TABLE OF CONTENTS-Continued

MERCURY

GENERAL SERVICE

GENERAL MOTORS CORP.—TAB 3

Page No.

BUICK

CADILLAC

CHEVROLET

GEO

OLDSMOBILE

PONTIAC

Page No.

GENERAL SERVICE

MOTOR
INFORMATION SYSTEMS

AUTO REPAIR MANUAL

DAIMLERCHRYSLER CORPORATION, FORD MOTOR COMPANY AND GENERAL MOTORS CORPORATION

63rd Edition, Volume 1

First Printing

John R. Lypen, SAE
Editorial Director

Marian A. Maasshoff, SAE
Executive Managing Editor

EDITORIAL DEVELOPMENT

Senior Editor
Warren Schildknecht, SAE

Quality Assurance Editor
Richard G. Glover, SAE

Assistant Special Projects Editor
Ron Lathrop

Technical Editors
Richard H. Sparkes, ASE
Duayn M. Verhelst, ASE
Michael A. Zimmerman, ASE
Gerald S. Athey
Jeff Finamore
Anthony W. Dutton
Uche-Uwa Ogu
Jim Jackovatz

EDITORIAL PRODUCTION

Production Manager
Richard C. Grunz, ASE

Production Assistant
Julie Andrews
Catherine Starzyk

PRODUCT SUPPORT

Product Support Specialist
Donald J. Schall, ASE

BOOK PRODUCTION

Director of Technology
Robert Jaramillo

Production Manager
Tina Wrubel

Production Group
Michele L. Hawley
Frank Jannaro
Christopher Mallory
Mike Stokes
Susan J. Verhelst
Ann Wittenbach

Published by
MOTOR

Published by Hearst Holdings, Inc.
A Unit Of The Hearst Corporation

5600 Crooks Road, Troy, MI 48098

Printed in the U.S.A.

ISBN 1-58251-026-1

VEHICLE IDENTIFICATION

INDEX

1st POSITION
COUNTRY
1 = United States
2 = Canada
3 = Mexico
4 = United States

2nd POSITION
MAKE
B = Dodge
C = Chrysler
E = Eagle
P = Plymouth

3rd POSITION
VEHICLE TYPE
3 = Passenger Car
4 = Multipurpose Vehicle
7 = Truck

4th POSITION
RESTRAINT/G.V.W.R.
RESTRAINT
A = Dual Air Bags
A = Air Bag
A = Auto Belts & Driver Air Bag
A = Manual Belts & Dual Air Bags
B = Automatic Belts
B = Manual Belts
C = Automatic Belts
C = Manual Belts
D = W/O Air Bags
E = Active Dual Air Bags
E = Active, Passenger Air Bag
E = Manual Belts & Dual Air Bags
F = Manual Belts (Mexico)
H = HYBRID Air Bag
H = Active Dual AirBag
X = Air Bag, Passenger Manual
Y = Air Bag, Passenger Automatic
G.V.W.R.
D = 1-3000 LB
E = 3001-4000 LB
F = 4001-5000 LB
G = 5001-6000 LB
H = 6001-7000 LB

5th POSITION
CARLINE
A = LeBaron LE/Landau
A = Spirit/Spirit LE
A = Acclaim
C = New Yorker
C = Chrysler "LHS"
C = New Yorker Salon
C = Dynasty/Dynasty LE
C = Town & Country
D = Concorde LX/LXI
D = Intrepid
D = Vision
D = New Yorker
D = Chrysler "LHS"
D = Caravan/Grand Caravan
E = Chrysler Vision
E = 300M
F = Laser/Talon (FWD)
G = Laser/Talon (AWD)
H = Minivan (FWD)
H = Intrepid
J = Stratus
J = Cirrus LX / LXI / Breeze
K = Minivan (AWD)
K = Talon / Talon ESI/ TSI (FWD)
L = Concorde
L = Sebring Convertible
L = Talon / Talon TSI(AWD)
L = Sebring (JX) (JXi)
M = Lebaren

5th POSITION (Cont'd)
CARLINE
P = Shadow/Shadow ES
P = Sundance/Duster
P = Minivan (FWD)
R = Viper, RT/10 & "GTS" Coupe
R = Durango 2WD
S = Laser/Talon (FWD)
S = Neon/Neon Sport
S = Durango 4WD
T = Laser/Talon (AWD)
T = Minivan (AWD)
U = LeBaron/LeBaron LS
U = LeBaron GTC/Convertible
U = Sebring/Avenger
V = Imperial
V = New Yorker Fifth Ave
W = Daytona/Daytona ES
W = Daytona IROC
W = Daytona IROC R/T
W = Prowler (RWD) Roadster
7 = R/T

6th POSITION
SERIES
1 = Economy (E)
2 = Low Line (L)
2 = Caravan / Grand Caravan
2 = Voyager / Grand Voyager
2 = Talon
2 = Durango & Durango SLT
3 = Medium Line (M)
4 = High Line (H)
4 = Talon ESI
4 = Avenger / Avenger ES
4 = Sebring LX
4 = SE Minivan
4 = Concorde/Intrepid
5 = Premium (P)
5 = Avenger ES
5 = Talon TSI (FWD)
5 = Talon Tsi Turbo FWD & AWD
5 = Sebring LXI
5 = Caravan / Grand Caravan LE /ES
5 = Voyager LE / SE & Grand Voyager LE / SE.
5 = Intrepid ES/LHS
6 = Special/Sport (S)
6 = Sebring LX
6 = Town & country LXI
7 = Performance / Image (X)
7 = Sport Utility (2WD)
8 = Talon TSI (AWD)
8 = Avenger ES
8 = Sport Utility (4WD)

7th POSITION
BODY STYLE
PASSENGER CAR
1 = 2 Door Coupe/Sedan
2 = 2 Door Pillared H.T.
4 = 2 Door Hatchback
4 = 3 Door Hatchback
4 = NS
5 = 2 Door Convertible
5 = NS
5 = Convertible - Open Body
6 = 4 Door Sedan
7 = 4 Door Pillared H.T.
8 = 4 Door Hatchback
9 = 4 Door Wagon
9 = 2 Door Specialty Coupe
TRUCK
1 = Van
4 = Extended Wagon/Van
5 = Wagon
8 = Sport Utility 4 Door

8th POSITION
ENGINE CODE
A = 2.2-L4, 16V Turbo III
A = 1.8-L4
B = 2.5-L4, TBI
B = 1.8-L4, MFI
B = 2.4-L4, 16V DOHC MPI
B = 2.0-L4, DOHC MPI
C = 2.0-L4, 16V SOHC
C = 2.2-L4, Turbo
D = 2.2-L4, TBI
E = 8.0-V10, MPI
E = 8.0-V10, SFI
E = 2.0-L4, MFI
E = 2.0-L4, MPI Turbo
F = 3.5-V6, 24V MPI
F = 2.0-L4, MFI Turbo
F = 2.0 DOHC_MPI Turbo
F = 2.0L-L4 Turbo T/C
G = 2.4-V6, MPI
G = 3.5-V6, SOHC 24 Valve
H = 2.5-L4, SPI
H = 2.5-V6, SOHC
J = 2.5-L4, Turbo
J = 3.3-V6, CNG
J = 3.2-V6, SOHC 24 Valve
K = 2.5-L4, TBI
L = 3.8-V6, MPI
L = 3.8-V6, SFI
M = 2.5-L4, Eurostar Diesel
N = 2.0-L4, SFI-SOHC
N = 2.5-V6, 24 Valve
N = 2.5 SOHC, MPI
P = 2.5-L4, SFI Turbo II
R = 3.3-V6, MPI
R = 2.0-L4, MPI
R = 2.7-V6, DOHC 24 Valve
S = 2.4-L4, DOHC Turbo
T = 1.8-L4, MPI
T = 3.3-V6, MPI
U = 2.0-L4, MPI Turbo
U = 3.3-V6, Flex Fuel MPI
V = 2.5-L4, Flex Fuel TBI
W = 2.5-L4, TBI
X = 2.4-L4, 16V DOHC
X = 3.9-V6
Y = 5.2-V8
Y = 2.0-L4, SFI-DOHC
Y = 2.0-L4, MPI
Z = 5.9-V8
2 = 2.5-L4, SFI Turbo
3 = 3.0-V6, MPI
9 = 54-KW, Electric

9th POSITION
CHECK DIGIT

10th POSITION
MODEL YEAR
N = 1992
P = 1993
R = 1994
S = 1995
T = 1996
V = 1997
W = 1998
X = 1999

11th POSITION
ASSEMBLY PLANT

12th Thru 17th POSITION
PRODUCTION SEQUENCE NUMBER

CR1139800577000X

Fig. 1 VIN Defined. DaimlerChrysler

1st POSITION
COUNTRY
1 = United States
2 = Canada
3 = Mexico
4 = United States
5 = United States
9 = Brazil
J = Japan
K = Korea
L = Taiwan

2nd POSITION
MAKE
B = Ford
C = Ford
F = Ford
F = Mazda
F = Mercury
L = Lincoln
M = Mercury
N = Continental
N = Ford
N = Nissan
Z = Ford

3rd POSITION
TYPE
A = Passenger Car
A = Imported Mercury Tracer
B = Bus
C = Basic, Stripped Chassis
D = Incomplete Vehicle
E = Passenger Car
E = Incomplete Vehicle
F = Equiped Without Power Train
F = Imported, Incomplete Truck
H = Incomplete Vehicle
I = Passenger Car
J = Incomplete Vehicle
J = Passenger Car
J = Imported Car, Aspire
M = Multi Purpose Vehicle
N = Passenger Car
P = Passenger Car, Imported
T = Basic, Complete
T = Truck, Complete
V = Passenger Car
W = Passenger Car
2 = Truck, Complete, Imported
2 = Multi Purpose Vehicle
3 = Incomplete Vehicle
4 = Truck, Complete
4 = Incomplete Vehicle, Imported

4th POSITION
RESTRAINT SYSTEM
A = Active Driver, Passive Passenger
A = Active Rear & Driver Air Bag
B = Active Belts
C = Air Bags & Active Belts
D = Active Belts
F = Active Belts, Second Generation Air Bags
H = Active Belts, Second Generation Air Bags
K = Active Belts, Second Generation Air Bags
L = Air Bags & Active Belts
P = Passive & Active Belts
R = Passive, Active & Driver Air Bag
S = Passive, Active & Dual Air Bags

5th POSITION
IDENTIFICATION
M = Lincoln/Mercury Make
P = Ford Make
T = Imported & Non-Ford Built

6th & 7th POSITION
BODY SERIES NUMBER
See The Body Series Pages

8th POSITION
ENGINE CODE
A = 2.0-L4, MFI, Mazda
A = 3.9-V8, MFI, DOHC
B = 2.5-V6, MFI, Mazda
C = 5.8-V8, MFI
D = 5.0-V8, MFI
G = 2.5L-V6, DOHC
H = 1.3-L4, MFI, Mazda
J = 1.9-L4, CVH SEFI
K = 1.9-L4, HO-CVH-SEFI
L = 2.5-V6, MFI
N = 3.4-V8, MFI, SHO-DOHC
P = 3.2-V6, SHO DOHC
P = 2.0-L4, SOHC, MFI, SPI 2000
R = 3.8-V6, SUPERCHARGED
S = 3.0-V6, MFI, DOHC
T = 5.0-V8, MFI, OHV
U = 3.0-V6, MFI
V = 4.6-V8, MFI, DOHC
W = 4.6-V8, MFI, SOHC
X = 2.3-L4, MFI, OHV
Y = 3.0-V6, MFI, Yamaha
Z = 1.6-L4, MFI, Mazda
1 = 3.0-V6, MFI Flex Fuel
3 = 2.0-L4, MFI-ZETA
4 = 3.8-V6, MFI-SEFI
6 = 1.6-L4, MFI/TC, Mazda
8 = 1.8-L4, MFI, Mazda
9 = 4.6-V8, Natural Gas

9th POSITION
CHECK DIGIT

10th POSITION
MODEL YEAR
S = 1995
T = 1996
V = 1997
W = 1998
X = 1999

11th POSITION
ASSEMBLY PLANT
A = Atlanta, GA
F = Dearborn, MI
G = Chicago, IL
H = Lorain, OH
K = Kansas City, MO
M = Cuautitlan
R = Hermosillo, Mexico
S = Allen Park, MI
W = Wayne, MI
X = St. Thomas, Canada
Y = Wixom, MI
5 = Flat Rock, MI
6 = Kia, Korea
8 = Broadmeadows, Australia

12th Thru 17th POSITION
PRODUCTION SEQUENCE NUMBER

FM1139700508000X

Fig. 2 VIN Defined. Ford Motor Co.

1st POSITION
COUNTRY
1 = United States
2 = Canada
3 = Mexico
4 = United States
J = Japan
W = Germany

2nd POSITION
MANUFACTURER
G = General Motors
C = CAMI
O = Opel
Y = Nummi
8 = Isuzu

3rd POSITION
DIVISION
4 = Buick
7 = GM of Canada

4th POSITION
CARLINE CODE
A = Century
B = Estate Wagon (RWD)
B = Coachbuilder Wagon
B = Roadmaster
C = Park Avenue (FWD)
E = Riviera
G = Riviera
H = LeSabre (FWD)
N = Somerset/Skylark
W = Regal
W = Century (1997-99)

5th POSITION
CARLINE SERIES
B = Regal Custom
B = Regal Gran Sport (2D)
B = Regal LS Sedan
B = Coachbuilder Wagon
D = Regal Limited
D = Riviera
F = Regal Gran Sport (4D)
G = Century Spl & Wagon
H = Century Custom/Wagon
J = Skylark
L = Century Limited Wagon
M = Skylark Gran Sport
N = Roadmaster
P = LeSabre Custom
R = LeSabre Limited
R = Roadmaster Est Wagon
S = Century Custom (1997-99)
T = Roadmaster Limited
U = Park Avenue - Ultra
V = Somerset
V = Skylark Custom
V = Skylark LTD/Gran Sport
W = Park Avenue
Y = Century Limited (1997-99)
Z = Riviera

6th POSITION
BODY TYPE
1 = 2 Door Coupe
2 = 2 Door
3 = 2 Door Convertable
4 = 2 Door Waqon
5 = 4 Door Sedan
6 = 4 Door
8 = 4 Door Wagon

7th POSITION
RESTRAINT SYSTEM
1 = Manual Belts
2 = Manual Belts (Dual Air Bags)
3 = Manual Belts (Driver Air Bag)
4 = Automatic Belts
4 = Manual Belts (Dual & Side Air Bags)
5 = Automatic Belts (Driver Air Bag)
6 = Automatic Belts (Dual Air Bags)
7 = Manual Driver Belt, Automatic Passenger Belt, (Dual Air Bags)

8th POSITION
ENGINE CODE
D = 2.3-L4, MFI
K = 3.8-V6, MFI
L = 3.8-V6, MFI
M = 3.1-V6, MFI
N = 3.3-V6, MFI
P = 5.7-V8, MFI
R = 2.5-L4, TBI
T = 3.1-V6, MFI (1993)
T = 2.4-L4, MFI (1996)
1 = 3.8-V6, MFI
3 = 2.3-L4, MFI
4 = 2.2-L4, MFI
7 = 5.7-V8, TBI

9th POSITION
CHECK DIGIT

10th POSITION
MODEL YEAR
P = 1993
R = 1994
S = 1995
T = 1996
V = 1997
W = 1998
X = 1999

11th POSITION
ASSEMBLY PLANT

12th Thru 17th POSITION
PRODUCTION SEQUENCE NUMBER

GC1139800734000X

Fig. 3 VIN Defined. Buick

1st POSITION
COUNTRY
1 = United States
2 = Canada
3 = Mexico Built
4 = United States
J = Japan Built
W = Germany

2nd POSITION
MANUFACTURER
G = General Motors
C = CAMI
O = Opel
Y = NUMMI
8 = Isuzu

3rd POSITION
DIVISION
6 = Cadillac
7 = GM of Canada

4th POSITION
CARLINE CODE
C = Fleetwood/DeVille (FWD)
C = Commercial Chassis
C = Sixty Special
C = DeVille/DeVille Touring
D = Fleetwood/DeVille (RWD)
D = Brougham
D = Commercial Chassis (RWD)
E = Eldorado
E = Eldorado Touring
J = Cimarron
K = Concours
K = DeVille
K = Seville
K = Seville Touring
V = Allante'
V = Catera

5th POSITION
CARLINE SERIES
B = Fleetwood (FWD)
B = Sixty Special
D = DeVille (FWD)
E = Deville D'Flegance
F = Concours
F = Fleetwood Limo
G = Cimarron
G = Fleetwood 60 Special
H = Fleetwood Limo
H = Commercial Chassis (RWD)
L = Eldorado
M = Deville (RWD)
R = Allante' Conv. & HT
R = Catera
S = Seville
S = Allante' Convertible
S = Fleetwood 60 Special
T = Eldorado Touring
T = DeVille Touring
W = Fleetwood Brougham
Y = Seville Touring Sedan
7 = Commercial Chassis

6 & 7th POSITION, 1985-86
BODY TYPE
19 = 4 Door Sedan
27 = 2 Door Coupe
35 = 4 Door Wagon
37 = 2 Door Coupe
47 = 2 Door Coupe
57 = 2 Door Coupe
67 = 2 Door Convertable
69 = 4 Door Sedan
77 = 2 Door Hatchback
87 = 2 Door Coupe

6th POSITION, 1987-99
BODY TYPE
1 = 2 Door Coupe
2 = 2 Door
3 = 2 Door Convertible
5 = 4 Door Sedan
6 = 4 Door
8 = 4 Door Station Wagon

7th POSITION, 1987-99
RESTRAINT SYSTEM
1 = Manual Belts
2 = Manual Belts (Built in Saftey)
2 = Manual Belts (Dual Air Bags)
3 = Manual Belts (Driver Air Bag)
4 = Automatic Belts
4 = Manual Belts (Dual & Side Air Bags)
5 = Automatic Belts (Dual Air Bag)
6 = Automatic Belts (Dual Air Bags)
7 = Manual Driver Belt, Automatic Passenger Belt (Dual Air Bags)

8th POSITION
ENGINE CODE
B = 4.9-V8, MFI
E = 5.0-V8, TBI
K = 3.8-V6, MFI
N = 5.7-V8, Diesel
P = 2.0-L4, EFI
P = 5.7-V8, MFI
R = 3.0-V6, MFI
W = 2.8-V6, MFI
Y = 5.0-V8, 4 Barrel
Y = 4.6-V8, MFI
3 = 4.5-V8, MFI
5 = 4.5-V8, Fuel Injected
6 = 4.5-V8, Fuel Injected
7 = 4.1-V8, Fuel Injected
7 = 5.7-V8, TBI
8 = 4.1-V8, DFI
8 = 4.5-V8, MFI
9 = 5.0-V8, 4 Barrel
9 = 4.6-V8, MFI

9th POSITION
CHECK DIGIT

10th POSITION
MODEL YEAR
F = 1985
G = 1986
H = 1987
J = 1988
K = 1989
L = 1990
M = 1991
N = 1992
P = 1993
R = 1994
S = 1995
T = 1996
V = 1997
W = 1998
X = 1999

11th POSITION
ASSEMBLY PLANT

12th Thru 17th POSITION
PRODUCTION SEQUENCE NUMBER

GC1139800735000X

Fig. 4 VIN Defined. Cadillac

1st POSITION
COUNTRY
1 = United States
2 = Canada
3 = Mexico
4 = United States
J = Japan
W = Germany

2nd POSITION
MANUFACTURER
C = CAMI
G = General Motors
O = Opel
Y = N.U.M.M.I.
8 = Isuzu

3rd POSITION
DIVISION
1 = Chevrolet
7 = GM of Canada

4th POSITION
CARLINE CODE
B = Impala
B = Caprice
F = Camaro
J = Cavalier
J = Toyota
L = Corsica, Beretta
M = Geo Metro & Metro LSI
N = Malibu
S = Geo Prizm
L = Lumina
W = Lumina
W = Monte Carlo
Y = Corvette

5th POSITION
CARLINE SERIES
C = Cavalier
D = Corsica
D = Malibu LX
E = Malibu LS
F = Cavalier Convertible
F = Cavalier Z24 & LS
G = Toyota (Sedan)
H = Toyota (Coupe & Sedan)
L = Impala SS
L = Caprice/Caprice Wagon
L = Lumina Sedan
L = Lumina LS
K = Geo Prizm LSi
N = Lumina LS
N = Lumina LTZ
P = Camaro Sport Coupe & Conv.
R = Geo Metro & Metro LSI
V = Beretta
W = Beretta Z26
W = Monte Carlo SS
W = Monte Carlo LS
X = Monte Carlo Z34
Y = Corvette & Convertible
Z = Corvette ZR1

6th POSITION
BODY TYPE
1 = 2 Door Coupe
2 = 2 Door
3 = 2 Door Convertable
4 = 2 Door Wagon
5 = 4 Door Sedan
6 = 4 Door
8 = 4 Door Wagon

7th POSITION
RESTRAINT SYSTEM
1 = Manual Belts
2 = Manual Belts (Dual Air Bags)
3 = Manual Belts (Driver Air Bag)
4 = Manual Belts (Dual & Side air Bags)
4 = Automatic Belts
5 = Automatic Belts (Driver Air Bag)
6 = Automatic Belts (Dual Air Bags)
7 = Manual Driver Belt, Automatic Passenger Belt, (Dual Air Bags)

8th POSITION
ENGINE CODE
D = 2.3-L4, MFI
G = 5.7-V8, MFI (1997-99)
J = 5.7-V8, MFI
K = 3.8-V6, MFI
M = 3.1-V6, MFI
P = 5.7-V8, MFI
S = 3.4-V6, MFI
T = 2.4-L4, MFI (96-99)
T = 3.1-V6,MFI
W = 4.3-V8, MFI
X = 3.4-V6, MFI
2 = 1.3-L4, MFI
4 = 2.2-L4, MFI
5 = 5.7-V8, MFI
6 = 1.0-L3, TBI
6 = 1.6-L4, MFI
8 = 1.8-L4, MFI
9 = 1.3-L4, TBI

9th POSITION
CHECK DIGIT

10th POSITION
MODEL YEAR
S = 1995
T = 1996
V = 1997
W = 1998
X = 1999

11th POSITION
ASSEMBLY PLANT

12th Thru 17th POSITION
PRODUCTION SEQUENCE NUMBER

GC1139800736000X

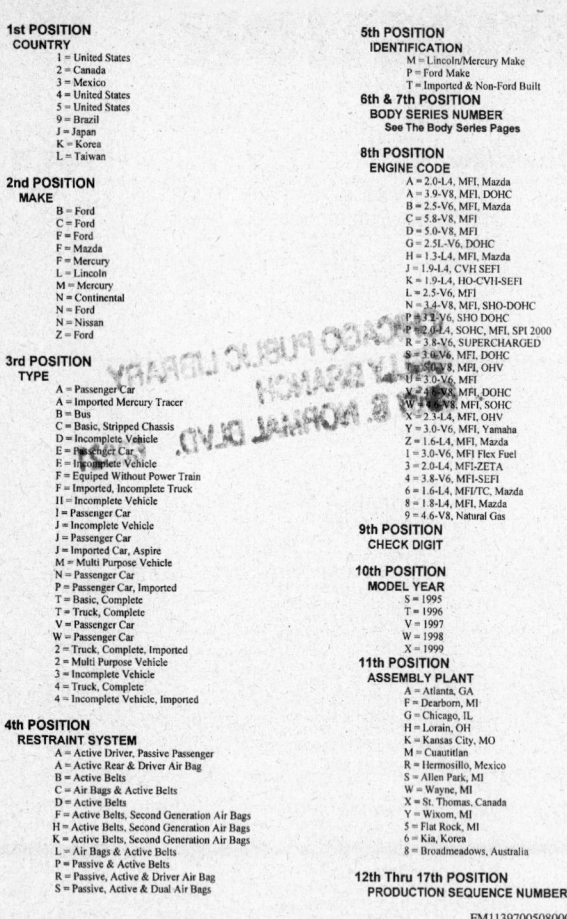

Fig. 5 VIN Defined. Chevrolet

1st POSITION
COUNTRY
1 = United States
2 = Canada
3 = Mexico
4 = United States
J = Japan
W = Germany

2nd POSITION
MANUFACTURER
C = CAMI
G = General Motors
O = Opel
Y = Nummi
8 = Isuzu

3rd POSITION
DIVISION
3 = Oldsmobile
7 = GM of Canada

4th POSITION
CARLINE CODE
A = Cutlass Ciera/Cruiser
B = 88 Custom Cruiser (RWD)
C = 98 Touring Sedan
C = 98 Regency/Elite
E = Toronado
E = Toronado Trofe'o
G = Aurora
H = 88 Royale/LS (FWD)
H = Regency
H = LSS
N = Achieva
N = Ciera
N = Cutlass
N = Alero
W = Cutlass
W = Intrigue

5th POSITION
CARLINE SERIES
B = Ciera
B = Cutlass
B = Cutlass GL
C = Regency
F = Achieva SL & SC
G = Cutlass
G = Cutlass Ciera S
G = Cutlass GLS
H = Intrigue
H = Cutlass Supreme SL
H = Cutlass Supreme S
J = Cutlass S/SL & Wagon
L = Cutlass Ciera S
L = Achieva SL & SC
L = Achieva S
L = Alero
M = Cutlass Ciera SL
M = Cutlass Cruiser SL Wagon
N = 88 LS
N = 88 Royale
P = Custom Crusier
R = Cutlass Supreme Int'l

5th POSITION (Cont'd)
CARLINE SERIES
R = Aurora
S = Intrigue
T = Cutlass Convertible
V = Toranado Trofe'o
V = 98 Touring Sedan
W = 98 Regency Elite
X = 98 Regency (FWD)
X = 98 Regency Elite
X = Intrigue
Y = LSS
Y = 88 Royale LS
Z = Toronado

6th POSITION
BODY TYPE
1 = 2 Door Coupe
2 = 2 Door
3 = 2 Door Convertible
4 = 2 Door Wagon
5 = 4 Door Sedan
6 = 4 Door
8 = 4 Door Wagon

7th POSITION
RESTRAINT SYSTEM
1 = Manual Belts
2 = Manual Belts (Dual Air Bags)
3 = Manual Belts (Driver Air Bag)
4 = Manual Belts (Dual & Side Air Bag)
4 = Automatic Belts
5 = Automatic Belts (Driver Air Bag)
6 = Automatic Belts (Dual Air Bags)
7 = Manual Driver Belt, Automatic Passenger Belt, (Dual Air Bags)

8th POSITION
ENGINE CODE
A = 2.3-L4, MFI
C = 4.0-V8, MFI
D = 2.3-L4, MFI
E = 5.0-V8, TBI
H = 3.5-V6, MFI
K = 3.8-V6, MFI
L = 3.8-V6, MFI
M = 3.1-V6, MFI
N = 3.3-V6, MFI
R = 2.5-L4, TBI
T = 2.4-L4, MFI (96-99)
T = 3.1-V6, MFI (1993)
X = 3.4-V6, MFI
1 = 3.8-V6, MFI
3 = 2.3-L4, MFI
4 = 2.2-L4, MFI
7 = 5.7-V8, TBI

9th POSITION
CHECK DIGIT

10th POSITION
MODEL YEAR
P = 1993
R = 1994
S = 1995
T = 1996
V = 1997
W = 1998
X = 1999

11th POSITION
ASSEMBLY PLANT
B = Lansing, MI
B = Baltimore, MD
C = Lansing, MI
C = Charlotte, MI
D = Doraville, GA
E = Linden, NJ
F = Flint, MI
F = Fairfax II, KS
G = Framingham, MA
H = Flint, MI
J = Janesville, WI
K = Leeds, MO
K = Linden, NJ
M = Lansing, MI
R = Arlington, TX
T = Shreveport, LA
U = Hamtramck, MI
W = Willow Run, MI
X = Fairfax, KS
Y = Wilmington, DE
Z = Spring Hill, TN
Z = Fremont, CA
Z = Fort Wayne, IN
1 = Wentzville, MO
1 = Oshawa #2, Canada
2 = Ste. Therese, Canada
2 = Moraine, OH
3 = Detroit, MI
4 = Orion, MI
5 = Bowling Green, KY
6 = Ingersoll, Canada
6 = Oklahoma, OK
7 = Lordstown, OH
8 = Shreveport, LA
9 = Oshawa #1, Canada

12th Thru 17th POSITION
PRODUCTION SEQUENCE NUMBER

GC1139800737000X

Fig. 6 VIN Defined. Oldsmobile

1st POSITION
COUNTRY
1 = United States
2 = Canada
3 = Mexico
4 = United States
J = Japan Built
W = Germany

2nd POSITION
MANUFACTURER
C = CAMI
G = General Motors
O = Opel
Y = Nummi
8 = Isuzu

3rd POSITION
DIVISION
2 = Pontiac
7 = GM of Canada

4th POSITION
CARLINE CODE
F = Firebird / Formula / Trans Am
H = Bonneville
J = Sunbird & Convertible
J = Sunfire
N = Grand Am
W = Grand Prix

5th POSITION
CARLINE SERIES
B = Sunbird SE & Convertible
B = Sunfire SE & Convertible
D = Sunfire GT
E = Grand Am SE
J = Grand Prix SE
L = Sunbird SE
M = Grand Prix
P = Grand Prix GT
S = Firebird & Convertible
V = Formula & Convertible
V = Trans Am
W = Grand Am GT
X = Bonneville SE
Z = Bonneville SSE / SSEI

6th POSITION
BODY TYPE
1 = 2 Door Coupe
2 = 2 Door
3 = 2 Door Convertible
4 = 2 Door Wagon
5 = 4 Door Sedan

6th POSITION (Cont'd)
6 = 4 Door
8 = 4 Door Wagon

7th POSITION
RESTRAINT SYSTEM
1 = Manual Belts
2 = Manual Belts (Dual Air Bags)
3 = Manual Belts (Driver Air Bag)
4 = Manual Belts (Dual & Side Air Bags)
4 = Automatic Belts
5 = Automatic Belts (Driver Air Bag)
6 = Automatic Belts (Dual Air Bags)
7 = Manual Driver Belt, Automatic Passenger Belt, (Dual Air Bags)

8th POSITION
ENGINE CODE
A = 2.3-L4, MFI
D = 2.3-L4, MFI
G = 5.7-V8, MFI
H = 2.0-L4, MFI
K = 3.8-V6, MFI
L = 3.8-V6, MFI
M = 3.1-V6, MFI
P = 5.7-V8, MFI
S = 3.4-V6, MFI
T = 3.1-V6, MFI (93-94)
T = 2.4-L4, MFI (96-99)
X = 3.4-V6, MFI
1 = 3.8-V6, MFI
3 = 2.3-L4, MFI
4 = 2.2-L4, MFI

9th POSITION
CHECK DIGIT

10th POSITION
MODEL YEAR
R = 1994
S = 1995
T = 1996
V = 1997
W = 1998
X = 1999

11th POSITION
ASSEMBLY PLANT

12th Thru 17th POSITION
PRODUCTION SEQUENCE NUMBER

GC1139800738000X

Fig. 7 VIN Defined. Pontiac

1st POSITION
COUNTRY
1 = United States

2nd POSITION
MANUFACTURER
G = General Motors

3rd POSITION
DIVISION
8 = Saturn

4th POSITION
CARLINE CODE
Z = SL, SL1&2, SC
Z = SC1&2, SW1&2

5th POSITION
CARLINE SERIES
B = SC2 Coupe, SW1 Wagon
B = SL Sedan, SL1 Sedan
C = SC1 Coupe
D = SL2 Sedan, SW2 Wagon
E = SC1 Coupe
F = SL Sedan, SC1 Coupe
G = SL1 Sedan, SC
G = SC2 Sedan, SW1 Wagon
H = SL1 Sedan, SC
H = SC2 Coupe, SW1 Wagon
J = SL2 Sedan, SW2 Wagon
K = SL2 Sedan, SW2 Wagon

6th POSITION
BODY TYPE
1 = 2 Door Coupe
2 = 2 Door
3 = 2 Door Convertible
4 = 2 Door Wagon
5 = 4 Door Sedan
6 = 4 Door
8 = 5 Door Wagon

7th POSITION
RESTRAINT SYSTEM
1 = Manual Belts
2 = Manual Belts (Dual Air Bags)
3 = Manual Belts (Driver Air Bag)
4 = Manual Belts (Dual & Side Air Bag)
4 = Automatic Belts
5 = Automatic Belts (Driver Air Bag)
6 = Automatic Belts (Dual Air Bags)
7 = Manual Driver Belt, Automatic Passenger Belt. (Dual Air Bags)

8th POSITION
ENGINE CODE
5 = AC EV (Electri Vehcle)
7 = 1.9-L4, MFI
8 = 1.9-L4, MFI
9 = 1.9-L4, TBI

9th POSITION
CHECK DIGIT

10th POSITION
MODEL YEAR
M = 1991
N = 1992
P = 1993
R = 1994
S = 1995
T = 1996
V = 1997
W = 1998
X = 1999

11th POSITION
ASSEMBLY PLANT
Z = Spring Hill, TN

12th Thru 17th POSITION
PRODUCTION SEQUENCE NUMBER

GC1139800739000X

Fig. 8 VIN Defined. Saturn

AIR BAG SYSTEM PRECAUTIONS

INDEX

DAIMLERCHRYSLER

DISARMING

It may be necessary to access and record all diagnostic trouble codes (DTCs) prior to disarming air bag system.

When arming and disarming air bag systems, ensure auxiliary batteries and power supplies are disabled if equipped.

1. Place ignition switch in lock position.
2. Disconnect battery ground cable connector.
3. **Wait at least two minutes after disconnecting battery ground cable before doing any further work on vehicle. The air bag system is designed to retain enough voltage to deploy air bag for a short time even after battery has been disconnected.**

ARMING

1. Connect battery ground cable.
2. From passenger side of vehicle, turn ignition switch to On position.
3. The SRS warning light should illuminate for six to eight seconds, then remain off for at least 45 seconds to indicate if SRS system is functioning correctly.
4. If SRS indicator does not perform as described, refer to **MOTOR's "Air Bag Manual."**

FORD MOTOR CO.

After the battery has been disconnected and reconnected, abnormal drive conditions may be present while the powertrain control module relearns its adaptive strategy. The vehicle may need to be driven 10 miles or more to relearn the strategy.

The following disarming and arming procedures require the disconnection or removal of the driver's and passenger's air bag modules to eliminate the possibility of deployment when performing diagnostic and testing and service procedures. While the air bag module is removed from the vehicle, an air bag simulator tool should be connected to the air bag module wiring harness connector, **Fig. 1.** The air bag simulator tool is a resistor which is used to simulate an air bag module connection. If the air bag simulator tool is not used while the air bag module is disconnected, a Diagnostic Trouble Code (DTC) will be set when diagnosis and testing procedures are performed.

DISARMING

ASPIRE

1. Disconnect battery ground cable. Allow at least one minute for back-up power supply to deplete.
2. Remove four bolts mounting air bag module to steering wheel.
3. Disconnect air bag electrical connector from slip ring/clockspring connectors and remove air bag assembly.
4. Connect Rotunda tool No. 105-00009, or equivalent, to vehicle harness at top of steering column.
5. Open glove compartment door, then remove two glove compartment mounting screws.
6. Remove glove compartment.
7. Remove four air bag module mounting bolts.
8. Push air bag module outward from inside instrument panel. **Do not handle air bag module by deployment doors.**
9. Disconnect electrical connector, then remove air bag module.
10. Connect Rotunda tool No. 105-00009, or equivalent, to passenger's air bag harness.
11. Connect battery ground cable.

CONTINENTAL

Prior to disconnecting battery, record USER 1 and USER 2 preset radio frequencies.

1997–98

1. Disconnect battery ground cable.
2. Wait one minute for back-up power supply to deplete.
3. Remove two air bag mounting bolt hole covers from steering wheel spokes.
4. Remove two air bag module mounting bolts, then carefully lift air bag module from steering wheel.
5. Disconnect driver's air bag module connector.
6. Attach Rotunda tool No. 105-00011, or equivalent, to air bag terminals on clockspring assembly to simulate air bag.
7. Open glove compartment and rotate downward past stops.
8. Disconnect passenger's air bag module electrical connector.
9. Remove three bolts mounting lower passenger's air bag module mounting bracket to instrument panel through glove compartment opening.
10. Remove passenger's air bag module by pushing module outward from inside instrument panel. Do not grab edges of deployment doors.
11. Attach Rotunda tool No. 105-00010, or equivalent, to air bag terminals on wiring harness side of passenger's air bag module connector.
12. Connect battery ground cable.

1999–2000

1. Disconnect and isolate battery ground cable.
2. **On models equipped with auxiliary batteries and power supplies,** disconnect and isolate these items, too.
3. **On all models,** wait one minute for back-up power supply to deplete.
4. Remove two steering wheel spoke bolt covers, if equipped.
5. Remove two air bag module to steering wheel.
6. Carefully lift air bag module away from steering wheel, then disconnect air bag module and horn to clockspring electrical connectors. **When carrying a live air bag module, ensure bag and trim cover are pointed away from your body. To prevent injury by accidental deployment, place module on a bench with trim cover facing upward.**
7. Remove air bag module.
8. Attach Rotunda air bag simulator tool No. 105-00012, or equivalent, to vehicle harness connector at top of steering column.
9. Open glove compartment, then push tabs in and rotate door downward past stops.
10. Disconnect passenger's air bag module electrical connector.
11. Attach Rotunda air bag simulator tool No. 105-00012, or equivalent, to passenger's air bag module electrical connector on vehicle wiring harness side.
12. Disconnect side air bag module electrical connector located beneath driver's seat.
13. Attach Rotunda air bag simulator tool No. 105-00012, or equivalent, to side air bag connector under driver's seat on vehicle wiring harness side
14. Disconnect side air bag module electrical connector located beneath passenger's seat.
15. Attach Rotunda air bag simulator tool No. 105-00012, or equivalent, to side air bag connector under passenger's seat on vehicle wiring harness side
16. Connect battery ground cable.

CONTOUR & MYSTIQUE

1997-98

1. Disconnect battery ground cable, then the positive cable. Allow at least one minute for back-up power supply to deplete.
2. Remove five mounting screws and steering column shrouds from column tube, then rotate steering wheel as necessary to access and remove air bag mounting bolts.
3. Disconnect driver's air bag module connector and carefully remove module. Place module on a bench with trim cover facing upward.
4. Connect Rotunda tool No. 105-00010, or equivalent, to air bag sliding contact connector at top of steering column.
5. Open glove compartment and lower compartment to floor by pressing inward on sides.
6. Remove four screws, then disconnect glove compartment lamp and remove glove compartment upper panel.
7. Remove A/C evaporator register duct and two mounting nuts from passenger's air bag module.
8. Remove two bolts from passenger's air bag module, then disconnect electrical connector and carefully remove module. **To prevent injury by accidental deployment, place module on a bench with trim cover facing upward.**
9. Connect second air bag simulator Rotunda tool No. 105-00010, or equivalent, to wiring harness in place of passenger's air bag.
10. Connect battery positive battery cable, then the ground cable.

1999-2000

Prior to disconnecting battery, record preset radio frequencies.

1. Disconnect and isolate battery ground cable.
2. Allow at least one minute for back-up power supply to deplete.
3. Remove two driver's air bag module Torx mounting screws at rear of steering wheel.
4. Lift driver's air bag module upward, and disconnect air bag module electrical connector.
5. Remove air bag module. **When carrying a live air bag module, ensure bag and trim cover are pointed away from your body. To prevent injury by accidental deployment, place module on a bench with trim cover facing upward.**
6. Connect Rotunda air bag simulator tool No. 105-R0012, or equivalent, to vehicle harness at top of steering column.
7. Open glove compartment and lower compartment to floor by pressing inward on sides.
8. Remove four glove compartment upper panel screws and disconnect glove compartment lamp.
9. Remove glove compartment upper panel.
10. Remove passenger's air vent duct.
11. Disconnect passenger's air bag module electrical connector.
12. Connect second Rotunda air bag simulator tool No. 105-R0012, or equivalent, to wiring harness in place of passenger's air bag.
13. Connect battery ground cable.

COUGAR

1997

Prior to disconnecting battery, record USER 1 and USER 2 preset radio frequencies.

1. Disconnect battery ground cable. Allow at least one minute for back-up power supply to deplete.
2. Remove two bolt cover plugs, then the two bolt and washer assemblies mounting driver's air bag assembly to steering wheel.
3. Disconnect driver's air bag connector and remove air bag from steering wheel. **To prevent injury by accidental deployment, place module on a bench with trim cover facing upward.**
4. Connect Rotunda tool No. 105-00010, or equivalent, to vehicle air bag wiring harness at top steering column.
5. Using a small screwdriver, detach dampening rod from righthand side of glove compartment.
6. Pull lefthand side of glove compartment inward and allow glove compartment to drop downward.
7. Remove mounting screws and air duct.
8. Remove two vertically positioned bolts from each side of air bag module.
9. Remove two remaining air bag module mounting bolts.
10. Push air bag module outward from instrument panel. **Do not handle air bag module by deployment doors.**
11. Disconnect electrical connector and remove air bag module. Place module on a bench with trim cover facing upward.
12. Connect Rotunda tool No. 105-00010, or equivalent, to vehicle air bag wiring harness in place of passenger's air bag module.
13. Connect battery ground cable.

1999-2000

Prior to disconnecting battery, record preset radio frequencies.

1. Disconnect and isolate battery ground cable.
2. Allow at least one minute for back-up power supply to deplete.
3. Remove two driver's air bag module Torx mounting screws at rear of steering wheel.
4. Lift driver's air bag module upward and disconnect air bag module electrical connector.
5. Remove air bag module. **When carrying a live air bag module, ensure bag and trim cover are pointed away from your body. To prevent injury by accidental deployment, place module on a bench with trim cover facing upward.**
6. Connect Rotunda air bag simulator tool No. 105-R0012, or equivalent, to vehicle harness at top of steering column.
7. Remove three glove compartment Torx mounting screws.
8. Open glove compartment and depress side stops to detach sides.
9. Remove four Torx screws and the glove compartment finish panel.
10. Remove passenger's air register duct.
11. Disconnect passenger's air bag module electrical connector.
12. Remove two bolts mounting passenger's air bag module to cross beam.
13. Lower front edge of passenger's air bag module, roll air bag module around cross beam. Lower air bag module to passenger's foot well and remove. **When carrying a live air bag module, ensure bag and trim cover are pointed away from your body. To prevent injury by accidental deployment, place module on a bench with trim cover facing upward.**
14. Connect second Rotunda air bag simulator tool No. 105-R0012, or equivalent, to wiring harness in place of passenger's air bag.
15. **On models with side air bags,** proceed as follows:
    a. From driver's and passenger's seats, remove seat back rest, cover and pad.
    b. Depress mounting tang at each side and disconnect side air bag module electrical connector at driver's and passenger's seats.
    c. At driver's and passenger's seats, remove two mounting nuts, then the side air bag module.
16. **On all models,** connect battery ground cable.

CROWN VICTORIA & GRAND MARQUIS

Prior to disconnecting battery, record USER 1 and USER 2 preset radio frequencies.

1997-98

1. Disconnect battery ground cable and wait one minute for back-up power supply to deplete.
2. Remove four bolt and washer assemblies mounting driver's air bag assembly to steering wheel.
3. Disconnect driver's air bag module connector.
4. Connect Rotunda tool No. 105-00010, or equivalent, to vehicle air bag wiring harness at top of steering column.
5. Remove instrument panel upper molding by disengaging snap-in tabs.
6. Open glove compartment, press sides inward and lower glove compartment to floor.
7. Working through glove compartment opening, remove two front air bag module screws.
8. Remove two rear air bag module mounting screws, then disconnect electrical connector and remove air bag module.
9. Attach Rotunda tool No. 105-00010, or equivalent, to harness side of passenger's air bag module connector.

1999-2000

1. Disconnect and isolate battery ground cable, then wait one minute for back-up power supply to deplete.
   a. Remove two bolts mounting air bag assembly to steering wheel.
   b. Carefully lift air bag module from steering wheel, then disconnect air bag module and horn switch electrical connectors. **When carrying a live air bag module, ensure bag and trim cover are pointed away from your body. To prevent injury by accidental deployment, place module on a bench with trim cover facing upward.**
2. Connect Rotunda air bag simulator tool No. 105-00012, or equivalent, to vehicle air bag wiring harness at top of steering column.
3. Open glove compartment and disconnect glove compartment locator.
4. Push inward on glove compartment door tabs and position door downward.
5. Detach trim panel located below air bag module from instrument panel by pulling straight out to release clips. Disconnect clock electrical connector and remove trim panel.
6. Disconnect passenger's air bag module electrical connector.
7. Remove two passenger's air bag module mounting bolts.
8. Remove two passengers air bag module mounting screws.
9. Place one hand in glove compartment opening and push passenger's air bag module from instrument panel. **When carrying a live air bag module, ensure bag and trim cover are pointed away from your body. To prevent injury by accidental deployment, place module on a bench with trim cover facing upward.**
10. Attach Rotunda air bag simulator tool No. 105-00012, or equivalent, to harness side of passenger's air bag module connector.
11. Connect battery ground cable.

ESCORT, TRACER & ZX2

Prior to disconnecting battery, record preset radio frequencies.

1. Disconnect battery ground cable and allow at least one minute for back-up power supply to be depleted.
2. Remove two air bag module bolts, then disconnect air bag sliding contact and horn electrical connectors.
3. Carefully lift module away from steering wheel.
4. Install air bag simulator tool No. T96P-50-AH, or equivalent, in place of driver's air bag module.
5. Push in on glove compartment door tabs and position downward and remove door.
6. Remove four air bag module bolts and carefully pull module out of instrument panel.
7. Disconnect air bag module electrical connector.
8. Install air bag simulator tool No. 105-00010, or equivalent, in place of passenger's air bag module.

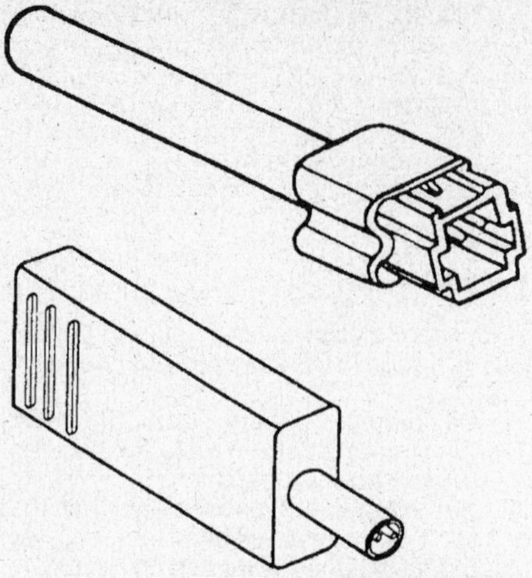

FM8019701901000X

Fig. 1 Air bag simulator tools

9. Connect battery ground cable.

LS

Prior to disconnecting battery, record USER 1 and USER 2 preset radio frequencies.

1. Disconnect battery ground cable.
2. Wait at least one minute for backup power supply in Restraints Control Module (RCM) to deplete its stored energy.
3. Remove driver's air bag module as described under " Component Service."
4. Install driver/passenger air bag simulator on wiring harness connector for driver air bag.
5. Remove righthand instrument panel insulator.
6. Remove righthand floor heat duct.
7. Release assist cable from glove compartment arm from under instrument panel.
8. Open glove compartment.
9. Remove instrument panel finish panel.
10. **On late build models,** push down on glove compartment arms and lower glove compartment door.
11. **On early build models,** proceed as follows:
    a. Release assist cable.
    b. Lower glove compartment.
    c. Release stops.
    d. If equipped with compact disc changer, remove mounting screws and glove compartment door inner panel.
12. **On all models,** remove mounting screws and glove compartment instrument panel finish panel, then disconnect electrical connectors.
13. Remove mounting bolts and glove compartment.
14. Disconnect glove compartment electrical connector.
15. Reaching over cross-car beam, slide passenger air bag connector lock downward.
16. Squeeze locking tabs and pull connector from passenger air bag.
17. Attach driver/passenger air bag simulator to passenger's air bag connector harness side.
18. Disconnect driver's side air bag module at connector beneath driver's seat.
19. Attach side air bag simulator tool No. 418-133, or equivalent, to driver's side air bag connector harness side
20. Repeat previous steps for passenger's side air bag connector.
21. Access driver's side safety belt retractor pretensioner in B-pillar.
22. Disconnect pretensioner electrical connector and attach pretensioner simulator tool No. 105-R0012, or equivalent.
23. Repeat previous steps for passenger's side safety belt retractor pretensioner.
24. Connect battery ground cable.

MARK VIII

Prior to disconnecting battery, record USER 1 and USER 2 preset radio frequencies.

1. Disconnect battery ground cable.
2. Wait one minute for back-up power supply to discharge.
3. Remove air bag module screw covers from rear of steering wheel.
4. Remove two screw and washer assemblies mounting driver's air bag module to steering wheel.
5. Disconnect driver's air bag module connector.
6. Connect Rotunda air bag simulator tool No. 105-00010, or equivalent, to vehicle harness at top of steering column.
7. Remove headlamp switch knob and shaft assembly.
8. Unsnap lefthand instrument panel finish panel from instrument panel finish panel. Detach bulb and socket, then remove finish panel.
9. Remove headlamp switch mounting screws, then the switch.
10. Remove two screws mounting lefthand end finish panel to instrument panel.
11. Remove two screws located at top of instrument cluster opening attaching instrument panel trim panel to instrument panel.
12. Remove two screws attaching lower lefthand insulator to instrument panel. Disconnect bulb and socket, then remove insulator.
13. Remove instrument panel steering column lower cover.
14. Remove upper and lower steering gear housings from steering column tube.
15. Remove upper shroud extension to instrument panel screws.
16. From righthand side, disengage instrument cluster trim panel retainers.
17. Open glove compartment, press insides inward and lower glove compartment to floor.
18. Remove two screws mounting side defroster duct.
19. Working through glove compartment, remove two lower air bag module mounting bolts.
20. Remove three remaining air bag module mounting screws from side of air bag cover.
21. Disconnect electrical connector attached to lefthand side of air bag while removing air bag module.

22. Install Rotunda tool No. 105-00010, or equivalent, on vehicle air bag harness connector in place of air bag. Harness connector will contain GY/O and PK/BK wires.
23. Connect battery ground cable.

MUSTANG

Prior to disconnecting battery, record USER 1 and USER 2 preset radio frequencies.

1997-98

1. Disconnect battery ground cable and allow at least one minute for back-up power supply to deplete.
2. Remove two rear cover plugs from steering wheel in order to access air bag module screws.
3. Remove driver's air bag module screws and washers, then disconnect electrical connector and carefully remove air bag module. **To prevent injury by accidental deployment, place module on a bench with trim cover facing upward.**
4. Connect Rotunda tool No. 105-00010, or equivalent, to vehicle air bag wiring harness at top steering column.
5. Open glove compartment, press sides inward to release it from instrument panel and lower glove compartment to floor.
6. Remove righthand A/C duct, then the passenger's air bag mounting bolts from instrument panel steel reinforcement.
7. Disconnect electrical connector at lower lefthand corner of passenger's air bag module and remove connector from instrument panel reinforcement.
8. Pull gently upon each corner of air bag cover to disengage from instrument panel and push air bag module out from behind instrument panel. **To prevent injury by accidental deployment, place module on a bench with trim cover facing upward.**
9. Install second air bag module simulator Rotunda tool No. 105-00010, or equivalent, on passenger's air bag harness.
10. Connect battery ground cable.

1999-2000

1. Disconnect and isolate battery ground cable, then allow at least one minute for back-up power supply to deplete.
2. Remove two rear cover plugs from steering wheel in order to access air bag module screws.
3. Remove driver's air bag module screws and washers, then disconnect electrical connector and carefully remove air bag module. **When carrying a live air bag module, ensure bag and trim cover are pointed away from your body. To prevent injury by accidental deployment, place module on a bench with trim cover facing upward.**
4. Connect Rotunda air bag simulator tool No. 105-00012, or equivalent, to vehicle air bag wiring harness at top steering column.
5. Open glove compartment, press sides inward to release it from instrument panel and lower glove compartment to floor.
6. Remove righthand A/C duct and remove passenger's air bag mounting bolts from instrument panel steel reinforcement.
7. Disconnect electrical connector at lower lefthand corner of passenger's air bag module and remove connector from instrument panel reinforcement.
8. Install second Rotunda air bag simulator tool No. 105-00012, or equivalent, on passenger's air bag harness on vehicle side of harness
9. Connect battery ground cable.

PROBE

1. Disconnect battery ground cable. Allow at least one minute for back-up power supply to deplete.
2. Remove four nut and washer assemblies mounting driver's air bag module to steering wheel.
3. Disconnect driver's air bag module connector.
4. Connect Rotunda tool No. 105-00009, or equivalent, to vehicle air bag wiring harness at top steering column.
5. Disconnect two passenger's air bag diagnostic module connectors under lefthand instrument panel pad.
6. Open glove compartment door, then press in sides to disengage retainers and lower glove compartment from instrument panel, then remove screws and glove compartment.
7. Remove screws from glove compartment upper cover.
8. Remove upper cover and disconnect passenger's air bag module electrical connectors.
9. Remove passenger's air bag module bolts, then the module by pressing outward from inside instrument panel. **Do not pull on wiring during removal or handling of air bag module. Place module on a bench with trim cover facing upward to avoid injury by accidental deployment.**
10. Connect second Rotunda tool No. 105-00009, or equivalent, to passenger's air bag harness.
11. Connect battery ground cable.

SABLE & TAURUS

Prior to disconnecting battery, record USER 1 and USER 2 preset radio frequencies.

1997-98

1. Disconnect battery ground cable.
2. Allow at least one minute for back-up power supply to deplete.
3. Remove two air bag mounting screw covers from rear of steering wheel.
4. Remove two screw and washer assemblies mounting driver's air bag module to steering wheel.
5. Attach Rotunda tool No. 105-00010, or equivalent, to air bag terminals on clockspring assembly to simulate air bag.
6. Unsnap passenger's air bag trim cover tabs.
7. Open glove compartment and press side inward and lower glove compartment to floor.
8. Working through glove compartment opening, remove two air bag module mounting screws.
9. Disconnect two air bag module electrical connectors.
10. Remove air bag module.
11. Connect Rotunda air bag simulator tool No. 105-00010, or equivalent, to wiring harness in place of passenger's air bag module. Connect tool to wiring harness having LB/O and PK/BK wire.
12. Connect battery ground cable.

1999

1. Disconnect and isolate battery ground cable.
2. Allow at least one minute for back-up power supply to deplete.
3. Remove two air bag mounting screw covers from sides of steering wheel.
4. Remove two screw and washer assemblies mounting driver's air bag module to steering wheel.
5. Disconnect air bag module electrical connector. **When carrying a live air bag module, ensure bag and trim cover are pointed away from your body. To prevent injury by accidental deployment, place module on a bench with trim cover facing upward.**
6. Attach Rotunda air bag simulator tool No. 105-00012, or equivalent, to air bag terminals on clockspring assembly to simulate air bag.
7. Unsnap passenger's air bag trim cover tabs.
8. Open glove compartment and press sides inward, then lower glove compartment to floor.
9. Working through glove compartment opening, remove two passenger's air bag module mounting screws.
10. Disconnect two air bag module electrical connectors.
11. Remove passenger's air bag module. **When carrying a live air bag module, ensure bag and trim cover are pointed away from your body. To prevent injury by accidental deployment, place module on a bench with trim cover facing upward.**
12. Connect Rotunda air bag simulator tool No. 105-00012, or equivalent, to wiring harness in place of passenger's air bag module.
13. Connect battery ground cable.

THUNDERBIRD

Prior to disconnecting battery, record USER 1 and USER 2 preset radio frequencies.

1. Disconnect battery ground cable. Allow at least one minute for back-up power supply to deplete.
2. Remove two bolt cover plugs, then the two bolt and washer assemblies mounting driver's air bag assembly to steering wheel.
3. Disconnect driver's air bag connector and remove air bag from steering wheel. **To prevent injury by accidental deployment, place module on a**

bench with trim cover facing upward.

4. Connect Rotunda tool No. 105-00010, or equivalent, to vehicle air bag wiring harness at top steering column.
5. Using a small screwdriver, detach dampening rod from righthand side of glove compartment.
6. Pull lefthand side of glove compartment inward and allow glove compartment to drop downward.
7. Remove mounting screws and air duct.
8. Remove two vertically positioned bolts from each side of air bag module.
9. Remove two remaining air bag module mounting bolts.
10. Push air bag module outward from instrument panel. **Do not handle air bag module by deployment doors.**
11. Disconnect electrical connector and remove air bag module. Place module on a bench with trim cover facing upward.
12. Connect Rotunda tool No. 105-00010, or equivalent, to vehicle air bag wiring harness in place of passenger's air bag module.
13. Connect battery ground cable.

TOWN CAR

Prior to disconnecting battery, record USER 1 and USER 2 preset radio frequencies.

1997-98

1. Disconnect battery ground cable and allow at least one minute for back-up power supply to deplete.
2. Remove air bag mounting screw covers from rear of steering wheel, then the two air bag module mounting screws.
3. Disconnect driver's air bag module connector.
4. Connect Rotunda tool No. 105-00010, or equivalent, to vehicle air bag wiring harness at top steering column.
5. Remove instrument panel moldings, instrument panel finish panel mounting screws, then the panel.
6. Open glove compartment and press side inward, then lower glove compartment to floor.
7. Working through glove compartment opening, remove two lower air bag module mounting bolts.
8. Remove two remaining air bag module mounting screws and disconnect air bag module electrical connector.
9. Connect second Rotunda air bag simulator tool No. 105-00010, or equivalent, to wiring harness in place of passenger's air bag module.
10. Connect battery ground cable.

1999-2000

1. Disconnect and isolate battery ground cable, then allow at least one minute for back-up power supply to deplete.
2. Remove two air bag module mounting screws.
3. Disconnect driver's air bag module and horn switch connectors. **When carrying a live air bag module, ensure bag and trim cover are pointed away from your body. To prevent injury by accidental deployment, place module on a bench with trim cover facing upward.**
4. Connect Rotunda air bag simulator tool No. 105-00012, or equivalent, to vehicle air bag wiring harness at top steering column.
5. Open glove compartment and disconnect glove compartment isolator.
6. Push in on glove compartment door tabs and position downward.
7. Disconnect passenger's air bag module electrical connector.
8. Connect second Rotunda air bag simulator tool No. 105-00012, or equivalent, to wiring harness in place of passenger's air bag module.
9. Disconnect side air bag module electrical connector located beneath driver's seat.
10. Attach Rotunda air bag simulator tool No. 105-00012, or equivalent, to side air bag connector under driver's seat on vehicle wiring harness side
11. Disconnect side air bag module electrical connector located beneath passenger's seat.
12. Attach Rotunda air bag simulator tool No. 105-00012, or equivalent, to side air bag connector under passenger's seat on vehicle wiring harness side
13. Connect battery ground cable.

ARMING

ASPIRE

1. Disconnect battery ground cable. Allow one minute for back-up power supply to deplete.
2. Remove air bag simulator from harness on top of steering column.
3. Connect air bag electrical connector to slip ring/clockspring connector.
4. Position driver's air bag on steering wheel and secure with four nut and bolt assemblies. Tighten nut and bolt assemblies to specifications.
5. Remove air bag simulator from passenger's air bag harness.
6. Connect air bag module electrical connector.
7. Position air bag module to instrument panel.
8. Install four air bag module mounting bolts. Tighten air bag module bolts to specifications.
9. Install glove compartment.
10. Connect battery ground cable.
11. Place ignition switch in Run position and note air bag warning lamp operation. Indicator lamp should illuminate for approximately six seconds, then turn off. **If warning lamp does not illuminate or remains illuminated continuously or flashes, refer to MOTOR's "Air Bag Manual."**

CONTINENTAL

1997-98

1. Disconnect battery ground cable. Allow at least one minute for back-up power supply to deplete.
2. Remove air bag simulator from clockspring connector at top of steering column.
3. Connect driver's air bag electrical connector.
4. Install driver's air bag module to steering wheel.
5. Tighten air bag module mounting bolts to specifications and install bolt covers.
6. Remove air bag simulator at passenger's air bag connector.
7. Position passenger's air bag module to instrument panel.
8. Through glove compartment opening, install three passenger's air bag module lower mounting bracket to instrument panel bolts. Install two forward bolts, then the center bolt. Tighten mounting bolts to specifications.
9. Connect passenger's air bag electrical connector and close glove compartment.
10. Connect battery ground cable.
11. Place ignition switch in Run position and note air bag warning lamp operation. Indicator lamp should illuminate for approximately six seconds, then turn off. **If warning lamp does not illuminate or remains illuminated continuously or flashes, refer to MOTOR's "Air Bag Manual."**

1999-2000

1. Disconnect battery ground cable. Allow at least one minute for back-up power supply to deplete.
2. Remove air bag simulator from harness connector at top of steering column.
3. Connect driver's air bag module and horn to clockspring electrical connectors.
4. Position driver's air bag module to steering wheel.
5. Install two driver's air bag module to steering wheel mounting bolts. Tighten mounting bolts to specifications.
6. Install two steering wheel spoke bolt covers, if equipped.
7. Remove air bag simulator at passenger's air bag connector.
8. Connect passenger's air bag electrical connector and close glove compartment.
9. Remove air bag simulator from side air bag connector located beneath driver's seat and connect side air bag electrical connector.
10. Remove air bag simulator from side air bag connector located beneath passenger's seat and connect side air bag electrical connector.
11. Connect battery ground cable.
12. Place ignition switch in Run position **from a safe location at side or below air bag modules** and note air bag warning lamp operation. Indicator lamp should light for approximately six seconds, then turn off. **If warning lamp does not light, remains illuminated continuously or flashes, refer to MOTOR's "Air Bag Manual."**

CONTOUR & MYSTIQUE

1997-98

1. Disconnect battery ground cable, then the positive cable. Allow at least one minute for back-up power supply to deplete.
2. Remove air bag simulator tool from driver's air bag sliding contact connector.
3. Connect driver's air bag connector and install air bag module to steering wheel. Tighten mounting bolts to specifications.
4. Remove air bag simulator tool from passenger's air bag wiring harness and position air bag module in instrument panel.
5. Install mounting bolts and nuts. Tighten mounting bolts and nuts to specifications.
6. Install A/C evaporator register duct and glove compartment upper cover, then connect glove compartment lamp and install screws.
7. Install glove compartment assembly in instrument panel.
8. Connect battery positive cable, then the ground cable.
9. Place ignition switch in Run position and note air bag warning lamp operation. Indicator lamp should illuminate for approximately six seconds, then turn off. **If warning lamp does not illuminate or remains illuminated continuously or flashes, refer to MOTOR's "Air Bag Manual."**

1999-2000

1. Disconnect and isolate battery ground cable.
2. Allow at least one minute for back-up power supply to deplete.
3. Remove air bag simulator tool from driver's air bag sliding contact connector.
4. Connect driver's air bag module electrical connector.
5. Position driver's air bag module to steering wheel.
6. Install two air bag module bolt and washer assemblies at rear or sides of steering wheel. Tighten mounting bolts to specifications.
7. Remove air bag simulator tool from passenger's air bag wiring harness.
8. Connect passenger's air bag module electrical connector.
9. Install passenger's air vent duct and glove compartment upper cover, then connect glove compartment lamp and install screws.
10. Install glove compartment assembly in instrument panel.
11. Connect battery ground cable.
12. Place ignition switch in Run position **from a safe location at sides or below air bag modules** and note air bag warning lamp operation. Indicator lamp should light for approximately six seconds, then turn off. **If warning lamp does not light or remains illuminated continuously or flashes, refer to MOTOR's "Air Bag Manual."**

COUGAR

1997

1. Disconnect battery ground cable. Allow at least one minute for back-up power supply to deplete.
2. Disconnect air bag simulator and connect driver's air bag connector to air bag module.
3. Position driver's air bag module to steering wheel and install mounting bolts and washers. Tighten mounting bolts to specifications.
4. Disconnect from passenger's air bag simulator and connect electrical connector to passenger's's air bag module.
5. Install passenger's air bag module. Connect battery ground cable.
6. Place ignition switch in Run position and note air bag warning lamp operation. Indicator lamp should illuminate for approximately six seconds, then turn off. **If warning lamp does not illuminate or remains illuminated continuously or flashes, refer to MOTOR's "Air Bag Manual."**

1999-2000

1. Disconnect and isolate battery ground cable.
2. Allow at least one minute for back-up power supply to deplete.
3. Remove air bag simulator tool from driver's air bag sliding contact connector.
4. Connect driver's air bag module electrical connector.
5. Position driver's air bag module to steering wheel.
6. Install driver's air bag module Torx mounting screws. Tighten mounting screws to specifications.
7. Remove air bag simulator tool from passenger's air bag wiring harness.
8. From passenger's foot well, roll passenger's air bag module around cross beam.
9. After positioning air bag module, install two air bag module to cross beam mounting bolts, Tighten mounting bolts to specifications.
10. Connect passenger's air bag module electrical connector.
11. Install passenger's air register duct.
12. Install glove compartment finish panel and secure with four Torx mounting screws.
13. Depress side stops to attach glove compartment sides and close glove compartment.
14. Install three glove compartment Torx mounting screws.
15. **On models with side air bags,** proceed as follows:
    a. At driver's and passenger's seats, install side air bag module. Tighten mounting nuts to specifications.
    b. Connect side air bag module electrical connector at driver's and passenger's seats.
    c. Install seat pads, covers and back rests.
16. **On all models,** connect battery ground cable.
17. Place ignition switch in Run position **from a safe location at sides or below air bag modules** and note air bag warning lamp operation. Indicator lamp should light for approximately three seconds, then turn off. **If warning lamp does not light or remains illuminated continuously or flashes, refer to MOTOR's "Air Bag Manual."**

CROWN VICTORIA & GRAND MARQUIS

1997-98

1. Disconnect battery ground cable and wait one minute for back-up power supply to deplete.
2. Remove air bag simulator from harness on top of steering column.
3. Connect driver's air bag connector.
4. Position driver's air bag on steering wheel and secure with four nut and washer assemblies. Tighten air bag module mounting nuts to specifications.
5. Remove air bag simulator from harness connector.
6. Connect electrical connector to air bag module and position air bag module in instrument panel.
7. Install two upper and two lower air bag module mounting screws. Tighten mounting screws to specifications and snap instrument panel upper molding into place.
8. Connect battery ground cable.
9. Place ignition switch in Run position and note air bag warning lamp operation. Indicator lamp should illuminate for approximately six seconds, then turn off. **If warning lamp does not illuminate or remains illuminated continuously or flashes, refer to MOTOR's "Air Bag Manual."**

1999-2000

1. Disconnect and isolate battery ground cable, then wait one minute for back-up power supply to deplete.
2. Remove air bag simulator from harness on top of steering column.
3. Connect driver's air bag and horn electrical connectors.
4. Position driver's air bag on steering wheel and secure with two mounting bolts. Tighten air bag module mounting screws to specifications.
5. Remove air bag simulator from passenger side air bag harness connector.
6. Position air bag module in instrument panel.
7. Install two passengers air bag module mounting screws. Tighten mounting screws to specifications.
8. Install two passengers air bag module mounting bolts. Tighten mounting bolts to specifications.
9. Connect passenger's air bag module electrical connector.
10. Connect clock electrical connector and position trim panel to instrument panel. Attach trim panel by pulling inward to seat clips.
11. Push inward on glove compartment door tabs then position door upward.

12. Install glove compartment locator.
13. Connect battery ground cable.
14. Place ignition switch in Run position **from a safe location at sides of or below air bag modules** and note air bag warning lamp operation. Indicator lamp should light for approximately six seconds, then turn off. **If warning lamp does not light or remains lit continuously or flashes, refer to MOTOR's "Air Bag Manual."**
15. Reset radio stations and clock.

ESCORT, TRACER & ZX2

1. Disconnect battery ground cable and allow at least one minute for back-up power supply to be depleted.
2. Disconnect air bag simulator tool from driver's air bag harness connector.
3. Position module in steering wheel and connect horn and air bag sliding contact connectors.
4. Install air bag module bolts and tighten to specifications.
5. Disconnect air bag simulator tool from passenger's air bag module harness connector.
6. Position air bag module in instrument panel and connect electrical connector.
7. Install four air bag module bolts and tighten to specifications.
8. Install glove compartment door.
9. Place ignition switch in On position while observing air bag indicator lamp. Lamp should remain lit for approximately six seconds, then go out.
10. If lamp fails to light, remains lit continuously or flashes, a malfunction is indicated; proceed to **MOTOR's "Air Bag Manual."Flashing may not occur until approximately 45 seconds after ignition switch activation.**
11. If air bag indicator is inoperative, five sets of five beeps will sound to indicate a system malfunction. Indicator must be repaired prior to further diagnosis.

LS

1. Disconnect battery ground cable.
2. Wait at least one minute for backup power supply in Restraints Control Module (RCM) to deplete its stored energy.
3. Remove pretensioner simulators from harness at safety belt pretensioners and restore pretensioner connections.
4. Remove driver/passenger air bag simulator from air bag sliding contact connector.
5. Install driver's air bag module.
6. Remove driver/passenger air bag simulator from passenger's air bag connector.
7. Connect passenger air bag electrical connector.
8. Install glove compartment.
9. Connect battery ground cable.
10. Turn ignition switch from to RUN position and visually monitor air bag indicator.
11. Place ignition switch in Run position **from a safe location at sides of or below air bag modules** and note air bag warning lamp operation. Indicator lamp should light for approximately six seconds, then turn off. **If warning lamp does not light or remains lit continuously or flashes, refer to MOTOR's "Air Bag Manual."**

MARK VIII

1. Disconnect battery ground cable.
2. Allow at least one minute for back-up power supply to deplete.
3. Remove air bag simulator from clockspring connector at top of steering column.
4. Connect driver's air bag electrical connector.
5. Position driver's air bag on steering wheel and secure with two screw and washer assemblies. Tighten mounting screws to specifications.
6. Remove air bag simulator from passenger harness connector.
7. Connect electrical connector to air bag module and position air bag module in instrument panel.
8. Install three upper mounting screws. Tighten mounting screws to specifications.
9. Install lower module mounting screws. Tighten mounting screws to specifications.
10. Install side defroster duct screws.
11. Reverse removal procedure to install glove compartment, instrument trim covers and steering column covers.
12. Connect battery ground cable.
13. Place ignition switch in Run position and note air bag warning lamp operation. Indicator lamp should illuminate for approximately six seconds, then turn off. **If warning lamp does not illuminate or remains illuminated continuously or flashes, refer to MOTOR's "Air Bag Manual."**

MUSTANG

1997-98

1. Disconnect battery ground cable and allow at least one minute for back-up power supply to deplete.
2. Remove air bag simulator tool from harness connector at top of steering column.
3. Connect driver's air bag connector.
4. Position driver's air bag on steering wheel and secure with four nut and bolt assemblies. Tighten mounting nut and bolt assemblies to specifications.
5. Remove air bag simulator tool from passenger's air bag module harness, then position module in instrument panel.
6. Attach connector to instrument panel reinforcement and connect to wiring harness.
7. Install passenger's air bag mounting bolts. Tighten mounting bolts to specifications.
8. Press gently upon air bag module corners to engage with instrument panel trim and install righthand side A/C duct.
9. Press sides of glove compartment assembly together and lift into position in instrument panel. Close glove compartment door.
10. Connect battery ground cable.
11. Place ignition switch in Run position and note air bag warning lamp operation. Indicator lamp should illuminate for approximately six seconds, then turn off.
12. If warning lamp does not illuminate, remains illuminated continuously or flashes, refer to **MOTOR's "Air Bag Manual."**

1999-2000

1. Disconnect and isolate battery ground cable.
2. Allow at least one minute for back-up power supply to deplete.
3. Remove air bag simulator tool from harness connector at top of steering column.
4. Connect driver's air bag electrical connector.
5. Position driver's air bag on steering wheel and secure with its bolts. Tighten mounting bolts to specifications.
6. Remove air bag simulator tool from passenger's air bag module harness and position module in instrument panel.
7. Attach connector to instrument panel reinforcement and connect to wiring harness.
8. Install righthand side A/C duct.
9. Press sides of glove compartment assembly together and lift into position in instrument panel. Close glove compartment door.
10. Connect battery ground cable.
11. Place ignition switch in Run position **from a safe location at side or below air bag modules** and note air bag warning lamp operation. Indicator lamp should light for approximately six seconds, then turn off. **If warning lamp does not light or remains lit continuously or flashes, refer to MOTOR's "Air Bag Manual."**
12. Reset radio stations and clock.

PROBE

1. Disconnect battery ground cable. Allow one minute for back-up power supply to deplete.
2. Remove air bag simulator from harness on top of steering column.
3. Connect driver's air bag connector.
4. Position driver's air bag on steering wheel and secure with four nut and bolt assemblies. Tighten mounting nut and bolt assemblies to specifications.
5. Disconnect passenger's air bag simulator from passenger's air bag harness.
6. Insert air bag module into instrument panel, aligning guide pins with guide holes and engage module tab with instrument panel clip. **Ensure wiring in not pinched between air bag module and instrument panel.**
7. Install air bag module bolts. Tighten mounting bolts to specifications. Connect air bag module electrical connectors securely.
8. Insert connector pin into hole on rear of air bag module.
9. Install glove compartment upper cover, then the glove compartment.
10. Connect two diagnostic module connectors.

11. Connect battery ground cable.
12. Place ignition switch in Run position and note air bag warning lamp operation. Indicator lamp should illuminate for approximately six seconds, then turn off. **If warning lamp does not illuminate or remains illuminated continuously or flashes, refer to MOTOR's "Air Bag Manual."**

SABLE & TAURUS

1997-98

1. Disconnect battery ground cable.
2. Wait one minute for back-up power supply to deplete.
3. Remove air bag simulator from clockspring connector.
4. Position driver's air bag on steering wheel and secure with screw and washer assemblies. Tighten mounting screws to specifications.
5. Remove air bag simulator from air bag module wiring harness connector.
6. Connect electrical connectors to air bag module in instrument panel.
7. Install air bag module mounting bolts. Tighten mounting screws to specifications.
8. Return glove compartment to correct position.
9. Connect battery ground cable.
10. Install air bag module trim cover.
11. Place ignition switch in Run position and note air bag warning lamp operation. Indicator lamp should illuminate for approximately six seconds, then turn off. **If warning lamp does not illuminate or remains illuminated continuously or flashes, refer to MOTOR's "Air Bag Manual."**

1999

1. Disconnect and isolate battery ground cable.
2. Wait one minute for back-up power supply to deplete.
3. Remove air bag simulator from clockspring connector.
4. Connect driver's air bag module electrical connector.
5. Position driver's air bag on steering wheel and secure with screw and washer assemblies. Tighten mounting screws to specifications.
6. Remove air bag simulator from air bag module wiring harness connector.
7. Connect electrical connectors to air bag module and position air bag module in instrument panel.
8. Install air bag module mounting bolts. Tighten mounting bolts to specifications.
9. Return glove compartment to normal position.
10. Install air bag module trim cover.
11. Connect battery ground cable.
12. Place ignition switch in Run position **from a safe location at side or below air bag modules** and note air bag warning lamp operation. Indicator lamp should light for approximately six seconds, then turn off. **If warning lamp does not light or remains lit continuously or flashes, refer to MOTOR's "Air Bag Manual."**
13. Reset radio stations and clock.

THUNDERBIRD

1. Disconnect battery ground cable. Allow at least one minute for back-up power supply to deplete.
2. Disconnect air bag simulator and connect driver's air bag connector to air bag module.
3. Position driver's air bag module to steering wheel and install mounting bolts and washers. Tighten mounting bolts to specifications.
4. Disconnect from passenger's air bag simulator and connect electrical connector to passenger's's air bag module.
5. Install passenger's air bag module. Connect battery ground cable.
6. Place ignition switch in Run position and note air bag warning lamp operation. Indicator lamp should illuminate for approximately six seconds, then turn off. **If warning lamp does not illuminate or remains illuminated continuously or flashes, refer to MOTOR's "Air Bag Manual."**

TOWN CAR

1997-98

1. Disconnect battery ground cable and wait one minute for back-up power supply to deplete.
2. Remove air bag simulator tool from harness connector at top of steering column.
3. Connect air bag connector.
4. Position driver's air bag on steering wheel and secure with two mounting screws. Tighten mounting screws to specifications. Install two mounting screw covers to rear of steering wheel.
5. Remove air bag simulator from passenger's harness connector.
6. Connect electrical connector to air bag module in instrument panel.
7. Install upper mounting screws and tighten to specifications.
8. Install two lower module mounting bolts. Tighten mounting bolts to specifications.
9. Return glove compartment to correct position and install instrument panel moldings.
10. Connect battery ground cable.
11. Place ignition switch in Run position and note air bag warning lamp operation. Indicator lamp should illuminate for approximately six seconds, then turn off. **If warning lamp does not illuminate or remains illuminated continuously or flashes, refer to MOTOR's "Air Bag Manual."**

1999-2000

1. Disconnect and isolate battery ground cable, then wait one minute for back-up power supply to deplete.
2. Remove air bag simulator tool from harness connector at top of steering column.
3. Connect air bag module electrical connector.
4. Position driver's air bag module on steering wheel and secure with two mounting screws. Tighten mounting screws to specifications.
5. Remove air bag simulator from passenger's harness connector.
6. Install two module mounting bolts. Tighten mounting bolts to specifications.
7. Connect electrical connector to air bag module in instrument panel.
8. Return glove compartment to proper position.
9. Remove air bag simulator from side air bag connector located beneath driver's seat and connect side air bag electrical connector.
10. Remove air bag simulator from side air bag connector located beneath passenger's seat and connect side air bag electrical connector.
11. Connect battery ground cable.
12. Place ignition switch in Run position **from a safe location at side or below air bag modules** and note air bag warning lamp operation. Indicator lamp should light for approximately six seconds, then turn off. **If warning lamp does not light or remains lit continuously or flashes, refer MOTOR's "Air Bag Manual."**
13. Reset radio stations and clock.

GENERAL MOTORS

On Buick, Cadillac, Chevrolet, Oldsmobile, Pontiac, Metro & Prizm models, the diagnostic energy reserve module or sensing and diagnostic module (DERM/SDM) can maintain enough voltage to cause air bag deployment for up to ten minutes after the ignition switch is turned off and the battery is disconnected. Servicing the SIR system during this period may result in accidental deployment and personal injury.

DISARMING

ACHIEVA, SKYLARK & 1997-98 GRAND AM

1. Ensure wheels are straight ahead.
2. Turn ignition switch to LOCK position and remove key from ignition switch.
3. Remove air bag fuse from fuse block.
4. Remove right and left lower instrument panel sound insulators.
5. Disconnect CPA and yellow connector at base of steering column.
6. Disconnect CPA and yellow connector located under righthand instrument panel.

ALERO, CUTLASS, MALIBU & 1999-2000 GRAND AM

1. Ensure wheels are straight ahead.
2. Turn ignition switch to Off position and remove key from ignition switch.
3. Remove AIR BAG fuse from lefthand instrument panel wiring harness junction block.
4. Remove CPA from driver yellow connector located above lefthand instrument panel wiring harness junction block.
5. Disconnect driver yellow connector located above lefthand instrument panel wiring harness junction block.
6. Remove CPA from passenger yellow

connector located above righthand instrument panel wiring harness junction block.
7. Disconnect passenger yellow connector located above righthand instrument panel wiring harness junction block.

AURORA & RIVIERA

1. Ensure front wheels are pointed straight ahead.
2. Turn ignition switch to LOCK position and remove AIR BAG fuse.
3. Remove left sound insulator. **If necessary, remove courtesy lamp from sound insulator.**
4. Disconnect Connector Position Assurance (CPA), then both yellow 2-way SIR electrical connectors at base of steering column.
5. Remove righthand sound insulator and disconnect CPA and yellow 2-way connector from passenger's inflator pigtail.
6. Wait at least 2 minutes before proceeding with diagnosis or service.

BONNEVILLE, LESABRE, LSS, PARK AVENUE, EIGHTY EIGHT, NINETY EIGHT & REGENCY

1. Ensure front wheels are pointed straight ahead.
2. Turn ignition switch to LOCK position and remove SIR or AIR BAG fuse.
3. Remove left sound insulator. **If necessary, remove courtesy lamp from sound insulator.**
4. Disconnect Connector Position Assurance (CPA) and yellow 2-way connector at base of steering column.
5. Remove righthand sound insulator and disconnect CPA and yellow 2-way connector from passenger's inflator pigtail.
6. Wait at least 2 minutes before proceeding with diagnosis or service.

CAMARO & FIREBIRD

1. Ensure front wheels are pointed straight ahead.
2. Turn ignition switch to LOCK position and remove SIR or AIR BAG fuse.
3. Remove left sound insulator. **If necessary, remove courtesy lamp from sound insulator.**
4. Disconnect Connector Position Assurance (CPA) and yellow 2-way connector at base of steering column.
5. **On 1997 models,** remove glove compartment door assembly, then CPA and yellow 2-way connector from passenger's inflator module.
6. **On 1998–2000 models,** remove right instrument panel insulator.
7. Wait at least 2 minutes before proceeding with diagnosis or service.

CATERA

1. Turn steering wheel to straight forward position and remove ignition key.
2. Wait one minute for SIR reserve energy to discharge.
3. Disconnect battery ground cable.
4. Remove center console, then disconnect sensing and diagnostic module.

CAVALIER & SUNFIRE

1. Ensure front wheels are pointed straight ahead.
2. Turn ignition switch to LOCK position and remove key.
3. Remove "AIR BAG" fuse from instrument panel fuse block, then remove lefthand lower trim panel.
4. Remove Connector Position Assurance (CPA), then disconnect both yellow 2-way SIR electrical connectors at base of steering column.
5. Wait at least 2 minutes before proceeding with diagnosis or service.

GRAND PRIX, INTRIGUE & REGAL

1. Ensure front wheels are pointed straight ahead.
2. Turn ignition switch to LOCK position and remove SIR or AIR BAG fuse.
3. Remove left sound insulator. **If necessary, remove courtesy lamp from sound insulator.**
4. Disconnect Connector Position Assurance (CPA) and yellow 2-way connector at base of steering column.
5. Remove CPA and disconnect 2–way connector at right of steering column.
6. **On all models,** wait at least 2 minutes before proceeding with diagnosis or service.

CORVETTE

1. Ensure front wheels are pointed straight ahead.
2. Turn ignition switch to LOCK position.
3. Remove front floor kick panel, then AIR BAG fuse from instrument panel fuse block, then remove trim panel from under steering column.
4. Remove Connector Position Assurance (CPA), then disconnect both yellow 2-way SIR electrical connectors at base of steering column.
5. Wait at least 2 minutes before proceeding with diagnosis or service.

DEVILLE, ELDORADO & SEVILLE

1. Ensure front wheels are pointed straight-ahead.
2. Turn ignition switch to Lock position, then remove key from switch.
3. **On 1997–98 models,** remove SIR fuse from trunk compartment.
4. **On 1999–2000 models,** remove rear seat to access fuse block, then remove SIR fuse.
5. **On all models,** remove lefthand sound insulator.
6. Disconnect CPA and yellow two-way SIR electrical connector at base of steering column.
7. Remove glove compartment.
8. Disconnect CPA and yellow two-way connector from passenger's inflator pigtail.
9. Remove right and lefthand front door panels.
10. Disconnect right and left CPA and yellow two-way connectors located near inflatable restraint side impact sensing module.

IMPALA, LUMINA, MONTE CARLO & 1997 CUTLASS SUPREME

1. Ensure front wheels are pointed straight ahead.
2. Turn ignition switch to LOCK position and remove key.
3. Remove AIR BAG fuse from instrument panel fuse block.
4. Remove trim panel from under steering column.
5. Disconnect Connector Position Assurance (CPA) and yellow 2-way connector at base of steering column.
6. Open glove compartment door and disconnect passenger side Connector Position Assurance (CPA) and yellow 2-way connector.
7. Wait at least 2 minutes before proceeding with diagnosis or service.

METRO

1. Ensure front wheels are pointed straight ahead.
2. Turn ignition switch to LOCK position.
3. Remove AIR BAG fuse from air bag fuse block.
4. Remove steering wheel side cover.
5. Remove Connector Position Assurance (CPA) and disconnect yellow connector for driver's inflator module.
6. Pull glove compartment out, while pushing inward on right and lefthand stoppers.
7. Remove Connector Position Assurance (CPA) and disconnect connector for passenger's inflator module.
8. Wait at least 10 minutes before proceeding with diagnosis or service.

PRIZM

1. Ensure front wheels are pointed straight ahead.
2. Turn ignition switch to LOCK position.
3. Remove CIG and IGN fuses from junction block.
4. Remove Connector Position Assurance (CPA) and disconnect yellow connector at base of steering column.
5. Open glove box door and gently pry off passenger's inflator module connector retainer.
6. Remove Connector Position Assurance (CPA) and disconnect yellow connector from passenger's inflator module.
7. Wait at least 10 minutes before proceeding with diagnosis or service.

ARMING

ACHIEVA, SKYLARK & 1997–98 GRAND AM

1. Remove key from ignition switch.
2. Connect CPA and yellow connector at base of steering column.
3. Connect CPA and yellow connector located under righthand instrument panel.
4. Install right and left sound insulators.
5. Install air bag fuse.
6. Turn ignition switch to RUN position and ensure air bag warning indicator flashes seven times, then turns off. If lamp operation is not as specified, refer to **MOTOR's "Air Bag Manual."**

ALERO, CUTLASS, MALIBU & 1999–2000 GRAND AM

1. Remove key from ignition switch.
2. Connect passenger yellow connector located above righthand instrument panel wiring harness junction block.
3. Install CPA to passenger yellow connector located above righthand instrument panel wiring harness junction block.
4. Connect driver yellow connector located above lefthand instrument panel wiring harness junction block.
5. Install CPA to driver yellow connector located above lefthand instrument panel wiring harness junction block.
6. Install AIR BAG fuse to lefthand instrument panel wiring harness junction block.
7. Turn ignition switch to RUN position and ensure air bag warning indicator flashes seven times, then turns off. If lamp operation is not as specified, refer to **MOTOR's "Air Bag Manual."**

AURORA & RIVIERA

1. Connect yellow 2-way connector to passenger's inflator pigtail, then install Connector Position Assurance (CPA).
2. Connect yellow 2-way SIR electrical connector at base of steering column, then install Connector Position Assurance (CPA).
3. Install lefthand sound insulator. **If necessary, install courtesy lamp to sound insulator.**
4. Install SIR fuse into fuse block, then turn ignition switch to the LOCK position and ensure "Inflatable Restraint" lamp flashes seven to nine times, then turns off. If lamp does not operate as specified, refer to MOTOR's "Air Bag Manual."

BONNEVILLE, LESABRE, LSS, PARK AVENUE, EIGHTY EIGHT, NINETY EIGHT & REGENCY

1. Connect yellow connector to passenger's inflator pigtail, then install Connector Position Assurance (CPA) and righthand sound insulator.
2. Connect yellow SIR electrical connector, then install Connector Position Assurance (CPA).
3. Install lefthand sound insulator. **If necessary, install courtesy lamp to sound insulator.**
4. Install SIR fuse, then turn ignition key to the RUN position and ensure the "Inflatable Restraint" lamp flashes seven to nine times and then turns off. If lamp does not operate as specified, refer to **MOTOR's "Air Bag Manual."**

CAMARO & FIREBIRD

1. Turn ignition key to the LOCK position and remove key.
2. Connect yellow 2-way connector to passenger's inflator module, then install Connector Position Assurance (CPA) and glove compartment door assembly.
3. Connect yellow 2-way SIR electrical connector, then install Connector Position Assurance (CPA) near base of steering column.
4. Install lefthand sound insulator. **If necessary, install courtesy lamp to sound insulator.**
5. Install SIR fuse, then turn ignition key to the RUN position and ensure the "Inflatable Restraint" lamp flashes seven to nine times and then turns off. If lamp does not operate as specified, refer to MOTOR's "Air Bag Manual."

CATERA

1. Connect sensing and diagnostic module, then install center console.
2. Connect battery ground cable.
3. Wait one minute for SIR system to charge.
4. Stay away from inflator modules and turn key to RUN. Verify that air bag warning lamp turns on for 3–4 seconds and then turns off.
5. If SIR system does not operate described , refer to **MOTOR's "Air Bag Manual."**

CAVALIER & SUNFIRE

1. With ignition in the LOCK position and key removed, connect both yellow SIR connectors at base of steering column.
2. Install Connector Position Assurance (CPA), then the lefthand lower trim panel.
3. Install "AIR BG 1" fuse into fuse block.
4. Turn ignition switch to the RUN position and ensure " AIR BAG" warning lamp flashes seven times, then turns off. If lamp does not operate as specified, refer to **MOTOR's "Air Bag Manual."**

GRAND PRIX, INTRIGUE & REGAL

1. Place ignition switch in LOCK position and remove key.
2. Connect yellow 2-way SIR electrical connector, then install Connector Position Assurance (CPA).
3. **On models equipped with passenger air bag,** connect passenger 2–way electrical connector, then install CPA.
4. **On all models,** install lefthand sound insulator. **If necessary, install courtesy lamp to sound insulator.**
5. Install SIR or AIR BAG fuse into fuse block.
6. Turn ignition switch to the RUN position and ensure AIR BAG lamp flashes seven times and then turns off. If lamp does not operate as specified, refer to **MOTOR's "Air Bag Manual."**

CORVETTE

1. Turn ignition to the LOCK position.
2. Connect both yellow SIR connectors, then install Connector Position Assurance (CPA).
3. Install trim panel under steering column.
4. Install AIR BAG fuse into instrument panel fuse block.
5. Turn ignition switch to the RUN position and ensure " AIR BAG" warning lamp flashes seven times, then turns off. If lamp does not operate as specified, refer to **MOTOR's "Air Bag Manual."**

IMPALA, LUMINA, MONTE CARLO & 1997 CUTLASS SUPREME

1. Turn ignition key to the LOCK position and remove key.
2. Open glove compartment door and connect yellow 2-way connector and Connector Position Assurance (CPA).
3. Connect yellow 2-way connector at base of steering column, then install Connector Position Assurance (CPA).
4. Install trim panel under steering column.
5. Install AIR BAG fuse into instrument panel fuse block.
6. Turn ignition key to the RUN position and verify that the AIR BAG/ INFLATABLE RESTRAINT warning lamp flashes seven times and then turns off. If lamp does not operate as specified, refer to **MOTOR's "Air Bag Manual."**

CUTLASS & MALIBU

1. Remove key from ignition switch.
2. Connect passenger 2–way connector, then install CPA.
3. Connect driver 2–way connector, then install CPA.
4. Install air bag fuse.
5. Turn ignition switch to RUN position. Ensure air bag warning lamp flashes seven times, then turns off. If lamp operation is not as specified, refer to **MOTOR's "Air Bag Manual."**

DEVILLE, ELDORADO & SEVILLE

1. Connect side impact yellow two-way connectors and install both front door panels.
2. Connect yellow two-way connector to passenger's inflator pigtail and install CPA.
3. Install glove compartment.
4. Connect yellow two-way SIR electrical connector at base of steering column and install CPA.
5. Install lefthand sound insulator. **If necessary, install courtesy lamp to sound insulator.**
6. Install SIR fuse into fuse block and turn ignition switch to Lock position.
7. Ensure SIR lamp flashes 7 times and turns off. If lamp does not operate as specified, refer to **MOTOR's "Air Bag Manual."**

METRO

1. Turn ignition key to the LOCK position.
2. Connect yellow connector for passenger's inflator module.
3. Install passenger's inflator Connector Position Assurance (CPA), then close glove compartment.
4. Connect yellow 2-way electrical connector inside inflator module housing.
5. Install driver's inflator Connector Position Assurance (CPA), then the steering wheel side cap.
6. Install Air Bag fuse into Air Bag fuse block.
7. Turn ignition switch to the RUN position and ensure " Inflatable Restraint" lamp flashes seven, then turns off. If

lamp does not operate as specified, refer to **MOTOR's "Air Bag Manual."**

PRIZM

1. Turn ignition key to the LOCK position.
2. Connect passenger's inflator module yellow 2-way connector and secure with Connector Position Assurance (CPA).
3. Connect yellow 2-way connector on the lower steering column and secure with Connector Position Assurance (CPA).
4. Install CIG and IGN fuses.
5. Turn ignition key to ACC or RUN position and verify that the air bag indicator illuminates steady for approximately six seconds and then turns off. If lamp does not operate as specified, refer to **MOTOR's "Air Bag Manual."**

SATURN

DISARMING

1997-99

The Sensing And Diagnostic Module (SDM) can maintain enough voltage to cause air bag deployment for up to ten seconds after the ignition switch is turned off and the battery is disconnected. Servicing the SIR system during this period may result in accidental deployment and personal injury.

1. Point front wheels straight ahead.
2. Turn ignition switch to the LOCK position and remove key.
3. Remove air bag fuse.
4. Remove Connector Position Assurance (CPA) device from yellow 2-way SIR connector at base of steering column, then disconnect connector.
5. Remove upper trim panel extension located on the top righthand side of the instrument panel.
6. Remove upper instrument panel screw caps, located on the top center of the instrument panel, then remove upper trim panel attaching screws.
7. Lift upper trim panel off of instrument panel, then remove upper trim panel insulator.
8. Remove Connector Position Assurance (CPA) device from yellow 2-way SIR connector, located on pigtail from passenger's inflator module.
9. Disconnect inflator module connector.

2000

S-Series

1. Turn steering wheel so that wheels point straight ahead.
2. Turn ignition switch to lock position and remove key.
3. Remove air bag fuse from instrument panel fuse block.
4. Disconnect driver yellow two-way connector, clipped to steering column.
5. **Do not remove upper trim panel,** passenger disconnect is accessible from underside of instrument panel.
6. Detach clip holding passenger yellow two-way connector to metal brace near heat & A/C fan.
7. Disconnect passenger yellow two-way connector.

L-Series

1. Turn steering wheel so that wheels are pointing straight ahead.
2. Turn ignition switch to Off position and remove key.
3. Remove IGN1 mini-fuse from under hood fuse block.
4. Remove lower left instrument panel closeout panel.
5. Push out clips that secure yellow two-way connectors to instrument panel brace.
6. Disconnect both yellow two way connectors.

ARMING

1997-99

1. Turn ignition key to LOCK position and remove key.
2. Connect yellow 2-way SIR connector at base of steering column and install Connector Position Assurance (CPA) device to connector.
3. Connect yellow 2-way SIR connector at pigtail of passenger's inflator module and install Connector Position Assurance (CPA) device to connector.
4. Install upper trim panel insulator. **Ensure all flaps are tucked in.**
5. Install upper trim panel into clips at base of windshield.
6. Lower panel and push down at clip locations.
7. Install upper trim panel attaching screws, then the screw caps.
8. Install upper trim panel extension.
9. Install air bag fuse.
10. Turn ignition switch to RUN position, ensure air bag lamp flashes seven times, then remains off. If lamp does not operate as specified, refer to **MOTOR's "Air Bag Manual."**

2000

S-Series

1. Connect passenger yellow two-way connector.
2. Attach connector clip to metal brace near heater A/C fan.
3. Connect driver yellow two-way connector and clip to steering column brace.
4. Install air bag fuse in instrument panel fuse block.
5. Verify air bag telltale operates properly.

L-Series

1. Turn steering wheel so that vehicles wheels are pointing straight ahead.
2. Turn ignition switch to Off position and remove key.
3. Connect both yellow two-way connectors.
4. Fasten clips on yellow two-way connectors to instrument panel brace.
5. Install IGN1 mini-fuse in under hood fuse block.
6. Turn ignition switch to On position and verify that air bag telltale operates properly.
7. Install lower left instrument panel closeout panel.

COMPUTER RELEARN PROCEDURE

INDEX

DAIMLERCHRYSLER

If battery cable has been disconnected, the PCM must relearn a new operating strategy. Connect battery cable and run engine until operating temperature is reached. After engine warm-up, drive vehicle under various operating conditions until PCM has relearned new strategy.

FORD MOTOR CO.

Disconnect negative battery cable for a minimum of five minutes. After clearing memory, it is necessary to drive vehicle a minimum of 10 miles to allow PCM time to relearn operating strategy.

GENERAL MOTORS

BODY CONTROL MODULE PROGRAMMING

CORVETTE

1. Ensure battery is fully charged.
2. Install a Tech 2 or equivalent and select NEW BCM SETUP and program BCM with correct RPO configuration.
3. Turn ignition switch to ON position and leave on for 11 minutes.
4. Turn ignition to OFF position for 30 seconds.
5. Place ignition to ON position for 11 minutes or until DTC P1630 sets.
6. Turn ignition OFF for 30 seconds.
7. Turn ignition to ON position for 30 seconds, then start engine.
8. If engine will start, proceed as follows:
   a. Clear DTC's, then turn ignition OFF for 30 seconds.
   b. Ensure engine starts and runs.
9. If engine cranks but will not start, refer to **MOTOR's Auto Engine Performance & Driveability Manual.**

CRANKSHAFT POSITION SYSTEM VARIATION LEARN

The crankshaft position system values are stored within PCM memory after a learn procedure is performed. If crankshaft position system variation is not within value stored in PCM memory, DTC P0300 may be set.

The crankshaft variation learn procedure must be performed under the following conditions: DTC P1336, PCM replacement, PCM reprogramming, engine replacement, crankshaft replacement, crankshaft damper replacement and crankshaft position sensor replacement.

When performing this procedure, ensure vehicle is at operating temperature, no DTC's other than P1336 are present and that no camshaft position sensor faults are present. Proceed as follows for CKP learn procedure:

1. Set parking brake.
2. Ensure engine is at operating temperature.
3. Install a suitable scan tool, then select CKP variation learn procedure from scan tool function list.
4. Follow scan tool instructions.
5. Monitor scan tool for DTC P1336. If scan tool indicates that DTC P1336 ran and passed, learn procedure is complete. If scan tool indicates DTC P1336 failed or not run, check for DTC's. If no DTC's other than P1336 exist, repeat procedure as necessary.

PASSKEY THEFT DETERRENT SYSTEM PASSWORD LEARN

On models equipped with the passkey theft deterrent system, a new password must be learned by the PCM when the BCM or PCM has been replaced. When the PCM is replaced, the EEPROM calibration is flashed into the new PCM. Refer to the latest GM Techline or equivalent information for PCM programming. After EEPROM calibration is complete, perform the following procedure:

EXCEPT PARK AVENUE

1. Attempt to start vehicle, vehicle will stall.
2. Leave ignition in ON position until THEFT SYSTEM warning lamp turns off.
3. Place ignition switch to OFF position.
4. Attempt to start vehicle, password is now learned and vehicle will now start.

PARK AVENUE

1. Insert valid coded unlearned ignition key into ignition lock cylinder and turn to RUN position.
2. When "SECURITY" lamp turns off, turn ignition switch to OFF position, then remove key and wait 10 seconds.
3. Repeat steps 1 and 2 two more times.
4. Insert key into ignition cylinder and turn to ON position. Ensure "SECURITY" indicator remains off.

PCM REPROGRAMMING

1. Ensure battery is fully charged.
2. Turn ignition switch to ON position, then connect a suitable scan tool to DLC.
3. Follow scan tool instructions for reprogramming.
4. If PCM fails to program, refer to GM Techline or equivalent information for PCM reprogramming.

THEFT DETERRENT SYSTEM PROGRAMMING

CUTLASS & MALIBU

1. Connect suitable scan tool to DLC.
2. Select "Service Programming" from scan tool menu.
3. Enter vehicle information, then choose "Request Info. " from menu. Disconnect scan tool from vehicle and connect to a Techline Terminal or equivalent.
4. Select "Service Programming System," then "Terminal" for terminal to scan tool programming.
5. Select "Done" then follow instructions on communications setup screen.
6. Select "Body Function Controller" and "Program" from screen menu. The terminal will download information to scan tool.
7. Disconnect scan tool from terminal and reconnect to vehicle.
8. Turn ignition switch to RUN position.
9. Select "Service Programming" from scan tool main menu.
10. Follow scan tool on screen instructions and reprogram PCM and theft deterrent system.

CAMARO, FIREBIRD, LUMINA & MONTE CARLO

1. Turn ignition to RUN position.
2. Start engine to verify system operation.
3. If SECURITY lamp illuminates for 5 seconds, then turns off, programming has been successfully completed.
4. If lamp flashes, programming is not

complete. Inspect theft deterrent circuit connections, ignition key resistor pellet and resistor sensing contacts.

SATURN

CRANKSHAFT LEARN PROCEDURE

The PCM uses crankshaft velocity calculations to determine engine misfire and to run misfire self-diagnostics. The PCM must know precisely the variability in crankshaft notches for this function. The PCM has a notch learn process that learns the variability between notches which must be reset if the crankshaft has been replaced. Using a suitable scan tool, the " Crankshaft Learn Procedure" can be set to "Relearn. "

CRANKSHAFT RELEARN PROCEDURE

Any time a PCM or crankshaft position sensor is replaced the PCM must relearn the crankshaft notches. Using a suitable scan tool, select Crankshaft Pos. Variation Learn under the SPECIAL FUNCTIONS menu and follow the on screen prompts. This procedure will not be initiated if a misfire has been detected. If misfire DTC's are present, diagnose and repair before proceeding with crankshaft relearn procedure.

PCM/ECM LEARNING PROCEDURE

If the battery is disconnected or if the PCM is replaced, the PCM must go through the learning process. To allow the PCM to relearn, the following steps must be performed:

1. Start vehicle and run until engine reaches normal operating temperature.
2. Drive vehicle at part throttle, with moderate acceleration and idle conditions until normal performance returns.
3. Park vehicle and engage parking brake with engine running.
4. **On models equipped with automatic transaxle,** place transaxle in Drive position.
5. **On models equipped with manual transaxle,** place transaxle in Neutral position.
6. **On all models,** allow vehicle to idle for approximately two minutes until engine idle stabilizes, ensure engine is at normal operating temperature.

PASSLOCK THEFT DETERRENT RELEARN PROCEDURE

There are two methods used to reprogram the Passlock security system, the Seed and Key method and the Auto Learn method. If no components were replaced or the Passlock sensor was the only component replaced, the Auto Learn technique may be used to program the security system. If the BCM or PCM were replaced then the Seed & Key method must be used.

SEED & KEY METHOD

1. Turn ignition switch to On position.
2. Using a suitable scan tool, inspect for body control module (BCM) or powertrain control module (PCM) diagnostic trouble codes (DTC's).
3. Record and repair DTC's.
4. Turn ignition switch to Off position.
5. Using Saturn Programming System or equivalent reprogramming tool, select Passlock Relearn option.
6. Wait for ten minutes, then observe security telltale changing from Flashing to On to Off.
7. If ignition is switched Off before telltale changes state, relearn procedure must be performed again.
8. Turn ignition switch Off.
9. Vehicle should start on next ignition switch cycle.

AUTO LEARN METHOD

1. Turn ignition switch to On position.
2. Momentarily rotate ignition switch to Crank position, do not start vehicle.
3. Wait for ten minutes.
4. Observe security telltale changing from Flashing to On to Off.
5. If ignition is turned Off before telltale changes state, procedure will have to be performed again.
6. Turn Ignition switch to Off position.
7. Repeat procedure two more times.
8. If vehicle does not start on next ignition switch cycle, repeat procedure.

REMOTE KEYLESS ENTRY SYNCHRONIZATION

The remote keyless entry system does not send the same signal twice. The body control module (BCM) will not execute a signal if it has been sent previously. To synchronize a transmitter with the BCM, simultaneously press and hold the Lock and Unlock buttons on the transmitter for approximately ten seconds near the vehicle. The doors locks will cycle to confirm synchronization.

SERVICE REMINDER & WARNING LAMP RESET PROCEDURES

INDEX

DAIMLERCHRYSLER

ANTI-LOCK WARNING LAMP

This lamp will be illuminated when the ignition switch is placed in the ON position. The lamp may be illuminated for as long as 30 seconds as a bulb and system check. If the lamp remains illuminated or comes on while operating the vehicle, a problem in the anti-lock brake system is indicated. When the lamp is illuminated, place ignition switch in the OFF position, then restart engine. If the lamp still remains illuminated, the anti-lock brake system should be serviced. The brake system will remain functional, but without the anti-lock function. After servicing the anti-lock brake system, the lamp will automatically reset. On some models, it may be necessary to operate the vehicle at a speed over 18 mph to reset the lamp.

AIR BAG WARNING LAMP

On models equipped with an air bag system, if the air bag warning lamp illuminates and stays on, diagnosis and repair of the air bag system will be necessary to reset the lamp. Erasing stored DTC's is not required.

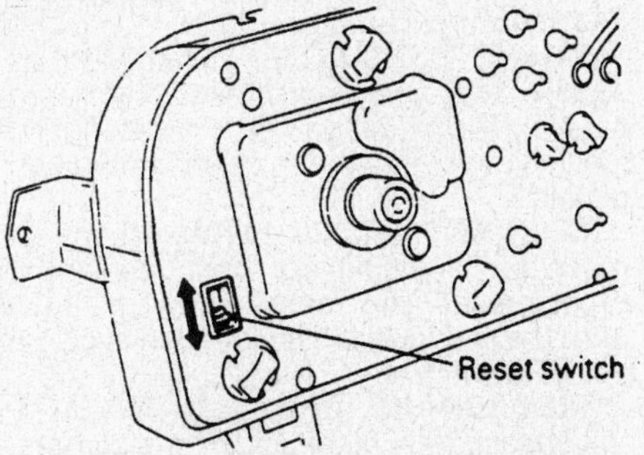

Fig. 1 EGR or Maintenance Reminder Lamp reset switch location. 1985-91 Colt Vista

BRAKE PAD WEAR WARNING LAMP

MEDALLION

When this message is displayed, the disc brake pads should be inspected and replaced as necessary. After completing service, the message will be reset automatically.

EGR WARNING LAMP

1985–87 COLT VISTA

This lamp will be illuminated every 50,000 miles to indicate the interval for EGR system service. After performing EGR system service, the lamp can be reset by moving the reset switch lever located at the rear of the instrument cluster, **Fig. 1.**

CHECK ENGINE LAMP

CHRYSLER, DODGE & PLYMOUTH

The Check Engine lamp will be illuminated for approximately three seconds after the ignition switch has been placed in the ON position as a bulb check. If incorrect or no signals are received by the Single Board Engine Controller (SBEC) from various sensors, the SBEC will illuminate the Check Engine lamp. After diagnosing and servicing the fuel injection system or emission related systems, the SBEC memory will be cleared after approximately 50 to 100 ignition key on-off cycles.

MEDALLION

This lamp will be illuminated during engine starting as a bulb check. Once the engine has started, the lamp should go off. If the lamp remains illuminated, the fuel injection and emission control system diagnosis should be performed using tester M.S. 1700. During the diagnosis and repair procedure with tester M.S. 1700, the Check Engine lamp will be reset.

MONACO & PREMIER

This lamp will be illuminated during engine starting as a bulb check. Once the engine has started, the lamp should go off. If the lamp remains illuminated, the fuel injection and emission control system diagnosis should be performed using tester DRB II. During the diagnosis and repair procedure with tester DRB II, the Check Engine lamp will be reset.

CHECK ENGINE OR MALFUNCTION INDICATOR LAMP

CHRYSLER, DODGE & PLYMOUTH EXCEPT COLT & SUMMIT

The powertrain control module monitors a variety of sensors in the fuel injection, ignition, emission and engines systems. Each time the ignition key is turned to the On position, the MIL lamp on the instrument panel should illuminate for approximately two seconds and then go out. If the PCM senses a problem with a monitored circuit often enough to indicate an actual problem, it stores a Diagnostic Trouble Code (DTC) in the PCM's memory. If the code applies to a non-emissions related components or system and the problem is repaired or ceases to exist, the PCM cancels the code after 40 warmup cycles. DTC's that affect vehicle emissions illuminate the MIL. Use a suitable scan tool to retrieve and erase DTC's and to reset the MIL.

COLT & SUMMIT

This lamp is used to monitor fuel injection and emission control system components for malfunctions. When the ignition switch is placed in the ON position, the lamp will illuminate for two to three seconds as a bulb check. If the lamp remains on, a malfunction in the fuel injection or emission control system is indicated. If malfunction is intermittent, the lamp will go off when the Electronic Control Unit (ECU) receives a normal signal from the malfunctioning component. If the ECU receives an improper signal from a malfunctioning component for a time longer than that programmed into the ECU, a code will be stored in the ECU memory and the Malfunction Indicator Lamp will be illuminated. After servicing the indicated component, the Malfunction Indicator Lamp can be reset by clearing the ECU memory. The ECU memory is cleared by using a suitable scan tool or disconnecting the battery ground cable for approximately ten seconds.

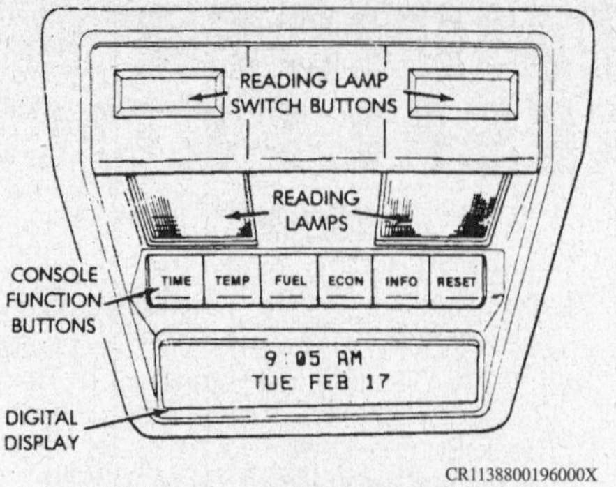

Fig. 2 Electronic Vehicle Information Center display console. 1988-89 Dynasty & New Yorker

ELECTRONIC MONITOR

1988-89 LEBARON

This system is an electronic monitor system with sensors, which displays messages on an instrument panel mounted console. If no messages are stored, the message "MONITORED SYSTEMS OK" will be displayed approximately six seconds after the ignition switch has been placed in the ON position. The system is actuated by depressing the check button located on the front of the message display. When this button is depressed, the system will sound a tone and cycle through the messages and then return to normal operation. If the monitor detects a fault, the component will be noted on the display. The fault messages are as follows:

BRAKE FLUID LOW—When this message is displayed, bring brake fluid to proper level. The message will be reset after the ignition switch has been cycled to the OFF position.

COOLANT LEVEL LOW—When this message is displayed, bring coolant to proper level. The message will be reset after the ignition switch has been cycled to the OFF position.

DISC BRAKE PADS WORN—When this message is displayed, the disc brake pads should be inspected and replaced as necessary. After completing service, the message will be reset after the ignition switch has been cycled to the OFF position.

DRIVER, PASSENGER OR HATCH AJAR—Close door or hatch indicated to cancel message.

ENGINE TEMPERATURE HIGH—This message will be indicated when an engine overheating condition is encountered. After repairing cause of engine overheating condition or when engine speed is less than 30 mph, the message will be automatically cancelled.

EXTERIOR LAMPS ON—This message will appear when the ignition switch is in OFF, LOCK OR ACC positions, the driver's door is open and the light switch is in the ON position. This message will be cancelled when the light switch is placed in the OFF position or the door is closed.

HEADLAMP, BRAKE OR TAIL LAMP OUT—The display will be illuminated when brake is applied or light switch is in the ON position and a burned out lamp bulb is present. To reset the message, replace burned out bulb, then actuate lamp circuit.

KEY IN IGNITION—This message will appear when the ignition switch is in the OFF, LOCK or ACC position and the driver's door is open. This message will be cancelled when the keys are removed or the door is closed.

LOW FUEL LEVEL—When this message is displayed, add fuel to vehicle to reset message.

LOW OIL PRESSURE—This message will be displayed when a low engine oil pressure condition exists. If message is encountered with vehicle operating at idle speed, increase engine mph. If message remains or if message is encountered while operating vehicle, the engine lubricating system should be checked and serviced immediately. After engine lubricating system has been serviced, the message will be automatically cancelled.

LOW TRANS PRESSURE—When this message is displayed, a problem in the automatic transaxle is present. After completing automatic transaxle service, the message will be reset after the ignition switch has been cycled to the OFF position.

VOLTAGE LOW—When this message is displayed, a problem in the charging or electrical system exists. After servicing, the message will be reset after the ignition switch has been cycled to the OFF position.

WASHER FLUID LOW—When this message is displayed, bring washer fluid to proper level to reset message.

ELECTRONIC VEHICLE INFORMATION CENTER

1988-93 DYNASTY, NEW YORKER & NEW YORKER LANDAU & 1990-93 FIFTH AVENUE & IMPERIAL

On 1988–89 models, this system is a computer controlled monitor system, which displays messages on an overhead console, **Fig. 2.** When the vehicle is started and no faults are present, the display will indicate "MONITORED SYSTEMS OK." If the monitor detects a fault, a tone will be sounded and component will be noted on the display.

On 1990–93 models, the Electronic Vehicle Information Center is a computer controlled warning system which monitors various sensors used on the vehicle. The system supplements the warning indicators in the instrument cluster. When a warning message has been activated, a tone will sound to attract the driver's attention. The warning message will then be displayed on the overhead console, **Fig. 3,** until the condition has been corrected or a new display function is called up. A tone will announce each new warning condition. The " Service Reminder" warning message will be indicated at 7,500 mile or 12 month intervals to indicate that required service is to be performed. After performing the required service, the Service Reminder message can be reset by using a DRB II diagnostic readout tool.

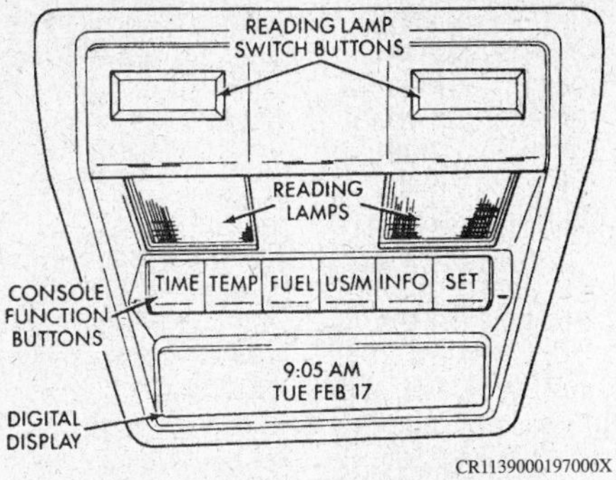

Fig. 3 Electronic Vehicle Information Center display console. 1990–93 Dynasty, New Yorker, Fifth Avenue & Imperial

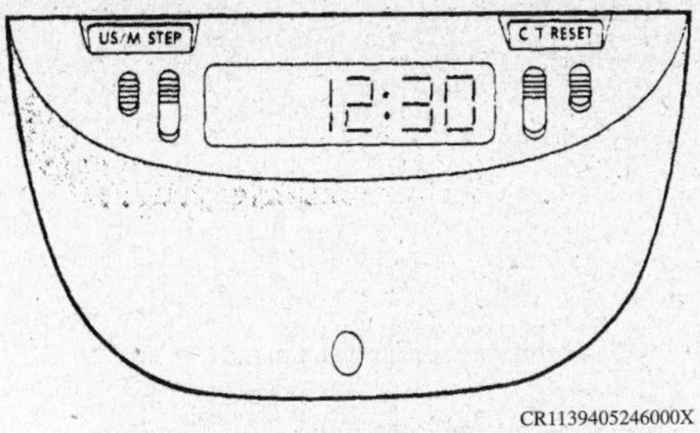

Fig. 4 Overhead Travel Information System (OTIS). Concorde, Intrepid, LHS, New Yorker, Vision & 300M

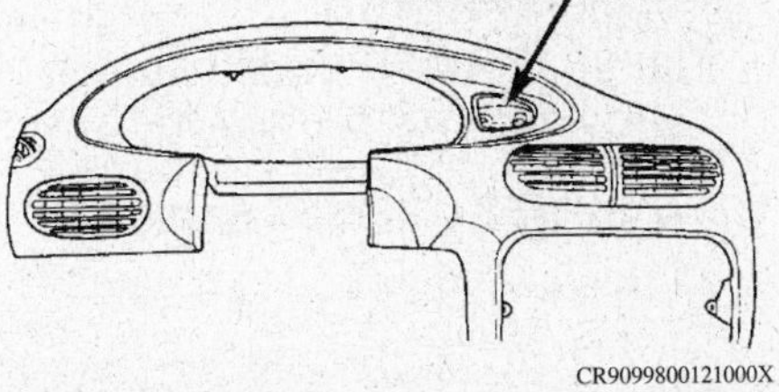

Fig. 6 Compass/temperature mini trip computer. Concorde, Intrepid, LHS, New Yorker, Vision & 300M

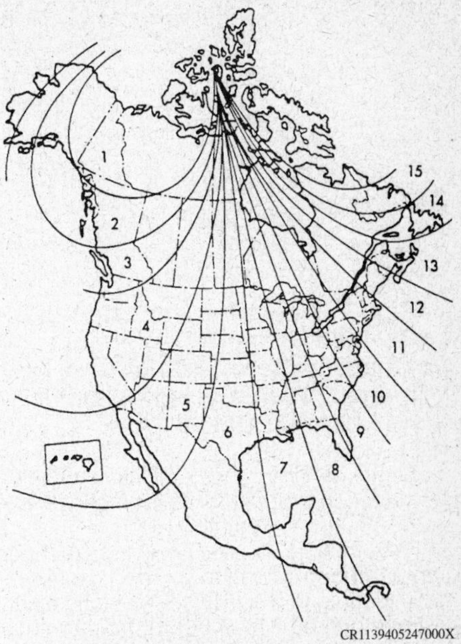

Fig. 5 Variance zone map. Concorde, Intrepid, LHS, New Yorker, Vision & 300M

OVERHEAD TRAVEL INFORMATION SYSTEM (OTIS)

CONCORDE, INTREPID, LHS, NEW YORKER, VISION & 300M

Overhead Travel Information System (OTIS) is a module with six informational displays and four buttons, **Fig. 4.** When the ignition switch is turned ON, OTIS blanks the display for one second, then returns to the display active when the vehicle was last turned OFF.

LOW OIL PRESSURE—This message will be displayed when a low engine oil pressure condition exists. If message is encountered with vehicle operating at idle speed, increase engine mph. If message remains or if message is encountered while operating vehicle, the engine lubricating system should be checked and serviced immediately. After engine lubricating system has been serviced, the message will be automatically cancelled.

SERVICE REMINDER—This message will be indicated at 7,500 mile or 12 month intervals to indicate that required service is to be performed. After performing the required service, with the Service Reminder message displayed, depress the Vehicle Electronic Information Center Reset button.

TURN SIGNAL ON—This message will be indicated when the turn signal is on and the vehicle has traveled a distance over ½ mile at a speed above 15 mph. The message will be reset when the turn signal has been placed in the OFF position.

VOLTAGE IMPROPER—When this message is displayed, a problem in the charging or electrical system exists. After servicing, the message will be reset after the ignition switch has been cycled to the OFF position.

WASHER FLUID LOW—When this message is displayed, bring washer fluid to proper level. This message will be reset after the ignition switch has been cycled to the OFF position.

The six informational displays on the OTIS are as follows:

1. Compass/temperature.
2. Average fuel economy.
3. Distance to empty.
4. Instantaneous fuel economy.
5. Trip odometer.
6. Elapsed time.

The four buttons on the OTIS are as follows:

1. STEP—Depress this button to select display modes except Compass/temperature.
2. C/T—Depress this button to display compass (vehicle direction) and temperature.
3. U/SM—Switches display information between English and Metric readings.
4. RESET—Depress this button to reset the current display (for displays that can be reset.)

Compass Calibration

Do not attempt to set compass calibration near large metal objects, such as other vehicles, buildings or bridges.

1. Remove all magnetic devices from roof panel.
2. Turn key to ON position.
3. Press C/T button to select Compass/Temperature display.
4. Depress and hold RESET button for about five seconds. The VAR symbol will light during this time.
5. Continue to hold RESET button for about ten seconds until CAL symbol illuminates.
6. Drive vehicle through three complete 360° turns in no less than 48 seconds. The compass will be calibrated when the CAL symbol is extinguished.
7. Reset compass variance as follows:
   a. Press and hold RESET button for about five seconds until VAR symbol is lit.
   b. The OTIS will display variance zone and VAR.
   c. Press STEP button to display variance zone, **Fig. 5.**
   d. Press RESET button to set new variance zone and resume normal operation.

COMPASS & TEMPERATURE MINI TRIP COMPUTER

CONCORDE, INTREPID, LHS, NEW YORKER, VISION & 300M

1. Set mini trip computer to Compass/Temperature mode, **Fig. 6.**
2. Press US/M and STEP buttons simultaneously until VAR and current variance zone number is displayed.
3. Press STEP until proper variance zone number is displayed, **Fig. 5.**
4. After 5 seconds of inactivity, displayed zone will be set automatically. Ensure accuracy of compass by pointing vehicle in N, S, E and W directions.

EMISSION MAINTENANCE REMINDER INDICATOR

1980–81 CONCORD, EAGLE, PACER & SPIRIT

On 1980–81 models, at 30,000 miles intervals, a warning lamp will be illuminated on the instrument panel to indicate oxygen sensor replacement. After performing the required service, the reminder lamp switch must be reset. The switch is located between the upper and lower speedometer cables in the engine compartment on the lefthand side of the dash panel. Rotate the reset screw located on the switch ¼ turn counterclockwise, **Fig. 7.**

1982–83 CONCORD & SPIRIT & 1982–87 EAGLE

The emission maintenance lamp, **Fig. 8,** will illuminate after 1000 hours of engine operation to indicate that the oxygen sensor must be replaced. After performing the

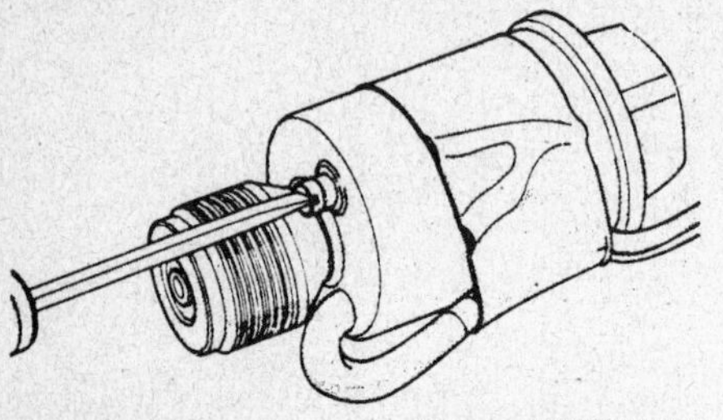

Fig. 7 Resetting emission or oxygen sensor maintenance reminder switch. 1979-80 Chrysler, Dodge & Plymouth (mechanical type) & 1980-81 AMC

required service, the emission maintenance E-Cell timer must be replaced for the next 1000 hour interval.

This timer is located in the passenger compartment, attached to the wiring harness leading to the MCU. To replace timer, remove printed circuit board, then remove timer from its enclosure and insert replacement timer.

1988 EAGLE 4 X 4

The emission maintenance timer will illuminate an indicator lamp on the instrument cluster when vehicle mileage has reached 82,500 miles. At this time, the oxygen sensor and PCV valve should be replaced, in addition to the other required emission maintenance scheduled for this mileage.

If the timer should fail before vehicle has accumulated 82,500 miles, the timer and oxygen sensor should both be replaced to maintain a proper sensor replacement interval.

After performing the required service, replace the emission maintenance timer as follows:

1. Remove emission maintenance timer to dash bracket attaching screws. The timer is located on the dash panel to the right of the steering column.
2. Remove timer from bracket, then disconnect electrical connector and remove timer from vehicle, **Fig. 9.**
3. Connect electrical connector to replacement timer, then position timer to mounting bracket and install and tighten attaching screws.

LOW COOLANT WARNING LAMP

1990-92 LASER & TALON

The Low Coolant Warning lamp will be illuminated whenever coolant level in the coolant reservoir is below a predetermined level. Add coolant to bring reservoir to proper level to turn lamp off.

MAINTENANCE REQUIRED LAMP

1988-91 COLT VISTA

This lamp will be illuminated at 50,000, 80,000, 100,000 and 150,000 miles to indicate interval for emission control system inspection. After performing emission control system inspection at the 50,000, 80,000 or

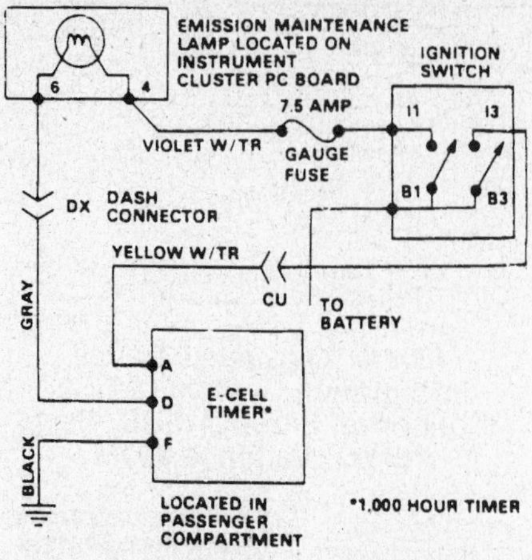

Fig. 8 Emission maintenance reminder indicator wiring schematic. 1982–83 Concord & Spirit & 1982–87 Eagle

Fig. 10 Maintenance Required Lamp bulb location. 1988-91 Colt Vista

100,00 mile interval, the lamp can be reset by moving the reset switch lever located at the rear of the instrument cluster, **Fig. 1.** At the 150,000 mile interval, after performing inspection, remove bulb from lamp socket, **Fig. 10.**

OXYGEN SENSOR MAINTENANCE REMINDER LAMP

1979 ASPEN & VOLARE w/3.7L CALIFORNIA ENGINE & 1980 CHRYSLER, DODGE & PLYMOUTH

At 30,000 miles intervals, a warning lamp will be illuminated on the instrument panel to indicate oxygen sensor replacement. The reminder can either be mechanical, **Fig. 11,** or electronic, **Fig. 12.** After performing the required service, the reminder lamp must be reset.

On the mechanical system, rotate the reset screw located on the switch counterclockwise until it stops, **Fig. 7.**

On the electronic system, remove 9 volt battery from module, which is located under the lefthand side of the instrument panel. Insert a suitable rod into hole on module case to reset switch. After resetting switch, install a replacement 9 volt battery.

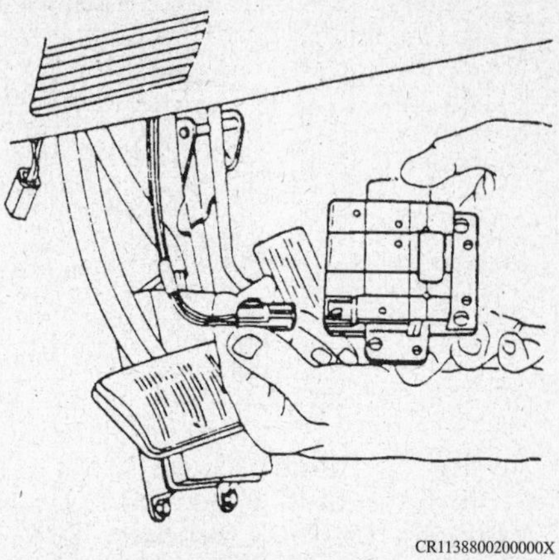

Fig. 9 Emission maintenance timer replacement. 1988 Eagle 4 X 4

POWER LOSS/LIMIT LAMP

CHRYSLER, DODGE & PLYMOUTH

The Power Loss/Limit lamp will be illuminated for approximately three seconds after the ignition switch has been placed in the ON position as a bulb check. If incorrect or no signals are received by the logic module from various sensors, the logic module will illuminate the Power Loss/Limit lamp. After diagnosing and servicing the fuel injection system or EGR system (California models with EGR sensor), the logic module memory can be cleared by disconnecting and reconnecting the battery quick disconnect.

VEHICLE MAINTENANCE MONITOR (VMM) SYSTEM

MONACO & PREMIER

This system, **Fig. 13,** monitors regular service and maintenance intervals, engine oil level, engine coolant level, windshield washer fluid level, brake and tail lamps, door ajar, transaxle (models w/4-150 engine) and oil, coolant and washer sensors.

When the vehicle is started and no faults are present, the display will indicate "MONITOR." If the monitor detects a fault, it will be noted on the display. If more than one fault is noted, the fault of the highest priority will be displayed first. The display will then note all existing faults and return to the fault of highest priority. The VMM fault messages are as follows:

DOOR—Door Ajar—Close door indicated on vehicle outline display to reset monitor.

LAMP—Brake or Tail Lamp Outage—The display will be illuminated when brake is applied or light switch is in the ON position and a burned out lamp bulb is present. To reset monitor, replace burned out bulb.

COOLANT—Low Engine Coolant Level—Bringing coolant to proper level will reset monitor.

OIL—Low Engine Oil Level—The system will check engine oil level approximately 12 minutes after the ignition switch has been placed in the OFF position. A low oil

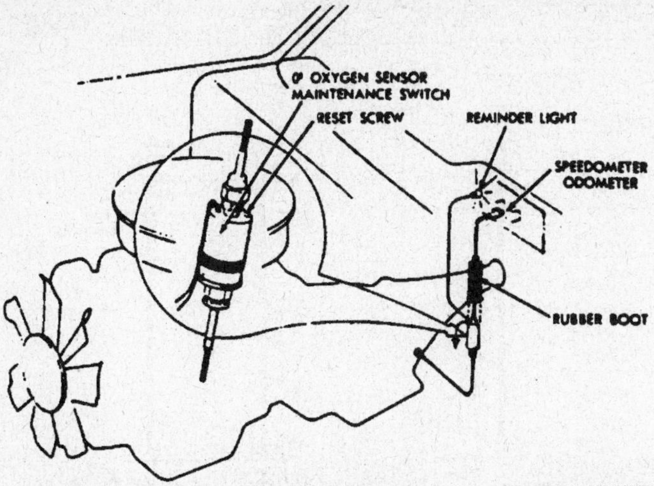

CR1138000202000X

Fig. 11 Oxygen sensor maintenance reminder system. 1979 Aspen & Volare w/3.7L California Engine & 1980 Chrysler, Dodge & Plymouth mechanical type

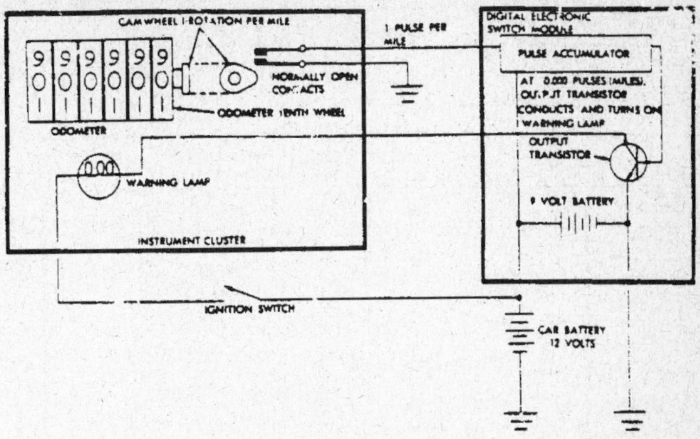

CR1138000203000X

Fig. 12 Oxygen sensor maintenance reminder system. 1979 Aspen & Volare w/3.7L California Engine & 1980 Chrysler, Dodge & Plymouth electronic type

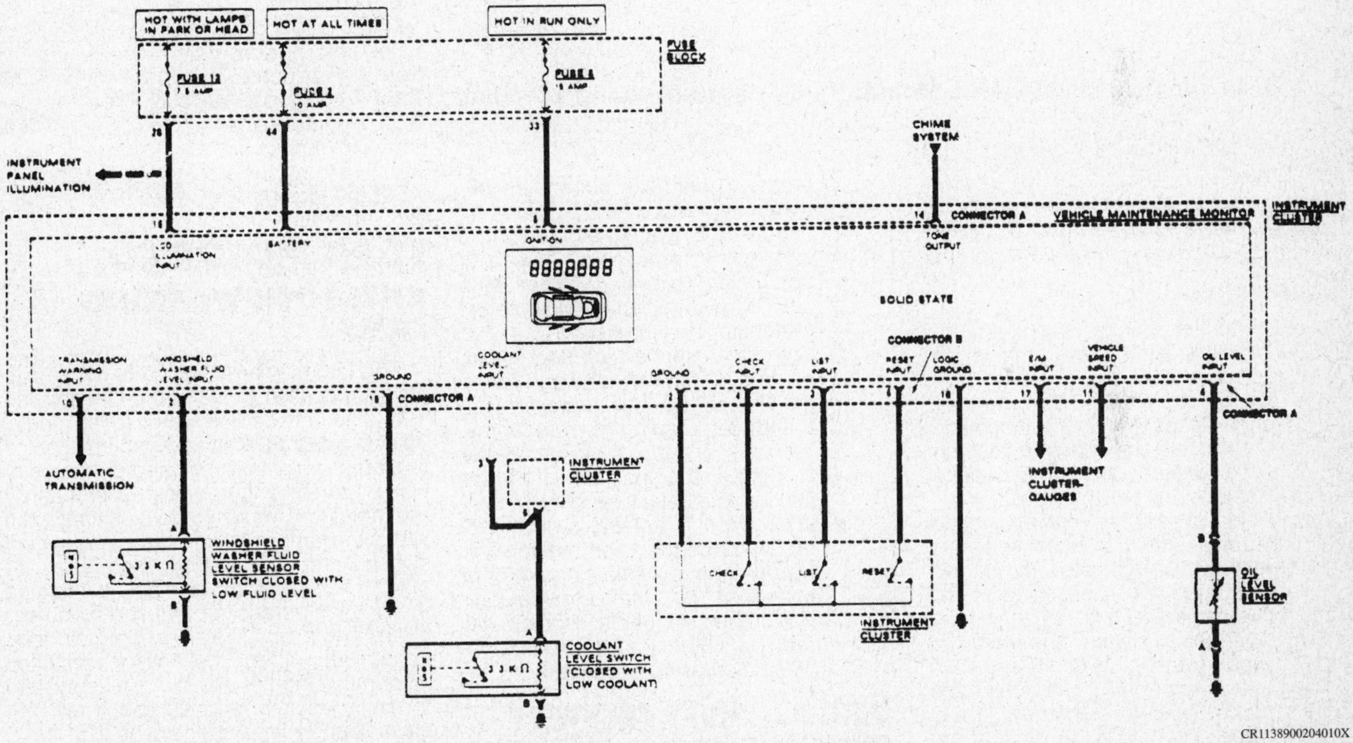

CR1138900204010X

Fig. 13 Vehicle Maintenance Monitor (VMM) System wiring schematic (Part 1 of 2). Monaco & Premier

level condition must be indicated three consecutive times before the monitor will display " Oil." To reset monitor, add oil to bring to proper level. Then, while display is indicating the "Oil" message, depress RESET select switch until a beep is noted. Even if RESET select switch is not depressed, the system will automatically reset monitor after three proper oil level readings have been obtained.

WASHER—Low Washer Fluid Level—Bringing washer fluid to proper level will reset monitor.

TRANS—Service Transaxle (Models w/4–150 Engine)—Indicates defect in automatic transaxle.

SERVICE—Perform Required Service and Maintenance—This message will be indicated at 7,500 mile intervals to indicate that required service is to be performed. After performing required service, depress the Reset select switch until a beep is noted.

SENSOR—This message will be indicated when a defect in the oil, coolant or washer sensor circuit is noted. Refer to "Self Diagnosis."

MILES (KMS)—Mile to next scheduled service interval.

Self Diagnosis

To diagnose, depress and hold the Check and List select switches, then place the ignition switch in the ON position. With the instrument cluster switch in the English mode, all diagnosis will be performed automatically in sequence. With the instrument cluster in the Metric mode, the Check select switch will have to be depressed to proceed to the next test. The display will indicate

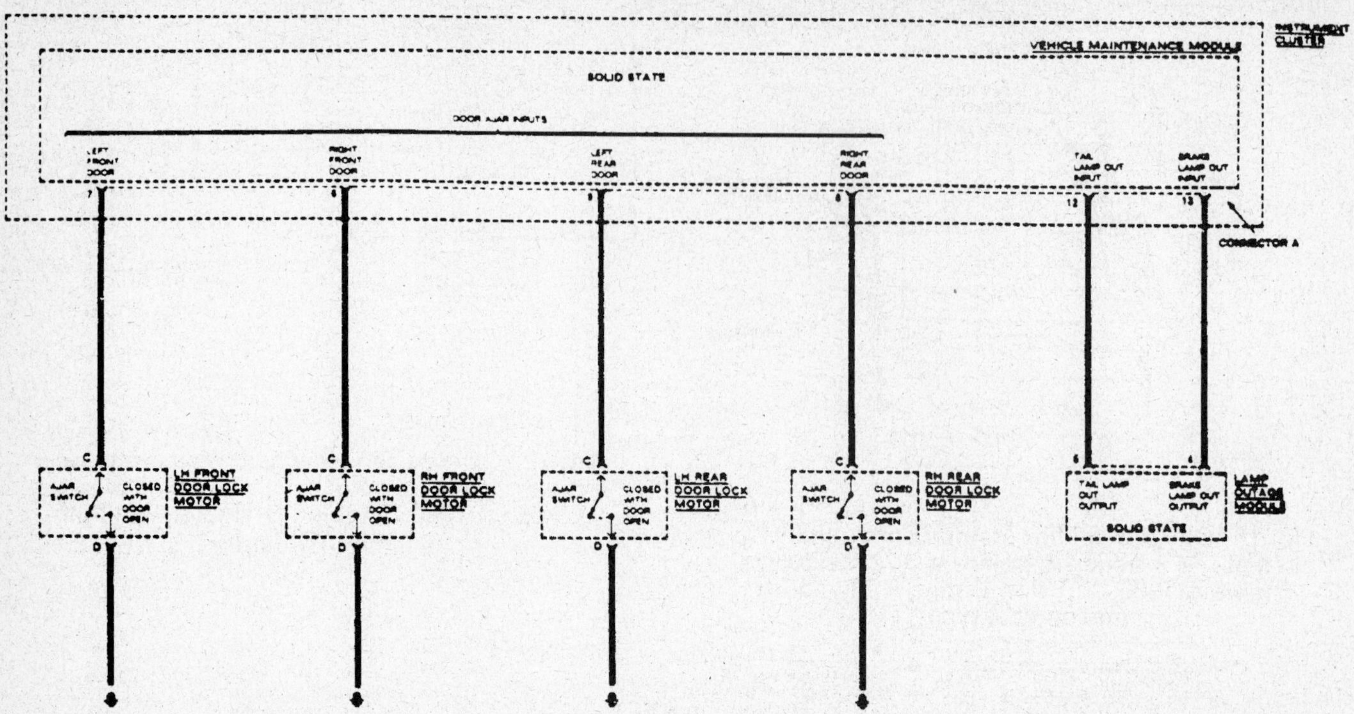

CR1138900204020X

Fig. 13 Vehicle Maintenance Monitor (VMM) System wiring schematic (Part 2 of 2). Monaco & Premier

which components are defective or satisfactory. Refer to **Fig. 14.** After completing diagnosis, depress Check and List select switches to exit diagnosis mode.

Troubleshooting

1. If a condition of no display or incorrect information exists, start engine and check the following:
   a. On models less passive restraint, check fuses 8 and 19 in fuse panel. On models with passive restraint, check fuses 2 and 8 in fuse panel. Replace any blown fuses.
   b. Using a suitable voltmeter, check terminal Nos. 1 and 5 of connector A, **Fig. 13.** Voltmeter should indicate battery voltage. If not, check for open circuit to fuse panel.
   c. Connect a suitable ohmmeter between terminal Nos. 15 and 18 of connector A, **Fig. 13.** Ohmmeter should indicate zero ohms. If a no display condition is present, replace monitor. If an incorrect information condition is present, refer to " Self Diagnosis." If reading is other than zero ohms, check for open circuit.
   d. With all doors closed, connect an ohmmeter between terminal Nos. 6, 7, 8 and 9 of connector A, **Fig. 13.** Ohmmeter should indicate an infinite reading. If reading is other than infinite, check for short circuit to ground.
2. If monitor fails to change modes, disconnect electrical connector B, **Fig. 13,** and proceed as follows:
   a. With Check select switch depressed, connect ohmmeter between terminal Nos. 2 and 4 of connector B. If ohmmeter reading is zero ohms, proceed to step b. If ohmmeter reading is other than zero ohms, replace mode select switches.
   b. With List select switch depressed, connect ohmmeter between terminal Nos. 2 and 3 of connector B. If ohmmeter reading is zero ohms, proceed to step c. If ohmmeter reading is other than zero ohms, replace mode select switches.
   c. With Reset select switch depressed, connect ohmmeter between terminal Nos. 2 and 5 of connector B. Ohmmeter reading should be zero ohms. If ohmmeter reading is other than zero ohms, replace mode select switches.

VEHICLE THEFT SECURITY SYSTEM (VTSS)

If the VTSS indicator LED comes on and stays on after the bulb test, it indicates that the Sentry Key Immobilizer Module (SKIM) has detected a system malfunction and/or that the Sentry Key Immobilizer System (SKIS) has become inoperative. If the SKIM detects an invalid key when the ignition switch is turned to the On position, it sends a message to the instrument cluster to flash the VTSS indicator LED. The SKIM can also send messages to the instrument cluster to flash the LED and to generate a single audible chime tone.

If the VTSS indicator LED comes on and stays on after the bulb test function, diagnosis of the SKIS should be performed with a suitable scan tool.

FORD MOTOR CO.

ANTI-LOCK WARNING LAMP

This lamp will be illuminated when the ignition switch is placed in the ON position. The lamp may be illuminated for as long as 30 seconds as a bulb and system check. If the lamp remains illuminated or comes on while operating the vehicle, a problem in the anti-lock brake system is indicated. When the lamp is illuminated, place ignition switch in the OFF position, then restart engine. If the lamp still remains illuminated, the anti-lock brake system should be serviced. The brake system will remain functional, but without the anti-lock function. After servicing the anti-lock brake system, the lamp will automatically reset when vehicle is operated at a speed over 25 mph.

AIR BAG WARNING LAMP

On models equipped with an air bag system, if the air bag warning lamp illuminates and stays on, diagnosis and repair of the air bag system will be necessary to reset the lamp.

AUXILIARY WARNING INDICATOR & GRAPHIC DISPLAY MODULE

MERKUR

This system monitors engine oil level, engine coolant level, windshield washer fluid level, brake pad wear, fuel level, seat

TEST 1 Initially, a number will be displayed on the monitor's screen. This number indicates the version of the maintenance module installed in the vehicle.

TEST 2

In Display	Meaning
"CAL O"	Monitor Bad
"CAL 1-7"	Monitor OK
"CAL F"	Monitor Bad

TEST 3 The module internal memory is tested.

In Display	Meaning
"RAM P"	Monitor OK
"RAM F"	Monitor Bad

TEST 4 The module program is tested.

In Display	Meaning
"ROM P"	Monitor OK
"ROM F"	Monitor Bad

TEST 5 The monitor's clocks are tested.

In Display	Meaning
"TIME P"	Monitor OK
"TIME F"	Monitor Bad

TEST 6 The monitor's storage capability is tested.

In Display	Meaning
"NVM P"	Monitor OK
"NVM F"	Monitor Bad

TEST 7 The monitor's internal synchronization is tested.

In Display	Meaning
"PAR 0"	Monitor OK
"PAR N"	Monitor Bad

TEST 8 The monitor's display screen is tested.

In Display	Meaning
All Segments ON	Monitor OK
All Segments OFF	Monitor OK
"0"	Monitor OK
"1"	Monitor OK
"10"	Monitor OK
"100"	Monitor OK
"1000"	Monitor OK
"10000"	Monitor OK
"100000"	Monitor OK
"111111"	Monitor OK
"122222"	Monitor OK
"133333"	Monitor OK
"144444"	Monitor OK
"155555"	Monitor OK
"166666"	Monitor OK
"177777"	Monitor OK
"188888"	Monitor OK
"199999"	Monitor OK

The graphic segments will light, one at a time, in the following order: the engine symbol, the car outline, right front door, right rear door, rear tail lamps, left rear door, and left front door. Any deviation from the above patterns signifies a bad monitor. Should any of the segments fail to light, the monitor is bad.

TEST 9 This test can only be performed while the test program is in the manual mode. OIL will flash. Release CHECK button and press and hold LIST button until OIL flashes three times, then release LIST button and OIL will stop flashing. There will be a 30-45 second delay while system is testing. Oil level faults are displayed at this time. The engine oil level is tested.

In Display	Meaning
"OIL H"	Monitor OK, Oil Level Normal
"OIL L"	Monitor OK, but Oil Level Is Low
"OIL O"	Monitor OK, but Oil Level Sensor Is Open
"OIL S"	Monitor OK, but Oil Level Sensor Is Shorted

TEST 10 The oil level probe is tested. The intermittent fault can be cleared in diagnostic program by pressing RESET switch while message is displayed.

In Display	Meaning
"OIL IF"	Intermittent Fault With Oil Sensor
NO MESSAGE	Monitor OK, Sensor OK

TEST 11 The washer fluid level is tested.

In Display	Meaning
"WASH H"	Washer Fluid Level Normal
"WASH L"	Washer Fluid Level Low
"WASH O"	Washer Fluid Level Probe Open

TEST 12 The washer level sensor is tested. The intermittent fault can be cleared in diagnostic program by pressing RESET switch while message is displayed.

In Display	Meaning
"WASHER IF"	Intermittent Fault With Washer Fluid Sensor
NO MESSAGE	Monitor OK, Sensor OK

TEST 13 The coolant fluid level is tested.

In Display	Meaning
"COOL H"	Coolant Fluid Level Is Normal
"COOL L"	Coolant Fluid Level Is Low
"COOL O"	Coolant Fluid Level Probe Is Open

TEST 14 The coolant fluid level sensor is tested. The intermittent fault can be cleared in diagnostic program by pressing RESET switch while message is displayed.

In Display	Meaning
"COOL IF"	Intermittent Fault With the Coolant Level Sensor
NO MESSAGE	Monitor OK, Sensor OK

TEST 15 The tail lamp circuit is tested.

In Display	Meaning
"TLO P"	Tail Lamp Circuit OK
"TLO F"	Tail Lamp Circuit Open

TEST 16 The brake lamp circuit is tested.

In Display	Meaning
"BLO P"	Brake Lamp Circuit OK
"BLO F"	Brake Lamp Circuit Open

TEST 17 The status of the transmission diagnostic module is tested.

In Display	Meaning
"TRANS P"	Transmission Module OK
"TRANS F"	Transmission Module Fault

TEST 18 The frequency of the road speed sensor is displayed. When in manual mode, continuous monitoring is possible.

In Display	Meaning
"SPD XXX"*	Frequency of Vehicle Speed Sensor

*Note: XXX will vary from 0 and increase as vehicle speed increases.

CR1139405248000X

Fig. 14 Vehicle Maintenance Monitor (VMM) System self diagnosis test chart. Monaco & Premier

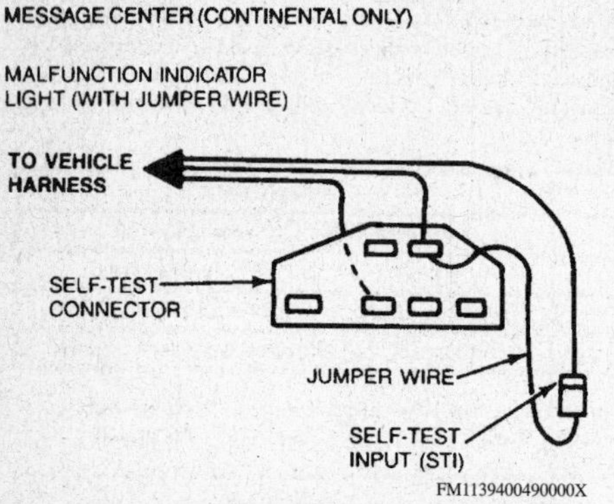

Fig. 15 Jumper wire connections for resetting Check Engine lamp. EEC-IV Except Festiva, Probe w/2.2L Engine & Escort & Tracer w/1.8L Engine

belt usage, headlamp, brake and tail lamps, door ajar, liftgate ajar and ambient temperature.

When ignition switch is placed in the ON position, the graphic display module and all warning indicators will illuminate for five seconds. After five seconds, all warning lamps should go off and the graphic display module should indicate the outline of the vehicle and the two brake lamps. The two brake lamp indications should go out once the brake pedal is depressed. If warning lamps remain illuminated or graphic display indicates a fault, check the following:

The low engine oil warning lamp is used to indicate when engine oil level is 12 mm or more below the specified level. The lamp will be illuminated during engine starting. If oil level is sufficient, the lamp will go off when engine is operating. If oil level is low, the lamp will remain on until engine oil is added and the ignition switch is placed in the OFF position. The module will take approximately three minutes to reset. If the engine is started during this period, the last recorded reading will be displayed.

The low coolant warning lamp will be illuminated whenever coolant level in the coolant recovery bottle is below the specified mark. Raise coolant level in recovery bottle to turn lamp off.

The low fuel warning lamp will be illuminated whenever fuel level drops below 1.4 gals. Add fuel to vehicle to turn lamp off.

The washer fluid warning lamp will be illuminated whenever fluid drops below the specified reservoir level. Raise washer fluid level in reservoir to turn lamp off.

The brake pad wear warning lamp will be illuminated when disc brake pads wear down to 1.5 mm. At 1.5 mm, a wire loop in the brake pad is exposed and severed, which in turn illuminates the brake pad warning lamp. To turn lamp off, replace brake pads.

Air temperature is monitored by a sensor located on the RH side of the vehicle, behind the front bumper. The signal from the sensor is evaluated by the control assembly, which controls the low air temperature (ICE) indication on the graphic display. When air temperature is approximately 39°F, the ICE indication will be illuminated in yellow. When temperature drops to 32°F, the triangle located around the ICE indication will be illuminated in red. If a short circuit in the wiring between the sensor and the control assembly is present, the ICE indication on the graphic will flash. If an open circuit between the sensor and control assembly exists, the triangle will flash.

The graphic display will indicate when doors and liftgate are closed (green) and when doors and liftgate are ajar (red). To cancel door or liftgate ajar indication, close door or liftgate indicated.

The graphic will also indicate lamp bulb outage. Replacement of the lamp bulb indicated will turn off graphic display indicator. A lamp out indication will also be present if an open or short circuit in the lamp wiring is present.

CHECK ENGINE LAMP

1987-93 MODELS w/EEC-IV

Except Festiva, Merkur, Probe w/2.2L Engine & Escort & Tracer w/1.8L Engine

This lamp will be illuminated when the ignition switch is placed in the ON position. After the engine is started, the lamp should go off, unless a problem is detected by the EEC-IV system. Following diagnosis and repair, the Check Engine/MIL lamp will automatically reset when the stored codes are cleared from the EEC-IV system memory. After diagnosis and repair, the EEC-IV memory may be cleared of stored codes as follows:

1. With ignition switch in the OFF position, connect a jumper wire between Self Test and Self Test Input (STI) connectors, **Fig. 15.** On Ford Crown Victoria, Mercury Grand Marquis and Lincoln Town Car models, the Self Test and STI connectors are gray in color and are located on the front of the LH fender apron, near the Electronic Engine Control (EEC) relay. On Ford Mustang models, the Self Test and STI connectors are gray in color and are located on the LH fender apron. On Ford Tempo, Topaz, 1987–90 Escort and Mercury Lynx, the Self Test connector is gray in color and the STI connector is black in color and they are both located on the RH fender apron, near the front of the strut tower. On Ford Taurus and Mercury Sable, the Self Test and STI connectors are gray in color and are located on the RH fender apron, near the front of the engine in the area of the AIR pump and alternator. On 1987–88 Ford Thunderbird and Mercury Cougar, the Self Test and STI connectors are gray in color and are located on the LH fender apron, near the strut tower. On 1989–93 Ford Thunderbird and Mercury Cougar, the Self Test and STI connectors are gray in color and are located on the RH fender apron, near the strut tower. On 1987 Lincoln Mark VIII and 1987–89 Continental, the Self Test and STI connectors are gray in color and are located on the RH side of the fender apron, near the ignition coil. On 1988–91 Lincoln Continental, the Self Test and STI connectors are attached to the Electronic Control Assembly, which is located in the engine compartment at the center of the firewall, below the TFI ignition module.
2. Position ignition switch in ON position, then disconnect jumper wire from test connector terminals. Disconnect jumper as soon as Check Engine lamp starts flashing.

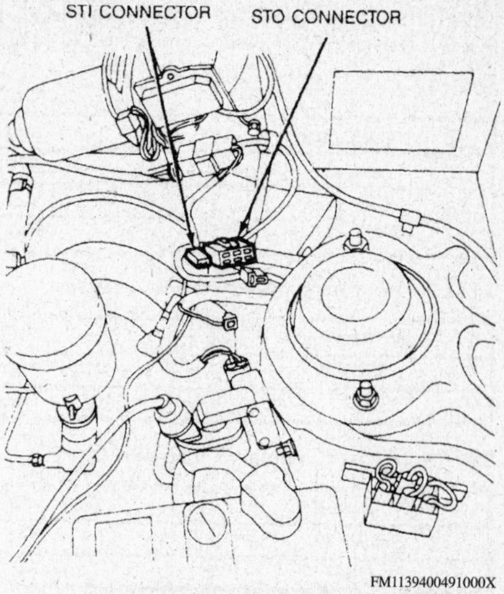

Fig. 16 STI connector location. 1988-90 Festiva

Festiva

The Check Engine Indicator lamp will be illuminated when the ignition switch is in the RUN position with the engine not operating. When the engine is started, the Check Engine lamp should go off. If the lamp remains on, a service code has been stored in the EEC-IV self test system memory. After diagnosis and repair, the self test memory may be cleared of stored codes as follows:

1. With ignition switch in OFF position, connect a jumper wire between Self Test Input (STI) connector terminal and ground. The STI connector is located in rear LH side of engine compartment, **Fig. 16.**
2. Position ignition switch in ON position, then disconnect and reconnect jumper wire connected between STI connector and ground.
3. Disconnect jumper from STI connector as soon as Check Engine lamp stops flashing.
4. Disconnect battery ground cable and depress brake pedal for approximately five to ten seconds.
5. Reconnect battery ground cable.

Merkur

This lamp will be illuminated when the ignition switch is placed in the ON position. After the engine is started, the lamp should go off, unless a problem is detected by the EEC-IV system. After diagnosis and repair, the Check Engine lamp will automatically reset when stored codes are cleared from the EEC-IV system memory. After diagnosis and repair, the EEC-IV memory may be cleared of stored codes as follows:

1. With ignition switch in OFF position,

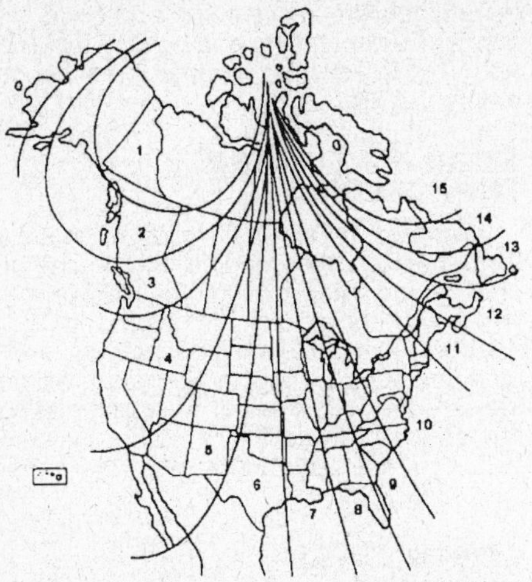

FM9099800928000X

Fig. 17 Magnetic zone map. Continental. Mark VIII & Town Car

connect a jumper wire between Self Test and Self Test Input (STI) connectors, **Fig. 15.** The Self Test and STI connectors are located on RH fender apron between strut tower and battery.
2. Position ignition switch in ON position, then disconnect jumper wire from test connector terminals. Disconnect jumper as soon as Check Engine lamp starts flashing.

Probe w/2.2L Engine & Escort & Tracer w/1.8L Engine

This lamp will be illuminated when the ignition switch is placed in the ON position. After engine is started, the lamp should go off, unless a problem is detected by the system. After diagnosis and repair, the Check Engine lamp will automatically reset when stored codes are cleared from the system memory as follows:

1. Disconnect battery ground cable, then depress brake pedal for approximately five to ten seconds.
2. Reconnect battery ground cable.

1995-97 MODELS w/EEC-IV

This lamp will be illuminated when the ignition switch is placed in the ON position. After engine is started, the lamp should go off, unless a problem is detected by the EEC-IV system. A diagnostic trouble code is stored in the PCM. Following diagnosis and repair, the Check Engine/MIL lamp will automatically reset when stored diagnostic trouble codes are cleared from PCM memory. The PCM reset procedure allows the scan tool to command the PCM to clear all diagnostic trouble codes.

PCM Reset Using Star Tester

1. Turn ignition to OFF position.
2. Perform necessary vehicle preparation and visual inspection.
3. Connect Star tester, then select vehicle model and year.
4. Follow operating instructions on tester screen. Select Generic OBD II Functions.
5. Press CONT button if all OBD II monitors are not complete.
6. Turn ignition switch to ON position.
7. Select Clear Diagnostic Codes and press Start key.

PCM Reset Using Generic Scan Tool

1. Turn ignition to OFF position.
2. Connect scan tool to DLC.
3. Turn ignition switch to ON position.
4. Perform scan tool reset, then turn ignition switch to the OFF position.

Keep Alive Memory (KAM) Reset & PCM Reset Less Electronic Tester

To clear KAM, disconnect battery ground cable for at least five minutes. This will also result in PCM reset.

MODELS w/EEC- V

1. Turn ignition to OFF position.
2. Connect scan tool to DLC.
3. Turn ignition switch to ON position.
4. Perform scan tool reset, then turn ignition switch to the OFF position.

ELECTRONIC COMPASS

CONTINENTAL

1. Determine magnetic zone, **Fig. 17.**
2. Insert a suitable rod into compass module, **Fig. 18,** and press internal switch until ZONE and current zone setting are displayed.
3. Turn ignition switch to ON position, then release switch.
4. Press internal switch until proper zone number is displayed, then release to exit zone setting mode and lock in zone.

MARK VIII

1. Press and hold COMPASS button, then the RESET button until ECO-ZONE and RSETCAL is displayed.
2. Press FUEL ECONOMY button to enter the zone set mode.
3. Refer to **Fig. 17** for proper compass zone selection.
4. Press RESET until correct zone is selected.
5. Press COMPASS button to end zone adjustment.

TOWN CAR

The compass module is located at the back of the rear view mirror.

1. Select compass magnetic zone, **Fig. 17.**
2. Press and hold reset button on top of compass module until message center display reads current magnetic zone setting.
3. Press calibration button on compass module to select proper zone setting.
4. To exit zone setting mode, do not press any buttons for 10 seconds.

LOW COOLANT WARNING SYSTEM

The low coolant warning lamp will be illuminated whenever the coolant level in the coolant recovery bottle is 1/4 to 3/4 inch or more below the cold full mark. Raise coolant level in recovery bottle to the cold full mark to turn lamp off.

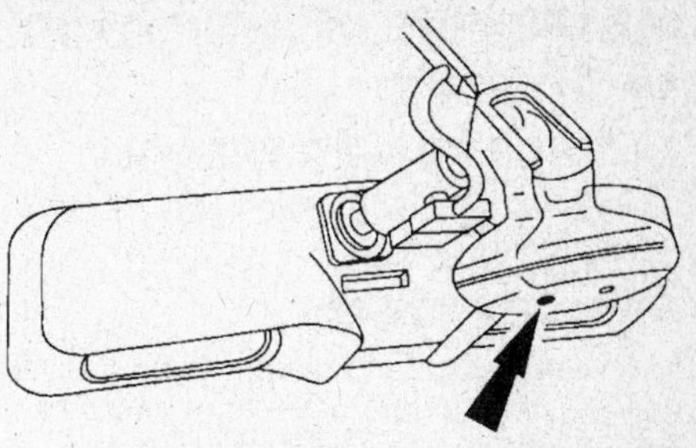

FM9099800929000X

Fig. 18 Compass module location. Continental

On models equipped with GEM module and low coolant level warning system, the low coolant level indicator illuminates for two seconds during engine start up or when ignition is turned to RUN. If coolant level falls below specification for more than 15 seconds, the GEM module generates a single one second tone. Raise coolant level in recovery bottle to specified level to turn lamp off.

LOW OIL LEVEL WARNING INDICATOR

This system is used to indicate when the engine oil level is 1½ quarts or more below the specified level. The lamp will be illuminated during engine starting. If the oil level is sufficient, the lamp will go off when the engine is operating. If the oil level is low, the lamp will remain on until engine oil is added and the ignition switch is placed in the OFF position. The module will take approximately five minutes to reset. If the engine is started during this period, the last recorded reading will be displayed.

MAINTENANCE REMINDER INDICATOR

This lamp is used on some models not equipped with electronic engine controls. The lamp will be illuminated after approximately 2,000 engine starts (60,000 miles of vehicle operation). After performing the required emission control service, the lamp maybe reset as follows:

1. Turn ignition switch to OFF position.
2. Install a suitable screwdriver through the .2 inch hole labeled Reset, then lightly press down and hold.
3. While pressing screwdriver down, turn ignition switch to RUN position. The advisory lamp will then come on. Hold screwdriver down for approximately five seconds.
4. Remove screwdriver and note advisory lamp. Lamp should go out within two to ten seconds indicating that a reset has occurred. If lamp does not go out, repeat procedure. Turn ignition switch to OFF position.
5. Turn ignition switch to RUN position. The advisory lamp should light for approximately two to ten seconds indicating that a proper reset has been accomplished.

MALFUNCTION INDICATOR LAMP (MIL)

EXCEPT 1988-89 TRACER

Refer to "Check Engine Lamp" for lamp reset procedure.

1988-89 TRACER

The malfunction indicator lamp is used only on EFI models. This lamp indicates a malfunction in the Electronic Engine Control (EEC) system. If a malfunction occurs, the lamp will illuminate. The malfunction detected may or may not be a noticeable driveability problem. The lamp will be automatically reset during diagnosis and repair of the system.

The indicator system monitors the following:

1. Air temperature sensor (ACT).
2. Barometric pressure (BP) sensor.
3. Clutch switch, manual transaxle.
4. Engine coolant temperature (ECT) sensor.
5. Engine coolant temperature (ECT) switch.
6. Exhaust gas oxygen (EGO) sensor.
7. Ignition coil (-) terminal.

MESSAGE CENTER

CROWN VICTORIA, GRAND MARQUIS & TOWN CAR

The message center is located to the right of the instrument cluster. It consists of three buttons: Select, E/M and Reset. The E/M button switches the display between English and Metric. The Reset button set data to zero of instantaneous information. The Select button cycles the message display through the following selections:

1. Average speed.
2. Fuel remaining.
3. Average fuel economy and instantaneous fuel economy.
4. Distance to empty.
5. Trip distance.

MARK VIII

Air Ride Switch Off

This warning message is displayed when the air suspension service switch, located in the LH side of the luggage compartment, is off.

Check Air Ride System

This warning message is displayed when an air suspension system diagnostic trouble code is detected by the air suspension/EVO control module.

Check Charging System

This warning message is displayed when the electrical system is not maintaining a proper voltage at the message center.

Check Engine Temp

This warning message is displayed when the coolant is overheating.

Low Engine Coolant

This warning message is displayed when the engine coolant level is below the cold line of the coolant recovery reservoir.

Check Exterior Lamps

This warning message is displayed when one of the following lamps is turned on and at least one is burned out: stop lamp, rear parking lamp or low beam headlamp.

Change Oil Soon Or Oil Change Required

The oil life functions include oil life, change oil soon and oil change required. The oil life is determined by three functions: Smart Tach pulses, miles driven and time elapsed.

When the oil life drops down to the range of 1–5%, the " Change Oil Soon" message will appear. When oil life is 0%, the "Oil Change Required" message will appear.

Depressing the oil change reset button will reset the oil life to 100%.

MULTIPLE FUNCTION WARNING INDICATOR

1987-89 MUSTANG GT

This system monitors engine oil, cooling system, fuel and washer reservoir levels for low fluid level conditions. During engine starting, the lamps will be illuminated for approximately three seconds as a bulb check out. After approximately three seconds, when the bulb check is completed, low fluid level conditions will be verified, if present.

The low engine oil warning lamp is used to indicate when the engine oil level is 1½ quarts or more below the specified level. The lamp will be illuminated during engine starting. If the oil level is sufficient, the lamp will go off when the engine is operating. If the oil level is low, the lamp will remain on until engine oil is added and the ignition switch is placed in the OFF position. The module will take approximately 90 to 150 seconds to reset. If the engine is started during this period, the last recorded reading will be displayed.

The low coolant warning lamp will be illuminated whenever the coolant level in the coolant recovery bottle is below the cold full mark. Raise the coolant level in the recovery bottle to the cold full mark to turn lamp off.

The low fuel warning lamp will be illuminated whenever the fuel level is ⅛ tank capacity or less. Add fuel to vehicle to turn lamp off.

The washer fluid warning lamp will be illuminated whenever the reservoir level is below ⅓ capacity. Raise washer fluid level in reservoir to turn lamp off.

SERVICE INTERVAL REMINDER

1985-88 COUGAR & THUNDERBIRD

At approximately 5,000 or 7,500 miles, depending on engine installation, the word Service will appear on the display for approximately 1 ½ miles to indicate time for service interval. After completing the required service, reset service interval reminder by depressing and holding the Trip and Trip Reset buttons until three beeps are heard, **Fig. 19.**

1989-93 COUGAR & THUNDERBIRD

At approximately 7,500 miles, for models less super charged engine, the engine oil change indicator on the Vehicle Maintenance Monitor will indicate an oil change is needed. On models with super charged engine, the need for engine oil change will be indicated at 5,000 miles. After completing the required service, the oil change indicate can be reset by depressing the reset switch, **Fig. 20.**

CONTINENTAL

After performing the require interval service, the service interval reminder mileage display on the instrument cluster can be reset as follows:

1. Depress System Check button on instrument panel, service interval reminder mileage should be displayed on fuel computer display, **Fig. 21.**
2. Depress Reset button, the service interval reminder mileage should start flashing.
3. Depress Reset and System Check buttons at the same time to reset mileage.

PROBE

Electronic Instrument Cluster

At 7,500 mile intervals, a Service Check message will be displayed under the System Scanner nomenclature on the instrument cluster for three minutes after engine starts, **Fig. 22.** After performing the required interval service, reset the service interval by depressing and holding the Service reset button, located on the speed alarm keyboard, until three tones have sounded, **Fig. 23.**

Vehicle Maintenance Monitor

On models with Vehicle Maintenance Monitor, at 7,500 mile intervals a Service lamp, located on the overhead map lamp console, will be illuminated for 3 minutes after engine start, **Fig. 24.** After performing the required interval service, reset the service interval. On models with speed alarm keypad, depress and hold the Service reset button, until three tones have sounded. On models less speed alarm keypad, locate reset hole in overhead console, then using a suitable tool depress the reset button located behind the hole.

1986-89 SABLE & TAURUS w/ELECTRONIC INSTRUMENT CLUSTER

At 7,200 mile intervals, a Service message will be displayed under the System Scanner nomenclature on the instrument cluster for 30 seconds after engine starts, **Fig. 25.** After performing the required interval service, reset the service interval by simultaneously depressing the ODO Sel and

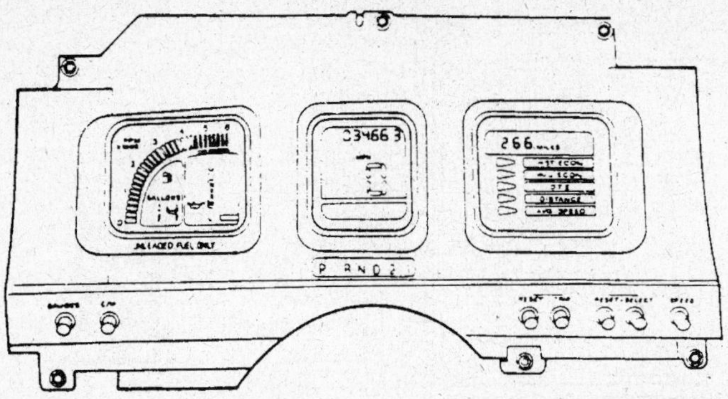

FM1138500149000X

Fig. 19 Trip & reset button locations. 1985–88 Cougar & Thunderbird

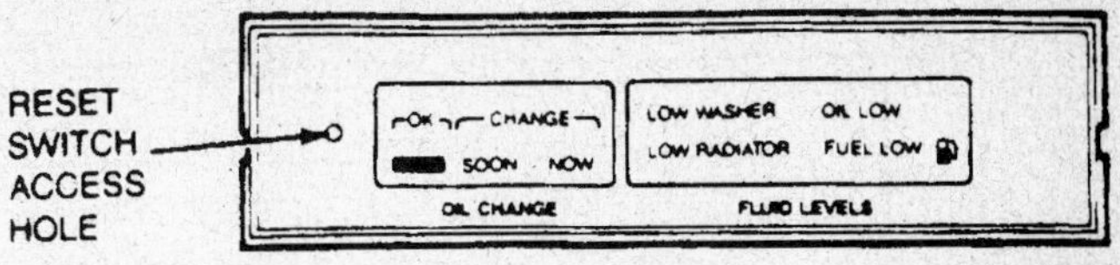

FM1138900150000X

Fig. 20 Oil change interval indicator reset switch access hole location. 1989–93 Cougar & Thunderbird

Trip Reset buttons located on the instrument panel. The word service will disappear from the display and three tones will sound to indicate the service interval has been reset.

GENERAL MOTORS

ANTI-LOCK WARNING LAMP

This lamp will be illuminated when the ignition switch is placed in the ON position. The lamp may be illuminated for as long as 30 seconds as a bulb and system check. If lamp remains illuminated or comes on while operating the vehicle, a problem in the anti-lock brake system is indicated. When lamp is illuminated, place ignition switch in OFF position, then restart engine. If lamp still remains illuminated, the anti-lock brake system should be serviced. The brake system will remain functional, but without the anti-lock function. After servicing the anti-lock brake system the lamp will automatically reset. On some models it may be necessary to operate vehicle at a speed over 18 mph to reset lamp or to clear stored DTC's with a suitable scan tool.

CHANGE ENGINE OIL MESSAGE

BUICK

1997 LeSabre & Park Avenue

After the engine oil has been changed, display the oil life index on the DIC, then hold the RESET button for five seconds. When a DIC message of RESET is displayed and the oil life index equals 100%, the reset is complete.

1998 LeSabre & Park Avenue & 1997-98 Riviera

1. Turn ignition switch to RUN position.
2. Press TRIP button on driver information center until OIL LIFE REMAINING is displayed.
3. Press and hold RESET for 6 seconds, then turn ignition off.

1999-2000 Park Avenue & LeSabre

1. **On 1999 models,** turn ignition On, then press TRIP button on driver information center (DIC) switch to view various menu choices.
   a. Select "OIL LIFE REMAINING."
   b. A message will display percentage of oil life remaining.
   c. Press and hold RESET button on DIC switch for at least 2 seconds.
   d. A message will display the percentage of oil life remaining as 99%.
2. **On 2000 models,** turn ignition switch to On position.
   a. Press the GAGE info button on driver's information center (DIC) switch to view OIL LIFE INDEX.
   b. Press and hold reset button on DIC until display reads OIL LIFE INDEX 100% NORMAL.
3. **On all models,** the engine oil life monitor is now reset.
4. Turn ignition Off.

1999 Riviera

1. Turn ignition to On, then press TRIP button on driver information center (DIC) switch to view various menu choices and stop on OIL LIFE REMAINING. A message will display percentage of oil life remaining.
2. Press and hold RESET button on DIC switch for at least 2 seconds. A message will display percentage of oil life remaining as 99%. The engine oil life monitor is now reset.
3. Turn ignition Off.

1997 Century & Regal

Ensure oil life indicator is displayed. Press and hold the RESET button until oil life display is returned to 100 percent.

1998-2000 Century & Regal

1. Turn ignition switch to RUN position. Do not start engine.
2. Press and release accelerator pedal 3 times within 5 seconds.
3. If CHANGE OIL SOON lamp flashes 2 times, system is reset. If system does not reset, repeat procedure.

Roadmaster

1. Turn ignition switch to On position, without starting engine.
2. Press accelerator pedal to wide open throttle (WOT) position and release three times within five seconds.
3. If "Change Oil" warning indicator goes out, system has been reset.
4. If "Change Oil" warning indicator does not reset, turn ignition switch Off and repeat procedure.

CADILLAC

When the engine oil life index has reached zero, the Change Engine Oil message will be indicated on the Driver Information Display. After performing the engine oil change, the engine Oil Life Index may be reset as follows:

Allante

Press RANGE button until oil index appears, then simultaneously press and hold the AVG SPD and RANGE buttons for a minimum of five seconds.

1989-91 Eldorado & Seville

Press and hold the ENG DATA and RANGE buttons, **Fig. 26,** for a minimum of 5 seconds.

1991-92 DeVille & Fleetwood FWD

Press RANGE and FUEL USED buttons simultaneously to display oil life index, then press the RANGE and RESET buttons until "Change Oil Soon" light flashes (approximately five seconds). The oil life index will not remain displayed.

1993 DeVille & Sixty Special

Reset the Engine Oil Life Index (EOLI) after each oil change by pressing the RANGE and RESET keys on the Fuel Data Center for 5–50 seconds. The "Change Oil Soon" lamp will flash four times to indicate that the index has been reset.

1992-98 Eldorado, 1992-97 Seville & 1994-99 DeVille

Press the INFORMATION button until Oil Life Index is displayed, then press and hold RESET button until Oil Life Index resets to 100 (approximately five seconds).

Fleetwood

1. Turn ignition switch to On position, without starting engine.
2. Press accelerator pedal to wide open throttle (WOT) position and release three times within five seconds.
3. If "Change Oil" warning indicator goes out, system has been reset.
4. If "Change Oil" warning indicator does not reset, turn ignition switch Off and repeat procedure.

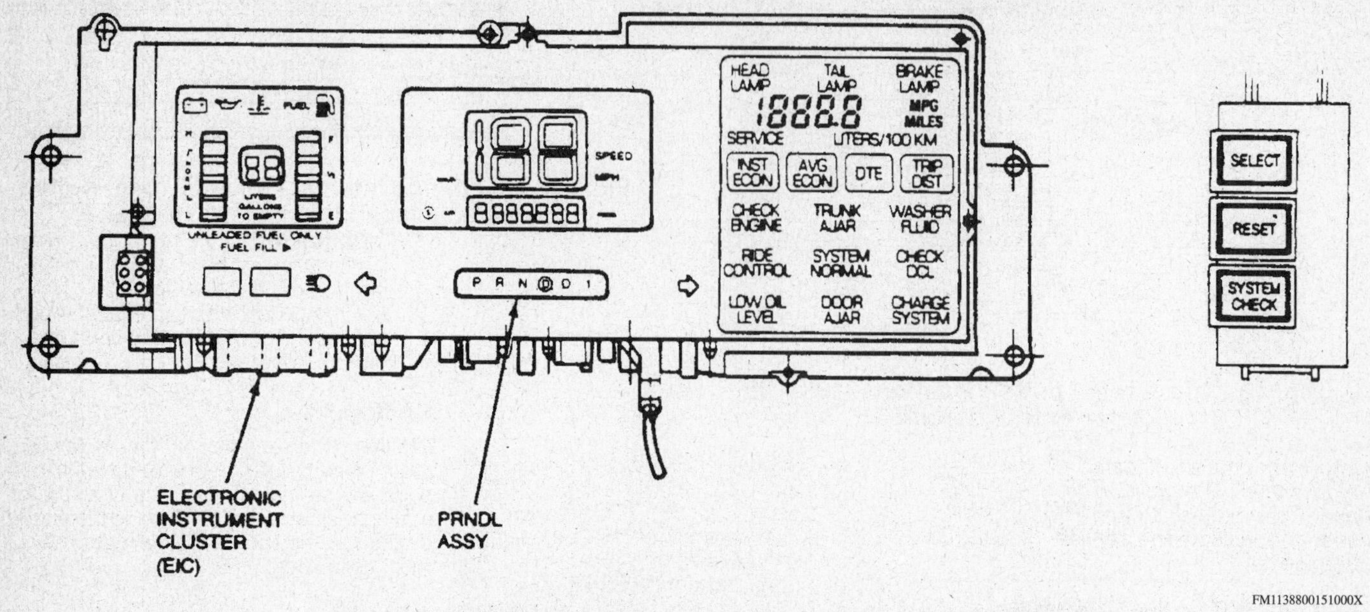

Fig. 21 Instrument cluster & message center. Continental

1995-96 Concours, DeVille, Eldorado & Seville

Press the INFORMATION button until oil life index is displayed, then press Reset button until oil life index resets to 100.

DeVille, Seville & Eldorado

1. Turn ignition On.
2. **On 1999 models,** press TRIP button on driver information center (DIC) switch to view various menu choices
   a. Stop on OIL LIFE REMAINING.
   b. A message will display percentage of oil life remaining.
   c. Press and hold RESET button on DIC switch for at least 2 seconds. A message will display the percentage of oil life remaining as 99%.
3. **On 2000 models,** press INFO button on driver's information center.
   a. Stop when display reads ENGINE OIL LIFE.
   b. Press and hold INFO RESET button on DIC until display reads 100% ENGINE OIL LIFE.
4. **On all models,** the engine oil life monitor is now reset.
5. Turn ignition Off.

CHEVROLET

1994 Caprice & Impala SS

After engine oil has been changed, the Change Oil Soon lamp must be reset. Remove the instrument panel fuse box cover. With ignition switch in the On position, depress the Oil Reset button for five seconds. The change oil lamp should go off.

1995-96 Caprice & Impala SS

1. Turn ignition switch to On position, without starting engine.
2. Press accelerator pedal to wide open throttle (WOT) position and release three times within five seconds.
3. If "Change Oil" warning indicator goes out, system has been reset.
4. If "Change Oil" warning indicator does not reset, turn ignition switch Off and repeat procedure.

1999-2000 Camaro

1. Turn ignition to Run, engine Off.
2. Press TRIP/OIL RESET button on instrument panel for 12 seconds. The OIL CHANGE light will start to flash to confirm that the system is reset. When reset is complete the light will go out.
3. Turn ignition Off.

1990-91 Corvette

After changing engine oil and filter, if necessary, reset service interval indicator as follows:

1. Turn ignition On, press ENG/MET button and release, then press ENG/MET button again within five seconds.
2. Within five seconds of step 1, press and hold the RANGE button until the "Change Oil" indicator begins to flash. Hold RANGE button until indicator stops flashing and goes out, approximately 10 seconds.
3. If indicator was not successfully reset, turn ignition Off and repeat reset procedure.

1992-96 Corvette

1. Turn ignition key to On position, without starting engine.
2. Press ENG MET button on the trip monitor and release, then press and release again within five seconds.
3. Within five seconds of step 2, press and hold GAUGES button on trip monitor. "Change Oil" lamp will flash.
4. Hold GAUGES button until "Change Oil" lamp stops flashing and goes out.
5. When light goes out, the engine oil life monitor is reset. If it does not reset, turn ignition switch Off and repeat procedure.

1997-2000 Corvette

1. Turn ignition key to Run position.
2. Press Trip button on the Driver Information Center (DIC) switch to view menu. Stop at Oil Life Remaining. A message will display the percentage of oil life remaining.
3. Press and hold the Reset button on the DIC switch for at least 2 seconds. A message will display the percentage of oil life remaining as 100%.
4. Place the ignition switch in the Off position.

1998-2000 Lumina & Monte Carlo

1. Turn ignition switch to RUN position. Do not start engine.
2. Press and release accelerator pedal 3 times within 5 seconds.
3. If CHANGE OIL SOON lamp flashes 2 times, system is reset. If system does not reset, repeat procedure as necessary.

OLDSMOBILE

Alero

1. Turn ignition to On position, engine Off.
2. Press RESET button and release. The CHANGE OIL indicator will start flashing.
3. Press and release RESET button again.

Except Aurora, LSS, Toronado & 1992-97 Eighty Eight & Ninety-Eight

When the engine oil life index has reached 10 or less, the Driver Information System display will indicate distance to oil change and sound a beep, when ignition switch is placed in the Run or Accessory position for the first time each day. When the engine oil life index has reached 0, the

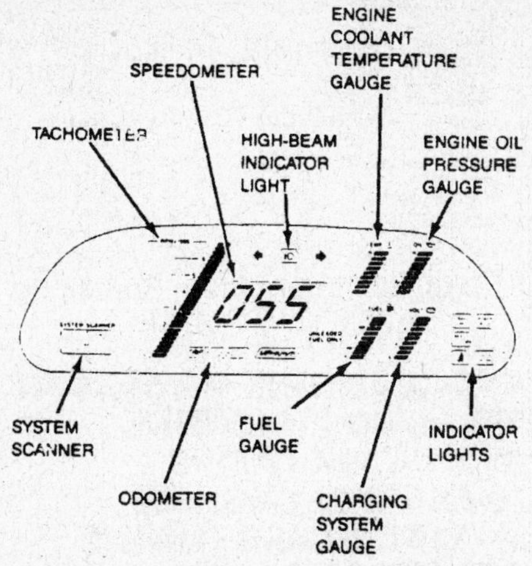

FM1138900152000X

Fig. 22 Electronic instrument cluster. Probe

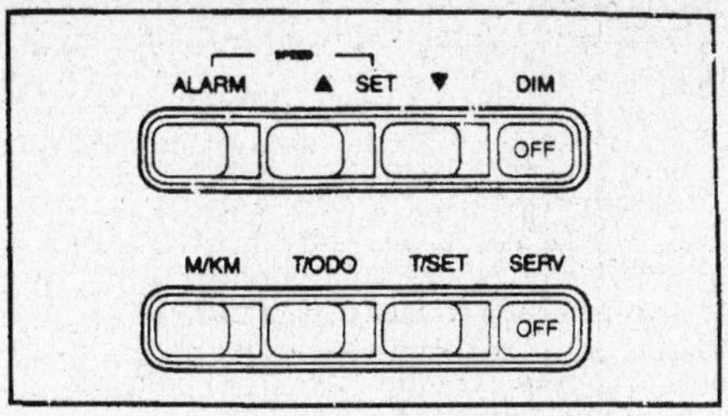

FM1138900153000X

Fig. 23 Speed alarm keyboard. Probe

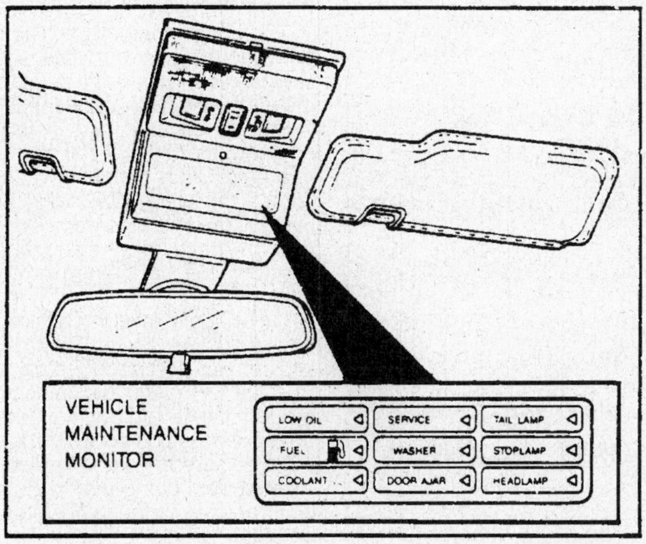

FM1138900154000X

Fig. 24 Vehicle maintenance monitor. Probe

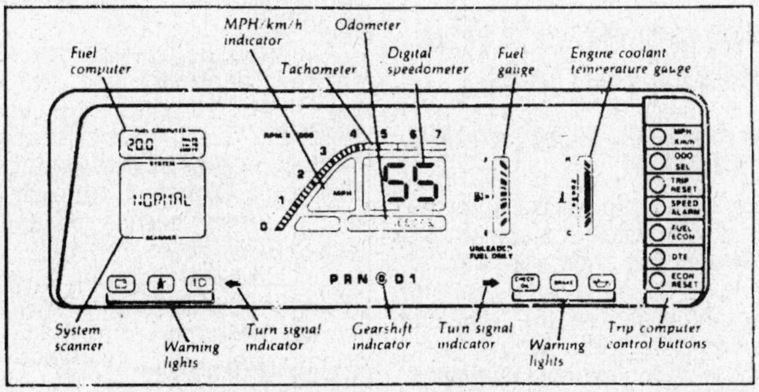

FM1138600155000X

Fig. 25 Instrument cluster & trip control buttons. 1986-89 Sable & Taurus

Driver Information System display will indicate Change Oil Now and sound a beep, when ignition switch is placed in the Run or Accessory position for the first time each day. After engine oil change has been performed, the oil life index may be reset by depressing and holding the Oil and Reset buttons for approximately 5 seconds, **Fig. 27.**

1986-89 Toronado

When the engine oil life index has reached 0, the Information System display will indicate Change Oil. After engine oil change has been performed, the oil life index may be reset by depressing and holding the Engine Data and Gauge buttons until Oil Index 100 message appears in Information Display panel, **Fig. 28.**

1990-92 Toronado

On vehicles less CRT Driver Information Display option, oil life is displayed by pressing the ENG DATA button on the Driver Information System (DIS) keypad several times. To reset the oil life index, press and hold the RESET/ENTER key for five seconds while the oil life is displayed.

On vehicles equipped with a Driver Information Display (option U68), oil life may be displayed by pressing the INFO button and then selecting the OIL LIFE option. Oil life is reset is reset by pressing RESET on the oil life display and then pressing YES on the confirmation screen. This will reset the oil life index and OIL LIFE INDEX 100. The Change Oil message will remain off until the next oil change is needed.

1995 Aurora, 1992-95 Eighty Eight & Ninety-Eight

When the engine oil life index has reached 10 or less, the Driver Information System display will indicate distance to oil change and sound a beep when the ignition switch is placed in the RUN or ACC position for the first time each day. When the engine oil life index has reached zero, the Driver Information System display will indicate "Change Oil Now" and sound a beep, when ignition switch is placed in the RUN or ACC position for the first time each day. After engine oil change has been performed, the oil life index may be reset as follows:

1. **On 1995 Aurora, 1992–93 Eighty Eight and Ninety-Eight,** depress the TEST button and release.
2. Depress OIL button and release.
3. **On 1994–95 Eighty-Eight and Ninety Eight,** select OIL menu by depressing MODE button.
4. **On all models,** depress and hold the RESET button for five to seven seconds.

1996-99 Aurora, LSS, Eighty-Eight & Ninety-Eight

After the engine oil has been changed, display the oil life index on the DIC, then hold the RESET button for six seconds. When a DIC message of RESET is displayed and the oil life index equals 100%, the reset is complete.

Intrigue

1. Turn ignition switch to RUN position. Do not start engine.
2. Press and release accelerator pedal 3

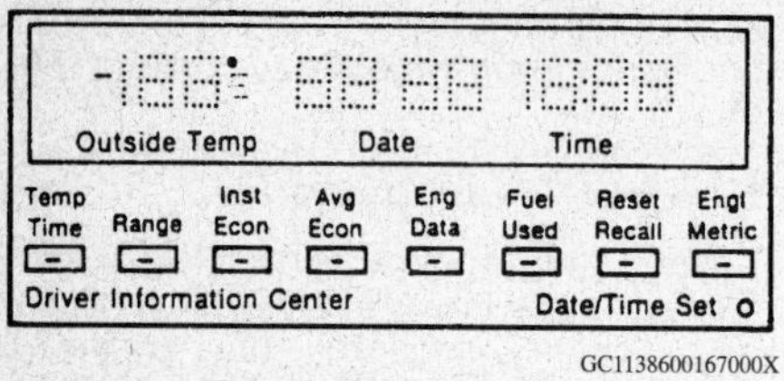

Fig. 26 Driver Information Center. 1986–92 Cadillac Eldorado & Seville

times within 5 seconds.

3. If CHANGE OIL SOON lamp flashes 2 times, system is reset. If system does not reset, repeat procedure as necessary.

PONTIAC

6000 & 1992-95 Bonneville

After changing engine oil and filter, if necessary, reset service interval indicator by depressing and releasing the service reminder button until the desired item is displayed. When the desired item is displayed, do not release service reminder button. After button has been depressed for approximately 10 seconds, the service interval mileage display will begin to count down in 500 mile intervals. When desired service interval mileage is reached, release button. The service interval reminder indicates miles to service, not miles from last service.

1996-97 Bonneville

After the engine oil has been changed, display the oil life index on the DIC, then hold the RESET button for five seconds. When a DIC message of RESET is displayed and the oil life index equals 99% or 100%, the reset is complete.

1998 Bonneville

1. Turn ignition switch to RUN position.
2. Press TRIP button on driver information center (DIC) switch to view menu choices.
3. Select OIL LIFE REMAINING.
4. Press and hold RESET button on DIC for more than five seconds until oil life changes to 100%.
5. Turn ignition switch to OFF position.

1999 Bonneville

1. Turn ignition switch to RUN position.
2. Press and hold reset button in glove compartment for at least five seconds but not more than 60 seconds.
3. After five seconds, observe the CHANGE OIL SOON light flash four times before light turns OFF.
4. Engine oil life monitor has been reset.

2000 Bonneville

1. Turn ignition switch to ON position.
2. Press MODE button on driver information center (DIC) until VIEW DATA is visible.
3. Press SELECT button until OIL LIFE % is visible.
4. Press and hold RESET button on DIC until display reads OIL LIFE 100% NORMAL.

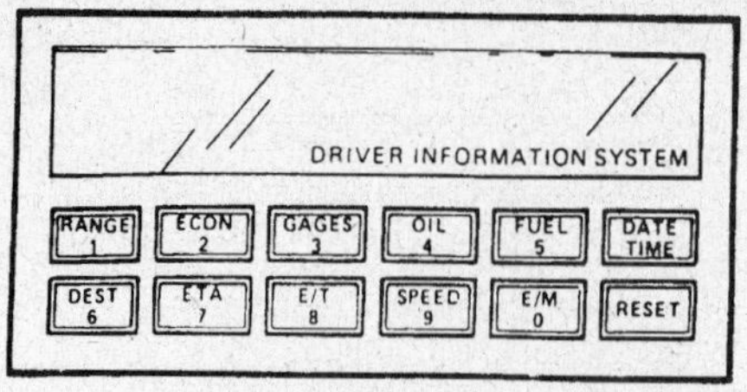

Fig. 27 Driver Information Center. Oldsmobile except Aurora, LSS, Toronado & 1992–97 Eighty Eight & Ninety-Eight

5. Engine oil life monitor is now reset.

1999 Firebird

1. Turn ignition to Run, engine Off.
2. Press TRIP/OIL RESET button on instrument panel for 12 seconds.
3. The OIL CHANGE light will start to flash to confirm that the system is reset. When reset is complete the light will go out.
4. Turn ignition Off.

1999-2000 Grand AM

1. Turn ignition to On position, engine Off.
2. Press RESET button and release. The CHANGE OIL indicator will start flashing.
3. Press and release RESET button again.

Grand Prix

Ensure oil life indicator is displayed. Press and hold the RESET button until oil life display is returned to 100 percent.

CHECK GAUGE WARNING LAMP

The "Check Gauge" warning lamp will illuminate to warn the driver to check the oil pressure gauge, engine coolant temperature gauge and the voltmeter. When lit, the "Check Gauge" lamp indicates that one of these gauges is operating in an abnormal range.

CHECK ENGINE INDICATOR LAMP (DIESEL ENGINE)

MODELS w/DIESEL ELECTRONIC CONTROL SYSTEM

The check engine lamp will be illuminated when the ignition switch is placed in the On position. When the engine is started, the lamp should go off. If the lamp remains On after the engine is started, the self diagnosis system has detected a problem and has stored a code in the system Electronic Control Module (ECM). After diagnosis and repair, the ECM memory can be cleared of codes when the ignition switch has been placed in the Off position. To clear codes, disconnect battery ground cable for approximately 30 seconds. It should be noted, when battery ground cable is disconnected to clear codes, components such as clocks, electronically tuned radios etc., will have to be reset.

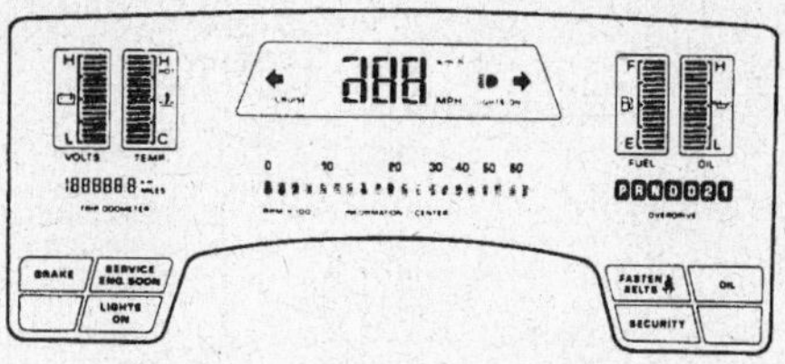

Fig. 28 Information Center. 1986–89 Toronado

CHECK ENGINE OR SERVICE NO w/SOON ENGINE INDICATOR LAMPS (GASOLINE ENGINES w/ELECTRONIC ENGINE CONTROLS OR EFI)

EXCEPT CHEVROLET SPECTRUM & SPRINT, GEO & PONTIAC LEMANS

The check engine lamp will be illuminated when the ignition switch is placed in the On position. When the engine is started, the lamp should go off. If the lamp remains On for 10 seconds or constantly after the engine is started, the self diagnosis system has detected a problem and has stored a code in the system Electronic Control Module (ECM) or Powertrain Control Module (PCM). After diagnosis and repair, the ECM memory can be cleared of codes as follows:

On models except Cadillac with DEFI and 1986–88 Buick Reatta/Riviera and Oldsmobile Toronado/Trofeo, remove the ECM/PCM fuse or disconnect the battery ground cable for approximately 30 seconds, with ignition switch in the Off position. If battery ground cable is disconnected to clear codes, components such as clocks, electronically tuned radios etc., will have to be reset.

On vehicle that are equipped as such, the ECM/PCM power feed is connected by a pigtail, inline fuse holder, at the positive battery terminal. To clear codes within the ECM/PCM system and protect the components that need resetting, disconnect the inline fuse.

On 1980–85 Cadillac models with DEFI engines, depress Electronic Climate Control Off and Hi buttons to clear codes. On 1986–92 Cadillac DeVille and Fleetwood models, depress Off and Lo button on the Electronic Climate Control to clear stored BCM codes. Depress Off and Hi to clear stored ECM codes.

On Cadillac Eldorado and Seville and 1986–88 Buick Reatta/Riviera and Oldsmobile Toronado/Trofeo models, the stored codes are cleared during the self-diagnostic procedure.

CHEVROLET SPECTRUM

The check engine lamp will be illuminated when the ignition switch is in the On position with engine not operating. When engine is started, the Check Engine lamp should go off. If lamp remains on, a code has been stored by the Electronic Control Module (ECM). After diagnosis and repair, place ignition switch in Off position, then clear codes stored in the ECM memory by removing the Emission or ECM fuse, located in the fuse box under the instrument panel on the lefthand side, for approximately 10 seconds.

CHEVROLET SPRINT

1987-88 Models Less Turbo Engine

The check engine lamp will be illuminated when the ignition switch is in the On position with engine not operating. When engine is started, the Check Engine lamp should go off. If lamp remains on, a code has been stored by the Electronic Control Module (ECM) memory. After diagnosis and repair, with diagnosis switch in Off position, start engine and allow to reach operating temperature. After engine hasreached operating temperature, the Check Engine lamp should be off while engine is operating.

1987-88 Models w/Turbo Engine

The check engine lamp will be illuminated when the ignition switch is in the On position with engine not operating. When engine is started, the Check Engine lamp should go off. If lamp remains on, a code has been stored by the Electronic Control Module (ECM) memory. After diagnosis and repair, place ignition switch in Off position, then clear codes stored in the ECM memory by disconnecting the battery ground cable, for approximately 20 seconds.

GEO METRO

The check engine lamp will be illuminated when the ignition switch is in the On position with engine not operating. When engine is started, the Check Engine lamp should go off. If lamp remains on, a code has been stored by the Electronic Control Module (ECM) memory. After diagnosis and repair, place ignition switch in Off position, then clear codes stored in the ECM memory by disconnecting the battery ground cable, for approximately 20 seconds.

GEO PRIZM

The check engine lamp will be illuminated when the ignition switch is in the On position with engine not operating. When engine is started, the Check Engine lamp should go off. If lamp remains on, a code has been stored by the Electronic Control Unit (ECU) memory. After diagnosis and repair, place ignition switch in Off position, then clear codes stored in the ECU memory by removing the Stop Fuse. The Stop fuse is located in a fuse panel, in the passenger compartment, on driver's side, behind kick panel, **Fig. 29.** The fuse must be removed for 10 seconds or longer, depending on ambient temperature. The lower the ambient temperature, the longer the fuse will have to be removed.

GEO STORM

The check engine lamp will be illuminated when the ignition switch is in the On position with engine not operating. When engine is started, the Check Engine lamp should go off. If lamp remains on, a code has been stored by the Electronic Control Module (ECM) memory. After diagnosis and repair, place ignition switch in Off position, then clear codes stored in the ECM memory by disconnecting the battery ground cable for approximately 30 seconds.

GEO SPECTRUM

The check engine lamp will be illuminated when the ignition switch is in the On position with engine not operating. When engine is started, the Check Engine lamp should go off. If lamp remains on, a code has been stored by the Electronic Control Module (ECM) memory. After diagnosis and repair, place ignition switch in Off position, then clear codes stored in the ECM memory by disconnecting the battery ground cable for approximately 30 seconds.

PONTIAC LEMANS

The check engine lamp will be illuminated when the ignition switch is placed in the On position. When the engine is started, the lamp should go off. If the lamp remains On for 10 seconds or constantly after the engine is started, the self diagnosis system has detected a problem and has stored a code in the system Electronic Control Module (ECM). After diagnosis and repair, the ECM memory can be cleared of codes, by disconnecting battery ground cable for 10 seconds, with ignition switch in the Off position.

CHECK INFO CENTER WARNING LAMP

1986-92 CADILLAC ELDORADO & SEVILLE

This lamp will be illuminated for a few seconds when the ignition switch is placed in the On position as a bulb check. If lamp remains illuminated, a message is store in the Driver Information Center. Refer to " Driver Information Center."

CHOKE OR OIL/CHOKE WARNING LAMP

CARBURETED ENGINE

On models less gauges, the oil/choke warning indicator lamp should be illuminated when the ignition switch is in the Run or Start position. When the engine is started, the choke warning indicator lamp should go off. If the lamp fails to illuminate with ignition switch in Run or Start position with engine not operating, a burned bulb or fuse or defect in choke electrical system is indicated. If lamp remains on after engine has been started, a problem in the engine oil pressure system or electrical choke system exist.

On models equipped with gauges, the choke warning indicator lamp should be illuminated when the ignition switch is in the Run or Start position. When the engine is started, the choke warning indicator lamp should go off. If fails to illuminate with ignition switch in Run or Start position with engine not operating, a burnt out bulb or fuse or defect in choke electrical system is indicated. If lamp remains on after engine has been started, a problem in the alternator circuit is indicated.

After service has been completed, the lamp operation should return to normal.

DRIVER INFORMATION CENTER

CADILLAC

1986-88 Eldorado & Seville

This system, **Fig. 26,** incorporates a warning lamp, located on the instrument cluster, that is illuminated when the ignition switch is in the On position. After a few seconds the lamp should go off, unless a message in The Driver Information System is present. The driver information center will display the following messages:

A/C Overheated—A/C Compressor Off—This message is displayed when excessive pressure in the refrigerant system is encountered. When this condition is encountered, the A/C compressor clutch will be de-energized and cool air will not be delivered to the vehicle interior. The message will continue to appear and the A/C compressor clutch will continue to be de-energized until the system pressure returns to normal range. If this message frequently appears, the A/C system should be serviced.

A/C Sensor Fault—This message will be displayed when the sensor controlling A/C compressor clutch cycling has failed. When this sensor has failed, the A/C compressor will not operate and the A/C system will emit warmer air. After servicing system and replacing sensor, the display message will be cancelled.

Battery Volts High—This message will appear when the charging system is overcharging the battery. After completing charging system diagnosis and repair, the message will be cancelled when battery voltage returns to 11.5 to 15.5 volts with engine operating. Battery voltage can be displayed on the Drive Information Center Display by depressing the Eng-Data button three times.

Battery Volts Low—If this message is displayed while driving the vehicle or after vehicle has been started, a problem in the charging system is present or battery has been drained. After diagnosing charging system or electrical system for cause of battery drain, the message will be cancelled when engine is operating and battery voltage is between 11.5 to 15.5 volts. Battery voltage can be displayed on the Drive Information Center Display by depressing the Eng-Data button three times.

Engine Hot—A/C Compressor Off—This message will appear when A/C system is on Auto or Defrost and engine coolant temperature is excessive. The A/C compressor clutch will be automatically de-energized when excessive engine coolant temperatures are encountered. When engine coolant temperature returns to normal, the A/C compressor clutch will be energized and the message on the display will be cancelled.

Front Or Rear Door Ajar—This message will appear when the transmission selector lever is moved out of the Park position and a door is not properly closed. The message can be cancelled by properly closing the indicated door.

Fuel Level Very Low—When low fuel level conditions are encountered this message will appear. To cancel message, add fuel.

Headlamps Or Parking Lamps On—This message will be displayed when the headlamp switch is On, vehicle is moving and the sensed level of outside light indicates that headlamps should not be illuminated. This message may be cancelled by placing the headlamp switch in the Off position.

Low A/C Refrigerant—A/C Compressor Off—This message will be displayed when the A/C system detects a refrigerant charge low enough to cause compressor damage. When this condition is encountered, the A/C compressor clutch is de-energized and the A/C system is switched from Auto to Econ. The system will remain in Econ until necessary repairs are made and system is recharged. After completing necessary repairs and recharging the system, A/C system operation will return to normal and the message on the display will be cancelled.

Low A/C Refrigerant—Service A/C Soon—This message will be displayed when the A/C system detects that refrigerant charge is low enough to cause a reduction in cooling capacity. This message will be displayed until system has been recharged.

Low Washer Fluid—This message will appear when windshield washer fluid level is low. To cancel message, refill windshield washer fluid reservoir.

Service Electrical System—This message will appear when a problem in the charging system is present. After repairing charging system, the message will be automatically cancelled.

Service Now Or Service Soon—This message will be displayed when a problem in one the engine monitored systems is present. After diagnosis and repair the message will be automatically cancelled.

System Problem—Service Car Soon—This message will be displayed when one or more of the vehicle computers supplying information to the Driver Information Center become defective. After diagnosis and repair of the defective computer, the message will be automatically cancelled.

Theft System Problem/Car May Not Start—This message will appear when the vehicle security system senses an improper ignition key has been placed in the ignition switch. After removal of key from ignition switch, the Driver Information Center display will indicate " Wait 3 Minutes," "Wait 2 Minutes," Wait 1 Minute and then "Start Car." When the " Start Car" message appears, insert ignition key and attempt to start vehicle. If message appears again, check ignition key for damage and replace as necessary. If key appears to be satisfactory, clean pellet contacts with a soft cloth and attempt to restart vehicle.

Trunk Open—This message will appear when the ignition switch is the Run position and the trunk is not properly closed. The message can be cancelled by properly closing the trunk.

1989-92 Eldorado & Seville

This system incorporates a warning lamp, located on the instrument cluster, that is illuminated when the ignition switch is in the On position. After a few seconds the lamp should go off, unless a message in The Driver Information System is present. The driver information center will display the following messages:

A/C Overheated—A/C Compressor Off—This message is displayed when excessive pressure in the refrigerant system is encountered. When this condition is encountered, the A/C Compressor clutch will be de-energized and cool air will not be delivered to the vehicle interior. The message will continue to appear and the A/C compressor clutch will continue to be de-energized until the system pressure returns to normal range. If this message frequently appears, the A/C system should be serviced.

A/C Sensor Fault—This message will be displayed when the sensor controlling A/C compressor clutch cycling has failed. When this sensor has failed, the A/C compressor will not operate and the A/C system will emit warmer air. After servicing system and replacing sensor, the display message will be cancelled.

Battery Volts High—This message will appear when the charging system is overcharging the battery. After completing charging system diagnosis and repair, the message will be cancelled when battery voltage returns to 11.5 to 15.5 volts with engine operating. Battery voltage can be displayed on the Drive Information Center Display by depressing the Eng-Data button three times.

Battery Volts Low—If this message is displayed while driving the vehicle or after vehicle has been started, a problem in the charging system is present or battery has been drained. After diagnosing charging system or electrical system for cause of battery drain, the message will be cancelled when engine is operating and battery voltage is between 11.5 to 15.5 volts. Battery voltage can be displayed on the Drive Information Center Display by depressing the Eng-Data button three times.

Change Engine Oil—When the engine oil life index has reached 0, the Change Engine Oil message will be indicated. After performing the engine oil change, the engine Oil Life Index may be reset by depressing and holding the Engine Data and Range buttons for at least 5 seconds

Cooling Fan Fault—This message will appear when the engine cooling fan system inoperative. After repairing cooling fan system the message will be automatically cancelled.

Engine Hot—A/C Compressor Off—This message will appear when A/C system is Auto or Defrost and engine coolant temperature is excessive. The A/C compressor clutch will be automatically de-energized when excessive engine coolant temperatures are encountered. When engine coolant temperature returns to normal, the A/C compressor clutch will be energized and the message on the display will be cancelled.

Front Or Rear Door Ajar—This message will appear when the transmission selector lever is moved out of the Park position and a door is not properly closed. The message can be cancelled by properly closing the indicated door.

Fuel Level Very Low—When low fuel level conditions are encountered this message will appear. To cancel message, add fuel.

Gear Select Problem—This message will appear if a problem in the transaxle gear select system is encountered while operating vehicle. After performing necessary service, the message will automatically be cancelled.

Headlamps Or Parking Lamps On—This message will be displayed when the headlamp switch is On, vehicle is moving and the sensed level of outside light indicates that headlamps should not be illuminated. This message may be cancelled by placing the headlamp switch in the Off position.

Headlamps Suggested—This message will be displayed when the Twilight Sentinel is in the Off position, vehicle is moving and the sensed level of outside light indicates that headlamps should be illuminated. This message may be cancelled by activating the Twilight Sentinel System.

Low A/C Refrigerant—A/C Compressor Off—This message will be displayed when the A/C system detects a refrigerant charge low enough to cause compressor damage. When this condition is encountered, the A/C compressor clutch is de-energized and the A/C system is switched from Auto to Econ. The system will remain in Econ until necessary repairs are made and system is recharged. After completing necessary repairs and recharging the system, A/C system operation will return to normal and the message on the display will be cancelled.

Low A/C Refrigerant—Service A/C Soon—This message will be displayed when the A/C system detects that refrigerant charge is low enough to cause a reduction in cooling capacity. This message will be displayed until system has been recharged.

Low Washer Fluid—This message will appear when windshield washer fluid level is low. To cancel message, refill windshield washer fluid reservoir.

Oil Life Index—The oil life index is a series of numerals ranging from 0–100. The 100 is indicated when engine oil has been drained and refilled. The 0 is an indication that the engine oil should be changed. The oil life index is accessed by depressing the Engine Data button four times.

Service Electrical System—This message will appear when a problem in the charging system is present. After repairing charging system, the message will be automatically cancelled.

Set Timing Mode—This message will appear if ignition timing is improperly set. After performing necessary service, the message will be automatically cancelled.

Starting Disabled/Due to Theft System/Remove Ignition Key—This message is an indication of a problem in the vehicle security system that may prohibit the vehicle from being restarted after the ignition switch has been placed in the Off position. After servicing the vehicle security system the message will be automatically cancelled.

System Satisfactory—This message will be displayed for approximately 5 seconds after ignition switch has been placed in the On position, unless a problem in the system has been detected. After approximately 5 seconds the display will return to the last display function selected.

System Problem—Service Car Soon—This message will be displayed when one or more of the vehicle computers supplying information to the Driver Information Center become defective. After diagnosis and repair of the defective computer, the message will be automatically cancelled.

Theft System Problem/Car May Not Start—This message will appear when the vehicle security system senses an improper ignition key has been placed in the ignition switch. After removing key from ignition switch, the Driver Information Center display will indicate " Wait 3 Minutes," "Wait 2 Minutes," Wait 1 Minute and then "Start Car." When the " Start Car" message appears, insert ignition key and attempt to start vehicle. If message appears again, check ignition key for damage and replace as necessary. If key appears to be satisfactory, clean pellet contacts with a soft cloth and attempt to restart vehicle.

Trunk Open—This message will appear when the ignition switch is the Run position and the trunk is not properly closed. The message can be cancelled by properly closing the trunk.

OLDSMOBILE

Aurora, 1992-93 Eighty-Eight & Ninety-Eight

The Driver Information Center Display, **Figs. 30 and 31,** is located on the instrument panel (Eighty-Eight and Ninety-Eight models with digital cluster or touring sedan gauge cluster). It provides traveling and performance information on the following:

1. Date and Time—This information is displayed for five seconds when the ignition is turned on. The DT/TM button may be depressed at any time to display current date and time.
2. Fuel Economy—The ECON button displays average fuel economy.
3. Remaining Fuel/Fuel Used—Depressing FUEL button displays amount of fuel used since reset button was last pressed. Depressing FUEL button a second time displays amount of fuel remaining.
4. Fuel Range—Depress RANGE to display distance that may be driven before refueling. To display amount of fuel used from a specific starting point, depress FUEL then RESET.
5. Average Speed—Depress SPEED to display average speed. To reset average speed, depress SPEED then RESET.
6. Remaining Oil Life and Oil Change Information—The OIL button displays information on oil life. Refer to "Change Oil Or Change Oil Now Message" for reset procedure.
7. Engine Coolant Temperature, Oil Pressure, Battery Voltage and Tachometer—Depressing GAGES once displays coolant temperature. Pressing GAGES a second time displays oil pressure. Pressing GAGES a third time displays battery voltage. Pressing GAGES a fourth time displays tachometer RPM.
8. Distance To Destination—Depress DEST then RESET and enter length of trip. Display will then count backwards to zero distance remaining. When the display reaches zero, "TRIP COMPLETE" is displayed. This message will clear when the TEST button is depressed or the ignition switch is turned off.
9. Estimated Time of Arrival—After entering distance to destination, Press ETA button to display time remaining to destination (based on average speed).
10. Elapsed Time—Depressing the E/T button activates a stopwatch that records up to 100 hours.

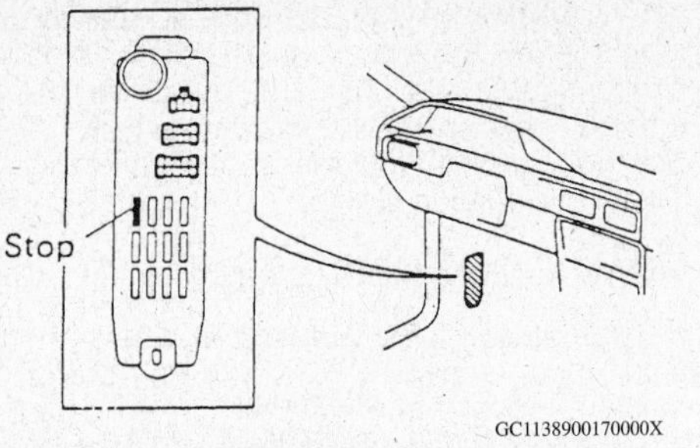

Fig. 29 Stop fuse location. Geo Prizm

LSS, 1994-96 Eighty-Eight & Ninety Eight

The Driver Information Center Display, **Fig. 32,** is located on the instrument panel. When the ignition switch is placed in the On position, the display will go through a system check while the message "Monitored Systems OK" is displayed. If no problems are detected, the screen returns to the mode displayed before the engine was turned off.

There are four buttons that control the functions of the driver information center:

1. The MODE button, when pressed, cycles through a series of displays in the following order:
   a. ECON—Average fuel economy and instantaneous fuel economy.
   b. FUEL—Amount of fuel used since last fuel-used reset, and fuel remaining.
   c. RANGE—Fuel range and low fuel range.
   d. OIL—Oil life index and next required oil change.
   e. GAGES—Oil pressure, tachometer and battery voltage information.
   f. ET—Elapsed time since last reset.
   g. DT/TM—Date and time.
2. The ON/OFF button is used to input numbers and to blank out the display.
3. The RESET button is used with other buttons to reset the system. Depressing this button once enters the reset mode. Pressing this button again aborts the reset.
4. The SEL button is used to select different displays within a specific mode. For example, when the SEL button is depressed while in the GAGES mode, the display will cycle from oil pressure to battery voltage to tachometer.

PONTIAC

6000 & Bonneville

The Driver Information Center Display, **Fig. 33,** is located on the instrument panel. When the ignition switch is placed in the On position, the display will go through a bulb check, in which the vehicle graph and message title will be displayed in sequence. After the sequence has been completed, all messages and vehicle graph will remain illuminated for approximately 2 seconds. After approximately 2 seconds, if all monitored systems are functioning properly, the message titles should go off and only the vehicle outline should be illuminated. If a problem in any of the monitored systems is present, the particular title for the monitored system will be illuminated and its approximate location on the vehicle graphic display will be illuminated. The following messages will be displayed:

1. **Function Monitor**—The coolant level, fuel level and windshield washer levels are monitored when ignition switch is the On position.
   a. Coolant Level—This message will be indicated when engine coolant level in the radiator drops below a predetermined level. To cancel message, check cooling system, then add coolant to bring system to proper level.
   b. Fuel Level—This message will be indicated when fuel level is 5 gallons or less. To cancel message add fuel to fuel tank.
   c. Washer Fluid—This message will be indicated when windshield washer fluid is at about 40% of capacity. To cancel message, add washer fluid to reservoir.
2. **Lamp Check**—The headlamps, tail lamps, brake lamps and turn signal lamps will be checked whenever the lamp system is activated. To cancel this message, replace bulb or check and repair electrical system as necessary for lamp system indicated.
3. **Security**—Door, Hood Or Trunk Ajar are monitored. This message will appear when the indicated component is open or improperly closed. To cancel message, properly close indicated component.

4. **Service Reminder**—Oil change, oil filter change, engine tune-up and tire rotation intervals are monitored.
   a. After the bulb check sequence has been completed, the service interval can be checked by depressing the service reminder button. Depressing the button once will display the Change Oil indication and mileage remaining to service interval. Depressing the button a second time, will display the Change Oil Filter indication and mileage remaining to service interval. Depressing the button a third time will display the Rotate Tires and mileage to service interval. Depressing the button a fourth time will display Tune-Up indication and mileage to service interval.
   b. After completing the required service, reset service interval indicator by depressing and releasing the service reminder button until the desired item is displayed. When the desired item is displayed, do not release service reminder button. After button has been depressed for approximately 10 seconds, the service interval mileage display will begin to count down in 500 mile intervals. When desired service interval mileage is reached, release button. The service interval reminder indicates miles to service, not miles from last service.

EMISSION OR SENSOR MAINTENANCE REMINDER FLAG

1980 MODELS & 1981–83 CADILLAC LIMOUSINE & COMMERCIAL CHASSIS

At 30,000 mile intervals, a Emission or Sensor reminder flag, if equipped, will appear across the odometer to indicate the need for oxygen sensor replacement. After performing the required service, the flag must be reset for the next 30,000 mile interval.

On models except Cadillac, this is accomplished by gaining access to the speedometer head and removing the speedometer lens. Using a suitable pointed tool, rotate edge of flag wheel detents downward, until flag wheel can no longer be rotated. Flag wheel alignment mark should center in odometer.

On Cadillac models, remove lower steering column cover, then lightly pull sensor reset cable to reset flag. The sensor reset cable is located to the left of the speedometer cluster.

ENGINE CONTROL SYSTEM WARNING LAMP

1986–88 CADILLAC ELDORADO & SEVILLE

This lamp will be illuminated for a few seconds when the ignition switch is placed in On position as a bulb check. If lamp remains on, a problem in one of the emission control systems is indicated. The Driver Information Center should indicate a Service Soon or Service Now message. Refer to " Driver Information Center."

LOW COOLANT LAMP

This lamp will be illuminated when engine coolant level in the radiator drops below a predetermined level. To turn lamp off, check cooling system, then add coolant to bring system to proper level.

LOW OIL LEVEL INDICATOR

The Low Oil indicator ground is controlled by the PCM. To check for a low oil condition, the PCM checks the low oil level sensor after the ignition switch has been turned to the Off or Lock position. The PCM checks for a low oil condition 32 minutes after the ignition switch is turned off if the previous ignition cycle was less than 12 minutes. The PCM checks for a low oil condition 3 minutes after the ignition switch is turned off if the previous ignition cycle was less than 12 minutes.

LOW WASHER FLUID INDICATOR

The windshield washer solvent tank has a switch that closes when the washer solvent level becomes low, illuminating the "Low Washer Fluid" indicator.

OXYGEN SENSOR MAINTENANCE REMINDER LAMP

1985–86 CHEVROLET SPRINT

A Sensor lamp is located on the instrument panel to indicate proper operation of the oxygen sensor feedback circuit. Every 30,000 miles of vehicle operation, the lamp will begin to flash. When the lamp begins to flash, the feedback circuit should be checked and the lamp reset using the following procedure.

1. Ensure ignition switch is off, remove fuse panel cover and move cancel switch to on position, **Fig. 34.**
2. Turn ignition switch to On position and observe Sensor lamp. If lamp does not light (without flashing), check for defective bulb or open feed circuit and repair as needed.
3. After illumination of lamp is confirmed, start engine and run until it reaches normal operating temperature.
4. Run engine at 1500–2000 RPM while observing lamp.
5. If lamp flashes, system is operating properly. If lamp does not flash, a problem in the Computer Controlled Emission Control System may be indicated.
6. After proper system operation has been verified, place cancel switch in off position to reset automatic indicator system.

SERVICE AIR COND LAMP

CADILLAC

This lamp will be illuminated when the A/C system detects a low refrigerant charge. The lamp will be illuminated for approximately 2 seconds after ignition switch has been placed in the On position as a bulb check.

If while operating vehicle, the lamp illuminates for approximately 60 seconds and then goes off, the refrigerant level is low enough to cause reduced cooling capacity. At this point the blower motor will increase speed to try to offset the loss in cooling capacity. The lamp will be automatically reset after system has been checked and refrigerant charge has been brought to proper level.

If lamp is illuminated for approximately 60 seconds after engine start up, the refrigerant charge may be low enough to cause A/C compressor damage. When this condition is encountered, the A/C compressor clutch is de-energized and the A/C system is switched from Auto to Econ. The system will remain in Econ until necessary repairs are made and system is recharged. After completing necessary repairs and recharging the system, A/C system operation will return to normal and the lamp will be automatically reset.

SERVICE ELECTRICAL SYSTEM LAMP

CADILLAC

This lamp will be illuminated when a problem in the charging system is present. The lamp will be illuminated during engine starting as a bulb check. If lamp is illuminated while engine is operating, the charging system should be checked. After repairing charging system, the lamp will be automatically reset.

WATER IN FUEL OR DRAIN FUEL FILTER WARNING LAMP

DIESEL ENGINE

The water in fuel indicator will be illuminated when excessive water has entered the fuel system. As the fuel filter becomes plugged, a low pressure sensor activates the lamp. The lamp will be illuminated during engine starting as a bulb check. Once the engine has started, the lamp should go off. If the lamp is illuminated intermittently, drain fuel filter. If lamp remains illuminated, drain fuel filter. If the lamp still remains on after fuel filter has been drained, replace fuel filter. If lamp is illuminated during high speed operation or during heavy acceleration, replace fuel filter. If after starting, the engine stalls and will not restart and lamp remains illuminated, check for plugged fuel filter or fuel lines. If this condition occurs immediately after refueling, check fuel tank for large concentration of water in fuel, and if necessary purge fuel tank and replace

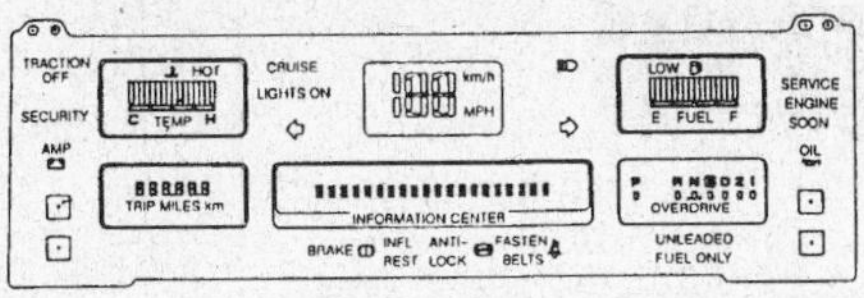

GC1139200518000X

Fig. 30 Driver information center. 1992-93 Eighty-Eight & Ninety-Eight

fuel filter. After performing the required service, the increased fuel pressure through the fuel filter will reset the water in fuel lamp.

SATURN

AIR BAG TELLTALE LAMP

During normal operation the air bag telltale lamp will notify the driver of correct system operation by flashing seven times when the ignition is first turned On. The telltale will turn Off if the system is functioning normally. The telltale lamp will illuminate to warn the operator of a SIR electrical system malfunction which could potentially affect the operation of the SIR system.

CHANGE OIL SOON TELLTALE LAMP

The PCM has the ability to calculate when the engine oil needs to be changed based on vehicle mileage, engine revolutions and engine coolant temperature. The PCM bases the engine oil change interval within a window of 3000–6000 miles regardless of engine revolutions and engine coolant temperature. To reset the PCM oil life monitor, depress the oil life reset switch located in the underhood fuse box for five seconds with the ignition switch in the On position.

ENGINE COOLANT TEMPERATURE TELLTALE LAMP

If the engine coolant temperature exceeds 244°F, or if the transaxle fluid temperature exceeds 284°F, the coolant temperature telltale lamp will illuminate. The PCM will turn the cooling fan On if an ECT DTC is active.

LOW OIL PRESSURE TELLTALE LAMP

The engine oil pressure switch is normally closed and open when engine oil pressure is 1.4–5.8 psi. If the lamp is illuminated with engine running, inspect wiring for oil pressure switch circuit and the engine lubrication system for proper oil pump output pressure.

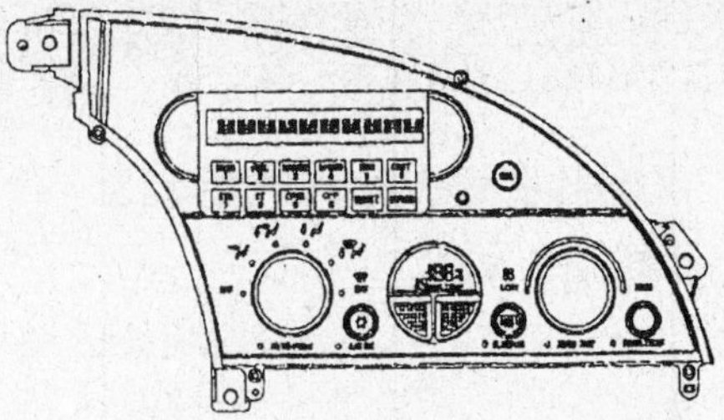

GC1139500519000X

Fig. 31 Driver information center. Aurora

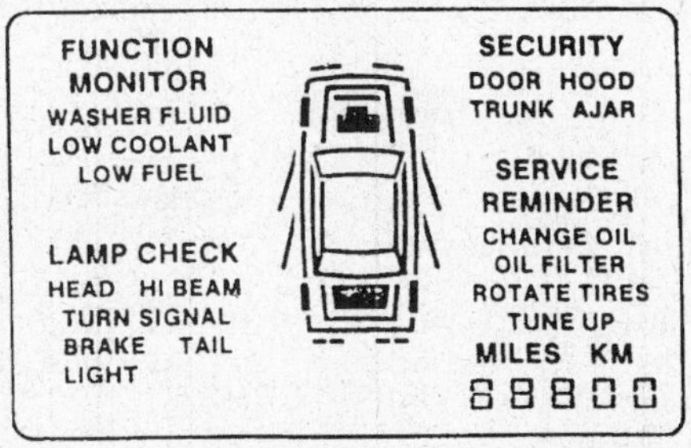

GC1138800171000X

Fig. 33 Driver Information Center. 1988–90 Pontiac 6000 STE & Bonneville SSE

MALFUNCTION INDICATOR LAMP (MIL)

As a bulb and system check, the lamp will come On with the key On and the engine not running. When the engine is started, the lamp will turn Off. If the lamp remains On, the self diagnostic system has detected a malfunction. If the malfunction is intermittent or the system is repaired, the lamp will go Off after three trips but a diagnostic trouble code (DTC) will be stored in the PCM. Use a suitable scan tool to retrieve and erase any DTC's using the "Clear DTC Information" option. If the lamp remains On while the engine is running or when a malfunction is suspected due to a driveability problem, perform and OBD system check. Scan the serial data stream using a suitable scan tool.

PASSLOCK TELLTALE LAMP

2000

The instrument panel cluster contains the security telltale lamp. The security telltale has three modes of operation, Off, Flashing & On. The security telltale will be Off if ignition is in the Off position or if the ignition is in the Run, Start or Acc position and the security system diagnostics have all passed. The security telltale will be On if the body control module (BCM) is performing a bulb test at vehicle start up, the security system diagnostics have not yet completed at vehicle start up or if a security system diagnostic trouble code (DTC) is set in the BCM or PCM. The security telltale will be flashing if the tamper hall effect has been triggered, there was incorrect Passlock sensor data to the BCM for more than five seconds during vehicle start, there was no Passlock sensor data to the BCM for more than five seconds during vehicle start or there was incorrect password from the BCM to the PCM after five seconds during vehicle start. Repair or replace components as necessary, and retrieve and clear any associated DTC's to reset the telltale lamp.

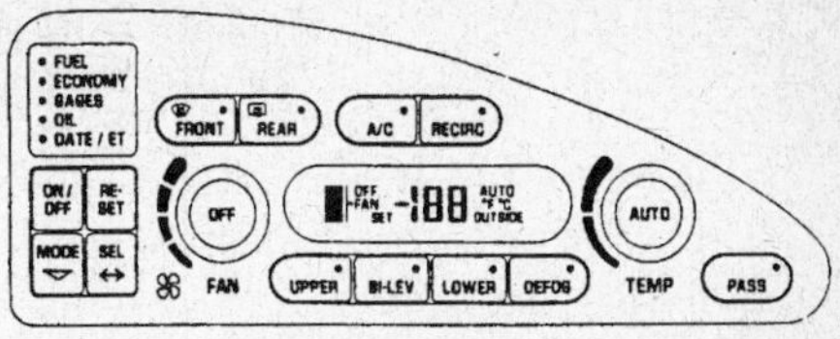

GC1139400520000X

Fig. 32 Driver information center. 1994-96 Eighty-Eight & Ninety-Eight

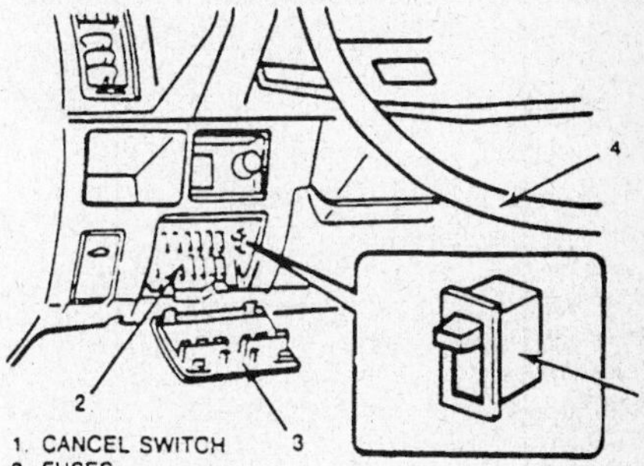

GC1138500172000X

Fig. 34 Oxygen sensor indicator lamp cancel switch. 1985–86 Chevrolet Sprint

SERVICE TELLTALE LAMP

The service telltale lamp is used for non-emissions related failures which without being serviced could lead to component damage to other sub systems. As a bulb check, the lamp will come On for two to three seconds and then turn Off. If the lamp remains On, the system has detected a fault. If the problem is intermittent or the system is repaired, the lamp will turn Off three seconds after the PCM diagnostic test passes. Any DTC's will be stored in the freeze frame/failure records. Use a suitable scan tool to retrieve and erase any DTC's using the "Clear DTC Information" option.

VEHICLE LIFT POINTS

TABLE OF CONTENTS

DaimlerChrysler

INDEX

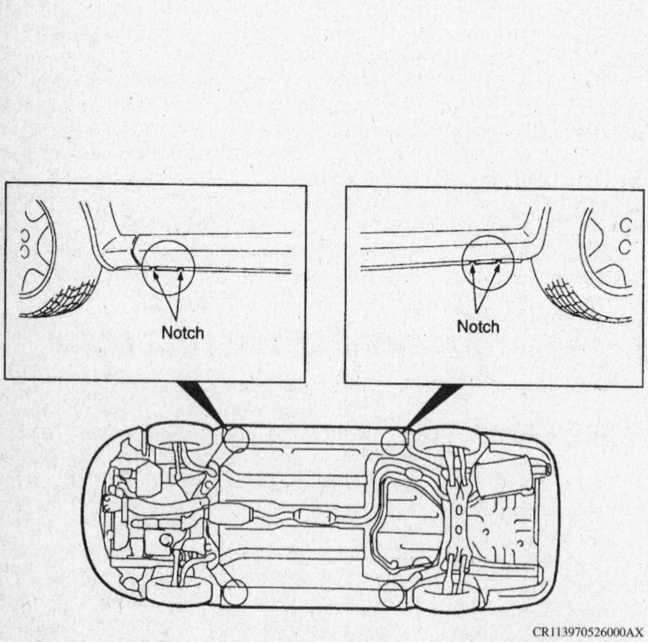

Fig. 1 Vehicle Lift Points (Part 1 of 2). Avenger & Sebring

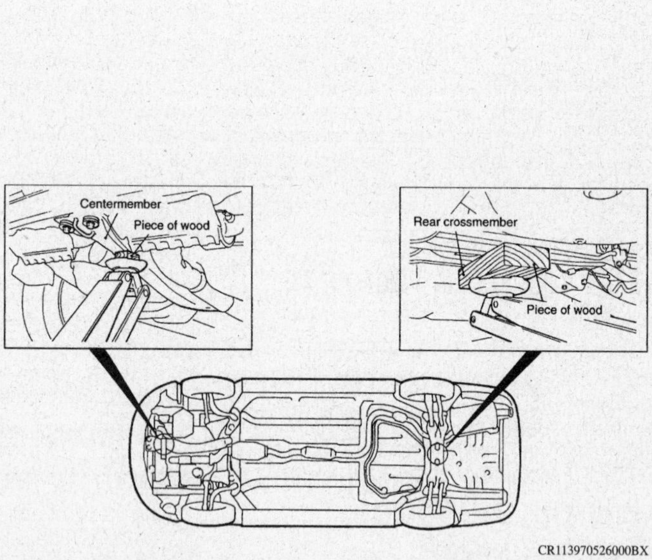

Fig. 1 Vehicle Lift Points (Part 2 of 2). Avenger & Sebring

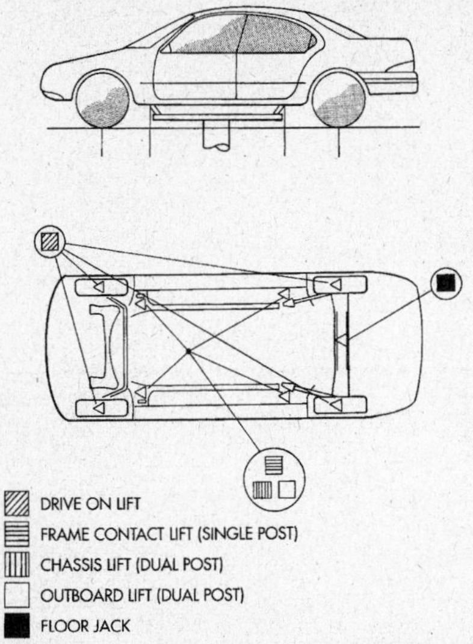

CAUTION: Do not position hoisting device on suspension components, damage to vehicle can result.

CR1139705263000X

Fig. 2 Vehicle Lift Points. Breeze, Cirrus & Stratus

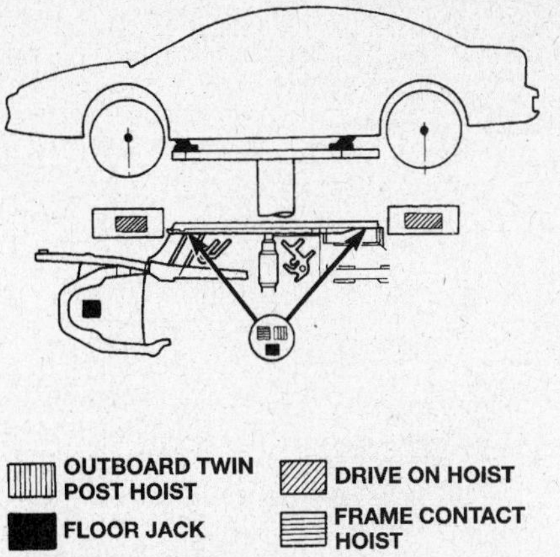

CAUTION: Do not position hoisting device on suspension components, damage to vehicle can result.

CR1139705264000X

Fig. 3 Vehicle Lift Points. 1997 Concorde, Intrepid, LHS & Vision

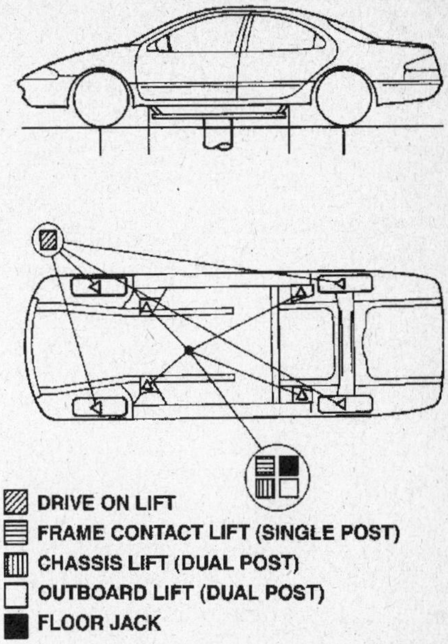

CR1139800576000X

Fig. 4 Vehicle Lift Points. 1998-2000 Concorde, Intrepid, LHS & 300M

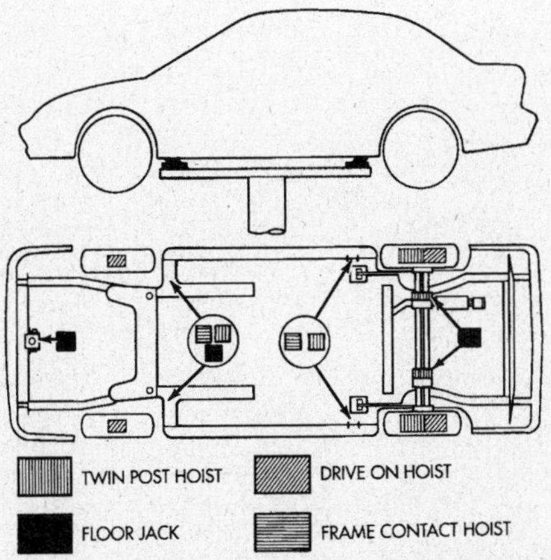

CR1139705265000X

Fig. 5 Vehicle Lift Points. Neon

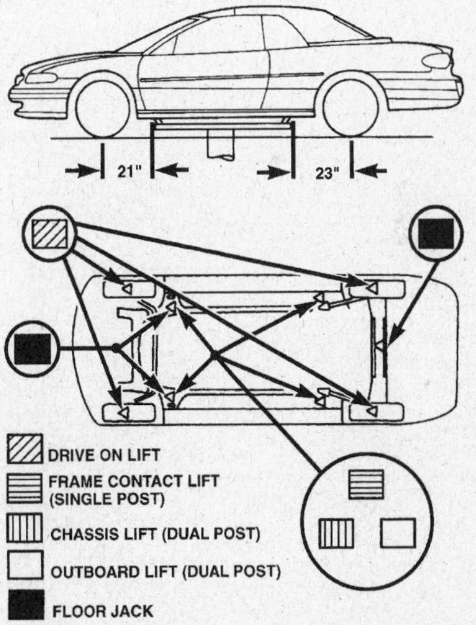

CR1139705266000X

Fig. 6 Vehicle Lift Points. Sebring Convertible

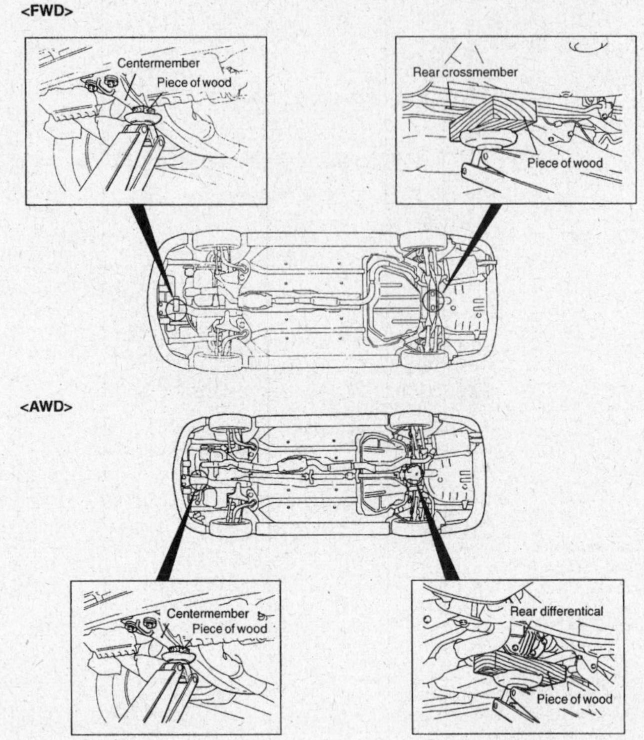

Caution
Never support any point other than the specified one, or it will be deformed.

CR113970526800AX

Fig. 7 Vehicle Lift Points (Part 1 of 2). Talon

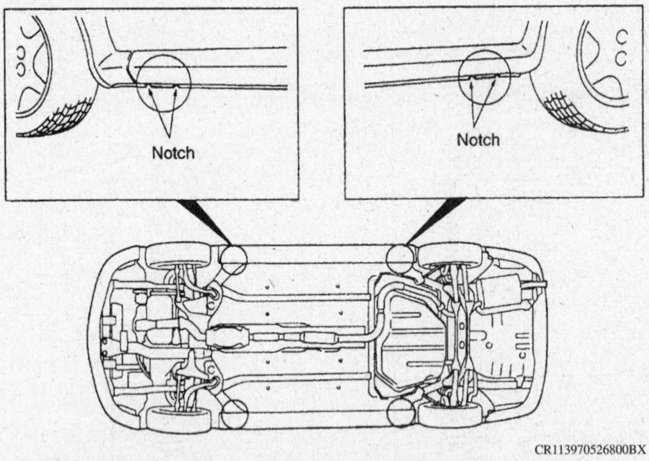

CR113970526800BX

Fig. 7 Vehicle Lift Points (Part 2 of 2). Talon

Ford Motor Co.

INDEX

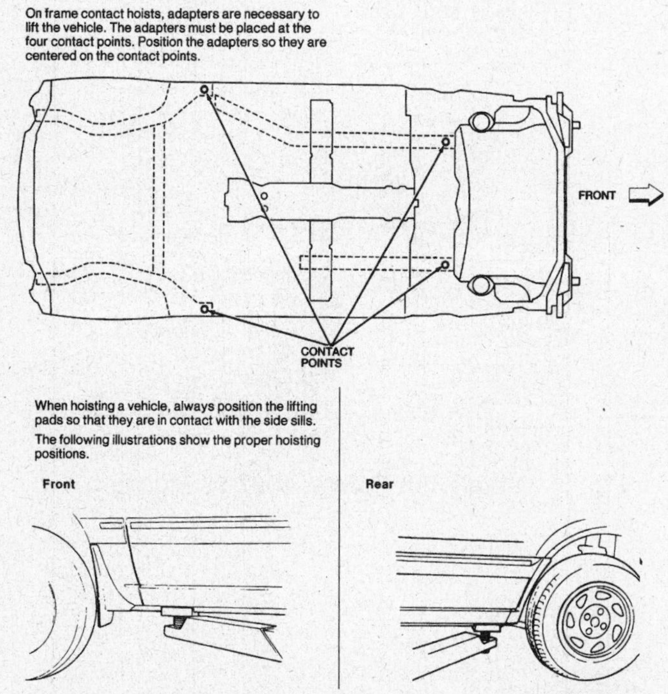

Fig. 1 Vehicle Lift Points (Part 1 of 2). Aspire

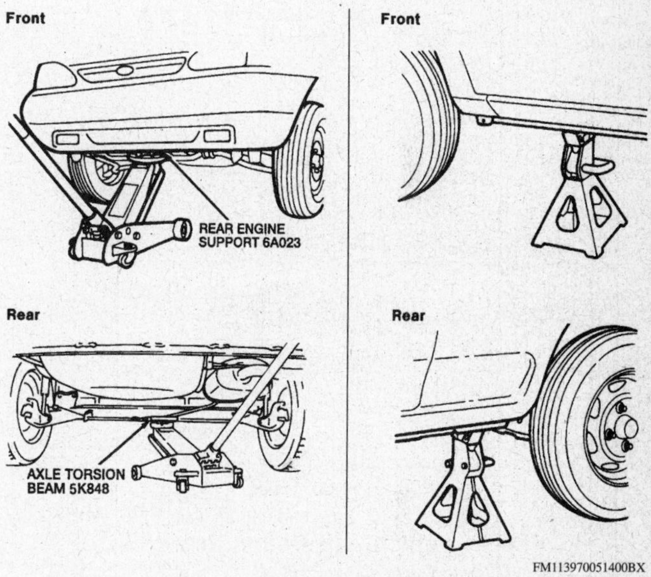

Fig. 2 Vehicle Lift Points (Part 2 of 2). Aspire

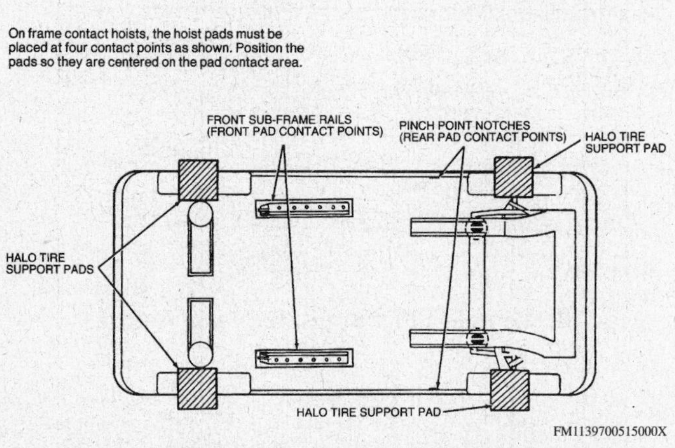

Fig. 3 Vehicle Lift Points. 1997 Continental

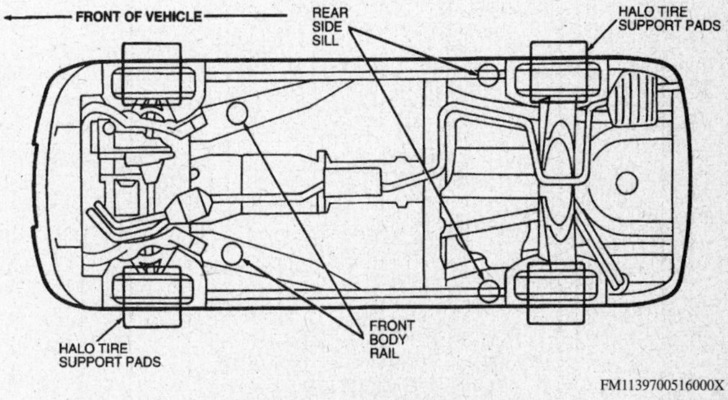

Fig. 4 Vehicle Lift Points. Contour, Mystique & 1999–2000 Cougar

On frame contact hoists, adapters are necessary to lift the vehicle. The adapters must be placed at four contact points. Position the adapters so they are centered on the adapter contact area.

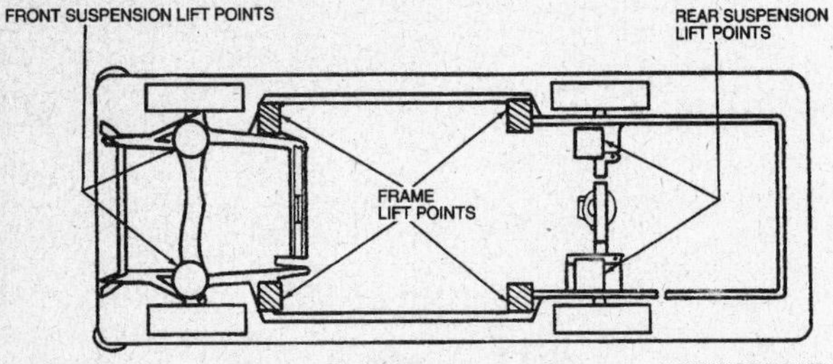

FM1139700517000X

Fig. 5 Vehicle Lift Points. Crown Victoria, Grand Marquis & Town Car

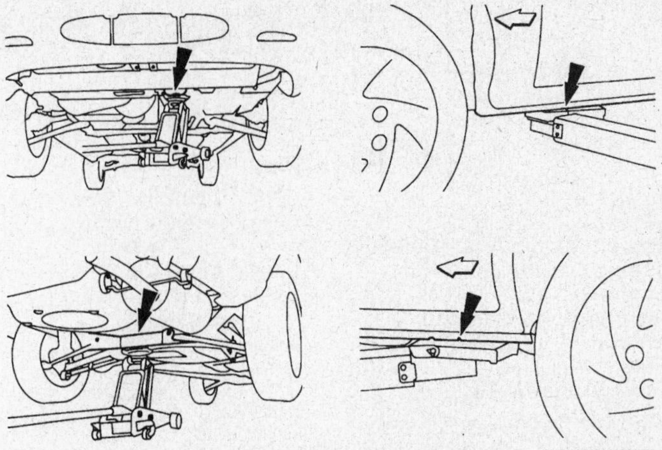

FM1139700518000X

Fig. 6 Vehicle Lift Points. Escort, Tracer & ZX2

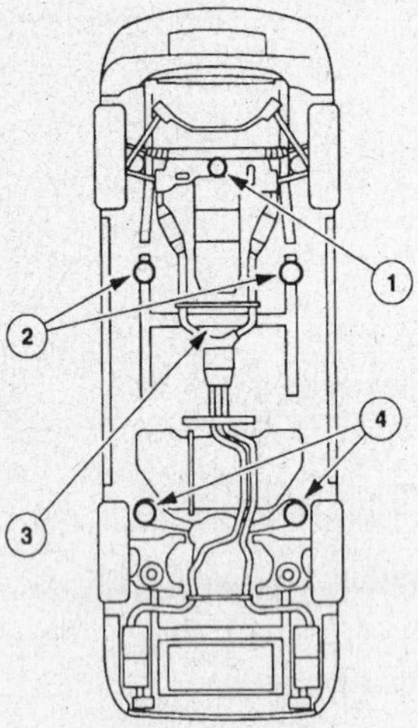

1 Front suspension lift point.
2 Front frame lift points.
3 No. 3 crossmember.
4 Rear frame lift points.

FM1139700519000A

Fig. 7 Vehicle Lift Points. Mark VIII

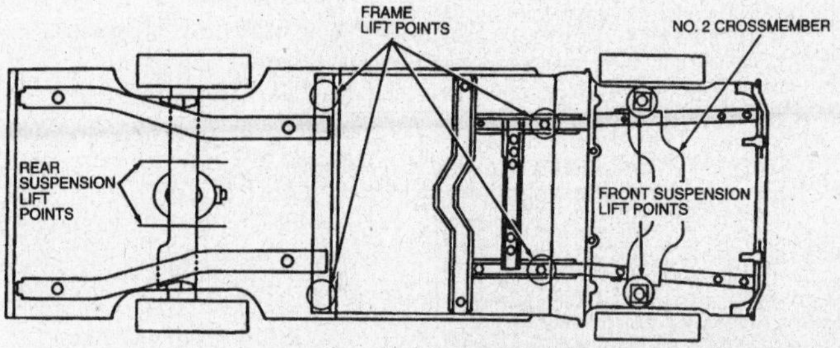

FM1139700520000X

Fig. 8 Vehicle Lift Points. 1997-98 Mustang

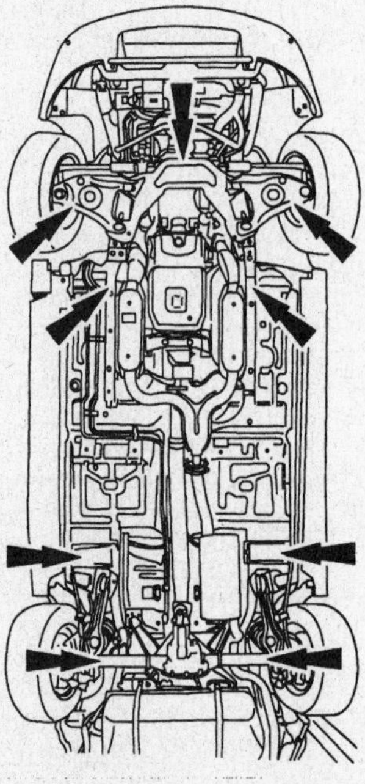

FM1139900926000X

Fig. 9 Vehicle lift points. 1999–2000 Mustang

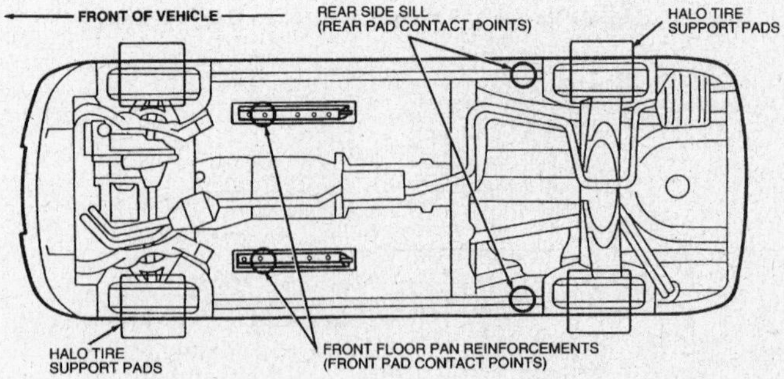

FM1139700522000X

Fig. 10 Vehicle Lift Points. Sable & Taurus

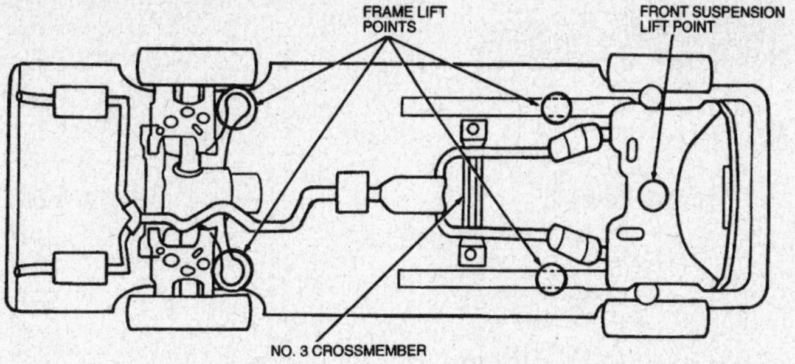

Fig. 11 Vehicle Lift Points. Thunderbird & 1997 Cougar

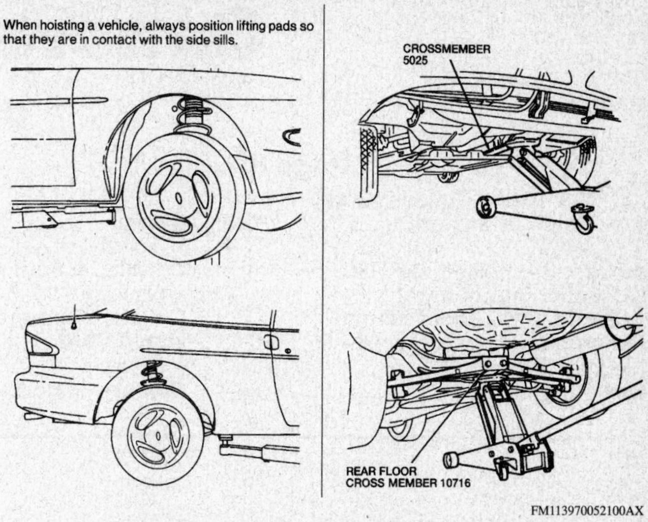

Fig. 12 Vehicle Lift Points(Part 1 of 2). Probe

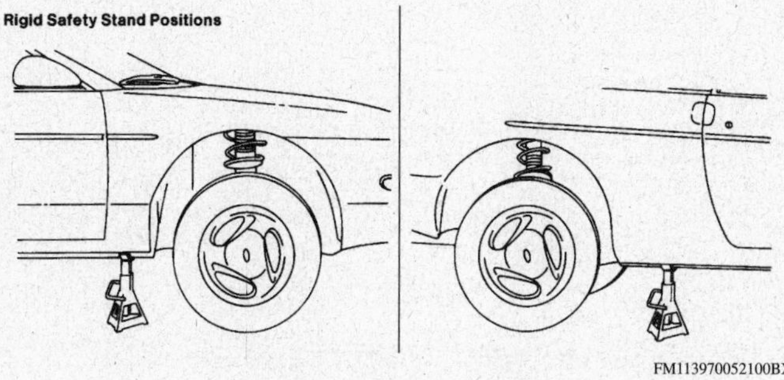

Fig. 12 Vehicle Lift Points (Part 2 of 2). Probe

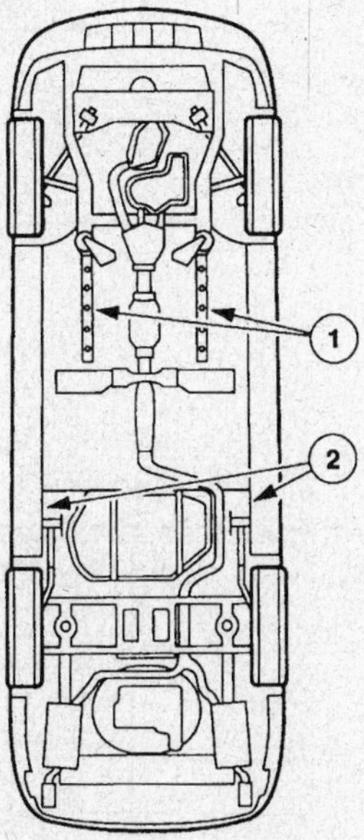

1 Front frame lift points.

2 Rear pinch point notches.

FM1139800564000X

Fig. 13 Vehicle Lift Points. 1998–2000 Continental

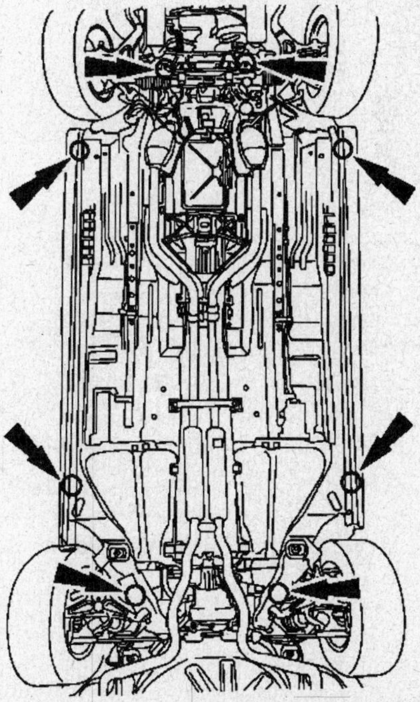

Fig. 14 Vehicle Lift Points. LS

General Motors

INDEX

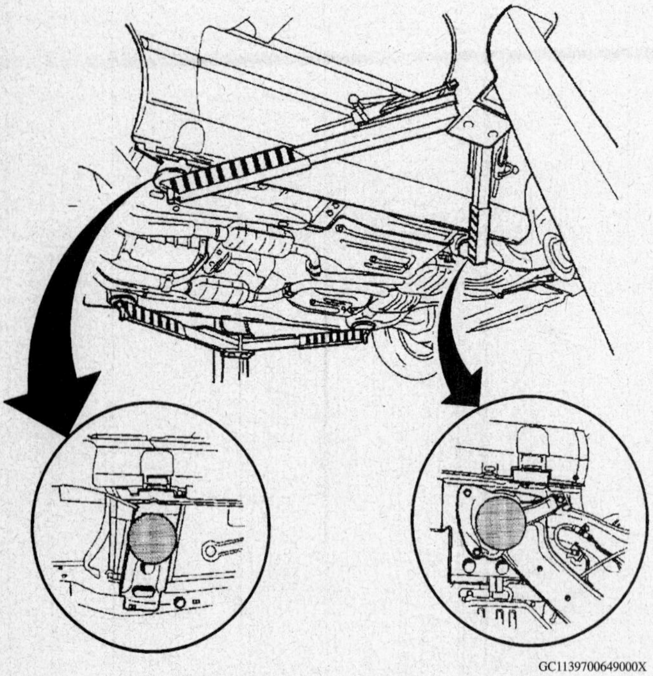

Fig. 1 Vehicle Lift Points. Catera

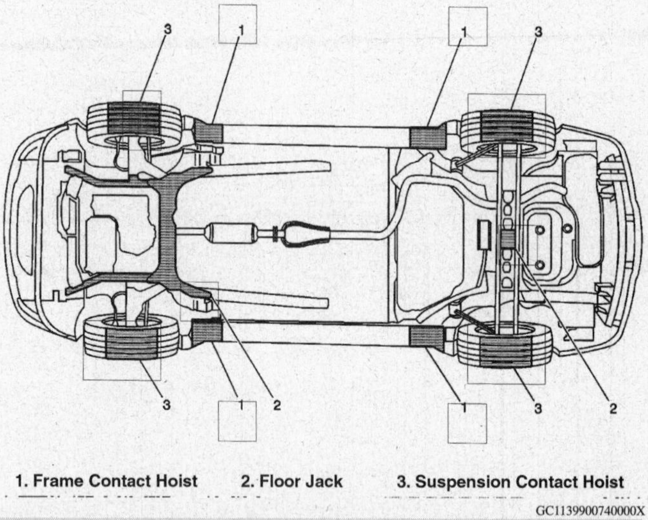

Fig. 2 Vehicle Lift Points. Achieva, Alero, Cutlass, Grand Am, Malibu & Skylark

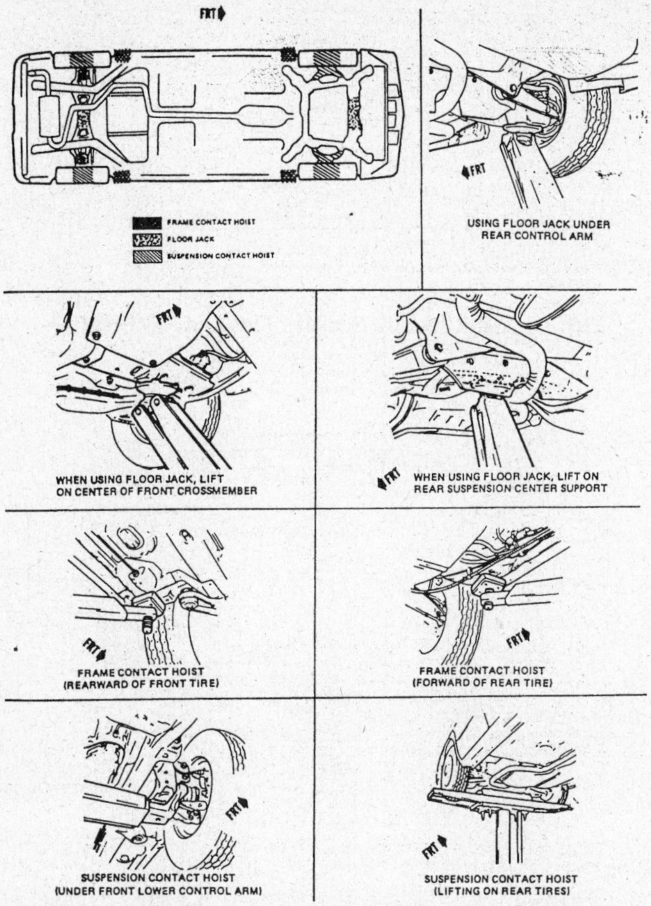

GC1139100175000X

Fig. 3 Vehicle Lift Points. Aurora, Bonneville, DeVille, Eldorado, Eighty-Eight, LeSabre, LSS, Park Avenue, Riviera, Regency & Seville

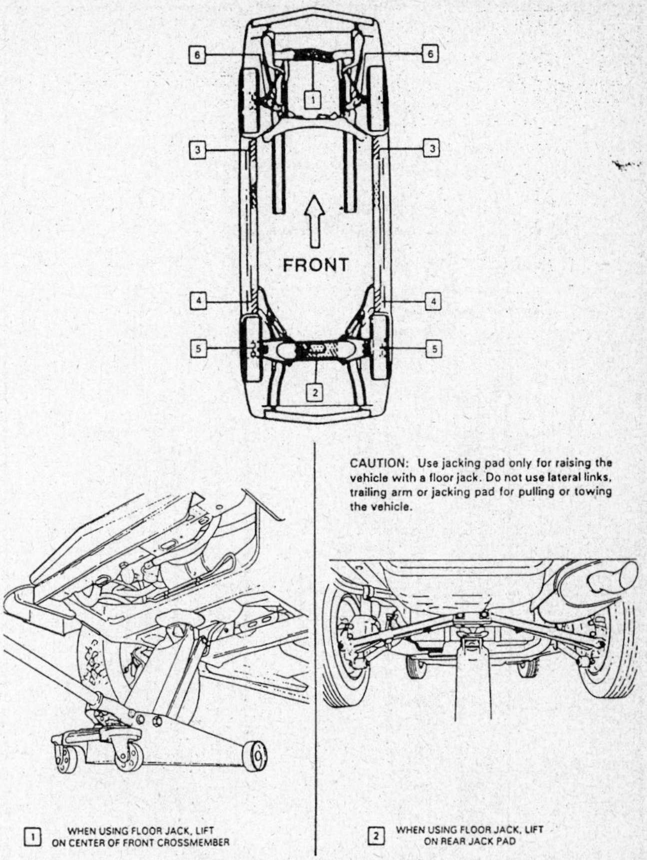

1
2
3
4
5
6
FRONT
CAUTION: Use jacking pad only for raising the vehicle with a floor jack. Do not use lateral links, trailing arm or jacking pad for pulling or towing the vehicle.
1 WHEN USING FLOOR JACK, LIFT ON CENTER OF FRONT CROSSMEMBER
2 WHEN USING FLOOR JACK, LIFT ON REAR JACK PAD

GC1139100178010X

Fig. 4 Vehicle Lift Points. Cutlass Supreme, Lumina & Monte Carlo (Part 1 of 2)

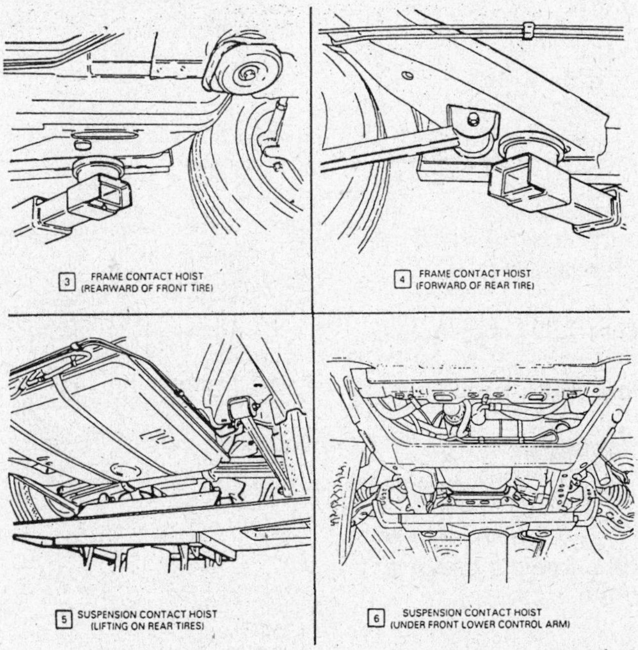

GC1139100178020X

Fig. 4 Vehicle Lift Points. Cutlass Supreme, Lumina & Monte Carlo (Part 2 of 2)

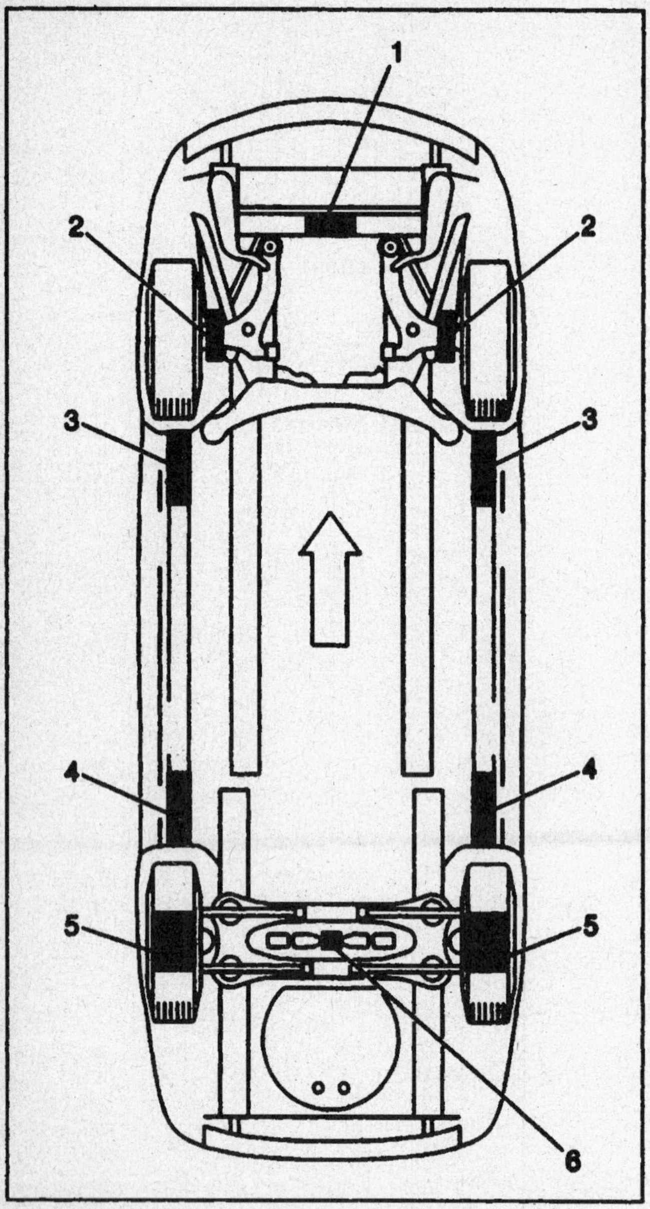

Legend

(1) Front Floor Jacking Location
(2) Front Suspension Contact to Suspension Automotive Lift Location
(3) Front Frame Contact Automotive Lift Location
(4) Rear Frame Contact Automotive Lift Location
(5) Rear Suspension Contact to Suspension Automotive Lift Location
(6) Rear Floor Jacking Location

GC1139700648000X

Fig. 5 Vehicle Lift Points. Century, Impala, Intrigue, Grand Prix & Regal

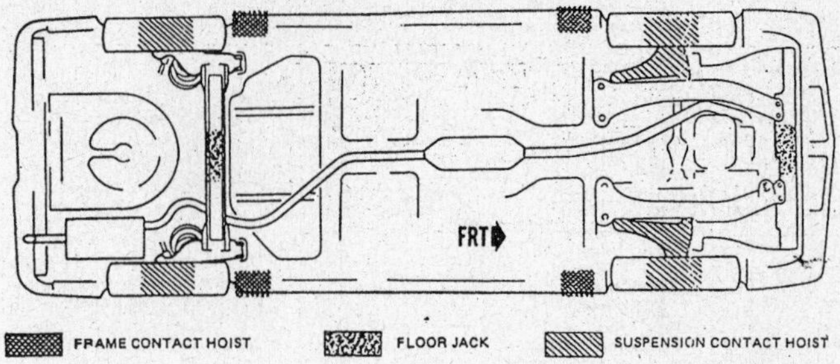

GC1139100179000X

Fig. 6 Vehicle Lift Points. Cavalier & Sunfire

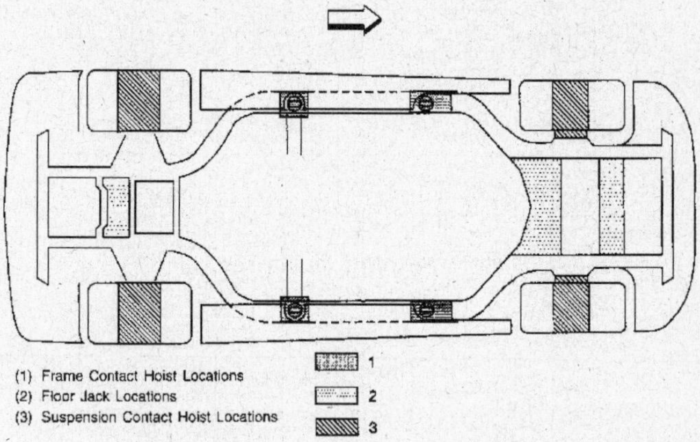

GC1139700674000X

Fig. 7 Vehicle Lift Points. Corvette

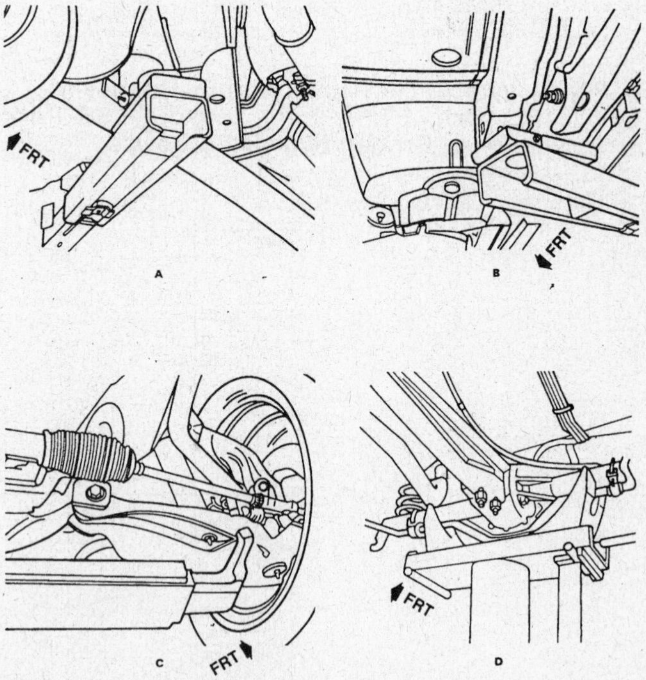

A USING FRAME CONTACT HOIST REARWARD OF FRONT TIRE
B USING FRAME CONTACT HOIST FORWARD OF REAR TIRE
C USING SUSPENSION CONTACT HOIST UNDER FRONT LOWER CONTROL ARM ASSEMBLY
D USING SUSPENSION CONTACT HOIST LIFTING ON REAR AXLE ASSEMBLY

GC1139500517000X

Fig. 8 Vehicle Lift Points. Camaro & Firebird

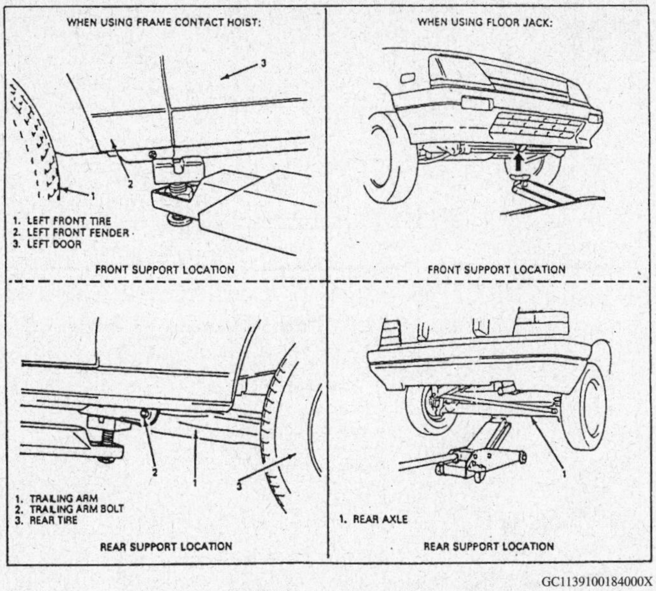

Fig. 9 Vehicle Lift Points. Metro

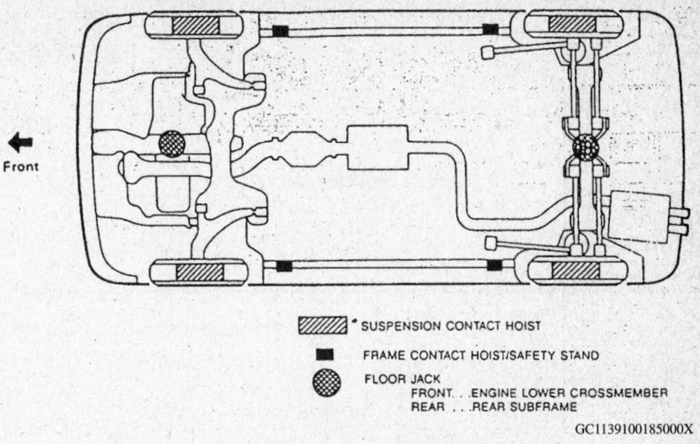

Fig. 10 Vehicle Lift Points. Prizm

Saturn

INDEX

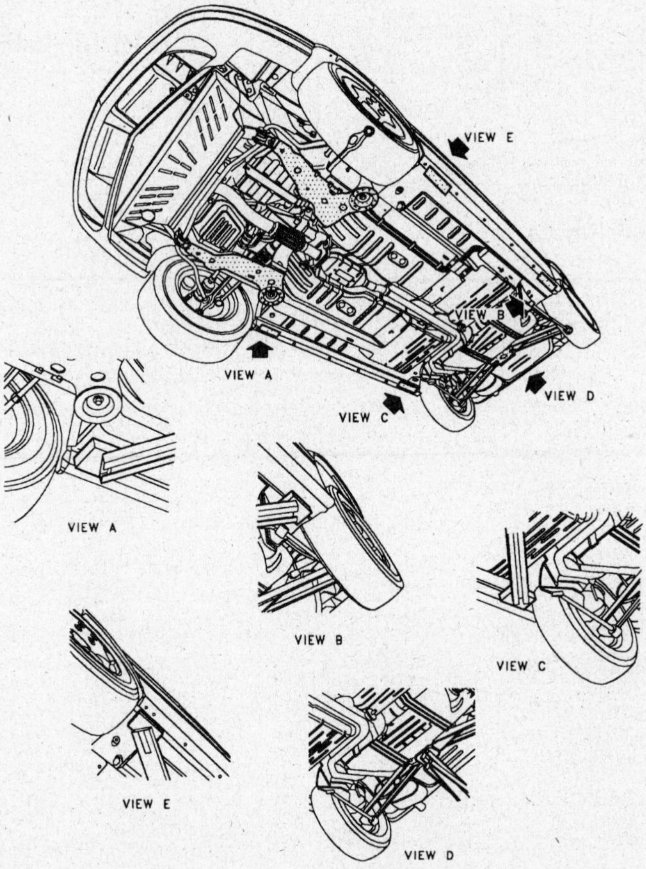

Fig. 1 Vehicle Lift Points. Saturn

ELECTRICAL SYMBOL & WIRE COLOR CODE IDENTIFICATION

TABLE OF CONTENTS

Electrical Symbol Identification

INDEX

Devices appearing in circuit diagrams are indicated by the following symbols.

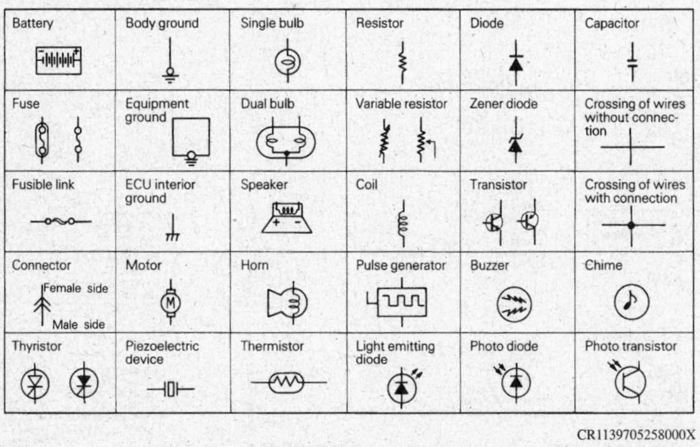

Fig. 1 Symbol Identification. 1997 DaimlerChrysler Imported

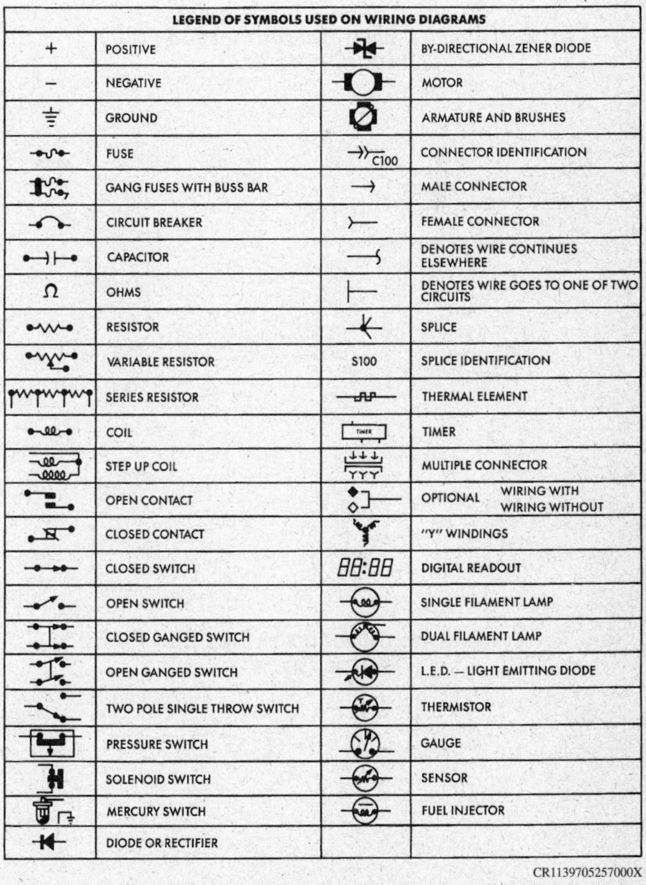

Fig. 2 Symbol Identification. 1997 DaimlerChrysler Domestic

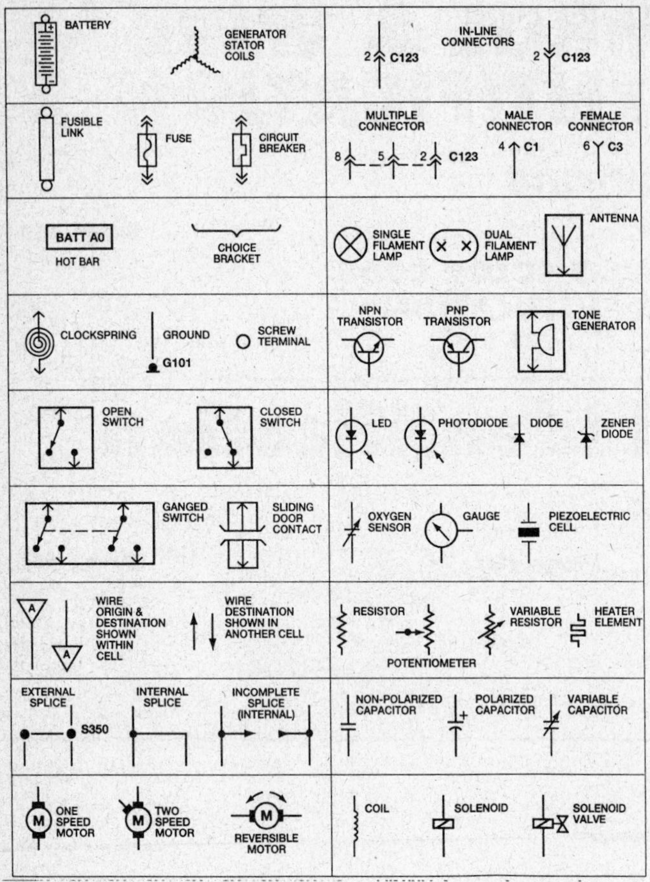

CR9049800087000X

Fig. 3 Symbol Identification. 1998–2000 DaimlerChrysler

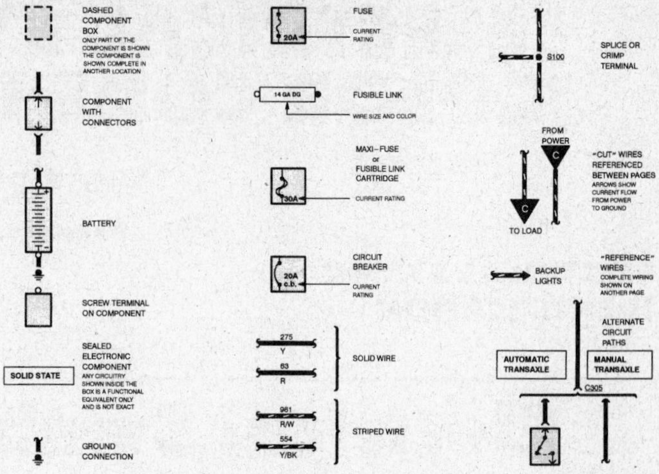

FM1139700510010X

Fig. 4 Symbol Identification (Part 1 of 2). Ford Motor Co.

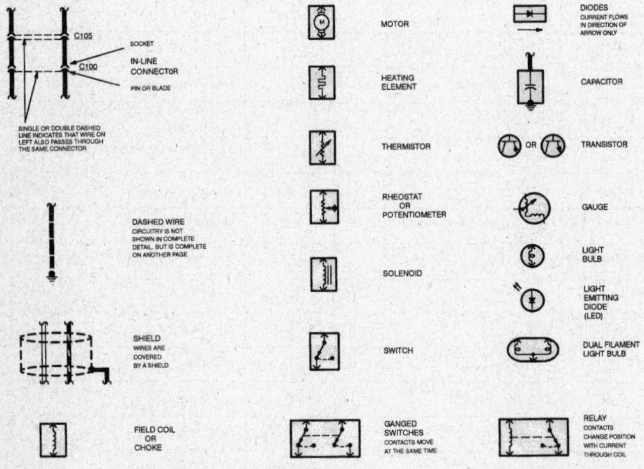

FM1139700510020X

Fig. 4 Symbol Identification (Part 2 of 2). Ford Motor Co.

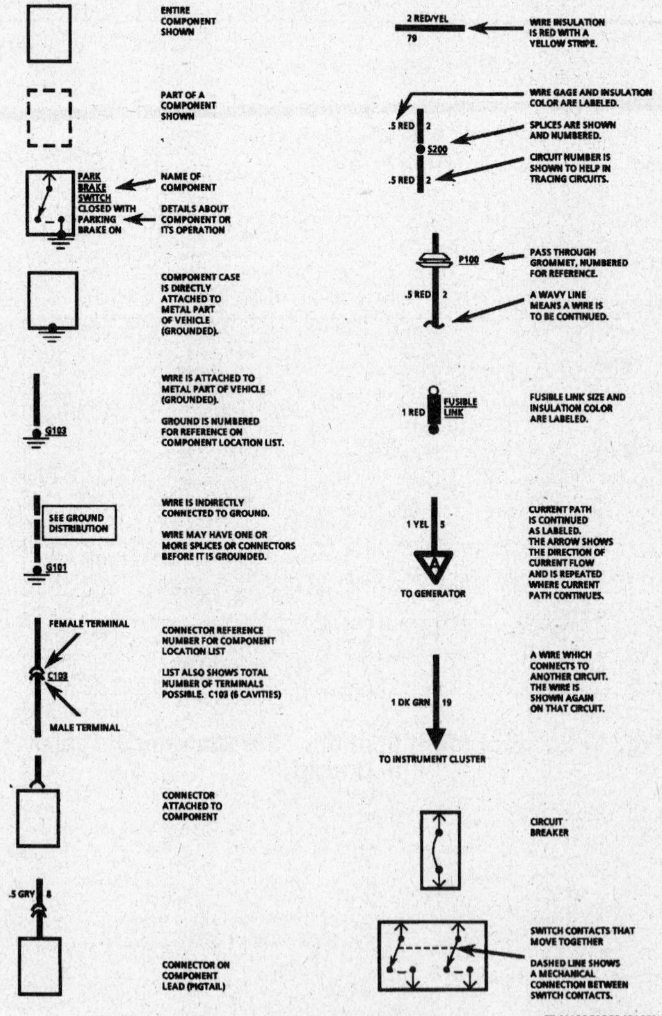

FM1139500524010X

Fig. 5 Symbol Identification (Part 1 of 3). General Motors Except Saturn

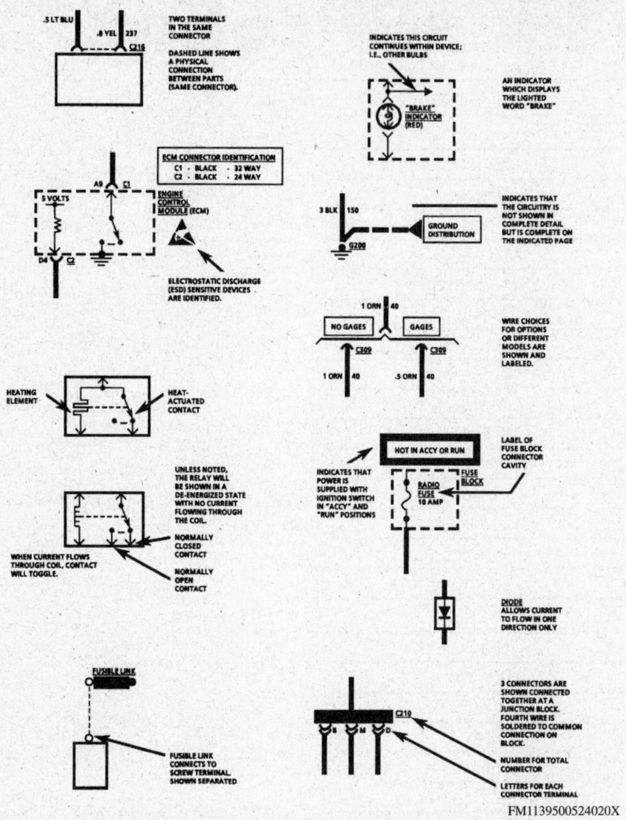

Fig. 5 Symbol Identification (Part 2 of 3). General Motors Except Saturn

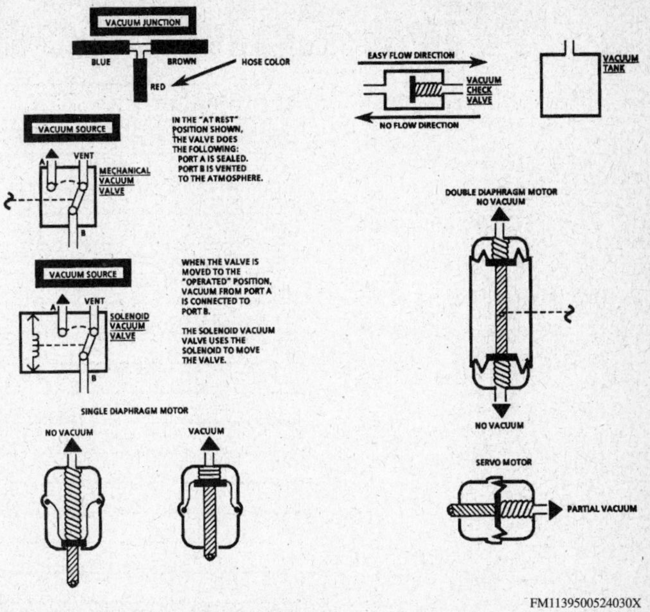

Fig. 5 Symbol Identification (Part 3 of 3). General Motors Except Saturn

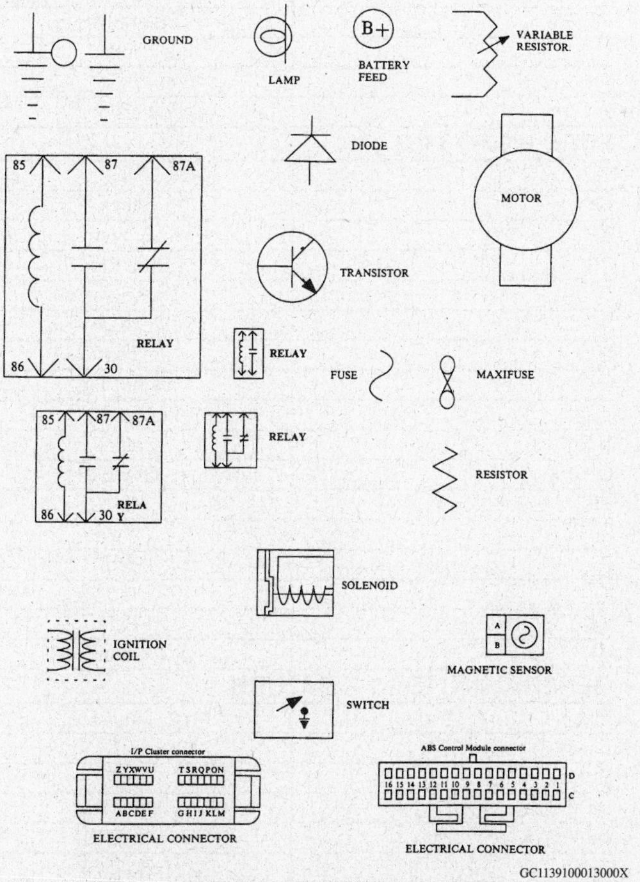

Fig. 6 Symbol Identification. Saturn

Wire Color Code Identification

Abbreviation	Wire Color
DAIMLERCHRYSLER DOMESTIC	
BL	Blue
BK	Black
BR	Brown
DB	Dark Blue
DG	Dark Green
GY	Gray
LB	Light Blue
LG	Light Green
OR	Orange
PK	Pink
RD	Red
TN	Tan
VT	Violet
WT	White
YL	Yellow
DAIMLERCHRYSLER IMPORTS	
B	Black
BR	Brown
G	Green
GR	Gray
L	Blue
LG	Light Green
O	Orange
P	Pink
R	Red
SB	Sky Blue
V	Violet
W	White
Y	Yellow
FORD MOTOR CO.	
BL	Blue
BK	Black
BR	Brown
DB	Dark Blue
DG	Dark Green
GN	Green
GY	Gray
LB	Light Blue
LG	Light Green
N	Natural
O	Orange
PK	Pink
P	Purple
R	Red
T	Tan
W	White
Y	Yellow
GENERAL MOTORS & SATURN	
Black	BLK
Blue	BLU
Brown	BRN
Dark Blue	DK BLU
Dark Green	DK GRN
Gray	GRA/GRY
Green	GRN

Continued

Abbreviation	Wire Color
GENERAL MOTORS & SATURN	
Light Blue	LT BLU
Light Green	LT GRN
Light Gray	LT GRAY
Orange	ORN
Pink	PNK
Purple	PPL
Red	RED
Tan	TAN
White	WHT
Yellow	YEL

VEHICLE MAINTENANCE SCHEDULES

TABLE OF CONTENTS

Chrysler Cirrus & Sebring Convertible, Dodge Neon & Stratus & Plymouth Breeze & Neon

Recommended Service & Intervals (Months)	Service Interval In Miles①																																							
	3000	6000	7500	9000	12000	15000	18000	21000	22500	24000	27000	30000	33000	36000	37500	39000	42000	45000	48000	51000	52500	54000	57000	60000	63000	66000	67500	69000	72000	75000	78000	81000	82500	84000	87000	90000	93000	96000	97500	99000
BODY																																								
Inspect Supplemental Restraint System												X												X												X				
BRAKES																																								
Inspect Brake Connections, Hoses & Lines	Normal Service Every 6 Months Or 7,500 Miles, Severe Service Every 3,000 Miles																																							
Inspect Brake Drums & Rotors (Normal Service Every 18 Mos.)					S				N	S				S				N		S				S			N		S					S		N		S		
Inspect Brake Pads, Linings & Wheel Bearings (Normal Service Every 18 Mos.), 1997-99					S				N	S				S				N		S				S			N		S					S		N		S		
Inspect Brake Pads, Linings & Wheel Bearings, 2000	Normal Service Every 22,500 Miles; Severe Every 12,000 Miles																																							
CLUTCH & TRANSMISSION																																								
Change Automatic Transaxle Filter, Fluid & Adjust Bands,1997-98						S						S						S						S						S						S				
Change Automatic Transaxle Filter, Fluid & Adjust Bands, Neon 2000	Normal Service Every 30,000 Miles; Severe Service Every 15,000 Miles																																							
Change Automatic Transaxle Filter, Fluid & Adjust Bands, 2000	Normal Service Every 100,000 Miles; Severe Service Every 48,000 Miles																																							
DRIVESHAFT																																								
Inspect CV Joints	S	S	X	S	S	X	S	S	X	S	S	X	S	S	X	S	S	X	S	S	X	S	S	X	S	S	X	S	S	X	S	S	X	S	S	X	S	S	X	S
ENGINE																																								
Change Engine Coolant, 1997-98	At 36 Months Or 45,000 Miles, Then At 60 Months Or 75,000 Miles																																							
Change Engine Coolant, 1999-2000	At 36 Months Or 45,000 Miles, Then Every 30,000 Miles Thereafter																																							
Change Engine Oil (Normal Service Every 6 Mos.)	S	S	N	S	S	X	S	S	N	S	S	X	S	S	N	S	S	X	S	S	N	S	S	X	S	S	N	S	S	X	S	S	N	S	S	X	S	S	N	S

Recommended Service & Intervals (Months)	Service Interval In Miles① 3000	6000	7500	9000	12000	15000	18000	21000	22500	24000	27000	30000	33000	36000	37500	39000	42000	45000	48000	51000	52500	54000	57000	60000	63000	66000	67500	69000	72000	75000	78000	81000	82500	84000	87000	90000	93000	96000	97500	99000
ENGINE																																								
Change Engine Oil Filter (Normal Service Every 12 Mos.), 1997-98		S			S	N	S			S		X		S			S	N	S			S		X		S			S	N	S			S		X		S		
Change Engine Oil Filter, 1999②	Normal Service Every 15,000 Miles; Severe Service Every 9000 Miles																																							
Change Engine Oil Filter, 2000	Normal Service Every 7500 Miles; Severe Service Every 3000 Miles																																							
Inspect Air Filter④						S						X						S						X						S						X				
Inspect Coolant Level	At Every Engine Oil Change																																							
Inspect EVAP & Fuel Systems Filler Pipe, Hoses, Lines, Tank & Cap												X												X												X				
Inspect Exhaust System	S	S	N	S	S	X	S	S	N	S	S	X	S	S	N	S	S	X	S	S	N	S	S	X	S	S	N	S	S	X	S	S	N	S	S	X	S	S	N	S
Inspect PCV Valve (Normal Service Every 48 Mos.)												S												X												S				
Inspect PCV Valve (Normal Service Every 48 Mos.), 2000④	Normal Service Every 60,000 Miles; Severe Service Every 30,000 Miles																																							
Inspect & Adjust Drive Belts,						X						X						X						X						X						X				
Replace Drive Belts	Every 60,000 Miles																																							
Replace Spark Plugs, 2.0L & 2.4LC												X												X												X				
Replace Spark Plugs, 2.0L	Every 30,000 Miles																																							
Replace Spark Plugs, 1997–2000 2.5L	Normal Service Every 100,000 Miles; Severe Service Every 75,000 Miles																																							
Replace Timing Belt	At 105,000 Miles																																							
STEERING, SUSPENSION & TIRES																																								
Inspect Ball Joints												X												X												X				
Lubricate Suspension & Steering Linkage												X												X												X				
Rotate Tires & Adjust Pressure,1997-99			X			X			X			X			X			X			X			X			X			X			X			X			X	
Rotate Tires & Adjust PressureV	Inspect And Rotate Tires Normal Service Every 7500 Miles; Severe Service Every 6000 Miles																																							

Mos. — Months
N — Normal Service
S — Severe Service
X — Normal Or Severe Service
① — After vehicles passes 99,000 mile mark return to beginning of mileage table & start cycle over again.
② — 2.0L & 2.4L engines.
③ — 1999 Breeze, Cirrus & Stratus w/2.0L & 2.4L engines w/California emissions.
④ — This maintenance is recommended by DaimlerChrysler Corporation to the owner but is not required to maintain the emissions warranty.

Chrysler Concorde, LHS, 300M & Dodge Intrepid & Eagle Vision

Service Interval In Miles①

Recommended Service & Intervals (Months)	3000	6000	7500	9000	12000	15000	18000	21000	22500	24000	27000	30000	33000	36000	37500	39000	42000	45000	48000	51000
BODY																				
Inspect Supplemental Restraint System												X								
BRAKES																				
Inspect Brake Connections, Hoses & Lines	Normal Service Every 6 Mos. Or 7,500 Miles; Severe Service Every 3,000 Miles																			
Inspect Brake Drums & Rotors					S				N	S				S				N	S	
Inspect Brake Pads, Linings					S				N	S				S				N	S	
CLUTCH & TRANSMISSION																				
Change Automatic Transaxle Fluid & Filter, 1997-98						S						S						S		
Change Automatic Transaxle Fluid & Filter, 1999																				
Change Automatic Transaxle Fluid & Filter, 2000	Normal Service At 100,000 Miles; Severe Service Every 48,000 Miles																			
DRIVESHAFT & CV JOINTS																				
Inspect CV Joints	S	S	N	S	S	X	S	S	N	S	S	X	S	S	N	S	S	X	S	S
ENGINE																				
Change Engine Coolant, 1997	First Interval, 36 Months Or 45,000 Miles; Subsequent Intervals 24 Months Or 30,000 Miles																			
Change Engine Coolant, 1998-2000	Every 60 Months Or 75,000 Miles																			
Change Engine Oil (Normal Service Every 6 Mos.)	S	S	N	S	S	X	S	S	N	S	S	X	S	S	N	S	S	X	S	S
Change Engine Oil Filter (Normal Service Every 12 Mos.), 1997-98		S			S	N	S			S		X		S			S	N	S	
Change Engine Oil Filter (Normal Service Every 12 Mos.), 1999	Normal Service Every 15,000 Miles; Severe Service Every 3000 Miles																			
Change Engine Oil Filter (Normal Service Every 6Mos.), 2000	Normal Service Every 7500 Miles; Severe Service Every 3000 Miles																			

Recommended Service & Intervals (Months)	52500	54000	57000	60000	63000	66000	67500	69000	72000	75000	78000	81000	82500	84000	87000	90000	93000	96000	97500	99000
BODY																				
Inspect Supplemental Restraint System				X												X				
BRAKES																				
Inspect Brake Connections, Hoses & Lines	Normal Service Every 6 Mos. Or 7,500 Miles; Severe Service Every 3,000 Miles																			
Inspect Brake Drums & Rotors				S			N		S					S		N		S		
Inspect Brake Pads, Linings				S			N		S					S		N		S		
CLUTCH & TRANSMISSION																				
Change Automatic Transaxle Fluid & Filter, 1997-98				S						S						S				
Change Automatic Transaxle Fluid & Filter, 1999					S															
Change Automatic Transaxle Fluid & Filter, 2000	Normal Service At 100,000 Miles; Severe Service Every 48,000 Miles																			
DRIVESHAFT & CV JOINTS																				
Inspect CV Joints	N	S	S	X	S	S	N	S	S	X	S	S	N	S	S	X	S	S	N	S
ENGINE																				
Change Engine Coolant, 1997	First Interval, 36 Months Or 45,000 Miles; Subsequent Intervals 24 Months Or 30,000 Miles																			
Change Engine Coolant, 1998-2000	Every 60 Months Or 75,000 Miles																			
Change Engine Oil (Normal Service Every 6 Mos.)	N	S	S	X	S	S	N	S	S	X	S	S	N	S	S	X	S	S	N	S
Change Engine Oil Filter (Normal Service Every 12 Mos.), 1997-98		S		X		S			S	N	S			S		X		S		
Change Engine Oil Filter (Normal Service Every 12 Mos.), 1999	Normal Service Every 15,000 Miles; Severe Service Every 3000 Miles																			
Change Engine Oil Filter (Normal Service Every 6Mos.), 2000	Normal Service Every 7500 Miles; Severe Service Every 3000 Miles																			

Recommended Service & Intervals (Months)	Service Interval In Miles①																																						
	3000	6000	7500	9000	12000	15000	18000	21000	22500	24000	27000	30000	33000	36000	37500	39000	42000	45000	48000	51000	52500	54000	57000	60000	63000	66000	67500	69000	72000	75000	78000	81000	82500	84000	87000	90000	93000	96000	97500	99000
ENGINE																																								
Inspect Air Filter						S						X						S						X						S						X				
Inspect EVAP & Fuel Systems Filler Pipe, Hoses, Lines, Tank & Cap												X												X												X				
Inspect Exhaust System	S	S	N	S	S	X	S	S	N	S	S	X	S	S	N	S	S	X	S	S	N	S	S	X	S	S	N	S	S	X	S	S	N	S	S	X	S	S	N	S
Inspect & Adjust Drive Belts						X						X						X						X						X						X				
Replace Drive Belts																								S																
Replace PCV Valve, 1997												S												X												X				
Replace PCV Valve, 1998-99												S												S												X				
Replace PCV Valve, 2000	Normal Service Replace at 60,000 Miles And Inspect Every 30,000 Thereafter; Severe Service Replace Every 30,000 Miles																																							
Replace Spark Plugs, 1997												X												X												X				
Replace Spark Plugs, 1998	Normal Service Every 84 Months Or 105,000 Miles; Severe Service Every 102,000 Miles																																							
Replace Spark Plugs, 1999-2000	Every 100,000 Miles																																							
Replace Timing Belt, 3.2L & 3.5L, 1997-98	At 105,000 Miles																																							
Replace Timing Belt, 3.2L & 3.5L, 1999-2000②	At 100,000 Miles																																							
Replace Timing Belt, 3.2L & 3.5L, 1999-2000③	At 105,000 Miles																																							
STEERING, SUSPENSION & TIRES																																								
Inspect Ball Joints		S	N		S	N	S		N	S		X		S	N		S	N	S		N	S		X		S	N		S	N	S		N	S		X		S	N	
Inspect Wheel Bearings, 1997–99				S			S		N		S			S				X				S			S		X		S			S				X				X
Lubricate Suspension & Steering Linkage						S						S						S						X						S						S				
Rotate Tires & Adjust Pressure, 1997-98		S	N		S	N	S		N	S		X		S	N		S	N	S		N	S		X		S	N		S	N	S		N	S		X		S	N	
Rotate Tires & Adjust Pressure, 1999-2000	Normal Service Inspect For Wear And Rotate Every 7,500 Miles; Severe Service Every 6000 Miles																																							

Mos. — Months
N — Normal Service
S — Severe Service
X — Normal Or Severe Service
① — After vehicles passes 99,000 mile mark return to beginning of mileage table & start cycle over again.
② — 1999 models w/Federal emissions.
③ — 1999 models w/California emissions.

Chrysler Sebring Coupe & Dodge Avenger

Recommended Service & Intervals (Months)	Service Interval In Miles① 3000	6000	7500	9000	12000	15000	18000	21000	22500	24000	27000	30000	33000	36000	37500	39000	42000	45000	48000	51000	52500	54000	57000	60000	63000	66000	67500	69000	72000	75000	78000	81000	82500	84000	87000	90000	93000	96000	97500	99000
BODY																																								
Inspect Supplemental Restraint System Components	Every 10 Years From Vehicle Build Date																																							
BRAKES																																								
Inspect Brake Connections, Hoses & Lines	Every 12 Months Or 15,000 Miles																																							
Inspect Disc Brake Pads (Every 12 Mos.)	Normal Service Check for Wear Every 15,000 Miles; Severe Service Every 6000 Miles																																							
Inspect Drum Brake Shoes (Every 24 Mos.)	Normal Service Check For Wear Every 30,000 Miles; Severe Service Every 15,000 Miles																																							
CLUTCH & TRANSMISSION																																								
Change Or Inspect Automatic Transaxle Fluid & Filter	Normal Service, Every 15,000 Miles; Severe Service, Change Every, Miles																																							
Change Manual Transaxle Lubricant												S												S												S				
DRIVESHAFT & CV JOINTS																																								
Inspect CV Joint Boots (Every 12 Mos.)						X						X						X						X						X						X				
ENGINE																																								
Change Engine Coolant	Every 24 Months Or 30,000 Miles																																							
Change Engine Oil (Normal Service Every 6 Mos./Severe Service Every 3 Mos.)	S	S	N	S	S	X	S	S	N	S	S	X	S	S	N	S	S	X	S	S	N	S	S	X	S	S	N	S	S	X	S	S	N	S	S	X	S	S	N	S
Change Engine Oil & Filter		S			S	N	S			S		X		S			S	N	S			S		X		S			S	N	S			S		X		S		
Inspect Air Filter						S						X						S						X						S						X				
Inspect Coolant Level	At Every Engine Oil Change																																							
Inspect Distributor Cap & Rotor																								X																
Inspect EVAP System																								X																
Inspect Exhaust System & Heat Shields	S	S	N	S	S	X	S	S	N	S	S	X	S	S	N	S	S	X	S	S	N	S	S	X	S	S	N	S	S	X	S	S	N	S	S	X	S	S	N	S
Inspect Fuel Filler Cap																								X																
Inspect Fuel Hoses, Lines & Connections																								X																
Inspect Fuel Tank																								X																
Inspect & Adjust Drive Belts						X						X						X						X						X						X				
Replace Spark Plugs, DOHC						S						X						S						X						S						X				

Recommended Service & Intervals (Months)	Service Interval In Miles①																																							
	3000	6000	7500	9000	12000	15000	18000	21000	22500	24000	27000	30000	33000	36000	37500	39000	42000	45000	48000	51000	52500	54000	57000	60000	63000	66000	67500	69000	72000	75000	78000	81000	82500	84000	87000	90000	93000	96000	97500	99000
ENGINE																																								
Replace Spark Plugs, 1997–99 SOHC	Every 100,000 Miles																																							
Replace Timing Belt																								X																
STEERING, SUSPENSION & TIRES																																								
Inspect Ball Joints & Steering Linkage Grease Seals (Every 24 Mos.)												X												X												X				
Lubricate Suspension & Steering Linkage (Every 24 Mos.)												X												X												X				
Rotate Tires & Adjust Pressure (Every 6 Mos.)			X			X			X			X			X			X			X			X			X			X			X			X			X	

Mos. — Months
N — Normal Service
S — Severe Service
X — Normal Or Severe Service
① — After vehicles passes 99,000 mile mark return to beginning of mileage table & start cycle over again.

Ford Aspire

Recommended Service	Service Interval In Miles①																														
	3000	5000	6000	7500	9000	10000	12000	15000	18000	20000	21000	22500	24000	25000	27000	30000	33000	35000	36000	37500	39000	40000	42000	45000	48000	50000	51000	52500	54000	55000	57000	60000
BODY																																
Inspect A/C Refrigerant Charge & System Operation	Before Warm Season Arrives Or Every 12 Months Or 15,000 Miles																															
Inspect Seat Belts, Anchors, Buckles & Retractors								X								X								X								X
Inspect & Tighten Body Fasteners								S								S								S								X
Lubricate Body Hardware & Hinges								X								X								X								X
BRAKES																																
Inspect Brake Discs & Pad								X								X								X								X
Inspect Brake Drums & Linings																X																X
Inspect Brake System Connections, Hoses & Lines								X								X								X								X

Recommended Service	Service Interval In Miles①																														
	3000	5000	6000	7500	9000	10000	12000	15000	18000	20000	21000	22500	24000	25000	27000	30000	33000	35000	36000	37500	39000	40000	42000	45000	48000	50000	51000	52500	54000	55000	57000	60000
CLUTCH & TRANSMISSION																																
Change Automatic Transaxle Fluid & Filter																X																X
Inspect Clutch Pedal Operation																X																X
Lubricate Transaxle Controls & Linkages								X								X								X								X
DRIVESHAFT																																
Inspect CV Joint Boots																X																X
ENGINE																																
Change Engine Coolant	Every 36 Months Or 30,000 Miles																															
Change Engine Oil & Filter	S		S	N	S		S	X	S		S	N	S		S	X	S		S	N	S		S	X	S		S	N	S		S	X
Inspect Cooling System & Protection Level								X								X								X								X
Inspect Coolant Hoses & Clamps	Every 12 Months																															
Inspect Drive Belts																X																X
Inspect Engine Air Filter Element								S																S								
Inspect EVAP System Connections, Hoses & Lines																																X
Inspect Exhaust System																X																X
Inspect Fuel System Connections, Hoses & Lines																X																X
Inspect Idle Speed																X																X
Inspect Ignition Timing, Aspire																																X
Replace Engine Air Filter Element	Normal Service Every 30,000 Miles; More Frequently In Severe Service Or Dusty Conditions																															
Replace Fuel Filter																																X
Replace Spark Plugs Less Turbocharger																X																X
Replace Spark Plugs, w/Turbocharger								X								X								X								X
Replace Timing Belt																																X
STEERING, SUSPENSION & TIRES																																
Inspect Steering Linkage, Rack Guides & Seal Boots, Tie Rod Ends & System Operation																X																X
Inspect Suspension Ball Joints																X																X
Inspect & Repack Front & Rear Wheel Bearings, Aspire & Festiva																																X
Inspect & Repack Rear Wheel Bearings, Capri																																X
Rotate Tires			S	N							S	N							S	N							S	N				

Mos. — Months
N — Normal Service
S — Severe Service
X — Normal Or Severe Service
① — After vehicle has passed 60,000 mile mark return to beginning of mileage table & start cycle over again.

Ford Probe

Recommended Service	Service Interval In Miles①																														
	3000	5000	6000	7500	9000	10000	12000	15000	18000	20000	21000	22500	24000	25000	27000	30000	33000	35000	36000	37500	39000	40000	42000	45000	48000	50000	51000	52500	54000	55000	57000	60000
BODY																																
Inspect A/C Refrigerant Charge & System Operation	Before Warm Season Arrives Or Every 12 Months Or 15,000 Miles																														
Inspect Seat Belts, Anchors, Buckles & Retractors								X								X								X								X
Inspect & Tighten Body Fasteners								S								X								S								X
Lubricate Body Hardware & Hinges								X								X								X								X
BRAKES																																
Inspect Brake Discs & Pad								S								X								S								X
Inspect Brake Drums & Linings								S								X								S								X
Inspect Brake System Connections, Hoses & Lines,																X																X
CLUTCH & TRANSMISSION																																
Change Automatic Transaxle Fluid & Filter																X																X
Lubricate Transaxle Controls & Linkages								X								X								X								X
DRIVESHAFT																																
Inspect CV Joint Boots																X																X
ENGINE																																
Change Engine Coolant	At 48 Months Or 50,000 Miles, Then Every 36 Months Or 30,000 Miles																														
Change Engine Oil & Filter, w/Turbocharger	S	N	S		S	N	S	X	S	N	S		S	N	S	X	S	N	S		S	N	S	X	S	N	S		S	N	S	X
Change Engine Oil & Filter, Less Turbocharger	S		S	N	S		S	X	S		S	N	S		S	X	S		S	N	S		S	X	S		S	N	S		S	X
Inspect Cooling System & Protection Level								X								X								X								X
Inspect Coolant Hoses & Clamps	Normal Service Every 36 Months Or 30,000 Miles; Severe Service Every 12 Months																														
Inspect Drive Belts																X																X
Inspect Engine Air Filter Element								S																S								
Inspect EVAP System Connections, Hoses & Lines																																X
Inspect Exhaust System																X																X
Inspect Fuel System Connections, Hoses & Lines																X																X
Inspect Idle Speed																X																X
Replace Engine Air Filter Element	Normal Service Every 30,000 Miles; More Frequently In Severe Service Or Dusty Conditions																														
Replace Fuel Filter																S																X
Replace PCV Valve																X																X
Replace Spark Plugs, Less Turbocharger																X																X
Replace Spark Plugs, w/Turbocharger								X								X								X								X
Replace Spark Plugs, Probe 3.0L																																X
Replace Timing Belt																																X

Recommended Service	Service Interval In Miles①																														
	3000	5000	6000	7500	9000	10000	12000	15000	18000	20000	21000	22500	24000	25000	27000	30000	33000	35000	36000	37500	39000	40000	42000	45000	48000	50000	51000	52500	54000	55000	57000	60000
STEERING, SUSPENSION & TIRES																																
Inspect Steering Linkage, Rack Guides & Seal Boots, Tie Rod Ends & System Operation																X																X
Inspect Suspension Ball Joints																X																X
Rotate Tires		N	S					X					S	N			S	N				N	S				S	N				
Tighten Chassis Fasteners								S								X								S								X

Mos. — Months
N — Normal Service
S — Severe Service
X — Normal Or Severe Service
① — After vehicle has passed 60,000 mile mark return to beginning of mileage table & start cycle over again.

Ford Contour & Mercury Mystique

Recommended Service	Service Interval In Miles①																														
	3000	5000	6000	7500	9000	10000	12000	15000	18000	20000	21000	22500	24000	25000	27000	30000	33000	35000	36000	37500	39000	40000	42000	45000	48000	50000	51000	52500	54000	55000	57000	60000
BODY																																
Inspect A/C Refrigerant Charge & System Operation	Every 12 Months Or 15,000 Miles, Before Warm Season Arrives																															
Inspect Instrument Panel Warning Lamps & Gauges	At Every Engine Oil Change																															
Lubricate Body Hardware & Hinges								X								X								X								X
Lubricate Hood Latch Pivot Points & All Contact Areas				X				X				X				X				X				X				X				X
Replace Passenger Compartment Pollen Filter								X								X								X								X
BRAKES																																
Inspect Brake Drums, Linings, Pads, Rotors, Lubricate Caliper Slide Rails, 1997-98					S	N			S	N					S	N			S			N		S		N			S			N
Inspect Brake Drums, Linings, Pads, Rotors, Lubricate Caliper Slide Rails, 1999	Normal Service Every 15,000 Miles; Severe Service Every 5000 Miles																															
Inspect Parking Brake System Operation								X								X								X								X
CLUTCH & TRANSMISSION																																
Change Automatic Transmission Fluid & Filter, 1997-98																S																S
Change Automatic Transmission Fluid & Filter, 1999	Normal Service Inspect Every 15,000 Miles; Severe Service Change Every 30,000 Miles.																															
Lubricate Transmission Control Linkage								X								X								X								X

Recommended Service	Service Interval In Miles①																														
	3000	5000	6000	7500	9000	10000	12000	15000	18000	20000	21000	22500	24000	25000	27000	30000	33000	35000	36000	37500	39000	40000	42000	45000	48000	50000	51000	52500	54000	55000	57000	60000
DRIVESHAFT																																
Inspect CV Joint Boots (Every 6 Mos.)								X								X								X								X
ENGINE																																
Change Engine Coolant, 1997–98	At 48 Months Or 50,000 Miles, Then Every 36 Months Or 30,000 Miles Thereafter																															
Change Engine Coolant, 1999	Replace Green If Equipped Every 45,000 Miles, Then Every 30,000 Miles Thereafter; Replace Orange If Equipped Every 150,000 Miles																															
Change Engine Oil & Filter	S	N	S		S	N	S	X	S	N	S		S	N	S	X	S	N	S		S	N	S	X	S	N	S		S	N	S	X
Inspect Cooling & Protection Level	Annually Or Every 15,000 Miles																															
Inspect Drive Belts, 1997-98																X																X
Inspect Drive Belts, 1999	Every 100,000 MIles																															
Inspect Exhaust Heat System																X																X
Inspect Fluid & Lubricant Levels	At Every Engine Oil Change																															
Inspect Fuel System Connections, Hoses & Lines								X								X								X								X
Replace Fuel Filter, 1999②	Every 30,000 Miles																															
Replace Air Filter																X																X
Replace PCV Valve, 1997																																X
Replace PCV Valve, 1998-99	Every 100,000 Miles																															
Replace PCV Valve, 1999	4 Cylinder Every 60,000 Miles; Except 4 Cylinder Every 100,000 Miles																															
Replace Spark Plugs, 1997 2.0L																																X
Replace Spark Plugs, 1997–99 2.5L	Normal Service Every 100,000 Miles; Severe Service Every 60,000 Miles																															
Replace Spark Plugs, 1998-99 2.0L	Every 100,000 Miles																															
STEERING, SUSPENSION & TIRES																																
Rotate Tires,1997-98		N	S					X					S	N			S	N					S	N			S			N		S
Rotate Tires,1999	Inspect For Wear And Rotate Every 5000 Miles																															

Mos. — Months
N — Normal Service
S — Severe Service
X — Normal Or Severe Service
① — After vehicle has passed 60,000 mile mark return to beginning of mileage table & start cycle over again.
② — On all vehicles equipped with California emissions.

Ford Crown Victoria & Mercury Grand Marquis

Recommended Service	Service Interval In Miles①																															
	3000	5000	6000	7500	9000	10000	12000	15000	18000	20000	21000	22500	24000	25000	27000	30000	33000	35000	36000	37500	39000	40000	42000	45000	48000	50000	51000	52500	54000	55000	57000	60000
BODY																																
Inspect A/C Refrigerant Charge & System Operation	Every 12 Months Or 15,000 Miles																															
Inspect Instrument Panel Warning Lamps & Gauges	At Every Engine Oil Change																															
Lubricate Body Hardware & Hinges								X								X								X								X
Lubricate Hood Latch Pivot Points & All Contact Areas				X				X				X				X				X				X				X				X
BRAKES																																
Inspect Brake Drums, Linings, Pads, Rotors, Lubricate Caliper Slide Rails, 1997-98	Normal Service Every 15,000 Miles; Severe Service Every 12,000 Miles																															
Inspect Brake Drums, Linings, Pads, Rotors, Lubricate Caliper Slide Rails, 1999	Normal Service Every 15,000 Miles; Severe Service Every 5000 Miles																															
Inspect Parking Brake System Operation								X								X								X								X
CLUTCH & TRANSMISSION																																
Change Automatic Transmission Fluid & Filter, 1997–98											S					N							S									N
Change Automatic Transmission Fluid & Filter, 1999	Normal Service Inspect Every 15,000 Miles; Severe Service Change Every 30,000 Miles.																															
Lubricate Transmission Control Linkage								X								X								X								X
DRIVE AXLE & DRIVESHAFT																																
Change Differential Lubricant	Every 100,000 Miles																															
Lubricate Driveshaft								X								X								X								X
ENGINE																																
Change Engine Coolant, 1997–98	At 48 Months Or 50,000 Miles, Then Every 36 Months Or 30,000 Miles Thereafter																															
Change Engine Coolant, 1999	Replace Green If Equipped Every 45,000 Miles, Then Every 30,000 Miles Thereafter. Replace Orange If Equipped Every 150,000 Miles.																															
Change Engine Oil & Filter	S		S	N	S		S	X	S		S	N	S		S	X	S		S	N	S		S	X	S		S	N	S		S	X
Inspect Cooling System & Protection Level	Annually Or Every 15,000 Miles																															
Inspect Drive Belts																																X
Inspect Exhaust System																X																X
Inspect Fluid & Lubricant Levels	At Every Engine Oil Change																															
Inspect Fuel System Connections, Hoses & Lines								X								X								X								X
Inspect & Clean Choke Linkage, 5.8L																X																X
Inspect & Replace Engine Air Filter								S								X								S								X
Replace Engine Air Filter	Every 30,000 Miles																															
Replace Fuel Filter Element & Housing O-Ring Seal , Drain Coalescent Filter Bowl, 1998-99 NGV	Every 120,000 Miles																															
Replace PCV Valve, 1997–98																																X
Replace PCV Valve, 1999	Every 100,000 Miles																															

Recommended Service	3000	5000	6000	7500	9000	10000	12000	15000	18000	20000	21000	22500	24000	25000	27000	30000	33000	35000	36000	37500	39000	40000	42000	45000	48000	50000	51000	52500	54000	55000	57000	60000
ENGINE																																
Replace Spark Plugs, NGV,																																X
Replace Spark Plugs, 1997–99 Except NGV	Normal Service Every 100,000 Miles; Severe Service Every 60,000 Miles																															
STEERING, SUSPENSION & TIRES																																
Inspect & Repack Front Wheel Bearings																X																X
Lubricate Steering & Suspension Components								X								X								X								X
Rotate Tires, 1997–98		N	S					X					S	N			S	N					S	N			S			N		S
Rotate Tires, 1999	Normal Service Inspect for Wear and Rotate Every 5,000 Miles.																															

Service Interval In Miles①

N — Normal Service
NGV — Natural Gas Vehicle
S — Severe Service
X — Normal Or Severe Service
① — After vehicle has passed 60,000 mile mark return to beginning of mileage table & start cycle over again.

Ford Mustang

Service Interval In Miles①

Recommended Service	3000	5000	6000	7500	9000	10000	12000	15000	18000	20000	21000	22500	24000	25000	27000	30000	33000	35000	36000	37500	39000	40000	42000	45000	48000	50000	51000	52500	54000	55000	57000	60000
BODY																																
Inspect A/C Refrigerant Charge & System Operation	Every 12 Months Or 15,000 Miles																															
Inspect Instrument Panel Warning Lamps & Gauges	At Every Engine Oil Change																															
Lubricate Body Hardware & Hinges								X								X								X								X
Lubricate Hood Latch Pivot Points & All Contact Areas				X				X				X				X				X				X				X				X
BRAKES																																
Inspect Brake Drums, Linings, Pads, Rotors, Lubricate Caliper Slide Rails, 1997-98	Normal Service Every 30,000 Miles; Severe Service Every 12,000 Miles																															
Inspect Brake Drums, Linings, Pads, Rotors, Lubricate Caliper Slide Rails, 1999-2000	Normal Service Every 15,000 Miles; Severe Service Every 5,000 Miles																															
Inspect Parking Brake System Operation								X								X								X								X
CLUTCH & TRANSMISSION																																
Adjust Clutch Pedal, 1998	S	N	S		S	N	S	X	S	N	S		S	N	S	X	S	N	S		S	N	S	X	S	N	S		S	N	S	X
Change Automatic Transmission Fluid & Filter, 1997–98											S					N							S									N

Recommended Service	Service Interval In Miles①																														
	3000	5000	6000	7500	9000	10000	12000	15000	18000	20000	21000	22500	24000	25000	27000	30000	33000	35000	36000	37500	39000	40000	42000	45000	48000	50000	51000	52500	54000	55000	57000	60000
CLUTCH & TRANSMISSION																																
Change Automatic Transmission Fluid & Filter, 1999-2000	Normal Service Inspect Every 15,000 Miles; Severe Service Change Every 30,000 Miles.																														
Lubricate Transmission Control Linkage								X								X								X								X
DRIVE AXLE & DRIVESHAFT																																
Change Differential Lubricant	Every 100,000 Miles																														
Lubricate Driveshaft								X								X								X								X
ENGINE																																
Change Engine Coolant, 1997–98	At 48 Months Or 50,000 Miles, Then Every 36 Months Or 30,000 Miles Thereafter																														
Change Engine Coolant, 1999-2000	Replace Green If Equipped Every 45,000 Miles, Then Every 30,000 Miles Thereafter. Replace Orange If Equipped Every 150,000 Miles.																														
Change Engine Oil & Filter	S	N	S		S	N	S	X	S	N	S		S	N	S	X	S	N	S		S	N	S	X	S	N	S		S	N	S	X
Inspect Cooling System & Protection Level	Annually Or Every 15,000 Miles																														
Inspect Drive Belts, 1997-98																																X
Inspect Drive Belts, 1999-2000	Every 100,000 Miles																														
Inspect Exhaust System																X																X
Inspect Fluid & Lubricant Levels	At Every Engine Oil Change																														
Inspect Fuel System Connections, Hoses & Lines								X								X								X								X
Inspect Timing Belt, 2.3L SOHC																																X
Inspect & Clean Choke Linkage, 5.8L																X																X
Inspect & Replace Engine Air Filter								S								X								S								X
Replace Engine Air Filter	Every 30,000 Miles																														
Replace Fuel Filter, 1999-2000②	Every 30,000 Miles																														
Replace PCV Valve, 1998																																X
Replace PCV Valve, 1999-2000	Every 100,000 Miles																														
Replace PCV Valve, 1998 3.8L																																
Replace Spark Plugs, 1997–2000	Normal Service Every 100,000 Miles; Severe Service Every 60,000 Miles																														
STEERING, SUSPENSION & TIRES																																
Inspect & Repack Front Wheel Bearings																X																X
Lubricate Steering & Suspension Components								X								X								X								X
Rotate Tires, 1997–98		N	S					X					S	N			S	N					S	N			S			N		S
Rotate Tires, 1999-2000	Normal Service Inspect for Wear And Rotate Every 5,000 Miles.																														

N — Normal Service
NGV — Natural Gas Vehicle
S — Severe Service
X — Normal Or Severe Service
① — After vehicle has passed 60,000 mile mark return to beginning of mileage table & start cycle over again.
② — On All vehicles equipped with California emissions.

Ford Thunderbird & Mercury Cougar

Recommended Service	Service Interval In Miles① 3000	5000	6000	7500	9000	10000	12000	15000	18000	20000	21000	22500	24000	25000	27000	30000	33000	35000	36000	37500	39000	40000	42000	45000	48000	50000	51000	52500	54000	55000	57000	60000
BODY																																
Inspect A/C Refrigerant Charge & System Operation	Every 12 Months Or 15,000 Miles																															
Inspect Instrument Panel Warning Lamps & Gauges	At Every Engine Oil Change																															
Lubricate Body Hardware & Hinges								X								X								X								X
Lubricate Hood Latch Pivot Points & All Contact Areas				X				X				X				X				X				X				X				X
BRAKES																																
Inspect Brake Drums, Linings, Pads, Rotors, Lubricate Caliper Slide Rails, Except 1997 Cougar & Thunderbird	Normal Service Every 30,000 Miles; Severe Service Every 12,000 Miles																															
Inspect Brake Drums, Linings, Pads, Rotors, Lubricate Caliper Slide Rails, 1997 Cougar & Thunderbird																S																X
Inspect Brake Drums, Linings, Pads, Rotors, Lubricate Caliper Slide Rails, 1999-2000 Cougar	Normal Service Every 15,000 Miles; Severe Service Every 5000 Miles																															
Inspect Parking Brake System Operation								X								X								X								X
CLUTCH & TRANSMISSION																																
Change Automatic Transmission Fluid & Filter, 1997											S					N							S									N
Change Automatic Transmission Fluid & Filter, 1999-2000	Normal Service Inspect Every 15,000 Miles; Severe Service change Every 30,000 Miles.																															
Lubricate Transmission Control Linkage								X								X								X								X
DRIVE AXLE & DRIVESHAFT																																
Change Differential Lubricant	Every 100,000 Miles																															
Lubricate Driveshaft								X								X								X								X
ENGINE																																
Change Engine Coolant, 1997	At 48 Months Or 50,000 Miles, Then Every 36 Months Or 30,000 Miles Thereafter																															
Change Engine Coolant, 1999-2000	Replace Green If Equipped Every 45,000 Miles, Then Every 30,000 Miles Thereafter. Replace Orange If Equipped Every 150,000 Miles.																															
Change Engine Oil & Filter,	S	N	S		S	N	S	X	S	N	S		S	N	S	X	S	N	S		S	N	S	X	S	N	S		S	N	S	X
Inspect Cooling System & Protection Level	Annually Or Every 15,000 Miles																															
Inspect Drive Belts, 1997																																X
Inspect Drive Belts, 1999-2000	Every 100,000 MIles																															
Inspect Exhaust System																X																X
Inspect Fluid & Lubricant Levels	At Every Engine Oil Change																															
Inspect Fuel System Connections, Hoses & Lines								X								X								X								X
Inspect & Replace Engine Air Filter								S								X								S								X
Replace Engine Air Filter	Every 30,000 Miles																															
Replace Filter, 1999-2000②	Every 30,000 Miles																															

Recommended Service	Service Interval In Miles①																															
	3000	5000	6000	7500	9000	10000	12000	15000	18000	20000	21000	22500	24000	25000	27000	30000	33000	35000	36000	37500	39000	40000	42000	45000	48000	50000	51000	52500	54000	55000	57000	60000
ENGINE																																
Replace PCV Valve, 1997 3.8L	Every 100,000 Miles																															
Replace PCV Valve, 1999-2000	4 Cylinder Every 60,000 Miles; V6 Every 100,000 Miles																															
Replace Spark Plugs	Normal Service Every 100,000 Miles; Severe Service Every 60,000 Miles																															
STEERING, SUSPENSION & TIRES																																
Lubricate Steering & Suspension Components								X								X								X								X
Rotate Tires, 1997		N	S					X					S	N			S	N					S	N			S			N		S
Rotate Tires, 1999-2000	Normal Service Inspect For Wear And Rotate Every 5000 Miles																															

N — Normal Service
NGV — Natural Gas Vehicle
S — Severe Service
X — Normal Or Severe Service
① — After vehicle has passed 60,000 mile mark return to beginning of mileage table & start cycle over again.
② — On all vehicles equipped with California emissions.

Ford Escort & Tempo & Mercury Topaz & Tracer

Recommended Service	Service Interval In Miles①																															
	3000	5000	6000	7500	9000	10000	12000	15000	18000	20000	21000	22500	24000	25000	27000	30000	33000	35000	36000	37500	39000	40000	42000	45000	48000	50000	51000	52500	54000	55000	57000	60000
BODY																																
Inspect A/C Refrigerant Charge & System Operation	Every 12 Months Or 15,000 Miles																															
Inspect Instrument Panel Warning Lamps & Gauges	At Every Engine Oil Change																															
Lubricate Body Hardware & Hinges								X								X								X								X
Lubricate Hood Latch Pivot Points & All Contact Areas				X				X				X				X				X				X				X				X
Tighten Body Fasteners								S								X								S								X
BRAKES																																
Inspect Brake Drums, Linings, Pads, Rotors, Lubricate Caliper Slide Rails, 1997-98	Normal Service Every 30,000 Miles; More Frequently In Severe Service																															
Inspect Brake Drums, Linings, Pads, Rotors, Lubricate Caliper Slide Rails, 1999 Escort and Tracer	Normal Service Every 15,000 Miles; Severe Service Every 5000Miles																															
Inspect Parking Brake System Operation								X								X								X								X

Recommended Service	Service Interval In Miles①																															
	3000	5000	6000	7500	9000	10000	12000	15000	18000	20000	21000	22500	24000	25000	27000	30000	33000	35000	36000	37500	39000	40000	42000	45000	48000	50000	51000	52500	54000	55000	57000	60000
CLUTCH & TRANSMISSION																																
Change Automatic Transmission Fluid & Filter, 1999 Escort & Tracer	Normal Service Inspect Every 15,000 Miles; Severe Service Change Every 30,000 Miles.																															
Inspect Clutch Pedal Operation, Escort & Tracer																X																X
Lubricate Transmission Control Linkage								X								X								X								X
DRIVESHAFT																																
Inspect CV Joint Boots								X								X								X								X
ENGINE																																
Change Engine Coolant, Escort & Tracer 1.9L, 1997-98	At 48 Months Or 50,000 Miles, Then Every 36 Months Or 30,000 Miles Thereafter																															
Change Engine Coolant, Escort & Tracer, 1999	Replace Green If Equipped Every 45,000 Miles, Then Every 30,000 Miles Thereafter. Replace Orange If Equipped Every 150,000 Miles																															
Change Engine Oil & Filter, 1997–98	S	N	S		S	N	S	X	S	N	S		S	N	S	X	S	N	S		S	N	S	X	S	N	S		S	N	S	X
Change Engine Oil & Filter, 1999	Normal Service Every 5000 Miles; Severe Service Every 3000 MIles																															
Inspect Cooling System & Protection Level	Annually Or Every 15,000 Miles																															
Inspect Drive Belts, 1997-98								S								X								S								X
Inspect Drive Belts, 1999	Every 100,000 Miles																															
Inspect Exhaust System																X																X
Inspect Fuel System Connections, Hoses & Lines								X								X								X								X
Inspect & Replace Engine Air Filter																X																X
Replace Fuel Filter, 1999②	Every 30,000 Miles																															
Replace PCV Valve, 1997–98 Escort & Tracer																																
Replace PCV Valve, 1999 Escort & Tracer	Cylinder Every 60,000 MIles; Except 4 Cylinder Every 100,000 Miles																															
Replace Spark Plugs, Tempo & Topaz 2.3L																X																X
Replace Spark Plugs, 1997–99	Every 100,000 Miles																															
STEERING, SUSPENSION & TIRES																																
Inspect & Repack Rear Wheel Bearings																X																X
Lubricate Steering & Suspension Components								X								X								X								X
Rotate Tires, 1997–98		N	S					X					S	N			S	N					S	N			S			N		S
Rotate Tires, 1999	Normal Service Inspect For Wear And Rotate Every 5000 Miles																															
Tighten Chassis Fasteners, Escort & Tracer								S								X								S								X

FFV — Flexible Fuel Vehicle
N — Normal Service
NGV — Natural Gas Vehicle
S — Severe Service
X — Normal Or Severe Service
① — After vehicle has passed 60,000 mile mark return to beginning of mileage table & start cycle over again.
② — On all vehicles equipped with California emissions.

Ford Taurus & Mercury Sable

Recommended Service	Service Interval In Miles①																														
	3000	5000	6000	7500	9000	10000	12000	15000	18000	20000	21000	22500	24000	25000	27000	30000	33000	35000	36000	37500	39000	40000	42000	45000	48000	50000	51000	52500	54000	55000	57000	60000
BODY																																
Inspect A/C Refrigerant Charge & System Operation	Every 12 Months Or 15,000 Miles, Before Warm Season Arrives																															
Inspect Instrument Panel Warning Lamps & Gauges	At Every Engine Oil Change																															
Lubricate Body Hardware & Hinges								X								X								X								X
Lubricate Hood Latch Pivot Points & All Contact Areas				X				X				X				X				X				X				X				X
Replace Passenger Compartment Pollen Filter, 1997–99								X								X								X								X
BRAKES																																
Inspect Brake Drums, Linings, Pads, Rotors, Lubricate Caliper Slide Rails, 1997-98							S						S			N			S						S							X
Inspect Brake Drums, Linings, Pads, Rotors, Lubricate Caliper Slide Rails, 1999	Normal Service Every 15,000 Miles; Severe Service Every 5000 Miles																															
Inspect Brake Lines & Hoses							S						S			N			S						S							X
Inspect Parking Brake System Operation								X								X								X								X
CLUTCH & TRANSMISSION																																
Change Automatic Transmission Fluid & Filter, 1997–98											S					N							S									N
Change Automatic Transmission Fluid & Filter, 1999	Normal Service Inspect Every 15,000 Miles; Severe Service Change Every 30,000 Miles.																															
Lubricate Transmission Control Linkage								X								X								X								X
DRIVESHAFT																																
Inspect CV Joint Boots								X								X								X								X
ENGINE																																
Change Engine Coolant, 1997–98	At 48 Months Or 50,000 Miles, Then Every 36 Months Or 30,000 Miles Thereafter																															
Change Engine Coolant, 1999	Replace Green If Equipped Every 45,000 Miles, Then Every 30,000 Miles Thereafter. Replace Orange If Equipped Every 150,000 Miles.																															
Change Engine Oil & Filter, 1997–99	S	N	S		S	N	S	X	S	N	S		S	N	S	X	S	N	S		S	N	S	X	S	N	S		S	N	S	X
Inspect Cooling System & Protection Level	Annually Or Every 15,000 Miles																															
Inspect Drive Belts 1997-98																X																X
Inspect Drive Belts 1999	Inspect Accesory Drive Belts Every 100,000 Miles.																															
Inspect Exhaust System																X																X
Inspect Fluid & Lubricant Levels	At Every Engine Oil Change																															
Inspect Fuel System Connections, Hoses & Lines								X								X								X								X
Inspect & Adjust Engine Valve Clearance, 1998 Taurus SHO	Every 100,000 Miles																															
Inspect & Replace Engine Air Filter																X																X
Replace Crankcase Emission Filter Or PCV Filter Element, 2.5L	Normal Service Every 30,000 Miles; More Frequently In Severe Service																															
Replace Fuel Filter, 1999②	Every 30,000 Miles																															
Replace PCV Valve, 1997–98	Normal Service Every 100,000 Miles; Severe service Every 90,000 Miles																															

Recommended Service	Service Interval In Miles①																														
	3000	5000	6000	7500	9000	10000	12000	15000	18000	20000	21000	22500	24000	25000	27000	30000	33000	35000	36000	37500	39000	40000	42000	45000	48000	50000	51000	52500	54000	55000	57000	60000
ENGINE																																
Replace PCV Valve, 1999	Every 100,000 Miles																															
Replace Spark Plugs, 1997–99	Normal Service Every 100,000 Miles; Severe Service Every 60,000 Miles																															
STEERING, SUSPENSION & TIRES																																
Lubricate Steering & Suspension Components								X								X								X								X
Rotate Tires, 1997–98		N	S					X					S	N			S	N					S	N			S			N		S
Rotate Tires, 1999	Normal Service Inspect For Wear And Rotate Every 5000 Miles																															

N — Normal Service
S — Severe Service
X — Normal Or Severe Service
① — After vehicle has passed 60,000 mile mark return to beginning of mileage table & start cycle over again.
② — On all vehicles equipped with California emissions.

Lincoln Passenger Cars

Recommended Service	Service Interval In Miles①																														
	3000	5000	6000	7500	9000	10000	12000	15000	18000	20000	21000	22500	24000	25000	27000	30000	33000	35000	36000	37500	39000	40000	42000	45000	48000	50000	51000	52500	54000	55000	57000	60000
BODY																																
Inspect A/C Refrigerant Charge & System Operation	Every 12 Months Or 15,000 Miles, Before Warm Season Arrives																															
Inspect Instrument Panel Warning Lamps & Gauges	At Every Engine Oil Change																															
Lubricate Body Hardware & Hinges								X								X								X								X
Lubricate Hood Latch Pivot Points & All Contact Areas				X				X				X				X				X				X				X				X
Replace Passenger Compartment Pollen Filter, 1997							S	N					S			N			S					N	S							X
Replace Passenger Compartment Pollen Filter, 1998					S			N	S						S	N			S					X					S			N
Replace Passenger Compartment Pollen Filter, 1999	Normal Service Every 15,000 Miles; Severe Service Inspect Every 3000 Miles And Change As Necessary																															
BRAKES																																
Inspect Brake Drums, Linings, Pads, Rotors, Lubricate Caliper Slide Rails, 1997-98	Normal Service Every 30,000 Miles; Severe Service Every 12,000 Miles																															
Inspect Brake Drums, Linings, Pads, Rotors, Lubricate Caliper Slide Rails, 1999	Normal Service Every 15,000 Miles; Severe Service Every 5000 Miles																															
Inspect Brake Lines & Hoses	Normal Service Every 30,000 Miles; Severe Service Every 12,000 Miles																															
Inspect Parking Brake System Operation								X								X								X								X

Recommended Service	Service Interval In Miles①																														
	3000	5000	6000	7500	9000	10000	12000	15000	18000	20000	21000	22500	24000	25000	27000	30000	33000	35000	36000	37500	39000	40000	42000	45000	48000	50000	51000	52500	54000	55000	57000	60000
CLUTCH & TRANSMISSION																																
Change Automatic Transmission Fluid & Filter, 1997–98 Town Car, 1997–98 Mark VIII & 1997–98 Continental											S					N							S									N
Change Automatic Transmission Fluid & Filter, 1999	Normal Service Inspect Every 15,000 Miles; Severe Service Change Every 30,000 Miles.																															
Lubricate Transmission Control Linkage								X								X								X								X
DRIVE AXLE & DRIVESHAFT																																
Change Differential Lubricant, Rear Wheel Drive Models④⑤	Every 100,000 Miles																															
Inspect CV Joint Boots								X								X								X								X
Lubricate Driveshaft								X								X								X								X
ENGINE																																
Change Engine Coolant, 1997–98	At 48 Months Or 50,000 Miles, Then Every 36 Months Or 30,000 Miles																															
Change Engine Coolant, 1999	Replace Green If Equipped Every 45,000 Miles, Then Every 30,000 Miles Thereafter. Replace Orange If Equipped Every 150,000 Miles.																															
Change Engine Oil & Filter, 1997–98 Town Car	S		S	N	S		S	X	S		S	N	S		S	X	S		S	N	S		S	X	S		S	N	S		S	X
Change Engine Oil & Filter, 1997–99 All	S	N	S		S	N	S	X	S	N	S		S	N	S	X	S	N	S		S	N	S	X	S	N	S		S	N	S	X
Inspect Cooling System & Protection Level	Annually Or Every 15,000 Miles																															
Inspect Drive Belts, 1997-98																X																X
Inspect Drive Belts, 1999	Every 100,000 Miles																															
Inspect Exhaust System																X																X
Inspect Fuel System Connections, Hoses & Lines								X								X								X								X
Inspect & Replace Engine Air Filter																X																X
Replace Crankcase Emission Filter, 5.0L								X								X								X								X
Replace Crankcase Emission Filter Or PCV Filter Element, 1990–91 Continental	Normal Service Every 30,000 Miles; More Frequently In Severe Service																															
Replace PCV Valve, 1997–98 Town Car																																X
Replace PCV Valve, Mark VIII																																X
Replace PCV Valve	Every 100,000 Miles																															
Replace PCV Valve, 1997-98 Continental	Normal Service Every 100,000 Miles; Severe Service Every 90,000 Miles																															
Replace PCV Valve, 1999	Every 100,00 Miles																															
Replace Spark Plugs, Mark VII																X																X
Replace Spark Plugs, 1997–2000 Continental & 1997–99 Mark VIII & Town Car	Normal Service Every 100,000 Miles; Severe Service Every 60,000 Miles																															

Recommended Service	Service Interval In Miles①																														
	3000	5000	6000	7500	9000	10000	12000	15000	18000	20000	21000	22500	24000	25000	27000	30000	33000	35000	36000	37500	39000	40000	42000	45000	48000	50000	51000	52500	54000	55000	57000	60000
STEERING, SUSPENSION & TIRES																																
Inspect & Repack Front Wheel Bearings, Mark VII & Town Car																X																X
Lubricate Steering & Suspension Components								X								X								X								X
Rotate Tires, 1997–98		N	S					X					S	N			S	N					S	N			S			N		S
Rotate Tires, 1999	Normal Service Inspect for Wear And Rotate Every 5000 Miles																														

N — Normal Service
S — Severe Service
X — Normal Or Severe Service
① — After vehicle has passed 60,000 mile mark return to beginning of mileage table & start cycle over again.
② — On vehicles equipped with California emissions.

Buick Century & Regal, Chevrolet Lumina & Monte Carlo, Oldsmobile Cutlass Supreme & Intrigue, Pontiac Grand Prix

Recommended Service	Service Interval In Miles①																																						
	3000	6000	7500	9000	12000	15000	18000	21000	22500	24000	27000	30000	33000	36000	37500	39000	42000	45000	48000	51000	52500	54000	57000	60000	63000	66000	67500	69000	72000	75000	78000	81000	82500	84000	87000	90000	93000	96000	97500	99000
BODY																																								
Inspect Lamps, Seat Belts & Warning Devices	At Least Once Every 6 Months																																							
Lubricate Hinges, Latches, Lock Cylinders & Strikers	At Engine Oil Changes Or At Least Every 12 Months																																							
Replace Passenger Compartment Air Filter						X						X						X						X						X						X				
BRAKES																																								
Inspect Brake System,	Every 6 Months																																							
Inspect Disc Brake Pads, Rotors, Shoes & Drums, 1997	At 5,000 Miles, Then Every 10,000 Miles																																							

Recommended Service	Service Interval In Miles①																																						
	3000	6000	7500	9000	12000	15000	18000	21000	22500	24000	27000	30000	33000	36000	37500	39000	42000	45000	48000	51000	52500	54000	57000	60000	63000	66000	67500	69000	72000	75000	78000	81000	82500	84000	87000	90000	93000	96000	97500	99000
BRAKES																																								
Inspect Disc Brake Pads, Rotors, Shoes & Drums, 1998-2000	At 7,500 Miles, Then Every 15,000 Miles																																							
Inspect Parking Brake Operation	At Least Once Every 12 Months																																							
Lubricate Parking Brake Cable Guides		S	N		S	N	S		N	S		X		S	N		S	N	S		N	S		X		S	N		S	N	S		N	S		X		S	N	
CLUTCH & TRANSAXLE																																								
Change Automatic Transmission Fluid & Filter	Normal Service Every 100,000 Miles; Severe Service Every 50,000 Miles																																							
Inspect Neutral Safety & BTSI & Lubricate Shift Linkage		S	N		S	N	S		N	S		X		S	N		S	N	S		N	S		X		S	N		S	N	S		N	S		X		S	N	
DRIVE AXLE & DRIVESHAFT																																								
Inspect CV Joint Boots	At Tire Rotations																																							
ENGINE																																								
Change Engine Coolant	Every 60 Months Or 150,000 Miles																																							
Change Engine Oil & Filter, Less Turbo②	S	S	N	S	S	X	S	S	N	S	S	X	S	S	N	S	S	X	S	S	N	S	S	X	S	S	N	S	S	X	S	S	N	S	S	X	S	S	N	S
Change Engine Oil & Filter, w/Turbo②	X	X		X	X	X	X	X		X	X	X	X	X		X	X	X	X	X		X	X	X	X	X		X	X	X	X	X		X	X	X	X	X		X
Inspect Drive Belts & EGR System, 1997-98												X												X												X				
Inspect Drive Belts & EGR System, 1999-2000	Inspect Every 60,000 Miles																																							
Inspect Exhaust System	At Engine Oil Changes																																							
Inspect Fuel Filler System & PCV												X												X												X				
Inspect Spark Plug Wires	At Spark Plug Changes																																							
Inspect TBI Unit Mounting Fastener Security		S	N																																					
Inspect Throttle Linkage Operation	At Air Cleaner Element Changes																																							
Replace Air Filter & PCV Filter						S						X						S						X						S						X				
Replace Spark Plugs	Every 100,000 Miles																																							
Replace Timing Belt, 3.4L																								X																
STEERING, SUSPENSION & TIRES																																								
Inspect Steering & Suspension System	At Tire Rotations																																							

Recommended Service	Service Interval In Miles① 3000	6000	7500	9000	12000	15000	18000	21000	22500	24000	27000	30000	33000	36000	37500	39000	42000	45000	48000	51000	52500	54000	57000	60000	63000	66000	67500	69000	72000	75000	78000	81000	82500	84000	87000	90000	93000	96000	97500	99000
STEERING, SUSPENSION & TIRES																																								
Lubricate Chassis & Suspension		S	N		S	N	S		N	S		X		S	N		S	N	S		N	S		X		S	N		S	N	S		N	S		X		S	N	
Rotate Tires, 1997–98		S	N				S		N			S			N		S				N	S					X					S	N				S		N	
Rotate Tires, 1999-2000	Inspect For Wear And Rotate Every 7,500 Miles																																							

N — Normal Service
S — Severe Service
X — Normal Or Severe Service
BTSI — Brake Transmission Shift Interlock
IAC — Idle Air Control
ISC — Idle Speed Control System
① — After vehicle passes 99,000 mile mark return to beginning of mileage table & start cycle over again.
② — If equipped, the engine oil life monitor will indicate when to change engine oil, usually 3000–10,000 miles. Under severe driving conditions, engine oil may need to be changed before 3000 miles. If vehicle is driven in a dusty area, change engine oil every 3000 miles.

Buick Electra & Park Avenue, Oldsmobile Eighty-Eight, LSS & Regency & Pontiac Bonneville

Recommended Service	Service Interval In Miles① 3000	6000	7500	9000	12000	15000	18000	21000	22500	24000	27000	30000	33000	36000	37500	39000	42000	45000	48000	51000	52500	54000	57000	60000	63000	66000	67500	69000	72000	75000	78000	81000	82500	84000	87000	90000	93000	96000	97500	99000
BODY																																								
Clean Power Antenna Mast		S	N		S	N	S		N	S		X		S	N		S	N	S		N	S		X		S	N		S	N	S		N	S		X		S	N	
Flush Vehicle Underside, Inspect Drain Holes	At Least Every 12 Months																																							
Inspect Lamps & Seat Belts & Warning Devices	At Least Once Every 6 Months																																							
Lubricate Hinges, Latches, Lock Cylinders & Strikers	At Engine Oil Changes Or At Least Every 12 Months																																							
Replace Passenger Compartment Air Filter						X						X						X						X						X						X				
BRAKES																																								
Inspect Brake Fluid Level	Every 6 Months																																							

Recommended Service	Service Interval In Miles①																																							
	3000	6000	7500	9000	12000	15000	18000	21000	22500	24000	27000	30000	33000	36000	37500	39000	42000	45000	48000	51000	52500	54000	57000	60000	63000	66000	67500	69000	72000	75000	78000	81000	82500	84000	87000	90000	93000	96000	97500	99000
BRAKES																																								
Inspect Brake System 1997	At 5,000 Miles, Then Every 10,000 Miles																																							
Inspect Brake System 1998	At 7,500 Miles, Then Every 15,000 Miles																																							
Inspect Brake System 1999-2000	Normal Service AT 7,500 Miles, Then Every 10,000 Miles Thereafter; Severe Service Every 7,500 Miles																																							
Inspect Parking Brake Operation	At Least Once Every 12 Months																																							
Lubricate Parking Brake Cable Guides		S	N		S	N	S		N	S		X		S	N		S	N	S		N	S		X		S	N		S	N	S		N	S		X		S	N	
CLUTCH & TRANSAXLE																																								
Inspect Neutral Safety & BTSI & Lubricate Shift Linkage		S	N		S	N	S		N	S		X		S	N		S	N	S		N	S		X		S	N		S	N	S		N	S		X		S	N	
DRIVESHAFT																																								
Inspect CV Joint Boots	At Engine Oil Changes & Tire Rotations																																							
ENGINE																																								
Change Engine Coolant③	Every 60 Months Or 150,000 Miles																																							
Change Engine Oil & Filter②	S	S	N	S	S	X	S	S	N	S	S	X	S	S	N	S	S	X	S	S	N	S	S	X	S	S	N	S	S	X	S	S	N	S	S	X	S	S	N	S
Inspect Drive Belts & EGR System												X												X												X				
Inspect Exhaust System	At Engine Oil Changes																																							
Inspect Fuel System & PCV Valve & Supercharger Lubricant Level③												X												X												X				
Inspect Spark Plug Wires	At Spark Plug Changes																																							
Inspect TBI Unit Mounting Fastener Security		S	N																																					
Inspect Thermostatically Controlled Air Cleaner Operation												X												X												X				
Inspect Throttle Linkage Operation	At Engine Oil Or Air Cleaner Element Changes																																							
Replace Air Filter & PCV Filter, 1997–98						S						X						S						X						S						X				
Replace Air Filter & PCV Filter, 1999-2000③	Every 30,000 Miles																																							
Replace Spark Plugs ③	Every 100,000 Miles																																							
STEERING, SUSPENSION & TIRES																																								
Inspect Power Steering Fluid Level & Suspension System	At Engine Oil Changes & Tire Rotations																																							

Recommended Service	Service Interval In Miles①																																							
	3000	6000	7500	9000	12000	15000	18000	21000	22500	24000	27000	30000	33000	36000	37500	39000	42000	45000	48000	51000	52500	54000	57000	60000	63000	66000	67500	69000	72000	75000	78000	81000	82500	84000	87000	90000	93000	96000	97500	99000
STEERING, SUSPENSION & TIRES																																								
Lubricate Chassis & Suspension		S	N		S	N	S		N	S		X		S	N		S	N	S		N	S		X		S	N		S	N	S		N	S		X		S	N	
Rotate Tires, 1997–98		S	N				S		N			S			N		S				N	S					X					S	N				S		N	
Rotate Tires, 1999-2000	Normal Service Inspect For Wear & Rotate Every 7,500 Miles; Severe Service Every 6000 Miles																																							

N — Normal Service
S — Severe Service
X — Normal Or Severe Service
BTSI — Brake Transmission Shift Interlock
IAC — Idle Air Control
ISC — Idle Speed Control System
① — After vehicle passes 99,000 mile mark return to beginning of mileage table & start cycle over again.
② — If equipped, the engine oil life monitor will indicate when to change engine oil, usually 3,000–10,000 miles. Under severe driving conditions, engine oil may need to be changed before 3000 miles. If vehicle is driven in a dusty area, change engine oil every 3000 miles.
③ — The U.S. Environmental Protection Agency or the California Air Resources Board has determined the failure to perform this maintenance item will not nullify the emission warranty or limit recall liability prior to the completion of the vehicle's useful life. We, however, urge that all recommended maintenance services be performed at the indicated intervals and the maintenance be recorded.

Oldsmobile Aurora & Buick Riviera

Recommended Service	Service Interval In Miles①																																							
	3000	6000	7500	9000	12000	15000	18000	21000	22500	24000	27000	30000	33000	36000	37500	39000	42000	45000	48000	51000	52500	54000	57000	60000	63000	66000	67500	69000	72000	75000	78000	81000	82500	84000	87000	90000	93000	96000	97500	99000
BODY																																								
Clean Power Antenna Mast		S	N		S	N	S		N	S		X		S	N		S	N	S		N	S		X		S	N		S	N	S		N	S		X		S	N	
Inspect Lamps, Seat Belts & Warning Devices	At Least Every 6 Months																																							
Lubricate Hinges, Latches, Lock Cylinders & Strikers	At Engine Oil Changes Or At Least Every 12 Months																																							
Replace Passenger Compartment Air Filter						X						X						X						X						X						X				
BRAKES																																								
Inspect Brake System, 1997	At 5,000 Miles, Then Every 10,000 Miles																																							
Inspect Brake System, 1998	At 7,500 Miles, Then Every 15,000 Miles																																							
Inspect Brake System, 1999	At 7,500 Miles, Then Every 10,000 Miles Thereafter; Severe Service Every 7,500 Miles																																							

Recommended Service	Service Interval In Miles① 3000	6000	7500	9000	12000	15000	18000	21000	22500	24000	27000	30000	33000	36000	37500	39000	42000	45000	48000	51000	52500	54000	57000	60000	63000	66000	67500	69000	72000	75000	78000	81000	82500	84000	87000	90000	93000	96000	97500	99000
BRAKES																																								
Inspect Parking Brake Operation	At Least Once Every 12 Months																																							
Lubricate Parking Brake Cable Guides		S	N		S	N	S		N	S		X		S	N		S	N	S		N	S		X		S	N		S	N	S		N	S		X		S	N	
CLUTCH & TRANSAXLE																																								
Change Automatic Transmission Fluid & Filter	No Normal Service Required; Severe Service Every 50,000 Miles																																							
Inspect Neutral Safety & BTSI Operation		S	N		S	N	S		N	S		X		S	N		S	N	S		N	S		X		S	N		S	N	S		N	S		X		S	N	
Lubricate Transmission Shift Linkage		S	N		S	N	S		N	S		X		S	N		S	N	S		N	S		X		S	N		S	N	S		N	S		X		S	N	
DRIVESHAFT																																								
Inspect CV Joint Boots	At Tire Rotations																																							
ENGINE																																								
Change Engine Coolant, 1997-99	Every 60 Months Or 100,000 (1996) Or 150,000 (1997-99) Miles																																							
Change Engine Oil & Filter	S	S	N	S	S	X	S	S	N	S	S	X	S	S	N	S	S	X	S	S	N	S	S	X	S	S	N	S	S	X	S	S	N	S	S	X	S	S	N	S
Inspect Drive Belts												X												X												X				
Inspect EGR System												X												X												X				
Inspect Exhaust System	At Engine Oil Changes																																							
Inspect Fuel Filler Cap												X												X												X				
Inspect Fuel System Hoses, Lines & Connections												X												X												X				
Inspect PCV Valve												X												X												X				
Inspect Spark Plug Wires	At Spark Plug Changes																																							
Inspect Supercharger Lubricant Level												X												X												X				
Inspect Throttle Body Bores & Plates, Remove Any Deposits, 4.0L						X												X												X										
Inspect Throttle Linkage Operation	At Air Cleaner Element Changes																																							
Replace Air Filter & PCV Filter, 1997–99						S						X						S						X						S						X				
Replace Spark Plugs	Every 100,000 Miles																																							
STEERING, SUSPENSION & TIRES																																								
Inspect Steering & Suspension System	At Tire Rotations																																							

Recommended Service	Service Interval In Miles①																																						
	3000	6000	7500	9000	12000	15000	18000	21000	22500	24000	27000	30000	33000	36000	37500	39000	42000	45000	48000	51000	52500	54000	57000	60000	63000	66000	67500	69000	72000	75000	78000	81000	82500	84000	87000	90000	93000	96000	97500	99000
STEERING, SUSPENSION & TIRES																																								
Lubricate Chassis & Suspension		S	N		S	N	S		N	S		X		S	N		S	N	S		N	S		X		S	N		S	N	S		N	S		X		S	N	
Rotate Tires, 1997–98		S	N				S		N			S			N		S				N	S					X					S	N				S		N	
Rotate Tires, 1999	Normal Service Inspect for Wear & Rotate Every 7,500 Miles; Severe Service Every 6,000 Miles																																						

N — Normal Service
S — Severe Service
X — Normal Or Severe Service
BTSI — Brake Transmission Shift Interlock
IAC — Idle Air Control
ISC — Idle Speed Control System
① — After vehicle passes 99,000 mile mark return to beginning of mileage table & start cycle over again.
② — The engine oil life monitor will indicate when to change engine oil, usually 3,000–10,000 miles. Under severe driving conditions, engine oil may need to be changed before 3000 miles. If vehicle is driven in a dusty area, change engine oil every 3000 miles.
③ — If vehicle is used in hilly or mountainous terrain, heavy city traffic where outside temperature reaches 90° F or higher or uses such high performance operation.

Buick Skylark, Chevrolet Malibu, Oldsmobile Achieva, Cutlass, Intrigue & Pontiac Grand Am

Recommended Service	Service Interval In Miles①																																						
	3000	6000	7500	9000	12000	15000	18000	21000	22500	24000	27000	30000	33000	36000	37500	39000	42000	45000	48000	51000	52500	54000	57000	60000	63000	66000	67500	69000	72000	75000	78000	81000	82500	84000	87000	90000	93000	96000	97500	99000
BODY																																								
Clean Power Antenna Mast		S	N		S	N	S		N	S		X		S	N		S	N	S		N	S		X		S	N		S	N	S		N	S		X		S	N	
Inspect Lamps, Seat Belts & Warning Devices	At Least Once Every 6 Months																																						
Lubricate Hinges, Latches, Lock Cylinders & Strikers	At Engine Oil Changes Or At Least Every 12 Months																																						
Replace Passenger Compartment Air Filter						X						X						X						X						X						X				
BRAKES																																								
Inspect Brake System, 1997	At 5,000 Miles, Then Every 10,000 Miles																																						
Inspect Brake System, 1998	At 7,500 Miles, Then Every 15,000 Miles																																						

Recommended Service	Service Interval In Miles①																																							
	3000	6000	7500	9000	12000	15000	18000	21000	22500	24000	27000	30000	33000	36000	37500	39000	42000	45000	48000	51000	52500	54000	57000	60000	63000	66000	67500	69000	72000	75000	78000	81000	82500	84000	87000	90000	93000	96000	97500	99000
BRAKES																																								
Inspect Brake System, 1999	Every 7500 Miles																																							
Inspect Parking Brake Operation	At Least Once Every 12 Months																																							
Lubricate Parking Brake Cable Guides		S	N		S	N	S		N	S		X		S	N		S	N	S		N	S		X		S	N		S	N	S		N	S		X		S	N	
CLUTCH & TRANSAXLE																																								
Change Automatic Transmission Fluid & Filter, 1997–99	No Normal Service Required; Severe Service Every 50,000 Miles																																							
Inspect Neutral Safety & BTSI Operation & Lubricate Shift Linkage		S	N		S	N	S		N	S		X		S	N		S	N	S		N	S		X		S	N		S	N	S		N	S		X		S	N	
DRIVESHAFT																																								
Inspect CV Joint Boots	At Engine Oil Changes & Tire Rotations																																							
ENGINE																																								
Change Engine Coolant, 1997-99	Every 60 Months Or 100,000 (1996) Or 150,000 (1997-99) Miles																																							
Change Engine Oil & Filter, Less Turbo②	S	S	N	S	S	X	S	S	N	S	S	X	S	S	N	S	S	X	S	S	N	S	S	X	S	S	N	S	S	X	S	S	N	S	S	X	S	S	N	S
Change Engine Oil & Filter, w/Turbo②	X	X		X	X	X	X	X		X	X	X	X	X		X	X	X	X	X		X	X	X	X	X		X	X	X	X	X		X	X	X	X	X		X
Inspect Drive Belts & EGR System, 1997-98												X												X												X				
Inspect Drive Belts & EGR System, 1999	Every 60,000 Miles																																							
Inspect Exhaust System	At Engine Oil Changes																																							
Inspect Spark Plug Wires	At Spark Plug Changes																																							
Inspect Thermostatically Controlled Air Cleaner Operation & Fuel & PCV System												X												X												X				
Inspect Throttle Linkage Operation	At Air Cleaner Element Changes																																							
Replace Air Filter & PCV Filter, 1997–98						S						X						S						X						S						X				
Replace Air Filter & PCV Filter, 1999③	Every 30,000 Miles																																							
Replace Spark Plugs③	Every 100,000 Miles																																							

Recommended Service	Service Interval In Miles①																																						
	3000	6000	7500	9000	12000	15000	18000	21000	22500	24000	27000	30000	33000	36000	37500	39000	42000	45000	48000	51000	52500	54000	57000	60000	63000	66000	67500	69000	72000	75000	78000	81000	82500	84000	87000	90000	93000	96000	97500	99000
ENGINE																																								
Replace Timing Belt																								X																
STEERING, SUSPENSION & TIRES																																								
Inspect Steering & Suspension System	At Tire Rotations																																							
Lubricate Chassis & Suspension		S	N		S	N	S		N	S		X		S	N		S	N	S		N	S		X		S	N		S	N	S		N	S		X		S	N	
Rotate Tires, 1997–98		S	N				S		N			S			N		S				N	S					X					S	N				S		N	
Rotate Tires, 1999	Inspect for Wear and Rotate Every 7500 Miles																																							

N — Normal Service
S — Severe Service
X — Normal Or Severe Service
BTSI — Brake Transmission Shift Interlock
IAC — Idle Air Control
ISC — Idle Speed Control System
① — After vehicle passes 99,000 mile mark return to beginning of mileage table & start cycle over again.
② — If equipped, the engine oil life monitor will indicate when to change engine oil, usually 3,000–10,000 miles. Under severe driving conditions, engine oil may need to be changed before 3000 miles. If vehicle is driven in a dusty area, change engine oil every 3000 miles.
③ — The U.S. Environmental Protection Agency or the California air Resources Board has determined the failure to perform this maintenance item will not nullify the emission warranty or limit recall liability prior to the completion of the vehicle's useful life. We, however, urge that all recommended maintenance services be performed at the indicated intervals and the maintenance be recorded.

Cadillac Catera

Recommended Service	Service Interval In Miles①																																						
	3000	6000	7500	9000	12000	15000	18000	21000	22500	24000	27000	30000	33000	36000	37500	39000	42000	45000	48000	51000	52500	54000	57000	60000	63000	66000	67500	69000	72000	75000	78000	81000	82500	84000	87000	90000	93000	96000	97500	99000
BODY																																								
Flush Vehicle Underside, Inspect Drain Holes	At Least Every 12 Months, Especially In Winter & Springtime																																							
Inspect Lamps, Seat Belts & Warning Devices	At Least Once Every 6 Months																																							
Lubricate Hinges, Latches, Lock Cylinders & Strikers	At Engine Oil Changes Or At Least Every 12 Months																																							

Recommended Service	Service Interval In Miles①																																							
	3000	6000	7500	9000	12000	15000	18000	21000	22500	24000	27000	30000	33000	36000	37500	39000	42000	45000	48000	51000	52500	54000	57000	60000	63000	66000	67500	69000	72000	75000	78000	81000	82500	84000	87000	90000	93000	96000	97500	99000
BODY																																								
Replace Passenger Compartment Air Filter						X						X						X						X						X						X				
BRAKES																																								
Inspect Brake System, 1997	At 5,000 Miles, Then Every 10,000 Miles																																							
Inspect Brake System, 1998	At 7,500 Miles, Then Every 15,000 Miles																																							
Inspect Brake System, 1999	Every 5000 Miles																																							
Inspect Parking Brake Operation	At Least Once Every 12 Months																																							
Lubricate Parking Brake Cable Guides		S	N		S	N	S		N	S		X		S	N		S	N	S		N	S		X		S	N		S	N	S		N	S		X		S	N	
CLUTCH & TRANSAXLE																																								
Change Automatic Transmission Fluid & Filter④	Every 50,000 Miles																																							
Inspect Neutral Safety & BTSI Operation		S	N		S	N	S		N	S		X		S	N		S	N	S		N	S		X		S	N		S	N	S		N	S		X		S	N	
Lubricate Transmission Shift Linkage		S	N		S	N	S		N	S		X		S	N		S	N	S		N	S		X		S	N		S	N	S		N	S		X		S	N	
ENGINE																																								
Change Engine Coolant	Every 60 Months Or 150,000 Miles																																							
Change Engine Oil & Filter	Normal Service Initially At 5000 Miles, Then Every 10,000 Miles Thereafter; Severe Service Every 5000 Miles																																							
Inspect Air Cleaner Element						X												X												X						X				
Inspect Drive Belts, 1997-98												X												X												X				
Inspect Drive Belts, 1999	Every 60,000Miles																																							
Inspect EGR System												X												X												X				
Inspect Exhaust System	At Engine Oil Changes																																							
Inspect Fuel Filler Cap												X												X												X				
Inspect Fuel System Hoses, Lines & Connections												X												X												X				
Inspect PCV Valve												X												X												X				
Inspect Spark Plug Wires	At Spark Plug Changes																																							
Replace Air Filter & PCV Filter, 1997-98						S						X						S						X						S						X				
Replace Air Filter & PCV Filter,1999	Every 30,000 Miles																																							
Replace Fuel Filter	Every 100,000 Miles																																							
Replace Fuel Filter	Inspect And Or Replace filter At 60,000 Miles, Then Every 30,000 Miles Thereafter																																							
Replace Spark Plugs	Every 100,000 Miles																																							

Recommended Service	Service Interval In Miles①																																							
	3000	6000	7500	9000	12000	15000	18000	21000	22500	24000	27000	30000	33000	36000	37500	39000	42000	45000	48000	51000	52500	54000	57000	60000	63000	66000	67500	69000	72000	75000	78000	81000	82500	84000	87000	90000	93000	96000	97500	99000
ENGINE																																								
Replace Timing Belt	Replace Every 100,000 Miles Under Normal Operating Conditions; Replace Every 60,000 Miles If Driven Without An Engine Coolant Heater At Ambient Temperatures Of –20°F Or Less, Then Inspect At 15,000 Mile Intervals.																																							
Replace Timing Belts , Reset Counter, 1999	Every 60,000Miles																																							
STEERING, SUSPENSION & TIRES																																								
Inspect Steering & Suspension System	At Tire Rotations																																							
Lubricate Chassis & Suspension		S	N		S	N	S		N	S		X		S	N		S	N	S		N	S		X		S	N		S	N	S		N	S		X		S	N	
Rotate Tires	Initial Service At 5000 Miles, Then Every 10,000 Miles Thereafter																																							

N — Normal Service
S — Severe Service
X — Normal Or Severe Service
BTSI — Brake Transmission Shift Interlock
IAC — Idle Air Control
ISC — Idle Speed Control System
① — After vehicle passes 99,000 mile mark return to beginning of mileage table & start cycle over again.
② — Replacement is not necessary if the vehicle is not operated under extreme cold conditions.
③ — On vehicles driven in temperatures above -20° F, or in vehicles driven in temperatures below this limit while using an engine coolant heater.
④ — If driven in heavy city traffic where temperature reaches 90° F, in hilly or mountainous terrain, frequent towing of a trailer or any high performance operation.

Chevrolet Cavalier & Pontiac Sunfire

Recommended Service	Service Interval In Miles①																																							
	3000	6000	7500	9000	12000	15000	18000	21000	22500	24000	27000	30000	33000	36000	37500	39000	42000	45000	48000	51000	52500	54000	57000		63000	66000	67500	69000	72000	75000	78000	81000	82500	84000	87000	90000	93000	96000	97500	99000
BODY																																								
Inspect Lamps, Seat Belt & Warning Devices	At Least Once Every 6 Months																																							
Lubricate Hinges, Latches, Lock Cylinders & Strikers	At Engine Oil Changes Or At Least Every 12 Months																																							
Replace Passenger Compartment Air Filter						X						X						X												X						X				

Recommended Service	3000	6000	7500	9000	12000	15000	18000	21000	22500	24000	27000	30000	33000	36000	37500	39000	42000	45000	48000	51000	52500	54000	57000	63000	66000	67500	69000	72000	75000	78000	81000	82500	84000	87000	90000	93000	96000	97500	99000
Service Interval In Miles①																																							
BRAKES																																							
Inspect Brake System, 1997	At 5,000 Miles, Then Every 10,000 Miles																																						
Inspect Brake System, 1998	At 7,500 Miles, Then Every 15,000 Miles																																						
Inspect Brake System, 1999-2000	Normal Service At 7,500 Miles, Then Every 10,000 Miles Thereafter; Severe Service Every 7,500 Miles																																						
Inspect Parking Brake Operation	At Least Once Every 12 Months																																						
Lubricate Parking Brake Cable Guides		S	N		S	N	S		N	S		X		S	N		S	N	S		N	S			S	N		S	N	S		N	S		X		S	N	
CLUTCH & TRANSAXLE																																							
Change Automatic Transmission Fluid & Filter	No Normal Service Required; Severe Service Every 50,000 Miles																																						
Inspect Neutral Safety & BTSI Operation & Lubricate Shift Linkage		S	N		S	N	S		N	S		X		S	N		S	N	S		N	S			S	N		S	N	S		N	S		X		S	N	
DRIVESHAFT																																							
Inspect CV Joint Boots	At Tire Rotations																																						
ENGINE																																							
Change Engine Coolant	Every 60 Months Or Or 150,000 Miles																																						
Change Engine Oil & Filter, Less Turbo	S	S	N	S	S	X	S	S	N	S	S	X	S	S	N	S	S	X	S	S	N	S	S	S	S	N	S	S	X	S	S	N	S	S	X	S	S	N	S
Change Engine Oil & Filter, w/Turbo	X	X		X	X	X	X	X		X	X	X	X	X		X	X	X	X	X		X	X	X	X		X	X	X	X	X		X	X	X	X	X		X
Inspect Drive Belts & EGR System & Fuel & PCV System												X																							X				
Inspect Exhaust System	At Engine Oil Changes																																						
Inspect Spark Plug Wires	At Spark Plug Changes																																						
Inspect Thermostatically Controlled Air Cleaner Operation												X																							X				
Inspect Throttle Linkage Operation	At Engine Oil Or Air Cleaner Element Changes																																						
Replace Air Filter & PCV Filter						S						X						S											S						X				
Replace Spark Plugs	Every 100,000 Miles																																						
STEERING, SUSPENSION & TIRES																																							
Inspect Steering & Suspension System	At Tire Rotations																																						
Lubricate Chassis & Suspension		S	N		S	N	S		N	S		X		S	N		S	N	S		N	S			S	N		S	N	S		N	S		X		S	N	
Rotate Tires, 1997–98		S	N				S		N			S			N		S				N	S				X					S	N				S		N	

Recommended Service	Service Interval In Miles①																																						
	3000	6000	7500	9000	12000	15000	18000	21000	22500	24000	27000	30000	33000	36000	37500	39000	42000	45000	48000	51000	52500	54000	57000		63000	66000	67500	69000	72000	75000	78000	81000	82500	84000	87000	90000	93000	96000	97500	99000
STEERING, SUSPENSION & TIRES																																								
Rotate Tires, 1999-2000	Normal Service Inspect For Wear & Rotate Every 7,500 Miles; Severe Service Every 6,000 Miles																																							

N — Normal Service
S — Severe Service
X — Normal Or Severe Service
BTSI — Brake Transmission Shift Interlock
IAC — Idle Air Control
ISC — Idle Speed Control System
① — After vehicle passes 99,000 mile mark return to beginning of mileage table & start cycle over again.

Chevrolet Camaro & Pontiac Firebird

Recommended Service	Service Interval In Miles①																																						
	3000	6000	7500	9000	12000	15000	18000	21000	22500	24000	27000	30000	33000	36000	37500	39000	42000	45000	48000	51000	52500	54000	57000	60000	63000	66000	67500	69000	72000	75000	78000	81000	82500	84000	87000	90000	93000	96000	97500	99000
BODY																																								
Clean Power Antenna Mast		S	N		S	N	S		N	S		X		S	N		S	N	S		N	S		X		S	N		S	N	S		N	S		X		S	N	
Flush Vehicle Underside, Inspect Drain Holes	At Least Every 12 Months																																							
Inspect Lamps, Seat Belts & Warning Devices	At Least Once Every 6 Months																																							
Lubricate Hinges, Latches, Lock Cylinders & Strikers	At Engine Oil Changes Or At Least Every 12 Months																																							
Replace Passenger Compartment Air Filter						X						X						X						X						X						X				
BRAKES																																								
Inspect Brake System, 1997	At 5,000 Miles, Then Every 10,000 Miles																																							
Inspect Brake System, 1998	At 7,500 Miles, Then Every 15,000 Miles																																							
Inspect Brake System, 1999-2000	Normal Service At 7,500 Miles, Then Every 10,000 Miles Thereafter; Severe Service Every 7,500 Miles																																							
Inspect Parking Brake Operation	At Least Once Every 12 Months																																							
Lubricate Parking Brake Cable Guides		S	N		S	N	S		N	S		X		S	N		S	N	S		N	S		X		S	N		S	N	S		N	S		X		S	N	

Service Interval In Miles①

Recommended Service	3000	6000	7500	9000	12000	15000	18000	21000	22500	24000	27000	30000	33000	36000	37500	39000	42000	45000	48000	51000	52500	54000	57000	60000	63000	66000	67500	69000	72000	75000	78000	81000	82500	84000	87000	90000	93000	96000	97500	99000
CLUTCH & TRANSAXLE																																								
Change Automatic Transmission Fluid & Filter, 1997-98	Normal Service Every 100,000 Miles; Severe Service Every 15,000 Miles																																							
Change Automatic Transmission Fluid & Filter, 1999-2000	Normal Service Every 100,000 Miles; Severe Service Every 50,000 Miles																																							
Inspect Neutral Safety & BTSI Operation		S	N		S	N	S		N	S		X		S	N		S	N	S		N	S		X		S	N		S	N	S		N	S		X		S	N	
Lubricate Transmission Shift Linkage		S	N		S	N	S		N	S		X		S	N		S	N	S		N	S		X		S	N		S	N	S		N	S		X		S	N	
ENGINE																																								
Change Engine Coolant	Every 60 Months Or 150,000 Miles																																							
Change Engine Oil & Filter	S	S	N	S	S	X	S	S	N	S	S	X	S	S	N	S	S	X	S	S	N	S	S	X	S	S	N	S	S	X	S	S	N	S	S	X	S	S	N	S
Inspect Drive Belts												X												X												X				
Inspect EGR System												X												X												X				
Inspect Exhaust System	At Engine Oil Changes																																							
Inspect Fuel Filler Cap												X												X												X				
Inspect Fuel System Hoses, Lines & Connections												X												X												X				
Inspect PCV Valve												X												X												X				
Inspect Spark Plug Wires	At Spark Plug Changes																																							
Inspect TBI Unit Mounting Fastener Security		S	N																																					
Inspect Thermostatically Controlled Air Cleaner Operation												X												X												X				
Inspect Throttle Linkage Operation	At Air Cleaner Element Changes																																							
Replace Air Filter & PCV Filter, 1997-98	Normal Service Every 36 Months Or 30,000 Miles; More Frequently In Severe Service Or Dusty Conditions																																							
Replace Air Filter & PCV Filter, 1999-2000②	Inspect and Replace If Necessary Every 10,000 Miles.																																							
Replace Spark Plugs	Every 100,000 Miles																																							
STEERING, SUSPENSION & TIRES																																								
Inspect Steering & Suspension System	At Tire Rotations																																							
Lubricate Chassis & Suspension		S	N		S	N	S		N	S		X		S	N		S	N	S		N	S		X		S	N		S	N	S		N	S		X		S	N	
Rotate Tires, 1997–98		S	N				S		N			S			N		S				N	S					X					S	N				S		N	

Recommended Service	Service Interval In Miles① 3000	6000	7500	9000	12000	15000	18000	21000	22500	24000	27000	30000	33000	36000	37500	39000	42000	45000	48000	51000	52500	54000	57000	60000	63000	66000	67500	69000	72000	75000	78000	81000	82500	84000	87000	90000	93000	96000	97500	99000
STEERING, SUSPENSION & TIRES																																								
Rotate Tires, 1999-2000	Normal Service Inspect For Wear & Rotate Every 7,500 Miles; Severe Service Every 6,000 Miles																																							

N — Normal Service
S — Severe Service
X — Normal Or Severe Service
BTSI — Brake Transmission Shift Interlock
IAC — Idle Air Control
ISC — Idle Speed Control System
① — After vehicle passes 99,000 mile mark return to beginning of mileage table & start cycle over again.
② — The U.S. environmental Protection Agency or the California Air Resources Board has determined the failure to perform this maintenance item will not nullify the emission warranty or limit recall liability prior to the completion of the vehicle's useful life. We, however, urge that all recommended maintenance services be performed at the indicated intervals and the maintenance be recorded.

Chevrolet Corvette

Recommended Service	Service Interval In Miles① 3000	6000	7500	9000	12000	15000	18000	21000	22500	24000	27000	30000	33000	36000	37500	39000	42000	45000	48000	51000	52500	54000	57000	60000	63000	66000	67500	69000	72000	75000	78000	81000	82500	84000	87000	90000	93000	96000	97500	99000
BODY																																								
Clean Power Antenna Mast		S	N		S	N	S		N	S		X		S	N		S	N	S		N	S		X		S	N		S	N	S		N	S		X		S	N	
Inspect Lamps, Seat Belts & Warning Devices	At Least Once Every 6 Months																																							
Lubricate Hinges, Latches, Lock Cylinders & Strikers	At Engine Oil Changes Or At Least Every 12 Months																																							
Replace Passenger Compartment Air Filter						X						X						X						X						X						X				
BRAKES																																								
Inspect Brake System, 1997	At 5,000 Miles, Then Every 10,000 Miles																																							
Inspect Brake System, 1998	At 7,500 Miles, Then Every 15,000 Miles																																							
Inspect Brake System, 1999-2000	Normal Service At 7,500 Miles, Then Every 10,000 Miles Thereafter; Severe Service Every 7,500 Miles																																							
Inspect Parking Brake Operation	At Least Once Every 12 Months																																							
Lubricate Parking Brake Cable Guides		S	N		S	N	S		N	S		X		S	N		S	N	S		N	S		X		S	N		S	N	S		N	S		X		S	N	

Recommended Service	Service Interval In Miles①																																							
	3000	6000	7500	9000	12000	15000	18000	21000	22500	24000	27000	30000	33000	36000	37500	39000	42000	45000	48000	51000	52500	54000	57000	60000	63000	66000	67500	69000	72000	75000	78000	81000	82500	84000	87000	90000	93000	96000	97500	99000
CLUTCH & TRANSAXLE																																								
Change Automatic Transmission Fluid & Filter	No Normal Service Required; Severe Service Every 50,000 Miles																																							
Inspect Neutral Safety & BTSI Operation & Lubricate Shift Linkage		S	N		S	N	S		N	S		X		S	N		S	N	S		N	S		X		S	N		S	N	S		N	S		X		S	N	
ENGINE																																								
Change Engine Coolant	Every 60 Months Or 150,000 Miles																																							
Change Engine Oil & Filter②	Normal Service Every 12 Months Or 10,000 Miles; Severe Service Every 3000 Miles																																							
Inspect Air Cleaner Element, 1997–98	Every 10,000 Miles, Replace Every 30,000 Miles																																							
Inspect Air Cleaner Element, 1999-2000②	Inspect At 15,000 Miles, Replace Every 30,000 Miles																																							
Inspect Drive Belts, EGR, Fuel & PCV System												X												X												X				
Inspect Exhaust System	At Engine Oil Changes																																							
Inspect Spark Plug Wires	At Spark Plug Changes																																							
Inspect TBI Unit Mounting Fastener Security		S	N																																					
Inspect Thermostatically Controlled Air Cleaner Operation												X												X												X				
Inspect Throttle Linkage Operation	At Air Cleaner Element Changes																																							
Replace Air Filter & PCV Filter, 1997–98						S						X						S						X						S						X				
Replace Spark Plugs	Every 100,000 Miles																																							
STEERING, SUSPENSION & TIRES																																								
Inspect Steering & Suspension System	At Tire Rotations																																							
Lubricate Chassis & Suspension		S	N		S	N	S		N	S		X		S	N		S	N	S		N	S		X		S	N		S	N	S		N	S		X		S	N	

N — Normal Service
S — Severe Service
X — Normal Or Severe Service
BTSI — Brake Transmission Shift Interlock
IAC — Idle Air Control
ISC — Idle Speed Control System
① — After vehicle passes 99,000 mile mark return to beginning of mileage table & start cycle over again.
② — The U.S. Environmental Protection Agency or the California air Resources Board has determined the failure to perform this maintenance item will no nullify the emissions warranty or limit recall liability prior to the completion of the vehicle's useful life. We, however, urge that all recommended maintenance services be performed at the indicated intervals and the maintenance be recorded.

Chevrolet & Geo Metro

Recommended Service	Service Interval In Miles①																																							
	3000	6000	7500	9000	12000	15000	18000	21000	22500	24000	27000	30000	33000	36000	37500	39000	42000	45000	48000	51000	52500	54000	57000	60000	63000	66000	67500	69000	72000	75000	78000	81000	82500	84000	87000	90000	93000	96000	97500	99000
BODY																																								
Inspect Seat Belts & Related Components & Lubricate Lock Cylinders	At Least Once Every 12 Months																																							
Inspect Supplemental Restraint System	10 Years From Vehicle Build Date																																							
Inspect Warning Lamps & Devices	S	S	N	S	S	X	S	S	N	S	S	X	S	S	N	S	S	X	S	S	N	S	S	X	S	S	N	S	S	X	S	S	N	S	S	X	S	S	N	S
Lubricate Door Hinges	At Every Engine Oil Change																																							
BRAKES																																								
Change Brake Fluid																								X																
Inspect Brake System		S	N		S				N	S				S	N				S		N			S			N		S				N	S				S	N	
CLUTCH & TRANSAXLE																																								
Change Automatic Transaxle Fluid & Filter	No Normal Service Interval Recommended By Manufacturer; Severe Service Every 50,000 Miles																																							
Change Manual Transaxle Lubricant					S					S		N		S					S					X					S					S		N		S		
Inspect Clutch Pedal Freeplay		S	N		S	N	S		N	S		X		S	N		S	N	S		N	S		X		S	N		S	N	S		N	S		X		S	N	
Inspect Neutral Safety & Shift Interlock Switch Operation	At Least Once Every 12 Months																																							
Inspect Transaxle Fluid & Shift Control Operation	At Every Engine Oil Change																																							
Replace Automatic Transaxle Fluid Cooler Hoses																		X																		X				
DRIVESHAFT																																								
Inspect CV Joint Boots		S	N		S	N	S		N	S		X			N		S	N	S		N	S		X		S	N		S	N	S		N	S		X		S	N	
ENGINE																																								
Change Engine Coolant & Inspect Ignition Coils												X												X												X				
Change Engine Oil & Filter	S	S	N	S	S	X	S	S	N	S	S	X	S		N	S	S	X	S	S	N	S	S	X	S	S	N	S	S	X	S	S	N	S	S	X	S	S	N	S
Inspect Air Filter Element	S	S		S	S	S	S	S		S	S	S	S			S	S	S	S	S		S	S	S	S	S		S	S	S	S	S		S	S	S	S	S		S
Inspect Distributor Cap & Rotor & Drive Belts & PCV valve						S						S						S						X						S						S				
Inspect Engine Valve Clearance						X						X						X						X						X						X				
Inspect Exhaust, Fuel & EVAP System & Coolant						X						X						X						X						X						X				

Recommended Service	Service Interval In Miles① 3000	6000	7500	9000	12000	15000	18000	21000	22500	24000	27000	30000	33000	36000	37500	39000	42000	45000	48000	51000	52500	54000	57000	60000	63000	66000	67500	69000	72000	75000	78000	81000	82500	84000	87000	90000	93000	96000	97500	99000
ENGINE																																								
Inspect Spark Plug Wires						S						S						S												S						S				
Inspect Warning Lamps	S	S	N	S	S	X	S	S	N	S	S	X	S		N	S	S	X	S	S	N	S	S	X	S	S	N	S	S	X	S	S	N	S	S	X	S	S	N	S
Replace Engine Air Filter Element & PCV Filter	Normal Service Every 30,000 Miles; More Frequently In Severe Service Or Dusty Conditions																																							
Replace EVAP Canister Filter, 1999-2000	Every 10 Years Or 120,000 Miles																																							
Replace Fuel Filter, 1997	Normal Service Every 105 Months Or 105,000 Miles; Severe Service Every 60 Months Or 60,000 Miles																																							
Replace Fuel Filter, 1998	Every 10 Years Or 120,000 Miles																																							
Replace Fuel Filter, 1999-2000	Every 100,000 Miles																																							
Replace Spark Plugs												X												X												X				
Replace Spark Plug Wires																								X																
STEERING, SUSPENSION & TIRES																																								
Inspect Power Steering , Steering & Suspension & Wheel Bearings		S	N		S	N	S		N	S		X			N		S	N	S		N	S		X		S	N		S	N	S		N	S		X		S	N	
Lubricate Chassis & Suspension	At Every Engine Oil Change																																							
Rotate Tires, 1997-98		S	N		S	N	S		N	S		X			N		S	N	S		N	S		X		S	N		S	N	S		N	S		X		S	N	
Rotate Tires, 1999-2000	Inspect For Wear And Rotate Every 6000 Miles																																							

N — Normal Service
S — Severe Service
X — Normal Or Severe Service
① — After vehicle passes 99,000 mile mark return to beginning of mileage table & start cycle over again.
② — The U.S. Environmental Protection Agency or the California Air Resources Board has determined the failure to perform this maintenance item will nullify the emission warranty or limit recall liability prior to the completion of the vehicle's useful life. We, however, urge that all recommended maintenance services be performed at the indicated intervals and the maintenance be recorded.

Chevrolet & Geo Prizm

Recommended Service	Service Interval In Miles①																																							
	3000	6000	7500	9000	12000	15000	18000	21000	22500	24000	27000	30000	33000	36000	37500	39000	42000	45000	48000	51000	52500	54000	57000	60000	63000	66000	67500	69000	72000	75000	78000	81000	82500	84000	87000	90000	93000	96000	97500	99000
BODY																																								
Inspect Body Fastener Security	Severe Service Every 5000 Miles																																							
Inspect Seat Belts & Related Components	At Least Once Every 12 Months																																							
Supplemental Restraint System	10 Years From Vehicle Build Date, Then Every 24 Months Thereafter																																							
Inspect Lamps & Warning Devices	S	S	N	S	S	X	S	S	N	S	S	X	S	S	N	S	S	X	S	S	N	S	S	X	S	S	N	S	S	X	S	S	N	S	S	X	S	S	N	S
Lubricate Lock Cylinders	At Least Once Every 12 Months																																							
BRAKES																																								
Inspect Brake System Hoses, Lines & Connections	Normal Service Every 15,000 Miles; Severe Service Every 5000 Miles																																							
CLUTCH & TRANSAXLE																																								
Change Automatic Transmission Fluid & Filter						X						X						X						X						X						X				
Change Differential & Manual Transaxle Lubricant						S						S						S						S						S						S				
Inspect Neutral Safety & Shift Interlock Switch Operation	At Least Once Every 12 Months																																							
Inspect Transaxle Lubricant Level	At Every Engine Oil Change																																							
DRIVESHAFT																																								
Inspect CV Joint Boots & Tighten Driveshaft Flange	Normal Service Every 15,000 Miles; Severe Service Every 5000 Miles																																							
ENGINE																																								
Change Engine Coolant②	Every 24 Months Or 30,000 Miles																																							
Change Engine Oil & Filter	Normal Service Every 7500 Miles; Severe Service Every 3 Months or 3000 Miles																																							
Inspect Cooling System & Drive Belts						X						X						X						X						X						X				
Inspect Engine Valve Clearance																								X																
Inspect EVAP Charcoal Canister	Every 72 Months Or 60,000 Miles																																							
Inspect EVAP & Fuel System						X						X						X						X						X						X				
Inspect Exhaust System					X						X						X						X						X						X					
Inspect Thermostatic Air Cleaner System Operation												X												X												X				
Replace Air Filter Element & PCV Filter	Normal Service Every 30,000 Miles; More Frequently In Severe Service Or Dusty Conditions																																							

Service Interval In Miles①

Recommended Service	3000	6000	7500	9000	12000	15000	18000	21000	22500	24000	27000	30000	33000	36000	37500	39000	42000	45000	48000	51000	52500	54000	57000	60000	63000	66000	67500	69000	72000	75000	78000	81000	82500	84000	87000	90000	93000	96000	97500	99000
ENGINE																																								
Replace Spark Plugs (Standard Type)												X												X												X				
Replace Spark Plugs (Platinum Tip Type)																								X																
Replace Timing Belt, 1997																								X																
STEERING, SUSPENSION & TIRES																																								
Inspect Chassis Fastener Security	Severe Service Every 5000 Miles																																							
Inspect Steering & Suspension			S			X			S			X			S			X			S			X			S			X			S			X			S	
Lubricate Chassis & Suspension & Rotate Tires	At Every Engine Oil Change																																							
Lubricate Chassis & Suspension & Rotate Tires	Every 6000 Miles																																							

N — Normal Service
S — Severe Service
X — Normal Or Severe Service
① — After vehicle passes 99,000 mile mark return to beginning of mileage table & start cycle over again.
② — The U. S. Environmental Protection Agency or the California Air Resources Board has determined that the failure to perform this maintenance item will not nullify the emission warranty or limit recall liability prior to the completion of the vehicle's useful life. We, however, urge that all recommended maintenance services be performed at the indicated intervals and the maintenance be recorded.

Geo Storm

Service Interval In Miles①

Recommended Service	3000	6000	7500	9000	12000	15000	18000	21000	22500	24000	27000	30000	33000	36000	37500	39000	42000	45000	48000	51000	52500	54000	57000	60000	63000	66000	67500	69000	72000	75000	78000	81000	82500	84000	87000	90000	93000	96000	97500	99000
BODY																																								
Inspect Seat Belts & Related Components	At Least Once Every 12 Months																																							
Inspect Warning Lamps & Devices	S	S	N	S	S	X	S	S	N	S	S	X	S	S	N	S	S	X	S	S	N	S	S	X	S	S	N	S	S	X	S	S	N	S	S	X	S	S	N	S
Lubricate Lock Cylinders	At Least Once Every 12 Months																																							

Recommended Service	Service Interval In Miles①																																							
	3000	6000	7500	9000	12000	15000	18000	21000	22500	24000	27000	30000	33000	36000	37500	39000	42000	45000	48000	51000	52500	54000	57000	60000	63000	66000	67500	69000	72000	75000	78000	81000	82500	84000	87000	90000	93000	96000	97500	99000
BRAKES																																								
Inspect Brake System		S	N					S	N					S	N					S	N					S	N					S	N					S	N	
CLUTCH & TRANSAXLE																																								
Change Transaxle Fluid & Filter						S						X						S						X						S						X				
Inspect Neutral Safety & Shift Interlock Switch Operation	At Least Once Every 12 Months																																							
Inspect & Adjust Clutch Pedal Freeplay, Lubricate Linkage	Every 5000 Miles																																							
DRIVESHAFT																																								
Inspect CV Joint Boots		S	N					S	N					S	N					S	N					S	N					S	N					S	N	
ENGINE																																								
Change Engine Coolant												X												X												X				
Change Engine Oil & Filter	S	S	N	S	S	X	S	S	N	S	S	X	S	S	N	S	S	X	S	S	N	S	S	X	S	S	N	S	S	X	S	S	N	S	S	X	S	S	N	S
Inspect Cooling System & Protection Level						X						X						X						X						X						X				
Inspect Drive Belts & PCV Valve						S						X						S						X						S						X				
Inspect Exhaust System	S	S	N	S	S	X	S	S	N	S	S	X	S	S	N	S	S	X	S	S	N	S	S	X	S	S	N	S	S	X	S	S	N	S	S	X	S	S	N	S
Inspect Fuel System						X						X						X						X						X						X				
Inspect Thermostatic Air Cleaner System Operation												X												X												X				
Replace Air Filter Element & PCV Filter	Normal Service Every 30,000 Miles; More Frequently In Severe Service Or Dusty Conditions																																							
Replace Spark Plugs												X												X												X				
Replace Timing Belt																								X																
STEERING, SUSPENSION & TIRES																																								
Inspect Power Steering Fluid Hoses & Lines																	S	N																S	N					
Lubricate Chassis & Suspension	At Every Engine Oil Change																																							
Rotate Tires		S	N					S	N					S	N					S	N					S	N					S	N					S	N	

N — Normal Service
S — Severe Service
X — Normal Or Severe Service
① — After vehicle passes 99,000 mile mark return to beginning of mileage table & start cycle over again.

Pontiac LeMans

Recommended Service	Service Interval In Miles① 3000	6000	7500	9000	12000	15000	18000	21000	22500	24000	27000	30000	33000	36000	37500	39000	42000	45000	48000	51000	52500	54000	57000	60000	63000	66000	67500	69000	72000	75000	78000	81000	82500	84000	87000	90000	93000	96000	97500	99000
BODY																																								
Flush Underside Of Vehicle & Inspect Drain Holes	At Least Once Every 12 Months																																							
Inspect Seat Belts & Related Components	At Least Once Every 12 Months																																							
Inspect Warning Lamps & Devices	S	S	N	S	S	X	S	S	N	S	S	X	S	S	N	S	S	X	S	S	N	S	S	X	S	S	N	S	S	X	S	S	N	S	S	X	S	S	N	S
Lubricate Lock Cylinders	At Least Once Every 12 Months																																							
BRAKES																																								
Inspect Brake System Hoses Lines & Connections		S	N					S	N					S	N					S	N					S	N					S	N					S	N	
Inspect Brake System Warning Lamp	S	S	N	S	S	X	S	S	N	S	S	X	S	S	N	S	S	X	S	S	N	S	S	X	S	S	N	S	S	X	S	S	N	S	S	X	S	S	N	S
Inspect Disc Brake Pads & Rotors		S	N					S	N					S	N					S	N					S	N					S	N					S	N	
Inspect Rear Brake Drums & Shoes		S	N					S	N					S	N					S	N					S	N					S	N					S	N	
CLUTCH & TRANSAXLE																																								
Inspect Neutral Safety & Shift Interlock Switch Operation	At Least Once Every 12 Months																																							
Inspect & Adjust Clutch Pedal Freeplay, Lubricate Linkage	Every 10,000 Miles																																							
DRIVESHAFT																																								
Inspect CV Joint Boots		S	N					S	N					S	N					S	N					S	N					S	N					S	N	
ENGINE																																								
Change Engine Coolant	Every 24 Months Or 30,000 Miles																																							
Change Engine Oil & Filter	S	S	N	S	S	X	S	S	N	S	S	X	S	S	N	S	S	X	S	S	N	S	S	X	S	S	N	S	S	X	S	S	N	S	S	X	S	S	N	S
Inspect Cooling System & Protection Level						X						X						X						X						X						X				
Inspect Drive Belts						S						X						S						X						S						X				
Inspect EVAP System Hoses, Lines & Connections						X						X						X						X						X						X				
Inspect Exhaust System	S	S	N	S	S	X	S	S	N	S	S	X	S	S	N	S	S	X	S	S	N	S	S	X	S	S	N	S	S	X	S	S	N	S	S	X	S	S	N	S
Inspect Fuel Filler Cap						X						X						X						X						X						X				
Inspect Fuel Hoses, Lines & Connections						X						X						X						X						X						X				

	Service Interval In Miles①																																							
Recommended Service	3000	6000	7500	9000	12000	15000	18000	21000	22500	24000	27000	30000	33000	36000	37500	39000	42000	45000	48000	51000	52500	54000	57000	60000	63000	66000	67500	69000	72000	75000	78000	81000	82500	84000	87000	90000	93000	96000	97500	99000
ENGINE																																								
Inspect Fuel Tank Mounting Straps						X						X						X						X						X						X				
Inspect Ignition Timing												X												X												X				
Inspect TBI Unit Fastener Security		S	N																																					
Inspect Thermostatic Air Cleaner System Operation												X												X												X				
Inspect Warning Lamps	S	S	N	S	S	X	S	S	N	S	S	X	S	S	N	S	S	X	S	S	N	S	S	X	S	S	N	S	S	X	S	S	N	S	S	X	S	S	N	S
Replace Air Filter Element & PCV Filter	Normal Service Every 30,000 Miles; More Frequently In Severe Service Or Dusty Conditions																																							
Replace Fuel Filter	Every 36 Months Or 30,000 Miles																																							
Replace Spark Plugs												X												X												X				
Replace Spark Plug Wires												X												X												X				
Replace Timing Belt	Manufacturer Does Not Recommend A Specific Maintenance Interval																																							
STEERING SUSPENSION & TIRES																																								
Lubricate Chassis & Suspension	At Every Engine Oil Change																																							
Rotate Tires		S	N					S	N					S	N					S	N					S	N					S	N					S	N	

N — Normal Service
S — Severe Service
X — Normal Or Severe Service
① — After vehicle passes 99,000 mile mark return to beginning of mileage table & start cycle over again.

Saturn

	Service Interval In Miles①																																							
Recommended Service	3000	6000	7500	9000	12000	15000	18000	21000	22500	24000	27000	30000	33000	36000	37500	39000	42000	45000	48000	51000	52500	54000	57000	60000	63000	66000	67500	69000	72000	75000	78000	81000	82500	84000	87000	90000	93000	96000	97500	99000
BODY																																								
Inspect Seat Belts & Restraint Systems	At Least Once Every 6 Months																																							
Inspect Wiper Blades & Inserts	At Least Once Every 6 Months																																							

Recommended Service	Service Interval In Miles①																																							
	3000	6000	7500	9000	12000	15000	18000	21000	22500	24000	27000	30000	33000	36000	37500	39000	42000	45000	48000	51000	52500	54000	57000	60000	63000	66000	67500	69000	72000	75000	78000	81000	82500	84000	87000	90000	93000	96000	97500	99000
BODY																																								
Lubricate Door Check Straps & Hinges		X		X		X		X		X		X		X		X		X		X		X		X		X		X		X		X		X		X		X		X
Lubricate Hood Latch		X		X		X		X		X		X		X		X		X		X		X		X		X		X		X		X		X		X		X		X
Lubricate Headlamp Doors		X		X		X		X		X		X		X		X		X		X		X		X		X		X		X		X		X		X		X		X
Lubricate Sunroof		X		X		X		X		X		X		X		X		X		X		X		X		X		X		X		X		X		X		X		X
BRAKES																																								
Inspect Disc Brake Calipers For Freedom Of Movement (Lubricate If Required)		X				X				X				X				X				X				X				X				X				X		
Inspect Disc Brake Pads & Rotors		X				X				X				X				X				X				X				X				X				X		
Inspect Brake Drums & Shoes		X				X				X				X				X				X				X				X				X				X		
Inspect Brake Hoses, Lines & Connections		X				X				X				X				X				X				X				X				X				X		
CLUTCH & TRANSAXLE																																								
Change Automatic Transaxle Fluid & Filter										X										X										X										X
Change Manual Transaxle Lubricant	Once Only At 6000 Miles																																							
DRIVESHAFT																																								
Inspect CV Joint Boots		X		X		X		X		X		X		X		X		X		X		X		X		X		X		X		X		X		X		X		X
ENGINE																																								
Change Engine Coolant & Inspect Pressure Cap	Every 60 Months Or 100,000 Miles																																							
Change Engine Oil & Filter	S	X	S	X	S	X	S	X	S	X	S	X	S	X	S	X	S	X	S	X	S	X	S	X	S	X	S	X	S	X	S	X	S	X	S	X	S	X	S	X
Inspect Cooling System & Protection Level						X						X						X						X						X						X				
Inspect Drive Belts						X						X						X						X						X						X				
Inspect Emission Hoses, Lines & Connections										X										X										X										X
Inspect Exhaust System		X		X		X		X		X		X		X		X		X		X		X		X		X		X		X		X		X		X		X		X
Inspect Fuel Hoses, Lines & Connections										X										X										X										X
Inspect Fuel Tank Filler Cap										X										X										X										X
Replace Air Filter	Normal Service Every 30,000 Miles; More Frequently In Severe Service Or Dusty Conditions																																							
Replace Fuel Filter, 1997																				X																				X
Replace Fuel Filter, 1999	Every 100,000 Miles																																							
Replace Spark Plugs										X										X										X										X

Recommended Service	Service Interval In Miles①																																							
	3000	6000	7500	9000	12000	15000	18000	21000	22500	24000	27000	30000	33000	36000	37500	39000	42000	45000	48000	51000	52500	54000	57000	60000	63000	66000	67500	69000	72000	75000	78000	81000	82500	84000	87000	90000	93000	96000	97500	99000
STEERING, SUSPENSION & TIRES																																								
Inspect Ball Joint Seals		X		X		X		X		X		X		X		X		X		X		X		X		X		X		X		X		X		X		X		X
Inspect Suspension		X		X		X		X		X		X		X		X		X		X		X		X		X		X		X		X		X		X		X		X
Rotate Tires		X				X				X				X				X				X				X				X				X				X		

N — Normal Service
S — Severe Service
X — Normal Or Severe Service
BTSI — Brake Transaxle Shift Interlock
① — After vehicle passes 120,000 mile mark return to beginning of mileage table & start cycle over again.

DAIMLERCHRYSLER CORP.

DAIMLERCHRYSLER CORP.

AVENGER & SEBRING COUPE

NOTE: Refer To The Rear Of This Manual For Vehicle Manufactures Special Service Tool Suppliers.

INDEX OF SERVICE OPERATIONS

Specifications

GENERAL ENGINE SPECIFICATIONS

Year	Engine		Fuel System	Bore x Stroke, Inches	Comp. Ratio	Net HP @ RPM	Maximum Torque, Ft. Lbs. @ RPM	Normal Oil Pressure @ Idle, psi
	Liter	VIN Code①						
1997–2000	2.0L	Y	SMFI	3.44 x 3.27	9.6	140 @ 6000	130 @ 4800	4.0
	2.5L	N	SMFI	3.29 x 2.99	9.5	163 @ 5500	170 @ 4400	11.4

SMFI — Sequential Multi-Port Fuel Injection

① — Eighth digit of Vehicle Identification Number (VIN) denotes engine code.

TUNE UP SPECIFICATIONS

Engine Liter	Spark Plug Gap, Inch	Firing Order Fig.④	Ignition Timing °BTDC			Curb Idle Speed①		Fuel Pump Pressure, psi.③	Valve Lash, Inch
			Man. Trans.	Auto. Trans.	Mark Fig.	Man. Trans.	Auto. Trans.		
2.0L	.048–.053	A	12②	12②	⑤	800⑥	800⑥	47–50	⑦
2.5L	.039–.043	B	—	10②	⑤	750⑥	750⑥	47–50	⑦

BTDC — Before Top Dead Center.

① — When adjusting idle speed, set parking brake & chock drive wheels.

② — Direct (Distributorless) Ignition System (DIS), not adjustable.

③ — Remove rear seat cushion, then the protector. Disconnect fuel pump connector. Start engine & let run until it stops naturally, then turn ignition to Off. Connect fuel pump connector, install protector & rear seat cushion. Remove cover from service valve on fuel rail. Connect suitable fuel pressure test gauge to service valve. Switch ignition in Run position, then use scan tool to activate fuel pump & pressurize system.

④ — Before disconnecting wires from coil unit, determine location of ignition wires in coil towers, as position may have been altered from that shown.

⑤ — Equipped w/crankshaft position sensor.

⑥ — Non-adjustable.

⑦ — Equipped w/hydraulic lash adjusters.

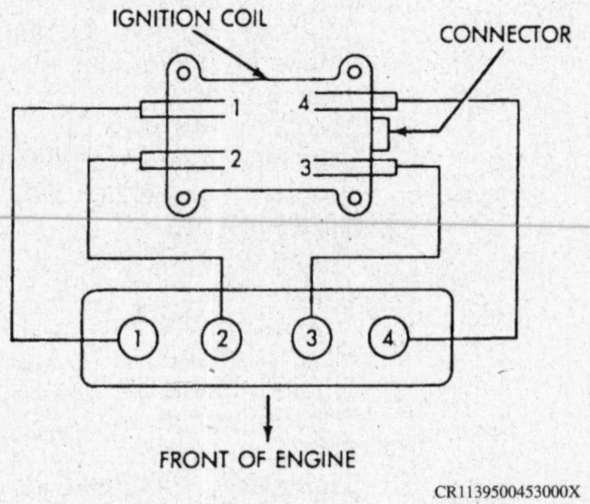

Fig. A

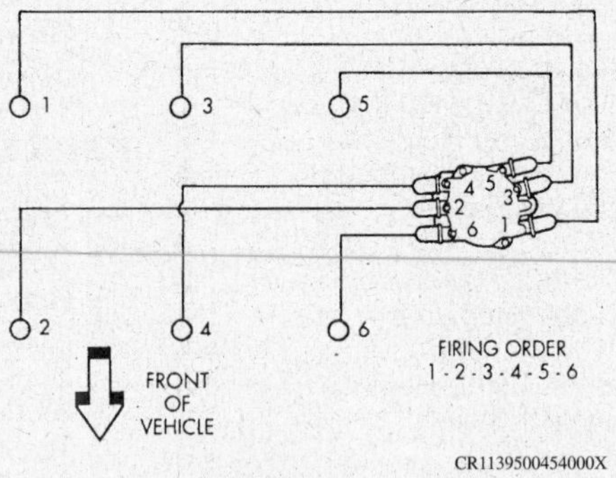

Fig. B

FRONT WHEEL ALIGNMENT SPECIFICATIONS

Year	Camber Angle, Degrees ①		Toe, Inch③		Caster, Degrees		Ball Joint Wear
	Limits	Desired	Limits	Desired	Limits	Desired	
1997–2000	-.5 to +.05	0	-.12 to +.12	0	+2.83 to +5.83	4.33	②

① — Not adjustable.

② — Refer to "Ball Joint Inspection" under "Front Suspension & Steering."

③ — Toe in (+); toe out (-).

REAR WHEEL ALIGNMENT SPECIFICATIONS

Year	Camber, Degrees			Total Toe, Inch①	
	Limits	Desired	Max. LH/RH Deviation	Limits	Desired
1997–2000	-1.83 to -.83	-1.33	.5	0 to +.24	+.12

① — Toe in (+); toe out (-).

FLUID CAPACITIES & COOLING SYSTEM DATA

Engine	Coolant Capacity, Qts.	Radiator Cap Relief Pressure, Lbs.	Thermo. Opening Temp. °F	Fuel Tank Capacity, Gals.	Engine Oil Refill, Qts.①	Transaxle Oil, Qts.	
						Manual	Auto.
2.0L	7.4	16	195	16.9	4	2.1	9.1
2.5L	7.4	11–15	180	16.9	4	—	9.1

① — Capacity without oil filter. Add additional 1/2 quart when changing filter.

LUBRICANT DATA

Year	Lubricant Type①			Brake System
	Transaxle		Power Steering	
	Manual	Automatic		
1997–2000	Mopar Type M.S. 9417	Mopar ATF Type 7176	Dexron II ATF	DOT 3 or 4

① — Automatic Transaxle Fluid.

Electrical

NOTE: Refer To "Air Bag System Precautions " Located In The Front Of This Manual For System Disarming & Arming Procedures.

NOTE: Refer To "Computer Relearn Procedures " Located In The Front Of This Manual For Computer Relearn Procedures.

INDEX

PRECAUTIONS

AIR BAG SYSTEMS

Refer to "Air Bag System Precautions" in the front of this manual for system disarming and arming procedures.

BATTERY GROUND CABLE

Prior to service, disconnect battery ground cable and isolate as required.

FUSE PANEL & FLASHER LOCATION

The fuse panel is located behind the lower lefthand side of the instrument panel. The turn signal and hazard flasher unit is located behind the center of the instrument panel, near the A/C and heater control panel.

FUEL PUMP RELAY LOCATION

The fuel pump relay is located in the rear lefthand corner of the engine compartment, behind the left shock tower, **Fig. 1.**

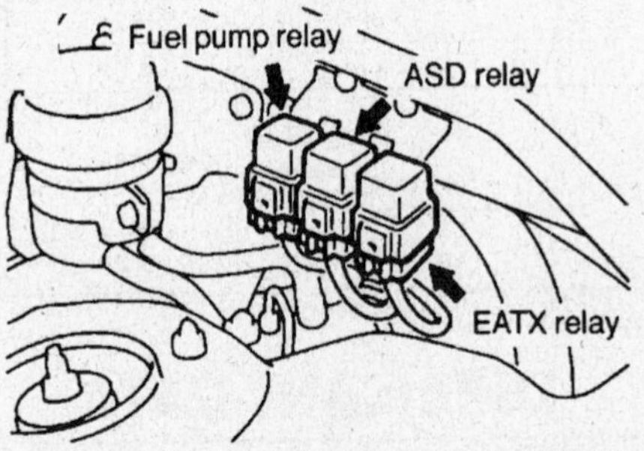

Fig. 1 Fuel pump relay location

STARTER

REPLACE

1. Disconnect starter terminal and electrical connector.
2. Remove starter from vehicle.
3. Reverse procedure to install, noting the following:
   a. **On models equipped with 2.0L engine, torque** starter mounting bolts to 40 ft. lbs.
   b. **On models equipped with 2.5L engine, torque** starter mounting bolts to 20–25 ft. lbs.

ALTERNATOR

REPLACE

2.0L ENGINE

1. Remove alternator drive belt, **Fig. 2.**
2. Disconnect alternator electrical connector.
3. Remove alternator bracket, then the alternator and brace.
4. Reverse procedure to install. **Torque** alternator mounting bolt to 45 ft. lbs.

2.5L ENGINE

1. Remove pump cover and A/C compressor drive belt, **Fig. 3.**
2. Remove power steering pump and alternator drive belt.
3. Remove intake manifold plenum.
4. Remove alternator bracket.
5. Remove intake manifold plenum stay.
6. Disconnect alternator electrical connector.
7. Remove alternator.
8. Remove tensioner pulley, then bracket.
9. Remove alternator bracket.
10. Reverse procedure to install.

DISTRIBUTOR

REPLACE

2.5L ENGINE

1. Remove spark plug wires.
2. Remove distributor mounting bolts, then distributor.
3. Remove distributor O-ring.
4. Reverse procedure to install.

COIL PACK

REPLACE

2.0L ENGINE

1. Remove spark plug wires.
2. Remove four coil pack mounting bolts, then coil pack.
3. Reverse procedure to install. **Torque** mounting bolts to 108 inch lbs.

IGNITION LOCK

REPLACE

1. Remove steering wheel as outlined under "Steering Wheel, Replace."
2. Remove lower instrument panel plug, **Fig. 4.**
3. Remove hood lock release handle.
4. Remove instrument panel under cover.
5. Remove steering column lower and upper covers.

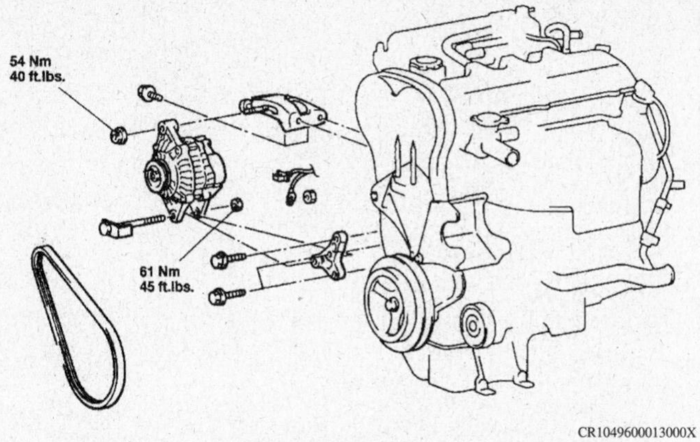

CR1049600013000X

Fig. 2 Alternator replacement. 2.0L engine

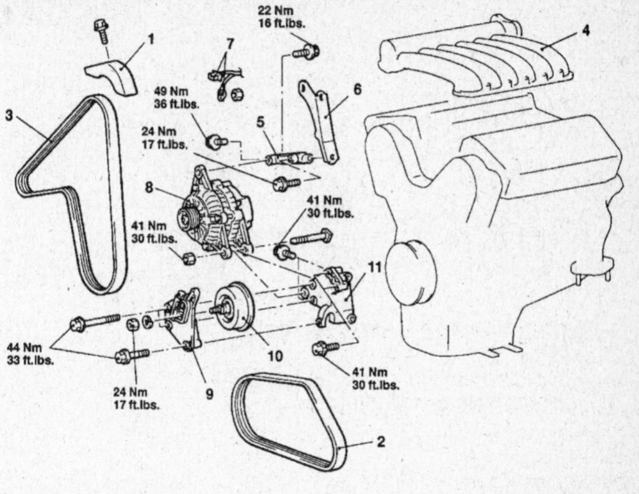

1. Pump cover
2. Drive belt (A/C compressor)
3. Drive belt (Power steering oil pump and generator)
4. Intake manifold plenum

5. Generator bracket
6. Intake manifold plenum stay
7. Generator harness connector
8. Generator
9. Tensioner pulley bracket
10. Tensioner pulley
11. Generator bracket

CR1049600014000X

Fig. 3 Alternator replacement. 2.5L engine

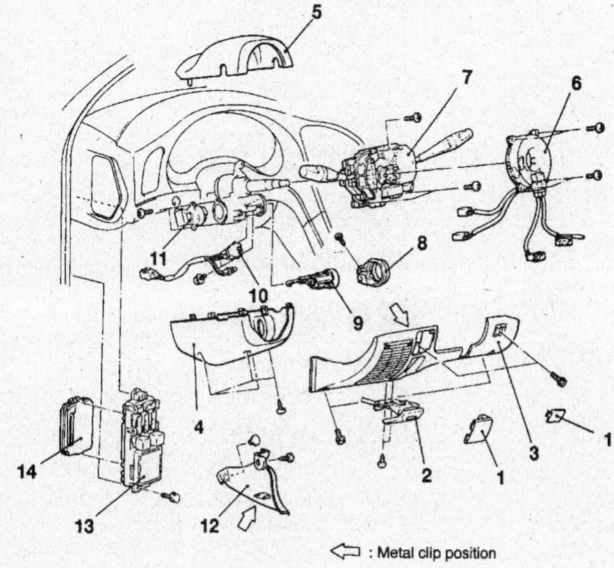

- Steering wheel

1. Plug
2. Hood lock release handle
3. Instrument under cover
4. Column cover lower
5. Column cover upper
6. Clock spring
7. Column switch
8. Ignition key illumination ring or ring cover
9. Steering lock cylinder

CR1049600015000X

Fig. 4 Ignition lock/switch & multi-function switch replacement

6. Remove clockspring.
7. Remove column multi-function switch.
8. Remove ignition key illumination ring or ring cover.
9. Insert key in steering lock cylinder and turn to ACC position.
10. Using screwdriver or suitable pointed tool, push lock pin of steering lock cylinder inward, then pull lock cylinder outward to remove.
11. Reverse procedure to install. Refer to "Supplemental Restraint Systems" for clockspring installation procedure.

IGNITION SWITCH

REPLACE

1. Remove steering wheel as described under "Steering Wheel, Replace."
2. Remove lower instrument panel plug, **Fig. 4.**
3. Remove hood lock release handle.
4. Remove instrument panel under cover.
5. Remove steering column lower and upper covers.
6. Remove clockspring.
7. Locate ignition switch attached to ignition lock cylinder.
8. Disconnect ignition switch electrical connector, then remove switch.
9. Reverse procedure to install. Refer to "Supplemental Restraint Systems" for clockspring installation procedure.

NEUTRAL SAFETY SWITCH

REPLACE

The neutral safety switch is located at the lower left side of the transaxle housing, under the air cleaner assembly, **Fig. 5.**

1. Disconnect neutral safety switch electrical connector.
2. Remove switch from transaxle case.
3. Reverse procedure to install.

MULTI-FUNCTION SWITCH

REPLACE

1. Remove steering wheel as described under "Steering Wheel, Replace."
2. Remove lower instrument panel plug, **Fig. 4.**
3. Remove hood lock release handle.
4. Remove instrument panel under cover.
5. Remove steering column lower and upper covers.
6. Remove clockspring.
7. Remove column multi-function switch.
8. Reverse procedure to install. Refer to

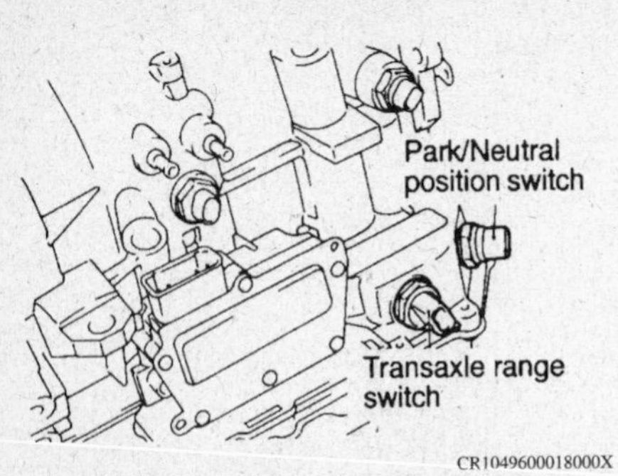

Fig. 5 Neutral safety switch

"Supplemental Restraint Systems" for clockspring installation procedure.

STEERING WHEEL

REPLACE

1. Remove air bag module mounting nut from back side of steering wheel.
2. Remove air bag module from steering wheel, **Fig. 6.**
3. Turn air bag module over and press air bag lock toward outer side to spread it open, then use a flat-tipped screwdriver to gently pry apart clockspring connector, **Fig. 7.**
4. Remove steering wheel nut and steering wheel using suitable steering wheel puller tool. **Do not use hammer to remove steering wheel as this may damage the collapsible shaft.**
5. Reverse procedure to install. **Torque** steering wheel nut to 30 ft. lbs.

INSTRUMENT CLUSTER

REPLACE

1. Remove steering wheel as outlined under "Steering Wheel, Replace."
2. Remove two screws from under top of instrument cluster bezel.
3. Remove instrument cluster bezel. It may be necessary to remove the steering column upper shroud.
4. Remove instrument cluster retaining screws at top of cluster.
5. Pull instrument cluster forward slightly, then disconnect electrical connectors from back of cluster.
6. Remove instrument cluster from instrument panel.
7. Reverse procedure to install.

RADIO

REPLACE

1. Remove instrument panel center panel, **Fig. 8.**
2. Remove radio and tape player or CD player. Disconnect electrical connectors.
3. Remove floor console assembly installer screws.
4. Pull upper part of floor bracket back slightly and remove radio bracket.
5. Reverse procedure to install.

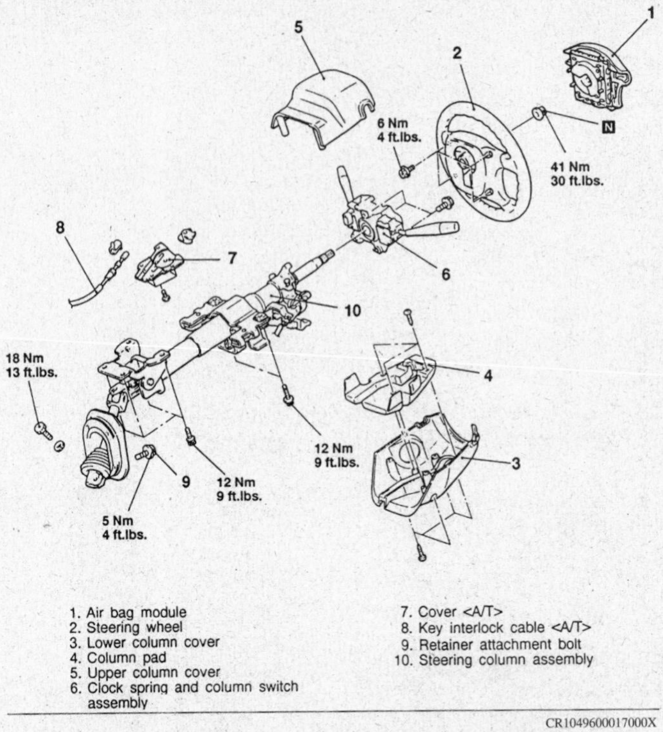

Fig. 6 Steering wheel replacement

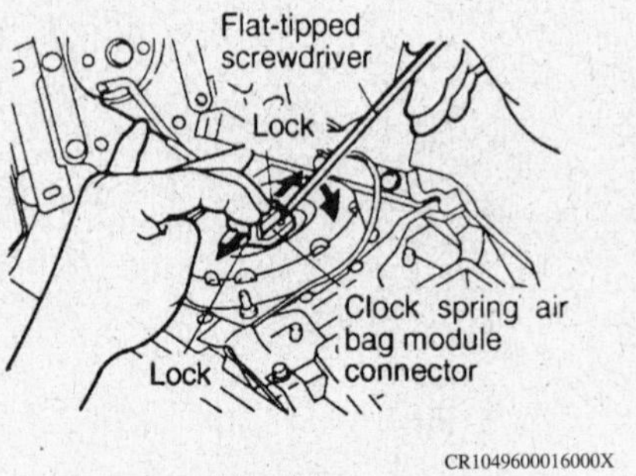

Fig. 7 Air bag module clockspring connector

WIPER MOTOR

REPLACE

1. Remove wiper arm and blade assembly.
2. Remove front deck garnish/cowl screen.
3. Remove wiper motor and link assembly and disconnect motor electrical connector.
4. Reverse procedure to install.

BLOWER MOTOR

REPLACE

1. Remove glove compartment.
2. **On models equipped with A/C,** remove automatic compressor ECM mounted under blower motor.
3. **On all models,** disconnect blower motor electrical connector.
4. Remove blower motor and fan assembly mounting screws and lower motor/fan assembly from blower unit.
5. Reverse procedure to install.

HEATER CORE

REPLACE

1. Recover as much coolant from cooling system as possible to prevent spillage when heater hoses are disconnected, then remove center console in numbered sequence shown in **Fig. 9.**
2. Remove steering wheel and column covers, **Fig. 10,** then the instrument panel in numbered sequence shown in **Fig. 11.**
3. Remove heater unit and core in numbered sequence shown in **Fig. 12,** noting the following:
   a. **On models equipped with manual transaxle,** ensure vehicle speed sensor is protected from coolant spillage when heater hoses are disconnected.
   b. **On all models,** use a suitable Philips head screwdriver to remove duct clips by pressing center of each clip inward approximately .08 inch while pulling outward. **Do not push pins in farther than necessary, grommet may be damaged or pins may fall through grommet holes.**
   c. It may be necessary to slide cooling unit outward slightly before removing heater unit.
4. Reverse to install noting the following:
   a. Install in numbered sequence shown in **Fig. 12.**
   b. Install instrument panel by reversing numbered sequence shown in **Fig. 11.**
   c. Refer to **Fig. 10** when installing steering wheel and column covers.
   d. Install center console by reversing

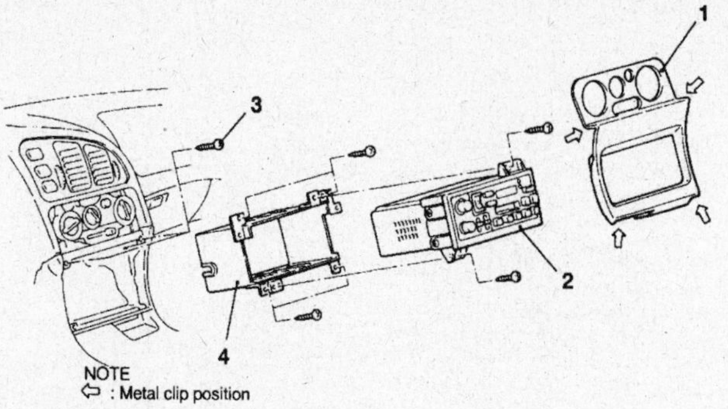

1. Center panel
2. Radio, radio with tape player or radio with tape player and CD player
3. Floor console assembly installer screws
4. Radio bracket

CR1049600019000X

Fig. 8 Radio removal

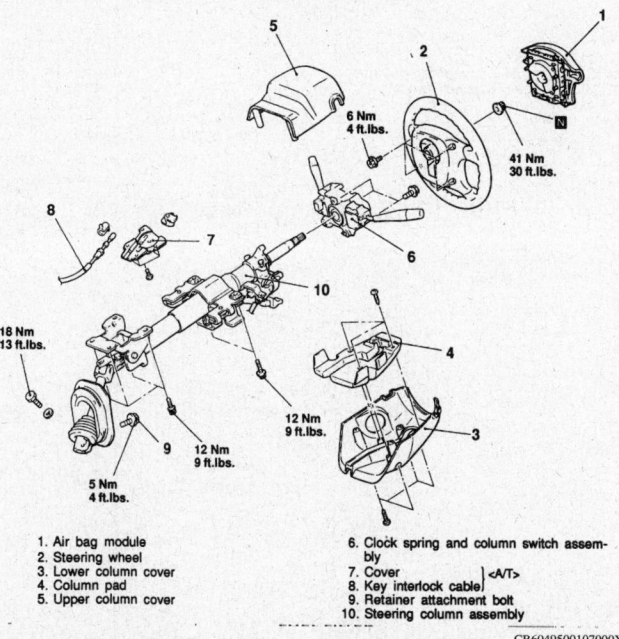

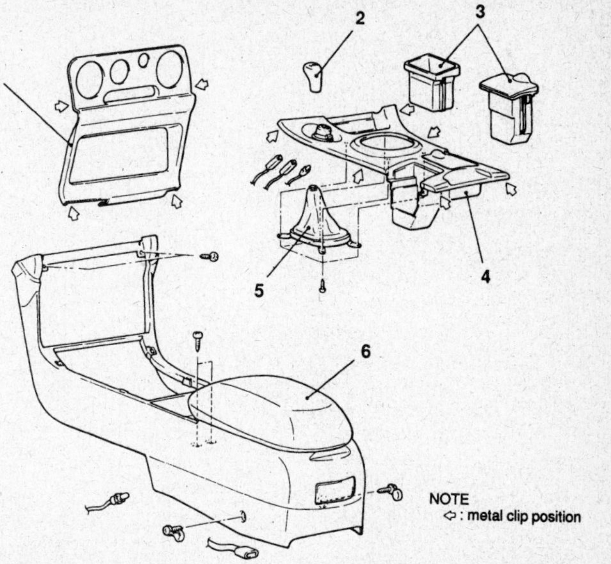

1. Center console panel
2. Shift knob
3. Accessory box or ashtray
4. Floor console panel assembly
5. Shift lever cover assembly
6. Floor console assembly

CR9149500060000X

Fig. 9 Center console replacement

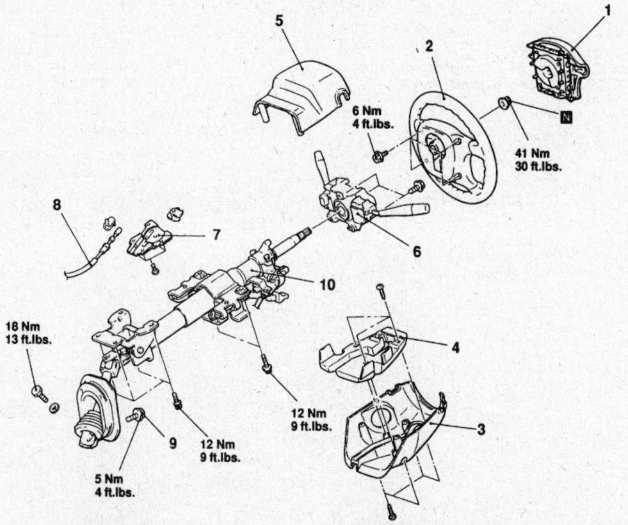

1. Air bag module
2. Steering wheel
3. Lower column cover
4. Column pad
5. Upper column cover
6. Clock spring and column switch assembly
7. Cover <A/T>
8. Key interlock cable <A/T>
9. Retainer attachment bolt
10. Steering column assembly

CR6049500107000X

Fig. 10 Exploded view of steering column & wheel assembly

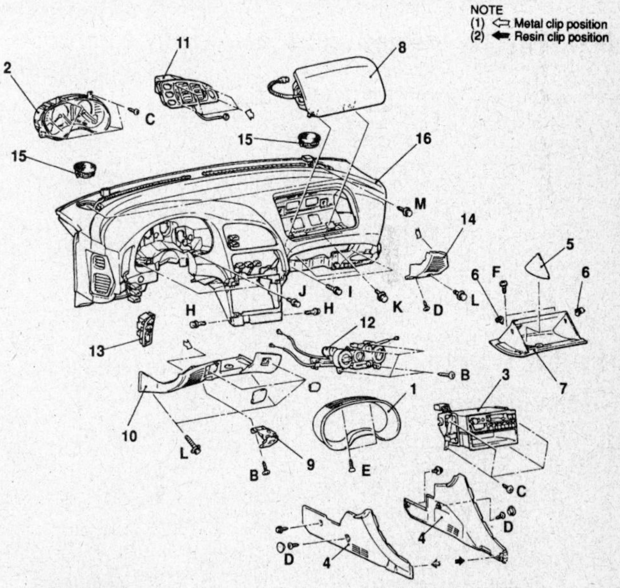

1. Meter bezel
2. Combination meter
3. Radio and tape player, and box
4. Console side cover
5. Sunglasses holder
6. Stopper
7. Glove box
8. Passenger's side air bag module assembly
9. Hood lock release handle
10. Instrument under cover L.H.
11. Center air outlet assembly
12. Heater control assembly
13. Instrument panel switch
14. Instrument under cover R.H.
15. Front speaker
16. Instrument panel assembly

CR9149500052000X

Fig. 11 Instrument panel replacement

numbered sequence shown in **Fig. 9.**

e. Refill cooling system and check for leaks.

EVAPORATOR CASE

REPLACE

1. Recover refrigerant as outlined in "Air Conditioning" section.
2. Disconnect A/C drain hose, **Fig. 13.**
3. Disconnect suction pipe and liquid pipe.
4. Remove glove compartment and instrument panel corner panel.
5. Remove glove compartment frame.
6. Remove righthand center console side cover.
7. Remove ABS-ECU cover and bracket.
8. Remove cooling unit retaining pin by pushing center of pin into grommet with a suitable screwdriver. Push pin inward to a depth of about .08 inch, then pull outward to remove.
9. Remove cooling unit from vehicle.
10. Reverse procedure to install.

EVAPORATOR CORE

REPLACE

1. Recover refrigerant as outlined under "Air Conditioning."
2. Remove evaporator case in numbered sequence shown in **Fig. 14.**
3. Use a suitable Phillips head screwdriver to remove evaporator case clips by pressing center of each clip inward approximately .08 inch while pulling outward.
4. Disassemble evaporator case in numbered sequence shown in **Fig. 15.**
5. Install evaporator and evaporator case by reversing numbered sequences shown in **Figs. 14 and 15.**

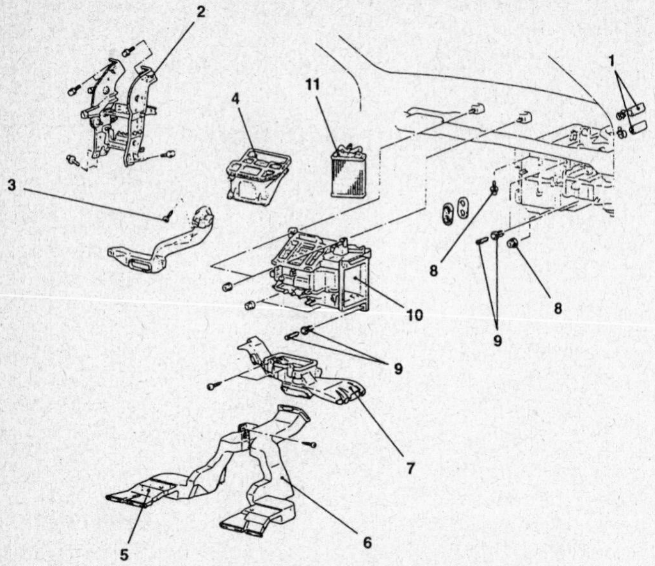

- Instrument panel
1. Heater hose connection
2. Center stay
3. Lap cooler duct mounting screw
4. Center duct
5. Rear heater duct (L.H.)
6. Rear heater duct (R.H.)
7. Foot distribution duct
8. Cooling unit mounting bolt and nut <Vehicles with A/C>
9. Clip
10. Heater unit
11. Heater core

CR7029500231000X

Fig. 12 Heater unit & core replacement

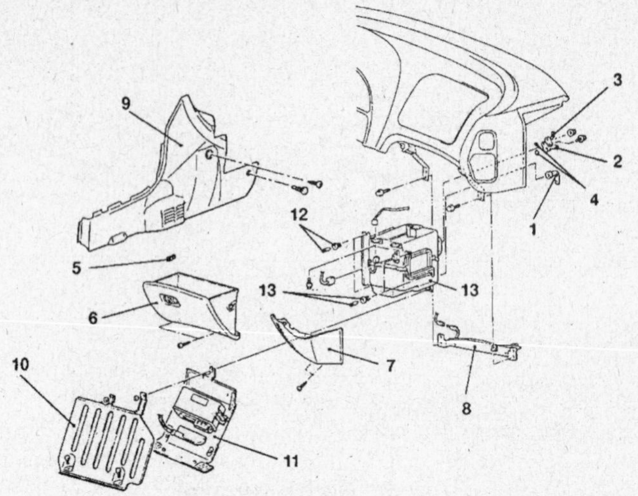

1. Drain hose
2. Suction pipe connection
3. Liquid pipe connection
4. O-ring
5. Stopper
6. Glove box
7. Corner panel
8. Glove box under frame
9. Console side cover <R.H.>
10. Control unit cover
11. ABS-ECU bracket
12. Clip
13. Cooling unit

CR7029600268000X

Fig. 13 Evaporator case removal

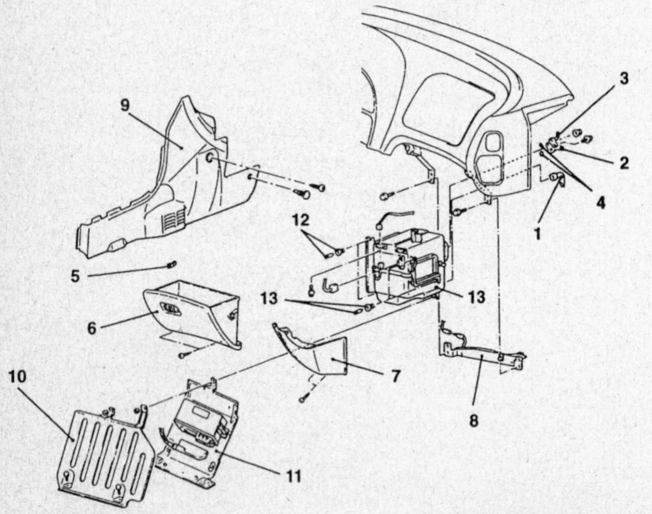

1. Drain hose
2. Suction pipe connection
3. Liquid pipe connection
4. O-ring
5. Stopper
6. Glove box
7. Corner panel
8. Glove box under frame
9. Console side cover <R.H.>
10. Control unit cover
11. ABS-ECU bracket
12. Clip
13. Cooling unit

CR7029500232000X

Fig. 14 Evaporator case replacement

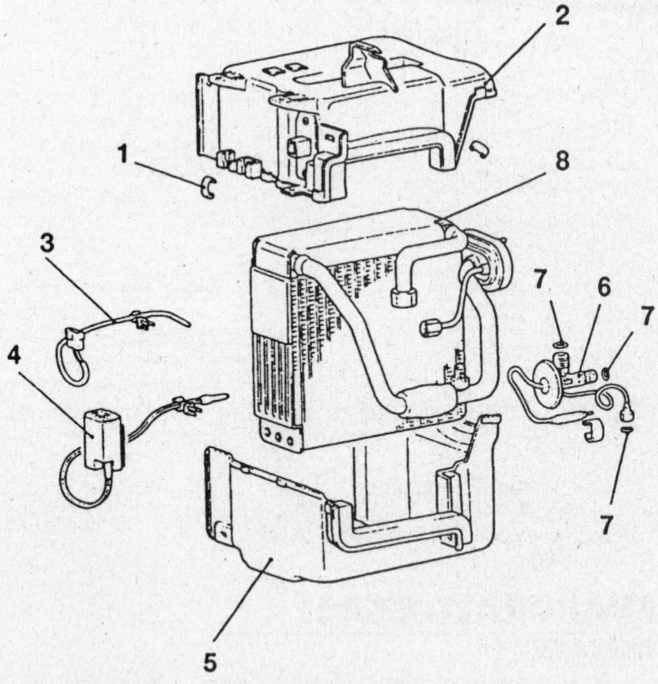

1. Clip
2. Evaporator case (upper)
3. Fin thermo sensor <DOHC>
4. Automatic compressor-ECM and fin thermo sensor assembly <SOHC>
5. Evaporator case (lower)
6. Expansion valve
7. O-ring
8. Evaporator

CR7029500233000X

Fig. 15 Evaporator case disassembly

2.0L Engine

NOTE: Refer To The "Talon" Chapter For Procedures Not Covered In This Section.

NOTE: Refer To "Air Bag System Precautions " Located In The Front Of This Manual For System Disarming & Arming Procedures.

NOTE: Refer To "Computer Relearn Procedures " Located In The Front Of This Manual For Computer Relearn Procedures.

NOTE: Prior To Performing Any Service Operations Listed In This Section, Consult The "Technical Service Bulletins " Section For Related Information.

INDEX

PRECAUTIONS

AIR BAG SYSTEMS

Refer to "Air Bag System Precautions" in the front of this manual for system disarming and arming procedures.

BATTERY GROUND CABLE

Prior to service, disconnect battery ground cable and isolate as required.

FUEL SYSTEM PRESSURE RELIEF

1. Remove rear seat cushion.
2. Remove protector to disconnect fuel pump connector.
3. Start engine and run until it stops naturally, then turn ignition switch off.
4. Connect fuel pump connector and install protector.
5. Install rear cushion.

COMPRESSION PRESSURE

Perform compression test with engine at normal operating temperature, spark plugs removed and throttle wide open. Standard compression pressure is 170–225 psi. The minimum compression pressure is 100 psi with a maximum variation between highest and lowest cylinders of 25 percent.

ENGINE MOUNT

REPLACE

1. Remove radiator coolant reserve tank.
2. Raise and support engine so there is no weight on the engine mount bracket insulator.
3. Remove engine mount insulator mounting bolt, **Fig. 1**.
4. Remove engine mount bracket and stopper.
5. Reverse procedure to install.

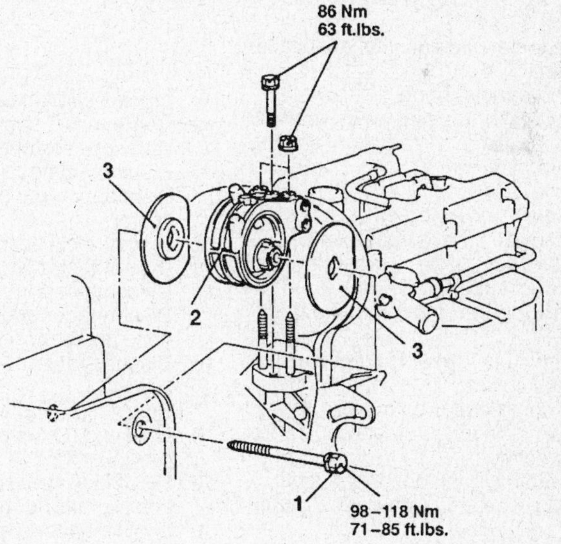

1. Engine mount insulator mounting bolt
2. Engine mount bracket
3. Engine mount stopper

CR1069600641000X

Fig. 1 Engine mount replacement

ENGINE

REPLACE

1. Relieve fuel system pressure as described under "Precautions."

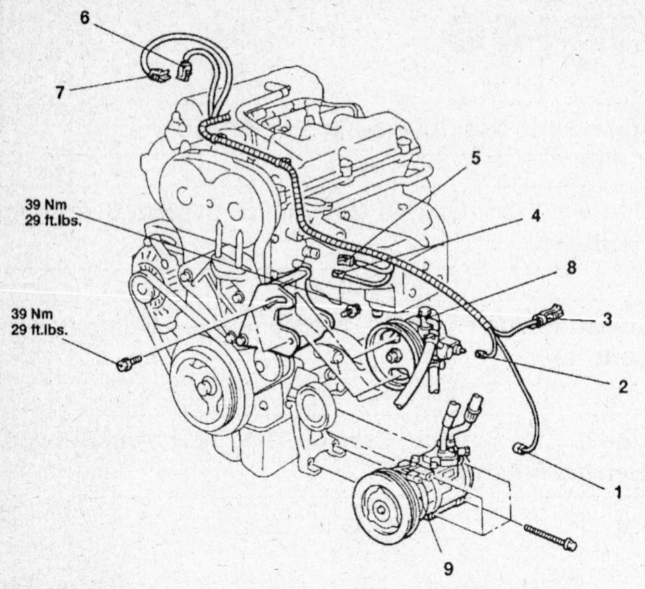

1. A/C compressor connector
2. Power steering pressure switch connector
3. Heated oxygen sensor connector
4. Engine coolant temperature gauge unit connector
5. Engine coolant temperature sensor connector
6. MAP sensor connector
7. Intake air temperature sensor connector
8. Power steering pump connection
9. A/C compressor connection

CR1069600642010X

Fig. 2 Engine removal (Part 1 of 3)

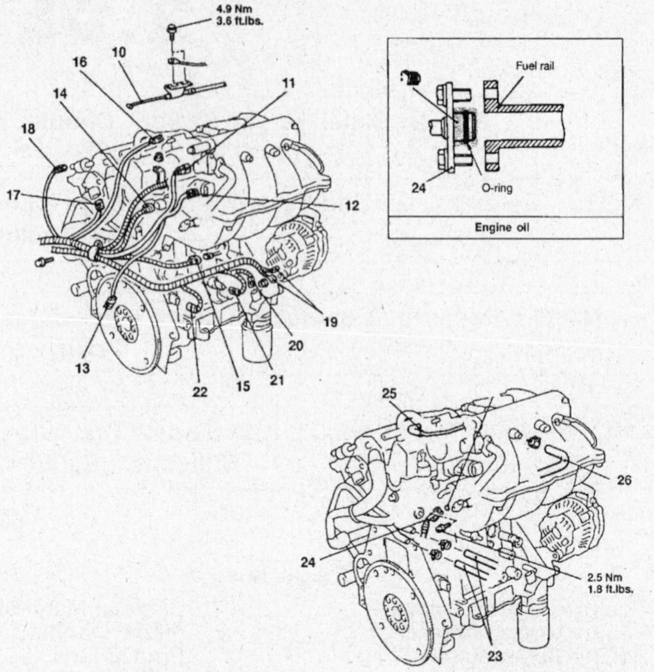

10. Accelerator cable connection
11. Throttle position sensor connector
12. Idle air control motor connector
13. Vehicle speed sensor connector <M/T>
14. Injector harness connector
15. Generator harness connector
16. Ignition coil connector
17. Camshaft position sensor connector
18. EGR solenoid valve connector
19. Generator connector
20. Crankshaft position sensor connector
21. Knock sensor connector
22. Oil pressure switch connector
23. Heater hose connection
24. High pressure fuel hose connection
25. Purge air hose connection
26. Brake booster vacuum hose connection

CR1069600642020X

Fig. 2 Engine removal (Part 2 of 3)

2. Drain engine coolant into a suitable container.
3. Mark and remove hood.
4. **On models equipped with manual transaxle,** remove transaxle assembly as outlined in "Clutch & Manual Transaxle" section.
5. **On models equipped with automatic transaxle,** remove transaxle as outlined in "Automatic Transmissions/ Transaxles " chapter.
6. **On all models,** remove engine under cover.
7. Disconnect the following electrical harness connectors:
   a. A/C compressor connector, **Fig. 2.**
   b. Power steering pressure switch connector.
   c. Heated oxygen sensor connector.
   d. Engine coolant temperature gauge unit connector.
   e. Engine coolant temperature sensor connector.
   f. Manifold Absolute Pressure (MAP) sensor connector.
   g. Intake air temperature sensor connector.
   h. Throttle position sensor connector.
   i. Idle air control connector.
   j. Vehicle speed sensor connector.
   k. Injector harness connector.
   l. Alternator harness connector.
   m. Ignition coil connector.
   n. Camshaft position sensor connector.
   o. Crankshaft position sensor connector.
   p. Knock sensor connector.
   q. EGR solenoid valve connector.
8. Remove power steering pump from bracket with hose attached.
9. Remove A/C compressor from bracket with hose attached.
10. Disconnect accelerator cable.
11. Disconnect oil pressure switch connector.
12. Disconnect heater hose connection.
13. Disconnect high pressure fuel hose.
14. Disconnect purge air hose.
15. Disconnect brake booster vacuum hose and vapor hose.
16. Disconnect front exhaust pipe connection.
17. Support engine with suitable jack.
18. Hold engine assembly with chain block or similar tool.
19. Place jack against engine oil pan with a piece of wood in between, then raise engine so the weight of the engine is no longer being applied to mounting bracket.
20. Remove mounting bracket.
21. Ensure all cables, hoses and harness connectors have been remove from engine, then lift chain block to remove engine from engine compartment.
22. Reverse procedure to install, noting the following:
   a. When connecting high pressure fuel hose to fuel rail, apply clean engine oil to hose union.
   b. Tighten all fasteners to specifications.

INTAKE MANIFOLD

REPLACE

1. Release fuel system pressure as described under " Precautions."
2. Drain engine coolant.
3. Disconnect air intake hose and breather hose, **Fig. 3.**
4. Disconnect accelerator cable and remove cable retaining clips.
5. Disconnect Manifold Absolute Pressure (MAP) sensor connector.
6. Disconnect intake air temperature sensor connector.
7. Disconnect vacuum hose connection.
8. Disconnect Throttle Position Sensor (TPS) connector.
9. Disconnect idle air control motor connector.
10. Remove control wiring harness.
11. Disconnect alternator wiring harness.
12. Remove Positive Crankcase Ventilation (PCV) hose assembly.
13. Disconnect vacuum hose.
14. Disconnect brake booster vacuum hose.
15. Disconnect EGR pipe.
16. Disconnect high pressure fuel hose.
17. Remove intake manifold stay and engine hanger.
18. Disconnect injector connector.
19. Remove throttle body.
20. Remove intake manifold plenum and gasket.
21. Remove fuel rail/injector/pressure regulator assembly.
22. Remove injector O-rings.
23. Remove intake manifold and gasket.
24. Reverse procedure to install. Tighten to specifications.

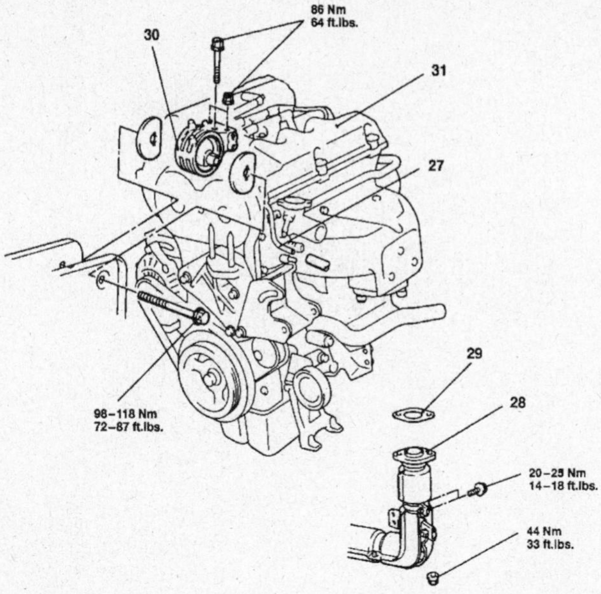

Fig. 2 Engine removal (Part 3 of 3)

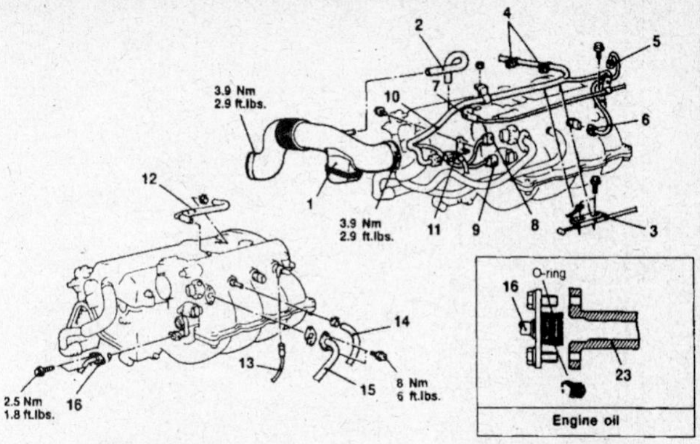

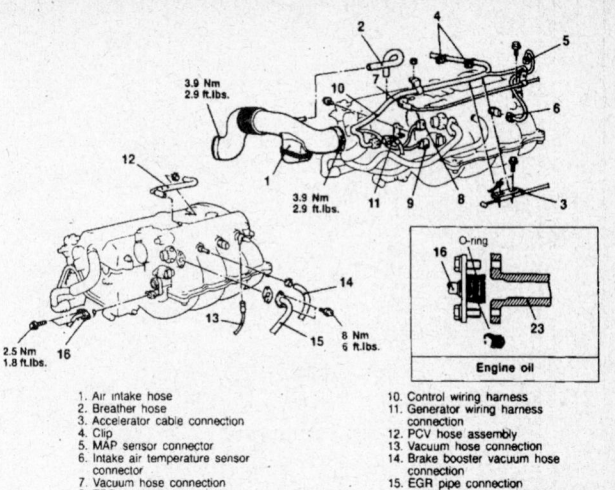

Fig. 3 Intake manifold removal (Part 1 of 2)

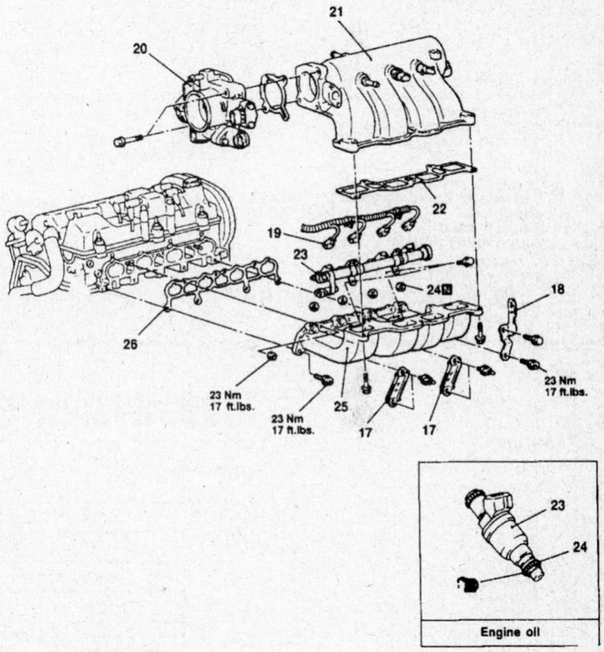

Fig. 3 Intake manifold removal (Part 2 of 2)

EXHAUST MANIFOLD

REPLACE

1. Drain engine coolant.
2. Remove air intake hose, **Fig. 4.**
3. Disconnect radiator upper hose connection.
4. Disconnect air hose and control wiring harness.
5. Remove water pipe assembly.
6. Remove engine oil dipstick.
7. Remove heat protector and engine hanger.
8. Disconnect front exhaust pipe.
9. Remove heat protector.
10. Remove exhaust manifold and gasket.
11. Reverse procedure to install. Tighten to specifications.

RADIATOR

REPLACE

1. Drain radiator.
2. Disconnect overflow hose, then remove reserve tank and bracket, **Fig. 5.**
3. Disconnect radiator upper hose and lower hose.
4. **On models equipped with automatic transaxle,** disconnect transaxle fluid cooler hose.
5. **On all models,** remove upper insulator.
6. Remove radiator assembly, then the lower insulator.
7. **On models equipped with A/C,** remove condenser fan motor assembly.
8. **On all models,** remove radiator fan motor assembly.
9. Remove fan, fan motor and shroud.
10. Reverse procedure to install.

TECHNICAL SERVICE BULLETINS

BELT NOISE OR IRREGULAR WEAR

1997

On these models the power steering belt may make noise or wear irregularly.

This condition may be caused by incorrect belt track. To correct this condition, proceed as follows:

1. Remove power steering belt, then the pump from bracket. Hang pump aside.
2. Remove bracket upper mounting bolt, then loosen but do not remove power steering bracket mounting bolt for engine block and engine mount front bolt.
3. Install one or two .039 inch shims between power steering pump bracket and front engine mount.
4. **Torque** bracket mounting bolts to 29 ft. lbs.
5. Install power steering pump and new belt. Using suitable gauge, tension belt to 93–115 lbs.
6. **Torque** power steering mounting bolts to 29 ft. lbs.

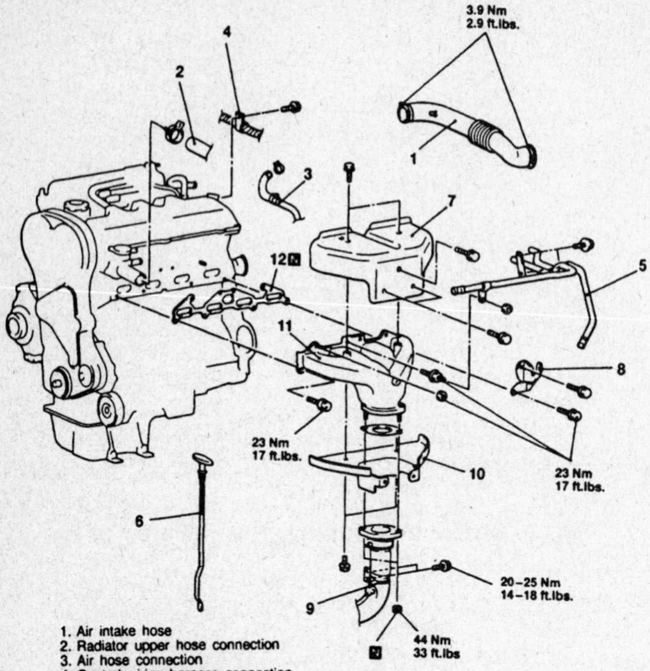

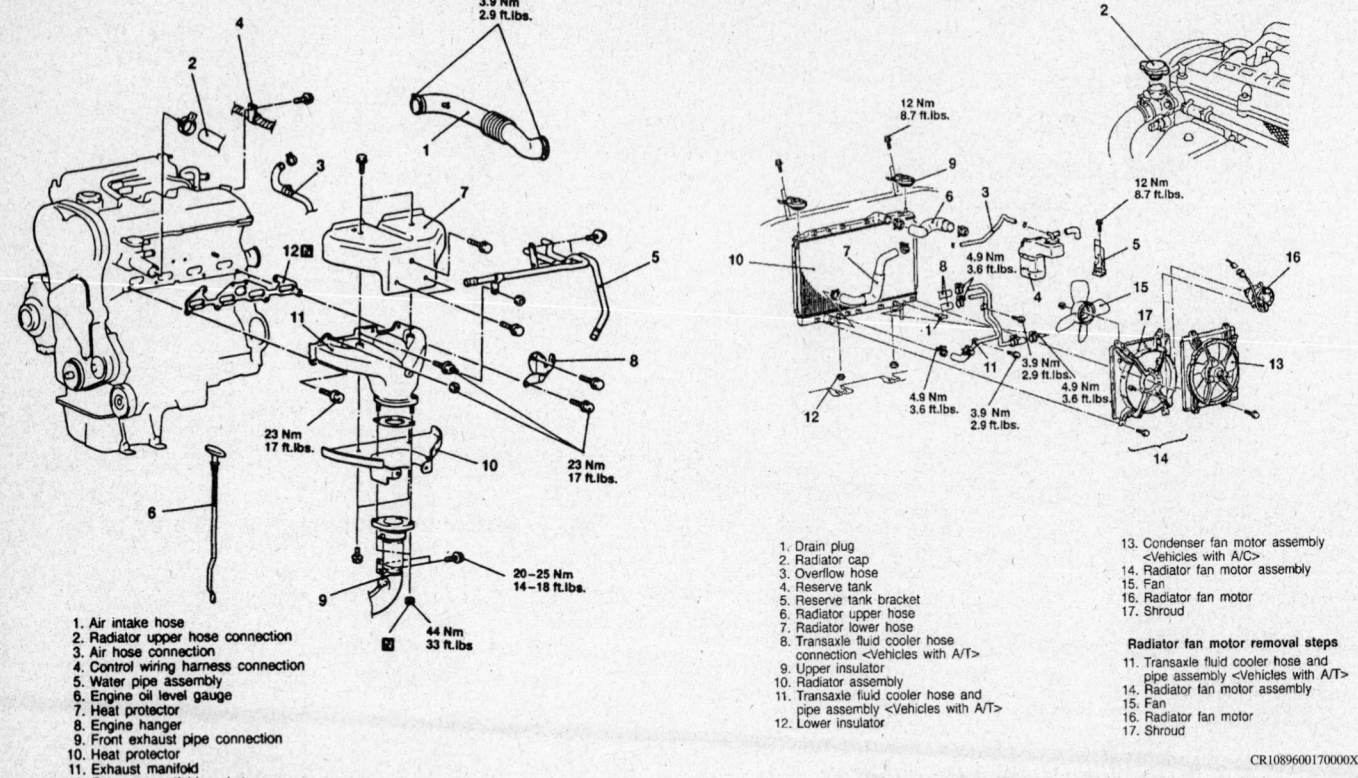

1. Air intake hose
2. Radiator upper hose connection
3. Air hose connection
4. Control wiring harness connection
5. Water pipe assembly
6. Engine oil level gauge
7. Heat protector
8. Engine hanger
9. Front exhaust pipe connection
10. Heat protector
11. Exhaust manifold
12. Exhaust manifold gasket

CR1059600116000X

Fig. 4 Exhaust manifold replacement

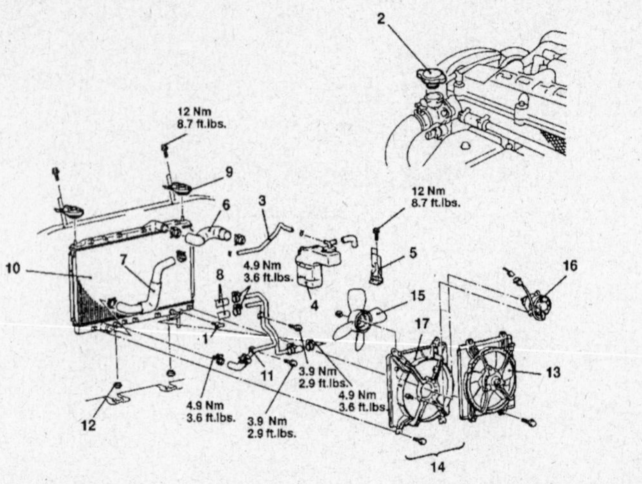

1. Drain plug
2. Radiator cap
3. Overflow hose
4. Reserve tank
5. Reserve tank bracket
6. Radiator upper hose
7. Radiator lower hose
8. Transaxle fluid cooler hose connection <Vehicles with A/T>
9. Upper insulator
10. Radiator assembly
11. Transaxle fluid cooler hose and pipe assembly <Vehicles with A/T>
12. Lower insulator
13. Condenser fan motor assembly <Vehicles with A/C>
14. Radiator fan motor assembly
15. Fan
16. Radiator fan motor
17. Shroud

Radiator fan motor removal steps

11. Transaxle fluid cooler hose and pipe assembly <Vehicles with A/T>
14. Radiator fan motor assembly
15. Fan
16. Radiator fan motor
17. Shroud

CR1089600170000X

Fig. 5 Radiator replacement

TIGHTENING SPECIFICATIONS

Year	Component	Torque/ Ft. Lbs.
1997-2000	Coolant Reserve Tank Bracket Bolt	108①
	Engine Mount Bracket Bolts	63
	Engine Mount Insulator Mounting Bolt	71–85
	Front Exhaust Pipe Connection Bolt	14–18
	Power Steering Pump Retaining Bolts	29
	Radiator Upper Insulator Mounting Bolts	108①

① — Inch lbs.

2.5L Engine

NOTE: Refer To The "Breeze, Cirrus, Sebring Convertible & Stratus" Chapter For Procedures Not Covered In This Section.

NOTE: Refer To "Air Bag System Precautions " Located In The Front Of This Manual For System Disarming & Arming Procedures.

NOTE: Refer To "Computer Relearn Procedures " Located In The Front Of This Manual For Computer Relearn Procedures.

INDEX

PRECAUTIONS

AIR BAG SYSTEMS

Refer to "Air Bag System Precautions" in the front of this manual for system disarming and arming procedures.

BATTERY GROUND CABLE

Prior to service, disconnect battery ground cable and isolate as required.

FUEL SYSTEM PRESSURE RELIEF

1. Remove rear seat cushion.
2. Remove protector to disconnect fuel pump connector.
3. Start engine and run until it stops naturally, then turn ignition switch off.
4. Connect fuel pump connector and install protector.
5. Install rear cushion.

COMPRESSION PRESSURE

Perform compression test with engine at normal operating temperature, spark plugs removed and throttle wide open. Standard compression pressure at cranking speed is 185 psi. The minimum compression pressure is 139 psi with a maximum variation between cylinders of 14 psi.

ENGINE MOUNT

REPLACE

1. Remove radiator coolant reserve tank.
2. Raise and support engine so there is no weight on the engine mount bracket insulator.
3. Remove engine mount insulator mounting bolt, **Fig. 1.**
4. Remove engine mount bracket.
5. Remove engine mount stopper.
6. Remove dynamic damper.
7. Reverse procedure to install. Tighten to specifications.

ENGINE

REPLACE

1. Release fuel pressure as described under "Precautions."
2. Mark and remove hood.
3. Remove radiator as described under "Radiator, Replace."
4. Remove front exhaust pipe.
5. Remove transaxle as outlined in "Automatic Transmissions/Transaxles" chapter.
6. Disconnect the following electrical connectors:
   a. Power steering pressure switch, **Fig. 2.**
   b. Intake air temperature sensor.
   c. Oxygen sensors.
   d. A/C compressor.
   e. Injectors.
   f. Engine coolant temperature gauge unit.
   g. Engine coolant temperature sensor.
   h. Ignition coil.
   i. Idle air control motor.
   j. Crankshaft position sensor.
   k. Alternator wiring harness.
   l. Throttle position sensor.
   m. Relay box.
7. Disconnect accelerator cable.
8. Disconnect brake booster vacuum hose.
9. Disconnect purge hose.
10. Disconnect high pressure fuel hose.
11. Disconnect heater hose.
12. Remove power steering pump cover.
13. Remove accessory drive belts.
14. Remove A/C compressor with hose attached.
15. Support engine with jack and hold engine with chain block or similar support tool.
16. Place jack under engine oil pan with piece of wood in between, then raise engine so the weight of the engine is no longer being applied to mounting bracket.
17. Remove engine mount bracket.
18. Remove power steering pump with hoses attached. Suspend pump with wire.
19. Ensure all cables, connectors and hoses have been disconnected, then raise engine slowly from engine compartment.
20. Reverse procedure to install. Tighten all fasteners to specifications.

TIMING BELT

REPLACE

With the timing belt removed, avoid turning the camshaft or crankshaft. If movement is required, exercise extreme caution to avoid valve damage caused by piston contact.

1. Remove cooling system reserve tank.
2. Remove A/C compressor drive belt, then the alternator and power steering pump drive belt.
3. Remove alternator bracket.
4. Remove front center undercover.
5. Support engine by positioning a suitable jack and wooden block under oil pan.
6. Using pulling tool Nos. MB998754 and MB990767, or equivalents, remove the crankshaft pulley, **Fig. 3.**
7. Disconnect oxygen sensor electrical connector.
8. Remove engine mount bracket and support bracket, **Fig. 3. Spray upper engine support bracket (reamer) bolt with lubricant and use care when removing, as bolt may be heat seized, Fig. 4.**
9. Remove power steering pump and bracket, then position aside with hoses attached.

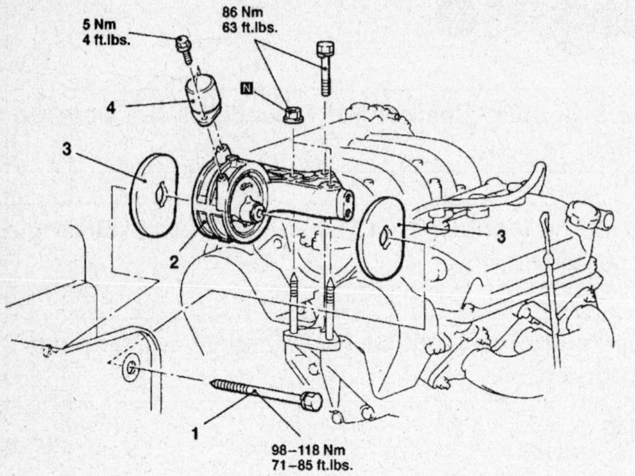

1. Engine mount insulator mounting bolt
2. Engine mount bracket
3. Engine mount stopper
4. Dynamic damper

CR1069600643000X

Fig. 1 Engine mount replacement

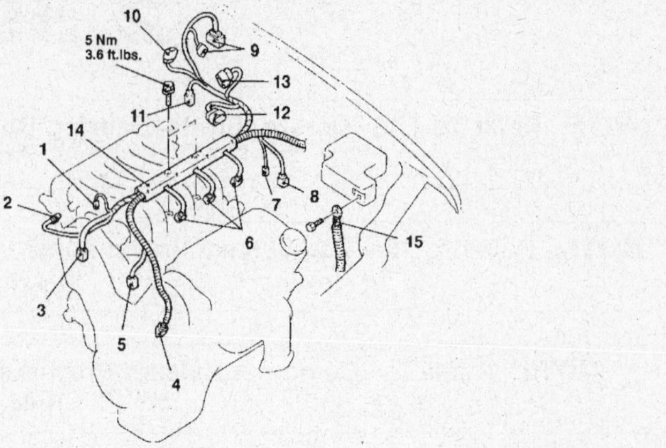

1. Power steering pressure switch connector
2. Intake air temperature sensor connector
3. Heated oxygen sensor connector
4. A/C compressor connector
5. Heated oxygen sensor connector
6. Injector connector
7. Engine coolant temperature gauge unit connector
8. Engine coolant temperature sensor connector
9. Ignition coil connector
10. Idle air control motor connector
11. Crankshaft position sensor connector
12. Generator wiring harness connector
13. TPS connector
14. Control wiring harness
15. Relay box and generator wiring harness connection

CR1069600644010X

Fig. 2 Engine replacement (Part 1 of 2)

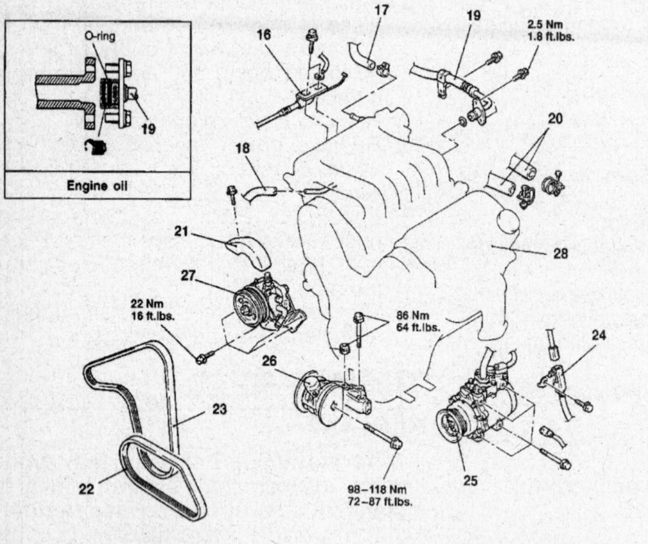

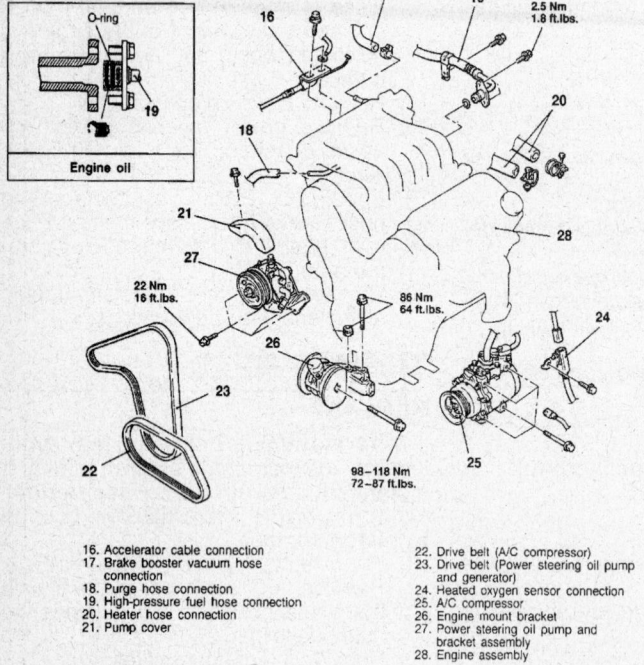

16. Accelerator cable connection
17. Brake booster vacuum hose connection
18. Purge hose connection
19. High-pressure fuel hose connection
20. Heater hose connection
21. Pump cover
22. Drive belt (A/C compressor)
23. Drive belt (Power steering oil pump and generator)
24. Heated oxygen sensor connection
25. A/C compressor
26. Engine mount bracket
27. Power steering oil pump and bracket assembly
28. Engine assembly

CR1069600644020X

Fig. 2 Engine replacement (Part 2 of 2)

10. Remove timing belt upper and lower covers.
11. Rotate crankshaft to align camshaft and crankshaft sprocket timing marks, **Fig. 5.**
12. Loosen timing belt tensioner pulley center bolt, then remove timing belt.
13. Remove timing belt tensioner attaching bolts, then the tensioner.
14. Inspect timing belt tensioner for leaks and tensioner push rod for cracks. Replace tensioner if leaks or cracks are present.
15. Position timing belt tensioner in a soft jawed vise.
16. Carefully press push rod into tensioner body. Press push rod into pump body until pin holes are aligned, **Fig. 6.**
17. Insert a .06 inch pin through tensioner body and push rod pin holes, **Fig. 7. Do not remove pin until after timing belt has been installed.**
18. Ensure camshaft and crankshaft sprocket timing marks are aligned, **Fig. 5.**
19. Position timing belt over crankshaft sprocket, idler pulley, front bank camshaft sprocket, water pump pulley, rear bank camshaft sprocket, then the timing belt tensioner pulley. **Do not to allow timing belt to slack during installation.** Use binder clips to hold timing belt in place during installation. After timing belt has been installed, remove binder clips.
20. Apply force in counterclockwise direction to rear bank camshaft sprocket until timing belt tension side is taut, **Fig. 8.** Ensure the camshaft and crankshaft sprocket timing marks are aligned, **Fig. 5.**
21. Carefully raise tensioner pulley so that timing belt does not sag, then tighten tensioner pulley center bolt, **Fig. 8.**
22. Rotate crankshaft ¼ turn counterclockwise, then turn crankshaft clockwise until camshaft and crankshaft timing marks are aligned, **Fig. 5.**
23. Loosen timing belt tensioner pulley center bolt.
24. Using holding tool No. MD998776, or equivalent, and a suitable torque wrench, apply 3.3 ft. lbs. of tension to the timing belt, **Fig. 9.** While applying tension to timing belt, torque tensioner pulley center bolt to 35 ft. lbs. **When tightening tensioner pulley center bolt, do not allow tensioner pulley to rotate.**
25. Remove .06 inch pin from tensioner push rod and tensioner body pin holes.
26. Rotate crankshaft two turns in clockwise direction.
27. Wait approximately five minutes, then check if .06 inch pin can be easily inserted through tensioner body and push rod pin holes. If pin cannot be easily inserted, check tensioner push rod projection, **Fig. 10.** Tensioner push

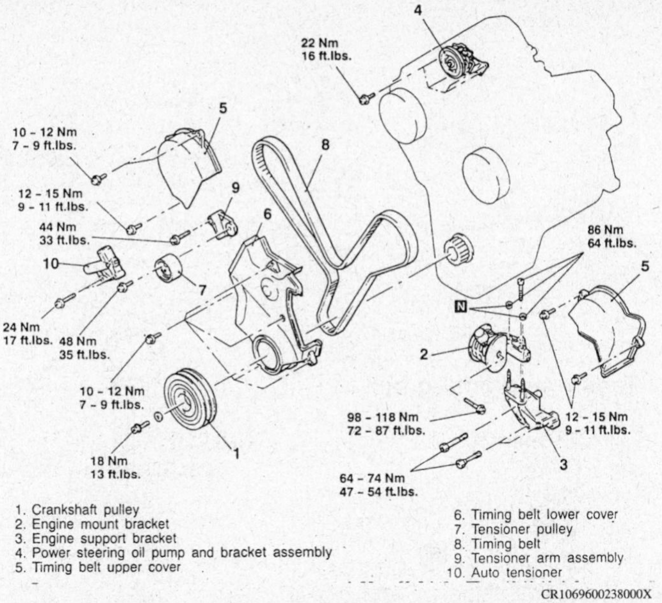

Fig. 3 Timing belt & components

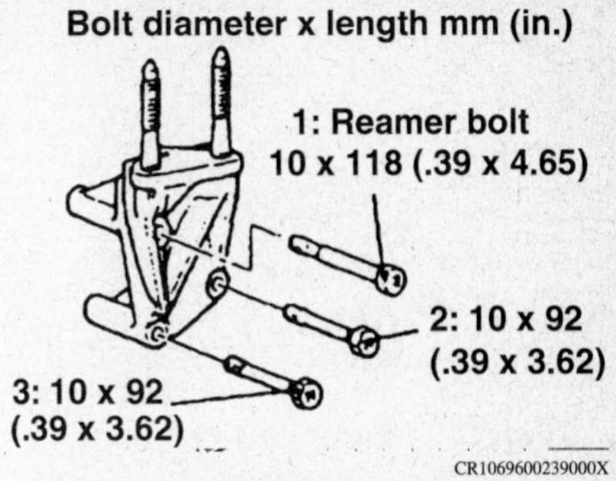

Fig. 4 Engine support bolt identification

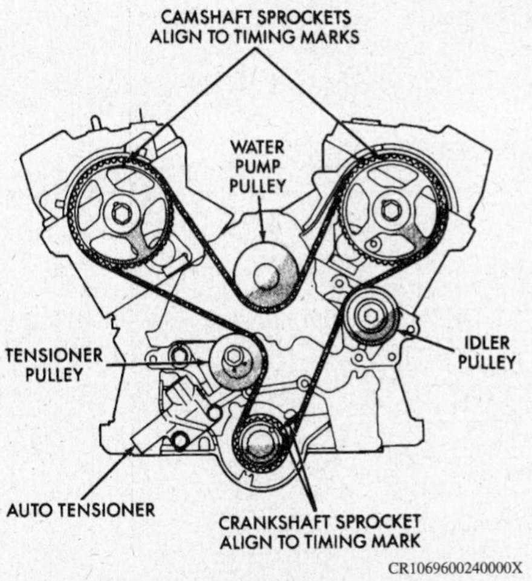

Fig. 5 Camshaft & crankshaft timing marks

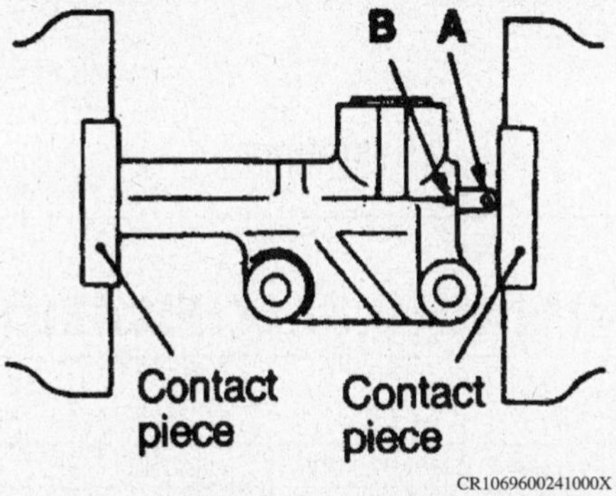

Fig. 6 Pressing tensioner push rod into tensioner housing

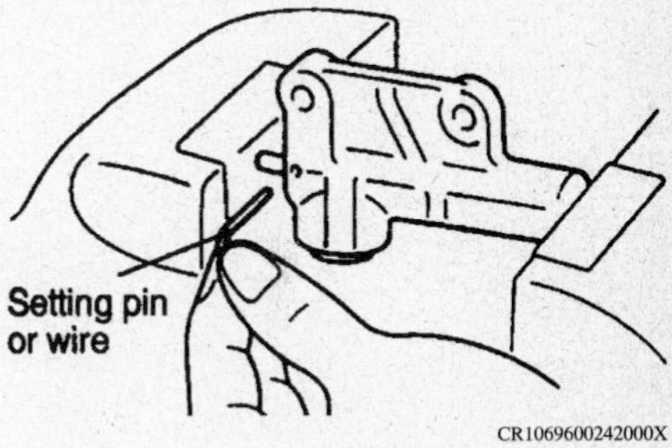

Fig. 7 Tensioner push rod pin installation

rod projection should be .149–.177 inch. If projection is not within limits, repeat previous six steps.

28. Ensure camshaft and crankshaft sprocket timing marks are aligned, **Fig. 5.**
29. Install timing belt lower and upper covers.
30. Install power steering pump and bracket.
31. Install engine mount bracket and support bracket, **Fig. 3. Spray upper engine support bracket bolt with lubricant and use care when installing. When installing engine mount bracket, ensure arrow on engine mount stopper is facing toward engine, Fig. 11.**
32. Using holding tool No. MB990767, or equivalent and a suitable torque wrench, install crankshaft pulley bolt. Tighten crankshaft pulley bolt to specifications.
33. Connect oxygen sensor electrical connector.
34. Remove jack and wooden block from under oil pan.
35. Install alternator bracket.
36. Install front center undercover.
37. Install alternator and power steering pump drive belt, then the A/C compressor drive belt.
38. Install cooling system reserve tank.
39. Check and adjust ignition timing as necessary.

RADIATOR

REPLACE

1. Remove radiator drain plug and drain engine coolant into a suitable container.
2. Remove radiator cap.
3. Disconnect overflow hose and remove coolant reserve tank.
4. Remove reserve tank bracket.
5. After making mating marks on radiator hoses and hose clamps, remove upper and lower radiator hoses.
6. Disconnect transaxle fluid cooler hose and pipe assembly. Plug radiator port to prevent foreign material from entering.
7. Remove upper insulator, then the radiator.
8. Remove lower insulator.
9. Remove condenser fan motor and fan.
10. Remove radiator fan motor and fan.
11. Remove radiator fan shroud.
12. Reverse procedure to install. Tighten to specifications.

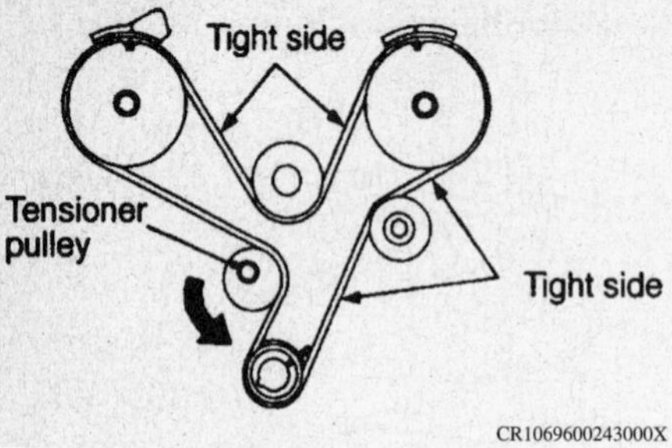

Fig. 8 Timing belt removal

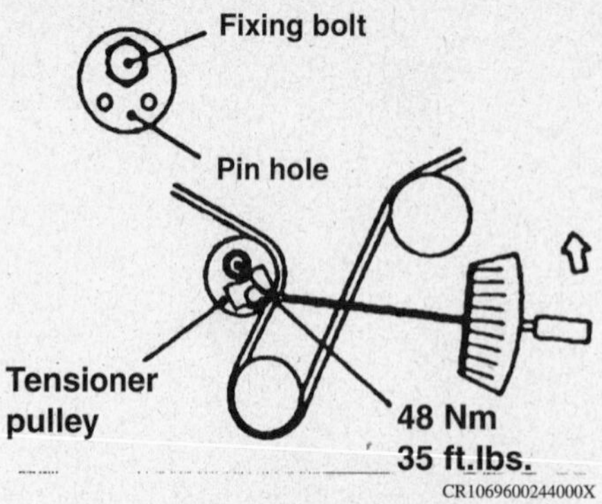

Fig. 9 Tensioning timing belt

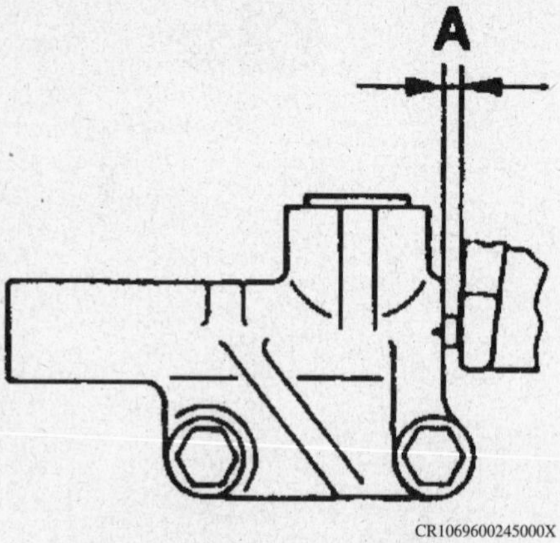

Fig. 10 Tensioner push rod protrusion inspection

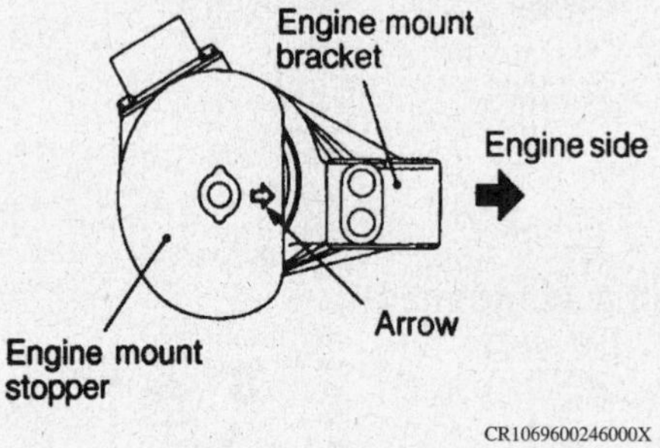

Fig. 11 Positioning engine mount stopper

TIGHTENING SPECIFICATIONS

Component	Torque/Ft. Lbs.
Coolant Reserve Tank Bracket Bolts	108①
Crankshaft Pulley Bolt	134
Dynamic Damper Bolt	48①
Engine Mount Bracket Bolt & Nut	63
Engine Mount Bracket/Stopper Through Bolt	71–85
Power Steering Pump Mounting Bolt	16
Upper Radiator Insulator Bolts	108①

① — Inch lbs.

Clutch & Manual Transaxle

INDEX

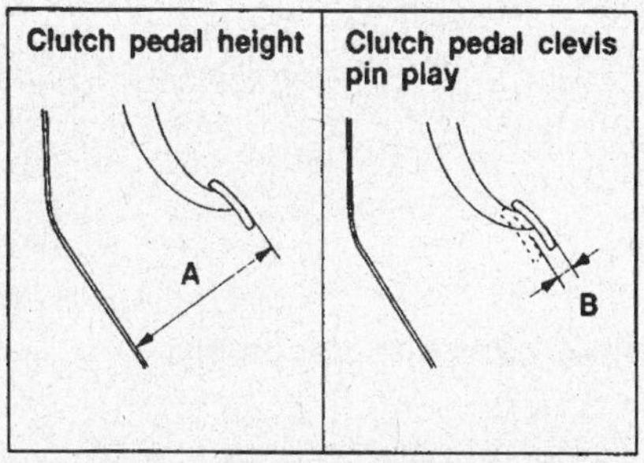

Fig. 1 Clutch pedal height measurement

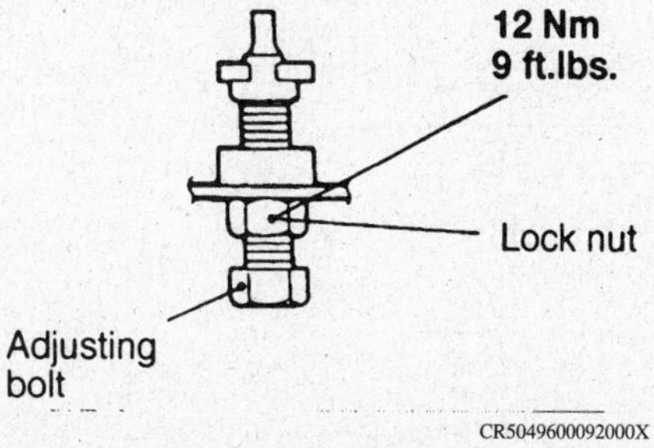

Fig. 2 Pedal height adjusting bolt

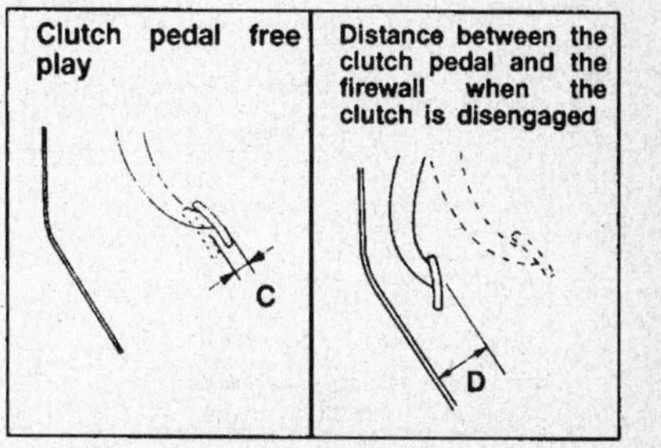

Fig. 3 Clutch pedal freeplay adjustment

ADJUSTMENTS

CLUTCH PEDAL

1. Turn up carpet under clutch pedal.
2. Measure clutch pedal height and clutch pedal clevis pin play, **Fig. 1.** Pedal height (A) should be 7.0–7.1 inches. Clevis pin play (B) should be .04–.12 inch.
3. If pedal height is outside standard limits, loosen locknut and adjust pedal height using adjusting bolt, **Fig. 2.**
4. If clutch pedal play is outside standard limits, adjust with push rod.
5. After completing adjustments, confirm pedal freeplay and distance between clutch pedal and firewall with clutch disengaged are within specifications. Referring to **Fig. 3,** freeplay (C) should be .24–.51 inch. Distance between clutch pedal and firewall (D) should be at least 2.76 inches.
6. If these measurements are not within specifications, it may be the result of air trapped in the hydraulic system or a faulty master cylinder and/or clutch.

INTERLOCK SWITCH

Ensure the interlock switch is as shown in **Fig. 4** when the clutch pedal is depressed at its full stroke. If necessary, loosen locknut to adjust switch.

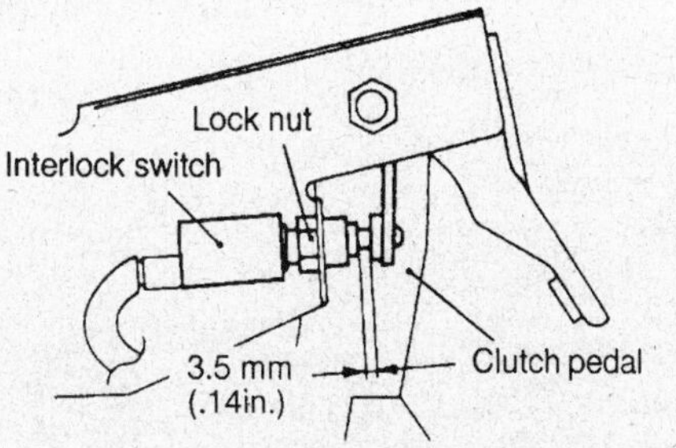

Fig. 4 Interlock switch adjustment

HYDRAULIC SYSTEM SERVICE

CLUTCH SYSTEM BLEED

1. Connect a clear plastic hose to slave cylinder bleeder screw valve and submerge other end of hose in a clear container of clean DOT 3 or 4 brake fluid.
2. With parking brake applied, pump clutch pedal several times, then fully release.
3. Open bleeder valve, then depress clutch pedal to floor and hold.
4. Close bleeder valve, then release pedal.
5. Repeat procedure until bubbles can no longer be seen emerging from bleeder valve. **Keep clutch master cylinder full of clean DOT 3 or 4 brake fluid.**
6. Ensure bleeder valve is closed, then inspect clutch operation.

COMPONENT REPLACEMENT

Master Cylinder, Slave Cylinder & Hydraulic Lines

1. Drain clutch hydraulic fluid into a suitable container.
2. Remove master cylinder, slave cylinder and/or hydraulic lines in numbered sequences shown, **Fig. 5.**
3. Reverse procedure to install, noting the following:
   a. Fill and bleed clutch hydraulic system as outlined under "Clutch System Bleed" in this section.
   b. Adjust clutch pedal as outlined under "Adjustments."
   c. Tighten all fasteners to specifications.

CLUTCH

REPLACE

The modular clutch assembly is comprised of a single, dry clutch disc, diaphragm style cover and flywheel. These components are not independently serviceable; the entire clutch module must be replaced as an assembly.

1. Drain clutch hydraulic fluid and transaxle fluid into suitable containers.
2. Remove transaxle as outlined under "Transaxle, Replace."
3. Remove clutch assembly in numbered sequence, **Fig. 6.**
4. Reverse procedure to install, noting the following:
   a. Apply Mitsubishi grease part No. 0101011, or equivalent, to contact points at ends of clutch release lever and to clutch disc splines. Use a suitable brush to force grease into splines.
   b. Fill and bleed clutch hydraulic system as outlined under "Hydraulic System Service."
   c. Fill transaxle with correct type of lubricant.

TRANSAXLE

REPLACE

1. Drain transaxle fluid into a suitable container, then remove battery.
2. Remove lower engine cover.
3. Remove air cleaner cover and air hose assembly, **Fig. 7.**
4. Remove air cleaner element, then the battery tray and stay.

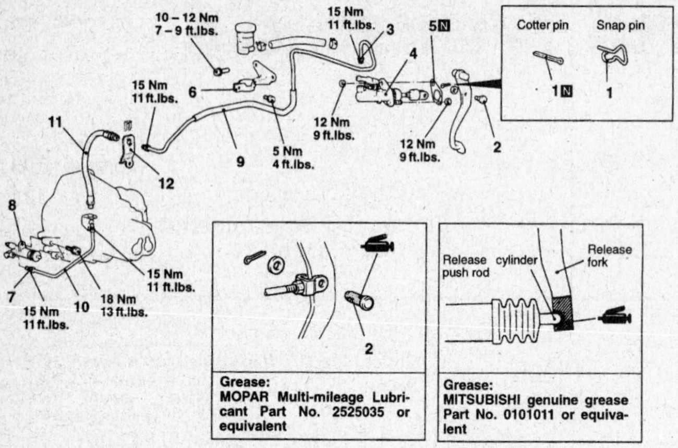

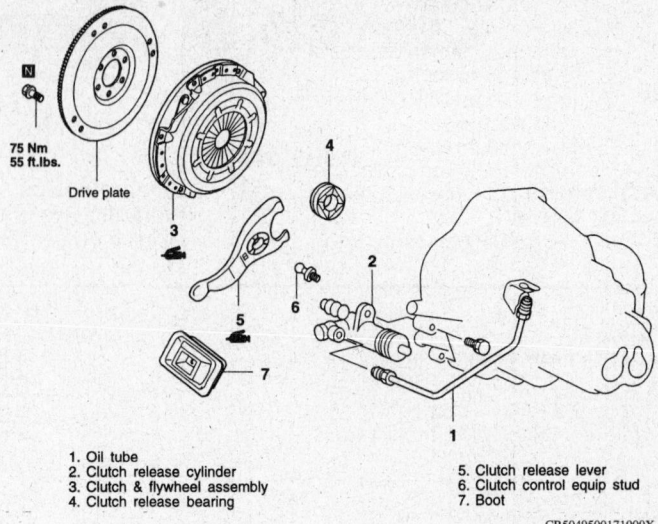

Clutch master cylinder removal steps
1. Cotter pin or snap pin
2. Clevis pin
3. Clutch pipe connection
4. Clutch master cylinder
5. Sealer
6. Reservoir bracket

Clutch release cylinder removal steps
7. Clutch pipe connection
8. Clutch release cylinder

Clutch line removal steps
9. Clutch pipe
10. Clutch pipe
11. Clutch hose
12. Clutch hose bracket

CR5049500172000X

Fig. 5 Clutch hydraulic system component replacement

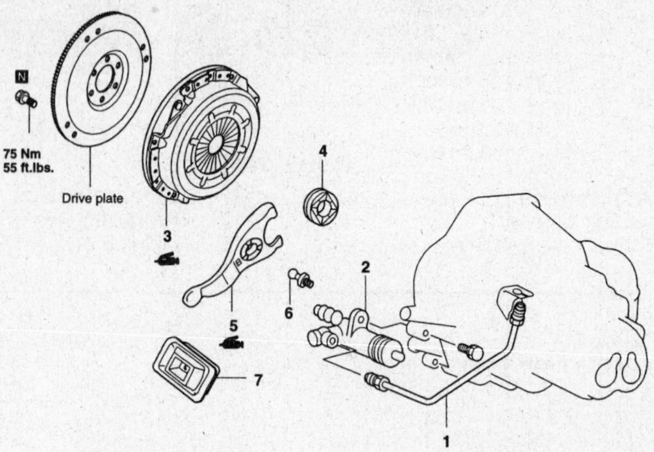

1. Oil tube
2. Clutch release cylinder
3. Clutch & flywheel assembly
4. Clutch release bearing
5. Clutch release lever
6. Clutch control equip stud
7. Boot

CR5049500171000X

Fig. 6 Modular clutch replacement

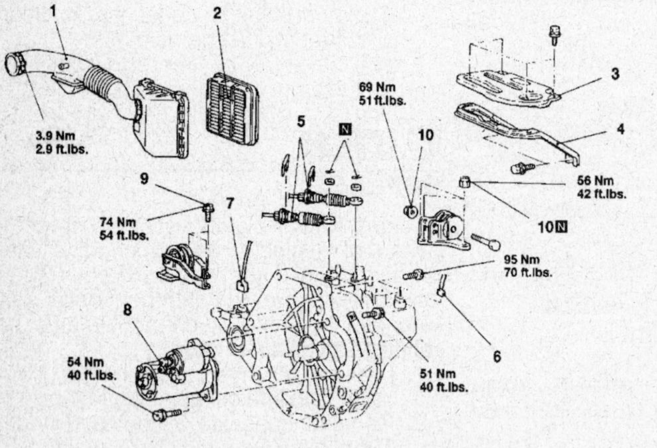

1. Air cleaner cover and air intake hose assembly
2. Air cleaner element
3. Battery tray
4. Battery tray stay
5. Shift cable and select cable connection
6. Backup light switch connector
7. Vehicle speed sensor connector
8. Starter motor
9. Rear roll stopper bracket mounting bolts
10. Transaxle mounting bracket mounting nuts

CR5039601006010X

Fig. 7 Transaxle removal (Part 1 of 2)

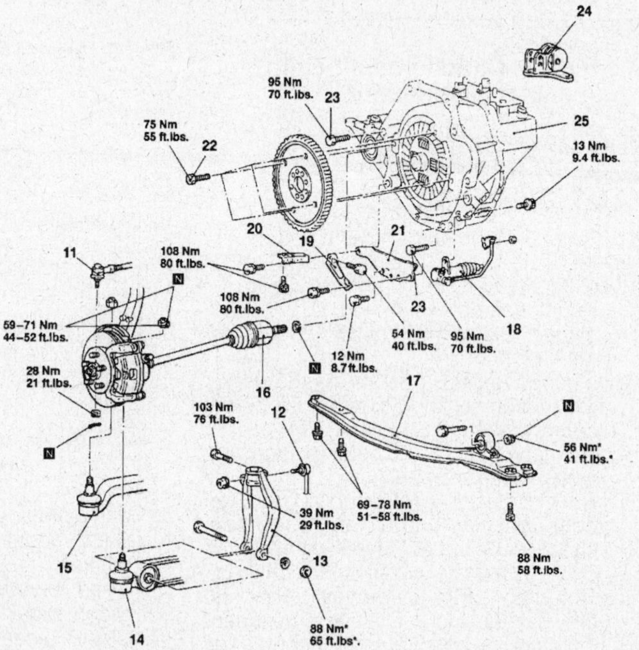

11. Tie rod end connection
12. Stabilizer link connection
13. Damper fork
14. Lateral lower arm connection
15. Compression lower arm connection
16. Drive shaft connection
17. Center member assembly
18. Clutch release cylinder connection
19. Front plate
20. Rear plate
21. Transaxle case lower cover
22. Flex plate connecting bolts
23. Transaxle assembly mounting bolts
24. Transaxle mounting
25. Transaxle assembly

Caution
***: Indicates parts which should be temporarily tightened, and then fully tightened with the vehicle on the ground in the unladen condition.**

CR5039601006020X

Fig. 7 Transaxle removal (Part 2 of 2)

5. Disconnect shift cable.
6. Disconnect back-up lamp switch and vehicle speed sensor connectors.
7. Remove starter motor.
8. Remove rear roll stopper bracket mounting bolts.
9. Raise transaxle with jack, then remove transaxle mounting bracket nuts.
10. Install engine support tool No. C-4852, or equivalent.
11. Raise and support vehicle, then loosen tie rod end nut.
12. Disconnect stabilizer link and remove damper fork.
13. Loosen end nuts on lateral lower arm and compression lower arm connections.
14. Insert pry bar between transaxle case and driveshaft, then remove driveshaft. Do not remove hub and knuckle from driveshaft.

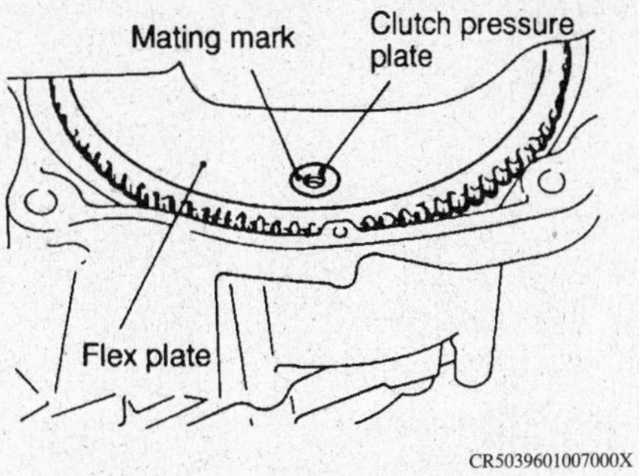

Fig. 8 Flex plate match marks

15. Suspend driveshaft with wire so there are no sharp bends in any of the joints.
16. Remove center member assembly.
17. Remove clutch release cylinder without disconnecting oil lines.
18. Remove front plate and rear plate.
19. Remove transaxle lower case, then support transaxle with suitable jack
20. Remove flex plate bolts while turning crankshaft.
21. Chalk mating marks on flex plate and clutch pressure plate for installation, **Fig. 8.**
22. Press clutch pressure plate into transaxle for easier removal.
23. Remove transaxle assembly mounting bolts and lower transaxle.
24. Reverse procedure to install. Tighten fasteners to specifications.

TIGHTENING SPECIFICATIONS

Year	Component	Torque/ Ft. Lbs.
1997-2000	Clutch Fluid Pipe Fittings	11
	Clutch Master Cylinder Bolts	108①
	Clutch Release Cylinder Bolts	13
	Damper Fork	65
	Flex Plate Bolts	55
	Reservoir Bracket Bolts	84–108①
	Stabilizer Link Nut	29
	Transaxle Mounting Bolts	70

① — Inch lbs.

Rear Suspension

NOTE: **Prior To Performing Any Service Operations Listed In This Section, Consult The "Technical Service Bulletins " Section For Related Information.**

INDEX

DESCRIPTION

The rear suspension is a modified double-wishbone design with coil springs and direct acting shock absorbers, **Fig. 1.** The rear axle consists of a knuckle, rear hub, unit bearing and axle shaft. The unit bearing is press-fitted to the rear axle shaft and bolted to the knuckle. On models equipped with ABS, a rotor for detecting vehicle speed is located on the axle shaft and a speed sensor is located on the knuckle.

HUB & BEARING

REPLACE

1. Raise and support vehicle.
2. **On models equipped with ABS,** remove rear speed sensor.
3. **On models equipped with rear disc brakes,** remove and suspend brake caliper assembly, **Fig. 2.**
4. **On all models,** remove brake drum or disc.
5. Remove clip mounting bolt.
6. Remove brake shoe and lining assembly.
7. Remove rear hub and ABS rotor.
8. Reverse procedure to install. Tighten to specifications.

SHOCK ABSORBER

REPLACE

1. Remove shock absorber cap.
2. Remove flange nuts under cap.

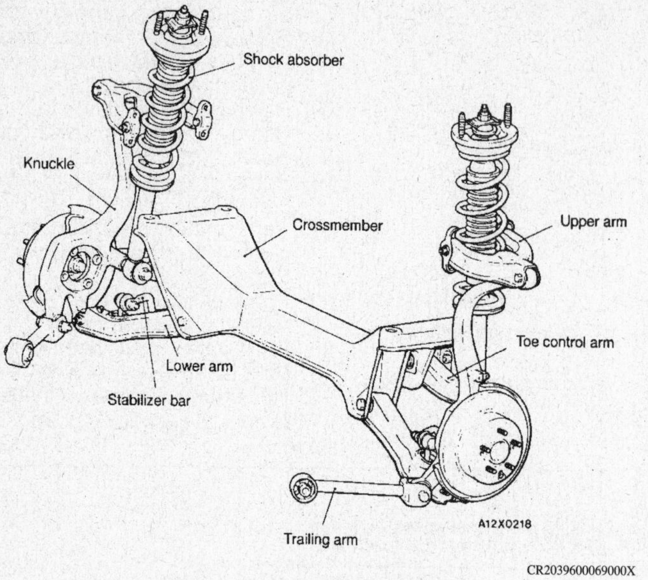

Fig. 1 Rear suspension

3. Remove shock absorber lower bolt and the shock absorber.
4. Reverse procedure to install. Tighten to specifications.

COIL SPRING

REPLACE

Remove shock absorber and coil spring assembly and disassemble as shown, **Fig. 3,** to replace coil spring. Compress coil spring using compressor tool Nos. MB991237 and MB991239, or equivalents.

CONTROL ARM

REPLACE

UPPER

1. Raise and support vehicle.
2. Remove upper arm and knuckle connecting bolt, **Fig. 4.**
3. Remove upper arm mounting bolt.
4. Remove upper arm assembly.
5. Remove upper arm bracket.
6. Reverse procedure to install. Tighten to specifications.

LOWER

1. Raise and support vehicle.
2. Remove stabilizer link, **Fig. 5.**
3. **On models equipped with ABS,** remove wheel speed sensor clamp bolts.
4. **On all models,** remove lower arm assembly and knuckle connecting bolt.
5. Remove lower arm mounting bolt.
6. Disconnect toe control arm ball joint from knuckle.
7. Remove toe control arm mounting bolt.
8. Remove toe control arm assembly.
9. Reverse procedure to install. Tighten to specifications.

KNUCKLE

REPLACE

1. Raise and support vehicle.
2. Remove rear hub as described under "Hub & Bearing, Replace."
3. Disconnect trailing arm, **Fig. 1.**
4. Disconnect lower arm.
5. Disconnect toe control arm. Loosen nut but do not remove.
6. Disconnect shock absorber.
7. Disconnect upper arm.
8. Remove knuckle.
9. **On models less ABS,** remove hub cap.
10. **On all models,** reverse procedure to install. Tighten to specifications.

TRAILING ARM

REPLACE

1. Raise and support vehicle.
2. Disconnect knuckle and trailing arm assembly connecting bolt.
3. Remove grommet.
4. Remove trailing arm assembly mounting bolt.
5. Remove stopper.
6. Remove trailing arm.
7. Reverse procedure to install. Tighten to specifications.

STABILIZER BAR

REPLACE

1. Raise and support vehicle.
2. Remove stabilizer link mounting nuts.
3. Remove stabilizer link.
4. Remove stabilizer bar brackets.
5. Remove stabilizer bar bracket bushings.
6. Remove stabilizer bar.
7. Reverse procedure to install. Tighten to specifications.

TECHNICAL SERVICE BULLETINS

THUMP, CHUCKLE OR CREAK

1997

On these models there may be a light thump, chuckle or creak from rear suspension while driving over small to medium bumps.

This conditions may be caused by rear shock absorbers. To correct this condition, replace rear shock absorbers with models with lot numbers of KJ15 or greater. Lot number is on shock absorber, below part number.

SQUEAKING OR HARD RUBBING

1997-98

On these models there may be a squeaking or hard rubbing noise on bumps.

This condition may be caused by trailing arm bushing stoppers. To correct this condition, replace one piece trailing arm bushing stoppers with upgraded, two-piece parts (outside part No. MR316383, inside part No. MR316384).

LIGHT KNOCKING OR TAPPING

1997-98

On these models there may be a light knocking or tapping from rear shock area on bumps.

This condition may be caused by rear shock bracket assembly. To correct this condition, replace rear shock bracket assembly with redesigned insulator (part No. MR311114).

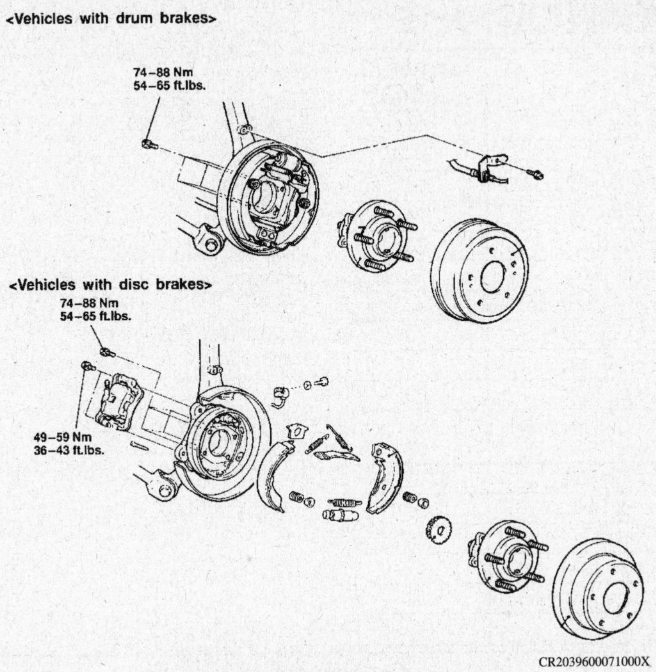

Fig. 2 Rear hub removal

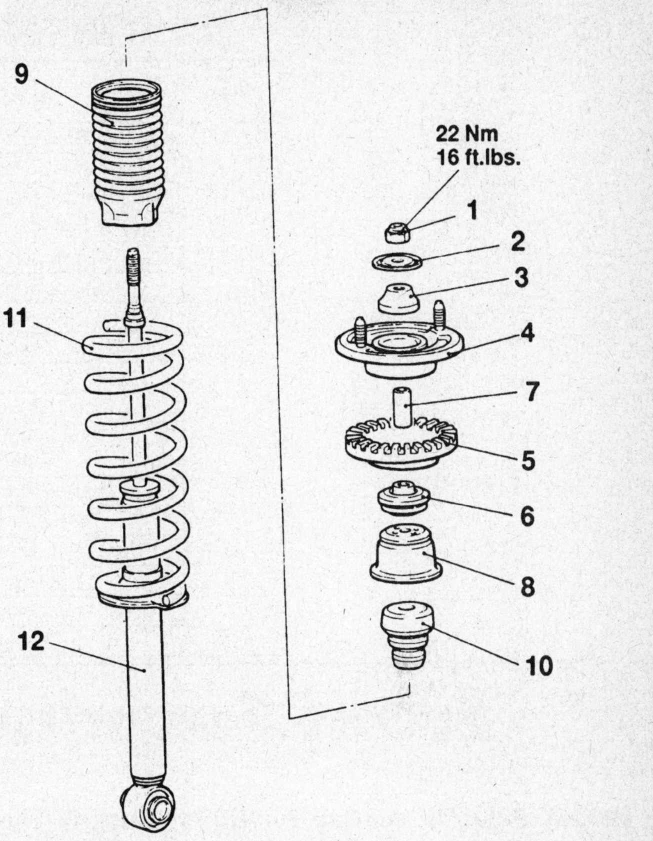

1. Self-locking nut
2. Washer
3. Upper bushing A
4. Bracket
5. Spring pad
6. Upper bushing B
7. Collar
8. Cup
9. Dust cover
10. Bump rubber
11. Coil spring
12. Shock absorber assembly

CR2039600073000X

Fig. 3 Coil spring replacement

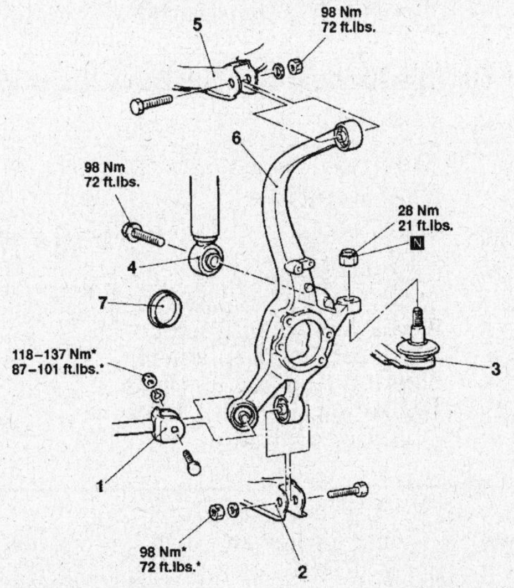

1. Trailing arm connection
2. Lower arm connection
3. Toe control arm connection
4. Shock absorber connection
5. Upper arm connection
6. Knuckle
7. Hub cap <Vehicles without ABS>

Caution
***: Indicates parts which should be temporarily tightened, and then fully tightened with the vehicle on the ground in the unladen condition.**

CR2039600072000X

Fig. 4 Knuckle removal

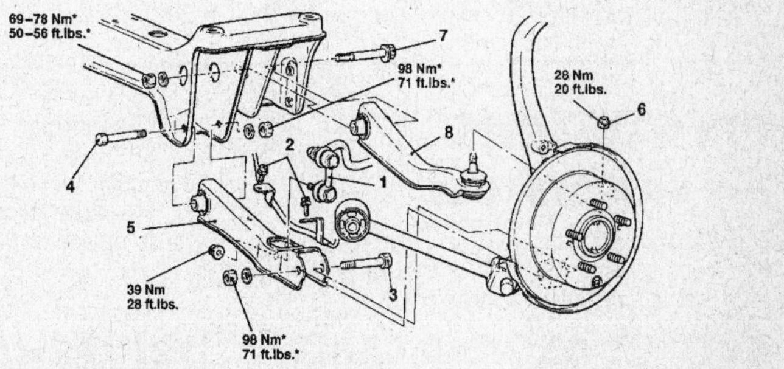

1. Stabilizer link
2. ABS wheel-speed sensor clamp bolts <Vehicles with ABS>
3. Lower arm assembly and knuckle connecting bolt
4. Lower arm assembly mounting bolt
5. Lower arm assembly
6. Toe control arm ball joint and knuckle connection
7. Toe control arm assembly mounting bolt
8. Toe control arm assembly

Caution
*** : Indicates parts which should be temporarily tightened, and then fully tightened with the vehicles on the ground in the unladen condition.**

CR2039600074000X

Fig. 5 Lower arm & toe control arm removal

TIGHTENING SPECIFICATIONS

Year	Component	Torque/Ft. Lbs.
1997-2000	Brake Hose Connection	11
	Caliper Mounting Bolts	36–43
	Crossmember Mounting Self-Locking Nuts	64
	Lower Arm & Knuckle Connecting Nut	71
	Lower Arm Mounting Nuts	71
	Shock Absorber Lower Bolt	72
	Shock Absorber Upper Flange Bolts	32
	Shock Tower Self-Locking Nut	16
	Stabilizer Bar Bracket Bolts	7–10
	Stabilizer Link Mounting Nuts	28
	Toe Control Arm Ball Joint & Knuckle Connecting Nut	20
	Trailing Arm Connecting Nut	87–101
	Trailing Arm Mounting Bolt	99–114
	Upper Arm Assembly Mounting Bolt	28
	Upper Arm Bracket Nuts	41
	Upper Arm & Knuckle Connecting Bolt	72
	Wheel Lug Nuts	87–101

Front Suspension & Steering

NOTE: Refer To "Air Bag System Precautions " Located In The Front Of This Manual For System Disarming & Arming Procedures.

INDEX

PRECAUTIONS

AIR BAG SYSTEMS

Refer to "Air Bag System Precautions" in the front of this manual for system disarming and arming procedures.

BATTERY GROUND CABLE

Prior to service, disconnect battery ground cable and isolate as required.

HUB & BEARING

REPLACE

1. Raise and support vehicle, then remove tire.
2. Remove driveshaft nut cotter pin.
3. Remove driveshaft end nut.
4. **On models equipped with ABS,** remove front speed sensor.
5. **On all models,** remove brake caliper assembly and suspend with wire.
6. Remove brake disc.
7. Disconnect upper arm from steering knuckle.
8. Remove hub assembly.
9. Reverse procedure to install. Tighten to specifications.

DRIVESHAFT

REPLACE

1. Raise and support vehicle.
2. Remove tire and wheel assembly.
3. Remove driveshaft nut, **Fig. 1.**
4. Disconnect tie rod end.
5. Disconnect stabilizer link.
6. Remove damper fork.
7. Disconnect lateral lower arm.
8. Disconnect compression lower arm.
9. Remove harness clip.
10. Remove driveshaft to transaxle bolt.
11. Tap center bearing bracket lightly with plastic hammer to remove drive shaft and inner shaft from transaxle.
12. Insert pry bar between transaxle case and driveshaft, then pry driveshaft from transaxle.
13. Reverse procedure to install. Tighten to specifications.

BALL JOINT INSPECTION

Use torque wrench tool No. MB990326, or equivalent, to measure ball joint breakaway torque. Breakaway torque should be as specified in **Fig. 2.**

COIL SPRING

REPLACE

Remove shock absorber as described under "Shock Absorber, Replace," then disassemble shock/coil spring unit as shown in **Fig. 3.**

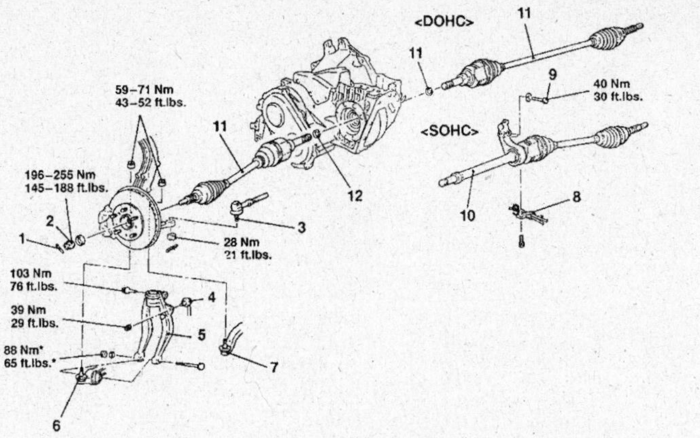

1. Cotter pin
2. Drive shaft nut
3. Tie rod end connection
4. Stabilizer link connection
5. Damper fork
6. Lateral lower arm connection
7. Compression lower arm connection
8. Harness clip
9. Bolt
10. Drive shaft and inner shaft (RH) <SOHC>
11. Drive shaft
12. Circlip

Caution
* : Indicates parts which should be temporarily tightened, and then fully tightened with the vehicle on the ground in the unladen condition.

CR2029600121000X

Fig. 1 Driveshaft replacement

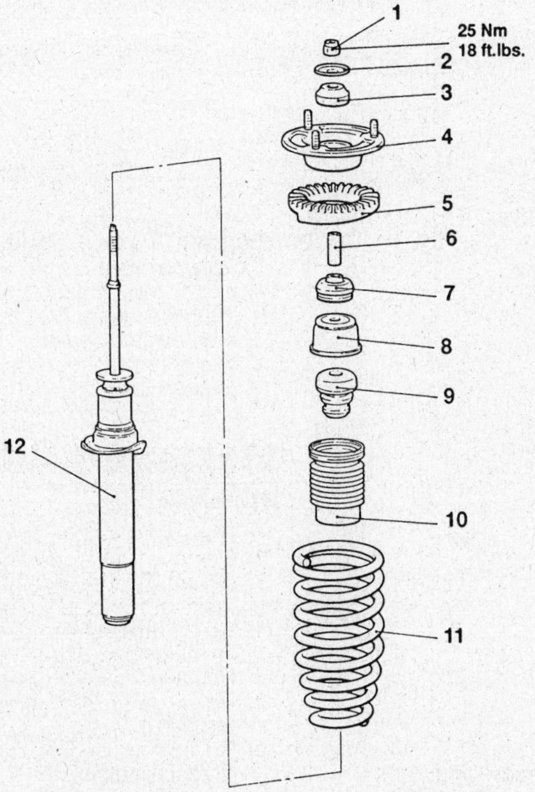

1. Self-locking nut
2. Washer
3. Upper bushing A
4. Upper bracket assembly
5. Upper spring pad
6. Collar
7. Upper bushing B
8. Cup assembly
9. Bump rubber
10. Dust cover
11. Coil spring
12. Shock absorber assembly

CR2029600115000X

Fig. 3 Coil spring replacement

Ball Joint	Breakaway Torque, Inch Lbs.
Compression Lower Arm	4–22
Lateral Lower Arm	9–13
Stabilizer Link	4–13
Upper Arm	3–13

Fig. 2 Ball joint specifications

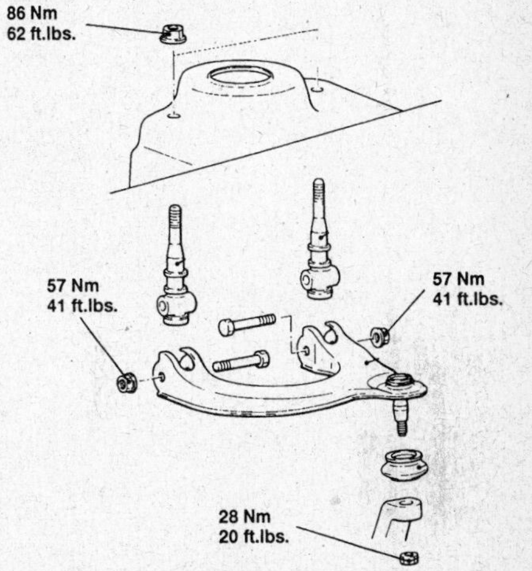

CR2029600116000X

Fig. 4 Upper arm replacement

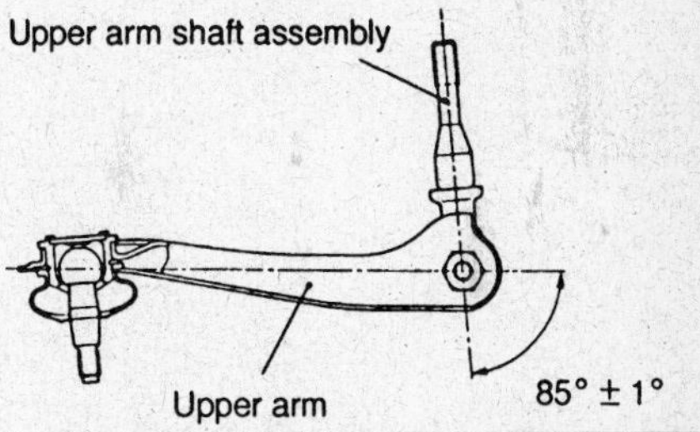

CR2029600117000X

Fig. 5 Upper arm shaft installation

SHOCK ABSORBER

REPLACE

1. Remove stabilizer link mounting nut.
2. From engine compartment, remove shock absorber upper mounting nuts.
3. Raise and support vehicle.
4. Remove shock absorber lower mounting bolt.
5. Remove damper fork mounting bolt and damper fork.
6. Remove shock absorber from vehicle.
7. Reverse procedure to install. Tighten to specifications.

CONTROL ARM

REPLACE

UPPER

1. Raise and support vehicle.
2. Disconnect upper arm ball joint from knuckle, **Fig. 4.**

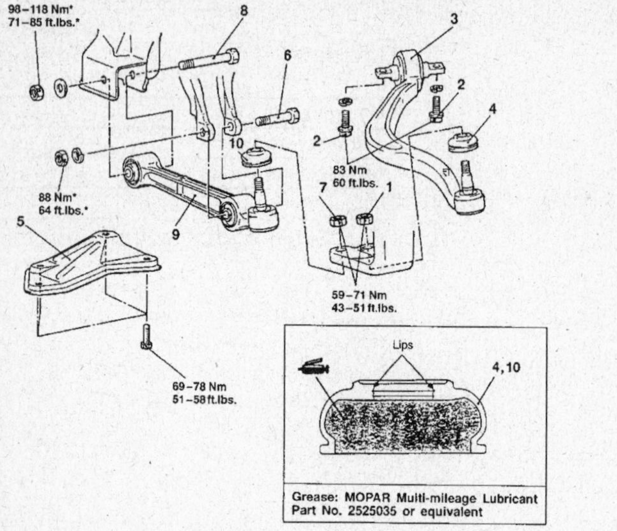

1. Compression lower arm ball joint and knuckle connection
2. Compression lower arm mounting bolt
3. Compression lower arm assembly
4. Dust cover
5. Stay
6. Shock absorber lower mounting bolt and nut
7. Lateral lower arm ball joint and knuckle connection
8. Lateral lower arm mounting bolt and nut
9. Lateral lower arm assembly
10. Dust cover

CR2029600118000X

Fig. 6 Compression lower arm & lateral lower arm

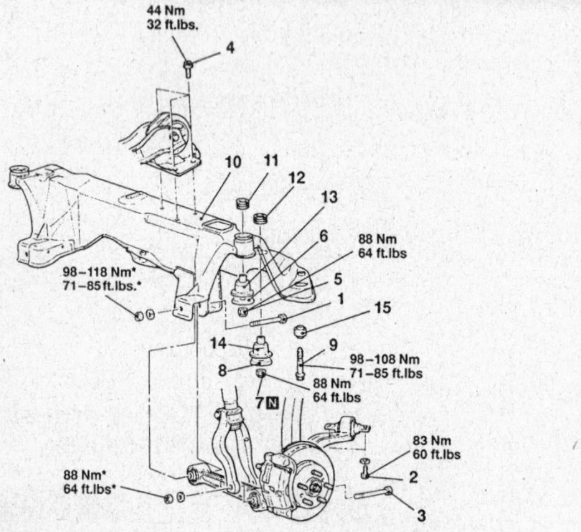

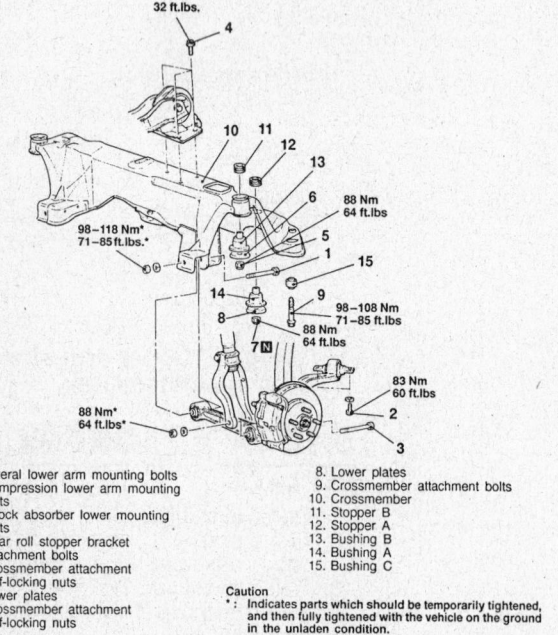

1. Lateral lower arm mounting bolts
2. Compression lower arm mounting bolts
3. Shock absorber lower mounting bolts
4. Rear roll stopper bracket attachment bolts
5. Crossmember attachment self-locking nuts
6. Lower plates
7. Crossmember attachment self-locking nuts
8. Lower plates
9. Crossmember attachment bolts
10. Crossmember
11. Stopper B
12. Stopper A
13. Bushing B
14. Bushing A
15. Bushing C

Caution
* : Indicates parts which should be temporarily tightened, and then fully tightened with the vehicle on the ground in the unladen condition.

CR2029600120000X

Fig. 8 Crossmember replacement

3. At engine compartment shock tower, remove self-locking nut for upper arm installation.
4. Remove upper arm assembly.
5. Remove dust cover.
6. Reverse procedure to install. Install upper arm shaft at angle shown in **Fig. 5,** and tighten to specifications.

LOWER

1. Raise and support vehicle.
2. Disconnect compression lower arm ball joint from knuckle, **Fig. 6.**
3. Remove compression lower arm mounting bolt.
4. Remove compression lower arm dust cover.
5. Remove lateral lower arm stay.
6. Remove shock absorber lower bolt and nut.
7. Disconnect lateral lower arm ball joint from knuckle.
8. Remove lateral lower arm mounting bolt and nut.

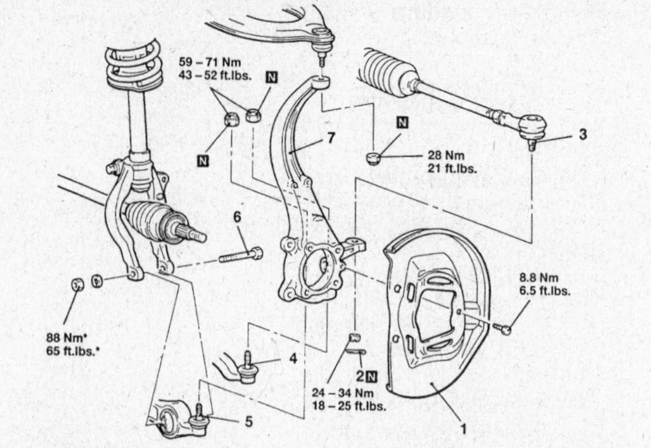

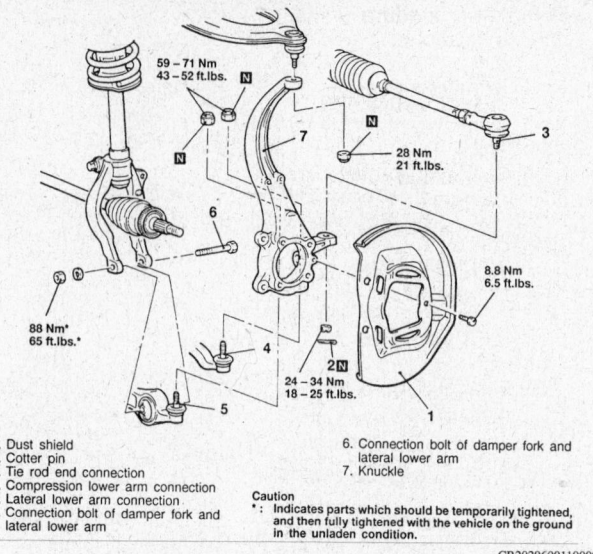

1. Dust shield
2. Cotter pin
3. Tie rod end connection
4. Compression lower arm connection
5. Lateral lower arm connection
6. Connection bolt of damper fork and lateral lower arm
6. Connection bolt of damper fork and lateral lower arm
7. Knuckle

Caution
* : Indicates parts which should be temporarily tightened, and then fully tightened with the vehicle on the ground in the unladen condition.

CR2029600119000X

Fig. 7 Steering knuckle replacement

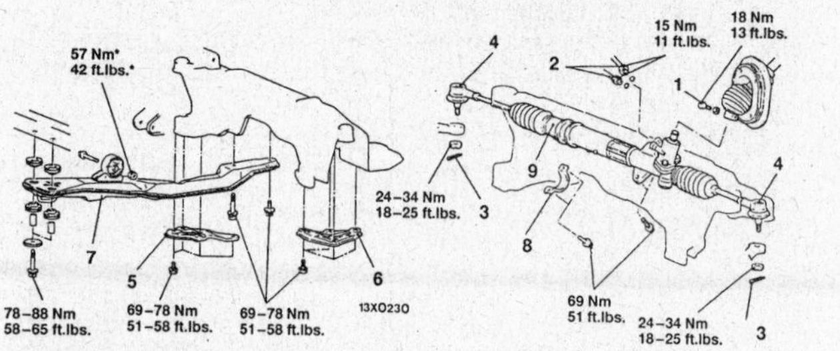

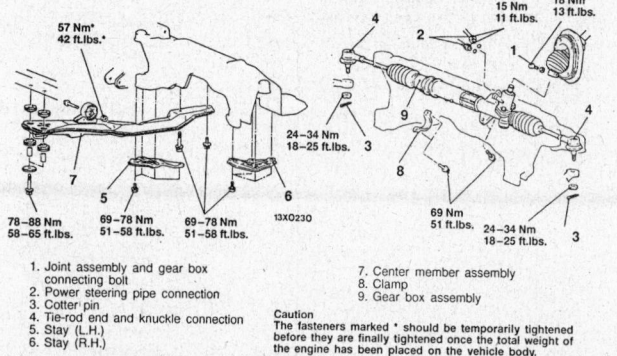

1. Joint assembly and gear box connecting bolt
2. Power steering pipe connection
3. Cotter pin
4. Tie-rod end and knuckle connection
5. Stay (L.H.)
6. Stay (R.H.)
7. Center member assembly
8. Clamp
9. Gear box assembly

Caution
The fasteners marked * should be temporarily tightened before they are finally tightened once the total weight of the engine has been placed on the vehicle body.

CR2029600122000X

Fig. 9 Center member & power steering gear replacement

9. Remove lateral lower arm assembly.
10. Remove dust cover.
11. Reverse procedure to install. Tighten to specifications.

STEERING KNUCKLE

REPLACE

1. Raise and support vehicle.
2. Remove front wheel and tire assembly.
3. **On models equipped with ABS,** remove front wheel speed sensor.
4. **On all models,** remove hub assembly as described under "Hub & Bearing, Replace."
5. Refer to **Fig. 7** for removal of steering knuckle.
6. Reverse procedure to install. Tighten to specifications.

STABILIZER BAR

REPLACE

1. Raise and support vehicle.
2. Remove stabilizer link mounting nut.
3. Remove stabilizer link.
4. Remove stabilizer bar bracket and bushing.
5. Remove stabilizer bar.

6. Reverse procedure to install. Tighten to specifications.

CROSSMEMBER

REPLACE

1. Raise and support vehicle.
2. Drain power steering fluid and remove steering gear as described under "Power Steering Gear, Replace."
3. Remove front exhaust pipe.
4. Remove stabilizer bar as described under "Stabilizer Bar, Replace."
5. Refer to **Fig. 8** to remove crossmember.
6. Reverse procedure to install. Tighten to specifications.

POWER STEERING GEAR

REPLACE

1. Drain power steering fluid.
2. Remove stabilizer bar as described under "Stabilizer Bar, Replace."
3. Remove windshield washer reservoir.
4. Remove steering gear, **Fig. 9.**
5. Reverse procedure to install, noting the following:
   a. Tighten bolts to specifications.
   b. Add power steering fluid and bleed system as described under " Power Steering System Bleed."

POWER STEERING PUMP

REPLACE

1. Drain power steering fluid into a suitable container.
2. Remove power steering pump drive belt.
3. Disconnect suction hose.
4. Disconnect pressure hose from pump.
5. Remove gasket or O-ring.
6. Disconnect pressure switch electrical connector.
7. Remove oil pump and bracket.
8. Reverse procedure to install and tighten to specifications. Add power steering fluid and bleed system as described under "Power Steering System Bleed."

POWER STEERING SYSTEM BLEED

1. Raise and support front wheels.
2. Manually turn oil pump pulley a few turns.
3. Turn steering wheel to full left and full right five or six times.
4. Disconnect high tension ignition cable, then while operating starter motor intermittently, turn steering wheel full left and full right five or six times.
5. Connect ignition cable, then start engine and run at idle.
6. Turn steering wheel to left and right until there are no bubbles in the reservoir.
7. Confirm fluid is not milky and that fluid level is up to specified position on dipstick.
8. Confirm there is very little change in fluid level when steering wheel is turned to left or right.

TIGHTENING SPECIFICATIONS

Year	Component	Torque/ Ft. Lbs.
1997-2000	Axle Nut	145–188
	Centermember Rear Assembly Bolts	64
	Centermember To Bracket Bolts	32
	Centermember To Crossmember Bolts	51–58
	Compression Lower Arm Ball Joint To Knuckle	43–51
	Compression Lower Arm Mounting Bolt	60
	Crossmember Lower Plate Bolts	71–85
	Crossmember To Rear Roll Bracket Bolts	32
	Damper Fork Mounting Bolt	75
	Damper Fork To Lateral Lower Arm Through Bolt	65
	Driveshaft Nut	145–188
	Driveshaft To Transaxle Bolt	30
	Hub Nut	145–188
	Joint Assembly & Steering Gear Connection	13
	Lateral Lower Arm Mounting Bolt & Nut	71–85
	Lateral Lower Arm To Knuckle Nuts	43–52
	Power Steering Gear Clamp Bolts	51
	Power Steering Pipe Connection	11
	Power Steering Pump Bracket Bolts (2.0L)	29
	Power Steering Pump Bracket Bolts (2.5L)	16
	Power Steering Pump Mounting Bolt (2.0L)	42
	Shock Absorber Lower Mounting Bolt	64
	Shock Absorber Upper Mounting Nut	32
	Stabilizer Bar Bracket	28
	Stabilizer Link Mounting Nut	28
	Tie Rod End To Steering Knuckle	18–25
	Upper Arm Self-Locking Nut	62
	Upper Arm Shaft To Control Arm	41

Wheel Alignment

INDEX

DESCRIPTION

Caster and camber are preset at the factory and cannot be adjusted. If camber is not within specifications, inspect and replace bent or damaged parts.

PRELIMINARY INSPECTION

Wheel alignment should be measured with alignment equipment on a level surface. The suspension, steering system and wheels should be serviced to normal condition prior to measurement of wheel alignment. Inspect wheel runout as follows:

1. Raise and support vehicle.
2. While slowly turning wheel, measure runout with dial indicator.
3. Radial and lateral runout should be .05 inch or less for steel wheel, and .04 inch or less for aluminum wheel.

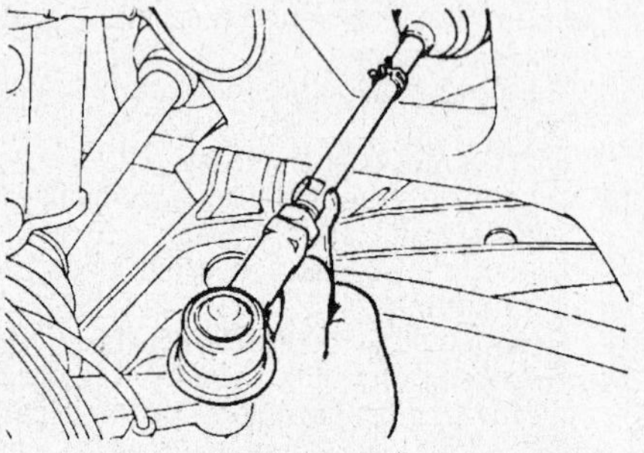

CR2049600057000X

Fig. 1 Front toe adjustment

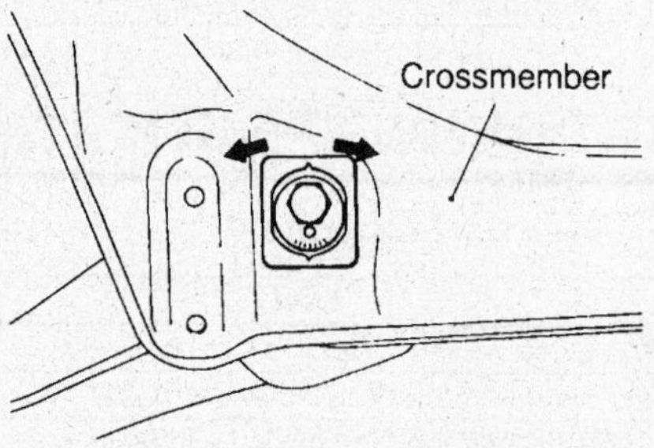

CR2049600058000X

Fig. 2 Rear toe adjustment

4. If wheel runout exceeds limit, replace wheel.

FRONT WHEEL ALIGNMENT

If toe measurement is not within specifications, adjust as follows:

1. Undo clips and turn left and right tie rod turnbuckles by the same amount in opposite directions, **Fig. 1.**
2. Toe will move out as left turnbuckle is turned toward front of vehicle and right turnbuckle is turned toward rear of vehicle.

REAR WHEEL ALIGNMENT

Toe is adjusted by turning the toe control arm mounting bolt to the left or right in equal amounts, **Fig. 2.** Turning the lefthand bolt clockwise adjusts in the toe-out direction. Turning the righthand bolt clockwise adjusts in the toe-in direction. Toe adjustments are made in graduations of .05 inch.

BREEZE, CIRRUS, SEBRING CONVERTIBLE & STRATUS

NOTE: Refer To The Rear Of This Manual For Manufacturer's Special Service Tool Supplies.

INDEX OF SERVICE OPERATIONS

Specifications

GENERAL ENGINE SPECIFICATIONS

Year	Engine		Fuel System	Bore & Stroke, Inches	Comp. Ratio	Net HP @ RPM	Maximum Torque, Ft. Lbs. @ RPM	Normal Oil Pressure, psi @ 3000 RPM
	Liter	VIN Code①						
1997–2000	2.0L	C	SMPI	3.45 x 3.27	9.8	132 @ 6000	129 @ 5000	25–80
	2.4L	X	SMPI	3.44 x 3.98	9.4	150 @ 5200	167 @ 4000	25–80
	2.5L	H	SMPI	3.29 x 2.99	9.4	168 @ 5800	170 @ 4350	35–75

SMPI — Sequential Multi-Port Injection

① — Eighth digit of Vehicle Identification Number (VIN) denotes engine code.

TUNE UP SPECIFICATIONS

Year	Engine	Spark Plug Gap, Inch	Ignition Timing			Minimum Air Flow Idle Speed, RPM②	Fuel Pump Pressure, psi	Valve Clearance
			Firing Order	Firing Order Fig.	°BTDC			
1997–2000	2.0L	.035	1-3-4-2	A	②	600–1300	49④	①
	2.4L	.050	1-3-4-2	A	②	600–1300	49④	①
	2.5L	.041	1-2-3-4-5-6	B	②	500–1100	47–51③	①

BTDC — Before Top Dead Center

① — Equipped w/hydraulic valve adjusters. No adjustment is necessary.

② — Controlled by PCM; not adjustable.

③ — Disconnect fuel rail wiring harness. Connect a jumper wire between 12 volt power source & A142 circuit terminal of fuel rail wiring harness connector. Connect one end of a jumper wire to ground, then connect other end of jumper wire to each injector terminal in harness. Disconnect fuel line from fuel rail & connect a suitable fuel pressure test gauge between fuel line & fuel rail. Connect DRB scan tool, or equivalent. Place ignition switch in On position, the use scan tool to activate ADSD fuel system test.

④ — Remove cap from fuel pressure test port on fuel rail. Connect a suitable fuel pressure test gauge to fuel rail test port. Connect DRB scan tool, or equivalent. Place ignition switch in On position, then use scan tool to activate ADSD fuel system test.

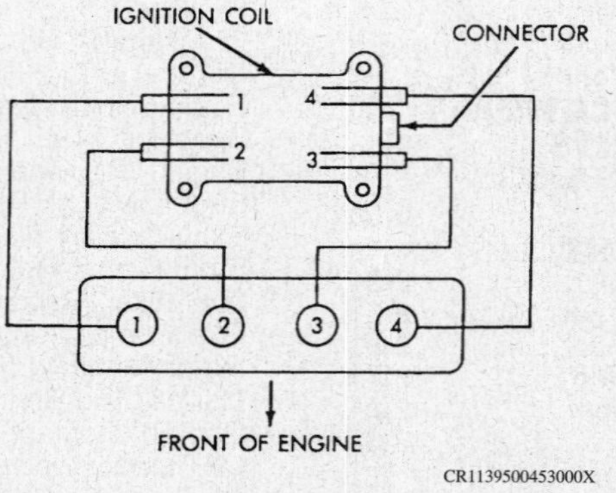

Fig. A

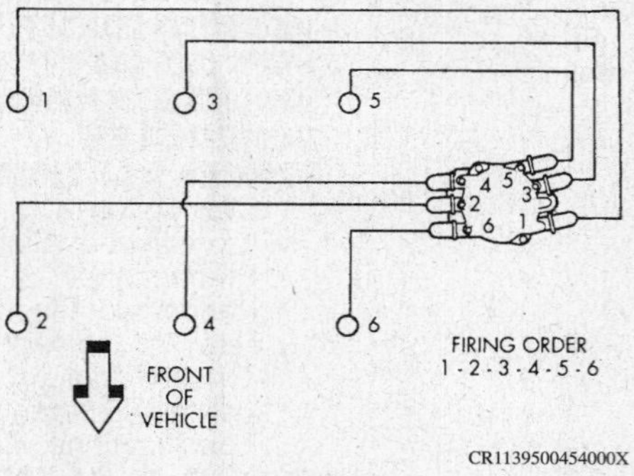

Fig. B

FRONT WHEEL ALIGNMENT SPECIFICATIONS

Year	Model	Camber Angle, Degrees		Toe, Degrees③		Caster, Degrees①	Ball Joint Wear
		Limits	Desired	Individual	Total		
1997–2000	Breeze, Cirrus & Stratus	-.6 to +.6	0	+.05	+.1	+3.3	②
	Sebring Convertible	-.5 to +.7	+.1	+.05	+.1	+3.1	②

① — Not adjustable.

② — Refer to "Ball Joint Inspection" in "Front Suspension & Steering" section.

③ — Toe in (+); toe out (-).

REAR WHEEL ALIGNMENT SPECIFICATIONS

Year	Model	Camber Angle, Degrees		Toe, Degrees①		Thrust Angle, Degrees	
		Limits	Desired	Individual	Total	Limits	Desired
1997–2000	Breeze, Cirrus & Stratus	-.6 to +.2	-.2	+.05	+.1	-.15 to +.15	0
	Sebring Convertible	-.5 to +.3	-.1	+.05	+.1	-.15 to +.15	0

① — Toe in (+); toe out (-).

FLUID CAPACITIES & COOLING SYSTEM DATA

Year	Engine	Coolant Capacity, Qts.	Radiator Cap Relief Pressure, Lbs.	Thermo. Opening Temp., °F	Fuel Tank Capacity, Gals.	Engine Oil Refill, Qts.①	Transaxle Oil, Qts.	
							Manual Trans.	Auto. Trans.
1997–2000	2.0L	8.5	14–18	192–199	16	4.5	4.4	②
	2.4L	9.0	14–18	192–199	16	5.0	4.4	②
	2.5L	10.5	14–18	192–199	16	4.5	4.4	②

① — Includes filter change.

② — Service fill, 4.0 qts.; overhaul fill w/torque converter, 9.1 qts.

LUBRICANT DATA

Year	Lubricant Type			
	Transaxle		Power Steering	Brake System
	Manual	Automatic		
1997–2000	Mopar Type M.S. 9417	Mopar ATF Type 7176	Mopar Part No. 4549617	DOT 3

Electrical

NOTE: Refer To "Air Bag System Precautions " Located In The Front Of This Manual For System Disarming & Arming Procedures.

NOTE: Refer To "Computer Relearn" Located In The Front Of This Manual For Computer Relearn Procedures.

INDEX

PRECAUTIONS

AIR BAG SYSTEMS

Refer to Air Bag System Precautions in the front of this manual for system disarming and arming procedures.

BATTERY GROUND CABLE

Prior to service, disconnect battery ground cable and isolate as required.

FUSE PANEL LOCATION

The interior accessory fuse panel is located between the instrument panel and the driver's side door. The door must be open to access the fuse panel. The fuse panel contains the headland relay, horn relay, rear window defogger relay, circuit breakers, and several fuses.

FUEL PUMP RELAY LOCATION

The fuel pump relay is located in the the Power Distribution Center (PDC), which is near the battery on the leftward side of the engine compartment.

RELAY CENTER LOCATION

The engine compartment relays are located in the Power Distribution Center (PDC) next to the battery. The PDC contains the starter relay, radiator fan relay, A/C compressor clutch relay, auto shutdown relay, wiper relay, back-up lamp relay, transvalue control relay, fuel pump relay and several fuses.

STARTER

REPLACE

2.0L ENGINE

Automatic Transaxle

Refer to the "2.4L Engine" starter replacement procedure.

Manual Transaxle

1. Remove air cleaner resonator.
2. Remove battery positive cable nut from starter, then remove the battery positive cable and alternator output wire from starter.
3. Disconnect push on solenoid connector.
4. Remove two bolts attaching starter to transvalue housing and remove starter from vehicle.
5. Reverse procedure to install. Clean corrosion from wire terminals before installation.

2.4L ENGINE

1. Remove air cleaner resonator.
2. Remove three Transvalue Control Module (TCM) mounting screws. Move TCM to provide access to top starter mounting bolt. **Do not disconnect TCM wiring.**
3. Remove bolt attaching starter to transvalue housing, then raise and support vehicle.
4. Remove battery cable nut from starter and remove cable.
5. Disconnect push on solenoid connector.
6. Remove top bolt attaching starter to transvalue housing, then the starter from vehicle.
7. Reverse procedure to install, noting the following:
   a. **Torque** starter mounting bolts to 40 ft. lbs.
   b. Clean corrosion from wire terminals before connecting wiring to solenoid.

2.5L ENGINE

1. Raise and support vehicle.
2. Remove oil filter.
3. Remove battery positive cable nut from starter and remove cable.
4. Disconnect push-on solenoid connector.
5. Remove three bolts attaching starter to transvalue housing and remove starter from vehicle.
6. Reverse procedure to install. Clean corrosion from wire terminals before installation.

ALTERNATOR

REPLACE

2.0L & 2.4L ENGINES

1. Unplug field circuit from alternator.
2. Remove B+ terminal cover by spreading the cover with a small flat blade tool.
3. Remove B+ terminal nut and wire.
4. Loosen adjusting Bolt, but do not remove.
5. Loosen pivot bolt, but do not remove.

6. Loosen adjusting bolt to allow removal of the alternator drive belt.
7. Remove adjusting Bolt.
8. Remove pivot bolt, do not drop spacer.
9. **On models equipped with 2.0L engine,** proceed as follows:
   a. Release alternator from mounting bracket and move it toward passenger headland bucket.
   b. Remove alternator from head lamp bucket area.
10. **On models equipped with 2.4L engine,** proceed as follows:
    a. Remove ABS braking unit by removing the two lower plate mounting bolts.
    b. Remove coolant overflow bottle.
    c. Remove by sliding alternator under air conditioning lines towards passenger side of vehicle.
11. **On all models,** reverse procedure to install.

2.5L ENGINE

1. Unplug field circuit from alternator.
2. Remove B+ terminal nut and wire.
3. Loosen top mounting ear bolt.
4. Loosen pivot bolt, but do not remove.
5. Loosen adjusting bolt on idler to allow removal of alternator drive belt.
6. Remove pivot bolt. Do not drop spacer.
7. Remove top mounting ear bolt.
8. Remove upper alternator bracket, then the alternator.
9. Reverse procedure to install.

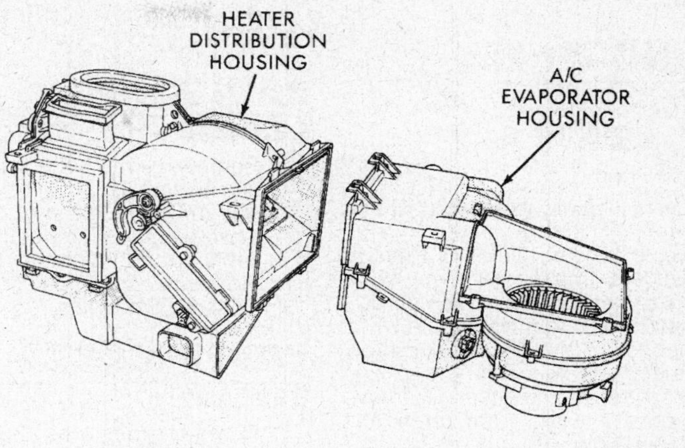

Fig. 1 A/C & Heater housing unit

DISTRIBUTOR

REPLACE

2.5L ENGINE

Removal

1. Remove bolt holding air inlet resonator to intake manifold.
2. Loosen clamps holding air cleaner cover to air cleaner housing.
3. Remove PCV air hose from air inlet tube.
4. Loosen hose clamp at throttle body.
5. Remove air inlet tube, resonator and air cleaner cover.
6. Remove EGR tube.
7. Remove spark plug cables from distributor cap.
8. Loosen distributor cap hold-down screws and remove cap.
9. Mark rotor position for installation reference, then remove rotor.
10. Remove two harness connectors from distributor.
11. Remove two sets of distributor hold-down nuts and washers from studs.
12. Remove bolt and spark plug cable mounting bracket from top of distributor housing.
13. Remove bolt and transvalue dipstick tube.
14. Carefully remove distributor from engine.

Installation

1. Install rotor on shaft.
2. Position distributor in engine and ensure Oaring is properly seated on distributor. Replace Oaring if it is cracked or nicked.
3. Carefully engage distributor drive with slotted end of camshaft. When the distributor is installed properly, the rotor will be in line with previously marked line on air intake plenum.
4. If engine was cranked while distributor was removed, establish proper relationship between distributor shaft and No. 1 piston position as follows:
   a. Rotate crankshaft until number one piston is at top of compression stroke.
   b. Rotate rotor to No. 1 rotor terminal.
   c. Lower distributor into opening, engaging distributor drive with drive on camshaft. With distributor fully seated on engine, rotor should be under No. 1 terminal.
5. Install distributor hold-down washers and nuts. **Torque** to 108 inch lbs.
6. Install spark plug cable bracket.
7. Install two harness connectors to distributor.
8. Install distributor cap.
9. Install transvalue dipstick tube.
10. Install EGR tube to intake manifold. **Torque** bolts to 96 inch lbs.

COIL PACK

REPLACE

2.0L & 2.4L ENGINES

1. Disconnect coil pack electrical connector.
2. Remove mounting nuts, then the coil pack.
3. Reverse procedure to install. If a new coil pack is to be installed, transfer spark plug cables to corresponding towers on new unit.

IGNITION LOCK

REPLACE

1. Remove upper steering column shroud.
2. Pull lower shroud down far enough to access lock cylinder retaining tab.
3. Place key cylinder in Run position. Depress retaining tab and remove key cylinder.
4. Reverse procedure to install.

IGNITION SWITCH

REPLACE

1. Remove fuse panel cover from left end of instrument panel. Remove screw holding end of instrument panel top cover.
2. Pull center bezel off.
3. Remove screws holding instrument panel top cover to center of instrument panel.
4. Pull instrument panel top cover up enough to gain access to knee bolster screws.
5. Remove lower knee bolster screws and knee bolster.
6. Remove screws from lower steering column shroud.
7. Pull lower shroud to clear ignition cylinder and key release, if equipped.
8. Hold tilt wheel lever down and slide lower shroud forward to remove it from column.
9. Tilt wheel to full down position and remove upper steering column shroud.
10. Remove screws holding multiplication switch to lock housing.
11. Place key cylinder in Run position. Depress lock cylinder retaining tab and remove key cylinder.
12. Disconnect electrical connectors from ignition switch.
13. Remove ignition switch mounting screw with a suitable Tore bit.
14. Depress retaining tabs and pull ignition switch from steering column.
15. Reverse procedure to install.

MULTI-FUNCTION SWITCH

REPLACE

1. Remove upper steering column cover.
2. Remove multiplication switch mounting screws.
3. Disconnect wire connectors. Lift switch straight up to remove.

4. Reverse procedure to install.

STEERING WHEEL

REPLACE

BREEZE, CIRRUS & STRATUS

1. Place front wheels in straight ahead position.
2. Remove air bag as outlined in "Passive Restraint Systems" section.
3. Remove speed control switch screws from back of steering wheel. Pull switch pods out and disconnect wires.
4. Disconnect horn wire from the air bag module mounting bracket. Remove speed control wires from under the bracket and from wire guides.
5. Remove steering wheel retaining nut.
6. Remove steering wheel with wheel a suitable fuller tool. Feed all wires through steering wheel armature to avoid damaging wires.
7. Reverse procedure to install, noting the following:
   a. **Torque** steering wheel retaining nut to 45 ft. lbs.
   b. **Torque** air bag module bolts to 84 inch. lbs.

SEBRING CONVERTIBLE

1. Place front wheels in straight ahead position, then rotate steering wheel 180° clockwise.
2. Lock steering column with ignition lock.
3. Remove and disconnect speed control switches, then air bag module as outlined in "Passive Restraint Systems" section.
4. Disconnect horn electrical connectors.
5. Remove steering wheel retaining nut, then use a suitable fuller to remove wheel, noting the following:
   a. **Do not hammer on end of steering shaft during removal.**
   b. Carefully feed wires through holes in clocking armature.
6. Reverse procedure to install, noting the following:
   a. **Torque** steering wheel retaining nut to 45 ft. lbs.
   b. **Torque** air bag module bolts to 96 inch. lbs.

INSTRUMENT CLUSTER

REPLACE

1. Remove instrument panel left end cap.
2. Tilt steering column down to its lowest position.
3. Remove instrument panel center bezel by disengaging four clips.
4. Remove instrument cluster hood by doing the following:
   a. Remove two screws adjacent radio.
   b. Remove screw below HVAC control in center.
   c. Remove screw at left end of panel.
   d. Pull on hood to disengage eight clips.
5. Remove instrument cluster from panel. Pull cluster rearward to disconnect wire connectors from base panel.
6. Reverse procedure to install.

RADIO

REPLACE

1. Remove center bezel and two radio retaining screws.
2. Pull radio straight out and disconnect both electrical connectors, antenna cable and radio ground strap, then remove radio from vehicle.
3. Reverse procedure to install.

WIPER MOTOR

REPLACE

1. Remove wiper arms and blades.
2. Remove cowl screen.
3. Remove wiper motor mounting screws, then lift assembly to access harness clip.
4. Disconnect harness clip at forward mounting leg, then disconnect motor electrical connector.
5. Disconnect drive linkage at motor output crank, then use a suitable ball joint separator tool to separate ball cap from ball.
6. Remove motor.
7. Reverse procedure to install. **Torque** mounting screws to 96–108 inch. lbs. and motor screws to 19–23 ft. lbs.

BLOWER MOTOR

REPLACE

1. Remove lower right under panel silencer duct.
2. Remove blower motor connector from resistor block.
3. Remove blower motor retaining screws.
4. Lower blower motor from housing and remove fan scroll from motor shaft.
5. Remove motor from case.
6. Reverse procedure to install.

HEATER CORE

REPLACE

1. Remove radio and climate control bezel, then the right instrument panel side trim.
2. Remove two screws at lower right side support beam.
3. Remove bolt for instrument panel support at A-pillar.
4. Remove left instrument panel side trim.
5. Remove upper instrument panel bezel.
6. Remove lower knee bolster.
7. Remove console screws at instrument panel.
8. Remove gearshift knob and shifter bezel.
9. Remove console screws at rear, then the rear half of console.
10. Remove front console screws, then the front half of console.
11. Remove right side instrument panel support strut.
12. Drain coolant.
13. Remove heater hoses at cowl.
14. Remove heater core cover screws and cover.
15. Remove heater core.
16. Reverse procedure to install.

EVAPORATOR CASE

REPLACE

1. Recover A/C system as outlined under "Air Conditioning. "
2. Remove air cleaner hose and air distribution duct from the engine.
3. Drain engine coolant into a suitable container.
4. Disconnect heater hoses at dash panel, then plug the heater core inlet and outlet tubes.
5. Remove both A/C lines from expansion valve using special disconnect tool No. 7193, or equivalent, to disconnect connectors on A/C lines.
6. Cap expansion valve openings and the A/C hose openings to prevent dirt or moisture from entering refrigerant system during servicing.
7. Remove trim bezel around radio and climate control module.
8. Remove cluster hood bezel retaining screws in the trim bezel opening.
9. Pry up cluster hood bezel a few inches to expose the cubby bin bezel and wiring.
10. Remove cubby bin bezel and wiring.
11. Remove control module retaining screws.
12. Drop the A/C control module into cubby bin bezel opening, then disconnect wiring on rear of control module.
13. Release cable clips from top of control module. Retain clips for installation.
14. Disconnect temperature control and recirculation control cables.
15. Remove control module.
16. Remove upper instrument panel bezel.
17. Remove right and left instrument panel end caps.
18. Remove left lower knee bolster. Disconnect mode door motor wiring.
19. Remove right and left interior door post kick panel.
20. Remove front and rear halves of floor console.
21. Remove radio as outlined under "Radio, Replace."
22. Remove right side lower silencer/duct.
23. Remove glove compartment assembly.
24. Remove right side vertical support strut brace.
25. Remove left side vertical support strut brace.
26. Remove center lower distribution housing.
27. Remove bolts securing heater-A/C housing to instrument panel metal frame.
28. Remove upper instrument panel cowl trim cover.

29. Disconnect steering column from instrument panel. Lower steering column.
30. Remove instrument panel bolts at cowl fence.
31. Remove bolts at lower A-posts.
32. Remove instrument frame and wiring.
33. Remove bolts securing Heater-A/C housing to cowl.
34. Reverse procedure to install. Verify cables are properly adjusted and control module is seated properly.

EVAPORATOR CORE

REPLACE

1. Remove evaporator case as described under "Evaporator Case, Replace."
2. Remove recirculation door inlet cover.
3. Remove evaporator temperature probe.
4. Remove clips retaining evaporator housing to heater/distribution housing.
5. Separate evaporator housing from heater/distribution housing, **Fig. 1.**
6. Remove seal around evaporator tube inlet.
7. Remove evaporator housing upper cover.
8. Lift evaporator out of lower housing.
9. Remove foam seal around evaporator.
10. Transfer evaporator sensor. Place the evaporator sensor in the same location as on the previous evaporator.
11. Reverse procedure to install.

2.0L & 2.4L Engines

NOTE: Refer To "Air Bag System Precautions " Located In The Front Of This Manual For System Disarming & Arming Procedures.

NOTE: Refer To "Computer Relearn" Located In The Front Of This Manual For Computer Relearn Procedures.

INDEX

PRECAUTIONS

AIR BAG SYSTEMS

Refer to "Air Bag System Precautions" in the front of this manual for system disarming and arming procedures.

BATTERY GROUND CABLE

Prior to service, disconnect battery ground cable and isolate as required.

FUEL SYSTEM PRESSURE RELIEF

2.0L & 2.4L Engines

1. Disconnect ground cable from auxiliary jumper terminal.
2. Remove fuel filler cap.
3. Remove protective cap from fuel pressure test port on fuel rail, **Fig. 1.**
4. Place open end of fuel pressure release hose tool No. C-4799-1, or equivalent, into a suitable gasoline container, then connect other hose end to fuel pressure test port. Fuel pressure should bleed off through hose into container.

2.5L Engine

1. Disconnect fuel rail electrical harness from engine harness.
2. Connect suitable jumper wire between fuel rail harness connector terminal A142 and 12 volt power source.
3. Connect another suitable jumper wire to ground source, then momentarily ground one injector harness connector terminal, to release fuel system pressure.
4. Repeat procedure for two to three injectors.

COMPRESSION PRESSURE

Compression pressure should be 170–225 psi with no more than a 25% variation in pressure between cylinders.

ENGINE MOUNT

REPLACE

RIGHT SIDE MOUNT

1. Raise and support vehicle, then remove the inner splash.
2. Remove right engine support assembly attaching bolts from frame rail, **Fig. 2.**
3. Lower vehicle and support engine assembly with floor jack to remove pressure on motor mounts.

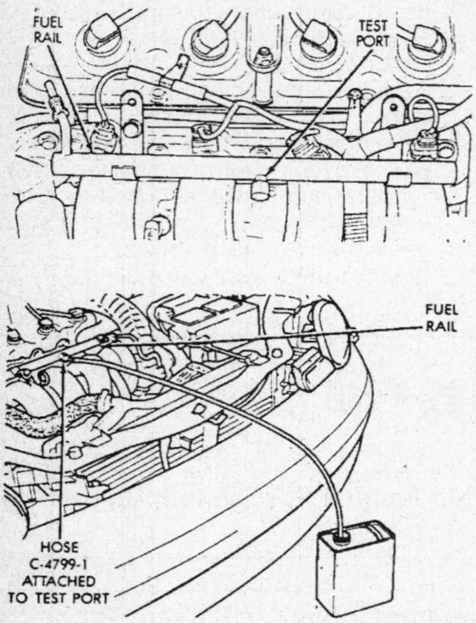

Fig. 1 Fuel system test port location & pressure relief equipment

4. Remove three engine support to engine bracket attaching bolts.
5. Reverse procedure to install. Tighten attaching nuts and bolts to specifications shown in **Fig. 2.**

ENGINE CRADLE (SUPPORT MODULE)

1. Raise and support vehicle, then remove rear mount through bolt and bolts securing cradle to crossover, **Fig. 3.**
2. Remove rear support strut bracket upper bolt and bolts securing cradle to lower radiator support.
3. With cooling module supported, remove lower radiator support.
4. Remove front through bolt, then the cradle.
5. Reverse procedure to install, noting the following:
   a. Do not tighten front through bolt until rear through bolt is installed and tightened.
   b. Tighten bolts to specifications.

LEFT SIDE MOUNT

1. Support transvalue with suitable jack.
2. Remove three engine mount to transvalue attaching bolts, **Figs. 4 and 5.**
3. Remove transvalue mount attaching bolts, then the mount.
4. Reverse procedure to install. Tighten attaching nuts and bolts to specifications shown in **Figs. 4 and 5.**

REAR MOUNT

1. Raise and support vehicle, then remove left front wheel.
2. Support transvalue with transvalue jack.
3. Remove mount and rear suspension crossover insulator attaching bolt, **Figs. 6 and 7.**
4. Remove four transvalue mount attaching bolts, then the mount.
5. Reverse procedure to install. Tighten attaching nuts and bolts to specifications shown in **Figs. 6 and 7.**

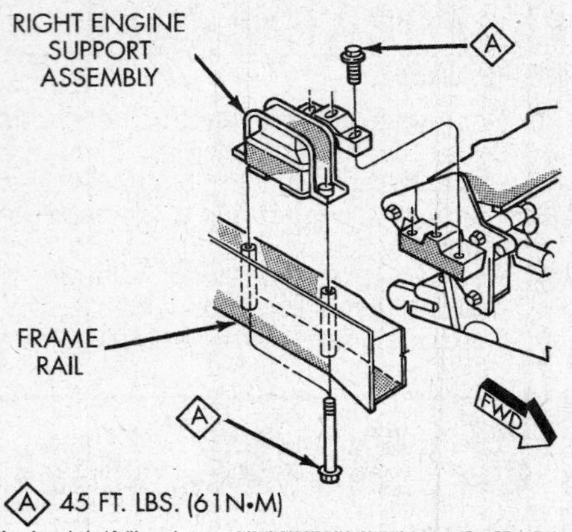

Fig. 2 Right side engine mount replacement

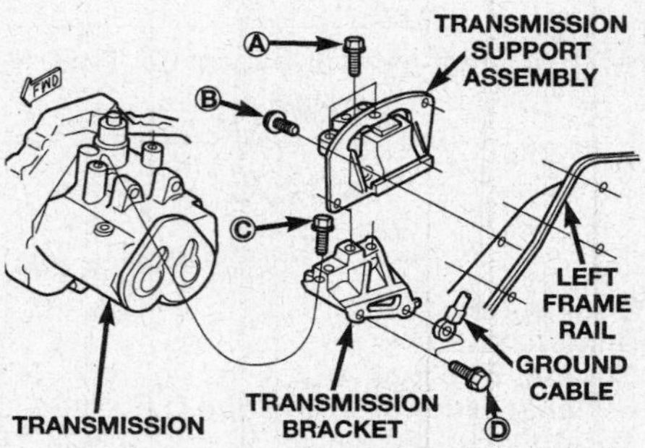

ITEM	DESCRIPTION	TORQUE
A	Bolt	61 N·m (45 ft. lbs.)
B	Bolt	33 N·m (24 ft. lbs.)
C	Bolt	61 N·m (45 ft. lbs.)
D	Bolt	61 N·m (45 ft. lbs.)

CR1069500597000X

Fig. 4 Left engine mount replacement. 2.0L engine

ENGINE

REPLACE

1. Relieve fuel system pressure as outlined under " Precautions."
2. Disconnect and remove battery and tray, then disconnect Pertain Control Module (PCM) electrical connector and position aside.
3. Drain coolant into a suitable container.
4. Remove upper radiator hose, fan module and radiator as outlined under "Radiator, Replace."
5. Remove lower radiator hose.
6. **On models equipped with manual transvalue,** disconnect clutch cable and shift linkage.
7. **On models equipped with automatic transvalue,** disconnect and plug transvalue cooler line.

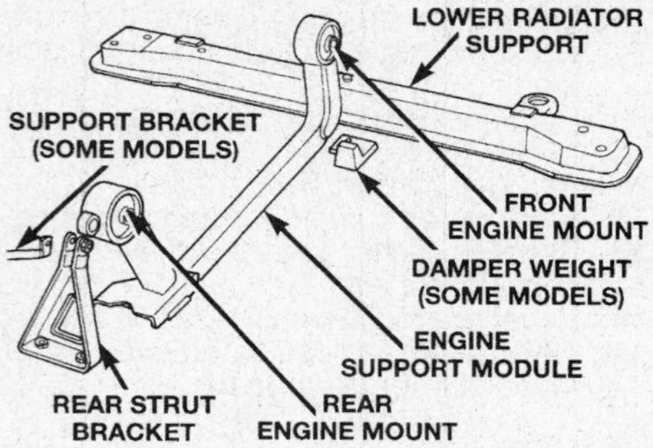

Fig. 3 Engine cradle (support module)

8. **On all models,** disconnect throttle body linkage.
9. Disconnect engine wiring harness electrical connectors.
10. Disconnect heater hoses.
11. Recover A/C refrigerant as outlined in "Air Conditioning " section.
12. Raise and support vehicle, then remove the right inner splash shield.
13. Remove accessory drive belts.
14. Remove axle shafts.
15. Disconnect exhaust pipe from manifold.
16. Remove front and rear engine mount bracket from the body.
17. Lower vehicle, then remove the air cleaner assembly.
18. Remove power steering pump and reservoir.
19. Remove A/C compressor.
20. Remove ground straps to body.
21. Raise and support vehicle to install engine dolly and cradle tool Nos. 6135 and 6710, or equivalents.
22. **On models equipped with 2.4L engine,** install post tool No. 6848, or equivalent.
23. **On all models,** loosen engine cradle mounts to position engine locating holes in belated, then lower the vehicle until engine rests on cradle mounts and tighten mounts to cradle frame to prevent mount movement.
24. Lower vehicle so weight of engine and transvalue is only on cradle.
25. Remove engine and transvalue mount attaching bolts.
26. Slowly raise and support vehicle, move engine and transvalue assembly on cradle to allow for removal around body flanges as required.
27. Reverse procedure to install.

INTAKE MANIFOLD

REPLACE

1. Relieve fuel system pressure as outlined under " Precautions."
2. Remove air inlet resonator.
3. Disconnect fuel supply line quick connect from fuel tube assembly.
4. Remove fuel rail assembly attaching screws, then the fuel rail assembly cover injector holes.
5. Remove accelerator, kickstand and speed control cables from throttle lever and bracket.
6. Disconnect Idle Air Control (IAC) motor

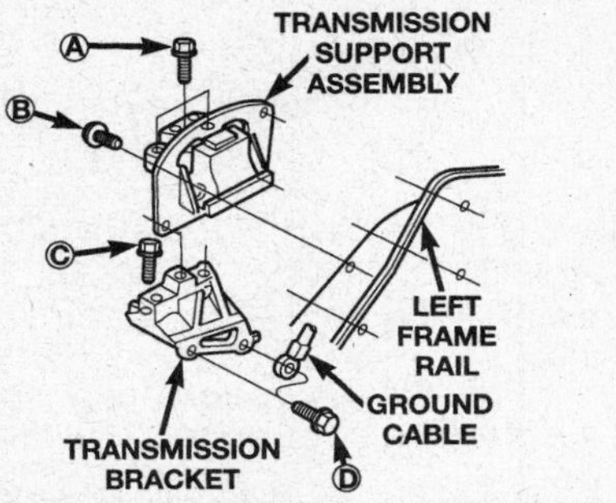

ITEM	DESCRIPTION	TORQUE
A	Bolt	61 N·m (45 ft. lbs.)
B	Bolt	33 N·m (24 ft. lbs.)
C	Bolt	61 N·m (45 ft. lbs.)
D	Bolt	61 N·m (45 ft. lbs.)

CR1069500598000X

Fig. 5 Left engine mount replacement. 2.4L engine

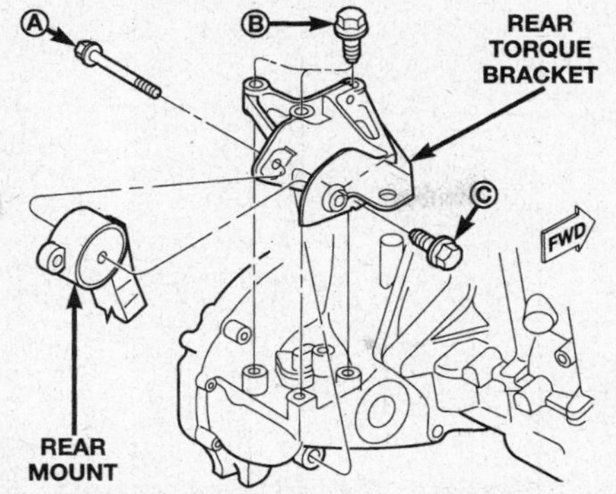

ITEM	DESCRIPTION	TORQUE
A	Bolt	61 N·m (45 ft. lbs.)
B & C	Bolt—w/Auto. Transaxle	110 N·m (80 ft. lbs.)
	Bolt—w/Manual Transaxle	61 N·m (45 ft. lbs.)

CR1069500599000X

Fig. 6 Rear engine mount replacement. 2.0L engine

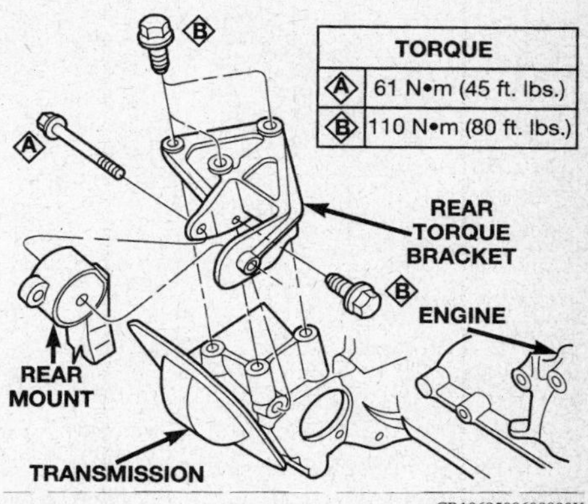

CR1069500600000X

Fig. 7 Rear engine mount replacement. 2.4L engine

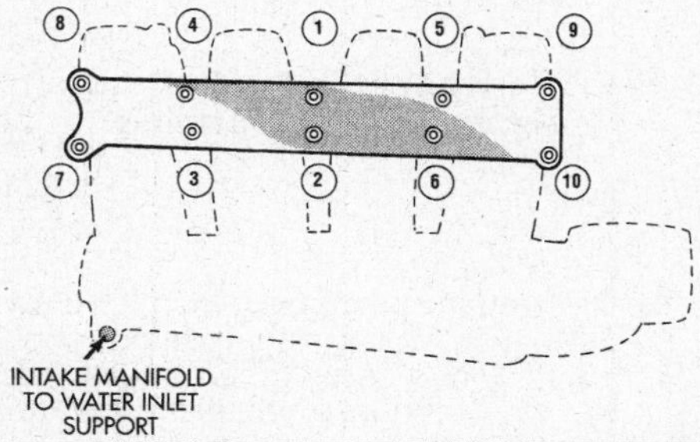

CR1059500096000X

Fig. 8 Intake manifold bolt tightening sequence. 2.0L engine

and Throttle Position Sensor (TPS) electrical connectors.

7. Disconnect vacuum hoses from throttle body.
8. Disconnect Manifold Absolute Pressure (MAP) intake air temperature electrical connectors.
9. Disconnect vapor and brake booster hoses.
10. Disconnect knock sensor electrical connector and harness from tab located on intake manifold .
11. Remove transvalue to throttle body support bracket bolts at throttle body and loosen bolt at transvalue.
12. Remove EGR tube attaching bolts, then the tube.
13. Remove intake manifold to inlet water tube support bolt and manifold support bracket, if required.
14. Remove ten intake manifold attaching bolts and washers, then the intake manifold.
15. Reverse procedure to install, noting the following:
    a. Clean all mating surfaces, then check for cracked or distorted manifold and torn or missing Rings.
    b. **On models equipped with 2.0L engine,** replace all seals, bolts and washers.
    c. **On all models,** tighten intake manifold attaching bolts in sequence, **Figs. 8 and 9,** to specifications.
    d. Tighten attaching nuts and bolts to specifications.

EXHAUST MANIFOLD

REPLACE

1. Raise and support vehicle.
2. Remove exhaust pipe from manifold. It may be necessary to remove entire exhaust system.
3. Remove exhaust manifold heat shield attaching bolts and heat shield.
4. Remove eight exhaust manifold attaching bolts and exhaust manifold.
5. Reverse procedure to install, noting the following:
    a. Install new manifold gasket.
    b. Tighten exhaust manifold and exhaust pipe attaching bolts to specifications.

CYLINDER HEAD

REPLACE

1. Relieve fuel system pressure as outlined under " Precautions," then drain cooling system.
2. Remove air cleaner and disconnect all vacuum lines, electrical harnesses and fuel lines from throttle body.
3. Remove throttle linkage.
4. Remove accessory drive belts.
5. Remove intake manifold power brake vacuum connection.
6. Raise and support vehicle, then remove exhaust pipe from manifold.
7. Remove and set aside power steering pump assembly.
8. Disconnect coil pack electrical connector and remove coil pack and bracket.
9. Remove cam sensor and fuel injector electrical connectors.
10. Remove timing belt and camshaft sprocket.
11. Remove valve cover.
12. Remove rocker arm shaft assemblies.
13. Remove cylinder head bolts.
14. Reverse procedure to install, noting the following:
    a. Apply oil to bolts before installing.
    b. Install four short bolts in positions 7, 8, 9 and 10, **Figs. 10 and 11.**
    c. Using sequence shown in **Figs. 10 and 11,** tighten cylinder head bolts in four steps. First step, **torque** bolts to 25 ft. lbs.; second step, **torque** bolts to 50 ft. lbs.; third step, **torque** bolts to 50 ft. lbs.; fourth step, tighten bolts an additional 1/4 turn without using a torque wrench.

VALVE COVER

REPLACE

2.0L ENGINE

1. Remove air cleaner inlet duct.
2. Remove coil pack as outlined in "Electrical" section, then remove valve cover bolts.
3. Remove valve cover bolts, then the cover from engine.
4. Reverse procedure to install, noting the following:
    a. Install a new valve cover gasket.
    b. Tighten valve cover bolts to specifications.

2.4L ENGINE

1. Disconnect engine ground strap, then remove ignition coil pack as outlined in "Electrical" section.
2. Remove valve cover fasteners, then the cover.
3. Reverse procedure to install, noting the following:
    a. Install new valve cover gaskets and spark plug seals. **Do not allow oil or solvents to contact timing belt.**
    b. Apply silicone rubber adhesive sealant to camshaft cap corners and at top edge of half-round seal.
    c. **Torque** valve cover fasteners in three steps: first to 40 inch lbs., then to 6–7 ft. lbs. and, finally, to 8–9 ft. lbs.

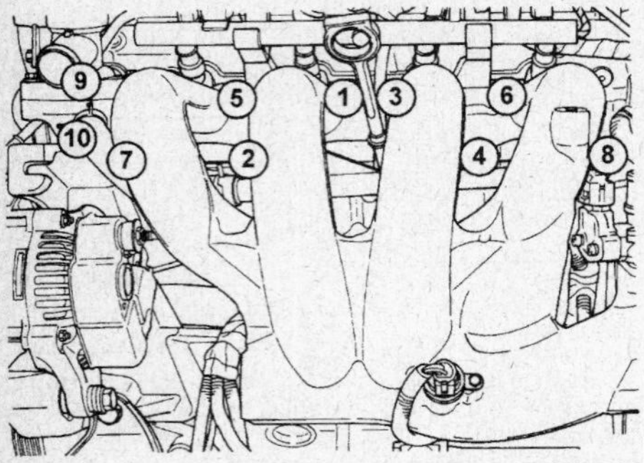
CR1069700677000X

Fig. 9 Intake manifold bolt tightening sequence. 2.4L engine

VALVE ARRANGEMENT

Intake valves are located on intake manifold side of engine and exhaust valves are located on exhaust manifold side of engine.

CAMSHAFT LOBE LIFT SPECIFICATIONS

Engine	Lift, Inch	
	Intake	Exhaust
1997		
2.0L	.307	.277
2.4L	.324	.256
1998–2000		
2.0L	.283	.277
2.4L	.324	.256

VALVE CLEARANCE SPECIFICATIONS

These engines are equipped with hydraulic lash adjusters designed to maintain zero lash at all times.

ROCKER ARMS

REPLACE

2.0L ENGINE

1. Remove valve cover as outlined under "Valve Cover, Replace."
2. Identify rocker are shaft assemblies, then remove attaching bolts and rocker arm shaft assemblies.
3. Reverse procedure to install, noting the following:
   a. Install rocker arm and shaft assemblies with notches on shafts facing up and toward timing belt side of engine, **Fig. 12.**
   b. Tighten bolts to specifications in sequence shown, **Fig. 13.**

FRONT COVER

REPLACE

1. Remove accessory drive belts.
2. Raise and support vehicle on a hoist and remove right inner splash shield.
3. **On models equipped with 2.0L engine,** remove crankshaft damper bolt,

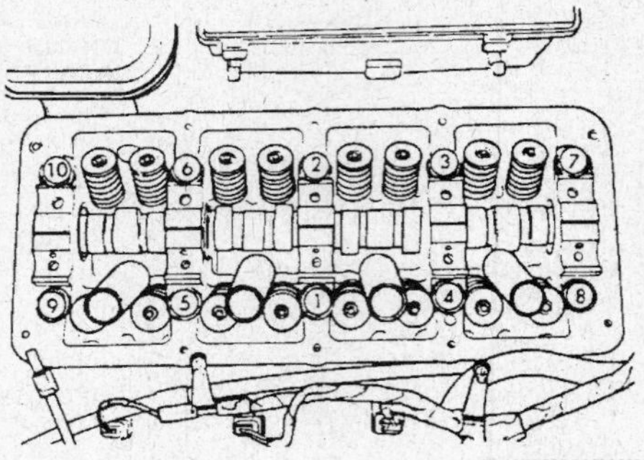
CR1069500564000X

Fig. 10 Cylinder head bolt tightening sequence. 2.0L engine

CR1069500567000X

Fig. 12 Rocker arm shaft notch alignment. 2.0L engine

then remove damper using fuller tool No. 1023 and insert tool No. C-4685-C2, or equivalents.

4. **On models equipped with 2.4L engine,** remove crankshaft damper bolt, then remove damper using fuller tool No. 1026 and insert tool No. 6827, or equivalents.
5. **On all models,** lower vehicle and place jack under engine.
6. Remove purge duty solenoid and wiring harness from right engine mount.
7. Remove right engine mount and bracket.
8. Remove upper timing belt cover attaching bolts, then the upper timing belt cover.
9. Remove lower timing belt cover attaching bolts, then the lower timing belt cover.
10. Reverse procedure to install.

TIMING BELT

REPLACE

2.0L ENGINE

The following procedure has been revised by a Technical Service Bulletin.

Removal

1. Remove timing belt front cover as described under " Front Cover, Replace."
2. Align crankshaft and camshaft sprocket marks, **Fig. 14,** then loosen timing belt pensioner attaching bolts.
3. Remove timing belt. If belt is to be reused, mark running direction on belt for installation reference.
4. Remove timing belt pensioner. **Pensioner pivot bolt, Fig. 15, should never be tightened, loosened or removed, as factory locking com-**

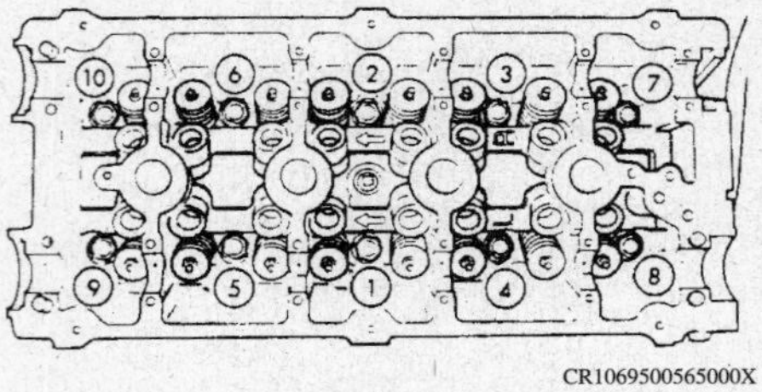
CR1069500565000X

Fig. 11 Cylinder head bolt tightening sequence. 2.4L engine

pound is not reusable. If pivot bolt is disturbed, entire pivot bracket assembly must be replaced (part No. 4777346).

5. Inspect timing belt for cracks, missing teeth, rubber hardening and abnormal wear and replace as necessary.

Installation

1. Position timing belt pensioner in a soft jawed vise, then slowly compress pensioner plunger into pensioner body.
2. With pensioner plunger compressed into body, insert a 5/64 inch hex wrench or other suitable locking pin through holes in pensioner body, **Fig. 16.** This will hold plunger in position until after pensioner has been installed on engine.
3. Align mark on crankshaft sprocket with arrow mark on oil pump housing, then back off to three sprocket teeth before Top Dead Center (TDC), **Fig. 17.**
4. Align camshaft sprocket mark with arrow mark on timing belt rear cover, **Fig. 14.**
5. Position crankshaft sprocket at ½ tooth before TDC, **Fig. 18.**
6. Position timing belt over crankshaft sprocket, around water pump sprocket, over camshaft sprocket, then around pensioner pulley.
7. Place crankshaft sprocket in TDC position to take up slack in timing belt.
8. Position timing belt pensioner on engine block, then loosely install attaching bolts. **Pensioner pivot bolt, Fig. 15, should never be tightened, loosened or removed, as factory locking compound is not reusable. If pivot bolt is disturbed, entire pivot bracket assembly must be replaced (part No. 4777346).**
9. Using a suitable torque wrench, apply a force of 20–21 ft. lbs. to timing belt pensioner pulley, **Fig. 14.**
10. While applying tension on pensioner pulley, move timing belt pensioner up against pensioner pulley bracket, then tighten pensioner attaching bolts to specifications.
11. Remove hex wrench or locking pin retaining pensioner plunger in body. Timing belt pretension is correct when wrench or pin can be freely removed from and installed in pensioner body holes.
12. Rotate crankshaft two revolutions in normal direction of rotation, then check crankshaft and camshaft sprocket timing mark alignment, **Fig. 14.** If timing marks are not properly aligned, repeat

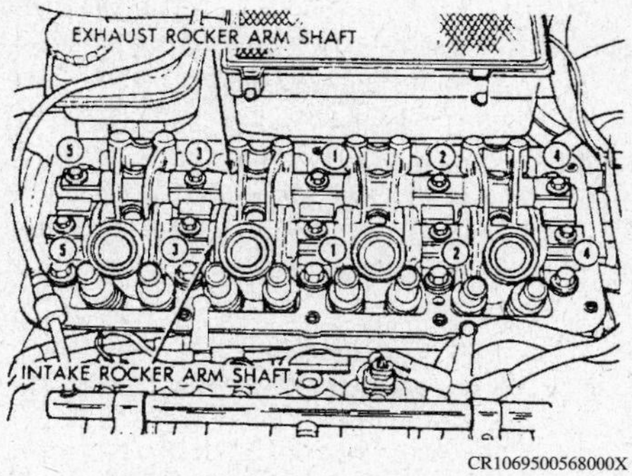

Fig. 13 Rocker arm shaft tightening sequence. 2.0L engine

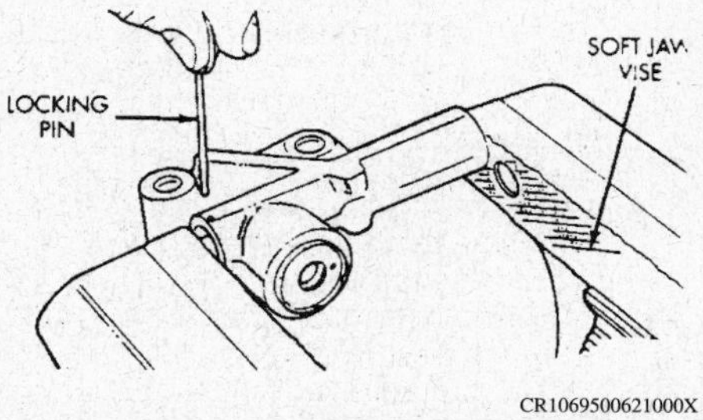

Fig. 16 Timing belt pensioner locking pin installation

belt installation procedure.

13. Install front cover as described under "Front Cover, Replace."
14. **After completing installation, perform camshaft and crankshaft alignment relearn procedure using DRB scan tool and attendant instructions. Failure to perform relearn will set Diagnostic Trouble Code P1390 and illuminate Check Engine lamp.**
15. Inspect valve timing as follows:
    a. Remove No. 1 spark plug from cylinder head.
    b. Using a suitable dial indicator, set No. 1 cylinder at TDC on its compression stroke.
    c. Remove access plug from timing belt front cover.
    d. Timing mark on camshaft sprocket should be aligned with arrow mark on timing belt rear cover, **Fig. 14.**

2.4L ENGINE

Removal

1. Remove timing belt front covers as outlined under " Front Cover, Replace."
2. Align crankshaft and camshaft sprocket timing marks, **Fig. 19.**
3. Position a 6mm hex head wrench to timing belt pensioner pulley and insert a 3mm hex head wrench into pensioner pulley pin hole, **Fig. 20.**
4. With 6mm hex head wrench, rotate pensioner pulley counterclockwise until 3mm hex head wrench can be inserted into locking hole on cylinder block.
5. Remove timing belt.

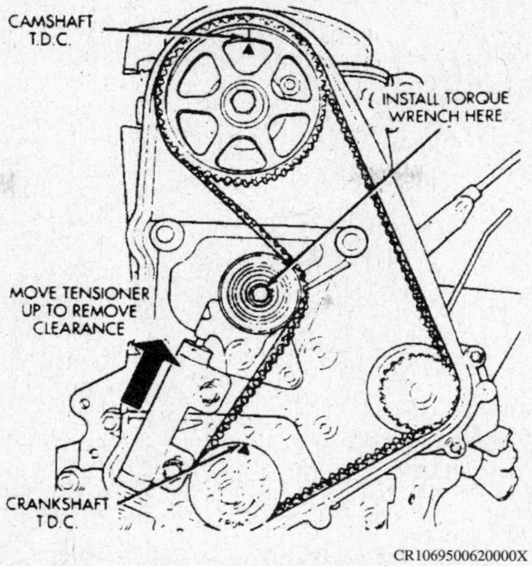

Fig. 14 Crankshaft & camshaft timing mark alignment. 2.0L engine

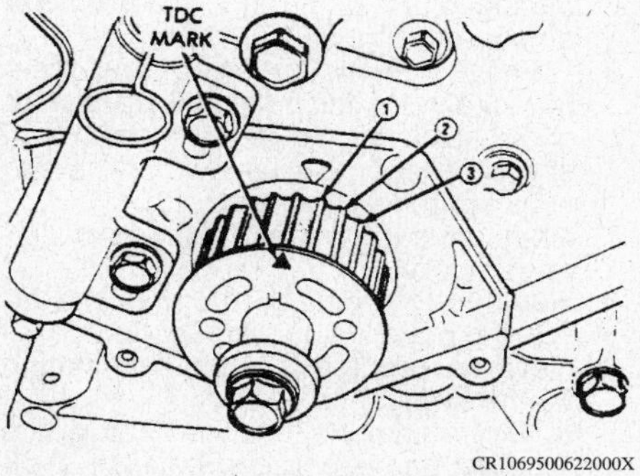

Fig. 17 Crankshaft sprocket & oil pump housing alignment marks. 2.0L engine

Installation

1. Ensure crankshaft sprocket timing mark is aligned.
2. Position camshaft sprockets so the exhaust sprocket is ½ notch below intake sprocket, **Fig. 21.**
3. Install timing belt over crankshaft sprocket, around water pump sprocket, idler pulley, camshaft sprockets and pensioner pulley.
4. Move exhaust camshaft sprocket counterclockwise and align timing marks, to remove slack from belt.
5. Remove 3 mm hex head wrench from cylinder block and pensioner.
6. Rotate crankshaft sprocket two revolutions in normal direction of engine rotation.
7. Ensure all timing marks are aligned, then install front covers as outlined under "Front Cover, Replace."

CAMSHAFT

REPLACE

2.0L ENGINE

1. Relieve fuel system pressure as outlined under " Precautions."
2. Remove valve cover, then mark rocker

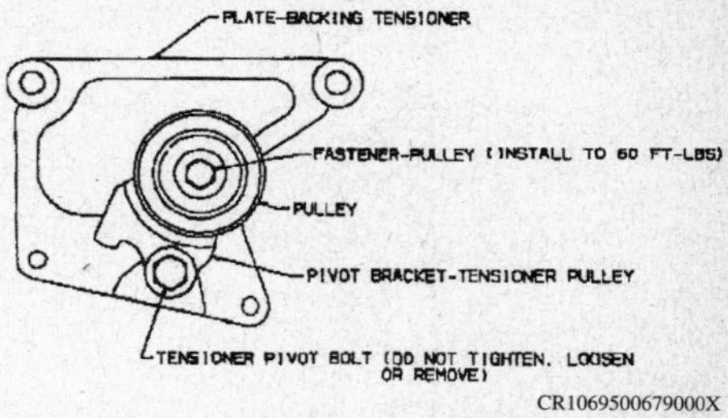

Fig. 15 Pensioner pivot bracket. 2.0L engine

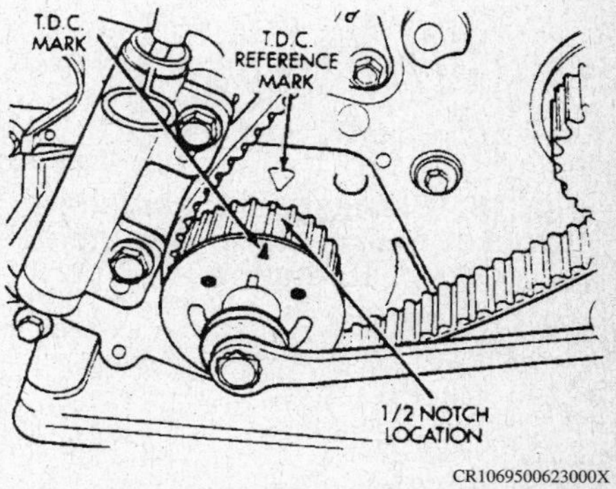

Fig. 18 Crankshaft sprocket ½ tooth rotation

arm shaft assemblies so that they can be installed in their original positions.

3. Remove rocker shaft bolts, then the timing belt front cover and belt as outlined under "Timing Belt, Replace."
4. Remove rear timing belt cover, then the cylinder head as outlined under "Cylinder Head, Replace."
5. Remove camshaft sensor and camshaft target magnet, then the camshaft sprocket bolt.
6. Remove sprocket from camshaft with modified sprocket removal tool No. C-4687-1, or equivalent, **Fig. 22.** Hold camshaft sprocket with modified tool while removing bolt.
7. Remove camshaft seal using camshaft seal remover tool No. C-4679, or equivalent.
8. Remove camshaft from rear of cylinder head.
9. Reverse procedure to install, noting the following:
    a. Install new camshaft seal with seal insertion tool No. MD998306, or equivalent.
    b. Install camshaft sprocket retaining bolt. Hold camshaft sprocket with tool No. C-4687 and adapter tool No. C-4687-1, or equivalents, and tighten to specifications.

2.4L ENGINE

1. Remove valve cover as outlined under "Valve Cover, Replace."
2. Remove timing belt, sprockets and covers as outlined under " Timing Belt, Replace."
3. Bearing caps are identified for location. Remove outside bearing caps L1, R1, L6 and R6 first.

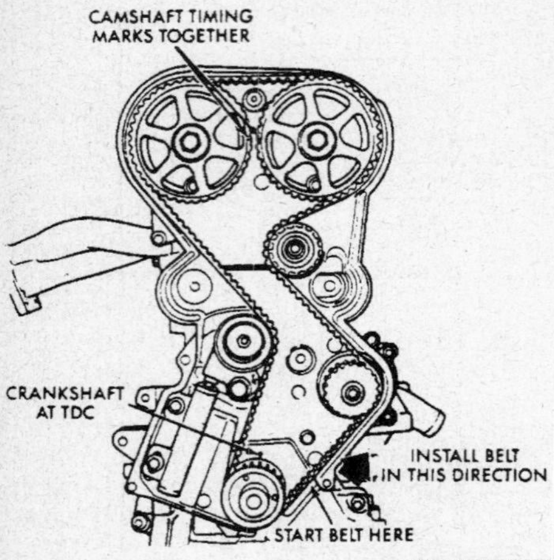

Fig. 19 Crankshaft & camshaft sprocket timing mark alignment. 2.4L engine

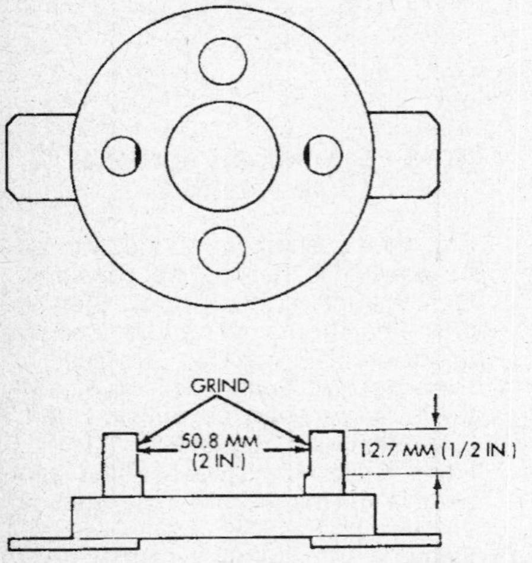

Fig. 22 Sprocket removal tool modification. 2.0L engine

4. Loosen camshaft bearing cap attaching bolts in sequence, **Fig. 23,** one camshaft at a time.
5. Identify camshafts before removing from head. Camshafts are not interchangeable.
6. Reverse procedure to install, noting the following:
   a. Install right and left inside camshaft bearing caps , and R6 outside camshaft bearing cap. **Tighten** caps in sequence, **Fig. 24,** to specifications, one camshaft at a time. **Outside camshaft bearing cap R6, is to be tightened as an inside bearing cap.**
   b. Install outside camshaft bearing caps L1, R1 and L6, tighten to specifications.

BALANCE SHAFT

REPLACE

2.4L ENGINE

1. Remove timing belt front cover as outlined under " Front Cover, Replace."

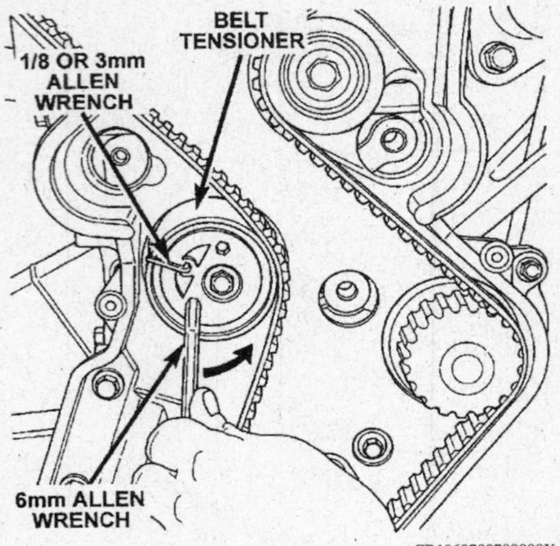

Fig. 20 Locking timing belt pensioner in release position. 2.4L engine

2. Remove gear cover double ended retaining stud, gear and chain covers and gears, **Fig. 25.**
3. Remove balance shaft gear and chain sprocket retaining bolts and crankshaft chain sprocket. To remove chain and sprocket assembly, use two pry bars to work sprocket back and forth.
4. Remove carrier rear cover and balance shafts.
5. Remove four carrier to crankcase attaching bolts to separate carrier.
6. Reverse procedure to install, noting the following:
   a. Dot marks on balance shaft gears must be aligned and balance shaft keys must face upward, **Fig. 26.**
   b. Balance shaft timing chain and gear timing marks must be aligned as shown in **Fig. 27.**
   c. When adjusting balance shaft timing chain tension, position a shim .039 inch thick by 2.75 inches long between pensioner and chain. Push pensioner and shim against timing chain with a force of 5.5–6.6 lbs., **Fig. 28.** With force applied to timing chain, tighten top pensioner bolt, then bottom pensioner bolt to specifications.

PISTON & ROD ASSEMBLY

The L or H stamping on the front portion of the piston must face toward the front of the engine. The connecting rod and cap are stamped on the side with a cylinder number identification. The numbered side of the connecting rod cap must be installed on the same side as the numbered side of the rod. When installing cap bolts, **torque** to 20 ft. lbs., then tighten an additional ¼ turn.

MAIN & ROD BEARINGS

2.0L ENGINE

Main and rod bearings are available in the standard size and in undersides of .025

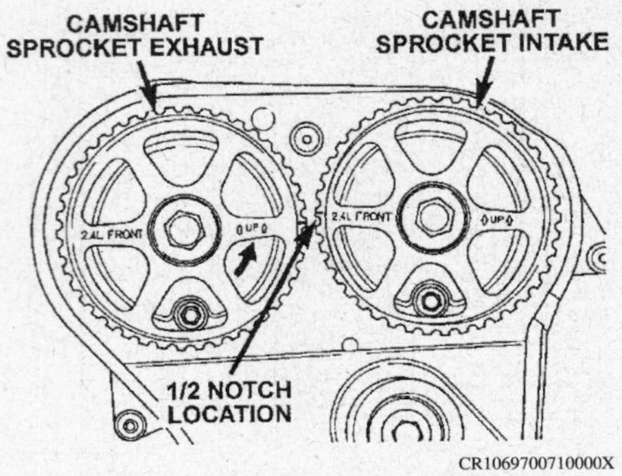

Fig. 21 Camshaft sprocket alignment. 2.4L engine

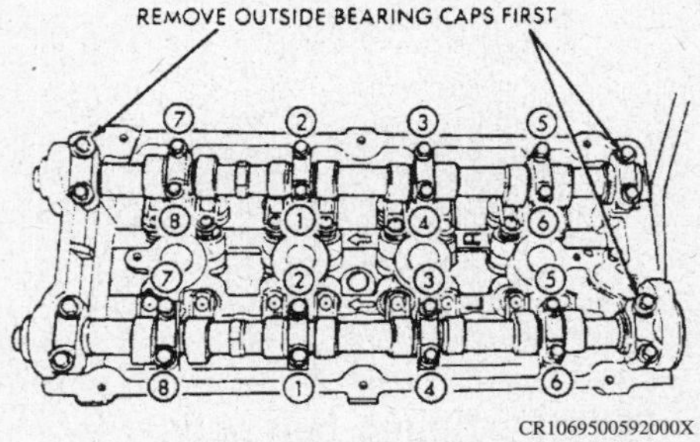

Fig. 23 Camshaft bearing cap removal

mm and .250 mm. **Torque** main bearing M8 cap bolts to 22–25 ft. lbs. and M11 bolts to 60 ft. lbs.

2.4L ENGINE

Main and rod bearings are available in the standard size and in undersides of .001, .002, .010, .011 and .012 inch. **Torque** main bearing M8 cap bolts to 20–21 ft. lbs. and M11 bolts to 30 ft. lbs. plus an additional ¼ turn.

CRANKSHAFT SEAL

REPLACE

1. Remove components to access crankshaft sprocket as outlined under "Timing Belt, Replace."
2. Remove crankshaft sprocket using sprocket remover tool No. 6793 and insert tool No. C-4685-C2, or equivalents, **Fig. 29.**
3. Remove seal using oil seal remover tool No. 6771, or equivalent, to remove front crankshaft oil seal, **Fig. 30.**
4. Reverse procedure to install, noting the following:
   a. Install new seal using seal installation tool No. 6780-1, or equivalent.
   b. Install crankshaft sprocket using tool No. 6792, or equivalent.

CRANKSHAFT REAR OIL SEAL

REPLACE

1. With transvalue separated from engine, pry out rear seal with screwdriver. Do not nick or damage crankshaft flange seal surface or retainer bore.

ACCESSORY DRIVE BELT		GAUGE
2.0/2.4L ENGINE		
AIR CONDITIONING COMPRESSOR/GENERATOR	NEW	150 LB.
	USED	80 LB.
POWER STEERING PUMP	NEW	130 LB.
	USED	80 LB.
2.5L ENGINE		
AIR CONDITIONING COMPRESSOR/GENERATOR	NEW	150 LB.
	USED	80 LB.
POWER STEERING PUMP	NEW	130 LB.
	USED	80 LB.

CR1089500140000X

Fig. 31 Belt tension chart. 1997

Accessory Drive Belts	Gauge
2.0/2.4/2.5L Engines	
Air Conditioning Compressor & Generator	NEW BELT: 150 LB.
Power Steering Pump	USED BELT: 90 LB.

CR1089800195000X

Fig. 32 Belt tension chart. 1998–2000

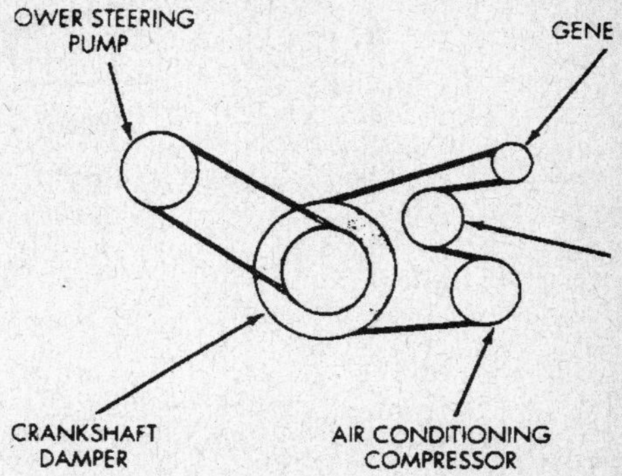

Fig. 33 Serpentine drive belt routing

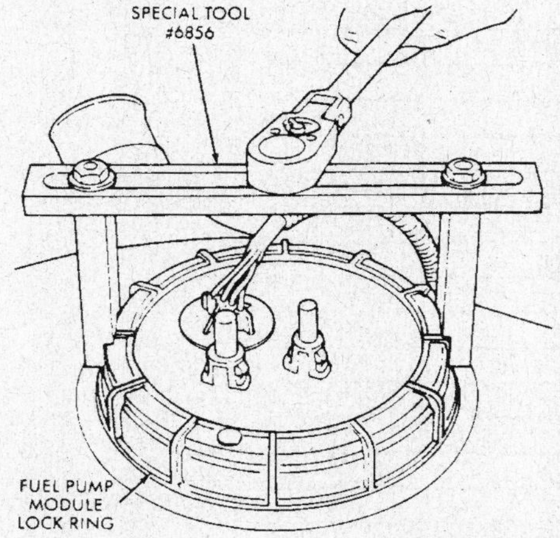

Fig. 34 Fuel pump module lockout

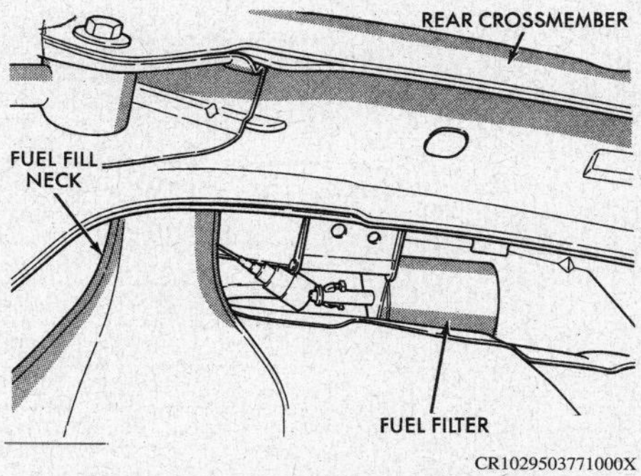

Fig. 35 Fuel filter location

5. Disconnect and plug automatic transvalue hoses at cooler.
6. Disconnect fan electrical connector.
7. Remove air conditioning condenser attaching screws located at front of radiator, if equipped.
8. Remove radiator from engine compartment by lifting upward.
9. Reverse procedure to install.

FUEL PUMP

REPLACE

The electric fuel pump is not serviceable. If the fuel pump requires service, the entire fuel pump module must be replaced.

1. Relieve fuel system pressure as outlined under " Precautions."
2. Drain and remove fuel tank.
3. Disconnect fuel filter lines at fuel pump module.
4. Clean top of tank to remove dirt and debris.
5. Remove lockout securing pump module with fuel pump module ring spanner tool No. 6856, or equivalent, **Fig. 34.**
6. Remove fuel pump module and Oaring from tank, then discard Oaring.
7. Reverse procedure to install, noting the following:
   a. Install new pump module Oaring.
   b. Tighten fuel pump module lock ring to specifications.

FUEL FILTER

REPLACE

1. Release fuel system pressure as outlined under " Precautions."
2. From inside trunk, disconnect fuel pump module wiring jumper from main body harness. Connector is located under leftward side of trunk mat, near base of shock tower.
3. Locate body grommet for jumper near base of rear seat and push grommet out, then feed jumper through hole in body.
4. Raise and support vehicle.
5. Position a suitable fuel container with a capacity of at least 16 gallons, under drain plug located on bottom left edge of tank.
6. Remove drain plug and allow fuel to drain.
7. When tank stops draining, install drain plug and tighten to specifications.
8. Remove driver's side fuel tank strap and loosen, but do not remove, passenger's side fuel tank strap, allowing fuel tank fill neck to touch rear suspension crossover.
9. Disconnect fuel lines from fuel pump module. These are quick connect fittings located on top of tank.
10. Disconnect fuel supply line from fuel brake module.
11. Remove fuel filter, **Fig. 35.**
12. Reverse procedure to install.

TIGHTENING SPECIFICATIONS

Year	Component	Torque/ Ft. Lbs.
1997–2000	Balance Shaft Timing Chain Pensioner (2.4L)	96–108⑤
	Camshaft Sprocket Bolt (2.0L)	85
	Camshaft Sprocket Bolt (2.4L)	75
	Connecting Rod Cap Bolt	②
	Coolant Outlet To Cylinder Head	108⑤
	Crankshaft Damper Bolt (2.0L)	105
	Crankshaft Pulley Bolt (2.4L)	100
	Cylinder Head	①
	EGR Tube	84–96⑤
	Engine Cradle Through Bolts	45
	Engine Mount Bracket	30
	Engine Mounts	③
	Exhaust Flange	20–21
	Exhaust Manifold Heat Shield	96–108⑤
	Exhaust Manifold To Cylinder Head	16–17
	Fuel Pump Module Lock Ring	40
	Fuel Rail To Intake Manifold	16–17
	Fuel Tank Drain Plug	32⑤
	Inside Camshaft Bearing Caps (2.4L)	10
	Intake Manifold (2.0L)	96–108⑤
	Intake Manifold (2.4L)	20
	Main Bearing Cap Bolts	④
	Oil Filter	15
	Oil Filter Adapter To Engine	40
	Oil Pan Drain Plug	25
	Oil Pan To Engine Block	96–108⑤
	Oil Pump Cover	96–108⑤
	Oil Pump Mounting Bolts	20
	Oil Pump Pickup Tube Screw	20
	Oil Pump Relief Valve Retaining Cap (2.0L)	30
	Oil Pump Relief Valve Retaining Cap (2.4L)	40
	Outside Camshaft Bearing Caps (2.4L)	21
	Rocker Arm And Shaft Assembly (2.0L)	20–21
	Serpentine Belt bolt	40
	Spark Plugs	20
	Thermostat Housing Bolts	16–17
	Throttle Body Support Bracket	96–108⑤
	Throttle Body To Intake	15–16
	Timing Belt Pensioner (2.0L)	23
	Timing Belt Pensioner (2.4L)	20
	Timing Belt Pensioner Pulley (2.4L)	30
	Valve Cover (2.0L)	96–108⑤
	Valve Cover (2.4L)	⑥
	Water Pump	96–108⑤

① — Refer to "Cylinder Head, Replace" for tightening procedure & specifications.

② — Refer to "Piston & Rod Assembly" for tightening procedure & specifications.

③ — Refer to "Engine Mount, Replace" illustrations for tightening specifications.

④ — Refer to "Main & Rod Bearings" for tightening procedure & specifications.

⑤ — Inch lbs.

⑥ — Refer to "Valve Cover, Replace" for tightening procedure & specifications.

2.5L Engine

NOTE: Refer To "Air Bag System Precautions " Located In The Front Of This Manual For System Disarming & Arming Procedures.

NOTE: Refer To "Computer Relearn" Located In The Front Of This Manual For Computer Relearn Procedures.

INDEX

PRECAUTIONS

AIR BAG SYSTEMS

Refer to "Air Bag System Precautions" in the front of this manual for system disarming and arming procedures.

BATTERY GROUND CABLE

Prior to service, disconnect battery ground cable and isolate as required.

FUEL SYSTEM PRESSURE RELIEF

1. Disconnect fuel rail electrical harness from engine harness.
2. Connect suitable jumper wire between fuel rail harness connector terminal A142 and 12 volt power source.
3. Connect another suitable jumper wire to ground source, then momentarily ground one injector harness connector terminal, to release fuel system pressure.
4. Repeat procedure for two to three injectors.

COMPRESSION PRESSURE

Compression pressure should be 178 psi at 250 RPM with no more than a 14 psi variation in pressure between cylinders.

ENGINE MOUNT

REPLACE

RIGHT SIDE MOUNT

1. Raise and support vehicle, then remove the inner splash.

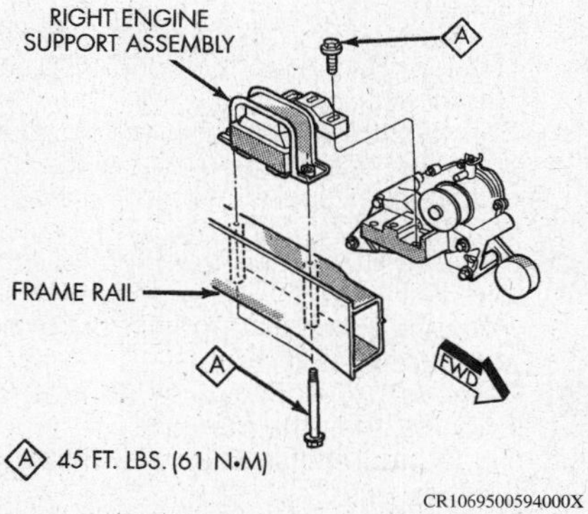

Fig. 1 Right side engine mount replacement

2. Remove right engine support assembly attaching bolts from frame rail, **Fig. 1.**
3. Lower vehicle and support engine assembly with floor jack to remove pressure on motor mounts.
4. Remove three engine support to engine bracket attaching bolts.
5. Reverse procedure to install. Tighten attaching nuts and bolts to specifications shown in **Fig. 1.**

ENGINE CRADLE (SUPPORT MODULE)

1. Raise and support vehicle, then remove rear mount through bolt and bolts securing cradle to crossover, **Fig. 3.**
2. Remove rear support strut bracket upper bolt and bolts securing cradle to lower radiator support.
3. With cooling module supported, remove lower radiator support.
4. Remove front through bolt, then the cradle.
5. Reverse procedure to install, noting the following:
   a. Do not tighten front through bolt until rear through bolt is installed and tightened.
   b. Tighten bolts to specifications.

ENGINE

REPLACE

1. Relieve fuel system pressure as outlined under " Precautions."
2. Disconnect and remove battery and tray, then disconnect Pertain Control Module (PCM) electrical connector and position aside.
3. Drain coolant into a suitable container.
4. Remove upper radiator hose, fan module and radiator as outlined under "Radiator, Replace."
5. Remove lower radiator hose.
6. **On models equipped with manual transvalue,** disconnect clutch cable and shift linkage.
7. **On models equipped with automatic transvalue,** disconnect and plug transvalue cooler line.
8. **On all models,** disconnect throttle body linkage.
9. Disconnect engine wiring harness electrical connectors.
10. Disconnect heater hoses.
11. Recover A/C refrigerant as outlined in "Air Conditioning " section.
12. Raise and support vehicle, then remove the right inner splash shield.

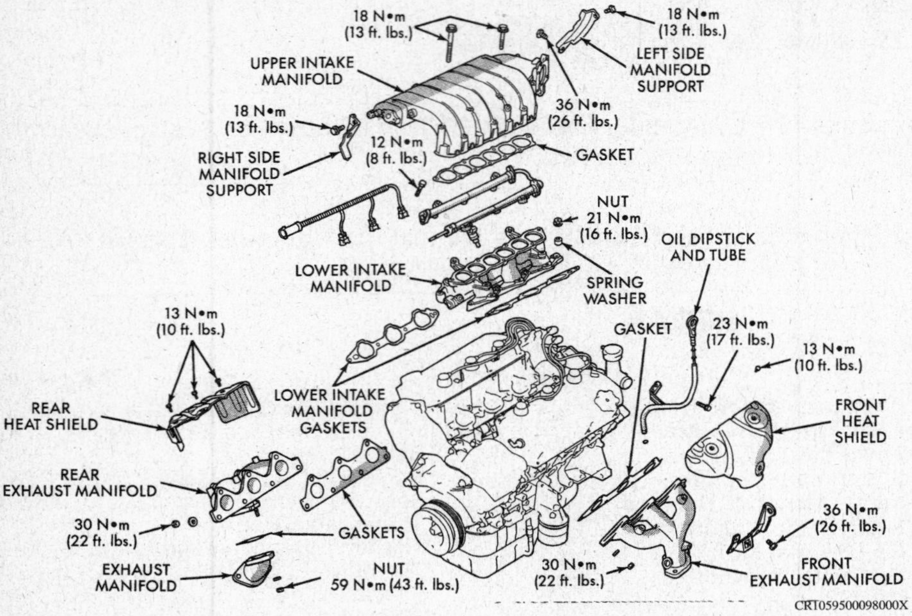

Fig. 2 Exploded view of intake & exhaust manifolds

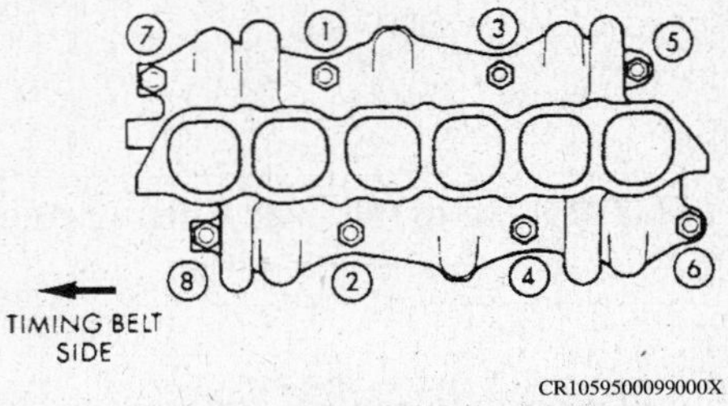

Fig. 3 Intake manifold bolt tightening sequence

13. Remove accessory drive belts.
14. Remove axle shafts.
15. Disconnect exhaust pipe from manifold.
16. Remove front and rear engine mount bracket from the body.
17. Lower vehicle, then remove the air cleaner assembly.
18. Remove power steering pump and reservoir.
19. Remove A/C compressor.
20. Remove ground straps to body.
21. Raise and support vehicle to install engine dolly and cradle tool Nos. 6135 and 6710, or equivalents.
22. Loosen engine cradle mounts to position engine locating holes in belated, then lower the vehicle until engine rests on cradle mounts and tighten mounts to cradle frame to prevent mount movement.
23. Lower vehicle so weight of engine and transvalue is only on cradle.
24. Remove engine and transvalue mount attaching bolts.
25. Slowly raise and support vehicle, move engine and transvalue assembly on cradle to allow for removal around body flanges as required.
26. Reverse procedure to install.

INTAKE MANIFOLD

REPLACE

1. Relieve fuel system pressure as outlined under " Precautions."
2. Disconnect fuel supply tube from rail, using a towel to catch any gasoline spillage.
3. Disconnect Manifold Absolute Pressure (MAP) and Intake Air Temperature (IAT) sensor electrical connectors.
4. Remove plenum support bracket bolt, located rearward of MAP sensor, **Fig. 2.**
5. Remove air inlet resonator to intake manifold bolt.
6. Loosen throttle body air inlet hose clamp, release snaps holding air cleaner housing cover to housing, then remove the air cleaner cover and inlet hoses.
7. Disconnect Throttle Position Sensor (TPS) and Idle Air Control (IAC) motor electrical connectors.
8. Depress throttle cable retainer tab and pull cable rearward out of bracket, then repeat for speed control cable, if equipped.
9. Remove EGR tube from intake manifold.
10. Remove plenum support bracket bolt, rearward of EGR tube.
11. Remove upper intake plenum attaching bolts, then the plenum.
12. Disconnect fuel injector electrical connectors.
13. Remove four fuel rail attaching bolts and spacers, then the fuel rail.
14. Remove lower intake manifold attaching bolts, then the intake manifold.
15. Reverse procedure to install, noting the following:
    a. Clean all mating surfaces, then inspect for cracked or distorted manifold and torn or missing Rings.
    b. Install intake manifold with new gaskets and install intake manifold onto cylinder head tightening to specifications in sequence shown in **Fig. 3.**
    c. Tighten attaching nuts and bolts to specifications.

EXHAUST MANIFOLD

REPLACE

1. Raise and support vehicle.
2. Disconnect exhaust pipe from rear exhaust manifold at flex joint. It may be necessary to remove entire exhaust system.
3. Remove crossover pipe to manifold attaching bolts, then remove assembly.
4. **On 1997 models,** disconnect oxygen sensor lead wire at rear exhaust manifold.
5. **On all models,** remove power steering pump bracket.
6. Remove rear manifold to cylinder head attaching nuts, then the manifold.
7. Lower vehicle, then remove front heat shield to manifold attaching screws.
8. **On 1997 models,** disconnect front heated oxygen sensor.
9. **On all models,** remove front manifold attaching nuts, then the manifold.
10. Reverse procedure to install, noting the following:
    a. Install new manifold gaskets.
    b. Tighten all attaching bolts and nuts to specifications.

CYLINDER HEAD

REPLACE

1. Relieve fuel system pressure as outlined under " Precautions," then drain cooling system.
2. Remove camshaft sprockets as outlined under " Timing Belt, Replace."
3. Remove rocker arms as outlined under " Rocker Arms, Replace."
4. Remove upper intake manifold assembly as outlined under " Intake Manifold, Replace."
5. Remove distributor as outlined in "Electrical" section.
6. Remove exhaust manifolds and crossover pipe as outlined under "Exhaust Manifold, Replace."
7. Remove cylinder head bolts and cylinder head.
8. Reverse procedure to install. Using sequence shown in **Fig. 4, torque** cylinder head bolts gradually in two or three steps to 80 ft. lbs.

VALVE COVER

REPLACE

1. Remove intake plenum as outlined under "Intake Manifold, Replace."
2. Cover lower intake manifold, then disconnect spark plug wires and position aside.
3. Remove bolts, then the valve cover.
4. Reverse procedure to install, noting the following:
    a. Install a new valve cover gasket.
    b. Tighten bolts to specifications.

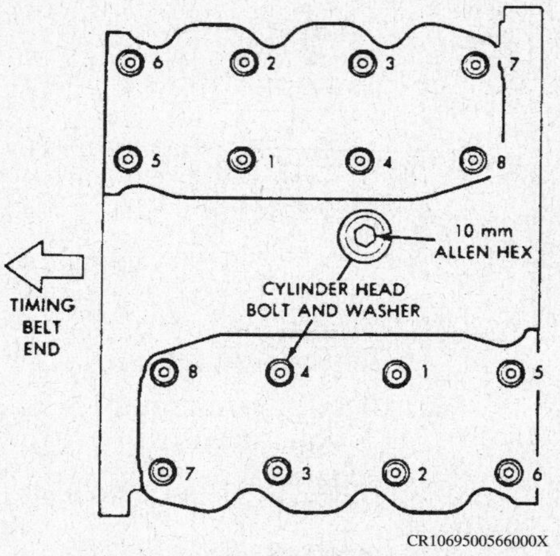

Fig. 4 Cylinder head bolt tightening sequence

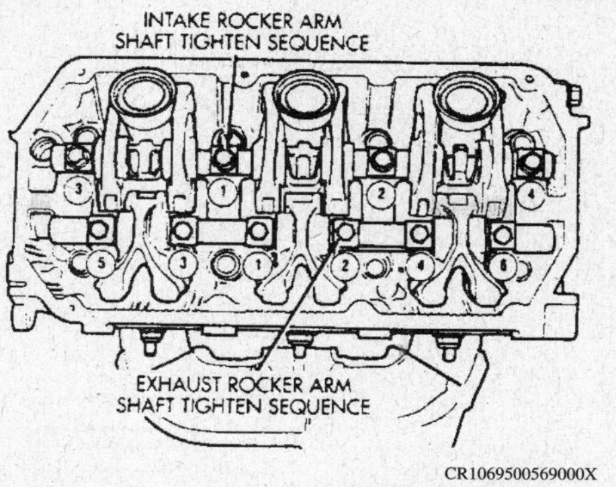

Fig. 5 Rocker arm shaft tightening sequence

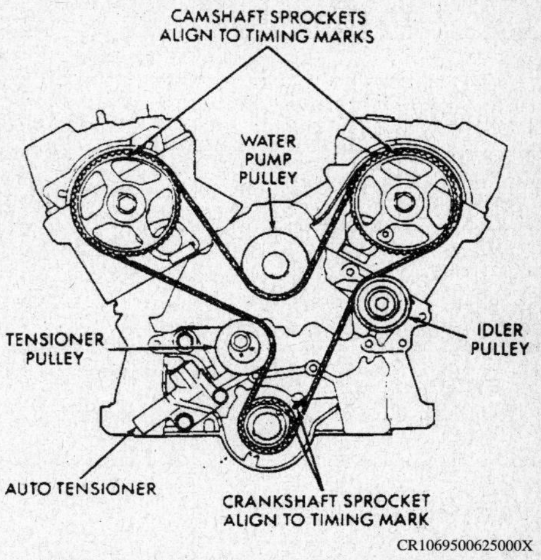

Fig. 6 Crankshaft & camshaft sprocket mark alignment

VALVE ARRANGEMENT

Intake valves are located on upper sides of cylinder heads and exhaust valves are on lower sides of cylinder heads.

VALVE CLEARANCE SPECIFICATIONS

These engines are equipped with hydraulic lash adjusters designed to maintain zero lash at all times.

ROCKER ARMS

REPLACE

1. Remove valve covers as outlined under "Valve Cover, Replace."
2. Identify rocker arm shaft assemblies before removal.
3. Install auto lash adjuster retainer tool No. MD998443, or equivalent. These retainers hold lash adjuster into position when rocker arms are serviced.
4. Remove rocker arm bolts and shaft assemblies.
5. Reverse procedure to install, noting the following:
   a. Install rocker arm and shaft assemblies with flat spot in rocker arm shafts facing toward timing belt side of engine for right cylinder head. For left cylinder head, install rocker arm and shaft assemblies with flat spot in rocker arm shafts facing toward transvalue side of engine. Install retainers and spring clips in their original positions on exhaust and intake shafts.
   b. Tighten bolts to specifications in sequence shown, **Fig. 5.**
   c. Remove lash adjuster retainers from rocker arms.

FRONT COVER

REPLACE

1. Remove radiator as outlined under "Radiator, Replace."
2. Remove right inner splash shield.
3. Remove accessory drive belts.

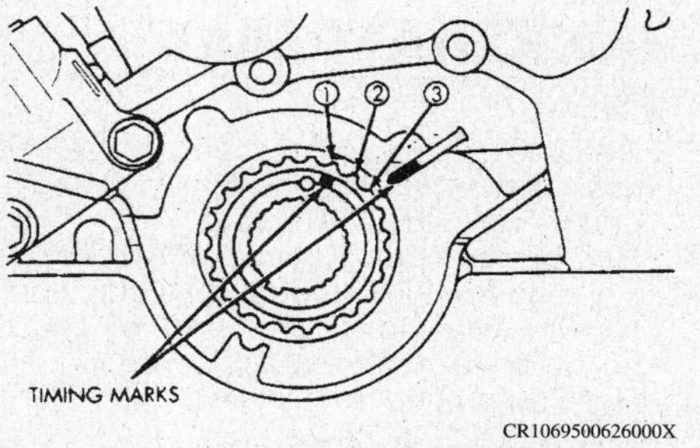

Fig. 7 Crankshaft sprocket teeth & mark location

4. Remove right engine mount as outlined under "Engine Mount, Replace."
5. Remove crankshaft damper.
6. Remove engine mount bracket.
7. Remove timing belt upper left cover, then upper right cover and, finally, lower cover.
8. Reverse procedure to install.

TIMING BELT

REPLACE

REMOVAL

1. Remove timing belt front cover as outlined under " Front Cover, Replace."
2. Align crankshaft and camshaft sprocket marks, **Fig. 6,** then loosen timing belt pensioner attaching bolts.
3. Remove timing belt and pensioner. If timing belt is to be reused, mark running direction for installation reference.
4. Inspect timing belt for cracks, missing teeth, hardened rubber and abnormal wear.

INSTALLATION

1. Position timing belt pensioner in a soft jawed vise, then slowly compress pensioner plunger into pensioner body.
2. With pensioner plunger compressed into body, insert a suitable locking pin through holes in pensioner body, **Fig. 16.** This will hold plunger in position until after pensioner has been installed on engine.
3. Align mark on crankshaft sprocket with arrow mark on oil pump housing, then back off to three sprocket teeth before Top Dead Center (TDC), **Fig. 7.**
4. Align camshaft sprocket marks with marks on valve covers, **Fig. 6.**
5. Install timing belt as follows:
   a. Position timing belt over rear camshaft sprocket. Use a binder clip to secure timing belt to camshaft sprocket.
   b. With timing belt held taut, install belt under water pump pulley, then over front camshaft sprocket. Use a binder clip to secure timing belt to camshaft sprocket.
   c. Align crankshaft sprocket TDC mark with mark on oil pump cover, **Fig. 6.**
   d. Install timing belt over idler pulley, crankshaft sprocket and pensioner pulley.
6. Apply rotating force in clockwise direction to crankshaft sprocket to remove timing belt slack. Ensure timing marks are aligned, **Fig. 6.**
7. Using a suitable torque wrench and torque wrench tool No. MD998767, or equivalent, apply a force of 39 inch lbs. to timing belt pensioner pulley, then **torque** pensioner pulley bolt to 35 ft. lbs.
8. With force still upon pensioner pulley, install timing belt pensioner to pensioner pulley bracket. **Torque** attaching bolts to 23 ft. lbs.
9. Remove locking pin retaining pensioner plunger in body.
10. Rotate crankshaft two revolutions in clockwise direction, then check camshaft and crankshaft sprocket mark alignment, **Fig. 6,** and ensure locking pin slides freely through pensioner body holes. If camshaft and crankshaft sprocket marks are not properly aligned and/or locking pin cannot slide freely through pensioner holes, repeat procedure.
11. Install front cover as outlined under "Front Cover, Replace."

CAMSHAFT

REPLACE

1. Remove timing belt, sprockets and

MAIN JOURNAL

SIZE	NEW	CURRENT
59.543 to 59.695 mm (2.344 to 2.350 in.)	2	WHITE ENAMEL
59.695 to 59.848 mm (2.350 to 2.356 in.)	1	NONE
59.848 to 60.000 mm (2.356 to 2.362 in.)	0	YELLOW ENAMEL

CONNECTING ROD JOURNAL

SIZE	NEW	CURRENT
49.492 to 49.619 mm (1.949 to 1.954 in.)	III	WHITE ENAMEL
49.619 to 49.873 mm (1.954 to 1.964 in.)	II	NONE
49.873 to 50.000 mm (1.964 to 1.969 in.)	I	YELLOW ENAMEL

CR1069500678000X

Fig. 8 Crankshaft journal markings

covers as outlined under "Timing Belt, Replace."

2. Remove valve covers as outlined under "Valve Cover, Replace."
3. Attach auto lash adjuster retainer tool No. MD998443, or equivalent.
4. Mark rocker arm shaft assemblies for installation reference.
5. Remove rocker arm shaft bolts as outlined under "Rocker Arms, Replace."
6. Remove cylinder head as outlined under "Cylinder Head, Replace."
7. Remove thrust case from left head assembly and camshaft from rear of head.
8. Remove distributor from right head assembly and camshaft from rear of head.
9. Reverse procedure to install. Tighten thrust case and camshaft sprocket to specifications.

PISTON & ROD ASSEMBLY

The pistons are stamped with a letter and an arrow. Pistons stamped "R" are installed in cylinders 1, 3 and 5; pistons stamped "L" are installed in cylinders 2, 4 and 6. When a piston is installed in the engine, its arrow mark must face the front of the engine. The connecting rod and cap are stamped on the side with a cylinder number identification. The numbered side of the connecting rod cap must be installed on the same side as the numbered side of the rod.

MAIN & ROD BEARINGS

Service replacement parts carry identification marks, but factory parts are unmarked. The crankshaft journal markings, **Fig. 8,** may aid in the selection of bearings.

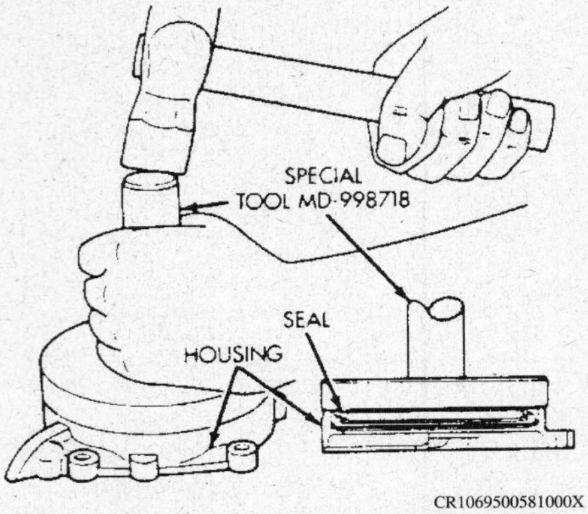

CR1069500581000X

Fig. 9 Rear oil seal installation

CRANKSHAFT SEAL

REPLACE

1. Remove components necessary to access crankshaft sprocket as outlined under "Timing Belt, Replace."
2. Remove crankshaft sprocket and key.
3. Pry out front oil seal with a flat tip screwdriver. **Cover the end of the screwdriver with a shop towel.**
4. Reverse procedure to install.

CRANKSHAFT REAR OIL SEAL

REPLACE

After the crankshaft rear oil seal housing and old seal have been removed, a new rear oil seal can be installed with seal installation tool No. MD998718, or equivalent, **Fig. 9.** Apply Molar silicon rubber adhesive sealant, or equivalent, to the oil seal housing and a light coating of engine oil to the entire circumference of the oil seal lip. Tighten bolts to specifications.

OIL PAN

REPLACE

1. Disconnect ground cable from remote battery jumper terminal.
2. Drain engine oil into a suitable container.
3. Remove dipstick tube, then the starter as outlined in "Electrical" section.
4. Remove engine to transvalue struts, then the transvalue inspection cover.
5. Remove oil pan attaching bolts, then the oil pan.
6. Clean oil pan and cylinder block gasket surfaces.
7. Reverse procedure to install, noting the following:
   a. Apply Molar silicone rubber adhesive sealant, or equivalent, as shown, **Fig. 10.**
   b. Tighten pan bolts to specifications.

OIL PUMP

REPLACE

1. Remove components to access oil pump as outlined under "Timing Belt, Replace."

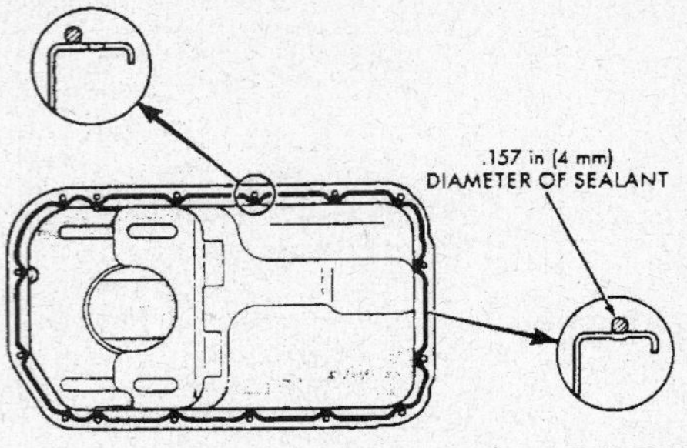

CR1069500578000X

Fig. 10 Oil pan sealant application

2. Remove oil pump attaching bolts, then the pump.
3. Reverse procedure to install. Tighten attaching bolts to specifications.

OIL PUMP SERVICE

DISASSEMBLE & INSPECTION

1. Inspect oil pump case for damage and remove rear cover.
2. Remove pump rotors and inspect case for excessive wear.
3. Insert rotor into oil pump case and measure clearance, **Figs. 11 and 12.**
4. Replace if out of specifications.

ASSEMBLE

1. Clean block and pump surfaces.
2. Assemble pump using new parts as required; lubricate with clean oil. Align marks on inner and outer rotors when assembling.
3. Install cover and tighten to specifications.
4. Install relief valve, spring, gasket and cap and tighten to specifications.
5. Prime oil pump before installation by filling rotor cavity with clean engine oil.

BELT TENSION DATA

Refer to **Figs. 31 and 32** for belt tension data.

SERPENTINE DRIVE BELT

Refer to "2.0L & 2.4L Engines" section for serpentine drive belt.

COOLING SYSTEM BLEED

Refer to "2.0L & 2.4L Engines" section for cooling system bleed procedure.

THERMOSTAT

REPLACE

Refer to "2.0L & 2.4L Engines" section for thermostat replacement procedure.

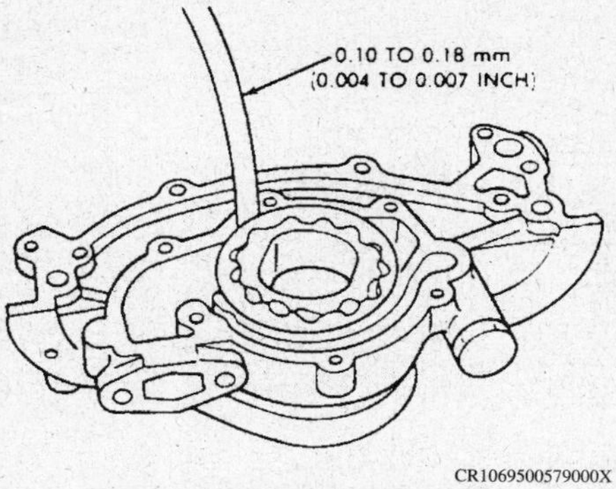

Fig. 11 Outer rotor & case clearance inspection

WATER PUMP

REPLACE

1. Remove timing belt as outlined under "Timing Belt, Replace."
2. Drain coolant into a suitable container.
3. Remove mounting bolts.
4. Separate pump from water inlet pipe and remove water pump.
5. Reverse procedure to install, noting the following:
   a. Inspect pump for cracks or leaks and replace if necessary.
   b. Install new water pipe Oaring and pump gasket.
   c. Tighten water pump mounting bolts to specifications.
   d. Fill and bleed cooling system as necessary.

RADIATOR

REPLACE

1. Remove air inlet resonator, then drain coolant into a suitable container.
2. Remove upper radiator crossover.
3. Remove hose clamps and hoses from radiator.
4. Disconnect engine block heater electrical wire, if equipped.
5. Disconnect and plug automatic transvalue hoses at cooler.
6. Disconnect fan electrical connector.
7. Remove air conditioning condenser attaching screws located at front of radiator, if equipped.
8. Remove radiator from engine compartment by lifting upward.
9. Reverse procedure to install.

FUEL PUMP

REPLACE

The electric fuel pump is not serviceable.

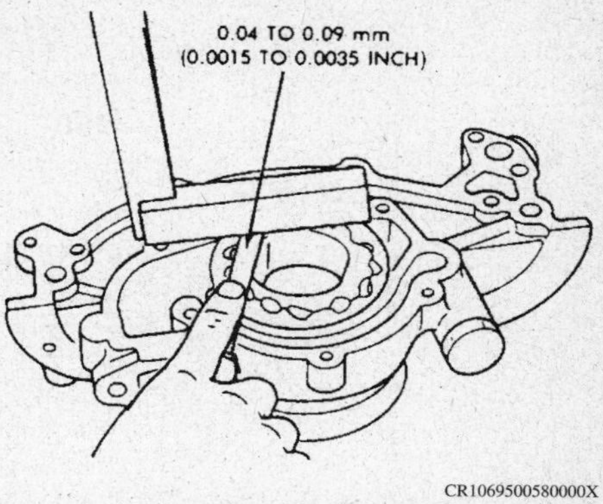

Fig. 12 Rotor end clearance inspection

If the fuel pump requires service, the entire fuel pump module must be replaced.

Refer to "2.0L & 2.4L Engines" section for fuel pump replacement procedure.

FUEL FILTER

REPLACE

Refer to "2.0L & 2.4L Engines" section for fuel filter replacement procedure.

TIGHTENING SPECIFICATIONS

Year	Component	Torque/ Ft. Lbs.
1997–2000	Air Intake Plenum	12–13
	Auto Pensioner Bolt	17
	Band Clamp	60
	Camshaft Sprocket	65
	Connecting Rod Cap Nut	37
	Coolant Inlet Elbow	96–108②
	Crankshaft Bolt	134
	Crankshaft Rear Oil Seal Retainer	96–108②
	Crossover	22
	Cylinder Head	①
	Engine Cradle Through Bolts	45
	Engine Support Bracket	33
	Exhaust Manifold	22
	Fuel Pump Module Lock Ring	40
	Fuel Tank Drain Plug	32②
	Heater Pipe Assembly	13
	Idler Pulley Bolt	33
	Intake Manifold	16
	Main Bearing Cap Bolts	69
	Oil Filter	10
	Oil Pan	48②
	Oil Pan Drain Plug	25
	Oil Pump Cover	84②
	Oil Pump Relief Valve Cap	30
	Oil Pump To Engine Block	17–19
	Oil Screen	13
	Rocker Arm And Shaft Assembly	16–17
	Serpentine Belt bolt	40
	Spark Plugs	18
	Pensioner Arm Assembly	33
	Pensioner Pulley Bolt	35
	Thermostat Housing	13
	Thrust Case	85
	Valve Cover	96–108②
	Water Inlet Pipe	10
	Water Pump	17

① — Refer to "Cylinder Head, Replace" for tightening procedure & specifications.

② — Inch lbs.

Clutch & Manual Transaxle

INDEX

PRECAUTIONS

AIR BAG SYSTEMS

Refer to "Air Bag System Precautions" in the front of this manual for system disarming and arming procedures.

BATTERY GROUND CABLE

Prior to service, disconnect battery ground cable and isolate as required.

ADJUSTMENTS

The clutch cable has a self-adjusting mechanism built into the cable which compensates for clutch disc wear. The cable requires no maintenance or lubrication and is not adjustable.

HYDRAULIC SYSTEM SERVICE

CLUTCH SYSTEM BLEED

The clutch hydraulic system must be bled whenever the system has been opened for any reason or when performance is not satisfactory.

1. Connect a clear plastic hose to slave cylinder bleeder screw valve and submerge other end of hose in a clear container of clean DOT 3 brake fluid.
2. With parking brake applied, pump clutch pedal several times, then fully release.
3. Open bleeder valve, then depress clutch pedal to floor and hold.
4. Close bleeder valve, then release pedal.
5. Repeat procedure until bubbles can no longer be seen emerging from bleeder valve. **Keep clutch master cylinder full of clean DOT 3 brake fluid.**
6. Ensure bleeder valve is closed, then inspect clutch operation.

CLUTCH

REPLACE

The modular clutch assembly used in these models consists of a single dry-type clutch disc and a diaphragm style clutch cover. The clutch assembly is serviced as a unit and cannot be disassembled.

1. Raise and support vehicle.
2. Remove starter wiring, then the starter assembly.
3. Remove transvalue as outlined under "Transvalue, Replace."

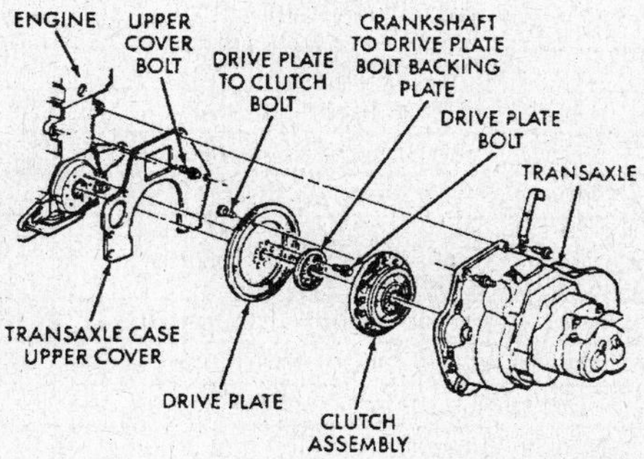

CR5049500082000X

Fig. 1 Exploded view of clutch assembly

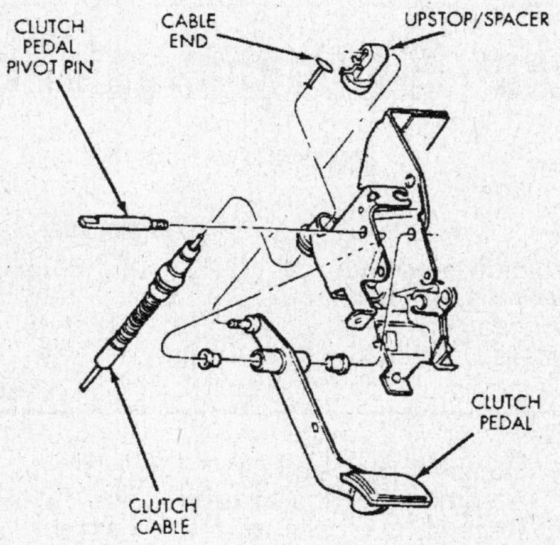

CR5049500084000X

Fig. 3 Clutch cable end separation from pedal assembly

4. Remove modular clutch assembly from transvalue input shaft, **Fig. 1. Handle carefully to avoid contaminating friction surfaces.**
5. Reverse procedure to install, noting the following:
   a. Install driveled mounting bolts in a crisscross pattern until all bolts are seated.
   b. Tighten bolts to specifications using same crisscross pattern.

SHIFT CABLE

REPLACE

1. Pull up and remove Power Distribution Center (PDC).
2. Remove air cleaner assembly, then the clutch cable inspection cover.

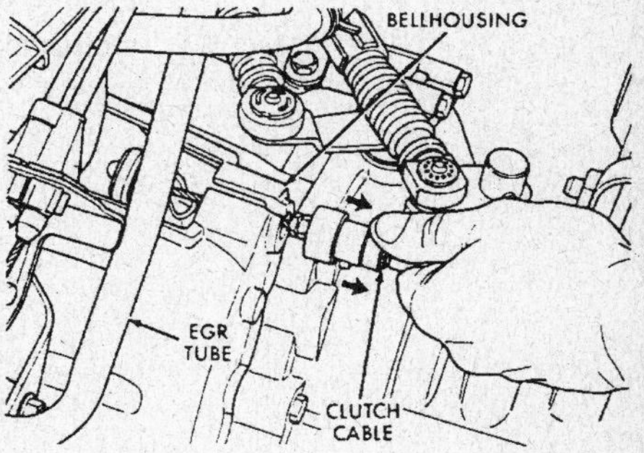

CR5049500083000X

Fig. 2 Clutch cable removal

3. Pull back on clutch cable housing and disengage cable from housing, **Fig. 2.**
4. Disconnect clutch cable up-stop/spacer with cable strand, **Fig. 3.** Depressing the clutch pedal provides access to clutch cable strand.
5. Disconnect cable up-stop/spacer from pedal pivot by wedging a suitable flat blade pry tool between pin and retaining tab.
6. Hold tab slightly away from pin, then pull the up-stop/spacer off pedal.
7. Remove cable end from up-stop/spacer.
8. Reverse procedure to install.

TRANSAXLE

REPLACE

1. Remove the air cleaner at throttle body inlet.
2. Remove clutch housing vent cap, exposing clutch cable end and release lever, then disconnect clutch cable at transvalue.
3. Remove selector cable lever at transvalue.
4. Remove crossover lever cable, then the shift cable mounting bracket.
5. Disconnect accelerator cables ends and bracket from throttle body.
6. Remove upper starter bolt and upper bellowing stud nut, then the throttle body support bracket.
7. Remove upper transaxle mounting bolts, then the upper bellhousing bolts.
8. Remove Vehicle Speed Sensor (VSS), then disconnect back-up lamp wiring at transaxle.
9. Install suitable engine bridge fixture and support engine.
10. Raise and support vehicle, then remove front wheels.
11. Drain transaxle fluid.

12. Remove both front driveshafts.
13. Remove left lower splash shield/ battery cover.
14. Remove left transaxle mount lower bracket bolts.
15. Remove engine lower crossbar retaining bolts.
16. Remove front engine steel mount bracket, then the bolts on front engine aluminum mount bracket.
17. Remove lower starter bolt, then the rear transaxle mount bracket.
18. Remove transaxle to rear lateral bending strut from engine and transaxle.
19. Remove lower dust shield screw.
20. Using suitable transaxle support jack, support transaxle.
21. Rotate engine crankshaft clockwise to gain access to driveplate clutch bolts, then remove driveplate clutch bolts.
22. Remove lower transaxle to engine bellhousing bolts, then the transaxle.
23. Reverse procedure to install.

TIGHTENING SPECIFICATIONS

Year	Component	Torque/ Ft. Lbs.
1997–2000	Back-Up Lamp Switch	18
	Clutch Pedal Pivot Shaft Nut	30
	Drive Plate To Crankshaft Bolts	70
	Drive Plate To Modular Clutch Bolts	55
	End Plate Cover Bolts	21
	Front Engine Mount To Transaxle	80
	Front Transaxle Mount Through Bolt	45
	Front Transaxle Mount To Engine Bolt	40
	Lateral Bending Strut To Engine	40
	Lateral Bending Strut To Transaxle	40
	Left Transaxle Mount Through Bolt	80
	Transaxle To Engine Bolts	70
	Transaxle To Engine Intake Bracket Stud	70

Rear Suspension

INDEX

DESCRIPTION

The rear suspension, **Fig. 1,** is a fully independent short and long arm style suspension. An upper control arm bolts to the top of each rear cast knuckle to the rear suspension crossmember. The movement of the rear knuckle is controlled laterally by two lower lateral links going from the front and rear of the knuckle to the rear crossmember and upper control arm. Fore and aft movement of the knuckle is controlled by a trailing arm.

HUB & BEARING

REPLACE

All models are equipped with permanently lubricated, sealed-for-life wheel bearings. There is no periodic lubrication or maintenance recommended for these units. If servicing is required, proceed as follows:

1. Raise and support vehicle, then remove rear wheel and tire assembly.
2. Remove brake drum.
3. Remove dust cap from hub/bearing assembly to spindle retaining nut.
4. Remove hub/bearing retainer assembly from spindle by pulling straight on spindle by hand.
5. Reverse procedure to install. Tighten hub/bearing assembly retaining nut to specifications.

SHOCK ABSORBER

REPLACE

1. Roll back carpeting on top of rear shock tower to access shock mounting bolts, then remove shock tower cover.
2. Remove two attaching nuts.
3. Raise and support vehicle.
4. Remove rear wheel and tire assembly, then the bolt attaching clevis bracket on shock to knuckle, **Fig. 2.**
5. Remove shock absorber clevis bracket from knuckle by pushing down on suspension.
6. Move shock absorber downward and tilt top of shock outward.
7. Remove shock from vehicle through top of wheelwell opening.
8. Reverse procedure to install.

COIL SPRING

REPLACE

1. Remove shock absorber as outlined under "Shock Absorber, Replace."
2. Position shock assembly in a vise, **Fig. 3,** clamping by clevis bracket at bottom of shock.
3. Mark coil spring and strut assembly right or left as needed.
4. Using coil spring compressor tool No. GP-2020-S2.5, or equivalent, compress coil spring.
5. Using a suitable tool, keep shock shaft rod from turning and remove shock shaft nut.
6. Remove washer, shock mounting bracket, washer on top of dust shield, then the dust shield.
7. Remove coil spring and spring compressor as an assembly.
8. Reverse procedure to install. Tighten mounting nuts to specifications.

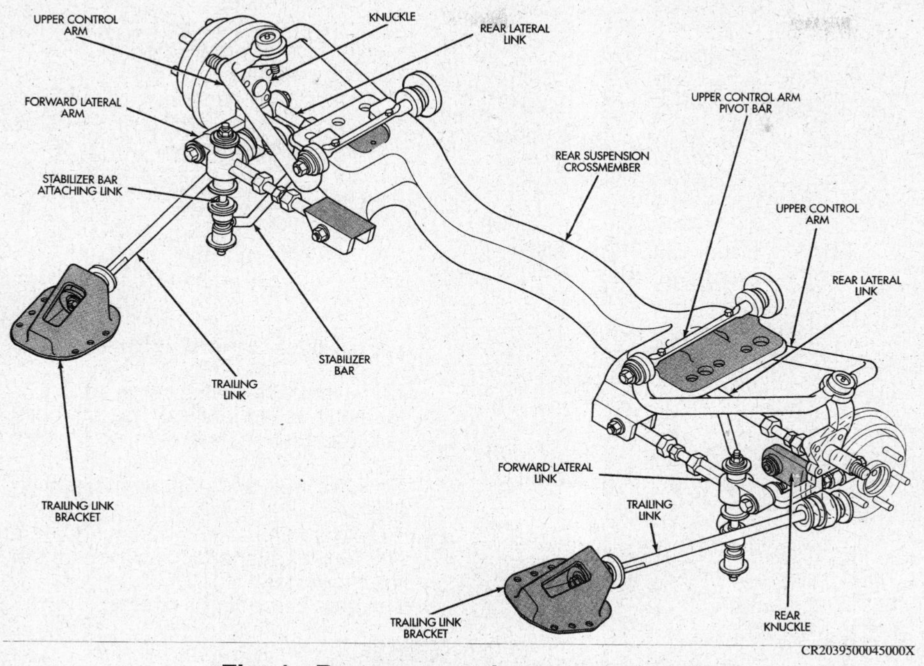

Fig. 1 Rear suspension components

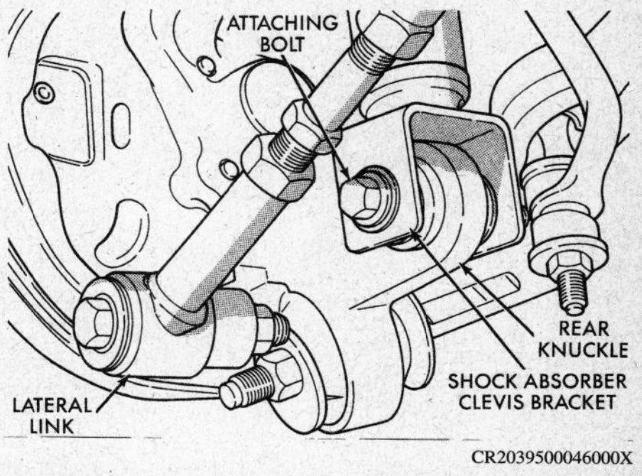

Fig. 2 Shock & knuckle location

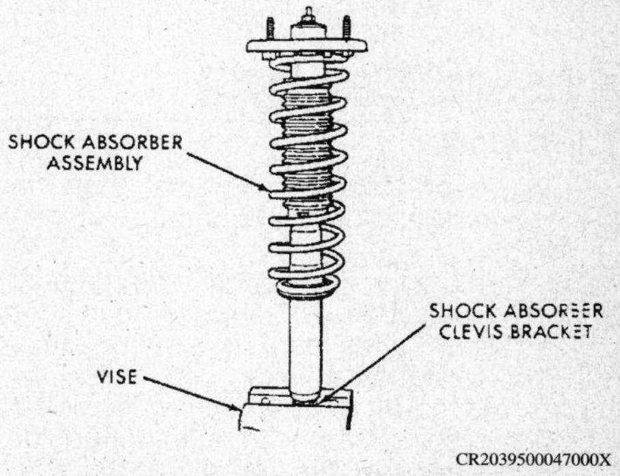

Fig. 3 Coil spring removal

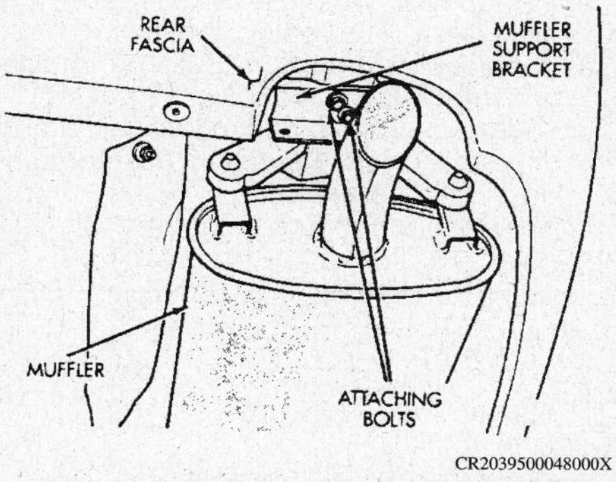

Fig. 4 Muffler support bracket

CONTROL ARM

REPLACE

1. Raise and support vehicle, then remove both rear wheel and tire assemblies.
2. Remove shock absorber clevis bracket as outlined under " Shock Absorber, Replace" on both sides of vehicle.
3. Remove muffler support bracket from rear frame, **Fig. 4.**
4. Remove rear exhaust pipe hanger bracket from rear suspension crossmember and move exhaust down far as possible.
5. Remove cotter pin and castle nut from ball joint.
6. On side of vehicle requiring control arm removal, separate control arm ball joint from rear knuckle using puller tool No. CT-1106, or equivalent. **Reinstall castle nut on ball joint stud to protect threads.**
7. Position a suitable floor jack and block of wood under center of rear suspension crossmember to support and lower crossmember during removal. **Do not put strain on brake flex hoses or damage may occur.**
8. Remove routing clips for wheel speed sensor cable from brackets on both upper control arms.
9. Remove four bolts securing rear suspension crossmember to rear frame rails.
10. Lower rear suspension crossmember far enough to access upper control arm pivot bar to crossmember attaching bolts, then the two bolts attaching upper control arm to crossmember, **Fig. 5.**
11. Remove control arm from vehicle.
12. Reverse procedure to install, noting the following:
    a. Align upper control arm pivot bar with mounting holes in rear suspension crossmember.
    b. Install the two pivot bar nuts to crossmember attaching bolts. Tighten to specifications.
    c. Using suitable jackstand, raise rear suspension crossmember up to frame rails and loosely install the four attaching nuts.
    d. Position appropriate size drift into position hole in each side of rear suspension crossmember and crossmember locating holes in frame rails, then tighten frame rail attaching bolts to specifications.
    e. Install upper ball joint stud in knuckle, then the ball join castle nut and tighten to specifications.

KNUCKLE

REPLACE

1. Raise and support vehicle, then remove rear wheel and tire assembly.
2. Remove brake drum or disc brake.
3. Remove rear wheel speed sensor.

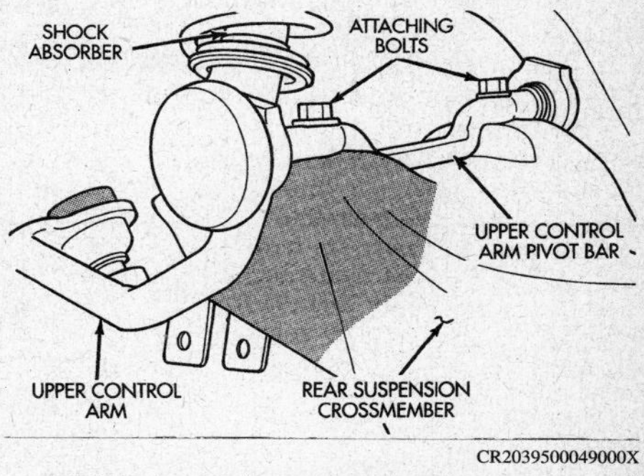

Fig. 5 Upper control arm & crossmember

4. Remove parking brake cable from brake actuator lever.
5. Remove parking brake cable as follows:
    a. Position a ½ inch box end wrench over cable retainer, **Fig. 6,** to collapse retaining tabs.
    b. Pull brake cable from brake support plate.
6. Remove rear hub/bearing assembly retaining nut, then the washer and hub/bearing assembly from knuckle.
7. Remove four attaching bolts from rear support plate and knuckle.
8. Remove brake support plate, brake shoes and wheel cylinder as an assembly from knuckle.
9. Remove attaching nuts and bolts holding forward and rear lateral links to knuckle.
10. Disconnect ball joint stud from knuckle following procedure outlined under "Control Arm, Replace."
11. Remove knuckle.
12. Reverse procedure to install.

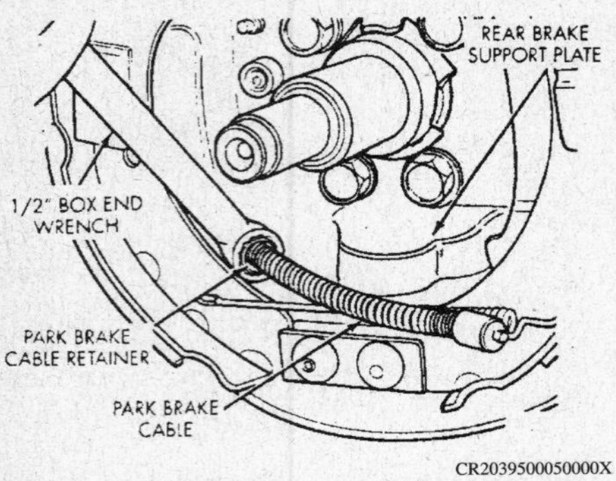

Fig. 6 Parking brake cable removal

STABILIZER BAR

REPLACE

1. Raise and support vehicle, then remove both rear wheel and tire assemblies.
2. Using a suitable wrench to keep stabilizer links from rotating, remove nuts attaching stabilizer link isolator bushings to stabilizer links.
3. Remove four bolts attaching stabilizer bar bushing clamps to rear suspension crossmember, **Fig. 7.**
4. Remove rear stabilizer bar to crossmember bushing clamps and bushings from stabilizer bar.
5. Remove stabilizer bar between exhaust pipe and rear suspension crossmember.
6. Reverse procedure to install.

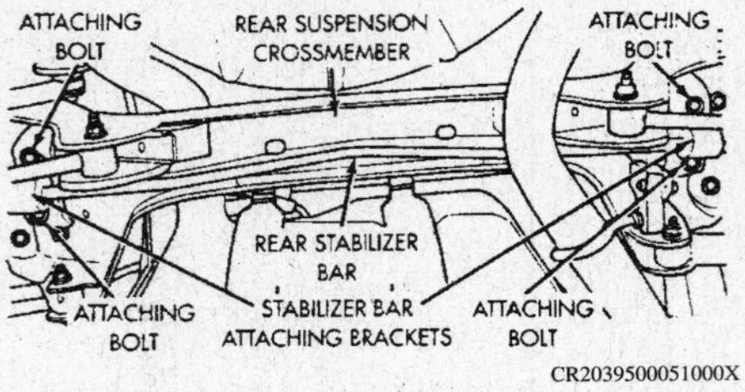

Fig. 7 Rear stabilizer bar components

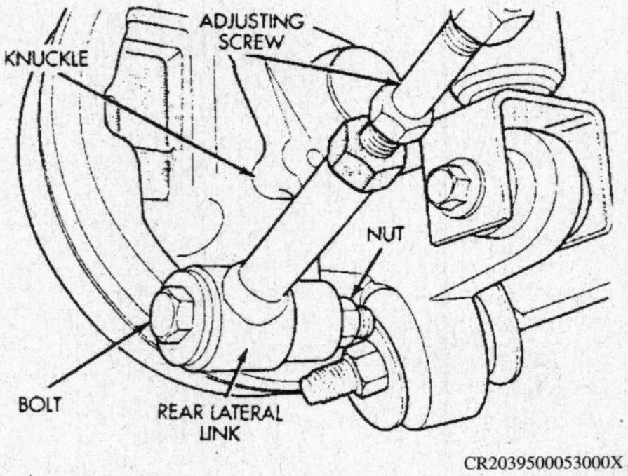

Fig. 9 Rear lateral link

LATERAL LINK

REPLACE

FORWARD

1. Raise and support vehicle, then remove rear wheel and tire assembly from side of car being serviced.

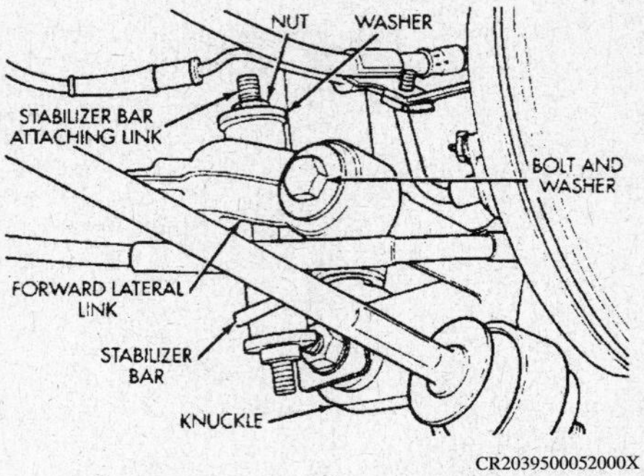

Fig. 8 Forward lateral link

2. Remove rear stabilizer bar attaching link from forward lateral link to knuckle, **Fig. 8.**
3. Remove nut, bolt and washer attaching lateral link to knuckle.
4. Remove nut and bolt attaching lateral link to rear suspension crossmember, then the lateral link.
5. Reverse procedure to install.

REAR

1. Raise and support vehicle, then remove rear wheel and tire assembly from side of car being serviced.
2. Remove nut, bolt and washer attaching lateral link to knuckle, **Fig. 9.**
3. Remove nut and bolt attaching lateral link to rear suspension crossmember, then the lateral link.
4. Reverse procedure to install.

TIGHTENING SPECIFICATIONS

Year	Component	Torque/ Ft. Lbs.
1997–2000	Brake Support Plate To Knuckle Mounting Bolts	45
	Hub & Bearing Assembly	184–185
	Lateral Link Attaching Nut	70
	Shock Assembly Clevis Bracket To Knuckle	70
	Shock Assembly Shaft Nut	①
	Shock Assembly To Body	25
	Sway Bar Isolator Bushing Retainer To Crossmember Bolt	20
	Sway Bar To Forward Lateral Link Attaching Link Nut	②
	Upper Ball Joint To Knuckle Castle Nut	63
	Upper Control Arm Pivot Bar To Crossmember	79
	Wheel Lug Nuts	80–110

①— 1997, 55 ft. lbs.; 1998–2000, 40 ft. lbs.

②— 1997, 40 ft. lbs.; 1998–2000, 24 ft. lbs.

Front Suspension & Steering

INDEX

WHEEL BEARING

ADJUST

These models are equipped with permanently–sealed front wheel bearings. There is no periodic lubrication or maintenance recommended.

HUB & BEARING

REPLACE

1. Raise and support vehicle.
2. Remove cotter pin, lock nut and spring washer from front stub axle.
3. Lower vehicle, then loosen hub nut while vehicle is on the ground and brakes are applied.
4. Raise and support vehicle, then remove from wheel and tire assembly.
5. Remove front disc brake caliper and brake disc assembly and support aside from steering knuckle.
6. **On models equipped with 15 inch wheels,** remove lower ball joint heat shield from lower control arm.
7. **On all models,** remove attaching outer tie rod end to steering knuckle.
8. Using remover tool No. MB-991113, or equivalent, remove tie rod end from steering knuckle.
9. Remove speed sensor cable routing bracket, **Fig. 1.**
10. Remove cotter pin and castle nut from stud of lower ball joint at steering knuckle.
11. Turn steering knuckle so front of steering knuckle is facing as far outboard in wheelwell as possible. Lightly tap boss on steering knuckle to separate from stud of lower ball joint. **Do not hit lower control arm or ball joint grease seal.**
12. Lift up on steering knuckle and separate from ball joint stud. **Support driveshaft so it does not hang by inner Constant Velocity (CV) joint.**
13. Separate steering knuckle from outer CV joint by pulling away, **Fig. 2.**
14. Remove cotter pin and nut from upper ball joint to steering knuckle attachment.
15. Remove upper ball joint stud using puller tool No. C3894-A, or equivalent, then the steering knuckle.
16. Mount steering knuckle securely in a vise, then remove three bolts attaching hub/bearing assembly to steering knuckle.

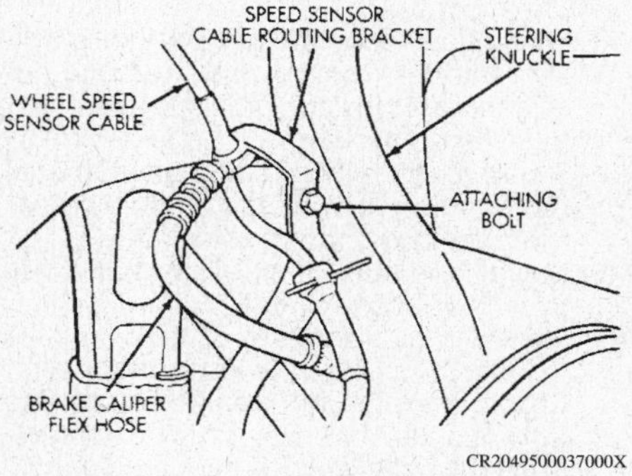

Fig. 1 Speed sensor cable routing bracket

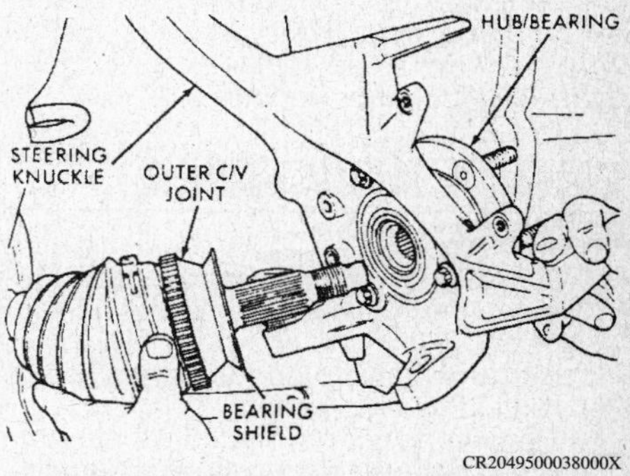

Fig. 2 Steering knuckle & outer CV joint

17. Remove hub/bearing assembly from steering knuckle. **If bearing does not come out, tap lightly using a rubber mallet.**
18. Before installing hub/bearing assembly, clean all mounting surfaces thoroughly.
19. Install hub/bearing assembly in steering knuckle aligning bolts in bearing flange with hole in steering knuckle.
20. Reverse remaining procedure to install.

DRIVESHAFT

REPLACE

1. Loosen, but do not remove, stub axle to hub/bearing retaining nut while vehicle is on floor and brakes applied, then raise and support vehicle and remove front wheel and tire assembly.
2. Remove brake caliper and support aside, then the brake disc.
3. Remove tie rod end attaching nut, then the tie rod end stud from steering knuckle using remover tool No. MB-991113, or equivalent.
4. Remove vehicle speed sensor cable routing bracket.
5. Remove cotter pin and castle nut from stud of lower ball joint at steering knuckle.
6. Turn steering knuckle so front of knuckle is facing as far outboard in wheelwell as possible. Lightly tap boss on steering knuckle to separate from stud of lower ball joint.
7. Pull steering knuckle assembly out and away from outer CV joint.
8. Support outer end of driveshaft assembly, then insert a pry bar between tripod joint and transaxle case side gear, **Fig. 3,** as far as possible by hand.
9. Hold inner tripod joint and interconnecting shaft of driveshaft assembly.
10. Remove inner tripod joint from transaxle by pulling it straight out of transaxle side gear.
11. Reverse procedure to install. Tighten all nuts and bolts to specifications.

BALL JOINT INSPECTION

LOWER

1. Raise and support vehicle.
2. Install dial indicator so it contacts top surface of steering knuckle near lower ball joint stud castle nut.
3. Grasp wheel and tire assembly and push it up and down firmly.
4. Record amount of up and down movement of steering knuckle from dial indicator.
5. Replace lower control arm if movement exceeds .059 inch.

UPPER

With the weight of the vehicle resting on its wheels, attempt to move the grease fitting with no mechanical assistance. If any movement of the grease fitting is detected, the ball joint is worn.

BALL JOINT

REPLACE

The ball joints are not a replaceable

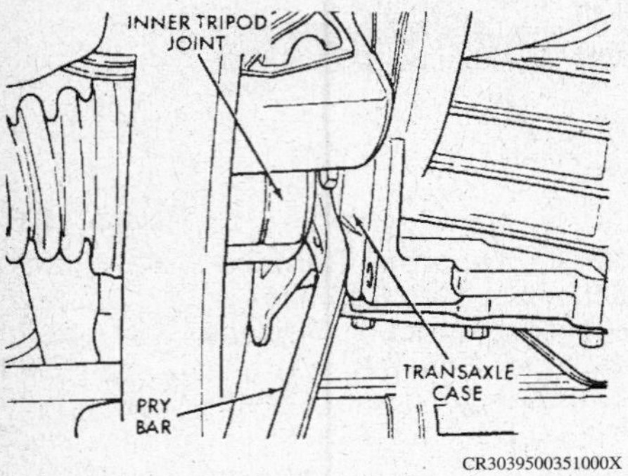

Fig. 3 Inner tripod joint removal

component of the control arms. If determined to be defective, the entire control arm will have to be replaced as outlined under "Control Arm, Replace."

SHOCK ABSORBER

REPLACE

1. Raise and support vehicle, then remove the front wheel and tire assembly.
2. Remove vehicle speed sensor cable routing bracket.
3. Remove cotter pin and castle nut from upper ball joint stud to steering knuckle attachment.
4. Remove upper ball joint stud from steering knuckle using pull tool No. C-3894–A, or equivalent, then position steering outward toward rear of wheelwell.
5. Remove pinch bolt attaching shock clevis to shock.
6. Remove through bolt attaching shock to lower control arm.
7. Remove clevis from shock by carefully tapping clevis with soft brass drift off shock fluid reservoir.
8. Remove four bolts attaching shock/upper control arm mounting bracket to shock tower.
9. Remove shock and upper control arm mounting bracket as an assembly through front area of wheelwell.
10. Reverse procedure to install. Tighten all nuts and bolts to specifications.

CONTROL ARM

REPLACE

LOWER

1. Raise and support vehicle, then remove the front wheel and tire assembly.
2. **On models equipped with 15 inch wheels,** remove lower ball joint heat shield.
3. **On all models,** remove disc brake caliper and support aside, then the brake disc.
4. Disconnect ball joint from steering knuckle, then turn steering knuckle so front of knuckle is facing as far outboard as possible.
5. Separate steering knuckle from lower ball joint by lightly tapping with a rubber mallet.

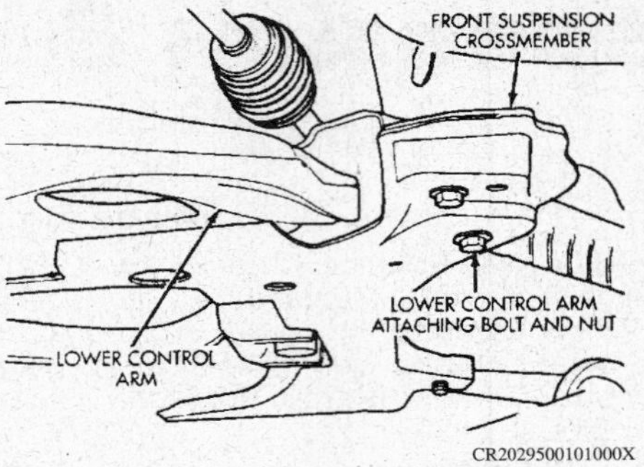

Fig. 4 Lower control arm removal

6. Remove shock absorber clevis from lower control.
7. Using an Allen wrench to prevent stabilizer bar link from rotating, remove nut attaching stabilizer bar link assembly to lower control arm.
8. Remove attaching bolts of stabilizer bar bushing to front suspension crossmember and body of vehicle.
9. Lower one side of stabilizer bar away from lower control arm.
10. Remove nut and bolt attaching rear isolator bushing of lower control arm, **Fig. 4,** then the nut and bolt attaching front isolator bushing of lower control arm.
11. Remove front isolator bushing of lower control arm to front suspension crossmember.
12. To remove lower control arm, proceed as follows:
    a. Remove front of lower control arm from front suspension crossmember first.
    b. Remove rear of lower control arm from between the top and bottom half of front suspension crossmember, keeping lower control arm as level as possible.
13. Reverse procedure to install.

UPPER

1. Raise and support vehicle, then remove the front wheel and tire assembly.
2. Remove vehicle speed sensor cable routing bracket.
3. Remove cotter pin and castle nut from upper ball joint stud to steering knuckle attachment.
4. Remove upper ball joint stud from steering knuckle using puller tool No. C-3894-A, or equivalent, then position the steering outward toward rear of wheelwell.
5. Remove pinch bolt attaching shock clevis to shock.
6. Remove through bolt attaching shock to lower control arm.
7. Remove clevis from shock by carefully tapping clevis with soft brass drift off shock fluid reservoir.
8. Remove four bolts attaching upper control arm/shock absorber mounting bracket to shock tower.
9. Remove shock absorber and upper control arm mounting bracket as an assembly.
10. Reverse procedure to install.

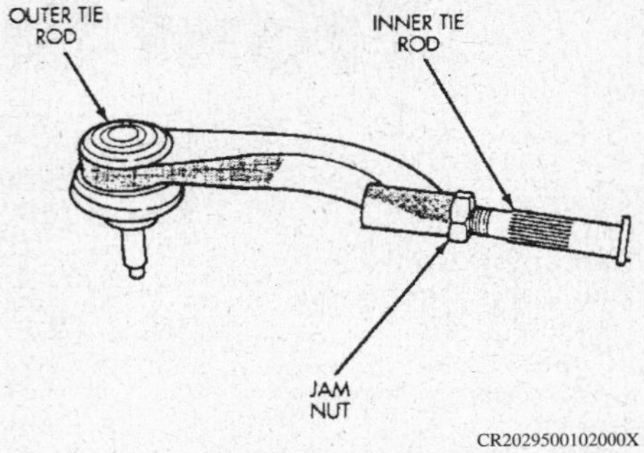

Fig. 5 Tie rod replacement

STEERING KNUCKLE

REPLACE

Refer to "Hub & Bearing, Replace" for knuckle replacement procedures.

STABILIZER BAR

REPLACE

1. Raise and support vehicle.
2. Using a suitable hex wrench to prevent stabilizer bar link from rotating, remove nut attaching stabilizer bar link assembly to lower control arm.
3. Remove attaching bolts of stabilizer bar bushing to front suspension crossmember and body of vehicle.
4. Remove bushings, bushing retainers, and attaching links, then the stabilizer bar.
5. Reverse procedure to install.

TIE ROD

REPLACE

1. Raise and support vehicle, then remove the front wheel and tire assembly.
2. Remove nuts attaching both outer tie rod ends to steering knuckle.
3. Using remover tool No. MB-991113, or equivalent, remove both tie rod end studs from steering knuckles.
4. Loosen inner to outer tie rod jam nut, **Fig. 5,** then remove the outer tie rod from inner tie rod.
5. Remove jam nut, then using pliers, expand tie rod boot, to inner tie rod clamp and remove from steering gear.
6. Reverse procedure to install.

POWER STEERING GEAR

REPLACE

1. Siphon power steering fluid from remote power steering reservoir
2. From interior of vehicle, remove retaining pin from intermediate shaft coupler pinch bolt, then the pinch bolt from intermediate shaft coupler.
3. Separate intermediate shaft coupler from gear shaft.
4. Raise and support vehicle, then remove both front wheel and tire assemblies.

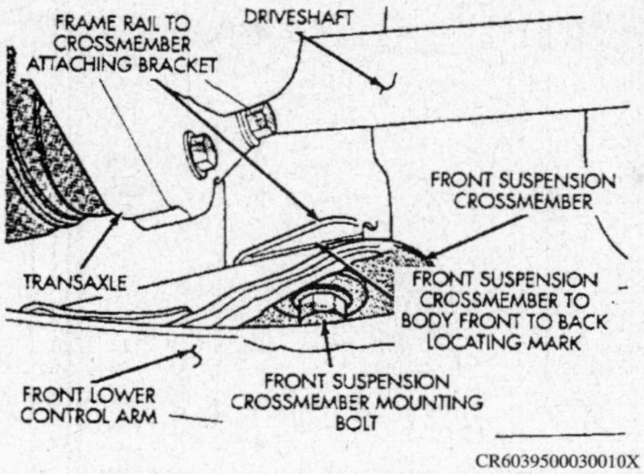

Fig. 6 Front suspension crossmember front to back locating mark (Part 1 of 2)

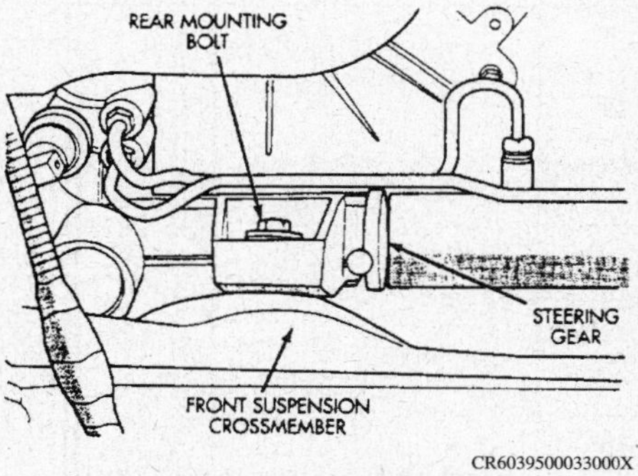

Fig. 8 Steering gear rear mounting isolator bolts

5. Remove nuts attaching both outer tie rod ends to steering knuckles.
6. Using remover tool No. MB-991113, or equivalent, remove both tie rod end studs from steering knuckles.
7. Using an awl, scribe a line on body, **Fig. 6,** marking the front to back installed location where front suspension crossmember is mounted on each side of vehicle.
8. Using an awl, scribe a line on front suspension crossmember, **Fig. 7,** marking side to side installed location where front suspension crossmember is mounted against body on both sides of vehicle.
9. Remove stabilizer bar bushing clamp to body attaching bolts only.
10. Remove three ABS control unit bolts, then secure unit to body for suspension crossmember removal. **Do not let unit hang by brake tubes.**
11. Remove bolts attaching shock absorber clevis to lefthand and righthand lower control arms.
12. Remove two bolt attaching engine support bracket to front suspension crossmember.
13. Position a suitable jackstand under center of front suspension crossmember.
14. Remove from both sides of vehicle front two bolts attaching front suspension crossmember to frame rail of vehicle, then the rear attaching bolts.
15. Using jackstand, lower front suspension crossmember enough to allow steering gear to be removed from crossmember. **Ensure crossmember is supported by jackstand to avoid damage.**

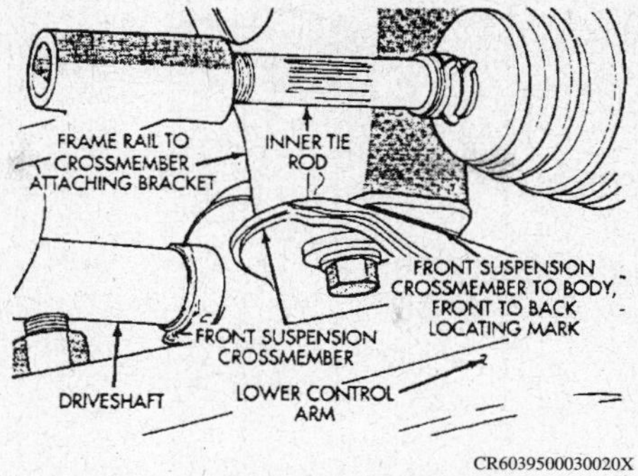

Fig. 6 Front suspension crossmember front to back locating mark (Part 2 of 2)

16. Drain power steering fluid, pressure and return hoses from power steering gear assembly.
17. Disconnect power steering harness connector from fluid reservoir switch.
18. Remove two bolts at isolators, **Figs. 8 and 9,** attaching steering gear assembly to front suspension crossmember, then the two bolts attaching steering gear saddle bracket to front suspension crossmember, **Fig. 10.**
19. Remove steering gear assembly.
20. Reverse procedure to install.

POWER STEERING PUMP

REPLACE

2.0L & 2.4L ENGINES

1. Siphon power steering fluid out of remote power steering fluid reservoir.
2. Raise and support vehicle, then remove righthand wheel and tire assembly.
3. Remove accessory drive splash shield from righthand front wheelwell.
4. Disconnect power steering fluid pressure hose from pressure fitting on power steering pump, then drain remaining power steering fluid.
5. Remove attaching hose clamp from power steering suction fitting, then the power steering supply hose.
6. Remove power steering pump adjusting nut, then the bolt attaching power steering pump to aluminum mounting bracket.
7. Remove ABS hydraulic control unit heat shield.
8. Remove speed sensor cable sealing grommet from inner fender, then disconnect the wheel speed sensor cable from wiring harness and secure aside. Pull through hole in inner fender and unclip wiring harness trough from frame rail.

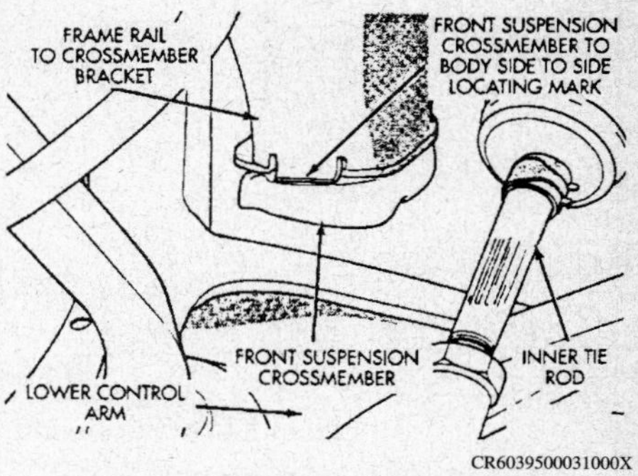

Fig. 7 Front suspension crossmember side to side locating mark

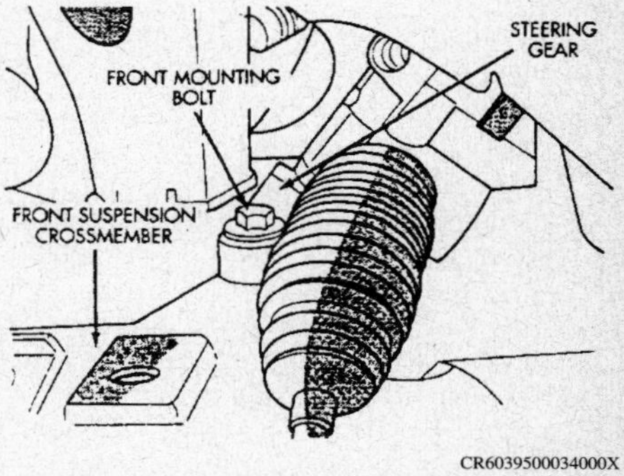

Fig. 9 Steering gear front mounting isolator bolts

9. Remove ABS sealing plug from hole in firewall.
10. Remove bolt attaching top of power steering pump front bracket to mounting bracket, **Fig. 11.**
11. Remove power steering pump drive belt.
12. Remove power steering pump and bracket as an assembly.
13. Reverse procedure to install.

2.5L ENGINE

1. Siphon power steering fluid out of remote power steering fluid reservoir.
2. Raise and support vehicle, then remove the righthand wheel and tire assembly.
3. Remove accessory drive splash shield from righthand front wheelwell.
4. Disconnect power steering fluid pressure hose from pressure fitting on power steering pump, then drain remaining power steering fluid.
5. Remove power steering pressure hose from fitting on pump.
6. Remove ABS hydraulic control unit heat shield.
7. Remove adjusting bolt in accessory drive mounting bracket.
8. Remove bolt at adjusting slot, **Fig. 12,** then the bolt from at top of power steering pump front mounting brackets.
9. Remove power steering drive belt.
10. Remove power steering pump.
11. Reverse procedure to install.

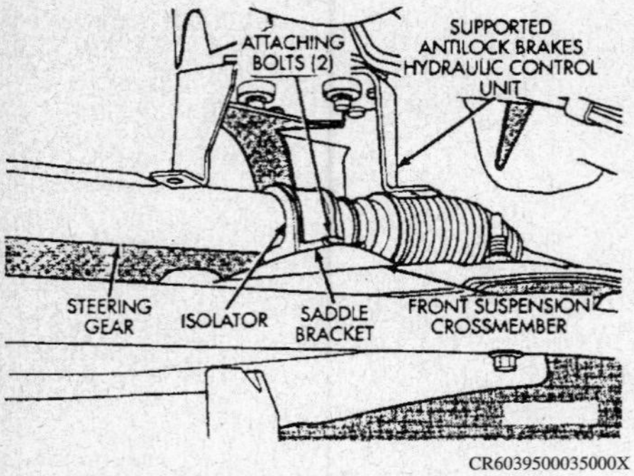

Fig. 10 Steering gear saddle bracket mounting bolts

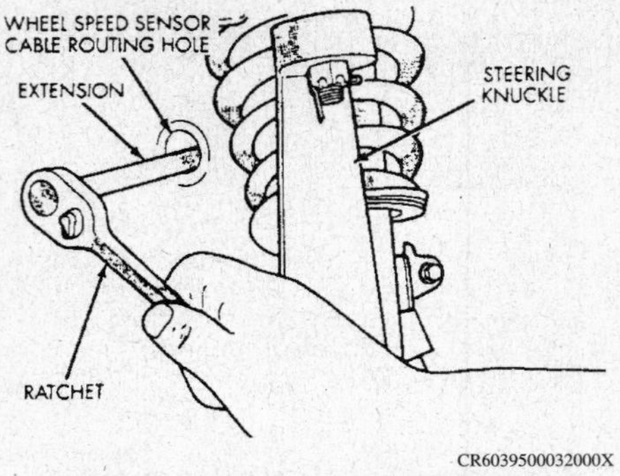

Fig. 11 Top bolt for power steering pump mounting bracket

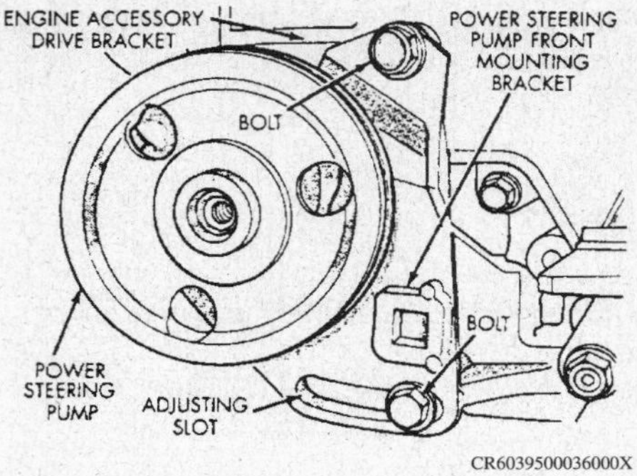

Fig. 12 Power steering pump front bracket

TIGHTENING SPECIFICATIONS

Year	Component	Torque/ Ft. Lbs.
1997–2000	Ball Joint Stud To Shock Tower Attaching Bolts	23
	Ball Joint Stud To Steering Gear Castle Nut	70
	Disc Brake Caliper Assembly To Steering Knuckle Bolts	16
	Front Crossmember Assembly To Body Mounting Nuts	120
	Front Stub Axle To Hub/Bearing Assembly	180
	Lower Control Arm To Crossmember Pivot Bolt	120
	Outer Tie Rod To Inner Tie Rod Lock Nut	55
	Power Steering Bracket To Engine Mounting Bolt	40
	Power Steering Pump Mounting To Front Bracket	40
	Power Steering & Return Hose	21–23
	Pressure Hose To Return Hose (2.0L & 2.4L)	7
	Pressure Hose To Return Hose (2.5L)	40
	Shock Absorber Shaft Nut	①
	Shock Assembly Clevis Bracket To Lower Control Arm Nut	②
	Stabilizer Bar Bushing Retainer To Crossmember Bolts	③
	Stabilizer Bar To Control Arm Attaching Link Nut	④
	Steering Gear To Crossmember Bolts	50
	Tie Rod End To Steering Knuckle Attaching Nut	45
	Wheel Lug Nuts	80–110

① — 1997, 55 ft. lbs.; 1998–2000, 40 ft. lbs.

② — 1997, 120 ft. lbs.; 1998–2000, 68 ft. lbs.

③ — 1997, 21 ft. lbs.; 1998–2000, 45 ft. lbs.

④ — 1997, 55 ft. lbs.; 1998–2000, 78 ft. lbs.

Wheel Alignment

INDEX

PRECAUTIONS

Vehicle hoisting equipment used must be frame contact type only. Use of equipment designed to lift vehicles by the rear axle cannot be used, as damage to rear suspension components will occur. Do not attempt to modify any suspension or steering components by heating or bending of the component.

DESCRIPTION

This vehicle is equipped with a non-adjustable front caster and camber suspension. Front caster and camber settings are determined at the time of design and require no adjustment during alignment. Though not adjustable, front caster and camber must be checked and components replaced when outside of vehicle specification. Inspect all components for damage or signs of bending and replace as required.

Prior to checking or adjusting front or rear suspension alignment, inspect suspension components and wheel bearings for damage or excessive wear and replace as needed. Ensure tire pressure is properly adjusted, then raise and release front or rear bumper several times to allow vehicle to assume ride height.

Toe, measured in degrees or inches, is the amount of difference in distance between the front and rear tire edges, **Fig. 1.**

Thrust angle is the average of the toe setting on each rear wheel, **Fig. 1.**

PRELIMINARY INSPECTION

1. Ensure gas tank is full.
2. Inspect tire pressure and inflate specification. Ensure tires are of same size and tread.
3. Inspect front wheel and tire radial runout.
4. Ensure all suspension fasteners are tightened properly.
5. Inspect ball joints and steering linkage for wear, looseness or damage.
6. Inspect all suspension component rubber bushings for wear or deterioration.

FRONT WHEEL ALIGNMENT

CAMBER

Camber adjustment is not normally required. Inspect all front suspension components for damage or wear, then check rear alignment setting prior to adjusting camber setting.

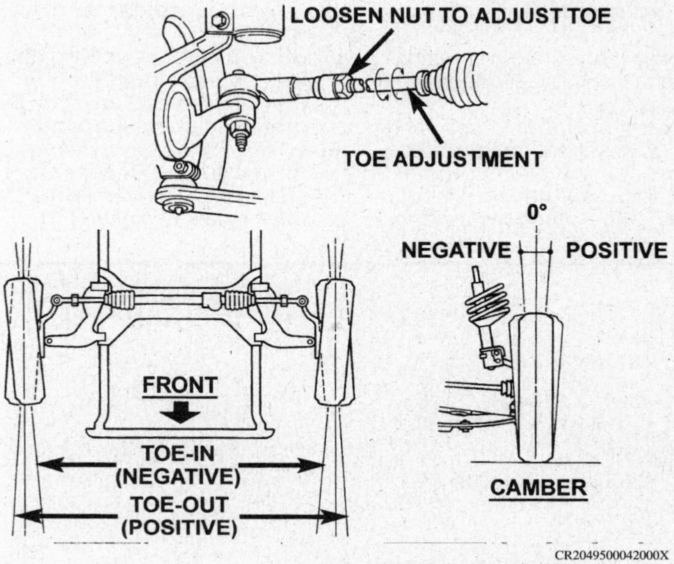

Fig. 1 Toe & camber angle adjustment

1. Mark position of all shock assembly mounting bolts on shock tower of side to be adjusted.
2. Raise and support vehicle by frame until front tires and suspension are not supporting vehicle.
3. Loosen shock mounting bolts on side to be adjusted. Only loosen far enough to allow removal of plastic locating pins that align upper mounting bracket with shock tower.
4. Remove both plastic retaining pins using suitable punch or pliers.
5. Position shock assembly inboard or outboard as required to adjust camber. Ensure fore and aft position is same as marked and that rearward and forward bolts are moved an equal length.
6. **Do not enlarge any existing holes to increase adjustment range.**
7. **Torque** upper shock assembly mounting bolts to 68 ft. lbs.
8. Lower vehicle, then bounce front and rear of vehicle an equal amount of times.
9. Recheck camber setting and readjust as necessary.

TOE

Prior to performing front alignment, check rear alignment.

1. **Perform rear wheel alignment as outlined under "Rear Wheel Alignment."**
2. Loosen front inner and outer tie rod jam nuts and rotate inner tie rod end, **Fig. 2,** at steering gear to set front toe.

REAR WHEEL ALIGNMENT

1. Center steering wheel and lock using a suitable steering wheel clamp.
2. Loosen adjusting screw jam nuts on four of the lateral arms and adjusting screws. Note each adjusting screw has one right-handed and one left-handed nut, **Fig. 3.** When setting rear camber and toe, the maximum lateral link lengths, **Fig. 4,** must not be exceeded. If exceeded, inadequate retention of adjustment link to inner and outer link may result.
3. Adjust rear lateral link adjusting screw, **Fig. 3,** to obtain approximate rear camber setting, then adjust forward

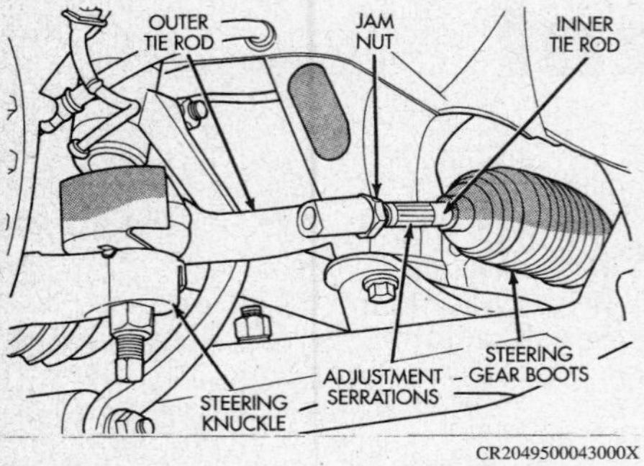

Fig. 2 Inner & outer tie rod adjustment

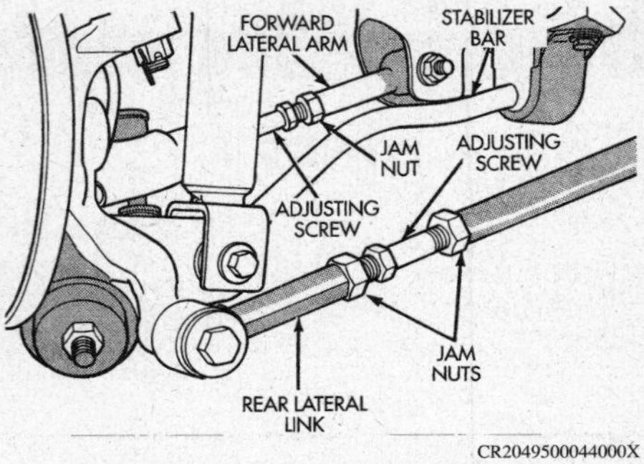

Fig. 3 Rear lateral arm adjustment

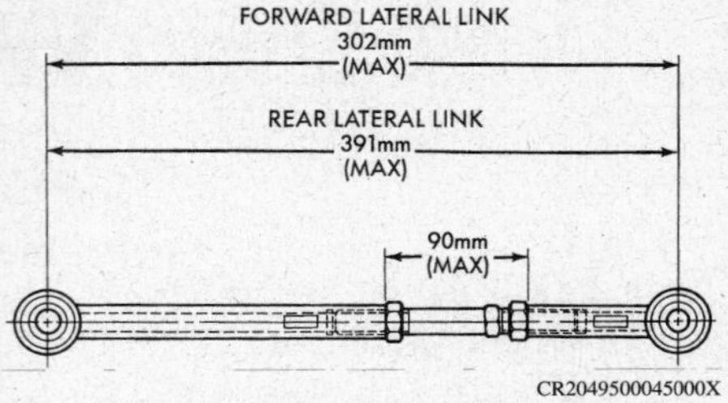

Fig. 4 Lateral link maximum length

lateral link adjusting screw in combination with rear lateral link to reach preferred specification.

4. Adjust forward lateral link adjusting screw, **Fig. 3,** to set preferred rear toe specification.
5. **Toe adjustment will cause a slight change in the camber setting. Should camber setting change during toe adjustment, continue to adjust camber and toe until both are at preferred specifications.**
6. Using crow foot and torque wrench, **torque** lateral link adjusting screw jam nuts to 48 ft. lbs., while holding adjustment screws from turning.

THRUST ANGLE

The thrust angle is the average of the toe settings on each rear wheel. If measurement is not within specifications, readjust rear wheel toe to provide each wheel with ½ of the total toe measurement. When readjusting, do not exceed the total toe specification.

CONCORDE, INTREPID, LHS, VISION & 300M

NOTE: Refer To Rear Of This Manual For Vehicle Manufacturer's Special Service Tool Suppliers.

INDEX OF SERVICE OPERATIONS

Specifications

GENERAL ENGINE SPECIFICATIONS

Engine	Engine Code①	Fuel System	Bore & Stroke, Inch	Comp. Ratio	Brake HP @ RPM	Maximum Torque, Ft. Lbs. @ RPM	Normal Oil Pressure, psi	
							Idle	3000 RPM
1997								
3.3L	T	SMPI	3.661 x 3.188	8.9	161 @ 5300	181 @ 3200	5	30–80
3.3L	U	SMPI/FF	3.661 x 3.188	8.9	—	—	5	30–80
3.5L	F	SMPI	3.780 x 3.189	9.6	214 @ 5800	221 @ 3100	5	25–80
1998								
2.7L	R	SMPI	3.386 x 3.091	9.7	200 @ 5800	190 @ 4850	5	30–80
3.2L	J	SMPI	3.622 x 3.189	9.5	225 @ 6300	225 @ 3800	5	30–80
1999								
2.7L	R	SMPI	3.386 x 3.091	9.7	200 @ 5800	190 @ 4850	5	30–80
3.2L	J	SMPI	3.622 x 3.189	9.5	225 @ 6300	225 @ 4000	5	30–80
3.5L	G	SMPI	3.780 x 3.189	9.9	253 @ 6400	255 @ 3950	5	30–80
2000								
2.7L	R	SMPI	3.386 x 3.091	9.7	200 @ 5800	190 @ 4850	5	25–105
3.2L	J	SMPI	3.622 x 3.189	9.5	225 @ 6300	225 @ 3800	5	25–105
3.5L	G	SMPI	3.780 x 3.189	9.9	253 @ 6400	255 @ 3950	5	25–105

SMPI: Sequential Multi-Port Fuel Injection.

FF: Flex fuel.

① — Eighth digit of VIN denotes engine code.

TUNE UP SPECIFICATIONS

Engine	Spark Plug Gap, Inch	Firing Order Fig.④	Ignition Timing		Idle Speed, RPM	Fuel Pump Pressure, psi⑥	Valve Clearance, Inch
			°BTDC	Mark			
1997							
3.3L	.048–.053	A	②	⑤	600–840N①	55	③
3.5L	.033–.038	A	②	⑤	750–1100N①	48	③
1998							
2.7L	.048–.058	B	②	⑤	350–700⑦	49	③
3.2L	.048–.053	B	②	⑤	350–700⑦	49	③
1999–2000							
2.7L	.048–.058	B	②	⑤	350–700⑦	49	③
3.2L	.048–.053	B	②	⑤	350–700⑦	49	③
3.5L	.048–.053	B	②	⑤	350–700⑦	49	③

BTDC — Before Top Dead Center

N — Neutral

① — Controlled by PCM.

② — Direct (Distributorless) Ignition System (DIS); not adjustable.

③ — Equipped w/hydraulic lash adjusters, no adjustment is necessary.

④ — Before disconnecting wires from coil unit, determine location of No. 1 wire, as position may have been altered from that shown in Fig. A.

⑤ — Equipped w/crankshaft position sensor.

⑥ — Remove cover from service valve on fuel rail. Connect suitable fuel pressure test gauge to service valve. With ignition switch in Run position, use Diagnostic Read-Out Box to activate fuel pump & pressurize system.

⑦ — Minimum air flow idle RPM.

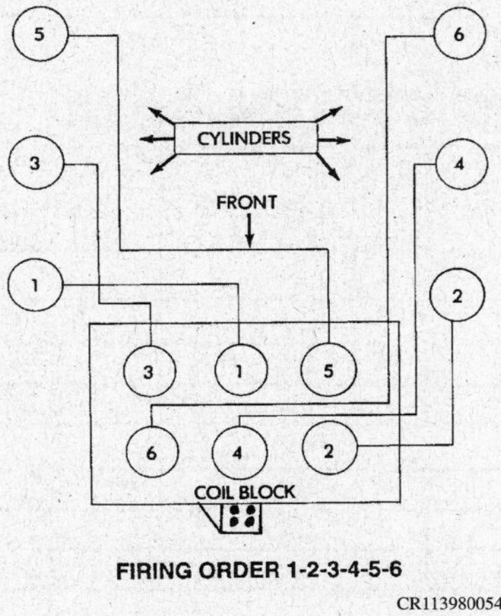

Fig. A

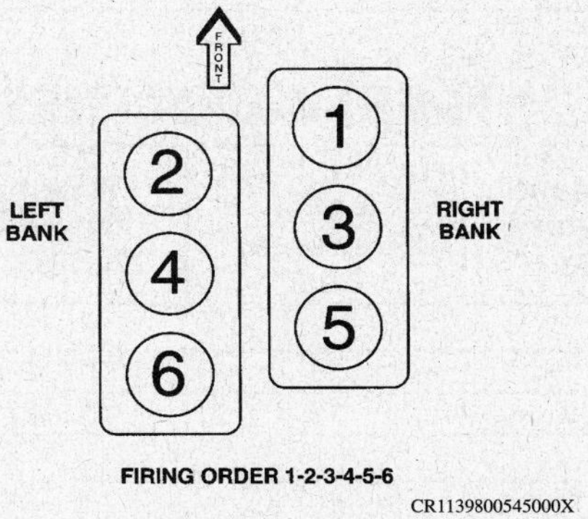

Fig. B

FRONT WHEEL ALIGNMENT SPECIFICATIONS

Year	Camber Angle, Degrees①		Caster Angle, Degrees①		Toe In, Degrees		Ball Joint Wear
	Limits	Desired	Limits	Desired	Limits	Desired	
1997	–.6 to +.6②	0	+2 to +4③	+3	+.4 to 0	+.2	④
1998–99	–.6 to +.6②	0	+2 to +4③	+3	+.3 to -.1	+.1	④
2000	–.6 to +.6②	0	+2 to +4③	+3	+.2 to -.2	0	④

① — Reference angle only; not adjustable.
② — Side to side differential not to exceed .7.°
③ — Side to side differential not to exceed 1.°
④ — Refer to "Ball Joint Inspection" in "Front Suspension & Steering."

REAR WHEEL ALIGNMENT SPECIFICATIONS

Year	Camber Angle, Degrees①		Toe In, Degrees		Thrust Angle①
	Limits	Desired	Limits	Desired	
1997–98	–.6 to +.4	–.1	-.2 to +.4	+.1	–.15 to +.15
1999–2000	–.7 to +.3	–.2	-.2 to +.4	+.1	–.15 to +.15

① — Reference angle only; not adjustable.

FLUID CAPACITIES & COOLING SYSTEM DATA

Engine	Coolant Capacity, Qts.	Radiator Cap Relief Pressure, Lbs.	Thermo. Opening Temp., °F	Fuel Tank, Gals.	Engine Oil Refill, Qts.①	Transaxle Oil, Qts.②	Differential Oil, Qts.
1997							
3.3L	11.09	18	215–220	18	5.0	9.9	1.0
3.5L	12.15	18	215–220	18	5.5	9.9	1.0
1998–99							
2.7L	11	18	215–220	17	5.0	9.9	1.0
3.2L	12	18	215–220	17	5.0	9.9	1.0
3.5L	12	18	215–220	17	5.5	9.9	1.0
2000							
2.7L	9.4	18	203–220	18	5.0	9.9	1.0
3.2L	9.4	18	203–220	18	5.0	9.9	1.0
3.5L	9.4	18	203–220	18	5.0	9.9	1.0

① — Includes oil filter.

② — Approximate; make final check w/dipstick. Includes torque converter sump.

LUBRICANT DATA

Year	Lubricant Type			
	Transaxle	Differential	Power Steering	Brake System
1997–2000	Mopar ATF Type 7176	Mopar 80W-90 Hypoid Gear Lubricant	Mopar P/N 4318055	DOT 3

Electrical

NOTE: Refer To "Air Bag System Precautions " Located In The Front Of This Manual For System Disarming & Arming Procedures.

NOTE: Prior To Performing Any Service Operations Listed In This Section, Consult The "Technical Service Bulletins " Section For Related Information.

NOTE: Refer To "Computer Relearn Procedure " Located In The Front Of This Manual For Computer Relearn Procedures.

INDEX

PRECAUTIONS

AIR BAG SYSTEMS

Refer to "Air Bag System Precautions" in the front of this manual for system disarming and arming procedures.

BATTERY GROUND CABLE

Prior to service, disconnect battery ground cable and isolate as required.

FUSE PANEL & FLASHER LOCATION

The fuse panel/junction block is located under the lefthand side of the instrument panel. The hazard flasher unit is located under the lefthand side of the instrument panel between the junction block and the brake pedal.

FUEL PUMP RELAY LOCATION

The fuel pump relay is located in the power distribution center. The power distribution center is located in the engine compartment next to the battery.

STARTER

REPLACE

1997

1. Raise and support vehicle.
2. Remove three bolts from starter.
3. Remove starter assembly from engine.
4. Disconnect electrical connections from starter solenoid.
5. Reverse procedure to install.

1998–2000

2.7L Engine

1. Remove battery negative remote cable from ground post, then raise and support vehicle.
2. Remove catalyst support bracket mounting nuts, then the battery feed and posi-lock wiring harness connectors.
3. Remove starter heat shield mounting bolts and nuts, then the starter mounting bolts.
4. Remove starter from transmission housing, then rotate starter solenoid toward engine and slide starter motor rear between catalyst and engine mount.
5. Reverse procedure install. **Torque** starter mounting bolts to 40 ft. lbs. and solenoid battery nut to 8 ft. lbs.

3.2L & 3.5L Engines

1. Remove battery negative remote cable from ground post, then raise and support vehicle.
2. Remove catalyst support bracket mounting nuts, then the battery feed wire.
3. Remove starter solenoid from transmission housing, then position starter to access posi-lock wiring connector.
4. Using suitable jack stand beneath engine, slightly lift engine to relieve lefthand engine mount pressure.
5. Remove lefthand engine mount mounting bolts.
6. Using suitable jack, raise engine slightly for starter maneuver room.
7. Slide starter motor rear between catalyst and engine mount, disconnect posi-lock starter solenoid connector and remove starter.
8. Reverse procedure install. **Torque** starter mounting bolts to 40 ft. lbs. and solenoid battery nut to 8 ft. lbs.

COIL PACK

REPLACE

1997

The electronic ignition coil pack attaches to the lefthand cylinder head on 3.3L engines or to the righthand cylinder head on 3.5L engines.

1. **On models equipped with 3.5L engine,** remove air cleaner hose.
2. **On all models,** disconnect electrical connector from coil pack.
3. Remove coil pack mounting screws.
4. Remove coil pack.
5. Transfer spark plug wires to new coil pack.
6. Reverse procedure to install.

1998–2000

These engines are equipped with a coil on plug ignition system. Each cylinder has a dedicated coil sitting atop each plug. No secondary wires are required and connection from the coil to plug is made with a boot that is attached to the coil.

1. Clean area around coil and spark plug with compressed air spray.
2. Remove electrical connector from ignition coil.
3. **On models equipped with 3.2L and 3.5L engines,** alternately loosen screws back and forth. **Do not lose spacers under coil.**
4. **On all models,** remove fasteners and ignition coil.
5. Reverse procedure to install, noting the following:
   a. **On models equipped with 2.7L engine, torque** mounting screws to 55 inch lbs.
   b. **On models equipped with 3.2L and 3.5L engines, torque** mounting screws to 60 inch lbs.

IGNITION LOCK

REPLACE

CYLINDER

1. Remove tilt lever.
2. Remove upper and lower column covers.
3. Turn ignition key to Run position, then depress lock cylinder mounting tab and slide cylinder out of housing, **Fig. 1.**
4. Reverse procedure to install.

HOUSING

1. Remove upper and lower column covers.
2. Remove tilt lever.
3. Remove ignition switch as outlined under "Ignition Switch, Replace."
4. Center punch tamper proof screws, **Fig. 2.**
5. Using a ¼ inch drill bit, drill out screw heads.
6. Remove lock cylinder housing from steering column.
7. Use suitable pliers to remove bolts from steering column.

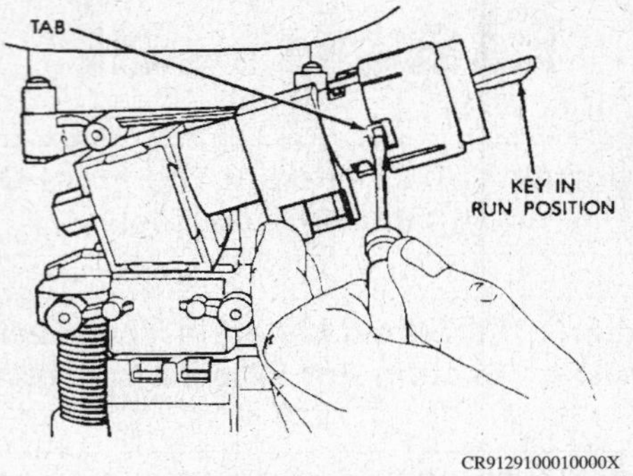

Fig. 1 Lock cylinder replacement

8. Reverse procedure to install. Tighten new tamper proof screws until heads twist off.

IGNITION SWITCH

REPLACE

1. Remove tilt lever, then upper and lower column covers.
2. Remove Sentry Key Immobilizer Module (SKIM), if equipped.
3. Remove multi-function switch.
4. Disconnect electrical connector from ignition switch.
5. Remove ignition switch mounting screws and ignition switch, **Fig. 3.**
6. Reverse procedure to install. Align tab on ignition switch with slot on lock housing.

HEADLAMP SWITCH

REPLACE

1. Open front door and remove lefthand end cover.
2. Remove screw from lefthand end of instrument panel and pull headlight bezel rearward to disengage clips.
3. Remove headlight switch screws and pull switch out to disconnect electrical connectors.
4. Remove headlight switch.
5. Reverse procedure to install.

STOP LIGHT SWITCH

REPLACE

REMOVAL

1. Press and hold brake pedal.
2. Rotate switch 30° counterclockwise, pull rearward and remove from bracket.
3. Disconnect wiring harness connector.

INSTALLATION

1. Hold stop lamp switch firmly in one hand, then using other hand, pull plunger outward until it ratches to its fully extended position.
2. Connect wiring harness connector.
3. Press brake pedal as far down as possible, then install switch in bracket by aligning switch index key with mounting bracket square hole slot.
4. When fully install, rotate switch 30° clockwise to lock.
5. Gently pull brake pedal back until pedal stops moving and switch plunger ratchets to correct position.

MULTI-FUNCTION SWITCH

REPLACE

1. Remove tilt lever, then upper and lower steering column covers.
2. Remove multi-function switch to column mounting screws.
3. Disconnect multi-function switch electrical connections.
4. Reverse procedure to install. **Torque** multi-function switch to column screws to 17 inch lbs.

TURN SIGNAL SWITCH

REPLACE

Refer to "Multi-Function Switch, Replace" for turn signal switch replacement.

DIMMER SWITCH

REPLACE

Refer to "Multi-Function Switch, Replace" for dimmer switch replacement.

STEERING WHEEL

REPLACE

REMOVAL

1. Lock steering column by turning steering wheel ½ turn (180°) clockwise from straight ahead position.
2. Place ignition in Off/Lock position and remove ignition key. This will ensure no damage occurs to clockspring.
3. Remove speed control switches from steering wheel to gain access to air bag module attaching screws. If vehicle is not equipped with speed control, pry out covers on sides of steering wheel for access.
4. Remove bolts attaching air bag module to steering wheel.
5. Lift air bag module from steering wheel, disconnecting wiring harness connections from rear of air bag module and remove module from steering wheel.
6. Remove steering wheel mounting nut from steering column shaft.
7. Remove steering wheel using steering wheel puller tool No. C-3428B, or equivalent.

INSTALLATION

1. Confirm that steering wheel position is a halt turn (180°) to the right. Column is locked with ignition cylinder lock.
2. Ensure turn signal stalk is in neutral, then pull all wires through larger opening of hub area on wheel.
3. Install steering wheel ensuring flats on hub align with clockspring.
4. Install steering wheel mounting nut and tighten nut to draw steering wheel onto column. **Torque** steering column shaft nut to 45 ft. lbs.
5. Connect wiring harness on air bag module.

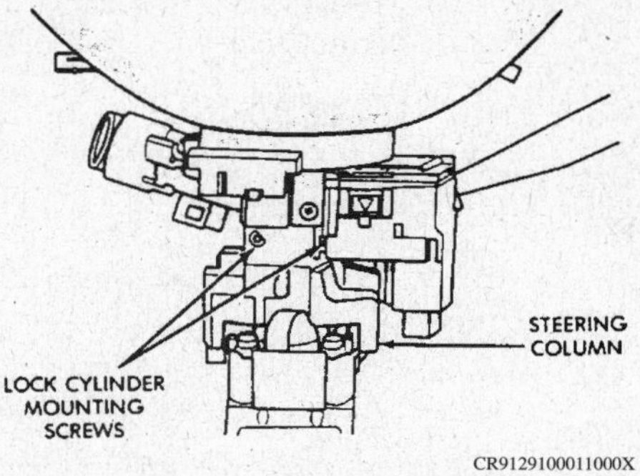

Fig. 2 Lock cylinder housing replacement

6. Install air bag module into steering wheel using care not to pinch any wires.
7. Install air bag mounting bolts, center air bag module and **torque** air bag module mounting bolts to 9–10 ft. lbs.
8. Connect speed control switches, then install switches on steering wheel. If vehicle is not equipped with speed control, install speed control switch covers. **Torque** mounting screws to 12–18 inch lbs.

INSTRUMENT CLUSTER

REPLACE

1. Remove instrument panel lefthand end cap.
2. Remove headlamp switch as previously described.
3. Remove instrument panel upper center bezel. Refer to "Dash Panel Service."
4. Remove hazard switch and steering column shroud, then tilt steering wheel down.
5. Remove instrument panel cluster bezel.
6. Remove instrument cluster screws and disengage upper latch.
7. Remove instrument cluster from panel. **The instrument panel wiring harness connectors are mounted directly to rear panel. A force of approximately 20 lbs. will be required to disengage cluster from connectors.**
8. Reverse procedure to install.

RADIO

REPLACE

1. Remove lower center bezel, radio mounting screws, then the remove radio, **Fig. 4.**
2. Pull radio straight out and disconnect electrical and antenna connections.
3. Remove radio ground strap, then the radio.
4. Reverse procedure to install.

WIPER MOTOR

REPLACE

1. Remove wiper arms and blades and disconnect hoses from inline connector.

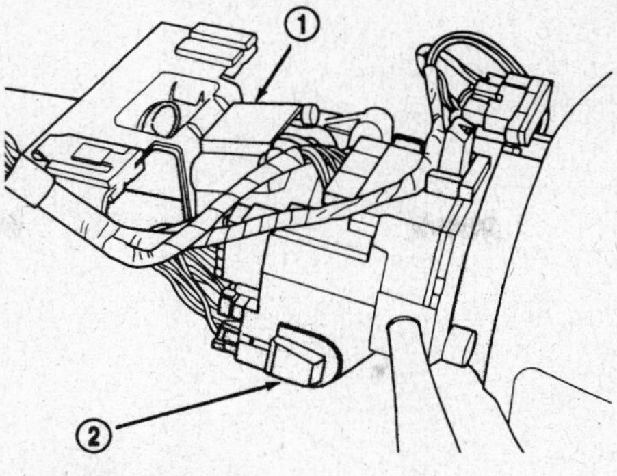

1 – STEERING COLUMN
2 – IGNITION SWITCH

Fig. 3 Ignition switch replacement

2. Remove rear hood seal with cowl top plastic screen and disconnect washer hose at inline connector.
3. Disconnect motor connector at back side of housing, **Fig. 5.**
4. Remove wiper housing mounting screws, then the wiper housing module.
5. Disconnect and remove wiper drive link from motor crank.
6. Remove motor mounting screws, then lift motor and mounting plate out of housing.
7. Disconnect motor harness grommet from housing.
8. Reverse procedure to install. **Torque** crank motor nut to 7–10 ft. lbs. and motor mounting screws to 7–9 ft. lbs.

WIPER SWITCH

REPLACE

Refer to "Multi-Function Switch, Replace" for wiper switch replacement.

BLOWER MOTOR

REPLACE

1. Remove lower righthand under panel silencer duct.
2. Remove blower motor housing cover.
3. Remove blower motor mounting screws, lower blower motor from housing.
4. Reverse procedure to install.

HEATER CORE

REPLACE

1. Remove heater and A/C housing as outlined under " Evaporator Case, Replace."
2. Pull back heater core mounting clips, then pull heater core out of housing.
3. Install new heater core.
4. Place mounting brackets over heater core and fasten with screws provided with new heater core, **Fig. 6.**
5. Install heater housing into vehicle as outlined under " Evaporator Case, Replace."

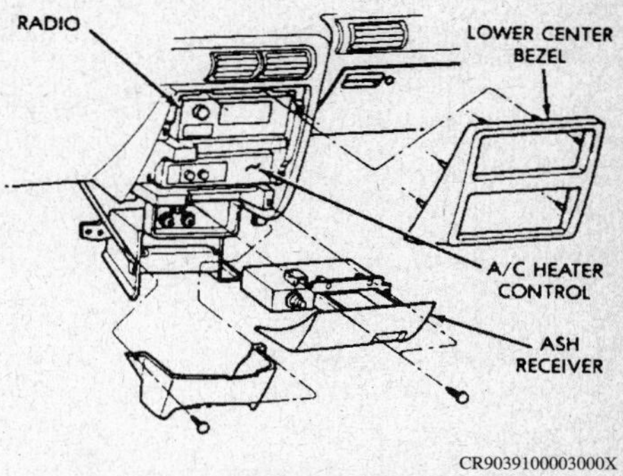

Fig. 4 Radio replacement

EVAPORATOR CASE

REPLACE

1997

Refer to procedures found under "Dash Panel Service " when servicing the dash panel.

1. Recover refrigerant as outlined under "Air Conditioning. "
2. Remove air cleaner hose and air distribution duct.
3. Drain engine cooling system.
4. Disconnect heater hoses at dash panel and plug heater core inlet tubes.
5. Remove both A/C lines from expansion valve, using line tool No. 7193, or equivalent.
6. Plug A/C lines and evaporator housing inlets.
7. Remove heater and A/C housing stud nuts.
8. Remove right and lefthand instrument panel end caps.
9. Remove right and lefthand interior door post kick panel.
10. Remove righthand side bezel from instrument panel.
11. Remove radio center bezel, then the radio and heater A/C control head.
12. Remove center instrument panel bezel.
13. Remove center console from vehicle.
14. Remove passenger side air bag as outlined under " Passive Restraints."
15. Remove lower bolster mounting screws.
16. Lower bolster, then disconnect luggage compartment release and glove box light wiring then remove bolster from vehicle.
17. Remove instrument panel top cover.
18. Remove windshield A pillar trim covers.
19. Remove instrument panel to cowl panel bolts.
20. Disconnect DRB scan tool connector brace.
21. Remove instrument panel ground strap from lower lefthand side of center console.
22. Remove knee blocker support bracket, under column duct and lefthand floor duct.
23. Disconnect 60-way connector and all related wiring connectors.
24. Disconnect fuse panel wiring connectors and brake light switch.
25. Remove steering column covers, then

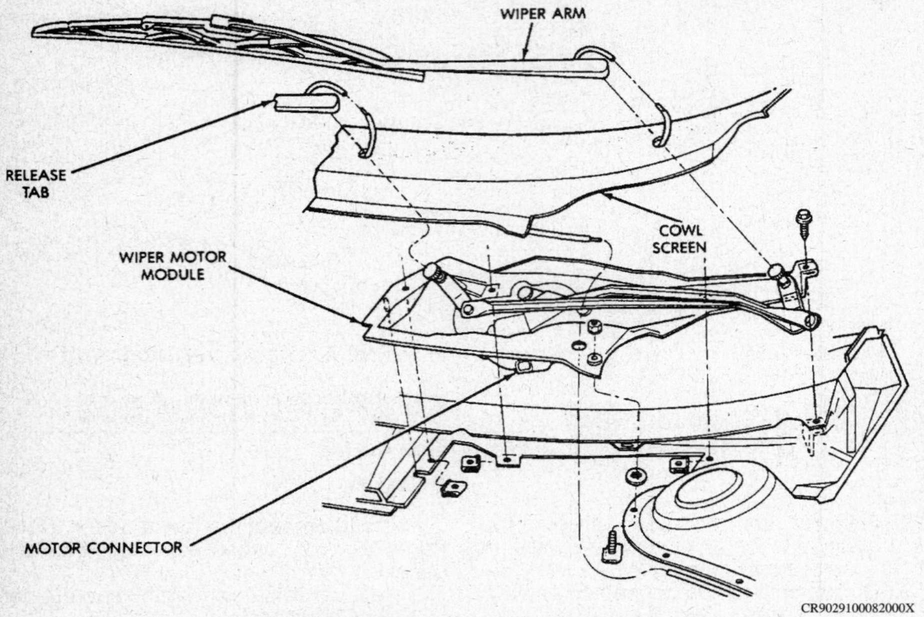

Fig. 5 Wiper motor & linkage module

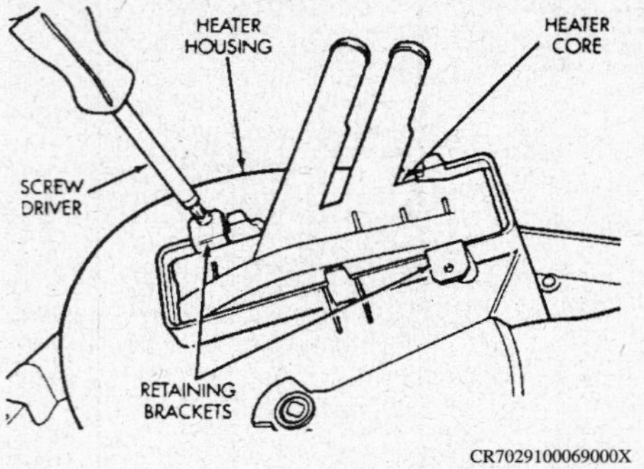

Fig. 6 Heater core replacement

the column mounting bolts and allow steering column to lower to floor.

26. Disconnect air bag connectors.
27. Remove righthand side floor air duct.
28. Disconnect 10-way blower module and blower motor connectors from heater and A/C housing.
29. Remove body controller.
30. Disconnect righthand side connector and antenna.
31. Remove right and lefthand side upper instrument panel mounting screws located in door jamb.
32. Remove upper instrument panel with all harnesses and gauges from vehicle.
33. Remove air duct for rear heater vents.
34. Remove air bag module and brace from vehicle.
35. Remove heater housing to dash panel bolts, then roll heater and A/C housing out of vehicle.
36. Remove drain tube from housing.
37. Reverse procedure to install. Install drain tube from underneath vehicle after heater housing is installed.

1998–2000

The heater- A/C housing unit must be removed from vehicle before performing this repair. The heater a/c unit housing need not be disassembled to remove heater core. Refer to "Heater Core, Replace."

Refer to procedures found under "Dash Panel Service " when servicing the dash panel.

1. Recover refrigerant as outlined under "Air Conditioning. "
2. Drain engine coolant into suitable container.
3. Remove air cleaner hose and distribution duct from engine.
4. Remove fasteners from heater hoses at dash panel and remove hoses from heater core.
5. Plug heater core inlet and outlet tubes to block coolant from entering interior.
6. Remove one nut at expansion valve retaining both A/C lines to expansion valve.
7. Cap expansion valve and A/C openings.
8. Remove three retaining nuts from studs from dash panel into engine compartment.
9. Remove two screws from defrost duct and remove duct.
10. Remove two nuts, two screws attaching housing to dash panel.
11. Remove four nuts retaining rear seat heat duct and remove duct.
12. Remove rear seat heat duct elbow push pin fastener.
13. Disconnect harness connector.
14. Gently pull unit housing rearward from dash panel.
15. Reverse procedures to install.

EVAPORATOR CORE

REPLACE

1. Remove heater and A/C housing as outlined under " Evaporator Case, Replace."
2. Remove recirculation door actuator.
3. Remove recirculation door and housing.
4. Remove upper housing mounting screws, then the upper half of heater housing.
5. Lift evaporator out of lower housing.
6. Transfer expansion valve onto new evaporator using new gaskets.
7. Reverse procedure to install.

TECHNICAL SERVICE BULLETINS

POOR HEATER PERFORMANCE

1998

2.7L Engine

On these models, heater performance may be poor.

This condition may be caused by heater outlet duct location or the engine thermostat. To correct this condition, proceed as follows:

1. Inspect and correct engine coolant level.
2. Ensure lefthand heater outlet duct faces down toward foot area. Remove and orient as necessary.
3. Fully warm engine at 1500–2000 RPM for 15–20 minutes.
4. Using suitable scan tool, ensure coolant temperature is above 180°F.
5. If coolant temperature is not above 180°F, remove thermostat.
6. Replace thermostat that is propped or stuck open.
7. If coolant temperature is above 180°F, but heater performance is still poor, conduct HVAC diagnosis as outlined in **MOTOR's " Air Conditioner & Heater Manual."**

3.2L Engine

On these models, heater performance may be poor.

This condition may be caused by heater outlet duct location, core sand contamination or the engine thermostat. To correct this condition, proceed as follows:

1. Inspect and correct engine coolant level.
2. Ensure lefthand heater outlet duct faces down toward foot area. Remove and orient as necessary.
3. Fully warm engine at 1500–2000 RPM for 15–20 minutes.
4. Using suitable scan tool, ensure coolant temperature is above 180°F.
5. If coolant temperature is above 180°F, but heater performance is still poor, conduct HVAC diagnosis as outlined in

MOTOR's "Air Conditioner & Heater Manual."

6. Shine suitable flashlight into plastic coolant hot bottle next to filler cap and view bottle bottom with adjustable mirror.
7. If there is a dark shadow larger than a quarter, there may be excessive core sand accumulation. Proceed to next step. If core sand accumulation is not excessive (all vehicles may show core sand accumulation), proceed as follows:
   a. If coolant temperature is not above 180°F, remove thermostat.
   b. Replace thermostat that is propped or stuck open.
8. At 65 mph shift transmission to low or 2nd gear and drive approximately ½ mile between 4500–6500 RPM. Engine temperature should drop. **This test is best perform at low ambient temperatures.**
9. Shift transmission into overdrive and maintain 65 mph for at least three miles.
10. If coolant temperature does not return 180°F, but continues to drop, thermostat has been held open by core sand. Proceed as follows:
    a. Replace thermostat.
    b. Flush cooling system.
    c. Clean coolant hot bottle.
11. If coolant temperature does return to 180°F, repeat 65 mph procedure three times. If temperature always returns to normal, core sand is not the problem.

FLAG SPEAKER BUZZ

1998

Infinity Audio System

On these models, a buzz noise may come from door flag speaker, most noticeably with deep male voices on talk radio.

This condition may be caused by flag speaker seal/gasket. To correct this condition, install revised front door flag speaker seal/gasket (part No. 05014669AA).

COURTESY LAMPS FLICKER

1999

On these models built between July 20, 1998 and October 23, 1998, the headliner mounted courtesy lamps may intermittently flicker when they would normally be "ON."

This condition may be caused by faulty wiring from the M-1 circuit and C-11 connector. To correct this condition proceed as follows:

1. Disconnect negative battery cable remote terminal.
2. Remove C-11 connector from fuse panel.
3. Lift locking wedge tab up 2 mm, remove pink M-1 circuit from connector using tool No. 6680–2, or equivalent.
4. Cut off existing terminal at base of terminal.
5. Strip off insulation from wire to expose ⅛ inch copper.
6. Carefully attach terminal (part No. 56019990) into wire using crimping tool No. PWC46, or equivalent.
7. Install pink M-1 wire/terminal into connector, reset locking wedge.
8. Install C-11 connector and verify lamp operation.

AM/FM RADIO RECEPTION

1998–99

AM/FM reception performance can be poor. These conditions can be caused by car phone antennas and rear window glass tint.

Car phone antennas mounted on the rear window glass, particularly at the top of the glass where AM grid resides. The grid design varies between models, but all provide adequate mounting area near the top of the glass to mount a car phone antenna base to the glass. Care must be exercised to avoid the car phone antenna mounting base from coming into contact with any of the antenna grid lines.

Conductive window tint film containing titanium applied to the rear window glass has the effect of grounding the AM antenna and altering the FM antenna signal. Customers who wish to have rear window glass film, should use only non-conductive tint film.

2.7L Engine

NOTE: On Air Bag Equipped Models, Refer To " Air Bag System Precautions" Located In The Front Of This Manual For System Disarming & Arming Procedures.

NOTE: Prior To Performing Any Service Operations Listed In This Section, Consult The "Technical Service Bulletins " Section For Related Information.

NOTE: Refer To "Computer Relearn Procedure " Located In The Front Of This Manual For Computer Relearn Procedures.

INDEX

PRECAUTIONS

AIR BAG SYSTEMS

Refer to "Air Bag System Precautions" in the front of this manual for system disarming and arming procedures.

BATTERY GROUND CABLE

Prior to service, disconnect battery ground cable and isolate as required.

FUEL SYSTEM PRESSURE RELIEF

1. Remove fuel pump relay for power distribution center.
2. Start and run engine until it stalls.
3. Attempt to start engine until it no longer runs.
4. Turn ignition switch to Off position.
5. Place rag or towel under fuel line quick-connector fitting at fuel rail.
6. Install fuel pump relay.
7. One or more Diagnostic Trouble Codes (DTCs) may have been stored because of removing fuel pump relay. Clear these DTCs with suitably programmed scan tool.

COMPRESSION PRESSURE

The minimum compression pressure should be no less than 100 psi and the maximum variation between cylinders should be no more than 25%.

ENGINE MOUNT

REPLACE

LEFT & RIGHTHAND

1. Raise and support vehicle.
2. Remove isolator mounting nuts.
3. Support engine with suitable jack and wood block across full width of oil pan.
4. Remove lower mounting nuts.
5. Raise engine carefully, then remove isolator with heat shield.
6. Reverse procedure to install. Tighten nuts to specifications.

REAR

1. Raise and support vehicle.
2. Support transaxle with suitable jack.
3. Remove mounting nut, then the crossmember bolts and mount.
4. Reverse procedure to install. Tighten bolts to specifications.

STRUCTURAL COLLAR

REPLACE

1. Raise and support vehicle.
2. Remove mounting bolts, then the structural collar from oil pan and transaxle housing.
3. Reverse procedure to install. Bolts must be installed and tightened in the following sequence:
   a. Install vertical collar oil pan bolts and **torque** to 10 inch lbs.
   b. Install collar to transaxle bolts and **torque** to 40 ft. lbs.
   c. Starting with center vertical bolt and working outward, **torque** mounting bolts to 40 ft. lbs.

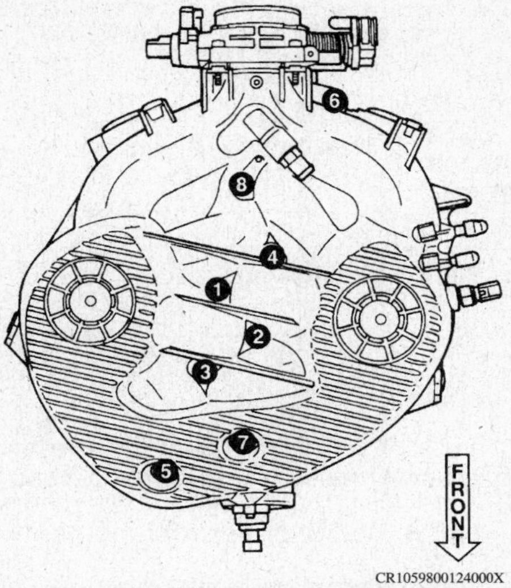

Fig. 1 Upper intake manifold tightening sequence

ENGINE

REPLACE

1. Relieve fuel pressure as described under "Precautions."
2. Mark hood position at hinges and remove, then drain cooling system into suitable container.
3. Remove wiper arms, right and lefthand cowl covers, then the cowl support.
4. Remove air cleaner assembly and air inlet hose, then the upper radiator crossmember.
5. Disconnect hood release cable from latch, then remove cooling fan module.
6. Disconnect upper radiator hose from engine and lower hose from radiator, then the transaxle cooler lines from radiator.
7. Remove A/C condenser to radiator fasteners, then the transaxle cooler lines support bracket and mounting screw on radiator lefthand side.
8. Remove radiator, then the accessory drive belts.
9. Remove mounting bolts and set power steering pump aside.
10. Disconnect electrical connector, remove mounting bolts and set A/C compressor aside.
11. Remove exhaust manifold V-band clamps, then disconnect throttle and speed control cables.
12. Disconnect coolant pressure bottle hoses, then the heater hoses.
13. Disconnect fuel line, then the vacuum lines, electrical connectors and engine ground straps.
14. Raise and support vehicle, then drain engine oil into suitable container.
15. Remove catalytic converter down pipe front and rear fasteners.
16. Remove mounting bolts and structural collar.
17. Mark flexplate to torque converter position and remove converter mounting bolts.
18. Disconnect transaxle cooler line brackets from engine, then remove starter.
19. Remove crankshaft position sensor and lower transaxle to block bolts.
20. Lower vehicle, then remove fuel line and electrical harness throttle body mounting screws.
21. Remove electrical harness attaching bracket and transaxle shift cable attaching bracket.
22. Remove throttle body support bracket fasteners from transaxle to block double-ended bolts.
23. Remove upper transaxle to block bolts, then the right and lefthand engine mount isolator to engine mount bracket mounting fasteners.
24. Remove cam sensor from lefthand cylinder head.
25. Attach suitable lifting device to engine, support transaxle with suitable floor jack, and remove engine.
26. Reverse procedure to install, noting the following:
    a. Tighten all fasteners to specifications.
    b. Do not tighten transaxle case to engine block bolts until all bolts have been started and mating surface are completely joined.

INTAKE MANIFOLD

REPLACE

UPPER

1. Remove air inlet resonator and inlet tube.
2. Remove throttle and speed control cables from throttle arm and bracket, then the bracket.
3. Disconnect Manifold Absolute Pressure (MAP), Intake Air Temperature (IAT), Throttle Position (TPS) sensors and Idle Air Control (IAC) motor electrical connectors.
4. Disconnect vapor purge, brake booster, speed control servo and Positive Crankcase Ventilation (PCV) hoses.
5. Remove Exhaust Gas Recirculation (EGR) tube.
6. Loosen throttle body support bracket upper fastener, then the support brackets upper fasteners at right and lefthand sides of the upper manifold.
7. Apply upward pressure to release retaining clip and remove engine name cover.
8. Remove mounting bolts and upper manifold.
9. Reverse procedure to install, noting the following:
    a. Ensure fuel injectors and wiring harnesses are positioned to not interfere with installation.
    b. Tighten manifold to specifications using sequence shown in **Fig. 1.**
    c. Tighten throttle body support bracket fasteners to specifications.

LOWER

1. Relieve fuel pressure as described under "Precautions."
2. Remove upper intake manifold as previously described.

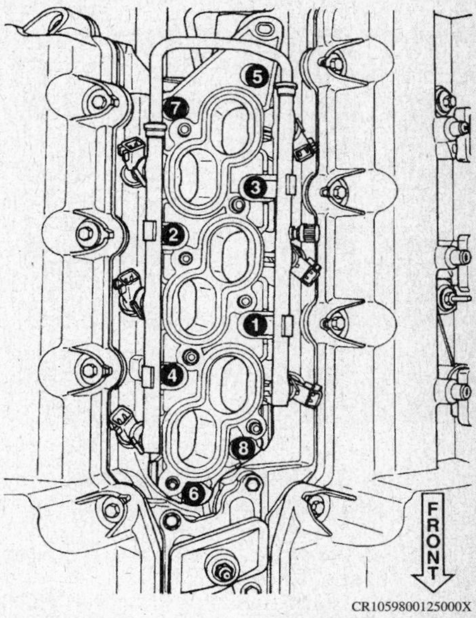

Fig. 2 Lower intake manifold tightening sequence

3. Remove fuel rail fuel supply hose, then the screw mounting fuel rail support bracket to throttle body support bracket.
4. Remove mounting bolts, then the fuel rail and injectors as an assembly.
5. Remove mounting bolts and lower intake manifold.
6. Reverse procedure to install, noting the following:
    a. To properly position manifold, install bolt 2–3 turns in rearmost attaching hole.
    b. Tighten mounting bolts to specifications using sequence shown in **Fig. 2.**
    c. Ensure fuel injectors are located in correct positions.

EXHAUST MANIFOLD

REPLACE

RIGHTHAND

1. Remove air intake plenum and air filter housing.
2. Remove battery cable housing tube to transmission housing mounting bolt.
3. Remove EGR tube to exhaust manifold and EGR valve mounting bolts.
4. Disconnect electrical connector, then remove exhaust manifold oxygen sensor.
5. Remove manifold to catalytic converter V-band clamp.
6. Remove mounting screws and heat shields.
7. Remove mounting bolts and exhaust manifold.
8. Reverse procedure to install, noting the following:
    a. Tighten exhaust manifold mounting bolts to specifications from center outwards.
    b. Tighten heat shield mounting screws to specifications.

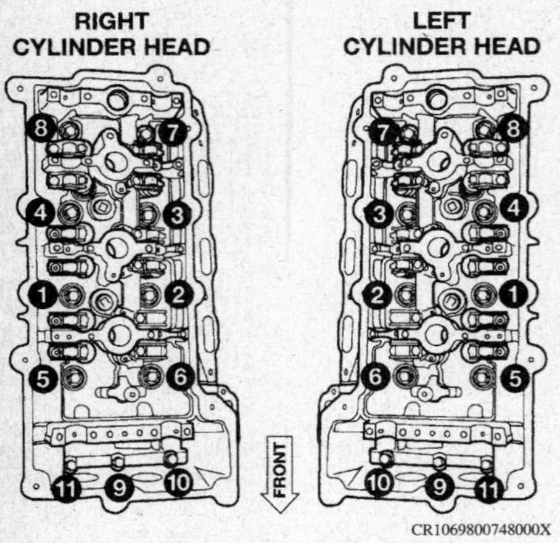

Fig. 3 Cylinder head bolt tightening sequence

c. Use new V-band clamp and tighten to specifications.
d. Use new gasket and tighten EGR tube mounting screws to specifications.

LEFTHAND

1. Raise and support vehicle.
2. Remove exhaust system, then the lefthand catalytic converter.
3. Remove transmission dipstick tube mounting bolt, then rotate housing away from engine.
4. Lower vehicle.
5. Disconnect electrical connectors and remove harness mounting screws from support bracket, then the engine wiring harness support bracket from cylinder head.
6. Disconnect connector and remove exhaust manifold oxygen sensor.
7. Remove engine oil dipstick tube.
8. Remove mounting screws and heat shield.
9. Remove mounting bolts and exhaust manifold.
10. Reverse procedure to install, noting the following:
    a. Tighten exhaust manifold mounting bolts to specifications from center working outward.
    b. Tighten heat shield mounting screws to specifications.
    c. Install new engine oil dipstick O-ring.
    d. Use new V-band clamp and tighten to specifications.

CYLINDER HEAD

REPLACE

1. Relieve fuel pressure as described under "Precautions."
2. Drain cooling system into suitable container and remove accessory drive belts.
3. Remove crankshaft damper as outlined under "Crankshaft Damper, Replace."
4. Remove upper and lower intake manifolds as previously described.
5. Remove cylinder head cover as outline under "Valve Cover, Replace" and timing chain cover as outlined under "Front Cover, Replace."
6. Remove water outlet connector.
7. Rotate crankshaft until crankshaft sprocket timing mark aligns with oil pump housing timing mark, then remove timing chain.
8. Remove camshafts as described under "Camshaft, Replace."
9. Remove catalytic converter pipe V-band clamps at exhaust manifold.
10. Remove cylinder head mounting bolts in reverse of tightening sequence, **Fig. 3,** then the cylinder heads.
11. Reverse procedure to install, noting the following:
    a. Because cylinder head bolts are tightened using torque plus angle procedure, bolts with stretched threads must be replaced.
    b. Use new cylinder head gasket.
    c. Ensure head is properly positioned over locating dowels.
    d. Lubricate bolt threads with clean engine oil.
    e. **Torque** cylinder head bolt Nos. 1–8 to 35 ft. lbs. in sequence, **Fig. 3.**
    f. **Torque** bolt Nos. 1–8 to 55 ft. lbs.
    g. **Torque** bolt Nos. 1–8 to 55 ft. lbs.
    h. **Torque** bolt Nos. 1–8 to 75 ft. lbs.
    i. Tighten cylinder head bolt Nos. 1–8 an additional 90.° Do not use torque wrench.
    j. **Torque** cylinder head bolt Nos. 9–11 to 21 ft. lbs.
    k. Use new V-band clamp and tighten to specifications.

VALVE COVER

REPLACE

1. Remove upper intake manifold as previously described, then the ignition coil electrical connectors.
2. Remove righthand cylinder head ground strap, then disconnect electrical and vacuum harness retaining clips from studs.
3. Remove ignition coil capacitor fasteners, then the right and lefthand upper intake manifold support brackets.
4. Loosen mounting bolts and remove cylinder head covers. Mounting bolts are captured in cover.
5. Reverse procedure to install, noting the following:
    a. Replace gaskets as necessary.
    b. Ensure double-ended studs are in correct locations, **Fig. 4.**
    c. Tighten mounting bolts to specifications.

VALVE ADJUSTMENT

Rocker arms are equipped with hydraulic lash adjusters. No adjustment is necessary.

ROCKER ARMS

REPLACE

REMOVAL

1. Remove valve cover(s) as previously described.
2. Turn crankshaft to rotate engine until cam lobe is on base circle (heel) of rocker arm being removed.
3. Using valve spring compressor tool No. 8215 and adapter tool No. 8216, or equivalents, depress valve spring only enough to release tension and remove rocker arm.
4. Identify rocker arm position.
5. Repeat procedure for each rocker arm being removed.

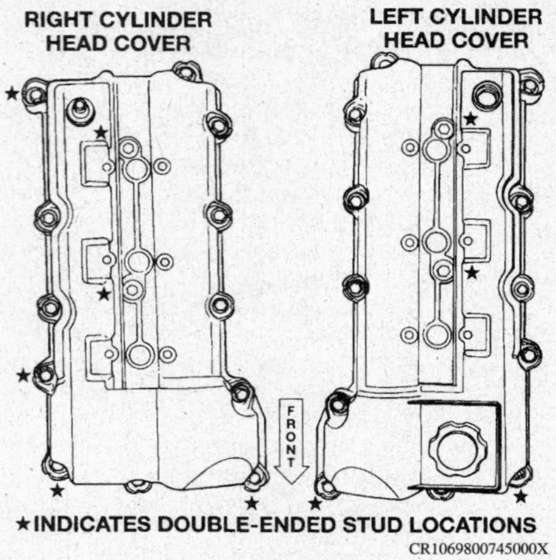

Fig. 4 Valve cover replacement

INSTALLATION

1. Lubricate rocker arm(s) with clean engine oil.
2. Turn crankshaft to rotate engine until cam lobe is on base circle (heel) of rocker arm being removed.
3. Using valve spring compressor tool No. 8215 and adapter tool No. 8216, or equivalents, depress valve spring only enough to release tension.
4. Install rocker arm in original position and release valve spring tension.
5. Repeat procedure for each rocker arm to be installed.
6. Install valve cover(s) as previously described.

VALVE SPRINGS

REPLACE

IN-VEHICLE

Ensure piston is at TDC on cylinder from which valve spring(s) is being removed.

1. Relieve fuel pressure as described under "Precautions."
2. Remove air cleaner housing cover and inlet hose.
3. Remove upper intake manifold as previously described.
4. Remove valve cover(s) as previously described.
5. Remove crankshaft damper as outlined under "Crankshaft Damper, Replace."
6. Remove timing chain as outlined under "Timing Chain, Replace."
7. Remove camshaft(s) as outlined under "Camshaft, Replace."
8. Install suitable spark plug adapter into

cylinder being serviced, then apply 90–100 psi air pressure to hold valves in place.

9. Using valve spring compressor tool No. MD-998772-A with adapter tool No. 6779, or equivalents, compress valve spring, then remove valve locks, retainer and spring.
10. Using suitable valve seal tool, remove valve stem seals.
11. Reverse procedure to install, noting the following:
    a. Push valve steam seal/seat firmly and squarely over valve guide with stem as guide.
    b. Do not force seal against guide top.
    c. When install retainer locks, compress spring only enough to install locks.

HEAD REMOVED

Removal

1. Using valve spring compressor tool No. C-3422-B, or equivalent, compress valve spring.
2. Remove valve retaining locks, valve spring retainers, valve springs and valve springs seat/stem seal assembly.
3. Identify valves for installation, then remove valve stem lock groove burrs.
4. Remove valves.

Installation

1. Coat with clean engine oil and install valve stems.
2. If valves and/or seats have been ground, proceed as follows:
    a. Measure valve tip height (A) from cylinder head surface to valve stem top, **Fig. 5.**
    b. If intake valve tip height is more than 1.8737 inches, grind tip to specifications.
    c. If exhaust valve tip height is more than 1.9347 inches, grind tip to specifications.
3. Install seal/spring seat assembly over valve guides.
4. Ensure garter spring is intact around rubber seal top, then install valve springs and retainers.
5. Compress valve springs with suitable valve spring compressor, then install locks and release tool.
6. If valves and/or seats have been ground, proceed as follows:
    a. Measure springs installed height (B) from spring seal to spring retainer bottom surface, **Fig. 5.**
    b. If height is more than 1.5256 inches, install .030 inch spacer in head counterbore under valve spring seat.

VALVE SEATS

Refer to "Valve Springs, Replace" for valve seat service.

HYDRAULIC LIFTERS

REPLACE

1. Remove rocker arm as previously described.

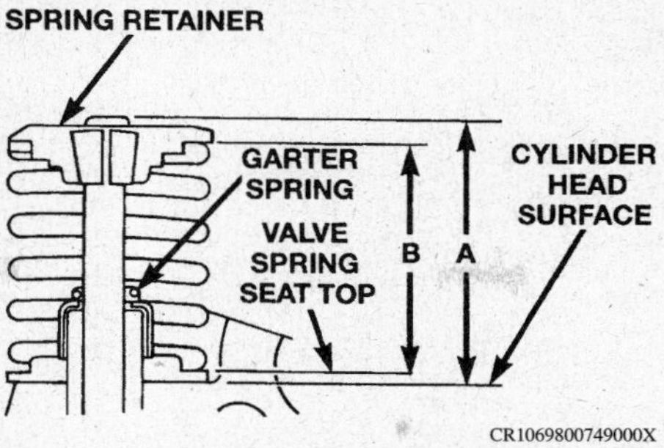

Fig. 5 Valve tip & spring installed heights inspection

2. Mark position for assembly.
3. Remove hydraulic lash adjuster.
4. Reverse procedure to install, ensure adjuster is at least partially full of oil.

CRANKSHAFT DAMPER

REPLACE

1. Remove upper radiator crossmember, then the fan module.
2. Remove accessory and air conditioning belts.
3. Using crankshaft damper holder tool No. 8191, or equivalent, and three-jaw puller tool No. 1023, or equivalent, remove damper.
4. Reverse procedure to install. Tighten center bolt to specifications.

FRONT COVER

REPLACE

1. Remove upper radiator support crossmember, then the fan module and accessory drive belts.
2. Remove crankshaft damper as previously described.
3. Remove power steering pump from mounting bracket, then the accessory drive belt tensioner pulley and bracket.
4. Remove mounting bolts and timing chain cover.
5. Reverse procedure to install, noting the following:
    a. If front crankshaft seal was bench installed, place crankshaft seal protection tool No. 6780-2, or equivalent, over nose.
    b. Apply ⅛ inch bead of suitable silicone rubber adhesive sealant to parting lines between oil pan and cylinder block.
    c. Tighten mounting bolts to specifications.
    d. If front crankshaft seal was not previously installed, use crankshaft seal installer and sleeve tool No. 6780-2, or equivalent, to install seal.

TIMING CHAIN

REPLACE

With the timing chain removed, avoid turning the camshaft or crankshaft. If movement is required, exercise caution to avoid valve damage caused by piston contact.

REMOVAL

1. Remove upper intake manifold, valve covers, crankshaft damper and front cover as previously described.
2. Rotate crankshaft to align crankshaft sprocket timing with oil pump housing marks. Cylinder No. 1 should be at 60° ATDC.
3. Remove primary timing chain tensioner from righthand cylinder head.
4. Remove camshaft position sensor from lefthand cylinder head, then the chain guide access plug.
5. Remove righthand camshaft sprocket mounting bolts. When bolts are removed, camshaft with rotate clockwise.
6. Remove camshaft damper and sprocket.
7. Remove mounting bolts and lefthand camshaft sprocket.

INSTALLATION

1. Align crankshaft sprocket and oil pump housing timing marks, **Fig. 6.**
2. Place lefthand side primary chain sprocket on chain so that timing mark is between two plated links.
3. Lower primary chain with lefthand side sprocket through lefthand cylinder head opening.
4. Loosely position lefthand side camshaft sprocket over camshaft hub.
5. Align plated link to crankshaft sprocket timing mark, **Fig. 7.**
6. Position primary chain onto water pump drive sprocket.
7. Align righthand camshaft sprocket timing mark to timing chain plated link and loosely position over camshaft hub.
8. Ensure all plated links are properly aligned to sprockets' timing marks.
9. Install lefthand lower chain guide and tensioner arm, then tighten to specifications.
10. Install chain guide access plug to lefthand cylinder head and tighten to specifications.
11. Remove tensioner from housing and place check ball end into shallow end of timing chain tensioner resetting gauge tool No. 8186, or equivalent.
12. Using hand pressure, slowly depress tensioner until oil is purged from cylinder, then install into housing.
13. Position cylinder plunger into deeper end of timing chain tensioner resetting gauge tool No. 8186, or equivalent, then apply downward force until tensioner bottoms against top edge of tool.
14. Install chain tensioner into righthand cylinder head.
15. Insert suitable ⅜ inch square drive extension with breaker bar into righthand cylinder bank intake camshaft drive hub, then rotate until camshaft hub aligns with camshaft sprocket and damper attaching holes.
16. Install sprocket mounting bolts and tighten to specifications.
17. Insert suitable ⅜ inch square drive extension with breaker bar into lefthand cylinder bank intake camshaft drive hub, then rotate until camshaft hub

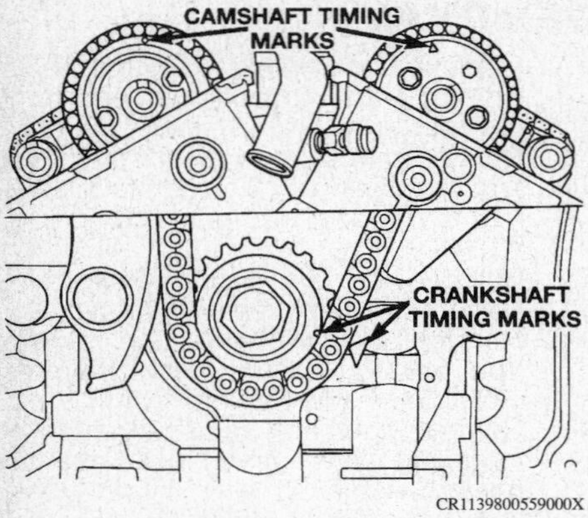

Fig. 6 Timing chain mark alignment

aligns with camshaft sprocket and damper attaching holes.
18. Install sprocket mounting bolts and tighten to specifications.
19. Rotate engine slightly clockwise to remove timing chain slack.
20. Using suitable flat bladed pry tool, gently pry tensioner arm toward tensioner slightly, then release tensioner arm and ensure tensioner extends and arms.
21. Install front cover, crankshaft damper, cylinder heads, camshaft position sensor, electrical connector and upper intake manifold.

TIMING CHAIN TENSIONER

REPLACE

Refer to "Timing Chain, Replace" for tensioner replacement.

TIMING CHAIN TENSIONER BLEED

Refer to "Timing Chain, Replace" for tensioner bleed.

CAMSHAFT

REPLACE

With the timing chain removed, avoid turning the camshaft or crankshaft. If movement is required, exercise caution to avoid valve damage caused by piston contact.

REMOVAL

1. Remove primary timing chain as outlined under "Timing Chain, Replace," then the secondary chain tensioner mounting bolts.
2. Loosen camshaft bearing cap bolts in reverse order of installation, **Fig. 8**, then remove bearing caps.
3. Remove camshafts, secondary chain and tensioner as an assembly.
4. Remove tensioner and chain from camshaft.

INSTALLATION

1. Assemble camshaft chain on cams

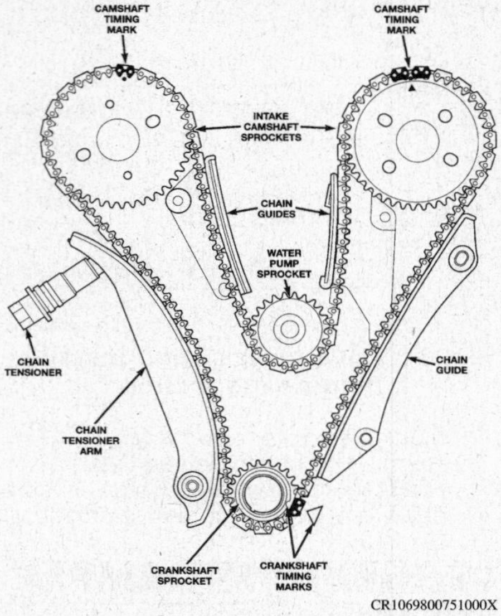

Fig. 7 Primary timing chain alignment marks

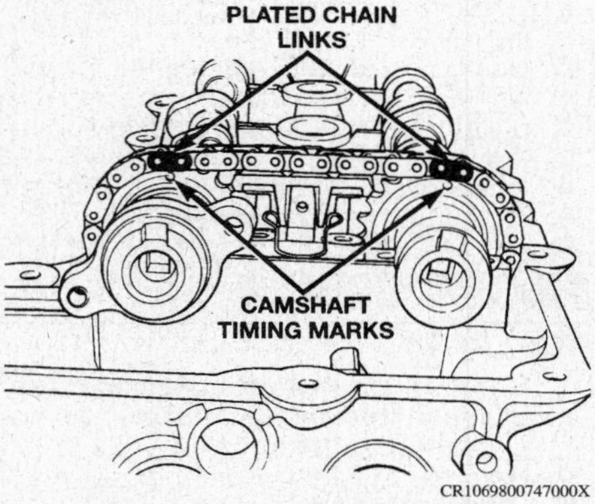

Fig. 9 Camshaft chain timing

with plated links facing front and aligned with camshaft sprocket dots, **Fig. 9.**

2. **On models equipped with early build tensioners that separate into subcomponents,** proceed as follows:
   a. Separate cylinder from tensioner housing.
   b. Carefully drain housing oil without removing internal components.
   c. Assemble plunger to housing.
   d. Compress tensioner with hand pressure and lock with fabricated lock pin.
3. **On models equipped with late build tensioners that do not separate into subcomponents,** proceed as follows:
   a. Place tensioner into suitable soft jaw vise.
   b. Slowly compress tensioner.
   c. Install fabricated lock pin.
   d. Remove compressed and locked tensioner from vise.
4. **On all models,** install compressed and locked camshaft chain tensioner between camshafts and chain.
5. Rotate cams so plated links and sprocket dots are at 12 o'clock position, then install to cylinder head. Ensure rocker arms are correctly seated

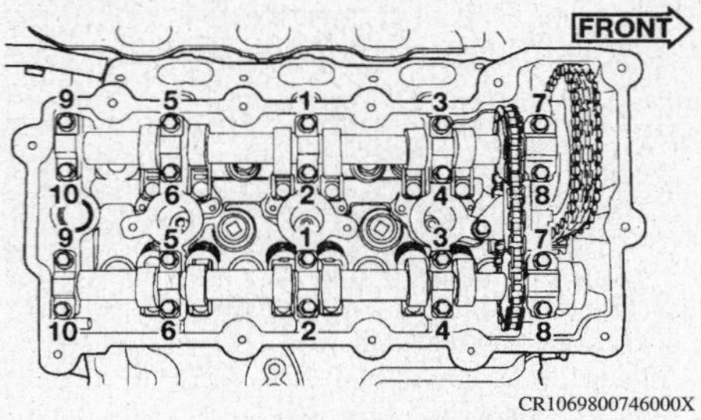

Fig. 8 Camshaft bearing cap tightening sequence

and in proper positions.

6. Install camshaft bearing caps in same position as removed.
7. **Torque** bearing caps gradually to 9 ft. lbs. in sequence, **Fig. 9.**
8. Install secondary chain tensioner mounting bolts and tighten to supplications.
9. Measure camshaft endplay.
10. Install primary timing chain as outlined under "Timing Chain, Replace."

PISTON & ROD ASSEMBLY

REMOVAL

1. Remove cylinder bores top ridge with suitable ridge reamer before removing pistons.
2. Rotate crankshaft so connecting rod is centered in cylinder bore.
3. Mark connecting rod and bearing caps with permanent ink marker or suitable scribe tool for assembly. Do not use stamp or punch to mark connecting rods.
4. Remove connecting rod cap.
5. Install connecting rod guide tools No. 8189, or equivalent, into connecting rod, then remove piston and rod assembly from top of cylinder block.
6. Install bearing cap on mating rod.

INSTALLATION

1. Install oil ring expander.
2. Place one end of upper side rail between piston ring groove and expander, then hold end firmly and press down portion to be installed until side rail is in position. **Do not use piston ring expander.**
3. Place one end of lower side rail between piston ring groove and expander, then hold end firmly and press down portion to be installed until side rail is in position. **Do not use piston ring expander.**
4. Install No. 2 intermediate piston ring. Ensure manufacturers I.D. dot mark faces up, towards top of piston, **Fig. 10.**
5. Install piston ring No. 1.
6. Position piston ring end gaps, **Fig. 11.**
7. Ensure compression ring gaps are staggered so neither is in line with oil ring rail gap.
8. Ensure oil ring expander ends are butted and rail gaps properly located before installing ring compressor.

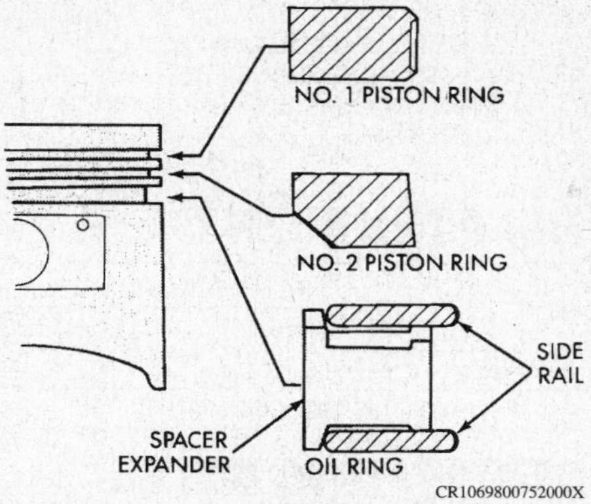

Fig. 10 Piston ring installation

9. Immerse piston head and rings in clean engine oil, slide ring compressor over piston and tighten. Ensure ring position does not change.
10. Position bearing onto connecting rod. Ensure bearing half hole aligns with connecting rod hole.
11. Lubricate bearing surface with engine oil.
12. Install connecting rod guide tools No. 8189, or equivalent.
13. Pistons are marked on top with arrow and F above pin boss. These marks must point toward front of engine in both cylinder banks.
14. Connecting rod oil squirt hole faces major thrust (righthand) side of block.
15. Rotate crankshaft so connecting rod journal is centered in cylinder bore, then insert rod and piston into bore and guide rod over crankshaft journal.
16. Using suitable hammer handle, tap piston down cylinder bore and guide connecting rod onto connecting rod journal.
17. Lubricate rod bolts and bearing surfaces with engine oil.
18. Install connecting rod cap and bearing. Tighten to specifications.

CRANKSHAFT

REPLACE

REMOVAL

1. Remove engine as previously described and mount on suitable stand.
2. Drain engine oil into suitable container and remove oil filter.
3. Remove oil pan as outlined under "Oil Pan, Replace " and oil pickup tube.
4. Remove accessory drive idler pulley bracket.
5. Remove upper intake manifold, valve covers, front cover and timing chain as previously described.
6. Remove crankshaft sprocket as outlined under "Crankshaft Sprocket, Replace."
7. Remove oil pump as outlined under "Oil Pump, Replace. "
8. Remove crankshaft rear oil seal retainer as outlined under " Crankshaft Rear Oil Seal. Replace"
9. Remove structural windage tray.
10. Using permanent ink marker or suitable scribe tool, mark connecting rod cap position for assembly. Do not use punch or stamp to mark connecting rods.
11. Remove connecting rod bearing caps.
12. Remove main bearing cap and tie bolts, then the main bearing caps.
13. Remove crankshaft.

INSTALLATION

Upper and lower bearing halves are not interchangeable.

1. Lubricate upper main bearing halves with engine oil.
2. Push crankshaft forward.
3. Roll lubricate front thrust washer onto machined shelf between No. 3 upper main bulk head and crankshaft thrust surface. Ensure crankshaft thrust washer coated and oil groove side faces crankshaft thrust surface.
4. Move crankshaft rearward.
5. Roll lubricate rear thrust washer onto machined shelf between No. 3 upper main bulk head and crankshaft thrust surface. Ensure crankshaft thrust washer coated and oil groove side faces crankshaft thrust surface.
6. Lubricate lower main bearings with engine oil, then install main bearings and caps.
7. Install inside main bearing cap bolts, then **torque** to 15 ft. lbs. and finally tighten an addition 1/4 turn.
8. Measure crankshaft endplay.
9. Install connecting rods and measure side clearance.
10. Install windage tray.
11. Lubricate windage tray mounting bolts with engine oil, then **torque** to 20 ft. lbs., and finally tighten an addition 1/4 turn.
12. Install main cap tie bolts and tighten to specifications.
13. Install rear crankshaft oil seal retainer and oil seal.
14. Install oil pump, crankshaft sprocket, timing chain, front cover and valve covers.
15. Install accessory drive idler pulley bracket, then the oil pickup tube and O-ring.
16. Install oil pan and filter, then the oil dipstick tube.
17. Install engine and fill crankcase with suitable oil.

CRANKSHAFT SPROCKET

REPLACE

With the timing chain removed, avoid turning the camshaft or crankshaft. If movement is required, exercise caution to avoid valve damage caused by piston contact.

REMOVAL

1. Remove timing chain as previously described.
2. Using crankshaft damper bolt and suitable puller, remove sprocket.

INSTALLATION

1. Using crankshaft seal and sprocket installer tool No. 6780-1 and crankshaft damper installer screw tool No. 8179, or equivalents, install sprocket until it bottoms against crankshaft step flange.
2. Measure from sprocket outer face to end of crankshaft. Ensure measurement is 1.5174–1.5574 inches.
3. Install primary timing chain.

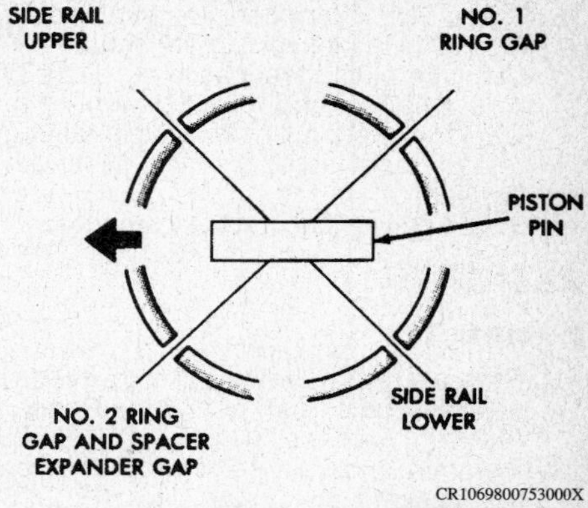

Fig. 11 Piston ring end gap positions

MAIN & ROD BEARINGS

Refer to "Crankshaft, Replace" for main and rod bearings service.

CRANKSHAFT SEAL

REPLACE

1. Remove crankshaft damper as previously described.
2. Insert crankshaft damper remover insert tool No. 8194, or equivalent, into crankshaft nose.
3. Using crankshaft seal remover tool No. 6771, or equivalent, remove seal.
4. Reverse procedure to install using crankshaft seal protector tool No. 6780-2, crankshaft seal and sprocket installer tool 6780-1 and crankshaft damper installer screw tool No. 8179, or equivalents.

CRANKSHAFT REAR OIL SEAL

REPLACE

SEAL

Removal

1. Remove transaxle and drive plate.
2. Insert suitable 3/16 inch wide flat bladed screwdriver between lip and seal metal case.
3. Angle screwdriver through dust lip against metal case and pry out seal. **Do not allow screwdriver blade to contact seal surface.**

Installation

1. Place magnetic base, crankshaft rear seal pilot guide tool No. 6926-1, or equivalent, on crankshaft.

2. Place seal over pilot tool and ensure seal lip faces towards crankshaft.
3. Using crankshaft rear seal installer tool No. 6926-2 and handle tool No. C-4171, or equivalents, drive seal into retainer housing until seal is flush with surface.
4. Install drive plate and transaxle.

RETAINER

Removal

1. Remove rear oil seal as previously described and oil pan as outlined under "Oil Pan, Replace."
2. Remove mounting screws, retainer and gasket.

Installation

1. Install gasket and loosen assemble seal retainer.
2. Attach crankshaft real seal retainer alignment fixture tools No. 8225, or equivalents to pan rail using oil pan fasteners. Ensure 2.7L stamped is facing cylinder block with flat side of tools against pan rail.
3. While applying firm pressure to seal with alignment fixture tools, tighten retainer screws to specifications.
4. Install oil pan and crankshaft rear oil seal.

OIL PAN

REPLACE

REMOVAL

1. Remove dipstick and tube, then raise and support vehicle.
2. Drain engine oil into suitable container, then remove oil filter.
3. Remove structural collar as previous described.
4. Remove mounting bolts, oil pan and gasket. Ensure timing cover to oil pan bolts are removed, before removing pan.

INSTALLATION

1. Apply ⅛ inch bead of suitable silicone rubber adhesive sealant to front T-joints, **Fig. 12.**
2. Install gasket to block.
3. Install oil pan, then finger tighten bolts and nuts until gasket's rubber seal is compressed.
4. Install timing chain cover and **torque** mounting bolts (4) to 9 ft. lbs.
5. **Torque** mounting bolts (2) to 21 ft. lbs.
6. **Torque** mounting nuts (1 and 3) to 9 ft. lbs.
7. Install structural collar as previously described.
8. Install oil filter and drain plug, then lower vehicle and install dipstick and tube.
9. Fill crankcase with suitable oil.

OIL PUMP

REPLACE

1. Remove crankshaft damper, front cover, timing chain, crankshaft sprocket and oil pan as previously described.

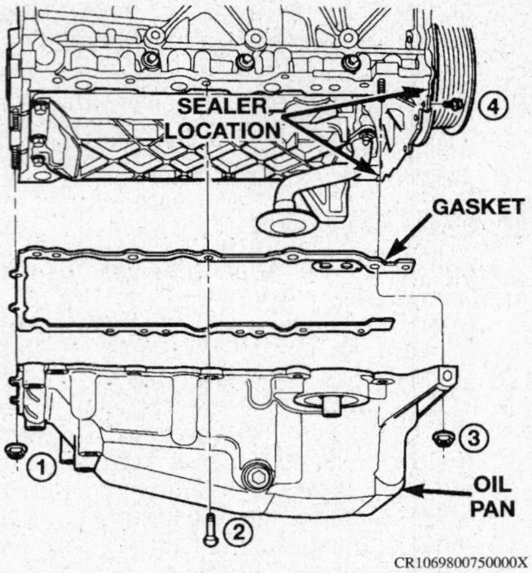

Fig. 12 Oil pan replacement

2. Remove oil pickup tube and O-ring.
3. Ensure crankshaft sprocket and oil pump marks align, with crankshaft position at cylinder No. 1 at 60° ATDC.
4. Remove mounting bolts and oil pump.
5. Reverse procedure to install, noting the following:
   a. Ensure pump is primed with oil before installation.
   b. Ensure crankshaft sprocket and oil pump marks align, with crankshaft position at cylinder No. 1 at 60° ATDC.
   c. Tighten mounting bolts to specifications.

OIL PUMP SERVICE

1. Remove retaining cap, spring and pressure relief valve.
2. Remove mounting screws and lift cover plate off.
3. Remove pump rotors.
4. Wash parts in suitable solvent, then inspect for damage or wear.
5. Lay straightedge across pump cover surface. If .001 inch feeler gauge can be inserted between cover and straight edge, replace cover.
6. Measure thickness and diameter of rotors.
7. If outer rotor thickness is less than .373 inch or diameter less than 3.5108 inches, replace rotor.
8. If inner rotor thickness is less than .373 inch, replace rotor.
9. Slide outer rotor into body, press to one side with fingers and measure clearance between rotor and body. If clearance is more than .015 inch, replace body.
10. Install inner rotor and measure clearance between rotors. If clearance is more than .003 inch, replace pump assembly.
11. Inspect oil pressure relief valve plunger for scoring and free operation in bore. Small marks may be removed with 400-grit wet or dry sandpaper.
12. Relief valve spring free length should be approximately 1.95 inches. Compress spring with 23–25 lbs. If length is not 1.34 inches, replace spring.
13. Reverse procedure to assemble. Tighten screws and retaining cap to specifications

BELT TENSION DATA

Belt	Belt Tension, Lbs.	
	New	Used
Accessory	180–200	120
A/C	140–160	120

SERPENTINE DRIVE BELT

1. Loosen tensioner pulley locking nut.
2. Loosen belt adjusting bolt.
3. Remove accessory drive belt.
4. Reverse procedure to install.

SEPARATED ACCESSORY DRIVE SYSTEM

AIR CONDITIONING

Removal

1. Remove alternator/power steering serpentine drive belt as previously described.
2. Loosen tensioner locking and pivot bolts. Do not remove.
3. Insert suitable ½ inch drive breaker bar into belt tensioner square opening, rotate tensioner counterclockwise until belt can be removed from pulleys.
4. Slowly rotate tensioner clockwise to relieve spring load.

Installation

1. Insert suitable ½ inch drive breaker bar into tensioner square opening, then hold counterclockwise pressure on tensioner while removing locking bolt.
2. Carefully release tensioner torsion spring load.
3. Remove pivot bolt, tensioner and spring from front timing cover.
4. Insert spring arm into appropriate New or Used tensioner belt position.
5. Install torsion spring, tensioner and pivot bolt. Tighten pivot bolt to specifications.
6. Using ½ inch drive breaker bar, apply counterclockwise pressure on tensioner until locking bolt can be installed.
7. Rotate tensioner counterclockwise until belt can be installed on pulleys.
8. Release tensioner and remove socket wrench, then tighten tensioner locking bolt to specifications.
9. Install accessory drive belt.

COOLING SYSTEM BLEED

1. Close radiator drain hand tight.

2. Attach approximately 48 inches of .250 inch I.D. clear hose to bleed valve.
3. Route hose away from accessory drive belt, drive pulleys and electrical cooling fan to clean container.
4. Open cooling system bleed valve, then attach filling aid funnel tool No. 8195, or equivalent, to pressure bottle filler neck.
5. Pinch overflow hose between coolant bottle chambers.
6. Pour 50/50 mix of suitable coolant and distilled water into large section of filling funnel.
7. Slowly fill until steady stream of coolant flows from bleed valve hose.
8. Close bleed valve and continue filling system to top of funnel.
9. Remove overflow hose clip and allow funnel to drain into overflow chamber.
10. Remove funnel and install coolant pressure bottle cap.
11. Remove bleed valve hose, then start and run engine until operating temperature is reached.
12. Shut off engine and allow to cool.
13. With engine cold, ensure pressure chamber level is between MIN and MAX marks. Adjust as necessary.

THERMOSTAT

REPLACE

1. Drain cooling system into suitable container.
2. Remove accessory drive belt, then raise and support vehicle.
3. Remove alternator mounting bolts, then position alternator aside.
4. Remove lower radiator and heater hoses from thermostat housing.
5. Remove mounting bolts, housing and thermostat.
6. Reverse procedure to install, noting the following:
   a. Install thermostat with bleed valve at 12 o'clock position.
   b. Tighten mounting bolts to specifications.

WATER PUMP

REPLACE

1. Drain cooling system into suitable container.
2. Remove upper radiator crossmember.
3. Disconnect fan module electrical connector, then remove mounting screws and fan module.
4. Remove accessory and air conditioning drive belts.
5. Remove crankshaft damper, front cover and primary timing chain as previously described, then the chain guides.
6. Remove mounting bolts and water pump.
7. Reverse procedure to install, tighten mounting bolts to specifications.

RADIATOR

REPLACE

1. Drain cooling system into suitable container.
2. Remove upper radiator crossmember, then the clamps and hoses from radiator.
3. Disconnect transmission hoses from cooler and plug.
4. Disconnect engine oil cooler lines.
5. Disconnect fan module electrical connector, then remove mounting bolts and fan module.
6. Remove air conditioning condenser mounting screws and the transmission cooler line bracket.
7. Lift condenser up enough to clear upper mounting clips, then rest condenser on lower radiator crossmember.
8. Remove radiator.
9. Reverse procedure to install. Tighten bolts and screws to specifications.

FUEL PUMP

REPLACE

1. Relieve fuel pressure as outlined under "Precautions."
2. Remove rear seat, then disconnect fuel pump electrical connector.
3. Raise and support vehicle, then drain fuel tank into suitable container.
4. Loosen brackets from body and swing rear stabilizer bar toward rear.
5. Remove fuel filler tube from tank, then disconnect fuel and EVAP lines.
6. Position suitable transmission jack under fuel tank, then remove fuel tank strap bolts, passenger side first.
7. Lower fuel tank, then remove purge and vent lines.
8. Depress quick connector retainers and disconnect fuel line from pump.
9. Slide fuel pump module electrical connector lock to unlock, then push connector retainer down and pull off module.
10. Using fuel pump removal/installation tool No. 6856, or equivalent, remove fuel pump module locknut.
11. Remove fuel pump and O-ring seal.
12. Reverse procedure to install, noting the following:
    a. Ensure underside alignment tabs on module flange sit on fuel tank notches.
    b. Use fuel pump removal/installation tool No. 6856, or equivalent, to tighten locking ring to specifications.

FUEL FILTER

REPLACE

A combination fuel filter/pressure regulator is located on top of fuel pump module. A separate frame mount filter is not used.

1. Relieve fuel pressure as outlined under "Precautions."
2. Lower fuel tank as outlined under "Fuel Pump, Replace."
3. Remove fuel tank purge and vent lines.
4. Disconnect pressure regulator fuel line, then push locking tab in from locking slot and turn pressure regulator to unlock.
5. Pull regulator straight up and remove.
6. Reverse procedure to install.

TECHNICAL SERVICE BULLETINS

EXHAUST DRONE

1998

On these models, there may be an exhaust drone between 1600–2000 RPM.

This condition may be caused by the lefthand exhaust pipe. If exhaust system is free and not grounded by body or suspension, proceed as follows:

1. Replace lefthand front exhaust pipe/catalytic converter (Federal emissions part No. 04581705AF; California emission part No. 04581707AF).
2. Use new V-band exhaust manifold clamp (part No. 04581013AC).
3. Remove and discard righthand front exhaust piper support bracket.

TIGHTENING SPECIFICATIONS

Year	Component	Torque, Ft. Lbs.
1997– 2000	A/C Belt Tensioner	21
	A/C Compressor	21
	A/C Condenser To Radiator	45①
	Alternator	30
	Alternator/Power Steering Belt Tensioner	40

Continued

TIGHTENING SPECIFICATIONS—Continued

Year	Component	Torque, Ft. Lbs.
1997-2000	Camshaft Bearing Cap	⑦
	Camshaft Chain Tensioner	108①
	Camshaft Sprocket	21①
	Condenser Inlet Tube	45①
	Connecting Rod Cap	③
	Cooling System Bleed	108①
	Crankshaft Damper	125
	Crankshaft Main Bearing Cap	②
	Crankshaft Main Bearing Cap, Tie	21
	Cylinder Head	④
	Cylinder Head Cover	108①
	Exhaust Manifold Heat Shield	108①
	Exhaust Manifold To Catalytic Converter	96①
	Exhaust Manifold To Cylinder Head	21
	Fan Blade	45①
	Fan Module	45①
	Fan Motor	25①
	Front Cover, M10	40
	Front Cover, M6	108①
	Fuel Pump Locking Ring	40
	Fuel Pump Module	40
	Fuel Rail	16
	Fuel Tank Straps	44
	Intake Manifold	108①⑤
	Oil Pan	⑧
	Oil Pan Drain Plug	25
	Oil Pan Filter	15
	Oil Pump	21
	Oil Pump Cover	108①
	Oil Pump Pickup Tube	21
	Oil Pump Pressure Relief Valve Cap	108①
	PCV Valve	60①
	Rear Crankshaft Seal Retainer	108①
	Spark Plug	15
	Starter	30
	Structural Collar	⑥
	Thermostat Housing	108①
	Throttle Body	108①
	Throttle Body Support Bracket, Lower	50①
	Throttle Body Support Bracket, Upper	108①
	Timing Chain Cover, M6	108①
	Timing Chain Cover, M10	40
	Timing Chain Guide	21
	Timing Chain Guide Access Plug	15
	Timing Chain Tensioner	40
	Water Pump	108①
	Water Outlet Housing	108①
	Water Outlet Housing Bleed	72①

① — Inch lbs.

② — Refer to "Crankshaft, Replace" for tightening specifications and sequence.

③ — Torque to 20 ft. lbs., then tighten an additional ¼ turn.

④ — Refer to "Cylinder Head, Replace" for tightening specifications and sequence.

⑤ — Refer to "Intake Manifold, Replace" for tightening sequence.
⑥ — Refer to "Structural Collar, Replace" for tightening specifications and sequence.
⑦ — Refer to "Camshaft, Replace" for tightening specifications and sequence.
⑧ — Refer to "Oil Pan, Replace" for tightening specifications and sequence.

3.2L & 3.5L VIN G Engines

NOTE: On Air Bag Equipped Models, Refer To " Air Bag System Precautions" Located In The Front Of This Manual For System Disarming & Arming Procedures.

NOTE: Prior To Performing Any Service Operations Listed In This Section, Consult The "Technical Service Bulletins " Section For Related Information.

NOTE: Refer To "Computer Relearn Procedure " Located In The Front Of This Manual For Computer Relearn Procedures.

INDEX

PRECAUTIONS

AIR BAG SYSTEMS

Refer to "Air Bag System Precautions" in the front of this manual for system disarming and arming procedures.

BATTERY GROUND CABLE

Prior to service, disconnect battery ground cable and isolate as required.

FUEL SYSTEM PRESSURE RELIEF

1. Remove fuel pump relay for power distribution center.
2. Start and run engine until it stalls.
3. Attempt to start engine until it no longer runs.
4. Turn ignition switch to Off position.
5. Place rag or towel under fuel line quick-connector fitting at fuel rail.
6. Install fuel pump relay.
7. One or more Diagnostic Trouble Codes (DTCs) may have been stored because of removing fuel pump relay. Clear these DTCs with suitably programmed scan tool.

COMPRESSION PRESSURE

The minimum compression pressure should be no less than 100 psi and the maximum variation between cylinders should be no more than 25%.

ENGINE MOUNT

REPLACE

Refer to "2.7L Engine" for engine mount replacement.

STRUCTURAL COLLAR

REPLACE

Refer to "2.7L Engine" for structural collar replacement.

ENGINE

REPLACE

1. Relieve fuel pressure as described under "Precautions."
2. Mark hood position at hinges and remove, then drain cooling system into suitable container.
3. Remove wiper arms, right and lefthand cowl covers, then the cowl support.
4. Remove air cleaner assembly and air inlet hose, then the upper radiator crossmember.
5. Disconnect hood release cable from

latch, then remove cooling fan module and accessory drive belts.
6. Disconnect upper radiator hose at engine and lower hose at radiator, then the engine oil and transaxle cooler lines at radiator.
7. Remove power steering line bracket at lefthand side of radiator, then the A/C condenser to radiator fasteners.
8. Remove radiator, then the accessory drive belts.
9. Remove alternator, then the power steering pump mounting bolts and set pump aside.
10. Remove mounting bolts and set A/C compressor aside.
11. Remove righthand exhaust manifold V-band clamps, then the righthand side catalytic converter down pipe front and rear support bracket fasteners.
12. Relieve fuel pressure as outlined under "Precautions, " then disconnect fuel line.
13. Disconnect throttle and speed control cables, then the coolant bottle hoses.
14. Disconnect vacuum lines and engine ground straps at both cylinder heads.
15. Remove upper intake manifold as described under " Intake Manifold, Replace."
16. Disconnect heater hoses, then remove rear throttle body support bracket.
17. Remove water piper fastener at transmission to block bolt, then the four upper transmission to block bolts.
18. Disconnect electrical connections, then raise and support vehicle.
19. Drain engine oil into suitable container, then remove mounting bolts and structural collar.
20. Mark flexplate to torque converter position and remove converter mounting bolts.
21. Disconnect transaxle cooler line brackets from engine.
22. Remove lefthand exhaust manifold V-band clamp, then the starter.
23. Remove left and righthand engine mount bolts.
24. Remove crankshaft position sensor and lower transaxle to block bolts.
25. Lower vehicle and attach suitable lifting device to engine.
26. Support transaxle with suitable floor jack and small block of wood, then remove engine.
27. Reverse procedure to install, noting the following:
    a. Tighten all fasteners to specifications.
    b. Do not tighten transaxle case to engine block bolts until all bolts have been started and mating surface are completely joined.

INTAKE MANIFOLD

REPLACE

UPPER

1. Remove air cleaner housing and inlet hose.
2. Remove throttle and speed control cables from throttle arm and bracket.
3. Disconnect Secondary Runner Valve (SRV), Manifold Tuning Valve (MTV), Throttle Position Sensor (TPS), Idle Air Control (IAC) and Intake Air Temperature/Manifold Absolute Pressure (TMAP) electrical connectors.
4. Disconnect SRV reservoir, speed control reservoir and Positive Crankcase Ventilation (PCV) vacuum hoses.
5. Remove right and left side intake manifold supports, then the support brackets at intake manifold front corners and MTV.
6. Remove EGR tubes mounting clips.
7. Remove mounting bolts and upper manifold.
8. Reverse procedure to install, noting the following:
    a. Hand start all intake manifold mounting bolts.
    b. Tighten manifold mounting bolts to specifications using sequence shown in **Figs. 1 and 2.**

LOWER

1. Relieve fuel pressure as described under "Precautions, " then drain cooling system into suitable container.
2. Remove upper intake manifold as previously described.
3. Disconnect fuel injectors and coolant temperature sensor electrical connectors, then the heater hose quick connect tee from heater tube.
4. Disconnect fuel rail fuel supply hose from fuel rail, then remove screw mounting fuel rail support bracket to throttle body support bracket.
5. Remove mounting bolts, then the fuel rail and injectors as an assembly.
6. Remove mounting bolts and lower intake manifold.
7. Reverse procedure to install. Gradually **torque** mounting bolts to 21 ft. lbs. in sequence, **Fig. 3.**

EXHAUST MANIFOLD

REPLACE

RIGHTHAND

1. Raise and support vehicle, then remove exhaust system.
2. Loosen converter pipe support mounting bolt at transaxle mount.
3. Loosen A/C drive belt, then lower vehicle.
4. Remove air cleaner housing and air inlet tube.
5. Remove manifold V-band clamp.
6. Remove mounting bolts and set A/C compressor aside.
7. Remove engine oil dipstick tube, then the A/C compressor bracket.
8. Disconnect electrical connector and remove oxygen sensor.
9. Remove mounting screws and heat shields.
10. Remove mounting bolts and exhaust manifold.
11. Reverse procedure to install, noting the following:
    a. Tighten exhaust manifold mounting bolts to specifications from center outwards.
    b. Tighten heat shield mounting screws to specifications.
    c. Use new V-band clamp and tighten to specifications.

LEFTHAND

1. Raise and support vehicle.
2. Remove exhaust system, then loosen converter pipe support mounting bolt at transaxle.
3. Lower vehicle and remove exhaust manifold connector V-band clamp.
4. Disconnect connector and remove exhaust manifold oxygen sensor.
5. Remove mounting screws and heat shield.
6. Remove mounting bolts and exhaust manifold.
7. Reverse procedure to install, noting the following:
    a. Tighten exhaust manifold mounting bolts to specifications from center working outward.
    b. Tighten heat shield mounting screws to specifications.
    c. Use new V-band clamp and tighten to specifications.

CYLINDER HEAD

REPLACE

1. Remove crankshaft damper as outlined under "Crankshaft Damper, Replace."
2. Remove timing belt covers as outlined under "Front Cover, Replace."
3. Remove camshaft sprockets as outlined under "Camshaft Sprocket, Replace."
4. Remove upper and lower intake manifolds as previously described.
5. Remove exhaust manifold to catalytic converter pipe connection V-band clamps.
6. Remove rear timing belt cover to cylinder head fasteners and rear covers.
7. Remove mounting bolts and cylinder heads.
8. Reverse procedure to install, noting the following:
    a. Cylinder head bolts are tightened using a torque plus angle procedure. **Bolts with stretched threads must be replaced.**
    b. Use new cylinder head gasket. Gaskets for 3.5L engine have perfectly round combustion sealing rings, for 3.2L engine, the combustion sealing rings are not perfectly round.
    c. Ensure head is properly positioned over locating dowels.
    d. Lubricate bolt threads with clean engine oil.
    e. **Torque** cylinder head bolts to 45 ft. lbs. in sequence, **Fig. 4.**
    f. **Torque** bolts to 65 ft. lbs.
    g. **Torque** bolts again to 65 ft. lbs.
    h. Tighten bolts an additional 90.° **Do not use torque wrench.**
    i. Final cylinder head bolt torque should be 90 ft. lbs. If not, replace bolts.
    j. Install new O-ring seal in righthand rear timing belt cover.
    k. Use new V-band clamp and tighten to specifications.

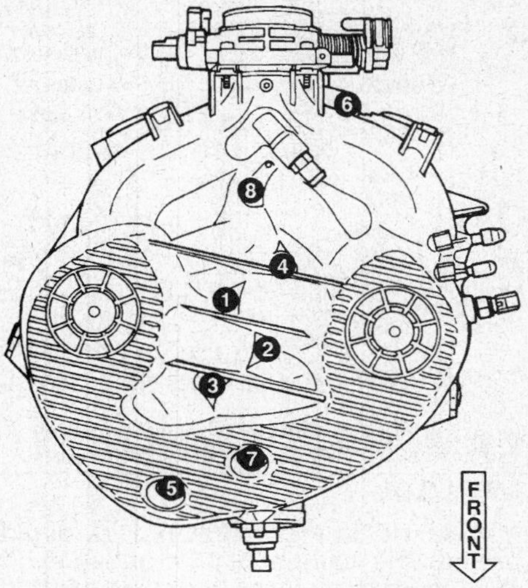

Fig. 1 Upper intake manifold tightening sequence. 1997–98

VALVE COVER

REPLACE

1. Remove air cleaner assembly, then the upper intake manifold plenum as previously described.
2. Cover lower intake manifold.
3. Disconnect electrical connectors and remove ignition coils.
4. Remove mounting bolts and cylinder head cover.
5. Reverse procedure to install, noting the following:
   a. Using suitable pry tool, remove spark plug tube seals.
   b. Position new seal with part number facing cylinder head cover and install with installer tool No. MB-998306, or equivalent.
   c. Tighten cylinder head cover mounting bolts to specifications.

SPARK PLUG TUBES

REPLACE

1. Remove cylinder head cover as previously described.
2. Using suitable locking pliers, remove tube from cylinder head.
3. Apply suitable stud and bearing mount to new tube approximately .039 inch from tube end, in .118 inch wide area.
4. Install seater end of tube into cylinder head, then carefully install tube using suitable hardwood block and mallet until seated into bore bottom.
5. Install cylinder head cover.

VALVE ADJUSTMENT

Rocker arms are equipped with hydraulic lash adjusters. No adjustment is necessary.

ROCKER ARMS

REPLACE

REMOVAL

1. Remove cylinder heads as previously described.
2. Identify rocker arm assembly and rocker arm for installation.
3. Remove mounting bolts and rocker arm assembly.
4. To prevent air ingestion into lash adjusters, avoid turning rocker arm assembly upside down.
5. Do not rest rocker arm assembly on lash adjusters.
6. Install screw, nut, spacer and washer into pin, tighten screw into pin, then loosen nut and pull out shaft support dowel, **Fig. 5.**
7. Remove rocker arms and pedestals in order.

INSTALLATION

1. Install rocker arms and pedestals into shaft. Rocker shaft notches face up. Righthand cylinder bank notches face toward rear and lefthand notches face toward front.
2. Press new dowel pins until they bottom against shaft in pedestal. Pins pass through pedestal into exhaust rocker shafts.
3. Rotate camshafts until lobes are in neutral position, **Fig. 6.**
4. Install rocker arm and shaft assembly. Ensure identification marks face engine front on lefthand head and toward rear on righthand head.
5. Tighten mounting bolts to specification using sequence shown in **Fig. 7.**

VALVE SPRINGS

REPLACE

IN-VEHICLE

Ensure piston is at TDC on cylinder from which valve spring(s) is being removed.

1. Relieve fuel pressure as described under "Precautions."
2. Remove air cleaner housing and hose.
3. Remove upper intake manifold as previously described.
4. Remove valve cover as previously described.
5. Remove rocker arm and shaft assembly as previously described.
6. Rotate crankshaft clockwise until piston No. 1 is at TDC.
7. Install suitable spark plug adapter into cylinder being serviced, then apply 90–100 psi air pressure to hold valves in place.
8. Using valve spring compressor tool No. MD-998772-A with adapter tool No. 6527, or equivalents, compress valve spring, then remove valve locks, retainer and spring.
9. Using suitable valve seal tool, remove valve stem seals.
10. Repeat procedure in firing sequence 1-2-3-4-5-6. **Ensure piston is at TDC on cylinder from which valve spring(s) is being removed.**
11. Reverse procedure to install, noting the following:
    a. Push valve steam seal/seat firmly and squarely over valve guide with stem as guide.

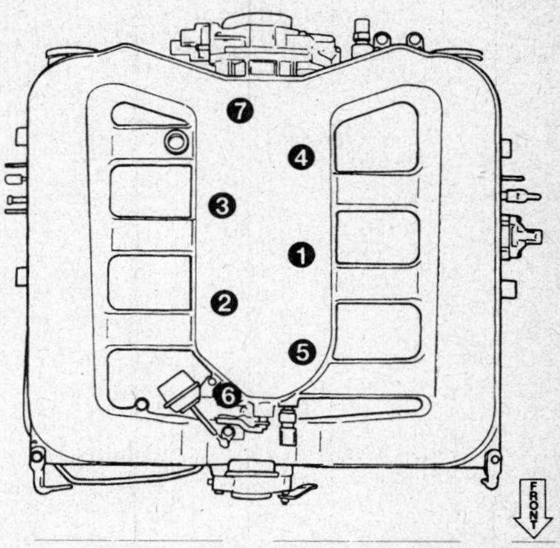

Fig. 2 Upper intake manifold tightening sequence. 1999–2000

    b. Do not force seal against guide top.
    c. When install retainer locks, compress spring only enough to install locks.

HEAD REMOVED

Removal

1. Using valve spring compressor tool No. C-3422-B, or equivalent, compress valve spring.
2. Remove valve retaining locks, valve spring retainers, valve springs and valve springs seat/stem seal assembly.
3. Identify valves for installation, then remove valve stem lock groove burrs.
4. Remove valves.

Installation

1. Coat with clean engine oil and install valve stems.
2. If valves and/or seats have been ground, proceed as follows:
   a. Measure valve tip height (A) form cylinder head surface to valve stem top, **Fig. 8.**
   b. If intake valve tip height is more than 1.7185 inches, grind tip to specifications.
   c. If exhaust valve tip height is more than 1.8102 inches, grind tip to specifications.
3. Install seal/spring seat assembly over valve guides.
4. Ensure garter spring is intact around rubber seal top, then install valve springs and retainers.
5. Compress valve springs with suitable valve spring compressor, then install locks and release tool.
6. If valves and/or seats have been ground, proceed as follows:
   a. Measure springs installed height (B) from spring seal to spring retainer bottom surface, **Fig. 5.**
   b. If height is more than 1.5256 inches, install .030 inch spacer in head counterbore under valve spring seat.

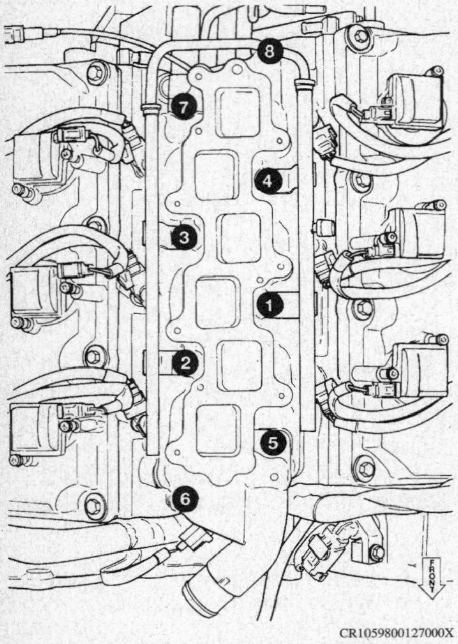

Fig. 3 Lower intake manifold tightening sequence

VALVE SEATS

Refer to "Valve Spring, Replace" for valve seat/seal replacement.

CRANKSHAFT DAMPER

REPLACE

1. Remove upper radiator crossmember, then the fan module.
2. Remove accessory drive belts.
3. Hold crankshaft damper with holder tool No. 8191, or equivalent, then remove center bolt.
4. Using three-jaw puller tool No. 1023 and crankshaft damper remover insert tool No. C-4685-C2, or equivalents, remove damper.
5. Reverse procedure to install. Tighten center bolt to specifications.

FRONT COVER

REPLACE

1. Remove upper radiator crossmember, then the cooling fan module and accessory drive belts.
2. Remove crankshaft damper as previously described.
3. Remove lower belt cover, stamped steel cover and lefthand cast cover.
4. Do not remove cover sealer. If some sealer is missing, replace with suitable silicone rubber adhesive sealant.
5. Reverse procedure to install.

TIMING BELT

REPLACE

With the timing belt removed, avoid turning the camshaft or crankshaft. If movement is required, exercise caution to avoid valve damage caused by piston contact.

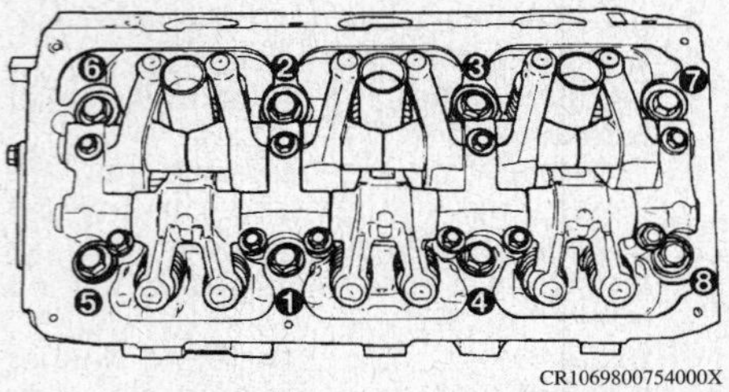

Fig. 4 Cylinder head tightening sequence

This procedure can only be used when camshaft sprockets have not been loosened or removed. If camshaft sprockets have been loosened or removed, refer to "Camshaft Timing, Adjust" for proper procedure.

REMOVAL

1. Remove upper radiator crossmember, then disconnect fan module electrical connector.
2. Remove fan module and accessory drive belts.
3. Remove crankshaft damper and front cover as previously described.
4. If reusing timing belt, mark rotational direction on belt.
5. Turn crankshaft clockwise until crankshaft mark aligns with oil pump housing TDC mark and camshaft sprocket timing marks are between rear cover marks, **Fig. 9.**
6. Using ink or paint, mark camshaft sprocket timing mark position to two rear timing cover timing marks.
7. Remove timing belt tensioner and store with plunger facing up.
8. Remove timing belt.

INSTALLATION

1. Place crankshaft sprocket with oil pump housing TDC mark, **Fig. 9.**
2. Align camshaft sprockets to reference marks between rear cover marks.
3. Slowly preload tensioner with suitable vise and install locking pin. Store pin with plunger facing up until ready to install.
4. Install timing belt starting at crankshaft sprocket and going in counterclockwise direction. Maintain tension on belt when positioned around tensioner pulley.
5. Ensure camshaft sprockets mark still fall between cover marks.
6. Hold tensioner pulley against belt, install tensioner and tighten to specifications.
7. Pull retaining pin and allow tensioner to extend to pulley bracket.
8. Ensure camshaft sprocket marks are still aligned.
9. Rotate crankshaft sprocket two revolutions and ensure timing marks align.
10. Install front covers and crankshaft damper, then accessory drive belts and cooling fan module.
11. Install upper radiator crossmember.

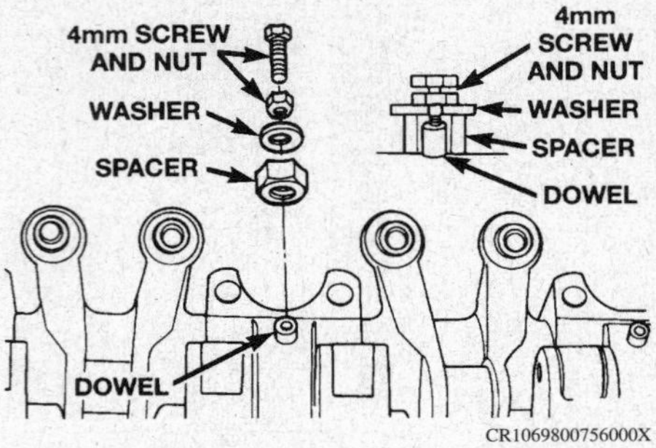

Fig. 5 Rocker arm dowel removal

CAMSHAFT SPROCKET

REPLACE

With the timing belt removed, avoid turning the camshaft or crankshaft. If movement is required, exercise caution to avoid valve damage caused by piston contact.

1. Hold camshaft sprocket with suitable box wrench, then remove bolt and washer. If engine is in vehicle, it may be necessary to lift engine side.
2. Remove camshaft sprocket.
3. Camshaft sprockets are not interchangeable. Lefthand sprocket has DIS pickup slots while righthand sprocket does not.
4. For installation, refer to "Camshaft Timing, Adjust."

CAMSHAFT

REPLACE

With the timing belt removed, avoid turning the camshaft or crankshaft. If movement is required, exercise caution to avoid valve damage caused by piston contact.

1. Remove camshaft sprocket(s) as previously described.
2. Remove cylinder head(s) as previously described.
3. Mark rocker arm and shaft assembly for installation, then remove.
4. Remove rear camshaft cover and O-ring.
5. Carefully remove camshaft from cylinder head rear.
6. Reverse procedure to install. Lubricate camshaft journals and cam with clean engine oil before installation.

CAMSHAFT OIL SEAL

REPLACE

1. Remove camshaft sprocket(s) as previously described.
2. Using camshaft seal remover tool No. C-3981B, or equivalent, remove oil seal.
3. Reverse procedure to install, noting the following:
   a. Lightly coat oil seal lip with clean engine oil.
   b. Use seal protector sleeve tool No. 6788 and seal installer tool No. 6052, or equivalents, to install oil seal.

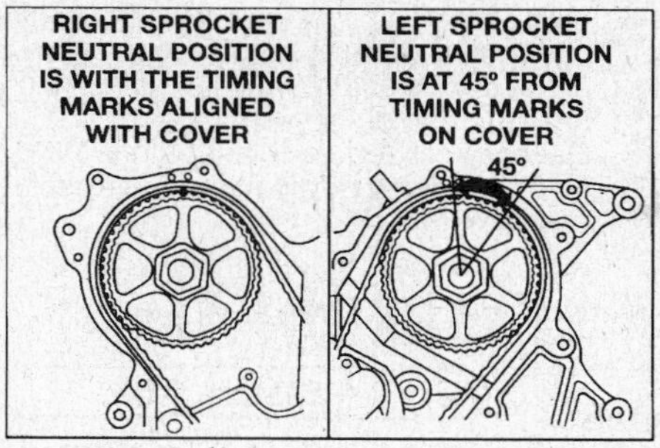

Fig. 6 Camshaft sprockets neutral position

CAMSHAFT TIMING

ADJUST

With the timing belt removed, avoid turning the camshaft or crankshaft. If movement is required, exercise caution to avoid valve damage caused by piston contact.

1. Place crankshaft sprocket with oil pump housing TDC mark, **Fig. 9.**
2. Install dial indicator in cylinder No. 1 and rotate crankshaft until piston is at exactly TDC.
3. Install camshaft alignment tools No. 6642, or equivalent, on each cylinder head rear.
4. Slowly preload tensioner with suitable vise and install locking pin. Store pin with plunger facing up until ready to install.
5. Install camshaft sprockets with timing mark between cover timing marks.
6. Install new mounting bolts. Lefthand mounting bolt is 10 inches long, righthand 8⅜ inches. Do not tighten at this time.
7. Install timing belt starting at crankshaft sprocket and going in counterclockwise direction. Maintain tension on belt when positioned around tensioner pulley.
8. Ensure camshaft sprockets mark still fall between cover marks.
9. Hold tensioner pulley against belt, install tensioner and tighten to specifications.
10. Pull retaining pin and allow tensioner to extend to pulley bracket.
11. Ensure No. 1 piston is at TDC, then hold camshaft sprocket hex with suitable wrench and tighten camshaft bolts to specifications.
12. Remove dial indicator and install spark plug.

TIMING BELT TENSIONER BLEED

Operate engine at 1600–2000 RPM for 10–15 minutes. This will purge air from tensioner and noise will dissipate.

PISTON & ROD ASSEMBLY

Refer to "2.7L Engine" for piston and rod assembly service.

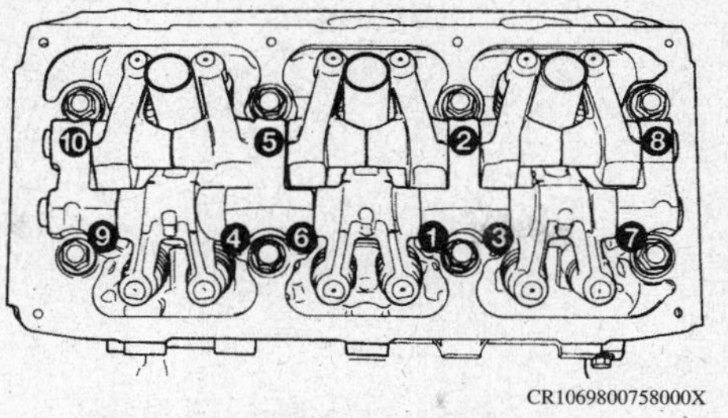

Fig. 7 Rocker arm & shaft assembly tightening sequence

CRANKSHAFT

REPLACE

REMOVAL

1. Remove engine as previously described.
2. Remove oil pan as described under "Oil Pan, Replace, " then the oil pickup tube.
3. Remove crankshaft damper as previously described.
4. Remove accessory drive belt idler pulley.
5. Remove front covers as previously described, then the tensioner and timing belt.
6. Remove crankshaft sprocket as outlined under "Crankshaft Seal, Replace."
7. Tap crankshaft dowel pin out, then remove oil pump assembly.
8. Remove rear oil seal retainer.
9. Mark connecting rod bearing caps for assembly, then remove.
10. Mark main bearing caps for assembly, then remove.
11. Remove crankshaft.

INSTALLATION

Upper and lower bearing halves are not interchangeable.

1. Lubricate upper main bearing halves with engine oil.
2. Push crankshaft forward.
3. Roll lubricate front thrust washer onto machined shelf between No. 2 upper main bulk head and crankshaft thrust surface.
4. Move crankshaft rearward.
5. Roll lubricate rear thrust washer onto machined shelf between No. 2 upper main bulk head and crankshaft thrust surface.
6. Lubricate lower main bearings with engine oil, then install main bearings and caps.
7. Install inside main bearing cap bolts and **torque** to 15 ft. lbs., then tighten an additional ¼ turn.
8. Measure crankshaft end play.
9. Install connecting rods and measure side clearance.
10. Install windage tray.
11. Lubricate windage tray mounting bolts with engine oil and **torque** to 20 ft. lbs., then tighten an additional ¼ turn.
12. Install main cap tie bolts and tighten to specifications.
13. Install rear crankshaft oil seal retainer and oil seal.

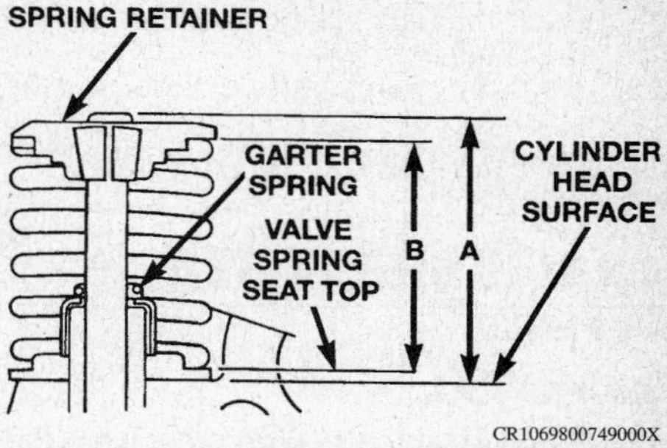

Fig. 8 Valve tip & spring installed heights inspection

14. Install oil pump, crankshaft dowel pin, crankshaft sprocket, timing belt, covers and crankshaft damper.
15. Install accessory drive idler pulley, then the oil pickup tube and pan.
16. Install engine and fill crankcase with suitable oil.

MAIN & ROD BEARINGS

REMOVAL

1. Remove oil pan as outlined under "Oil Pan, Replace, " then the oil pickup tube and windage tray.
2. Mark bearing caps for assembly.
3. Remove bearing caps one at a time.
4. Insert main bearing tool No. C-3059, or equivalent, into crankshaft oil hole, rotate crankshaft clockwise and force bearing shell upper half out.

INSTALLATION

When installing new upper bearing shells, slightly chamfer sharp edges from plain side.

1. Lubricate main bearing with clean engine oil.
2. Start bearing in place and insert main bearing tool No. C-3059, or equivalent, into crankshaft oil hole.
3. Slowly rotate crankshaft counterclockwise, sliding bearing into place, then remove tool.
4. Lubricate and install lower bearing half.
5. Lubricate main bearing cap bolts and finger tighten.
6. Move crankshaft to forward travel limit.
7. Roll lubricate front thrust washer onto machined shelf between No. 2 upper main bulk head and crankshaft thrust surface.
8. Move crankshaft rearward.
9. Roll lubricate rear thrust washer onto machined shelf between No. 2 upper main bulk head and crankshaft thrust surface.
10. Install main bearing cap and tighten inner bolts finger tight.
11. **Torque** inside main bearing cap bolts to 15 ft. lbs., then an additional ¼ turn.
12. Measure crankshaft end play.
13. Install windage tray.
14. Lubricate windage tray mounting bolts with engine oil and **torque** to 20 ft. lbs., then an additional ¼ turn.

15. Install main cap tie bolts and tighten to specifications.
16. Install oil pump, pickup tube and oil pan.
17. Install engine and fill crankcase with suitable oil.

CRANKSHAFT SEAL

REPLACE

REMOVAL

1. Remove timing belt as previously described.
2. Using crankshaft sprocket puller tool No. L-4407-A, or equivalent, remove crankshaft sprocket.
3. Tape dowel pin out of crankshaft.
4. Using crankshaft seal remover tool No. 6341A, or equivalent, remove seal.

INSTALLATION

1. Using crankshaft seal installer tool No. 6342, or equivalent, install crankshaft seal.
2. Install crankshaft dowel pin to .047 inch protrusion.
3. Using crankshaft sprocket installer tool No. 6641 or crankshaft damper installer bolt tool No. C-4685-C1, or equivalents, install crankshaft sprocket.
4. Install timing belt.

CRANKSHAFT REAR OIL SEAL

REPLACE

Refer to "2.7L Engine" for crankshaft rear oil seal and retainer replacement.

OIL PAN

REPLACE

1. Remove dipstick and tube, then raise and support vehicle.
2. Drain engine oil into suitable container.
3. Remove structural collar as previous described.
4. Remove engine oil cooler line, then transmission oil cooler line clips.
5. Remove mounting bolts, oil pan and gasket.
6. Reverse procedure to install, noting the following:
   a. Apply ⅛ inch bead of suitable silicone rubber adhesive sealant to parting line of oil pump housing and rear seal retainer.
   b. Tighten mounting bolts to specifications.

OIL PUMP

REPLACE

1. Drain cooling system into suitable container, then remove fan module and accessory drive belts.
2. Remove crankshaft damper and front cover as previously described.
3. Remove crankshaft sprocket as outline under "Crankshaft Seal, Replace."
4. Remove oil pan as previously described, then the oil pickup tube.

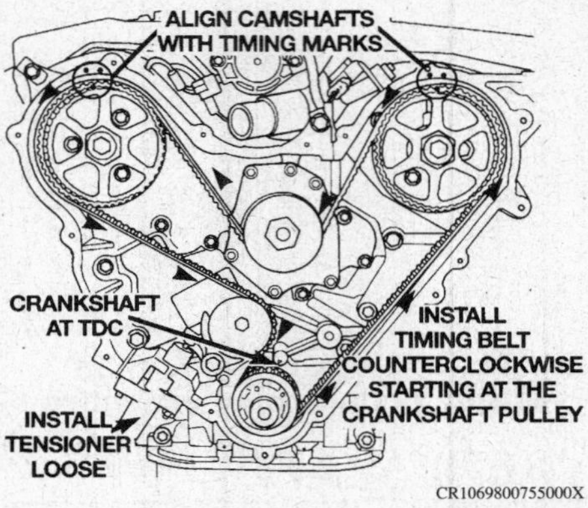

Fig. 9 Camshaft sprocket timing mark alignment

5. Remove mounting bolts, then the oil pump and gasket.
6. Reverse procedure to install, noting the following:
   a. Prime oil pump before installing.
   b. Tighten mounting bolts to specifications.
   c. Install new O-ring with oil pickup tube.

OIL PUMP SERVICE

1. Remove cotter pin and drill ⅛ inch hole into relief valve retainer cap, then insert self-threading sheet metal screw into cap.
2. Clamp screw into suitable vise, support oil pump body and remove cap by tapping on body with suitable soft hammer.
3. Discard cap, then remove spring and pressure relief valve.
4. Remove mounting screws and lift cover plate off.
5. Remove pump rotors.
6. Wash parts in suitable solvent, then inspect for damage or wear.
7. Lay straightedge across pump cover surface. If .001 inch feeler gauge can be inserted between cover and straight edge, replace cover.
8. Measure thickness and diameter of rotors.
9. If outer rotor thickness is less than .563 inch or diameter less than 3.141 inches, replace rotor.
10. If inner rotor thickness is less than .563 inch, replace rotor.
11. Slide outer rotor into body, press to one side with fingers and measure clearance between rotor and body. If clearance is more than .015 inch, replace body.
12. Install inner rotor and measure clearance between rotors. If clearance is more than .008 inch, replace pump assembly.
13. Place straightedge across body face between bolt holes. If clearance between rotors and straightedge is more than .003 inch replace pump assembly.
14. Inspect oil pressure relief valve plunger for scoring and free operation in bore. Small marks may be removed with 400-grit wet or dry sandpaper.
15. Relief valve spring free length should be approximately 1.95 inches. Compress spring with 23–25 lbs. If length is not 1.34 inches, replace spring.
16. Reverse procedure to assembly. Tighten screws and retaining cap to specifications

BELT TENSION DATA

Belt	Tension, Lbs.	
	New	Used
Accessory	180–200	120
A/C	140–160	120

SERPENTINE DRIVE BELT

1. Remove tensioner pulley locking nut.
2. Raise and support vehicle.
3. Remove push clips attaching lower air shield to engine cradle, then the air shield.
4. Loosen tensioner adjusting bolt until belt can be removed.
5. Reverse procedure to install. Tighten belt to specifications.

SEPARATED ACCESSORY DRIVE SYSTEM

AIR CONDITIONING

1. Remove accessory drive belt as previously described.
2. Loosen tensioner pulley lock nut, then tensioner pulley adjusting screw until belt can be removed.
3. Reverse procedure to install, tighten tensioner nut to specification.

COOLING SYSTEM BLEED

Refer to procedure under "2.7L Engine" for cooling system bleed procedure.

THERMOSTAT

REPLACE

1. Drain cooling system into suitable container, then raise and support vehicle.
2. Disconnect engine oil pressure and power steering pressure switch electrical connectors.
3. Disconnect radiator and heater hoses from thermostat.
4. Remove mounting bolts, housing, thermostat and gasket.
5. Reverse procedure to install. Tighten mounting bolts to specifications.

WATER PUMP

REPLACE

1. Drain cooling system into suitable container.
2. Remove accessory drive belts.

3. Remove timing belt components necessary to access water pump as outlined under "Timing Belt, Replace."
4. Remove mount bolt and water pump.
5. Reverse procedure to install, noting the following:
   a. Apply suitable dielectric grease to O-ring.
   b. Tighten mounting bolts to specifications.

RADIATOR

REPLACE

Refer to procedure under "2.7L Engine" for radiator replacement.

FUEL PUMP

REPLACE

Refer to "2.7L Engine" for fuel pump replacement.

FUEL FILTER

REPLACE

Refer to "2.7L Engine" for fuel filter replacement.

TECHNICAL SERVICE BULLETINS

EXHAUST DRONE

1998

On some of these models, there may be an exhaust drone between 1600–2000 RPM.

This condition may be caused by the lefthand exhaust pipe. If exhaust system is free and not grounded by body or suspension, proceed as follows:

1. Replace lefthand front exhaust pipe/catalytic converter (Federal emissions part No. 04581701AF; California emission part No. 04581703AF).
2. Use new V-band exhaust manifold clamp (part No. 04581013AC).
3. Remove and discard righthand front exhaust piper support bracket.

TIGHTENING SPECIFICATIONS

Year	Component	Torque, Ft. Lbs.
1997–2000	A/C Belt Tensioner	40
	A/C Compressor To Bracket	21
	A/C Compressor To Engine Block	40
	A/C Condenser	45①
	A/C Condenser Inlet Tube Bracket	45①
	Alternator	40
	Camshaft Sprocket	②
	Camshaft Thrust Plate	21
	Cooling System Bleed	72①
	Connecting Rod Cap	③
	Crankshaft Damper	75
	Crankshaft Main Bearing Cap	③
	Crankshaft Main Bearing Cap, Tie Bolts	21
	Cylinder Head	⑥
	Cylinder Head Cover	108①
	Engine Mount Bracket	45
	Engine Mount Isolator	40
	Exhaust Manifold Heat Shield	108①
	Exhaust Manifold To Cylinder Head	17
	Exhaust Pipe Flange	25
	Fan Blade	45①
	Fan Module	45①
	Fan Motor	25①
	Fuel Pump Module	40
	Fuel Rail, 3.2L	16
	Fuel Rail, 3.5L	96①
	Fuel Tank Straps	40
	Intake Manifold, Lower	④
	Intake Manifold, Upper	9④
	Oil Pan	108①
	Oil Pan Drain Plug	25
	Oil Pan Filter	15
	Oil Pump Cover	108①

Continued

TIGHTENING SPECIFICATIONS—Continued

Year	Component	Torque, Ft. Lbs.
1997-2000	Oil Pump Pick-Up Tube	21
	PCV Valve	60①
	Rear Crankshaft Seal Retainer	108①
	Rocker Arm & Shaft	23⑥
	Spark Plug	20
	Spark Plug Tube	45
	Structural Collar	⑤
	Thermostat Housing	108①
	Throttle Body	108①
	Timing Belt Cover, M6	108①
	Timing Belt Cover, M8	21
	Timing Belt Cover, M10	40
	Timing Belt Tensioner	21
	Timing Belt Tensioner Pulley	45
	Water Pump	108①
	Water Outlet Housing	72①

① — Inch Lbs.
② — Righthand side, 75 ft. lbs., then an additional ¼ turn; lefthand side, 85 ft. lbs., then an additional ¼.
③ — Refer to "Crankcase, Replace" for tightening specifications and sequence.
④ — Refer to "Intake Manifold, Replace" for tightening procedure.
⑤ — Refer to "Structural Collar, Replace" for tightening specifications and sequence.
⑥ — Refer to "Rocker Arm, Replace" for tightening sequence.

3.3L Engine

NOTE: Refer To "Air Bag System Precautions " Located In The Front Of This Manual For System Disarming & Arming Procedures.

NOTE: Prior To Performing Any Service Operations Listed In This Section, Consult The "Technical Service Bulletins " Section For Related Information.

NOTE: Refer To "Computer Relearn Procedure " Located In The Front Of This Manual For Computer Relearn Procedures.

INDEX

PRECAUTIONS

AIR BAG SYSTEMS

Refer to "Air Bag System Precautions" in the front of this manual for system disarming and arming procedures.

BATTERY GROUND CABLE

Prior to service, disconnect battery ground cable and isolate as required.

FLEXIBLE FUEL SYSTEM

Flexible Fuel engine control systems allow engines to run on mixtures of methanol and unleaded gasoline. The system allows optimum engine operation with various mixtures of up to 85 percent methanol 15 percent unleaded gasoline.

A Methanol Concentration Sensor (MCS), containing a microprocessor, is used to sample fuel as it is pumped to the fuel injection system and determine the percentage of methanol and unleaded gasoline. This sensor sends a real-time correction signal to the Powertrain Control Module (PCM). The PCM then adjusts ignition and fuel injection functions to provide optimum engine performance. In the event of MCS failure, the PCM remembers the last correction signal and will use that information to enable a limp home mode.

Flexible Fuel Vehicles (FFV) use unique methanol-compatible components. These items may be identified by either, a green tag or sticker or the component itself will be colored green.

Certain gasoline only (uncolored) components may appear identical to these FFV components. Under no circumstances may these components be interchanged.

FUEL SYSTEM PRESSURE RELIEF

When releasing fuel pressure on Flexible Fuel Vehicles (FFV) use methanol resistant gloves and eye protection. Avoid prolonged skin contact with liquid or breathing of vapors.

Persons taking medications containing DISULFIRAM such as ANTIBUSE should avoid contact with liquids or vapors from methanol based fuels.

1. Remove fuel filler cap.
2. Remove protective cap from fuel pressure test port on fuel rail, **Fig. 1.**
3. Place open end of fuel pressure release hose tool No. C-4799-1, or equivalent, into approved container.
4. Connect other end of hose to pressure test port.
5. Fuel pressure will bleed off through hose into container.

COMPRESSION PRESSURE

The minimum compression pressure should be no less than 100 psi and the maximum variation between cylinders should be no more than 25%.

ENGINE MOUNT

REPLACE

FRONT

1. Remove insulator attaching nuts from top of mounting bracket.
2. Raise and support vehicle.
3. Support engine using suitable jack stand and a block of wood across full width of oil pan.
4. Remove lower attaching nuts from bottom of insulator to frame, **Fig. 2.**
5. Raise engine enough to remove insulator.
6. Reverse procedure to install, tightening mount to specification.

REAR

1. Raise and support vehicle.
2. Support transaxle with suitable transmission jack.

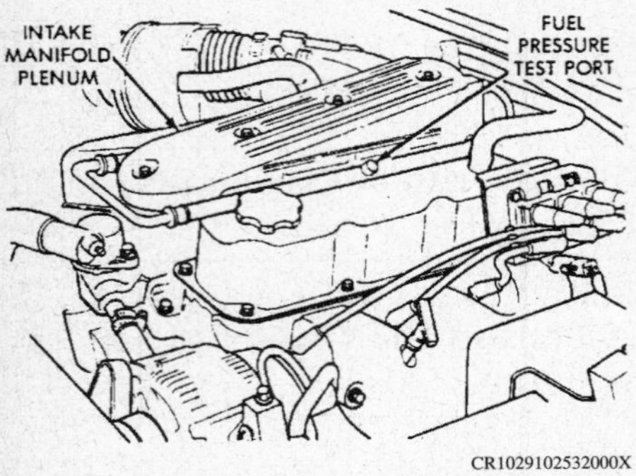

Fig. 1 Fuel pressure test port

3. Remove insulator through bolt from mount.
4. Remove rear mount retainers and remove mount.
5. Reverse procedure to install, tightening bolts to specifications.

ENGINE

REPLACE

1. Release fuel system pressure as outlined under " Precautions."
2. Mark hood position at hinges then remove.
3. Drain cooling system.
4. Disconnect all electrical connections.
5. Remove coolant hoses from radiator and engine.
6. Remove radiator and fan assembly.
7. Disconnect fuel lines and accelerator cable.
8. Remove air cleaner assembly.
9. Raise and support vehicle then drain engine oil.
10. Remove air conditioning compressor mounting bolts and position compressor aside. **Do not allow compressor to hang by hoses, support using suitable wire to frame.**
11. Disconnect exhaust pipe at manifold.
12. Remove transaxle inspection cover and mark flexplate to torque converter position.
13. Remove bolts holding torque converter to flexplate and attach a C-clamp on bottom of converter housing to prevent torque converter from coming out.
14. Remove power steering pump mounting bolts and position pump aside. **Do not allow pump to hang by hoses, support using suitable wire to frame.**
15. Remove lower transmission to engine block bolts.
16. Remove starter assembly as outlined under "Electrical."
17. Lower vehicle and disconnect vacuum lines and ground straps.
18. Support transaxle using suitable floor jack.
19. Attach engine lifting device and support engine.
20. Remove upper transaxle to engine block bolts.
21. Remove front engine mounts as previously described.
22. Remove engine from vehicle.
23. Reverse procedure to install, noting the following:

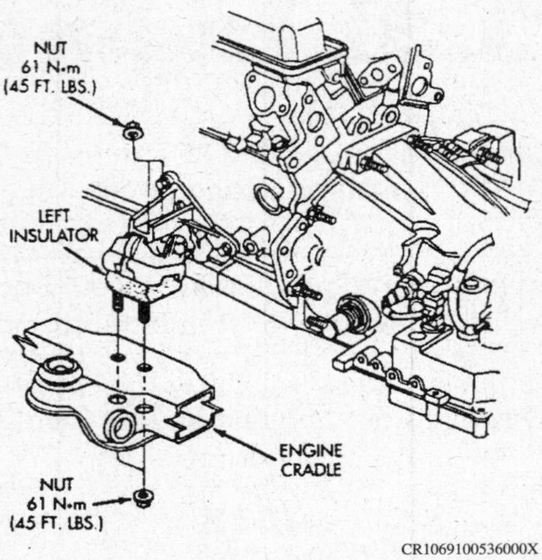

Fig. 2 Front lefthand engine mount replacement

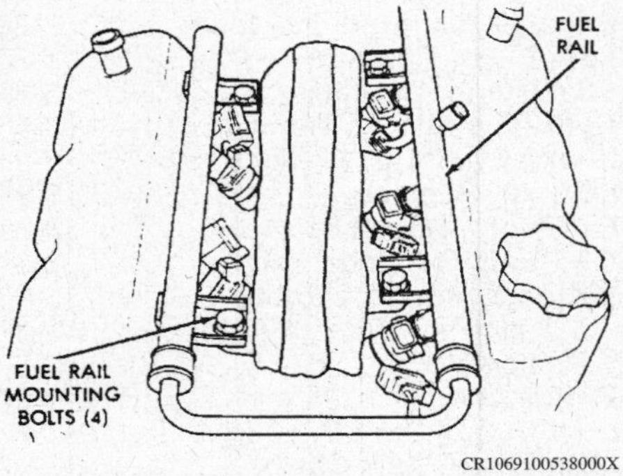

Fig. 4 Fuel rail replacement

a. Tighten all fasteners to specifications.
b. Refer to "Cooling System Bleed" when filling cooling system with coolant.

INTAKE MANIFOLD

REPLACE

1. Release fuel system pressure as outlined under " Precautions."
2. Drain cooling system.
3. Disconnect air tube from air cleaner and throttle body.
4. Hold throttle lever in wide open position then remove throttle and speed control cables from lever.
5. Compress locking tabs on throttle and speed control cables then remove cables from bracket.
6. Disconnect electrical connector from EGR solenoid valve transducer and MAP sensor.
7. **On models equipped with flexible fuel system,** disconnect electrical connector from Intake Air Temperature (IAT) sensor.
8. **On all models,** disconnect PCV valve, brake booster, throttle body purge and fuel pressure regulator hoses.
9. Disconnect throttle position sensor and idle air control motor.
10. Remove EGR tube mounting screws at intake manifold.

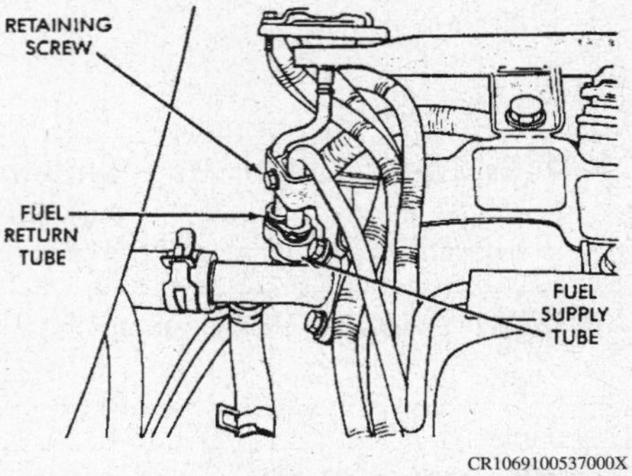

Fig. 3 Fuel supply & return tubes replacement

11. Remove intake manifold plenum bolts, then lift plenum up off engine.
12. Disconnect fuel supply and return tube quick disconnect fittings at rear of intake manifold, **Fig. 3.**
13. Remove screw from fuel tube clamp then separate fuel tubes from the bracket.
14. Rotate injectors toward center of engine, tag injector connectors with their cylinder number then disconnect each injector.
15. Remove fuel rail bolts, then lift fuel rail and injectors straight up and off engine, **Fig. 4.**
16. Remove upper radiator and rear intake manifold hoses.
17. Remove intake manifold bolts, then the intake manifold, **Fig. 5.**
18. Remove intake manifold seal retainer screws, then the intake manifold gasket, **Fig. 6.**
19. Inspect for damage and cracks of each section.
20. Inspect for clogged water passages in end crossovers and for clogged gas passages.
21. Reverse procedure to install, noting the following:
    a. Clean all surfaces of cylinder block and heads.
    b. Place a 1/4 inch drop of Mopar Silicone Rubber Adhesive Sealant, or equivalent, onto each manifold to cylinder head gasket corners, **Fig. 7.**
    c. Install intake manifold gasket, then tighten seal retainers to specifications.
    d. Install intake manifold and tighten bolts in sequence, **Fig. 5.**
    e. **Torque** bolts in sequence to 10 inch lbs.
    f. **Torque** bolts in sequence to 16–17 ft. lbs.
    g. Ensure bolts are **torqued** to 16–17 ft. lbs. in sequence .
    h. Ensure seal and gasket are in correct place.
    i. Apply a light coat of clean engine oil to O-ring on each injector prior to installation.
    j. **Torque** plenum bolts to 20–21 ft. lbs. in sequence, **Fig. 8.**
    k. Bleed cooling system as outlined under "Cooling System Bleed."

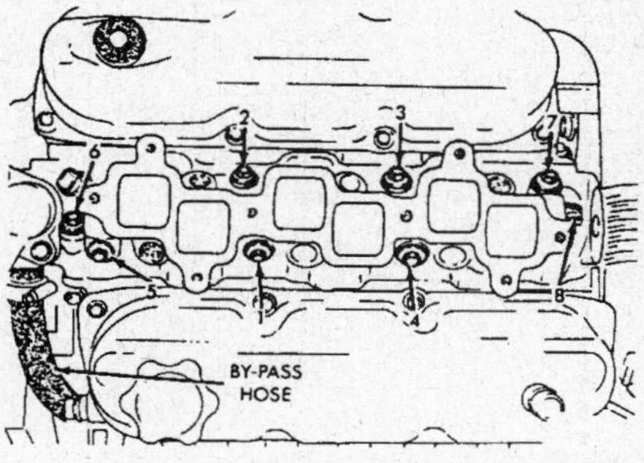

CR1059100081000X

Fig. 5 Intake manifold bolt tightening sequence

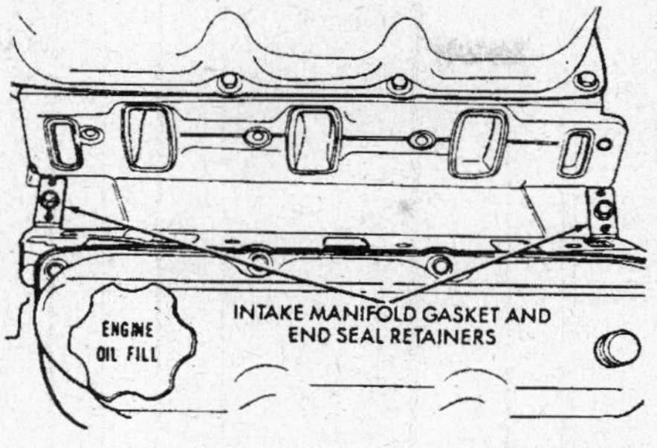

CR1059100082000X

Fig. 6 Intake manifold seal retainer screws replacement

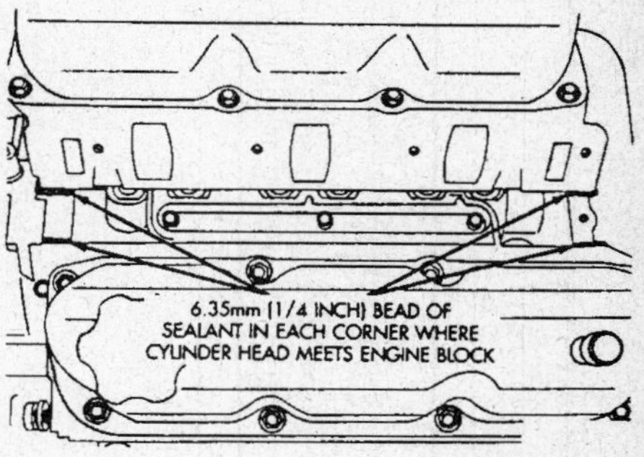

CR1059100083000X

Fig. 7 Intake manifold sealant

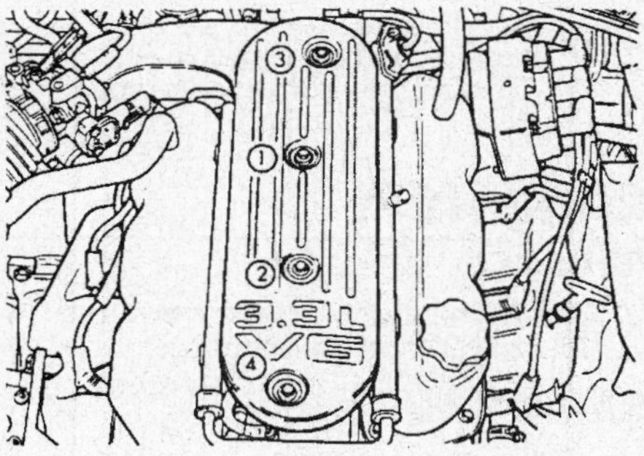

CR1059100084000X

Fig. 8 Intake plenum bolt tightening sequence

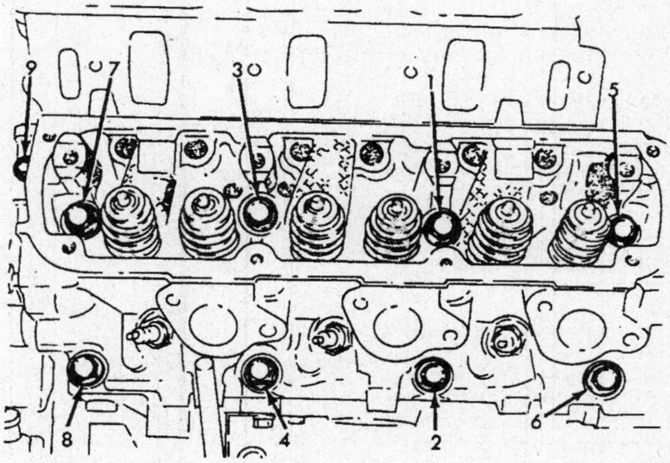

CR1069100539000X

Fig. 9 Cylinder head bolt tightening sequence

EXHAUST MANIFOLD

REPLACE

1. Raise and support vehicle, then disconnect exhaust pipe at manifold.
2. Separate EGR tube from manifold and disconnect heated oxygen sensor lead.
3. Remove manifold heat shield, then the manifold mounting bolts.
4. Remove manifold from cylinder head.
5. Reverse procedure to install. Tighten manifold bolts and exhaust pipe nuts to specifications.

CYLINDER HEAD

REPLACE

REMOVAL

1. Drain coolant from radiator.
2. Remove intake manifold and throttle body as previously described.
3. Disconnect coil wires, sending unit wire, heater hoses and bypass hose from engine block.
4. Remove closed ventilation system, then evaporation control system.
5. Remove valve covers as outlined under "Valve Cover, Replace," then the exhaust manifold as previously described.
6. Remove rocker arm and shaft assemblies as outlined under " Rocker Arms, Replace."
7. Remove cylinder head mounting bolts, then cylinder head from cylinder block.
8. Clean cylinder block and cylinder head mating surfaces, then inspect for cracks, damage and leakage.

INSTALLATION

1. Install new gaskets on cylinder block.
2. Tighten cylinder head bolts 1–8 in sequence, **Fig. 9,** using four-step procedure. **Cylinder head bolts are tightened using Torque To Yield (TTY) method and should be inspected before reuse. If threads are stretched or are not straight, bolts must be replaced.**
3. **Torque** cylinder head mounting bolts in sequence to 45 ft. lbs.
4. **Torque** cylinder head mounting bolts again in sequence to 65 ft. lbs.
5. **Torque** cylinder head mounting bolts again in sequence to 65 ft. lbs.
6. Tighten cylinder head bolts ¼ turn. **Do not use a torque wrench for this step.**
7. Ensure head bolt **torque** is more than 90 ft. lbs.; if not, replace bolt.
8. After head bolts 1–8 have been tightened to specifications, **torque** head bolt No. 9 to 25 ft. lbs.
9. Install pushrods in their original positions, then rocker arm and shaft assemblies. Tighten rocker arm shaft mounting bolts to specifications.
10. Install valve covers, then intake manifold.

VALVE COVER

REPLACE

1. Disconnect air cleaner to throttle body air tube.
2. Remove intake manifold plenum previously described.
3. If lefthand cover is to be replaced, remove coil pack as outlined under "Electrical."
4. Remove valve cover bolts, then the cover. Discard gasket.
5. Reverse procedure to install, using new valve cover gasket. Tighten mounting bolts to specifications.

VALVE ADJUSTMENT

This engine is equipped with hydraulic valve lash adjusters which are not adjustable.

ROCKER ARMS

REPLACE

1. Remove upper intake manifold as previously described, then identify and carefully disconnect spark plug wires.
2. Disconnect closed ventilation and evaporation control systems at valve cover, then remove cover and gasket as previously described.

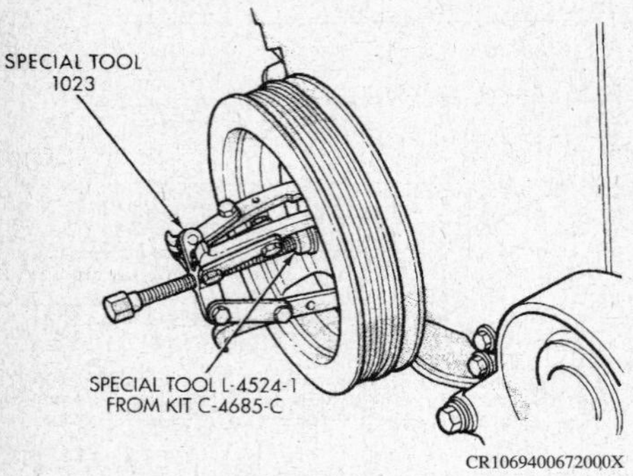

Fig. 10 Crankshaft damper removal

3. Remove rocker shaft bolts and retainers, then lift out arms and shaft as an assembly.
4. If rocker arms and shaft are to be disassembled, note arm positions for assembly reference.
5. Reverse procedure to install. Tighten rocker shaft bolts to specifications.

HYDRAULIC LIFTERS

REPLACE

1. Remove cylinder head as previously described.
2. Remove yoke retainer and aligning yokes, then using tool No. C-4129, , or equivalent, remove lifter from bore. **Identify lifter components for installation reference.**
3. Reverse procedure to install, noting the following:
   a. If a lifter or bore is damaged or if sticking is indicated, ream bore to next larger size and install corresponding size lifter.
   b. Lubricate lifter prior to installation. Tighten yoke retainer screws to specifications.
   c. **Do not run engine above fast idle until all lifters have filled with oil and are quiet.**

CRANKSHAFT DAMPER

REPLACE

1. Remove fan module.
2. Remove drive belts as outlined under "Serpentine Drive Belt" and "Separated Accessory Drive System, " then secure damper with tool No. C-3281, or equivalent.
3. Remove damper center bolt, then install special damper removal tools and remove damper, **Fig. 10.**
4. Reverse procedure to install. Tighten center crankshaft bolt to specifications.

TIMING CHAIN

REPLACE

1. Remove oil pan as outlined under "Oil Pan, Replace, " then the oil pump pickup tube.
2. Remove power steering pump from

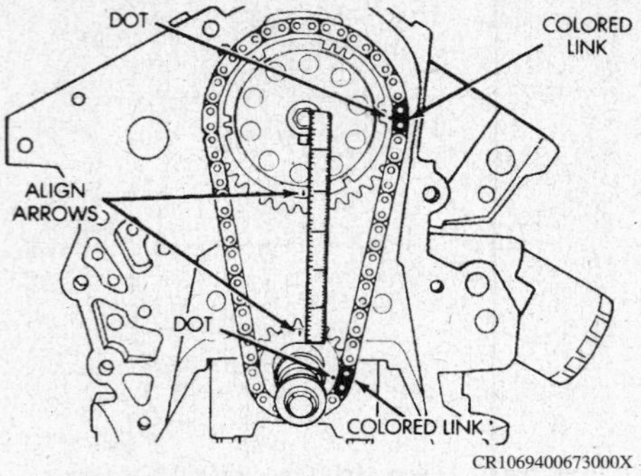

Fig. 11 Crankshaft & camshaft timing

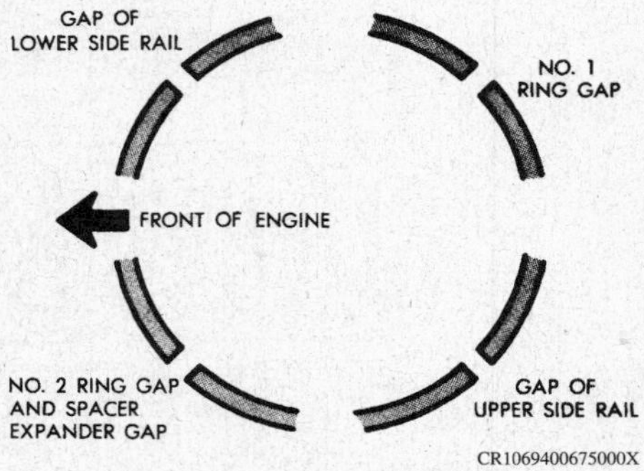

Fig. 13 Piston ring orientation

engine and position aside, then the crankshaft damper as previously described.

3. Remove tensioner pulley bracket and cam sensor, then the chain cover.
4. Remove camshaft sprocket bolt, then the sprocket and timing chain.
5. Remove crankshaft sprocket using suitable puller.
6. Reverse procedure to install chain, note the following:
   a. Rotate crankshaft until timing arrow is in 12 o'clock position, then position timing chain around camshaft sprocket and set timing arrow to 6 o'clock position so that crankshaft and camshaft arrows point to one another.
   b. Align dark colored timing chain links with camshaft and crankshaft sprocket dots, **Fig. 11,** then install camshaft sprocket.
   c. Ensure camshaft and crankshaft arrows are pointing to one another, then install camshaft sprocket bolt and tighten to specifications.
   d. Rotate crankshaft through two full revolutions and inspect sprocket alignment. If marks do not line up, remove camshaft sprocket and correct alignment.
   e. Measure camshaft endplay. If endplay excess .012 inch, replace thrust plate.
   f. Use new cover gasket and O-rings.
   g. Rotate crankshaft until oil pump drive flats are vertical, then position oil pump inner rotor so that mating flats correspond. **Inspect alignment of flats during installation of timing chain cover; otherwise,**

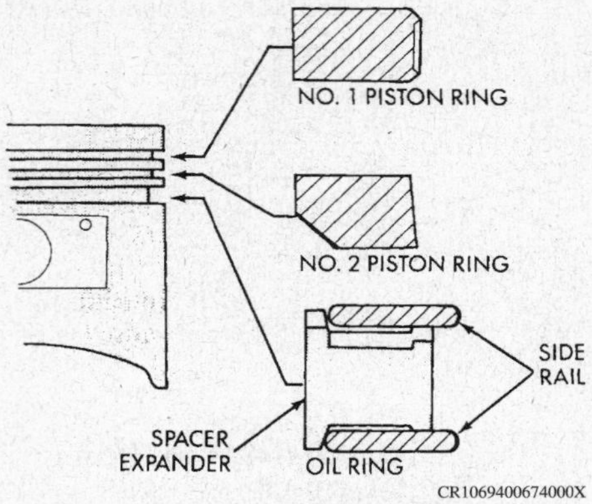

Fig. 12 Piston ring installation

severe damage may result.

   h. Tighten cover screws to specifications.

CAMSHAFT

REPLACE

The engine must be removed from the vehicle to replace the camshaft.

REMOVAL

1. Remove cylinder heads as previously described, then the timing chain with camshaft sprocket.
2. Remove pushrods and lifters as previously described, then the camshaft thrust plate.
3. Thread long bolt into front of camshaft to facilitate removal.
4. Remove camshaft. **Do not damage bearings with cam lobes.**

INSTALLATION

1. Lubricate camshaft lobes and bearing journals, then insert camshaft to within two inches of its final position in block.
2. Install camshaft thrust plate and tighten screws to specifications.
3. Set crankshaft and camshaft timing as outlined under " Timing Chain, Replace."
4. Install pushrods and lifters, then the cylinder head as previously described. **All lifters must be replaced whenever a new camshaft is installed.**

PISTON & ROD ASSEMBLY

REMOVAL

1. Cover piston tops, then use suitable ridge reaming tool to remove top ridges of cylinder bores.
2. Identify pistons, rods and caps for installation reference.
3. Rotate crankshaft until each connecting rod is centered in cylinder bore, then remove connecting rod cap and install rod bolt protectors.
4. Push each piston and rod assembly out through top of block. **Be careful not to damage crankshaft journals.**
5. After removal, install bearing cap on corresponding rod.

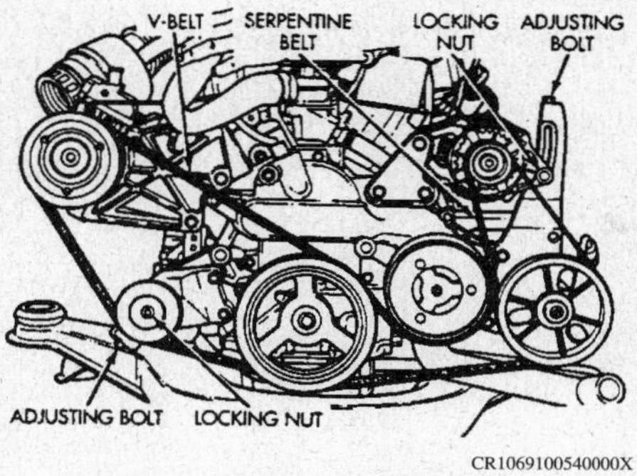

Fig. 14 Drive belt routing

INSTALLATION

1. Install piston rings on piston, noting the following:
   a. No. 1 and No. 2 piston rings have a different cross section, **Fig. 12.** Install with manufacturer's identification mark facing upward.
   b. Install oil ring expander first, followed by upper oil ring side rail, lower side rail, No. 2 (intermediate) piston ring and, finally, No. 1 (upper) piston ring.
   c. **Do not use a piston ring expander to install oil ring side rails.** Install by placing one end between piston ring groove and expander, then holding end firmly and pressing down around rail circumference until installation is complete.
   d. Ensure ring end gaps are positioned, **Fig. 13,** with oil ring expander gap at least 45° from side rail gaps but not on piston pin center or thrust direction.
2. Immerse piston head and rings in clean engine oil, then slide suitable ring compressor tool over piston and tighten. **Ensure ring orientation does not change.**
3. Rotate crankshaft until connecting rod journal is located at center of cylinder bore.
4. With connecting rod bolt protectors installed, insert rod and piston assembly into cylinder bore and carefully guide end of rod over crankshaft journal. **Ensure notch on top of piston faces front (belt side) of engine.**
5. Use a hammer handle to tap piston into bore; ensure connecting rod end meets crankshaft journal properly.
6. Install rod caps with cleaned and oiled rod bolts and tighten to specifications.

CRANKSHAFT SEAL

REPLACE

1. Remove fan module and drive belts as outlined under " Serpentine Drive Belt."
2. Remove crankshaft damper as previously described.
3. Using crankshaft seal removal tool No. 6341A, or equivalent, remove oil seal. Exercise caution to avoid scratching sealing surface.
4. Reverse procedure to install, noting the following:

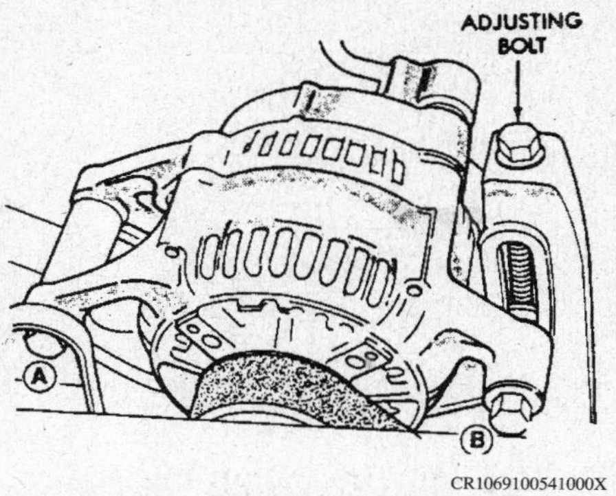

Fig. 15 Serpentine drive belt adjustment bolt

   a. Use crankshaft seal installation tool No. C-4992, or equivalent, to install seal.
   b. Ensure seal spring faces engine and seal is installed flush with cover.

CRANKSHAFT REAR OIL SEAL

REPLACE

REMOVAL

1. With transaxle assembly removed, insert suitable 3⁄16 inch flat blade pry tool between crankshaft dust seal and metal casing.
2. Angle pry tool through dust lip against metal casing and pry seal out. **Do not allow pry tool blade to contact sealing surface.**
3. Inspect crankshaft chamfer for burrs or scratches; if present, clean with 400 grit sandpaper to prevent damage to new seal.

INSTALLATION

1. Install seal pilot tool No. C-4681, or equivalent, on crankshaft.
2. Apply thin coat of Loctite Stud 'n' Bearing Mount, or equivalent, to outer diameter of seal.
3. Position seal over pilot tool and tap into place with suitable plastic hammer.

OIL PAN

REPLACE

1. Remove engine oil dipstick tube.
2. Raise and support vehicle, then drain engine oil into suitable container.
3. Disconnect sway bar and position aside, then remove transaxle support bracket and inspection cover.
4. Remove oil pan bolts, then the pan. Discard pan gasket.
5. Reverse procedure to install, noting the following:
   a. Apply a 1⁄8 inch bead of suitable silicone rubber adhesive sealant along parting line of chain case cover and rear seal retainer.
   b. Install new pan gasket and tighten pan bolts to specifications.

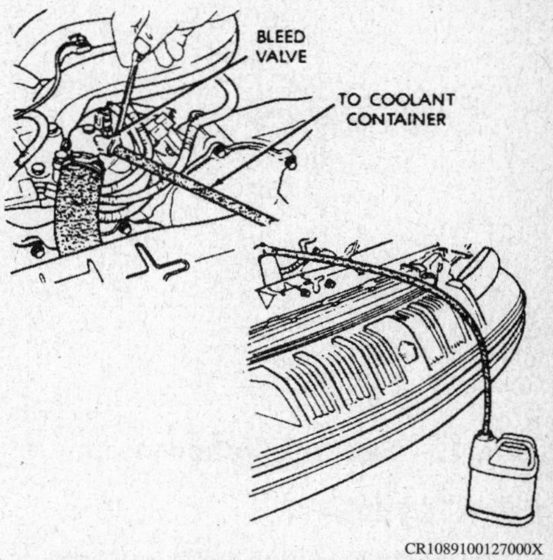

Fig. 16 Cooling system bleed screw location

   c. Ensure crankcase is filled with oil prior to operation.

OIL PUMP

REPLACE

1. Remove oil pan as previously described, then the oil pickup tube.
2. Remove timing chain cover as previously described.
3. Reverse procedure to install. Fill oil pump rotor cavity with oil prior to installation to facilitate pump priming.

OIL PUMP SERVICE

1. Drill 1⁄8 inch hole into relief valve retainer cap and install self-threading sheet metal screw in hole.
2. Clamp screw in vise, then support chain case cover and tap with suitable soft hammer to remove retainer cap.
3. Discard retainer cap, then remove spring and relief valve.
4. Remove oil pump cover screws, then the cover.
5. Remove pump rotors and wash all components in suitable solvent.
6. Carefully inspect all oil pump components for damage or wear; replace as necessary.
7. Assemble oil pump, installing new retainer cap.

BELT TENSION DATA

Use belt tensioning kit tool No. C-4162, or equivalent, to tighten used belts to 120 lbs. and new belts to 140–160 lbs.

SERPENTINE DRIVE BELT

ROUTING

Refer to **Fig. 14,** for serpentine drive belt routing.

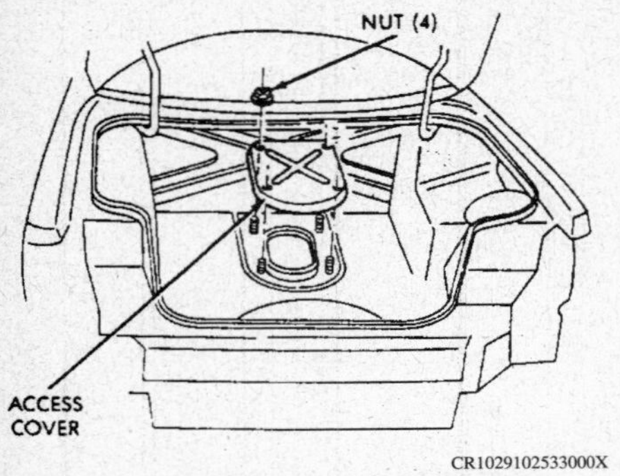

Fig. 17 Fuel pump access panel

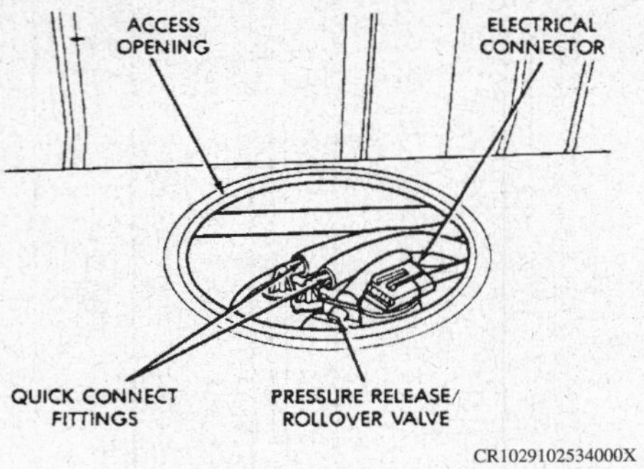

Fig. 18 Fuel pump module connections

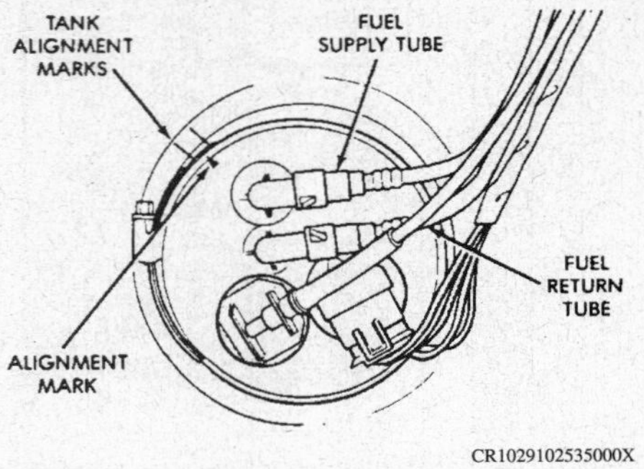

Fig. 19 Fuel pump alignment marks

ADJUSTMENT

The drive belt is provided with an adjusting screw on the alternator mounting bracket, **Fig. 15,** to maintain proper belt tension.

REPLACEMENT

1. Release tension by loosening alternator mounting bolt (A).
2. Loosen adjusting bolt locknut and loosen adjusting bolt.
3. Reverse procedure to tighten belt to specified tension.

SEPARATED ACCESSORY DRIVE SYSTEM

AIR CONDITIONING

Routing

Refer to **Fig. 14,** for A/C drive belt routing.

Replacement

The drive belt is provided with an adjustable tensioner pulley, **Fig. 14,** to maintain proper belt tension.

1. Remove serpentine drive belt as previously described.
2. Release tension by loosening tensioner pulley locking nut, then the adjustment bolt.
3. Remove belt.
4. Reverse procedure to install, noting the following:
   a. Tension belt as previously described.
   b. Tighten tensioner locking nut to specifications.

COOLING SYSTEM BLEED

1. Close radiator drain.
2. Install cylinder block drain plugs.
3. Attach one end of .250 inch ID clear hose that is 48 inches long to bleed screw on thermostat housing, **Fig. 16.**
4. Route hose away from accessory drive belts and cooling fan and place into a clean suitable container.
5. Open bleed screw.

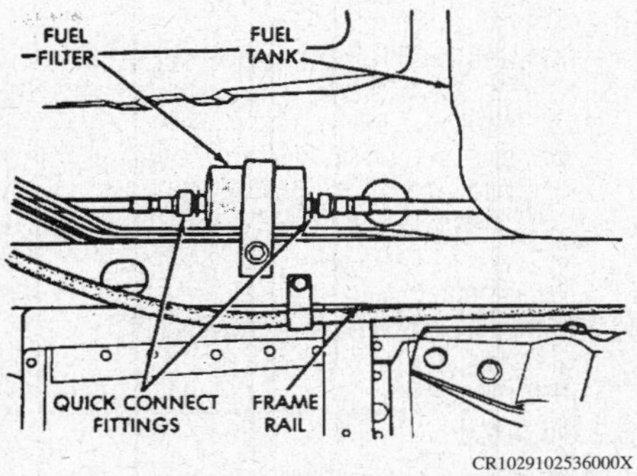

Fig. 20 Fuel filter location

6. Slowly fill coolant pressure bottle until a steady stream of coolant flows from hose.
7. Gently squeeze upper radiator hose until all air is removed from system.
8. Close bleed valve and continue filling to proper fill line of coolant pressure bottle.
9. Install cap on coolant pressure bottle remove hose from bleed screw.

THERMOSTAT

REPLACE

1. With suitable container placed below draincock, drain engine coolant until it is below level of thermostat.
2. Remove thermostat housing bolts, then the housing.
3. Remove thermostat and gasket, then discard gasket and clean mating surfaces.
4. Reverse procedure to install, noting the following:
   a. Dip new gasket in water prior to installation
   b. Place new gasket on water box surface and center thermostat in intake manifold opening.
   c. Tighten bolts to specifications.

WATER PUMP

REPLACE

The water pump is equipped with a "weep hole," which may emit a small amount of engine coolant and stain the pump body slightly. This condition is normal and does not warrant replacement. However, should the coolant discharge become excessive, a shaft seal failure is indicated and pump replacement is necessary.

1. Drain engine coolant into suitable container, then remove drive belts as previously described.
2. Remove water pump pulley bolts, pulley and pump mounting bolts.
3. Remove pump from vehicle and discard O-ring seal.
4. Reverse procedure to install, noting the following:
   a. Carefully clean O-ring sealing groove and install new seal.
   b. Tighten pump and pulley mounting bolts to specifications.
   c. After installation, rotate pump by hand to ensure it moves freely.

RADIATOR

REPLACE

1. Drain cooling system.
2. Remove upper radiator crossmember, then the coolant hose clamps and hoses from radiator.
3. Disconnect automatic transaxle cooler lines from radiator.
4. **On models equipped with an auxiliary transaxle cooler,** disconnect rubber auxiliary cooler lines.
5. **On all models,** disconnect radiator fan wiring from RFI module.
6. Disconnect upper radiator mounting screws.
7. **On models equipped with engine block heater,** disconnect wiring.
8. **On all models,** remove condenser to radiator mounting screws.
9. Using caution not to bend condenser inlet tube or damage cooling fins, lean condenser forward against bumper.
10. Lift radiator free of vehicle.
11. **On models equipped with an auxiliary transaxle cooler,** remove plastic mounting straps and remove cooler.
12. **On all models,** reverse procedure to install, noting the following:
    a. Tighten A/C condenser mounting screws and to radiator hose clamps specifications.
    b. Refill and bleed cooling system as previously described.
    c. Check automatic transaxle oil level and replenish as necessary.

FUEL PUMP

REPLACE

1. Release fuel system pressure as outlined under " Precautions."
2. Remove luggage compartment liner, access panel and gasket, **Fig. 17.**
3. Disconnect electrical connector from top of pump module.
4. Disconnect fuel supply and return hoses and pressure relief/roll over valve, **Fig. 18.**
5. Loosen band clamp until fuel pump module rises up from tank.
6. Place shop towels around access opening to absorb possible fuel spillage.
7. Without removing module, tip module backward to allow fuel to drain back into tank.
8. Tilt fuel pump module to prevent fuel level gauge float from catching on fuel tank when removing module.
9. Reverse procedure to install, noting the following:
   a. Align marks on module and tank when installing module, **Fig. 19.**
   b. Seat module into tank by pushing top down. Ensure gasket does not slip over outside or inside edge of fuel tank lip.
   c. Tighten fuel pump module band clamp to specifications. **Do not over-tighten band clamp.**
   d. Pressurize fuel system and test for leaks.

FUEL FILTER

REPLACE

The fuel filter is located on the frame rail in front of fuel tank, **Fig. 20.** The inlet and outlet ends of the filter are marked for correct installation.

1. Release fuel system pressure as outlined under " Precautions."
2. Disconnect quick connect fitting from fuel filter.
3. Remove fuel filter mounting bracket and filter.
4. Reverse procedure to install.

TECHNICAL SERVICE BULLETINS

RUSTY ENGINE LEVEL INDICATOR TUBE

1997

On these models, the oil level indicator tube may rust causing dip stick to adhere to interior walls or handle to break off.

This condition may be caused by tube or dip stick materials. To correct this condition, replace tube and dip stick with revised parts (part Nos. 04663180 and 04663601).

TIGHTENING SPECIFICATIONS

Year	Component	Torque/Ft. Lbs.
1997–2000	A/C Belt Tensioner	40
	A/C Compressor Bracket To Water Pump Bolt	30
	A/C Compressor Support Bolts	30
	A/C Compressor To Bracket Bolt	16–17
	A/C Condenser To Radiator Bolt	45①
	Alternator Adjusting Strap Bolt	16–17
	Alternator Adjusting Strap Mounting Bolt	30
	Alternator Bracket Bolt	30
	Alternator Mounting Pivot Nut	30
	Camshaft Sprocket Bolt	40
	Camshaft Thrust Plate	96-108①
	Chain Case Cover Bolt (8 mm)	20
	Chain Case Cover Bolt (10 mm)	40
	Condenser Inlet Tube Bracket	45①
	Connecting Rod Bolt	40②
	Crankshaft Pulley To Crankshaft Bolt	40
	Cylinder Head Bolt	③
	Cylinder Head Cover Bolt	108①
	Engine Mount	45
	Exhaust Crossover Pipe Flange Nut/Bolt	25
	Exhaust Front Down Pipes To Exhaust Support Bracket Screw	35
	Exhaust Manifold Heat Shield Mounting Screws	16–17
	Exhaust Manifold Mounting Bolts	16–17
	Exhaust Manifold Nuts To Front Down Pipes	20
	Exhaust Module Body Bracket Support	18
	Exhaust Support Bracket To Transaxle Screw	35
	Exhaust U-Bolt In Front Of Under Floor Converter Nut	24
	Fan Blade Nut	45①

Continued

TIGHTENING SPECIFICATIONS—Continued

Year	Component	Torque/Ft. Lbs.
1997-2000	Fan Module To Radiator	45①
	Fan Motor To Shroud Lefthand Side Screws	45①
	Fan Motor To Shroud Righthand Side Screws	25①
	Heat Shield Mounting Screws	16–17
	Insulator Mounting Bolts	16–17
	Intake Manifold Bolts	④
	Intake Manifold Gasket Retainer Screws	96-108①
	Intake Plenum Bolts	④
	Lifter Retainer Yoke Screw	96-108①
	Main Bearing Cap Bolt	30②
	Muffler Heat Shield Mounting Nuts	45①
	Oil Filter Attaching Nipple	30
	Oil Level Sensor Plug	30
	Oil Pan Drain Plug	25
	Oil Pan Screw	8–9
	Oil Pressure Gauge Sending Unit	5
	Oil Pump Cover Bolt	96-108①
	Oil Pump Pickup Tube Screw	20–21
	Radiator To Body Screws	96-108①
	Radiator Hose Clamps	22①
	Receiver/Drier Swivel Nut	45①
	RFI Harness To Shroud Screw	25①
	Rocker Shaft Bracket Bolt	20–21
	Spark Plug	20
	Starter Mounting Bolt	50
	Strut Intake Manifold To Cylinder Head Bolt	40
	Tappet Retainer Yoke Screw	96-108①
	Temperature Gauge Sending Unit	60①
	Thermostat Bleed Screw	60-72①
	Thermostat Housing Bolts	20–21
	Upper Radiator Crossmember Bolts	20–21
	Valve Cover Bolt	108①
	Water Pump Mounting Bolts	96-108①
	Water Pump Pulley Bolts	20–21
	Water Pump To Chain Case Cover Bolt	96-108①

① — Inch lbs.

② — Plus an additional 1/4 turn.

③ — Refer to "Cylinder Head, Replace" for tightening procedure & specifications.

④ — Refer to "Intake Manifold, Replace" for tightening procedure & specifications.

3.5L VIN F Engine

NOTE: Refer To "Air Bag System Precautions " Located In The Front Of This Manual For System Disarming & Arming Procedures.

NOTE: For Procedures Not Found In This Section, Refer To The "3.3L Engine" Section In This Chapter.

NOTE: Refer To "Computer Relearn Procedure " Located In The Front Of This Manual For Computer Relearn Procedures.

INDEX

PRECAUTIONS

AIR BAG SYSTEMS

Refer to "Air Bag System Precautions" in the front of this manual for system disarming and arming procedures.

BATTERY GROUND CABLE

Prior to service, disconnect battery ground cable and isolate as required.

FUEL SYSTEM PRESSURE RELIEF

1. Remove fuel filler cap.
2. Remove protective cap from fuel pressure test port on fuel rail, **Fig. 1.**
3. Place open end of fuel pressure release hose tool No. C-4799-1, or equivalent, into approved container.
4. Connect other end of hose to pressure test port.
5. Fuel pressure will bleed off through hose into container.

COMPRESSION PRESSURE

Compression pressure should be 155–170 psi and the maximum variation between cylinders should be no more than 25%.

INTAKE MANIFOLD

REPLACE

1. Release fuel system pressure as outlined under " Precautions."
2. Drain cooling system.

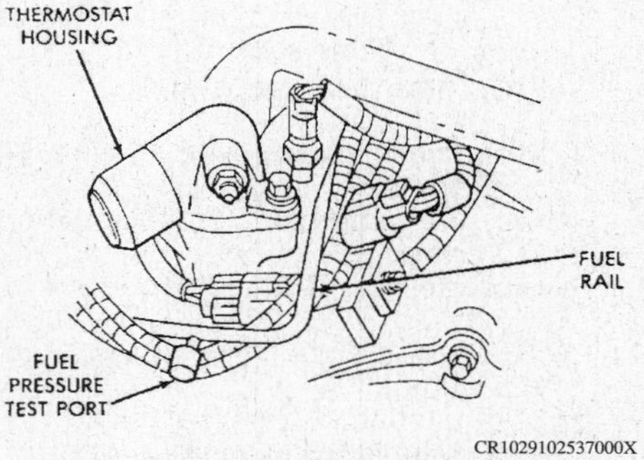

Fig. 1 Fuel pressure test port

3. Remove engine cover from top of plenum.
4. Remove accelerator cable and speed control cable from throttle arm, **Fig. 2.**
5. Disconnect electrical connector from idle air control motor and charge air temperature sensor then remove vacuum hose from Manifold Tuning Valve (MTV), **Fig. 3.**
6. Remove ground screw from intake manifold.
7. Disconnect electrical connector from Manifold Absolute Pressure (MAP) sensor and Throttle Position Sensor (TPS), **Fig. 4.**
8. Disconnect purge hose from throttle bodies.
9. Disconnect PCV make up air hose and idle air control motor supply hose, then remove air inlet plenum from behind manifold.
10. Disconnect PCV, brake booster and remaining vacuum hoses from intake manifold.
11. Remove EGR tube mounting bolts at intake manifold plenum.
12. Remove air plenum support bracket on each side of manifold.
13. Remove intake manifold plenum mounting bolts. Plenum uses two different length bolts, **Fig. 5.**
14. Remove intake manifold plenum.
15. Remove upper radiator hose from thermostat housing and heater hose from rear of intake manifold.
16. Remove intake manifold attaching bolts in sequence, **Fig. 6,** then the intake manifold.
17. Reverse procedure to install noting the following:
    a. Bleed cooling system after refilling cooling system.
    b. **Torque** intake manifold bolts in sequence, **Fig. 6** to 20–21 ft. lbs.

CYLINDER HEAD

REPLACE

1. Release fuel system pressure as outlined under " Precautions."
2. Remove crankshaft damper.
3. Remove camshaft sprockets as outlined under "Camshaft, Replace."
4. Remove intake manifold as previously described.
5. Remove timing belt cover to cylinder head fasteners, **Fig. 7.**
6. If righthand side timing belt cover is removed, there are O-rings located behind it for water pump passages, **Fig. 8.**
7. Remove cylinder head bolts, then the cylinder head.
8. Check for cracks, leaks or damage.
9. Clean mating surfaces of cylinder head and engine block.
10. Clean cylinder head and oil passages.

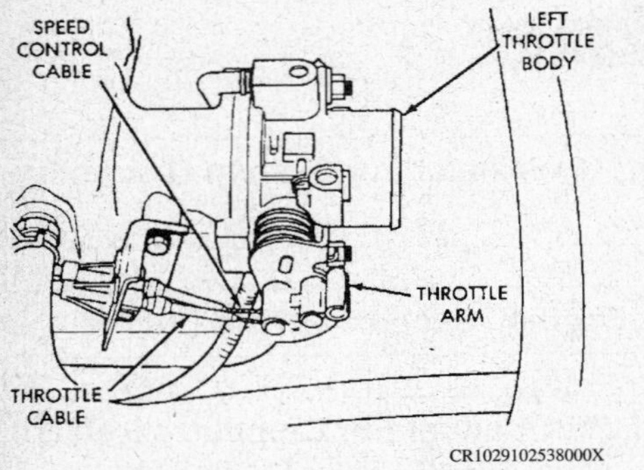

Fig. 2 Throttle lever

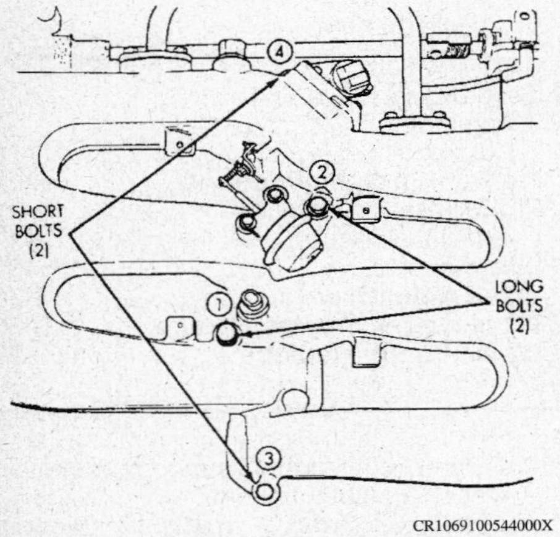

Fig. 5 Intake plenum bolt length identification

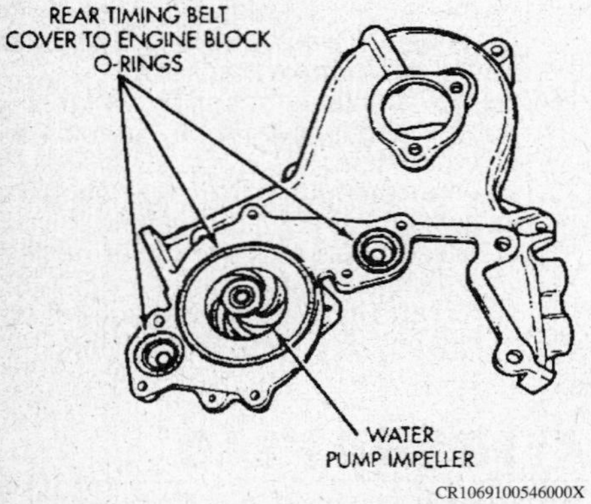

Fig. 8 Water pump O-rings

11. Ensure cylinder head flatness is within .002 inch.
12. Check cylinder head bolts for necking by holding a scale or straightedge against threads. If all threads do not contact scale, bolts should be replaced, **Fig. 9.**
13. Reverse procedure to install, noting the following:
    a. Lightly coat threads of cylinder head bolts with engine oil.
    b. Install cylinder head gasket, **Fig. 10.**
    c. **Cylinder head bolts are tightened using a Torque To Yield (TTY) procedure.** Tighten cylinder

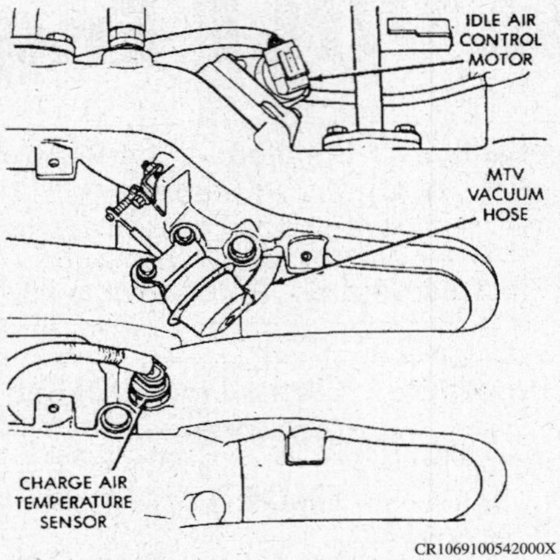

Fig. 3 Idle air control motor, charge air temperature sensor & MTV component location

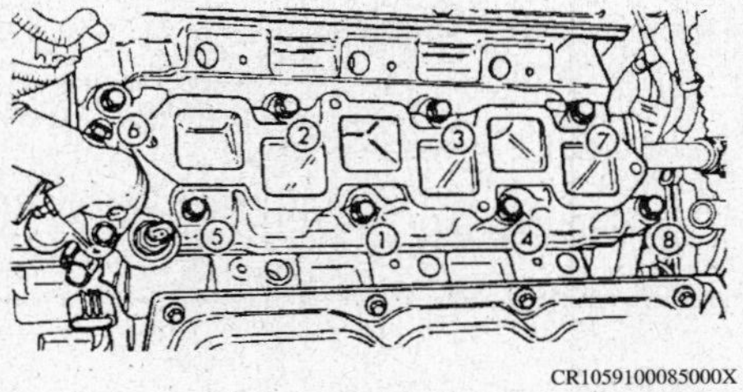

Fig. 6 Intake manifold replacement sequence

head bolts in sequence, **Fig. 11,** in four steps.
    d. **Torque** head bolts in sequence to 45 ft. lbs.
    e. **Torque** head bolts in sequence to 65 ft. lbs.
    f. **Torque** head bolts in sequence to 65 ft. lbs.
    g. Tighten head bolts an additional ¼ turn without using a torque wrench.
    h. Ensure bolt **torque** is more than 90 ft. lbs. If not, replace bolt.

VALVE COVER

REPLACE

1. Remove air cleaner assembly and intake manifold plenum as outlined under "Intake Manifold, Replace."
2. Cover lower intake manifold during service.
3. Disconnect and relocate spark plug wires.
4. Loosen A/C compressor mounting bracket and pull away from cylinder head.
5. Remove spark plug tube nut and O-ring.
6. Remove rocker cover screws and remove cover.
7. Reverse procedure to install.

VALVE ADJUSTMENT

This engine is equipped with hydraulic valve lash adjusters which are not adjustable.

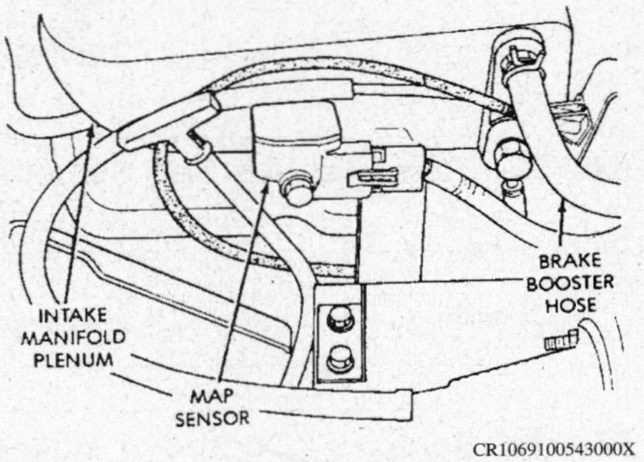

Fig. 4 MAP location

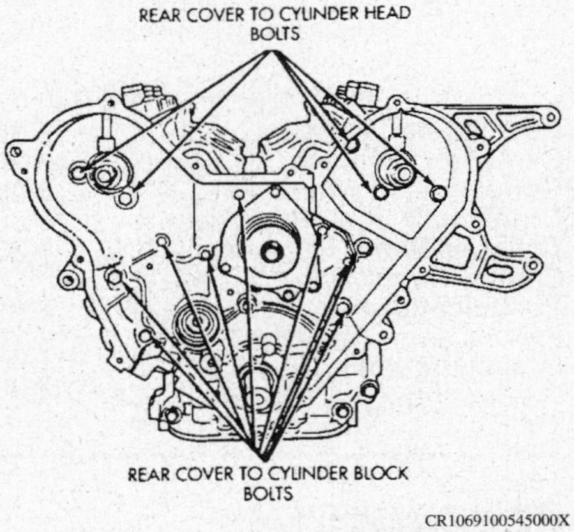

Fig. 7 Rear timing belt cover bolts

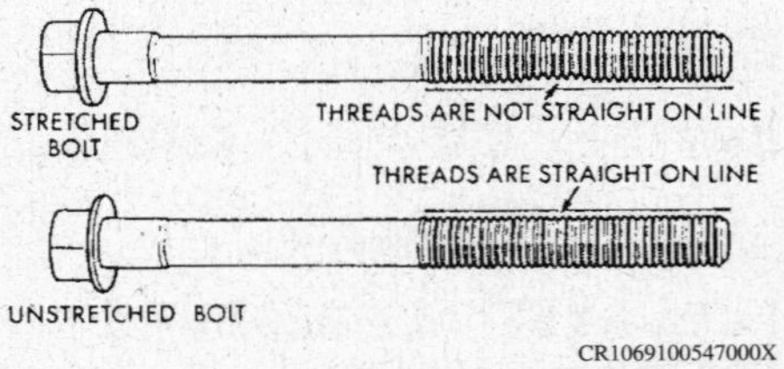

Fig. 9 Cylinder head bolt inspection

ROCKER ARMS

REPLACE

REMOVAL

1. Remove cylinder head covers as previous described.
2. Identify and mark rocker arm assembly and rocker arms before disassembly, **Fig. 12.**
3. Remove rocker arm assembly bolts, then the rocker arms.
4. Check rocker arms for following wear or damage:
    a. Roller scuffing or wear.
    b. Bore scuffing or wear.
    c. Swivel pad on lash adjuster missing or broken.
    d. Rocker arm showing signs of fatigue or cracking.
    e. Roller axle protruding from arm.
5. Remove dowel pin using a 4 mm screw, nut, spacer and washer installed into pin, **Fig. 13.**

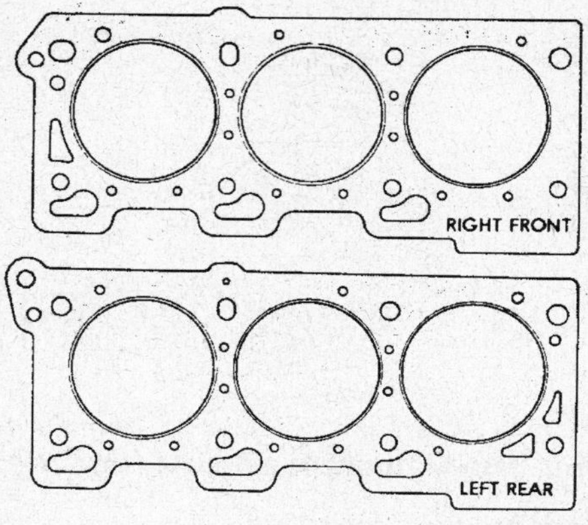

CR1069100548000X

Fig. 10 Cylinder head gasket identification

CR1069100558000X

Fig. 13 Dowel pin removal

6. Remove rocker arms and pedestals in order, **Fig. 14.**
7. Check rocker arm mounting portion of shafts for wear or damage.
8. Check oil holes for clogging with small wire, clean as required.

INSTALLATION

1. Install rocker arms and pedestals onto shaft.
2. Install dowel pins in correct locations, **Fig. 14.** Dowel pins pass through pedestal into rocker shafts. Dowel pins should be pressed until they bottom out in pedestal.
3. Rotate camshaft placing lobes in a neutral position (no load on valves).
4. Install rocker arm assembly with identification marks toward front of engine.
5. Install oil feed bolt into correct location on rocker shaft retainer, then **torque** bolts in sequence, **Fig. 15,** to 22–23 ft. lbs.
6. Install cylinder head covers as previously described.

FRONT COVER

REPLACE

1. Remove upper radiator crossmember, then the fan module.
2. Remove accessory drive belts.
3. Use holding tool No. C-3281, or equivalent, to hold crankshaft damper, remove center bolt.
4. Remove stamped steel, cast and lower

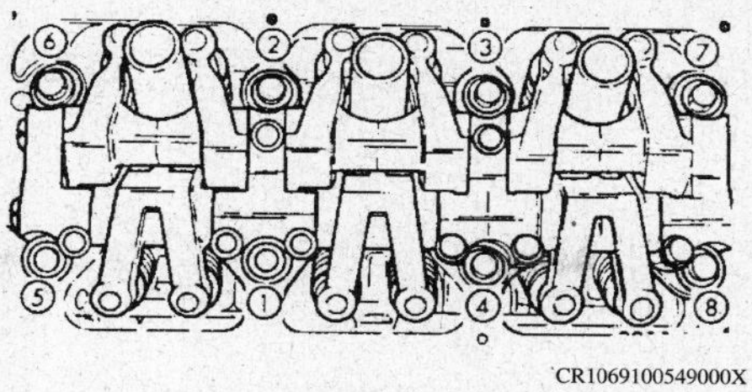

CR1069100549000X

Fig. 11 Cylinder head bolt tightening sequence

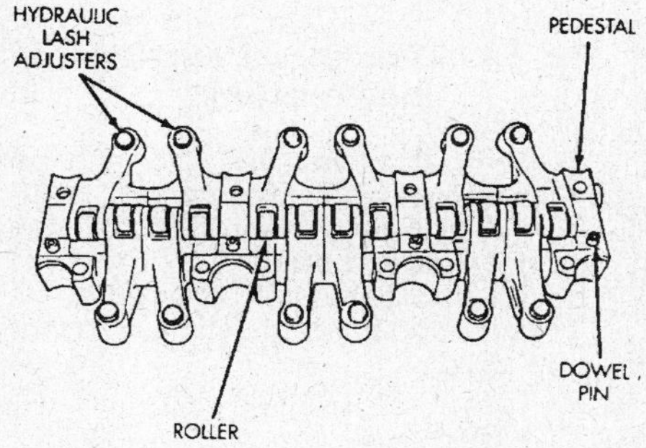

CR1069100559000X

Fig. 14 Rocker arms & shaft assembly

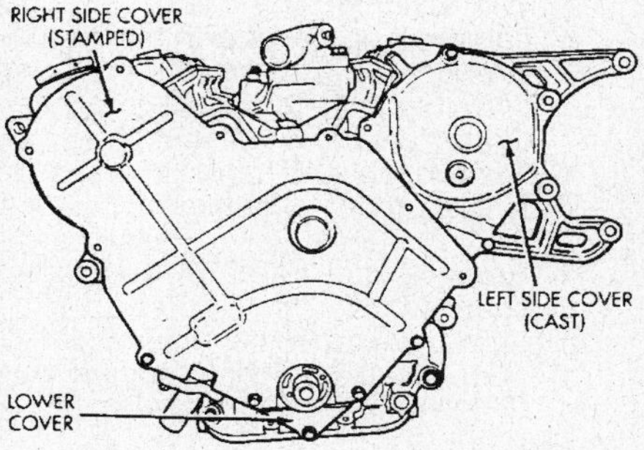

CR1069100550000X

Fig. 16 Timing belt covers

covers, **Fig. 16. Do not remove sealer on steel cover; it is reusable.**

5. Remove lefthand cast cover, then lower belt cover behind crankshaft damper.
6. Reverse procedure to install.

TIMING BELT

REPLACE

REMOVAL

1. Release fuel system pressure as outlined under " Precautions."
2. Remove front cover as previously described.
3. Mark belt running direction for installation.
4. Align camshaft sprockets with marks on rear covers, **Fig. 17.**
5. Remove timing belt tensioner and timing belt.

INSTALLATION

1. Place tensioner into suitable vise and slowly compress plunger, **Fig. 18.**
2. When plunger is compressed into tensioner body, install pin through body and plunger to retain plunger in place until tensioner is installed.
3. **If camshaft sprockets have been removed, align camshafts prior to installing timing belt as outlined under "Camshaft, Replace."**
4. Align crankshaft sprocket with Top Dead Center (TDC) mark on oil pump cover, **Fig. 17.**
5. Align camshaft sprockets between marks on covers.
6. Install timing belt starting at crankshaft sprocket in a counterclockwise direction. After belt is installed on righthand sprocket keep tension on belt until it is past tensioner pulley.
7. Holding tensioner pulley against belt, install tensioner into housing and tighten to specifications.
8. When tensioner is in place, pull mounting pin to allow tensioner to extend to pulley bracket.
9. Rotate crankshaft sprocket two revolutions and check timing marks on camshafts and crankshaft. If marks do not line up, repeat procedure.

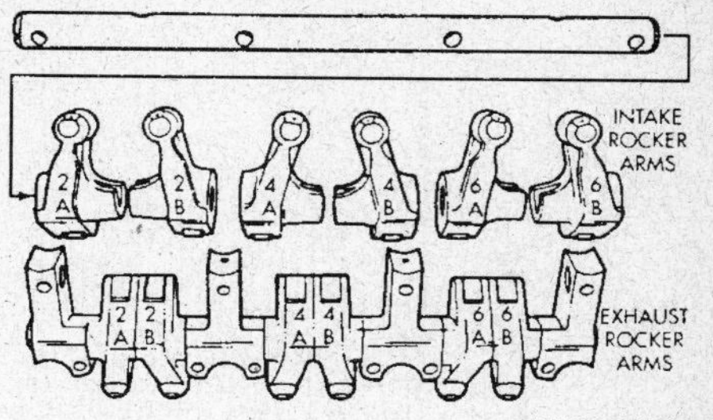

CR1069100557000X

Fig. 12 Rocker arms & shaft identification

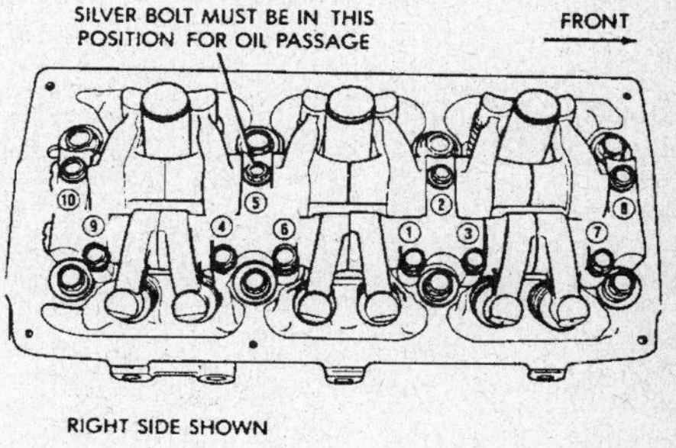

CR1069100560000X

Fig. 15 Rocker arm shaft bolt tightening sequence

CAMSHAFT

REPLACE

1. If camshaft sprockets are to be removed, proceed as follows:
   a. Remove timing belt as previously described.
   b. Hold camshaft sprocket with 1 7/16 inch box wrench, loosen, then remove sprocket bolt and washer. **To remove bolt with engine in vehicle, it may be necessary to lift that side of engine to gain access for bolt removal.**
   c. Remove camshaft sprocket from

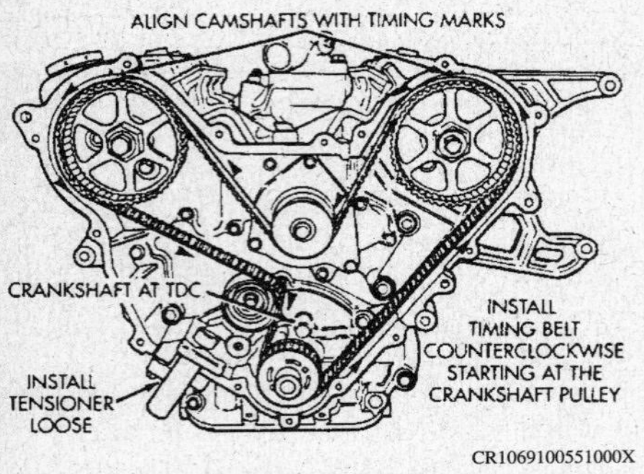

Fig. 17 Timing belt installation

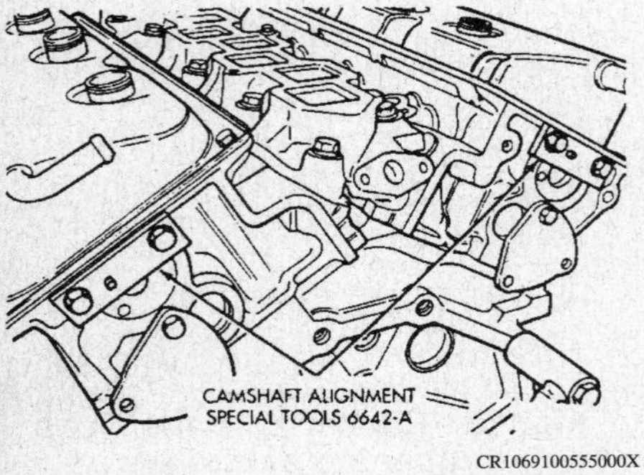

Fig. 20 Camshaft alignment tool

camshaft. Each sprocket had " D" shaped hole that allows it to rotate several degrees in each direction on its shaft. **This design must be timed with engine to ensure proper engine performance.**

2. If camshaft oil seals are to be removed, sprockets must be removed and oil seal remover tool No. C-3981B, or equivalent, must be used, **Fig. 19.**
3. Remove cylinder head as previously described.
4. Mark, then remove rocker arm assemblies as previously described.
5. Remove rear camshaft cover and O-ring from head.
6. Carefully remove camshaft from rear of cylinder head. **Use care not to damage, nick or scratch camshaft journals when removing camshafts.**
7. Reverse procedure to install, ensure camshaft and journals are lubricated with clean engine oil. **If camshaft sprockets were removed, they must be installed and timed to engine as follows:**
   a. Place crankshaft sprocket at TDC mark on oil pump housing.
   b. Install camshaft alignment tool No. 6642-A, or equivalent, to rear of cylinder heads, **Fig. 20.**
   c. Preload tensioner with vise and install locking pin as outlined under "Timing Belt, Replace."
   d. If camshaft oil seals were removed, lubricate prior to installation and install using seal installer tool No. 6052, or equivalent.
   e. Install camshaft sprockets on camshafts.
   f. Apply Loctite sealer No. 277, or equivalent, to ends of bolts. Ten-

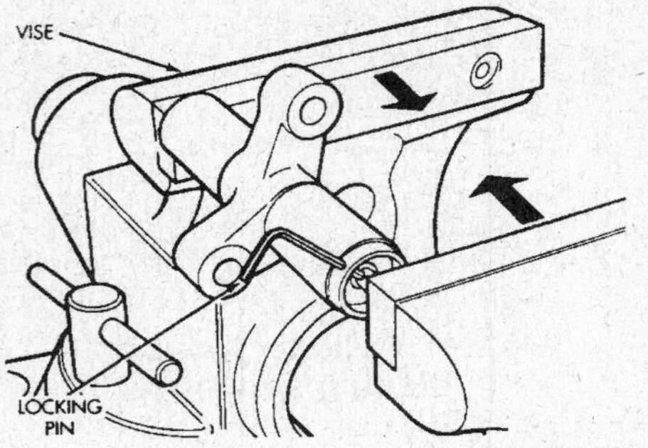

Fig. 18 Timing belt tensioner compression

inch bolt is installed into lefthand camshaft and $8\frac{3}{8}$-inch bolt is installed into righthand camshaft. **Do not tighten bolts.**

   g. Position camshaft sprocket mark should be between marks on cover, **Fig. 17.**
   h. Install timing belt as previously described.
   i. Install suitable dial indicator in cylinder No. 1 to check TDC of piston, **Fig. 21.** Rotate crankshaft until piston is at TDC exactly.
   j. With cylinder No. 1 at TDC, hold camshaft sprocket with a $1\frac{7}{16}$ inch wrench and **torque** righthand sprocket bolt to 75 ft. lbs., then tighten an additional 90.°
   k. **Torque** lefthand sprocket bolt to 85 ft. lbs., then tighten an additional 90.°
   l. Remove dial indicator and install spark plugs.
   m. Remove camshaft alignment tool and install camshaft covers and O-rings.

CRANKSHAFT SEAL

REPLACE

1. Remove timing belt as previously described.
2. Using pulley puller tool No. L-4407-A, or equivalent, remove crankshaft sprocket, **Fig. 22.**
3. Tap dowel pin out of crankshaft.
4. Using seal remover tool No. 6341, or equivalent, remove crankshaft seal.
5. Shaft seal lip must be free of varnish, dirt or nicks. Polish with 400 grit paper if necessary.
6. Using seal installer tool No. 6342, or equivalent, install crankshaft seal.
7. Install dowel pin into crankshaft .047 inch.
8. Using sprocket tool No. C-4685-C1, or equivalent, install crankshaft sprocket.
9. Install timing belt and covers.

BELT TENSION DATA

Use tensioning special tool kit No. C-4162, or equivalent, to tighten used belts to 120 lbs. and new belts to 140–160 lbs.

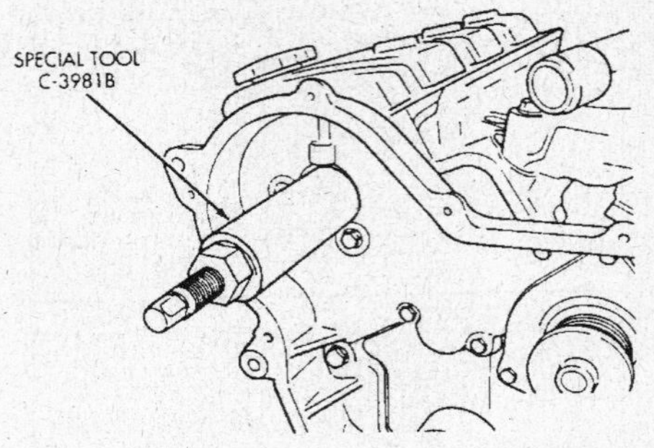

Fig. 19 Camshaft oil seal removal

Fig. 21 No. 1 cylinder positioning at TDC

SERPENTINE DRIVE BELT

ROUTING

Refer to **Fig. 23,** for serpentine drive belt routing.

ADJUSTMENT

The drive belt is provided with an adjustable tensioner pulley on the timing belt cover, **Fig. 23,** to maintain proper belt tension. Release tension by loosening the tensioner pulley nut and adjustment bolt. Reverse procedure to tighten belt to specified tension.

SEPARATED ACCESSORY DRIVE SYSTEM

AIR CONDITIONING

The drive belt is provided with an adjustable tensioner pulley, **Fig. 23,** to maintain proper belt tension.

1. Remove serpentine drive belt.
2. Release tension by loosening tensioner pulley locking nut, then the adjustment bolt.
3. Remove belt.
4. Reverse procedure to install, noting the following:
   a. Tension belt as outlined under "Belt Tension Data."

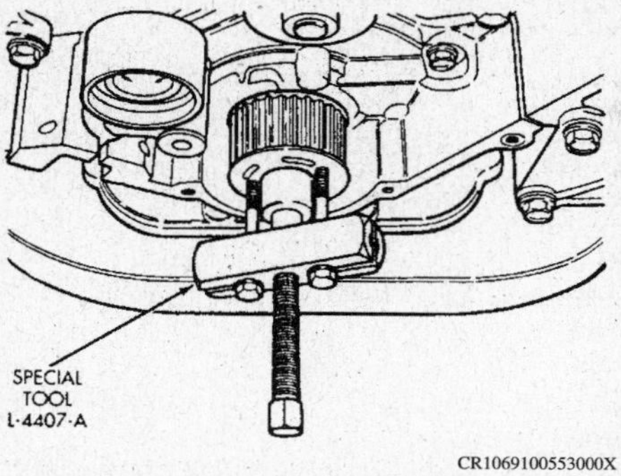

Fig. 22 Crankshaft sprocket removal

b. Tighten tensioner locking nut to specifications.

WATER PUMP

REPLACE

1. Drain engine coolant into suitable container.
2. Remove timing belt previously described.
3. Remove water pump mounting bolts, then the water pump, **Fig. 24.**
4. Reverse procedure to install.

RADIATOR

REPLACE

1. Drain engine coolant into suitable container.
2. **On 1997 LHS models,** proceed as follows:

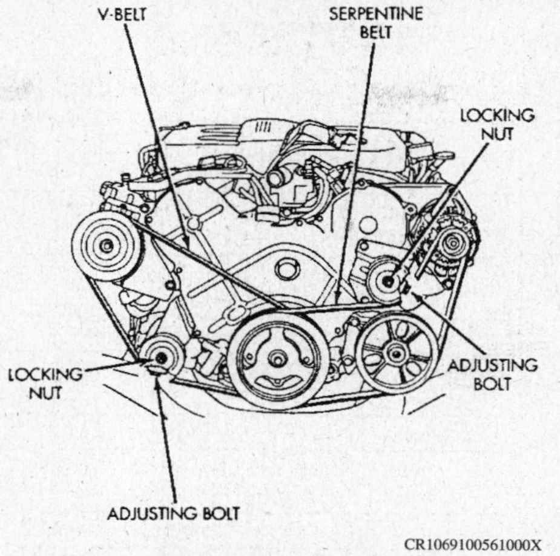

Fig. 23 Drive belt routing

a. Remove sight shields, then right and lefthand headlamp modules.
b. Recover A/C refrigerant as outlined in "Air Conditioning. "

3. **On all models,** remove upper radiator crossmember, then the coolant hose clamps and hoses from radiator.
4. Disconnect automatic transaxle cooler lines from radiator.
5. **On models equipped with auxiliary transaxle cooler,** disconnect rubber auxiliary cooler lines.
6. **On all models,** disconnect radiator fan wiring from RFI module.
7. Disconnect upper radiator mounting screws.
8. **On models equipped with engine**

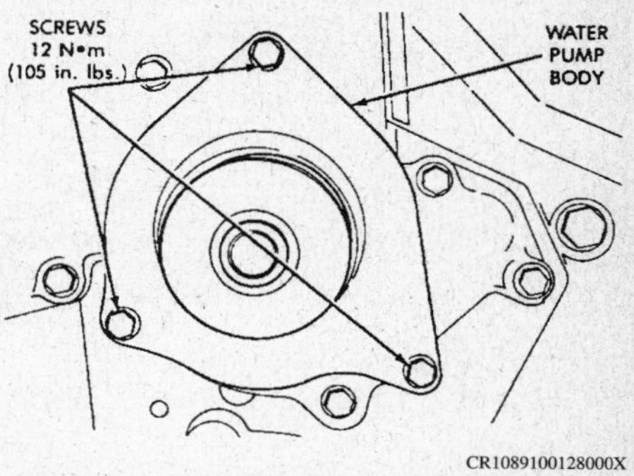

Fig. 24 Water pump replacement

block heater, disconnect wiring.

9. **On all models,** remove condenser to radiator mounting screws.
10. Using caution not to bend condenser inlet tube or damage cooling fins, lean condenser forward against bumper.
11. Lift radiator out of vehicle.
12. **On models equipped with auxiliary transaxle cooler,** remove plastic mounting straps and remove cooler.
13. **On all models,** reverse procedure to install, noting the following:

a. Tighten A/C condenser mounting screws and radiator hose clamps to specifications.
b. Refill and bleed cooling system as outlined under "Cooling System Bleed."
c. Check automatic transaxle oil level and replenish as necessary.
d. Recharge air conditioning system as outlined in "Air Conditioning."

TIGHTENING SPECIFICATIONS

Year	Component	Torque/Ft. Lbs.
1997–2000	A/C Compressor To Bracket	16–17
	A/C Compressor To Engine Block	30
	A/C Condenser To Radiator Bolt	45①
	A/C Drive Belt Tensioner Locking Nut	40
	Alternator Bracket Bolts	30
	Alternator Mounting Bolt (8 mm)	22–23
	Camshaft Sprocket Bolt (Lefthand Side)	85②
	Camshaft Sprocket Bolt (Righthand Side)	75②
	Camshaft Thrust Plate	20–21
	Condenser Inlet Tube Bracket	45①
	Connecting Rod Cap Nuts	40②
	Crankshaft Damper Bolt	85
	Crankshaft Main Bearing Cap Bolts	30②
	Crankshaft Main Bearing Tie Bolts	40
	Cylinder Head Bolts	③
	Cylinder Head Cover	96-108①
	Engine Mount Bracket To Block Bolts	65
	Engine Mount Insulator Nuts	45

Continued

TIGHTENING SPECIFICATIONS—Continued

Year	Component	Torque/Ft. Lbs.
1997-2000	Exhaust Front Down Pipes To Exhaust Support Bracket Screw	35
	Exhaust Manifold Heat Shield Mounting Screws	8–11
	Exhaust Manifold Mounting Screws	16–17
	Exhaust Manifold Nuts To Front Down Pipes	20
	Exhaust Manifold To Cylinder Head	16–17
	Exhaust Module Body Bracket Support	18
	Exhaust Pipe Flange	25
	Exhaust Support Bracket To Transaxle Screw	35
	Exhaust U-Bolt In Front Of Under Floor Converter Nut	24
	Fan Blade Nut	45①
	Fan Module To Radiator	45①
	Fan Motor To Shroud Lefthand Side Screws	45①
	Fan Motor To Shroud Righthand Side Screws	25①
	Insulator Mounting Bolts	16–17
	Intake Manifold Attaching Screws	④
	Intake Plenum Attaching Screws	④
	Muffler Heat Shield Mounting Nuts	45①
	Oil Filter	15
	Oil Pan Bolts	96-108①
	Oil Pan Drain Plug	25
	Oil Pump Cover Bolts	96-108①
	Oil Pump Pickup Tube Bolt	20–21
	PCV Valve	60①
	Radiator Hose Clamp	22①
	Radiator To Body Screws	96-108①
	Rear Crankshaft Seal Retainer Bolts	96-108①
	Rear Insulator To Crossmember Support Bracket Nut	30
	Rear Support Bracket To Crossmember Flange Nuts	30
	Receiver/Drier Swivel Nut	45①
	RFI Harness To Shroud Screw	25①
	Rocker Arm Shaft Retaining Bolts	⑤
	Spark Plugs	20
	Spark Plug Tubes	45
	Spark Plug Tube Nuts	60①
	Starter Mounting Bolts	30
	Thermostat Bleed Screw	60-72①
	Thermostat Housing Bolts	108①
	Throttle Body Bolts	96-108①
	Timing Belt Cover Bolts (6 mm)	96-108①
	Timing Belt Cover Bolts (8 mm)	20–21
	Timing Belt Cover Bolts (10 mm)	40
	Timing Belt Tensioner Bolts	20–21
	Timing Belt Tensioner Pulley Assembly Bolts	45
	Upper Radiator Crossmember Bolts	20–21

Continued

TIGHTENING SPECIFICATIONS—Continued

Year	Component	Torque/Ft. Lbs.
1997-2000	Water Inlet Connector	20–21
	Water Pump Mounting Bolts	96-108①
	Water Pump Pulley Bolts	20–21
	Water Pump To Timing Belt Cover	96-108①

① — Inch lbs.
② — Plus an additional 1/4 turn.
③ — Refer to "Cylinder Head, Replace" for tightening procedure & specifications.
④ — Refer to "Intake Manifold, Replace" for tightening specifications.
⑤ — Refer to "Rocker Arms, Replace" for tightening specifications.

Rear Axle & Suspension

NOTE: Refer To "Computer Relearn Procedure " Located In The Front Of This Manual For Computer Relearn Procedures.

INDEX

REAR WHEEL SPINDLE

REPLACE

1. Raise and support vehicle, then remove rear tire and wheel assemblies.
2. **On models equipped with rear disc brakes,** proceed as follows:
   a. Remove rear caliper assembly and support to frame using suitable wire.
   b. Remove rear disc brake rotor.
3. **On models equipped with rear drum brakes,** proceed as follows:
   a. Remove brake flex hose bracket from support plate and wheel cylinder.
   b. Remove brake drum.
4. **On all models,** remove rear hub and bearing assembly.
5. **On models equipped with drum brakes,** remove rear brake support plate with parking brake cable attached.
6. **On all models,** remove speed sensor head from rear disc brake adapter.
7. Remove speed sensor cable routing tube from trailing arm.
8. **On models equipped with rear disc brakes,** remove disc brake adapter, disc shield, park brake shoes and park brake cable as an assembly.
9. **On all models,** disconnect trailing arm from trailing arm bracket.
10. Disconnect lateral rod from spindle.
11. Loosen and remove rear spindle to strut assembly pinch bolt.
12. Tap suitable center punch into hole on spindle until punch is jammed into hole, **Fig. 1. Do not punch hole in strut with center punch.**
13. Using suitable hammer, tap on top surface of spindle, driving it down and off strut assembly, **Fig. 2.**
14. Remove spindle from vehicle.
15. Reverse procedure to install, noting the following:
    a. Install spindle assembly onto bottom of strut assembly. Push or tap spindle assembly onto strut until notch in spindle is tightly seated against locating tab on strut assembly.
    b. Check rear toe as outlined under "Wheel Alignment. "

STRUT

REPLACE

1. **On 1998–2000 models,** proceed as follows:
   a. Remove rear seat cushion and back assembly.
   b. Remove upper and lower quarter trim panels.
   c. Remove rear parcel shelf trim panel.
   d. Remove rear speakers and mounting plates, then disconnect speaker wiring.
2. **On all models,** raise and support vehicle, then remove rear wheel and tire assembly.
3. **On models equipped with rear disc brakes,** proceed as follows:
   a. Remove rear caliper assembly and support to frame using suitable wire.
   b. Remove rear disc brake rotor.
   c. Remove speed sensor cable routing tube on trailing arm bracket to spindle.
4. **On models equipped with rear drum brakes,** remove brake flex hose bracket from support plate and wheel cylinder.
5. **On all models,** remove bolt attaching lateral link to rear spindle assembly, **Fig. 3.**
6. Remove rear strut assembly to stabilizer bar attaching link at stabilizer bar.
7. Loosen and remove rear spindle to strut assembly pinch bolt.
8. Tap suitable center punch into hole on spindle until punch is jammed into hole, **Fig. 1. Do not punch hole in strut with center punch.**
9. Using suitable hammer, tap on top surface of spindle, driving it down and off strut assembly, **Fig. 2.**

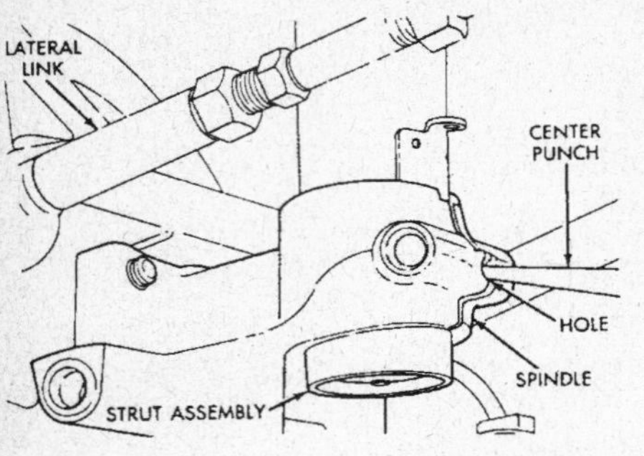

CR2039100041000X

Fig. 1 Center punch installed in spindle

10. Let rear spindle and assembled components hang from trailing arm while strut is out of vehicle.
11. Lower vehicle.
12. Remove rear upper strut mount from vehicle by accessing upper strut mount tower and removing three attaching nuts from luggage compartment of vehicle.
13. Remove strut from vehicle.
14. Reverse procedure to install, noting the following:
    a. Install spindle assembly onto bottom of strut assembly.
    b. Push or tap spindle assembly onto strut until notch in spindle is tightly seated against locating tab on strut assembly.
    c. Check rear toe as outlined under "Wheel Alignment."

STRUT SERVICE

1. Remove strut assembly from vehicle as previously described.
2. Position strut assembly in suitable vise.
3. Mark strut assembly lower spring isolator, spring and upper strut mount for indexing.
4. Position spring compressor tool No. 7520, or equivalent, on strut assembly spring and compress coil spring until all load is removed from upper strut mount assembly.
5. Install strut rod ratchet socket tool No. 6864, or equivalent, on strut nut.
6. Insert an 8 mm Allen wrench into end of strut shaft and remove shaft nut from shaft.
7. Remove upper strut mount assembly from strut shaft.
8. Remove coil spring, plate, spring compressor, dust shield, jounce bumper and lower spring isolator.
9. Inspect all components for signs of abnormal wear or failure, replacing any component as required.
10. Reverse procedure to install. Align marks made during disassembly.

REAR CROSSMEMBER

REPLACE

1997

1. Raise and support vehicle, then remove rear tire and wheel assemblies.
2. Position suitable jack under fuel tank just forward of crossmember to help support fuel tank when crossmember is removed.
3. Disconnect lateral link from spindle, **Fig. 3.**
4. Remove bolts attaching crossmember to frame rails.
5. Lower crossmember and lateral links out of vehicle as an assembly.
6. Reverse procedure to install. Install lateral link mounting bolts with heads facing vehicle front.

1998–2000

Removal

1. Open fuel filler door and remove filler neck mounting screws and cap.
2. Raise and support vehicle, then remove rear tire and wheel assemblies.
3. Remove lateral links mounting bolts and nuts. Lefthand front lateral link bolt cannot be removed until crossmember is lowered.
4. Remove brake tubes mounting screws from lefthand stabilizer bar isolator bushing retainer.
5. Remove stabilizer bar isolation bushing retaining frame rail mounting bolts and allow bar to hang down.
6. Remove tensioner from intermediate parking brake cable, then from lefthand rear parking brake cable.
7. Remove righthand rear parking brake cable from intermediate parking brake cable.
8. Remove retainer clips and rear parking brake cables from crossmember.
9. Remove brake proportioning valve mounting nuts.
10. Position suitable transmission jack under muffler.
11. Disconnect exhaust resonator hanger from rear frame rail, then the muffler hangers on each side of muffler.
12. Lower jack and muffler enough to access crossmember.
13. Remove fuel filler neck lefthand frame rail mounting screw.
14. Remove crossmember rear corner mounting bolts, then lower crossmember as low as possible to access lateral link mounting bolt at lefthand front corner.
15. Remove mounting bolt and link, then the crossmember.

Installation

1. Install rear suspension crossmember above muffler. Ensure brake tubes are properly routed as crossmember is installed.
2. Install rear proportioning valve mounting brackets and nuts, then the intermediate parking brake cable routing clip.
3. Attach lefthand front lateral link to crossmember, then install mounting bolt through front of crossmember. Do not install nut at this time.
4. Raise crossmember against frame rails and install, but do not tighten two rear mounting bolts at this time.
5. Raise exhaust into place, then install hangers.

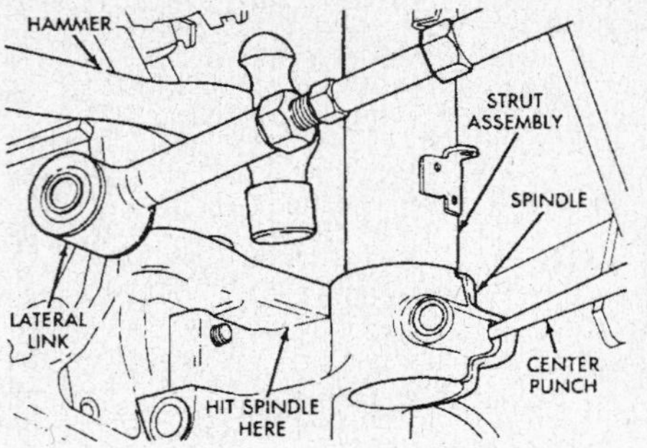

CR2039100042000X

Fig. 2 Spindle removal

6. Install mounting screw and attach fuel filler neck to lefthand frame rail.
7. Position rear parking brake cables into crossmember alignment holes, then install retaining clips.
8. Connect righthand rear parking brake cable to intermediate parking brake cable, then install parking brake cable tensioner.
9. Install stabilizer bar isolator bushing retainer mounting bolts and tighten to specifications.
10. Tighten rear suspension crossmember rear mounting bolts to specifications.
11. Install brake tubes mounting screws.
12. Install remaining lateral links and mounting bolts. Forward mounting bolts must point towards the rear and rear mounting bolts should point towards the front.
13. Install lateral link mounting nuts but do not tighten now. **Tighten mounting bolts when vehicle is at curb riding height.**
14. Install tire and wheel assemblies. Tighten wheel mounting stud nuts to half specification, then to specifications.
15. Lower vehicle, then install filler neck mounting screws and fuel filler cap.
16. Tighten lateral arm to crossmember mounting bolts to specifications.
17. Inspect and set rear wheel toe to specifications.

STABILIZER BAR

REPLACE

1997

1. Raise and support vehicle, then remove rear tire and wheel assemblies.
2. Position suitable jack under fuel tank just forward of crossmember to help support fuel tank when crossmember is removed.
3. Remove crossmember to frame rail bolts.
4. Release fuel system pressure as outlined in appropriate engine section, then drain fuel tank into suitable container.
5. Pull exhaust pipe hangers rubber insulators off mounting studs on frame rail from rear of vehicle and front of fuel tank.
6. Place alignment marks on fuel filler

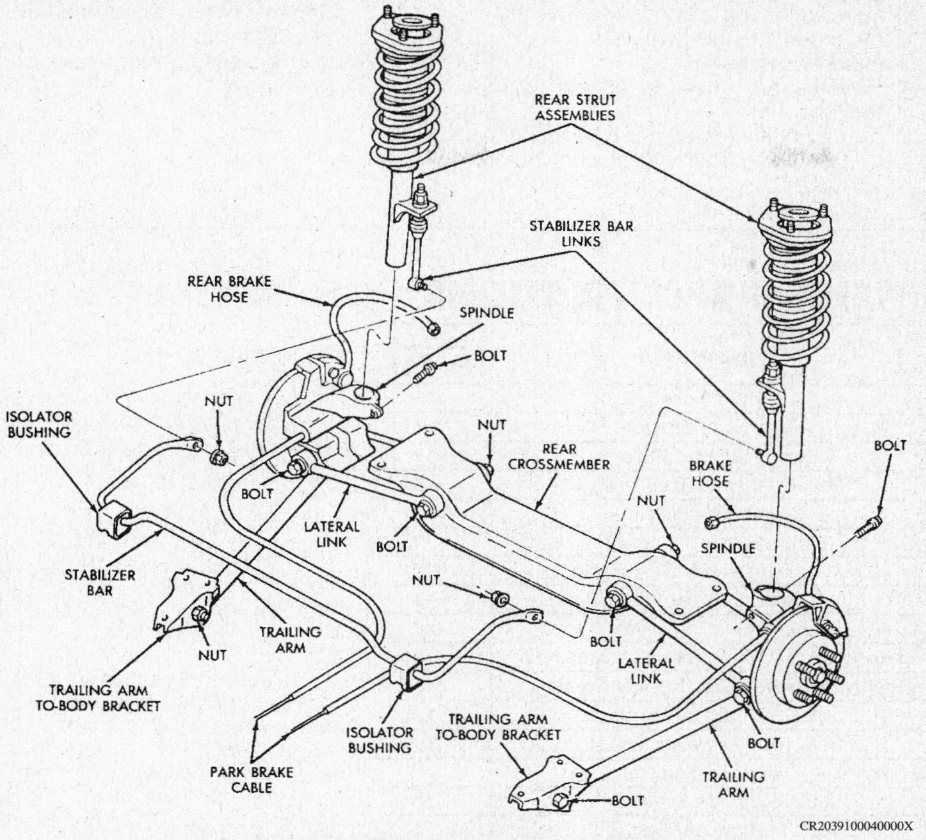

Fig. 3 Exploded view of rear suspension

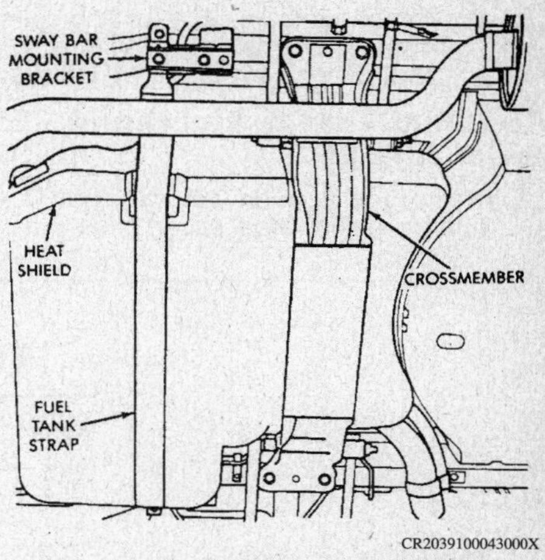

Fig. 4 Fuel tank heat shield & tank strap removal. 1997

hose, filler tube vent hose and vent tube, then remove fuel filler and vent hoses.

7. Disconnect fuel supply tube from fuel filter, then the fuel return and vent tube near fuel filter.
8. Disconnect both ends of stabilizer bar from links.
9. Mark position of crossmember on frame rails, then pull crossmember down until it stops.
10. Loosen, do not remove, stabilizer mounting bracket bolts, then remove heat shield and fuel tank strap, **Fig. 4**.
11. Disconnect fuel pump module.
12. Slightly lower front of fuel tank, then slide tank away from crossmember while pushing filler vent and fill tube over crossmember.
13. Lower tank from vehicle.
14. Remove stabilizer bar and isolator bushings as an assembly from vehicle.
15. Reverse procedure to install, aligning marks made during removal.

1998–2000

1. Raise and support vehicle.
2. Using suitable thin wrench to keep attaching link stud from turning, remove stabilizer bar to strut attaching link stud nuts.
3. Remove links from stabilizer bar.
4. Remove stabilizer bar isolator bushing retainers mounting bolts, then the stabilizer bar.
5. Mount bar in suitable soft jawed vise, then carefully pry back upper bushing retainer wider end tabs from lower half.
6. Using suitable hammer and brass drift punch, tap bushing retainer upper half forward, then off of lower half and bushing.
7. Remove bushing retainer lower half, then the bushing.
8. Remove bar from vise and repeat procedure to remove other bushing.
9. Reverse procedure to install, noting the following:
   a. Bushing slit points toward front of vehicle.
   b. Tighten mounting bolts to specifications.

LATERAL LINK

REPLACE

1997

Lefthand

1. Raise and support vehicle, then remove tire and wheel assembly.
2. Disconnect lateral links from spindle.
3. Disconnect lateral links from crossmember, then remove lateral links.
4. Reverse procedure to install, noting the following:
   a. Install solid lateral link toward front of vehicle and adjustable link toward rear of vehicle.
   b. Install lateral link bolts with head toward front of vehicle.
   c. Adjust rear toe as outlined under "Wheel Alignment."

Righthand

1. Raise and support vehicle, then remove tire and wheel assembly.
2. Disconnect lateral links from spindle.
3. Position suitable transmission jack under fuel tank.
4. Remove crossmember to frame rail bolts and lower crossmember enough to allow lateral link bolts to clear fuel tank.
5. Disconnect lateral links from crossmember, then remove lateral links.
6. Reverse procedure to install, noting the following:
   a. Install solid lateral link toward front of vehicle and adjustable link toward rear of vehicle.
   b. Install lateral link bolts with head toward front of vehicle.
   c. Adjust rear toe as outlined under "Wheel Alignment."

1998–2000

Lefthand Front

1. Raise and support vehicle, then remove lefthand rear tire and wheel assembly.
2. Remove lateral link to spindle mounting nut and bolt.
3. Remove link to rear crossmember mounting nut. Bolt cannot be removed now.
4. Remove brake tubes to lefthand stabilizer bar isolator bushing retainer mounting screws.
5. Remove stabilizer bar isolator bushing retainers mounting bolts.
6. Remove fuel filler neck to frame rail mounting screw, then position suitable transmission jack under fuel tank.
7. Remove righthand, then the lefthand fuel tank mounting strap mounting bolts, allow straps to hang.
8. Lower fuel tank enough to remove lateral link to crossmember mounting bolt, then the lefthand front lateral link.
9. Reverse procedure to install, noting the following:
   a. Do not tighten lateral link mounting bolt until vehicle is at curb riding height.

b. Tighten mounting screws and bolts to specifications.
c. Inspect and correct rear wheel toe.

Lefthand Rear & Righthand Front & Rear

1. Raise and support vehicle, then remove tire and wheel assemblies.
2. Remove lateral link to rear crossmember mounting nuts and bolts.
3. Remove lateral links.
4. Reverse procedure to install, noting the following:
   a. Do not tighten lateral link mounting bolt until vehicle is at curb riding height.
   b. Tighten mounting screws and bolts to specifications.
   c. Inspect and correct rear wheel toe.

TIGHTENING SPECIFICATIONS

Year	Component	Torque/ Ft. Lbs.
1997	Brake Hose	35
	Brake Hose Bracket	17
	Brake Support Plate	80
	Caliper Adapter To Spindle	85
	Caliper To Adapter	16
	Crossmember To Body	70
	Hub & Bearing Assembly To Spindle	125
	Lateral Link Jam Nut	48
	Lateral Link To Spindle	105
	Lateral Link To Suspension Crossmember	105
	Stabilizer Bar Isolator Bushing Retainer	40
	Stabilizer Bar Link To Strut	17
	Strut Rod To Upper Mount	50
	Strut To Body	21
	Strut To Spindle Pinch Bolt	70
	Strut To Stabilizer Bar Link	17
	Trailing Arm	75
	Trailing Arm Bracket To Body	50
	Wheel Lug Nut	80–110
1998–2000	Brake Hose	35
	Brake Hose Bracket	17
	Brake Support Plate	80
	Caliper Adapter To Spindle	85
	Caliper To Adapter	16
	Crossmember To Body	75
	Hub & Bearing Assembly To Spindle	125
	Lateral Link Jam Nut	65
	Lateral Link To Spindle	100
	Lateral Link To Suspension Crossmember	70
	Stabilizer Bar Isolator Bushing Retainer	30
	Stabilizer Bar To Strut Link	70
	Strut Shaft To Upper Mount	55
	Strut To Body	19
	Strut To Spindle Pinch Bolt	40
	Strut To Stabilizer Bar Link	17
	Trailing Arm	75
	Trailing Arm Bracket	80
	Trailing Arm Bracket To Body	45
	Wheel Lug Nut	80–110

Front Suspension & Steering

NOTE: On Air Bag Equipped Models, Refer To " Air Bag System Precautions" Located In The Front Of This Manual For System Disarming & Arming Procedures.

NOTE: Prior To Performing Any Service Operations Listed In This Section, Consult The "Technical Service Bulletins " Section For Related Information.

NOTE: Refer To "Computer Relearn Procedure " Located In The Front Of This Manual For Computer Relearn Procedures.

INDEX

PRECAUTIONS

AIR BAG SYSTEMS

Refer to "Air Bag System Precautions" in the front of this manual for system disarming and arming procedures.

BATTERY GROUND CABLE

Prior to service, disconnect battery ground cable and isolate as required.

HUB & BEARING

REPLACE

1. Raise and support vehicle, then remove tire and wheel.
2. Remove front caliper assembly and rotor from steering knuckle as outlined under "Disc Brakes."
3. Remove hub and bearing to stub axle mounting nut.
4. Remove hub bolts, then the hub and bearing assembly from steering knuckle by sliding it straight off end of hub axle. **CAUTION: When removing hub and bearing assembly from steering knuckle, be careful not to damage the flinger disc on the hub and bearing assembly. If flinger disc becomes damaged, hub and bearing assembly must be replaced with a new hub and bearing assembly, Fig. 1.**
5. If hub and bearing will not slide out of knuckle, insert suitable pry bar between hub and steering knuckle, **Fig. 2.**
6. Reverse procedure to install, noting the following:
   a. Use new stub shaft nut when installing.
   b. Tighten stub shaft nut, then lower vehicle, with brakes applied, tighten stub shaft to specifications.

BALL JOINT INSPECTION

The lower ball joint is serviced with the lower control arm.

1. Raise and support front of vehicle.
2. Grasp tire at top and bottom then apply an in and out force.
3. While applying force to tire, look for movement between lower ball joint and lower control arm.
4. If there is any movement, replace lower control arm.

CONTROL ARM

REPLACE

LOWER

1. Raise and support vehicle, then remove tire and wheel assembly.
2. Remove ball joint stud to steering knuckle clamp nut and bolt, **Fig. 3.**
3. Insert suitable pry bar between lower control arm and steering knuckle to separate ball joint stud from steering knuckle, **Fig. 4. Pulling steering knuckle out away from vehicle after releasing from ball joint can separate inner tripod joint.**
4. Remove and discard tension strut to cradle nut and washer from end of tension strut, **Fig. 5. Never reuse tension strut nut.**
5. Loosen and remove lower control arm pivot bushing bolt.
6. Separate lower control arm and tension strut from cradle as an assembly by first removing pivot bushing from cradle and then sliding tension strut out of isolator bushing, **Fig. 6.**
7. Reverse procedure to install, tightening lower control arm pivot bushing to cradle bracket attaching bolt with full weight of vehicle on suspension.

STEERING KNUCKLE

REPLACE

1. Raise and support vehicle, then remove tire and wheel assembly.
2. Remove brake caliper and rotor as outlined under " Caliper, Replace" in "Disc Brakes."
3. Remove ABS speed sensor screw.
4. Carefully remove speed sensor head from knuckle. If sensor has seized due to corrosion use a hammer and a punch to tap edge of sensor ear, rocking sensor until free, **Fig. 7. Do not use pliers on sensor head.**
5. Remove hub and bearing as outlined under "Hub & Bearing, Replace."
6. Remove ball joint stud to steering knuckle clamp nut and bolt, **Fig. 3.**
7. Insert suitable pry bar between lower control arm and steering knuckle to separate ball joint stud from steering knuckle, **Fig. 4. Do not pull steering knuckle out away from vehicle after releasing from ball joint as this can separate inner tripod joint.**
8. Remove strut assembly to steering knuckle attaching bolts. **Strut bolts have a serrated shaft for a tight fit into steering knuckle. Turn nut on bolts only, do not turn bolts.**
9. Remove steering knuckle from vehicle.
10. Reverse procedure, noting the following:

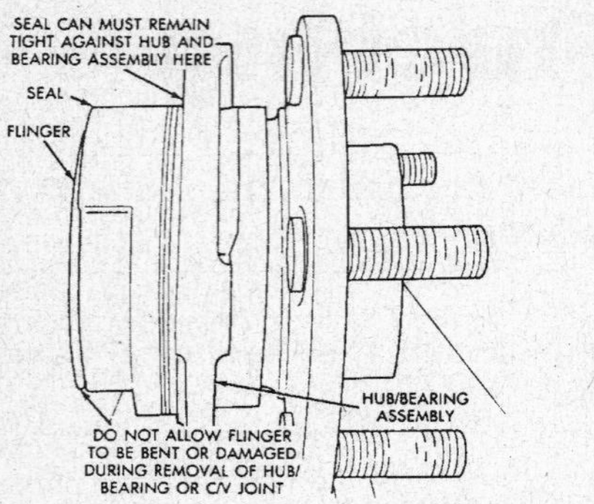
SEAL CAN MUST REMAIN TIGHT AGAINST HUB AND BEARING ASSEMBLY HERE
SEAL
FLINGER
HUB/BEARING ASSEMBLY
DO NOT ALLOW FLINGER TO BE BENT OR DAMAGED DURING REMOVAL OF HUB/ BEARING OR C/V JOINT
CR3039100346000X

Fig. 1 Hub & bearing assembly

a. **Strut bolts have a serrated shaft so do not turn bolts in steering knuckle. Turn nut on bolts do not turn bolts.**
b. Coat speed sensor head with high temperature multi-purpose EP grease before installing.
c. Tighten new stub shaft mounting nut, then lower vehicle and with brake applied, tighten to specifications.

STABILIZER BAR

REPLACE

1997

When removing the front stabilizer bar, it is necessary to support engine assembly and remove the entire front cradle module, **Fig. 8.**

1. **On models equipped with 3.3L engine,** proceed as follows:
   a. Mount engine support fixture tool No. 7137, or equivalent, across engine compartment, **Fig. 9.**
   b. Remove bolt attaching A/C compressor bracket to front of engine.
   c. Install webbing material hook on A/C compressor bolt, then install bolt and tighten, **Fig. 10.**
   d. Loosen, but do not remove, generator to engine bolt, then remove spacer between generator and engine.
   e. Install webbing material hook between generator and engine, then install and tighten bolt.
   f. Remove electronic ignition coil and mounting bracket bolt from rear of engine.
   g. Install webbing material hook on bracket bolt, then install and tighten bolt. **Route webbing material between fuel injector rail and valve cover.**
   h. Mount remaining piece of webbing material to threaded hole on back of lefthand cylinder head using suitable bolt.
   i. Securely attach pieces of webbing material to hook on engine holding fixture. Tighten hook on fixture until all slack is removed from all webbing material.
2. **On models equipped with 3.5L engine,** proceed as follows:
   a. Mount engine support fixture tool No. 7137, or equivalent, across engine compartment, **Fig. 11.**
   b. Remove bolt attaching timing belt housing to front of engine, **Fig. 12.**
   c. Install webbing material hook on bolt, then install bolt and tighten.
   d. Remove generator to generator mounting bracket nut and bolt.
   e. Install webbing material hook on generator mounting bolt, then install and tighten nut and bolt, **Fig. 13.**
   f. Mount remaining pieces of webbing material to threaded hole on back of each cylinder head using suitable bolt.
   g. Securely attach pieces of webbing material to hook on engine holding fixture. Tighten hook on fixture until all slack is removed from webbing material.
3. **On all models,** raise and support vehicle, then remove tire and wheel assemblies.
4. Remove ball joint stud to steering knuckle clamp nut and bolt, **Fig. 3.**
5. Insert suitable pry bar between lower control arm and steering knuckle to separate ball joint stud from steering knuckle, **Fig. 4. Pulling steering knuckle out away from vehicle after releasing from ball joint can separate inner tripod joint.**
6. Remove ground strap from cradle assembly.
7. Disconnect motor and transmission mounts from cradle assembly, **Fig. 14.**
8. Disconnect stabilizer bushing retainer from cradle, **Fig. 15.**
9. Position suitable jack stand under front of cradle and at center of transaxle cradle assembly mount. Raise jack stand at transaxle mount until transaxle just lifts off cradle assembly, **Fig. 16.**
10. Loosen, but do not remove, two rear cradle assembly to body bolts, **Fig. 14.**
11. Remove two front cradle assembly to body attaching bolts. **Ensure jack stand is properly placed under front of cradle to support cradle weight.**
12. With rear of cradle supported and jack stand supporting transaxle, remove two rear cradle bolts and slowly lower front jack stand until weight of engine is supported by engine support fixture and motor bolts are clear of cradle assembly.
13. Lift front of cradle off jack stand and remove cradle from vehicle.
14. Remove stabilizer bar to link attaching nuts, **Fig. 17.**
15. Remove stabilizer bar assembly from vehicle.
16. Reverse procedure to install.

1998–2000

1. Remove righthand upper mount to strut tower mounting nut and washer.
2. Raise and support vehicle, then remove righthand front tire and wheel assembly.
3. Remove mounting nut and righthand stabilizer bar attaching link at strut.

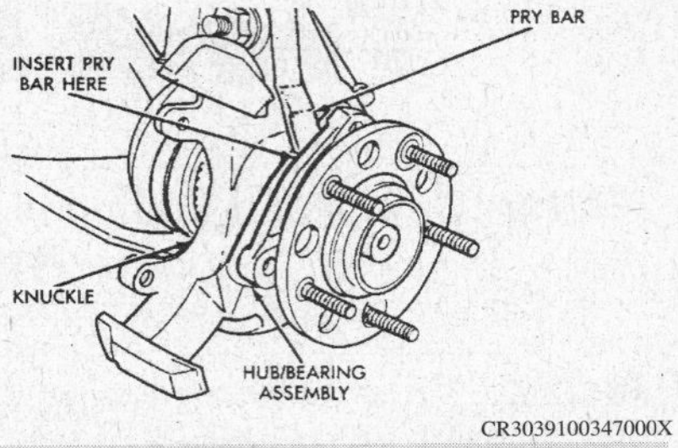
PRY BAR
INSERT PRY BAR HERE
KNUCKLE
HUB/BEARING ASSEMBLY
CR3039100347000X

Fig. 2 Hub & bearing removal

4. Remove mounting nut and lefthand stabilizer bar attaching link at strut.
5. Loosen but do not remove righthand outer tie rod end to strut arm mounting nut.
6. Using puller tool No. C-3894A, or equivalent, release righthand outer tie rod end from strut steering arm, then remove nut and tire rod.
7. **On models equipped with ABS,** remove speed sensor cable routing bracket.
8. **On all models,** remove strut to steering knuckle mounting bolts, then the righthand front strut.
9. Remove structural collar to engine oil pan mounting bolts, then the stabilizer bushing retainers to cradle mounting bolts.
10. Remove stabilizer bar isolator bushing retainers and bushings.
11. Position suitable transmission jack under engine oil pan with a wood block buffer between jack and oil pan.
12. Carefully raise jack until motor mounts clear cradle.
13. Rotate stabilizer bar and remove out righthand wheel opening, routing it in front righthand half-staff than between knuckle. **Be careful to not pull knuckle outward.**
14. Reverse procedure to install. Tighten mounting bolts to specifications.

STRUT DAMPNER

REPLACE

1. Raise and support vehicle, then remove tire and wheel assembly.
2. Remove stabilizer bar link at strut assembly, **Fig. 17.**
3. Loosen, but do not remove, outer tie rod end nut, then remove outer tie rod end using suspension component puller tool No. C-3894A, or equivalent.
4. Remove speed sensor cable routing bracket from strut assembly.
5. Remove brake caliper and brake rotor as outlined under " Disc Brakes." Suspend caliper from frame using suitable wire.
6. Disconnect lower strut from steering knuckle. **Strut bolts have a serrated shaft for a tight fit into steering knuckle. Turn nut on bolts only, do not turn bolts.**
7. Disconnect upper strut from shock tower and remove strut assembly from vehicle.

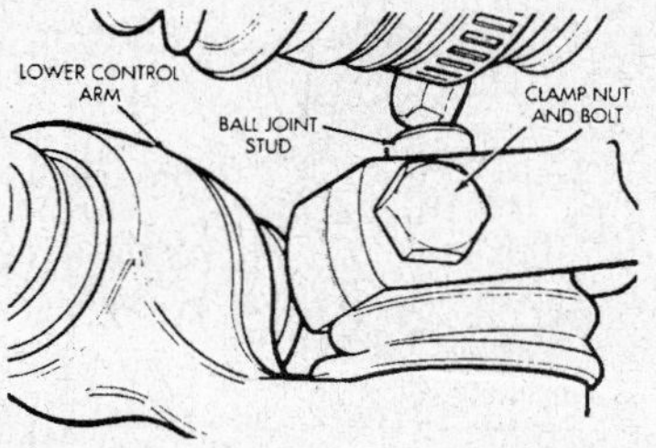

Fig. 3 Ball joint stud to steering knuckle clamp nut & bolt removal

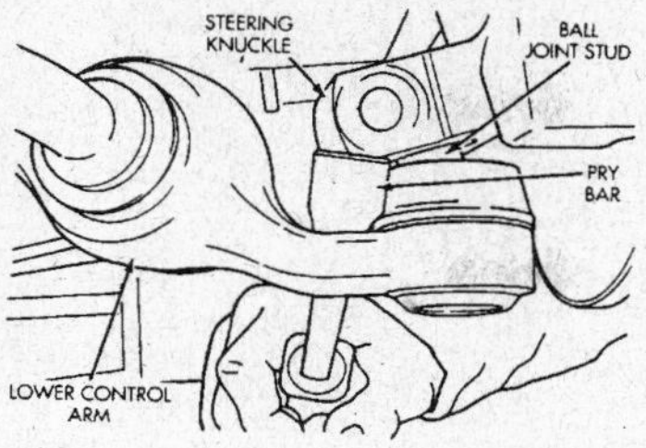

Fig. 4 Ball joint separation from steering knuckle

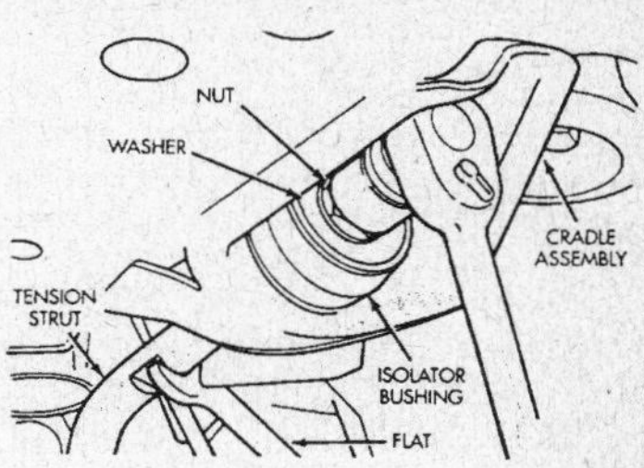

Fig. 5 Tension strut to cradle mounting

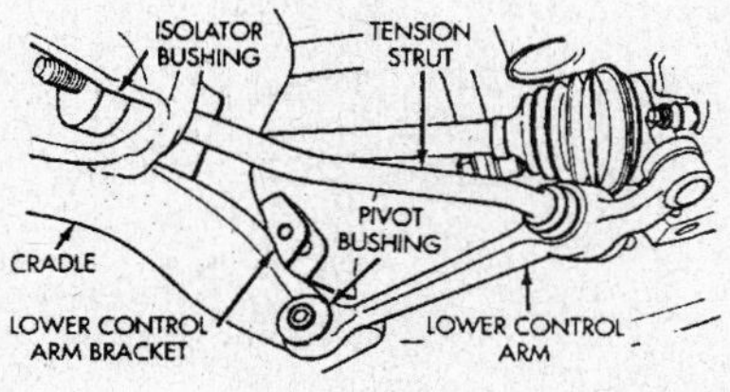

Fig. 6 Lower control arm removal

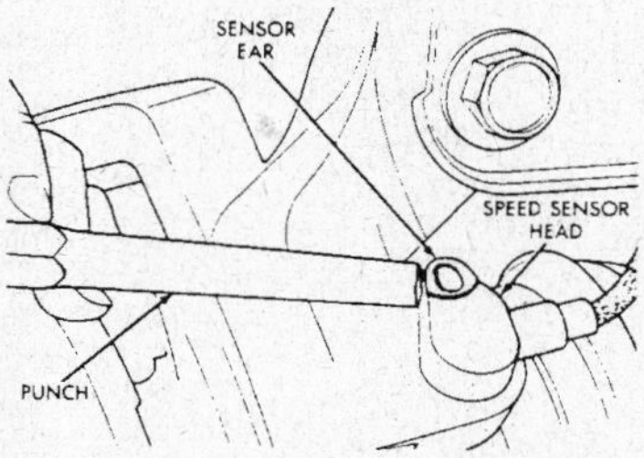

Fig. 7 Speed sensor removal

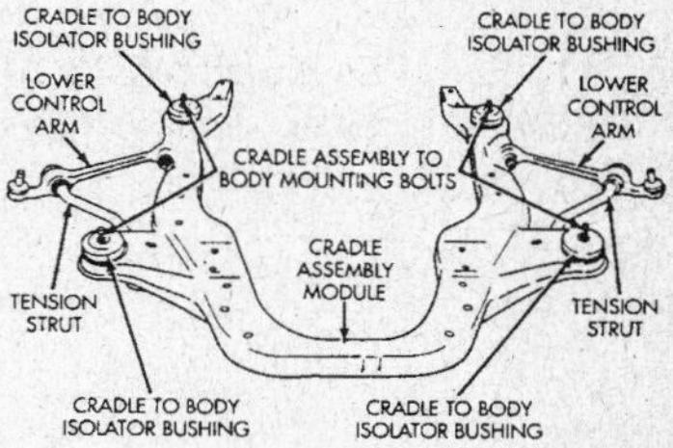

Fig. 8 Front cradle assembly. 1997

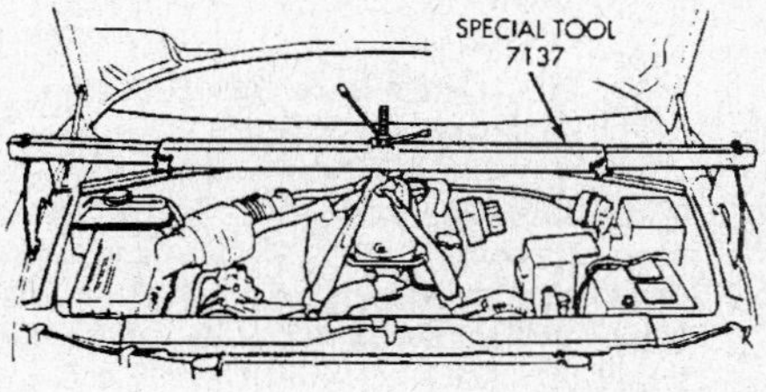

Fig. 9 Engine support fixture installation. 1997 3.3L engine

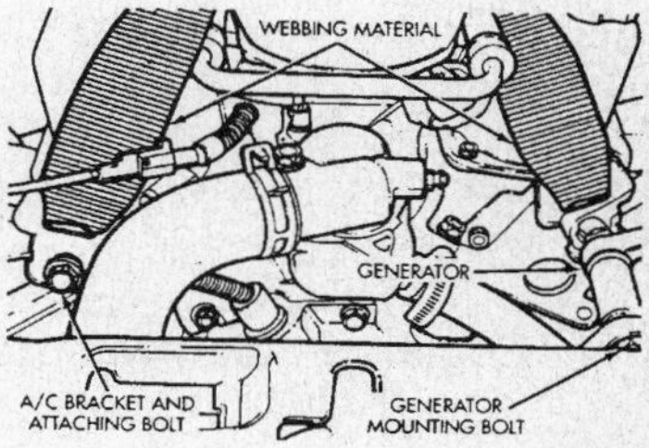

Fig. 10 Webbing material installation. 1997 3.3L engine

8. If damper is to be serviced, proceed as follows:
   a. Position strut assembly in suitable vise by clamping strut by steering arm.
   b. Mark strut unit, lower spring isolator, spring and upper strut mount for indexing of parts during assembly.
   c. Install spring compressor tool No. 7520, or equivalent, on coil spring and compress coil spring to release all load from upper strut mount assembly.
   d. Install strut rod socket tool No. 6864, or equivalent, on strut shaft nut; then, using a 10 mm socket on strut shaft end, remove strut shaft nut.
   e. Remove upper strut mount, jounce bumper, seat/bearing, dust shield, coil spring and lower spring mount from strut.
   f. Reverse procedure to assemble, aligning marks made during disassembly.
9. Reverse procedure to install. **Strut bolts have a serrated shaft; do not turn bolts in steering knuckle. Turn nut on bolts instead of turning bolts.**

TENSION STRUT

REPLACE

1. Remove lower control arm as previously described.
2. Separate tension strut from lower control arm.
3. Install replacement tension strut into lower control arm. Position tension strut with word Front stamped in strut positioned away from control arm, **Fig. 18.**
4. Install lower control arm and tension strut into vehicle.
5. Install washer and new nut on tension strut.
6. Install tire and wheel assembly.
7. Tighten lower control arm pivot bushing to cradle bracket attaching bolt with full weight of vehicle on suspension.

POWER STEERING GEAR

REPLACE

1997

Removal

1. Raise and support vehicle.
2. Disconnect gear shift cable from lever on transaxle, then remove cable off transaxle.
3. Lower vehicle.
4. **On models equipped with 3.5L engine,** disconnect throttle cable from throttle body and remove from cable bracket.
5. **On all models,** remove both wiper arm assemblies from pivots.
6. Remove cowl closure panel and weatherstrip as an assembly from cowl, **Fig. 19.**
7. Disconnect air plenum from throttle bodies, PCV make up air tube and idle air control motor.
8. Remove plenum from righthand side of vehicle, **Fig. 20.**
9. Remove wiper module assembly as outlined under " Electrical."
10. Remove vacuum supply hose for power brake booster at intake manifold and position hose aside.
11. Turn front wheels to full lefthand turn position, then turn wheels back until roll pin is steering coupler is accessible, **Fig. 21.** Lock steering column in place using ignition key.
12. Mark steering coupler and gear shaft for assembly.
13. Remove steering coupler roll pin using correct pin punch.
14. Remove pedal travel sensor from brake booster as follows:
    a. Pump brake pedal 20 times to evacuate stored vacuum.
    b. Remove wiring harness connector from sensor.
    c. Using a small screwdriver, lift mounting ring from notch, then remove mounting ring from grommet, **Fig. 22.**
    d. Remove pedal travel sensor from brake booster by carefully pulling it out of its grommet. **Do not twist.**
15. Remove brake master cylinder with lines connected from brake booster.
16. Carefully position master cylinder against lefthand shock tower.
17. Remove power steering pressure and return hoses from power steering gear.

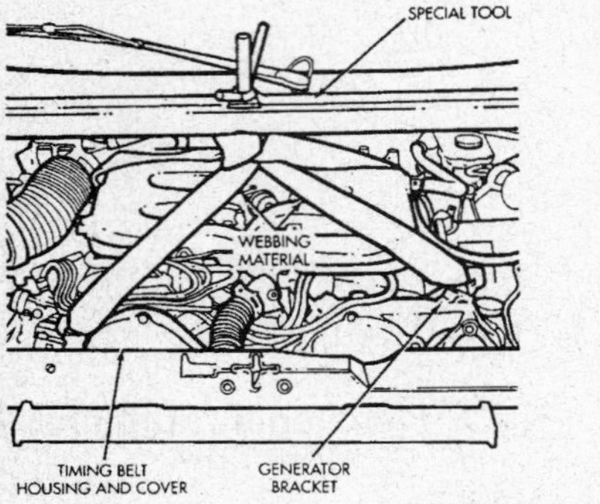

Fig. 11 Engine support fixture installation. 1997 3.5L engine

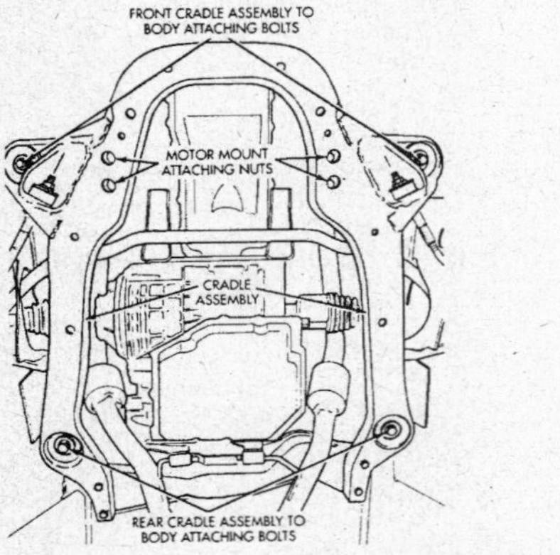

Fig. 14 Engine cradle assembly. 1997

18. Bend back mounting tabs on bolt attaching tie rods to steering gear then loosen and remove bolts attaching tie rods to steering gear. Lay tie rods, bolts and plate as an assembly on bellhousing of transaxle, **Fig. 23.**
19. Remove bolts attaching steering gear assembly to crossmember.
20. Slide steering gear forward in vehicle to disengage steering coupler. **After steering gear is disengaged from steering column, do not rotate steering gear shaft.**
21. Remove steering gear through area in cowl wiper module removal provided.

Installation

If a replacement steering gear assembly is being installed, the replacement gear will need to be positioned prior to installation.

1. Install steering gear assembly in vehicle through opening in cowl.
2. When reusing original gear, align paint marks on steering coupler and gear shaft then insert gear shaft into coupling.
3. When using a replacement gear, position gear by carefully grasping shaft of steering gear and rotating until steering gear is in a full left turn position.
4. Align steering gear with mounting holes in crossmember then install gear mounting bracket bolts. **Ensure brake line routing clip is installed under lefthand steering gear mounting bracket.**

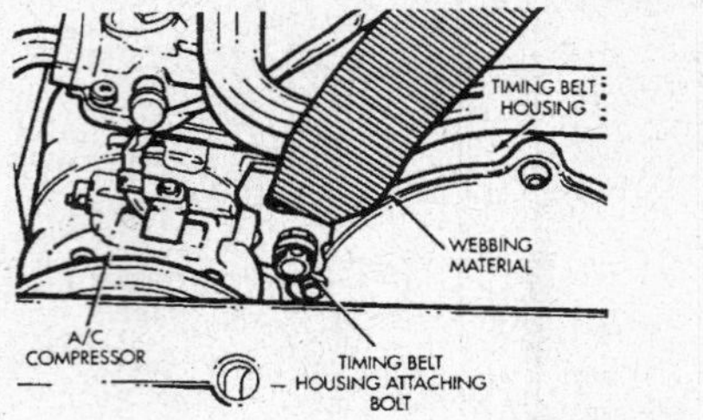

Fig. 12 Webbing material to timing belt cover installation. 1997 3.5L engine

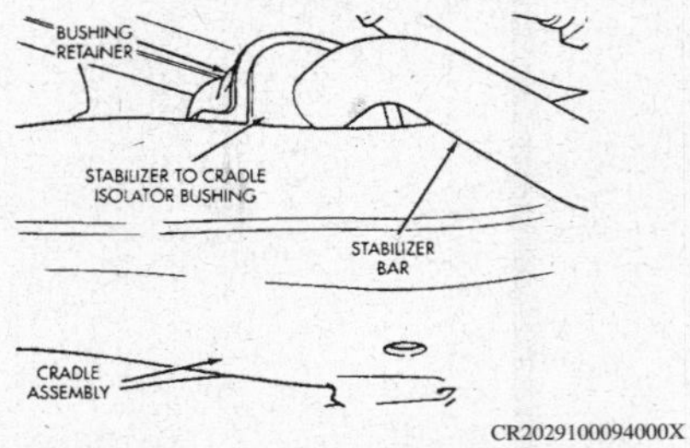

Fig. 15 Stabilizer bar isolator bushing & bracket. 1997

5. Install steering gear coupler mounting roll pin flush with top of steering coupler.
6. Attach power steering fluid pressure and return lines to proper ports of steering gear.
7. **On models equipped with 3.5L engine,** correct orientation of power steering pressure hose at power steering pump must be maintained. Ensure power steering hose is installed in orientation clip at power steering pump prior to tightening tube fitting.
8. **On all models,** align center take off on power steering gear with tie rod assemblies, then install tie rod bolts and washers, **Fig. 23.**
9. After tie rod bolts have been tightened to specification, bend lock tabs against bolt heads.
10. Install pedal travel sensor retainer ring on sensor grommet with tab on ring located in top notch of mounting grommet.
11. Sparingly lubricate pedal travel sensor O-ring with fresh brake fluid then install sensor into grommet by pushing it straight into grommet. **Ensure sensor is installed into grommet until tab on sensor is past mounting ring on grommet.**
12. Install master cylinder on brake booster.
13. Install vacuum supply hose for brake booster on intake manifold.
14. Install windshield wiper module system.
15. Connect wiring harness from windshield wiper module into wiring harness.
16. **On models equipped with 3.5L engine,** connect air intake plenum to throttle bodies, PCV make up air tube and idle air control motor.
17. **On all models,** install cowl closer panel and weather strip.

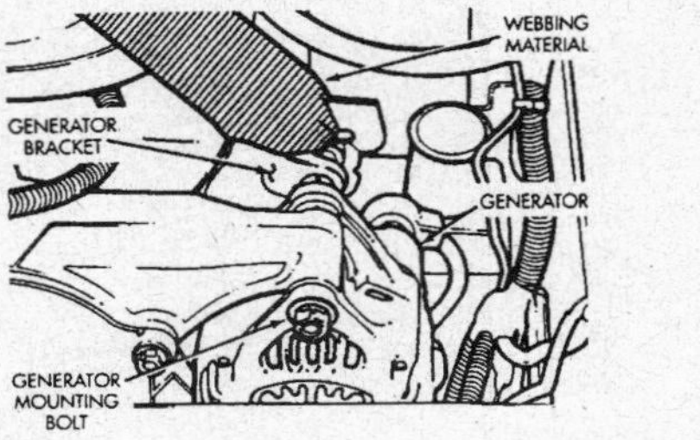

Fig. 13 Webbing material to generator bracket installation. 1997 3.5L engine

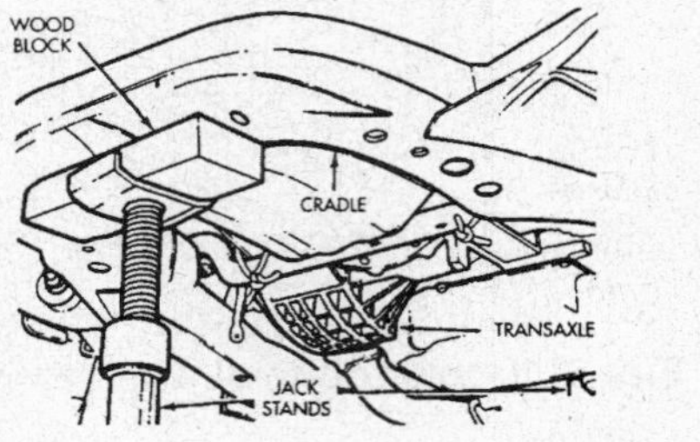

Fig. 16 Cradle & transaxle support. 1997

18. Install washer hoses on wiper arms then both wiper arms on pivots.
19. **On models equipped with 3.5L engine,** install throttle cable in throttle cable bracket and on throttle body.
20. **On all models,** raise and support vehicle.
21. Install gear shift cable on shift lever and mounting bracket.
22. Install tire and wheel assemblies then lower vehicle.
23. Connect battery ground cable.
24. Bleed system as outlined under "Power Steering System Bleed."
25. Adjust toe as outlined under "Wheel Alignment."

1998-2000

1. Position wheels straight ahead, then raise and support vehicle.
2. Remove caps, mounting nuts and wiper arms, then the wiper module and cowl covers.
3. Remove mounting bolts, then the reinforcement.
4. Remove inline resonator and inlet hose from throttle body, then the air inlet hose from air cleaner housing.
5. Using suitable clamp, lock steering wheel.
6. Remove steering column coupler retaining pin and bolt, then separate intermediate steering shaft from column coupler.
7. Bend back tie rod to steering gear mounting bolts' mounting plate retaining tabs.
8. Remove mounting bolts, mounting plate and washers, then lay tie rods on top of transaxle bell housing.
9. Using suitable siphon pump, remove as much power steering fluid as possible from reservoir.
10. Remove power steering fluid pressure

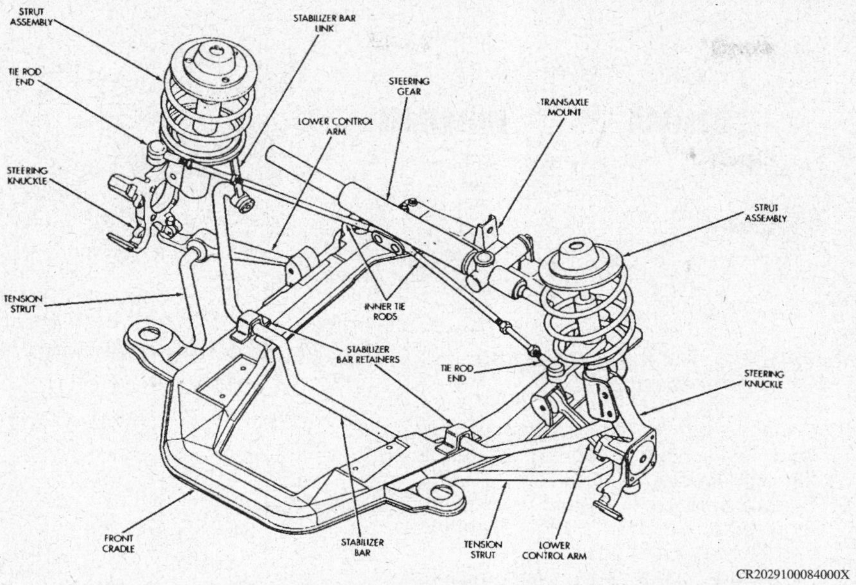

Fig. 17 Front suspension component location.

and return hoses from steering gear.

11. **On models equipped with speed proportional steering gear,** remove solenoid wiring harness connector.
12. **On all models,** remove mounting nuts, then the master cylinder with brake tubes connected from vacuum booster. Carefully position master cylinder upright on lefthand side valve cover.
13. Remove steering gear to crossmember lefthand, then righthand side mounting bolts. Loosen righthand mounting bracket mounting bolts to clear air conditioning lines, if necessary.
14. Slide steering gear and intermediate shaft into engine compartment to access intermediate shaft flex coupler roll pin.
15. Using roll pin remover tool No. 6831-A, or equivalent, remove roll pin and separate intermediate steering shaft from steering gear.
16. Raise and support vehicle, then remove righthand front tire and wheel assembly.
17. Remove tie rod end to steering arm mounting nut, then, using puller tool No. C-3894-A, or equivalent, remove tie rod.
18. **On models equipped with 2.7L engine,** turn front of lefthand front tire and wheel assembly as far outward as possible.
19. **On all models,** slide steering gear end through righthand side inner fender tie rod hole until approximately half the gear is through hole.
20. Lift lefthand end of gear up between engine and cowl, then pull gear out.
21. Reverse procedure to install, noting the following:
    a. Tighten mounting bolts to specifications.
    b. Ensure tie rod spacer block inside steering gear bellows is aligned with steering gear and gear bellows' holes.
    c. Adjust toe.

POWER STEERING PUMP

REPLACE

1997

1. Loosen and remove power steering drive belt as outlined in appropriate engine section.
2. Raise and support vehicle.
3. Drain power steering fluid from reservoir into suitable container.
4. Loosen and remove power steering pressure hose from pump discharge fitting.
5. Loosen and remove bolts attaching pump to pump bracket through holes in pump drive pulley.
6. Remove pump and pulley as an assembly from vehicle through bottom of engine compartment.
7. Reverse procedure to install, noting the following:
    a. **On models equipped with 3.5L engine,** correct orientation of power steering pressure hose at power steering pump must be maintained. Ensure power steering hose is installed in orientation clip at power steering pump prior to tightening tube fitting.
    b. **On all models,** install power steering drive belt as outlined in appropriate engine section.
    c. Bleed system as outlined under "Power Steering System Bleed."

1998–2000

1. Using suitable siphon pump, remove as much power steering fluid as possible from power steering reservoir.
2. Remove power steering fluid return

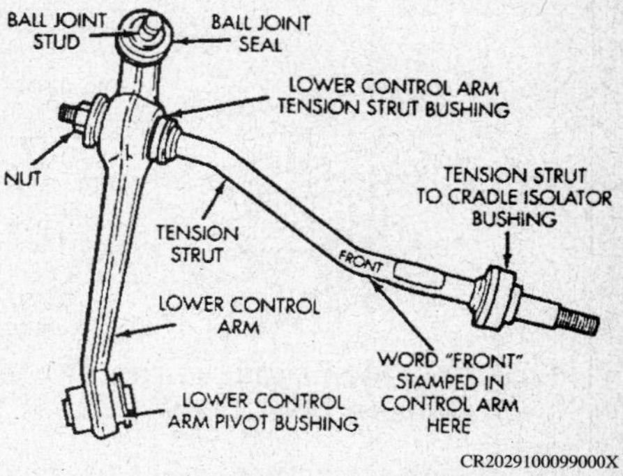

Fig. 18 Tension strut removal from control arm

hose from reservoir, then let fluid drain from reservoir and pump into suitable container.

3. Cap power steering fluid reservoir open nipple.
4. Remove pressure hose from power steering pump and let remaining fluid drain from pump into container.
5. **On models equipped with 3.2 and 3.5L engines,** remove power steering pressure switch wiring harness connector.
6. **On all models,** loosen serpentine drive belt tensioner locknut, then, using adjustment bolt, remove power steering pump drive belt tension.
7. Remove drive belt from power steering pump pulley.
8. Remove pump mounting bolts through pulley face holes.
9. Insert suitable screwdriver between pump and tensioner bracket sleeve, then push sleeve forward in tensioner bracket until it is flush with tensioner bracket back.
10. Remove pump and pulley as an assembly. On 2.7L engines, the reservoir is part of the pump.
11. Reverse procedure to install, noting the following:
    a. Long mounting bolt is install in tensioner bracket sleeve.
    b. Ensure return hose clamp is installed past nipple upset bead.
    c. Tighten mounting bolts to specifications.

POWER STEERING SYSTEM BLEED

During bleeding procedure, keep fluid in reservoir at correct level.

1. Raise and support front of vehicle.
2. Manually turn oil pump pulley a few times.
3. Turn steering wheel from stop to stop five or six times.
4. Disconnect high tension cable then operate starter motor intermittently while turning steering wheel from stop to stop five or six times.
5. Connect high tension cable and start engine.
6. Turn steering wheel from stop to stop until no bubbles appear in reservoir.
7. Ensure fluid is not milky and that at proper level.

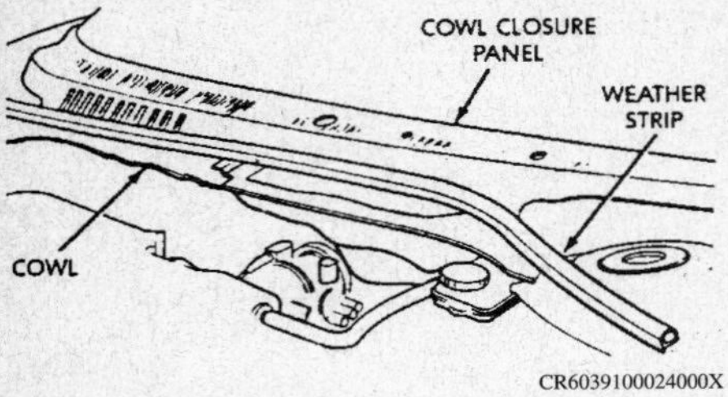

Fig. 19 Cowl closure panel replacement. 1997

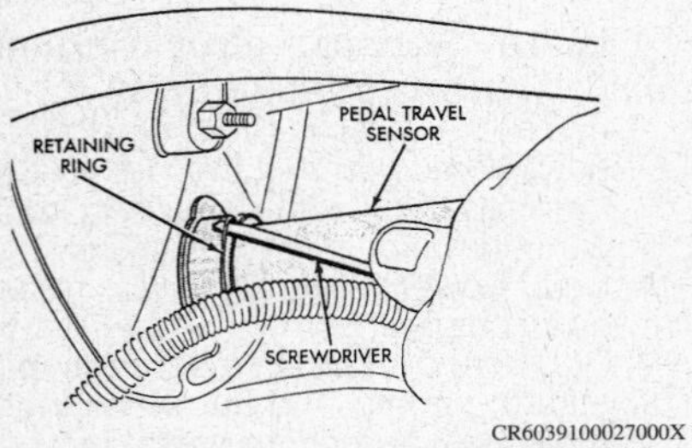

Fig. 22 Pedal sensor mounting ring removal. 1997

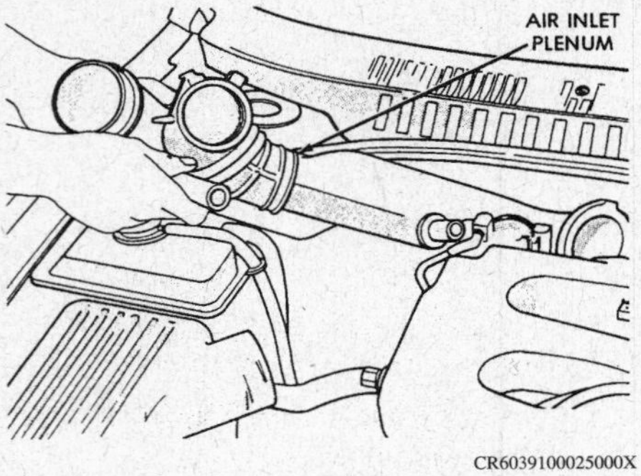

Fig. 20 Air intake plenum removal. 1997

8. Confirm there is little or no change in fluid level when steering wheel is turned from stop to stop.
9. Ensure difference in fluid level is no more than .2 inch with engine running and when it is stopped.
10. If fluid level is not as specified, system is not completely bled. Repeat procedure.

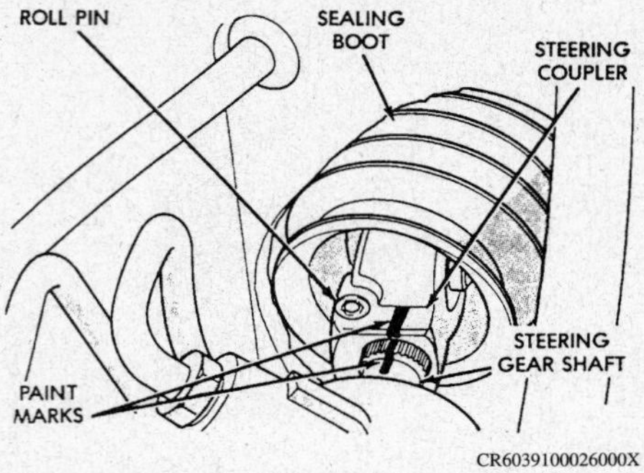

Fig. 21 Steering gear coupler pin removal. 1997

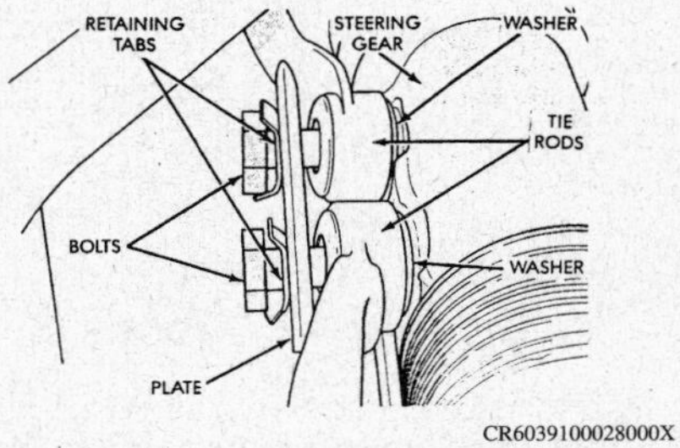

Fig. 23 Tie rod attachment to steering gear. 1997

TIGHTENING SPECIFICATIONS

Year	Component	Torque/Ft. Lbs.
1997–2000	Ball Joint Stud To Steering Knuckle	40
	Disc Brake Caliper	16
	Driveshaft Nut	120
	Front Cradle Assembly To Body (1997)	115
	Front Cradle Assembly To Body (1998–2000)	120
	Front Stub Axle To Hub & Bearing	135
	Hub & Bearing Assembly To Steering Knuckle	80
	Inner Tie Rod To Adjustment Sleeve Jam Nut	55
	Lower Control Arm To Cradle Pivot (1997)	90
	Lower Control Arm To Cradle Pivot (1998–2000)	105
	Outer Tie Rod To Adjustment Sleeve Jam Nut	55
	Power Steering Fluid Pressure Hose To Discharge Fitting (1997)	55
	Power Steering Fluid Pressure Hose To Discharge Fitting (1998–2000)	62
	Power Steering Pressure Hose Tube (1997)	23
	Power Steering Pressure Hose Tube (1998–2000)	35
	Power Steering Pressure Switch	15
	Power Steering Pump To Bracket Bolts (1997)	35
	Power Steering Pump To Bracket Bolts (1998–2000)	21
	Return Tube	23

Continued

TIGHTENING SPECIFICATIONS—Continued

Year	Component	Torque/Ft. Lbs.
1997-2000	Stabilizer Bar Attaching Link To Strut	17
	Stabilizer Bar Bushing Retainer To Cradle (1997)	40
	Stabilizer Bar Bushing Retainer To Cradle (1998–2000)	45
	Stabilizer Link	70
	Steering Gear To Crossmember (1997)	50
	Steering Gear To Crossmember (1998–2000)	43
	Strut Assembly Shaft	70
	Strut Assembly To Shock Tower	28
	Strut Assembly To Steering Knuckle	125①
	Stub Shaft	②
	Sway Bar To Strut Link	70
	Tension Strut (1997)	110
	Tension Strut (1998–2000)	95
	Tie Rod End Adjusting Sleeve	25
	Tie Rod End To Strut Steering	27
	Tie Rod To Steering Gear	57
	Wheel Lug Nut	80–110

① — Strut bolts have a serrated shaft so do not turn bolts in steering knuckle. Turn nuts on bolts. Do not turn bolts.
② — Refer to "Hub & Bearing, Replace" for tightening procedure & specifications.

Wheel Alignment

NOTE: Prior To Performing Any Service Operations Listed In This Section, Consult The "Technical Service Bulletins " Section For Related Information.

INDEX

PRELIMINARY INSPECTION

Before any attempt is made to change or correct front wheel alignment, the following inspections and necessary corrections must be made.

1. Ensure tire pressure is at recommended pressure, all tires should be same size and in good condition and have approximately same wear.
2. Check front wheels and tire assembly for radial runout.
3. Inspect lower ball joint and steering linkage for looseness.
4. Check for broken or damaged front and rear springs.
5. **Just prior to each alignment reading, then vehicle should be jounced (rear first, then front) by grasping bumper at center and jouncing each end of vehicle an equal number of times. Always release bumpers at bottom of down cycle.**

FRONT WHEEL ALIGNMENT

CAMBER

If front camber is not within specifications, and strut and steering knuckles are not bent or damaged, use following procedure to modify strut clevis bracket to adjust camber.

1. Raise and support front of vehicle, then remove tire and wheel assemblies.
2. Remove stabilizer bar link from strut, then loosen, but do not remove outer tie rod end nut.
3. Using puller tool No. C-3894-A, or equivalent, remove tie rod end from steering arm.
4. Remove ABS wheel speed sensor routing bracket from strut.
5. Remove mounting bolts, then separate strut from steering knuckle and position knuckle out of way.
6. Using suitable grinder and cutting tool, elongate bottom strut bracket mounting hole .0789 inch left and right.
7. Install steering knuckle and loosely install bolts attaching strut to knuckle.

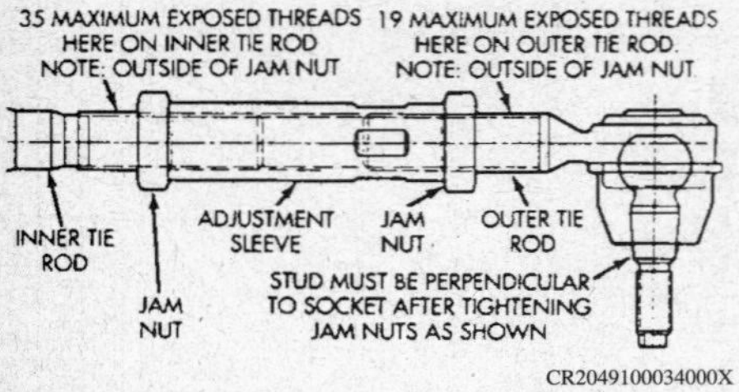

Fig. 1 Front tie rod adjustment dimensions

8. Install speed sensor bracket.
9. Install outer tie rod and tighten nut to specifications.
10. Install stabilizer bar attaching link and tighten nut to specifications.
11. Install tire and wheel assemblies.
12. Lower vehicle, then jounce front and rear of vehicle equal number of times.
13. Adjust front camber to preferred specifications by pushing in or pulling out on top of tire and wheel assembly.
14. Tighten upper and lower mounting bolts enough to not allow steering knuckle to move, then jounce front and rear of vehicle equal number of times.
15. Ensure camber is with specifications, then tighten mounting bolts to specifications.
16. Inspect and correct toe as necessary.

TOE

1. Prepare vehicle as previously described.
2. Center steering wheel and hold with steering wheel clamp.
3. Loosen tie rod adjustment sleeve jam nuts. Rotate adjustment sleeve to align tore to specifications.
4. **When setting toe, maximum threads exposed on inner and outer tie rod can not exceed amounts shown in Fig. 1.**
5. When tightening adjustment sleeve jam nuts, following procedure must be followed to ensure adequate tightening and retention of adjustment sleeve jam nut is obtained.
   a. Install correct size open end wrench on flat of adjustment sleeve.
   b. While holding adjustment sleeve, **torque** outer tie rod to adjusting sleeve jam nut to 55 ft. lbs.
   c. While holding adjustment sleeve from turning, **torque** inner tie rod to adjustment sleeve jam nut to 55 ft. lbs.
6. **Torque** tie rod adjustment sleeve locknuts to 55 ft. lbs.
7. Remove steering wheel clamp.

REAR WHEEL ALIGNMENT

TOE

1. Prepare vehicle as previously described.
2. Loosen lateral link adjustment link jam nuts.
3. Rotate adjustment link as required to set rear wheel toe to specification.
4. **Do not exceed maximum length dimension of lateral links, Fig. 2. Both dimensions must be checked.**
5. **Torque** lateral links locknuts to 55 ft. lbs.

TECHNICAL SERVICE BULLETINS

LEADS OR PULLS ON FLAT NON-CROWNED ROADS

On these models from 1993–99, the vehicle leads or pulls on a flat non-crowned road.

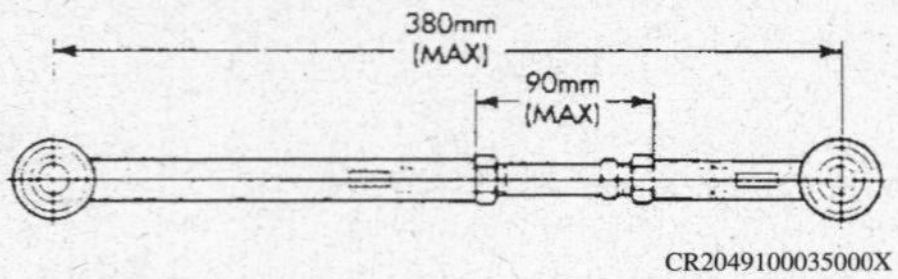

Fig. 2 Rear tie rod adjustment dimensions

This condition may be caused by caster bias. To correct this condition, proceed as follows:

1. Loosen engine cradle to frame bolts.
2. **If vehicle leads left,** rotate cradle to increase lefthand caster .8° and reduce righthand caster .8°.
3. **If vehicle leads right,** rotate cradle to increase righthand caster .8° and reduce lefthand caster .8°.
4. **On all models, torque** engine cradle to frame bolts to 129 ft. lbs.
5. Center steering wheel and set toe. If condition still exists, proceed to next step.
6. raise and support vehicle, then remove tire and wheel assemblies.
7. Remove strut clevis to knuckle bolts and nuts.
8. Loosely assembly new clevis to knuckle bolts (part No. 06505363AA) and nuts (part No. 06505363AA).
9. Install tire and wheel assemblies, then lower vehicle.
10. Adjust front camber to preferred setting by physically pushing or pulling on top of tire.
11. When camber is correct, **torque** upper then lower strut clevis bolt to 160 ft. lbs.
12. Set front toe to specifications.
13. Road test vehicle.
14. If vehicle still drifts or leads, repeat camber adjustment procedure but bias cross camber setting opposite lead tendency. If vehicle leads left, set front lefthand camber to minus .3° and front righthand camber to plus .6°.

NEON

NOTE: Refer To The Rear Of This Manual For Manufacturer's Special Service Tool Supplies.

INDEX OF SERVICE OPERATIONS

Specifications

GENERAL ENGINE SPECIFICATIONS

Engine	Engine VIN Code①	Fuel System	Bore & Stroke, Inches	Compres-sion Ratio	Net HP @ RPM	Maximum Torque, Ft. Lbs. @ RPM	Normal Oil Pressure, psi	
							Curb Idle	3000 RPM
1997–99								
DOHC	Y	SMPI	3.45 X 3.27	9.6	150 @ 6500	133 @ 5500	4	25–80
SOHC	C	SMPI	3.45 X 3.27	9.8	132 @ 6000	129 @ 5000	4	25–80
2000								
SOHC	C	SMPI	3.45 X 3.27	9.8	132 @ 5600	130 @ 4600	4	25–80

DOHC — Dual Overhead Cam
SMPI — Sequential Multi-Port Fuel Injection
SOHC — Single Overhead Cam
① — Eighth digit of VIN denotes engine code.

TUNE UP SPECIFICATIONS

Engine	Spark Plug Gap, Inch	Ignition Timing		Curb Idle Speed	Fuel Pump Pressure, psi	Valve Clearance, Inch
		Firing Order ④	°BTDC			
1997–99						
2.0L	.033–.038	1-3-4-2	①	③	48②	⑤
2000						
2.0L	.033–.038	1-3-4-2	①	550–1300	48.7–49.7	⑤

BTDC — Before Top Dead Center
① — Direct Ignition System (DIS); not adjustable.
② — Less vacuum applied to pressure regulator.
③ — Below 1000 miles, 550–1300 RPM. Above 1000 miles, 600–1300 RPM.
④ — Refer to **Fig. A** for spark plug wire connections.
⑤ — Equipped w/non-adjustable hydraulic lash adjusters.

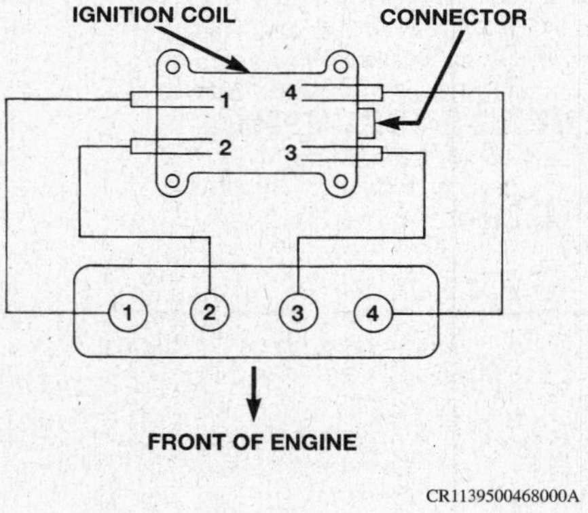

Fig. A

FRONT WHEEL ALIGNMENT SPECIFICATIONS

Year	Camber, Degrees①		Caster, Degrees①		Toe In, Degrees		Ball Joint Wear
	Limits	Desired	Limits	Desired	Limits	Desired	③
1997–99	–0.4 to +0.4	0	+1.8 to +3.8②	+2.8	–0.1 to +0.3	+0.1	③
2000	–0.4 to +0.4	0	+1.6 to +3.6②	+2.6	–0.1 to +0.3	+0.1	③

① — Reference angle only; not adjustable.

② — Side to side differential not to exceed .1.°

③ — Refer to "Ball Joint Inspection" under "Front Suspension & Steering."

REAR WHEEL ALIGNMENT SPECIFICATIONS

Year	Camber Angle, Degrees①		Total Toe, Degrees①		Thrust Angle, Degrees①
	Limits	Desired	Limits	Desired	
1997–99	–.75 to +.25	–.25	–.1 to +.3	+.1	–.1 to +.1
2000	–.65 to +.15	–.25	–.1 to +.5	+.3	–.1 to +.1

① — Reference angle only. Nonadjustable.

FLUID CAPACITIES & COOLING SYSTEM DATA

Year	Coolant Capacity, Qts.	Radiator Cap Relief Pressure, Lbs.	Thermo. Opening Temp., °F	Fuel Tank, Gals.	Engine Oil Refill, Qts.③	Auto. Transaxle Oil, Qts.②	Man. Transaxle Oil, Pts.
1997–99	7.4	16	195	12.5	4.5	①	4.0–4.6
2000	6.5	14–18	192–199	12.5	4.5	④	4.0–4.6

① — Fluid change only, 4.0 qts. After overhaul: except fleet models, 8.9 qts.; fleet models, 9.2 qts.

② — Approximate. Make final inspection w/dipstick.

③ — Includes oil filter.

④ — Fluid change only, 4.0 qts. After overhaul, 8.9 qts.

LUBRICANT DATA

Year	Transaxle		Power Steering	Brake System
	Automatic	Manual		
1997–98	Mopar ATF Type 7176	Mopar Type MS 9417	Mopar No. 4318055	DOT 3
1999	Mopar ATF Type 7176	Mopar Type MS 9417	Mopar No. 5010304AA	DOT 3
2000	Mopar ATF+4 Type 9602	Mopar Type MS 9417	Mopar No. 5010304AA	DOT 3

Electrical

NOTE: Refer To "Air Bag System Precautions" Located In The Front Of This Manual For System Disarming & Arming Procedures.

NOTE: Refer To "Computer Relearn" Located In The Front Of This Manual For Computer Relearn Procedures.

INDEX

PRECAUTIONS

AIR BAG SYSTEMS

Refer to "Air Bag System Precautions" in the front of this manual for system disarming and arming procedures.

BATTERY GROUND CABLE

Prior to service, disconnect battery ground cable and isolate as required.

FUSE PANEL LOCATION

On 1997–99 models, the fuse panel is located behind the lefthand side of the instrument panel, to the left of the steering column.

On 2000 models, the fuse block is positioned on a mounting bracket up and under the lefthand side of the instrument panel, secured by two screws. It can be accessed by removing the instrument panel end cap.

FUEL PUMP RELAY LOCATION

The fuel pump relay is located in the Power Distribution Center (PDC), at the lefthand side of the engine compartment near the battery.

RELAY CENTER LOCATION

The relay center is located on the lefthand side of the engine compartment, next to the battery.

STARTER

REPLACE

1. Raise and support vehicle.
2. **On 1997–99 models equipped with A/C,** proceed as follows:
   a. Using a floor jack or jack stand, support engine and transaxle so it will not rotate.
   b. Remove front engine mount through-bolt from insulator and front crossmember mounting bracket.
   c. Lower engine to rotate assembly forward for access to starter.
3. **On all models,** remove starter to transaxle housing attaching bolts.
4. Remove starter from transaxle to access electrical connectors.
5. Note locations of wiring and electrical connectors at starter and solenoid, then remove as required.
6. **On 1997–99 models,** position starter vertically with flange pointed downward, then reposition A/C lines for clearance.
7. **On all models,** lower starter from engine compartment.
8. Reverse procedure to install, noting the following:
   a. **Torque** starter mounting bolts to 40 ft. lbs.
   b. **Torque** front engine mount through-bolt to 40 ft. lbs.

ALTERNATOR

REPLACE

1. Loosen alternator adjustment nut.
2. **On 1997–99 models,** turn front wheels fully to right.
3. **On all models,** raise and support vehicle.
4. Remove lower splash shield.
5. Disconnect alternator wiring.
6. Loosen alternator pivot bolt.
7. Remove alternator drive belt.
8. Remove three bolts from pivot bracket.
9. Remove pivot nut from T-bolt while supporting alternator.
10. Lower alternator and remove through wheelwell.
11. Reverse procedure to install, noting the following:
    a. **Torque** alternator mounting bolts to 40 ft. lbs.
    b. **Torque** alternator feed terminal nut to 6 ft. lbs.

COIL PACK

REPLACE

1. Disconnect coil pack electrical connector and remove mounting nuts.
2. Remove coil pack from valve cover.
3. Reverse procedure to install, noting the following:
   a. **On 1997–99 models, torque** coil pack to valve cover bolts to 16.6 ft. lbs.
   b. **On 2000 models, torque** coil pack to valve cover bolts to 8.8 ft. lbs.
   c. **On all models,** transfer spark plug wires to corresponding coil pack towers.

IGNITION LOCK

REPLACE

Refer to "Ignition Switch, Replace" for ignition lock replacement procedure.

IGNITION SWITCH

REPLACE

1. Turn ignition to Run position.
2. Using suitable tool, depress lock cylinder retaining tab through hole in lower column shroud and remove lock cylinder.
3. Remove steering column upper and lower shrouds as required.
4. Disconnect ignition switch electrical connectors.
5. Remove ignition switch mounting screw.
6. Depress retaining tabs, then pull ignition switch from steering column.
7. Reverse procedure to install, ensuring ignition switch and actuator rod in lock housing are both in Run position.

CLUTCH START SWITCH

REPLACE

1997–99

1. Disconnect electrical connector from switch.
2. Depress tabs on switch and push through mounting bracket.
3. Reverse procedure to install.

2000

1. Remove instrument panel as outlined in "Dash Panel Service" chapter.
2. **Note clutch interlock/upstop switch wiring routing. This is critical to avoid interference with pedals.**
3. Disconnect clutch interlock/upstop switch electrical connector.
4. Depress four plastic wing tabs on switch, then remove the switch.
5. Reverse procedure to install, noting the following:
   a. **On models equipped with tilt steering,** do not release tilt lever from locked position until after steering column has been securely installed on instrument panel.
   b. **On all models, torque** two steering column lower mounting nuts, then the upper nuts in this order to 12.5 ft. lbs.
   c. **Torque** column pinch bolt to 20.8 ft. lbs.
   d. **Torque** steering wheel retaining nut to 45 ft. lbs.
   e. **Torque** driver's air bag module to steering wheel bolts to 90 inch lbs.

HEADLAMP SWITCH

REPLACE

1997–99

1. Remove steering column cover and liner.

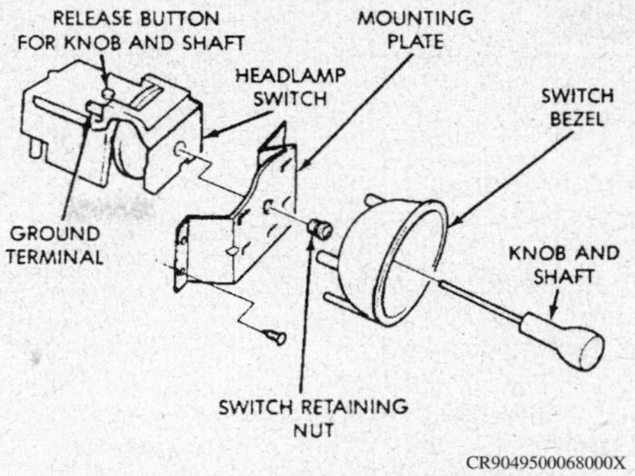

Fig. 1 Headlamp switch replacement. 1997–99

2. Remove three screws securing headlamp switch mounting plate to instrument panel.
3. Pull headlamp switch assembly rearward from instrument panel opening.
4. Disconnect two electrical connectors from switch.
5. Depress button on bottom of switch, then pull control knob out of switch, **Fig. 1.**
6. Unsnap headlamp switch bezel from mounting plate for access to retaining nut.
7. Remove retaining nut and mounting plate from switch.
8. Reverse procedure to install.

2000

Refer to "Combination Switch, Replace" for procedures.

STOP LIGHT SWITCH

REPLACE

1. Depress brake pedal and rotate switch counterclockwise approximately 30°.
2. Pull switch rearward and remove from mounting bracket.
3. Disconnect electrical connector from switch.
4. Pull switch plunger head out until ratchet sound stops.
5. Reverse procedure to install.

COMBINATION SWITCH

REPLACE

1. Remove steering column upper and lower shrouds.
2. Disconnect all electrical connectors from combination switch.
3. Remove combination switch mounting screws, then the switch.
4. Reverse procedure to install. Transfer any components from old to new switch as required.

TURN SIGNAL SWITCH

REPLACE

Refer to "Combination Switch, Replace" for procedure.

DIMMER SWITCH

REPLACE

Refer to "Combination Switch, Replace" for procedure.

STEERING WHEEL

REPLACE

1. Place front wheels in straight-ahead position.
2. Rotate steering wheel 180° clockwise.
3. Lock steering with column lock cylinder.
4. Remove speed control switch and connector.
5. Remove air bag as outlined in "Passive Restraint Systems" section.
6. Remove steering wheel retaining nut and vibration damper if equipped.
7. Using appropriate puller tool, remove steering wheel while avoiding damage to clockspring wiring.
8. Reverse procedure to install, noting the following:
   a. Install steering wheel ensuring flats on hub align with clockspring.
   b. **Torque** steering wheel mounting nut to 45 ft. lbs.

INSTRUMENT CLUSTER

REPLACE

1. **On 2000 models,** using trim stick tool No. C-4755, or equivalent, remove A-pillar moldings.
2. **On all models,** remove instrument panel top cover and cluster bezel.
3. Remove four screws attaching cluster housing to base panel.
4. Pull cluster rearward to disconnect from base panel.
5. Remove cluster assembly.
6. Reverse procedure to install.

RADIO

REPLACE

1. Remove instrument panel center module bezel.
2. Remove radio mounting screws, then pull radio out from instrument panel.
3. Disconnect electrical connectors, ground wire and antenna lead from radio.
4. Reverse procedure to install.

WIPER MOTOR

REPLACE

1997–99

1. Remove wiper arms and blades.
2. Remove rear hood seal and cowl screen.
3. Remove electrical connector at wiper motor.
4. Remove mounting screws from wiper assembly.
5. Disconnect wiper linkage from bellcrank on wiper motor.
6. Reverse procedure to install.

2000

1. Remove wiper arms and blades.
2. Remove cowl cover to cowl screws at base of windshield opening.
3. Remove hood to cowl seal at leading edge of cowl cover. Pull seal toward front of vehicle.
4. Remove cowl cover.
5. Disconnect electrical connectors at wiper motor.
6. Remove windshield wiper module from vehicle.
7. Remove linkage from motor crank by inserting a suitable screwdriver between crank and linkage, then twisting and lifting straight up on linkage.
8. Remove windshield wiper motor mounting screws, then separate motor from linkage.
9. Reverse procedure to install, noting the following:
   a. Add a suitable "unilube" grease to socket.
   b. **Torque** motor mounting screws to 45–55 inch lbs.
   c. **Torque** drive link nut to 98–106 inch lbs.

WIPER SWITCH

REPLACE

1997–99

1. Remove three screws from steering column shroud and remove upper half of shroud.
2. Remove mounting screws on switch and remove switch.
3. Disconnect electrical connector from switch.
4. Reverse procedure to install.

2000

Refer to "Combination Switch, Replace" for procedures.

BLOWER MOTOR

REPLACE

1. **On models less A/C,** disconnect blower motor electrical connector, then remove blower motor by turning motor approximately 1/8 turn counterclockwise while pulling down locking tab.

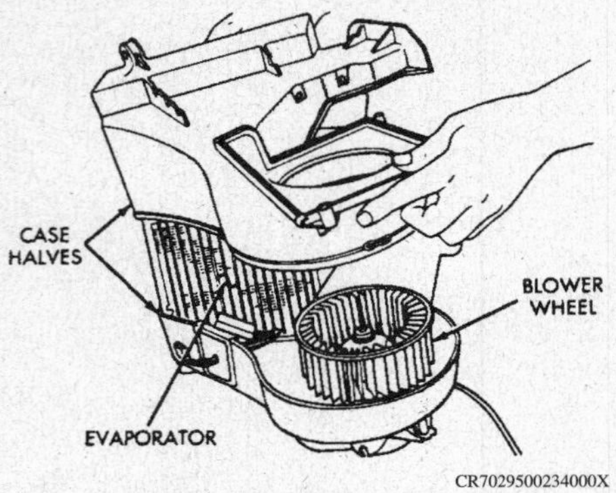

Fig. 2 Typical evaporator case separation

2. **On models equipped with A/C,** remove righthand side scuff plate, then pull back carpet.
3. **On 1997–99 models,** cut wheel housing silencer in line with blower motor wiring.
4. **On all models,** disconnect blower motor wiring connector.
5. Remove blower motor retaining screws, then lower blower motor assembly from unit housing.
6. Reverse procedure to install, taping silencer in position.

HEATER CORE

REPLACE

1997–99

1. Drain coolant into a suitable container.
2. Remove instrument panel as outlined in "Dash Panel Service" chapter.
3. Disconnect heater hoses at dash panel.
4. Plug heater core outlets to prevent coolant spillage during housing removal.
5. **On models equipped with A/C,** evacuate and recover A/C refrigerant.
6. **On all models,** remove suction line at expansion valve. Plug refrigerant lines to prevent contamination of system.
7. Remove expansion valve from evaporator.
8. Remove drain hose from evaporator case.
9. Remove three retaining nuts on firewall in engine compartment.
10. Remove righthand retaining screw from heater case.
11. Disconnect blue five-way connector from plenum.
12. Remove heater case assembly from vehicle.
13. Remove clips and screws to separate air distribution and evaporator/blower modules.
14. Remove panel opening, demister opening and heater core tube foam seals from unit.
15. Remove clips and screws holding housing halves together.
16. Turn unit upside down and separate module halves, then lift heater core out of case.
17. Reverse procedure to install.

2000

1. Drain coolant into a suitable container.
2. Remove instrument panel as outlined in "Dash Panel Service" chapter.
3. Disconnect heater hoses at dash panel.
4. Plug heater core outlets to prevent coolant spillage during housing removal.
5. **On models equipped with A/C,** evacuate and recover A/C refrigerant.
6. **On all models,** remove coolant reservoir fasteners, then position reservoir aside.
7. Remove suction line at expansion valve. Plug refrigerant lines to prevent contamination of system.
8. Remove expansion valve from evaporator. Plug all fittings.
9. Remove rubber drain tube extension from evaporator drain.
10. Disconnect vacuum harness at brake booster.
11. Unsnap and remove defroster duct.
12. Remove three housing retaining nuts on engine side of firewall.
13. Remove righthand side retaining screw.
14. Remove one remaining nut located on dash panel stud.
15. Disconnect electrical connectors as required.
16. Remove unit housing assembly from vehicle.
17. Separate air distribution outlet foam seals at case halves.
18. Remove foam seals at evaporator and heater core tubes.
19. Remove retaining clips and screws holding halves together.
20. Separate the housing halves.
21. Carefully lift heater core out of unit housing.
22. Reverse procedure to install.

EVAPORATOR CORE

REPLACE

1. Remove unit housing as outlined under "Heater Core, Replace."
2. Remove clips and screws to separate evaporator/blower case.
3. Remove evaporator case foam seal.
4. Remove four retaining screws from air duct and remove air duct with recirculation door assembly.
5. Disconnect fin sensing switch from harness.
6. Remove upper and lower clips and screws, then separate case halves, **Fig. 2.**
7. Remove evaporator from case.
8. Reverse procedure to install.

2.0L Engine

NOTE: On Models Equipped With Dual Overhead Cam (DOHC) Engine, Refer To The "2.0L Engine" Chapter In The "Talon " Section Of This Manual For Any Procedures Not Covered In This Section.

NOTE: On Models Equipped With Single Overhead Cam (SOHC) Engine, Refer To The "2.0L Engine" Section In The "Breeze, Cirrus & Sebring Convertible & Stratus" Chapter Of This Manual For Any Procedures Not Covered In This Section.

NOTE: Refer To "Air Bag System Precautions " Located In The Front Of This Manual For System Disarming & Arming Procedures.

NOTE: Refer To "Computer Relearn Procedures " Located In The Front Of This Manual For Computer Relearn Procedures.

INDEX

PRECAUTIONS

AIR BAG SYSTEMS

Refer to "Air Bag System Precautions" in the front of this manual for system disarming and arming procedures.

BATTERY GROUND CABLE

Prior to service, disconnect battery ground cable and isolate as required.

FUEL SYSTEM PRESSURE RELIEF

1997–99

1. Disconnect ground cable from auxiliary jumper terminal.
2. Remove fuel filler cap.
3. Remove protective cap from fuel pressure test port on fuel rail.
4. Place open end of fuel pressure release hose tool No. C-4799-1, or equivalent, into a suitable gasoline container, then connect other hose end to fuel pressure test port. Fuel pressure should bleed off through hose into container.

2000

1. Remove fuel pump relay from Power Distribution Center (PDC).
2. Start engine and allow it to run until it stalls from lack of fuel.
3. Attempt to start engine until it will not start.
4. Turn ignition Off.

COMPRESSION PRESSURE

Proper compression pressure is 170–225 psi and should not vary more than 25% from cylinder to cylinder.

ENGINE MOUNT

REPLACE

FRONT

1. Raise and support vehicle, then support engine and transaxle with suitable floor jack.
2. Remove front engine mount through bolt from insulator and crossmember mounting bracket.
3. Remove mass damper, front mount nuts and insulator assembly.
4. Remove front mounting bracket
5. Reverse procedure to install.

LEFT

1997–99

1. Raise and support vehicle, then remove lefthand front tire.
2. Remove power distribution center and place aside.
3. Support transaxle with suitable jack, then remove the insulator through bolt from mount.
4. Remove transaxle mount fasteners, then the mount.
5. Reverse procedure to install.

2000

Removal

1. Remove air cleaner assembly.
2. Remove battery and tray.
3. Loosen lefthand front wheel lugnuts.
4. Raise and support vehicle approximately one foot on a suitable hoist.
5. Support transaxle with a suitable jack.
6. Remove lefthand front wheel.
7. Remove lefthand front splash shield.
8. Remove through-bolt access plug at lefthand side outer frame rail.
9. Remove mount through-bolt.
10. Disconnect transaxle shift cable from lefthand mount and transaxle linkage.
11. Remove lefthand mount bracket to body frame rail fasteners.
12. Remove mount attaching bolts, then the mount.

Installation

1. Install mount and attaching fasteners. Tighten to specifications.
2. Install engine mount to body frame rail fasteners. Tighten to specifications.
3. Position engine and transaxle for through-bolt installation. Tighten to specifications.
4. Remove jack from transaxle.
5. Install through-bolt access plug.
6. Install lefthand splash shield and wheel.

7. Connect transaxle shift linkage.
8. Lower vehicle.
9. Tighten lugnuts in order to half specification. Repeat procedure and tighten to full specification.
10. Install battery and tray.
11. Install air cleaner assembly.

RIGHT

1997–99

1. Remove purge duty solenoid from engine mount bracket.
2. Remove righthand engine mount insulator vertical fasteners from frame rail.
3. Carefully support engine/transaxle assembly to relieve pressure on mount.
4. Remove through bolt from insulator, then the insulator.
5. Reverse procedure to install.

2000

Removal

1. Remove engine accessory drive belts.
2. Remove righthand splash shield.
3. Using three-jaw puller tool No. 1026 and insert No. 6827-A, or equivalents, remove crankshaft damper.
4. Remove upper and lower engine torque struts.
5. Support engine using a suitable jack.
6. Remove righthand engine mount bolt access cover, then the bolt.
7. Using a permanent ink marker or paint crayon, mark position of engine mount to body frame rail.
8. Remove mount to body attaching bolts.
9. Remove mount between engine and body frame rail. This might require lowering or raising engine to provide clearance.

Installation

1. Position mount in its original location on body frame rail.
2. If mount location was not marked before removal or if frame rail has been replaced, proceed as follows:
   a. Insert new mount loosely in frame rail.
   b. Align mount's four holes with mating holes in rail so they are concentric and centered.
   c. Using a permanent ink marker or paint crayon, mark position of engine mount to body frame rail.
3. Ensure mount stays put in its original location. Tighten bolts to specifications.
4. Install engine mount bracket. Tighten bolts to specifications.
5. Using washer, thrust bearing and nut from tool No. 6792 and a suitable M12 × 1.75 × 150 mm bolt, install crankshaft damper.
6. While holding crankshaft damper in place with holder tool No. 6847, or equivalent, install damper bolt. Tighten bolt to specifications.
7. Install righthand splash shield.
8. Install engine accessory drive belts.

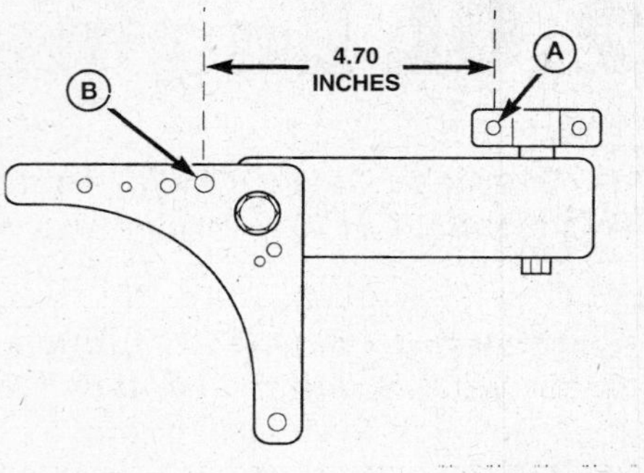

Fig. 1 Engine mount bracket stud alignment. 2000

TORQUE STRUTS

REPLACEMENT

Lower

1. Raise and support vehicle on hoist.
2. Remove righthand splash shield.
3. Remove lower strut to crossmember and strut bracket bolts.
4. Remove lower torque strut.
5. Reverse procedure to install. Refer to "Adjustment" for adjustment procedure.

Upper

1. Remove upper torque strut mounting bolts.
2. Remove upper torque strut.
3. Reverse procedure to install. Refer to "Adjustment" for adjustment procedure.

ADJUSTMENT

The lower and upper torque struts require adjustment together whenever a mounting bolt has been loosened. Proceed as follows:

1. Loosen upper and lower torque strut attaching bolt at suspension crossmember and strut tower bracket.
2. Position a suitable floor jack and wood block under forward edge of transaxle bellhousing.
3. Carefully exert upward force, allowing upper engine to rotate rearward until distance between center of rearmost engine mount bracket attaching stud, point "A," **Fig. 1,** and center of strut tower bracket washer hose clip hole, point "B," is 4.70 inches (119 mm).
4. Hold engine in this position, then tighten torque strut bolts to specifications.
5. Remove floor jack.

ENGINE

REPLACE

1997–99

1. Relieve fuel system pressure as outlined under " Precautions."
2. Disconnect and remove battery and tray, then disconnect the Powertrain Control Module (PCM) electrical connector and position aside.
3. Drain coolant into a suitable container.
4. Remove upper radiator hose and radiator fan module.
5. Remove lower radiator hose.
6. **On models equipped with automatic transaxle,** disconnect oil cooler lines.
7. **On models equipped with manual transaxle,** disconnect clutch cable, transaxle and throttle body linkage.
8. **On all models,** disconnect engine wiring harness electrical connectors.
9. Disconnect heater hoses.
10. Recover A/C refrigerant as outlined in "Air Conditioning " section.
11. Raise and support vehicle, then remove the righthand inner splash shield.
12. Remove accessory drive belts.
13. Remove axle shafts.
14. Disconnect exhaust pipe from manifold.
15. Remove front and rear engine mount bracket from the body.
16. Lower vehicle, then remove the air cleaner assembly.
17. Remove power steering pump and reservoir.
18. Remove A/C compressor.
19. Remove ground straps to body.
20. Raise and support vehicle to install engine dolly and cradle tool Nos. 6135, 6710 and 6810, or equivalents.
21. Loosen cradle engine mounts, to position engine locating holes to bed plate, then lower the vehicle until engine rests on cradle mounts, tighten mounts to cradle frame to prevent mount movement.
22. Lower vehicle so weight of engine and transaxle is only on cradle.
23. Remove engine and transaxle mount attaching bolts.
24. Slowly raise and support vehicle, move engine and transaxle assembly on cradle to allow for removal around body flanges as required.
25. Reverse procedure to install.

2000

1. Relieve fuel system pressure as outlined under " Precautions."
2. Drain coolant into a suitable container.
3. Remove battery and tray.
4. Recover A/C refrigerant as outlined in "Air Conditioning " section.
5. Disconnect air intake duct at intake manifold.
6. Disconnect throttle cables.
7. Disconnect electrical connectors at throttle body and air cleaner housing.
8. Remove air cleaner housing assembly.
9. Remove upper radiator hose.
10. Remove fan module.
11. Remove lower radiator hose.
12. **On models equipped with automatic transaxle,** disconnect and plug fluid cooler lines.
13. **On models equipped with manual transaxle,** proceed as follows:
    a. Disconnect shift linkage.
    b. Disconnect transaxle electrical connectors.
    c. Disconnect clutch cable.
14. **On all models,** disconnect engine wiring harness.

15. Disconnect positive cable from PDC and ground wire from vehicle body.
16. Disconnect ground wire from vehicle body to engine at righthand strut tower.
17. Disconnect heater hoses.
18. Disconnect vacuum hose from brake booster.
19. Disconnect coolant reserve and recovery hose.
20. Remove engine accessory drive belts.
21. Remove power steering pump and reservoir. Position them aside with hoses intact.
22. Loosen front wheel lugnuts.
23. Raise and support vehicle on hoist.
24. Drain engine oil into an approved container.
25. Remove righthand inner splash shield.
26. Remove front wheels.
27. Remove axle shafts.
28. Disconnect exhaust system at exhaust manifold.
29. Disconnect downstream HO2S sensor electrical connector.
30. Remove engine lower torque strut.
31. Lower vehicle, then remove A/C compressor.
32. Raise vehicle just enough so engine dolly tool No. 6135 and cradle tool No. 6710, or their equivalents can be installed under vehicle.
33. Loosen engine support posts to allow movement for positioning onto engine locating holes and flange on engine bedplate.
34. Lower vehicle and position cradle until engine is resting on support posts. Tighten mounts to cradle frame.
35. Install safety straps around engine to cradle. Tighten straps and lock them into position. **Safety straps must be used in this step.**
36. Raise vehicle enough to ensure straps are tight enough to hold cradle to engine.
37. Lower vehicle so engine and transaxle's weight only is on cradle assembly.
38. Remove engine upper torque strut.
39. Remove righthand and lefthand engine and transaxle through-bolts.
40. Raise vehicle slowly until body is approximately six inches above normal engine mounting locations.
41. Remove alternator, its lower bracket and mounting bolt.
42. Continue slowly raising vehicle until powertrain clears engine compartment. Movement of powertrain might be required to steer it clear of body flanges.
43. Reverse procedure to install.

RADIATOR

REPLACE

1997-99

1. Drain cooling system into an approved container, then remove hose clamps from radiator.
2. Disconnect automatic transaxle hoses from cooler and plug off.
3. Remove radiator to battery strut, then fan module assembly by disconnecting fan motor electrical connector.
4. Remove fan shroud retaining screws located on top of shroud.
5. Lift shroud up and out of bottom shroud attachment clips separating shroud from radiator.
6. **On models equipped with dual cooling fans,** the lefthand fan module may be removed first, then the righthand side module.
7. **On all models,** remove upper radiator isolator bracket mounting screws, then the engine block heater, if equipped.
8. Remove air conditioning condenser attaching screws located at front of radiator, if equipped. Do not discharge air conditioning system.
9. Remove radiator from engine compartment by lifting upward.
10. Reverse procedure to install.

2000

1. Drain coolant into an approved container.
2. Disconnect upper hose at radiator.
3. **On models equipped with automatic transaxle,** disconnect and cap fluid cooler lines.
4. **On all models,** disconnect cooling fan motor electrical connector.
5. Remove cooling fan module retaining screws on top side of shroud.
6. Lift shroud up and out of lower shroud clips.
7. Remove lower radiator hose.
8. Remove upper radiator isolator bracket mounting screws.
9. **On models equipped with engine block heater,** disconnect block heater wiring.
10. **On all models,** remove A/C condenser attaching screws at front of radiator, allowing condenser to lean forward. **Discharging and recovering refrigerant is not required for this step.**
11. Carefully lift radiator up and out of engine compartment.
12. Reverse procedure to install, noting the following:
    a. Radiator requires approximately .20–.31 inch upward clearance after installation.
    b. Align hoses and clamps to prevent them from interfering with engine components or hood movement.
    c. Close radiator petcock, fill cooling system and inspect for leaks.

FUEL PUMP

REPLACE

1997-99

1. Relieve fuel system pressure as outlined under " Precautions," then drain fuel from tank into a suitable container.
2. Disconnect fuel pump module fuel line quick connect fitting, then disengage electrical connector lock.
3. Disconnect electrical connector, then use a suitable transmission jack to support fuel tank.
4. Remove fuel tank strap bolts and lower tank slightly.
5. Using tool No. 6856, or equivalent, remove fuel pump module locknut.
6. Lift fuel pump module and O-ring seal away from fuel tank, noting the following:
    a. Discard O-ring seal.
    b. **Residual fuel may spill out of fuel pump module reservoir during removal. Exercise caution to prevent injury or damage.**
7. Reverse procedure to install, noting the following:
    a. Use a new O-ring seal.
    b. Tighten fuel pump module locknut to specifications.

2000

1. Relieve fuel system pressure as outlined under " Precautions."
2. Raise and support vehicle on hoist.
3. Disconnect vapor line from EVAP canister tube.
4. Remove EVAP canister.
5. Remove drain port cap, then drain fuel into an approved container. **Replace cap after fuel has drained.**
6. Disconnect fuel pump module electrical connector and ground wire.
7. Disconnect fuel tube from fuel filter and regulator assembly.
8. Disconnect fuel filler tube and filler vent tube from filler hose at tank.
9. Support tank with a suitable transmission jack.
10. Loosen tank mounting straps, then slightly lower tank.
11. Remove tank mounting straps, then the tank from vehicle.
12. Using locknut wrench tool No. 6856, or equivalent, remove fuel pump module locknut.
13. Remove fuel pump and O-ring from fuel tank. Discard O-ring.
14. Reverse procedure to install, noting the following:
    a. Ensure tank's O-ring surface is clean.
    b. Install a new O-ring.
    c. Position fuel pump in tank, ensuring alignment on pump's underside flange sits in fuel tank notch.
    d. Tighten locknut using locknut wrench tool to specifications. **Do not overtighten.**
    e. Ensure tank mounting straps do not twist or bend.

TIGHTENING SPECIFICATIONS

Year	Component	Torque/ Ft. Lbs.
1999	Engine Mount Bracket Attaching Bolts	30
	Fuel Pump Module Locknut	40–41
	Oil Drain Plug	25
	Radiator Isolator Mounting Bracket	72①
	Wheel Lugnuts	95
2000	Crankshaft Damper	100
	Engine Mount Bracket To Body Frame Rail	20.8
	Engine Mount Through-Bolt	87
	Engine Mount Torque Strut Bolts	87
	Fuel Pump Module Locknut	40–41
	Fuel Tank Strap Bolts	16.7
	LH Engine Mount Attaching Bolts	50
	Oil Drain Plug	20
	Radiator Isolator Mounting Bracket	90①
	RH Engine Mount Bracket Bolts	45
	Wheel Lugnuts	100

① — Inch lbs.

Clutch & Manual Transaxle

NOTE: Refer To "Air Bag System Precautions " Located In The Front Of This Manual For System Disarming & Arming Procedures.

NOTE: Refer To "Computer Relearn" Located In The Front Of This Manual For Computer Relearn Procedures.

INDEX

PRECAUTIONS

AIR BAG SYSTEMS

Refer to "Air Bag System Precautions" in the front of this manual for system disarming and arming procedures.

BATTERY GROUND CABLE

Prior to service, disconnect battery ground cable and isolate as required.

ADJUSTMENTS

CLUTCH

The clutch cable used on these vehicles incorporates a self adjusting mechanism within the cable outer housing at the pedal end of the cable. A preload spring is used to take up slack in the cable and to keep the release bearing tensional against the fingers of the clutch pressure plate.

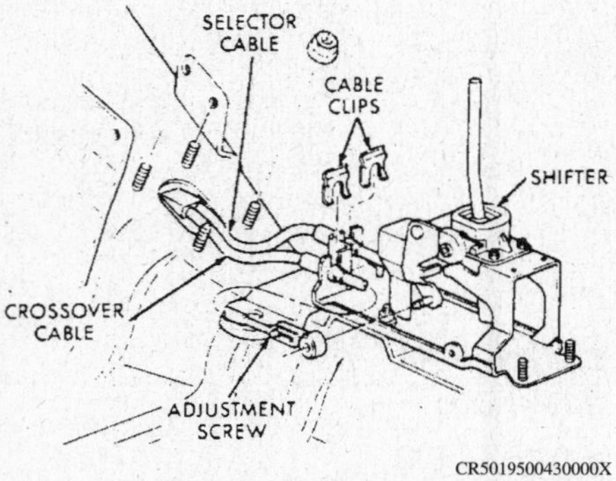

Fig. 1 Gearshift crossover cable adjustment

GEARSHIFT

The gearshift selector cable is not adjustable. If adjustment is required, only the crossover cable may be adjusted.

1. Remove gearshift console from vehicle.
2. Loosen crossover cable adjustment screw, **Fig. 1.**
3. Using a ¼ inch drill bit or suitable equivalent, pin crossover cable lever to transaxle, **Fig. 2.** Ensure drill bit engages through crossover lever into transaxle case at least ½ inch.
4. Ensure shift lever is in the spring loaded neutral position. If necessary, move lever forward and back, then allow lever to fall into its natural neutral position.
5. Without allowing movement in either cable or lever, hand tighten crossover cable adjustment screw, then tighten screw to specifications.
6. Remove pin from transaxle crossover

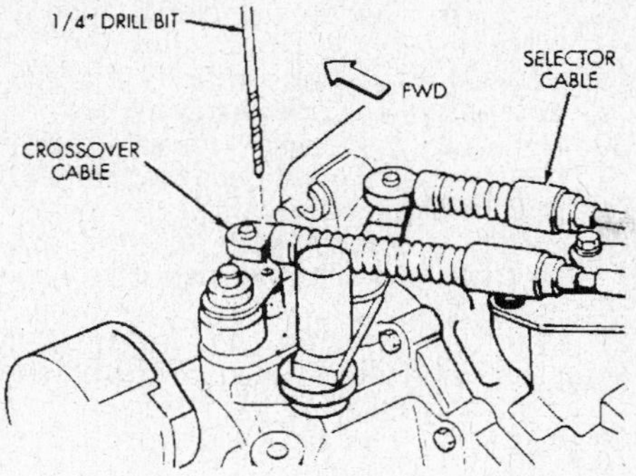

CR5019500431000X

Fig. 2 Crossover lever attachment to transaxle

lever, then inspect transaxle shift functions.

7. Install gearshift console.

CLUTCH

REPLACE

Two types of clutches are used on these vehicles. A single, conventional dry disc with a diaphragm cover is used on 1997–99 models produced at the Toluca assembly plant. On 1997–99 models produced at the Belvidere plant and all 2000 models, a modular clutch assembly is used. The modular clutch assembly can only be serviced as a unit. The two types of clutches can be identified by the 11th digit of the Vehicle Identification Number (VIN). The Belvidere plant is identified by the letter " D." The Toluca plant is identified by the letter " T."

CONVENTIONAL

1. Remove transaxle as outlined under "Transaxle, Replace. "
2. Mark clutch cover for possible later installation.
3. Support clutch disc with clutch pilot tool No. 6724, or equivalent, during removal to prevent damage.
4. Loosen clutch cover bolts in a cross pattern about two turns at a time to prevent clutch cover damage.
5. Remove clutch cover and clutch plate from flywheel, **Fig. 3.**
6. Reverse procedure to install, noting the following:
   a. The flywheel is manufactured with a slightly tapered surface and the clutch cover may have a concave taper of 0–.0039 inch.
   b. All surfaces must be clean and free of oil or corrosion.
   c. Align clutch disc to flywheel using clutch pilot tool No. 6724, or equivalent.
   d. Tighten clutch cover bolts to specifications in an alternating pattern, about two turns at a time, to prevent clutch cover damage.

MODULAR

1997–99

1. Remove starter as outlined in "Electrical" section.

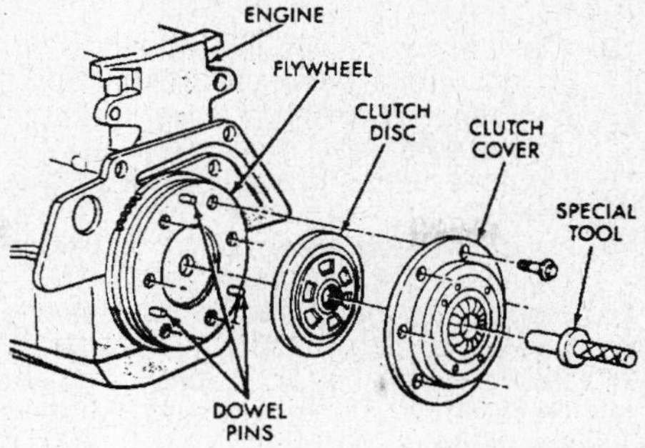

CR5049500085000X

Fig. 3 Conventional clutch assembly

2. Remove front and rear transaxle support brackets.
3. Remove modular clutch retaining bolts, then remove transaxle as outlined under "Transaxle, Replace" in this section. **Transaxle and clutch are removed as an assembly.**
4. Remove modular clutch assembly from transaxle input shaft. **Do not allow friction surfaces to become contaminated.**
5. Reverse procedure to install, noting the following:
   a. Inspect engine rear main and transaxle input shaft seals for leakage. Correct any leaks prior to installing new clutch assembly.
   b. Install new clutch to flywheel bolts and tighten to specifications in an alternating pattern.

2000

1. Remove transaxle from vehicle as outlined under " Transaxle, Replace."
2. Remove clutch assembly from transaxle input shaft.
3. Reverse procedure to install, noting the following:
   a. Install new flywheel to clutch bolts and tighten in a criss-cross pattern until clutch assembly is evenly seated. Tighten to specifications.
   b. Raise engine and transaxle with screw jack until upper mount through-bolt hole aligns with hole in mount bracket. Tighten to specifications.
   c. When installing structural collar, position collar and install all bolts finger tight. **Torque** collar to oil pan bolts to 30 inch lbs. **Torque** collar to transaxle bolts to 80 ft. lbs. **Torque** collar to oil pan bolts to 40 ft. lbs.

TRANSAXLE

REPLACE

1997–99

The transaxle may be removed from the vehicle without removing the engine.

1. Disconnect battery positive cable, then pull power distribution center up and out of its holding bracket and position aside.
2. Remove battery heat shield, battery and battery tray from vehicle.

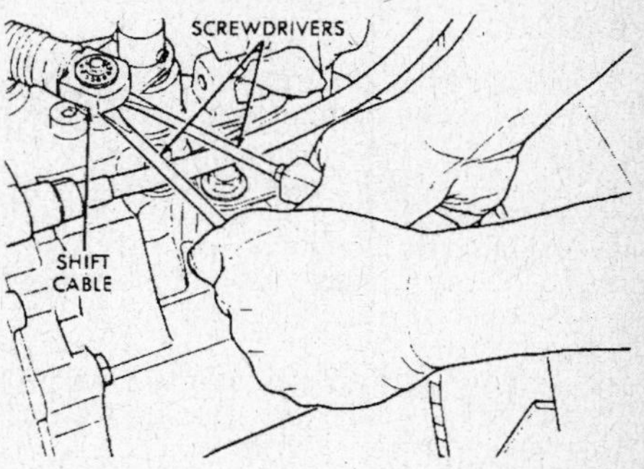

CR5039500504000X

Fig. 4 Shift cable disconnection

3. **On models equipped with cruise control,** disconnect cruise control.
4. **On all models,** disconnect back-up lamp switch and speed sensor wiring connectors from transaxle.
5. Using two suitable pry bars and applying equal pressure to each side of shift cable end and crossover cable end, pry cable ends from transaxle shift levers, **Fig. 4.**
6. Remove clutch housing cap to expose clutch cable and release lever, then pull back on clutch cable outer housing to unseat cable from transaxle and then disconnect cable from release lever.
7. Remove shift cable mounting bracket from transaxle housing, then the intake manifold support bracket and upper starter bolt.
8. Remove upper bellhousing bolts.
9. Install a suitable engine support bridge fixture, then adjust support bridge to relieve tension from engine and transaxle mounts.
10. Raise and support vehicle, then remove front wheels.
11. Drain transaxle oil into a suitable container.
12. Remove both front drive axles as outlined under " Driveshaft, Replace" in the "Front Wheel Drive Axles " section of this manual.
13. Remove engine damper and bracket.
14. Disconnect starter wiring, then remove lower starter bolt and remove starter.
15. Remove engine to transaxle braces.
16. Remove lower bellhousing dust shield bolts.
17. Support transaxle with a suitable jack.
18. Remove front motor mount through bolt, then the front motor mount bolts from engine and transaxle.
19. Remove lefthand transaxle mount to frame through bolt, then the mount from transaxle.
20. Lower transaxle and remove from vehicle.
21. Reverse procedure to install, noting the following:
    a. Tighten bolts to specifications.
    b. Fill transaxle to bottom of filler plug hole with oil listed in "Specifications" section.
    c. When installing front drive axles, always use new driveshaft retaining clips.

2000

1. Remove battery and tray.
2. Remove air cleaner and throttle body unit.
3. Disconnect back-up lamp switch electrical connector.
4. Remove bellhousing cap.
5. Disconnect clutch cable from release lever, then remove cable from transaxle.
6. Remove shift cable to bracket clips.
7. Disconnect shift selector and crossover cable from levers.
8. Remove shift selector and crossover cables, then position them aside.
9. Disconnect vehicle speed sensor electrical connector.
10. Raise and support vehicle on hoist.
11. Remove transaxle lubricant drain plug and allow lubricant to drain in an approved container.
12. Remove lefthand and righthand axle shafts.
13. Remove bellhousing lower structural collar.
14. Remove lefthand engine to transaxle lateral bending brace.
15. Remove bellhousing inspection cover.
16. Remove righthand engine to transaxle lateral bending brace.
17. Remove starter as outlined under "Starter, Replace " in "Electrical" section.
18. Remove flywheel to clutch module bolts.
19. Support engine at oil pan with a suitable screw jack and wooden block.
20. Remove transaxle upper mount through-bolt. This is accessed through driver's side wheelhouse.
21. Carefully lower engine and transaxle on screw jack until sufficient clearance is obtained.
22. Have an assistant hold transaxle in place, then remove transaxle to engine mounting bolts.
23. Carefully remove transaxle from vehicle.

TIGHTENING SPECIFICATIONS

Year	Component	Torque/ Ft. Lbs.
1997–99	Clutch Cover (Conventional)	20–21
	Clutch Pedal Pivot Shaft	30
	Clutch To Flywheel (Modular)	55
	Crossover Cable Adjustment Screw	72①
	Flywheel To Crankshaft (Conventional)	70
	Flywheel To Crankshaft (Modular)	70
	Front Engine Mount To Transaxle	80
	LH Mount To Transaxle	40
	Transaxle Drain Plug	22
	Transaxle To Engine	70
	Wheel Lugnuts	95
2000	Clutch To Flywheel	65
	Crossover Cable Adjustment Screw	72①
	Flywheel To Crankshaft	70
	RH Lateral Bending Brace	60
	Transaxle Drain Plug	20.8
	Transaxle To Engine	70
	Wheel Lugnuts	100

① — Inch lbs.

Rear Suspension

INDEX

DESCRIPTION

Due to the construction of this type of suspension, only frame contact or wheel lift type hoisting equipment should be used to raise vehicle.

Rear suspension components which become damaged must be replaced. No attempt should be made to repair these components.

The rear suspension is a fully independent strut type, **Figs. 1 and 2.** A forged spindle knuckle is bolted to the strut assembly. Lateral links and tension struts are used to control position and movement of the rear suspension.

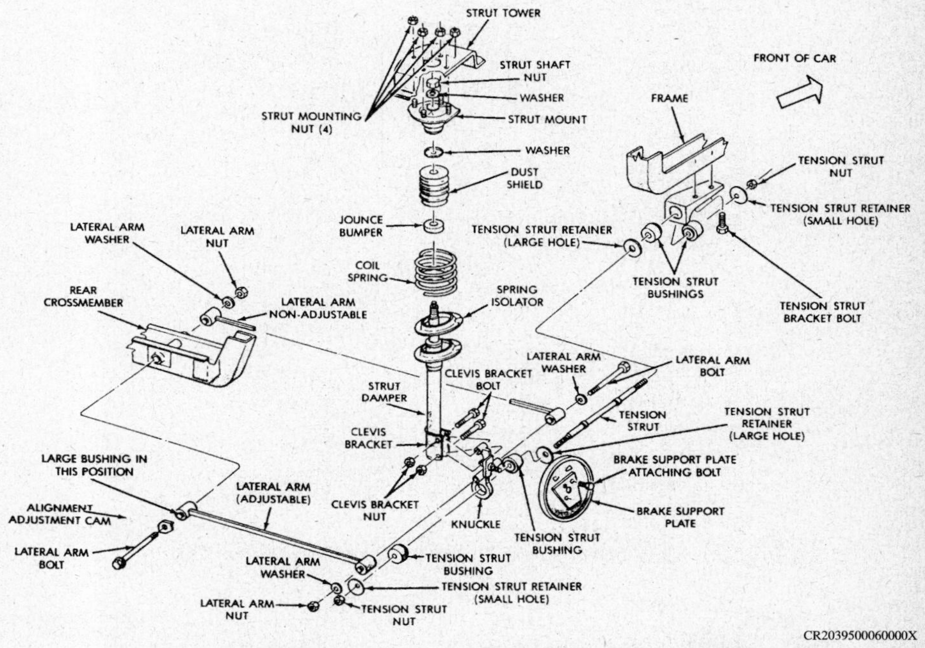

Fig. 1 Exploded view of rear suspension. 1997–99

HUB & BEARING

REPLACE

The rear hub and bearing are serviced as an assembly.

1. Raise and support vehicle, then remove wheel and tire.
2. **On models equipped with rear disc brakes,** remove caliper and disc as outlined in the "Disc Brakes" chapter.
3. **On models equipped with rear drum brakes,** remove drum as outlined in the "Drum Brakes" chapter of this manual.
4. **On all models,** remove the hub retaining nut, then the hub and bearing assembly. Discard retaining nut.
5. Reverse procedure to install. Tighten new retaining nuts and bolts to specifications.

SPINDLE KNUCKLE

REPLACE

1997–99

1. Remove rear hub and bearing as outlined under "Hub & Bearing, Replace."
2. **On models equipped with ABS,** remove retaining bolt, then the speed sensor, **Figs. 3 and 4.** If speed sensor is seized, do not use pliers to remove. Gently tap on mounting ear with a suitable punch and hammer to loosen sensor.
3. **On models equipped with rear drum brakes,** remove brake support plate mounting bolts, then without disconnecting brake fluid hose, position and support assembly aside. **Do not allow assembly to hang from the brake fluid hose.**
4. **On models equipped with rear disc brakes,** remove disc brake adapter plate mounting bolts, then without disconnecting brake fluid hose, position and support assembly aside. **Do not allow assembly to hang from the brake fluid hose.**
5. **On all models,** loosen but do not remove spindle knuckle to strut clevis nuts. **The spindle knuckle to strut clevis bolts are serrated for a tight fit into the knuckle. Do not turn bolt when loosening. Turn nut only, or damage to knuckle or bolt will occur.**
6. Remove lateral link to knuckle bolt. Then using a suitable adjustable wrench to prevent tension strut from turning, remove tension strut nut, washer and bushing, **Fig. 5.**
7. Remove spindle knuckle to strut clevis bolts that were previously loosened, then pull spindle knuckle straight out of strut and rotate off tension strut.
8. Reverse procedure to install, noting the following:
   a. Tighten bolts and nuts to specifications.
   b. When tightening spindle knuckle to strut clevis bolts, do not turn bolts. Tighten by turning nuts only.
   c. **The lateral link to spindle knuckle bolt must be installed with head of bolt towards front of vehicle.**
   d. Lateral link bolts must be tightened to specifications with suspension supporting vehicle weight.
   e. Refer to **Fig. 6** when installing tension strut retainer washers and bushings.
   f. Inspect and adjust rear wheel alignment as outlined under the " Wheel Alignment" section of this chapter.

2000

Removal

1. Remove rear hub and bearing as outlined under "Hub & Bearing, Replace."
2. **On models equipped with ABS,** remove sensor bracket to strut screw.
3. **On models equipped with rear drum brakes,** proceed as follows:
   a. Remove four brake support plate to

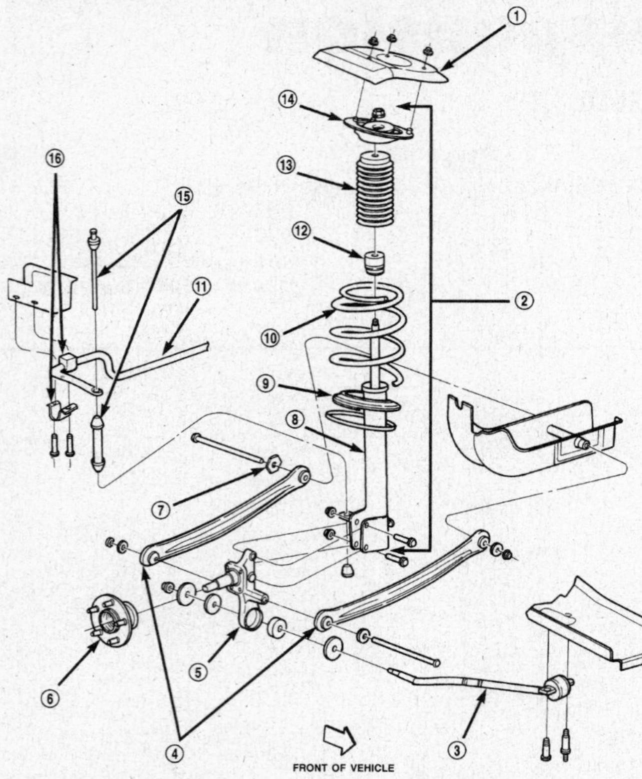

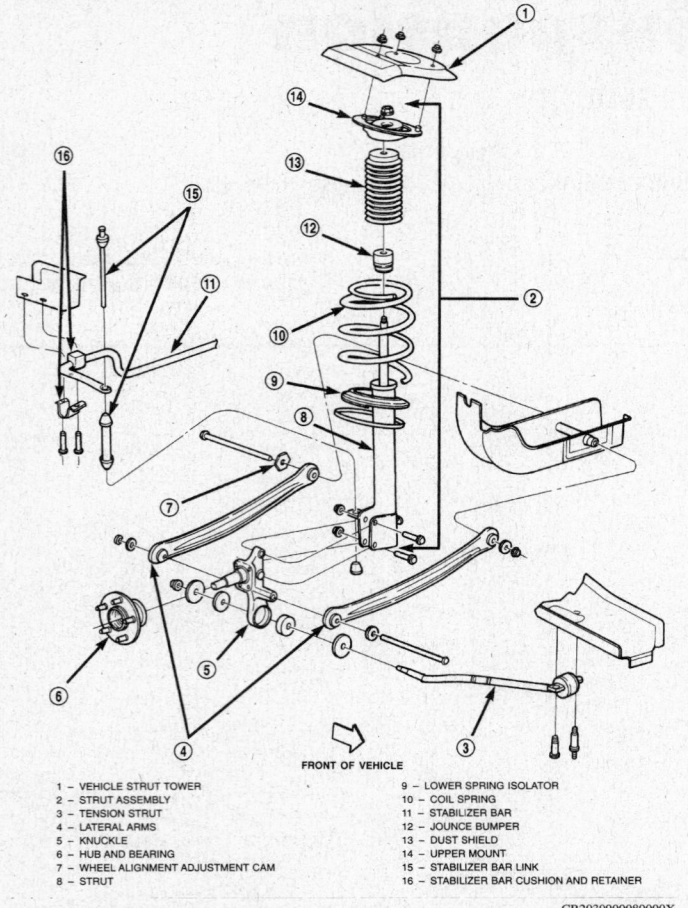

1 – VEHICLE STRUT TOWER
2 – STRUT ASSEMBLY
3 – TENSION STRUT
4 – LATERAL ARMS
5 – KNUCKLE
6 – HUB AND BEARING
7 – WHEEL ALIGNMENT ADJUSTMENT CAM
8 – STRUT
9 – LOWER SPRING ISOLATOR
10 – COIL SPRING
11 – STABILIZER BAR
12 – JOUNCE BUMPER
13 – DUST SHIELD
14 – UPPER MOUNT
15 – STABILIZER BAR LINK
16 – STABILIZER BAR CUSHION AND RETAINER

CR2039900089000X

Fig. 2 Exploded view of rear suspension. 2000

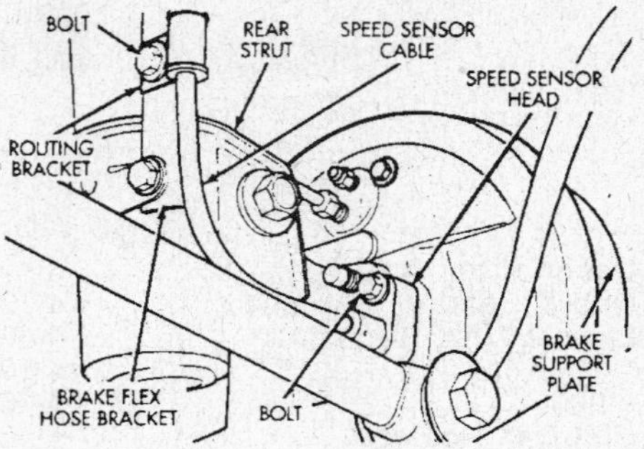

CR2039500054000X

Fig. 3 ABS speed sensor location. 1997–99 w/rear drum brakes

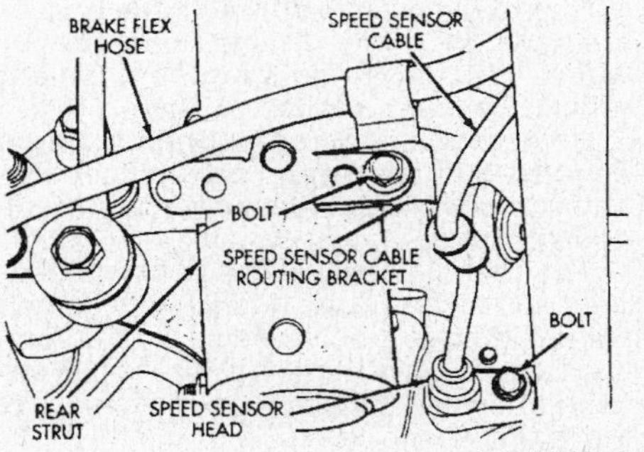

CR2039500055000X

Fig. 4 ABS speed sensor location. 1997–99 w/rear disc brakes

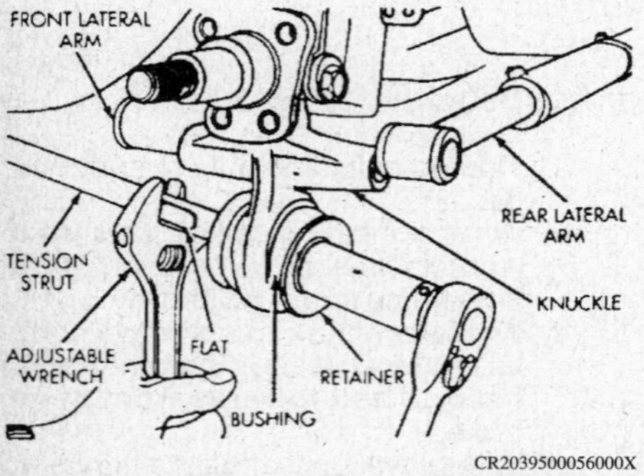

CR2039500056000X

Fig. 5 Tension strut removal. 1997–99

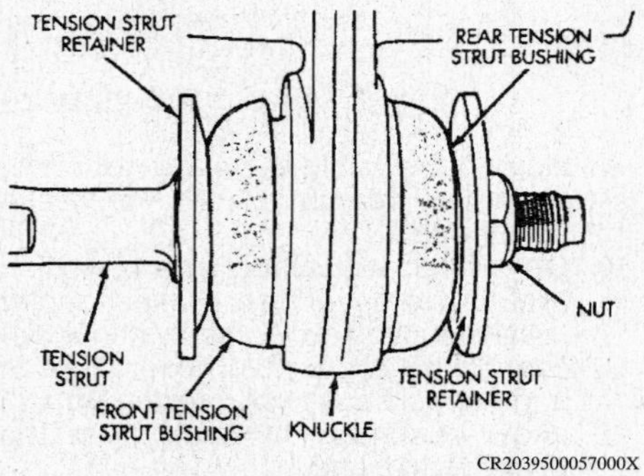

CR2039500057000X

Fig. 6 Tension strut bushings. 1997–99

knuckle bolts.

b. Remove brake support plate, brake shoes and wheel cylinder as an assembly from knuckle. Leave brake hose intact.
c. Tie assembly aside with a suitable cord or string. **Avoid overextending brake hose.**

4. **On models equipped with rear disc brakes,** proceed as follows:
   a. Remove four brake adapter to knuckle bolts.
   b. Remove adapter, rotor shield, parking brake shoes and cable as an assembly.
   c. Tie this assembly aside with a suitable cord or string.
5. **On all models,** loosen, but do not completely remove, two knuckle to strut nuts and bolts. **These bolts are serrated and must not be turned during removal. Hold bolts in place in knuckle while removing nuts, then tap bolts out using a suitable pin punch.**
6. Remove rear knuckle to lateral arm nuts and bolt.
7. Prevent tension strut from turning by using a suitable wrench on the strut's flat, then remove nut from rear of tension strut.
8. Remove tension strut retainer.
9. Remove rear tension strut bayonet bushing from strut.
10. Remove two nuts and bolts attaching rear knuckle to strut. Tap out bolts using a suitable pin punch.
11. Remove knuckle from vehicle.

Installation

1. Align hole in lower end of rear knuckle with forward bayonet bushing on tension strut. Ensure bushing's stepped area seats squarely into knuckle's hole.
2. Rotate knuckle until its upper mounting holes align with holes in strut's clevis bracket.
3. Install two bolts attaching strut to rear knuckle from front side. Install nuts on bolts. Tighten to specifications.
4. Align lateral arms with hole in center of knuckle. Install arm to knuckle bolts. Start bolt from front side. Install nut, but do not tighten completely.
5. Install rear bayonet bushing onto tension strut. Ensure stepped area seats squarely into hole in knuckle.
6. Install rear tension strut retainer, then the nut. Tighten to specifications while holding strut in place with a wrench on flat area.
7. Install brake support plate or adapter onto knuckle. Tighten fasteners to specifications.

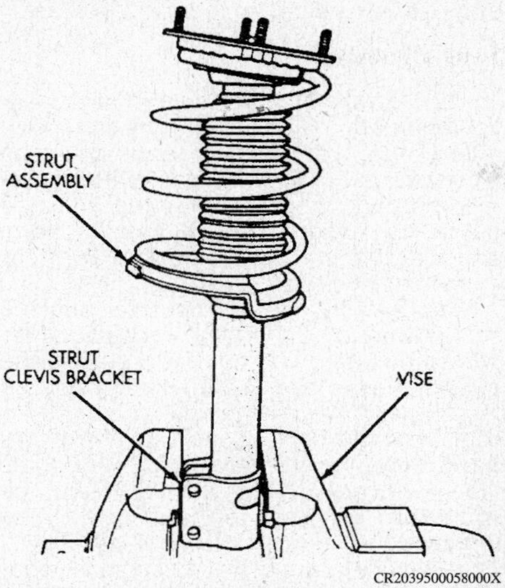

Fig. 7 Strut assembly mounted in vise

8. **On models equipped with ABS,** install sensor bracket to strut screw. Tighten to specifications.
9. **On all models,** install tire and wheel. Tighten lugnuts in proper sequence to half specification. Repeat sequence again to full specification.
10. Lower vehicle to ground, then rock it to bring to curb height.
11. Tighten lateral arm to knuckle mounting bolt to specifications.
12. Inspect and adjust rear toe. Refer to "Rear Wheel Alignment Specifications" in "Specifications" section.

STRUT

REPLACE

1997–99

1. Raise and support vehicle, then remove wheel.
2. Remove brake fluid hose support bracket from strut.
3. **On models equipped with ABS,** remove speed sensor cable and routing clip from strut.
4. **On all models,** loosen but do not remove spindle knuckle to strut clevis bolts. **The spindle knuckle to strut clevis bolts are serrated for a tight fit into the knuckle. Do not turn bolt when loosening. Turn nut only, or damage to knuckle or bolt will occur.**
5. Lower vehicle, then access four upper strut to strut tower mounting nuts. Removing carpeting and dust shield as required.
6. Loosen but do not remove upper strut to tower mounting nuts.
7. Using a suitable device, support suspension. **Do not allow suspension components to hang after removing strut. Do not place support under lateral links or tension strut as they may bend.**
8. Remove previously loosened upper strut mounting nuts and strut to spindle knuckle bolts.
9. Slide strut straight back off spindle knuckle, then lower strut from vehicle.
10. Reverse procedure to install, noting the following:
    a. Tighten bolts and nuts to specifications.
    b. **Do not turn bolts when tightening spindle knuckle to strut clevis bolts. Tighten by turning nuts only.**
    c. Inspect and adjust rear wheel alignment as outlined under " Wheel Alignment."

2000

1. Raise and support vehicle.
2. Remove wheel and tire.
3. **On models equipped with rear drum brakes,** remove brake hose bracket to strut screw.
4. **On models equipped with ABS,** remove wheel speed sensor bracket to strut screw.
5. **On all models,** remove nut from end of rear stabilizer bar link bolt. Pull bolt out through top of link, then remove link.
6. **On models equipped with rear disc brakes,** proceed as follows:
    a. Remove four brake adapter to knuckle bolts.
    b. Remove adapter, rotor shield, parking brake shoes and cable as an assembly.
    c. Tie this assembly aside with a suitable cord or string.
7. **On all models,** remove two knuckle to strut nuts and bolts. **These bolts are serrated and must not be turned during removal. Hold bolts in place in knuckle while removing nuts, then tap bolts out using a suitable pin punch.**
8. Lower vehicle only enough to climb into luggage compartment without tires reaching ground.
9. Remove carpeting from top of strut tower inside luggage compartment.
10. Loosen, but do not completely remove, three strut to tower nuts.
11. Hold strut firmly in place, then remove the three nuts from tower.
12. Remove strut assembly from knuckle by sliding it away from knuckle, lowering it between two lateral arms, then angling top outward and out through wheelwell opening.
13. Reverse procedure to install, noting the following:
    a. Tighten three tower nuts to specifications.
    b. Align holes in strut clevis bracket on strut's lower end with knuckle's mounting holes.
    c. Install tire and wheel. Tighten lugnuts in proper sequence to half specification. Repeat sequence again to full specification.
    d. Lower vehicle to ground, then rock it to bring to curb height.
    e. Tighten stabilizer bar link nut to specifications.
    f. Inspect and adjust rear toe. Refer to "Rear Wheel Alignment Specifications" in "Specifications" section.

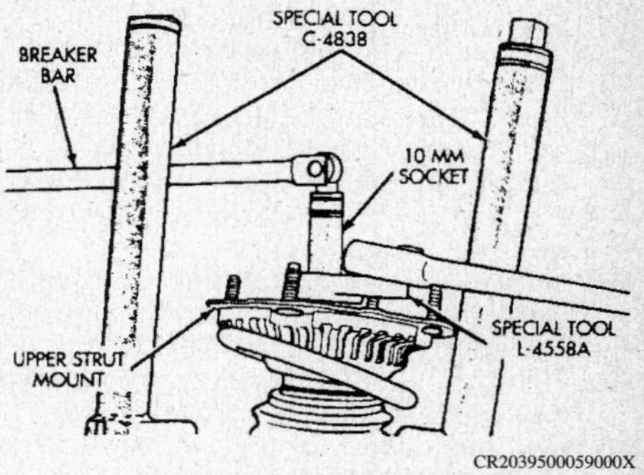

Fig. 8 Strut shaft nut replacement

STRUT SERVICE

Coil springs on these models are available in different load rates. Spring rates may be different on each side of the vehicle depending on how the vehicle is equipped. Ensure proper spring rates are chosen during assembly.

The gas-charged strut damper cannot be rebuilt and is serviced as a unit.

1997–99

1. Remove strut assembly as outlined under "Strut, Replace."
2. Using a suitable marker or paint, place match marks on components of strut assembly to aid in assembly alignment.
3. Place strut assembly into a suitable vise, **Fig. 7. Do not clamp body of strut into vise.**
4. Using coil spring compressor tool No. C-4838, or equivalent, compress spring until tension is removed from upper strut mount assembly.
5. Using strut nut wrench tool No. L-4558A, or equivalent, **Fig. 8** and a 10 mm socket and breaker bar to hold strut shaft, remove strut shaft nut.
6. Remove outer washer, upper strut mount, coil spring, inner washer, dust shield, jounce bumper and spring isolator from strut **Fig. 1.**
7. Reverse procedure to install, noting the following:
    a. Tighten nuts to specifications.
    b. Install inner strut shaft washer with raised edge up and outer strut shaft washer with raised edge down.
    c. Transfer alignment marks to any replaced component. Ensure alignment of all components during assembly.

2000

1. Remove strut assembly as outlined under "Strut, Replace."
2. Note orientation of all markings, letters and assembly tips before proceeding.
3. Using a suitable marker or paint, place match marks on components of strut assembly to aid in assembly alignment.
4. Position strut assembly in compressor tool No. PSE W-7200, or equivalent following tool manufacturer's instructions.

5. Compress coil spring until all spring tension is off upper mount.
6. After spring has compressed, install strut nut socket tool No. 6864, or equivalent on strut shaft retaining nut.
7. Install a socket on hex on shaft's end.
8. Prevent strut shaft from turning, then remove shaft nut.
9. Remove upper mount from strut shaft.
10. Remove clamp from bottom of spring.
11. Pull strut through bottom of spring.
12. Remove dust shield and jounce bumper by pulling them straight up.
13. Remove lower spring isolator from strut's lower spring seat.
14. If coil spring is being replaced, proceed as follows:
    a. Make note of spring's position in compressor tool for easier assembly.
    b. Back off compressor drive completely to release spring tension.
    c. Push hooks back, then remove spring.
15. Reverse procedure to install, noting the following:
    a. Mount coil spring into original position noted during disassembly.
    b. Inspect upper mount before installation. Ensure proper mount is being installed. Righthand mounts are marked with an "R," while lefthands have an "L" marking.
    c. Tighten all fasteners to specifications.

TENSION STRUT

REPLACE

1. Remove wheel and tire as required.
2. Using a suitable wrench on flat to prevent tension strut from turning, remove nuts from both ends of tension strut.
3. Note orientation of tension strut bushings and washers.
4. Remove bushings and washers from tension strut, then the tension strut.
5. Reverse procedure to install, noting the following:
    a. Tighten nuts to specifications.
    b. **On 1997–99 models,** refer to **Fig. 6** when installing tension strut bushings and washers.
    c. **On all models,** inspect and adjust rear wheel alignment as outlined under the " Wheel Alignment" section of this chapter.

ROLL BAR

REPLACE

1. Raise and support vehicle, then remove both rear wheels.
2. Disconnect roll bar from attaching links at each side, then swing bar down to clear links.
3. Remove bolts from roll bar attaching brackets, then remove roll bar from vehicle. **Note orientation of bushings at this time.**
4. Reverse procedure to install, noting the following:
    a. Tighten nuts and bolts to specifications.
    b. Ensure bushings are installed in original positions noted during removal.

LATERAL LINK

REPLACE

1997–99

Rear suspension lateral link bushings are not replaceable. They are serviced as a unit.

The lateral links are not interchangeable. The forward link is non-adjustable, and both bushing sleeves are the same size. The rearward link is adjustable. The small bushing sleeve must be placed at the spindle knuckle to allow for toe adjustments.

1. Raise and support vehicle, then remove rear wheels.
2. Remove lateral link attachment bolt and washers at the spindle knuckle.
3. Remove lateral link attachment bolt, washers and adjustment cams at the cross member, then remove lateral links.
4. Reverse procedure to install, noting the following:
    a. Tighten nuts and bolts to specifications.
    b. Forward lateral links have same size bushing sleeves at each end.
    c. Rearward lateral links have two different size bushing sleeves, **small bushing sleeve must be installed at spindle knuckle end.**
    d. The short mounting bolt is used at the spindle knuckle end, **and must be installed with head of bolt towards front of vehicle.**
    e. The long mounting bolt is used at the crossmember end, **and must be installed with head of bolt towards rear of vehicle.**
    f. Lateral link bolts must be tightened to specifications with suspension supporting vehicle weight.
    g. Inspect and adjust rear wheel alignment as outlined under "Wheel Alignment."

2000

Removal

1. Raise and support vehicle.
2. Remove tire and wheel.
3. Remove lateral link to knuckle nut, bolt and washers.
4. Remove nut, washer, bolt and wheel alignment cam attaching lateral arms to rear crossmember.
5. Remove lateral arms from vehicle.

Installation

The lateral arms have a specific installation orientation. The arm with identical size bushing sleeves on both ends must be mounted on the forward side of the crossmember and knuckle with the trimmed outer edge facing rearward. This front arm also displays the word "FORWARD. " This side must face forward.

The arm with differing size bushing sleeves mounts on the rearward side of the crossmember and knuckle. Position the smaller sleeve end at the knuckle and the larger end at the rear crossmember. **If the rear arm will be mounted on the righthand side,** the trimmed outer edge must face rearward. **If the rear arm will be mounted on the lefthand side,** the trimmed outer edge must face forward.

1. Place forward lateral arm against leading edge of knuckle.
2. Install short lateral arm mounting bolt with a washer through lateral arm and knuckle and out trailing end of knuckle.
3. Install small sleeved end of rear lateral arm onto end of bolt installed in previous step.
4. Install washer and nut onto end of mounting bolt, but do not tighten completely.
5. Install an alignment cam on long arm mounting bolt.
6. Hold rear lateral arm up against crossmember and install long mounting bolt with adjustment cam through lateral arm bushing and rear crossmember. Ensure bolt is installed with alignment cam's notch pointing straight up.
7. Position forward lateral arm against rear crossmember hole.
8. Route long mounting bolt through lateral arm bushing sleeve.
9. Install washer and nut onto end of mounting bolt at rear crossmember, but do not tighten completely.
10. When properly installed, each lateral arm will have the bow in its length facing downward. Both righthand side arms will have trimmed outer edges facing rear of vehicle. Lefthand side arms will have trimmed outer edges facing each other. Mounting bolt at knuckle will have nut at rear, while mounting bolt at crossmember will have nut at front.
11. Install tire and wheel. Tighten lugnuts in proper sequence to half specification. Repeat sequence again to full specification.
12. Lower vehicle to ground, then rock it to bring to curb height.
13. Tighten lateral arm mounting bolt nut at knuckle to specifications.
14. Tighten lateral arm mounting bolt nut at crossmember to specifications.
15. Inspect and adjust rear toe. Refer to "Rear Wheel Alignment Specifications" in "Specifications" section.

TIGHTENING SPECIFICATIONS

Year	Component	Torque/ Ft lbs.
1997–99	Brake Hose	35
	Brake Hose Bracket	17
	Brake Plate To Spindle Knuckle	50
	Caliper To Disc Brake Adapter	16
	Disc Brake Adapter To Spindle Knuckle	50
	Hub And Bearing To Spindle Knuckle	124
	Lateral Link	70
	Roll Bar Isolator Bracket To Frame	25
	Roll Bar To Rear Strut Link	25
	Strut Assembly Shaft Nut	55
	Strut Assembly To Spindle Knuckle Clevis	70
	Strut Assembly To Tower	25
	Tension Strut Shaft	70
	Tension Strut To Body Attaching Bracket	70
	Wheel Lugnuts	95
2000	Brake Hose Bracket Bolt	23
	Brake Support Plate Bolts	55
	Disc Brake Adapter Bolts	55
	Hub & Bearing To Knuckle Nut	160
	Knuckle Attaching Bolts	65
	Lateral Arm Nut At Crossmember	65
	Lateral Arm Nut At Knuckle	70
	Parking Brake Cable Nut	20.8
	Roll Bar Cushion Retainer Bolts	25
	Roll Bar Link Bolt Nut	16.7
	Strut Assembly Shaft Nut	55
	Tension Strut Frame Rail Bolts	70
	Tension Strut Rear Nut	70
	Tower Attaching Nuts	25
	Wheel Lugnuts	100①

① — Tighten lugnuts in proper sequence to half specification. Repeat sequence again to full specification.

Front Suspension & Steering

INDEX

DESCRIPTION

This suspension is a gas pressurized strut system used in place of front suspension upper ball joint and upper control arm. The bottom of the strut is attached directly to the steering knuckle using two attaching bolts and nuts going through the clevis bracket and steering knuckle, **Figs. 1 and 2.**

A cast lower arm assembly is attached to the front suspension crossmember using two rubber isolator bushings and to the steering knuckle by means of a ball joint.

A sealed for life front hub and bearing assembly is attached to the front steering knuckle. The outer CV joint assembly is splined to the front hub and bearing assembly.

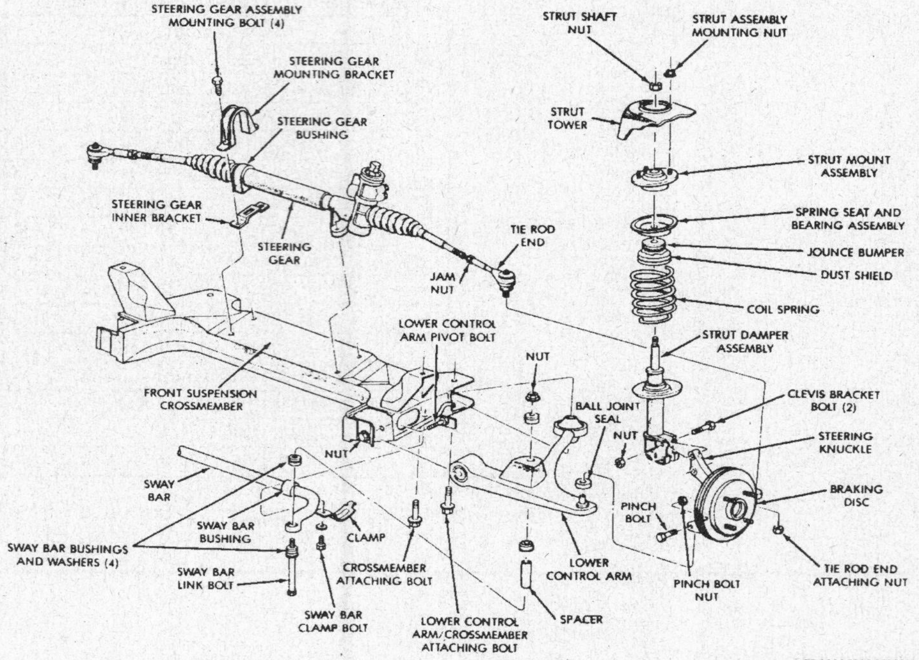

Fig. 1 Exploded view of front suspension. 1997–99

HUB & BEARING

REPLACE

1997–99

1. Remove cotter pin, castle nut and hub nut while vehicle is still on floor with brakes applied.
2. Raise and support vehicle, then remove front tire and wheel assembly.
3. Remove front disc brake caliper and place aside. **Do not let caliper assembly hang by hose.**
4. Remove front disc brake, then disconnect tie rod from steering knuckle using removal tool No. MB-990635, or equivalent.
5. Separate ball joint stud from steering knuckle by prying down on lower control arm. **Ensure ball joint seal is not damaged.**
6. Pull steering knuckle assembly out and away from outer CV joint of driveshaft assembly.
7. Remove two steering knuckle to strut damper attaching bolts, then the steering knuckle and hub/bearing assembly from vehicle.
8. Reverse procedure to install. **Torque** clamp bolt to 70 ft. lbs.

2000

The cartridge type front wheel bearing on these models is not transferable to a new knuckle. If a new knuckle does not arrive with a new bearing, a new bearing must be installed. This must be done before the knuckle is installed on the vehicle.

1. Apply and hold brakes.
2. Raise and support vehicle.
3. Remove tire and wheel.
4. Keep brakes applied, then loosen and remove hub nut on end of driveshaft.
5. Remove two caliper to knuckle guide pin bolts.
6. Remove caliper from knuckle, then position it aside with a suitable cord or wire. **Do not let it hang by the brake hose.**
7. Remove any clips from wheel studs.
8. Remove rotor from hub.
9. Remove outer tie rod to knuckle nut.
10. Using tie rod remover tool No. MB991113, or equivalent, remove tie rod end from knuckle.
11. Remove tie rod heat shield.
12. Remove ball joint stud to knuckle nut and pinch bolt.
13. Remove two strut to knuckle bolts. **These bolts are serrated and must not be turned during removal. Hold bolts in place in knuckle while removing nuts, then tap bolts out using a suitable pin punch.**
14. Separate ball joint from knuckle by prying down on lower control arm and up against ball joint knuckle boss. Avoid cutting or tearing the seal.
15. Pull knuckle off driveshaft outer CV joint splines, then remove knuckle. Do not let driveshaft hang by inner CV joint. Support it with a suitable cord.
16. Refer to "Hub & Bearing Service" for continuation of bearing replacement procedure.

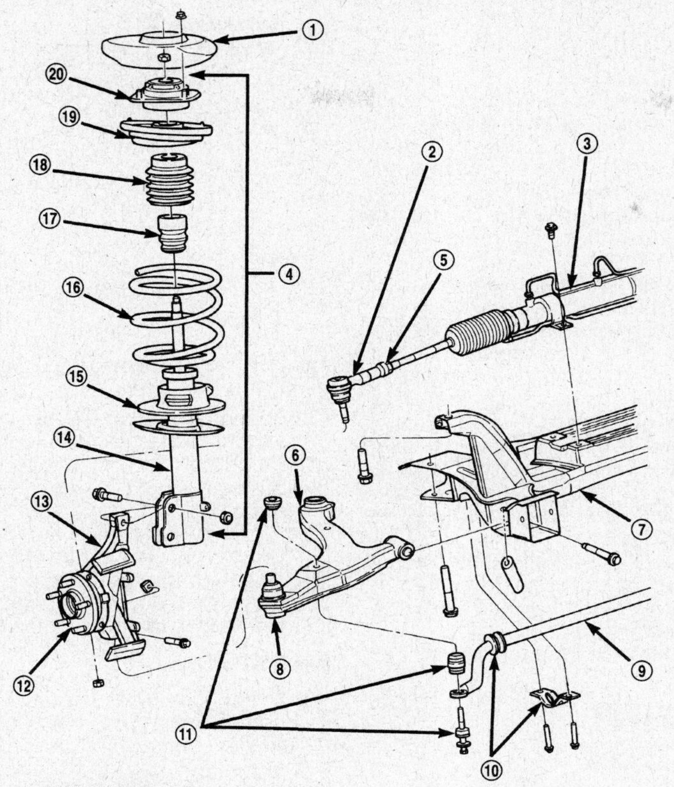

1 – VEHICLE STRUT TOWER
2 – OUTER TIE ROD
3 – STEERING GEAR
4 – STRUT ASSEMBLY
5 – JAM NUT
6 – LOWER CONTROL ARM
7 – CROSSMEMBER
8 – BALL JOINT
9 – STABILIZER BAR
10 – STABILIZER BAR CUSHION AND RETAINER
11 – STABILIZER BAR LINK
12 – HUB
13 – KNUCKLE
14 – STRUT
15 – LOWER SPRING ISOLATOR
16 – COIL SPRING
17 – JOUNCE BUMPER
18 – DUST SHIELD
19 – SPRING SEAT AND BEARING
20 – UPPER MOUNT

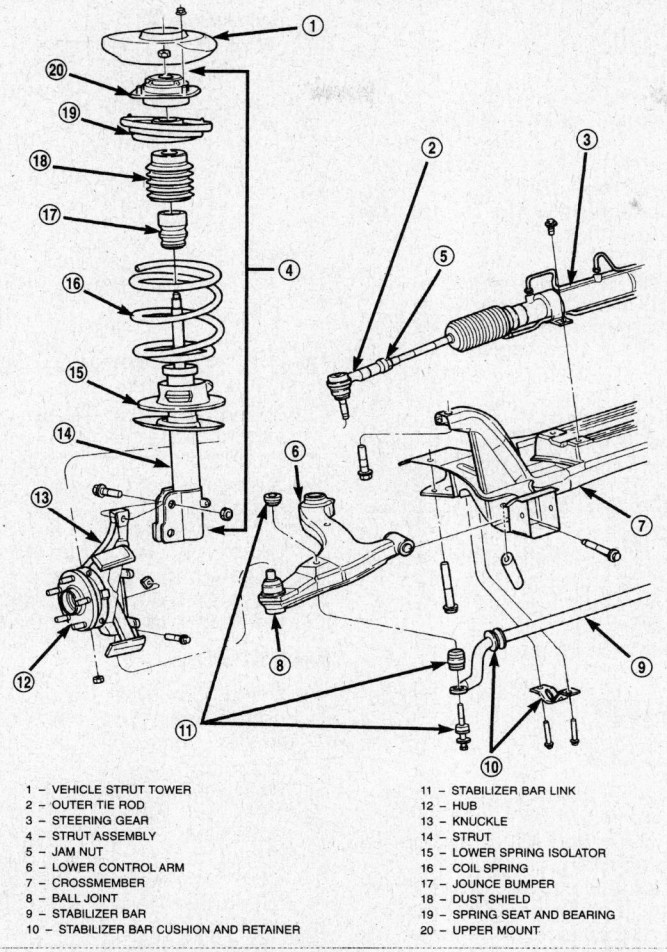

Fig. 2 Exploded view of front suspension. 2000

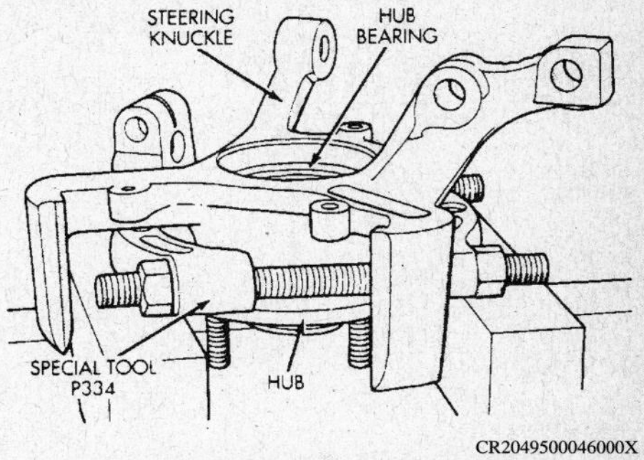

Fig. 3 Hub, bearing & steering knuckle supported for removal of hub

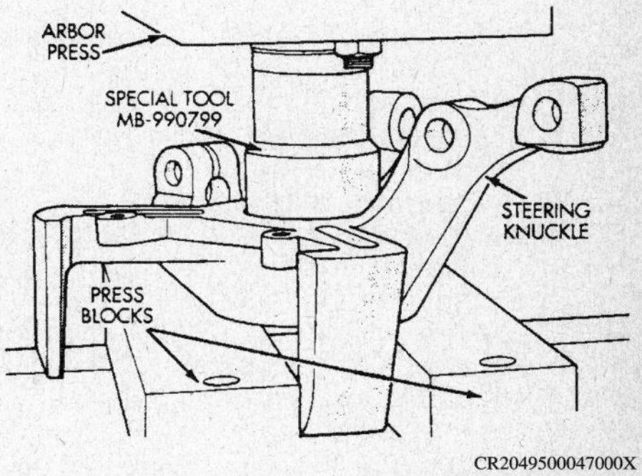

Fig. 4 Hub bearing removal

HUB & BEARING SERVICE

DISASSEMBLE

1997–99

All steps of the hub bearing removal from steering knuckle must be done using a hydraulic arbor press.

1. Install bearing splitter tool No. P334, or equivalent, on steering knuckle and hub/bearing assembly to support steering knuckle when pressing out bearing.
2. Position steering knuckle and hub/bearing assembly in vise, **Fig. 3,** supported by splitter tool.
3. Position driver tool No. 6644-2, or equivalent, on small end of hub, then press hub from bearing. The one bearing race may come out with hub when hub is removed from bearing.
4. Remove bearing splitter from steering knuckle, then place steering knuckle is press supported by press blocks, **Fig. 4.**
5. Place bearing driver tool No. MB-990799, or equivalent, on outer race of hub bearing, then press hub bearing completely out of steering knuckle.
6. Install bearing splitter tool on hub so it is between flange of hub and bearing race remaining on hub.
7. Install assembly into press, then place driver tool on end of hub and press hub out of hub bearing race, **Fig. 5.**

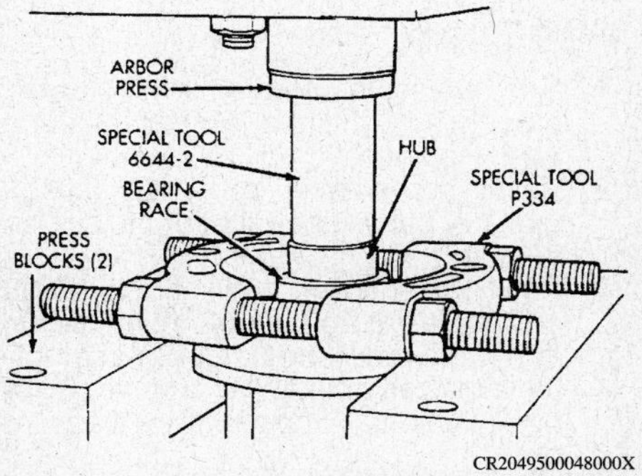

Fig. 5 Hub bearing race removal

2000

The cartridge type front wheel bearing on these models is not transferable to a new knuckle. If a new knuckle does not arrive with a new bearing, a new bearing must also be installed. This must be done before the knuckle is installed on the vehicle.

1. Using stud remover tool No. 4150A, or equivalent, press one wheel stud out of hub flange.
2. Rotate hub until removed stud aligns with bearing retainer plate notch.
3. Remove stud from hub.
4. Rotate hub until open stud hole faces away from caliper lower rail on knuckle.
5. Install one half of bearing splitter tool No. 1130, or equivalent between hub and bearing plate.
6. Align threaded hole in first half of bearing splitter with caliper rail on knuckle.
7. Install remaining portions of splitter. Hand tighten nuts to hold splitter in place on knuckle.
8. After splitter is completely installed, ensure three retainer plate to knuckle bolts are contacting splitter. The retainer plate should not support knuckle or contact splitter.
9. Mount knuckle in an arbor press supported by the bearing splitter as shown, **Fig. 3.**
10. Position driver tool No. 6644-2, or equivalent on hub's small end.
11. Use arbor press to remove hub from wheel bearing. Outer race normally comes out bearing when hub is pressed.
12. Remove bearing splitter tool from knuckle.
13. Remove three bearing retainer plate to knuckle bolts, then the plate.
14. Mount knuckle in arbor press again,

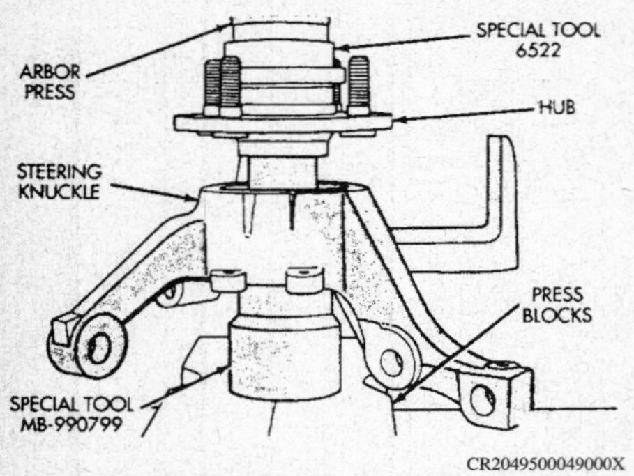

Fig. 6 Hub bearing installation

supported by press blocks, **Fig. 4.** Ensure press blocks do not obstruct knuckle bore or bearing will not slide out.
15. Place bearing driver tool No. MB-990799, or equivalent on bearing's outer race.
16. Press bearing out of knuckle.
17. Install bearing splitter tool on hub in such a way so it is between hub flange and outer bearing race.
18. Place hub, race and splitter in arbor press as shown in **Fig. 5.**
19. Place driver tool on end of hub.
20. Press hub out of bearing race.

ASSEMBLE

1997–99

1. Install new bearing into bore of steering knuckle so it is square with bore, then place steering knuckle in press with receiver tool No. C-4698-2, or equivalent, supporting steering knuckle.
2. Place driver tool No. 5052, or equivalent, on outer race of hub, then press hub bearing into steering knuckle until it is fully bottom in bearing bore of steering knuckle.
3. Install hub bearing retaining snap ring into groove in hub bearing bore of steering knuckle. **Ensure snap ring is fully seated.**
4. Place steering knuckle with hub bearing installed in press with receiver tool No. MB-990799, or equivalent, supporting inner race of hub bearing, **Fig. 6.**
5. Place hub into hub bearing ensuring it is square with bearing.
6. Place driver tool No. 6522, or equivalent, on front face of hub, then press hub into bearing until it bottoms in hub bearing.

2000

The cartridge type front wheel bearing on these models is not transferable to a new knuckle. If a new knuckle does not arrive with a new bearing, a new bearing must also be installed. This must be done before the knuckle is installed on the vehicle.
1. Wipe knuckle bore clean with a clean, dry lint free towel. Ensure no dirt or grease remains.
2. Place new bearing into knuckle bore, perfectly square.
3. Place knuckle in arbor press with receiver tool No. C-4698-2, or equivalent supporting knuckle.
4. Place driver tool 5052, or equivalent, on bearing outer race.
5. Press bearing into knuckle until it has fully bottomed. Remove knuckle from press.
6. Install bearing retainer plate onto knuckle **with the three original or exact replacement bolts. Do not use any substitutions.** Tighten to specifications.
7. Place previously removed wheel stud back into hub flange.
8. Place hub in arbor press supported by tool No. C-4698-1, or equivalent.
9. Press stud into hub flange until it seats fully against flange's rear side. Remove hub from press.
10. Place knuckle with its newly installed bearing back into arbor press with receiver tool No. MB-990799, or equivalent supporting bearing inner race as shown in **Fig. 6.**
11. Place hub in bearing, ensuring it is square with inner race.
12. Press hub into bearing until it fully bottoms in bearing.
13. Remove knuckle from press.

BALL JOINT INSPECTION

With weight of vehicle resting on wheels, grasp grease fitting and, with no mechanical assistance or added force, attempt to move grease fitting, **Fig. 7.**

If the ball joint is worn the grease fitting will move easily. If movement is noted, replacement of ball joint is recommended.

BALL JOINT

REPLACE

1997–99

1. Remove lower control arm following procedure outlined under "Control Arm, Replace."
2. Using screwdriver or other suitable tool, pry ball joint seal boot off joint assembly.
3. Position receiving cup tool No. 6758, or equivalent, to support lower control arm while receiving ball joint assembly.
4. Install receiver/installer tool No. 6804, or equivalent, in top of ball joint assembly.
5. Using suitable press equipment, press ball joint assembly completely out of control arm.
6. Reverse procedure to install.

2000

Removal

1. Remove lower control arm following procedure outlined under " Control Arm, Replace."
2. Using screwdriver or other suitable tool, pry ball joint seal boot off ball joint assembly.
3. Position receiver tool No. 6908-2, or equivalent, on a hydraulic press to support lower control arm while receiving ball joint assembly.
4. Place control arm on top of receiver tool so bottom of ball joint sits in receiver cup.
5. Place larger end of adapter tool No. 6804, or equivalent on top of ball joint.
6. Use hydraulic press to press ball joint completely out of control arm.
7. Remove arm and all tools from press.

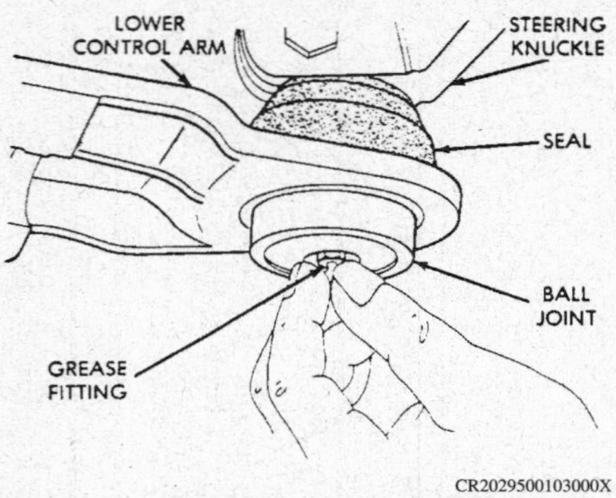

Fig. 7 Ball joint wear inspection

Installation

1. Position new ball joint by hand into its control arm bore, with notch in stud facing control arm front isolator bushing, to ease assembly to knuckle. Ensure it moves in straight and square.
2. Position installer tool No. 6758, or equivalent on hydraulic press to support control arm. Place control arm on top of installer in upside-down position, aligning ball joint stud squarely with installer cup.
3. Place larger end of adapter tool No. 6804, or equivalent on top of ball joint.
4. Use hydraulic press to press ball joint into control arm until joint's shoulder bottoms in its bore. **Do not apply excessive pressure after joint has bottomed.**
5. Remove all tools and control arm from press.
6. Install a new ball joint seal over stud. Position upward lip on outside perimeter of seal boot outward away from control arm once installed. Start installation by hand.
7. Position installer tool No. 6758, or equivalent over boot's outer diameter. Use hand pressure on top of tool until boot is pressed squarely down against top surface of control arm.
8. Install lower control arm following procedure outlined under " Control Arm, Replace."

STRUT

REPLACE

1997–99

1. Loosen wheel lugnuts, then raise and support vehicle.
2. Remove wheel and tire assembly, then disconnect the hydraulic brake hose routing bracket from strut bracket.
3. **On models equipped with ABS,**

speed sensor is combined with hydraulic hose routing bracket.
4. **On all models,** remove two strut assembly clevis bracket to steering knuckle attaching bolts.
5. Remove three nuts attaching strut assembly upper mount to strut tower, then the strut.
6. Reverse procedure to install.

2000

Removal

1. Raise and support vehicle on hoist.
2. Remove tire and wheel.
3. Mark strut assemblies if both lefthand and righthand units will be replaced.
4. Remove ground wire screw at rear of strut.
5. **On models equipped with ABS,** remove ABS sensor bracket screw at rear of strut.
6. **On all models,** remove two strut to knuckle bolts. **These bolts are serrated and must not be turned during removal. Hold bolts in place in knuckle while removing nuts, then tap bolts out using a suitable pin punch.**
7. Lower vehicle enough to open hood, but do not let tires reach ground.
8. Remove three strut to tower mounting nuts.
9. Remove strut assembly from vehicle.

Installation

1. Install new strut into tower. Ensure three studs align with tower holes. Tighten nuts to specifications.
2. Close hood.
3. Position lower end of strut assembly in line with upper end of knuckle and align mounting holes.
4. Install two strut to knuckle bolts with nuts facing front of vehicle. **These bolts are serrated and must not be turned during removal. Hold bolts in place in knuckle while installing nuts.** Tighten nuts to specifications, then rotate an additional 90°.
5. **On models equipped with ABS,** mount wheel speed sensor to rear ear of strut. Tighten to specifications.
6. **On all models,** attach ground wire to rear of strut. Tighten to specifications.
7. Install tire and wheel. Tighten lugnuts in proper sequence to half specification. Repeat sequence again to full specification.

STRUT SERVICE

1997-99

1. Clamp strut assembly by the clevis bracket into suitable vise.
2. Scribe coil spring and strut assembly as to righthand or lefthand, then using compressor tool No. C-4838, or equivalent, compress coil spring, **Fig. 8.**
3. Install socket strut nut tool No. L4558A, or equivalent, on strut shaft retaining nut.
4. Install 10 mm socket on hex head of strut shaft and remove nut while holding strut to keep from rotating.

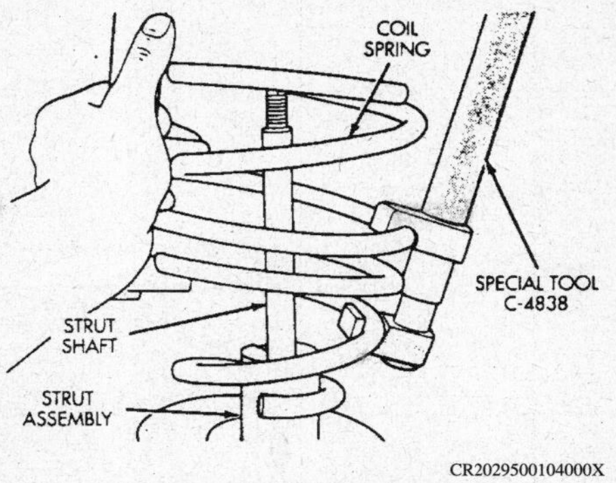

Fig. 8 Coil spring removal

5. Remove upper spring seat, pivot bearing and dust shield as an assembly.
6. Remove coil spring.
7. Reverse procedure to install.

2000

Removal

1. Remove strut assembly as outlined under "Strut, Replace " section in this chapter.
2. Position strut assembly into coil spring compressor tool No. PSE W-7200, or equivalent following manufacturer's instructions. Set lower hooks, then the uppers.
3. Place a clamp on lower end of spring to hold strut in place when shaft nut is removed. **Do not remove strut shaft nut until after spring has been compressed.**
4. Compress spring until all tension is gone from upper mount.
5. When spring has been sufficiently compressed, install strut nut socket tool No. 6864, or equivalent on nut.
6. Install a suitable socket on hex end of strut shaft, then hold shaft in place and remove nut.
7. Remove upper spring seat and bearing with upper spring isolator as a unit from top of coil spring by pulling them straight up. Isolator can be separated after removal from vehicle.
8. Remove dust shield, then the jounce bumper by pulling them straight up.
9. If coil spring is being replaced, release spring tension by completely backing off compressor drive. Push hooks back and remove spring.

Installation

1. Place coil spring into compressor tool following manufacturer's instructions.
2. Rotate spring so end of top coil is directly in rear.
3. Slowly compress spring until strut assembly can be assembled.
4. Install lower spring isolator on strut's lower spring seat.
5. Install strut through bottom of spring until clevis bracket is positioned straight outward away from compressor.
6. Install clamp on lower end of spring and strut so strut stays in place.
7. Install jounce bumper on strut shaft, with smaller end pointing downward toward lower seat.
8. Install dust shield on strut shaft. Shield's bottom will snap past retainer on top of strut housing.
9. Install upper spring isolator on upper spring seat and bearing.
10. Install upper spring seat and bearing on top of spring. Position notch in upper edge of seat straight out away from compressor.
11. Install strut upper mount over strut shaft, onto top of upper spring seat and bearing.
12. Loosely install strut shaft retaining nut.
13. Install strut nut socket tool No. 6864, or equivalent on strut shaft retaining nut.
14. Install a suitable socket on hex end of strut shaft, then hold shaft in place and tighten nut to specifications.
15. Slowly release coil spring tension by completely backing off tensioner drive. Ensure upper mount, seat and bearing properly align, and upper mount does not bind.
16. Remove clamp from lower end of spring and strut. Push hooks back and remove strut assembly from compressor.
17. Install strut assembly as outlined under "Strut, Replace" section in this chapter.

CONTROL ARM

REPLACE

1997-99

1. Raise and support vehicle, then remove wheel and tire assembly.
2. Remove steering knuckle ball joint ball stud, clamping nut and bolt.
3. Remove attaching links connecting sway bar to lower control arm, then loosen, but do not remove, bolts attaching sway bar retainers to front suspension crossmember. Rotate sway bar away from lower control arm.
4. Using a pry bar, separate steering knuckle from ball joint stud, then remove front lower control arm bushing to crossmember attaching nut and bolt.
5. Remove rear lower control arm to crossmember and frame attaching bolt, then the lower control arm, **Fig. 9.**
6. Reverse procedure to install.

2000

This procedure has been revised by a Technical Service Bulletin.

1. Raise and support vehicle.
2. Remove tires and wheels.
3. Remove stabilizer links.
4. Rotate forward ends of stabilizer bar downward. Loosen bar cushion retainers if required.
5. Remove ball joint stud nut and pinch bolt at knuckle. **Do not pull outward on knuckle. This might separate inner CV joint on driveshaft.**
6. Carefully separate ball joint stud from knuckle, avoiding cuts and tears to seals. Pry downward on control arm and up against knuckle's ball joint boss.

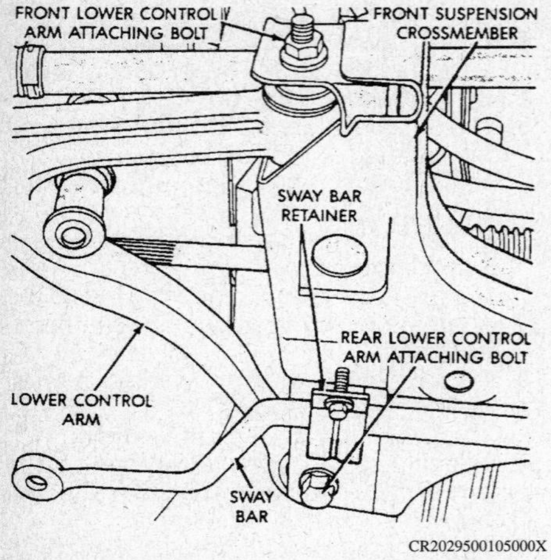

Fig. 9 Lower control arm removal

7. On righthand control arm, remove engine torque strut mounting bolts, then the torque strut.
8. Remove control arm front pivot bolt at crossmember.
9. Remove control arm rear pivot bolt at crossmember and frame rail.
10. remove control arm from crossmember.
11. Reverse procedure to install, noting the following:
    a. Position control arm into crossmember.
    b. Install rear pivot bolt at crossmember and frame rail, but do not fully tighten at this time.
    c. Install control arm front pivot bolt at crossmember.
    d. Tighten control arm rear pivot bolt, then the front pivot bolt to specifications.
    e. If righthand control arm was replaced, install engine torque strut and adjust as outlined under "Adjustment" in " Engine Mount, Replace" section.
    f. Install a new ball joint pinch bolt and tighten to specifications.
    g. Lower vehicle to ground, then rock it to bring to curb height.
    h. If original stabilizer link bolts are being installed, clean all grease, oil and loose material from them, then apply two drops of Mopar Lock And Seal part No. 4318031, or equivalent to last ½ inch of each bolt's threads.
    i. Tighten stabilizer link bolts to specifications.

STEERING KNUCKLE

REPLACE

Refer to "Hub & Bearing, Replace" for procedure.

POWER STEERING GEAR

REPLACE

1997–99

1. Disconnect steering gear coupler from steering column shaft coupler, **Fig. 10.**

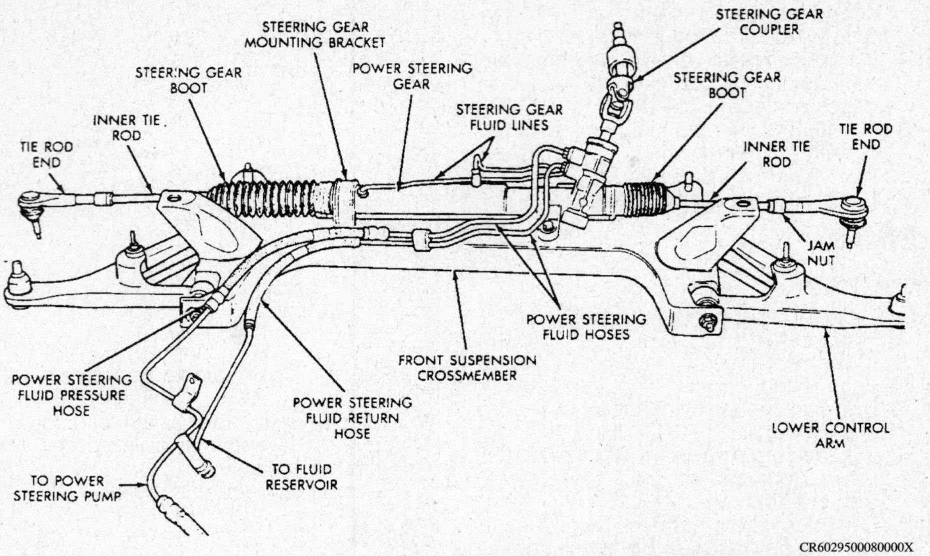

Fig. 10 Power steering gear assembly. 1997–99

2. Raise and support vehicle, then remove both front wheel and tire assemblies.
3. Remove engine/transaxle dampener.
4. Remove attaching nuts from both tie rod ends.
5. Remove both tie rod end studs from steering knuckle using remover tool No. MB-990635, or equivalent, then disconnect wiring harness connector from power steering fluid pressure switch.
6. Remove power steering pressure and return hose routing bracket from front suspension crossmember.
7. Remove power steering fluid, pressure and return hoses from power steering gear assembly.
8. Scribe a line marking the location of where front suspension crossmember is mounted against body.
9. Position a transaxle jack beneath the center of the front suspension crossmember, then remove two bolts attaching front suspension crossmember to frame rails of vehicle.
10. Loosen both rear bolts and lower control arm to body of vehicle.
11. Using transaxle jack lower front suspension crossmember enough to allow steering gear to be removed.
12. Remove four bolts attaching steering gear assembly to front suspension crossmember, then the steering gear assembly.
13. Reverse procedure to install.

2000

1. Ensure front wheels are in straight-ahead position, then lock it using a steering wheel holder tool.
2. Remove steering column coupler retainer pin inside passenger compartment.
3. Back off coupling pinch bolt nut, then remove pinch bolt.
4. Separate steering column upper and lower couplings.
5. Raise and support vehicle.
6. Remove both front tires and wheels.
7. Remove both outer tie rod to knuckle nuts. Hold tie rods stationary while removing nuts.
8. Using tie rod remover tool No. MB991113, or equivalent, remove outer tie rods from knuckles.
9. Remove tie rod heat shield.
10. Release power steering fluid pressure switch wiring electrical connector locking tab, then disconnect connector from switch.
11. Back out tube nut securing power steering fluid pressure hose to gear.
12. **On models less power steering fluid cooler,** disconnect fluid return hose from gear, then remove return hose from C-clamps on outside of two routing clips on gear's front side.
13. **On models equipped with power steering fluid cooler,** disconnect cooler hose from steering gear.
14. **On all models,** remove pressure hose from front of steering gear.
15. **On models equipped with power steering fluid cooler,** remove two screws attaching cooler to crossmember, then allow cooler to hang aside.
16. **On all models,** remove engine torque strut to righthand forward corner of crossmember.
17. Using a suitable awl, scribe alignment marks to ease crossmember to body installation and avoid losing front wheel caster and camber settings.
18. Position a suitable transmission jack under center of front crossmember, then raise it to support bottom of crossmember.
19. Loosen and completely remove two front crossmember to frame rail bolts.
20. Loosen, but do not remove, two rear crossmember to frame rail bolts.
21. Lower the front crossmember with jack enough to allow steering gear removal from rear of crossmember. **Do not allow crossmember to hang from control arms. Let the jack take the weight.**

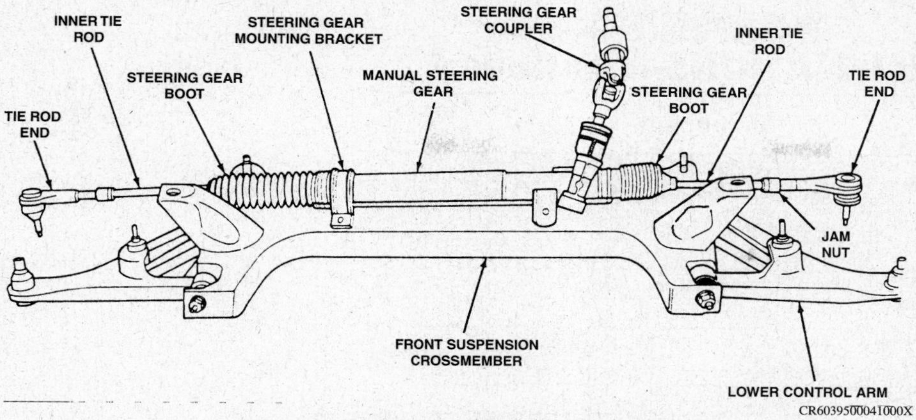

Fig. 11 Manual steering gear assembly

22. Using a suitable punch, remove roll pin where steering column lower coupling meets pinion shaft. Push lower coupling up and off pinion shaft.
23. Release pinion shaft firewall cover seal from tabs cast into steering gear housing, then remove seal from gear.
24. Loosen and remove four steering gear to crossmember bolts.
25. Carefully remove steering gear from front crossmember.
26. Reverse procedure to install, noting the following:
    a. Start the two rear crossmember mounting bolts into tapping plates on body.
    b. Install two front crossmember to frame rail mounting bolts.
    c. Temporarily tighten all four bolts to 20 inch lbs.
    d. Using a suitable soft-faced hammer, tap crossmember back into alignment with scribe marks made during removal. When it is in proper position, tighten two rear bolts, the rear control arm bolts, then front two crossmember bolts to specifications.
    e. Ensure grease is present on dash to coupling seal lip where it meets coupling's plastic collar.
    f. Fill and bleed power steering fluid system.
    g. Inspect and adjust front toe setting as outlined under the "Wheel Alignment" section of this chapter.

POWER STEERING PUMP

REPLACE

1997–99

1. Disconnect power steering pressure hose from power steering pump.
2. Remove power steering fluid supply hose to power steering suction fitting, then the power steering fluid supply hose.
3. Remove two power steering pump to cast bracket mounting and adjusting bolts.
4. Loosen bolt attaching front power steering pump mounting bracket to front engine mount only far enough to slide bracket from behind bolt.
5. Remove drive belt, then the power steering pump and bracket as an assembly.
6. Reverse procedure to install.

2000

1. Siphon all possible power steering fluid from pump reservoir.
2. Remove steering pump drive belt.
3. Disconnect fluid return hose from reservoir.
4. Disconnect fluid pressure hose from steering pump.
5. Remove steering pump to rear support bracket bolt.
6. Loosen two support bracket to engine block bolts.
7. Working through pump pulley holes, remove three pump to cast bracket bolts.
8. Remove power steering pump with reservoir from engine.
9. Reverse procedure to install, noting the following:
    a. Tighten all fasteners to specifications.
    b. Fill and bleed power steering fluid system.
    c. Inspect for and correct any leaks.

MANUAL STEERING GEAR

REPLACE

Refer to "Power Steering Gear, Replace" and **Fig. 11** for service procedures.

TIGHTENING SPECIFICATIONS

Year	Component	Torque/ Ft. Lbs.
1997– 99	Lower Control Arm To Crossmember	120
	Outer Tie Rod To Inner Tie Rod Locknut	45
	Power Steering Pressure Hose Banjo Fitting	25
	Power Steering Pressure & Return Hose Tube Nuts	23
	Power Steering Pump To Rear Bracket Mounting Bolts	40
	Stabilizer Bar To Crossmember	21
	Steering Gear To Crossmember Bolts	50
	Strut Assembly Shaft Nut	55
	Strut Assembly To Shock Tower Mounting Bolts	25
	Tie Rod End To Steering Knuckle Nut	45
	Tie Rod To Steering Knuckle	45
	Wheel Lugnuts	95

Continued

TIGHTENING SPECIFICATIONS—Continued

Year	Component	Torque/ Ft. Lbs.
2000	ABS Wheel Speed Sensor Bolt	10
	Ball Joint Pinch Bolt Nut	70
	Brake Caliper Guide Bolts	16
	Control Arm Front Pivot Bolt	120
	Control Arm Rear Pivot Bolt	150
	Driveshaft Hub Nut	180
	Front Crossmember Front Mounting Bolts	105
	Front Crossmember Rear Mounting Bolts	150
	Ground Wire To Strut	10
	Hub Bearing Retainer Plate Bolts	20.8
	PS Cooler Mounting Screws	90①
	PS Fluid Pressure Switch	70①
	PS Hose Tube Nuts	25
	PS Pump Mounting Bolts	20.8
	PS Pump Pressure Fitting	65
	PS Pump Pressure Hose Tube Nut	25
	PS Pump Rear Support Bracket To Engine Bolts	40
	Stabilizer Bar Cushion Bolts	20.8
	Stabilizer Link Bolts	21.7
	Steering Column Lower Coupling Pinch Bolt	20.8
	Strut Shaft Nut	55
	Strut To Knuckle Bolts	40②
	Strut To Tower Nuts	25
	Wheel Lugnuts	100③

① — Inch lbs.

② — Rotate an additional 90° after specification has been reached.

③ — Tighten lugnuts in proper sequence to half specification. Repeat sequence again to full specification.

Wheel Alignment

INDEX

PRELIMINARY INSPECTION

Ensure vehicle has a full tank of gas when wheel alignment specifications are inspected or adjusted. If tank is not full, this change in weight will affect curb height of vehicle and alignment specifications. Inspect and adjust tire pressure. Ensure all tires are the same size. Inspect all suspension components for looseness or damage. Components showing signs of wear or damage should be replaced before alignment.

FRONT WHEEL ALIGNMENT

Caster and camber settings are determined by the location of vehicle's suspension components, **Fig. 1.** No adjustment of caster and camber is possible after vehicle is built or when servicing suspension components. Caster and camber are not normally considered an adjustable specification when performing an alignment on these models.

CASTER

If caster is not within specifications, inspect for damaged suspension components or body damage causing component locations to change. No adjustment is possible for caster.

CAMBER

1. Properly position vehicle on alignment rack and install all required equipment per alignment equipment specifications.
2. Center steering wheel and lock in place using steering wheel clamp.
3. Jounce vehicle, then read front alignment settings and compare to specifications.
4. If camber readings obtained are not within specifications, a Mopar Service Kit will be required. Different kits are designed for front and rear suspension. **On 2000 models, this procedure should only be used on vehicles less ACR Competition Package.**
5. Raise and support vehicle, then remove original upper bolt attaching front strut clevis bracket to steering knuckle. **These bolts are serrated and must not be turned during removal. Hold bolts in place in knuckle while removing nuts, then tap bolts out using a suitable pin punch.**
6. Loosen lower bolt attaching strut clevis bracket to steering knuckle only enough to allow knuckle to move in clevis bracket.
7. Install bolt from service kit into upper strut clevis bracket to steering knuckle mounting hole.
8. Install nut provided by service kit on replacement bolt.
9. Tighten upper bolt and nut from service kit until snug, but still allowing movement between strut clevis bracket and knuckle.
10. Remove original lower bolt and install bolt from service kit into lower strut clevis bracket hole. Install nut and tighten until snug.
11. Lower vehicle until full weight is supported by suspension, then jounce front and rear of vehicle an equal number of times.
12. Adjust camber to preferred setting by pushing or pulling top of tire.
13. Tighten upper and lower strut clevis bracket bolts.
14. Jounce vehicle an equal number of times and verify rear camber setting. When vehicle is at proper setting, **torque** both front strut clevis brackets to 40 ft. lbs. plus an additional ¼ turn.

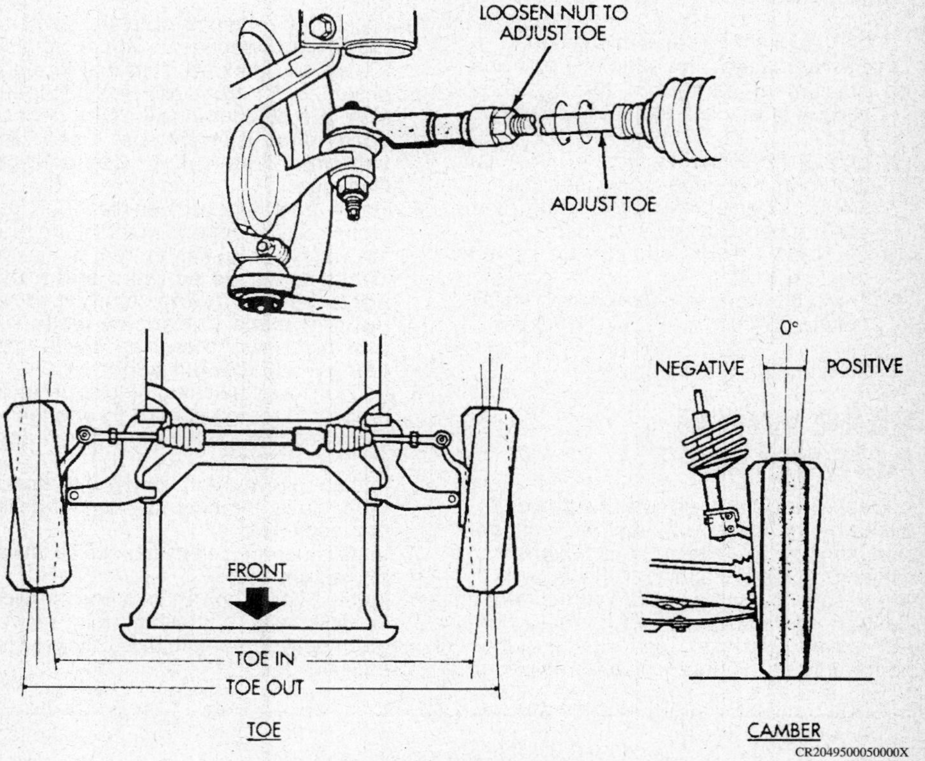

Fig. 1 Camber & toe alignment

TOE

Rear wheel toe must be set prior to setting front wheel toe. Proceed as follows:

1. Center steering wheel and lock in place using a steering wheel clamp.
2. Loosen nuts on attaching bolts for left-hand and righthand lateral links to rear crossmember, **Fig. 2.**
3. Rotate lateral link adjustment cams, **Fig. 3,** until preferred rear toe specification is obtained.
4. While holding toe adjustment cams from turning, tighten righthand and left-hand lateral links to rear crossmember attaching bolt nuts. This will securely

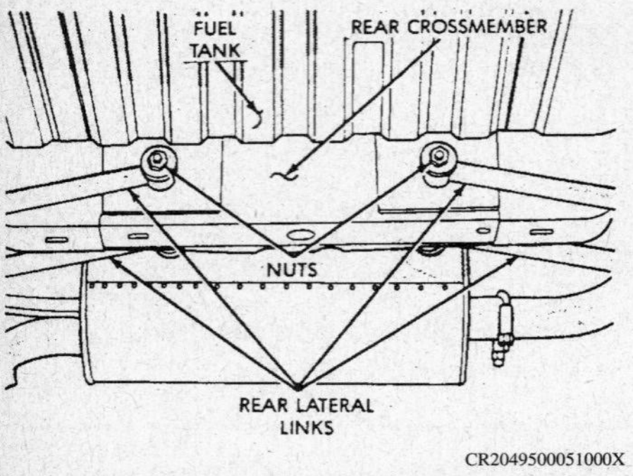

Fig. 2 Rear lateral link toe setting

hold adjustment cams in position.

5. Prevent lateral link attaching bolt and adjustment cam from turning, then **torque** lateral link attaching bolt to 70 ft. lbs.
6. Loosen front inner tie rod end jam nuts, then grasp inner tie rods at serration.
7. Rotate inner tie rods of steering gear and set front toe specifications.
8. **On 1997–99 models, torque** tie rod locknuts to 45 ft. lbs.
9. **On 2000 models, torque** tie rod locknuts to 55 ft. lbs.

REAR WHEEL ALIGNMENT

Caster and camber settings are determined by the location of vehicle's suspension components, **Fig. 1.** No adjustment of caster is possible after vehicle is built or when servicing suspension components. Caster and camber are not normally considered an adjustable specification when performing an alignment on this vehicle.

CASTER

If caster is not within specifications, inspect for damaged suspension components or body damage causing component locations to change. No adjustment is possible for caster.

CAMBER

1. Properly position vehicle on alignment rack and install all required equipment, per alignment equipment specifications.
2. Jounce vehicle and read rear alignment settings and compare to specifications.
3. If camber readings obtained are not within specifications, a Mopar Service Kit will be required. Different kits are designed for front and rear suspension. **On 2000 models, this procedure should only be used on vehicles less ACR Competition Package.**
4. Raise and support vehicle, then remove original upper bolt attaching rear strut clevis bracket to rear knuckle. **These bolts are serrated and must not be turned during removal. Hold bolts in place in knuckle while removing nuts, then tap bolts out using a suitable pin punch.**
5. Loosen lower bolt attaching strut clevis bracket to rear knuckle only enough to allow knuckle to move in clevis bracket.
6. Install bolt from service kit into upper strut clevis bracket to rear knuckle mounting hole.
7. Install nut provided by service kit on replacement bolt.
8. Tighten upper bolt and nut from service kit until snug, but still allowing movement between strut clevis bracket and knuckle.

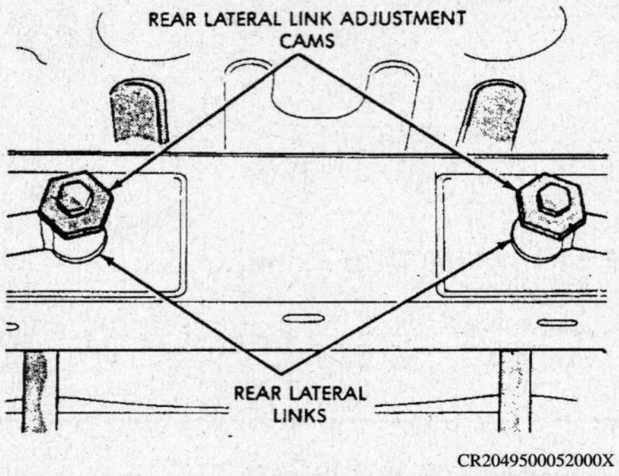

Fig. 3 Rear wheel toe adjustment cams

9. Remove original lower bolt and install bolt from service kit into lower strut clevis bracket hole. Install nut and tighten until snug.
10. Lower vehicle until full weight is supported by suspension, then jounce front and rear of vehicle an equal number of times.
11. Adjust camber to preferred setting by pushing or pulling top of tire.
12. Tighten upper and lower strut clevis bracket bolts.
13. Jounce vehicle an equal number of times and verify rear camber setting. When vehicle is at proper setting, **torque** rear strut clevis brackets to 70 ft. lbs.

TOE

Rear wheel toe must be set prior to setting front wheel toe. Refer to "Front Wheel Alignment" in this section for front and rear wheel toe setting procedures.

TALON

NOTE: Refer To The Rear Of This Manual For Manufacturer's Special Service Tool Supplies.

INDEX OF SERVICE OPERATIONS

Specifications

GENERAL ENGINE SPECIFICATIONS

Year	Engine		Fuel System	Bore and Stroke, Inch	Compression Ratio	Net HP @ RPM ②	Maximum Torque, Ft. Lbs. @ RPM	Minimum Oil Pressure, psi @ RPM
	Liter	VIN①						
1997–98	2.0L④	Y	MFI③	3.44 x 3.27	9.6	140 @ 6000	130 @ 4800	4.0 @ 800
	2.0L⑤	F	MFI③	3.35 x 3.46	8.5	⑥	⑦	11.4 @ 750

① — Eighth digit of VIN denotes engine code.
② — Ratings are net as installed in vehicle.
③ — Multi-Port Fuel Injection.
④ — Non-turbocharged.
⑤ — Turbocharged.
⑥ — 210 @ 6000 w/manual transaxle; 205 @ 6000 w/automatic transaxle.
⑦ — 214 @ 3000 w/manual transaxle; 220 @ 3000 w/automatic transaxle.

TUNE UP SPECIFICATIONS

Year & Engine (VIN Code)①	Spark Plug Gap	Ignition Timing ° BTDC				Curb Idle Speed, RPM		Fast Idle Speed, RPM		Fuel Pump Pressure, psi.	Valve Clearance, inch
		Firing Order Fig.④	Man. Trans.	Auto. Trans.	Mark Fig.	Man. Trans.	Auto Trans.	Man. Trans.	Auto. Trans.		
1997-98											
2.0L (Y)⑧	.050	B	⑥	⑥	A	800②	800②	②	②	47–50③	⑦
2.0L (F)⑤	.030	C	⑥	⑥	A	750②	750②	②	②	42–45⑨	⑦

BTDC — Before Top Dead Center

N — Neutral

① — The eighth digit of the Vehicle Identification Number (VIN) denotes engine code.

② — Controlled by the idle air control motor.

③ — Disconnect fuel pump electrical connector, located at fuel tank. Start engine & operate until it stalls. Disconnect battery ground cable, then connect fuel pump electrical connector. Install suitable fuel pressure gauge to fuel pressure test port on fuel rail. Connect battery, then place ignition switch in the On position & use scan tool to perform fuel system pressure test. Note fuel pressure reading.

④ — Before disconnecting wires from distributor cap, determine location of No. 1 wire in cap, as distributor position may have been altered from that shown at the end of this chart.

⑤ — Turbocharged.

⑥ — Ignition timing is electronically controlled, and is not adjustable.

⑦ — Equipped w/hydraulic lash adjusters. No periodic adjustment is needed.

⑧ — Non-turbocharged.

⑨ — Disconnect fuel pump electrical connector, located at fuel tank. Start engine & operate until it stalls. Disconnect battery ground cable, then reconnect fuel pump electrical connector. Place shop towels around fuel high pressure hose at fuel delivery pipe side, then disconnect hose. Install suitable fuel pressure gauge between fuel delivery pipe & high pressure hose. Disconnect & plug vacuum hose from fuel pressure regulator. Connect battery ground cable & inspect fuel pressure w/engine idling.

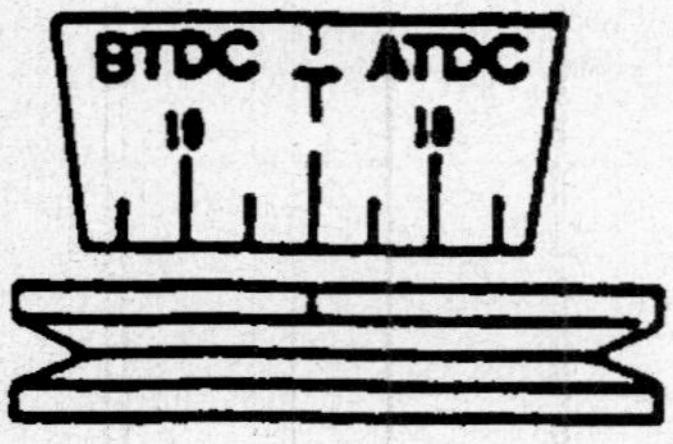

CR1139000316000X

Fig. A

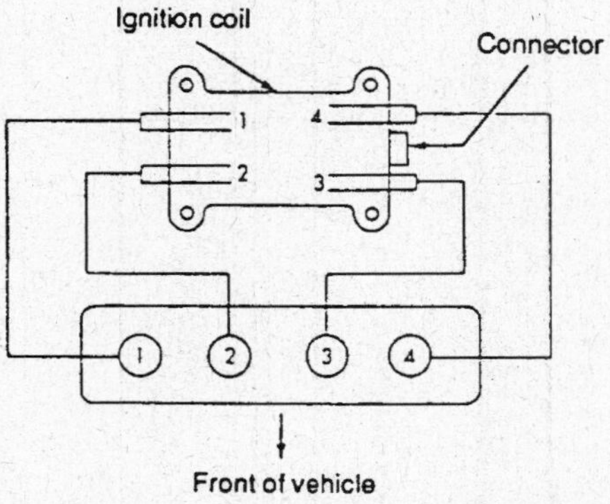

CR1139500475000X

Fig. B

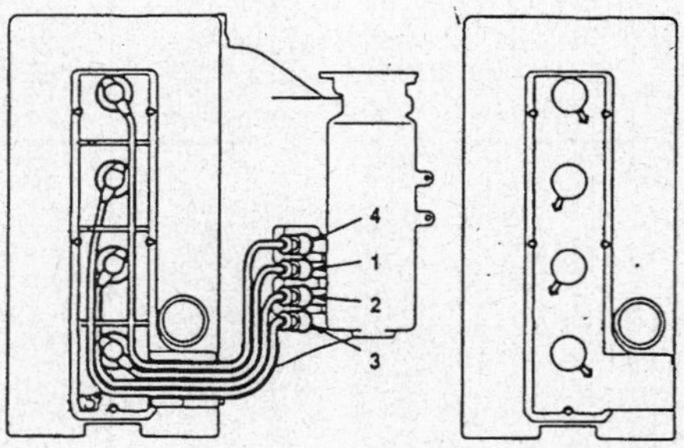

CR1139500476000X

Fig. C

FRONT WHEEL ALIGNMENT SPECIFICATIONS

Year	Model	Camber Angle, Degrees②		Caster Angle, Degrees②		Toe In, Inch	Ball Joint Wear
		Limits	Desired	Limits	Desired		
1997	③	-5/6 to +1/6	-1/3	+3 1/6 to +6 1/6	+4 2/3	0④	①
	⑨	-7/12 to +5/12	-1/12	+3 1/6 to +6 1/6	+4 2/3	0④	①
1998	③	-5/6 to +1/6	-1/3	+3 1/6 to +6 1/6	+4 2/3	0④	①
	⑤	-7/12 to +5/12	-1/12	+3 1/6 to +6 1/6	+4 2/3	0④	①

① — Ball joint breakaway torque for the compression lower arm ball joint should be 4–22 inch lbs. Ball joint breakaway torque for the lateral lower arm ball joint should be 9–30 inch lbs. when under a load of 838 lbs.
② — Reference angle only. Non adjustable.
③ — FWD models & models w/16 inch wheels.
④ — Plus or minus .12 inch.
⑤ — AWD models & models w/14 inch wheels.

REAR WHEEL ALIGNMENT SPECIFICATIONS

Year	Model	Camber Angle, Degrees		Toe In, Inch	Ball Joint Wear
		Limits	Desired		
1997	②	-1 5/6 to -5/6①	-1 1/3①	.12⑤	③
	④	-2 1/6 to -1 1/6	-1 2/3①	.12⑤	③
1998	②	-1 5/6 to -5/6①	-1 1/3①	.12⑤	③
	④	-2 1/6 to -1 1/6	-1 2/3①	.12⑤	③

① — Reference angle only. Non adjustable.
② — FWD models w/14 inch wheels & AWD models.
③ — Ball joint breakaway torque for the lower arm and toe control ball joints should be 1–23 inch lbs. Ball joint breakaway torque for the stabilizer link ball joint should be 4–13 inch lbs.
④ — FWD models w/16 inch wheels.
⑤ — Plus or minus .12 inch.

FLUID CAPACITIES & COOLING SYSTEM DATA

Year	Liter	VIN Code	Coolant Capacity, Qts.	Radiator Cap Relief Pressure, Lbs.	Thermo. Opening Temp., °F	Fuel Tank, Gals.	Engine Oil Refill, Qts.	Transaxle Oil		Rear Axle, Pts.
								5 Speed, Pts.	Auto. Trans., Qts.①	
1997-98	2.0L⑤	Y	7.4	16	195	15.9	4.0③	4.2	9.1	—
	2.0L②	F	7.4	13	180	15.9	4.2④	4.6⑥	7.1⑥	1.8

① — Approximate. Make final inspection w/dipstick.
② — Turbocharged engine.
③ — With filter change add .5 qt.
④ — With filter change add .5 qt. Oil cooler capacity, .5 qt.
⑤ — Non-turbocharged engine.
⑥ — Transfer, .63 qts.

LUBRICANT DATA

Year	Model	Lubricant Type					
		Transaxle		Transfer Case	Rear Axle	Power Steering	Brake System
		Manual	Automatic				
1997–98	All	③	①	75W–90 API GL-4	80W–90 API GL-5	②	DOT 3 or 4

① — Mopar ATF type 7176, Dia. ATF SP or equivalent.
② — Mopar ATF type 7176, Dia. ATF SP, Dexron or Dexron II.
③ — Non-turbocharged, Mopar MS9417 MTX fluid, or equivalent; turbocharged, 75W-90 GL-4, or 75W–85W GL-4.

Electrical

NOTE: On Air Bag Equipped Models, Refer To " Air Bag System Precautions" Located In The Front Of This Manual For System Disarming & Arming Procedures.

NOTE: Refer To "Computer Relearn Procedure " Located In The Front Of This Manual For Computer Relearn Procedures.

INDEX

PRECAUTIONS

AIR BAG SYSTEMS

Refer to "Air Bag System Precautions" in the front of this manual for system disarming and arming procedures.

BATTERY GROUND CABLE

Prior to service, disconnect battery ground cable and isolate as required.

FUSE PANEL & FLASHER LOCATION

The multi-purpose fuse panel and dedicated fuse panel are located under the driver's side instrument panel.

The hazard and turn signal flasher are located behind the center console.

On non-turbocharged models, the No. 1–12 dedicated fuse panel/power distribution block is located in the front lefthand side of the engine compartment.

On turbocharged models, the No. 1–12 dedicated fuse panel/power distribution block is located in the righthand side of the engine compartment.

On all models, the No. 13 dedicated fuse is located in the interior relay box under the driver's side instrument panel.

FUEL PUMP RELAY LOCATION

NON-TURBOCHARGED ENGINE

The fuel pump relay is located in the LH rear corner of the engine compartment.

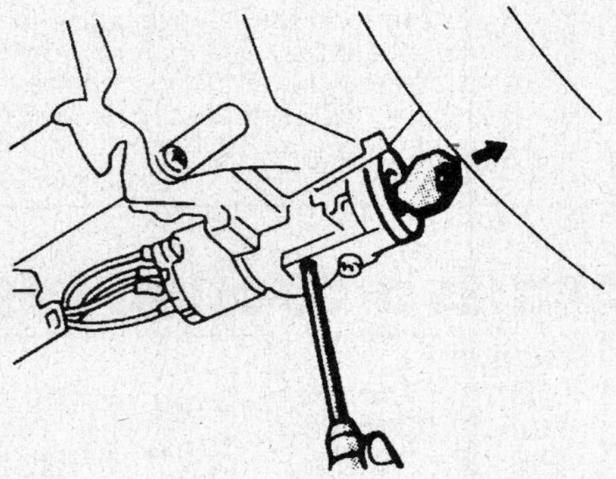

CR9129100008000X

Fig. 1 Ignition lock release

TURBOCHARGED ENGINE

The fuel pump relay is located behind the center dash panel.

STARTER

REPLACE

1. Raise and support vehicle.
2. **On non-turbocharged models with manual transmission,** remove aspirator assembly.
3. **On turbocharged models,** remove air hose.
4. **On all models,** remove starter terminal and connector.
5. Remove starter.
6. Reverse procedure to install.

DISTRIBUTOR

REPLACE

2.0L ENGINE

This engine uses a direct ignition system (DIS), with a coil pack rather than a distributor. Refer to "Coil Pack Replace" for replacement procedure.

COIL PACK

REPLACE

2.0L ENGINE

1. **On turbocharged models,** remove center cover.
2. **On all models,** disconnect spark plug cables from ignition coil. **Label cables for installation reference.**
3. Remove coil pack mounting screws, then the coil pack.
4. Reverse procedure to install.

IGNITION LOCK

REPLACE

1. Remove upper and lower steering column covers.
2. Insert key in steering lock cylinder, then turn to Accessory position.
3. Using suitable screwdriver, push lockpin, **Fig. 1,** of steering lock cylinder inward and pull lock cylinder out of housing.
4. Reverse procedure to install.

IGNITION SWITCH

REPLACE

1. Remove instrument panel undercover, **Fig. 2.**

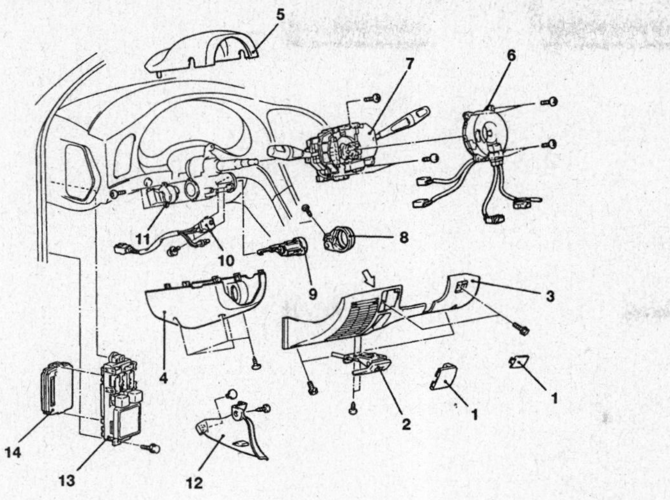

Steering lock cylinder removal steps

1. Plug
2. Hood lock release handle
3. Instrument under cover
4. Column cover lower
5. Column cover upper
6. Clock spring
7. Column switch
8. Ignition key illumination ring or ring cover
9. Steering lock cylinder

Key reminder switch segment or key hole illumination light removal steps

4. Column cover lower
5. Column cover upper
10. Key reminder switch segment or key hole illumination light

Ignition switch segment removal steps

4. Column cover lower
5. Column cover upper
11. Ignition switch segment

ETACS-ECU removal steps

12. Cowl side trim (L.H.)
13. Junction block
14. ETACS-ECU

CR9049500067000X

Fig. 2 Ignition switch removal

2. Remove upper and lower column covers.
3. Disconnect ignition switch wiring connector.
4. Remove ignition switch.
5. Reverse procedure to install.

HEADLAMP SWITCH

REPLACE

Refer to "Combination Switch, Replace" for procedure.

COMBINATION SWITCH

REPLACE

1. Remove air bag module as described under "Air Bag System."
2. Remove steering wheel as described under "Steering Wheel, Replace."
3. Remove column switch in numbered sequence, **Fig. 2.**
4. Reverse procedure to install.

DIMMER SWITCH

REPLACE

Refer to "Combination Switch, Replace" for procedure.

STEERING WHEEL

REPLACE

1. Remove air bag module as described under "Air Bag System."
2. Remove steering wheel attaching bolt, **Fig. 3.**
3. Remove steering wheel using suitable wheel puller. **Do not use hammer as this may damage the collapsible mechanism.**
4. Reverse procedure to install.

INSTRUMENT CLUSTER

REPLACE

1. Remove instrument cluster bezel.
2. Remove screws holding cluster to dash.
3. Gently pull cluster outward enough to remove connectors and clips from rear of cluster, allowing it to be removed.
4. Reverse procedure to install.

RADIO

REPLACE

1. Use suitable plastic trim tool to pry lower part of radio panel out of console.
2. Remove floor console assembly.
3. Remove radio bracket.
4. Gently pull outward on radio assembly enough to remove connectors from rear of unit.
5. Reverse procedure to install.

WIPER MOTOR

REPLACE

FRONT

Remove front windshield wiper motor and transmission in numbered sequence, **Fig. 4,** noting the following:

1. Mark position of wiper arms before removal.
2. Reverse procedure to install.

REAR

Remove rear windshield wiper motor and transmission in numbered sequence, **Fig. 5,** noting the following:

1. Mark position of wiper arm before removal.
2. Reverse procedure to install

WIPER TRANSMISSION

REPLACE

Refer to "Wiper Motor, Replace" for procedure.

BLOWER MOTOR

REPLACE

Remove blower motor in numbered sequence, **Fig. 6,** noting the following:

1. Clean blower case before installation.
2. Reverse procedure to install.

HEATER CORE

REPLACE

Remove heater unit in numbered sequence, **Fig. 7,** noting the following:

1. Drain engine coolant.
2. Remove instrument panel as outlined in the "Dash Panel Service" section.
3. Reverse procedure to install. Fill up engine coolant.

EVAPORATOR CORE

REPLACE

Remove evaporator unit in numbered sequence, **Figs. 8 and 9,** noting the following:

1. Properly recover refrigerant from A/C system as described in the "Air Conditioning" section.
2. Plug refrigerant lines to prevent air from mixing when disconnecting them.
3. **On non-turbocharged models,** refill evaporator with 1.35 fl. oz. ND-OIL 8 compressor oil, or equivalent, before replacing evaporator.
4. **On turbocharged models,** refill evaporator with 2.03 fl. oz. SUN PAG 56 compressor oil, or equivalent, before replacing evaporator.
5. **On all models,** reverse procedure to install. Be sure A/C system is properly charged as described in the " Air Conditioning" section.

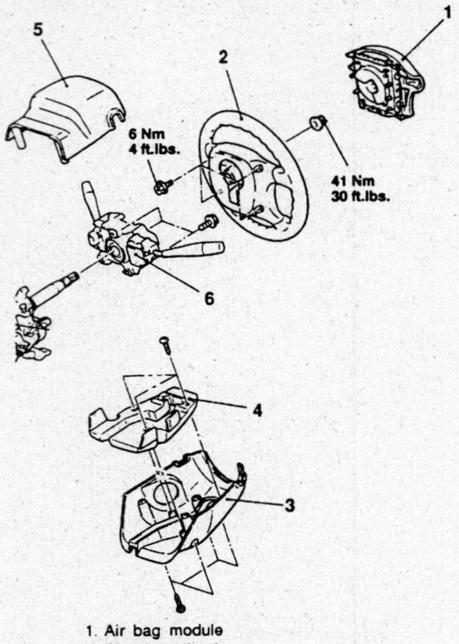

1. Air bag module
2. Steering wheel
3. Lower column cover
4. Column pad
5. Upper column cover
6. Clock spring and column switch assembly

CR6049500104000X

Fig. 3 Steering wheel removal

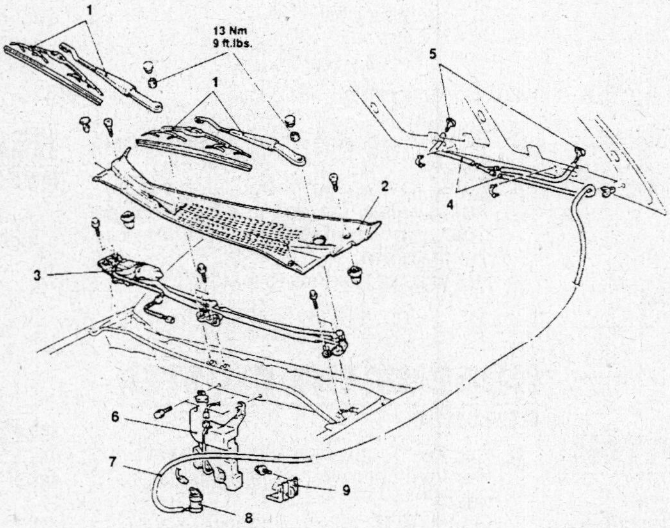

Motor and link assembly removal steps

1. Wiper arm and blade assembly
2. Front deck garnish
3. Motor and link assembly

Washer nozzle removal steps

4. Washer hose connection
5. Washer nozzle

Washer tank removal steps

6. Windshield washer tank
7. Washer hose
8. Washer motor
9. Washer tank bracket

CR9029500132000X

Fig. 4 Front wiper motor & transmission replacement

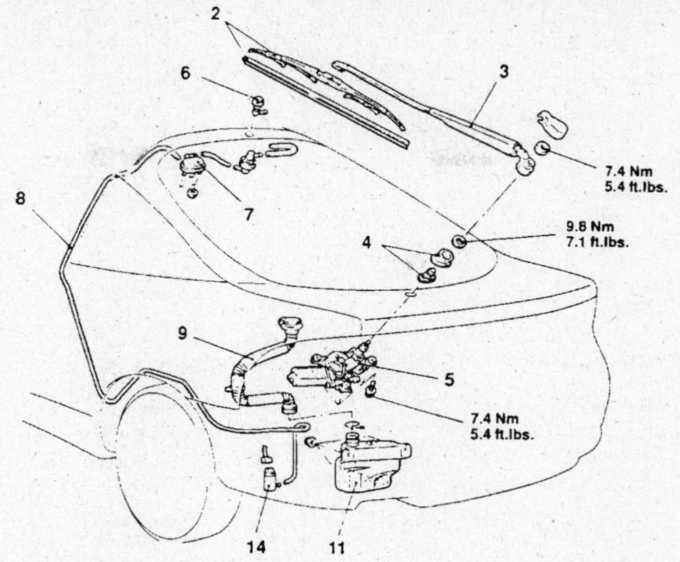

Rear wiper motor removal steps

2. Wiper blade
3. Wiper arm
4. Spacer assembly
• Liftgate lower trim

5. Rear wiper motor

Rear washer tank and hose removal steps

• Quarter upper trim (LH)
• Quarter lower trim (LH)
• Rear end trim
• Rear side trim
• Liftgate upper trim
6. Washer nozzle
7. Joint assembly
8. Tube assembly
9. Hose assembly
11. Rear washer tank
14. Rear washer motor

CR9029500133000X

Fig. 5 Rear wiper motor & transmission replacement

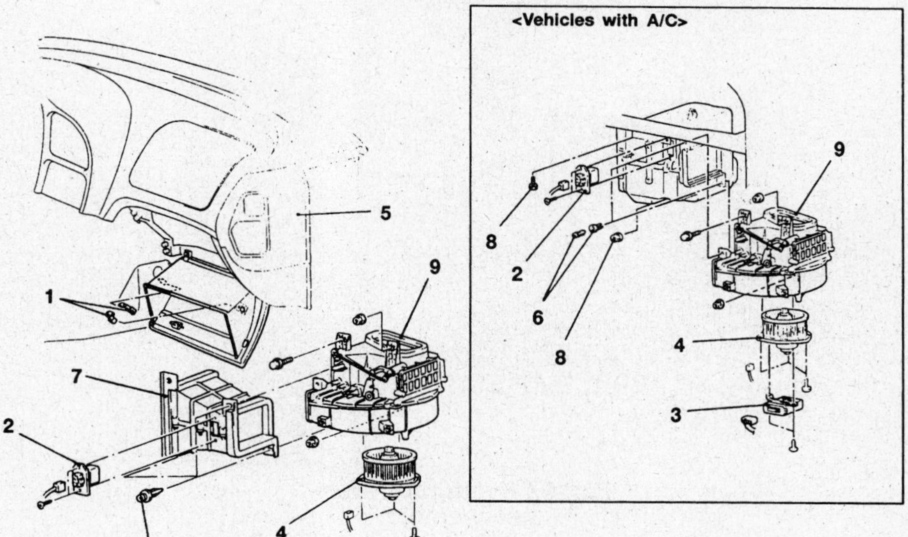

Resistor removal steps

1. Stopper
2. Resistor

Blower fan and motor removal steps

3. Automatic compressor – ECM <Vehicles with A/C for non-turbo>
4. Blower fan and motor

Blower unit removal steps

5. Instrument panel
6. Clip
7. Joint duct <Vehicles without A/C>
8. Cooling unit installation bolts and nuts <Vehicles with A/C>
9. Blower unit assembly

CR7029500230000X

Fig. 6 Blower motor replacement

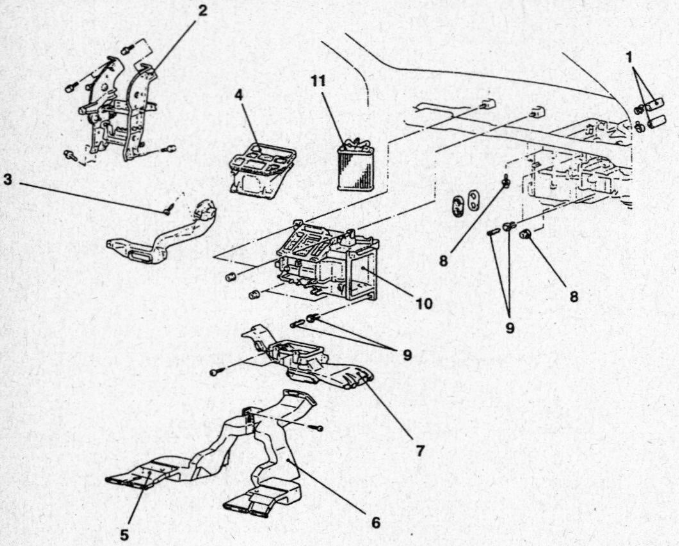

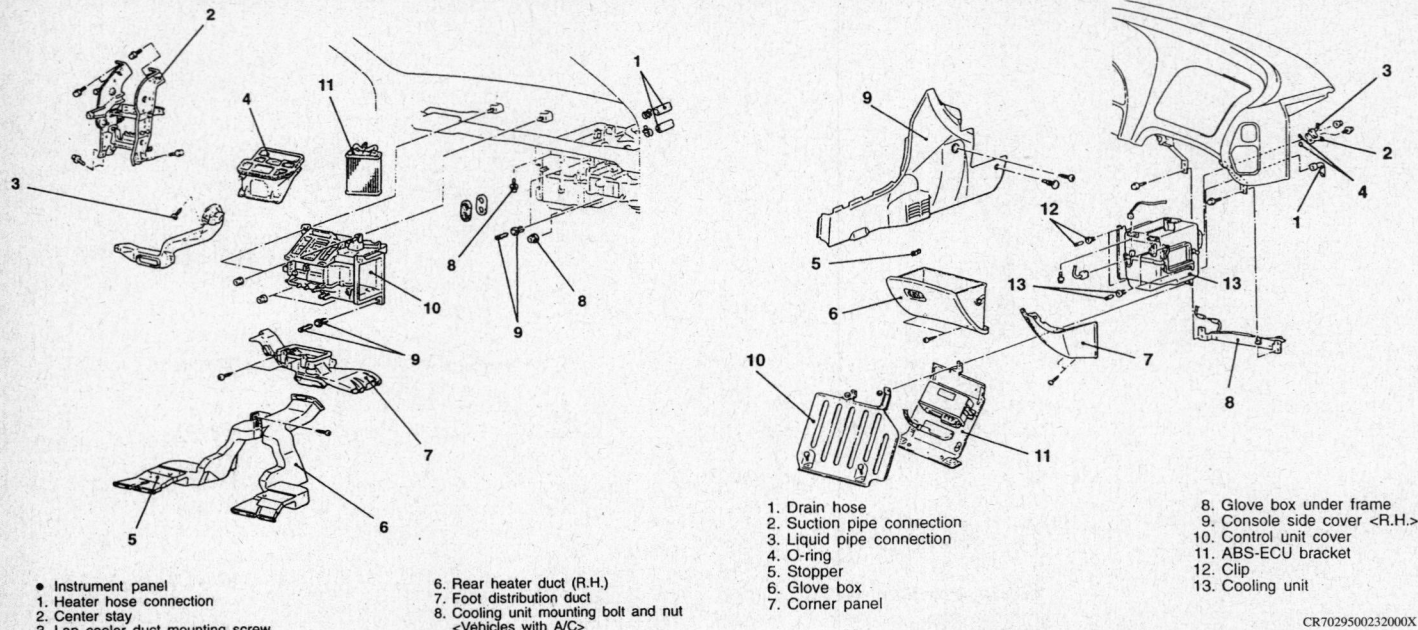

- Instrument panel
1. Heater hose connection
2. Center stay
3. Lap cooler duct mounting screw
4. Center duct
5. Rear heater duct (L.H.)
6. Rear heater duct (R.H.)
7. Foot distribution duct
8. Cooling unit mounting bolt and nut <Vehicles with A/C>
9. Clip
10. Heater unit
11. Heater core

CR7029500231000X

Fig. 7 Heater unit removal

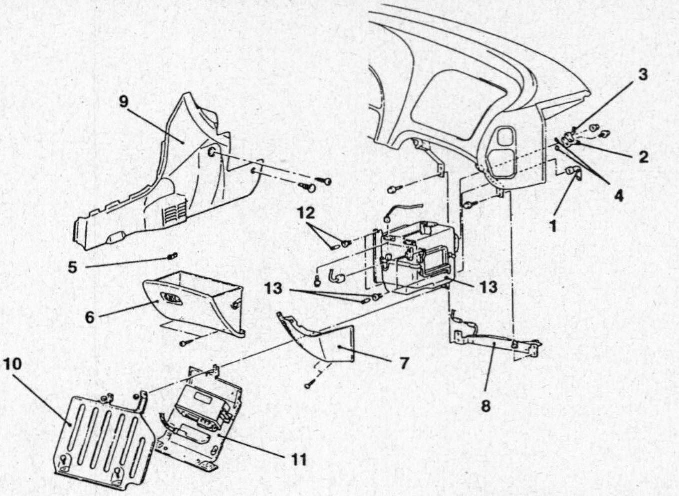

1. Drain hose
2. Suction pipe connection
3. Liquid pipe connection
4. O-ring
5. Stopper
6. Glove box
7. Corner panel
8. Glove box under frame
9. Console side cover <R.H.>
10. Control unit cover
11. ABS-ECU bracket
12. Clip
13. Cooling unit

CR7029500232000X

Fig. 8 Evaporator replacement

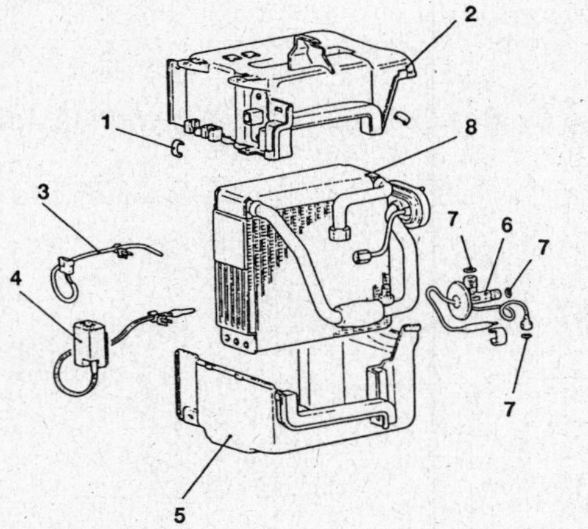

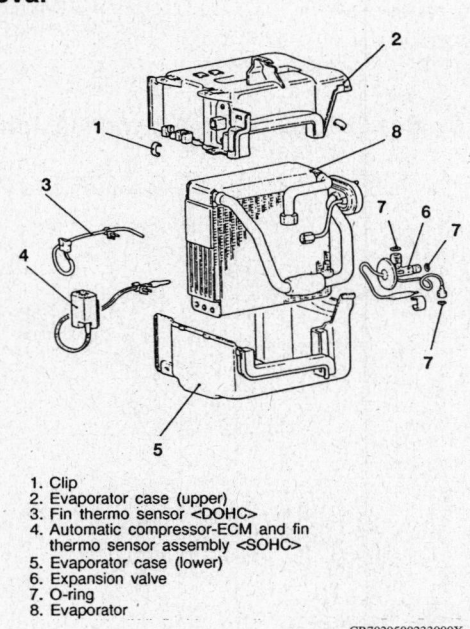

1. Clip
2. Evaporator case (upper)
3. Fin thermo sensor <DOHC>
4. Automatic compressor-ECM and fin thermo sensor assembly <SOHC>
5. Evaporator case (lower)
6. Expansion valve
7. O-ring
8. Evaporator

CR7029500233000X

Fig. 9 Evaporator unit disassemble

2.0L Engine

NOTE: Refer To "Computer Relearn Procedure " Located In The Front Of This Manual For Computer Relearn Procedures.

INDEX

PRECAUTIONS

FUEL SYSTEM PRESSURE RELIEF

1. Disconnect fuel pump harness connector at fuel tank.
2. Start engine and let it run until it stalls, then turn ignition switch to off.
3. Reconnect fuel pump harness connector.

BATTERY GROUND CABLE

Prior to service, disconnect battery ground cable and isolate as required.

COMPRESSION PRESSURE

Refer to **Fig. 1** for compression pressure data.

Year	Engine	Compression Pressure, psi①	Minimum Pressure, psi	Max. Variation Between Cylinders, psi
1997–98	2.0L②	170-225	100	④
	2.0L③	178	133	14

① — At 250–400 psi.
② — Non-turbocharged engine.
③ — Turbocharged engine.
④ — 25 maximum variation between cylinders.

Fig. 1 Compression pressure data

ENGINE MOUNT

REPLACE

UPPER MOUNT

Remove engine mount in numbered sequence, **Fig. 2,** noting the following:

1. Slightly raise and support engine, removing weight of engine from mount.
2. Inspect insulators for damage or cracks and replace as necessary.
3. Inspect brackets and replace if deformed or damaged.
4. When installing mounting stoppers, ensure arrow on stopper faces center of engine, **Fig. 3.**
5. Reverse procedure to install. Tighten to specifications.

ENGINE ROLL STOPPER

Remove engine roll stoppers in numbered sequence, **Fig. 4,** noting the following:

1. Slightly raise and support engine, removing weight of engine from mount.
2. Inspect insulators for damage or cracks and replace as necessary.
3. Inspect brackets and replace if deformed or damaged.
4. Inspect front roll stopper bracket assembly. If the dimension shown in **Fig. 5** is not 1.57–1.81 inches when the weight of the engine is on the body, replace the front roll stopper assembly.
5. When installing mounting stoppers, ensure arrow on stopper faces center of engine, **Fig. 3.**
6. Reverse procedure to install. Tighten to specifications.

ENGINE

REPLACE

1. Relieve fuel pressure as outlined

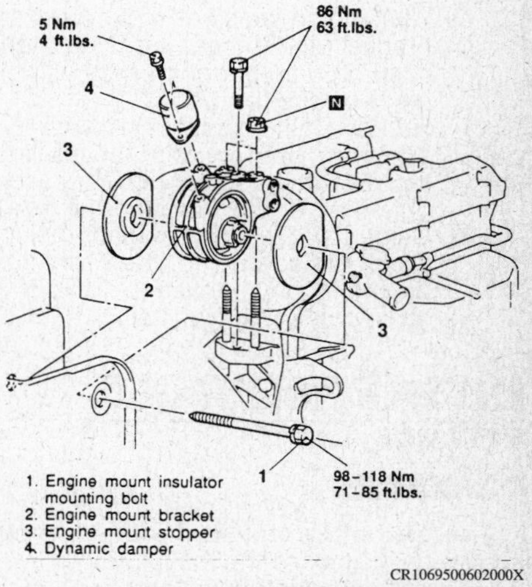

Fig. 2 Engine upper mount replacement

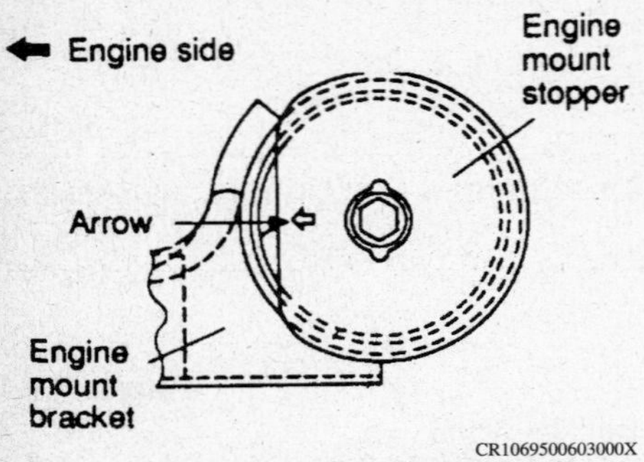

Fig. 3 Engine mount stopper installation

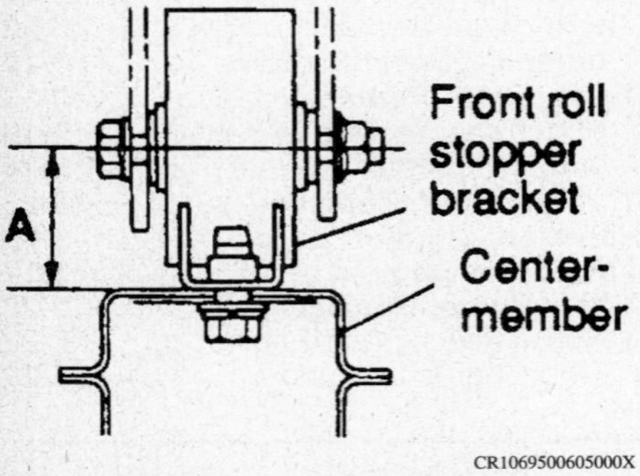

Fig. 5 Front roll stopper clearance

under "Precautions."
2. Remove hood.
3. Drain coolant into a suitable container as follows:
   a. Place instrument panel temperature control lever in Hot position.
   b. Carefully remove radiator cap.
   c. Remove radiator drain plug.
4. Remove transaxle assembly.
5. Remove radiator as outlined under "Radiator, Replace."
6. Remove engine in numbered sequence, **Figs. 6 and 7,** noting the following:
   a. Remove power steering pump from bracket with hoses attached, then secure pump out of the way with a piece of wire.
   b. Remove air conditioner compressor from bracket with hoses attached, then secure compressor out of the way with a piece of wire.
   c. Using a suitable engine hoist, slightly raise engine, then remove engine mount bracket.
7. Reverse procedure to install.

INTAKE MANIFOLD

REPLACE

REMOVAL

Remove intake manifold in numbered sequence, **Fig. 8,** noting the following:

1. Drain coolant into a suitable container as follows:
   a. Place instrument panel temperature control lever in Hot position.
   b. Carefully remove radiator cap.
   c. Remove radiator drain plug.

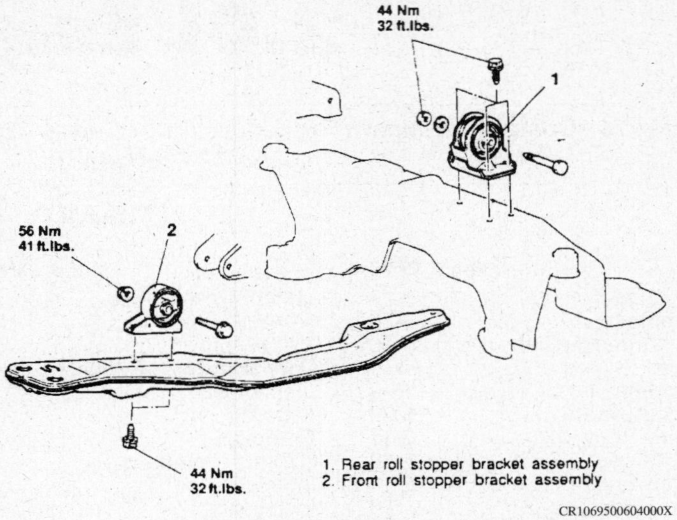

Fig. 4 Engine roll stopper replacement

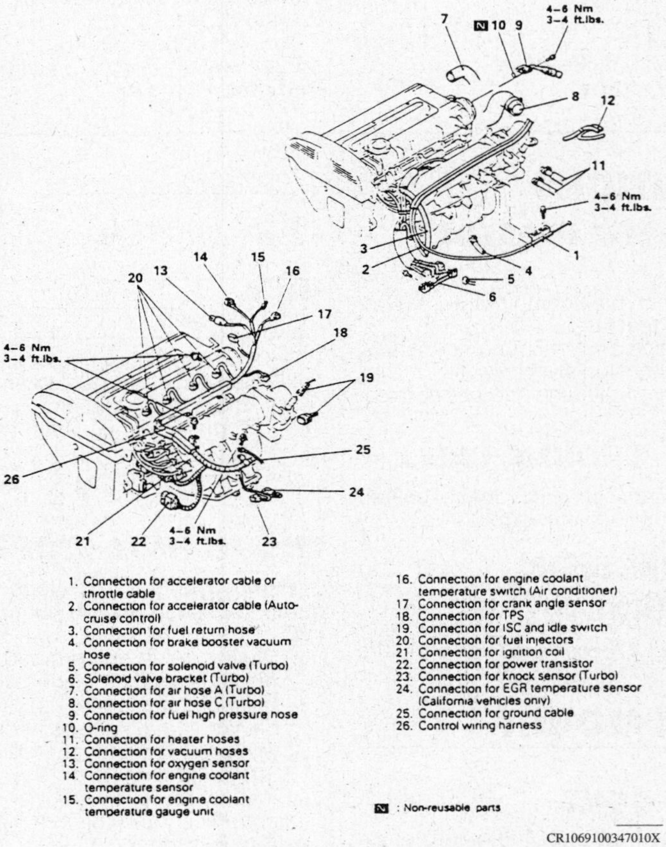

Fig. 6 Engine replacement (Part 1 of 2). Non-turbocharged engine

2. Before disconnecting high pressure fuel line, release fuel pressure as outlined under "Precautions."
3. Remove delivery pipe, fuel injector and regulator as an assembly.

INSPECTION

Inspect intake manifold and air intake plenum (if equipped) as follows:

1. Inspect for damage, cracks or defects.
2. Ensure coolant and jet air passages are clear.
3. Inspect installation surfaces with a straightedge. Replace if deflection exceeds .012 inch.

INSTALLATION

Reverse removal procedure to install. When installing throttle body, refer to bolt length chart, **Fig. 9.**

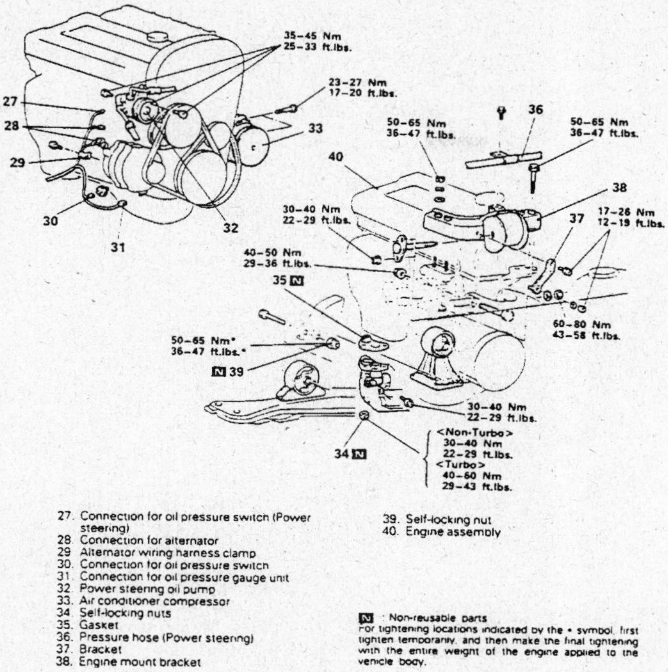

Fig. 6 Engine replacement (Part 2 of 2). Non-turbocharged engine

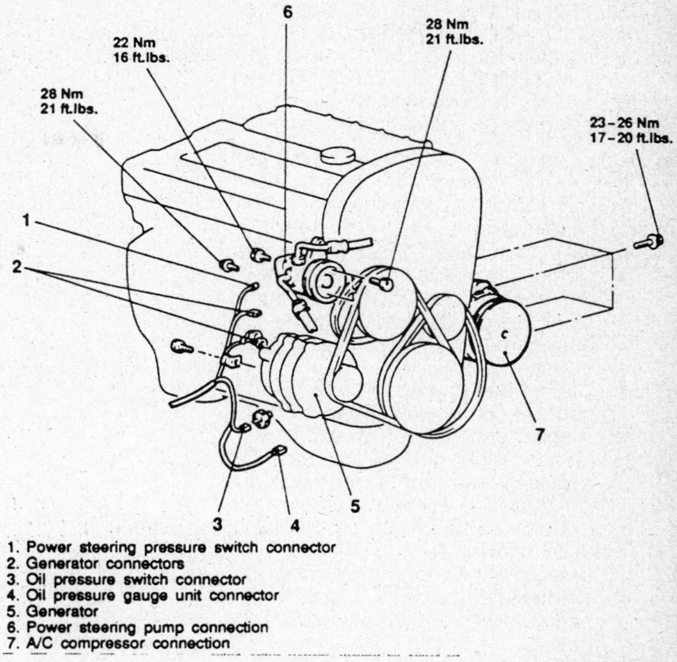

Fig. 7 Engine replacement (Part 1 of 2). Turbocharged engine

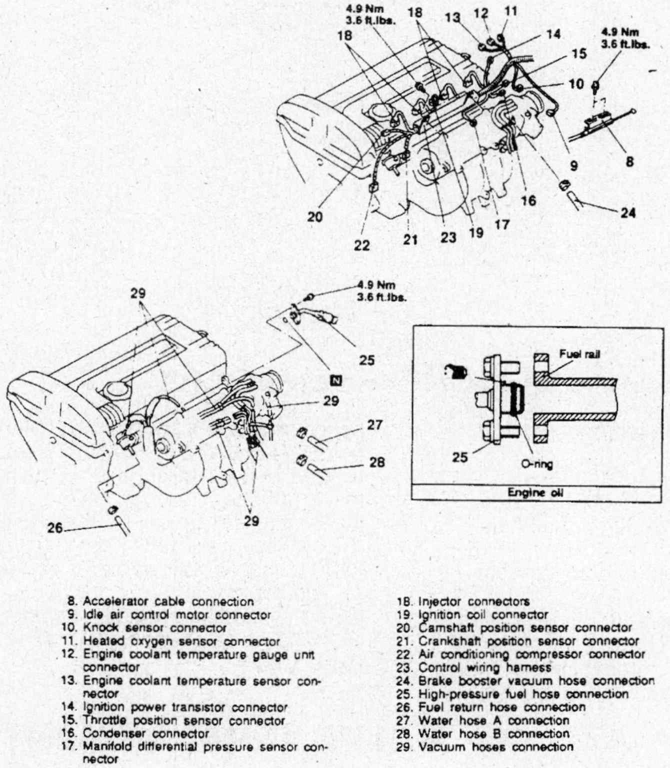

Fig. 7 Engine replacement (Part 2 of 2). Turbocharged engine

EXHAUST MANIFOLD

REPLACE

Remove exhaust manifold in numbered sequence, referring to **Figs. 10 and 11,** noting the following:

1. **On turbocharged models,** drain engine oil and coolant prior to removing exhaust manifold. To drain coolant into a suitable container, proceed as follows:
   a. Place instrument panel temperature control lever in Hot position.
   b. Carefully remove radiator cap.
   c. Remove radiator drain plug.
2. **On all models,** use oxygen sensor socket tool No. MD998703, or equivalent, to remove oxygen sensor.
3. **On turbocharged models,** leave power steering hoses attached when disconnecting power steering pump. Position pump out of the way and secure with a piece of wire.
4. **On all models,** reverse procedure to install. On turbocharged engine, apply machine oil to inner surface pipe flare prior to installing water pipe (18), **Fig. 11.**

CYLINDER HEAD

REPLACE

TURBOCHARGED ENGINE

Removal

Remove cylinder head in numbered sequence, **Fig. 12,** noting the following:

1. Before disconnecting high pressure fuel line, release fuel pressure as outlined under "Precautions."
2. Before removing upper radiator hose, mark hose clamp in relation to hose for assembly reference, then drain coolant into a suitable container as follows:
   a. Place instrument panel temperature control lever in Hot position.
   b. Carefully remove radiator cap.
   c. Remove radiator drain plug.

3. Remove timing belt as described under "Timing Belt, Replace."
4. Using cylinder head bolt wrench tool No. MD998051, or MB991654, or equivalent, remove cylinder head bolts in sequence as shown in **Fig. 13.**

Installation

Reverse removal procedure to install, noting the following:

1. Install cylinder head gasket as follows:
   a. Using a suitable scraper, remove old gasket material from cylinder block, using care not to allow old gasket material to fall into cylinder or passages.
   b. Clean head and block surfaces that come in contact with head gasket.
   c. Place head gasket on block with identification mark at top front. **Do not apply sealant to head gasket.**
2. When installing cylinder head, install head bolt washers, then tighten head bolts as follows:
   a. Inspect shank length of each bolt before installation. If shank length exceeds 3.91 inch, then replace the bolt.
   b. **Torque** bolts to 58 ft. lbs. in order shown in **Fig. 14.**
   c. Fully loosen bolts in order shown in **Fig. 13.**
   d. **Torque** bolts to 14–15 ft. lbs. in order shown in **Fig. 14,** then tighten in sequence an additional 180° in 90° increments.
3. When installing semi-circular packing, apply liberal amount of gasket sealant onto circumference of packing.
4. When installing rocker cover, apply gasket sealant to area as shown in **Fig. 15.**
5. Install timing belt as described under "Timing Belt, Replace."
6. When installing high pressure fuel line (5), apply small amount of gasoline to hose union. Use care to avoid damaging O-ring.

NON-TURBOCHARGED ENGINE

1. Relieve fuel system pressure as described under " Precautions."
2. Drain engine coolant, then drain crankcase.
3. Disconnect electrical connectors from A/C compressor clutch, power steering pump switch, oxygen sensor, engine coolant temperature switch and sensor, MAP sensor and intake air temperature sensor.
4. Disconnect accelerator cable.
5. Disconnect TPS, IAC motor and injector harness electrical connectors.
6. Disconnect ignition coil, camshaft position sensor and EGR solenoid electrical connectors.
7. Disconnect heater hose, upper radiator hose, overflow tube and water hose connection. **Mark relationship between radiator hose and clamp for installation reference.**
8. Disconnect fuel high pressure and return hoses.
9. Disconnect purge air hose.

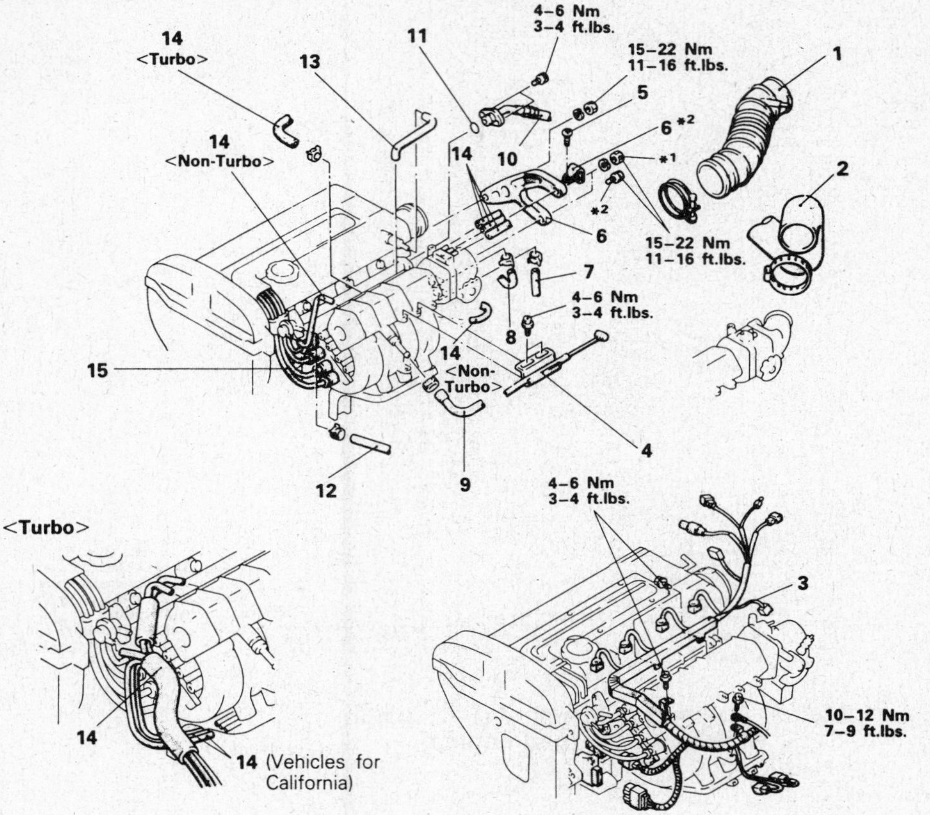

1. Air intake hose <Non-Turbo>
2. Air hose C <Turbo>
3. Connection for control harness
4. Connection for accelerator cable
5. Ground plate installation screw
6. Throttle body stay and ground plate
7. Connection for water by-pass hose
8. Connection for water hose
9. Connection for brake booster vacuum hose
10. Connection for fuel high pressure hose
11. O-ring
12. Connection for fuel return hose
13. Connection for PCV hose
14. Connection for vacuum hoses
15. Connection for spark plug cable

(4) *1: <Non-Turbo>
(5) *2: <Turbo>

CR1059100061010X

Fig. 8 Intake manifold replacement (Part 1 of 2)

10. Disconnect power brake booster vacuum hose connection.
11. Remove intake manifold stay.
12. Remove intake and exhaust camshafts as described under " Camshaft, Replace."
13. Disconnect exhaust pipe from exhaust manifold.
14. Remove cylinder head attaching bolts, then remove cylinder head and gasket. After cylinder head removal, remove intake and exhaust manifold as necessary.
15. Reverse procedure to install, noting the following:
    a. Prior to installation, inspect cylinder head bolts for stretching by placing a straightedge against bolt threads. If all threads do not contact straightedge, replace bolt.
    b. Clean bolt threads and lubricate with clean engine oil.
    c. Tighten cylinder head bolts in sequence shown in **Fig. 16. Torque** bolts 1 through 6 to 25 ft. lbs., and bolts 7 through 10 to 20 ft. lbs. Next, **torque** bolts 1 through 6 to 50 ft. lbs. and bolts 7 through 10 to 20 ft. lbs. Again, **torque** bolts 1 through 6 to 50 ft. lbs., then bolts 7 through 10 to 20 ft. lbs. Finally, tighten all bolts an additional 90.°
    d. When installing radiator hoses, align marks on clamps and respective hoses.

VALVE ARRANGEMENT

Intake valves are on the righthand side of the engine. The exhaust valves are on the lefthand side of the engine.

VALVE ADJUSTMENT

Hydraulic lash adjusters are used. No periodic adjustment is necessary.

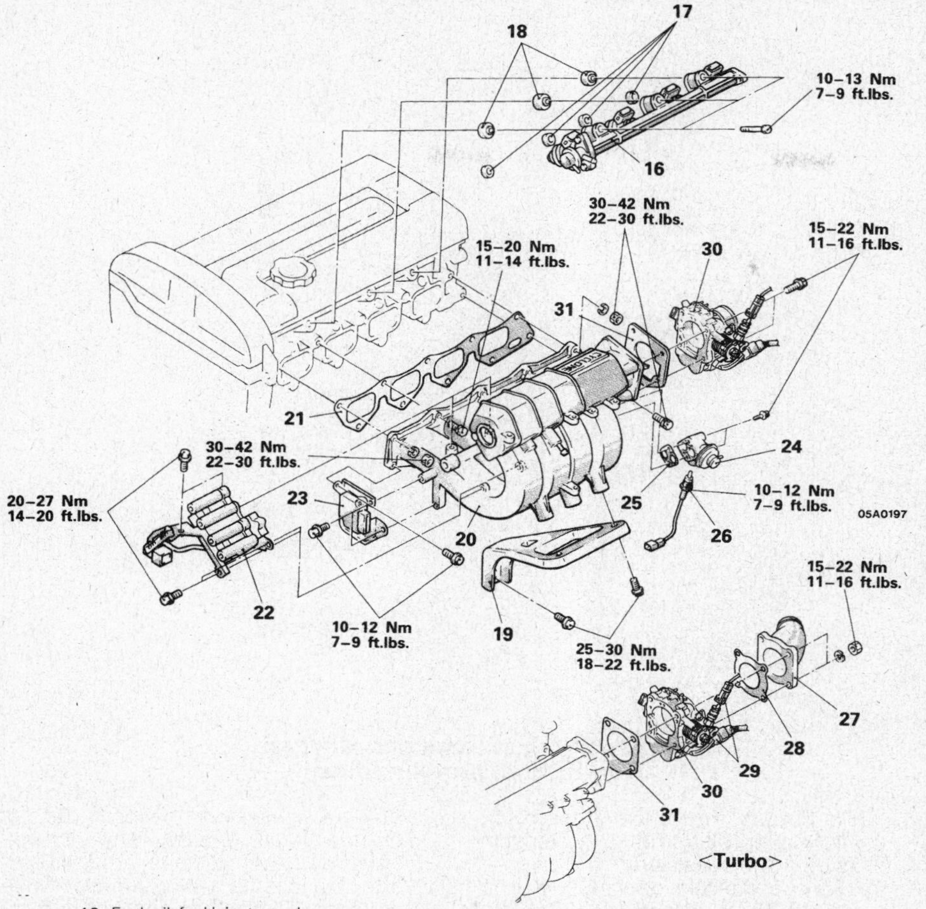

16. Fuel rail, fuel injector and pressure regulator
17. Insulator
18. Insulator
19. Intake manifold stay
20. Intake manifold
21. Intake manifold gasket
22. Ignition coil
23. Ignition power transistor unit
24. EGR valve
25. Gasket
26. EGR temperature sensor <Vehicles for California>
27. Air fitting <Turbo>
28. Gasket <Turbo>
29. Connection for control harness
30. Throttle body
31. Gasket

CR1059100061020X

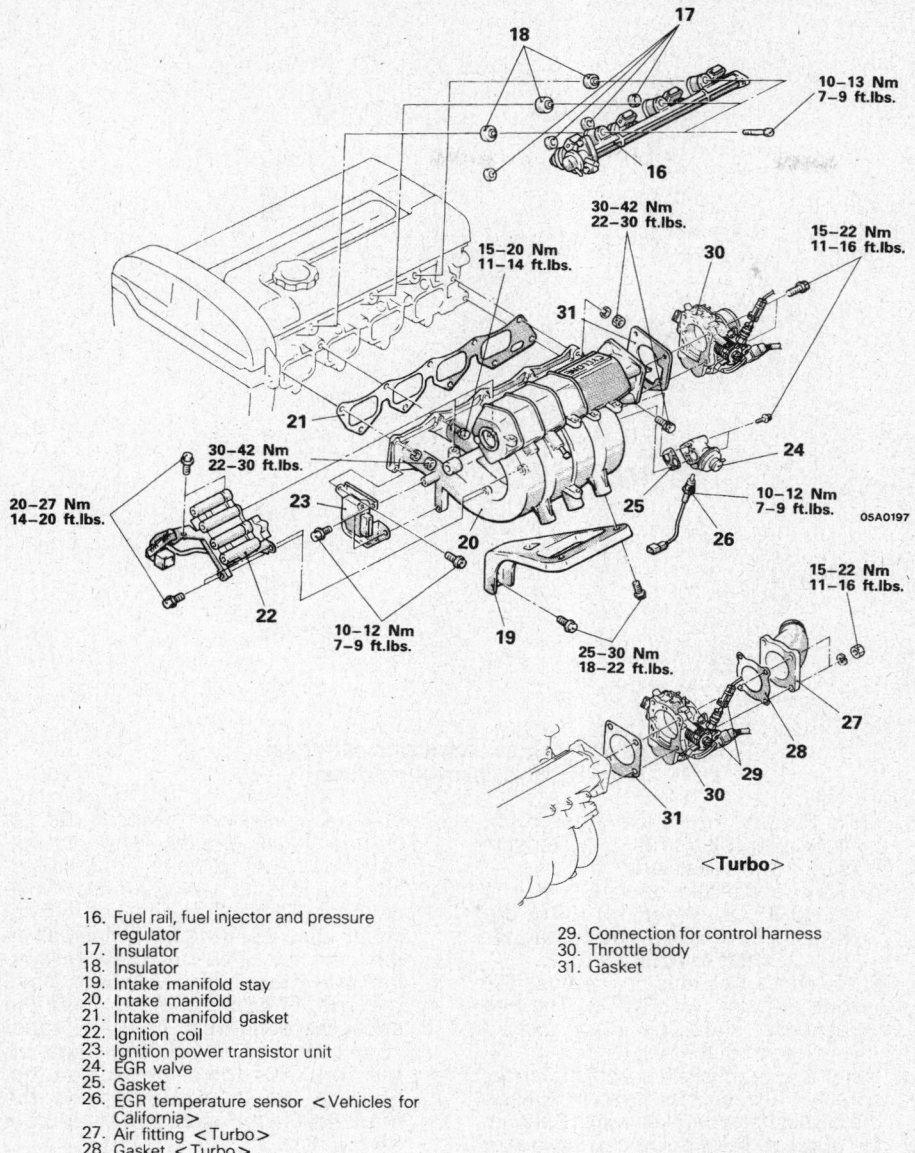

Fig. 8 Intake manifold replacement (Part 2 of 2)

ROCKER ARMS

Refer to "Camshaft, Replace" for rocker arm and rocker arm shaft replacement procedures.

TIMING BELT

REPLACE

NON-TURBOCHARGED ENGINE

With the timing belt removed, avoid turning the camshaft or crankshaft. If movement is required, exercise extreme caution to avoid valve damage caused by piston contact.

1. Remove the cooling system reserve tank.
2. Remove the under cover.
3. Remove the A/C compressor and power steering pump drive belt.
4. Remove the alternator drive belt.
5. Remove the crankshaft pulley.
6. Remove the power steering pump from the bracket with the hoses attached and position out of way.
7. Support engine by positioning a suitable jack and wooden block under the engine oil pan.
8. Remove the engine mount bracket assembly, **Fig.17**
9. Remove the timing belt front cover.
10. Align the camshaft and crankshaft sprocket timing marks, **Fig. 18.**
11. Loosen the timing belt tensioner, then remove the timing belt.
12. Remove the timing belt tensioner.
13. Position the timing belt tensioner in a soft jawed vise, then carefully compress the plunger. After the plunger has been compressed, insert a pin through the tensioner body to hold the plunger in place, **Fig. 19.**
14. Ensure the crankshaft sprocket mark

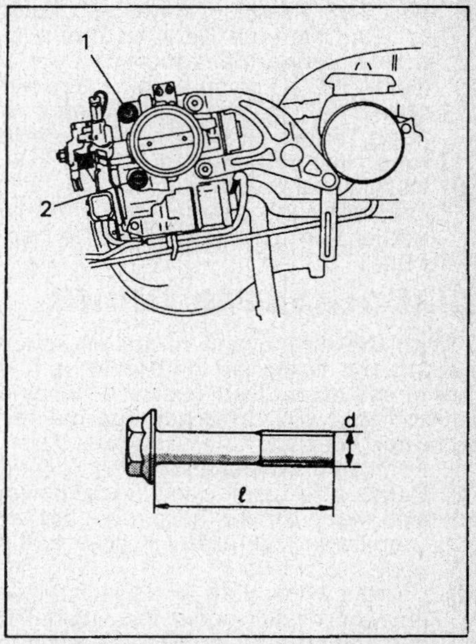

No.	d × ℓ mm (in.)
1	8 × 30 (.31 × 1.18)
2	8 × 55 (.31 × 2.16)

CR1059100062000X

Fig. 9 Throttle body attaching bolts

is aligned with mark on oil pump housing and the camshaft timing marks are aligned, **Fig. 18.**

15. Move the crankshaft sprocket to 1/2 notch before TDC, **Fig. 20.**
16. Install the timing belt over the crankshaft sprocket, water pump sprocket, idler pulley, camshaft sprockets and tensioner pulley.
17. Move the crankshaft sprocket 1/2 notch, aligning the crankshaft sprocket mark with mark on oil pump housing.
18. Install the timing belt tensioner onto the engine. Do not tighten the attaching bolts.
19. Using a suitable torque wrench, apply a torque of 21 ft. lbs. to the tensioner pulley, **Fig. 21.**
20. While applying torque to the tensioner pulley, move the tensioner up against the pulley bracket and tighten the attaching bolts, **Fig. 21. Torque** the tensioner attaching bolts to 23 ft. lbs.
21. Remove the pin from the tensioner body. Pretension is correct when the pin can be removed and installed.
22. Rotate crankshaft two turn in the normal direction of rotation. Check if crankshaft and camshaft timing marks are aligned, **Fig. 18.** If marks are not aligned, the timing belt must be removed and re-installed.
23. Install the timing belt front cover.
24. Install the engine mount bracket assembly, **Fig. 17.**
25. Remove jack and wooden block from under the engine oil pan.
26. Install the power steering pump to the bracket.
27. Install the crankshaft pulley. **Torque** the crankshaft pulley bolt to 105 ft. lbs.

28. Install the alternator drive belt. **Refer to "Belt Tension Data" in this section for proper belt tension.**
29. Install the A/C compressor and power steering pump drive belt. **Refer to "Belt Tension Data" in this section for proper belt tension.**
30. Install the undercover.
31. Install the cooling system reserve tank. Add engine coolant to system as necessary

TURBOCHARGED ENGINE

With the timing belt removed, avoid turning the camshaft or crankshaft. If movement is required, exercise extreme caution to avoid valve damage caused by piston contact.

1. Remove the undercover.
2. Remove the clamp securing the power steering pressure hose and the air conditioner high pressure hose to the body.
3. Using a wood block and a jack, place the wood block under the engine oil pan and raise the engine only enough to relieve tension on the top engine mount, then remove the mount and the bracket.
4. Remove the accessory drive belts. **Prior to removing the water pump drive belt, loosen the water pump pulley bolts.**
5. Remove the tensioner pulley and the bracket.
6. Remove the crankshaft pulley, then the water pump pulley.
7. Remove the upper and lower timing covers.
8. Rotate the crankshaft clockwise to bring No. 1 cylinder to top dead center of the compression stroke. **Rotate the crankshaft only in the clockwise direction.** The No. 1 cylinder is at top dead center of the compression stroke when the timing marks on the camshaft sprockets are aligned with the upper surface of the cylinder head and the dowel pins on the camshaft sprockets are facing up as shown, **Fig. 22.**
9. Remove the auto-tensioner.
10. Remove the timing belt.
11. Remove the tensioner pulley and arm, then the idler pulley.
12. Remove the crankshaft sprocket bolt, special washer, sprocket and the flange.
13. Remove the tensioner "B," then the timing belt "B."
14. Ensure the timing marks of the balance shaft sprocket and the crankshaft sprocket "B" are aligned, **Fig. 23,** then install the timing belt " B" over both sprockets and ensure the belt has no slack.
15. Adjust the timing belt "B" tension as follows:
    a. Temporarily install the timing belt "B" tensioner so that the center of the tensioner pulley is to the left and above the center of the installation bolt, then temporarily attach the tensioner pulley so that the flange is toward the front of engine, **Fig. 24.**
    b. Hold the timing belt "B" tensioner up in the direction shown by the arrow in, **Fig. 25,** then place pressure on the timing belt so that the tension side of the belt is taut.
    c. **Torque** the tensioner "B "" bolt to 11-16 ft. lbs. **When torquing the bolt, do not allow the tensioner pulley shaft to rotate.**
    d. To check belt tension, depress the belt at point (A), **Fig. 26.** The belt deflection should be .20-.28 inch . If not, readjust the belt tension.
16. Install the crankshaft sprocket flange, sprocket and special washer. **Torque** the crankshaft sprocket bolt to 80-94 ft. lbs. **Ensure the flange and sprocket are correctly installed as shown Fig. 27.**
17. Install the auto-tensioner. If the tensioner rod is fully extended, proceed as follows:
    a. Position the auto-tensioner level in a soft jawed vise. If the plug at the bottom of the tensioner protrudes, apply a plain washer to prevent the plug from direct contact with the vise.
    b. Slowly push the tensioner rod in, using the vise, until the set hole (A) is aligned with the hole (B) in the tensioner cylinder, **Fig. 28.**
    c. Insert a .055 inch wire into the set holes, then remove the auto-tensioner from the vise.
    d. Install the auto-tensioner, then **torque** the retaining bolt to 14-20 ft. lbs. **Leave the wire installed in the auto-tensioner.**
18. Install the tensioner pulley onto the tensioner arm, position the hole in pulley shaft to the left of the center bolt, then tighten the center bolt finger tight.
19. Ensure the camshaft sprockets dowel pins are located on top, then ensure the timing marks are facing each other and are aligned with the top surface of cylinder head, **Fig. 29.** When the exhaust camshaft is released, it will rotate one tooth in the counterclockwise direction. This should be taken into account when installing the timing belt on the sprockets. **The camshaft sprockets are interchangeable and have two sets of timing marks. When the sprocket is mounted on the exhaust camshaft, use the timing mark on the right with dowel pin hole on top. For the intake sprocket, use the mark on the left with dowel pin hole on top, Fig. 30.**
20. Ensure the crankshaft sprocket and the oil pump sprocket timing marks align as shown, **Fig. 31.**
21. With the oil pump sprocket timing marks aligned, remove the plug from the lefthand side of cylinder block and insert a screwdriver with a shaft diameter of .3 inch, **Fig. 32.** If the screwdriver can be inserted 2.4 inches or more, alignment is correct. If the screwdriver can be inserted only 1 inch, rotate the oil pump sprocket one revolution and realign the timing marks. Ensure the screwdriver can be inserted 2.4 inches or more. This check is performed to ensure the balance shaft and the oil pump sprocket are properly positioned. Leave the screwdriver inserted in the hole until after the timing belt has been installed.
22. Install the timing belt as follows:
    a. Install the timing belt around the tensioner pulley and the crankshaft sprocket. Hold the timing belt on the tensioner pulley with your left hand.
    b. Pulling the timing belt with your right hand, install the belt around

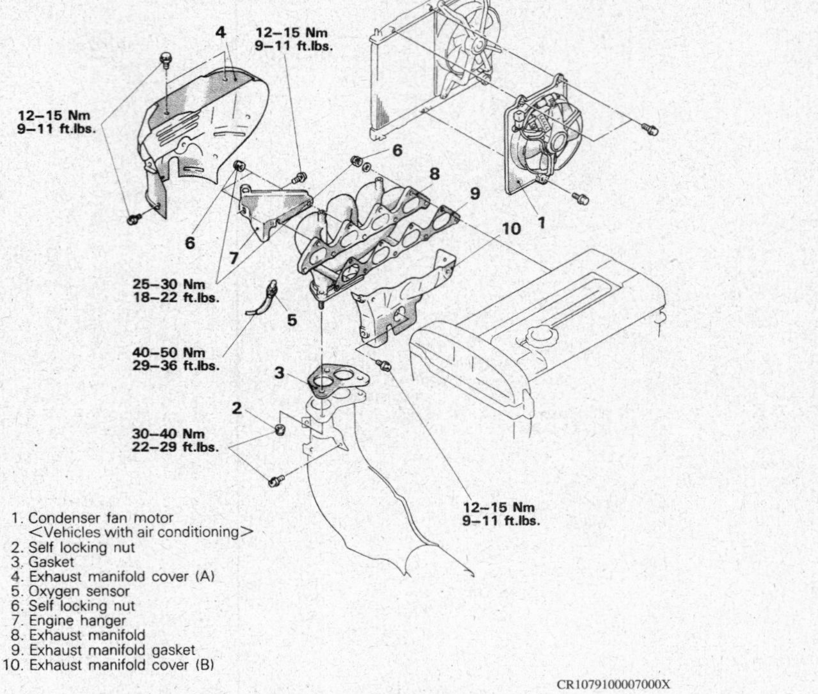

Fig. 10 Exhaust manifold removal. Non-turbocharged engine

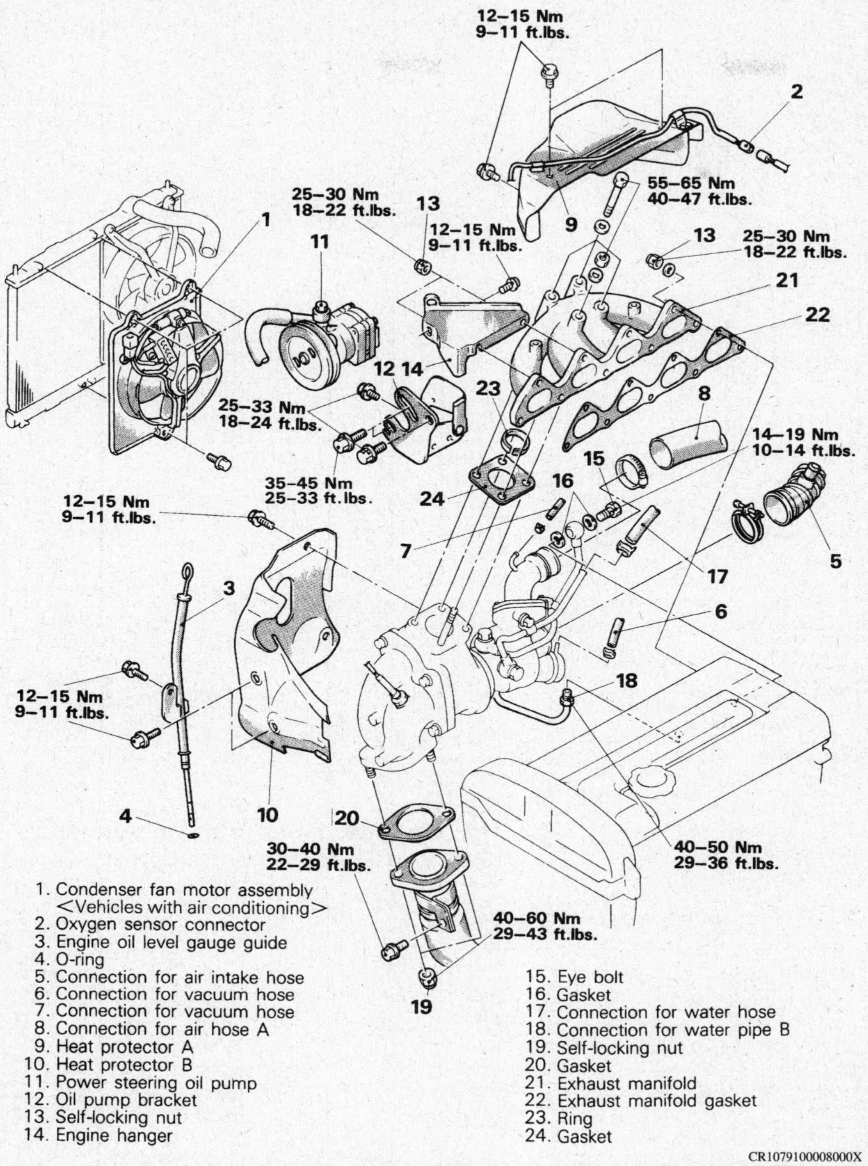

Fig. 11 Exhaust manifold removal. Turbocharged engine

the oil pump sprocket.

c. Install the timing belt around the idler pulley, then around the intake camshaft sprocket.
d. Rotate the exhaust camshaft sprocket one tooth clockwise to align the timing mark with cylinder head top surface, then pulling the belt with both hands, install around the exhaust camshaft sprocket.
e. Gently raise the tensioner pulley in the direction shown by the arrow in **Fig. 33** so the belt does not sag, then temporarily tighten the center bolt.

23. Adjust the timing belt tension as follows:
    a. Remove the screwdriver from hole in lefthand side of cylinder block and install the plug.
    b. Rotate the crankshaft 1/4 turn counterclockwise, then rotate clockwise to move No. 1 cylinder to TDC.
    c. Loosen the tensioner pulley center bolt. Use Chrysler wrench tool No. MD998767, or equivalent, and a torque wrench, apply a torque of 30 inch lbs. to the tensioner pulley, **Fig. 34.** Use a torque wrench capable of measuring within a range of 0-30 inch lbs. If the vehicle body interferes with the torque wrench, use a suitable jack to slightly raise the engine.
    d. While holding the tensioner pulley with the tool, **torque** the pulley center bolt to 31-40 ft. lbs.
    e. Screw Chrysler set screw tool No. MD998738, or equivalent, into the left engine support bracket until the end of tool makes contact with the tensioner arm, **Fig. 35.** Turn the tool enough to relieve the tension on the auto-tensioner rod, then remove the set wire previously installed in the auto-tensioner.
    f. Remove the set screw tool.
    g. Rotate the crankshaft clockwise two complete turns, then let sit for 15 minutes.
    h. Measure clearance (A) between the tensioner arm and the auto-tensioner body, **Fig. 36.** If clearance is not .15-.18 inch, repeat steps a to g until the clearance is correct.
    i. If clearance (A) can not be measured with the engine in the vehicle, screw in Chrysler set screw No. MD998738 or equivalent, until the end of tool makes contact with the tensioner arm.
    j. Starting in this position, count the number of turns of the tool required to bring the tensioner arm in contact with the auto-tensioner body. Ensure contact is made within 2.5–3 turns, then remove the tool.
    k. Install the rubber plug into the timing belt rear cover.
24. Install the upper and lower timing covers.
25. Install the crankshaft pulley and the water pump pulley.
26. Install the tensioner pulley and the bracket.
27. Install the accessory drive belts. **Refer to "Belt tension Data" in this section for proper belt tension.**
28. Install the engine mount and the bracket.
29. Remove the jack and wooden block positioned under the oil pan.
30. Install the clamp securing the power steering pressure hose and the air conditioner high pressure hose to the body.
31. Install the undercover. Check and adjust the ignition timing as necessary.

CAMSHAFT

REPLACE

TURBOCHARGED ENGINE

Removal

Remove camshaft in numbered sequence, **Fig. 37,** noting the following:

1. Remove timing belt as outlined under "Timing Belt, Replace."
2. Remove camshaft sprockets as follows:
    a. While holding camshaft in position with a crescent wrench at hexagon between No. 2 and No. 3 journals, remove camshaft sprocket bolt.
    b. Remove camshaft sprockets.
3. Remove camshaft oil seals using a suitable screwdriver.
4. Remove camshaft bearing caps by loosening installation bolts in two or three steps. If bearing cap is difficult to remove, gently tap on the rear portion of the camshaft with a plastic hammer.

Installation

Reverse removal procedure to install, noting the following:

1. Install the camshafts on the cylinder

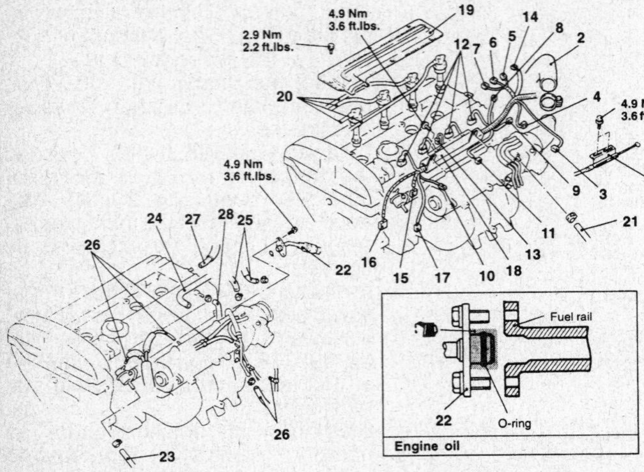

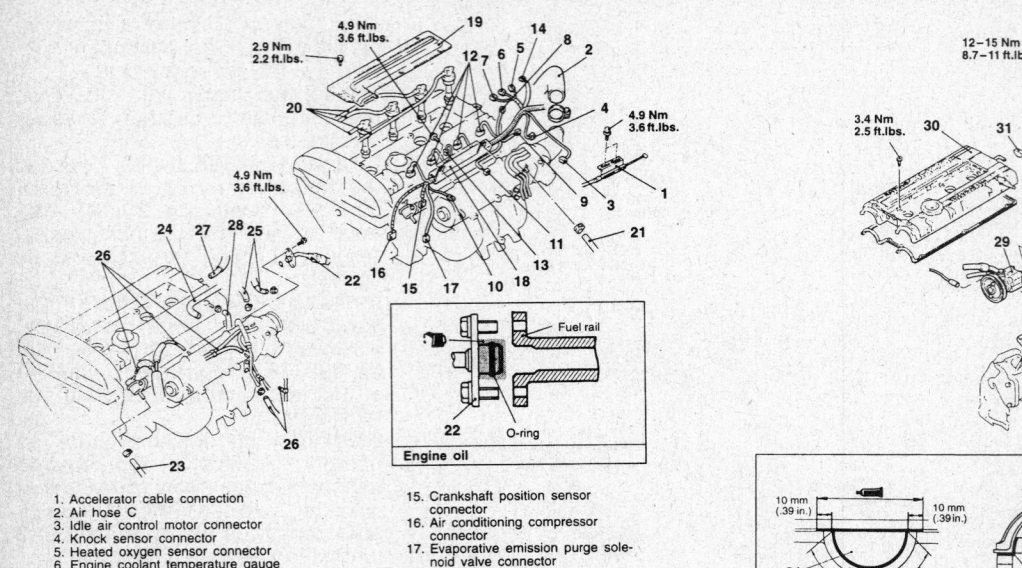

1. Accelerator cable connection
2. Air hose C
3. Idle air control motor connector
4. Knock sensor connector
5. Heated oxygen sensor connector
6. Engine coolant temperature gauge unit connector
7. Engine coolant temperature sensor connector
8. Ignition power transistor connector
9. Throttle position sensor connector
10. Capacitor connector
11. Manifold differential pressure sensor connector
12. Injector connectors
13. Ignition coil connector
14. Camshaft position sensor connector
15. Crankshaft position sensor connector
16. Air conditioning compressor connector
17. Evaporative emission purge solenoid valve connector
18. Control wiring harness
19. Center cover
20. Spark plug cable
21. Brake booster vacuum hose connection
22. High-pressure fuel hose connection
23. Fuel return hose connection
24. By-pass valve hose connection
25. Water hose connection
26. Vacuum hoses connection
27. Breather hose connection
28. PCV hose connection

CR1069100352010X

Fig. 12 Cylinder head removal sequence (Part 1 of 2). Turbocharged engine

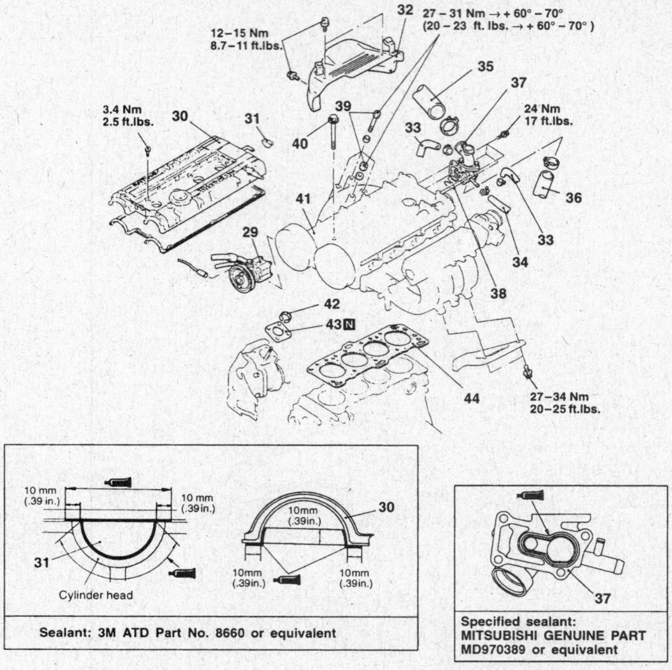

- Timing belt
29. Power steering pump
30. Rocker cover
31. Semi-circular packing
32. Heat protector (A)
33. Water hose connection
34. Water hose A connection
35. Radiator upper hose connection
36. Radiator lower hose connection
37. Thermostat case assembly
38. O-ring
39. Flange bolts and flange nut
40. Cylinder head bolt
41. Cylinder head assembly
42. Ring
43. Gasket (A)
44. Cylinder head gasket

CR1069100352020X

Fig. 12 Cylinder head removal sequence (Part 2 of 2). Turbocharged engine

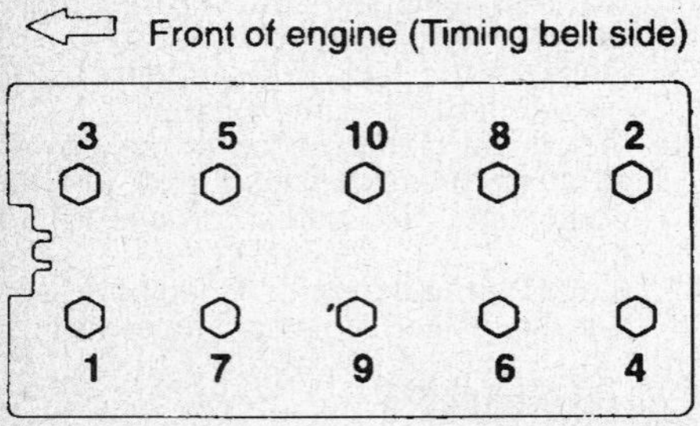

CR1069100353000X

Fig. 13 Cylinder head bolt loosening sequence. Turbocharged engine

head. **Ensure intake side camshaft is installed on intake side and exhaust side camshaft is installed on exhaust side.** Intake side camshaft has a slot machined in the back end to drive the crank angle sensor. Once installed, the camshaft dowel pins should be in the positions as shown in **Fig. 38.**

2. When installing camshaft bearing caps, tighten evenly, in two or three steps.
3. When installing camshaft oil seal, use oil seal guide tool No. MD998307 and oil seal installation tool No. MD998306, or equivalents, as shown, **Fig. 39.**
4. Install crank angle sensor as follows:
   a. Ensure mating mark on housing of crank angle sensor is aligned with notch in plate.
   b. Ensure crank angle sensor does not move when tightening attaching nut.
5. When installing semi-circular packing, apply liberal amount of gasket sealant onto circumference of packing.
6. When installing rocker cover, apply gasket sealant to area as shown in **Fig. 15.**

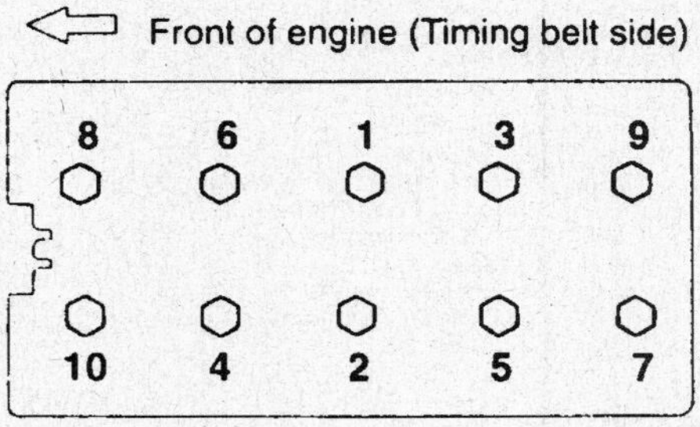

CR1069100354000X

Fig. 14 Cylinder head bolt tightening sequence. Turbocharged engine

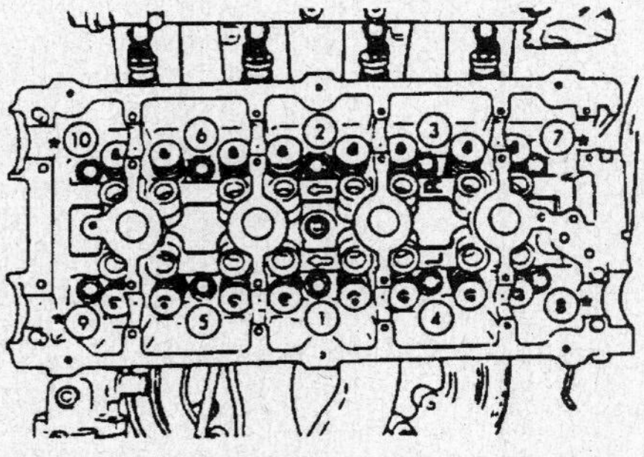

*Location of 110 mm (4.330 in.) short bolts.

CR1069500631000X

Fig. 16 Cylinder head bolt tightening sequence. Non-turbocharged engine

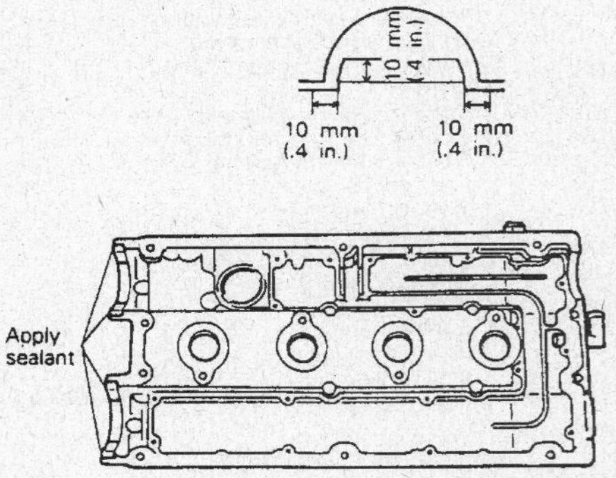

CR1069100355000X

Fig. 15 Rocker cover installation. Turbocharged engine

NON-TURBOCHARGED ENGINE

Removal

Remove camshaft in numbered sequence, **Fig. 40,** noting the following:

1. Use camshaft sprocket holder and adapter tools No. C-4687 and C-4687–

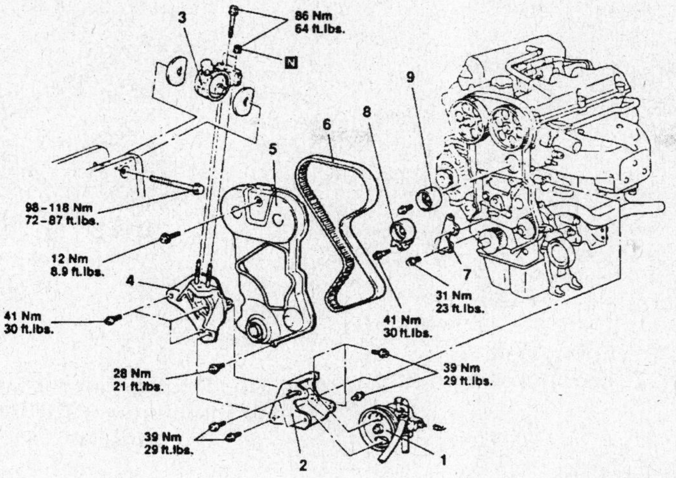

1. Power steering oil pump connection
2. Power steering oil pump bracket
3. Engine mount bracket assembly
4. Engine mount bracket
5. Front timing belt cover
6. Timing belt
7. Timing belt tensioner
8. Tensioner pulley
9. Idle pulley

CR1069500160000X

Fig. 17 Timing belt & components. Non-turbocharged engine

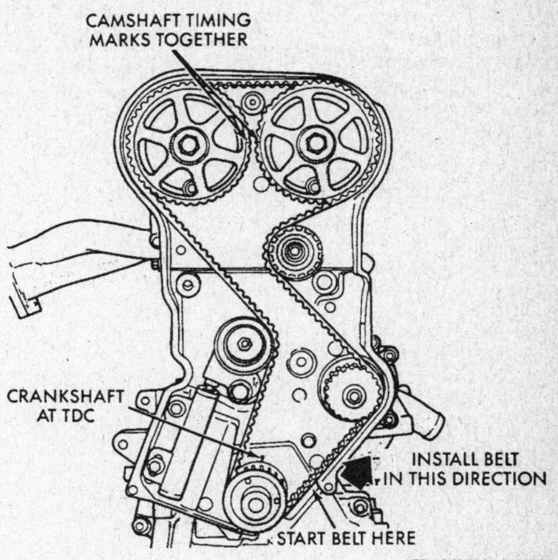

CR1069500161000X

Fig. 18 Camshaft & crankshaft sprocket timing marks. Non-turbocharged engine

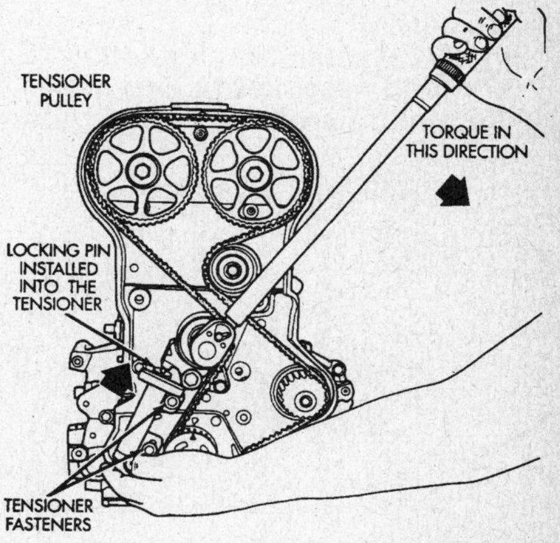

CR1069500164000X

Fig. 21 Adjusting timing belt tension. Non-turbocharged engine

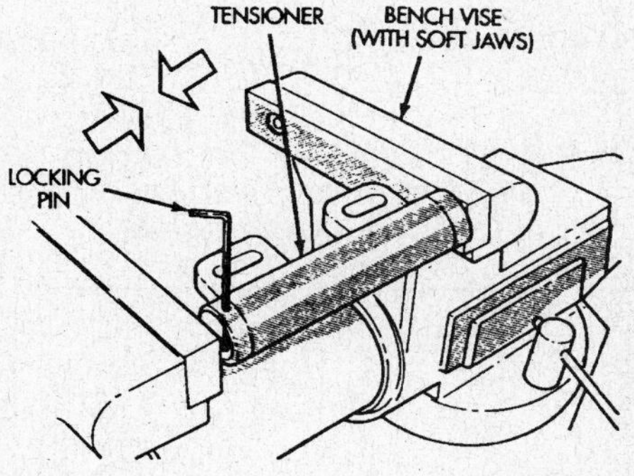

CR1069500162000X

Fig. 19 Compressing timing belt tensioner rod. Non-turbocharged engine

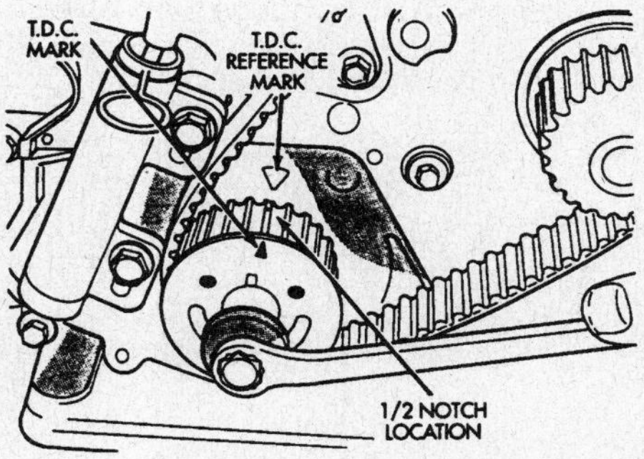

CR1069500163000X

Fig. 20 Positioning crankshaft sprocket 1/2 notch from top dead center. Non-turbocharged engine

1, or equivalent, to ensure camshaft sprockets do not turn during removal.

2. Mark and identify intake camshaft and exhaust camshaft before removal as they are not interchangeable.
3. Loosen camshaft bearing cap attaching bolts in sequence shown in **Fig. 41,** one camshaft at a time.
4. Remove camshaft oil seals using suitable screwdriver to pry seal out.

Installation

1. Install new camshaft oil seals using special oil seal seating tools No. MB991554 and MB998713, or equivalents, **Fig. 42.**
2. **Ensure piston is not at top dead center when installing camshaft.**
3. Install camshaft bearing cap attaching bolts in sequence shown in **Fig. 41,** one camshaft at a time. Tighten to specifications.
4. Use camshaft sprocket holder and adapter tools No. C-4687 and C-4687–1, or equivalents, to ensure camshaft sprockets do not turn during installation.
5. Install cylinder head cover assembly to head and tighten in sequence shown in **Fig. 43. Torque** in three steps; first to 3.3 ft. lbs., then to 6.6 ft. lbs., finally to 8.9 ft. lbs.

SILENT SHAFT

REPLACE

DISASSEMBLE

Disassemble front case, oil pump and silent shaft in numbered sequence, **Fig. 44,** noting the following:

1. Use oil pressure switch socket tool No. MD998054, or equivalent, to remove oil pressure switch.
2. Remove oil pan as outlined under "Oil Pan & Oil Screen, Replace."
3. Use plug cap socket No. tool No. MD998162, or equivalent, to remove front case plug cap (17).
4. When removing oil pump driven gear bolt, insert a Phillips screwdriver into plug hole, **Fig. 45,** to block the silent shaft.
5. Using silent shaft bearing puller tool No. MD998371, or equivalent, remove silent shaft front bearing as shown, **Fig. 46.**
6. Using silent shaft bearing puller tool No. MD998372, or equivalent, remove righthand silent shaft rear bearing as shown, **Fig. 47.**
7. Using silent shaft bearing puller tool No. MD998374, or equivalent, remove lefthand silent shaft rear bearing as shown, **Fig. 48.**

INSPECTION

1. Inspect front case for the following:
   a. Clogged oil passages.

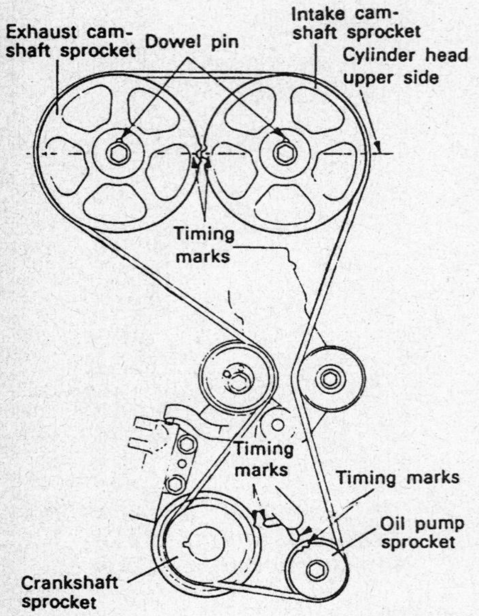

CR1069000165000X

Fig. 22 Camshaft, crankshaft & oil pump sprocket timing mark alignment. Turbocharged engine

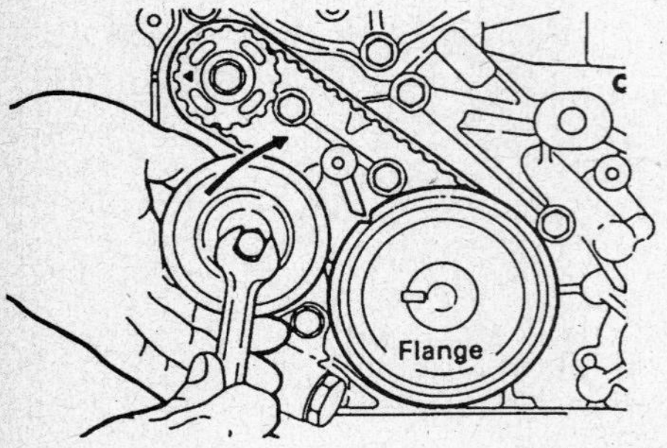

CR1069000168000X

Fig. 25 Tensioning timing belt "B." Turbocharged engine

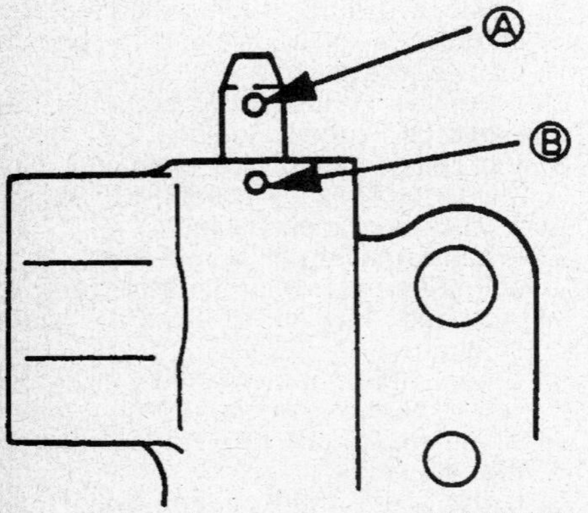

CR1069000171000X

Fig. 28 Tensioner rod alignment. Turbocharged engine

b. Damaged or seized lefthand silent shaft front bearing section.
c. Cracks or other signs of damage on case.

2. Inspect oil seal lip for wear or damage, replacing as necessary.

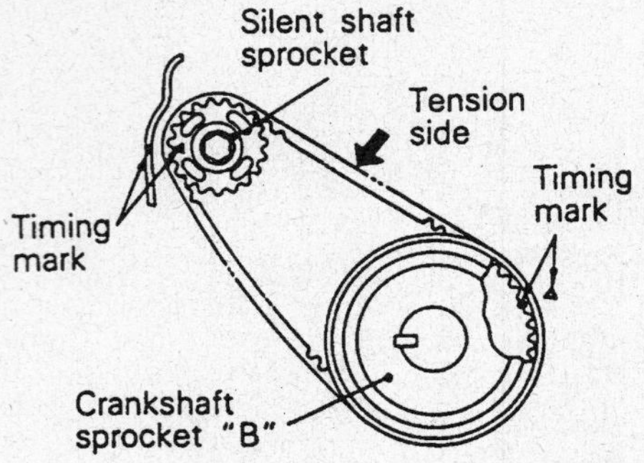

CR1069000166000X

Fig. 23 Timing belt "B" installation. Turbocharged engine

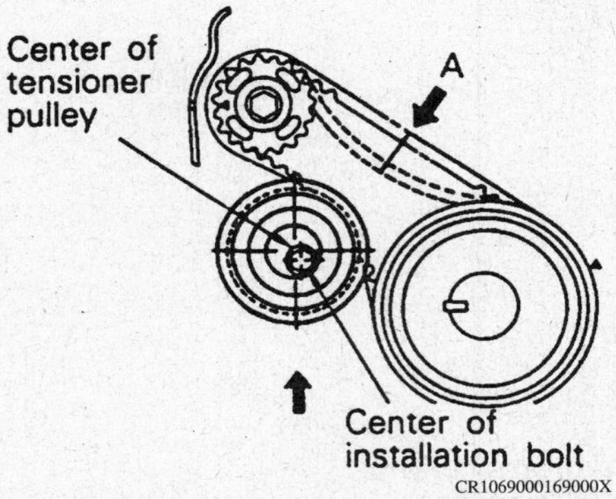

CR1069000169000X

Fig. 26 Checking timing belt "B" tension. Turbocharged engine

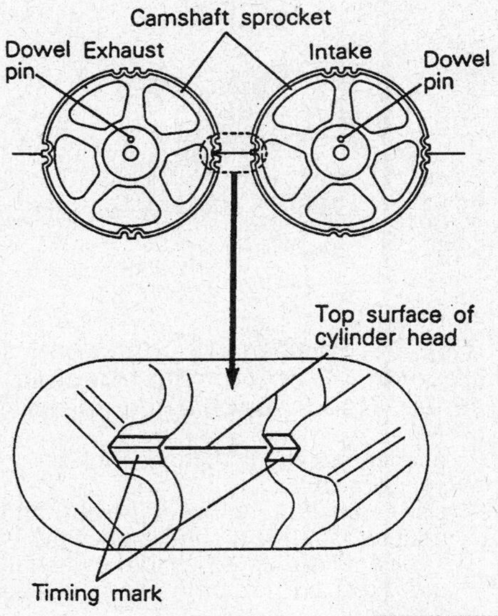

CR1069000172000X

Fig. 29 Camshaft sprocket timing mark alignment. Turbocharged engine

3. Inspect oil switch as follows:
   a. Connect an ohmmeter between switch terminal and switch body.
   b. If ohmmeter reads no continuity, replace switch. If ohmmeter reads continuity, proceed to following step.
   c. Insert a fine wedge into oil switch hole. Ohmmeter should read no continuity when wedge is slightly pressed into hole. If ohmmeter reads continuity, replace switch.

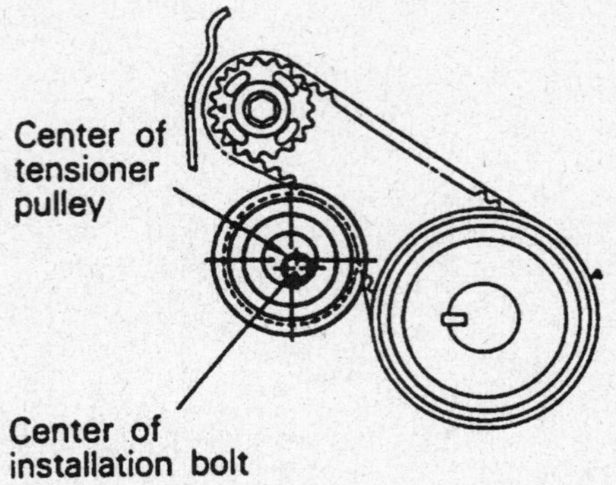

CR1069000167000X

Fig. 24 Timing belt "B" tensioner pulley installation. Turbocharged engine

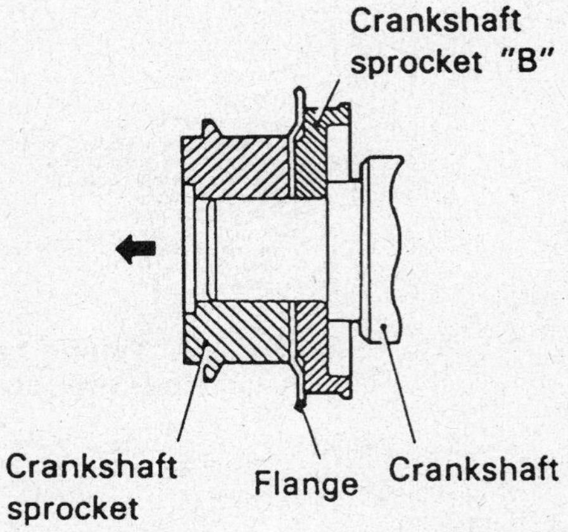

CR1069000170000X

Fig. 27 Flange & crankshaft sprocket installation. Turbocharged engine

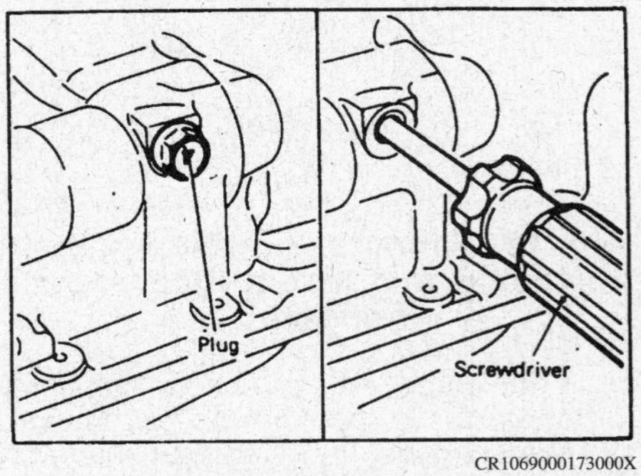

CR1069000173000X

Fig. 30 Positioning camshaft sprockets. Turbocharged engine

4. **On turbocharged models,** inspect oil cooler bypass valve as follows:
   a. Ensure valves move smoothly.
   b. Measure dimension L on bypass valve, **Fig. 49.** At room temperature, dimension L should be 1.358 inches.
   c. Dip valve in engine oil heated to

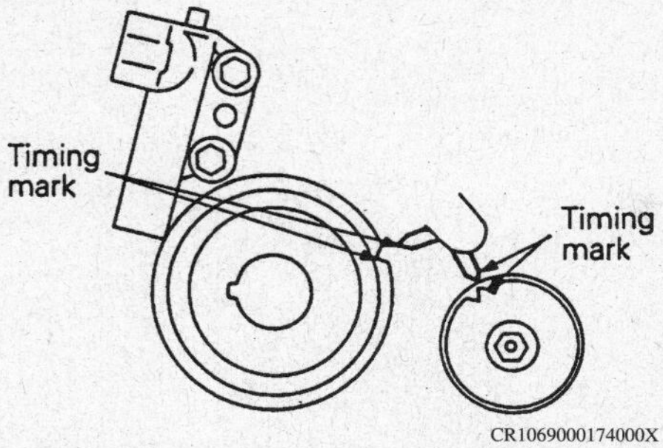

CR1069000174000X

Fig. 31 Crankshaft & oil pump sprocket alignment. Turbocharged engine

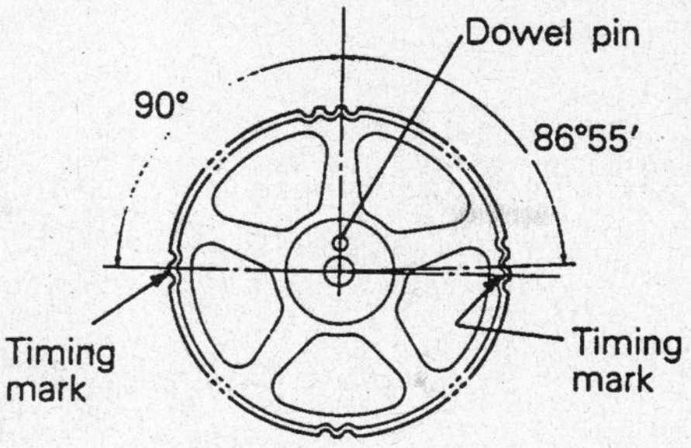

CR1069000175000X

Fig. 32 Checking oil pump sprocket alignment. Turbocharged engine

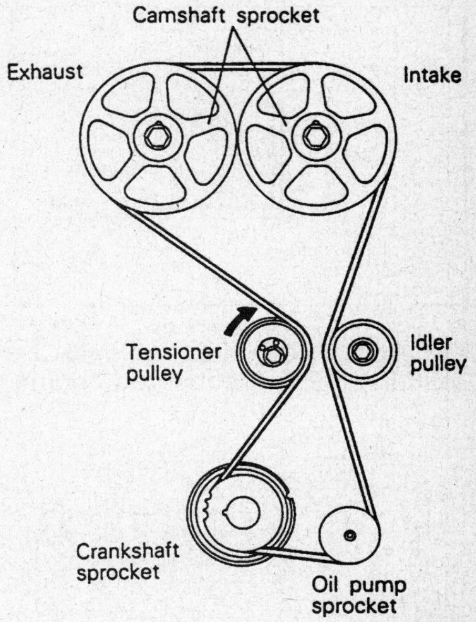

CR1069000176000X

Fig. 33 Timing belt installation. Turbocharged engine

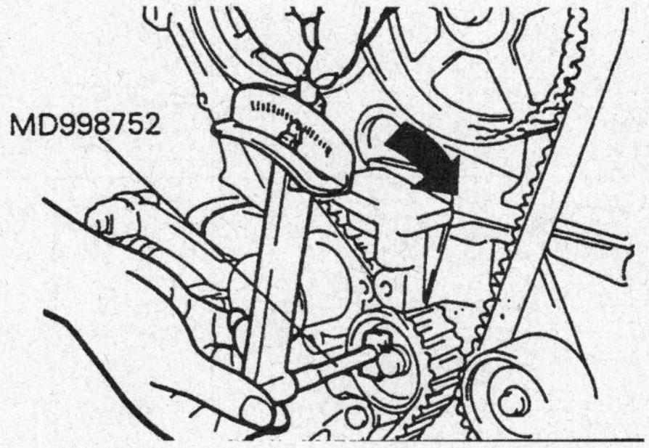

CR1069000177000X

Fig. 34 Tightening tensioner pulley center bolt. Turbocharged engine

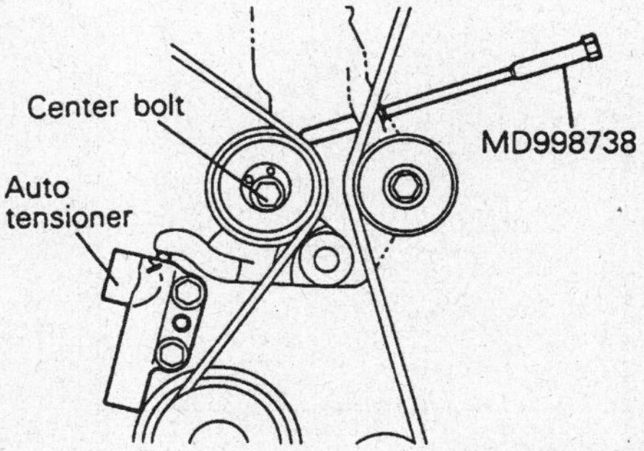

CR1069000178000X

Fig. 35 Set screw tool installation. Turbocharged engine

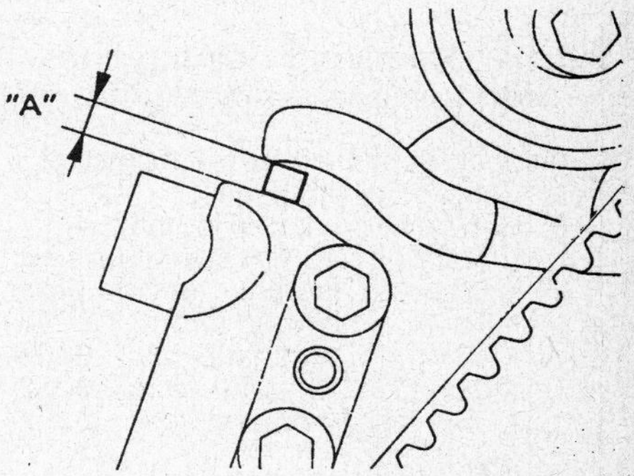

CR1069000179000X

Fig. 36 Auto-tensioner protrusion measurement. Turbocharged engine

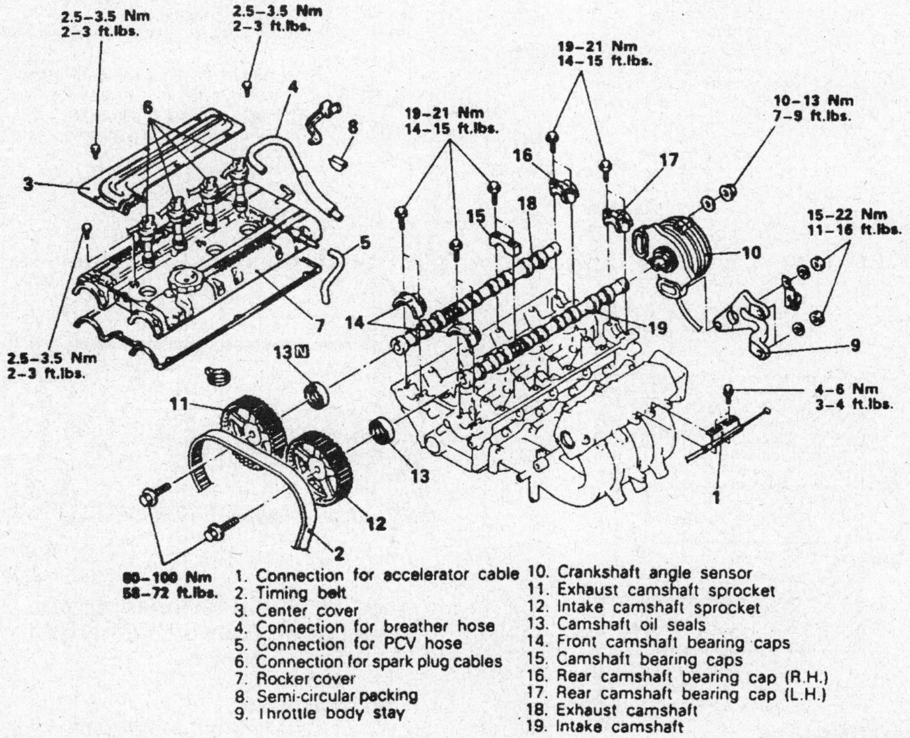

1. Connection for accelerator cable
2. Timing belt
3. Center cover
4. Connection for breather hose
5. Connection for PCV hose
6. Connection for spark plug cables
7. Rocker cover
8. Semi-circular packing
9. Throttle body stay
10. Crankshaft angle sensor
11. Exhaust camshaft sprocket
12. Intake camshaft sprocket
13. Camshaft oil seals
14. Front camshaft bearing caps
15. Camshaft bearing caps
16. Rear camshaft bearing cap (R.H.)
17. Rear camshaft bearing cap (L.H.)
18. Exhaust camshaft
19. Intake camshaft

CR1069100400000X

Fig. 37 Camshaft replacement. Turbocharged engine

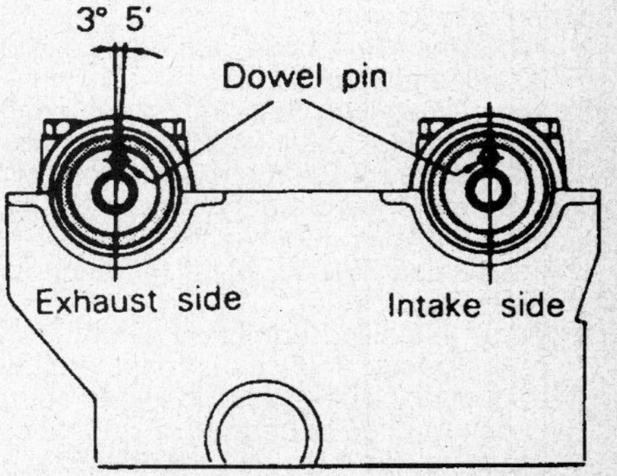

CR1069100401000X

Fig. 38 Camshaft installation. Turbocharged engine

212°F. Dimension L should now be at least 1.570 inches.

5. **On all models,** inspect oil pump as follows:
   a. Install oil pump gears in front case and rotate gears. Ensure smooth rotation without excessive looseness.
   b. Inspect for ridge wear on surface of oil pump cover.
   c. Inspect drive gear and driven gear tip clearance.
   d. Inspect side clearance of gears.

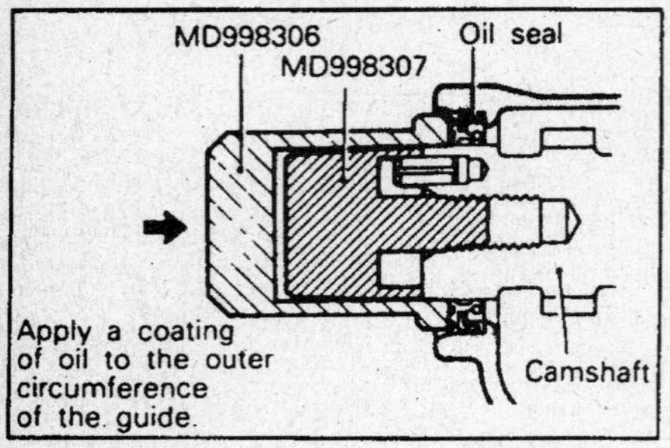

Fig. 39 Camshaft oil seal installation. Turbocharged engine

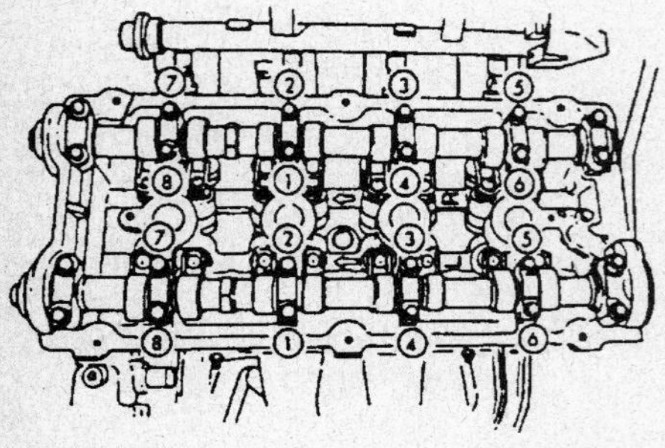

Fig. 41 Camshaft bearing caps. Non-turbocharged engine

6. Inspect silent shaft for the following:
   a. Clogged oil passages.
   b. Seized or damaged journal.
   c. Ensure oil clearance is within specifications. Clearance should be as follows: righthand front, .0008–.0024 inch; righthand rear, .0008–.0021 inch; lefthand front, .0002–.0036 inch; lefthand rear, .0017–.0033 inch.
7. Inspect oil jet and check valve for clogging or damage.

ASSEMBLE

Reverse removal procedure to install, noting the following:

1. When installing oil jet, ensure nozzle is installed toward the piston.
2. When installing lefthand silent shaft rear bearing, apply clean engine oil to engine block bearing hole and to outer circumference of bearing. Using bearing installation tool No. MD998374, or equivalent, **Fig. 50,** install bearing into cylinder block.
3. When installing righthand silent shaft rear bearing, apply clean engine oil to engine block bearing hole and to outer circumference of bearing. Using bearing installation tool No. MD998373 or equivalent, **Fig. 51,** install bearing into cylinder block. **Ensure oil hole in bearing is aligned with oil hole in cylinder block.**
4. When installing silent shaft front bearing, apply clean engine oil to engine block bearing hole and to outer circumference of bearing. Using bearing installation tool No. MD998373, or equivalent, **Fig. 52,** install bearing into cylinder block. **Ensure oil hole in bearing is aligned with oil hole in cylinder block.**
5. When installing oil pump gears, coat gears with clean engine oil, then align mark on drive gear notch with mark on driven gear tooth.
6. Install crankshaft oil seal using oil seal installation tool No. MD998375, or equivalent.
7. Install oil seal (22) and silent shaft oil

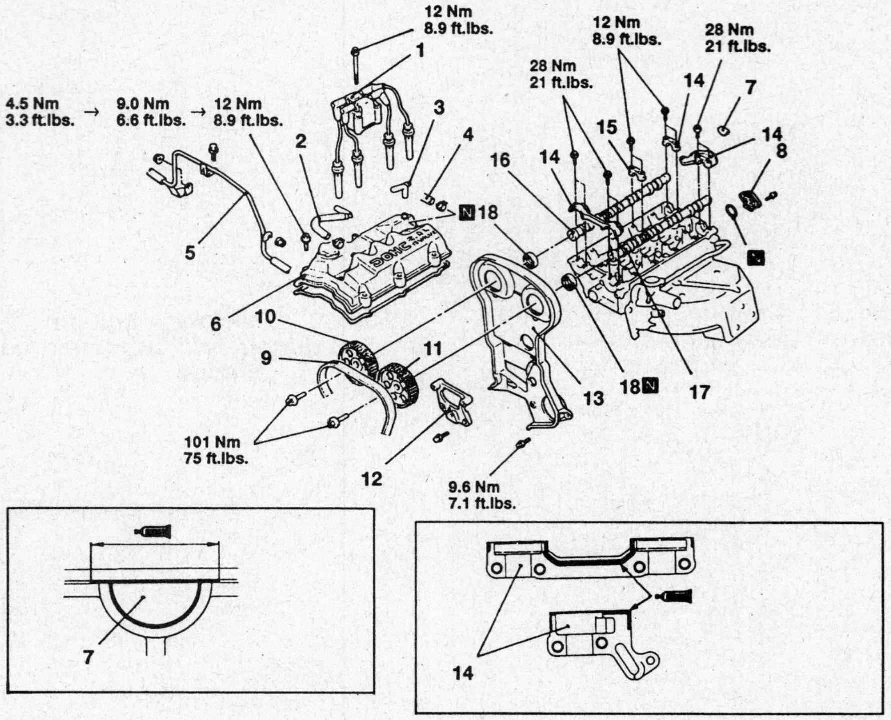

Camshaft removal steps
1. Ignition coil pack
2. PCV hose
3. Breather hose
4. Air hose
5. Vapor hose and pipe assembly connection
6. Cylinder head cover
7. Semi–circular packing
8. Camshaft position sensor
9. Timing belt
10. Intake camshaft sprocket
11. Exhaust camshaft sprocket
12. Bracket
13. Rear timing belt cover
14. Outside camshaft bearing cap
15. Camshaft bearing cap
16. Intake camshaft
17. Exhaust camshaft

Camshaft oil seal removal steps
9. Timing belt
10. Intake camshaft sprocket
11. Exhaust camshaft sprocket
12. Bracket
13. Rear timing belt cover
18. Camshaft oil seal

CR1069500614000X

Fig. 40 Camshaft replacement. 2.0L non-turbocharged engine

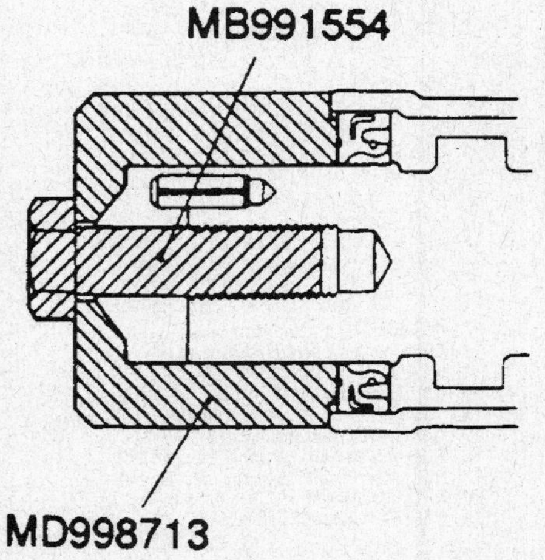

Fig. 42 Camshaft oil seal installation. Non-turbocharged engine

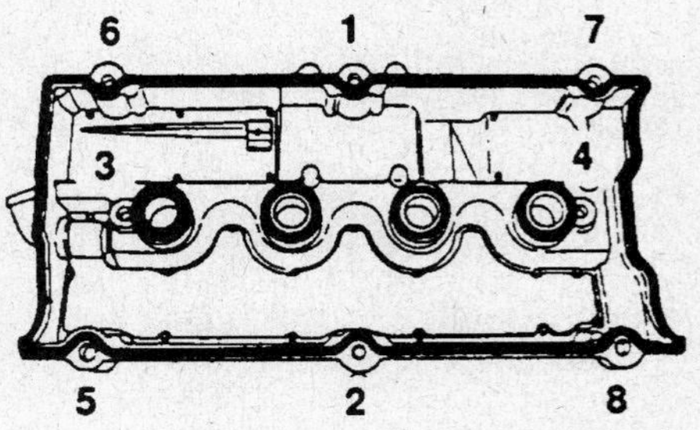

Fig. 43 Cylinder head cover installation. Non-turbocharged engine

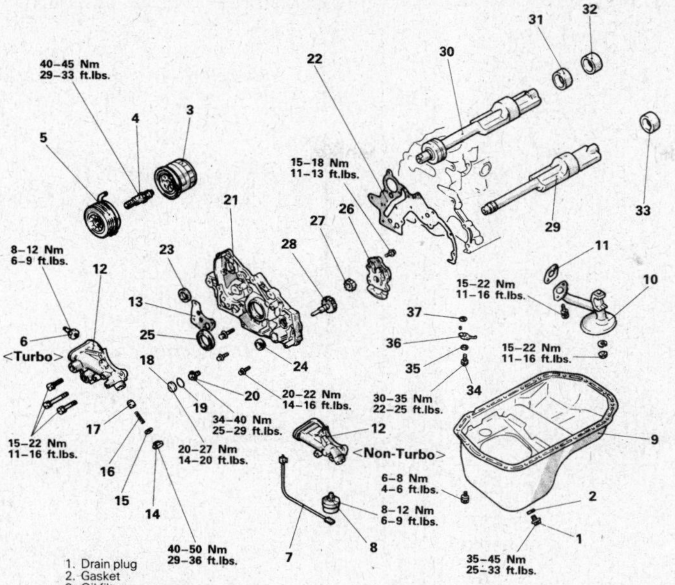

1. Drain plug
2. Gasket
3. Oil filter
4. Oil cooler bolt (Turbo)
5. Oil cooler (Turbo)
6. Oil pressure switch
7. Harness assembly
8. Oil pressure gauge unit
9. Oil pan
10. Oil screen
11. Gasket
12. Oil filter bracket
13. Gasket
14. Relief plug
15. Gasket
16. Relief spring
17. Relief plunger
18. Plug cap
19. O-ring
20. Driven gear bolt
21. Front case
22. Gasket
23. Oil seal
24. Silent shaft oil seal
25. Crankshaft front oil seal
26. Oil pump cover
27. Oil pump driven gear
28. Oil pump drive gear
29. Left silent shaft
30. Right silent shaft
31. Silent shaft front bearings
32. Right silent shaft rear bearing
33. Left silent shaft rear bearing
34. Check valve (Turbo)
35. Gasket (Turbo)
36. Oil jet (Turbo)
37. Gasket (Turbo)

CR1069100368000X

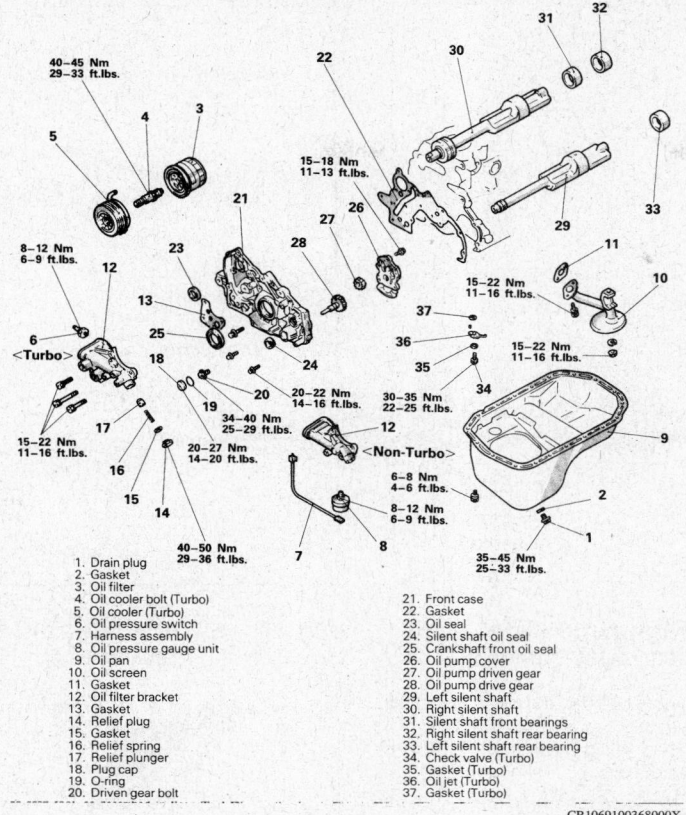

Fig. 44 Front case, oil pump & silent shaft assembly

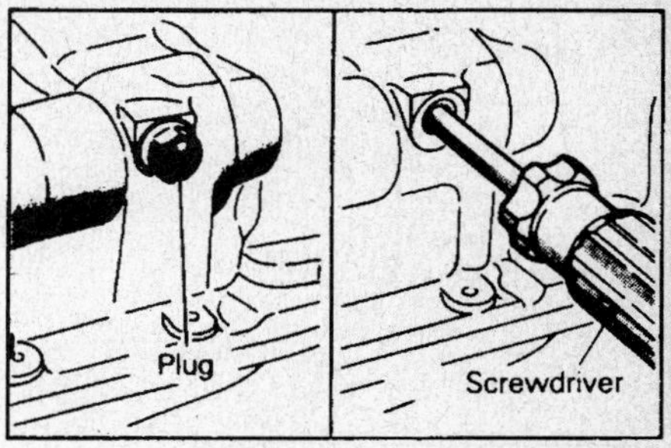

CR1069100369000X

Fig. 45 Blocking silent shaft for oil pump sprocket removal

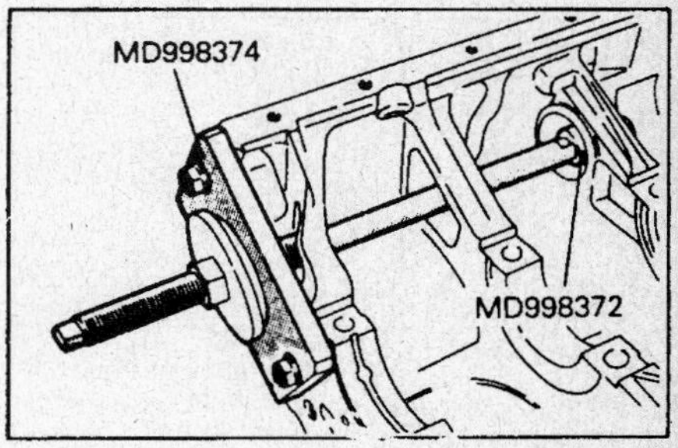

CR1069100370000X

Fig. 48 Lefthand silent shaft rear bearing removal

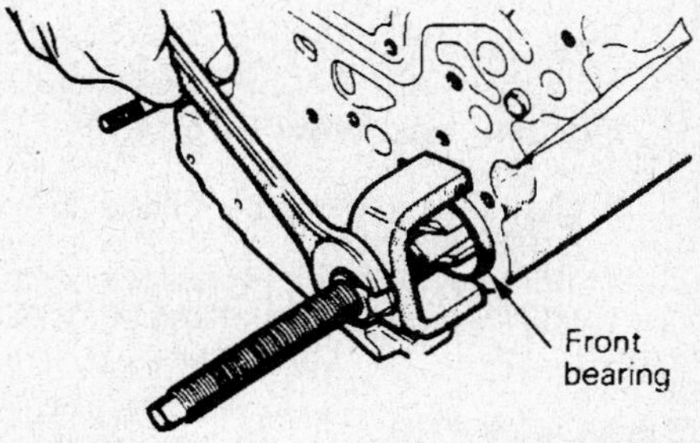

CR1069100363000X

Fig. 46 Silent shaft front bearing removal

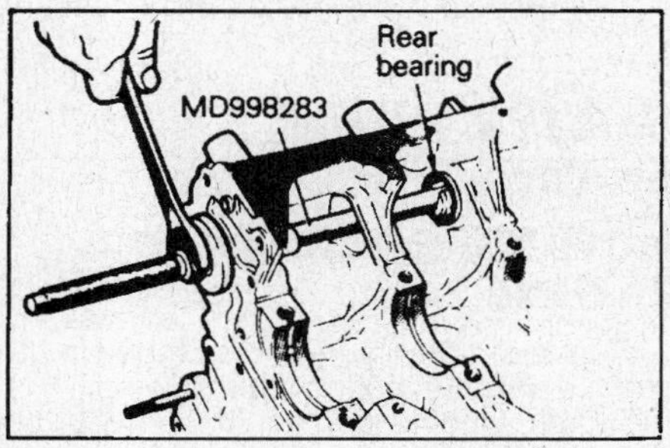

CR1069100364000X

Fig. 47 Silent shaft rear bearing removal

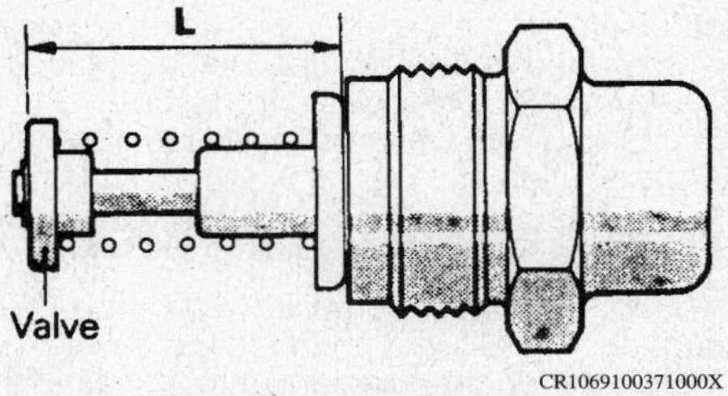

CR1069100371000X

Fig. 49 Oil cooler bypass valve

seal (23) by placing a socket over the top of the seal and pressing it into the case.

8. Install front case as follows:
   a. Place crankshaft front oil seal guide No. MD998285, or equivalent, over front end of crankshaft, then apply engine oil to outer circumference of guide.
   b. Install front case over top of guide, onto cylinder block. Temporarily tighten all bolts except the filter bracket attaching bolts, referring to bolt length chart, **Fig. 53.**
   c. Install oil filter bracket and the four attaching bolts.
   d. Tighten all bolts to specifications.
9. When installing driven gear bolt (19), insert a Phillips screwdriver into plug hole on lefthand side of cylinder block, **Fig. 45,** to block the silent shaft.
10. When installing plug cap, place a new O-ring into groove of case, then use plug cap socket No. MD998162 or equivalent to tighten cap.
11. Install oil pan as outlined under "Oil Pan, Replace."
12. When installing oil pressure switch, coat threads of switch with gasket adhesive. **Do not allow hole in end of switch to be covered with adhesive.** Install switch using oil pressure switch socket tool No. MD998054, or equivalent.

PISTON & ROD ASSEMBLY

When installing piston and rod assembly, arrow on top of piston must face toward timing belt side of engine, **Fig. 54.**

OIL PAN

REPLACE

REMOVAL

Remove oil pan and oil screen in numbered sequence, referring to **Figs. 55 through 57 ,** noting the following:

1. Once all oil pan bolts are removed, use oil pan separator tool No. MD998727, or equivalent, and a hammer to loosen pan. **Do not use a screwdriver or a chisel to perform this task, as damage to oil pan flange may result.**
2. Remove pan by placing a brass bar at corner of separator tool and striking it with a hammer.

INSPECTION

Replace the oil pan if damaged or cracked. Ensure screen is not clogged, cracked or damage.

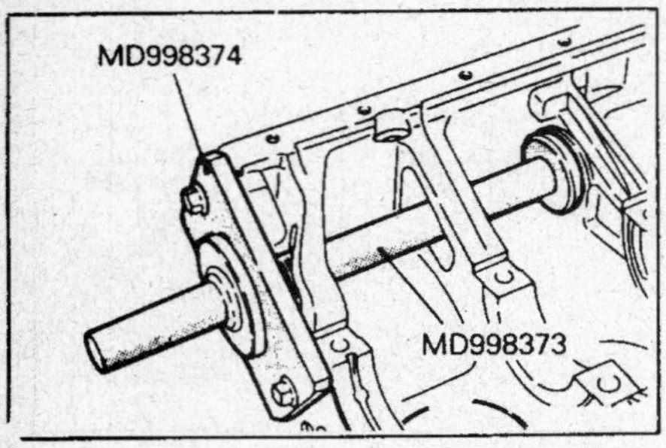

CR1069100372000X

Fig. 50 Lefthand silent shaft rear bearing installation

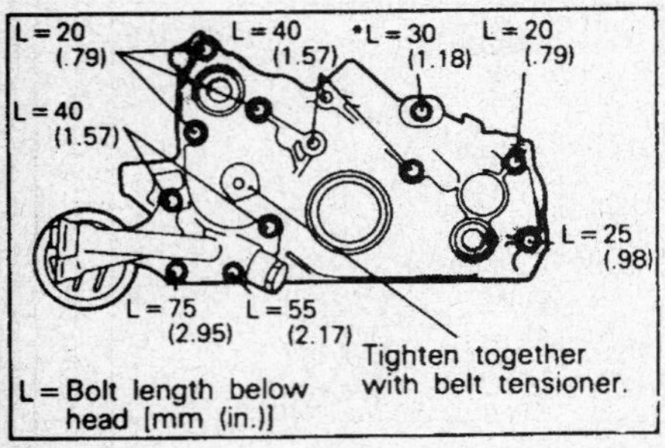

CR1069100375000X

Fig. 53 Front case attaching bolts

INSTALLATION

Reverse removal procedure to install. When installing oil pan, ensure mating surfaces are clean, then apply gasket adhesive into groove in oil pan flange. Do not allow adhesive to cover bolt holes.

OIL PUMP

REPLACE

Refer to "Silent Shaft, Replace" for procedure.

BELT TENSION DATA

Refer to **Fig. 58** for belt tension data.

COOLING SYSTEM BLEED

These engines do not require a specified bleed procedure. After filling cooling system, run engine to operating temperature with radiator/pressure cap off. Air will then be automatically bled through cap opening.

THERMOSTAT

REPLACE

Do not remove pressure cap while engine is hot or under pressure.

Remove thermostat in numbered sequence, **Fig. 59,** noting the following:

1. Drain coolant to below level of thermostat housing.
2. Mark and note the position of the hose clamps before removal.
3. Clean mating surfaces.

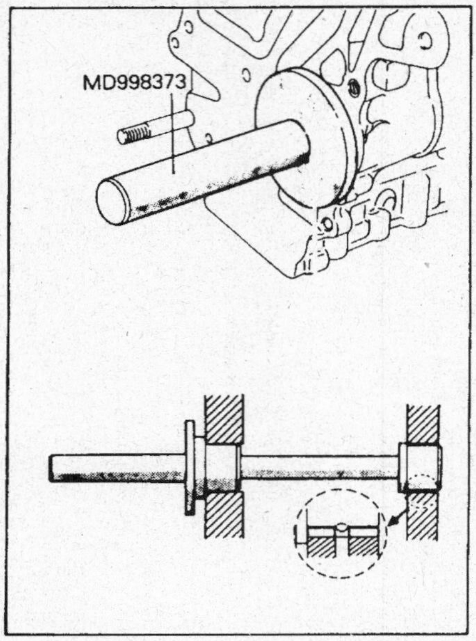

CR1069100373000X

Fig. 51 Righthand silent shaft rear bearing installation

4. Reverse procedure to install, noting the following:
   a. Install retaining bolts and tighten to specifications.
   b. Align hose clamps in position as marked.
   c. Ensure drain is closed, then fill up coolant. Replace cap, start engine until warm. Inspect for leaks, then inspect coolant and fill if necessary.

WATER PUMP

REPLACE

NON-TURBOCHARGED ENGINE

Remove water pump in numbered sequence, **Fig. 60,** noting the following:

1. Drain engine coolant into a suitable container as follows:
   a. Place instrument panel temperature control lever in Hot position.
   b. Carefully remove radiator cap.
   c. Remove radiator drain plug.
2. Remove timing belt rear cover as described under " Timing Belt, Replace."
3. Reverse procedure to install. Coat O-ring with water or coolant to ease installation.

TURBOCHARGED ENGINE

Remove water pump in numbered sequence, **Fig. 61,** noting the following:

1. Drain engine coolant into a suitable container as follows:
   a. Place instrument panel temperature control lever in Hot position.
   b. Carefully remove radiator cap.
   c. Remove radiator drain plug.
2. Remove timing belt rear cover as described under " Timing Belt, Replace."
3. Reverse procedure to install, noting the following:

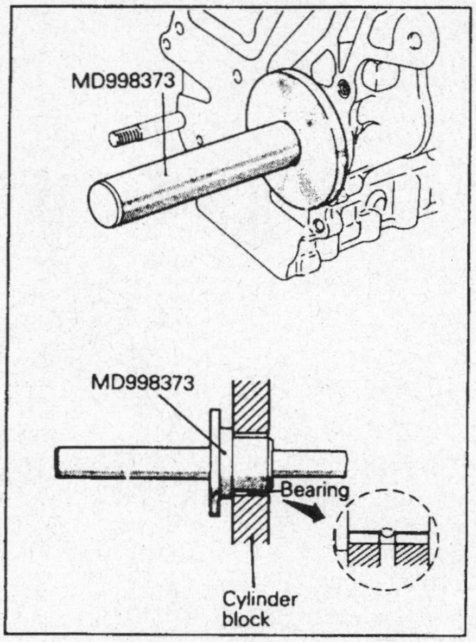

CR1069100374000X

Fig. 52 Silent shaft front bearing installation

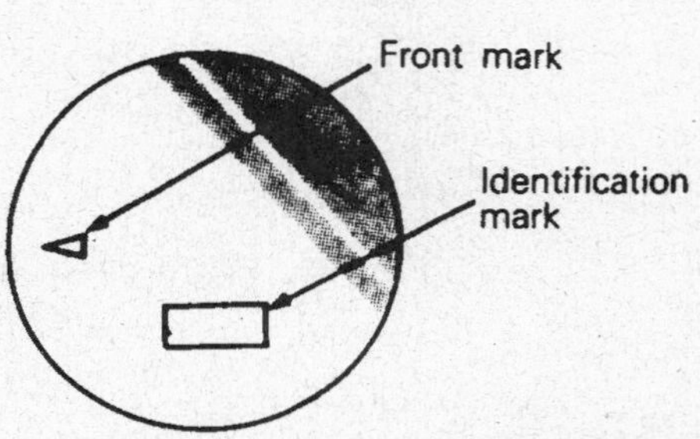

CR1069100403000X

Fig. 54 Top view of piston

a. Coat O-ring with water or coolant to ease installation.
b. Refer to bolt inset, **Fig. 61,** when installing water pump attaching bolts.

RADIATOR

REPLACE

Remove radiator in numbered sequence, **Figs. 62 and 63,** noting the following:

1. Drain engine coolant into a suitable container as follows:
   a. Place instrument panel temperature control lever in Hot position.
   b. Carefully remove radiator cap.
   c. Remove radiator drain plug.
2. Mark and note the position of the hose clamps before removal.
3. **On turbocharged models,** remove air cleaner bracket.
4. **On models equipped with automatic transaxle,** plug or cover nipples and hoses for cooling lines to ensure dust, dirt or other contaminants do not enter lines.
5. **On all models,** reverse procedure to install, noting the following:
   a. Align hose clamps in position as marked.

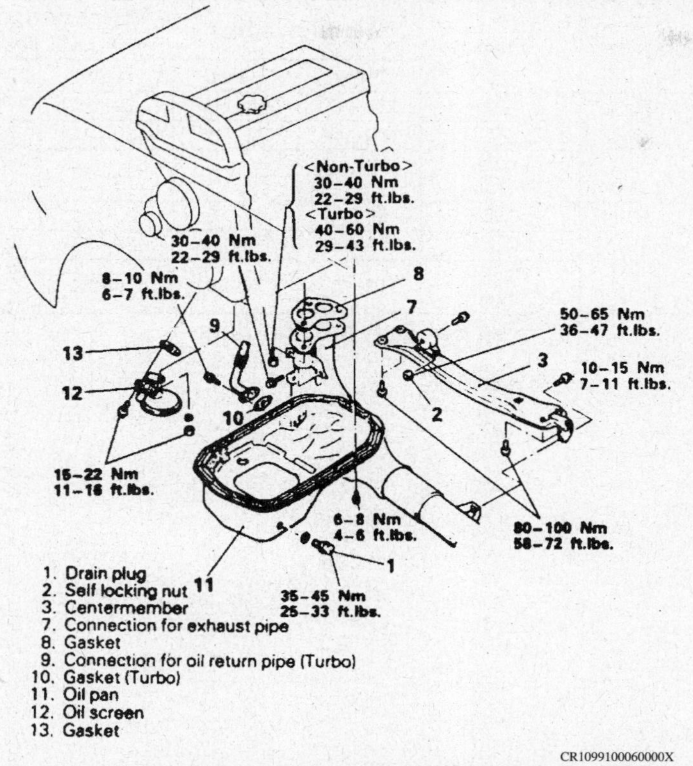

Fig. 55 Oil pan & screen replacement. Turbo FWD models

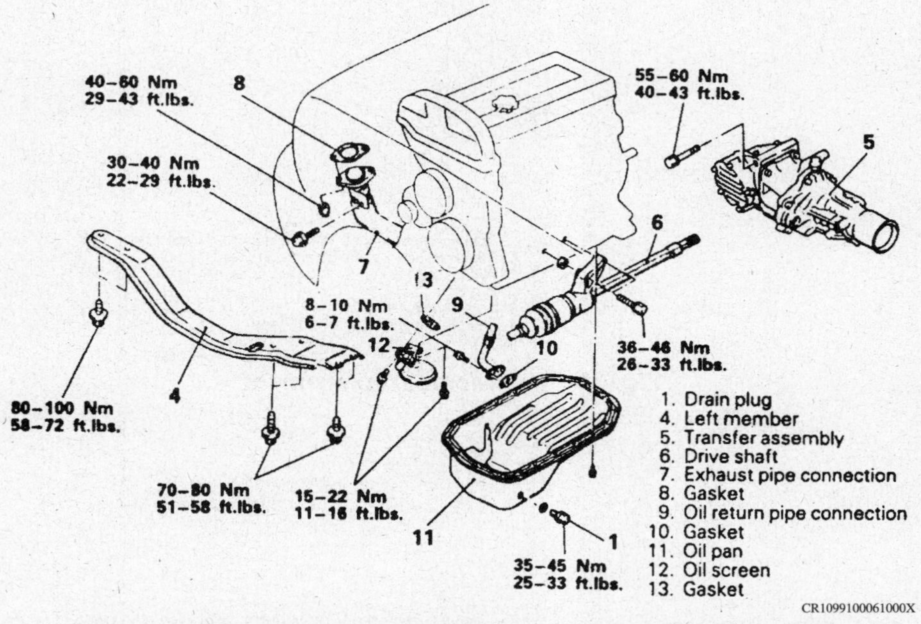

Fig. 56 Oil pan & screen replacement. Turbo AWD models

b. **On turbocharged models,** install air cleaner bracket
c. **On models equipped with automatic transaxle,** install cooling lines.
d. **On all models,** ensure drain is closed, then fill up coolant. Replace cap, then run engine until warm. Inspect for leaks, then inspect coolant level and fill if necessary.

FUEL PUMP

REPLACE

FWD MODELS

Removal

Remove fuel pump in numbered sequence, **Fig. 64.**

1. Relieve fuel pressure as outlined under "Precautions."
2. Remove fuel from fuel tank into a suitable container.
3. When disconnecting high pressure fuel line, cover fuel line connection with rags to prevent spraying of fuel.
4. Remove rear seat cushion and floor plate for access to fuel pump.
5. Disconnect hoses and connectors to remove fuel pump

Installation

Reverse removal procedure to install, noting the following:

1. Align packing position projections with holes in fuel pump assembly.
2. Ensure fuel pump assembly and hoses are not leaking.
3. Before installing hole cover plate, apply suitable sealant to rear floor pan.

AWD MODELS

Removal

Relieve fuel pressure as outlined under "Precautions."

Remove fuel pump in numbered sequence, **Fig. 65.**

1. Remove fuel from fuel tank into a suitable container.
2. When disconnecting high pressure fuel line, cover fuel line connection with rags to prevent spraying of fuel.
3. Remove rear seat cushion and floor plate for access to fuel pump.
4. Disconnect hoses and connectors to remove fuel pump

Installation

Reverse removal procedure to install, noting the following:

1. Ensure packing seal is not damaged or deformed.
2. Apply soapy water to fuel tank threads, then install fuel pump and cap.
3. Using special cap tightening tool No. MB991480, or equivalent, **Fig. 66, torque** cap to 36 ft. lbs.
4. Ensure fuel pump assembly and hoses are not leaking.

FUEL FILTER

REPLACE

Relieve fuel pressure as outlined under "Precautions."

1. When replacing fuel filter, refer to **Fig. 67** for removal and installation procedure.
2. **On turbocharged models,** remove battery and air intake hose to access fuel filter.
3. **On all models,** reverse procedure to install.

TURBOCHARGER

REPLACE

Remove turbocharger in numbered sequence, **Fig. 68,** noting the following:

1. Drain engine cooling system into a suitable container as follows:
   a. Place temperature control lever in hot position.

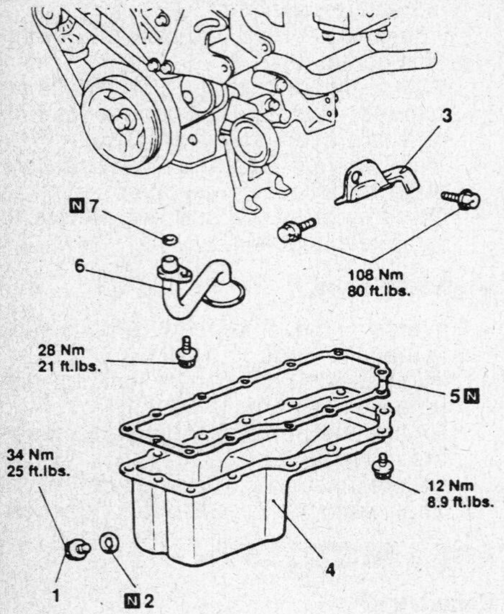

1. Drain plug
2. Gasket
3. Front plate
4. Oil pan
5. Oil pan gasket
6. Oil screen
7. O-ring

CR1069500618000X

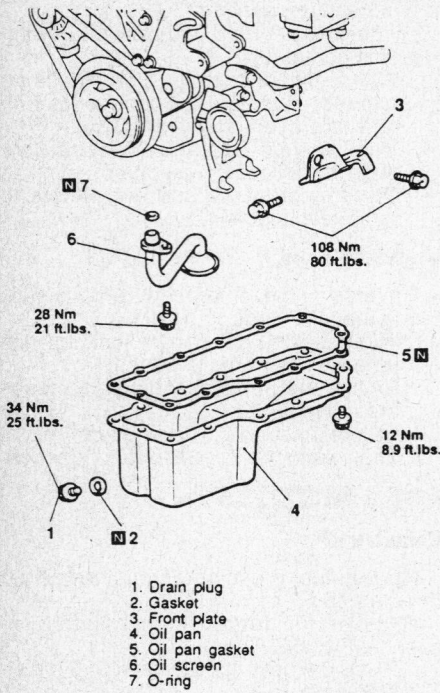

Fig. 57 Oil pan & screen replacement. Non-turbocharged engine

b. Carefully remove radiator cap.
c. Remove radiator drain plug.
2. Drain engine oil.
3. Disconnect oxygen sensor electrical connector, then using oxygen sensor socket tool No. MD998748, or equivalent, and an offset box-end wrench, remove oxygen sensor.
4. Remove power steering pump from bracket with hoses attached, then secure pump aside with a piece of wire.
5. Remove turbocharger assembly with water pipes A and B and oil pipe attached. **After disconnecting oil pipe, ensure foreign material does not enter oil passage hole of turbocharger.**
6. Reverse procedure to install, noting the following:
   a. Prior to installing turbocharger assembly, pour a small quantity of clean engine oil into oil supply pipe fitting hole in turbocharger.
   b. Clean alignment surfaces of turbocharger. **Use caution not to allow gasket or other foreign material to enter oil passage hole.**
   c. Use new gaskets, locknuts and O-rings.
   d. Install oxygen sensor using oxygen sensor socket tool No. MD998748, or equivalent, and an offset box-end wrench, then connect oxygen sensor electrical connector.

Year	Engine	Belt	Tension Lbs.		Deflection, Inch @ 22 lbs.	
			New	Used	New	Used
1997–98	Non-Turbo	A/C	137–159	93–115	.32–.35	.39–.43
		Alt.	110–160	90–110	.30–.41	.35–.47
		Power Steering	110–160	90–110	.26–.37	.43–.55
	Turbo	A/C	86–99	57–75	.22–.24	.26–.30
		Alt.	110–154	88	.30–.35	.39
		Power Steering	110–154	77–99	.18–.22	.24–.28

Fig. 58 Belt tension data

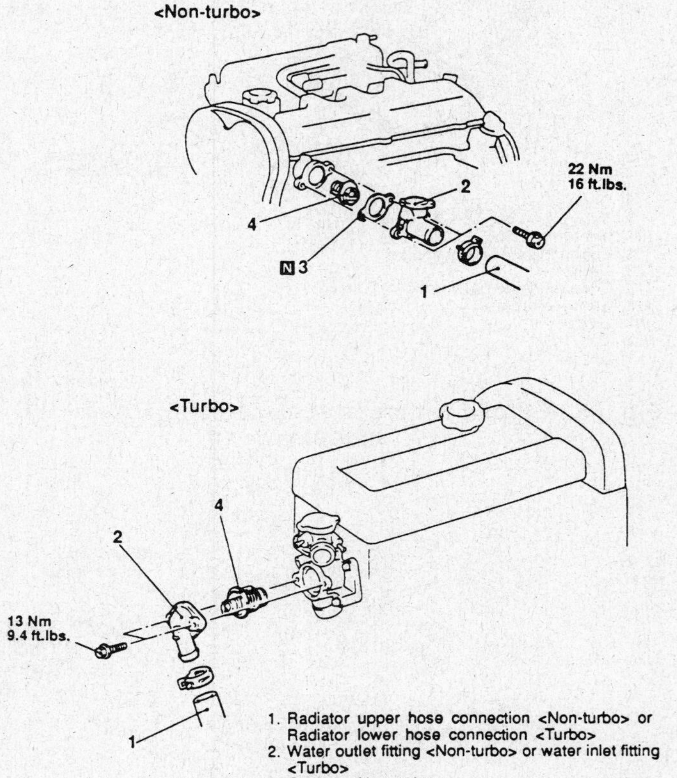

1. Radiator upper hose connection <Non-turbo> or Radiator lower hose connection <Turbo>
2. Water outlet fitting <Non-turbo> or water inlet fitting <Turbo>
3. Gasket <Non-turbo>
4. Thermostat

CR1089500145000X

Fig. 59 Thermostat replacement

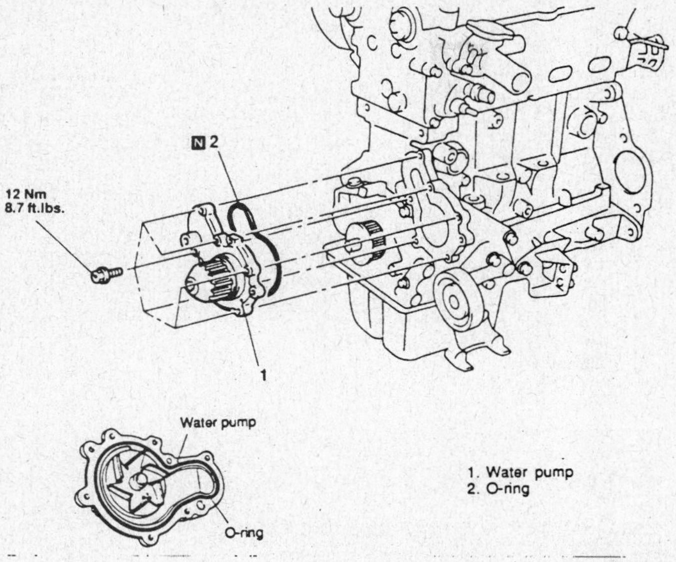

1. Water pump
2. O-ring

CR1089500146000X

Fig. 60 Water pump removal. Non-turbocharged engine

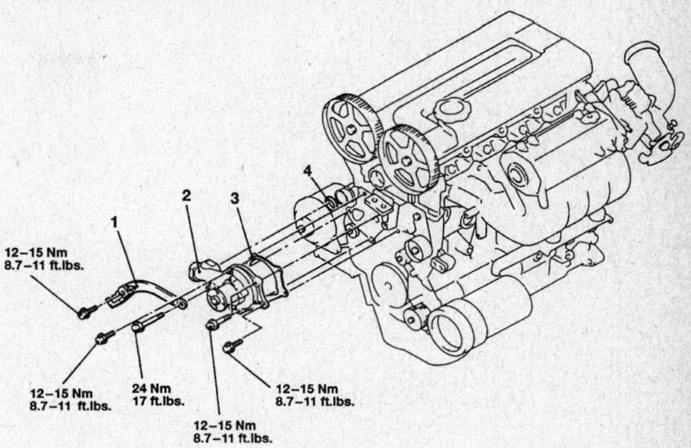

1. Generator brace
2. Water pump
3. Water pump gasket
4. O-ring

CR1089500147000X

Fig. 61 Water pump removal. Turbocharged engine

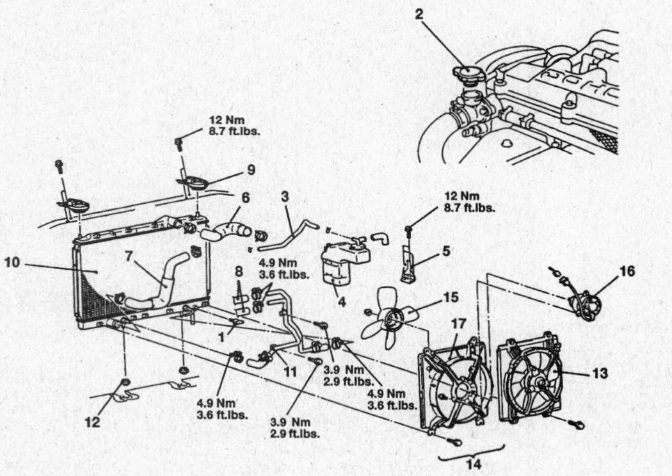

Radiator removal steps

1. Drain plug
2. Radiator cap
3. Overflow tube
4. Reserve tank
5. Reserve tank bracket
6. Radiator upper hose
7. Radiator lower hose
8. Transaxle fluid cooler hose connection <Vehicles with A/T>
9. Upper insulator
10. Radiator assembly
11. Transaxle fluid cooler hose and pipe assembly <Vehicles with A/T>
12. Lower insulator
13. Condenser fan motor assembly <Vehicles with A/C>
14. Radiator fan motor assembly
15. Fan
16. Radiator fan motor
17. Shroud

Radiator fan motor removal steps

11. Transaxle fluid cooler hose and pipe assembly <Vehicles with A/T>
14. Radiator fan motor assembly
15. Fan
16. Radiator fan motor
17. Shroud

CR1089500149000X

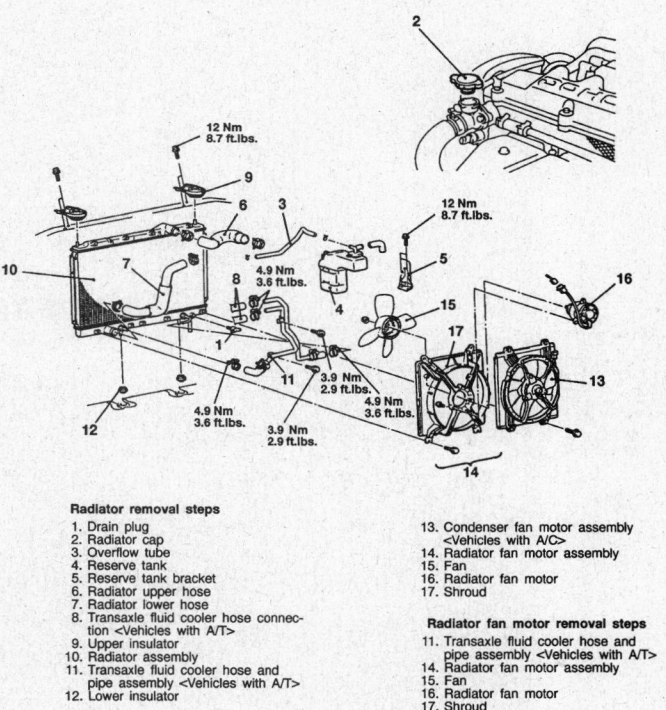

Fig. 62 Radiator replacement. Non-turbocharged engine

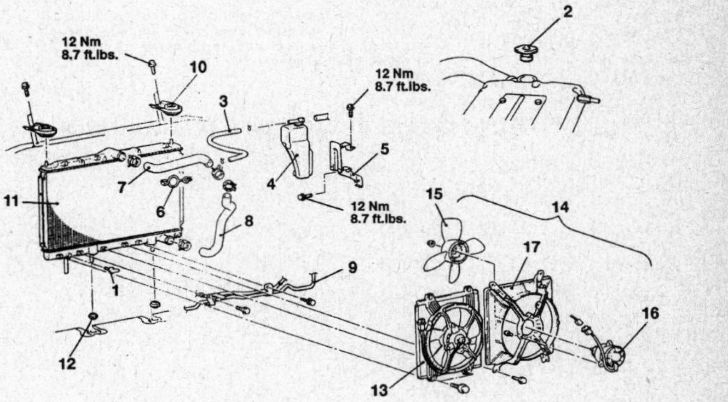

Radiator removal steps

1. Drain plug
2. Radiator cap
3. Overflow tube
4. Reserve tank
5. Reserve tank bracket
6. Clip
7. Radiator upper hose
8. Radiator lower hose
9. Transaxle fluid cooler hose and pipe assembly <Vehicles with A/T>
10. Upper insulator
11. Radiator assembly
12. Lower insulator
13. Condenser fan motor assembly <Vehicles with A/C>
14. Radiator fan motor assembly
15. Fan
16. Radiator fan motor
17. Shroud

Radiator fan motor removal steps

4. Reserve tank
9. Transaxle fluid cooler hose and pipe assembly <Vehicles with A/T>
14. Radiator fan motor assembly
15. Fan
16. Radiator fan motor
17. Shroud

CR1089500150000X

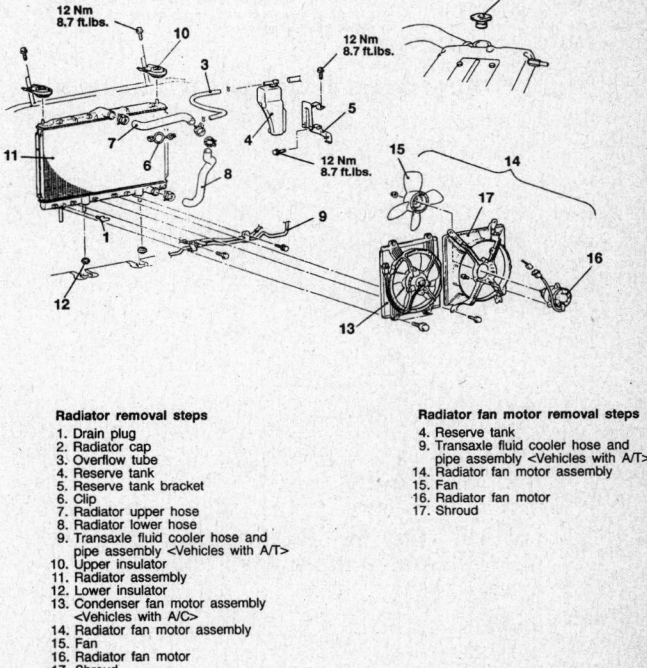

Fig. 63 Radiator replacement. Turbocharged engine

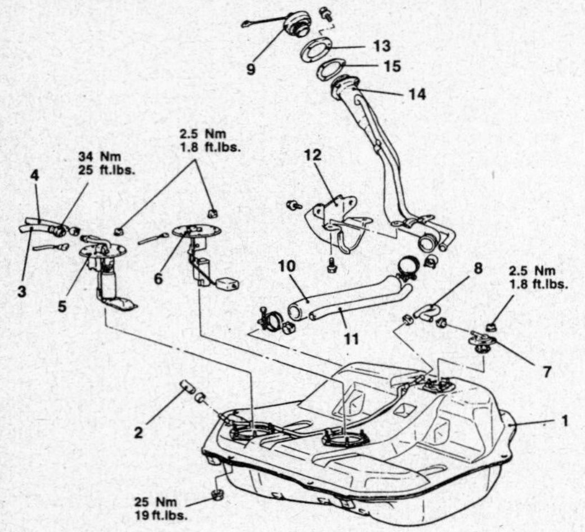

1. Fuel tank
2. Vapor hose
3. High-pressure fuel hose
4. Return hose
5. Fuel pump assembly
6. Fuel gauge unit
7. Fuel cut-off valve assembly
8. Vapor hose
9. Fuel tank filler tube cap
10. Filler hose
11. Vapor hose
12. Fuel tank filler tube protector
13. Reinforcement
14. Fuel tank filler tube assembly
15. Packing

NOTE
When replacing the fuel pump assembly or the fuel gauge unit only, it is possible to work from the service holes underneath the rear seat cushion without having to remove the fuel tank.

CR1029503772000X

Fig. 64 Fuel pump removal. FWD models

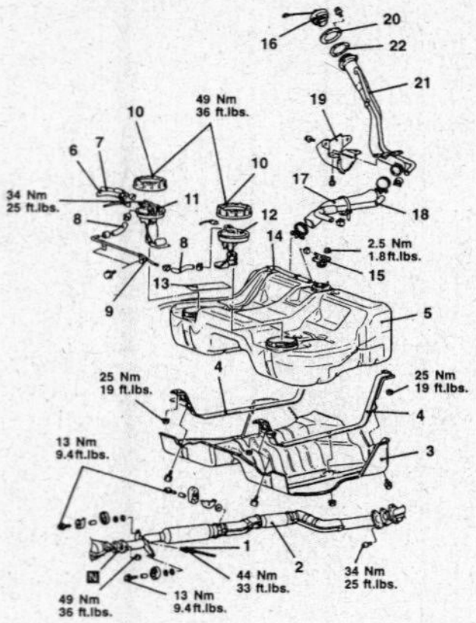

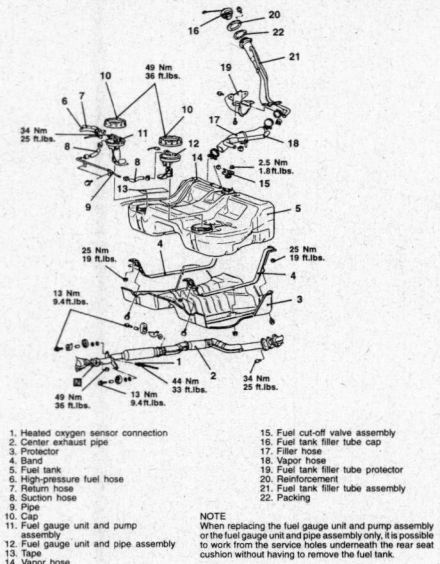

1. Heated oxygen sensor connection
2. Center exhaust pipe
3. Protector
4. Band
5. Fuel tank
6. High-pressure fuel hose
7. Return hose
8. Suction hose
9. Pipe
10. Cap
11. Fuel gauge unit and pump assembly
12. Fuel gauge unit and pipe assembly
13. Tape
14. Vapor hose
15. Fuel cut-off valve assembly
16. Fuel tank filler tube cap
17. Filler hose
18. Vapor hose
19. Fuel tank filler tube protector
20. Reinforcement
21. Fuel tank filler tube assembly
22. Packing

NOTE
When replacing the fuel gauge unit and pump assembly or the fuel gauge unit and pipe assembly only, it is possible to work from the service holes underneath the rear seat cushion without having to remove the fuel tank.

CR1029503773000X

Fig. 65 Fuel pump removal. AWD models

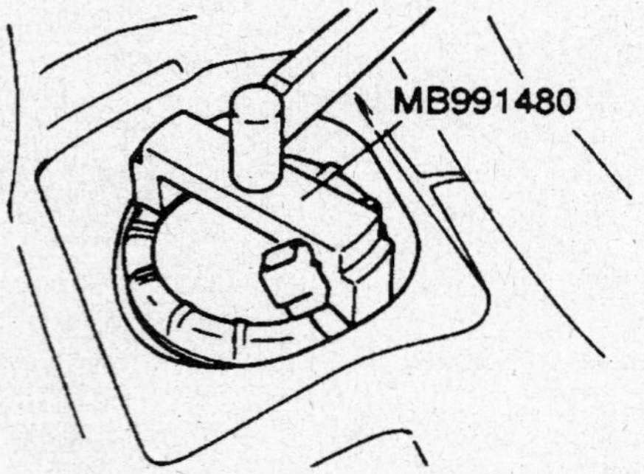

CR1029503774000X

Fig. 66 Fuel pump cap installation. AWD models

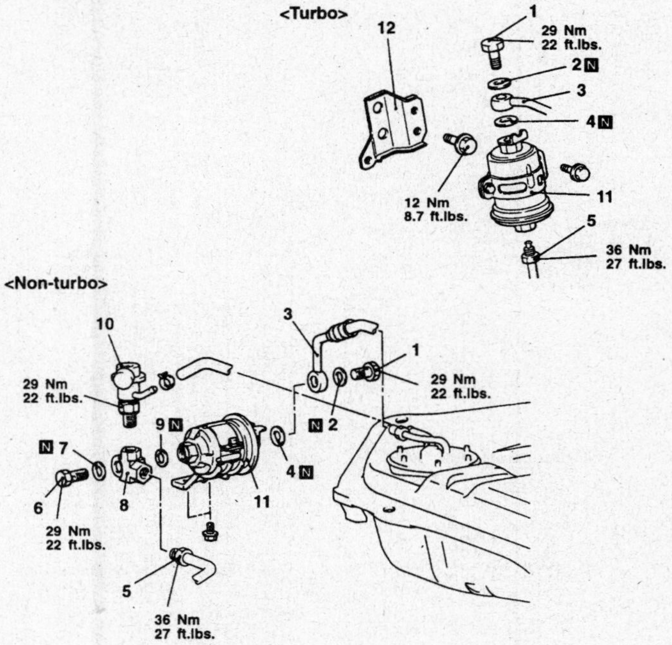

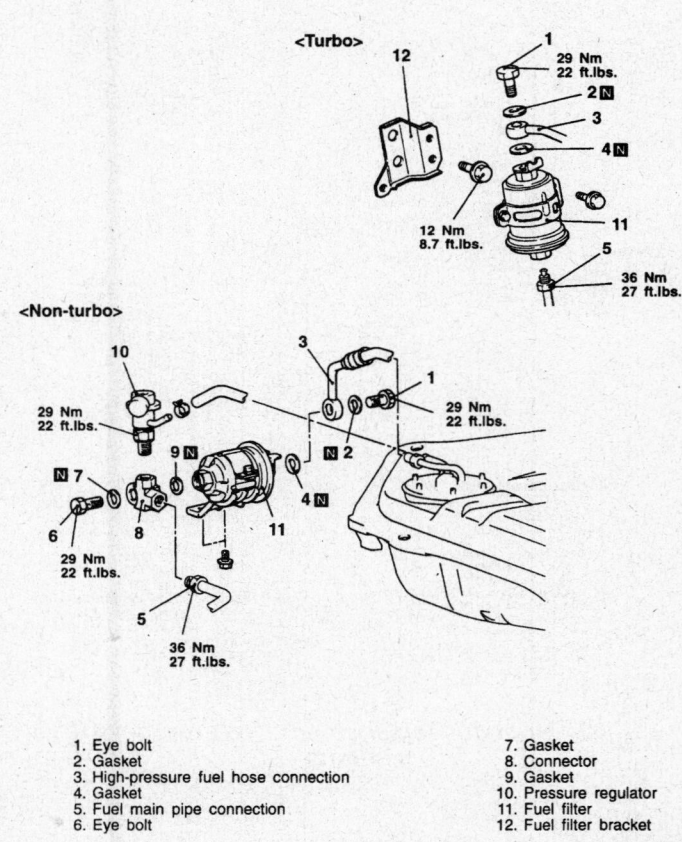

1. Eye bolt
2. Gasket
3. High-pressure fuel hose connection
4. Gasket
5. Fuel main pipe connection
6. Eye bolt
7. Gasket
8. Connector
9. Gasket
10. Pressure regulator
11. Fuel filter
12. Fuel filter bracket

CR1029607304000X

Fig. 67 Fuel filter replacement

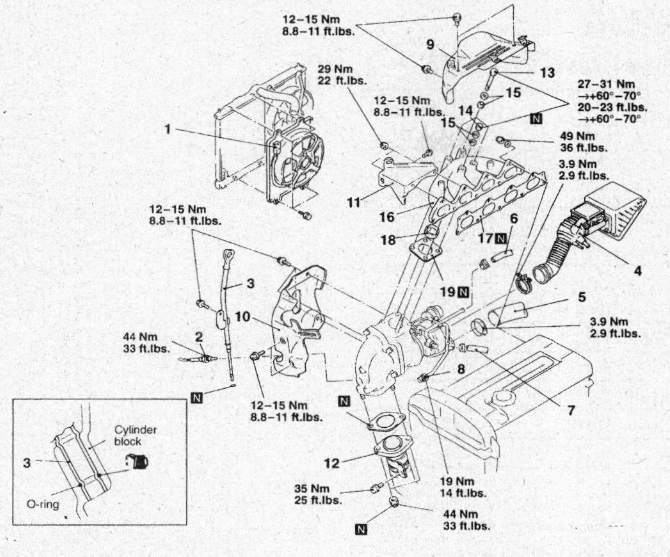

1. Condenser fan motor assembly <Vehicles with air conditioning>
2. Heated oxygen sensor <front>
3. Engine oil level gauge guide
4. Air cleaner and air intake hose assembly
5. Air hose (A) connection
6. Water hose connection
7. Water hose connection
8. Oil pipe (A) connection
9. Heat protector (A)
10. Heat protector (B)
11. Engine hanger
12. Front exhaust pipe connection
13. Flange bolts
14. Flange nut
15. Coned disc spring
16. Exhaust manifold
17. Exhaust manifold gasket
18. Ring
19. Gasket (A)

CR1059600119010X

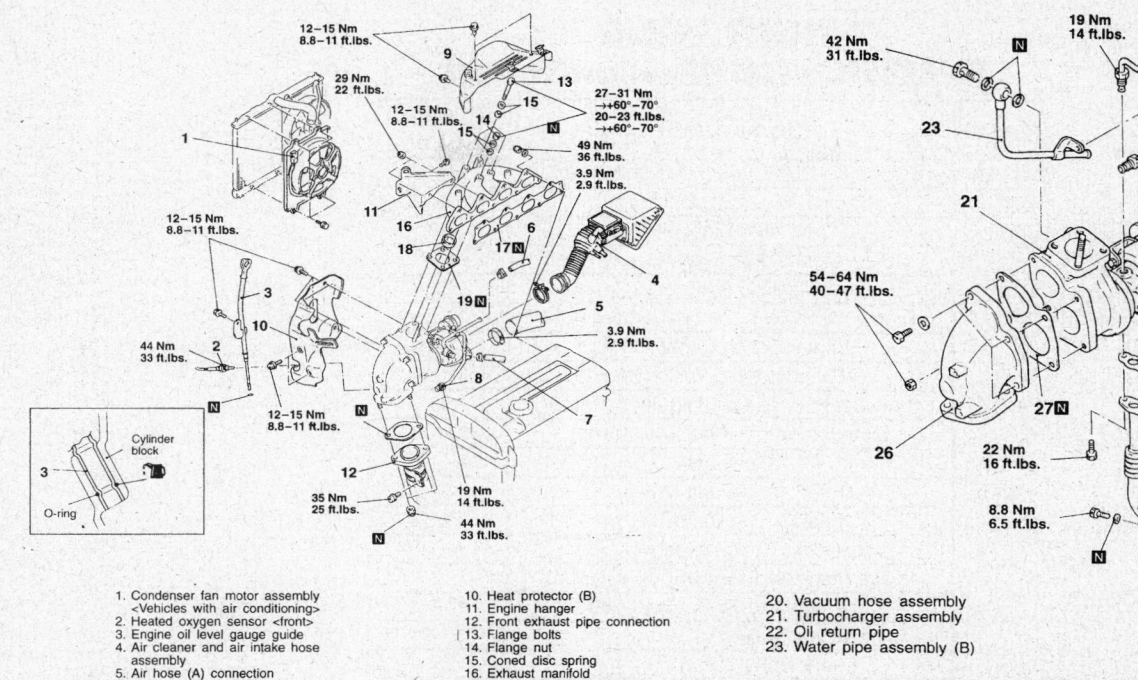

Fig. 68 Turbocharger removal (Part 1 of 2)

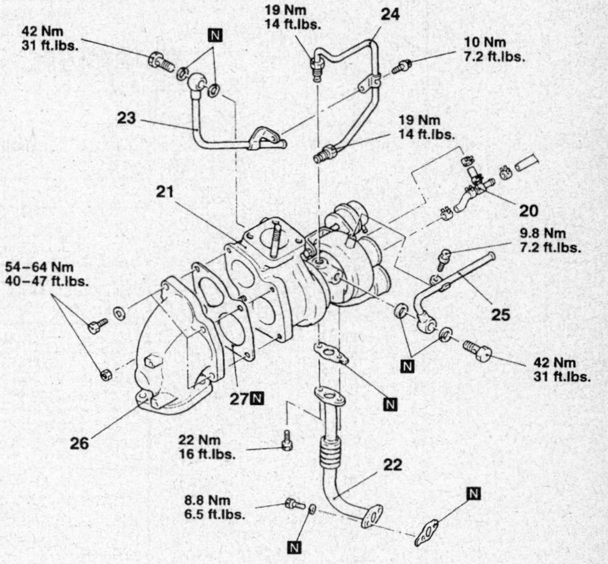

20. Vacuum hose assembly
21. Turbocharger assembly
22. Oil return pipe
23. Water pipe assembly (B)
24. Oil pipe assembly
25. Water pipe assembly (A)
26. Exhaust manifold fitting
27. Gasket

CR1059600119020X

Fig. 68 Turbocharger removal (Part 2 of 2)

TIGHTENING SPECIFICATIONS

Year	Component	Torque/ Ft. Lbs.
1997–98	A/C Compressor Bracket	17–20
	Air Cleaner-to-Body	72–84⑤
	Auto Tensioner (Non-Turbo)	23
	Auto Tensioner (Turbo)	17
	Camshaft Bearing Cap Bolt-Main (Non-Turbo)	21
	Camshaft Bearing Cap Bolt-Small (Non-Turbo)	108⑤
	Camshaft Bearing Cap Bolt (Turbo)	14–15
	Camshaft Sprocket (Non-Turbo)	75
	Camshaft Sprocket (Turbo)	65
	Center Cover (Turbo)	26⑤
	Connecting Rod Bearing Caps (Turbo)	15③
	Connecting Rod Bearing Caps (Non-Turbo)	20⑥
	Crankshaft Bearing Caps Inner (Non-Turbo)	55
	Crankshaft Bearing Caps- Outer (Non-Turbo)	20
	Crankshaft Bearing Cap (Turbo)	18③
	Crankshaft Pulley (Non-Turbo)	105
	Crankshaft Pulley (Turbo)	18
	Crankshaft Sprocket (Turbo)	80–94
	Cylinder Head Bolt	①
	EGR Valve	16
	Electric Fuel Pump (Bolt)	22⑤
	Engine Coolant Temperature Sensor	60⑤
	Engine Mount Insulator Mounting Bolt	49
	Engine Mount Stopper Bolt	71–85

Continued

TIGHTENING SPECIFICATIONS—Continued

Year	Component	Torque/ Ft. Lbs.
1997-98	Engine Oil Cooler Mounting Bolt (Turbo)	29–33
	Engine Roller Stopper (Front)	41
	Engine Roller Stopper (Rear)	32
	Exhaust Manifold To Engine (Non-Turbo)	17
	Exhaust Manifold To Engine (Turbo)	22
	Exhaust Manifold To Turbocharger (Turbo)	②
	Exhaust Pipe Clamp Bolt	113⑤
	Exhaust Pipe To Hanger	113⑤
	Exhaust Pipe To Manifold (Non-Turbo)	33
	Exhaust Pipe To Manifold (Turbo)	33–36
	Flywheel	94–101
	Fuel Gauge Unit (AWD)	36
	Fuel Gauge Unit (FWD)	22⑤
	Heat Shield To Exhaust Manifold (Turbo)	9–11
	Intake Manifold To Engine (Non-Turbo)	17
	Intake Manifold To Engine (Turbo)	14
	Oil Filter Bracket (Turbo)	11–16
	Oil Pan (Non-Turbo)	108⑤
	Oil Pan (Turbo)	60⑤
	Oil Pan Drain Plug (Non-Turbo)	25
	Oil Pan Drain Plug (Turbo)	29
	Oil Pressure Gauge Unit (Turbo)	84⑤
	Oil Pressure Switch (Turbo)	84⑤
	Oil Pump Cover (Non-Turbo)	17
	Oil Pump Cover (Turbo)	9–12
	Oil Pump Driven Gear (Turbo)	84⑤
	Oil Return Pipe To Oil Pan (Turbo)	78
	Oil Screen (Non-Turbo)	21
	Oil Screen (Turbo)	14
	Oxygen Sensor	22
	Tensioner Pulley Bracket (Turbo)	17–20
	Throttle Body	11–16
	Timing Belt B Tensioner Bolt (Turbo)	14
	Timing Belt Front Cover, Bottom (Non-Turbo)	21
	Timing Belt Front Cover, Top (Non-Turbo)	108⑤
	Timing Belt Front Cover (Turbo)	④
	Timing Belt Tensioner (Turbo)	17–20
	Timing Belt Tensioner Pulley (Non-Turbo)	30
	Water Pump (Non-Turbo)	104⑤
	Water Pump (Turbo)	9–11

① — Refer to "Cylinder Head, Replace" for procedure.

② — Refer to "Exhaust Manifold, Replace" for procedure.

③ — Tighten an additional 90–100.°

④ — Refer to "Timing Belt, Replace" for procedure.

⑤ — Inch lbs.

⑥ — Tighten an additional 90.°

Clutch & Manual Transaxle

INDEX

ADJUSTMENTS

CLUTCH PEDAL

1. Measure clutch pedal height or clevis pin play as shown, **Fig. 1.**
2. If height is higher than 7.0–7.1 inches, refer to **Fig. 2** for adjustment.
3. If pedal height is lower than 7.0–7.1 inches, proceed as follows:
   a. Loosen bolt or clutch switch and turn pushrod until pedal height is proper, **Fig. 3. Do not move pushrod toward master cylinder.**
   b. After adjustment, tighten bolt or clutch switch to reach pedal stopper, then lock with locknut.
4. If clevis pin play is not .04–.12 inch, turn pushrod until clevis pin play is proper.
5. Ensure interlock switch is as shown, **Fig. 4,** when clutch pedal is fully depressed, and if necessary, adjust.
6. Confirm clutch pedal freeplay, **Fig. 5,** is .24 –.51 inches.
7. Confirm distance between clutch pedal and firewall, when clutch is disengaged, **Fig. 5,** is 2.7 inches or more. If distance is not as specified, problem may be the result of air in hydraulic system or faulty master cylinder or clutch.

HYDRAULIC SYSTEM SERVICE

HYDRAULIC CLUTCH SYSTEM BLEED

Whenever the any component of the hydraulic clutch system has been removed, bleeding must be performed.

Ensure clutch hydraulic cylinder is full, have helper depress clutch pedal and hold, open bleeder screw on hydraulic cylinder, then close bleeder screw. Repeat procedure until all air is bled from system.

CLUTCH SLAVE CYLINDER, REPLACE

1. Drain clutch fluid into a suitable container.
2. Disconnect clutch slave cylinder tube connections.
3. Remove slave cylinder retaining bolts then the slave cylinder.
4. Reverse procedure to install, noting the following:
   a. Apply multi-purpose grease to slave cylinder pushrod where it contacts the release fork.

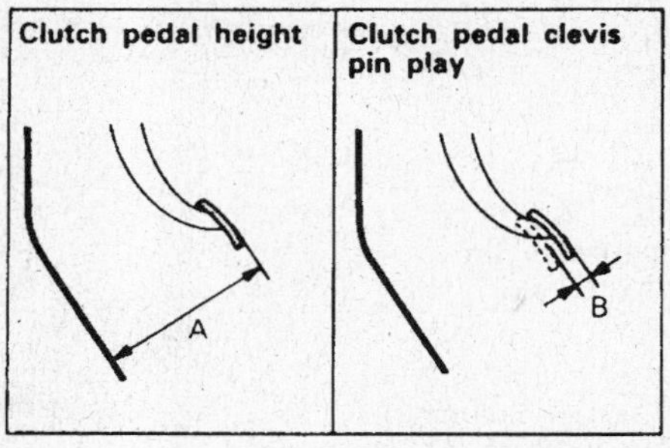

Fig. 1 Clutch pedal inspection

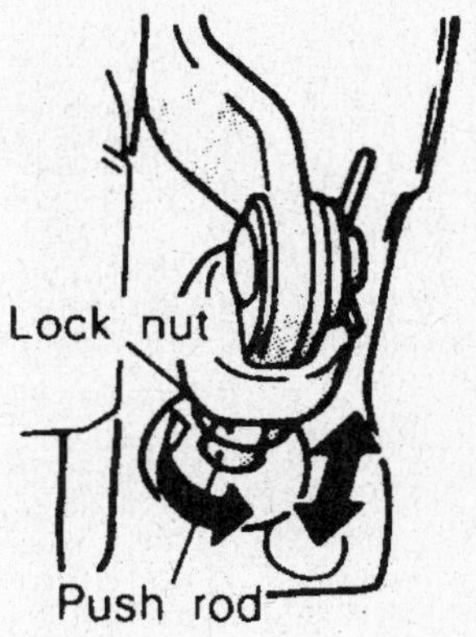

Fig. 3 Pushrod adjustment

   b. Bleed hydraulic clutch system as outlined under " Hydraulic Clutch System Bleeding."

CLUTCH

REPLACE

Replace clutch in numbered sequence **Fig. 6,** noting the following:

1. Remove transaxle as outlined under "Transaxle, Replace."
2. Diagonally loosen clutch cover bolts in two or three steps.
3. Support clutch cover and remove cover bolts, lowering clutch and clutch cover.
4. Slide release fork in direction of arrow as shown in **Fig. 7** and disengage fulcrum from clip to release fork. **Do not push the release fork in direction other than arrow or remove with force as clip may be damaged.**
5. Reverse procedure to install. Use special clutch positioning tool No. MD998126, or equivalent, to install clutch disc on flywheel, **Fig. 8.**

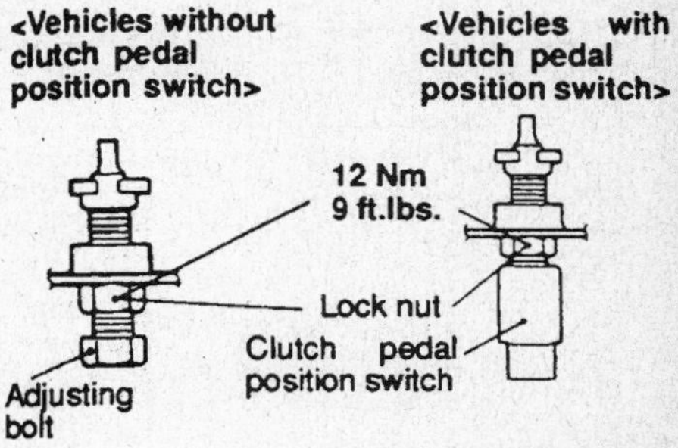

Fig. 2 Clutch pedal adjustment

TRANSAXLE

REPLACE

Remove transaxle in numbered sequence, **Fig. 9** for non-turbocharged models, **Fig. 10** for turbocharged models with Front Wheel Drive (FWD), and **Fig. 11** for turbocharged models with All Wheel Drive (AWD), noting the following:

1. Remove battery.
2. Raise and support vehicle.
3. Drain transaxle oil.
4. Remove undercover.
5. **On AWD models,** remove transfer case.
6. **On all models,** using a suitable jack, slightly raise transaxle, then remove mounting bracket nuts. **Do not tilt transaxle assembly.**
7. Use special engine support tool No. MZ203827, or equivalent, to support engine assembly, **Fig. 12.**
8. Using special tool No. MB991113, or equivalent, remove tie rod ends, lateral lower arms, and compression lower arms, **Figs. 13 through 15. Loosen but do not remove nuts. Suspend special tool by cord to hold in place.**
9. **On AWD models,** remove driveshaft nut using special tool No. MB990767, or equivalent, **Fig. 16.**
10. **On all models,** disconnect driveshaft as follows:
    a. Insert pry bar between transaxle case and driveshaft, **Fig. 17,** then pry driveshaft from transaxle. **Do not pull on driveshaft, as doing so will damage inboard joint. Do not insert pry bar so deep as to damage oil seal.** Suspend driveshaft with suitable wire.
11. **On AWD models,** lightly tap center bearing bracket using a suitable plastic hammer to remove inner shaft from transaxle, **Fig. 18.**

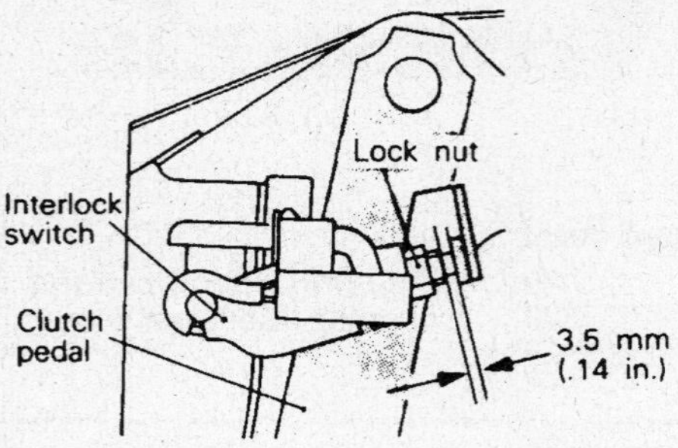

CR5049100066000X

Fig. 4 Interlock switch adjustment

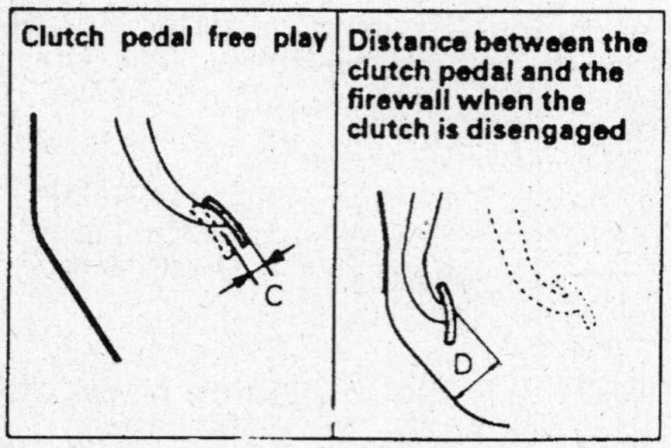

CR5049100067000X

Fig. 5 Clutch pedal operation inspection

12. **On all models,** remove clutch release cylinder without disconnecting fluid line and suspend it nearby with suitable wire.
13. **On FWD models,** remove flexplate connecting bolts and transaxle assembly mounting bolts, ensuring the following:
    a. Transaxle must be solidly supported by suitable jack.
    b. Chalk mating marks on the flex plate and clutch pressure plate for easier installation, **Fig. 19.**
    c. Press clutch pressure plate into the transaxle for easier removal.
14. **On all models,** reverse procedure to install noting;
    a. Inspect front roll stopper. If dimension shown in **Fig. 20** is not 1.57–1.81 inches, replace roll stopper bracket assembly.
    b. Ensure serrated part of driveshaft does not damage oil seal lip.
    c. **On AWD models,** install driveshaft nut washer as shown in **Fig. 21.** Using special tool No. MB990767, or equivalent, tighten driveshaft nut as specified in **Fig. 21.** Ensure there is no load on wheel bearings.

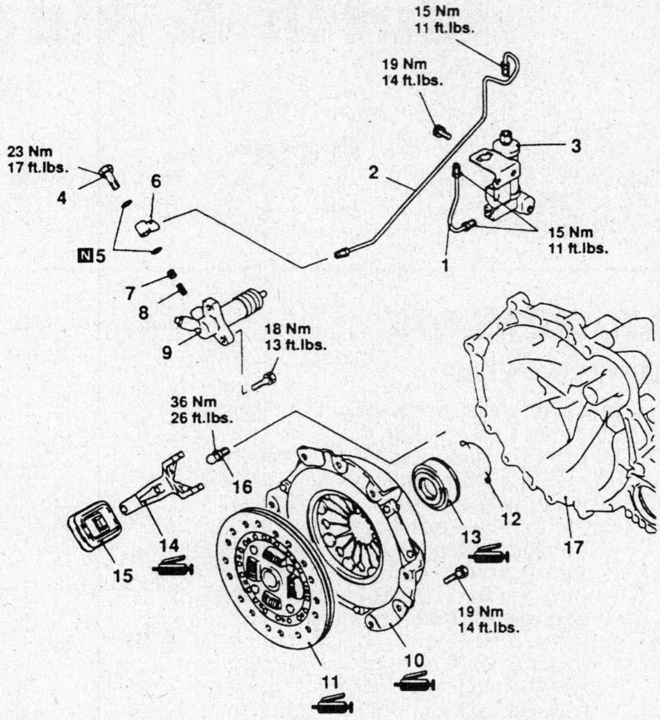

1. Clutch oil tube (A)
2. Clutch oil tube
3. Clutch oil fluid chamber
4. Union bolt
5. Gasket
6. Union
7. Valve plate
8. Valve plate spring
9. Clutch release cylinder
10. Clutch cover
11. Clutch disc
12. Return clip
13. Clutch release bearing
14. Release fork
15. Release fork boot
16. Fulcrum
17. Transaxle

CR5049500087000X

Fig. 6 Clutch assembly replacement

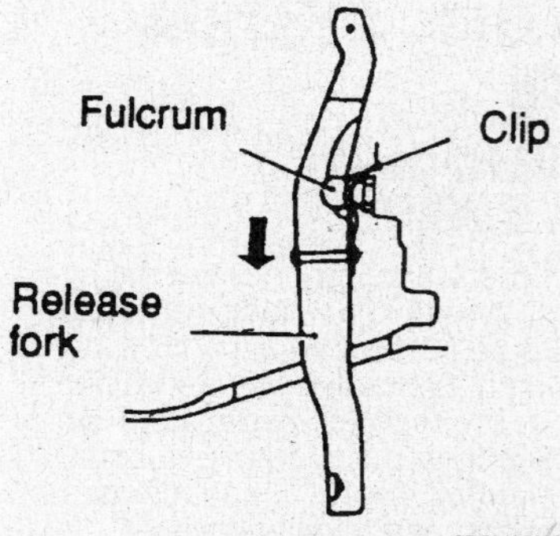

CR5049500088000X

Fig. 7 Release fork removal

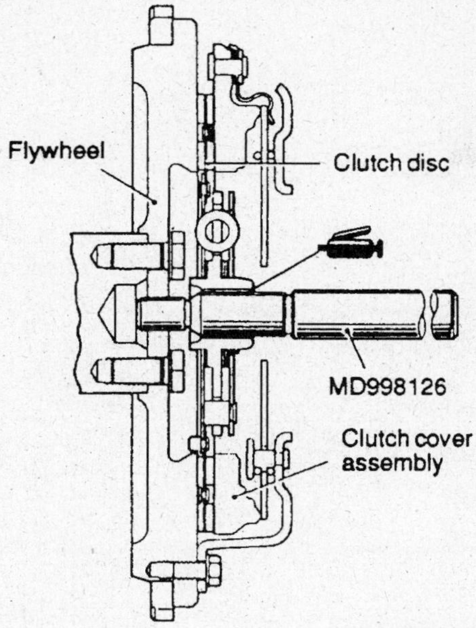

CR5049500089000X

Fig. 8 Clutch disc installation

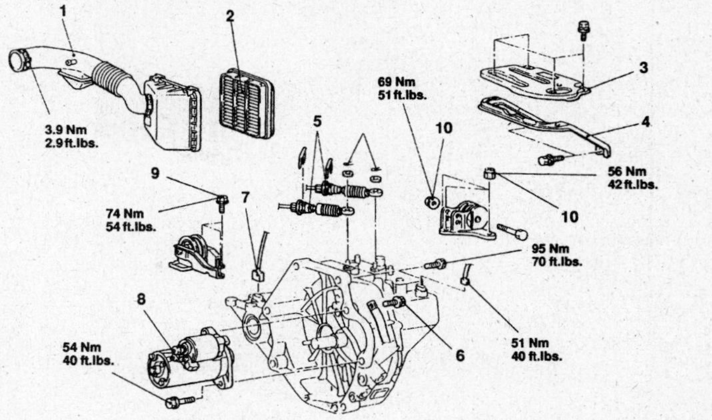

1. Air cleaner cover and air intake hose assembly
2. Air cleaner element
3. Battery tray
4. Battery tray stay
5. Shift cable and select cable connection
6. Backup light switch connector
7. Vehicle speed sensor connector
8. Starter motor
9. Rear roll stopper bracket mounting bolts
10. Transaxle mounting bracket mounting nuts

CR5039500925010X

Fig. 9 Transaxle removal (Part 1 of 2) Non-turbocharged engine

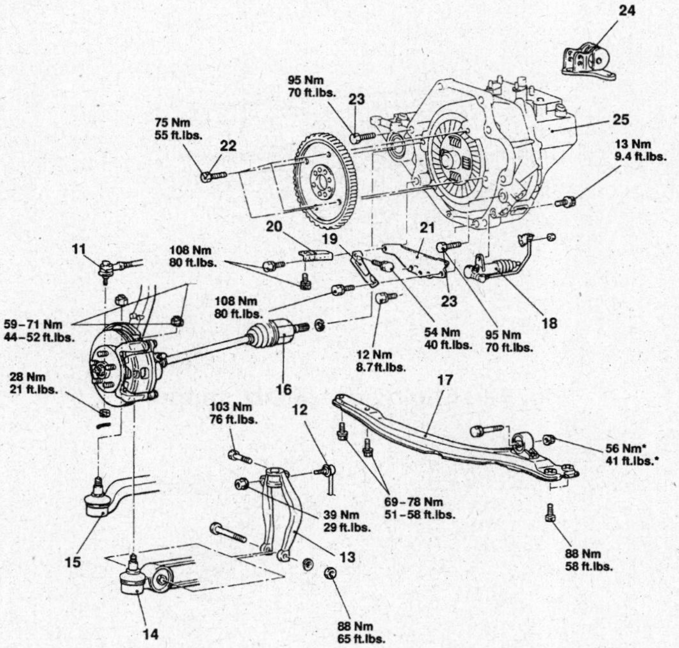

Lifting up of the vehicle

11. Tie rod end connection
12. Stabilizer link connection
13. Damper fork
14. Lateral lower arm connection
15. Compression lower arm connection
16. Drive shaft connection
17. Center member assembly
18. Clutch release cylinder connection
19. Front plate
20. Rear plate
21. Transaxle case lower cover
22. Flex plate connecting bolts
23. Transaxle assembly mounting bolts
24. Transaxle mounting
25. Transaxle assembly

CR5039500925020X

Fig. 9 Transaxle removal (Part 2 of 2). Non-turbocharged engine

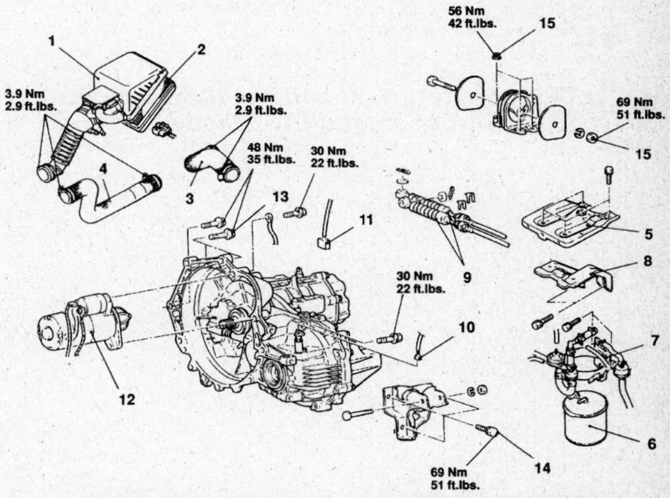

1. Air cleaner cover and air intake hose assembly
2. Air cleaner element
3. Air hose C
4. Air hose A
5. Battery tray
6. Evaporative emission canister
7. Evaporative emission canister holder
8. Battery tray stay
9. Shift cable and select cable connection
10. Backup light switch connector
11. Vehicle speed sensor connector
12. Starter motor
13. Transaxle assembly mounting bolts
14. Rear roll stopper bracket mounting bolts
15. Transaxle mounting bracket mounting nuts

CR5039500926010X

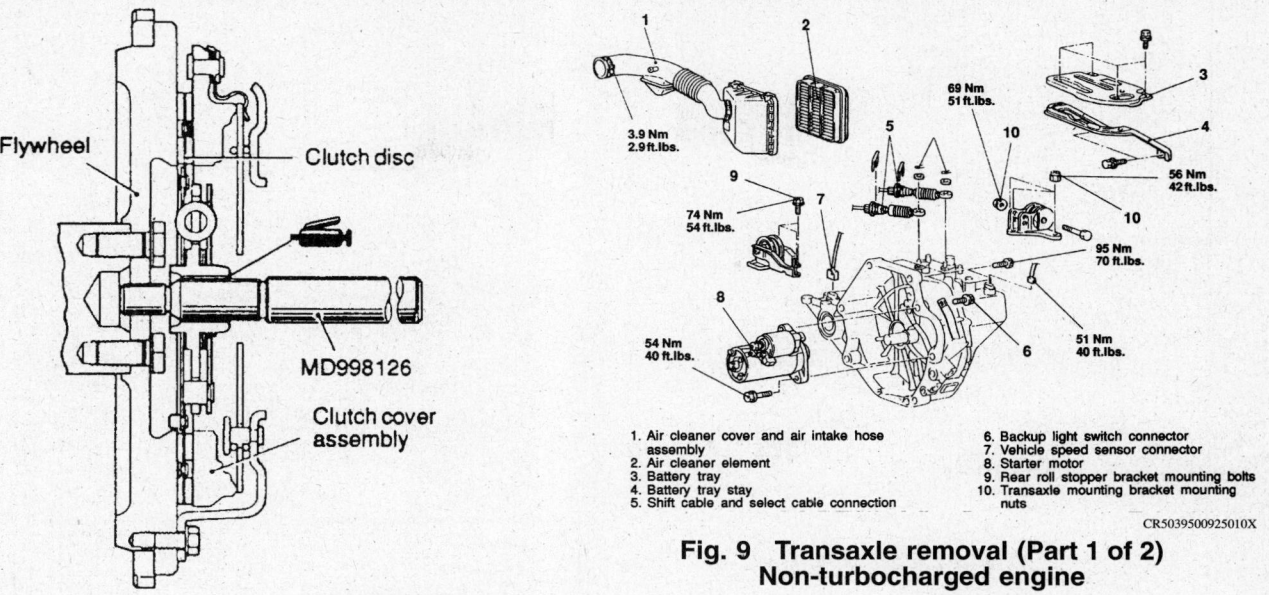

Fig. 10 Transaxle removal (Part 1 of 2). Turbocharged FWD models

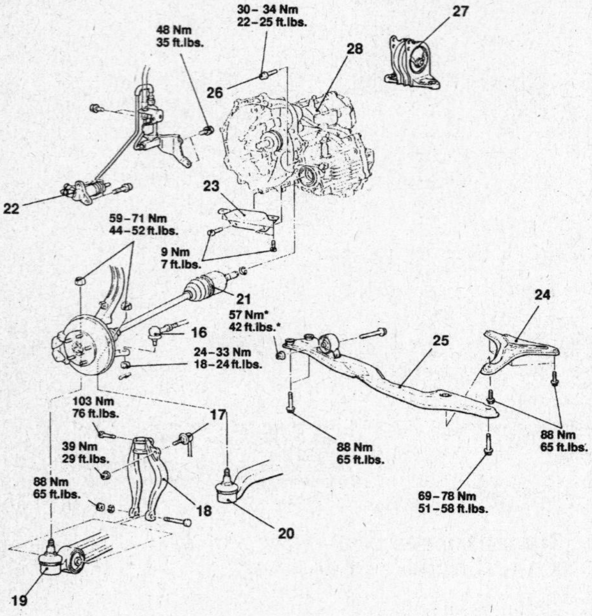

Lifting up of the vehicle

16. Tie rod end connection
17. Stabilizer link connection
18. Damper fork
19. Lateral lower arm connection
20. Compression lower arm connection
21. Drive shaft connection
22. Clutch release cylinder connection
23. Bell housing cover
24. Stay (R.H.)
25. Center member assembly
26. Transaxle assembly mounting bolt
27. Transaxle mounting
28. Transaxle assembly

CR5039500926020X

Fig. 10 Transaxle removal (Part 2 of 2). Turbocharged FWD models

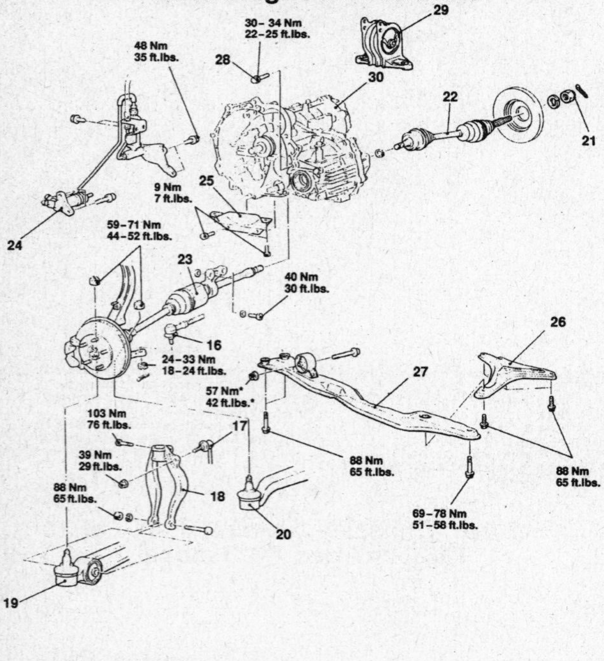

Lifting up of the vehicle

16. Tie rod end connection
17. Stabilizer link connection
18. Damper fork
19. Lateral lower arm connection
20. Compression lower arm connection
21. Drive shaft nut
22. Drive shaft
23. Drive shaft connection
24. Clutch release cylinder connection
25. Bell housing cover
26. Stay (R.H.)
27. Center member assembly
28. Transaxle assembly mounting bolt
29. Transaxle mounting
30. Transaxle assembly

CR5039500927020X

Fig. 11 Transaxle removal (Part 2 of 2). Turbocharged AWD models

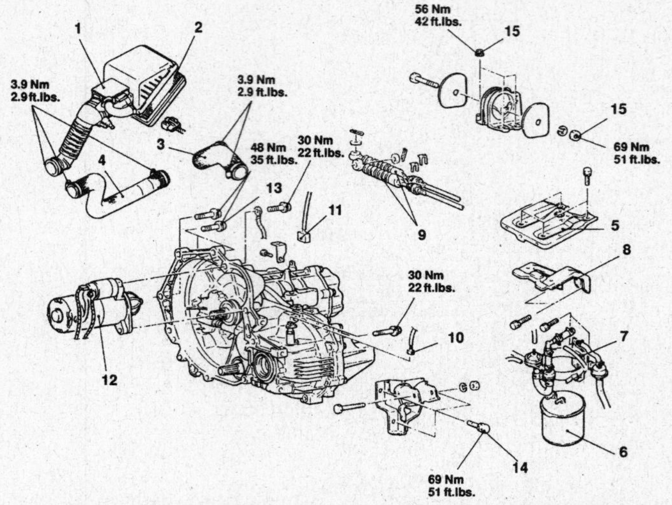

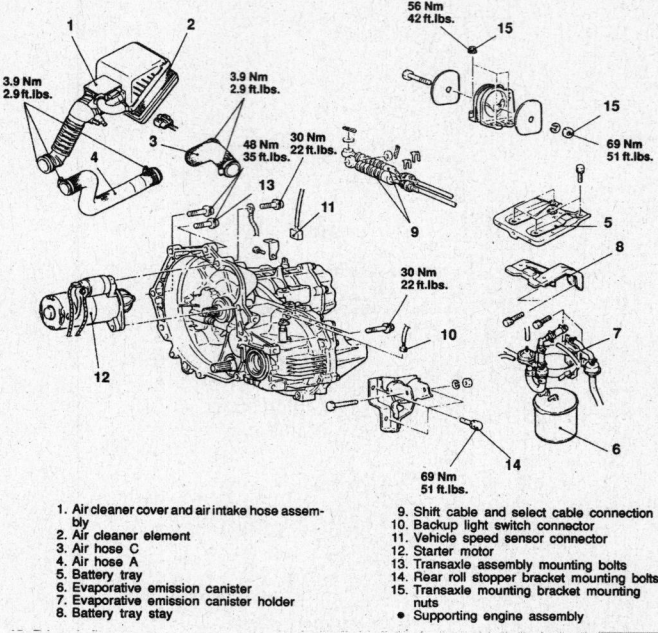

1. Air cleaner cover and air intake hose assembly
2. Air cleaner element
3. Air hose C
4. Air hose A
5. Battery tray
6. Evaporative emission canister
7. Evaporative emission canister holder
8. Battery tray stay
9. Shift cable and select cable connection
10. Backup light switch connector
11. Vehicle speed sensor connector
12. Starter motor
13. Transaxle assembly mounting bolts
14. Rear roll stopper bracket mounting bolts
15. Transaxle mounting bracket mounting nuts

• Supporting engine assembly

CR5039500927010X

Fig. 11 Transaxle removal (Part 1 of 2). Turbocharged AWD models

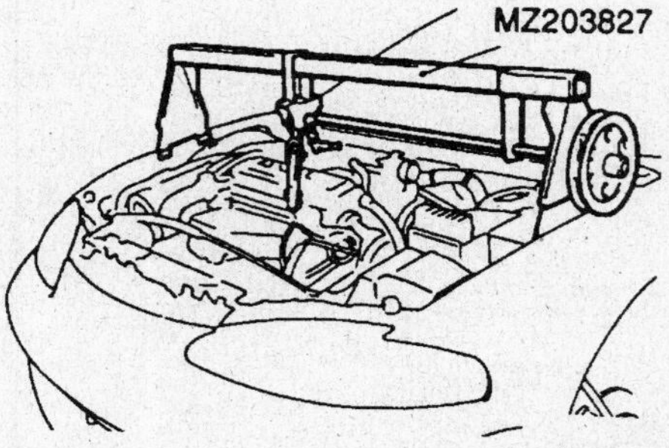

CR5039500928000X

Fig. 12 Engine assembly support

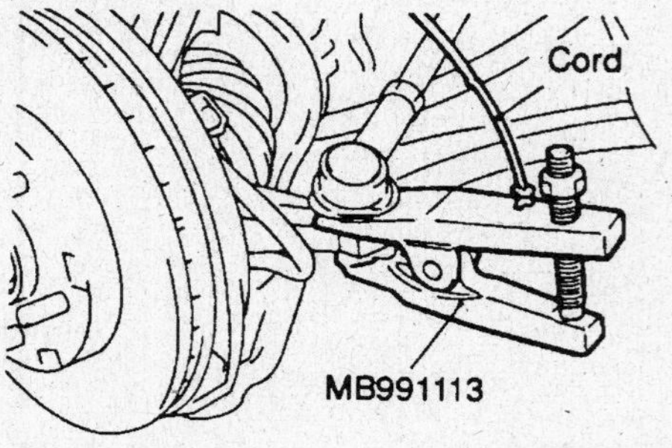

CR5039500929000X

Fig. 13 Tie rod end removal

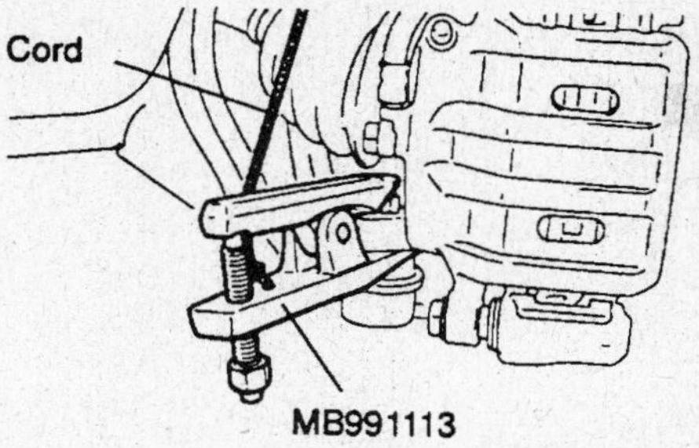

CR5039500930000X

Fig. 14 Lateral lower arm removal

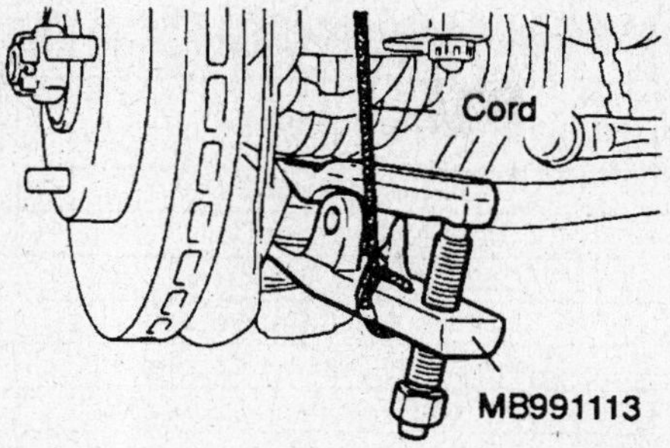

CR5039500931000X

Fig. 15 Compression lower arm removal

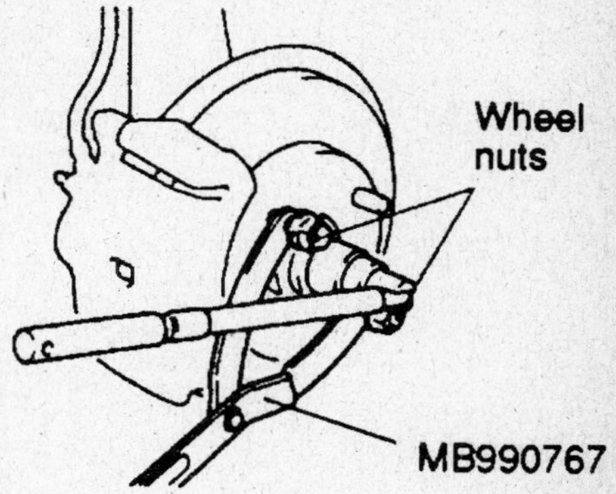

CR5039500932000X

Fig. 16 Driveshaft nut removal. AWD models

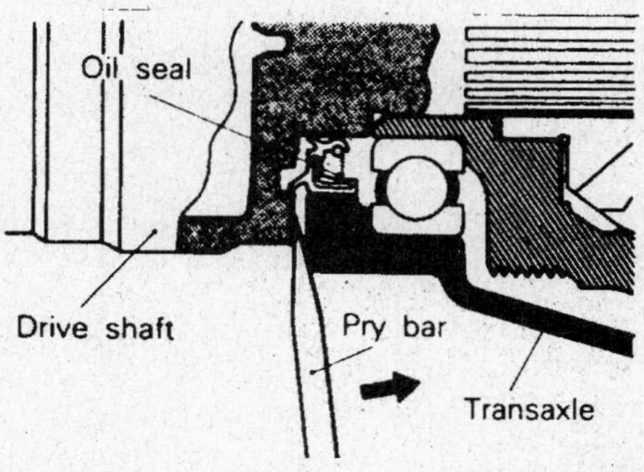

CR5039100916000X

Fig. 17 Driveshaft removal

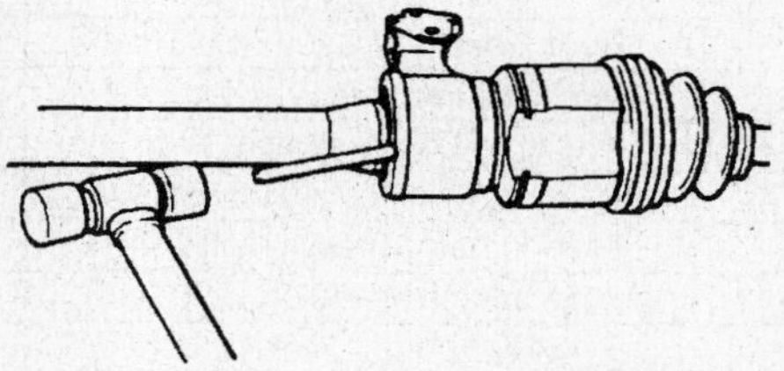

CR5039500933000X

Fig. 18 Inner shaft removal. AWD models

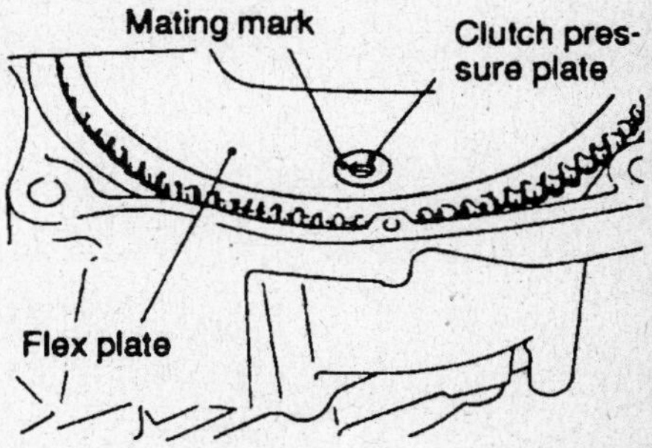

CR5039500934000X

Fig. 19 Flex plate mating marks. FWD models

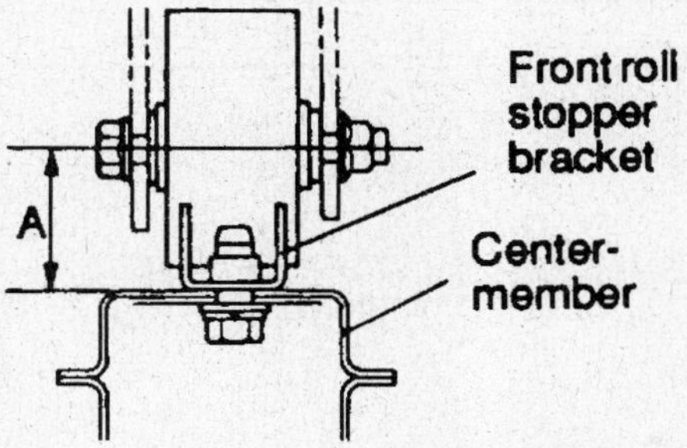

CR5039500935000X

Fig. 20 Front roll stopper inspection

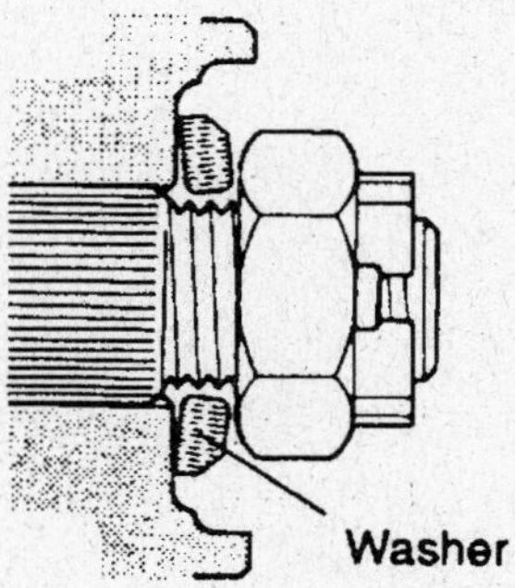

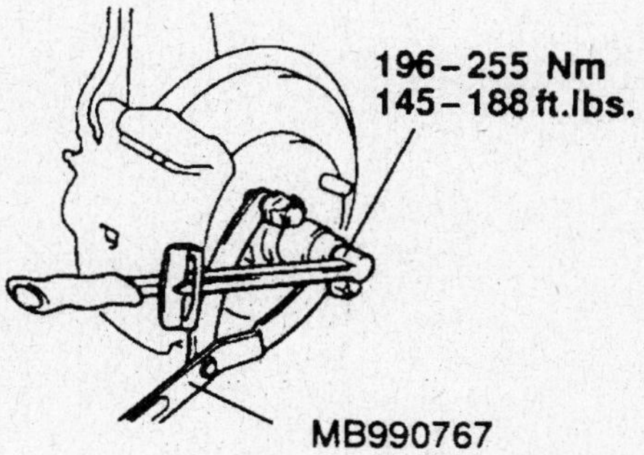

CR5039500936000X

Fig. 21 Driveshaft nut installation. AWD models

TIGHTENING SPECIFICATIONS

Year	Component	Torque/ Ft. Lbs.
1997–98	Back-Up Lamp Switch	22
	Bearing Retainer Bolt	14
	Clutch Cover Assembly	11–16
	Clutch Pedal Bracket	72–108①
	Clutch Pedal Support Bracket	72–108①
	Clutch Pedal To Support Bracket	14–18
	Clutch Release Cylinder	11–16
	Compression Lower Arm	44–52
	Flywheel Bolts	55
	Lower Arm Ball Joint To Knuckle	44–52
	Poppet Plug	27
	Rear Housing Cover Bolt	14
	Rear Roll Stopper Bracket	51
	Restrict Ball Assembly	24
	Shift & Select Cable To Transaxle	11–16
	Speedometer Sleeve Bolt	36①
	Starter Motor Mounting Bolt	40
	Stop Lamp Switch	24
	Tie Rod End To Knuckle	18–24
	Transaxle Case Tightening Bolt	29
	Transaxle Mounting Bolt	35
	Transfer Assembly Mounting Bolt	40–44
	Wheel Lug Nut	88–108

① — Inch lbs.

Rear Axle & Suspension

INDEX

REAR AXLE SHAFT

REPLACE

Remove rear driveshaft in numbered sequence, **Fig. 1** noting the following:

1. Remove driveshaft nut using removal tool No. MB990767, or equivalent.
2. Remove driveshaft by pushing the lower part of the knuckle to the outside of the vehicle, then separate the driveshaft from the differential carrier. At this time, use a suitable tire lever or similar tool to separate the driveshaft connection.
3. Reverse procedure to install, noting the following:
   a. Ensure proper driveshaft placement. The righthand driveshaft has an orange boot band, while the lefthand driveshaft has a green boot band.
   b. Ensure differential carrier oil seal is not damaged by driveshaft spline.
   c. Using special tool No. MB990767, or equivalent, tighten driveshaft nut to specifications. Ensure there is no load on wheel bearings.

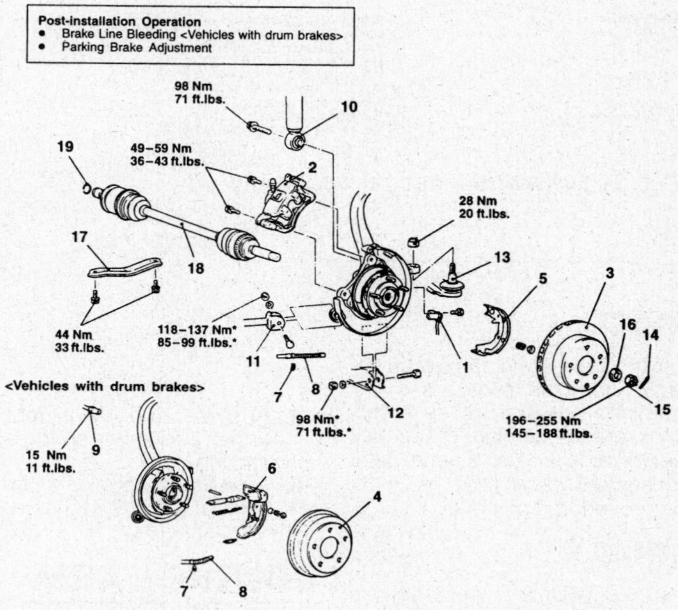

1. Rear wheel speed sensor <Vehicles with ABS>
2. Caliper assembly
3. Brake disc
4. Brake drum
5. Shoe and lever assembly
6. Shoe and lever assembly
7. Clip
8. Parking brake cable
9. Brake pipe connection
10. Shock absorber connection
11. Trailing arm connection
12. Lower arm connection
13. Toe control arm ball joint and knuckle connection
14. Cotter pin
15. Drive shaft nut
16. Washer
17. Differential mount support
18. Drive shaft
19. Circlip

Caution

1. **For vehicles with ABS, be careful not to damage the drive shaft rotor.**
2. ***: Indicates parts which should be temporarily tightened, and then fully tightened with the vehicle on the ground in the unladen condition.**

CR3039500356000A

Fig. 1 Driveshaft replacement

DIFFERENTIAL CARRIER

REPLACE

Replace differential carrier in numbered sequence shown in **Fig. 2,** noting the following:

1. Remove rear axle shaft as described under "Rear Axle Shaft, Replace."
2. Mark with mating marks, then disconnect propeller shaft assembly.
3. Suspend propeller shaft out of the way.
4. Support differential carrier with suitable jack for removal.
5. Reverse procedure to install.

HUB & BEARING

REPLACE

FWD MODELS

Remove rear axle hub in numbered sequence, **Fig. 3,** noting the following:

1. Remove rear speed sensor.
2. Remove and suspend caliper assembly with a piece of wire. **Do not hang caliper by brake hose.**
3. Reverse procedure to install.

BALL JOINT INSPECTION

AWD MODELS

Inspect ball joint for proper starting torque as follows:

1. Move ball joint stud from side to side several times.
2. Mount two nuts on ball joint, then using a suitable torque wrench measure starting torque. Starting torque should be within 17–78 inch lbs. for lower arm and upper arm ball joints, and 15–28 inch lbs. for stabilizer link ball joint.
3. If starting torque exceeds upper limit, replace lower arm assembly.
4. If starting torque is below lower limit, the ball joint may still be reused unless it has drag or excessive play.

WHEEL BEARING

ADJUST

1. To inspect bearing endplay, proceed as follows:
   a. Place hub in suitable vise, protected by wood blocks, **Fig. 4.**
   b. Place dial gauge against hub surface, then move hub in axial direction.
   c. If endplay exceeds .002 inch, use special wheel bearing installer tool No. MB990998, or equivalent, to tighten bearing. **Torque** special tool to 145–188 ft. lbs.
2. Replace hub bearing unit if adjustment cannot be made to within limit.

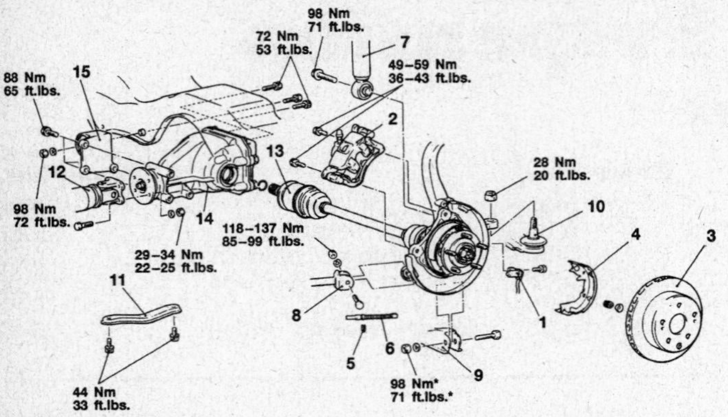

1. Rear wheel speed sensor <Vehicles with ABS>
2. Caliper assembly
3. Brake disc
4. Shoe and lining assembly
5. Clip
6. Parking brake cable
7. Shock absorber connection
8. Trailing arm connection
9. Lower arm connection
10. Toe control arm ball joint and knucle connection
11. Differential mount support
12. Propeller shaft connection
13. Drive shaft connection
14. Differential carrier
15. Differential mount bracket assembly

CR3039500357000X

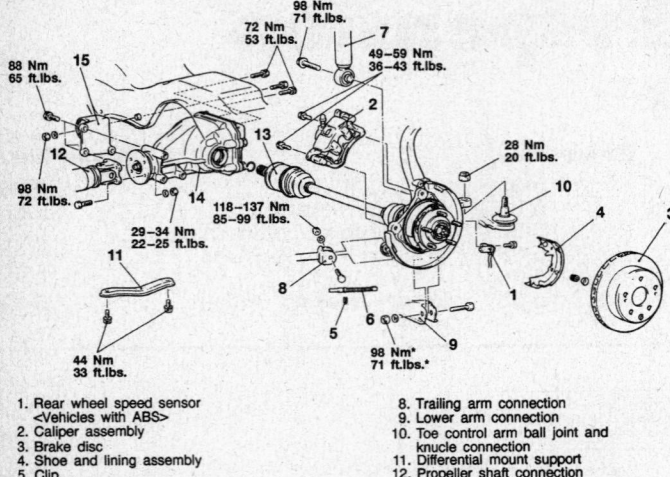

Fig. 2 Differential carrier assembly

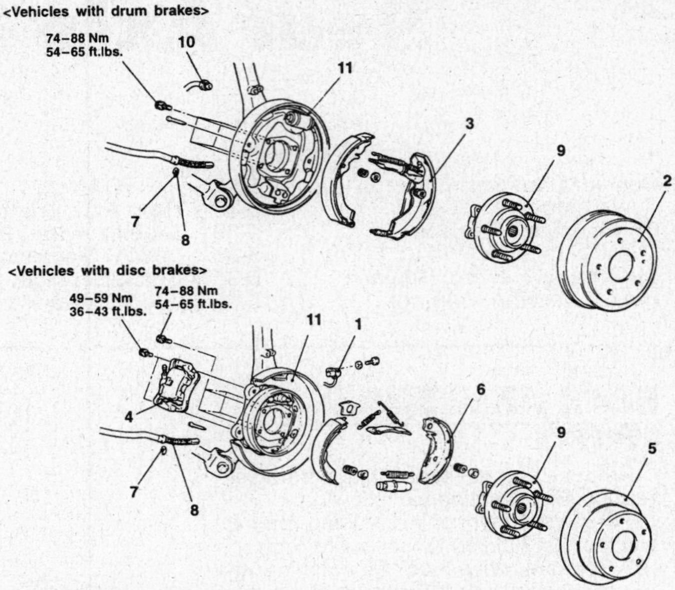

1. Rear wheel speed sensor <Vehicles with ABS>
2. Brake drum
3. Shoe and lever assembly
4. Caliper assembly
5. Brake disc
6. Shoe and lining assembly
7. Clip
8. Parking brake cable
9. Rear hub assembly
10. Brake pipe connection
11. Dust seal

Caution
The rear hub assembly should not be disassembled.

CR3039500358000A

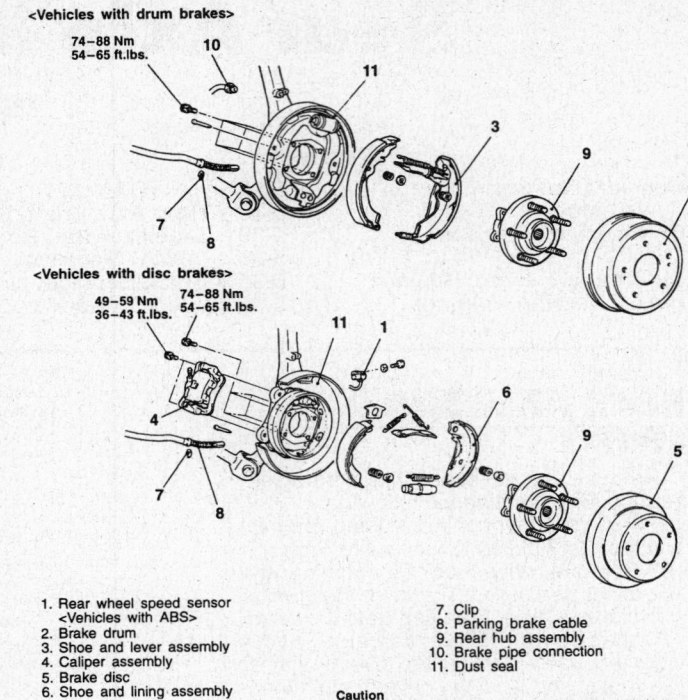

Fig. 3 Rear axle hub replacement. FWD models

STRUT

REPLACE

FWD MODELS

Remove strut assembly in numbered sequence, **Fig. 5,** noting the following:

1. Jack up torsion axle and arm assembly in order to release tension. Place jack at center of axle beam. Ensure jack does not contact lateral rod
2. Reverse procedure to install.

AWD MODELS

Remove shock absorber assembly in numbered sequence, **Fig. 5,** noting the following:

1. Jack up torsion axle and arm assembly in order to release tension. Place jack at center of axle beam. Ensure jack does not contact lateral rod.
2. Reverse procedure to install.

STRUT SERVICE

Disassemble strut assembly in numbered sequence shown in **Fig. 6,** noting the following:

1. Compress spring using spring compression tools No. MB991237 and MB991239, or equivalents, to ease in disassembly and assembly.
2. Ensure spring is properly seated in upper and lower spring seat when installing.
3. Install strut upper bracket as shown in **Fig. 7,** then tighten strut rod nut to specifications.

CONTROL ARM

REPLACE

AWD MODELS

Remove upper and lower arm in numbered sequences, **Figs. 8 and 9,** noting the following:

1. Loosen, but do not remove self-locking nut.
2. Inspect all bushings and bolts for wear and damage.
3. Reverse procedures to install.

TRAILING ARM

REPLACE

AWD MODELS

Remove trailing arm in numbered sequence, **Fig. 10,** noting the following:

1. Inspect bushings and bolts for wear or damage.
2. Inspect trailing arm for bends or damage.
3. Reverse procedure to install.

STABILIZER BAR

REPLACE

AWD MODELS

Remove stabilizer bar in numbered sequence, **Fig. 11,** noting the following:

1. Reverse procedure to install, noting the following:
   a. Set stabilizer bar so identification mark is at the left.
   b. Install the bushing, ensure the dimension is as shown in **Fig. 12.**

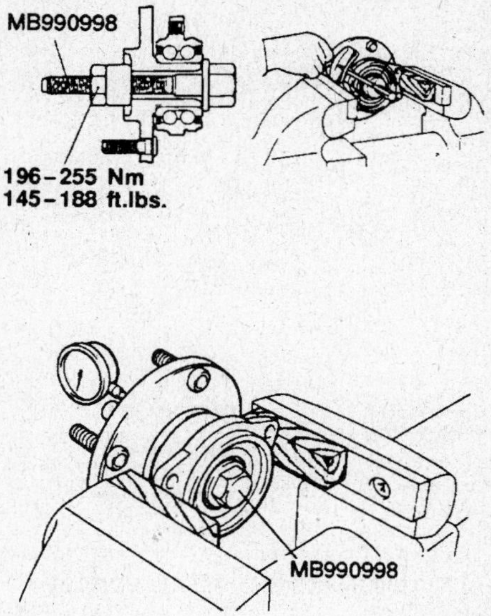

Fig. 4 Hub endplay adjustment

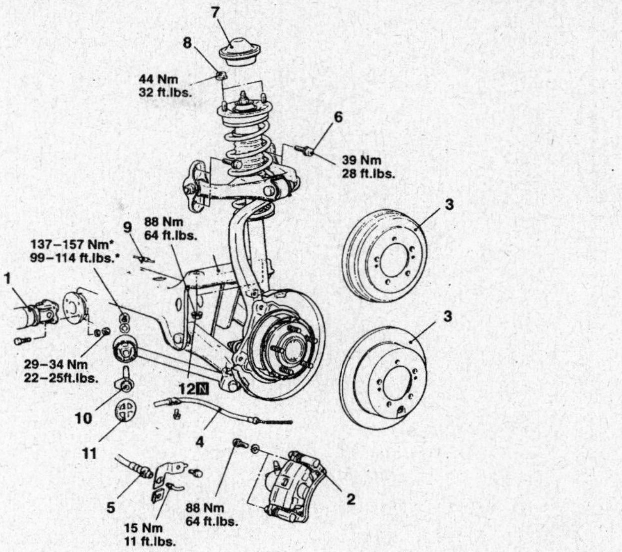

1. Propeller shaft connection <AWD>
2. Brake caliper assembly
3. Brake disc <Vehicles with disc brakes> or brake drum <Vehicles with drum brakes>
4. Parking brake cable end
5. Brake hose connection <Vehicles with drum brakes>
6. Upper arm bracket mounting bolts
7. Cap
8. Shock absorber mounting nuts
9. Rear wheel-speed sensor connector <Vehicles with ABS>
10. Grommet
11. Trailing arm mounting bolt
12. Crossmember mounting self-locking nuts
13. Rear suspension assembly

Caution
*** : indicates parts which should be temporarily tightened, and then fully tightened with the vehicles on the ground in the unladen condition.**

CR2039500061000A

Fig. 5 Strut assembly removal

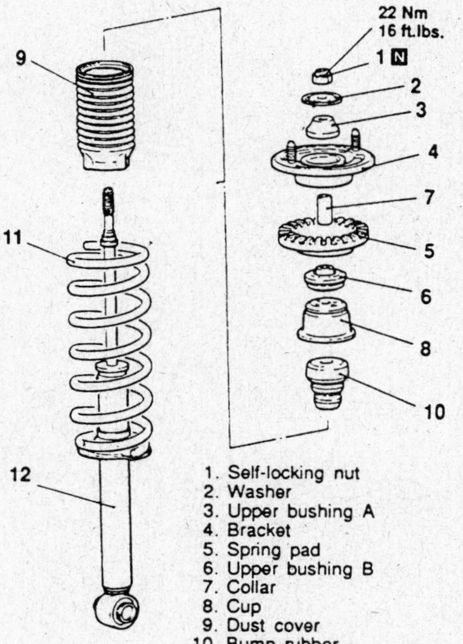

1. Self-locking nut
2. Washer
3. Upper bushing A
4. Bracket
5. Spring pad
6. Upper bushing B
7. Collar
8. Cup
9. Dust cover
10. Bump rubber
11. Coil spring
12. Shock absorber assembly

CR2039500062000X

Fig. 6 Exploded view of strut assembly

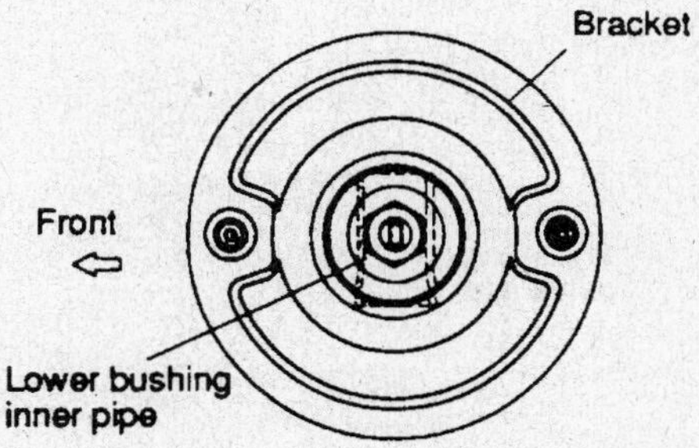

CR2039500063000X

Fig. 7 Upper spring mount installation

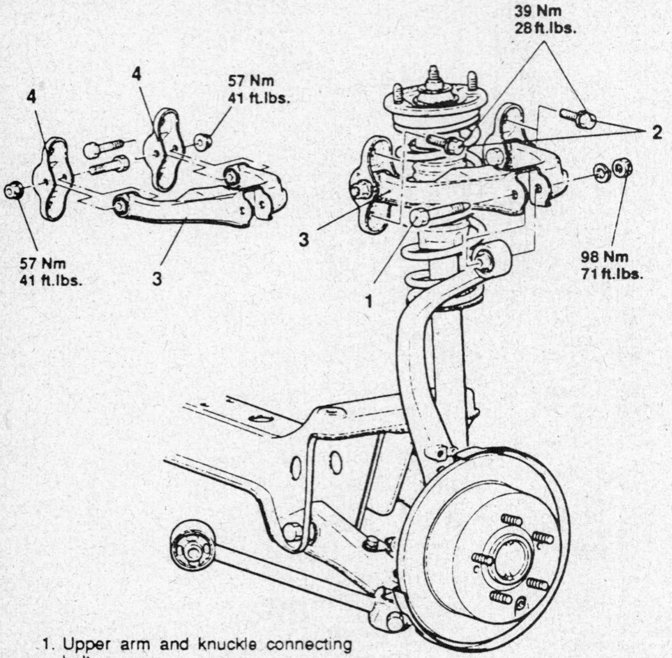

1. Upper arm and knuckle connecting bolt
2. Upper arm assembly mounting bolts
3. Upper arm assembly
4. Upper arm bracket

CR2039500064000X

Fig. 8 Upper arm replacement. AWD models

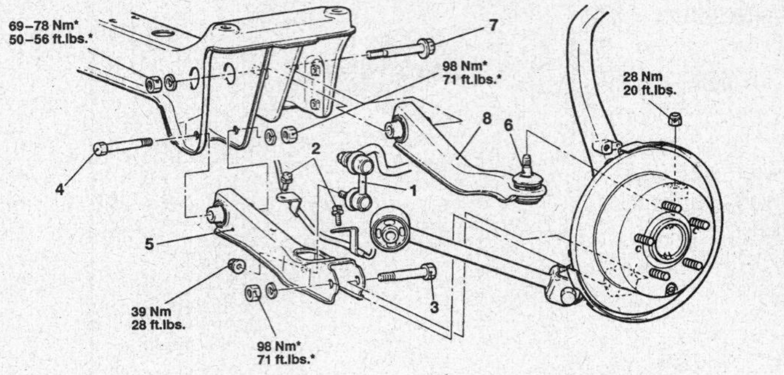

Lower arm assembly removal steps

1. Stabilizer link ball joint and lower arm connection
2. ABS wheel-speed sensor clamp bolts <Vehicles with ABS>
3. Lower arm assembly and knuckle connecting bolt
4. Lower arm assembly mounting bolt
5. Lower arm assembly

Toe control arm assembly removal steps

6. Toe control arm ball joint and knuckle connection
7. Toe control arm assembly mounting bolt
8. Toe control arm assembly

CR2039500065000X

Fig. 9 Lower arm replacement. AWD models

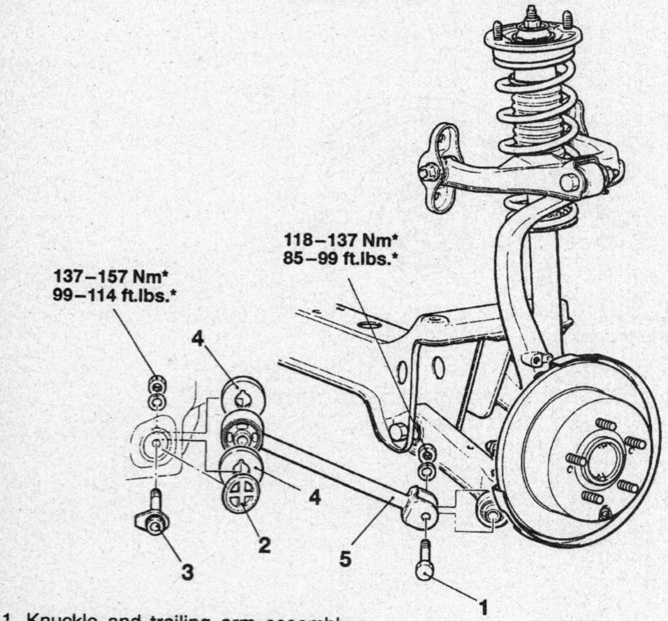

1. Knuckle and trailing arm assembly connecting bolt
2. Grommet
3. Trailing arm assembly mounting bolt
4. Stopper
5. Trailing arm assembly

CR2039500066000X

Fig. 10 Trailing arm assembly. AWD models

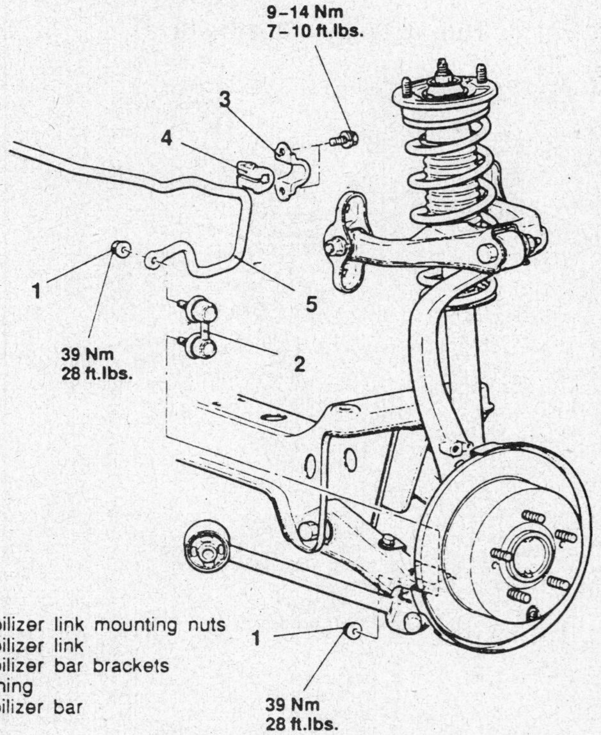

1. Stabilizer link mounting nuts
2. Stabilizer link
3. Stabilizer bar brackets
4. Bushing
5. Stabilizer bar

CR2039500067000X

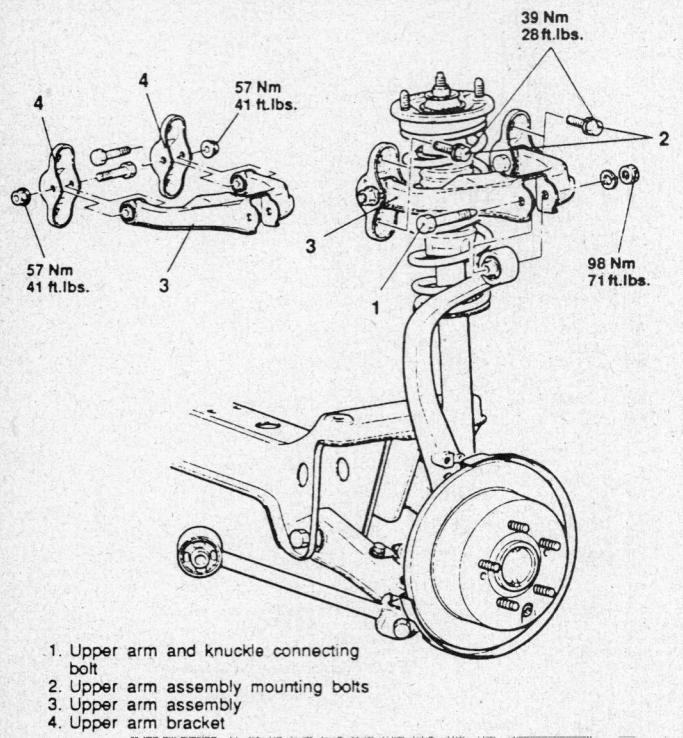

Fig. 11 Stabilizer bar replacement. AWD models

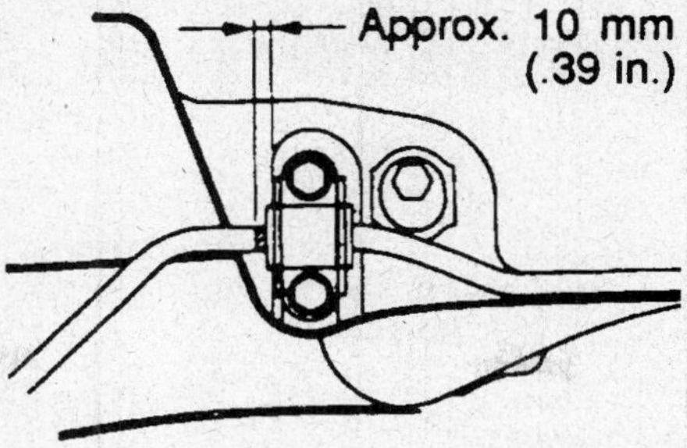

Fig. 12 Stabilizer bar bushing alignment. AWD models

TIGHTENING SPECIFICATIONS

Year	Component	Torque/Ft. Lbs.
1997–98	Axle Nut	145–188
	Brake Caliper Assembly	36–43
	Differential Mounting Bracket To Crossmember	72
	Differential Mounting Bracket To Differential	65
	Differential Mount Support Bolts	33
	Driveshaft Nut	145-188
	Hub Nut	145–188
	Lower Arm To Crossmember	71
	Lower Arm To Knuckle	71–72
	Lower Shock Absorber Mounting Bolt	71–72
	Piston Rod Tightening Nut	16
	Propeller Shaft To Differential	22–25
	Rear Hub To Knuckle	54–65
	Stabilizer Bar Mounting Bracket	7–10
	Stabilizer Link To Lower Arm	28
	Stabilizer Link To Stabilizer Bar	28
	Toe Control Arm To Crossmember	50–56
	Toe Control Arm To Knuckle	20–21
	Trailing Arm To Body	99–114
	Trailing Arm To Knuckle	85–101
	Upper Arm Bracket To Body	28
	Upper Arm Bracket To Upper Arm	41
	Upper Arm To Knuckle	71
	Upper Shock Absorber Mounting Nut	32
	Wheel Lug Nut	88-108

Front Suspension & Steering

INDEX

WHEEL HUB & STEERING KNUCKLE

REPLACE

REMOVAL

Remove knuckle and hub assembly in numbered sequence, **Fig. 1,** noting the following:

1. Loosen driveshaft nut with vehicle on floor and brakes applied.
2. Loosen, but do not remove tie rod end nut.
3. Remove and suspend caliper assembly out of the way using a piece of wire.
4. Shift the knuckle to the outside in order to maintain the clearance between the front hub assembly mounting bolts and the driveshaft. **Do not damage the ball joint boot.**
5. **On models with ABS,** ensure to not damage rotor.

DISASSEMBLE & ASSEMBLE

The front hub assembly should not be disassembled. If required by damage or wear, it should be replaced.

Disassemble knuckle assembly in numbered sequence, **Fig. 2,** noting the following:

1. Loosen, but do not remove tie rod end nut.
2. Loosen, but do not remove compression lower arm nut.
3. Loosen, but do not remove lateral lower arm nut.

INSTALLATION

Reverse removal procedure to install, noting the following:

1. Ensure to install driveshaft washer as shown, **Fig. 3.**
2. After installing wheel, lower vehicle to ground, then final-tighten driveshaft nut.
3. If cotter pin holes do not line up, **torque** nut up to 188 ft. lbs.

BALL JOINT INSPECTION

Inspect ball joint for proper starting torque as follows:

1. Move ball joint stud from side to side several times.

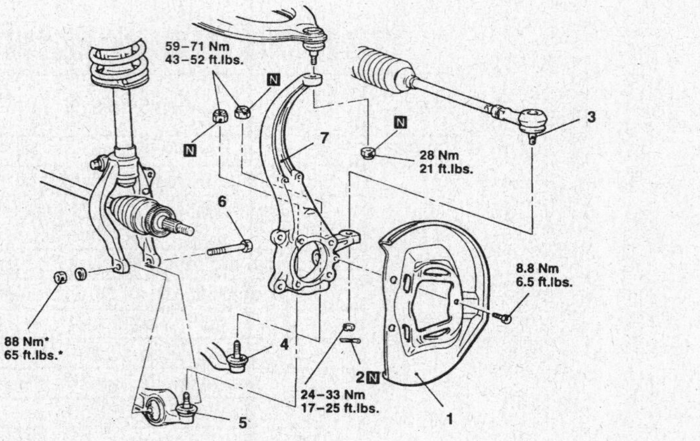

1. Dust shield
2. Cotter pin
3. Tie rod end ball joint and knuckle connection
4. Compression lower arm ball joint and knuckle connection
5. Lateral lower arm ball joint and knuckle connection
6. Connecting bolt of damper fork and lateral lower arm
7. Knuckle

Caution
* : Indicates parts which should be temporarily tightened, and then fully tightened with the vehicles on the ground in the unladen condition.

CR3039500360000A

Fig. 1 Hub & knuckle assembly removal

2. Mount two nuts on ball joint, then using a suitable torque wrench measure starting torque.
3. Starting torque should be within 3–13 inch lbs. for upper arm ball joint, and 4–13 inch lbs. for stabilizer link ball joint.
4. If starting torque exceeds upper limit, replace lower arm assembly.
5. If starting torque is below lower limit, the ball joint may still be reused unless it has drag or excessive play.

STRUT

REPLACE

REMOVAL

Remove strut assembly in numbered sequence, **Fig. 4.**

DISASSEMBLE & ASSEMBLE

Disassemble strut in numbered sequence, **Fig. 5** noting the following:

1. Compress spring using spring compression tools No. MB991237 and MB991239, or equivalents, to ease in disassembly and assembly.

INSTALLATION

Reverse removal procedure to install, noting the following:

1. Ensure spring is properly seated in upper and lower spring seat when installing.
2. Install strut upper bracket as shown in **Fig. 6,** then tighten strut rod nut to specifications.

CONTROL ARM

REPLACE

LOWER

Remove compression and lateral lower control arms in numbered sequence, **Fig. 7,** noting the following:

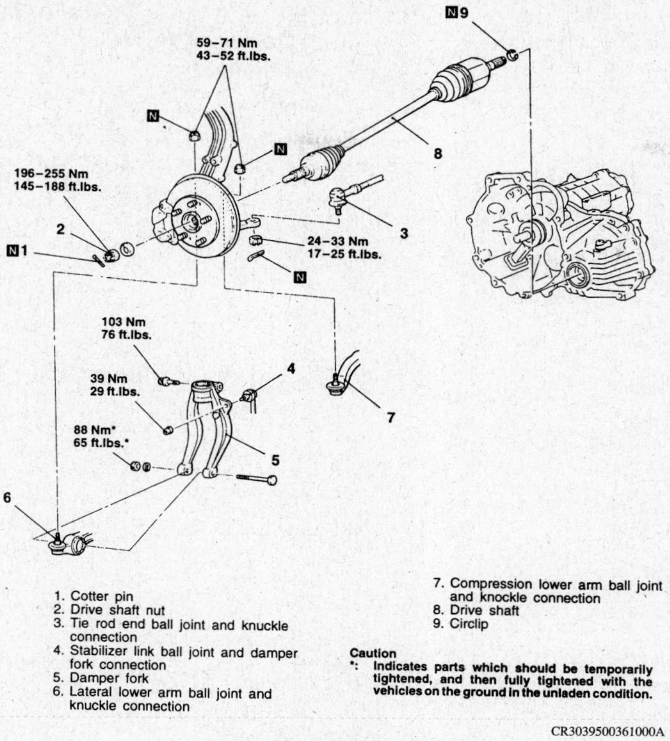

Fig. 2 Knuckle assembly

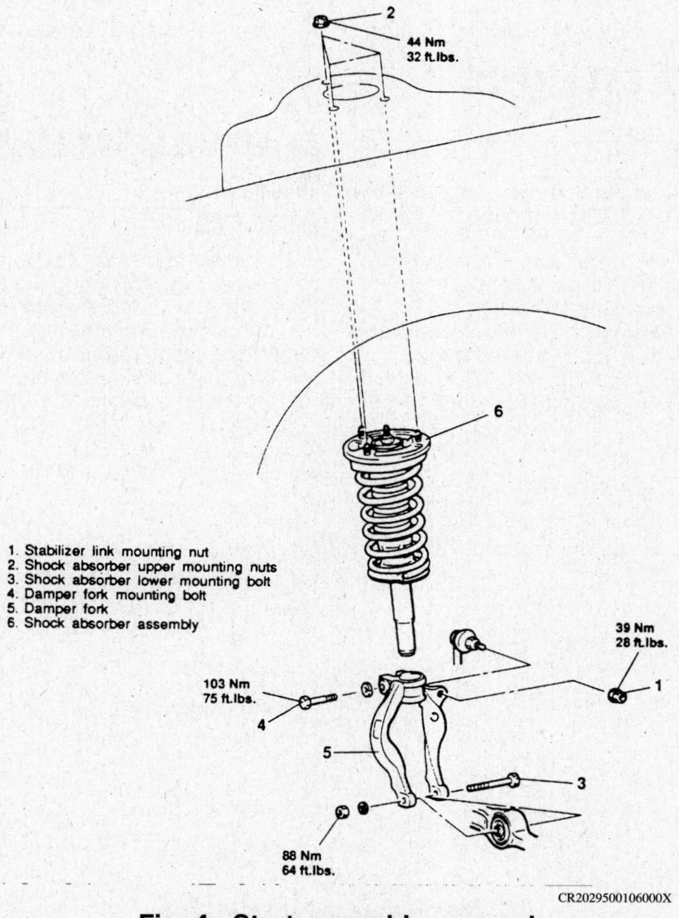

Fig. 4 Strut assembly removal

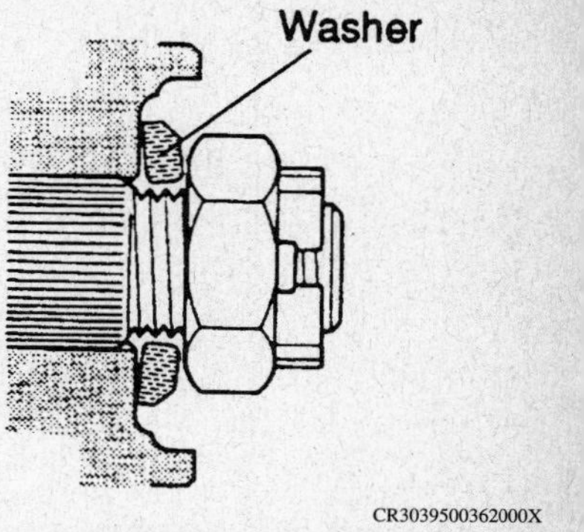

Fig. 3 Driveshaft washer installation

1. Loosen but do not remove compression lower arm ball joint.
2. Inspect compression lower arm ball joint breakaway torque. This should be 4–22 inch lbs. If reading exceeds specified amount, replace lower arm assembly.
3. Loosen but do not remove knuckle/lateral lower arm ball joint.
4. Inspect lateral lower arm ball joint breakaway torque. This should be 9–30 inch lbs. If reading exceeds specified amount, replace lower arm assembly.

UPPER

Remove upper control arm in numbered sequence, **Fig. 8,** noting the following:

1. Use ball joint separator tool No. MB991113, or equivalent, to loosen, **but not remove,** tie rod end mounting nut.
2. Inspect ball joint as follows:
   a. Inspect ball joint starting torque, which should be within 3–22 inch lbs. Replace ball joint if torque exceeds specifications.
   b. Inspect ball joint dust cover, and replace control arm assembly if any cracks or tears are found.
   c. Install upper arm shaft assembly at angle shown, **Fig. 9.**
   d. When upper arm shaft is installed as shown, **Fig. 9,** inspect upper arm for bends or other damage, **Fig. 10.** Replace arm if needed.
3. Reverse procedure to install.

STABILIZER BAR

REPLACE

FWD MODELS

Remove stabilizer bar in numbered sequence, **Fig. 11,** noting the following:

1. Reverse procedure to install, noting the following:
   a. Set stabilizer bar so identification mark is at the left.
   b. Install bushing, ensure the dimension is as shown in **Fig. 12.**

AWD MODELS

1. Remove stabilizer bar in numbered sequence, **Fig. 11.**
2. Reverse procedure to install. Ensure

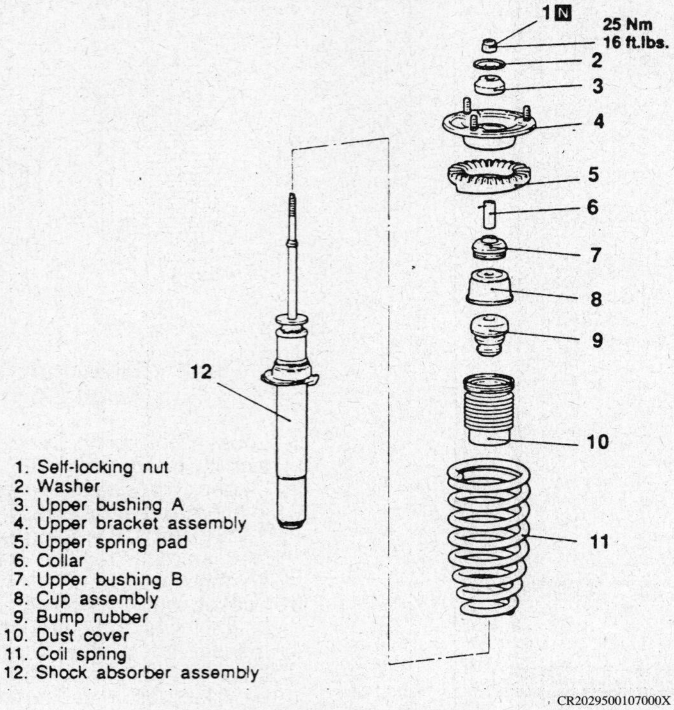

Fig. 5 Strut disassembly

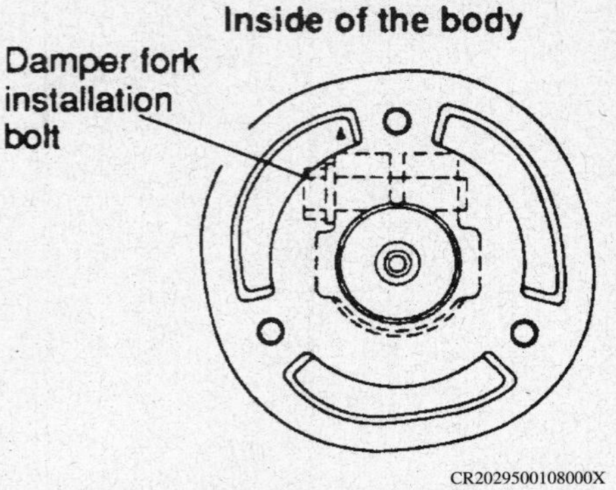

Fig. 6 Upper bracket installation

stabilizer bar is set so identification mark is at the left. Install bushing, ensure the dimension is as shown in **Fig. 12.**

POWER STEERING GEAR

REPLACE

Remove rack and pinion in numbered sequence, **Fig.13,** noting the following:

1. Turn rack completely to righthand, the disconnect gearbox from crossmember.
2. While tilting gearbox downward, remove from lefthand side.
3. Reverse procedure to install.

POWER STEERING PUMP

REPLACE

Remove steering pump in numbered sequence, **Figs. 14 and 15** noting the following:

1. Remove reservoir cap and disconnect return hose to drain fluid.
2. Raise and support vehicle.
3. Cover alternator (located under oil pump) if any hoses are removed
4. Reverse procedure to install. Ensure oil pump is installed in position toward front of bracket. Adjust belt tension using air conditioning tension pulley.

MANUAL STEERING GEAR

REPLACE

Remove rack and pinion in numbered sequence, **Fig. 16,** noting the following:

1. Turn rack completely to right, the disconnect gearbox from crossmember.
2. While tilting gearbox downward, remove from lefthand side.
3. Reverse procedure to install.

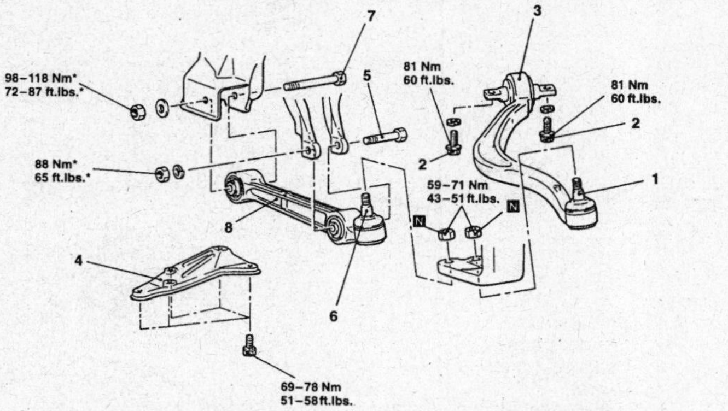

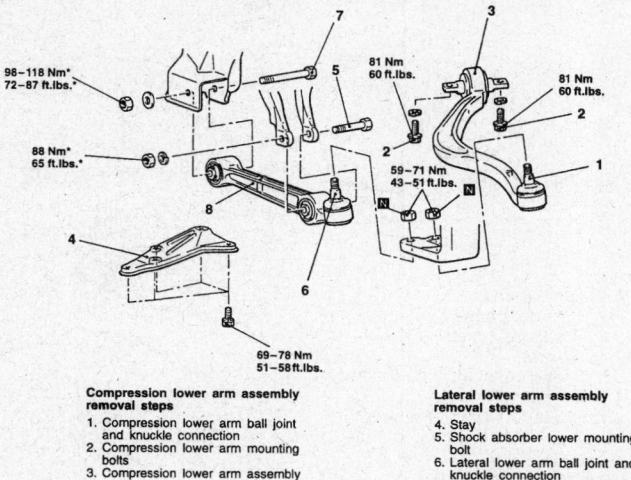

Compression lower arm assembly removal steps

1. Compression lower arm ball joint and knuckle connection
2. Compression lower arm mounting bolts
3. Compression lower arm assembly

Lateral lower arm assembly removal steps

4. Stay
5. Shock absorber lower mounting bolt
6. Lateral lower arm ball joint and knuckle connection
7. Lateral lower arm mounting bolt
8. Lateral lower arm assembly

Caution
*: **Indicates parts which should be temporarily tightened, and then fully tightened with the vehicle on the ground in the unladen condition.**

CR2029500109000A

Fig. 7 Compression & lateral lower arm assemblies

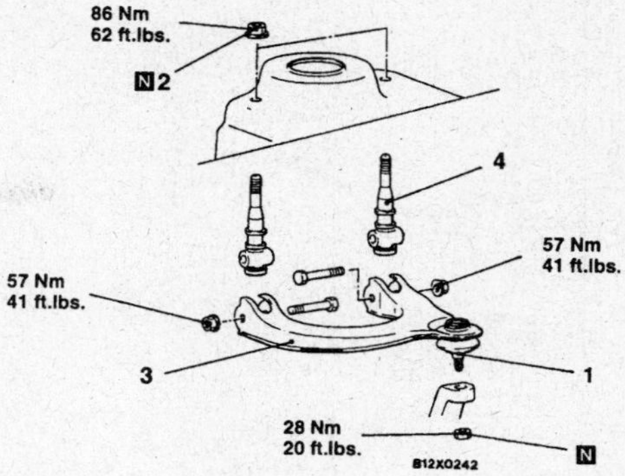

1. Upper arm ball joint and knuckle connection
2. Upper arm self-locking nut
3. Upper arm assembly
4. Upper arm shaft assembly

CR2029500144000X

Fig. 8 Upper control arm removal

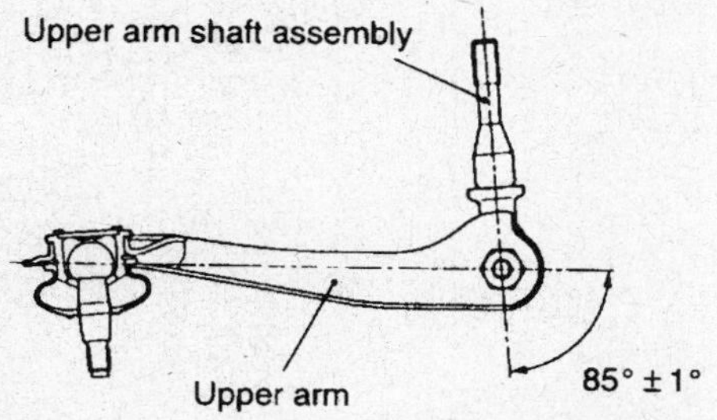

CR2029500145000X

Fig. 9 Upper arm shaft assembly installation

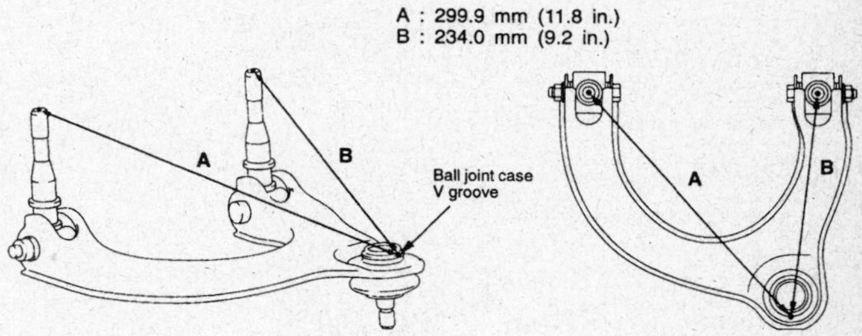

CR2029500146000X

Fig. 10 Upper arm dimensions inspection

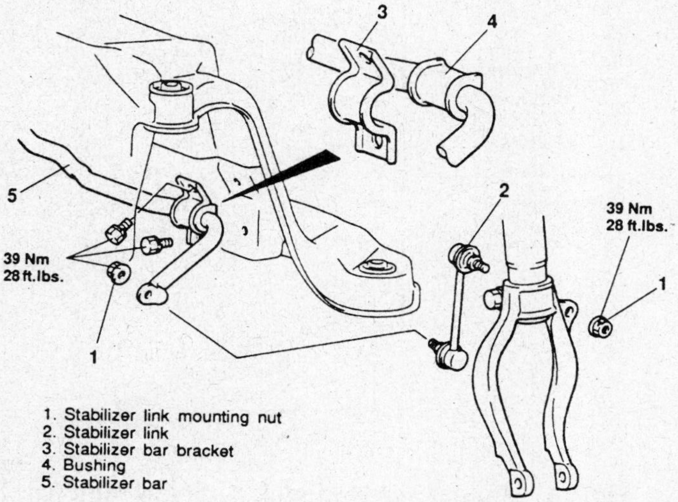

1. Stabilizer link mounting nut
2. Stabilizer link
3. Stabilizer bar bracket
4. Bushing
5. Stabilizer bar

CR2029500110000X

Fig. 11 Stabilizer bar removal. FWD models

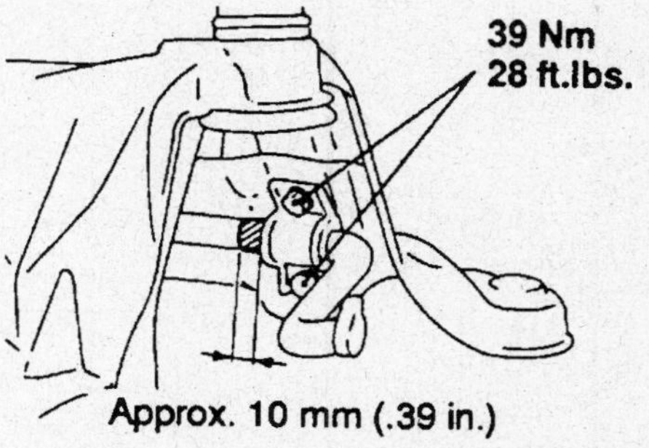

CR2029500111000X

Fig. 12 Stabilizer bar bushing alignment. FWD models

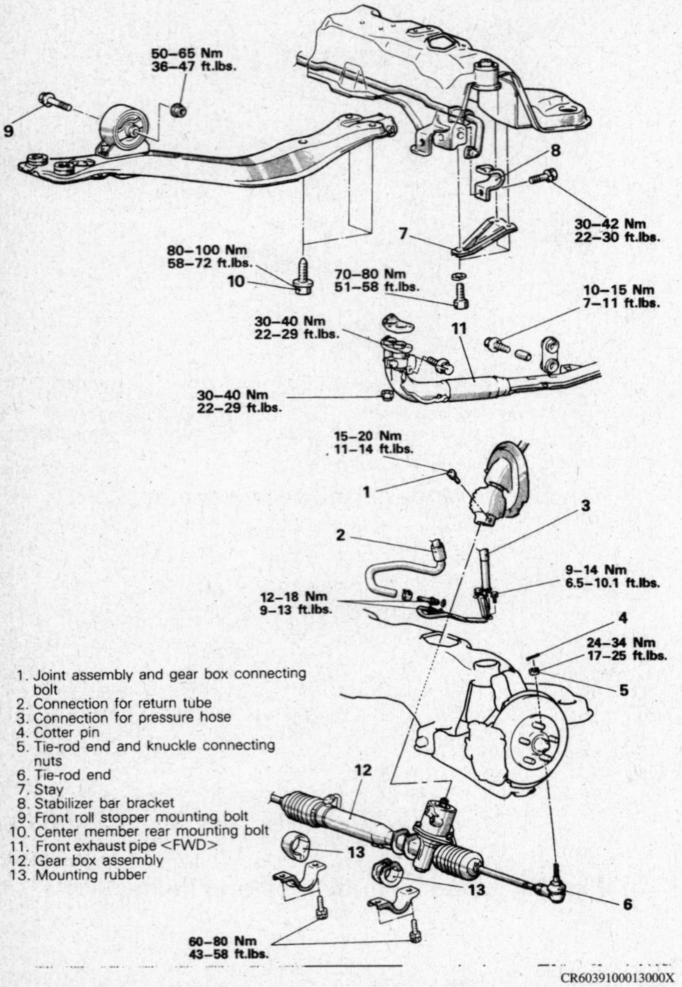

Fig. 13 Power steering rack & pinion removal

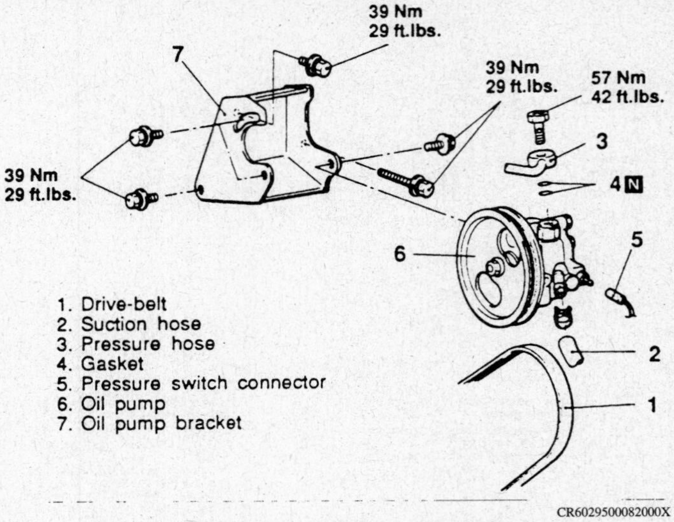

Fig. 14 Power steering pump removal. Non-turbocharged engine

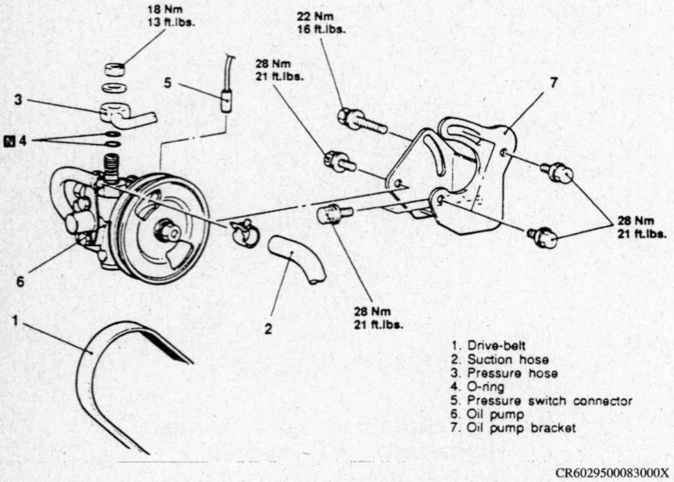

Fig. 15 Power steering pump removal. Turbocharged engine

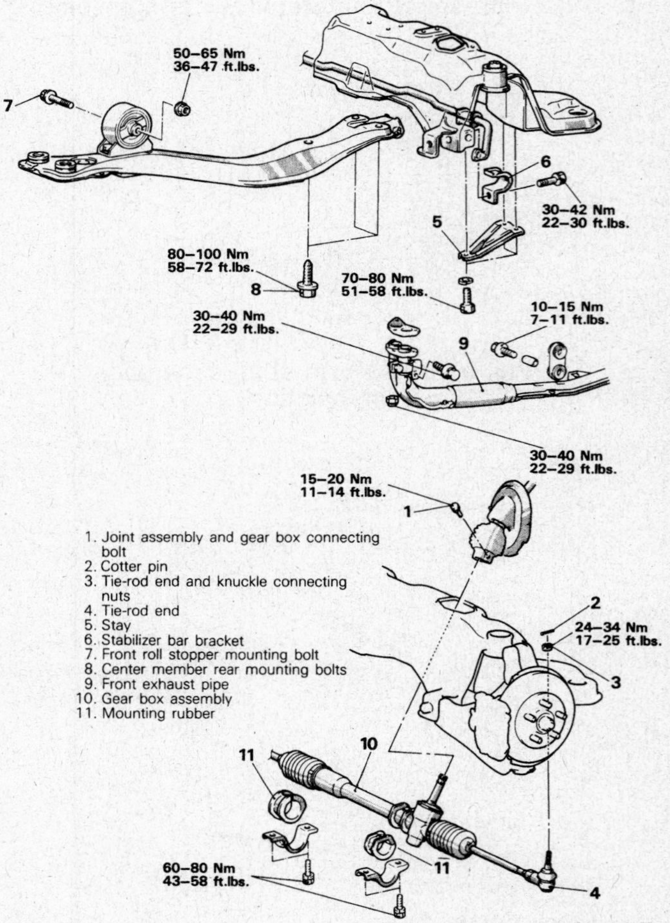

Fig. 16 Manual steering rack & pinion removal

TIGHTENING SPECIFICATIONS

Year	Component	Torque/Ft. Lbs.
1997-98	Axle Nut	145–188
	Caliper Assembly Mounting Bolt	65
	Center Member To Body	58–65
	Compression Lower Arm To Crossmember	60
	Compression Lower Arm To Knuckle	43–52
	Driveshaft Nut	145–188
	Dust Shield To Knuckle	78①
	Hub Assembly To Knuckle	65
	Hub Nut	145–188
	Joint Assembly & Gear Box Bolt	13
	Knuckle To Compression Lower Arm	43–52
	Knuckle Upper Mounting	21
	Lateral Lower Arm To Crossmember	71–85
	Lateral Lower Arm To Damper Fork	65
	Lateral Lower Arm To Knuckle	43–52
	Power Steering Brackets To Crossmember	51
	Power Steering Oil Pump To Bracket	21–29
	Power Steering Pipe Connections	11
	Power Steering Pressure Hose To Pump (Non-Turbo)	42
	Power Steering Pressure Hose To Pump (Turbo)	13
	Stabilizer Bar Bracket	28
	Stabilizer Link To Dampener Fork	28
	Stabilizer Link To Stabilizer Bar	28
	Stay To Crossmember	51–58
	Strut Lower Mounting	75
	Strut Top End Nut	16
	Strut Upper Mounting Nut	32
	Tie Rod End To Knuckle	17–25
	Upper Arm To Knuckle	17–25
	Wheel Lug Nuts	88–108

① — Inch lbs.

Wheel Alignment

INDEX

PRELIMINARY INSPECTION

1. Prior to wheel alignment, ensure tires are at recommended pressure, are of equal size and have approximately the same wear pattern.
2. Inspect front wheel and tire assembly for radial runout and inspect lower ball joints and steering linkage for looseness
3. Inspect front and rear springs for sagging or damage.
4. Front suspension inspections should be performed on a level floor or alignment rack with fuel tank at capacity and vehicle free of luggage and passenger compartment load. The vehicle should be bounced an equal number of times from the center of the bumper alternately, first from the rear, then the front, releasing at the bottom of down cycle.

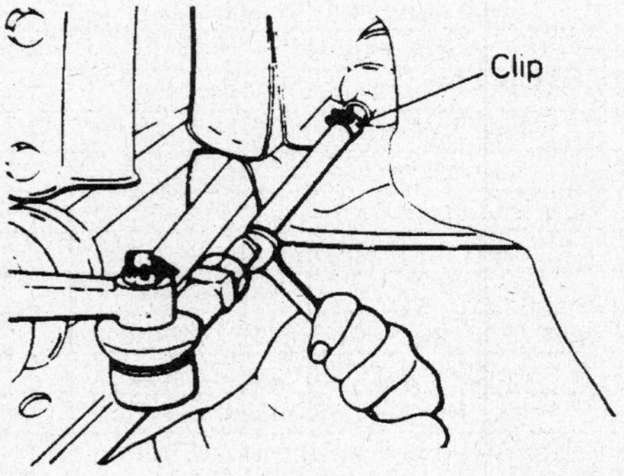

Fig. 1 Toe-in adjustment

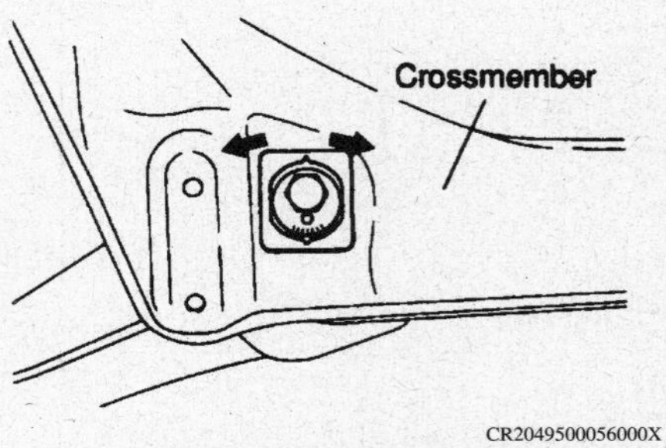

Fig. 2 Rear wheel toe-in adjustment

FRONT WHEEL ALIGNMENT

CASTER & CAMBER

Caster and camber are preset at the factory and cannot be adjusted. If caster or camber are not within specifications, replace bent or damaged components.

TOE-IN

Adjust toe-in by undoing clips and turning each tie rod turnbuckle an equal amount in opposite directions, **Fig. 1.** Toe will move out as the lefthand turnbuckle is turned toward front of vehicle and the righthand turnbuckle is turned toward rear of vehicle. For each half turn, toe-in will increase or decrease .24 inch.

REAR WHEEL ALIGNMENT

CAMBER

Camber is preset at the factory and cannot be adjusted. If camber is not within specifications, replace bent or damaged components.

TOE-IN

1. Measure toe-in using a toe-in gauge.
2. If toe-in is not within specifications, adjust by turning toe control arm mounting bolt on crossmember to left or right by equal amounts, **Fig. 2.**
3. Toe adjustments can be made at graduations of .05 inch.

AIR CONDITIONING

TABLE OF CONTENTS

System Testing

INDEX

PRECAUTIONS

BATTERY GROUND CABLE

Prior to service, disconnect battery ground cable and isolate as required.

R-134A SYSTEMS

R-134a refrigerant is a non-toxic, non-flammable, clear, colorless, odorless liquefied gas.

R-134a refrigerant is not compatible with R-12 refrigerant. Even small amounts of R-12 in an R-134a system will cause lubricant contamination, compressor failure, or improper A/C performance. Never add R-12 to an R-134a system.

New service ports have been added to the compressor to prevent charging the system with R-12 refrigerant. **R-134a systems require a special compressor lubricant. Use PAG compressor oil when servicing system.**

Avoid breathing A/C R-134a refrigerant and lubricant vapor or mist. Exposure may irritate eyes, nose and throat. Use only approved service equipment to discharge R-134a systems.

Always wear eye protection when servicing the air conditioning system. Serious injury may result from eye contact with refrigerant. If this happens, seek prompt medical attention.

EXERCISE SYSTEM

A/C units must be used periodically. Manufacturers caution that when the air conditioner is not used regularly, particularly during cold months, it should be turned on for a few minutes once every two or three weeks while the engine is running. This keeps the system in good operating condition.

Inspecting the system for effects of infrequent usage before the onset of summer is one of the most important aspects of A/C servicing.

First, clean out the condenser core, in all cases in front of the radiator. All obstructions such as leaves, bugs and dirt must be removed, as they will reduce heat transfer and impair the efficiency of the system. Ensure the space between the condenser and the radiator is also free of foreign matter.

Ensure evaporator water drain is open. The evaporator cools and dehumidifies the air before it enters the passenger compartment. At that point, the refrigerant is changed from a liquid to a vapor. As the core cools the air, moisture condenses on it but is prevented from collecting in the evaporator by the water drain.

PERFORMANCE TEST

AVENGER & SEBRING COUPE

Vehicle should not be in direct sunlight when performing this test.

1. Connect manifold gauge set to vehicle, then start engine.
2. Set A/C controls as follows:
   a. A/C switch to MAX A/C.
   b. Mode selection to face position.
   c. Air to recirculation position.
   d. Temperature control to maximum cool.
   e. Blower on High.
3. Adjust idle to 1000 RPM with A/C clutch engaged. Engine should be at normal operating temperature. Doors and windows should be closed.
4. Insert thermometer in left center A/C outlet and operate the engine for 20 minutes.
5. With A/C clutch engaged, compare discharge air temperature to A/C performance temperature charts, **Figs. 1 and 2.**
6. If discharge air temperature fails to meet specifications, further diagnosis of air conditioning system should be performed.

TALON

1. Connect a suitable manifold gauge set and tachometer.
2. Set controls of air conditioner as follows:
   a. Air conditioning switch to A/C On position.
   b. Place mode selection lever in Face position.
   c. Place temperature control lever in Max. cooling position.
   d. Place air selection lever in Recirculation position.
   e. Place blower switch to high position.
3. Start engine, then adjust idle to 1000 RPM with compressor clutch engaged.
4. Vehicle doors should be closed, windows up and engine should be at normal operating temperature.
5. Insert a thermometer in the left center vent and allow engine to run for 20 minutes.

6. Note discharge temperature and compare with chart, **Fig. 3. Reading should be taken with compressor clutch engaged.**

CONCORDE, INTREPID, LHS, VISION & 300M

1. Connect a suitable manifold gauge set and tachometer.
2. Start engine and hold at a steady 1000 RPM.
3. **On models with manual air conditioning,** set air conditioner controls as follows:
   a. Air conditioning switch to A/C On position.
   b. Place air selection lever in Panel-Recirculation position.
   c. Place temperature control lever in Max. cooling position.
   d. Place blower switch to High position.
4. **On models with automatic temperature control,** set controls of air conditioner as follows:
   a. Air conditioning switch to A/C On position.
   b. Rotate blower knob to High, full clockwise position.
   c. Rotate temperature control knob to full cool, counterclockwise position.
   d. Push panel mode button.
   e. Push Recirculation button. A/C and REC buttons should now be lit.
5. **On all models,** close all vehicle windows and doors, then allow engine to reach operating temperature.
6. Insert a thermometer in the lefthand center vent and allow engine to run for five minutes. The A/C clutch may cycle depending on ambient conditions.
7. Note discharge temperature and compare with chart, **Figs. 4 and 5. Reading should be taken with compressor clutch engaged.**

BREEZE, CIRRUS, NEON, SEBRING CONVERTIBLE & STRATUS

1. Connect a suitable manifold gauge set and tachometer.
2. Attach a suitable thermocouple to evaporator inlet line.
3. Set controls to PANEL, FULL COOL, RECIRC, HIGH BLOWER with A/C on.
4. Start engine, then adjust idle to 1000 RPM with compressor clutch engaged.
5. Vehicle doors should be closed, windows up and engine should be at normal operating temperature.
6. Insert a thermometer in the lefthand center vent and allow engine to run for five minutes. The A/C clutch may cycle depending on ambient conditions.
7. **On Breeze, Cirrus, Sebring Convertible and Stratus models,** compare discharge air temperature to evaporator inlet line temperature. The inlet line reading should not be more than 10°F cooler than discharge temperature.
8. **On Neon models,** note discharge temperature and compare with chart, **Fig. 6. Reading should be taken with compressor clutch engaged.**

Garage ambient temperature °C (°F)	20 (68)	25 (77)	35 (95)	40 (104)
Discharge air temperature °C (°F)	2.0–7.0 (36–45)	3.0–7.0 (37–45)	6.0 (43)	12 (54)
Compressor high pressure kPa (psi)	1,089–1,304 (158.0–189.2)	1,422–1,579 (206.3–229.1)	1,863 (270.3)	2,167 (314.4)
Compressor low pressure kPa (psi)	177–304 (25.7–44.1)	206–226 (29.9–32.8)	265 (38.4)	343 (49.8)

CR7029500259000X

Fig. 1 Performance temperature chart. Avenger & Sebring Coupe w/2.0L engine

Garage ambient temperature °C (°F)	20 (68)	25 (77)	35 (95)	40 (104)
Discharge air temperature °C (°F)	2.5–5.0 (37–41)	3.0–6.0 (37–43)	3.5–7.5 (38–46)	4.0–8.0 (39–46)
Compressor high pressure kPa (psi)	892 (129.4)	892 (129.4)	1,422 (206.3)	1,824 (264.6)
Compressor low pressure kPa (psi)	186 (27.0)	186 (27.0)	206 (29.9)	275 (39.9)

CR7029500260000X

Fig. 2 Performance temperature chart. Avenger & Sebring Coupe w/2.5L engine

Garage ambient temperature °C (°F)	20 (68)	25 (77)	35 (95)	40 (104)
Discharge air temperature °C (°F)	2.5–5.0 (37–41)	3.0–6.0 (37–43)	3.5–7.5 (38–46)	4.0–8.0 (39–46)
Compressor high pressure kPa (psi)	700–900 (101.6–130.6)	740–1,100 (107.4–159.6)	750–1,350 (108.8–195.4)	960–1,570 (139.3–227.8)
Compressor low pressure kPa (psi)	140 (20.3)	140–210 (20.3–30.5)	140–220 (20.3–31.9)	150–230 (21.8–33.4)

CR7029500261000X

Fig. 3 Performance temperature chart. Talon

Ambient Temperature	21°C (70°F)	26.5°C (80°F)	37.5°C (90°F)	37.5°C (100°F)	43°C (110°F)
Maximum Allowable Air Temperature at Center Left Panel Outlet	7°C (45°F)	9°C (49°F)	12°C (54°F)	13°C (56°F)	15°C (59°F)
Compressor Discharge Pressure	772-1448 kPa (112-210 PSI)	903-1475 kPa (131-214 PSI)	1241-1482 kPa (180-215 PSI)	1400-1986 kPa (203-288 PSI)	1600-2282 kPa (232-331 PSI)
Compressor Suction Pressure	69-255 kPa (10-37 PSI)	117-262 kPa (17-38 PSI)	145-324 kPa (21-47 PSI)	193-352 kPa (28-51 PSI)	207-365 kPa (30-53 PSI)

CR7029300227000X

Fig. 4 Performance temperature chart. 1997 Concorde, Intrepid, LHS & Vision

LEAK TEST

Do not pressure test R-134a systems with compressed air. Some mixtures of air and R-134a have been shown to be combustible at higher pressures.

A leak detector designed for R-12 will not detect leaks in an R-134a system.

Park vehicle in a wind-free work area, then proceed as follows:

1. Inspect charge level as described under "Performance Test" in this section.
2. When performing this test with original discharge pressure less than 30 psi, reclaim remaining refrigerant, then connect suitable vacuum pump and evacuate system to lowest vacuum possible.
3. Ensure system holds vacuum reading for at least 15 minutes. If system holds

AMBIENT TEMPERATURE	21°C (70°F)	26.5°C (80°F)	32.5°C (90°F)	37°C (100°F)	43°C (110°F)
MAXIMUM ALLOWABLE AIR TEMPERATURE AT CENTER LEFT PANEL OUTLET	6°C (42°F)	7°C (45°F)	10°C (50°F)	12°C (54°F)	15°C (59°F)
COMPRESSOR DISCHARGE PRESSURE	1379–1585 kPa (200–230 psi)	1448–1723 kPa (210–250 psi)	1654–1930 kPa (240–280 psi)	1930–2206 kPa (280–320 psi)	2206–2516 kPa (320–365 psi)
COMPRESSOR SUCTION PRESSURE	103–172 kPa (15–25 psi)	139–208 kPa (20–30 psi)	172–241 kPa (25–35 psi)	208–276 kPa (30–40 psi)	241–310 kPa (35–45 psi)

CR7029900528000X

Fig. 5 Performance temperature chart. 1998–2000 Concorde, Intrepid, LHS & 300M

Ambient Temperature	21°C (70°F)	26.5°C (80°F)	32°C (90°F)	37°C (100°F)	43°C (110°F)
Air Temperature at Left Center Panel Outlet	1-8°C (34-46°F)	3-9°C (37-49°F)	4-10°C (39-50°F)	6-11°C (43-52°F)	7-18°C (45-65°F)
Compressor Discharge Pressure After the Filter Drier	1034-1724 kPa (150-250 PSI)	1517-2275 kPa (220-330 PSI	1999-2620 kPa (290-380 PSI)	2068-2965 kPa (300-430 PSI)	2275-3421 kPa (330-496 PSI)
Evaporator Suction Pressure	103-207 kPa (15-30 PSI)	117-221 kPa (17-32 PSI)	138-241 kpa (20-35 PSI)	172-269 kpa (25-39 PSI)	207-345 kPa (30-50 PSI)

CR7020000584000X

Fig. 6 Performance temperature chart. Neon

vacuum for 15 minutes a leak is probably not present. If vacuum did not hold for 15 minutes proceed as follows:

a. Ensure transaxle is in Park.
b. Run engine for five minutes, then ensure engine is idling at 700 RPM.
c. Charge system with 10 ounces of R-134a refrigerant.
d. Set A/C control to 100% outside air.
e. Set panel mode to full cool.
f. Set blower to high speed.
g. Place A/C button in ON position.
h. Open vehicle windows.

4. Turn engine Off, wait approximately 5 minutes, then use a suitable electronic leak detector designed for R-134a refrigerant systems and inspect system for leakage. If a leak is found repair as required. If no leak was found fill system as outlined under "Performance Test" in this section.

DISCHARGING SYSTEM

The use of refrigerant recovery and recycling stations allows the recovery and reuse of refrigerant after contaminants and moisture have been removed.

When using a recovery or recycling station, follow the manufacturer's operating instructions, noting the following:

1. **Use extreme caution and observe all safety and service precautions related to use of refrigerants.**
2. Connect refrigerant recycling station hose(s) to vehicle A/C service port(s) and recovery station inlet fitting. Hoses used should have shutoff devices or check valve within 12 inches of hose ends to minimize introduction of air into recycling station and to minimize amount of refrigerant released when hose(s) is disconnected.
3. Turn recycling station On to start recovery process. Allow recycling station to pump refrigerant from A/C system until station pressure gauge indicates vacuum. Vacuum gauge should read 26 inches for at least 45 minutes.
4. After vehicle A/C system has been evacuated, close station inlet valve, if equipped.
5. Turn station Off. With some stations, pump will automatically be turned Off by a low pressure switch.
6. Allow vehicle A/C system to remain closed for approximately two minutes. Observe vacuum level indicated on gauge. If pressure does not rise, disconnect recycling station hose(s).
7. If system pressure rises, repeat steps 3 through 6 until vacuum level remains stable for two minutes.
8. Service A/C system as required, then evacuate and recharge A/C system.

SYSTEM EVACUATION

USING VACUUM PUMP

Vacuum pumps suitable for removing air and moisture from A/C systems are commercially available. A specification for system pump-down used here is 26–29½ inches of vacuum. This reading can be attained at or near sea level only. For each 1000 feet of altitude this operation is being performed, the vacuum reading will be 1 inch lower. As an example, at 5000 feet elevation, only 21–24½ inches of vacuum can be obtained.

The system must be completely discharged before it can be evacuated. Damage to vacuum pump may result if pressurized refrigerant is allowed to enter.

1. With gauges connected into system, remove cap from vacuum hose connector. Install center hose from gauge manifold to vacuum pump connector. Mid-position the high and low side compressor service valves (if used). Open high and low side gauge manifold hand valves.
2. Operate vacuum pump a minimum of 30 minutes for air and moisture removal. Watch compound gauge that system pumps down into a vacuum. System will reach 26–29½ inches vacuum in 5 minutes or less. If system does not pump down, inspect all connections and leak-test if required.
3. Close gauge manifold hand valves and shutoff vacuum pump.
4. Inspect ability of system to hold vacuum. Watch compound gauge to ensure gauge does not rise at a faster rate than 1 inch of vacuum every 4 or 5 minutes. If compound gauge rises at too rapid a rate, install partial charge and leak-test, then evacuate system as outlined above.
5. If system holds vacuum, charge system with refrigerant.

USING CHARGING STATION

On systems using R-134a refrigerant use a charging station designed for R-134a refrigerant systems.

A vacuum pump is built into the charging station and is constructed to withstand repeated and prolonged use without damage. Complete moisture removal from the system is possible only with a vacuum pump constructed for the purpose.

The system must be completely discharged before it can be evacuated. Damage to the vacuum pump may result if pressurized refrigerant is allowed to enter.

1. Connect hose to vacuum pump if system was discharged through charging station.
2. Open high and low side gauge valves of charging station.
3. Connect station to proper electrical outlet.
4. Engage "Off-On" switch to vacuum pump according to directions of specific station being used.
5. System should pump down into a 28–29½ inches vacuum in 5 minutes or less. If system fails to meet this specification, repair as required.
6. Operate pump a minimum of 30 minutes to remove all air and moisture.
7. Close high and low side gauge valves. Open switch to turn off pump.
8. Inspect ability of system to hold vacuum by watching compound gauge to ensure it does not rise at a rate higher than 1 inch of vacuum every 4 or 5 minutes. If rise rate is not within specifications, repair system as required. If rise rate is within specifications, charge system with refrigerant.

CHARGING SYSTEM

AVENGER, SEBRING COUPE & TALON

Never use cans to charge into high pressure side of system (compressor discharge port) or into system at high temperature, as high system pressure transferred into charging can may cause it to explode.

1. Attach center hose from manifold gauge set to refrigerant dispensing manifold. Turn refrigerant manifold valves completely counterclockwise to open fully, and remove protective caps from refrigerant manifold.
2. Screw refrigerant cans into manifold. Ensure gasket is in place and in good condition. **Torque** can and manifold nuts to 6–8 ft. lbs.
3. Turn refrigerant manifold valves clockwise to puncture cans and close manifold valves.
4. Loosen charging hose at gauge set manifold and turn a refrigerant valve counterclockwise to release refrigerant and purge air from charging hose. When refrigerant gas escapes from loose connection, tighten hose again.
5. Fully open all refrigerant manifold

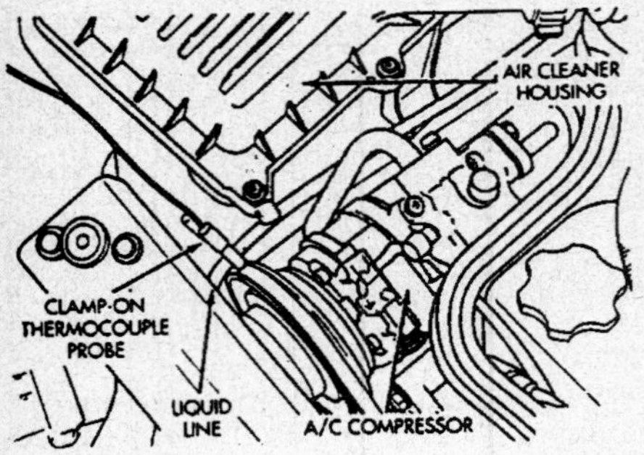

Fig. 7 Thermocouple clamp attachment to liquid line. Concorde, Intrepid, LHS, Vision & 300M

valves being used and place refrigerant cans into pan of hot water at 125°F to aid transfer of refrigerant gas. **Do not heat refrigerant cans over 125°F as they may explode. Place water pan and refrigerant cans on scale and note weight.**

6. Start engine and turn A/C On, then index blower switch to low position.
7. Low pressure cutout switch will prevent clutch from engaging until refrigerant is added to system. If clutch does engage, replace switch before continuing.
8. Charge through suction side of system by slowly opening suction manifold valve. Adjust valve so charging pressure does not exceed 50 psi.
9. Adjust engine speed to fast idle of 1400–1550 RPM.
10. After specified refrigerant charge has entered system, close gauge set manifold valves and refrigerant manifold valves, then connect wiring.

CONCORDE, INTREPID, LHS, VISION & 300M

1. Connect suitable pressure gauge to discharge side of compressor, then attach clamp on thermocouple part No. PSE 66-324-0014, or 80PK-1A, or equivalent to liquid line as shown in **Fig. 7.** It must be attached as close to condenser as possible to read liquid line temperature.
2. With transaxle in Park and engine idling at 700 RPM, set air conditioning controls as follows:
   a. A/C control set to outside air.
   b. Set panel mode to full cool.
   c. Blower to high speed.
   d. A/C button in On position.
   e. **On models equipped with ATC,** turn Recirc button Off.
3. **On all models,** open all vehicle windows, operate system and allow to stabilize, then set system pressure to 260 psi by placing a piece of cardboard over part of condenser to obtain specified gauge reading.
4. Observe discharge pressure and liquid line temperature, then refer to charge determination graph, **Figs. 8 and 9,** to determine system charge.
5. If charge is not within specification, add or reclaim two ounces of refrigerant at a time, then read gauge pressure and liquid line temperature. Continue procedure until proper charge area on chart determination graph is obtained, **Figs. 8 and 9.**

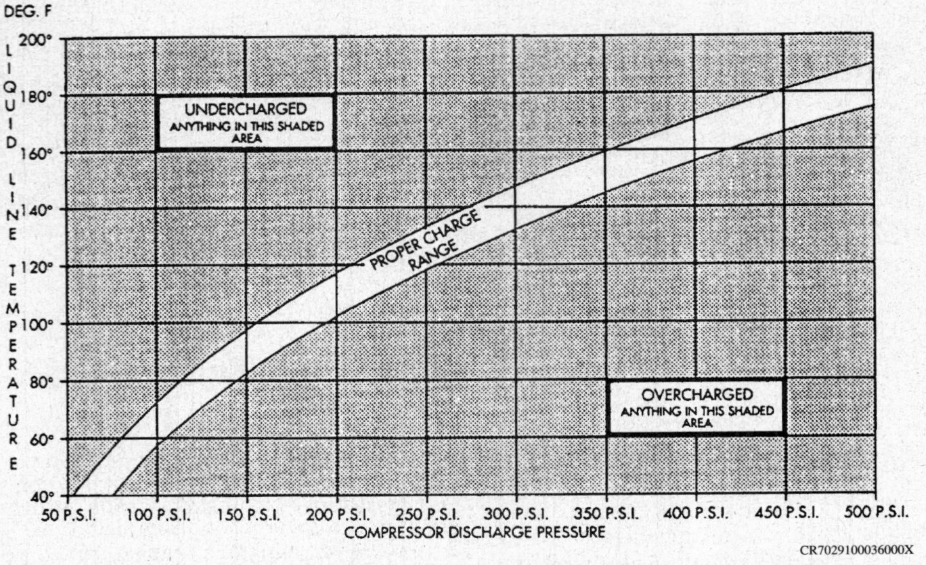

Fig. 8 Charge determination chart. 1997 Concorde, Intrepid, LHS & Vision

BREEZE, CIRRUS, SEBRING CONVERTIBLE & STRATUS

This test can be accomplished using a manifold gauge set or a DRB scan tool.

1. Connect a manifold gauge set to discharge side of compressor or connect a DRB, or equivalent scan tool, to Diagnostic Link Connector (DLC) and set scan tool to "Partial Charge Test."
2. Attach a clamp on thermocouple part No. PSE 66-324-0014, or equivalent, onto liquid line as close to condenser outlet as possible, to observe liquid line temperature.
3. With transaxle in Park, engine idling at 700 RPM and windows open, set air conditioning controls as follows:
   a. Controls set to "Outside Air."
   b. Panel mode to full cool.
   c. Blower on high.
   d. A/C button in ON position.
4. Operate system for a couple of minutes to allow system to stabilize.
5. Set system pressure to about 260 psi, by blocking off airflow to front grille area. This will maintain a constant pressure and stop the cooling fans from alternating between high and low speeds.
6. **When using a manifold gauge set,** proceed as follows:
   a. Observe discharge pressure and liquid line temperature, using graph shown in **Fig. 10** to determine where the system is currently operating.
   b. If system is in undercharged region of graph, add two ounces of refrigerant to system and inspect readings again.
   c. If system is in overcharged region of graph, drain two ounces of refrigerant from system and inspect readings again.
   d. Repeat steps "b" and "c" until readings are within proper operating range.
7. **When using a DRB or equivalent scan tool,** it is not necessary to use a graph. Scan tool will calculate proper liquid line temperature automatically.

NEON

1. Connect suitable pressure gauge to discharge side of compressor, then attach thermocouple part No. PSE 66-324-0014, or equivalent, to liquid line as close to filter-dryer as possible.
2. With transaxle in Park and engine idling, set air conditioning controls as follows:
   a. A/C control set to outside air.
   b. Set panel mode to full cool.
   c. Blower to high speed.
   d. A/C button in On position, with windows and doors closed.
3. Operate system for a few minutes to allow system to stabilize.
4. Observe filter-dryer pressure and liquid line temperature.
5. Using the chart in **Fig. 11,** determine where system is currently operating. If the system is not in the proper range, reclaim all the refrigerant and recharge per A/C label, using suitable refrigerant recovery and charging equipment.

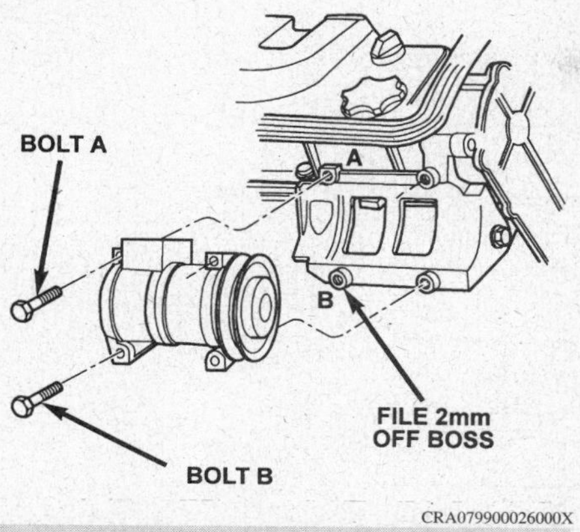

Fig. 9 A/C compressor mounting & bracket boss modification

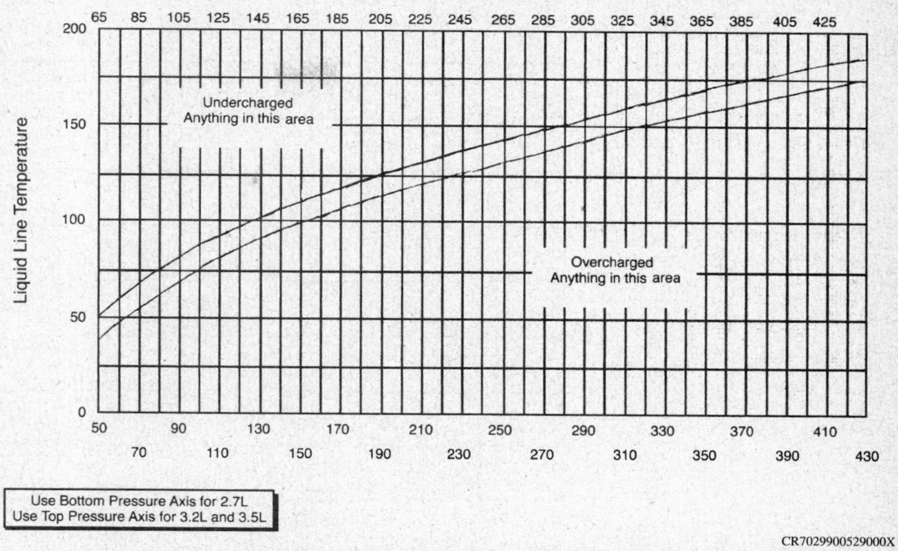

Fig. 10 Charge determination chart. 1998–2000 Concorde, Intrepid, LHS & 300M

TECHNICAL SERVICE BULLETINS

A/C COMPRESSOR LOCK-UP AT LOW MILEAGE

1998–2000 Neon

On these models the A/C compressor may lock-up, leading to a drive belt slip and squeal condition. The temporary lock-up does not always indicate the compressor has failed.

This condition may be caused by the normal refrigerant movement within the A/C system caused by temperature differences between the various components. This washes the refrigerant oil out of the compressor.

The A/C system should be operated for a minimum of five minutes in the Fresh Air A/C High Blower Mode, with the engine idling, prior to taking a vehicle out of operation or storing it for more than two weeks. This ensures adequate oil flow-back to the compressor.

To determine the extent of this condition, start and operate the engine at idle. Turn the A/C system On and listen for the squealing drive belt. **If the belt squeal starts, immediately turn the A/C system Off.** If the squealing stops, proceed as follows:

1. Using an oil filter strap wrench, grasp outer diameter of A/C clutch hub that houses rubber donut. While facing compressor, attempt to rotate hub clockwise, then counterclockwise. If hub will not rotate, replace compressor. If hub rotates, proceed to next step.
2. Turn hub clockwise 5 complete revolutions, then remove strap wrench.
3. Start and operate engine at idle, then turn A/C system On.
4. Observe A/C system and compressor for proper operation for cool-down and noise levels.
5. If A/C operation is within specifications, allow system to operate at idle for 5 minutes.
6. If A/C system operates acceptably for 5 minutes, compressor is still serviceable. Inspect drive belt for damage and replace if required.
7. If A/C system does not operate acceptably, or if compressor is internally damaged, replace compressor.

A/C COMPRESSOR MOAN AT 2000 RPM

1998–99 Concorde, Intrepid, LHS & 300M

On these models, equipped with 3.2L or 3.5L engines, this condition may occur with the compressor clutch engaged and the engine running at 2000 RPM.

To determine the proper procedure to correct this condition, remove compressor mounting bolt "A," **Fig. 11.** If the moan is greatly reduced or eliminated, perform the repair procedure. If the moan is still present, install bolt "A" and **torque** to 16.7–25 ft. lbs. Remove bolt "B" and listen for the moaning again. If the moan is greatly reduced or eliminated, perform repair procedure as follows:

1. Remove A/C compressor drive belt.
2. Remove air cleaner housing and frame rail air cleaner housing mounting stud.
3. Remove compressor mounting bolts, then position compressor aside with hoses intact.
4. Remove compressor bracket from engine block.
5. File 2 mm off A/C bracket boss "B," then remove threads in bracket with a 3/8 inch drill bit.
6. Install bracket back onto block. **Torque** bolts to 30–50 ft. lbs.
7. Install compressor onto bracket, but do not use bolt "B." **Torque** remaining three bolts to 16.7–25 ft. lbs.
8. Install compressor drive belt. Adjust tension as outlined under "Belt Tension."

UNWANTED AUTOMATIC TEMPERATURE CONTROL CHANGE TO MANUAL OPERATION

1998–99 Concorde, Intrepid, LHS & 300M

On these models, built before 7/20/98, this condition may occur if left in "Auto" mode when the ignition was turned Off and may appear when the ignition is turned back On.

This condition may be caused by servicing the A/C or radio without disconnecting and isolating the battery ground cable. This will set an erroneous DTC of "In-Car Temperature Sensor Failure" in the Body Control Module (BCM). This DTC's presence will result in the unrequested Auto to Manual change. This can be prevented by disconnecting and isolating the battery ground cable during electrical system service, then corrected by erasing the DTC.

This condition may also be caused by changing the blower speed while the ignition is turned Off. This is a normal ATC system operation and should be explained to the vehicle's owner.

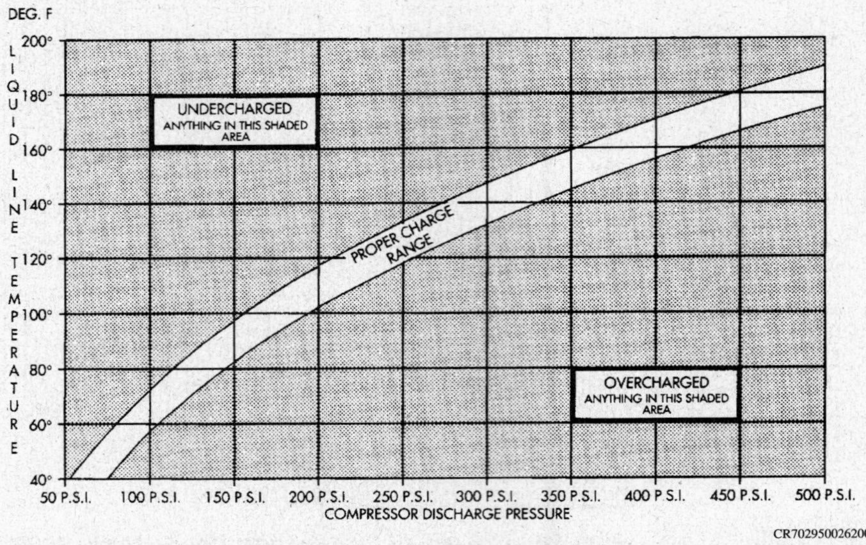

Fig. 11 Charge determination chart. Breeze, Cirrus, Stratus & 1997–99 Sebring Convertible

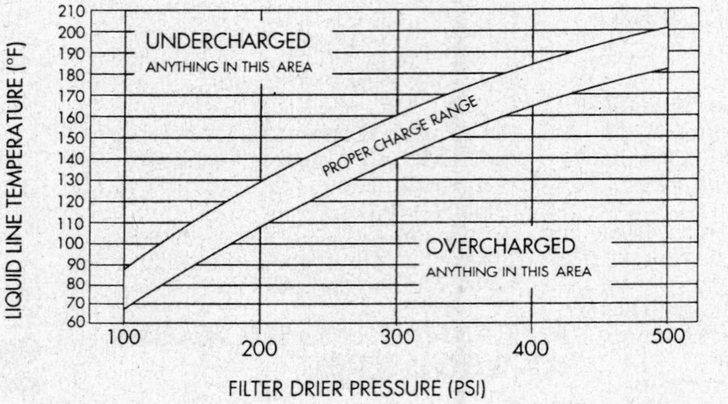

Fig. 12 Charge determination chart. Neon

System Service

INDEX

OIL CHARGE

Model	Year	Compressor	Component	Oil①④
Avenger & Sebring Coupe	1997–99	10PA17C⑤	Condenser	1.35
			Evaporator	1.35
			Receiver-Dryer	.34
			Lines	.34
	1997–2000	MSC105CVS⑥	Condenser	.51
			Evaporator	2.03
			Receiver-Dryer	.34
			Lines	.34
Breeze, Cirrus, Sebring Convertible & Stratus	1997–2000	TRS90	Condenser	1
			Evaporator	2
			Receiver-Dryer	1
			Line	1.5
Concorde, Intrepid, LHS, Vision & 300M②	1997–2000	10PA17-R-134a③	Evaporator	2
			Condenser	1
			Receiver-Dryer	1
			Lines	1.5
Neon	1997–99	10PA17-R-134a③	Condenser	1
			Evaporator	2
			Receiver-Dryer	1
			Lines	1.5
	2000	Nippondenso 10S17	Condenser	1
			Evaporator	2
			Lines	1.5
			Receiver-Dryer	1.0
Talon	1997–98	10PA17C⑦	Condenser	1.35
			Evaporator	1.35
			Receiver-Dryer	.34
			Lines	.34
		MSC105CVS⑧	Condenser	.51
			Evaporator	2.03
			Receiver-Dryer	.34
			Lines	.34

① — Ounces.
② — When components of an A/C system utilizing R-134a refrigerant are replaced, use only ND8 PSG compressor oil No. 82300101, or equivalent.
③ — The 10PA17–R12 compressor looks the same & has the same bolt pattern as the 10PA17–R134a compressor. Ensure proper compressor is used when replacement is required.
④ — Refer to A/C Specifications for refrigerant oil type.
⑤ — 2.0L engine.
⑥ — 2.5L engine.
⑦ — Less turbo.
⑧ — Turbo.

OIL LEVEL CHECK

The oil level of these compressors should be inspected whenever refrigerant has been lost due to leakage or through normal system servicing.

Specifications

INDEX

A/C SPECIFICATIONS

Year	Model	Refrigerant		Viscosity	Total System Capacity, Ounces	Compressor Oil Check	Compressor Clutch Air Gap, Inch
		Capacity, Lbs.	Type				
1997	Avenger DOHC	1.54	R-134a	ND8 PAG	2.7	①	.014–.026
	Avenger SOHC	1.54	R-134a	SUN PAG 56	5.7	①	.016–.024
	Breeze	1.75	R-134a	SP15 PAG	5.0	①	.013–.025
	Cirrus	1.75	R-134a	SP15 PAG	5.0	①	.013–.025
	Concorde	1.75	R-134a	ND8 PAG	5.0	①	.014–.026
	Intrepid	1.75	R-134a	ND8 PAG	5.0	①	.014–.026
	LHS	1.75	R-134a	ND8 PAG	5.0	①	.014–.026
	Neon	1.57	R-134a	ND8 PAG	6.8	①	.014–.026
	Sebring Coupe DOHC	1.54	R-134a	ND8 PAG	2.7	①	.014–.026
	Sebring Coupe SOHC	1.54	R-134a	SUN PAG 56	5.7	①	.016–.024
	Sebring Convertible	1.75	R-134a	SP15 PAG	5.0	①	.013–.025
	Stratus	1.75	R-134a	SP15 PAG	5.0	①	.013–.025
	Talon Non-Turbo	1.54	R-134a	ND8 PAG	2.7	①	.014–.026
	Talon w/Turbo	1.54	R-134a	SUN PAG 56	5.7	①	.016–.026
	Vision	1.75	R-134a	SP15 PAG	5.0	①	.014–.026
1998	Avenger DOHC	1.54–1.63	R-134a	ND8 PAG	2.7	①	.016–.024
	Avenger SOHC	1.54–1.63	R-134a	SUN PAG 56	5.7	①	.016–.024
	Breeze	1.63	R-134a	ND8 PAG	5.0	①	.013–.025
	Cirrus	1.63	R-134a	ND8 PAG	5.0	①	.013–.025
	Concorde	1.56	R-134a	ND8 PAG	5.0	①	.014–.026
	Intrepid	1.56	R-134a	ND8 PAG	5.0	①	.014–.026
	Neon	1.57	R-134a	ND8 PAG	6.8	①	.014–.026
	Sebring Coupe DOHC	1.54–1.63	R-134a	ND8 PAG	2.7	①	.016–.024
	Sebring Coupe SOHC	1.54–1.63	R-134a	SUN PAG 56	5.7	①	.016–.024
	Sebring Convertible	1.75	R-134a	ND8 PAG	5.0	①	.013–.025
	Stratus	1.63	R-134a	ND8 PAG	5.0	①	.013–.025
	Talon Non-Turbo	1.54–1.63	R-134a	ND8 PAG	2.7	①	.014–.026
	Talon w/Turbo	1.54–1.63	R-134a	SUN PAG 56	5.7	①	.016–.026
1999	Avenger DOHC	1.54–1.63	R-134a	ND8 PAG	2.7	①	.016–.024
	Breeze	1.25	R-134a	ND8 PAG	5.0	①	.013–.025
	Cirrus	1.25	R-134a	ND8 PAG	5.0	①	.013–.025
	Neon	1.57	R-134a	ND8 PAG	6.8	①	.014–.026
	Sebring Coupe DOHC	1.54–1.63	R-134a	ND8 PAG	2.7	①	.016–.024
	Stratus	1.25	R-134a	ND8 PAG	5.0	①	.013–.025

Continued

A/C SPECIFICATIONS—Continued

Year	Model	Refrigerant		Viscosity	Total System Capacity, Ounces	Compressor Oil Check	Compressor Clutch Air Gap, Inch
		Capacity, Lbs.	Type				
1999–2000	Avenger SOHC	1.54–1.63	R-134a	SUN PAG 56	5.7	①	.016–.024
	Concorde	1.56	R-134a	ND8 PAG	5.0	①	.014–.026
	Intrepid	1.56	R-134a	ND8 PAG	5.0	①	.014–.026
	LHS	1.56	R-134a	ND8 PAG	5.0	①	.014–.026
	Sebring Convertible	1.75	R-134a	ND8 PAG	5.0	①	.013–.025
	Sebring Coupe SOHC	1.54–1.63	R-134a	SUN PAG 56	5.7	①	.016–.024
	300M	1.56	R-134a	ND8 PAG	5.0	①	.014–.026
2000	Breeze	1.19	R-134a	SP-15 PAG	5.0	①	.016–.031
	Cirrus	1.19	R-134a	SP-15 PAG	5.0	①	.016–.031
	Neon	1.69	R-134a	ND8 PAG	6.1	①	.014–.026
	Stratus	1.19	R-134a	SP-15 PAG	5.0	①	.016–.031

① — Oil Level cannot be inspected. Refer to total capacity in ounces.

CHARGING VALVE LOCATION

AVENGER, BREEZE, CIRRUS, SEBRING CONVERTIBLE, SEBRING COUPE & STRATUS

The low side valve is located on the suction line. The high side valve is located on the high pressure line.

CONCORDE, INTREPID, LHS, VISION & 300M

On models equipped with 2.7L engines, the high pressure gauge port is located on the liquid line and the low pressure gauge port is located on the suction line. On models equipped with 3.2L and 3.5L engines, the high and low side pressure connectors are located on the A/C compressor.

NEON

The low side valve is located on the suction line. The high side valve is located on the filter-dryer.

TALON

The low side valve is located on the suction line. The high side valve is located on the high pressure line.

BELT TENSION

AVENGER & SEBRING COUPE

2.0L Engine

1. Install a suitable belt tension gauge in middle of belt span, **Fig. 1.**
2. Proper belt tension is 93–114 lbs.
3. Adjust belt tension as follows:
   a. Loosen tension pulley nut.
   b. Adjust tension using adjusting bolt.

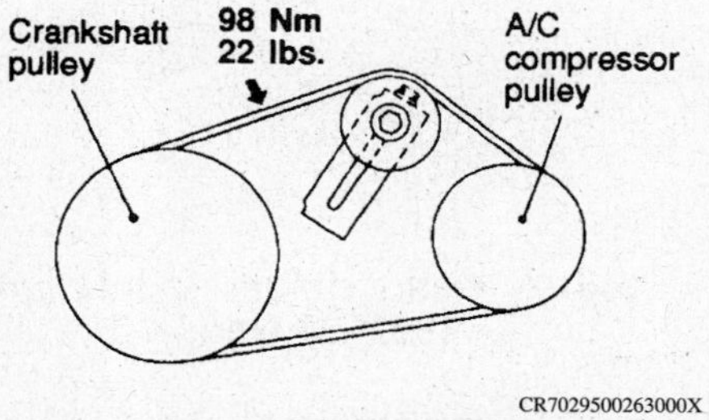

Fig. 1 Belt tension inspection. Avenger & Sebring Coupe w/2.0L engine

   c. Adjust new belt to 137–158 lbs. and used belt to 93–114 lbs.
   d. Tighten pulley nut.

2.5L Engine

1. Install a suitable belt tension gauge in middle of belt span, **Fig. 2.**
2. Proper belt tension is 66–86 lbs.
3. Adjust belt tension as follows:
   a. Loosen tension pulley nut.
   b. Adjust tension using adjusting bolt.
   c. Adjust new belt to 110–132 lbs. and used belt to 66–86 lbs.
   d. Tighten pulley nut.

BREEZE, CIRRUS, SEBRING CONVERTIBLE & STRATUS

1. Install a suitable belt tension gauge in middle of belt span.
2. Proper belt tension is 66–86 lbs.
3. Adjust belt tension as follows:
   a. Loosen locking nut and pivot bolt, **Fig. 3.**
   b. Adjust tension by tightening adjusting bolt.
   c. Adjust new belt to 150 lbs. and used belt to 80 lbs.
   d. **Torque** locking nut and pivot bolt to 40 ft. lbs.

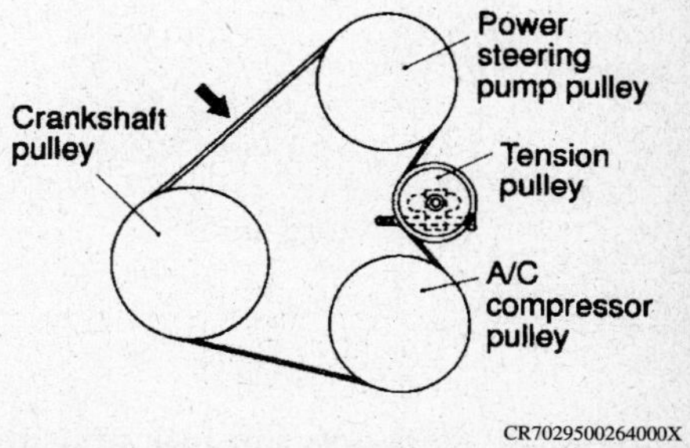

Fig. 2 Belt tension inspection. Avenger & Sebring Coupe w/2.5L engine

CONCORDE, INTREPID, LHS, VISION & 300M

1. Use belt tensioning tool No. C-7198, or equivalent, to measure A/C compressor belt tension.
2. With new belts, tension should be 140–160 lbs.
3. With used belts, tension should be 120 lbs.
4. If not within specification, tighten belt as follows:
   a. Loosen tensioner pulley locking nut, **Figs. 4 through 6.**
   b. Adjust tension to specification with adjusting bolt, 140–160 lbs. for a new belt and 120 lbs. for a used belt.
   c. **Torque** locking nut to 40 ft. lbs.
5. Inspect belt tension after driving vehicle.

NEON

1997–99

1. Using belt tensioning tool No. C-4162, or equivalent, ensure belt tension is 100 lbs. If not within specification, tighten belt as follows:

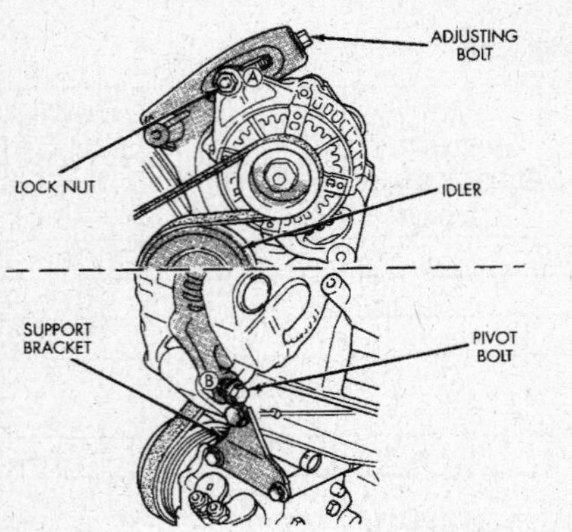

CR7029500267000X

Fig. 3 Belt tension adjustment. Breeze, Cirrus, Sebring Convertible & Stratus

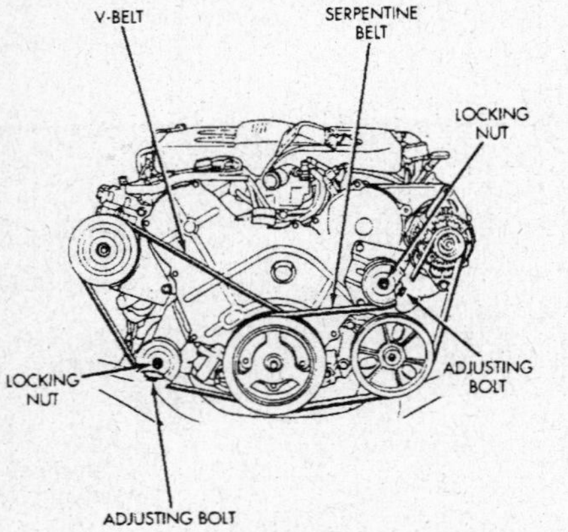

CR7029400225000X

Fig. 6 Belt tension inspection. Concorde, Intrepid, LHS, Vision & 300M w/3.2L & 3.5L engines

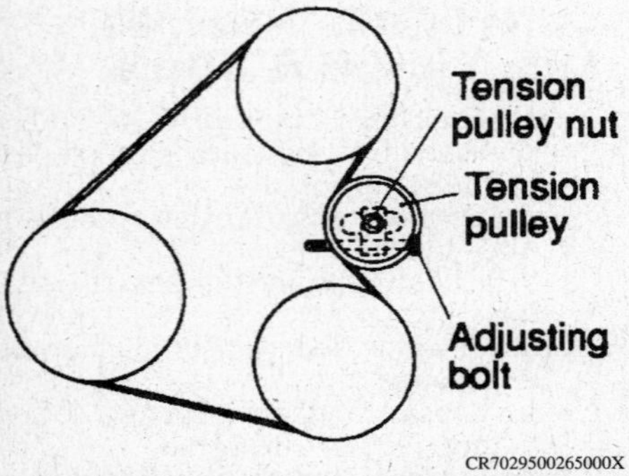

CR7029500265000X

Fig. 9 Belt tension inspection. Talon less turbocharged engine

a. Loosen power steering pump locking bolts A and B **Fig. 7,** then loosen pivot bolt C.
b. Adjust tension by applying torque to square hole on idler bracket. A new belt should be set to 135 lbs. Used belts should be set to 100 lbs.
c. **Torque** in order, locking bolt A, then locking bolt B to 20 ft. lbs. Finally, **torque** pivot bolt C to 40 ft. lbs.

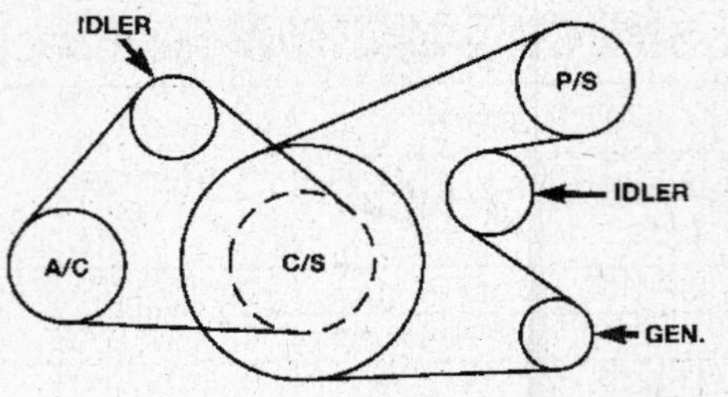

CR7029900530000X

Fig. 4 Belt tension inspection. Concorde, Intrepid, LHS & 300M w/2.7L engine

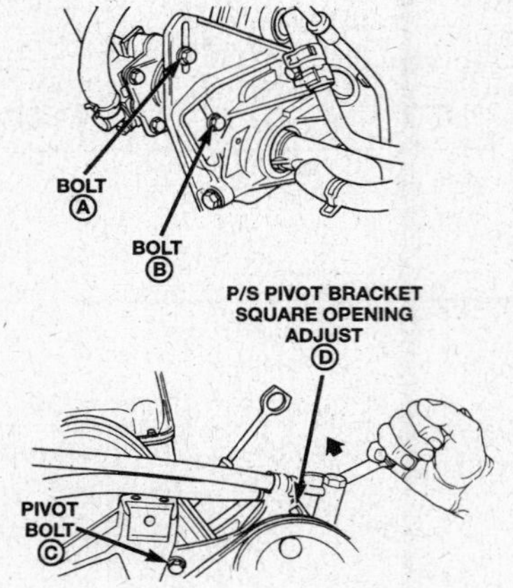

CR7029500226000X

Fig. 7 Belt tension inspection. 1997–99 Neon

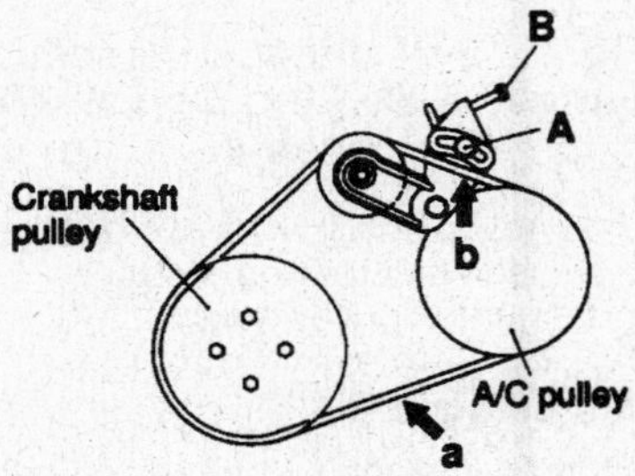

CR7029500266000X

Fig. 10 Belt tension inspection. Talon w/turbocharged engine

2. Inspect belt tension after driving vehicle.

2000

On these models an automatic belt tensioning device is incorporated with the engine mount bracket assembly, **Fig. 8.** The tensioner pulley is a serviceable component.

Slight tensioner arm axial movement is normal. Ensure the arm moves freely and can maintain 50–70 lbs. of tension on the belt.

TALON

Non-Turbocharged Engine

1. Using a suitable belt tension gauge, measure drive belt deflection by pulling or pushing at midpoint of the belt between pulleys as shown in **Fig. 9,** with a force of 22 lbs.
2. Deflection should be .39–.43 inch. If deflection is not within specifications, tighten belt as follows:
   a. Loosen tension pulley securing nut.
   b. Adjust tension to specification with adjusting bolt, .32–.35 inch for a new belt and .39–.43 inch for used belt.
   c. Tighten securing nut.
3. Inspect belt tension after driving vehicle.

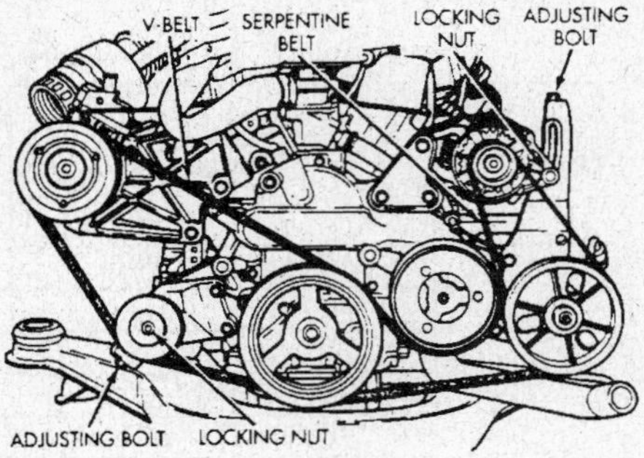

CR7029400224000X

Fig. 5 Belt tension inspection. Concorde, Intrepid & LHS w/3.3L engine

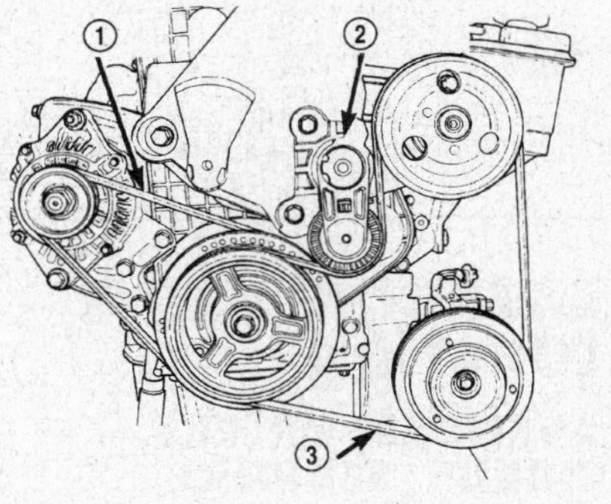

1 – GENERATOR BELT
2 – AUTOMATIC BELT TENSIONER
3 – POWER STEERING PUMP/A/C COMPRESSOR BELT

CR7020000585000X

Fig. 8 Belt tensioning system. 2000 Neon

Turbocharged Engine

1. Using a suitable belt tension gauge, measure drive belt deflection by pulling or pushing at midpoint of the belt between pulleys as shown in **Fig. 10,** with a force of 22 lbs.
2. Deflection should be .26–.30 inch. If deflection is not within specifications, tighten belt as follows:
   a. Loosen tension pulley fixing bolt A.
   b. Adjust tension to specification with adjusting bolt B, .22–.24 inch for a new belt and .26–.30 inch for used belt.
   c. **Torque** fixing nut to 17–20 ft. lbs.
3. Inspect belt tension after driving vehicle.

COOLING FANS

NOTE: Electrical Symbol And Wire Color Code Identification Located In Front Of This Manual Can Be Used As An Aid When Using Wiring Circuits Found In This Section.

NOTE: On Air Bag Equipped Models, Refer To " Air Bag System Precautions" Located In The Front Of This Manual For System Disarming & Arming Procedures.

NOTE: Refer To "Computer Relearn Procedures " Located In The Front Of This Manual For Computer Relearn Procedures.

INDEX

PRECAUTIONS

AIR BAG SYSTEMS

Refer to "Air Bag System Precautions" in the front of this manual for system disarming and arming procedures.

BATTERY GROUND CABLE

Prior to service, disconnect battery ground cable and isolate as required.

DESCRIPTION

AVENGER, SEBRING COUPE & TALON

Refer to **Figs. 1 through 3** for fan operation modes.

BREEZE, CIRRUS & STRATUS

1997-98

Fan control is accomplished in two ways. The fan always runs when the A/C pressure reaches 265 psi. The fan is also turned on by the temperature of the coolant which is sensed by the coolant temperature sensor. The sensor sends this temperature reading to the engine controller. The engine controller then turns on the fan through the fan relay. Refer to **Figs. 4 through 6** for fan operating modes.

1999-2000

Fan control is accomplished in three ways. The fans come on when the air conditioning pressure reaches a predetermined pressure as listed in **Figs. 4 through 6.** The fan is also activated by coolant temperature. Coolant temperature is sensed by a coolant sensor which sends a signal to the Powertrain Control Module (PCM). On models equipped with an automatic transaxle, the transmission fluid thermister also can turn on the fan.

CONCORDE, INTREPID, LHS, VISION & 300M

Radiator fan control is accomplished in two ways. A pressure transducer on the compressor discharge line sends a signal to the Powertrain Control Module (PCM) which activates the fans. The fans are also activated when the coolant temperature sensor sends a signal to the PCM. The engine controller then sends a signal to the fan relay which turns the coolant fans on.

Refer to **Figs. 7 through 10,** for specific fan operating modes.

NEON

Fan control is accomplished in two ways. The fan always runs when the compressor clutch is engaged. The fan is also activated by the temperature of the coolant which is sensed by the coolant temperature sensor. The coolant temperature sensor sends this signal to the engine controller which turns the fan on through the fan relay. Switching through the engine controller provides fan control for the following conditions:

1. Fan will not run when cranking engine no matter what coolant temperature is.
2. Fan will run when A/C clutch engaged and low pressure cutout switch is closed.
3. **At vehicle speeds over 40 mph,** fan will run only if coolant temperature reaches 230°F and fan will turn off when temperature drops to 220°F.
4. **At vehicle speeds under 40 mph,** fan

Switch conditions		Vehicle speed sensor km/h (mph)	Engine coolant temperature sensor °C (°F)	Fan revolving operation condition		
Air conditioning switch	Dual pressure switch			Radiator fan motor		Condenser fan motor
	Turn to ON at 1770 kPa (256 psi) or more			M/T	A/T	
OFF	OFF	45 (28) or less	95 (203) or less	OFF	OFF	OFF
			95 (203)–100 (210)	HIGH	Medium	OFF
			100 (210) or more	HIGH	HIGH	Medium
		45 (28)–80 (50)	90 (194) or less	OFF	OFF	OFF
			90 (194)–100 (210)	HIGH	Medium	OFF
			100 (210) or more	HIGH	HIGH	Medium
		80 (50) or more	100 (210) or less	OFF	OFF	OFF
			100 (210) or more	HIGH	HIGH	OFF
ON	OFF	19 (12) or less	100 (210) or less	HIGH	Medium	Medium
			100 (210)–115 (242)	HIGH	HIGH	HIGH
			115 (242) or more	HIGH	HIGH	HIGH
		19 (12)–80 (50)	100 (210) or less	HIGH	Medium	Medium
			100 (210)–115 (242)	HIGH	HIGH	HIGH
			115 (242) or more	HIGH	HIGH	HIGH
		80 (50) or more	100 (210) or less	OFF	OFF	OFF
			100 (210)–115 (242)	HIGH	HIGH	HIGH
			115 (242) or more	HIGH	HIGH	HIGH

CR1089500134000X

Fig. 1 Fan operating mode conditions. Avenger, Sebring Coupe & Talon w/2.0L engine less turbocharged engine

Switch conditions		Vehicle speed sensor km/h (mph)	Engine coolant temperature sensor °C (°F)	Fan revolving operation condition	
Air conditioning switch	Dual pressure switch			Radiator fan motor	Condenser fan motor
	Turn to ON at 1770 kPa (256 psi) or more				
OFF	OFF	45 (28) or less	95 (203) or less	OFF	OFF
			95 (203)–100 (210)	LOW	LOW
			100 (210) or more	HIGH	HIGH
		45 (28)–80(50)	90 (194) or less	OFF	OFF
			90 (194)–100 (210)	LOW	LOW
			100 (210) or more	HIGH	HIGH
		80 (50) or more	100 (210) or less	OFF	OFF
			100 (210) or more	HIGH	HIGH
ON	OFF	19 (12) or less	100 (210) or less	LOW	OFF
			100 (210)–115 (242)	HIGH	LOW
			115 (242) or more	HIGH	HIGH
		19 (12)–80(50)	100 (210) or less	LOW	OFF
			100 (210)–115 (242)	HIGH	LOW
			115 (242) or more	HIGH	HIGH
		80 (50) or more	100 (210) or less	OFF	OFF
			100 (210)–115 (242)	HIGH	HIGH
			115 (242) or more	HIGH	HIGH

CR1089500161000X

Fig. 2 Fan operating mode conditions. Avenger & Sebring Coupe w/2.5L engine

will run when coolant temperature reaches 215°F and fan will turn off when temperature drops 200°F.

5. **At idle speed,** to prevent steaming, the fan will run only for three minutes, when ambient temperature is below 60°F and coolant temperature is between 100–195°F.

SEBRING CONVERTIBLE

The radiator has a single cooling fan, with a two speed motor. The fan is controlled by the Powertrain Control Module (PCM) which activates the cooling fan relays.

Refer to **Figs. 11 through 13** for fan operating mode conditions.

SYSTEM DIAGNOSIS & TESTING

Wiring Diagrams

AVENGER & SEBRING COUPE

Refer to **Figs. 14 through 17** for cooling fan wiring diagrams.

BREEZE, CIRRUS & STRATUS

Refer to **Fig. 18** for cooling fan wiring diagrams.

NEON

Refer to **Figs. 19 and 20** for cooling fan wiring diagrams.

SEBRING CONVERTIBLE

Refer to **Figs. 21 through 23** for cooling fan wiring diagrams.

TALON

Refer to **Figs. 24 through 31** for cooling fan wiring diagrams.

CONCORDE, INTREPID, LHS, VISION & 300M

Refer to **Figs. 32 through 34** for cooling fan wiring diagrams.

COMPONENT DIAGNOSIS & TESTING

Coolant Temperature Sensor

AVENGER, SEBRING COUPE & TALON

1. Disconnect engine coolant temperature sensor electrical connector and connect an ohmmeter between sensor terminals.
2. Measure resistance between terminals. When coolant temperature is at 77°F, resistance should be 9.0–11.0 kohms. When coolant temperature is at 212°F, resistance should be 600–800 ohms.
3. If resistance is not as specified, replace sensor.

BREEZE, CIRRUS & STRATUS

1. Ensure ignition switch is in the OFF position, then disconnect wiring harness at coolant temperature sensor and connect an ohmmeter between sensor terminals.
2. Measure resistance between sensor terminals. Resistance should be 7.0–13.0 kohms.
3. Run engine until coolant temperature reaches approximately 200°F, then measure resistance. Resistance should be 700–1000 ohms.
4. Measure wiring harness resistance between Powertrain Control Module (PCM) terminal 26 and coolant sensor harness connector. Resistance should not exceed 1 ohm.
5. If resistance is not as specified, replace coolant sensor or repair wiring harness.

CONCORDE, INTREPID, LHS, VISION & 300M

1. With ignition in the OFF position, disconnect coolant temperature sensor connector.
2. Measure resistance between sensor terminals when engine is at 200°F.
3. If resistance is not 700–1000 ohms, replace sensor.

NEON

1. Ensure ignition is in the OFF position, then disconnect coolant temperature sensor electrical connector and connect a digital volt/ohmmeter between sensor terminals.
2. Measure resistance between sensor terminals. Resistance should be 7.0–13.0 kohms.
3. Run engine until coolant temperature reaches approximately 200°F, then measure resistance. Resistance should be 700–1000 ohms.
4. Measure wiring harness resistance between Powertrain Control Module (PCM) terminal 28 and coolant sensor harness connector. Resistance should not exceed 1 ohm.
5. Measure wiring harness resistance between PCM terminal 51 and coolant sensor harness connector. Resistance should not exceed 1 ohm.

Switch conditions		Vehicle speed sensor km/h (mph)	Engine coolant temperature sensor °C (°F)	Fan revolving operation condition		
Air conditioning switch	Dual pressure switch			Radiator fan motor		Condenser fan motor
	Turn to ON at 1770 kPa (256 psi) or more			M/T	A/T	
OFF	OFF	45 (28) or less	95 (203) or less	OFF	OFF	OFF
			95 (203)-100 (210)	Medium	LOW	LOW
			100 (210) or more	HIGH	HIGH	HIGH
		45 (28)-80(50)	90 (194) or less	OFF	OFF	OFF
			90 (194)-100 (210)	Medium	LOW	LOW
			100 (210) or more	HIGH	HIGH	HIGH
		80 (50) or more	100 (210) or less	OFF	OFF	OFF
			100 (210) or more	HIGH	HIGH	HIGH
ON	OFF	19 (12) or less	100 (210) or less	Medium	LOW	OFF
			100 (210)-115 (242)	HIGH	HIGH	LOW
			115 (242) or more	HIGH	HIGH	HIGH
		19 (12)-80(50)	100 (210) or less	Medium	LOW	OFF
			100 (210)-115 (242)	HIGH	HIGH	LOW
			115 (242) or more	HIGH	HIGH	HIGH
		80 (50) or more	100 (210) or less	OFF	OFF	OFF
			100 (210)-115 (242)	HIGH	HIGH	HIGH
			115 (242) or more	HIGH	HIGH	HIGH

CR1089500135000X

Fig. 3 Fan operating mode conditions. Talon w/turbocharged engine

Radiator Fan Control			A/C Pressure	
A/C Off	**Low**	**High**		
Fan On:	104°C (220°F)	110°C (230°F)		
Fan Off:	99°C (210°F)	104°C (220°F)		
A/C On	Low	High	Low	High
Fan On:	99°C (210°F)	110°C (230°F)	1,466 Kpa (209 psi)	1,717 Kpa (249 psi)
Fan Off:	93°C (200°F)	104°C (220°F)	1,172 Kpa (170 psi)	1,579 Kpa (229 psi)
EATX Fluid Temperature			**Low Speed**	**High Speed**
Fan On:			116°C (240°F)	120°C (248°F)
Fan Off:			109°C (228°F)	116°C (240°F)

CR1089900256000X

Fig. 4 Fan operating mode conditions. Breeze & Stratus w/2.0L engine

Radiator Fan Control			A/C Pressure	
A/C Off	**Low**	**High**		
Fan On:	104°C (219°F)	110°C (230°F)		
Fan Off:	99°C (210°F)	105°C (221°F)		
A/C On	**Low**	**High**	**Low**	**High**
Fan On:	99°C (210°F)	110°C (230°F)	1,448 Kpa (210 psi)	1,718 Kpa (249 psi)
Fan Off:	93°C (199°F)	105°C (221°F)	1,207 Kpa (175 Psi)	1,585 Kpa (229 Psi)
EATX Fluid Temperature			**Low Speed**	**High Speed**
Fan On:			118°C (244°F)	122°C (252°F)
Fan Off:			116°C (240°F)	118°C (244°F)

CR1089900257000X

Fig. 5 Fan operating mode conditions. Breeze & Stratus w/2.4L engine

Radiator Fan Control			A/C Pressure	
A/C Off	**Low**	**High**		
Fan On:	104°C (220°F)	110°C (230°F)		
Fan Off:	98°C (208°F)	105°C (221°F)		
A/C On	Low	High	Low	High
Fan On:	99°C (210°F)	110°C (230°F)	1,448 Kpa (210 psi)	1,718 Kpa (249 psi)
Fan Off:	93°C (199°F)	105°C (221°F)	1,207 Kpa (175 psi)	1,585 kpa (229 psi)
EATX Fluid Temperature			**Low Speed**	**High Speed**
Fan On:			118°C (244°F)	122°C (252°F)
Fan Off:			116°C (240°F)	118°C (244°F)

CR1089900258000X

Fig. 6 Fan operating mode conditions. Cirrus & Stratus w/2.5L engine

RADIATOR COOLING FAN OPERATION	ENGINE COOLANT TEMPERATURE AND A/C COMPRESSOR PRESSURES		
	A/C OFF	A/C ON	A/C Compressor Pressure
Low Speed Fan ON	(210°F)	(210°F)	1,446.57 Kpa (209.8 psi)
Low Speed Fan OFF	(199°F)	(199°F)	861.87 Kpa (125 psi)
High Speed Fan ON	(230°F)	(230°F)	1,723.75 Kpa (250 psi)
High Speed Fan OFF	(219°F)	(219°F)	1,585.85 Kpa (230 psi)

CR1089500160000X

Fig. 7 Fan operating mode conditions. 1997 Concorde, Intrepid, LHS & Vision

Radiator Fan Control			A/C Pressure	
A/C Off	Low	High		
Fan On:	110°C (230°F)	113°C (235°F)		
Fan Off:	104°C (219°F *)	111°C (231°F)		
***109°C (228°F) @ Vehicle speed greater than 12.8 Kmh (8 mph).**				
A/C On	Low	High	Low	High
Fan On:	105°C (221°F)	110°C (230°F)	1,448 Kpa (210 psi)	1,717 Kpa (249 psi)
Fan Off:	102°C (216°F)	106°C (223°F)	1207 Kpa (175 psi)	1,579 Kpa (229 psi)

CR1089800214000X

Fig. 8 Fan operating mode. 1998 Concorde & Intrepid

6. If resistance is not as specified, replace coolant sensor or repair wiring harness.

SEBRING CONVERTIBLE

1. With key off, disconnect connector from coolant sensor.
2. Connect one lead of digital volt/ohm meter to each terminal of sensor.
3. With engine sensor at normal operating temperature of approximately 200°F, reading should be 700–1000 ohms.
4. With engine sensor at room temperature of approximately 70°F, reading should be 7–13 k ohms.
5. If sensor measurements are not as indicated, replace sensor.

Engine Coolant Temperature Switch

TALON

1. Place sensor in oil up to mounting thread.
2. Connect a suitable ohmmeter across terminals of coolant temperature switch, then increase oil temperature.
3. Ensure switch is switched OFF when oil temperature at 234–244°F, replace sensor if necessary.

Thermo Sensor

TALON

1. Place sensor in hot water up to mounting thread.
2. Check for continuity between terminals on sensor.
3. Continuity should exist with water temperature at 180–190°F. Continuity should not exist with water temperature at 172°F or less.
4. If continuity is not as specified, replace sensor.

ENGINE COOLANT TEMPERATURE							INTAKE (CHARGE) TEMPERATURE	
	A/C Off		A/C On		Engine @ Idle<2 Km/h (1 MPH) Vehicle Speed			
Fan Speed	Low	High	Low	High	Low	High	Low	High
Fan On:	106°C (223°F)	110°C (230°F)	105°C (221°F)	110°C (230°F)	99°C (210°F) - After 2nd Fan Cycle	110°C (230°F)	63°C (145°F) if coolant<93°C (199°F) 60°C (140°F) if coolant>99°C (210°F)	67°C (153°F)
Fan Off:	102°C (216°F)	107°C (225°F)	102°C (216°F)	106°C (223°F)	Fan on time = 4 minutes*	105°C (221°F)	Fan on time = 8 minutes*	Fan on time = 4 minutes*

*Minimum fan on time = 90 seconds

	A/C PRESSURE		TRANSMISSION OIL TEMPERATURE	
Fan Speed	Low	High	Low	High
Fan On:	1,448 Kpa (210 psi)	1,717 Kpa (249 psi)	109°C (228°F)	111°C (232°F)
Fan Off:	1,207 Kpa (175 psi)	1,503 Kpa (218 psi)	104°C (220°F)	109°C (228°F)

CR1089800262000X

Fig. 9 Fan operating mode conditions. 1999–2000 Concorde & Intrepid w/2.7L engine

Radiator Fan Control			A/C Pressure	
A/C Off	Low	High		
Fan On:	102°C (215°F)	107°C (225°F)		
Fan Off:	96°C (205°F)	96°C (205°F)		
A/C On	Low	High	Low	High
Fan On:	102°C (215°F)	107°C (225°F)	1,448 Kpa (210 psi)	1,718 Kpa (249 psi)
Fan Off:	96°C (205°F)	96°C (205°F)	1,207 Kpa (175 Psi)	1,585 Kpa (229 Psi)
EATX Fluid Temperature			**Low Speed**	**High Speed**
Fan On:			118°C (244°F)	122°C (252°F)
Fan Off:			116°C (240°F)	118°C (244°F)

CR1089900260000X

Fig. 11 Fan operating mode conditions. Sebring Convertible w/2.4L engine

ENGINE COOLANT TEMPERATURE					INTAKE (CHARGE) AIR TEMPERATURE	
	A/C Off/On		Engine @ Idle <2 Km/h (1 MPH) Vehicle Speed			
Fan Speed	Low	High	Low	High	Low	High
Fan On:	102°C (216°F)	110°C (230°F)	99°C (210°F) - After 2nd Fan Cycle	110°C (230°F)	63°C (145°F) if coolant<93°C (199°F) 60°C (140°F) if coolant>99°C (210°F)	67°C (153°F)
Fan Off:	99°C (210°F)	105°C (221°F)	Fan on time = 4 minutes*	105°C (221°F)	Fan on time = 8 minutes*	Fan on time = 4 minutes*

*Minimum fan on time = 90 seconds

	A/C PRESSURE		TRANSMISSION OIL TEMPERATURE	
Fan Speed	Low	High	Low	High
Fan On:	1,448 Kpa (210 psi)	1,717 Kpa (249 psi)	102°C (216°F)	109°C (228°F)
Fan Off:	1,207 Kpa (175 psi)	1,510 Kpa (219 psi)	98°C (208°F)	107°C (224°F)

CR1089800263000X

Fig. 10 Fan operating mode conditions. 1999–2000 Concorde, Intrepid, LHS & 300M w/3.2L & 3.5L engines

Radiator Fan Control			A/C Pressure	
A/C Off	Low	High		
Fan On:	102°C (215°F)	107°C (224°F)		
Fan Off:	96°C (205°F)	101°C (213°F)		
A/C On	Low	High	Low	High
Fan On:	102°C (215°F)	107°C (224°F)	1,448 Kpa (210 psi)	1,718 Kpa (249 psi)
Fan Off:	96°C (205°F)	101°C (213°F)	1,207 Kpa (175 psi)	1,585 Kpa (229 psi)
EATX Fluid Temperature			**Low Speed**	**High Speed**
Fan On:			118°C (244°F)	122°C (252°F)
Fan Off:			116°C (240°F)	118°C (244°F)

CR1089500194000X

Fig. 12 Fan operating mode conditions. 1997–98 Sebring Convertible w/2.5L engine

Radiator Fan Control			A/C Pressure	
A/C Off	Low	High		
Fan On:	102°C (215°F)	107°C (224°F)		
Fan Off:	96°C (205°F)	103°C (217°F)		
A/C On	Low	High	Low	High
Fan On:	102°C (215°F)	107°C (224°F)	1,448 Kpa (210 psi)	1,718 Kpa (249 psi)
Fan Off:	96°C (205°F)	101°C (213°F)	1,207 Kpa (175 psi)	1,585 Kpa (229 psi)
EATX Fluid Temperature			**Low Speed**	**High Speed**
Fan On:			118°C (244°F)	122°C (252°F)
Fan Off:			116°C (240°F)	118°C (244°F)

CR1089900261000X

Fig. 13 Fan operating mode conditions. 1999–2000 Sebring Convertible w/2.5L engine

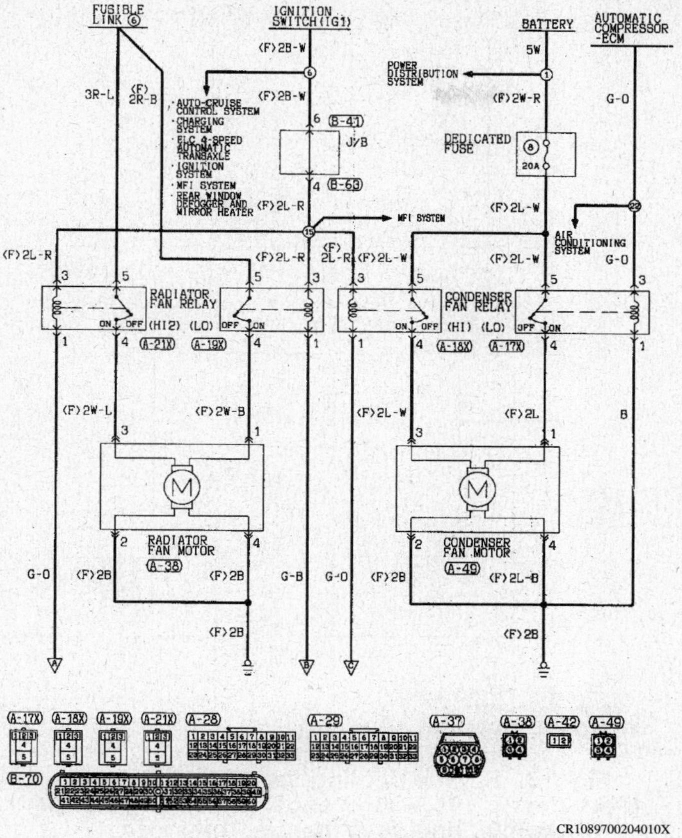

Fig. 14 Engine cooling fan wiring diagram (Part 1 of 2). 1997–98 Avenger & Sebring Coupe w/2.0L engine & automatic transaxle

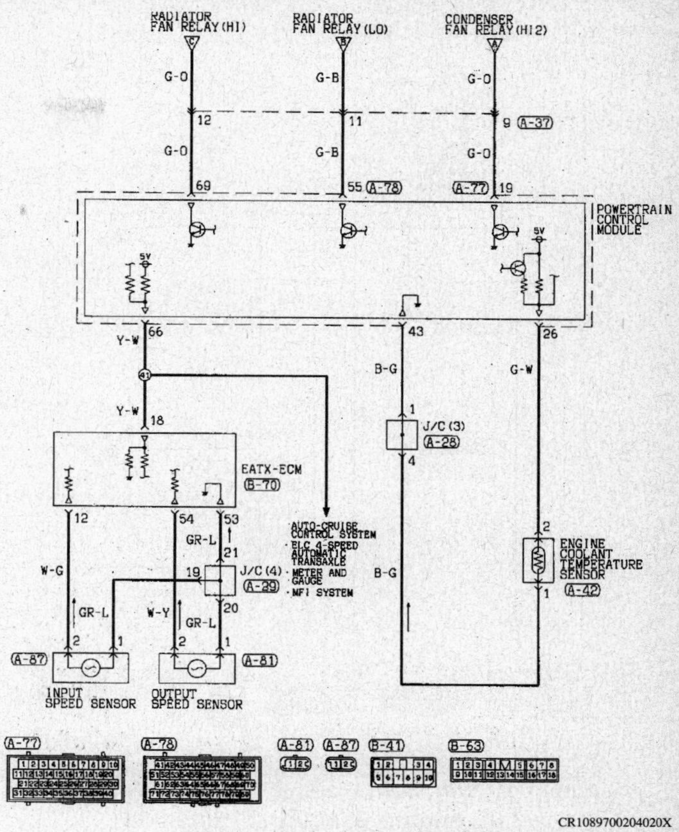

Fig. 14 Engine cooling fan wiring diagram (Part 2 of 2). 1997–98 Avenger & Sebring Coupe w/2.0L engine & automatic transaxle

Fan Motor Relay

AVENGER, SEBRING COUPE & TALON

Refer to **Fig. 35** when performing this test.

1. Remove radiator fan motor relay from relay box inside engine compartment.
2. Check for continuity between terminals 1 and 3. Continuity should exist.
3. Check for continuity between terminals 4 and 5. Continuity should not exist.
4. Connect 12 power supply between terminals 1 and 3.
5. Check for continuity between terminals 4 and 5. Continuity should exist.
6. If continuity is not as specified, replace relay.

NEON

Refer to **Fig. 36** for coolant fan control relay circuit test.

Radiator Fan Motor

AVENGER & SEBRING COUPE

1. Connect battery positive and negative terminals to fan motor connector terminals as shown in **Figs. 37 and 38.**
2. If fan motor does not operate normally, replace fan motor assembly.

BREEZE, CIRRUS & STRATUS

1. Disconnect fan motor electrical connector.
2. Check low speed coolant fan motor as follows:
   a. Connect battery voltage to fan motor connector terminal No. 3.
   b. If low speed coolant fan operates, proceed to next step. If coolant fan does not operate, check circuit between connector terminal No. 1 and ground. If ground circuit is satisfactory, replace fan motor.
   c. Check circuit and relays for open or short.
3. Check high speed coolant fan motor as follows:
   a. Connect battery voltage to fan motor connector terminal No. 4.
   b. If high speed coolant fan operates, proceed to next step. If coolant fan does not operate, check circuit between connector terminal No. 2 and ground. If ground circuit is satisfactory, replace fan motor.
   c. Check circuit and relays for open or short.

CONCORDE, INTREPID, LHS, VISION & 300M

1997

1. Disconnect fan motor electrical connector.
2. Check low speed coolant fan motor as follows:
   a. Connect battery voltage to fan motor connector terminal No. 1.
   b. If low speed coolant fan operates, proceed to next step. If coolant fan does not operate, check circuit between connector terminal No. 3 and ground. If ground circuit is satisfactory, replace fan motor.
   c. Check circuit and relays for open or short.
3. Check high speed coolant fan motor as follows:
   a. Connect battery voltage to fan motor connector terminal No. 2.
   b. If high speed coolant fan operates, proceed to next step. If coolant fan does not operate, check circuit between connector terminal No. 3 and ground. If ground circuit is satisfactory, replace fan motor.
   c. Check circuit and relays for open or short.

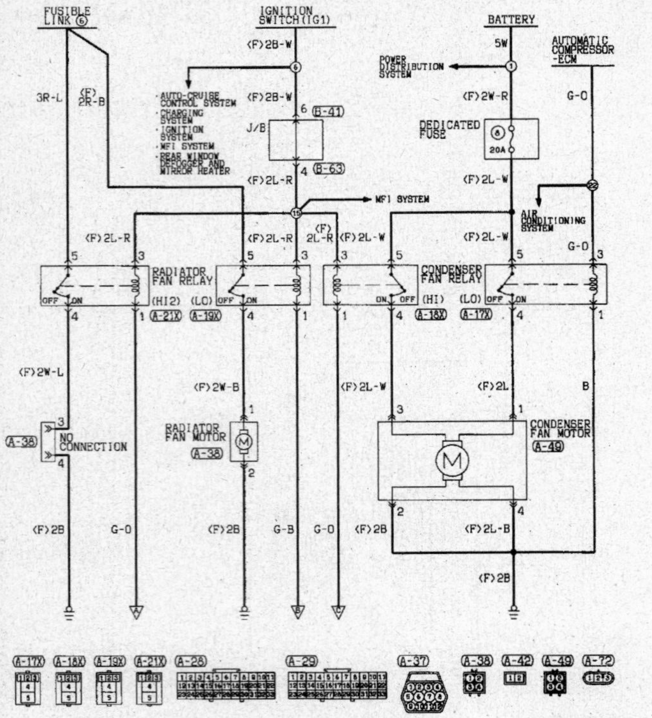

CR1089700205010X

Fig. 15 Engine cooling fan wiring diagram (Part 1 of 2). 1997–98 Avenger & Sebring Coupe w/2.0L engine & manual transaxle

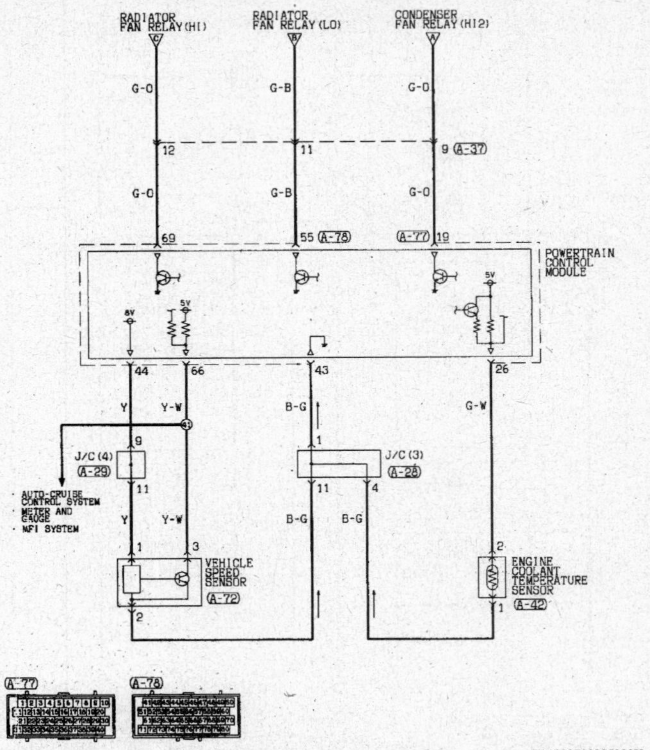

CR1089700205020X

Fig. 15 Engine cooling fan wiring diagram (Part 1 of 2). 1997–98 Avenger & Sebring Coupe w/2.0L engine & manual transaxle

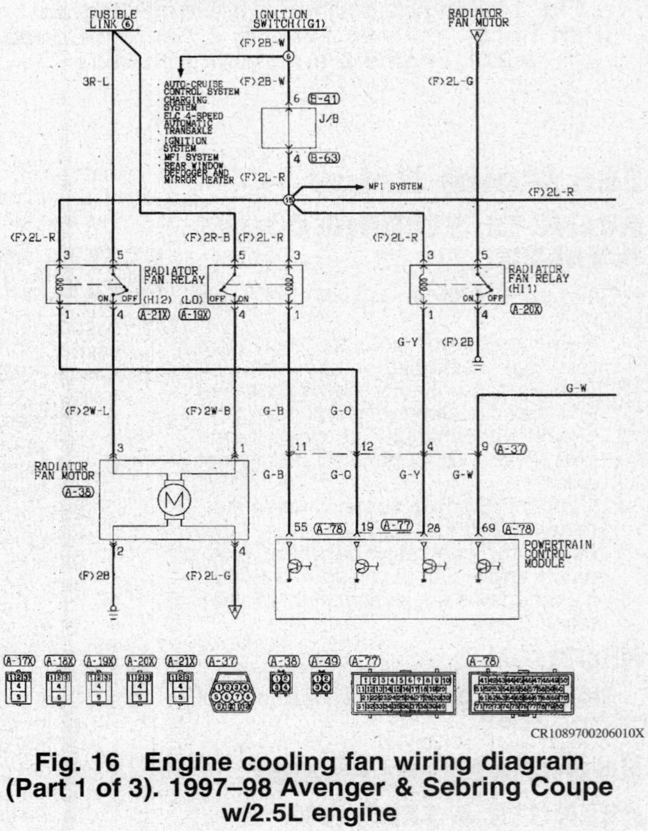

CR1089700206010X

Fig. 16 Engine cooling fan wiring diagram (Part 1 of 3). 1997–98 Avenger & Sebring Coupe w/2.5L engine

1998–2000

Refer to **Figs. 39 and 40,** for coolant fan motor connector view and diagnostic test.

NEON

1. Disconnect fan motor electrical connector.
2. Connect a 14 gauge jumper wire from battery positive terminal to fan motor terminal No. 1.
3. If fan motor does not operate normally, check circuit between fan motor electrical connector terminal No. 2 and ground.
4. If ground circuit is satisfactory, replace fan motor.

SEBRING CONVERTIBLE

1. Disconnect fan motor electrical connector.
2. Check low speed fan operation as follows:
   a. Connect a jumper wire from battery positive terminal to fan motor terminal No. 2.
   b. If fan motor operates at low speed, proceed to next step. If fan motor does not operate normally, check circuit between fan motor electrical connector terminal No. 1 and ground. If ground circuit is satisfactory, replace fan motor.
   c. Check circuit and relay for open or short.
3. Check high speed fan operation as follows:
   a. Connect a jumper wire from battery positive terminal to fan motor terminal No. 3.
   b. If fan motor operates at high speed, proceed to next step. If fan motor does not operate normally, check circuit between fan motor electrical

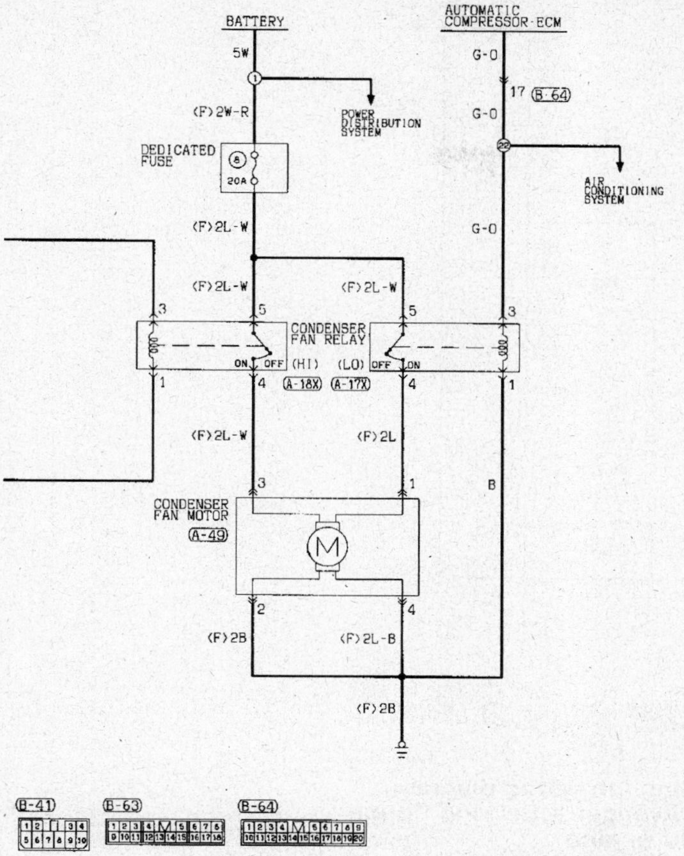

CR1089700206020X

Fig. 16 Engine cooling fan wiring diagram (Part 2 of 3). 1997–98 Avenger & Sebring Coupe w/2.5L engine

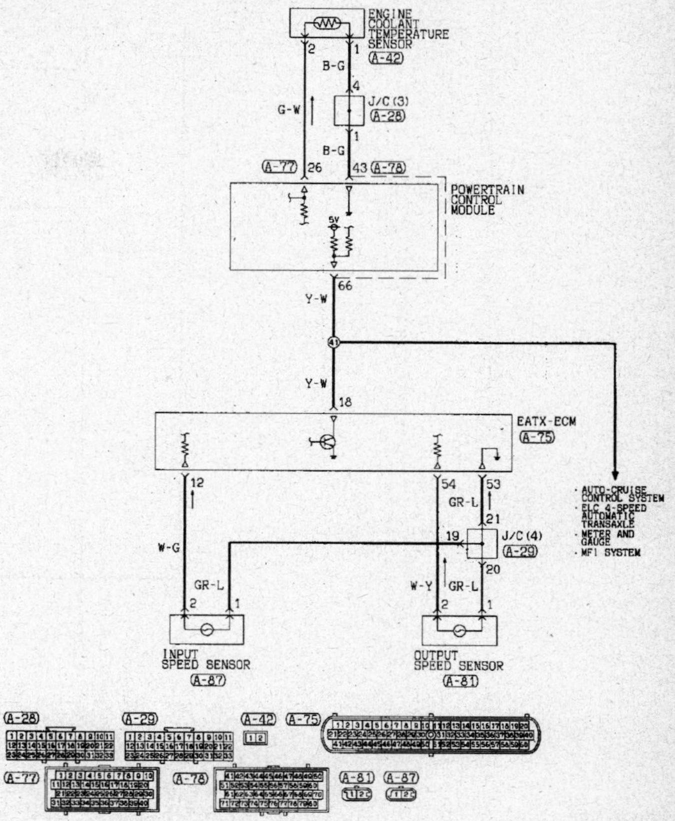

CR1089700206030X

Fig. 16 Engine cooling fan wiring diagram (Part 3 of 3). 1997–98 Avenger & Sebring Coupe w/2.5L engine

connector terminal No. 1 and ground. If ground circuit is satisfactory, replace fan motor.

c. Check circuit and relay for open or short.

4. Check low speed fan operation as follows:
   a. Connect a jumper wire from battery positive terminal to fan motor terminal No. 2.
   b. If fan motor operates at low speed, proceed to next step. If fan motor does not operate normally, check circuit between fan motor electrical connector terminal No. 1 and ground. If ground circuit is satisfactory, replace fan motor.
   c. Check circuit and relay for open or short.

TALON

1. Disconnect fan motor connector and connect to battery positive and negative using jumper wires as shown, **Fig. 41.**
2. If fan does not run normally or makes abnormal noises, replace fan motor assembly.

Low Speed Fan Control Relay

AVENGER, BREEZE, CIRRUS, SEBRING CONVERTIBLE, SEBRING COUPE, STRATUS & TALON

Refer **Figs. 42 through 45,** for low coolant fan relay circuit connectors. Refer to **Fig. 46** for low coolant fan relay diagnostic procedures.

CONCORDE, INTREPID, LHS, VISION & 300M

1997

Refer to **Fig. 47** for low speed coolant fan relay circuit diagnostic test.

1998–2000

Refer to **Figs. 48 and 49** for low speed coolant fan relay connector views. Refer to **Figs. 50 and 51** for relay diagnostic procedures.

High Speed Fan Control Relay

AVENGER, BREEZE, CIRRUS, SEBRING, STRATUS & TALON

Refer to **Figs. 52 through 57,** for circuit connector views. Refer to **Fig. 58** for high speed coolant fan relay circuit diagnostic test.

CONCORDE, INTREPID, LHS, VISION & 300M

1997

Refer to **Fig. 59** for high speed coolant fan relay circuit diagnostic test.

1998–2000

Refer to **Figs. 60 through 62,** for high speed coolant fan relay connector view and diagnostic test.

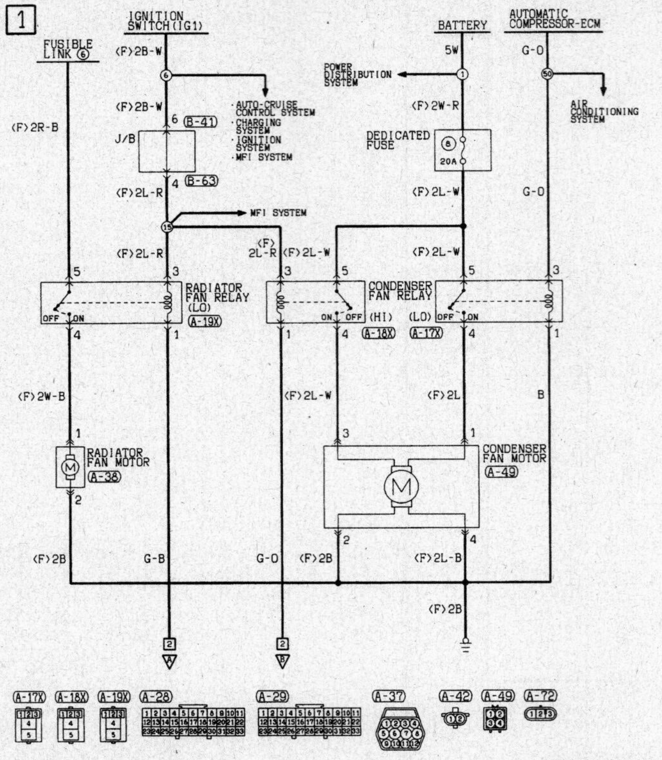

CR1089900255010X

Fig. 17 Engine cooling fan wiring diagram (Part 1 of 2). 1999–2000 Avenger & Sebring Coupe w/DOHC engine

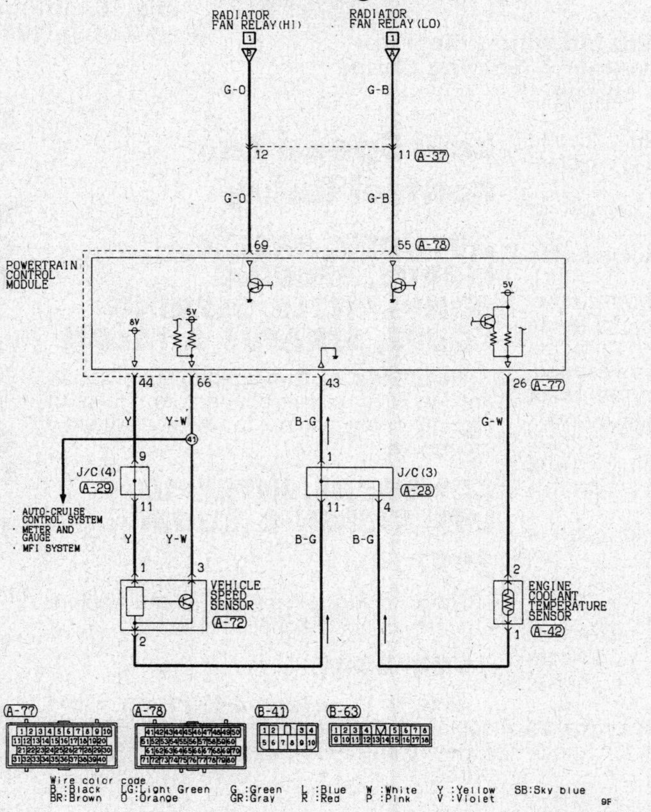

CR1089900255020X

Fig. 17 Engine cooling fan wiring diagram (Part 2 of 2). 1999–2000 Avenger & Sebring Coupe w/DOHC engine & automatic transmission

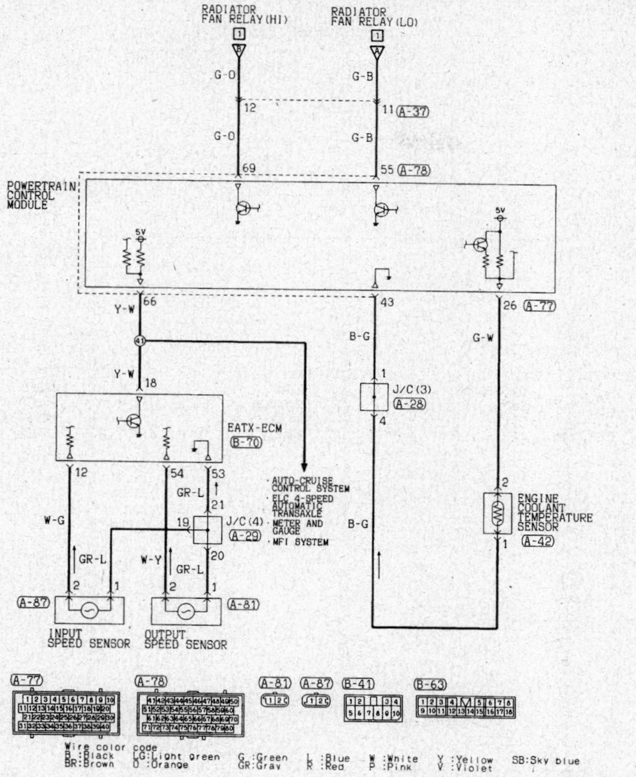

CR1089900255030X

Fig. 17 Engine cooling fan wiring diagram (Part 2 of 2). 1999–2000 Avenger & Sebring Coupe w/DOHC engine & manual transmission

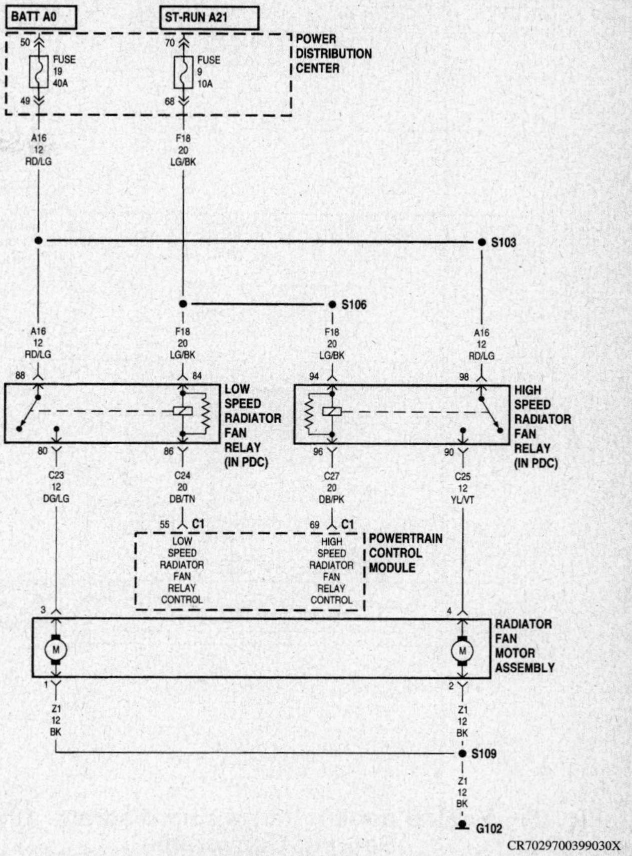

CR7029700399030X

Fig. 18 Engine cooling fan wiring diagram. Breeze, Cirrus & Stratus

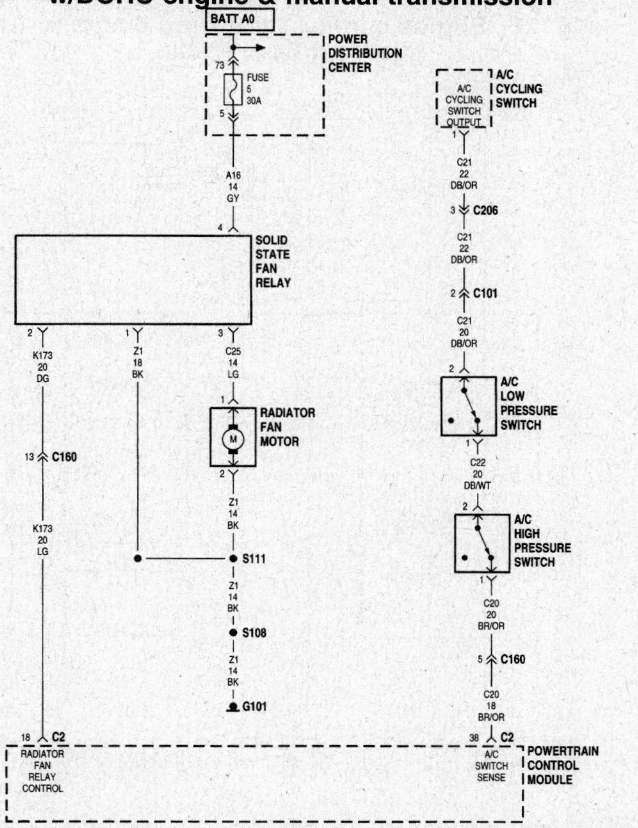

CR7029700405010X

Fig. 19 Engine cooling fan wiring diagram. 1997–99 Neon

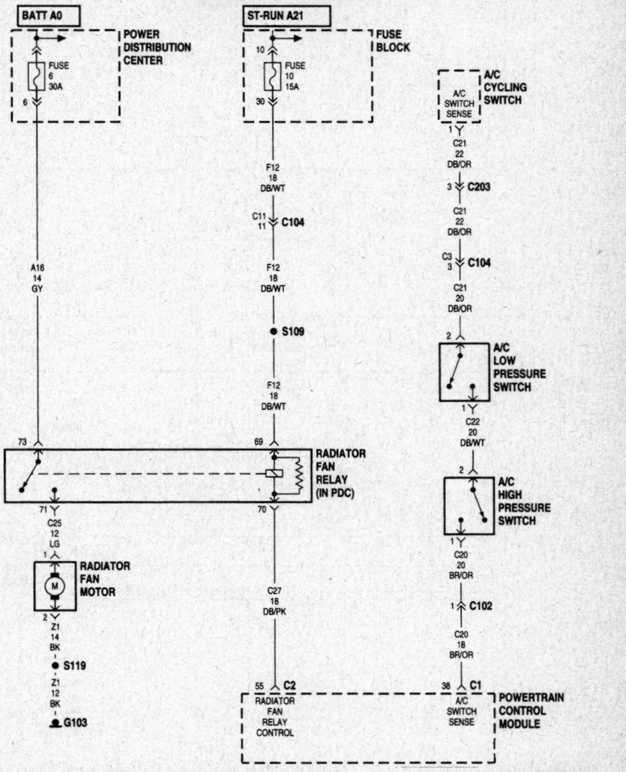

CR1080000275000X

Fig. 20 Engine cooling fan wiring diagram. 2000 Neon

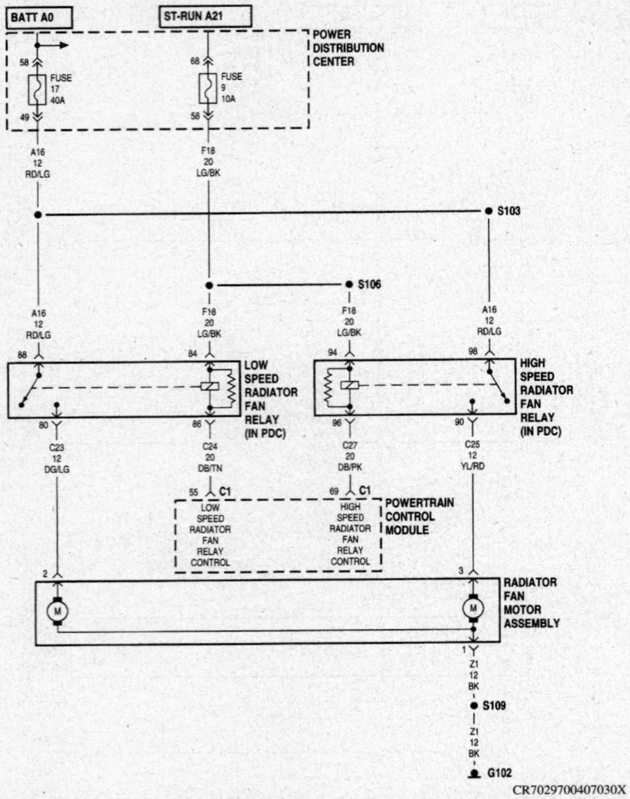

Fig. 21 Engine cooling fan wiring diagram. 1997–98 Sebring Convertible

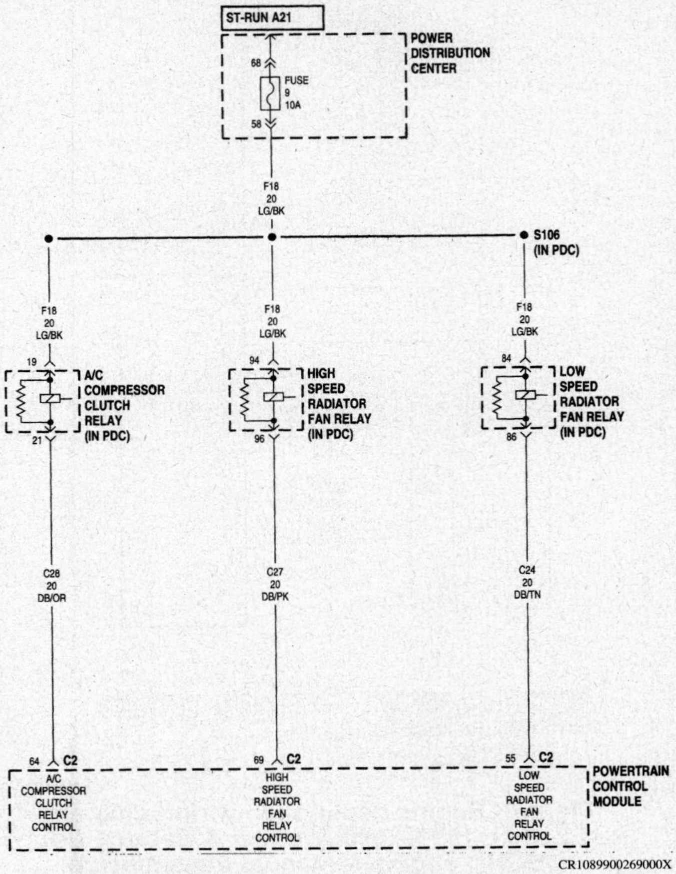

Fig. 22 Engine cooling fan wiring diagram. 1999 Sebring Convertible

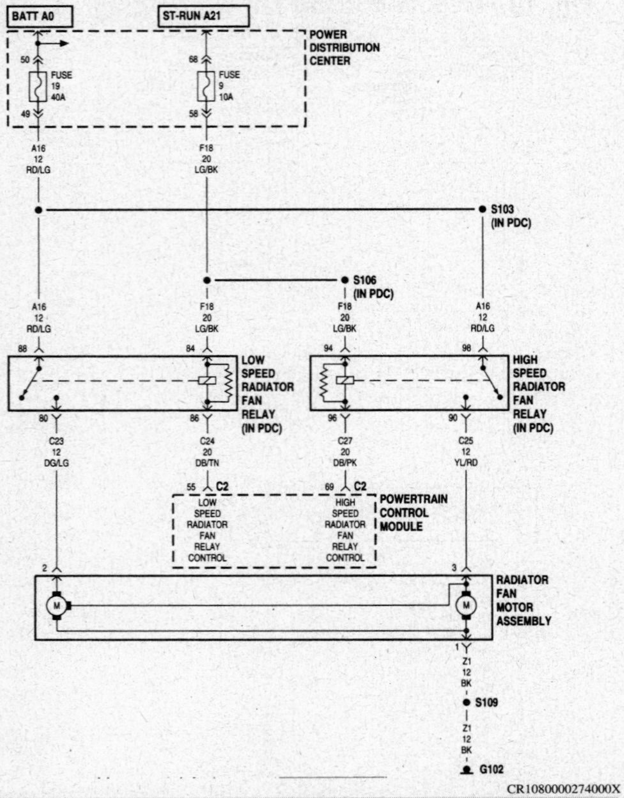

Fig. 23 Engine cooling fan wiring diagram. 2000 Sebring Convertible

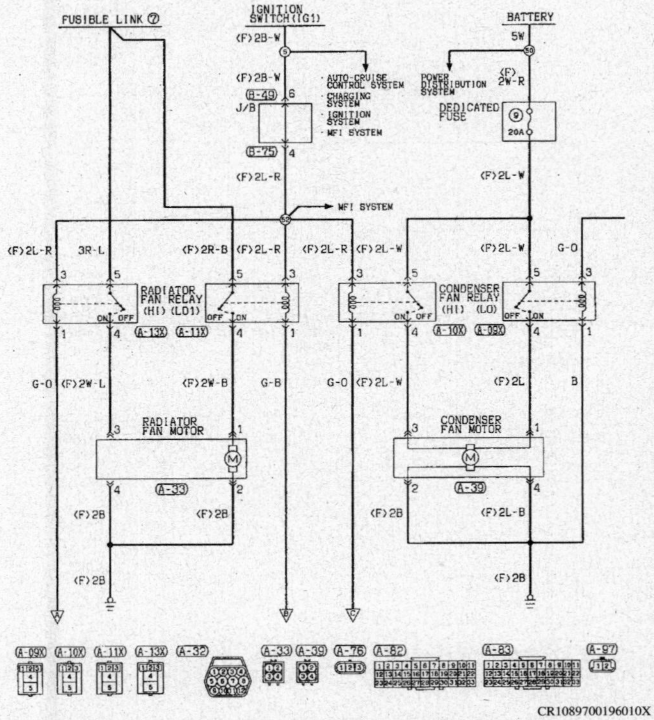

Fig. 24 Engine cooling fan wiring diagram (Part 1 of 2). 1997 Talon less turbo w/manual transaxle

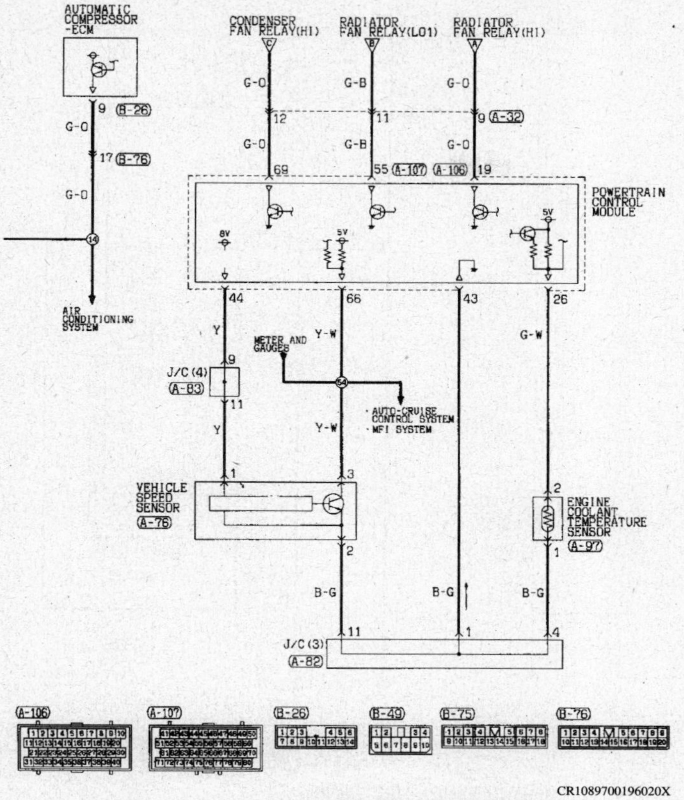

Fig. 24 Engine cooling fan wiring diagram (Part 2 of 2). 1997 Talon less turbo w/manual transaxle

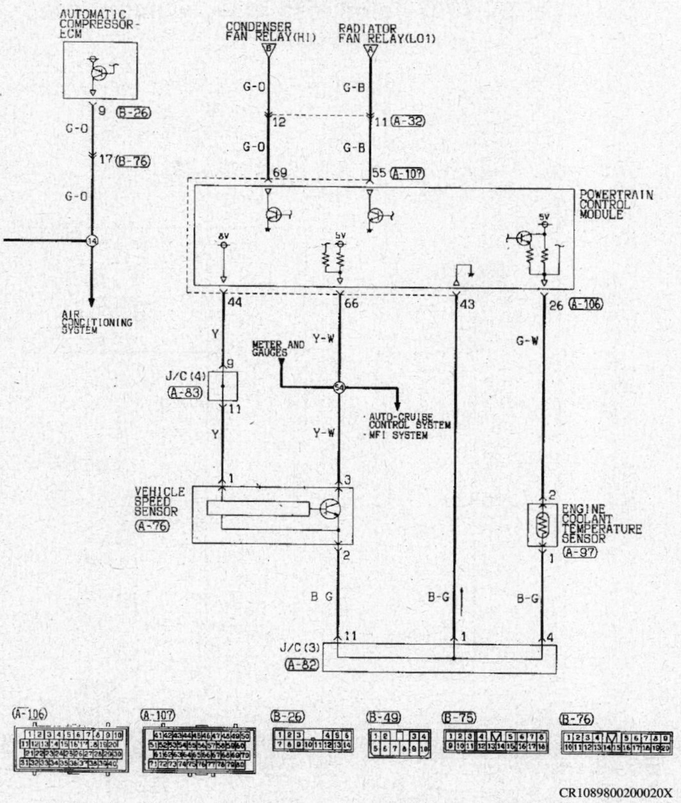

Fig. 25 Engine cooling fan wiring diagram (Part 2 of 2). 1998 Talon less turbo w/manual transaxle

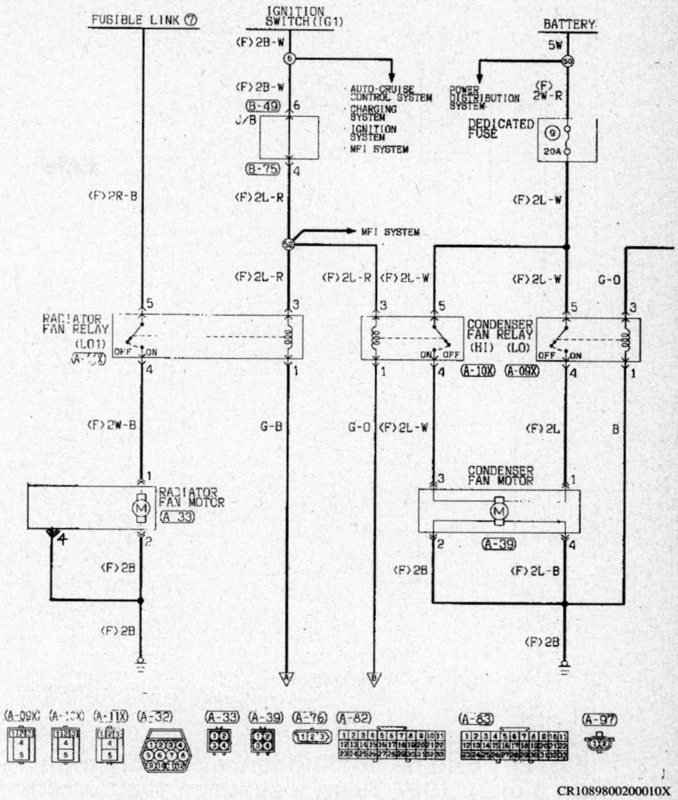

Fig. 25 Engine cooling fan wiring diagram (Part 1 of 2). 1998 Talon less turbo w/manual transaxle

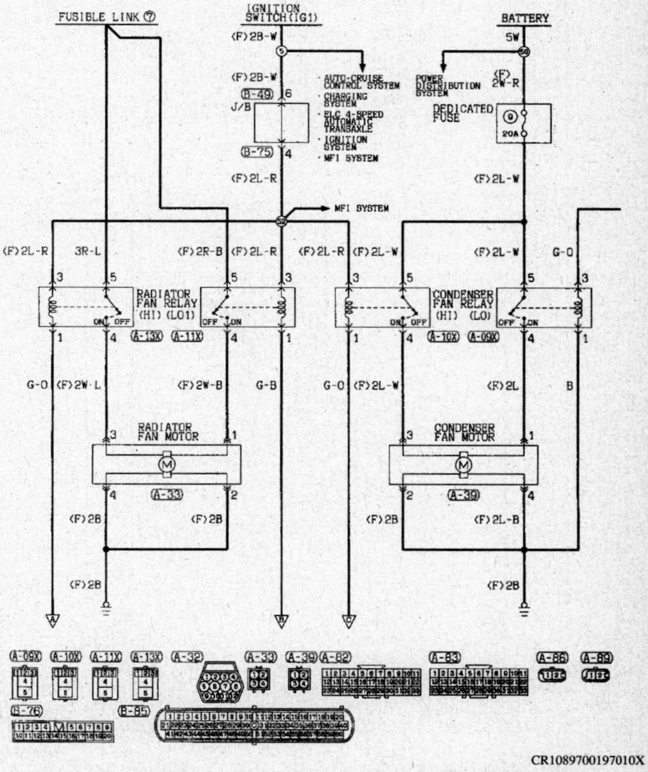

Fig. 26 Engine cooling fan wiring diagram (Part 1 of 2). 1997 Talon less turbo w/automatic transaxle

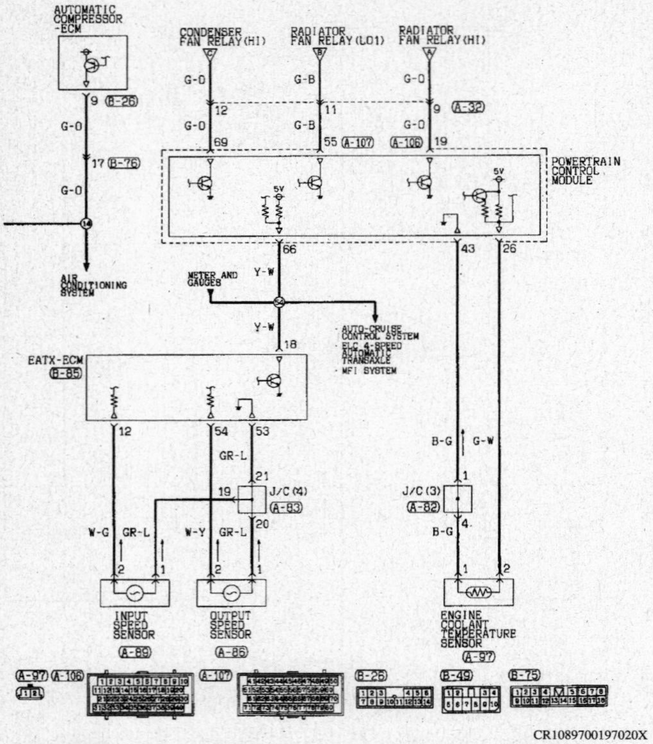

Fig. 26 Engine cooling fan wiring diagram (Part 2 of 2). 1997 Talon less turbo w/automatic transaxle

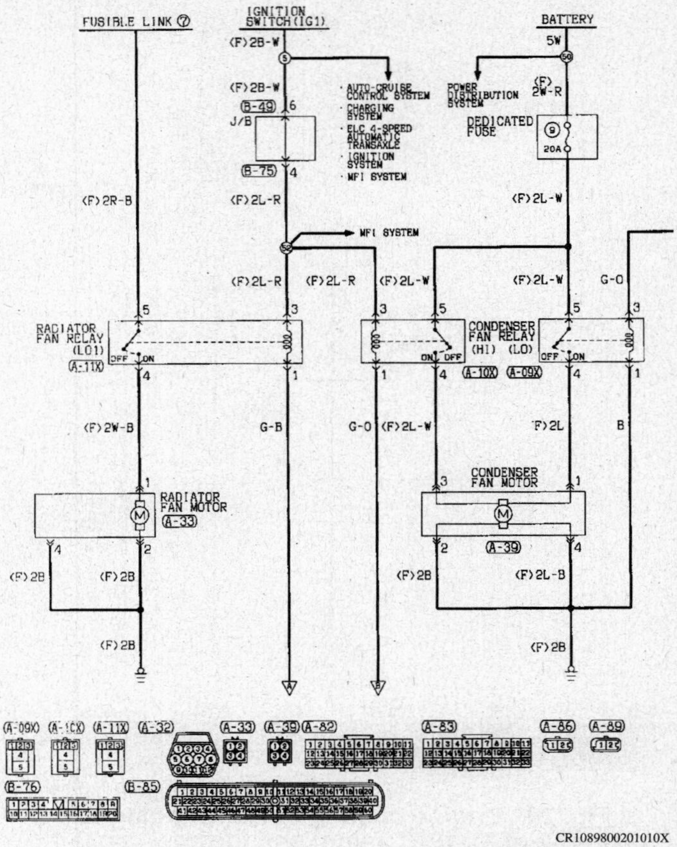

Fig. 27 Engine cooling fan wiring diagram (Part 1 of 2). 1998 Talon less turbo w/automatic transaxle

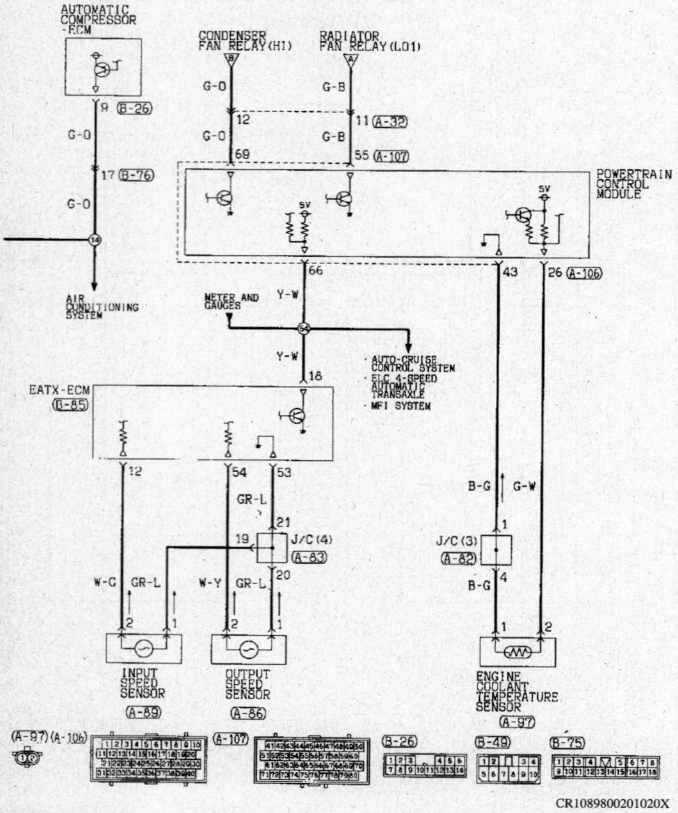

Fig. 27 Engine cooling fan wiring diagram (Part 2 of 2). 1998 Talon less turbo w/automatic transaxle

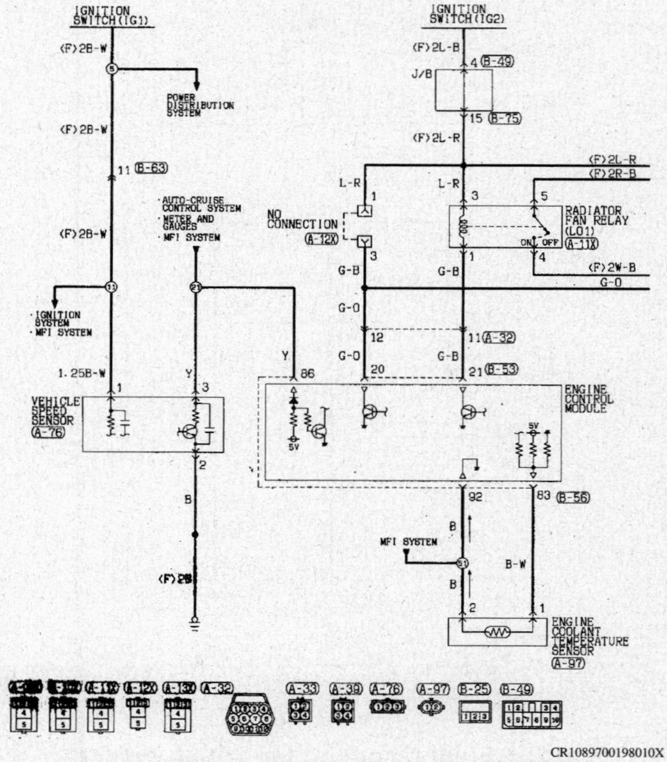

Fig. 28 Engine cooling fan wiring diagram (Part 1 of 2). 1997 Talon w/turbo & manual transaxle

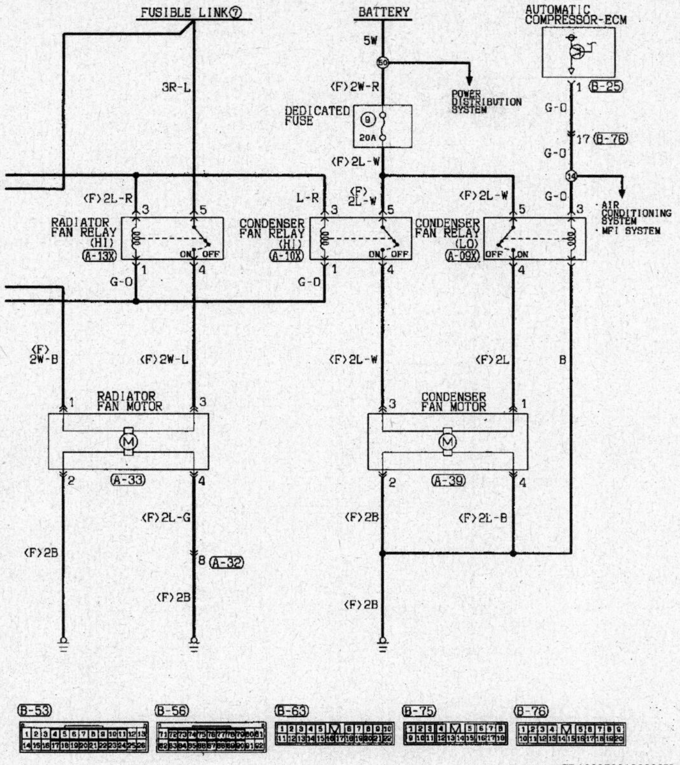

CR1089700198020X

Fig. 28 Engine cooling fan wiring diagram (Part 2 of 2). 1997 Talon w/turbo & manual transaxle

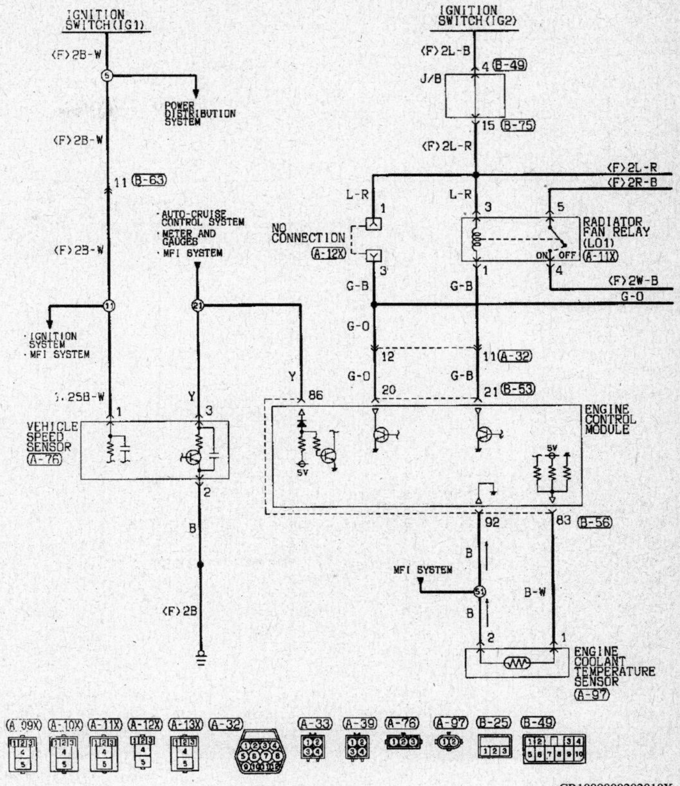

CR1089800202010X

Fig. 29 Engine cooling fan wiring diagram (Part 1 of 2). 1998 Talon w/turbo & manual transaxle

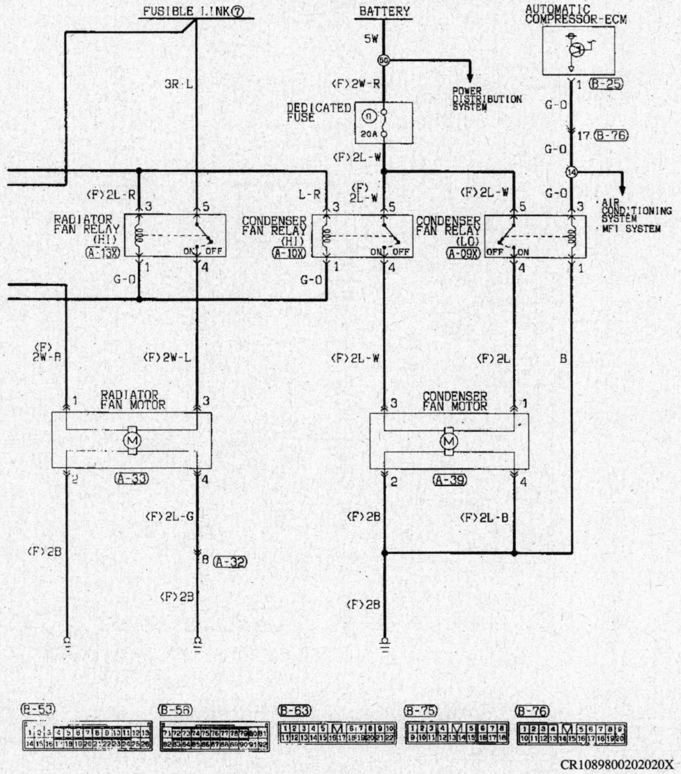

CR1089800202020X

Fig. 29 Engine cooling fan wiring diagram (Part 2 of 2). 1998 Talon w/turbo & manual transaxle

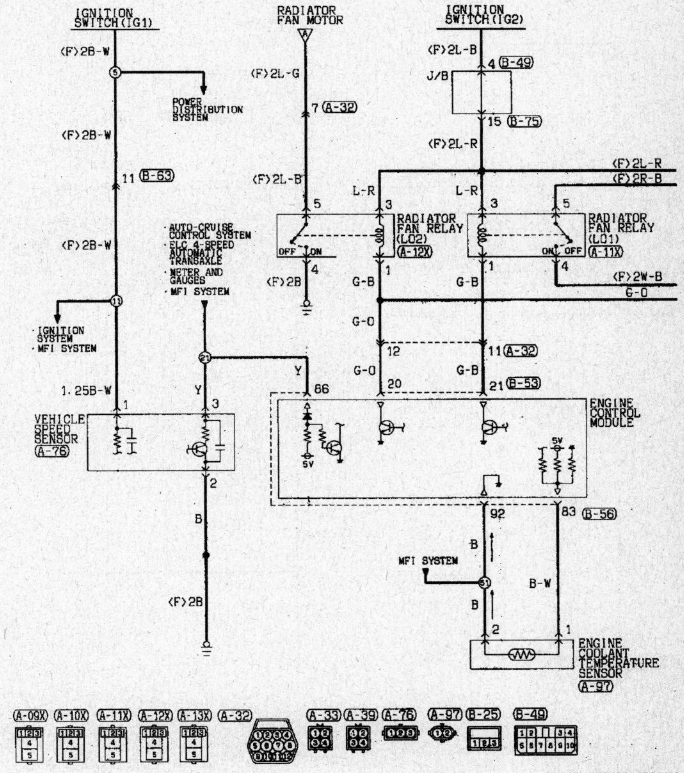

CR1089700199010X

Fig. 30 Engine cooling fan wiring diagram (Part 1 of 2). 1997 Talon w/turbo & automatic transaxle

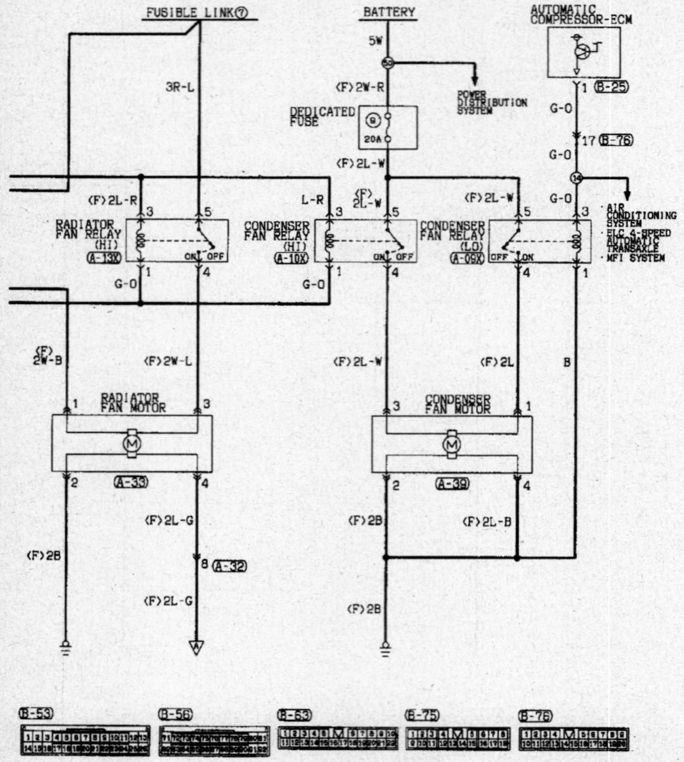

CR1089700199020X

Fig. 30 Engine cooling fan wiring diagram (Part 2 of 2). 1997 Talon w/turbo & automatic transaxle

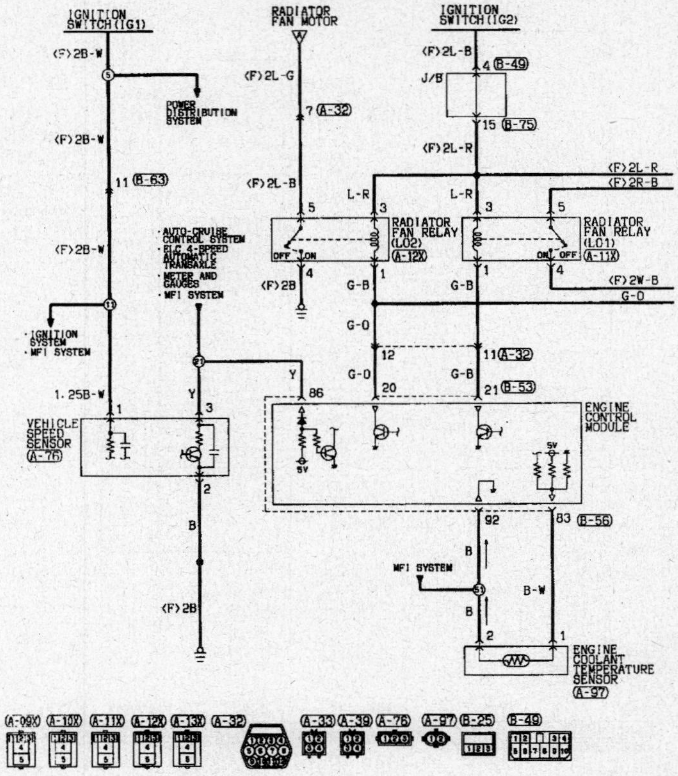

CR1089800203010X

Fig. 31 Engine cooling fan wiring diagram (Part 1 of 2). 1998 Talon w/turbo & automatic transaxle

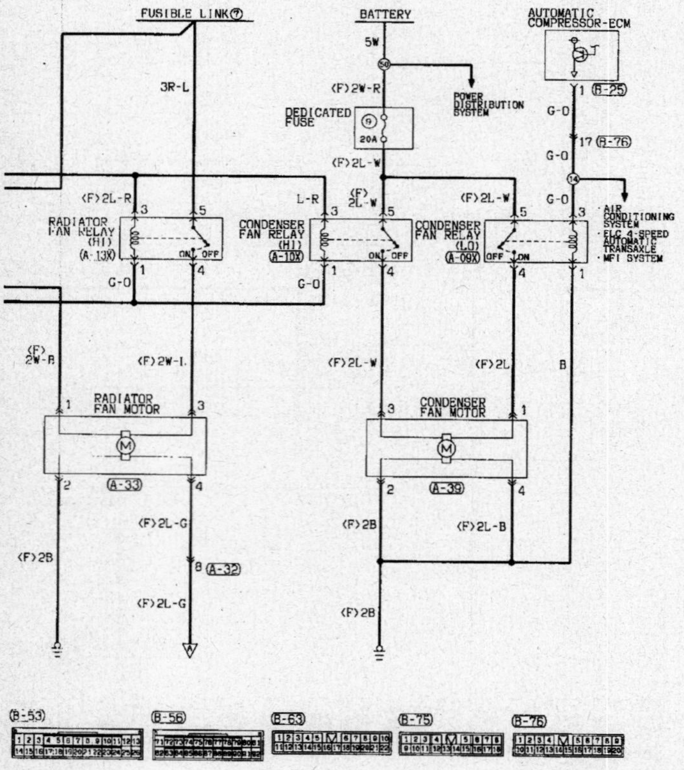

CR1089800203020X

Fig. 31 Engine cooling fan wiring diagram (Part 2 of 2). 1998 Talon w/turbo & automatic transaxle

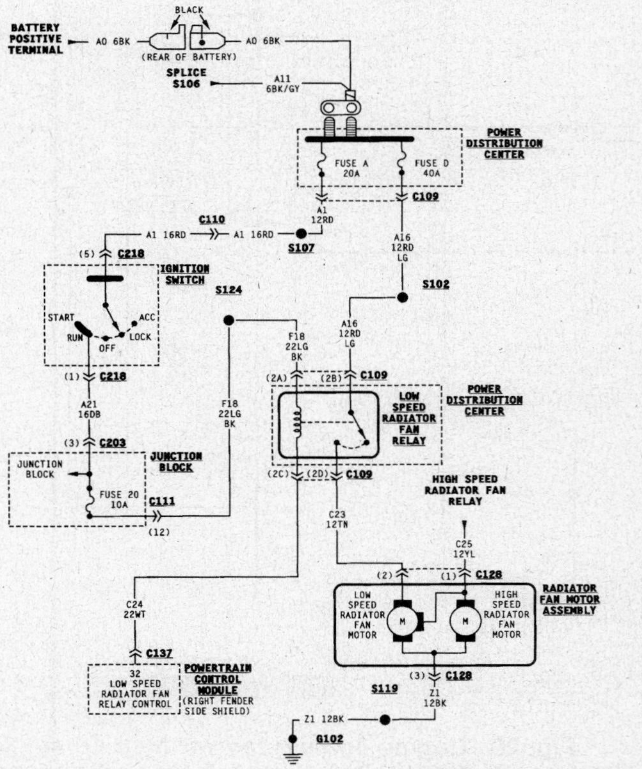

CR1089500162010X

Fig. 32 Engine cooling fan wiring diagram (Part 1 of 2). 1997 Concorde, Intrepid & Vision

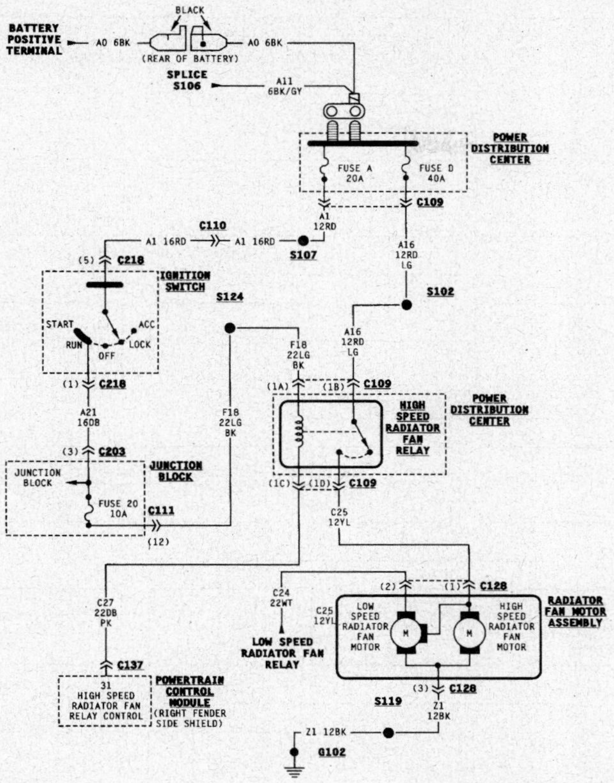

CR1089500162020X

Fig. 32 Engine cooling fan wiring diagram (Part 2 of 2). 1997 Concorde, Intrepid, LHS & Vision

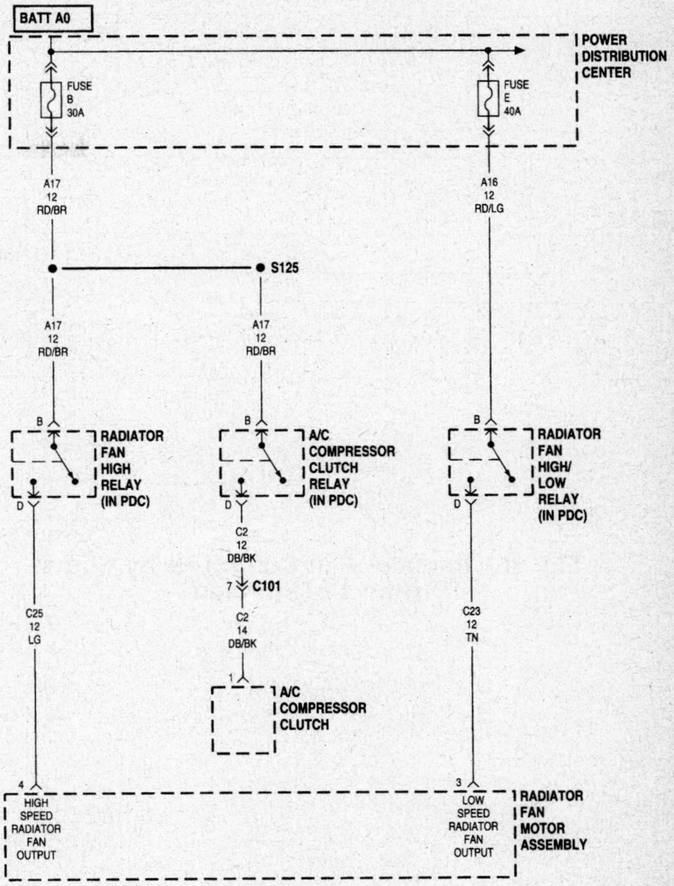

CR1089800215000X

Fig. 33 Engine cooling fan wiring diagram. 1998–99 Concorde, Intrepid, LHS & 300M

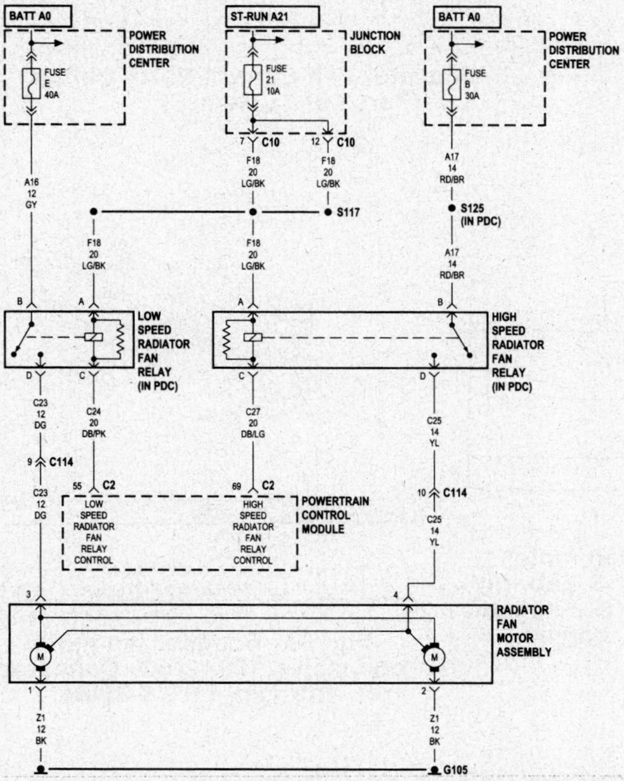

CR1080000272000X

Fig. 34 Engine cooling fan wiring diagram. 2000 Concorde, Intrepid, LHS & 300M

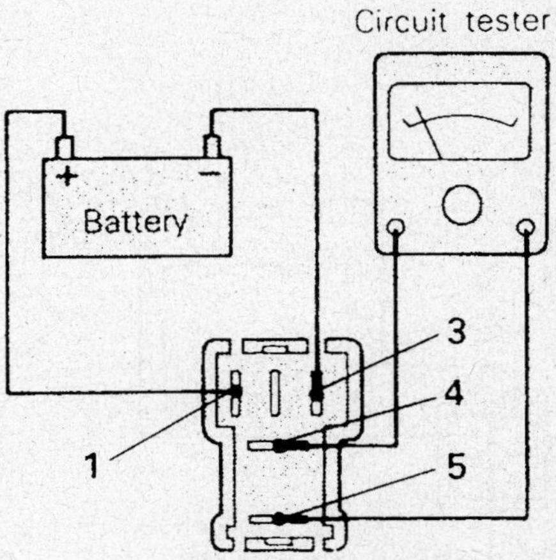

CR1089300080000X

Fig. 35 Radiator fan motor relay test. Avenger, Sebring Coupe & Talon

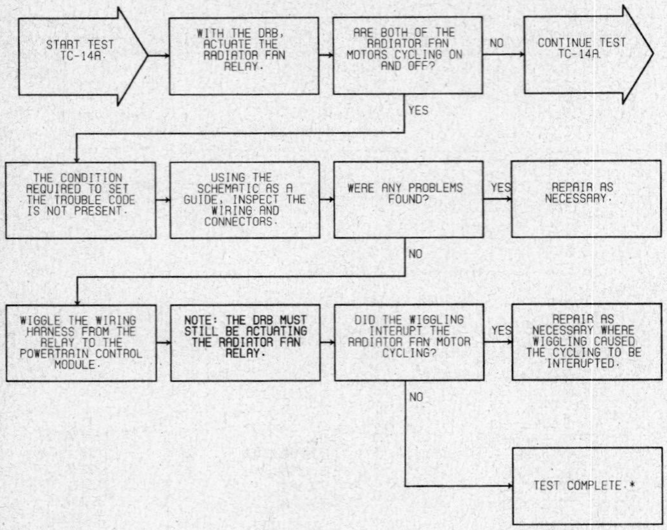

CR1029807611010X

Fig. 36 Radiator Fan Control Relay Circuit (Part 1 of 2). Neon

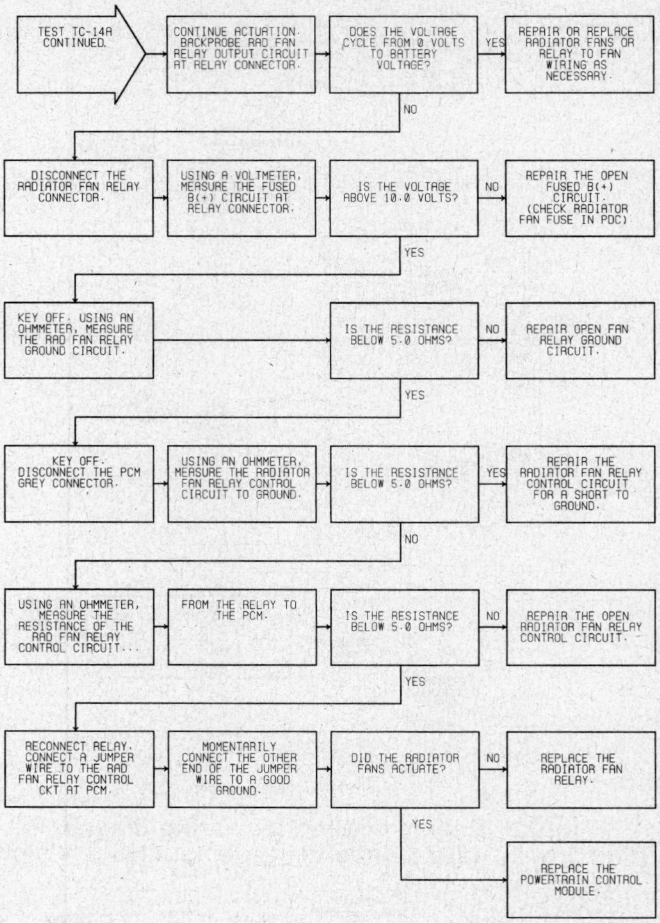

CR1029807611020X

Fig. 36 Radiator Fan Control Relay Circuit (Part 2 of 2). Neon

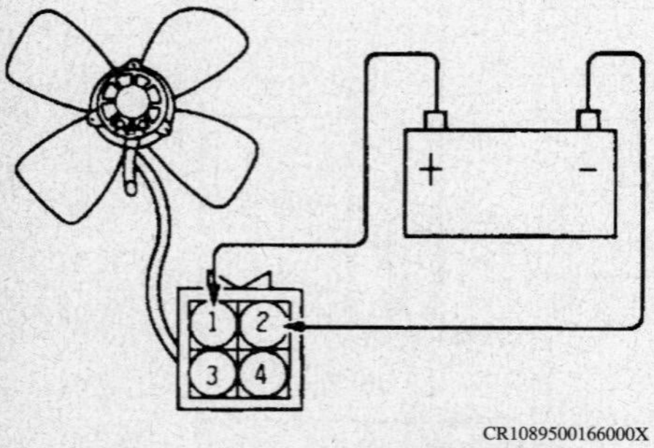

CR1089500166000X

Fig. 37 Cooling fan motor inspection. Avenger & Sebring Coupe w/2.0L engine & manual transaxle

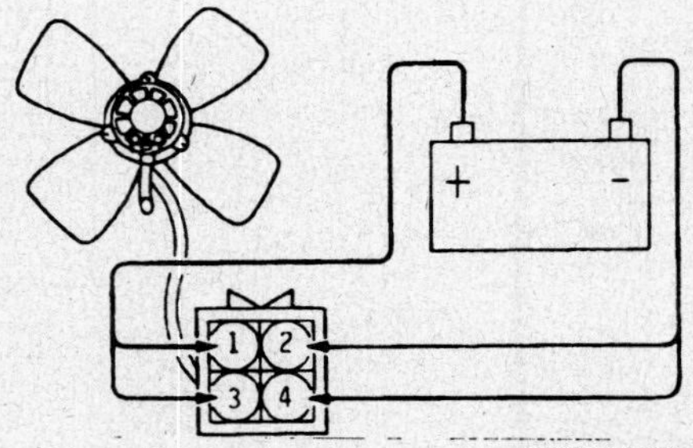

CR1089500167000X

Fig. 38 Cooling fan motor inspection. Avenger & Sebring Coupe w/2.0L engine & automatic transaxle & 2.5L engine

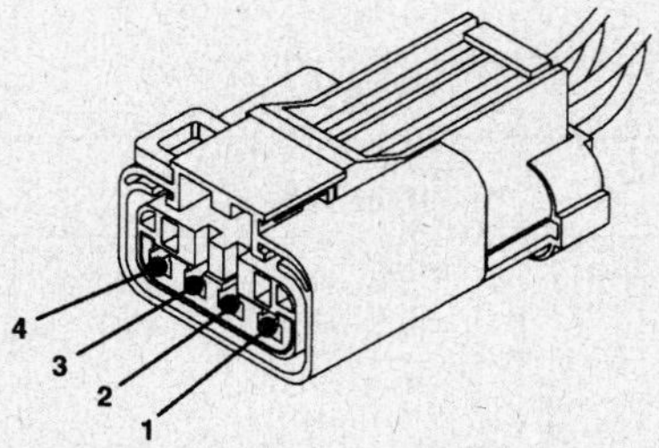

CAV	COLOR	FUNCTION
1	BK	GROUND
2	BK	GROUND
3	TN	LO SPEED RAD FAN RELAY OUTPUT
4	LG	HI SPEED RAD FAN RELAY OUTPUT

CR1089800249000X

Fig. 39 Radiator fan motor connector. 1998–2000 Concorde, Intrepid, LHS & 300M

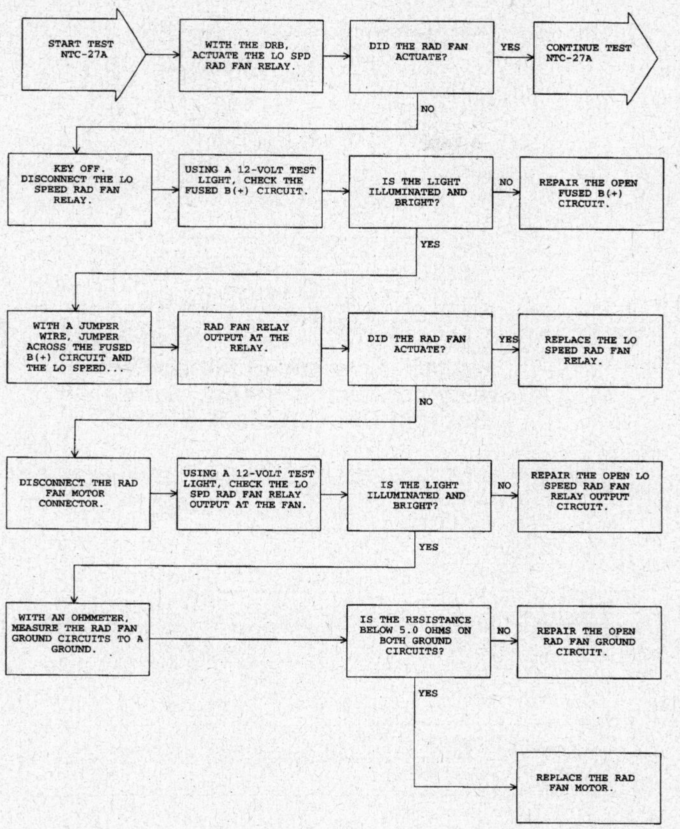

START TEST NTC-27A
WITH THE DRB, ACTUATE THE LO SPD RAD FAN RELAY.
DID THE RAD FAN ACTUATE?
YES
CONTINUE TEST NTC-27A
NO
KEY OFF. DISCONNECT THE LO SPEED RAD FAN RELAY.
USING A 12-VOLT TEST LIGHT, CHECK THE FUSED B(+) CIRCUIT.
IS THE LIGHT ILLUMINATED AND BRIGHT?
NO
REPAIR THE OPEN FUSED B(+) CIRCUIT.
YES
WITH A JUMPER WIRE, JUMPER ACROSS THE FUSED B(+) CIRCUIT AND THE LO SPEED...
RAD FAN RELAY OUTPUT AT THE RELAY.
DID THE RAD FAN ACTUATE?
YES
REPLACE THE LO SPEED RAD FAN RELAY.
NO
DISCONNECT THE RAD FAN MOTOR CONNECTOR.
USING A 12-VOLT TEST LIGHT, CHECK THE LO SPD RAD FAN RELAY OUTPUT AT THE FAN.
IS THE LIGHT ILLUMINATED AND BRIGHT?
NO
REPAIR THE OPEN LO SPEED RAD FAN RELAY OUTPUT CIRCUIT.
YES
WITH AN OHMMETER, MEASURE THE RAD FAN GROUND CIRCUITS TO A GROUND.
IS THE RESISTANCE BELOW 5.0 OHMS ON BOTH GROUND CIRCUITS?
NO
REPAIR THE OPEN RAD FAN GROUND CIRCUIT.
YES
REPLACE THE RAD FAN MOTOR.

CR1089800251010X

Fig. 40 Radiator fan motor test (Part 1 of 2). 1998–2000 Concorde, Intrepid, LHS & 300M

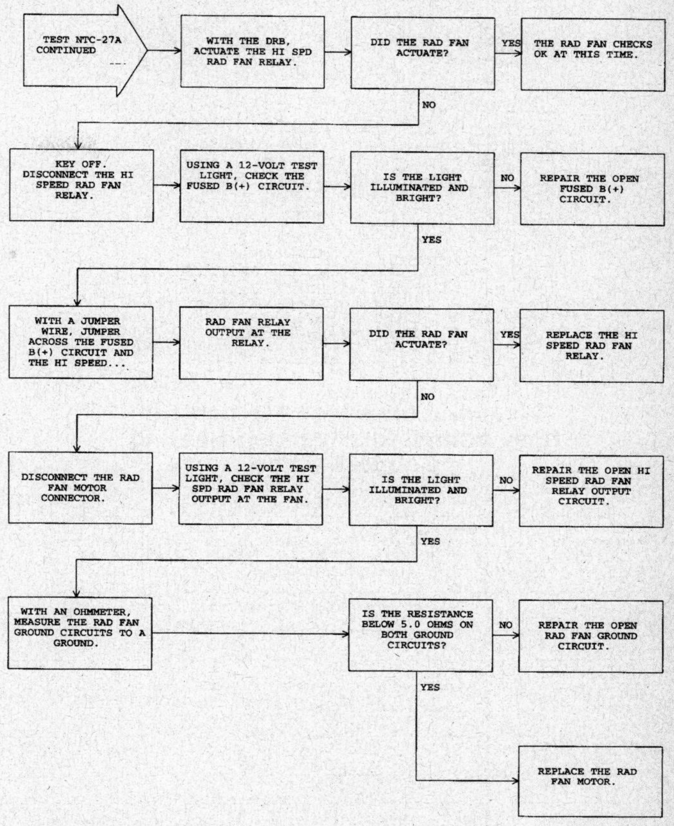

TEST NTC-27A CONTINUED
WITH THE DRB, ACTUATE THE HI SPD RAD FAN RELAY.
DID THE RAD FAN ACTUATE?
YES
THE RAD FAN CHECKS OK AT THIS TIME.
NO
KEY OFF. DISCONNECT THE HI SPEED RAD FAN RELAY.
USING A 12-VOLT TEST LIGHT, CHECK THE FUSED B(+) CIRCUIT.
IS THE LIGHT ILLUMINATED AND BRIGHT?
NO
REPAIR THE OPEN FUSED B(+) CIRCUIT.
YES
WITH A JUMPER WIRE, JUMPER ACROSS THE FUSED B(+) CIRCUIT AND THE HI SPEED...
RAD FAN RELAY OUTPUT AT THE RELAY.
DID THE RAD FAN ACTUATE?
YES
REPLACE THE HI SPEED RAD FAN RELAY.
NO
DISCONNECT THE RAD FAN MOTOR CONNECTOR.
USING A 12-VOLT TEST LIGHT, CHECK THE HI SPD RAD FAN RELAY OUTPUT AT THE FAN.
IS THE LIGHT ILLUMINATED AND BRIGHT?
NO
REPAIR THE OPEN HI SPEED RAD FAN RELAY OUTPUT CIRCUIT.
YES
WITH AN OHMMETER, MEASURE THE RAD FAN GROUND CIRCUITS TO A GROUND.
IS THE RESISTANCE BELOW 5.0 OHMS ON BOTH GROUND CIRCUITS?
NO
REPAIR THE OPEN RAD FAN GROUND CIRCUIT.
YES
REPLACE THE RAD FAN MOTOR.

CR1089800251020X

Fig. 40 Radiator fan motor test (Part 2 of 2). 1998–2000 Concorde, Intrepid, LHS & 300M

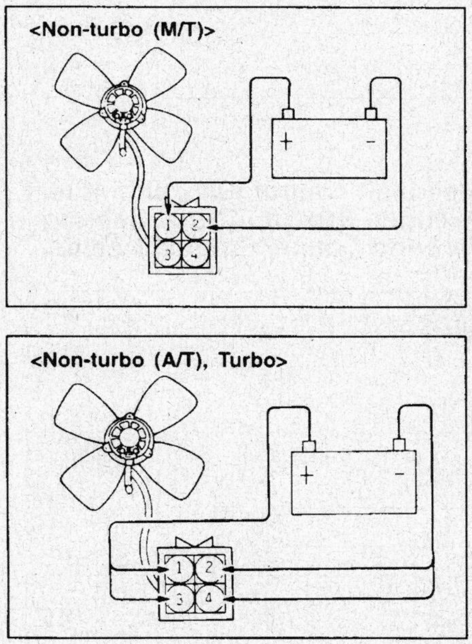

<Non-turbo (M/T)>
<Non-turbo (A/T), Turbo>

CR1089800207000X

Fig. 41 Fan motor terminal identification. Talon

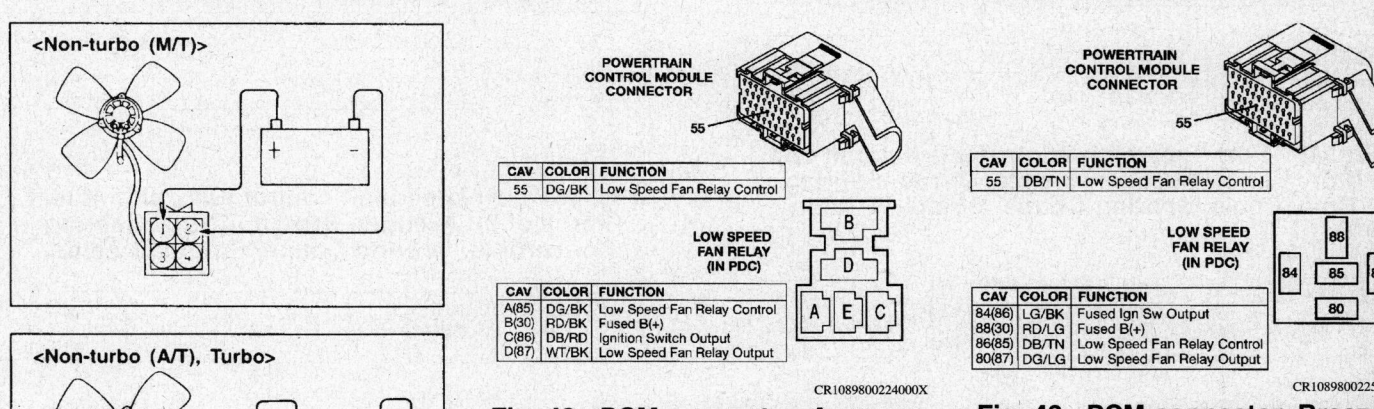

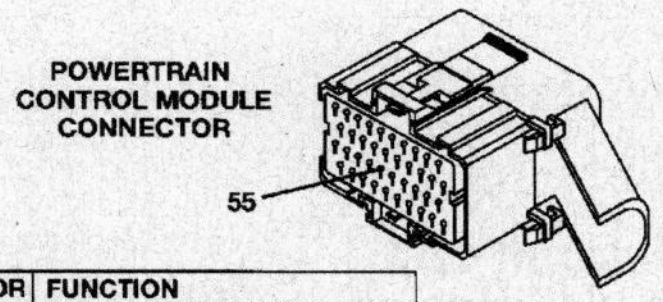

POWERTRAIN CONTROL MODULE CONNECTOR
55

CAV	COLOR	FUNCTION
55	DG/BK	Low Speed Fan Relay Control

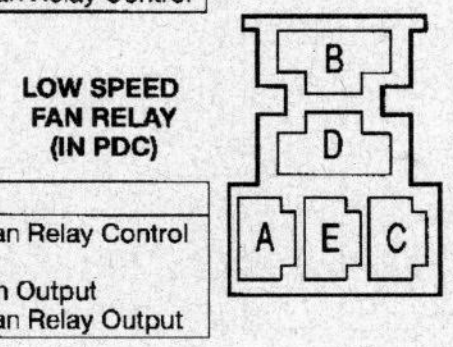

LOW SPEED FAN RELAY (IN PDC)
B
D
A
E
C

CAV	COLOR	FUNCTION
A(85)	DG/BK	Low Speed Fan Relay Control
B(30)	RD/BK	Fused B(+)
C(86)	DB/RD	Ignition Switch Output
D(87)	WT/BK	Low Speed Fan Relay Output

CR1089800224000X

Fig. 42 PCM connector. Avenger, Sebring Coupe & Talon

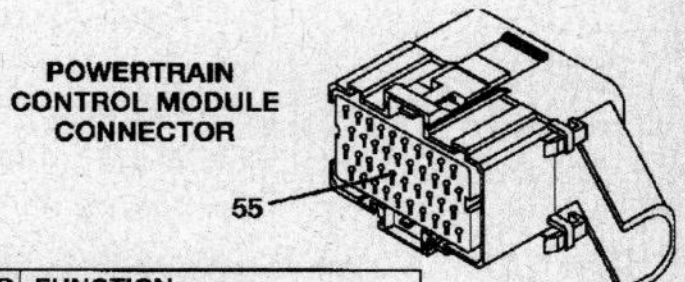

POWERTRAIN CONTROL MODULE CONNECTOR
55

CAV	COLOR	FUNCTION
55	DB/TN	Low Speed Fan Relay Control

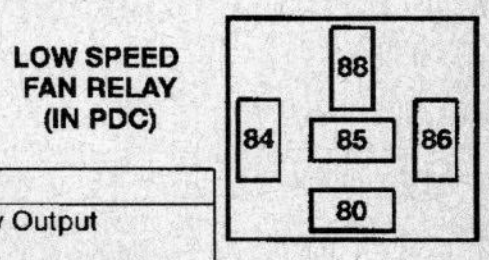

LOW SPEED FAN RELAY (IN PDC)
88
84
85
86
80

CAV	COLOR	FUNCTION
84(86)	LG/BK	Fused Ign Sw Output
88(30)	RD/LG	Fused B(+)
86(85)	DB/TN	Low Speed Fan Relay Control
80(87)	DG/LG	Low Speed Fan Relay Output

CR1089800225000X

Fig. 43 PCM connector. Breeze, Cirrus, Sebring Convertible & Stratus

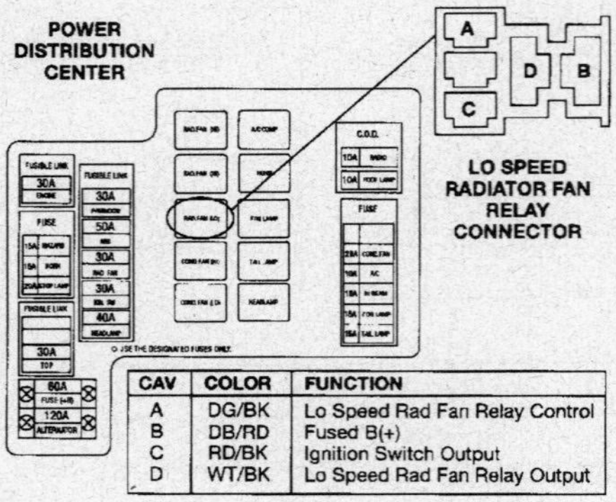

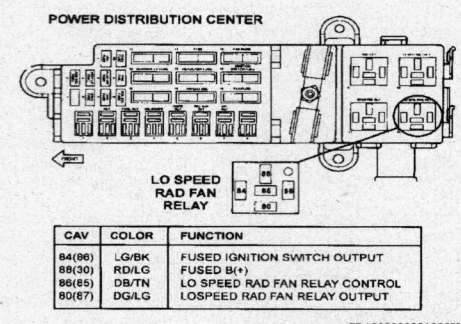

CAV	COLOR	FUNCTION
A	DG/BK	Lo Speed Rad Fan Relay Control
B	DB/RD	Fused B(+)
C	RD/BK	Ignition Switch Output
D	WT/BK	Lo Speed Rad Fan Relay Output

CR1089800220000X

Fig. 44 Low speed fan control relay connector. Avenger, Sebring Coupe & Talon

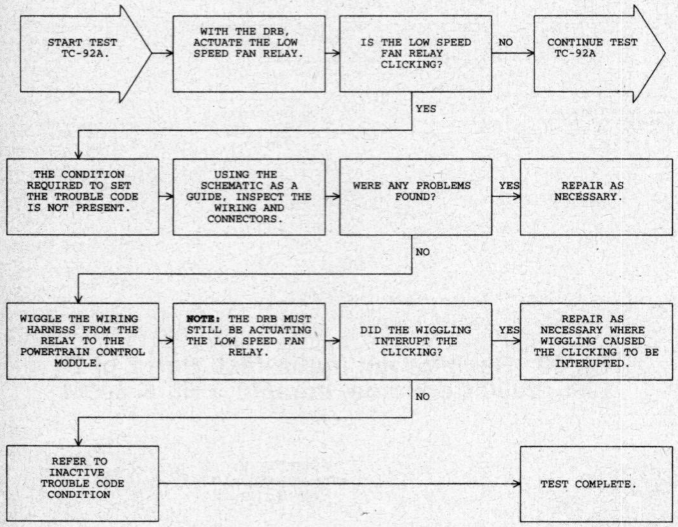

CR1089800219010X

Fig. 46 Low speed fan control relay circuit test (Part 1 of 3). Avenger, Breeze, Cirrus, Sebring Convertible, Sebring Coupe, Stratus & Talon

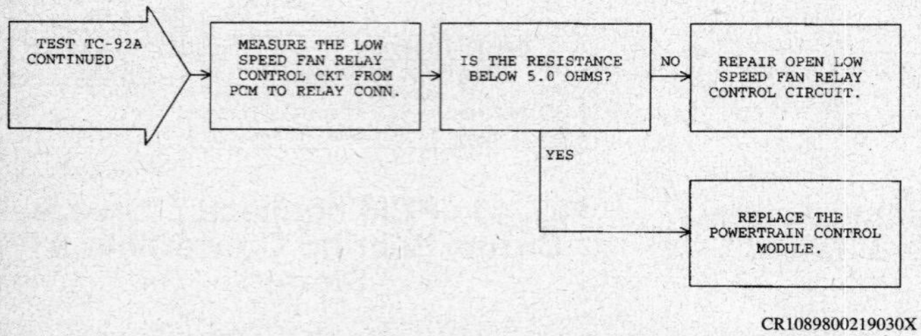

CR1089800219030X

Fig. 46 Low speed fan control relay circuit test (Part 3 of 3). Avenger, Breeze, Cirrus, Sebring Convertible, Sebring Coupe, Stratus & Talon

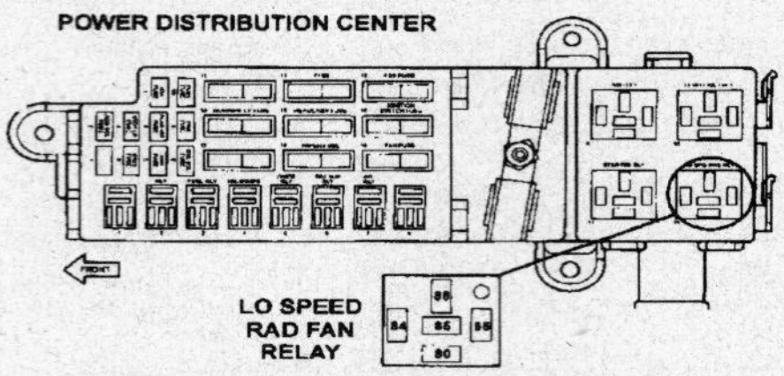

CAV	COLOR	FUNCTION
84(86)	LG/BK	FUSED IGNITION SWITCH OUTPUT
88(30)	RD/LG	FUSED B(+)
86(85)	DB/TN	LO SPEED RAD FAN RELAY CONTROL
80(87)	DG/LG	LOSPEED RAD FAN RELAY OUTPUT

CR1089800221000X

Fig. 45 Low speed fan control relay connector. Breeze, Cirrus, Sebring Convertible & Stratus

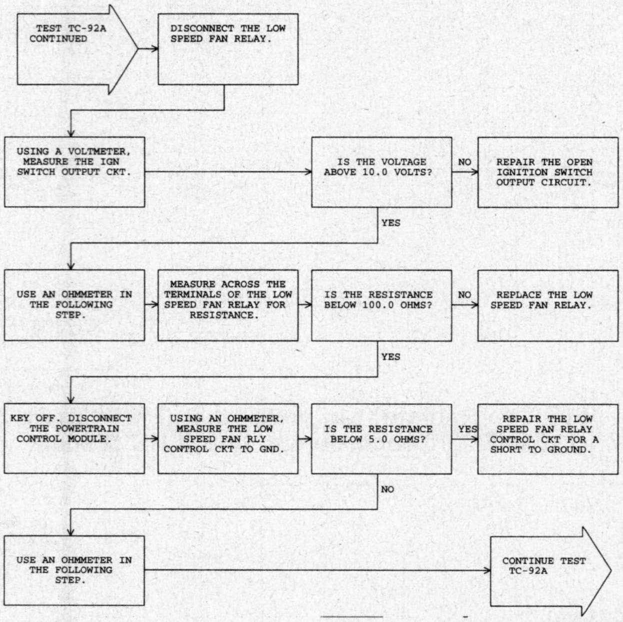

CR1089800219020X

Fig. 46 Low speed fan control relay circuit test (Part 2 of 3). Avenger, Breeze, Cirrus, Sebring Convertible, Sebring Coupe, Stratus & Talon

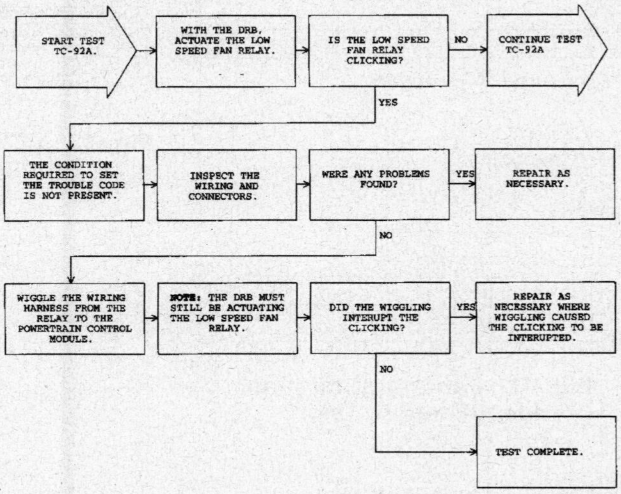

CR1029807674010X

Fig. 47 Low Speed Coolant Fan Relay Circuit (Part 1 of 3). 1997 Concorde, Intrepid, LHS & Vision

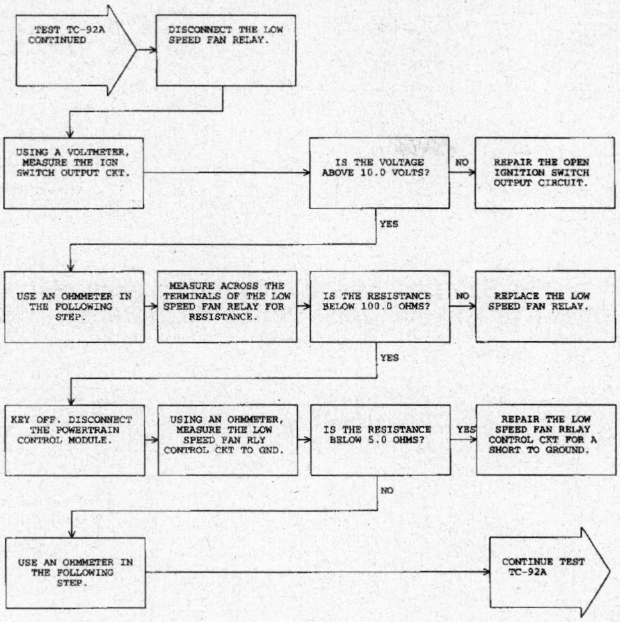

CR1029807674020X

Fig. 47 Low Speed Coolant Fan Relay Circuit (Part 2 of 3). 1997 Concorde, Intrepid, LHS & Vision

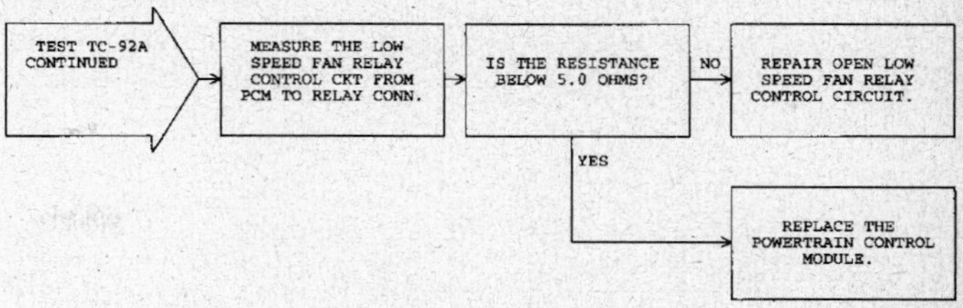

CR1029807674030X

Fig. 47 Low Speed Coolant Fan Relay Circuit (Part 3 of 3). 1997 Concorde, Intrepid, LHS & Vision

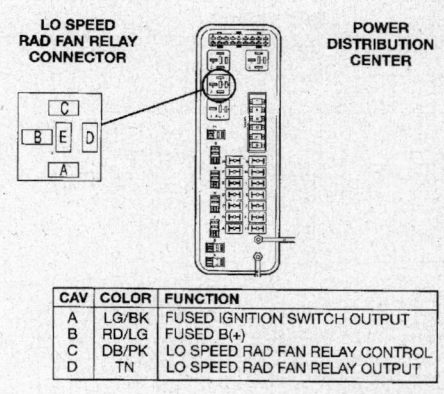

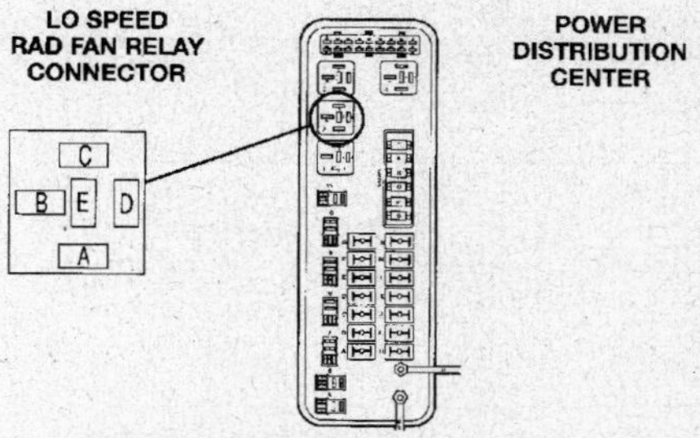

CAV	COLOR	FUNCTION
A	LG/BK	FUSED IGNITION SWITCH OUTPUT
B	RD/LG	FUSED B(+)
C	DB/PK	LO SPEED RAD FAN RELAY CONTROL
D	TN	LO SPEED RAD FAN RELAY OUTPUT

CR1089800241000X

Fig. 48 Low speed fan relay connector. 1998–2000 Concorde, Intrepid, LHS & 300M

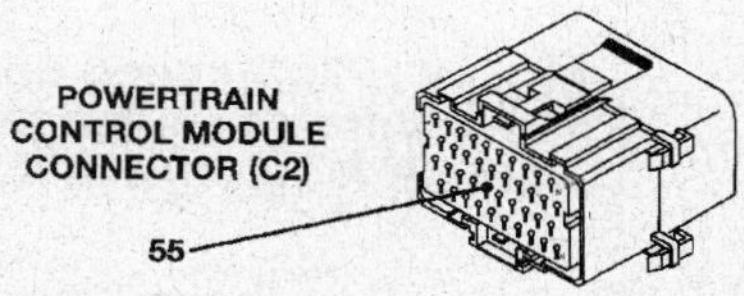

CAV	COLOR	FUNCTION
55	DB/PK	LOW SPEED FAN RELAY CONTROL

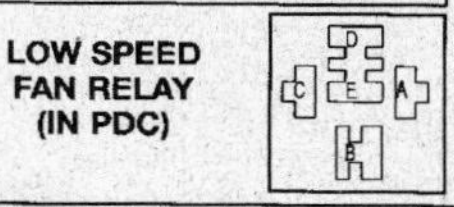

CAV	COLOR	FUNCTION
A	LG/BK	FUSED IGNITION SW OUTPUT
B	RD/LG	FUSED B(+)
C	DB/PK	LOW SPEED FAN RELAY CONTROL
D	TN	LOW SPEED FAN RELAY OUTPUT

CR1089800243000X

Fig. 49 PCM connector. 1998–2000 Concorde, Intrepid, LHS & 300M

INACTIVE TROUBLE CODE CONDITION

You have just attempted to simulate the condition that initially set the trouble code message. The following additional checks may assist you in identifying a possible intermittent problem:

— Visually inspect related wire harness connectors. Look for broken, bent, pushed out, or corroded terminals.

— Visually inspect the related harnesses. Look for chafed, pierced, or partially broken wire.

— Refer to any hotlines or technical service bulletins that may apply.

CR1089800239000X

Fig. 50 Inactive trouble code condition. 1998–2000 Concorde, Intrepid, LHS & 300M

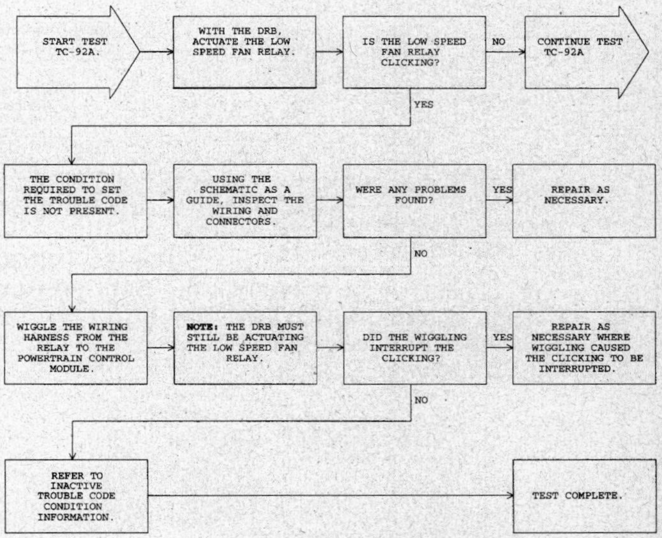

CR1089800240010X

Fig. 51 Low speed fan control relay test (Part 1 of 3). 1998–2000 Concorde, Intrepid, LHS & 300M

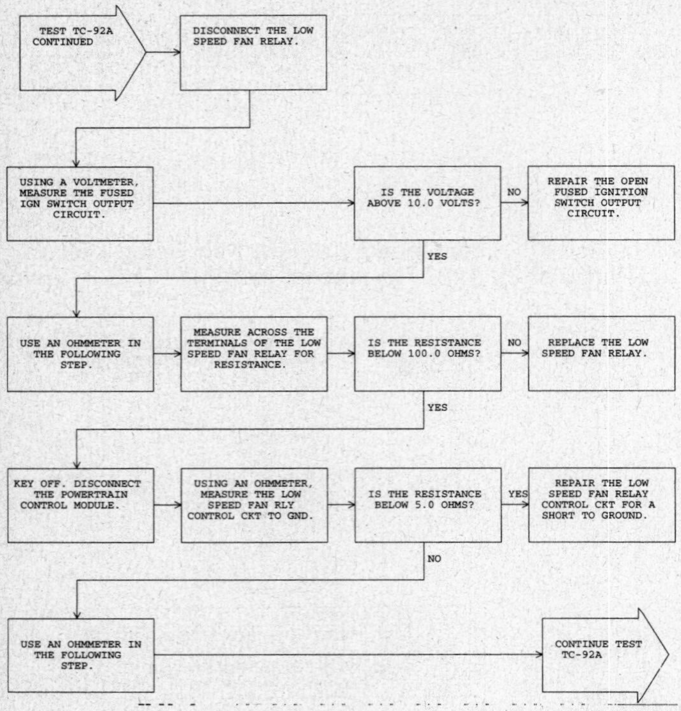

CR1089800240020X

Fig. 51 Low speed fan control relay test (Part 2 of 3). 1998–2000 Concorde, Intrepid, LHS & 300M

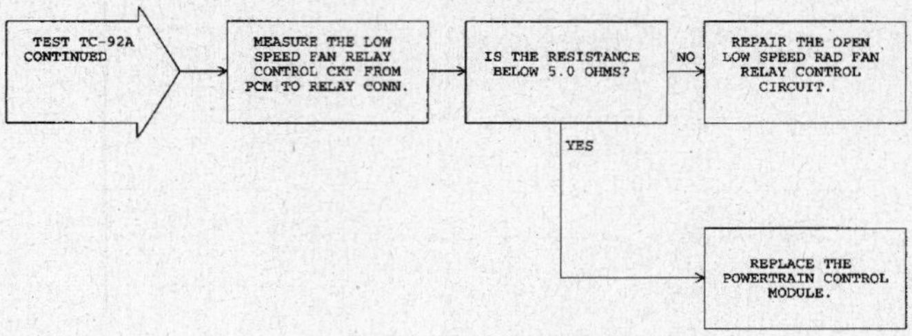

CR1089800240030X

Fig. 51 Low speed fan control relay test (Part 3 of 3). 1998–2000 Concorde, Intrepid, LHS & 300M

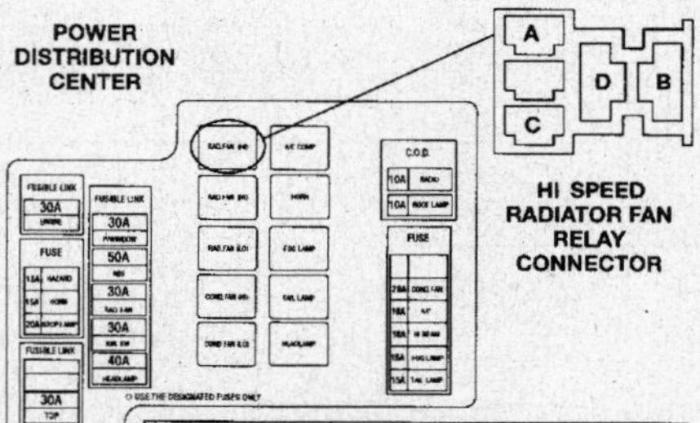

CAV	COLOR	FUNCTION
A	DG/OR	Hi Spd Rad Fan Relay Control
B	RD/DB	Fused B(+)
C	DB/RD	Ignition Switch Output
D	WT/DB	Hi Spd Rad Fan Relay Output

CR1089800230000X

Fig. 52 High speed coolant fan relay connector. Avenger, Sebring Coupe & Talon w/2.0L engine

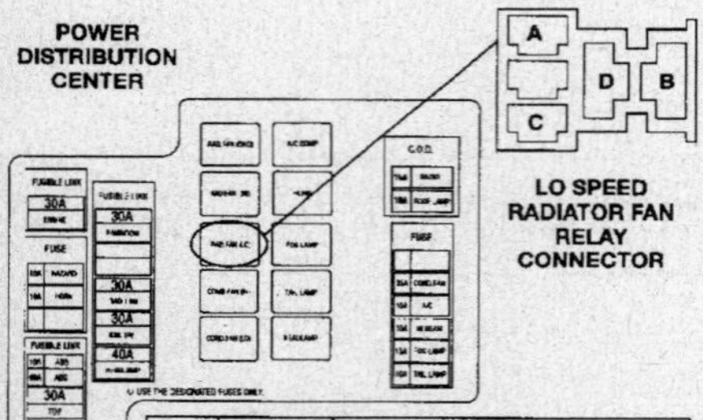

CAV	COLOR	FUNCTION
A	DG/BK	Lo Speed Rad Fan Relay Control
B	DB/YL	Ignition Switch Output
C	DB/RD	Fused B(+)
D	DB/BK	Lo Speed Rad Fan Relay Output

CR1089800231000X

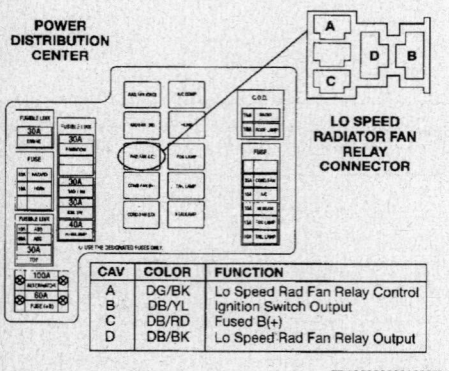

Fig. 53 High speed coolant fan relay connector. Avenger & Sebring Coupe w/2.5L engine

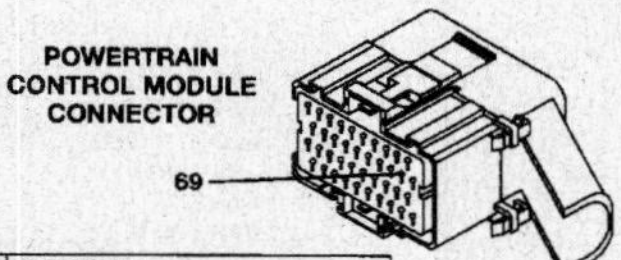

CAV	COLOR	FUNCTION
69	DG/OR	High Speed Fan Relay Control

HIGH SPEED FAN RELAY (IN PDC)

CAV	COLOR	FUNCTION
A (85)	DG/OR	High Speed Fan Relay Ctrl
B (30)	RD/DB	Fused B(+)
C (86)	DB/RD	Ignition Switch Output
D (87)	WT/DB	High Speed Fan Relay Output

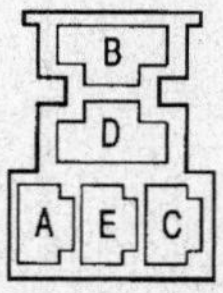

CR1089800234000X

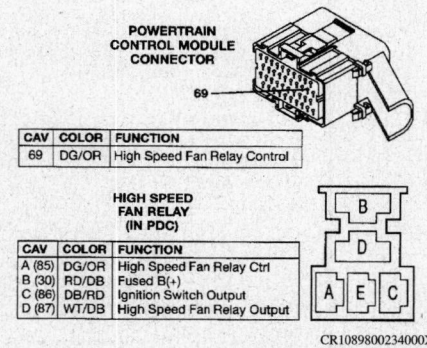

Fig. 54 PCM connector. Avenger, Sebring Coupe & Talon w/2.0L engine

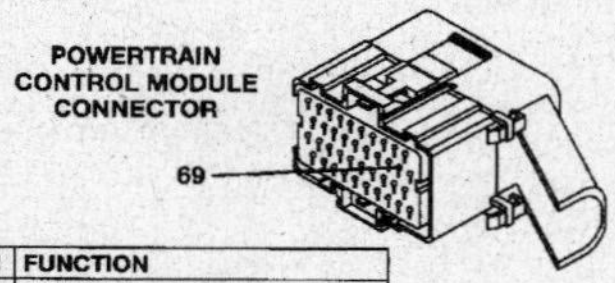

CAV	COLOR	FUNCTION
69	DG/OR	High Speed Fan Relay Control

HIGH SPEED FAN RELAY (IN PDC)

CAV	COLOR	FUNCTION
A (85)	DG/OR	High Speed Fan Relay Ctrl
B (30)	RD/DB	Fused B(+)
C (86)	DB/RD	Ignition Switch Output
D (87)	WT/DB	High Speed Fan Relay Output

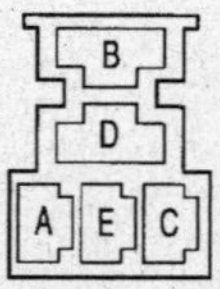

CR1089800235000X

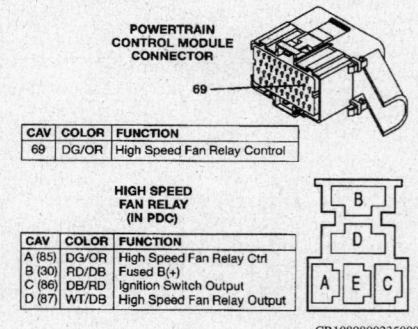

Fig. 55 PCM connector. Avenger & Sebring Coupe w/2.5L engine

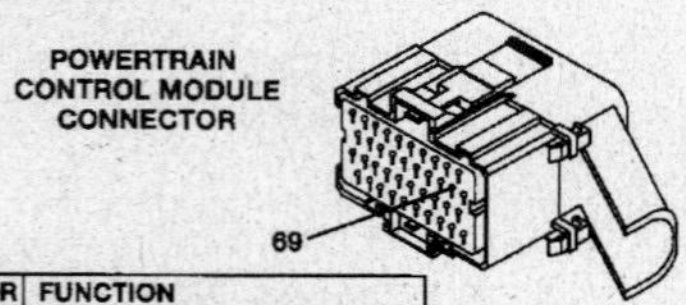

CAV	COLOR	FUNCTION
69	DB/PK	High Speed Fan Relay Control

HIGH SPEED FAN RELAY (IN PDC)

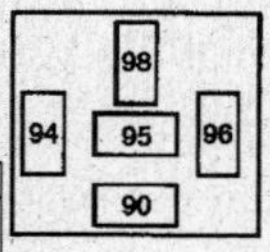

CAV	COLOR	FUNCTION
94(86)	LG/BK	Fused Ignition Switch Output
98(30)	RD/LG	Fused B(+)
96(85)	DB/PK	High Speed Fan Relay Control
90(87)	YL/VT	High Speed Fan Relay Output

CR1089800236000X

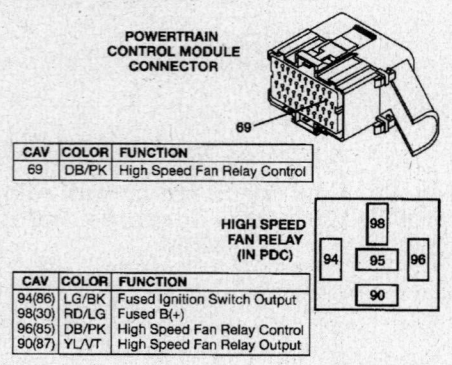

Fig. 56 PCM connector. Breeze, Cirrus & Stratus

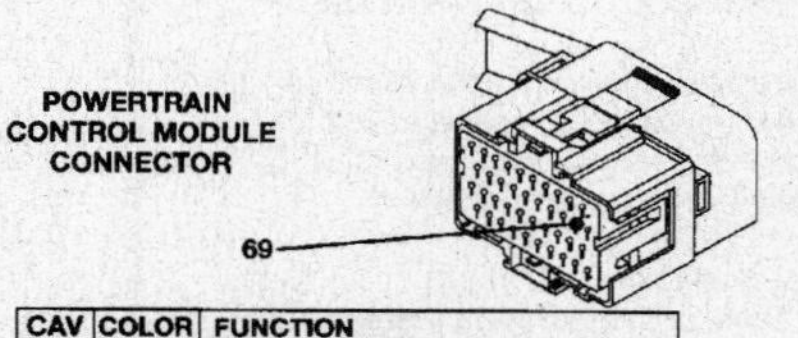

CAV	COLOR	FUNCTION
69	DB/PK	HIGH SPEED FAN RELAY CONTROL

HIGH SPEED FAN RELAY (IN PDC)

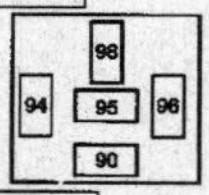

CAV	COLOR	FUNCTION
94(86)	LG/BK	FUSED IGNITION SWITCH OUTPUT
98(30)	RD/LG	FUSED B(+)
96(85)	DB/PK	HIGH SPEED FAN RELAY CONTROL
90(87)	YL/RD	HIGH SPEED FAN RELAY OUTPUT

CR1089800237000X

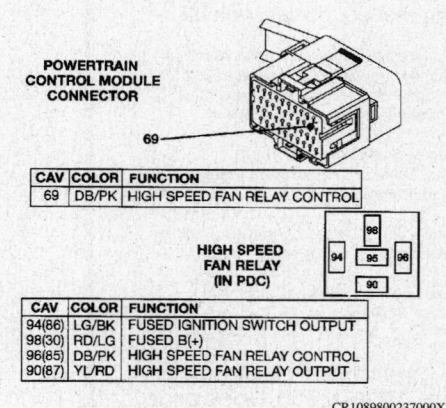

Fig. 57 PCM connector. Sebring Convertible

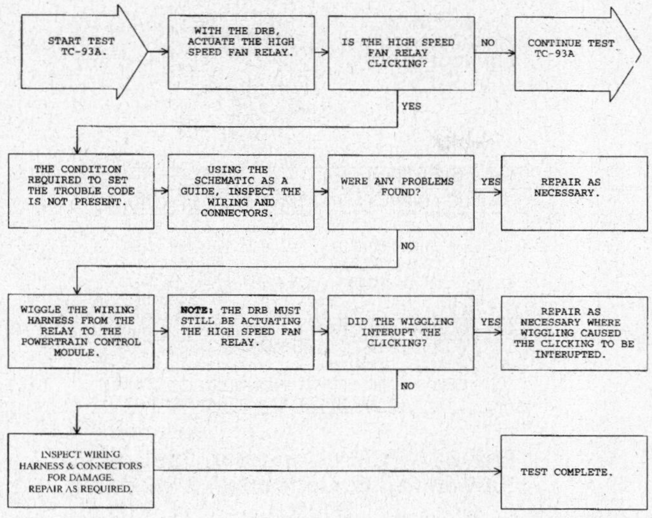

CR1089800229010X

Fig. 58 High speed fan control relay circuit test (Part 1 of 3). Avenger, Breeze, Cirrus, Sebring Convertible, Sebring Coupe, Stratus & Talon

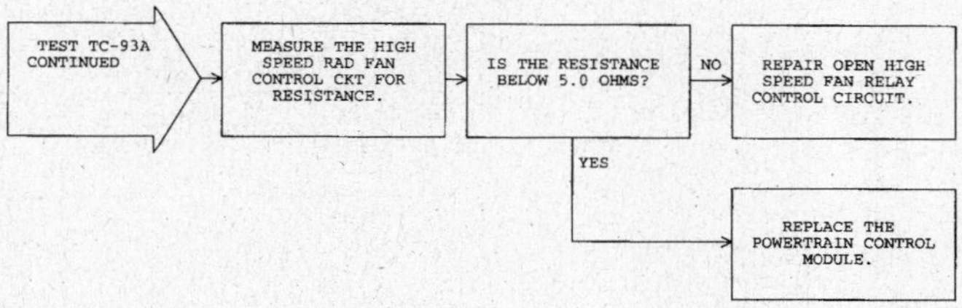

CR1089800229030X

Fig. 58 High speed fan control relay circuit test (Part 3 of 3). Avenger, Breeze, Cirrus, Sebring Convertible, Sebring Coupe, Stratus & Talon

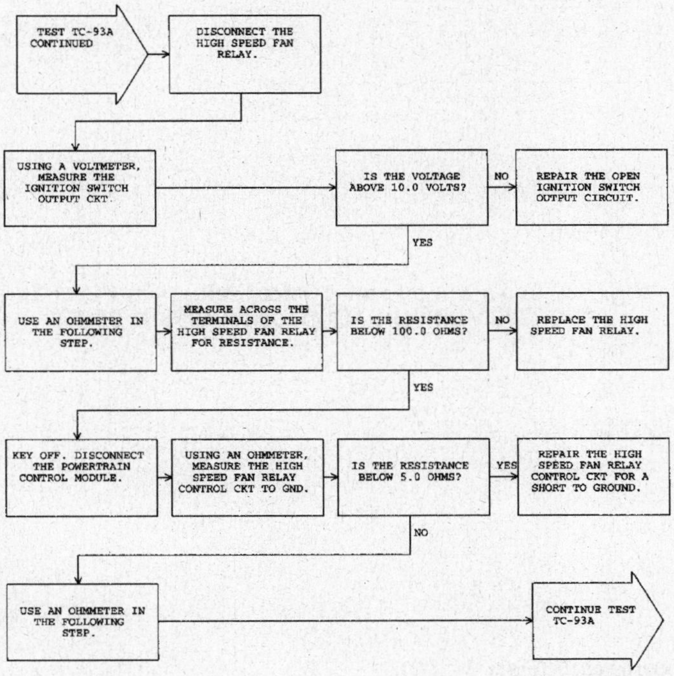

CR1029807675020X

Fig. 59 High Speed Coolant Fan Relay Circuit (Part 2 of 3). 1997 Concorde, Intrepid, LHS & Vision

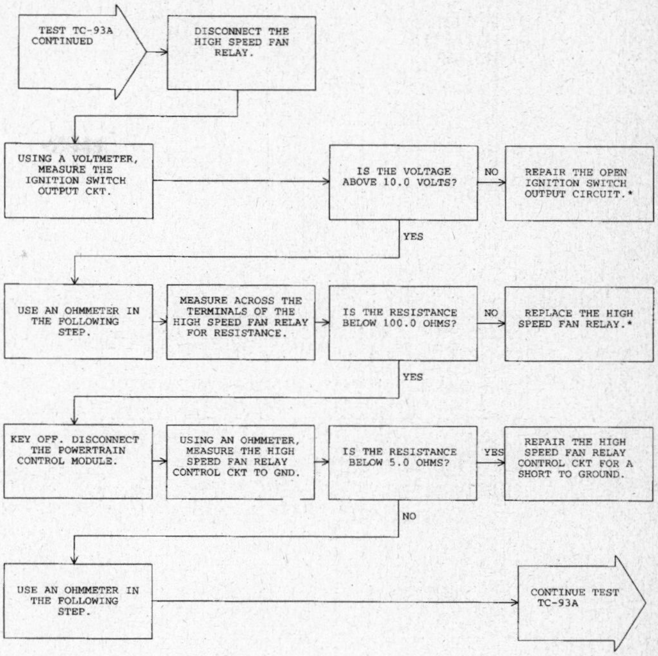

CR1089800229020X

Fig. 58 High speed fan control relay circuit test (Part 2 of 3). Avenger, Breeze, Cirrus, Sebring Convertible, Sebring Coupe, Stratus & Talon

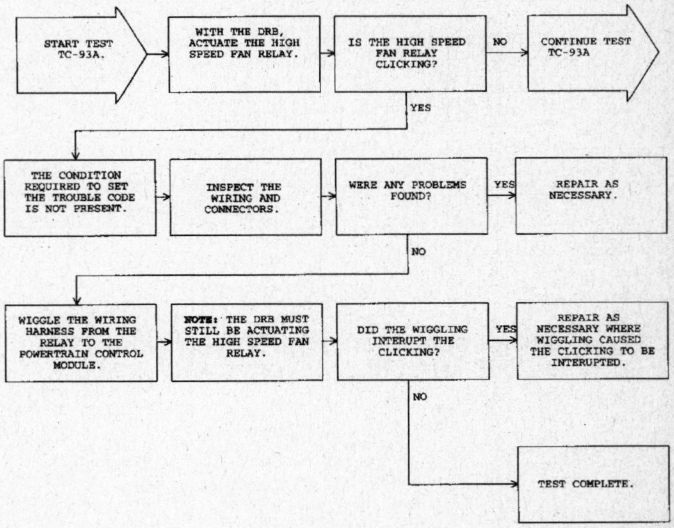

CR1029807675010X

Fig. 59 High Speed Coolant Fan Relay Circuit (Part 1 of 3). 1997 Concorde, Intrepid, LHS & Vision

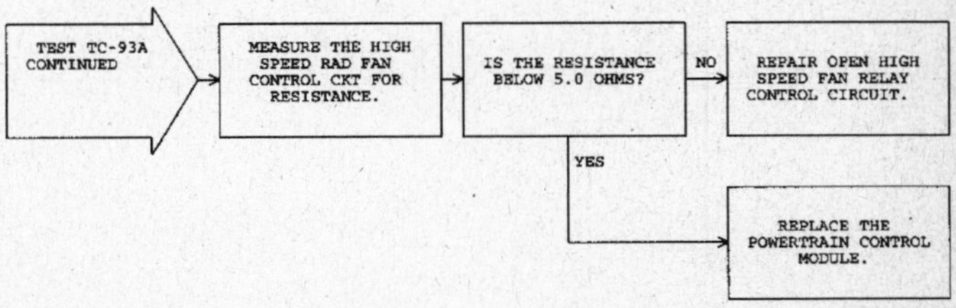

CR1029807675030X

Fig. 59 High Speed Coolant Fan Relay Circuit (Part 3 of 3). 1997 Concorde, Intrepid, LHS & Vision

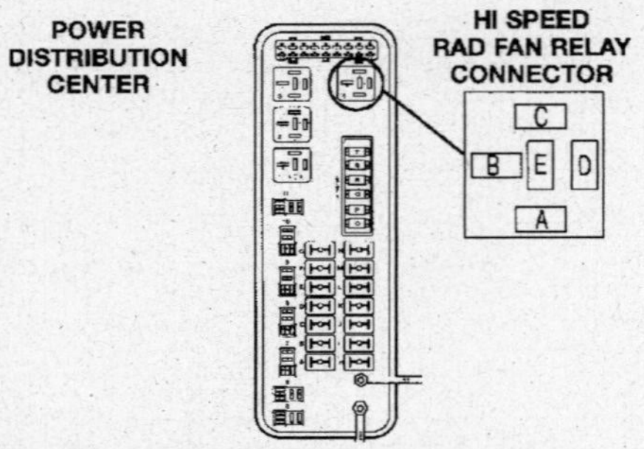

CAV	COLOR	FUNCTION
A	LG/BK	FUSED IGNITION SWITCH OUTPUT
B	RD/BR	FUSED B(+)
C	DB/LG	HI SPEED RAD FAN RELAY CONTROL
D	LG	HI SPEED RAD FAN RELAY OUTPUT

CR1089800246000X

Fig. 60 High speed relay connector. 1998–2000 Intrepid, Concorde, LHS & 300M

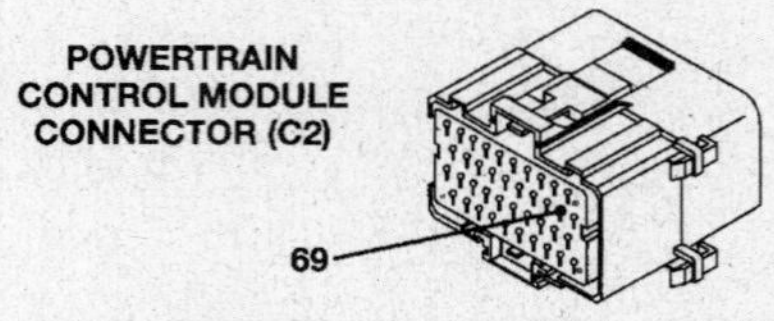

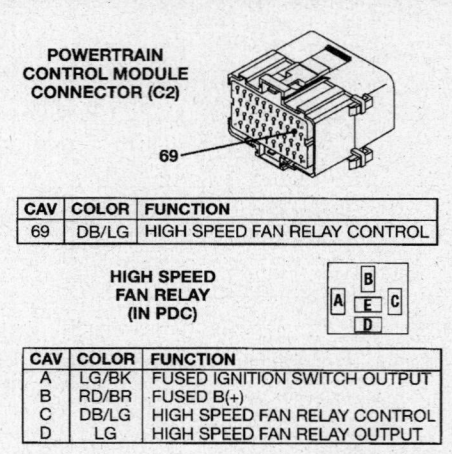

CAV	COLOR	FUNCTION
69	DB/LG	HIGH SPEED FAN RELAY CONTROL

CAV	COLOR	FUNCTION
A	LG/BK	FUSED IGNITION SWITCH OUTPUT
B	RD/BR	FUSED B(+)
C	DB/LG	HIGH SPEED FAN RELAY CONTROL
D	LG	HIGH SPEED FAN RELAY OUTPUT

CR1089800247000X

Fig. 61 PCM connector. 1998–2000 Intrepid, Concorde, LHS & 300M

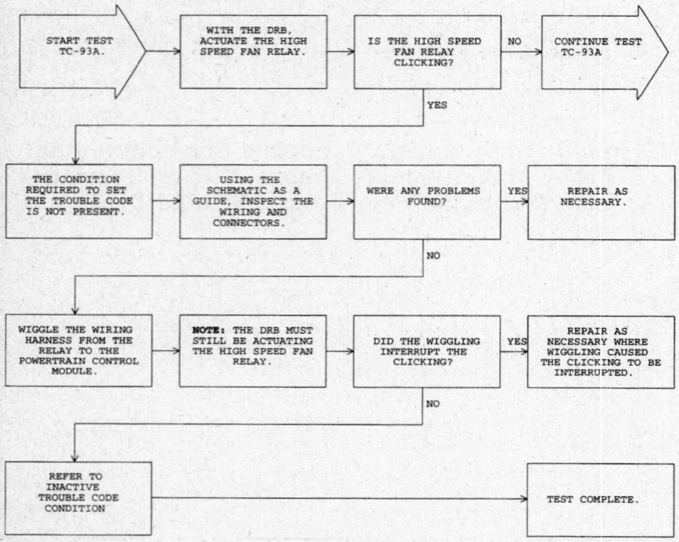

CR1089800245010X

Fig. 62 High speed fan control relay (Part 1 of 3). 1998–2000 Intrepid, Concorde, LHS & 300M

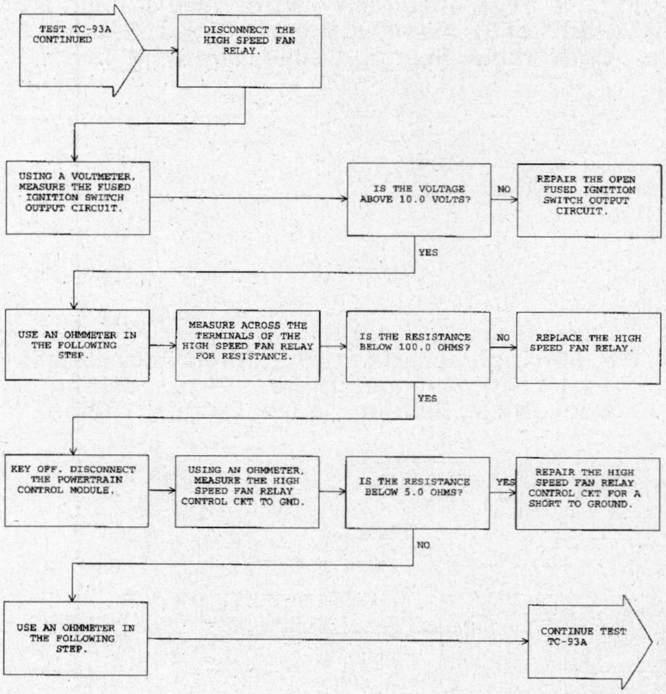

CR1089800245020X

Fig. 62 High speed fan control relay (Part 2 of 3). 1998–2000 Intrepid, Concorde, LHS & 300M

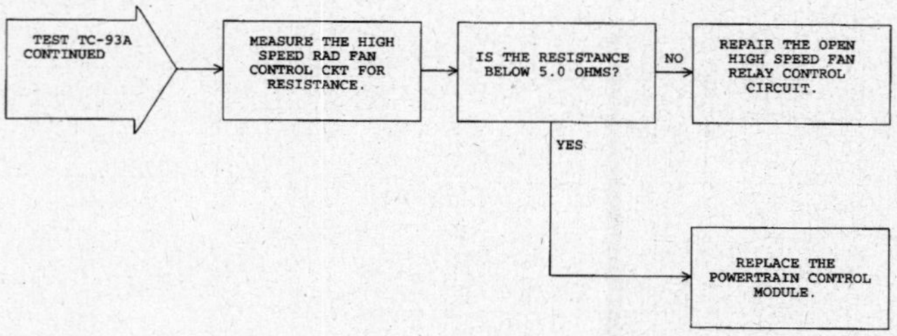

CR1089800245030X

Fig. 62 High speed fan control relay (Part 3 of 3). 1998–2000 Intrepid, Concorde, LHS & 300M

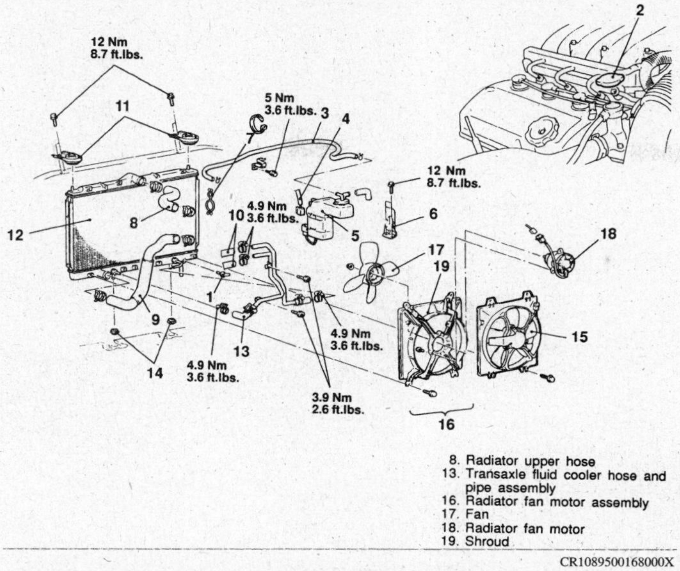

Fig. 63 Cooling fan & fan motor removal. Avenger & Sebring Coupe

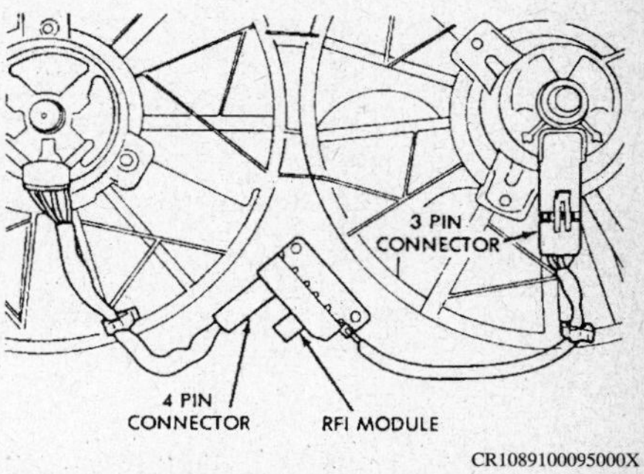

Fig. 64 RFI module location. 1997 Concorde, Intrepid, LHS & Vision

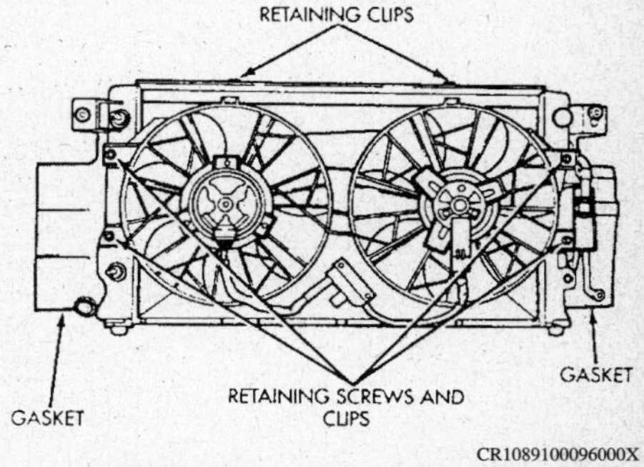

Fig. 65 Fan module removal. 1997 Concorde, Intrepid, LHS & Vision

COMPONENT REPLACEMENT

Fan Motor

AVENGER & SEBRING COUPE

1. Drain engine coolant into a suitable container.
2. Remove cooling fan motor, **Fig. 63.**
3. Reverse procedure to install.

BREEZE, CIRRUS & STRATUS

1. Remove fan shroud and retaining clip at end of fan motor shaft, then slide fan from shaft. **Do not bend or strike fan blades during removal.**
2. Disconnect fan motor electrical connectors, then remove fan motor fasteners from motor support.
3. Separate motor from support.
4. Reverse procedure to install, noting the following:
   a. **Torque** short fasteners to 25 inch lbs.
   b. **Torque** long fasteners to 45 inch lbs.
   c. **Torque** fan shroud fasteners to 5.5 ft. lbs.

CONCORDE, INTREPID, LHS, VISION & 300M

1. Disconnect electrical connector, **Fig. 64.**
2. Remove fan module to radiator clips and fasteners, **Figs. 65 and 66.**
3. Remove assembly from radiator, then remove fan blades as follows:
   a. Bench support motor and motor shaft.
   b. Remove fan retaining clip or nut. Surface or burr removal may be necessary before removing fans from shaft. **Do not let fan blades touch bench when removing.**
4. Remove motor fasteners from support, then motor from support.
5. Reverse procedure to install, noting the following:
   a. **Torque** right fan motor fasteners to 25 inch lbs. and left fan motor fasteners to 45 inch lbs.
   b. **Torque** shroud to radiator fasteners to 45 inch lbs.

NEON

1. Disconnect electrical connector from motor.
2. Drain cooling system below upper radiator hose level.
3. Remove upper radiator hose from radiator.
4. Remove radiator to battery strut.
5. **On models equipped with dual fan modules,** remove battery and battery tray.
6. **On all models,** remove fan module fasteners from radiator.
7. Lift fan shroud up and out of lower shroud attachment clips.
8. Reverse procedure to install.

SEBRING CONVERTIBLE

1. Remove upper radiator crossmember.
2. Disconnect fan motor electrical connector.
3. Remove fasteners attaching fan module to radiator.
4. Remove fan from motor shaft.
5. Remove motor fasteners from motor support, then the motor.
6. Reverse procedure to install, **torque** fasteners to 45 inch lbs.

TALON

Refer to **Figs. 67 and 68** for radiator fan motor replacement.

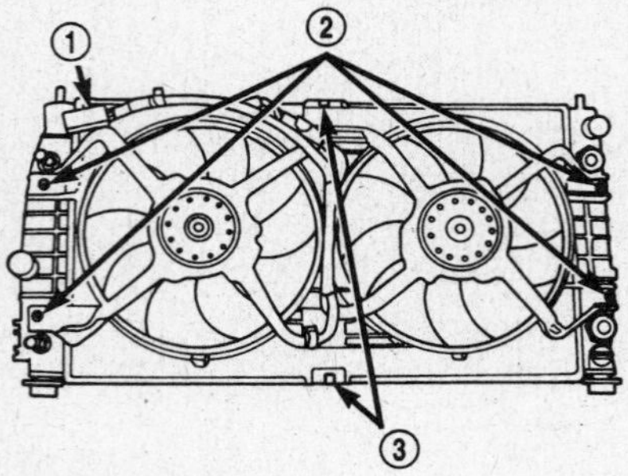

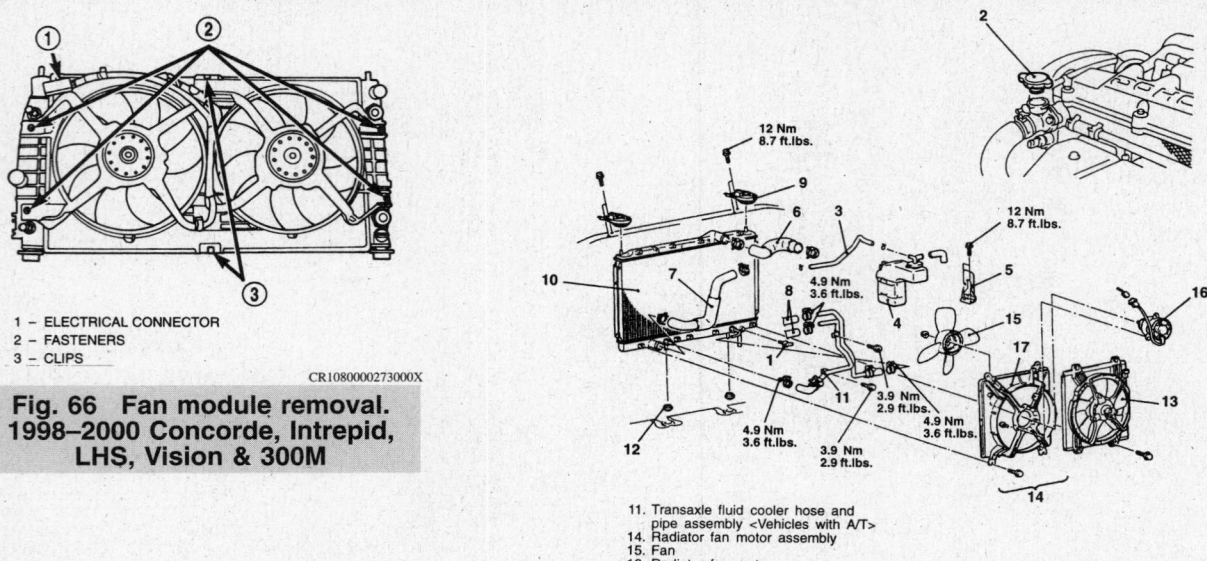

1 – ELECTRICAL CONNECTOR
2 – FASTENERS
3 – CLIPS

CR1080000273000X

Fig. 66 Fan module removal. 1998–2000 Concorde, Intrepid, LHS, Vision & 300M

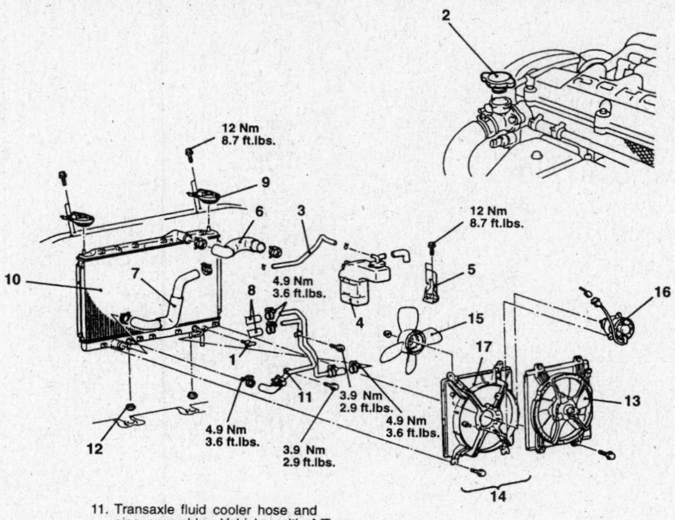

11. Transaxle fluid cooler hose and pipe assembly <Vehicles with A/T>
14. Radiator fan motor assembly
15. Fan
16. Radiator fan motor
17. Shroud

CR1089700266000X

Fig. 67 Radiator fan motor replacement. Talon less turbocharged engine

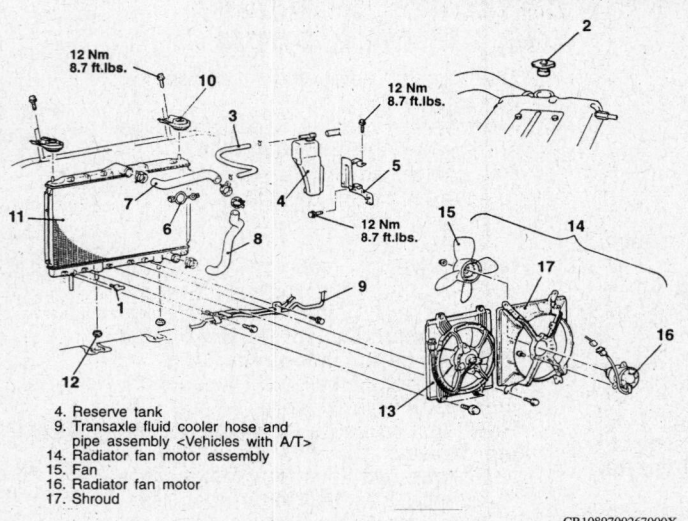

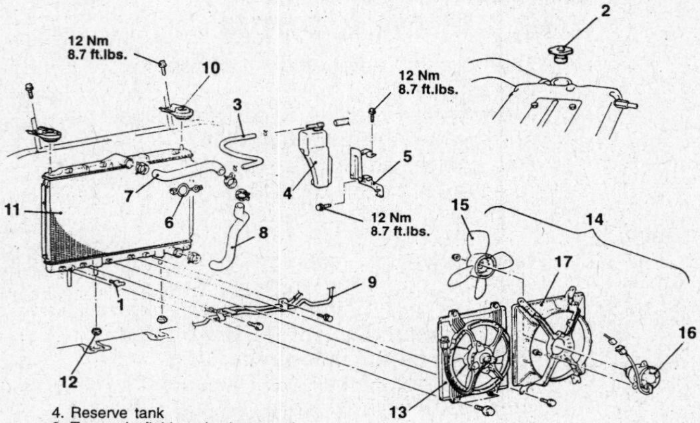

4. Reserve tank
9. Transaxle fluid cooler hose and pipe assembly <Vehicles with A/T>
14. Radiator fan motor assembly
15. Fan
16. Radiator fan motor
17. Shroud

CR1089700267000X

Fig. 68 Radiator fan motor replacement. Talon w/turbocharged engine

STARTER MOTORS

NOTE: On Air Bag Equipped Models, Refer To " Air Bag System Precautions" Located In The Front Of This Manual For System Disarming & Arming Procedures.

NOTE: Refer To "Computer Relearn" Located In The Front Of This Manual For Computer Relearn Procedures.

TABLE OF CONTENTS

Application Chart

Model	Year	Engine	Starter	
			Manufacturer	Type
Avenger & Sebring Coupe	1997–2000	2.0L	Mitsubishi	Direct Drive
		2.5L	Mitsubishi	Gear Reduction
Breeze, Cirrus & Stratus	1997–99	2.0L	Bosch	Gear Reduction
		2.4L	Nippondenso	Gear Reduction
		2.5L	Melco	Gear Reduction
	2000	2.0L	Bosch	Direct Drive
		2.4L	Nippondenso	Gear Reduction
		2.5L	Melco	Direct Drive
Concorde, Intrepid, LHS, Vision & 300M	1997	3.3L	Nippondenso	Gear Reduction
		3.5L	Nippondenso	Gear Reduction
	1998–99	2.7L	Nippondenso	Direct Drive
		3.2L	Nippondenso	Gear Reduction
		3.5L	Melco	Gear Reduction
	2000	2.7L	Melco	Direct Drive
		3.2L	Nippondenso	Gear Reduction
		3.5L	Nippondenso	Gear Reduction
Neon	1997–99	2.0L	Bosch	Gear Reduction
	2000	2.0L	Bosch	Gear Reduction
Sebring Convertible	1997–2000	2.4L	Nippondenso	Gear Reduction
		2.5L	Melco	Gear Reduction
Talon	1997–98	2.0L①	Mitsubishi	Direct Drive
		2.0L②	Mitsubishi	Gear Reduction

① — Non-turbocharged engine. ② — Turbocharged engine.

Bosch Starter Motors

INDEX

DESCRIPTION

Bosch starter motors incorporate an overrunning clutch type starter drive. A solenoid switch is mounted on the starter motor, **Fig. 1.**

The Bosch starter is a gear reduction type. It uses six permanent magnets in place of conventional wound field magnets to save weight, eliminate field winding to case shorts and improve cold start performance. The gear reduction system uses a planetary gear train to transmit armature rotation to the pinion shaft. A solenoid switch is mounted on the starter motor drive end shield.

TROUBLESHOOTING

Refer to **Fig. 2** when troubleshooting the starting system.

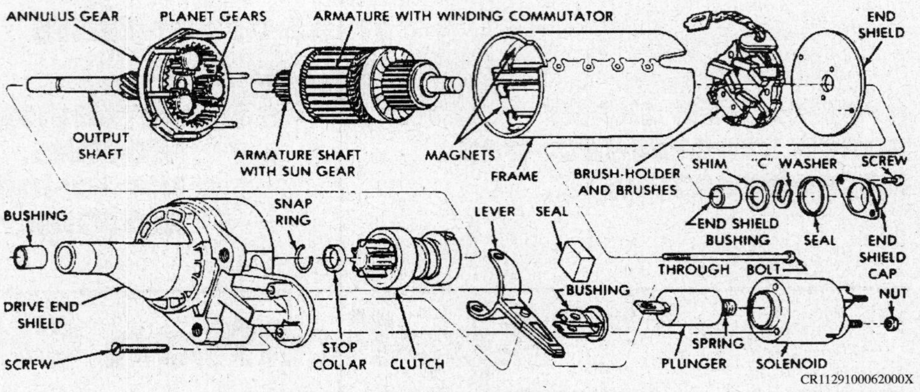

Fig. 1 Bosch starter motor

SYMPTOM STARTER FAILS TO ENGAGE. NO SOUNDS	SYMPTOM STARTER FAILS TO ENGAGE. SOLENOID OR RELAY CLICKS	SYMPTOM STARTER ENGAGES, FAILS TO TURN ENGINE. DOME LIGHT DIMS	SYMPTOM STARTER ENGAGES, DRIVE CLUTCH SPINS OUT	SYMPTOM STARTER DOES NOT DISENGAGE AFTER ENGINE STARTS
POSSIBLE CAUSE STARTER CONTROL CIRCUIT FAULTY IGNITION SWITCH FAULTY NEUTRAL SAFETY SWITCH (AUTO TRANS.) FAULTY OR MISADJUSTED CLUTCH PEDAL SWITCH (MANUAL TRANS.) FAULTY OR MISADJUSTED STARTER RELAY FAULTY STARTER ASSEMBLY FAULTY	POSSIBLE CAUSE RESISTANCE TOO HIGH IN STARTER FEED CIRCUIT STARTER CONTROL CIRCUIT FAULTY STARTER SOLENOID FAULTY STARTER ASSEMBLY FAULTY	POSSIBLE CAUSE RESISTANCE TOO HIGH IN STARTER FEED CIRCUIT ENGINE SEIZED STARTER ASSEMBLY FAULTY	POSSIBLE CAUSE DRIVE CLUTCH FAULTY BROKEN TEETH ON RING GEAR STARTER ASSEMBLY FAULTY	POSSIBLE CAUSE IGNITION SWITCH FAULTY STARTER RELAY FAULTY STARTER ASSEMBLY FAULTY
	REFER TO PROPER SERVICE AND TEST PROCEDURES FOR THE COMPONENTS INVOLVED			

CR1129200128000X

Fig. 2 Starting system troubleshooting chart

DIAGNOSIS & TESTING

IN-VEHICLE TESTS

Before starting any tests, ensure the battery is fully charged and all connections are secure.

STARTER FEED CIRCUIT TEST

The following test will require a suitable volt-ohmmeter tester, accurate to .10 volt.

On models equipped with manual transaxle, apply parking brake and depress clutch pedal whenever a test step calls for turning the ignition to Start position.

1. Connect tester to battery remote terminals following manufacturer's instructions.
2. **On Breeze, Cirrus, Stratus and Neon,** disable ignition and fuel systems by disconnecting automatic shutdown (ASD) relay in power distribution center (PDC).
3. **On all models,** ensure all electrical accessories are off, transmission is in Park or Neutral position and parking brake is set.
4. Turn ignition to Start and observe tester.
5. **On 1997–99 models,** if voltage reads between 9.6 and 12.4 volts and amperage draw reads above 250 amps, perform test outlined under " Starter Feed Circuit Resistance Test."
6. **On 2000 models,** if voltage reads between 9.6 and 12.4 volts and amperage draw reads above 280 amps, perform test outlined under "Starter Feed Circuit Resistance Test. "
7. **On all models,** if voltage reads 12.4 volts or more and amperage reads 0–10 amps, perform "Starter Control Circuit Test" in this section.
8. After starting system conditions have been corrected, ensure battery is fully charged.
9. **On 2000 models,** if voltage reads below 9.6 volts and amperage draw reads above 300 amps, replace starter motor as outlined under "Starter Motor, Replace."
10. **On all models,** disconnect all testing equipment and connect ignition system.
11. Start vehicle several times to ensure system is operating properly.

STARTER FEED CIRCUIT RESISTANCE (VOLTAGE DROP) TEST

Neon

Ensure when performing this test that

wiring harnesses and components are connected properly. The following test will require a voltmeter accurate to .10 volt.

On models equipped with manual transaxle, apply parking brake and depress clutch pedal whenever a test step calls for turning the ignition to Start position.

1. Disable ignition and fuel system by disconnecting Automatic Shutdown (ASD) relay in power distribution center.
2. Connect negative lead of voltmeter to battery ground post, then the positive lead to negative battery cable clamp.
3. Turn ignition to Start and observe voltmeter.
4. If voltage is detected, correct poor contact between cable clamp and post.
5. Connect positive lead of voltmeter to positive battery terminal and negative lead to battery positive cable clamp.
6. Turn ignition to Start and observe voltmeter.
7. If voltage is detected, correct poor contact between cable clamp and post.
8. Connect negative lead of voltmeter to battery ground terminal, and positive lead to engine block near battery cable attaching point.
9. Turn ignition to Start.
10. If voltage reads above .2 volt, correct poor contact at ground cable attaching point.
11. If voltage reading is still above .2 volt after correcting poor contacts, replace ground cable.
12. Remove starter heat shield if required.
13. Connect positive voltmeter lead to starter motor housing and negative lead to battery ground terminal.
14. Turn ignition to Start.
15. If voltage reads above .2 volt, correct poor starter to engine ground.
16. Connect positive voltmeter lead to battery positive terminal, and negative lead to battery cable terminal on starter solenoid.
17. Turn ignition to Start.
18. If voltage reads above .2 volt correct poor contact at battery cable to solenoid connection.
19. If reading is still above .2 volt after correcting poor contacts, replace battery positive cable.
20. **On 1997–99 models,** if resistance tests do not detect feed circuit failures, remove starter motor and Perform Bench Test. Refer to "Bench Tests" in this section.
21. **On 2000 models,** if resistance tests do not detect feed circuit failures, replace starter motor as outlined under "Starter Motor, Replace."

Breeze, Cirrus, Sebring Convertible & Stratus

Ensure when performing this test that wiring harnesses and components are connected properly. The following test will require a voltmeter accurate to .10 volt.

On models equipped with manual transaxle, apply parking brake and depress clutch pedal whenever a test step calls for turning the ignition to Start position.

1. Disable ignition and fuel systems by disconnecting automatic shutdown relay in power distribution center.
2. Connect negative lead of voltmeter to remote battery ground terminal, and positive lead to engine block near battery cable attaching point.
3. Turn ignition to Start.
4. If voltage reads above .2 volt, clean or repair poor contact at ground cable attaching points.
5. If voltage reading is still above .2 volt after correcting poor contacts, replace ground cable.
6. Connect positive voltmeter lead to remote battery positive terminal, and negative lead to remote battery positive cable terminal on starter solenoid.
7. Turn ignition to Start.
8. If voltage reads above .2 volt, clean or repair poor contact at:
    a. Battery cable to solenoid connection.
    b. Battery cable to remote terminal.
    c. Battery cable to battery.
9. If reading is still above .2 volt after correcting poor contacts, replace battery positive cable.
10. If resistance tests do not detect feed circuit failure, replace starter as outlined under "Starter Motor, Replace."

STARTER CONTROL CIRCUIT TEST

The starter control circuit consists of the starter solenoid, starter relay, ignition switch, neutral safety switch and all related wiring and connections. Always perform the Starter Solenoid Test before the performing the Starter Relay Test.

On models equipped with manual transaxle, apply parking brake and depress clutch pedal whenever a test step calls for turning the ignition to Start position.

Starter Solenoid Test

1. Ensure battery is fully charged and in good condition.
2. Raise and support vehicle.
3. Inspect starter and starter solenoid for corrosion or loose wiring.
4. Lower vehicle and remove starter relay from connector.
5. Connect a remote starter switch or a jumper wire between battery remote positive post and terminal 87 on starter relay connector.
6. If engine cranks, starter and starter solenoid are operating properly. Perform starter relay test as described under "Starter Relay Test."
7. If engine does not crank or solenoid chatters, inspect wiring and connectors from relay to starter for loose or corroded connections.
8. Repeat test and, if engine still does not crank properly, repair or replace starter or starter solenoid as required.

Starter Relay Test

1. Remove starter relay from power distribution center.
2. With relay in de-energized position, continuity should exist between terminals 87A and 30, but not between terminals 87 and 30.
3. Measure resistance between terminals 85 and 86, which should be 70–80 ohms.
4. Connect battery positive lead to terminal 86 and ground lead to terminal 85. Relay should click.
5. With relay in energized position, continuity should exist between terminals 30 and 87, but not between terminals 87A and 30.
6. If any one inspection failed, replace relay.

Ignition Switch Test

After testing starter solenoid and relay, test ignition switch and wiring. Inspect all wiring for opens and shorts and all connectors for looseness or corrosion.

BENCH TESTS

STARTER SOLENOID

1. Disconnect field coil wire from field coil terminal.
2. Inspect for continuity between solenoid terminal and field coil terminal. Continuity should exist.
3. Inspect for continuity between solenoid terminal and solenoid housing. Continuity should exist.
4. If continuity does not exist in either test, replace solenoid assembly.

STARTER SPECIFICATIONS

Year	Free Speed Test			Minimum RPM	Cranking Amp Draw Test①
	Power Rating, KW	Max. Amps	Volts		
1997–99	.95	.95	12	—	150–280
2000	1.1	—	12	—	150–280

① — With engine @ operating temperature.

Mitsubishi Starter Motors

INDEX

DESCRIPTION

Mitsubishi starters are either direct drive or gear reduction type. The unit shown in **Fig. 1** is a direct drive starter motor with an overrunning clutch type starter drive. A solenoid switch is mounted on the starter motor. The unit shown in **Fig. 2** is a gear reduction type utilizing a planetary gear assembly to obtain higher rotational speeds with the same torque output.

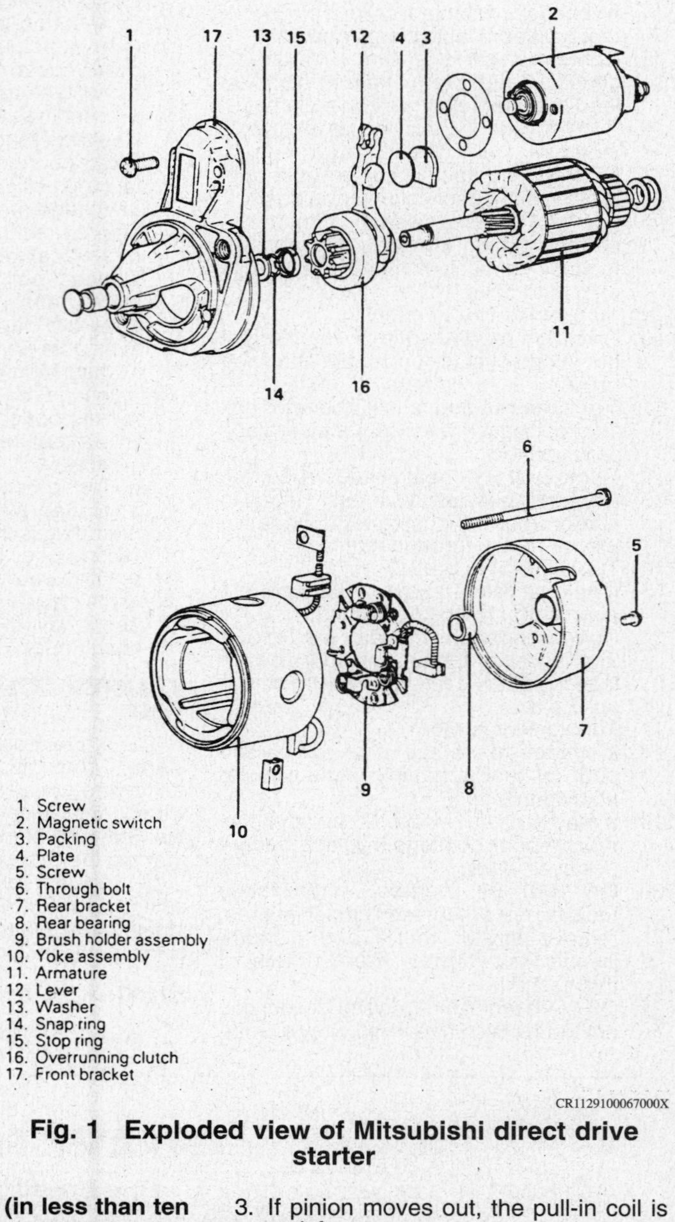

Fig. 1 Exploded view of Mitsubishi direct drive starter

TROUBLESHOOTING

STARTER MOTOR DOES NOT OPERATE AT ALL

1. Inspect starter coil.
2. Inspect for poor contact at battery terminals and starter.
3. Inspect park/neutral position switch.
4. Inspect clutch pedal position switch.
5. Inspect starter relay.
6. Inspect theft alarm starter relay.
7. Inspect key reminder switch.

DIAGNOSIS & TESTING

STARTER SOLENOID CONTINUITY INSPECTION

Direct Drive Starter

1. Disconnect wire from M (motor) terminal, **Fig. 3.**
2. Inspect for continuity between S (solenoid) terminal and M (motor) terminal. Continuity should exist.
3. Inspect for continuity between S terminal and solenoid housing. Continuity should exist.
4. If continuity is detected in both tests, solenoid is operating properly.
5. If continuity is not detected in either one of the tests, solenoid is faulty. Replace starter motor.

MAGNETIC SWITCH PULL-IN TEST

Gear Reduction Starter

1. Disconnect field coil wire from "M" terminal, **Figs. 4 and 5.**
2. Connect a 12 volt battery between terminals S and M. **This test must be performed quickly (in less than ten seconds) to prevent coil from burning.**
3. If pinion moves out, the pull-in coil is satisfactory.
4. If pinion does not move out, replace magnetic switch.

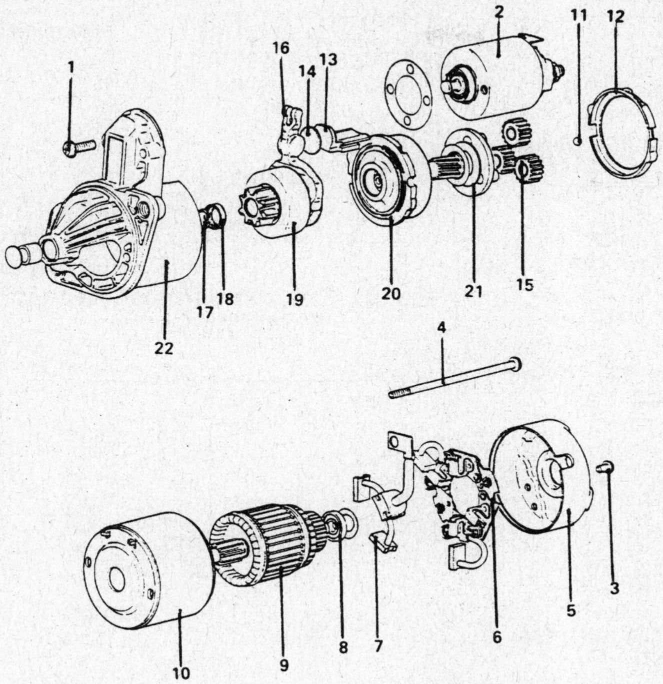

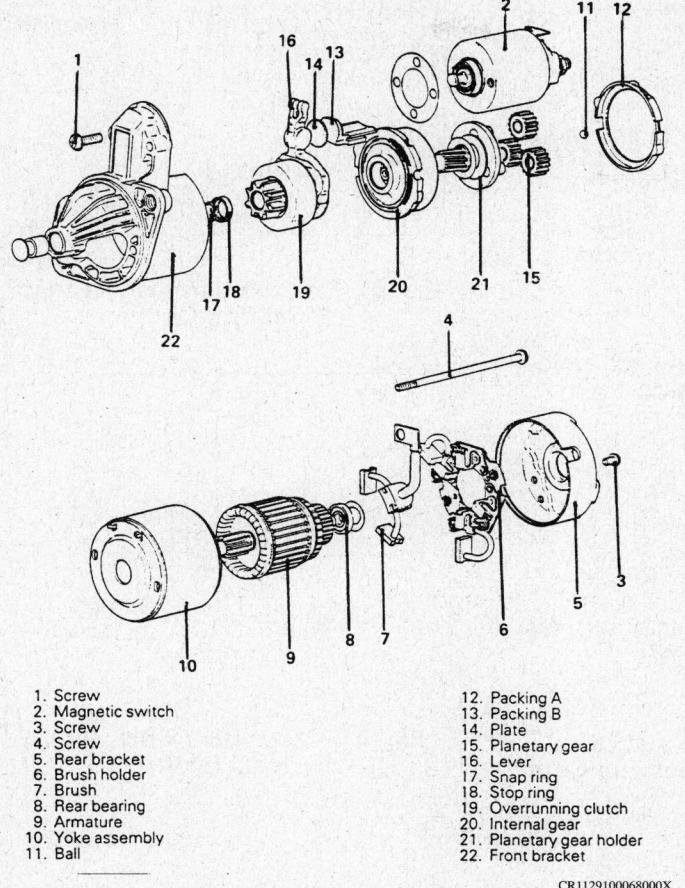

1. Screw
2. Magnetic switch
3. Screw
4. Screw
5. Rear bracket
6. Brush holder
7. Brush
8. Rear bearing
9. Armature
10. Yoke assembly
11. Ball
12. Packing A
13. Packing B
14. Plate
15. Planetary gear
16. Lever
17. Snap ring
18. Stop ring
19. Overrunning clutch
20. Internal gear
21. Planetary gear holder
22. Front bracket

CR1129100068000X

Fig. 2 Exploded view of Mitsubishi gear reduction starter

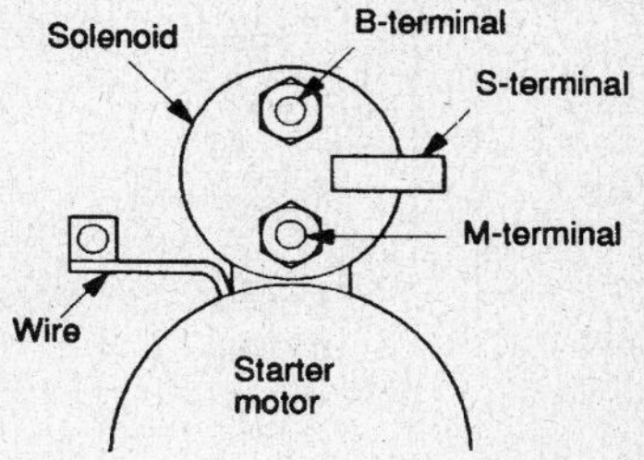

CR1129500193000X

Fig. 3 Starter solenoid continuity inspection. Direct drive starter

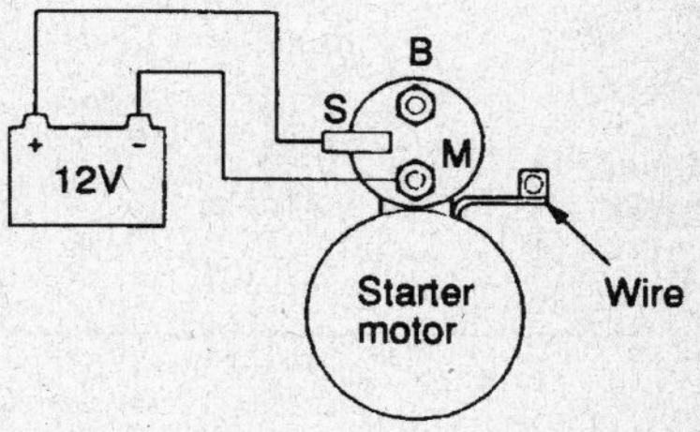

CR1129500185000X

Fig. 4 Magnetic switch pull-in test. Avenger & Sebring Coupe

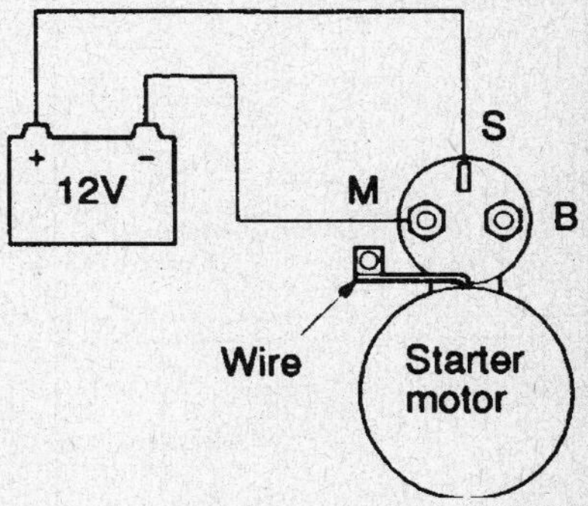

CR1129500186000X

Fig. 5 Magnetic switch pull-in test. Talon

MAGNETIC SWITCH HOLD-IN TEST

Gear Reduction Starter

1. Disconnect field coil wire from terminal M of switch, **Figs. 6 and 7.**
2. Connect a 12 volt battery between terminal S and starter body. **This test must be performed quickly (in less than ten seconds) to prevent coil from burning.**
3. Pull out pinion by hand until it hits stopper.
4. If pinion remains out, switch is operating properly.
5. If pinion moves in, hold-in circuit is open. Replace magnetic switch.

FREE RUNNING TEST

1. Place starter motor assembly in a soft-jawed vise.
2. Connect a test voltmeter (100 ampere scale) and carbon pile rheostat in series with positive post of fully charged battery and starter motor terminal, **Figs. 8 and 9.**
3. Connect a voltmeter (15 volt scale) across starter motor.
4. Rotate carbon pile to full resistance position.
5. Connect battery ground cable to starter body.
6. Adjust rheostat until battery voltage shown by voltmeter matches voltage listed in "Starter Specifications" chart.
7. Confirm amperage is as indicated in "Starter Specifications " chart and starter motor turns smoothly and freely.

MAGNETIC SWITCH RETURN TEST

Gear Reduction Starter

1. Disconnect field coil wire from terminal M from magnetic switch, **Figs. 10 and 11.**
2. Connect a 12 volt battery between terminals M and starter body. **This test must be performed quickly (in less than ten seconds) to prevent coil from burning.**
3. Pull pinion out and release.
4. If pinion quickly returns to original position, switch is operating properly.
5. If pinion does not quickly return to original position, replace magnetic switch.

STARTER RELAY TEST

Refer to **Fig. 12** for starter relay location, **Figs. 13 and 14** for starter relay terminal identification and **Figs. 15 and 16** for starter relay continuity tests.

THEFT ALARM STARTER RELAY TEST

Refer to **Fig. 12** for theft alarm starter relay location, **Figs. 17 and 18** for starter relay terminal identification, then to **Figs. 19 and 20** for theft alarm starter relay continuity tests.

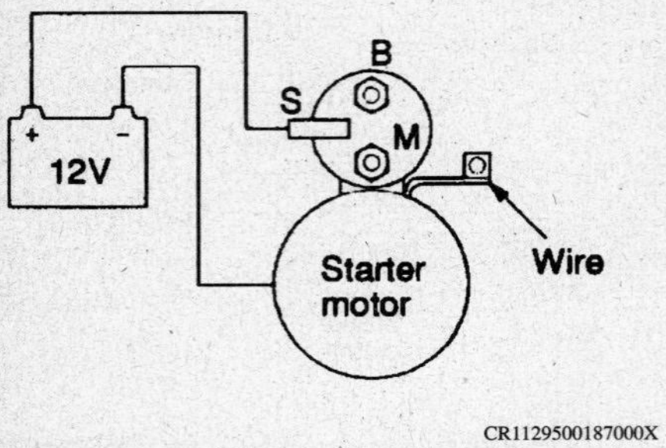

Fig. 6 Magnetic switch hold-in test. Avenger & Sebring Coupe

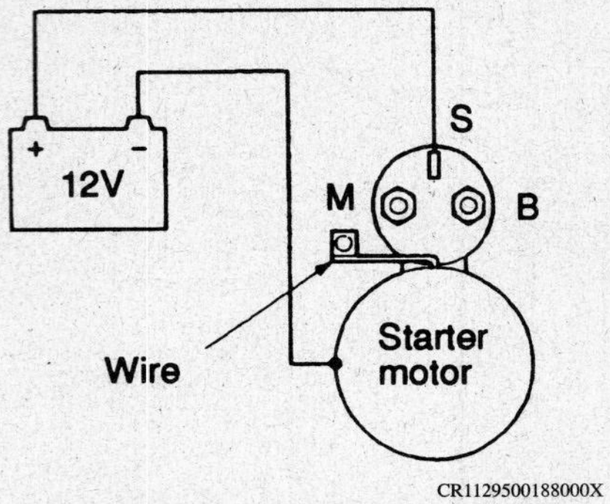

Fig. 7 Magnetic switch hold-in test. Talon

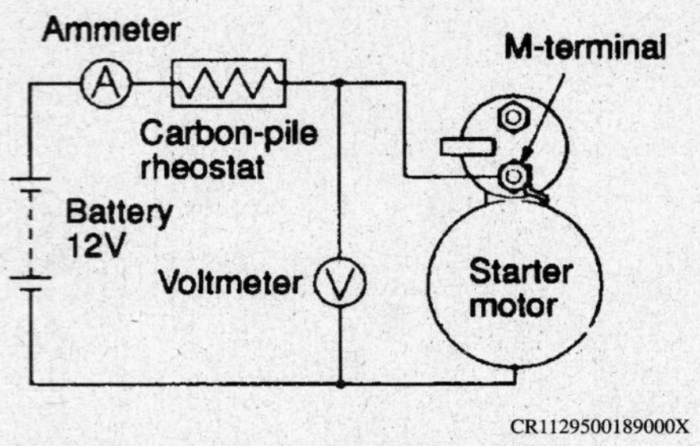

Fig. 8 Free running test. Avenger & Sebring Coupe

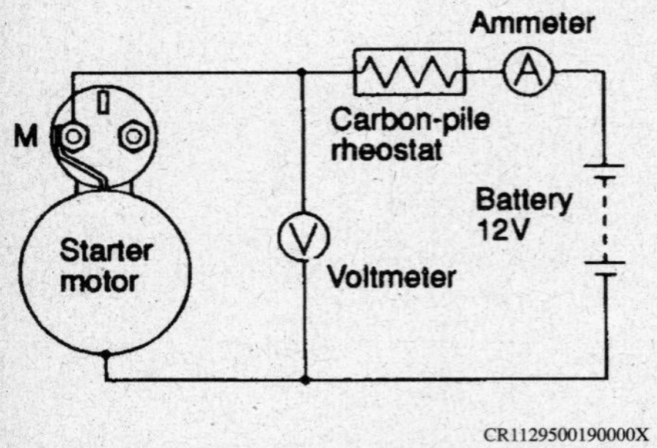

Fig. 9 Free running test. Talon

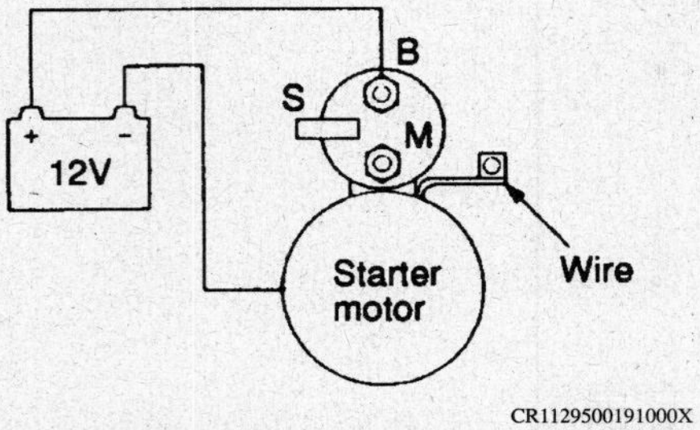

Fig. 10 Magnetic switch return test. Avenger & Sebring Coupe

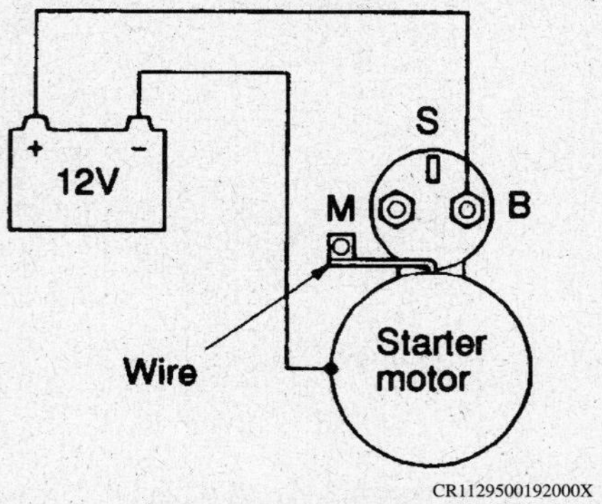

Fig. 11 Magnetic switch return test. Talon

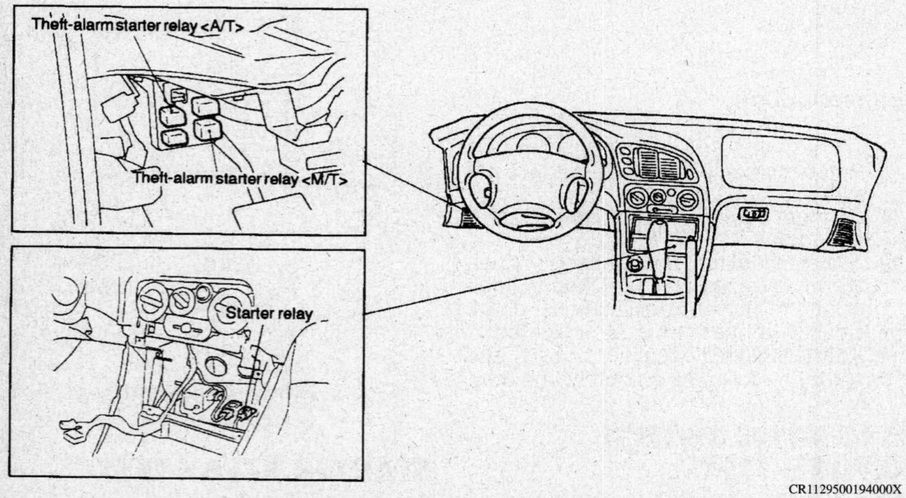

Fig. 12 Starter relay & theft alarm starter relay locations

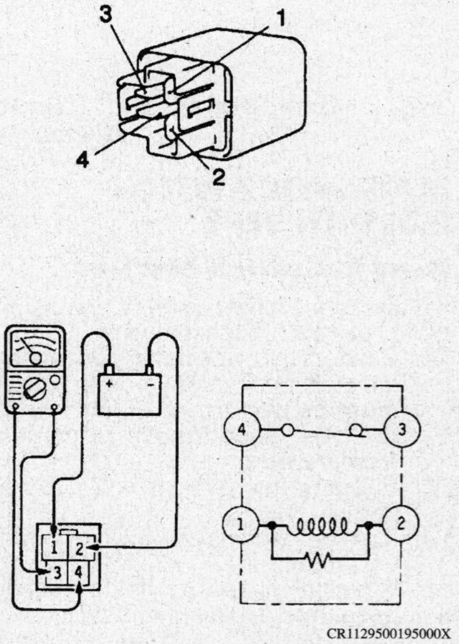

Fig. 13 Starter relay terminal identification. Manual transaxle

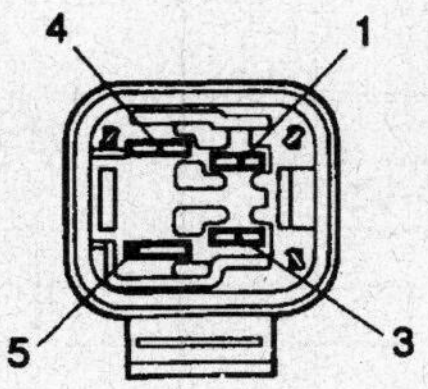

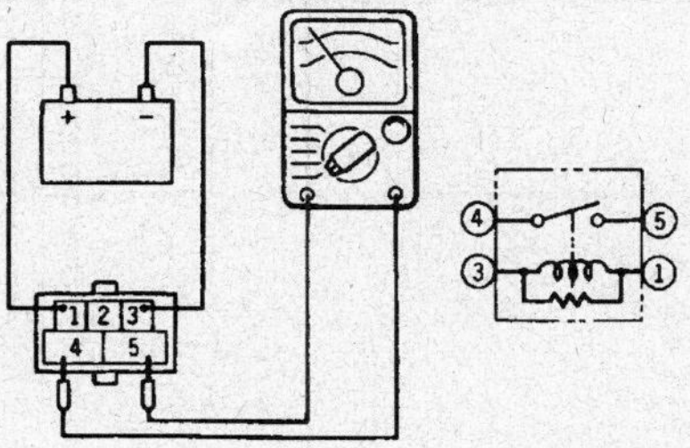

CR1129500196000X

Fig. 14 Starter relay terminal identification. Automatic transaxle

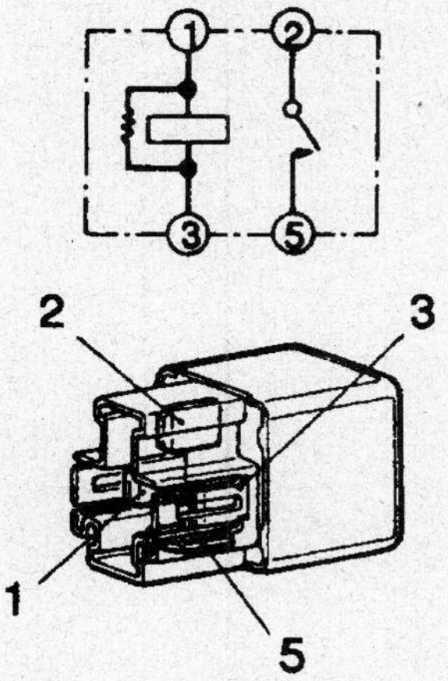

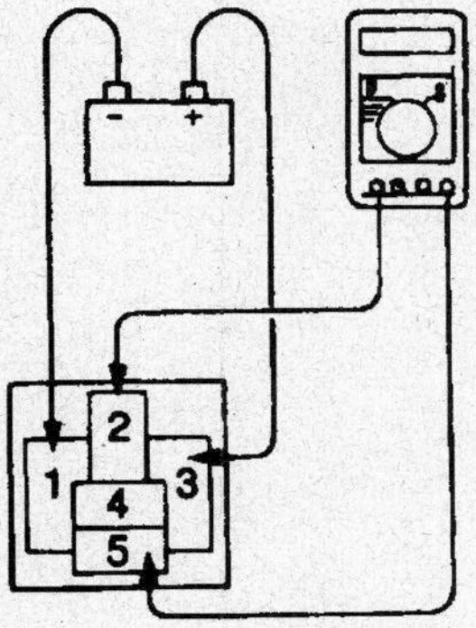

CR1129500199000X

Fig. 17 Theft alarm starter relay terminal identification. Manual transaxle

Battery voltage	Terminal 1	2	3	4
Not applied	O—	—O	O—	—O
Applied	⊕- -	- -⊖		

NOTE
O—O indicates that there is continuity between the terminals.
⊕- -⊖ indicates terminals to which battery voltage is applied.

CR1129500197000X

Fig. 15 Starter relay test. Manual transaxle

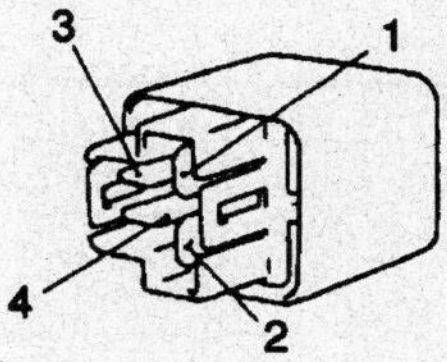

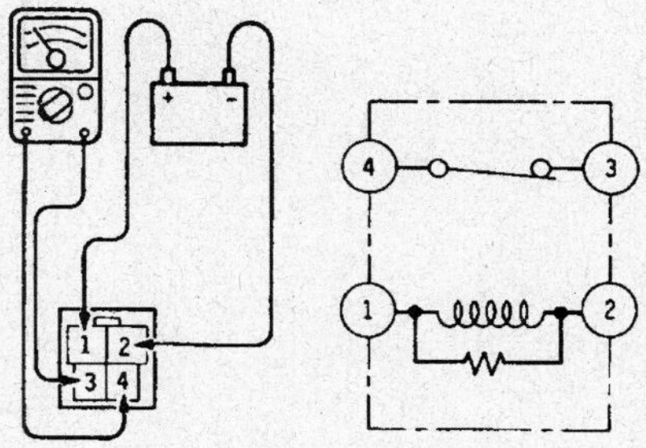

CR1129500200000X

Fig. 18 Theft alarm starter relay terminal identification. Automatic transaxle

Battery voltage	Terminal 1	2	3	4	5
Not applied	O—	—	—O		
Applied	⊕- -	- -	- -⊖	O—	—O

NOTE
O—O indicates that there is continuity between the terminals.
⊕- -⊖ indicates terminals to which battery voltage is applied.

CR1129500198000X

Fig. 16 Starter relay test. Automatic transaxle

Battery voltage	Terminal 1	2	3	5
Not applied	O—	—	—O	
Applied	⊖- -	- -	- -⊕	
		O—	—	—O

NOTE
O—O indicates that there is continuity between the terminals.
⊕- -⊖ indicates terminals to which battery voltage is applied.

CR1129500201000X

Fig. 19 Theft alarm starter relay test. Manual transaxle

Battery voltage	Terminal 1	2	3	4
Not applied	O—	—O	O—	—O
Applied	⊕- -	- -⊖		

NOTE
O—O indicates that there is continuity between the terminals.
⊕- -⊖ indicates terminals to which battery voltage is applied.

CR1129500202000X

Fig. 20 Theft alarm starter relay test. Automatic transaxle

STARTER SPECIFICATIONS

Model	Engine	Free Speed Test			Minimum RPM
		Power Rating	Max. Amps	Volts	
Avenger & Sebring Coupe	2.0L	.95 kw	—	—	—
	2.5L	1.20 kw	—	—	—
Talon	2.0L①	.95 kw	—	—	—
	2.0L②	1.20 kw	—	—	—
Avenger & Sebring Coupe	2.0L	.95 kw	—	—	—
	2.5L	1.20 kw	—	—	—

① — Maximum, Turbocharged engine.

② — Minimum, Non-turbocharged engine.

Nippondenso Starter Motors

INDEX

DESCRIPTION

Nippondenso starters, **Figs. 1 and 2,** are either direct drive or gear reduction types. The direct drive starter has an overrunning clutch type starter drive and a solenoid switch is mounted on the starter motor. The structure of the gear reduction type starter differs from that of the direct drive type, but the electrical wiring is the same for both types.

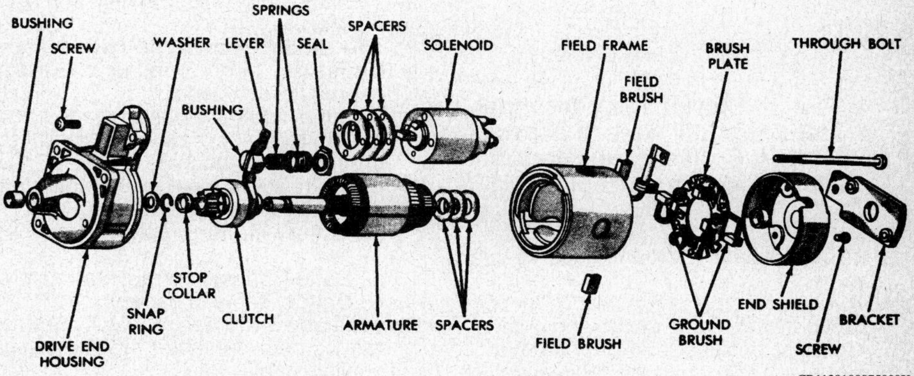

Fig. 1 Exploded view of Nippondenso direct drive starter

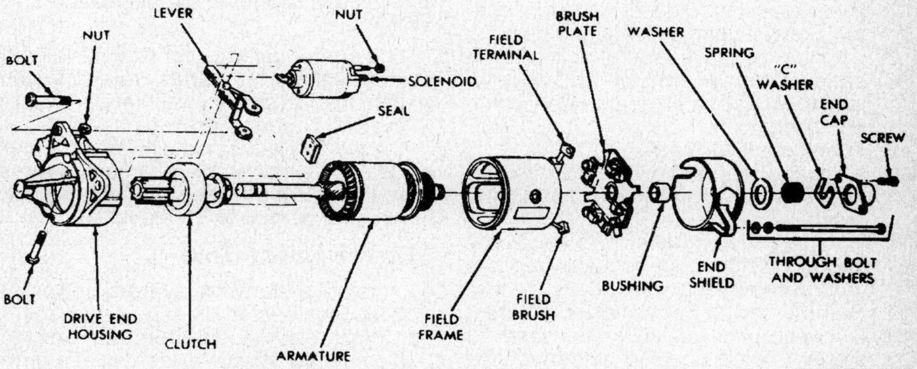

Fig. 2 Exploded view of Nippondenso gear reduction starter

DIAGNOSIS & TESTING

IN-VEHICLE TESTS

Before starting any tests, ensure the battery is fully charged and that all connections are good, then disable ignition system as follows:

On models equipped with manual transaxle, apply parking brake and depress clutch pedal whenever a test step calls for turning the ignition to Start position.

1. **On models equipped with distributor ignition system,** disconnect ignition coil cable from distributor cap, then connect a suitable jumper wire between coil cable end terminal and a good body ground.
2. **On models equipped with direct ignition system,** disconnect ignition coils electrical connector.
3. **On 2000 models,** disconnect Automatic Shutdown (ASD) relay in Power Distribution Center (PDC).

STARTER FEED CIRCUIT TEST

Ensure when performing this test that wiring harnesses and components are connected properly. The following test will require a voltmeter accurate to .10 volt.

On models equipped with manual transaxle, apply parking brake and depress clutch pedal whenever a test step calls for turning the ignition to Start position.

1. Connect tester to battery terminals following manufacturer's instructions.
2. Ensure all electrical accessories are off, transmission is in Park or Neutral and parking brake is set.
3. Turn ignition to Start and observe tester.
4. **On 1997–99 models,** if voltage reads between 9.6 and 12.4 volts and amperage draw reads above 250 amps, perform test outlined under "Starter Feed Circuit Resistance (Voltage Drop) Test."
5. **On 2000 models,** if voltage reads above 9.6 volts and amperage draw reads above 280 amps, inspect for engine seizure or a faulty starter.
6. **On 1997–99 models,** if voltage reads 12.4 volts or more and amperage reads 0–10 amps, perform test outlined under "Starter Control Circuit Test."
7. **On 2000 models,** if voltage reads 12.4 volts or more and amperage reads 0–10 amps, inspect and correct corroded cables and poor connections. If voltage reads below 9.6 volts and amperage reads above 300 amps, replace starter motor as outlined under "Starter Motor, Replace."
8. **On all models,** after starting system fault conditions have been corrected, ensure battery is fully charged.
9. Disconnect all testing equipment and connect ignition system.
10. Start vehicle several times to ensure system is operating properly.

STARTER FEED CIRCUIT RESISTANCE (VOLTAGE DROP) TEST

Concorde, Intrepid, LHS, Vision & 300M

Ensure when performing this test that wiring harnesses and components are connected properly. The following test will require a voltmeter accurate to .10 volt.

On models equipped with manual transaxle, apply parking brake and depress clutch pedal whenever a test step calls for turning the ignition to Start position.

1. Disconnect Automatic Shutdown (ASD) relay in Power Distribution Center (PDC).
2. Connect negative lead of voltmeter to battery ground post, then the positive lead to negative battery cable clamp.

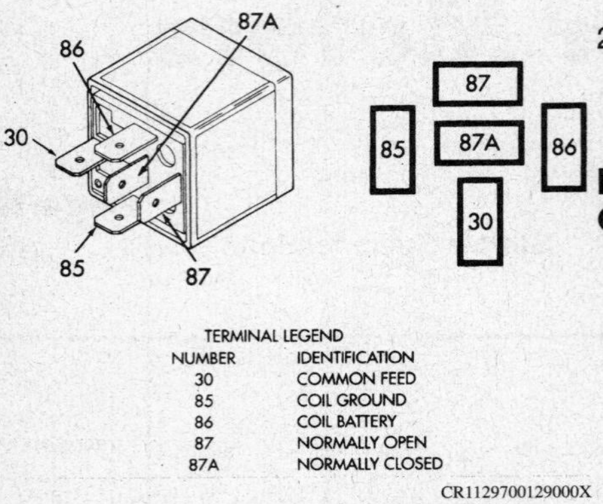

Fig. 3 Starter relay terminal identification. Breeze, Cirrus, Sebring Convertible, Stratus & 1997 Concorde, Intrepid, LHS & Vision

3. Turn ignition to Start and observe voltmeter.
4. If voltage is detected, correct poor contact between cable clamp and post.
5. Connect positive lead of voltmeter to positive battery terminal and negative lead to battery positive cable clamp.
6. Turn ignition to Start and observe voltmeter.
7. If voltage is detected, correct poor contact between cable clamp and post.
8. Connect negative lead of voltmeter to battery ground terminal, and positive lead to engine block near battery cable attaching point.
9. Turn ignition to Start.
10. If voltage reads above .2 volt, correct poor contact at ground cable attaching point.
11. If voltage reading is still above .2 volt after correcting poor contacts, replace ground cable.
12. Remove starter heat shield if required.
13. Connect positive voltmeter lead to starter motor housing and negative lead to battery ground terminal.
14. Turn ignition to Start.
15. If voltage reads above .2 volt, correct poor starter to engine ground.
16. Connect positive voltmeter lead to battery positive terminal, and negative lead to battery cable terminal on starter solenoid.
17. Turn ignition to Start.
18. If voltage reads above .2 volt correct poor contact at battery cable to solenoid connection.
19. If reading is still above .2 volt after correcting poor contacts, replace battery positive cable.
20. If resistance tests do not detect feed circuit failures, replace starter motor as outlined under "Starter Motor, Replace."

Breeze, Cirrus, Sebring Convertible & Stratus

1. Connect negative lead of voltmeter to battery ground terminal, and positive lead to engine block near battery cable attaching point.
2. Turn and hold ignition switch in START position.
3. **On models equipped with manual transaxle,** apply parking brake and depress clutch pedal.
4. **On all models,** if voltage reads above .2 volt, clean or repair poor contact at ground cable attaching points.
5. If voltage still reads above .2 volt, clean or repair poor contact at:
   a. Battery cable to solenoid connection.
   b. Battery cable to remote terminal.
   c. Battery cable to battery.
6. If reading is still above .2 volt after correcting poor contacts, replace battery positive cable.
7. If resistance tests do not detect feed circuit failures, replace starter motor.

STARTER CONTROL CIRCUIT TEST

The starter control circuit consists of the starter solenoid, starter relay, ignition switch, neutral safety switch and all related wiring and connections.

On models equipped with manual transaxle, apply parking brake and depress clutch pedal whenever a test step calls for turning the ignition to Start position.

Starter Relay Test

1. Remove starter relay from power distribution center.
2. With relay in de-energized position, continuity should exist between terminals 87A and 30, but not between terminals 87 and 30.
3. Measure resistance between terminals 85 and 86, which should be 70–80 ohms.
4. Connect battery positive lead to terminal 86 and ground lead to terminal 85. Relay should click.
5. With relay in energized position, continuity should exist between terminals 30 and 87, but not between terminals 87A and 30.
6. If any one inspection failed, replace relay.

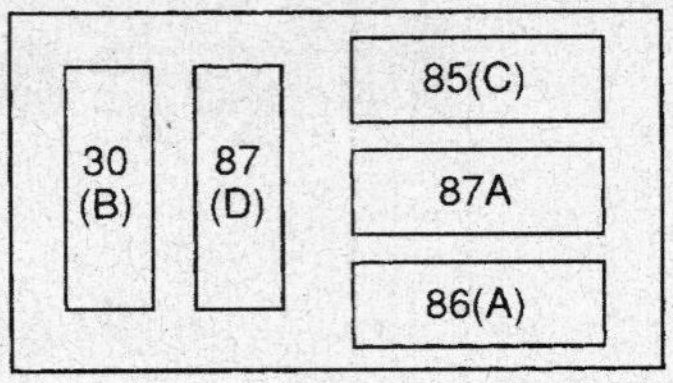

Starter Relay Pinout

CAV	COLOR	FUNCTION
30 (B)	RD	B (+)
85 (C)	TN	P/N POSITION SW.SENSE (AUTO)
86 (A)	YL	IGNITION SWITCH OUTPUT
87 (D)	LG	STARTER RELAY OUTPUT

CR1129100065000X

Fig. 4 Starter relay terminal identification. 1998–2000 Concorde, Intrepid, LHS & 300M

Starter Solenoid Test

1. Ensure battery is fully charged and in good condition.
2. Raise and support vehicle.
3. Inspect starter and starter solenoid for corrosion or loose wiring.
4. Lower vehicle.
5. Remove starter relay from connector.
6. Connect a remote starter switch or a jumper wire between battery positive post and terminal 87, **Figs. 3 and 4.**
7. If engine cranks, starter and starter solenoid are operating properly.
8. Perform starter relay test as described under "Starter Control Circuit Test."
9. If engine does not crank or solenoid chatters, inspect wiring and connectors from relay to starter for loose or corroded connections.
10. Repeat test and, if engine still does not crank properly, repair or replace starter or starter solenoid as required.

Ignition Switch Test

After testing starter solenoid and relay, test ignition switch and wiring. Inspect all wiring for opens or shorts and all connectors for looseness or corrosion.

BENCH TESTING

STARTER SOLENOID

Refer to "Bench Tests" in the " Bosch Starter Motors" section.

STARTER SPECIFICATIONS

Engine	Free Speed Test			Minimum RPM	Cranking Amp Draw Test①
	Power Rating, KW	Max. Amps	Volts		
2.4L	1.4	—	12	—	150–280
2.7L	1.4	—	12	—	150–280
3.2L	1.4	—	12	—	150–280
3.3L	1.2	—	12	—	150–280
3.5L	1.2	—	12	—	150–280

① — With engine @ operating temperature.

Melco Starters

INDEX

DESCRIPTION

Melco starters may be direct drive or gear reduction type starters. They have an overrunning clutch starter drive and a solenoid switch mounted on the starter motor.

DIAGNOSIS & TESTING

Refer to the "Nippondenso Starter Motors" section for Melco starter diagnosis and testing procedures.

STARTER SPECIFICATIONS

Engine	Free Speed Test		Cranking Amp Draw Test①
	Power Rating, KW	Volts	
2.5L	1.2	12	150–280
2.7L	1.4	12	150–280
3.5L	1.2	12	150–280

① — With engine @ operating temperature.

ALTERNATORS

NOTE: On Air Bag Equipped Models, Refer To " Air Bag System Precautions" Located In The Front Of This Manual For System Disarming & Arming Procedures.

NOTE: Refer To "Computer Relearn Procedures" Located In The Front Of This Manual For Computer Relearn Procedures.

TABLE OF CONTENTS

Melco & Nippondenso

NOTE: "Electrical Symbol & Wire Color Code Identification" Located In The Front Of This Manual May Be Used As An Aid When Using Wiring Circuits Found In This Section.

INDEX

APPLICATION CHART

Model & Year	Engine	Type	Model No.	ID. No.
1997				
Breeze, Cirrus, Sebring Convertible & Stratus	2.0L & 2.4L	Nippondenso	—	4609415
Cirrus, Sebring Convertible & Stratus	2.5L	Melco	—	4609320
Concorde, Intrepid, LHS & Vision	All	Nippondenso	90HS	4609034
Neon	All	Melco	—	4793190
1998				
Breeze, Cirrus & Stratus	2.0L & 2.4L	Nippondenso	—	4609415
Cirrus & Stratus	2.5L	Melco	—	4609320
Concorde & Intrepid	2.7L	Nippondenso	—	—
	3.2L & 3.5L	Melco	—	—
Neon	All	Melco	—	4793190
Sebring Convertible	All	Nippondenso	—	4609415
1999				
Breeze, Cirrus & Stratus	2.0L & 2.4L	Nippondenso	—	—
Cirrus & Stratus	2.5L	Melco	—	—
Concorde, Intrepid, LHS & 300M	2.7L	Nippondenso	—	—
	3.2L & 3.5L	Melco	—	—
Neon	All	Melco	—	—
Sebring Convertible	All	Nippondenso	—	—

Continued

APPLICATION CHART—Continued

Model & Year	Engine	Type	Model No.	ID. No.
2000				
Breeze, Cirrus & Stratus	2.0L & 2.4L	Nippondenso	—	—
Cirrus & Stratus	2.5L	Melco	—	—
Concorde, Intrepid, LHS & 300M	2.7L	Denso	—	—
	3.2L & 3.5L	Melco	—	—

PRECAUTIONS

BATTERY GROUND CABLE

Prior to service, disconnect battery ground cable and isolate as required.

GENERAL INFORMATION

The power source of the charging system is the alternator. Current is transmitted from the field terminal of the regulator through a slip ring to the field coil and back to ground through another slip ring. The strength of the field regulates the output of the alternating current. This alternating current is then transmitted from the alternator to the rectifier where it is converted to direct current.

These alternators employ a three-phase stator winding in which the phase windings are electrically 120° apart. The rotor consists of a field coil encased between interleaved sections producing a magnetic field with alternate north and south poles. By rotating the rotor inside the stator, the alternating current is induced in the stator windings. This alternating current is rectified (changed to DC) by silicon diodes and brought out to the output terminal of the alternator.

DIODE RECTIFIERS

Six or more silicon diode rectifiers are used and act as electrical one-way valves. One half of the diodes have ground polarity and are pressed or screwed into a heat sink which is grounded. The other diodes (ungrounded) are pressed or screwed into and insulated from the end head. These diodes are connected to the alternator output terminal.

Since the diodes have a high resistance to the flow of current in one direction and a low resistance in the opposite direction, they may be connected in a manner which allows current to flow from the alternator to the battery in the low resistance direction. The high resistance in the opposite direction prevents the flow of current from the battery to the alternator. Because of this feature no circuit breaker is required between the alternator and battery.

SERVICE PRECAUTIONS

1. Ensure battery polarity is proper when servicing units. Reversed battery polarity will damage rectifiers and regulators.
2. If booster battery is used for starting, use proper polarity in hookup.
3. When a fast charger is used to charge a vehicle battery, vehicle battery cables should be disconnected unless fast charger is equipped with a special alternator protector, in which case vehicle battery cables need not be disconnected. Also, fast chargers should never be used to start a vehicle, as damage to rectifiers will result.
4. Lead connections to grounded rectifiers (negative) should never be soldered, as excessive heat may damage rectifiers.
5. Unless system includes a load relay or field relay, grounding alternator output terminal will damage alternator and/or circuits. This is true even when system is not in operation, since no circuit breaker is used and battery voltage is applied to alternator output terminal at all times. Field or load relay acts as a circuit breaker in that it is controlled by ignition switch.
6. Before making any in-vehicle tests of alternator or regulator, battery should be inspected and circuit inspected for faulty wiring or insulation, loose or corroded connections and poor ground circuits.
7. Inspect alternator belt tension to ensure belt is tight enough to prevent slipping under load.
8. To prevent system damage, turn ignition Off before making any test connections.
9. The vehicle battery must be fully charged or a fully charged battery may be installed for test purposes.

DESCRIPTION

The main components of the alternator are the rotor, stator, rectifier, end shields and drive pulley. Direct current is available at the output B terminal.

Alternator output is controlled by voltage regulator circuitry contained within the power and logic modules of the engine controller.

DIAGNOSIS & TESTING

WIRING DIAGRAMS

Breeze, Cirrus, Sebring Convertible & Stratus

Refer to **Figs. 1 through 3** for wiring diagrams.

Concorde, Intrepid, LHS, Vision & 300M

Refer to **Figs. 4 and 5** for wiring diagrams.

1997-99 Neon

Refer to **Fig. 6** for wiring diagram.

2000 Neon

These models are equipped with Mitsubishi alternators. Refer to the Mitsubishi alternator section in this chapter for wiring diagrams and diagnostic procedures.

DIAGNOSTIC TESTS

Refer to **Figs. 7 through 28** for diagnostic tests.

OUTPUT WIRE VOLTAGE DROP TEST

1997-98

1. Prepare vehicle for test as follows:
   a. Ensure battery is in good condition and fully charged.
   b. Ensure battery cables are clean.
   c. Start engine and allow it to reach normal operating temperature.
   d. Turn engine off, then connect engine to a tachometer.
   e. Fully engage parking brake.
2. Start engine, then place heater blower in High position.
3. Place headlamps in high-beam position.
4. Turn vehicle interior lamps on.
5. Start engine, then bring engine speed up to 2400 RPM and hold.
6. Test positive circuitry as follows:
   a. Using a voltmeter, touch negative lead directly to battery positive.
   b. Touch positive lead to battery positive terminal stud on alternator. There should be no higher than .6 volts.
   c. If voltage is higher than .6 volts, touch test lead to terminal mounting stud nut and then to wiring connector. If voltage is now below .6 volts, inspect for dirty, loose or poor connection and condition of alternator output wire to battery bullet connector.
7. Test ground circuitry as follows:
   a. Touch positive lead of voltmeter directly to battery ground post.
   b. Touch negative lead of voltmeter to alternator case. Voltage should be no higher than .3 volts.
   c. If voltage is higher than .3 volts,

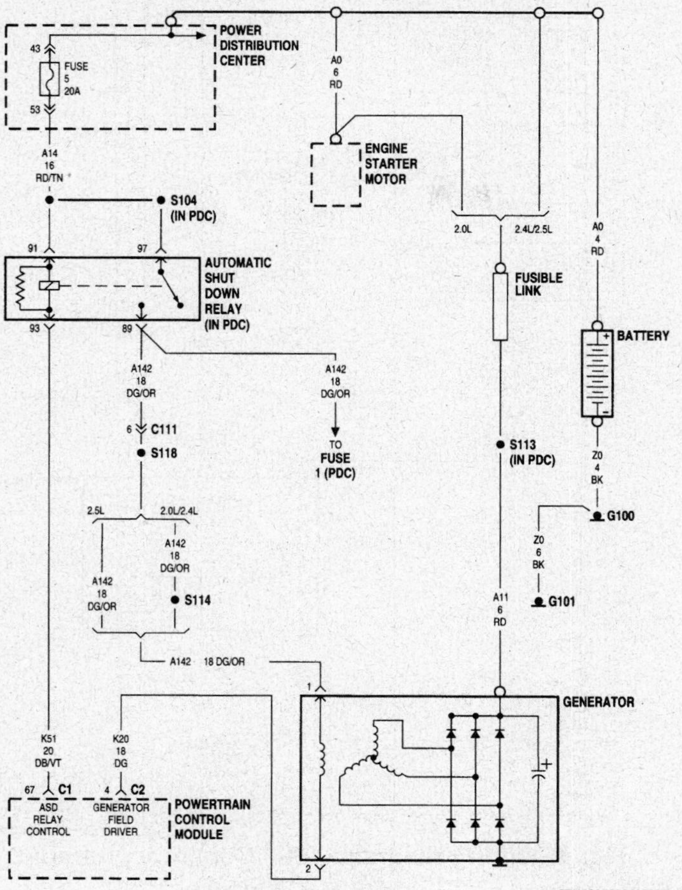

Fig. 1 Wiring diagram. 1997–98 Breeze, Cirrus, Sebring Convertible & Stratus

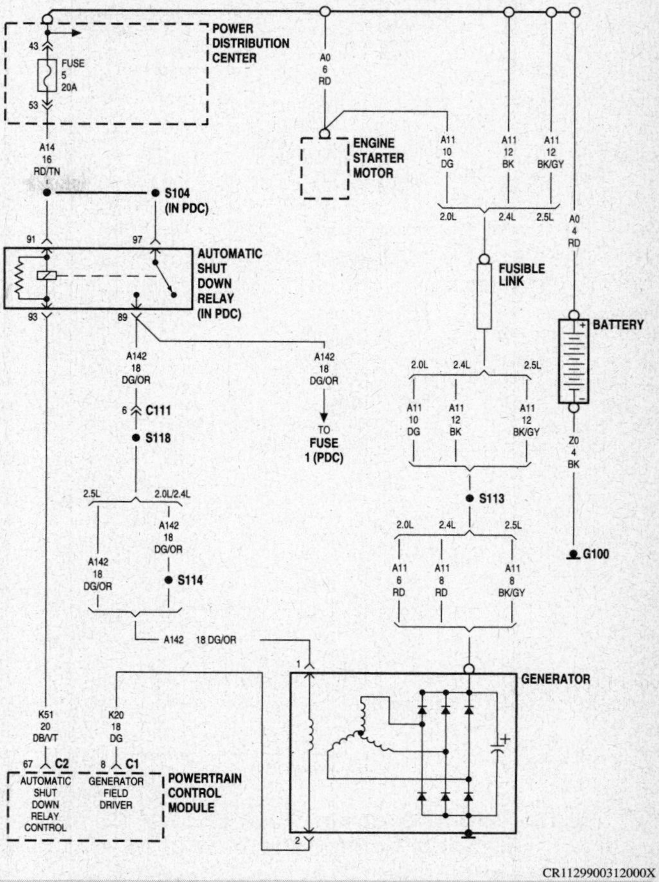

Fig. 2 Wiring diagram. 1999 Breeze, Cirrus, Sebring Convertible & Stratus

touch test lead to alternator case and then to engine block. If voltage is now below .3 volts, inspect for dirty, loose or poor connection.

CURRENT OUTPUT TEST

1997–98

A volt/amp tester equipped with both a battery load control (Carbon pile rheostat) and an inductive type pickup clamp are required for this test.

1. Prepare vehicle for test as follows:
   a. Ensure battery is in good condition and fully charged.
   b. Ensure battery cables are clean.
   c. Ensure alternator drive belt is properly tensioned.
   d. Start engine and allow it to reach normal operating temperature.
   e. Turn off engine, then turn off all electrical accessories and all vehicle lighting.
   f. Fully engage parking brake.
2. Connect volt/amp tester leads to battery post or jump start posts. Ensure carbon pile rheostat control is in Open or Off position before connecting leads.
3. Connect inductive clamp, then a tachometer to engine.
4. Fully apply parking brake.
5. Start engine and bring speed to 2500 RPM.
6. With engine speed held at 2500 RPM, slowly adjust rheostat control on tester to obtain highest amperage reading. **Do not allow voltage to drop below 12 volts. This load test must be performed within 15 seconds to prevent damage to test equipment.**
7. Record reading. If amperage does not meet specification, refer to "Diagnostic Tests" in this section. Refer to "Alternator Specifications" in this section for specifications.
8. Rotate load control to Off position.
9. Continue holding engine speed at 2500 RPM. If electronic voltage regulator circuitry is in good condition, amperage should drop below 15-20 amps.
10. Remove volt amp tester. If amperage does not meet specification, refer to "Diagnostic Tests" in this section.

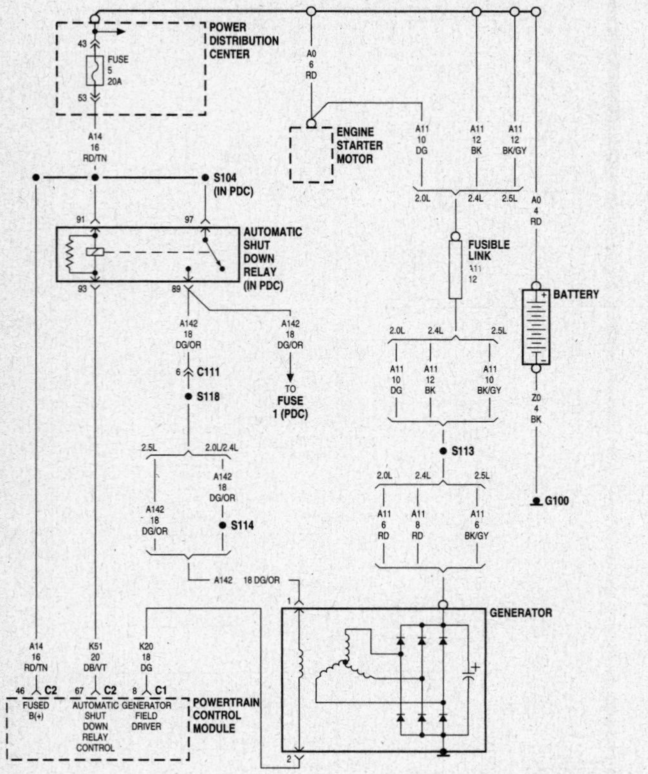

CR1120000313000X

Fig. 3 Wiring diagram. 2000 Breeze, Cirrus, Sebring Convertible & Stratus

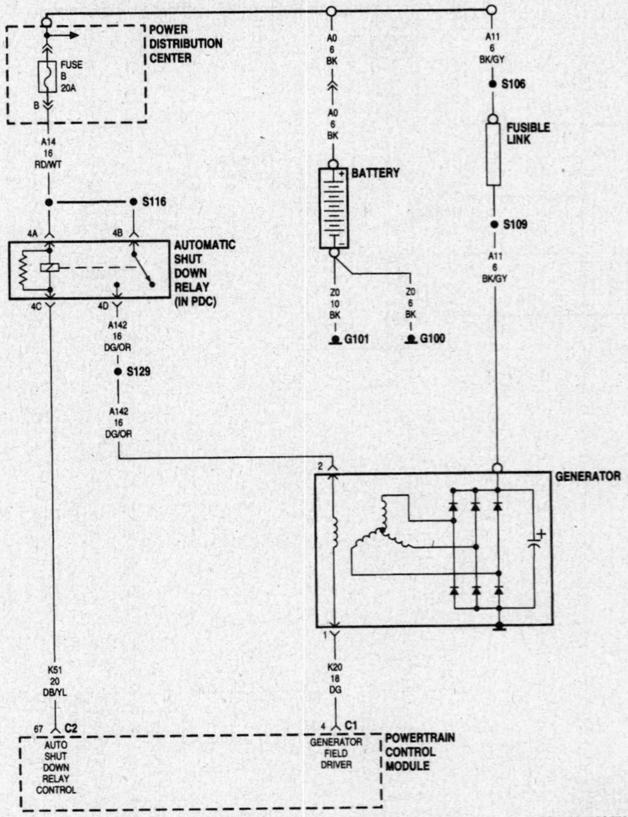

CR1129700257000X

Fig. 4 Wiring diagram. 1997 Concorde, Intrepid, LHS & Vision

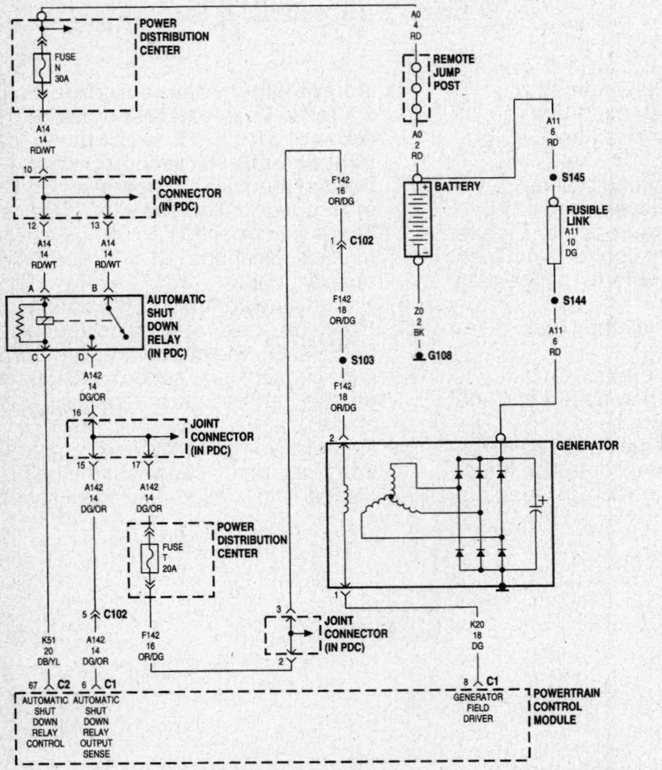

CR1129900258000X

Fig. 5 Wiring diagram. 1998–2000 Concorde, Intrepid, LHS & 300M

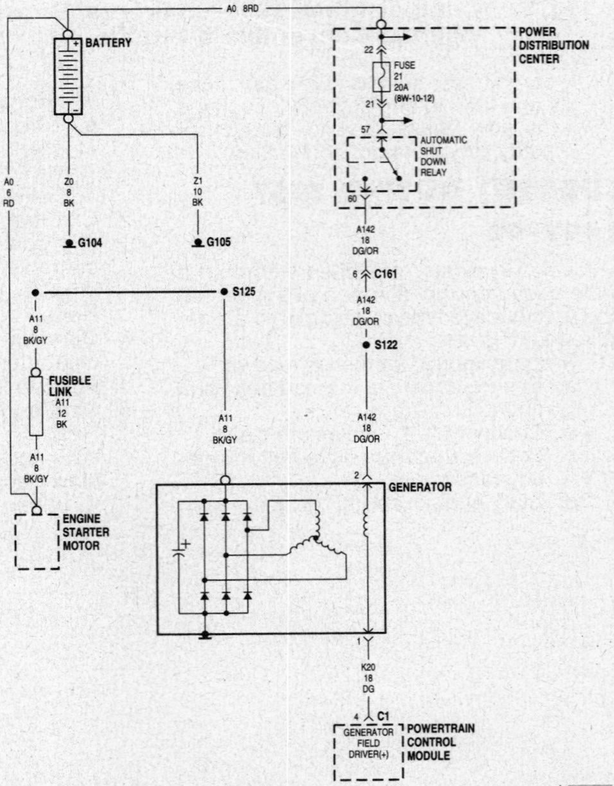

CR1129700260000X

Fig. 6 Wiring diagram. 1997–99 Neon

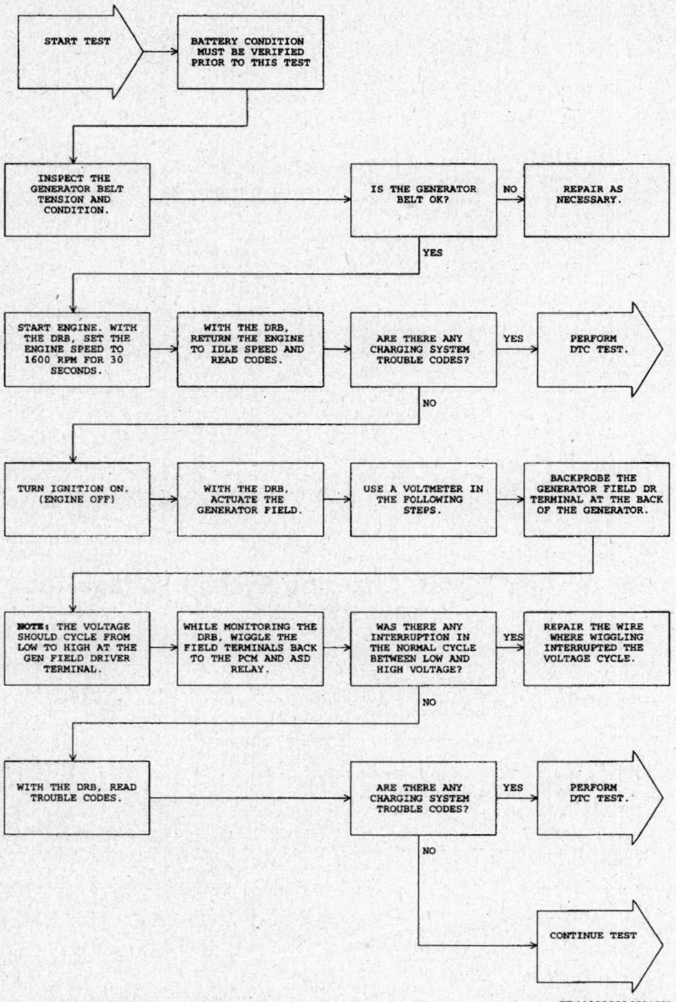

Fig. 7 Test CH-1A: Charging System No Code Test (Part 1 of 3). 1997–98

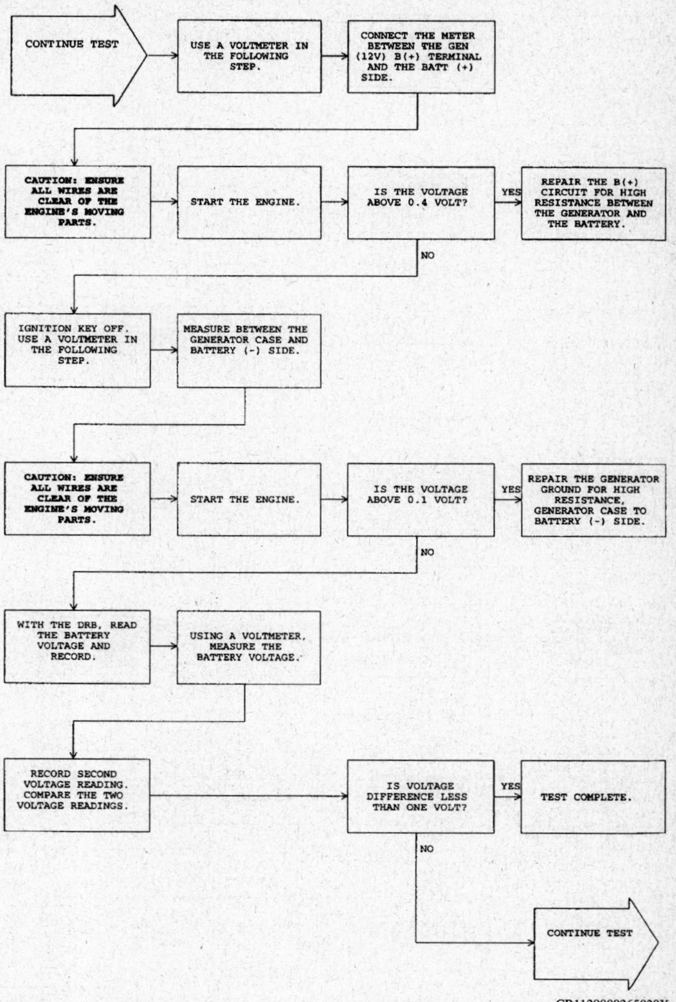

Fig. 7 Test CH-1A: Charging System No Code Test (Part 2 of 3). 1997–98

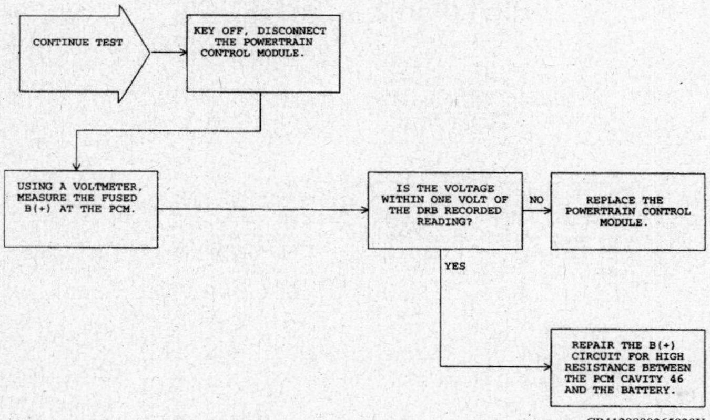

Fig. 7 Test CH-1A: Charging System No Code Test (Part 3 of 3). 1997–98

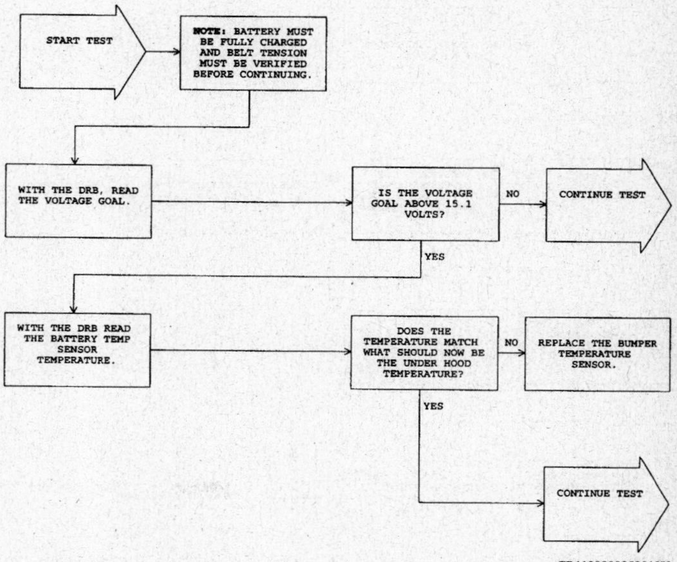

Fig. 8 Test TC-5A: Charging System Voltage Too Low (Part 1 of 2). 1997–98

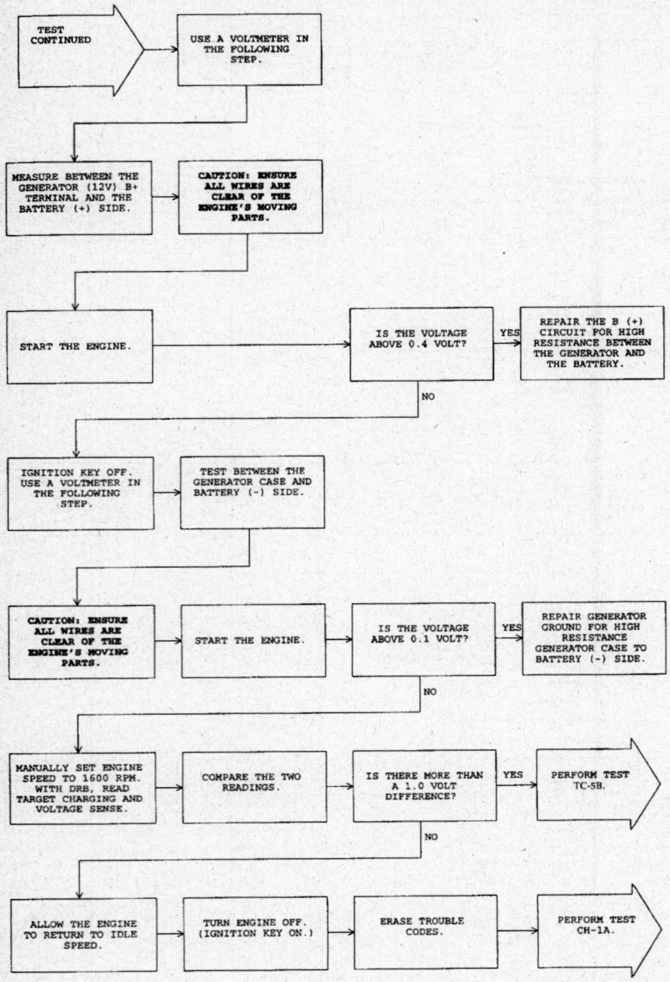

CR1129800252020X

Fig. 8 Test TC-5A: Charging System Voltage Too Low (Part 2 of 2). 1997–98

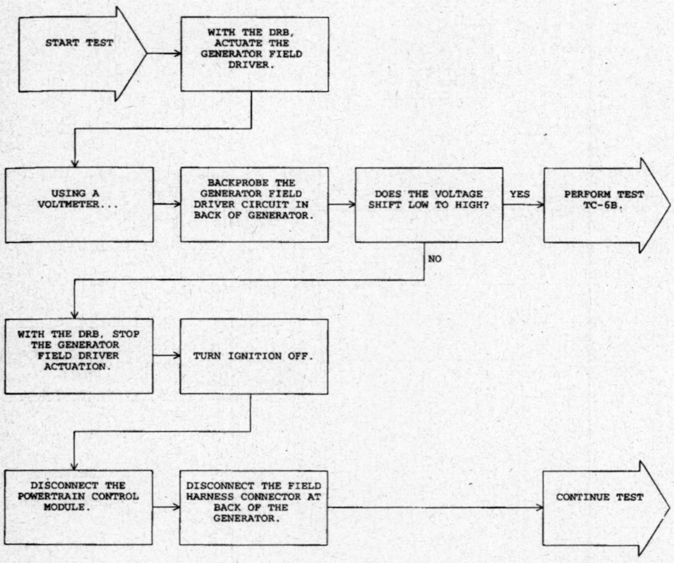

CR1129800254010X

Fig. 10 Test TC-6A: Charging System Voltage Too High (Part 1 of 2). 1997–98

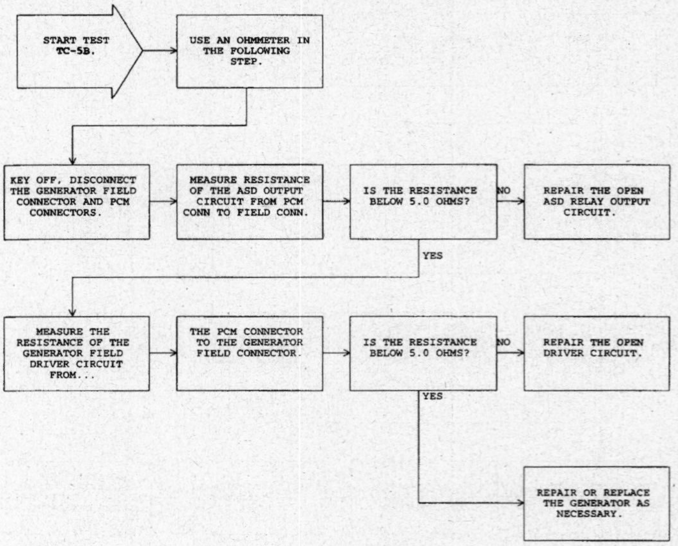

CR1129800253000X

Fig. 9 Test TC-5B: Charging System Voltage Too Low. 1997–98

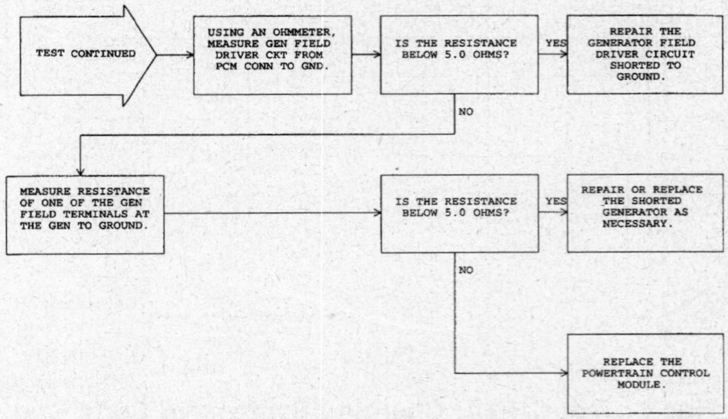

CR1129800254020X

Fig. 10 Test TC-6A: Charging System Voltage Too High (Part 2 of 2). 1997–98

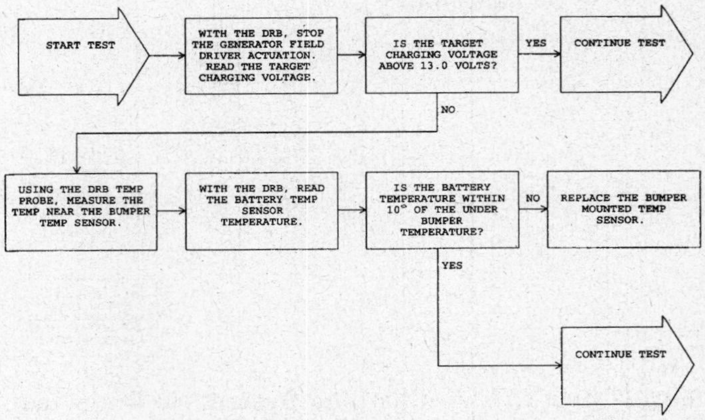

CR1129800255010X

Fig. 11 Test TC-6B: Charging System Voltage Too High (Part 1 of 2). 1997–98

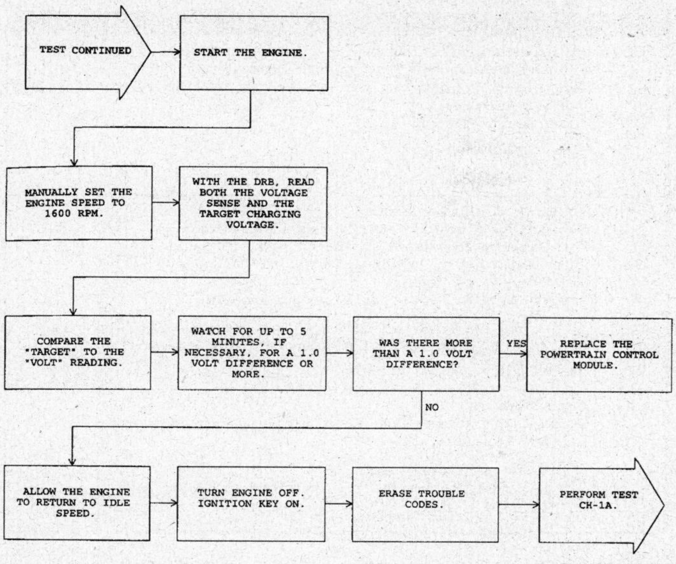

CR1129800255020X

Fig. 11 Test TC-6B: Charging System Voltage Too High (Part 2 of 2). 1997–98

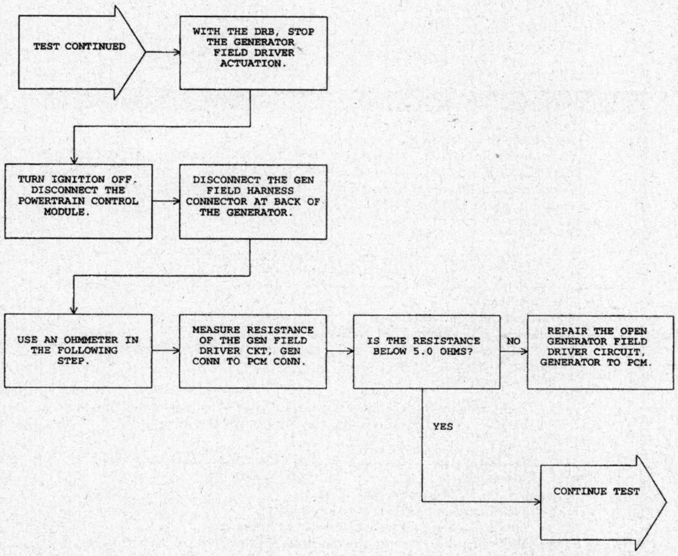

CR1129800256020X

Fig. 12 Test TC-11A: Alternator Field Not Switching Properly (Part 2 of 3). 1997–98

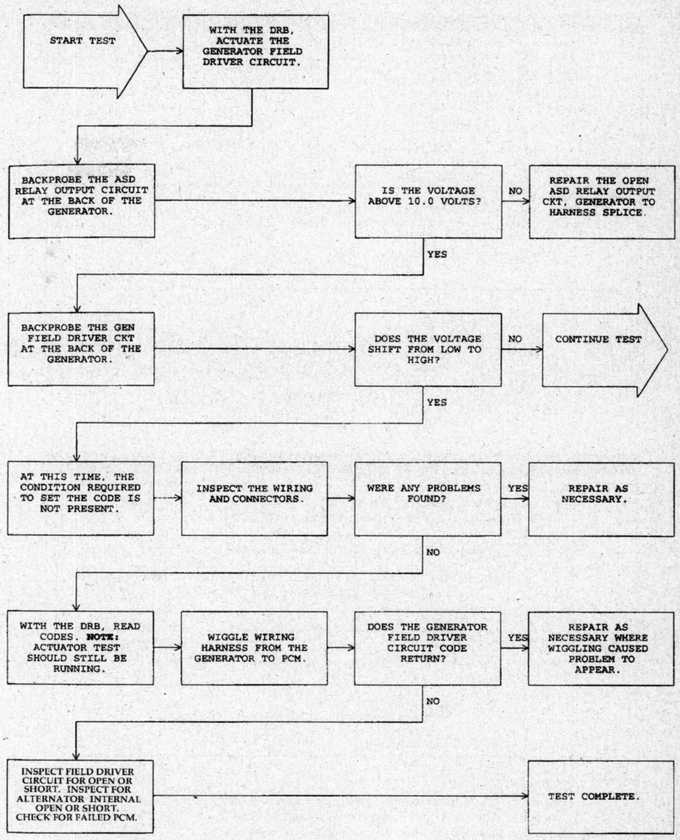

CR1129800256010X

Fig. 12 Test TC-11A: Alternator Field Not Switching Properly (Part 1 of 3). 1997–98

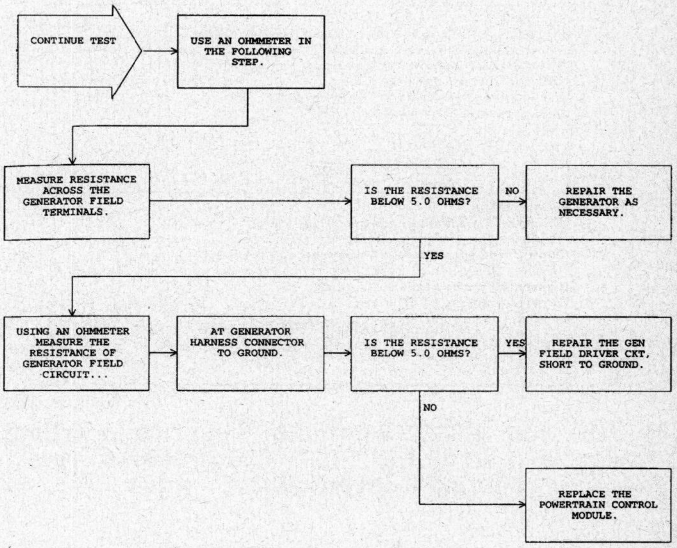

CR1129800256030X

Fig. 12 Test TC-11A: Alternator Field Not Switching Properly (Part 3 of 3). 1997–98

TEST	ACTION	APPLICABILITY
1	Ignition On, Engine Not Running With the DRB, erase trouble codes. With the DRB, actuate the Generator Field Driver Circuit. Backprobe the ASD Relay Output Circuit at the back of the Generator. Record all DTC's and Freeze Frame Data. Is the voltage above 10.0 volts? Yes → Go To 2 No → Repair the open ASD Relay Output Circuit, Generator to Harness splice. Perform Powertrain Verification Test VER-3A.	All
2	Ignition On, Engine Not Running With the DRB, actuate the Generator Field Driver Circuit. Backprobe the Generator Field Driver Circuit at the back of the Generator. Does the voltage shift from low to high? Yes → Go To 3 No → Go To 5	All

CR1120000314010X

Fig. 13 Code P0622: Alternator Field Not Switching Properly (Part 1 of 3). 1999–2000 Breeze, Cirrus, Sebring Convertible & Stratus

TEST	ACTION
3	Ignition On, Engine Not Running Actuate the Generator Field Driver Circuit. Wiggle Wiring Harness from the Generator to the PCM. Read codes. Does the Generator Field Driver circuit code return? Yes → Repair as necessary where wiggling caused problem to appear. Perform Powertrain Verification Test VER-3A. No → Go To 4
4	Ignition Off Using the schematic as a guide, inspect the Wiring and Connectors. Were any problems found? Yes → Repair as necessary. Perform Powertrain Verification Test VER-3A. No → Test Complete.
5	Ignition Off Disconnect the PCM. **Note: Check connectors - Clean/repair as necessary.** Disconnect the Generator Field Harness Connector at the back of the Generator. **Note: Check connectors - Clean/repair as necessary.** Using an Ohmmeter, measure the resistance across the Generator Field Terminals. Is the resistance below 5.0 ohms? Yes → Go To 6 No → Repair the Generator as necessary. Perform Powertrain Verification Test VER-3A.
6	Ignition Off Disconnect the Powertrain Control Module Harness Connector. Disconnect the Generator Field Harness Connector at the back of the Generator. **Note: Check connectors - Clean/repair as necessary.** Using an Ohmmeter, test the resistance of the Generator Field Driver Circuit from the Generator Connector to the PCM Connector. Is the resistance below 5.0 ohms? Yes → Go To 7 No → Repair open Generator Field Driver Circuit, Generator to PCM. Perform Powertrain Verification Test VER-3A.
7	Ignition Off Disconnect the Powertrain Control Module Harness Connector. Disconnect the Generator Field Harness Connector at the back of the Generator. **Note: Check connectors - Clean/repair as necessary.** Using an Ohmmeter, measure the resistance of the Generator Field Circuit at the Generator Harness Connector to ground. Is the resistance below 5.0 ohms? Yes → Repair the Generator Field Driver Circuit short to ground. Perform Powertrain Verification Test VER-3A. No → Go To 8

CR1120000314020X

Fig. 13 Code P0622: Alternator Field Not Switching Properly (Part 2 of 3). 1999–2000 Breeze, Cirrus, Sebring Convertible & Stratus

TEST	ACTION	APPLICABILITY
8	If there are no potential causes remaining, replace the PCM. View repair options. Repair Replace the Powertrain Control Module. Perform Powertrain Verification Test VER-3A.	All

CR1120000314030X

Fig. 13 Code P0622: Alternator Field Not Switching Properly (Part 3 of 3). 1999–2000 Breeze, Cirrus, Sebring Convertible & Stratus

TEST	ACTION
1	Ignition On, Engine Not Running With the DRB actuate the Generator Field Driver Circuit. Using a 12-volt test light, backprobe the Generator Field Driver Circuit at the back of the Generator. Did the light blink? Yes → Go To 2 No → Go To 4
2	Ignition On, Engine Not Running With the DRB actuate the Generator Field Driver Circuit. **Note: Actuator Test should still be running.** Wiggle Wiring Harness from the Generator to PCM. With the DRB, read Codes. Does the Generator Field Driver (-) Circuit code return? Yes → Repair as necessary where wiggling caused problem to appear. Perform the Powertrain Verification Test - Ver 3 No → Go To 3
3	Turn ignition off. Using the schematic as a guide, inspect the Wiring and Connectors. Were any problems found? Yes → Repair as necessary. Perform the Powertrain Verification Test - Ver 3 No → Test Complete.

CR1129900321010X

Fig. 14 Code P0622: Alternator Field Not Switching Properly (Part 1 of 2). 1999–2000 Concorde, Intrepid, LHS & 300M

TEST	ACTION
4	Ignition On, Engine Not Running Record all DTC's and freeze frame data, now erase Codes. Carefully inspect all Connectors for corrosion or spread Terminals before continuing. With the DRB actuate the Generator Field Driver Circuit. Backprobe the ASD Relay Output Circuit at back of Generator. Is the voltage above 10.0 volts? Yes → Go To 5 No → Repair the open ASD Relay Output Circuit. Perform the Powertrain Verification Test - Ver 3
5	Turn ignition off. Disconnect the PCM Connectors. Disconnect the Generator Field harness connector. Using an Ohmmeter, measure the Generator Field Driver Circuit from PCM Connector to ground. Is the resistance below 5.0 ohms? Yes → Repair the Generator Field Driver Circuit shorted to ground. Perform the Powertrain Verification Test - Ver 3 No → Go To 6
6	Turn ignition off. Disconnect the PCM harness connectors. Disconnect the Generator Field harness connector. **Note: Check Connectors - Clean/repair as necessary.** Using an Ohmmeter, measure the Generator Field Driver Circuit from PCM to Generator. Is the resistance below 5.0 ohms? Yes → Go To 7 No → Repair the open Generator Field Driver Circuit. Perform the Powertrain Verification Test - Ver 3
7	Turn ignition off. Disconnect the Generator Field harness connector at back of the Generator. **Note: Check connectors - Clean/repair as necessary.** Use an Ohmmeter in the following steps. Measure resistance across the Generator Field Terminals at the Generator. Is the resistance below 5.0 ohms? Yes → Repair the Generator as necessary. Perform the Powertrain Verification Test - Ver 3 No → Go To 8
8	If there are no possible causes remaining, replace the Powertrain Control Module. View repair options. Repair Replace the Powertrain Control Module. Perform the Powertrain Verification Test - Ver 3

CR1129900321020X

Fig. 14 Code P0622: Alternator Field Not Switching Properly (Part 2 of 2). 1999–2000 Concorde, Intrepid, LHS & 300M

TEST	ACTION
1	The Powertrain Control Module is reporting an internal trouble code and must be replaced. View repair options. Repair Replace the Powertrain Control Module.

CR1129900322000X

Fig. 15 Code P1478: Battery Temperature Sensor Voltage Out Of Limit. 1999–2000 Concorde, Intrepid, LHS & 300M

TEST	ACTION
2	Ignition On, Engine Not Running Disconnect the Battery Temperature Sensor (BTS). **Note: Check connectors - Clean/repair as necessary.** With the DRB, read the BTS voltage. Is the BTS voltage above 4.0 volts? Yes → Replace the BTS. Perform Powertrain Verification Test VER-2A. No → Go To 3
3	Ignition Off Disconnect the Battery Temperature Sensor (BTS). **Note: Check connectors - Clean/repair as necessary.** Disconnect the Powertrain Control Module. **Note: Check connectors - Clean/repair as necessary.** With an Ohmmeter, measure the BTS Sensor Signal Ckt at BTS Conn to ground. Is the resistance below 5.0 ohms? Yes → Repair the Sensor Signal Circuit for a short to ground. Perform Powertrain Verification Test VER-2A. No → Go To 4
4	If there are no potential causes remaining, replace the Powertrain Control Module. View repair options. Repair Replace the Powertrain Control Module. Perform Powertrain Verification Test VER-2A.
5	Ignition On, Engine Not Running With the DRB, read the Battery Temperature Sensor (BTS) voltage. Is the BTS voltage above 4.9 volts? Yes → Go To 6 No → Go To 11
6	Ignition Off Disconnect the BTS Electrical Connector. **Note: Check connectors - Clean/repair as necessary.** Disconnect the PCM Connector. **Note: Check connectors - Clean/repair as necessary.** Using an Ohmmeter, measure the resistance of the Sensor Ground Circuit between the BTS and the Powertrain Control Module. Is the resistance below 5.0 ohms? Yes → Go To 7 No → Repair the open BTS Sensor Ground Circuit. Perform Powertrain Verification Test VER-2A.

CR1120000315020X

Fig. 16 Codes P1492 & P1493: Battery Temperature Sensor Voltage Out Of Range (Part 2 of 4). 1999–2000 Breeze, Cirrus, Sebring Convertible & Stratus

TEST	ACTION
12	Ignition Off Using the schematic as a guide, inspect the Wiring and Connectors. Were any problems found? Yes → Repair as necessary. Perform Powertrain Verification Test VER-2A. No → Test Complete.

CR1120000315040X

Fig. 16 Codes P1492 & P1493: Battery Temperature Sensor Voltage Out Of Range (Part 4 of 4). 1999–2000 Breeze, Cirrus, Sebring Convertible & Stratus

TEST	ACTION
1	Ignition On, Engine Not Running With the DRB, read the Battery Temperature Sensor (BTS) voltage. Is the BTS voltage below 0.4 volt? Yes → Go To 2 No → Go To 5

CR1120000315010X

Fig. 16 Codes P1492 & P1493: Battery Temperature Sensor Voltage Out Of Range (Part 1 of 4). 1999–2000 Breeze, Cirrus, Sebring Convertible & Stratus

TEST	ACTION
7	Ignition On, Engine Not Running Disconnect the Battery Temperature Sensor (BTS). **Note: Check connectors - Clean/repair as necessary.** Connect a jumper wire between the BTS Signal and Sensor Ground at BTS Connectors. With the DRB, read the BTS voltage. Is the voltage below 1.0 volt? Yes → Replace the BTS. Perform Powertrain Verification Test VER-2A. No → Go To 8
8	Ignition Off Disconnect the Battery Temperature Sensor (BTS). **Note: Check connectors - Clean/repair as necessary.** Using a Voltmeter, measure the BTS Signal Circuit voltage. Is the voltage above 5.0 volts? Yes → Repair the BTS Signal Circuit for a short to voltage. Perform Powertrain Verification Test VER-2A. No → Go To 9
9	Ignition Off Disconnect the Battery Temperature Sensor (BTS). **Note: Check connectors - Clean/repair as necessary.** Disconnect the Powertrain Control Module. **Note: Check connectors - Clean/repair as necessary.** Using an Ohmmeter, measure the BTS Signal Circuit from the Sensor Connector to the PCM. Is the resistance below 5.0 ohms? Yes → Go To 10 No → Repair the open BTS Signal Circuit. Perform Powertrain Verification Test VER-2A.
10	If there are no remaining causes known, replace the PCM. View repair options. Repair Replace the PCM. Perform Powertrain Verification Test VER-2A.
11	Ignition On, Engine Not Running With the DRB, read the Battery Temperature Sensor (BTS) voltage. Using the schematic as a guide, wiggle the BTS Connector and Harness. Monitor the DRB display. Was there any BTS voltage change? Yes → Repair the Harness or Connector that caused the voltage change. Perform Powertrain Verification Test VER-2A. No → Go To 12

CR1120000315030X

Fig. 16 Codes P1492 & P1493: Battery Temperature Sensor Voltage Out Of Range (Part 3 of 4). 1999–2000 Breeze, Cirrus, Sebring Convertible & Stratus

TEST	ACTION
1	Turn ignition on. With the DRBIII®, read DTC's. Is the DTC Global Good Trip Counter displayed and equal to zero? Yes → Go To 2 No → Go To 11

CR1129900323010X

Fig. 17 Codes P1492 & P1493: Ambient/Battery Temperature Sensor Voltage Out Of Range (Part 1 of 3). 1999–2000 Concorde, Intrepid, LHS & 300M

TEST	ACTION
2	Disconnect the Ambient Temperature Sensor. Remove the Ambient Temperature Sensor. Using an ohmmeter, measure the resistance of the Ambient Temperature Sensor across the Sensor. Compare the readings with the Ambient Temp Sensor Specifications Do the readings compare with the values listed? Yes → Go To 3 No → Replace the Ambient Temperature Sensor. Perform the Powertrain Verification Test - Ver 5
3	Turn the ignition off. Disconnect the Ambient Temperature Sensor connector. Close all doors , insure all lights are off, then wait one minute. Measure the resistance of the sensor ground circuit to ground. Is the resistance below 30 ohms? No → Go To 4 Yes → Go To 6
4	Turn ignition off. Disconnect the Ambient Temperature Sensor connector. Disconnect the BCM connector. Measure the resistance of the Sensor Ground circuit between the Ambient Temperature Sensor connector and the BCM. Is the resistance below 5.0 ohms? No → Repair the open Sensor Ground circuit. Perform the Powertrain Verification Test - Ver 5 Yes → Go To 5
5	If there are no possible causes remaining, replace the BCM. View repair options. Repair Replace the BCM. Perform the Powertrain Verification Test - Ver 5
6	Turn ignition off. Disconnect the Ambient Temperature Sensor connectors. Disconnect the BCM connectors. Using an Ohmmeter, measure the resistance of the Ambient Temperature Sensor Signal circuit from the Sensor connector to the BCM connector. Is the resistance below 5.0 ohms? No → Repair the open circuit. Perform the Powertrain Verification Test - Ver 5 Yes → Go To 7

CR1129900323020X

Fig. 17 Codes P1492 & P1493: Ambient/Battery Temperature Sensor Voltage Out Of Range (Part 2 of 3). 1999–2000 Concorde, Intrepid, LHS & 300M

TEST	ACTION
7	Turn ignition off. Disconnect the Ambient Temperature Sensor connector. Disconnect the BCM connector. Using an Ohmmeter, measure the resistance between the Sensor Ground circuit and ground at the BCM. Is the resistance below 500K (500,000) ohms? No → Go To 8 Yes → Repair the Sensor Ground circuit for a partial short to ground. Perform the Powertrain Verification Test - Ver 5
8	Turn ignition off. Disconnect the Ambient Temperature Sensor connector. Disconnect the BCM connector. Using an Ohmmeter, measure the Ambient Temperature Sensor Signal circuit to ground. Is the resistance below 50K (50,000) ohms? Yes → Repair the Ambient Temperature Sensor signal circuit for a partial short to ground. Perform the Powertrain Verification Test - Ver 5 No → Go To 9
9	Turn ignition off. Disconnect the Ambient Temperature Sensor connector. Disconnect the BCM connector. Using an Ohmmeter, measure the resistance between the Ambient Temperature Sensor Signal circuit and the Sensor Ground circuit. Is the resistance below 50K (50,000) ohms? Yes → Repair the Ambient Temperature Sensor Signal Circuit for a short to the Sensor Ground Circuit. Perform the Powertrain Verification Test - Ver 5 No → Go To 10
10	If there are no possible causes remaining, replace the BCM. View repair options. Repair Replace the BCM. Perform the Powertrain Verification Test - Ver 5
11	Turn ignition off. **Note: Visually inspect the related wiring harness. Look for any chafed, pierced, pinched, or partially broken wires.** **Note: Visually inspect the related wire harness connectors. Look for broken, bent, pushed out, or corroded terminals.** **Note: Refer to any Technical Service Bulletins (TSB) that may apply.** Were any problems found? Yes → Repair wiring harness/connectors as necessary. Perform the Powertrain Verification Test - Ver 5 No → Test Complete.

CR1129900323030X

Fig. 17 Codes P1492 & P1493: Ambient/Battery Temperature Sensor Voltage Out Of Range (Part 3 of 3). 1999–2000 Concorde, Intrepid, LHS & 300M

TEST	ACTION
1	Ignition On, Engine Not Running. **Note: Battery must be fully charged.** **Note: Generator Belt tension and condition must be checked before continuing.** With the DRB, actuate the Generator Field Driver. Using a voltmeter, backprobe the Generator Field Driver Circuit at the Generator. Does the voltage shift low to high? Yes → Go To 2 No → Go To 5
2	Ignition On, Engine Not Running. **Note: Battery must be fully charged.** **Note: Generator Belt tension and condition must be checked before continuing.** With the DRB, read the target charging voltage. Is the target charging voltage above 13.0 volts? Yes → Go To 4 No → Go To 3
3	Ignition On, Engine Not Running. Using the DRB temperature probe, measure the under hood temperature near PCM. With the DRB, read the Battery Temperature Sensor temperature. Is the battery temperature within 10F of the under hood temperature? Yes → Go To 4 No → Replace the Powertrain Control Module. Perform Powertrain Verification Test VER-3A.

CR1120000316010X

Fig. 18 Code P1594: Charging System Voltage Too High (Part 1 of 2). 1999–2000 Breeze, Cirrus, Sebring Convertible & Stratus

TEST	ACTION
4	Start the engine. Manually set the engine speed to 1600 RPM. With the DRB, read both the voltage and the target charging voltage. Compare the "target" to the "volt" reading. Watch for up to 5 minutes, if necessary, for a 1.0 volt difference or more. Was there more than a 1.0 volt difference? Yes → Replace the PCM. Perform Powertrain Verification Test VER-3A. No → Refer to symptom * CHARGING SYSTEM NO CODE in the CHARGING category.
5	Ignition Off Disconnect the Powertrain Control Module. **Note: Check connectors - Clean/repair as necessary.** Disconnect the Field Harness Connector at back of Generator. **Note: Check connectors - Clean/repair as necessary.** Using an ohmmeter, measure the Generator Field Driver Circuit from PCM Connector to ground. Is the resistance below 5.0 ohms? Yes → Repair the Generator Field Driver Circuit shorted to ground. Perform Powertrain Verification Test VER-3A. No → Go To 6
6	Ignition Off Disconnect the Powertrain Control Module. **Note: Check connectors - Clean/repair as necessary.** Disconnect the Field Harness Connector at back of Generator. **Note: Check connectors - Clean/repair as necessary.** Using an ohmmeter, measure resistance of one of the Gen Field Terminals at the Gen to ground. Is the resistance below 5.0 ohms? Yes → Repair or replace the shorted Generator as necessary. Perform Powertrain Verification Test VER-3A. No → Go To 7
7	If there are no potential causes remaining, replace the PCM. View repair options. Repair Replace the Powertrain Control Module. Perform Powertrain Verification Test VER-3A.

CR1120000316020X

Fig. 18 Code P1594: Charging System Voltage Too High (Part 2 of 2). 1999–2000 Breeze, Cirrus, Sebring Convertible & Stratus

TEST	ACTION
4	Turn ignition off. **Note: Battery must be fully charged.** **Note: Generator Belt tension and condition must be checked before continuing.** Start engine and allow it to reach operating temperature. With the DRB, read the BTS temperature. Using a Thermometer, measure under hood temperature. Is the temperature within 10 F degrees of Battery temperature? Yes → Test Complete. No → Replace Powertrain Control Module. Perform the Powertrain Verification Test - Ver 3
5	Turn ignition off. Disconnect the PCM Connectors. Disconnect the Generator Field harness connector. Using an Ohmmeter, measure the Generator Field Driver Circuit from PCM Connector to ground. Is the resistance below 5.0 ohms? Yes → Repair the Generator Field Driver Circuit shorted to ground. Perform the Powertrain Verification Test - Ver 3 No → Go To 6
6	Turn ignition off. Disconnect the Field Harness Connector at back of the Generator. **Note: Check connectors - Clean/repair as necessary.** Measure resistance of the Generator Field Driver Circuit at the Generator to Ground. Is the resistance below 5.0 ohms? Yes → Repair or replace the shorted Generator as necessary. Perform the Powertrain Verification Test - Ver 3 No → Go To 7
7	If there are no possible causes remaining, replace the Powertrain Control Module. View repair options. Repair Replace the Powertrain Control Module. Perform the Powertrain Verification Test - Ver 3

CR1129900324020X

Fig. 19 Code P1594: Charging System Voltage Too High (Part 2 of 2). 1999–2000 Concorde, Intrepid, LHS & 300M

TEST	ACTION
1	Ignition On, Engine Not Running With DRB, actuate the Generator Field Driver. With a 12-volt test light, backprobe the Generator Field Driver Circuit in back of Generator. Did the light blink? Yes → Go To 2 No → Go To 5
2	Ignition On, Engine Not Running With the DRB, actuate the Generator Field Driver. With DRB, stop the Generator Field Driver actuation. With DRB, read the Target Charging voltage. Is the Target Charging voltage above 13 volts? Yes → Go To 3 No → Go To 4
3	Start the engine. Manually set the engine speed to 1600 RPM. With DRB, read both the Battery voltage and the Target Charging voltage. Compare the "Target Voltage" to the "Battery Voltage" reading. Monitor voltage for 5 minutes, if necessary. Look for a 1.0 volt difference or more. Was there more than a 1.0 volt difference? Yes → Replace the Powertrain Control Module. Perform the Powertrain Verification Test - Ver 3 No → Test Complete.

CR1129900324010X

Fig. 19 Code P1594: Charging System Voltage Too High (Part 1 of 2). 1999–2000 Concorde, Intrepid, LHS & 300M

TEST	ACTION
1	Ignition On, Engine Not Running. **Note: Battery must be fully charged.** With the DRB, read the target charging voltage. Is the voltage goal above 15.1 volts? Yes → Go To 2 No → Go To 6
2	**Note: Battery must be fully charged.** Start the Engine. Manually set Engine Speed to 1600 rpm. With the DRB, read target charging voltage and charging voltage. Compare the two readings. Is there more than a 1.0 volt difference? Yes → Go To 3 No → Refer to CHARGING SYSTEM NO CODE

CR1120000317010X

Fig. 20 Code P1682: Charging System Voltage Too Low (Part 1 of 3). 1999–2000 Breeze, Cirrus, Sebring Convertible & Stratus

TEST	ACTION
3	Ignition Off **Note: Battery must be fully charged.** **Caution: Ensure all Wires are clear of the Engine's moving parts.** Using a Voltmeter, measure between the Generator (12V) B+ Terminal and the Battery (+) side. Start the Engine. Is the voltage above 0.4 volt? Yes → Repair the B (+) Circuit for high resistance between the Generator and Battery. Perform Powertrain Verification Test VER-3A. No → Go To 4
4	Ignition Key Off **Note: Battery must be fully charged.** **Caution: Ensure all Wires are clear of the Engine's moving parts.** With a Voltmeter, measure between the Generator Case and Battery (-) side. Start the Engine. Is the voltage above 0.1 volt? Yes → Repair Generator Ground for high resistance Generator Case to Battery (-) Side. Perform Powertrain Verification Test VER-3A. No → Go To 5
5	**Note: Battery must be fully charged.** Ignition On, Engine Not Running. With the DRB, read the Battery Temperature Sensor (BTS) temperature. Does the temperature match the under hood temperature? Yes → Go To 9 No → Replace the Battery Temperature Sensor. Perform Powertrain Verification Test VER-3A.
6	**Note: Battery must be fully charged.** Start the Engine. With the DRBIII, set Engine Speed to 1600 rpm. With the DRB, read target charging voltage and charging voltage. Compare the two readings. Is there more than a 1.0 volt difference? Yes → Go To 7 No → Refer to CHARGING SYSTEM NO CODE
7	Ignition Off **Note: Battery must be fully charged.** **Caution: Ensure all Wires are clear of the Engine's moving parts.** Using a Voltmeter, measure between the Generator (12V) B+ Terminal and the Battery (+) side. Start the Engine. Is the voltage above 0.4 volt? Yes → Repair the B (+) Circuit for high resistance between the Generator and Battery. Perform Powertrain Verification Test VER-3A. No → Go To 8

CR1120000317020X

Fig. 20 Code P1682: Charging System Voltage Too Low (Part 2 of 3). 1999–2000 Breeze, Cirrus, Sebring Convertible & Stratus

TEST	ACTION
1	Turn Ignition Off. **Note: Battery must be fully charged.** **Note: Generator Belt tension and condition must be checked before continuing.** Start Engine. With the DRB, read the target charging voltage. Is the target charging voltage above 15.1 volts? Yes → Go To 2 No → Go To 3
2	Turn ignition off. **Note: Battery must be fully charged.** **Note: Generator Belt tension and condition must be checked before continuing.** Start engine and allow it to reach operating temperature. With the DRB, read the BTS temperature. Using a Thermometer, measure under hood temperature. Is the temperature within 10 F degrees of Battery temperature? Yes → Go To 3 No → Replace the PCM. Perform the Powertrain Verification Test - Ver 3

CR1129900325010X

Fig. 21 Code P1682: Charging System Voltage Too Low (Part 1 of 3). 1999–2000 Concorde, Intrepid, LHS & 300M

TEST	ACTION
8	Ignition Off **Note: Battery must be fully charged.** **Caution: Ensure all Wires are clear of the Engine's moving parts.** With a Voltmeter, measure between the Generator Case and Battery (-) side. Start the Engine. Is the voltage above 0.1 volt? Yes → Repair Generator Ground for high resistance Generator Case to Battery (-) Side. Perform Powertrain Verification Test VER-3A. No → Go To 9
9	Ignition Off Disconnect the Generator Field Connector. Disconnect the Powertrain Control Module Connectors. **Note: Check connectors - Clean/repair as necessary.** Using an Ohmmeter, measure resistance of the ASD Output Circuit from PCM Connector to Field Connector. Is the resistance below 5.0 ohms? Yes → Go To 10 No → Repair the ASD Relay Output Circuit open. Perform Powertrain Verification Test VER-3A.
10	Ignition Off Disconnect the Generator Field Connector. **Note: Check connectors - Clean/repair as necessary.** Disconnect the Powertrain Control Module Connectors. **Note: Check connectors - Clean/repair as necessary.** Using an Ohmmeter, measure resistance of the Generator Field Driver Circuit from PCM Connector to Generator Field Connector. Is the resistance below 5.0 ohms? Yes → Go To 11 No → Repair the open Driver Circuit. Perform Powertrain Verification Test VER-3A.
11	Turn Ignition off. If there are no potential causes remaining, replace the Generator. View repair options. Repair Replace the Generator. Perform Powertrain Verification Test VER-3A.

CR1120000317030X

Fig. 20 Code P1682: Charging System Voltage Too Low (Part 3 of 3). 1999–2000 Breeze, Cirrus, Sebring Convertible & Stratus

TEST	ACTION
3	Turn ignition on, engine not running. Using a Voltmeter, measure voltage between the Generator B(+) Terminal and the Battery (+) Post. **Caution: Ensure all wires are clear of the engine's moving parts.** Start engine. Is the voltage above 0.4 volt? Yes → Repair the B(+) Circuit for high resistance between the Generator and Battery. Perform the Powertrain Verification Test - Ver 3 No → Go To 4
4	Start engine. Warm the engine to operating temperature. **Caution: Ensure all wires are clear of the engine's moving parts.** Using a Voltmeter, measure voltage between the Generator case and Battery (-) Post. Is the voltage above 0.1 volt? Yes → Repair Generator Ground for high resistance, Generator Case to Battery (-) side. Perform the Powertrain Verification Test - Ver 3 No → Go To 5
5	Start engine. Turn on all accessories, manually set engine speed to 1600 RPM. With DRB, read Target Charging and Charging voltage. Compare the two readings. Is there more than a 1.0 volt difference? Yes → Go To 6 No → Test Complete.
6	Ignition On, Engine Not Running With the DRB, actuate the Generator Field. Using a Voltmeter, measure the voltage at both Generator Field Terminals. Is the voltage below 3.0 volts at either Terminal? Yes → Go To 7 No → Test Complete.
7	Ignition On, Engine Not Running Record all DTC's and freeze frame data, now erase Codes. Carefully inspect all Connectors for corrosion or spread Terminals before continuing. With the DRB actuate the Generator Field Driver Circuit. Backprobe the ASD Relay Output Circuit at back of Generator. Is the voltage above 10.0 volts? Yes → Go To 8 No → Repair the open ASD Relay Output Circuit. Perform the Powertrain Verification Test - Ver 3

CR1129900325020X

Fig. 21 Code P1682: Charging System Voltage Too Low (Part 2 of 3). 1999–2000 Concorde, Intrepid, LHS & 300M

TEST	ACTION
8	Turn ignition off. Disconnect the PCM Connectors. Disconnect the Generator Field harness connector. Using an Ohmmeter, measure the Generator Field Driver Circuit from PCM Connector to ground. Is the resistance below 5.0 ohms? Yes → Repair the Generator Field Driver Circuit shorted to ground. Perform the Powertrain Verification Test - Ver 3 No → Go To 9
9	Turn ignition off. Disconnect ASD Relay Connector. **Note: Check connectors - Clean/repair as necessary.** Disconnect the generator field connector. **Note: Check Connectors - Clean/repair as necessary.** Using an Ohmmeter, measure the ASD Relay Output Circuit from ASD Relay Connector to ground. Is the resistance below 5.0 ohms? Yes → Repair the ASD Relay Output Circuit shorted to ground. Perform the Powertrain Verification Test - Ver 3 No → Go To 10
10	Turn ignition off. Disconnect the PCM harness connectors. Disconnect the Generator Field harness connector. **Note: Check Connectors - Clean/repair as necessary.** Using an Ohmmeter, measure the Generator Field Driver Circuit from PCM to Generator. Is the resistance below 5.0 ohms? Yes → Go To 11 No → Repair the open Generator Field Driver Circuit. Perform the Powertrain Verification Test - Ver 3
11	If there are no possible causes remaining, replace the Powertrain Control Module. View repair options. Repair Replace the Powertrain Control Module. Perform the Powertrain Verification Test - Ver 3

CR1129900325030X

Fig. 21 Code P1682: Charging System Voltage Too Low (Part 3 of 3). 1999–2000 Concorde, Intrepid, LHS & 300M

TEST	ACTION
5	Ignition Off **Caution: Ensure all wires are clear of the engine's moving parts.** Start the engine. Using a Voltmeter, measure the voltage between the Generator Case and Battery (-) side. Is the voltage above 0.1 volt? Yes → Repair Generator Ground High Resistance Generator Case to Battery (-) side. Perform Powertrain Verification Test VER-3A. No → Go To 6
6	Ignition Off Connect voltmeter between the Generator (12V) B+ Terminal and the Batt (+) side. **Caution: Ensure all Wires are clear of the Engine's moving parts.** Start the Engine. Is the voltage above 0.4 volt? Yes → Repair B+ Circuit for high resistance between the Generator and the Battery. Perform Powertrain Verification Test VER-3A. No → Go To 7
7	Ignition On, Engine Not Running With the DRB, read the Battery voltage and record. Using a Voltmeter, measure the Battery voltage B(+) to B(-) Terminal. Record second voltage reading. Compare the two voltage readings. Is the voltage difference less than one volt? Yes → Test Complete. No → Go To 8
8	Ignition On, Engine Not Running With the DRB, read the Battery voltage and record. Key off. Disconnect the Powertrain Control Module. **Note: Check connectors - Clean/repair as necessary.** Using a Voltmeter, measure the Fused B(+) at PCM. Is the voltage within one volt of the DRB recorded reading? Yes → Repair the B+ Circuit for high resistance between the PCM and the Battery. Perform Powertrain Verification Test VER-3A. No → Go To 9
9	Turn Ignition off. If there are no potential causes remaining, replace the PCM. View repair options. Repair Replace the PCM. Perform Powertrain Verification Test VER-3A.

CR1120000318020X

Fig. 22 Charging System Diagnosis w/No Code (Part 2 of 2). 1999–2000 Breeze, Cirrus, Sebring Convertible & Stratus

TEST	ACTION
1	Ignition Off **Note: Battery condition must be verified prior to this test.** Inspect the Generator Belt tension and condition. Is the Generator Belt OK? Yes → Go To 2 No → Repair as necessary.
2	Engine Running With the DRB, set the engine speed to 1600 RPM for 30 seconds. With the DRB, return the engine to idle speed and read codes. Are there any Charging System trouble codes? Yes → Refer to Symptom list for further diagnostic tests. Perform Powertrain Verification Test VER-3A. No → Go To 3
3	Ignition On, Engine Not Running With DRB, actuate the Generator Field. Using a Voltmeter, backprobe the Generator Field DR Terminal at the back of the Generator. **Note: The voltage should cycle from 0 to Battery voltage every 1.4 seconds at both terminals.** While monitoring the DRB, wiggle the field terminals back to the PCM and ASD relay. Was there any interruption in the normal cycle between 0 and Battery voltage? Yes → Repair the Wire where wiggling interrupted the voltage cycle. Perform Powertrain Verification Test VER-3A. No → Go To 4
4	Ignition On, Engine Running With DRB, read trouble codes. Are there any Charging System trouble codes? Yes → Refer to Symptom list for further diagnostic tests. No → Go To 5

CR1120000318010X

Fig. 22 Charging System Diagnosis w/No Code (Part 1 of 2). 1999–2000 Breeze, Cirrus, Sebring Convertible & Stratus

TEST	ACTION
1	Turn ignition off. **Note: Battery condition must be verified prior to this test.** Inspect the Generator Belt tension and condition. Is the Generator Belt OK? Yes → Go To 2 No → Repair as necessary. Perform the Powertrain Verification Test - Ver 3
2	Start the Engine. Turn on all accessories. Raise engine speed to 2000 RPM for 30 seconds then return to idle. With the DRB III read DTC's. Are there any "Charging System" Trouble Codes? Yes → Refer to Symptom list for problems related to Charging. Perform the Powertrain Verification Test - Ver 3 No → Go To 3
3	Ignition On, Engine Not Running With the DRB, actuate the Generator Field. Using a 12-volt test light, backprobe the Generator Field Driver Terminal at the back of the Generator. **Note: The test light should blink On and Off every 1.4 seconds.** While monitoring the 12-volt test light, wiggle the Field Terminals back to the PCM and ASD Relay. Was there any interruption in the normal cycle of the test light? Yes → Repair the wire where wiggling interrupted the voltage cycle. Perform the Powertrain Verification Test - Ver 3 No → Go To 4

CR1129900326010X

Fig. 23 Charging System Diagnosis w/No Code (Part 1 of 3). 1999–2000 Concorde, Intrepid, LHS & 300M

TEST	ACTION
4	Ignition On, Engine Not Running With the DRB, read trouble codes. Are there any "Charging System" trouble codes? Yes → Refer to Symptom list for problems related to Charging. Perform the Powertrain Verification Test - Ver 3 No → Go To 5
5	Turn ignition on, engine not running. Using a Voltmeter, measure voltage between the Generator B(+) Terminal and the Battery (+) Post. **Caution: Ensure all wires are clear of the engine's moving parts.** Start engine. Is the voltage above 0.4 volt? Yes → Repair the B(+) Circuit for high resistance between the Generator and Battery. Perform the Powertrain Verification Test - Ver 3 No → Go To 6
6	Start engine. Warm the engine to operating temperature. **Caution: Ensure all wires are clear of the engine's moving parts.** Using a Voltmeter, measure voltage between the Generator case and Battery (-) Post. Is the voltage above 0.1 volt? Yes → Repair Generator Ground for high resistance, Generator Case to Battery (-) side. Perform the Powertrain Verification Test - Ver 3 No → Go To 7
7	Ignition On, Engine Not Running. With the DRB, read the Battery voltage and record the results. Using a Voltmeter, measure Battery voltage B(+) to B(-) Terminal and record the results. Compare the two voltage readings. Is the voltage difference less than one volt? Yes → Test Complete. No → Go To 8
8	Ignition On, Engine Not Running With the DRB, read the Battery voltage and record the results. Turn Ignition off. Disconnect the PCM. **Note: Check connectors - Clean/repair as necessary.** Turn Ignition on, with the engine off. Using a Voltmeter, measure the Fused B(+) at PCM Connector. Is the voltage within one volt of the DRB recorded reading? Yes → Go To 9 No → Repair the B(+) Circuit for high resistance between the PCM and the Battery. Perform the Powertrain Verification Test - Ver 3

CR1129900326020X

Fig. 23 Charging System Diagnosis w/No Code (Part 2 of 3). 1999–2000 Concorde, Intrepid, LHS & 300M

TEST	ACTION
1	Turn ignition off. **Note: Visually inspect the related wiring harness. Look for any chafed, pierced, pinched, or partially broken wires.** **Note: Visually inspect the related wire harness connectors. Look for broken, bent, pushed out, or corroded terminals.** **Note: Refer to any Technical Service Bulletins (TSB) that may apply.** Were any problems found? Yes → Repair wiring harness/connectors as necessary. Perform the Powertrain Verification Test - Ver 5 No → Go To 2
2	Turn ignition on. With the DRB in sensors, read the "Ambient/Bat Tmp Deg" value and record the reading. Using a temp probe, measure the air temperature near the BTS. Is the recorded BTS temperature value within 10° of the temperature probe reading? Yes → Test Complete. No → Replace the BTS. Perform the Powertrain Verification Test - Ver 5

CR1129900327000X

Fig. 24 Ambient/Battery Temperature Sensor Diagnosis. 1999–2000 Concorde, Intrepid, LHS & 300M

TEST	ACTION
9	If there are no possible causes remaining, replace the Powertrain Control Module. View repair options. Repair Replace the PCM. Perform the Powertrain Verification Test - Ver 3

CR1129900326030X

Fig. 23 Charging System Diagnosis w/No Code (Part 3 of 3). 1999–2000 Concorde, Intrepid, LHS & 300M

VERIFICATION TEST VER-2A
1. Road Test For Non-OBD II **2. Note: If the PCM has been changed and the correct VIN and mileage have not been programmed, a DTC will be set in the ABS and Air Bag modules. In addition, if the vehicle is equipped with a SKIM; Secret Key data must be updated to enable starting.** 3. For ABS and Air Bag Systems: ACTION: Enter correct VIN and mileage in PCM. Erase codes in ABS and Air Bag modules. 4. For SKIM Theft Alarm: ACTION: 5. Connect DRB to data link connector. 6. Go to Theft Alarm, SKIM, misc. and place SKIM in secured access mode, by using appropriate PIN code for vehicle. 7. 3. Select Update Secret Key data. Data will be transferred from SKIM to PCM. 8. Inspect the vehicle to ensure that all engine components are connected. 9. If there are any DTCs that have not been repaired, return to the symptom list and follow the path specified for that symptom. After all DTCs have been repaired, return to the appropriate Verification Test. **10. Note: If this verification procedure is being performed after a NO TROUBLE CODE test, do the following:** 11. Check to see if the initial symptom still exists. 12. If the initial or another symptom exists, the repair is not complete. Check for any Technical Service Bulletins or flash updates and return to the symptom list and restart diagnostic testing for this symptom if necessary. 13. Connect the DRB to the data link connector. 14. Using the DRB, erase any DTCs and reset all values. 15. Road test vehicle, use all accessories that may be related to this repair. 16. Using the DRB, read Global Good Trips. If Global Good Trips is zero, the repair is not complete. Check for any Technical Service Bulletins or flash updates and return to the symptom list and restart diagnostic testing for that symptom. 17. If another trouble code has set, return to the symptom list and restart diagnostic testing and follow the path specified for that symptom. 18. If there are no trouble codes or the Global Good Trip is not zero, the repair was successful and is now complete. Repair is not complete, refer to appropriate symptom.

CR1120000320000X

Fig. 25 Verification Test VER-2A. 1999–2000 Breeze, Cirrus, Sebring Convertible & Stratus

POWERTRAIN VERIFICATION TEST VER - 3
1. Inspect the vehicle to ensure that all engine components are properly installed and connected. Reassemble and reconnect components as necessary. 2. Connect the DRB to the Data Link Connector and erase the codes. 3. If the PCM has been replaced perform steps 4 through 6 then continue the verification. 4. If PCM has been changed and correct VIN and mileage have not been programmed, a DTC will be set in ABS and Air bag modules. In addition, if vehicle is equipped with a Sentry Key Immobilizer Module (SKIM), Secret Key data must be updated to enable start. 5. For ABS and Air Bag systems: Enter correct VIN and Mileage in PCM. Erase codes in ABS and Air Bag modules. 6. For SKIM theft alarm: Connect DRB to data link conn. Go to Theft Alarm, SKIM, Misc. and place SKIM in secured access mode, by using the appropriate PIN code for this vehicle. Select Update the Secret Key data. Data will be transferred from SKIM to PCM. 7. Ensure no other charging system problems remain by doing the following: Start the engine. Perform generator output per service manual. 8. Raise the engine speed to 2000 rpm for at least 30 seconds. 9. Allow the engine to idle. 10. Turn the engine off. 11. Turn the ignition key on. 12. With the DRB, read trouble code messages. 13. If repaired code has reset, or any other one has set, check all pertinent Technical Service Bulletins and return to Symptom List if necessary. 14. If there are no codes, the repair is now complete. Repair is not complete, refer to appropriate symptom.

CR1129900328000X

Fig. 26 Verification Test VER-3. 1999–2000 Concorde, Intrepid, LHS & 300M

VERIFICATION TEST VER-3A

1. Charging Verification
2. Note: If the PCM has been changed and the correct VIN and mileage have not been programmed, a DTC will be set in the ABS and Air Bag modules. In addition, if the vehicle is equipped with a SKIM, Secret Key data must be updated to enable starting.
3. For ABS and Air Bag Systems: ACTION: Enter correct VIN and mileage in PCM. Erase codes in ABS and Air Bag modules.
4. For SKIM Theft Alarm: ACTION:
5. Connect DRB to data link connector.
6. Go to Theft Alarm, SKIM, misc. and place SKIM in secured access mode, by using appropriate PIN code for vehicle.
7. Select Update Secret Key data. Data will be transferred from SKIM to PCM.
8. Inspect the vehicle to ensure that all engine components are connected. Reassemble and reconnect components as necessary.
9. Connect the DRB to the PCM data link connector and erase codes.
10. Note: Ensure no other Charging System problems remain by doing the following:
11. Start the engine.
12. Perform generator output test
13. Raise the engine speed to 2000 RPM for at least 30 seconds.
14. Allow the engine to idle.
15. Turn the engine off.
16. Turn the ignition key on.
17. With the DRB, read trouble code messages.
18. If the repaired code has reset, or any other one has set, check all pertinent Technical Service Bulletins and return to the symptom list and restart diagnostic testing for this symptom if necessary.
19. If there are no codes, the repair is now complete.

Repair is not complete, refer to appropriate symptom.

CR1120000319000X

Fig. 27 Verification Test VER-3A. 1999–2000 Breeze, Cirrus, Sebring Convertible & Stratus

POWERTRAIN VERIFICATION TEST VER - 5

1. Inspect the vehicle to ensure that all engine components are properly installed and connected. Reassemble and reconnect components as necessary.
2. If any existing diagnostic trouble codes have not been repaired, go to Symptom List and follow path specified.
3. Connect the DRBIII® to the data link connector.
4. Ensure the fuel tank has at least a quarter tank of fuel. Turn off all accessories.
5. Perform steps 6 through 8 if the PCM has been replaced. Then proceed with the verification. If the PCM has not been replaced skip those steps and continue verification.
6. If PCM has been changed and correct VIN and mileage have not been programmed, a DTC will be set in ABS and Air bag modules. In addition, if vehicle is equipped with a Sentry Key Immobilizer Module (SKIM), Secret Key data must be updated to enable start.
7. For ABS and Air Bag systems: Enter correct VIN and Mileage in PCM. Erase codes in ABS and Air Bag modules.
8. For SKIM theft alarm: Connect DRB to data link conn. Go to Theft Alarm, SKIM, Misc. and place SKIM in secured access mode, by using the appropriate PIN code for this vehicle. Select Update the Secret Key data. Data will be transferred from SKIM to PCM.
9. If a Comprehensive Component DTC was repaired, perform steps 10-13. If a Major OBDII Monitor DTC was repaired skip those steps and continue verification.
10. After the ignition has been off for at least 10 seconds, restart the vehicle and run 2 minutes.
11. If the Good Trip counter changed to one or more and there are no new DTC's, the repair was successful and is now complete. Erase DTC's and disconnect the DRBIII®.
12. If the repaired DTC has reset, the repair is not complete. Check for any related TSB's or flash updates and return to the Symptom list.
13. If another DTC has set, return to the Symptom List and follow the path specified for that DTC.
14. With the DRBIII®, monitor the appropriate pre-test enabling conditions until all conditions have been met. Once the conditions have been met, switch screen to the appropriate OBDII monitor, (Audible beeps when the monitor is running).
15. If the monitor ran, and the Good Trip counter changed to one or more, the repair was successful and is now complete. Erase DTC's and disconnect the DRBIII®.
16. If the repaired OBDII trouble code has reset or was seen in the monitor while on the road test, the repair is not complete. Check for any related technical service bulletins or flash updates and return to Symptom List.
17. If another DTC has set, return to the Symptom List and follow the path specified for that DTC.

Repair is not complete, refer to appropriate symptom.

CR1129900329000X

Fig. 28 Verification Test VER-5. 1999–2000 Concorde, Intrepid, LHS & 300M

ALTERNATOR SPECIFICATIONS

Model & Year	Engine	Type	Rated Output Amps
1997			
Breeze, Cirrus, Sebring Convertible & Stratus	2.0L & 2.4L	Nippondenso	74
Cirrus, Sebring Convertible & Stratus	2.5L	Melco	74
Concorde, Intrepid, LHS & Vision	All	Nippondenso	90
Neon	All	Melco	75
1998			
Breeze, Cirrus & Stratus	2.0L & 2.4L	Nippondenso	74
Cirrus & Stratus	2.5L	Melco	74
Concorde & Intrepid	2.7L	Nippondenso	105
	3.2L & 3.5L	Melco	110
Neon	All	Melco	75
Sebring Convertible	All	Nippondenso	74
1999			
Breeze, Cirrus & Stratus	2.0L & 2.4L	Nippondenso	74
Cirrus & Stratus	2.5L	Melco	74
Concorde, Intrepid, LHS & 300M	2.7L	Nippondenso	105
	3.2L & 3.5L	Melco	110
Neon	All	Melco	75
Sebring Convertible	All	Nippondenso	74
2000			
Breeze, Cirrus & Stratus	2.0L & 2.4L	Nippondenso	74
Cirrus & Stratus	2.5L	Melco	74
Concorde, Intrepid, LHS & 300M	2.7L	Nippondenso	105
	3.2L & 3.5L	Melco	110
Sebring Convertible	All	Nippondenso	74

Mitsubishi

NOTE: "Electrical Symbol & Wire Color Code Identification" Located In The Front Of This Manual May Be Used As An Aid When Using Wiring Circuits Found In This Section.

INDEX

APPLICATION CHART

Model	Part No.
1997–98	
Avenger & Sebring Coupe	①
Talon	②
1999–2000	
Avenger & Sebring Coupe	①
2000	
Neon	③

① — 2.0L engine, M04661998; 2.5L engine, M04609075.
② — Less turbocharged engine, M04661998; turbocharged engine, MD327513.
③ — 4794222AA.

PRECAUTIONS

BATTERY GROUND CABLE

Prior to service, disconnect battery ground cable and isolate as required.

GENERAL INFORMATION

The power source of the charging system is the alternator. Current is transmitted from the field terminal of the regulator through a slip ring to the field coil and back to ground through another slip ring. The strength of the field regulates the output of the alternating current. This alternating current is then transmitted from the alternator to the rectifier where it is converted to direct current.

These alternators employ a three-phase stator winding in which the phase windings are electrically 120° apart. The rotor consists of a field coil encased between interleaved sections producing a magnetic field with alternate north and south poles. By rotating the rotor inside the stator the alternating current is induced in the stator windings. This alternating current is rectified (changed to D.C.) by silicon diodes and brought out to the output terminal of the alternator.

DIODE RECTIFIERS

Six or more silicon diode rectifiers are used and act as electrical one-way valves. One half of the diodes have ground polarity and are pressed or screwed into a heat sink which is grounded. The other diodes (ungrounded) are pressed or screwed into and insulated from the end head. These diodes are connected to the alternator output terminal.

Since the diodes have a high resistance to the flow of current in one direction and a low resistance in the opposite direction, they may be connected in a manner which allows current to flow from the alternator to the battery in the low resistance direction. The high resistance in the opposite direction prevents the flow of current from the battery to the alternator. Because of this feature no circuit breaker is required between the alternator and battery.

SERVICE PRECAUTIONS

1. Ensure battery polarity is proper when servicing units. Reversed battery polarity will damage rectifiers and regulators.
2. If booster battery is used for starting, use proper polarity in hookup.
3. When a fast charger is used to charge a vehicle battery, vehicle battery cables should be disconnected unless fast charger is equipped with a special alternator protector, in which case vehicle battery cables need not be disconnected. Also, fast chargers should never be used to start a vehicle, as damage to rectifiers will result.
4. Lead connections to grounded rectifiers (negative) should never be soldered, as excessive heat may damage rectifiers.
5. Unless system includes a load relay or field relay, grounding alternator output terminal will damage alternator and/or circuits. This is true even when system is not in operation, since no circuit breaker is used and battery is applied to alternator output terminal at all times. Field or load relay acts as a circuit breaker in that it is controlled by ignition switch.
6. Before making any in-vehicle tests of alternator or regulator, battery should be inspected and circuit inspected for faulty wiring or insulation, loose or corroded connections and poor ground circuits.
7. Inspect alternator belt tension to ensure belt is tight enough to prevent slipping under load.
8. To prevent system damage, turn ignition Off before making any test connections.
9. The vehicle battery must be fully charged or a fully charged battery may be installed for test purposes.

DESCRIPTION

On these units, the regulator is incorporated into the alternator rear housing. The electronic voltage regulator has the ability to vary regulated system voltage upward or downward as temperature changes. No voltage regulator adjustments are required on these units.

DIAGNOSIS & TESTING

WIRING DIAGRAMS

Refer to **Figs. 1 through 4** for wiring diagrams when diagnosing the charging system.

ALTERNATOR OUTPUT WIRE VOLTAGE DROP TEST

Avenger, Sebring Coupe & Talon

1. Disconnect alternator output lead from alternator B terminal, **Figs. 5 and 6,** then connect a DC ammeter between terminal B and disconnected output lead, noting the following:
   a. Connect positive lead of ammeter to B terminal.
   b. Connect negative lead to disconnected output wire.
2. Connect a digital voltmeter between alternator B terminal and battery positive terminal, noting the following:
   a. Connect positive lead wire of voltmeter to B terminal.
   b. Connect negative lead wire to positive battery terminal.
3. Connect battery ground cable and leave hood open.

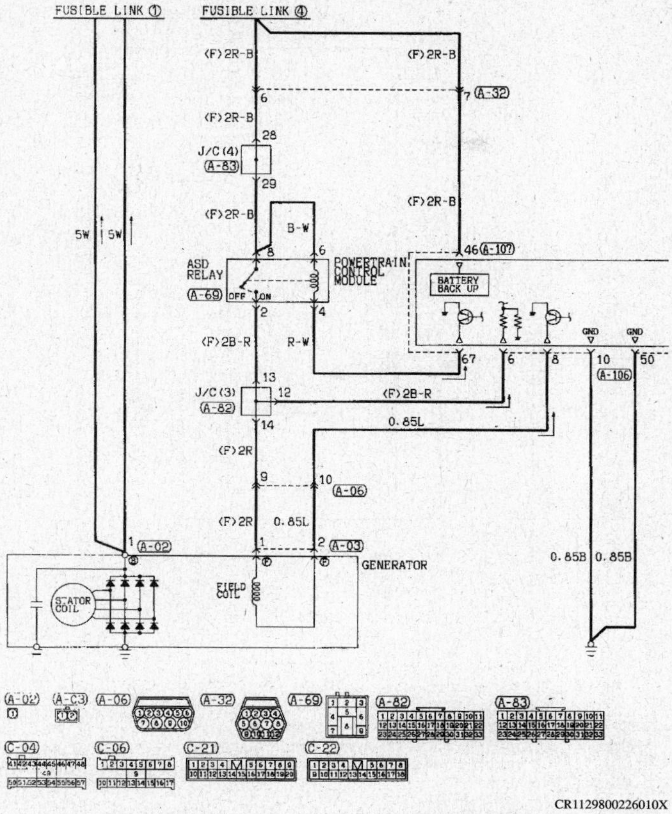

Fig. 1 Wiring diagram (Part 1 of 2). Talon less turbocharged engine & Avenger & Sebring Coupe w/2.0L engine

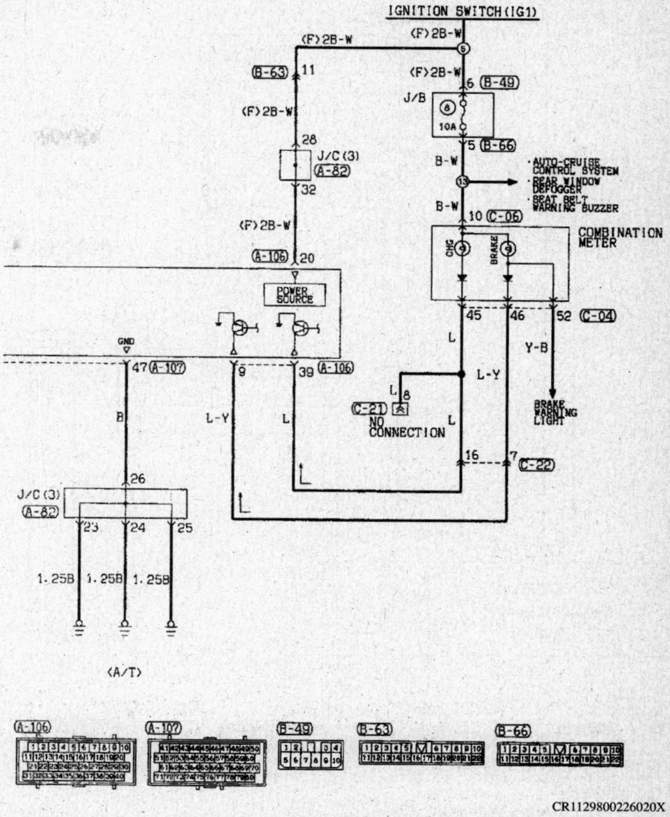

Fig. 1 Wiring diagram (Part 2 of 2). Talon less turbocharged engine & Avenger & Sebring Coupe w/2.0L engine

4. With engine running at approximately 2500 RPM, turn headlamps and other lamps on and off to adjust alternator load on ammeter to slightly above 30 amps.
5. Decrease engine speed gradually until value displayed on ammeter is 30 amps, then take a reading on voltmeter, noting the following:
   a. **On Talon less turbocharged engine, Avenger and Sebring Coupe,** limit value should be .5 volts maximum.
   b. **On Talon with turbocharged engine,** limit value should be .3 volts maximum.
6. **On all models,** if alternator output is high and value does not decrease to 30 amps, set value at 40 amps and take a voltmeter reading, noting the following:
   a. Limit value should be .7 volts maximum.
   b. If value is still above limit value, a malfunction in alternator output wire may exist.
   c. Inspect wiring between alternator B terminal and battery positive terminal, including fusible link.
   d. If a terminal is not sufficiently tight or if harness has become discolored due to overheating, repair and test again.
7. Run engine at idle.
8. Turn all lamps and ignition Off.
9. Disconnect battery ground cable, then the ammeter and voltmeter.
10. Connect alternator output wire to alternator B terminal.

CURRENT OUTPUT TEST

Avenger, Sebring Coupe & Talon

1. Turn ignition Off, then disconnect battery cables.
2. Disconnect wire from terminal B of alternator, **Figs. 7 and 8,** then connect an ammeter between B terminal and disconnected output wire, noting the following:
   a. Connect positive lead of ammeter to B terminal.
   b. Connect negative lead of ammeter to disconnected output wire.
3. Connect a voltmeter between alternator and ground, noting the following:
   a. Connect positive lead of voltmeter to B terminal.
   b. Connect negative lead of voltmeter to ground.
4. Connect battery ground cable. Leave hood open.
5. Ensure voltmeter reading is equal to battery voltage. If voltage is 0 volts, the cause is probably an open circuit in wire or fusible link between alternator B terminal and battery positive terminal.
6. Start engine and turn headlamps on.
7. Switch headlamps to high beam, turn heater blower switch to High, increase engine speed to approximately 2500 RPM and read maximum current output. Limit should be 70% of rated output.
8. Reading should be above limit value. If reading is below limit value and alternator output wire is in good condition, replace alternator.
9. Run engine at idle speed.
10. Turn ignition Off.
11. Disconnect battery ground cable, then the ammeter and voltmeter.
12. Connect alternator output wire to generator B terminal.
13. Connect battery ground terminal.

VOLTAGE REGULATOR TEST

Talon Less Turbocharged Engine & Avenger & Sebring Coupe

1. Turn ignition Off, then connect a digital voltmeter as shown in **Fig. 9,** noting the following:
   a. Connect positive lead of voltmeter to battery positive terminal.
   b. Connect negative lead of voltmeter to a secure ground or battery ground terminal.
2. Disconnect alternator output wire from alternator B terminal, then connect a DC ammeter in series between B terminal and output wire, noting the following:
   a. Connect positive lead of ammeter

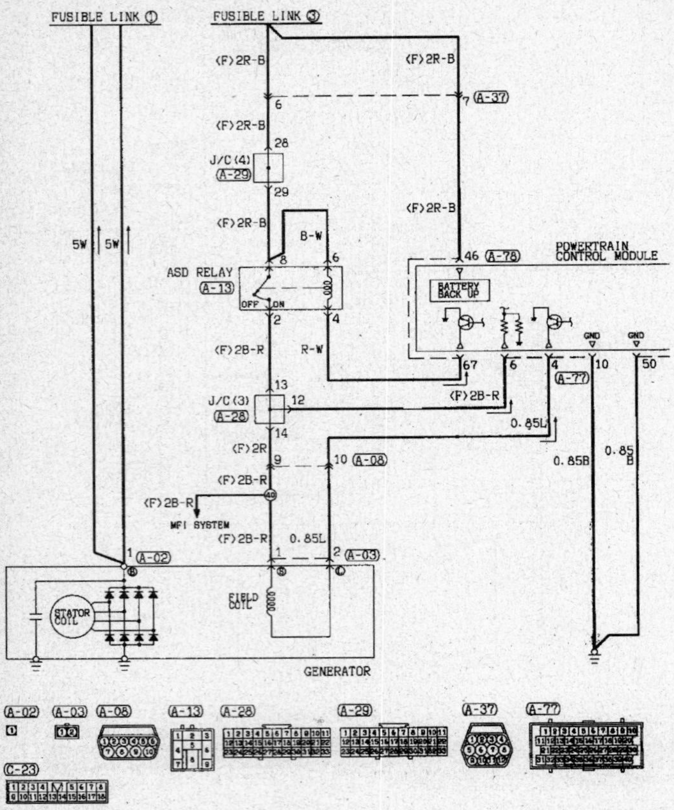

CR1129700225010X

Fig. 2 Wiring diagram (Part 1 of 2). Avenger & Sebring Coupe w/2.5L engine

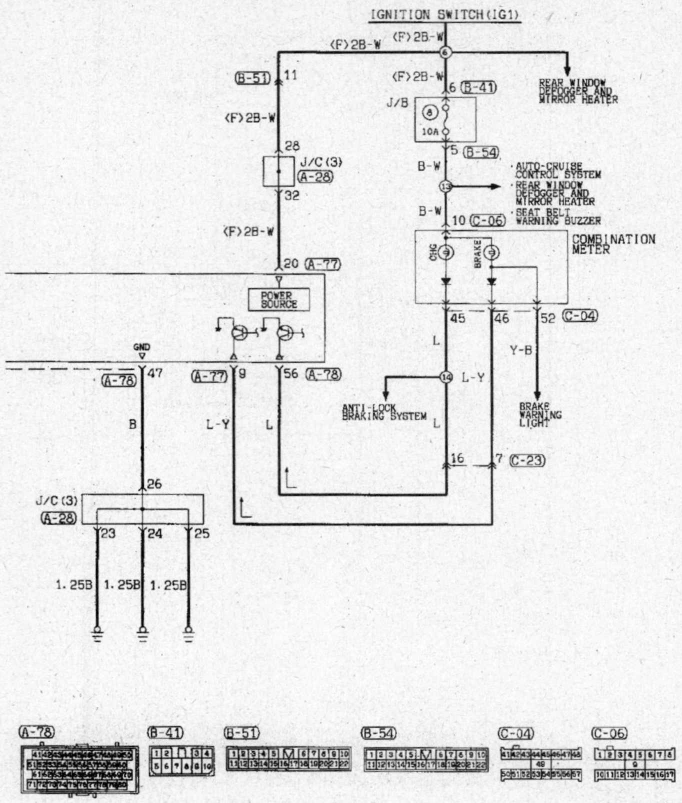

CR1129700225020X

Fig. 2 Wiring diagram (Part 2 of 2). Avenger & Sebring Coupe w/2.5L engine

to B terminal.
  b. Connect negative lead to output wire.
3. Connect battery ground cable, then ensure all lamps and accessories are off.
4. Connect a tachometer and start engine.
5. Increase engine speed to approximately 2500 RPM.
6. Read voltmeter when current output by alternator becomes 10 amps or less, noting the following:
   a. If voltage reading is as specified in **Fig. 10,** voltage regulator is operating properly.
   b. If voltage is not within specification, a voltage regulator or alternator malfunction exists.
7. Lower engine speed to idle speed.
8. Turn ignition Off.
9. Disconnect battery ground cable, then the ammeter, voltmeter and tachometer.
10. Connect alternator output wire to B terminal.

Talon w/Turbocharged Engine

1. Turn ignition Off.
2. Connect a digital voltmeter between alternator S terminal and ground, **Fig. 11,** noting the following:
   a. Connect positive lead of voltmeter to S terminal.
   b. Connect negative lead of voltmeter to a secure ground or to battery ground terminal.
3. Disconnect alternator output wire from alternator B terminal.
4. Connect a DC ammeter in series between B terminal and disconnected output wire, noting the following:
   a. Connect positive lead of ammeter to B terminal.
   b. Connect negative lead of ammeter to disconnect output wire.
5. Connect a tachometer to engine.
6. Connect battery ground terminal.
7. Turn ignition On.
8. Ensure reading on voltmeter is equal to battery voltage. If there is 0 volts, the cause is probably an open circuit in wire or fusible link between alternator S terminal and battery positive terminal.
9. Ensure all lamps and accessories are off.
10. Start engine and increase engine speed to approximately 2500 RPM.
11. Read voltmeter when current output by alternator becomes 10 amps or less, noting the following:
    a. If voltage is as specified in **Fig. 12,** voltage regulator is operating properly.
    b. If voltage is not as specified, a voltage regulator or alternator malfunction exists.

DIAGNOSTIC TESTS

2000 Neon

Refer to **Figs. 13 through 17** for diagnostic tests.

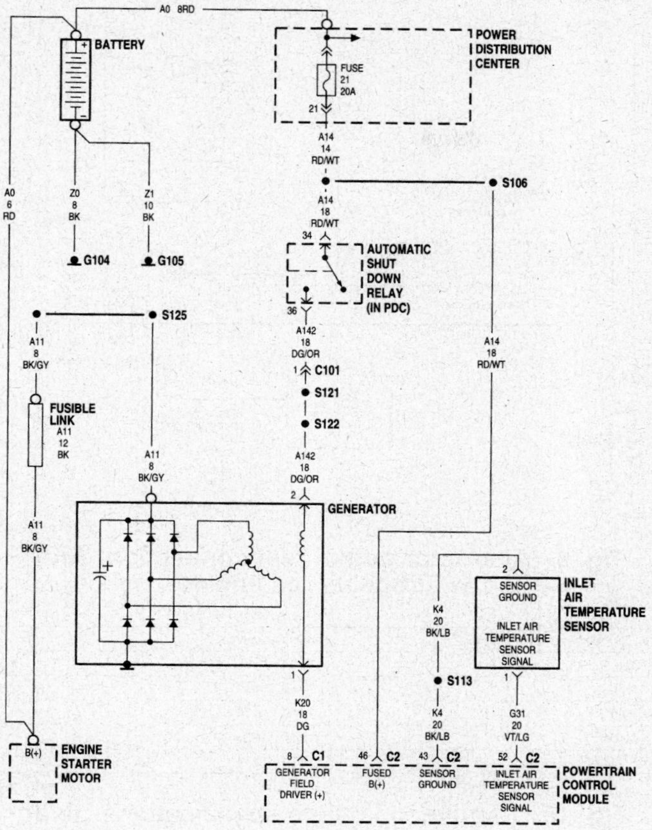

CR1120000330000X

Fig. 3 Wiring diagram. 2000 Neon

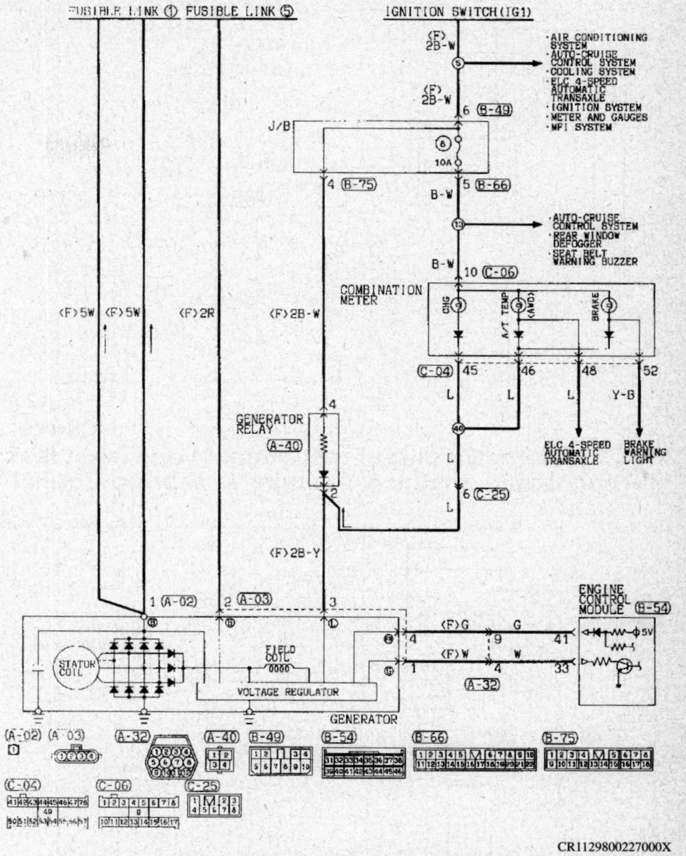

CR1129800227000X

Fig. 4 Wiring diagram. Talon w/turbocharged engine

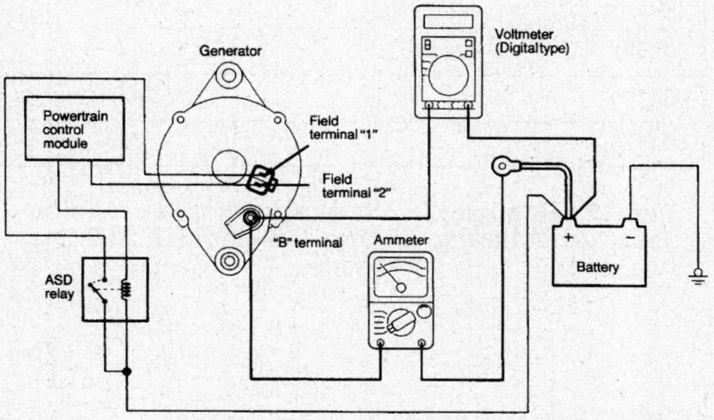

CR1129100122000A

Fig. 5 Alternator output wire voltage drop test connection. Talon less turbocharged engine & Avenger & Sebring Coupe

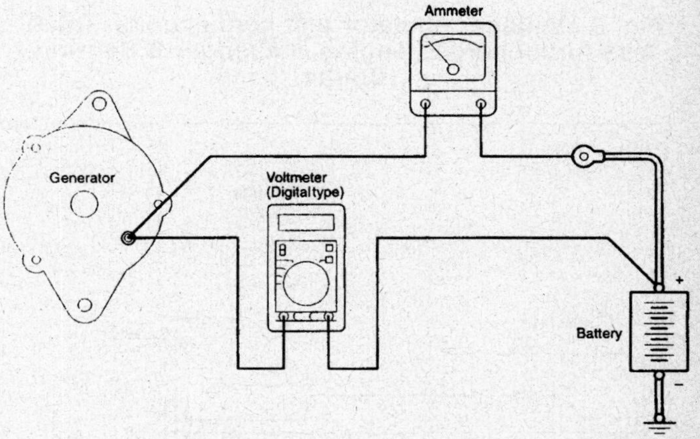

CR1129800261000X

Fig. 6 Alternator output wire voltage drop test connection. Talon w/turbocharged engine

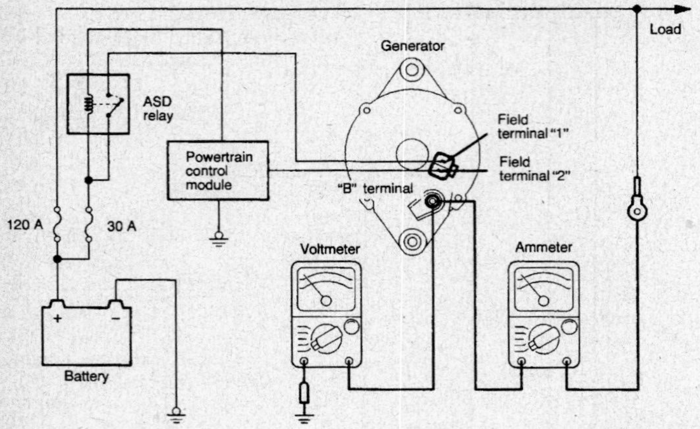

CR1129100123000A

Fig. 7 Alternator output test connection. Talon less turbocharged engine & Avenger & Sebring Coupe

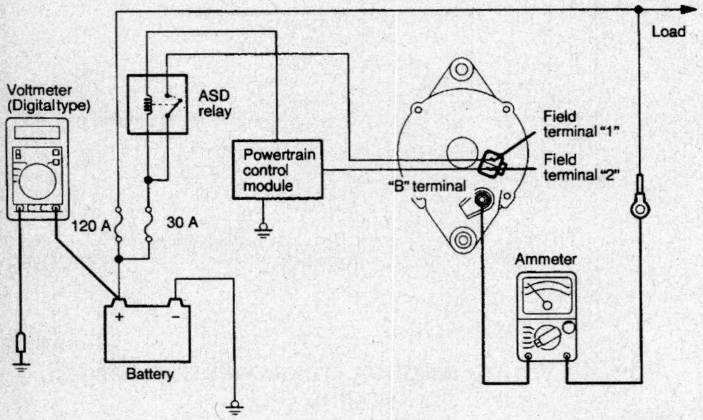

CR1129100124000A

Fig. 9 Voltage regulator test connections. Talon less turbocharged engine & Avenger & Sebring Coupe

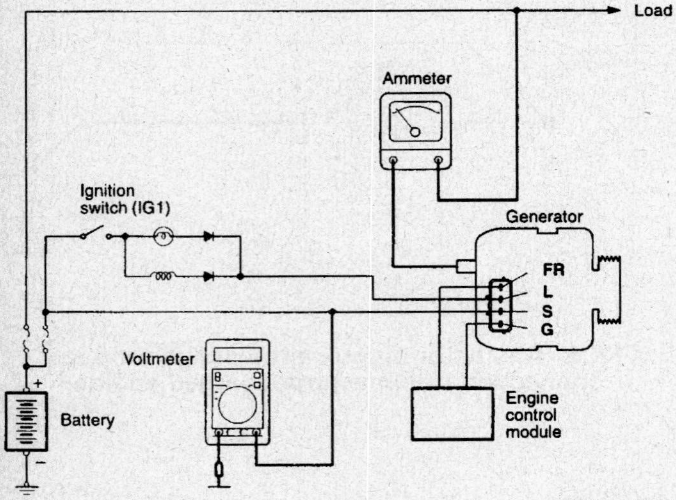

CR1129800263000X

Fig. 11 Voltage regulator test connections. Talon w/turbocharged engine

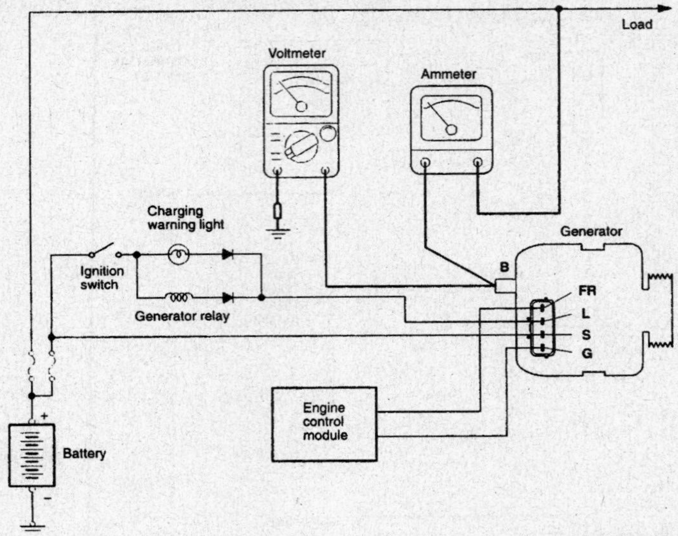

CR1129800262000X

Fig. 8 Alternator output test connection. Talon w/turbocharged engine

Battery ambient temperature °C (°F)	Standard value V
–20 (–4)	14.07 – 15.07
0 (32)	13.89 – 14.89
20 (68)	13.58 – 14.58
40 (104)	13.15 – 14.15
62 (143.6)	12.84 – 13.84

CR1129900261000X

Fig. 10 Regulated voltage specifications. Talon less turbocharged engine & Avenger & Sebring Coupe

Battery ambient temperature °C (°F)	Standard value V
–20 (–4)	14.2–15.4
20 (68)	13.9–14.9
60 (140)	13.4–14.6
80 (176)	13.1–14.5

CR1129800264000X

Fig. 12 Regulated voltage specifications. Talon less turbocharged engine & Avenger & Sebring Coupe

TEST	ACTION
1	Ignition On, Engine Not Running With the DRB actuate the Generator Field Driver Circuit. Using a 12-volt test light, backprobe the Gen Field Driver Circuit at the back of the Generator. Did the light blink? Yes → Go To 2 No → Go To 4
2	Ignition On, Engine Not Running With the DRB actuate the Generator Field Driver Circuit. **Note: Actuator Test should still be running.** Wiggle Wiring Harness from the Generator to PCM. With the DRB, read Codes. Does the Generator Field Driver (-) Circuit code return? Yes → Repair as necessary where wiggling caused problem to appear. Perform Powertrain Verification Test VER-3A. No → Go To 3
3	Turn ignition off. Using the schematic as a guide, inspect the Wiring and Connectors. Were any problems found? Yes → Repair as necessary. Perform Powertrain Verification Test VER-3A. No → Test Complete.
4	Ignition On, Engine Not Running Record all DTC's and freeze frame data, now erase Codes. Carefully inspect all Connectors for corrosion or spread Terminals before continuing. With the DRB actuate the Generator Field Driver Circuit. Backprobe the ASD Relay Output Circuit at back of Generator. Is the voltage above 10.0 volts? Yes → Go To 5 No → Repair the open ASD Relay Output Circuit. Perform Powertrain Verification Test VER-3A.
5	Turn ignition off. Disconnect the PCM Connectors. **Note: Check connectors - Clean/repair as necessary.** Disconnect the generator field connector. **Note: Check Connectors - Clean/repair as necessary.** Using an Ohmmeter, measure the Generator Field Driver Circuit from PCM Connector to ground. Is the resistance below 5.0 ohms? Yes → Repair the Generator Field Driver Circuit shorted to ground. Perform Powertrain Verification Test VER-3A. No → Go To 6

CR1120000331010X

Fig. 13 Code P0622: Alternator Field Not Switching Properly (Part 1 of 2). 2000 Neon

TEST	ACTION
6	Turn ignition off. Disconnect the PCM Connectors. Disconnect the generator field connector. **Note: Check Connectors - Clean/repair as necessary.** Using an Ohmmeter, measure the Generator Field Driver Circuit from PCM to Generator. Is the resistance below 5.0 ohms? Yes → Go To 7 No → Repair the open Generator Field Driver Circuit. Perform Powertrain Verification Test VER-3A.
7	Turn ignition off. Disconnect the Gen Field Harness Connector at back of the Generator. **Note: Check connectors - Clean/repair as necessary.** Use an Ohmmeter in the following steps. Measure resistance across the Generator Field Terminals at the Generator. Is the resistance below 5.0 ohms? Yes → Repair the Generator as necessary. Perform Powertrain Verification Test VER-3A. No → Go To 8
8	If there are no potential causes remaining, the PCM is assumed to be defective. View repair options. Repair Replace the Powertrain Control Module. Perform Powertrain Verification Test VER-3A.

CR1120000331020X

Fig. 13 Code P0622: Alternator Field Not Switching Properly (Part 2 of 2). 2000 Neon

TEST	ACTION
9	Ignition On, Engine Not Running With DRB, actuate the Generator Field Driver. With a 12-volt test light, backprobe the Generator Field Driver Circuit in back of Generator. Did the light blink? Yes → Go To 10 No → Go To 13
10	Ignition On, Engine Not Running With the DRB, actuate the Generator Field Driver. With DRB, stop the Generator Field Driver actuation. With DRB, read the Target Charging voltage. Is the Target Charging voltage above 13 volts? Yes → Go To 11 No → Go To 12
11	Start the engine. Manually set the engine speed to 1600 RPM. With DRB, read both the Battery voltage and the Target Charging voltage. Compare the "Target Voltage" to the "Battery Voltage" reading. Monitor voltage for 5 minutes, if necessary. Look for a 1.0 volt difference or more. Was there more than a 1.0 volt difference? Yes → Replace the Powertrain Control Module. Perform Powertrain Verification Test VER-3A. No → Test Complete.
12	Turn ignition off. **Note: Battery must be fully charged.** **Note: Generator Belt tension and condition must be checked before continuing.** Start engine and allow it to reach operating temperature. With the DRB, read the BTS temperature. Using a Thermometer, measure under hood temperature. Is the temperature within 10 F degrees of Battery temperature? Yes → Test Complete. No → Replace Powertrain Control Module. Perform Powertrain Verification Test VER-3A.
13	Turn ignition off. Disconnect the PCM Connectors. **Note: Check connectors - Clean/repair as necessary.** Disconnect the generator field connector. **Note: Check Connectors - Clean/repair as necessary.** Using an Ohmmeter, measure the Generator Field Driver Circuit from PCM Connector to ground. Is the resistance below 5.0 ohms? Yes → Repair the Generator Field Driver Circuit shorted to ground. Perform Powertrain Verification Test VER-3A. No → Go To 14

CR1120000332010X

Fig. 14 Code P1594: Charging System Voltage Too High (Part 1 of 2). 2000 Neon

TEST	ACTION
14	Turn ignition off. Disconnect the Field Harness Connector at back of the Generator. **Note: Check connectors - Clean/repair as necessary.** Measure resistance of the Generator Field Driver Circuit at the Generator to Ground. Is the resistance below 5.0 ohms? Yes → Repair or replace the shorted Generator as necessary. Perform Powertrain Verification Test VER-3A. No → Go To 15
15	If there are no potential causes remaining, the Powertrain Control Module is assumed to be defective. View repair options. Repair Replace the Powertrain Control Module. Perform Powertrain Verification Test VER-3A.

CR1120000332020X

Fig. 14 Code P1594: Charging System Voltage Too High (Part 2 of 2). 2000 Neon

TEST	ACTION
16	Turn Ignition Off. **Note: Battery must be fully charged.** **Note: Generator Belt tension and condition must be checked before continuing.** Start Engine. With the DRB, read the target charging voltage. Is the target charging voltage above 15.1 volts? Yes → Go To 17 No → Go To 18
17	Turn ignition off. **Note: Battery must be fully charged.** **Note: Generator Belt tension and condition must be checked before continuing.** Start engine and allow it to reach operating temperature. With the DRB, read the BTS temperature. Using a Thermometer, measure under hood temperature. Is the temperature within 10 F degrees of Battery temperature? Yes → Go To 18 No → Replace the PCM. Perform Powertrain Verification Test VER-3A.
18	Turn ignition on, engine not running. Using a Voltmeter, measure voltage between the Generator B(+) Terminal and the Battery (+) Post. **Caution: Ensure all wires are clear of the engine's moving parts.** Start engine. Is the voltage above 0.4 volt? Yes → Repair the B(+) Circuit for high resistance between the Generator and Battery. Perform Powertrain Verification Test VER-3A. No → Go To 19
19	Start engine. Warm the engine to operating temperature. **Caution: Ensure all wires are clear of the engine's moving parts.** Using a Voltmeter, measure voltage between the Generator case and Battery (-) Post. Is the voltage above 0.1 volt? Yes → Repair Generator Ground for high resistance, Generator Case to Battery (-) side. Perform Powertrain Verification Test VER-3A. No → Go To 20
20	Start engine. Turn on all accessories, manually set engine speed to 1600 RPM. With DRB, read Target Charging and Charging voltage. Compare the two readings. Is there more than a 1.0 volt difference? Yes → Go To 21 No → Test Complete.

CR1120000333010X

Fig. 15 Code P1682: Charging System Voltage Too Low (Part 1 of 3). 2000 Neon

TEST	ACTION
26	If there are no potential causes remaining, the PCM is assumed to be defective. View repair options. Repair Replace the Powertrain Control Module. Perform Powertrain Verification Test VER-3A.

CR1120000333030X

Fig. 15 Code P1682: Charging System Voltage Too Low (Part 3 of 3). 2000 Neon

TEST	ACTION
21	Ignition On, Engine Not Running With the DRB, actuate the Generator Field. Using a Voltmeter, measure the voltage at both Generator Field Terminals. Is the voltage below 3.0 volts at either Terminal? Yes → Go To 22 No → Test Complete.
22	Ignition On, Engine Not Running Record all DTC's and freeze frame data, now erase Codes. Carefully inspect all Connectors for corrosion or spread Terminals before continuing. With the DRB actuate the Generator Field Driver Circuit. Backprobe the ASD Relay Output Circuit at back of Generator. Is the voltage above 10.0 volts? Yes → Go To 23 No → Repair the open ASD Relay Output Circuit. Perform Powertrain Verification Test VER-3A.
23	Turn ignition off. Disconnect the PCM Connectors. **Note: Check connectors - Clean/repair as necessary.** Disconnect the generator field connector. **Note: Check Connectors - Clean/repair as necessary.** Using an Ohmmeter, measure the Generator Field Driver Circuit from PCM Connector to ground. Is the resistance below 5.0 ohms? Yes → Repair the Generator Field Driver Circuit shorted to ground. Perform Powertrain Verification Test VER-3A. No → Go To 24
24	Turn ignition off. Disconnect ASD Relay Connector. **Note: Check connectors - Clean/repair as necessary.** Disconnect the generator field connector. **Note: Check Connectors - Clean/repair as necessary.** Using an Ohmmeter, measure the ASD Relay Output Circuit from ASD Relay Connector to ground. Is the resistance below 5.0 ohms? Yes → Repair the ASD Relay Output Circuit shorted to ground. Perform Powertrain Verification Test VER-3A. No → Go To 25
25	Turn ignition off. Disconnect the PCM Connectors. Disconnect the generator field connector. **Note: Check Connectors - Clean/repair as necessary.** Using an Ohmmeter, measure the Generator Field Driver Circuit from PCM to Generator. Is the resistance below 5.0 ohms? Yes → Go To 26 No → Repair the open Generator Field Driver Circuit. Perform Powertrain Verification Test VER-3A.

CR1120000333020X

Fig. 15 Code P1682: Charging System Voltage Too Low (Part 2 of 3). 2000 Neon

TEST	ACTION
27	Turn ignition off. **Note: Battery condition must be verified prior to this test.** Inspect the Generator Belt tension and condition. Is the Generator Belt OK? Yes → Go To 28 No → Repair as necessary. Perform Powertrain Verification Test VER-3A.
28	Start the Engine. Turn on all accessories. Raise engine speed to 2000 RPM for 30 seconds then return to idle. With the DRB III read DTC's. Are there any "Charging System" Trouble Codes? Yes → Refer to Symptom list for problems related to Charging. Perform Powertrain Verification Test VER-3A. No → Go To 29
29	Ignition On, Engine Not Running With the DRB, actuate the Generator Field. Using a 12-volt test light, backprobe the Generator Field Driver Terminal at the back of the Generator. **Note: The test light should blink On and Off every 1.4 seconds.** While monitoring the 12-volt test light, wiggle the Field Terminals back to the PCM and ASD Relay. Was there any interruption in the normal cycle of the test light? Yes → Repair the wire where wiggling interrupted the voltage cycle. Perform Powertrain Verification Test VER-3A. No → Go To 30
30	Ignition On, Engine Not Running With the DRB, read trouble codes. Are there any "Charging System" trouble codes? Yes → Refer to Symptom list for problems related to Charging. Perform Powertrain Verification Test VER-3A. No → Go To 31
31	Turn ignition on, engine not running. Using a Voltmeter, measure voltage between the Generator B(+) Terminal and the Battery (+) Post. **Caution: Ensure all wires are clear of the engine's moving parts.** Start engine. Is the voltage above 0.4 volt? Yes → Repair the B(+) Circuit for high resistance between the Generator and Battery. Perform Powertrain Verification Test VER-3A. No → Go To 32

CR1120000334010X

Fig. 16 Charging System Diagnosis w/No Code (Part 1 of 2). 2000 Neon

TEST	ACTION
32	Start engine. Warm the engine to operating temperature. **Caution: Ensure all wires are clear of the engine's moving parts.** Using a Voltmeter, measure voltage between the Generator case and Battery (-) Post. Is the voltage above 0.1 volt? Yes → Repair Generator Ground for high resistance, Generator Case to Battery (-) side. Perform Powertrain Verification Test VER-3A. No → Go To 33
33	Ignition On, Engine Not Running. With the DRB, read the Battery voltage and record the results. Using a Voltmeter, measure Battery voltage B(+) to B(-) Terminal and record the results. Compare the two voltage readings. Is the voltage difference less than one volt? Yes → Test Complete. No → Go To 34
34	Ignition On, Engine Not Running With the DRB, read the Battery voltage and record the results. Turn Ignition off. Disconnect the PCM. **Note: Check connectors - Clean/repair as necessary.** Turn Ignition on, with the engine off. Using a Voltmeter, measure the Fused B(+) at PCM Connector. Is the voltage within one volt of the DRB recorded reading? Yes → Go To 35 No → Repair the B(+) Circuit for high resistance between the PCM and the Battery. Perform Powertrain Verification Test VER-3A.
35	If there are no potential causes remaining, the PCM is assumed to be defective. View repair options. Repair Replace the PCM. Perform Powertrain Verification Test VER-3A.

CR1120000334020X

Fig. 16 Charging System Diagnosis w/No Code (Part 2 of 2). 2000 Neon

VERIFICATION TEST VER-3A

1. Inspect the vehicle to ensure that all engine components are properly installed and connected. Reassemble and reconnect components as necessary.
2. Connect the DRB to the Data Link Connector and erase the codes.
3. If the PCM has been replaced perform steps 4 through 6 then continue the verification.
4. If PCM has been changed and correct VIN and mileage have not been programmed, a DTC will be set in ABS and Air bag modules. In addition, if vehicle is equipped with a Sentry Key Immobilizer Module (SKIM), Secret Key data must be updated to enable start.
5. For ABS and Air Bag systems: Enter correct VIN and Mileage in PCM. Erase codes in ABS and Air Bag modules.
6. For SKIM theft alarm: Connect DRB to data link conn. Go to Theft Alarm, SKIM, Misc. and place SKIM in secured access mode, by using the appropriate PIN code for this vehicle. Select Update the Secret Key data. Data will be transferred from SKIM to PCM.
7. Ensure no other charging system problems remain by doing the following: Start the engine. Perform generator output per service manual.
8. Raise the engine speed to 2000 rpm for at least 30 seconds.
9. Allow the engine to idle.
10. Turn the engine off.
11. Turn the ignition key on.
12. With the DRB, read trouble code messages.
13. If repaired code has reset, or any other one has set, check all pertinent Technical Service Bulletins and return to Symptom List if necessary.
14. If there are no codes, the repair is now complete.

CR1120000335000X

Fig. 17 Verification Test VER-3A. 2000 Neon

ALTERNATOR SPECIFICATIONS

Model	Engine	Type	Rated Output Amps
Avenger & Sebring Coupe	2.0L	Mitsubishi	90
	2.5L	Mitsubishi	110
Neon	2.0L	Mitsubishi	85
Talon	2.0L①	Mitsubishi	75
	2.0L②	Mitsubishi	90

① — Turbocharged engine.
② — Less turbocharged engine.

STEERING COLUMNS

NOTE: On Air Bag Equipped Models, Refer To " Air Bag System Precautions" Located In The Front Of This Manual For System Disarming & Arming Procedures.

NOTE: Prior To Performing Any Service Operations Listed In This Section, Consult The "Technical Service Bulletins " For Related Information.

NOTE: Refer To "Computer Relearn Procedures " Located In The Front Of This Manual For Computer Relearn Procedures.

INDEX

PRECAUTIONS

AIR BAG SYSTEMS

Refer to "Air Bag System Precautions" in the front of this manual for system disarming and arming procedures.

BATTERY GROUND CABLE

Prior to service, disconnect battery ground cable and isolate as required.

COLUMN SERVICE

When servicing collapsible steering columns, care should be exercised since they are extremely susceptible to damage. Dropping of or leaning on column or striking sharp blows on end of steering shaft or shift levers could loosen or shear plastic fasteners which maintain column rigidity.

It is important that only the specified screws, bolts and nuts be used during the mandatory reassembly sequence and tightened to specifications to ensure proper breakaway action of column under impact. Avoid using excessively long bolts, as they may prevent a portion of the steering column from collapsing under impact.

If there is evidence of a sheared plastic shift tube injection, a new shift tube must be installed. If plastic injections are sheared but steering shaft is not bent, repairs may be possible using a service steering shaft repair kit containing instructions and dimensions for all steering columns. On some models, the retaining brackets will shear under impact and must also be replaced.

STEERING COLUMN

REPLACE

AVENGER, SEBRING COUPE & TALON

Refer to **Fig. 1,** for steering column removal. Remove steering wheel using puller tool No. MB–990803, or equivalent.

BREEZE, CIRRUS, SEBRING CONVERTIBLE & STRATUS

1. Place front wheels in straight ahead position.
2. Remove fuse panel cover from left-hand end of instrument panel and instrument panel cover mounting screw from behind fuse panel.
3. Remove center bezel from top cover and top cover of instrument panel.
4. Remove knee bolster.
5. Remove speed control switches from steering wheel, then disconnect clockspring and horn ground wire.
6. Remove Torx head mounting bolts from steering wheel and air bag module.
7. Disconnect clockspring electrical connection from air bag module.
8. Remove steering wheel retaining nut and steering wheel using puller tool No. C-J2001-P, or equivalent.
9. Remove upper shroud from steering column, **Fig. 2,** then tilt column to its highest position and remove lower shroud.
10. Remove wiring harness connectors from clockspring, halo light and ignition switch.
11. **On models equipped with automatic transmission,** place key cylinder in Off position and remove shifter/ignition interlock cable from key lock housing.
12. **On all models,** remove pinch bolt and separate steering coupler from steering gear.
13. Ensure steering column tilt lever is in locked position and insert a 7/32 drill bit in each locking pin hole on upper steering column bracket.
14. Remove upper and lower steering column support bracket mounting nuts.
15. Remove steering column assembly.
16. Reverse procedure to install, noting the following:
    a. Depress two clockspring locking pins to disengage clockspring locking mechanism.
    b. With clockspring locking mechanism disengaged, rotate clockspring rotor fully clockwise until it does not turn. **Do not over tighten.**
    c. Rotate clockspring rotor counterclockwise until yellow appears in clockspring centering window.
    d. Engage clockspring locking mechanism.

1997 CONCORDE, INTREPID, LHS & VISION

1. Turn steering wheel ½ turn from straight ahead position and remove key from lock cylinder, **Fig. 3.**
2. **On models equipped with speed control,** remove speed control switches from steering wheel.
3. **On models less speed control,** remove steering wheel side covers.
4. **On all models,** remove air bag module mounting bolts and slightly lift module.

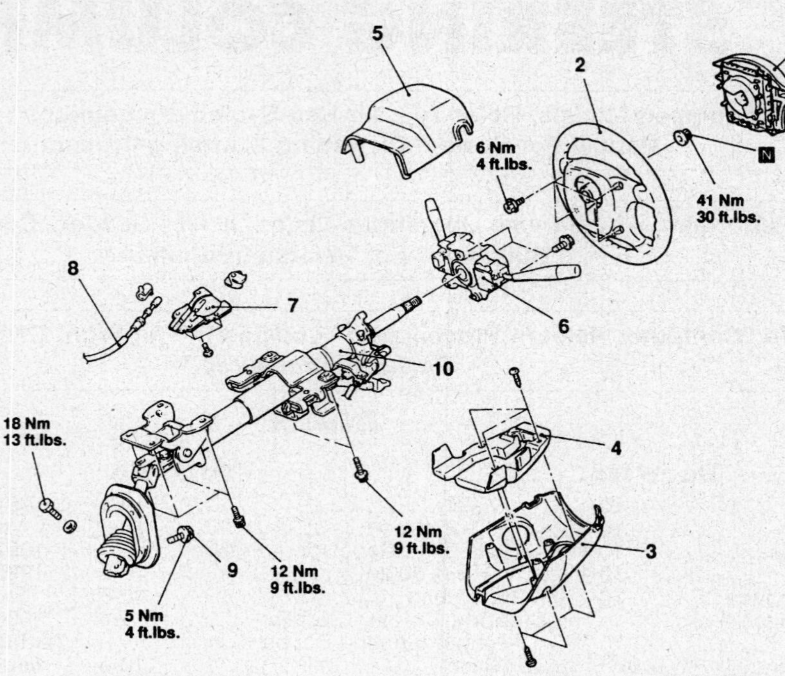

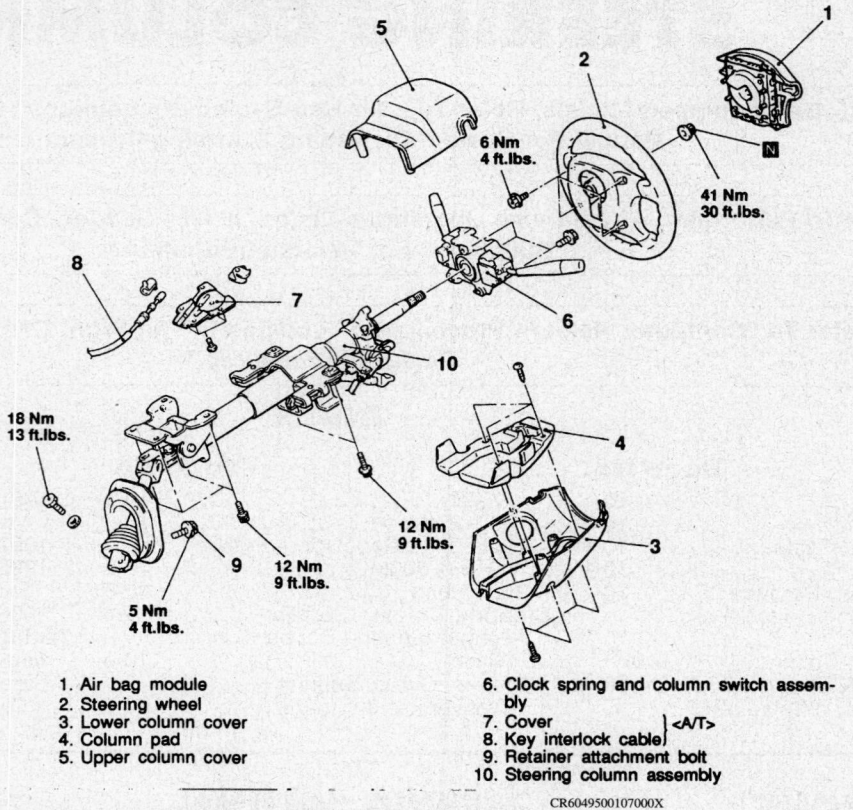

1. Air bag module
2. Steering wheel
3. Lower column cover
4. Column pad
5. Upper column cover
6. Clock spring and column switch assembly
7. Cover } <A/T>
8. Key interlock cable }
9. Retainer attachment bolt
10. Steering column assembly

CR6049500107000X

Fig. 1 Steering column replacement. Avenger, Sebring Coupe & Talon

5. Disconnect module electrical connectors and remove module from steering wheel.
6. Remove retaining nut and steering wheel using puller tool No. C-3428-B, or equivalent. Do not bump or hammer on steering column shaft to remove wheel.
7. Remove instrument panel end covers, and air bag fuse Nos. 7 and 19 from fuse panel.
8. Remove cowl trim panels, console or instrument panel lower center cover and ashtray.
9. Remove lefthand silencer/duct under instrument panel and lower dash panel assembly.
10. Remove under steering column air outlet duct and tilt steering column to full down position.
11. Remove tilt lever and steering column shrouds.
12. **On models equipped with column shift lever,** remove shift cable as follows:
    a. Install tilt lever and tilt steering column to full up position.
    b. Pry shift cable off shifter pin and remove shift cable retaining clip at shift cable support bracket. Do not bend cable bracket.
    c. Remove tilt lever.
13. **On all models,** turn ignition key to Run position, unlocking steering column.
14. Depress tab and remove floor shift interlock cable from steering column socket.

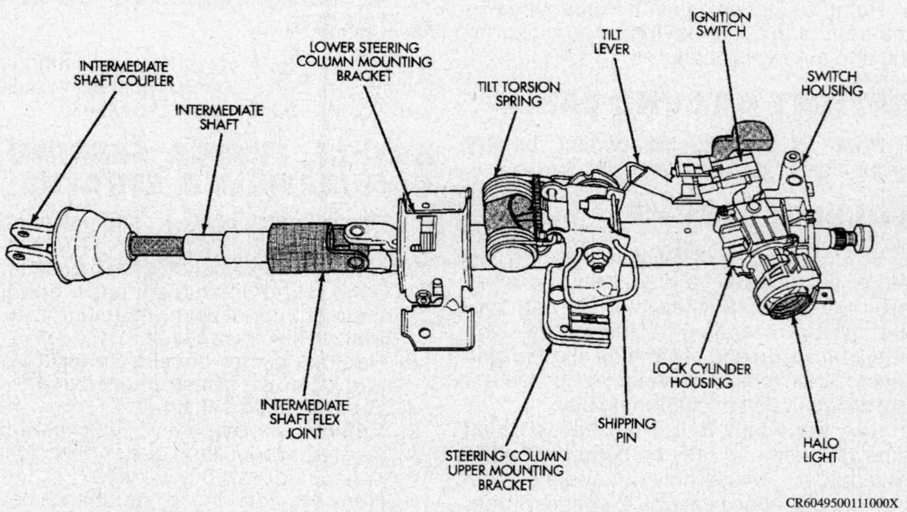

CR6049500111000X

Fig. 2 Steering column assembly replacement. Breeze, Cirrus, Sebring Convertible & Stratus

15. Remove retaining pin from lower steering column coupler bolt.
16. Remove coupler bolt and separate coupler from intermediate shaft.
17. Loosen two bolts retaining lower steering column assembly bracket to mount bracket.
18. While supporting weight of steering column, remove two nuts retaining upper steering column mounting bracket.
19. Remove steering column assembly from its mounting bracket and lay it on floor of vehicle.
20. Disconnect turn signal/multi-function switch and ignition switch wiring harness connectors.
21. Disconnect halo light and clockspring wiring harness connectors, then depress tab to remove steering column wiring trough from its mounting bracket.

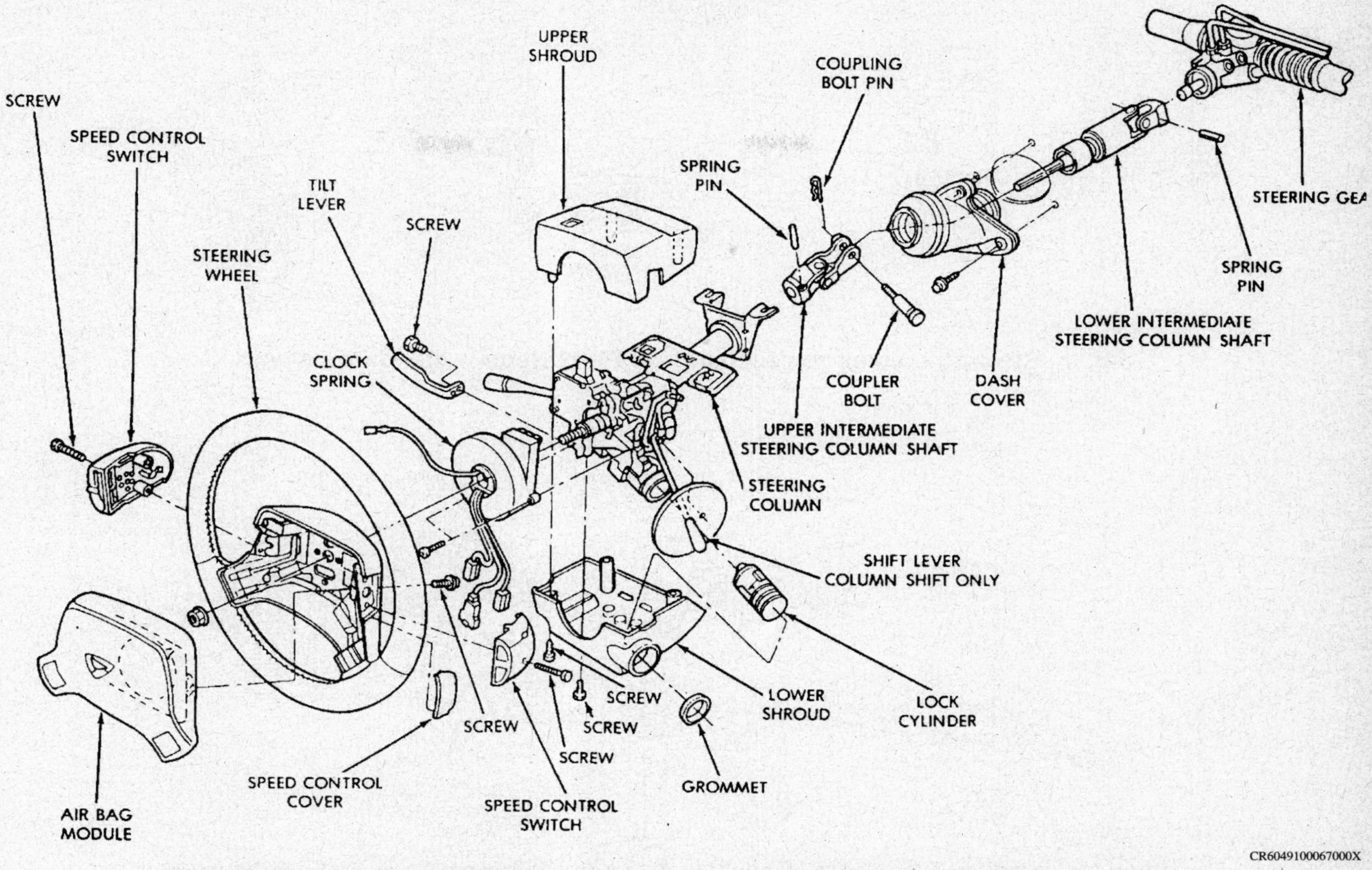

Fig. 3 Steering column assembly replacement. 1997 Concorde, Intrepid, LHS & Vision

22. Remove steering column from vehicle.
23. Reverse procedure to install, noting the following:
    a. Ensure ground clip is installed on lefthand capsule slot.
    b. Ensure both breakaway capsules are fully seated in slots of steering column upper support bracket. **Torque** bolts to 8 ft. lbs.
    c. **On models equipped with column shift,** a new interlock cassette must be installed.
    d. **On all models, torque** steering wheel nut to 45 ft. lbs.

1998–2000 CONCORDE, INTREPID, LHS & 300M

The steering column has been designed to be serviced as an assembly. The steering column must be replaced whenever the vehicle is involved in an accident which deploys the air bag or if vehicle is involved in an impact when front suspension or under carriage results in any type of damage to front suspension crossmember.

If the column is to be removed as one assembly, or without removing the steering wheel, the steering wheel must be turned from the straight ahead position to the right 180° and locked in place.

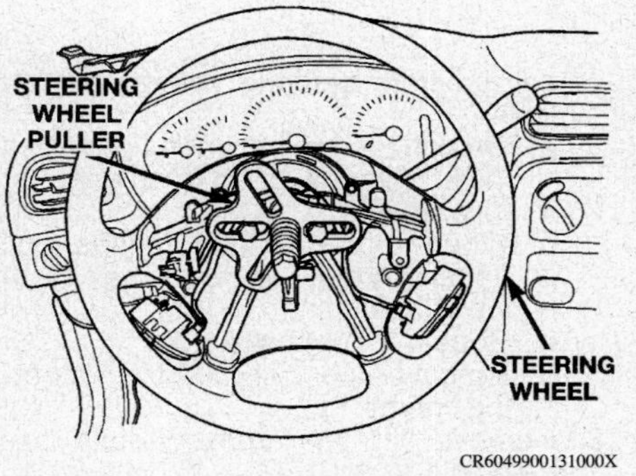

Fig. 4 Steering wheel removal. 1998–2000 Concorde, Intrepid, LHS & 300M

1. Remove remote ground cable from ground stud on shock tower, then isolate ground cable from vehicle by installing isolator on stud.
2. Remove fuse panel cover from left end of instrument panel.
3. Remove two screws from behind fuse panel cover retaining lower instrument panel cover to instrument panel mounting bracket.
4. Remove lower instrument panel cover.
5. Remove wiring harness connector from trunk release switch in lower instrument panel cover.
6. Remove park release cable from release handle in lower instrument panel cover.
7. Remove four reinforcement to instrument panel retaining bolts, then the reinforcement from instrument panel.
8. Remove diagnostic connector from reinforcement.
9. Ensure front wheels are in a straight ahead position.
10. Remove speed control switches from steering wheel.
11. **Wait a minimum of two minutes before starting to remove air bag from steering wheel. This will allow air bag system capacitor to de-energize.** Remove two air bag module to steering wheel retaining bolts, then the air bag module.
12. Remove connector lock from air bag electrical lead connector. **Do not twist connector lock when removing it from air bag.**
13. Disconnect electrical connector from back of air bag module. **Do not twist connector lock when removing it from air bag.**

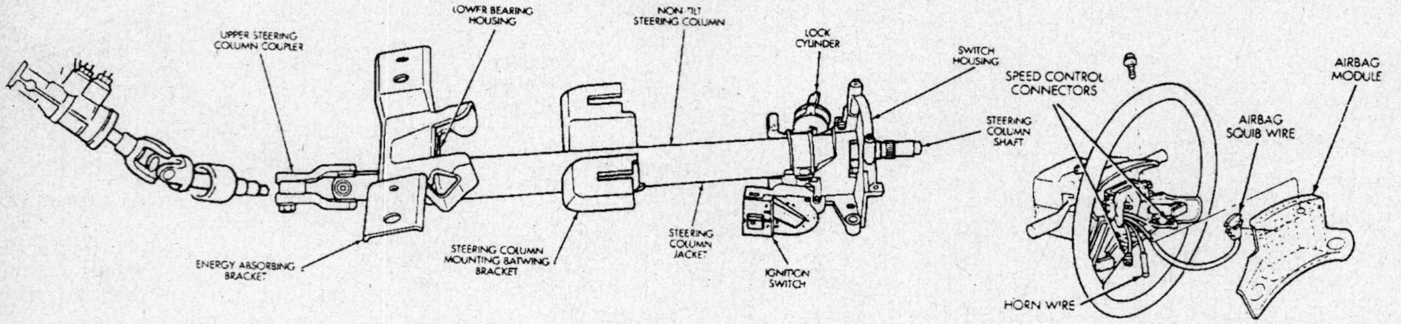

CR6049500097000X

Fig. 5 Steering column replacement. 1997–99 Neon w/standard column

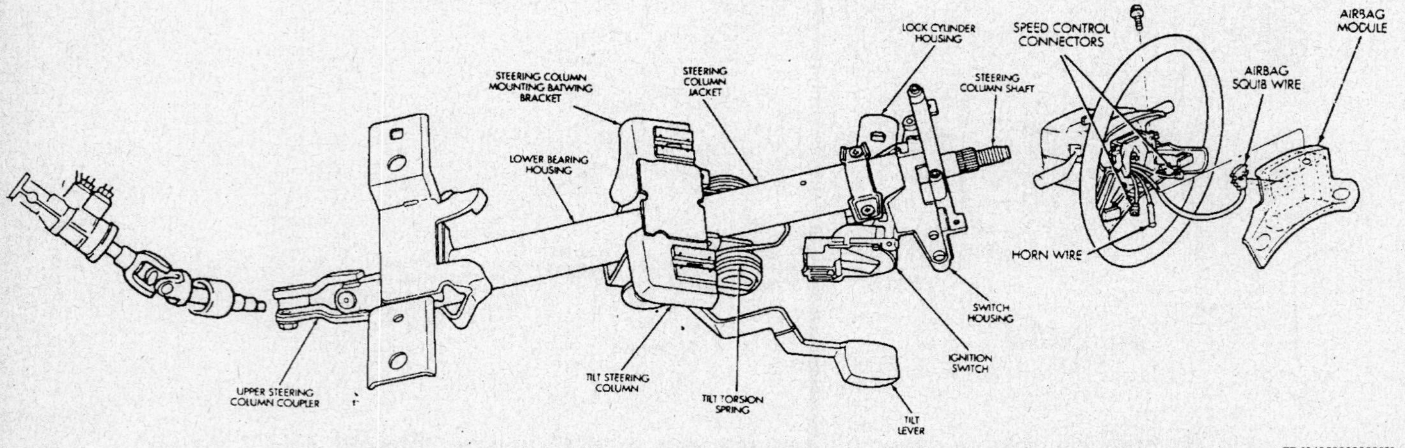

CR6049500098000X

Fig. 6 Steering column replacement. 1997–99 Neon w/tilt column

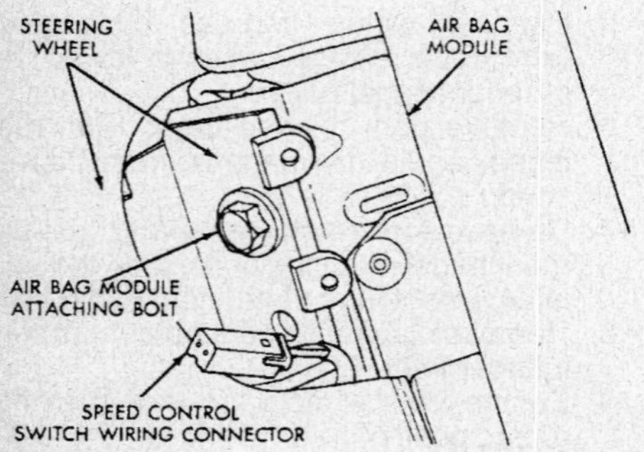

CR6049500099000X

Fig. 7 Air bag module mounting bolt locations. 1997–99 Neon

14. Remove horn switch wire from clockspring horn wire.
15. Remove steering wheel retaining nut from column shaft, then install puller on steering wheel as shown in **Fig. 4. When installing wheel puller on steering wheel, ensure puller bolts are fully seated in threaded holes in steering wheel.**
16. Remove steering wheel from steering column shaft.
17. Remove steering column upper shroud from steering column as follows:
    a. On right seam, between upper and lower shrouds, push in on seam at forward end.
    b. When upper shroud unsnaps, pull upper shroud upward away from lower.
    c. Repeat for opposite side.
    d. Remove upper shroud from steering column.
18. Remove tilt lever from steering column.
19. Remove two lower shroud to steering column retaining screws, then the lower shroud.
20. Remove wiring harness connectors from clockspring.
21. Remove two clockspring to steering column retaining screws, then the clockspring.
22. Disconnect wire harness connector at module, then remove retaining screw and unclip module from key cylinder halo bezel.
23. Remove wiring harness from routing clip on top of multi-function switch.
24. Remove two multi-function switch to steering column retaining screws, then the multi-function switch.

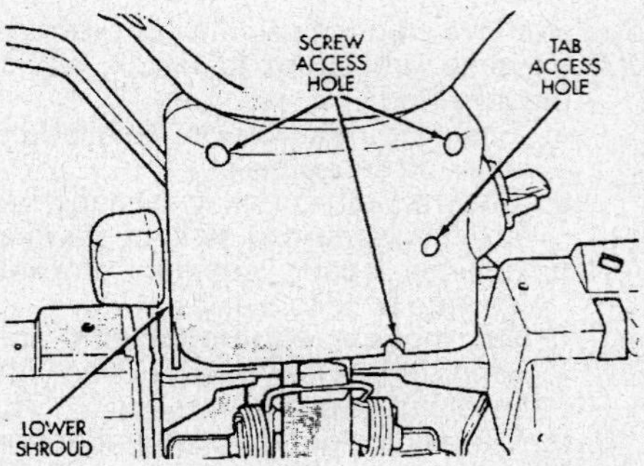

CR6049500100000X

Fig. 8 Ignition key lock cylinder retaining tab access hole location. 1997–99 Neon

25. Remove two ignition switch to steering column retaining screws, then the ignition switch.
26. **On models equipped with floor mounted shifter,** depress lock tab on shifter/ignition interlock cable, then remove cable from key lock housing.
27. **On models equipped with steering column mounted shifter,** proceed as follows:

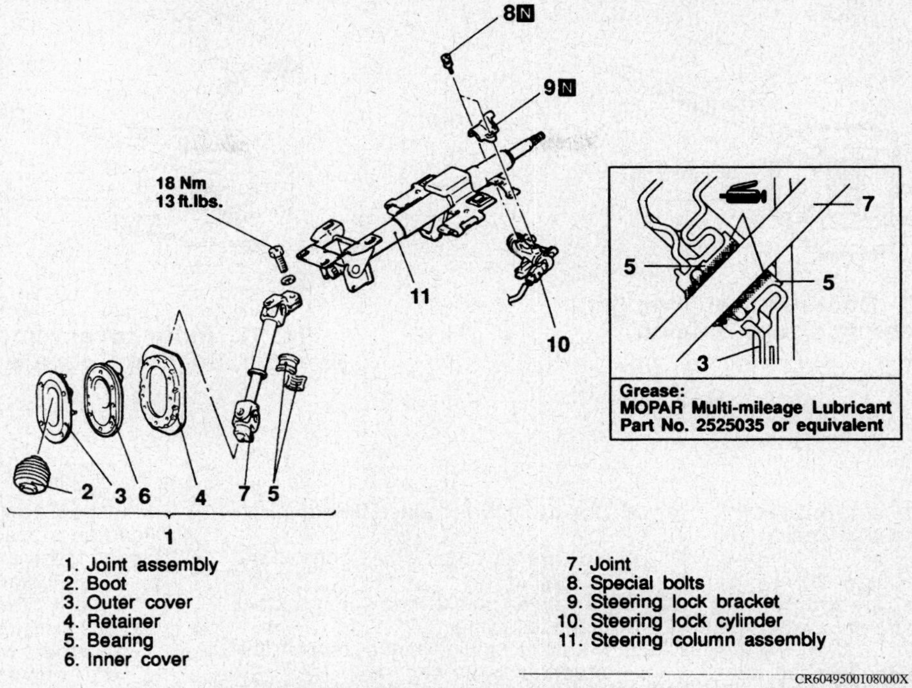

Fig. 9 Exploded view of steering column. Avenger, Sebring Coupe & Talon

  a. Remove shift cable from shifter mechanism.
  b. Unlock cable lock, then remove shift cable by inserting a screwdriver between shift cable and shifter mechanism and prying cable off pin.

28. **On all models,** remove two shift cable mounting bracket retaining screws from steering column, then the mounting bracket.
29. Remove two air ducts from under steering column.
30. Remove retaining pin in steering column coupler pinch bolt, then the pinch bolt from steering column coupler.
31. Remove two upper mounting bracket to support bracket retaining nuts, then loosen two bolts attaching steering column lower mounting bracket to support bracket.
32. Remove steering column from support bracket by pulling it rearward, then out of car.
33. Reverse procedure to install, noting the following:
    a. **Torque** bracket to support bracket fasteners to 8 ft. lbs.
    b. **Torque** coupler pinch bolt to 20 ft. lbs.
    c. **Torque** steering wheel retaining nut to 45 ft. lbs.
    d. **Torque** air bag module bolts to 6 ft. lbs

1997–99 NEON

1. Ensure front wheels are directed straight ahead.
2. Remove steering column cover trim panel and cover liner from lower instrument panel, **Figs. 5 and 6.**
3. Remove steering wheel trim covers and, if necessary, speed control switches from steering wheel.
4. Remove bolts securing air bag module to steering wheel, **Fig. 7,** then lift module carefully from center of steering wheel and disconnect clockspring electrical connector from rear of module.
5. Disconnect clockspring electrical connectors from horn switches, then remove steering wheel retaining nut and dampener weight.
6. Install steering wheel puller tool No. C-3428-B, or equivalent, and tighten tool center bolt until wheel can be slid from steering shaft. **Do not hammer on tool or steering wheel during removal.**
7. Place key lock cylinder in On position and use a small screwdriver or other suitable tool to depress lock cylinder retaining tab through tab access hole, **Fig. 8.**
8. Remove key lock cylinder assembly from steering column, then the steering column lower shroud.
9. Tilt steering column to lowest position, then remove upper shroud and slip retaining pin out of upper to lower column pinch bolt.
10. Remove pinch bolt nut, then separate upper and lower coupler shafts. **Pinch bolt cannot be removed from coupler assembly.**
11. Remove through bolt from lower steering column bearing housing and mounting bracket, then the upper steering column assembly bracket bolts.
12. Lower steering column in instrument panel access opening, then disconnect wiring harness at wiper and multifunction switches and disengage from clips.
13. Remove wiring harness connectors from ignition switch and clockspring, then lift steering column assembly out of vehicle through driver's door.
14. Reverse procedure to install, noting the following:
    a. **Torque** upper steering column bracket to support bolts to 9 ft. lbs.
    b. **Torque** pinch bolt nut to 21 ft. lbs. and ensure its retaining pin is installed.
    c. **Torque** steering wheel retaining nut to 45 ft. lbs.
    d. Use only original or correct replacement bolts when installing air bag module. **Torque** bolts to 7–8 ft. lbs.

2000 NEON

1. Ensure front wheels are in straight ahead position.
2. Remove screw to left end of instrument panel above left end cap.
3. Remove instrument panel top cover

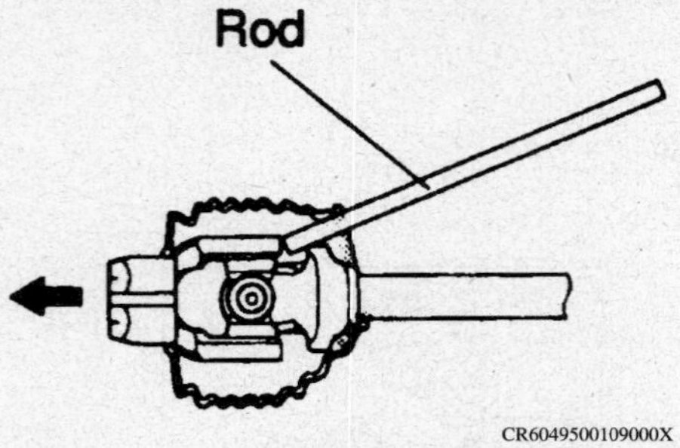

Fig. 10 Boot removal. Avenger, Sebring Coupe & Talon

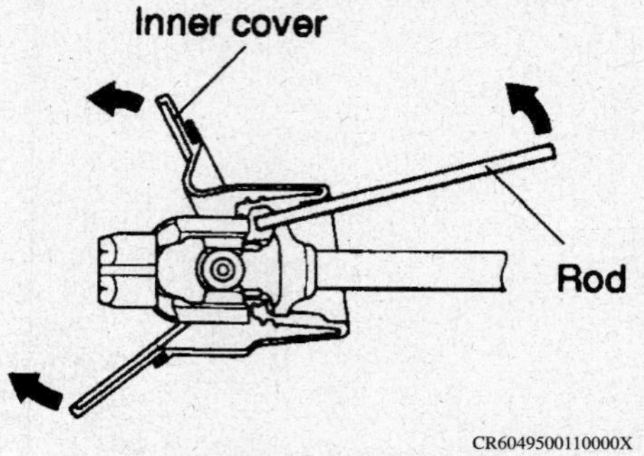

Fig. 11 Inner cover removal. Avenger, Sebring Coupe & Talon

from driver side first, removing retaining clip to allow access to instrument panel.
4. Remove instrument cluster bezel.
5. Remove screws and clips from column covers, pull covers straight away from instrument panel.
6. Remove speed control switches from steering wheel (if equipped).
7. Remove trim caps on either side of steering wheel rear cover.
8. Remove mounting screws from steering wheel, attaching air bag module.
9. Disconnect clockspring and electrical connectors from air bag module, remove air bag module.
10. Remove steering wheel retaining nut, install suitable puller tool, remove steering wheel from steering column shaft.
11. Remove ignition key from cylinder.
12. Remove upper and lower column shroud.
13. Remove steering column coupling retainer pin, coupling bolt and separate upper and lower steering column couplings.
14. **On models equipped with automatic transmission,** disconnect automatic transaxle ignition interlock cable from steering column.
15. **On all models,** remove upper and lower mounting nuts attaching steering column to instrument panel, lowering steering column away from instrument panel.
16. Disconnect wiring electrical connectors from clockspring, multi-function switch, windshield wiper switch and ignition switch.
17. **On models equipped Sentry Key Immobilzer Module (SKIM),** disconnect electrical connector.
18. **On all models,** remove steering column from vehicle.
19. Reverse procedures to install noting the following:
    a. **Torque** mounting screws for SKIM to 24 in.lbs.
    b. **Torque** mounting nuts to instrument panel 13 ft. lbs.
    c. **Torque** coupler pinch bolt to 20 ft. lbs.
    d. **Torque** air bag module bolts to 90 in. lbs.
20. When replacing steering column, perform the following:
    a. Remove ignition key cylinder from steering column.
    b. Remove clockspring from steering column.
    c. Remove multi-function switch straight away from steering column.
    d. If equipped with SKIM, remove mounting screws and slide off nonhalo ring.
    e. Remove ignition switch straight away from column ignition housing.

STEERING COLUMN SERVICE

AVENGER, SEBRING COUPE & TALON

1. Remove steering column as outlined under "Steering Column, Replace."
2. Disassemble steering column in sequence shown, **Fig. 9,** noting the following:
    a. Apply grease to inside lip of boot and remove boot while using a suitable rod to widen lip of boot, **Fig. 10.**
    b. Apply grease to inside lip of inner cover and cover joint while using a suitable rod to widen lip section, and widen inner cover from behind with a suitable rod and pull cover to remove from joint, **Fig. 11.**
    c. If steering lock cylinder is to be removed, cut special bolts at bracket side with a hacksaw.
3. Inspect steering column as follows:
    a. Inspect steering shaft for play and round movement.
    b. Inspect joints for play, damage, or rough movement.
    c. Inspect joint bearing for wear and damage.
    d. Inspect dust shield for damage.
4. Reverse procedure to assemble, noting the following:
    a. When installing steering lock cylinder and steering lock bracket, temporarily install steering lock in alignment with column boss.
    b. After ensuring steering lock operates correctly, tighten special bolts until heads twist off.
    c. Cover inside lip of inner cover with grease and pull outside of cover onto joint.
    d. Fill inside of bearing with multipurpose grease and install bearings to shaft on joint assembly.
    e. Wrap vinyl tape 1½ times around concave circumferences of bearings, and press fit bearing into cover assembly.
    f. Apply grease to inside of lip section of boot and install boot to joint.

BREEZE, CIRRUS, SEBRING CONVERTIBLE & STRATUS

The steering column used on this model, **Fig. 2,** has been designed to be serviced as an assembly except for wiring, switches, shrouds and the steering wheel. Most steering column components can be serviced without removing the column from the vehicle.

The only other serviceable component is the steering column shaft coupler. If the coupler requires replacement because of a seized bearing, insufficient bearing staking or improper bearing seating, proceed as follows:

1. Remove steering column assembly as described under "Steering Column, Replace."
2. Install puller tool No. 6831-A, or equivalent, through center of roll pin in flex joint and install knurled nut.
3. Using a suitable screw driver inserted between flex joint and steering column lower mounting bracket, pry flex joint off of steering column shaft.
4. Reverse procedure to install.

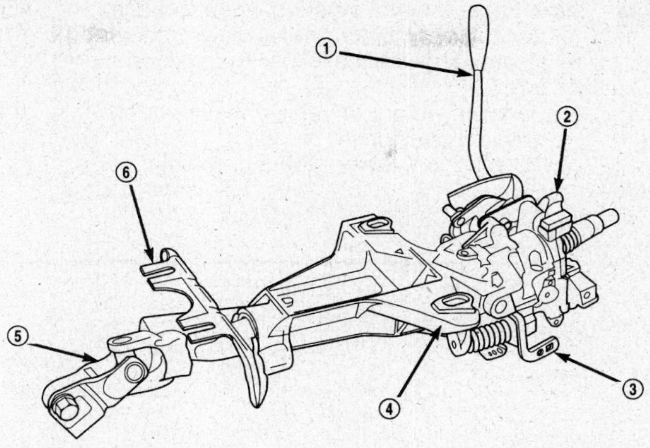

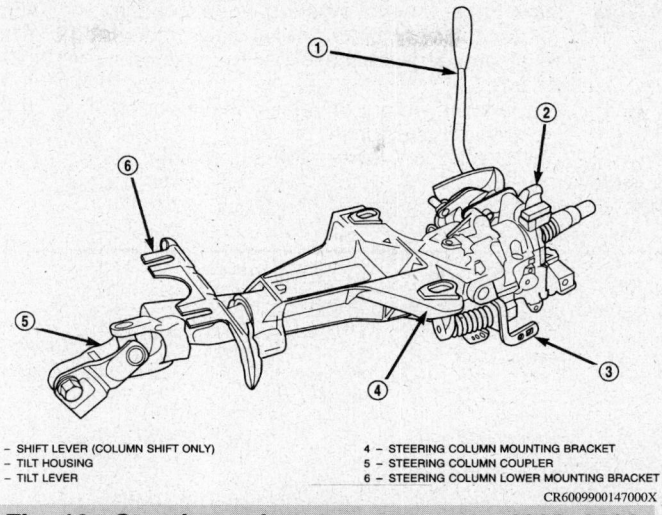

1 – SHIFT LEVER (COLUMN SHIFT ONLY)
2 – TILT HOUSING
3 – TILT LEVER
4 – STEERING COLUMN MOUNTING BRACKET
5 – STEERING COLUMN COUPLER
6 – STEERING COLUMN LOWER MOUNTING BRACKET

CR6009900147000X

Fig. 12 Steering column components. 1998–2000 Concorde, Intrepid, LHS & 300M

1997 CONCORDE, INTREPID, LHS & VISION

This steering column has been designed to be serviced as an assembly except for wiring, switches, shrouds and steering wheel. Also, most steering column components can be serviced without removing the column from the vehicle, **Fig. 3.**

The only other serviceable components are as follows:

1. **On models equipped with column shift,** replace gear shift lever assembly as follows:
   a. Remove gear shift cable from retaining pin on gear shift assembly and unlock shift cable adjuster.
   b. Remove three Torx head screws retaining shifter assembly to tilt housing.
   c. Remove shifter assembly from tilt housing and unhook interlock cable from shifter assembly.
   d. Remove and discard interlock cassette from steering column.
   e. Reverse procedure to install.
2. **On all models,** replace steering column jacket bushing assembly as follows:
   a. Remove steering column as outlined under "Steering Column, Replace."
   b. Remove steering coupler from steering shaft by removing spring pin from coupler and sliding coupler off end of steering shaft. Steering column shaft must be supported during removal of spring pin.
   c. Separate steering column bracket from jacket bushing by depressing retaining tabs on bushing and lifting bracket off bushing.
   d. Using a pin punch, lightly tap jacket bushing off end of steering column jacket and steering shaft.
   e. Reverse procedure to install. Use an arbor press and installer tool No. MB-990800, or equivalent, to install bushing. Ensure three retaining tabs are expanded out past edge of lower bracket.

1998–2000 CONCORDE, INTREPID, LHS & 300M

The steering column used on these vehicles has been designed to be serviced as an assembly; less wiring, switches, clockspring, gear shift lever, shift ignition interlock, brake lock solenoid, shrouds and steering wheel. **Fig. 12.**

The steering column shaft upper coupler is shown to be defective due to seized bearing, loose bearing stake or bearing nor seated properly. The steering column intermediate shaft must be replaced as an entire assembly.

1997–99 NEON

The steering column used on this model, **Figs. 5 and 6,** has been designed to be serviced as an assembly except for wiring, switches, shrouds and the steering wheel. Most steering column components can be serviced without removing the column from the vehicle.

The only other serviceable component is the steering column shaft coupler. If the coupler requires replacement because of a seized bearing, insufficient bearing staking or improper bearing seating, proceed as follows:

1. Remove steering column assembly as described under "Steering Column, Replace."
2. Remove spring pin from coupler and slide coupler from end of steering shaft. **Ensure lower shaft coupler is supported during spring pin removal and installation to prevent bearing damage.**
3. Reverse procedure to install.

2000 NEON

The steering column on these models has been designed to be serviced only as a complete assembly. The shaft, bearings and upper coupling are all serviced with the column.

The replaceable components on the steering column are the key cylinder, ignition switch, multi-function switch, trim shrouds, steering wheel, air bag module and the clockspring.

TECHNICAL SERVICE BULLETINS

STEERING WHEEL SHAKE AT IDLE

1997 Breeze, Cirrus & Stratus

On these models built after January 1, 1997, and equipped with 2.0L or 2.4L engines, the steering wheel may shake at idle as if engine is running rough. This occurs with or without the air conditioning running.

This condition may be caused by lack of steering wheel and column damping. To correct this condition, ensure there are no engine system Diagnostic Trouble Codes (DTCs). If no DTCs exist, install steering wheel damper (part No. 04649160AB).

STEERING WHEEL/COLUMN CLUNKING OR RATTLING

1997-98 Breeze, Cirrus, Neon, Sebring Convertible & Stratus

Steering wheel/column clunking or rattle is more frequent while hitting bumps or hard turns. Inspect steering wheel/column for any rattle or clunking noise. If symptoms exist, proceed with the following repair procedure.

1. Ensure weight of vehicle is supported by tires/suspension.
2. Disconnect lower steering column intermediate shaft from steering gear shaft. This allows steering column preload to reset.
3. Install intermediate shaft to steering gear using new bolt part No. 06502413. **Torque** bolt to 20 ft. lbs.
4. Install retaining pin into bolt.

MANUAL STEERING GEARS

NOTE: On Air Bag Equipped Models, Refer To "Air Bag System Precautions" Located In The Front Of This Manual For System Disarming & Arming Procedures.

INDEX

PRECAUTIONS

AIR BAG SYSTEMS

Refer to "Air Bag System Precautions" in the front of this manual for system disarming and arming procedures.

BATTERY GROUND CABLE

Prior to service, disconnect battery ground cable and isolate as required.

STEERING GEAR SERVICE

TALON

Disassemble

1. Place steering gear assembly in a suitable soft-jawed vise.
2. Remove outer tie rod ends and locking nuts, then place tie rod ends in a suitable soft-jawed vise and remove dust covers using a hammer and screwdriver.
3. Remove bellows clips, bands, and bellows.
4. Separate tab washers from inner tie rods using a chisel, then remove inner tie rods and tab washers.
5. Remove rack support cover locknut, rack support cover, rack support spring, cushion rubber and rack support.
6. Remove top plug locknut, top plug, pinion oil seal, pinion collar, then the pinion and bearing assembly, **Fig. 1.**
7. Remove pinion bearing from pinion using a suitable press and steering/pinion gear replacement tool No. MB990783, or equivalent.
8. Remove rack from gear housing by pulling in direction shown in **Fig. 2. If rack is pulled from housing in wrong direction, rack bushing in gear housing may be damaged by rack threads.**
9. Remove rack bushing from rack housing.
10. Inspect rack support for uneven wear or damage, rack support spring for deterioration, rack pinion tooth surfaces for wear or damage, pinion bearing for noise, uneven rotation or damage and rack bushing for damage. Replace as necessary.

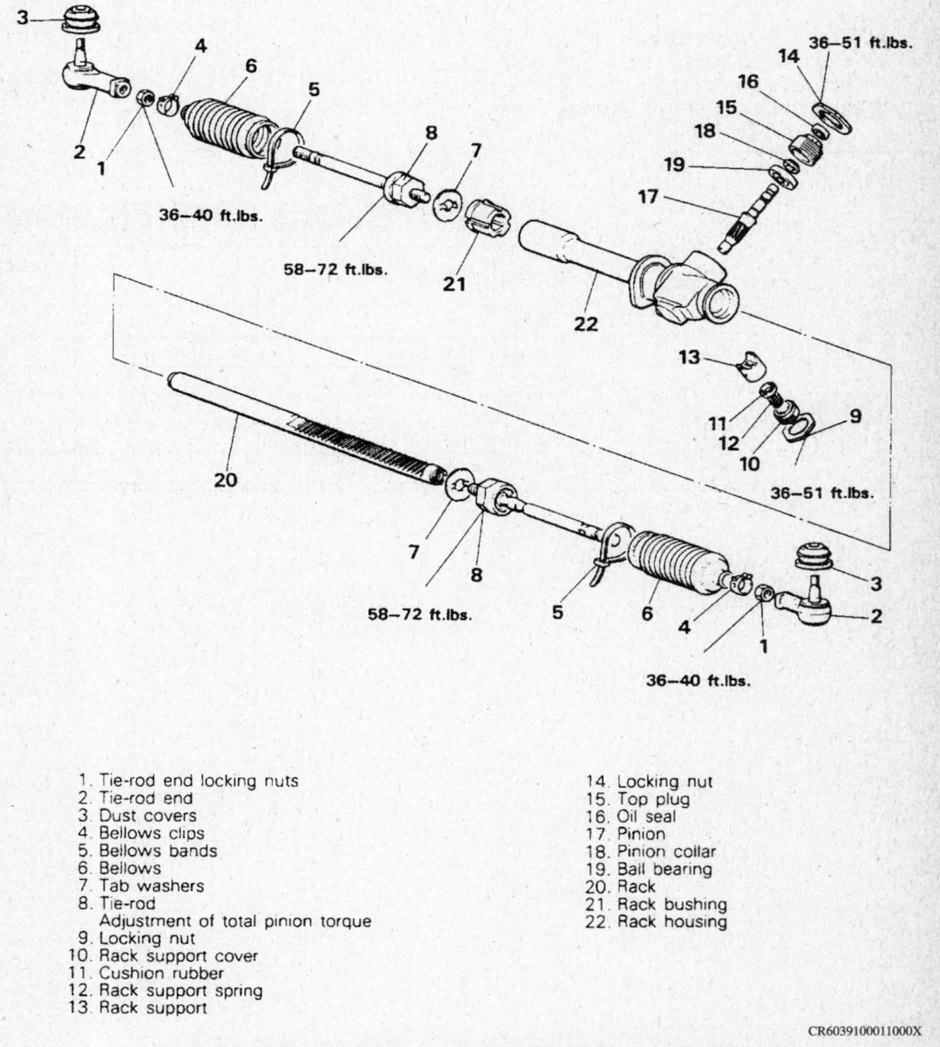

Fig. 1 Manual steering gear assembly. Talon

Assemble

1. Apply Mopar multi-mileage lubricant part No. 2525035, or equivalent, to rack tooth surfaces, rack bushing and pinion needle bearing in rack housing.
2. Install rack bushing, then the rack into gear housing opposite of removal.
3. Press pinion bearing onto pinion using steering/pinion gear remover/installer tool No. MB990783, or equivalent.
4. Apply multi-mileage lubricant to toothed surface of pinion, install pinion and bearing assembly into housing, then the pinion collar.
5. Press oil seal into top plug, apply semi-drying sealant to threaded portion of top plug, install top plug, then the top plug locking nut and tighten to specifications.
6. Apply multi-mileage lubricant to surface of rack support that contacts rack,

then install rack support to rack housing.

7. Apply multi-mileage lubricant to inner side of rack support spring, then install rack support spring to rack housing.
8. Install rubber cushion to rack support cover, apply a coating of semi-drying sealant to threaded part of rack support cover, install rack support cover to rack housing, then the locknut.
9. With rack placed in center position, tighten cover to specifications.
10. In a neutral position, rotate pinion shaft at a rate of one revolution every 4 to 6 seconds using preload socket tool No. CT-1108, or equivalent, and a suitable torque wrench. Return rack support cover 30–60° and adjust torque as follows:
    a. From 0–90,° **torque** should be 5–11 inch lbs.; from 90–650,° **torque** should be 2–9 inch lbs.
11. When adjusting, set at highest value, ensure there is no ratcheting or catching when operating rack towards shaft direction.
12. If specified values cannot be obtained, check rack support cover components and replace as necessary.
13. Install and tighten locking nut to specifications.
14. Install tab washers and inner tie rods, then tighten inner tie rods to specifications.
15. Secure inner tie rods by bending tab washers onto tie rod stepped portions.
16. Pack tie rod bellows lock groove with suitable silicone grease, install bellows into position and ensure they are not twisted, then the clips and bands.
17. Fill inside and lip of dust covers with multi-mileage lubricant, apply semi-drying sealant to dust covers, then press dust covers onto tie rod ends using front axle base tool No. MB990776-A, or equivalent.
18. Install outer tie rod end locknuts, then the tie rod ends.
19. Adjust so length between outer lip of bellows and inner side of tie rod end is 7.24–7.32 inches, then tighten locknuts to specifications and recheck length.

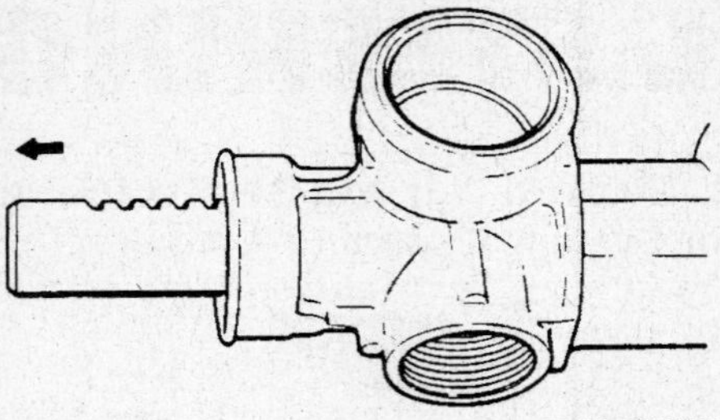

Fig. 2 Rack removal direction

TIGHTENING SPECIFICATIONS

Component	Torque/Ft. Lbs.
TALON	
Inner Tie Rod End	58–72
Outer Tie Rod End Locknut	36–40
Rack Support Cover	11
Rack Support Cover Locknut	36–51
Top Cover Locknut	36–51

POWER STEERING

TABLE OF CONTENTS

Power Steering Pressure Specifications

Model	Year	Power Steering Pump Pressure, psi			Output Flow, Gallons Per Minute④
		Test Valve		Max Relief Pressure	
		Open	Closed		
Avenger, Sebring Coupe & Talon	1997–2000	114–142	1209–1309③	1209–1309	—
Breeze, Cirrus, Sebring Convertible & Stratus	1997–99	50–80①	1195–1293②	1195–1293	⑤
	2000	50–80①	1195–1293②	1195–1293	1.3–1.6
Concord, Intrepid, LHS, Vision & 300M	1997	50–80①	1250–1350②	1250–1350	1.7
	1998	50–80①	1250–1350②	1250–1350	2.1–2.5
	1999–2000	50–125①	1250–1350②	1250–1350	2.1–2.5
Neon	1997–99	50–80①	1195–1293②	1195–1293	1.3–1.4
	2000	50–80①	1350–1450②	1350–1450	1.1–1.3

① — Initial pressure.
② — Do not leave valve closed for more than five seconds.
③ — Do not leave valve closed for more than 10 seconds.
④ — At 1500 RPM & minimum pressure.
⑤ — Models built prior to 1/7/97, 1.3–1.4 gallons per minute; models built after 1/7/97, 1.5–2.0 gallons per minute.

Avenger, Sebring Coupe & Talon

NOTE: On Air Bag Equipped Models, Refer To " Air Bag System Precautions" Located In The Front Of This Manual For System Disarming & Arming Procedures.

NOTE: Prior To Performing Any Service Operations Listed In This Section, Consult The "Technical Service Bulletins " For Related Information.

INDEX

PRECAUTIONS

AIR BAG SYSTEMS

Refer to "Air Bag System Precautions" in the front of this manual for system disarming and arming procedures.

BATTERY GROUND CABLE

Prior to service, disconnect battery ground cable and isolate as required.

DESCRIPTION

POWER STEERING PUMP

A vane type oil pump with a fluid flow control system is used on these models. Two different type pumps are used. One type is used on 2.0L engines, **Fig. 1**, the other on 2.5L engines, **Fig. 2**.

STEERING GEAR

The steering gear and linkage are an integral rack and pinion type, **Fig. 3**.

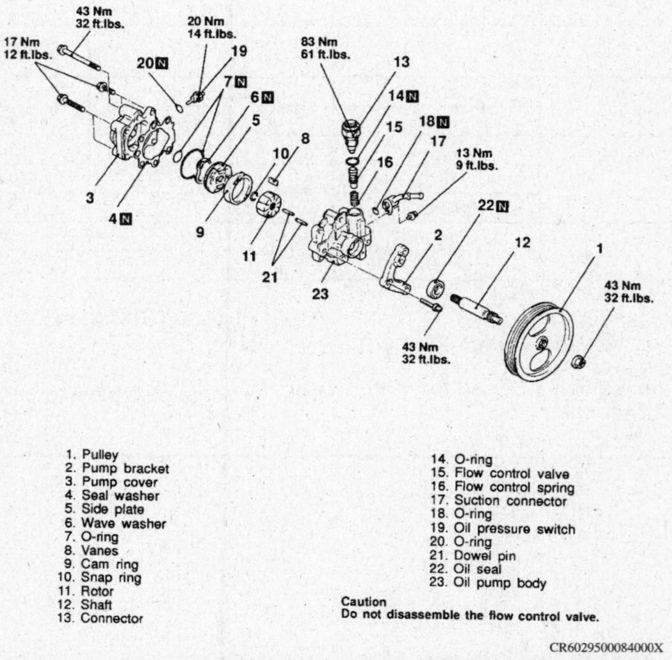

Fig. 1 Exploded view of power steering pump. 2.0L engine

DIAGNOSIS & TESTING

ACCESSING DIAGNOSTIC TROUBLE CODES

A DRB, or equivalent scan tool, is required to access the speed proportional power steering diagnostic trouble codes. Connect the scan tool to the Data Link Connector (DLC) under the lefthand side of the instrument panel. The diagnostic cycle begins when the ignition is turned On.

CONNECTOR TERMINAL IDENTIFICATION

Refer to **Fig. 4** for connector terminal identifications.

DIAGNOSTIC TESTS

Refer to "Breeze, Cirrus, Sebring Convertible & Stratus" for power steering system diagnostic tests.

CLEARING DIAGNOSTIC TROUBLE CODES

Record existing codes for future reference prior to clearing DTCs. To clear diagnostic trouble codes, select the "Erase DTCs" data screen on the DRB scan tool.

COMPONENT TESTING

Oil Pump Relief Pressure Test

1. Disconnect the pressure hose from the oil pump, then connect the oil pump pressure test tools, **Fig. 5.**
2. Bleed air, then turn steering wheel several times while vehicle is not moving.
3. Start engine and idle at 900–1100 RPM.
4. Fully close shutoff valve on pressure gauge, then measure oil pump relief

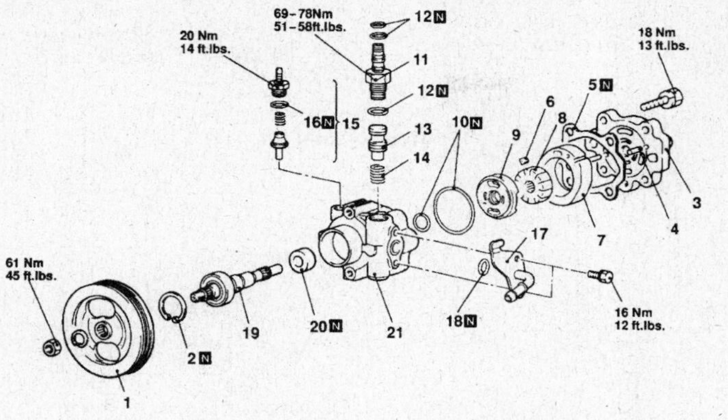

Disassembly steps
1. Pulley
2. Snap ring
3. Pump cover
4. Dowel pin
5. Seal washer
6. Vanes
7. Cam ring
8. Rotor
9. Side plate
10. O-ring
11. Connector
12. O-ring
13. Flow control valve
14. Flow control spring
15. Pressure switch assembly
16. O-ring
17. Suction connector
18. O-ring
19. Shaft assembly
20. Oil seal
21. Oil pump body

Caution
Do not disassemble the flow control valve.

CR6029500085000X

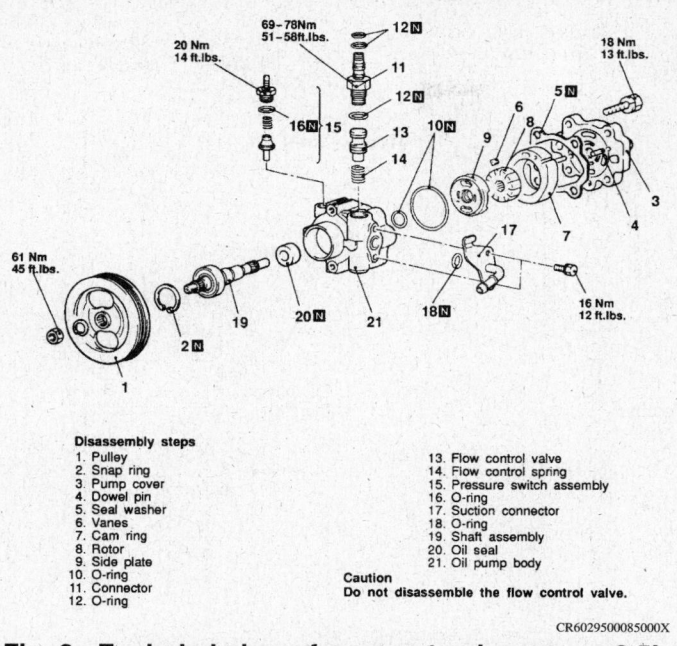

Fig. 2 Exploded view of power steering pump. 2.5L engine

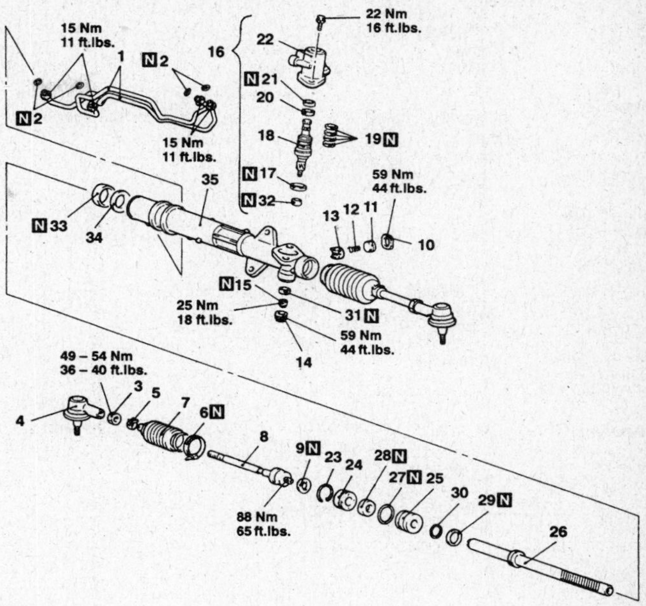

1. Feed tube
2. O-ring
3. Tie rod end locking nut
4. Tie rod end
5. Bellows clip
6. Bellows band
7. Bellows
8. Tie rod
9. Tab washer
- Total pinion torque adjustment
10. Locking nut
11. Rack support cover
12. Rack support spring
13. Rack support
14. End plug
15. Self-locking nut
16. Valve housing assembly
17. Oil seal
18. Pinion and valve assembly
19. Seal ring
20. Ball bearing
21. Oil seal
22. Valve housing
23. Circlip
24. Rack stopper
25. Rack bushing
26. Rack
27. O-ring
28. Oil seal
29. Seal ring
30. O-ring
31. Ball bearing
32. Needle roller bearing
33. Oil seal
34. Back-up washer
35. Rack housing

CR6029700191000X

Fig. 3 Exploded view of power steering gear

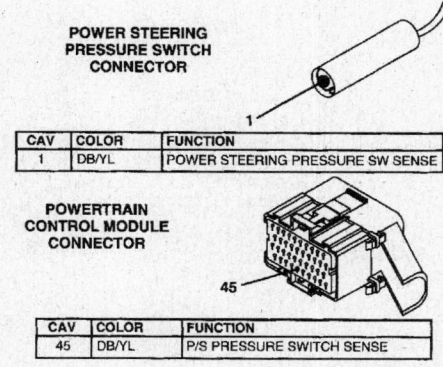

pressure to confirm that it is within 1209–1309 psi. **Pressure gauge shutoff valve must not remain closed for more than 10 seconds.**

5. If pressure is not as specified, replace oil pump.
6. Remove pressure test tools, then tighten pressure hose to specifications.
7. Bleed system.

No-Load Condition Pressure Test

1. Disconnect pressure hose from oil pump, then connect no-load condition pressure test tools, **Fig. 6.**
2. Bleed air, then turn steering wheel several times while vehicle is not moving so fluid temperature rises.
3. Start engine and idle at 900–1100 RPM.
4. Inspect and ensure hydraulic pressure is at standard value of 114–142 psi when no-load conditions are created by fully opening pressure gauge shutoff valve.
5. If pressure is not as specified, condition's probable cause is oil line or steering gearbox. Inspect and repair as required.
6. Remove pressure test tools, then tighten pressure hose to specifications.
7. Bleed system.

Steering Gear Retention Hydraulic Pressure Test

1. Disconnect pressure hose from oil pump, then connect retention hydraulic pressure test tools, **Fig. 7.**
2. Bleed air, then turn steering wheel several times while vehicle is not moving so fluid temperature rises.
3. Start engine, then idle at 900–1100 RPM.

POWER STEERING PRESSURE SWITCH CONNECTOR

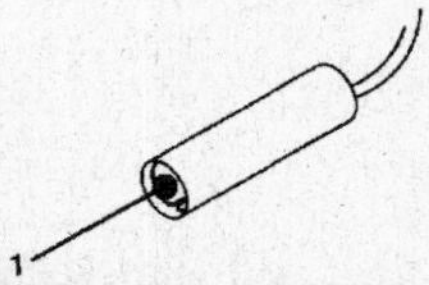

CAV	COLOR	FUNCTION
1	DB/YL	POWER STEERING PRESSURE SW SENSE

POWERTRAIN CONTROL MODULE CONNECTOR

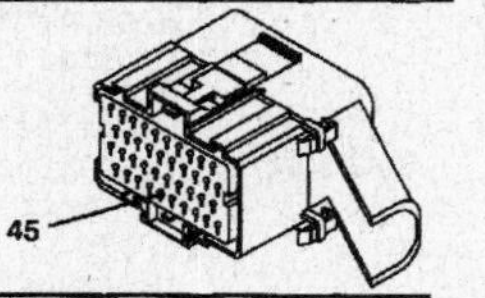

CAV	COLOR	FUNCTION
45	DB/YL	P/S PRESSURE SWITCH SENSE

CR6029800151000X

Fig. 4 Connector terminal identification

4. Fully close, then fully open shutoff valve on pressure gauge.
5. Turn steering wheel all the way to left or right, then ensure retention hydraulic pressure is at standard value of 1209–1309 psi.
6. If pressure is not within standard value, overhaul steering gearbox.
7. Measure fluid pressure again.
8. Remove tools, then tighten pressure hose to specifications.
9. Bleed system.

Power Steering Pressure Switch Inspection

1. Disconnect pressure hose from oil pump, then connect power steering pressure switch test tools, **Fig. 8.**
2. Bleed air, then turn steering wheel several times while vehicle is not moving so fluid temperature rises.
3. Idle engine.
4. Disconnect pressure switch connector, then place ohmmeter in position, **Fig. 8.**
5. Gradually close shutoff valve at pressure gauge and increase hydraulic pressure.
6. Ensure hydraulic pressure activates the switch at standard value of 213–284 psi.
7. Gradually open shutoff valve and reduce hydraulic pressure.
8. Ensure hydraulic pressure deactivates the switch at standard value of 114 psi or less.
9. Remove tools, then tighten pressure hose to specifications.
10. Bleed system.

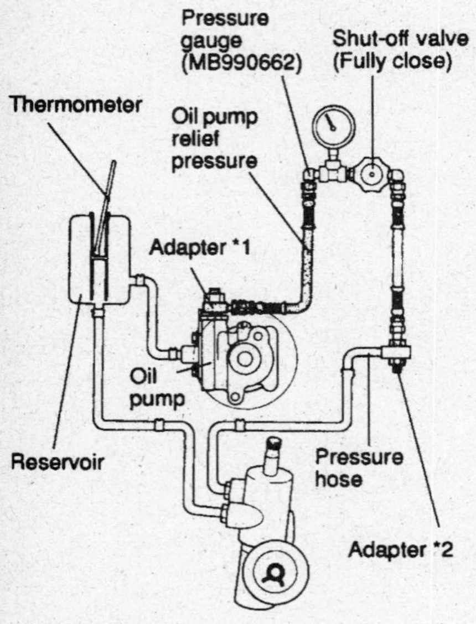

NOTE
*1: MB990993 or MB991217 <SOHC>
MB991548 <DOHC>
*2: MB990994 <SOHC>
MB991549 <DOHC>

CR6029500087000X

Fig. 5 Oil pump relief pressure test tool installation

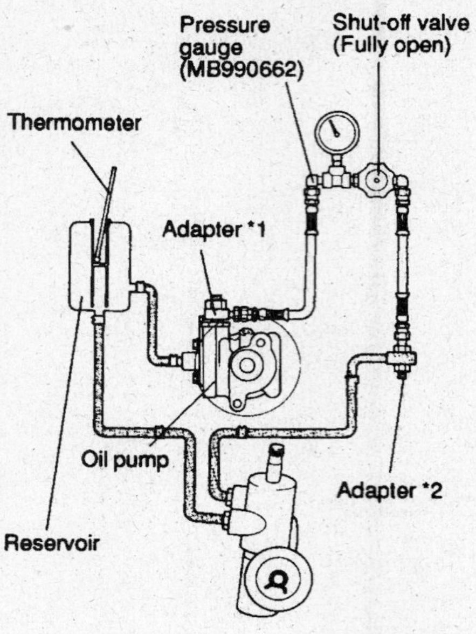

NOTE
*1: MB990993 or MB991217 <SOHC>
MB991548 <DOHC>
*2: MB990994 <SOHC>
MB991549 <DOHC>

CR6029500088000X

Fig. 6 No-load pressure test tool installation

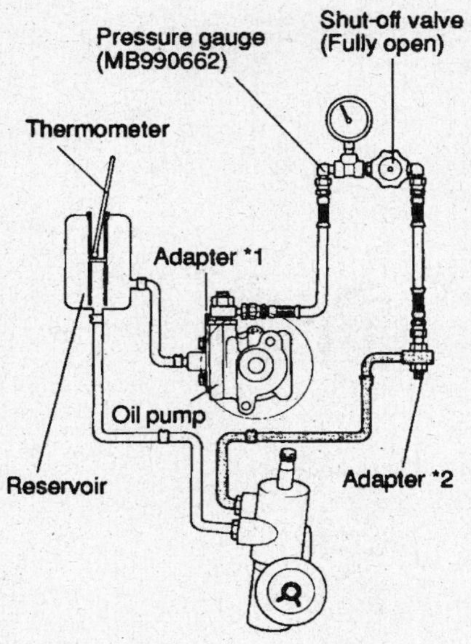

NOTE
*1: MB990993 or MB991217 <SOHC>
MB991548 <DOHC>
*2: MB990994 <SOHC>
MB991549 <DOHC>

CR6029500089000X

Fig. 7 Retention pressure test tool installation

POWER STEERING SYSTEM SERVICE

Power Steering System Bleed

1. Raise and support front wheels.
2. Manually turn oil pump pulley several times.
3. Turn steering wheel all the way left and right five or six times.
4. Disconnect high-tension cable, then crank starter motor intermittently, while turning steering wheel fully to left and right, five or six times for 15–20 seconds.
5. **Refill the fluid supply during air bleeding so level never falls below lower position of the filter.**
6. **If air bleeding is done while engine is running, air will be broken up and absorbed into the fluid. Ensure bleeding is done only while cranking.**
7. Connect high-tension cable, then start engine.
8. Turn steering wheel to left and right until there are no air bubbles in reservoir.
9. Ensure fluid is not milky, then inspect fluid level.
10. Ensure level does not change when steering wheel is turned left or right.

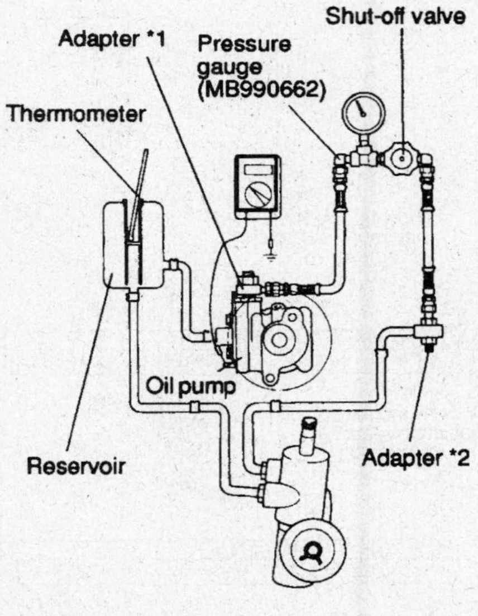

NOTE
*1: MB990993 or MB991217 <SOHC>
MB991548 <DOHC>
*2: MB990994 <SOHC>
MB991549 <DOHC>

CR6029500090000X

Fig. 8 Pressure switch test tool installation

11. Ensure level is within .2 inch when engine is stopped compared to when it is running.
12. **If fluid level variation is more than .2 inch, air still exists in the system, requiring additional bleeding.**
13. If bleeding procedure is not complete, abnormal noises may be emitted from pump and flow control valve which may reduce pump life.

Component Service

OUTER TIE ROD & BOOT REPLACEMENT

Removal

Refer to **Fig. 9** for tie rod and boot removal.

Installation

1. Using pliers, apply pressure to concave section of bellows band and tighten, **Fig. 10.**
2. Using a plastic hammer, bend convex section of bellows band, **Fig. 11.**
3. Pack tie rod dust cover with multi purpose grease, then apply specified sealant, 3M ATD Part No. 8663, or equivalent, **Fig. 12.**
4. Using tool No. MB990776, or equivalent, **Fig. 12,** install dust cover to tie rod end ball joint.

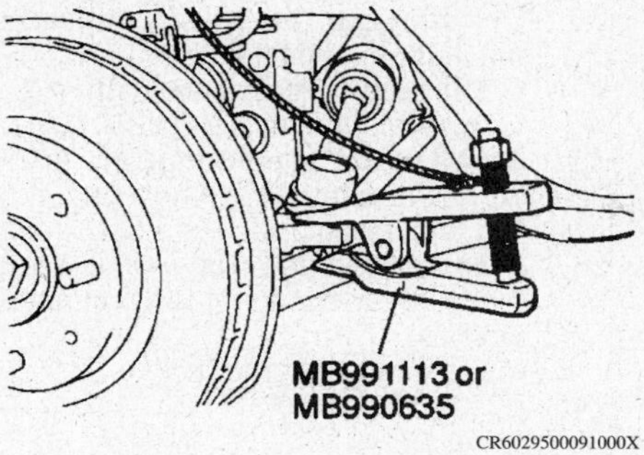

Fig. 9 Tie rod removal

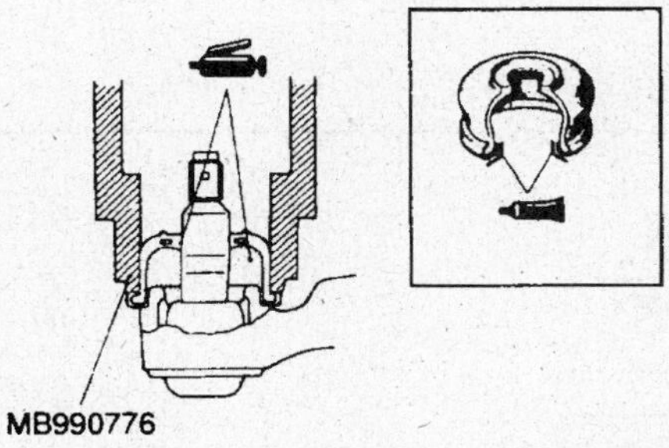

Fig. 12 Dust cover sealant application

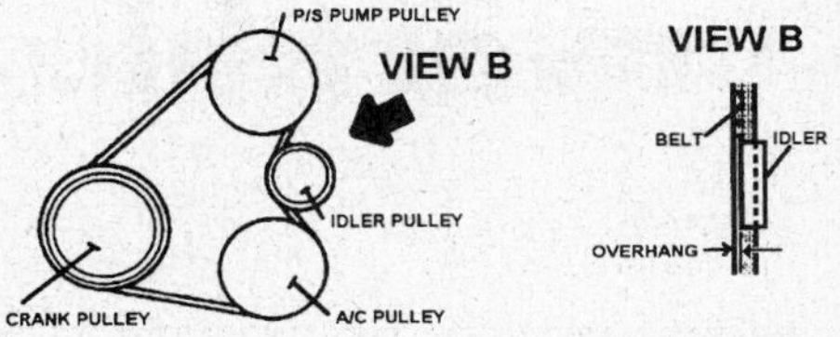

Fig. 15 PS pump pulley & idler pulley alignment inspection. With A/C

5. Install tie rod end to specified dimension, **Fig. 13, then tighten tie rod to specifications.**

TECHNICAL SERVICE BULLETINS

BELT NOISE OR IRREGULAR WEAR

1997–99

On these models, equipped with 2.0L non-turbocharged engines, the power steering belt may make noise or wear irregularly. These conditions may be caused by power steering pump pulley misalignment.

On models less A/C, visually inspect pump pulley alignment to the crankshaft pulley. If improper alignment is not clearly visible, use a suitable straightedge. The pump pulley should be close to parallel with the crankshaft pulley, **Fig. 14.**

On models equipped with A/C, inspect pulley alignment by observing the way the belt rides on the idler pulley. If the belt rides

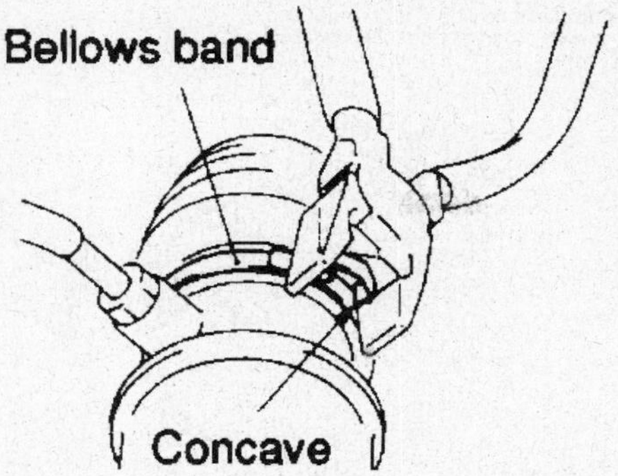

Fig. 10 Concave section of band adjustment

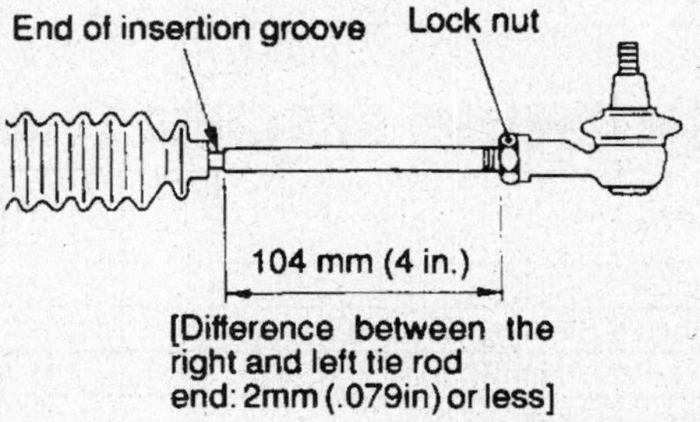

Fig. 13 Tie rod replacement dimension

over the idler's edge, the pump pulley will be misaligned, **Fig. 15.**

If misalignment is discovered, perform repair procedures listed below.

1. On models built prior to September 19, 1997, proceed as follows:
   a. Remove power steering belt, then the pump from bracket. Position pump aside.
   b. Remove and discard pump bracket, **Fig. 16.**
   c. Install replacement bracket part No. MR403066, then **torque** bolts to 29 ft. lbs.
   d. **On models equipped with A/C,** remove and discard idler pulley assembly. Install replacement pulley part No. MR398887, then **torque** bolts to 21–30 ft. lbs. **This new pulley went into production on models built after February 2, 1998.**
   e. **On all models,** install PS pump onto bracket.
   f. **On models equipped with A/C, torque** pump mounting bolts to 29 ft. lbs.
   g. **On models less A/C,** do not tighten bolts until after belt tension has been properly adjusted.
   h. **On all models,** install a new PS belt (less A/C, part No. M04668223; with A/C, part No. MB878687).
   i. Using a suitable belt tension gauge, adjust tension at middle of belt to 93–115 lbs.
   j. **On models less A/C, torque** bolts to 29 ft. lbs.
   k. **On all models,** proper belt tension

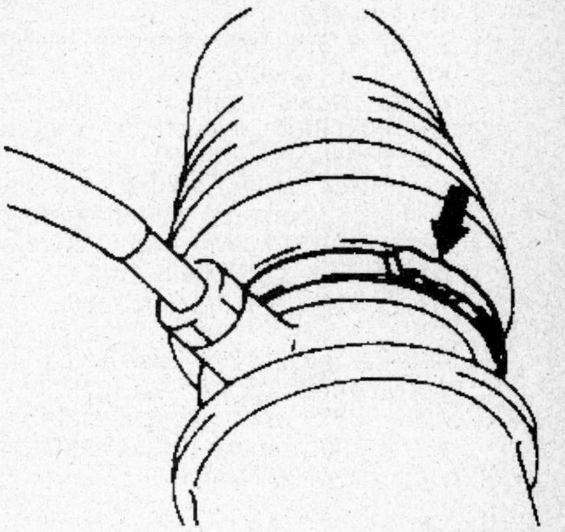

Fig. 11 Convex section of band adjustment

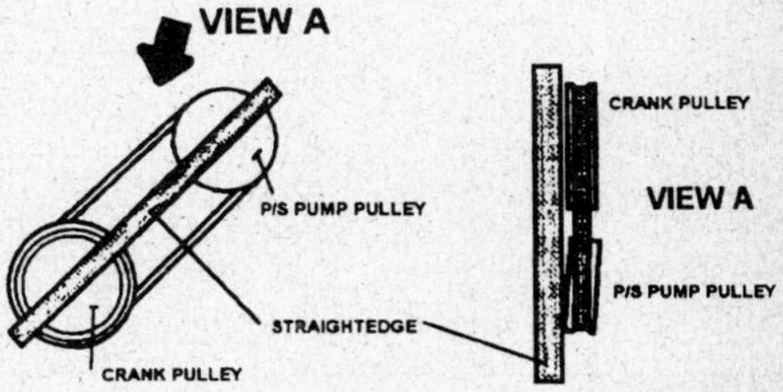

Fig. 14 PS pump pulley & crankshaft pulley alignment inspection. Less A/C

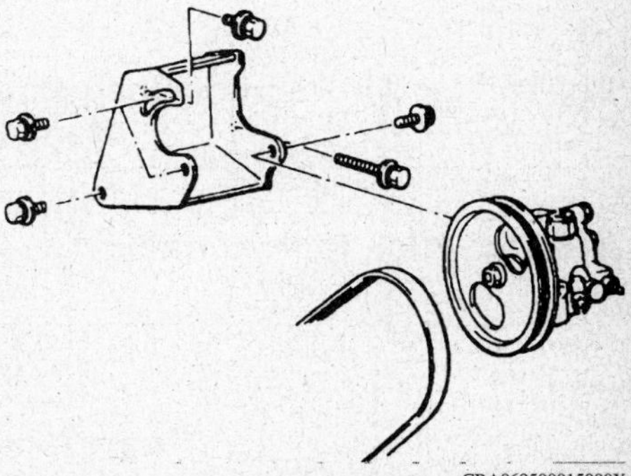

Fig. 16 PS pump bracket. Models built prior to 9/19/97

is critical. If installing a new belt, adjust tension to upper end of specifications. Start and run engine, then turn it off and inspect tension once again.
   l. Inspect belt alignment. **If misalignment condition is not completely corrected, proceed to next step.**
2. **On 1998 models built between September 19, 1997 and November 1, 1997, and earlier models which were not cured with previous procedure,** proceed as follows:
   a. Remove power steering belt, then the pump from bracket. Position

pump aside.

b. Remove bracket upper mounting bolt, then loosen, but do not remove, power steering bracket mounting bolt and engine mount front bolt.

c. Install one or two shims part No. MA111832 between power steering pump bracket and front engine mount, **Fig. 17** Usually two shims will be enough to correct the condition.

d. Install a new PS belt (less A/C, part No. M04668223; with A/C, part No. MB878687) and, using a suitable belt tension gauge, adjust tension at middle of belt to 93–115 lbs.

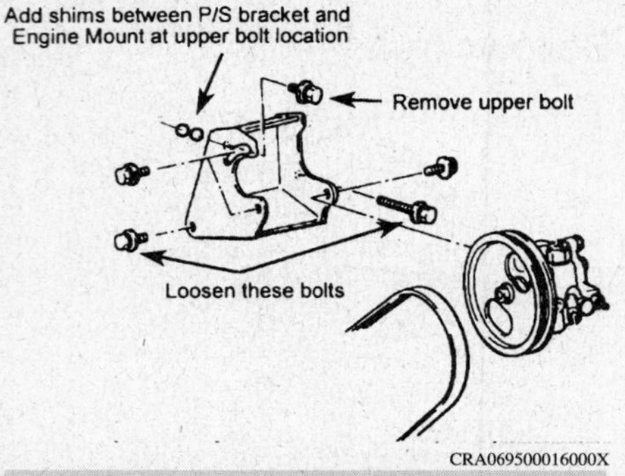
Add shims between P/S bracket and
Engine Mount at upper bolt location
Remove upper bolt
Loosen these bolts
CRA069500016000X

Fig. 17 PS pump bracket. Models built between 9/19/97 & 11/1/97

e. **On models less A/C, torque** bracket bolts to 29 ft. lbs.

f. **On models equipped with A/C, torque** idler pulley bolts to 29 ft. lbs.

g. **On all models,** proper belt tension is critical. If installing a new belt, adjust tension to upper end of specifications. Start and run engine, then turn it off and inspect tension once again.

h. Inspect belt alignment.

TIGHTENING SPECIFICATIONS

Component	Torque/Ft. Lbs.
Outer Tie Rod End Locknut	36–40
Outer Tie Rod To Steering Knuckle	18–25
Pressure Hose To Pump (2.0L)	42
Pressure Hose To Pump (2.5L)	13

Breeze, Cirrus, Sebring Convertible & Stratus

NOTE: On Air Bag Equipped Models, Refer To " Air Bag System Precautions" Located In The Front Of This Manual For System Disarming & Arming Procedures.

NOTE: Prior To Performing Any Service Operations Listed In This Section, Consult The "Technical Service Bulletins " For Related Information.

INDEX

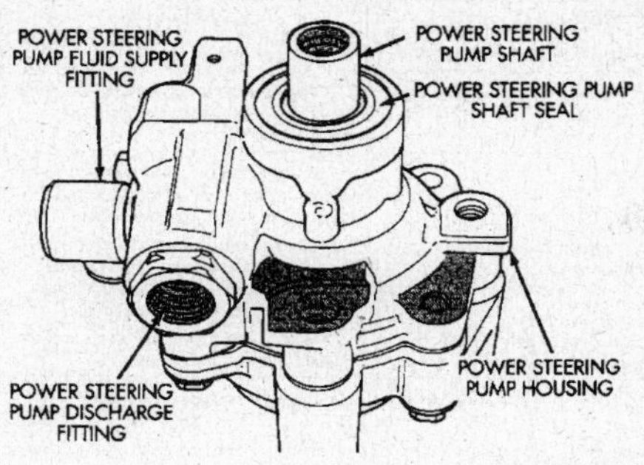

Fig. 1 Exploded view of power steering pump

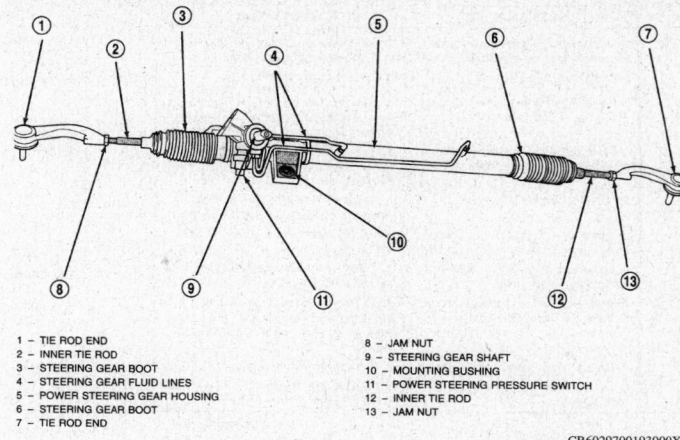

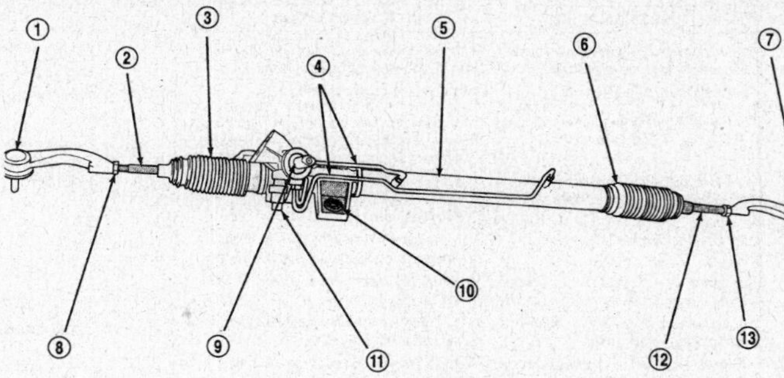

1 – TIE ROD END
2 – INNER TIE ROD
3 – STEERING GEAR BOOT
4 – STEERING GEAR FLUID LINES
5 – POWER STEERING GEAR HOUSING
6 – STEERING GEAR BOOT
7 – TIE ROD END
8 – JAM NUT
9 – STEERING GEAR SHAFT
10 – MOUNTING BUSHING
11 – POWER STEERING PRESSURE SWITCH
12 – INNER TIE ROD
13 – JAM NUT

CR6029700193000X

Fig. 2 Power steering gear assembly

PRECAUTIONS

AIR BAG SYSTEMS

Refer to "Air Bag System Precautions" in the front of this manual for system disarming and arming procedures.

BATTERY GROUND CABLE

Prior to service, disconnect battery ground cable and isolate as required.

DESCRIPTION

POWER STEERING PUMP

Constant Displacement

On models equipped with a TTA constant displacement, vane type pump, **Fig. 1,** the pump utilizes a remote fluid reservoir, mounted at the rear of the cylinder head on the passenger side of the vehicle. In the event of a power steering failure, manual control can be maintained. However, under these conditions, steering effort will be significantly increased. No repairs are to be done on internal components of the TTA power steering pumps.

All vehicles equipped with this pump have a remote mounted power steering fluid reservoir. On models equipped with 2.0L and 2.4L engines the reservoir is mounted to the rear of the cylinder head on the passenger side of the vehicle. On models equipped with 2.5L engines the reservoir is mounted to the front side of the engine between the cylinder heads.

Rectangular pumping vanes in the shaft driven rotor move power steering fluid from the intake to the cam ring pressure cavities of the pump. As the rotor begins to turn, centrifugal force throws the vanes against the inside surface of the cam ring to pickup residual oil. This oil is then forced into the cavities of the thrust plate through two crossover holes in the cam ring and pressure plate. The crossover holes empty into the high pressure area between the pressure plate and the housing end cover.

As the high pressure is filled, oil flows under the vanes in the rotor slots, forcing the vanes to follow the inside surface of the cam ring. As the vanes reach the restricted area of the cam ring, oil is forced out from between the vanes. When excess oil flow is generated during high speed operation, a regulated amount of oil returns to the pump intake side through a flow control valve. The flow control valve reduces the power required to drive the pump and holds down temperature buildup.

When steering conditions exceed maximum pressure requirements, such as when the wheels are turned against the stops, pressure built up in the steering gear exerts pressure on the spring end of the flow control valve. The high pressure lifts the relief valve ball from its seat and allows oil to flow through a trigger orifice located in the outlet fitting. This reduces pressure on the spring end of the flow control valve which then opens and allows the oil to return to the intake side of the pump. This action limits maximum pressure output of the pump to a safe level.

Under normal power steering pump operating conditions, pressure requirements of the pump are below maximum, causing the pressure relief valve to remain closed.

Variable Assist

Cirrus and Stratus models with speed proportional steering built before January 7, 1997, are equipped with an electronically controlled speed sensitive variable assist power steering system. Vehicles built on or after January 7, 1997, are equipped with the droop flow speed sensitive variable assist power steering system used on the Sebring Convertible. The drop flow pump is a constant displacement, but variable flow rate vane type pump.

The system provides additional steering assist while the vehicle is stationary and at low driving speeds. This additional power steering assist reduces the steering effort required by the driver for low speed driving and parking maneuvers. Variable assist speed proportional power steering then provides less power steering assist at highway speeds to maintain the firm responsive feel of the non-variable assist speed proportional power steering system.

The operational range of the variable assist speed proportional power steering system is from 0–60 mph. Maximum available power steering assist is provided at zero miles per hour. The power steering assist is then gradually reduced from vehicle speeds greater than zero to a maximum speed of 60 mph. The minimum power steering assist available is reached at a vehicle speed of approximately 60 mph.

Variable assist power steering is provided by controlling fluid pressure at the power steering gear. The pressure is controlled by regulating fluid flow from the steering gear back to the pump. A solenoid valve located on the steering gear is used to control power steering pressure by varying the size of an orifice which controls fluid flow from the steering gear back to the pump.

The variable assist speed proportional solenoid control valve is controlled by the steering gear mounted electronic solenoid control module (SCM). The SCM receives the vehicle speed signal sent from the transmission control module (TCM). Upon receiving the vehicle speed signal from the TCM, the SCM converts that speed signal into an electrical current usable by the solenoid control valve for controlling the variable assist of the power steering system.

STEERING GEAR

The power steering system consists of these six major components: the power steering gear, pump, fluid reservoir, supply and pressure hose, return hose and oil cooler. Turning of the wheel is converted into linear travel through the meshing of helical pinion teeth with rack teeth, **Fig. 2.** Power assisted steering is provided by an open center, rotary type control valve which directs oil from the pump to either side of integral rack piston.

Road feel is controlled by the diameter of a torsion bar which initially steers the vehicle. This movement directs oil behind the integral rack piston which, in turn, builds up hydraulic pressure and assists in turning effort.

The drive tangs on the pinion of the power steering pump mate loosely with a stub shaft. This is to permit manual steering control to be maintained if the drive belt on the pump should break. However, under these conditions, steering effort will be increased.

TROUBLESHOOTING

Refer to **Fig. 3** when troubleshooting the power steering system.

CONDITION	POSSIBLE CAUSES	CORRECTION
OBJECTIONABLE HISS OR WHISTLE*	1. Damaged or mispositioned steering column shaft/coupling dash panel seal.	1. Reposition or replace steering column shaft/coupling dash panel seal.
	2. Noisy valve in power steering gear.	2. Replace power steering gear.
RATTLE OR CLUNK	1. Power steering gear loose on front suspension crossmember.	1. Inspect power steering gear mounting bolts. Replace as necessary. Tighten to the specified torque.
	2. Front suspension crossmember mounting fasteners loose at frame.	2. Tighten the front suspension crossmember mounting fasteners to the specified torque.
	3. Loose tie rod (outer or inner).	3. Check tie rod pivot points for wear. Replace worn/loose parts as required.
	4. Loose lower control arm mounting bolts at front suspension crossmember.	4. Tighten control arm mounting bolts to the specified torques.
	5. Loose shock assembly mounting fasteners at shock tower.	5. Tighten shock assembly fasteners to the specified torques.
	6. Power steering fluid pressure hose touching the body of the vehicle.	6. Adjust hose to proper position by loosening, repositioning, and tightening fitting to specified torque. Do not bend tubing.
	7. Internal power steering gear noise.	7. Replace power steering gear.
	8. Damaged front suspension crossmember.	8. Replace front suspension crossmember.

CR6029700192010X

Fig. 3 Power steering pump troubleshooting (Part 1 of 6)

CONDITION	POSSIBLE CAUSES	CORRECTION
STEERING WHEEL/ COLUMN CLICKING, CLUNKING OR RATTLING.	1. Steering column preload is not set properly.	1. Loosen steering column coupling pinch bolt to reset steering column preload. Replace pinch bolt and torque to specifications.
	2. Loose steering coupling pinch bolt.	2. Replace pinch bolt and torque to specifications.
	3. Steering column bearings.	3. Replace steering column.
STEERING WHEEL HAS FORE AND AFT LOOSENESS.	1. Steering wheel retaining nut not properly tightened and torqued.	1. Tighten the steering wheel retaining nut to its specified torque.
	2. Steering column preload is not set properly.	2. Loosen steering column coupling pinch bolt to reset steering column preload. Replace pinch bolt and torque to specifications.
	3. Steering column lower bearing spring retainer slipped on steering column shaft.	3. Replace steering column.
STEERING WHEEL OR DASH VIBRATES DURING LOW SPEED OR STANDSTILL STEERING MANEUVERS.	1. Air in the fluid of the power steering system.	1. Bleed air from system following the power steering pump initial operation service procedure.*
	2. Tires not properly inflated.	2. Inflate tires to the specified pressure.
	3. Excessive engine vibration.	3. Ensure that the engine is running properly.
	4. Loose tie rod end jam nut.	4. Tighten the inner to outer tie rod jam nut to the specified torque.
	5. Overcharged air conditioning system.	5. Check air conditioning pump head pressure and correct as necessary.
STEERING CATCHES, STICKS IN CERTAIN POSITIONS OR IS DIFFICULT TO TURN.	1. Low power steering fluid level.	1. Fill power steering fluid reservoir to specified level and check for leaks.
	2. Tires not inflated to specified pressure.	2. Inflate tires to the specified pressure.
	3. Lack of lubrication in front suspension control arm ball joints.	3. Lubricate ball joints if ball joints are not a lubricated-for-life type ball joint. If ball joint is a lubricated-for-life ball joint, replace ball joint or control arm.
	4. Worn upper or lower control arm ball joint.	4. Replace ball joint or control arm.
	5. Lack of lubrication in steering gear outer tie rod ends.	5. Lubricate tie rod ends if they are not a lubricated-for-life type. If tie rod end is a lubricated-for-life type, replace tie rod end.

CR6029700192030X

Fig. 3 Power steering pump troubleshooting (Part 3 of 6)

CONDITION	POSSIBLE CAUSES	CORRECTION
POPPING NOISE	1. Worn outer tie rod.	1. Replace outer tie rod.
CHIRP OR SQUEAL (POWER STEERING PUMP)	1. Loose power steering pump drive belt.	1. Check and adjust power steering pump drive belt to specifications. Replace belt if worn or glazed.
WHINE OR GROWL (POWER STEERING PUMP)**	1. Low fluid level.	1. Fill power steering fluid reservoir to proper level and check for leaks (make sure all air is bled from the system fluid).
	2. Power steering hose touching vehicle body or frame.	2. Adjust hose to proper position by loosening, repositioning, and tightening fitting to specified torque. Do not bend tubing. Replace hose if damaged.
	3. Extreme wear of power steering pump internal components.	3. Replace power steering pump and flush system as necessary.
SUCKING AIR SOUND	1. Loose clamp on power steering fluid return hose.	1. Tighten or replace hose clamp.
	2. Missing O-Ring on power steering hose connection.	2. Inspect connection and replace O-Ring as required.
	3. Low power steering fluid level.	3. Fill power steering fluid reservoir to proper level and check for leaks.
	4. Air leak between power steering fluid reservoir and power steering pump.	4. Replace power steering pump (with reservoir).
SQUEAK OR RUBBING SOUND	1. Steering column shroud rubbing.	1. Realign shrouds as necessary.
	2. Steering column shaft rubbing.	2. Move or realign item rubbing shaft.
	3. Clockspring noisy.	3. Remove clockspring. Reinstall wheel. If noise is gone, replace clockspring.
	4. Steering gear internally noisy.	4. Replace steering gear.
SCRUBBING OR KNOCKING NOISE.	1. Incorrect tire or wheel size.	1. Replace incorrect size tire or wheel with size used as original equipment.
	2. Interference between steering gear and other vehicle components.	2. Check for bent or misaligned components and correct as necessary.
	3. Steering gear internal stops worn excessively allowing tires to be steered excessively far.	3. Replace steering gear.

CR6029700192020X

Fig. 3 Power steering pump troubleshooting (Part 2 of 6)

CONDITION	POSSIBLE CAUSES	CORRECTION
	6. Loose power steering pump drive belt.	6. Tighten the power steering pump drive belt to specifications. If drive belt is worn or glazed, replace belt.
	7. Faulty power steering pump flow control (Perform Power Steering System Flow and Pressure Test).	7. Replace power steering pump.
	8. Excessive friction in steering column or intermediate shaft.	8. Isolate and correct condition.
	9. Binding upper or lower control arm ball joint.	9. Replace the upper or lower ball joint.
	10. Excessive friction in power steering gear.	10. Replace power steering gear.
STIFF, HARD TO TURN, SURGE, MOMENTARY INCREASE IN EFFORT WHEN TURNING.	1. Tires not properly inflated.	1. Inflate tires to specified pressure.
	2. Low power steering fluid level.	2. Add power steering fluid as required to power steering fluid reservoir to obtain proper level. Check for leaks.
	3. Loose power steering pump drive belt.	3. Tighten the power steering pump drive belt to specifications. If drive belt is worn or glazed, replace belt.
	4. Lack of lubrication in control arm ball joints.	4. Lubricate ball joints if ball joints are not a lubricated-for-life type ball joint. If ball joint is a lubricated-for-life ball joint, replace ball joint or control arm.
	5. Low power steering pump pressure (Perform Power Steering System Flow and Pressure Test).	5. Replace the power steering pump as necessary.
	6. High internal leak in power steering gear (Perform Power Steering System Flow and Pressure Test).	6. Replace power steering gear.
STEERING WHEEL DOES NOT RETURN TO CENTER POSITION.	1. Tires not inflated properly.	1. Inflate tires to specified pressure.
	2. Improper front wheel alignment.	2. Check and adjust wheel alignment as necessary.
	3. Lack of lubrication in front suspension control arm ball joints.	3. Lubricate ball joints if ball joints are not a lubricated for life type of ball joint. If ball joint is a lubricated for life ball joint, replace ball joint or control arm.
	4. Steering column coupling joints misaligned.	4. Realign steering column coupling joints.
	5. Steering wheel rubbing.	5. Adjust steering column shrouds to eliminate rubbing condition.

CR6029700192040X

Fig. 3 Power steering pump troubleshooting (Part 4 of 6)

CONDITION	POSSIBLE CAUSES	CORRECTION
	6. Damaged, mis-positioned or un-lubricated steering column coupler to dash seal.**	6. Replace, reposition, or lubricate dash seal.
	7. Binding upper or lower control arm ball joint.	7. Replace the upper or lower control arm ball joint.
	8. Tight shaft bearing in steering column.	8. Replace the steering column.
	9. Excessive friction in steering column coupling.	9. Replace steering column coupling.
	10. Excessive friction in power steering gear.	10. Replace power steering gear.
EXCESSIVE STEERING WHEEL KICKBACK OR TOO MUCH STEERING WHEEL FREE PLAY.	1. Air in the fluid of the power steering system.	1. Bleed air from system following the the power steering pump initial operation service procedure.*
	2. Power steering gear loose on front suspension crossmember.	2. Inspect power steering gear mounting bolts. Replace as necessary. Tighten to the specified torque.
	3. Steering column coupling worn, broken or loose.	3. Replace steering column coupling.
	4. Free play in steering column.	4. Check all components of the steering system and repair or replace as required.
	5. Worn control arm ball joints.	5. Replace ball joint or control arm as required.
	6. Loose steering knuckle to ball joint stud pinch bolt.	6. Inspect pinch bolts, replace as necessary, and tighten to specified torque.
	7. Front wheel bearings loose or worn.	7. Replace wheel bearing or knuckle as necessary.
	8. Loose outer tie rod ends.	8. Replace outer tie rod ends that have excessive free play.
	9. Loose inner tie rod ends.	9. Replace power steering gear.
	10 Defective steering gear rotary valve.	10. Replace power steering gear.

NOTE: * Steering shudder can be expected in new vehicles and vehicles with recent steering system repairs. Shudder should dissipate after the vehicle has been driven several weeks.

CR6029700192050X

Fig. 3 Power steering pump troubleshooting (Part 5 of 6)

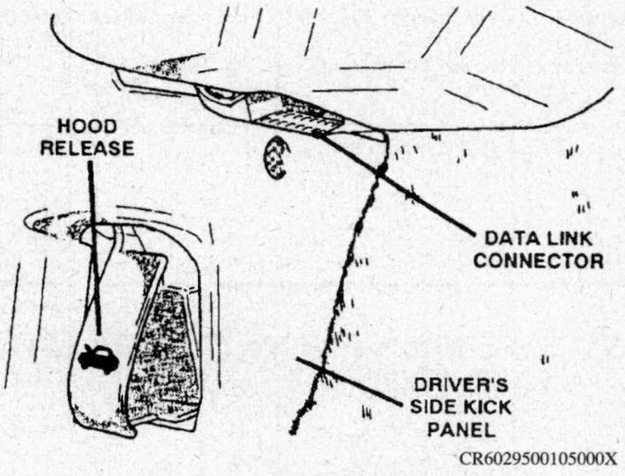

Fig. 4 DLC location

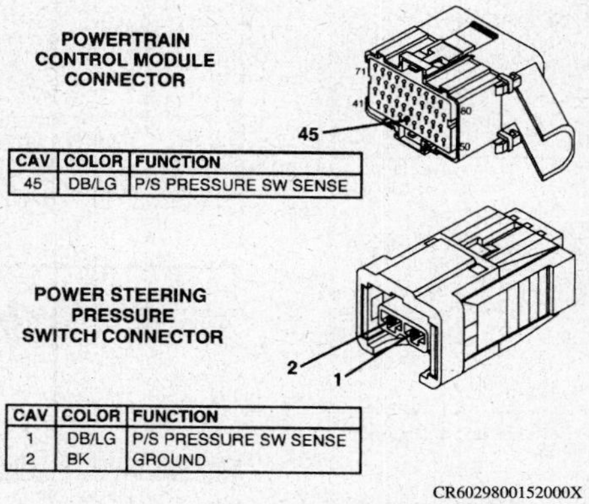

POWERTRAIN
CONTROL MODULE
CONNECTOR
45
CAV COLOR FUNCTION
45 DB/LG P/S PRESSURE SW SENSE
POWER STEERING
PRESSURE
SWITCH CONNECTOR
2
1
CAV COLOR FUNCTION
1 DB/LG P/S PRESSURE SW SENSE
2 BK GROUND
CR6029800152000X

Fig. 5 Connector terminal identification

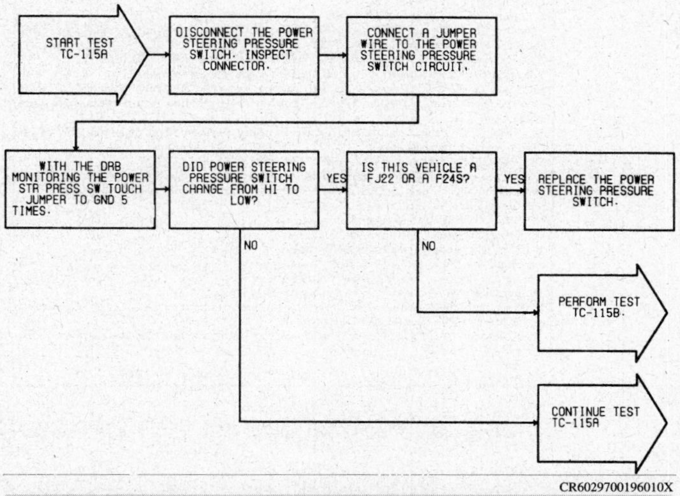

Fig. 6 Test TC-115A: PS Switch Failure (Part 1 of 2). 1997–98

CONDITION	POSSIBLE CAUSES	CORRECTION
LOW FLUID LEVEL WITH VISIBLE LEAK.	1. Loose power steering hose fittings.	1. Tighten the fitting to its specified torque.
	2. Damaged or missing fitting seal, gasket, or O-ring.	2. Replace as necessary.
	3. Power steering pump or power steering gear leaking.	3. Repair or replace the leaking component as required.
AERATED FLUID.	1. Low fluid level.*	1. Fill power steering fluid reservoir to proper level.
	2. Air leak between power steering fluid reservoir and pump.	2. Inspect for proper sealing. Replace the power steering pump (with reservoir).
	3. Cracked power steering pump housing.	3. Replace the power steering pump.
RESERVOIR FLUID OVERFLOW AND FLUID THAT IS MILKY IN COLOR	1. Water contamination.	1. Drain the power steering fluid from the system. Flush the system with fresh clean power steering fluid, drain, then refill to the proper level.

CR6029700192060X

Fig. 3 Power steering pump troubleshooting (Part 6 of 6)

DIAGNOSIS & TESTING

ACCESSING DIAGNOSTIC TROUBLE CODES

A DRB or equivalent scan tool is required to access the speed proportional power steering diagnostic trouble codes. Connect the scan tool to the Data Link Connector (DLC), **Fig. 4**. The diagnostic cycle begins when the ignition is turned On.

CONNECTOR TERMINAL IDENTIFICATION

Refer to **Fig. 5** for connector terminal identification.

DIAGNOSTIC TESTS

Refer to **Figs. 6 through 9** for diagnostic and testing procedures.

CLEARING DIAGNOSTIC TROUBLE CODES

Record existing codes for future reference prior to clearing DTCs. To clear diagnostic trouble codes, select the "Erase DTCs" data screen on the DRB scan tool.

POWER STEERING SYSTEM SERVICE

Power Steering System Bleed

To avoid personal injury, power steering fluid level should be inspected with engine Off. Use only approved fluid. Do not use automatic transmission fluid. Do not overfill fluid system.

1. Wipe filler cap clean, then inspect fluid level.
2. Dipstick should indicate "Full Cold" when fluid is at normal temperature approximately 70–80°F.
3. Fill power steering pump fluid reservoir to proper level with approved power steering fluid.
4. Start and run engine for a few seconds, then turn engine Off.
5. Add fluid as required.
6. Repeat previous procedure until fluid level remains constant after running engine.

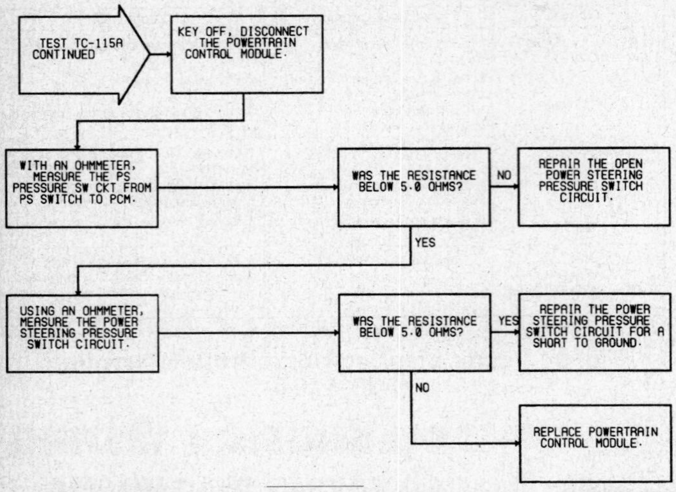

Fig. 6 Test TC-115A: PS Switch Failure (Part 2 of 2). 1997–98

TEST	ACTION
1	Ignition Off Disconnect the Power Steering Pressure Switch. **Note: Check connectors - Clean/repair as necessary.** Ignition on, engine not running. Connect a jumper wire to the Power Steering Pressure Switch Circuit. With the DRB monitoring the Power Steering Pressure Switch, touch jumper to ground 5 times. Did the Power Steering Pressure Switch change from high to low? Yes → Go To 2 No → Go To 4
2	Ignition Off Disconnect the Power Steering Pressure Switch. **Note: Check connectors - Clean/repair as necessary.** Using an Ohmmeter, measure the resistance of the Ground Circuit at the Power Steering Pressure Switch Connector. Is the resistance below 5.0 ohms? Yes → Go To 3 No → Repair the open Ground Circuit. Perform Powertrain Verification Test VER-5A.
3	If there are no potential causes remaining, replace the Power Steering Pressure Switch. View repair options. Repair Replace the Power Steering Pressure Switch. Perform Powertrain Verification Test VER-2A.

CR6029900194010X

Fig. 8 DTC P0551: PS Switch Failure (Part 1 of 2). 1999–2000

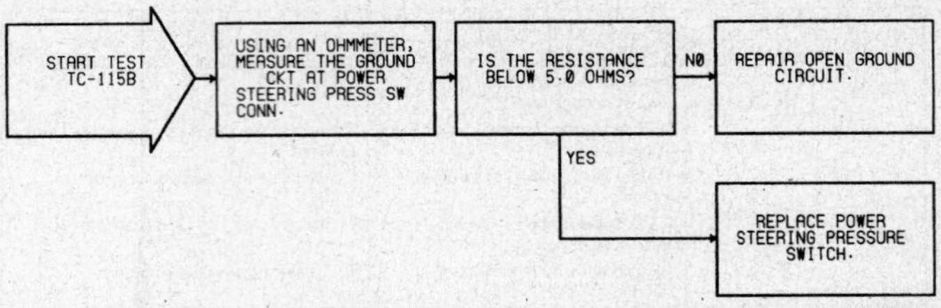

Fig. 7 Test TC-115B: PS Switch Failure. 1997–98

TEST	ACTION
4	Ignition Off Disconnect the Power Steering Pressure Switch. **Note: Check connectors - Clean/repair as necessary.** Disconnect the PCM. **Note: Check connectors - Clean/repair as necessary.** With an Ohmmeter, measure the Power Steering Pressure Switch Circuit from power steering switch to PCM. Was the resistance below 5.0 ohms? Yes → Go To 5 No → Repair the open Power Steering Pressure Switch Circuit. Perform Powertrain Verification Test VER-2A.
5	Ignition Off Disconnect the Power Steering Pressure Switch. **Note: Check connectors - Clean/repair as necessary.** Disconnect the PCM. **Note: Check connectors - Clean/repair as necessary.** Using an Ohmmeter, measure the Power Steering Pressure Switch Circuit resistance from power steering switch to ground. Was the resistance below 5.0 ohms? Yes → Repair the Power Steering Pressure Switch Circuit for a short to ground. Perform Powertrain Verification Test VER-2A. No → Go To 6
6	There are no other potential causes remaining. View repair options? Repair Replace the PCM. Perform Powertrain Verification Test VER-2A.

CR6029900194020X

Fig. 8 DTC P0551: PS Switch Failure (Part 2 of 2). 1999–2000

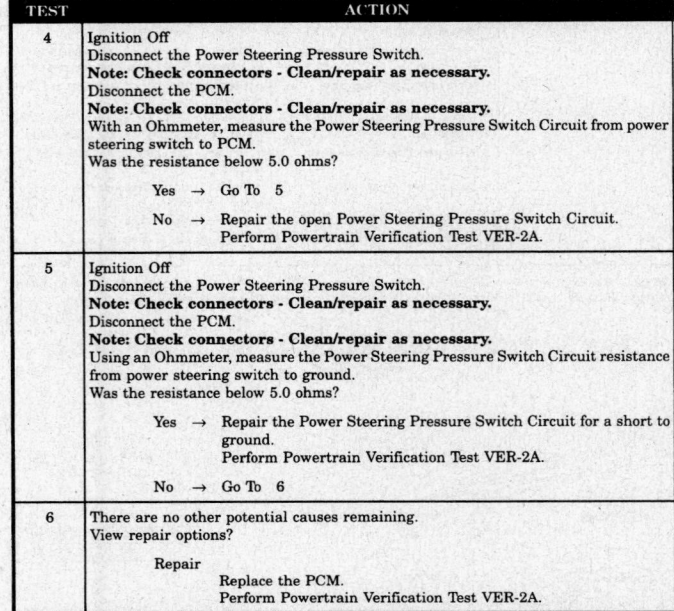

VERIFICATION TEST VER-2A	APPLICABILITY
1. Road Test For Non-OBD II **2. Note: If the PCM has been changed and the correct VIN and mileage have not been programmed, a DTC will be set in the ABS and Air Bag modules. In addition, if the vehicle is equipped with a SKIM; Secret Key data must be updated to enable starting.** 3. For ABS and Air Bag Systems: ACTION: Enter correct VIN and mileage in PCM. Erase codes in ABS and Air Bag modules. 4. For SKIM Theft Alarm: ACTION: 5. Connect DRB to data link connector. 6. Go to Theft Alarm, SKIM, misc. and place SKIM in secured access mode, by using appropriate PIN code for vehicle. 7. 3. Select Update Secret Key data. Data will be transferred from SKIM to PCM. 8. Inspect the vehicle to ensure that all engine components are connected. 9. If there are any DTCs that have not been repaired, return to the symptom list and follow the path specified for that symptom. After all DTCs have been repaired, return to the appropriate Verification Test. **10. Note: If this verification procedure is being performed after a NO TROUBLE CODE test, do the following:** 11. Check to see if the initial symptom still exists. 12. If the initial or another symptom exists, the repair is not complete. Check for any Technical Service Bulletins or flash updates and return to the symptom list and restart diagnostic testing for this symptom if necessary. 13. Connect the DRB to the data link connector. 14. Using the DRB, erase any DTCs and reset all values. 15. Road test vehicle, use all accessories that may be related to this repair. 16. Using the DRB, read Global Good Trips. If Global Good Trips is zero, the repair is not complete. Check for any Technical Service Bulletins or flash updates and return to the symptom list and restart diagnostic testing for that symptom. 17. If another trouble code has set, return to the symptom list and restart diagnostic testing and follow the path specified for that symptom. 18. If there are no trouble codes or the Global Good Trip is not zero, the repair was successful and is now complete. Repair is not complete, refer to appropriate symptom.	ENGINE - 2.5L V6, ENGINE - 2.0L I-4 SOHC and/or ENGINE - 2.4L I-4 DOHC

CR6029900195000X

Fig. 9 Verification Test VER-2A. 1999–2000

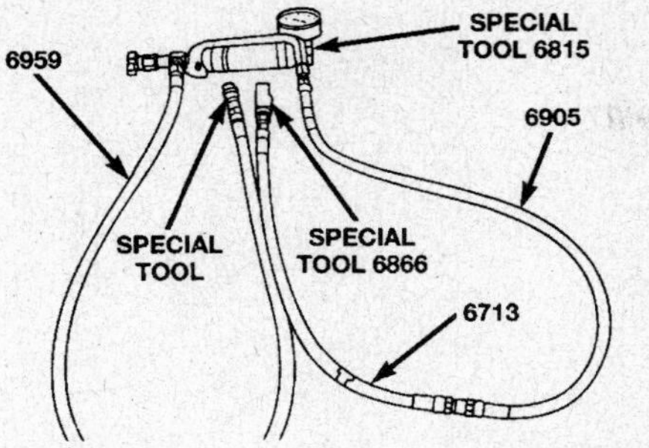

Fig. 10 Power steering flow/ pressure tester & fittings

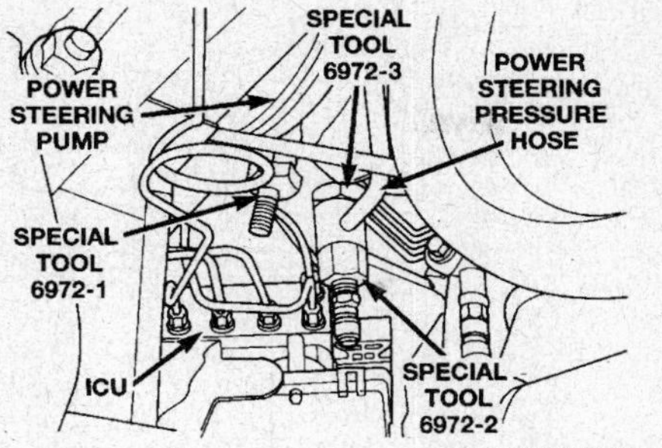

Fig. 11 Adapter fitting installation

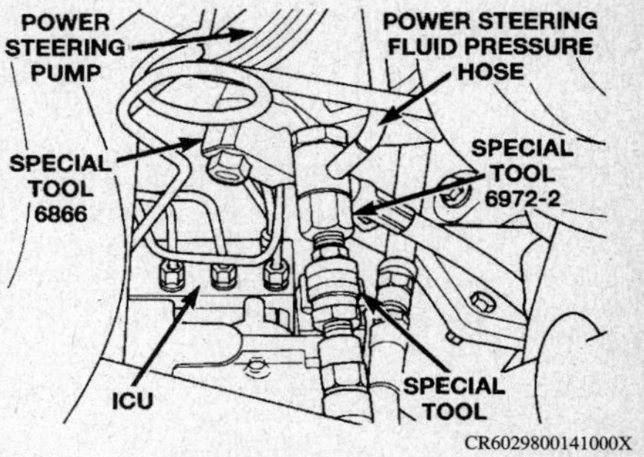

Fig. 12 Flow/pressure tester connections

7. Raise front wheels off ground, then start engine.
8. Slowly turn steering wheel right and then left, lightly contacting the wheel stops.
9. Turn engine off and add fluid as required.
10. Lower vehicle and start engine.
11. Turn steering wheel slowly from lock to lock.
12. Stop engine, then inspect fluid and refill as required.
13. If fluid is extremely foamy, wait a few minutes, then repeat entire bleeding procedure.

Pump Pressure Inspection

NON-VARIABLE & ELECTRONICALLY CONTROLLED VARIABLE ASSIST

1. Inspect power steering pump drive belt tension and adjust as required.
2. Disconnect power steering fluid pressure hose at power steering pump.
3. Connect inlet hose on pressure gauge tool No. 6815, or equivalent, using required adapter to pressure fitting on power steering pump.
4. Connect pressure hose which was removed from power steering pump, using required adapter fitting, to outlet port of pressure gauge. **Pressure gauge is to be installed in series with power steering pressure hose, between pump and steering gear. It must also be installed so it is in proper direction of fluid flow.**
5. Completely open valve on gauge.
6. Start engine and let idle long enough to circulate fluid through flow/pressure test and get air out of fluid.
7. Turn off engine, then inspect fluid level and add as required.
8. Start engine and observe pressure gauge, which should read below 125 psi. If reading is above specification, inspect hoses for restrictions.
9. Initial pressure reading should be 50–80 psi and flow meter should read 1.3–1.6 GPM.
10. Close pressure gauge valve fully three times and record highest pressure each time. Readings must be above specification and within 50 psi of each other. **Do not leave valve closed for more than five seconds as pump could be damaged.**
11. Open test valve, then turn steering wheel to left and right positions until against stops, recording highest pressure at each position. **Do not force pump to operate against stops for more than 2–4 seconds as pump damage will result.**
12. Compare pressure gauge readings to pump specifications.
13. If highest output pressures are not same against either stop, steering gear is leaking internally and must be replaced.

DROOP FLOW VARIABLE ASSIST

1. Set up power steering analyzer as follows:
   a. Connect together pressure hose tool No. 6713 and 6905, or equivalents, **Fig. 10.**
   b. Install adapter tool No. 6866, or equivalent, on end of pressure hose, then the quick disconnect.
   c. Install pressure hose in inlet and outlet fitting of pressure/flow tester.
2. Inspect power steering pump drive belt tension and adjust as required.
3. Disconnect power steering fluid pressure hose at pump.
4. Install adapter tool No 6972-1, or equivalent, in pressure fitting on pump, then adapter tool No 6972-2, or equivalent, in banjo fitting on power steering fluid pressure hose and nut tool No. 6972-3, or equivalent, on adapter tool 6972-2 in banjo fitting, **Fig. 11.**
5. Connect inlet hose of pressure/flow tester tool No. 6815, or equivalent, to pressure fitting on pump using adapter tool No. 6866 that was installed in pressure hose tool No. 6713, or equivalent, **Fig. 12.**
6. Connect outlet hose on pressure/flow tester to adapter tool No. 6972-2, or equivalent, installed in pressure hose using quick disconnect.
7. Completely open valve on pressure/ flow tester.
8. Start engine and idle long enough to circulate fluid through tester and extract air from fluid, then turn off engine.
9. Inspect and adjust fluid level as required, then start and idle engine.
10. Pressure gauge should read below 125 psi. If reading is above specification, inspect hoses for restrictions.
11. Initial pressure reading should be 50–80 psi and flow meter should read 1.3–1.6 GPM.
12. Close pressure gauge valve fully three times and record highest pressure each time. Readings must be above specification and within 50 psi of each other. **Do not leave valve closed for more than 2–4 seconds as pump will be damaged.**
13. Open test valve, then turn steering wheel to left and right positions until against stops, recording highest pressure at each position. **Do not force pump to operate against stops for more than 2–4 seconds as pump damage will result.**
14. Compare pressure gauge readings to pump specifications. If highest output pressures are not same against either stop, steering gear is leaking internally and must be replaced.

Component Service

POWER STEERING PUMP

On these models, the power steering pump is not serviceable except for the following items:

1. Power steering pump oil seals except for the pump shaft seal.
2. Power steering pump reservoirs and related components.
3. Power steering pump reservoir filler cap/dipstick.
4. Power steering pump pulley.

Pulley, Replace

The power steering pump must be removed from the vehicle when removing the power steering pump pulley. Refer to "Power Steering Pump, Replace" section for removal procedure.

1. Remove power steering pump from engine.
2. Place power steering pump in a vise while using puller tool No. C-4068, or C-4333, or equivalents, **Fig. 13,** to remove pulley. **Ensure pump shaft does not turn. Do not hammer on pulley or shaft.**
3. Install pulley, noting the following:
   a. Place power steering pump in vise using power steering pump bracket.
   b. Place power steering pump pulley

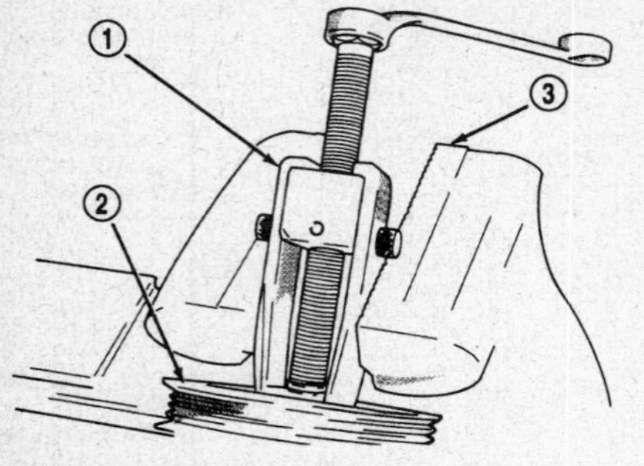

1 – SPECIAL TOOL C-4333 OR C-4068
2 – POWER STEERING PUMP PULLEY
3 – VISE

CR6029700198000X

Fig. 13 Power steering pump pulley removal

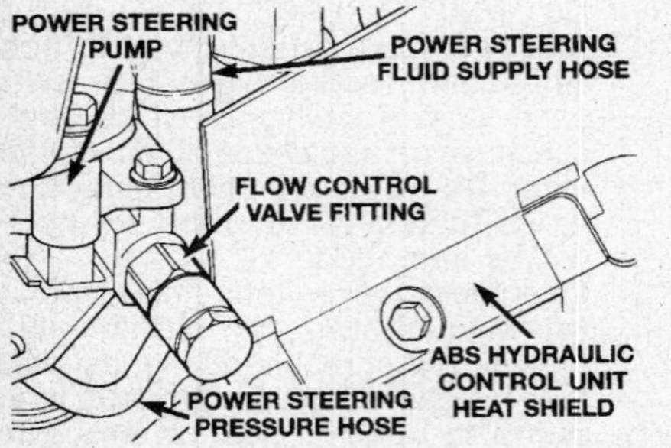

CR6029800137000X

Fig. 16 Power steering pressure hose replacement. With droop flow variable assist power steering

squarely on end of power steering pump shaft.

c. Install spacer tool No. 6936, or equivalent, on top of pulley, **Fig. 14.**

d. Place installer tool No. C-4063B, or equivalent, in internal threads of power steering pump shaft and against spacer on power steering pump pulley, **Fig. 15.**

e. Ensuring installer tool and pulley remain aligned with pump shaft, install pulley onto power steering pump shaft until spacer is against end of shaft. **When spacer is against the shaft, the power steering pump tool will no longer be able to turn.**

f. Remove installation tool, then install pump. Refer to " Power Steering Pump, Replace" for installation procedures.

g. Refill fluid and bleed system of air. Refer to " Power Steering System Bleed" for air bleeding procedure.

Flow Control Valve Fitting O-Ring, Replace

The power steering pump does not require removal from the engine for flow control valve O-ring replacement.

1. Remove power steering fluid pressure hose from power steering pump pressure fitting, **Figs. 16 and 17.**
2. Remove pump discharge/flow control valve fitting from power steering pump housing, **Figs. 18 and 19. Prevent**

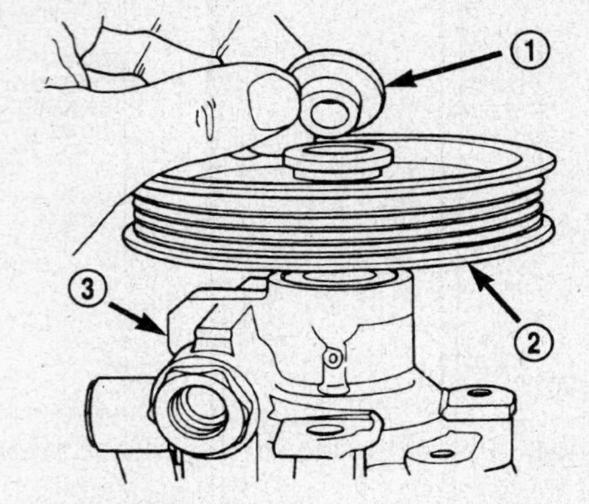

1 – SPECIAL TOOL 6936
2 – POWER STEERING PUMP PULLEY
3 – POWER STEERING PUMP

CR6029700199000X

Fig. 14 Power steering pump pulley spacer

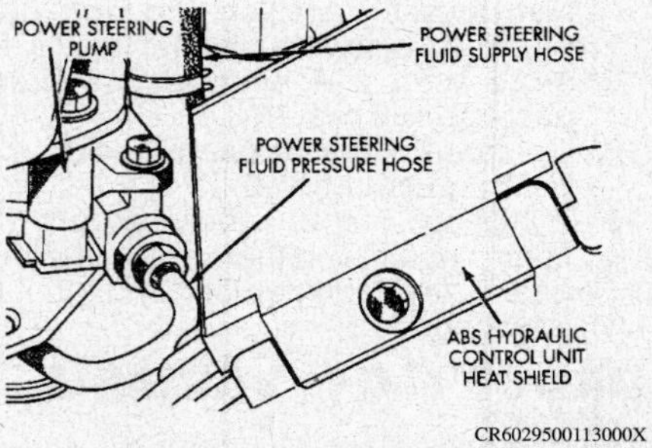

CR6029500113000X

Fig. 17 Power steering pressure hose replacement. Less droop flow assisted power steering

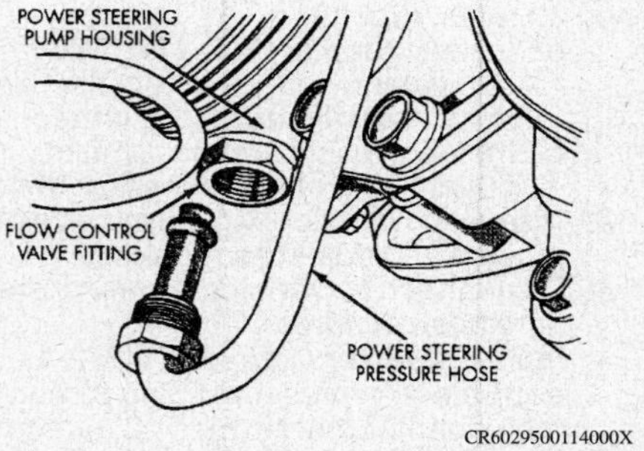

CR6029500114000X

Fig. 19 Flow control valve replacement. Less droop flow assisted power steering

flow control valve and spring from sliding out of housing bore.

3. Remove and discard O-ring.
4. Reverse procedure to install, noting the following:
   a. Clean and install flow control valve and spring in pump housing bore if required.
   b. Install new O-ring seal on fitting.
   c. Install pump discharge/flow control valve fitting in pump and tighten to specifications.
   d. Install power steering pressure hose on flow control valve fitting, then tighten tube nut to specifications.
   e. Refill fluid and bleed system of air. Refer to " Power Steering System Bleed" for air bleeding procedure.

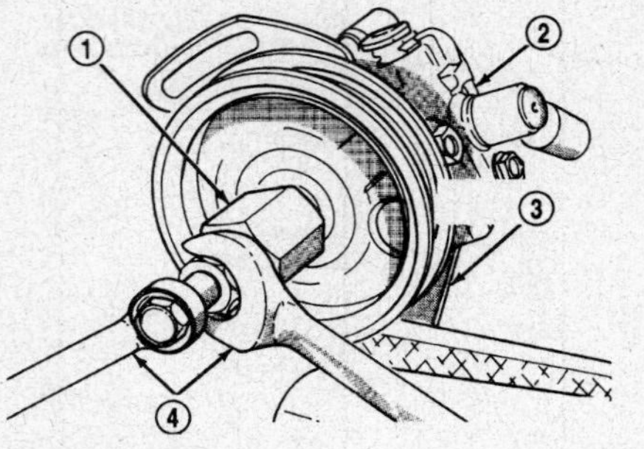

1 – SPECIAL TOOL C-4063
2 – POWER STEERING PUMP
3 – POWER STEERING PUMP BRACKET
4 – WRENCHES

CR6029700200000X

Fig. 15 Power steering pulley installer tool

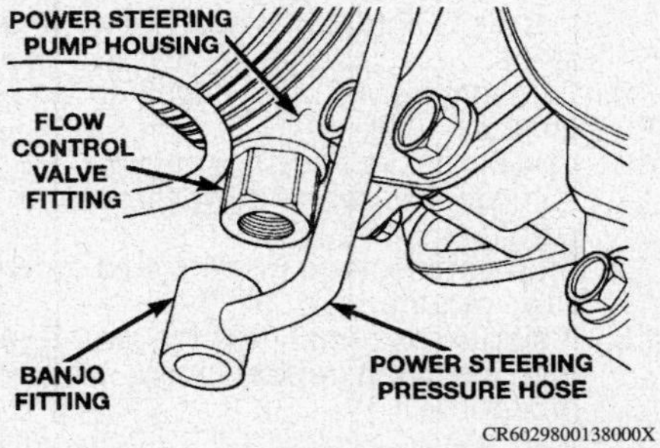

CR6029800138000X

Fig. 18 Flow control valve replacement. With droop flow assisted power steering

Suction Port O-Ring Seal, Replace

The power steering pump must be removed from the vehicle for replacement of the suction port O-ring seal. Refer to "Power Steering Pump, Replace" section for removal procedure.

1. Remove power steering fluid supply hose from power steering pump suction port fitting.
2. Remove suction port fitting attaching bolt, **Fig. 20.**
3. Remove and discard O-ring seal from suction port fitting.
4. Reverse procedure to install, noting the following:
   a. Install new O-ring on suction fitting.
   b. Install suction port fitting to power steering pump. Install and securely tighten suction port fitting attaching bolt.
   c. Install power steering fluid supply hose on suction port fitting, ensure hose clamp is installed on hose past upset bead on suction port fitting.
   d. Refill fluid and bleed system of air. Refer to " Power Steering System Bleed" for air bleeding procedure.

Fluid Reservoir, Replace

Use care when replacing power steering fluid hoses on power steering reservoir. Avoid excessive force when removing or installing hoses, as nipples on reservoir may break off.

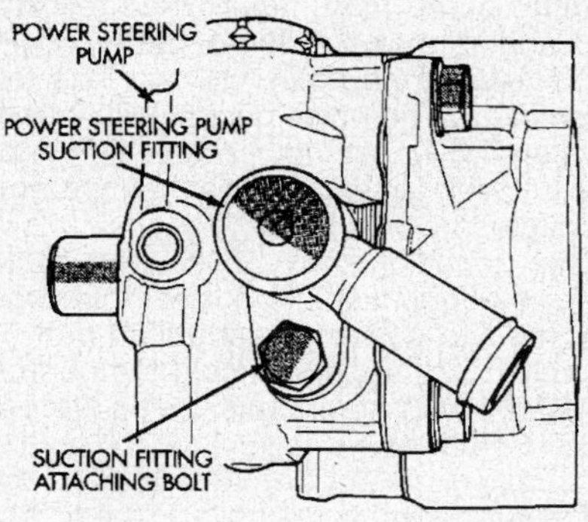

CR6029500115000X

Fig. 20 Suction port fitting replacement

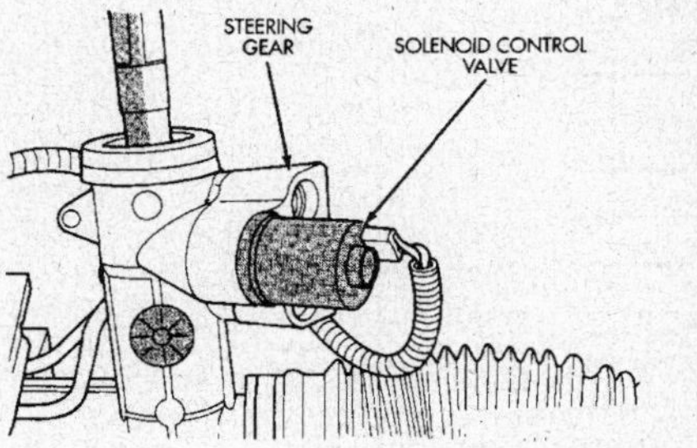

CR6029500118000X

Fig. 23 Solenoid module electrical connectors. Breeze, Cirrus, Sebring Convertible & Stratus

1. Using a siphon pump, remove fluid from power steering fluid reservoir.
2. Raise and support vehicle.
3. Remove power steering fluid supply hose at power steering pump.
4. Drain fluid remaining fluid from supply hose and power steering fluid reservoir until empty.
5. Lower vehicle.
6. Remove power steering fluid return and supply hose from power steering reservoir.
7. Remove reservoir attaching bolts on engine, then reservoir.
8. Reverse procedure to install, noting the following:
   a. When installing return and supply hoses, ensure both hose clamps are installed on hose past upset bead on steering gear steel tube.
   b. Refill fluid and bleed system of air. Refer to " Power Steering System Bleed" for air bleeding procedure.

POWER STEERING PRESSURE SWITCH, REPLACE

Models equipped with power steering use a power steering pressure switch, **Fig. 21,** to improve engine idle quality. The switch maintains idle speed when required due to increased power steering system pressure. Otherwise, this higher pressure would slow down the power steering pump, decreasing engine idle speed.

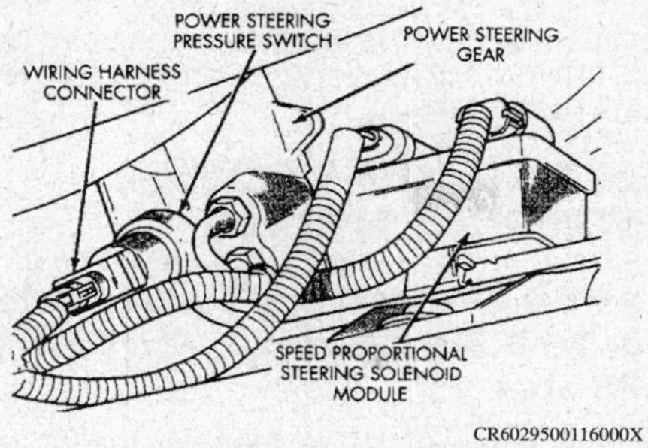

CR6029500116000X

Fig. 21 Pressure switch replacement. Breeze, Cirrus, Neon, Sebring Convertible & Stratus

The pressure switch signals the Powertrain Control Module (PCM) that additional engine load is being applied by the power steering system. Engine idle is compensated for load by the signal from the pressure switch. As steering load increases or decreases, engine idle speed and quality are maintained.

The pressure switch is mounted directly on the power steering gear.

1. Raise and support vehicle.
2. Locate power steering switch on rear side of power steering gear, then disconnect its electrical connector.
3. Using a crowfoot and long extension, or equivalent, remove pressure switch from steering gear.
4. Reverse procedure to install, noting the following:
   a. Install and hand tighten switch into gear until fully seated.
   b. Using a crowfoot and extension, or equivalent, tighten switch to specifications. **Do not overtighten. This may result in damage to switch port threads on steering gear.**
   c. Connect pressure switch electrical connector, ensuring the latch is securely engaged with locking tab.
   d. Refill fluid and bleed system of air. Refer to " Power Steering System Bleed" for air bleeding procedure.
   e. Inspect system for fluid leaks.

SOLENOID CONTROL MODULE, REPLACE

Replacement of the solenoid control module, **Fig. 22,** can be done without removing steering gear from vehicle. The solenoid control module is mounted on the steering gear assembly fluid lines.

1. Disconnect solenoid control module electrical connectors, **Fig. 23.**
2. Unclip locking tab, holding module to fluid lines, on bottom side of control module.
3. Rotate module upward, then remove the two upper attaching clips from steering gear.
4. Reverse procedure to install, noting the following:
   a. Hook upper tabs on solenoid control module to upper steering gear fluid lines.

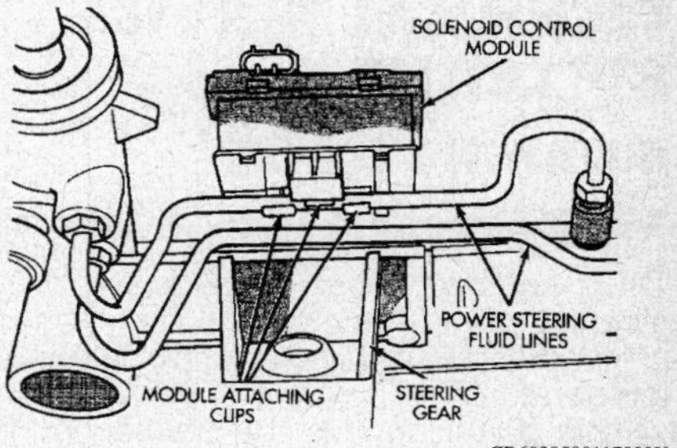

CR6029500117000X

Fig. 22 Solenoid control module replacement. Breeze, Cirrus, Sebring Convertible & Stratus

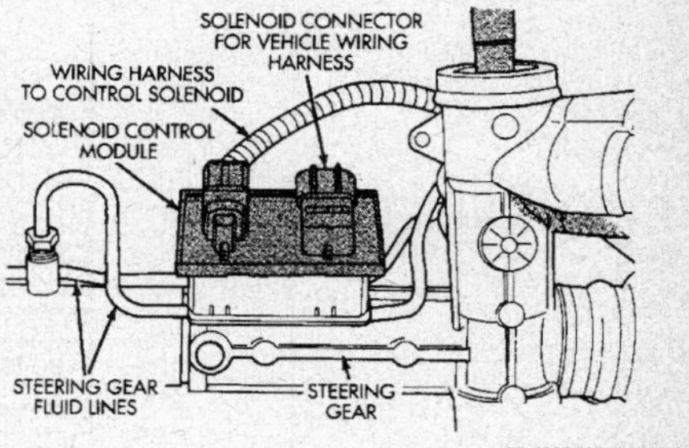

CR6029500119000X

Fig. 24 Solenoid control valve replacement. Breeze, Cirrus, Sebring Convertible & Stratus

   b. Rotate module downward until locking tab on bottom of module is locked on lower power steering gear fluid line.
   c. Connect control module electrical connectors. Ensure connector seal is in good condition prior to installation.

SOLENOID CONTROL VALVE, REPLACE

Removal of the steering gear assembly from the vehicle is required when replacing the solenoid control valve, **Fig. 24.** Refer to "Front Suspension & Steering" for power steering gear replacement procedures.

1. Disconnect solenoid control valve electrical connector at solenoid control module, **Fig. 22.**
2. Using a 1 5/16 inch crowfoot or equivalent, remove solenoid from steering gear.
3. Inspect O-ring seals on solenoid control valve for damage replace as required. Coat with fresh clean power steering fluid prior to installation.
4. Install solenoid control valve by hand until fully seated, then using crowfoot tool or equivalent, tighten to specifications.
5. Connect solenoid electrical connectors. Ensure connector seal is in good condition prior to installation.
6. Road test vehicle or test using DRB scan tool, or equivalent to confirm proper operation of variable assist speed proportional power steering gear.

TECHNICAL SERVICE BULLETINS

MOANING NOISE

1997 Breeze, Cirrus & Stratus

On some of these models, the power steering pump may moan. The moaning noise increases with steering input and temperature.

This condition may be caused by the pressure hose. To correct this condition, replace the power steering pressure hose with revised unit (2.0L/2.4L engine part No. AR-04764347AA; for 2.5L engine part No. AR-04764349AA).

COLD ENGINE POWER STEERING NOISE

1996-98 Sebring Convertible & 1997-98 Breeze, Cirrus & Stratus

On some of these models, the power steering pump may make noise following cold engine starts at temperatures below 10°F. Usually the noise will last less than one minute. The noise occurs with or without steering wheel input, increasing in duration and intensity as temperature decreases.

This condition may be caused by the power steering fluid. To correct this condition, replace power steering fluid part No. MS-5931 with improved cold temperature property power steering fluid part No. MS-9933 (5010304AA).

TIGHTENING SPECIFICATIONS

Component	Torque/Ft. Lbs.
Discharge/Flow Control Valve Fitting	55
Hose Tube Nuts	23
Outer Tie Rod To Inner Tie Rod Lock Nut	55
Pressure Switch	12
Reservoir To Engine Bracket	21
Solenoid Control Valve	10
Steering Pump Bracket	40
Tie Rod To Steering Knuckle	45

Concorde, Intrepid, LHS, Vision & 300M

NOTE: On Air Bag Equipped Models, Refer To " Air Bag System Precautions" Located In The Front Of This Manual For System Disarming & Arming Procedures.

NOTE: Prior To Performing Any Service Operations Listed In This Section, Consult The "Technical Service Bulletins " For Related Information.

INDEX

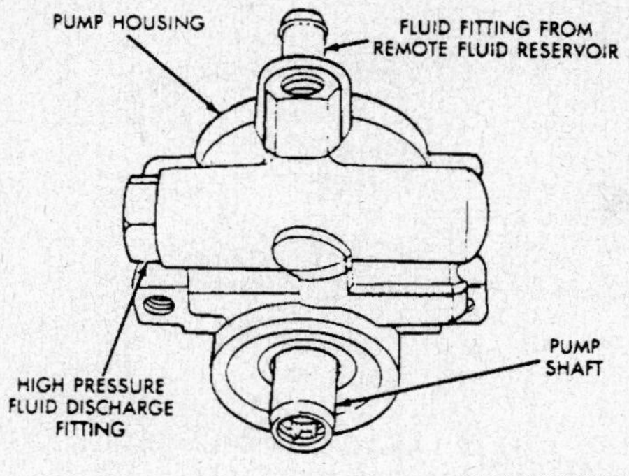

Fig. 1 Saginaw CB style power steering pump. 1997

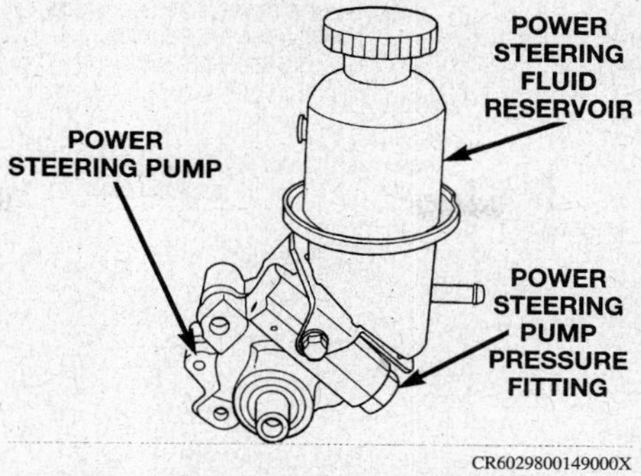

Fig. 2 Power steering pump. 1998–2000 2.7L engine

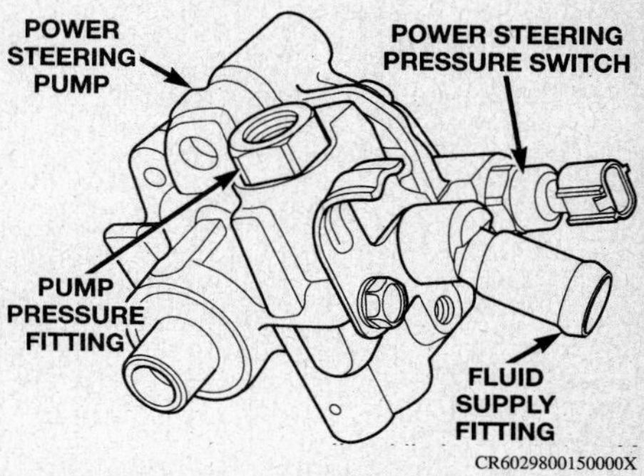

Fig. 3 Power steering pump. 1998–2000 3.2 & 3.5L engines

PRECAUTIONS

AIR BAG SYSTEMS

Refer to "Air Bag System Precautions" in the front of this manual for system disarming and arming procedures.

BATTERY GROUND CABLE

Prior to service, disconnect battery ground cable or negative remote cable and isolate as required.

DESCRIPTION

Power assist is provided by an open center, rotary type control valve. It is used to direct oil from the power steering pump to either side of the integral steering rack piston. These vehicles may be equipped with three different types of power steering. They are base, firm-feel and speed-proportional power steering.

POWER STEERING PUMP

1997

The belt driven power steering pump is a constant flow rate and displacement vane type.

These models use a Saginaw CB stye power steering pump, **Fig. 1,** with a remote mounted power steering fluid reservoir. The reservoir is mounted to the lefthand frame rail, just to the rear of the battery tray.

1998–2000

2.7L Engine

This belt driven constant flow rate power steering pump has an integral power steering fluid reservoir, **Fig. 2.**

3.2L & 3.5L Engines

The belt driven power steering pump is a constant flow rate and displacement vane type. This power steering pump has a remotely mounted power steering fluid reservoir, **Fig. 3.**

STEERING GEAR

The standard and firm-feel steering gears only differ internally, **Figs. 4 and 5.**

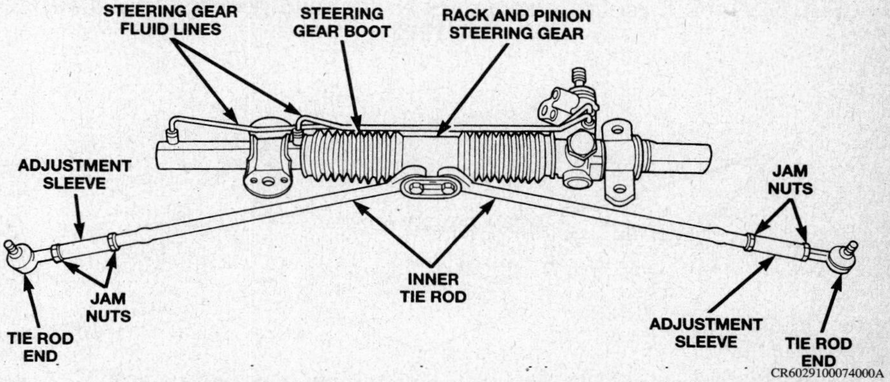

Fig. 4 Rack & pinion steering gear less speed proportional steering. 1997

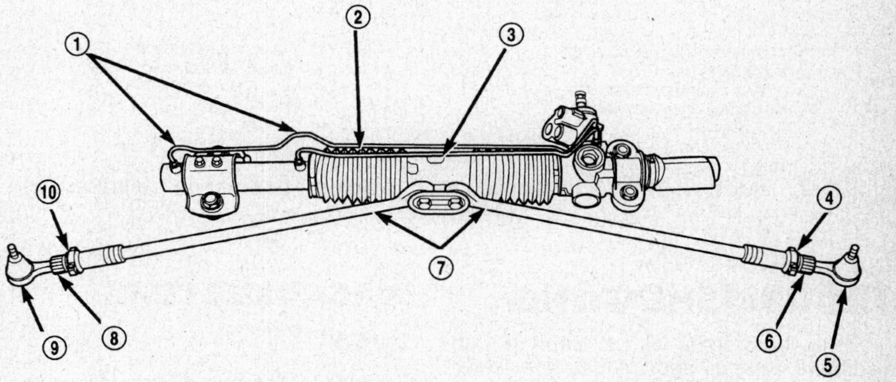

1 – STEERING GEAR FLUID LINES
2 – STEERING GEAR BOOT
3 – RACK AND PINION STEERING GEAR
4 – CLAMP
5 – TIE ROD END
6 – ADJUSTMENT SLEEVE
7 – INNER TIE ROD
8 – ADJUSTMENT SLEEVE
9 – TIE ROD END
10 – CLAMP

CR6029800201000X

Fig. 5 Rack & pinion steering gear less speed proportional steering. 1998–2000

The speed-sensitive variable-effort, speed-proportional steering is an electronically controlled, variable-effort type system. The speed-proportional steering gear has an externally mounted control valve which varies steering effort at different speeds in conjunction with mechanical components, **Figs. 6 and 7.**

The rack and pinion power steering gear used on these models should not be serviced or adjusted. If a malfunction or internal fluid leak should occur, the complete steering gear must be replaced.

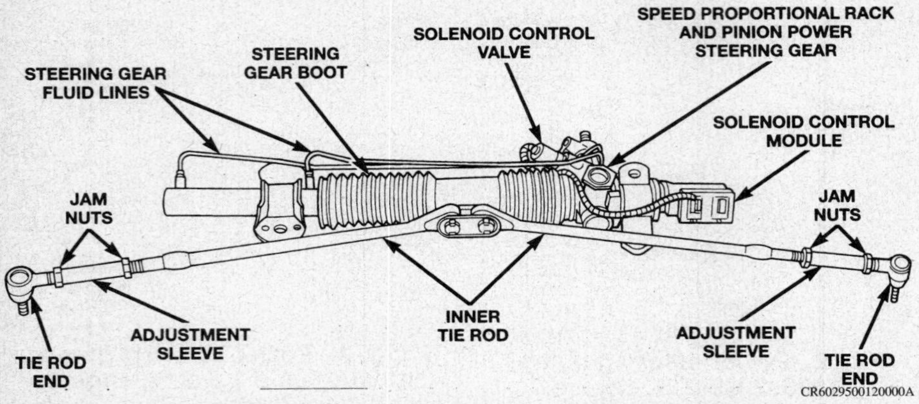

Fig. 6 Rack & pinion steering gear w/speed proportional steering. 1997

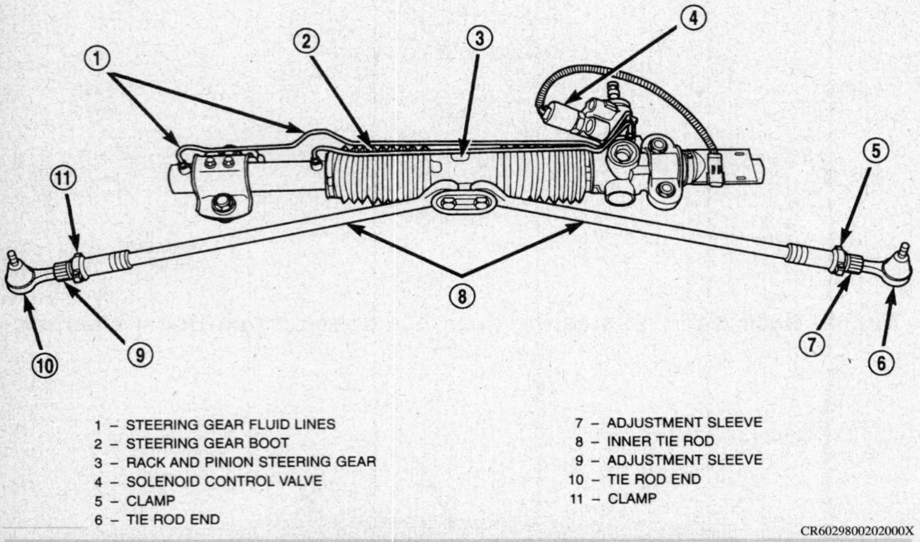

Fig. 7 Rack & pinion steering gear w/speed proportional steering. 1998–2000

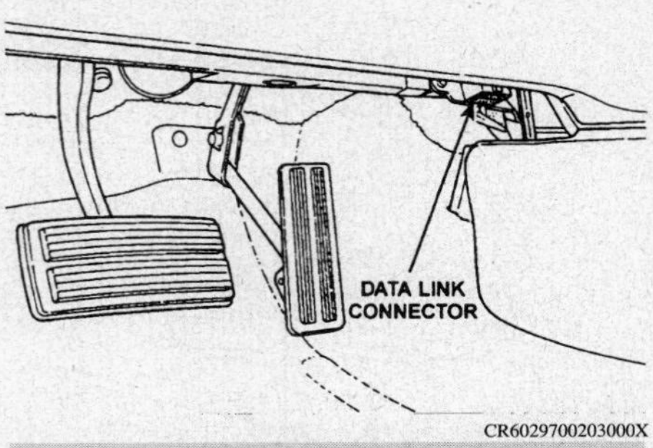

Fig. 8 Data link connector location. 1997

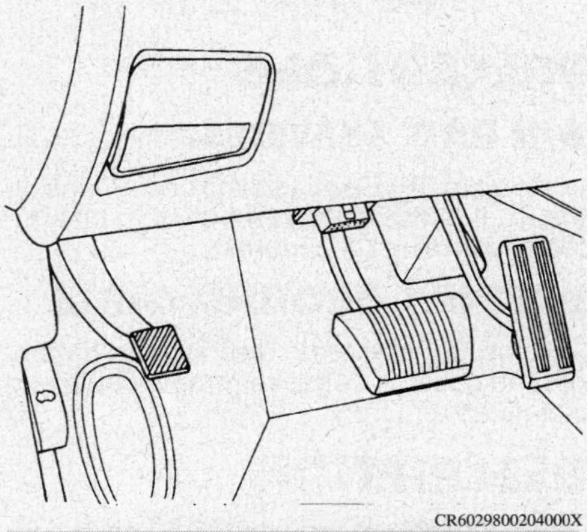

Fig. 9 Data link connector location. 1998–2000

TROUBLESHOOTING

Refer to "Breeze, Cirrus, Sebring Convertible & Stratus" section for power steering system troubleshooting.

DIAGNOSIS & TESTING

ACCESSING DIAGNOSTIC TROUBLE CODES

A DRB III or equivalent scan tool is required to access the speed proportional power steering diagnostic trouble codes. Connect the scan tool to the Data Link Connector (DLC), **Figs. 8 and 9.** The diagnostic cycle begins when the ignition is turned On.

CONNECTOR TERMINAL IDENTIFICATION

Refer to **Fig. 10** for connector terminal identification.

DIAGNOSTIC TESTS

1997

Refer to "Breeze, Cirrus, Sebring Convertible & Stratus" section for power steering system diagnostic tests.

1998

Refer to **Fig. 11** for diagnostic test.

1999–2000

Refer to **Figs. 12 and 13** for diagnostic tests.

CLEARING DIAGNOSTIC TROUBLE CODES

Record existing codes for future reference prior to clearing DTCs. To clear diagnostic trouble codes, select the "Erase DTCs" data screen on the DRB scan tool.

COMPONENT TESTING

Power Steering Pump Less Speed Proportional Steering

Refer to "Neon" section for power steering pump diagnosis and testing procedures.

POWER STEERING SYSTEM SERVICE

Power Steering System Bleed

1. Ensure power steering fluid remote reservoir is full, then start engine and turn steering wheel from stop to stop several times.
2. Stop engine and inspect fluid level again. If required, add fluid until proper fluid level is reached.
3. Repeat procedure until fluid level is consistent. Inspect system for leaks.

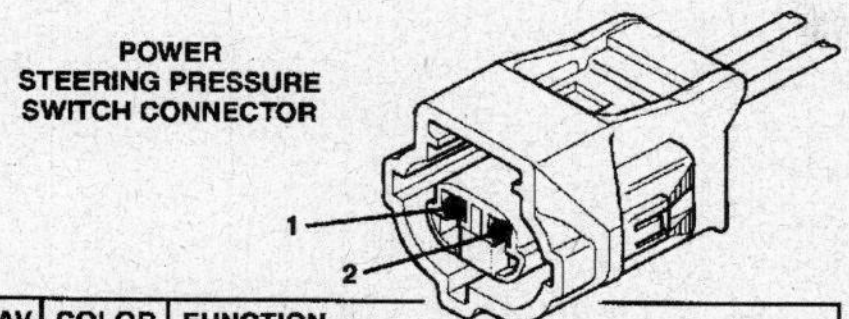

CAV	COLOR	FUNCTION
2	DB/LG	POWER STEERING PRESSURE SWITCH SENSE

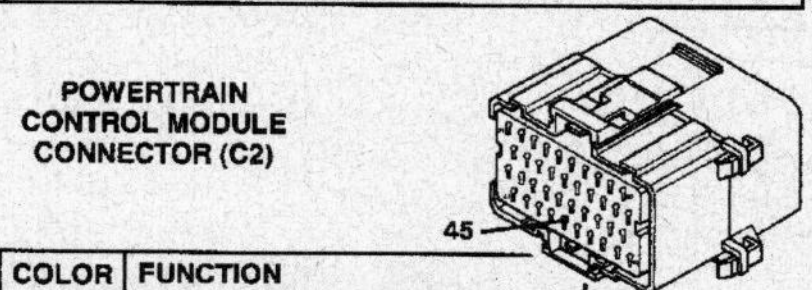

CAV	COLOR	FUNCTION
45	DB/LG	PS PRESSURE SWITCH SENSE

CR6029800155000X

Fig. 10 Connector terminal identification

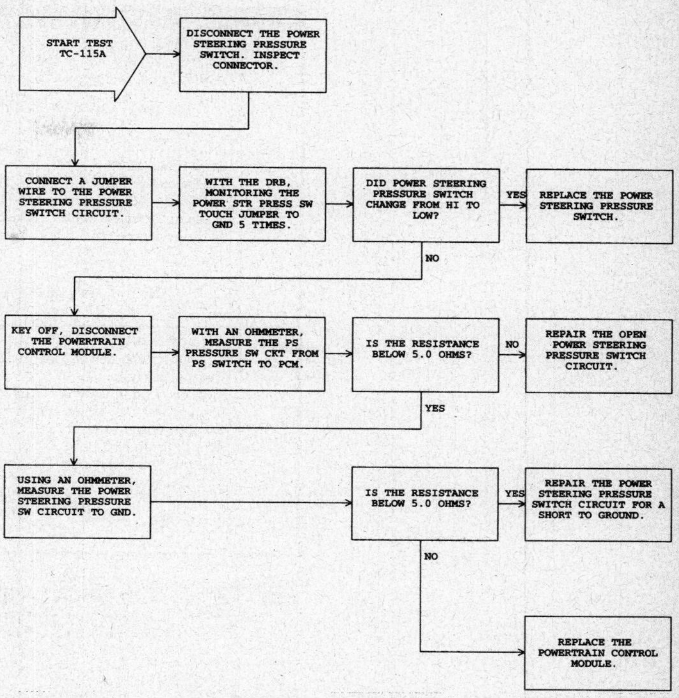

CR6029800205000X

Fig. 11 Test TC-115A: Power Steering Switch Failure. 1998

Component Service

FLUID COOLER, REPLACE

1997

1. Using suitable siphon pump, remove as much power steering fluid as possible from reservoir.
2. Remove hose clamps, then drain power steering fluid from hoses and cooler into suitable container.
3. Using suitable grinder and cutter, remove power steering fluid cooler mounting rivet heads. Use extreme care to not damage air conditioning condenser.
4. Using suitable punch, remove rivets from bracket and bumper reinforcement, then remove cooler.
5. Reverse procedure to install, noting the following:
   a. Use 1/4–20 bolts and nuts to mount cooler to reinforcement.
   b. **Torque** mounting bolts to 7 ft. lbs.

1998–2000

1. Using suitable siphon pump, remove as much power steering fluid as possible from reservoir.
2. Raise and support vehicle on a frame contact hoist or with suitable jack stands.
3. **On 300M models,** remove front fascia.
4. **On all models,** remove clamp and lower hose, then drain fluid into suitable container.
5. Remove clamp and upper hose.
6. Remove mounting clips and air dam from lower radiator support.
7. Remove mounting nuts and cooler.
8. Reverse procedure to install, noting the following:
   a. Install air dam with new retaining clips.
   b. Ensure clamps are installed on hoses past the cooler retention beads.
   c. Tighten mounting nuts to specifications.
   d. Fill and bleed power steering fluid.

RESERVOIR, REPLACE

1997

1. Raise and support vehicle.
2. Remove reservoir hoses and drain fluid into suitable container.
3. Lower car, then remove battery, mounting bolts and battery tray.
4. Remove mounting screw and reservoir.
5. Reverse procedure to install, noting the following:

TEST	ACTION
1	Turn Ignition On. With the DRB, read the DTC's. Is the Global Good Trip Counter displayed and equal to zero? Yes → Go To 2 No → Go To 7
2	Turn Ignition Off Disconnect the Power Steering Pressure Switch connector. Using an Ohmmeter, measure the resistance of the Ground Circuit at the Power Steering Pressure Switch connector to a good Ground. Is the resistance below 5.0 ohms? Yes → Go To 3 No → Repair the open Power Steering Pressure Switch Ground Circuit. Perform the Powertrain Verification Test - Ver 5.
3	Turn ignition off. Disconnect the Power Steering Pressure Switch Connector. Turn ignition on. Connect a Jumper Wire to the Power Steering Pressure Switch Sense Circuit. Using the DRB, while monitoring the Power Steering Pressure Switch, touch the Jumper Wire to the Ground Circuit at the Power Steering Pressure Switch harness connector several times. Did the Power Steering Pressure Switch status change from Hi to Low? Yes → Replace the Power Steering Pressure Switch. Perform the Powertrain Verification Test - Ver 5. No → Go To 4

CR6020000206010X

Fig. 12 DTC P0551: PS Switch Failure (Part 1 of 2). 1999–2000

a. Ensure reservoir bottom tab is inserted into frame rail hole.

b. Tighten mounting screw to specifications.

TEST	ACTION
4	Turn Ignition Off. Disconnect the Power Steering Pressure Switch Connector. Disconnect the Powertrain Control Module connector. With an Ohmmeter, measure the Power Steering Pressure Switch Sense Circuit to ground at the PCM connector. Is the resistance below 5.0 ohms? Yes → Repair the Power Steering Pressure Switch Sense Circuit for a short to ground. Perform the Powertrain Verification Test - Ver 5. No → Go To 5
5	Turn Ignition Off. Disconnect the Power Steering Pressure Switch Connector. Disconnect the Powertrain Control Module connector. Using an Ohmmeter, measure resistance of Power Steering Pressure Switch Sense circuit from PCM connector to Sensor Connector. Is the resistance below 5.0 ohms? Yes → Go To 6 No → Repair the open Power Steering Switch Sense Circuit. Perform the Powertrain Verification Test - Ver 5.
6	If there are no possible causes remaining, replace the Powertrain Control Module. View repair options. Repair Replace the Powertrain Control Module. Perform the Powertrain Verification Test - Ver 5.
7	Turn ignition off. **Note: Visually inspect the related wiring harness. Look for any chafed, pierced, pinched, or partially broken wires.** **Note: Visually inspect the related wire harness connectors. Look for broken, bent, pushed out, or corroded terminals.** **Note: Refer to any Technical Service Bulletins (TSB) that may apply.** Were any problems found? Yes → Repair wiring harness/connectors as necessary. Perform the Powertrain Verification Test - Ver 5. No → Test Complete.

CR6020000206020X

Fig. 12 DTC P0551: PS Switch Failure (Part 2 of 2). 1999–2000

POWERTRAIN VERIFICATION TEST VER - 5

1. Inspect the vehicle to ensure that all engine components are properly installed and connected. Reassemble and reconnect components as necessary.
2. If any existing diagnostic trouble codes have not been repaired, go to Symptom List and follow path specified.
3. Connect the DRBIII® to the data link connector.
4. Ensure the fuel tank has at least a quarter tank of fuel. Turn off all accessories.
5. Perform steps 6 through 8 if the PCM has been replaced. Then proceed with the verification. If the PCM has not been replaced skip those steps and continue verification.
6. If PCM has been changed and correct VIN and mileage have not been programmed, a DTC will be set in ABS and Air bag modules. In addition, if vehicle is equipped with a Sentry Key Immobilizer Module (SKIM), Secret Key data must be updated to enable start.
7. For ABS and Air Bag systems: Enter correct VIN and Mileage in PCM. Erase codes in ABS and Air Bag modules.
8. For SKIM theft alarm: Connect DRB to data link conn. Go to Theft Alarm, SKIM, Misc. and place SKIM in secured access mode, by using the appropriate PIN code for this vehicle. Select Update the Secret Key data. Data will be transferred from SKIM to PCM.
9. If a Comprehensive Component DTC was repaired, perform steps 10-13. If a Major OBDII Monitor DTC was repaired skip those steps and continue verification.
10. After the ignition has been off for at least 10 seconds, restart the vehicle and run 2 minutes.
11. If the Good Trip counter changed to one or more and there are no new DTC's, the repair was successful and is now complete. Erase DTC's and disconnect the DRBIII®.
12. If the repaired DTC has reset, the repair is not complete. Check for any related TSB's or flash updates and return to the Symptom list.
13. If another DTC has set, return to the Symptom List and follow the path specified for that DTC.
14. With the DRBIII®, monitor the appropriate pre-test enabling conditions until all conditions have been met. Once the conditions have been met, switch screen to the appropriate OBDII monitor, (Audible beeps when the monitor is running).
15. If the monitor ran, and the Good Trip counter changed to one or more, the repair was successful and is now complete. Erase DTC's and disconnect the DRBIII®.
16. If the repaired OBDII trouble code has reset or was seen in the monitor while on the road test, the repair is not complete. Check for any related technical service bulletins or flash updates and return to Symptom List.
17. If another DTC has set, return to the Symptom List and follow the path specified for that DTC.

Repair is not complete, refer to appropriate symptom.

CR6020000207000X

Fig. 13 Verification Test VER-5. 1999–2000

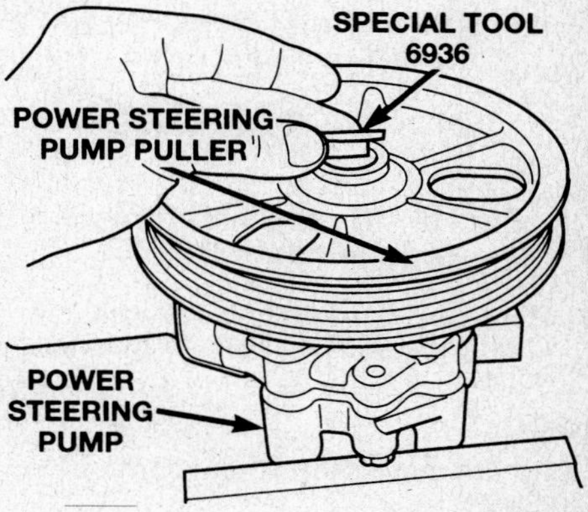

Fig. 14 Spacer tool installation into pulley. 1998–2000

1998–2000

2.7L Engine

1. Remove power steering pump as outlined in "Front Suspension & Steering" under "Concorde, Intrepid, LHS, Vision & 300M."
2. Remove mounting bolts and reservoir.
3. Reverse procedure to install, noting the following:
   a. Lubricate reservoir O-ring seal with fresh clean power steering fluid.
   b. Press reservoir nipple straight into pump without rotating or twisting.
   c. Tighten fasteners to specifications.

3.2 & 3.5L Engines

1. Raise and support vehicle on a frame contact hoist or with suitable jack stands.
2. Remove reservoir hoses and drain fluid into suitable container.
3. Lower vehicle, then rotate reservoir's rear side toward engine, out of its bracket, then remove reservoir.
4. Reverse procedure to install, noting the following:
   a. Ensure reservoir bottom tab is inserted into frame rail hole.
   b. Ensure clamps are installed on hoses past the retention beads.
   c. Tighten mounting screw to specifications.

DRIVE PULLEY, REPLACE

REMOVAL

1. Remove power steering pump as described under "Front Suspension & Steering" section.
2. Mount pump by mounting boss in suitable vise. Do not clamp pump body.
3. Using puller tool No. C-4333, or equivalent, remove pulley. **Do not use press or hammer on pump shaft.**

INSTALLATION

1. Place pulley squarely on shaft end and install spacer provided with pump or pulley into pulley hub.
2. **On 1998–2000 models,** install spacer tool No. 6936, or equivalent into pulley hub, **Fig. 14.**
3. **On all models,** thread installer tool No. C-4063, or equivalent, into pump shaft.
4. Holding installer tool with one wrench, turn installer hex down threaded rod pushing pulley onto shaft. Ensure tool and pulley remain aligned.
5. Ensure spacer is fully seated against shaft front, then remove tool and spacer.
6. Tighten all fasteners to specifications.

FLOW CONTROL VALVE, REPLACE

1997

1. If required, remove pulley as previously described.
2. Remove pump housing fitting. **Do not allow flow control valve and spring to slide out of housing.**
3. Remove O-ring seal and discharge fitting.
4. Reverse procedure to install. Tighten fitting to specifications.

PRESSURE FITTING, REPLACE

1998–99

1. Remove power steering pump as outlined in "Front Suspension & Steering" section.
2. Remove pressure fitting.

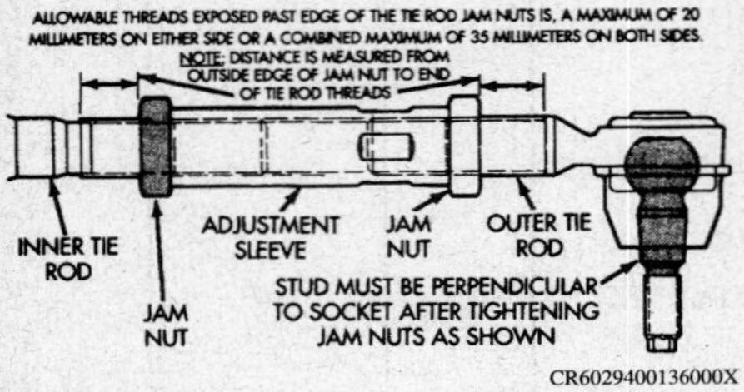

Fig. 15 Tie rod end thread requirements. 1997

3. Reverse procedure to install with new O-ring seal. Tighten fitting to specifications.

2000

On these models this is not a serviceable component.

PRESSURE SWITCH, REPLACE

1998–2000

1. **On models equipped with 3.2 and 3.5L engines,** raise and support vehicle.
2. **On all models,** disconnect wire harness electrical connector, then remove power steering pressure switch.
3. Reverse procedure to install. Tighten to specifications.

OUTER TIE ROD & BOOT, REPLACE

1. Raise and support vehicle, then remove tire and wheel assembly.
2. Loosen tie rod adjustment sleeve locknut.
3. Loosen, but do not remove, outer tie rod to steering arm nut.
4. **On 1997 models,** using tie rod remover tool No. MB990635, or equivalent, remove tie rod end from steering arm.
5. **On 1998–2000 models,** using tie rod remover tool No. C-3894-A, or equivalent, remove tie rod end from steering arm.
6. Remove tie rod from adjustment sleeve.
7. Reverse procedure to install, noting the following:
   a. Inspect toe setting prior to tightening adjustment sleeve locknut.
   b. Ensure maximum exposed thread requirements are not exceeded, **Figs. 15 and 16.**

SOLENOID CONTROL VALVE CONTROL MODULE, REPLACE

1. Remove electrical connector from control module.
2. Depress two locking tabs on bottom of control module, then detach control module from steering gear end cap.
3. Rotate control module upward, until retaining tabs can be removed from steering gear end cap. Remove control module from steering gear.
4. Reverse procedure to install.

SOLENOID CONTROL VALVE, REPLACE

1. Remove solenoid control valve electrical connector from control module.
2. Remove power steering pressure and return hoses from steering gear, allowing fluid to drain into an approved container.
3. Using a 1$\frac{5}{16}$ inch crowfoot wrench, loosen solenoid control valve from steering gear.
4. Remove control valve from steering gear.
5. Reverse procedure to install. Tighten valve to specifications.

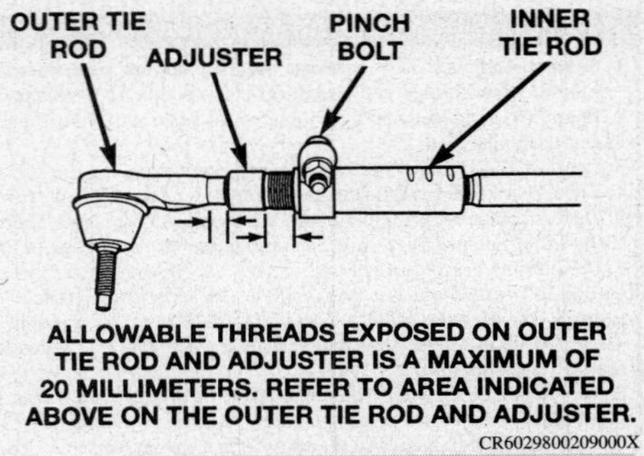

Fig. 16 Tie rod end thread requirements. 1998–2000

TECHNICAL SERVICE BULLETINS

COLD ENGINE POWER STEERING NOISE

1998 Concorde & Intrepid & 1998–99 Concorde, Intrepid, LHS & 300M Built Through 7/31/98

On these models, the power steering pump may make noise following cold engine starts at temperatures below 10°F. The noise usually last less than one minute, occurring with and without steering wheel input and increasing in duration and intensity as temperatures decrease.

This condition may be caused by the power steering fluid. To correct this condition, replace power steering fluid with improved cold temperature property power steering fluid part No. MS-9933, (5010304AA) or equivalent.

TIGHTENING SPECIFICATIONS

Year	Component	Torque/ Ft. Lbs.
1997	Discharge Fitting	55
	Gear To Crossmember	45
	Hose Tube Nut	23
	Outer To Inner Tie Rod Jam	55
	Pump To Bracket	35
	Reservoir Mounting	5
	Solenoid Control Valve	12
	Tie Rod To Steering Gear	66
	Tie Rod To Strut Steering Arm	27
1998–2000	Discharge Fitting	62
	Gear To Crossmember	43
	Hose Tube Nuts	35
	Pressure Switch	17
	Pump Mounting	21
	Reservoir Mounting (3.2 & 3.5L Engines)	9
	Reservoir Mounting, Pulley Side (2.7L Engine)	10
1998–2000	Reservoir Mounting, Rear (2.7L Engine)	18
	Solenoid Control Valve	12
	Tie Rod Adjuster Pinch (1998)	25
	Tie Rod Adjuster Pinch (1999–2000)	33
	Tie Rod Steering Arm	27
	Tie Rod Steering Gear	60

Neon

NOTE: On Air Bag Equipped Models, Refer To " Air Bag System Precautions" Located In The Front Of This Manual For System Disarming & Arming Procedures.

NOTE: Prior To Performing Any Service Operations Listed In This Section, Consult The "Technical Service Bulletins " For Related Information.

INDEX

PRECAUTIONS

AIR BAG SYSTEMS

Refer to "Air Bag System Precautions" in the front of this manual for system disarming and arming procedures.

BATTERY GROUND CABLE

Prior to service, disconnect battery ground cable and isolate as required.

POWER STEERING PUMP APPLICATIONS

Due to the unique shaft bearings, flow control levels and pump displacements, the power steering pumps used on these models may not be interchanged with pumps from other vehicles.

On 2000 models, the only serviceable power steering pump components are the pulley and the pump itself. The reservoir is serviced with the pump.

DESCRIPTION

POWER STEERING PUMP

This model is equipped with a TTA constant displacement, vane type pump, **Figs. 1 and 2** a remote fluid reservoir mounts at the rear of the cylinder head on the passenger side of the vehicle. **On 2000 models,** the reservoir is serviced with the pump.

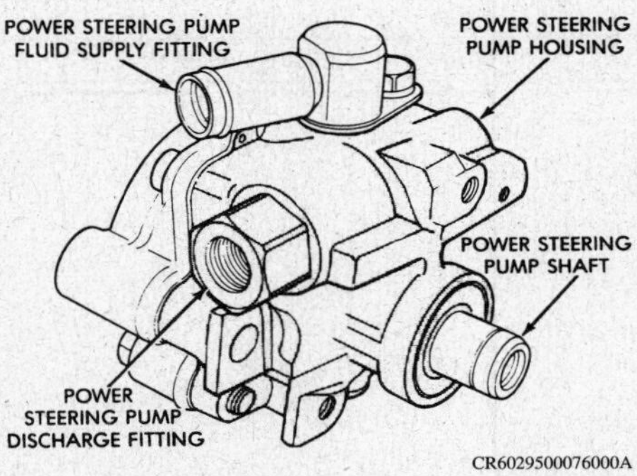

Fig. 1 TTA power steering pump. 1997–99

STEERING GEAR

The rack and pinion power steering gear used on these models should not be serviced or adjusted. If a malfunction or fluid leak should occur, the complete steering gear must be replaced.

TROUBLESHOOTING

Refer to "Breeze, Cirrus, Sebring Convertible & Stratus" section for power steering system troubleshooting.

DIAGNOSIS & TESTING

ACCESSING DIAGNOSTIC TROUBLE CODES

A DRB or equivalent scan tool is required to access the speed proportional power steering diagnostic trouble codes. Connect the scan tool to the Data Link Connector (DLC) under lefthand side of instrument panel. The diagnostic cycle begins when the ignition is turned On.

CONNECTOR TERMINAL IDENTIFICATION

Refer to **Fig. 3** for connector terminal identification.

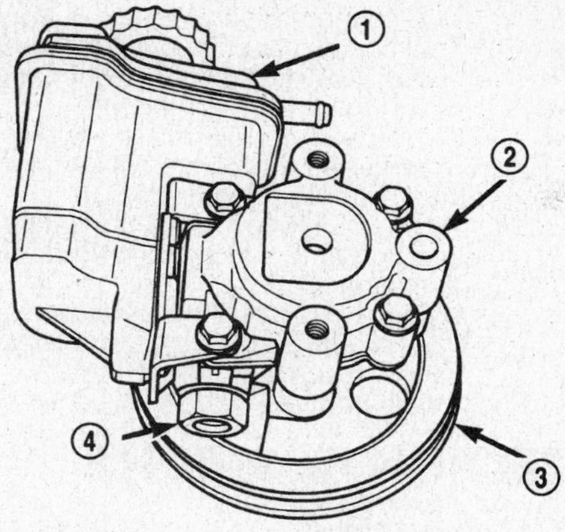

1 – POWER STEERING FLUID RESERVOIR
2 – POWER STEERING PUMP
3 – PULLEY
4 – PUMP PRESSURE FITTING

CR6020000210000X

Fig. 2 TTA power steering pump. 2000

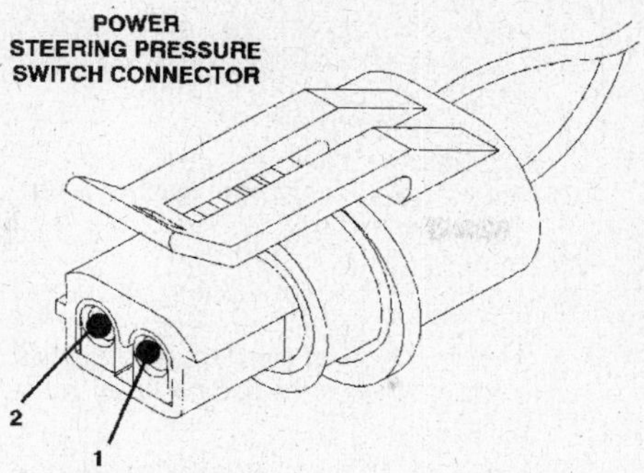

CAV	COLOR	FUNCTION
1	WT	POWER STEERING PRESSURE SWITCH SENSE
2	BK/TN	GROUND

CR6029800154000X

Fig. 3 Connector terminal identification

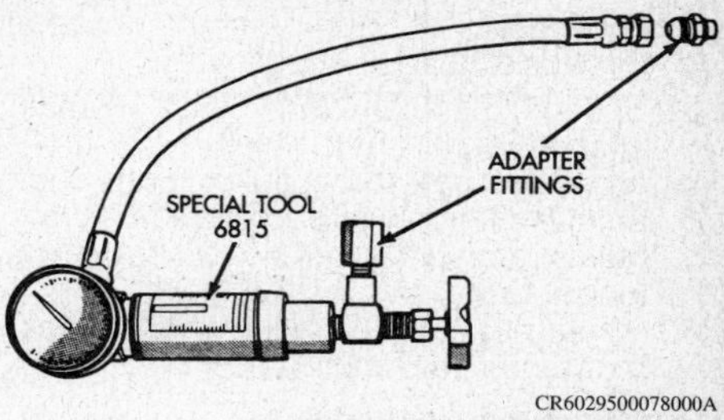

Fig. 4 Pressure gauge tool connections. 1997–99

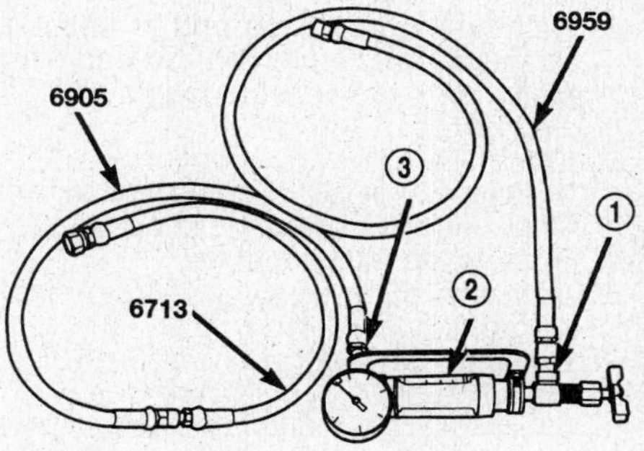

1 – OUTLET
2 – SPECIAL TOOL 6815
3 – INLET

CR6020000211000X

Fig. 5 Pressure gauge tool connections. 2000

DIAGNOSTIC TESTS

Refer to "Breeze, Cirrus, Sebring Convertible & Stratus" section for power steering system diagnostic tests.

CLEARING DIAGNOSTIC TROUBLE CODES

Record existing codes for future reference prior to clearing DTCs. To clear diagnostic trouble codes, select the "Erase DTCs" data screen on the DRB scan tool.

COMPONENT TESTING

Pump Pressure Inspection

1. Inspect power steering pump drive belt tension and adjust as required.
2. Disconnect power steering fluid pressure hose at steering gear or power steering pump.
3. Connect pressure/flow tester tool No C-6815, or equivalent, to both hoses using proper adapter fittings, **Figs. 4 and 5.**
4. Connect spare pressure hose to gear or pump.
5. Open valve on pressure/flow tester to fully open position.
6. Start engine and let idle, then inspect steering fluid level and add as required.
7. Gauge should read below 125 psi. If pressure is not as specified, inspect hoses for restrictions. Initial pressure should be 50–80 psi.
8. Close valve fully three times and record highest pressure indicated each time. **Do not leave valve closed for more than five seconds as pump damage could occur.**
9. All three readings must be above specifications and within 50 psi of each other.
10. Open test valve and turn steering wheel left and right until against stops, then record highest indicated pressure at each position.
11. Compare pressure gauge readings to power steering pump specifications.
12. If highest output pressures are not the same against either stop, steering gear is leaking internally and must be replaced.

POWER STEERING SYSTEM SERVICE

Power Steering System Bleed

1. Ensure power steering fluid reservoir is full, then start and run engine.
2. If fluid level drops after engine has been run, fill and run again until level remains constant.
3. Raise and support front of vehicle, then start engine and turn steering wheel slowly from stop to stop.
4. Stop engine and add fluid as required, then lower vehicle and start engine.
5. Turn steering wheel slowly from stop to stop, then stop engine again and add fluid as required.
6. Inspect fluid condition. If it appears extremely foamy, do not disturb vehicle for several minutes, then repeat bleed procedure. Inspect for leaks.

Component Service

POWER STEERING PRESSURE SWITCH

1. Raise and support vehicle.
2. Locate power steering switch on rear side of power steering gear, then disconnect its electrical connector.
3. **On 1998–2000 models,** using a suitable 7/8 inch deepwell socket, remove pressure switch from steering gear.
4. **On all models,** reverse procedure to install, noting the following:
   a. Install and hand tighten switch into gear until fully seated.
   b. Using deepwell socket, tighten switch to specifications. **Do not overtighten. This may result in damage to switch port threads on steering gear.**
   c. Connect pressure switch electrical connector, ensuring the latch is securely engaged with locking tab.
   d. Refill fluid and bleed system of air. Refer to " Power Steering System Bleed" for air bleeding procedure.
   e. Inspect system for fluid leaks.

POWER STEERING PUMP

On 1997–99 models, the power steering pump is not serviceable except for the pulley, reservoirs and related components, filler cap/dipstick and any oil seals other than the pump shaft seal.

On 2000 models, the only serviceable power steering pump components are the pulley and the pump itself. The reservoir is serviced with the pump.

POWER STEERING PUMP PULLEY

The power steering pump must be removed from the vehicle when removing the power steering pump pulley. Refer to "Power Steering Pump, Replace" section for removal procedure.

1. Remove power steering pump from engine.
2. Place power steering pump in a vise while using puller tool No. C-4333, or equivalent to remove pulley, **Ensure pump shaft does not turn. Do not hammer on pulley or shaft.**
3. Place new pulley squarely on end of pump shaft.
4. Mount installer tool No. C-4063, or

equivalent in pump shaft internal threads and against pulley.

5. Ensure installer and pulley remain aligned with shaft, then turn tool's outer nut and force pulley onto shaft until it is flush with end of shaft. When pulley is flush the tool's outer nut will no longer turn.
6. Install pump onto engine. tighten fasteners to specifications.

STEERING GEAR

OUTER TIE ROD & BOOT REPLACEMENT

1997–99

1. Raise and support vehicle.
2. Remove required wheel and tire.
3. Loosen inner to outer tie rod jam nut.
4. **On 1998–99 models,** thread jam nut far enough up inner tie rod to pull collar away from outer tie rod end, then pull collar of end of outer tie rod.
5. **On all models,** remove outer tie rod end to knuckle attaching nut by holding rod end stud stationary using an 11⁄32 inch socket, then removing nut with a wrench.
6. Using tie rod end remover tool No. MB990635, or equivalent, disconnect tie rod end from steering knuckle.
7. Unthread outer tie rod end from inner tie rod.
8. Reverse procedure to install, noting the following:
   a. Install outer tie rod onto inner tie rod, ensuring jam nut is on inner tie rod. **Do not tighten nut at this time.**
   b. **On 1998–99 models,** ensure collar is installed on inner tie rod with flat end against jam nut and open end facing outer tie rod.
   c. **On all models,** install tie rod end into knuckle.
   d. Start tie rod end to knuckle attaching nut onto rod end stud.
   e. While holding rod end stud stationary, tighten tie rod end to knuckle attaching nut.
   f. Using a crowfoot wrench and an 11⁄32 inch socket, tighten attaching nut to specifications. **Avoid twisting steering gear boot.**
   g. Adjust front toe setting.
   h. Tighten tie rod jam nut to specifications.
   i. Adjust steering gear to inner tie rod boots at inner tie rods if they have twisted.

2000

1. Raise and support vehicle.
2. Remove required wheel and tire.
3. Loosen inner to outer tie rod jam nut.
4. Thread jam nut far enough up inner tie rod to pull collar away from outer tie rod end, then pull collar of end of outer tie rod.
5. Remove outer tie rod end to knuckle attaching nut by holding rod end stud stationary and loosening nut with a wrench.
6. Using tie rod end remover tool No. MB991113, or equivalent, disconnect tie rod end from steering knuckle.
7. Remove tie rod heat shield.
8. Unthread outer tie rod end from inner tie rod.
9. Reverse procedure to install, noting the following:
   a. Ensure jam nut is in place on inner tie rod.
   b. Thread outer tie rod end into inner tie rod.
   c. Position collar around end of outer tie rod.
   d. Thread jam nut down inner tie rod far enough to keep collar in place. Do not tighten nut at this time.
   e. Place heat shield on knuckle's steering arm. Ensure shield's hole is aligned with knuckle's hole and tangs on outside of shield with outside configuration of steering arm. The shield should now face outboard, away from steering gear and tie rod.
   f. Install outer tie rod end to knuckle.
   g. Start tie rod end to knuckle attaching nut onto rod end stud.
   h. While holding rod end stud stationary, tighten tie rod end to knuckle attaching nut.
   i. Using a suitable crowfoot wrench, tighten attaching nut to specifications.
   j. Adjust front toe setting.

TECHNICAL SERVICE BULLETINS

WHISTLE OR HISS

1997

On some of these models, the power steering pump may whistle or hiss on right-hand turns.

This condition may be caused by the power steering gear assembly. To correct this condition, replace the power steering gear assembly with revised unit (part No. 04897187AA).

COLD ENGINE POWER STEERING NOISE

1997–98

On these models, power steering pump may make noise following cold engine starts at temperatures below 10°F. The noise usually lasts less than one minute, occurring with or without steering wheel input and increasing in duration and intensity as temperature decreases.

This condition may be caused by the power steering fluid. To correct this condition, replace power steering fluid with improved cold temperature property power steering fluid part No. MS-9933 (5010304AA), or equivalent.

TIGHTENING SPECIFICATIONS

Component	Torque/Ft. Lbs.
Outer Tie Rod End To Knuckle Nut	40
Outer Tie Rod End Locknut (1997–99)	45
Outer Tie Rod End Locknut (2000)	55
Power Steering Hose Tube Nuts (1997–99)	23
Power Steering Hose Tube Nuts (2000)	25
Power Steering Pressure Switch	70①
Power Steering Pump Relief Valve Ball Seat	48①
Pressure Hose Banjo Bolt	25

① — Inch lbs.

DISC BRAKES

TABLE OF CONTENTS

Application Chart

Model	Year	Disc Brake Type
FRONT		
Avenger & Sebring Coupe	1997–2000	6
Cirrus, Breeze & Stratus	1997–2000	3
Concorde, Intrepid, LHS, Vision & 300M	1997–2000	4
Neon	1997–2000	4
Sebring Convertible	1997–2000	3
Talon AWD	1997–98	1
Talon FWD	1997–98	6
REAR		
Avenger & Sebring Coupe	1997–2000	2
Concorde, Intrepid, LHS, Vision & 300M	1997–2000	5
Neon	1997–2000	5
Talon	1997–98	2

Type 1–MR56W & MR57W Dual Piston Floating Caliper Disc Brake, Front

INDEX

TROUBLESHOOTING

Refer to **Fig. 1,** for brake system troubleshooting.

LATERAL RUNOUT INSPECTION

1. Remove caliper support bolts, then the caliper.
2. Inspect disc surface for grooves, cracks and rust.
3. Place a dial gauge approximately .2 inch from outer circumference of brake rotor.
4. Measure runout of rotor. Refer to "Disc Brake Specifications."
5. If runout of rotor is equal to or exceeds limit specified, change phase of rotor and hub then, measure runout again noting following:
   a. Before removing brake rotor, chalk both sides of wheel stud on side at which runout is greatest.
   b. Remove brake rotor and place dial gauge as shown in **Fig. 2.**
   c. Move hub in axial direction and measure play. If play exceeds .0020 inch disassemble hub knuckle and check each part.
   d. If play does not exceed limit specification, install brake rotor 180° away from chalk marks.
6. Check runout of brake rotor again.
7. If runout cannot be corrected by changing phase of rotor, replace or machine rotor.

PARALLELISM INSPECTION

1. Using a suitable micrometer, measure rotor thickness at eight positions, approximately 45° apart and .39 inch in from outer edge of disc.
2. If rotor is beyond limits for thickness, replace.
3. If thickness variation exceeds specification, replace or resurface brake rotor with an on vehicle type brake lathe tool No. Accuturn-8750, or equivalent.

Symptom	Probable cause	Remedy
Vehicle pulls to one side when brakes are applied	Grease or oil on pad or lining surface	Replace
	Inadequate contact of pad or lining	Correct
	Auto adjuster malfunction	Adjust
	Drum out of round or uneven wear	Repair or replace as necessary
Insufficient braking power	Low or deteriorated brake fluid	Refill or change
	Air in brake system	Bleed air from system
	Overheated brake rotor due to dragging of pad or lining	Correct
	Inadequate contact of pad or lining	
	Brake booster malfunction	
	Clogged brake line	
	Grease or oil on pad or lining surface	Replace
	Proportioning valve malfunction	
	Auto adjuster malfunction	Adjust
Increased pedal stroke (Reduced pedal to floorboard clearance)	Air in brake system	Bleed air from system
	Worn lining or pad	Replace
	Broken vacuum hose	
	Faulty master cylinder	
	Brake fluid leaks	Correct
	Auto adjuster malfunction	Adjust
	Excessive push rod to master cylinder clearance	
Brake drag	Incomplete release of parking brake	Correct
	Clogged master cylinder return port	
	Incorrect parking brake adjustment	Adjust
	Incorrect push rod to master cylinder clearance	
	Faulty master cylinder piston return spring	Replace
	Worn brake pedal return spring	
	Broken rear drum brake shoe return spring	
	Lack of lubrication in sliding parts	Lubricate

CR4079100038010X

Fig. 1 Brake system troubleshooting (Part 1 of 3)

Symptom	Probable cause	Remedy
Insufficient parking brake function	Worn brake lining	Replace
	Grease or oil on lining surface	
	Parking brake cable sticking	
	Stuck wheel cylinder or caliper piston	
	Excessive parking brake lever stroke	Adjust the parking brake lever stroke or check the parking brake cable routing
	Auto adjuster malfunction	Adjust
Scraping or grinding noise when brakes are applied	Worn brake lining or pad	Replace
	Caliper to wheel interference	Correct or replace
	Dust cover to disc interference	
	Bent brake backing plate	
	Cracked drums or brake disc	
Squealing, groaning or chattering noise when brakes are applied	Missing or damaged brake pad anti-squeak shim	Replace
	Brake drums and linings, discs and pads worn or scored	Correct or replace
	Incorrect parts	
	Burred or rusted calipers	Clean or deburr
	Dirty, greased, contaminated or glazed linings	Clean or replace
	Drum brakes-weak, damaged or incorrect shoe hold-down springs, loose or damaged shoe hold-down pins and springs	Correct or replace
	Incorrect brake pedal or booster push rod setting	Adjust
Squealing noise when brakes are not applied	Bent or warped backing plate causing interference with drum	Replace
	Drum brakes-weak, damaged or incorrect shoe-to-shoe spring	
	Poor return of brake booster, master cylinder or wheel cylinder	
	Loose or extra brake parts	Retighten

CR4079100038020X

Fig. 1 Brake system troubleshooting (Part 2 of 3)

Symptom	Probable cause	Remedy
Squealing noise when brakes are not applied	Improper positioning of pads in caliper	Correct
	Improper installation of support mounting to caliper body	
	Improper machining of drum causing interference with backing plate or shoe	Replace drum
	Disc brakes-rusted, stuck	Lubricate or replace
	Worn, damaged or insufficiently lubricated wheel bearings	
	Incorrect brake pedal or booster push rod setting	Adjust
Groaning clicking or rattling noise when brakes are not applied	Stones or foreign material trapped inside wheel covers	Remove stones, etc.
	Loose wheel nuts	Retighten
	Disc brakes-loose installation bolt	
	Worn, damaged or dry wheel bearings	Lubricate or replace
	Disc brakes-failure of anti-rattle shim	Replace
	Disc brakes-wear on sleeve	
	Incorrect brake pedal or booster push rod setting	Adjust

CR4079100038030X

Fig. 1 Brake system troubleshooting (Part 3 of 3)

BRAKE SYSTEM BLEED

Bleeding the hydraulic brake system is necessary if air has entered the system. Symptoms can be noted by loss of brake operation, and/or a low or spongy brake pedal.

Pressure bleeding is recommended for all hydraulic brake systems. However, if pressure bleeding equipment is not available, the hydraulic system may be bled as described under "Manual Bleed."

PRESSURE BLEED

1. Use bleeder tank tool No. C-3496-B, or equivalent, with required adapter for master cylinder reservoir.
2. Attach clear plastic hose to bleeder screw and feed hose into clear jar containing enough brake fluid to submerge end of hose.
3. Bleed system using sequence as follows:
   a. Left rear.
   b. Right front.
   c. Right rear.
   d. Left front.
4. Open bleeder screw one full turn or more to obtain steady stream.
5. Close bleeder screw after 4–8 ounces of air free fluid is bled into jar.
6. Repeat procedure to all remaining bleeder screws.

MANUAL BLEED

Refer to **Fig. 3,** for bleeding sequence of the brake hydraulic system.

1. Attach clear plastic hose to bleeder screw and feed hose into clear jar containing enough brake fluid to submerge end of hose.
2. Pump brake pedal three to four times, hold pedal down.
3. Open bleeder screw at least one full turn.
4. Close bleeder screw and release brake pedal.
5. Repeat four to five times at each bleeder screw.
6. If pedal travel is excessive, repeat previous steps until all air is bled from system.
7. Test drive vehicle, ensure brakes are operating correctly.

BRAKE PAD SERVICE

The brake pads have wear indicators that contact the brake rotor when the brake pad thickness becomes .08 inch. The wear indicators emit a squealing sound to warn the driver to have the pads replaced and brake system checked.

1. Remove guide pin, **Fig. 4.**
2. Lift caliper assembly, then slide the assembly toward inside of wheel well until separated from lock pin.
3. Remove pad and wear indicator assemblies, inner and outer shims, then the clip from caliper support.
4. Remove drive shaft.
5. Set tool No. MB990998, or equivalent, into front hub assembly.
6. Securely attach pad clip to caliper support.

7. Clean piston and insert into cylinder with tool No. MB990520, or equivalent.
8. Apply grease to attaching faces of pad and inner shim and to attaching faces of inner and outer shims.
9. Ensure piston boot does not catch and tear as caliper assembly and lockpin are installed.
10. Reverse procedure to install.

CALIPER SERVICE

REPLACEMENT

1. Raise and support vehicle, then remove wheel and tire assembly.
2. Disconnect brake hose at caliper strut and brake caliper, then cap brake line.
3. Remove brake pads as outlined under "Brake Pad Service."
4. Remove caliper support to steering knuckle attaching bolts, then caliper support.
5. Reverse procedure to install, noting the following:
   a. Tighten bolts to specifications.
   b. Bleed brakes as outlined under "Brake System Bleed."

OVERHAUL

1. Remove caliper assembly as described under "Caliper, Replace."
2. Remove lockpin, bushing, caliper support, pin boot and boot ring, **Fig. 4.**
3. Using compressed air, remove two piston boots and pistons. **To prevent damage to pistons, place a suitable block of wood in caliper when removing pistons.**
4. Using finger tip, remove piston seal.
5. Reverse procedure to assemble, noting the following:
   a. Inspect cylinders and pistons for wear, damage and/or corrosion.
   b. Inspect caliper body and sleeve for wear.
   c. Apply suitable brake fluid to cylinders, then install piston seals into cylinder groove. **Do not wipe grease from piston seal.**
   d. Apply brake fluid to pistons and insert into cylinders by pushing downward into caliper. **Do not twist pistons into caliper.**
   e. Fill piston edges with grease supplied with seal and boot repair kit, then install piston boots.
   f. Lubricate sliding surface of guide, lockpins and boots with grease supplied with seal and boot repair kit.
   g. Install guide and lockpins. Ensure head marks match identification marks on caliper body.

ROTOR

REPLACE

Remove caliper as outlined under "Caliper Service," then remove rotor. If necessary use a suitable soft face hammer to tap rotor free of hub.

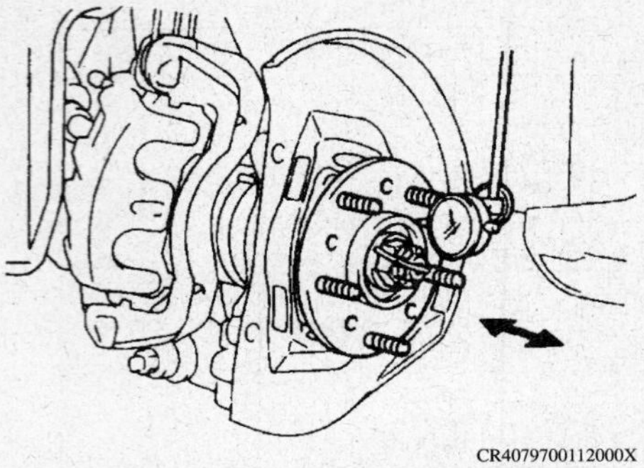

CR4079700112000X

Fig. 2 Dial gauge mounting

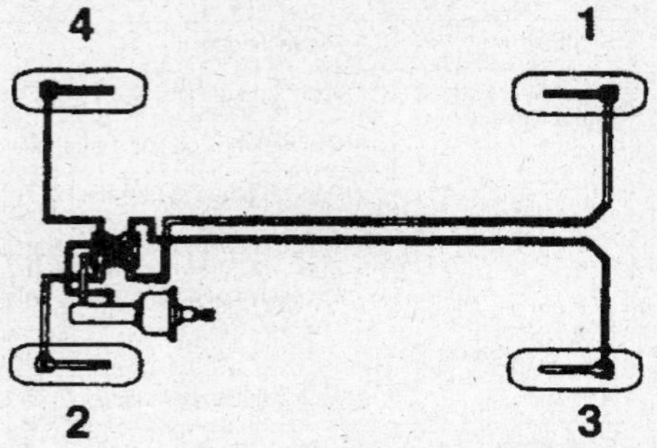

CR4079700111000X

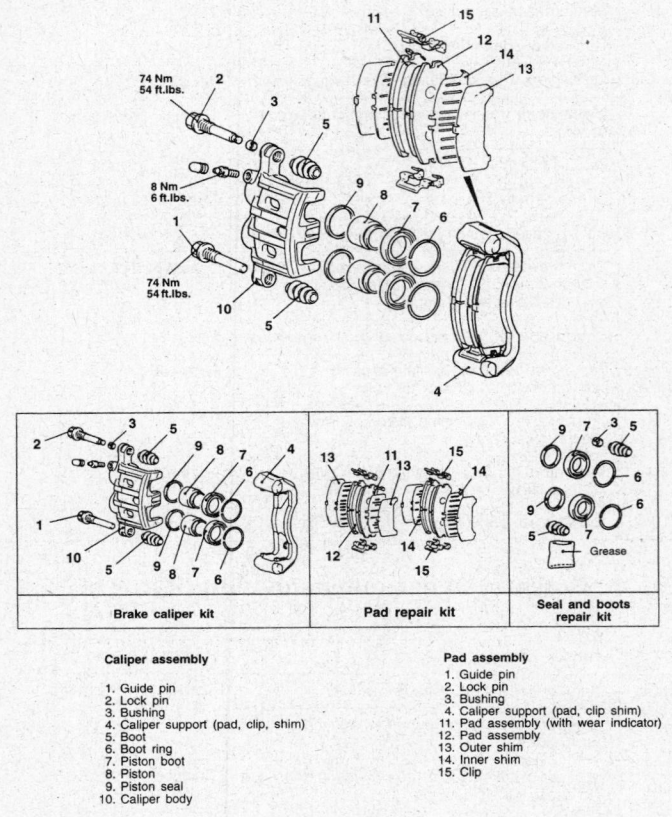

Fig. 3 Bleed sequence

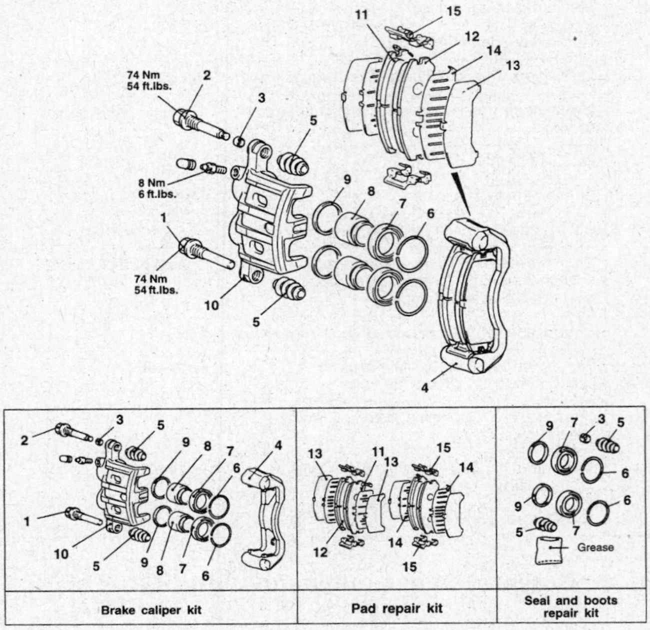

Caliper assembly

1. Guide pin
2. Lock pin
3. Bushing
4. Caliper support (pad, clip, shim)
5. Boot
6. Boot ring
7. Piston boot
8. Piston
9. Piston seal
10. Caliper body

Pad assembly

1. Guide pin
2. Lock pin
3. Bushing
4. Caliper support (pad, clip shim)
11. Pad assembly (with wear indicator)
12. Pad assembly
13. Outer shim
14. Inner shim
15. Clip

CR4079100043000X

Fig. 4 MR56W & MR57W dual piston floating caliper disc brake assembly

TECHNICAL SERVICE BULLETINS

ABS LIGHT ON, CANNOT COMMUNICATE w/DRB III

1998 Talon AWD

When performing ABS diagnostics, early model vehicles may not be able to communicate with the DRB III due to a miswired data link connector.

1. Remove 16 way data link connector from mounting bracket.
2. Remove pin No. 8 (yellow/red) from connector. Cut female terminal from wire and strip ½ of insulation from end of wire.
3. Remove pin No. 7 (pink) from data link connector. Make a center splice approximately one inch behind the female terminal. Remove ½ inch of insulation.
4. Wrap yellow/red wire around center splice of pink wire. Solder splice with rosin core solder.
5. Slide a piece of shrink tubing over splice and heat until it is shrunk and glue flows from both ends.

6. Reverse procedure to install.

ALTERNATE ABS DIAGNOSTIC CODE RETRIEVAL

1998 Avenger, Sebring & Talon

ABS diagnostic trouble codes can be accessed by actuating a procedure where the ABS warning light will blink the DTC. Follow the procedure listed below to retrieve and erase ABS trouble codes.

1. Connect pin No. 1 of the 16 way data link connector to ground.
2. Turn ignition switch ON. Diagnostic trouble codes will begin to flash on the amber ABS warning light. The first digit of the code will be represented by slow flashes and the second digit will be represented by quick flashes.
3. Diagnostic trouble code can be erased by turning ignition switch ON while the brake pedal is depressed. Quickly operate brake pedal 10 times in succession. Each pedal depression must be within 1 second of the last pedal depression. data link connector pin No. 1 must be connected to ground.
4. When code is erased, ABS warning lamp will flash quickly and continuously.

DISC BRAKE SPECIFICATIONS

ROTOR SPECIFICATIONS

Model	Year	Nominal Thickness, Inch	Minimum Allowable Thickness, Inch	Thickness Variation Parallelism, Inch	Lateral Runout (T.I.R.), Inch
Talon AWD	1997–98	.940	.880	.0006	.0031

CALIPER SPECIFICATIONS

Model	Year	Caliper Bore Dia. Inch
Talon AWD	1997–98	1.6875 x 2

TIGHTENING SPECIFICATIONS

Component	Torque/Ft. Lbs.
Bleed Screws	60-84①
Caliper Guide & Lockpins	54
Caliper Support To Front Axle	58–72
Wheel Lug Nuts	87–101

① — Inch lbs.

Type 2–MR45S, MR45V & MR58V Dual Pin Floating Caliper Disc Brake, Rear

INDEX

TROUBLESHOOTING

Refer to "Type 1–MR56W & MR57W Dual Piston Floating Caliper Disc Brake, Front" for system troubleshooting.

BRAKE SYSTEM BLEED

Bleeding the hydraulic brake system is necessary if air has entered the system. Symptoms can be noted by loss of brake operation, and/or a low or spongy brake pedal.

The hydraulic fluid is bled or flushed from the system through bleeder valves located on the calipers, wheel cylinders, and some master cylinders. Use only specified brake fluid when bleeding the system. **Never reuse brake fluid that was removed from the system.**

PRESSURE BLEED

Refer to "Type 1–MR56W & MR57W Dual Piston Floating Caliper Disc Brake, Front" for bleeding procedures.

MANUAL BLEED

Refer to "Type 1–MR56W & MR57W Dual Piston Floating Caliper Disc Brake, Front" for bleeding procedures.

BRAKE PAD SERVICE

Refer to **Fig. 1,** for MR45S and MR45V dual pin floating caliper disc brake assembly.

Refer to "Type 1-MR56W & MR57W Dual Piston Floating Caliper Disc Brake, Front" for brake pad service procedures.

CALIPER SERVICE

REPLACEMENT

1. Raise and support vehicle, then remove wheel assembly.
2. Disconnect brake hose.
3. Remove brake assembly attaching bolts, then the brake assembly.
4. Remove brake pads and shims, then separate caliper body from caliper support, **Fig. 1.**
5. Reverse procedure to install.

OVERHAUL

1. Remove caliper assembly as described under "Caliper Replace."
2. Remove caliper support, **Fig. 1.**
3. Remove pin boots and boot ring.
4. Position a suitable wood block in caliper body, then apply compressed air through the brake hose fitting hole to remove piston and dust boot. **Apply air gently.**
5. Using finger tip, remove piston seal.
6. Reverse procedure to assemble, noting the following:
   a. Inspect cylinder and piston for wear, damage and/or corrosion. Inspect caliper body and sleeve for wear.
   b. Apply brake fluid to inner cylinder, then install piston seal into cylinder groove. **Do not wipe grease from piston seal.**
   c. Apply brake fluid to pistons and insert into cylinders by pushing downward into caliper. **Do not twist pistons into caliper.**
   d. Fill piston edge with grease from seal and boot repair kit, then install piston boot.
   e. Lubricate bushing, pin boot and slide pins with grease from seal and boot repair kit.
   f. Install guide and lockpins. Ensure head marks match with identification marks on caliper body.

ADJUSTMENTS

PARKING BRAKE LEVER

Avenger, Sebring Coupe & Talon

1. Pull parking brake lever with a force of approximately 45 ft. lbs. and count number of notches. Standard value is 5–7 notches for vehicles with drum brakes, and 3–5 notches on vehicles with drum in disc brakes.
2. If parking brake lever stroke is not as specified, adjust as follows:
   a. Remove inner compartment mat of floor console.
   b. Loosen adjusting nut to end of cable rod to free cable.
   c. Remove adjustment hole plug, then use a flat tipped screwdriver, or equivalent, to turn adjuster.
   d. Turn adjuster in direction of arrow (Direction which expands shoes) so disc will not rotate.
   e. Return adjuster five notches in opposite direction.
   f. Turn adjusting nut to adjust parking brake lever stroke within standard value. **If the number of brake lever notches engaged is less than the standard value, the cable has been excessively pulled.**
   g. Check to ensure there is no play between adjusting nut and pin.
   h. Raise and support rear of vehicle.
   i. Turn rear wheel with parking brake in released position to confirm rear brakes are not dragging.

PARKING BRAKE SHOE

1. Raise and support vehicle, then remove rear wheels.
2. **On AWD models,** disconnect drive axles from companion flange.
3. **On all models,** firmly apply, then release parking brake lever several times to seat and center parking brake shoes.
4. Remove adjusting hole plug from hub of brake disc.
5. Using a suitable tool, turn adjusting nut until brake disc cannot be turned by hand.
6. Back off adjusting nut five notches.
7. Repeat above steps on opposite side.
8. **On AWD models,** connect drive axles to companion flange.
9. **On all models,** firmly apply, then release parking brake lever several times to seat and center parking brake shoes.
10. Adjust parking brake lever as outlined under "Parking Brake Lever, Adjust"
11. Install rear wheels, then lower vehicle.

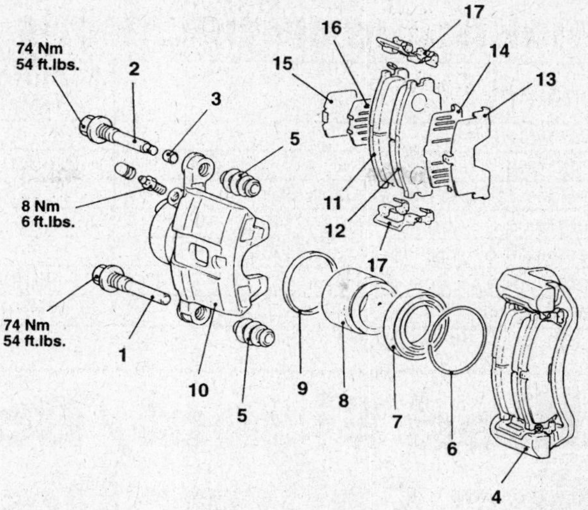

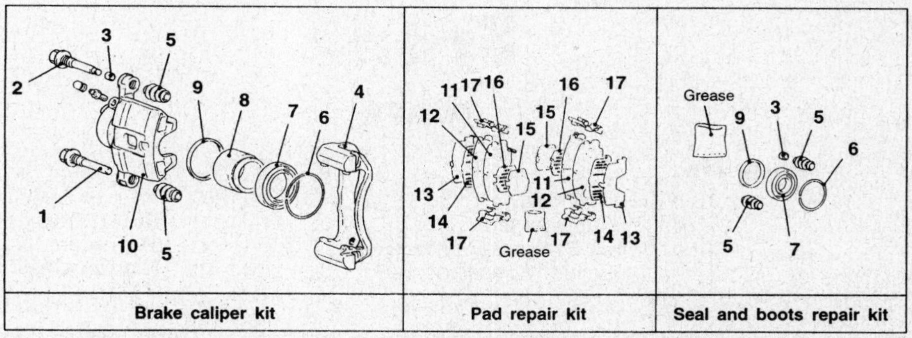

Caliper assembly

1. Guide pin
2. Lock pin
3. Bushing
4. Caliper support (pad, clip, shim)
5. Boot
6. Boot ring
7. Piston boot
8. Piston
9. Piston seal
10. Caliper body

Pad assembly

1. Guide pin
2. Lock pin
3. Bushing
4. Caliper support (pad, clip, shim)
11. Pad and wear indicator assembly
12. Pad assembly
13. Outer shim (stainless)
14. Outer shim (coated with rubber)
15. Inner shim (stainless)
16. Inner shim (coated with rubber)
17. Clip

CR4079100045000X

Fig. 1 Disc brake assembly. Avenger, Sebring Coupe & Talon

ROTOR

REPLACE

1. Remove caliper as outlined under "Caliper Service."
2. Remove parking brake adjustment hole plug from brake disc hub.
3. Using a suitable tool, turn parking brake adjusting nut until brake disc can be removed.
4. Reverse procedure to install. Adjust parking brake as outlined under "Adjustments."

DISC BRAKE SPECIFICATIONS

ROTOR SPECIFICATIONS

Model	Year	Nominal Thickness, Inch	Minimum Allowable Thickness, Inch	Lateral Runout (T.I.R.), Inch
Avenger, Sebring Coupe & Talon	1997–2000	.390	.330	.0031

CALIPER SPECIFICATIONS

Model	Caliper Bore Dia., Inch
All	1.375

TIGHTENING SPECIFICATIONS

Component	Torque/Ft. Lbs.
Backing Plate Bolts	36–43
Bleed Screws	60-84①
Brake Hose To Rear Caliper Banjo Bolt	18–25
Caliper Guide & Lockpins, Rear (MR45V & MR45S)	20
Caliper Guide & Lockpins, Rear (MR58V)	32
Caliper Support To Rear Axle	36–43
Wheel Lug Nuts	87–101

① — Inch lbs.

Type 3–Allied Signal/Bosch Dual Pin Floating Caliper Disc Brake, Front

INDEX

TROUBLESHOOTING

Refer to **Fig. 1,** for brake system troubleshooting procedures.

BRAKE SYSTEM BLEED

Bleeding the hydraulic brake system is necessary if air has entered the system. Symptoms can be noted by loss of brake operation, and/or a low or spongy brake pedal.

The hydraulic fluid is bled or flushed from the system through bleeder valves located on the calipers, wheel cylinders, and some master cylinders. Use only specified brake fluid when bleeding the hydraulic brake system. **Never reuse old brake fluid removed from the system.**

PRESSURE BLEED

Refer to "Type 1–MR56W & MR57W Dual Piston Floating Caliper Disc Brake, Front" for bleeding procedures.

MANUAL BLEED

Refer to "Type 1–MR56W & MR57W Dual Piston Floating Caliper Disc Brake, Front" for bleeding procedures.

BRAKE PAD SERVICE

1. Raise and support vehicle, then remove front wheel and tire assembly.
2. Remove caliper to steering knuckle attaching bolts.
3. Remove caliper from steering knuckle by rotating free end of caliper away from steering knuckle, then slide opposite end of caliper out from under machined abutment on steering knuckle. Support caliper on upper control arm. Do not allow it to hang on flex hose.
4. Remove front brake rotor, then the outboard pad by prying the pad retaining clip over raised area on caliper, **Fig. 2.**
5. Pull inboard brake pad away from piston until retaining clip is free from cavity in piston.
6. Press caliper piston back into piston bore of caliper.
7. Lubricate both steering knuckle abutments with a suitable multi-purpose grease.
8. Install front rotor on hub.
9. Install inboard brake pad into caliper piston, then slide new outboard brake pad assembly onto caliper assembly.
10. Carefully position caliper and brake pad assembly over brake rotor by hooking lower end of caliper over the steering knuckle, then rotate caliper into position at top of steering knuckle. Ensure caliper guide pin bolts, bushings and sleeves are clear of steering knuckle bosses.
11. Install caliper guide pin bolts and tighten to specifications.
12. Install wheel and tire assembly, then lower vehicle.
13. Apply brake pedal several times, then inspect master cylinder brake fluid level and add fluid if necessary.

CALIPER SERVICE

REPLACEMENT

1. Raise and support vehicle.
2. Remove front wheel and tire assembly.
3. Remove two caliper to steering knuckle guide pin bolts.
4. Remove brake caliper from steering knuckle as follows:
   a. Rotate bottom end of caliper away from knuckle.
   b. Slide top of caliper down from machined abutment on steering knuckle.
5. Support caliper to prevent weight from being applied to brake hose.

OVERHAUL

1. Remove caliper from brake rotor and brake pads from caliper as described in "Brake Pad Service."
2. Hang caliper on a wire away from rotor.
3. Place a small piece of wood between piston and caliper fingers.
4. Carefully depress brake pedal to hydraulically push piston out of bore, then apply and hold-down brake pedal to any position beyond the first inch of

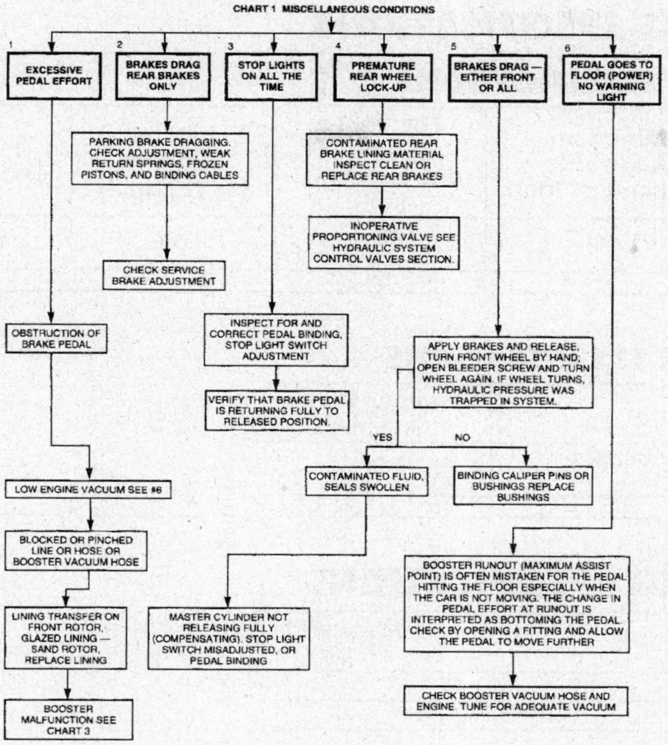

Fig. 1 Brake system troubleshooting

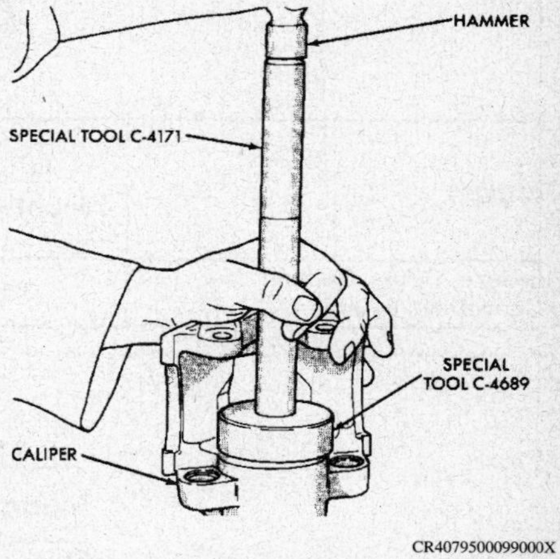

Fig. 3 Piston caliper boot installation

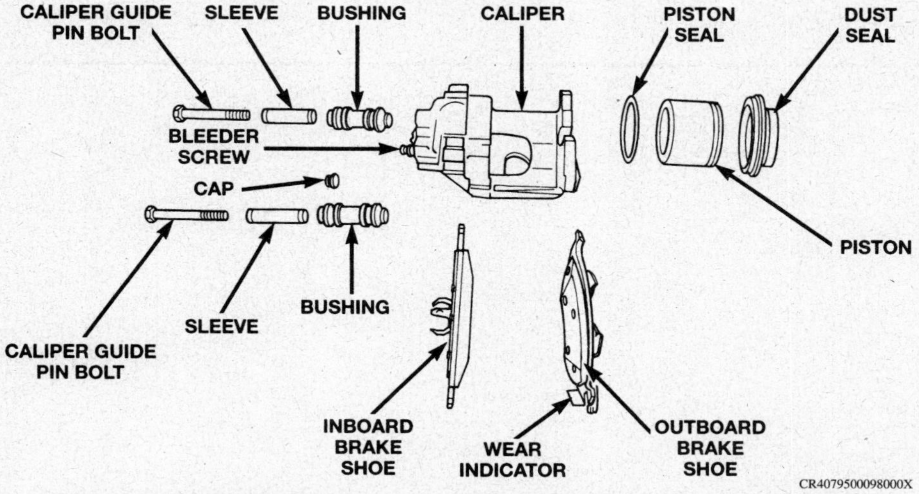

Fig. 2 Allied Signal/Bosch dual pin floating caliper disc brake assembly

brake travel. This will prevent master cylinder brake fluid loss.

5. Disconnect brake line from caliper. Plug brake line to avoid any additional brake fluid loss.
6. Mount brake caliper assembly in soft jawed vise. **Excessive vise pressure will cause bore distortion and binding of piston.**
7. Remove guide pin bushings from caliper.
8. Remove piston dust boot from caliper and discard.
9. Using a plastic trim stick, work piston seal out of its groove in caliper piston bore. **Do not use a screw driver or other metal tool for this procedure, because of the possibility of scratching piston bore or burring edges of seal groove.**
10. Clean all parts using alcohol or a suitable solvent and wipe dry using a lint free cloth. **No lint residue can be left in the caliper bore.**
11. Inspect piston bore for scoring or pitting. Light scratches or corrosion can usually be cleared from the bores using crocus cloth. Bores that show deep scratches or scoring should be honed. **Bore diameter should not be honed more than .001 inch. If bore does not clean up within this specification, a new caliper housing should be installed.**
12. When honing brake caliper housing, coat stones and bore with brake fluid.
13. After honing bore, clean seal and boot grooves with a stiff non-metallic rotary brush. **Use extreme care in cleaning caliper after honing. Remove all dirt and grit by flushing caliper with brake fluid, wipe dry with a lint free cloth.**
14. Replace caliper piston if there is any pitting, scratches, or physical damage.
15. Dip new piston seal in clean brake fluid and install in caliper bore groove. Seal should be positioned at one area in groove and gently worked around the groove, using only your fingers until properly seated. **Never reuse old piston seal.**
16. Coat new piston boot with clean brake fluid leaving a generous amount inside boot.
17. Coat dust boot with clean brake fluid, the position over piston.
18. Install piston into caliper bore pushing it past piston seal until it bottoms in caliper bore.
19. Position dust boot in counterbore of caliper piston bore.
20. Using a hammer and piston caliper boot installer No. C-4689 and handle No. C-4171, or their equivalents, drive boot into counterbore of the caliper, **Fig. 3.**
21. Install guide pin bushings and dust boots.
22. Attach hydraulic brake line to caliper. **Always use new seal washers when installing brake line to caliper.**
23. Install brake pads and caliper assembly as described in "Caliper, Replace."
24. Bleed brake system as described in "Brake System Bleed."

ROTOR

REPLACE

Refer to "Brake Pad Service" for rotor replacement procedures.

DISC BRAKE SPECIFICATIONS

ROTOR SPECIFICATIONS

Model	Nominal Thickness, Inch	Minimum Allowable Thickness, Inch	Thickness Variation (Parallelism), Inch	Lateral Runout (T.I.R.), Inch	Finish, Micro-Inch
Breeze, Cirrus, Sebring Convertible & Stratus	.900–.911	.843	.0005	.005	15–80

CALIPER SPECIFICATIONS

Model	Caliper Piston O.D., Inch
Breeze, Cirrus, Sebring Convertible & Stratus	2.125

TIGHTENING SPECIFICATIONS

Component	Torque/Ft. Lbs.
Bleeder Screw	84①
Caliper Banjo Bolt	35
Caliper Guide Pin Bolts	16
Hydraulic Brake Line Fitting	26
Wheel Lug Nuts	100

① — Inch lbs.

Type 4–Kelsey-Hayes Dual Pin Floating Caliper Disc Brake, Front

INDEX

DESCRIPTION

The single piston, floating caliper disc brake assembly, **Fig. 1,** consists of the rotor, caliper, pads and the driving hub. The caliper is mounted to the steering knuckle using bushings, sleeves and 2 thru bolts which thread directly into the steering knuckle.

This assembly has an anti-rattle clip attached to the outer pad and an inner pad-piston retainer clip.

All of the braking force is taken directly by the adapter. The caliper is a one piece casting with the inboard side containing a single piston cylinder bore.

A square cut rubber piston seal is located in a machined groove in the caliper bore and provides a seal between piston and caliper bore.

A molded rubber dust boot installed in a groove in the cylinder bore and piston keeps contamination from the caliper bore and piston. The boot mounts in the caliper bore and in a groove in the piston.

TROUBLESHOOTING

Refer to **Fig. 2,** for system troubleshooting.

LATERAL RUNOUT INSPECTION

Refer to "Disc Brake Specifications" for runout specifications.

1. Raise and support vehicle, then remove wheels.
2. If applicable, ensure wheel bearings are properly adjusted.
3. Using suitable spacers install lug nuts or bolts, then tighten to specifications.
4. Mount a dial indicator to vehicle, then position dial indicator plunger so it contacts the rotor at a point one inch from the outer edge.
5. Rotate the rotor and note the dial indicator readings. Perform this inspection on both inboard and outboard rotor faces.
6. If runout exceeds specifications proceed as follows:
   a. Position rotor on the hub, then inspect runout.
   b. If runout still exceeds specifications, replace or machine the rotor.

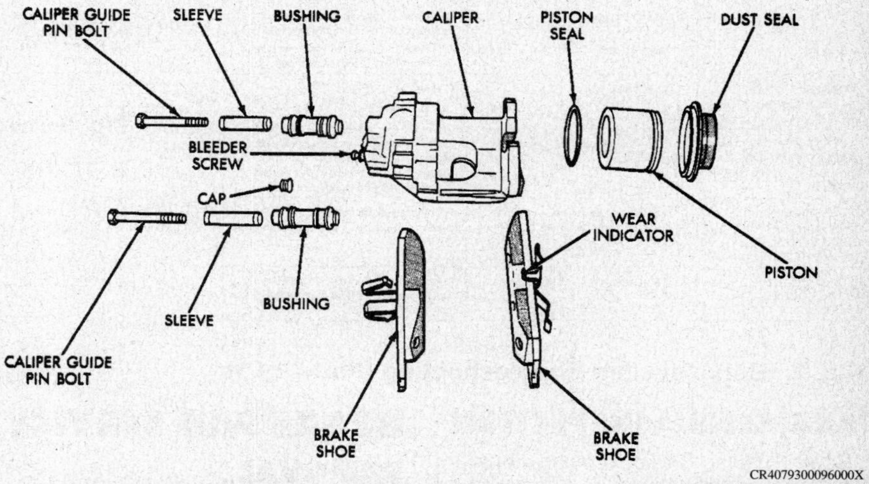

Fig. 1 Kelsey Hayes dual pin floating caliper disc brake assembly

RED BRAKE WARNING LAMP

CONDITION	POSSIBLE CAUSES	CORRECTION
RED BRAKE WARNING LAMP ON	1. Parking brake lever not fully released.	1. Release parking brake lever.
	2. Parking brake warning lamp switch on parking brake lever.	2. Inspect and replace switch as necessary.
	3. Brake fluid level low in reservoir.	3. Fill reservoir. Check entire system for leaks. Repair or replace as required.
	4. Brake fluid level switch.	4. Disconnect switch wiring connector. If lamp goes out, replace switch.
	5. Mechanical instrument cluster (MIC) problem.	5. Refer to Chassis Diagnostic Procedures manual.

BRAKE NOISE

CONDITION	POSSIBLE CAUSES	CORRECTION
DISC BRAKE CHIRP	1. Excessive brake rotor runout.	1. Follow brake rotor diagnosis and testing. Correct as necessary.
	2. Lack of lubricant on brake caliper slides.	2. Lubricate brake caliper slides.
DISC BRAKE RATTLE OR CLUNK	1. Broken or missing anti-rattle spring clips on shoes.	1. Replace brake shoes.
	2. Caliper guide pins loose.	2. Tighten guide pins.
DISC BRAKE SQUEAK AT LOW SPEED (WHILE APPLYING LIGHT BRAKE PEDAL EFFORT)	1. Brake shoe linings.	1. Replace brake shoes.
SCRAPING (METAL-TO-METAL).	1. Foreign object interference with brakes.	1. Inspect brakes and remove foreign object.
	2. Brake shoes worn out.	2. Replace brake shoes. Inspect rotors. Reface or replace as necessary.

CR4079900136010X

Fig. 2 Brake system troubleshooting (Part 1 of 3)

OTHER BRAKE CONDITIONS

CONDITION	POSSIBLE CAUSES	CORRECTION
BRAKES CHATTER	1. Disc brake rotor has excessive thickness variation.	1. Isolate condition as rear or front. Reface or replace brake rotors as necessary.
BRAKES DRAG (FRONT OR ALL)	1. Contaminated brake fluid. 2. Binding caliper pins or bushings. 3. Binding master cylinder. 4. Binding brake pedal.	1. Check for swollen seals. Replace all system components containing rubber. 2. Replace pins and bushings 3. Replace master cylinder. 4. Replace brake pedal.
BRAKES DRAG (REAR ONLY)	1. Parking brake cables binding or froze up. 2. Parking brake cable return spring not returning shoes. 3. Obstruction inside the center console preventing full return of the parking brake cables.	1. Check cable routing. Replace cables as necessary. 2. Replace cables as necessary. 3. Remove console and remove obstruction.
BRAKES GRAB	1. Contaminated brake shoe linings. 2. Improper power brake booster assist.	1. Inspect and clean, or replace shoes. Repair source of contamination. 2. Refer to Power Brake Booster in the diagnosis and testing section.
EXCESSIVE PEDAL EFFORT	1. Obstruction of brake pedal. 2. Low power brake booster assist. 3. Glazed brake linings. 4. Brake shoe lining transfer to brake rotor.	1. Inspect, remove or move obstruction. 2. Refer to power brake booster in the diagnosis and testing section. 3. Reface or replace brake rotors as necessary. Replace brake shoes. 4. Reface or replace brake rotors as necessary. Replace brake shoes.
EXCESSIVE PEDAL TRAVEL (VEHICLE STOPS OK)	1. Air in brake lines.	1. Bleed brakes.
EXCESSIVE PEDAL TRAVEL (PEDAL GOES TO FLOOR - CAN'T SKID WHEELS)	1. Power brake booster runout (vacuum assist).	1. Check booster vacuum hose and engine tune for adequate vacuum supply. Refer to power brake booster in the diagnosis and testing section.
EXCESSIVE PEDAL TRAVEL (ONE FRONT WHEEL LOCKS UP DURING HARD BRAKING)	1. One of the two hydraulic circuits to the front brakes is malfunctioning.	1. Inspect system for leaks. Check master cylinder for internal malfunction.
PEDAL PULSATES/ SURGES DURING BRAKING	1. Disc brake rotor has excessive thickness variation.	1. Isolate condition as rear or front. Reface or replace brake rotors as necessary.

CR4079900136020X

Fig. 2 Brake system troubleshooting (Part 2 of 3)

CONDITION	POSSIBLE CAUSES	CORRECTION
PEDAL IS SPONGY	1. Air in brake lines. 2. Power brake booster runout (vacuum assist).	1. Bleed brakes. 2. Check booster vacuum hose and engine tune for adequate vacuum supply. Refer to power brake booster in the diagnosis and testing section.
PREMATURE REAR WHEEL LOCKUP	1. Contaminated brake shoe linings. 2. Inoperative proportioning valve. 3. Improper power brake booster assist.	1. Inspect and clean, or replace shoes. Repair source of contamination. 2. Test proportioning valves folowing procedure listed in diagnosis and testing section. Replace valves as necessary. 3. Refer to power brake booster in the diagnosis and testing section.
STOP LAMPS STAY ON	1. Brake lamp switch out of adjustment. 2. Brake pedal binding. 3. Obstruction in pedal linkage. 4. Power Brake Booster not allowing pedal to return completely.	1. Adjust brake lamp switch. 2. Inspect and replace as necessary. 3. Remove obstruction. 4. Replace power brake booster.
VEHICLE PULLS TO RIGHT OR LEFT ON BRAKING	1. Frozen brake caliper piston. 2. Contaminated brake shoe lining. 3. Pinched brake lines. 4. Leaking piston seal. 5. Suspension problem.	1. Replace frozen piston or caliper. Bleed brakes. 2. Inspect and clean, or replace shoes. Repair source of contamination. 3. Replace pinched line. 4. Replace piston seal or brake caliper. 5. Refer to the Suspension group.
PARKING BRAKE - EXCESSIVE LEVER TRAVEL	1. Rear parking brake shoes out of adjustment.	1. Adjust rear parking brake shoes.

CR4079900136030X

Fig. 2 Brake system troubleshooting (Part 3 of 3)

PARALLELISM INSPECTION

Refer to "Disc Brake Specifications" for parallelism specifications.

1. Using a suitable micrometer, measure the rotor at 12 equally spaced points at a radius approximately one inch from edge of disc.
2. **If measurements exceed specifications,** resurface or replace rotors as necessary.

BRAKE SYSTEM BLEED

Bleeding the hydraulic brake system is necessary if air has entered the system. Symptoms can be noted by loss of brake operation, and/or a low or spongy brake pedal.

The hydraulic fluid is bled or flushed from the system through bleeder valves located on the calipers, wheel cylinders, and some master cylinders. Use only specified brake fluid when bleeding the system. **Never reuse old brake fluid removed from the system.**

PRESSURE BLEED

Refer to "Type 1–MR56W & MR57W Dual Piston Floating Caliper Disc Brake, Front" for bleeding procedures.

MANUAL BLEED

Refer to "Type 1–MR56W & MR57W Dual Piston Floating Caliper Disc Brake, Front" for bleeding procedures.

BRAKE PAD SERVICE

REMOVAL

1. Raise and support vehicle.
2. Remove front wheel and tire assembly.
3. Remove two caliper assembly to steering knuckle guide pin bolts.
4. Remove caliper assembly from steering knuckle as follows:
   a. Rotate top of caliper away from steering knuckle.
   b. Lift caliper off bottom machined abutment on steering knuckle.
5. Support caliper to prevent damage of flexible brake hose.
6. Remove outboard brake shoe by prying shoe retaining clip over raised area of caliper.
7. Pull inboard brake shoe away from piston until retaining clip is free from cavity in piston.

CALIPER SERVICE

REPLACEMENT

1. Raise and support vehicle.
2. Remove front wheel and tire assembly.
3. Remove two caliper to steering knuckle guide pin bolts.
4. Remove brake caliper from steering knuckle as follows:
   a. Rotate bottom end of caliper away from knuckle.
   b. Slide top of caliper down from machined abutment on steering knuckle.
5. Support caliper to prevent weight from being applied to brake hose.

OVERHAUL

Disassemble

1. Remove caliper assembly as described under "Brake Pad, Service."
2. Place a wood block between caliper piston and caliper fingers. With brake hose attached to caliper, carefully depress brake pedal to push piston out of caliper bore. Prop brake pedal to any position below first inch of brake pedal travel to prevent brake fluid loss.
3. If pistons are to be removed from both calipers, disconnect brake hose at frame bracket after removing piston, then cap brake line and repeat procedure to remove piston from other caliper.
4. Disconnect brake hose from caliper.
5. Mount caliper in a soft jawed vise.
6. Support caliper, then remove and discard dust boot.
7. Using a small wooden or plastic stick, remove seal from groove in piston bore and discard. **Do not use a screwdriver or other metal tool, as this may scratch caliper bore.**
8. Remove caliper bushings.

Assemble

1. Mount caliper in a soft jawed vise.
2. Lubricate piston seal with clean brake fluid and install seal in caliper bore groove. Ensure seal is properly seated.
3. Lubricate piston boot with clean brake fluid and position over piston.
4. Install piston and boot assembly, pushing it past piston seal until it bottoms in caliper bore.
5. Using a hammer and dust boot installer No. C-4689 with handle No. C-4171, or equivalents, drive dust boot into counterbore until properly seated.

6. On models where bushings require replacement, compress flanges of bushings and install on caliper housing. Ensure bushing flanges extend evenly over caliper housing on both sides. Remove Teflon sleeves from guide pin bushings prior to installing bushings into caliper. After bushings are installed into caliper, reinstall Teflon sleeves into bushings.
7. Connect brake hose to brake line at frame bracket.
8. Install caliper on vehicle as described under "Brake Pad Service."
9. Bleed brakes as outlined under "Brake System Bleed."

ROTOR

REPLACE

Remove caliper as outlined under "Caliper Service," then remove rotor. Use a suitable soft face hammer if necessary to tap rotor free of hub.

DISC BRAKE SPECIFICATIONS

ROTOR SPECIFICATIONS

Model	Year	Nominal Thickness, Inch	Minimum Refinish Thickness, Inch	Thickness Variation (Parallelism), Inch	Lateral Runout (T.I.R.), Inch	Finish, Micro-Inch
Concorde, Intrepid, LHS & Vision	1997–2000	1.019–1.029	.960	.0005	.003	15–80
Neon	1997–99	.782–.792	.724	.0005	.005	15–80
	2000	.861–.871	.803	.0005	.005	15–80

CALIPER SPECIFICATIONS

Model	Caliper Piston O.D., Inch
Concorde, Intrepid, LHS & Vision	2.360
Neon	2.125

TIGHTENING SPECIFICATIONS

Component	Torque/Ft. Lbs.
Bearing Retainer Bolts	21
Bleed Screws	10
Brake Hose To Caliper Banjo Bolt	35
Brake Line Fitting	12
Caliper Mounting Bolts	16
Caliper Guide Pins	30
Front Brake Hose Intermediate Bracket	9
Wheel Lug Nuts	85–110

Type 5–Kelsey-Hayes Dual Pin Floating Caliper Disc Brake, Rear

INDEX

DESCRIPTION

This single piston, floating caliper rear disc brake assembly, **Fig. 1,** includes a hub assembly, adapter, rotor, caliper, shoes and pads. The parking brake system consists of a small duo-servo brake mounted to an adapter which expands out against the hat section on the inside of the rotor. The caliper has either a 1.338 or 1.42 inch piston located on the inboard side.

The caliper floats on rubber bushings with metal sleeves on two bolts that are threaded into the adapter. Two machined abutments on the adapter position and align the caliper and brake pads for movement fore and aft.

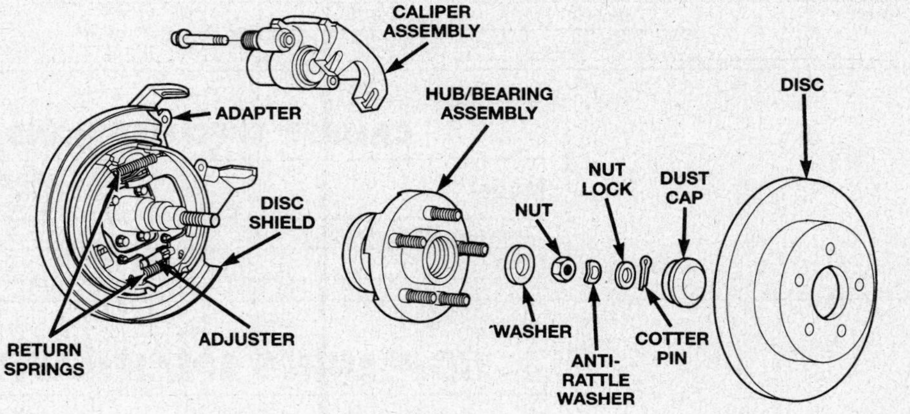

Fig. 1 Kelsey-Hayes dual pin floating caliper disc brake assembly

TROUBLESHOOTING

Refer to "Type 1–MR56W & MR57W Dual Piston Floating Caliper Disc Brake Front" for system troubleshooting.

LATERAL RUNOUT INSPECTION

Refer to "Disc Brake Specifications" for runout specifications.

1. Raise and support vehicle, then remove wheels.
2. If applicable, ensure wheel bearings are properly adjusted.
3. Using suitable spacers install lug nuts or bolts, then tighten to specifications.
4. Mount a dial indicator to vehicle, then position dial indicator plunger so it contacts the rotor at a point one inch from the outer edge.
5. Rotate the rotor and note the dial indicator readings. Perform this inspection on both inboard and outboard rotor faces.
6. If runout exceeds specifications, proceed as follows:
   a. Position rotor on the hub, then inspect runout.
   b. If runout still exceeds specifications, replace or machine the rotor.

PARALLELISM INSPECTION

Refer to "Disc Brake Specifications" for parallelism specifications.

1. Using a suitable micrometer, measure the rotor at 12 equally spaced points at a radius approximately one inch from edge of disc.
2. **If measurements exceed specifications,** resurface or replace rotor as necessary.

BRAKE SYSTEM BLEED

Bleeding the hydraulic brake system is necessary if air has entered the system. Symptoms can be noted by loss of brake operation, and/or a low or spongy brake pedal.

The hydraulic fluid is bled or flushed from the system through bleeder valves located on the calipers, wheel cylinders, and some master cylinders. Use only specified brake fluid when bleeding the system. **Never reuse old brake fluid removed from the system.**

PRESSURE BLEED

Refer to "Type 1–MR56W & MR57W Dual Piston Floating Caliper Disc Brake, Front" for bleeding procedures.

MANUAL BLEED

Refer to "Type 1–MR56W & MR57W Dual Piston Floating Caliper Disc Brake, Front" for bleeding procedures.

BRAKE PAD SERVICE

Refer to "Type 6–Kelsey-Hayes Dual Pin Floating Caliper Disc Brake, Front" for service procedures.

CALIPER SERVICE

REPLACEMENT

1. Raise and support vehicle.
2. Remove rear wheel and tire assembly.
3. Remove two caliper assembly to adapter guide pin bolts.
4. Remove caliper from adapter as follows:
   a. Rotate top of caliper away from adapter.
   b. Lift caliper off bottom abutment on adapter.
5. Support caliper assembly from rear strut to prevent flexible brake hose damage.
6. Remove rear rotor from hub by pulling it straight off wheel mounting studs.

OVERHAUL

1. Remove caliper from rotor as described under "Brake Pad Service."
2. Place a small piece of wood between piston and caliper fingers, then carefully depress brake pedal to hydraulically push piston out of bore. Prop brake pedal to any position below first inch of brake pedal travel to prevent brake fluid loss.
3. If pistons are to be removed from both calipers, disconnect brake hose at frame bracket after removing piston, then cap brake line and repeat procedure to remove piston from other caliper.
4. Disconnect brake hose from caliper.
5. Mount caliper in a soft jawed vise.
6. Support caliper, then remove and discard dust boot.
7. Using a small wooden or plastic stick, remove seal from groove in piston bore and discard. **Do not use a screwdriver or other metal tool, as this may scratch caliper bore.**
8. If necessary, remove bushing and sleeve assembly, as follows:
   a. Using fingers, push inner sleeve until it pops out of bushing, then pull inner sleeve completely out of bushing.
   b. Using fingers collapse one side of bushing. Pull opposite side of bushing to remove from caliper.
9. Using denatured alcohol or equivalent, thoroughly clean piston and caliper grooves, caliper housing and bushing mounting surfaces.
10. Dip new piston seal in clean brake fluid and install in groove in bore.
11. Coat new piston boot with clean brake fluid leaving a generous amount inside boot.
12. Coat piston with clean brake fluid, then position dust boot over piston.
13. Install piston into bore pushing it past piston seal until it bottoms in bore.
14. Position dust boot in counterbore, then using a hammer and installer No. C-4383-7, or equivalent, drive boot into counterbore of caliper.
15. If removed, install guide pin sleeve bushings as follows:
    a. Fold bushing in half lengthwise at solid middle section.
    b. Using fingers, insert folded bushing into caliper. Do not use sharp object to perform this step.
    c. Using wooden dowel, unfold bushing until it is fully seated in caliper. Flanges should be seated evenly on both sides of bushing hole.
16. If removed, install guide pin sleeve as follows:
    a. Hold end of bushing, then push sleeve through bushing until end of bushing is fully seated into seal groove of sleeve.
    b. Holding sleeve in place, install other end of bushing into seal groove.
    c. Ensure bushing is in seal groove on both sides.
17. Install brake fluid line, then install caliper as outlined under "Brake Pad Service."
18. Bleed brakes as outlined under "Brake System Bleed."

PARKING BRAKE SERVICE

PARKING BRAKE SHOES, REPLACE

1. Remove rear disc brake caliper assembly, as described under "Caliper Service," from adapter and rotor.
2. Remove rear rotor from hub, then the dust cap.
3. Remove cotter pin, nut retainer, wave washer and rear hub/bearing assembly retaining nut and washer from rear spindle.
4. Remove rear hub and bearing assembly from rear spindle.
5. **On Neon, Concord, LHS, Intrepid and Vision models,** remove rear brake shoe assembly hold-down clip.
6. **On all models,** turn brake shoe adjuster wheel until adjuster is at shortest length.
7. Remove adjuster assembly from parking brake assembly.
8. **On Neon, Concord, LHS, Intrepid and Vision models,** remove lower shoe to shoe spring.
9. **On all models,** pull front parking brake shoe away from anchor pin, then remove front parking brake shoe and lower spring.
10. **On Neon, Concord, LHS, Intrepid and Vision models,** pull rear brake shoe assembly away from anchor.
11. **On all models,** remove rear brake shoe and upper spring.
12. **On Neon, Concord, LHS, Intrepid and Vision models,** remove front brake shoe hold-down clip, then the brake shoe assembly.

ADJUSTMENTS

PARKING BRAKE

1. Release parking brake.
2. Raise and support vehicle.
3. Adjust parking brake cable until there is slack in the cable.
4. Tighten adjusting nut until a slight drag is felt when rotating the rear wheels.
5. Back off adjusting nut two full turns past the point when both rear wheels rotate freely.
6. Inspect parking brake operation.

ROTOR

REPLACE

1. Remove caliper as outlined under "Caliper Service."
2. Remove parking brake adjustment hole plug from hub of brake disc.
3. Using a suitable tool, turn parking brake adjusting nut until brake disc can be removed.
4. Reverse procedure to install. Adjust parking brake as outlined under "Adjustments."

TECHNICAL SERVICE BULLETINS

HOWL FROM REAR BRAKES DURING LOW SPEED STOP

1997 Neon

This bulletin applies to all non-ABS equipped vehicles. Vehicles with ABS did not come with rear drum brakes.

A howl type noise coming from rear brakes during a low speed (10 mph or less) brake apply in a forward direction. The condition may be more frequent in cold/damp weather during the first few stops with cold brakes.

While traveling at 10 mph, lightly apply the brakes and listen for a low pitched howl from the rear. If the noise is heard, perform the following procedure.

1. Raise vehicle and support vehicle.
2. Remove rear wheel and tire, then the brake drum.
3. Remove dust cap from rear hub bearing.
4. Remove retaining nut holding rear bearing/hub assembly to spindle, then the spindle.
5. Remove brake shoes from brake support plate.
6. Disconnect rear brake flex hose tube from wheel cylinder.
7. Remove park brake actuator lever from park brake cable.
8. Position a ½ inch wrench over retainer fingers on end of parking brake cable. Compress cable housing retaining fingers and start cable housing out of support plate. Remove wrench when retainer is free from park brake cable mounting hole in rear of brake shoe support plate.
9. Remove four brake support plate to knuckle attaching bolts. Separate brake shoe support from rear suspension knuckle.
10. Transfer all brake hardware to new backing plate.
11. New brake shoe support plate comes with wheel cylinder attached. Do not loosen wheel cylinder attaching bolts. Positioning of rear wheel cylinder is critical.
12. Install brake support plate and gasket to rear suspension. **Torque** support plate bolts to 55 ft. lbs.
13. Install parking brake cable end into brake support plate.
14. Install brake cylinder hydraulic hose to wheel cylinder. **Torque** to 12 ft. lbs.
15. Attach parking brake cable to actuator, then install brake shoe assemblies.
16. Install rear bearing and hub assembly. Install new nut and **torque** to 13 ft. lbs.
17. Install remaining components in reverse order of removal.

DISC BRAKE SPECIFICATIONS

ROTOR SPECIFICATIONS

Model	Year	Nominal Thickness, Inch	Minimum Allowable Thickness, Inch	Thickness Variation (Parallelism), Inch	Lateral Runout (T.I.R.), Inch	Finish, Micro-Inch
Concorde, Intrepid, LHS & Vision	1997–2000	.458–.478	.409	.0005	.005	15–80
Neon	1997–99	.782–.792	.724	.0005	.005	15–80
	2000	.344–.364	.285	.0005	.005	15–80

CALIPER SPECIFICATIONS

Rotor Type	Caliper Piston O.D., Inch
Solid	1.34
Vented	1.42

TIGHTENING SPECIFICATIONS

Component	Torque/Ft. Lbs.
Bearing Retainer Bolts	21
Bleed Screws	10
Brake Hose To Caliper Banjo Bolt	35
Brake Line Fitting	12
Caliper Guide Pins	30
Caliper Mounting Bolts	16
Support Plate To Rear Axle	80
Wheel Lug Nuts	85–110

Type 6-MR31S, MR34V, MR44V & MR46V Dual Pin Floating Caliper Disc Brake, Front

INDEX

TROUBLESHOOTING

Refer to "Type 1–MR56W & MR57W Dual Piston Floating Caliper Disc Brake, Front" for system troubleshooting.

LATERAL RUNOUT INSPECTION

Refer to "Type 1–MR56W & MR57W Dual Piston Floating Caliper Disc Brake, Front" for system troubleshooting.

PARALLELISM INSPECTION

Refer to "Type 1–MR56W & MR57W Dual Piston Floating Caliper Disc Brake, Front" for system troubleshooting.

BRAKE SYSTEM BLEED

Bleeding the hydraulic brake system is necessary if air has entered the system. Symptoms can be noted by loss of brake operation, and/or a low or spongy brake pedal.

The hydraulic fluid is bled or flushed from the system through bleeder valves located on the calipers, wheel cylinders, and some master cylinders. Use only specified brake fluid when bleeding the system. **Never reuse old brake fluid removed from the system.**

PRESSURE BLEED

Refer to "Type 1–MR56W & MR57W Dual Piston Floating Caliper Disc Brake, Front" for bleeding procedures.

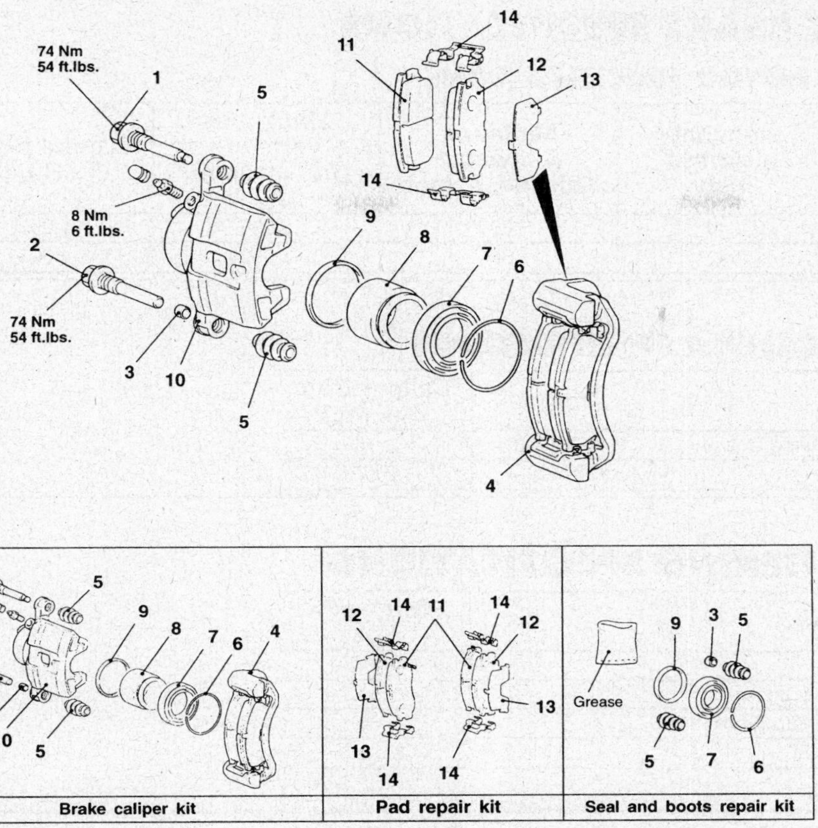

Caliper assembly

1. Guide pin
2. Lock pin
3. Bushing
4. Caliper support (pad, clip, shim)
5. Boot
6. Boot ring
7. Piston boot
8. Piston
9. Piston seal
10. Caliper body

Pad assembly

1. Guide pin
2. Lock pin
3. Bushing
4. Caliper support (pad, clip, shim)
11. Pad and wear indicator assembly
12. Pad assembly
13. Outer shim
14. Clip

CR4079100060000X

Fig. 1 Disc brake assembly. Avenger & Sebring Coupe.

MANUAL BLEED

Refer to "Type 1–MR56W & MR57W Dual Piston Floating Caliper Disc Brake, Front" for bleeding procedures.

BRAKE PAD SERVICE

1. Remove approximately ⅓ of brake fluid from master cylinder.
2. Raise and support vehicle, then remove tire and wheel assembly.
3. Remove guide pin, **Fig. 1,** then lift caliper body upward and secure with wire.
4. Remove inner shims, anti-squeak shims, brake pad assemblies and pad clips from support mounting.
5. Press caliper piston into caliper bore with suitable tool.
6. Install upper and lower pad clips, pad assemblies, inner shims and anti-squeak shims into support mounting.
7. Lower caliper body, then install lockpin.
8. Depress brake pedal several times to seat pads, then inspect and replenish brake fluid as necessary.
9. Install wheel and tire assembly, then lower vehicle.

CALIPER SERVICE

REPLACEMENT

1. Raise and support vehicle, then remove wheel and tire assembly.
2. Disconnect brake hose at caliper strut, then at the brake caliper. Cap vehicle brake line.
3. Remove brake pads as outlined under "Brake Pad Service."
4. Remove caliper support to steering knuckle attaching bolts, then caliper support.
5. Reverse procedure to install, noting the following:
   a. Tighten bolts to specifications.
   b. Bleed brakes as outlined under "Brake System Bleed."

OVERHAUL

Avenger & Sebring Coupe

1. Remove caliper assembly as described under "Caliper, Replace."
2. Remove lockpin, bushing, caliper support, guide pin and lockpin boots, **Fig. 1.**
3. Remove boot ring using a suitable flat blade screwdriver.
4. Position a shop towel in caliper body, then apply compressed air through the brake hose fitting hole to remove piston and dust boot. **Apply air gently.**
5. Remove piston seal using finger tips. **Do not use screwdriver or other tool to prevent damage to inner cylinder.**
6. Reverse procedure to assemble, noting the following:
   a. Inspect cylinder and piston for wear or damage and/or corrosion. Inspect caliper body and sleeve for wear.
   b. Apply suitable brake fluid to inner cylinder, then install piston seal into cylinder groove. **Do not wipe special grease from piston seal.**
   c. Apply suitable brake fluid to piston and insert into cylinder without twisting.
   d. Fill piston edge with grease from seal and boot repair kit or equivalent, then install piston boot.
   e. Lubricate sliding surface of lockpin and guide pin boots, caliper support and bushing with grease from seal and boot repair kit.
   f. Install guide and lockpins with their head marks matched with identification marks on caliper body.

ROTOR

REPLACE

Remove caliper as outlined under "Caliper Service," then remove rotor. Use a suitable soft face hammer if necessary to tap rotor free of hub.

DISC BRAKE SPECIFICATIONS

ROTOR SPECIFICATIONS

Model	Year	Nominal Thickness, Inch	Minimum Allowable Thickness, Inch	Thickness Variation (Parallelism), Inch	Lateral Runout (T.I.R.), Inch
Avenger & Sebring Coupe	1997–2000	.940	.880	.0006	.0031
Talon	1997–98	.940	.880	.0006	.0031

CALIPER SPECIFICATIONS

Model	Year	Caliper Bore Dia. Inch
Avenger & Sebring Coupe	1997–2000	2.375
Talon FWD	1997–98	2.375

TIGHTENING SPECIFICATIONS

Component	Torque/Ft. Lbs.
Bleed Screws	50-84①
Caliper Guide & Lockpins	54
Caliper Support To Front Axle	65
Wheel Lug Nuts	87–101

① — Inch lbs.

DRUM BRAKES

TABLE OF CONTENTS

Application Chart

Model	Type	Drum Brake Type
Avenger & Sebring Coupe	—	2
Breeze, Cirrus & Stratus	Varga	1
Concorde, Intrepid, LHS & Vision	Varga	1
Neon	Kelsey-Hayes	1
Sebring Convertible	Kelsey-Hayes	1

Type 1: Kelsey-Hayes & Varga Leading-Trailing Drum Brakes

INDEX

PRECAUTIONS

When working on or around brake assemblies, care must be taken to prevent breathing asbestos dust. During routine service operations, the amount of asbestos dust from brake lining wear is at a low level due to a chemical breakdown during use. A few precautions will minimize exposure.

Do not sand or grind brake linings unless suitable exhaust ventilation equipment is used to prevent excessive asbestos exposure.

1. Wear a suitable respirator approved for asbestos dust use during all repair procedures.
2. When cleaning brake dust from brake parts, use a vacuum cleaner with a highly efficient filter system. If a suitable vacuum cleaner is not available, use a water soaked rag. **Do not use compressed air or dry brush to clean brake parts.**
3. Keep work area clean using same equipment as for cleaning brake parts.
4. Properly dispose of rags and vacuum cleaner bags by placing them in plastic bags.
5. Do not smoke or eat while working on brake systems.
6. Never use any fluid containing mineral oil to clean brake system components. This will damage the rubber caps and seals. If system contamination is suspected, inspect brake fluid in the reservoir for dirt, discoloration, or separation (breakdown) of the brake fluid into distinct layers. Drain and flush the hydraulic system with clean brake fluid if contamination is suspected.

INSPECTION

BRAKE DRUMS

Any time the brake drums are removed for brake service, the braking surface diameter should be inspected with a suitable brake drum micrometer at several points to determine if they are within the safe oversize limit stamped on the brake drum outer surface. If the braking surface diameter exceeds specifications, the drum must be replaced. If the braking surface diameter is within specifications, drums should be cleaned and inspected for cracks, scores, deep grooves, taper, out of round and heat spotting. If drums are cracked or heat spotted, they must be replaced. Scoring and grooves in the braking surface can only be removed by machining with special equipment, as long as the braking surface is within specifications. Any brake drum showing taper or sufficient out of round to cause vehicle vibration or noise while braking should also be machined, removing only enough stock to true up the drum.

After a brake drum is machined, wipe the braking surface diameter with a denatured alcohol soaked cloth. If one brake drum is machined, the other should also be machined to the same diameter to maintain equal braking forces.

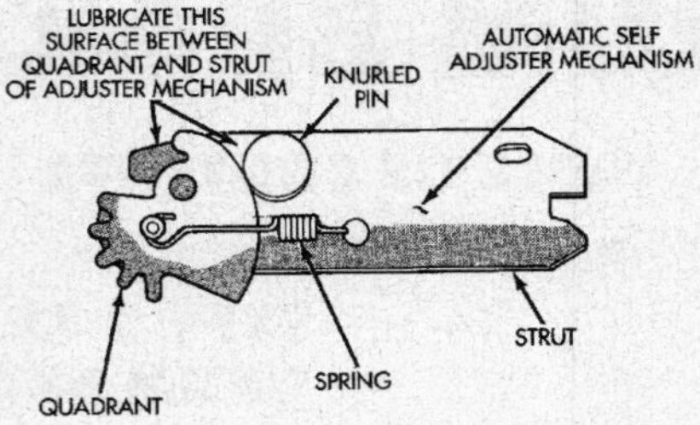

CR4089800040010X

Fig. 1 Automatic self-adjuster mechanism. Breeze, Cirrus & Stratus

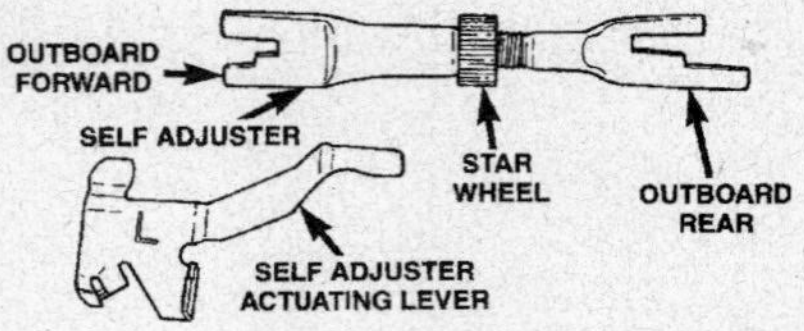

CR4089800040020X

Fig. 2 Automatic self-adjuster mechanism. Except Breeze, Cirrus & Stratus

BRAKE LININGS & SPRINGS

Inspect brake linings for excessive wear, damage, oil, grease or brake fluid contamination. If any of the above conditions exist, brake linings should be replaced as an axle set to maintain equal braking forces. Examine brake shoe webbing, hold-down and return springs for signs of overheating indicated by a slight blue color. Any component which exhibits overheating signs should be replaced. Overheated springs lose their pull and could cause brake linings to wear out prematurely. Inspect all springs for sags, bends and external damage and replace as required.

Inspect hold-down retainers and pins for bends, rust and corrosion. Replace faulty components as required.

WHEEL CYLINDER

With brake drum removed, inspect the wheel cylinder for fluid leaks. Inspect wheel cylinder boots for cuts, tears, or heat cracks. Replace faulty components as required.

BACKING PLATE

Inspect backing plate shoe contact surface for grooves that may restrict shoe movement and cannot be removed by lightly sanding with emery cloth or other suitable abrasive. If backing plate exhibits above condition, it should be replaced. Also inspect for signs of cracks, warpage and excessive rust, indicating need for replacement.

ADJUSTER MECHANISM

Inspect the adjuster assembly, **Figs. 1 and 2.** Use the following procedure to ensure adjuster mechanism operates properly:

1. Ensure quadrant rotates freely throughout its tooth contact range.
2. Ensure quadrant slides freely entire length of its mounting slot.
3. Inspect quadrant spring for any signs of damage.
4. Ensure knurled pin is securely attached to adjuster mechanism and teeth are not damaged.
5. Examine adjuster mechanism for excessive wear or damage. Replace as required.
6. If adjuster mechanism will be used again, apply a light coat of multipurpose lubricant, or equivalent, between quadrant and strut of adjuster mechanism.

SYMPTOM	CHART 1 MISC. COND.	CHART 2 WARNING LIGHT	CHART 3 POWER BRAKES	CHART 4 BRAKE NOISE	CHART 5 WHEEL BRAKES
Brake Warning Light On		X	NO	NO	
Excessive Pedal Travel	6	X	NO		O
Pedal Goes To The Floor	6	X			
Stop Light On Without Brakes	3				
All Brakes Drag	5				
Rear Brakes Drag	2	NO	NO		
Grabby Brakes			O		X
Spongy Brake Pedal		X	NO		
Premature Rear Brake Lockup	4	NO	NO		O
Excessive Pedal Effort	1		O		
Rough Engine Idle		NO	O		
Brake Chatter (Rough)		NO	NO		X
Surge During Braking		NO	NO		X
Noise During Braking		NO	NO	X	
Rattle Or Clunking Noise		NO	NO	X	
Pedal Pulsates During Braking		NO	NO		X
Pull To Right Or Left		NO	NO		X
No: Not A Possible Cause	X: Most Likely Cause		O: Possible Cause		

CR4089700045010X

Fig. 3 Brake system troubleshooting (Part 1 of 6). 1997–98

PARKING BRAKE CABLE

Inspect parking brake cable end for kinks, fraying and elongation and replace as required. Use a small hose clamp to compress clamp where it enters backing plate during removal.

TROUBLESHOOTING

Refer to **Figs. 3 and 4** for brake system troubleshooting.

BRAKE SERVICE

REMOVAL

Breeze, Cirrus & Stratus

1. Raise and support vehicle on jack stands or centered on a hoist.
2. Remove rear wheel and tire assemblies.
3. Remove rubber plug from top of brake support plate.
4. Insert a suitable screwdriver into hole and turn adjuster towards front of car until it stops. This will fully release rear brake adjuster.
5. Remove brake drum.
6. Remove brake drum to hub/bearing retaining nuts, then the rear brake drum from hub and bearing assembly.
7. Remove actuator spring from automatic adjuster mechanism and trailing brake shoe, **Fig. 5.**
8. Remove upper and lower return springs.
9. Remove brake shoe retainer and pin from leading brake shoe.
10. Remove leading brake shoe and adjuster mechanism as an assembly from brake support plate.
11. Remove brake shoe retainer and pin from trailing brake shoe.
12. Remove trailing brake shoe assembly from brake support plate.
13. Remove park brake cable from actuating lever. **Do not attempt to remove actuating lever from brake shoe assembly.**
14. Fully extend automatic adjuster mechanism in direction shown in **Fig. 6,** then rotate and remove adjuster mechanism from leading brake shoe assembly.

Concorde, Intrepid, LHS & Vision

1. Remove dust cap from hub and bearing assembly.
2. Remove cotter pin, nut retainer, wave washer, retaining nut and washer from rear spindle.
3. Remove hub and bearing assembly from spindle.
4. Remove automatic adjuster spring from adjuster lever.
5. Rotate automatic adjuster screw assembly until each shoe assembly is free from wheel cylinder boots.

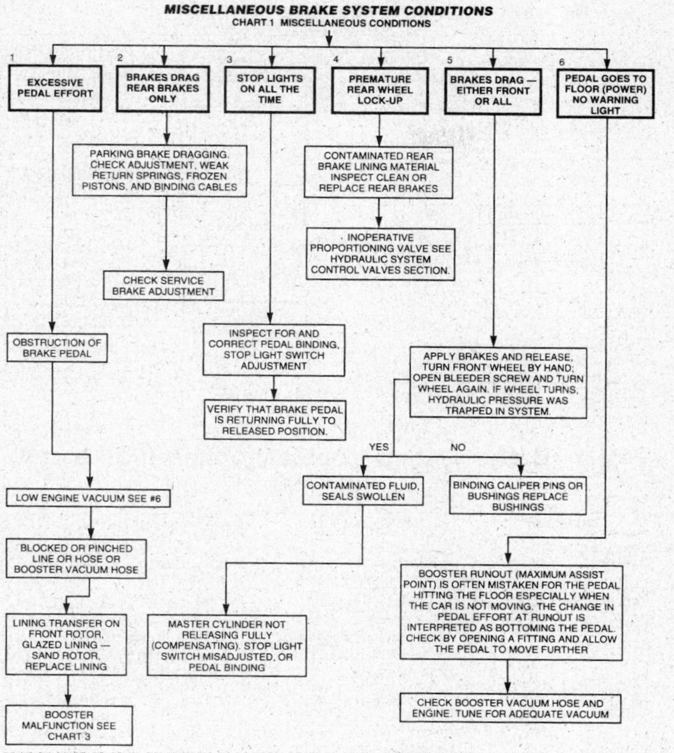

CR4089700045020X

Fig. 3 Brake system troubleshooting (Part 2 of 6). 1997–98

6. Disconnect parking brake cable from lever.
7. Remove lower brake shoe assembly to anchor plate springs.
8. Remove brake shoe assembly to support plate hold-down springs.
9. Remove upper brake shoe return spring, then the automatic adjuster and adjuster lever from brake shoe support plate.
10. Separate brake shoes from automatic adjuster mechanism.
11. Remove automatic adjuster lever from leading brake shoe.

Sebring Convertible & 1997-99 Neon

Due to the automatic adjustment feature of the parking brake, only remove brake shoes from one side of the vehicle at a time. If the brake shoes are removed from both sides of vehicle at the same time the adjuster will remove all slack from park brake cables making shoe installation very difficult.

1. Raise and support vehicle.
2. Remove rear wheel and tire assemblies.
3. Remove rear brake drum to hub retaining clips (if equipped), then the drum from hub and bearing assembly.
4. Remove automatic adjuster lever actuating spring from leading shoe, then the automatic adjuster actuating lever.
5. Thread automatic adjuster star wheel all the way into adjuster.
6. Remove upper return spring from brake shoes.
7. Remove brake shoe lower return spring.
8. Remove hold-down spring and attaching pin from leading brake shoe.
9. Remove leading brake shoe from brake support plate.
10. Remove automatic adjuster from trailing brake shoe and parking brake actuating lever.
11. Remove park brake actuating lever to trailing brake retaining clip.
12. Remove pin and hold-down spring from trailing brake shoe.

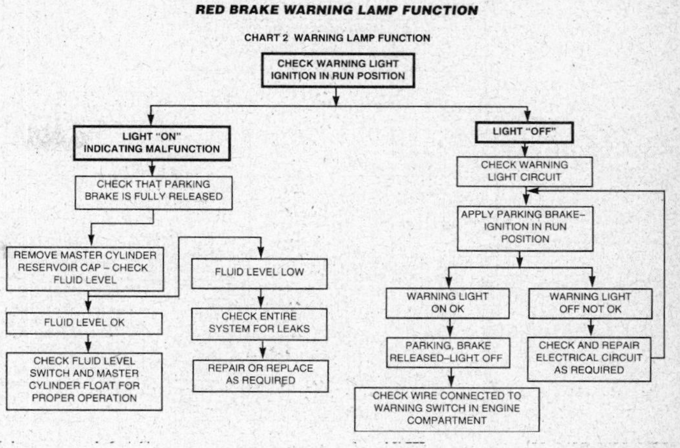

CR4089700045030X

Fig. 3 Brake system troubleshooting (Part 3 of 6). 1997–98

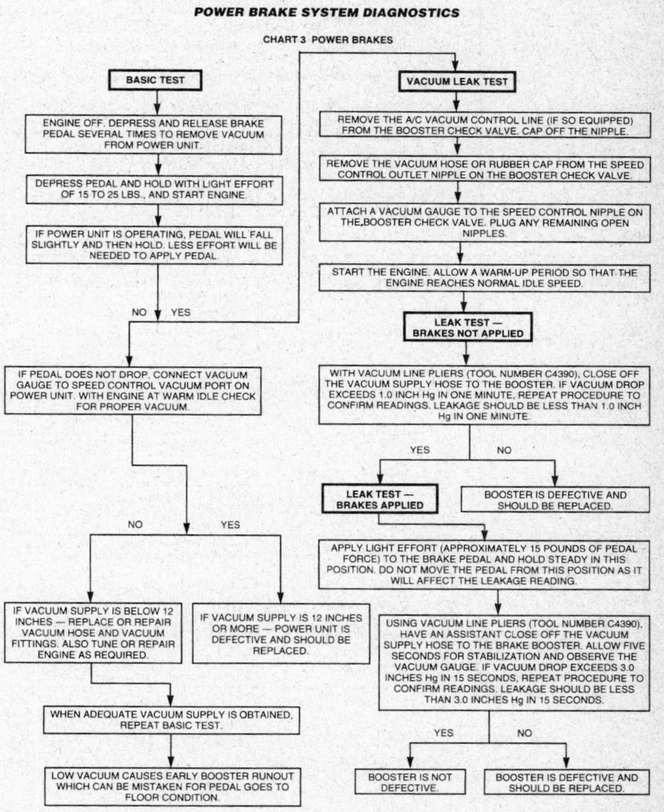

CR4089700045040X

Fig. 3 Brake system troubleshooting (Part 4 of 6). 1997–98

13. Remove trailing brake shoe from brake support plate and parking brake actuating lever.

2000 Neon

Due to the automatic adjustment feature of the parking brake, only remove brake shoes from one side of the vehicle at a time. If the brake shoes are removed from both sides of vehicle at the same time the adjuster will remove all slack from park brake cables making shoe installation very difficult.

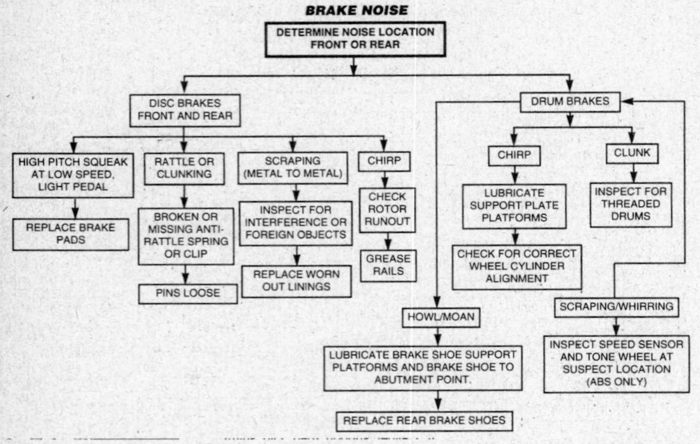

Fig. 3 Brake system troubleshooting (Part 5 of 6). 1997–98

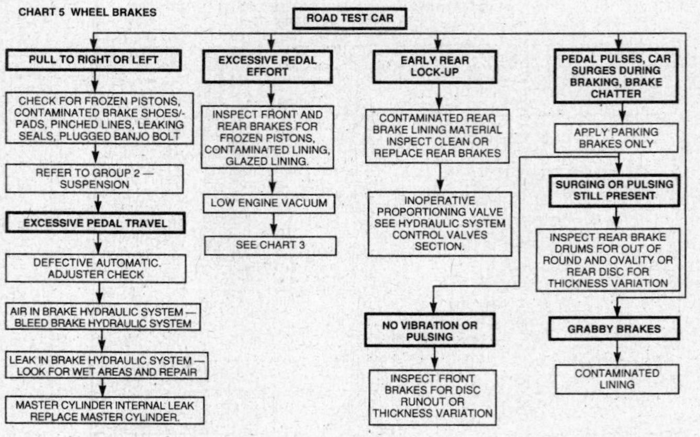

Fig. 3 Brake system troubleshooting (Part 6 of 6). 1997–98

RED BRAKE WARNING LAMP

CONDITION	POSSIBLE CAUSES	CORRECTION
RED BRAKE WARNING LAMP ON	1. Parking brake lever not fully released.	1. Release parking brake lever.
	2. Parking brake warning lamp switch on parking brake lever.	2. Inspect and replace switch as necessary.
	3. Brake fluid level low in reservoir.	3. Fill reservoir. Check entire system for leaks. Repair or replace as required.
	4. Brake fluid level switch.	4. Disconnect switch wiring connector. If lamp goes out, replace switch.
	5. Mechanical instrument cluster (MIC) problem.	5. Diagnose Instrument Cluster Fault Condition.
	6. ABS EBD malfunction.	6. Refer to ABS section

BRAKE NOISE

CONDITION	POSSIBLE CAUSES	CORRECTION
DISC BRAKE CHIRP	1. Excessive brake rotor runout.	1. Follow brake rotor diagnosis and testing. Correct as necessary.
	2. Lack of lubricant on brake caliper slides.	2. Lubricate brake caliper slides.
DISC BRAKE RATTLE OR CLUNK	1. Broken or missing anti-rattle spring clips on shoes.	1. Replace brake shoes.
	2. Caliper guide pins loose.	2. Tighten guide pins.
DISC BRAKE SQUEAK AT LOW SPEED (WHILE APPLYING LIGHT BRAKE PEDAL EFFORT)	1. Brake shoe linings.	1. Replace brake shoes.
DRUM BRAKE CHIRP	1. Lack of lubricant on brake shoe support plate where shoes ride.	1. Lubricate shoe contact areas on brake shoe support plates.
	2. Wheel cylinder out of alignment.	2. Loosen wheel cylinder mounting bolts, realign wheel cylinder with brake shoes and tighten mounting bolts.
DRUM BRAKE CLUNK	1. Drum(s) have threaded machined braking surface.	1. Reface or replace drake drums as necessary.
DRUM BRAKE HOWL OR MOAN	1. Lack of lubricant on brake shoe support plate where shoes ride and at the anchor.	1. Lubricate shoe contact areas on brake shoe support plates and at the anchor.
	2. Rear brake shoes.	2. Replace rear brake shoes.
DRUM BRAKE SCRAPING OR WHIRRING	1. ABS wheel speed sensor or tone wheel.	1. Inspect, correct or replace faulty component(s).
SCRAPING (METAL-TO-METAL).	1. Foreign object interference with brakes.	1. Inspect brakes and remove foreign object.
	2. Brake shoes worn out.	2. Replace brake shoes. Inspect rotors and drums. Reface or replace as necessary.

CR4089900044010X

Fig. 4 Brake system troubleshooting (Part 1 of 3). 1999–2000

CONDITION	POSSIBLE CAUSES	CORRECTION
BRAKES CHATTER	1. Rear brake drum out of round or disc brake rotor has excessive thickness variation.	1. Isolate condition as rear or front. Reface or replace brake drums or rotors as necessary.
BRAKES DRAG (FRONT OR ALL)	1. Contaminated brake fluid.	1. Check for swollen seals. Replace all system components containing rubber.
	2. Binding caliper pins or bushings.	2. Replace pins and bushings
	3. Binding master cylinder.	3. Replace master cylinder.
	4. Binding brake pedal.	4. Replace brake pedal.
BRAKES DRAG (REAR ONLY)	1. Parking brake cables binding or froze up.	1. Check cable routing. Replace cables as necessary.
	2. Parking brake cable return spring not returning shoes.	2. Replace cables as necessary.
	3. Service brakes not adjusted properly (rear drum brakes only).	3. Follow the procedure listed in the adjustment section.
	4. Obstruction inside the center console preventing full return of the parking brake cables.	4. Remove console and remove obstruction.
BRAKES GRAB	1. Contaminated brake shoe linings.	1. Inspect and clean, or replace shoes. Repair source of contamination.
	2. Improper power brake booster assist.	2. Refer to power brake booster in the diagnosis and testing section.
EXCESSIVE PEDAL EFFORT	1. Obstruction of brake pedal.	1. Inspect, remove or move obstruction.
	2. Low power brake booster assist.	2. Refer to power brake booster in the diagnosis and testing section.
	3. Glazed brake linings.	3. Reface or replace brake rotors as necessary. Replace brake shoes.
	4. Brake shoe lining transfer to brake rotor.	4. Reface or replace brake rotors as necessary. Replace brake shoes.
EXCESSIVE PEDAL TRAVEL (VEHICLE STOPS OK)	1. Air in brake lines.	1. Bleed brakes.
	2. Rear drum brake auto-adjuster malfunctioning.	2. Inspect and replace drum brake components as necessary. Adjust rear brakes.
EXCESSIVE PEDAL TRAVEL (PEDAL GOES TO FLOOR - CAN'T SKID WHEELS)	1. Power brake booster runout (vacuum assist).	1. Check booster vacuum hose and engine tune for adequate vacuum supply. Refer to power brake booster in the diagnosis and testing section.
EXCESSIVE PEDAL TRAVEL (ONE FRONT WHEEL LOCKS UP DURING HARD BRAKING)	1. One of the two hydraulic circuits to the front brakes is malfunctioning.	1. Inspect system for leaks. Check master cylinder for internal malfunction.

CR4089900044020X

Fig. 4 Brake system troubleshooting (Part 2 of 3). 1999–2000

1. Raise and support vehicle.
2. Remove rear wheel and tire assemblies.
3. Remove brake drum retaining clips, then the drum from hub/bearing assembly.
4. remove self-adjuster lever to brake shoe spring.
5. Remove self-adjustment lever from shoe.
6. Remove brake shoe to support plate hold-down clips and pins.
7. Remove lower brake shoe to anchor plate return spring.
8. Remove park brake lever pin to shoe retaining clip.
9. Remove leading and trailing brake shoes, upper return spring and self-adjuster screw from support plate as an assembly for disassembly on a workbench.

INSTALLATION

Sebring Convertible & 1997–99 Neon

1. Using Mopar Multi-Purpose Lubricant, or equivalent, lubricate all brake shoe contact areas on brake support plate and anchor, **Fig. 7.**
2. Install wave washer on pin of parking brake actuating lever.
3. Install trailing brake shoe on parking brake actuating lever, then on the brake support plate.
4. Install parking brake actuating lever to trailing brake shoe retaining clip.
5. Install trailing brake shoe attaching pin and hold-down spring.
6. Install park brake actuating lever to trailing brake shoe retaining clip.
7. Install automatic adjuster on trailing brake shoe and parking brake actuating lever.
8. Install leading brake shoe on brake

CONDITION	POSSIBLE CAUSES	CORRECTION
PEDAL PULSATES/SURGES DURING BRAKING	1. Rear brake drum out of round or disc brake rotor has excessive thickness variation.	1. Isolate condition as rear or front. Reface or replace brake drums or rotors as necessary.
PEDAL IS SPONGY	1. Air in brake lines.	1. Bleed brakes.
	2. Power brake booster runout (vacuum assist).	2. Check booster vacuum hose and engine tune for adequate vacuum supply. Refer to power brake booster in the diagnosis and testing section.
PREMATURE REAR WHEEL LOCKUP	1. Contaminated brake shoe linings.	1. Inspect and clean, or replace shoes. Repair source of contamination.
	2. Inoperative proportioning valve (non-ABS vehicles only).	2. Test proportioning valves folowing procedure listed in diagnosis and testing section. Replace valves as necessary.
	3. ABS EBD not functioning.	3. Refer to the ABS section
	4. Improper power brake booster assist.	4. Refer to power brake booster in the diagnosis and testing section.
STOP LAMPS STAY ON	1. Brake lamp switch out of adjustment.	1. Adjust brake lamp switch.
	2. Brake pedal binding.	2. Inspect and replace as necessary.
	3. Obstruction in pedal linkage.	3. Remove obstruction.
	4. Power Brake Booster not allowing pedal to return completely.	4. Replace power brake booster.
VEHICLE PULLS TO RIGHT OR LEFT ON BRAKING	1. Frozen brake caliper piston.	1. Replace frozen piston or caliper. Bleed brakes.
	2. Contaminated brake shoe lining.	2. Inspect and clean, or replace shoes. Repair source of contamination.
	3. Pinched brake lines.	3. Replace pinched line.
	4. Leaking piston seal.	4. Replace piston seal or brake caliper.
	5. Suspension problem.	5. Refer to the Suspension section.
PARKING BRAKE - EXCESSIVE HANDLE TRAVEL	1. Rear brakes out of adjustment.	1. Adjust rear drum brake shoes, or rear parking brake shoes on vehicles with rear disc brakes.

CR4089900044030X

Fig. 4 Brake system troubleshooting (Part 3 of 3). 1999–2000

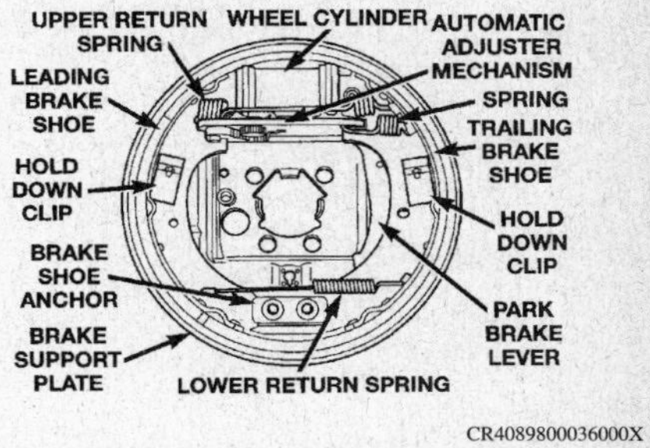

Fig. 5 Brake assembly. Breeze, Cirrus & Stratus

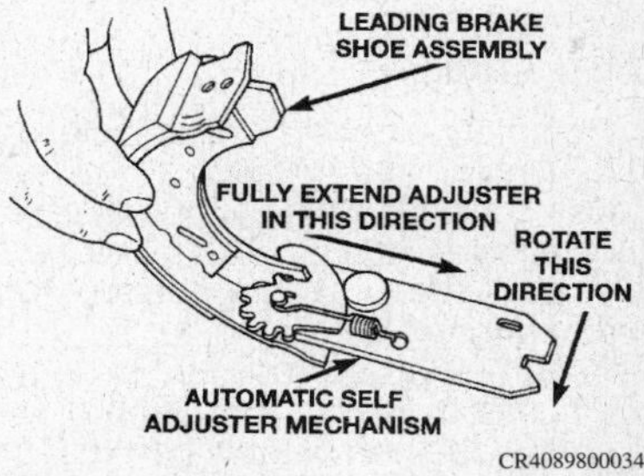

Fig. 6 Adjuster mechanism removal. Breeze, Cirrus & Stratus

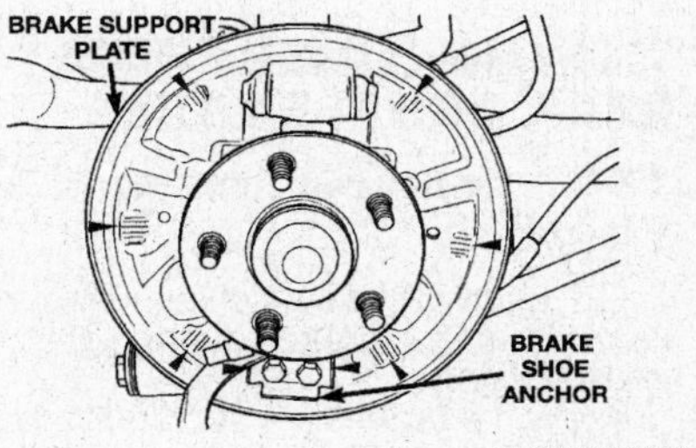

Fig. 7 Brake shoe contact areas. Neon & Sebring Convertible

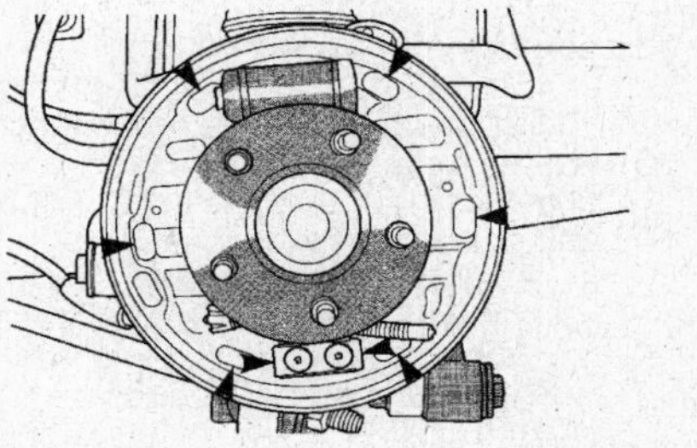

Fig. 8 Brake shoe contact areas. Except Neon & Sebring Convertible

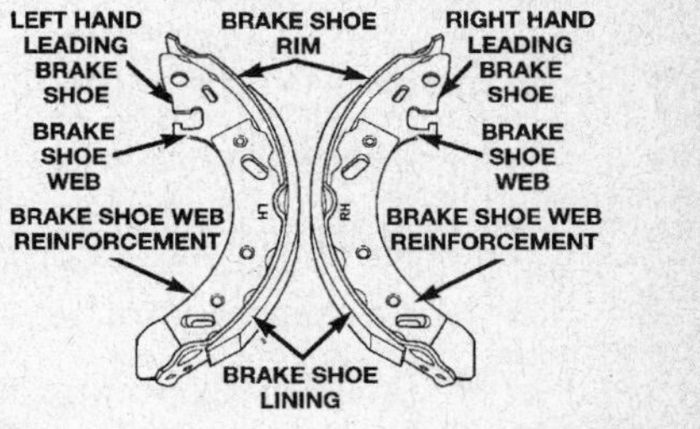

Fig. 9 Brake shoe installation. Breeze, Cirrus & Stratus

support with its attaching pin and hold-down spring.

9. Install brake shoe lower and upper return springs.
10. Install automatic adjuster actuating lever and spring on leading brake shoe.
11. Manually adjust brake shoes outward as far as possible, but not so far as to interfere with drum installation.
12. Install rear brake drums on hub, then adjust rear brake shoes as outlined under "Adjustments."
13. Install wheel and tire assembly. Tighten lugnuts in proper sequence to half specification, then repeat procedure and tighten in sequence to full specification.
14. Road test vehicle.

Breeze, Cirrus & Stratus

1. Using Mopar Multi-Purpose Lubricant, or equivalent, lubricate brake shoe contact areas on support plate, **Fig. 8.**
2. Install park brake cable on park brake actuating lever of trailing brake shoe.
3. Install trailing brake shoe on support plate so it is squarely on shoe contact areas. **The leading and trailing shoes used on these models are unique for lefthand and righthand vehicle sides. When properly installed, the shoe web reinforcement plates will be facing toward brake support plates. The park brake actuating lever will be positioned behind brake shoe web, Fig. 9.**
4. Install automatic self-adjuster on leading brake shoe assembly.
5. Install leading brake shoe and adjuster mechanism as an assembly on brake support plate.
6. Install brake retainer on retainer pin.
7. Install lower return spring onto leading and trailing brake shoes.
8. Install upper return spring (blue righthand side, green lefthand side) on leading brake shoe, then on trailing shoe.
9. Install automatic adjuster actuator spring on trailing shoe, then hook it onto the adjuster mechanism.
10. Install rear brake drums on hubs, then the wheel and tire assembly.
11. Adjust rear brake shoes as outlined under "Adjustments."

Concorde, Intrepid, LHS & Vision

1. Lubricate shoe contact areas on support plate and anchor, **Fig. 8.**
2. Assemble leading and trailing brake shoe assemblies, top shoe to shoe spring, automatic adjuster lever and adjuster, before mounting on vehicle. **Be sure automatic adjuster ends are above extruded pins in web of brake shoes.**
3. Install pre-assembled brake shoe assembly on support plate.
4. Install both lower brake shoe assembly to anchor plate return springs.
5. Install park brake cable on park brake lever of trailing brake shoe.
6. Rotate adjuster nut to remove free play from adjuster assembly.
7. Install automatic adjuster lever spring on leading brake shoe and automatic adjuster lever.
8. Install rear hub and bearing assembly on rear spindle.
9. Install wave washer, nut lock and cotter pin on spindle, then the dust cap.
10. Install brake drums, then the wheel and tire assemblies.

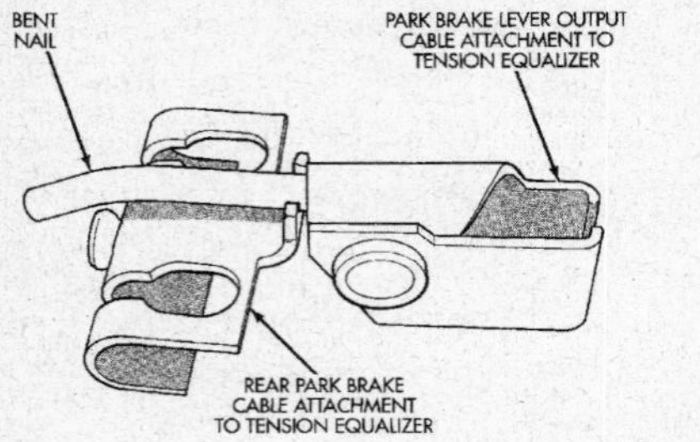

CR4089800037000X

Fig. 10 Bent nail park brake cable tension equalizer. Breeze, Cirrus & Stratus

2000 Neon

1. Complete one side of vehicle before moving on to the other.
2. Using Mopar Multi-Purpose Lubricant, or equivalent, lubricate all brake shoe contact areas on brake support plate and anchor, **Fig. 7.**
3. Assemble front and rear shoes, self-adjuster screw, and upper return spring as an assembly before installation on vehicle.
4. Install brake shoe components assembly onto vehicle.
5. Install wave washer on park brake lever pin.
6. Install both shoe to support plate hold-down pins and clips.
7. Install lower shoe to anchor plate return spring.
8. Install self-adjustment lever on leading brake shoe.
9. Install self-adjustment lever to shoe spring.
10. Adjust shoes out until drum drags lightly when installed. Do not over-adjust.
11. Install brake drum.
12. Repeat procedures on opposite side of vehicle.

ADJUSTMENTS

SERVICE BRAKE

Breeze, Cirrus & Stratus

These vehicles are equipped with a fully automatic adjustment mechanism. In the event of brake shoe replacement the following initial adjustment procedure must be completed prior to driving the vehicle.

1. Ensure parking brake lever is fully released.
2. Depress brake pedal as far as possible 2–3 times. This will cause automatic adjuster to properly adjust rear brakes.
3. Apply and release park brake lever one time after service brakes have been adjusted.

Concorde, Intrepid, LHS, Neon, Sebring Convertible & Vision

1. Ensure parking brake is in its fully released position.
2. Raise and support vehicle with a frame contact hoist or jack stands.
3. Remove brake adjusting hole plug from rear brake shoe support plate.
4. Insert a brake adjustment tool or a suitable thin screwdriver through adjusting hole in support plate and against star wheel of adjustment screw.
5. Rotate adjuster downward until a slight drag is felt when wheel is rotated.
6. Insert a thin screwdriver or welding rod into adjustment hole, then push adjustment lever out of engagement with star wheel. **Do not bend adjusting lever or distort lever spring.**
7. If brakes are now over-adjusted, insert a second screwdriver and engage it with star wheel while holding adjuster actuator lever away from star wheel.
8. Back off star wheel until there is no brake shoe drag. Repeat adjustment procedure.
9. Install brake adjusting hole plug.
10. Repeat procedure at other rear wheel.

PARKING BRAKE

Breeze, Cirrus & Stratus

These vehicles use a bent nail type park brake cable tensioner equalizer, **Fig. 10.** The bent nail tension equalizer is to be used only one time to set cable tension. If park brake cables require adjustment during the life of vehicle a new tension equalizer must be installed.

1. Remove three screws attaching rear of center console.
2. **On models equipped with automatic transaxle,** remove shift knob from shifter using a suitable hex wrench.
3. **On models equipped with manual transaxle,** remove gearshift knob and shifter boot as follows:
   a. Push boot down to expose clips on shift knob and the handle's roll pin.
   b. Using a suitable flat pry tool, pry knob clips away from roll pin.
   c. Pull straight up on shifter knob to remove it from handle.
   d. Squeeze shifter boot bezel base together, then pull upward on boot.
4. **On all models,** remove two screws attaching front of center console to gear selector or shifter.
5. Raise parking brake hand lever halfway up and remove center console from vehicle.
6. Lower the park brake lever handle.
7. Loosen adjusting nut on park brake cable output cable.
8. Using a screwdriver unlatch park brake output cable retainer, then the cable retainer from cable tension equalizer.
9. Remove cable tension equalizer from lever output cable and rear cables, **Fig. 11.**
10. Install a new park brake cable tension equalizer on lever output cable and rear cables.
11. Install new park brake lever output cable to tension equalizer retaining clip.
12. Adjust cable tension as follows:
    a. Position park brake lever in its fully released position.
    b. Tighten adjusting nut on park brake lever output cable until ½ inch of thread is past top of adjusting nut.
    c. Pull park brake lever to its fully applied position one time, then release. **This will yield bent nail portion of tension equalizer approximately ¼ inch.** Maximum travel is 21 clicks.
13. Reverse procedures to install.

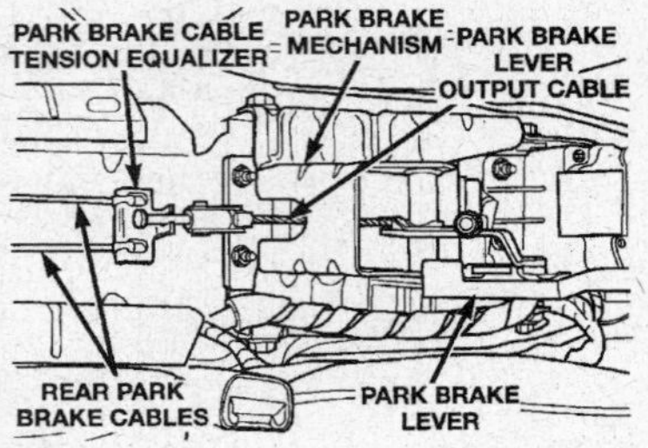

CR4089800038000X

Fig. 11 Park brake assembly. Breeze, Cirrus & Stratus

Concorde, Intrepid, LHS, Neon, Sebring Convertible & Vision

Due to the self-adjusting feature of the parking brake lever, adjustment of the parking brake system relies on proper brake shoe adjustment. Refer to "Adjustments."

TECHNICAL SERVICE BULLETINS

TICKING NOISE FROM REAR DRUM BRAKES

1997 Concorde, Intrepid & Vision

On these models a ticking noise may be heard from rear brakes during light to moderate braking.

Apply the brakes lightly from 30 mph to a complete stop. If there is a ticking noise coming from the rear brakes, perform following repair procedure:

1. Apply parking brake pedal three clicks.
2. Drive vehicle at 20 mph for 1.5 miles.
3. Release parking brake.
4. Apply brakes from 30 mph to a complete stop. If no brake noise is present, vehicle is repaired.
5. If brake noise is still present, repeat steps 1 through 4, but only for 1 mile.
6. If brake noise is still present, resurface brake drum.

HOWL FROM REAR BRAKES DURING LOW SPEED STOPS

1997 Neon

This bulletin applies to all non-ABS equipped vehicles.

A howl type noise is heard from the rear brakes during a low speed (10 mph or less) during brake application in forward direction. The condition may be more frequent in cold or damp weather during the first few stops with cold brakes.

To correct this condition, install replacement brake backing plates part No. 5011628AA for righthand, and part No. 5011629AA for lefthand. Support plate gaskets part No. 4509544 and hub/bearing retaining nuts part No. 6502432 are also required. Proceed as follows:

1. Raise and support vehicle on jack stands or a frame contact type hoist.
2. Remove rear wheel and tire, then the brake drum.
3. Remove dust cap from rear hub/bearing.
4. Remove retaining nut, then the hub/bearing from the spindle.
5. Remove rear brake shoes from brake support plate.
6. Disconnect rear brake flex hose tube from wheel cylinder.
7. Remove rear park brake actuator lever from park brake cable.
8. Position a ½ inch wrench over retainer fingers on end of parking brake cable. Compress cable housing retaining fingers and start cable housing out of support plate.
9. Remove wrench when retainer is free from park brake cable mounting hole in support plate.
10. Remove four support plate attaching bolts. Separate brake shoe support plate from rear suspension knuckle.
11. Transfer all brake hardware to the new backing plate.
12. The new brake shoe support plate comes with the wheel cylinder attached. **Do not remove or loosen the wheel cylinder attaching bolts. Rear wheel cylinder positioning is critical.**
13. Install new brake support plate and gasket on rear suspension knuckle. **Torque** mounting bolts to 55 ft. lbs.
14. Install parking brake cable end fitting into brake support plate.
15. Install hydraulic brake hose tube fitting into wheel cylinder. **Torque** to 12 ft. lbs.
16. Attach parking brake cable to parking brake actuator.
17. Install rear brake shoe assemblies.
18. Install rear bearing/hub assembly.
19. Install new nut and **torque** to 160 ft. lbs.
20. Install remaining components in reverse order of removal.

DRUM BRAKE SPECIFICATIONS

Year	Model	Brake Drum Inside Dia. Inch	Rear Wheel Cylinder Bore Dia. Inch
1997–98	Concorde, Intrepid, LHS & Vision	①	—
1997–2000	Breeze, Cirrus, Neon, Sebring Convertible & Stratus	①	—

① — Maximum refinishing diameter is stamped on outer face of drum.

TIGHTENING SPECIFICATIONS

Component	Torque/Ft. Lbs.
BREEZE, CIRRUS, SEBRING CONVERTIBLE & STRATUS	
Bearing Retainer Bolts	185
Brake Line Fittings	12
Support Plate To Rear Axle	46
Wheel Cylinder Bleed Screws	79②
Wheel Cylinder To Backing Plate	97②
Wheel Lugnuts	100①
CONCORDE, INTREPID, LHS, VISION	
Bearing Retainer Bolts	124
Brake Line Fittings	12
Support Plate To Rear Axle	80
Wheel Cylinder Bleed Screws	72②
Wheel Cylinder To Support Plate	72②
Wheel Lugnuts	85–115
NEON	
Bearing Retainer Bolts	160
Brake Line Fittings	12
Support Plate To Rear Axle (1997–99)	85
Support Plate To Rear Axle (2000)	55
Wheel Cylinder Bleed Screws	80②
Wheel Cylinder To Backing Plate (1997–99)	72②
Wheel Cylinder To Backing Plate (2000)	115②
Wheel Lugnuts	100①

① — Tighten in proper sequence to half specification, then repeat procedure and tighten to full specification.
② — Inch lbs.

Type 2–Leading-Trailing Drum Brakes

INDEX

PRECAUTIONS

When working on or around brake assemblies, care must be taken to prevent breathing asbestos dust. During routine service operations, the amount of asbestos dust from brake lining wear is at a low level due to a chemical breakdown during use. A few precautions will minimize exposure.

Do not sand or grind brake linings unless suitable local exhaust ventilation equipment is used to prevent excessive asbestos exposure.

1. Wear a suitable respirator approved for asbestos dust use during all repair procedures.
2. When cleaning brake dust from brake parts, use a vacuum cleaner with a highly efficient filter system. If a suitable vacuum cleaner is not available, use a water soaked rag. **Do not use compressed air or dry brush to clean brake parts.**
3. Keep work area clean using same equipment as for cleaning brake parts.
4. Properly dispose of rags and vacuum cleaner bags by placing them in plastic bags.
5. Do not smoke or eat while working on brake systems.
6. Never use any fluid containing mineral oil to clean brake system components. This will damage the rubber caps and seals. If system contamination is suspected, inspect brake fluid in the reservoir for dirt, discoloration, or separation (breakdown) of the brake fluid into distinct layers. Drain and flush the hydraulic system with clean brake fluid if contamination is suspected.

Symptom	Probable cause	Remedy
Vehicle pulls to one side when brakes are applied	Grease or oil on pad or lining surface	Replace
	Inadequate contact of pad or lining	Correct
	Auto adjuster malfunction	Adjust
	Drum out of round or uneven wear	Repair or replace as necessary
Insufficient braking power	Low or deteriorated brake fluid	Refill or change
	Air in brake system	Bleed air from system
	Overheated brake rotor due to dragging of pad or lining	Correct
	Inadequate contact of pad or lining	
	Brake booster malfunction	
	Clogged brake line	
	Grease or oil on pad or lining surface	Replace
	Proportioning valve malfunction	
	Auto adjuster malfunction	Adjust
Increased pedal stroke (Reduced pedal to floorboard clearance)	Air in brake system	Bleed air from system
	Worn lining or pad	Replace
	Broken vacuum hose	
	Faulty master cylinder	
	Brake fluid leaks	Correct
	Auto adjuster malfunction	Adjust
	Excessive push rod to master cylinder clearance	
Brake drag	Incomplete release of parking brake	Correct
	Clogged master cylinder return port	
	Incorrect parking brake adjustment	Adjust
	Incorrect push rod to master cylinder clearance	
	Faulty master cylinder piston return spring	Replace
	Worn brake pedal return spring	
	Broken rear drum brake shoe return spring	
	Lack of lubrication in sliding parts	Lubricate

CR4089200019010X

Fig. 1 Brake system troubleshooting (Part 1 of 3)

INSPECTION

BRAKE DRUMS

Any time the brake drums are removed for brake service, the braking surface diameter should be inspected with a suitable brake drum micrometer at several points to determine if they are within the safe oversize limit stamped on the brake drum outer surface. If the braking surface diameter exceeds specifications, the drum must be replaced. If the braking surface diameter is within specifications, drums should be cleaned and inspected for cracks, scores, deep grooves, taper, out of round and heat spotting. If drums are cracked or heat spotted, they must be replaced. Scoring and grooves in the braking surface can only be removed by machining with special equipment, as long as the braking surface is within specifications. Any brake drum showing taper or sufficiently out of round to cause vehicle vibration or noise while braking should also be machined, removing only enough stock to true up the drum.

After a brake drum is machined, wipe the braking surface diameter with a denatured alcohol soaked cloth. If one brake drum is machined, the other should also be machined to the same diameter to maintain equal braking forces.

BRAKE LININGS & SPRINGS

Inspect brake linings for excessive wear, damage, oil, grease or brake fluid contamination. If any of the above conditions exist, brake linings should be replaced as an axle set to maintain equal braking forces. Examine brake shoe webbing, hold-down and return springs for signs of overheating indicated by a slight blue color. Any component which exhibits overheating signs should be replaced. Overheated springs

Symptom	Probable cause	Remedy
Insufficient parking brake function	Worn brake lining	Replace
	Grease or oil on lining surface	
	Parking brake cable sticking	
	Stuck wheel cylinder	
	Excessive parking brake lever stroke	Adjust the parking brake lever stroke or check the parking brake cable routing
	Auto adjuster malfunction	Adjust
Scraping or grinding noise when brakes are applied	Worn brake lining or pad	Replace
	Caliper to wheel interference	Correct or replace
	Dust cover to disc interference	
	Bent brake backing plate	
	Cracked drums or brake disc	
Squealing, groaning or chattering noise when brakes are applied	Missing or damaged brake pad anti-squeak shim	Replace
	Brake drums and linings, discs and pads worn or scored	Correct or replace
	Incorrect parts	
	Burred or rusted calipers	Clean or deburr
	Dirty, greased, contaminated or glazed linings	Clean or replace
	Drum brakes-weak, damaged or incorrect shoe hold-down springs, loose or damaged shoe hold-down pins and springs	Correct or replace
	Incorrect brake pedal or booster push rod setting	Adjust
Squealing noise when brakes are not applied	Bent or warped backing plate causing interference with drum	Replace
	Drum brakes-wear, damaged or incorrect shoe-to-shoe spring	
	Poor return of brake booster, master cylinder or wheel cylinder	
	Loose or extra brake parts	Retighten

CR4089200019020X

Fig. 1 Brake system troubleshooting (Part 2 of 3)

Symptom	Probable cause	Remedy
Squealing noise when brakes are not applied	Improper positioning of pads in caliper	Correct
	Improper installation of support mounting to caliper body	
	Improper machining of drum causing interference with backing plate or shoe	Replace drum
	Disc brakes-rusted, stuck	Lubricate or replace
	Worn, damaged or insufficiently lubricated wheel bearings	
	Incorrect brake pedal or booster push rod setting	Adjust
Groaning clicking or rattling noise when brakes are not applied	Stones or foreign material trapped inside wheel covers	Remove stones, etc.
	Loose wheel nuts	Retighten
	Disc brakes-loose installation bolt	
	Worn, damaged or dry wheel bearings	Lubricate or replace
	Disc brakes-failure of anti-rattle shim	Replace
	Disc brakes-wear on sleeve	
	Incorrect brake pedal or booster push rod setting	Adjust

CR4089200019030X

Fig. 1 Brake system troubleshooting (Part 3 of 3)

lose their pull and could cause brake linings to wear out prematurely. Inspect all springs for sags, bends and external damage and replace as required.

Inspect hold-down retainers and pins for bends, rust and corrosion. If any of the above is found, replace as required.

BACKING PLATE

Inspect backing plate shoe contact surface for grooves that may restrict shoe movement and cannot be removed by lightly sanding with emery cloth or other suitable abrasive. If backing plate exhibits above condition, it should be replaced. Also inspect for signs of cracks, warpage and excessive rust, indicating need for replacement.

ADJUSTER MECHANISM

Inspect all components for rust, corrosion, bends and fatigue. Replace as required. On adjuster mechanism equipped with adjuster cable, inspect cable for kinks, fraying or elongation of eyelet and replace as required.

PARKING BRAKE CABLE

Inspect parking brake cable end for kinks, fraying and elongation and replace as required. Use a small hose clamp to compress clamp where it enters backing plate to remove.

TROUBLESHOOTING

Refer to **Fig. 1** for brake system troubleshooting.

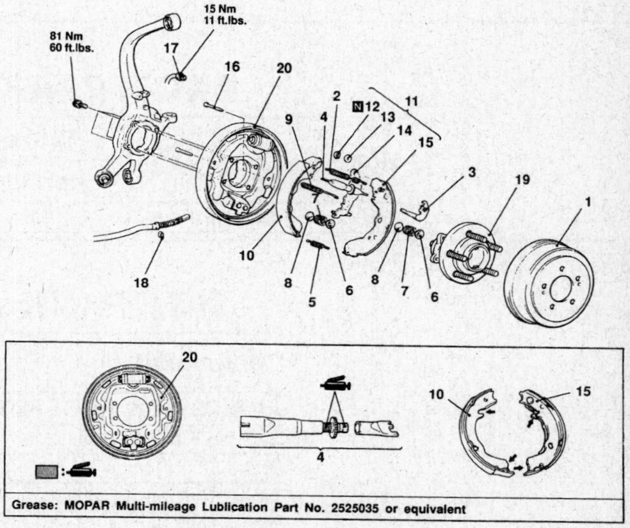

1. Brake drum
2. Shoe-to-lever spring
3. Adjuster lever
4. Auto adjuster assembly
5. Retainer spring
6. Shoe hold-down cup
7. Shoe hold-down spring
8. Shoe hold-down cup
9. Shoe-to-shoe spring
10. Shoe and lining assembly
11. Shoe and lever assembly
12. Retainer
13. Wave washer
14. Parking lever
15. Shoe and lining assembly
16. Shoe hold-down pin
17. Brake pipe connection
18. Snap ring
19. Rear hub assembly
20. Backing plate

CR4089500024000X

Fig. 2 Leading trailing drum brake assembly. Avenger & Sebring Coupe

BRAKE SERVICE

For drum brake service procedures, refer to **Figs. 2 and 3.**

ADJUSTMENTS

PARKING BRAKE

These brakes are equipped with self adjusting mechanisms. Periodic adjustments are not required. If stopping power is insufficient, or if brake pedal travel is excessive, brakes and self adjusting mechanism should be cleaned and inspected.

After performing brake service, adjust parking brake as follows:

1. Apply parking brake lever with a force of approximately 45 lbs. while counting number of clicks. Lever should click five to seven times.
2. If not within specifications, release parking brake lever and remove center console, if equipped.
3. Loosen adjusting nut on parking brake lever to free parking brake cables, then depress brake pedal several times to ensure shoe to drum clearance is properly maintained by self-adjusters.
4. Tighten adjusting nut until brake lever can be raised five to seven notches with a force of approximately 45 lbs. **If adjusting nut is tightened excessively, self-adjuster mechanism will be inoperative.**
5. After adjustment, raise rear of vehicle, ensuring brakes do not drag with parking brake lever released.

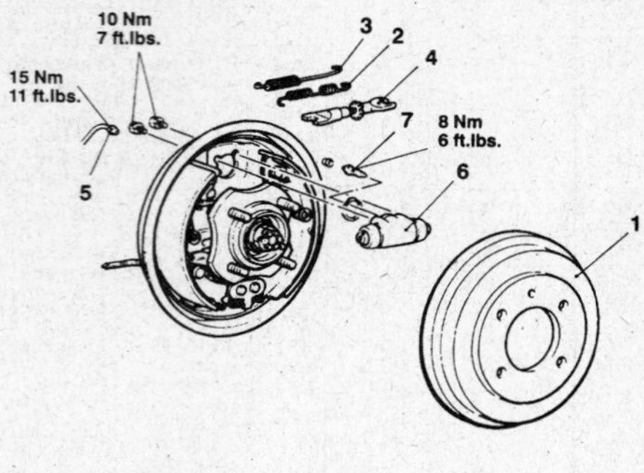

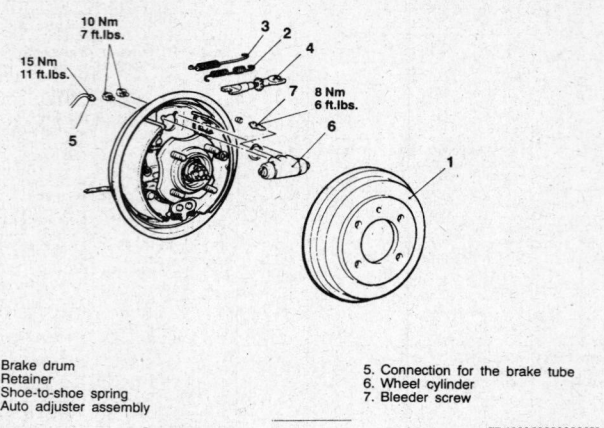

1. Brake drum
2. Retainer
3. Shoe-to-shoe spring
4. Auto adjuster assembly
5. Connection for the brake tube
6. Wheel cylinder
7. Bleeder screw

CR4089500023000X

Fig. 3 Rear drum brake wheel cylinder. Avenger & Sebring Coupe

DRUM BRAKE SPECIFICATIONS

Model	Brake Drum I.D. Inch		Rear Wheel Cylinder Bore I.D. Inch
	Standard	Maximum	
Avenger & Sebring Coupe	9.0	9.08	.750

TIGHTENING SPECIFICATIONS

Component	Torque/Ft. Lbs.
AVENGER & SEBRING COUPE	
Backing Plate To Rear Axle	60
Brake Line Fittings	11
Wheel Cylinder Bleed Screw	96①
Wheel Cylinder To Backing Plate	84①
Wheel Lugnuts	65–80

① — Inch lbs.

HYDRAULIC BRAKE SYSTEMS

NOTE: Refer To "Anti-Lock Brakes" Chapter When Servicing ABS System.

INDEX

MASTER CYLINDER APPLICATIONS

Model	Year	Type No.
Avenger & Sebring	1997–2000	1
Breeze	1997–2000	2
Cirrus & Stratus	1997–2000	2
Concorde & Intrepid	1997–2000	3
LHS & Vision	1997	3
LHS & 300M	1999–2000	3
Neon	1997–2000	2
Sebring Convertible	1997–2000	2
Talon	1997–98	1

HYDRAULIC CONTROLS APPLICATIONS

Model	Year	Type No.
Avenger & Sebring	1997–2000	1
Breeze	1997–2000	2
Cirrus & Stratus	1997–2000	2
Concorde, Intrepid	1997–98	3
	1999–2000	4
LHS & Vision	1997	3
LHS & 300M	1999–2000	4
Neon	1997–2000	2
Sebring Convertible	1997–2000	2
Talon	1997–98	1

DESCRIPTION

FRONT & REAR SPLIT HYDRAULIC BRAKE SYSTEMS

When the brake pedal is depressed, both the primary (front brake) and the secondary (rear brake), master cylinder pistons are moved simultaneously to exert hydraulic fluid pressure on their respective independent hydraulic systems. The fluid displacement of the two master cylinders is proportioned to fulfill the requirements of each of the two independent hydraulic brake systems, **Fig. 1.**

If a failure of a rear (secondary) brake system occurs, initial brake pedal movement causes the unrestricted secondary piston to bottom in the master cylinder bore. Primary piston movement displaces hydraulic fluid in the primary section of the dual master cylinder to actuate the front brake system.

If the front (primary) brake system fails, initial brake pedal movement causes the unrestricted primary piston to bottom out against the secondary piston. Continued downward movement of the brake pedal moves the secondary piston to displace hydraulic fluid in the rear brake system to actuate the rear brakes.

The increased pedal travel and the increased pedal effort required to compensate for the loss of the failed portion of the brake system provides a warning that a partial brake system failure has occurred. When the ignition switch is turned on, a brake warning light on the instrument panel illuminates.

Should a failure of either the front or rear brake hydraulic system occur, the hydraulic fluid pressure differential resulting from pressure loss of the failed brake system forces the valve toward the low pressure area to light the brake warning lamp.

DIAGONALLY SPLIT HYDRAULIC BRAKE SYSTEMS

This system operates on the same principles as conventional front and rear split systems using primary and secondary master cylinders moving simultaneously to exert hydraulic pressure on their respective systems.

The hydraulic brake lines on this system have been diagonally split front to rear (left front to right rear and right front to left rear) in place of separate lines to the front and rear wheels, **Fig. 2.**

In the event of a system failure, the remaining functional system applies the braking force to one front wheel and the opposite rear wheel maintaining 50% of the total braking force. The hydraulic pressure loss would result in a pressure differential in the system and activate a dash warning light.

MASTER CYLINDERS

Type 1

Master cylinders of this type are serviceable. They consist of plastic reservoirs mounted on cast bodies and use replaceable springs, grommets and O-rings.

Type 2

This master cylinder utilizes screw-in proportioning valves at the master cylinder instead of a combination valve. The chassis brake tubes connect directly from the master cylinder to the brake flex hose.

Vehicles not equipped with ABS use a standard compensating port design, vehicles equipped with ABS use a center valve design. The non-ABS master cylinders are a four outlet design with two screw-in proportioning valves attached directly to the inboard side of the master cylinder housing, **Fig. 3.**

The ABS master cylinders are a two outlet design with the screw-in proportioning valves attached to the ABS Hydraulic Control Unit (HCU), **Fig. 4.** Vehicles equipped with rear drum brakes use a master cylinder with a 21 mm bore, while vehicles equipped with rear disc brakes use a 7/8 inch bore master cylinder.

The only serviceable component on both master cylinders are the reservoir and the sealing grommets. Neither of the master cylinder assemblies can be serviced, and must be replaced as an assembly.

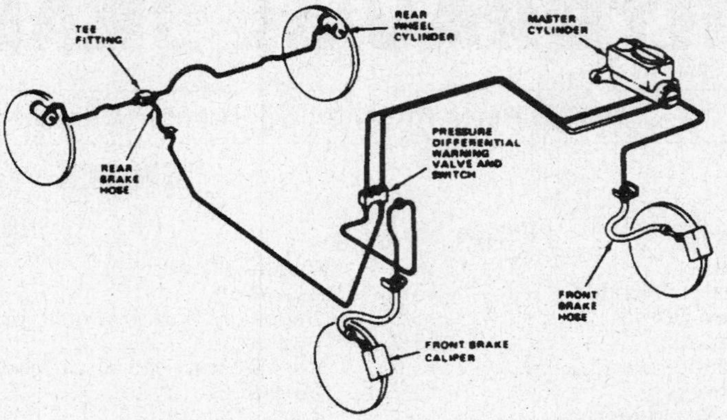

CR4099100011000X

Fig. 1 Hydraulic front & rear split brake system schematic

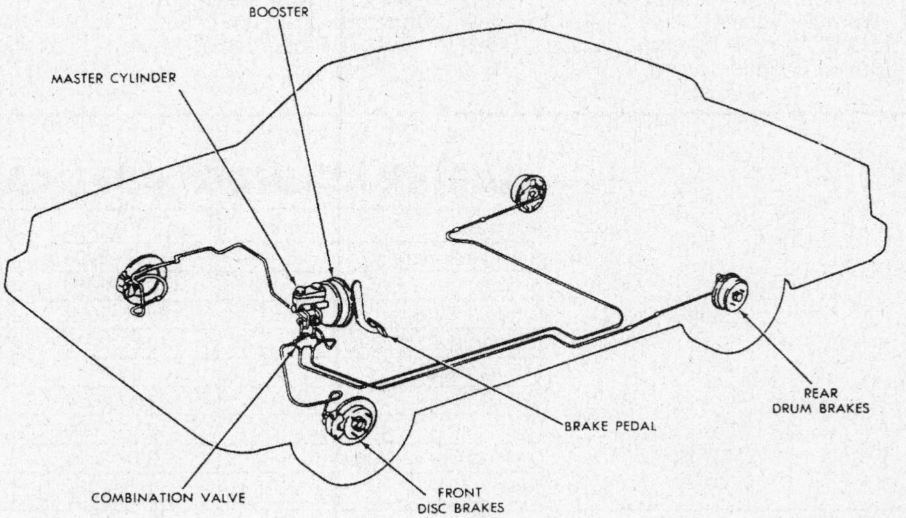

CR4099100012000X

Fig. 2 Hydraulic diagonally split brake system schematic

On non-ABS master cylinders, the primary outlet ports supply hydraulic pressure to the left front and right rear brakes. The secondary outlet ports supply hydraulic pressure to the right front and left rear brakes, **Fig. 5.**

On ABS master cylinders, the primary outlet ports supply hydraulic pressure to the right front and left rear brakes. The secondary outlet ports supply hydraulic pressure to the left front and right rear brakes, **Fig. 6.**

Type 3

The only serviceable component on both master cylinders are the reservoir and the sealing grommets. Neither of the master cylinder assemblies can be serviced, and must be replaced as an assembly.

TROUBLESHOOTING

Refer to "Troubleshooting" in "Disc Brakes" for troubleshooting of the hydraulic brake system.

DIAGNOSIS & TESTING

TYPE 3 MASTER CYLINDER

1. Ensure master cylinder vents at both ports.
2. With engine running apply slight pressure to brake pedal, check for fluid squirting or swirling into reservoir. A special baffle reduces amount of fluid entering secondary reservoir, so only a small disturbance may be noticed.

ADJUSTMENTS

TYPE 1 MASTER CYLINDER

Brake Booster Pushrod To Primary Piston Clearance

1. With master cylinder removed from vehicle, as described under "Component Replacement," proceed with following procedure.
2. Measure distance between master cylinder end face and piston, **Fig. 7.**
3. Position a square (straight scale) against edge of master cylinder, then

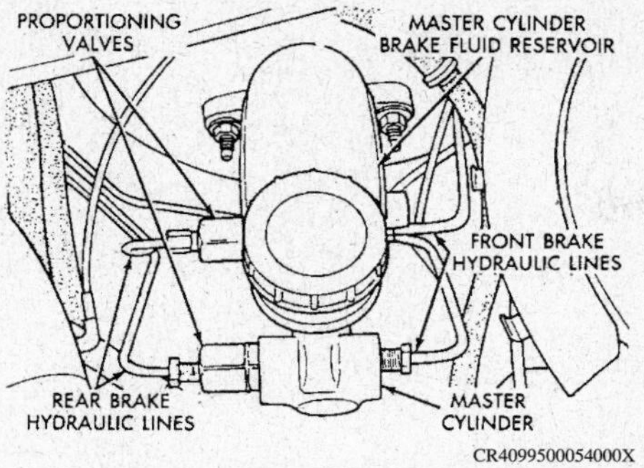

Fig. 3 Type 2 master cylinder. Less ABS

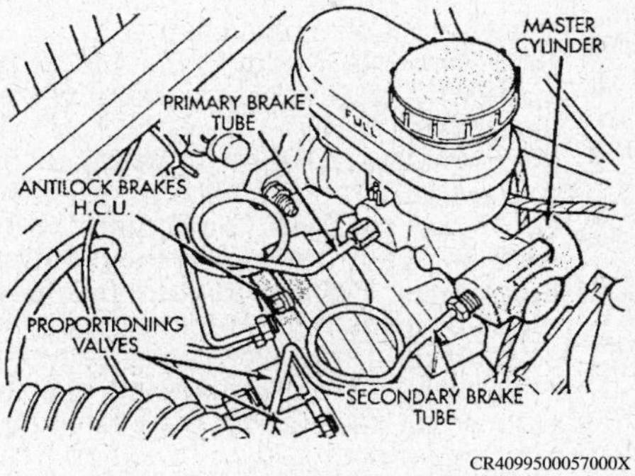

Fig. 6 Type 2 primary & secondary output ports. With ABS

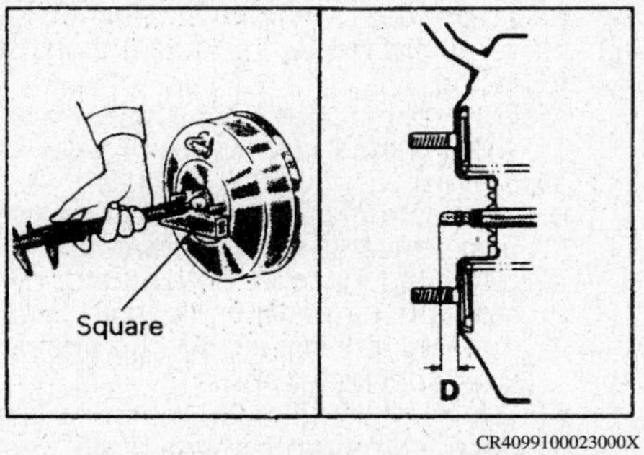

Fig. 9 Master cylinder mounting surface to pushrod end distance measurement. Type 1

measure and subtract thickness of square to determine dimension B.

4. Find dimension C by measuring distance between brake booster mounting surface and end face, **Fig. 8.**
5. Measure distance between master cylinder mounting surface and pushrod end, **Fig. 9.**
6. Find dimension D by subtracting the square's thickness from the measurement taken.
7. Find brake booster-to-primary piston clearance dimension A, **Fig. 10,** using the formula A = B–C–D. Refer to "Hydraulic Brake System Specifications" chart for proper clearance specifications.
8. If dimension A is not as specified, adjust brake booster pushrod as shown, **Fig. 11.**

Brake Pedal Height

1. Measure brake pedal height dimen-

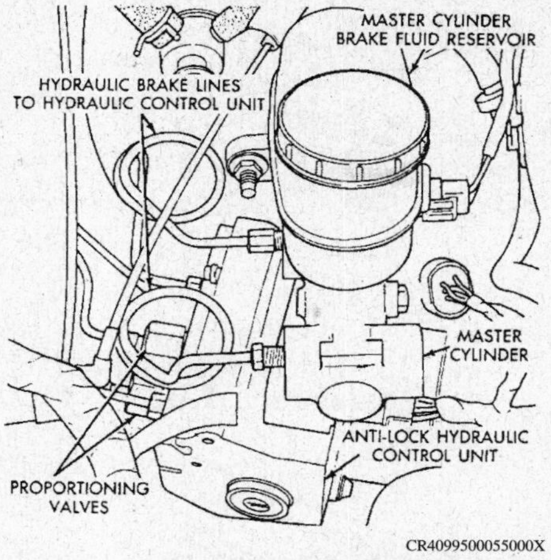

Fig. 4 Type 2 master cylinder. With ABS

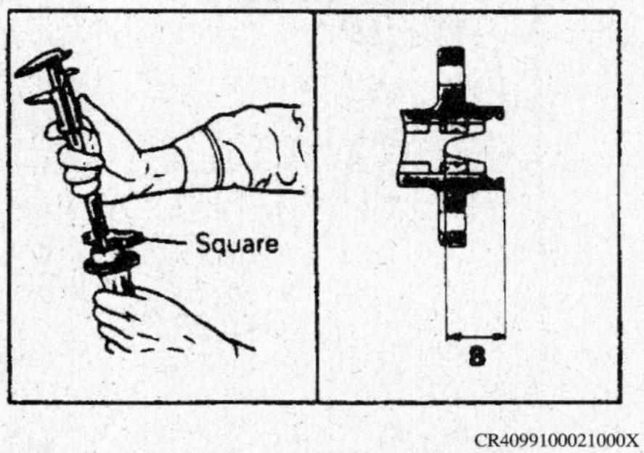

Fig. 7 Master cylinder end face to piston measurement. Type 1

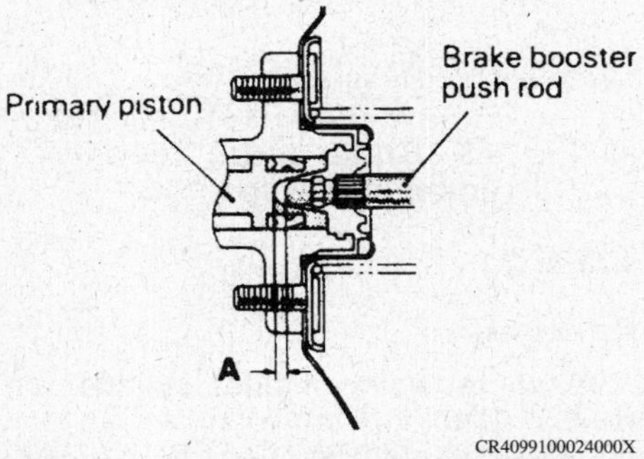

Fig. 10 Brake booster to primary piston clearance dimension A. Type 1

sion "A,." as shown in **Fig. 12.**

2. Standard height is 6.9–7.1 inches on Avenger, Talon and Sebring models.
3. If pedal height is not within specification, adjust using following procedure.
4. Disconnect stop light switch electrical connector, then loosen locknut and move stop light switch to a position were it does not contact brake pedal arm.
5. Adjust brake pedal height by turning operating rod with pliers, **Fig. 13,** until correct brake pedal height is obtained.
6. Screw in stop light switch until it contacts brake pedal stopper, ensure brake pedal does not move, then return stop light switch ½–1 turn and secure by tightening locknut.

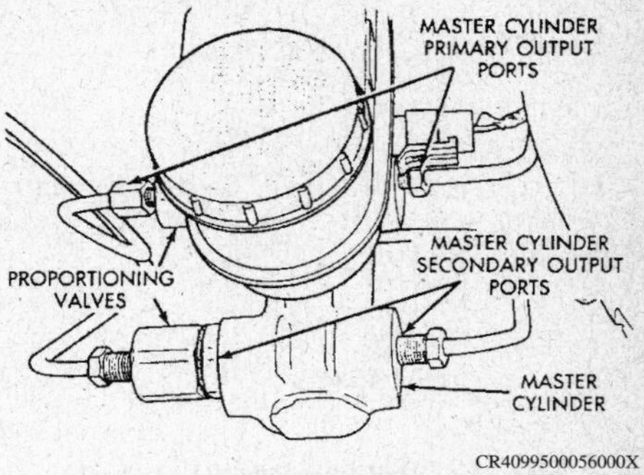

Fig. 5 Type 2 primary & secondary output ports. Less ABS

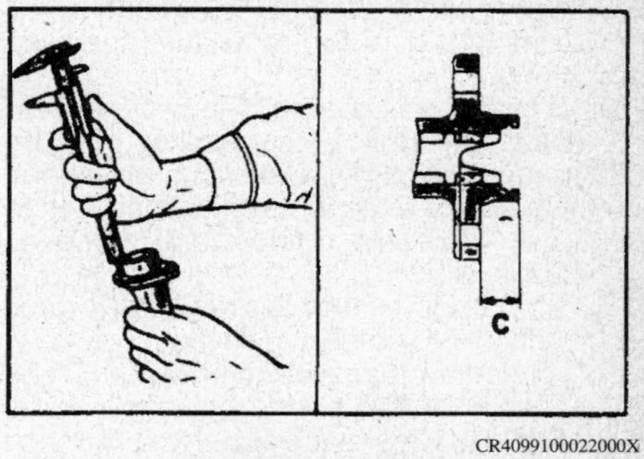

Fig. 8 Brake booster mounting surface to end face distance measurement. Type 1

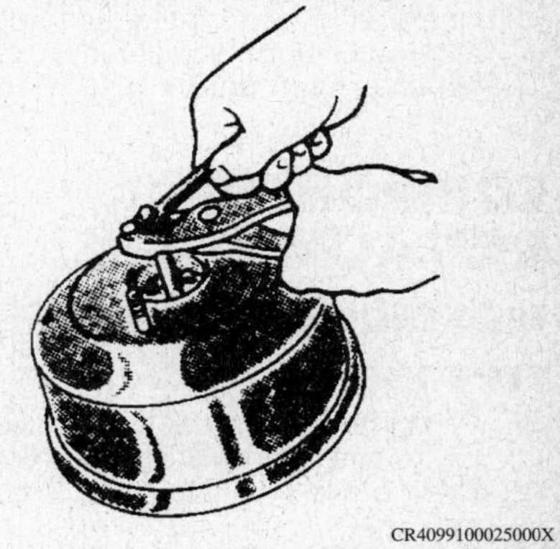

Fig. 11 Brake booster pushrod adjustment. Type 1

7. Connect stop light switch electrical connector and ensure stop light is not illuminated with brake pedal unpressed.
8. Check reference dimension "B" as shown in, **Fig. 14,** distance should be .02–.04 inch.
9. **On models with shift lock mechanism,** check adjustment of shift lock after brake pedal height has been adjusted, refer to "Automatic Transaxles" section and adjust if necessary.
10. **On all models,** with engine stopped, depress brake pedal two or three times to eliminate vacuum in power brake booster.
11. Press pedal down by hand and confirm that amount of freeplay, dimension "C," **Fig. 15,** before resistance is felt is within .1–.3 inch.
12. If freeplay is less than .1 inch, ensure

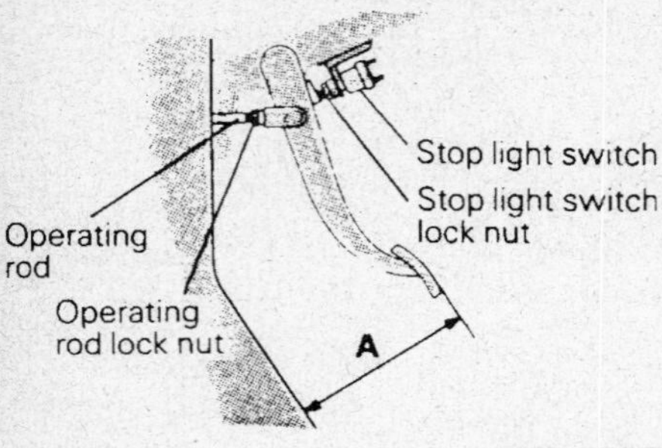

CR4099100026000X

Fig. 12 Brake pedal height dimension "A. Type 1"

clearance between stop light switch and brake pedal is within specifications.

13. If freeplay is greater than .4 inch, it is probably due to excessive play between clevis pin and brake pedal arm. Check for excessive clearance and replace defective components as necessary.
14. Start engine, then depress brake pedal with approximately 110 lbs. of force.
15. Measure clearance dimension "D" between brake pedal and floorboard, **Fig. 16.** Clearance should be 3.1 inches or more.
16. If clearance is less than 3.1 inches, check for air trapped in brake lines, fluid leaks, excessive brake shoe clearance due to faulty self-adjusters and repair or replace defective components as necessary.

COMPONENT REPLACEMENT

MASTER CYLINDER

TYPE 1

1. Disconnect brake fluid sensor connector from master cylinder reservoir.
2. Drain brake fluid into suitable container.
3. **On models with separately mounted reservoir,** disconnect reservoir hoses from the master cylinder.
4. **On all models,** use a suitable wrench to disconnect brake lines from the master cylinder. Plug all lines and fittings.
5. Remove master cylinder-to-brake booster attaching nuts.
6. Pull master cylinder outward and away from brake booster.
7. Reverse procedure to install noting the following:
   a. Prior to master cylinder installation, check brake booster pushrod to primary piston clearance as described under "Adjustments, " and adjust if necessary.
   b. Fill master cylinder reservoir, then bleed hydraulic system as described under "Brake System Bleed."
   c. Check adjustment of brake pedal as described under " Adjustments," and adjust if necessary.

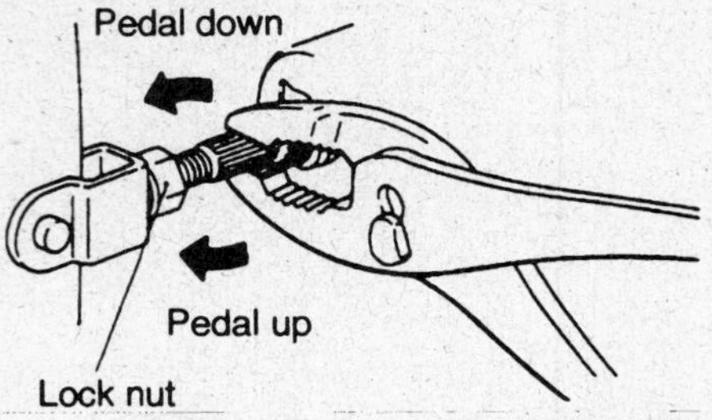

CR4099100027000X

Fig. 13 Brake pedal height adjustment. Type 1

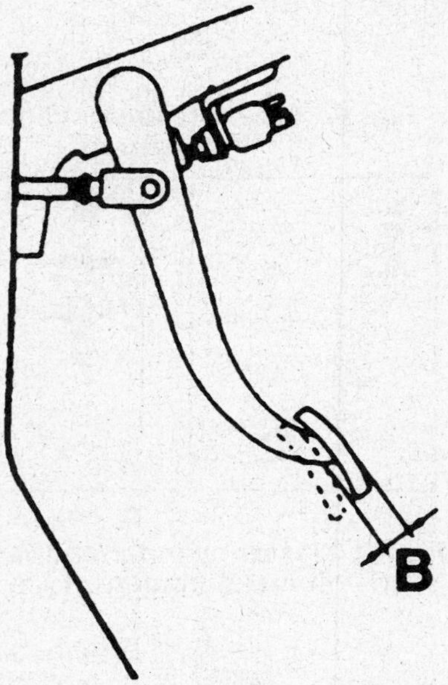

CR4099100029000X

Fig. 15 Brake pedal freeplay dimension. Type 1"C"

TYPE 2

Removal

When replacing master cylinder on Neon models equipped with ABS, vacuum in power booster must be pumped down before removing master cylinder to prevent booster from drawing in contaminants. This can be done by pumping the brake pedal until it is firm, with the ignition off.

1. **On Neon models equipped with ABS,** ensure engine is not running and brake pedal has been pumped until firm.
2. **On all models,** remove wiring harness connector from brake fluid level sensor mounted on fluid reservoir.
3. Disconnect the primary and secondary brake tubes from master cylinder housing.
4. Install suitable plugs at all open brake tube outlets on master cylinder assembly.
5. **On Neon models equipped with ABS and all Breeze, Cirrus, Sebring Convertible and Stratus models,** clean area where master cylinder attaches to power brake vacuum booster

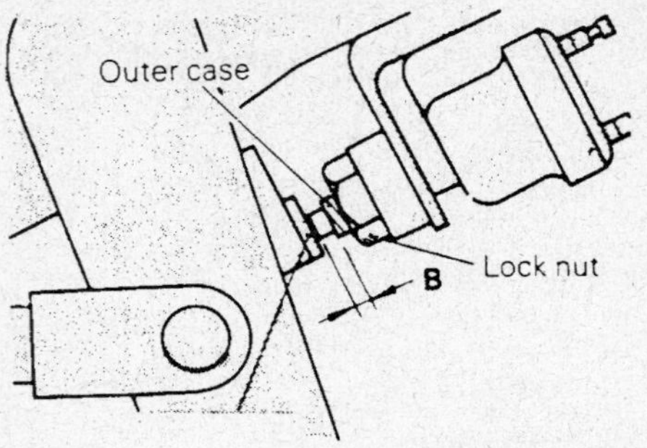

CR4099100028000X

Fig. 14 Stop light switch reference dimension "B. Type 1"

using a suitable brake cleaner.

6. **On all models,** remove nuts attaching master cylinder to power brake vacuum booster.
7. Slide master cylinder forward out of power brake vacuum booster.
8. **On Neon models equipped with ABS, the vacuum seal in the front of the power brake vacuum booster must be replaced.** Remove vacuum seal in front of power brake vacuum booster by carefully inserting a suitable, small, screwdriver between master cylinder push rod and vacuum seal and prying seal out of booster, **Fig. 17. Do not attempt to pry seal out by inserting screwdriver between seal and booster.**
9. Reverse procedure to install noting the following:
   a. **On Neon models equipped with ABS,** install new vacuum seal as follows:
   b. Lubricate master cylinder push rod using suitable silicone lubricant.
   c. Slide vacuum seal onto master cylinder push rod with notches on seal pointing toward and seated against master cylinder housing.
   d. **On all models,** slide master cylinder assembly into power brake vacuum booster and position on mounting studs.
   e. Install mounting nuts and **torque** to 21 ft. lbs.

TYPE 3

1. Disconnect primary and secondary brake lines from master cylinder, then install plugs at brake line outlets.
2. Remove master cylinder attaching nuts, then slide cylinder away from brake booster.
3. Reverse procedure to install noting the following:
   a. **Torque** master cylinder to brake booster attaching nuts to 21 ft. lbs.
   b. Connect brake lines to master cylinder, then **torque** to 12 ft. lbs.

FLUID RESERVOIR

TYPE 2

1. Clean master cylinder housing and brake fluid reservoir.
2. Remove reservoir cap and remove as much brake fluid as possible using suitable syringe or similar tool.

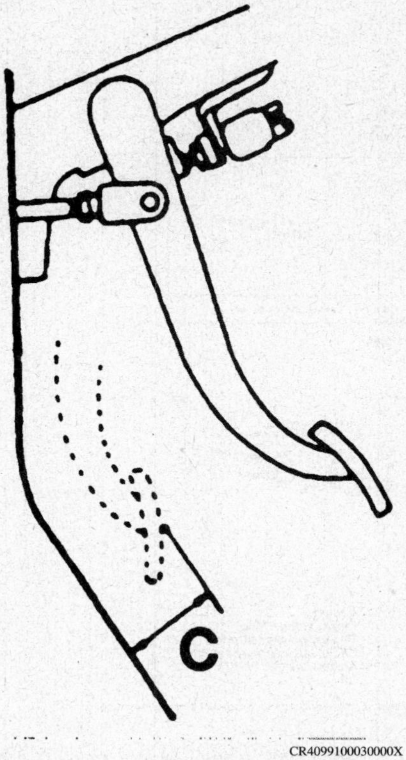

Fig. 16 Clearance between brake pedal & floor board dimension "D." Type 1

3. Rock reservoir from side to side while pulling upward to remove from master cylinder housing, **Fig. 18.** Do not pry off using a tool as damage to reservoir may result.
4. Replace grommets in master cylinder housing.
5. Reverse procedure to install.

TYPE 3

1. Clean master cylinder housing, then remove reservoir caps.
2. Using a suitable tool remove brake fluid from reservoir, then secure master cylinder in a suitable vise.
3. Remove two reservoir to master cylinder retaining pins, **Fig. 19.**
4. Rock reservoir from side to side and remove from master cylinder. **Do not use any tools when removing reservoir from master cylinder, damage to reservoir may result.**
5. Remove sealing grommets.
6. Reverse procedure to install noting the following:
   a. Lubricate new sealing grommets with brake fluid.
   b. Ensure reservoir is seated properly against sealing grommets.
   c. Refer to "Brake System Bleed" to bench bleed master cylinder. **The Type 3 models use ISO style flares that are of metric dimension. Use ISO style tubing flares and metric tubing when performing any repairs.**

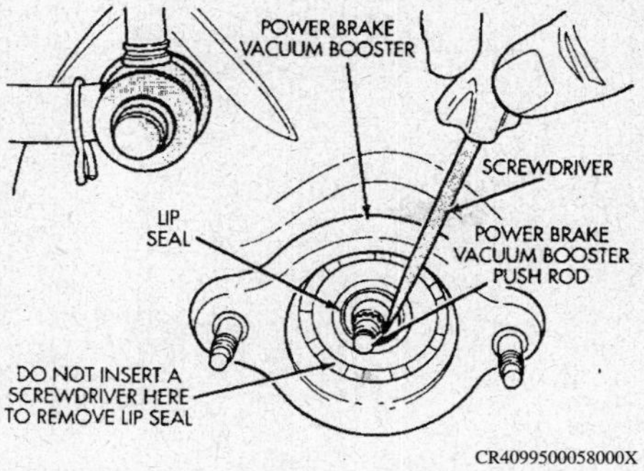

Fig. 17 Type 2 vacuum seal removal. Neon w/ABS

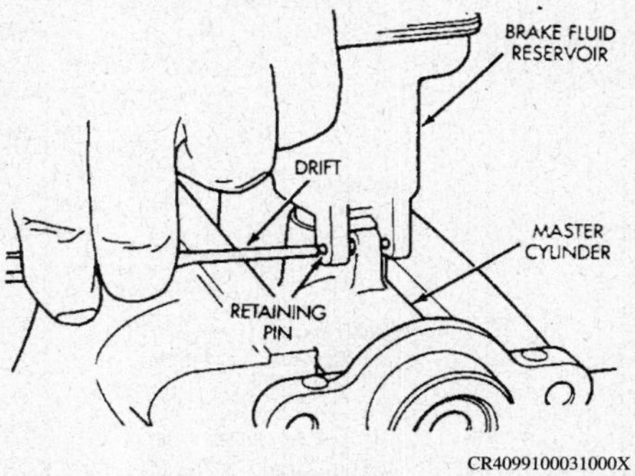

Fig. 19 Type 3 reservoir retaining pin removal

WHEEL CYLINDER

REMOVAL

1. Remove wheel, drum and brake shoes.
2. Loosen brake line fitting at wheel cylinder. Do not pull metal line away from cylinder.
3. Remove screws holding cylinder to backing plate.
4. Separate wheel cylinder from brake line and backing plate by pulling the cylinder outward and away from backing plate.

INSTALLATION

1. Wipe end of hydraulic line to remove any foreign matter.
2. Position wheel cylinder to backing plate. Install brake line to cylinder and start connecting fitting.
3. Secure wheel cylinder to backing plate, then complete tightening of brake line fitting.
4. Install brake shoes, drum and wheel.
5. Bleed system as outlined previously, and adjust brakes.

COMPONENT SERVICE

MASTER CYLINDER

When disassembling the master cylinder, note the position of all parts as they are removed for proper installation. When disassembled, wash all parts in denatured alcohol or clean brake fluid only. Use an air hose to blow out all passages, orifices and valve holes. Air dry and place parts on clean paper or lint-free cloth.

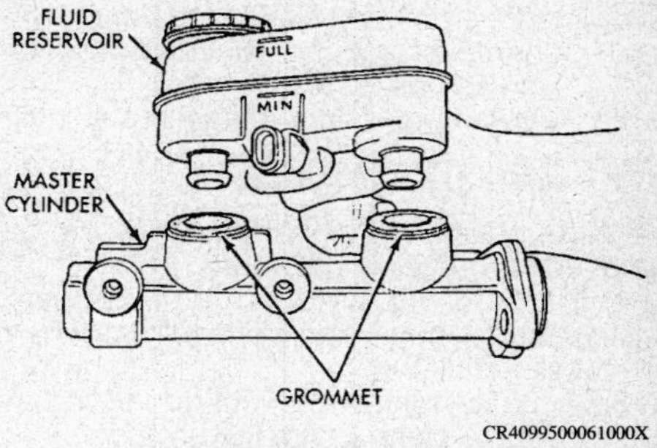

Fig. 18 Type 2 brake fluid reservoir removal

Inspect master cylinder bore for scoring, rust, pitting or etching. Any of these conditions will require replacement of the housing. Never hone the bore of the master cylinder as this will remove the anodized surface. Inspect master cylinder pistons for scoring, pitting or distortion. Replace piston if any of these conditions exist. If either the master cylinder housing or piston is replaced, clean the new parts with denatured alcohol or clean brake fluid, and blow out all passages with air hose.

Examine reservoirs for foreign matter and check all passages for restrictions. If there is any indication of contamination or evidence of corrosion, service the hydraulic system as needed, and flush the entire system as described under "Brake System Bleed."

When reassembling the master cylinder, use all parts contained in the repair kit. Dip all component parts in clean brake fluid, and place them on a clean surface. To prevent faulty operation, when installing seals inspect through side outlet of the dual master cylinder housing to make certain cup lips do not hang up on edge of hole or turn back. A piece of 3⁄16 inch rod with an end rounded off will be helpful in guiding cups past the hole.

When performing overhaul procedures, refer to **Fig. 20.**

When disassembling the master cylinder, note the position of all parts as they are removed for proper installation.

1. Use a wooden stick or dowel to depress primary piston into cylinder bore.
2. With pushrod depressed, remove piston stopper bolt, then piston stopper ring.
3. Release pushrod, then remove piston assemblies. If secondary piston assembly is stuck in the bore, apply a light amount of compressed air to the secondary outlet port until piston assembly works free.
4. Examine reservoirs for foreign matter and check all passages for restrictions. If there is any indication of contamination or evidence of corrosion, service the hydraulic system as needed, then flush the entire system as described under "Brake System Bleed."
5. Wash all parts in denatured alcohol or clean brake fluid. Use an air hose to blow out all passages, orifices and valve holes. Air dry and place parts on clean paper or lint-free cloth.

6. Inspect master cylinder bore and components for scoring, rust and pits. Replace as necessary.
7. Reverse procedure to assemble.

WHEEL CYLINDER

Note position of all parts as they are removed for proper installation.

1. Refer to **Fig. 21,** then remove boots, pistons, cups and spring from wheel cylinder.
2. Wipe cylinder walls with denatured alcohol or clean brake fluid.
3. Examine cylinder bore. A scored bore may be honed providing the bore diameter is not increased more than .005 inch. Replace as necessary.
4. Check pistons for wear or damage. Replace as necessary.
5. Use all parts contained in repair kit. Lubricate cylinder wall and rubber cups with brake fluid.

HYDRAULIC TUBING

Never use copper tubing as a replacement for steel tubing. Copper tubing is subject to fatigue cracking and corrosion which could result in brake system failure.

Steel tubing is used to transfer hydraulic pressure to the brakes. All fittings, tubing and hose should be inspected for rust, damage or defective flared seats. The tubing is equipped with a double flare/inverted seat or ISO flare to ensure more positive seating in the fitting.

DOUBLE FLARE/INVERTED SEAT

1. Using the tool shown in **Fig. 22,** or equivalent, cut off the damaged seat or damaged tubing.
2. Ream out any burrs or rough edges on inside edges of tubing. Before flaring tubing, place a compression nut on tubing.
3. Open handles of flaring tool and rotate jaws of tool until mating jaws of tubing size are centered in area between vertical posts.
4. Slowly close handles with tubing inserted in jaws but do not apply heavy pressure to handle as this will lock tubing in place.
5. Referring to **Fig. 22,** place gauge on edge over end of tubing and push tubing through jaws until end of tubing contacts recessed notch of gauge matching size of tubing.
6. Squeeze handles of flaring tool and lock tubing in place.
7. Place proper size plug of gauge down in end of tubing.
8. Swing compression disc over gauge and center tapered flaring screw in recess in disc.
9. Lubricate taper of flaring or screw and screw in until plug gauge has seated in jaws of flaring tool. This action has started to invert the extended end of tubing.
10. Remove gauge and apply lubricant to tapered end of flaring screw and continue to screw down until tool is firmly seated in tubing.

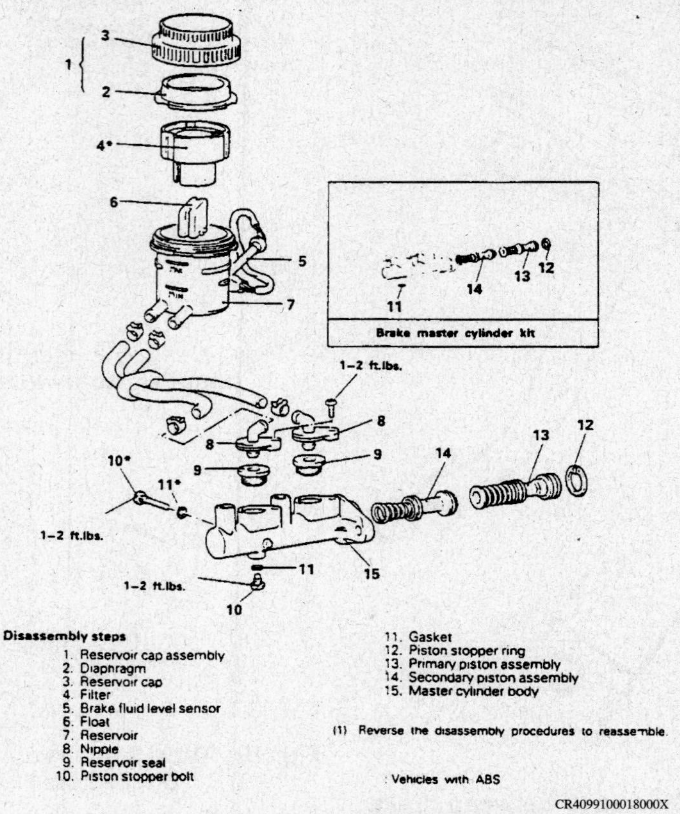

Fig. 20 Type 1 master cylinder. Talon

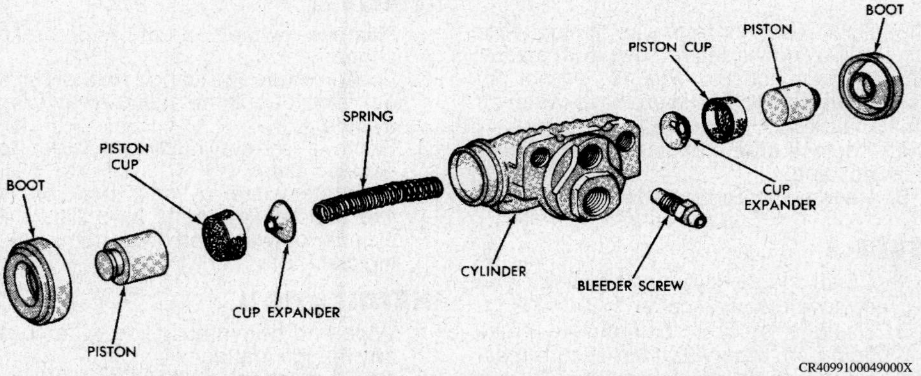

Fig. 21 Disassembled view of typical wheel cylinder

11. Remove tubing from flaring tool and inspect the seat. If seat is cracked, cut off cracked end and repeat flaring operation.

ISO STYLE TUBE FLARING

All ISO style tubing flares are of metric dimensions. When performing any service procedures on a vehicle using ISO style tubing flares, metric size tubing of 4.75 mm must be used.

1. Using tool shown in **Fig. 22,** or equivalent, cut off damaged seat or damaged tubing.
2. Open jaws of flaring tool, then align jaws around tubing.
3. Close jaws of flaring tool, but do not lock tubing in place.
4. Position tubing in jaws of flaring tool so that it is flush with top surface of tool bar assembly, **Fig. 23.**
5. Install brake tubing on feed screw of yoke assembly.
6. Center yoke and adapter over end of tubing and apply lubricant to adapter area that contacts brake tubing.
7. Ensure adapter pilot is fully inserted in end of brake tubing.
8. Tighten screw on yoke assembly until adapter has seated squarely on surface of bar assembly.

BRAKE SYSTEM BLEED

Bleeding the hydraulic brake system is necessary if air has entered the system. Symptoms can be noted by an improper or loss of brake operation, and/or a low or spongy brake pedal.

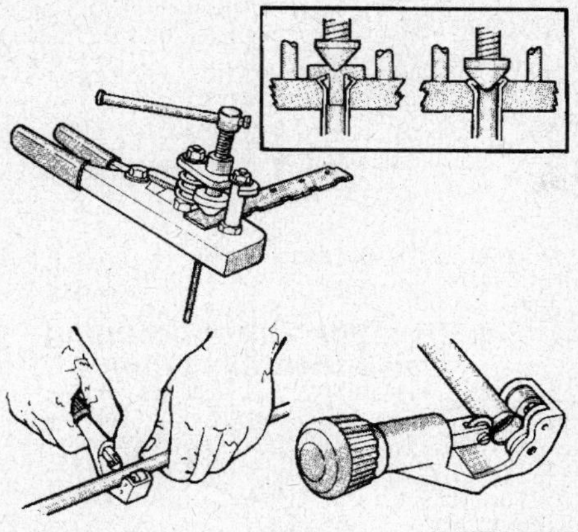

Fig. 22 Flaring hydraulic brake tubing

The hydraulic fluid is bled or flushed from the system through bleeder valves located on the calipers, wheel cylinders, and some master cylinders. When bleeding the hydraulic brake system, use only specified brake fluid, never reuse old brake fluid removed from the system.

Use bleeder tank tool No. C-3496-B, or equivalent, and adapter tool No. BB400-9A, or equivalent, to pressurize hydraulic system.

PRESSURE BLEED

1. Attach a clear plastic hose to bleeder screw and submerge other end into clear container containing clean brake fluid.
2. Open bleeder screw at least one full turn.
3. Bleed 4–8 ounces of fluid through system until an air free flow is maintained.
4. Repeat procedure at all bleeder screws.
5. If pedal travel is excessive or has not improved, repeat procedure.

PRECAUTIONS

Normal pressure from the pressure bleeder should not be greater than about 35 psi. On vehicles equipped with plastic reservoirs, do not exceed 25 psi bleeding pressure.

On models with hold-off valves contained in the combination valve, the valve stem on the outside of the combination valve must be held in position during bleeding using valve holding tool No. C-4121, or equivalent.

MANUAL BLEED

On models with power brakes, if bleeding the hydraulic system without the engine running, first reduce vacuum in the power unit to zero by pumping the brake pedal several times with the engine off.

1. Remove rubber dust caps from all four bleeder screws.
2. Attach clear plastic tubing to bleeder screw and submerge other end of tube into a clear container of clean brake fluid.
3. Pump brake pedal three or four times and hold it down.
4. Open bleeder screw at least one full turn.
5. Release brake pedal only after bleeder screw is closed.
6. Repeat procedure four or five times at all bleeder screw locations. **Ensure fluid level in master cylinder stays at proper level.**
7. Test drive vehicle after a solid pedal is obtained.

MASTER CYLINDER BLEED

Refer to "Bench Bleed" procedure first if the master cylinder has been removed from the vehicle for service or replacement.

ON-VEHICLE SERVICE

Master cylinders may be bled manually or by pressure bleeding. It is recommended that the master cylinder be bled before bleeding the wheel cylinders and calipers.

Pressure Bleed

1. Ensure master cylinder reservoir is full. Add suitable brake fluid as needed.
2. Install pressure bleeder according to manufacturer specifications.
3. Position a drain pan under master cylinder.
4. Loosen brake lines, or bleeder valves if equipped, at master cylinder.
5. Watch for air bubbles in the fluid and listen for air escaping from the system.
6. Retighten brake lines or bleeder valves.
7. Bleed master cylinder until all air is removed.
8. Inspect master cylinder fluid level, top up as necessary.

Manual Bleed

1. Ensure master cylinder reservoir is full. Add suitable brake fluid as needed, and securely reinstall the master cylinder cap.
2. Position a drain pan under the master cylinder.
3. Have an assistant depress the brake pedal with a slow even pressure and hold it. **Do not depress brake pedal fully to end of master cylinder stroke. This may cause damage to master cylinder.**
4. Loosen brake lines, or bleeder valves if equipped, at master cylinder.
5. Watch for air bubbles in fluid and listen for air escaping from the system. **While bleeding the system, recheck brake fluid supply in the master cylinder often so as not to allow the master cylinder to run dry.**
6. With brake pedal still depressed, tighten the brake lines or bleeder valves.
7. Bleed the master cylinder until all air is removed. Inspect master cylinder fluid level, top up as necessary.

Bench Bleed

When replacing or overhauling a master cylinder it is advisable to bleed it before installing it on the car.

1. Properly support master cylinder assembly and attach special bleeding tubes as shown in **Fig. 24.**
2. Fill reservoir with approved brake fluid.

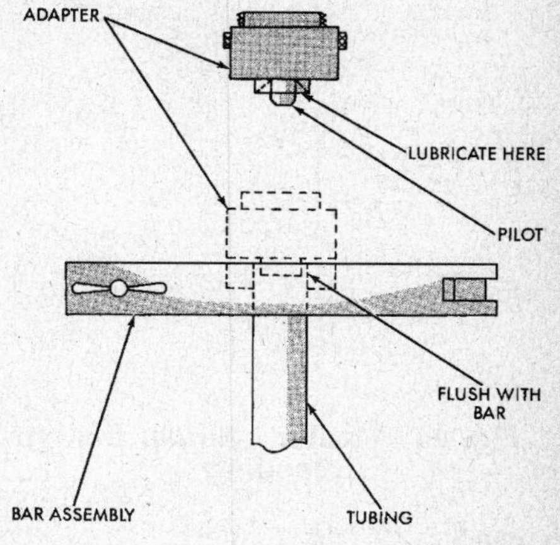

Fig. 23 ISO tubing flare tool

3. Using a wooden stick or dowel (cars with power brakes) depress pushrod slowly and allow the pistons to return under pressure of the springs. Do this several times until all air bubbles are expelled.
4. Remove bleeding tubes from cylinder and install reservoir cover.
5. Install master cylinder onto vehicle as described under " Component Replacement."
6. Bleed the hydraulic system as described previously.

HYDRAULIC BRAKE SYSTEM CONTROLS

Type 1 Proportioning Valve

TESTING

1. Install suitable pressure gauges, one each on input side and output side of proportioning valve as shown in **Fig. 25.**
2. Bleed brake line and pressure gauge, then gradually depress brake pedal and observe gauge readings. Refer to "Hydraulic Brake Controls Specifications" chart.
3. Observe left and right output pressures.
4. Pressure difference between left and right should not be greater than 57 psi.
5. If gauge readings are not within specifications, replace proportioning valve.

Type 2 Proportioning Valves

DESCRIPTION

This system uses proportioning valves to balance front to rear braking by controlling, at a given ratio, the increase in rear brake system hydraulic pressure above a preset level. Under light pedal application, the proportioning valves allow full hydraulic pressure to be applied to the rear brakes.

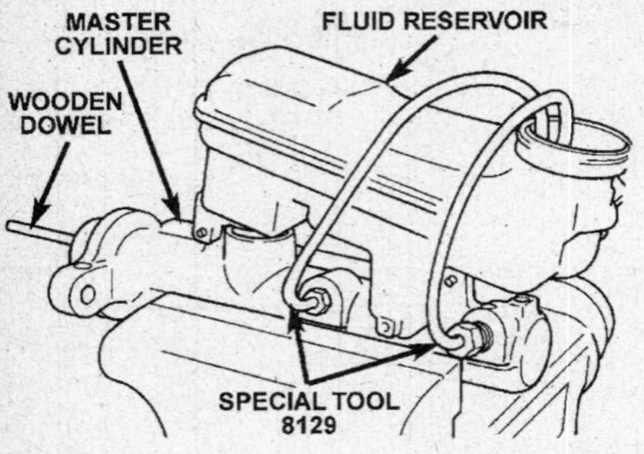

Fig. 24 Master cylinder bench bleeding

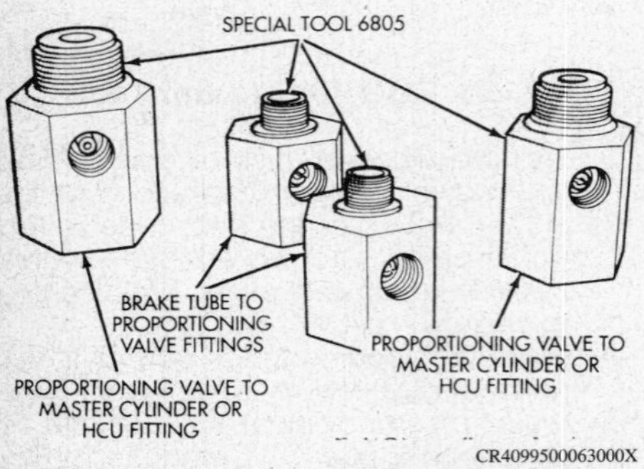

Fig. 27 Type 2 proportioning valve pressure test fittings

There are two proportioning valve assemblies used in each vehicle. Due to differences in thread size, each valve has a different part number. During any service procedures, identify valve assemblies by part number or color code, **Fig. 26.**

TESTING

The in-line proportioning valves used require special pressure fittings to test for proper valve function, **Fig. 27.** The fittings are installed before and after the proportioning valve being tested to verify valve is maintaining the required hydraulic pressure to the rear wheel brake which it controls. The pressure gauges used for testing the in-line proportioning valves on both non-ABS and ABS systems is Pressure Gauge Set No. C-4007–A, or equivalent

If a condition of premature wheel skid occurs on a vehicle, the proportioning valve should always be tested prior to being replaced as there are conditions other than a faulty proportioning valve that can cause premature wheel skid, such as worn, contaminated or improper brake linings.

LESS ANTI-LOCK BRAKE SYSTEM

Neon Less ABS, 1997 Breeze, Cirrus, Sebring Convertible & Stratus

1. Road test vehicle to determine which rear wheel exhibits premature wheel skid. Refer to **Fig. 28 and 29,** to determine which proportioning valve needs to be tested.
2. Remove hydraulic brake line from proportioning valve to be tested, then remove valve from master cylinder outlet port.

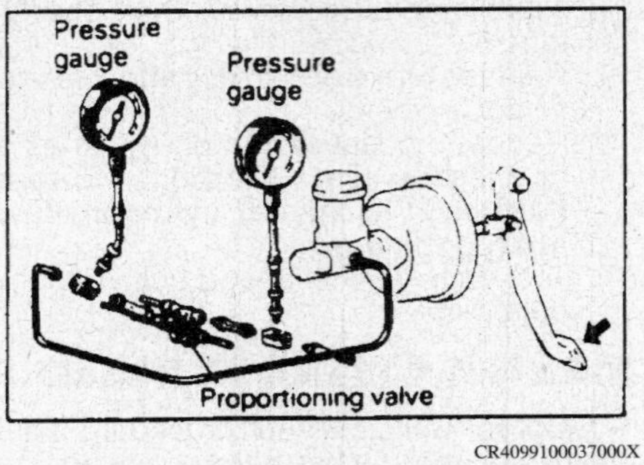

Fig. 25 Type 1 proportioning valve pressure gauge test connection

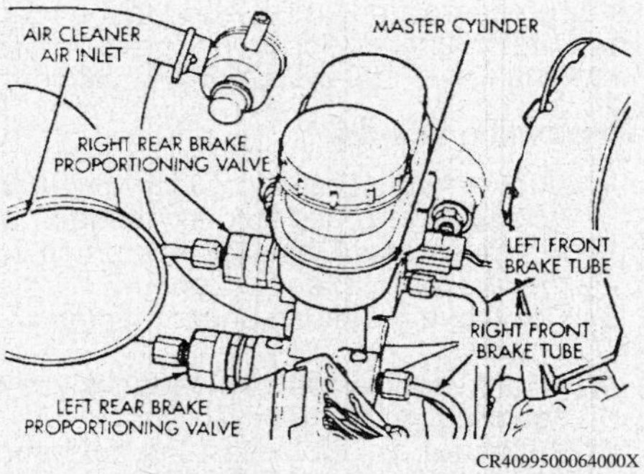

Fig. 28 Type 2 proportioning valve location. Neon Less ABS

3. **On Neon models,** install pressure test fitting tool No. 6805–1 or 6805–2, or equivalent, into outlet port of master cylinder.
4. **On Breeze, Cirrus, Sebring Convertible and Stratus models,** install pressure test fitting tool No. 6805–1 or 6805–2, or equivalent, into rear brake tube.
5. **On all models,** install proportioning valve into pressure test fitting.
6. Install pressure test fitting tool No. 6805–3 or 6805–4, or equivalent, into outlet port of proportioning valve.
7. Connect brake hydraulic line onto pressure test fitting on proportioning valve.
8. Install pressure gauge set tool No. C-4007–A, or equivalent, into test fitting and bleed air from pressure gauge hose.
9. Apply pressure to brake pedal until reading on proportioning valve inlet test fitting is appropriate, then check the pressure reading on the outlet test fitting.
10. If proportioning valve outlet pressure is not within specifications when inlet pressure is obtained, replace valve.
11. **On Neon models,** install proportioning valve into master cylinder body until O-ring is seated, then **torque** proportioning valve to 30 ft. lbs.
12. **On Breeze, Cirrus, Sebring Convertible and Stratus models,** install proportioning valve and hand tighten until installed, then **torque** proportioning valve to 12 ft. lbs.

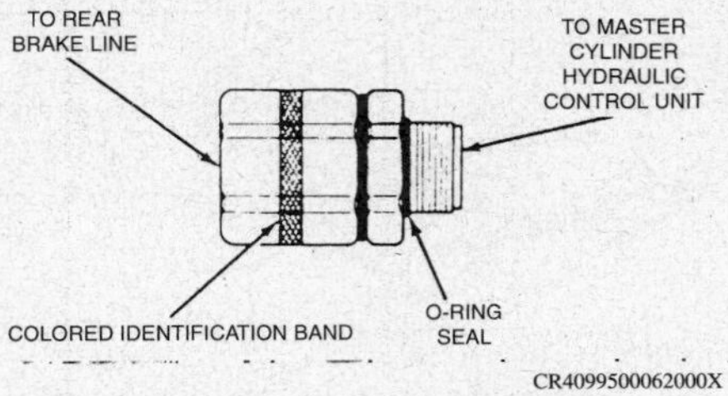

Fig. 26 Type 2 proportioning valve identification

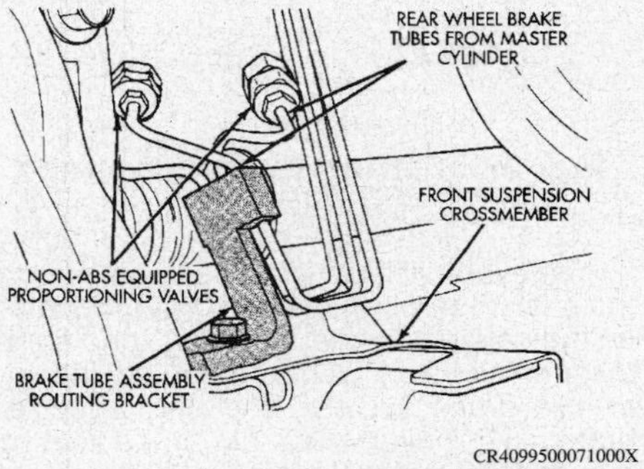

Fig. 29 Type 2 proportioning valve location. 1997 Breeze, Cirrus, Sebring Convertible & Stratus

13. **On all models,** install brake tube onto proportioning valve and **torque** tube nut to 12 ft. lbs.
14. Bleed brake line as outlined under "Brake System Bleed."

1998–2000 Breeze, Cirrus, Sebring Convertible & Stratus

1. Road test vehicle to determine which rear wheel exhibits premature wheel skid.
2. Remove hydraulic brake line from proportioning valve that controls rear wheel which has premature skid, **Fig. 30.**
3. Remove proportioning valve from rear brake chassis tube.
4. Install pressure test fitting tool No. 8187, or equivalent, in inlet port of proportioning valve and **torque** tube nuts to 12 ft. lbs.
5. Install pressure test fitting tool No. 8187-2, or equivalent, in outlet port of proportioning valve and **torque** tube nuts to 12 ft. lbs, **Fig. 31.**
6. Install proportioning valve with pressure test fittings installed, in chassis brake tube and **torque** tube nuts to 12 ft. lbs.
7. Install pressure gauge tool No. C-4007-A, or equivalent, into each pressure test fitting.
8. Bleed air out of hose from pressure test fitting to pressure gauge to remove trapped air in hose.
9. Apply pressure to brake pedal until reading on proportioning valve inlet gauge is within specifications.

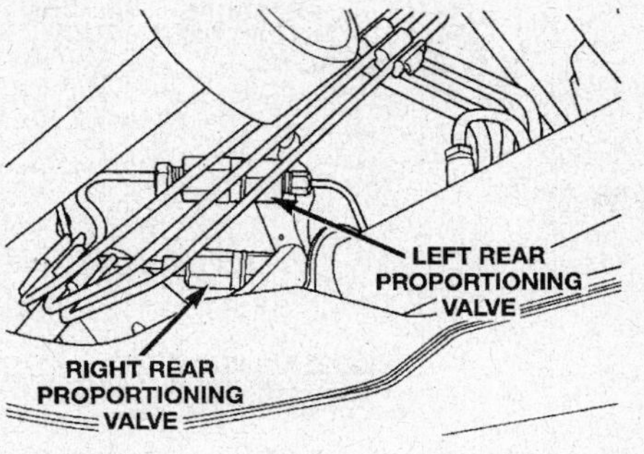

CR4099800076000X

Fig. 30 Type 2 proportioning valve location. 1998–2000 Breeze, Cirrus, Sebring Convertible & Stratus less ABS

10. Check pressure reading on proportioning valve outlet gauge. If outlet pressure is not within specifications when inlet pressure is obtained, replace valve.
11. Check rear wheel brake shoe linings for contamination, replace as necessary.
12. Install proportioning valve in rear brake line and hand tighten both tube nuts until fully seated in valve.
13. **Torque** both tube nuts at proportioning valve to 12 ft. lbs.
14. Bleed affected brake line as described under "Brake System Bleed."

ANTI-LOCK BRAKE SYSTEM

Neon, 1997 Breeze, Cirrus, Sebring Convertible, & Stratus

1. Road test vehicle to determine which rear wheel exhibits premature wheel skid. Refer to **Figs. 32 and 33,** to determine which proportioning valve needs to be tested.
2. Remove hydraulic brake line from proportioning valve to be tested, then remove valve from master cylinder outlet port.
3. Install pressure test fitting tool No. 6805–1 or 6805–2, or equivalent, into outlet port of master cylinder.
4. Install proportioning valve into pressure test fitting in master cylinder outlet port.
5. Install pressure test fitting tool No. 6805–3 or 6805–4, or equivalent, into outlet port of proportioning valve.
6. Connect brake hydraulic line onto pressure test fitting on proportioning valve.
7. Install pressure gauge set tool No. C-4007–A, or equivalent, into test fitting and bleed air from pressure gauge hose.
8. Apply pressure to brake pedal until reading on proportioning valve inlet test fitting is appropriate, then check the pressure reading on the outlet test fitting.
9. If the pressure on the outlet test fitting is not within specifications, replace proportioning valve.
10. Install proportioning valve into master cylinder body until O-ring is seated,

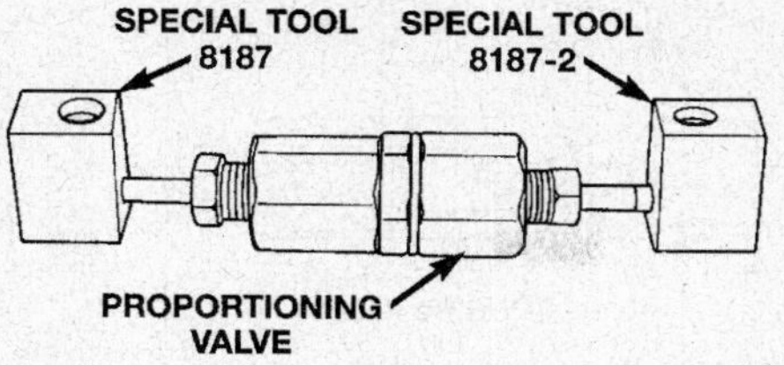

CR4099800079000X

Fig. 31 Pressure test fittings 8187 & 8187-2 installed. Type 2

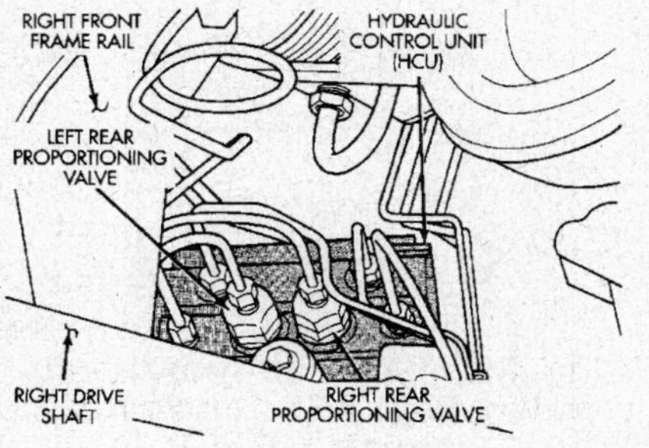

CR4099500072000X

Fig. 33 Type 2 proportioning valve location. 1997 Cirrus, Sebring Convertible, Stratus & 1997 Breeze w/ABS

then **torque** proportioning valve to 30 ft. lbs.

11. Install brake tube onto proportioning valve and **torque** tube nut to 12 ft. lbs.
12. Bleed brake line as outlined under "Brake System Bleed."

1998–2000 Breeze, Cirrus, Sebring Convertible & Stratus

1. Remove cover securing chassis brake tubes and fuel lines to vehicle floor pan.
2. Remove chassis brake tubes from proportioning valve controlling rear wheel which has premature wheel skid, **Fig. 34.**
3. Remove proportioning valve from rear brake chassis tube.
4. Remove routing clips for chassis brake tubes and fuel lines from floor pan.
5. Remove chassis brake tube that requires testing of its proportioning valve from routing clips.
6. Install pressure test fitting tool No.6833-1, or equivalent, in inlet port of proportioning valve.
7. Install pressure test fitting tool No. 8187-2, or equivalent, in outlet port of valve and **torque** tube nuts to 12 ft. lbs, **Fig. 35.**
8. Install proportioning valve with pressure test fittings installed, in chassis brake tube. **Torque** tube nuts to 12 ft. lbs.
9. Install pressure gauge tool No. C-4007-A, or equivalent, into each pressure fitting, **Fig. 36.**
10. Apply pressure to brake pedal until reading on proportioning valve inlet gauge is within specifications.
11. Check pressure reading on proportioning valve outlet gauge.

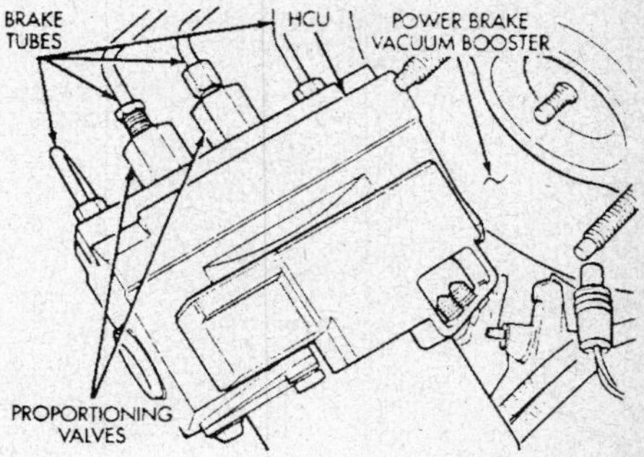

CR4099500068000X

Fig. 32 Type 2 proportioning valve location. Neon w/ABS

12. If outlet pressure is not within specifications when inlet pressure is obtained, replace valve.
13. Check rear wheel brake shoe linings for contamination, replace as necessary.
14. Install chassis brake tube in routing clips.
15. Install routing clips for chassis brake tubes and fuel lines on floor pan.
16. Install cover securing chassis brake tubes and fuel lines to vehicle floor pan.
17. Install proportioning valve in chassis brake tube and **torque** valve to 12 ft. lbs.
18. Install brake tube on proportioning valve and **torque** to 12 ft. lbs.
19. Bleed affected brake line as described under "Brake System Bleed."

Type 3 Proportioning Valves

DESCRIPTION

This dual proportioning valve assembly, **Fig. 37,** is used on non-ABS models except Transitional Low Emission Vehicles (TLEV) with two front catalytic converters.

The proportioning valve transfers full braking force to the rear brakes until a preset ratio called the split point is achieved. At this point the pressure increase is routed away from the rear brake system to prevent rear wheel lock-up.

On models with ABS and non-ABS with TLEV, two screw in proportioning valves are used, **Fig. 38.** The proportioning valves are attached to the rear brake outlets of the hydraulic control unit (HCU).

The brake warning light will come on when the parking brake is applied with the ignition turned On. The same light will also come on when one of the two service brake systems fail.

TESTING

LESS ABS EXCEPT MODELS w/TLEV

If premature rear wheel skid occurs on hard brake application, it could be an indication of a malfunctioning proportioning valve unit.

The proportioning valve is designed with two separate systems. One half controls

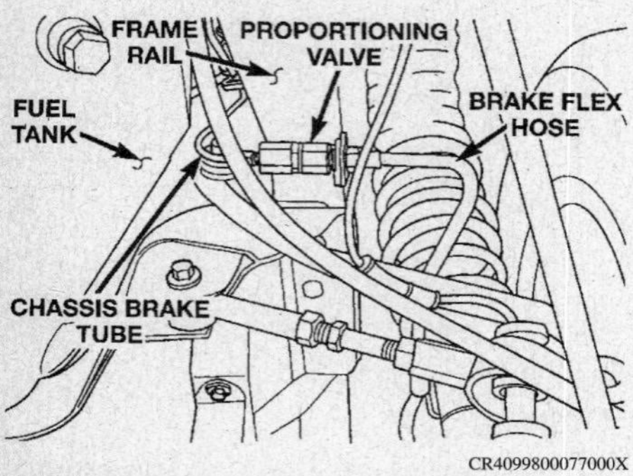

Fig. 34 Type 2 proportioning valve location. 1998–2000 Breeze, Cirrus, Sebring Convertible & Stratus w/ABS

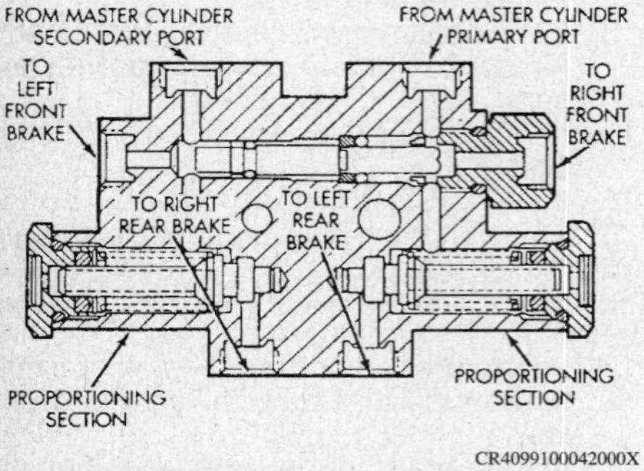

Fig. 37 Type 3 proportioning valve. Less ABS except models w/TLEV

the right rear brake, and the other half controls the left rear brake. A road test to determine which rear brake slides first must be performed.

1. If right rear wheel slides first, leave front brakes connected to valve, then proceed with following procedure.
2. Install one gauge of set tool No. C-4007A, or equivalent, between brake line from master cylinder secondary port and brake valve assembly, **Fig. 39.**
3. Install second gauge of set tool No. C-4007A, or equivalent, as shown in **Fig. 39.** A special adapter may be fabricated from a short piece of brake tube and one 3/8 X 24 tube nuts and one M10 X 1 tube nut.
4. Bleed the hose and gauge set.
5. While watching pressure gauges, have an assistant depress the brake pedal. Note gauge readings, then refer to "Hydraulic Brake Controls Specifications" chart.
6. If left rear wheel slides first, leave front brakes connected to valve, then proceed with following procedure.
7. Install one gauge of set tool No. C-4007A, or equivalent, between brake line from master cylinder secondary port and brake valve assembly, **Fig. 40.**
8. Install gauge set tool No. C-4007A, or equivalent, as shown in **Fig. 40.** A special adapter may be fabricated from a M12x1 tube nut, a short piece of brake tube and a 3/8 X 24 tube nut.

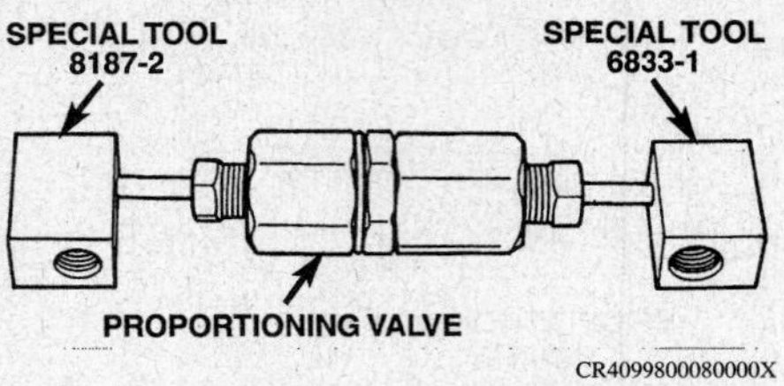

Fig. 35 Pressure test fittings 8187-2 & 6833-1 installation. 1998–2000 Breeze, Cirrus, Sebring Convertible & Stratus

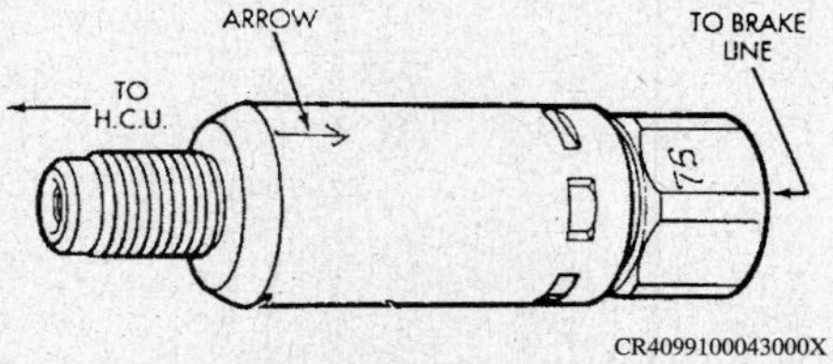

Fig. 38 Type 3 proportioning valve. With ABS & non-ABS models w/TLEV

9. Bleed hose and gauge set.
10. While watching pressure gauges, have an assistant depress the brake pedal. Note gauge readings, then refer to "Hydraulic Brake Controls Specifications" chart.
11. If pressure readings are not as specified for left or right rear wheel, replace the combination valve. After installing a new combination valve, bleed hydraulic brake system as described under "Brake System Bleed."

WITH ABS & NON-ABS w/TLEV

On vehicles with Teves Mark IV ABS system refer to "Anti-Lock Brakes" section for testing procedures.

All ABS components use an ISO type tubing flare. Ensure proper adapters with ISO type flare are used when installing test gauges.

1. Install one gauge of set tool No. C-700A, or equivalent, between hydraulic assembly and male end (inlet) of valve.
2. Install second gauge of set tool No. C-700A, or equivalent, at female end (outlet) of valve, **Fig. 41.**
3. While watching inlet and outlet pressure gauges, have an assistant depress the brake pedal. Note gauge readings, then refer to "Hydraulic Brake Controls Specifications" chart.
4. If pressures are not within specifications replace proportioning valve.

Type 4

DESCRIPTION

Two inline proportioning valves are used on both anti-lock and non anti-lock systems. One valve is used for each rear brake hydraulic circuit.

On light brake applications, equal brake pressure will be transmitted to the front and rear brakes. On heavy pedal applications,

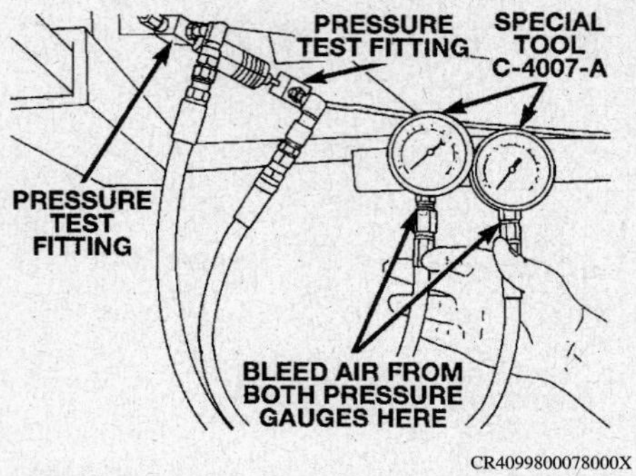

Fig. 36 Pressure gauge C-4007-A installation. 1998–2000 Breeze, Cirrus, Sebring Convertible & Stratus

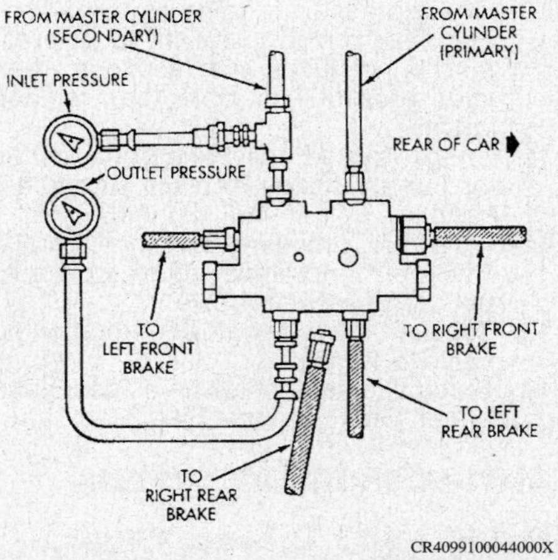

Fig. 39 Type 3 proportioning valve pressure gauge test connections (Right wheel fault). Less ABS except models w/TLEV

the pressure transmitted to the rear will be lower than the front brakes. This action prevents premature rear wheel skid. If hydraulic pressure is lost in one half of the diagonally split system, the operation of the proportioning valve in the remaining half is not effected. These valves are only serviced as a unit.

TESTING

Not all components use the same type tubing flare. The tube leading into the proportioning valve has an ISO flare, while the flex hose coming out of proportioning valve has a standard double-inverted flare. Ensure correct adapters when installing gauges to test proportioning valves.

On vehicles with and without anitlock brakes, are equipped with two proportioning valves. One valve is connected to each rear flex hose. One proportioing valve controls the right rear brake and the other controls the left rear brake.

On vehicles without ABS, if premature wheel skid occurs on hard brake application, it could be an indication that a malfunction has occured with one of the two rear brake proportioing valves. Test valve that controls the side that the skid occured on.

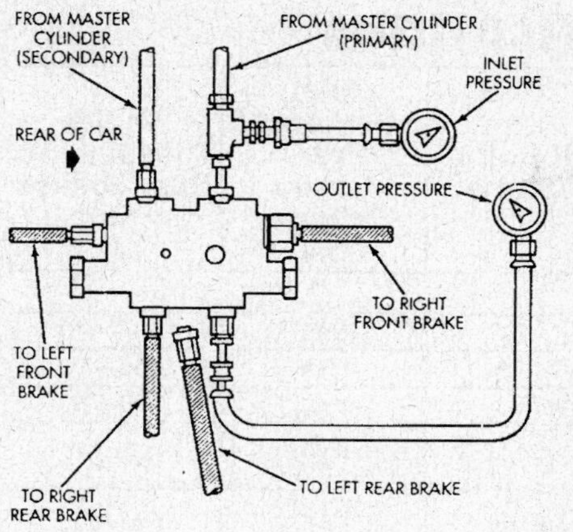

Fig. 40 Type 3 proportioning valve pressure gauge test connections (Left wheel fault). Less ABS except models w/TLEV

On vehicles with ABS, if premature rear wheel ABS cycling occurs on a hard brake application, it could be an indication that a malfunction has occured with one of the two proportioning valves. Since ABS cycles both rear brakes together, both valves must be tested to isolate the suspected proportioning valve.

1. Clean any debris away from proportioing valve, connections.
2. Remove chassis brake tube from proportioing valve. **Fig. 42.**

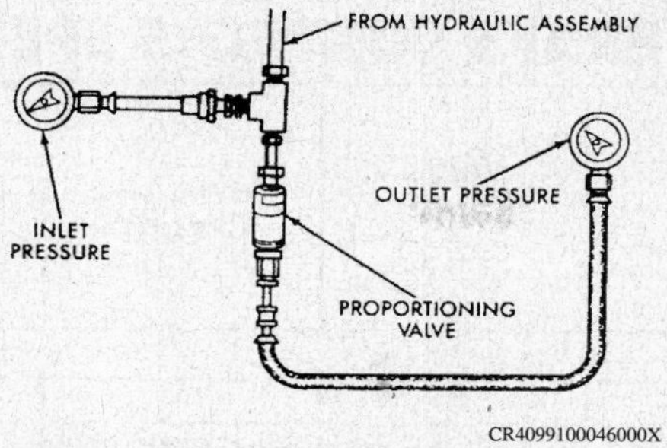

Fig. 41 Type 3 proportioning valve pressure gauge test connections. With ABS & Non-ABS w/TLEV

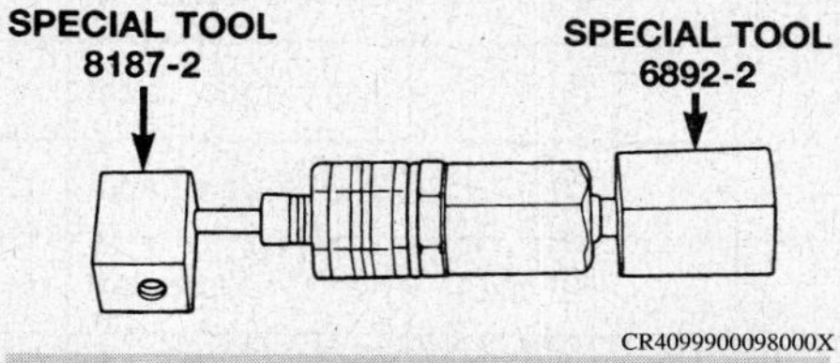

Fig. 43 Proportioning Valve Fittings

3. Remove proportioning valve from rear flex hose, then remove retainer clip securing rear flex hose from its bracket.
4. Install pressure fittings into inlet and outlet ports of proportioning valve. **Fig. 43.**

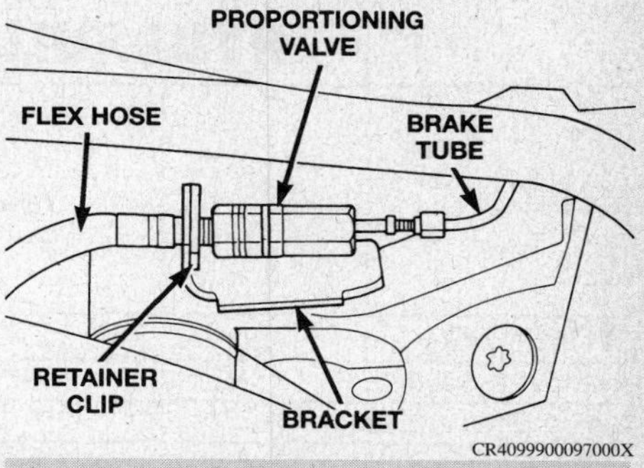

Fig. 42 Proportioning Valve Assembly

5. Install proportioning valve and pressure test fittings as an assembly back into chassis brake tube. Connect Special Tool No. 6892–2 or equivalent, to the chassis brake tube, and Special Tool No. 8187–2 or equivalent, to the brake flex hose.
6. Install pressure gauge Special Tool No. C-4007–A or equivalent, into each pressure test fitting. Bleed any air out of system, from pressure gauge on.
7. While watching inlet and outlet pressure gauges, have an assistant depress brake pedal. Note gauge readings, if correct pressure is not obtained, replace proportioning valve.

HYDRAULIC BRAKE SYSTEM SPECIFICATIONS

Model	Year	Master Cylinder Bore Dia. Inch	Booster to Primary Piston Clearance Inch	Wheel Bleed Sequence
Avenger & Sebring	1997–2000	1.001	.0255–.0334	LR, RF, RR, LF
Breeze	1997–2000	.874	—	LR, RF, RR, LF
Cirrus & Stratus	1997–2000	.874	—	LR, RF, RR, LF
Concorde & Intrepid	1997–2000	.937	—	RR, LF, LR, RF
Vision	1997	.938	—	RR, LF, LR, RF
LHS & 300M	1999–2000	.937	—	RR, LF, LR, RF
Neon②	1997–99	.875	—	LR, RF, RR, LF
Neon①	1997–99	.827	—	LR, RF, RR, LF
Neon	2000	③	—	LR, RF, RR, LF
Sebring Convertible	1997–2000	.874	—	LR, RF, RR, LF
Talon	1997–98	1.001	.0255–.0334	LR, RF, RR, LF

① — Front and rear disc brakes. ② — Front disc and rear drum brakes. ③ — With ABS .937; w/out ABS ..875.

HYDRAULIC BRAKE CONTROLS SPECIFICATIONS

Model	Year	Valve Identification	Valve Tag Color①	Split Point psi/Slope	Inlet Pressure From Master Cylinder psi	Outlet Pressure To Rear Brakes psi
WITH ABS						
Avenger & Sebring	1997–2000	③	—	391–462	996	569–640
Cirrus, Stratus & Breeze⑧	1997–2000	③	Bar Coded Label	500/.43	1000	600–700
Cirrus, Stratus & Breeze⑨	1999–2000	③	Bar Coded Label	400/.34	1000	600–700
Concord, Intrepid, LHS & Vision⑥	1997–98	③	Bar Coded Label	435/.43	1000	560–640
Concord, Intrepid, LHS & Vision⑦	1997–98	③	Bar Coded Label	435/.43	1000	525–600
Concorde, Intrepid, LHS & 300M⑨	1999	③	Bar Coded Label	400	1000	600–700
Concorde, Intrepid, LHS & 300M④	1999	③	Bar Coded Label	500	1000	650–750
Concorde, Intrepid, LHS & 300M⑪	2000	③	Bar Coded Label	350/.34	1000	525–625
Neon ②	1997	③	Gold Or Bar Coded Label	400/.34	1000	550–650
Neon②	1998–99	③	Bar Coded Label	300/.34	1000	550–650
Neon②	2000	③	Black Band	300/.34	1000	550–650
Sebring Convertible⑧	1997–2000	③	Bar Coded Label	600/.59	1000	800–900
Sebring Convertible②	1999–2000	③	Bar Coded Label	500/.43	1000	600–700
Talon⑤	1997–98	③	—	391–462	—	569–640
LESS ABS						
Avenger & Sebring	1997–2000	③	—	320–391	925	462–533
Breeze	1997–2000	③	—	500/.43	1000	600–700
Cirrus & Stratus	1997–2000	③	—	500/.43	1000	600–700
Concorde, Intrepid, LHS & Vision⑩	1997–98	③	White Or Bar Coded Label	500/.43	1000	725–850
Concorde, Intrepid & LHS & 300M	1999	③	Bar Coded Label	400	1000	600–700
Concorde, Intrepid, LHS & 300M	2000	③	Bar Coded Label	350/.34	1000	525–625
Neon⑧	1997–99	③	Black	400/.43	1000	600–700
Neon②	1997	③	Gold	400/.34	1000	550–650
Neon②	1998–99	③	Bar Code Label	300/.34	1000	550–650
Neon⑩	2000	③	Bar Code Band	400/.43	1000	600–700
Sebring Convertible⑧	1997–2000	③	Black /Gold Stripe Or Bar Coded Label	600/.59	1000	800–900
Talon⑤	1997–98	③	—	320–391	—	462–533

① — Color tag located under boot of valve stem.
② — 14 inch disc-disc.
③ — Proportioning Valve.
④ — 16 inch disc-disc system w/ABS & TCS. Sales code BR4.
⑤ — FWD.
⑥ — With ABS & Less TCS.
⑦ — With TCS & ABS
⑧ — 14 inch disc-drum.
⑨ — 15 & 16 inch disc-disc systems, w/ABS & w/ABS & TCS. Sales codes BRG, BR3 & BR3 + BNM.
⑩ — Disc-drum.
⑪ — All Sales Codes.

POWER BRAKE UNITS

INDEX

DESCRIPTION

SYSTEM

These units are of the vacuum suspended type. Some units are of the single diaphragm type, while others are of the tandem diaphragm type, both single piston and double piston or split system type master cylinders are used.

The vacuum suspended diaphragm type units utilize engine manifold vacuum and atmospheric pressure for its power. It consists of three basic elements combined into a single power unit. The three basic elements of the single diaphragm type are:

1. A vacuum power section which includes a front and rear shell, a power diaphragm, a return spring and a pushrod.
2. A control valve, built integral with the power diaphragm and connected through a valve rod to the brake pedal, controls the degree of brake application or release in accordance with the pressure applied to the brake pedal.
3. A hydraulic master cylinder, attached to the vacuum power section which contains all the elements of the conventional brake master cylinder except for the pushrod, supplies fluid under pressure to the wheel brakes in proportion to the pressure applied to the brake pedal.

OPERATION

Upon application of the brakes, the valve rod and plunger move to the left in the power diaphragm to close the vacuum port and open the atmospheric port to admit air through the air cleaner and valve at the rear diaphragm chamber. With vacuum present in the rear chamber, a force is developed to move the power diaphragm, hydraulic pushrod and hydraulic piston or pistons to close the compensating port or ports and force fluid under pressure through the residual check valve or valves and lines into the front and rear wheel cylinders to actuate the brakes.

As pressure is developed within the master cylinder a counter force acting through the hydraulic pushrod and reaction disc against the vacuum power diaphragm and valve plunger sets up a reaction force opposing the force applied to the valve rod and plunger. This reaction force tends to close the atmospheric port and reopen the vacuum port. Since this force is in opposition to the force applied to the brake pedal by the driver it gives the driver a "feel" of the amount of brake applied. The proportion of reactive force applied to the valve plunger through the reaction disc is designed into the Master-Vac to ensure maximum power consistent with maintaining pedal feel. The reaction force is in direct proportion to the hydraulic pressure developed within the brake system.

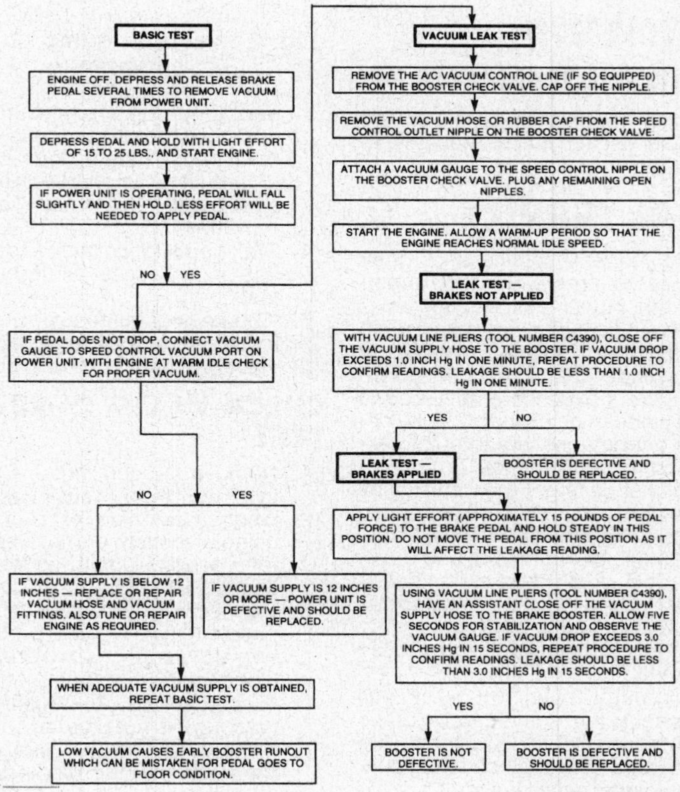

CR4099700074000X

Fig. 1 Power brake system diagnosis

TROUBLESHOOTING

DECREASING BRAKE PEDAL TRAVEL

If a decreasing brake pedal is encountered, the power brake unit may be binding internally. To test the power brake unit for this condition proceed as follows:

1. Place transmission shift lever into Neutral and start engine.
2. Increase engine speed to approximately 1500 RPM, close throttle and completely depress brake pedal.
3. Slowly release brake pedal and stop engine.
4. Remove vacuum check valve and hose from power brake unit. Observe for backward movement of brake pedal.
5. If brake pedal moves backward, power brake unit has internal binding. Replace power brake unit.

HARD BRAKE PEDAL

An internal bind or a failed vacuum check valve would cause this condition. Refer to previous to test power brake unit for an internal bind. To check for a failed vacuum check valve proceed as follows:

1. Start engine and increase engine speed to approximately 1500 RPM, then close throttle and stop engine.
2. Wait 90 seconds, then try brake action.

3. If brakes are not vacuum assisted for two or more applications, replace check valve.

DRAGGING BRAKES

If slow or incomplete release of brakes (dragging brakes) is encountered the power brake unit has an internal bind condition. Test for an internal bind condition as outlined under "Decreasing Brake Pedal Travel."

DIAGNOSIS & TESTING

Refer to **Fig. 1,** for diagnostic flowchart.

ADJUSTMENTS

PUSHROD ADJUSTMENT

Refer to "Adjustments" in the "Hydraulic Brake Systems" section for pushrod adjustment procedure.

GENERAL SERVICE

In order to properly service and repair available brake systems, a thorough understanding of the power assist systems is necessary. The vacuum assist diaphragm assembly multiplies the force exerted on the master cylinder piston in order to increase the hydraulic pressure delivered to the wheel cylinders or calipers while decreasing the effort necessary to obtain acceptable stopping performance.

Vacuum assist units get their energy by opposing engine vacuum to atmospheric pressure. A piston, cylinder and flexible diaphragm utilize this energy to provide brake assistance. The diaphragm is balanced with engine vacuum until the brake pedal is depressed, allowing atmospheric pressure to unbalance the unit and apply force to the brake system.

Brakes will operate even if the power unit fails. This means the conventional brake system and the power assist system are completely separate. Troubleshooting conventional and power assist systems are exactly the same until the power unit is reached. As with conventional hydraulic brakes, a spongy pedal still means air is trapped in the hydraulic system. Power brakes give higher line pressure, making leaks more critical.

BRAKE BOOSTER OPERATION TEST

1. Run engine for one or two minutes, then shut off.
   a. If brake pedal depresses fully first time but gradually becomes higher when depressed succeeding times, booster is operating properly.
   b. If pedal height remains unchanged, booster is defective.
2. With engine stopped, step on brake pedal several times, then step on brake pedal and start engine.
   a. If pedal moves downward slightly, booster is in good condition.
   b. If there is no change in pedal, booster is defective.
3. With engine running, step on brake pedal and stop engine, then hold pedal depressed for 30 seconds.
   a. If pedal height does not change, booster is in good condition.
   b. If pedal height rises, booster is defective.
4. Brake booster performance is satisfactory if it passes all three operating tests.
5. If brake booster does not pass all three tests, there may be a fault in check valve, vacuum hose or in booster itself.

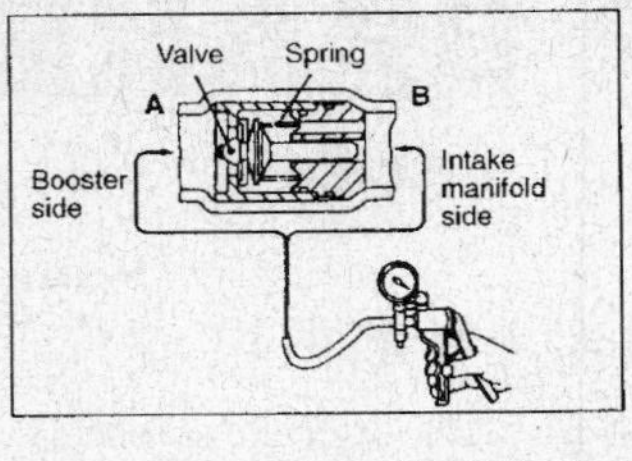

Vacuum pump connection	Accept/reject criteria
Connection at the brake booster side (A)	A negative pressure (vacuum) is created and held.
Connection at the intake manifold side (B)	A negative pressure (vacuum) is not created.

CR4099700073000X

Fig. 2 Vacuum pump connection locations

CHECK VALVE OPERATION TEST

1. Remove vacuum hose. **Check valve is press fitted inside vacuum hose.**
2. Check operation of check valve by using a vacuum pump. Refer to **Fig. 2,** for vacuum pump connection locations.
3. Connect vacuum pump at brake booster side (A). A negative pressure (vacuum) should be created and held.
4. Connect vacuum pump at intake manifold side (B). A negative pressure (vacuum) is not created.
5. If check valve is defective, replace it as an assembly unit together with vacuum hose.

POWER BRAKE UNIT SERVICE

POWER BOOSTER, REPLACE

AVENGER, SEBRING & TALON

Refer to **Figs. 3 and 4,** for removal procedures.

CONCORDE, INTREPID, VISION, LHS & 300M

Two different power brake vacuum boosters are used. For standard brake and ABS applications a Bendix booster is used. For traction control ABS applications a Teves booster is used, **Fig. 5.**

Do not attempt to disassemble or service power brake unit. Brake unit is serviced only as a complete unit.

1. Remove both wiper arm assemblies, then cowl panel cover from cowl.
2. Remove five screws that attach windshield wiper module from dash panel.
3. Remove two master cylinder to brake booster attaching nuts, then slide master cylinder off mounting studs.
4. Disconnect vacuum hose from booster check valve. **Do not remove check valve from booster.**
5. From under instrument panel, position small screwdriver between center tang of booster input rod to brake pedal pin retaining clip, then rotate screwdriver so retainer clip center tang passes over end of brake pedal pin and pull retainer clip off. Discard old retainer clip.
6. From under instrument panel remove four booster attaching nuts, slide booster up and to right on dash panel, then tilt outward and up to remove.
7. Reverse procedure to install noting the following:
   a. **Torque** booster to dash panel and master cylinder to booster attaching nuts to 21 ft. lbs.
   b. When connecting booster input rod to brake pedal pin use new retainer clip.
   c. Ensure brake lights work properly.

NEON

When repairing vehicles equipped with ABS systems, the vacuum in the power booster must be pumped down before removing the master cylinder to avoid drawing in any contamination. This can be done simply by pumping the brake with ignition off until a firm pedal is achieved.

1. **On models with ABS systems,** ensure ignition switch is Off and brake pedal has been pumped until firm.
2. **On 2000 models,** disconnect positive cable from battery, remove battery from tray, then remove both the air cleaner box and battery tray.
3. **On all models,** disconnect wiring harness from brake fluid level sensor mounted on fluid reservoir.
4. Disconnect primary and secondary brake tubes from master cylinder housing and plug outlets on master cylinder.
5. **On models with ABS systems,** clean area where master cylinder attaches to power booster using a suitable cleaner.
6. **On all models,** remove mounting nuts and slide master cylinder forward out of booster.
7. **On models equipped with ABS, the vacuum seal in the front of the power brake vacuum booster must be replaced.** Remove vacuum seal in front of power brake vacuum booster by carefully inserting a small screwdriver between the master cylinder push rod and vacuum seal and prying the seal out of the booster. **Do not attempt to pry seal out by inserting screwdriver between seal and booster.**
8. **On all models,** disconnect vacuum hoses from power booster check valve. **Do not remove check valve from power booster.**
9. **On models with ABS systems,** remove Hydraulic Control Unit (HCU).
10. **On all models,** locate power booster input rod to brake pedal attachment

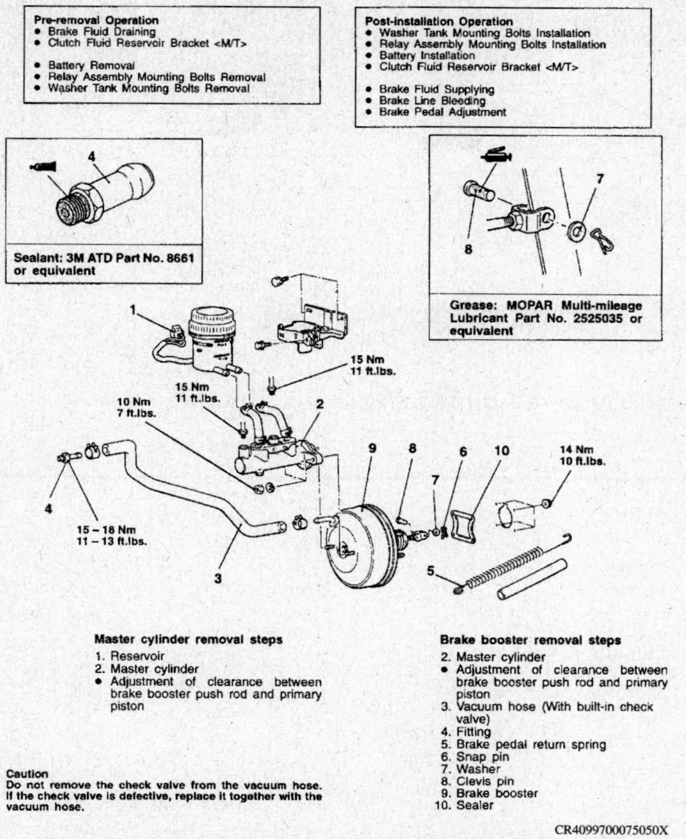

Fig. 3 Brake booster & master cylinder removal. Avenger & Sebring

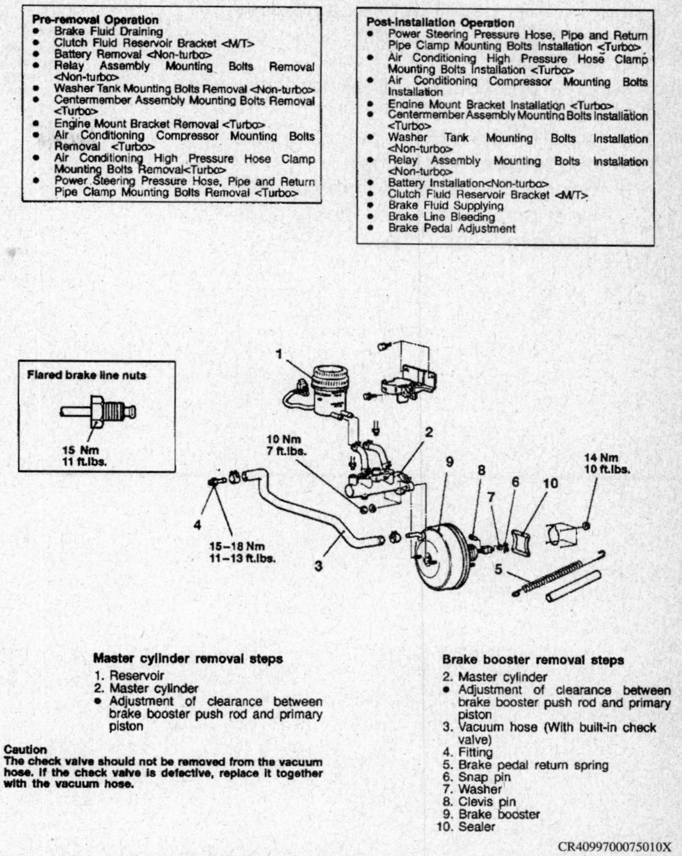

Fig. 4 Brake booster & master cylinder removal. Talon

under instrument panel.

11. Position a suitable small screwdriver between center tang on input rod to brake pedal pin retaining clip.
12. Rotate screwdriver to allow retaining clip center tang to pass over end of brake pedal pin. Discard retaining clip.
13. Remove power booster mounting nuts holding unit to dash panel.
14. Slide power booster forward until mounting studs clear dash, then tilt unit upward to remove.
15. Reverse procedure to install noting the following:
    a. **On models with ABS,** install new vacuum seal by lubricating master cylinder push rod using suitable silicone lubricant and slide vacuum seal onto master cylinder push rod with notches on seal pointing toward and seated against master cylinder housing.
    b. **On all models,** install mounting nuts and **torque** to 21 ft. lbs.
    c. Connect brake tubes to master cylinder primary and secondary ports and **torque** tube nuts to 12 ft. lbs.

BREEZE, CIRRUS & STRATUS

2.0L & 2.4L Engines

1. Remove remote ground cable from stud located on lefthand strut tower, then remove wiring harness connector from speed control servo.
2. Remove two speed control servo mounting bracket nuts, then move speed control servo out of way. **Do not remove speed control cable from servo.**
3. Remove vacuum harness connector and electrical connector from purge control solenoid.
4. Remove purge control solenoid bracket bolt, then remove purge control solenoid.
5. Remove vacuum hoses from check valve located on brake booster, then remove EGR transducer assembly and vacuum hoses.
6. Remove master cylinder assembly from brake booster. **Do not remove brake lines from master cylinder.**
7. Disconnect brake booster input rod from brake pedal pin.
8. Remove brake booster mounting nuts and brake booster.
9. Reverse procedure to install. Install brake booster mounting nuts and **torque** to 21 ft. lbs.

2.5L Engine

1. Remove remote ground cable from stud located on lefthand strut tower, then remove wiring harness connector from speed control servo.
2. Remove PCV hose from intake manifold.
3. Remove bolt attaching air chamber to intake manifold and loosen clamp attaching air inlet hose to throttle body.
4. Remove air inlet hose, air cleaner lid and air chamber as an assembly.
5. Remove throttle cable and speed control cable from throttle body, then remove vacuum hose from throttle body.
6. Remove wiring harness connectors from AIS motor and throttle position sensor, then remove throttle body from intake manifold.
7. Remove throttle cable and speed control cable mounting bracket from intake manifold. **Do not remove cables from bracket.**
8. Remove EGR tube from intake manifold and EGR valve.
9. Remove two speed control servo mounting bracket nuts, then move speed control servo out of way. **Do not remove speed control cable from servo.**
10. Remove primary and secondary brake tubes from master cylinder assembly, then remove master cylinder from brake booster.
11. Remove vacuum harness connector and electrical connector from purge control solenoid.
12. Remove purge control solenoid bracket bolt, then remove purge control solenoid.
13. Remove dipstick and dipstick tube from transaxle as an assembly.
14. Remove vacuum hoses from check valve located on brake booster.
15. Disconnect brake booster input rod

from brake pedal pin, then remove brake booster mounting nuts and brake booster.

16. Reverse procedure to install noting the following:
    a. Install brake booster mounting nuts and **torque** to 21 ft. lbs.
    b. Connect brake tubes to master cylinder primary and secondary ports and **torque** tube nuts to 12 ft. lbs.

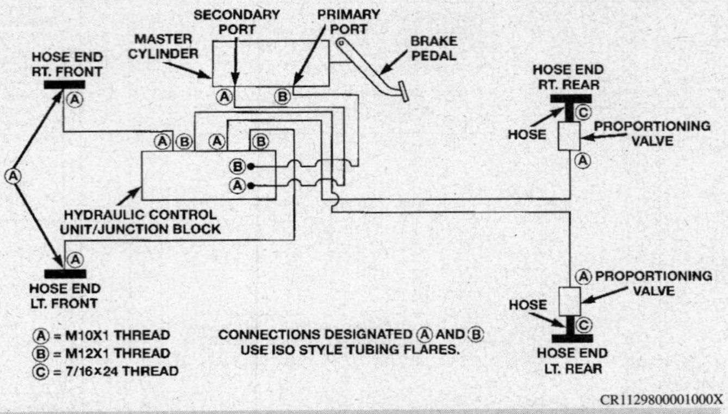

Fig. 5 Brake tube nut thread size & tube routing

AUTOMATIC TRANSAXLES

TABLE OF CONTENTS

Application Chart

Model	Year	Automatic Transmission/Transaxle
Avenger	1997–2000	F4AC1
Breeze	1997–2000	41TE
Cirrus	1997–2000	41TE
Concorde	1997–2000	42LE
Intrepid	1997–2000	42LE
LHS	1997 & 1999–2000	42LE
Neon	1997–2000	31TH
Sebring Convertible	1997–2000	41TE
Sebring Coupe	1997–2000	F4AC1
Stratus	1997–2000	41TE
Talon	1997–98	F4AC1, F4A33, W4A33
Vision	1997	42LE
300M	1999–2000	42LE

F4A33 & W4A33 Automatic Transaxles

NOTE: On Air Bag Equipped Models, Refer To " Air Bag System Precautions" Located In The Front Of This Manual For System Disarming & Arming Procedures.

NOTE: Refer To "Computer Relearn Procedures " Located In The Front Of This Manual For Computer Relearn Procedures.

INDEX

PRECAUTIONS

AIR BAG SYSTEMS

Refer to "Air Bag System Precautions" in the front of this manual for system disarming and arming procedures.

BATTERY GROUND CABLE

Prior to service, disconnect battery ground cable and isolate as required.

IDENTIFICATION

The transaxle identification number is located at the top of the bellhousing, **Fig. 1.**

DESCRIPTION

The Mitsubishi F4A33 is a fully automatic four-speed electronically controlled transaxle. This transaxle is used on the Talon equipped with FWD and turbocharged engines.

The Mitsubishi W4A33 is a fully automatic four-speed electronically controlled transaxle. This transaxle is used on the Talon equipped with AWD and turbocharged engines.

TROUBLESHOOTING

TRANSAXLE

Refer to **Fig. 2,** when troubleshooting the transaxle.

MAINTENANCE

FLUID CHECK

With vehicle on level surface, start engine and operate at idle speed. With parking brake applied, move shift lever through each gear, then place selector lever in N. Remove dipstick and check fluid level. Transmission should be at operating temperature when checking fluid level (160–180°F). Fluid level should be within the Hot range on dipstick. If necessary, add Mopar ATF type 7176 Dia. ATFSP, or equivalent, automatic transmission fluid to bring fluid level within the Hot range.

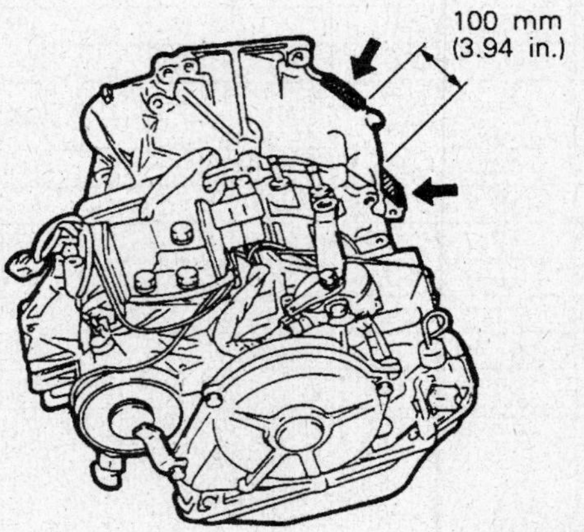

Fig. 1 Transaxle identification

FLUID CHANGE

The automatic transaxle fluid should be changed every 30,000 miles on these units. When refilling transaxle, add only Mopar ATF type 7176 Dia. ATFSP, or equivalent, automatic transaxle fluid.

1. Remove drain plug from bottom of differential and drain fluid into a suitable container.
2. Loosen transaxle oil pan attaching bolts, then tap pan at one corner to break loose and drain fluid into a suitable container.
3. Remove oil pan and drain residual fluid.
4. Inspect oil filter for damage or obstructions and replace if necessary.
5. Install drain plug with a new gasket and tighten to specifications.
6. Clean transaxle case and oil pan mating surfaces, then install oil pan with a new gasket and tighten attaching bolts to specifications.
7. Add 4.2 quarts Mopar ATF type 7176 Dia. ATFSP, or equivalent, automatic transmission fluid to transaxle through dipstick hole.
8. Run engine at idle for at least two minutes, then shift transaxle through all ranges and recheck fluid level.
9. Add sufficient fluid to bring level to lower mark on dipstick, then run engine until normal operating temperature is reached. Recheck dipstick and ensure fluid level is within Hot range.

ADJUSTMENTS

KICKDOWN SERVO

1. Thoroughly clean area around kickdown servo cover.
2. Remove snap ring, then kickdown servo switch.
3. Install holding fixture tool No. MD998918 and adapter tool No. MD998915, or equivalents, as shown in **Fig. 3.** Ensure piston is not pushed in by tool. When installing adapter to brake pressure output port, tighten only by hand.
4. Loosen locknut past V channel in adjuster rod, then tighten tool No. MD998916, or equivalent, (inner) until there is contact with locknut **Fig. 4.**
5. Attach tool No. MD998916 (outer), or equivalent, to locknut. Turn outer tool to left and inner tool to right to lock locknut and inner tool.
6. Install torque wrench to inner tool. **Torque** locknut to 7 ft. lbs., then loosen locknut and **torque** to 43 inch lbs. Back off inner tool by 2–2¼ turns.
7. Attach outer tool to locknut. Turn outer tool to right and inner tool to left to unlock locknut and inner tool.

		Problem / Presumed cause	Driving impossible or abnormal (before start-off): Starter motor won't function	Forward/backward movement impossible	Forward movement impossible	Backward movement impossible	Engine stalls when N → D or R	Clutch slips at D (stall rpm too high)	Clutch slips at R (stall rpm too high)	Stall rpm too low	Vehicle moves at P or N	Engine starts, or vehicle moves, between N R or N-D	Parking doesn't hold	Abnormal vibration-shock when shift to D-2-L-R
Engine	1	Abnormal idling rpm					⊗							×
Engine	2	Performance malfunction					×			×				
Transaxle (power train)	3	Improper adjustment of manual linkage	×	⊗	⊗	⊗		⊗	⊗		⊗	⊗	⊗	⊗
Transaxle (power train)	4	Malfunction of torque convertor		×	×	×				×				
Transaxle (power train)	5	Operation malfunction of oil pump		×	×	×		×	×					
Transaxle (power train)	6	Malfunction of one-way clutch			×			×						
Transaxle (power train)	7	Damaged or worn gear or other rotating part, or improper adjustment of the preload												
Transaxle (power train)	8	Malfunction of parking mechanism									×		×	
Transaxle (power train)	9	Cracked drive plate, or loose bolt		×										
Transaxle (power train)	10	Worn inside diameter of front clutch retainer				×			×					
Oil pressure system (including friction elements)	11	Low fluid level		⊗	⊗	⊗		×	×					
Oil pressure system (including friction elements)	12	Line pressure too low (seal damaged, leakage, looseness, etc.)		⊗	⊗	⊗		⊗	⊗					
Oil pressure system (including friction elements)	13	Malfunction of valve body (sticking valve, working cavity, adjustment, etc.)		⊗	⊗	⊗	×	×	×		×	×		×
Oil pressure system (including friction elements)	14	Malfunction of front clutch or piston				×			×					×
Oil pressure system (including friction elements)	15	Malfunction of rear clutch or piston			⊗			×						×
Oil pressure system (including friction elements)	16	Malfunction of kickdown band or piston												
Oil pressure system (including friction elements)	17	Improper adjustment of kickdown servo												
Oil pressure system (including friction elements)	18	Malfunction of low-reverse brake or piston		×		×			×					×
Oil pressure system (including friction elements)	19	O-ring of low-reverse brake circuit between valve body and case not installed				×			×					
Oil pressure system (including friction elements)	20	Malfunction of end clutch or piston (check ball hole, other)												
Electronic control system	21	Malfunction of inhibitors switch, damaged or disconnected wiring, or improper adjustment	×								×	×		×
Electronic control system	22	Malfunction of TPS; or improper adjustment												×
Electronic control system	23	Pulse generator (A) damaged or disconnected wiring, or short-circuit												
Electronic control system	24	Pulse generator (B) damaged or disconnected wiring, or short-circuit				×								
Electronic control system	25	Malfunction of kickdown servo switch												
Electronic control system	26	SCSV-A or B damaged or disconnected wiring, or short-circuit or sticking (valve open)												
Electronic control system	27	Malfunction of ignition signal system												
Electronic control system	28	Incorrectly grounded ground strap												
Electronic control system	29	PCSV damaged or disconnected wiring, or short-circuit												
Electronic control system	30	PCSV damaged or disconnected wiring (valve open)		⊗	⊗	⊗		×	×					
Electronic control system	31	DCCSV damaged or disconnecting wiring (valve closed)												
Electronic control system	32	DCCSV short-circuit or sticking (valve open)					⊗							
Electronic control system	33	Malfunction of overdrive control switch												
Electronic control system	34	Malfunction of accelerator switch, or improper adjustment												×
Electronic control system	35	Malfunction of oil-temperature sensor												
Electronic control system	36	Malfunction of lead switch												
Electronic control system	37	Poor contact of ignition switch												
Electronic control system	38	Malfunction of transaxle control unit												×

NOTE: ⊗ indicates items of high priority during inspection.
Abbreviations: TPS = Throttle position sensor SCSV = Shift control solenoid valve

CR5019000166010X

Fig. 2 Transaxle troubleshooting (Part 1 of 2)

	Transaxle malfunction of shift-shock (after start-off): Won't shift from 2nd to 3rd	Won't shift to 4th	Overdrive control switch doesn't function	Doesn't shift according to shift pattern (shifting is possible)	Improper start-off (starts off from 2nd, etc.)	Excessive creeping or idling vibration	Excessive vibration-shock when shift 1-2 or 3-4	Excessive vibration-shock when shift 2-3 or 4-3	Excessive vibration-shock during upshift	Excessive vibration-shock during D-2 downshift	Sudden engine rpm increase during upshift	Sudden engine rpm increase during 3-2 shift, excessive vibration	Excessive vibration-shock only when cold	Excessive vibration-shock (other than already described)	Damper clutch won't function	Abnormal vibration in high-load region in low gear (approx. 1 Hz)	Abnormal noise, other: Abnormal noise from convertor housing together with engine rpm	Mechanical noise (clatter noise) from convertor housing	Abnormal noise inside transaxle case	3rd gear is held
1						×														
2					×		×	×	×	×			×	×		×				
3		×			×															×
4					×										×	×				
5												×					×			
6																				
7																			×	
8																				
9																		×		
10	×	×									×	×								×
11												×								×
12											⊗	⊗		×						×
13	×			×	×		×	×	×	×	×	×	×	×	×	×				×
14	×							×	×		×									×
15																				×
16							×				×	×								×
17							×				×	×		×						×
18										×										×
19																				×
20		⊗					×				×									×
21		×			×															×
22				⊗			×	×	⊗	×	⊗	×		×	×	×				
23							×	×	×	×	×	×		×	×	×				×
24				×											×	×				×
25							×					×								×
26																				×
27							×	×	×	×	×	×		×	×					
28																				×
29																				×
30	×	×									×	×								×
31															×					
32																×				×
33		×	×																	
34					×	×									×					
35														×	×	×				
36																				×
37				×																×
38	×	×	×	×	×	×	×	×	×	×	×	×	×	×	×	×	×			×

PSCV = Pressure control solenoid valve
DCCSV = Damper clutch control solenoid valve

CR5019000166020X

Fig. 2 Transaxle troubleshooting (Part 2 of 2)

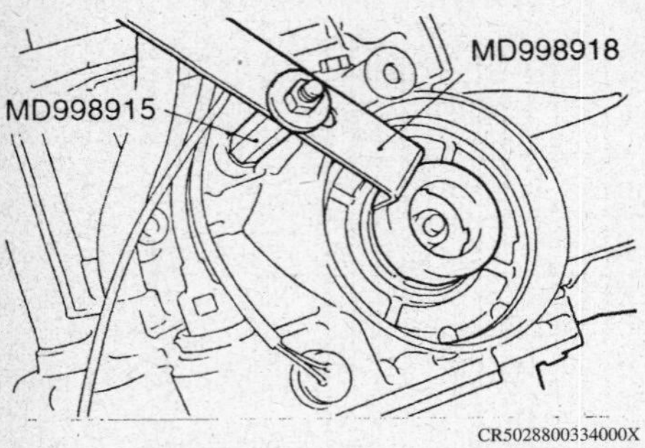

Fig. 3 Kickdown servo tools

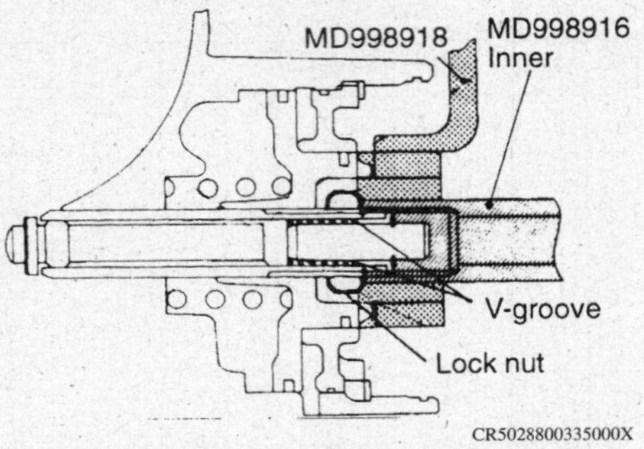

Fig. 4 Installing inner & outer adjustment tools

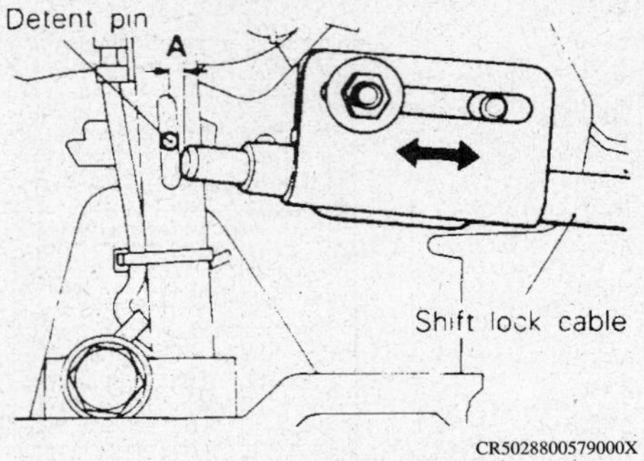

Fig. 5 Shift lock cable adjustment

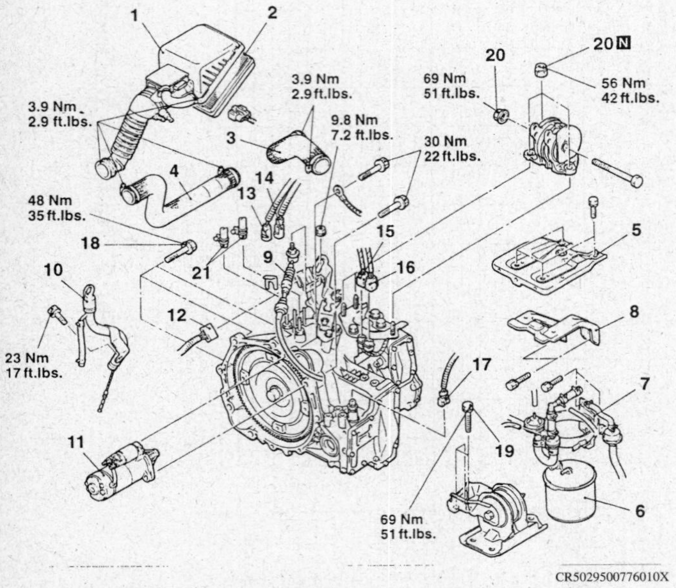

Fig. 6 Transaxle replacement (Part 1 of 2)

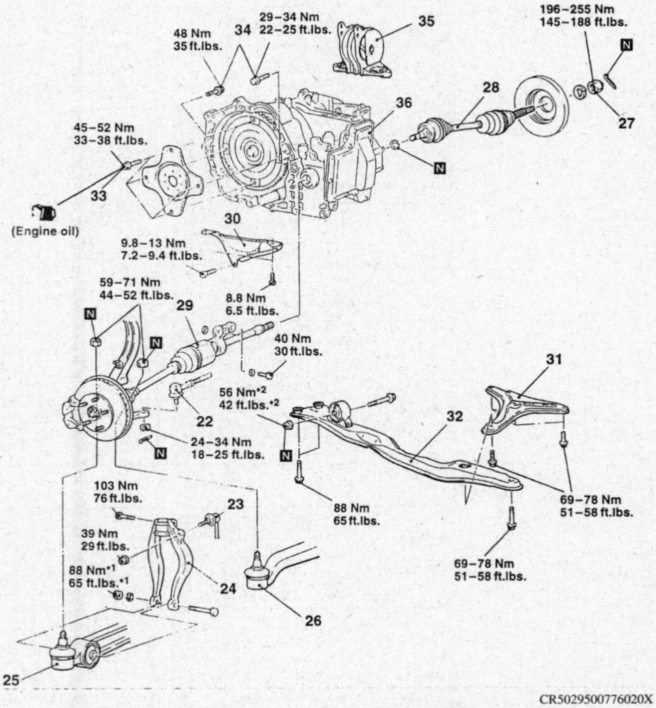

Fig. 6 Transaxle replacement (Part 2 of 2)

8. Tighten locknut by hand until it contacts piston. Using torque wrench, **torque** locknut to 18–23 ft. lbs.
9. Remove holding fixture, then install a plug to outlet of low reverse pressure port.

SHIFT LOCK CONTROL

1. Move select lever to Reverse position, then clamp shift lock cable.
2. Connect shift lock cable to select lever assembly and temporarily tighten nut.
3. Slide shift lock cable so distance between select lever assembly's detent pin and end of shift lock cable (distance A) is .04–.15 inch, **Fig. 5.**

TRANSAXLE

REPLACE

1. Drain transaxle fluid.
2. Remove transaxle assembly in numbered sequence shown in **Fig. 6,** noting the following:
   a. Raise transaxle assembly using suitable transmission jack to relieve weight off of mounts, then remove transaxle mount insulator bolt.
   b. Support engine using engine support fixture tool No. MZ203827, or equivalent.
   c. Loosen, but do not remove tie rod ends, lateral lower arm, and compression lower arm using ball joint puller tool No. MB991113-01, or equivalent.
   d. Remove driveshaft by applying pry bar to protrusion. **Remove driveshaft as an assembly together with hub and knuckle**
   e. Remove inner shaft assembly from transaxle by tapping on center bearing bracket a suitable plastic hammer.
   f. Support transaxle assembly with a suitable transaxle stand, then rotate crankshaft and remove four torque converter bolts.
   g. After removing bolts, push torque converter toward transaxle.
   h. Remove coupling bolt at bottom of transaxle assembly, then lower transaxle assembly.
3. Reverse procedure to install.

TIGHTENING SPECIFICATIONS

Component	Torque/Ft. Lbs.
Air Intake Hose Connections	36①
Bell Housing Cover	84–108①
Compression Arm Connection	44–52
Crossmember To Body	51–58
Crossmember To Righthand Stay	51–58
Crossmember To Transaxle	42
Damper Fork to Lateral Lower Arm	65
Drain Plug	22–25
Driveplate Connecting Bolt	33–38
Lateral Lower Arm Connection	44–52
Mounting Bracket To Body	51
Mounting Bracket To Transaxle	42
Oil Level Gauge Bracket	17
Oil Pan	96①
Rear Roll Stopper Bracket	51
Stabilizer Link To Damper Fork	29
Starter Motor to Transaxle	22
Tie Rod End Nut	18–25
Torque Converter Connecting Bolt	33–38
Transaxle Control Cable Connection	84①
Transaxle Lower Coupling Bolts	35
Transaxle Upper Coupling Bolts	22–25

① — Inch lbs.

F4AC1 Automatic Transaxle

NOTE: On Air Bag Equipped Models, Refer To " Air Bag System Precautions" Located In The Front Of This Manual For System Disarming & Arming Procedures.

NOTE: Refer To "Computer Relearn Procedures " Located In The Front Of This Manual For Computer Relearn Procedures.

INDEX

PRECAUTIONS

AIR BAG SYSTEMS

Refer to "Air Bag System Precautions" in the front of this manual for system disarming and arming procedures.

BATTERY GROUND CABLE

Prior to service, disconnect battery ground cable and isolate as required.

IDENTIFICATION

The vehicle information code plate **Fig. 1,** is mounted onto the bulkhead of the engine compartment. This plate shows model code (1), engine model (2 and 3), transaxle model (4) and vehicle color code (5).

DESCRIPTION

The F4AC1 automatic transaxle is a fully adaptive, electronically controlled four speed full automatic transaxle. The F4AC1 transaxle uses a three element type torque converter with torque converter clutch.

The F4AC1 transaxle provides four forward speeds with ratios of 2.84:1, 1.57:1, 1.00:1 and .069:1. Reverse ratio is 2.21:1 and the final gear ratio is 4.08:1. The F4AC1 transaxle **Fig. 2,** consists of damper, under drive, reverse, 2/4, and low/reverse clutches. It is also equipped with output and input speed sensors.

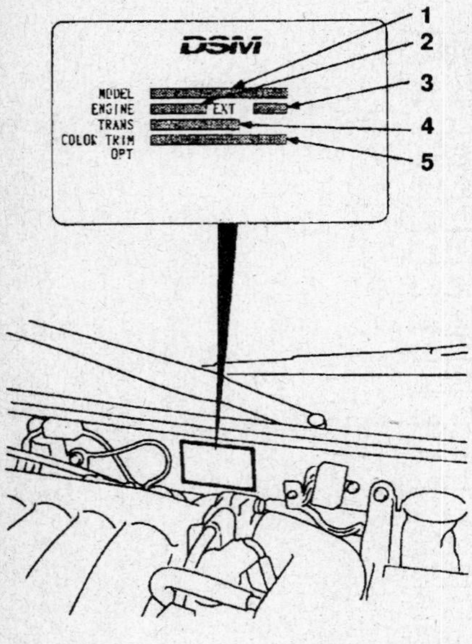

Fig. 1 Transaxle identification

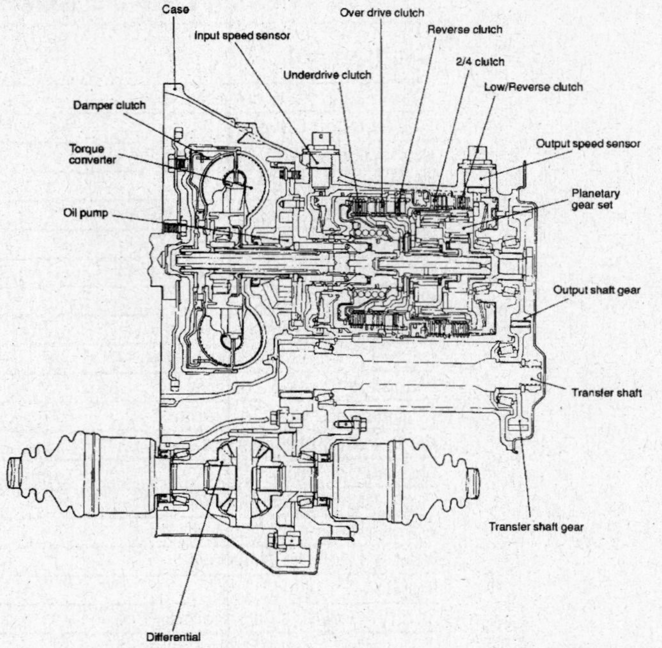

Fig. 2 Cross-sectional view of F4AC1 automatic transaxle

TROUBLESHOOTING

Refer to **Fig. 3,** when troubleshooting the transaxle.

MAINTENANCE

FLUID CHECK

Place vehicle on level surface, start engine and operate at idle speed. Shift transaxle through all gear ranges and return to park. With parking brake applied, place selector lever in N, then remove dipstick and check fluid level. Transmission should be at operating temperature when checking fluid level (160–180°F). Fluid level should be between Add and Full lines on dipstick. If necessary, add Dexron II automatic transmission fluid to bring fluid level within Add and Full lines on dipstick.

FLUID CHANGE

The automatic transaxle fluid should be changed every 30,000 miles on these units. When refilling transaxle, add only Mopar ATF Plus (Type 7176), or equivalent.

1. Raise and support front of vehicle, then position drain pan under transaxle.
2. Loosen transaxle oil pan bolts and tap pan at one corner to break it loose allowing fluid to drain.
3. Install a new filter and O-ring on bottom of valve body and clean oil pan and magnet.
4. Install oil pan and tighten mounting bolts to specifications.
5. Add 4.0 qts. of transaxle fluid through filler tube.
6. Start engine and check fluid level as outlined under " Fluid Level Inspection."

ADJUSTMENTS

SHIFT LOCK CABLE

1. Place selector lever in Park position.
2. Install cable so it is above red marking, **Fig. 4.**

THROTTLE CONTROL CABLE

1. Ensure choke lever is away from cam follower.
2. Raise throttle cable (B) upward, then loosen cable lower mounting bracket bolt, **Fig. 5.**
3. Move cable lower mounting bracket until clearance between nipple and top of cable cover (A) is .02-.06 inch, then tighten cable lower mounting bracket bolt to specifications.
4. With throttle lever in wide open position, pull throttle cable upward to ensure cable has freedom of movement.

INHIBITOR SWITCH & CONTROL CABLE

1. Place selector lever in Neutral position.
2. Loosen transaxle control cable to manual control cable lever coupling nut to free cable and lever.
3. Place manual control lever in Neutral position.
4. Turn inhibitor switch body to align end of manual control lever to flange of inhibitor switch body, **Fig. 6.**
5. Tighten inhibitor switch mounting bolts to specifications.
6. Loosen nut shown in **Fig. 7,** and lightly pull end of transaxle control cable in direction F. Tighten nut to specifications.
7. Ensure selector lever is in Neutral position.
8. Ensure switch operates properly.

IN-VEHICLE REPAIRS

TRANSAXLE CONTROL CABLE

Refer to **Fig. 8,** when replacing transaxle control cable.

KEY INTERLOCK & SHIFT LOCK CABLES

Refer to **Fig. 9,** when replacing key interlock or shift lock cables.

TRANSAXLE

REPLACE

2.0L ENGINE

1. Remove transaxle assembly in numbered sequence shown in **Fig. 10,** noting the following:
   a. Support transaxle with a suitable transaxle jack when removing mounting bracket nuts.
   b. Support engine using engine support fixture tool No. 7137, or equivalent.
   c. Loosen, but do not remove nut from tie rod ends, lateral lower arm and compression lower arm joints using ball joint puller tool No. MB990635, or equivalent.
   d. Remove driveshaft by applying pry bar between transaxle case and

Probable cause		Harsh engagement from Neutral(N) to Drive(D)	Harsh engagement from Neutral(N) to Reverse(R)	Delayed engagement from Neutral(N) to Drive(D)	Delayed engagement from Neutral(N) to Reverse(R)	Poor shift quality	Shifts erratically	Dives in Neutral(N)	Drags or locks	Grating, scraping, growling noise	Knocking noise	Buzzing noise during shifts only	Hard to fill oil blows out filler tube	Transaxle overheats	Harsh upshift	No upshift into overdrive	No torque converter control	Harsh downshifts	High shift efforts	Harsh torque converter control shift
Engine performance				X			X								X				X	X
Worn or faulty clutch(es)	Underdrive clutch			X									X	X	X			X		X
	Overdrive clutch					X	X						X	X	X					
	Reverse clutch												X	X			X		X	
	2-4 clutch			X			X						X		X					
	Low/Reverse clutch			X									X		X				X	X
Clutch(es) dragging														X						
Insufficient clutch plate clearance								X						X						
Damaged clutch seal				X													X	X		
Worn or damaged accumulator sealing (s)				X													X	X	X	X
Faulty cooling system								X												
Engine coolant temperature too low					X	X														
Incorrect gear shift control linkage adjustment								X						X	X		X	X		
Shift linkage damaged			X																	
Chipped or damaged gear teeth												X	X							
Planetary gear sets broken or seized												X	X							
Bearings worn or damaged												X	X							
Driveshaft(s) bushing(s) worn or damaged												X								
Worn or broken reaction shaft support sealing				X											X	X	X	X		
Worn or damaged input shaft sealing					X												X	X		
Valve body malfunction or leakage			X	X	X						X			X	X	X	X	X	X	X
Hydraulic pressures too low					X		X	X							X	X	X	X		
Hydraulic pressures too high				X			X												X	X
Faulty oil pump					X			X							X		X	X		
Oil filter clogged									X						X	X	X	X		
Low fluid level				X	X			X			X				X	X	X	X		
High fluid level								X	X											
Aerated fluid				X	X			X	X		X				X	X	X	X		
Engine idle too low																	X	X		
Engine idle too high				X				X											X	X
Normal solenoid operation										X										
Solenoid sound cover loose										X										
Sticking lockup piston		X																		
Torque converter failure					X			X												X

CR5029500782000X

Fig. 3 Troubleshooting symptoms chart

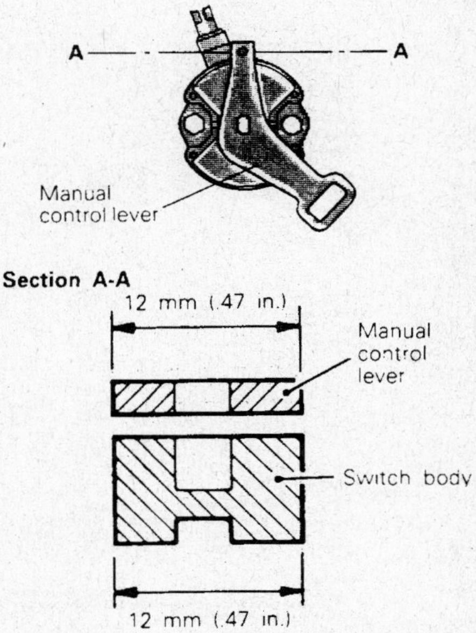

CR5028800575000X

Fig. 6 Inhibitor switch adjustment

driveshaft. **Remove driveshaft as an assembly together with hub and knuckle**

e. Support transaxle assembly with a suitable transaxle stand, then rotate crankshaft and remove four torque converter bolts.
f. After removing bolts, push torque converter toward transaxle.
g. Remove coupling bolt at bottom of transaxle assembly, then lower transaxle assembly.

2. Reverse procedure to install.

2.5L ENGINE

1. Remove battery, then the washer fluid reservoir.
2. Remove radiator, then the under cover.
3. Remove transaxle assembly in numbered sequence shown in **Fig. 11,** noting the following:
   a. Raise transaxle assembly using suitable transmission jack to relieve weight off of mounts, then remove transaxle mount insulator bolt.
   b. Support engine using engine support fixture tool No. 7137, or equivalent.
   c. Loosen, but do not remove nut from tie rod ends, lateral lower arm and compression lower arm joints using ball joint puller tool No. MB990635, or equivalent.
   d. Remove driveshaft by applying pry bar between transaxle case and driveshaft. **Remove driveshaft as an assembly together with hub and knuckle**
   e. Support transaxle assembly with a suitable transaxle stand, then rotate crankshaft and remove four torque converter bolts.
   f. After removing bolts, push torque converter toward transaxle.
   g. Remove coupling bolt at bottom of transaxle assembly, then lower transaxle assembly.
4. Reverse procedure to install.

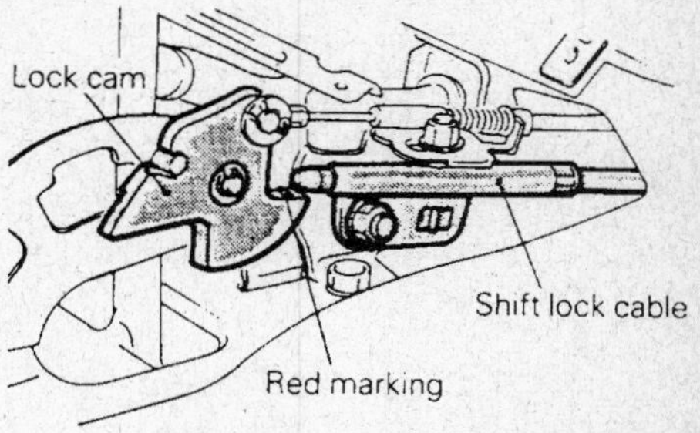

CR5028800569000X

Fig. 4 Shift lock cable adjustment

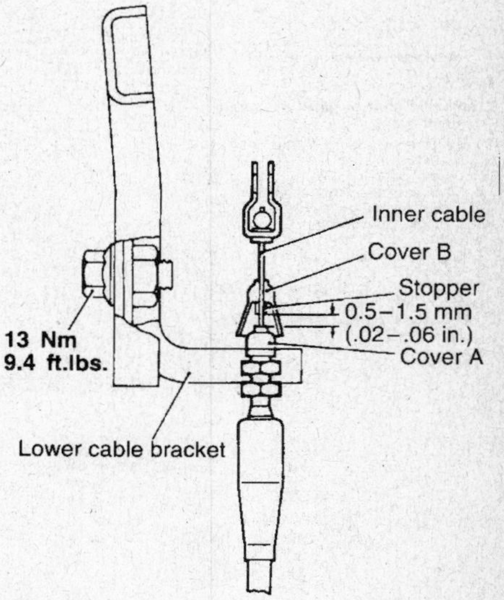

CR5029500772000X

Fig. 5 Throttle control cable adjustment

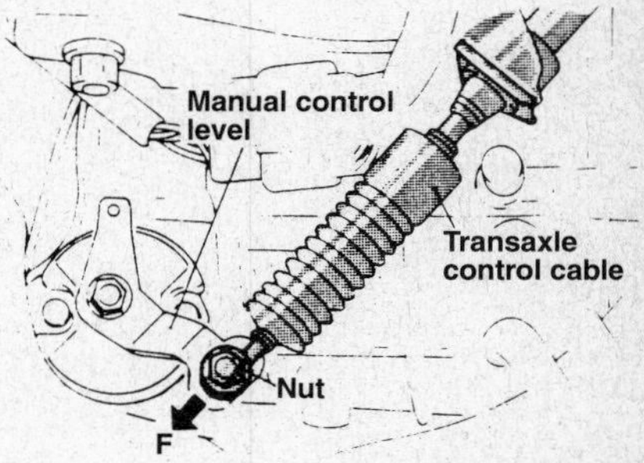

CR5028800576000X

Fig. 7 Control cable adjustment

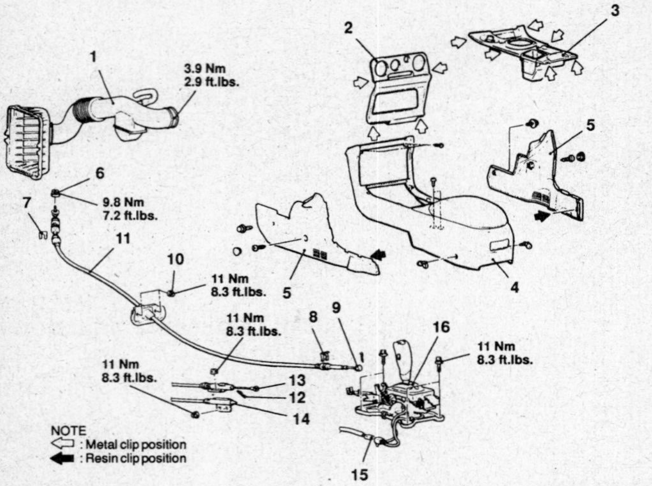

Transaxle control cable assembly removal steps

1. Air cleaner and air intake hose assembly
2. Center panel
3. Floor console panel assembly
4. Floor console assembly
5. Console side cover
6. Nut
7. Clip
8. Clip
9. Transaxle control cable connection
10. Nut
11. Transaxle control cable assembly

Selector lever assembly removal steps

2. Center panel
3. Floor console panel assembly
4. Floor console assembly
5. Console side cover
8. Clip
9. Transaxle control cable connection
12. Snap pin
13. Key interlock cable connection
14. Shift lock cable connection
15. Overdrive switch/position indicator light connector
16. Selector lever assembly

CR5029500783000X

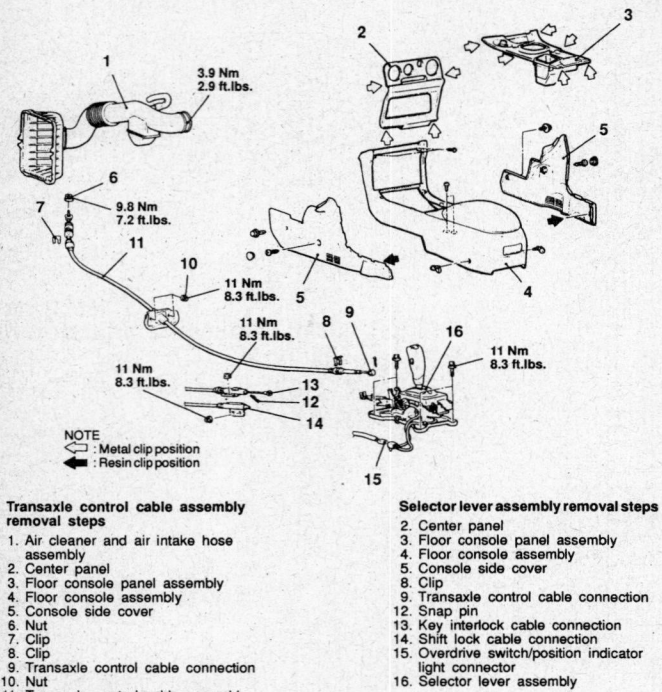

Fig. 8 Transaxle control cable replacement

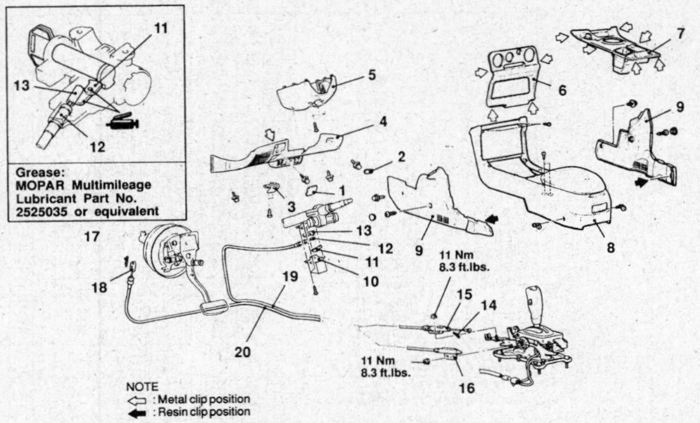

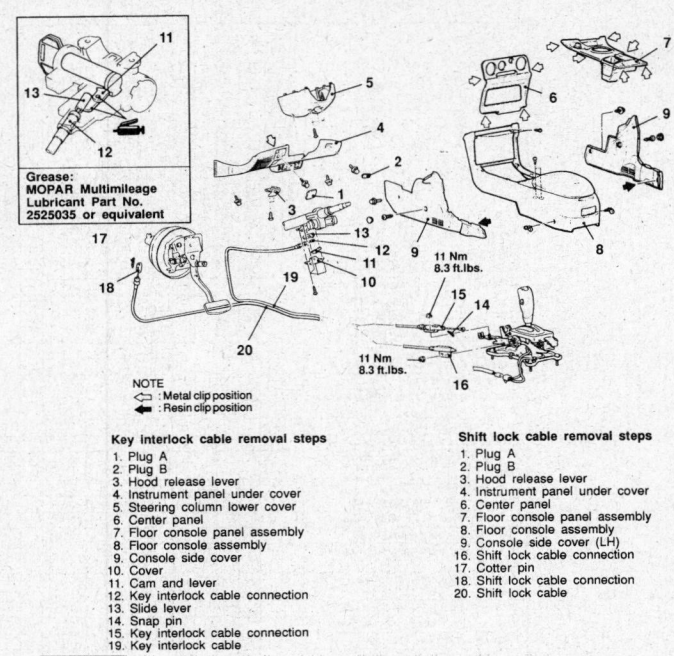

Key interlock cable removal steps

1. Plug A
2. Plug B
3. Hood release lever
4. Instrument panel under cover
5. Steering column lower cover
6. Center panel
7. Floor console panel assembly
8. Floor console assembly
9. Console side cover
10. Cover
11. Cam and lever
12. Key interlock cable connection
13. Slide lever
14. Snap pin
15. Key interlock cable connection
19. Key interlock cable

Shift lock cable removal steps

1. Plug A
2. Plug B
3. Hood release lever
4. Instrument panel under cover
6. Center panel
7. Floor console panel assembly
8. Floor console assembly
9. Console side cover (LH)
16. Shift lock cable connection
17. Cotter pin
18. Shift lock cable connection
20. Shift lock cable

CR5029500784000X

Fig. 9 Key interlock & shift lock cable replacement

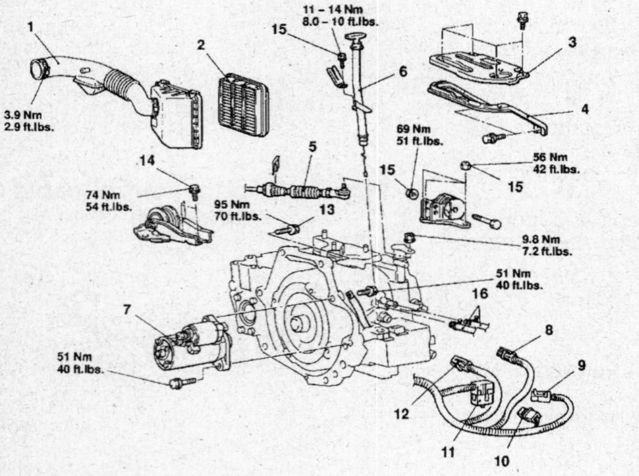

Removal steps

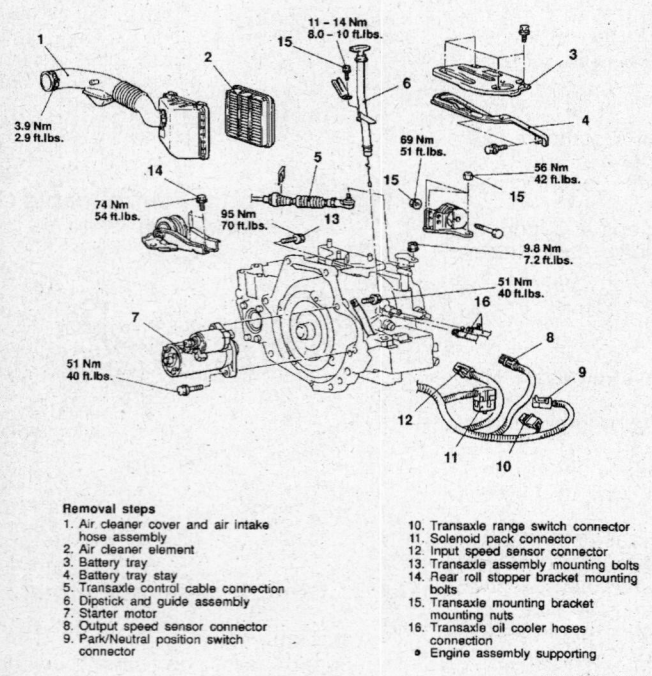

1. Air cleaner cover and air intake hose assembly
2. Air cleaner element
3. Battery tray
4. Battery tray stay
5. Transaxle control cable connection
6. Dipstick and guide assembly
7. Starter motor
8. Output speed sensor connector
9. Park/Neutral position switch connector
10. Transaxle range switch connector
11. Solenoid pack connector
12. Input speed sensor connector
13. Transaxle assembly mounting bolts
14. Rear roll stopper bracket mounting bolts
15. Transaxle mounting bracket mounting nuts
16. Transaxle oil cooler hoses connection

- Engine assembly supporting

CR5029500785010X

Fig. 10 Transaxle replacement (Part 1 of 2). Avenger & Sebring & 1997–98 Talon w/2.0L engine

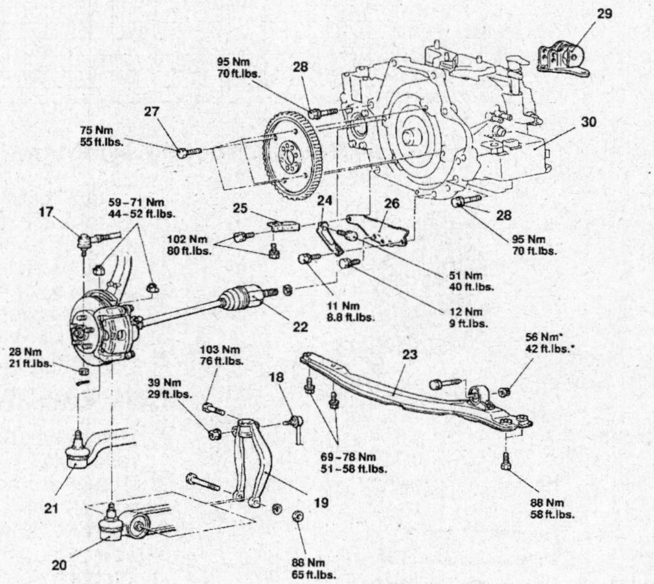

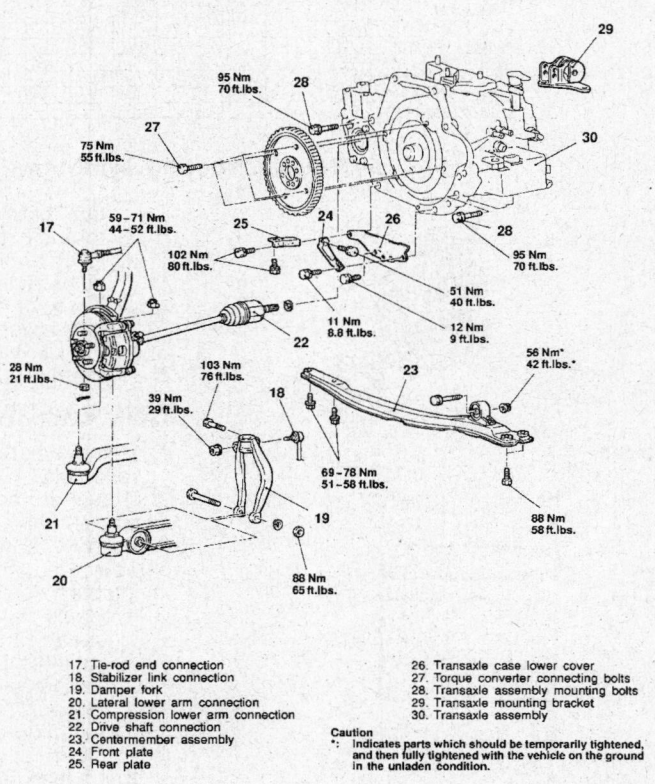

17. Tie-rod end connection
18. Stabilizer link connection
19. Damper fork
20. Lateral lower arm connection
21. Compression lower arm connection
22. Drive shaft connection
23. Centermember assembly
24. Front plate
25. Rear plate
26. Transaxle case lower cover
27. Torque converter connecting bolts
28. Transaxle assembly mounting bolts
29. Transaxle mounting bracket
30. Transaxle assembly

Caution
*: Indicates parts which should be temporarily tightened, and then fully tightened with the vehicle on the ground in the unladen condition.

CR5029500785020X

Fig. 10 Transaxle replacement (Part 2 of 2). Avenger & Sebring & 1997–98 Talon w/2.0L engine

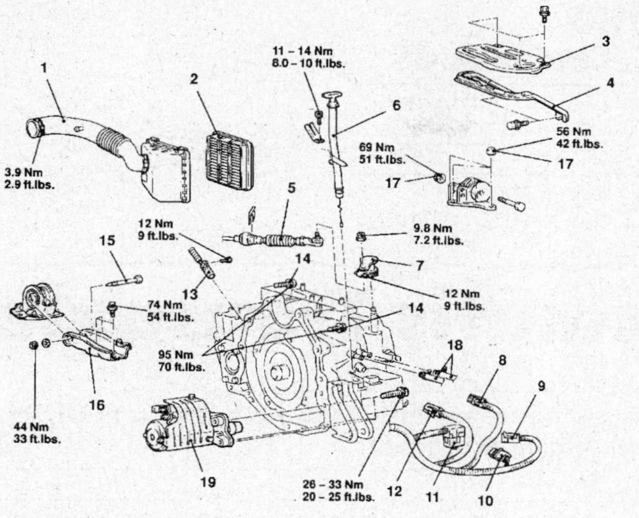

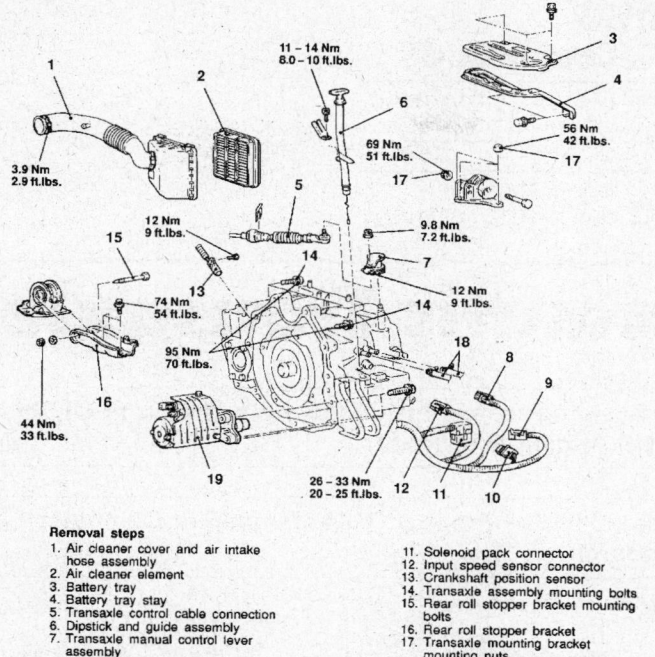

Removal steps

1. Air cleaner cover and air intake hose assembly
2. Air cleaner element
3. Battery tray
4. Battery tray stay
5. Transaxle control cable connection
6. Dipstick and guide assembly
7. Transaxle manual control lever assembly
8. Output speed sensor connector
9. Park/Neutral position switch connector
10. Transaxle range switch connector
11. Solenoid pack connector
12. Input speed sensor connector
13. Crankshaft position sensor
14. Transaxle assembly mounting bolts
15. Rear roll stopper bracket mounting bolts
16. Rear roll stopper bracket
17. Transaxle mounting bracket mounting nuts
18. Transaxle oil cooler hoses connection
- Engine assembly supporting
19. Starter motor

CR5029500786010X

Fig. 11 Transaxle replacement (Part 1 of 2). Avenger & Sebring w/2.5L engine

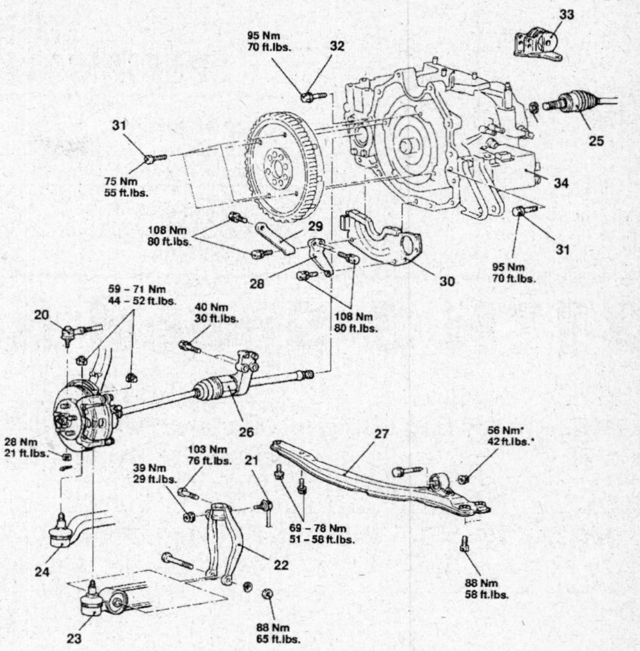

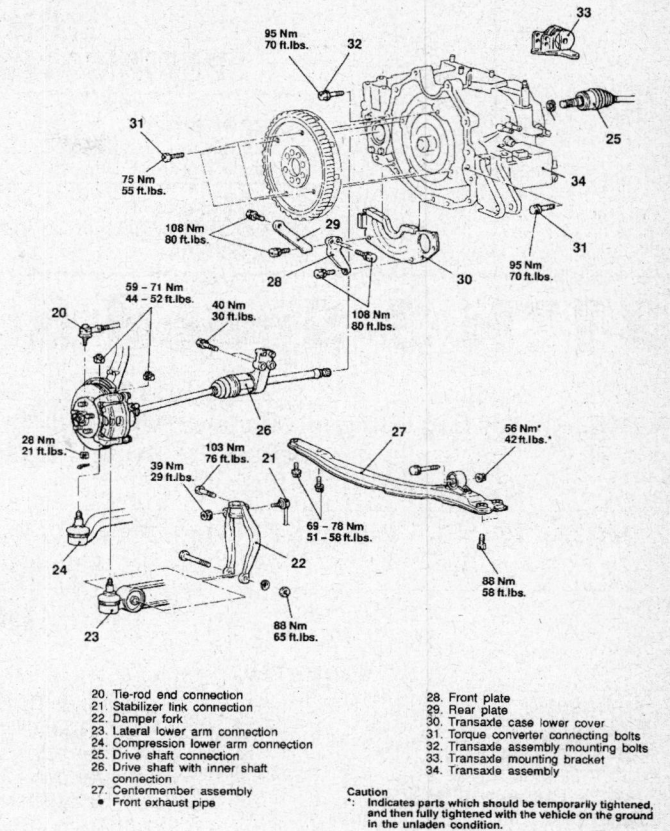

20. Tie-rod end connection
21. Stabilizer link connection
22. Damper fork
23. Lateral lower arm connection
24. Compression lower arm connection
25. Drive shaft connection
26. Drive shaft with inner shaft connection
27. Centermember assembly
- Front exhaust pipe
28. Front plate
29. Rear plate
30. Transaxle case lower cover
31. Torque converter connecting bolts
32. Transaxle assembly mounting bolts
33. Transaxle mounting bracket
34. Transaxle assembly

Caution
*: Indicates parts which should be temporarily tightened, and then fully tightened with the vehicle on the ground in the unladen condition.

CR5029500786020X

Fig. 11 Transaxle replacement (Part 2 of 2). Avenger & Sebring w/2.5L engine

TIGHTENING SPECIFICATIONS

Component	Torque/Ft. Lbs.
Air Intake Hose Clamp	36③
Centermember Assembly To Body	51–58
Centermember Assembly To Transaxle	42
Compression Lower Arm Nut	44–52
Damper Fork To Lateral Lower Arm	65
Damper Fork To Stabilizer	29
Dipstick Guide Bracket	8–10
Front Plate To Lower Cover	①
Inhibitor Switch Mounting Bolts	84–96③
Lateral Lower Arm Nut	44–52
Lower Cover To Transaxle	108③
Mounting Bracket To Body	51
Mounting Bracket To Transaxle	42
Oil Pan	14
Rear Plate To Lower Cover	80
Rear Roll Stopper To Transaxle	54
Roll Stopper Bracket To Body	33
Starter Mounting Bolts	②
Throttle Cable Lower Mounting Bracket	10
Tie Rod Nut	21
Torque Converter Bolts	55
Transaxle Assembly Bolts	70

Continued

TIGHTENING SPECIFICATIONS—Continued

Component	Torque/Ft. Lbs.
Transaxle Control Cable	84③

① — DOHC engine 40 ft. lbs., SOHC engine 80 ft. lbs.
② — DOHC engine 40 ft. lbs., SOHC engine 20–25 ft. lbs.
③ — Inch lbs.

31TH 3-Speed Automatic Transaxle

NOTE: On Air Bag Equipped Models, Refer To " Air Bag System Precautions" Located In The Front Of This Manual For System Disarming & Arming Procedures.

NOTE: Refer To "Computer Relearn Procedures " Located In The Front Of This Manual For Computer Relearn Procedures.

INDEX

PRECAUTIONS

AIR BAG SYSTEMS

Refer to "Air Bag System Precautions" in the front of this manual for system disarming and arming procedures.

BATTERY GROUND CABLE

Prior to service, disconnect battery ground cable and isolate as required.

IDENTIFICATION

A seven digit part number is stamped on a pad located at the rear of the transaxle on the transaxle oil pan flange. This number must be referred to when servicing the transaxle due to differences in some internal components.

DESCRIPTION

These transaxles combine a torque converter, three speed automatic transaxle, final drive gearing and differential combined into one unit. The torque converter, transaxle and differential assemblies are housed in an integral aluminum diecast housing, **Fig. 1. The differential oil sump is integral with the transaxle sump. Separate filling of the differential is not necessary.**

The torque converter is connected to the crankshaft through a flexible driveplate. Converter cooling is accomplished by an oil-to-water type cooler, located in the radiator side tank. The torque converter cannot be disassembled.

The transaxle consists of two multiple disc clutches, an overrunning clutch, two servos, a hydraulic accumulator, two bands and two planetary gear assemblies to provide three forward and one reverse gear. The sun gear is connected to the front clutch retainer. The hydraulic system consists of an oil pump, and a single valve body which contains all of the valves except the governor valves. Output torque from the main drive gears is transferred through helical gears to the transfer shaft. An integral ring gear on the transfer shaft drives the differential ring gear.

All vehicles except turbocharged models are equipped with a lock-up torque converter. The lock-up mode is activated only in direct drive (3rd gear) and is controlled by the engine control computer. A lock-up solenoid on the valve body transfer plate is powered by the computer to activate torque converter lock-up.

TROUBLESHOOTING

Refer to **Fig. 2,** when troubleshooting transaxle.

MAINTENANCE

FLUID CHECK

To check fluid level, apply the parking brake and operate engine at idle speed with transaxle in N or P position. Add fluid as necessary.

FLUID CHANGE

Fluid and filter changes are not required for average passenger car use. Severe usage such as commercial type usage or prolonged operation in city traffic, requires that fluid be changed and bands adjusted every 15,000 miles.

Whenever the factory fill fluid is changed, only fluids of the type labeled Mopar ATF Plus (Type 9602) should be used. Dexron II automatic transmission fluid should be used only if the recommended fluid is not available.

1. Raise vehicle and place a suitable drain pan under transaxle oil pan.
2. Loosen transaxle oil pan attaching bolts and allow fluid to drain, then remove oil pan.
3. Replace oil filter and adjust bands if necessary, then install oil pan and gasket.
4. Add four quarts of approved automatic transaxle fluid through the filler tube.
5. Start engine and allow to idle for at least two minutes, then with parking

brake applied move selector lever momentarily to each position. Place selector lever in N or P and check fluid level. Add fluid to bring level to Add mark.

6. Recheck fluid level after transaxle has reached operating temperature. The level should be between Add and Full marks.

ADJUSTMENTS

BANDS

Kickdown Band

1. Loosen locknut and back off nut approximately five turns, **Fig. 3.**
2. Ensure adjusting screw turns freely in transaxle case.
3. Using wrench tool No. C-3880-A and adapter tool No. C-3705, or equivalents, **torque** band adjusting screw to 72 inch lbs. If adapter tool No. C-3705 is not used, **torque** adjusting screw to 6 Ft. lbs.
4. Back off adjusting screw 2¼ turns. Tighten locknut to specifications while preventing adjusting screw from turning.

Low-Reverse Band

1. Loosen locknut and back off nut approximately five turns.
2. **Torque** adjusting nut to 41 inch lbs.
3. Back off adjusting nut 3½ turns.
4. Tighten locknut to specifications.

GEARSHIFT LINKAGE

1. Set parking brake, then remove floor console.
2. Place gear selector lever in (P) park position, then unsnap collar at shifter cable.
3. Move gear selector lever on transaxle to park position, then verify that both shifter lever and transaxle are in park position.
4. Rotate collar on shift cable adjuster until it seats against plastic housing, **Fig. 4. Collar must seat against plastic housing to achieve required detent lock position.**
5. Inspect adjustment as follows:
   a. Detent position for neutral and drive should be within limits of hand lever gate stops.
   b. Key start must occur only when shift lever is in neutral or park positions.

THROTTLE PRESSURE LINKAGE

1. Ensure engine is at operating temperature.
2. Release cross-lock on cable assembly by pulling upward.
3. Ensure cable is able to slide freely towards the engine, against its stop.
4. Move transaxle throttle control lever fully clockwise, against its internal stop.
5. Press cross-lock downward into locked position.

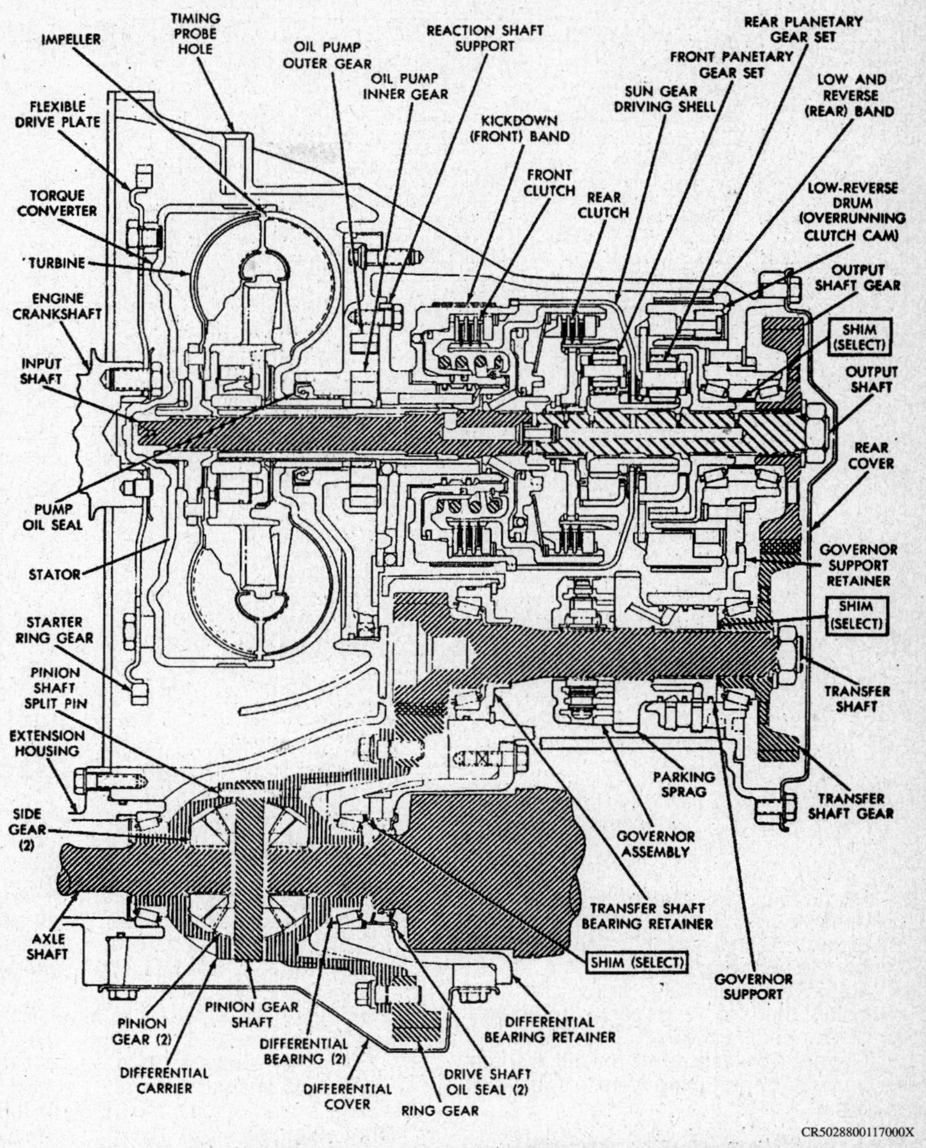

Fig. 1 Cross-sectional view of 31TH automatic transaxle

6. Ensure proper operation of throttle cable.

SHIFT INTERLOCK SYSTEM

1. Remove console assembly.
2. Remove gearshift knob set screw and knob.
3. Remove gearshift indicator bezel and indicator lamp, then install gearshift knob.
4. Place shifter in Park position.
5. **On 1997–99 models,** place ignition in Lock or Accessory position. **If cable is out of adjustment, then grasp slug on interlock cable with a suitable pair of pliers and pull back on cable. This will allow ignition to be placed in position.**
6. Ensure interlock cable is completely seated into shifter interlock lever, then ensure ignition is in Lock or Accessory position.
7. Pry up adjuster lock on interlock cable. **Spring on interlock cable should automatically adjust for slack in cable.**
8. Snap interlock cable adjuster lock onto cable.
9. Remove gearshift knob set screw and knob.
10. **On 2000 models,** adjust interlock cable/system by prying up on cable adjuster lock to release and allow cable to self adjust. Lock cable adjustment by pressing down on adjuster lock until bottomed at cable housing.
11. **On all models,** install indicator lamp, gearshift bezel and gearshift knob.

IN-VEHICLE REPAIRS

VALVE BODY, REPLACE

1. Loosen transaxle oil pan attaching bolts and allow transaxle to drain, then remove oil pan.

CONDITION	POSSIBLE CAUSES	CORRECTION
HARSH ENGAGEMENT (FROM NEUTRAL TO DRIVE OR REVERSE)	1. Fluid Level Low	1. Add Fluid
	2. Throttle Linkage Misadjusted	2. Adjust linkage - setting may be too long.
	3. Excessive Pinion Backlash	3. Correct as needed.
	4. Hydraulic Pressure Incorrect	4. Check pressure. Remove, overhaul or adjust valve body as needed.
	5. Band Misadjusted.	5. Adjust rear band.
	6. Valve Body Check Balls Missing.	6. Inspect valve body for proper check ball installation.
	7. Clutch, band or planetary component Damaged.	7. Remove, disassemble and repair transmission as necessary.
	8. Converter Clutch (if equipped) Faulty.	8. Replace converter and flush cooler and line before installing new converter.
DELAYED ENGAGEMENT (FROM NEUTRAL TO DRIVE OR REVERSE)	1. Fluid Level Low.	1. Correct level and check for leaks.
	2. Filter Clogged.	2. Change filter.
	3. Gearshift Linkage Misadjusted.	3. Adjust linkage and repair linkage if worn or damaged.
	4. Rear Band Misadjusted.	4. Adjust band.
	5. Valve Body Filter Plugged.	5. Replace fluid and filter. If oil pan and old fluid were full of clutch disc material and/or metal particles, overhaul will be necessary.
	6. Oil Pump Gears Worn/Damaged.	6. Remove transmission and replace oil pump.
	7. Hydraulic Pressure Incorrect.	7. Perform pressure test, remove transmission and repair as needed.
	8. Reaction Shaft Seal Rings Worn/Broken.	8. Remove transmission, remove oil pump and replace seal rings.
	9. Rear Clutch/Input Shaft, Rear Clutch Seal Rings Damaged.	9. Remove and disassemble transmission and repair as necessary.
	10. Governor Valve Stuck.	10. Remove and inspect governor components. Replace worn or damaged parts.
	11. Regulator Valve Stuck.	11. Clean.

CR5029901214010X

Fig. 2 Transaxle troubleshooting chart. (Part 1 of 7)

CONDITION	POSSIBLE CAUSES	CORRECTION
NO DRIVE RANGE (REVERSE OK)	1. Fluid Level Low.	1. Add fluid and check for leaks if drive is restored.
	2. Gearshift Linkage/Cable Loose/Misadjusted.	2. Repair or replace linkage components.
	3. Rear Clutch Burnt.	3. Remove and disassemble transmission and rear clutch and seals. Repair/replace worn or damaged parts as needed.
	4. Valve Body Malfunction.	4. Remove and disassemble valve body. Replace assembly if any valves or bores are damaged.
	5. Transmission Overrunning Clutch Broken.	5. Remove and disassemble transmission. Replace overrunning clutch.
	6. Input Shaft Seal Rings Worn/ Damaged.	6. Remove and disassemble transmission. Replace seal rings and any other worn or damaged parts.
	7. Front Planetary Failed Broken.	7. Remove and repair.
NO DRIVE OR REVERSE (VEHICLE WILL NOT MOVE)	1. Fluid Level Low.	1. Add fluid and check for leaks if drive is restored.
	2. Gearshift Linkage/Cable Loose/Misadjusted.	2. Inspect, adjust and reassemble linkage as needed. Replace worn/damaged parts.
	3. Filter Plugged.	3. Remove and disassemble transmission. Repair or replace failed components as needed. Replace filter. If filter and fluid contained clutch material or metal particles, an overhaul may be necessary. Perform lube flow test. Flush oil. Replace cooler as necessary.
	4. Oil Pump Damaged.	4. Perform pressure test to confirm low pressure. Replace pump body assembly if necessary.
	5. Valve Body Malfunctioned.	5. Check press and inspect valve body. Replace valve body (as assembly) if any valve or bore is damaged. Clean and reassemble correctly if all parts are in good condition.
	6. Transmission Internal Component Damaged.	6. Remove and disassemble transmission. Repair or replace failed components as needed. Remove and disassemble transmission. Repair or replace failed components as needed.
	7. Park Sprag not Releasing - Check Stall Speed, Worn/Damaged/Stuck.	7. Remove, disassemble, repair.
	8. Torque Converter Damage.	8. Inspect and replace as required.

CR5029901214020X

Fig. 2 Transaxle troubleshooting chart. (Part 2 of 7)

2. Remove oil filter attaching screws and oil filter.
3. Using a screwdriver, remove E-clip, then the parking rod.
4. Remove seven valve body attaching bolts, then remove valve body and governor oil tubes.
5. Reverse procedure to install. Tighten valve body attaching bolts to specifications.

GOVERNOR & TRANSFER SHAFT OIL SEAL, REPLACE

The governor assembly can be removed for reconditioning or replacement without removing the transfer gear cover, transfer gear and governor support. To remove governor, drain transaxle fluid and remove transaxle oil pan. Remove valve body, unbolt governor from governor support, then remove governor.

When cleaning or assembling the governor assembly, ensure governor valves move freely in governor body bores.

1. Remove rear cover attaching bolts and rear cover.
2. Using transfer shaft gear tool No. L-4434, or equivalent, remove transfer shaft gear retaining nut, **Fig. 5.**
3. Using transfer shaft gear puller tool No. L-4407, or equivalent, remove transfer shaft gear and shim, **Fig. 6.**
4. Remove governor support retainer, then remove low-reverse band anchor pin.
5. Remove governor assembly.
6. Remove transfer shaft retainer snap ring, then using transfer shaft and bearing retainer removal tool No. L-4512, or equivalent, and a suitable puller, remove transfer shaft and retainer assembly.
7. Remove transfer shaft retainer from shaft.
8. Using a screwdriver, remove oil seal from transfer shaft retainer.
9. Using suitable tool, tap oil seal into shaft retainer.
10. Reverse procedure to install. Tighten transfer shaft gear retaining nut to specifications.

SHIFT INTERLOCK CABLE

1. Remove console assembly.
2. Remove gearshift knob set screw and knob.
3. Remove gearshift bezel and indicator lamp.
4. Pry up adjuster lock on interlock cable, remove cable core from plastic cam and release cable from shifter bracket.
5. Pull cable up and out of gearshift assembly.
6. Remove lower steering column cover and liner.
7. Lift top cover and cluster bezel until clips disengage to provide clearance.
8. Place ignition in On position.
9. Insert a screwdriver into access hole in lower shroud and depress cylinder button while rotating cylinder to disengage it from column.
10. Remove upper and lower shrouds.
11. Disconnect interlock cable from interlock assembly, then remove interlock cable.
12. Reverse procedure to install. Adjust interlock cable as described under "Adjustments."

SHIFT INTERLOCK ASSEMBLY

1. Remove lower steering column cover and liner.
2. Lift top cover and cluster bezel until clips disengage to provide clearance.
3. Place ignition in On position.
4. Insert a screwdriver into access hole in lower shroud and depress cylinder button while rotating cylinder to disengage it from column.
5. Remove upper and lower shrouds.
6. Disconnect interlock cable from interlock assembly.
7. Remove interlock assembly mounting screws, then assembly.
8. Reverse procedure to install. **Torque** interlock assembly mounting screws to 21 inch lbs.

TRANSAXLE

REPLACE

The transaxle and converter must be removed as an assembly to prevent damage to the torque converter driveplate, pump bushing and oil seal. **The driveplate will not support a load. Do not allow the weight of the transaxle to rest on the driveplate.**

CONDITION	POSSIBLE CAUSES	CORRECTION
SHIFTS DELAYED OR ERRATIC (ALSO SHIFTS HARSH AT TIMES)	1. Fluid Level Low/High.	1. Correct fluid level and check for leaks if low.
	2. Fluid Filter Clogged.	2. Replace filter. If filter and fluid contained clutch material or metal particles, an overhaul may be necessary. Perform lube flow test.
	3. Throttle Linkage Misadjusted.	3. Adjust linkage as described in service section.
	4. Throttle Linkage Binding.	4. Check cable for binding. Check for return to closed throttle at transmission.
	5. Gearshift Linkage/Cable Misadjusted.	5. Adjust linkage/cable as described in service section.
	6. Governor Valve Sticking.	6. Inspect, clean or repair.
	7. Governor Seal Rings Worn/ Damaged.	7. Inspect/replace.
	8. Clutch or Servo Failure.	8. Remove valve body and air test clutch, and band servo operation. Disassemble and repair transmission as needed.
	9. Front Band Misadjusted.	9. Adjust band.
	10. Pump Suction Passage Leak.	10. Check for excessive foam on dipstick after normal driving. Check for loose pump bolts, defective gasket. Replace pump assembly if needed.
NO REVERSE (D RANGES OK)	1. Gearshift Linkage/Cable Misadjusted/Damaged.	1. Repair or replace linkage parts as needed.
	2. Rear Band Misadjusted/Worn.	2. Adjust band; replace.
	3. Valve Body Malfunction.	3. Remove and service valve body. Replace valve body if any valves or valve bores are worn or damaged.
	4. Rear Servo Malfunction.	4. Remove and disassemble transmission. Replace worn/damaged servo parts as necessary.
	5. Direct Clutch in Overdrive Worn	5. Disassemble overdrive. Replace worn or damaged parts.
	6. Front Clutch Burnt.	6. Remove and disassemble transmission. Replace worn, damaged clutch parts as required.
HAS FIRST/REVERSE ONLY (NO 1-2 OR 2-3 UPSHIFT)	1. Governor Valve, Shaft, Weights or Body Damaged/Stuck.	1. Remove governor assembly and clean or repair as necessary.
	2. Valve Body Malfunction.	2. Stuck 1-2 shift valve or governor plug.
	3. Front Servo/Kickdown Band Damaged/Burned.	3. Repair/replace.
MOVES IN 2ND OR 3RD GEAR, ABRUPTLY DOWNSHIFTS TO LOW	1. Valve Body Malfunction.	1. Remove, clean and inspect. Look for stuck 1-2 valve or governor plug.
	2. Governor Valve Sticking.	2. Remove, clean and inspect. Replace faulty parts.

CR5029901214030X

Fig. 2 Transaxle troubleshooting chart. (Part 3 of 7)

CONDITION	POSSIBLE CAUSES	CORRECTION
NO LOW GEAR (MOVES IN 2ND OR 3RD GEAR ONLY)	1. Governor Valve Sticking.	1. Remove governor, clean, inspect and repair as required.
	2. Valve Body Malfunction.	2. Remove, clean and inspect. Look for sticking 1-2 shift valve, 2-3 shift valve, governor plug or broken springs.
	3. Front Servo Piston Cocked in Bore.	3. Inspect servo and repair as required.
	4. Front Band Linkage Malfunction	4. Inspect linkage and look for bind in linkage.
NO KICKDOWN OR NORMAL DOWNSHIFT	1. Throttle Linkage Misadjusted.	1. Adjust linkage.
	2. Accelerator Pedal Travel Restricted.	2. Floor mat under pedal, accelerator cable worn or brackets bent.
	3. Governor/Valve Body Hydraulic Pressures Too High or Too Low Due to Sticking Governor, Valve Body Malfunction or Incorrect Hydraulic Control Pressure Adjustments.	3. Perform hydraulic pressure tests to determine cause and repair as required. Correct valve body pressure adjustments as required.
	4. Valve Body Malfunction.	4. Perform hydraulic pressure tests to determine cause and repair as required. Correct valve body pressure adjustments as required.
	5. Valve Body Malfunction.	5. Sticking 1-2, 2-3 shift valves, governor plugs, 3-4 solenoid, 3-4 shift valve, 3-4 timing valve.
STUCK IN LOW GEAR (WILL NOT UPSHIFT)	1. Throttle Linkage Misadjusted/ Stuck.	1. Adjust linkage and repair linkage if worn or damaged. Check for binding cable.
	2. Gearshift Linkage Misadjusted.	2. Adjust linkage and repair linkage if worn or damaged.
	3. Governor/Valve Body, Governor Valve Stuck Closed; Loose Output Shaft Support or Governor Housing Bolts, Leaking Seal Rings or Valve Body Problem (i.e., Stuck 1- 2 Shift Valve/Gov. Plug).	3. Check line and governor pressures to determine cause. Correct as required.
	4. Front Band Out of Adjustment.	4. Adjust Band.
	5. Clutch or Servo Malfunction.	5. Air pressure check operation of clutches and bands. Repair faulty component.
CREEPS IN NEUTRAL	1. Gearshift Linkage Misadjusted.	1. Adjust linkage.
	2. Rear Clutch Dragging/Warped Welded.	2. Disassemble and repair.
	3. Valve Body Malfunction.	3. Perform hydraulic pressure test to determine cause and repair as required.

CR5029901214040X

Fig. 2 Transaxle troubleshooting chart. (Part 4 of 7)

1. Pull Power Distribution Center (PDC) up and out of holding bracket. Position PDC aside.
2. Remove battery heat shield, then the battery and battery tray from engine compartment.
3. Disconnect cruise control, if equipped.
4. Disconnect vehicle speed sensor wiring, then the neutral safety switch and torque converter control wiring at transaxle.
5. Disconnect gear shift cable end from transaxle shift lever, then remove bracket bolt at transaxle.
6. Remove throttle pressure control cable from lever, then the bracket bolts at transaxle.
7. Remove dipstick tube.
8. Remove transaxle cooler lines, then plug lines to prevent fluid leakage.
9. Remove throttle pressure control cable support bracket bolts, then the upper bellhousing bolts and upper starter bolt.
10. Install engine bridge fixture and support engine.
11. Raise and support vehicle, then remove front wheels.
12. Remove both front driveshafts. **When reinstalling driveshafts, new driveshaft retaining clips must be used. Failure to use new clips may result in disengagement of inner constant-velocity joint.**
13. Remove exhaust flex joint to exhaust manifold retaining bolts, then disconnect exhaust pipe from manifold.
14. Remove transaxle to rear lateral bending strut from engine and transaxle.
15. Remove lower starter bolt, then the lower dust shield screw.
16. Rotate engine clockwise to gain access to converter bolts, then remove torque converter bolts. Mark converter to flex plate for installation reference.
17. Support transaxle using a suitable transaxle jack.
18. Remove left mount through bolt, then the left mount bolts from transaxle.
19. Remove left transaxle mount from transaxle, then the rear engine bolt at transaxle.
20. Carefully work transaxle and torque converter assembly rearward off engine block dowels, then disengage converter hub from end of crankshaft. **Attach a small C-clamp to edge of bellhousing to hold torque converter in place during transaxle removal.**
21. Reverse procedure to install.

CONDITION	POSSIBLE CAUSES	CORRECTION
BUZZING NOISE	1. Fluid Level Low	1. Add fluid and check for leaks.
	2. Shift Cable Misassembled.	2. Route cable away from engine and bell housing.
	3. Valve Body Misassembled.	3. Remove, disassemble, inspect valve body. Reassemble correctly if necessary. Replace assembly if valves or springs are damaged. Check for loose bolts or screws.
	4. Pump Passages Leaking	4. Check pump for porous casting, scores on mating surfaces and excess rotor clearance. Repair as required. Loose pump bolts.
	5. Cooling System Cooler Plugged.	5. Flow check cooler circuit. Repair as needed.
	6. Overrunning Clutch Damaged.	6. Replace clutch.
SLIPS IN REVERSE ONLY	1. Fluid Level Low.	1. Add fluid and check for leaks.
	2. Gearshift Linkage Misadjusted.	2. Adjust linkage.
	3. Rear Band Misadjusted.	3. Adjust band.
	4. Rear Band Worn.	4. Replace as required.
	5. Hydraulic Pressure Too Low.	5. Perform hydraulic pressure tests to determine cause.
	6. Rear Servo Leaking.	6. Air pressure check clutch-servo operation and repair as required.
	7. Band Linkage Binding.	7. Inspect and repair as required.
SLIPS IN FORWARD DRIVE RANGES	1. Fluid Level Low.	1. Add fluid and check for leaks.
	2. Fluid Foaming.	2. Check for high oil level, bad pump gasket or seals, dirt between pump halves and loose pump bolts. Replace pump if necessary.
	3. Throttle Linkage Misadjusted.	3. Adjust linkage.
	4. Gearshift Linkage Misadjusted.	4. Adjust linkage.
	5. Rear Clutch Worn.	5. Inspect and replace as needed.
	6. Low Hydraulic Pressure Due to Worn Pump, Incorrect Control Pressure Adjustments, Valve Body Warpage or Malfunction, Sticking Governor, Leaking Seal Rings, Clutch Seals Leaking, Servo Leaks, Clogged Filter or Cooler Lines	6. Perform hydraulic and air pressure tests to determine cause.
	7. Rear Clutch Malfunction, Leaking Seals or Worn Plates.	7. Air pressure check clutch-servo operation and repair as required.
	8. Overrunning Clutch Worn, Not Holding (Slips in 1 Only).	8. Replace Clutch.
SLIPS IN LOW GEAR "D" ONLY, BUT NOT IN 1 POSITION	Overrunning Clutch Faulty.	Replace overrunning clutch.

CR5029901214050X

Fig. 2 Transaxle troubleshooting chart. (Part 5 of 7)

CONDITION	POSSIBLE CAUSES	CORRECTION
NO REVERSE (OR SLIPS IN REVERSE)	1. Direct Clutch Pack (front clutch) Worn.	1. Disassemble unit and rebuild clutch pack.
	2. Rear Band Misadjusted.	2. Adjust band.
	3. Front Clutch Malfunctioned/Burnt.	3. Air pressure test clutch operation. Remove and rebuild if necessary.
OIL LEAKS (ITEMS LISTED REPRESENT POSSIBLE LEAK POINTS AND SHOULD ALL BE CHECKED.	1. Fluid Lines and Fittings Loose/ Leaks/Damaged.	1. Tighten fittings. If leaks persist, replace fittings and lines if necessary.
	2. Filler Tube (where tube enters case) Leaks/Damaged.	2. Replace tube seal. Inspect tube for cracks in tube.
	3. Pressure Port Plug Loose Loose/Damaged.	3. Tighten to correct torque. Replace plug or reseal if leak persists.
	4. Pan Gasket Leaks.	4. Tighten pan screws to 150 inch pounds. If leaks persist, replace gasket. Do no over tighten screws.
	5. Valve Body Manual Lever Shaft Seal Leaks/Worn.	5. Replace shaft seal.
	6. Rear Bearing Access Plate Leaks.	6. Replace gasket. Tighten screws.
	7. Gasket Damaged or Bolts are Loose.	7. Replace bolts or gasket or tighten both.
	8. Adapter/Extension Gasket Damaged Leaks/Damaged.	8. Replace gasket.
	9. Neutral Switch Leaks/Damaged.	9. Replace switch and gasket.
	10. Converter Housing Area Leaks.	10. Check for leaks at seal caused by worn seal or burr on converter hub (cutting seal), worn bushing, missing oil return, oil in front pump housing or hole plugged. Check for leaks past O-ring seal on pump or past pump-to-case bolts; pump housing porous, oil coming out vent due to overfill or leak past front band shaft access plug.
	11. Pump Seal Leaks/Worn/ Damaged.	11. Replace seal.
	12. Torque Converter Weld Leak/Cracked Hub.	12. Replace converter.
	13. Case Porosity Leaks.	13. Replace case.

CR5029901214070X

Fig. 2 Transaxle troubleshooting chart. (Part 7 of 7)

CONDITION	POSSIBLE CAUSES	CORRECTION
GROWLING, GRATING OR SCRAPING NOISES	1. Drive Plate Broken.	1. Replace.
	2. Torque Converter Bolts Hitting Dust Shield.	2. Dust shield bent. Replace or repair.
	3. Planetary Gear Set Broken/ Seized.	3. Check for debris in oil pan and repair as required.
	4. Overrunning Clutch Worn/Broken.	4. Inspect and check for debris in oil pan. Repair as required.
	5. Oil Pump Components Scored/ Binding.	5. Remove, inspect and repair as required.
	6. Output Shaft Bearing or Bushing Damaged.	6. Remove, inspect and repair as required.
	7. Clutch Operation Faulty.	7. Perform air pressure check and repair as required.
	8. Front and Rear Bands Misadjusted.	8. Adjust bands.
DRAGS OR LOCKS UP	1. Fluid Level Low.	1. Check and adjust level.
	2. Clutch Dragging/Failed	2. Air pressure check clutch operation and repair as required.
	3. Front or Rear Band Misadjusted.	3. Adjust bands.
	4. Case Leaks Internally.	4. Check for leakage between passages in case.
	5. Servo Band or Linkage Malfunction.	5. Air pressure check servo operation and repair as required.
	6. Overrunning Clutch Worn.	6. Remove and inspect clutch. Repair as required.
	7. Planetary Gears Broken.	7. Remove, inspect and repair as required (look for debris in oil pan).
WHINE/NOISE RELATED TO ENGINE SPEED	1. Fluid Level Low.	1. Add fluid and check for leaks.
	2. Shift Cable Incorrect Routing.	2. Check shift cable for correct routing. Should not touch engine or bell housing.
TORQUE CONVERTER LOCKS UP IN SECOND AND/OR THIRD GEAR	Lockup Solenoid, Relay or Wiring Shorted/Open.	Test solenoid, relay and wiring for continuity, shorts or grounds. Replace solenoid and relay if faulty. Repair wiring and connectors as necessary.
HARSH 1-2 OR 2-3 SHIFTS	Lockup Solenoid Malfunction.	Remove valve body and replace solenoid assembly.
NO START IN PARK OR NEUTRAL	1. Gearshift Linkage/Cable Misadjusted.	1. Adjust linkage/cable.
	2. Neutral Switch Wire Open/Cut.	2. Check continuity with test lamp. Repair as required.
	3. Neutral Switch Faulty.	3. Refer to service section for test and replacement procedure.
	4. Neutral Switch Connect Faulty.	4. Connectors spread open. Repair.
	5. Valve Body Manual Lever Assembly Bent/Worn/Broken.	5. Inspect lever assembly and replace if damaged.

CR5029901214060X

Fig. 2 Transaxle troubleshooting chart. (Part 6 of 7)

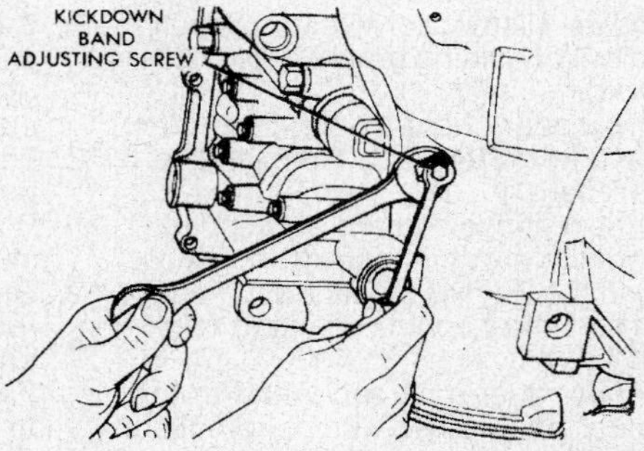

CR5028800122000X

Fig. 3 Kickdown band adjustment

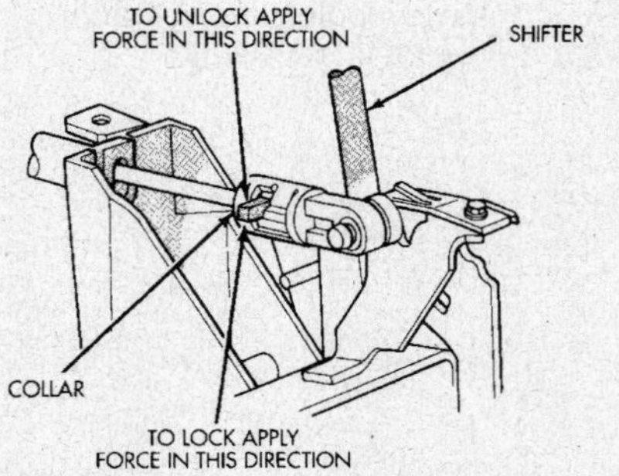

CR5029500770000X

Fig. 4 Gearshift linkage adjustment

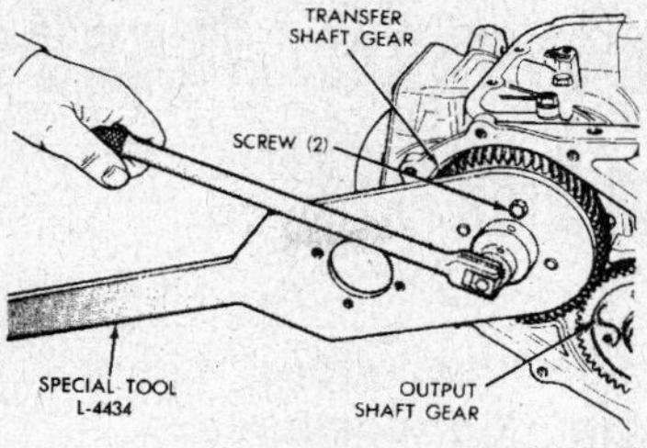

Fig. 5 Transfer shaft gear nut removal

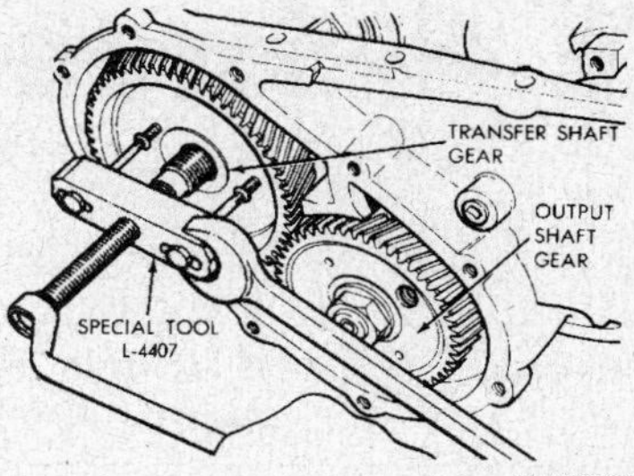

Fig. 6 Transfer shaft gear removal

TIGHTENING SPECIFICATIONS

Component	Torque/Ft. Lbs.
Bellhousing Cover Bolt	108①
Connector Assembly Cooler Line	21
Cooler Hose Connector To Radiator	108①
Differential Bearing Retainer To Case Bolt	21
Differential Cover To Case Screw Assembly	14
Differential Extension Housing To Case Bolt	21
Differential Ring Gear Screw	70
Flexplate To Crankshaft Bolt	70
Flexplate To Torque Converter	50
Front Motor Mount Bolt	40
Governor Counterweight Screw Assembly	21
Governor To Support Bolt	60①
Kickdown Band Adjustment Locknut	35
Left Motor Mount Bolt	40
Low Reverse Band Adjustment Locknut	10
Lower Bellhousing Cover Screw Assembly	30
Manual Cable To Transaxle Case Bolt	21
Manual Control Lever Screw Assembly	108①
Neutral Safety Switch	25
Output Shaft Nut	200
Pressure Check Plug	45①
Pump To Case Bolt Assembly	23
Reaction Shaft Assembly Bolt	21
Rear Cover To Case Screw Assembly	14
Reverse Band Shaft Plug	60①
Speedometer To Extension Screw Assembly	60①
Starter To Transaxle Bellhousing Bolt	40
Throttle Cable To Transaxle Case Bolt	108①
Throttle Lever To Transaxle Shaft Bolt	108①
Transaxle Oil Pan To Case	14
Transaxle To Cylinder Block Screw Assembly	70
Transaxle To Engine Bolts	70
Transfer Shaft Gear Retaining nut	200
Valve Body Attaching Bolts	108①
Valve Body Filter Screw Assembly	45①
Valve Body Reverse Band Adjusting Locknut	10
Valve Body Screw Assembly	45①
Valve Body Sprag Retainer To Transfer Case Bolt	21
Valve Body Transfer Plate Screw Assembly	45①
Valve Body Transfer Plate To Case Screw	108①

① — Inch lbs.

41TE 4-Speed Electronic Automatic Transaxle

NOTE: On Air Bag Equipped Models, Refer To " Air Bag System Precautions" Located In The Front Of This Manual For System Disarming & Arming Procedures.

NOTE: Refer To "Computer Relearn Procedures " Located In The Front Of This Manual For Computer Relearn Procedures.

NOTE: Prior To Performing Any Service Operations Listed In This Section, Consult The "Technical Service Bulletins " Section For Related Information.

INDEX

PRECAUTIONS

AIR BAG SYSTEMS

Refer to "Air Bag System Precautions" in the front of this manual for system disarming and arming procedures.

BATTERY GROUND CABLE

Prior to service, disconnect battery ground cable and isolate as required.

IDENTIFICATION

During production, the transaxle identification number (TIN) is stamped on a boss located on the transaxle housing. In addition to the TIN, each transaxle carries an assembly part No. which is on a pad just above the oil pan at the rear of the transaxle. This assembly number must be referenced when ordering transaxle replacement parts.

DESCRIPTION

The 41TE electronic four speed transaxle is a fully adaptive transaxle. The 41TE transaxle uses feedback sensors to adjust functions on a real time basis, similar to electronic anti-lock brake controls.

The 41TE transaxle provides four forward speeds with ratios of 2.84:1, 1.57:1, 1.00:1 and .069:1, and with torque converter lock-up available in second, direct, or overdrive gear. Reverse ratio is 2.21:1. The 41TE, **Fig. 1,** consists of three multiple disc input clutches, two multiple disc grounded clutches, four hydraulic accumulators and two planetary gear sets to provide four forward speeds and reverse ratio. Electrical solenoids provide the transaxles shifting control. Sensors on the transaxle send control inputs to the electronic control unit located under the hood in a potted, diecast aluminum housing. The system can be diagnosed by accessing information from the electronic control unit memory. The transaxle and differential sump have a common oil sump with a communicating opening between the two.

TROUBLESHOOTING

Before attempting any repair on the 41TE transaxles, general engine performance, transmission fluid level and shift linkage must first be checked and adjusted if necessary. Diagnosis of the Powertrain Control Module (PCM) must also be performed in the following steps: verification of complaint, verification of any related symptoms, symptom analysis, problem isolation, repair of isolated problem and verification of proper operation.

MAINTENANCE

FLUID CHECK

Oil level should be checked every six months. To check oil level, start engine and let idle with transaxle in Park or Neutral for at least one minute. Oil level, when properly filled, will read near the Add mark when oil is cold, (70°F), and in the Hot zone when oil is at normal operating temperature (180°F). Add as necessary.

FLUID CHANGE

Fluid and filter changes are not required for average passenger vehicle usage. If the vehicle is subjected to severe usage, the fluid and filter should be changed at 15,000 mile intervals. The magnet on the inside of the oil pan should also be cleaned with a clean, dry cloth at this time. Fluid and filter change procedure is as follows:

1. Raise vehicle on a suitable hoist and place a wide drain pan container under transaxle oil pan.
2. Loosen pan bolts and tap pan at one corner to break seal and allow fluid to drain, then remove pan.
3. Install new filter and O-ring on bottom of valve body, then clean the oil pan and magnet.
4. Reinstall pan using Mopar Silicone Adhesive sealant and **torque** pan bolts to 13.8 ft. lbs.
5. Add four quarts of Mopar ATF Plus Type 9602 automatic transmission fluid through the fill tube.
6. Start engine and allow to idle for at least one minute, then with parking and service brakes applied, move selector lever through it's range, pausing momentarily at each position. Return lever to P or N position.
7. Add fluid to bring level ⅛ inch below the Add mark. Recheck fluid level after

transaxle is at normal operating temperature.

ADJUSTMENTS

GEARSHIFT LINKAGE

Breeze, Cirrus, Sebring Convertible & Stratus

1. Set parking brake, then remove gearshift knob set screw and knob.
2. Remove gearshift selector bezel and lamp wiring.
3. Install gearshift knob and set screw.
4. Place gearshift in P park position, then loosen gearshift cable adjuster nut at shifter assembly.
5. Ensure shifter and transaxle are in P park position, then tighten nut at shifter assembly.
6. Inspect adjustment as follows:
   a. Detent position for neutral and drive should be with in limits of hand lever gate stops.
   b. Key start must occur only when shift lever is in park or neutral positions.

SHIFT INTERLOCK SYSTEM

1. Remove gearshift knob set screw and knob.
2. Remove floor console assembly.
3. Loosen adjustment nut on interlock lever, then place ignition in On position.
4. Remove interlock cable from shifter housing, then slide cable out of groove in interlock lever.
5. Inspect interlock cable as follows:
   a. With ignition in Off position and key removed, interlock cable should not move.
   b. With ignition in On position cable should slide freely when pulled and return to bottomed out position when released.
   c. If cable does not operate as specified, then cable is improperly installed or kinked.
6. Place shifter in P park position, then slide interlock cable into groove on adjustment lever.
7. Slip cable into housing until it snaps in place, then ensure shift lever remains in P position and remove key from ignition.
8. Loosen interlock cable adjustment nut. **When adjustment nut is loosened cable automatically indexes itself to correct position.**
9. Tighten adjustment nut, then install gearshift knob and set screw.

IN-VEHICLE REPAIRS

SHIFT INTERLOCK CABLE, REPLACE

1. Remove gearshift knob set screw and knob.
2. Remove floor console assembly.
3. Unsnap interlock cable from groove in gearshift lever, then pull cable up and out of gearshift assembly.
4. Remove fuse panel cover from left end of instrument panel, then remove screw holding instrument panel top cover.
5. Remove center bezel, then remove screw holding instrument panel top cover to center of instrument panel.
6. Pull instrument panel top cover up enough to gain access to knee bolster screws.
7. Remove knee bolster screws and knee bolster.
8. Remove screws from lower steering column shroud, then pull lower shroud to clear ignition cylinder.
9. Hold tilt wheel lever down, then slide lower shroud forward and remove.
10. Tilt wheel to full down position and remove upper steering column shroud.
11. Place ignition in On position, then remove interlock cable from interlock housing.
12. Remove interlock cable from underside of instrument panel.
13. Reverse procedure to install. Adjust interlock cable as described in "Adjustments."

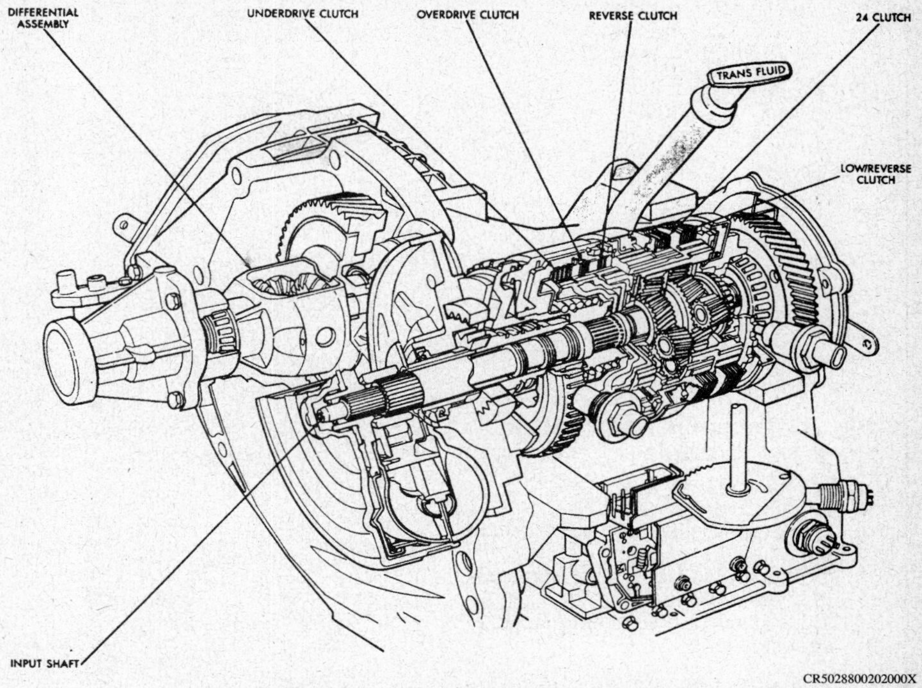

Fig. 1 Cross-sectional view of transaxle

SHIFT INTERLOCK ASSEMBLY, REPLACE

1. Remove fuse panel cover from left end of instrument panel, then remove screw holding instrument panel top cover.
2. Remove center bezel, then remove screw holding instrument panel top cover to center of instrument panel.
3. Pull instrument panel top cover up enough to gain access to knee bolster screws.
4. Remove knee bolster screws and knee bolster.
5. Remove screws from lower steering column shroud, then pull lower shroud to clear ignition cylinder.
6. Hold tilt wheel lever down, then slide lower shroud forward and remove.
7. Tilt wheel to full down position and remove upper steering column shroud.
8. Place ignition in On position, then remove interlock cable from interlock housing.
9. Remove interlock assembly to steering column mounting screws, then remove interlock assembly.
10. Reverse procedure to install. Tighten interlock assembly mounting screws to specifications.

SOLENOID ASSEMBLY, REPLACE

1. Remove air cleaner assembly.
2. Remove Transmission Control Module (TCM) **Fig. 2.**
3. Disconnect and remove input speed sensor **Fig. 3.**
4. Disconnect transmission cooler lines, then capping off fittings.
5. Disconnect and remove solenoid pressure switch assembly connector to transaxle case bolts **Fig. 4.**
6. Remove solenoid pressure switch gasket.
7. Reverse procedures to install.

VALVE BODY, REPLACE

1. Raise and support vehicle.
2. Drain transaxle fluid as described under "Maintenance. "
3. Remove oil pan attaching bolts and oil pan.
4. Remove oil filter, then the valve body attaching bolts.
5. Push park rod rollers from guide bracket, **Fig. 5,** then remove valve body.
6. Reverse procedure to install, noting the following:

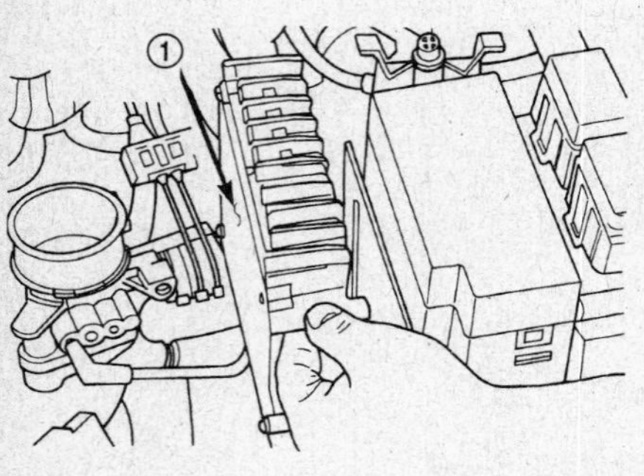

1 – TRANSMISSION CONTROL MODULE

CR5029901213000X

Fig. 2 Transmission control module

a. Guide park rollers into guide bracket.
b. Tighten valve body attaching bolts to specifications.
c. Tighten oil pan attaching bolts to specifications.

TRANSAXLE

REPLACE

BREEZE, CIRRUS, SEBRING CONVERTIBLE & STRATUS

1. Remove air cleaner duct.
2. Remove transaxle control module and wiring, then the solenoid pack connector.
3. Remove dipstick tube and oil cooler lines, then shift cable at lever and at clamp on transaxle.
4. Install engine support fixture, then remove left upper transaxle mounting bolts.
5. Raise and support vehicle, then remove front wheels and both drive shafts.
6. Remove splash shields, then remaining left upper mount bolts.
7. Remove engine oil filter, then starter and wiring.
8. Remove front motor mount bracket, then rear mount bracket through-bolt.
9. Remove center member bolts, then rear mount bracket bolts and rear mount bracket.
10. Remove radiator lower crossmember, then front and rear lateral bending strut brackets.
11. Remove flex plate cover.
12. Rotate lower engine pulley to line up converter bolts, then remove converter bolts. **Mark converter for installation reference.**
13. Remove crank position sensor, if equipped.
14. Remove transaxle wiring, then loosen right side steering gear bolts and right side K-frame bolts.
15. Remove sway bar mounts.
16. Support transaxle with suitable transmission jack and safety chain.

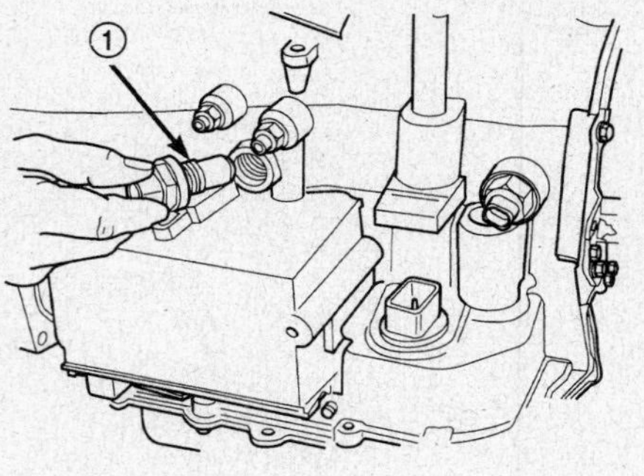

1 – INPUT (TURBINE) SPEED SENSOR

CR5028800206000A

Fig. 3 Input speed sensor removal

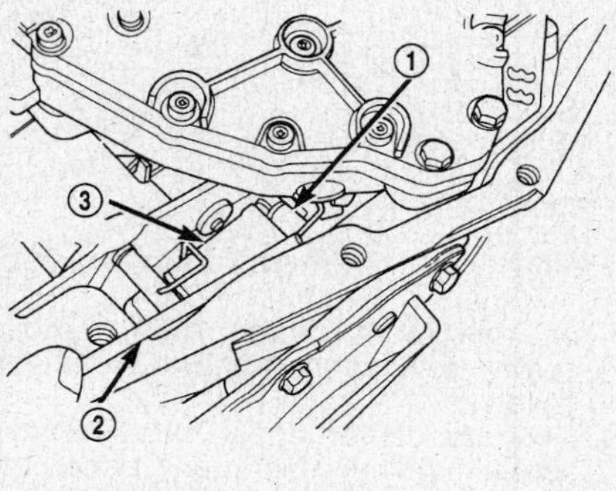

1 – PARK SPRAG ROLLERS
2 – SCREWDRIVER
3 – PARK SPRAG GUIDE BRACKET

CR5028800208000X

Fig. 5 Park rod rollers from guide bracket removal

17. Remove upper and lower bell housing bolts, then move K-frame rearward and lower transaxle assembly from vehicle.
18. Reverse procedure to install.

TECHNICAL SERVICE BULLETINS

TRANSAXLE SHUDDER DURING AN EMCC SHIFT

1997

Some of these transaxles may shudder during a 3rd gear to 3rd gear partial Electronically Modulated Converter Clutch (EMCC) engagement, 3rd gear partial EMCC to 4th gear partial EMCC engagement, or 4th gear to 4th gear EMCC engagement. Vehicle speed will be above 40 mph to obtain these shift points. This condition can be the result of worn out automatic transaxle fluid, using additives in transaxle fluid, or from using the wrong type fluid in transaxle.

To diagnose this condition, bring the vehicle to normal operating temperatures.

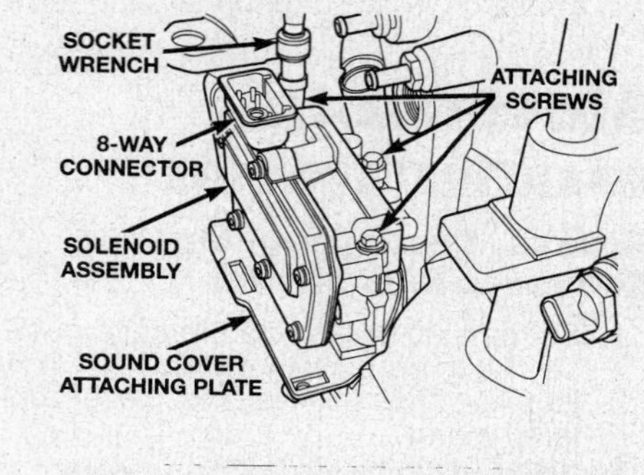

CR5028800207000X

Fig. 4 Solenoid assembly removal

Drive the vehicle on a smooth road while accelerating through the gears with light throttle application. Pay particular attention during the EMCC shifts that take place between 3rd and 4th gears above 40 mph. If vehicle shudder is noticed during the shifts, proceed with the following repair procedure.

1. Raise and support vehicle.
2. Clean transaxle oil pan area and adjoining surfaces.
3. Loosen transaxle oil pan and drain fluid into a suitable container.
4. Remove oil pan and clean all sealant from pan and transaxle mating surfaces.
5. Separate filter and O-ring from valve body. Inspect O-ring for cuts or improper installation.
6. Install a new oil filter and replace O-ring as necessary.
7. Apply a 1/8 inch bead of Mopar RTV sealant 82300234, or equivalent, to mounting flange of transaxle oil pan and to underside of oil pan retaining bolts.
8. Install oil pan to transaxle. Tighten bolts to specification.
9. Lower vehicle and add 4 quarts of Mopar ATF + 2 type 7176 transaxle fluid through fill tube.
10. Start engine and allow it to idle for a minimum of one minute.
11. With parking brake applied, press brake pedal and cycle transaxle from Park to all gear positions ending in Neutral or Park position.
12. Check transaxle fluid level and add appropriate amount to bring level to 1/8 inch below ADD mark on dipstick.
13. Recheck fluid level after transaxle is at normal operating temperature. Level should be in HOT range.
14. Drive vehicle for a minimum of 10 miles, then repeat steps 1 through 4.
15. Separate filter from valve body to allow additional fluid to drain from transaxle, then inspect filter O-ring for any damage and replace as necessary.
16. After transaxle has stopped draining, re-install filter and O-ring.
17. Repeat steps 7 through 13 for reassembly procedure.

DIFFERENTIAL FLUID LEAKAGE

1997-98 Concorde, Intrepid, LHS, New Yorker & Vision

An auxiliary vent tube assembly has been released for service to provide improved differential case venting. In cold climate areas, under certain driving conditions, pressure can build up in the differential case forcing fluid out through the primary vent tube at the top of the differential. Fluid can collect on the top of the differential case and/or drip to the ground.

1. Clean all fluid from the differential case.
2. Drain differential fluid by removing differential drain and fill plugs.
3. Install differential drain plug. **Torque** plug to 5 ft. lbs.
4. Fill differential with 32 ounces of Mopar 75W-90 Gear Lubricant 04549624, or equivalent.
5. Install new differential fill plug from vent tube kit part No. 05011589AA. **Torque** plug to 35 ft. lbs.
6. Install a new vent tube assembly into fill plug and orient tube between ribs on differential cover.

SHIFT SCHEDULE CHANGES/ENHANCEMENTS

On these models, the 4–3 coast down shift point was moved to a higher speed. The speed at which this occurs is 30 mph. The higher coast point allows transaxle to achieve lower gear quicker, thus improving overall performance.

On certain kick down conditions, Electronically Modulated Converter Clutch (EMCC) will be delayed to increase performance. For standard transaxles (non-autostick) after a 4–3 kick down from D to 3, there will be approximately 6 second delay before EMCC is applied. Autostick applications on a 4–3 downshift, there will be approximately a 10 second delay before EMCC application.

TIGHTENING SPECIFICATIONS

Component	Torque/Ft. Lbs.
Cooler Line Fittings	108①
Differential Cover	13–14
Differential Ring Gear	70
Differential Bearing Retainer	21
Driveplate To Crankshaft	70
Driveplate To Torque Converter	55
Extension Housing	21
Input Speed Sensor	20
L/R Clutch Retainer	36–48①
Neutral Safety Switch	25
Oil Pan To Case	14
Output Gear Bolt	200
Output Speed Sensor	20
Pressure Taps	45①
PRNDL Switch	25
Pump To Case	20
Reaction Shaft To Pump	20
Shift Interlock Assembly Mounting Screws	21①
Solenoid Assembly To Case	96–108①
Transfer Gear Nut (1.25 Inch Hex)	200
Transfer Plate To case	96–108①
Valve Body & Transfer Plate	36–48①
Vent Assembly	108①
8-Way Solenoid Connector	36①
60-Way EATX Connector	36①

① — Inch lbs.

42LE 4-Speed Electronic Automatic Transaxle

NOTE: On Air Bag Equipped Models, Refer To " Air Bag System Precautions" Located In The Front Of This Manual For System Disarming & Arming Procedures.

NOTE: Refer To "Computer Relearn Procedures " Located In The Front Of This Manual For Computer Relearn Procedures.

NOTE: Prior To Performing Any Service Operations Listed In This Section, Consult The "Technical Service Bulletins " Section For Related Information.

INDEX

PRECAUTIONS

AIR BAG SYSTEMS

Refer to "Air Bag System Precautions" in the front of this manual for system disarming and arming procedures.

BATTERY GROUND CABLE

Prior to service, disconnect battery ground cable and isolate as required.

IDENTIFICATION

The 42LE four speed transaxle identification code is printed on a bar code label. This label is located on the transaxle case, **Fig. 1.**

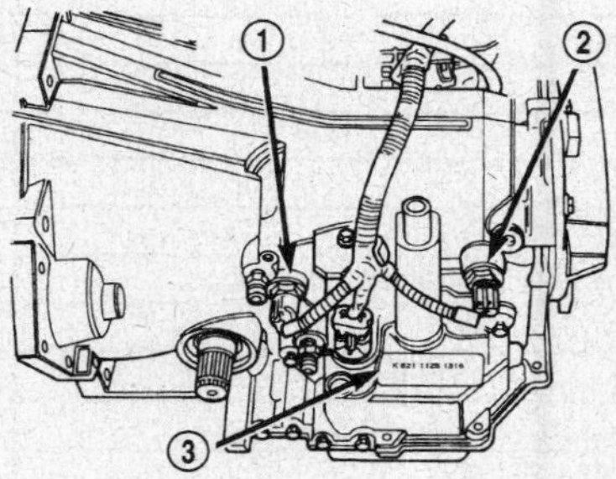

Fig. 1 Transaxle identification tag location

DESCRIPTION

The 42LE transaxle provides forward ratios of 2.84, 1.57, 1.00 and .69 with torque converter clutch available in second, direct or overdrive gear. The reverse ratio is 2.21. The shift lever is conventional with six positions. When overdrive is selected the transaxle shifts normally through all four speeds with the torque converter clutch operational in third and overdrive; this position is recommended for most driving. The third position is tailored for use in hilly or mountainous driving. When third is selected, the transaxle uses only first, second and direct gear with second-direct shift delayed to 40 mph or greater. When operating in third or low positions, torque converter clutch application occurs in direct gear. If high engine coolant temperature occurs, the torque converter clutch will also engage in second gear.

TROUBLESHOOTING

Prior to attempting any repair on the 42LE transaxle, general engine performance, transaxle fluid level and shift linkage must first be checked and adjusted, if necessary. For specific symptom diagnosis, refer to **Figs. 2 through 5.**

MAINTENANCE

FLUID CHECK

With vehicle on level surface, start engine and operate at idle speed for a minimum of one minute. Move selector through all transaxle ranges, then place selector lever in Park position. Remove dipstick and check fluid level. Transaxle should be at operating temperature when checking fluid level (160–180°F). Fluid level should be within the Hot range on dipstick. If necessary, add Mopar ATF Plus (Type 9602) automatic transmission fluid to bring fluid level within the Hot range.

The differential sump is checked separately from the transaxle. A fill plug located on the side of the transaxle must be removed to check fluid level, **Fig. 6.** Fluid should be level with bottom of the fill hole. If necessary, add Mopar petroleum based hypoid gear lubricant 75W-90 to bring level to bottom of fill hole. Synthetic gear lubricants should not be used.

FLUID CHANGE

1. To change transaxle fluid and filter, proceed as follows:
   a. Raise and support vehicle, then

place drain container under transaxle oil pan.

b. Loosen pan bolts and tap pan at one corner to break it loose allowing fluid to drain, then remove oil pan and filter.
c. Install new filter and O-ring on bottom of valve body. Tighten filter mounting bolts to specifications.
d. Clean and install oil pan and magnet. Tighten oil pan bolts to specifications.
e. Install four quarts of Mopar ATF Plus (Type 9602) automatic transmission fluid through dipstick opening.
f. Start engine and allow to idle for at least one minute. With parking and service brakes applied, move selector lever momentarily to each position, ending in Park or Neutral position.
g. **On 1997–98 models,** add fluid to bring level 1/4 inch above bottom hole of dipstick.
h. **On 1999–2000 models,** add fluid to bring level 1/8 inch below the ADD mark on dipstick.
i. **On all models,** recheck fluid level after transaxle has reached normal operating temperature.

2. To change differential fluid, proceed as follows:
   a. Raise and support vehicle.
   b. Remove differential drain plug located on the bottom of the differential housing. Allow fluid to drain into suitable container.
   c. Remove differential fill plug located on differential side cover.
   d. Install drain plug and tighten to specifications.
   e. Fill differential with Mopar petroleum based hypoid gear lubricant 75W-90. Fluid should be level with bottom of fill hole. Differential capacity is approximately 32 ounces.
   f. Install fill plug and tighten to specifications.

ADJUSTMENTS

GEARSHIFT LINKAGE

COLUMN SHIFT

1. Remove upper steering column shroud, then rotate cable adjuster into unlock position.
2. Ensure transaxle shift lever (at transaxle) is in the Park position.
3. Tilt steering column to full down position, then place shifter in Park position with key removed.
4. Adjust by rotating adjuster to lock position.
5. Install upper steering column shroud.
6. Check shifter for proper operation. Vehicle should start in Park or Neutral only.

FLOOR SHIFT

1. Remove shifter handle and console bezel, then loosen nut on shifter cable adjuster.

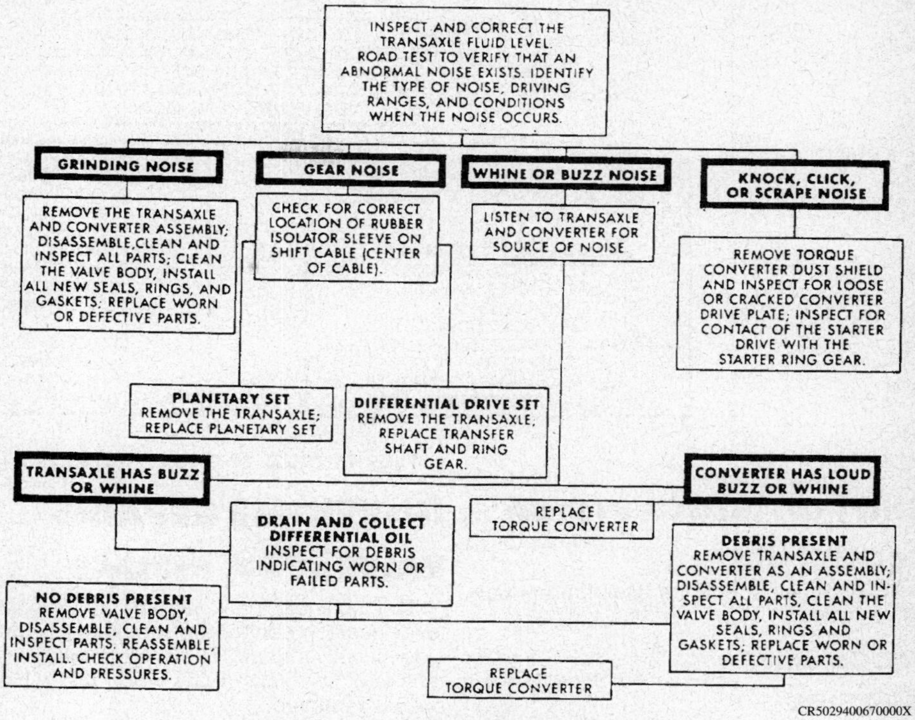

Fig. 2 Abnormal noise diagnosis

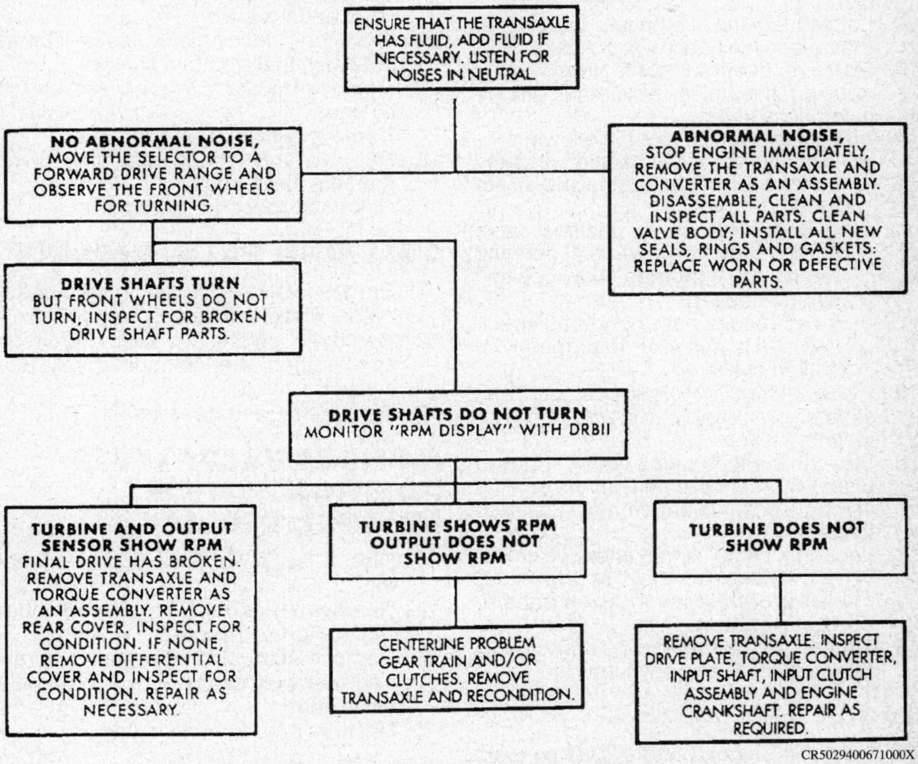

Fig. 3 Vehicle will not move diagnosis

2. Set shift lever assembly in Park (most rearward) position at transaxle.
3. Place shifter in Park position, then place ignition in lock with key removed.
4. Tighten adjuster nut at shifter.
5. Install console bezel and shifter handle.
6. Check shifter for proper operation. Vehicle should start in Park or Neutral only.

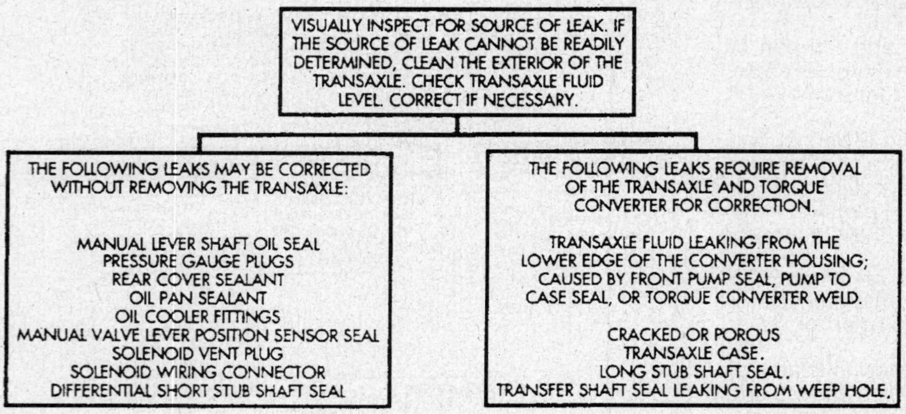
VISUALLY INSPECT FOR SOURCE OF LEAK. IF THE SOURCE OF LEAK CANNOT BE READILY DETERMINED, CLEAN THE EXTERIOR OF THE TRANSAXLE. CHECK TRANSAXLE FLUID LEVEL. CORRECT IF NECESSARY.
THE FOLLOWING LEAKS MAY BE CORRECTED WITHOUT REMOVING THE TRANSAXLE:
MANUAL LEVER SHAFT OIL SEAL
PRESSURE GAUGE PLUGS
REAR COVER SEALANT
OIL PAN SEALANT
OIL COOLER FITTINGS
MANUAL VALVE LEVER POSITION SENSOR SEAL
SOLENOID VENT PLUG
SOLENOID WIRING CONNECTOR
DIFFERENTIAL SHORT STUB SHAFT SEAL
THE FOLLOWING LEAKS REQUIRE REMOVAL OF THE TRANSAXLE AND TORQUE CONVERTER FOR CORRECTION.
TRANSAXLE FLUID LEAKING FROM THE LOWER EDGE OF THE CONVERTER HOUSING; CAUSED BY FRONT PUMP SEAL, PUMP TO CASE SEAL, OR TORQUE CONVERTER WELD.
CRACKED OR POROUS TRANSAXLE CASE.
LONG STUB SHAFT SEAL.
TRANSFER SHAFT SEAL LEAKING FROM WEEP HOLE.

CR5029400672000X

Fig. 4 Fluid leak diagnosis

SHIFT INTERLOCK SYSTEM

COLUMN SHIFT

Adjust column shift as described under "In-Vehicle Repairs."

FLOOR SHIFT

1997-99

1. Remove gearshift knob and console bezel.
2. Loosen locking clip on interlock cable, then place ignition in On position.
3. Remove interlock cable from shifter housing, then slide cable out of groove in interlock lever.
4. Inspect interlock cable as follows:
   a. With ignition in Off position and key removed, interlock cable should not move.
   b. With ignition in On position cable should slide freely when pulled and return to bottomed out position when released.
   c. If cable does not operate as specified, then cable is improperly installed or kinked.
5. Place shifter in P park position, then slide interlock cable into groove on adjustment lever.
6. Slip cable into housing until it snaps in place, then ensure shift lever remains in P park position and remove key from ignition.
7. Loosen locking clip on interlock cable. **When adjustment nut is loosened cable automatically indexes itself to correct position.**
8. Tighten adjustment nut, then install gearshift knob and set screw.

2000

1. Remove shifter handle and console bezel.
2. Move gear shifter to PARK and ignition key to LOCK position. **Fig. 7.**
3. If interlock cable is replaced, remove pin to allow cable to self adjust. **Fig. 8.**
4. If interlock cable is not being replaced, loosen locking clip **Fig. 8,** on interlock cable to allow cable to self adjust. Press locking clip to secure adjustment.

IN-VEHICLE REPAIRS

VALVE BODY, REPLACE

The solenoid pack and manual valve lever position sensor are mounted on top side of valve body. They will remain attached to the valve body when the valve body is removed.

1. Disconnect MVLPS/TRS wiring connector, then the shift cable from shift lever at transaxle.
2. Move shift lever clockwise as far as possible, then remove shift lever.
3. Remove transaxle pan bolts, then the oil pan.
4. Remove oil filter from valve body.
5. Remove valve body attaching bolts, then the valve body.
6. Reverse procedure to install.

SOLENOID PACK, REPLACE

1. Remove valve body as outlined under "Valve Body, Replace."
2. Remove solenoid pack retaining screw, then the solenoid pack and screen.
3. Reverse procedure to install.

MANUAL VALVE LEVER POSITION SENSOR (MVLPS), REPLACE

1. Disconnect MVLPS electrical connector.
2. Remove valve body as outlined under "Valve Body, Replace."
3. Remove manual shaft retaining screw and seal, then slide MVLPS off manual valve shaft.
4. Reverse procedure to install.

TRANSMISSION RANGE SENSOR (TRS), REPLACE

1. Disconnect TRS electrical connector.
2. Remove valve body as outlined under "Valve Body, Replace."
3. Remove manual shaft retaining screw and seal, then slide TRS off manual valve shaft.
4. Reverse procedure to install.

INPUT SPEED SENSOR, REPLACE

1. Disconnect electrical connector from input speed sensor. Ensure weather seal stays attached to connector.
2. Unscrew and remove sensor from transaxle.
3. Inspect speed sensor O-ring, replace if necessary.
4. Reverse procedure to install. Tighten sensor to specifications.

OUTPUT SPEED SENSOR, REPLACE

1. Disconnect electrical connector from output speed sensor. Ensure weather seal stays attached to connector.
2. Unscrew and remove sensor from transaxle.
3. Inspect speed sensor O-ring, replace if necessary.
4. Reverse procedure to install. Tighten sensor to specifications.

SHORT (RIGHT) STUB SHAFT SEAL, REPLACE

1. Place vehicle in Neutral position, then raise and support vehicle.
2. Remove short driveshaft, then place alignment mark on outer adjuster and housing.
3. Remove outer adjuster lock.
4. Using tool No. 6503, or equivalent, loosen outer adjuster, then retighten to alignment mark using a torque wrench. Record amount of torque required to return alignment marks to their original location. Remove adjuster.
5. Using press and seal remover tool No. 6558, or equivalent, replace oil seal.
6. Inspect stub shaft for corrosion.
7. Lubricate O-ring, threads on adjuster, seal protector and seal lips with gear oil.
8. Install outer adjuster into transaxle case. **Torque** adjuster to within 10 ft. lbs. of torque reading recorded in step 4.
9. Rotate ring gear four revolutions in both directions to seat differential bearings.
10. Continue tightening outer adjuster until

POSSIBLE CAUSE / CONDITION	HARSH ENGAGEMENT FROM NEUTRAL TO D	R	DELAYED ENGAGEMENT FROM NEUTRAL TO D	R	POOR SHIFT QUALITY	SHIFTS ERRATIC	DRIVES IN NEUTRAL	DRAGS OR LOCKS	GRATING, SCRAPING, GROWLING NOISE	ENGINE MISFIRE	BUZZING NOISE	BUZZING NOISE DURING SHIFTS ONLY	HARD TO FILL OIL BLOWS OUT FILLER TUBE	TRANSAXLE OVERHEATS	HARSH UPSHIFT	NO UPSHIFT INTO OVERDRIVE	NO TORQUE CONVERTER CLUTCH	HARSH DOWNSHIFTS	HIGH SHIFT EFFORTS	HARSH CONVERTER CLUTCH
Engine Performance	X	X				X									X			X		
Worn or faulty clutch(es)	X	X	X	X		X	X	X							X	X		X		
— Underdrive clutch	X		X			X	X	X										X		
— Overdrive clutch						X	X	X							X	X				
— Reverse clutch		X		X			X	X												
— 2/4 clutch						X		X							X			X		
— Low/reverse clutch	X	X				X		X										X		
Clutch(es) dragging							X													
Insufficient clutch plate clearance							X							X						
Damaged clutch seals			X	X														X		
Worn or damaged accumulator seal ring(s)	X	X	X	X														X		
Faulty cooling system														X						
Engine coolant temp. too low																X	X			
Incorrect gearshift control linkage adjustment			X	X		X	X							X						
Shift linkage damaged																			X	
Chipped or damaged gear teeth								X	X											
Planetary gear sets broken or seized								X	X											
Bearings worn or damaged								X	X											
Driveshaft(s) bushing(s) worn or damaged									X											
Worn or broken reaction shaft support seal rings			X	X	X	X												X		
Worn or damaged input shaft seal rings			X	X													X			
Valve body malfunction or leakage	X	X	X	X	X	X	X				X						X	X	X	
Hydraulic pressures too low			X	X	X	X								X	X		X			
Hydraulic pressures too high	X	X													X			X		
Faulty oil pump			X	X		X								X			X			
Oil filter clogged			X	X	X	X							X							
Low fluid level			X	X	X	X					X			X			X	X		
High fluid level													X	X						
Aerated fluid			X	X	X	X					X		X	X			X	X		
Engine idle speed too low			X	X																
Engine idle speed too high	X	X												X				X		
Normal solenoid operation												X								
Solenoid sound cover loose												X								
Sticking torque converter clutch position																				X
Torque Converter Failure	X													X			X			X
Drive Plate cracked or bent									X	X										

CR5029400673000X

Fig. 5 Symptom diagnosis chart

alignment marks line up in there original location, then install adjuster lock.

11. Install new driveshaft retaining circlip and O-ring on stub shaft, then the driveshaft.
12. Check fluid level in differential. Adjust as necessary.

SHIFT INTERLOCK SYSTEM

COLUMN SHIFT

The interlock cassette slides into the housing behind the lock cylinder and the cable at the rear of the cassette attaches to a locking arm on the shifter assembly. **The column shift interlock system is adjusted only after installing a new cassette. It can not be adjusted more than once. If the system operates incorrectly, install and adjust a new interlock cassette.**

Removal

1. Remove steering column upper and lower cover.
2. Depress tab on top of cassette.
3. Slide interlock cassette out of housing.
4. Remove cable from locking arm on shifter assembly.

Installation

1. Ensure latch rotates freely on shifter gate.
2. Place shifter in P position, then install cable over hook on locking arm of shifter assembly.
3. Slide cassette into housing until it locks into place.
4. Push adjustment tab in until it stops. **Tab will click as it moves into position. Ensure tab is fully depressed.**
5. Install steering column upper and lower covers.

FLOOR SHIFT

1. Remove gearshift knob.
2. Remove bezel from shifter console, then remove driver side under panel.
3. Remove tilt lever attaching screw, then remove tilt lever.
4. Remove upper and lower steering column covers, then loosen locking clip on interlock cable.
5. Remove ignition key, then remove interlock cable from shifter housing sliding cable out of groove in interlock lever.
6. **On 2000 models,** remove Brake Transmission Shift Interlock (BTSI) solenoid connector.
7. **On all models,** remove interlock cable

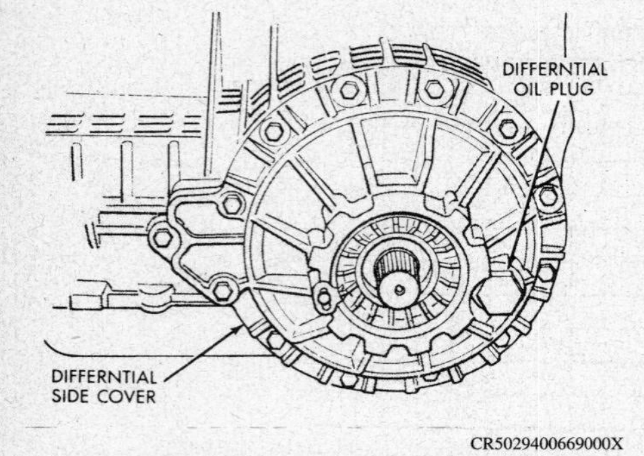

Fig. 6 Differential oil fill plug location

from lock cylinder, then remove interlock cable.

8. Reverse procedure to install. Adjust interlock cable as described under "Adjustments."

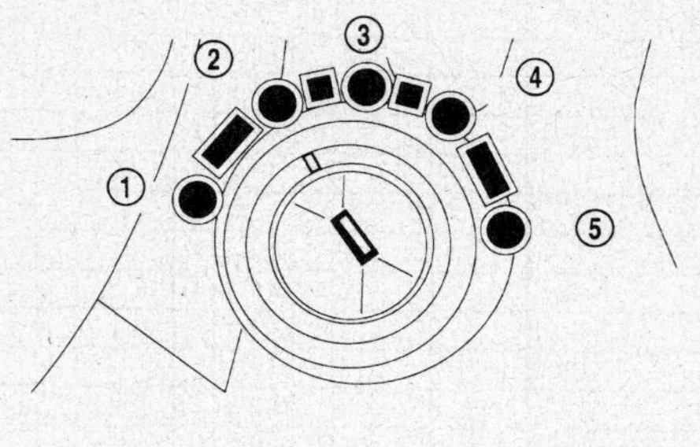

Fig. 7 Ignition key switch points. 2000

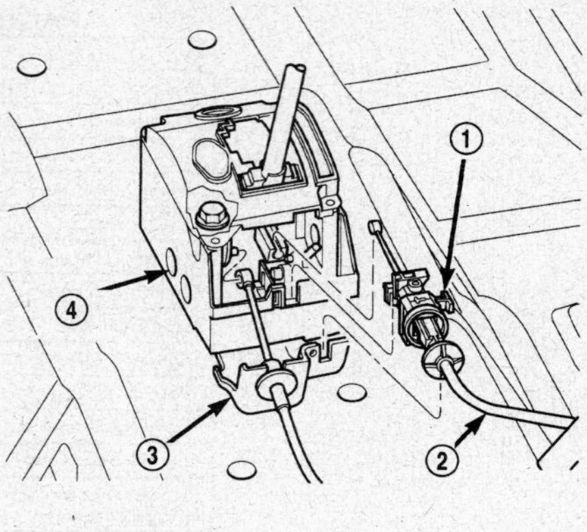

Fig. 8 Interlock cable assembly. 2000

TRANSAXLE

REPLACE

1997

1. Remove air inlet tube.
2. Disconnect crankshaft position sensor connector, then remove sensor. Sensor is located on upper right side of transaxle bellhousing.
3. Disconnect transaxle wiring connector located on right shock tower.
4. Raise and support vehicle, then remove front wheels.
5. Remove strut to steering knuckle bolts on both sides of vehicle.
6. Remove ABS wheel speed sensor, if equipped.
7. Using pry bar, disconnect inner CV joint from transaxle.
8. Pull top of knuckle and driveshaft outward to allow clearance during removal. Do not allow inner CV joint to hang unsupported.
9. Remove engine to transaxle brackets, then the bellhousing cover.
10. Place alignment mark on torque converter and flex plate, then remove torque converter bolts.
11. Remove starter attaching bolts, then the starter and position aside.
12. Disconnect transaxle cooler lines at transaxle, then the gear selector cable from transaxle.
13. Disconnect exhaust system at manifolds, then remove exhaust system.
14. Place and secure transmission jack under transaxle, then slightly raise transaxle to relieve weight on rear transaxle mount.
15. Remove transaxle mount through bolt, then the rear crossmember mounting bolts.
16. Pry transaxle mount rearward to separate mount from transaxle.
17. Remove rear crossmember, then lower rear of transaxle to gain access to bellhousing bolts.
18. Remove bellhousing bolts, then the dipstick tube from transaxle.
19. Remove engine to transaxle bolts, then the transaxle from vehicle.
20. Reverse procedure to install. Adjust gearshift cable if necessary.

1998–2000

1. Remove wiper blades, then the right and left wiper module covers.
2. Remove steel cowl/strut support.
3. Remove engine air inlet tube.
4. Remove transaxle harness connectors at cowl area.
5. Remove upper bell housing stud nuts from bell housing studs, then disconnect heater hose tube and throttle body support bracket.
6. Remove upper bell housing studs.
7. Raise and support vehicle.
8. Loosen clamps at intersection of rear exhaust system to front catalytic converter pipes, then separate rear exhaust from left catalytic converter pipe and right extension pipe.
9. Remove rear exhaust system, then the exhaust pipes to transmission mount retaining nuts.
10. Loosen clamp at right extension at right catalytic converter, then remove right extension.
11. Disconnect crankshaft position sensor connector, then remove sensor.
12. Remove dipstick tube.
13. Disconnect gear selector cable from transaxle.
14. Disconnect transmission range sensor connector, then the input and output speed sensor connector.
15. Disconnect and plug transaxle cooler lines at transaxle.
16. Remove lower control arm pinch bolts, then pry lower control arms down and out of steering knuckles. **Do not allow drive shaft or CV joint to hang freely. Internal joint damage may occur.**
17. Using a pry bar, disconnect inner tripod joints from transaxle.
18. Pull bottom of knuckles and drive shafts outward to allow clearance during transaxle removal. Drive shafts do not have to be completely removed from vehicle.
19. Disconnect oxygen sensor wiring, then remove left catalytic converter pipe.
20. Remove starter retaining bolts, then place starter between engine and frame.
21. Remove engine oil pan collar.
22. Remove torque converter bolts. Torque converter is indexed to flex plate. Mark torque converter location to ensure converter is installed correctly. **Driveplate to torque converter bolts and driveplate to crankshaft bolts must not be reused.**
23. Place a suitable transmission jack under transaxle, then secure it to jack.
24. Raise transaxle slightly to relieve weight on rear transaxle mount.
25. Remove rear crossmember bridge bolts, then the rear mount adapter plate retaining bolts.
26. Remove rear crossmember bridge, mount and adapter plate as an assembly, then lower rear of transaxle to gain access to bell housing bolts.
27. Remove side bell housing bolts, then the dipstick tube from transaxle. **Be prepared to plug dipstick hole when removing dipstick to prevent fluid from spilling out of transaxle.**
28. Remove connector on top of transaxle for solenoid pack, then the transaxle from vehicle.
29. Reverse procedure to install.

TECHNICAL SERVICE BULLETINS

TRANSAXLE SHUDDER DURING AN EMCC SHIFT

1997

Some of these transaxles may shudder during a 3rd gear to 3rd gear partial Electronically Modulated Converter Clutch (EMCC) engagement, 3rd gear partial EMCC to 4th gear partial EMCC engagement, or 4th gear to 4th gear EMCC engagement. Vehicle speed will be above 40 mph to obtain these shift points. This condition can be the result of worn out automatic transaxle fluid, using additives in transaxle fluid, or from using the wrong type fluid in transaxle.

To diagnose this condition, bring the vehicle to normal operating temperatures. Drive the vehicle on a smooth road while accelerating through the gears with light throttle application. Pay particular attention during the EMCC shifts that take place between 3rd and 4th gears above 40 mph. If vehicle shudder is noticed during the shifts, proceed with the following repair procedure.

1. Raise and support vehicle.
2. Clean transaxle oil pan area and adjoining surfaces.
3. Loosen transaxle oil pan and drain fluid into a suitable container.
4. Remove oil pan and clean all sealant from pan and transaxle mating surfaces.
5. Separate filter and O-ring from valve body. Inspect O-ring for cuts or improper installation.
6. Install a new oil filter and replace O-ring as necessary.
7. Apply a 1/8 inch bead of Mopar RTV sealant 82300234, or equivalent, to mounting flange of transaxle oil pan and to underside of oil pan retaining bolts.
8. Install oil pan to transaxle. Tighten bolts to specification.
9. Lower vehicle and add 4 quarts of Mopar ATF + 2 type 7176 transaxle fluid through fill tube.
10. Start engine and allow it to idle for a minimum of one minute.
11. With parking brake applied, press brake pedal and cycle transaxle from Park to all gear positions ending in Neutral or Park position.
12. Check transaxle fluid level and add appropriate amount to bring level to 1/8 inch below ADD mark on dipstick.
13. Recheck fluid level after transaxle is at normal operating temperature. Level should be in HOT range.
14. Drive vehicle for a minimum of 10 miles, then repeat steps 1 through 4.
15. Separate filter from valve body to allow additional fluid to drain from transaxle, then inspect filter O-ring for any damage and replace as necessary.
16. After transaxle has stopped draining, re-install filter and O-ring.
17. Repeat steps 7 through 13 for reassembly procedure.

DIFFERENTIAL FLUID LEAKAGE

1997-98 Concorde, Intrepid, LHS, New Yorker & Vision

An auxiliary vent tube assembly has been released for service to provide improved differential case venting. In cold climate areas, under certain driving conditions, pressure can build up in the differential case forcing fluid out through the primary vent tube at the top of the differential. Fluid can collect on the top of the differential case and/or drip to the ground.

1. Clean all fluid from the differential case.
2. Drain differential fluid by removing differential drain and fill plugs.
3. Install differential drain plug. **Torque** plug to 5 ft. lbs.
4. Fill differential with 32 ounces of Mopar 75W-90 Gear Lubricant 04549624, or equivalent.
5. Install new differential fill plug from vent tube kit part No. 05011589AA. **Torque** plug to 35 ft. lbs.
6. Install a new vent tube assembly into fill plug and orient tube between ribs on differential cover.

SHIFT SCHEDULE CHANGES/ENHANCEMENTS

1998 Concorde & Intrepid

On these models, the 4–3 coast down shift point was moved to a higher speed. The speed at which this occurs is 30 mph. The higher coast point allows transaxle to achieve lower gear quicker, thus improving overall performance.

On certain kick down conditions, Electronically Modulated Converter Clutch (EMCC) will be delayed to increase performance. For standard transaxles (non-autostick) after a 4–3 kick down from D to 3, there will be approximately 6 second delay before EMCC is applied. Autostick applications on a 4–3 downshift, there will be approximately a 10 second delay before EMCC application.

TIGHTENING SPECIFICATIONS

Component	Torque/Ft. Lbs.
Adjuster Lock Bracket Screws	45①
Cooler Line Connector	13
Differential Cover To Case	21
Differential Drain Plug	60①
Differential Fill Plug	35
Driveplate To Crankshaft Bolts	75
End Cover To Case Screw	21
Filter Retainer	45①
Input Sensor To Case	20
Manual Lever To Valve Body	45①
Oil Pan To Case Screw	14
Output Sensor To Case	20
Output Shaft Stake Nut	200
Park Sprag Retention Screw	45①
Pressure Check Plug (Wet)	53①
Pump To Case Bolt	22
Solenoid Assembly To Transfer Plate	53①
Solenoid Wiring Connector Retainer	53①
Torque Converter To Driveplate	60
Transfer Plate To Case	108①
Valve Body Screw	45①
Wiring Harness Tie Down Bolt	53①

① — Inch lbs.

FRONT WHEEL DRIVE AXLES

TABLE OF CONTENTS

Application Chart

Model	Year	Type No.
Avenger	1997–2000	1
Breeze	1997–2000	2
Cirrus	1997–2000	2
Concorde	1997–2000	2
Intrepid	1997–2000	2
LHS	1997–2000	2
Neon	1997–2000	2
Sebring Convertible	1997–2000	2
Sebring Coupe	1997–2000	1
Stratus	1997–2000	2
Talon	1997–98	1
Vision	1997	2
300M	1999–2000	2

Type 1

INDEX

DRIVESHAFT

REPLACE

AVENGER & SEBRING COUPE

2.0L Engine

Do not apply vehicle load to the wheel bearing after removal of the driveshaft. If a load must be applied to the bearing in moving the vehicle, temporarily secure bearing with stub axle replacement tool No. MB-990998, or equivalent, Fig. 1.

1. Remove center cap and drive axle nut.
2. Raise and support vehicle, then remove front wheel.
3. Disconnect tie rod end connection, stabilizer link connection and compression lateral lower arm using steering linkage puller tool No. MB-991113, or equivalent.
4. Insert a suitable pry bar between transaxle case and outer case of double offset joint, then withdraw drive axle, **Fig. 2.** Cover drive axle opening in transaxle. **Pry bar should not be inserted deeply between transaxle case and joint, as damage to oil seal may result.**
5. Reverse procedure to install. Position drive axle so raised inner diameter of washer is facing nut, then install and tighten drive axle nut to specifications.

2.5L Engine

Do not apply vehicle load to wheel bearing after removal of the driveshaft. If a load must be applied to the bearing in moving the vehicle, temporarily secure bearing with stub axle replacement tool No. MB-990998, or equivalent, Fig. 1.

1. Remove center cap and drive axle nut.
2. Raise and support vehicle, then remove front wheel.
3. Disconnect tie rod end connection, stabilizer link connection and compression lateral lower arm using steering linkage puller tool No. MB-991113, or equivalent.
4. When removing righthand driveshaft, lightly tap center bearing bracket with a plastic hammer and disconnect driveshaft and inner shaft from transaxle.
5. When removing lefthand driveshaft, insert a suitable pry bar to projecting part of driveshaft, then withdraw drive axle, **Fig. 2.** Cover drive axle opening in transaxle.
6. Reverse procedure to install. Tighten drive axle nut to specifications.

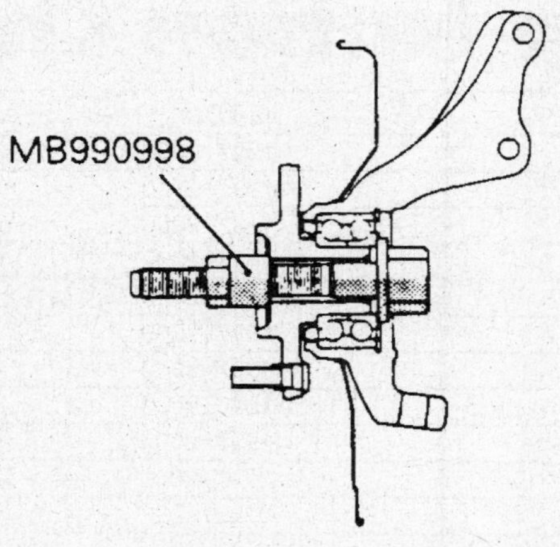

Fig. 1 Wheel bearing support tool installation

TALON

All Wheel Drive (AWD)

Do not apply vehicle load to wheel bearing after removal of the driveshaft. If a load must be applied to bearing in moving the vehicle, temporarily secure bearing with stub axle replacement tool No. MB-990998, or equivalent, Fig. 1.

1. Remove center cap and drive axle nut.
2. Raise and support vehicle, then remove front wheel.
3. Disconnect tie rod end connection, stabilizer link connection and compression lateral lower arm using steering linkage puller tool No. MB-991113, or equivalent.
4. When removing lefthand driveshaft, lightly tap center bearing bracket with a plastic hammer and disconnect driveshaft and inner shaft from transaxle.
5. When removing righthand driveshaft, insert a suitable pry bar to projecting part of driveshaft, then withdraw drive axle, **Fig. 2.** Cover drive axle opening in transaxle.
6. Reverse procedure to install. Tighten drive axle nut to specifications.

Front Wheel Drive (FWD)

Do not apply vehicle load to wheel bearing after removal of the driveshaft. If a load must be applied to the bearing in moving the vehicle, temporarily secure bearing with stub axle replacement tool No. MB-990998, or equivalent, Fig. 1.

1. Remove center cap and drive axle nut.
2. Raise and support vehicle, then remove front wheel.
3. Disconnect tie rod end connection, stabilizer link connection and compression lateral lower arm using steering linkage puller tool No. MB-991113, or equivalent.
4. Insert a suitable pry bar between transaxle case and outer case of double offset joint, then withdraw drive axle, **Fig. 2.** Cover drive axle opening in transaxle. **Pry bar should not be inserted deeply between transaxle case and joint, as damage to oil seal may result.**
5. Reverse procedure to install. Position drive axle so raised inner diameter of washer is facing nut, then install and Tighten drive axle nut to specifications.

DRIVESHAFT SERVICE

AVENGER, SEBRING COUPE & TALON w/FRONT WHEEL DRIVE (FWD)

DOUBLE OFFSET JOINT TYPE

When servicing the drive axle, do not disassemble the Birfield bell type or Rzeppa type constant velocity joint, as components on this type joint are precision fitted and are replaced only as a unit.

Disassemble

1. Remove Double Offset Joint (DOJ) boot bands, then remove circlip using a suitable screwdriver, **Fig. 3.**
2. Remove DOJ outer race from DOJ joint assembly.
3. Remove snap ring, then remove DOJ inner race, cage and balls as an assembly. Clean bearing assembly without disassembling them.
4. Wind tape around drive axle splines, then remove DOJ and Birfield joint boot band and slide boots from drive axle. When inspecting Birfield joint, note amount of grease removed for reassembly.

Assemble

A special grease containing Molybdenum is used to lubricate the drive axle double offset joint and the Birfield joint. This special grease is included in the drive axle repair kit and must be used.

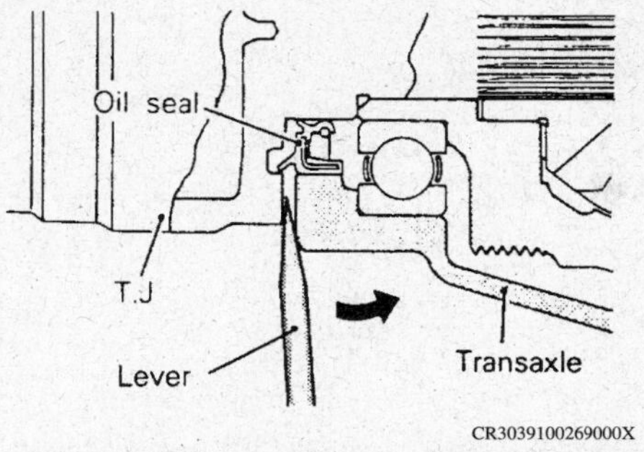

Fig. 2 Front drive axle removal

1. Wrap tape around drive axle splines to prevent damage to boots, then install Birfield joint and DOJ boots.
2. Apply special grease to DOJ joint assembly.
3. Install DOJ joint assembly on drive axle with chamfered side of cage facing splined end of shaft, then install snap ring.
4. Apply 1.4–2.1 ounces of special molybdenum grease to double offset joint outer race, then position outer race on drive axle.
5. Apply an additional .7–1.4 ounce of special molybdenum grease to DOJ boot, then install clip.
6. Add amount of special molybdenum grease to Birfield joint as removed during disassembly and inspection.
7. Install boots and boot bands for each joint. When installing boot bands for DOJ, position bands, **Fig. 4,** so dimension "A" is 3.5 inches on two wheel drive models or 3.3 inches on four wheel drive models.

TRIPOD JOINT TYPE DRIVESHAFT

When servicing the drive axle, do not disassemble the Birfield bell type or Rzeppa type constant velocity joint, as components of this type joint are precision fitted and are replaced only as a unit.

Disassemble

1. Remove boot clamps, then remove boot from tripod joint housing and position on drive axle, **Fig. 5 and 6.**
2. Pull drive axle from tripod joint housing, then remove snap ring and lift tripod joint spider from housing. Clean tripod joint spider and inspect for wear and damage. Also inspect joint needle roller bearings for smooth operation. **Do not disassemble tripod joint spider.**
3. Wind tape around drive axle splines, then remove bands for Rzeppa type joint and remove boots from drive axle. If Rzeppa joint is to be reused, do not wipe away grease. Inspect grease for contamination and clean and replace grease only if required. Note amount of grease removed for use during reassembly.
4. **On models with inner shaft,** continue disassembly as follows:
   a. Using press and support fixture No. MB-991248, or equivalent, press inner shaft and seal plate out of Tripod case.
   b. Using two inch steel pipe as support, **Fig. 7,** press inner shaft from center bearing support.
   c. Using screwdriver, remove driveshaft side dust seal, then using same steel pipe press out center bearing and differential side dust seal.

Assemble

A special grease is used to lubricate the drive axle tripod joint and Rzeppa joint. This grease is included in the drive axle repair kit and must be used.

1. Press fit center bearing into center bearing support, then lubricate and press fit dust seals into center bearing.
2. Press fit inner shaft into center bearing, then the inner shaft assembly into Tripod case.
3. Apply grease to drive axle, then install boots.
4. Position tripod joint spider on drive axle, then install snap ring.
5. Apply 2.8–3.2 ounces of special grease to tripod joint housing, then insert drive axle and spider into housing.
6. Apply another 2.8–3.2 ounces of special grease to tripod joint boot.
7. Apply as much special grease as removed to Rzeppa joint, if required.
8. Install bands and boots for each joint. When installing boot bands for tripod joint, bands (dimension "A") must be positioned 3.1 inches apart, **Fig. 4.**

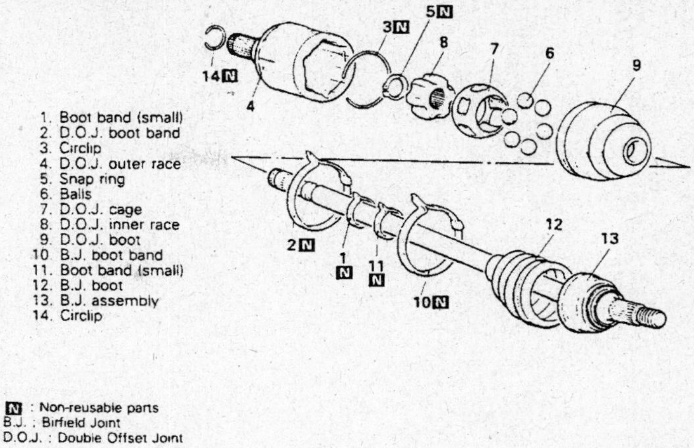

Fig. 3 Exploded view of double offset joint type front drive axle

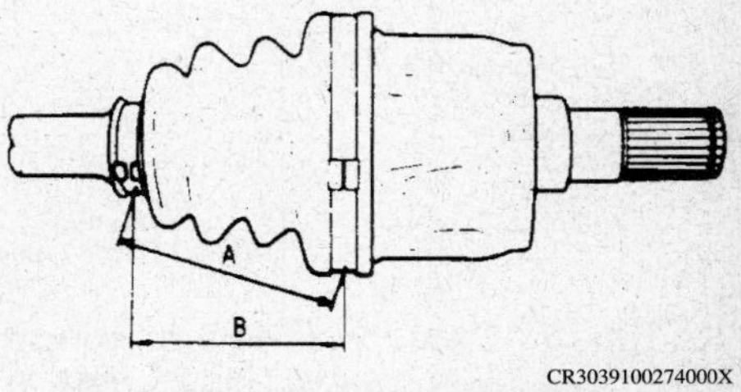

Fig. 4 Double offset joint or tripod joint boot length measurement

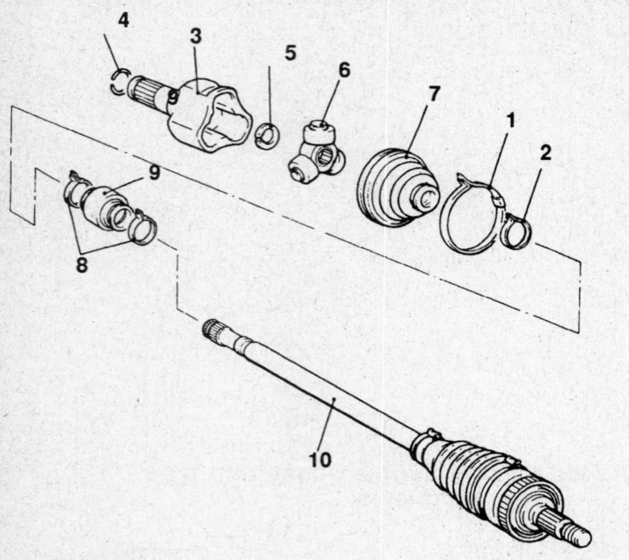

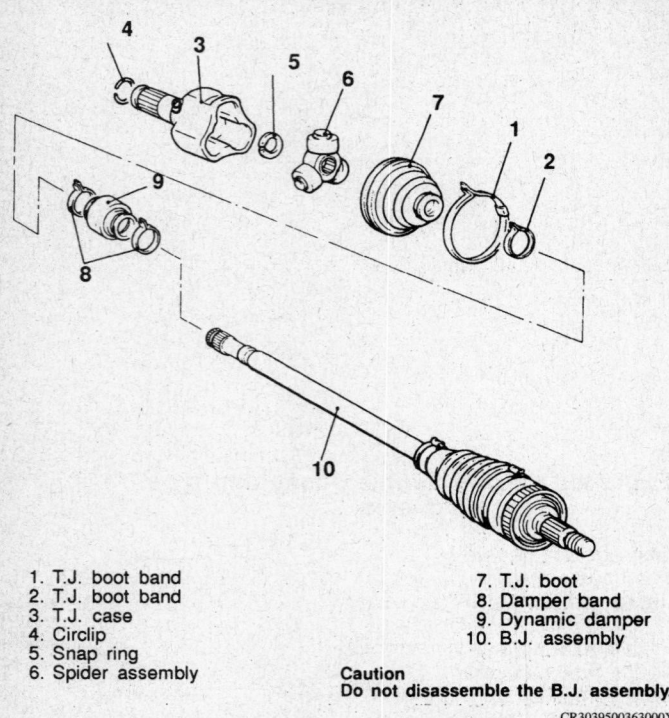

1. T.J. boot band
2. T.J. boot band
3. T.J. case
4. Circlip
5. Snap ring
6. Spider assembly
7. T.J. boot
8. Damper band
9. Dynamic damper
10. B.J. assembly

Caution
Do not disassemble the B.J. assembly.

CR3039500363000X

Fig. 5 Exploded view of tripod type front drive axle. Less inner shaft

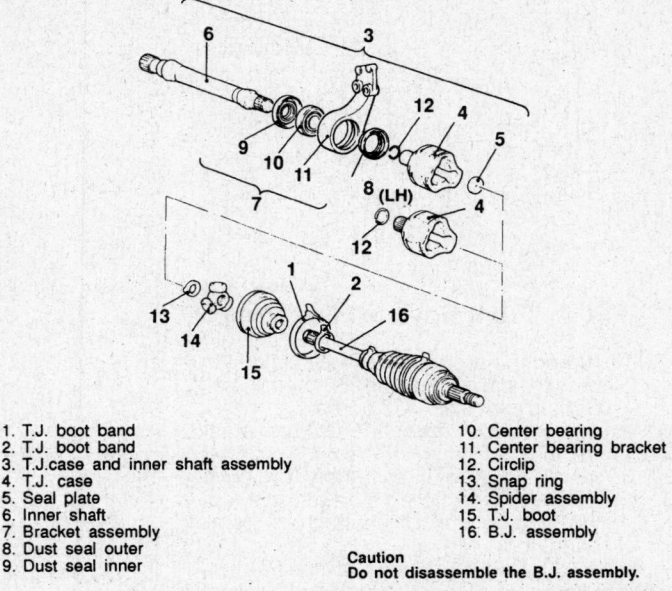

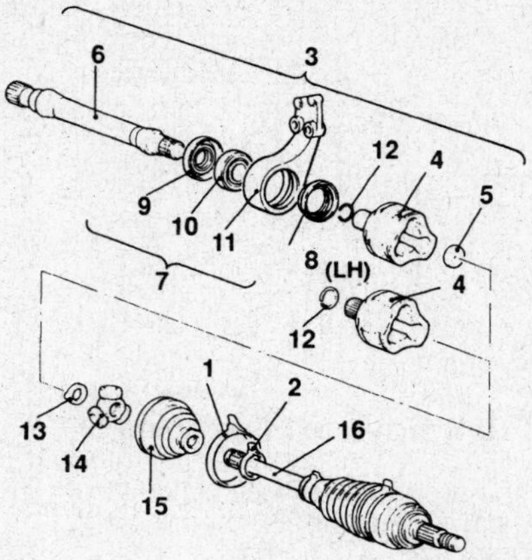

1. T.J. boot band
2. T.J. boot band
3. T.J.case and inner shaft assembly
4. T.J. case
5. Seal plate
6. Inner shaft
7. Bracket assembly
8. Dust seal outer
9. Dust seal inner
10. Center bearing
11. Center bearing bracket
12. Circlip
13. Snap ring
14. Spider assembly
15. T.J. boot
16. B.J. assembly

Caution
Do not disassemble the B.J. assembly.

CR3039500364000X

Fig. 6 Exploded view of tripod type front drive axle. With inner shaft

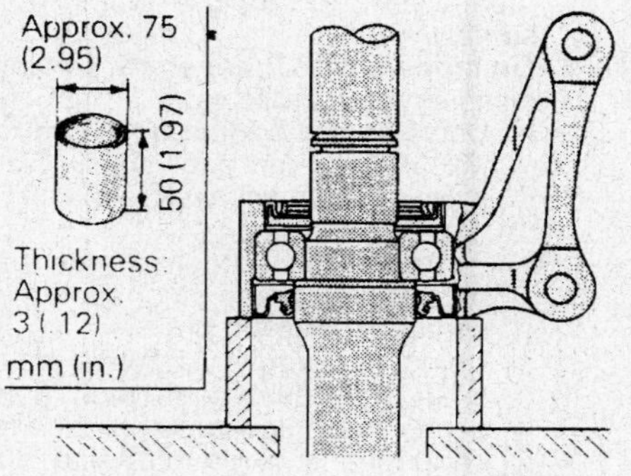

CR3039100277000X

Fig. 7 Inner shaft removal

TIGHTENING SPECIFICATIONS

Component	Torque Ft. Lbs.
Damper Fork To Lateral Lower Arm	65
Driveshaft Nut	145–188
Lateral Lower Arm Ball Joint & Knuckle Connection	43–52
Stabilizer Link Ball Joint & Damper Fork Connection	30
Tie Rod End Ball Joint & Knuckle Connection	17–25

Type 2

INDEX

DRIVESHAFT IDENTIFICATION

These models use an "unequal length" system. The "unequal length" system has a short solid interconnecting shaft on one side with a longer tubular interconnecting shaft on the other, **Figs. 1 through 4.**

DRIVESHAFT

REPLACE

BREEZE, CIRRUS, SEBRING CONVERTIBLE & STRATUS

1. Remove cotter pin, locknut and spring washer from end of outer CV joint stub axle.
2. Apply service brakes, loosen hub bearing retaining nut, then raise and support vehicle.
3. Remove wheel and tire assemblies.
4. Remove brake caliper assembly as outlined under the " Disc Brakes" section.
5. Remove brake rotor from front hub.
6. Remove tie rod end to steering knuckle attaching nut, then the tie rod end from steering knuckle using removal tool No. MB-991113, or equivalent.
7. **On models equipped with ABS,** remove speed sensor cable routing bracket from strut assembly.
8. **On all models,** remove cotter pin and castle nut from stud of lower ball joint at steering knuckle.
9. Turn knuckle so front of knuckle is facing as far outboard as possible, then using a suitable hammer strike steering boss until steering knuckle separates from stud of lower ball joint. **Do not hit lower control arm or ball joint seal. No tool is to be inserted between steering knuckle and lower ball joint to separate them. Do not separate inner CV joint at this time. The driveshaft must be supported. Do not allow it to hang by inner CV joint.**
10. Pull steering knuckle aside and away from outer CV joint.
11. Insert suitable pry bar between transmission case and driveshaft, then pry driveshaft from transmission. **Do not pull on interconnecting shaft, nor insert pry bar deep enough to damage oil seal.** Pry against inner tripod joint until tripod snap ring is disengaged.

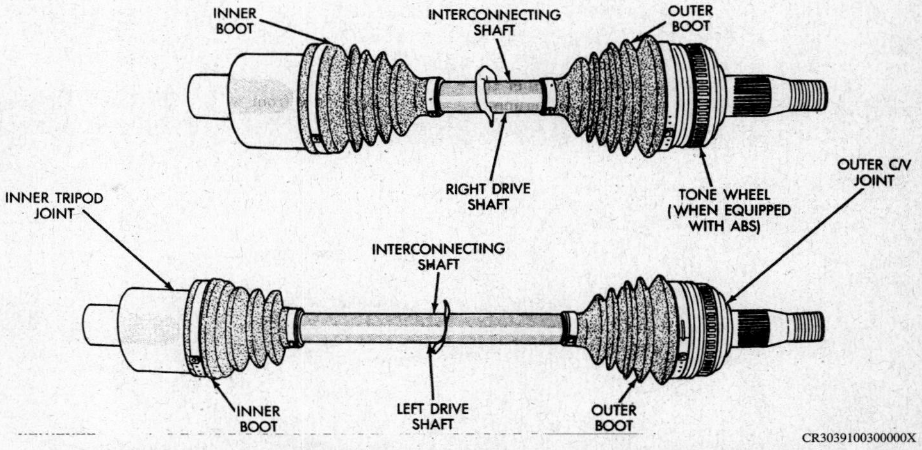

Fig. 1 Driveshaft identification. Concorde, Intrepid, LHS, Vision & 300M

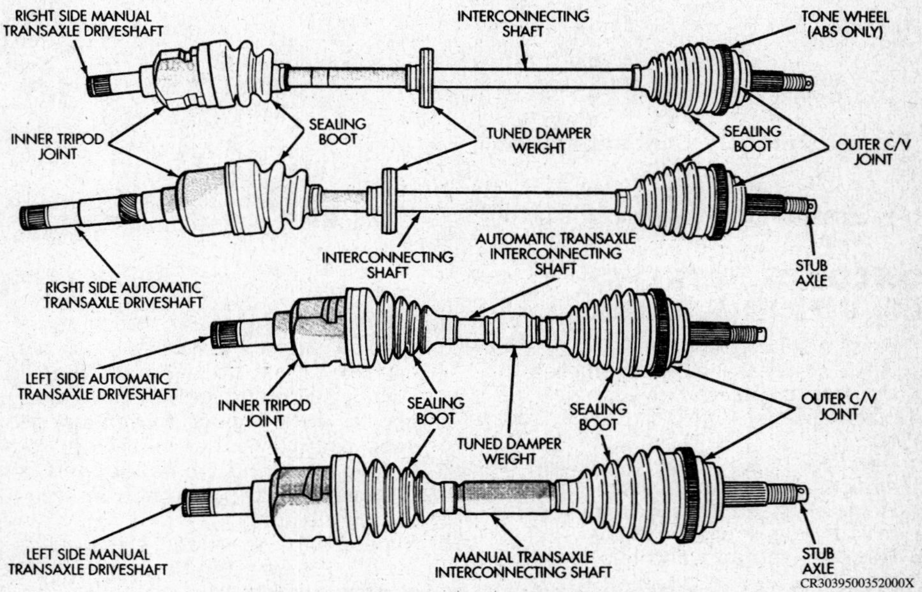

Fig. 2 Driveshaft identification. 1997 Neon

12. Hold inner tripod joint and interconnecting shaft of driveshaft assembly, then remove inner tripod joint from transaxle by pulling straight out. **Avoid letting spline or snap ring drag across transaxle to tripod joint oil seal lip.**
13. Reverse procedure to install, noting the following:
    a. Ensure snap rings are securely seated in their grooves.
    b. Tighten steering knuckle to ball joint stud castle nut to specifications.
    c. Tighten tie rod end to steering knuckle attaching nut to specifications.
    d. Apply vehicle brakes when tightening hub nut to specifications.

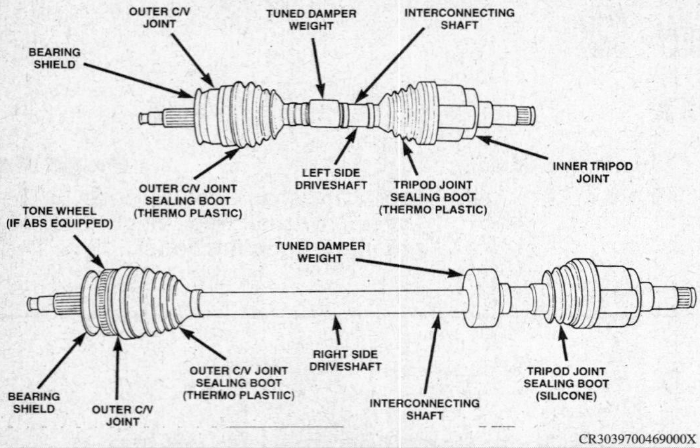

Fig. 3 Driveshaft identification. 1997–99 Breeze, Cirrus, Sebring Convertible & Stratus

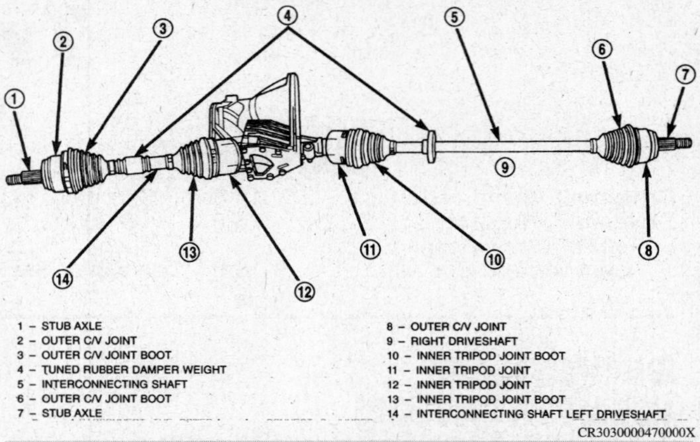

Fig. 4 Driveshaft identification. 1998–99 Neon & 2000 Breeze, Cirrus, Neon, Sebring Convertible & Stratus

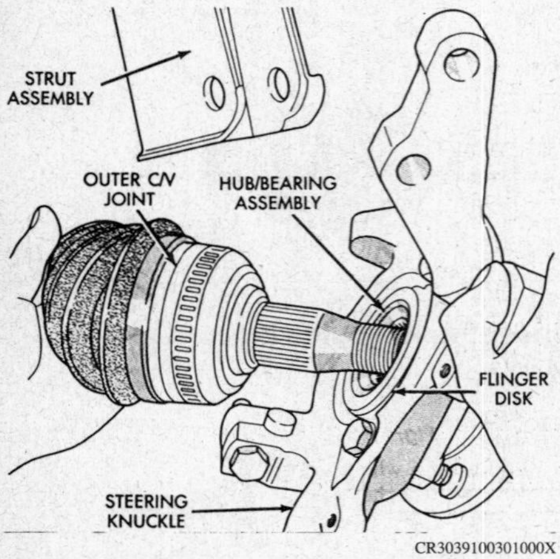

Fig. 5 Outer CV joint separation from hub

e. Ensure transaxle fluid is up to proper level.

CONCORDE, INTREPID, LHS, VISION & 300M

1. Raise and support vehicle.
2. Remove wheel and tire assemblies.
3. Remove brake caliper assembly as outlined under the " Disc Brakes" section.
4. Remove brake rotor by pulling it straight off mounting studs.
5. Remove speed sensor cable routing bracket from strut assembly.
6. Remove stub axle and hub retaining nut.
7. Install puller tool No. 6790, or equivalent on hub and bearing assembly using wheel lugnuts to secure it in place.
8. Install a lugnut on a wheel stud to protect its threads.
9. Insert a suitable flat-bladed pry tool to prevent hub from turning.
10. Using puller tool, force outer stub axle from hub and bearing assembly.
11. Dislodge inner tripod joint from stub shaft retaining ring on transaxle assembly.

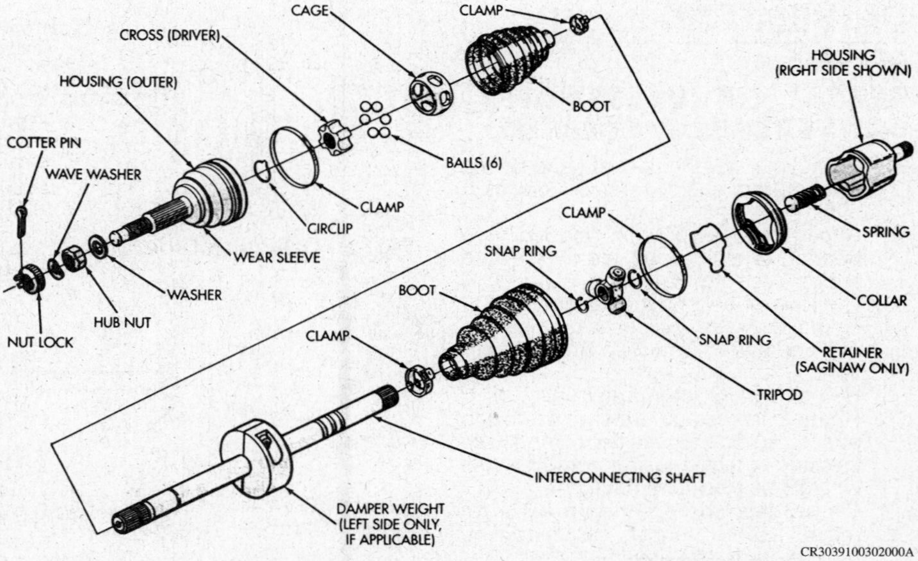

Fig. 6 Exploded view of driveshaft assembly

12. Insert suitable pry bar between transmission case and driveshaft, then pry driveshaft from transmission, **Fig. 5. Do not pull on driveshaft, nor insert pry bar deep enough to damage oil seal. Only pry inner joint from retaining snap ring. Do not attempt to remove inner tripod joint from transaxle stub shaft.**
13. Support steering knuckle, then disconnect and remove strut assembly from steering knuckle.
14. Hold outer CV joint assembly with one hand, grasp steering knuckle with the other hand and rotate it out and to the rear of the vehicle, until outer CV joint clears hub and bearing assembly.
15. Remove driveshaft inner tripod joint from transaxle stub shaft. **Do not pull on interconnecting shaft to remove inner tripod joint from stub shaft.**
16. Reverse procedure to install, noting the following:
    a. Install new O-ring seal and tripod joint retaining circlip.
    b. Apply a thin, even bead of Mopar Multi-Purpose Lubricant, or equivalent grease, around inner tripod joint splines where O-rings seats against joint.
    c. When installing outer CV joint into hub and bearing assembly, do not allow flinger disc, **Fig. 6,** to become damaged.
    d. Tighten strut attaching bolts to specifications. **Strut bolts have a serrated shaft so do not turn bolts in steering knuckle. Turn nut on bolts, but do not turn bolts.**
    e. Install a new hub and bearing stub shaft retaining nut. Tighten, but do not torque nut at this time.
    f. Apply vehicle brakes and tighten new hub and bearing stub shaft nut to specifications. **Do not exceed the maximum specification as damage to driveshaft may occur.**

NEON

1997–99

If the vehicle will be moved on its wheels when a driveshaft has been removed, install a properly sized bolt and nut through the front hub. **On 1997 models, torque** to 135 ft. lbs. **On 1998–99 models, torque** to 150 ft. lbs. This ensures the hub bearing will not loosen.

1. Remove cotter pin, locknut and spring washer from end of outer CV joint stub axle.
2. Apply service brakes, then loosen hub bearing retaining nut.
3. Raise and support vehicle.
4. Remove wheel and tire assemblies.
5. Remove brake caliper assembly as outlined in the " Disc Brakes" section.
6. Remove brake rotor from front hub. Support caliper with suitable cord or wire. **Do not let it hang by brake hose.**
7. Remove tie rod end to steering knuckle attaching nut, then remove tie rod end from steering knuckle using removal tool No. MB-990635, or MB-991113, or equivalent.
8. Remove nut and bolt clamping ball joint into steering knuckle, then separate ball joint stud from steering knuckle by prying down on lower control arm. **Do not damage ball joint seal. Do not separate inner CV joint at this time. Do not allow driveshaft to hang by inner CV joint. Driveshaft must be supported.**
9. Remove hub and bearing to stub axle retaining nut.
10. **On 1997 models,** proceed as follows:
    a. Insert suitable pry bar between transmission case and driveshaft, then pry driveshaft from transmission. **Do not pull on interconnecting shaft, nor insert pry bar deep enough to damage oil seal.**
    b. Pry against inner tripod joint until tripod snap ring is disengaged.
11. **On 1998–99 models,** proceed as follows:
    a. Install puller tool No. 6790, or equivalent on hub and bearing assembly using lugnuts to secure it in place.
    b. Install a lugnut on stud to protect threads.
    c. Insert a suitable flat-bladed pry tool to prevent hub from turning.
    d. Using puller tool, force outer stub axle from hub and bearing assembly.
12. **On all models,** pull steering knuckle aside and away from outer CV joint.
13. Hold inner tripod joint and interconnecting shaft of driveshaft assembly, then remove inner tripod joint from transaxle by pulling straight out. **Do not let spline or snap ring damage oil seal.**
14. Reverse procedure to install, noting the following:
    a. Tighten new steering knuckle to ball joint stud castle nut to specifications.
    b. Tighten tie rod end to steering knuckle attaching nut to specifications.
    c. Apply vehicle brakes and tighten hub nut to specifications.

2000

If the vehicle will be moved on its wheels when a driveshaft has been removed, install a properly sized bolt and nut through the front hub. Torque to 150 ft. lbs. This ensures the hub bearing will not loosen.

1. Disconnect and isolate battery ground cable.
2. Place transaxle in gated Park.
3. Raise and support vehicle on hoist.
4. Remove wheel and tire assembly.
5. **On models equipped with ABS,** disconnect front wheel speed sensor, then position harness aside.
6. **On all models,** remove ball joint to knuckle retaining nut and bolt.
7. Separate ball joint stud from knuckle by prying down on lower control arm. **Avoid damaging joint seal.**
8. Remove driveshaft from knuckle by pulling outward on knuckle while pressing in on driveshaft. Support outer end of driveshaft. If separation is difficult, proceed as follows:
    a. Install puller tool No. 6790, or equivalent on hub and bearing using lugnuts to secure it in place.
    b. Install a lugnut to protect threads.
    c. Insert a suitable flat-bladed pry tool to prevent hub from turning.
    d. Using puller tool, force driveshaft outer stub axle from hub and bearing assembly.
    e. Pull knuckle assembly out and away from outer CV joint.
9. Support outer end of driveshaft assembly.
10. Remove inner tripod joints from transaxle side gears using a punch to dislodge inner joint retaining ring from side gear. For righthand side joint removal, position punch against inner joint. For lefthand side joint removal, position punch in joint groove.
11. Position a suitable oil resistant container under driveshaft where it enters transaxle.
12. Hold inner tripod joint and driveshaft interconnecting shaft.
13. Remove inner joint from transaxle by pulling it straight out of side gear and oil seal. **Do not let spline or snap ring drag across oil sealing lip.**
14. Reverse procedure to install, noting the following:
    a. Ensure snap ring is fully seated in its groove. The tripod joint will not be removable by hand when snap ring is properly installed.
    b. Install a new knuckle to ball joint stud bolt and nut. Tighten to specifications.
    c. Clean all dirt and debris from driveshaft outer stub shaft threads. Tighten hub nut to specifications.
    d. Inspect transaxle fluid level and correct as required.

DRIVESHAFT SERVICE

The driveshaft assembly, **Fig. 6,** is a non-serviceable item, except for the inner and outer driveshaft boots. If any failure of internal components is diagnosed during a road test or disassembly, the driveshaft will need to replaced as an assembly.

INNER DRIVESHAFT BOOT, REPLACE

REMOVAL

1. Remove driveshaft as outlined under "Driveshaft, Replace."
2. Remove inner joint boot clamps, then slide boot down interconnecting shaft.
3. Remove interconnecting shaft and spider assembly out of joint housing. **Do not pull on interconnecting shaft.**
4. Remove snap ring, then spider assembly from interconnecting shaft using a brass drift if required. **Hold bearings in place on spider trunnions to prevent them from falling away. Do not hit outer tripod bearings when removing spider assembly.**
5. Remove joint boot from interconnecting shaft.
6. Clean and inspect spider assembly, tripod joint housing and interconnecting shaft for any signs of excessive wear. **If any excessive wear is present, replacement of entire driveshaft will be required.**

INSTALLATION

Two different types of boots are used on these models. First is a high temperature, soft and pliable type. The other is a normal temperature, stiff and rigid type. The replacement boot must be of the same type which was removed.

1. **On Concorde, Intrepid, LHS, Vision and 300M models,** install new boot clamps and boot onto interconnecting shaft. **Boot must be positioned on interconnecting shaft so only thinnest shaft groove is visible.**
2. **On Breeze, Cirrus, Neon, Sebring Convertible and Stratus models,** install new boot clamps and boot onto interconnecting shaft. **Boot must be positioned so raised bead on inside of boot is in groove on interconnecting shaft.**
3. **On all models,** install spider assembly onto interconnecting shaft, then the retaining snap ring. **Ensure retaining snap ring is fully installed and seated into its shaft groove.**
4. Distribute ½ the amount of grease provided in boot service package into tripod housing and the remaining amount into boot. **Do not use any other type of grease.**
5. Install spider assembly into tripod housing.
6. Position boot over boot retaining groove on interconnecting shaft and install boot retaining clamp using crimper tool No. C-4975-A, or equivalent.

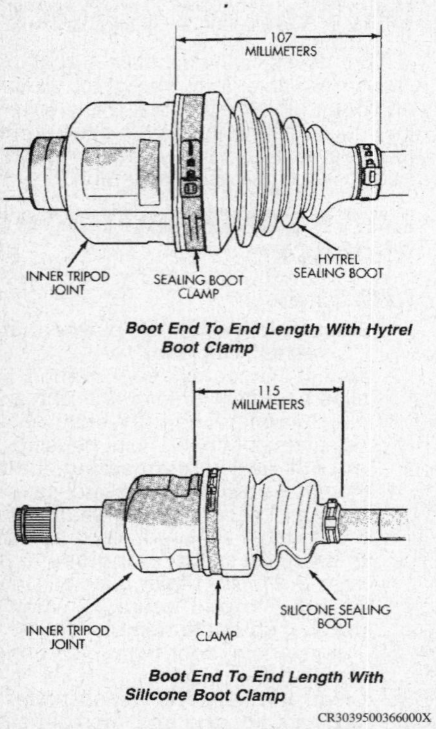

Fig. 7 Proper inner tripod joint stroke position. Neon

7. Position boot into tripod housing retaining groove.
8. **On Breeze, Cirrus, Neon, Sebring Convertible and Stratus models,** proceed as follows:
   a. Insert a trim stick between joint and boot to vent inner joint assembly. If inner joint has a hard plastic boot, the trim stick must be inserted between soft rubber insert and joint housing.
   b. With trim stick inserted between sealing boot and tripod joint housing, position interconnecting shaft so it sits in center of its travel in tripod joint housing.
   c. Remove trim stick.
   d. Position trilobal boot to interface with tripod housing. Boot lobes must be properly aligned with tripod housing recesses.
9. **On Neon and 1997 Concorde, Intrepid, LHS & Vision models,** prior to crimping boot clamp, the inner tripod joint must be at proper stroke position as shown in **Figs. 7 and 8.** This ensures proper amount of air is inside sealing boot before clamp is crimped. **Failure to perform this step will result in inner boot failure.**
10. **On models equipped with crimp type boot clamp,** proceed as follows:
    a. Clamp sealing boot onto tripod housing using crimper tool No. C-4975-A, or equivalent.
    b. Place crimping tool over clamp bridge.
    c. Tighten nut on crimper tool until tool's jaws are completely closed together, face to face.
11. **On models equipped with latching

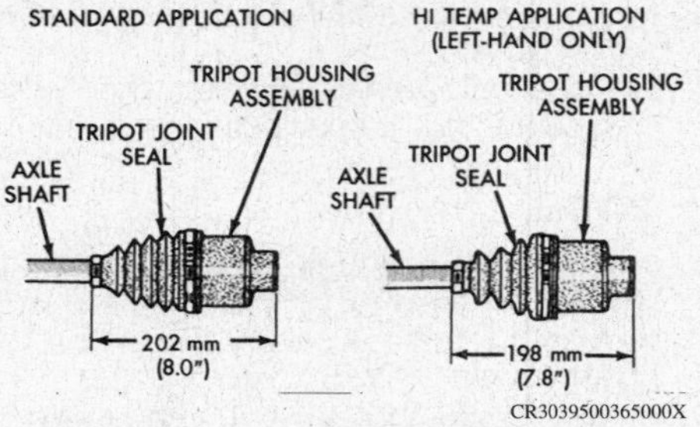

Fig. 8 Proper inner tripod joint stroke position. 1997 Concorde, Intrepid, LHS & Vision

type boot clamp,** proceed as follows:
    a. Clamp sealing boot onto tripod housing using clamp locking tool No. YA3050, or equivalent.
    b. Place tool's prongs in clamp hole.
    c. Squeeze tool together until clamp's top band is latched behind two tabs on lower clamp band.
12. **On all models,** install driveshaft as outlined under "Driveshaft, Replace."

OUTER DRIVESHAFT BOOT, REPLACE

CONCORDE, INTREPID, LHS, VISION & 300M

Removal

1. Remove driveshaft as outlined under "Driveshaft, Replace."
2. Remove outer joint boot clamps, then slide boot down interconnecting shaft.
3. Remove grease to expose outer CV joint retaining ring, **Fig. 9.**
4. Spread retaining ring and slide CV joint assembly off interconnecting shaft.
5. Remove and discard failed boot and clamps.
6. Clean and inspect spider assembly, CV joint and interconnecting shaft for any signs of excessive wear. **If any excessive wear is present, entire driveshaft replacement will be required.**

Installation

1. Install new boot clamps and boot onto interconnecting shaft.
2. Install CV joint onto interconnecting shaft by pushing shaft into CV joint until retaining snap ring is seated in groove on shaft, **Fig. 9.**
3. Distribute ½ the amount of grease provided in boot service package into CV joint assembly and remaining amount into boot.
4. Position boot over boot retaining grove on interconnecting shaft. **Boot must be positioned on interconnecting shaft so only thinnest shaft groove is visible.**
5. Install boot retaining clamp using crimper tool No. C-4975-A, or equivalent.
6. Position boot over boot retaining grove on CV joint housing and install boot retaining clamp using crimper tool. Ensure seal is not dimpled, stretched or distorted in any way.

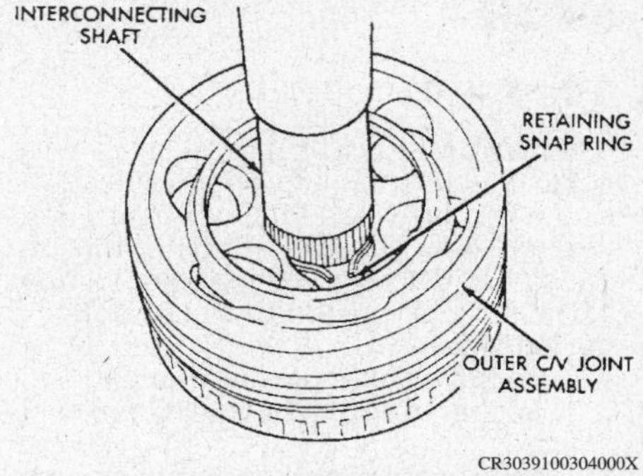

Fig. 9 Outer CV joint retaining snap ring location. Concorde, Intrepid, LHS, Vision & 300M

7. Install driveshaft as outlined under "Driveshaft, Replace."

1997 BREEZE, CIRRUS & STRATUS

The outer driveshaft boot on these models is not a serviceable part. In the event of outer CV boot failure the driveshaft must be serviced as quarter shaft by replacing the outer CV joint/boot, interconnecting shaft and vibration damper. Refer to "Inner Driveshaft Boot, Replace" in this section for outer CV joint/boot assembly replacement procedure.

Outer CV Joint Bearing Shield

The front hub/bearing shield on the outer CV joint is a serviceable component of the outer CV joint/boot assembly. Refer to the following procedure for replacement of the Outer CV Joint Bearing Shield.

1. Remove driveshaft as outlined under "Driveshaft, Replace."
2. Clamp driveshaft by interconnecting shaft into a suitable vice.
3. Using a suitable drift, tap around entire edge of shield until removed.
4. Install bearing shield by hand onto outer CV joint so it is seated squarely on CV joint.
5. Position Installation tool No. C-4698, or equivalent, on face of bearing shield, then using a suitable hammer, drive the bearing shield onto outer CV joint until flush.

NEON, SEBRING CONVERTIBLE & 1998–2000 BREEZE, CIRRUS & STRATUS

Removal

1. Remove driveshaft as outlined under "Driveshaft, Replace."
2. Remove and discard large boot clamp retaining CV joint sealing boot to CV joint housing.
3. Remove and discard small clamp that retains outer CV joint sealing boot to interconnecting shaft.
4. Slide sealing boot from outer CV joint housing and slide it down interconnecting shaft.
5. Wipe away grease to expose outer CV joint and interconnecting shaft.
6. Remove outer CV joint from interconnecting shaft as follows:

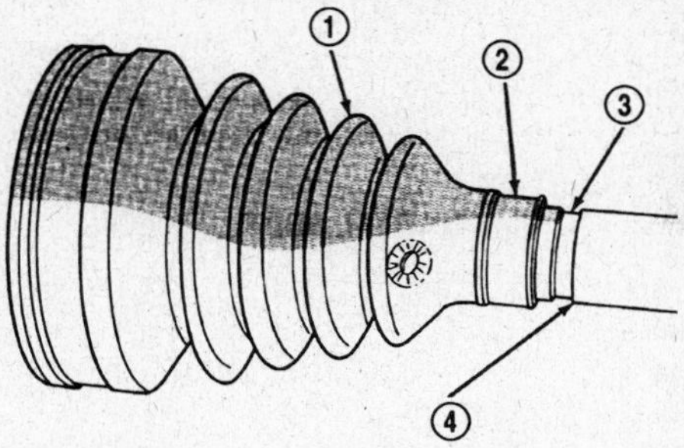

1 – SEALING BOOT
2 – RAISED BEAD IN THIS AREA OF SEALING BOOT
3 – GROOVE
4 – INTERCONNECTING SHAFT

CR3039800401000A

Fig. 10 Outer sealing boot installation. Neon, Sebring Convertible & 1998–2000 Breeze, Cirrus & Stratus

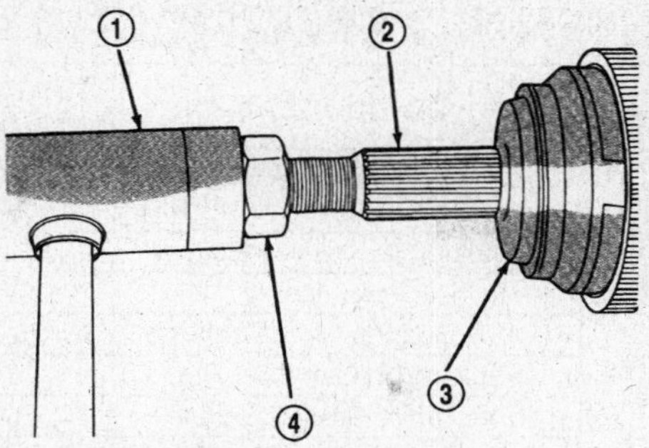

1 – SOFT FACED HAMMER
2 – STUB AXLE
3 – OUTER C/V JOINT
4 – NUT

CR3039800402000A

Fig. 11 Outer CV joint assembly installation. Neon, Sebring Convertible & 1998–2000 Breeze, Cirrus & Stratus

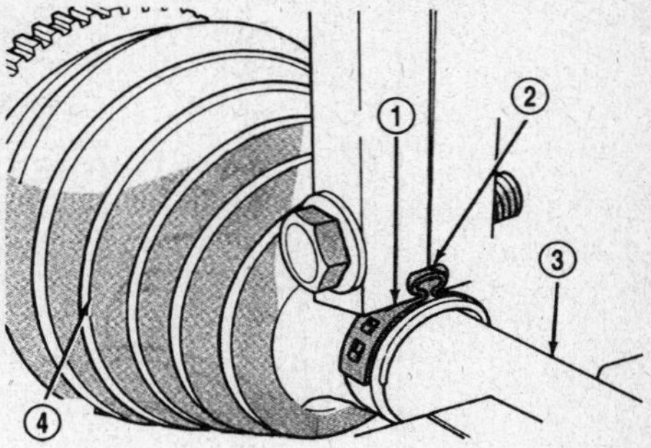

1 – CLAMP
2 – JAWS OF SPECIAL TOOL C-4975A MUST BE CLOSED COMPLETELY TOGETHER HERE
3 – INTERCONNECTING SHAFT
4 – SEALING BOOT

CR3039800403000A

Fig. 12 CV boot clamp installation. Neon, Sebring Convertible & 1998–2000 Breeze, Cirrus & Stratus

a. Support interconnecting shaft in a suitable soft jawed vice with protective jaw caps.
b. Using a suitable soft faced hammer, strike end of CV joint housing to dislodge housing from internal circlip on interconnecting shaft.
c. CV joint may have to be tapped off interconnecting shaft using a suitable soft faced hammer.

7. Remove large circlip from interconnecting shaft.
8. Slide boot off interconnecting shaft.
9. Thoroughly clean and inspect outer CV joint assembly and interconnecting joint for any signs of excessive wear. **If any components show signs of excessive wear, replace driveshaft assembly.**

Installation

1. Slide new sealing boot to interconnecting shaft retaining clamp and onto interconnecting shaft, **Fig. 10. Ensure seal boot is positioned on interconnecting shaft so raised bead on inside of seal boot is in groove on interconnecting shaft.**
2. Align splines on interconnecting shaft with splines on cross of outer CV joint assembly and start outer CV joint onto interconnecting shaft.
3. Use a suitable soft faced hammer to install outer CV joint assembly onto interconnecting shaft, **Fig. 11.**
4. Distribute ½ amount of grease provided in seal boot service package into outer CV joint assembly housing. **Do not use any other type of grease.**
5. Put remaining amount into sealing boot.
6. Install outer CV joint boot to interconnecting shaft clamp evenly on sealing boot.
7. Clamp sealing boot onto interconnecting shaft using clamp crimper tool No. C-4975-A, or equivalent, **Fig. 12.**
8. Position outer CV joint sealing boot into its retaining groove on outer CV joint housing.
9. Install sealing boot to outer CV joint retaining clamp evenly on sealing boot.
10. Clamp sealing boot onto CV joint housing using clamp crimper tool No. C-4975-A, or equivalent. **Ensure jaws of crimper tool are closed completely together.**
11. Install driveshaft as outlined under " Driveshaft, Replace."

TIGHTENING SPECIFICATIONS

Car/Year	Component	Torque Ft. Lbs.
BREEZE, CIRRUS, SEBRING CONVERTIBLE & STRATUS		
1997-99	Caliper To Knuckle Bolts	23
	Driveshaft Nut	180
	Hub & Bearing Stub Shaft Nut	70–90
	Knuckle To Ball Stud Nut	70
	Knuckle To Strut Bolt Nuts	125
	Tie Rod End To Knuckle	45
	Wheel Lugnuts	100
2000	Driveshaft Nut	105
	Hub & Bearing Stub Shaft Nut	70–90
	Knuckle To Ball Stud Nut	70
	Knuckle To Strut Bolt Nuts	125
	Tie Rod End To Knuckle	45
	Wheel Lugnuts	100
CONCORDE, INTREPID, LHS, VISION & 300M		
1997-99	Caliper To Knuckle Bolts	14
	Driveshaft Nut	120
	Hub & Bearing Stub Shaft Nut	70–90
	Knuckle To Ball Stud Nut	70
	Knuckle To Strut Bolt Nuts	125
	Tie Rod End To Knuckle	45
	Wheel Lugnuts	100
2000	Driveshaft Nut	105
	Hub & Bearing Stub Shaft Nut	70–90
	Knuckle To Ball Stud Nut	70
	Knuckle To Strut Bolt Nuts	125
	Tie Rod End To Knuckle	45
	Wheel Lugnuts	100
NEON		
1997-99	Driveshaft Nut	135
	Hub & Bearing Stub Shaft Nut	70–90
	Knuckle To Ball Stud Nut	70
	Knuckle To Strut Bolt Nuts (1997)	70
	Knuckle To Strut Bolt Nuts (1998-99 Less ACR Package)	40①
	Knuckle To Strut Bolt Nuts (1999 With ACR Package)	75①
	Tie Rod End To Knuckle	45
	Wheel Lugnuts	100
2000	Caliper To Knuckle Bolts	16
	Driveshaft Nut	180
	Hub & Bearing Stub Shaft Nut	70–90
	Knuckle To Ball Stud Nut	70
	Knuckle To Strut Bolt Nuts	40①
	Tie Rod End To Knuckle	45
	Wheel Lugnuts	100

① — Rotate an additional 90°

ALL WHEEL DRIVE SYSTEMS

NOTE: Refer To "Front Drive Axles " For Procedures Not Found In This Section.

INDEX

DESCRIPTION

This system used on Talon is a full time All Wheel Drive (AWD) system. It has an optional limited slip differential for increased traction. The main components used in this system are the transfer case, rear drive axle, axle shafts and driveshaft.

TROUBLESHOOTING

Refer to **Fig. 1,** when troubleshooting system malfunctions.

AXLE SHAFT

REPLACE

Refer to "Rear Axle Hub & Carrier Service" for procedure.

DRIVESHAFT

REPLACE

Remove rear driveshaft in numbered sequence, **Fig. 2,** noting the following:

1. Remove drive shaft nut using removal tool No. MB990767, or equivalent.
2. Remove driveshaft by pushing the lower part of the knuckle to the outside of the vehicle, then separate the driveshaft from the differential carrier. At this time, use a suitable tire lever or similar tool to separate the driveshaft connection.
3. Reverse procedure to install noting the following:
   a. Ensure proper driveshaft placement. The right driveshaft has an orange boot band, while the left driveshaft has a green boot band.
   b. Ensure differential carrier oil seal is not damaged by driveshaft spline.
   c. Using special tool No. MB990767, or equivalent, tighten driveshaft nut to specifications shown in **Fig. 2.** Ensure there is no load on wheel bearings.

AXLE SHAFT

Symptom	Probable cause	Remedy
Noise while wheels are rotating	Brake drag	Replace
	Bent axle shaft	
	Worn or scarred axle shaft bearing	
Grease leakage	Worn or damaged oil seal	
	Malfunction of bearing seal	

DRIVE SHAFT

Symptom	Probable cause	Remedy
Noise	Wear, play or seizure of ball joint	Replace
	Excessive drive shaft spline looseness	

DIFFERENTIAL (LIMITED SLIP DIFFERENTIAL)

Symptom	Probable cause	Remedy
Abnormal noise during driving or gear changing*1	Excessive drive gear backlash	Adjust
	Insufficient drive pinion preload	
	Excessive differential gear backlash	Adjust or replace
	Worn spline of a side gear	Replace
	Loose companion flange self-locking nut	Retighten or replace
Abnormal noise when cornering	Damaged differential gears	Replace
	Damaged pinion shaft	
	Insufficient gear oil quantity	Replenish
Gear noise	Improper drive gear tooth contact adjustment	Adjust or replace
	Incorrect drive gear backlash	Adjust
	Improper drive pinion preload adjustment	

CR3039100178010X

Fig. 1 AWD troubleshooting chart (Part 1 of 2)

DRIVESHAFT SERVICE

DISASSEMBLE

1. Remove Tripod Joint boot bands, **Fig. 3.**
2. Remove Tripod joint case.
3. Remove snap ring off Tripod joint end of driveshaft.
4. Remove spider assembly off driveshaft. **Do not service spider assembly.**
5. Wrap vinyl tape around splines of driveshaft then remove Tripod joint boot.
6. Remove Birfield joint bands.
7. Wrap vinyl tape around splines of driveshaft then remove Birfield joint boot.
8. Remove Birfield joint. **Do not service Birfield joint.**

INSPECTION

1. Check driveshaft for damage, bending or corrosion.
2. Check driveshaft spline for wear or damage.
3. Check Birfield joint for entry of water or foreign material.
4. Check spider assembly for roller rotation, wear or corrosion.
5. Check Birfield joint outer race for damage or corrosion.
6. Check boots for damage, cracking or wear.

ASSEMBLE

Reverse disassembly procedure to assemble, noting the following:

1. Wrap vinyl tape around spline on driveshaft then install Birfield joint and Tripod joint boots.
2. Fill inside of Birfield joint and Birfield joint boot with half of grease included in repair kit.
3. Secure boot bands with driveshaft at a 0° angle.
4. Apply grease to spider assembly then install spider assembly with chamfered spline end first.
5. Install Tripod joint on driveshaft.
6. Set Tripod joint boot bands 3.23–4.47 inches apart to adjust amount of air inside boot then tighten Tripod joint boot band securely.

DIFFERENTIAL CARRIER

REPLACE

1. Remove driveshafts as described in "Driveshaft, Replace."
2. Position a suitable jack under rear axle assembly, then drain differential gear oil.
3. Remove center exhaust system components as necessary.
4. Scribe mating marks on differential companion flange and flange yoke for assembly reference.
5. Remove differential to propeller shaft connection, then support propeller shaft with wire.
6. Remove dynamic damper to differential support member bolts.
7. Remove differential support member bolts, then the carrier.
8. Reverse procedure to install, tighten bolts to specifications shown in **Fig. 4.**

CARRIER INSPECTION & SERVICE

REAR AXLE TOTAL BACKLASH

If vehicle vibrates and has a booming sound due to system driveline imbalance. Total axle backlash should be checked. To check backlash, proceed as follows:

1. Place gearshift in neutral, apply parking brake, then raise and support vehicle.
2. Manually turn propeller shaft clockwise as far as it will go and scribe mating mark on companion flange dust cover and differential carrier, **Fig. 5.**
3. Manually turn shaft counterclockwise as far as it will go and measure movement of mating marks.
4. If axle total backlash is less than .2 inch (5 mm), backlash is satisfactory.
5. If backlash is more than .2 inch (5 mm), adjust as necessary.

Symptom	Probable cause	Remedy
Gear noise	Damaged, broken, and/or seized tooth surfaces of the drive gear and drive pinion	Replace
	Damaged, broken, and/or seized drive pinion bearings	
	Damaged, broken, and/or seized side bearings	
	Damaged differential case	
	Inferior gear oil	
	Insufficient gear oil quantity	Replenish
Gear oil leakage	Worn or damaged front oil seal, or an improperly installed oil seal	Replace
	Damaged gasket	
	Loose companion flange self-locking nut	Retighten or replace
	Loose filler or drain plug	Retighten or apply adhesive
	Clogged or damaged vent plug	Clean or replace
Seizure	Insufficient drive gear backlash	Adjust
	Excessive drive pinion preload	
	Excessive side bearing preload	
	Insufficient differential gear backlash	
	Excessive clutch plate preload	
	Inferior gear oil	Replace
	Insufficient gear oil quantity	Replenish
Breakdown	Incorrect drive gear backlash	Adjust
	Insufficient drive pinion preload	
	Insufficient side bearing preload	
	Excessive differential gear backlash	
	Loose drive gear clamping bolts	Retighten
The limited slip differential does not function (on snow, mud, ice, etc.)	The limited slip device is damaged	Disassemble, check the functioning and replace the damaged parts

CR3039100178020X

Fig. 1 AWD troubleshooting chart (Part 2 of 2)

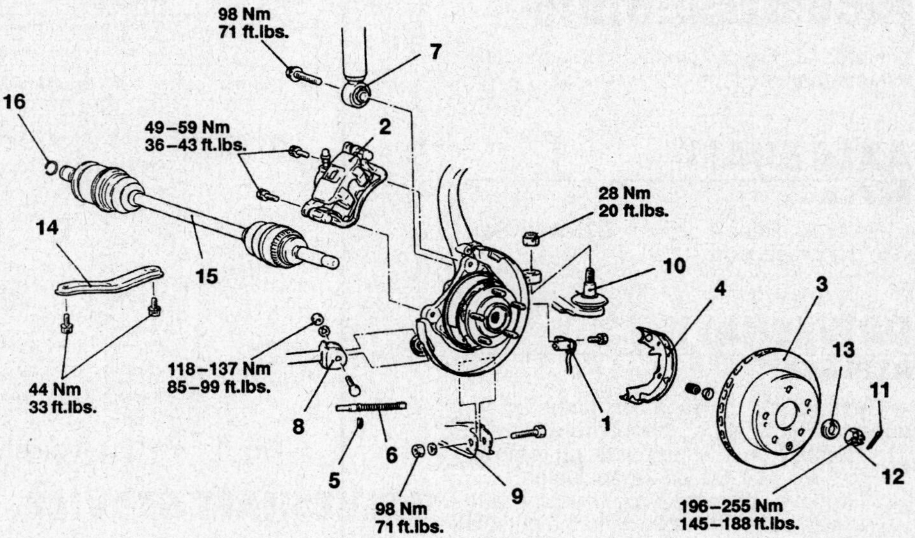

1. Rear wheel speed sensor <Vehicles with ABS>
2. Caliper assembly
3. Brake disc
4. Shoe and lining assembly
5. Clip
6. Parking brake cable
7. Shock absorber connection
8. Trailing arm connection
9. Lower arm connection
10. Toe control arm ball joint and knuckle connection
11. Cotter pin
12. Drive shaft nut
13. Washer
14. Differential mount support
15. Drive shaft
16. Circlip

CR3039500356000X

Fig. 2 Driveshaft replacement

GEAR OIL LEVEL CHECK

1. Remove filler plug and check oil level.
2. If oil level reaches bottom of filler plug hole, oil level is satisfactory.
3. If level does not reach bottom of filler plug hole, fill differential with Mopar Hypoid Gear Oil API classification GL-5, or equivalent.

REAR WHEEL BEARING ENDPLAY CHECK

1. Raise and support vehicle on axle stands.
2. Remove rear wheel and tire assembly, then disconnect parking brake cable from rear brake.
3. Remove caliper assembly and brake disc.
4. Position a dial indicator as shown in **Fig. 6** and measure endplay when axle is moved in an axial direction.
5. If endplay is less than .002 inch, endplay is satisfactory.
6. If endplay exceeds .002 inch, replace rear wheel bearing.

REAR WHEEL BEARING ROTATION SLIDING RESISTANCE CHECK

1. Raise and support vehicle, then remove driveshaft as described under "Driveshaft, Replace."
2. Use bolt tool No. MB990998, or equivalent to mount rear hub onto lower arm as shown in **Fig. 7.**
3. **Torque** nut of special bolt to 145–188 ft. lbs.
4. Rotate rear hub to seat bearing.
5. With bolt tool installed, measure wheel bearing starting torque using torque wrench, adapter and socket tool Nos. MB990998, MB990685 and MB990326, or equivalents.
6. Starting torque should be 9 inch lbs. or less and bearing must not feel rough when rotated.

LIMITED-SLIP DIFFERENTIAL CHECK

1. Block front wheels and move shift lever to neutral.
2. Release parking brake completely, then raise rear wheels and support with rigid jack stand.
3. Disconnect coupling of differential and propeller shaft.
4. Rotate one wheel slowly, ensure wheel on opposite side turns in the same direction.
5. If wheel turns in the opposite direction, replace viscous unit.

DIFFERENTIAL CARRIER SERVICE

EXCEPT LIMITED-SLIP

Pre-Disassemble Inspection

1. Support working base in a vise, and attach differential carrier to working base, **Fig. 8.**

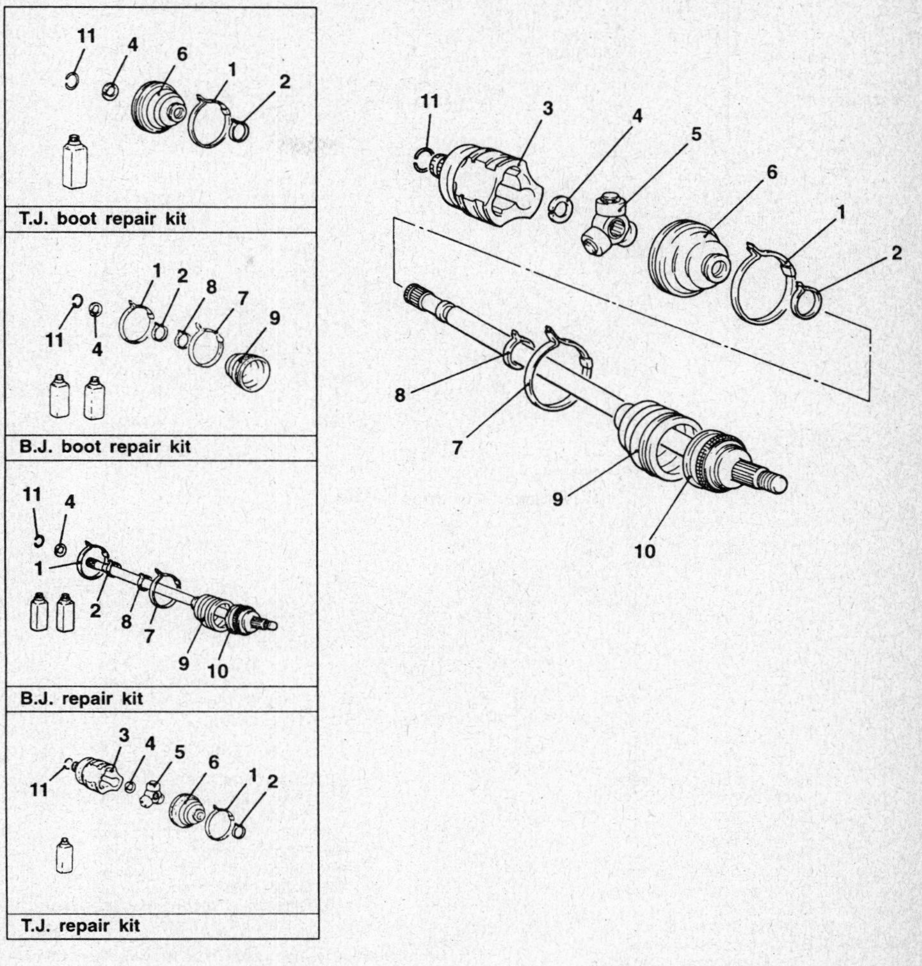

1. T.J. boot band (large)
2. T.J. boot band (small)
3. T.J. case
4. Snap ring
5. Spider assembly
6. T.J. boot
7. B.J. boot band (large)
8. B.J. boot band (small)
9. B.J. boot
10. B.J. assembly
11. Circlip

Caution
Do not disassemble the B.J. assembly.

Fig. 3 Exploded view of driveshaft

2. Check final drive gear backlash as follows:
   a. Lock drive pinion in place, then mount dial indicator as shown in **Fig. 9.**
   b. Measure backlash at four points or more on the circumference of the drive gear. Backlash should be within .004–.006 inch.
3. Mount dial indicator as shown in **Fig. 10,** then measure drive gear runabout at the shoulder on the reverse side of drive gear. Runabout should not exceed .002 inch.
4. Lock side gear with a wedge as shown in **Fig. 11,** then measure differential gear backlash with dial indicator on pinion gear. Differential gear backlash should not exceed .008 inch.
5. Check final drive gear tooth contact as follows:
   a. Apply a thin, uniform coat of machine blue to both surfaces of drive gear teeth as shown in **Fig. 12.**
   b. Insert a brass rod between differential carrier and differential case, then rotate companion flange by hand (once in normal direction, and once in reverse direction) while applying a load to drive gear, so revolution torque applied to the drive pinion is approximately 28–33 inch lbs., **Fig. 13.**
   c. Compare and adjust tooth contact pattern as shown in **Fig. 14.**
   d. If correct tooth pattern cannot be obtained by adjustment, drive gear and drive pinion have exceeded their usage limit and both gears should be replaced as a set.

Disassemble

1. Support working base in a vise, and attach differential carrier to working base.
2. Remove differential cover and vent plug, **Fig. 15.**

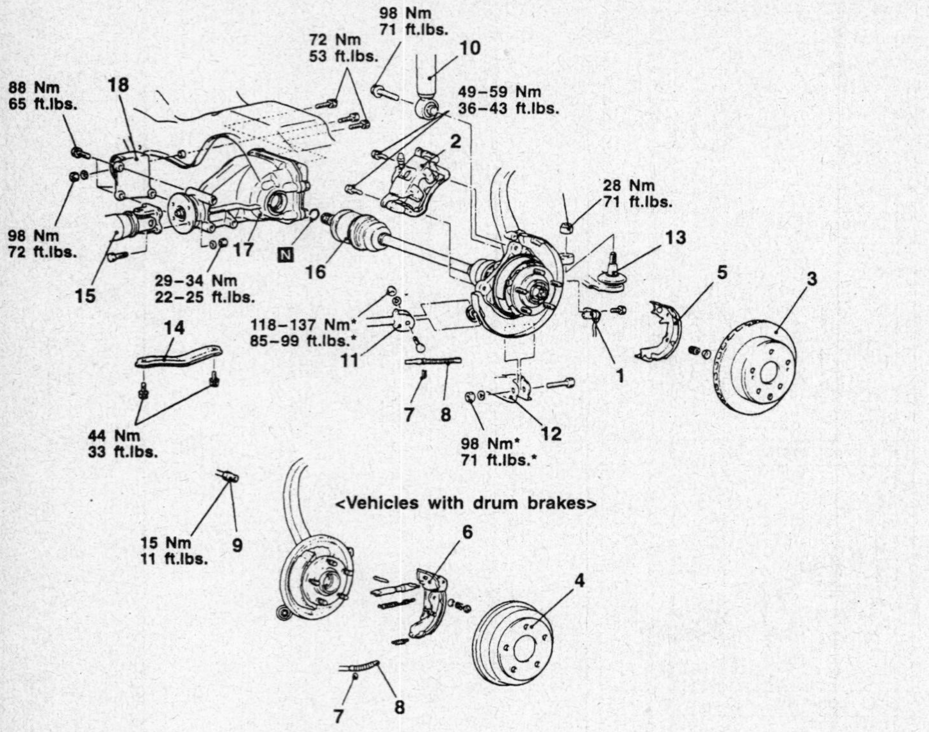

1. Rear wheel speed sensor <Vehicles with ABS>
2. Caliper assembly
3. Brake disc
4. Brake drum
5. Shoe and lever assembly
6. Shoe and lever assembly
7. Clip
8. Parking brake cable
9. Brake pipe connection
10. Shock absorber connection
11. Trailing arm connection
12. Lower arm connection
13. Toe control arm ball joint and knucle connection
14. Differential mount support
15. Propeller shaft connection
16. Drive shaft connection
17. Differential carrier
18. Differential mount bracket assembly

Caution

***: Indicates parts which should be temporarily tightened, and then fully tightened with the vehicle on the ground in the unladen condition.**

CR3039500398000X

Fig. 4 Differential carrier removal

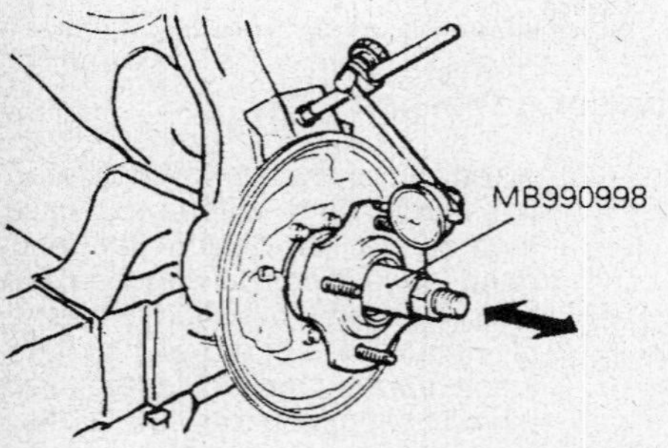

CR3039200184000X

Fig. 6 Rear wheel bearing endplay check

3. Using two hammer shafts, or equivalent, slowly and carefully pry differential case assembly out of gear carrier. **Ensure side bearing outer race is not dropped when removing differential case assembly. Keep right and left side bearings separate, so they do not become mixed at time of reassembly.**
4. Using side bearing puller tool No. MB990810 and side bearing cup tool No. MB990811, or equivalents, pull out

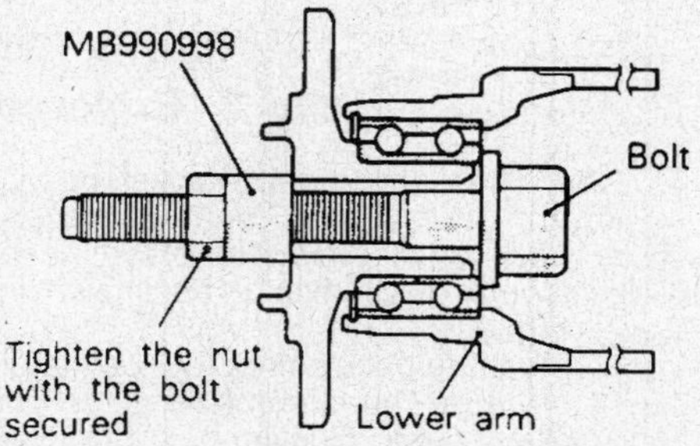

CR3039200183000X

Fig. 7 Bolt tool installation

side bearing inner races, **Fig. 16.**

5. Scribe mating marks on differential case and drive gear, then loosen drive gear attaching bolts in diagonal sequence to remove drive gear.
6. Drive out lockpin with a punch and remove pinion gears, pinion washers, side gears, side gear spacers and differential case.
7. Scribe mating marks on drive pinion and companion flange. **Mating marks should not be made to contact surfaces of companion flange and propeller shaft.**

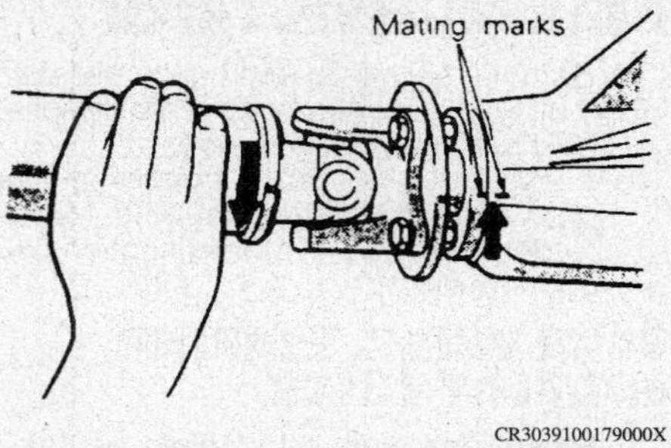

CR3039100179000X

Fig. 5 Rear axle total backlash check

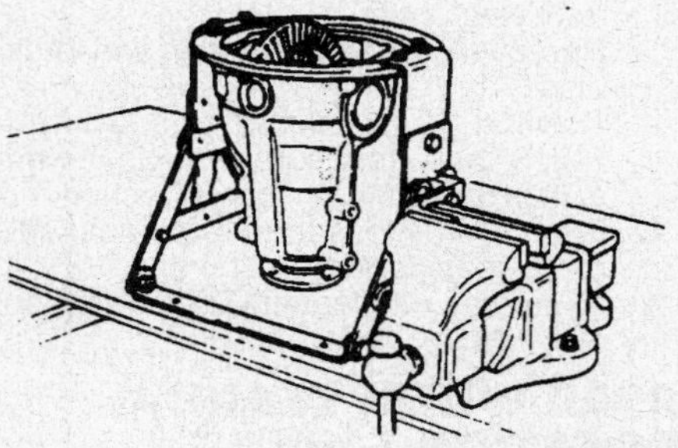

CR3039100203000X

Fig. 8 Differential carrier positioned in working base. Less limited-slip

8. Using side bearing puller tool No. MB990810, or equivalent, drive out drive pinion together with drive pinion spacer and drive pinion front shims.
9. Mount companion flange attached to taper roller bearing puller tool No. C-293-PA and bearing remover tool No. C-293-45, or equivalents in a vise as shown in **Fig. 17.** Pull drive pinion rear bearing inner race out of companion flange.
10. Remove drive pinion rear shim used for drive pinion height adjustment and drive pinion.
11. Remove oil seal, then drive out drive pinion front bearing from gear carrier.
12. Drive out drive pinion rear bearing outer race from gear carrier.

Inspection

1. Check companion flange for wear or damage.
2. Check oil seal for wear or deterioration.
3. Check bearing for wear and discoloration.
4. Check gear carrier for cracks.
5. Check drive pinion and drive gear for wear or cracks.
6. Check side gears, pinion gears and pinion shaft for wear or damage.
7. Check side gear spline for wear or damage.

Assemble

1. Apply multipurpose grease to lip of oil seal, then using installer bar tool No. C-4171 and oil seal installer tool No. MB991115, or equivalents, press seal into gear carrier.
2. Using installer handle tool No. C-4171

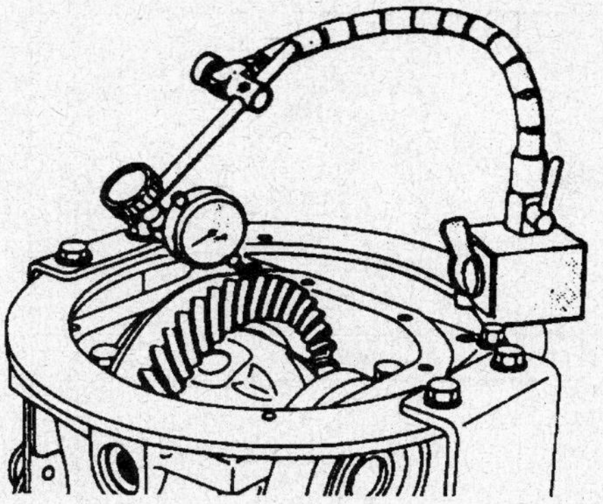

CR3039100204000X

Fig. 9 Final drive gear backlash measurement. Less limited-slip

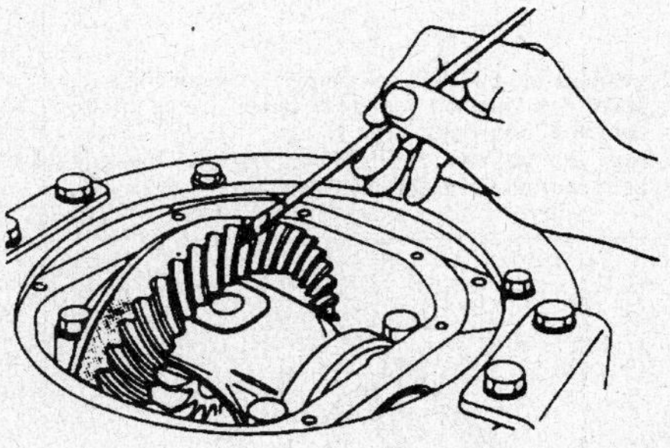

CR3039100207000X

Fig. 12 Final drive gear to check tooth contact marking. Less limited-slip

and bearing installer tool Nos. MB990932 and MB990935, or equivalents, press drive pinion rear and front bearing outer races into gear carrier.

3. Adjust drive pinion height as follows:
   a. Install a pinion height gauge set tool Nos. MB990835 and MB990836, or equivalent, and drive pinion front and rear bearing inner races on gear carrier as shown in **Fig. 18. Apply a thin coat of multipurpose grease to mating surface on washer of tool.**
   b. Tighten handle of special tool until standard value of drive pinion turning torque is obtained. Refer to **Fig. 19.**
   c. Measure drive pinion turning torque (without oil seal).
   d. Position special tool No. MB990835, or equivalent, in side bearing seat of gear carrier as shown in **Fig. 20.** Select a drive pinion rear shim of a thickness which corresponds to the gap between special tools. **Clean side bearing seat thoroughly. When positioning special tool, ensure cutout sections of tool are in position shown in Fig. 20, and that special tool is in close contact with side bearing seat. When selecting drive pinion rear shims, keep number of drive shims to a minimum.**
   e. Fit selected drive pinion rear shims to drive pinion, then using bearing installer tool No. MB990728, or equivalent, press rear bearing inner race onto drive pinion as shown in **Fig. 21.**

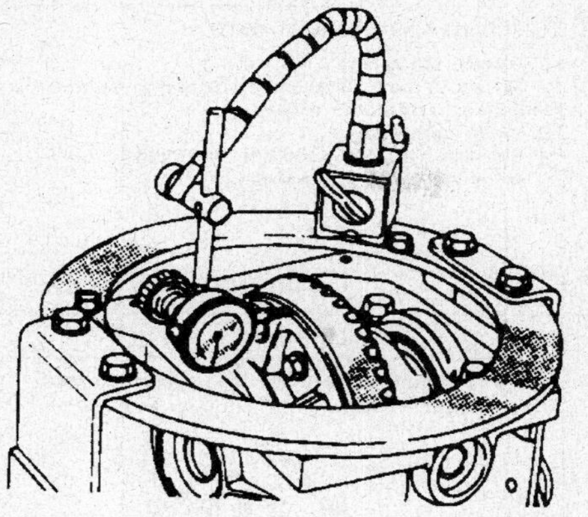

CR3039100205000X

Fig. 10 Drive gear runout measurement. Less limited-slip

4. Adjust drive pinion preload as follows:
   a. Fit drive pinion front shims between drive pinion spacer and drive pinion front bearing inner race.
   b. **Torque** companion flange nut to 116–159 ft. lbs. using end yoke holder tool No. MB990767, or equivalent. **Do not install oil seal.**
   c. Using a torque wrench, measure drive pinion turning torque as shown in **Fig. 22.**
   d. Compare measurement. Refer to **Fig. 19.** If turning torque is not within specification, adjust by replacing drive pinion front shims or drive pinion spacer. **If a number of shims will be required to bring preload within specified value, reduce the number of shims by replacing the spacer.**
   e. Remove companion flange and drive pinion, then drive oil seal into gear carrier front lip. Apply a thin coat of multipurpose grease to the oil seal lip.
   f. Apply a thin coat of multipurpose grease to companion flange washer contacting surface prior to installing drive pinion.
   g. Install drive pinion assembly and companion flange with mating marks aligned, and **torque** companion flange self-locking nut to 116–159 ft. lbs.
   h. Measure drive pinion turning torque, and compare with specified value. Refer to **Fig. 23.** If turning torque is not within specified value, ensure companion flange self-locking nut is tightened within specification and oil seal is correctly installed.
5. Clean drive gear attaching bolts, then using a M10 X 1.25 tap, remove adhesive adhering to threaded holes of drive gear. Clean remaining material out of drive gear using compressed air.
6. Apply multipurpose adhesive Mopar Loctite No. 271, or equivalent to threaded holes of drive gear.

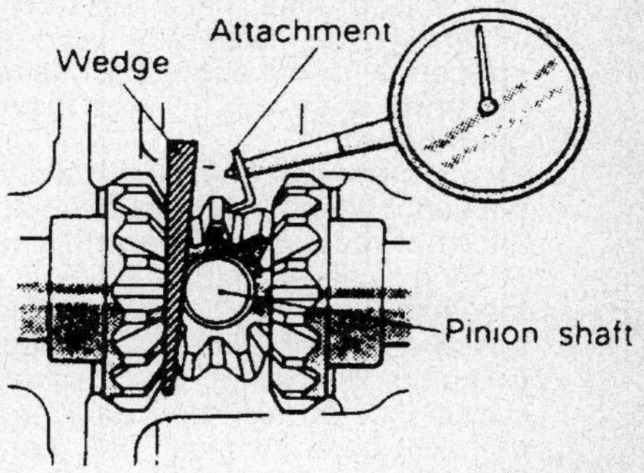

CR3039100206000X

Fig. 11 Differential gear backlash measurement. Less limited-slip

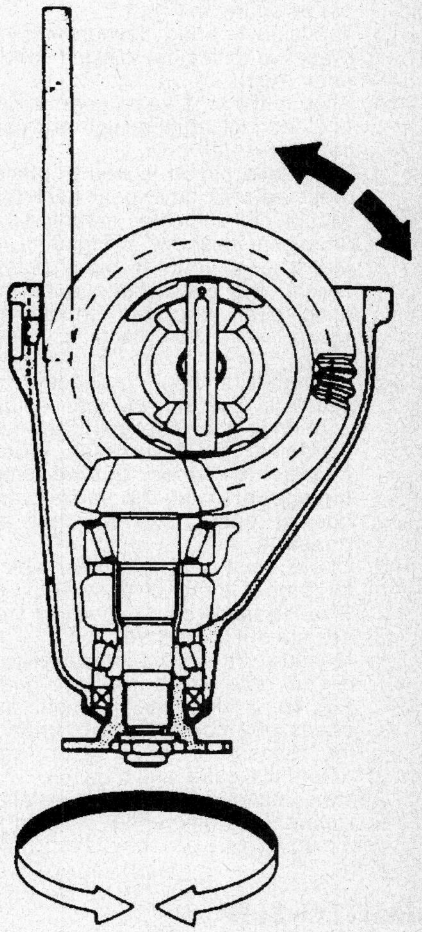

CR3039100208000X

Fig. 13 Final drive gear rotation. Less limited-slip

7. Install drive gear onto differential case with mating marks aligned. **Torque** drive gear attaching bolts in a diagonal sequence to 58–65 ft. lbs.
8. Using bearing installer tool No. MB990728, or equivalent, press side bearing inner races to differential case.
9. Adjust final drive gear backlash as follows:
   a. Install side bearing spacers, which are thinner than those removed, to side bearing outer races and then

mount differential case assembly into gear carrier. **Use side bearing spacers with the same thickness for both drive pinion and drive gear sides.**

b. Push differential case to one side of the gear carrier and measure clearance between gear carrier and side bearing as shown in **Fig. 24.**

c. Measure thickness of side bearing spacers on one side, then select two pairs of spacers which correspond to that thickness plus one half of clearance plus .002 inch, **Fig. 25.** Install one pair each to drive pinion side and drive gear side.

d. Install side bearing spacers and differential case assembly to gear carrier as shown in **Fig. 26.**

e. Tap side bearing spacers with a brass bar to fit them to side bearing outer race.

f. Align mating marks on gear carrier and bearing cap, then tighten bearing cap.

g. With drive pinion locked in place, measure final drive gear backlash with a dial indicator mounted on drive gear as shown in **Fig. 9.**

h. Measure at four or more points around the circumference of the drive gear, backlash should be within .004–.006 inch (.11–.16 mm).

i. Change side bearing spacers as shown in **Fig. 27,** and then adjust final drive gear backlash between drive gear and drive pinion. **When increasing number of side bearing spacers, use the same number of each, and as few as possible.**

j. Check drive gear and drive pinion for proper tooth contact, refer to "Pre-Disassemble Inspection" for adjustment procedure.

k. Measure drive gear runout at shoulder on reverse side of drive gear, **Fig. 10.** If drive gear runout exceeds .002 inch, reinstall by changing phase of drive gear and differential case, and measure.

10. Apply a semi-drying sealant to installation surface of differential cover and vent plug, **torque** cover bolts to 22–30 ft. lbs.

LIMITED-SLIP

Pre-Disassemble Inspection

1. Secure differential case assembly in a vise so differential side gear (right) is facing upward as shown in **Fig. 28.**
2. Insert a .0012 inch (.03 mm) feeler gauge at two places (diagonally) between differential case B and thrust washer, **Fig. 29. Do not insert feeler gauge in oil groove of differential case B.**
3. Insert side gear holding tool No. MB990990, or equivalent, at spline part of differential case B (right) and ensure side gear rotates, **Fig. 30.**
4. Insert a .0035 inch (.09 mm) feeler gauge to replace .0012 inch (.03 mm) feeler gauge.
5. Insert side gear holding tool No. MB990990, or equivalent, at spline part of differential case B (right) and ensure side gear does not rotate, **Fig. 30.**
6. Differential gear backlash (clearance in thrust direction of side gear) should be within .0012–.0035 inch (.03 mm–.09 mm). If clearance in the thrust direction of the side gear is within standard value range, backlash of differential gear is normal.
7. If clearance in thrust direction of side gear is not within specification, remove differential case A and make adjustment by adjusting thickness of the thrust washer (left).

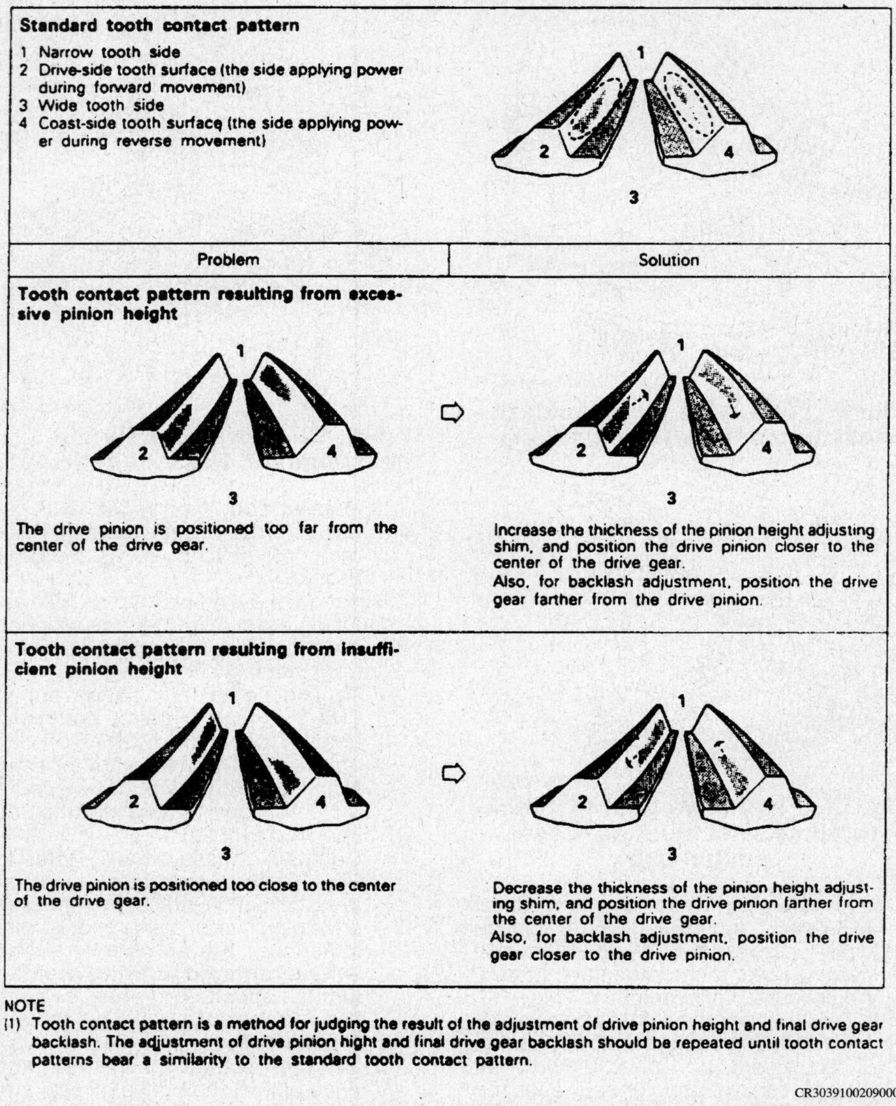
Standard tooth contact pattern
1 Narrow tooth side
2 Drive-side tooth surface (the side applying power during forward movement)
3 Wide tooth side
4 Coast-side tooth surface (the side applying power during reverse movement)
Problem
Solution
Tooth contact pattern resulting from excessive pinion height
The drive pinion is positioned too far from the center of the drive gear.
Increase the thickness of the pinion height adjusting shim, and position the drive pinion closer to the center of the drive gear.
Also, for backlash adjustment, position the drive gear farther from the drive pinion.
Tooth contact pattern resulting from insufficient pinion height
The drive pinion is positioned too close to the center of the drive gear.
Decrease the thickness of the pinion height adjusting shim, and position the drive pinion farther from the center of the drive gear.
Also, for backlash adjustment, position the drive gear closer to the drive pinion.
NOTE
(1) Tooth contact pattern is a method for judging the result of the adjustment of drive pinion height and final drive gear backlash. The adjustment of drive pinion hight and final drive gear backlash should be repeated until tooth contact patterns bear a similarity to the standard tooth contact pattern.
CR3039100209000X

Fig. 14 Final drive gear & drive pinion adjustment. Less limited-slip

Disassemble

1. Remove attaching screw from differential case A, **Fig. 31.**
2. Remove differential case B.
3. Remove left thrust washer. **Since thrust washer from left side is of a different thickness than the right side, it will be necessary to mark the washer in some manner for assembly reference.**
4. Remove viscous unit, pinion mate washer, differential pinion mate, pinion shaft and rightward differential side gear.
5. Remove right thrust washer. **Since thrust washer from right side is of a different thickness than the left side, it will be necessary to mark the washer for assembly reference.**

Inspection

1. Check gears and differential pinion shaft for unusual wear or damage.
2. Check spline part of right side differential gear for stepped wear or damage.
3. Check thrust washer and pinion mate washer for unusual wear of contact surfaces, heat damage or other damage.
4. Check contact surfaces of differential

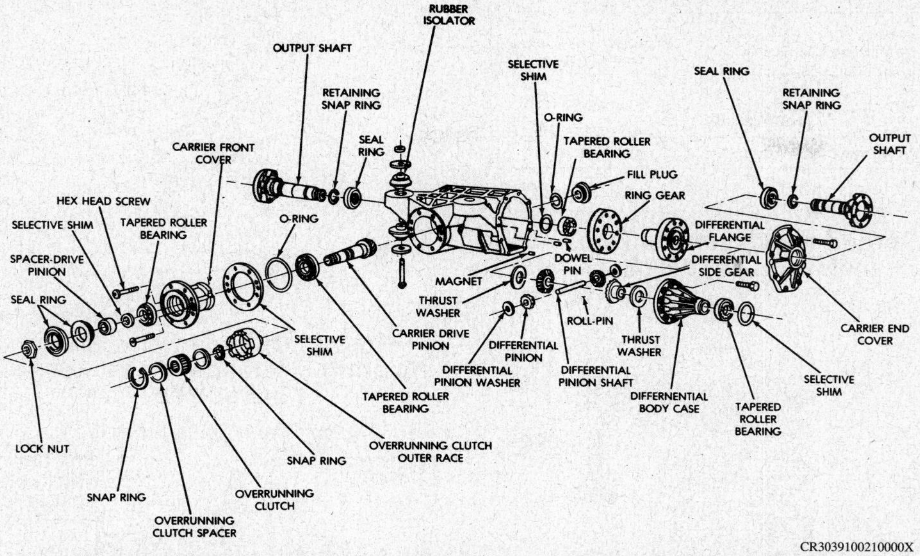

CR3039100210000X

Fig. 15 Exploded view of differential carrier. Less limited-slip

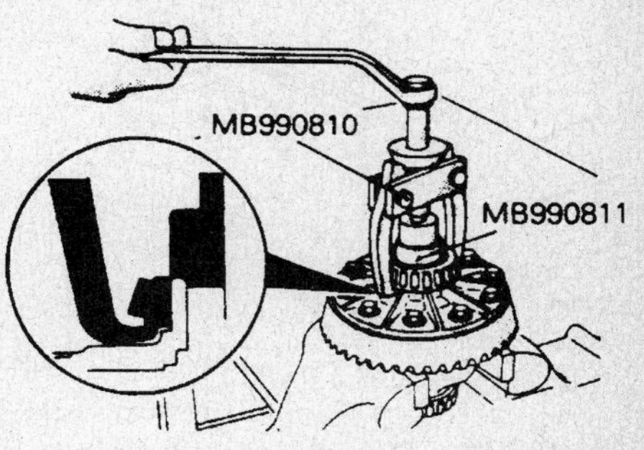

CR3039100211000X

Fig. 16 Side bearing inner race removal. Less limited-slip

Bearing classification	Bearing lubrication	Rotation torque (starting friction torque) Nm (in.lbs.)
New	None (with rust-prevention oil)	0.9–1.2 (8–10)
New/reused	Oil application	0.4–0.5 (3–4)

NOTE
(1) Gradually tighten the nut of the special tool while checking the drive pinion turning torque.
(2) Because the special tool cannot be turned one turn, turn it several times within the range that it can be turned; then, after fitting to the bearing, measure the rotation torque.

CR3039100215000X

Fig. 19 Drive pinion turning torque specifications (less oil seal installed). Less limited-slip

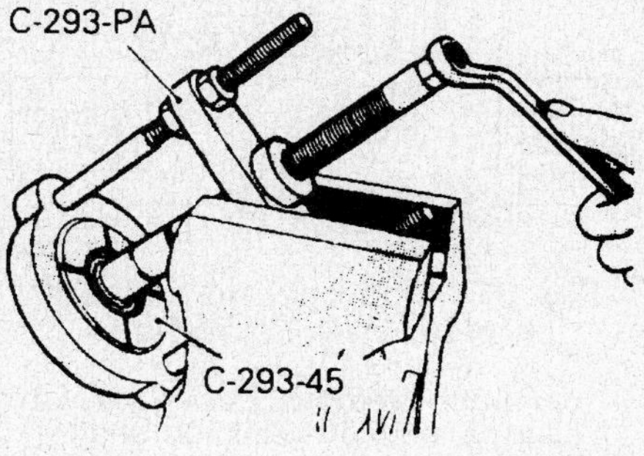

CR3039100212000X

Fig. 17 Rear bearing inner race removal. Less limited-slip

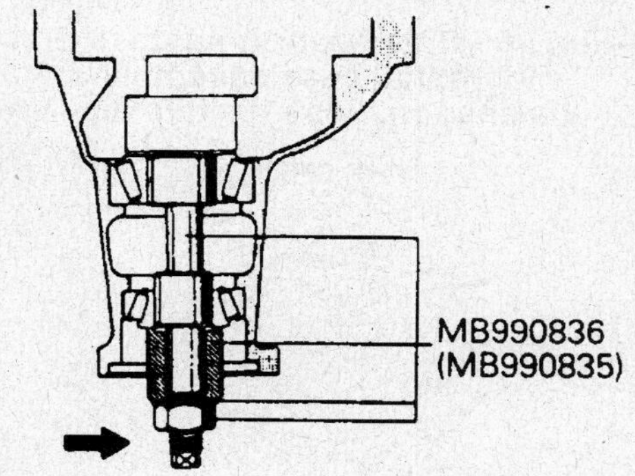

CR3039100214000X

Fig. 18 Drive pinion height adjustment. Less limited-slip

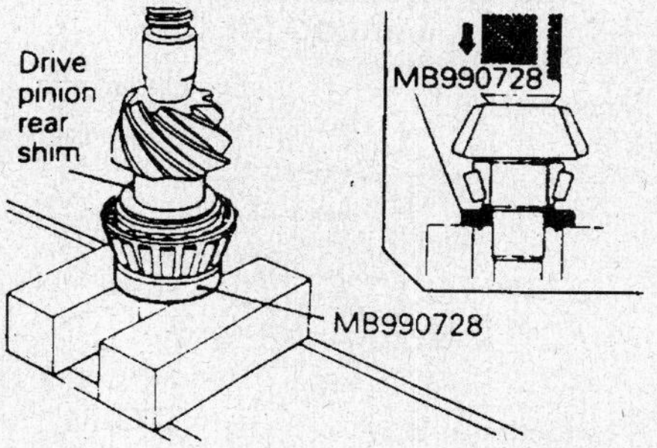

CR3039100217000X

Fig. 21 Drive pinion inner race installation. Less limited-slip

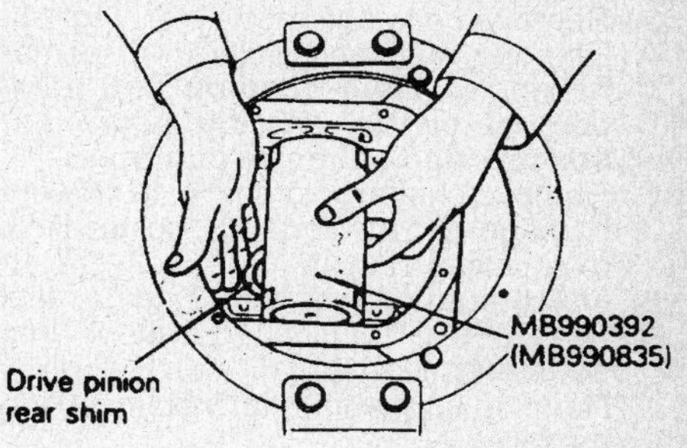

CR3039100216000X

Fig. 20 Selecting drive pinion adjustment shims. Less limited-slip

cases A and B for damage or wear, **Fig. 32.**

5. Check spline part of viscous unit for stepped wear or damage, and check contact surface with differential case B.
6. Check left side gear of viscous unit for unusual wear or damage.

Assemble

1. With pinion mate washer in position shown in **Fig. 33,** install to differential pinion mate to differential pinion shaft, and then install to differential case B.
2. If differential side gear and pinion mate gear have been replaced, select left side thrust washer as follows:
   a. Wash differential side gear and pinion mate gear in unleaded gasoline to remove all foreign material.
   b. Install previously used thrust washers (matching left and right sides), together with gears, viscous unit, pinion mate washer and pinion shaft to differential cases A and B. Using screws, secure temporarily.
   c. Secure differential case assembly in a vise so right side differential side gear is facing upward, **Fig. 28. Do not hold differential case too tightly.**
   d. Insert a .0012 inch feeler gauge at two places (diagonally) between differential case B and right side thrust washer. **Do not insert feeler gauge in oil groove of differential case B.**
   e. Insert side gear holding tool No. MB990990, or equivalent, at spline part of differential case B (right) and ensure side gear does not rotate, **Fig. 30.**
   f. Differential gear backlash (clearance in thrust direction of side gear) should be within .0012–.0035 inch (.03 mm–.09 mm). If clearance in the thrust direction of the side gear is within standard value range, backlash of differential gear is normal.
   g. If clearance in thrust direction of side gear is not within specification, remove differential case A and make adjustment by selecting appropriate thrust washer from chart shown in **Fig. 34.**
3. After installing thrust washers, align mating marks of differential cases and reassemble.

PROPELLER SHAFT

REPLACE

1. Place suitable match marks on all propeller shaft components where disassembly will occur.
2. Place suitable supports under shaft

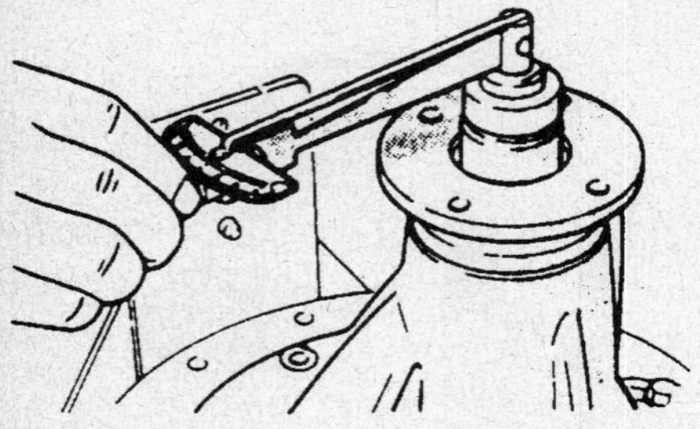

CR3039100218000X

Fig. 22 Drive pinion turning torque check. Less limited-slip

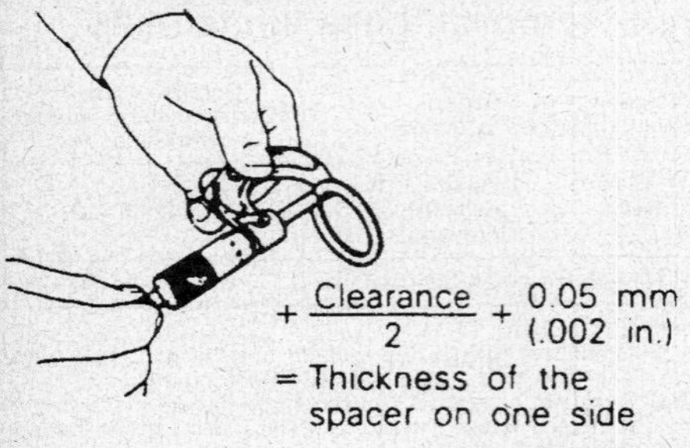

+ Clearance/2 + 0.05 mm (.002 in.)
= Thickness of the spacer on one side

CR3039100223000X

Fig. 25 Side bearing spacers selection. Less limited-slip

Bearing classification	Bearing lubrication	Rotation torque (starting friction torque) Nm (in.lbs.)
New	None (with rust-prevention oil)	1.0–1.3 (9–11)
New/reused	Oil application	0.5–0.6 (4–5)

CR3039100219000X

Fig. 23 Drive pinion turning torque specifications (w/oil seal installed). Less limited-slip

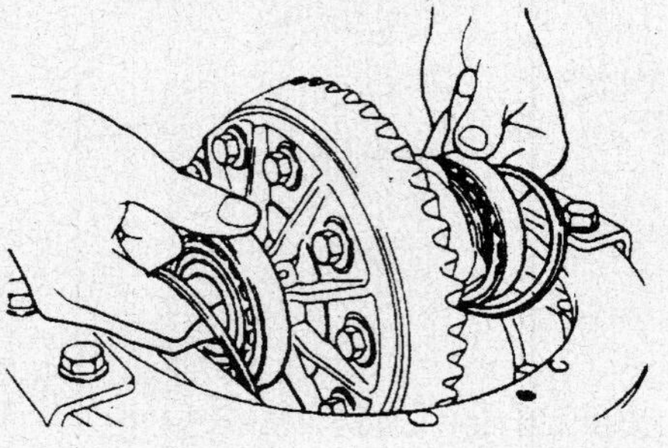

CR3039100224000X

Fig. 26 Side bearing spacers & differential case assembly installation. Less limited-slip

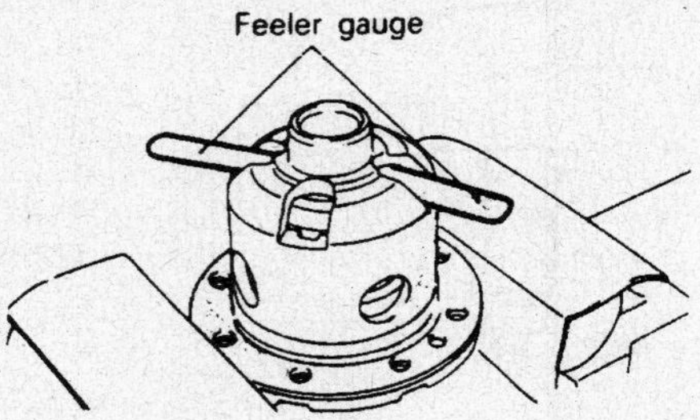

CR3039100233000X

Fig. 28 Differential case assembly mounting in vise. Limited-Slip

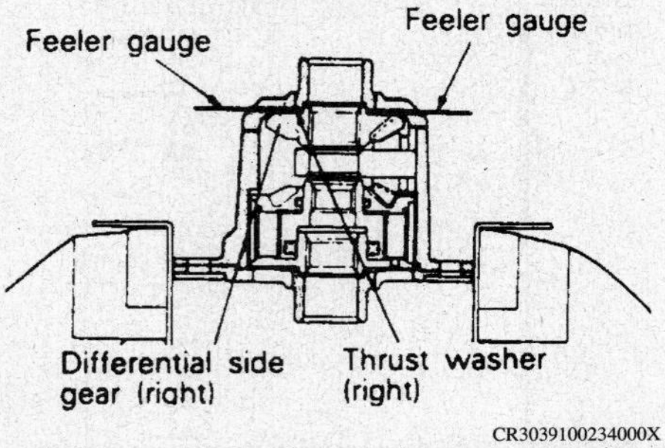

CR3039100234000X

Fig. 29 Feeler gauge insertion into differential case. Limited-Slip

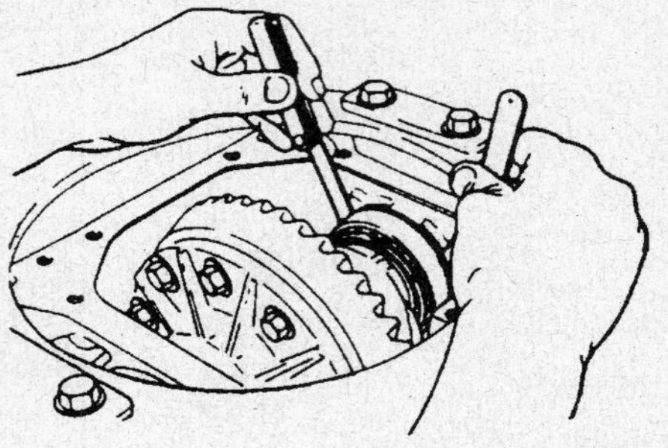

CR3039100222000X

Fig. 24 Gear carrier & side bearing clearance check. Less limited-slip

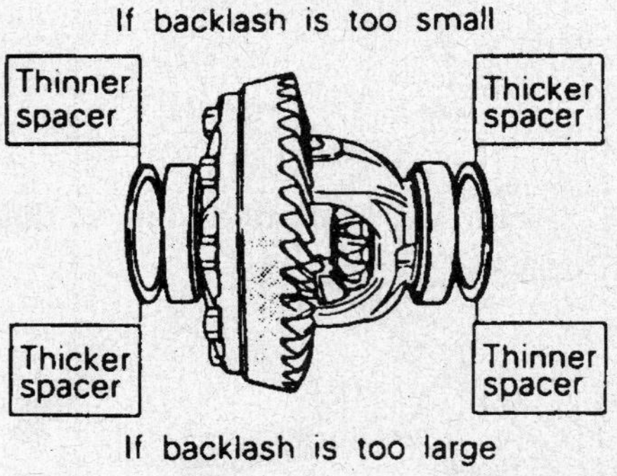

CR3039100225000X

Fig. 27 Side bearing spacers change. Less limited-slip

sections to prevent over flexing of components during removal.

3. Remove bolts at flange yoke, **Fig. 35.**
4. Remove nuts and bolts from center bearing(s). **Note position and location of center bearing alignment spacers and shims as equipped.**
5. Remove shaft from vehicle, to prevent damage to joints and boot, do not allow over flexing of shaft.
6. Install output shaft blocker plug, tool No. MB991193, or equivalent into transfer assembly.
7. Reverse procedure to install, noting the following:
   a. Ensure alignment of all match marks.
   b. **Torque** differential flange yoke bolts to 22–25 ft. lbs.
   c. **Torque** center bearing mount nuts and bolts to 22 ft. lbs.

PROPELLER SHAFT SERVICE

LOBO JOINT, JOINT BOOT & COMPANION FLANGE

Removal

1. Place suitable match marks on all components to be disassembled **Fig. 35.**
2. Remove bolts retaining Lobo joint to companion flange, then separate joint from flange.
3. Using a suitable screwdriver, tap flange edge of boot off Lobo joint outer race.
4. **On models where outer race of joint can be removed,** proceed as follows:
   a. Place match marks on all components and note position of balls.
   b. Tilt edge of outer race until balls can removed from cage, then remove balls.
   c. Remove outer race and cage, then snap ring retaining inner race to shaft.
   d. Using a suitable fuller, remove inner race from shaft.
5. **On models where outer race of joint can not be removed,** remove snap ring retaining joint to shaft.
6. **On models where outer race of joint can not be removed,** using a suitable fuller carefully pull joint from shaft.
7. **On all models,** remove boot clamp then boot and if equipped, boot washer.

Cleaning & Inspection

Do not use solvents to clean boot, wipe clean only.

1. Using a suitable solvent, clean, then dry joint components.
2. Check splines of shaft and joint for wear or damage.
3. Check ball grooves and balls for uneven wear, damage or rust.
4. Check cage for wear, rust or damage.
5. Inspect boot for tears, deterioration and chafing.

Installation

Note position of bosses in small end I.D. of boot for later assembly. These are used to ventilate boot and joint.

Ensure seat area on shaft for small end of joint is grease free when installing boot. Grease in this area will prevent proper ventilation of joint.

1. Place tape over shaft spline to protect boot during installation, then, as equipped, install boot washer, boot clamp and boot. Remove tape.
2. **On models where joint was disassembled,** reassemble joint, ensure match marks are aligned. Joint boot flange recess on outer race, spline recess of inner race and chamfer of cage should all be assembled on same side of joint.

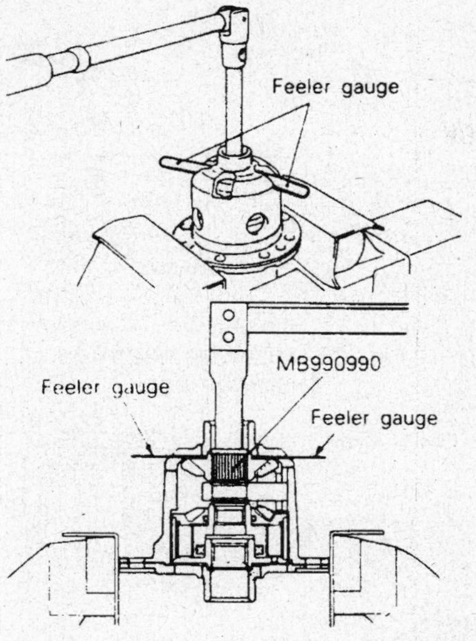

Fig. 30 Differential gear backlash check. Limited-Slip

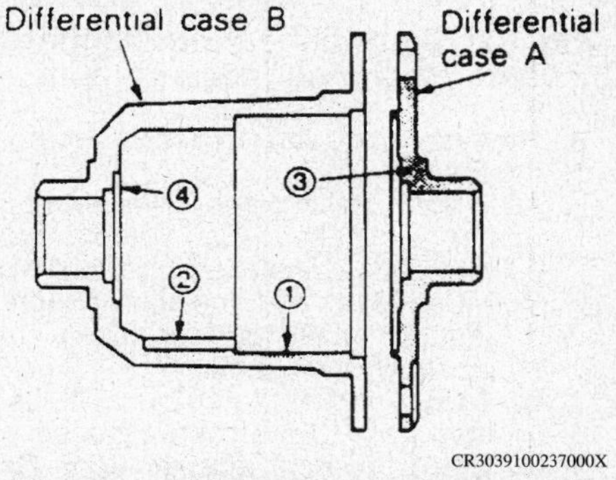

Fig. 32 Differential case contact surfaces. Limited-Slip

3. **On all models,** pack joint and boot with 1.6–2.0 oz. of a suitable joint grease.
4. Using a suitable adhesive, position and secure joint gaskets.
5. Place joint on shaft splines so that bolt holes of boot flange and joint align, then using a suitable socket or tube and hammer drive joint onto shaft and install snap ring.
6. Tighten boot clamp, ensure clip of clamp is on opposite side of bosses on inside of boot small end used for ventilation of joint.
7. Align match marks on companion flange and joint, install bolts, then **torque** bolts as shown in **Figs. 35.**

UNJOINTED JOURNALS

Removal

1. Place match marks on all components to be disassembled, then remove snap rings retaining journal bearing, **Fig. 35.**
2. Remove journal bearings using press tool as shown in **Fig. 36** or equivalent.
3. Remove journal from yoke.

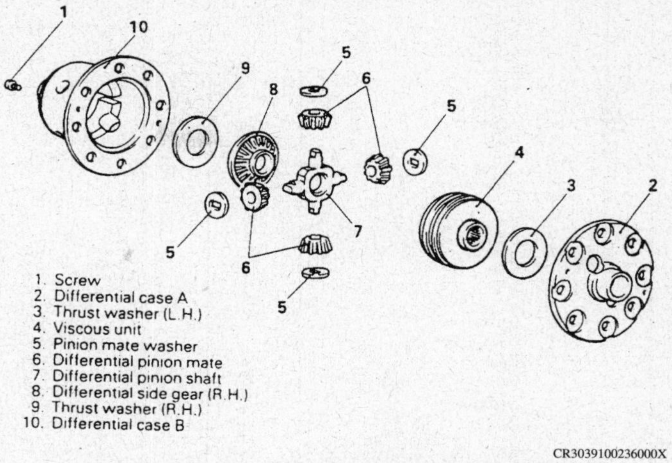

Fig. 31 Exploded view of differential carrier. Limited-Slip

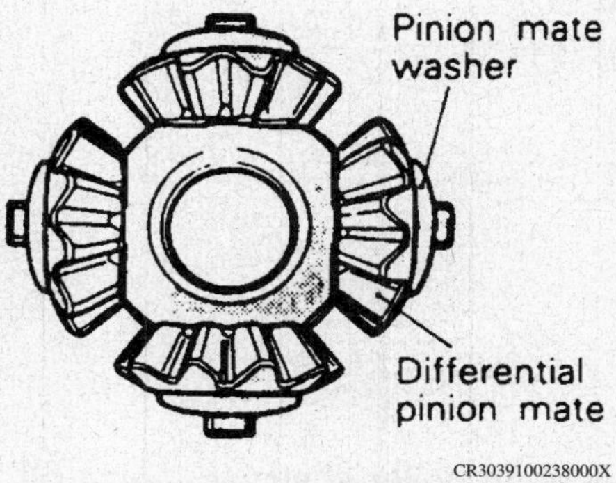

Fig. 33 Differential pinion mate installation. Limited-Slip

Installation

1. Position journal and journal bearings into yoke, then using press tool shown in **Fig. 36,** or equivalent. Press journal bearings into yoke and onto journal.
2. Install and seat snap rings into yoke, then using a suitable brass punch and hammer, tap journal and bearings until seated against one snap ring.
3. Using a suitable feeler gauge, measure resulting clearance, standard value dimension (A), between journal bearing cap and snap ring, **Fig. 37.**
4. If standard value dimension is less than or exceeds .0008–.0024 inch, select a new PAIR of snap rings from table **Fig. 38,** to set clearance to standard value.
5. Center journal bearing in yoke and install snap rings.

CENTER BEARINGS

1. Remove Unjointed journal or Lobo joint as described under "Lobo Joint, Joint Boot & Companion Flange" or " unjointed Journals" in this section.
2. Remove nut retaining companion flange or yoke, **Fig. 35.**
3. Using a suitable fuller, remove companion flange or yoke from shaft.
4. Using a suitable fuller, remove center bearing from shaft.

Thrust washer (left)	
Part No.	Thickness mm (in.)
MB569243	0.8 (.031)
	0.9 (.035)
	1.0 (.039)
	1.1 (.043)
	1.15 (.045)
	1.2 (.047)
	1.25 (.049)
	1.3 (.051)
	1.35 (.053)
	1.4 (.055)
	1.5 (.059)

CR3039100239000X

Fig. 34 Thrust washer thickness chart. Limited-Slip

5. Reverse procedure to install, noting the following
   a. Using a suitable socket or tube and hammer, drive center bearing then companion flange or yoke onto shaft.
   b. Install washer and nut, then **torque** nut as shown in **Fig. 35.**

REAR AXLE HUB & CARRIER SERVICE

Hub and carrier are serviceable as an assembly only.

1. Remove driveshaft as described under "Driveshaft, Replace" in this section.
2. Remove brake components as described under "Brakes " in the chassis section of this manual.
3. Remove bolts retaining hub & carrier to knuckle, then hub.
4. Reverse procedure to install, **torque** hub and carrier bolts to 54–65 ft. lbs.

POWER TRANSFER UNIT

REPLACE

1. Remove two front exhaust pipe attaching nuts and lower exhaust pipe, **Fig. 39.**

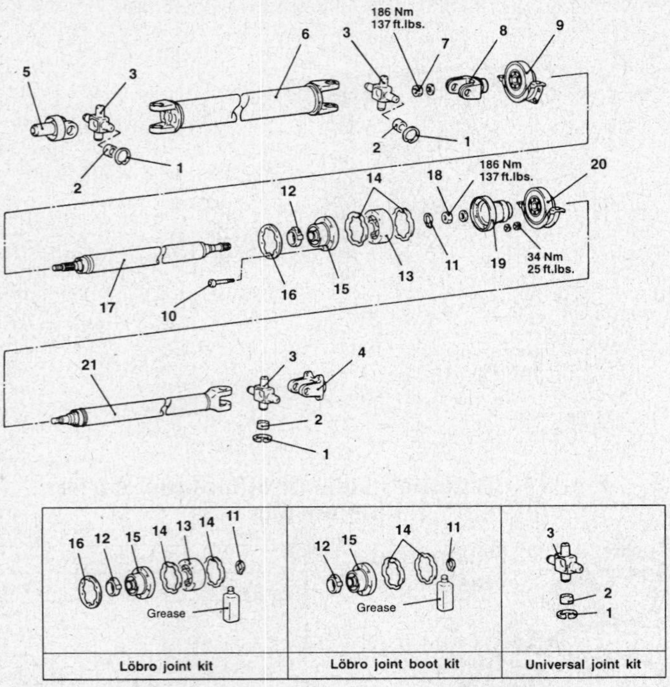

1. Snap ring
2. Journal bearing
3. Journal
4. Flange yoke
5. Sleeve yoke assembly
6. Front propeller shaft
7. Self-locking nut
8. Center yoke
9. Center bearing assembly
10. Bolts
11. Snap ring
12. Boot band
13. Löbro joint assembly
14. Rubber packing
15. Löbro joint boot
16. Washer
17. Center propeller shaft
18. Self-locking nut
19. Companion flange
20. Center bearing assembly
21. Rear propeller shaft

CR3039400393000X

Fig. 35 Exploded view of propeller shaft

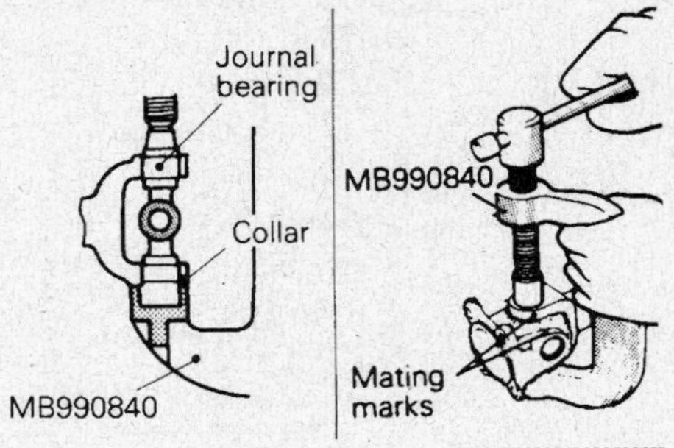

CR3039400395000X

Fig. 36 Journal bearings replacement

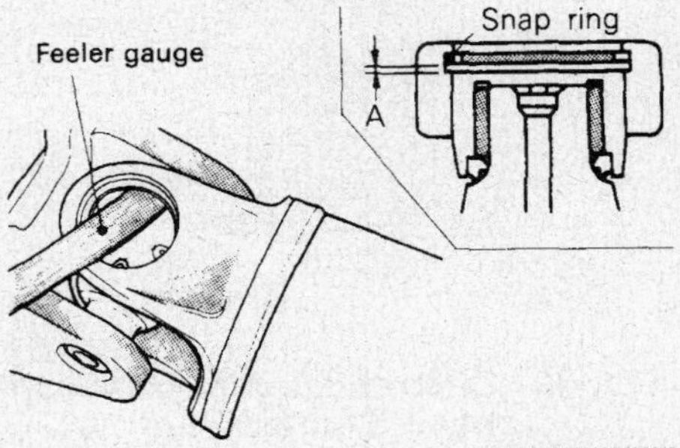

CR3039400396000X

Fig. 37 Journal bearing standard value clearance measurement

2. Remove transfer assembly mounting bolts.
3. Remove driveshaft by moving transfer assembly to the left and lowering the front side. Suspend driveshaft with a piece of wire.
4. Reverse procedure to install, noting the following:
   a. **Torque** transfer assembly mounting bolts to 40–43 ft. lbs.
   b. **Torque** front exhaust pipe attaching nuts to 29–43 ft. lbs.

POWER TRANSFER UNIT SERVICE

DISASSEMBLE

1. Remove cover and cover gasket, **Fig. 40.**
2. Remove extension housing assembly and transfer case subassembly.
3. Remove spacer, Oaring and transfer case adapter subassembly.

SUBASSEMBLY SERVICE

Extension Housing Assembly

1. Remove air breather, **Fig. 41.**
2. Remove dust shield guard and oil seal from extension housing assembly.
3. Reverse procedure to assemble, noting the following:
   a. Use oil seal installer tool No. MD998304, or equivalent, when installing oil seal.
   b. Prior to installing air breather, apply 3M Super Weatherstripped No. 8001 or equivalent to air breather.

Transfer Case Subassembly

1. Remove transfer cover, **Fig. 42.**
2. Remove Oaring, spacer and outer race.
3. Remove drive bevel gear assembly, spacer and oil seal.
4. Reverse procedure to assemble, noting the following:
   a. Use oil seal installer tool No. MD998323, or equivalent, when installing oil seal.
   b. Using reload socket tool No. MB990326 and side gear holding tool No. MB990900, or equivalents, check turning torque of the drive bevel gear assembly as shown in **Fig. 43.** If turning torque is not within 1.23–1.81 ft. lbs., adjust by installing new spacers. Select spacers of nearly same thickness on both sides.

Transfer Case Adapter Subassembly

1. Onstage lockout and using special spanner tool No. MB991013, or equivalent, remove lockout, **Fig. 44.**
2. Using a press, remove driven gear bevel assembly.
3. Remove taper roller bearing, spacer, collar and outer races.
4. Reverse procedure to assemble, noting the following:
   a. When installing taper roller bearing, use installer cap tool No. MD998812, installer tube tool No. MD998814 and installer adapter tool No. MD998820, or equivalent, as shown in **Fig. 45.**
   b. **Torque** lockout to 102–115 ft. lbs., then stake lockout at two places.
   c. Using wrench adapter tool No. MD998806 and suitable torque wrench, or equivalents, check turning torque of the driven bevel gear assembly as shown in **Fig. 46.** If turning torque is not within .72–1.23 ft. lbs., adjust with adjusting spacer.

Drive Bevel Gear Assembly

1. Using bearing removal tool No. MD998801, or equivalent, remove taper roller bearings and drive bevel gear as shown in **Fig. 47.**
2. Using installer cap tool No. MD998812 and installer adapter tool No. MD998827, or equivalent, install taper roller bearing above drive bevel gear, **Fig. 48.**
3. Using bearing installation tool No. MD998350, or equivalent, install taper roller bearing at opposite end drive bevel gear, **Fig. 48.**

Driven Bevel Gear Assembly

1. Using bearing removal tool No. MD998801, or equivalent, remove taper roller bearing from driven gear assembly, **Fig. 49.**
2. Use collar to install taper roller bearing onto driven bevel gear.

Snap Ring Thickness	Color
.0503	—
.0516	Yellow
.0528	Blue
.0539	Purple
.0551	Brown

Fig. 38 Journal bearing snap ring selection table

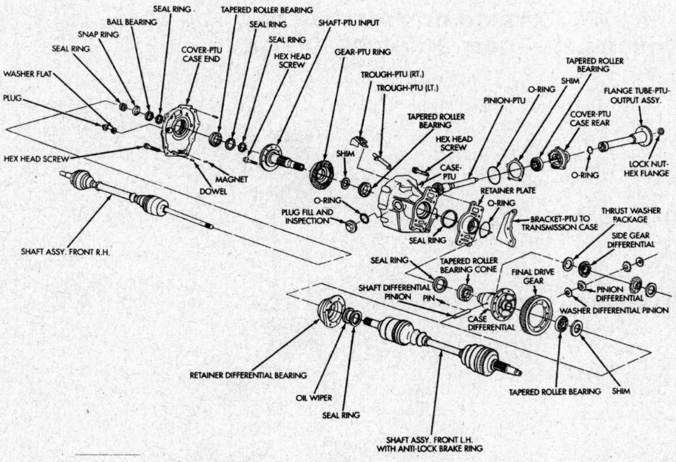

CR3039100243000X

Fig. 40 Exploded view of transfer assembly

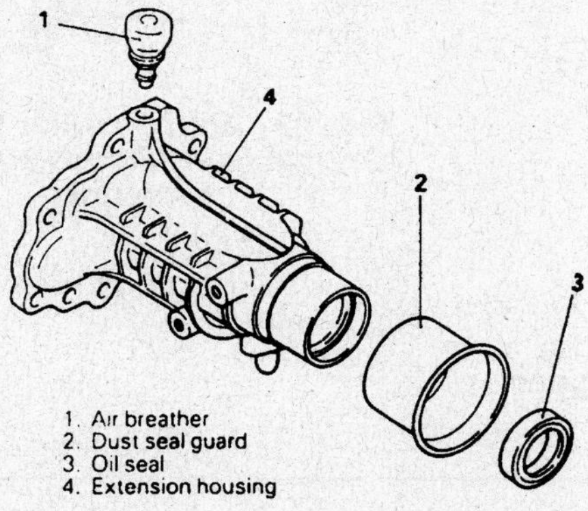

CR3039100244000X

Fig. 41 Extension housing assembly

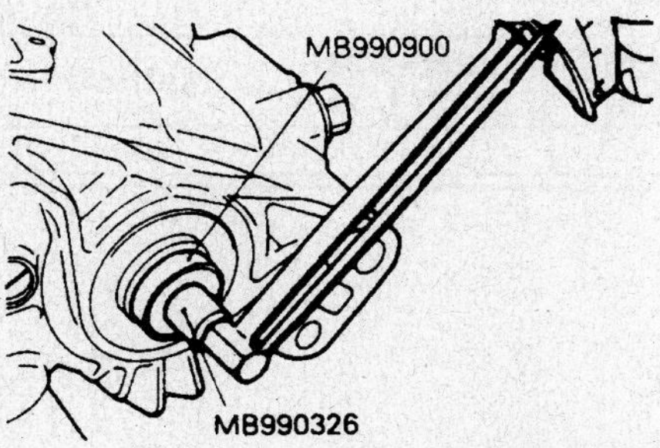

CR3039100246000X

Fig. 43 Turning drive torque of drive bevel gear assembly check

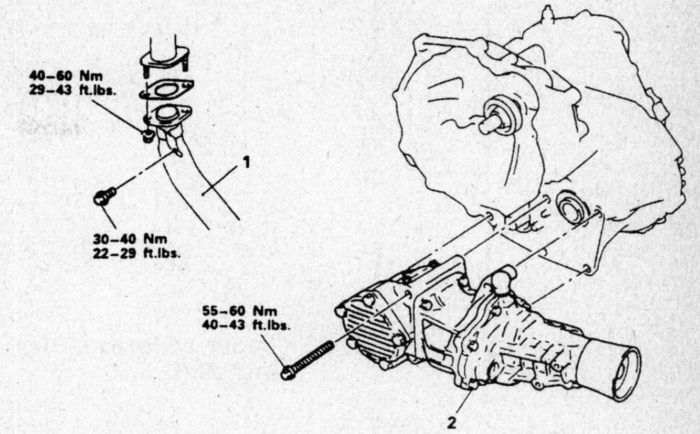

1. Front exhaust pipe connection
2. Transfer assembly

CR3039100191000X

Fig. 39 Transfer assembly removal

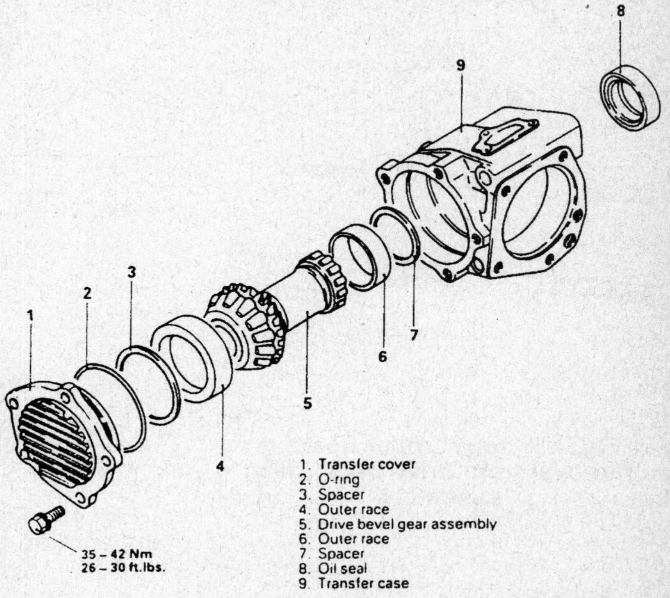

1. Transfer cover
2. O-ring
3. Spacer
4. Outer race
5. Drive bevel gear assembly
6. Outer race
7. Spacer
8. Oil seal
9. Transfer case

CR3039100245000X

Fig. 42 Transfer case subassembly

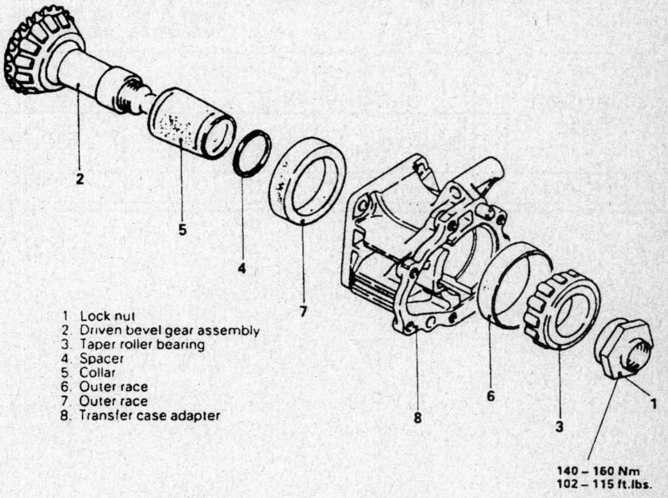

1. Lock nut
2. Driven bevel gear assembly
3. Taper roller bearing
4. Spacer
5. Collar
6. Outer race
7. Outer race
8. Transfer case adapter

CR3039100247000X

Fig. 44 Transfer case adapter subassembly

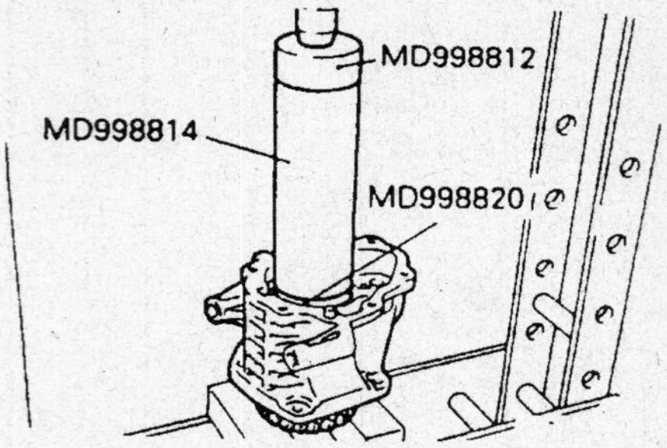

CR3039100248000X

Fig. 45 Taper roller bearing installation

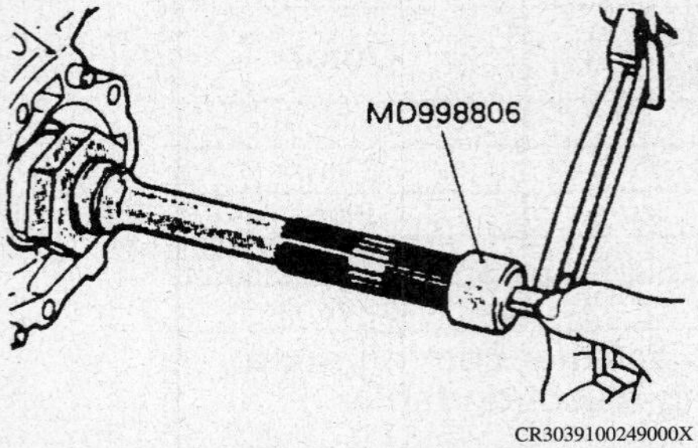

CR3039100249000X

Fig. 46 Turning drive torque of driven bevel gear assembly check

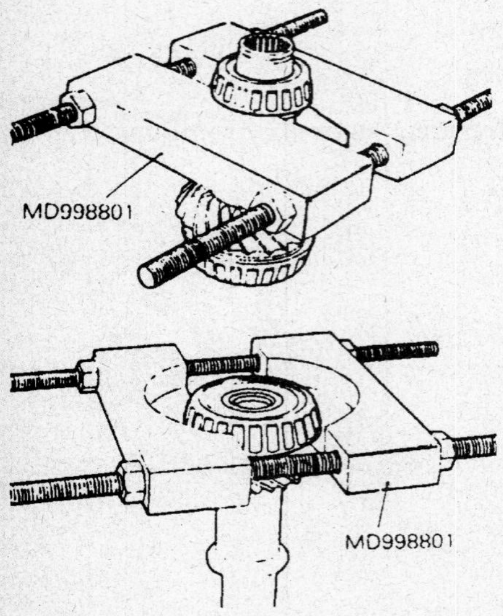

CR3039100250000X

Fig. 47 Taper roller bearing removal from drive bevel gear assembly

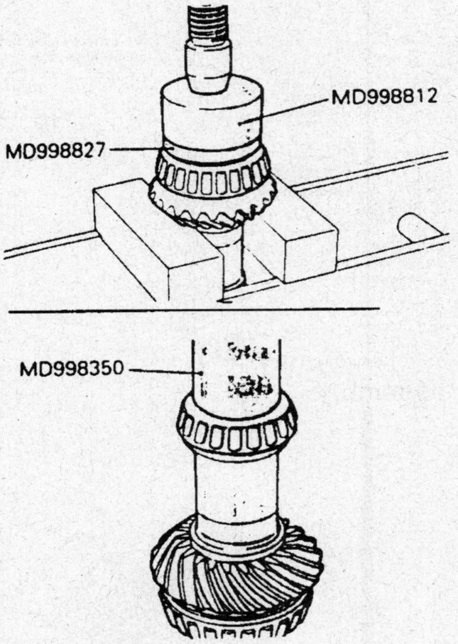

CR3039100251000X

Fig. 48 Taper roller bearing installation on drive bevel gear assembly

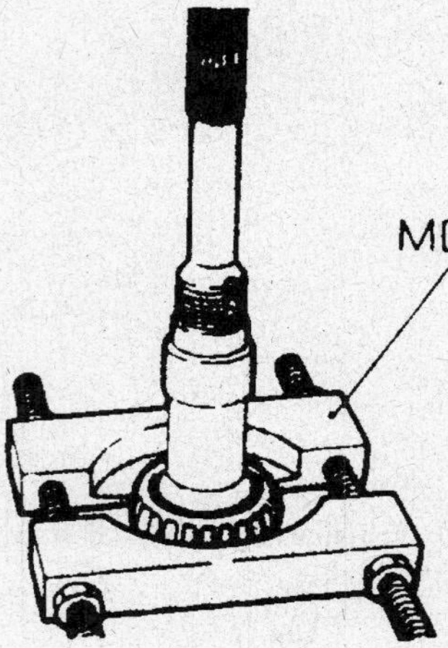

CR3039100252000X

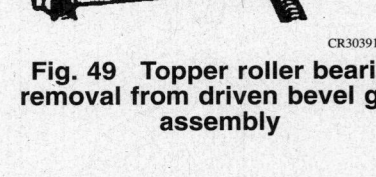

Fig. 49 Topper roller bearing removal from driven bevel gear assembly

REAR AXLE SPECIFICATIONS

Carrier Type	Ring Gear & Pinion Backlash		Pinion Bearing Reload			Differential Bearing Reload	
	Method	Adjustment	Method	With Seal Inch Lbs.	Less Seal Inch Lbs.	Method	Adjust-mend
Removal	Shim	.004–.006	Shim	—	8–10	Shim	.002

ENGINE REBUILDING SPECIFICATIONS

NOTE: For Engine Tightening Specifications, Refer To The Engine Section In The Appropriate Chassis Chapter Of This Manual.

INDEX

CYLINDER HEAD, VALVE GUIDE & VALVE SEATS

All measurements given in inches, unless otherwise specified.

Engine Liter	Year	Cylinder Head Warpage Limit	Cylinder Head Overall Thick-ness①	Valve Guides (Standard)			Valve Seats			
				Inside Diameter	Stem To Guide Clearance		Angle	Width		Runout
					Intake	Exhaust		Intake	Exhaust	
2.0L③	1997	.002	—	.2350–.2360	.0018–.0025	.0029–.0037	45.00°	.035—.051	.035—.051	.002
2.0L③	1998-99	.002	—	.2350–.2360	.0018–.0025	.0029–.0037	45.00°	.030—.049	.030—.049	.002
2.0L③	2000	.002	—	.2350–.2360	.0018–.0025	.0029–.0037	45.00°	.035—.051	.035—.051	.002
2.0L DOHC⑤	1997–99	.002	—	.2350–.2360	.0009–.0025	.0020–.0037	44.50–45.00°	.035–.051	.035– .051	.002
2.0L Non-Turbo④	1997–98	.004	—	.2352–.2362	.0009–.0025	.0020–.0037	45.00–45.50°	.035–.051	.035– .051	.002
2.0L Non-Turbo④	1999	.004	—	.2352–.2362	.0009–.0025	.0020–.0037	45.00–45.50°	.035—.051	.030—.049	.002
2.0L SOHC⑤	1997–2000	.002	—	.2350–.2360	.0018–.0025	.0029–.0037	45.00°	.035–.051	.035– .051	.002
2.0L Turbo④	1997–98	.008	5.193–5.201	.2600	.0008–.0020	.0020–.0035	—	.035–.051	.035– .051	—
2.0L②	1997–2000	.004	—	.2352–.2362	.0009–.0026	.0020–.0037	45.00–45.50°	.035–.051	.035– .051	.002
2.4L	1997–2000	.002	—	.2350–.2360	.0018–.0025	.0029–.0037	45.00°	.035-.051	.035– .051	.002
2.5L③	1997–2000	.004	—	.2360	.0008–.0020	.0016–.0028	44.00–44.50°	.035–.051	.035– .051	—
2.5L②	1997–2000	.008	4.720–4.730	.2360	.0008–.0020	.0016–.0028	45.00–45.50°	.035–.051	.035– .051	—
2.7L	1998–2000	.003	—	.2353–.2363	.0009–.0026	.0020–.0037	45.00–45.50°	.039—.059	.049—.069	.002
3.2L	1998–2000	.003	—	.2746–.2756	.0009–.0025	.0020–.0037	44.50–45.00°	.030—.049	.049—.069	.002
3.3L	1997	.008	—	.3140–.3150	.0010–.0030	.0020–.0060	45.00–45.50°	.069—.088	.057—.078	.003
3.5L	1997, 1999–2000	.003	—	.2746–.2756	.0009–.0026	.0020–.0037	45.00–45.50°	.029—.049	.049—.069	.002

DOHC — Dual Overhead Cam
SOHC — Single Overhead Cam
① — Minimum thickness is overall thickness, less warpage limit, combined w/amount of grinding of cylinder block gasket surface.
② — Avenger & Sebring Coupe.
③ — Breeze, Cirrus, Sebring Convertible & Stratus.
④ — Talon.
⑤ — Neon.

VALVE SPRINGS

All measurements given in inches, unless otherwise specified.

Engine	Year	Free Length		Installed Height	Spring Pressure, Lbs. @ Inches		Maximum Straightness Deviation
		Intake	Exhaust		Intake	Exhaust	
2.0L ②	1997	1.747	1.747	1.580	75@1.540	75@1.540	—
	1998-99	1.747	1.747	1.580	67@1.57	67@1.57	—
	2000	1.747	1.747	1.580	70@1.57	70@1.57	—
2.0L DOHC③	1997–99	1.811	1.811	1.496	55–60 @ 1.496	55–60 @ 1.496	—
2.0L SOHC③	1997–99	1.747	1.747	1.540	75 @ 1.540	75 @ 1.540	—
2.0L SOHC③	2000	1.840	1.840	1.580	70 @ 1.570	70 @ 1.570	—
2.0L Non-Turbo①	1997–2000	1.811	1.811	1.496	55–60 @ 1.496	55–60 @ 1.496	—
2.0L Non-Turbo④	1997–98	1.811	1.811	1.496	55–60 @ 1.496	55–60 @ 1.496	—
2.0L Turbo④	1997–98	1.850	1.850	1.570	54 @ 1.570	54 @ 1.570	4°
2.4L	1997–2000	1.905	1.905	1.496	76 @ 1.496	76 @ 1.496	—
2.5L①②	1997–2000	2.010	2.010	1.740	60 @ 1.740	60 @ 1.740	4°
2.7L	1998–2000	1.797	1.797	1.496	56–64 @ 1.496	56–64 @ 1.496	—
3.2L	1998–99	1.720	1.745	1.496	69.5–80.5 @ 1.496	56-64@1.496	—
3.2L	2000	1.720	1.745	1.496	69.5–80.5 @ 1.496	70-81@1.496	—
3.3L	1997	1.909	1.909	1.622–1.681	95–100 @ 1.570	95–100 @ 1.570	—
3.5L	1997	1.781	1.799	1.496	90–100 @ 1.496	81–89 @ 1.496	—
	1999	1.719	1.744	1.496	70–81 @ 1.496	56-64@1.496	—
	2000	1.719	1.744	1.496	70–81 @ 1.496	71-79@1.496	—

DOHC — Dual Overhead Cam
SOHC — Single Overhead Cam
① — Avenger & Sebring Coupe.
② — Breeze, Cirrus, Sebring Convertible & Stratus.
③ — Neon.
④ — Talon.

VALVES

All measurements given in inches, unless otherwise specified.

Engine	Year	Stem Diameter		Clearance		Stem Tip Height		Maximum Tip Refinish	Face Angle	Margin (Minimum)	
		Intake	Exh-aust	In-take	Exh-aust	Intake	Exh-aust			Intake	Exh-aust
2.0L①	1997–2000	.2340	.2330	—	—	1.891	1.889	—	44.5–45.0°	.050–.063	.038–.051
2.0L②	1997	.2340	.2330	—	—	1.891	1.889	—	45.0–45.5°	.045–.058	.058–.071
2.0L②	1998–2000	.2340	.2330	—	—	1.77-1.81	1.71-1.75	—	45.0–45.5°	.045–.058	.058–.071
2.0L③	1997–2000	.2340	.2330	—	—	1.770–1.810	1.710–1.750	—	45.0–45.5°	.045–.058	.058–.071
2.0L Non-Turbo④	1997–98	.2330	.2340	—	—	1.891	1.889	—	44.5–45.0°	.050–.063	.038–.050
2.0L Turbo④	1997–98	.2600	.2590	—	—	—	—	—	45.0–45.5°	.039	.059
2.4L	1997–2000	.2340	.2330	—	—	1.891	1.889	—	44.5–45.0°	.050–.063	.038–.051
2.5L①	1997–2000	.2360	.2360	—	—	—	—	—	45.0–45.5°	.039	.047
2.5L②	1997–2000	.2360	.2360	—	—	1.940	1.940	—	45.0°	.039	.047
2.7L	1998–2000	.2337–.2344	.2326–.2333	—	—	1.837–1.874	1.898–1.935	—	45.0–45.5°	—	—
3.2L	1998–2000	.2730–.2737	.2719–.2726	—	—	1.668–1.719	1.760–1.811	—	44.5–45.0°	—	—
3.3L	1997	.3120–.3130	.3112–.3119	—	—	1.950–2.018	1.950–2.018	—	44.5–45.0°	.031	.047
3.5L	1997, 1999–2000	.2730–.2737	.2719–.2726	—	—	1.668–1.719	1.760–1.811	—	44.5–45.0°	.040	.057

① — Avenger & Sebring Coupe.
② — Breeze, Cirrus, Sebring Convertible & Stratus.
③ — Neon.
④ — Talon.

CAMSHAFT

All measurements given in inches, unless otherwise specified.

Engine	Year	Camshaft Journal Diameter	Camshaft Bearing Clearance	Camshaft Endplay	Lifter Bore Diameter	Lifter Diameter	Lifter To Bore Clearance
2.0L DOHC⑤	1997–99	1.0210–1.0220	.0027–.0030	.0019–.0066	—	—	—
2.0L SOHC④⑤	1997–2000	②	.0027–.0030	_	—	—	—
2.0L SOHC,1997-98	–	–	–	.0059			
2.0L SOHC,1999	_	_	_	.002-.006			
2.0L SOHC,2000	_	_	_	.002-.015			
2.0L Non-Turbo③	1997–2000	1.0217–1.0224	.0027–.0028	.0060	—	—	—
2.0L Non-Turbo⑥	1997–98	1.0217–1.0224	.0027–.0028	.0060	—	—	—
2.0L Turbo⑥	1997–98	1.0220	—	—	—	—	—
2.4L	1997–2000	_	.0027–.0030	.0019–.0066	—	—	—
2.4L, 1997-99	1997–2000	1.024-1.025	.0027–.0030	.0019–.0066	—	—	—
2.4L, 2000	1997–2000	1.021-1.022	.0027–.0030	.0019–.0066	—	—	—
2.5L③	1997–2000	1.7689	—	—	—	—	—
2.5L④	1997–2000	1.7689	—	—	—	—	—
2.7L	1998–2000	.9449–.9441	.0020–.0035	.0051–.0110	.9469–.9476	—	—
3.2L	1998–2000	1.6905–.16913	.0030–.0047	.004–.014	—	—	—
3.3L	1997	①	.0010–.0040	.0050–.0120	.9051–.9059	.9035–.9040	.0011–.0024
3.5L	1997, 1999–2000	1.6905–1.6913	.0030–.0047	.0040–.0140	—	—	—

DOHC — Dual Overhead Cam

SOHC — Single Overhead Cam

① — No. 1, 1.9970–1.9990 inches; No.

2, 1.9809–1.9829 inches; No. 3, 1.9659–1.9679 inches; No. 4, 1.9499–1.9520 inches.
② — Bearing journal No. 1, 1.6190–1.6199 inches; No. 2, 1.6340–1.6350 inches; No. 3, 1.6500–1.6510 inches; No. 4, 1.6660–1.6680 inches; No. 5, 1.6820–1.6829 inches.
③ — Avenger & Sebring Coupe.
④ — Breeze, Cirrus, Sebring Convertible & Stratus.
⑤ — Neon.
⑥ — Talon.

CRANKSHAFT, BEARINGS & RODS

All measurements given in inches, unless otherwise specified.

Engine	Year	Crankshaft				Bearing Clearance		Connecting Rods		Crankshaft Endplay
		Main Bearing Journal Diameter	Connecting Rod Journal Diameter	Max. Out Of Round (All)	Max. Taper (All)	Main Bearings	Connecting Rod Bearings	Pin Bore Diameter	Side Clearance	
2.0L②③	1997–2000	2.0469–2.0475	1.8894–1.8900	.0001	.0001	.0008–.0024	.0010–.0023	.8252–.8260	.0050–.0150	.0035–.0094
2.0L④	1997–98	2.0469–2.0475	1.8894–1.8900	.0001	.0001	.0008–.0024	.0010–.0023	.8252–.8260	.0050–.0150	.0035–.0094
2.0L①	1997–2000	2.0469–2.0475	1.8894–1.8900	.0001	.0001	.0009–.0024	.0010–.0023	.8252–.8260	.0050–.0150	.0035–.0094
2.0L Turbo④	1997–98	2.2400	—	.0004	.0004	.0008–.0016	—	—	.0039–.0098	.0020–.0071
2.4L	1997–2000	2.3610–2.3625	1.9670–1.9685	.0001	.0001	.0007–.0023	.0009–.0027	.8252–.8260	.0051–.0150	.0035–0094
2.5L①	1997–2000	2.3600	—	—	—	.0008–.0016	—	—	.0039–.0098	.0020–.0098
2.5L②	1997–2000	2.3620	—	—	—	.0008–0016	—	—	.0039–.0098	.0020–.0100
2.7L	1998–2000	2.4997–2.5004	2.1067–2.1060	.0006	.0006	.0014–.0021	.0010–.0026	.8665–.8668	.0052–.0150	.0019–.0108
3.2L	1998–2000	2.5190–2.5200	2.2830–2.2840	.0006	.0006	.0007–.0030	.0007–.00340	.9452–.9455	—	.0040–0120
3.3L	1997	2.5190	2.2830	.0010	.0010	.0007–.0022	.0007–.0030	—	.0050–.0150	.0030–.0090
3.5L	1997	2.5190–2.5200	2.2820–2.2830	.0001	.0002	.0007–.0022	.0007–.0034	.9823–.9451	.0050–.0150	.0040–.0120
	1999–2000	2.5190–2.520	2.2830–2.2840	.0006	.0006	.0007–.0030	.0007–.0034	.9452–.9455	.0157	.0040–.0120

① — Avenger & Sebring Coupe.
② — Breeze, Cirrus, Sebring Convertible & Stratus.
③ — Neon.
④ — Talon.

PISTONS, PINS & RINGS

All measurements given in inches, unless otherwise specified.

Engine	Year	Piston Diameter (Std.)	Piston Clearance	Piston Pin Diameter	Piston Pin To Piston Clearance	Piston Ring End Gap (Minimum)			Piston Ring Side Clearance		
						Compression		Oil	Compression		Oil
						Top	2nd		Top	2nd	
2.0L DOHC⑥	1997–2000	3.4434–3.4441	.0007–.0020②	.8267–.8269	.0003–.0008	.0090–.0200	.0190–.0310	.0090–.0260	.0010–.0026	.0010–.0026	.0002–.0070
2.0L⑤	1997–99	3.4434–3.4441	.0004–.0017②	.8267–.8269	.0003–.0008	.0090–.0200	.0190-.0310	.0090–.0260	.0010–.0026	.0010–.0026	.0002–.0070
2.0L SOHC⑥	1997–2000	3.4434–3.4441	.0008–.0020②	.8267–.8269	.0003–.0008	.0090–.0200	.0190–.0310	.0090–.0260	.0010–.0026	.0010–.0026	.0002–.0070
2.0L Non-Turbo⑦	1997–98	3.4434–3.4441	.0005–.0017②	.8267–.8269	.0003–.0008	.0090–.0200	.0190–.0310	.0090–.0260	.0010–.0026	.0010–.0026	.0002–.0070
2.0L Turbo⑦	1997–98	3.3340	.0012–.0020	.8700	—	.0098–.0138	.0157–.0217	.0039–.0157	.0016–.0031	.0008–.0028	—
2.4L	1997–2000	3.4434–3.4441	.0009–.0022⑧	.8660–.8662	.0001–.0007	.0098–.0200	.0090–.0180	.0098–.0250	.0011–.0031	.0011–.0031	.0004–.0070
2.5L④⑤	1997–2000	3.2900	.0008–.0016	—	—	.010–.016	.016–.022	.006–.019	.0012–.0028	.0007–.0024	—
2.7L	1998–2000	3.3845–3.3857	.0001–.0016	.8661–.8662	.0001–.0004	.0080–.0140	.0146–.0249	.0100–.0300	.0016–.0031	.0016–.0031	.0025–.0082
3.2L	1998–2000	3.6205–3.6221	-.0003–.0018	.9448–.9449	.0002–.0006	.0080–.0140	.0087–.0193	.0100–.0300	.0016–.0031	.0016–.0031	.0015–.0073
3.3L	1997	3.6594–3.6602③	.0009–.0022	.9007–.9009	.0002–.0007	.0118–.0217	.0118–.0217	.0098–.0394	.0010–.0030	.0010–.0030	.0006–.0089
3.5L	1997	3.7800–3.7778①	.0007–.0020	.9448–.9449	.0002–.0006	.0120–.0180	.0120–.0220	.0100–.0300	.0012–.0031	.0012–.0031	.0019–.0077
	1999–2000	3.7780–3.7796	-.0003–.0018	.9448–.9449	.0003–.0008	.0080–.0140	.0091–.0197	.0100–.0300	.0014–.0034	.0014–.0034	.0015–.0073

DOHC — Dual Overhead Cam
SOHC — Single Overhead Cam
① — Measured at right angle to piston pin, .394 inches from bottom of piston.
② — Measured at 11/16 inch from bottom of skirt.
③ — Measured at right angle to piston pin, 1.65 inches from top of piston.
④ — Avenger & Sebring Coupe.
⑤ — Breeze, Cirrus, Sebring Convertible & Stratus.
⑥ — Neon.
⑦ — Talon.
⑧ — Measured at 9/16 inch from bottom of skirt.

CYLINDER BLOCK

All measurements given in inches, unless otherwise specified.

Engine	Year	Cylinder Bore Diameter (Std.)	Cylinder Bore Taper (Max.)	Cylinder Bore Out Of Round (Max.)
2.0L (Except Turbo)	1997–2000	3.4446–3.4452	.002	.002
2.0L (Turbo)	1997–98	3.3500	—	—
2.4L	1997–2000	3.4440–3.4452	.002	.002
2.5L	1997–2000	3.2900	—	—
2.7L	1998–2000	3.3859	.002	.003
3.2L	1998–2000	3.6220	.002	.003
3.3L	1997	3.6600	.002	.003
3.5L	1997	3.7800	.002	.003
	1999–2000	3.7797–3.7803	.002	.003

OIL PUMP

All measurements given in inches, unless otherwise specified.

Engine	Year	Rotor Backlash	Rotor To Body Cleara-nce	Rotor Endplay ①	Rotor Thickness (Minimum)		Outer Rotor Diameter (Mini-mum)	Maximum Cover Flat-ness Vari-ation	Relief Spring Free Length	Relief Spring Pressure, Lbs. @ Inches
					Inner	Outer				
2.0L (Except Turbo)	1997–2000	.0080②	.0150	.0040	.301	.301	3.148	.003	2.390	18.0–19.0 @ 1.600
2.0L (Turbo)	1997–98	—	③	—	—	—	—	—	—	—
2.4L	1997–2000	.0080	.0150	.0040	.370	.370	3.148	.001	—	—
2.5L	1997–2000	.0024–.0071	.0039–.0071	.0015–.0035	—	—	—	—	—	—
2.7L	1998–2000	.0080	.0150	—	.373–.374	.373–.374	3.511	.001	—	—
3.2L	1998–2000	.0080	.0150	—	.5630	.5630	3.149	.001	—	—
3.3L	1997	.0080	.0220	—	.301	.301	3.141	.003	—	—
3.5L	1997	.0007	.0070	—	.370	.370	3.149	.003	—	—
	1999–2000	.0080	.0150	—	.5630	.5630	3.149	.001	—	—

① — Measured between pump cover mounting surface & end of gear using straightedge & feeler gauge.

② — Maximum inner & outer rotor tip clearance.

③ — Drive gear, .0031–.0055 inch; driven gear, .0024–.0047 inch

FORD MOTOR COMPANY

FORD MOTOR COMPANY

ASPIRE

NOTE: Refer To The Rear Of This Manual For Manufacturer's Special Service Tool Suppliers.

INDEX OF SERVICE OPERATIONS

Specifications

GENERAL ENGINE SPECIFICATIONS

Year	Engine		Fuel System	Bore x Stroke, Inches	Comp. Ratio	Net HP @ RPM③	Maximum Torque, Ft. Lbs. @ RPM	Normal Oil Pressure, psi
	Liter	VIN Code②						
1997	1.3L	H	EFI①	2.78 x 3.29	9.7	63 @ 5000	74 @ 3000	50–64④

① — Aisin Kogyo port fuel injection.
② — The eighth digit of the VIN denotes engine code.
③ — Ratings are net, as installed in vehicle.
④ — At 3000 RPM w/engine hot.

TUNE UP SPECIFICATIONS

Engine	Spark Plug Gap	Ignition Timing, °BTDC				Curb Idle Speed		Fast Idle Speed		Fuel Pump Pressure, psi	Valve Clear-ance, Inch
		Firing Order, Fig.	Man. Trans.	Auto. Trans.	Mark Fig.	Man. Trans.	Auto. Trans.	Man. Trans.	Auto. Trans.		
1.3L	.041	A	10④	10④	B⑤	650–750	700–800	②	②	38–46③	①

BTDC — Before Top Dead Center
N — Neutral
P — Park
① — Equipped w/hydraulic valve lash adjusters; no adjustment required.
② — Controlled by Electronic Control Assembly (ECA).
③ — Remove fuel tank filler cap & allow fuel tank pressure to release. Start engine, then disconnect fuel pump relay connector. After engine has stalled, place ignition switch in Off position & connect fuel pump relay connector. Connect fuel pressure test gauge to fuel hose between fuel filter & fuel rail. Connect jumper wire between DCL F/P terminal & GND terminal, **Fig. C.**
④ — With jumper wire connected between DCL TEN & GND terminals. Refer to **Fig. C.**
⑤ — Align pointer w/yellow mark.

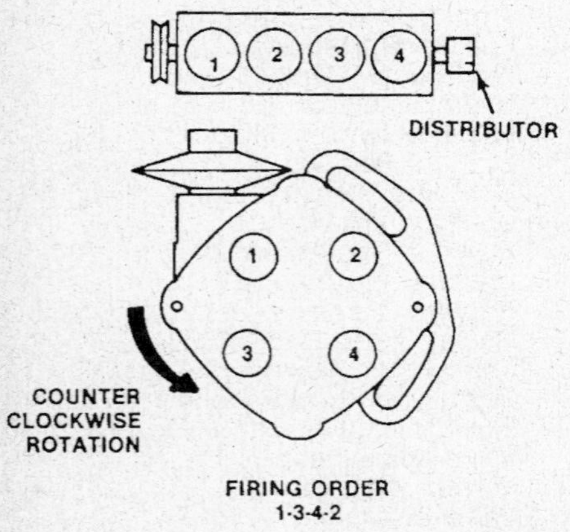

Fig. A

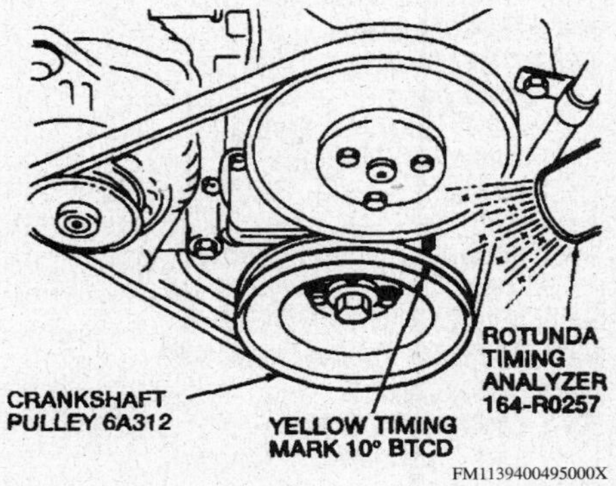

Fig. B

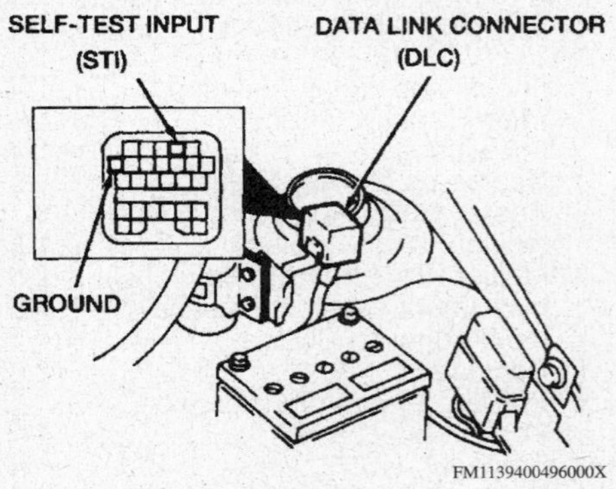

Fig. C

FRONT WHEEL ALIGNMENT SPECIFICATIONS

Year	Caster Angle, Degrees		Camber Angle, Degrees				Toe-In, Inch	Kingpin Inclination, Degrees	Ball Joint Wear
			Limits		Desired				
	Limits	Desired	Left	Right	Left	Right			
1997	+1 5/12 to +2 5/12	+1 2/3	+1/12 to +1 7/12	+1/12 to +1 7/12	+5/6	+5/6	+.2 to +.26	14	①

① — Refer to "Ball Joint Inspection" under "Front Suspension & Steering."

REAR WHEEL ALIGNMENT SPECIFICATIONS

Year	Camber		Toe-In, Inch
	Limits	Desired	
1997	-1 to +1/2	-1/4	0 to +.24

FLUID CAPACITIES & COOLING SYSTEM DATA

Year	Coolant Capacity, Qts.		Radiator Cap Relief Pressure, Lbs.	Thermo. Opening Temp.	Fuel Tank, Gals.	Engine Oil Refill, Qts.①	Transaxle Oil	
	Less A/C	With A/C					Man. Trans., Pts.	Auto. Trans., Qts.②
1997	5.8	6.3	13	③	10	3.4	5.2	5.6

① — Includes filter change.

② — Approximate, make final check w/dipstick.

③ — Sub-valve, 185° main valve, 190.°

LUBRICANT DATA

Year	Lubricant Type			
	Transaxle		Power Steering	Brake System
	Manual	Automatic		
1997	Mercon	Mercon	Type F ATF	DOT 3

Electrical

NOTE: On Air Bag Equipped Models, Refer To " Air Bag System Precautions" Located In The Front Of This Manual For System Disarming & Arming Procedures.

NOTE: Refer To "Computer Relearn Procedures " Located In The Front Of This Manual For Computer Relearn Procedures.

INDEX

PRECAUTIONS

AIR BAG SYSTEMS

Refer to "Air Bag System Precautions" in the front of this manual for system disarming and arming procedures.

BATTERY GROUND CABLE

Prior to service, disconnect battery ground cable and isolate as required.

FUSE PANEL & FLASHER LOCATION

The fuse panel is located left side of the steering column, behind access panel. The flashers are located below instrument panel in upper left hand corner, behind ECA.

FUEL PUMP RELAY LOCATION

The fuel pump relay is located behind the instrument panel, at the lefthand cowl.

RELAY CENTER LOCATION

The relay center is located near the main fuse panel in the engine compartment, next to the battery.

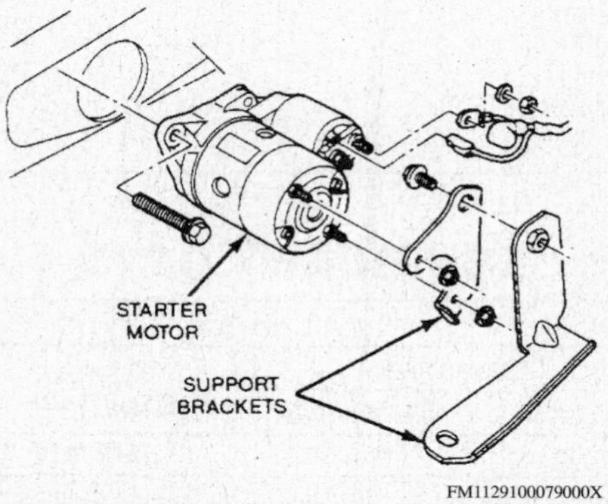

Fig. 1 Starter motor replacement

STARTER

REPLACE

AUTOMATIC TRANSAXLE

1. Remove two upper starter motor mounting bolts.
2. Raise and support vehicle.
3. Remove two manifold to cylinder block bracket bolts, then the bracket.
4. Remove mounting bracket to support bracket bolt.
5. Remove support bracket.
6. Remove two nuts and washers that secure mounting bracket to starter motor.
7. Disconnect the "B" and " S" terminal connectors at starter solenoid.
8. Remove lower starter motor mounting bolt.
9. Remove starter motor.
10. Reverse procedure to install. **Torque** starter motor retaining bolts to 23–34 ft. lbs.

MANUAL TRANSAXLE

1. Raise and support front of vehicle.
2. Disconnect all electrical connections at starter, **Fig. 1.**
3. Remove starter motor support bracket to transaxle attaching bolts.
4. Remove starter motor attaching bolts and the starter motor.
5. Reverse procedure to install. **Torque** starter motor retaining bolts to 23–34 ft. lbs.

DISTRIBUTOR

REPLACE

1. Disconnect coil wire from distributor.
2. Remove distributor cap attaching screws.
3. Pull off distributor cap and swing it aside.
4. Disconnect distributor electrical connector.
5. If the distributor is not being replaced, scribe a reference mark across distributor base flange and cylinder head. This reference mark will allow installation without changing timing.
6. Remove distributor unit, then O-ring at base of distributor.
7. Reverse procedure to install, noting the following:
   a. Install new O-ring.
   b. During installation of distributor, ensure offset tangs engage with camshaft slots.
   c. If distributor unit was not replaced,

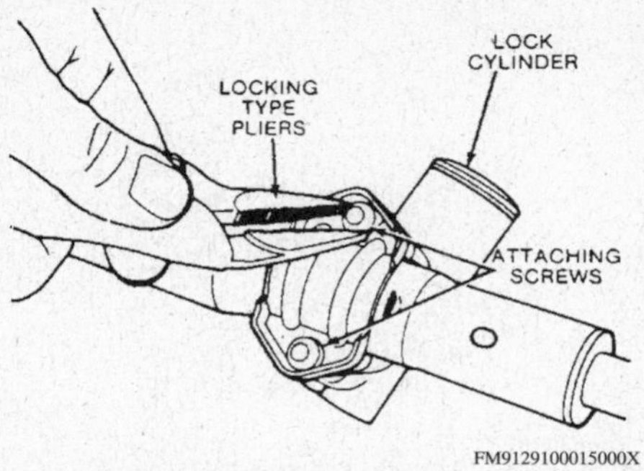

Fig. 2 Ignition lock removal

align scribe marks made during removal and **torque** mounting bolts to 14–18 ft. lbs.

d. If a new distributor is being installed, the ignition timing should be checked and adjusted.

IGNITION LOCK

REPLACE

1. Remove steering wheel as outlined under "Steering Wheel, Replace." Remove ignition switch as outlined under " Ignition Switch, Replace." Remove multi-function switch as outlined under "Multi-Function Switch, Replace."
2. Using suitable locking pliers, remove attaching screws, then the mounting cap and lock housing from steering column jacket, **Fig. 2.**
3. To install ignition lock, proceed as follows:
   a. Position lock housing on steering column jacket, then install mounting cap and new attaching screws. Tighten screws only enough to hold lock housing in position on column jacket.
   b. Turn lock mechanism with ignition key to verify correct operation of lock. If lock binds, reposition on jacket slightly until mechanism functions properly.
   c. Tighten attaching screws until heads break off, then reinstall parts removed in step 1 to complete installation.

IGNITION SWITCH

REPLACE

1. Remove upper and lower steering column trim covers.
2. Disengage switch harness from retaining clip, then remove retaining screw and ignition switch from lock housing, **Fig. 3.**
3. To install switch, proceed as follows:
   a. Push ignition switch into lock housing bore until switch tang engages lock cylinder. **If necessary, turn lock cylinder with ignition key until switch tang aligns with switch slot.**
   b. Install switch retaining screw, position wire harness as necessary, then close harness retaining clip.
   c. Reinstall upper and lower trim covers.

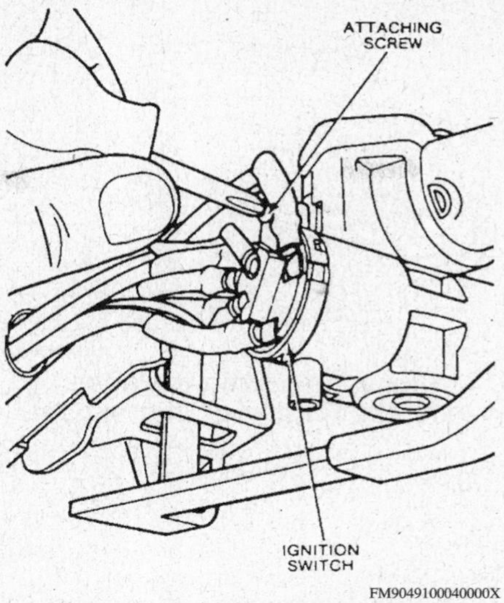

Fig. 3 Ignition switch screw location

HEADLAMP SWITCH

REPLACE

The headlamp/turn signal switch is mounted on the steering column as part of the multi-function switch assembly.

1. Remove multi-function switch as outlined under " Multi-Function Switch, Replace."
2. Remove attaching screws, then separate headlamp/turn signal switch from multi-function switch.
3. Rotate switch handle to parking light detent.
4. Remove switch handle attaching screws and plate, then rotate handle out of switch body. **Use care to prevent loss of detent balls and springs.**
5. Reverse procedure to install.

STOP LIGHT SWITCH

REPLACE

1. Disconnect wiring from switch.
2. Remove locknut, then the switch from brake pedal support, **Fig. 4.**
3. Install switch and locknut, then adjust switch as follows:
   a. Connect ohmmeter across switch terminals.
   b. Rotate switch toward brake pedal until ohmmeter indicates infinite resistance.
   c. Rotate switch toward brake pedal an additional ½ turn, then tighten locknut and reconnect wiring.

MULTI-FUNCTION SWITCH

REPLACE

1. Remove steering wheel as described under "Steering Wheel, Replace."
2. Remove upper and lower steering column shrouds.
3. Apply two strips of tape across sliding

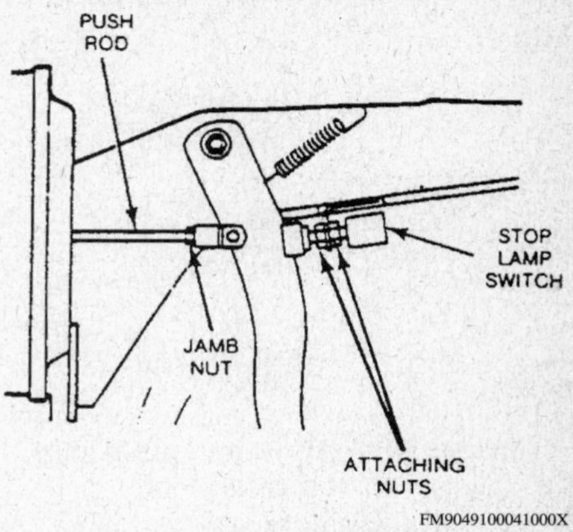

Fig. 4 Stop light switch replacement

contact to prevent accidental rotation, then proceed as follows:
   a. Remove three air bag sliding contact screws and pull sliding contact off steering column.
   b. Remove air bag sliding contact ground wire, then disconnect the air bag sliding contact electrical connector.
   c. Remove air bag sliding contact.
4. Remove multi-function switch screws, then disconnect the multi-function switch electrical connectors.
5. Slide multi-function switch off steering column.
6. Reverse procedure to install.

TURN SIGNAL SWITCH

REPLACE

Refer to "Headlamp Switch, Replace," for turn signal switch replacement procedure.

STEERING WHEEL

REPLACE

1. Remove air bag module as outlined under "Passive Restraint Systems."
2. Remove two screws from back of steering wheel, then disconnect horn wire.
3. Remove steering wheel cover, then steering wheel retaining nut.
4. Mark steering wheel and column shaft for assembling.
5. Remove steering wheel with steering wheel puller tool No. T67L-3600-A, or equivalent.
6. Reverse procedure to install. **Torque** steering wheel retaining nut to 29–36 ft. lbs.

INSTRUMENT CLUSTER

REPLACE

1. Remove instrument cluster bezel attaching screws and pull bezel away from instrument cluster.
2. Disconnect speedometer cable at transaxle.
3. Remove four instrument cluster screw, then pull instrument cluster away from instrument panel.

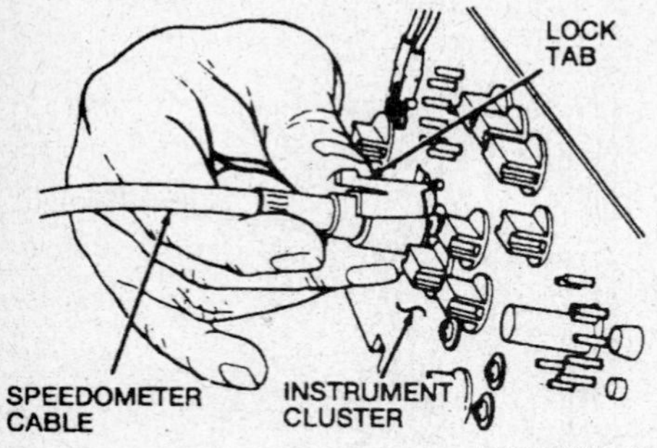

Fig. 5 Speedometer cable clip removal

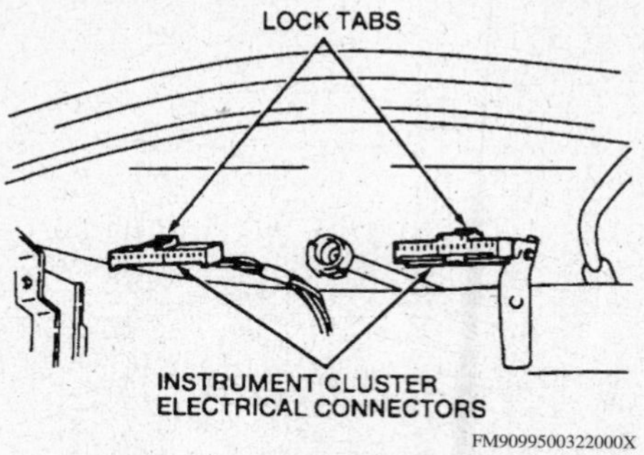

Fig. 6 Instrument cluster electrical connector clip removal

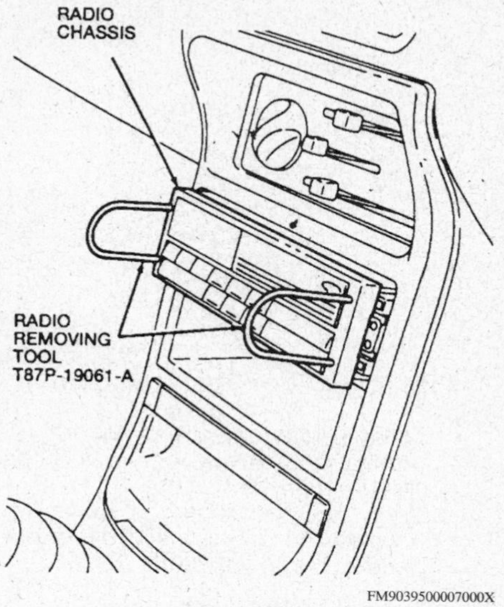

Fig. 7 Radio removal

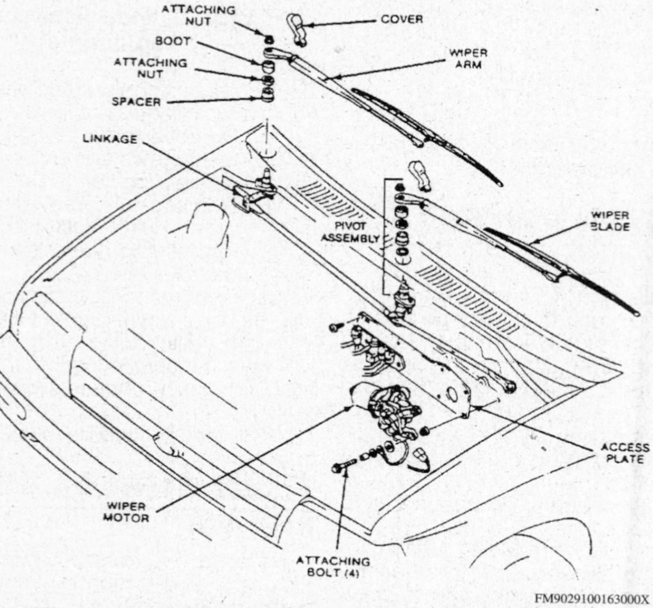

Fig. 8 Windshield wiper motor replacement

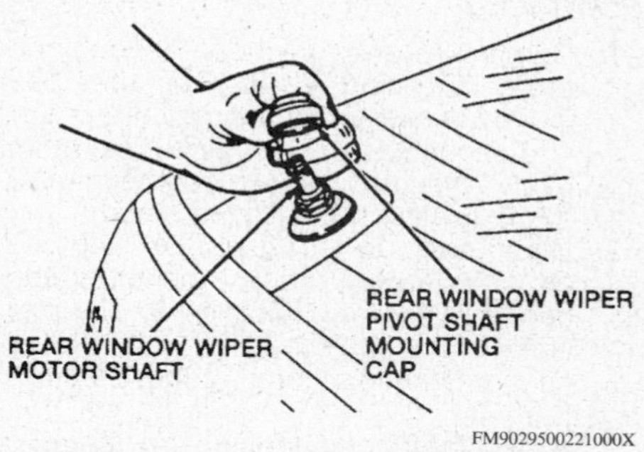

Fig. 9 Rear wiper motor pivot shaft

4. By pressing individual locking tabs, **Figs. 5 and 6,** disconnect speedometer cable and electrical connectors from back of cluster and remove cluster.
5. Reverse procedure to install.

RADIO

REPLACE

1. Using radio removing tool No. T87P-19061-A, or equivalent, pull radio chassis to access electrical connections and antenna, **Fig. 7.**
2. **On models equipped with amplifier,** disconnect electrical connector.
3. **On all models,** remove radio.
4. Reverse procedure to install

WIPER MOTOR

REPLACE

FRONT

1. Disconnect electrical connector, then remove wiper motor to dash panel attaching bolts, **Fig. 8.**
2. Remove mounting plate attaching screws and pull plate away from dash panel.
3. Remove two EGR solenoid vacuum valve bracket nuts and slide intake manifold vacuum outlet fitting and cap off access plate.
4. Using suitable tool, pry linkage pivot from motor output arm, then remove wiper motor from vehicle.
5. Reverse procedure to install. Ensure ground wire is fastened to left upper attaching bolt of motor.

REAR

1. Remove rear wiper pivot arm, then the rear wiper pivot shaft mounting cap from shaft, **Fig. 9.**
2. Remove two rear wiper pivot shaft cowl nuts, then the mounting spacer.
3. Remove rear wiper motor cover, then the liftgate trim panel.
4. Disconnect wiper motor electrical connectors.
5. Remove four wipers motor bolts, then the rear wiper motor.
6. Reverse procedure to install.

WIPER SWITCH

REPLACE

WINDSHIELD WIPER SWITCH/INTERVAL WIPER MODULE

The wiper switch and interval wiper module (if equipped) are mounted on the steering column as part of the multi-function switch assembly.

1. Remove multi-function switch as outlined previously.
2. Remove wiper switch/interval wiper module attaching screws, then disengage switch from multi-function switch, **Fig. 10.**
3. Using a thin screwdriver, disengage switch handle lock tab and pull handle from switch assembly.
4. Remove plunger, spring and O-ring from handle.
5. Reverse procedure to install.

REAR WIPER

1. **On models equipped with tilt steering column,** release tilt lock, then lower steering column to seat.
2. **On models equipped with conventional steering column,** remove

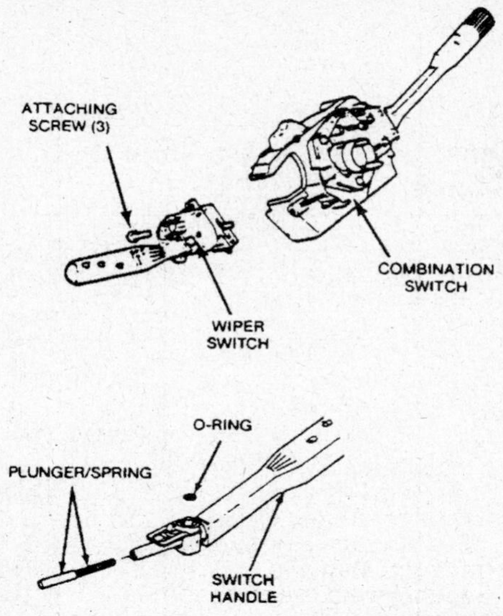

FM9029100165000X

Fig. 10 Windshield wiper switch & interval wiper module replacement

upper and lower steering column trim covers.

3. **On all models,** remove cluster bezel attaching screws and pull bezel away from cluster.
4. Depress switch lock tabs, then disconnect electrical connector and remove switch from bezel, **Fig. 8.**
5. Reverse procedure to install.

WIPER TRANSMISSION

REPLACE

1. Remove front wiper motor as outlined previously.
2. Remove wiper arms, then the pivot assembly protective boots, **Fig. 8.**
3. Remove pivot attaching nuts and spacers, then the linkage through opening in access panel.
4. Reverse procedure to install.

BLOWER MOTOR

REPLACE

1. Remove instrument panel spacer brace and air flow duct located below steering column.
2. Remove lower lefthand nut and pull blower motor housing out from behind evaporator case.
3. Remove blower motor attaching screws and the blower motor.
4. Remove blower wheel circlip, then pull wheel off blower motor shaft.
5. Remove three blower motor cover retaining screws, then the cover.
6. Reverse procedure to install.

HEATER CORE

REPLACE

1. Drain engine coolant.
2. Disconnect inlet and outlet heater hoses in engine compartment.

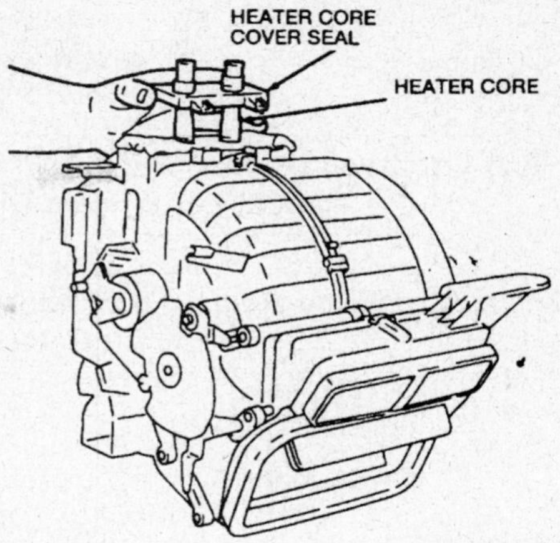

FM7029500223000X

Fig. 11 Heater core replacement

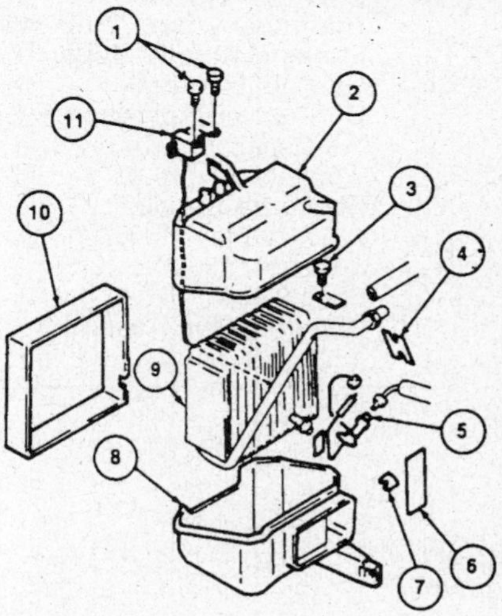

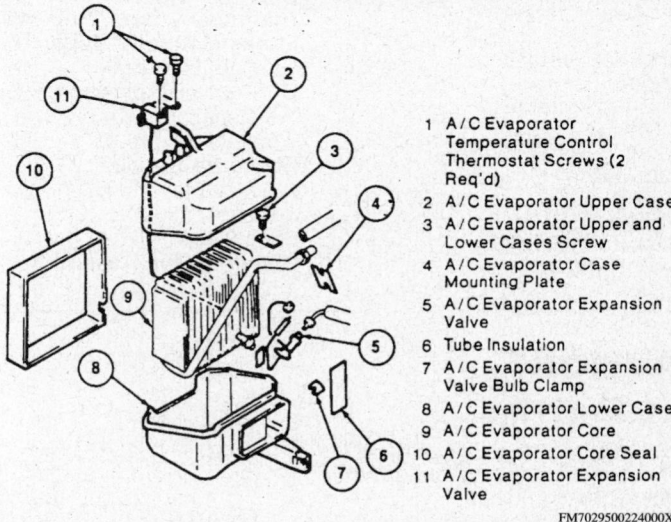

1 A/C Evaporator Temperature Control Thermostat Screws (2 Req'd)
2 A/C Evaporator Upper Case
3 A/C Evaporator Upper and Lower Cases Screw
4 A/C Evaporator Case Mounting Plate
5 A/C Evaporator Expansion Valve
6 Tube Insulation
7 A/C Evaporator Expansion Valve Bulb Clamp
8 A/C Evaporator Lower Case
9 A/C Evaporator Core
10 A/C Evaporator Core Seal
11 A/C Evaporator Expansion Valve

FM7029500224000X

Fig. 12 Exploded view of evaporator assembly

3. Remove instrument panel, then disconnect wiring harness and antenna from routing bracket on front of heater core case.
4. Loosen clamp securing evaporator register duct to heater core case.
5. Remove two retaining nuts from upper and lower right side of heater core case.
6. Remove lower left side nut, then disconnect heater core case from windshield defroster nozzle connectors and remove heater core case.
7. Remove four heater core cover seal screws and seal, then the heater core, **Fig. 11.**
8. Reverse procedure to install.

EVAPORATOR CORE

REPLACE

1. Recover A/C system refrigerant as outlined in "Air Conditioning" section.
2. Working from inside engine compartment, disconnect low and high pressure lines from evaporator outlet fitting.
3. Remove two glove box retaining screws, then glove box assembly.
4. Disconnect two electrical connectors from thermostat.
5. Disconnect cable from thermostat.
6. Disengage wire harness retaining clamps from top of evaporator housing.
7. Loosen clamp screw securing connector duct to evaporator housing.
8. Disconnect drain hose from evaporator housing on lower evaporator case.
9. Remove evaporator housing.
10. Remove the six clips securing the upper evaporator housing to lower housing.
11. Remove upper evaporator housing, **Fig. 12.**
12. Remove evaporator core from lower case.
13. Reverse procedure to install. Install new O-ring seals.

1.3L Engine

NOTE: On Air Bag Equipped Models, Refer To " Air Bag System Precautions" Located In The Front Of This Manual For System Disarming & Arming Procedures.

NOTE: Refer To "Computer Relearn Procedures " Located In The Front Of This Manual For Computer Relearn Procedures.

INDEX

PRECAUTIONS

AIR BAG SYSTEMS

Refer to "Air Bag System Precautions" in the front of this manual for system disarming and arming procedures.

FUEL SYSTEM PRESSURE RELIEF

1. Remove fuel pump relay.
2. Run engine, then disconnect fuel pump electrical connector and allow engine to run until it stalls.
3. After engine has stalled, turn ignition switch OFF.

BATTERY GROUND CABLE

Prior to service, disconnect battery ground cable and isolate as required.

COMPRESSION PRESSURE

The compression pressure check should be performed with the engine at normal operating temperature, wide open throttle, spark plugs removed and the distributor electrical connector disconnected. Compression pressures between the highest cylinder and the lowest should be within 75 percent of each other.

ENGINE MOUNT

REPLACE

REAR MOUNT

1. Support engine using engine support

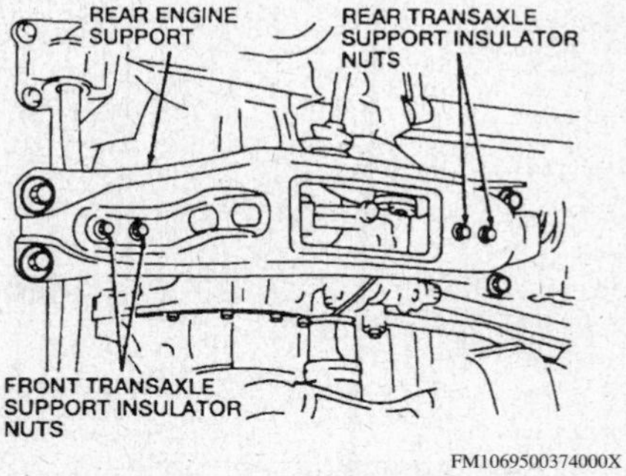

Fig. 1 Rear engine support

tool No. 014–00750, or equivalent, then raise and support vehicle.
2. Remove two front transaxle support insulator nuts from rear engine mount, **Fig. 1.**
3. Remove four rear engine support mount bolts, **Fig. 2,** then the engine support.
4. Reverse procedure to install tightening bolts to specifications.

RIGHT MOUNT

1. Remove engine air cleaner assembly, then support engine with suitable jack.
2. Remove three engine mount nuts and washers.
3. Remove engine mount through bolt, then the engine mount, **Fig. 3.**
4. Reverse procedure to install. Tighten to specifications.

ENGINE

REPLACE

The engine and transaxle must be removed as an assembly.

1. Relieve fuel system pressure as outlined under " Precautions," then remove battery and battery tray.
2. Scribe alignment marks on hood and hood hinges to facilitate installation, then remove hood.
3. Drain cooling system, crankcase and transaxle fluid, then recover A/C system refrigerant as outlined in "Air Conditioning" section.
4. Remove air cleaner and oil dipstick.
5. Disconnect electrical connectors and hoses, then remove cooling fan and radiator as an assembly.
6. Disconnect accelerator cable at carburetor and bracket.
7. Disconnect speedometer cable and remove bracket.
8. Disconnect and mark all remaining hoses, lines and electrical connections that will interfere with engine/transaxle removal.
9. **On models with automatic transaxle,** disconnect Park/Neutral position switch, kickdown solenoid electrical connector and transaxle ground, then the shift cable and bracket.
10. **On models equipped with power steering,** remove two power steering bolts and separate pump from engine.

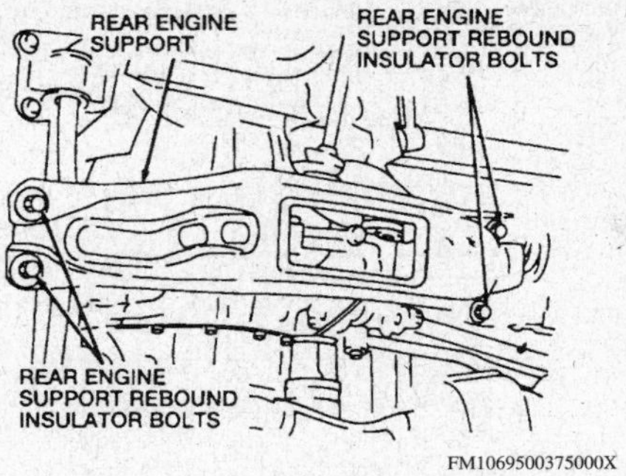

Fig. 2 Rear engine support removal

Disconnect power steering lines from engine.

11. **On all models,** raise and support vehicle, then drain transaxle fluid.
12. Disconnect exhaust inlet pipe.
13. Remove A/C compressor.
14. Disconnect lower control arms from steering knuckles.
15. Separate halfshafts from transaxle and install suitable holding tool for differential side gear
16. **On models with automatic transaxle,** remove six transaxle case to cylinder block front bracket and rear case bracket bolts, then the four flywheel to torque converter nuts.
17. **On models with manual transaxle,** remove six transaxle case to cylinder block front bracket and rear case bracket bolts, then disconnect clutch control cable, then the shift control rod from transaxle.
18. **On all models,** disconnect stabilizer bar from transaxle, then support engine using suitable tool.
19. Remove rear transaxle crossmember to chassis attaching bolts.
20. Remove two front transaxle crossmember nuts.
21. Remove rear engine mount to crossmember attaching nut.
22. Remove crossmember to chassis attaching bolts, then lower and remove crossmember from vehicle.
23. Lower vehicle, attach suitable hoist to engine, then raise vehicle again to gain clearance for engine/transaxle removal.
24. Remove right engine mount through bolt, raise engine/transaxle assembly slightly, then guide assembly out through bottom of vehicle.
25. Reverse procedure to install. Tighten to specifications.

INTAKE MANIFOLD

REPLACE

1. Relieve fuel system pressure as outlined under " Precautions," then drain cooling system.
2. Remove air cleaner assembly, then disconnect accelerator cable from carburetor.
3. Disconnect and mark all hoses, lines and electrical connections that will interfere with manifold removal.

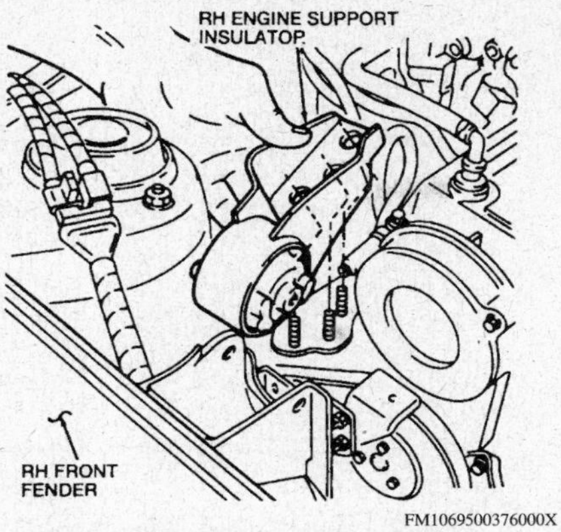

Fig. 3 Right engine mount removal

4. Remove retaining bolts, then the intake manifold.
5. Clean manifold and cylinder head mating surfaces.
6. Reverse procedure to install using a new manifold gasket. Tighten to specifications.

EXHAUST MANIFOLD

REPLACE

1. Relieve fuel system pressure as outlined under " Precautions," then raise and support vehicle.
2. Remove catalytic converter inlet pipe to manifold and pulse air tube to inlet pipe attaching nuts and washers.
3. Remove inlet pipe support bracket attaching bolts, then lower vehicle.
4. Remove air cleaner assembly, then the exhaust manifold heat shroud.
5. Remove oxygen sensor wiring from routing bracket, then disconnect sensor electrical connector.
6. Remove pulse air tube routing bracket attaching bolt and clamp, then the pulse air tube and gaskets.
7. Remove exhaust manifold to cylinder head attaching nuts, then the manifold.
8. Reverse procedure to install, using new gaskets. Tighten to specifications.

CYLINDER HEAD

REPLACE

1. Drain engine coolant.
2. Remove timing belt covers and timing belt as outlined under " Timing Belt, Replace."
3. Remove rocker arm cover.
4. Remove intake and exhaust manifolds.
5. Disconnect spark plug wires and remove spark plugs from cylinder head.
6. Disconnect distributor electrical connections, scribe alignment marks on distributor base flange and cylinder head, then remove distributor mounting bolts and the distributor.
7. Remove front and rear engine lifting eyes, then disconnect ground wire from cylinder head.
8. Disconnect all remaining electrical wiring that will interfere with cylinder head removal.

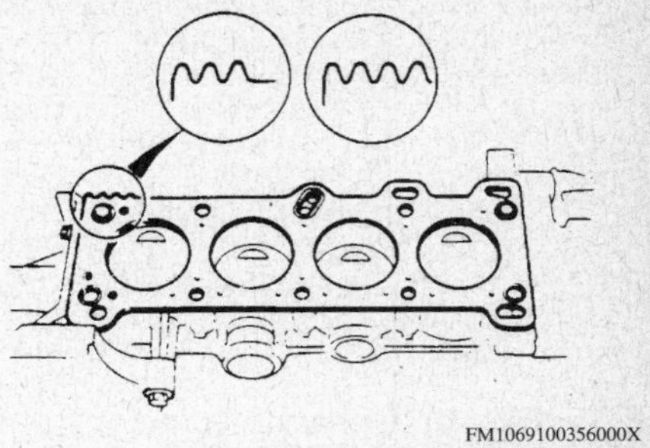

Fig. 4 Head gasket position

9. Remove upper radiator hose, then the bypass hose and bracket.
10. Remove cylinder head attaching bolts, cylinder head and gasket.
11. Reverse procedure to install, noting the following:
    a. Ensure cylinder head and block mating surfaces are clean and free of gasket material.
    b. When installing head gasket, ensure serrated edges of gasket are positioned as shown, **Fig. 4.**
    c. Install cylinder head bolts, then using tightening sequence shown in **Fig. 5, torque** in two steps; first step to 35–40 ft. lbs. and second step to 56–60 ft. lbs.

VALVE ARRANGEMENT

FRONT TO REAR

1.3L ....I-E-I-E-E-I-E-I

VALVE CLEARANCE SPECIFICATIONS

This engine is equipped with hydraulic valve lash adjusters, no adjustment is required.

VALVE ADJUSTMENT

These engines are equipped with hydraulic valve lash adjusters, **Fig.6,** which are not adjustable.

ROCKER ARMS

REPLACE

1. Remove rocker arm cover.
2. Alternately and evenly loosen rocker shaft attaching bolts, then carefully lift rocker shaft assemblies from cylinder head. **Do not remove hydraulic valve lash adjusters from rocker arms unless necessary.**
3. Remove rocker arms and springs from rocker shaft.
4. Measure outside diameter of rocker shaft and inside diameter of rocker arm shaft bore. The maximum difference between these two measurements should not exceed .004 inch. Check hydraulic valve lash adjuster for wear and damage and replace as necessary.
5. Pour engine oil into rocker reservoir, then apply engine oil to hydraulic valve lash adjuster and install in rocker arm,

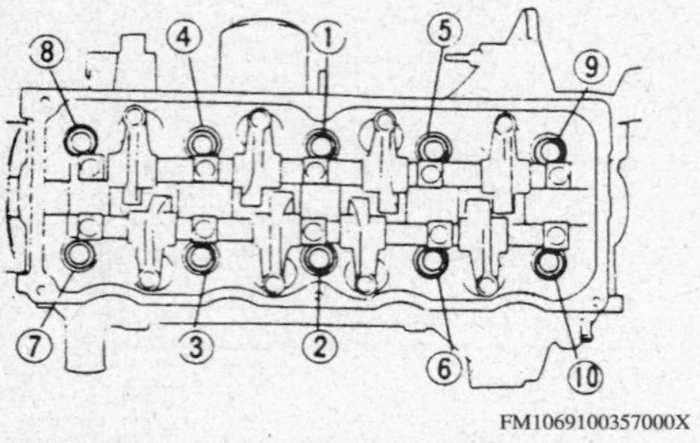

Fig. 5 Cylinder head bolt tightening sequence

if removed. Use care not to damage O-ring when installing.

6. Assemble rocker arms and springs to rocket shaft, **Fig. 7.** Rocker arms and shafts can be identified as shown in **Fig. 8.**
7. Install assembled rocker shaft assemblies, with oil holes facing down, to cylinder head and tighten attaching bolts alternately and evenly in sequence shown in **Fig. 7** to specifications. When tightening rocker shaft attaching bolts, pull back on rocker arm springs.

VALVE GUIDES

Valve guides can be replaced using valve guide remover tool No. T87C-6510-A, or equivalent. When removing valve guide, drive out toward camshaft side of cylinder head. When installing valve guide, drive in until clip just contacts cylinder head, **Fig. 9.**

HYDRAULIC LIFTERS

REPLACE

The hydraulic valve lash adjusters are located in the rocker arms, **Fig. 6.** Refer to " Rocker Arms, Replace" procedure.

FRONT COVER

REPLACE

1. Relieve fuel system pressure as outlined under " Precautions," then remove accessory drive belts.
2. Remove water pump pulley to pump hub attaching bolts, then the pulley.
3. Remove right inner fender panel to gain access to crankshaft pulley.
4. Remove outer crankshaft pulley attaching bolts, then the outer stiffener/spacer and outer pulley, **Fig. 10.**
5. Remove inner stiffener/spacer, attaching screws, inner pulley and baffle plate.
6. Remove attaching bolts, then the upper and lower timing covers.
7. Reverse procedure to install. When installing crankshaft pulley, ensure curved lip on baffle plate and deep recess of inner pulley face outward.

TIMING BELT

REPLACE

1. Remove timing belt covers as outlined under "Front Cover, Replace."
2. Remove timing belt tensioner pulley

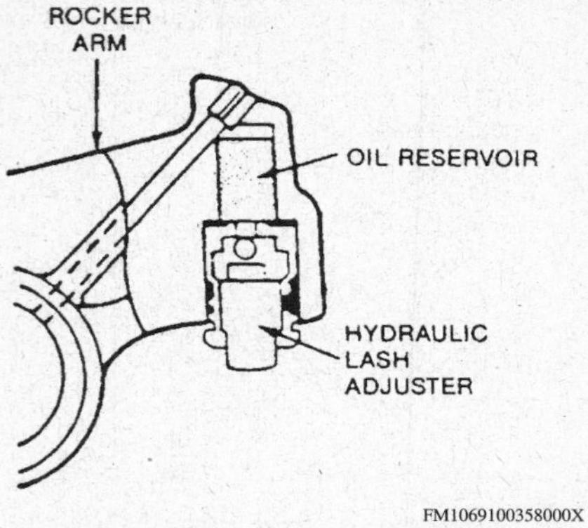

Fig. 6 Hydraulic valve lash adjuster assembly

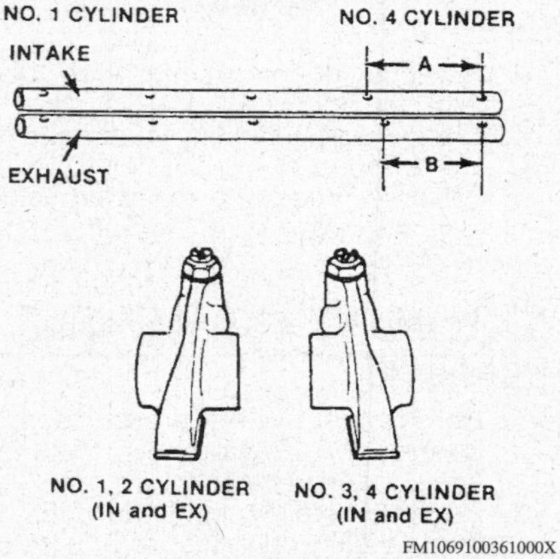

Fig. 8 Rocker arm & shaft identification

attaching bolt, then the tensioner pulley, spring and spring cover, **Fig. 11.**

3. If reusing old belt, mark direction of rotation on belt to aid installation.
4. Remove timing belt from crankshaft and camshaft sprockets.
5. Check crankshaft and camshaft sprockets, tensioner pulley and timing belt for wear or damage. Replace components as necessary.
6. Align camshaft and crankshaft sprocket timing marks with marks on cylinder head and oil pump housing, **Figs. 12 and 13.**
7. Install timing belt. If reusing old belt, ensure belt is installed so that direction of rotation mark made during removal is positioned correctly.
8. Install spring and spring cover onto tensioner pulley, **Fig. 11,** then install pulley and attaching bolt. Do not tighten bolt at this time.
9. Install tensioner spring onto anchor tightening pulley attaching bolt to specifications.
10. Time camshaft and crankshaft as follows:
    a. Align crankshaft pulley timing notch with TC mark on timing belt cover tab.
    b. Remove timing belt upper cover.
    c. Camshaft timing marks should be aligned, **Figs. 12 and 13.** If camshaft timing cannot be viewed, rotate crankshaft pulley one

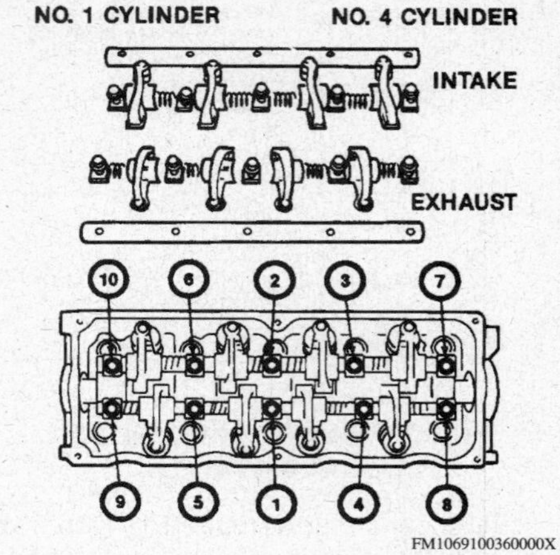

Fig. 7 Rocker arm assembly bolt tightening sequence

revolution, aligning notch with timing cover TC mark.

    d. If camshaft timing marks are aligned, the camshaft is properly timed to the crankshaft. If camshaft timing marks are not properly aligned, repeat procedure.

11. Reinstall timing belt covers.

CAMSHAFT

REPLACE

1. Remove rocker arm shaft assembly retaining bolts, then the rocker shaft assemblies.
2. Remove timing belt as outlined under "Timing Belt, Replace."
3. To prevent camshaft rotation, position suitable open end wrench on flats on front part of camshaft, then remove camshaft sprocket retaining bolt and camshaft sprocket.
4. If camshaft oil seal requires replacement, use a suitable tool to drive camshaft front seal into cylinder head, then cut seal with side cutters and remove seal. Use caution to prevent damaging bearing surface.
5. Remove camshaft thrust plate attaching bolt, then the thrust plate, **Fig. 14.**
6. Carefully slide camshaft out of lefthand side of cylinder head.
7. Lubricate camshaft journals and lobes.
8. Install camshaft and thrust plate.
9. Reverse procedure to install. If camshaft oil seal is to be replaced, install as follows:
    a. Lubricate front seal bore and seal lip with engine oil.
    b. Drive new seal into cylinder head using tool No. T87C-6019-A, or equivalent, **Fig. 15.**

PISTON & ROD ASSEMBLY

Assemble piston to connecting rod so that "F" mark on piston pin bore and oil groove on connecting rod face toward front of engine, **Fig. 16.** After installing connecting rod, check side clearance with feeler gauge. Clearance should not exceed .012 inch.

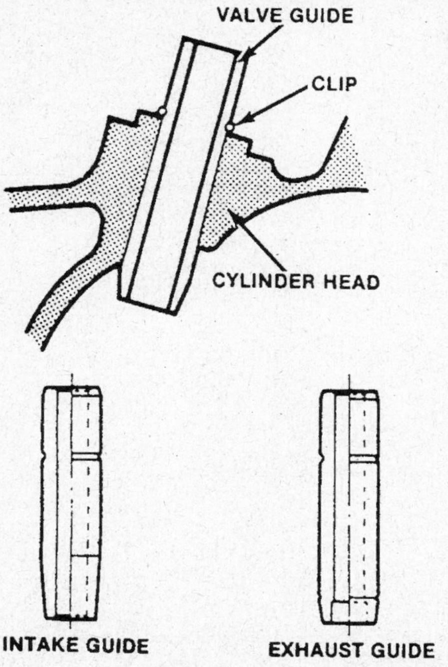

Fig. 9 Valve guide replacement

CRANKSHAFT SEAL

REPLACE

1. Remove timing belt as outlined under "Timing Belt, Replace."
2. Position shift lever in 4th gear, then apply parking brake.
3. Remove crankshaft sprocket retaining bolt, then the sprocket and key.
4. Using suitable tool, pry old seal from oil pump assembly.
5. Clean seal bore, then lubricate and press in new seal using suitable tool, **Fig. 17.**
6. Reinstall key and sprocket onto crankshaft.
7. Coat sprocket retaining bolt threads with non-hardening type sealer, then install bolt.
8. Reinstall timing belt.

CRANKSHAFT REAR OIL SEAL

REPLACE

1. Remove transaxle as outlined in "Clutch & Manual Transaxle" section.
2. Remove flywheel attaching bolts and flywheel, then the engine rear cover plate, **Fig. 18.**
3. Remove seal retainer attaching bolts and seal retainer, then carefully pry out oil seal using suitable tool.
4. Reverse procedure to install, noting the following:
   a. Tighten to specifications.
   b. Lubricate, then install seal using suitable tool. **Ensure hollow side of seal faces toward engine.**
   c. Install seal retainer and tighten to specifications. Trim off excess gasket material after installation.

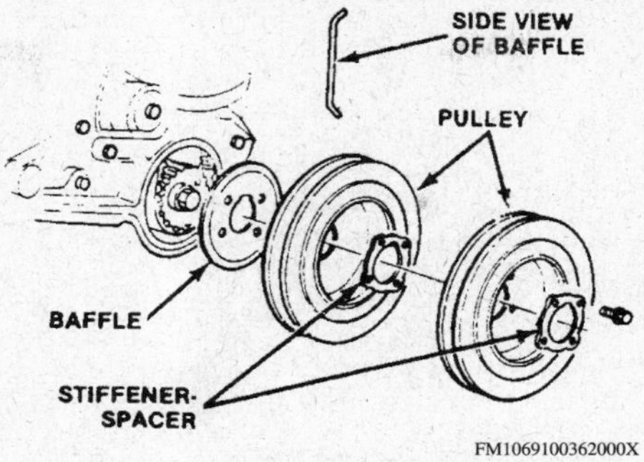

Fig. 10 Crankshaft pulley assembly

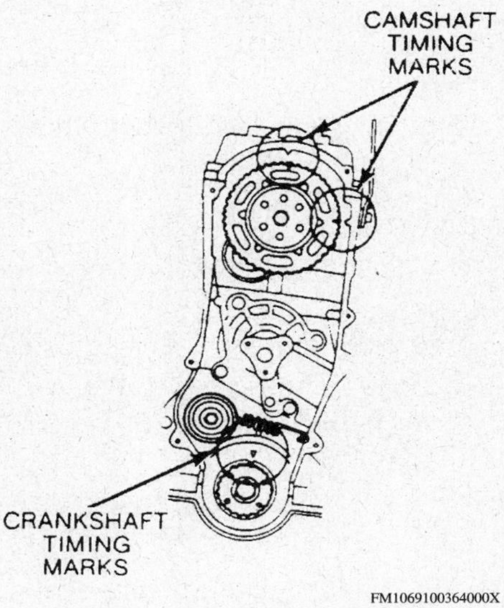

Fig. 12 Valve timing mark alignment

OIL PAN

REPLACE

1. Raise and support vehicle, then drain crankcase.
2. Remove flywheel housing dust cover.
3. Remove exhaust inlet pipe.
4. Remove oil pan to cylinder block attaching bolts, nuts and stiffeners, **Fig. 19.**
5. Remove oil pan from vehicle. **If crankshaft interferes with pan removal, it may be necessary to rotate the crankshaft to provide clearance between pan and counterweights.**
6. Remove oil pan baffle.
7. Reverse procedure to install, noting the following:
   a. Before installing pan, ensure pan and cylinder block mating surfaces are free from oil and old gasket material.
   b. Apply suitable sealer across joint line of cylinder block and front and rear engine covers as shown in **Fig. 20.**

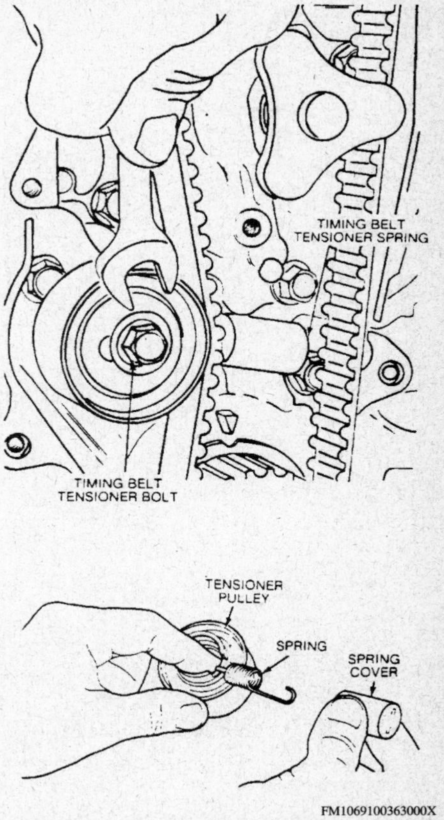

Fig. 11 Timing belt tensioner assembly

OIL PUMP

REPLACE

REMOVAL

1. Raise and support vehicle, then drain engine oil.
2. Remove crankshaft sprocket as outlined under "Crankshaft Front Seal, Replace."
3. Remove oil pan as outlined under "Oil Pan, Replace."
4. Remove oil pump to cylinder block attaching bolts, then the oil pump.

INSTALLATION

1. Ensure oil pump and cylinder block mating surfaces are clean and free from old gasket material.
2. Apply a thick film of sealer to both sides of oil pump gasket, then install gasket, oil pump and attaching bolts.
3. Install pickup tube and screen assembly using new gasket.
4. Install crankshaft sprocket and oil pan.

OIL PUMP SERVICE

DISASSEMBLE

1. Remove pickup tube and screen assembly.

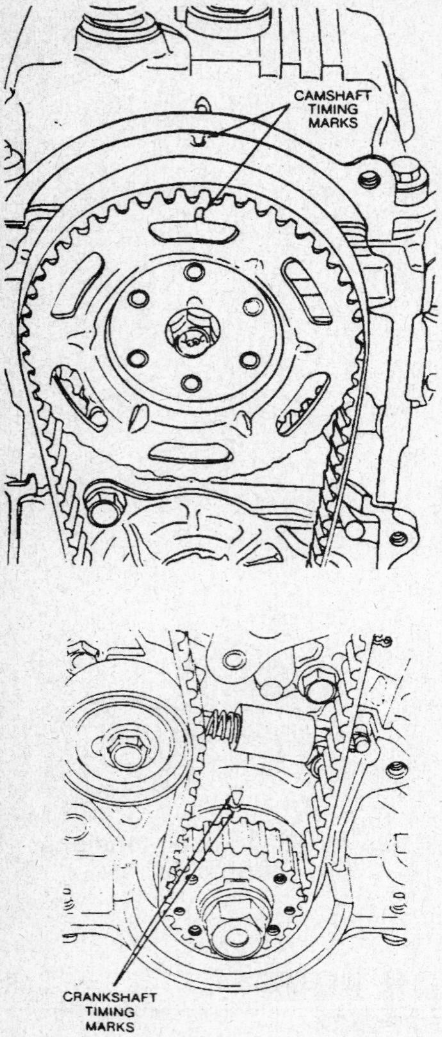

Fig. 13 Camshaft & crankshaft valve timing marks

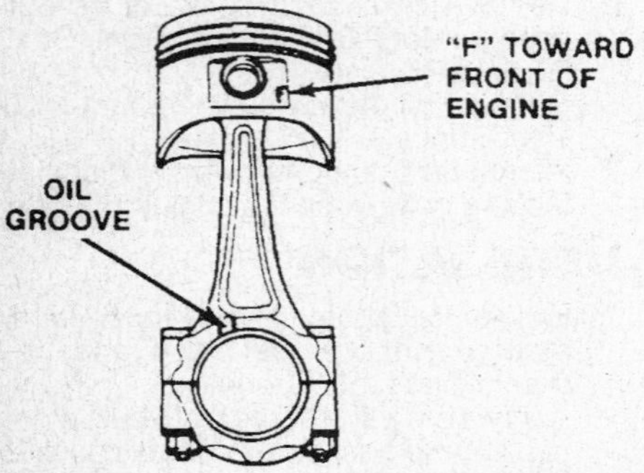

Fig. 16 Piston & rod assembly

2. Remove oil pump cover attaching bolts, then the cover and inner and outer gears, **Fig. 21.**
3. If necessary, pry oil seal from pump body.
4. Remove split pin, then the relief valve plunger assembly from pump body.

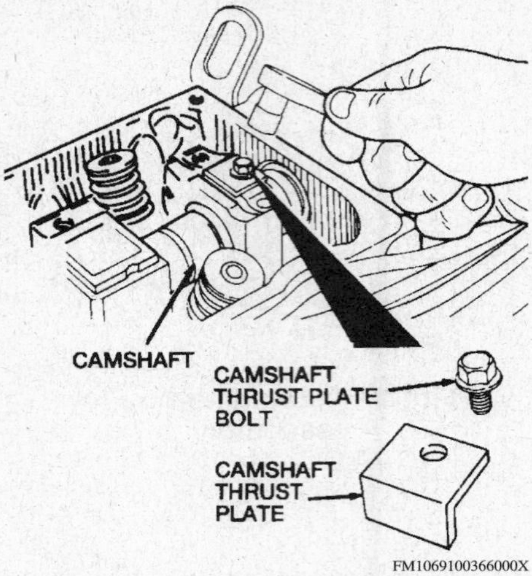

Fig. 14 Camshaft thrust plate

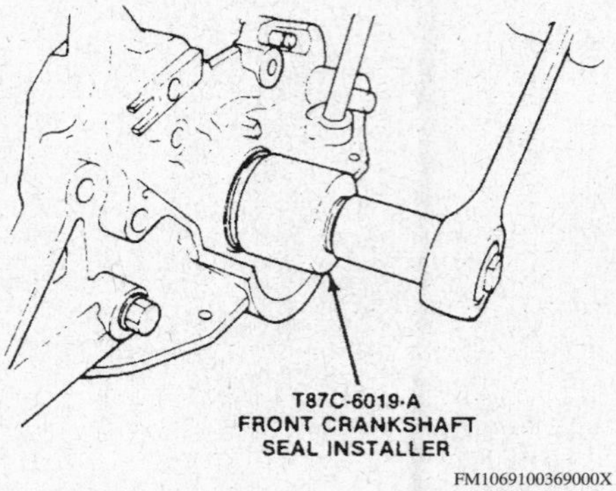

Fig. 17 Crankshaft front seal installation

INSPECTION

1. Inspect pump body gear pocket and relief valve bore for excessive wear or scoring. Replace pump body, if necessary.
2. Inspect relief valve plunger assembly for scoring, burrs or excessive wear. Replace plunger assembly as necessary.
3. Reinstall inner and outer gears into pump body.
4. Measure clearance between inner gear tip and outer gear as shown in **Fig. 22.** Clearance should not exceed .0078 inch.
5. Measure outer gear to pump body clearance. Clearance should not exceed .0087 inch.
6. Using a suitable straightedge, measure gear endplay as shown in **Fig. 22.** endplay should not exceed .0055 inch.
7. If above clearances are beyond specified limits, replace gears or pump body as required.

ASSEMBLE

1. Place relief valve plunger assembly into pump body, then install split pin.
2. If oil seal was removed, drive in new seal using seal installing tool No. T87C-6019-A, or equivalent.

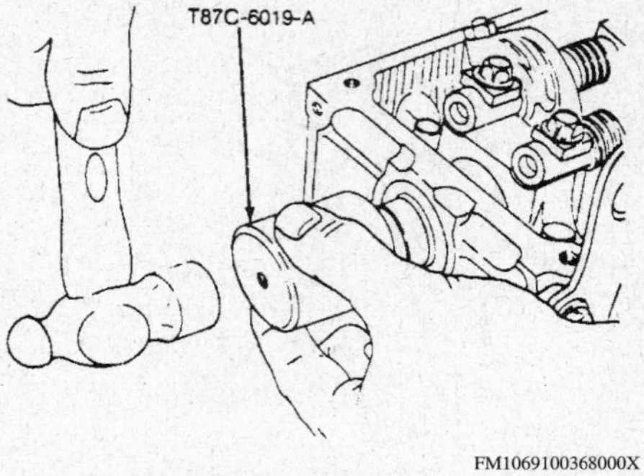

Fig. 15 Camshaft front oil seal installation

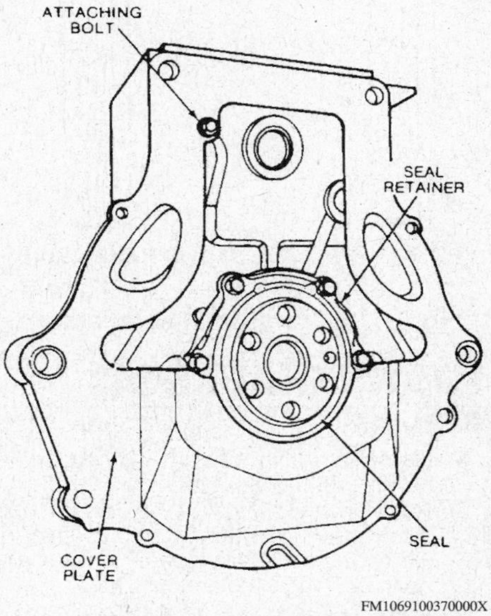

Fig. 18 Rear cover assembly

3. Lubricate, then install gears into pump body.
4. Install pump cover and attaching bolts. Coat bolt threads with Loctite, or equivalent, before installation.

BELT TENSION DATA

Belt	Tension, Inch Lbs.	
	New	Used
A/C Comp.	110–132	95–110
Alternator	86–103	68–86

COOLING SYSTEM BLEED

This engine does not require a specified bleed procedure. After filling cooling system, run engine to operating temperature with radiator/pressure cap off. Air will then automatically be bled through cap opening.

THERMOSTAT

REPLACE

To avoid possibility of personal injury or damage to vehicle, ensure ignition

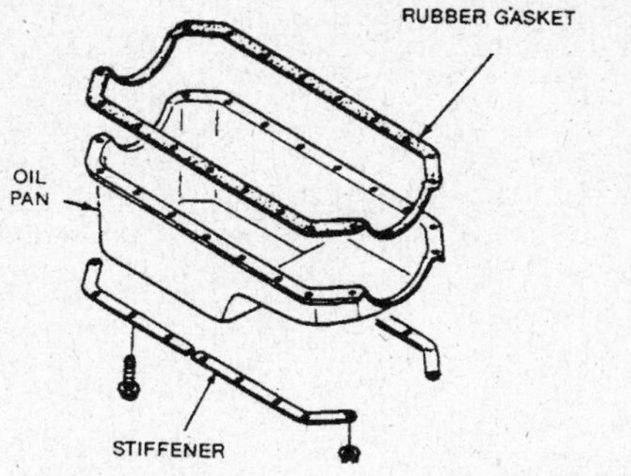

FM1099100065000X

Fig. 19 Oil pan replacement

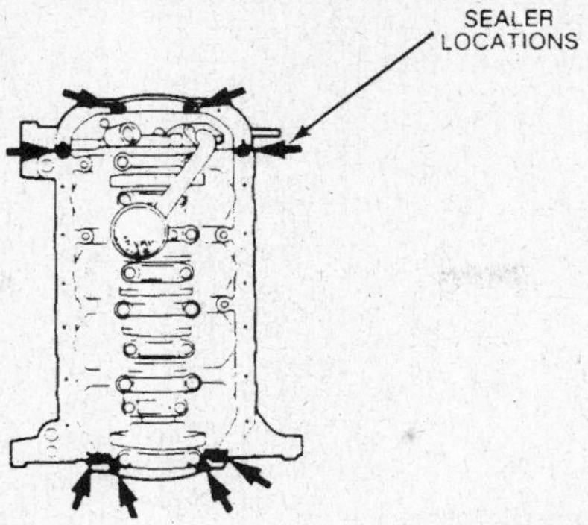

FM1099100066000X

Fig. 20 Cylinder block sealant application

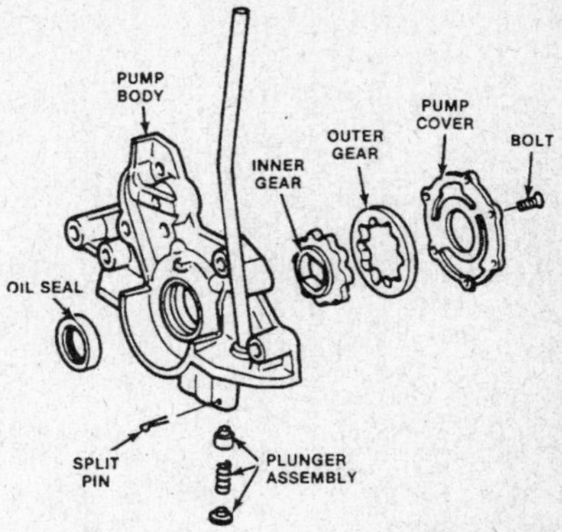

FM1099100067000X

Fig. 21 Exploded view of oil pump assembly

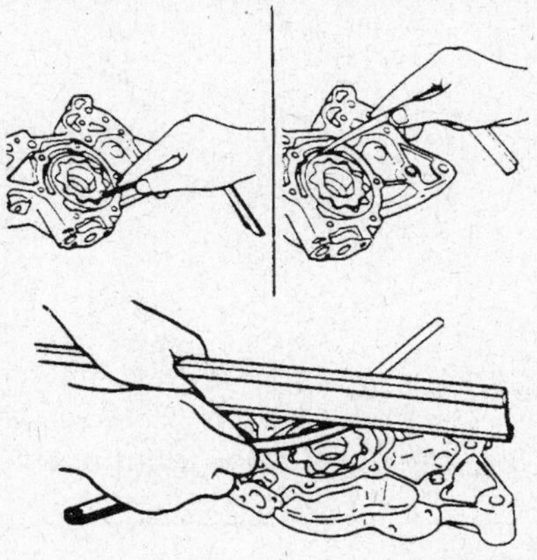

FM1099100068000X

Fig. 22 Oil pump clearance inspection

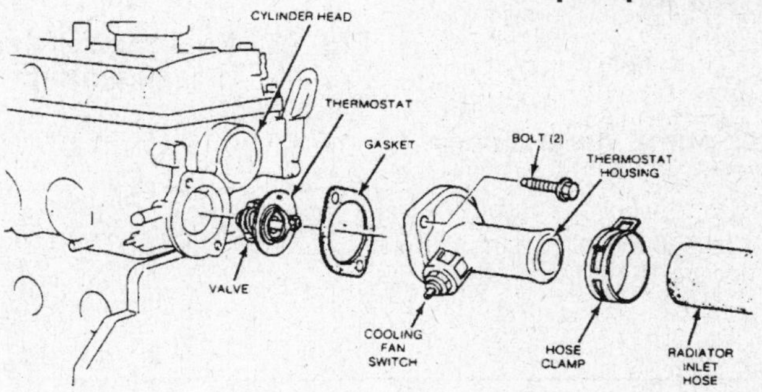

FM1089100068000X

Fig. 23 Thermostat replacement

switch is in Off position before disconnecting wire from cooling fan temperature switch. If wire is disconnected from temperature switch with ignition switch in On position, cooling fan will turn On.

1. Remove radiator pressure cap from radiator filler neck.
2. Drain coolant level below radiator upper hose.
3. Disconnect electrical connector from cooling fan switch on thermostat housing, **Fig. 23.**
4. Disconnect upper radiator hose at thermostat housing, then remove two thermostat housing retaining bolts from cylinder head.
5. Remove thermostat housing and gasket.
6. Remove thermostat.
7. Reverse procedure to install. Tighten to specifications.

WATER PUMP

REPLACE

1. Drain cooling system.
2. Remove timing belt as outlined previously.
3. Disconnect lower radiator and heater hoses from water pump inlet.
4. Remove water pump attaching bolts and the water pump, **Fig. 24.**
5. Ensure water pump and cylinder block mating surfaces are clean and free from old gasket material.
6. Coat both sides of water pump gasket with suitable sealer, then install gasket, water pump and attaching bolts. Tighten to specifications.
7. Connect lower radiator and heater hoses to pump inlet.
8. Install timing belt.

RADIATOR

REPLACE

1. Disconnect cooling fan motor electrical connector.
2. Remove radiator cap, then drain engine coolant.
3. Disconnect all coolant hoses to radiator.
4. **On models with automatic transaxle,** disconnect oil cooler lines.
5. **On all models,** disconnect wiring harness from routing clamps on fan shroud.
6. Remove four radiator support upper bracket securing bolts.
7. Remove upper radiator support brackets, then the radiator and fan shroud as an assembly.
8. Reverse procedure to install.

FUEL PUMP

REPLACE

1. Relieve fuel system pressure as outlined under " Precautions."
2. Disconnect and cap fuel supply and return lines.
3. Remove rear seat, then fold carpet forward until sending unit/fuel pump access plate is revealed.
4. Remove sending unit/fuel pump assembly to fuel tank attaching bolts, then remove sending unit/fuel pump assembly and gasket from tank, **Fig. 25.**
5. Remove fuel filter from fuel pump, then disconnect fuel pump electrical leads from sending unit.
6. Remove retaining clamp screw, then remove fuel pump outlet hose clamp.
7. Remove fuel pump from sending unit.
8. Reverse procedure to install.

FUEL FILTER

REPLACE

INLINE FILTER

1. Relieve fuel system pressure as outlined under " Precautions."
2. Remove fuel filter inlet tube clamp, plug end to prevent fuel spillage or contamination, **Fig. 26.**
3. Remove fuel filter outlet attaching bolts, then filter from bracket.
4. Reverse procedure to install. **Torque** fuel filter outlet attaching bolts to 18–25 ft. lbs.

IN-TANK FILTER

1. Relieve fuel system pressure as outlined under " Precautions."
2. Remove fuel pump as outlined under "Fuel Pump, Replace. "
3. Pull filter from fuel pickup tube end, **Fig. 26.**
4. Reverse procedure to install.

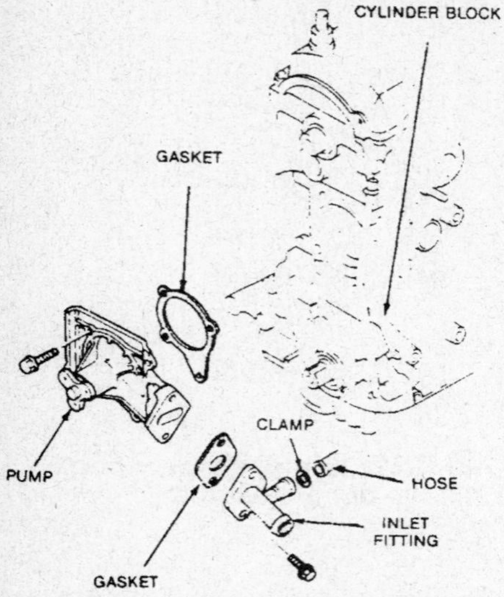

FM1089100069000X

Fig. 24 Water pump replacement

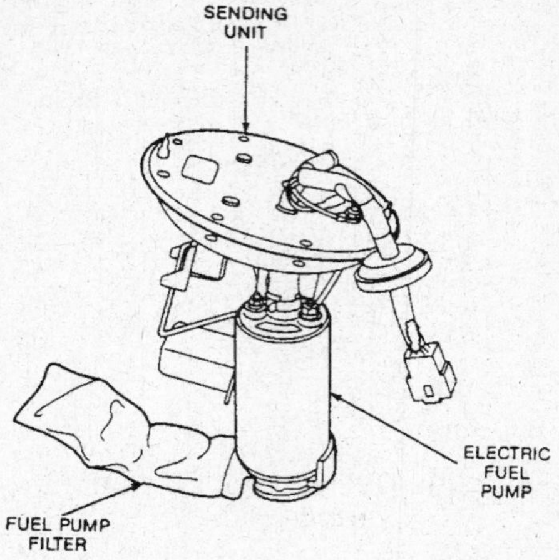

FM1029100154000X

Fig. 25 Fuel pump & sending unit assembly

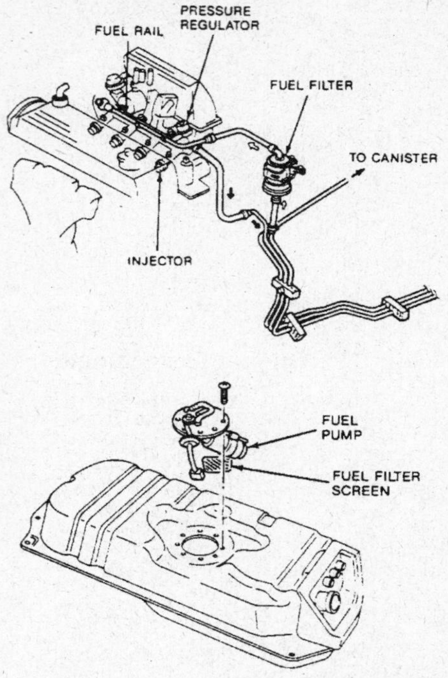

FM1029100153000X

Fig. 26 Fuel filter locations

TIGHTENING SPECIFICATIONS

Year	Component	Torque/Ft. Lbs.
1997	Camshaft Sprocket	36–45
	Connecting Rod Cap Bolts	①
	Cover Plate	72–96③
	Crankshaft Pulley Bolts	9–12
	Crankshaft Rear Seal Retainer	72–96③
	Crankshaft Sprocket	80–87
	Crossmember Bolts	47–66
	Cylinder Head Bolts	②
	Engine Mount (Front) To Crossmember Nuts	32–38
	Engine Mount (Rear) To Crossmember Nut	21–34
	Engine To Transaxle	41–59
	Exhaust Manifold To Cylinder Head	12–17
	Flywheel Cover	72–84③
	Flywheel To Crankshaft	71–76
	Gusset Plate	27–38
	Heat Shroud Bolts	12–17
	Intake Manifold To Cylinder Head	14–20
	Main Bearing Cap Bolts	40–43
	Oil Pan To Engine	72–84③
	Oil Pump Attaching Bolts	14–19
	Oil Pump Inlet Tube	72–96③
	Rocker Arm Shaft	16–21
	Side Mount Nuts	28–40
	Spark Plug	15–22
	Tensioner Bolt	14–19

Continued

TIGHTENING SPECIFICATIONS—Continued

Year	Component	Torque/Ft. Lbs.
1997	Thermostat Housing Attaching Bolts	14–22
	Timing Belt Cover Attaching Bolts	72–96③
	Torque Converter To Flex Plate	26–36
	Water Pump Pulley Attaching Bolts	36–45
	Water Pump To Engine	14–19

① — Torque bolts to 11–13 ft. lbs., then to 22–25 ft. lbs.
② — Refer to "Cylinder Head, Replace" for tightening procedure.
③ — Inch lbs.

Clutch & Manual Transaxle

NOTE: On Air Bag Equipped Models, Refer To " Air Bag System Precautions" Located In The Front Of This Manual For System Disarming & Arming Procedures.

NOTE: Refer To "Computer Relearn Procedures " Located In The Front Of This Manual For Computer Relearn Procedures.

INDEX

PRECAUTIONS

AIR BAG SYSTEMS

Refer to "Air Bag System Precautions" in the front of this manual for system disarming and arming procedures.

BATTERY GROUND CABLE

Prior to service, disconnect battery ground cable and isolate as required.

ADJUSTMENTS

CLUTCH PEDAL HEIGHT

1. Disconnect clutch cable at release lever so that cable will not interfere with measurement.
2. Move carpeting and insulation away from pedal area.
3. Measure distance from upper center of pedal to dash panel as shown in **Fig. 1.**
4. Measurement should be 8.075 inches.
5. If distance is not as specified, proceed to next step.
6. Inspect clutch pedal mounting for damaged, worn or missing parts. Replace parts as necessary. If pedal mounting is satisfactory, proceed to next step.
7. Remove instrument panel bracket and air duct located underneath steering column.

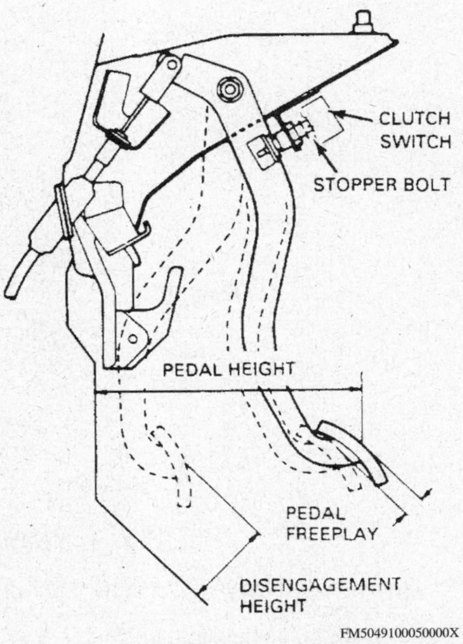

Fig. 1 Clutch pedal adjustments

8. Loosen clutch switch locknut, then turn switch in or out as required until pedal height is as specified previously. Tighten locknut.
9. Reconnect clutch cable to release lever, then adjust pedal freeplay as outlined below.
10. Recheck pedal height measurement. If height adjustment is not within specification, check clutch cable for binding or damage.
11. Reinstall air duct and instrument panel bracket.

PEDAL FREEPLAY

1. Move clutch pedal back and forth and measure freeplay, **Fig. 1.**
2. Pedal freeplay should be .350–.590 inch. If freeplay is not as specified, proceed to next step.
3. Pull back on release lever, then measure clearance between lever and cable pin, **Fig. 2.** Clearance should be .060–.100 inch.
4. If clearance is not as specified, thread adjuster in or out until specified clearance is obtained.
5. Recheck freeplay. If freeplay is still not within specified limits, inspect clutch release components for damage.

CLUTCH

REPLACE

1. Remove transaxle as described further on in this section.
2. If pressure plate will be reused, scribe

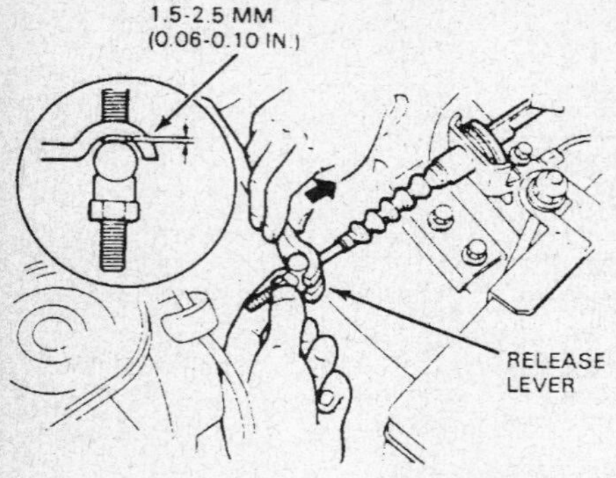

FM5049100051000X

Fig. 2 Clearance check between release lever & cable pin

alignment marks on pressure plate and flywheel to aid installation.

3. Prevent flywheel from turning using suitable tool, then loosen pressure plate attaching bolts one turn at a time until all spring tension is released.
4. Remove attaching bolts, pressure plate and clutch disc, **Fig. 3.**
5. If new clutch disc is being installed, sand friction surfaces of pressure plate and flywheel with medium grit emery cloth to break glaze on surface. After sanding is completed, remove grit with an alcohol soaked shop towel.
6. Install clutch disc with damper springs facing away from flywheel, then install pressure plate and attaching bolts.
7. Install suitable clutch alignment tool, then **torque** attaching bolts evenly to 17 ft. lbs. Remove tool.
8. Reinstall transaxle. Tighten to specifications.

TRANSAXLE

REPLACE

1. Raise and support vehicle.
2. Disconnect all electrical wiring and speedometer cable from transaxle.
3. Loosen clutch cable adjuster nut and disengage cable from release lever.
4. Remove starter motor, then the two bolts located at top of clutch housing, **Fig. 4**
5. Support engine using suitable support fixture.
6. Remove shift rod to input shaft rail attaching nut and bolt.
7. Remove lower control arm to steering knuckle attaching nuts and bolts, then disengage halfshafts from transaxle. Install differential plug tool No. T87C-7025-C, or equivalent, into transaxle to prevent movement of side gears.
8. Remove NVH bracket attaching bolts and bracket, then the crossmember.
9. Position suitable transmission jack under transaxle, then secure transaxle to jack with safety chain.
10. Remove remaining attaching bolts, then pull transaxle away from engine and lower out of vehicle.

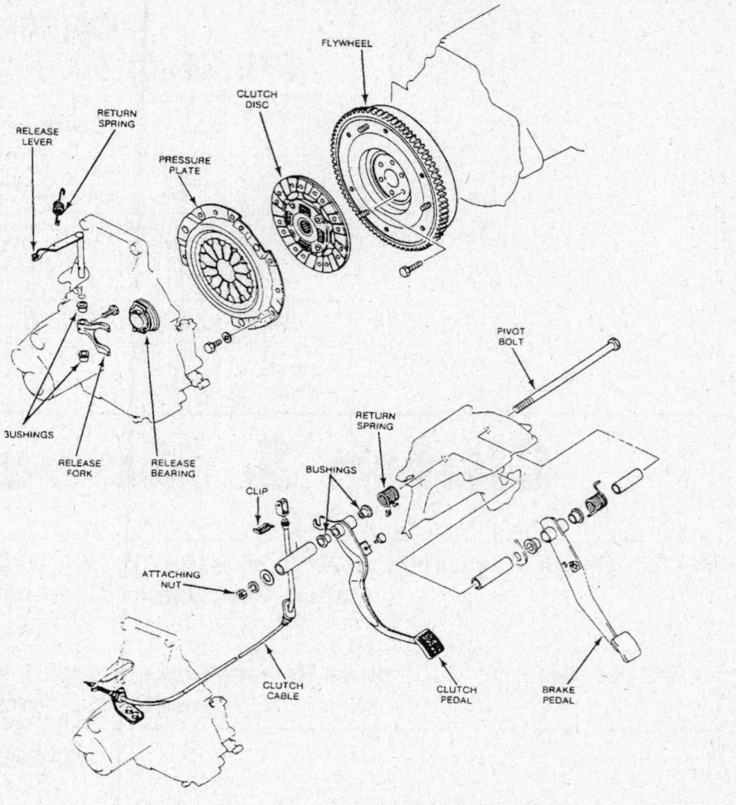

FM5049100052000X

Fig. 3 Clutch system components

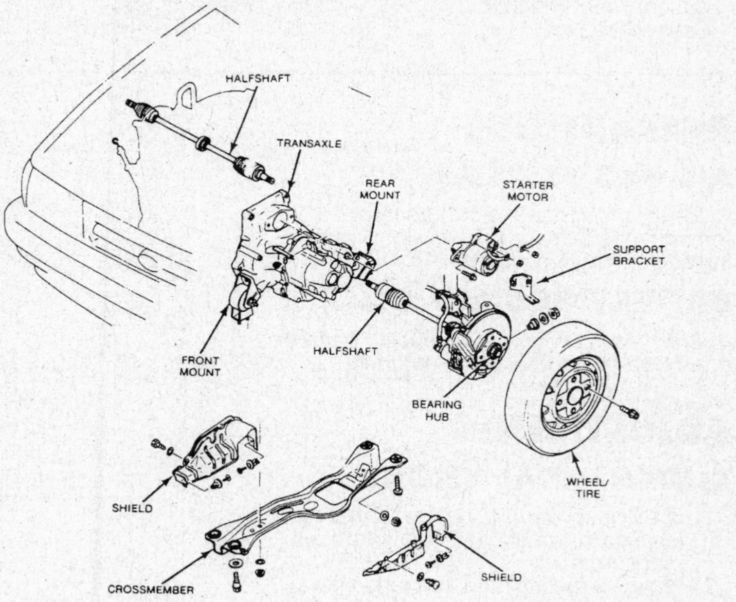

FM5039100564000X

Fig. 4 Manual transaxle replacement

11. Reverse procedure to install, noting the following:
    a. Tighten to specifications.
    b. When installing halfshafts, use new circlips.
    c. **Torque** clutch housing to engine attaching bolts to 57 ft. lbs.
12. After installation is completed, adjust clutch pedal freeplay.

TIGHTENING SPECIFICATIONS

Year	Component	Torque/Ft. Lbs.
1997	Back-Up Lamp Switch	15–22
	Baffle Plate	72–96①
	Clutch Pedal Pivot Bolt	14–25
	Detent Plug	11–15
	Flywheel	71–76
	Oil Guide	72–96①
	Pressure Plate	13–20
	Release Bearing Fork	26–30
	Release Fork	26–30
	Reverse Detent Plate	72–96①
	Shift Gate Frame	72–96①
	Shift Lever Housing	60–84①
	Shift Rod To Shift Lever	12–17
	Shift Rod To Transaxle	23–34
	Stabilizer Rod	23–34
	Transaxle Case	14–19
	Transaxle Mount	14–19
	Transaxle Stud Nut	23–34
	Transaxle To Engine	27–38
	Wheel Lug Nuts	65–87

① — Inch lbs.

Rear Axle & Suspension

INDEX

DESCRIPTION

The rear suspension, **Fig. 1,** is of the MacPherson strut design, with the strut at each wheel seated in a tower in the cargo compartment. Suspension action is carried out through the use of semi-independent trailing arms, which are integral with the torsion beam type rear axle.

The torsion beam axle provides positive control of trailing arm alignment, while doubling as a stabilizer to limit sway during hard cornering. Bushings and rubber insulators, installed at key attachment points, keep vibration and road noise to a minimum.

The brake drum and bearing hub is an integral assembly which rides on a spindle attached to the trailing arms. The assembly is supported by opposed tapered roller bearings located within the bearing hub.

REAR AXLE

REPLACE

1. Raise and support rear of vehicle so that struts are fully extended, then remove rear wheels.
2. Remove struts as outlined under "Strut, Replace."
3. Disconnect all brake lines that will interfere with axle removal.
4. Disconnect parking brake cable at backing plates, then remove equalizer and cables from axle.
5. If necessary, remove backing plates and spindles from trailing arms.
6. Remove axle assembly to body bracket pivot bolts, then lower axle assembly out of vehicle.
7. If axle bushings require replacement, proceed as follows:
   a. Using bushing remover tool No. D80L-1002-L, or equivalent, press bushings out of trailing arm from inboard side.
   b. Lubricate new bushings with soapy water, then position on outboard edges of trailing arm. Ensure marks on bushing face are aligned parallel with trailing arm axis, **Fig. 2.** Press bushings into trailing arms using tool mentioned in previous step. **To distinguish between right and left bushings, note the " F" and "R" marks molded into the bushing. When properly installed, the letters should be right side up with the " F" facing toward front of vehicle.**
8. Raise axle assembly, then align pivot bolt holes and install pivot bolts. Do not tighten bolts at this time.
9. If removed, install backing plates and spindles.
10. Install parking brake equalizer assembly on axle, then connect parking brake cables to parking brake levers at backing plates.
11. Connect brake lines at routing brackets and clip in place.
12. Install struts and rear wheels, then lower vehicle to allow suspension to reach normal ride height.
13. With vehicle on level surface, tighten pivot bolts.
14. After installation is completed, check rear suspension alignment as follows:
    a. Mark center of underbody at a position equidistant between left and right body bracket inboard mounting bolts.
    b. Measure distance from center mark obtained in previous step to centers of right and left strut lower mounting bolts.

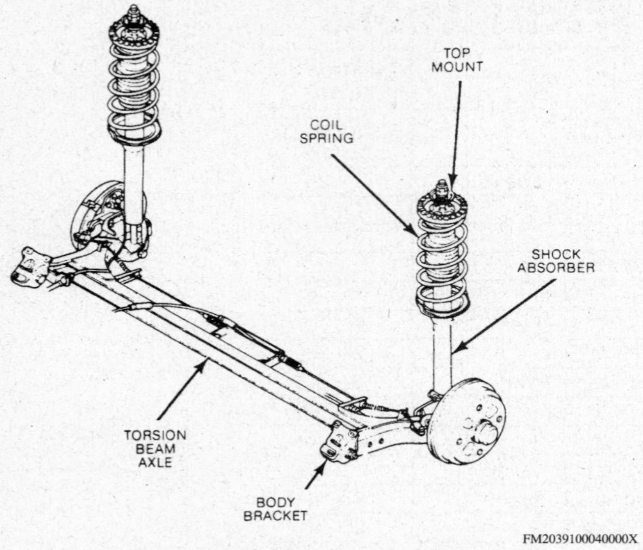

Fig. 1 Rear axle & suspension

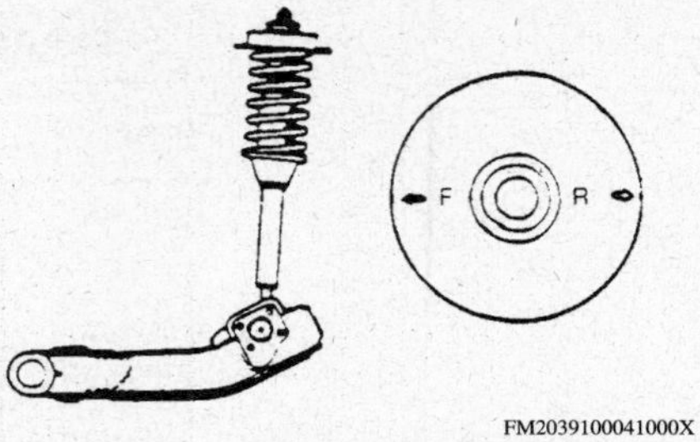

Fig. 2 Bushing on trailing arm position

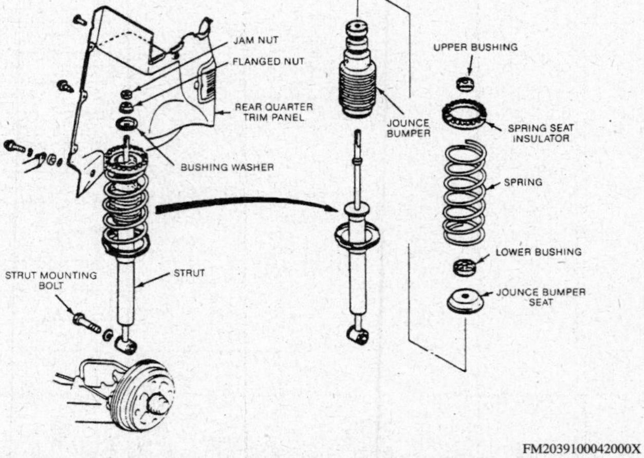

Fig. 3 Exploded view of strut assembly

c. If measurement obtained on right and left sides are not within .200 inch, shift body brackets side to side to center suspension.
d. After adjustment is completed, tighten upper body bracket bolts.

HUB & BEARING

REPLACE

1. Raise and support vehicle, then remove rear wheel.
2. Remove brake drum as follows:
   a. Remove grease cap, then pry upward on staked portion of locknut using suitable tool.
   b. Remove and discard locknut. **The locknut on the right side of the vehicle has lefthand threads. Turn locknut clockwise to remove.**
   c. Remove washer, outer wheel bearing and brake drum from spindle.
3. Pry seal from drum using suitable tool, then remove inner wheel bearing from drum.
4. Clean bearings with suitable solvent and inspect for scoring, pitting or heat damage. Replace bearings as necessary.
5. Pack bearings and hub area with suitable grease, then install inner wheel bearing.
6. Lubricate new seal, then install into drum using suitable driver.
7. Install drum, outer wheel bearing, washer and locknut.
8. Adjust wheel bearing preload as outlined under " Wheel Bearings, Adjust" procedure.
9. Install grease cap and rear wheel, then lower vehicle.

WHEEL BEARING

ADJUST

1. Raise and support vehicle, then remove rear wheel and grease cap.
2. While rotating brake drum, **torque** locknut to 18–22 ft. lbs.
3. Loosen locknut until it can be turned by hand, then measure seal drag as follows:
   a. Install a lug nut onto brake drum and place nut at 12 o'clock position.
   b. Using an inch lb. torque wrench, measure amount of force needed to start rotation of drum. Record seal drag measurement.
4. To determine specified preload, add seal drag measurement recorded in previous step to required bearing preload of 1.3–4.3 inch lbs.
5. Tighten locknut slightly, then measure amount of force needed to start rotation of drum.
6. Continue to tighten locknut until preload determined in step 4 is reached.
7. After adjustment is completed, stake locknut to spindle with a drift. **If splitting or cracking occurs after staking, replace locknut.**
8. Install grease cap and rear wheel, then lower vehicle.

SPINDLE KNUCKLE

REPLACE

1. Raise and support vehicle, then remove brake drum.
2. Wire backing plate in position, then working from rear side of plate, remove spindle attaching nuts. **Do not confuse mounting stud nuts with spindle nuts. The spindle nuts are located underneath the vehicle on the inboard side of the trailing arm.**
3. Position backing plate, then install spindle. Tighten spindle attaching nuts.
4. Reinstall brake drum, then lower vehicle.

STRUT

REPLACE

REMOVAL

1. Raise and support vehicle, then remove rear wheel.
2. Compress spring using suitable tool.
3. Working from cargo compartment, remove rear quarter trim panel.
4. Remove jam and flanged nuts from strut rod, then the bushing washer and upper bushing, **Fig. 3.**
5. Remove lower mounting bolt, then pull strut downward and separate it from spring and seat insulator.
6. Remove lower bushing and jounce bumper seat from strut rod, then slide jounce bumper and shield off strut.
7. Inspect all bushings, bumpers and insulators for damage or deterioration. Replace components as necessary.

INSTALLATION

1. Slide jounce bumper, shield, bumper seat and lower bushing onto strut rod.
2. If upper spring seat insulator requires replacement, install insulator onto upper end of spring so that end of coil seats firmly against step in insulator.
3. Position spring on strut, ensure end of coil seats firmly against step in strut spring seat.

4. Compress spring, then working from wheelwell area, guide upper end of strut rod into tower mounting hole.
5. Line up lower end of strut with mounting hole in trailing arm, then install lower mounting bolt several turns to hold strut in position.
6. Install upper bushing, bushing washer and flanged nut onto upper end of strut rod. Tighten flanged nut, then lock in position with jam nut.
7. Tighten lower mounting bolt, then remove spring compressor.
8. Install wheel, then lower vehicle.

TIGHTENING SPECIFICATIONS

Year	Component	Torque/Ft. Lbs.
1997	Body Bracket Lower Mounting Bolt	69–86
	Body Bracket Upper Mounting Bolt	40–50
	Brake Backing Plate	32–45
	Strut Lower Attaching Bolt	50–60
	Strut Rod Upper Nut	12–18
	Torsion Beam Pivot Bolt	69–86
	Wheel Lug Nuts	65–87
	Wheel Spindle Support Nut	32–45

Front Suspension & Steering

NOTE: On Air Bag Equipped Models, Refer To " Air Bag System Precautions" Located In The Front Of This Manual For System Disarming & Arming Procedures.

NOTE: Refer To "Computer Relearn Procedures " Located In The Front Of This Manual For Computer Relearn Procedures.

INDEX

PRECAUTIONS

BATTERY GROUND CABLE

Prior to service, disconnect battery ground cable and isolate as required.

DESCRIPTION

The front suspension, **Fig. 1,** is of the strut design, utilizing single pivot lower control arms with integral ball joints. The front wheels ride on forged steering knuckles, which are clamped to the ball joints on the lower end, and bolted to the lower bracket of the strut assembly on the upper end. A front stabilizer bar, connected to the lower control arms, is used to limit body sway during hard cornering and doubles as a trailing arm to maintain lower control arm alignment.

HUB & BEARING

REPLACE

Refer to "Steering Knuckle, Replace," for hub and bearing replacement procedure.

BALL JOINT INSPECTION

Check for ball joint wear by raising vehicle until the wheel is off the ground. Support the suspension arm so there is no load on the suspension strut. Attempt to rock the wheel top-to-bottom. If any wobble is felt, look for movement between the suspension lower arm and the wheel knuckle. Any movement indicates ball joint wear.

BALL JOINT

REPLACE

The ball joint is integral with the control arm and not serviceable. If the ball joint is worn, refer to "Control Arm, Replace " for replacement of the front suspension lower control arm.

STRUT

REPLACE

REMOVAL

1. Raise and support vehicle, ensure strut is fully extended, then remove front wheel.
2. Remove brake line clip, then disengage brake line from strut assembly.

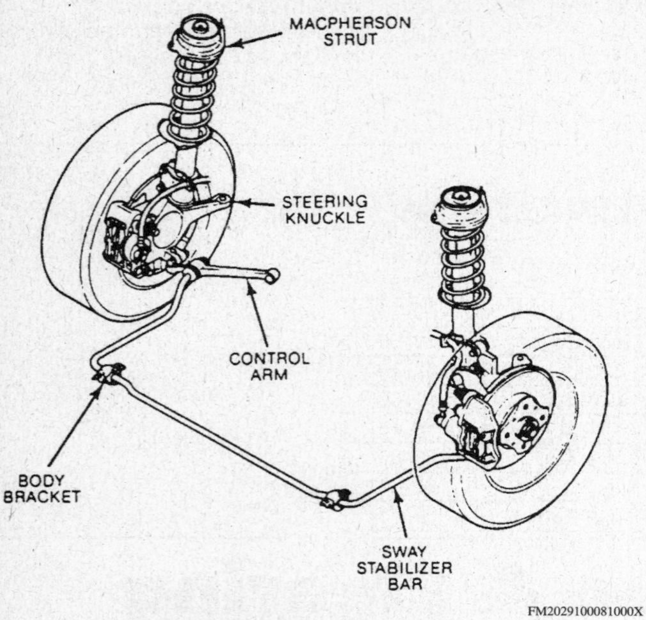

Fig. 1 Front suspension

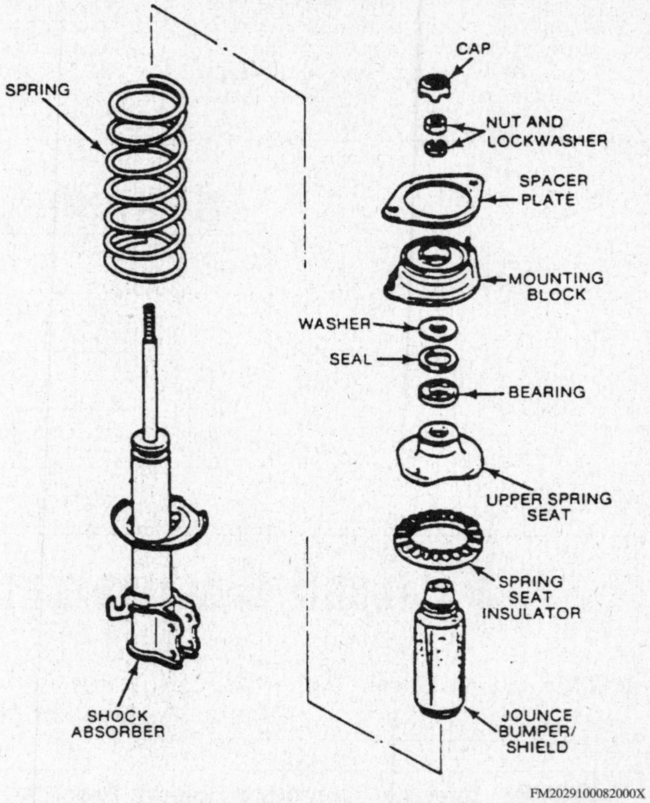

Fig. 2 Exploded view of front strut assembly

3. Remove strut to steering knuckle attaching bolts and nuts.
4. Working from engine compartment, remove nuts securing strut mounting block to shock tower.
5. Pull lower end of strut outward to disengage strut from steering knuckle, then lower strut assembly and remove from vehicle.

INSTALLATION

1. Position strut, together with spacer plate, into shock tower, ensure white alignment mark faces outward.
2. Install mounting block attaching nuts.
3. Connect steering knuckle to lower strut bracket, then install attaching bolts and nuts. Tighten to specifications.
4. Position brake line in cutout in strut lower bracket, then install retaining clip.
5. Install front wheel, then lower vehicle.

STRUT SERVICE

DISASSEMBLE

1. Remove strut as outlined previously.
2. Compress spring using suitable spring compressor.
3. Pry out mounting block cap, then remove upper attaching nut and lock washer, **Fig. 2.**
4. Remove spacer plate, mounting block, washer, seal and bearing from strut rod.
5. Remove upper spring seat, seat insulator and spring, then the jounce bumper and shield.
6. Inspect all components for excessive wear or damage. Replace components as necessary.

ASSEMBLE

1. Slide jounce bumper and shield over strut rod and onto main body of strut assembly.
2. Compress spring using suitable spring compressor, then install spring, seat insulator and upper seat. Ensure spring ends are positioned against steps in seats.
3. Install bearing, seal and washer on strut rod.
4. Install mounting block, ensure that white alignment mark is positioned on same side of strut as steering knuckle mounting bracket.
5. Install spacer plate, lock washer and attaching nut.
6. Remove spring compressor, then install mounting block cap.
7. Reinstall strut assembly into vehicle.

CONTROL ARM

REPLACE

REMOVAL

1. Raise and support vehicle, then remove pivot bolt at frame bracket.
2. Remove ball joint clamp bolt and nut at steering knuckle.
3. Remove stabilizer bar bushing retaining nut from rear of control arm, then remove bushing washer and bushing.
4. Pry ball joint stud out of steering knuckle, then disengage control arm from stabilizer bar and remove from vehicle.

INSPECTION

1. Check control arm for cracks and pivot bushing for deterioration. If bushing requires replacement, remove and install bushing using suitable tools.
2. Check ball joint stud rotating torque with suitable torque wrench. Rotating **torque** should be 16–27 inch lbs. If rotating torque is not as specified, replace control arm.

INSTALLATION

1. Install stabilizer bar into control arm. If removed, ensure front bushing washer is positioned with dished side facing front of vehicle.
2. Raise inner part of control arm and install pivot bolt. Do not tighten bolt at this time.
3. Connect ball joint stud to steering knuckle, then install clamp bolt and nut.
4. Install rear stabilizer bar bushing and washer. Ensure rear washer is positioned with dished side facing rear of vehicle, then install attaching nut.
5. Tighten pivot bolt and ball joint clamp bolt attaching nuts to specifications.

STEERING KNUCKLE

REPLACE

1. Raise and support vehicle, then remove front wheel.
2. Unstake halfshaft attaching nut using suitable chisel, apply brakes to prevent hub assembly from turning, then remove and discard attaching nut.
3. Remove brake hose to strut bracket retaining clip.
4. Remove cotter pin and tie rod attaching nut, then separate tie rod from steering knuckle using suitable tool.

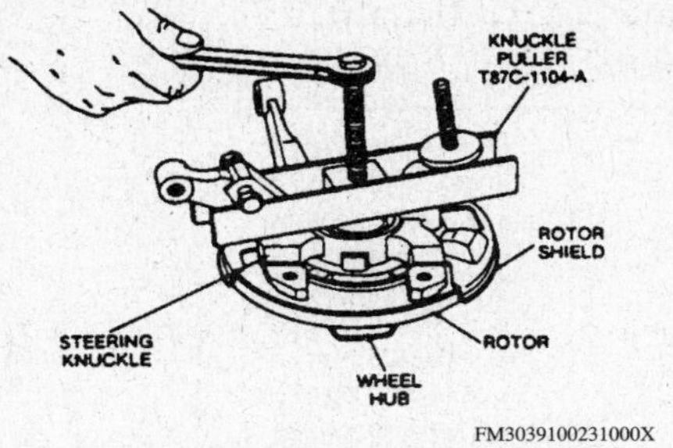

Fig. 3 Hub & rotor/steering knuckle separation

5. Remove brake caliper attaching bolts, then lift caliper assembly off steering knuckle. **Do not allow caliper to hang unsupported from brake hose. Wire caliper in place as required.**
6. Remove ball joint to steering knuckle clamp bolt and nut, then pry downward on control arm and disconnect joint from knuckle.
7. Remove steering knuckle to strut bracket attaching bolts and nuts, then slide hub/rotor assembly together with steering knuckle off end of halfshaft. If difficulty is encountered separating hub from halfshaft, tap end of shaft with plastic mallet to facilitate removal.
8. Separate hub/rotor assembly from steering knuckle using tool shown in **Fig. 3.**
9. Remove bearing preload spacer from hub, **Fig. 4. The spacer is pre-selected to yield correct bearing preload. Save spacer to use during assembling.**
10. Clamp hub/rotor assembly in soft jaw vise, scribe alignment marks on hub and rotor, then remove hub to rotor attaching bolts and separate rotor from hub.
11. Using suitable bearing remover, press hub shaft from outer bearing, then remove outer grease seal from hub.
12. Using suitable seal remover, pry inner grease seal from steering knuckle bore, then remove inner bearing.
13. Inspect bearings, hub, steering knuckle and dust shield for damage or excessive wear. Replace components as necessary.
14. If original bearings and steering knuckle are being used, proceed to step 15. If bearings or steering knuckle require replacement, proceed as follows to select proper bearing preload spacer:
    a. Drive new inner and outer bearing races into steering knuckle using suitable tools.
    b. Lubricate races and new bearings with engine oil, then install bearings into steering knuckle.
    c. Install spacer selection tool kit T87C-1104-B, original spacer and hardware shown in **Fig. 5** onto steering knuckle, then clamp steering knuckle in soft jaw vise.
    d. Tighten center bolt in increments. After bolt is tightened to specification, remove assembly from vise and rotate steering knuckle to seat bearings.

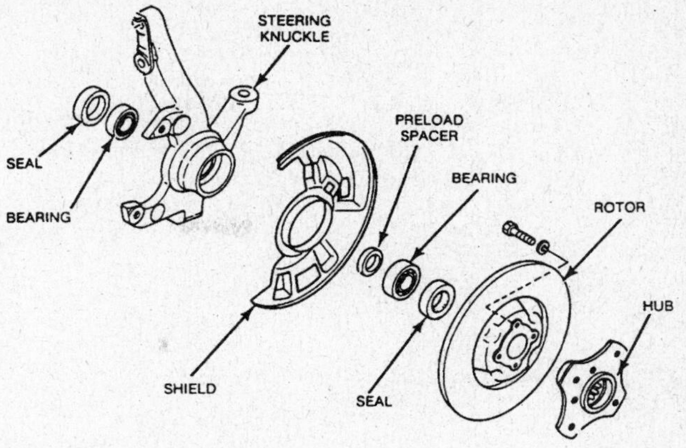

Fig. 4 Exploded view of steering knuckle & hub/rotor assembly

    e. Again clamp steering knuckle in vise, then measure the amount of torque necessary to start rotation of center bolt using an inch lb. torque wrench.
    f. If torque reading is 2.2–10.4 inch lbs., spacer is correct thickness. If torque reading is less than 2.2 inch lbs., a thinner spacer must be used. If torque reading is greater than 10.4 inch lbs., a thicker spacer must be used. Twenty one spacers of various thicknesses are available for service. Each spacer has a number stamped on it for identification purposes, **Fig. 6.** Changing the spacer by one number, either up or down, will result in a 1.7–3.5 inch lb. change in bearing preload.
15. Pack bearings and hub with suitable high temperature grease, then install inner bearing into steering knuckle.
16. Lubricate seal lip, then install new inner seal using suitable tool.
17. Place original bearing preload spacer, or spacer selected in step 14, into steering knuckle.
18. Lubricate seal lip, then install outer wheel bearing and new outer seal into knuckle.
19. Position rotor onto hub, aligning marks made during disassembling, then install attaching bolts.
20. Place hub/rotor assembly into steering knuckle bore, then press assembly fully into knuckle using suitable tools.
21. Follow steps 1 through 7 in reverse order to complete installation and note the following:
    a. Apply a thin coat of grease to halfshaft splines before installing steering knuckle and hub/rotor assembly.
    b. When installing new halfshaft attaching nut, apply brakes to prevent hub assembly from turning. Stake nut into groove on halfshaft after tightening.
    c. Tighten tie rod end to steering knuckle attaching nut, then install new cotter pin. **If holes in attaching nut do not line up with hole in ball stud, tighten nut as required until cotter pin can be installed. Never loosen nut when installing cotter pin.**

STABILIZER BAR

REPLACE

1. Raise and support vehicle.
2. Remove stabilizer bar mounting bracket attaching nuts, then the brackets and split bushings.
3. Remove stabilizer bar to control arm attaching nuts, then the rear washers and bushings.
4. Pull stabilizer bar forward and remove from vehicle. If necessary, remove front bushings and washers from bar.
5. Reverse procedure to install, noting the following:
    a. When installing bushing washers, ensure front washer is installed with dished side facing front of vehicle and rear washer is positioned with dished side facing rear of vehicle.
    b. When installing split bushings, ensure split side faces forward and that bushings are positioned next to white locating marks on bar.

TIE ROD END

REPLACE

OUTER

1. Remove and discard cotter pin and nut from tie rod end, then use tie rod end remover tool No. 3290-D, or equivalent, to separate tie rod end from steering knuckle.
2. While holding tie rod end with a suitable wrench, loosen jam nut slightly. **Allow jam nut to remain as close to its original position as possible for tie rod end installation depth reference.**
3. Using suitable pliers, remove tie rod end from tie rod.
4. Reverse procedure to install, noting following:
    a. Thread new tie rod end onto tie rod only until it reaches jam nut, then secure with jam nut until wheel alignment can be inspected and set.

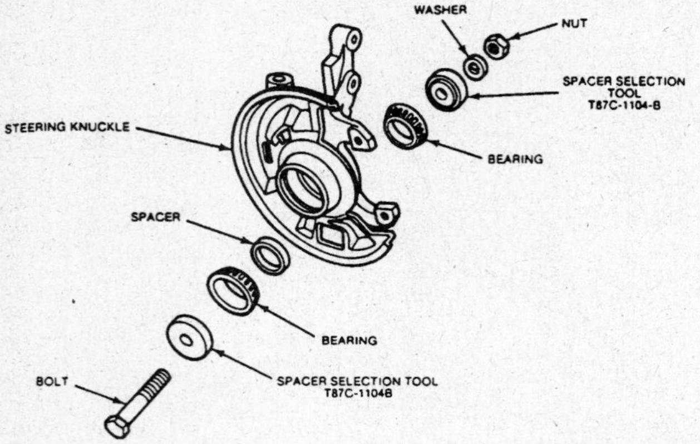

FM3039100233000X

Fig. 5 Bearing preload spacer selection tool installation

Stamped mark	Thickness
1	6.285 mm (0.2474 in)
2	6.325 mm (0.2490 in)
3	6.365 mm (0.2506 in)
4	6.405 mm (0.2522 in)
5	6.445 mm (0.2538 in)
6	6.485 mm (0.2554 in)
7	6.525 mm (0.2570 in)
8	6.565 mm (0.2586 in)
9	6.605 mm (0.2602 in)
10	6.645 mm (0.2618 in)
11	6.685 mm (0.2634 in)
12	6.725 mm (0.2650 in)
13	6.765 mm (0.2666 in)
14	6.805 mm (0.2682 in)
15	6.845 mm (0.2698 in)
16	6.885 mm (0.2714 in)
17	6.925 mm (0.2730 in)
18	6.965 mm (0.2746 in)
19	7.005 mm (0.2762 in)
20	7.045 mm (0.2778 in)
21	7.085 mm (0.2794 in)

FM3039100234000X

Fig. 6 Bearing preload spacer identification chart

b. Install a new tie rod end stud nut and cotter pin.
c. Tighten tie rod end to knuckle nut and tie rod end jam nut to specifications.
d. Set front wheel toe to specifications as described in " Wheel Alignment" section.

INNER

Refer to "Power Steering" for procedure.

POWER STEERING GEAR

REPLACE

REMOVAL

1. Remove steering column tube boot retainer and pry up boot.
2. Remove steering column gear input shaft coupling bolt, then raise and support vehicle.
3. Remove power steering hose bracket and disconnect power steering return hose.
4. Remove front wheel and tire assemblies, then tie rod cotter pins and end nuts.
5. Separate tie rod ends from steering knuckles using appropriate tool, then remove the tie rod splash shields.
6. Remove front catalytic converter front inlet exhaust pipe and lower for easier access.
7. Place alignment marks on tie rod end, jam nut, and tie rod to ease installation.
8. Loosen jam nut and remove right tie rod end.
9. Remove four steering gear mounting bolts and washers.
10. Slide steering gear to the left and pull right tie rod through fender opening, then the steering gear.

INSTALLATION

1. Position steering gear in its mounting location.
2. Attach intermediate shaft to steering gear pinion and **torque** bolt to 13–20 ft. lbs.
3. Guide intermediate shaft into steering column hole, then lower vehicle.

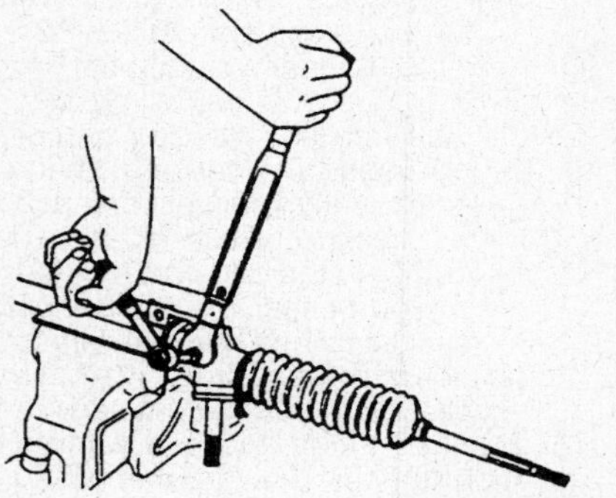

FM3039100235000X

Fig. 7 Rack yoke preload adjustment

4. With assistance in lifting the steering gear, align intermediate shaft with universal joint and install mounting bolt.
5. Raise and support vehicle, then install the four steering gear washer and bolts. **Torque** mounting bolts to 23–34 ft. lbs.
6. Install right tie rod end and attach tie rod ends to steering knuckles. **Torque** tie rod end nuts to 23–34 ft. lbs.
7. Install catalytic converter, tie rod splash shields and front wheel and tire assemblies.
8. Lower vehicle and attach power steering lines.
9. Add power steering fluid and bleed system following procedure outlined under "Power Steering System Bleed."

MANUAL STEERING GEAR

REPLACE

1. Remove battery.
2. Scribe alignment marks on steering column lower universal joint and steering gear pinion shaft, then remove steering column as follows:
   a. Working from underneath steering column, remove instrument panel brace and air duct.
   b. Remove upper and lower steering column covers, release harness clip, then disconnect harness connectors from back of multi-function switch.
   c. Remove ignition switch as outlined in the "Electrical, " section of this manual.
   d. Remove steering column upper mounting bracket to instrument panel attaching nuts, then lower column.
   e. Scribe alignment marks on column shaft and intermediate shaft upper universal joint, then remove clamp screw from joint.
   f. Remove steering column hinge bracket to pedal support attaching nuts, then pull steering column rearward and remove from vehicle.
3. Cut plastic tie strap securing steering column boot to steering gear.
4. Raise and support vehicle, then remove front wheels.
5. Remove tie rod to steering knuckle attaching nuts, then separate tie rods from knuckle.
6. Remove catalytic converter.
7. Remove tie rod splash shield from right inner fender.
8. Remove steering gear mounting bolts and lower gear until free from steering column boot.
9. Slide steering gear to the right until left tie rod is clear of inner fender, then lower gear and remove through left side of vehicle. **When sliding gear as required, guide gear carefully to prevent damage to boots.**
10. Reverse procedure to install, aligning all marks made during removal. Adjust

rack yoke preload, as follows:

a. Remove steering gear as previously described.
b. With rack centered, measure pinion rotating torque. Pinion **torque** should be 8–12 inch lbs. within 90 degrees of centered position, and should not exceed 13 inch lbs. when turned beyond 90° of center.
c. If pinion rotating torque is not as specified in previous step, loosen yoke adjusting bolt locknut and turn adjusting bolt as required until specified rotational torque is reached, **Fig. 7.**
d. After adjustment is completed, hold adjusting bolt in position and tighten locknut.

POWER STEERING SYSTEM BLEED

1. Add specified power steering fluid to "L" mark on power steering reservoir dip stick.
2. Start engine and run until reaching normal operating temperature.
3. Turn steering wheel from lock to lock 10 times, then turn off engine with wheels in straight ahead position.
4. Check fluid level and add if necessary to between the " L" and "H" mark on power steering reservoir dip stick.

TIGHTENING SPECIFICATIONS

Year	Component	Torque/Ft. Lbs.
1997	Ball Joint Pinch Bolt	32–40
	Control Arm Bushing Retaining Nuts	47–57
	Control Arm Frame Bracket Pivot Bolt	32–40
	Disc Brake Caliper Attaching Bolts	29–36
	Halfshaft Nut	116–174
	Rotor Attaching Bolts	33–40
	Stabilizer Mounting Bracket Nuts	40–50
	Stabilizer Rear Bushing Nut	43–52
	Steering Gear Mounting Bolts	23–34
	Steering Knuckle Bolts	69–86
	Steering Rack Support Cover	29–43
	Strut Rod Nut	40–50
	Tie Rod Ball Joints	43–58
	Tie Rod End Jam Nut	25–36
	Tie Rod End Nut	31–42
	Upper Mounting Block Bolts	22–27
	Wheel Lug Nuts	65–87

Wheel Alignment

INDEX

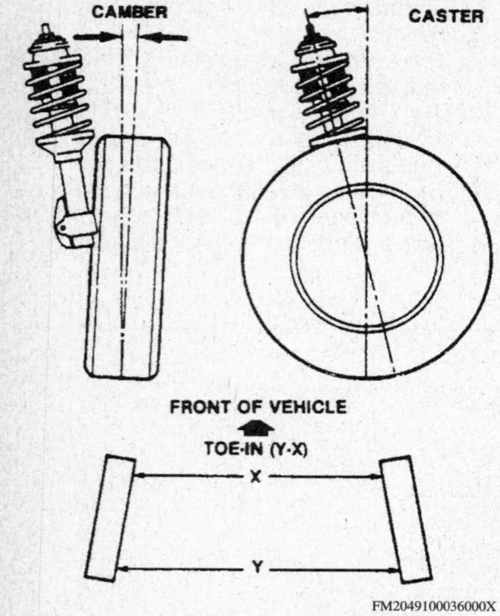

Fig. 1 Front wheel alignment settings

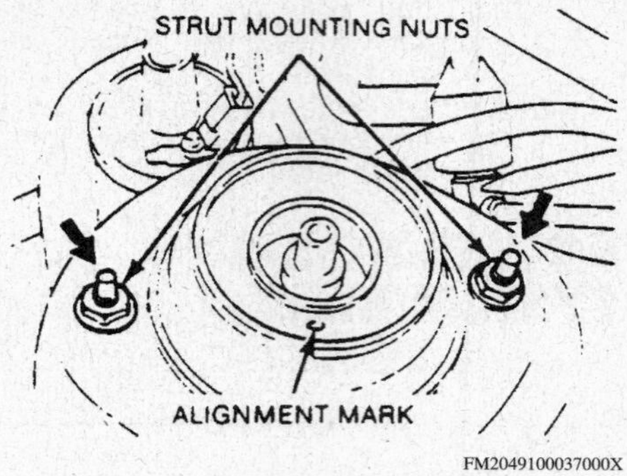

Fig. 2 Front strut camber alignment mark

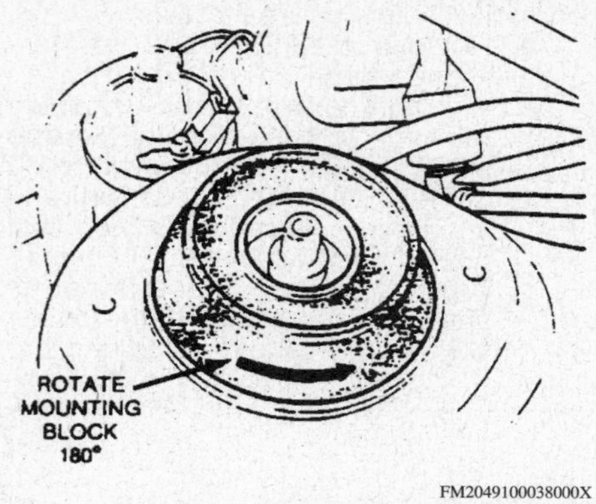

Fig. 3 Front camber adjustment

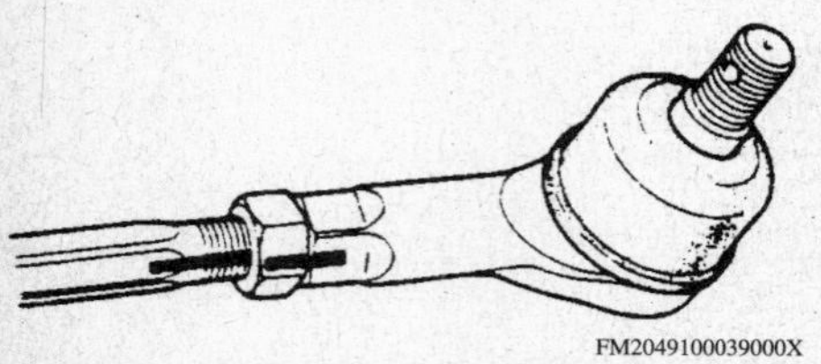

Fig. 4 Tie rod, tie rod end & jam nut position marking

PRELIMINARY INSPECTION

1. Inspect tires for proper inflation and similar tread wear.
2. Inspect hub and bearing for excessive wear, repair as required.
3. Inspect ball joints.
4. Inspect tie rod ends for excessive looseness.
5. Check wheel and tire runout.
6. Inspect vehicle ride height.
7. Inspect rack and pinion for looseness at frame.
8. Ensure proper strut operation.
9. Check suspension and steering components for damage, replace as required.

FRONT WHEEL ALIGNMENT

CASTER

Caster is not adjustable, **Fig. 1.** If caster angles are not within specification, check for damaged or bent suspension components, deteriorated bushings, or distorted body mounting points.

CAMBER

Camber angle, **Fig. 1,** is controlled by the position of the strut mounting block in the shock tower. The mounting block can be positioned in the tower in two ways, resulting in a camber variation of approximately ½.° If the camber setting has not been changed previously, the white alignment mark on the mounting block will be positioned on the outboard side of the strut assembly, **Fig. 2.** Changing the position of the alignment mark 180° will increase camber angle approximately ½°, **Fig. 3.** If the alignment mark is already positioned inboard of the strut, changing the mounting block position can only result in camber being reduced by approximately ½.° To adjust camber setting, proceed as follows:

1. Raise and support vehicle and remove front wheels.
2. Remove upper strut attaching nuts.
3. Lower strut sufficiently so that mounting studs clear tower, then rotate mounting block 180° as necessary.
4. Reposition strut in tower, then install attaching nuts and **torque** to 32–45 ft. lbs.

TOE-IN

1. Ensure tires are properly inflated, then position vehicle on suitable alignment rack.
2. Bounce vehicle several times to normalize ride height, then check toe setting. If toe setting is not within specification, proceed to next step.
3. Mark relationship between tie rods, tie rod ends and jam nuts, then loosen tie rod boot clamps to prevent twisting or damage to boots, **Fig. 4.**
4. Adjust toe-in by turning both tie rods in or out an equal amount until toe setting is within specification.
5. After adjustment is completed, tighten jam nuts and boot clamps.

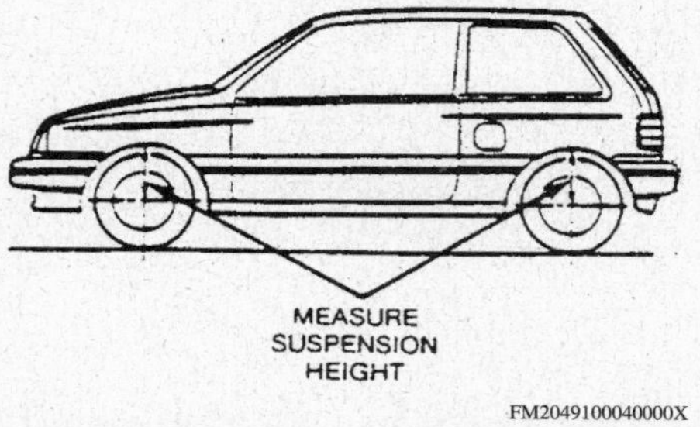

Fig. 5 Vehicle ride height measurement

REAR WHEEL ALIGNMENT

Rear camber and toe-in are determined by the configuration of the trailing arms on the torsion beam rear axle. No provision for adjustment is provided. The only rear suspension adjustment possible is the lateral positioning of the rear axle. This adjustment should only be performed if replacing the rear axle assembly. Refer to "Axle Assembly, Replace" procedure in "Rear Axle & Suspension" section for adjustment procedure.

VEHICLE RIDE HEIGHT

Prior to checking suspension height, remove heavy items from vehicle, such as tool boxes etc. Suspension height is measured from ground to the fender cut out above the center of the wheel and tire assembly, **Fig. 5.** This measurement should be performed at all four wheels. Readings from side to side and front to rear should not vary by more than .4 inch. **It should be noted that uneven tire wear will increase the variance in the measurements and should be taken into consideration. If variance is more than .4 inch, check springs and suspension components for wear and damage.**

CONTOUR, MYSTIQUE & 1999–2000 COUGAR

NOTE: Refer To The Rear Of This Manual For Manufacturer's Special Service Tool Suppliers.

INDEX OF SERVICE OPERATIONS

Specifications

GENERAL ENGINE SPECIFICATIONS

Year	Engine Liter (VIN) ①	Fuel System	Bore & Stroke, Inches	Compression Ratio	Net HP @ RPM②	Maximum Torque, Ft. Lbs. @ RPM	Normal Oil Pressure, psi
1997-2000	2.0	SEFI	3.34 X 3.46	9.6	125 @ 5500	130 @ 4000	③
	2.5④	SEFI	3.25 X 3.13	9.7	170 @ 6250	165 @ 4250	③
1998–2000	2.5⑤	SEFI	3.25 X 3.13	10.0	195 @ 6625	165 @ 5625	—

SEFI — Sequential Electronic Fuel Injection
① — Eighth digit of Vehicle Identifications Number (VIN) denotes engine code.
② — Net rating, as installed on vehicle.
③ — 1997–98 2.0L engine & 1999–2000 2.5L engine; 20–45 psi w/engine hot @ 1500 RPM. 1999–2000 w/2.0L engine; 35–65 psi w/engine hot @ 2000 RPM.
④ — Except Contour SVT.
⑤ — Contour SVT.

TUNE UP SPECIFICATIONS

Engine (Code)⑩	Spark Plug Gap, Inch	Ignition Timing; °BTDC				Curb Idle Speed⑦		Fast Idle Speed⑦		Fuel Pump Pressure, psi ②	Valve Clearance, Inch
		Firing Order Fig.①	Man. Trans.	Auto Trans.	Mark Fig.	Man. Trans.	Auto Trans.	Man. Trans.	Auto Trans.		
1997											
2.0L (3)	.050	A	10③	10③	C	880⑤	800⑤	⑤	⑤	39-43	⑥
2.5 (L)	.054	B	10③	10③	D	650⑤	650⑤	⑤	⑤	39-43	⑥
1998–2000											
2.0L (3)	.052	—	⑧	⑧	④	⑤	⑤	⑤	⑤	30-45	⑨
2.5L (L)	.052	—	⑧	⑧	④	⑤	⑤	⑤	⑤	45-60	⑥

BTDC — Before Top Dead Center
① — Before disconnecting wires from distributor coil unit, determine location of ignition wires, as position may have been altered from that shown at end of this chart.
② — Wrap shop towel around diagnostic valve to prevent fuel spillage. Connect suitable fuel pressure gauge to fuel diagnostic valve. Place ignition switch in On position to energize fuel pump & check pressure gauge reading.
③ — Non-adjustable. Check w/inline spout connector disconnected.
④ — Equipped w/crankshaft position sensor.
⑤ — Controlled by Idle air control valve.
⑥ — Valve clearance is hydraulically controlled, no adjustment is necessary.
⑦ — When adjusting idle speed, set parking brake & chock drive wheels.
⑧ — Non-adjustable
⑨ — Intake, .0043–.0071 inch; exhaust, .0106–.0134 inch.
⑩ — Eighth digit of Vehicle Identification Number (VIN) denotes engine code.

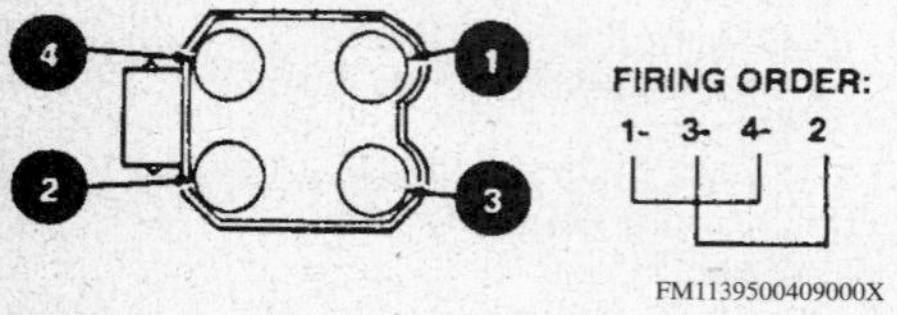

Fig. A

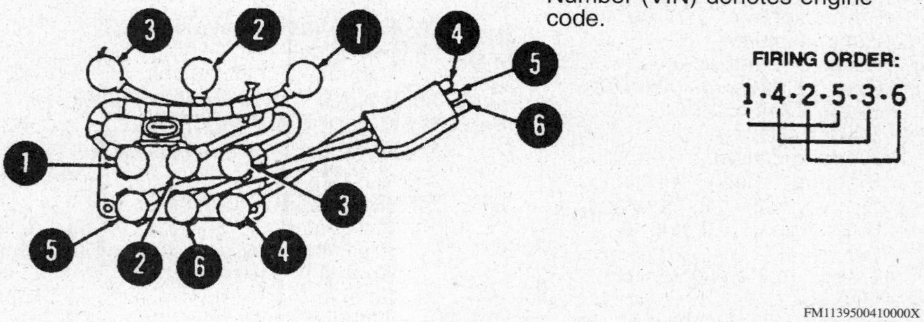

Fig. B

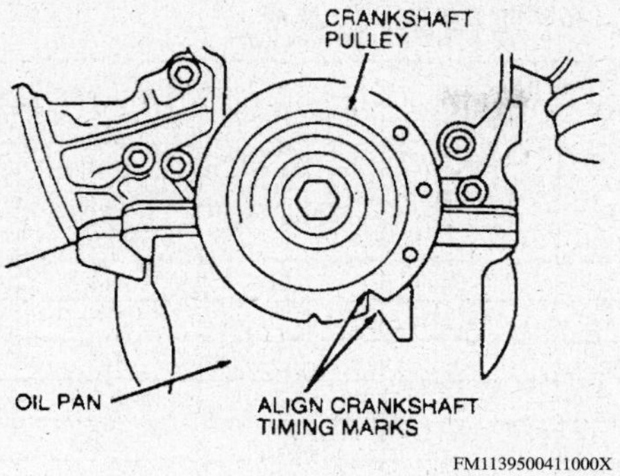

Fig. C

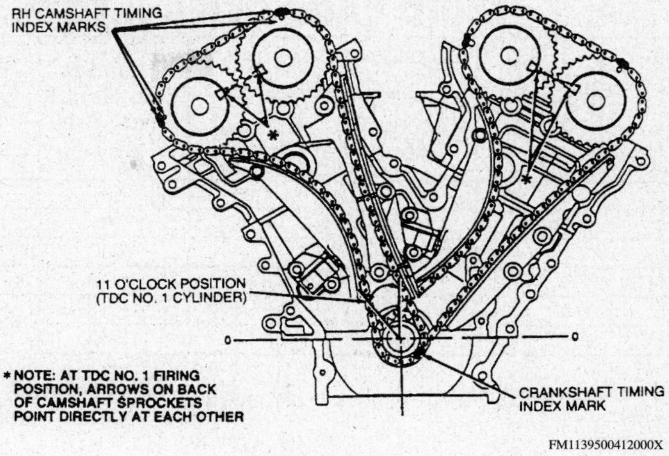

Fig. D

FRONT WHEEL ALIGNMENT SPECIFICATIONS

Model	Caster Angle, Degrees		Camber Angle, Degrees		Total Toe, Inch①		Toe-Out On Turns, Degrees		Ball Joint Wear, Inch
	Limits	Desired	Limits	Desired	Limits	Desired	Outer Wheel	Inner Wheel	
1997									
Except Contour SE	+1.30 to +3.30	+2.30	-1.71 to +.79	-.46	-.138 to +.059	0	18.25	20	.015②
Contour SE	+1.40 to +3.40	+2.40	-1.80 to +.70	-.55	-.138 to +.059	0	18.25	20	.015②
1998–2000									
Contour & Mystique	+1.23 to +3.31	+2.27	-1.83 to +.77	-.53	-.170 to +.170	0	—	—	.015②
Cougar	+1.23 to +3.31	+2.27	-1.83 to +.77	-.53	-.170 to +.170	0	—	—	.015②

① — Toe-in (+), toe-out (-).

② — Refer to “Ball Joint Inspection,” in “Front Suspension & Steering” section, for inspection procedure.

REAR WHEEL ALIGNMENT SPECIFICATIONS

Model	Camber Angle, Degrees		Total Toe, Degrees①	
	Limits	Desired	Limits	Desired
1997				
Except Contour SE	-1.40 to +.60	-.40	0 to +.56	+.28
Contour SE	-1.53 to +.47	-.53	0 to +.65	+.28
1998-2000				
All	-1.82 to +.76	-.53	+.12 to +.52	+.32

① — Toe-in (+), toe-out (-).

FLUID CAPACITIES & COOLING SYSTEM DATA

Year	Engine (Code)③	Coolant Capacity, Qts.		Radiator Cap Relief Pressure, Lbs.	Thermo Opening Temp., Dreg. F	Fuel Tank, Gals.	Engine Oil Refill, Qts.②	Transaxle Oil	
		Automatic Trans.	Manual Trans.					Manual Trans., Pts.	Automatatic Trans., Qts.①
1997	2.0L	7.5	7.0	16	191	14.5	4.5	5.5	9.0
	2.5L	9.1	8.9	16	187	14.5	5.5	5.5	10.3
1998	2.0L	7.5	7	13-18	191	15	4.5	4.2	9
	2.5L	9.1	8.9	13-18	187	15	5.5	4.2	10
1999- 2000	2.0L	7.5	7	13-18	191	④	4	2.9	9
	2.5L	9.1	8.9	13-18	187	④	5.8	2.9	10

① — Approximate. Make final check w/dipstick.
② — Includes filter.
③ — Eighth digit of Vehicle Identification Number (VIN) denotes engine code.
④ — Cougar; 15.5 gallons. Contour & Mystique; 15 gallons.

LUBRICANT DATA

Year	Model	Lubricant Type				
		Transaxle		Hydraulic Clutch Fluid	Power Steering	Brake System
		Manual	Automatic			
1997	All	Emerson	Emerson	DOT 3	Premium Power Steering Fluid①	DOT 3 or 4
1998–2000	All	Emerson	Emerson	DOT 3	Premium Power Steering Fluid①	DOT 3

① — Premium power steering fluid meeting Ford specification number ESW-M2C-33–F.

Electrical

NOTE: Refer To "Air Bag System Precautions" Located In The Front Of This Manual For System Disarming & Arming Procedures.

NOTE: Refer To "Computer Relearn Procedures" Located In The Front Of This Manual For Computer Relearn Procedures.

INDEX

PRECAUTIONS

BATTERY GROUND CABLE

Prior to service, disconnect battery ground cable and isolate as required.

AIR BAG SYSTEMS

Refer to "Air Bag System Precautions" in front of this manual for system disarming and arming procedures.

FUEL PRESSURE RELIEF

1. Remove air cleaner outlet tube.
2. Remove Scraper valve cap.
3. Connect fuel pressure gauge tool No. T80L-9974-B, or equivalent, to Scraper valve.
4. When relieving fuel pressure, catch any displaced fuel in a suitable container. Turn tap on fuel pressure gauge fully counterclockwise to relieve the fuel pressure.

FUSE PANEL & FLASHER LOCATION

Fuse junction panel is located to left of steering column and is attached to instrument panel

Indicator flasher is located at turn and emergency warning indicator switch at steering column tube.

FUEL PUMP RELAY LOCATION

Fuel pump relay is located in front left-hand corner of engine compartment, in engine compartment fuse box.

RELAY CENTER LOCATION

Relays are contained in power distribution box, located in engine compartment on lefthand fender apron.

STARTER

REPLACE

CONTOUR & MYSTIQUE

2.0L Engine

1. Remove air cleaner.
2. The engine ground cable is secured by one of the starter motor bolts. Remove starter motor upper bolts.
3. Cut cable ties, then raise and support vehicle.
4. Disconnect starter motor electrical connectors.
5. Remove starter motor.
6. Reverse procedure to install. **Torque** starter motor bolts to 15–20 ft. lbs.

2.5L Engine

1. Remove engine air cleaner.
2. Remove fuel supply and return tubes from fuel tube support bracket located on accelerator cable bracket and fuel tube support bracket.
3. **On models with automatic transaxle,** remove gear selector cable and gear shift cable bracket from transaxle.
4. **On all models,** remove engine air cleaner mounting bracket from engine and transaxle support.
5. Remove connector retaining nut from starter solenoid.
6. Remove starter motor to transaxle case retaining bolt at rear of start motor.
7. Remove two starter motor retaining bolts from top of starter.
8. Lift starter motor to disengage alignment pins from transaxle case. Carefully remove starter motor from vehicle.
9. Reverse procedure to install, noting the following:
   a. **Torque** starter motor bolts to 15-21 ft. lbs.
   b. **Torque** engine air cleaner mounting bracket to engine and transaxle support insulator bolts to 15-21 ft. lbs.
   c. **Torque** B terminal nut to 6-10 ft. lbs.
   d. **Torque** S terminal nut to 40-55 inch lbs.

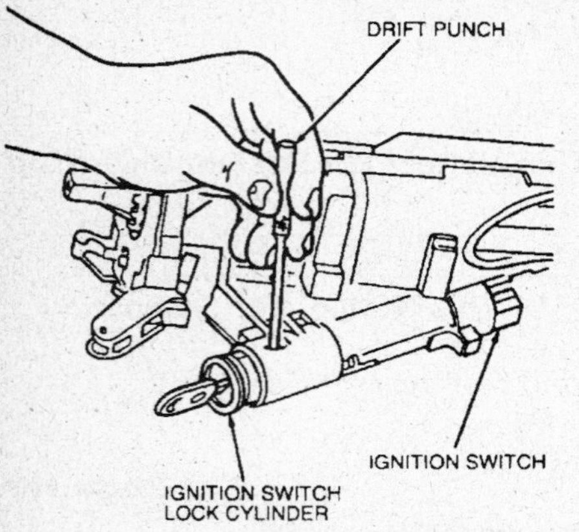

Fig. 1 Ignition lock cylinder removal. 1997 w/functional lock

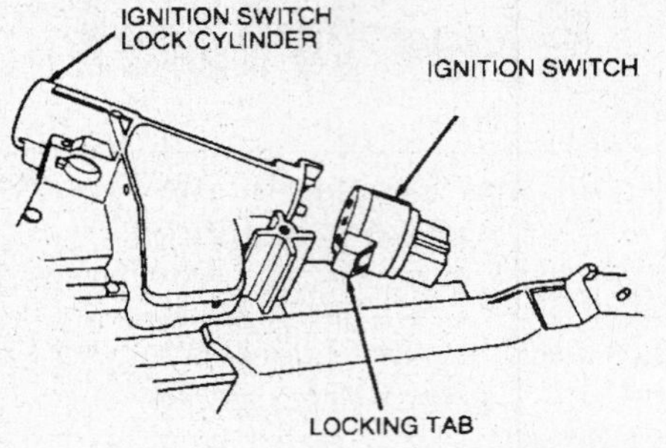

Fig. 2 Ignition switch replacement. 1997

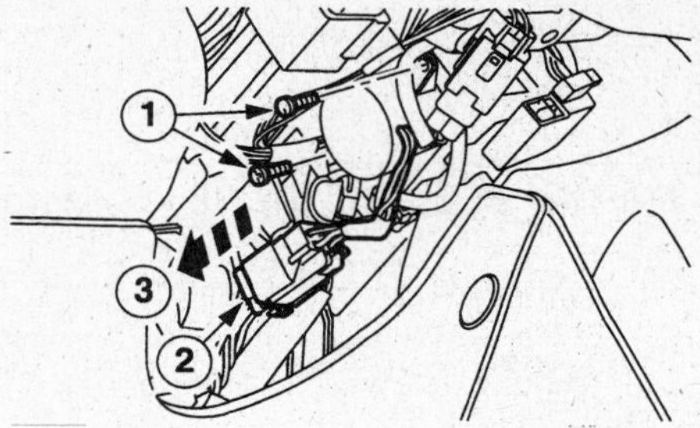

Fig. 3 Ignition switch replacement. 1998–2000

COUGAR

2.0L Engine

Refer to "Contour & Mystique" for replacement procedure.

2.5L Engine

1. Remove air cleaner, then the air cleaner bracket.
2. Disconnect starter motor electrical connectors.
3. Remove shift cable bracket bolts, then disconnect shift cable.
4. Remove starter motor support bracket.
5. Relieve fuel pressure as outlined in "Precautions."
6. Using fuel line tool No. 310-D005 or 310-D004, or equivalents, disconnect fuel return and supply lines.
7. Remove starter motor bolts and starter motor.
8. Reverse procedure to install, noting the following:
   a. **Torque** starter bolts and starter bracket bolts to 18 ft. lbs.
   b. **Torque** B terminal nut to 108 inch lbs.
   c. **Torque** S terminal nut to 40-55 inch lbs.

ALTERNATOR

REPLACE

2.0L ENGINE

1997

1. Remove engine air intake resonator, mass air flow sensor and air cleaner outlet tube assembly from throttle body and air cleaner assembly.
2. Disconnect wire harness attachments to integral alternator/voltage regulator, then raise and support vehicle.
3. Remove alternator drive belt from alternator pulley, then alternator mounting bracket bolts and alternator bracket.
4. Lower vehicle, then remove power steering pressure hose bracket nut and bolt.
5. Remove power steering pressure hose bracket from engine lifting eye, then the alternator bolts and alternator.
6. Reverse procedure to install, noting following:
   a. **Torque** power steering pressure hose bracket nut and bolt to 72–108 inch lbs.
   b. **Torque** alternator bracket bolts to 15–22 ft. lbs.
   c. **Torque** alternator mounting bolts to 15-22 ft. lbs.

1998–2000

1. Remove the intake air resonator as follows:
   a. Disconnect air cleaner outlet tube.
   b. Remove bolts and nuts, then the resonator.
2. **On Cougar models,** detach coolant hose from the retaining clip.
3. **On all models,** disconnect vacuum pipe underneath.
4. Remove radiator splash shield.
5. Disconnect cable and wiring from alternator.
6. Disconnect ground cable on eye hook, then raise and support vehicle.
7. Remove radiator splash shield.
8. Remove right front wheel, then splash shield bolts and splash shield.
9. Remove accessory drive belt, then alternator lower retaining bolts.
10. Lower vehicle and remove alternator upper retaining bolt.
11. There is a very limited amount of space in which to remove the alternator. Do not overdress or damage any hoses or cables. Lift alternator clear of engine.
12. Reverse procedure to install. **Torque** alternator bolt to 33 ft. lbs.

2.5L ENGINE

1. Remove alternator drive belt form alternator pulley.
2. Raise and support vehicle, then remove righthand wheel and tire.
3. Remove righthand outer tie rod end from righthand spindle.
4. Remove exhaust system Y pipe as follows:
   a. Remove front and rear Y pipe flange fasteners from exhaust manifolds.
   b. Remove stud bolt and nut retainer from oil pan, then remove two remaining nuts and bolts from U pipe outlet connection.
   c. Discard exhaust converter inlet gasket, then remove Y pipe.
5. Disconnect wire harness attachments to integral alternator/voltage regulator, then remove alternator brace bolts and brace from alternator.
6. Remove righthand halfhearted as described in "Front Wheel Drive Axles" section.
7. Remove alternator bolts from bracket, then rotate alternator and remove through righthand side of vehicle.
8. Remove bracket bolts and bracket from cylinder block.
9. Reverse procedure to install, noting following:
   a. **Torque** alternator bracket bolts to 15–22 ft. lbs.
   b. **Torque** alternator bolts to 29–40 ft. lbs.
   c. **Torque** alternator brace bolts to 15–22 ft. lbs.
   d. **Torque** output terminal nut to 84–96 inch lbs.

COIL PACK

REPLACE

1997

2.0L Engine

1. Remove engine intake air resonators, then disconnect fuel charging or engine control sensor wiring from ignition coil.
2. Squeezing locking tabs and twisting while pulling to disconnect ignition wires.
3. Remove retaining bolts or screws and ignition coil.
4. Reverse procedure to install, noting following:
   a. **Torque** mounting bolts to 13–17 ft. lbs.
   b. Apply silicone dielectric compound No. D7AZ-19A331-A, or equivalent, to ignition wire boots.

2.5L Engine

1. Disconnect fuel charging wiring from radio ignition interference capacitor, then remove EGR vacuum regulator solenoid from upper intake manifold.
2. Squeezing locking tabs and twisting while pulling to disconnect ignition wires.
3. Remove retaining bolts or screws and ignition coil.

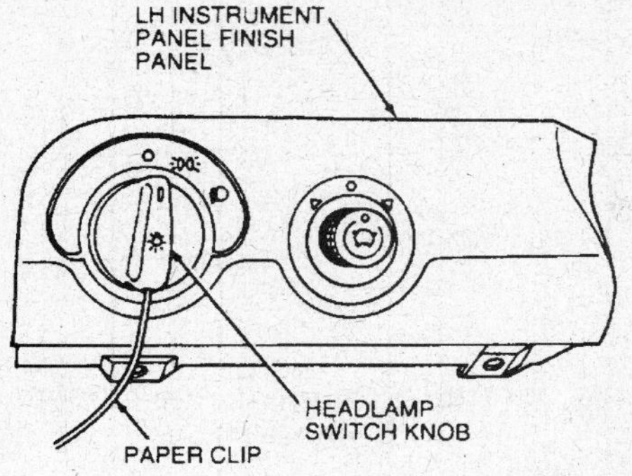

Fig. 4 Headland switch knob removal

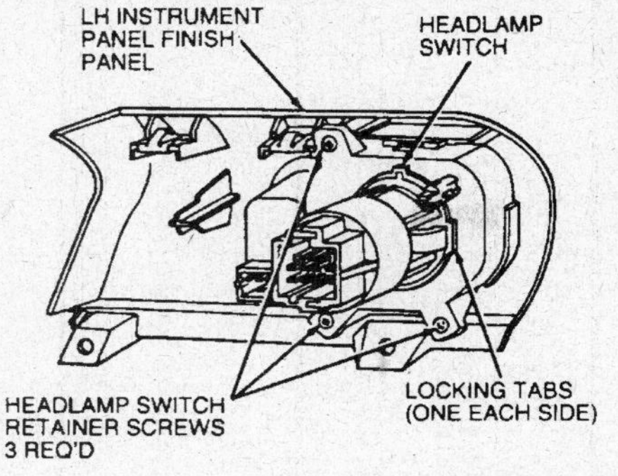

Fig. 5 Headland switch removal

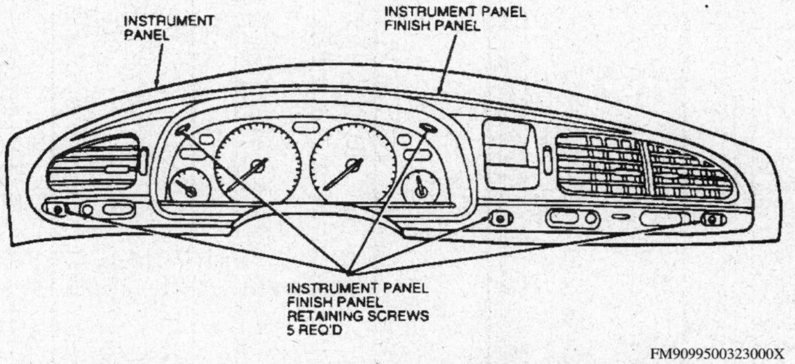

Fig. 6 Instrument panel finish panel removal. 1997

4. Remove radio ignition interference capacitor and disconnect coil ground wire.
5. Reverse procedure to install, noting following:
   a. **Torque** mounting bolts to 40–61 inch lbs.
   b. Apply silicone dielectric compound No. D7AZ-19A331-A, or equivalent, to ignition wire boots.

1998–2000

1. Disconnect ignition coil electrical connector and spark plug wires from coil.
2. Remove ignition coil mounting screws.
3. Reverse procedure to install. **Torque** coil mounting screws to 48 inch lbs.

IGNITION LOCK

REPLACE

FUNCTIONAL LOCK CYLINDER

1997

Removal

Following procedure applies to vehicles with a functional ignition switch lock cylinder. Lock cylinder keys are available for these vehicles, or lock cylinder key can be made. Place ignition key in lock cylinder.

1. Remove three upper and lower steering column shroud screws, then shrouds.
2. Turn ignition switch lock cylinder to accessory position.
3. Place ⅛ inch diameter wire pin or small drift punch in hole at top of lock cylinder housing, **Fig. 1.**
4. Press ignition switch lock cylinder pin while pulling lock cylinder from housing.

Installation

1. Install new ignition lock cylinder by turning it to accessory position and pressing in pin.
2. Insert lock cylinder into housing, then turn cylinder to Off position. This permits pin to extend into lock cylinder housing hole.
3. Rotate lock cylinder, using key, to check operation.
4. Install steering column shrouds, then shroud screws.
5. Connect battery ground cable.

1998–2000

1. Remove steering column lower shroud.
2. Remove anti-theft system transceiver screw and transceiver.
3. Insert and turn the key to accessory, then depress the retainer and remove ignition switch lock cylinder.
4. Reverse procedure to install.

NON-FUNCTIONAL LOCK CYLINDER

1997

Removal

Following procedure is for vehicles in which ignition switch lock cylinder is inoperative and ignition switch lock cylinder cannot be rotated due to a lost or broken lock cylinder key, unknown key number or with an ignition switch lock cylinder cap damaged and/or broken to extent key cannot be rotated.

1. Remove upper and lower steering column shroud screws, then shrouds.
2. Using ⅛ inch drill, drill out ignition switch lock cylinder pin.
3. Pull lock cylinder from steering column housing, then inspect housing for damage. If damaged, replace steering column as described in "Steering Columns" section.

Installation

1. Thoroughly clean all drill shavings and other foreign materials from steering column housing.
2. Install new lock cylinder by turning it to accessory position and pressing in pin.
3. Insert ignition switch lock cylinder into lock cylinder housing, then turn lock cylinder to OFF position. This permits pin to extend into lock cylinder housing hole.
4. Rotate lock cylinder, using key, to check for proper operation.
5. Install steering column shrouds, then shroud screws.
6. Connect battery ground cable.

IGNITION SWITCH

REPLACE

1. Remove steering column shroud screws, then shrouds.
2. Disconnect ignition switch electrical connector
3. **On 1997 models,** depress locking tabs to remove switch, **Fig. 2.**
4. **On 1998–2000 models,** remove two ignition switch attaching screws, then the ignition switch, **Fig. 3.**
5. **On all models,** reverse procedure to install.

CLUTCH START SWITCH

REPLACE

1997

1. Disconnect harness connector from clutch pedal position switch.
2. Rotate switch approximately 45° and pull switch from bracket.
3. Reverse procedure to install.

TRANSAXLE RANGE SENSOR

REPLACE

1. Place manual control lever in NEUTRAL position.
2. **On 1997 models,** remove engine intake air resonators and mass air flow sensor.
3. **On 1998–2000 models,** remove battery tray.
4. **On all models,** disconnect electrical harness from sensor, remove two retaining bolts and sensor.
5. Reverse procedure to install, noting following:
   a. Ensure manual control lever is in NEUTRAL position.

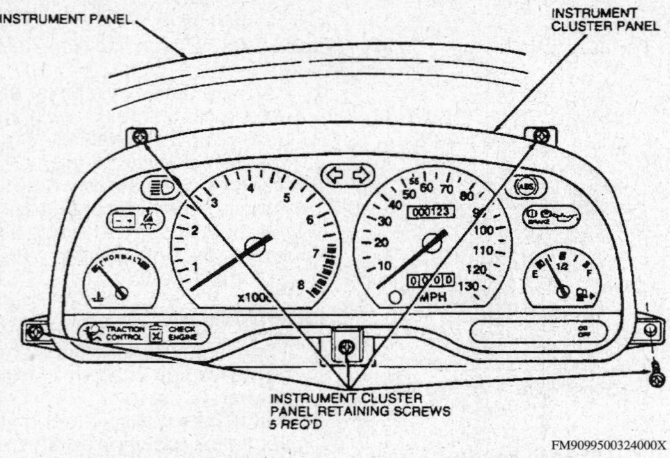

Fig. 7 Instrument cluster removal. 1997

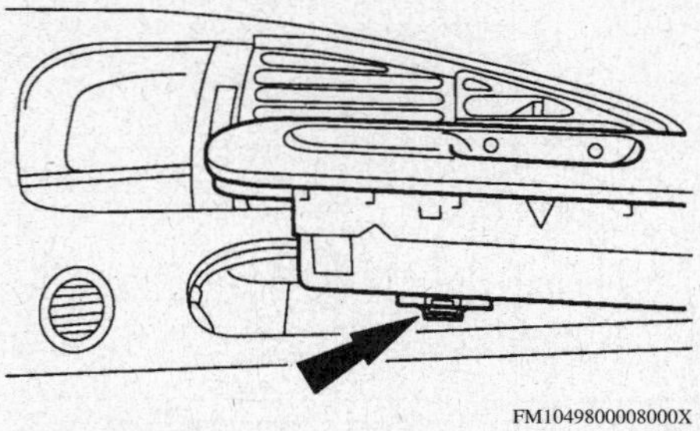

Fig. 8 Clock removal. 1998–2000 Contour

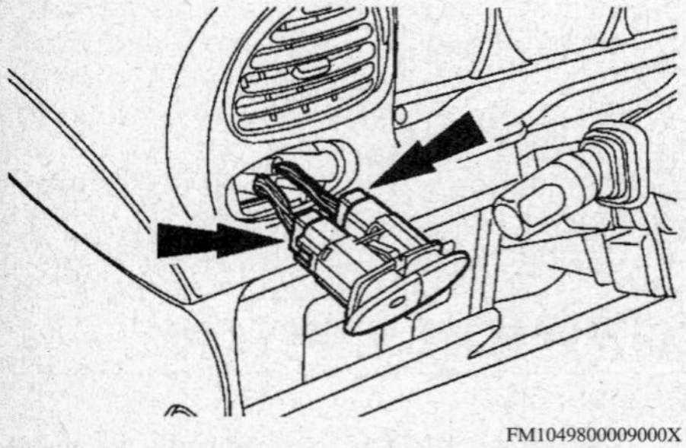

Fig. 9 Rear window defroster switch panel. 1998–2000 Contour

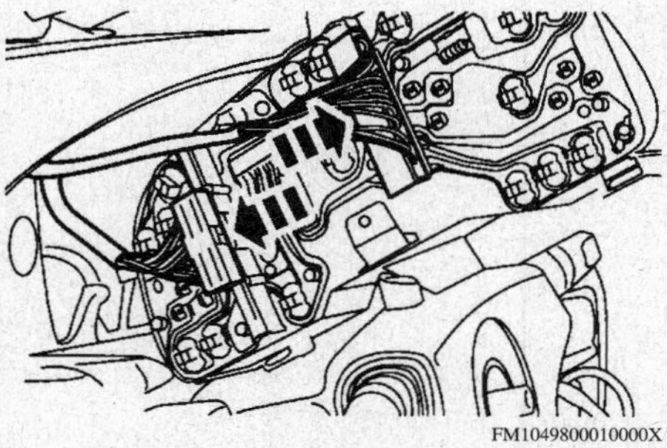

Fig. 10 Instrument cluster removal. 1998–2000 Contour

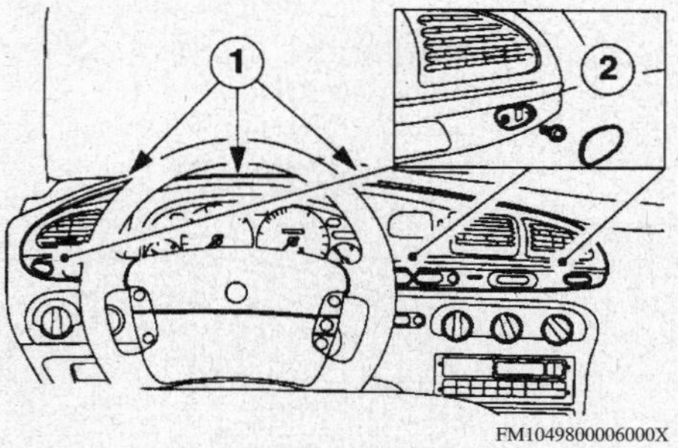

Fig. 11 Instrument cluster bezel removal. 1998–2000 Mystique

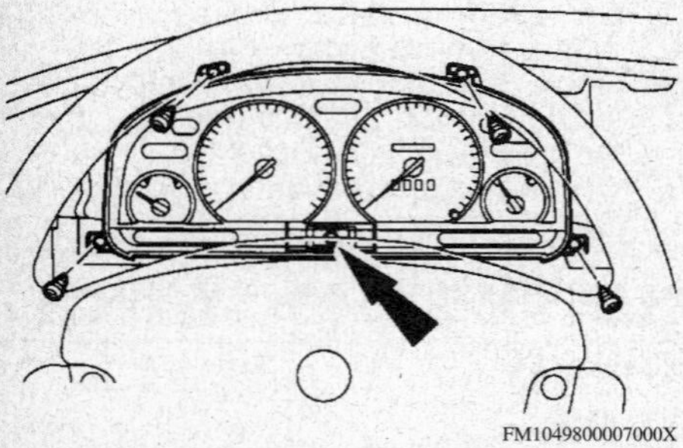

Fig. 12 Instrument cluster removal. 1998–2000 Mystique

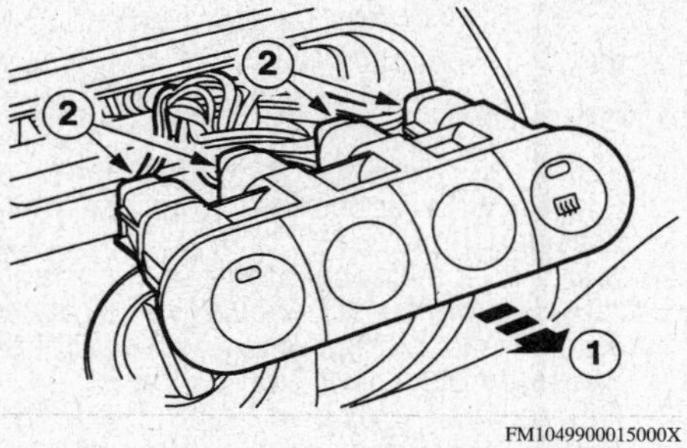

Fig. 13 Center switch removal. Cougar

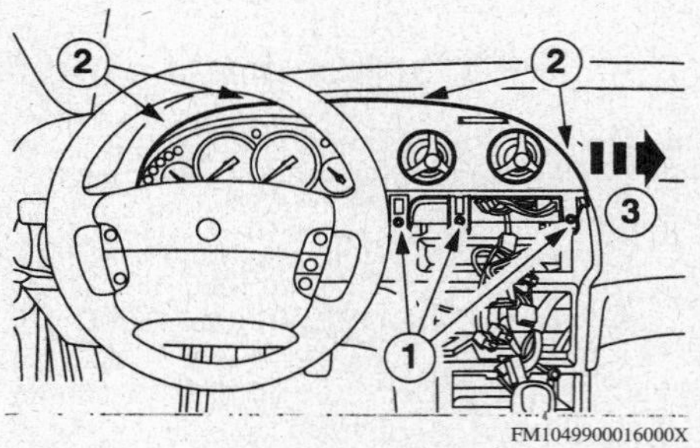

Fig. 14 Instrument cluster bezel removal. Cougar

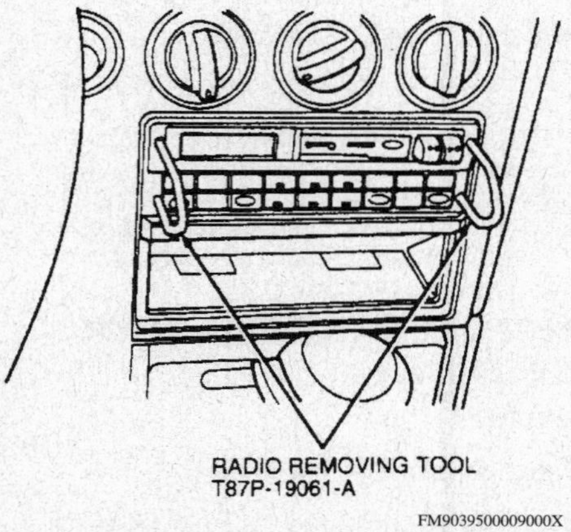

Fig. 15 Radio chassis removal

b. Align TR sensor slots using TR sensor tool No. T94P-70010-AH, or equivalent.
c. **Torque** TR sensor bolts to 84–108 inch lbs.
d. **Torque** MAF sensor bolts to 25 inch lbs.
e. **Torque** engine air cleaner tube clamps to 24–48 inch lbs.

HEADLAMP SWITCH

REPLACE

CONTOUR & MYSTIQUE

1. Remove two lefthand finish panel to instrument panel screws.
2. Pull straight outward on lefthand finish panel to release finish panel clips.
3. Grasp headland switch knob and slide small pin into hole in bottom of headland switch knob to release locking tab, **Fig. 4.**
4. Pull knob straight away from headland switch, then remove three headland switch retainer to lefthand instrument panel finish panel screws.
5. Press locking tabs on headland switch retainer and separate retainer, **Fig. 5.**
6. Press locking tabs on headland switch and remove headland switch from headland switch retainer.
7. Reverse procedure to install.

COUGAR

1. Remove instrument panel lower panel.
2. Remove lamp switch panel screws and detach instrument panel from clips.
3. Disconnect electrical connectors and remove switch.
4. Reverse procedure to install.

STOP LIGHT SWITCH

REPLACE

1. Disconnect stop lamp switch electrical connector.

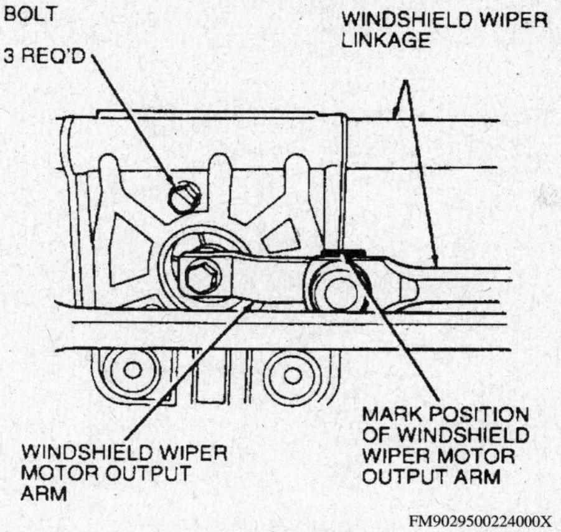

Fig. 16 Wiper pivot arm position marking

2. Remove switch by rotating 90° counterclockwise and pulling toward rear of vehicle.
3. Reverse procedure to install.

MULTI-FUNCTION SWITCH

REPLACE

1. Remove steering column upper shroud screws, then upper shroud.
2. Press multi-function switch locking tab, then slide switch up and off of steering column.
3. Press locking tabs on multi-function switch electrical connector and remove connector from switch.
4. Reverse procedure to install.

STEERING WHEEL

REPLACE

1. Remove air bag module screws and air bag module.
2. Disconnect air bag wire harness from driver side air bag module, then remove module from steering wheel.
3. Center front wheels to straight ahead position, then disconnect speed control wire harness from steering wheel.
4. Remove steering wheel bolt.
5. Route air bag sliding contact assembly wire harness through steering wheel opening while lifting steering wheel off shaft.
6. Reverse procedure to install, noting following:
   a. Ensure front wheels are in straight-ahead position.
   b. Ensure steering wheel and steering shaft alignment marks are aligned and air bag contact wire is not pinched.
   c. **Torque** new steering wheel bolt to 37 ft. lbs.
   d. **Torque** air bag module screws to 8–10 ft. lbs.
   e. Verify air bag warning indicator.

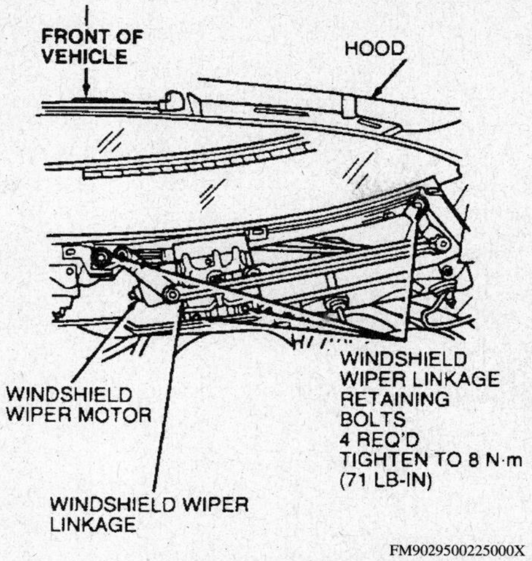

Fig. 17 Wiper linkage removal

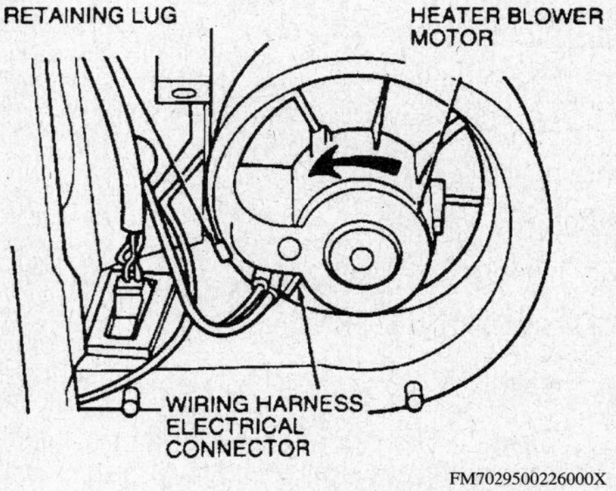

Fig. 19 Blower motor replacement

INSTRUMENT CLUSTER

REPLACE

CONTOUR & MYSTIQUE

1997

1. Remove instrument panel finish panel as follows:
   a. Remove three instrument panel finish panel screw covers, then the screws, **Fig. 6.**
   b. Remove six screws retaining instrument panel finish panel cluster to instrument panel.
   c. Pull finish panel away from instrument panel, then disconnect wiring harness connectors from indicator lamps, heated back window switch and light and traction assist switch.
   d. Remove cluster instrument panel finish panel.
2. Remove five instrument cluster panel screws, **Fig. 7.**
3. Pull instrument cluster away from instrument panel, then disconnect two cluster printed circuit connectors from instrument cluster back plate.
4. Reverse procedure to install.

1998–2000

Contour

1. Disconnect and remove clock, **Fig. 8.**

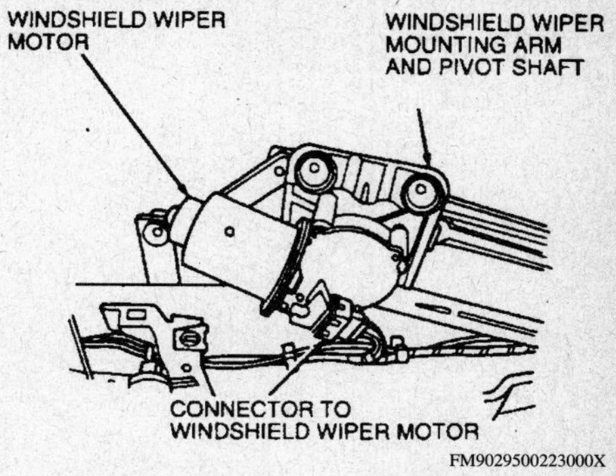

Fig. 18 Wiper motor removal

2. Remove lefthand lower instrument panel trim panel.
3. Remove headland switch panel.
4. Push rear window defroster switch panel outward and disconnect electrical connectors, **Fig. 9.**
5. Remove five instrument cluster bezel retaining screws, then the bezel.
6. Remove instrument cluster and disconnect electrical connectors, **Fig. 10.**
7. Reverse procedures to install.

Mystique

1. Remove instrument cluster bezel attaching screws, then the cluster bezel, **Fig. 11.**
2. Disconnect electrical connectors.
3. Remove instrument cluster, then disconnect electrical connectors, **Fig. 12.**
4. Reverse procedure to install.

COUGAR

1. Remove ashtray and cigar lighter bezel, then the radio.
2. Remove center switch assembly and disconnect electrical connectors, **Fig. 13.**
3. Remove heater control panel and radio unit bezel.
4. Remove heater control radio unit bezel, then disconnect electrical connectors and vacuum line.
5. Remove instrument panel lower trim panel.
6. Remove lamp switch panel and disconnect electrical connectors.
7. Remove instrument cluster bezel screws, release the clips and bezel, **Fig. 14.**
8. Pull instrument cluster forward, then release locking tangs and disconnect electrical connectors.
9. Remove cluster from vehicle.
10. Reverse procedure to install.

RADIO

REPLACE

1. Record preset stations.
2. Install radio removing tool No. T87P-19061-A, or equivalent, into radio chassis, then push tools in approximately 1 inch to release retaining clips, **Fig. 15. Do not use excessive force when installing radio removing tool to avoid damaging retaining clips. Damaging clips will make removing**

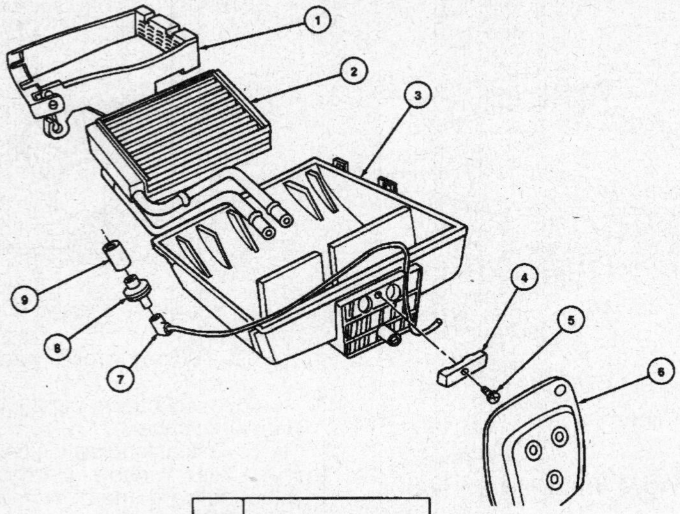

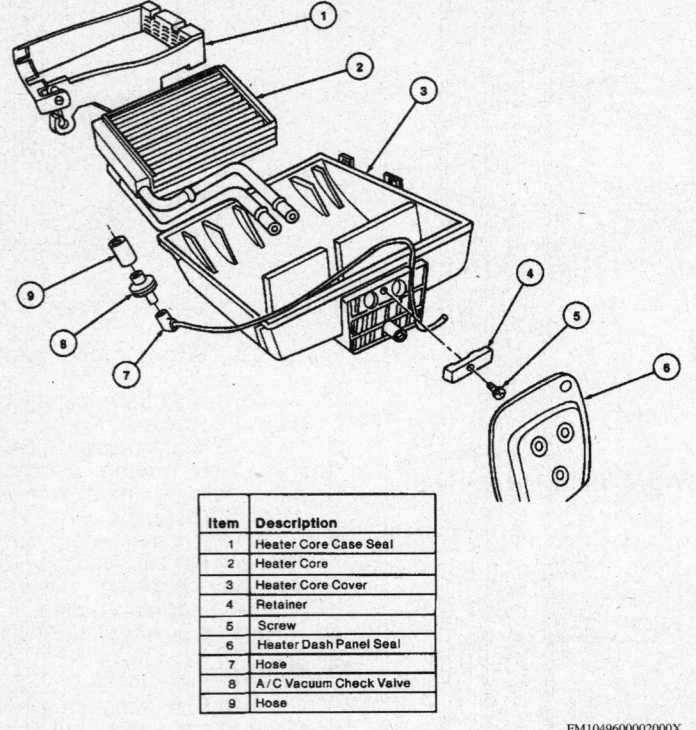

Item	Description
1	Heater Core Case Seal
2	Heater Core
3	Heater Core Cover
4	Retainer
5	Screw
6	Heater Dash Panel Seal
7	Hose
8	A/C Vacuum Check Valve
9	Hose

FM1049600002000X

Fig. 20 Heater core replacement. 1997

radio chassis difficult and may cause damage.

3. Apply light spreading force on tools and pull radio chassis out of instrument panel.
4. Disconnect wiring connectors and antenna cable.
5. Reverse procedure to install. Check radio chassis operation, then reset preset radio stations.

WIPER MOTOR

REPLACE

FRONT

1. Ensure wiper motor is in the park position, then wiper arms.
2. Remove cowl grille, then the wiper motor and linkage.
3. Mark position of wiper pivot arm in relation to wiper motor mounting bracket, **Fig. 16,** then remove windshield wiper linkage to upper cowl panel bolts, **Fig. 17.**
4. Remove wiper motor nut and bolt from mounting plate and linkage.
5. Disconnect harness from wiper motor, **Fig. 18.**
6. Reverse procedure to install, noting the following:
   a. **Torque** wiper motor mounting plate bolts to 72–108 inch lbs.
   b. **Torque** wiper motor output arm bolt to 19 ft. lbs.
   c. **Torque** wiper linkage bolts to 72 inch lbs.
   d. **Torque** wiper pivot arm nuts to 18 ft. lbs.
   e. **Torque** wiper motor bolts to 72–108 inch lbs.

REAR

1. Open wiper cover and loosen the nut.
2. Open liftgate and remove liftgate trim panel.
3. Loosen ground connection and bolts, then disconnect rear wiper motor electrical connector.
4. Remove rear window wiper motor.
5. Reverse procedure to install.

WIPER SWITCH

REPLACE

Refer to "Multi-Function Switch, Replace" for replacement.

CENTRAL TIMER MODULE

REPLACE

1997

1. Pull central timer module straight away from fuse junction panel, then remove from vehicle.
2. Reverse procedure to install.

BLOWER MOTOR

REPLACE

1. Working from inside vehicle, remove push pins and upper foothill trim panel from passenger side.
2. Disconnect blower motor wire harness electrical connector.
3. Carefully lift retaining lug on A/C blower motor flange, **Fig. 19,** and rotate blower motor counterclockwise approximately 30° to disengage it from A/C evaporator housing.

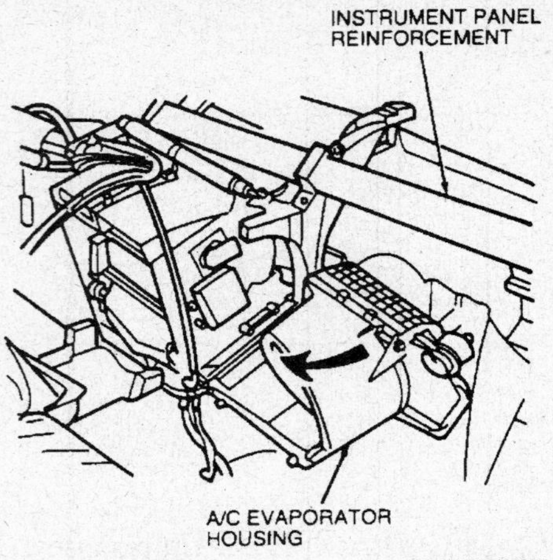

FM7029500229000X

Fig. 21 Evaporator housing replacement. 1997

4. Pull blower motor out of A/C evaporator housing.
5. Reverse procedure to install. After inserting blower motor into A/C evaporator housing, turn clockwise until retaining lug engages.

HEATER CORE

REPLACE

1997

1. Remove heater outlet floor duct.
2. Disconnect heater water hoses from heater core inlet and outlet tubes.
3. Disconnect vacuum supply hose (black) from vacuum service in engine compartment.
4. Disconnect vacuum supply hose (black) from A/C vacuum reservoir tank and bracket.
5. Remove four heater core cover retaining tabs and two clips, then the heater core cover.
6. Remove heater dash panel seal, then disconnect vacuum hose from heater core cover, **Fig. 20.**
7. Remove heater core mounting bracket retaining screw, then the bracket from cover.
8. Remove heater core from cover.
9. Reverse procedures to install.

1998–2000

1. Drain coolant into a suitable container.
2. Raise and support vehicle, then disconnect heater hoses from heater core.
3. Disconnect vacuum line from engine.
4. Lower vehicle.
5. Remove floor console as follows:
   a. **On models with manual transaxle,** remove gearshift knob, spring, damping sleeve and gearshift lever boot.
   b. **On models with armrest,** raise armrest to gain access.
   c. **On models less armrest,** remove rear cup holder to gain access.

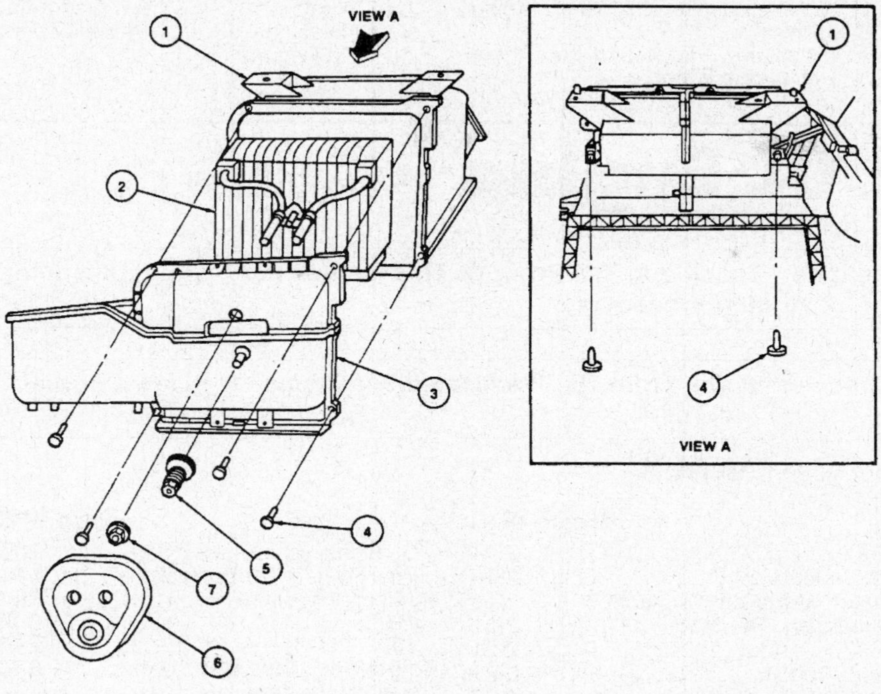

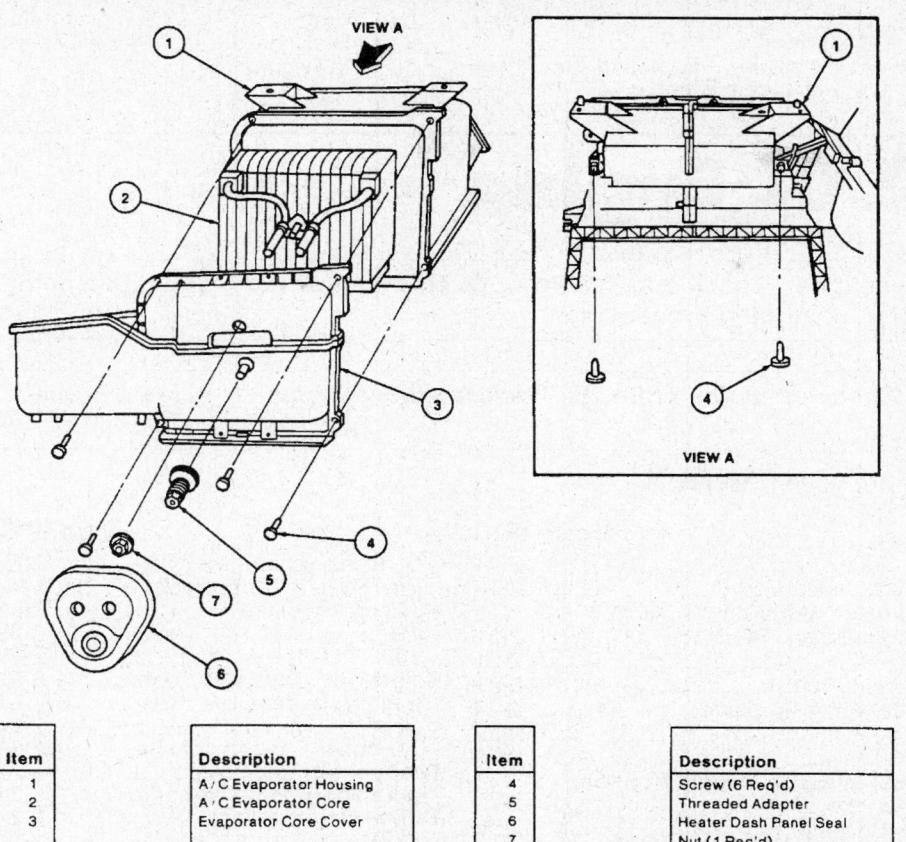

Item	Description
1	A/C Evaporator Housing
2	A/C Evaporator Core
3	Evaporator Core Cover
4	Screw (6 Req'd)
5	Threaded Adapter
6	Heater Dash Panel Seal
7	Nut (1 Req'd)

FM7029500230000X

Fig. 22 Evaporator core replacement. 1997

d. **On all models,** remove ashtray and cigar lighter bezel.
e. Remove stowage tray by pushing down on the power socket aperture and pulling out stowage tray.
f. Remove floor console front screws.
g. Fully raise parking brake control lever, then remove console and disconnect cigar lighter/power socket electrical connector.

6. Remove air bag diagnostic monitor and position to one side.
7. Disconnect vacuum supply line from vacuum reservoir tank.
8. Remove screws from heater outlet floor duct.
9. Remove heater outlet floor duct screw from heater/evaporator core housing, then slide air duct upwards and release retaining tabs on each side and remove the heater outlet floor duct.
10. Remove four heater core cover retaining clips, then the cover and core.
11. Reverse procedure to install.

EVAPORATOR CORE

REPLACE

1997

When replacing an A/C evaporator core, replace suction accumulator/drier.

1. Remove instrument panel as outlined in "Dash Panel Service."
2. Place drain pan or suitable container under heater water hose connections at cowl panel.
3. Recover refrigerant from A/C system as outlined in " Air Conditioning" section.
4. Raise and support vehicle.
5. Disconnect heater water hoses from heater core inlet and outlet tubes. Plug water hoses and cap heater core tubes to prevent coolant loss.
6. Disconnect vacuum supply hose (black) from vacuum source in engine compartment.
7. Disconnect discharge line using spring lock coupling disconnect tool No. T81P-19623-G2, or equivalent.
8. Disconnect discharge line to jumper line from evaporator core inlet and outlet tubes at cowl panel using spring lock coupling disconnect tool No. T83P-19623-C, or equivalent.
9. Remove A/C evaporator housing to cowl panel nut, then, working from inside vehicle, remove nut from upper crossover brace.
10. Remove bottom bracket bolt, then the crossover brace.
11. Pull off A/C plenum Demeter adapter from right and left sides of evaporator housing.
12. Remove two ram air intake duct to evaporator housing screws.
13. Release retaining clips and remove intake duct from evaporator housing.
14. Remove A/C vacuum reservoir tank bracket to evaporator housing screw.
15. Disconnect vacuum hoses from vacuum reservoir tank and bracket, then remove A/C vacuum reservoir tank and bracket from housing.
16. Remove air bag diagnostic monitor bracket from heater outlet floor duct.
17. Remove air transfer duct to heater outlet floor duct screw, then push transfer duct up inside of heater outlet floor duct.
18. Remove heater outlet floor duct to heater core cover screws, then release tab on each side of heater outlet floor duct and remove floor duct from heater core cover.
19. Release tabs and remove heater core, cover and vacuum hose from A/C evaporator housing, **Fig. 21.**
20. Remove amplifier and power radio booster equalizer amplifier bracket from vehicle.
21. Remove A/C evaporator housing to instrument panel reinforcement screws, then rotate housing away from reinforcement and remove from vehicle, **Fig. 21.**
22. Remove A/C recirculating air duct.
23. Remove heater dash panel seal and evaporator retaining nut.
24. Remove two screws from rear and four screws from front of A/C evaporator housing.
25. Separate evaporator housing and remove evaporator core, **Fig. 22.**
26. Reverse procedure to install.

1998–2000

1. Recover refrigerant from A/C system as outlined in " Air Conditioning" section.
2. Drain coolant into a suitable container.
3. Remove instrument panel as outlined in "Dash Panel Service."
4. Raise and support vehicle, then disconnect heater hoses from heater core and vacuum line from engine.
5. Lower vehicle and disconnect blower motor and resistor electrical connector.
6. **On models with 2.5L engine,** remove ignition.
7. **On all models,** pull clips off air conditioning lines.
8. Disconnect line to accumulator/drier at the evaporator using tool No. T84L-19623-B, or equivalent. Seal line and evaporator with plugs.
9. Disconnect line from condenser at the evaporator using tool No. T84L-19623-B, or equivalent.
10. Remove nut on heater/evaporator core housing.
11. Remove lower defroster air duct screw from heater/evaporator core housing and release retaining tabs.
12. Disconnect right and lefthand air hose from heater/evaporator core housing.
13. Disconnect air distributor from heater/air conditioning assembly.
14. Remove heater/evaporator core housing.
15. Separate heater/air conditioning housing.
16. Remove screws at front of heater/air conditioning housing and rubber seal.

17. Remove evaporator nut, unclip vacuum hose and disconnect housing parts.
18. Remove evaporator.
19. Reverse procedure to install, noting the following:
    a. Install new Rings and coat them with refrigerant oil.
    b. When installing a new evaporator, install gaskets as they were on the old evaporator.

2.0L Engine

NOTE: Refer To "Air Bag System Precautions " Located In The Front Of This Manual For System Disarming & Arming Procedures.

NOTE: Refer To "Computer Relearn" Located In The Front Of This Manual For Computer Relearn Procedures.

INDEX

PRECAUTIONS

BATTERY GROUND CABLE

Prior to service, disconnect battery ground cable and isolate as required.

AIR BAG SYSTEMS

Refer to "Air Bag System Precautions" in front of this manual for system disarming and arming procedures.

COOLING SYSTEM

This engine has an aluminum cylinder head and requires a special corrosion inhibiting coolant to avoid cooling system damage. Use only specified coolant in this engine.

FUEL SYSTEM PRESSURE RELIEF

1. Remove engine air intake resonators from air cleaner assembly.
2. Connect multipolar Fuel Injection (MFI) fuel pressure gauge tool No. T80L-9974-B, or equivalent, to fuel pressure relief valve cap on fuel injection supply manifold.
3. Open manual valve on gauge tool to relieve fuel system pressure.

COMPRESSION PRESSURE

Compression pressure should be checked with engine at normal operating temperature, spark plugs removed and throttle plate wide open. Cylinder compression pressure is considered within specification if lowest reading cylinder is within 75 percent of highest reading and no reading is lower than 101 psi.

ENGINE MOUNT

REPLACE

UPPER

Removal

1. Remove engine air intake resonators from air cleaner assembly.
2. Install three bar engine support tool No. D88L-6000-A, or equivalent, to existing engine lifting eyes and support engine.

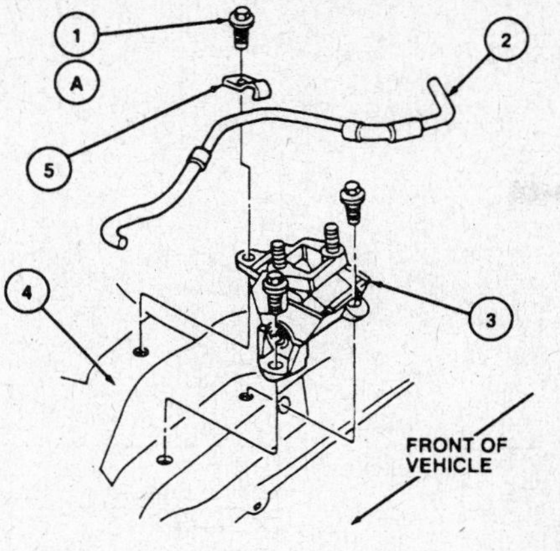

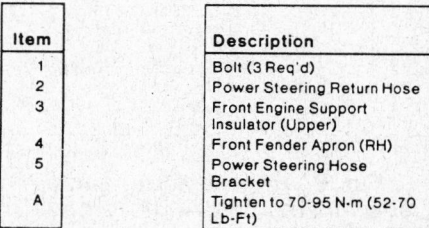

Item	Description
1	Bolt (3 Req'd)
2	Power Steering Return Hose
3	Front Engine Support Insulator (Upper)
4	Front Fender Apron (RH)
5	Power Steering Hose Bracket
A	Tighten to 70-95 N·m (52-70 Lb-Ft)

FM1069500380000X

Fig. 1 Upper front engine support insulator replacement. 1997

3. Remove front engine support self-locking nuts and discard nuts. **Engine support nuts are self-locking and must be replaced.**
4. Remove upper front engine support bracket.
5. Remove radiator coolant recovery reservoir bolts and position reservoir aside.
6. Remove front engine support insulator bolts, then the insulator from righthand front fender apron, **Fig. 1.**

Installation

If upper front engine support insulator or front engine support bracket has been removed, engine and transaxle position MUST BE REALIGNED to front suffrage. Failure to realign engine and transaxle may result in possible component damage.

1. Raise and support vehicle, then remove two front suffrage through bolts and lefthand front engine support insulator.
2. Install pertain alignment gauge tool No. T94P-6000-AH, or equivalent, to transaxle bracket and front suffrage, **Fig. 2.** Tighten vertical and through bolts to specifications.
3. Loosen righthand front engine support insulator through bolt, then lower vehicle.
4. Position power steering hose bracket and return hose onto upper front support insulator, then install upper front engine support insulator and bolts to righthand front fender apron.
5. Install radiator coolant recovery reservoir.
6. Install upper front engine support bracket onto engine and upper front engine support insulator. Tighten new self-locking upper front engine support bracket nuts to specifications

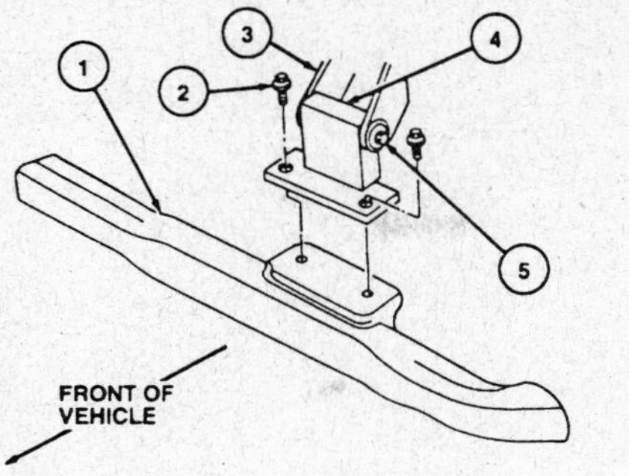

Item	Description
1	Front Sub-Frame
2	Bolt (2 Req'd)
3	Front Engine Support Bracket (LH)
4	Powertrain Alignment Gauge
5	Through Bolt

FM1069500381000X

Fig. 2 Pertain alignment gauge tool installation. 1997

7. Remove engine support tool, then tighten upper front engine support bracket nuts to specifications.
8. Raise and support vehicle, then observe position of righthand front engine support insulator. Insulator must be centered in transaxle bracket and in perfect front-to-rear alignment.
9. Tighten righthand front engine support insulator through bolt to specifications.
10. Remove three gauge tool bolts and gauge tool.
11. Install lefthand front engine support insulator to front suffrage, then **torque** bolts to 84 inch lbs. Observe insulator to ensure perfect front-to-rear alignment, then **torque** bolts to 30–40 ft. lbs.
12. Install lefthand front engine support insulator through bolt and tighten to specifications.
13. Install engine air intake resonators.
14. Fill power steering system.
15. Run engine and check for leaks.

LEFTHAND

1. Raise and support vehicle.
2. Remove lefthand front engine support insulator to front suffrage bolts, **Fig. 3.**
3. Remove lefthand front engine support insulator through bolt, then the insulator.
4. If necessary, remove lefthand front engine support bracket bolts and lefthand front engine support bracket from transaxle case.
5. Reverse procedure to install, noting the following:
   a. **Torque** front engine support insulator to front suffrage bolts to 84 inch lbs.
   b. Ensure engine support insulator is aligned properly, then **torque** bolts to 75–102 ft. lbs.

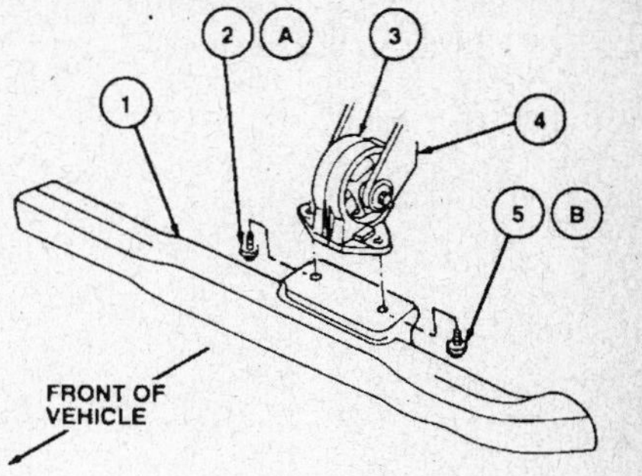

Item	Description
1	Front Sub-Frame
2	Bolt (2 Req'd)
3	Front Engine Support Insulator (LH)
4	Front Engine Support Bracket (LH)
5	Through Bolt
A	Tighten to 41-55 N·m (30-40 Lb-Ft)
B	Tighten to 103-137 N·m (75-102 Lb-Ft)

FM1069500382000X

Fig. 3 Lefthand front engine support insulator replacement. 1997

RIGHTHAND

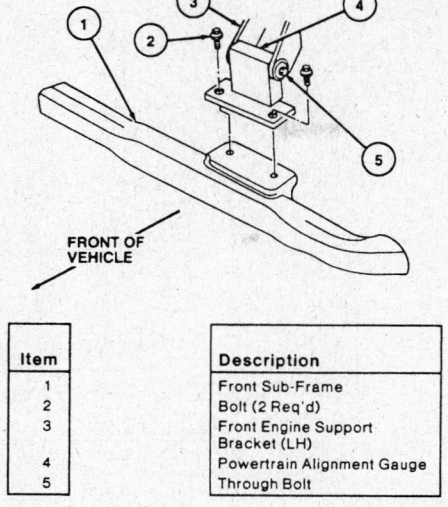

1. Raise and support vehicle.
2. Remove through bolt from righthand front engine support insulator, **Figs. 4 and 5.**
3. Remove righthand front engine support insulator to front suffrage bolts, then insulator, noting following:
   a. **When removing righthand front engine support insulator, always disconnect battery ground cable prior to removal. Contact of righthand front engine support insulator to alternator output terminal with battery connected may short alternator and battery to ground, causing possible injury and damage to vehicle.**
   b. **On models equipped with 2.5L engine and automatic transaxle,** remove insulator through bottom of righthand side of front suffrage, past righthand exhaust manifold and alternator.
4. **On all models,** if necessary, remove righthand front engine support bracket from transaxle.
5. Reverse procedure to install, noting the following:
   a. Install pertain alignment gauge tool No. T94P-600-AH, or equivalent, **Fig. 2,** to transaxle bracket and front suffrage, **Fig. 2. Torque** two vertical bolts, then through bolt to 20 ft. lbs.
   b. **Torque** righthand front engine support insulator bolts to front suffrage to 84 inch lbs.
   c. **Torque** righthand front engine support insulator through bolt to 75–102 ft. lbs.
   d. Install lefthand front engine support insulator to front suffrage with two

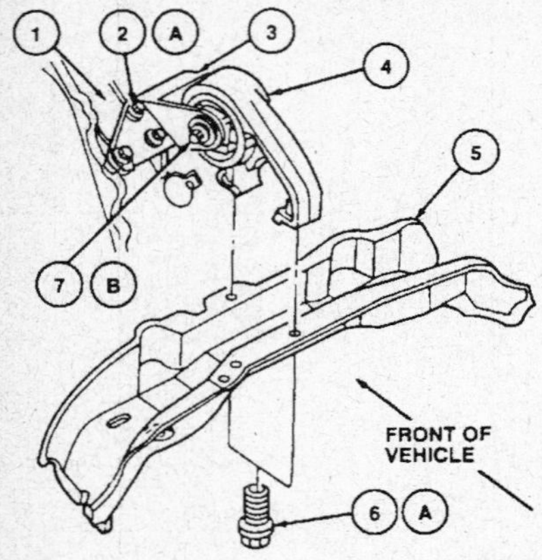

Item	Description
1	Transaxle
2	Bolt (3 Req'd)
3	Front Engine Support Bracket (RH)
4	Front Engine Support Insulator (RH)
5	Front Sub-Frame
6	Bolt (2 Req'd)
7	Through Bolt
A	Tighten to 41-55 N·m (30-40 Lb-Ft)
B	Tighten to 103-137 N·m (75-102 Lb-Ft)

FM1069500383000X

Fig. 4 Righthand front engine support insulator replacement. 1997 w/automatic transaxle

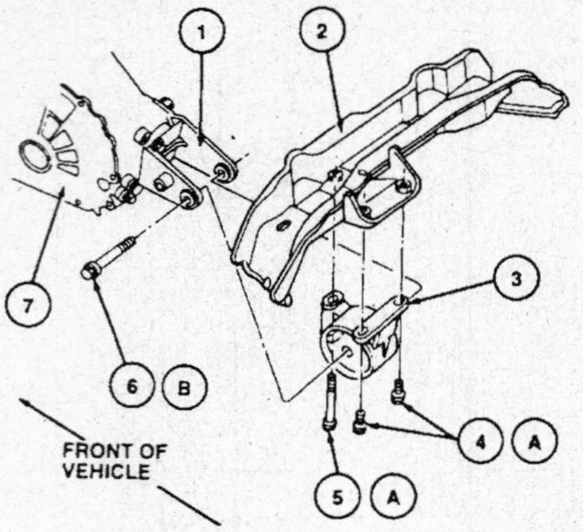

Item	Description
1	Front Engine Support Bracket (RH)
2	Front Sub-Frame
3	Front Engine Support Insulator (RH)
4	Bolt (2 Req'd)
5	Bolt
6	Through Bolt
7	Transaxle
A	Tighten to 41-55 N·m (30-40 Lb-Ft)
B	Tighten to 103-137 N·m (75-102 Lb-Ft)

FM1069500384000X

Fig. 5 Righthand front engine support insulator replacement. 1997 w/manual transaxle

bolts. **Torque** bolts to 84 inch lbs. Observe position of lefthand front engine support insulator to ensure perfect front-to-rear alignment. **Torque** lefthand front engine support insulator bolts to 30–40 ft. lbs.

ENGINE & TRANSAXLE SUPPORT INSULATOR, REPLACE

Engine and transaxle position must be realigned to front suffrage. Failure to realign engine and transaxle may result in component damage.

1. Remove engine air intake resonators from air cleaner assembly.
2. Disconnect engine control sensor wiring connector from Mass Air Flow (MAF) sensor, then engine control sensor wiring from Intake Air Temperature (IAT) sensor.
3. Remove engine air cleaner to body Oaring.
4. Remove engine air cleaner body and intake tube from bracket and intake tube and duct.
5. **On models equipped with 2.5L engine,** remove battery and battery tray.
6. **On all models,** remove air cleaner mounting bracket from engine and transaxle support insulator.
7. **On models equipped with 2.5L engine,** remove water pump pulley shield screws, then the shield.
8. **On all models,** install three bar engine support tool D88L-6000-A, or equivalent, to engine lifting eyes and support engine and transaxle.

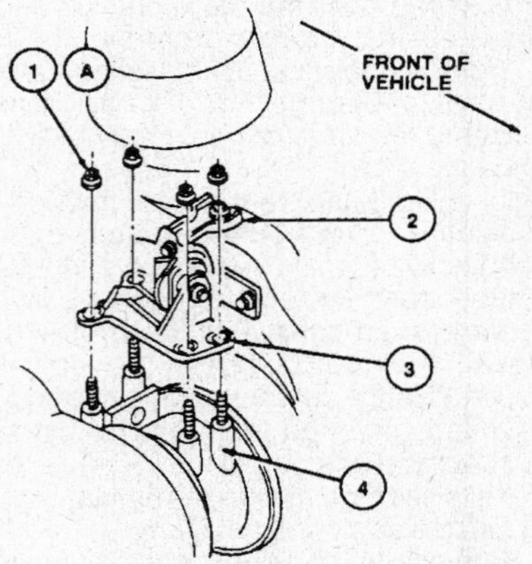

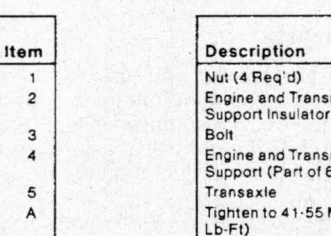

Item	Description
1	Nut (4 Req'd)
2	Engine and Transmission Support Insulator
3	Bolt
4	Engine and Transmission Support (Part of 6F063)
5	Transaxle
A	Tighten to 41-55 N·m (30-40 Lb-Ft)

FM1069500386000X

Fig. 7 Engine & transaxle support insulator replacement. 1997 w/automatic transaxle

9. Remove engine and transaxle support insulator to lefthand front fender apron bolts, **Fig. 6.**
10. Remove engine and transaxle support

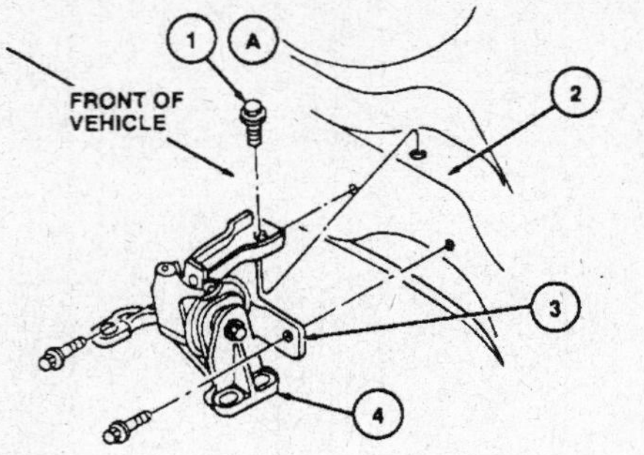

Item	Description
1	Bolt (3 Req'd)
2	Front Fender Apron (LH)
3	Engine and Transmission Support Insulator
4	Bolt
5	Engine and Transmission Support
A	Tighten to 70-95 N·m (52-70 Lb-Ft)

FM1069500385000X

Fig. 6 Engine & transaxle support insulator bolt removal. Automatic transaxle, manual transaxle similar. 1997

insulator nuts, then the insulator, **Figs. 7 and 8.** Discard nuts.

11. Reverse procedure to install, noting the following:
    a. Install pertain alignment gauge tool No. T94P-6000-AH, or equivalent, to transaxle bracket and front suffrage. vertical bolts, then through bolt to specification.
    b. Install new engine and transaxle support insulator nuts and tighten to specification.
    c. Remove engine support, then **torque** engine and transaxle support insulator nuts to specification.
    d. **Check position of righthand front engine support insulator. It must be centered in transaxle bracket and in perfect front-to-rear alignment.**

ENGINE

REPLACE

1997

1. Remove pinch bolt and disconnect steering shaft and joint at cowl in vehicle.
2. Remove engine air intake resonators from air cleaner assembly.
3. Recover air conditioning system refrigerant as outlined in " Air Conditioning" section.
4. Raise and support vehicle, then remove splash shield from front of suffrage and body.
5. Remove outlet flange nuts, then the muffler and exhaust converter outlet gasket from converter.
6. Remove EGR valve to exhaust manifold tube, bracket and clamp from converter.

7. Lower vehicle and remove heat shield and converter nuts from exhaust manifold.
8. Remove converter and exhaust converter inlet gasket from exhaust manifold. Discard exhaust converter inlet gasket.
9. Drain cooling system.
10. Remove front wheel and tire assemblies.
11. Remove cotter pins and nuts, then separate lefthand and righthand stabilizer bar links from front stabilizer bar.
12. Remove lefthand and righthand tie rod end nuts, then separate ends from front wheel knuckles using tie rod end remover tool No. 3290–D, or equivalent.
13. Remove pinch bolts, then separate lefthand and righthand front suspension lower arms from front wheel knuckles at ball joint.
14. Remove lefthand and righthand front axle wheel hub retainer from halfshaft ends, then halfshafts from knuckles.
15. Remove A/C accumulator screws from front subframe.
16. Disconnect vehicle speed sensor wiring harness at connector, then disconnect speedometer drive cable from transaxle.
17. **On models equipped with automatic transaxle,** proceed as follows:
    a. Remove righthand splash shield from front fender apron to access crankshaft pulley.
    b. Remove access plug from engine rear plate, then torque converter nuts.
    c. Push torque converter into transaxle front pump support and gear.
18. **On all models,** disconnect engine control sensor wiring from knock sensor and oil pressure sensor located on righthand side of cylinder block.
19. Lower vehicle, then secure radiator and engine cooling fan motor, fan blade and fan shroud assembly to radiator support with safety wire.
20. Disconnect accelerator cable and speed control actuator from throttle body and accelerator cable bracket, then the engine control sensor connector located near the fuel pressure regulator.
21. Remove engine control sensor wiring retaining screws from intake manifold.
22. Remove power steering pump auxiliary reservoir from bracket and position aside. Disconnect return hose from reservoir, then plug hose.
23. Disconnect power steering return hose from power steering pump.
24. Disconnect engine control sensor wiring from power steering pressure switch and alternator.
25. Remove ground strap from alternator mounting bracket, then disconnect vacuum supply hose from fitting on rear of intake manifold.
26. Disconnect coolant hoses from radiator coolant reservoir, then the hoses from A/C compressor.
27. Disconnect fuel supply lines from fuel injection supply manifold, then the vacuum supply hose from EGR valve.

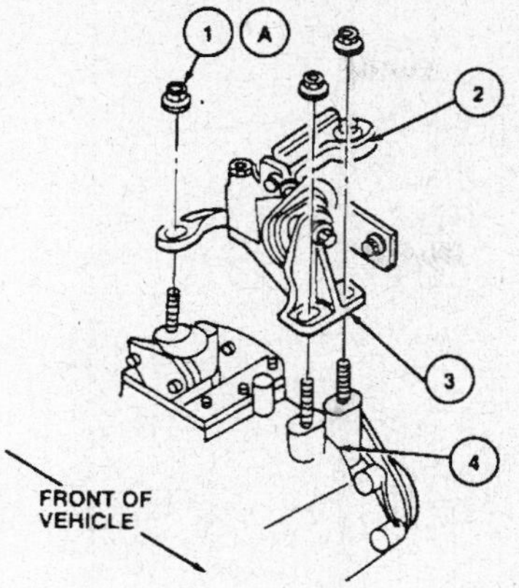

Item	Description
1	Nut (3 Req'd)
2	Engine and Transmission Support Insulator
3	Bolt
4	Engine and Transmission Support (Part of 6F063)
5	Transaxle
A	Tighten to 70-95 N·m (52-70 Lb-Ft)

FM1069500387000X

Fig. 8 Engine & transaxle support insulator replacement. 1997 w/manual transaxle

28. Disconnect EGR pressure sensor vacuum hoses at exhaust manifold tube.
29. **On models equipped with automatic transaxle,** proceed as follows:
    a. Pry shift cable from stud, then remove two bolts and shift cable and bracket from transaxle.
    b. Disconnect transaxle Range (TR) sensor connector, then remove shift cable, bracket and bolts from transaxle.
30. **On all models,** disconnect ground strap from transaxle case.
31. Disconnect ignition coil and radio ignition interference capacitor connector, then position wiring aside.
32. Disconnect vacuum supply line from power brake booster, then the upper radiator hose from radiator.
33. Disconnect evaporative emission hose from connector located near radio interference capacitor, then the heater water hose near EGR valve.
34. Disconnect positive and negative battery cable retainer from battery tray.
35. **On models equipped with manual transaxle,** remove retainer and disconnect clutch hydraulic line from clutch actuator pipe at transaxle case.
36. **On all models,** disconnect block heater power supply wiring from lefthand side of radiator support, then raise and support vehicle.
37. Disconnect heater water hose at heater water tube located under engine.
38. **On models equipped with automatic transaxle,** remove transaxle oil cooler lines from transaxle, then the oil cooler return line from bracket on lefthand side of transaxle.
39. **On models equipped with manual transaxle,** remove shift rod bolt and nut from stabilizer bar, then the bar.
40. **On all models,** disconnect lower radiator hose from radiator, then remove lower radiator support to front subframe bolts and rotate support forward.
41. Disconnect A/C compressor, heated oxygen sensor, engine coolant temperature sensor and crankshaft position sensor connectors.
42. Remove bumper cover brace screws from left and right sides of front subframe, then rotate braces forward.
43. Disconnect power steering oil cooler hoses at righthand front of front subframe, then drain power steering system.
44. Partially lower vehicle, then position and secure any hoses, lines and components to be removed with engine.
45. Install powertrain and subframe support bracket tool No. 134–00250, or equivalent, to Rotunda powertrain lift tool No. 134–00251, or equivalent.
46. Rotate transaxle adapters for transaxle removal, then position bracket and lift tools to provide proper contact at powertrain lift points.
47. Remove front subframe to body bolts.
48. Remove upper front engine support bracket, then the engine and transaxle support insulator nuts. Discard nuts.
49. Lower engine and transaxle with front subframe as an assembly.
50. Support engine with Rotunda floor crane positioning sling tool No. 014–00036, and Rotunda floor crane tool No. 014–00071, or equivalents, from engine lifting eyes.
51. Remove left and right halfshafts from transaxle as outlined in "Front Wheel Drive Axles" section.
52. Remove left and right front engine support insulators from front subframe and transaxle as outlined under "Engine Mount, Replace. "
53. Raise and support engine and transaxle assembly, then remove front subframe and lift tool.
54. Support transaxle with suitable transaxle jack
55. Remove starter motor bolts, then the starter motor.
56. Remove battery ground cable from engine to transaxle stud bolt.
57. Remove transaxle to engine bolts, then separate transaxle from engine.
58. Reverse procedure to install, noting the following:
    a. Install powertrain alignment gauge tool No. T94P-6000-AH, or equivalent, to lefthand front engine support bracket and front subframe. Tighten vertical and through bolt to specifications.
    b. Ensure engine and transaxle are firmly seated against front and rear brackets. **Torque** engine support bracket and transaxle support insulator nuts to 84 inch lbs.
    c. Install subframe alignment pin set tool No. 94P-2100-AH, or equivalent, into front subframe, **Fig. 9.**
    d. Install front subframe bolts and tighten to specifications. Remove pin set tool.
    e. Using new nuts, install upper front

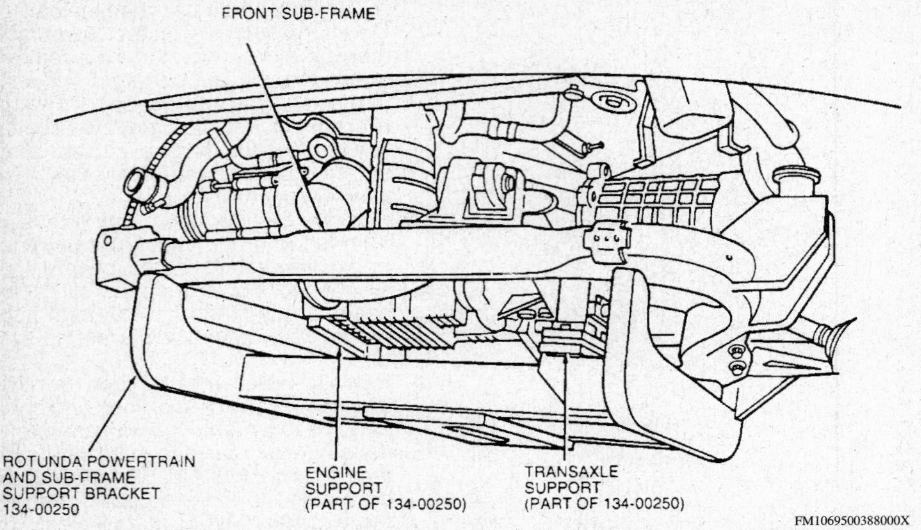

Fig. 9 Powertrain & subframe support bracket tool installation. 1997

engine support bracket and engine and transaxle support insulator.

f. Remove gauge tool, then install lefthand front engine support insulator to front subframe with bolts. Tighten bolts to specification. Observe lefthand front engine support insulator to ensure perfect front-to-rear alignment. Tighten bolts to specification.

g. Install driveshafts as described in "Front Wheel Drive Axles" section.

1998–2000

Automatic Transaxle

1. Move selector lever to "D."
2. Raise and support vehicle and remove front wheels.
3. Remove radiator splash shield and brace on both sides.
4. Drain engine coolant into a suitable container.
5. Lower vehicle and remove battery.
6. Remove air intake tube, then disconnect mass air flow and intake air temperature sensor connectors.
7. Remove air cleaner and crankcase ventilation hose.
8. Secure condenser core on hood lock panel.
9. Using an allen key to stop the piston rod from turning, loosen suspension strut locknuts five turns on both sides. Hold the suspension strut steady.
10. Disconnect engine wiring harness and automatic transaxle ground cable, then remove cable tie.
11. Unclip the wiring harness and disconnect transaxle range switch electrical connector.
12. Disconnect crankshaft position sensor and engine coolant temperature sensor electrical connectors.
13. Remove selector cable abutment bracket, then unclip selector cable from the selector lever and disconnect selector cable.
14. Disconnect throttle cable by pulling out the clip and unhooking the cable.
15. Remove upper accessory drive belt cover, then raise and support vehicle.
16. Remove righthand splash shield, then loosen and remove accessory drive belt.
17. Disconnect lower suspension arm ball joints and the stabilizer link rods, then ABS wiring harness bracket from the suspension strut. **Do not damage boot and ABS sensor ring.**
18. Disconnect radiator at the bottom and both heated oxygen sensor electrical connectors. Cut cable ties.
19. Remove power steering hoses from subframe.
20. Remove vehicle speed sensor retaining clip bolt, then vehicle speed sensor.
21. Disconnect brake booster vacuum line from of intake manifold.
22. Remove righthand engine support insulator bolts and engine support insulator.
23. Remove steering gear heat shield, then power steering line bracket and coolant line bracket.
24. Remove front exhaust tube and discard the gasket.
25. Using tool No. T97P-3504-A, or equivalent, remove steering gear two bolts and secure it with wire out of the way.
26. If necessary raise automatic transaxle slightly with a transmission jack to remove lefthand engine support insulator nuts, center bolt and insulator.
27. Remove suction accumulator bolts.
28. Remove subframe. Take out rubber guides from the lower radiator supports. Support subframe using a suitable powertrain lift.
29. Drain automatic transmission fluid into a suitable container and install drain plug.
30. Using a slide hammer tool No. T50T-100-A and halfshaft remover tool No. T86P-3514-A, or equivalents, remove lefthand halfshaft, **Fig. 10. To avoid damage to the halfshaft joints and boots, do not bend the inner halfshaft joint more than 18 degrees and the outer one no more than 45 degrees.**

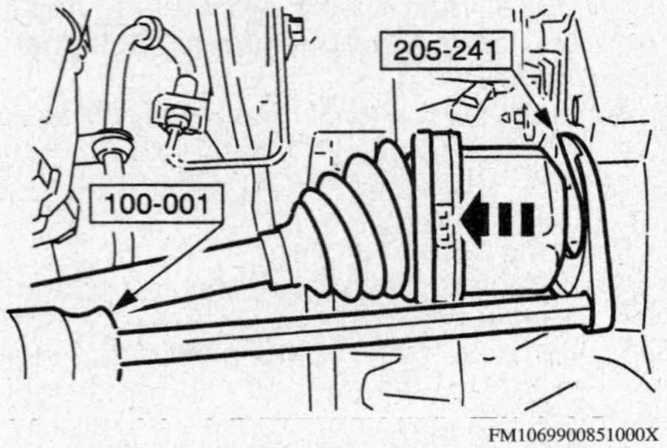

Fig. 10 Halfshaft removal. Cougar & 1998–2000 Contour & Mystique

31. Disconnect fluid tube and close off openings with suitable plugs.
32. Disconnect turbine shaft speed (sensor electrical connector.
33. Remove fluid cooler tube from transaxle.
34. Remove righthand drive halfshaft and intermediate shaft. Secure righthand drive halfshaft out of the way with mechanics wire.
35. Disconnect coolant hose from heater coolant tube and remove the bracket.
36. Disconnect lower coolant hose and lower vehicle.
37. Disconnect the two ground cables and hoses from oil cooler.
38. Disconnect fan motor and power steering pressure switch electrical connectors, then remove upper coolant hose.
39. Remove tube/hose (A/C) bracket and the power steering line.
40. Remove upper bolts from the power steering pump, wiring clamp from the fender apron panel and coolant hoses.
41. Raise and support vehicle and disconnect A/C compressor electrical connector.
42. Separate radiator from condenser core.
43. Remove A/C compressor bolts, then secure the compressor with mechanics wire and position it to one side.
44. Remove power steering pump and position it to one side.
45. Disconnect heater coolant hose, then lower the vehicle.
46. Remove power steering reservoir (push fit) and lay it to one side, then disconnect main wiring harness from the powertrain control module.
47. Disconnect vacuum hoses from intake manifold.
48. Relieve fuel pressure as outlined in "Precautions, " then disconnect fuel lines using quick disconnect connect tool Nos. D87L-9280-A or D87L-9280-B, or equivalents.
49. Raise and support vehicle.
50. Carefully lower vehicle and place engine/transaxle assembly on powertrain lift and secure it with retaining straps.
51. Remove coolant expansion tank and position it to one side. Disconnect speed control cable (if equipped) from the coolant expansion tank.

52. Remove front engine mounting bracket nuts and loosen bolts two turns.
53. Remove rear engine mounting bracket.
54. Raise vehicle and pull out powertrain lift with the engine/automatic transaxle assembly from underneath the vehicle.
55. Reverse procedure to install.

Contour & Mystique w/Manual Transaxle

1. Put gearshift lever into neutral, then using gear lever alignment tool No. T97P-7025-A, or equivalent, lock shifter into neutral, **Fig. 11.**
2. Raise and support vehicle, then remove both front tires.
3. Remove radiator splash shield and brace on both sides.
4. Drain engine coolant into a suitable container, then lower vehicle.
5. Remove battery, then disconnect mass air flow and intake air temperature sensor connectors.
6. Remove air cleaner body, crankcase ventilation hose and air hose.
7. Tie up air conditioning condenser on hood lock panel.
8. Loosen suspension strut locknuts five turns on both sides.
9. Disconnect engine wiring harness connector and automatic transaxle ground cable. Remove cable tie.
10. Brake fluid may leak out. Pull out clip and pull off the pipe and remove slave cylinder pipe from the transaxle and tie it up.
11. Pull out the clip and disconnect accelerator cable.
12. Remove upper drive belt cover and raise and support vehicle.
13. Remove lower wheel arch trim panels.
14. Loosen and remove drive belt.
15. Disconnect lower suspension arm ball joints and the stabilizer link rods, then ABS wiring harness bracket from suspension strut. **Do not damage boot and ABS sensor ring.**
16. Disconnect radiator at the bottom and disconnect both heated oxygen sensor connectors. Cut cable ties.
17. Remove power steering hoses from subframe.
18. Disconnect brake booster vacuum line from the intake manifold.
19. Remove steering gear bolt using steering gear wrench tool No. T97P-3504-A, or equivalent and righthand engine roll restrictor.
20. Remove bracket for righthand engine roll restrictor from transaxle.
21. Remove steering gear heat shield using steering gear heat shield wrench tool No. 21-066, or equivalent. Secure steering gear with mechanic's wire out of the way.
22. Disconnect front exhaust tube and remove the gasket.
23. If necessary raise transaxle slightly with a transmission jack and remove the lefthand engine roll restrictor nuts, center through bolt and roll restrictor.
24. Disconnect air conditioning dehydrator.

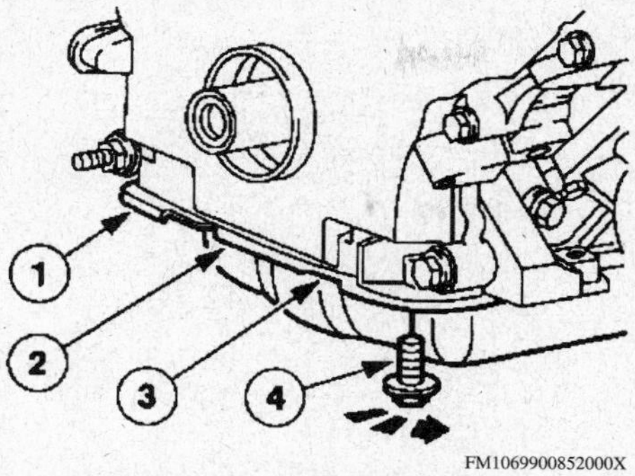

Fig. 11 Manual gear lever alignment tool installation. Cougar & 1998–2000 Contour & Mystique

25. Support subframe using a suitable powertrain lift. Remove subframe and take out rubber guides from the lower radiator supports.
26. **To avoid to damage the halfshaft joints and boots, do not bend the inner halfshaft joint more than 18 degrees and the outer one no more than 45 degrees.**
27. Using slide hammer tool No. T50T-100-A and halfshaft remover tool No. T86-P3514-A, or equivalents, remove left and righthand halfshafts, **Fig. 10.** Secure halfshafts with wire.
28. Disconnect coolant hose from heater coolant tube and remove bracket.
29. Disconnect lower coolant hose and lower vehicle.
30. Disconnect two ground cables, then the fan motor and power steering pressure switch connectors.
31. Remove A/C line bracket and the power steering hose.
32. Remove upper bolts from power steering pump, then the wiring clamp from fender apron panel and coolant hoses.
33. Raise and support vehicle.
34. Disconnect A/C compressor electrical connector.
35. Separate radiator from condenser by disconnecting electrical connector from fan motor ballast resistor and removing one bolt on each side. Lower radiator to remove.
36. Remove A/C compressor and secure it out of the way with mechanics wire.
37. Remove power steering pump and secure it out of the way with mechanics wire.
38. Disconnect shift cable from the transaxle, release abutment bracket by twisting it counterclockwise and remove the cable from the bracket.
39. Disconnect shift cable from gear selector lever, release abutment bracket by twisting it counterclockwise remove the cable from the bracket.
40. Lower vehicle.
41. Remove power steering reservoir (push fit) and lay it to one side, then disconnect main wiring harness from PCM.
42. Disconnect vacuum hoses from intake manifold.
43. Disconnect battery leads and connectors, and cut cable ties.
44. Relieve fuel pressure as outlined in "Precautions."
45. Using fuel line quick disconnect tool No. D87L-9280-A/B, equivalent, disconnect fuel lines.
46. Raise and support vehicle.
47. Carefully lower vehicle and place the engine/transaxle assembly on Montagetisch GV2166, or equivalent and secure it with straps.
48. Disconnect coolant recovery tank and lay it to one side, then the speed control cable (if equipped) from the coolant recovery tank.
49. Remove front engine mounting bracket nuts and loosen bolts two turns.
50. Remove rear engine mounting bracket.
51. Raise vehicle and pull out powertrain lift with the engine/transaxle assembly from underneath the vehicle.
52. Separate transaxle from the engine.
53. Reverse procedure to install.

Cougar w/Manual Transaxle

1. Put gearshift lever into neutral, then using gear lever alignment tool No. T97P-7025-A, or equivalent, lock shifter into neutral, **Fig. 11.**
2. Disconnect hose and remove hood bolts and hood.
3. Use an allen key to stop piston rod from turning and loosen suspension strut locknut five turns on both sides.
4. Raise and support vehicle, then remove front wheels.
5. Remove radiator splash shield and brackets on both sides.
6. Drain engine coolant into a suitable container.
7. Disconnect mass air flow and intake air temperature sensor electrical connectors, then remove air intake tube.
8. Remove crankcase ventilation hose and air hose.
9. Unhook rubber ring and remove the air cleaner.
10. Remove battery, then loosen central junction box and position it to one side.
11. Remove four battery bracket bolts and two ground cables.
12. Remove power steering reservoir (push fit) and position it to one side, then disconnect main wiring harness from PCM.
13. Remove ground cable from engine lifting eye and disconnect power steering pressure switch.
14. Disconnect speed control cable from throttle valve, then gently move cable up and down and pull it out off the retaining bush. Press retaining bush out of bracket.
15. Disconnect throttle cable by unhooking cable and pulling off plastic clip, then lay throttle cable to one side.
16. Disconnect vacuum hoses from intake manifold.
17. Remove heat shield, coolant hose brackets, then pull out the engine oil level indicator tube.
18. Remove coolant hose from coolant pipe and the coolant hose from the water pump.
19. Remove three-way catalytic converter from exhaust manifold.

20. Disconnect A/C compressor electrical connector.
21. Disconnect engine coolant temperature sensor electrical connector.
22. Disconnect fan motor electrical connector and remove upper coolant hoses.
23. Remove clamp from fender apron panel and coolant hoses.
24. Remove upper accessory drive belt cover.
25. Pull out clip, then disconnect from slave cylinder, then remove slave cylinder from transaxle and tie it up.
26. Disconnect ground cable from transaxle.
27. Raise and support vehicle.
28. Remove righthand fender splash shields.
29. Loosen and remove accessory drive belt, then disconnect brake booster vacuum line from the intake manifold.
30. Remove radiator brackets and disconnect both heated oxygen sensor (HO2S) electrical connectors. Cut cable ties.
31. Disconnect front exhaust tube and discard the gasket.
32. Disconnect lower suspension arm ball joints from the wheel knuckles and ABS wiring harness bracket from suspension strut. **Do not damage boot and ABS sensor ring.**
33. **To avoid to damage the halfshaft joints and boots, do not bend the inner halfshaft joint more than 18 degrees or outer halfshaft no more than 45 degrees.**
34. Using slide hammer tool No. T50T-100-A and halfshaft remover tool No. T86-P3514-A, or equivalents, remove left and right halfshafts, **Fig. 10.** Secure halfshafts with wire.
35. Remove righthand engine support insulator center bolt and engine support insulator.
36. Remove bracket for righthand engine support insulator from transaxle.
37. If necessary raise transaxle slightly with a transmission jack, then remove lefthand engine support insulator and three way catalytic converter (TWC).
38. Remove suction accumulator bracket bolts, then the lower coolant hose.
39. Disconnect heater coolant hoses, then remove compressor bolts and position compressor with mechanics wire to one side.
40. Disconnect shift cable from gear shift lever, then release abutment bracket by turning it counterclockwise and removing cable from bracket.
41. Disconnect shift cable from gear selector lever, then release abutment bracket by turning it counterclockwise and removing cable from bracket. Release adjustment mechanism by pressing it in.
42. Lower vehicle, then relieve fuel pressure as outlined under " Precautions."
43. Using fuel line quick disconnect tool No. D87L-9280-A/B, or equivalent, disconnect fuel lines.
44. Disconnect coolant expansion tank and position it to one side, then the speed control cable (if equipped) from

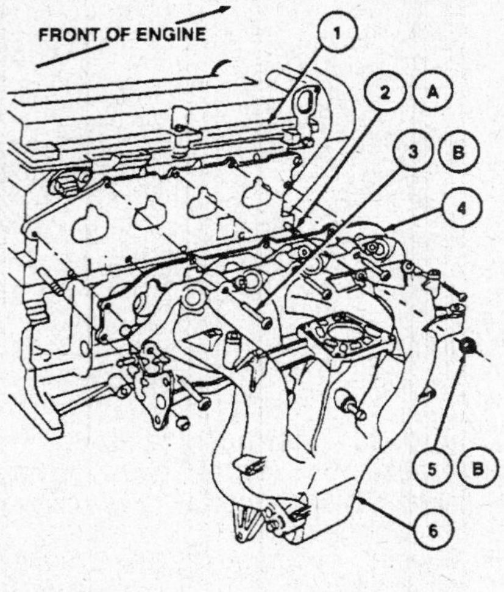

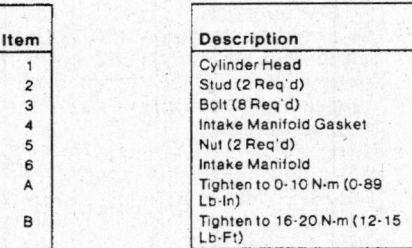

Item	Description
1	Cylinder Head
2	Stud (2 Req'd)
3	Bolt (8 Req'd)
4	Intake Manifold Gasket
5	Nut (2 Req'd)
6	Intake Manifold
A	Tighten to 0-10 N-m (0-89 Lb-In)
B	Tighten to 16-20 N-m (12-15 Lb-Ft)

FM1069500389000X

Fig. 12 Intake manifold replacement

the coolant expansion tank.

45. Remove TWC bracket.
46. Install lifting bracket tool No. T70P-6000 and spreader bar tool No. D93P–6001-A3, or equivalents, and a suitable floor crane, raise engine/transaxle assembly slightly to remove pressure from the support insulator.
47. Remove front engine support insulator nuts and loosen bolts two turns.
48. Mark up position, then remove rear transaxle support insulator nuts and bolts.
49. Raise engine/transaxle assembly, until power steering pump is accessible, then remove power steering pump bolts and position pump aside with mechanics.
50. Remove engine/transaxle assembly.
51. Separate transaxle from engine.
52. Reverse procedure to install.

INTAKE MANIFOLD

REPLACE

1. Remove air cleaner outlet tube.
2. Disconnect throttle position sensor, idle air control and engine control sensor wiring.
3. Relieve fuel system pressure as outlined under " Precautions."
4. Remove fuel supply manifold.
5. Remove engine wiring harness screws and position aside.
6. Disconnect vacuum supply hoses from the intake manifold by squeezing tabs, twisting hoses and pulling away from intake manifold.
7. Disconnect brake booster vacuum line from intake manifold.
8. Remove fuel charging wiring, then accessory drive belt.
9. Remove alternator bolts and position out of the way.
10. Remove intake manifold bolts and intake manifold, **Fig.12.**
11. Remove manifold gasket and discard.
12. Reverse procedure to install.

EXHAUST MANIFOLD

REPLACE

1. Remove the heat shield, coolant hose bracket and engine lifting eye and pull out engine oil dipstick tube.
2. **when repairing exhaust system or removing exhaust components, disconnect heated oxygen sensor (HO2S) at the wiring harness to prevent damage to sensors and the harness.** Disconnect HO2S wiring connector.
3. Remove catalytic converter from exhaust manifold.
4. Raise and support vehicle.
5. Loosen catalytic converter bracket bolt and drop converter down so the studs clear the exhaust manifold.
6. Lower vehicle.
7. Remove exhaust manifold bolts, manifold and gasket.
8. Reverse procedure to install.

FUEL INJECTION SUPPLY MANIFOLD

REPLACE

1. Remove fuel tank filler cap.
2. Relieve fuel pressure as described under "Precautions. "
3. Remove engine air intake resonators.
4. Disconnect fuel charging wiring from fuel injectors and position wiring aside, then disconnect vacuum line at fuel pressure regulator.
5. Remove fuel line coupling retainer clip from fuel supply and return fittings, then disconnect fuel supply and return hoses using spring lock coupling disconnect tool No. D87L-9280-A (3/8 inch) or D87L-9280-B (1/2 inch), or equivalent.
6. Disconnect fuel supply and return hoses from intake manifold bracket.
7. Remove fuel injection supply manifold bolts.
8. Disengage fuel injection supply manifold with fuel injectors and remove fuel injection supply manifold. It may be easier to remove fuel injectors with fuel injection supply manifold as an assembly.
9. Use light, twisting motion to remove fuel injectors and clip from fuel injection supply manifold.
10. Reverse procedure to install, noting the following:
    a. Lubricate O-rings lightly with clean engine oil, then install fuel injector retainer clip to fuel injectors.
    b. Install fuel injectors to fuel injection manifold with light twisting and pushing motion.

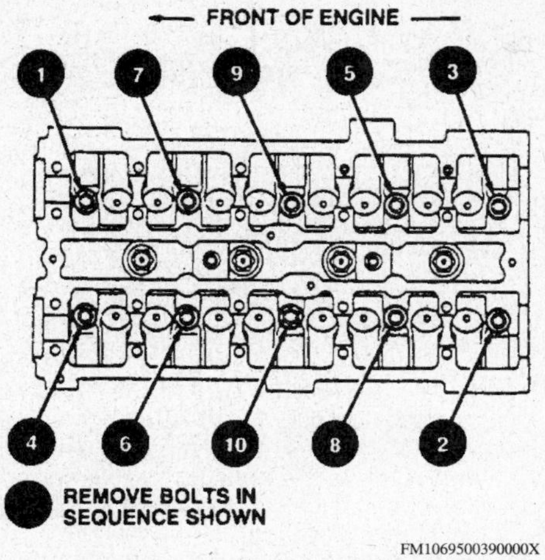

Fig. 13 Cylinder head bolt loosening sequence. 1997

c. Push fuel injection supply manifold down to ensure all fuel injector O-rings are fully seated in fuel injection supply manifold cups and lower intake manifold.
d. Ensure O-rings and washers are properly seated so no fuel leaks exist.

CYLINDER HEAD

REPLACE

1997-98

1. Drain engine coolant from radiator and cylinder block drain plugs.
2. Remove intake manifold as outlined under "Intake Manifold, Replace."
3. Remove exhaust manifold as outlined under "Exhaust Manifold, Replace."
4. Remove camshafts as outlined under "Camshaft, Replace."
5. Remove valve tappets from cylinder head, then support front of engine with wood block between crankshaft pulley and front subframe.
6. Remove righthand engine lifting eye bolt, then the righthand eye.
7. Remove power steering pump mounting and cylinder head support brackets.
8. Remove camshaft timing belt tensioner pulley, then the front cover from front of cylinder head.
9. Remove thermostat housing as outlined under "Thermostat, Replace."
10. Disconnect ignition coil electrical connectors by squeezing locking tabs and twisting while pulling upward.
11. Remove ignition coil attaching bolts, then the coil and bracket.
12. Remove spark plugs from cylinder head, then the cylinder head bolts in sequence, **Fig. 13. Discard cylinder head bolts.**
13. Remove cylinder head and head gasket from cylinder block.
14. If necessary, remove lefthand engine lifting eye from cylinder head.
15. Inspect cylinder head and cylinder block, then replace components as required.
16. Reverse procedure to install, noting following:
    a. Clean intake manifold, valve cover and cylinder head gasket surfaces.
    b. **On 1997 models,** using sequence shown in **Fig. 14, torque** new cylinder head bolts in three steps; first step to 15–22 ft. lbs., second step to 30–37 ft. lbs. and third step an additional 90–120.°
    c. **On 1998 models,** using sequence in **Fig. 14, torque** cylinder head bolts in three steps. First step 18 ft. lbs., second step 33 ft. lbs, then an additional 105.°

1999-2000

The maximum amount by which the engine management system will adjust the camshaft timing (VCT control unit) is limited to 2 degrees. As a result of this an extremely high degree of accuracy is required for any work which affects the valve timing.

1. Raise and support vehicle.
2. Remove engine undershield and front righthand wheel.
3. Remove radiator splash shield and drain coolant into a suitable container.
4. Remove righthand lower wheel arch cover.
5. Loosen water pump belt pulley bolts, then working clockwise, loosen and remove drive belt.
6. Remove water pump belt pulley and drive belt idler pulley.
7. Remove crankshaft vibration damper, then the lower timing belt cover.
8. It should be possible to insert locating pins free of strain in subframe and body locating bores. Check position of subframe and realign later if necessary.
9. **On models equipped with manual transaxle,** loosen bolts of righthand engine roll restrictor two turns.
10. **On models equipped with automatic transaxle,** loosen bolt of righthand engine roll restrictor two turns.
11. **On all models,** align subframe, if necessary as follows:
    a. Remove locating pins.
    b. Loosen subframe bolts two turns.
    c. Subframe must not move during tightening operation.
    d. With locating pins fitted, tighten four bolts, diagonally.
12. Remove lower power steering pump bolts, then disconnect brake booster line and crankcase ventilation hose from intake manifold.
13. Disconnect oil pressure switch connector and knock sensor.
14. Lower vehicle.
15. Remove intake pipe, pull out plug of mass air flow sensor and intake air temperature sensor.
16. Remove air cleaner, disconnect crankcase ventilation hose and intake hose.
17. Disconnect speed control cable from throttle valve. Move cable up and down slightly and pull it out of the retaining bush.
18. Disconnect accelerator cable, unhook cable and remove plastic clip, then position cable to one side.
19. Disconnect cylinder head wiring harness connector and vacuum hoses, then remove upper wiring rail bolts from intake manifold.

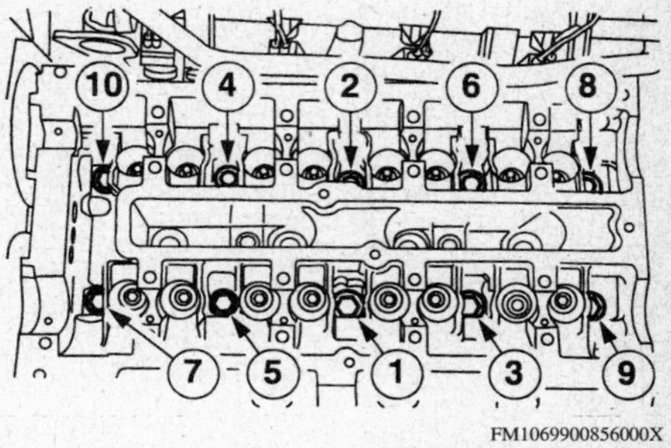

Fig. 14 Cylinder head bolt tightening sequence

20. Remove undershield, then disconnect starter motor positive lead. **Do not bend fusible element when removing the nut as there is a risk of it breaking.**
21. Disconnect radio interference suppressor, ignition coil, engine coolant temperature sensor and power steering pressure switch. Position wiring to one side.
22. Disconnect coolant hoses and lay them to one side.
23. Remove thermostat housing and disconnect connector from camshaft position sensor.
24. Remove bracket for PCV line.
25. Remove upper bolts, coolant hose bracket and engine lifting eye, pull out engine oil dipstick tube, bracket for the tube/hose (A/C), lower bolts and heat shield.
26. Disconnect catalytic converter from exhaust manifold, then remove heated oxygen sensor.
27. Remove belt pulley cover.
28. Remove power steering pump, coolant expansion tank, power steering pump bracket from cylinder head.
29. Remove alternator bolts, alternator and alternator bracket.
30. Raise and support vehicle.
31. **On models equipped with a manual transaxle,** remove lefthand engine roll restrictor and bracket.
32. **On models equipped with automatic transaxle,** slightly lifting engine with a transmission jack, remove left hand engine roll restrictor.
33. **On all models,** install gauge tool No. T94P-6000-AH, or equivalent, in place of lefthand engine roll restrictor.
34. Lower vehicle and support engine with a jack.
35. Remove front engine mounting, then the upper timing belt cover.
36. Disconnect solenoid valve connector and remove the cylinder head cover plate.
37. Using sequence, **Fig. 15,** remove cylinder head cover.
38. Remove center timing belt cover/front engine mounting bracket.
39. Loosen bolt and release timing belt tensioner by turning it clockwise. Loosen bolt four turns and unhook the timing belt tensioner.

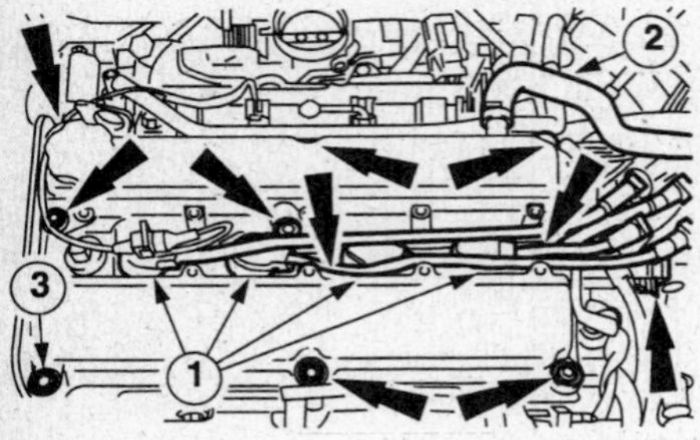

Fig. 15 Valve cover loosening sequence. 1999–2000

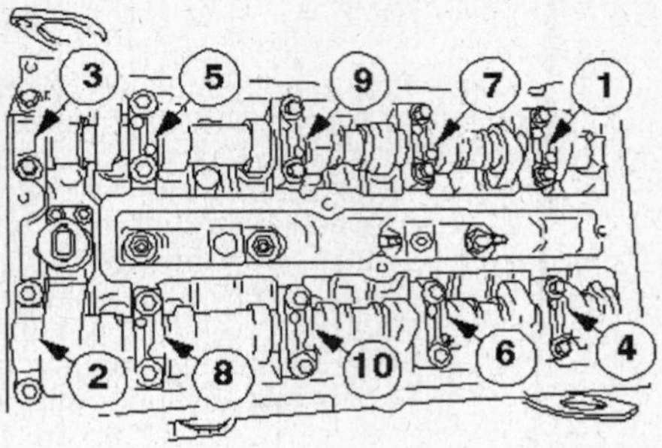

Fig. 16 Camshaft bearing caps loosening sequence. 1999–2000

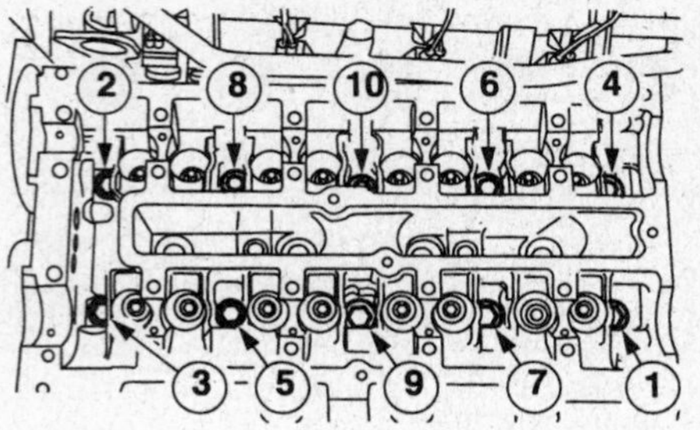

Fig. 17 Cylinder head removal sequence. 1998–2000

40. Remove timing belt, unscrew blanking plug from exhaust camshaft timing belt pulley. **Hold the camshaft by the hexagon with an open ended wrench to stop it from turning.**
41. Using timing belt pulley holding tool, tool No. T74P-6256-B, or equivalent to stop timing belt pulley from turning, remove exhaust camshaft timing belt pulley. .
42. Remove intake camshaft timing belt pulley.
43. Remove bolts from the VCT oil feed flange and upper timing case.
44. Loosen camshaft bearing caps in sequence, **Fig. 16.** Working evenly in several stages, loosen each bolt two turns at a time.
45. Remove intake camshaft and exhaust camshaft with VCT control unit.
46. Remove valve tappets.
47. Remove cylinder head bolts in sequence, **Fig. 17.**
48. Remove cylinder head from block.
49. Reverse procedure to install, noting the following:
    a. **Cylinder head bolts must be replaced with new bolts.**
    b. Using sequence in **Fig. 14, torque** cylinder head bolts in three steps. First step 18 ft. lbs., second step 33 ft. lbs, then an additional 105.°

VALVE COVER

REPLACE

1997

1. Remove engine air intake resonators from air cleaner assembly.
2. Disconnect crankcase ventilation tube from valve cover fitting.
3. Remove ignition wires and ignition wire separators from valve cover, then disconnect wires from spark plugs.
4. Remove power steering pressure hose bracket bolt and position hose aside.
5. Remove upper camshaft timing belt cover.
6. Remove valve cover outer attaching bolts, then the inner bolts.
7. Remove valve cover with gasket from cylinder head, **Fig. 18.**
8. Reverse procedure to install, noting following:
    a. Inspect valve cover gasket and O-rings for damage or signs of leakage, replace as necessary.

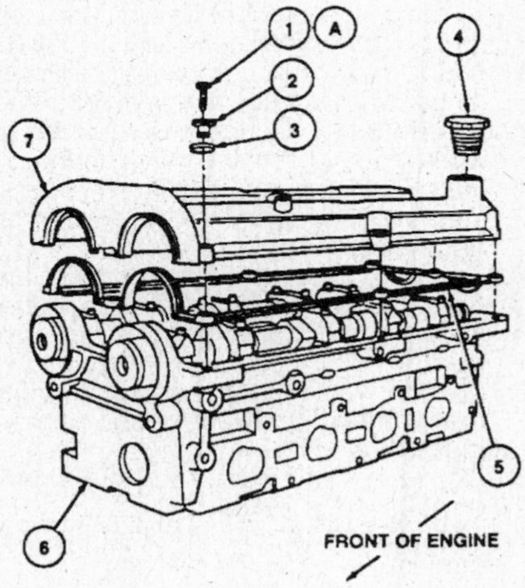

Item	Description
1	Bolt (10 Req'd)
2	Spacer (10 Req'd)
3	O-ring (10 Req'd)
4	Oil Filler Cap
5	Valve Cover Gasket
6	Cylinder Head
7	Valve Cover
A	Tighten to 6-8 N-m (53-71 Lb-In)

FM1069500399000X

Fig. 18 Valve cover replacement. 1997

    b. **Torque** valve cover bolts, beginning in center of valve cover and working to outside of valve cover to 53-71 inch lbs.
    c. Tighten upper camshaft timing belt cover bolts to specifications.
    d. Securely tighten power steering pressure hose bracket bolt and nut.

1998–2000

1. Disconnect oil feed sensor connector, then remove crankcase ventilation tube.
2. Position throttle cable out of the way and speed control cable if equipped, then remove eight bolts and appearance cover.
3. Remove spark plug wires.
4. Remove four bolts and position front cover out of the way.
5. Position throttle cable and the speed control cable if equipped out of the way, remove the bolts and valve cover. Refer to loosening sequence in "Cylinder Head, Replace."
6. Reverse procedure to install, noting the following:
    a. Inspect valve cover gasket and O-rings for damage or signs of leakage, replace as necessary.
    b. Tighten all bolts to specification.

CAMSHAFT LOBE LIFT SPECIFICATIONS

Camshaft lobe lift for intake and exhaust is .245 inch.

VALVE CLEARANCE SPECIFICATIONS

1997

Valve clearance is automatically controlled and not adjustable.

1998–2000

Intake valve clearance is .004–.007 inch, exhaust valve clearance is .010–.013.

VALVE ADJUSTMENT

1997

Valve clearance is automatically controlled and not adjustable.

1998–2000

1. Remove valve covers as described under "Valve Cover, Replace."
2. Rotate crankshaft until camshaft reaches base circle and measure valve clearance with a feeler gauge, **Fig. 19.**
3. Repeat for all valves and note measurement.
4. If valve clearance is not within specifications, remove camshafts as outlined under "Camshaft, Replace."
5. Measure and insert shim, **Fig. 20,** of required thickness as follows:
    a. Intake valve: required shim = current shim + measured clearance –.006 inch.
    b. Exhaust valve: required shim = current shim + measured clearance –.012 inch.
6. Install camshaft as outlined under "Camshaft, Replace. "

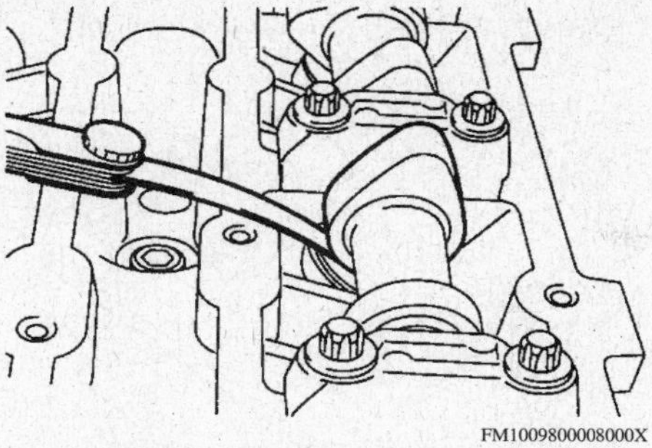

FM1009800008000X

Fig. 19 Valve clearance measurement. 1998–2000

7. Install valve cover as outlined under "Valve Cover, Replace." and tighten bolts to specification.

HYDRAULIC VALVE TAPPETS

REPLACE

1. Remove camshafts as described under "Camshaft, Replace."
2. If camshafts and valve tappets are to be reused, mark tappet locations for assembly.
3. Remove valve tappets.
4. If valve tappet is pitted, scored, excessively worn or if plunger is not free in body, replace tappet.
5. Reverse procedure to install.

FRONT COVER

REPLACE

1997

1. Remove engine air intake resonators as described under "Engine Air Intake Resonators, Replace."
2. Disconnect power steering pressure hose bracket from engine lifting eye and position bracket aside.
3. Remove upper camshaft timing belt cover bolts, then the cover from engine, **Fig. 21.**
4. Mark location of upper front engine support bracket, then remove bracket nuts and bracket from upper front engine support insulator.
5. Disconnect wire harness from low coolant level sensor connector at radiator coolant recovery reservoir.
6. Remove radiator coolant recovery reservoir retainers and position reservoir aside.
7. Remove upper front engine support insulator as described under "Engine Mount, Replace."
8. Set radiator coolant recovery reservoir into position, then loosely install bolt.
9. Loosen water pump pulley bolts. Do not remove bolts completely.
10. Remove serpentine drive belt as described under "Serpentine Drive Belt."
11. Remove drive belt idler pulley bolt and pulley from alternator bracket, then water pump pulley from water pump.
12. Remove center timing belt cover bolts, then cover from engine.

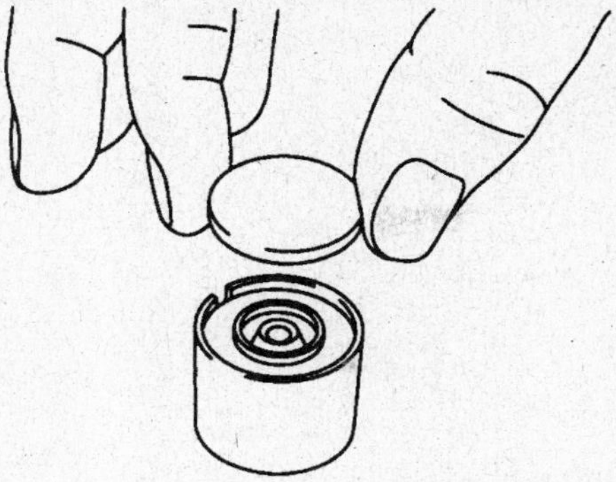

FM1009800009000X

Fig. 20 Shim installation. 1998–2000

13. Raise and support vehicle, then remove crankshaft pulley.
14. Remove lower timing belt cover bolts and lower cover from engine.
15. Reverse procedure to install.

1998–2000

1. Remove bolts and position power steering line out of the way.
2. Remove front engine support insulator.
3. Remove upper engine front cover studs, bolts and cover.
4. Remove splash shields bolts and splash shields.
5. Loosen but do not remove water pump pulley bolts.
6. Turn belt tensioner clockwise and remove accessory drive belt.
7. Remove idler pulley and water pump pulley.
8. Remove center engine front cover bolts and center engine front cover.
9. Remove bolt and crankshaft pulley.
10. Remove bolts and lower engine front cover.
11. Reverse procedure to install.

TIMING BELT

REPLACE

1997

Removal

With timing belt removed, avoid turning camshaft or crankshaft. If movement is required, exercise extreme caution to avoid valve damage caused by piston contact.

1. Remove bracket attaching power steering hoses to engine lifting bracket.
2. Install engine support bar D88L-6000-A, or equivalent to engine lifting brackets.
3. Remove upper timing belt cover attaching screws, then the cover, **Fig. 22.**
4. Mark location of front upper engine support bracket for use during installation, then remove retaining nuts and bracket.
5. Disconnect low coolant level sensor electrical connector, if equipped.

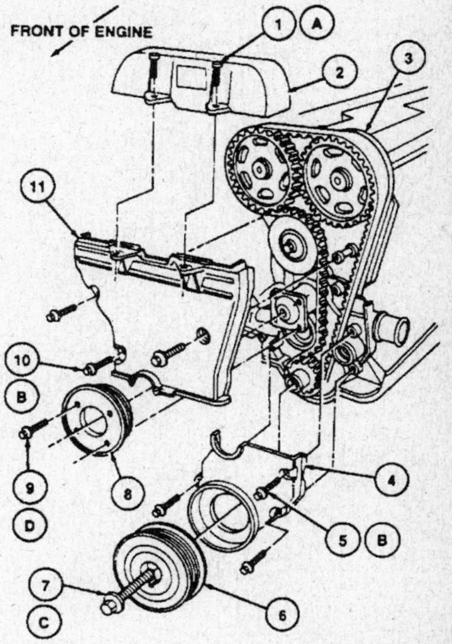

Item	Description
1	Bolt (2 Req'd)
2	Upper Camshaft Timing Belt Cover
3	Cylinder Block
4	Lower Camshaft Timing Belt Cover
5	Bolt (3 Req'd)
6	Crankshaft Pulley
7	Bolt
8	Water Pump Pulley
9	Bolt (4 Req'd)
10	Bolt (3 Req'd)
11	Center Camshaft Timing Belt Cover
A	Tighten to 3-5 N-m (27-44 Lb-In)
B	Tighten to 6-8 N-m (53-71 Lb-In)
C	Tighten to 110-120 N-m (81-89 Lb-Ft)
D	Tighten to 10-14 N-m (89-124 Lb-In)

FM1069500404000X

Fig. 21 Timing belt cover replacement. 1997

6. Remove coolant reservoir attaching bolts, then position reservoir out of way.
7. Remove front upper engine support insulator.
8. Position coolant reservoir to vehicle and loosely install attaching bolts.
9. Loosen water pump pulley attaching screws.
10. Remove accessory drive belts.
11. Remove accessory drive belt idler pulley from alternator bracket.
12. Remove water pump pulley attaching screws and water pump pulley.
13. Remove center timing belt cover attaching screws, then the cover.
14. Loosen front righthand wheel lugnuts, then raise and support front of vehicle on jackstands.
15. Remove righthand front wheel and tire assembly, then the splash shield.
16. Remove crankshaft pulley attaching bolts, then the pulley.

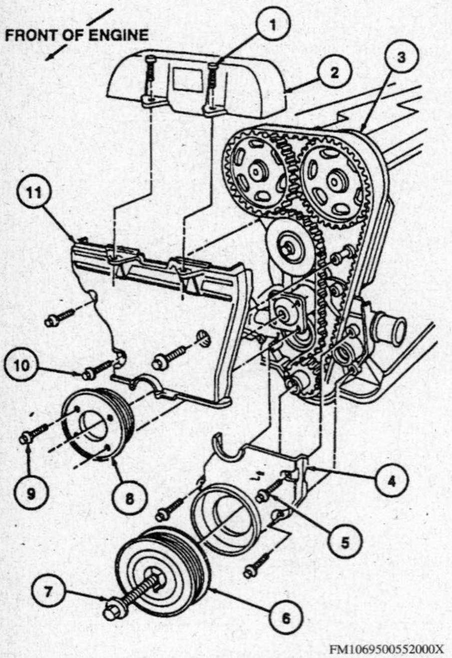

Fig. 22 Timing belt covers. 1997

17. Remove lower camshaft cover attaching screws, then the cover.
18. Disconnect ignition leads, n remove spark plugs. Tag ignition wires so can be installed at same locations.
19. Position crankshaft at No. 1 cylinder TDC compression stroke, then align crankshaft timing mark as shown in **Fig. 23.**
20. Disconnect PCV hose from cylinder head cover fitting.
21. Remove ignition wires and brackets from cylinder head cover.
22. Remove cylinder head cover attaching screws and cylinder head cover. Loosen cylinder head cover attaching screws alternately and evenly. Start at outer ends and work inward.
23. Install Ford camshaft alignment tool No. T94P-6256-CH, or equivalent, into alignment slots on rear of camshafts, **Fig. 23.**
24. Loosen timing belt tensioner pulley bolt, n move pulley away from timing belt to relieve tension. Tighten pulley bolt to hold tensioner in released position.
25. Remove timing belt.

Installation

1. Install crankshaft pulley and ensure crankshaft timing marks are properly aligned, **Fig. 23.**
2. Ensure camshafts are properly aligned, **Fig. 24.**
3. If timing belt has not been changed previously, a timing belt tensioner spring must be installed onto tensioner pulley. Install tensioner spring to tensioner pulley and attaching bolt to front of engine, **Fig. 25. Torque attaching bolt to 71-97 inch lbs. If tensioner spring is not installed, premature timing belt wear or damage may result.**

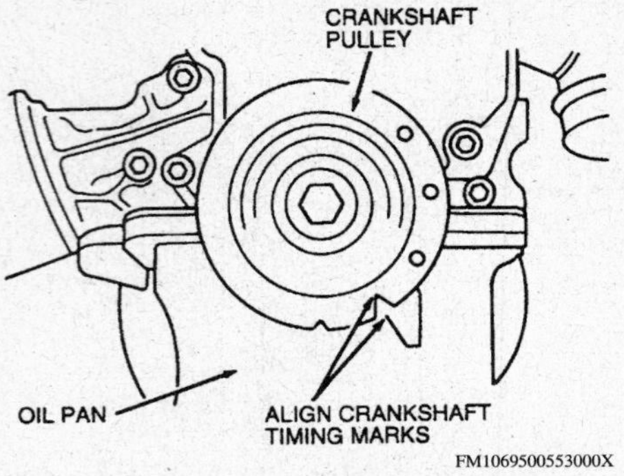

Fig. 23 Crankshaft timing marks. 1997

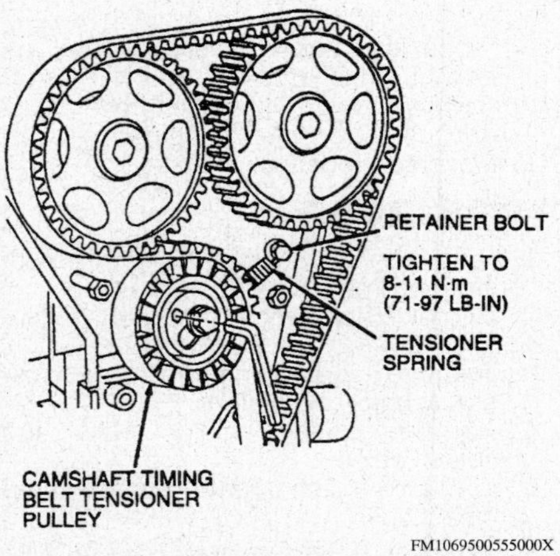

Fig. 25 Timing belt tensioner spring installation. 1997

4. Remove crankshaft pulley.
5. Install new timing belt over crankshaft sprocket, exhaust camshaft sprocket and intake camshaft sprocket, then the under tensioner pulley. **Ensure timing belt span between crankshaft sprocket and exhaust camshaft sprocket is taut. Also ensure timing belt is properly seated on all sprockets.**
6. Install timing belt lower cover. **Torque** attaching screws to 53-71 inch lbs.
7. Apply a suitable silicone gasket sealer to crankshaft keyway, then install crankshaft pulley. **Torque** crankshaft pulley attaching bolt to 81-89 ft. lbs.
8. Ensure crankshaft timing marks are aligned, **Fig. 23.**
9. Loosen timing belt tensioner pulley bolt and allow tensioner spring to tension timing belt.
10. Remove camshaft alignment tool, then rotate crankshaft two turns clockwise.
11. **Torque** timing belt tensioner pulley bolt to 26-30 ft. lbs.
12. Ensure crankshaft timing marks are aligned, **Fig. 23.** Using camshaft alignment tool, ensure camshafts are aligned, **Fig. 24.**
13. If crankshaft and camshafts are slightly out of alignment, camshaft can be moved slightly. Proceed as follows:
    a. Attach camshaft sprocket holding tool No. T74P-6256-B, or equivalent, to camshaft sprocket.

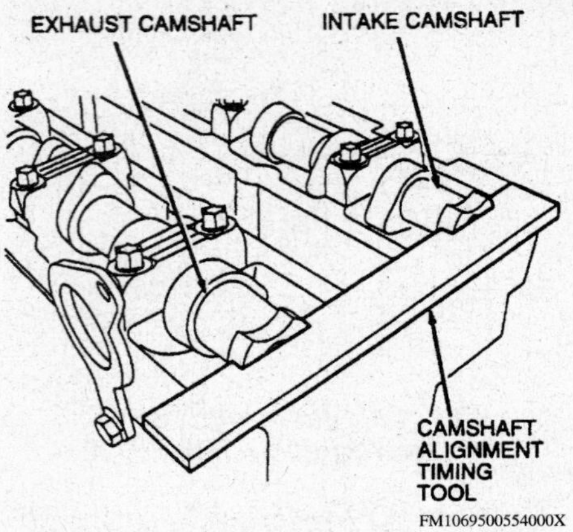

Fig. 24 Camshaft alignment. 1997–2000

    b. Loosen camshaft sprocket retaining bolt, then turn camshaft slightly until camshaft alignment tool can be installed, **Fig. 24.**
    c. Ensure crankshaft timing marks are aligned, **Fig. 23.**
    d. While holding camshaft sprocket in place with holding tool, **torque** retaining bolt to 47-53 ft. lbs., then remove camshaft holding tool.
14. Remove camshaft alignment tool, then rotate crankshaft two turns in clockwise direction.
15. Ensure crankshaft timing marks are aligned, **Fig. 23.** Using camshaft alignment tool, ensure camshafts are aligned, **Fig. 24.**
16. Install cylinder head cover. Tighten cylinder head cover attaching screws alternately and evenly. Start at center and work outward. **Torque** attaching screws to 53-71 inch lbs.
17. Attach ignition wires and brackets to cylinder head cover.
18. Connect PCV hose to cylinder head cover fitting.
19. Install spark plugs and connect ignition wires.
20. Install splash shield, then the wheel and tire.
21. Remove jackstands and lower vehicle, then tighten lugnuts.
22. Install center timing belt cover. **Torque** attaching screws to 53-71 inch lbs.
23. Install water pump pulley and hand tighten attaching screws.
24. Install accessory drive belt idler pulley to alternator bracket.
25. Install accessory drive belts.
26. Tighten water pump pulley attaching screws.
27. Install front upper engine support insulator. **Torque** attaching bolts to 52-70 ft. lbs.
28. Install engine coolant reservoir.
29. Connect low coolant level sensor electrical connector, if equipped.
30. Install front upper support bracket. Align marks made prior to support bracket removal. Use new self locking retaining nuts. **Torque** retaining nuts to 52-70 ft. lbs.
31. Install upper timing belt cover. **Torque**

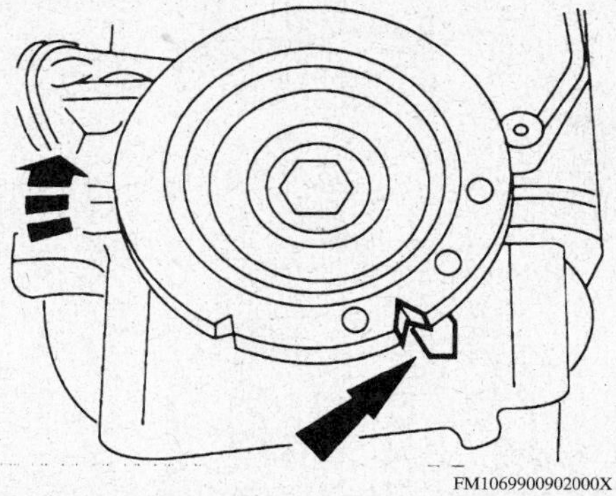

Fig. 26 Crankshaft timing marks. 1998–2000 Contour, Escort ZX2, Mystique & 1999–2000 Cougar

attaching screws to 53-71 inch lbs.
32. Remove engine support bar fixture.
33. Install bracket attaching power steering hoses to engine lifting bracket.
34. Connect battery ground cable. Inspect and adjust engine coolant level as necessary.

1998

Removal

With timing belt removed, avoid turning camshaft or crankshaft. If movement is required, exercise extreme caution to avoid valve damage caused by piston contact.

1. Rotate crankshaft until No. 1 cylinder reaches TDC, **Fig. 26.**
2. Remove power steering line retaining bolts, then position line out of way.
3. Remove engine front support insulator.
4. Remove engine front upper cover retaining bolts and studs, then the cover.
5. Loosen righthand front wheel lugnuts.
6. Raise and support vehicle with jackstands.
7. Remove righthand front wheel and tire.
8. Remove righthand front splash shield.
9. Loosen, but do not remove water pump pulley bolts.
10. Rotate serpentine belt tensioner clockwise, then remove belt.
11. Remove idler pulley.
12. Remove water pump pulley bolts and pulley.
13. Remove engine front center cover retaining bolts, then the cover.
14. Remove crankshaft pulley retaining bolt, then the pulley by using a suitable puller tool.
15. Remove engine front lower cover retaining bolts, then the cover.
16. Disconnect oil feed sensor connector.
17. Remove crankcase ventilation tube.
18. Position throttle and speed control cables aside.
19. Remove engine appearance cover retaining bolts, then the cover.
20. Tag spark plug wires, then disconnect them at spark plugs.
21. Remove four upper front cover bolts, then position cover aside.
22. Remove nine valve cover retaining bolts, then the cover.
23. Note timing belt tensioner's alignment marks, then loosen tensioner pulley bolt.
24. Rotate tensioner pulley clockwise, then remove timing belt.

Installation

1. Install camshaft alignment tool No. T94P-6256-CH, or equivalent, **Fig. 24.**
2. Remove blanking plug at side of engine block, n install timing peg tool No. T97P-6000-A, or equivalent, **Fig. 27. Torque** peg to 18 ft. lbs.
3. Ensure camshafts are properly positioned with alignment tool in place.
4. Install new timing belt, starting at crankshaft.
5. Rotate timing belt tensioner and ensure marks are properly aligned, then **torque** tensioner bolt to 18 ft. lbs.
6. Remove timing peg tool and install blanking plug into block. **Torque** plug to 18 ft. lbs.
7. Remove camshaft alignment tool.
8. Install valve cover. **Torque** retaining bolts to 60 inch lbs.
9. Install upper front cover.
10. Connect spark plug wires at spark plugs.
11. Install engine appearance cover.
12. Connect throttle and speed control cables.
13. Install crankcase ventilation tube.
14. Connect oil feed sensor connector.
15. Install crankshaft pulley. **Torque** retaining bolt to 83 ft. lbs.
16. Install water pump pulley. **Torque** bolts to 17 ft. lbs.
17. Install idler pulley. **Torque** retaining bolt to 34 ft. lbs.
18. Rotate serpentine belt tensioner clockwise, then install belt.
19. Install righthand front splash shield.
20. Install righthand front wheel and tire.
21. Lower vehicle to ground, then tighten wheel lugnuts.
22. Install engine front upper cover.
23. Install engine front support insulator.
24. Move power steering line back to its original position, then tighten retaining bolts.
25. Connect battery ground cable.
26. Start engine and inspect for proper operation. **Some abnormal drive symptoms may appear for approximately 10 miles while vehicle relearns its adaptive strategy.**

1999-2000

Removal

With timing belt removed, avoid turning camshaft or crankshaft. If movement is required, exercise extreme caution to avoid valve damage caused by piston contact.

1. Loosen righthand front wheel lugnuts.
2. Raise and safely support vehicle.
3. Remove righthand front wheel and tire.
4. Remove righthand front splash shield.
5. **On Cougar models,** remove engine undercover.
6. **On all models,** remove serpentine belt.
7. Loosen water pump pulley bolts.
8. Loosen belt tensioner in a clockwise direction, then remove tensioner.

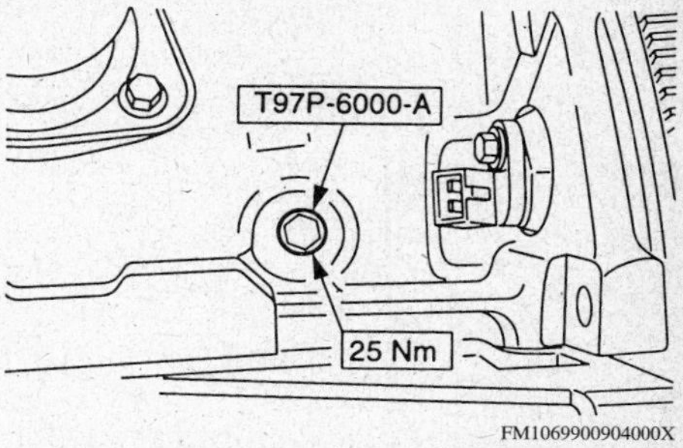

Fig. 27 1998–2000 Contour, Escort XZ2, Mystique & 1999–2000 Cougar

9. Remove water pump and belt idler pulleys.
10. Insert a suitable tool into access hole in bottom of transaxle case to prevent engine rotation.
11. Using a suitable puller tool, remove crankshaft pulley.
12. Remove lower portion of engine front cover.
13. Loosen righthand engine support insulator center bolt two turns.
14. Loosen lefthand engine support insulator center bolt two turns.
15. Lower vehicle.
16. Remove coolant expansion tank fasteners, then position tank aside.
17. Disconnect speed control cable from coolant expansion tank.
18. Position a suitable floor jack and a block of wood under engine oil pan.
19. Mark engine front support insulator mounting position.
20. Raise up slightly on floor jack to take pressure off engine front support insulator, then remove insulator.
21. Disconnect power steering pipe bracket from engine lifting eye.
22. Remove upper and center portions of engine front cover.
23. Unhook throttle and speed control cables from engine appearance cover.
24. Disconnect solenoid valve electrical connector.
25. Remove engine appearance cover.
26. Tag spark plug wires, then disconnect at spark plugs.
27. Disconnect crankcase ventilation hose.
28. Working diagonally from outside to inside, remove valve cover attaching bolts, then the valve cover.
29. Remove spark plugs.
30. Rotate crankshaft until No. 1 cylinder is approximately at TDC position.
31. Note timing belt tensioner alignment marks, then loosen tensioner bolt.
32. Rotate belt tensioner clockwise to release tension.
33. Loosen belt tensioner bolt four turns, then unhook tensioner.
34. Using a suitable wrench, hold camshafts by hexagons.
35. Remove blanking plug (1), **Fig. 28,** from exhaust camshaft sprocket.
36. Loosen exhaust camshaft sprocket (2), then the intake camshaft sprocket (3).
37. Remove timing belt.

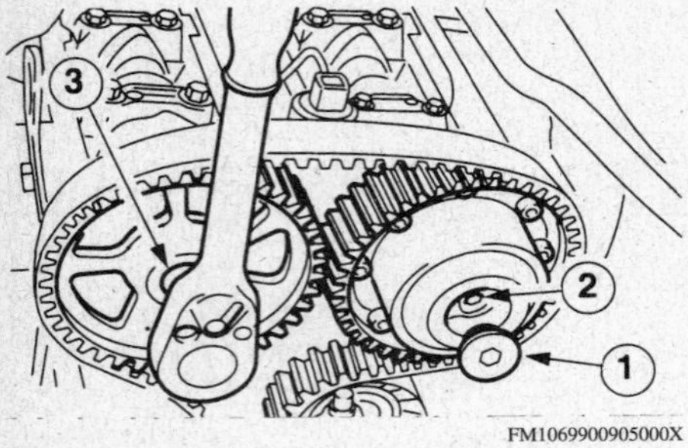

Fig. 28 Loosening camshaft sprockets. 1999–2000 Contour, Cougar & Mystique

Installation

1. Remove tool from access hole in bottom of transaxle case.
2. Rotate crankshaft until No. 1 cylinder reaches TDC, **Fig. 26.**
3. Using a suitable wrench (1), **Fig. 29,** hold camshafts by hexagons and turn in direction of engine rotation.
4. Install camshaft alignment tool No. T94P-6256-CH, or equivalent, **Fig. 24.**
5. Ensure crankshaft is still resting against timing peg. **Do not rotate crankshaft.**
6. Ensure timing belt tensioner lug is not hooked in sheet metal cover during belt installation.
7. Install new timing belt. Start at crankshaft sprocket, work in a counterclockwise direction and keep belt under tension, **Fig. 30.**
8. Hook belt tensioner into sheet metal cover and loosely turn bolt in.
9. Rotate belt tensioner counterclockwise until pointer and mark are properly aligned. **Torque** tensioner bolt to 18 ft. lbs.
10. Use holding tool No. T74P-6256-B, **Fig. 31,** or equivalent to prevent intake camshaft sprocket from turning.
11. **Torque** intake camshaft sprocket to 50 ft. lbs.
12. Using a suitable wrench, hold exhaust camshaft by its hexagon. **Torque** exhaust camshaft sprocket to 44 ft. lbs.
13. Remove timing peg and install blanking plug. **Torque** to 18 ft. lbs.
14. Remove camshaft locking tool.
15. Hold exhaust camshaft by its hexagon. **Torque** exhaust camshaft sprocket again to 89 ft. lbs.
16. Ensure camshaft timing is properly set by installing aligning tool No. T94P-6256-CH, or equivalent, onto camshafts. If aligning tool refuses to fit into both slots, loosen tensioner and both camshaft sprocket bolts, then tension timing belt again.
17. Install a new blanking plug onto exhaust camshaft sprocket. **Torque** to 27 ft. lbs.
18. Install valve cover. **Torque** mounting bolts to 62 inch lbs.
19. Install spark plugs. **Torque** to 11 ft. lbs.
20. Connect crankcase ventilation hose.
21. Connect spark plug wires.
22. Install engine appearance cover.
23. Connect solenoid valve electrical connector.

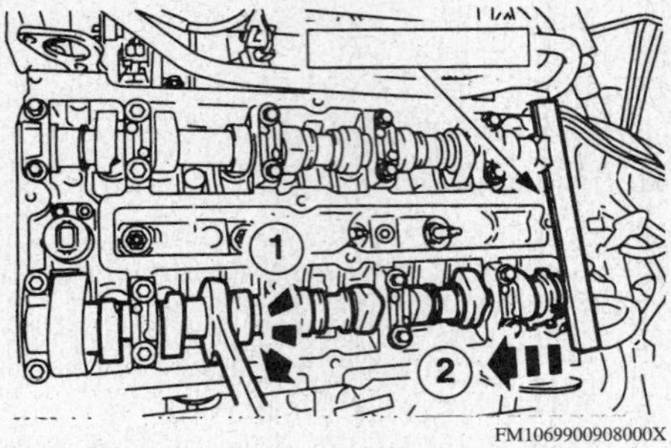

Fig. 29 Camshaft locking tool installation. 1999–2000 Contour, Cougar & Mystique

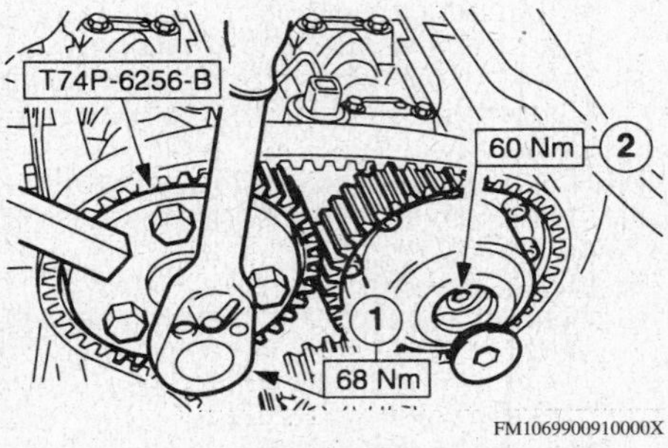

Fig. 31 Tightening camshaft sprockets. 1999–2000 Contour, Cougar & Mystique

24. Hook throttle and speed control cables at engine appearance cover.
25. Install center and upper portions of engine front cover.
26. Connect power steering pipe bracket at engine lifting eye.
27. Raise up slightly on floor jack, then install engine support insulator. **Torque** fasteners to 60 ft. lbs.
28. Install coolant expansion tank.
29. Connect speed control cable at coolant expansion tank.
30. Raise and safely support vehicle.
31. **On models equipped with automatic transaxle,** ensure center bolt is properly centered in righthand engine support insulator. **Torque** bolt to 86 ft. lbs.
32. **On models equipped with manual transaxle,** ensure center bolt is properly centered in righthand engine support insulator. **Torque** bolt to 34 ft. lbs.
33. **On all models,** ensure center bolt is properly centered in lefthand engine support insulator. **Torque** bolt to 86 ft. lbs.
34. Install lower portion of engine front cover.
35. Insert a suitable tool into access hole in bottom of transaxle case to prevent engine rotation.
36. Install crankshaft pulley. **Torque** retaining bolt to 85 ft. lbs.
37. Install serpentine belt idler and water pump pulleys.
38. Rotate serpentine belt tensioner clockwise and install belt.
39. **Torque** water pump pulley bolts to 13 ft. lbs.
40. **On Cougar models,** install engine undercover.

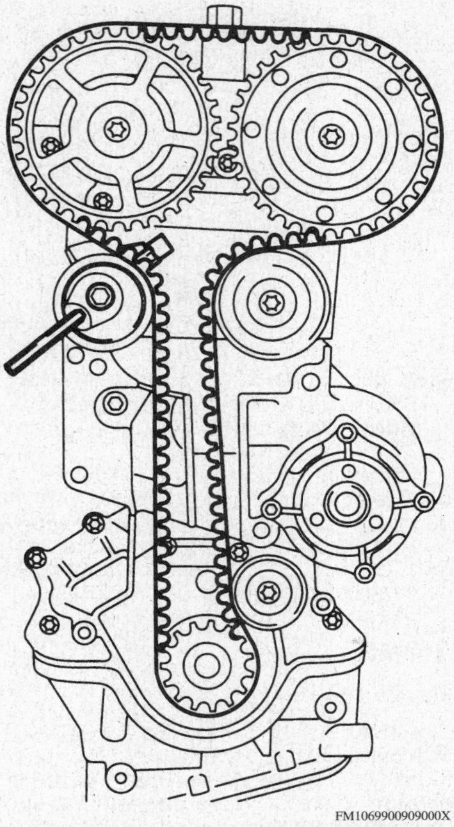

Fig. 30 Timing belt installation. 1999–2000 Contour, Cougar & Mystique

41. **On all models,** install righthand splash shield.
42. Install righthand front wheel and tire.
43. Lower vehicle to ground.
44. Tighten righthand front wheel lugnuts.
45. Connect battery ground cable.
46. Start engine and inspect for proper operation. **Some abnormal drive symptoms may appear for approximately 10 miles while vehicle relearns its adaptive strategy.**

CAMSHAFT

REPLACE

REMOVAL

1. **On 1998–2000 models,** before removal of camshaft, measure valve clearance as outlined in "Valve Adjustment."
2. **On all models** remove timing belt as described under "Timing Belt, Replace."
3. Remove camshaft sprockets.
4. Remove valve cover as described under "Valve Cover, Replace."
5. Mark cylinder head camshaft journal cap number on outside edge of camshaft journal caps and cylinder head. **Cylinder head camshaft journal caps and cylinder head should be numbered to ensure they are assembled in original positions. Keep**

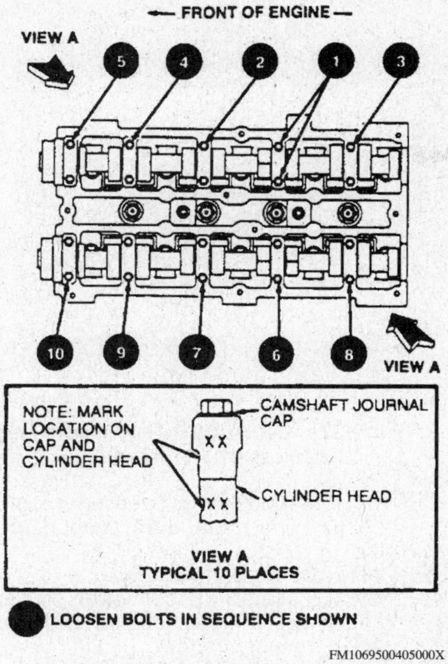

Fig. 32 Camshaft journal cap removal sequence. 1997

camshaft journal caps from cylinder head together. Do not mix with camshaft journal caps from another cylinder head. Failure to do so may result in engine damage.

6. Remove cylinder head camshaft journal cap bolts in pairs, loosening one turn at a time, beginning at rear of cylinder head, **Figs. 32 and 33.** Remove cylinder head camshaft journal thrust caps last to ensure proper camshaft position in cylinder head.
7. Remove intake and exhaust camshaft and camshaft front seals from cylinder head, **Fig. 34.**
8. Inspect camshafts and cylinder head for wear or damage. Replace components as required.

INSTALLATION

1. Ensure crankshaft is at Top Dead Center (TDC) of No. 1 cylinder.
2. Lubricate camshafts with engine assembly lubricant part No. D9AZ-19579-D, or equivalent.
3. Install camshafts into cylinder head. Camshafts are marked for identification. Intake camshaft also has additional cam lobe for camshaft position sensor.
4. Apply a ⅛ inch bead of silicone gasket and sealant part No. F1AZ-19562-A, or equivalent, to sealing surfaces of camshaft journal thrust caps and cylinder head.
5. Loosely install cylinder head camshaft journal caps and bolts. **Install camshaft journal thrust caps last.**
6. **Torque** camshaft journal cap bolts in sequence, **Figs. 35 and 36,** in several steps, with final step to 11 ft. lbs.
7. Install valve cover as described under "Valve Cover, Replace."
8. Install camshaft front seals as described under " Camshaft Front Seals, Replace."
9. Install camshaft sprockets.
10. Install timing belt as described under "Timing Belt, Replace."

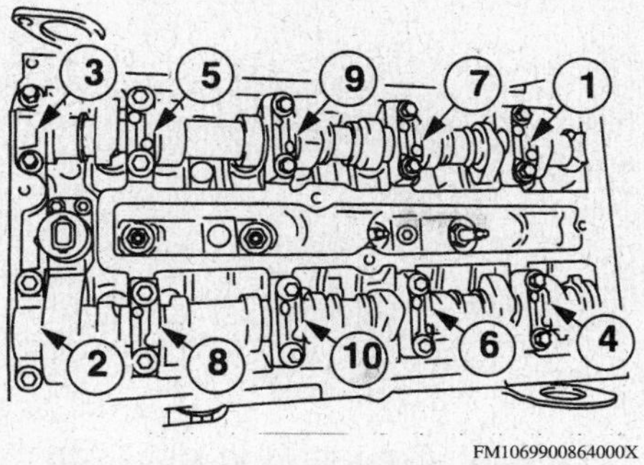

Fig. 33 Camshaft journal cap removal sequence. 1998–2000

CAMSHAFT FRONT SEALS

REPLACE

1997–98

1. Remove timing belt as described under "Timing Belt, Replace."
2. Remove camshaft sprockets, then using seal remover tool No. T92C-6700-CH, or equivalent, remove camshaft front oil seal from camshaft journal thrust caps.
3. Lubricate camshaft front oil seals with clean engine oil.
4. Using camshaft seal replacer tool No. T81P-6700-A, or equivalent, and rubber mallet, install camshaft front oil seals into camshaft journal thrust caps, **Fig. 37.**
5. Install camshaft sprockets.
6. Install timing belt as described under "Timing Belt, Replace."

1999–2000

1. Remove timing belt as described under "Timing Belt, Replace."
2. Remove camshaft sprockets, camshaft bearing cap No. 5, then the camshaft oil seals,
3. Reverse procedure to install, noting the following:
   a. Thinly coat camshaft bearing cap No. 5 with sealer.
   b. Bring oil feed ring hole right to the top.
   c. If lug is not centered between oil bores and mark, install a new exhaust camshaft timing belt pulley.

CRANKSHAFT SEAL

REPLACE

1. Remove timing belt as described under "Timing Belt, Replace," then the crankshaft sprocket and washer.
2. Using seal remover tool No. T92C-6700-CH, or equivalent, remove crankshaft front seal from oil pump.
3. Clean and inspect oil pump crankshaft front seal bore.

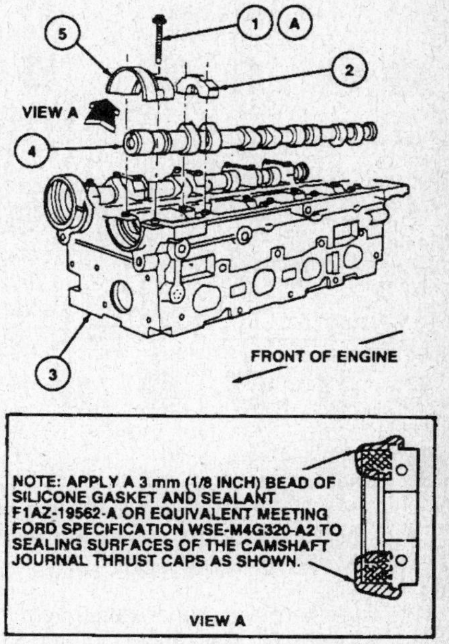

Item	Description
1	Bolt (20 Req'd)
2	Camshaft Journal Cap (8 Req'd
3	Cylinder Head
4	Camshaft
5	Camshaft Journal Thrust Cap (2 Req'd)
A	Tighten to 17-21 N·m (13-15 Lb-Ft)

FM1069500406000X

Fig. 34 Camshaft replacement

4. Lubricate oil pump crankshaft front oil seal bore and crankshaft front seal with engine assembly lubricant D9AZ-19579-D, or equivalent.
5. Using oil pump seal replacer tool No. T81P-6700-A, or equivalent, install crankshaft front seal into oil pump.
6. Install crankshaft timing sprocket, then timing belt as described under "Timing Belt, Replace."

CRANKSHAFT REAR OIL SEAL

REPLACE

1997

Removal

1. **On models equipped with automatic transaxle,** remove transaxle as described in "Automatic Transaxle/Transmission " section.
2. **On models equipped with manual transaxle,** remove transaxle, then clutch pressure plate and clutch disc as described under "Clutch & Manual Transaxle."
3. **On all models,** observe position of flywheel on crankshaft flange, then remove flywheel bolts, flywheel and reinforcement plate.

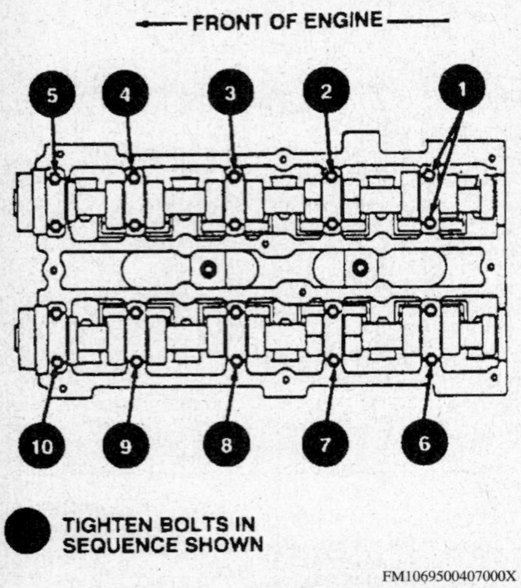

Fig. 35 Camshaft journal cap tightening sequence. 1997

4. Using sharp awl, punch hole in crankshaft rear oil seal metal surface between seal lip and seal retainer. Screw threaded end of jet plug remover tool No. T77L-9533-B, or equivalent, into oil seal and remove seal from retainer.
5. If necessary, remove crankshaft rear oil seal retainer as follows:
   a. Remove oil pan as described under "Oil Pan, Replace."
   b. Remove crankshaft rear oil seal retainer to cylinder block bolts, then the seal retainer and retainer gasket.

Installation

1. Clean and inspect crankshaft, seal retainer and cylinder block sealing surfaces.
2. Using a straight edge, install seal retainer with new gasket flush to cylinder block at oil pan sealing surface.
3. Install and tighten bolts. Cylinder block oil pan sealing surface to crankshaft rear oil seal retainer oil pan sealing surface clearance should not exceed .012–.031 inch.
4. Lubricate crankshaft flange and crankshaft rear oil seal bore with engine assembly lubricant D9AZ-19579-D, or equivalent.
5. Using crankshaft rear seal replacer tool No. T88P-6701-B1, or equivalent, and a suitable rubber mallet, install seal, **Fig. 38.**
6. Coat flywheel bolt threads with oil resistant pipe sealant part No. D8AZ-019554-A, or equivalent, then position flywheel on crankshaft.
7. **On models equipped with automatic transaxle,** install flywheel reinforcement plate.
8. **On all models,** install and tighten bolts to specifications in alternating sequence.
9. **On models equipped with manual transaxle,** install clutch disc, clutch pressure plate and transaxle as described under "Clutch & Manual Transaxle."
10. **On models equipped with automatic transaxle,** install transaxle as described in "Automatic Transaxle/ Transmission" section.
11. **On all models,** run engine and check for leaks.

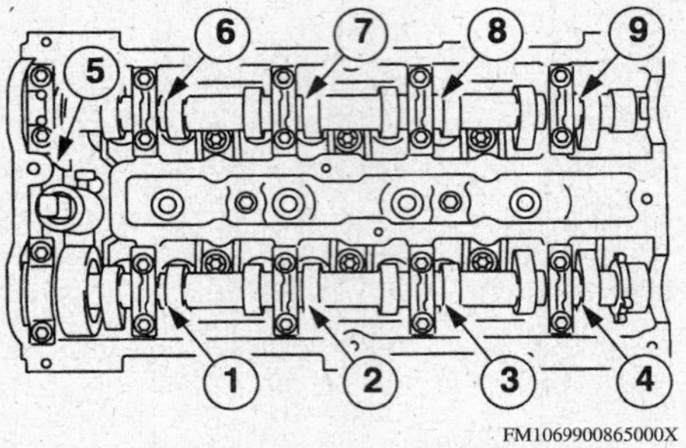

Fig. 36 Camshaft journal cap tightening sequence. 1998–2000

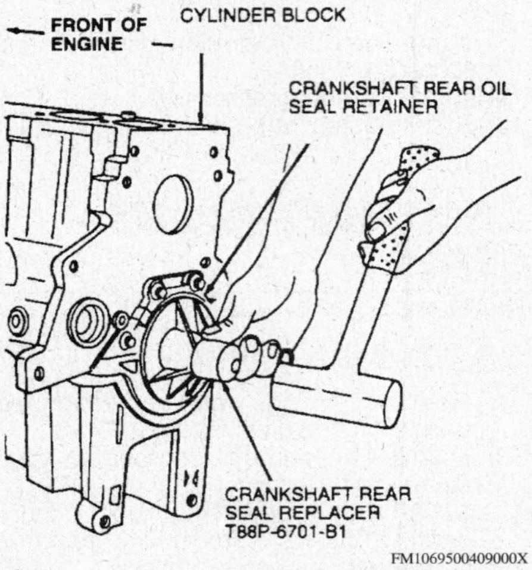

Fig. 38 Crankshaft rear oil seal installation. 1997

1998–2000

1. **On models equipped with automatic transaxle,** remove transaxle as described in "Automatic Transaxle/ Transmission" section.
2. **On models equipped with manual transaxle,** remove transaxle, then clutch pressure plate and clutch disc as described under "Clutch & Manual Transaxle."
3. **On all models,** observe position of flywheel on crankshaft flange, then remove flywheel bolts, flywheel and reinforcement plate.
4. Using seal remover tool No. T92C-6700-CH, or equivalent, remove rear oil seal.
5. Reverse procedure to install. Install oil seal using crankshaft rear seal replacer tool No. T88P-6701-B1, or equivalent, and three flywheel bolts.

OIL PAN

REPLACE

1997

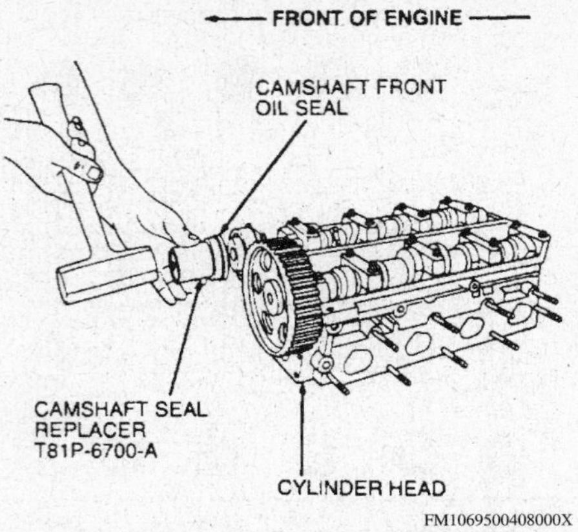

Fig. 37 Camshaft front seal installation. 1997–98

1. Install three bar engine support tool No. D88L-6000-A, or equivalent, onto engine lifting eyes, then support engine.
2. Raise and support vehicle.
3. Remove catalytic converter outlet flange nuts, then the converter outlet gasket from converter.
4. Remove exhaust manifold tube, bracket and clamp from converter.
5. Lower vehicle, then remove heat shield and converter nuts from exhaust manifold.
6. Raise and support vehicle.
7. Remove converter and converter inlet gasket from exhaust manifold. Discard inlet gasket.
8. Disconnect engine control sensor wiring from low oil level sensor.
9. Remove heater water tube bolt from bottom of oil pan and position heater water tube aside.
10. Remove engine oil pan drain plug and drain oil from engine, then install drain plug with new gasket and tighten to specifications.
11. Remove oil pan bolts from transaxle housing, then the lower engine rear plate.
12. Remove left and right front engine support insulator through bolts as outlined under "Engine Mount, Replace."
13. Lower vehicle.
14. Mark location of upper front engine support bracket, then remove bracket from upper front engine support insulator.
15. Raise engine enough to remove oil pan.
16. Raise and support vehicle, then remove oil pan attaching bolts.
17. Remove oil pan and oil pan gasket.
18. Reverse procedure to install, noting the following:
    a. Clean oil pan to cylinder block sealing surfaces with shop towel and metal brake parts cleaner part No. E6AZ-19579-BA, or equivalent.
    b. Apply ⅛ inch bead of silicone gasket and sealant part No. F1AZ-19562-A, or equivalent, to parting lines of oil pump and crankshaft rear main seal retainer on cylinder block at oil pan sealing surfaces, **Fig. 39.**

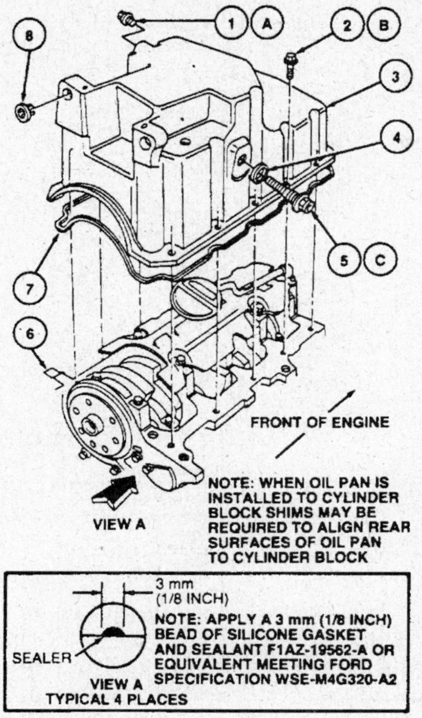

Item	Description
1	Oil Pan Drain Plug
2	Bolt (10 Req'd)
3	Oil Pan
4	Low Oil Level Sensor Washer
5	Low Oil Level Sensor
6	Cylinder Block
7	Oil Pan Gasket
8	Oil Pan Spacer (As Req'd)
A	Tighten to 21-28 N·m (15-21 Lb-Ft)
B	Tighten to 20-24 N·m (15-18 Lb-Ft)
C	Tighten to 20-34 N·m (15-25 Lb-Ft)

FM1099500070000X

Fig. 39 Oil pan installation. 1997

1998–2000

1. Remove heat shield and coolant hose bracket.
2. Remove engine lifting eye and pull out the engine oil dipstick tube.
3. Remove catalytic converter from exhaust manifold.
4. Raise vehicle.
5. Remove bolt and retaining clip for catalytic converter, then the catalytic converter from exhaust system.
6. Disconnect heated oxygen sensor connector, then remove catalytic converter from bracket.
7. Drain engine oil into a suitable container.
8. Remove oil pan bolts in sequence, **Fig. 40.**
9. Reverse procedure to install, noting the following:
   a. **Do not damage mating faces.** Using a spatula or scraper remove any traces of sealer or gasket residue from mating faces.

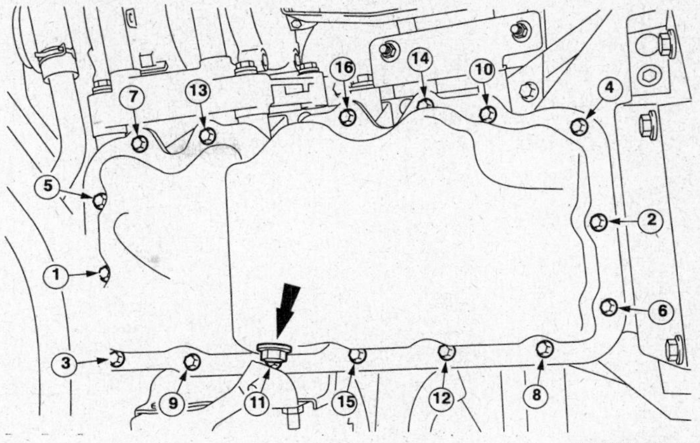

Fig. 40 Oil pan bolts removal sequence. 1998–2000

   b. The mating faces must be free of oil and gasket residue. Clean oil pan to remove any oil residue or sludge.
   c. Apply a 3 mm bead of sealer to mating face of the oil pan, then install oil pan within 10 minutes of applying the sealer.
   d. Using sequence, **Fig. 41** and **torque** oil pan bolts to 84 inch lbs.

OIL PUMP

REPLACE

1. Remove timing belt as described under "Timing Belt, Replace," then the crankshaft sprocket.
2. Remove oil pan as described under "Oil Pan, Replace. "
3. Remove oil pump screen cover and tube as described under " Oil Pump Service."
4. **On 1997 models,** remove oil bypass filter.
5. **On 1998–2000 models,** proceed as follows:
   a. Remove lower A/C bracket bolts, then lower crankcase to transmission bolts.
   b. Remove lower crankcase to upper crankcase bolts and lower crankcase.
6. **On all models,** remove oil pump bolts, then the pump from cylinder block.
7. Reverse procedure to install, noting following:
   a. Clean oil pump to cylinder block gasket sealing surfaces with wire brush. Use care to prevent damaging sealing surfaces.
   b. Rotate oil pump inner rotor to align with flats on crankshaft, then install pump with new gasket flush to cylinder block at oil pan sealing surface, using straight edge. Clearance between oil pan and oil pump sealing surfaces should not exceed .012–.031 inch.
   c. Fill crankcase to proper level with specified engine oil, then run engine and check for leaks.

OIL PUMP SERVICE

OIL PUMP SCREEN COVER & TUBE, REPLACE

1. Remove oil pan as described under "Oil Pan, Replace. "
2. Remove oil pump screen cover and tube nut from crankshaft main bearing cap stud bolt.
3. Remove oil pump screen cover and tube bolts from oil pump, then the screen cover and tube from engine, **Fig. 42.**
4. Reverse procedure to install. Install new screen cover and tube support nut to crankshaft main bearing cap stud bolt, then tighten to specifications.

BELT TENSION DATA

Drive belts have an automatic drive belt tensioner and do not require adjustment.

Automatic belt tensioner has a drive belt wear indicator mark, **Fig. 43.** If indicator mark is not between tabs on front cover, belt is worn or an incorrect belt is installed.

SERPENTINE DRIVE BELT

ROUTING

Refer to **Fig. 44** for belt routing.

BELT REPLACEMENT

Minor cracks in V-grooved portion of drive belt are considered normal and acceptable. Drive belt should be replaced if it has chunks missing from ribs, severe glazing or frayed cords.

1. Raise and support vehicle.
2. Using a 13 mm wrench, loosen drive belt tensioner pulley mounting bolt, then rotate drive belt tensioner away from accessory drive belt.
3. Lift belt over pulley flanges and remove.
4. Reverse procedure to install. Ensure drive belt is properly installed on each pulley, with all V-grooves making proper contact with each pulley, **Fig. 45.**

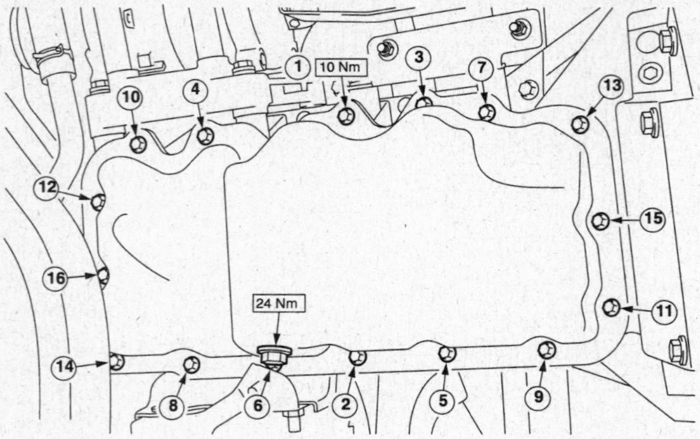

FM1069900867000X

Fig. 41 Oil pan tighten sequence. 1998–2000

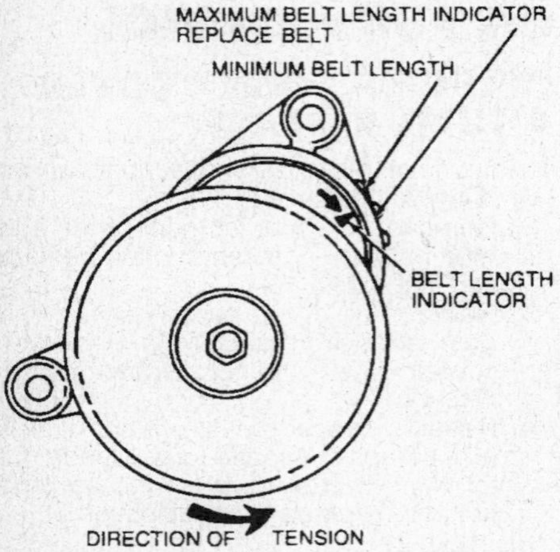

FM1069500412000X

Fig. 43 Drive belt wear indicator mark

TENSIONER REPLACEMENT

1. Remove drive belt as described under "Belt Replace."
2. Loosen belt tensioner bolts completely, then remove tensioner from front of engine.
3. Install tensioner and bolts to front of engine, then tighten bolts to specifications.
4. Install drive belt as described under "Belt Replace."

COOLING SYSTEM BLEED

These engines do not require a specific bleed procedure. To ensure coolant level is satisfactory, start the engine, turn heater control to its maximum heat and vent positions. After engine reaches normal operating temperature, hot air should be blowing from the A/C vents. If cool air is blowing from the vents, coolant level is low, turn engine off and add coolant as necessary.

THERMOSTAT

REPLACE

1. Remove engine air intake resonators from air cleaner assembly.
2. Drain engine cooling system so engine coolant level is below thermostat, then disconnect upper radiator hose and overflow hose from water hose connection.
3. Remove water outlet connection bolts, then the connection from thermostat housing, **Fig. 46.**
4. Remove thermostat and seal from housing.
5. Reverse procedure to install.

WATER PUMP

REPLACE

1997

1. Drain engine cooling system, then raise and support vehicle.
2. Remove lower radiator hose form water pump, then lower vehicle.
3. Remove timing belt as described under "Timing Belt, Replace."
4. Remove water pump bolts, water pump housing gasket and water pump from cylinder block, **Fig. 47.**
5. Reverse procedure to install, noting following:
   a. Clean water pump and cylinder block gasket sealing surfaces with wire brush.
   b. Install new water pump housing gasket.
   c. Lubricate lower radiator hose with silicone lubricant part No. D7AZ-19553-AA, or equivalent before installing hose to water pump.

1998–2000

1. Drain engine coolant into a suitable container.
2. Remove righthand front wheel and lower splash shield.
3. Lower vehicle.
4. Disconnect hoses and remove coolant expansion tank.
5. Install engine support tool No. D88L-6000-L, or equivalent.
6. Remove front engine support bracket nuts, bolts and bracket.
7. Loosen water pump pulley bolts, then remove accessory drive belt.
8. Remove water pump pulley bolts and pulley.

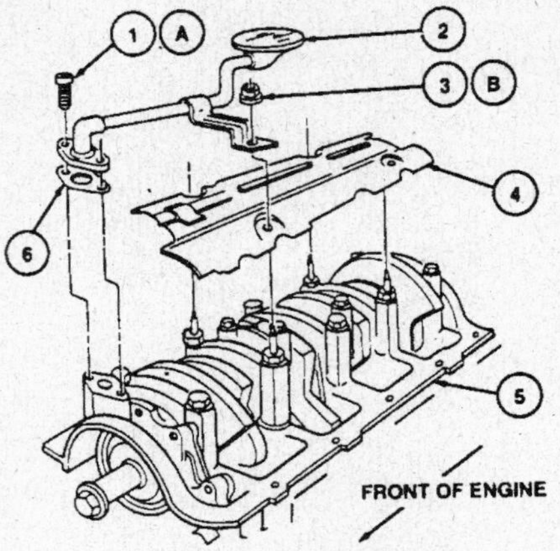

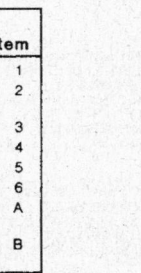

Item	Description
1	Bolt (2 Req'd)
2	Oil Pump Screen Cover and Tube
3	Nut (4 Req'd)
4	Oil Pan Baffle
5	Cylinder Block
6	Oil Pump Inlet Tube Gasket
A	Tighten to 8-11 N·m (71-97 Lb-In)
B	Tighten to 17-21 N·m (13-15 Lb-Ft)

FM1099500071000X

Fig. 42 Oil pump screen cover & tube replacement

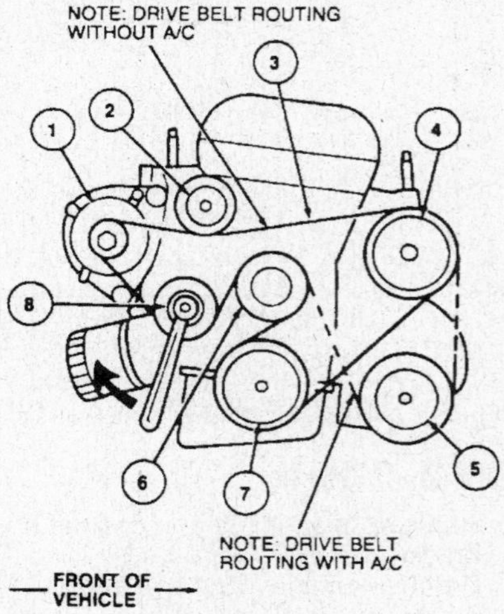

Item	Description
1	Generator
2	Drivebelt Idler Pulley
3	Accessory Drive Belt
4	Power Steering Pump Pulley
5	A/C Compressor
6	Water Pump Pulley
7	Crankshaft Pulley
8	Drive Belt Tensioner

FM1069500410000X

Fig. 44 Drive belt routing

9. Remove water pump bolts, then the water pump. Pump must be turned 180 to remove from the vehicle.
10. Reverse procedure to install.

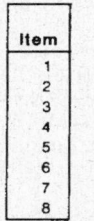

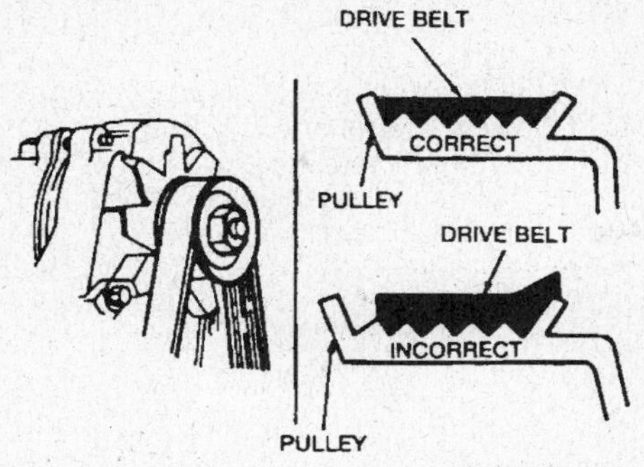

FM1069500411000X

Fig. 45 Drive belt installation

RADIATOR

REPLACE

1997

1. Drain engine cooling system, then remove upper radiator hose from radiator.
2. **On models with 2.5L engine,** remove radiator overflow hose from radiator.
3. **On models with automatic transaxle,** remove transaxle oil cooler tube from oil cooler inlet fitting.
4. **On all models,** remove fan shroud to radiator nut, then raise and support vehicle.
5. Remove lower radiator hose from radiator.
6. **On models with automatic transaxle,** remove oil cooler tube from oil cooler outlet fitting on radiator by loosening tubes while holding connector with back-up wrench.
7. **On all models,** support fan shroud, radiator and A/C condenser core with suitable jack stand, then remove lower radiator supports from front subframe and radiator.
8. Position jack stands aside and carefully remove radiator.
9. Reverse procedure to install.

1998-2000

Contour & Mystique

1. Drain engine coolant into a suitable container.
2. Disconnect fan resistor, cooling fan, A/C and A/C low pressure electrical connectors.
3. Disconnect ground cable from frame.
4. **On models equipped with automatic transaxle,** disconnect transaxle upper and lower cooling lines.
5. **On all models,** disconnect radiator upper and lower hoses.
6. Secure A/C condenser and remove bolts
7. Remove radiator four bolts and radiator.
8. Reverse procedure to install.

Cougar

1. Drain engine coolant into a suitable container.
2. Remove motor, fan and shroud.
3. Remove upper shield and secure condenser.

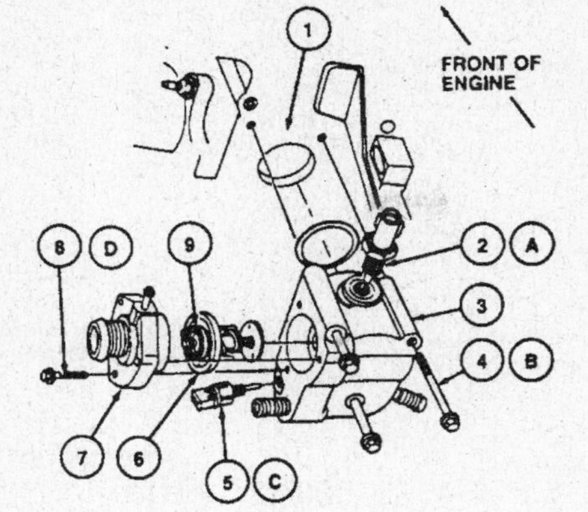

Item	Description
1	Cylinder Block
2	Engine Coolant Temperature Sensor
3	Water Thermostat Housing
4	Bolt (3 Req'd)
5	Water Temperature Indicator Sender Unit
6	O-Ring
7	Water Hose Connection
8	Bolt (3 Req'd)
9	Water Thermostat
A	Tighten to 10-14 N·m (89-124 Lb-In)
B	Tighten to 18-22 N·m (13-16 Lb-Ft)
C	Tighten to 7-10 N·m (62-89 Lb-In)
D	Tighten to 8-11 N·m (71-97 Lb-In)

FM1089500091000X

Fig. 46 Thermostat replacement

4. Disconnect radiator upper cooling hose.
5. **On models equipped with automatic transaxle,** disconnect radiator upper cooling hose.
6. **On all models,** disconnect radiator lower cooling hose and detach air conditioning condenser.
7. Remove radiator.
8. Reverse procedure to install.

FUEL PUMP

REPLACE

CONTOUR & MYSTIQUE

1. Relieve fuel system pressure as described under " Precautions."
2. Remove rear seat cushion.
3. Remove plastic grommet from floor pan, then disconnect fuel pump module electrical connector.
4. Disconnect fuel and vapor return tubes from fuel pump module.
5. Disconnect fuel lines by compressing tabs on both sides of each nylon push connect fitting and ease fuel line out of module.
6. Turn pump locking retainer ring counterclockwise using fuel tank sender wrench tool No. D84P-9275-A, or equivalent.
7. Remove fuel pump module, then immediately cover opening in fuel tank in order to prevent fuel system contamination.

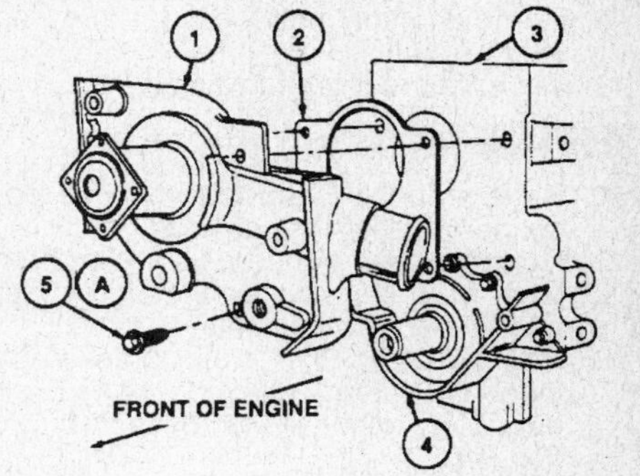

Item	Description
1	Water Pump
2	Water Pump Housing Gaskets
3	Cylinder Block
4	Oil Pump
5	Bolt (4 Req'd)
A	Tighten to 16-20 N·m (12-15 Lb-Ft)

FM1089500092000X

Fig. 47 Water pump replacement. 1997

8. Remove fuel pump module O-ring seal and discard.
9. Reverse procedure to install, noting the following:
   a. Apply light coat of premium long-life grease part No. XG-1-C,-K, or equivalent, on new O-ring seal, then install seal to groove on fuel tank.
   b. Ensure locating keys are in keyways and O-ring seal remains in place.
   c. Ensure all locking tabs are under fuel tank lock ring tabs.
   d. Install multi-port fuel pressure gauge tool No. T80L-9974-B, or equivalent, to fuel pressure relief valve cap on fuel supply injection manifold.
   e. Turn ignition switch to Run position for three seconds, five to 10 times until pressure gauge reads at least 30 psi, then check for leaks at fittings.

COUGAR

1. Remove fuel tank.
2. Fuel supply line connectors are white or are identified by a white band. Fuel return line connectors are red or are identified by a red band. Disconnect fuel feed pipe.
3. Remove fuel pump locking ring using fuel sender ring wrench tool No. D84P-9275-A, or equivalent.
4. Remove fuel pump.
5. Reverse procedure to install. Install new O-ring.

FUEL FILTER

REPLACE

IN-TANK

1. Remove fuel pump as described under "Fuel Pump, Replace."

2. Remove filter mounted on fuel pump inlet.
3. Reverse procedure to install.

INLINE

1. Relieve fuel system pressure as described under " Precautions."
2. Remove push connect fittings at both ends of fuel filter, then install retainer clips in each connect fitting.
3. Remove fuel filter from bracket by loosening worm gear mounting clamp enough to allow filter to pass through, **Fig. 48.**

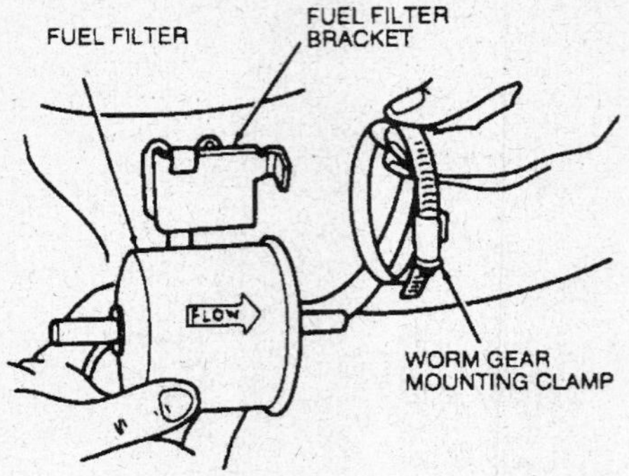

Fig. 48 Inline fuel filter replacement

4. Reverse procedure to install, noting the following:
   a. Locate fuel filter against tab at lower end of bracket. Ensure proper direction of fuel flow, **Fig. 48.**
   b. Tighten worm gear mounting clamp to specifications.

TIGHTENING SPECIFICATIONS

Year	Component	Torque/Ft. Lbs.
1997–2000	Accelerator Cable Bracket	72–108①
	Air Cleaner Bracket	15–22
	Battery Ground Cable To Engine At Transaxle Stud Bolt Nut	15–22
	Camshaft Journal Cap	④
	Camshaft Sprocket Bolt	47–53
	Catalytic Converter Bracket Bolts	72–108①
	Catalytic Converter Clamp Bolt	15–22
	Catalytic Converter To Exhaust Manifold Nuts	26–33
	Center & Lower Timing Belt Cover Bolts	60-72①
	Crankshaft Pulley Bolt	81–89
	Cylinder Head Bolts	②
	Drive Belt Idler Pulley Bolt	35
	Drive Belt Tensioner Bolts	15–22
	EGR Valve To Exhaust Manifold Tube Nut	44
	Engine Air cleaner Tube Clamps	24–48①
	Engine & Transaxle Support Insulator Nuts	84①
	Engine & Transaxle Support Insulator To Front Fender Apron Bolts	52–70
	Engine Lifting Eye	⑥
	Engine Rear Plate Bolts	79–86③
	Exhaust Manifold Heat Shield Nuts	72–108①
	Exhaust Manifold Nuts	13–16
	Exhaust Manifold Shield Retainers	72–108①
	Flywheel Bolts	81–86
	Flywheel Nuts	54–64③
	Front Engine Support Bracket To Front Sub-Frame Bolts	20
	Front Engine Support Bracket To Transaxle Bolts	⑤
	Front Engine Support Insulator Bolt	20
	Front Engine Support Insulator Through Bolt	20

Continued

TIGHTENING SPECIFICATIONS—Continued

Year	Component	Torque/Ft. Lbs.
1997-2000	Front Stabilizer Bar Link To Stabilizer Bar Nuts	35
	Heated Oxygen Sensor	44
	Heater Water Tube Bolt	72–108①
	Lower Engine Rear Plate Bolts	72–108①
	Main Bearing Cap Bolts	55-60
	Oil Level Indicator Tube Bolt	72–108①
	Oil Pan Drain Plug	15–21
	Oil Pan To Transaxle Case Bolts	15–18
	Oil Pan To Transaxle Housing Bolts	25–34
	Oil Pump Screen Cover & Tube Bolts	72–96①
	Power Steering Pump Mounting Bracket Support Bracket Bolts	29–41
	Radiator Coolant Recovery Reservoir Bolts	72–108①
	Radiator Supports To Front Sub-Frame Bolts	72–96①
	Righthand Front Engine Support Insulator Through Bolt	75–102
	Self-Locking Oil Pump Screen Cover & Tube Support Nut	13–15
	Shift Cable Bracket Bolts	15–19
	Shift Rod Bolt	17
	Stabilizer Nut	41
	Steering Shaft To Joint Bolt	18
	Thermostat Housing	15
	Throttle Body Bolts & Nuts	72–108①
	Tie Rod End Stud Nuts	⑧
	Timing Belt Pulley	26–30
	Timing Belt Tensioner Pulley	72–96①
	Transaxle Oil cooler Lines	18–22
	Transaxle To Engine Bolts	25–34
	Upper Front Engine Support Bolts	52–70
	Upper Front Engine Support Bracket Self-Locking Nuts	52-70
	Upper Timing Belt Cover Bolts	27–44①
	Valve Cover Bolts	⑦
	VCT Oil Feed Flange To Cylinder Head	84①
	Water Hose Connection Bolts	71–97
	Water Pump Pulley Bolts	89–124
	Wheel Knuckle To Lower Arm Bolts	37–43
	Wheel Lug Nuts	62
	Worm Gear Mounting Clamp	15–25①

① — Inch lbs.
② — Refer to "Cylinder Head, Replace."
③ — Tighten in alternating sequence.
④ — Refer to "Camshaft, Replace" for procedure.
⑤ — Lefthand side, 30–40 ft. lbs.; righthand side, 40–55 ft. lbs.
⑥ — Lefthand side, 10–13 ft. lbs.; righthand side, 30–40 ft. lbs.
⑦ — Refer to "Valve Cover, Replace" for procedure.
⑧ — Refer to "Engine, Replace" for procedure.

2.5L Engine

NOTE: Refer To "Air Bag System Precautions " Located In The Front Of This Manual For System Disarming & Arming Procedures.

NOTE: Refer To "Computer Relearn Procedures" Located In The Front Of This Manual For Computer Relearn Procedures.

INDEX

PRECAUTIONS

BATTERY GROUND CABLE

Prior to service, disconnect battery ground cable and isolate as required.

AIR BAG SYSTEMS

Refer to "Air Bag System Precautions" in front of this manual for system disarming and arming procedures.

COOLING SYSTEM

This engine has an aluminum cylinder head and requires a special corrosion inhibiting coolant to avoid cooling system damage. Use only specified coolant in this engine.

FUEL SYSTEM PRESSURE RELIEF

Fuel supply lines will remain pressurized for long periods of time after engine shutdown. Pressure must be relieved before servicing fuel system.

1. Remove engine air cleaner as follows:
   a. Remove engine air intake resonators.
   b. Disconnect engine control sensor wiring connectors from Mass Air Flow (MAF) sensor and Intake Air Temperature (IAT) sensor.
   c. Remove engine air cleaner to body O-ring retainer.
   d. Remove engine air cleaner body and intake tube from bracket and intake tube and duct.
2. Connect Multi-Port Fuel Injection (MFI) fuel pressure gauge tool No. T80L-9974-B, or equivalent, to fuel pressure relief valve cap on fuel injection supply manifold.
3. Open manual valve on gauge tool to relieve fuel system pressure.

COMPRESSION PRESSURE

Compression pressure should be checked at normal operating temperature with spark plugs removed and throttle plate wide open. Cylinder compression pressure is considered within specification if lowest reading cylinder is within 75 percent of highest reading.

ENGINE MOUNT

REPLACE

UPPER

1. Remove water pump pulley shield screws, then the shield.
2. Install three bar engine support tool No. D88L-6000-A, or equivalent, to existing engine lifting eyes and support engine.
3. Disconnect engine control sensor wiring from power steering pump switch connector, then remove power steering pressure hose bracket bolt from upper front engine support bracket.
4. Place towel below power steering pressure hose line to pump connection, then disconnect pressure hose from pump and position hose aside. **Do not allow power steering fluid to contact drive belt.**
5. Position ignition wires away from upper front engine support bracket.
6. Remove front engine support self-locking nuts and discard nuts. **Engine support nuts are self-locking and must be replaced.**
7. Remove upper front engine support bracket from vehicle.
8. Remove coolant recovery reservoir bolts and position reservoir aside.
9. Remove front engine support insulator bolts, then the insulator from righthand front fender apron, **Fig. 1.**
10. Reverse procedure to install. **Engine and transaxle position must be realigned to front subframe. Failure to realign engine and transaxle may**

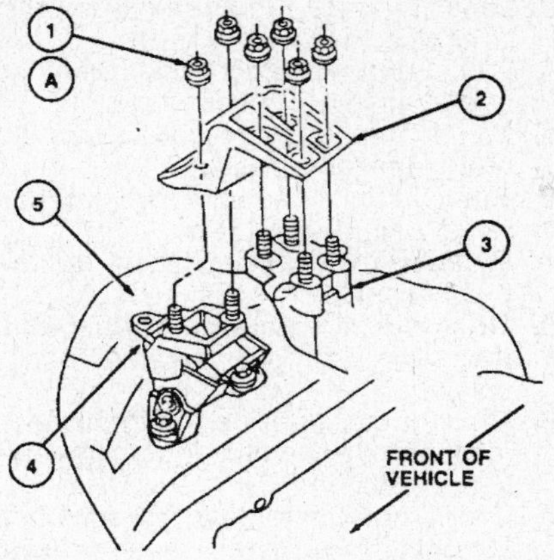

Item	Description
1	Nut (6 Req'd)
2	Front Engine Support Bracket (Upper)
3	Power Steering Pump Bracket
4	Front Engine Support Insulator (Upper)
5	Front Fender Apron (RH)
A	Tighten to 70-95 N·m (52-70 Lb-Ft)

FM1069500413000X

Fig. 1 Upper front engine support insulator replacement

result in possible component damage. To align engine and transaxle, proceed as follows:

a. Raise and support vehicle, then remove two front subframe through bolt bolts and lefthand front engine support insulator.
b. Install powertrain alignment gauge tool No. T94P-6000-AH, or equivalent, to transaxle bracket and front subframe, **Fig. 2. Torque** vertical bolts and through bolt to 20 ft. lbs.
c. Ensure righthand front engine support insulator is centered in transaxle bracket and is in perfect front-to-rear alignment.
d. Ensure lefthand front engine support insulator is in perfect front-to-rear alignment.

LEFTHAND

Refer to "2.0L Engine" section for lefthand front engine support insulator replacement.

RIGHTHAND

Refer to "2.0L Engine" section for righthand front engine support insulator replacement.

ENGINE & TRANSAXLE SUPPORT INSULATOR

Refer to "2.0L Engine" section for engine and transaxle support insulator replacement.

ENGINE

REPLACE

1997

1. Remove water pump pulley shield to lefthand valve cover attaching bolts, then the shield.
2. Disconnect positive battery cable and wiring from battery.
3. Remove pinch bolt, then disconnect steering shaft and joint in vehicle.
4. Remove air cleaner as follows:
   a. Loosen engine air cleaner tube clamps on outlet tube, then disconnect crankcase ventilation hoses and IAC valve tube from air cleaner outlet tube fitting.
   b. Remove air cleaner outlet tube from MAF sensor and throttle body.
   c. Disconnect engine control sensor wiring connector form MAF and IAT sensor.
   d. Remove engine air cleaner to body O-ring retainer, then the air cleaner body and intake tube from bracket.
   e. Remove engine air cleaner intake tube and duct.
5. **On models equipped with air conditioning,** recover air conditioning system as described in "Air Conditioning" section.
6. **On all models,** raise and support vehicle.
7. Remove converter outlet flange nuts, then the muffler and converter outlet gasket from converter.
8. Remove converter nuts and exhaust pipe flange hold down springs.
9. Remove converter and inlet gasket from Y pipe, then discard gasket.
10. Remove front and rear Y pipe flange fasteners from exhaust manifolds.
11. Remove stud bolt and nut retainer from oil pan, then the Y pipe.
12. Drain engine cooling system.
13. Remove stabilizer bar link cotter pins and nuts, then separate stabilizer bar links from front stabilizer bar.
14. Remove front suspension lower arm pinch bolts, then separate front suspension lower arms from front steering knuckles.
15. Remove tie rod end cotter pins and nuts, then separate tie rod ends from front steering knuckles with tie rod end remover tool No. 3290–D, or equivalent.
16. Remove axle wheel hub retainer from halfshaft ends, then the halfshafts.
17. Remove A/C accumulator screws from front subframe.
18. Disconnect speedometer drive cable from vehicle speed sensor on transaxle, then the sensor wiring harness at connector.
19. **On models with automatic transaxle,** proceed as follows:
   a. Remove engine rear plate access plug, then the torque converter nuts.
   b. Push torque converter into transaxle front pump support and gear.
20. **On all models,** lower vehicle, then secure radiator and engine cooling fan motor, fan blade and fan shroud assembly to radiator support with safety wire.
21. Disconnect accelerator cable and speed control actuator from throttle body, then remove accelerator cable bracket from throttle body.

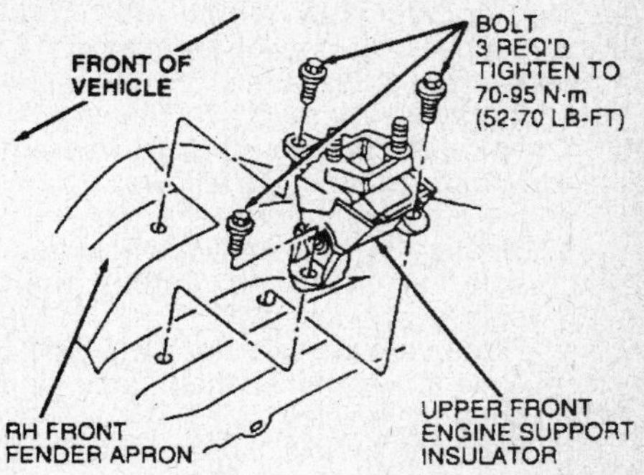

FM1069500414000X

Fig. 2 Powertrain alignment gauge tool installation

22. Remove three engine control sensor wiring connectors from bracket on lefthand front fender apron, then disconnect wiring at connectors.
23. Remove engine control sensor wiring retainer from air cleaner bracket.
24. Disconnect ignition control module electrical connector by carefully lifting up on connector finger ends while grasping connector body and pulling away from module
25. Remove ignition module screws, then the module from bracket.
26. Remove ignition control module bracket.
27. Remove power steering pump auxiliary reservoir from bracket and position over engine assembly.
28. Disconnect return hose from reservoir. Plug hose end.
29. Disconnect power steering pressure hose from power steering pump. **Do not allow power steering fluid to contact drive belt.**
30. Disconnect engine control sensor wiring from Powertrain Control Module (PCM) and retainer on righthand side of dash panel.
31. Remove engine control sensor wiring ground strap from righthand front fender apron.
32. Disconnect coolant hoses from radiator coolant recovery reservoir, then fuel and supply lines from fuel injection supply manifold.
33. **On models with automatic transaxle,** pry shift cable from stud, then remove shift cable bracket screws, bracket and cable.
34. **On all models,** disconnect ground strap from transaxle case.
35. Remove vacuum supply line from power brake booster, then the upper radiator hose from radiator.
36. Disconnect positive battery cable retainer from battery tray.
37. **On models equipped with manual transaxle,** remove clutch hydraulic retainer, then disconnect line from clutch actuator pipe at transaxle case.
38. **On models equipped with block heater,** disconnect block heater power supply wiring from righthand side of radiator support.
39. **On all models,** raise and support vehicle, then disconnect heater water hoses from heater core.

40. **On models with air conditioning,** disconnect A/C suction hose from A/C condenser core, then the A/C discharge hose from A/C accumulator.
41. **On models equipped with manual transaxle,** proceed as follows:
    a. Remove gearshift lever knob.
    b. Unsnap console applique from console assembly and remove gearshift lever boot.
    c. Remove gearshift stabilizer bar to case cover bolts, then raise and support vehicle.
    d. Remove middle under body heat shield nuts, then the shield.
    e. Remove transaxle gear shift rod and clevis from transaxle, then the stabilizer bar to bracket nut at righthand transaxle support insulator.
    f. Remove gearshift stabilizer bar from vehicle.
42. **On models with automatic transaxle,** remove transaxle oil cooler lines from transaxle, then the return line from bracket on lefthand side of transaxle.
43. **On all models,** disconnect lower radiator hose from radiator.
44. Remove lower radiator support to front subframe bolts, then rotate radiator supports forward.
45. **On models with air conditioning,** disconnect A/C compressor wire harness at connectors.
46. **On all models,** remove two bumper cover brace to left and right front subframe attaching screws. Rotate bumper cover braces forward.
47. Partially lower vehicle, then position and secure any hoses, lines and components to be removed with engine.
48. Install powertrain and subframe support bracket tool No. 134-00250, or equivalent, to Rotunda powertrain lift tool No. 134-00251, or equivalent, then rotate transaxle adapters for transaxle removal.
49. Remove four subframe bolts.
50. Remove upper front engine support bracket and engine and transaxle support insulator as described under "Engine Mount, Replace."
51. With assistance, lower engine and transaxle with front subframe as an assembly.
52. Support engine with Rotunda floor crane positioning sling tool No. 014-00036 and Rotunda floor crane tool No. 014-00071, or equivalents, from engine lifting eyes.
53. Remove halfshafts from transaxle as described under " Front Wheel Drive Axles."
54. Remove front engine support insulators from subframe and transaxle.
55. Raise engine and transaxle assembly and remove front subframe and lift tool, then support transaxle with Rotunda transmission jack tool No. 066-00016, or equivalent.
56. Remove starter motor bolts, then the starter motor.
57. Disconnect engine control sensor wiring from transaxle at connectors, then remove engine control sensor wiring to transaxle case clips and position engine control sensor wiring aside.

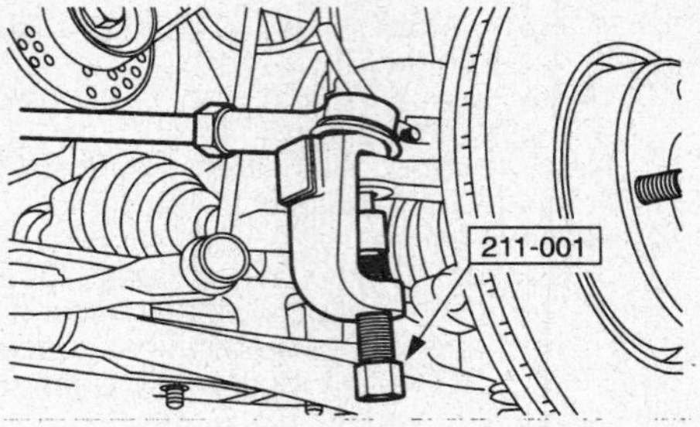

Fig. 3 Tie rod end removal. Cougar

58. Remove battery ground cable from engine to transaxle retaining stud bolt.
59. Remove transaxle to engine bolts and separate transaxle from engine.
60. **On models equipped with manual transaxle,** remove clutch pressure plate bolts, then the pressure plate and clutch disc.
61. **On all models,** reverse procedure to install, noting the following:
    a. Ensure engine and transaxle are firmly seated against front and rear insulator brackets.
    b. **Torque** righthand front engine support insulator to subframe bolt to 84 inch lbs. Ensure righthand front engine support insulator is centered in bracket and in perfect front-to-rear alignment. **Torque** insulator to subframe bolt to 30–40 ft. lbs.
    c. Fill and bleed hydraulic system as described in " Clutch & Manual Transaxle" section.
    d. Run engine and check for oil, coolant or fuel leaks, then verify proper cooling fan motor and A/C system operation.

1998–2000

CONTOUR & MYSTIQUE

1. Remove air intake box assembly, then the battery cables from retaining clips.
2. Use wire or tie strap to secure radiator.
3. Recover A/C system as outlined in "Air Conditioning " section.
4. Remove coolant and power steering reservoir caps.
5. Raise and support vehicle, then remove both front wheels.
6. Remove lower radiator splash shield and drain engine coolant into a suitable container.
7. **On models equipped with automatic transaxle,** remove drain plug and drain transaxle fluid, then disconnect lower transaxle cooler line.
8. **On all models,** disconnect power steering cooler lines and drain fluid.
9. Disconnect lower radiator hose and A/C compressor electrical connector.
10. Remove lower radiator support brackets.
11. **On models equipped with manual transaxle,** disconnect exhaust after converter pipe and remove the hanger.
12. **On models equipped with automatic transaxle,** disconnect exhaust after flex pipe and remove hanger.
13. **On all models,** remove exhaust crossover pipe.
14. Disconnect A/C condenser tube/hose and remove front heat shield.
15. Disconnect heater core hoses and drain remaining coolant.
16. Remove bolts and right side, front and rear inner splash shield.
17. Remove bolt and position bumper bracket aside.
18. **On models equipped with manual transaxle,** remove flywheel access cover.
19. **On models equipped with automatic transaxle,** remove four torque converter nuts.
20. **On all models,** remove A/C accumulator drier bolts, then the intermediate shaft pinch bolt.
21. Disconnect left and right stabilizer bar link rod and position stabilizer bar link rod out of the way.
22. Remove left and right wheel speed sensors and brake calipers.
23. Lower vehicle and remove water pump pulley cover.
24. Relieve fuel pressure as outlined in "Precautions. "
25. Remove safety clips and disconnect fuel lines using fuel line disconnect tool Nos. D87L-9280-A (3/8 inch) or D87L-9280-B (1/2 inch), or equivalent.
26. **On SVT models,** disconnect accelerator and speed control cables.
27. **On all models,** disconnect bulkhead connector.
28. Drain power steering fluid reservoir, then pull it out (push fit) and lay to one side.
29. Disconnect PCM electrical connector module.
30. Disconnect coolant expansion tank hoses.
31. Disconnect power steering line and position it out of the way.
32. **On models equipped with automatic transaxle,** remove shifter cable and position out of the way.
33. **On all models,** disconnect upper intake vacuum supply lines.
34. Disconnect upper radiator hose and heater control vacuum hoses.
35. Remove A/C accumulator tub/hose from bracket, then safety clip away from the A/C accumulator tube/hose.
36. **On models equipped with manual transaxle,** disconnect clutch slave cylinder hydraulic pipe.
37. **On all models,** raise and support vehicle.
38. Position powertrain fixture tool No. 134-00250, or equivalent under supporting plate and raise the jack.
39. Remove left and right subframe bolts.
40. Remove spark plug wiring rail from front engine mounting bracket.
41. Remove upper front engine support bracket nuts, then the rear transaxle mount nuts.
42. **On models equipped with manual transaxle,** disconnect shifter cables and position shifter bracket aside.
43. **On all models,** remove left and right strut pinch bolts,
44. Lower engine/transaxle assembly

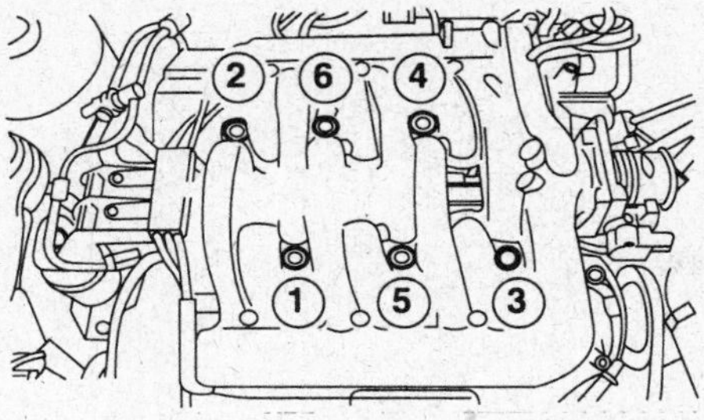

FM1069900869000X

Fig. 4 Upper intake removal sequence

from vehicle, or raise vehicle off of the assembly.

45. Remove left and right halfshaft.
46. Remove front rear roll restrictor through bolts.
47. Lift engine/transaxle assembly off of subframe with a suitable floor crane.
48. Do not let torque converter drop out of transaxle. Separate transaxle from engine.
49. Reverse procedure to install.

COUGAR

Automatic Transaxle

1. Remove front wheels, battery and hood.
2. Remove coolant hose from clip, then the water pump pulley cover bolts and cover.
3. Remove air cleaner, then drain engine coolant into a suitable container.
4. Disconnect accelerator and speed control cables from bracket.
5. Remove transaxle selector cable bolts and cable.
6. Remove bolt from bulkhead connector and disconnect electrical connector.
7. Loosen central junction box and position it to one side.
8. Disconnect ground cable and fan motor connector.
9. Remove four battery bracket bolts, battery bracket and two ground cables.
10. Relieve fuel pressure as outlined in "Precautions."
11. Disconnect fuel lines using fuel line disconnect tool Nos. D87L-9280-A (3/8 inch) or D87L-9280-B (1/2 inch), or equivalent.
12. Disconnect all heater hoses.
13. Disconnect suction accumulator electrical connector and evaporative emission hose.
14. Loosen both suspension strut nuts five turns.
15. Disconnect upper intake vacuum supply line and heater control vacuum hoses.
16. Drain power steering fluid reservoir into a suitable container, then pull reservoir out (push fit) and position it to one side.
17. Disconnect power steering lines and position to one side.
18. Disconnect PCM and ground cable.
19. Disconnect coolant expansion tank hoses, then remove the tank.
20. Remove upper transaxle cooling tube. Close off openings with plugs for transaxle opening

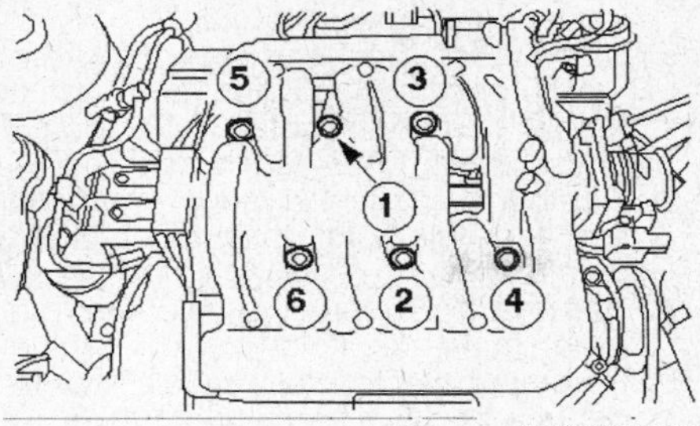

FM1069900870000X

Fig. 5 Upper intake manifold bolt tightening sequence

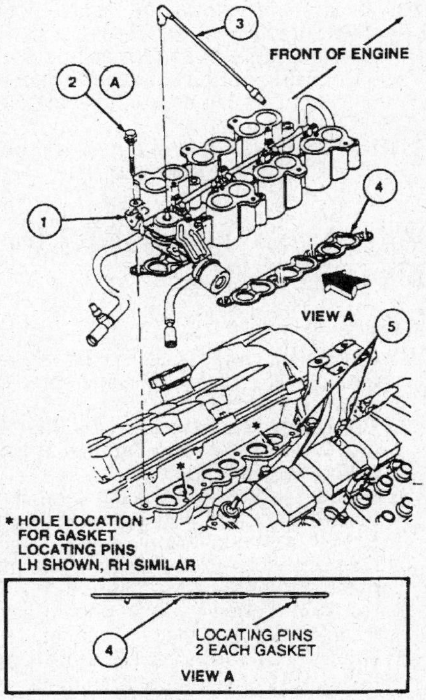

Item	Description
1	Lower Intake Manifold
2	Bolt (8 Req'd)
3	Main Emission Vacuum Control Connector
4	Intake Manifold Gasket (2 Req'd)
5	Cylinder Head (2 Req'd)
A	Tighten to 8-12 N·m (71-106 Lb-In)

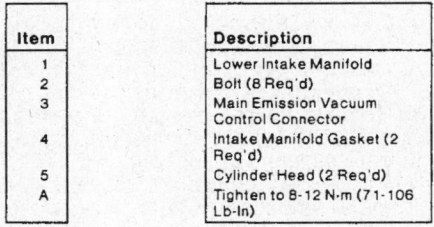

FM1059500073000X

Fig. 7 Lower intake manifold replacement

21. Remove fan, then raise and support vehicle.
22. Drain engine oil into a suitable container.
23. Disconnect heated oxygen sensor electrical connector.
24. Remove dual converter Y-pipe, then righthand fender splash shields.
25. Remove righthand control arm, then intermediate shaft bearing with the righthand front drive halfshaft from the transaxle and tie it up using cable ties.
26. Disconnect stabilizer link rod, then using the stabilizer link rod tool No. 211-001, or equivalent, **Fig. 3,** remove tie rod end.

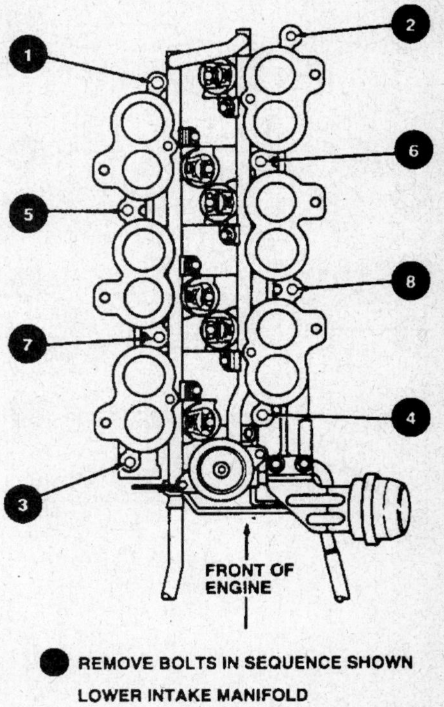

FM1059500072000X

Fig. 6 Lower intake manifold bolt removal sequence

27. Disconnect ABS wiring harness bracket from suspension strut. **Do not damage boot and ABS sensor ring.**
28. Remove lefthand front drive halfshaft from transaxle and hang it up.
29. Disconnect and remove HO2S electrical connector.
30. Remove transaxle cooling lines.
31. Remove coolant hose from the radiator.
32. Disconnect A/C compressor electrical connector.
33. Remove condenser core and tie it up.
34. Remove radiator and disconnect HO2S sensor.
35. Remove coolant pipe.
36. Remove accessory drive belt, then the compressor heat shield.
37. Remove compressor bracket bolts and secure compressor to one side with mechanics wire.
38. Remove lefthand support insulator nuts, center bolt and insulator.
39. Remove center bolt from righthand support insulator.
40. Lower vehicle.
41. Using lifting bracket tool No. T70P-6000, or equivalent, and a suitable floor crane raise engine slightly to remove pressure from support insulator.
42. Remove upper front support insulator from side member, then rear support insulator from side member.
43. Remove engine and transaxle as an assembly.
44. Separate transaxle from engine.
45. Reverse procedure to install.

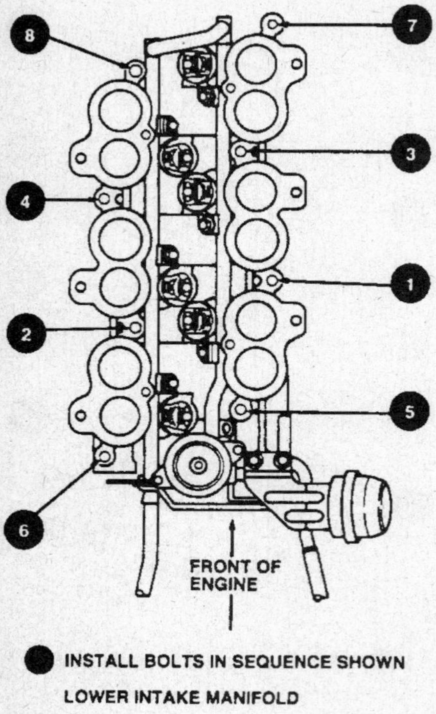

FM1059500074000X

Fig. 8 Intake manifold bolt tightening sequence

INTAKE MANIFOLD

REPLACE

UPPER

1. Remove air cleaner and water pump pulley shield.
2. Disconnect exhaust gas recirculation valve, accelerator and speed control cables, then remove accelerator cable bracket.
3. Disconnect black retainer, two vacuum supply lines from the upper intake and vacuum regulator solenoid vacuum hose.
4. Disconnect positive crankcase ventilation hose, throttle position sensor and Idle air control valve electrical connector.
5. Disconnect EGR vacuum regulator solenoid electrical connector.
6. Remove intake bolts in sequence, **Fig. 4.**
7. Reverse procedure, noting the following:
   a. New gaskets must be used, position gasket on the lower intake manifold.
   b. **Torque** bolts in sequence to 84 inch lbs., **Fig. 5.**

LOWER

1. Relieve fuel system pressure as described under " Precautions."
2. Remove upper intake manifold as outlined previously.
3. Disconnect fuel supply and return lines from fuel injection supply manifold.
4. Disconnect engine control sensor wiring from fuel injectors and valve cover studs. Position wiring aside.
5. Disconnect vacuum supply line from fuel pressure regulator and Intake Manifold Runner Control (IMRC) vacuum solenoid. Position line aside.
6. Remove fuel injection supply manifold and fuel injectors from lower intake manifold.
7. Remove IMRC vacuum solenoid from lower intake manifold.
8. Remove lower intake manifold to cylinder head bolts in sequence, **Fig. 6.**
9. Remove lower intake manifold from cylinder heads, then the intake manifold gaskets from cylinder heads, **Fig. 7.** Discard gaskets.
10. Reverse procedure to install, noting following:
    a. Verify IMRC vacuum solenoid and plate operation using hand vacuum pump. Install new intake manifold gaskets.
    b. **Torque** lower intake manifold bolts in sequence, **Fig. 8,** to 72–108 inch lbs.

EXHAUST MANIFOLD

REPLACE

RIGHTHAND

1. Disconnect engine control sensor extension wire from righthand heated oxygen sensor.
2. Raise and support vehicle, then remove alternator and bracket as described under "Electrical."
3. Remove converter outlet flange nuts, then the muffler and converter outlet gasket from converter.
4. Remove converter nuts and exhaust pipe flange hold down springs.
5. Remove converter and inlet gasket from Y pipe, then discard gasket.
6. Remove front and rear Y pipe flange fasteners from exhaust manifolds.
7. Remove stud bolt and nut retainer from oil pan, then the Y pipe.
8. Remove righthand halfshaft support bearing bracket from support bearing and cylinder block as described in "Front Wheel Drive Axles " section.
9. Remove heated oxygen sensor from righthand exhaust manifold using oxygen sensor wrench tool No. T94P-9472-A, or equivalent. If excessive force is necessary to remove sensor, lubricate sensor with penetrating oil before removal.
10. Loosen EGR valve to exhaust manifold tube from exhaust manifold.
11. Remove exhaust manifold nuts from cylinder head studs, then the manifold and manifold gasket from engine.
12. Reverse procedure to install, noting following:
    a. **Torque** exhaust manifold nuts in sequence, **Fig. 9,** to 13–16 ft. lbs.
    b. Tighten EGR valve to exhaust manifold tube nuts and heated oxygen sensor to specifications.

LEFTHAND

1. Disconnect lefthand heated oxygen sensor from engine control sensor wiring.

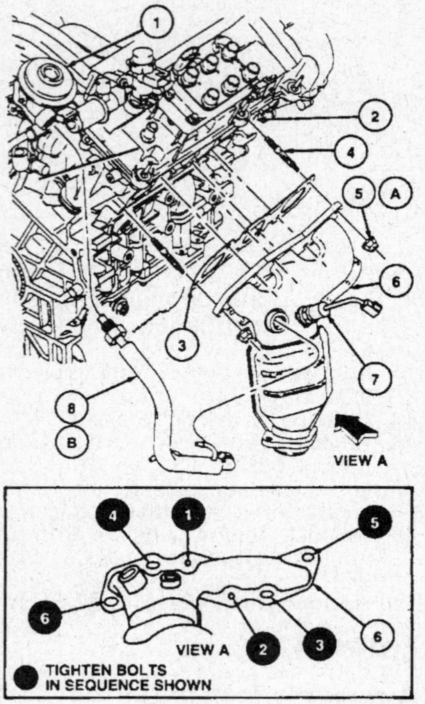

Item	Description
1	EGR Valve
2	RH Cylinder Head
3	Exhaust Manifold Gasket
4	Stud Bolt (6 Req'd)
5	Nut (6 Req'd)
6	RH Exhaust Manifold
7	Heated Oxygen Sensor
8	EGR Valve to Exhaust Manifold Tube
A	Tighten to 18-22 N·m (13-16 Lb-Ft)
B	Tighten to 35-45 N·m (26-33 Lb-Ft)

FM1079500016000X

Fig. 9 Exhaust manifold tightening sequence

2. Raise and support vehicle.
3. Remove front and rear flange pipe fasteners from exhaust manifolds, then the stud bolt and nut retainer from oil pan.
4. Remove two remaining nuts and bolts from Y-pipe outlet connection.
5. Discard exhaust converter inlet gasket, then remove Y-pipe.
6. Remove lower radiator hose tube bracket nuts from stud bolts, then the exhaust manifold nuts from lefthand cylinder head studs.
7. Position lower radiator hose tube aside, then remove lefthand exhaust manifold and gasket from engine.
8. Remove heated oxygen sensor from lefthand exhaust manifold using oxygen sensor wrench tool No. T94P-9472-A, or equivalent. If excessive force is necessary to remove sensor, lubricate sensor with penetrating oil before removal.
9. Reverse procedure to install. **Torque** lefthand exhaust manifold nuts in sequence, **Fig. 9,** to 13–16 ft. lbs.

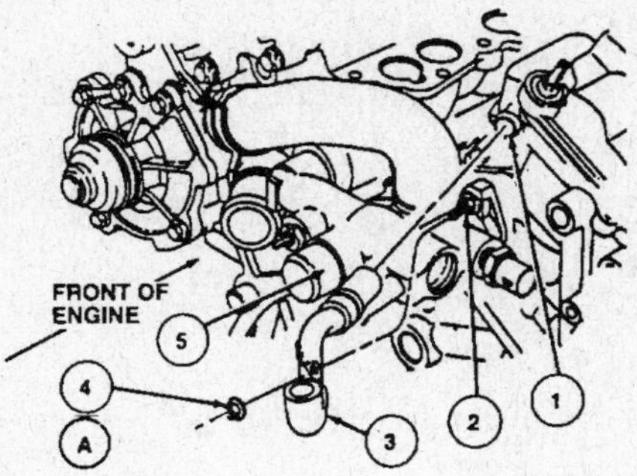

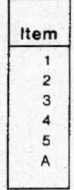

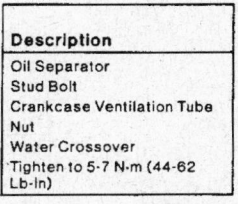

Item	Description
1	Oil Separator
2	Stud Bolt
3	Crankcase Ventilation Tube
4	Nut
5	Water Crossover
A	Tighten to 5-7 N·m (44-62 Lb-In)

FM1069500416000X

Fig. 10 Cylinder head replacement

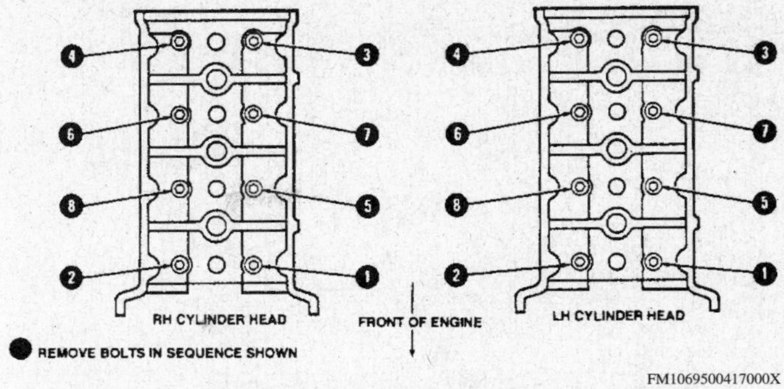

Fig. 11 Cylinder head bolt removal sequence

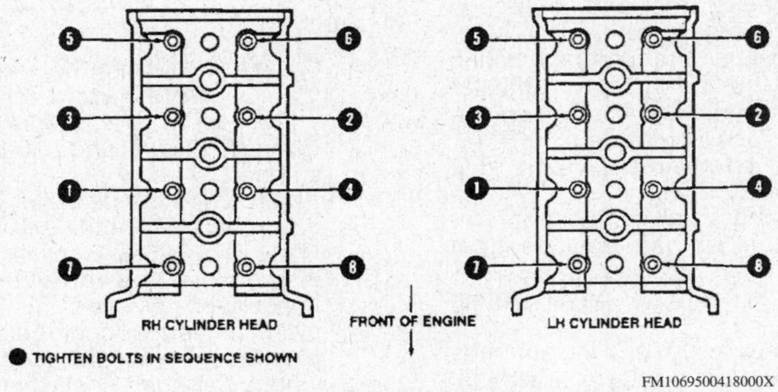

Fig. 12 Cylinder head bolt tightening sequence

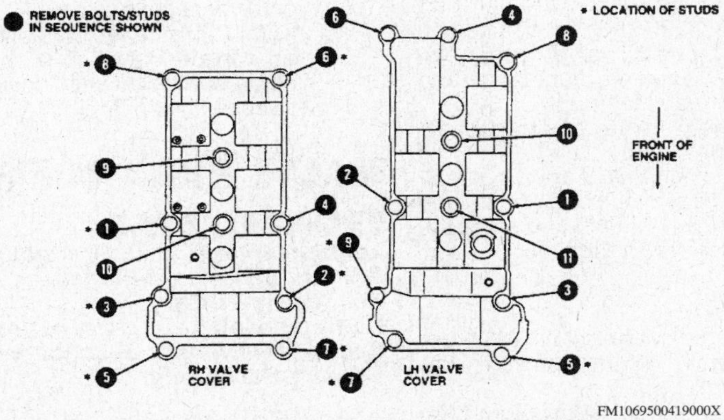

Fig. 13 Valve cover bolt removal sequence

CYLINDER HEAD

REPLACE

1. Drain engine coolant from radiator and cylinder block drain plugs.
2. Remove upper and lower intake manifolds as described under " Intake Manifold, Replace."
3. Remove oil pan as described under "Oil Pan, Replace. "
4. Remove alternator and alternator bracket as outlined in "Electrical" section.
5. Remove heated oxygen sensor from righthand exhaust manifold using oxygen sensor wrench tool No. T94P-9472-A, or equivalent. If excessive force is necessary to remove sensor, lubricate sensor with penetrating oil before removal.
6. **On lefthand cylinder head,** remove lefthand exhaust manifold as outlined under "Exhaust Manifold, Replace, " then the water pump as described under "Water Pump, Replace."
7. **On both cylinder heads,** remove front cover as described under "Front Cover, Replace."
8. Remove camshafts as described under "Camshaft, Replace, " then the valve tappets as described under "Hydraulic Valve Tappets, Replace."
9. Install upper front engine support insulator and front engine support bracket to front of engine and righthand front fender apron.
10. Remove three bar engine support tool No. D88L-6000-A, or equivalent.
11. **On righthand cylinder head,** proceed as follows:
    a. Disconnect hoses from EGR pressure sensor to exhaust manifold tube, then the pressure sensor electrical connector.
    b. Disconnect interior vacuum source hose from main emission vacuum harness, then the fuel vapor hose from PCV valve.
    c. Disconnect EGR transducer electrical connector.
    d. Remove EGR exhaust manifold tube from vehicle, then the fuel charging wiring bracket from EGR transducer bracket.
12. **On both cylinder heads,** loosen engine air cleaner tube clamps on outlet tube, then disconnect crankcase ventilation hoses and IAC valve tube from air cleaner outlet tube fitting.
13. Remove air cleaner outlet tube from MAF sensor and throttle body.
14. Disconnect engine control sensor wiring connector form MAF and IAT sensor.
15. Remove engine air cleaner to body O-ring retainer, then the air cleaner body and intake tube from bracket.
16. Remove engine air cleaner intake tube and duct.
17. Remove crankcase ventilation tube from water crossover and oil separator, **Fig. 10.**
18. Remove water crossover bolt and stud bolt from righthand cylinder head, then the crossover, position aside.
19. **On lefthand cylinder head,** remove oil level dipstick.
20. **On both cylinder heads,** remove cylinder head bolts in sequence, **Fig. 11.**
21. Remove cylinder heads. Remove righthand cylinder head with exhaust

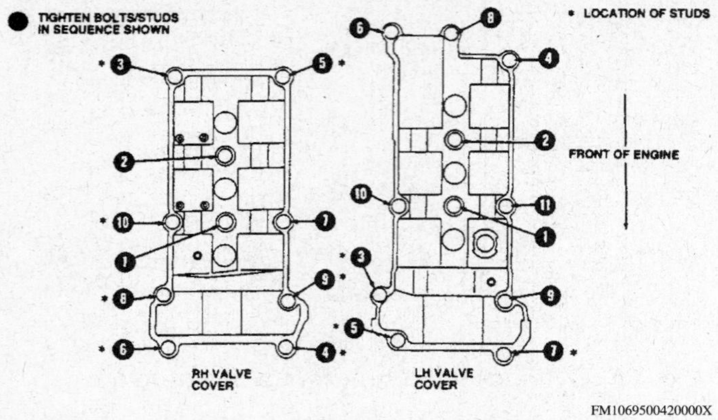

Fig. 14 Valve cover bolt tightening sequence

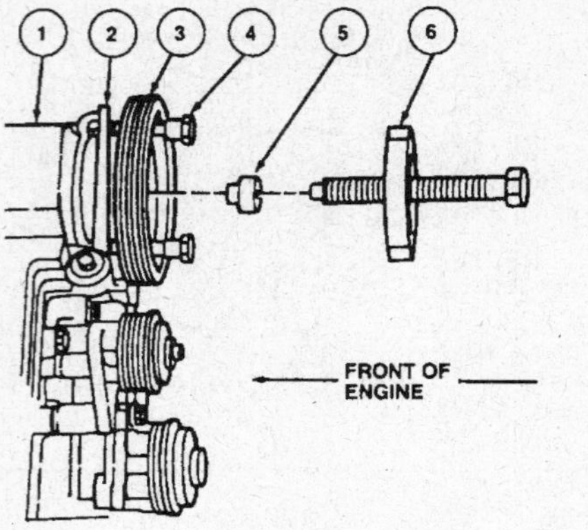

Item	Description
1	Valve Cover
2	Water Pump Pulley Remover/Replacer
3	Water Pump Drive Pulley
4	Screw (2 Req'd)
5	Shaft Protector
6	Crankshaft Damper Remover

FM1069500421000X

Fig. 15 Water pump drive pulley removal

manifold and EGR transducer bracket attached.

22. Remove exhaust manifold and EGR transducer bracket from righthand cylinder head.
23. Reverse procedure to install, noting following:
    a. Clean cylinder heads, lower intake manifold valve cover and cylinder gasket surfaces. If cylinder heads were removed to replace cylinder gasket, check flatness of cylinder heads and cylinder block gasket surfaces.
    b. Install new head gaskets on cylinder block.
    c. **Cylinder head bolts are torque-to-yield designed and must be replaced with new bolts. If reused, damage to engine may occur.**
    d. Using sequence shown in **Fig. 12,** tighten cylinder head bolts in six steps: first step, **torque** bolts 29 ft. lbs.; second step, tighten bolts an additional 90°; third step, loosen bolts one full turn; fourth step, **torque** bolts to 29 ft. lbs.; fifth step, tighten bolts an additional 90°; sixth step, tighten bolts an additional 90.°
    e. Inspect water crossover O-rings for wear or damage.
    f. Lubricate water crossover O-rings with specified engine coolant.

VALVE COVER

REPLACE

RIGHTHAND

1. Remove upper intake manifold as described under " Intake Manifold, Replace."
2. Remove ignition wires from ignition coils and spark plugs.
3. Disconnect engine control sensor wiring from ignition coil and radio ignition interference capacitor.
4. Remove EGR vacuum regulator control from upper intake manifold.
5. Disconnect ignition wires by squeezing locking tabs and twisting while pulling upward.
6. Remove ignition coil attaching bolts, then the ignition coil.
7. Remove radio ignition interference capacitor, then disconnect coil ground wire.
8. Remove crankcase ventilation tube from righthand valve cover.
9. Remove fuel charging wiring retainer and inline connector wiring bracket nuts and bracket from righthand valve cover stud bolts. Position bracket and fuel charging wiring aside.
10. Remove engine control sensor wiring nuts, then the wiring from righthand valve cover stud bolts. Position engine control sensor wiring aside.
11. Loosen valve cover bolts and stud bolts in sequence, **Fig. 13.**
12. Carefully remove valve cover from cylinder head, then the gaskets from cover.
13. Reverse procedure to install, noting following:
    a. Clean valve cover sealing surfaces using shop towel and suitable metal cleaner.
    b. Apply .31 inch diameter bead of black silicone rubber sealant, part No. F4AZ-19562-B, or equivalent, at two places on valve cover sealing surfaces where front cover and cylinder heads contact.
    c. Install new valve cover gaskets onto valve cover.
    d. Within six minutes of applying sealer, **torque** valve cover bolts and studs to 72–108 inch lbs. using sequence shown in **Figs. 14.**

LEFTHAND

1. Remove upper intake manifold as described under " Intake Manifold, Replace."
2. Remove crankcase ventilation tube from lefthand valve cover, then fuel charging wiring brackets from lefthand valve cover stud bolts. Position fuel charging wiring aside.
3. Remove ignition wires from spark plugs and valve cover, then loosen valve cover bolts and stud bolts in sequence, **Fig. 13.**
4. Carefully remove valve cover from lefthand cylinder head, then gaskets from cover.
5. Reverse procedure to install, noting following:
    a. Clean valve cover sealing surfaces using shop towel and suitable metal cleaner.
    b. Apply .31 inch diameter bead of black silicone rubber sealant, part No. F4AZ-19562-B, or equivalent, at two places on valve cover sealing surfaces where front cover and cylinder heads contact and two places on rear of cylinder head where camshaft seal retainer contacts cylinder head.
    c. Install new valve cover gaskets onto valve cover.
    d. Within six minutes of applying sealer, **torque** valve cover bolts and studs to 72–108 inch lbs. using sequence shown in **Fig. 14.**

VALVE ARRANGEMENT

FRONT TO REAR

Lefthand Intake: ....Secondary-Primary-Secondary-Primary-Secondary-Primary.
Righthand Intake: ....Primary-Secondary-Primary-Secondary-Primary-Secondary.

CAMSHAFT LOBE LIFT SPECIFICATIONS

Camshaft lobe lift for primary and secondary intake and exhaust is .188 inch with zero allowable lobe lift loss.

VALVE CLEARANCE SPECIFICATIONS

Valve clearance is hydraulically controlled and not adjustable.

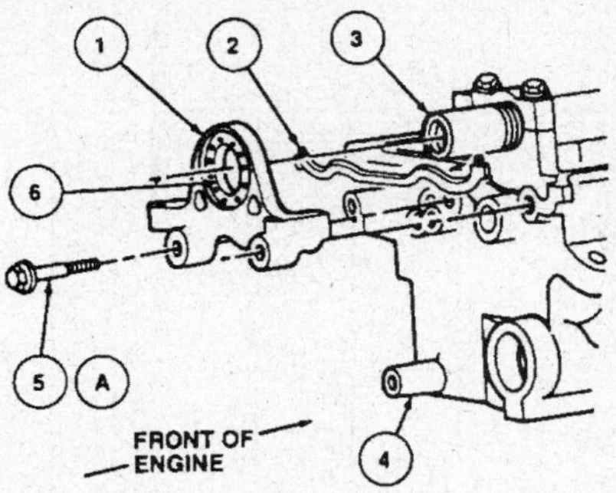

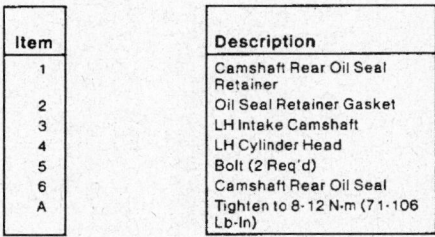

Item	Description
1	Camshaft Rear Oil Seal Retainer
2	Oil Seal Retainer Gasket
3	LH Intake Camshaft
4	LH Cylinder Head
5	Bolt (2 Req'd)
6	Camshaft Rear Oil Seal
A	Tighten to 8-12 N·m (71-106 Lb-In)

FM1069500422000X

Fig. 16 Rear camshaft rear oil seal retainer removal

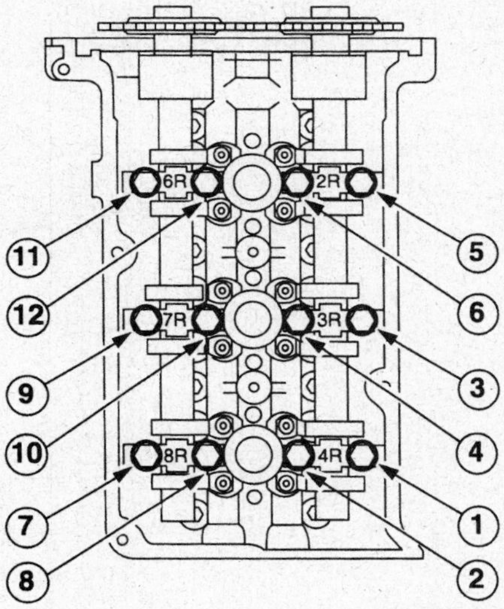

FM1069900871000X

Fig. 18 Right camshaft journal cap bolt removal sequence. 1998–2000

VALVE ADJUSTMENT

Valve clearance is hydraulically controlled and not adjustable.

CAMSHAFT FOLLOWERS

REPLACE

1. Remove valve covers and gaskets as described under "Valve Cover, Replace."
2. Remove crankshaft pulley bolt from front of crankshaft, then rotate crankshaft to position crankshaft keyway to 11 o'clock position and No. 1 cylinder at Top Dead Center (TDC).

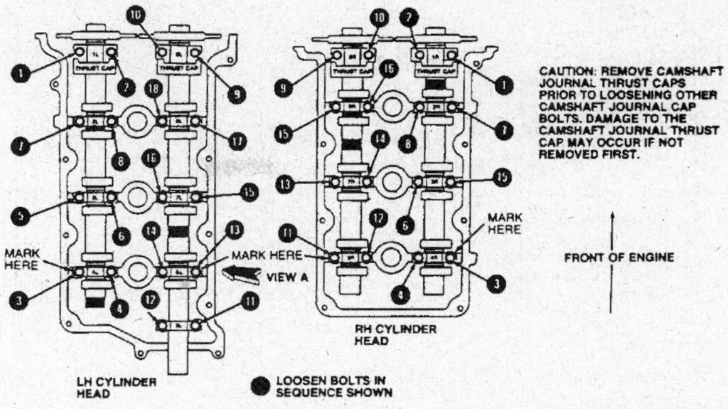

FM1069500423000X

Fig. 17 Camshaft journal cap bolt removal sequence. 1997

3. Verify alignment arrows on camshafts are aligned. If arrows are not aligned, rotate crankshaft one complete revolution.
4. Rotate crankshaft to position crankshaft keyway to three o'clock location. This will position righthand cylinder head camshafts to neutral position (base circle).
5. Rotate water pump drive belt tensioner clockwise to release water pump drive belt tension, remove water pump drive belt, then carefully release drive belt tensioner.
6. Remove battery, then using crankshaft damper remover tool No. T58P-6316-D and water pump pulley remover/replacer tool No. T94P-6312-AH, or equivalents, with shaft protector and screw, remove water pump drive pulley from lefthand intake camshaft, **Fig. 15.**
7. Remove camshaft rear oil seal bolts, then the retainer and gasket from lefthand cylinder head, **Fig. 16.**
8. Remove cylinder head camshaft journal thrust cap bolts and thrust caps from righthand cylinder head. **Remove cylinder head camshaft journal thrust caps first to prevent damage to cylinder head camshaft journal thrust caps. Cylinder head camshaft journal caps are numbered to ensure they are assembled in their original position. Do not mix camshaft journal caps.**
9. Loosen remaining righthand cylinder head camshaft journal cap bolts seven to eight turns in sequence, **Figs. 17 through 19,** in several passes (approximately one to two turns each pass) to allow camshafts to be raised from righthand cylinder head. Do not completely remove bolts.
10. With righthand cylinder head camshaft journal caps and camshafts loose on righthand cylinder head, remove rocker arms. **If camshaft followers are to be reused, mark position or rocker arms to ensure they are assembled in original positions.**
11. Rotate crankshaft two revolutions and position crankshaft keyway to 11 o'clock location. This will position lefthand cylinder head camshafts to neutral position (base circle).
12. Verify alignment arrows on camshafts are aligned.
13. Remove cylinder head camshaft journal thrust cap bolts and thrust caps from lefthand cylinder head. **Remove cylinder head camshaft journal thrust caps first to prevent damage to cylinder head camshaft journal thrust caps. Cylinder head camshaft journal caps are numbered to ensure they are assembled in their original position. Do not mix camshaft journal caps.**
14. Loosen remaining lefthand cylinder head camshaft journal cap bolts seven to eight turns in sequence, **Figs. 17 through19,** in several passes (approximately one to two turns each pass) to allow camshafts to be raised from lefthand cylinder head. Do not remove bolts completely.
15. With lefthand cylinder head camshaft journal caps and camshafts loose on lefthand cylinder head, remove rocker arms. **If camshaft followers are to be reused, mark positions of rocker**

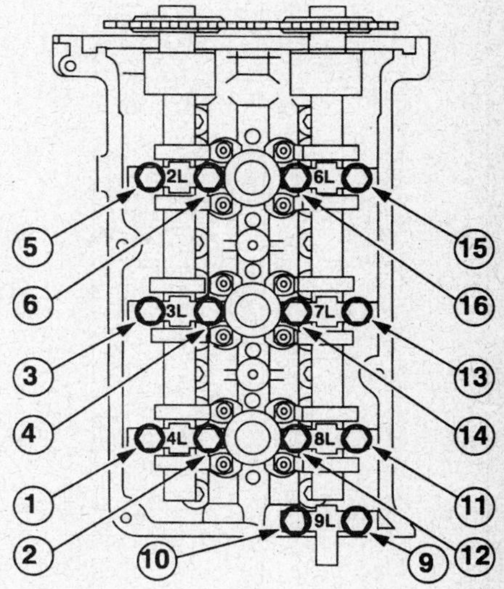

FM1069900872000X

Fig. 19 Left camshaft journal cap bolt removal sequence. 1998–2000

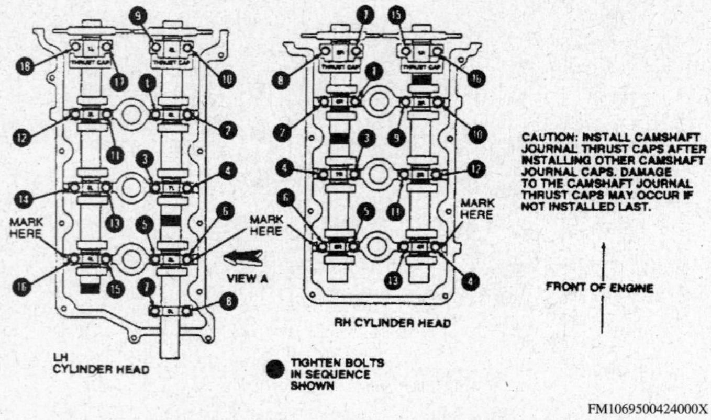

Fig. 20 Camshaft journal cap bolt tightening sequence. 1997

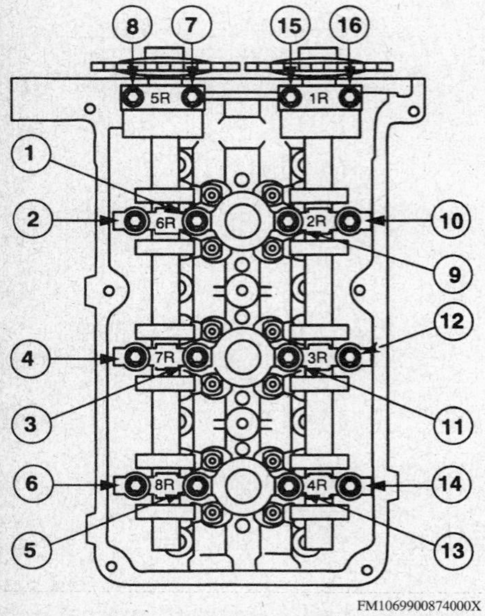

Fig. 22 Righthand camshaft journal cap bolt tighten sequence. 1998–2000

arms to ensure they are assembled in original positions.

16. Reverse procedure to install, noting the following:
    a. **Ensure camshaft followers are installed in original locations. Crankshaft keyway must be at 11 o'clock position before installing followers. Failure to do so may lead to engine damage.**
    b. Lubricate rocker arms with suitable engine assembly lubricant, then install rocker arms onto lefthand cylinder head under camshafts.
    c. With lefthand cylinder head rocker arms installed under camshafts, **torque** lefthand cylinder head camshaft journal cap bolts in sequence, **Figs. 17 through21,** in several passes, to 6–9 ft. lbs.
    d. With righthand cylinder head rocker arms installed under camshafts, **torque** righthand cylinder head camshaft journal cap bolts in sequence, **Figs. 20 and 22,** in several passes, to 6–9 ft. lbs. Install cylinder head camshaft journal thrust cap last to ensure damage to No. 1 journal cap does not occur.
    e. Using power steering pump pulley replacer tool No. T91P-3A733-A, screw tool No. T94P-6312-AH and replacer cup tool No. T94P-6312-AH, or equivalents, install water pump drive pulley on lefthand intake camshaft, **Fig. 23.**
    f. Tighten crankshaft pulley bolt in four steps: first step, **torque** bolt to 89 ft. lbs.; second step, loosen bolt one full turn; third step, **torque** bolt to 35–39 ft. lbs.; fourth step, tighten an additional 85–95.°

HYDRAULIC LASH ADJUSTER

REPLACE

If valve tappets and camshaft followers are to be reused, mark position of camshaft followers and valve tappets to ensure they are assembled in original positions.

1. Remove camshaft followers as described under "Camshaft Followers, Replace."
2. Remove valve tappets from cylinder heads.
3. Lubricate valve tappets with suitable engine assembly lubricant, then install tappets into cylinder heads. Ensure valve tappets are installed in original positions.
4. Install rocker arms as described under "Camshaft Followers, Replace."

FRONT COVER

REPLACE

1997

1. Remove lefthand and righthand valve covers as described under "Valve Cover, Replace."
2. Install three bar engine support tool No. D88L-6000-A, or equivalent, onto engine lifting eyes and support engine.
3. Remove power steering pressure hose bracket bolt from upper front engine support bracket.

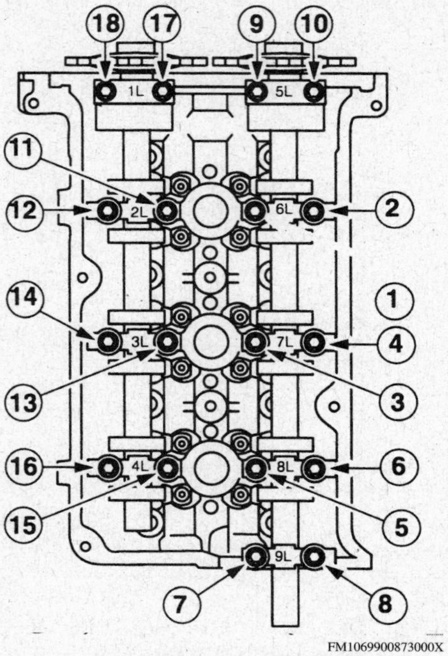

Fig. 21 Lefthand camshaft journal cap bolt tightening sequence. 1998–2000

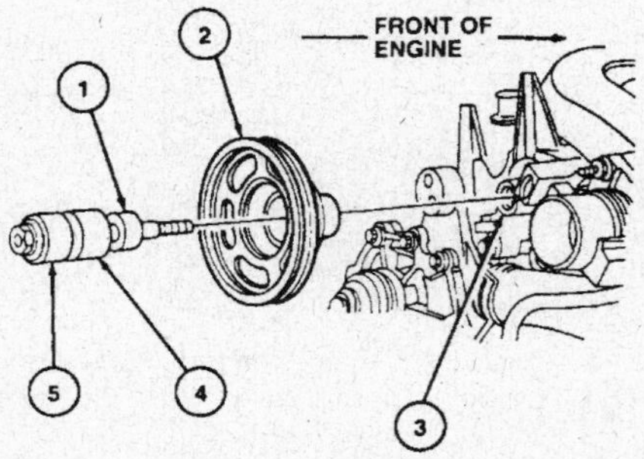

Item	Description
1	Screw
2	Water Pump Drive Pulley
3	LH Intake Camshaft
4	Replacer Cup
5	Power Steering Pump Pulley Replacer

FM1069500425000X

Fig. 23 Water pump drive pulley installation

4. Disconnect power steering pressure hose from power steering pump, then position hose aside.
5. Remove upper front engine support bracket nuts and front engine support bracket from engine and upper front engine support insulator as described under "Engine Mount, Replace." Mark location of upper front engine support bracket before removal.
6. Disconnect low coolant level sensor connector from wire harness.

7. Remove coolant recovery reservoir retainers and position reservoir aside.
8. Remove front engine support insulator as described under " Engine Mount, Replace."
9. Set coolant recovery reservoir into position, then disconnect fuel charging wiring at three connectors on inline connector bracket on front of righthand cylinder head. Position wiring aside.
10. Loosen power steering pump pulley bolts. Do not completely remove bolts.
11. Remove drive belt as described under "Serpentine Drive Belt."
12. Remove power steering pump pulley from pump.
13. Remove power steering pump and pump support attaching nuts and bolts, then the pump and pump support.
14. Raise and support vehicle, then remove oil pan drain plug and drain engine oil.
15. Remove through bolt for front engine support insulators as described under "Engine Mount, Replace."
16. Lower vehicle, then raise engine to gain access for oil pan removal.
17. Position alternator aside, then remove alternator bracket from engine.
18. Remove crankshaft pulley, then disconnect fuel charging wiring from CKP and CMP sensor electrical connectors.
19. Remove oil pan as described under "Oil Pan, Replace. "
20. **On models with air conditioning,** loosen A/C compressor bolts and position compressor aside to gain access to front cover bolt.
21. **On all models,** lower vehicle, then remove fuel charging wiring bracket retainers and A/C hose bracket from front cover stud bolts. Position fuel charging wiring aside.
22. Remove front cover bolts in sequence, **Fig. 24.** It may be necessary to raise and lower vehicle several times to follow bolt removal sequence.
23. Remove front cover and gaskets from vehicle. Discard gaskets.
24. Reverse procedure to install, noting the following:
    a. Clean front cover to cylinder block and cylinder head sealing surfaces.
    b. Apply .118 inch diameter bead, approximately .472 inch long of black silicone rubber part No. F4AZ-19562-B, or equivalent to cylinder block in six locations, **Fig. 25.**
    c. Install front cover bolts and stud bolts in proper locations and sequence, **Fig. 26.** Tighten cover bolts ¼ turn after cover contacts cylinder block and cylinder heads. **Install bolts and stud bolts no more than six minutes after applying sealer.**
    d. **Torque** front cover bolts and stud bolts in sequence, **Fig. 25,** to 15–22 ft. lbs.

1998–2000

1. Remove lefthand and righthand valve covers as described under "Valve Cover, Replace."
2. Remove oil pan as described under "Oil Pan, Replace. "
3. Remove alternator and power steering pump.
4. Disconnect camshaft and crankshaft position sensor electrical connectors and remove.
5. Remove front cover bolts and studs in sequence, **Fig. 27,** then the cover.
6. Reverse procedure to install, noting the following:
    a. Prior to applying sealer clean front cover to cylinder block and cylinder head sealing surfaces with metal surface cleaner F4AZ-19A536-RA.
    b. Engine front cover must be installed in a two step sequence.
    c. Install bolts and studs in the indicated sequence, **Fig. 26** tighten in two steps. First tighten seven bolts and studs one quarter turn (90°) after engine front cover contacts cylinder block and cylinder heads.
    d. Second, install remaining engine front cover bolts and studs and **torque** in sequence, **Fig. 28** to 18 ft. lbs.
    e. Lubricate new O-rings with engine oil before installation.
    f. Install position sensors and bolts.

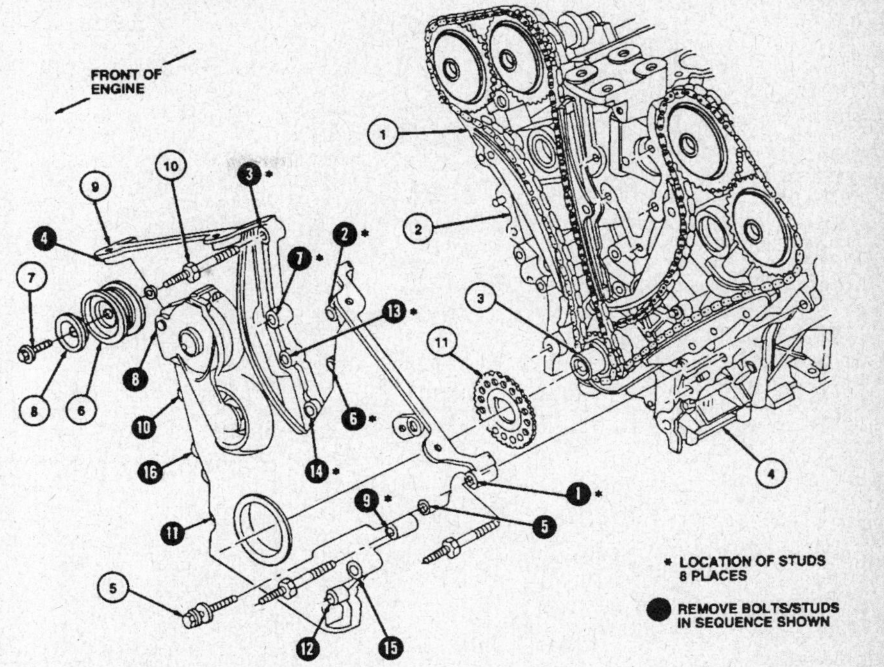

Item	Description	Item	Description
1	Cylinder Head, RH	6	Drive Belt Idler Pulley
2	Upper Cylinder Block	7	Bolt
3	Crankshaft	8	Dust Cover
4	Lower Cylinder Block	9	Engine Front Cover
5	Bolt (8 Req'd)	10	Stud Bolt (8 Req'd)
		11	Crankshaft Position Sensor Pulse Ring

FM1069500427000X

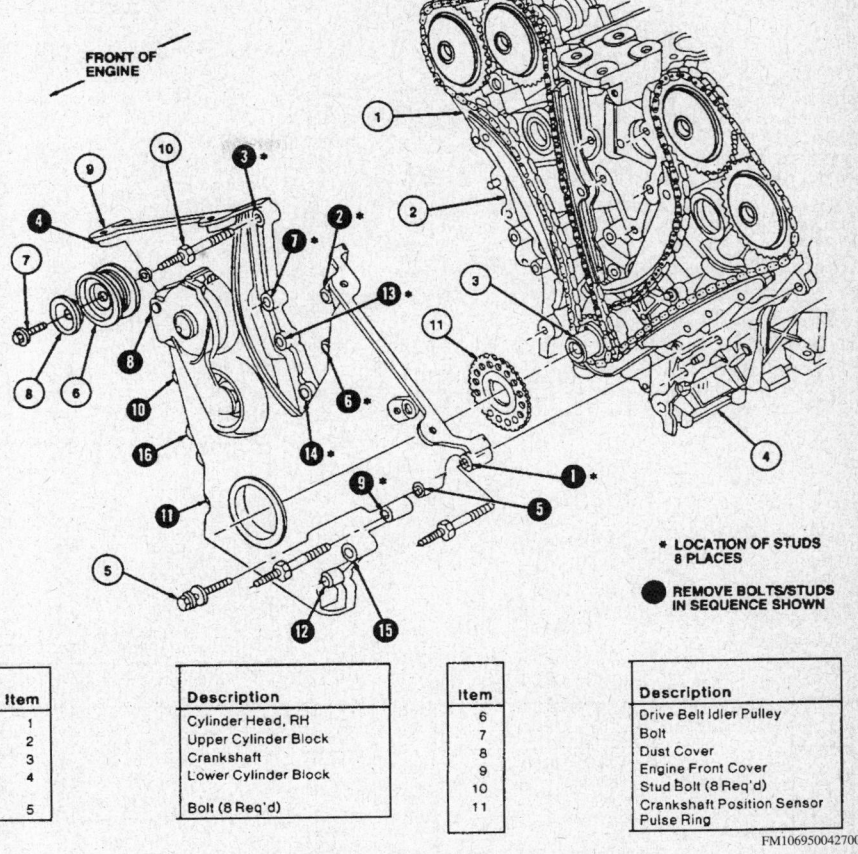

Fig. 24 Front cover removal. 1997

TIMING CHAIN

REPLACE

1997

1. Remove front cover as described under "Front Cover, Replace."
2. Rotate crankshaft keyway to 11 o'clock location to position crankshaft at Top Dead Center (TDC) No. 1 cylinder.
3. Verify alignment arrows on camshafts are aligned. If arrows are not aligned, rotate crankshaft one complete revolution.
4. Rotate crankshaft to position crankshaft keyway to 3 o'clock position. This will position righthand cylinder head camshafts to neutral position (base circle).
5. Remove righthand timing chain tensioner bolts, then the tensioner.
6. Remove cylinder head camshaft journal thrust cap bolts, thrust caps, camshaft journal bolts and rocker arms from righthand cylinder head as outlined under "Rocker Arms, Replace." If valve tappets and roller rocker arms are to be reused, mark position of rocker arms and valve tappets to ensure

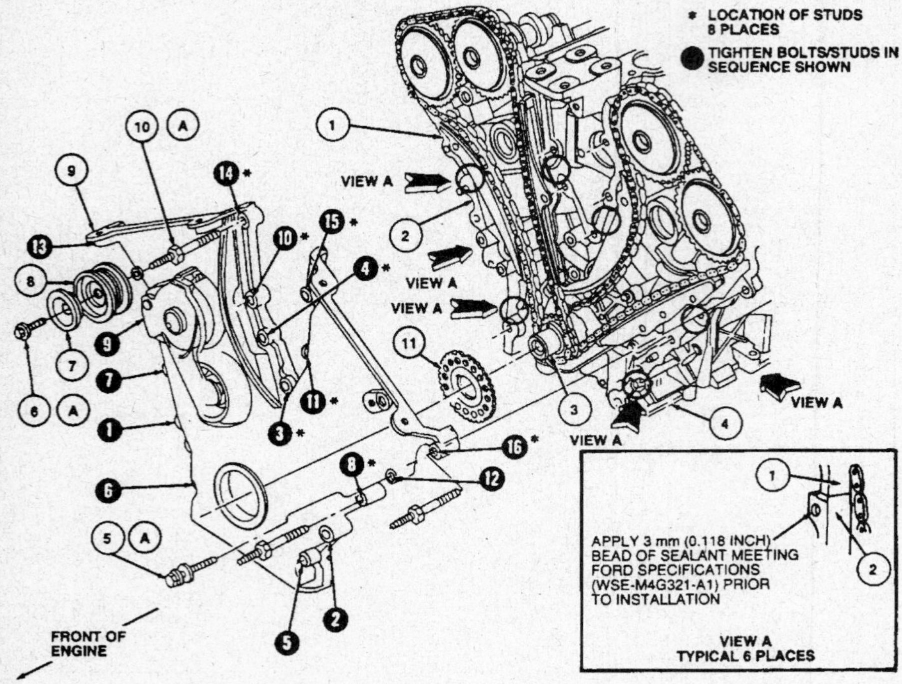

Item	Description	Item	Description
1	Cylinder Head, RH	8	Drive Belt Idler Pulley
2	Cylinder Block	9	Engine Front Cover
3	Crankshaft	10	Stud Bolt (8 Req'd)
4	Cylinder Block	11	Crankshaft Position Sensor Pulse Ring
5	Bolt (8 Req'd)		
6	Bolt	A	Tighten to 20-30 N·m (15-22 Lb-Ft)
7	Dust Cover		

FM1069500429000X

Fig. 25 Front cover installation. 1997

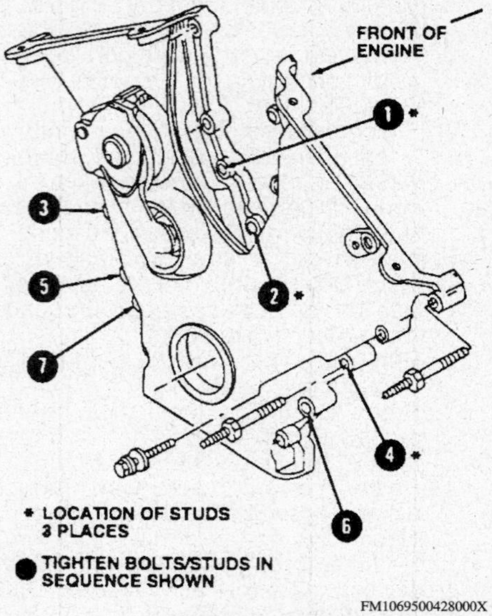

FM1069500428000X

Fig. 26 Front cover bolt & stud bolt installation sequence

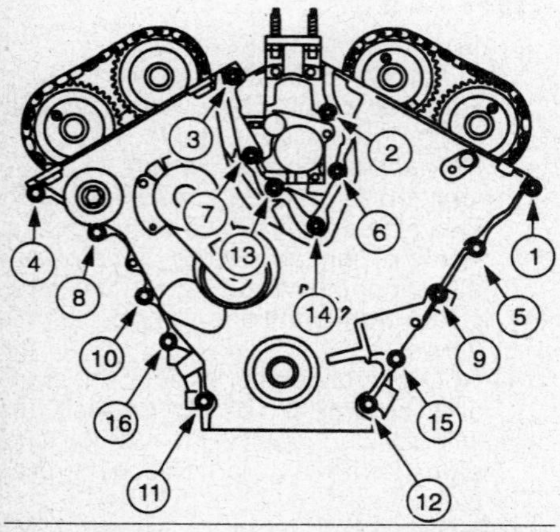

FM1069900875000X

Fig. 27 Front engine cover bolt removal sequence. 1998–2000

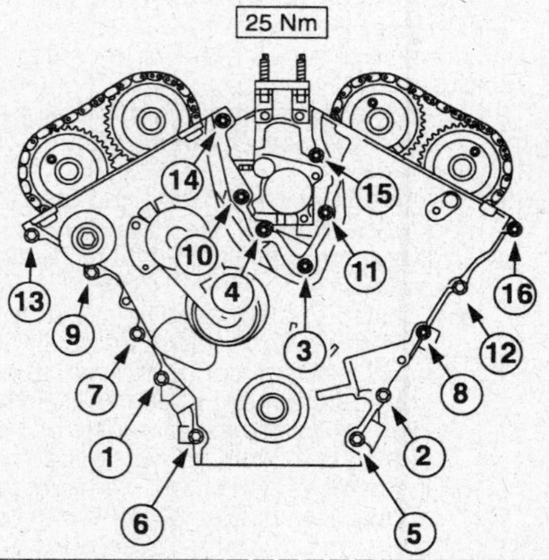

FM1069900876000X

Fig. 28 Front engine cover tightening sequence. 1998–2000

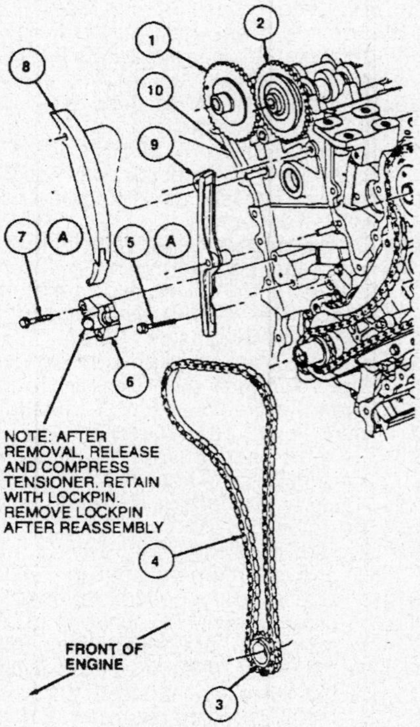

Item	Part Number	Description
1	6250	RH Exhaust Camshaft
2	6250	RH Intake Camshaft
3		RH Timing Chain Crankshaft Sprocket
4		RH Timing Chain
5		Bolt (2 Req'd)
6		Timing Chain Tensioner
7		Bolt (2 Req'd)
8		Timing Chain Tensioner Arm
9		Timing Chain Guide
10		RH Cylinder Head
A		Tighten to 20-30 N·m (15-22 Lb-Ft)

FM1069500426000X

Fig. 29 Timing chain replacement. 1997

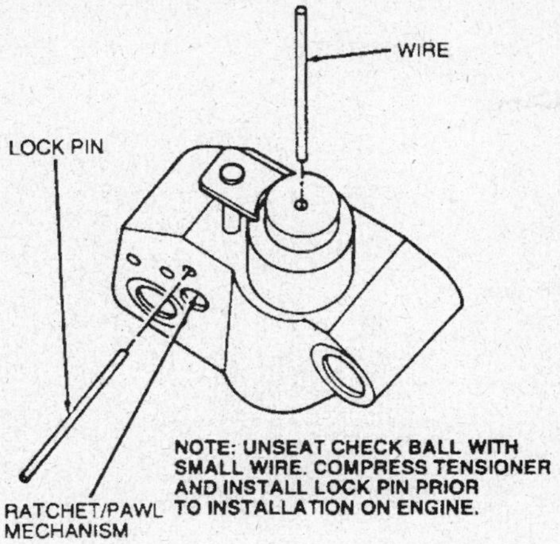

FM1069500430000X

Fig. 30 Timing chain tensioner compression. 1997

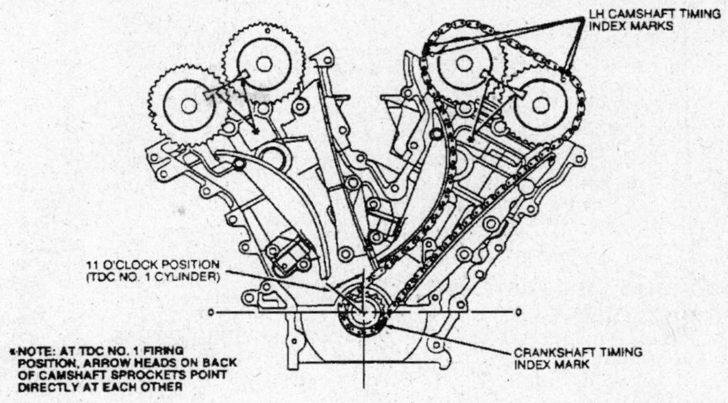

FM1069500431000X

Fig. 31 Lefthand timing chain index mark alignment. 1997

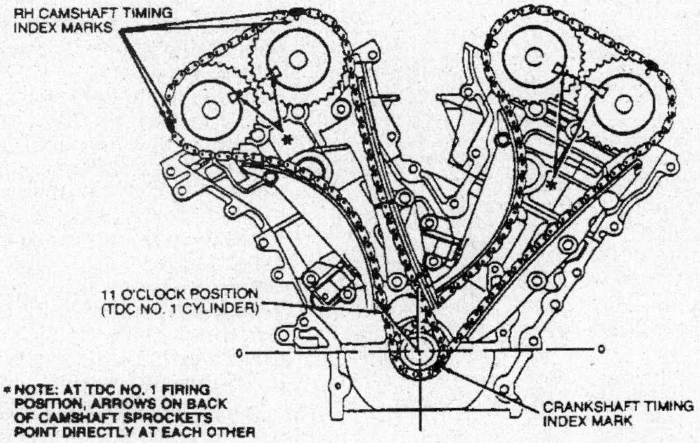

FM1069500432000X

Fig. 32 Righthand timing chain index mark alignment. 1997

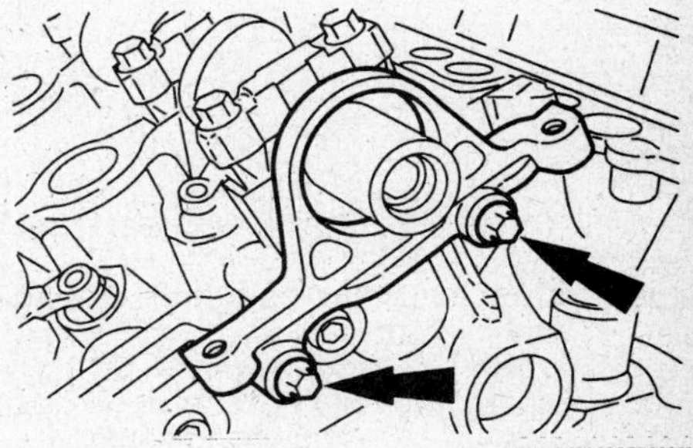

FM1069900877000X

Fig. 33 Camshaft oil seal removal. 1998–2000

they are assembled in original positions.

7. Remove righthand timing chain tensioner arm and righthand timing chain. **If righthand tensioner arm and chain guide are to be reused, mark position of tensioner arm and chain guide to ensure they are assembled in original positions.**
8. Remove righthand timing chain guide bolts, then the guide, **Fig. 29.**
9. Remove righthand timing chain crankshaft sprocket, then rotate crankshaft two revolutions and position crankshaft keyway to 11 o'clock location. This will position lefthand cylinder head camshafts to neutral position (base circle).
10. Remove cylinder head camshaft journal thrust cap bolts, thrust caps and rocker arm from lefthand cylinder head as outlined under " Rocker Arms, Replace." If valve tappets and roller rocker arms are to be reused, mark position of rocker arms and valve tappets to ensure they are assembled in original positions.
11. Verify alignment arrows on camshaft are aligned, then remove lefthand

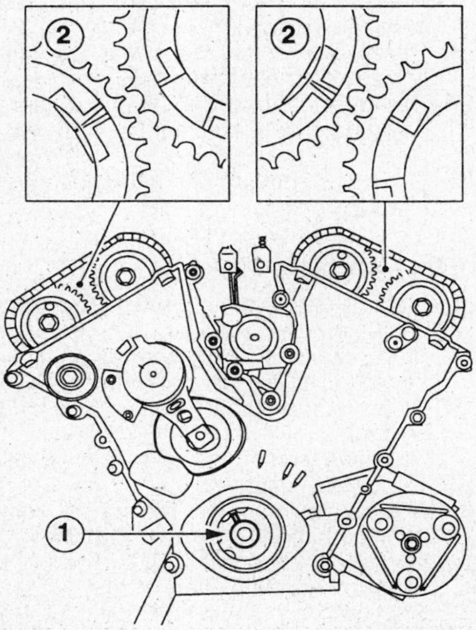

FM1139700545000A

Fig. 34 Crankshaft & camshaft alignment. 1998–2000

timing chain tensioner bolts and tensioner.

12. Remove lefthand timing chain tensioner arm and lefthand timing chain. **If lefthand tensioner arm and chain guide are to be reused, mark position of tensioner arm and chain guide to ensure they are assembled in original positions.**
13. Remove lefthand timing chain guide bolts, then the guide.
14. Remove lefthand timing chain crankshaft sprocket.
15. Using small screwdriver, release timing chain tensioner ratchet/pawl mechanism through access hole in tensioners.
16. Compress tensioner rack and piston into tensioner housing by inserting small wire into top of piston and gently unseat oil check ball, then compress tensioners by hand.
17. With tensioner rack and piston compressed, install .06 inch drill bit or wire into small hole above ratchet, engaging lock groove in rack of timing chain tensioners, **Fig. 30. Timing tensioners must be installed onto engine while compressed and locked. Failure to compress timing chain before installing may cause engine damage.**
18. Reverse procedure to install, noting the following:
    a. Ensure crankshaft keyway is at 11 o'clock location. **Crankshaft keyway must be at 11 o'clock location before assembly. If not in**

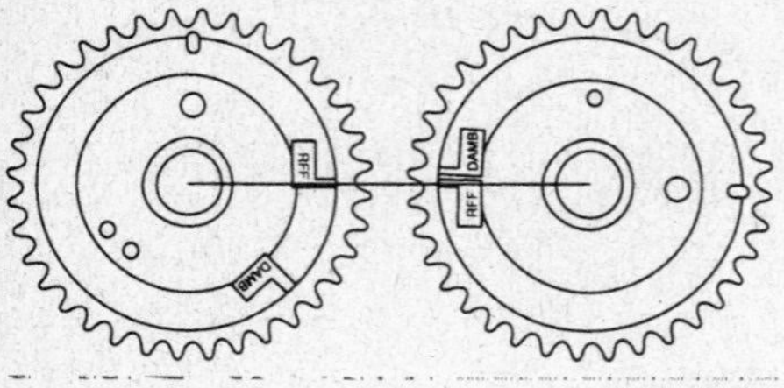

FM1069900878000X

Fig. 35 Lefthand camshaft flag alignment. 1998–2000

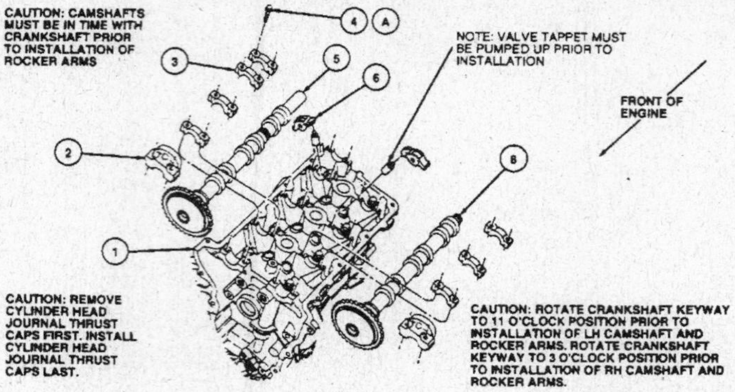

CAUTION: CAMSHAFTS MUST BE IN TIME WITH CRANKSHAFT PRIOR TO INSTALLATION OF ROCKER ARMS
NOTE: VALVE TAPPET MUST BE PUMPED UP PRIOR TO INSTALLATION
FRONT OF ENGINE
CAUTION: REMOVE CYLINDER HEAD JOURNAL THRUST CAPS FIRST. INSTALL CYLINDER HEAD JOURNAL THRUST CAPS LAST.
CAUTION: ROTATE CRANKSHAFT KEYWAY TO 11 O'CLOCK POSITION PRIOR TO INSTALLATION OF LH CAMSHAFT AND ROCKER ARMS. ROTATE CRANKSHAFT KEYWAY TO 3 O'CLOCK POSITION PRIOR TO INSTALLATION OF RH CAMSHAFT AND ROCKER ARMS.

FM1069500433010X

Fig. 36 Camshaft replacement (Part 1 of 2). 1997

Item	Description
1	Cylinder Head
2	Camshaft Journal Thrust Cap (2 Req'd)
3	Camshaft Journal Thrust Cap (7 Req'd)
4	Bolt (18 Req'd)
5	LH Intake Camshaft
6	Rocker Arm (12 Req'd Each Side)
7	Valve Tappet (12 Req'd Each Side)
8	LH Exhaust Camshaft
A	Tighten to 8-12 N·m (71-106 Lb-In)

FM1069500433020X

Fig. 36 Camshaft replacement (Part 2 of 2). 1997

this location, engine damage may result.

b. Verify alignment arrows on camshafts are aligned with each other prior to installing timing chain.
c. Verify timing index marks on lefthand timing chain are in alignment with timing index marks on lefthand crankshaft sprocket and camshaft sprockets, **Fig. 31.**
d. Verify timing index marks on righthand timing chain are in alignment with timing index marks on righthand crankshaft sprocket and camshaft sprockets, **Fig. 32.**
e. Install rocker arms as outlined under "Camshaft followers, Replace."
f. Install cylinder heads as outlined under "Cylinder Head, Replace."
g. Install front cover as outlined under "Front Cover, Replace."

1998–2000

Removal

1. Remove front cover as described under "Front Cover, Replace."
2. Remove camshaft oil seal retainer, **Fig. 33.**
3. Remove crankshaft position sensor pulse wheel, then install pulse wheel with keyway in slot.
4. Install crankshaft pulley bolt and washer and rotate crankshaft keyway clockwise to the 11 o'clock position. Roller finger follower marks on back of the camshaft sprockets must line up with one another, **Fig. 34.**
5. Rotate crankshaft clockwise to position crankshaft keyway in 3 o'clock position.
6. Mark position of all chain drive components to ensure they are assembled in their original positions.
7. Remove righthand chain tensioner and tensioner arm bolts, chain tensioner and tensioner adapter plate.
8. Remove righthand timing chain guide and timing chain.
9. Remove righthand camshafts as outlined in "Camshaft, Replace."
10. Remove righthand camshaft followers as outlined in " Camshaft Follower, Replace."
11. Rotate crankshaft clockwise two revolutions until keyway is in the 11 o'clock position.
12. Remove crankshaft pulley bolt and washer.
13. Remove lefthand chain tensioner and tensioner arm.
14. Remove lefthand timing chain fixed chain guide and timing chain.
15. Remove lefthand camshafts as outlined in "Camshaft, Replace."
16. Remove lefthand camshaft followers as outlined in " Camshaft Follower, Replace."
17. Remove righthand and lefthand timing chain sprockets.

Installation

1. Install righthand and lefthand timing chain sprocket, washer and bolt.
2. Turn crankshaft clockwise to position key to the 11 o'clock position.
3. Remove crankshaft pulley bolt and washer.
4. Lubricate camshafts with engine assembly lubricator.
5. Align timing flags on the rear of lefthand camshaft sprockets, **Fig. 35.**
6. Install lefthand chain guide and bolts (black material), then timing chain. **The colored links of timing chain and the marks on the timing sprockets must line up.**
7. Set tensioner as follows:
   a. Position timing chain tensioner in a vise with jaw protectors.
   b. During tensioner compression, do not release ratchet stem until tensioner piston is fully bottomed in its bore or damage to the ratchet stem will result.
   c. Hold timing chain tensioner ratchet lock mechanism away from the ratchet stem with a small pick.
   d. Slowly compress timing chain tensioner. **Piston should retract with minimal force. If binding occurs, reposition tensioner to eliminate side loading.**
   e. Retain piston with a paper clip. **Wire must remain in timing chain tensioner until tensioner is installed onto engine with the piston bottomed in the bore.**
8. Install lefthand tensioner arm (black material), tensioner adapter plate and timing chain tensioner.
9. Install righthand chain guide and bolts (tan material), then timing chain. **The colored links of timing chain and the marks on the timing sprockets must line up.**
10. Set tensioner as outlined in set 7.
11. Install righthand tensioner arm (tan material), tensioner adapter plate and timing chain tensioner.
12. Install lefthand camshaft as outlined in "Camshaft, Replace."
13. Install crankshaft pulley bolt and washer.
14. Rotating crankshaft counterclockwise may cause the timing chains to bind and may cause engine damage. Rotate engine clockwise to locate crankshaft keyway to 3 o'clock position.
15. Install righthand camshaft as outlined in "Camshaft, Replace."
16. Remove righthand and lefthand chain tensioner retaining wires.
17. Remove crankshaft pulley bolt and washer, then install camshaft oil seal retainer.
18. Install camshaft oil seal.
19. Install engine front cover as outlined.

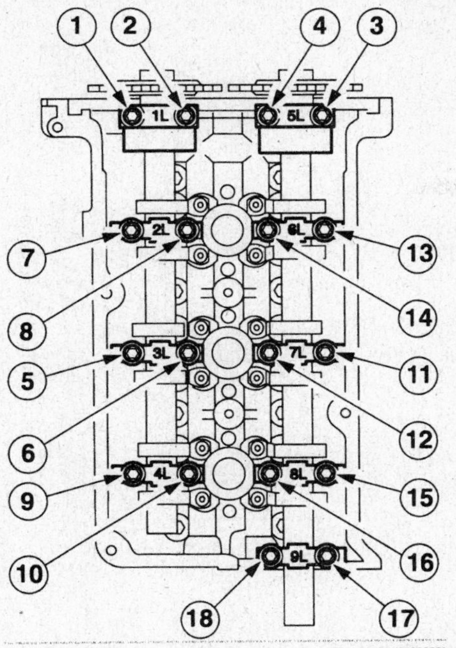

FM1069900879000X

Fig. 37 Lefthand camshaft cap bolt loosening sequence. 1998–2000

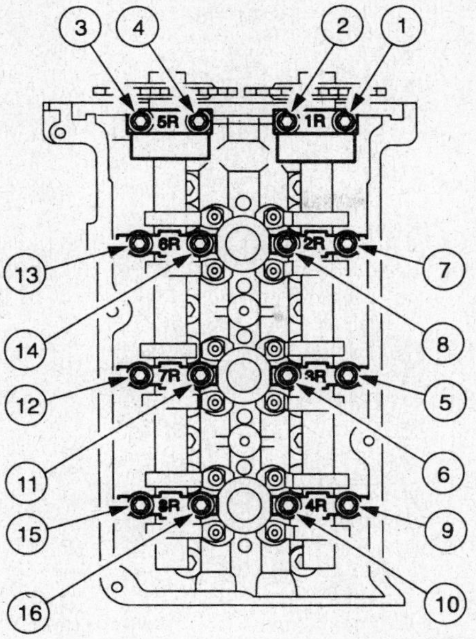

FM1069900880000X

Fig. 38 Righthand camshaft cap bolts loosening sequence. 1998–2000

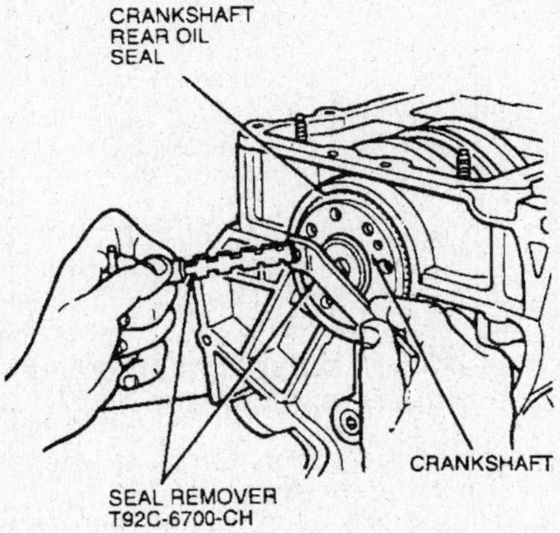

FM1069500435000X

Fig. 40 Crankshaft rear oil seal removal. 1997

TIMING CHAIN TENSIONER

REPLACE

Refer to "Timing Chain, Replace."

CAMSHAFT

REPLACE

1997

1. Remove timing chains and rocker arms as described under "Timing Chain, Replace."
2. Remove intake and exhaust camshafts from cylinder heads, **Fig. 36.**
3. Inspect camshafts and cylinder heads for wear or damage. Replace components as necessary.
4. If camshaft damper replacement is necessary, proceed as follows:
   a. Wrap righthand intake camshaft with shop towel, heater hose or similar item, then install in suitable vice with jaw protectors, or equivalent. **Do not overtighten vise or holding fixture.**
   b. If damper does not have attachment holes, drill two 3/16 inch holes, .35 inch deep, .393 inch from outside of center hub, 180° apart and tap with 6 x 1 mm thread tap, .35 inch deep.
   c. Install crankshaft damper remover tool No. T58P-6316-D, or equivalent, with two 6 x 1 x 6.9 mm bolts and pilot tool No. T94P-6312-AH2, or equivalent.
   d. Turn puller screw clockwise and remove damper.
   e. Install camshaft damper onto nose of camshaft.
   f. Install camshaft damper replacer tool No. T94P-6256-DH with water pump pulley remover/replacer screw tool No. T94P-6312-AH3 and nut from power steering pump pulley replacer tool No. T91P-3A73-A, or equivalents, onto camshaft.
   g. Install camshaft damper until fully seated against camshaft nose shoulder.
5. **Ensure camshaft keyway is at 11 o'clock position before installing. Failure to do so may lead to engine damage.**
6. Lubricate camshafts with engine assembly lubricant, then install camshafts into cylinder heads with timing marks on camshaft sprockets aligned.
7. Install timing chains and rocker arms as described under "Timing Chain, Replace."

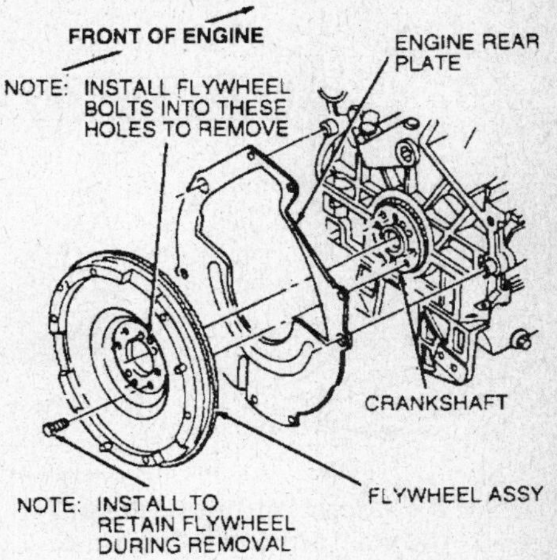

FM1069500434000X

Fig. 39 Flywheel retaining bolt installation. 1997

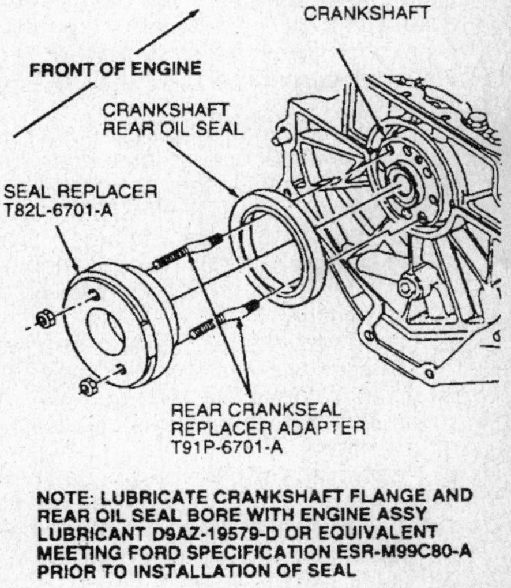

FM1069500436000X

Fig. 41 Crankshaft rear oil seal installation

1998-2000

1. Remove timing chains and rocker arms as described under " Timing Chain, Replace."
2. Remove camshaft cap bolts in sequence, **Figs. 37 and 38.**
3. Reverse procedure to install.

CRANKSHAFT SEAL

REPLACE

1. Raise and support vehicle, then remove righthand front wheel and tire assembly.
2. Remove righthand splash shield from fender apron for access to crankshaft pulley.
3. Remove accessory drive belt as described under " Serpentine Drive Belt."
4. Remove crankshaft pulley bolt and washer from crankshaft, then, using crankshaft damper remover tool No.

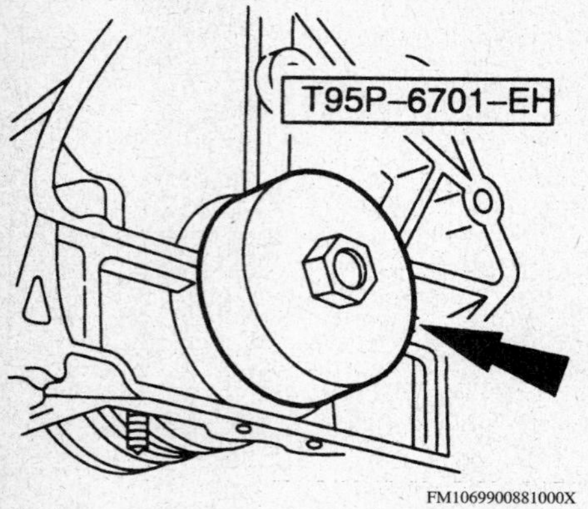

Fig. 42 Rear crankshaft seal remover tool installation. 1998–2000

T58P-6316-D, or equivalent, remove crankshaft pulley from crankshaft.

5. Using seal remover tool No. T92C-6700-CH, or equivalent, remove crankshaft front seal from front cover.
6. Reverse procedure to install, noting following:
   a. Lubricate seal sealing surfaces with suitable engine assembly lubricant, then, using crankshaft seal replacer tool No. T88T-6701-A and crankshaft damper replacer tool No. T74P-7316-B, or equivalents, install crankshaft front seal into front cover.
   b. Clean crankshaft pulley sealing surfaces with suitable metal cleaner to remove all residues which could interfere with sealer's ability to adhere.
   c. Apply black silicone rubber part No. F4AZ-19562-B, or equivalent, to front of crankshaft on inside diameter surface of pulley at keyway.
   d. Install crankshaft pulley using crankshaft damper replacer tool No. T74P-6316-B, or equivalent, and washer from bolt.
   e. **Torque** crankshaft pulley bolt to 89 ft. lbs., loosen bolt one full turn, **torque** bolt to 35–39 ft. lbs., then rotate bolt an additional 85–95.°

CRANKSHAFT REAR OIL SEAL

REPLACE

1997

1. **On models with manual transaxle,** remove transaxle and clutch assembly as outlined under "Clutch & Manual Transaxle" section.
2. **On models with automatic transaxle,** remove transaxle as outlined in "Automatic Transaxle/Transmission " section.
3. **On all models,** observe position of flywheel on crankshaft flange, then remove flywheel bolts.
4. Install one flywheel bolt loosely to retain flywheel during removal, then install flywheel bolts into holes, **Fig. 39.**

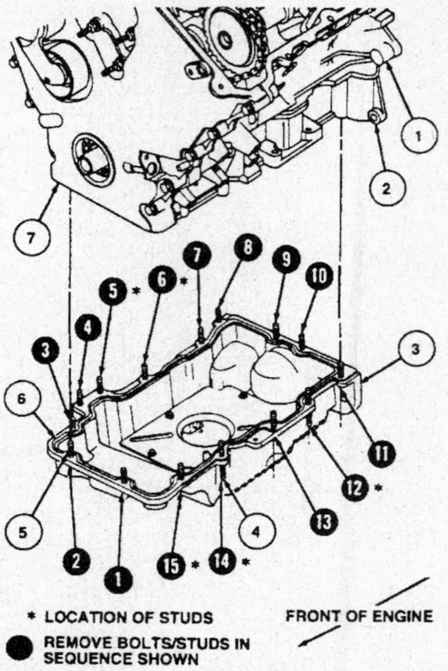

Item	Description
1	Upper Cylinder Block
2	Lower Cylinder Block
3	Oil Pan
4	Stud Bolt (5 Req'd)
5	Bolt (10 Req'd)
6	Oil Pan Gasket
7	Engine Front Cover

FM1099500072000X

Fig. 43 Oil pan bolt removal sequence. 1997

5. Tighten bolts to unseat flywheel from crankshaft, then remove bolt and flywheel from engine.
6. Using seal remover tool No. T92C-6700-CH, or equivalent, and piece of thin copper shim stock, .01 inch thick between crankshaft and seal remover tool, remove crankshaft rear oil seal from cylinder block, **Fig. 40.**
7. Reverse procedure to install, noting the following:
   a. Clean and inspect crankshaft rear oil seal sealing surfaces on crankshaft and cylinder block, then lubricate crankshaft flange and crankshaft rear oil seal bore with suitable engine assembly lubricant.
   b. Install crankshaft rear oil seal using rear main seal replacer tool No. T82L-6701-A and rear crank seal replacer adapters tool No. T91P-6701-A, or equivalents, **Fig. 41.** Alternate bolt tightening to properly seat oil seal .02–0 inch flush to rear of cylinder block.
   c. Position flywheel on crankshaft flange, then install and tighten bolts in alternating sequence to specifications.
   d. Run engine and check for leaks.

1998–2000

1. **On models with manual transaxle,** remove transaxle and clutch assembly

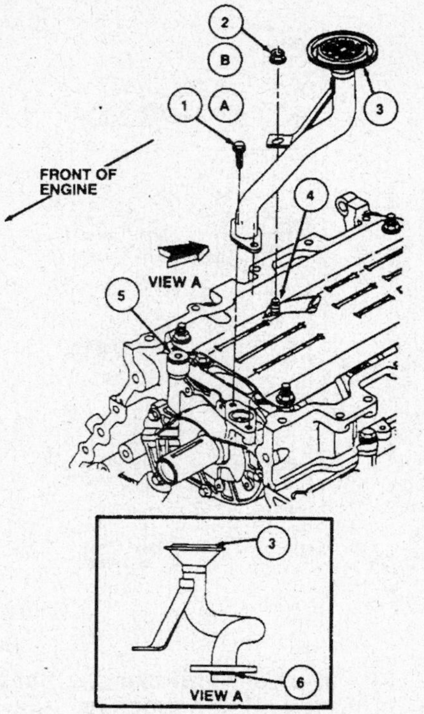

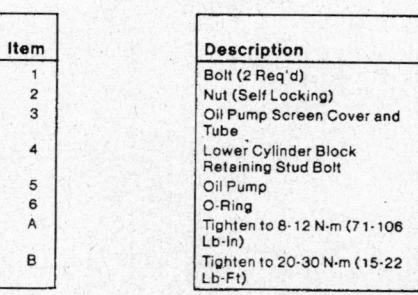

Item	Description
1	Bolt (2 Req'd)
2	Nut (Self Locking)
3	Oil Pump Screen Cover and Tube
4	Lower Cylinder Block Retaining Stud Bolt
5	Oil Pump
6	O-Ring
A	Tighten to 8-12 N·m (71-106 Lb-In)
B	Tighten to 20-30 N·m (15-22 Lb-Ft)

FM1099500073000X

Fig. 44 Oil pump screen cover and tube replacement. 1997

as outlined under "Clutch & Manual Transaxle" section.

2. **On models with automatic transaxle,** remove transaxle as outlined in "Automatic Transaxle/Transmission " section.
3. **On all models,** observe position of flywheel on crankshaft flange, then remove flywheel bolts.
4. Install rear crankshaft seal remover tool No. T95P-6701-EH, or equivalent, **Fig. 42.** Install slide hammer and remove rear crankshaft seal. **Avoid scratching or damaging the oil seal sealing surfaces on the crankshaft and cylinder block.**
5. Reverse procedure to install, noting the following:
   a. Clean and inspect crankshaft rear oil seal sealing surfaces.
   b. Lubricate crankshaft flange, crankshaft rear oil seal bore and oil seal lip with Engine Assembly Lubricant D9AZ - 19579 - D, or equivalent.
   c. Alternately tighten bolt until crankshaft rear oil seal is flush with the cylinder block, using rear main seal

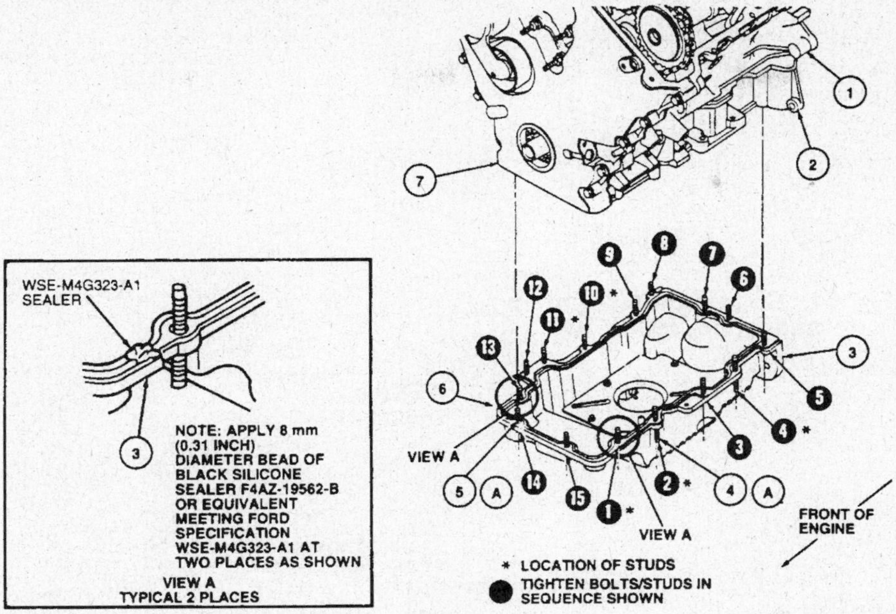

Item	Description	Item	Description
1	Upper Cylinder Block	5	Bolt (10 Req'd)
2	Lower Cylinder Block	6	Oil Pan Gasket
		7	Engine Front Cover
3	Oil Pan	A	Tighten to 20-30 N·m (15-22 Lb-Ft)
4	Stud Bolt (5 Req'd)		

FM1099500074000X

Fig. 45 Oil pan installation. 1997

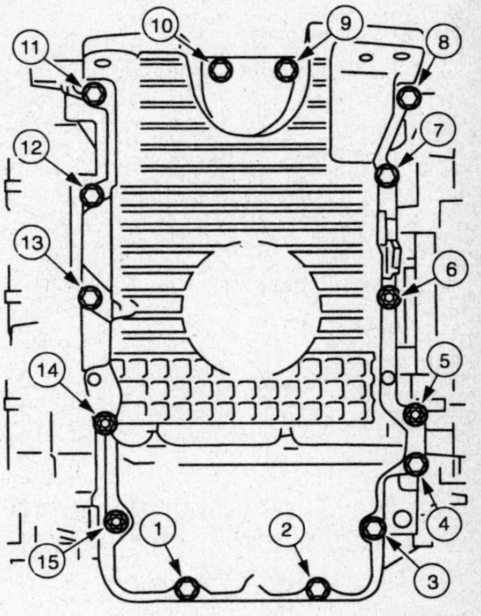

FM1069900882000X

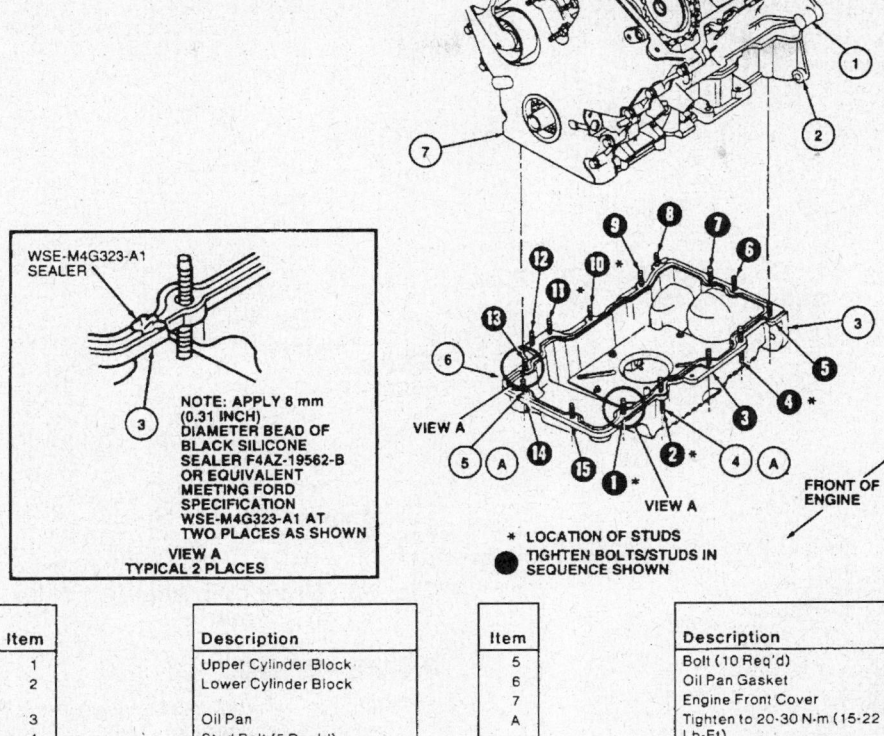

Fig. 46 Oil pan removal sequence. 1998–2000

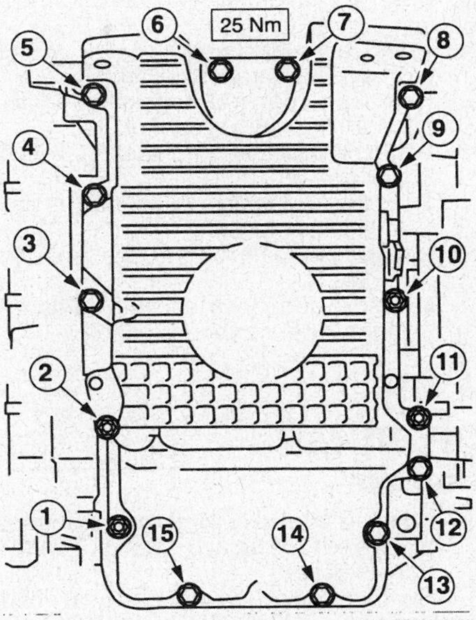

FM1069900883000X

Fig. 47 Oil pan tightening sequence. 1998–2000

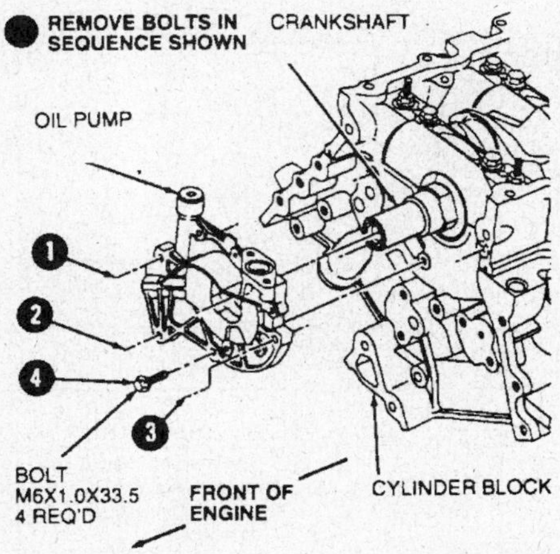

FM1099500075000X

Fig. 48 Oil pump bolt removal sequence. 1997

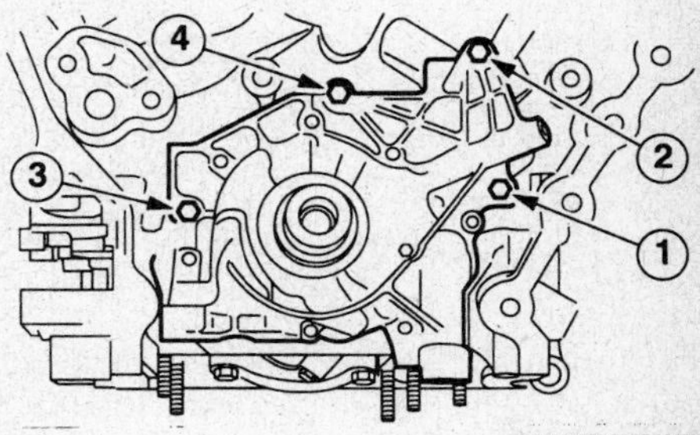

FM1099900080000X

Fig. 49 Oil pump bolt removal sequence. 1998–2000

replacer tool No. T82L-6701-A, or equivalent, **Fig. 41.**

OIL PAN

REPLACE

1997

1. Remove water pump pulley shield bolts from lefthand valve cover, then the water pump pulley shield from engine.
2. Install three bar engine support tool No. D88L-6000-A, or equivalent, onto engine lifting eyes and support engine.
3. Raise and support vehicle.
4. Remove front and rear Y-pipe flange fasteners from exhaust manifold, then the stud bolt and nut retainer from oil pan.
5. Remove two remaining nuts and bolts from Y-pipe outlet connection, then discard exhaust converter inlet gasket.
6. Remove Y-pipe.
7. Remove exhaust heat shield nuts, then the heat shields from lefthand side of oil pan.
8. Remove oil pan drain plug and drain engine oil from engine.
9. Install oil pan drain plug with new gasket and tighten to specifications.
10. Remove oil pan retaining bolts from transaxle housing.
11. **On models equipped with automatic transaxle,** remove engine rear plate access plug.
12. **On all models,** remove left and right front engine support insulator through bolt as described under "Engine Mount, Replace."
13. Lower vehicle, then mark location of upper front engine support bracket.
14. Remove upper front engine support bracket nuts from upper front engine support insulator as described under "Engine Mount, Replace."
15. Raise engine enough to gain clearance for oil pan removal.
16. Raise and support vehicle, then remove oil pan retaining bolts, in sequence, from lower cylinder block, **Fig. 43.**
17. Remove oil pan and gasket, then discard gasket.
18. Remove oil pump screen cover and

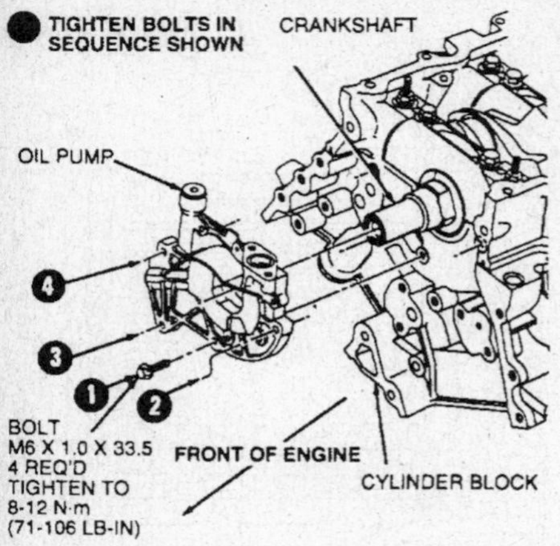

FM1099500076000X

Fig. 50 Oil pump bolt tightening sequence. 1997

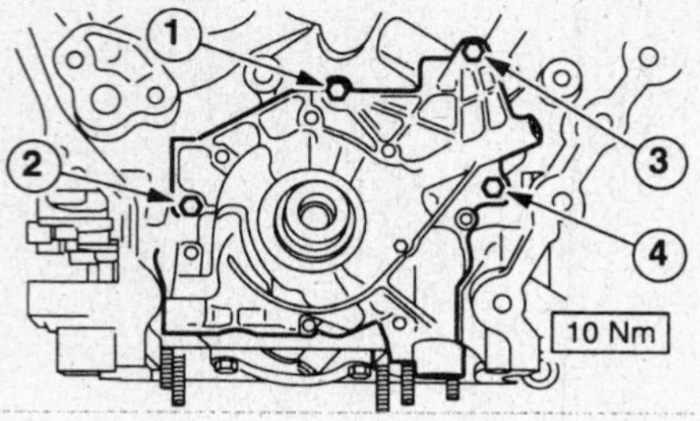

FM1099900081000X

Fig. 51 Oil pump bolt tightening sequence. 1998–2000

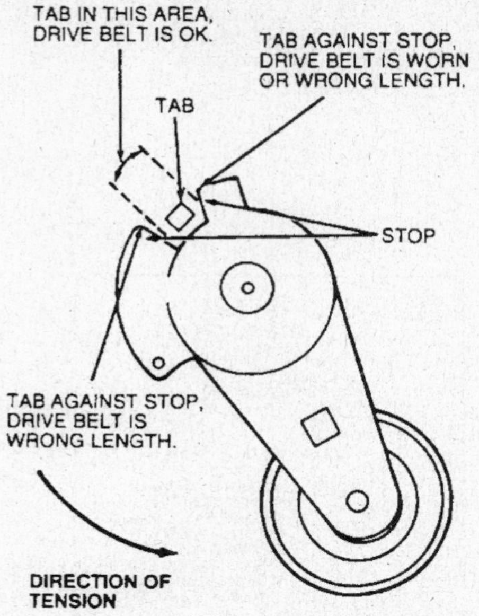

FM1069500437000X

Fig. 52 Drive belt wear indicator mark

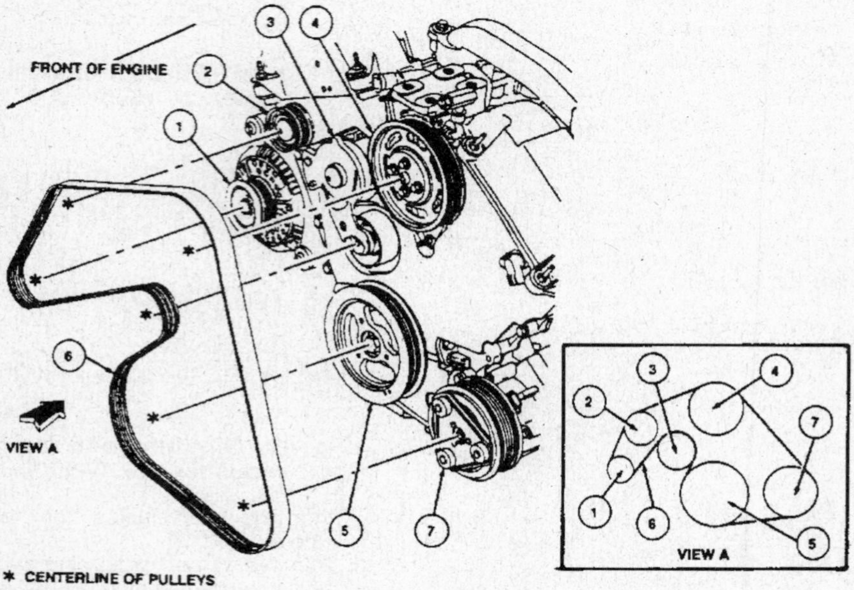

* CENTERLINE OF PULLEYS

Item	Description
1	Generator
2	Drive Belt Idler Pulley
3	Drive Belt Tensioner
4	Power Steering Pump Pulley
5	Crankshaft Pulley
6	Accessory Drive Belt
7	A/C Compressor

FM1069500438000X

Fig. 53 Accessory drive belt routing. With A/C

tube nut from lower cylinder block stud bolt.

19. Remove oil pump screen cover and tube bolts from oil pump, then the cover and tube from engine, **Fig. 44.**
20. Reverse procedure to install, noting following:
    a. Inspect oil pump screen cover and tube O-ring for damage and wear. Replace O-ring as necessary.
    b. Install new self-locking oil pump screen cover and tube support nut to lower cylinder block stud. Tighten nut to specifications.
    c. Clean oil pan with suitable soap and water solution, then dry completely with compressed air. Inspect oil pan for damage and replace as necessary.
    d. Clean oil pan to lower cylinder block sealing surfaces with shop towel and suitable metal surface cleaner to remove all residues which may interfere with sealer's ability to adhere.
    e. Apply .31 inch diameter bead of suitable sealer on oil pan gasket, **Fig. 45,** then install new oil pan gasket.
    f. **Torque** oil pan retaining bolts and studs in sequence, **Fig. 45,** to 15–22 ft. lbs.
    g. Tighten oil pan to transaxle housing bolts to specifications.

1998–2000

1. Remove exhaust Y-pipe, then the exhaust support bracket nuts and support bracket.
2. Remove A/C compressor heat shield nuts and heat shield.
3. Drain engine oil into a suitable container.
4. Remove flywheel access cover and oil pan bolts from transaxle housing.
5. Remove oil pan bolts and studs in sequence, **Fig. 46.** Discard gasket
6. Reverse procedure to install, noting the following:
    a. Position oil pan and loosely install bolts and studs.
    b. Install oil pan to transaxle housing bolts.
    c. Using sequence shown in **Fig. 47** tighten bolts to specification.

OIL PUMP

REPLACE

1. Remove oil pan and oil pump screen cover and tube as described under "Oil Pan, Replace."
2. Remove front cover as described under "Front Cover, Replace."
3. Remove timing chains as described under "Timing Chain, Replace."
4. Remove crankshaft sprocket, then the oil pump bolts in sequence, **Figs. 48 and 49.**
5. Remove pump from cylinder block.
6. Reverse procedure to install, noting the following:
    a. **Torque** oil pump bolts in sequence, **Figs. 50 and 51,** to 72–108 inch lbs.
    b. Fill crankcase to proper level with specified engine oil, then run engine and check for leaks.

OIL COOLER

REPLACE

1998-2000

Contour SVT

1. Drain engine coolant into a suitable container.
2. Raise and support vehicle.
3. Remove lower radiator splash shield push pins, bolts and splash shield.
4. Drain engine oil into a suitable container, then remove oil filter.
5. Disconnect oil cooler lines, then remove oil cooler insert and oil cooler.
6. Reverse procedure to install. Use a new oil drain plug gasket to prevent leaks.

BELT TENSION DATA

Drive belts have an automatic drive belt tensioner and do not require adjustment.

The automatic belt tensioner is a spring loaded device which sets and maintains drive belt tension. Drive belts should not require tension adjustment for the life of the drive belt.

The automatic belt tensioner has a drive belt wear indicator mark, **Fig. 52.** If the indicator mark is not approximately in between the tabs on the front cover, the belt is worn or an incorrect belt is installed.

SERPENTINE DRIVE BELT

ROUTING

Refer to **Figs. 53 through 55** for belt routing.

BELT REPLACEMENT

Water Pump

1. Remove engine cover, then rotate drive belt tensioner clockwise by hand.
2. Lift drive belt over pulley flanges and remove.
3. Reverse procedure to install.

Accessory Drive

1. Raise and support vehicle.
2. Use a breaker bar installed in the ⅜ inch square hole in drive belt tensioner to rotate the drive belt.
3. Lift drive belt over the pulley flanges and remove.
4. Reverse procedure to install.

TENSIONER REPLACEMENT

Accessory Drive

1. Remove drive belt as described under "Belt Replace."
2. Loosen belt tensioner bolts completely, then remove tensioner from front of engine.
3. Align drive belt tensioner spring to slot in front cover, then install tensioner onto front cover. Tighten tensioner bolt to specifications.
4. Install drive belt as described under "Belt Replace."

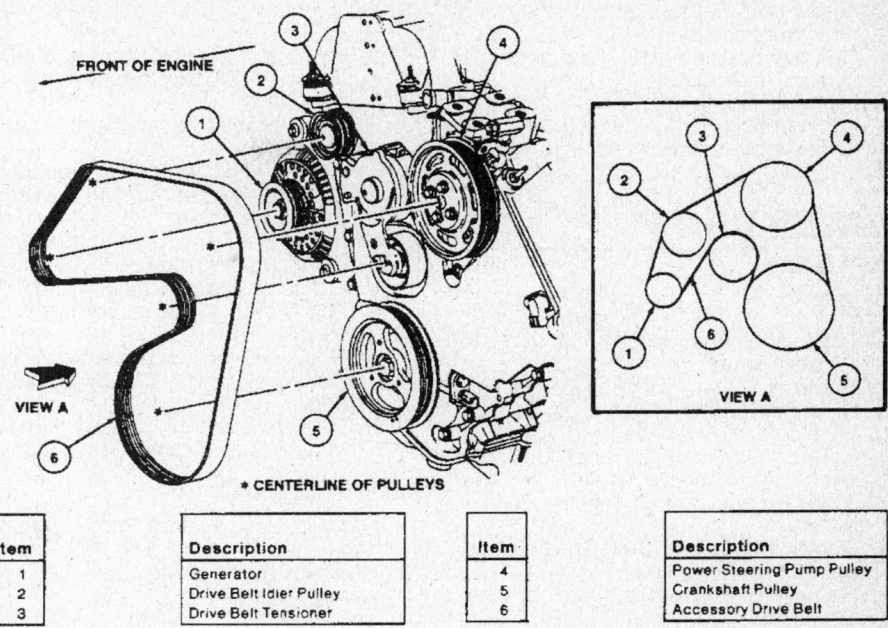

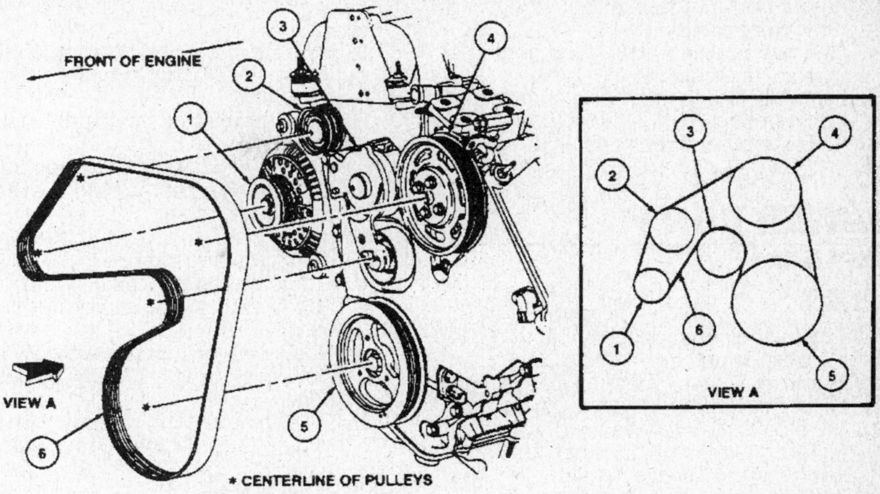

Item	Description
1	Generator
2	Drive Belt Idler Pulley
3	Drive Belt Tensioner
4	Power Steering Pump Pulley
5	Crankshaft Pulley
6	Accessory Drive Belt

FM1069500439000X

Fig. 54 Accessory drive belt routing. Less A/C

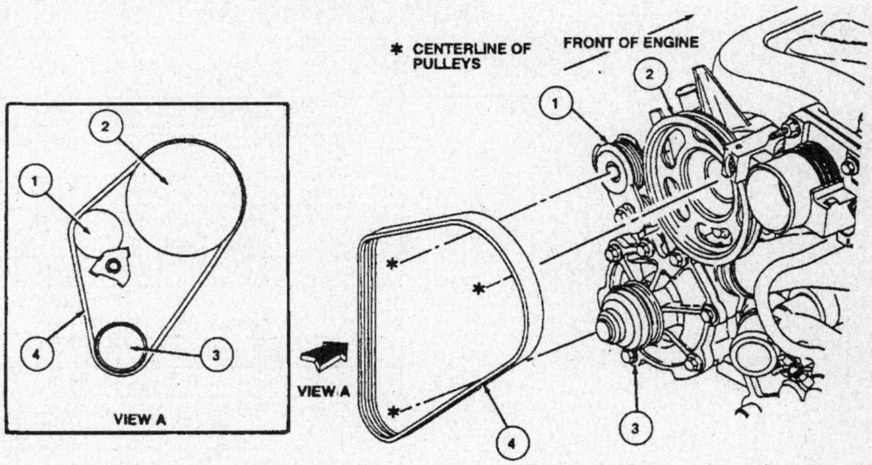

Item	Description
1	Drive Belt Tensioner
2	Water Pump Drive Pulley
3	Water Pump
4	Water Pump Drive Belt

FM1069500440000X

Fig. 55 Water pump drive belt routing

Water Pump

1. Remove tensioner bolt and tensioner from water pump.
2. Align tab on tensioner with hole in mounting area on water pump, then install tensioner onto pump. Tighten bolts to specifications.

COOLING SYSTEM BLEED

These engines do not require a specific bleed procedure. To ensure coolant level is satisfactory, start the engine, turn heater control to its maximum heat and vent positions. After engine reaches normal operating temperature, hot air should be blowing from the A/C vents. If cool air is blowing from the vents, coolant level is low, turn engine off and add coolant as necessary.

THERMOSTAT

REPLACE

1. Drain engine cooling system so engine coolant level is below water thermostat.
2. **On 1997 models,** remove battery.
3. **On all model,** disconnect radiator

hoses from thermostat housing, then remove housing.
4. Remove housing bolts, then separate thermostat housings.
5. Remove O-ring seal and thermostat from housing.
6. Reverse procedure to install.

WATER PUMP

REPLACE

1997

1. Drain engine cooling system into a suitable container.
2. Remove water pump pulley shield bolts from lefthand valve cover, then the shield from vehicle.
3. Rotate water pump drive belt tensioner clockwise to relieve tension on drive belt, then remove belt from pump drive pulley.
4. Remove inlet and outlet hoses from pump.
5. Remove pump to lefthand cylinder head bolts, then the pump from engine.
6. Separate water pump housing and remove water pump drive belt tensioner, if necessary.
7. Reverse procedure to install, noting following:
   a. Clean water pump to water pump housing gasket sealing surfaces using wire brush.
   b. Install new water pump to water pump housing gasket.
   c. Lubricate pump inlet and outlet hoses with suitable silicone lubricant.
   d. Rotate water pump drive belt tensioner clockwise when installing belt.
   e. Fill engine cooling system, then run engine and check for coolant leaks.

1998–2000

1. Drain cooling system into a suitable container.
2. Remove water pump drive belt tensioner.
3. Raise and support vehicle.
4. Remove water pump bolts, pump and gasket.
5. Reverse procedure to install.

RADIATOR

REPLACE

Refer to "2.0L Engine" for radiator replacement.

FUEL PUMP

REPLACE

Refer to " 2.0L Engine" for fuel pump replacement.

FUEL FILTER

REPLACE

Refer to " 2.0L Engine" for fuel filter replacement

TIGHTENING SPECIFICATIONS

Year	Component	Torque/Ft. Lbs.
1997–2000	A/C Compressor Bolts	15–22
	A/C Condenser Core To Radiator Bolts	60①
	A/C Hose Bracket To Front Cover Nut	72–108①
	Accelerator Cable Bracket To Throttle Body Bolts	72–108①
	Accessory Drive Belt Tensioner Bolt	15–22
	Battery Ground Cable To Engine/ Transaxle Stud Nut	15–22
	Camshaft Journal Cap Bolts	72–108①
	Camshaft Journal Thrust Cap Bolts	72–108①
	Camshaft Rear Oil Seal Retainer Bolts	72–108①
	Crankcase Ventilation Tube	44–62①
	Crankshaft Pulley Bolt	⑦
	Cylinder Head Bolts	②
	Drive Belt Idler Pulley Bolt	15–22
	EGR Valve To Exhaust Manifold Tube Nut	26–33
	Engine Air Cleaner Tube Clamps	24–48①
	Engine Rear Plate Bolts	54–64③
	Engine & Transaxle Support Insulator Nuts	④
	Exhaust Manifold Nuts	13–16
	Fan Shroud Nuts	24–48①
	Flywheel Bolts	54–64③
	Front Engine Support Bracket Nuts	52–70
	Front Engine Support Bracket To Sub-Frame Bolts	20
	Front Stabilizer Link To Front Stabilizer Bar Nuts	35
	Front Tie Rod End Nuts	⑥
	Front Wheel Knuckle To Front Suspension Lower Arm Bolts	37–43
	Heated Oxygen Sensor	26–34

Continued

TIGHTENING SPECIFICATIONS—Continued

Year	Component	Torque/Ft. Lbs.
1997-2000	Inline Fuel Filter Worm Gear Mounting Clamp	15–25①
	Intake Manifold Bolts	⑧
	Lower Radiator Hose Tube Nuts	72–108①
	Lower Radiator Support Bolts	72–96①
	Muffler Inlet Flange Nuts	26–33
	Oil Pan Drain Plug	16–22
	Oil Pan Retaining Bolts & Studs (1997)	15-22
	Oil Pan Retaining Bolts & Studs (1998–99)	18
	Oil Pan To Transaxle Bolts	25–34
	Oil Pan To Transaxle Housing Bolts	25–34
	Oil Pump Bolts	72–108①
	Oil Pump Screen Cover & Tube Bolts	72–108①
	Oil Pump Screen Cover & Tube Support Nut	15–22
	Power Steering Pressure Hose Bracket Bolt	72–108①
	Power Steering Pump Bolts	15-22
	Power Steering Pump Pulley Bolts	15–22
	Power Steering Pump Support Nuts	72–108①
	Radiator To Front Sub-Frame Bolts	72–96①
	Shift Cable Bracket Bolts	15–19
	Shift Rod Bolt	17
	Stabilizer Bar Nut	41
	Steering Shaft Pinch Bolt	18
	Thermostat Housing Bolts	15-22
	Three-Way Catalytic Converter Nuts	22–30
	Transaxle Oil Cooler Line Bracket Nuts	18–22
	Transaxle Oil Cooler Tube To Fitting	18–23
	Transaxle Stabilizer Bar Nut	41
	Transaxle To Engine Bolts	25–34
	Torque Converter To Flywheel Nuts	54–64
	Upper Intake Manifold Bolts	72–108①
	Valve Cover Bolts	72–108①
	Water Crossover Pipe (Bypass Tube) To Cylinder Head Bolts	72–108①
	Water Pump Bolts	⑤
	Water Pump Drive Belt Tensioner Bolt	72–108①
	Water Pump To Lefthand Cylinder Head Bolts	11-13⑨
	Water Pump To Water Pump Housing Bolts	16–18
	Wheel Lug Nuts	62

① — Inch lbs.
② — Refer to "Cylinder Head, Replace."
③ — Tighten in an alternating sequence.
④ — Automatic transaxle, 30–41 ft. lbs.; manual transaxle, 52–70 ft. lbs.
⑤ — Refer to "Water Pump, Replace."
⑥ — Refer to "Engine, Replace."
⑦ — Refer to "Crankshaft Seal, Replace."
⑧ — Refer to "Intake Manifold, Replace."
⑨ — On 1997 models, rotate an additional 85–95.°

Clutch & Manual Transaxle

NOTE: Refer To "Air Bag System Precautions " Located In The Front Of This Manual For System Disarming & Arming Procedures.

NOTE: Refer To "Computer Relearn Procedures" Located In The Front Of This Manual For Computer Relearn Procedures.

INDEX

PRECAUTIONS

BATTERY GROUND CABLE

Prior to service, disconnect battery ground cable and isolate as required.

AIR BAG SYSTEMS

Refer to "Air Bag System Precautions" in front of this manual for system disarming and arming procedures.

FUEL SYSTEM PRESSURE RELIEF

Fuel supply lines will remain pressurized for long periods of time after engine shutdown. Pressure must be relieved before servicing fuel system.

1. Remove engine air cleaner as follows:
    a. Remove engine air intake resonators as described under " Engine Air Intake Resonators, Replace."
    b. Disconnect engine control sensor wiring connectors from Mass Air Flow (MAF) sensor and Intake Air Temperature (IAT) sensor.
    c. Remove engine air cleaner to body O-ring retainer.
    d. Remove engine air cleaner body and intake tube from bracket and intake tube and duct.
2. Connect Multi-Port Fuel Injection (MFI) fuel pressure gauge tool No. T80L-9974-B, or equivalent, to fuel pressure relief valve cap on fuel injection supply manifold.
3. Open manual valve on gauge tool to relieve fuel system pressure.

ADJUSTMENTS

CLUTCH PEDAL

1997-98

Clutch pedal mechanism is self-adjusting, no adjustment is required.

1999-2000

1. Turn steering wheel from straight ahead position approximately 30° to left.
2. Attach cable ties to clutch pedal (second groove from the bottom) and tighten.
3. Install a steel rule with cable ties and pass through the steering wheel.
4. Read measurement, depress clutch pedal as far as the stop and read the measurement again, **Fig. 1.**
5. Pedal travel should not be restricted by mats or the clutch master cylinder.
6. Adjust clutch pedal travel to 5–5¼ inches at pedal stop screw.

HYDRAULIC SYSTEM SERVICE

HYDRAULIC SYSTEM BLEED

Pump clutch pedal at least 30 times to ensure no air is in system.

1. Clean top and side of fluid reservoir to avoid fluid contamination.
2. Remove air cleaner outlet tube and mass air flow sensor assembly.
3. Attach suitable hose to bleeder valve at clutch slave cylinder, then submerge other end in suitable container of clean brake fluid. **Ensure clutch reservoir is full at all times.**
4. While depressing clutch, slightly open bleeder valve, then observe air bubbles in fluid at end of hose.
5. Close bleeder valve before releasing clutch pedal.
6. Repeat previous steps, until no bubbles are seen in fluid.
7. Top off fluid in brake master cylinder reservoir, then install diaphragm and reservoir cap.
8. Replace air cleaner outlet tube and MAF sensor assembly.

CLUTCH SLAVE CYLINDER, REPLACE

1. Remove transaxle as outlined under "Transaxle, Replace. "
2. Disconnect slave cylinder to clutch master cylinder tube.
3. Remove clutch slave cylinder attaching bolts, then the cylinder.
4. Remove clutch slave cylinder bleed tube.
5. Reverse procedure to install. Bleed hydraulic system

CLUTCH

REPLACE

REMOVAL

1. Remove transaxle as described under "Transaxle, Replace. "
2. Mark assembled position of clutch pressure plate to flywheel.
3. Loosen clutch pressure plate retaining bolts evenly until clutch pressure plate spring pressure is released, then remove clutch pressure plate and clutch disc, **Fig. 2.**

INSTALLATION

1. Clean clutch pressure plate and flywheel surfaces. **Do not use cleaners with a petroleum base.**
2. Install the clutch disc using clutch aligner tool No. T74P-6375–A, or equivalent, **Fig. 3.**
3. Install the clutch pressure plate, then holding flywheel in place using flywheel holding tool No. T74P-6375–A, or equivalent, tighten pressure plate attaching bolts to specification, **Fig. 4.**
4. Connect slave cylinder tube coupling.
5. Install transaxle as outlined under "Transaxle, Replace. "
6. Bleed clutch hydraulic system.

TRANSAXLE

REPLACE

1997-98

1. Disconnect battery positive cable and remove battery.

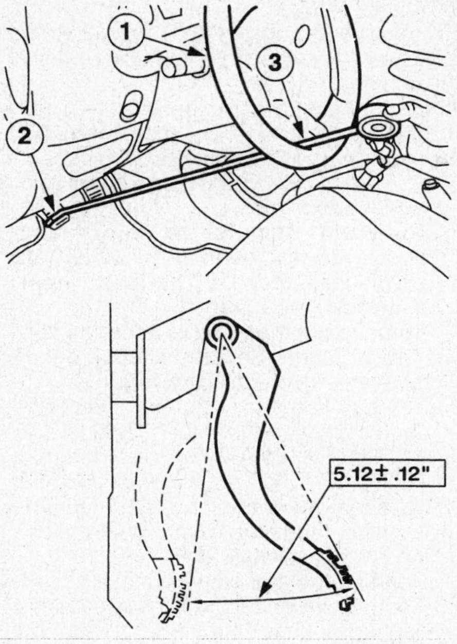

Fig. 1 Clutch pedal adjustment. 1999–2000

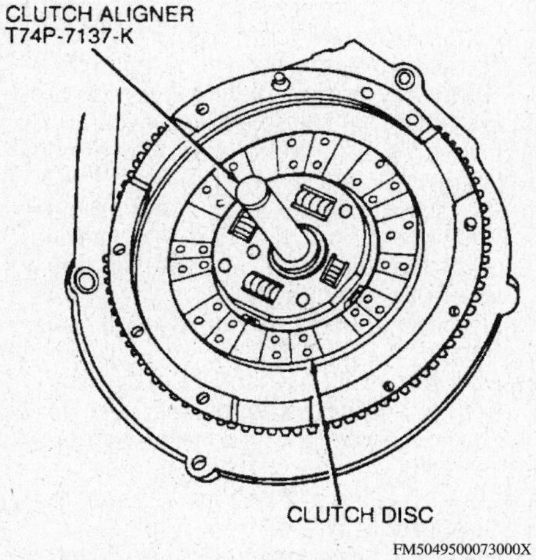

Fig. 3 Clutch aligning tool

2. Secure radiator and engine cooling fan motor, fan blade and shroud to radiator support with suitable wire.
3. Loosen but do not remove upper shock absorber mounting nuts.
4. Remove mass air flow sensor and air cleaner outlet tube with resonator.
5. Remove engine air cleaner and lower bracket.
6. Install engine support tool No. D88L-6000-A, or equivalent.
7. Disconnect back-up lamp electrical connector.
8. Remove bolt holding ground strap to transaxle, then the engine and transaxle support insulator
9. Disconnect hydraulic line and grommet from bracket.
10. Remove rubber inspection cover from transaxle clutch housing.
11. Disconnect hydraulic line fitting and position aside.

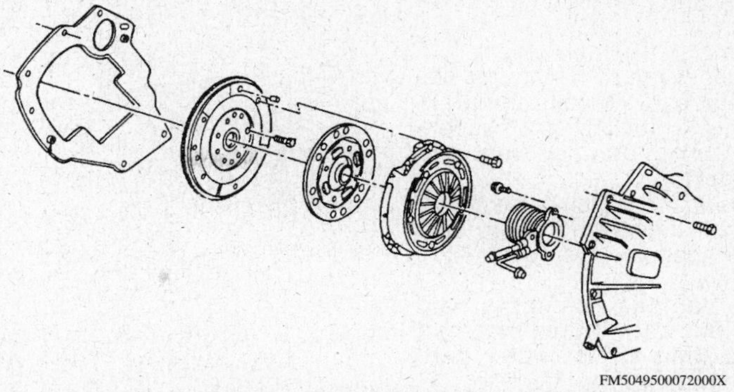

Fig. 2 Exploded view of clutch assembly

12. Remove upper transaxle to engine bolt, then the upper starter bolts and ground strap.
13. **On models with 2.0L engine,** remove exhaust manifold heat shield and disconnect catalytic converter at exhaust manifold.
14. **On all models,** remove front tire and wheel assemblies.
15. Raise and support vehicle.
16. **On models with 2.0L engine,** remove catalytic converter.
17. **On models with 2.5L engine,** remove catalytic converter Y-pipe.
18. **On all models,** remove vehicle speed sensor electrical connector and remove speedometer cable.
19. Remove lower radiator air deflector.
20. Push shift rod completely forward and remove shift rod pinch bolt, then pull shift rod back and remove from transaxle.
21. Remove shift control stabilizer bar and bracket from righthand engine support insulator bracket.
22. Remove underbody heat shield from under shift control.
23. Position and secure shift rod and stabilizer bar to allow transaxle removal.
24. Remove suction accumulator/drier from front subframe.
25. Remove left and right side halfshafts and intermediate shafts.
26. Remove righthand engine support insulator bracket.
27. Remove lefthand engine support insulator through-bolt.
28. Lower vehicle.
29. Adjust engine support tool No. D88L-6000-A, or equivalent, to remove tension at righthand front engine support bracket.
30. Remove righthand engine support bracket through-bolt.
31. Raise and properly support vehicle, then remove front subframe.
32. Lower vehicle and loosen front mount nuts five turns.
33. Using suitable floor jack and wood block under transaxle, release tension from engine support tool. Lower transaxle to limits of front engine mount movement.
34. Adjust engine support tool No. D88L-6000-A, or equivalent, to hold engine.
35. Remove floor jack and wood block
36. Secure transmission jack No. 014–002, or equivalent, to transaxle.

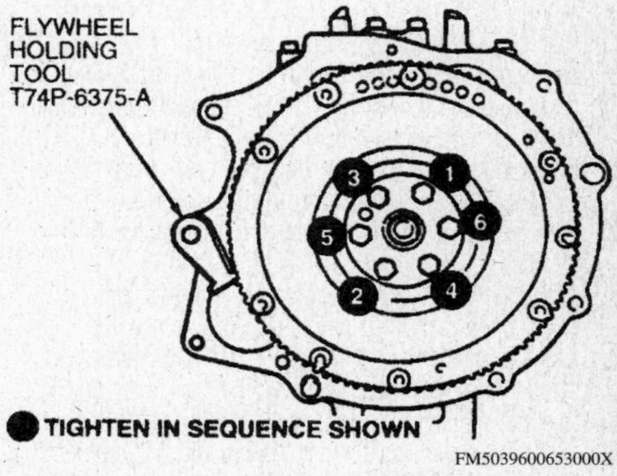

Fig. 4 Flywheel holding tool

37. Remove remaining starter bolts and position aside, support starter motor with suitable wire.
38. Remove engine oil pan to transaxle bolts.
39. Remove remaining bolts and separate transaxle from engine and remove from vehicle.
40. Reverse procedure to install.

1999–2000

2.0L Engine

1. Remove battery and engine air cleaner.
2. Loosen suspension strut nut five turns on both sides.
3. Disconnect intake air temperature sensor electrical connector.
4. Remove air cleaner outlet tube clamp and air cleaner outlet tube.
5. Use wire or tie strap to secure radiator.
6. Disconnect ground cable from transaxle and position it aside.
7. Disconnect reverse lamp switch connector.
8. Remove clip and disconnect clutch slave cylinder hydraulic line. **Be careful not to spill brake fluid onto painted surfaces.**
9. Disconnect clutch slave cylinder hydraulic line from bracket, then remove push pin and position aside.
10. Remove upper bellhousing and upper starter motor bolts.
11. Install support bar as shown, **Fig. 5.**
12. Remove lefthand transaxle support insulator nuts, bolts and insulator.
13. Remove lefthand transaxle support insulator studs.

14. Raise and support vehicle and remove both wheels.
15. Remove lower wheel arch covers.
16. Disconnect lower suspension arm ball joints and stabilizer link rods, then ABS wiring harness bracket from suspension strut. **Do not damage boot and ABS sensor ring.**
17. Remove righthand halfshaft and intermediate shaft. Secure righthand halfshaft out of the way with mechanic's wire.
18. **To avoid damage to joints and boots, do not bend inner halfshaft joint more than 18° or outer halfshaft more than 45.°**
19. Remove lefthand halfshaft using halfshaft remover tool Nos. T86P-3514-A1, T86P-3514-A2 and slide hammer T50T-100-A, or equivalents.
20. Secure halfshaft out of the way with mechanic's wire, then plug transmission openings with auxiliary plugs.
21. Remove rear and front roll restrictor bolts and the rear roll restrictors.
22. Remove suction accumulator bracket bolts.
23. Remove radiator splash shield and radiator support brackets.
24. Disconnect starter motor connectors and remove starter motor.
25. Remove three-way catalytic converter.
26. Disconnect shifter cables and bracket.
27. Disconnect VSS connector.
28. Remove power steering hose bracket bolt and nut.
29. Remove power steering line bracket bolt, then steering gear to subframe bolt.
30. Secure steering gear using mechanics wire, then remove subframe bolts and subframe.
31. Position a suitable hi-lift transmission jack and secure holding strap to transaxle.
32. Remove lower front bellhousing bolts, then the remaining bellhousing bolts.
33. Separate transaxle from engine.
34. Reverse procedure to install.

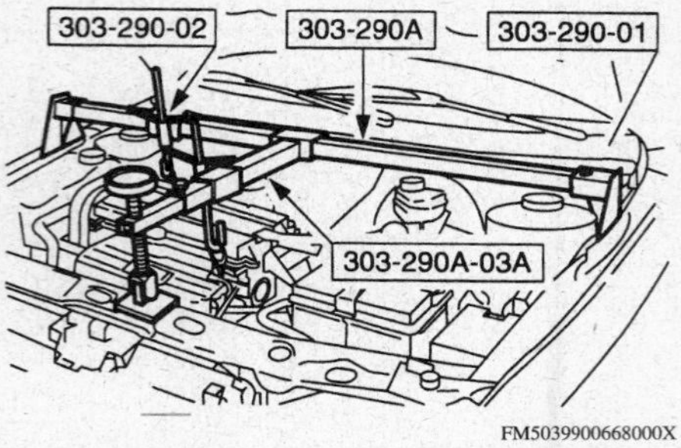

Fig. 5 Engine support bar tool installation. 1999–2000

2.5L Engine

1. Remove battery, then loosen both front nuts five turns.
2. Lock steering wheel, then using wire or tie strap to secure radiator.
3. Remove engine air cleaner, then the water pump cover.
4. Disconnect accelerator and speed control cables.
5. Disconnect ground cable from transaxle and position it aside.
6. Disconnect power steering reservoir hose and drain power steering reservoir.
7. Disconnect vehicle speed sensor and reverse lamp switch connectors.
8. Relieve fuel pressure as outlined in "Precautions."
9. Remove safety clips and disconnect fuel lines, using fuel line disconnect tool Nos. D87L-9280-A (3/8 inch) or D87L-9280-B (1/2 inch), or equivalent.
10. Disconnect starter motor connectors, then remove air cleaner bracket and starter motor bracket.
11. Remove clutch slave cylinder hydraulic pipe. **Do not spill brake fluid onto painted surfaces.**
12. Install engine support bar, **Fig. 5.**
13. Remove lefthand transaxle support insulator nuts, bolts and support insulator.
14. Remove lefthand transaxle support insulator studs.
15. Remove four upper bellhousing bolts.
16. Raise and support vehicle and remove both front wheels.
17. Disconnect lower suspension arm ball joints and stabilizer link rods, then ABS wiring harness bracket from suspension strut. **Do not damage boot and ABS sensor ring.**
18. **To avoid damage to joints and boots, do not bend inner halfshaft joint more than 18° and the outer halfshaft more than 45.°**
19. Remove righthand halfshaft and intermediate shaft. Secure halfshaft out of the way with mechanic's wire.
20. Remove lefthand halfshaft using halfshaft remover tool Nos. T86P-3514-A1, T86P-3514-A2 and slide hammer T50T-100-A, or equivalents. Secure halfshaft out of the way with mechanic's wire, then plug transmission openings with auxiliary plugs.
21. Remove radiator splash shield.
22. Remove secondary three way catalytic converter, then the radiator support brackets.
23. Remove bolt and position bumper bracket aside.
24. Remove suction accumulator bracket bolts, then the heated oxygen sensor connector from subframe.
25. Remove intermediate shaft pinch bolt.
26. Remove front and rear roll restrictors.
27. Remove rear roll restrictor bracket.
28. Loosen subframe bolts and lower subframe.
29. Disconnect shifter cables and bracket.
30. Remove power steering line bracket bolt and disconnect power steering line from steering gear.
31. Remove subframe bolts and subframe.
32. Position hi lift transmission jack and secure holding strap to transaxle.
33. Remove lower rear and front bellhousing bolts.
34. Lower engine and transaxle assembly.
35. Separate transaxle from engine.
36. Reverse procedure to install.

TIGHTENING SPECIFICATIONS

Year	Component	Torque/Ft. Lbs.
1997-2000	Back-Up Lamp Switch	84②
	Clutch Bleed Screw	84–108②
	Clutch Bleed Tube Fitting	10
	Clutch Master Cylinder Nuts	84②
	Clutch Pressure Plate To Flywheel	①
	Clutch Slave Cylinder Mounting	7–14
	Flywheel Attaching Bolts	83
	Front Engine Support Bracket	61
	Front Shock Absorber Upper Mounting	34
	RH Engine Support Bracket	62

Continued

TIGHTENING SPECIFICATIONS—Continued

Year	Component	Torque/Ft. Lbs.
1997-2000	Selector Housing	96②
	Shift Stabilizer Bar	28–38
	Shift Rod	14–18
	Starter Motor Bolts	35
	Transaxle Case To Clutch Housing	28–38
	Transaxle To Engine	28–38
	Wheel Lug Nuts	62

① — 1997, 13–18 ft. lbs.; 1998–2000, 22 ft. lbs.
② — Inch lbs.

Rear Suspension

INDEX

DESCRIPTION

Rear suspension has a quadralink design, **Fig. 1,** This is basically two horizontal, pressed steel, lateral arms each side of the vehicle, attached to a pressed steel crossmember at the inner pivots and cast iron spindle assemblies at the outer pivots. The lateral arms control the toe change of the rear wheels. The third link of the quadralink system is a tie bar which connects the wheel spindle to a forward body mounted bracket. The fourth link is a MacPherson strut mounted on top of the wheel spindle. The strut controls the camber and reacts to braking torque. The tie bar and lateral arms connect through rubber bushes, the strut is mounted to the spindle assembly. The rear lateral arm joint to the crossmember allows toe adjustment by rotation of a cam bolt. The system has additional roll control by use of a stabilizer bar, connected between the crossmember and the front lateral arms. A hub and bearing assembly runs on the wheel spindle and locates on the brake drum or disc, and the wheel.

HUB & BEARING

REPLACE

1. Raise and support vehicle, then remove wheel.
2. **On models with rear disc brakes,** remove caliper and brake rotor. **It is not necessary to disconnect hydraulic line from caliper; support caliper aside to prevent hydraulic line damage.**
3. **On models with rear drum brakes,** remove brake drum retainer, then drum.
4. **On all models,** remove and discard rear axle wheel hub retainer, then remove wheel hub. **Do not use an impact wrench to loosen retainer; spindle damage may result.**
5. Reverse procedure to install. Tighten new retainer and wheel lug nuts to specifications.

WHEEL BEARING

ADJUST

Wheel bearings are pre-greased and sealed; as a result, they require no periodic maintenance. Their cartridge design prohibits adjustment.

REAR WHEEL SPINDLE

REPLACE

1. Raise and support vehicle, then remove wheel and rear brake anti-lock sensor.
2. Remove rear wheel hub and bearing assembly as described under "Hub & Bearing, Replace."
3. **On models with rear disc brakes,** remove disc brake shield.
4. **On models with rear drum brakes,** proceed as follows:
   a. Remove brake backing plate and position aside.
   b. Disconnect stabilizer bar link from lateral arm.
5. **On all models,** disconnect rear suspension tie rod and bushing at spindle, **Fig. 2.**
6. Disconnect rearward and forward suspension arms with bushings from spindle, then remove strut to spindle pinch bolt.
7. Remove spindle from strut assembly.
8. Reverse procedure to install, noting the following:
   a. When installing rear suspension arms, tie rods and their respective bushings on the spindle, tighten bolts snugly, but do not tighten to specifications until all other components have been installed and vehicle weight is on the wheels.
   b. **Do not use an impact wrench to tighten new wheel hub retainer, as spindle damage may result.**
   c. Tighten all bolts and nuts to specifications.

STRUT

REPLACE

1. Raise and support vehicle, then remove wheel.
2. Detach anti-lock brake sensor wiring from strut assembly, then remove sensor.
3. **On models equipped with drum brakes,** clamp and disconnect rear brake hose from brake tube, then remove hose and retainer from strut assembly.
4. **On models equipped with disc brakes,** remove brake hose.
5. **On all models,** remove wheel spindle to suspension unit pinch bolt.
6. Remove wheel spindle from suspension unit.
7. Raise suspension unit of a jack and remove suspension unit from crossmember.

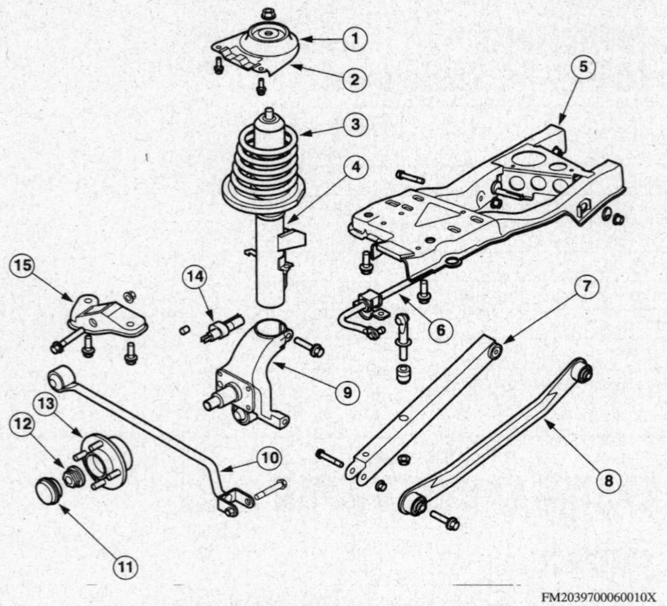

Fig. 1 Exploded view of rear suspension (Part 1 of 2)

Item	Part Number	Description
1	–	Body mounting cup
2	–	Spring seat
3	–	Spring
4	–	Strut
5	–	Crossmember
6	–	Stabilizer bar
7	–	Front lower arm
8	–	Rear lower arm
9	–	Wheel spindle
10	–	Tie-bar
11	–	Dust cap
12	–	Hub retaining nut
13	–	Hub and bearing assembly
14	–	Wheel speed sensor
15	–	Tie-bar mounting bracket

FM2039700060020X

Fig. 1 Exploded view of rear suspension (Part 2 of 2)

8. Remove suspension unit.

STRUT SERVICE

1. Position strut assembly in Rotunda strut spring compressor tool No. 014–00781, or equivalent, then compress spring.
2. Remove top nut, bracket, bushing and spring seat, **Fig. 3,** then slowly release spring compressor tool.
3. Remove spring, dust shield and jounce bumper.
4. Reverse procedure to assemble. Tighten top nut to specifications.

CONTROL ARM

REPLACE

LOWER

Front Arm

1. Raise and support vehicle, then remove wheel.
2. Remove stabilizer bar link and bushing from front lateral arm, then front lateral arm from spindle.
3. Remove tie bar from spindle carrier, then release three exhaust mounting and support exhaust system.
4. Support crossmember and remove crossmember bolts and lower.
5. Reverse procedure to install, noting following:
   a. When installing forward arm and bushing to crossmember bolt and nut, ensure bolt head faces fuel tank. Tighten bolt and nut snugly, but do not final tighten until vehicle weight is resting upon rear wheels.
   b. Tighten all bolts and nuts to specifications.

Rear Arm

1. Raise and support vehicle, then remove wheel and disconnect rear arm from spindle.
2. Remove rear lateral arm from crossmember.
3. Reverse procedure to install, noting following:
   a. When installing rearward arm, connect to spindle and tighten bolts and nuts snugly, but do not final tighten until vehicle weight is resting upon rear wheels. **Tighten wheel lug nuts to specifications before lowering vehicle.**
   b. After vehicle weight is resting on rear wheels, tighten rearward arm bolts and nuts to specifications.

TIE ROD

REPLACE

1. Raise and support vehicle, then remove wheel and disconnect parking brake cable and conduit from forward tie rod bracket.
2. Remove exhaust rubber from tie bar bracket.
3. Remove tie strap securing parking brake rear cable and conduit to rear suspension tie rod and bushing.
4. Disconnect tie rod and bushing assembly at spindle.
5. Remove bolts, tie rod and bushing assembly, then the front bracket from vehicle.

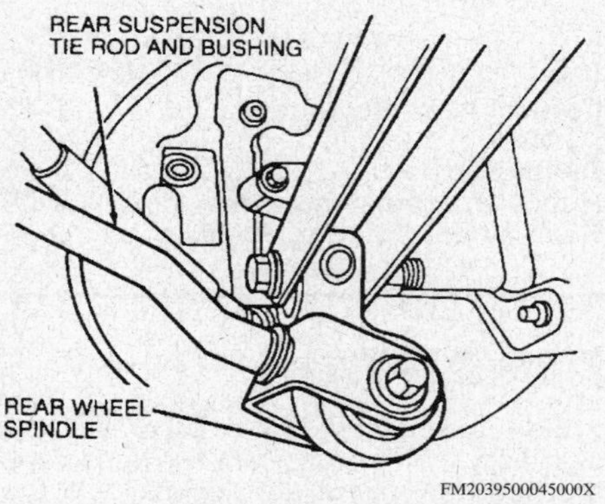

Fig. 2 Rear spindle assembly

6. Remove bolt and tie rod and bushing assembly from front bracket.
7. Reverse procedure to install.

STABILIZER BAR

REPLACE

1997

1. Raise and support vehicle, then remove wheel and disconnect stabilizer bar ends at lower arms, **Fig. 4.**
2. Remove stabilizer bar bracket, **Fig. 5,** then the stabilizer bar.
3. Remove lower suspension arm stabilizer bar insulators from stabilizer bar.
4. Reverse procedure to install. Tighten all bolts and nuts to specifications.

1998-2000

1. Raise and support vehicle.
2. Remove stabilizer bar links and bushings from front lateral arms.
3. Remove stabilizer bar bushings.
4. Remove righthand tie bar from wheel spindle, then the stabilizer bar.
5. Reverse procedure to install.

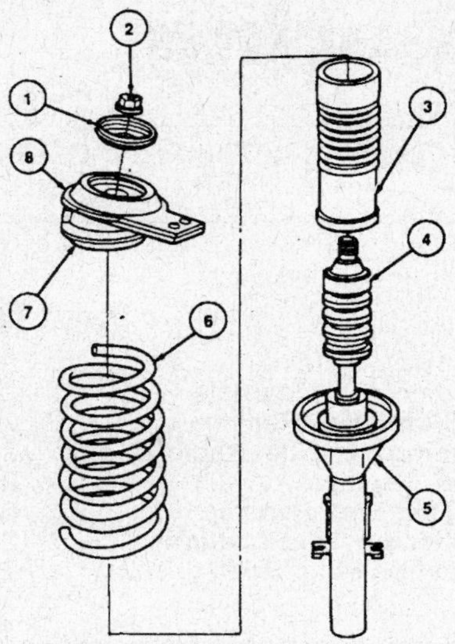

Item	Description
1	Rear Shock Absorber Bracket
2	Shock Absorber Mounting Nut
3	Rear Shock Absorber Dust Boot
4	Rear Suspension Jounce Bumper
5	Shock Absorber
6	Rear Spring
7	Spring Seat
8	Shock Absorber Bushing

FM2039500047000X

Fig. 3 Exploded view of strut assembly

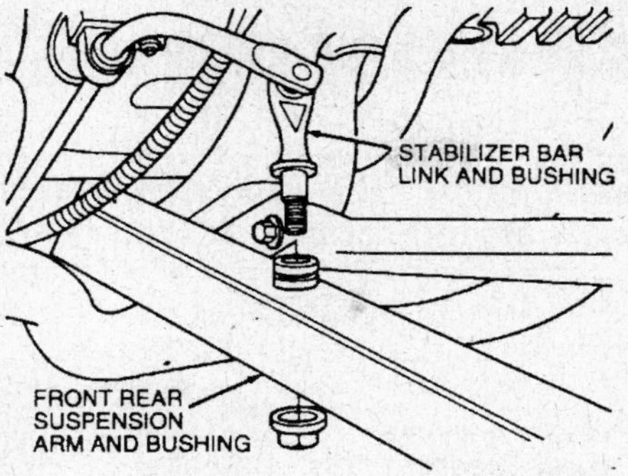

FM2039500046000X

Fig. 4 Stabilizer bar link & forward rear suspension arm. 1997

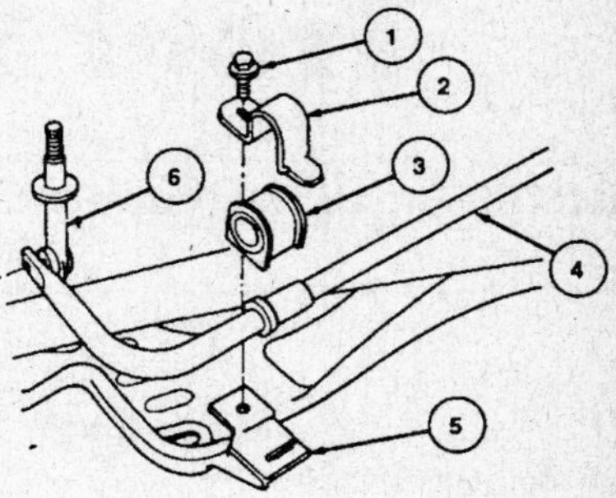

Item	Description
1	Bolt (4 Req'd)
2	Stabilizer Bar Bracket (2 Req'd)
3	Stabilizer Bar Insulator (2 Req'd)
4	Rear Stabilizer Bar
5	Rear Crossmember
6	Stabilizer Bar End

FM2039500048000X

Fig. 5 Exploded view of stabilizer bar, insulator & bracket assembly. 1997

TIGHTENING SPECIFICATIONS

Year	Component	Torque/Ft. Lbs.
1997-2000	Anti-Lock Sensor Bolt	84–96①
	Drum Brake Backing Plate Bolts	33–40
	Rearward Rear Suspension Arm To Crossmember Bolt	52–79
	Spindle To Forward Rear Suspension Arm Bolt	52–79
	Spindle To Rearward Rear Suspension Arm Bolt	75–102
	Stabilizer Bar Bracket Bolts	14–19
	Stabilizer Bar Link To Rear Suspension Arm	22–30
	Strut Mounting Bolts	17–22
	Strut Top Nut	30–43
	Strut To Spindle Pinch Bolt	52–72
	Tie Rod Forward Bracket To Body Bolts	75–102
	Tie Rod To Spindle Bolt	75–102
	Wheel Hub Retainer	170–192
	Wheel Lug Nuts	62

① — Inch lbs.

Front Suspension & Steering

NOTE: On Air Bag Equipped Models, Refer To "Air Bag System Precautions" Located In The Front Of This Manual For System Disarming & Arming Procedures.

INDEX

PRECAUTIONS

BATTERY GROUND CABLE

Prior to service, disconnect battery ground cable and isolate as required.

AIR BAG SYSTEMS

Refer to "Air Bag System Precautions" in front of this manual for system disarming and arming procedures.

DESCRIPTION

Front suspension utilizes McPherson struts, a stabilizer bar, lower control arms and a tubular perimeter frame. Steering control is maintained by an integral power rack and pinion steering gear coupled with a belt driven, vane type power steering pump. Power steering fluid is contained in a remote reservoir.

WHEEL BEARING

ADJUST

Wheel bearings are pre-greased and sealed; as a result, they require no periodic maintenance. Their cartridge design prohibits adjustment.

HUB & BEARING

REPLACE

1. Raise and support vehicle, then remove wheel, caliper and rotor. **It is not necessary to disconnect brake hydraulic line to caliper, but it is necessary to prevent caliper from hanging on brake hose by supporting it from vehicle chassis.**
2. Remove front brake anti-lock sensor and tie rod end cotter pin, then loosen tie rod end to knuckle nut.
3. Separate tie rod end from knuckle using rod end remover tool No. 3290-D, or equivalent, then insert steel rod into front disc brake rotor to prevent turning and remove front axle wheel hub retaining nut.
4. Separate halfshaft from wheel hub using special tools as shown in **Fig. 1. Support halfshaft during separation from wheel hub.**
5. Reverse procedure to install. Tighten bolts and nuts to specifications.

BALL JOINT INSPECTION

1. Raise and support vehicle.
2. Attach dial indicator with bracketry tool No. 4201-C, or equivalent, at ball joint to be checked.
3. To measure lateral movement between front wheel knuckle and front suspension arm lower ball joint, grasp tire at top and bottom and slowly move tire in and out.
4. Record radial play from dial indicator. If reading exceeds .015 inch, replace ball joint.

BALL JOINT

REPLACE

REMOVAL

1. Raise and support vehicle, then remove wheel and lower arm as described under "Control Arm, Replace."
2. Drill a .118 inch pilot hole through each rivet, **Fig. 2,** then drill a .354 inch hole in rivets to a depth of .472 inch.
3. Using a .275–.314 inch diameter punch, drive rivets out, then remove ball joint from vehicle.

INSTALLATION

1. Allow protective cover to remain on ball joint to protect seal, then position ball joint in lower arm.
2. Install three bolts and nuts in lower arm as shown, **Fig. 3,** to replace rivets.
3. Install lower arm as described under "Control Arm, Replace," then install wheel and lower vehicle.

STRUT

REPLACE

1. Raise and support vehicle, then remove wheel and, while holding piston rod with a hex wrench as shown in **Fig. 4,** remove strut top nut.
2. Disconnect stabilizer bar link from strut assembly, then disengage brake hose and anti-lock brake sensor wiring from strut brackets.
3. Remove strut to knuckle pinch bolt, then strut assembly.
4. Reverse procedure to install, noting following:
   a. Install strut top nut as shown in **Fig. 4** before tightening strut to knuckle pinch bolt.
   b. During stabilizer bar link installation, avoid damaging ball joint seal.
   c. Tighten bolts and nuts to specifications.

COIL SPRING & STRUT SERVICE

1. Remove strut assembly as described under "Strut, Replace," then position assembly in Rotunda spring compressor tool No. 086–00029, or equivalent.
2. Compress coil spring and remove thrust bearing retainer nut, thrust bearing, spring seat and dust shield, **Fig. 5.**
3. Release spring compressor tension and remove coil spring from strut assembly, then remove jounce bumper, **Fig. 5.**
4. Reverse procedure to assemble, noting following:
   a. Compress coil spring for installation using Rotunda spring compressor tool No. 086-0029B, or equivalent.
   b. Ensure coil spring seats properly in spring seat notch.
   c. Tighten thrust bearing nut to specifications.

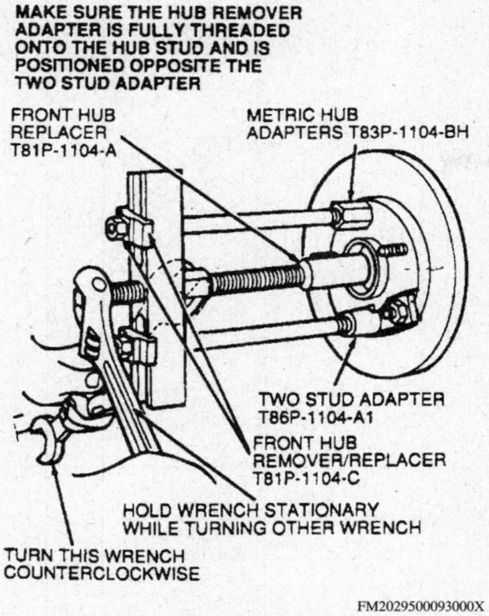

Fig. 1 Hub assembly removal

CONTROL ARM

REPLACE

LOWER

Left Side

1. Support radiator assembly.
2. **On models with 2.0L engine,** remove heat shield and catalytic converter retaining nuts from exhaust manifold.
3. **On all models,** raise and support vehicle, then remove 3–way catalytic converter, then disconnect steering column lower yoke.
4. **On models with manual transaxle,** disconnect gearshift rod and clevis.
5. **On all models,** remove lower front radiator cover, radiator supports and ball joint to knuckle pinch bolts.
6. Remove lower arm ball joints from knuckle, then disconnect power steering cooler lines at righthand front subframe and stabilizer bar link at front stabilizer bar.
7. Remove front and rear engine mount through bolts, then position Rotunda powertrain lift tool No. 014–00765, or equivalent, under front subframe.
8. Remove lower arm bushing to subframe nuts, then lower subframe to gain access to lower suspension mounting bolts.
9. Remove four lower arm to subframe bolts and nuts, **Fig. 6,** then separate lower arm from subframe.
10. Reverse procedure to install, noting following:
    a. Install lower arm bolts as shown, **Fig. 6.**
    b. Tighten all bolts and nuts to specifications.

Right Side

1. Raise and support vehicle, then remove wheel and ball joint to knuckle pinch bolt.
2. Separate lower arm ball joint from knuckle, then remove four lower arm

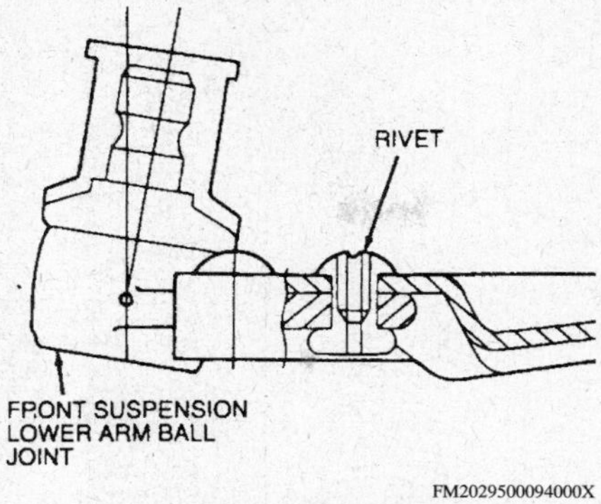

Fig. 2 Ball joint rivets

bushing to subframe bolts, **Fig. 6.**
3. Reverse procedure to install, noting following:
    a. Install lower arm bolts as shown, **Fig. 6.**
    b. Tighten all bolts and nuts to specifications.

STEERING KNUCKLE

REPLACE

1. Remove hub as described under "Hub & Bearing, Replace," then remove pinch bolt securing knuckle to lower arm ball joint.
2. Remove strut to knuckle pinch bolt, then knuckle, **Fig. 7.**
3. Reverse procedure to install, noting following:
    a. Install new pinch bolts and nuts on knuckle mounts.
    b. Tighten all bolts and nuts to specifications.

STABILIZER BAR

REPLACE

1. Raise and support vehicle, then remove both front wheels.
2. Remove stabilizer bar link from strut assembly, **Fig. 8,** then use ball joint remover tool No. D88L-3006-A, or equivalent, to remove link from stabilizer bar. **Avoid damaging stabilizer bar link ball joint seal during removal. Link assembly must be replaced if seal is damaged.**
3. Remove four stabilizer bar insulator bracket to subframe bolts, then stabilizer bar.
4. Reverse procedure to install, noting following:
    a. **Avoid damaging stabilizer bar link ball joint seal during installation. Link assembly must be replaced if seal is damaged.**
    b. Tighten bolts and nuts to specifications.

TIE ROD END

REPLACE

1. Remove and discard cotter pin and nut from tie rod end, then use tie rod end remover tool No. 3290-D, or equivalent, to separate tie rod end from steering knuckle.

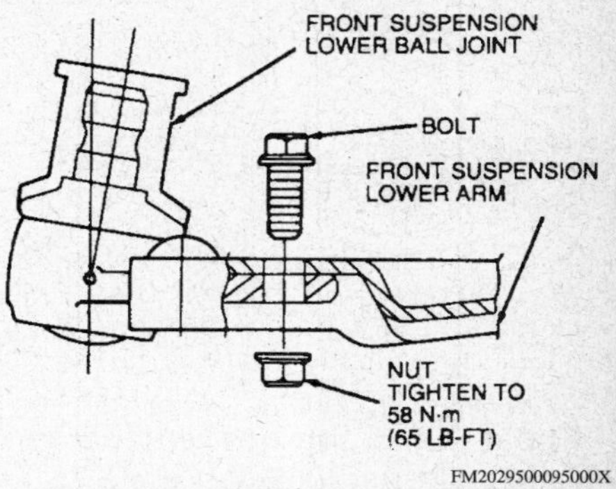

Fig. 3 Ball joint bolt installation

2. While holding tie rod end with a suitable wrench, loosen jam nut slightly. **Allow jam nut to remain as close to its original position as possible for tie rod end installation depth reference.**
3. Using suitable pliers, remove tie rod end from tie rod.
4. Reverse procedure to install, noting following:
    a. Thread new tie rod end onto tie rod only until it reaches jam nut, then secure with jam nut until wheel alignment can be inspected and set.
    b. Install a new tie rod end stud nut and cotter pin.
    c. Tighten tie rod end to knuckle nut and tie rod end jam nut to specifications.
    d. Set front wheel toe to specifications as described in "Wheel Alignment" section.

POWER STEERING GEAR

REPLACE

1. Center the steering wheel and lock in position.
2. Working from inside passenger compartment, remove clamp plate bolt securing steering column shaft to flex coupling.
3. Rotate clamp plate to disengage from steering gear pinion shaft, then carefully remove floor seal.
4. Remove pinch bolt from flex coupling, then slide coupling from steering gear pinion shaft.
5. Using a suction gun, or equivalent fluid suction tool, remove as much power steering fluid from pump auxiliary reservoir as possible.
6. Disconnect power steering return hose from pump auxiliary reservoir, then raise and support vehicle.
7. Remove front subframe assembly, then remove steering gear cover plate from subframe as shown, **Fig. 9.**
8. Disconnect pressure and return hose unions from power steering gear, then remove two bolts securing gear to subframe.
9. Separate steering gear from subframe. **Do not attempt to disassemble any part of steering gear. If any**

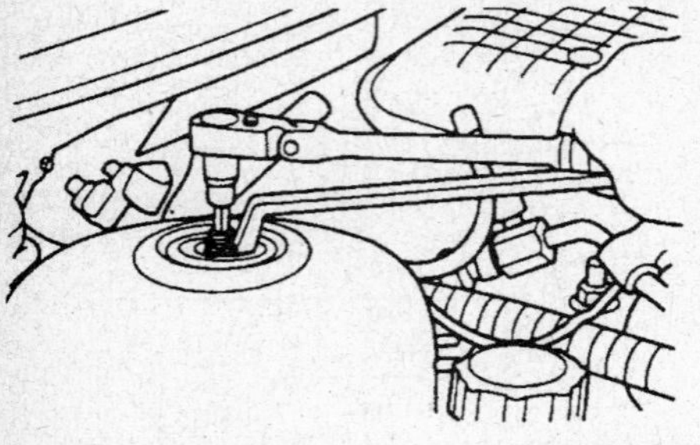

FM2029500096000X

Fig. 4 Strut top nut replacement

steering gear service is necessary, entire unit must be replaced.

10. Remove spindle connecting rods and boots from steering gear assembly.
11. Reverse procedure to install, noting following:
    a. Install new plastic seals on hydraulic lines.
    b. Tighten all bolts and nuts to specifications.
    c. Refill power steering fluid reservoir and bleed system as described under "Power Steering System Bleed."
    d. If tie rod ends were loosened during procedure, inspect and adjust wheel alignment as described in "Wheel Alignment" section.

POWER STEERING PUMP

REPLACE

2.0L ENGINE

1997

1. Remove exhaust manifold heat shield.
2. Disengage power steering pump reservoir hose from pump bracket and engine lifting bracket, then disconnect return hose and reservoir pump hose from pump.
3. Allow fluid to drain into a suitable container, then raise and support vehicle.
4. Remove lower belt guard, then rotate drive belt tensioner clockwise as viewed from direction shown, **Fig. 10.** and remove accessory drive belt.
5. Lower vehicle, then remove traction assist module bolts and position module aside.
6. Rotate power steering pump pulley to gain access to each pump front mounting bolt, then remove three front bolts and one rear bolt and lift pump from vehicle.
7. If it is necessary to separate pulley from power steering pump, proceed as follows:
    a. install power steering pump pulley remover tool No. T69L-10300-B, or equivalent, on pulley hub.
    b. Clamp hex head of tool in a suitable vise, then hold power steering pump in place while turning tool nut counterclockwise. **Do not apply inward or outward force on power steering pump shaft; internal pump damage may result.**

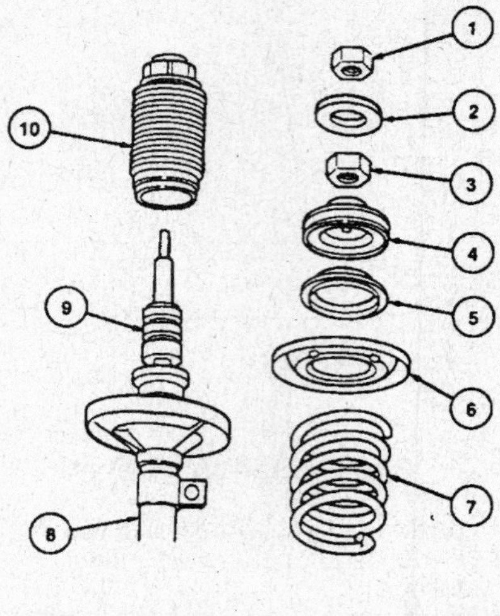

Item	Description
1	Nut
2	Retainer
3	Upper Mount Retainer Nut
4	Upper Mount
5	Bearing
6	Spring Seat
7	Front Coil Spring
8	Front Shock Absorber
9	Jounce Bumper
10	Dust Shield

FM2029500097000X

Fig. 5 Exploded view of strut assembly

    c. Slide pulley from power steering pump shaft.

8. Reverse procedure to install, noting following:
    a. If pulley and power steering pump were separated, install pulley on pump shaft using power steering pump pulley replacer tool No. T91P-3A733-A, or equivalent. **Ensure threads on end of tool are fully engaged in power steering pump shaft and end of shaft is within .010 inch of being flush with pulley surface.**
    b. When placing pump in vehicle, install rear mounting bolt first, but do not tighten until three front bolts are in position.
    c. Rotate drive belt tensioner clockwise as viewed from direction shown in **Fig. 10** to install accessory drive belt.
    d. Tighten all bolts, nuts and fittings to specifications.
    e. Refill power steering fluid reservoir and bleed system as described under "Power Steering System Bleed."

1998–2000

1. Raise and support vehicle, then remove lower splash shield.
2. Rotate drive belt tensioner clockwise and remove drive belt.
3. Disconnect power steering pump high pressure line union and drain fluid into suitable container.
4. Disconnect power steering low pressure hose.

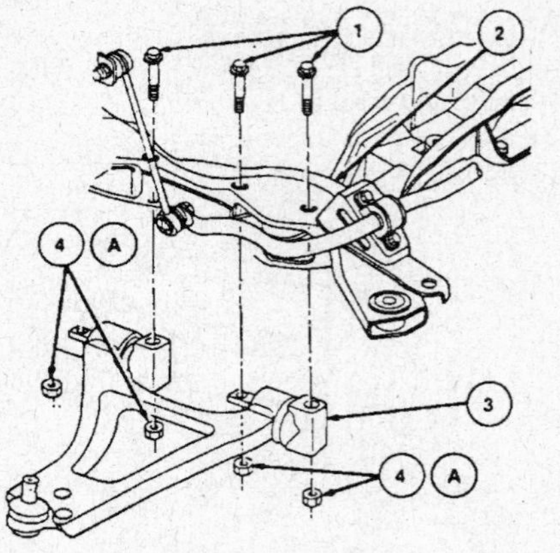

Item	Description
1	Bolts (4 Req'd)
2	Sub-frame
3	Front Suspension Lower Arm
4	Nuts (4 Req'd)
A	Tighten to 130 N·m (96 Lb-Ft)

FM2029500098000X

Fig. 6 Lower arm replacement

5. Remove four power steering pump bolts, then the pump.
6. Reverse procedures to install.

2.5L ENGINE

1997

1. Remove bolt securing power steering pressure hose to upper engine mount.
2. Disconnect power steering pressure hose from pump and allow fluid to drain into a suitable container, then position hose and ignition wire organizer aside.
3. Remove engine front support insulator, then loosen (but do not remove) power steering pump pulley bolts.
4. Rotate drive belt tensioner clockwise as viewed from drive belt side of engine, then remove accessory drive belt and power steering pump pulley.
5. Disconnect power steering reservoir pump hose from power steering pump, then remove pressure hose clamp from pump bracket.
6. Remove power steering pump bracket nuts and bolts, then bracket and pump, **Fig. 11. Do not attempt to disassemble any part of power steering pump. If service is required, entire pump assembly must be replaced.**
7. Reverse procedure to install, noting following:
    a. Do not tighten power steering pump pulley bolts to specifications until accessory drive belt has been installed.
    b. When installing accessory drive belt, rotate tensioner assembly clockwise as viewed from belt side of engine.
    c. Tighten all bolts, nuts and fittings to specifications.
    d. Refill power steering fluid reservoir and bleed system as described under "Power Steering System Bleed."

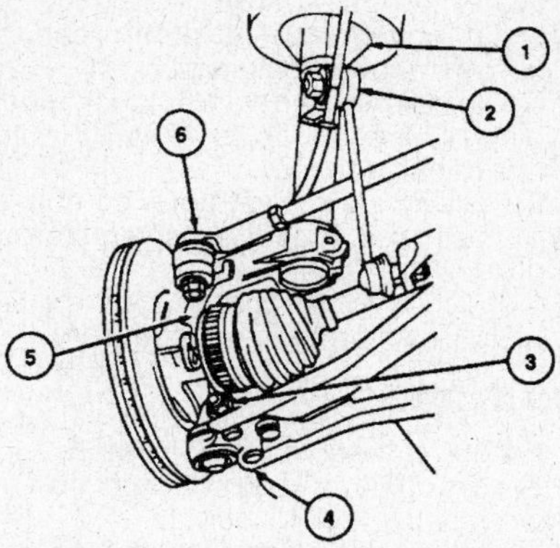

Item	Description
1	Front Shock Absorber
2	Stabilizer Bar Link
3	Lower Ball Joint-To-Knuckle Pinch Bolt
4	Front Suspension Lower Arm
5	Front Wheel Knuckle
6	Front Wheel Spindle Connecting Rod

FM2029500099000X

Fig. 7 Knuckle assembly

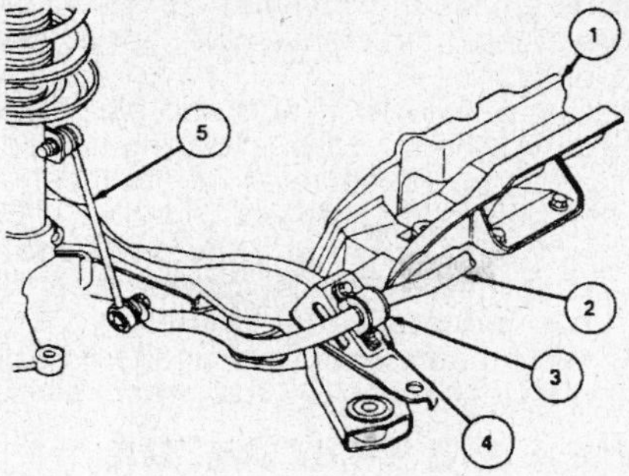

Item	Description
1	Front Sub-Frame
2	Stabilizer Bar
3	Stabilizer Bar Bracket
4	Stabilizer Bar Bracket Bolt (4 Req'd)
5	Stabilizer Bar Link

FM2029500100000X

Fig. 8 Stabilizer bar assembly

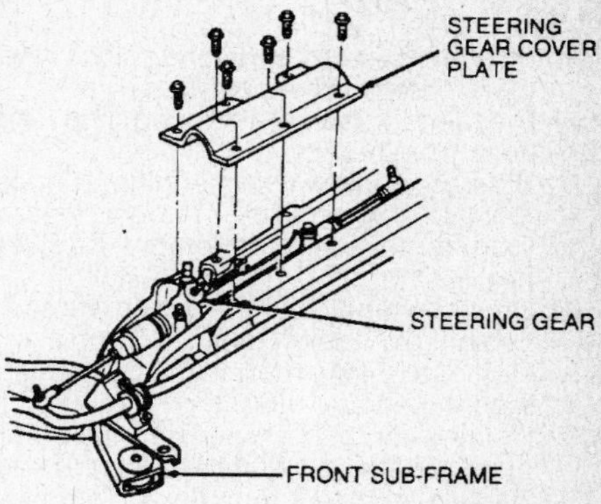

FM6029500193000X

Fig. 9 Steering gear cover plate removal

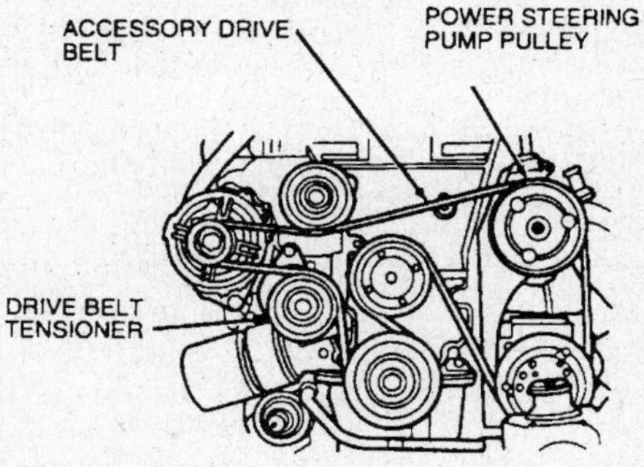

FM6029500194000X

Fig. 10 Accessory drive belt & tensioner. 1997 2.0L engine

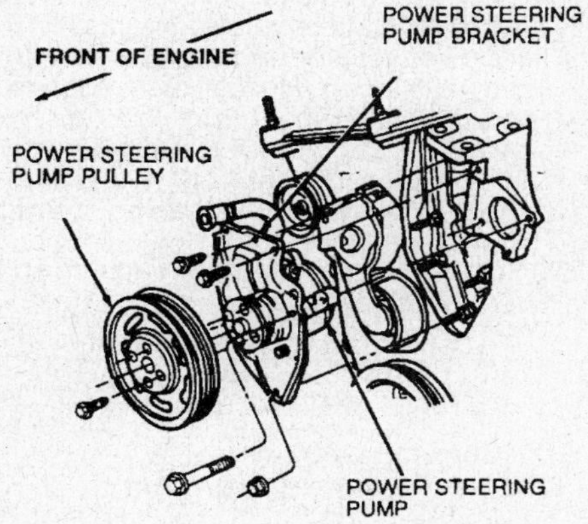

FM6029500195000X

Fig. 11 Power steering pump pulley & bracket. 1997 2.5L engine

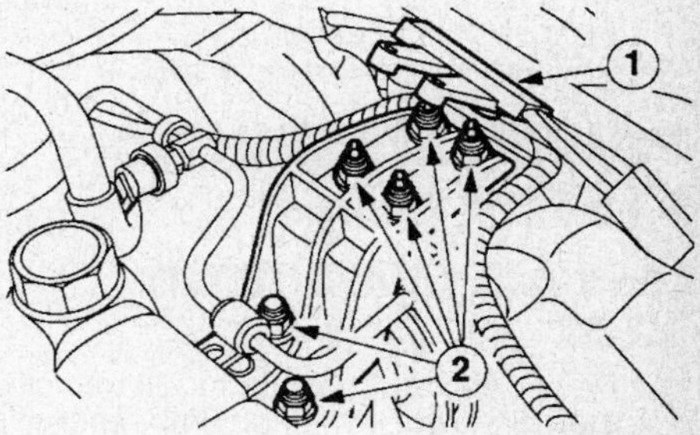

FM2029800140000X

Fig. 12 Engine mount bracket. 1998–2000 2.5L engine

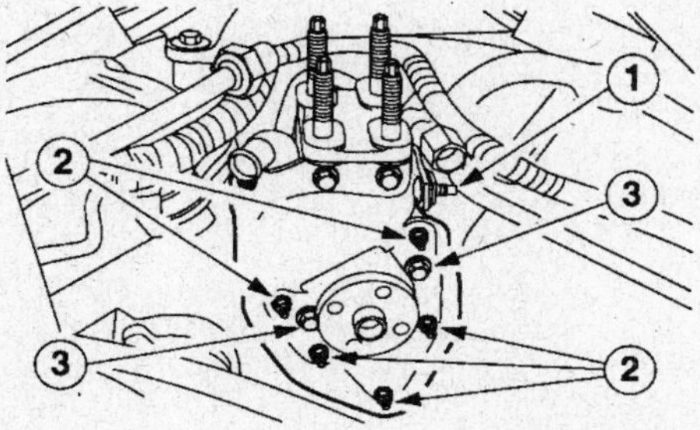

FM2029800141000X

Fig. 13 Retaining plate & bracket. 1998–2000 2.5L engine

1998–2000

1. Rotate drive belt tensioner clockwise, then remove drive belt.
2. Disconnect power steering line and hose from pump.
3. Support engine using engine support tool No. D88L–6000–A, or equivalent, then remove engine mount bracket, **Fig. 12.**
4. Drain cooling system , then remove coolant expansion tank.
5. Remove engine mount attaching bolts, then the engine mount.
6. Holding center of power steering pump pulley with a suitable hex head wrench, remove four power steering pump attaching bolts.
7. Remove pump bracket attaching bolt, then the retaining plate nuts and bolts, **Fig. 13.**
8. Remove power steering pump attaching bolts, then the pump.
9. Reverse procedures to install.

POWER STEERING SYSTEM BLEED

LESS AIR EVACUATOR TOOL

1. Raise and support front of vehicle, then fill power steering pump reservoir until fluid level is between MIN and MAX marks.
2. Disconnect Ignition Control Module (ICM) lead to prevent engine from starting, then crank engine for 30 seconds.
3. Check fluid level and add as necessary; then, while cranking engine again for 30 seconds, rotate steering wheel from lock to lock repeatedly. **Do not hold wheel at either lock more than five seconds, power steering pump damage may result.**
4. Check and add fluid as necessary, then reconnect ICM and lower vehicle.

WITH AIR EVACUATOR TOOL

1997

1. Raise and support front of vehicle, then insert air evacuator rubber stopper securely into power steering pump reservoir opening.
2. Start and idle engine, then apply 20–25 inches Hg vacuum for a minimum of three minutes.
3. Release vacuum and remove evacuator, then add fluid to reservoir until level is between MIN and MAX marks.
4. Install evacuator and apply a vacuum of 20–25 inches Hg to system, then rotate steering wheel from lock to lock every 30 seconds for approximately five minutes. **Do not hold wheel at either lock; power steering pump damage may result.**
5. Stop engine, then release vacuum and remove air evacuator.
6. Lower front of vehicle to ground, then install power steering pump reservoir cap and start engine again.
7. Cycle steering wheel from lock to lock every 30 seconds for approximately five minutes.
8. If system has not yet been completely purged of air, repeat evacuation procedure.
9. Inspect all hose connections for fluid leakage and repair as necessary.

1998–2000

1. Fill pump reservoir to MAX mark.
2. Start engine and slowly turn steering wheel from lock to lock
3. Switch engine off and check fluid level, add fluid as necessary.
4. Connect a suitable stopper to hand vacuum pump tube and insert into reservoir filler neck.
5. Start engine and slowly turn steering wheel to right, just off stop.
6. Turn engine off and apply 5 inches Hg of vacuum pressure until air is purged from system, minimum of five minutes. If pressure drops by more than 2 inches Hg in five minutes, system should be checked for leaks.
7. Depressurize system at vacuum pump, then repeat bleed operation turning steering wheel to left, just off stop.
8. If noise level is still unacceptable, leave vehicle standing overnight then repeat bleed procedure.

TIGHTENING SPECIFICATIONS

Year	Component	Torque/Ft. Lbs.
1997-2000	Engine Mount Through Bolts	40–55
	Exhaust Manifold Heat Shield Bolts & Nuts	53①
	Lower Arm To Subframe Bolts	96
	Lower Ball Joint Pinch Bolt	65
	Power Steering Hose To Bracket Bolts & Nut	53①
	Power Steering Hose To Power Steering Pump Fittings	48
	Power Steering Hose Union To Steering Gear	23
	Power Steering Pump Mounting Bolts	18
	Power Steering Pump Pulley Bolts (2.5L)	96①
	Stabilizer Bar Insulator Mounting Bracket To Subframe Bolts	37
	Stabilizer Bar Link Nut	37
	Steering Gear Cover Plate To Subframe	37
	Steering Gear To Subframe Bolts	101
	Steering Shaft Clamp Plate Bolt	18
	Steering Shaft Flex Coupling Pinch Bolt	21
	Strut Thrust Bearing Nut	44
	Strut To Front Wheel Knuckle Pinch Bolt	62
	Strut Top Mounting Nut	37
	Tie Rod End Jam Nut	35–50
	Tie Rod End To Knuckle Nut	18–22
	Traction Assist Module Bolts	53①
	Wheel Hub Retainer	210
	Wheel Lug Nuts	②

① — Inch lbs.

② — 1997, 62 ft. lbs; 1998–2000, 94 ft. lbs.

Wheel Alignment

INDEX

PRELIMINARY INSPECTION

1. Ensure all tires are inflated to proper pressure.
2. Inspect tire for wear patterns that may indicate improper wheel alignment, tire imbalance or damage due to bulges or separation.
3. Inspect suspension for modifications such as trailer towing equipment or heavy duty handling components.
4. Inspect vehicle for signs of overloading or sagging; ensure luggage compartment does not contain heavy objects.
5. Road test vehicle to isolate area of concern.

FRONT WHEEL ALIGNMENT

All wheel alignment inspections must be performed on an alignment rack leveled to within 1⁄16 inch side to side and front to rear. Alignment equipment must be capable of compensating for wheel runout and of measuring left and right front wheel toe independently.

CASTER & CAMBER

Front wheel caster and camber are preset by manufacturer and are not adjustable. If caster and camber are not as indicated under "Front Wheel Alignment Specifications," inspect suspension components for damage, modification or excessive wear.

TOE

1. Start engine and rotate steering wheel back and forth several times, then place it in its centered position (wheels straight ahead).
2. Stop engine and lock steering wheel in position, then loosen steering ball stud dust seal outer clamp and slide off end of seal to prevent seal from twisting during adjustment.
3. Loosen tie rod end jam nuts, then adjust left and right tie rod ends until each wheel's toe measurement is ½ of total toe as specified under "Front Wheel Alignment Specifications."
4. **Torque** tie rod end jam nuts to 35–46 ft. lbs., then position steering ball stud dust seal outer clamp over seal and tighten securely. **Ensure seal is not twisted.**

REAR WHEEL ALIGNMENT

1. Loosen bolt attaching rear suspension arm and bushing to subframe.
2. Rotate alignment cam to obtain specified toe.
3. **Torque** rear suspension arm and bushing retaining nut to 62 ft. lbs.

VEHICLE RIDE HEIGHT

Vehicle ride height is preset by manufacturer and is not adjustable. If vehicle ride height appears incorrect, check for damaged, modified or excessively worn suspension components.

CROWN VICTORIA, GRAND MARQUIS, THUNDERBIRD & 1997 COUGAR

NOTE: Refer To Rear Of This Manual For Vehicle Manufacturer's Special Service Tool Suppliers.

INDEX OF SERVICE OPERATIONS

Specifications

GENERAL ENGINE SPECIFICATIONS

Engine Liter (VIN Code)②	Fuel System	Bore & Stroke	Compression Ratio	Net H.P. @ RPM③	Maximum Torque Ft. Lbs. @ RPM	Normal Oil Pressure, psi
1997						
3.8L (4)	SEFI	3.80 x 3.40	9.0	145 @ 4000	215 @ 2750	40–60④
4.6L (W)⑥	SEFI	3.55 x 3.54	9.0	190 @ 4250	265 @ 3250	20–45⑨
4.6L (W)①⑧	SEFI	3.55 x 3.54	9.0	205 @ 4250	280 @ 3000	20–45⑨
4.6L (W)⑦⑧	SEFI	3.55 x 3.54	9.0	210 @ 4250	275 @ 3250	20–45⑨
4.6L (9)⑤	SEFI	3.55 x 3.54	10.0	175 @ 4500	235 @ 3500	—
1998–99						
4.6L (W)⑦	SEFI	3.55 x 3.54	9.0	⑩	⑪	—
4.6L (9)⑤	SEFI	3.55 x 3.54	10.0	175 @ 4500	235 @ 3500	—
2000						
4.6L (W)⑦	SEFI	3.55 x 3.54	9.0	—	—	40–70⑫
4.6L (9)⑤	SEFI	3.55 x 3.54	10.0	—	—	40–70⑫

SEFI — Sequential Multi-Port Electronic Fuel Injection

① — Cougar & Thunderbird.

② — The eighth digit of VIN denotes engine code.

③ — Ratings are net-as installed in vehicle.

④ — At 2500 RPM w/engine @ operating temperature.

⑤ — Natural Gas Vehicle (NGV).

⑥ — Single exhaust.

⑦ — Crown Victoria & Grand Marquis.

⑧ — Dual exhaust.

⑨ — At 1500 RPM w/engine @ operating temperature.

⑩ — 200 @ 4250 RPM w/single exhaust; 215 @ 4500 RPM w/dual exhaust.

⑪ — 275 @ 3000 RPM w/single exhaust; 285 @ 3000 RPM w/dual exhaust.

⑫ — At 200° F.

TUNE UP SPECIFICATIONS

Engine Liter (VIN Code)①	Spark Plug Gap	Ignition Timing, BTDC				Curb Idle Speed, RPM③		Fast Idle Speed, RPM③		Fuel Pump Pressure, psi	Valve Clearance, Inch
		Firing Order Fig.	Man. Trans.	Auto. Trans.	Mark Fig.	Man. Trans.	Auto. Trans.	Man. Trans.	Auto. Trans.		
1997											
3.8L (4)	.054	B⑪	—	10⑤	—	—	⑥	—	⑥	35–40⑦	⑧
4.6L (W)	.054	A⑩	—	10⑤	②	—	⑥	—	⑥	35–40⑦	⑧
4.6L (9)	.044	A⑩	—	10⑤	②	—	⑥	—	⑥	100–135⑦	⑧
1998–2000											
4.6L (W)	.054	A⑫	—	10⑤	②	—	⑥	—	⑥	30–45⑦	⑧
4.6L (9)⑨	.044	A⑫	—	10⑤	②	—	⑥	—	⑥	80–120④	⑧

BTDC — Before Top Dead Center

① — The eighth digit of Vehicle Identification Number (VIN) denotes engine code.

② — Equipped w/crankshaft sensor.

③ — When checking idle speed, set parking brake & block drive wheels.

④ — Locate vehicle in a well ventilated area away from heat, spark & flame producing equipment. Using extreme caution, connect a suitable natural gas approved fuel pressure gauge to the fuel pressure schrader valve. Release fuel pressure in fuel injection supply manifold back to fuel tanks. Place ignition switch in On position, then start engine if possible. Place ignition switch in Off position. After 2 minutes, check fuel pressure reading on gauge.

⑤ — Non-adjustable.

⑥ — Idle speed is controlled by an automatic idle speed control. No adjustment is necessary.

⑦ — Wrap shop towel around fuel diagnostic valve to prevent fuel spillage. Connect suitable fuel pressure gauge to fuel diagnostic valve. Place ignition switch in On position to energize fuel pump & check pressure gauge reading.

⑧ — Equipped w/hydraulic valve tappets.

⑨ — Natural Gas Vehicle.

⑩ — Cylinder numbering front to rear, right bank, 1, 2, 3, 4; left bank, 5, 6, 7, 8. Firing order, 1–3–7–2–6–5–4–8.

⑪ — Cylinder numbering front to rear, right bank, 1, 2, 3; left bank, 4, 5, 6. Firing order, 1–4–2–5–3–6.

⑫ — Equipped w/coil on spark plug ignition. Cylinder numbering front to rear, right bank, 1–2–3–4; left bank 5–6–7–8. Firing order, 1–3–7–2–6–5–4–8.

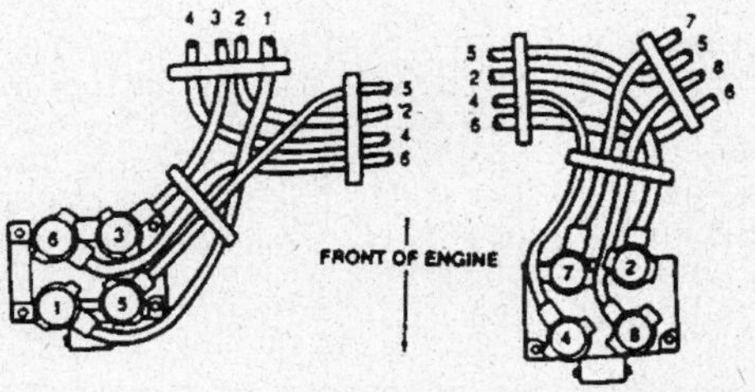

FM1139500504000X

Fig. A

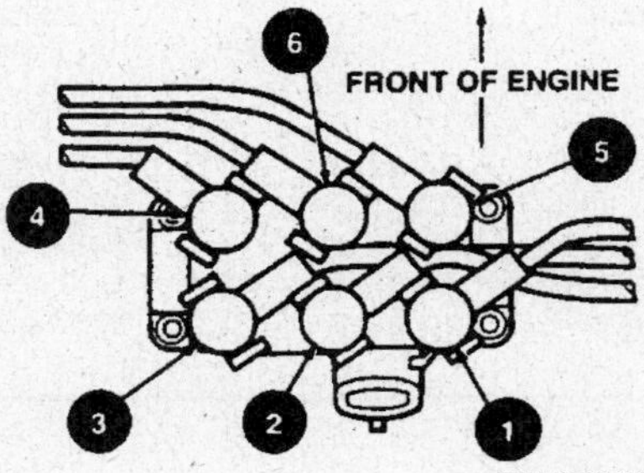

FM1139500505000X

Fig. B

FRONT WHEEL ALIGNMENT SPECIFICATIONS

Year	Caster Angle, Degrees		Camber Angle, Degrees				Total Toe-In, Inch	Toe Out on Turns, Deg.		Ball Joint Wear
	Limits	Desired	Limits		Desired			Outer Wheel	Inner Wheel	
			Left	Right	Left	Right				
COUGAR & THUNDERBIRD										
1997	+4.75 to +6.25	+5.5	−1.25 to +.25	−1.25 to +.25	−.5	−.5	1/16	19.73	20	.0015
CROWN VICTORIA & GRAND MARQUIS										
1997–2000	+4.75 to +6.25	+5.5	−1.25 to +.25	−1.25 to +.25	−.5	−.5	1/16	18.51	20	①

① — Refer to "Ball Joint Inspection" under "Front Suspension & Steering."

REAR WHEEL ALIGNMENT SPECIFICATIONS

Year	Camber Angle, Degrees						Total Toe-In Inch
	Limits		Desired		Maximum Difference (Left Minus Right)		
	Left	Right	Left	Right	Limits	Desired	
COUGAR & THUNDERBIRD							
1997	−1 to 0	−1 to 0	−.5	−.5	-.5 to +.5	0	1/16

FLUID CAPACITIES & COOLING SYSTEM DATA

Engine	Coolant Capacity, Qts.	Radiator Cap Relief Pressure, psi	Thermo. Opening Temp.	Fuel Tank Gals.	Engine Refill Qts.	Transmission Oil		
						Man. Trans. Pts.	Auto. Trans. Qts.①	Rear Axle Oil Pts.
1997								
3.8L	12.6	16	196	18	5②	—	13.9	④
4.6L	14.1	16	196	⑤	5②	—	13.9	③
1998–2000								
4.6L	⑥	16	192	19	5②	—	13.9⑥	3.75

① — Approximate, make final check w/dipstick.
② — Includes filter. Final check is made w/dipstick.
③ — Cougar & Thunderbird, 7.5 inch ring gear conventional, 3 pts.; 7.5 inch ring gear Traction-Lok, 2.85 pts.; 8.8 inch ring gear conventional, 3.5 pts.; 8.8 inch ring gear Traction-Lok, 3.25 pts. Crown Victoria & Grand Marquis, 3.75 pts.
④ — 7.5 inch ring gear conventional, 3 pts.; 7.5 inch ring gear Traction-Lok, 2.85 pts.; 8.8 inch ring gear conventional, 3.5 pts.; 8.8 inch ring gear Traction-Lok, 3.25 pts.
⑤ — Cougar & Thunderbird, 18 gals.; Crown Victoria & Grand Marquis, 20 gals. Some Crown Victoria & Grand Marquis may be equipped w/18 gal. tank.
⑥ — 2000 model police applications, 12.8 qts.

LUBRICANT DATA

Year	Model	Lubricant Type				
		Transmission		Rear Axle	Power Steering	Brake System
		Manual	Automatic			
1997	All	—	Mercon	80-90W①③	②	DOT 3
1998–2000	All	—	Mercon V	80-90W①④	②	DOT 3

① — Traction-Lok axles, add 4 oz. of Ford Motor Co. Friction Modifier C8AZ-19B546-A, or equivalent.
② — 1997–98 models, premium power steering fluid meeting Ford Specification ESW-M2C33–F; 1999–2000 models, Mercon ATF fluid.
③ — Hypoid premium gear lubricant.
④ — Premium thermally stable rear axle lubricant part No. XY-80W90–QL, or equivalent, meeting Ford specification WSP-M2C197–A.

Electrical

NOTE: On Air Bag Equipped Models, Refer To " Air Bag System Precautions" Located In The Front Of This Manual For System Disarming & Arming Procedures.

NOTE: Refer To "Computer Relearn Procedures " Located In The Front Of This Manual For Computer Relearn Procedures.

INDEX

PRECAUTIONS

AIR BAG SYSTEMS

Refer to "Air Bag System Precautions" in the front of this manual for system disarming and arming procedures.

BATTERY GROUND CABLE

Prior to service, disconnect battery ground cable and isolate as required.

FUSE PANEL & FLASHER LOCATION

COUGAR & THUNDERBIRD

The fuse panel is on the left side of the lower instrument panel.

The electronic flasher is located behind lefthand side of instrument panel, left of steering column.

CROWN VICTORIA & GRAND MARQUIS

The fuse panel is located behind the left side of the instrument panel.

The emergency flashers are located on the lefthand rear of the trunk, front flasher is located right rear of engine compartment and the rear flasher is located center rear of trunk.

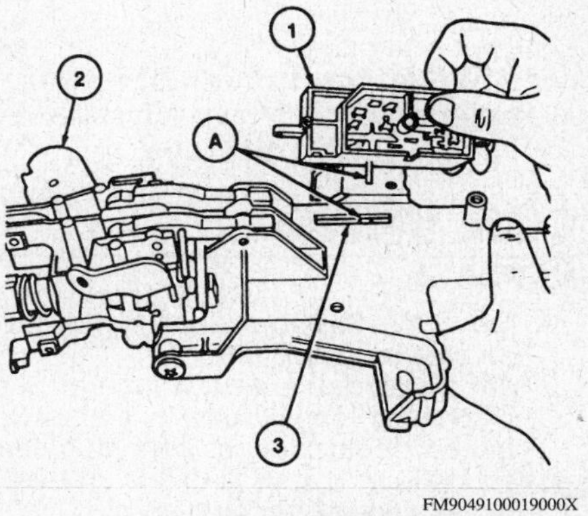

Fig. 1 Ignition switch replacement. Cougar & Thunderbird

FUEL PUMP RELAY LOCATION

COUGAR & THUNDERBIRD

The fuel pump relay is located in the relay center on the front lefthand side of the engine compartment.

CROWN VICTORIA & GRAND MARQUIS

The fuel pump relay is located on the lefthand side of engine compartment, in the relay center.

RELAY CENTER LOCATION

The relay center is located on the lefthand side of the engine compartment.

STARTER

REPLACE

COUGAR & THUNDERBIRD

1. Raise and support front of vehicle.
2. Disconnect starter cable and connector S-terminal from starter solenoid.

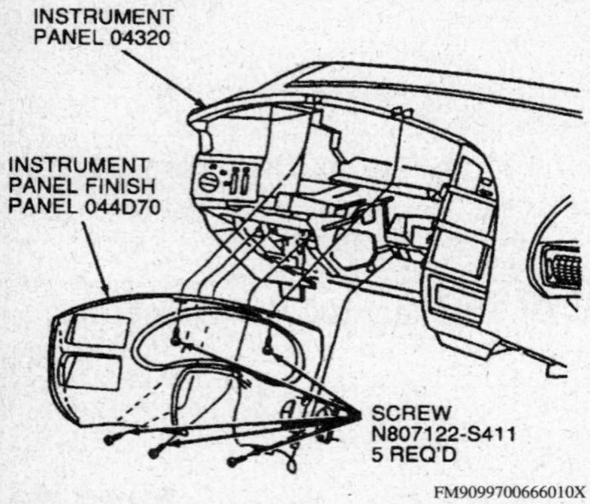

Fig. 2 Instrument cluster replacement (Part 1 of 2). Cougar & Thunderbird

3. Remove upper bolt.
4. **On models with 3.8L engines,** remove one lower bolt.
5. **On models with 4.6L engines,** remove two lower bolts.
6. **On all models,** reverse procedure to install. **Torque** starter bolts to 15–20 ft. lbs. and solenoid connector nut to 44 inch lbs.

CROWN VICTORIA & GRAND MARQUIS

1. Raise and support front of vehicle.
2. Remove the starter motor solenoid terminal cover. Disconnect starter cables from starter solenoid.
3. Remove bolt and position the transmission cooler lines and bracket out of the way.
4. Remove two upper mounting bolts using a ¼ inch drive ratchet with swivel-type 10 mm socket.
5. Remove lower mounting bolt and starter.
6. Reverse procedure to install, noting the following:
   a. **Torque** starter bolts to 15–20 ft. lbs.
   b. **Torque** S-terminal cable eyelet with washer nut to 40–57 inch lbs.
   c. **Torque** starter cable nut to starter B-terminal nut to 72–120 inch ft. lbs.
   d. **Torque** transmission cooler line bracket bolt to 84 inch lbs.

COIL PACK

REPLACE

1. Disconnect engine control sensor wiring from ignition coil and radio ignition interference capacitor.
2. Disconnect ignition wires by squeezing locking tabs and twisting while pulling upward.
3. Remove ignition coil mounting screws and ignition coil with radio ignition interference capacitor.
4. Reverse procedure to install. **Torque** coil pack mounting bolts to 40–61 inch lbs. and apply Dielectric Compound part No. D7AZ-19A331-A, or equivalent, to ignition wire boots.

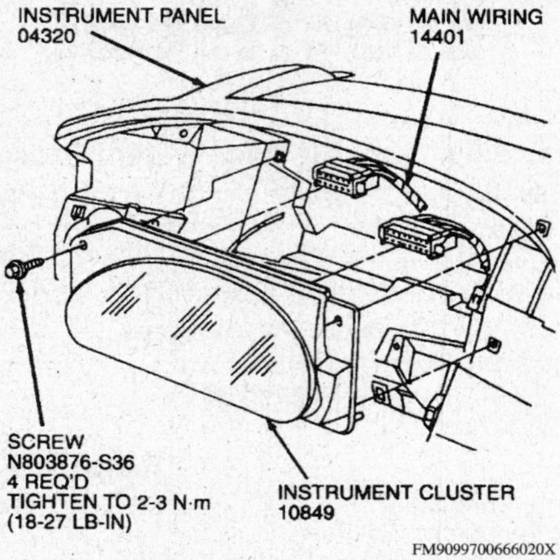

Fig. 2 Instrument panel replacement (Part 2 of 2). Cougar & Thunderbird

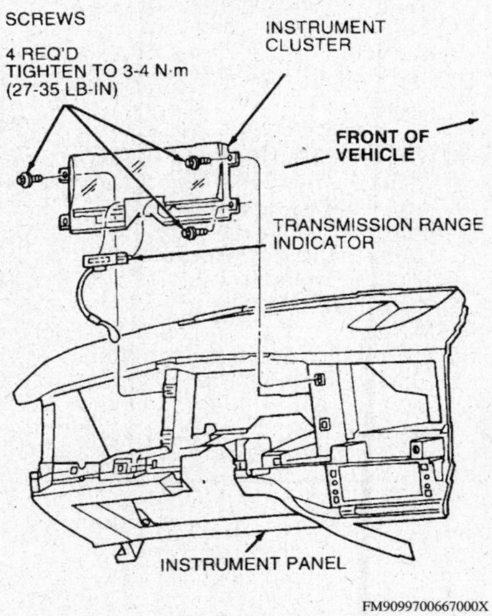

Fig. 4 Instrument cluster replacement. Crown Victoria & Grand Marquis

COIL UNITS

REPLACE

1. **On 1999–2000 models,** remove the air cleaner outlet tube.
2. **On all models,** remove fuel rail, then disconnect engine control sensor wiring connector from coil per plug units.
3. Remove coil per plug unit retaining bolts, then coil per plug units.
4. Reverse procedure to install. **Torque** retaining bolts to 72–108 inch lbs.

IGNITION LOCK

REPLACE

FUNCTIONAL

The following procedures are for vehicles that have a functioning ignition switch lock cylinder, ignition key is available, or the lock cylinder key numbers are known and key can be made.

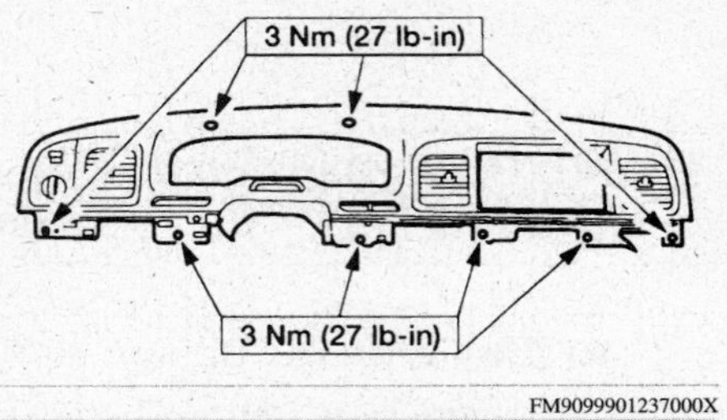

Fig. 3 Instrument panel cluster finish trim panel. 1999–2000 Crown Victoria & Grand Marquis

Cougar & Thunderbird

1. **On models equipped with tilt column,** remove upper extension shroud by detaching from retaining clip at 9 o'clock position.
2. **On all models,** remove both trim shroud halves.
3. Disconnect key warning switch electrical connector.
4. Turn ignition key to Run. Place gear selector lever in Park if equipped with column shift.
5. Insert a ⅛ inch diameter wire pin into hole in casting around lock cylinder. Remove lock cylinder while depressing retaining pin with wire.
6. Reverse procedure to install. Lock cylinder must be in Run and retaining pin depressed during installation. Following installation, turn key to check for correct operation in all positions.

Crown Victoria & Grand Marquis

1. Turn lock cylinder to Run position.
2. Insert a ⅛ inch diameter wire pin or small drift punch in hole in trim shroud under lock cylinder. Depress retaining pin while pulling out on lock cylinder to remove from column housing.
3. Install lock cylinder by turning to Run position and depressing retaining pin. Insert lock cylinder into housing. Ensure cylinder is fully seated and aligned in interlocking washer before turning key to " OFF." This will permit cylinder retaining pin to extend into cylinder housing hole.
4. Using key, rotate lock cylinder. Ensure correct mechanical operation in all positions.

NON-FUNCTIONAL

The following procedure is for vehicles that have a inoperative ignition lock cylinder and the ignition switch cannot be rotated due to a lost or broken lock cylinder key, unknown key number, or an ignition switch cap that has been damaged to the extent that the key cannot be rotated.

1. Remove steering wheel as described in "Steering Wheel, Replace."
2. Using channel lock or vise-grip type pliers, twist ignition cap or bezel until it separates from ignition switch.
3. Using a ⅜ inch diameter drill, drill down middle of key slot approximately

1 and ¾ inches, until ignition switch lock cylinder breaks loose from breakaway base of ignition switch lock cylinder.

4. Remove lock cylinder and drill shavings from steering column tube flange.
5. Remove steering column upper bearing retainer, steering column lock housing bearing, ignition switch lock cylinder and steering column lock gear. Thoroughly clean all drill shavings and other foreign material from casting.
6. Install new ignition lock cylinder as described in " Lock Cylinder, Functional."

IGNITION SWITCH

REPLACE

COUGAR & THUNDERBIRD

1. Remove steering column lower shroud, then remove four nuts holding column assembly to column mounting bracket.
2. Remove steering column shroud attaching screws, then the steering column shroud.
3. Disconnect ignition switch electrical connector, **Fig. 1,** then rotate ignition key lock cylinder to Run position.
4. Remove switch to lock cylinder attaching screws.
5. Remove ignition switch from actuator pin.
6. Adjust ignition switch by sliding carrier to Run position. **A new replacement switch assembly will be preset in Run position.**
7. Place ignition key lock cylinder in Run position by rotating cylinder approximately 90° from Lock position.
8. Install ignition switch on actuator pin. **Slightly move switch back and forth to align mounting holes with column lock housing threaded holes.**
9. Install switch to lock cylinder attaching bolts and **torque** bolts to 50–60 inch lbs.
10. Connect switch electrical connector.
11. Install steering column trim shrouds, then check ignition for proper operation.

CROWN VICTORIA & GRAND MARQUIS

1997–98

1. Remove steering column shroud by removing self-tapping screws, then tilt lever if equipped.
2. Remove instrument panel lower steering column cover.
3. Disconnect ignition switch electrical connector.
4. Rotate ignition key lock cylinder to Run position, then remove two screws retaining ignition switch.
5. Disconnect ignition switch from actuator.
6. Reverse procedure to install, noting the following:
   a. If necessary, move switch slightly back and forth to align mounting holes with column mounting holes.

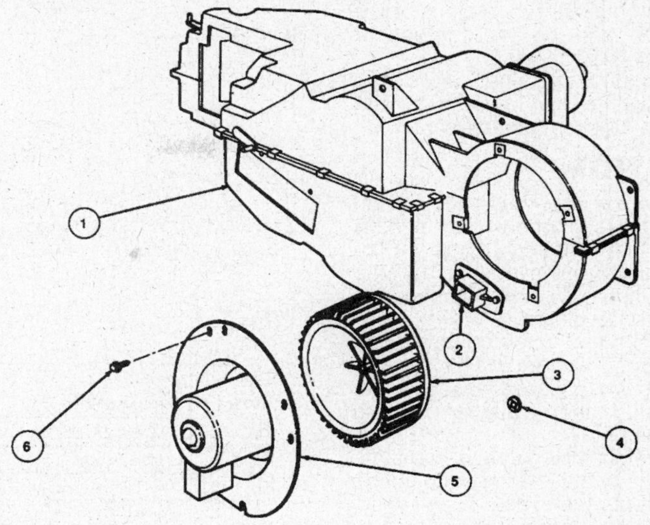

Item	Description
1	A / C Evaporator Housing
2	Heater Blower Motor Switch Resistor
3	Blower Motor Wheel
4	Pushnut
5	Blower Motor
6	Screw (4 Req'd)

FM7029700508000X

Fig. 5 Blower motor replacement. Cougar & Thunderbird

   b. Ensure proper operation of ignition switch in all positions.

1999–2000

1. Remove instrument panel pin type retainers, then position lefthand instrument panel insulator aside.
2. Disconnect courtesy lamp, then remove lefthand instrument panel insulator.
3. Remove lower instrument panel steering column opening cover.
4. Remove five bolts to remove instrument panel steering column opening cover reinforcement.
5. Disconnect ignition switch electrical connector.
6. Ignition key should be in the Off position, then remove ignition switch bolts and switch.
7. Reverse procedure to install, noting the following:
   a. **Torque** ignition switch bolts to 7–11 inch lbs.
   b. **Torque** reinforcement bolts to 31–45 inch lbs.
   c. **Torque** instrument panel insulator bolts to 19–26 inch lbs.

HEADLAMP SWITCH

REPLACE

COUGAR & THUNDERBIRD

1. Remove instrument panel finish panel.
2. Remove light switch knob by pulling off.
3. Remove hex nut retaining instrument panel finish panel to headlamp switch, then the instrument panel finish panel.
4. Remove two screws retaining headlamp switch to instrument panel.
5. Pull headlamp switch away from instrument panel far enough to disconnect wiring.
6. Reverse procedure to install.

CROWN VICTORIA & GRAND MARQUIS

1997–98

1. Remove light switch knob from headlamp switch by grasping knob and pulling out.
2. Remove instrument panel finish panel from instrument panel.
3. Disconnect main wiring connectors from headlamp switch.
4. Remove nut retaining headlamp switch to headlamp switch bracket, then the switch.
5. Reverse procedure to install.

1999–2000

1. Remove instrument panel cluster finish panel.
2. Unclip switch and remove headlamp switch.
3. Reverse procedure to install.

STOP LIGHT SWITCH

REPLACE

REMOVAL

Locking tab on connector must be lifted before connector can be removed. The switch side plate nearest brake pedal is slotted, it is not necessary to remove brake master cylinder push rod and one spacer washer from brake pedal pin.

1. Remove hairpin retainer and slide switch, pushrod, nylon washers and bushings away from brake pedal.

INSTALLATION

1. Position switch so that U-shaped side is nearest brake pedal and directly over or under the pin. Slide switch down or up trapping master cylinder pushrod and black bushing between switch and side plates.
2. Push switch and pushrod assembly firmly toward brake pedal arm. Assemble outside white plastic washer to pin and install hairpin retainer to trap whole assembly.
3. Ensure switch wire harness has sufficient length to travel with switch during full stroke of brake pedal.
4. Check switch for proper operation.

MULTI-FUNCTION SWITCH

REPLACE

COUGAR & THUNDERBIRD

1. Tilt column to lowest position and remove key release lever.
2. Remove ignition switch lock cylinder as described under "Ignition Lock, Replace"
3. Remove steering column upper and lower shrouds.
4. Remove screws retaining multi-function switch, then gently pull switch out of casting.
5. Disconnect wiring connectors.
6. Reverse procedure to install. **Torque** retaining screws to 18–26 inch lbs.

CROWN VICTORIA & GRAND MARQUIS

1. Tilt column to lowest position and remove tilt lever, if equipped.
2. Remove ignition lock cylinder.
3. Remove shroud screws, then remove upper and lower shrouds.
4. Remove two screws attaching multi-function switch to steering column casting. Disengage switch from casting.
5. Disconnect two electrical connectors.
6. Reverse procedure to install, **torque** retaining screws to 18–26 inch lbs.

TURN SIGNAL SWITCH

REPLACE

Refer to "Multi-Function Switch, Replace" for procedure.

STEERING WHEEL

REPLACE

1. Center front wheels to straight ahead position.
2. Remove air bag module from steering wheel.
3. Disconnect speed control wire harness from steering wheel.

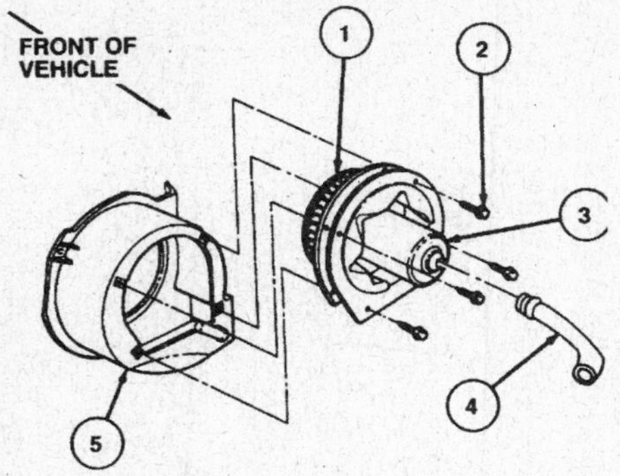

Item	Description
1	A/C Blower Wheel
2	Screw (4 Req'd)
3	A/C Blower Motor
4	Blower Motor Housing Tube
5	A/C Evaporator Core Housing

FM7029800509000X

Fig. 6 Blower motor replacement. 1997–98 Crown Victoria & Grand Marquis

4. Remove and discard steering wheel retaining bolt.
5. **On 1997–98 models,** install steering wheel puller tool No. T67L-3600-A, or equivalent, and remove steering wheel.
6. **On 1999–2000 models,** install steering wheel puller tool No. T77F-4220-B1, or equivalent, and remove steering wheel.
7. **On all models,** route contact assembly wire harness through steering wheel as wheel is lifted off of shaft.
8. Reverse procedure to install, noting the following:
   a. Route contact assembly wire harness through steering wheel opening at three o'clock position. Steering wheel and shaft alignment marks should be aligned.
   b. Ensure air bag contact wire is not pinched and speed control wiring does not get trapped between steering wheel and contact assembly.
   c. **Torque** steering wheel retaining bolt to 25–34 ft. lbs.
   d. **On 1997 Crown Victoria and Grand Marquis models, torque** air bag module retaining nuts to 36–47 inch lbs.
   e. **On 1998–2000 Crown Victoria and Grand Marquis models, torque** air bag module retaining nuts to 108 inch lbs.
   f. **On Cougar and Thunderbird models, torque** air bag module retaining nuts to 7–10 ft. lbs.

INSTRUMENT CLUSTER

REPLACE

COUGAR & THUNDERBIRD

1. Remove three screws along bottom of lower instrument panel.
2. Pull on panel to release three clips across top of instrument panel steering column cover, then remove cover.
3. Remove steering column shrouds.
4. Remove two screws retaining cluster finish panel above the instrument cluster face, **Fig. 2.**
5. Pull cluster instrument panel finish panel to unsnap one retaining clip above the lefthand A/C register.
6. Pull cluster finish panel to unsnap three retaining clips on right side vertical edge.
7. Pull cluster finish panel away from instrument panel far enough to disconnect the wiring connectors. Remove the finish panel.
8. Remove four screws retaining the instrument cluster to the instrument panel.
9. Pull instrument cluster out far enough to disconnect wiring and hoses.
10. Remove instrument cluster.
11. Reverse procedure to install.

CROWN VICTORIA & GRAND MARQUIS

STANDARD CLUSTER

1997–98

1. Remove lefthand instrument panel molding and righthand instrument panel molding.
2. **On Crown Victoria models,** remove six retaining screws and lower instrument panel steering column cover.
3. **On Grand Marquis models,** remove five retaining screws and instrument panel steering column cover.
4. **On all models,** remove screws and lower steering column shroud.
5. Remove screw fastening transmission range indicator column bracket to steering column. Detach cable loop from pin on shift lever. Remove column bracket from steering column.
6. Disconnect instrument cluster connectors from instrument cluster back plate and instrument cluster.
7. Reverse procedure to install. Adjust transmission range indicator as follows:
   a. Place transmission selector lever arm and support on steering column in "1" position.
   b. Place loop on indicator cable assembly over retainer pin on shift lever and secure cable bracket with screw.
   c. Shift selector lever arm and support into overdrive position. Adjust thumb wheel on steering column so entire width of pointer falls within letter D (overdrive).
   d. When properly adjusted, the entire width of pointer must fall within width of letter D (overdrive) and must touch remaining letters or numerals when viewed parallel to center line of steering column from driver's position.

1999–2000

1. Remove instrument cluster finish panel as follows:

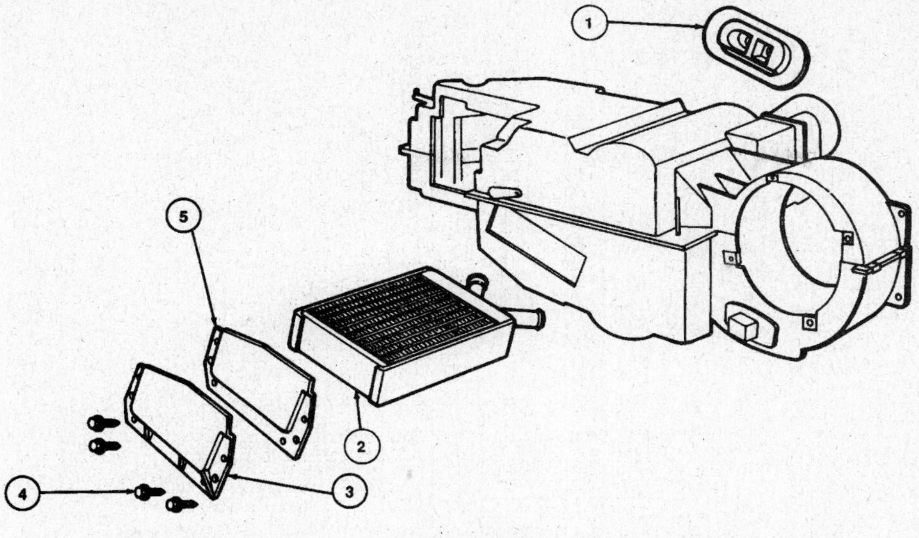

Item	Description	Item	Description
1	Heater Core Tube Gasket	3	Heater Core Cover
2	Heater Core	4	Screw (4 Req'd)
		5	Heater Core Cover Seal

FM7029700244000X

Fig. 7 Heater core replacement. Cougar & Thunderbird

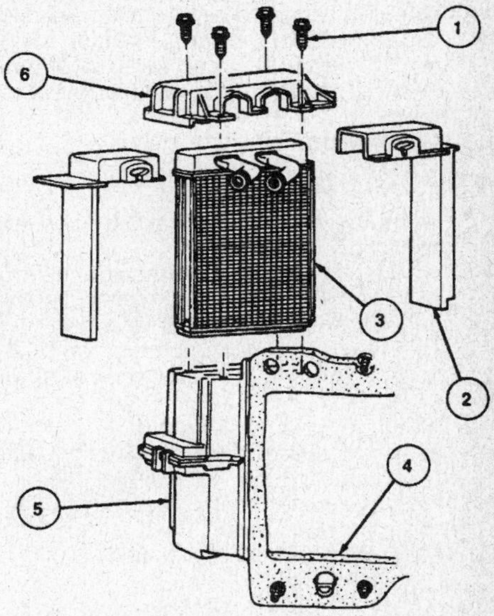

Item	Description
1	Screw (4 Req'd)
2	Heater Core Case Seal
3	Heater Core
4	Heater Dash Gasket
5	Heater Air Plenum Chamber
6	Heater Core Cover

FM7029800510000X

Fig. 8 Heater core replacement. Crown Victoria & Grand Marquis

a. Remove audio unit.
b. Remove right and left hand instrument panel finish panels and disconnect electrical connectors.
c. Place gearshift lever in No. 1 position.
d. Place steering column in full tilt position.
e. Remove screws, **Fig. 3,** then disconnect electrical connectors and remove instrument panel cluster finish panel.

2. Remove lower steering column cover.
3. Remove instrument panel steering column opening cover reinforcement.
4. Disconnect transmission range indicator cable and position out of way.
5. Remove four attaching screws, then the instrument cluster.
6. Reverse procedure to install.

ELECTRONIC CLUSTER

1997–98

1. Set parking brake.
2. Unsnap center molding on left and right sides of instrument panel.
3. Remove steering column cover and column shroud.
4. Remove knobs from auto dim and auto lamp switches, if equipped.
5. Remove 13 screws retaining instrument panel and pull panel out.
6. Move shift lever to 1 position for access.
7. Disconnect electrical connectors from warning lamp module, switch module and center panel switches, if equipped.
8. Remove instrument panel carefully to prevent damaging cluster lens.
9. Disconnect electrical connector from front of cluster.
10. Disconnect PRNDL assembly from cluster by carefully bending bottom tab down and pulling PRNDL assembly forward.
11. Pull cluster out and disconnect electrical connectors on rear of cluster.
12. Remove instrument cluster, **Fig. 4.**
13. Reverse procedure to install.

1999–2000

1. Remove instrument cluster finish panel as follows:
   a. Remove audio unit.
   b. Remove right and left hand instrument panel finish panels and disconnect electrical connectors.
   c. Place gearshift lever in No. 1 position.
   d. Place steering column in full tilt position.
   e. Remove screws, **Fig. 3,** then disconnect electrical connectors and remove instrument panel cluster finish panel.
2. Remove instrument panel lower steering column opening cover and reinforcement.
3. Disconnect transmission shift cable loop from shift tube hook.
4. Loosen steering column assembly.
5. Remove four attaching screws, pull cluster assembly slightly forward to disconnect electrical connectors, then remove cluster from vehicle.
6. Reverse procedure to install.

NATURAL GAS VEHICLE

Refer to procedures as outlined in "Standard Cluster " under "Crown Victoria & Grand Marquis."

RADIO

REPLACE

1. Install radio removal tools No. T87P-19061-A, or equivalent, into face plate. Push tools in to release retaining clips.
2. Slightly spread tools and pull radio from dash.
3. Disconnect power, antenna and speaker leads from radio.
4. Reverse procedure to install. Ensure rear bracket is engaged on lower support rail.

WIPER MOTOR

REPLACE

COUGAR & THUNDERBIRD

1. Remove wiper arm and blade assembly.
2. Remove motor retaining nuts, then motor.
3. Reverse procedure to install.

CROWN VICTORIA & GRAND MARQUIS

1997–98

1. Remove wiper arm and blade assembly.
2. Unsnap and remove windshield wiper motor and linkage cover.

3. Remove retaining clip from windshield wiper motor output arm by lifting locking tab and pulling clip away from pin.
4. Remove retaining screws and wiper motor.
5. Reverse procedure to install.

1999-2000

1. Remove mounting arm and pivot shaft assembly as follows:
   a. Remove cowl top vent panel.
   b. Remove evaporative emission canister purge valve and set aside.
   c. Remove attaching bolts, then position mounting arm and pivot shaft aside.
2. Remove wiper motor cover.
3. Remove clip and disconnect linkage from wiper motor.
4. Remove wiper motor mounting bolts, then the wiper motor.
5. Reverse procedure to install.

WIPER SWITCH

REPLACE

Refer to "Multi-Function Switch, Replace" for procedure.

BLOWER MOTOR

REPLACE

COUGAR & THUNDERBIRD

1. Remove glove compartment liner, then disconnect blower motor wire connector.
2. Remove four screws and pull blower motor outward, **Fig. 5.**
3. Remove push nuts from blower motor shaft and slide blower wheel off shaft.
4. Reverse procedure to install.

CROWN VICTORIA & GRAND MARQUIS

1997-98

1. Working in righthand wheel opening, remove three nuts securing radiator coolant recovery reservoir to fender splash panel and move radiator coolant recovery reservoir away from blower motor.
2. Disconnect blower motor from main wiring harness at snap lock connector.
3. Depress locking tab and slide two harness connectors from face of blower motor.
4. Remove blower motor housing tube from blower motor, **Fig. 6.**
5. Remove four retaining screws from blower motor mounting plate, then wiring support bracket.
6. Turn blower motor and A/C blower wheel assembly slightly to the right so bottom edge of mounting plate follows contour of front fender splash panel. While still in A/C evaporator core housing, lift blower motor up and maneuver if out of housing.
7. Reverse procedure to install.

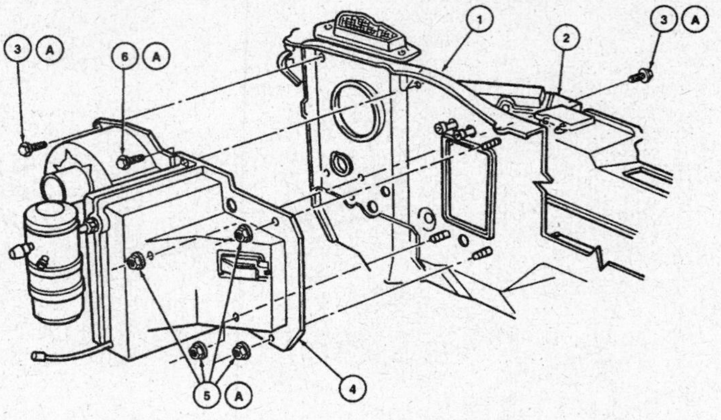

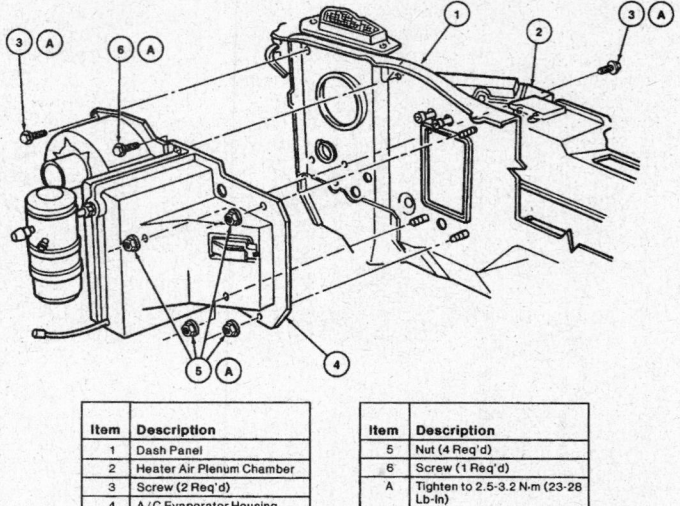

Item	Description
1	Dash Panel
2	Heater Air Plenum Chamber
3	Screw (2 Req'd)
4	A/C Evaporator Housing

Item	Description
5	Nut (4 Req'd)
6	Screw (1 Req'd)
A	Tighten to 2.5-3.2 N·m (23-28 Lb-In)

FM7029800511000X

Fig. 9 A/C evaporator core housing removal. Crown Victoria & Grand Marquis

1999-2000

1. Disengage wire harness connectors from retainer, then disconnect connectors.
2. Remove hose, then the screws retaining blower motor and the blower motor.
3. Prior to removing a wheel that is to be reused, clean any corrosion from the blower motor shaft to prevent damage to the wheel mounting shaft. Remove push clip, then blower motor wheel.
4. Reverse procedure to install.

HEATER CORE

REPLACE

COUGAR & THUNDERBIRD

1. Partially drain cooling system into a suitable container.
2. Remove instrument panel as outlined in " Dash Panel Service."
3. Remove A/C electronic blend door actuator.
4. Remove four heater core access cover retaining screws and access cover from housing.
5. Slide heater core and seals from housing, **Fig. 7.**
6. Reverse procedure to install.

CROWN VICTORIA & GRAND MARQUIS

1. Remove heater air plenum chamber as follows:
   a. Remove heater outlet floor duct.
   b. Remove instrument panel as outlined in " Dash Panel Service"
   c. Disconnect heater water hoses from heater core tubes. Plug ends of heater water hoses to prevent coolant loss.
   d. Plug heater core tubes securely to prevent coolant leakage from heater core.
   e. Remove one nut retaining upper lefthand corner of A/C evaporator core housing to instrument panel.
   f. Disconnect two vacuum supply hoses from vacuum source. Push grommet and vacuum supply hose into passenger compartment.
   g. Disconnect wiring harness from A/C electronic blend door actuator.
   h. Disconnect white vacuum hose from heater and A/C air inlet duct door vacuum control motor.
   i. Remove nuts from studs along lower flange of heater air plenum chamber.
   j. Disconnect connectors to A/C electronic blend door actuator and module on side of heater air plenum chamber.
   k. Remove heater air plenum chamber by pulling rearward.
2. Remove four retaining screws from heater core cover, then the heater core cover, **Fig. 8.**
3. Pull heater core assembly from heater air plenum chamber assembly.
4. Reverse procedure to install. Visually check to ensure heater core case seal is properly positioned.

EVAPORATOR CORE

REPLACE

COUGAR & THUNDERBIRD

Whenever an A/C evaporator core is replaced, it will be necessary to replace suction accumulator/drier.

1. Remove A/C evaporator housing as follows:
   a. Remove instrument panel as outlined in "Dash Panel Service"
   b. Recover A/C refrigerant system as outlined in "Air Conditioning"
   c. Remove high and low pressure hoses and plug ends.
   d. Disconnect liquid line and suction accumulator/drier inlet tube from A/C evaporator core at instrument panel. Cap refrigerant lines and A/C

evaporator core to prevent entrance of dirt and excessive moisture.

e. Remove suction accumulator/drier and bracket.
f. If necessary, remove throttle cable bracket and position out of the way.
g. Disconnect heater water hoses from heater core tubes and plug hoses.
h. Disconnect vacuum supply hose from in line A/C vacuum check valve in engine compartment.
i. Working under the hood, remove three nuts retaining A/C evaporator housing to instrument panel.
j. In passenger compartment, remove screw retaining A/C evaporator housing support bracket to cowl top panel.
k. Remove four nuts retaining A/C evaporator housing.
l. Carefully pull A/C evaporator housing away from instrument panel and remove A/C evaporator housing assembly from vehicle.

2. Remove heater core from A/C evaporator housing as described.
3. Remove A/C recirculating air duct.
4. **On models with semi automatic temperature controls,** remove electro-vacuum solenoid.
5. **On all models,** remove vacuum hose harness from its attachment points on A/C evaporator housing.
6. Remove heater air damper door vacuum control motor.
7. Remove heater blower motor switch resistor.
8. Remove blower motor, then heater outlet floor duct.
9. Remove A/C evaporator drain tube seal from A/C evaporator housing.
10. Reverse procedure to install.

CROWN VICTORIA & GRAND MARQUIS

Whenever an A/C evaporator core is replaced, it will be necessary to replace suction accumulator/drier.

1. Remove A/C evaporator housing as follows:
   a. Recover A/C refrigerant system as outlined in "Air Conditioning"
   b. Remove heater blower motor switch resistor.
   c. Disconnect evaporator to compressor suction line from suction accumulator/drier using spring lock coupling disconnect tools No. T81P-19623-G1 3/8 inch, T81P-19623-G2 1/2 inch, T83P-19623-C 5/8 inch or T85L-19623-A 3/4 inch, or equivalents. Plug openings to prevent dirt and excessive moisture from entering. Position hose away from suction accumulator/drier assembly.
   d. Disconnect condenser to evaporator tube from A/C evaporator core inlet tube using spring lock coupling disconnect tools No. T81P-19623-G1 3/8 inch, T81P-19623-G2 1/2 inch, T83P-19623-C 5/8 inch or T85L-19623-A 3/4 inch, or equivalents. Position condenser to evaporator tube away from A/C evaporator core housing assembly.

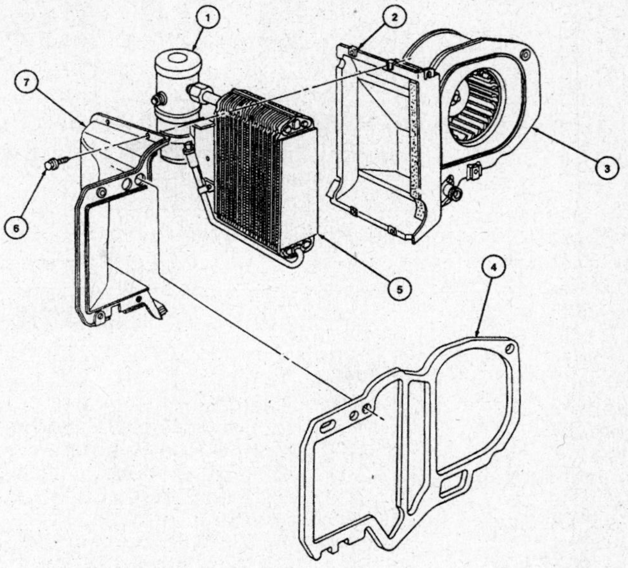

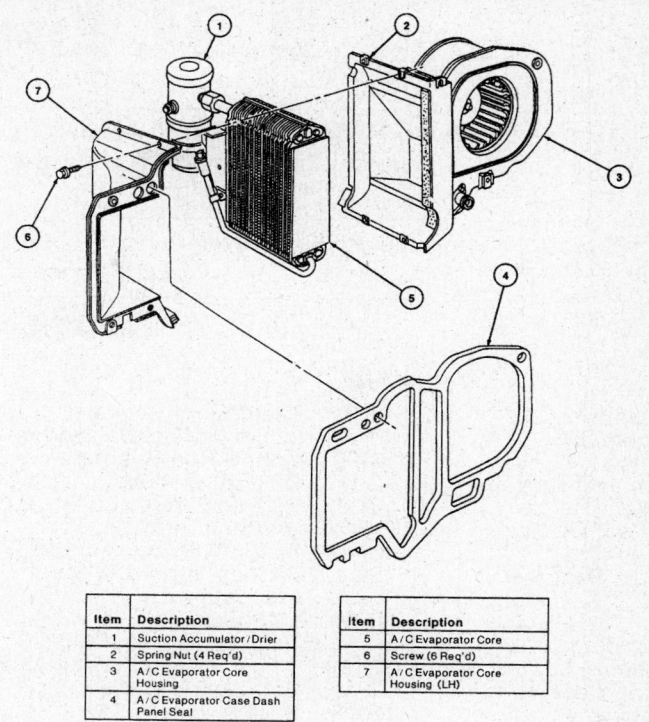

Item	Description
1	Suction Accumulator/Drier
2	Spring Nut (4 Req'd)
3	A/C Evaporator Core Housing
4	A/C Evaporator Case Dash Panel Seal

Item	Description
5	A/C Evaporator Core
6	Screw (6 Req'd)
7	A/C Evaporator Core Housing (LH)

FM7029800512000X

Fig. 10 A/C evaporator core replacement. Crown Victoria & Grand Marquis

   e. Drain coolant from radiator into a suitable container. Save coolant for reuse.
   f. Loosen hose clamps and disconnect heater water hoses from heater core tubes.
   g. Remove two nuts retaining purge valve mounting bracket to cowl top extension. Position purge valve and bracket away from A/C evaporator core housing.
   h. Remove radiator coolant recovery reservoir. Position forward, away from A/C evaporator core housing.
   i. Disconnect A/C blower motor lead assembly from main wiring harness and remove hard shell connector from A/C blower motor speed control and A/C cycling switch.
   j. Disconnect main wire harness (which crosses A/C evaporator core housing) at hard shell connecting point and position it away from A/C evaporator core housing.
   k. Remove instrument panel lower insulator from bottom of instrument panel on passenger side by disengaging four push pins and disconnecting power point electrical connector.
   l. Fold carpeting back on righthand side of floor. Remove bottom lefthand screw that supports A/C recirculating air duct.
   m. Raise and support vehicle, then remove righthand front tire.
   n. Remove retaining bolts from rear of righthand fender apron. Position apron down in rear to improve access to A/C evaporator core housing.
   o. From engine side of instrument panel, remove three nuts from evaporator assembly mounting studs. Also two screws from top of A/C evaporator core housing, **Fig. 9.**
   p. Pull bottom of A/C evaporator core housing assembly away from instrument panel to disengage two bottom studs. Move top of A/C evaporator core housing away from instrument panel, disengage it from top stud and maneuver case up and over fender apron.
2. Remove six screws retaining two halves of A/C evaporator core housing together, **Fig. 10.**
3. Separate two halves of A/C evaporator core housing and using a razor blade carefully cut A/C evaporator case instrument panel seal at the seams.
4. Disconnect suction accumulator/drier inlet from evaporator core outlet tube.
5. Remove retaining screw from suction accumulator/drier and evaporator core mounting bracket and suction accumulator/drier from A/C evaporator core.
6. Remove retaining screw from inlet tube bracket and A/C evaporator core.
7. Reverse procedure to install.

3.8L Engine

NOTE: On Air Bag Equipped Models, Refer To " Air Bag System Precautions" Located In The Front Of This Manual For System Disarming & Arming Procedures.

NOTE: Refer To "Computer Relearn Procedures " Located In The Front Of This Manual For Computer Relearn Procedures.

INDEX

PRECAUTIONS

AIR BAG SYSTEMS

Refer to "Air Bag System Precautions" in the front of this manual for system disarming and arming procedures.

BATTERY GROUND CABLE

Prior to service, disconnect battery ground cable and isolate as required.

FUEL SYSTEM PRESSURE RELIEF

Release pressure from fuel system at the fuel pressure relief valve using tool No. T80L-9974-B, or equivalent. When relieving fuel pressure, crank engine with fuel pump electrical connector disconnected.

COMPRESSION PRESSURE

1. Ensure oil in crankcase is of correct viscosity and at proper level and battery is properly charged. Operate vehicle until engine is at normal operating temperature. Turn ignition switch Off, then remove all spark plugs.
2. Install compression gauge, Rotunda Compression Tester 014-00707, or equivalent, in No. 1 cylinder.
3. Install an auxiliary starter switch in starting circuit. With ignition switch Off and using auxiliary starter, crank engine a minimum of five compression strokes and record highest reading. Note approximate number of compression strokes required to obtain highest reading.
4. Repeat test on each cylinder, cranking engine approximately same number of compression strokes.
5. The indicated compression pressures are considered within specification if the lowest reading cylinder is within 75% of highest reading. Refer to **Fig. 1** for compression pressure limit chart.

Maximum PSI	Minimum PSI	Maximum PSI	Minimum PSI	Maximum PSI	Minimum PSI	Maximum PSI	Minimum PSI
924 kPa (134 PSI)	696 kPa (101 PSI)	1131 kPa (164 PSI)	848 kPa (123 PSI)	1338 kPa (194 PSI)	1000 kPa (146 PSI)	1544 kPa (224 PSI)	1158 kPa (168 PSI)
938 kPa (136 PSI)	703 kPa (102 PSI)	1145 kPa (166 PSI)	855 kPa (124 PSI)	1351 kPa (196 PSI)	1014 kPa (147 PSI)	1558 kPa (226 PSI)	1165 kPa (169 PSI)
952 kPa (138 PSI)	717 kPa (104 PSI)	1158 kPa (168 PSI)	869 kPa (126 PSI)	1365 kPa (198 PSI)	1020 kPa (148 PSI)	1572 kPa (228 PSI)	1179 kPa (171 PSI)
965 kPa (140 PSI)	724 kPa (106 PSI)	1172 kPa (170 PSI)	876 kPa (127 PSI)	1379 kPa (200 PSI)	1034 kPa (150 PSI)	1586 kPa (230 PSI)	1186 kPa (172 PSI)
979 kPa (142 PSI)	738 kPa (107 PSI)	1186 kPa (172 PSI)	889 kPa (129 PSI)	1303 kPa (202 PSI)	1041 kPa (151 PSI)	1600 kPa (232 PSI)	1200 kPa (174 PSI)
933 kPa (144 PSI)	745 kPa (109 PSI)	1200 kPa (174 PSI)	903 kPa (131 PSI)	1407 kPa (204 PSI)	1055 kPa (153 PSI)	1055 kPa (153 PSI)	1207 kPa (175 PSI)
1007 kPa (146PSI)	758 kPa (110 PSI)	1214 kPa (176 PSI)	910 kPa (132 PSI)	1420 kPa (206 PSI)	1062 kPa (154 PSI)	1627 kPa (154 PSI)	1220 kPa (177 PSI)
1020 kPa (148 PSI)	765 kPa (111 PSI)	1227 kPa (178 PSI)	917 kPa (133 PSI)	1434 kPa (208 PSI)	1075 kPa (156 PSI)	1641 kPa (238 PSI)	1227 kPa (178 PSI)

FM1069800546010X

Fig. 1 Compression pressure limit chart (Part 1 of 2)

Maximum PSI	Minimum PSI	Maximum PSI	Minimum PSI	Maximum PSI	Minimum PSI	Maximum PSI	Minimum PSI
1034 kPa (150 PSI)	779 kPa (113 PSI)	1241 kPa (18 PSI)	931 kPa (135 PSI)	1448 kPa (210 PSI)	1083 kPa (157 PSI)	1655 kPa (240 PSI)	1241 kPa (180 PSI)
1048 kPa (152 PSI)	786 kPa (114 PSI)	1255 kPa (182 PSI)	936 kPa (136 PSI)	1462 kPa (212 PSI)	1089 kPa (158 PSI)	1669 kPa (242 PSI)	1248 kPa (181 PSI)
1062 kPa (154 PSI)	793 kPa (115 PSI)	1269 kPa (184 PSI)	952 kPa (138 PSI)	1476 kPa (214 PSI)	1103 kPa (160 PSI)	1682 kPa (244 PSI)	1262 kPa (183 PSI)
1076 kPa (156 PSI)	807 kPa (117 PSI)	1282 kPa (186 PSI)	965 kPa (140 PSI)	1489 kPa (216 PSI)	1117 kPa (162 PSI)	1696 kPa (246 PSI)	1269 kPa (184 PSI)
1089 kPa (158 PSI)	814 kPa (118 PSI)	1296 kPa (188 PSI)	972 kPa (141 PSI)	1503 kPa (218 PSI)	1124 kPa (163 PSI)	1710 kPa (248 PSI)	1282 kPa (186 PSI)
1103 kPa (160 PSI)	827 kPa (120 PSI)	1310 kPa (190 PSI)	75=982 kPa (142 PSI)	1517 kPa (220 PSI)	1138 kPa (165 PSI)	1724 kPa (250 PSI)	1293 kPa (187 PSI)
1110 kPa (161 PSI)	834 kPa (121 PSI)	1324 kPa (192 PSI)	993 kPa (144 PSI)	1631 kPa (222 PSI)	1223.25 kPa (166 PSI)		

FM1069800546020X

Fig. 1 Compression pressure limit chart (Part 2 of 2)

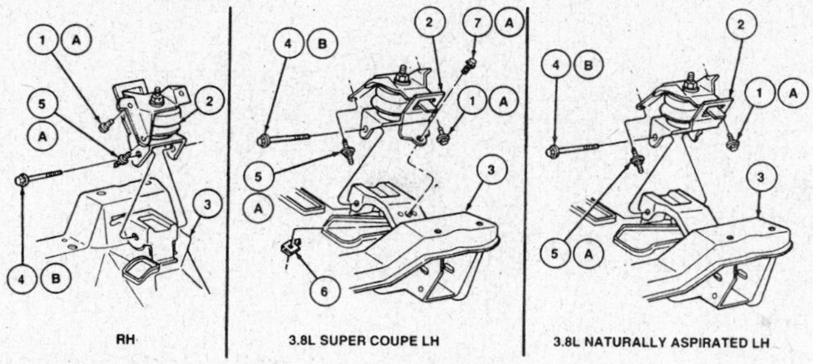

Item	Part Number	Description
1	N803098-S100	Bolt (2 Req'd)
2	6038	Front Engine Support Insulator
3	5C145	Front Sub-Frame
4	N805748-S36	Bolt
5	N805803-S36	Stud

Item	Part Number	Description
6	N805968-S36	U-Nut
7	N605918-S56	Bolt
A	—	Tighten to 34-47 N·m (25-35 Lb-Ft)
B	—	Tighten to 47-68 N·m (35-50 Lb-Ft)

FM1069100113000X

Fig. 2 Engine mount removal

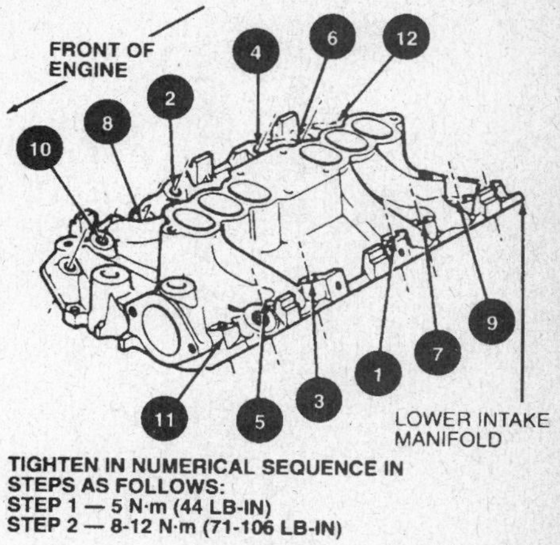

FM1059800155000X

Fig. 3 Lower intake manifold tightening sequence

6. If one or more cylinders reads low, squirt approximately on tablespoon of clean engine oil meeting Ford specification WSS-M2C153-F on top of pistons in low reading cylinders, then repeat compression pressure check on these cylinders.
7. If compression improves considerably, piston rings are faulty.
8. If compression does not improve, valves are sticking or seating poorly.
9. If two adjacent cylinders indicate low compression pressures and squirting oil on piston does not increase compression, head gasket may be leaking between cylinders. Engine oil and or coolant in cylinders could result from this condition.

ENGINE MOUNT

REPLACE

Whenever self-locking mounting bolts and nuts are removed, they must be replaced with new self-locking bolts and nuts.

1. Remove fan shroud attaching screws, then the air tube from remote air cleaner.
2. Raise and support vehicle, then support engine using a jack and wood block placed below engine.
3. Remove insulator to front subframe through bolts, **Fig. 2.**
4. Disconnect shift linkage, then raise engine enough to clear front sub-frame brackets.
5. Remove accessories and oil cooler line attaching clips from engine support brackets.
6. Remove bolts attaching insulator bracket assembly to engine, then remove insulator and bracket.
7. Reverse procedure to install. Tighten to specifications.

ENGINE

REPLACE

1. Drain engine coolant into a suitable container.
2. Disconnect underhood lamp wiring connector, then mark position of hood hinges and remove hood.
3. Remove left cowl vent screen and wiper module.
4. Disconnect alternator to voltage regulator wiring harness.
5. Remove radiator upper sight shield, release belt tension and remove belts.
6. Remove air cleaner to throttle body tube assembly, then disconnect cooling fan and motor assembly connector.
7. Disconnect constant control relay module at wiring connector and remove radiator coolant recovery reservoir.
8. Remove fan motor, fan blade and fan shroud assembly, then the upper radiator hose.
9. Disconnect automatic transmission oil cooler tubes from radiator, then the heater hoses.
10. Disconnect lower radiator hose at water pump, then remove radiator retaining bolts and radiator assembly.
11. Disconnect power steering pump hoses, remove power steering pump bracket and move aside.
12. Disconnect power steering pressure switch, then A/C clutch connector.
13. Recover A/C system as outlined in "System Evacuation " under "Air Conditioning ".
14. Disconnect A/C compressor lines. Cap or plug open A/C lines.
15. Remove A/C compressor retaining bolts, then the compressor.
16. Remove wiring shield, then disconnect accelerator cable mounting bracket and position aside.
17. Release fuel system pressure, as outlined in "Fuel System Pressure Relief," then disconnect fuel inlet and return hose.
18. Disconnect fuel charging wiring from engine control sensor wiring at 40 pin connector, then the main vacuum source hose.
19. Disconnect evaporative emission hose, then remove A/C compressor mounting bracket with drive belt tensioner attached.
20. Raise and support vehicle, then drain oil into suitable container and remove oil filter.
21. Remove exhaust pipe-to-manifold nuts, then remove left exhaust shield.
22. Disconnect heated exhaust gas oxygen (HEGO) sensor assembly.
23. Remove inspection plug, then the torque converter bolts.
24. Remove engine to transmission bolts, then remove engine mount bolts.
25. Remove crankshaft pulley assembly.
26. Remove starter motor assembly, ground cable and starter harness retainers from left and right sides.
27. Disconnect oil level indicator sensor. Partially lower vehicle, then disconnect oil pressure sending unit gauge assembly.
28. Position floor jack under transmission.
29. Install Rotunda Engine Lifting Brackets 014-00792 and Separator Bar 014-00793, or equivalents. Position engine lifting equipment and remove engine assembly from vehicle.
30. Reverse procedure to install. Tighten to specifications.

INTAKE MANIFOLD

REPLACE

1. Remove air cleaner outlet tube.
2. Disconnect accelerator cable at throttle body assembly, then the speed control cable, if equipped.
3. Remove retaining bolts from accelerator cable and position cables aside.
4. Disconnect vacuum lines at upper intake manifold.
5. Disconnect necessary electrical connectors.
6. Disconnect crankcase ventilation tube at upper intake manifold and at positive crankcase ventilation valve.
7. Remove throttle body if necessary, then EGR valve from upper intake manifold.
8. Remove nut and bolt retaining engine support and wiring retainer bracket located at lefthand front of intake manifold and set aside with ignition wires.
9. Remove upper intake manifold retaining bolts and studs, then upper intake manifold and manifold upper gasket.

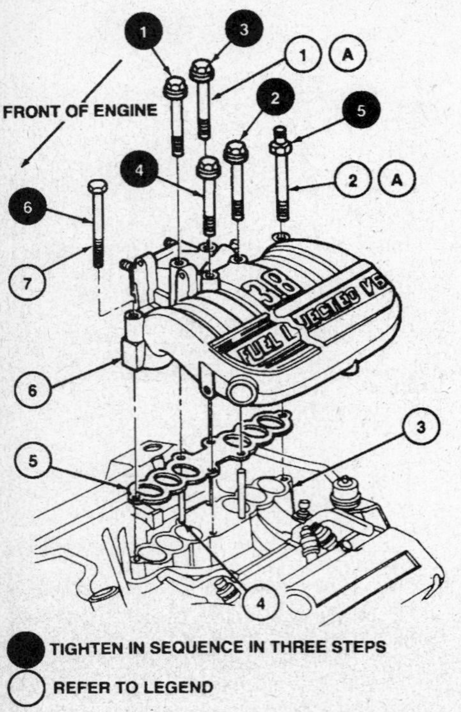

Item	Description
1	Bolt (4 Req'd)
2	Stud Bolt
3	Intake Manifold, Lower
4	Locating Pins (2 Req'd)
5	Intake Manifold Upper Gasket
6	Upper Intake Manifold
7	Bolt
A	Tighten in sequence in three steps: ● 10 N·m (8 Lb-Ft) ● 20 N·m (15 Lb-Ft) ● 32 N·m (24 Lb-Ft)

FM1059800154000X

Fig. 4 Upper intake manifold tightening sequence

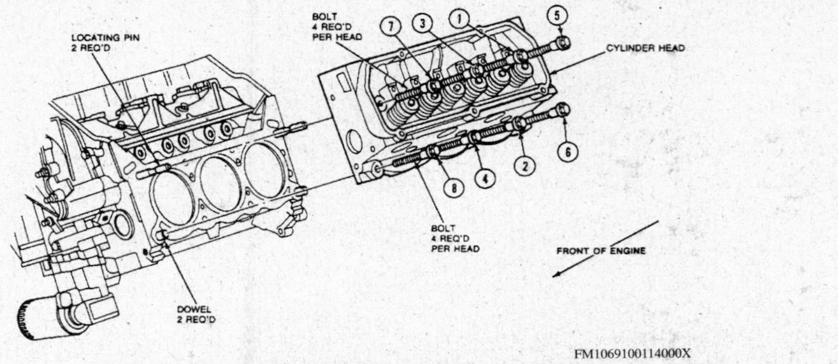

Fig. 5 Cylinder head tightening sequence

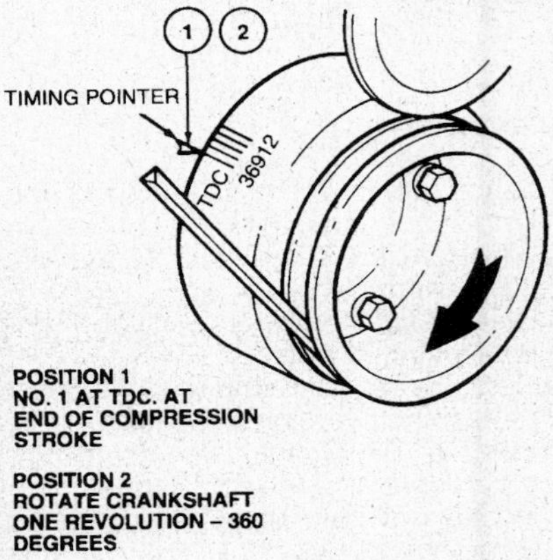

Cyl. No.	Set Gap of Valves Noted — Crankshaft Position 1	2
1	Int—Exh	None
2	Exh	Int
3	Int	Exh
4	Exh	Int
5	None	Int—Exh
6	Int	Exh

FM1059800156000X

Fig. 6 No 1 piston positioning

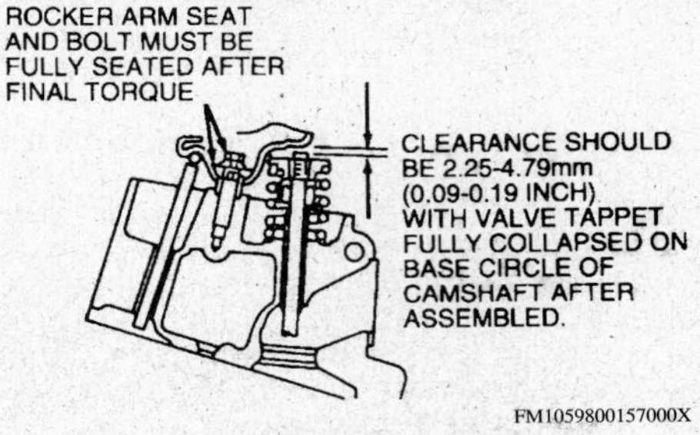

Fig. 7 Valve clearance adjustment

10. Drain engine coolant into a suitable container.
11. Remove fuel injectors and fuel injection supply manifold.
12. Remove heater water inlet and outlet hoses.
13. Remove lower intake manifold retaining bolts and studs.
14. Remove lower intake manifold. **The manifold is sealed at each end with RTV-type sealer. To break seal, it may be necessary to pry on front of manifold with a screwdriver blade. Use care to prevent damage to machined surfaces when prying with screwdriver.**
15. Remove and discard water hose connections and end seals.
16. If lower intake manifold is to be disassembled, perform the following:
    a. Remove water hose connection and water thermostat.
    b. Remove engine coolant temperature sensor and heater elbow.
    c. Remove all vacuum and electrical fittings.
17. Reverse procedure to install, noting the following:
    a. Clean all cylinder head/block to intake manifold contact areas.
    b. Apply a dab of gasket and trim adhesive part No. 19B508-AA, or equivalent, to each cylinder head mating surface. Press new intake manifold gasket into place over locating dowels.
    c. Apply a ⅛ inch bead of silicone sealer D6AZ-19562-B, , or equivalent, at each corner where cylinder head joins the cylinder block.
    d. Install front and rear intake manifold end seals, then carefully lower intake manifold into position on cylinder block and cylinder heads. Use locating dowels as necessary to guide manifold.
    e. Install attaching bolts and studs. **Torque** in two steps; first to 44 inch lbs., then to 72–108 inch lbs., in sequence, **Fig. 3.**
    f. **Torque** upper intake bolts in sequence, **Fig. 4** in three steps; first to 8 ft. lbs, then 15 ft. lbs and finally to 24 ft. lbs.
    g. Tighten EGR valve assembly mounting bolts and throttle body mounting bolts to specifications.

CYLINDER HEAD

REPLACE

REMOVAL

1. Drain engine coolant into suitable container.
2. Remove air cleaner outlet tube from throttle body.
3. Loosen drive belt tensioner, then remove drive belt.
4. If left cylinder head is being removed, proceed as follows:
    a. Remove oil filler cap and power steering pump front mounting bracket attaching bolts.
    b. Remove alternator assembly and accessory drive belt idler pulley.
    c. Remove power steering pump/alternator bracket attaching bolts.
5. If right cylinder head is being removed, proceed as follows:
    a. Remove drive belt.
    b. If equipped with A/C, remove mounting bracket retaining bolts. Leave hoses connected and position A/C compressor aside. If not equipped with A/C, remove A/C belt idler pulley.
    c. Remove positive crankcase ventilation valve.
6. Remove upper intake manifold.
7. Remove valve cover.
8. Remove fuel injection supply manifold, then lower intake manifold.

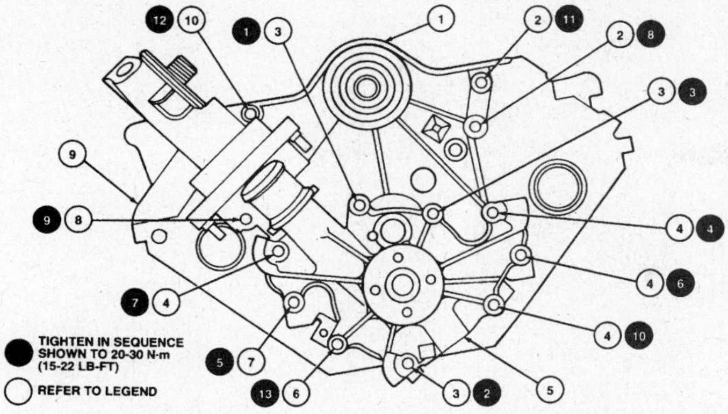

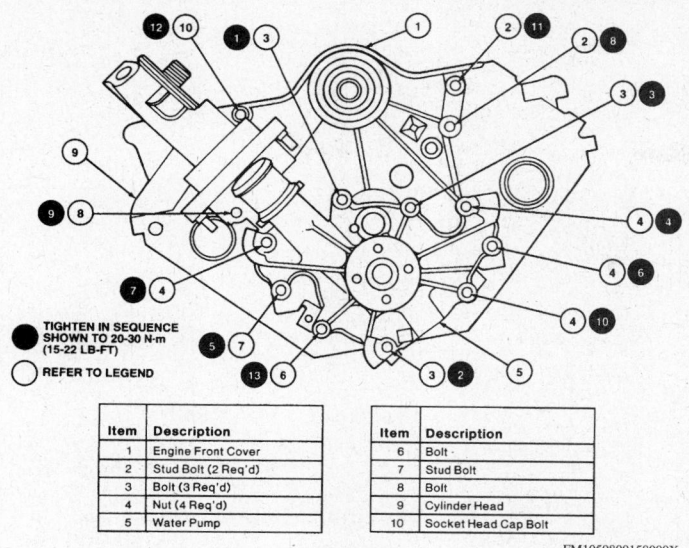

Item	Description
1	Engine Front Cover
2	Stud Bolt (2 Req'd)
3	Bolt (3 Req'd)
4	Nut (4 Req'd)
5	Water Pump

Item	Description
6	Bolt
7	Stud Bolt
8	Bolt
9	Cylinder Head
10	Socket Head Cap Bolt

FM1059800158000X

Fig. 8 Front cover tightening sequence

9. Remove exhaust manifolds, then loosen rocker arm seat retaining bolts enough to allow rocker arms to be lifted off push rods and rotated to one side.
10. Remove pushrods. Identify position of each rod for installation. Pushrods must be installed in original position.
11. Remove and discard cylinder head retaining bolts, then remove cylinder head.

INSTALLATION

Always use new cylinder head bolts. Torque retention with used bolts can vary, which may result in coolant or compression leakage at cylinder head mating surface.

1. Position cylinder head and new gasket on dowels for alignment.
2. Apply a thin coating of Pipe Sealant w/Teflon part No. D8AZ-19554-A, , or equivalent, to threads of short cylinder head bolts. **Do not apply to long bolts.**
3. **Torque** cylinder head bolts in sequence shown in **Fig. 5,** to 15 ft. lbs., then to 30 ft. lbs. and then to 37 ft. lbs. Tighten each bolt individually in sequence as follows:
   a. **Torque** long bolts to 30–37 ft. lbs., then tighten an additional 175–185°.
   b. **Torque** short bolts to 15–22 ft. lbs., then tighten an additional 175–185°.
4. Dip each pushrod end in Oil Conditioner D9AZ-19579-CA, or equivalent, then install each pushrod in original position.
5. For each valve, rotate crankshaft until valve lifter rests on heel (base circle) of camshaft lobe. **Torque** fulcrum attaching bolts to initial value of 43 inch lbs.
6. Lubricate all rocker arm assemblies with Oil Conditioner D9AZ-19579-CA, , or equivalent, heavy engine oil. Final **torque** fulcrum bolts to 19–25 ft. lbs.
7. Install exhaust manifolds and lower intake manifold. Tighten to specifications.
8. Install injector fuel rail assembly.
9. Install gasket and valve cover. Tighten to specifications.
10. Install upper intake manifold. Tighten to specifications.
11. Reverse remainder of removal procedure to complete installation. Tighten to specifications.

VALVE ARRANGEMENT

FRONT TO REAR

Right Side ....I-E-I-E-I-E
Left Side ....E-I-E-I-E-I

VALVE TAPPET, HYDRAULIC

REPLACE

REMOVAL

Before replacing a valve tappet for noisy operation, make sure the noise is not caused by improper valve to rocker arm clearance or by worn rocker arms or pushrods.

1. Disconnect ignition wires at spark plugs. To avoid damaging ignition wires use Spark Plug Wire Remover T74P-666-A, or equivalent.
2. Remove ignition wire routing clips from studs on valve cover retaining bolts. Lay ignition wires with routing clips toward front of engine.
3. Remove upper intake manifold.
4. Remove valve covers, then the lower intake manifold.
5. Sufficiently loosen each rocker arms seat retaining bolt to allow rocker arm to be lifted off pushrod and rotated to one side.
6. Remove pushrods and mark for installation reference. When engine is assembled, pushrod should be installed in their original locations.
7. Remove four bolts holding two tappet guide plates and retainers in place (bolts are held captive in retainers). Remove six valve tappet guide plates from adjacent valve tappets.
8. Remove valve tappets using a magnet and mark for installation reference When engine is assembled, valve tappets should be installed their original locations.
9. If valve tappets are stuck in bores due to excessive varnish or gum deposits, it may be necessary to use a claw type tool to aid removal. When using a remover tool, rotate valve tappet back and forth to loosen it from gum or varnish that may have formed on the valve tappet.

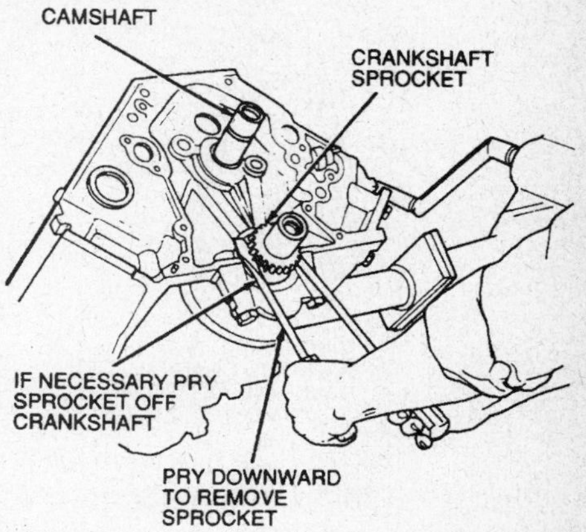

FM1059800159000X

Fig. 9 Camshaft sprocket, crankshaft sprocket & timing chain removal

INSTALLATION

1. Using a solvent, clean cylinder head and valve sealing surfaces.
2. Lightly oil all bolts and stud threads before installation, except those specifying special sealant.
3. Lubricate each valve tappet and bore with Engine Assembly Lubricant D9AZ-19579-D, or equivalent.
4. Install each valve tappet in bore from which it was removed. If new valve tappets are being installed, check for free fit in bore into which they are to be installed.
5. Align flats on side of valve tappets and install six valve tappet guide plates between adjacent valve tappets (make sure word " up" is showing). Install two tappet guide plates and retainers and torque four captive bolts to 84–120 inch lbs.
6. Dip each push rod end in Engine Assembly Lubricant D9AZ-19579-D, or equivalent meeting Ford specification ESR-M99C80-A. Install pushrods in their original location.
7. Lubricate all rocker arms with Engine Assembly Lubricant D9AZ-19579-D, , or equivalent, meeting Ford specification ESR-M99C80-A.
8. **Rocker arm seats must be fully seated in cylinder heads and pushrods must be seated in rocker arm sockets prior to final tightening or**

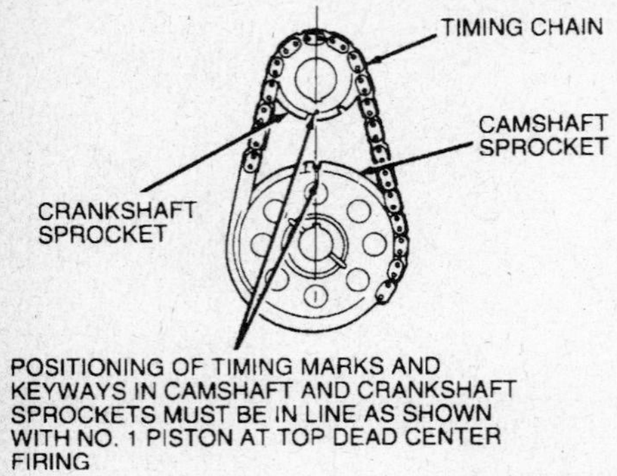

Fig. 10 Timing chain alignment marks

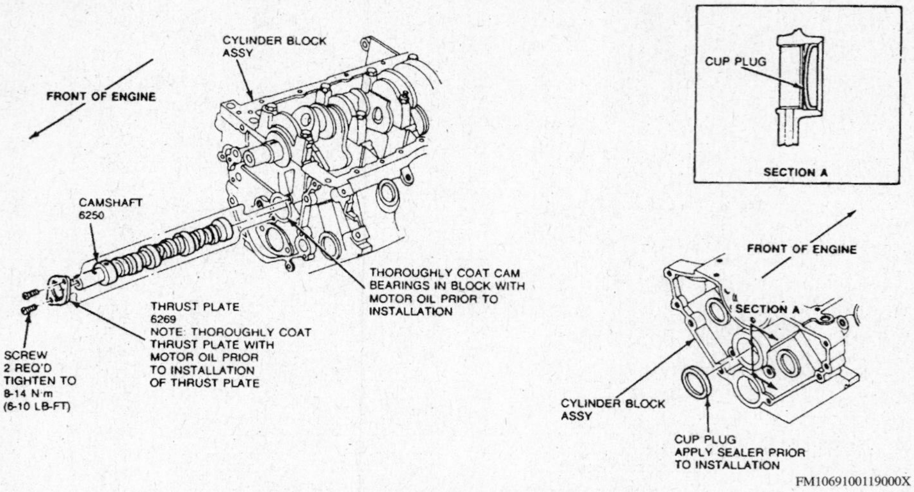

Fig. 11 Camshaft installation

possible damage to engine may occur. For each valve, rotate crankshaft until valve tappet rests onto heel (base circle) of camshaft lobe. Position rocker arms over push rods. Install rocker arm seats. Initially **torque** rocker arm seat retaining bolts to 44 inch lbs. Final **torque** rocker arm seat bolts to 22–29 ft. lbs. For final tightening, camshaft may be in any position.

9. Install lower intake manifold, then rocker arms.
10. Install upper intake manifold.
11. Install ignition wire routing clips and connect ignition wires to spark plugs.

VALVE LIFT SPECIFICATIONS

Engine	Intake, Inch	Exhaust, Inch
3.8L	.424	.447

CAMSHAFT LOBE LIFT SPECIFICATIONS

Engine	Intake, Inch	Exhaust, Inch
3.8L	.245	.259

VALVE CLEARANCE SPECIFICATIONS

Correct valve clearance is .09–.19 inch.

VALVE ADJUSTMENT

1. With No. 1 piston on top dead center (TDC) of compression stroke check following valves, **Fig. 6.**
2. When compressing valve spring to remove pushrod, make sure piston in individual cylinder is below TDC to avoid contact between valve and piston. To replace a pushrod, it will be necessary to loosen rocker arm seat retaining bolt and rotate arm to side.
3. After replacement of a pushrod, rocker arm or hydraulic valve tappet, the engine should not be cranked or rotated until valve tappets have an opportunity to leak down to their normal operating position. The leak down rate can be accelerated by using a valve tappet bleed down wrench or rocker arm and applying pressure in a direction to collapse valve tappet, **Fig. 7.**

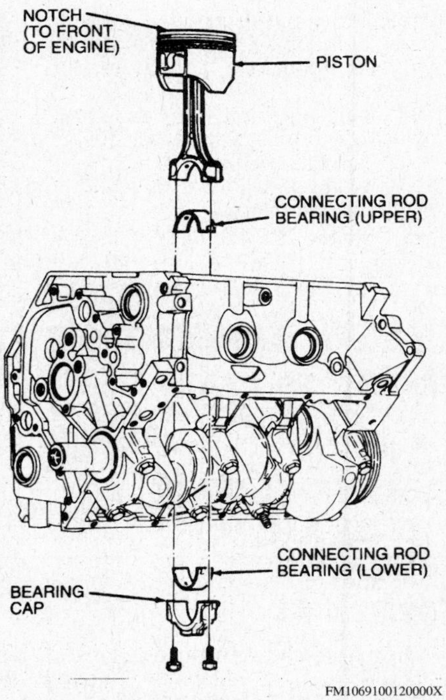

Fig. 12 Piston & rod assembly

ROCKER ARMS

1. Remove valve covers.
2. Remove rocker arm seat retaining bolts from cylinder head, then the rocker arms.
3. Reverse procedure to install, noting the following:
   a. Lubricate all rocker arms with Engine Assembly Lubricant D9AZ-19579-D, , or equivalent.
   b. **Rocker arm seats must be fully seated in cylinder head and pushrods must be seated in rocker arm sockets prior to final tightening or damage to engine may occur.** For each valve, rotate crankshaft until valve tappet rests onto heel (base circle) of camshaft lobe. Position rocker arms over pushrods. Install rocker arm seats. Tighten rocker arm seat retaining bolts to specifications.
   c. Final **torque** rocker arm seat bolts to 22–29 ft. lbs. For final tightening, camshaft may be in any position.
   d. Install valve cover.

VALVE GUIDES

Valve guides consist of holes bored in the cylinder head. For service the guide holes can be reamed oversize to accommodate valves with oversize stems of .015 and .030 inch.

FRONT COVER

REPLACE

REMOVAL

To replace seal in timing gear cover, it is necessary to remove cover as outlined below.

1. Drain cooling system into a suitable container.
2. Remove engine air cleaner and air cleaner outlet tube.
3. Remove cooling fan motor, fan blade and fan shroud assembly.
4. Remove drive belts and water pump pulley.
5. Remove power steering pump mounting bracket bolts. Leave hoses connected and position pump assembly aside.
6. Remove A/C compressor support bracket, if equipped. Leave compressor in place.
7. Remove heater water outlet tube retaining bolts, heater water outlet tube and O-ring from water pump.
8. Disconnect upper radiator hose at water hose connection.

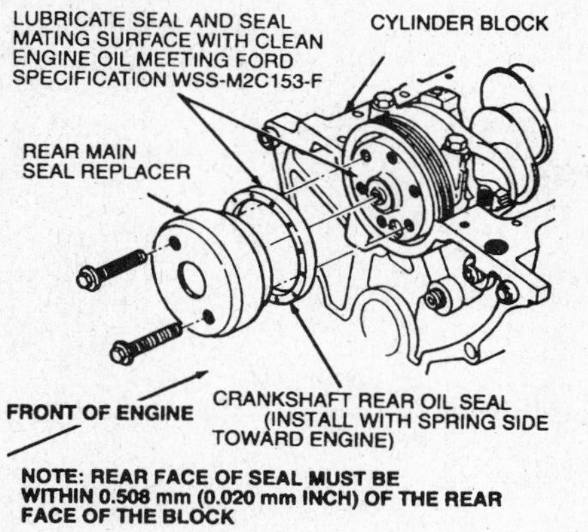

Fig. 13 Crankshaft rear seal installation

9. Disconnect fuel charging wiring from camshaft position sensor.
10. Remove hold down clamp and lift camshaft position sensor and housing out of engine front cover.
11. Raise and support vehicle.
12. Remove crankshaft pulley using crankshaft damper removal tool No. T85P-6316-D and vibration damper removal adapter tool No. T82L-6316-B, or equivalents.
13. Remove oil bypass filter, then disconnect lower radiator hose from water pump.
14. Remove oil pan as described under "Oil Pan, Replace."
15. Lower vehicle and remove front cover attaching bolts. **A front cover attaching bolt is located behind oil filter adapter. Identify bolts as they are removed so that they can be installed at same location.**
16. Remove front cover and water pump as an assembly.
17. If necessary, remove engine front cover gasket and discard.
18. If necessary, remove crankshaft position sensor shield and crankshaft position sensor.
19. If necessary, remove oil pump and filter body.

INSTALLATION

1. Lightly oil all bolt and stud threads before installation except those specifying special sealant. Clean gasket surfaces on engine front cover and cylinder blocks. If reusing engine front cover, replace crankshaft front seal.
2. If a new engine cover is to be installed, install the following:
   a. Install oil pump and filter body, install crankshaft position sensor and shield. Tighten crankshaft bolt and crankshaft position sensor shield nut to specifications.
   b. Clean water pump gasket surface. Position a new water pump housing gasket on engine front cover and install water pump. Install water pump retaining bolts, stud bolts and nuts. Tighten bolts and stud bolts and retaining nuts to specifications.

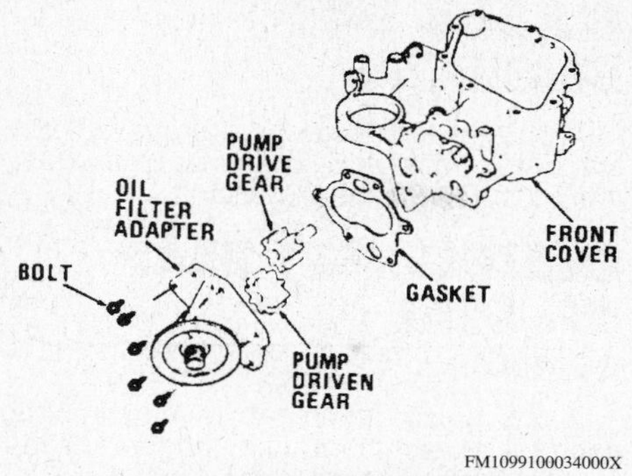

Fig. 14 Oil pump replacement

3. Lubricate crankshaft front seal with clean engine oil.
4. Position a new engine front cover gasket on cylinder block and install engine front cover and water pump as an assembly using dowels for proper alignment.
5. Install front cover retaining bolts, tighten to specifications, **Fig. 8.**
6. Raise vehicle, then install oil pan.
7. Connect lower radiator hose and tighten clamp securely.
8. Install oil bypass filter.
9. Coat crankshaft pulley and vibration damper sealing surface with clean engine oil.
10. Prior to applying sealer, clean sealing surfaces with Metal Surface cleaner F4AZ-19A536-RA, or equivalent, to remove all residues that may interfere with sealer's ability to adhere.
11. Apply a small amount of Silicone Gasket and Sealant F6AZ-19562-AA, or equivalent to crankshaft keyway.
12. Position crankshaft in crankshaft keyway.
13. Install crankshaft pulley and vibration damper using Damper Front Cover Seal Replacer T82L-6316-A, or equivalent.
14. Install crankshaft pulley retaining washer and bolt. Tighten bolt to specification.
15. Install crankshaft pulley to vibration damper if removed. Tighten bolt to specification.
16. Lower vehicle and inspect heater water outlet tube O-ring (replace as necessary). Install heater water outlet tube and O-ring into water pump. Install and tighten retaining bolts to specification.
17. Install camshaft position sensor and connect upper radiator hose at water hose connection. Tighten clamp securely.
18. If vehicle is equipped with A/C, install A/C compressor and mounting brackets. Tighten bolts to specification.
19. Install power steering pump and mounting bracket. Tighten bolts to specification.
20. Position drive belt over pulleys.
21. Install water pump pulley to water pump and cross tighten retaining bolts to specification.
22. Install cooling fan motor, fan blade and fan shroud assembly. Tighten bolts to specification and connect cooling fan motor.
23. Install drive belt and fill crankcase to proper level with engine oil.
24. Fill cooling system and install engine air cleaner.

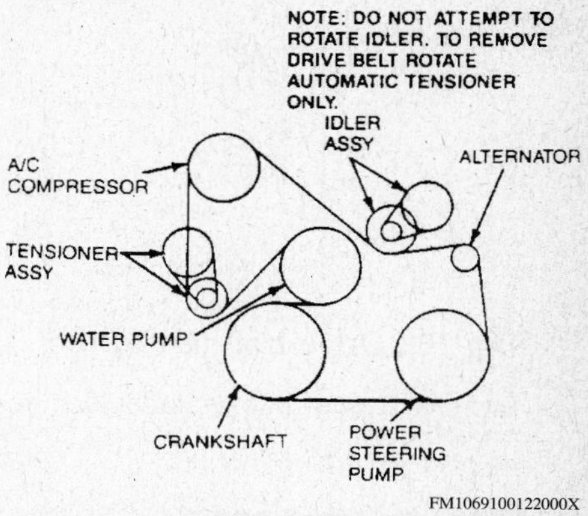

Fig. 15 Serpentine drive belt routing

TIMING GEARS

REPLACE

REMOVAL

The front cover contains the oil pump gears and the water pump. If a new front cover is to be installed, remove water pump and oil pump gears from old front cover.

1. Remove front cover as outlined in "Front Cover, Replace."
2. Remove camshaft sprocket retainer bolt and washer from end of camshaft.
3. Remove distributor drive gear.
4. If crankshaft sprocket is difficult to remove, loosen crankshaft sprocket by prying, using a pair of large pry bars positioned on both sides of crankshaft sprocket.
5. Remove camshaft sprocket, crankshaft sprocket and timing chain at the same time, **Fig. 9.**
6. Remove timing chain vibration damper from front of cylinder blocks. This requires pulling back on ratcheting mechanism and then installing pin through hole in bracket to relieve tension.

INSTALLATION

1. With timing chain vibration damper in compressed position, install timing chain vibration damper and retaining bolts to front of cylinder blocks. Tighten to specification.
2. Rotate crankshaft as necessary to position No. 1 piston at top dead center (TDC) and keyway at 12 o'clock position.
3. Lubricate timing chain with clean engine oil. Install camshaft sprocket, crankshaft sprocket and timing chain at same time. Ensure timing marks are positioned as indicated, **Fig. 10.**
4. Install distributor drive gear.
5. Install retaining bolt and washer at end of camshaft. Tighten bolts to specification.

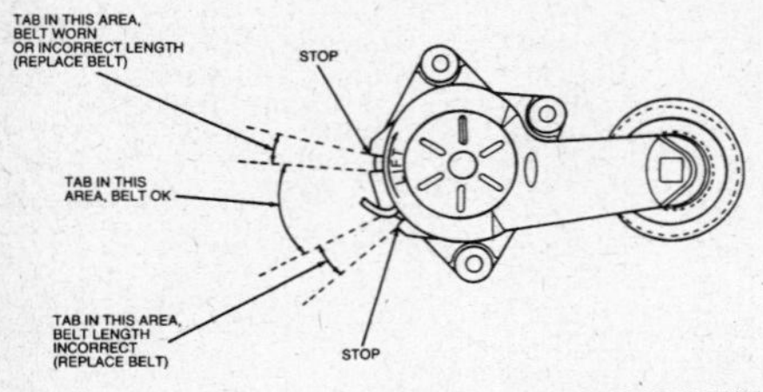

FM1069100124000X

Fig. 16 Drive belt tensioner

6. Remove timing chain vibration damper retaining pin.
7. Install front cover.

TIMING CHAIN

REPLACE

Refer to "Timing Gears, Replace" for timing chain replacement procedure.

CAMSHAFT

REPLACE

1. Drain cooling system into a suitable container and remove radiator and grille.
2. Recover refrigerant as outlined in "System Evacuation " under "Air Conditioning " and remove condenser.
3. Remove camshaft position sensor and housing.
4. Remove upper and lower intake manifold.
5. Remove valve tappet, valve tappet guide plate and tappet guide plate retainer.
6. Remove front cover, timing chain and camshaft sprocket spacer.
7. Remove oil pan and camshaft thrust plate.
8. Carefully remove camshaft by pulling toward front of engine, **Fig. 11. Use care to avoid damaging camshaft bearings.**
9. Reverse procedure to install, noting the following:
   a. Lubricate cam lobes and bearing surfaces with Oil Conditioner D9AZ-19579-D, , or equivalent.
   b. Tighten to specifications.

PISTON & ROD ASSEMBLY

When installed, piston and rod assembly should have the notch or arrow in piston head toward front of engine with connecting rod numbers positioned as shown, **Fig. 12.** Check side clearance between connecting rods at each crankshaft journal. Correct side clearance is .0047–.0114 Inch.

PISTONS, PINS & RINGS

Pistons are available in standard sizes and oversizes of .003, .020, .030 and .040 inch. Piston rings are available in standard sizes and oversizes of .020, .030 and .040 inch. Piston pins are available in standard size and oversizes of .001 and .002 inch.

MAIN & ROD BEARINGS

Main and rod bearings are available in standard sizes and undersizes of .001, .002, .010, .020 and .030 inch.

CRANKSHAFT REAR OIL SEAL

REPLACE

A one piece crankshaft rear oil seal is used for replacement on all engines. If replacement is necessary, this type of crankshaft rear oil seal must be used. The complete crankshaft rear oil seal can be replaced without removing crankshaft.

1. Remove transmission.
2. Using a sharp tool, punch one hole into crankshaft rear oil seal metal surface between lip and cylinder blocks.
3. Screw in threaded end of Jet Plug Remover T77L-9533-B, or equivalent, and remove oil seal.
4. Lubricate new seal with clean engine oil and install using seal installation tool No. T82L-6701-A, or equivalent. Tighten bolts alternately to seat seal properly, **Fig. 13.**

OIL PAN

REPLACE

1. Remove air cleaner outlet tube.
2. Remove two bolts attaching sight shield and position shield aside.
3. Remove hood weather seal and wiper assemblies.
4. Remove left cowl vent screen and wiper module.
5. Install engine lifting eyes, then engine support fixture D88L-6000-A, or equivalent.
6. Raise and support vehicle.
7. Remove engine mount through bolts.
8. Partially lower vehicle, then raise engine at support fixture.
9. Raise vehicle and remove starter motor assembly.
10. Drain engine oil, then remove oil filter.
11. Remove wire loom, ground strap and automatic transmission cooler lines.
12. Remove oil pan-to-bellhousing bolts, then the crankshaft position sensor shield bolts.
13. Remove remaining oil pan retaining bolts.
14. Remove steering shaft pinch bolts and separate steering shaft.
15. Position a transmission jack under front of subframe.
16. Remove six rearward bolts on front of subframe, then loosen two front subframe bolts.
17. Remove lower strut to control arm bolts and nuts on both sides of vehicle.
18. Lower subframe, then remove oil pan.
19. Reverse procedure to install. Tighten to specifications.

OIL PUMP

REPLACE

On these engines, the oil pump is contained within the front cover, **Fig. 14.** To replace oil pump, remove front cover as described under "Front Cover, Replace. "

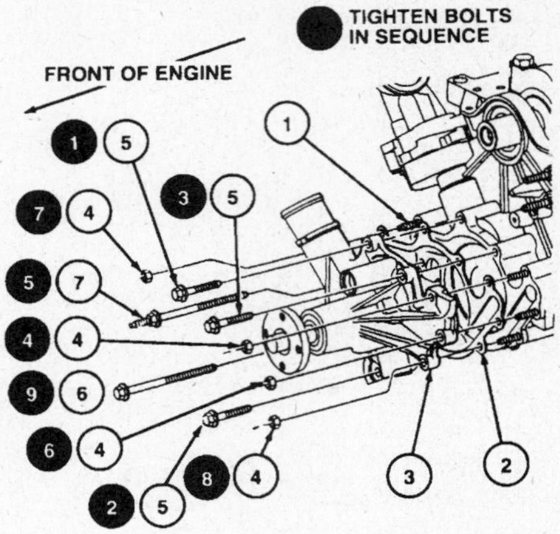

Item	Description
1	Stud (4 Req'd)
2	Water Pump Housing Gasket
3	Water Pump
4	Nut (4 Req'd)
5	Bolt (3 Req'd)
6	Bolt
7	Stud Bolt

FM1059800161000X

Fig. 17 Water pump tightening sequence

OIL PUMP SERVICE

Referring to **Fig. 14,** disassemble pump. To remove oil pressure relief valve, insert a self-threading sheet metal screw of the proper diameter into oil pressure relief valve chamber cap and pull cap out of chamber. Remove spring and plunger.

The inner rotor, shaft and outer race are serviced as an assembly. One part should not be replaced without replacing the other.

SERPENTINE DRIVE BELT

ROUTING

Refer to **Figs. 15** for serpentine drive belt routing.

ADJUSTMENT

Automatic belt tensioners are spring loaded devices which set and maintain the drive belt tension. The drive belt does not require tension adjustment. Automatic tensioners have belt wear indicator marks. If the indicator mark is not between the indicator lines, the belt is worn or an incorrect belt is installed.

If the indicator marks are difficult to view, locate the tab on the tensioner face plate, **Fig. 16.** The tab should be approximately between the stops.

TENSION DATA

Belt tension should be checked at the middle of longest accessible span. Belt tension should be 74 lbs.

Incorrect belt installation will cause excessive belt wear and may cause the belt to come off the drive pulleys.

REPLACEMENT

1. Rotate automatic tensioner away from belt.
2. Remove old belt from pulleys.
3. Install new belt over pulleys. Ensure all V-grooves make proper contact with pulleys.
4. **Incorrect belt installation will cause excessive belt wear and may cause the belt to come off the drive pulleys.**

COOLING SYSTEM BLEED

These engines do not require a specific bleed procedure. After filling cooling system, start engine and allow to reach operating temperature with radiator cap removed. Air in system will then be automatically bled through cap opening.

THERMOSTAT

REPLACE

1. Partially drain cooling system into a suitable container.
2. Disconnect upper radiator hose at thermostat housing.
3. Remove two mounting bolts, housing and gaskets.
4. Reverse procedure to install. Tighten to specifications.

WATER PUMP

REPLACE

1. Drain cooling system into a suitable container, then remove cooling fan motor, fan blade and fan shroud assembly.
2. Rotate drive belt tensioner and drive belt.
3. Remove retaining bolts and water pump pulley, then power steering pump pulley and water pump to power steering pump brace.
4. Remove heater water outlet tube retaining bolts and clutch pressure plate from water pump.
5. Remove water pump retaining bolts, stud bolts and nuts, then the water pump. Discard old water pump housing gasket.
6. Reverse procedure to install. Tighten bolts in sequence to specification, **Fig. 17.**

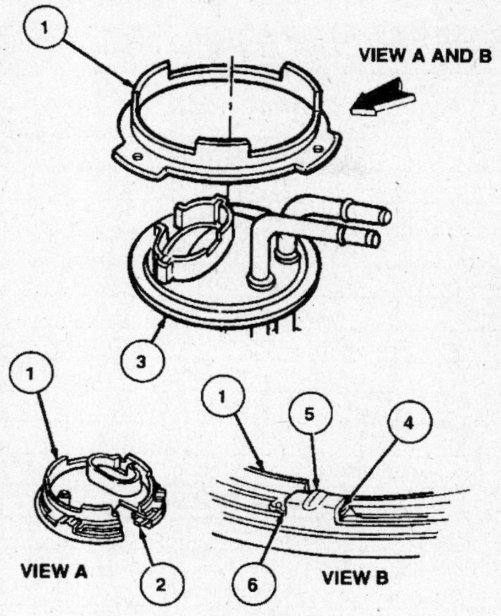

Item	Description
1	Fuel Pump Locking Retainer Ring
2	Fuel Pump Mounting Gasket
3	Fuel Pump Module
4	Stop
5	Tab
6	Detent

FM1029100137000A

Fig. 18 Fuel pump ring removal

RADIATOR

REPLACE

1. Drain coolant into a suitable container.
2. Disconnect upper, lower and overflow hose from radiator.
3. Disconnect automatic transmission fluid cooler inlet and outlet lines from radiator.
4. Remove two upper fan shroud to radiator support attaching bolts.
5. Lift fan shroud enough to disengage lower retaining clips and lay shroud back over fan.
6. Remove radiator upper support attaching bolts, then lift radiator from vehicle.
7. Reverse procedure to install.

FUEL PUMP

REPLACE

1. Relieve fuel pressure as described under "Precautions."
2. Remove fuel tank from vehicle as follow:
   a. Drain fuel tank into suitable container.
   b. Raise and support vehicle, then disconnect and cap fuel and vent lines from fuel tank. Tag lines so they can be installed in same locations. It may be necessary to remove exhaust pipe and shield to gain access to fuel tank.
   c. Disconnect electrical connectors from fuel sender and fuel pump. Tag electrical connections so they can be installed in same locations.
   d. Disconnect fuel filler tube.
   e. Remove fuel tank support straps, then lower fuel tank from vehicle.
3. Rotate fuel pump lock ring counterclockwise using Fuel Tank Sender Wrench T74P-9275-A, or equivalent, **Fig. 18.** Remove fuel pump.
4. Reverse procedure to install.

FUEL FILTER

REPLACE

1. Turn engine off and relieve fuel system pressure as described under "Precautions."
2. Raise and support vehicle.
3. Remove push connect fittings at both ends of the filter. Install new retaining in each push connect fitting.
4. Remove fuel filter from bracket by loosening worm gear clamp. Note direction of flow arrow as installed in bracket to ensure proper direction of fuel flow through replacement filter.
5. Reverse procedure to install. Tighten fuel filter worm gear clamp to specifications.

TIGHTENING SPECIFICATIONS

Year	Component	Torque/ Ft. Lbs.
1997	A/C Compressor Mounting	30–45
	A/C Lower Mounting Bracket	30–45
	Alternator Pivot Bolt	45–57
	Camshaft Sprocket	30–37
	Camshaft Thrust Plate	72–120②
	Connecting Rod	30③
	Coolant Temperature Switch	8–12
	Crankshaft Dampner	104–132
	Crankshaft Position Sensor	72–108 ②
	Crankshaft Pulley To Dampner	20–28
	Crankshaft Position Sensor Shield Nuts	18–35②
	Crankshaft Stud Bolt	72–102②
	Cylinder Head	④
	Dual Converter Y-Pipe To Exhaust Manifold Nuts	16–23
	ECT Sensor	11–14
	EGR Valve To Intake Manifold	15–22
	EGR Valve To Manifold Tube Connector	34–47
	Fan Clutch Assembly	12–18
	Fan Shroud	24–48②
	Flywheel	54–64
	Front Cover	15–22
	Fuel Rail Assembly Bolt	72–96②
	Fulcrum Bolt	①
	Heater Tube Support Bracket	15–22
	HEGO Sensor	28–33
	Intake Manifold	①
	Intake Manifold Retaining Strap	34–44
	Low Oil Level Sensor	20–30
	Main Bearing Cap	82–88
	Oil Drain Plug	15–25
	Oil Filter Adapter To Front Cover	18–22
	Oil Inlet Tube To Cylinder Block	15–22
	Oil Inlet Tube To Main Bearing Cap	30–40
	Oil Pan Bolts	80–106②
	Oil Pickup Tube	15–22
	Power Steering Lower Brace Bolt	18–24
	Power Steering Upper Brace Bolt	30–45
	Rocker Arm Cover	7–9
	Spark Plug	5–11
	Thermostat Housing	15–22
	Throttle Body Nut	15–22
	Valve Lifter Guide Plate	7–10
	Water Pump	15–22

① — Refer to “Intake Manifold, Replace.”

② — Inch lbs.

③ — Tighten an additional 90–120.°

④ — Refer to “Cylinder Head, Replace.”

4.6L Engine

NOTE: On Air Bag Equipped Models, Refer To " Air Bag System Precautions" Located In The Front Of This Manual For System Disarming & Arming Procedures.

NOTE: Refer To "Computer Relearn Procedures " Located In The Front Of This Manual For Computer Relearn Procedures.

INDEX

PRECAUTIONS

Air Bag Systems

Refer to "Air Bag System Precautions" in the front of this manual for system disarming and arming procedures.

Battery Ground Cable

Prior to service, disconnect battery ground cable and isolate as required.

Fuel System Pressure Relief, Gasoline Engines

The fuel system remains under high pressure even when the engine is not running. To avoid injury or fire, release pressure from the fuel system before disconnecting any fuel line. Proceed as follows:

1. Remove fuel tank cap to release residual fuel pressure from tank.
2. Connect fuel pressure gauge tool No. T80L-9974-B, or equivalent, to valve located on the fuel rail.
3. Gradually open testing kit valve to relieve fuel pressure in system. Drain fuel into suitable container or return to fuel tank.
4. To avoid unnecessary fuel spillage and fire hazard, any time fuel lines are disconnected, ignition switch should be in Off position.
5. When repair is completed, turn ignition On and Off several times to pressurize fuel system. Do not start engine.
6. Inspect for fuel leaks at pressure regulator, fuel injectors and fuel fittings. Repair as required.

Fuel System Pressure Relief, Natural Gas Engines

When servicing any component of the fuel charging system, fuel pressure should be released using the following procedures.

When venting fuel system, venting into a vent stack is recommended, **Fig. 1.** If using a vent stack, ensure local regulations are followed. Before venting occurs, battery should be disconnected and isolated as necessary.

Natural gas O-rings are identified with a yellow stripe. Do not use unapproved O-rings.

Before performing pressure relief

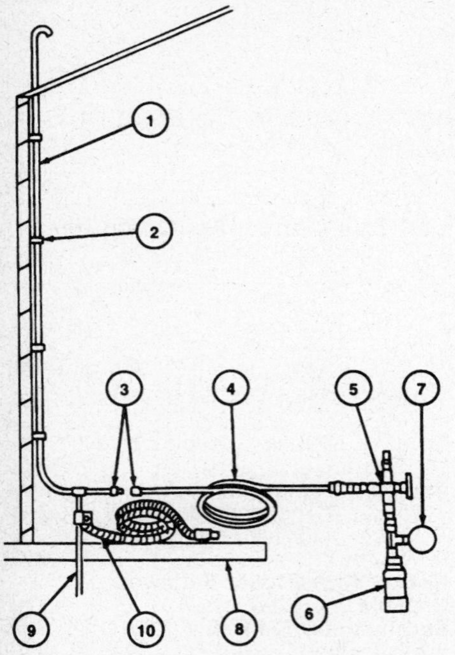

Item	Description
1	1/2 Inch Pipe
2	Vent Stack Support
3	Vent Stack Connectors
4	Rotunda Venting Hose
5	Rotunda Fuel Filter Neck Venting Kit
6	Fill Valve Connector
7	Gauge
8	Building Floor
9	Support/Grounding Rod
10	Grounding Cable

FM1029900308000X

Fig. 1 Typical vent stack installation

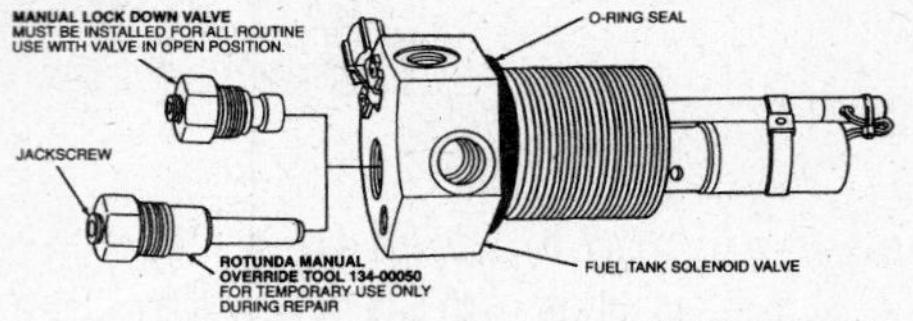

FM1029900309000X

Fig. 2 Fuel tank solenoid valve

Condition	Possible Source	Action
• Unable to Vent Fuel Tanks or Fuel Lines	• Damaged fuel tank solenoids. • Damaged lines or hoses. • Circuitry.	• GO to Pinpoint Test A.

FM1029900301000X

Fig. 3 NGV fuel tank solenoid valve symptom chart

procedures, refer to "NGV Fuel Tank Solenoid Valve Test" to determine status of fuel tank solenoid valves.

If a manual override tool has been used to open fuel tank solenoid valve, solenoid valve must be replaced, Fig. 2.

Do not vent fuel tank unless tank or fuel tank solenoid valve is being replaced. Unnecessary venting of good tanks will damage fuel tank solenoid valve.

NGV Fuel Tank Solenoid Valve Test

Prior to relieving fuel pressure on NGV vehicles, the following diagnosis should be performed to determine whether or not the fuel tank solenoid valve is stuck open or closed.

1. Inspect fuel system and determine if any of the following apply:
   a. Damaged fuel tanks.
   b. Damaged fuel tank solenoid valve.
   c. Damaged lines or hoses.
   d. Damaged fuse or relay.
   e. Damaged power distribution box.
   f. Damaged, loose or corroded electrical connections.
2. If any of the preceding conditions were found during visual inspection, repair as necessary. If none of the preceding conditions were found during visual inspection, refer to symptom chart, **Fig. 3.** For pinpoint test "A" on 1997–98 Crown Victoria models, refer to **Fig. 4.** For pinpoint test "A" on 1999 Crown Victoria and Grand Marquis models, refer to **Fig. 5.**
3. If fuel tank solenoid valve requires replacement, refer to appropriate **MOTOR's "Domestic Engine Performance Manual"** for procedure.

Fuel Line Pressure Relief, Natural Gas Engines

1997–98 CROWN VICTORIA w/NATURAL GAS ENGINE

1. Remove fuel pump relay from power distribution box.
2. When using fuel tester kit, ensure tester kit valve is closed. Connect fuel rail pressure test and venting kit tool No. 134-00116 and Rotunda venting hose assembly tool No. 134-00118, or equivalents, to schrader valve on fuel supply manifold.
3. Connect rotunda grounding cable tool No. 134-00121, or equivalent, to fuel supply manifold and earth ground.
4. Slowly open testing kit valve to relieve fuel pressure. **Five psi of fuel pressure will remain in fuel supply manifold. High pressure still exists in fuel tanks and upstream of quarter turn manual fuel line shut of valve if closed.**
5. **If fuel tubes continue to vent or pressure remains after one minute, fuel tank solenoids are stuck open. Do not disconnect fuel tubes while still under pressure.** Close bleed valve on fuel rail pressure tester and remove from vehicle.
6. After service is complete, inspect all connections at fuel injection supply manifold, fuel injectors and fuel line push connect fittings.
7. Using a jumper wire constructed of 6 inches of 18 gauge wire and two spade terminals, connect wire sockets 87 and 30 in fuel pump relay socket of power distribution box.
8. Inspect fuel system for leaks using Rotunda combustible gas detector tool No. 055-00107, or equivalent. Service all leaks as necessary.
9. Start engine and inspect for presence of any leaks.
10. Perform PCM self test as outlined under "Diagnosis & Testing."
11. Inspect coolant for presence of natural gas. If present, replace fuel pressure regulator.
12. Install fuel pump relay to power distribution box.

1999 CROWN VICTORIA & GRAND MARQUIS w/NATURAL GAS ENGINE

1. Connect grounding cable tool No. 134–00121, or equivalent, to fuel supply manifold and earth ground.
2. Ensure bleed valve on fuel rail pressure test kit is closed before installing.
3. Install fuel rail pressure test kit tool No. 134–00116, or equivalent, to fuel supply manifold schrader valve.
4. Connect vent hose to pressure test kit and vent stack.
5. Slowly open bleed valve of fuel rail pressure tester and allow fuel lines to vent to atmosphere for one minute. If pressure gauge still registers 95–125 psi, diagnose fuel tank solenoid valves

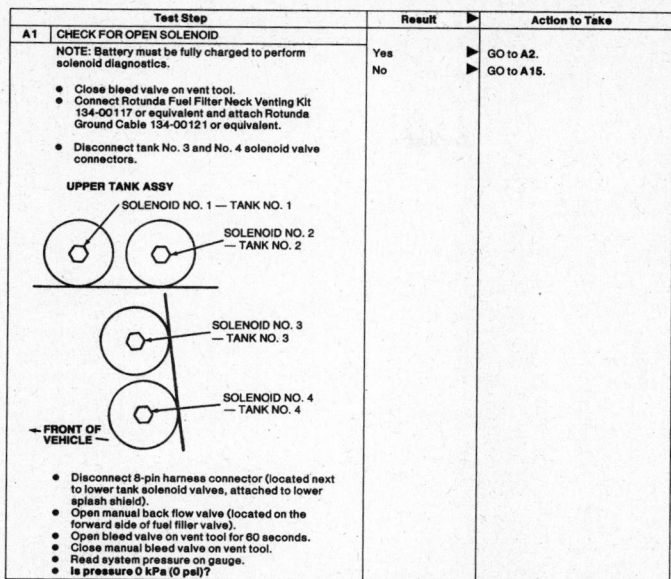

	Test Step	Result ▶	Action to Take
A1	CHECK FOR OPEN SOLENOID		
	NOTE: Battery must be fully charged to perform solenoid diagnostics. • Close bleed valve on vent tool. • Connect Rotunda Fuel Filter Neck Venting Kit 134-00117 or equivalent and attach Rotunda Ground Cable 134-00121 or equivalent. • Disconnect tank No. 3 and No. 4 solenoid valve connectors. 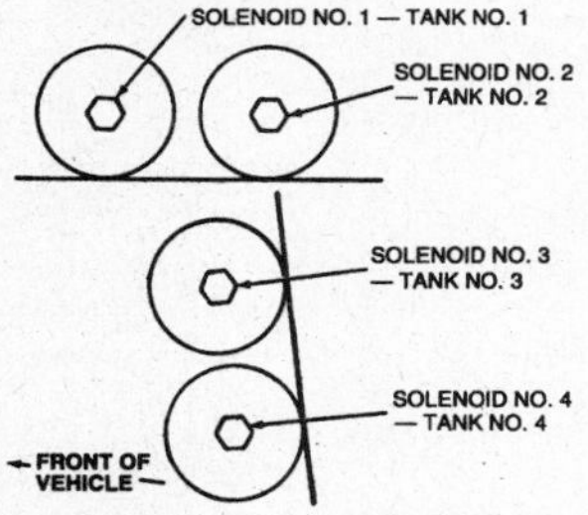 • Disconnect 8-pin harness connector (located next to lower tank solenoid valves, attached to lower splash shield). • Open manual back flow valve (located on the forward side of fuel filler valve). • Open bleed valve on vent tool for 60 seconds. • Close manual bleed valve on vent tool. • Read system pressure on gauge. • **Is pressure 0 kPa (0 psi)?**	Yes ▶ No ▶	GO to **A2**. GO to **A15**.

FM1029900302010X

Fig. 4 Pinpoint Test A: Fuel Tank Solenoid Valve Diagnosis (Part 1 of 9). 1997–98 Crown Victoria

	Test Step	Result ▶	Action to Take
A2	CHECK FUEL TANK NO. 4 SOLENOID VALVE		
	• Connect fuel tank No. 4 solenoid valve connector. • Connect Rotunda New Generation Star (NGS) Tester 007-00500 or equivalent to data link connector. • Select PCM. • Select ACTIVE COMMAND MODES. • Select OUTPUT TEST MODE. • Make sure manual lock down valve on fuel tank No. 4 solenoid valve is open. 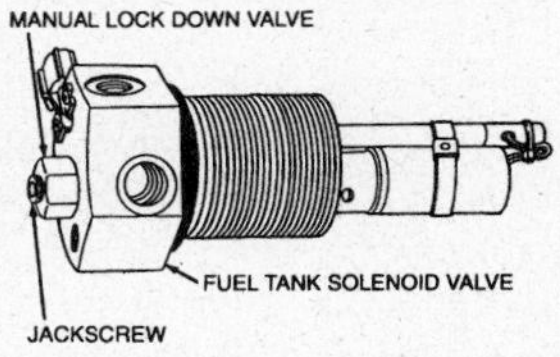 • NOTE: This procedure will supply power to the fuel tank solenoid valve for approximately 30-60 seconds. If time expires, cycle START/STOP button on NGS to restore power. • Push START button. • Read system pressure on Rotunda Fuel Filter Neck Venting Kit 134-00117 or equivalent. • Push STOP button. • Disconnect fuel tank No. 4 solenoid valve connector. • **Did system pressure read 0 kPa (0 psi) when triggered ON?**	Yes ▶ No ▶	GO to **A3**. MARK fuel tank No. 4 solenoid valve as "Good" and GO to **A5**.

FM1029900302020X

Fig. 4 Pinpoint Test A: Fuel Tank Solenoid Valve Diagnosis (Part 2 of 9). 1997–98 Crown Victoria

as outlined under "Fuel Injection."

Fuel Tank Pressure Relief, Natural Gas Engines

1997–98 CROWN VICTORIA

Stuck Open Or Normally Functioning Solenoid

When venting fuel tanks, tanks must be vented according to solenoid operation in the following sequence; stuck open, functioning normally, stuck closed or inoperative.

1. Ensure all solenoid valves are in locked position.
2. Connect Rotunda fuel filter neck venting kit tool No. 134–00117 and vent hose tool No. 134–00118, or equivalents, to vent stack, then to vehicle fuel fill valve.
3. Connect Rotunda grounding cable tool No. 134–00121, or equivalent, to rear of fuel filler valve assembly and to earth ground.
4. Remove fuel pump relay from power distribution box.
5. Using a jumper wire constructed of 6 inches of 18 gauge wire and two spade terminals, connect wire sockets 87 and 30 in fuel pump relay socket of power distribution box.
6. Slowly open manual lockout valve on affected tank.
7. Slowly open manual backflow valve on fuel filler valve.
8. Pressure on fuel filter neck venting kit gauge should read tank pressure is solenoid valve was identified as stuck open.
9. Slowly open bleed valve on fuel filter neck venting kit and allow tank to vent to atmosphere. Venting process may take 1 hour or more.
10. Close bleed valve on filter neck venting kit and ensure fuel line pressure is 0 psi.
11. Remove manual lockdown valve.
12. **Ensure jackscrew in manual override tool is retracted fully (counterclockwise) prior to installation into fuel tank solenoid valve. If tool is installed in vent position, fuel will be immediately released.**
13. Install Rotunda manual override tool No. 134-00050, or equivalent, to tank solenoid and **torque** to 28–31 ft. lbs.
14. Turn override tool jackscrew clockwise until fuel flows.
15. Vent system until fuel flow stops.
16. Remove override tool.
17. Install manual lockdown valve into fuel tank solenoid valve and **torque** to 28–31 ft. lbs.
18. **Torque** manual valve lockdown valve jackscrew to 62–79 inch lbs.
19. Repeat procedure on remaining tanks as necessary.
20. Close manual backflow valve on fuel filter valve when tank contents have vented and **torque** to 62–79 inch lbs.

Stuck Closed Or Inoperative Solenoid

When venting fuel tanks, tanks must be vented according to solenoid operation in the following sequence; stuck open, functioning normally, stuck closed or inoperative.

1. Ensure all solenoid valves should be in locked position.
2. Connect Rotunda fuel filter neck venting kit tool No. 134–00117 and vent hose tool No. 134–00118, or equivalents, to vent stack, then to vehicle fuel fill valve.
3. Connect Rotunda grounding cable tool No. 134–00121, or equivalent to rear of fuel filler valve assembly and to earth ground.
4. Remove manual lockout from solenoid valve.
5. **Ensure jackscrew in manual override tool is retracted fully (counterclockwise) prior to installation into fuel tank solenoid valve. If tool is installed in vent position, fuel will be immediately released.**
6. Install Rotunda manual override tool No. 134–00050, or equivalent and **torque** to 28–31 ft. lbs.
7. Turn override tool jackscrew clockwise until fuel flows.
8. Ensure pressure reading of fuel filler neck vent kit gauge reads tank pressure.
9. Slowly open bleed valve on neck vent kit and bleed tank to atmosphere. Vent process may take 1 hour or more.
10. Remove manual override tool from solenoid valve.
11. Retract manual lock down jackscrew, then install lockdown and **torque** to 62–79 inch lbs.
12. Close bleed valve on neck vent kit. Ensure tank pressure reads 0 psi.
13. Close manual backflow valve on fuel filler valve and **torque** to 62–79 inch lbs.
14. Remove neck vent kit from vehicle and vent stack.
15. Repeat vent procedure on remaining tanks as necessary.

1999 CROWN VICTORIA & GRAND MARQUIS

Normally Operating Solenoid

1. Remove vapor vent box from fuel tank as necessary.
2. Disconnect fuel tank electrical connectors and **torque** manual lockdown jackscrews to 80 inch lbs. on fuel tanks

Test Step		Result	Action to Take
A3	CHECK POWER SUPPLY TO FUEL TANK NO. 4 SOLENOID VALVE		
	• Connect NGS or equivalent to data link connector. • Select PCM. • Select ACTIVE COMMAND MODES. • Select OUTPUT TEST MODE. • Using a voltmeter connected to ground, connect second lead to fuel tank No. 4 solenoid connector Circuit 787 (PK / BK). 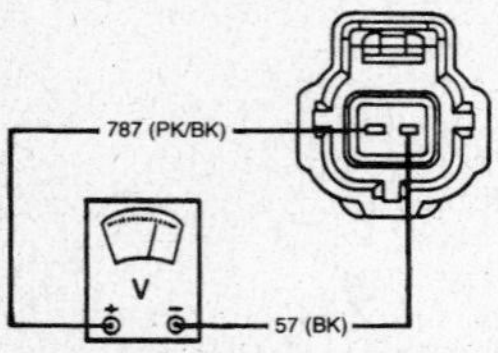 • NOTE: This procedure will supply power to the fuel tank solenoid valve for approximately 30-60 seconds. If time expires, cycle START/ STOP button on NGS Tester to restore power. • Push START button. • Read voltage. • Push STOP button. • **Is voltage B+?**	Yes ▶ No ▶	GO to **A4**. SERVICE Circuit 787 (PK / BK) for open. REPEAT Step A2.
A4	CHECK CIRCUIT 57 (BK) AT FUEL TANK NO. 4 SOLENOID		
	• Using an ohmmeter connected to ground, measure resistance at fuel tank No. 4 solenoid connector Circuit 57 (BK). • **Is resistance 5 ohms or less?**	Yes ▶ No ▶	MARK fuel tank No. 4 solenoid valve "Stuck Closed." Solenoid will be replaced after completing diagnostics. GO to **A5**. SERVICE Circuit 57 (BK) for open. REPEAT Step A2.
A5	CHECK FUEL TANK NO. 3 SOLENOID		
	• Open manual bleed valve on Rotunda Fuel Filter Neck Venting Kit 134-00117 or equivalent and vent system pressure to 0 kPa (0 psi). • Close manual bleed valve on Rotunda Fuel Filter Neck Venting Kit 134-00117 or equivalent. • Connect fuel tank No. 3 solenoid connector. • Connect NGS to data link connector. • Select PCM. • Select ACTIVE COMMAND MODES. • Select OUTPUT TEST MODE. • Make sure manual lock down on fuel tank No. 3 solenoid valve is open. • NOTE: This procedure will supply power to the fuel tank solenoid valve for approximately 30-60 seconds. If time expires, cycle START/ STOP button on NGS to restore power. • Push START button. • Read system pressure on Rotunda Fuel Filter Neck Venting Kit 134-00117 or equivalent gauge. • Push STOP button. • Disconnect fuel tank No. 3 solenoid connector. • **Did pressure read 0 kPa (0 psi) when triggered ON?**	Yes ▶ No ▶	GO to **A6**. MARK fuel tank No. 3 solenoid as "Good" and GO to **A8** .

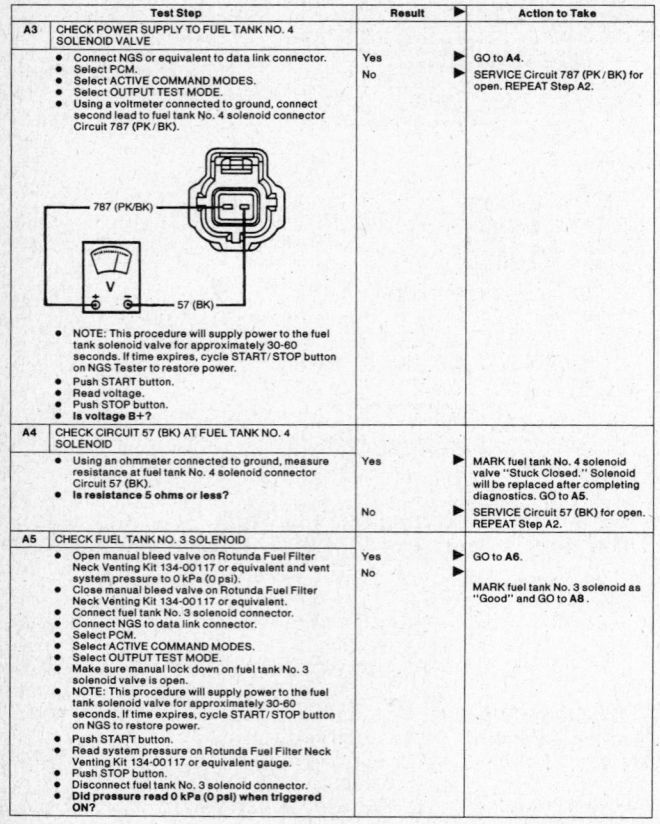

FM1029900302030X

Fig. 4 Pinpoint Test A: Fuel Tank Solenoid Valve Diagnosis (Part 3 of 9). 1997–98 Crown Victoria

Test Step		Result	Action to Take
A6	CHECK POWER SUPPLY TO FUEL TANK NO. 3 SOLENOID VALVE		
	• Connect NGS to data link connector. • Select PCM. • Select ACTIVE COMMAND MODES. • Select OUTPUT TEST MODE. • Using a voltmeter connected to ground, connect second lead to Circuit 787 (PK / BK) at fuel tank solenoid connector. • NOTE: This procedure will supply power to the fuel tank solenoid valve for approximately 30-60 seconds. If time expires, cycle START/ STOP button on NGS to restore power. • Push START button. • Read voltage. • Push STOP button. • **Is voltage B+?**	Yes ▶ No ▶	GO to **A7**. SERVICE Circuit 787 (PK / BK) for open. REPEAT Step A5.
A7	CHECK CIRCUIT 57 (BK) AT FUEL TANK NO. 3 SOLENOID VALVE		
	• Using an ohmmeter connected to ground, measure resistance at fuel tank No. 3 solenoid connector Circuit 57 (BK). • **Is resistance 5 ohms or less?**	Yes ▶ No ▶	MARK fuel tank No. 3 solenoid valve "Stuck Closed." Solenoid will be replaced after completing diagnostics. GO to**A8**. SERVICE Circuit 57 (BK) for open. REPEAT Step A5.
A8	CHECK FUEL TANK NO. 2 SOLENOID VENT		
	NOTE: Battery must be fully charged to perform solenoid diagnostics. • Open manual bleed valve on Rotunda Fuel Filter Neck Venting Kit 134-00117 or equivalent and vent system pressure to 0 kPa (0 psi) • Close manual bleed valve on vent tool. • Install Rotunda Electrical Harness for Venting Tanks 134-00120 or equivalent between upper tank assembly 8-pin and harness connectors. • Connect NGS to data link connector. • Select PCM. • Select ACTIVE COMMAND MODES. • Select OUTPUT TEST MODE. • Hold Rotunda Electrical Harness for Venting Tanks 134-00120 or equivalent to tank No. 2 position. • NOTE: This procedure will supply power to the fuel tank solenoid valve for approximately 30-60 seconds. If time expires, cycle START/ STOP button on NGS to restore power. • Push START button. • Read system pressure on Rotunda Fuel Filter Neck Venting Kit 134-00117 or equivalent gauge. • Release Rotunda Electrical Harness for Venting Tanks 134-00120 or equivalent switch. • Push STOP button. • **Did pressure read 0 kPa (0 psi) when triggered ON?**	Yes ▶ No ▶	NOTE: Fuel tank No. 2 solenoid valve may be "Stuck Closed". GO to **A9**. MARK fuel tank No. 2 solenoid valve as "Good". GO to **A9**.

FM1029900302040X

Fig. 4 Pinpoint Test A: Fuel Tank Solenoid Valve Diagnosis (Part 4 of 9). 1997–98 Crown Victoria

not to be vented. If neither of rear or upper tanks need to be vented, rear upper fuel tank rack harness connector may be disconnected without removing rear or upper fuel tank rack vent box.

3. Connect grounding cable 134-00121, or equivalent, to back side of fuel fill valve at fuel line connection and earth ground.
4. Ensure manual bleed valve on fuel vent kit is closed before connecting to fuel filler valve.
5. Connect fuel filler neck venting kit tool No. 134-00117, or equivalent, to fuel filler valve.
6. Connect vent hose tool No. 134-00118 to filler neck vent kit and vent stack.
7. Remove fuel valve relay from power distribution box.
8. Using a jumper wire constructed of 6 inches of 18 gauge wire and two spade terminals, connect wire sockets 87 and 30 in fuel pump relay socket of power distribution box.
9. Slowly open manual backflow valve on fuel filler valve using a suitable 3⁄16 inch allen wrench.
10. Ensure gauge on fuel filler neck vent kit indicates tank pressure.
11. Slowly open bleed valve on fuel filler neck vent kit and allow fuel tank to vent to atmosphere. Venting process may take 1 hour or more.
12. Close bleed valve on fuel filler neck vent kit and ensure gauge pressure is 0 psi.
13. Remove fuel tank solenoid manual lockdown valve.
14. **Ensure jackscrew in manual override tool is retracted fully (counterclockwise) prior to installation into fuel tank solenoid valve. If tool is installed in vent position, fuel will be immediately released.**
15. Install Rotunda manual override tool No. 134-00050, or equivalent, to tank solenoid and **torque** to 30 ft. lbs.
16. Turn override tool jackscrew clockwise until fuel flows.
17. Vent system until fuel flow stops.
18. Close manual backflow valve on fuel filler valve after tank has been vented.
19. Vent fuel lines as outlined under "Fuel Line Pressure Relief, Natural Gas Engines."
20. Remove manual override tool from fuel tank solenoid valve.
21. Install fuel tank solenoid manual lockdown valve and **torque** to 30 ft. lbs.
22. **Torque** manual lockdown valve jackscrew on fuel tank solenoid valve to 80 inch lbs.
23. Repeat procedure until affected tanks are vented.

Stuck Open Solenoid

1. Disconnect fuel tank electrical connectors and **torque** manual lockdown jackscrews to 80 inch lbs. on fuel tanks not to be vented. If neither of rear or upper tanks need to be vented, rear upper fuel tank rack harness connector may be disconnected without removing rear or upper fuel tank rack vent box.
2. Remove vent box from upper fuel tank rack as necessary.
3. Connect grounding cable tool No. 134–00121, or equivalent, to back side of fuel fill valve and earth ground.
4. Ensure manual bleed valve on fuel filler neck vent kit is closed before connecting to fuel filler valve.
5. Connect fuel filler vent kit tool No. 134-00117, or equivalent, to fuel filler valve.
6. Connect vent hose tool No. 134-00118, or equivalent, to filler neck vent kit and vent stack.
7. Slowly open manual backflow valve on fuel filler valve.
8. Ensure filler neck vent kit pressure gauge indicates tank pressure.
9. Slowly open bleed valve on filler neck vent kit and allow contents of fuel tank to vent to atmosphere. Vent process may take 1 hour or more.
10. Close bleed valve on fuel filler neck vent kit ensuring pressure gauge indicates 0 psi.
11. Remove fuel tank solenoid manual

Test Step		Result	Action to Take
A9	CHECK POWER SUPPLY TO FUEL TANK NO. 1 SOLENOID VALVE		
	• Open manual bleed valve on Rotunda Fuel Filter Neck Venting Kit 134-00117 or equivalent and vent system pressure 0 kPa (0 psi). • Close manual bleed valve on Rotunda Fuel Filter Neck Venting Kit 134-00117 or equivalent. • Connect NGS to data link connector. • Select PCM. • Select ACTIVE COMMAND MODES. • Select OUTPUT TEST MODE. • Switch Rotunda Electrical Harness for Venting Tanks 134-00120 or equivalent to tank No. 1 position. • NOTE: This procedure will supply power to the fuel tank solenoid valve for approximately 30-60 seconds. If time expires, cycle START/STOP button on NGS to restore power. • Push START button. • Read system pressure on Rotunda Fuel Filter Neck Venting Kit 134-00117 or equivalent gauge. • Release Rotunda Electrical Harness for Venting Tanks 134-00120 switch. • Push STOP button. • **Did pressure read 0 kPa (0 psi) when triggered ON?**	Yes ▶ No ▶	NOTE: Fuel tank No. 1 solenoid valve may be "Stuck Closed." GO to **A10**. MARK fuel tank No. 1 solenoid valve "Good." REPLACE all solenoids marked stuck closed. If fuel tank No. 2 solenoid valve was marked may be "Stuck Closed," GO to **A10**. If all solenoids were marked "Good," solenoids operating properly at this time. RETURN to venting procedure.
A10	CHECK CIRCUIT 57 (BK) TO UPPER TANK ASSEMBLY		
	• Open manual bleed valve on Rotunda Fuel Filter Neck Venting Kit 134-00117 or equivalent and vent system pressure to 0 kPa (0 psi). • Close manual bleed valve on Rotunda Fuel Filter Neck Venting Kit 134-00117 or equivalent. • Remove upper fuel tank rack assembly vapor vent box as described. • Using an ohmmeter, measure resistance of Circuit 57 (BK) between fuel tank No. 1 and No. 2 solenoid valve connectors and upper tank assembly 8-pin harness connector Pin 1. • **Is resistance 5 ohms or less on both circuits?**	Yes ▶ No ▶	GO to **A11**. SERVICE Circuit 57 (BK) for open. Install upper tank assembly as described. GO to **A8**.
A11	CHECK CIRCUIT 787 (PK/BK)		
	• Using an ohmmeter, measure resistance between upper tank assembly 8-pin harness connector Pin 6 and fuel tank No. 2 solenoid valve connector Circuit 787 (PK/BK) and upper tank assembly 8-pin harness connector Pin 5 and fuel tank No. 1 solenoid valve connector Circuit 787 (PK/BK). • **Is resistance 5 ohms or less for each circuit?**	Yes ▶ No ▶	GO to **A12**. SERVICE suspect circuit for open. Install upper tank assembly as described. GO to **A8**.
A12	CHECK FUEL TANK SOLENOID VALVE FOR MANUAL LOCK DOWNS		
	• Install upper tank assembly without vent box installed, make all fuel line and electrical connections as described in the installation procedure. • Check fuel tank No. 1 and No. 2 solenoid valves manual lock downs. • **Are manual lock downs open?**	Yes ▶ No ▶	REPLACE all solenoids marked "Stuck Closed." If fuel tank No. 1 or No. 2 solenoid valve was marked may be "Stuck Closed," REPLACE at this time. RESTORE vehicle. RETEST system. GO to **A13**.

FM1029900302050X

Fig. 4 Pinpoint Test A: Fuel Tank Solenoid Valve Diagnosis (Part 5 of 9). 1997–98 Crown Victoria

Test Step		Result	Action to Take
A13	CHECK FUEL TANK NO. 2 SOLENOID VALVE MANUAL LOCK DOWN		
	• Make sure bleed valve on Rotunda Fuel Filter Neck Venting Kit 134-00117 or equivalent is closed. • Open fuel tank No. 2 solenoid valve manual lock down. • Open bleed valve on Rotunda Fuel Filter Neck Venting Kit 134-00117 or equivalent for 60 seconds. • Close bleed valve on Rotunda Fuel Filter Neck Venting Kit 134-00117 or equivalent . • Read system pressure. • **Is system pressure 0 kPa (0 psi)?**	Yes ▶ No ▶	If fuel tank No. 1 solenoid valve manual lock down is open, GO to **A8**. If closed GO to **A14**. Mark fuel tank No. 2 solenoid valve "Stuck Open." GO to **A15**.
A14	CHECK FUEL TANK NO. 1 SOLENOID LOCK DOWN		
	• Using a 3/16 allen wrench, tighten manual lock down jackscrew on fuel tank No. 2 solenoid valve to within 7-9 N·m (62-79 lb-in). • Open fuel tank No. 1 solenoid valve manual lock down. • Open bleed valve on Rotunda Fuel Filter Neck Venting Kit 134-00117 or equivalent for 60 seconds. • Close bleed valve on Rotunda Fuel Filter Neck Venting Kit 134-00117 or equivalent. • Read system pressure. • **Is system pressure 0 kPa (0 psi)?**	Yes ▶ No ▶	GO to **A8**. MARK fuel tank No. 1 solenoid valve "Stuck Open." GO to **A15**.
A15	CHECK FOR SHORT TO B+		
	• Ignition switch OFF. • Using a voltmeter, measure for voltage at tank side of 8-pin harness connector Pin 1, Circuit 57 (BK), Pin 5, Circuit 787 (PK/BK) and Pin 6, Circuit 787 (PK/BK). • Measure for voltage at fuel tank No. 3 and No. 4 solenoid connectors Circuit 787 (PK/BK). 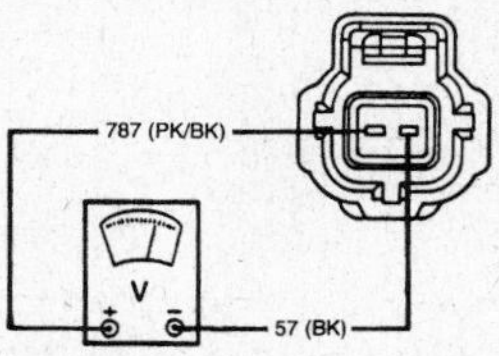 • **Is voltage B+ on any circuit?**	Yes ▶ No ▶	SERVICE suspect circuit for short to B+. GO to **A1**. GO to **A16**.

FM1029900302060X

Fig. 4 Pinpoint Test A: Fuel Tank Solenoid Valve Diagnosis (Part 6 of 9). 1997–98 Crown Victoria

lockdown valve.

12. **Ensure jackscrew in manual override tool is retracted fully (counterclockwise) prior to installation into fuel tank solenoid valve. If tool is installed in vent position, fuel will be immediately released.**
13. Install Rotunda manual override tool No. 134–00050, or equivalent, to tank solenoid and **torque** to 30 ft. lbs.
14. Turn override tool jackscrew clockwise until fuel flows.
15. Open manual bleed valve on fuel filler neck vent kit and vent system until fuel flow stops.
16. Close manual backflow valve on fuel filler valve after tank has been vented.
17. Vent fuel lines as outlined under "Fuel Line Pressure Relief, Natural Gas Engines."
18. Remove manual override tool from fuel tank solenoid valve.
19. Install fuel tank solenoid manual lockdown valve and **torque** to 30 ft. lbs.
20. **Torque** manual lockdown valve jackscrew on fuel tank solenoid valve to 80 inch lbs.
21. Repeat procedure until affected tanks are vented.

Stuck Closed Solenoid

1. Disconnect fuel tank electrical connectors and **torque** manual lockdown jackscrews to 80 inch lbs. on fuel tanks not to be vented. If neither of rear or upper tanks need to be vented, rear upper fuel tank rack harness connector may be disconnected without removing rear or upper fuel tank rack vent box.
2. Remove vent box from upper fuel tank rack as necessary.
3. Connect grounding cable tool No. 134-00121, or equivalent, to back side of fuel fill valve and earth ground.
4. Ensure manual bleed valve on fuel filler neck vent kit is closed before connecting to fuel filler valve.
5. Connect fuel filler vent kit tool No. 134-00117, or equivalent, to fuel filler valve.
6. Connect vent hose tool No. 134-00118, or equivalent, to filler neck vent kit and vent stack.
7. Open manual bleed valve on fuel filler neck vent kit for one minute to bleed residual fuel system pressure. Close manual bleed valve.
8. Remove manual lockdown valve from fuel tank solenoid valve of fuel tank to be vented.
9. **Ensure jackscrew in manual override tool is retracted fully (counterclockwise) prior to installation into fuel tank solenoid valve. If tool is installed in vent position, fuel will be immediately released.**
10. Install Rotunda manual override tool No. 134-00050, or equivalent, to tank solenoid and **torque** to 30 ft. lbs.
11. Turn override tool jackscrew clockwise until fuel flows.
12. Slowly open manual backflow valve on fuel filler valve and ensure pressure gauge on vent kit reads tank pressure.
13. Slowly open bleed valve on fuel filler neck vent kit and allow tank to vent to atmosphere. Vent process may take 1 hour or more.
14. Vent tank until fuel flow stops.
15. Close manual backflow valve on fuel filler valve when tank venting is complete.
16. Vent fuel lines as outlined under "Fuel Line Pressure Relief, Natural Gas Engines."
17. Remove manual override tool from fuel tank solenoid valve.
18. Install fuel tank solenoid manual lockdown valve and **torque** to 30 ft. lbs.
19. **Torque** manual lockdown valve jackscrew on fuel tank solenoid valve to 80 inch lbs.
20. Repeat procedure until affected tanks are vented.

COMPRESSION PRESSURE

Cylinder compression pressure should range between 134–250 psi at an engine cranking speed of 180 RPM minimum. The compression in each cylinder should fall within the specified compression pressure range with no more than a 75% variance in compression.

ENGINE MOUNT

REPLACE

COUGAR & THUNDERBIRD

1. Remove engine appearance cover.
2. Remove air cleaner outlet tube to engine air cleaner.

	Test Step	Result ▶	Action to Take
A16	CHECK FOR OPEN FUEL TANK SOLENOID IN UPPER TANK ASSEMBLY		
	• Using a 3/16 allen wrench, tighten manual lock down jackscrew on fuel tank No. 3 and No. 4 solenoid valves to within 7-9 N·m (62-79 lb-in). • Open bleed valve on Rotunda Fuel Filter Neck Venting Kit 134-00117 or equivalent for 60 seconds. • Close bleed valve on Rotunda Fuel Filter Neck Venting Kit 134-00117 or equivalent. • Read pressure on Rotunda Fuel Filter Neck Venting Kit 134-00117 or equivalent gauge. 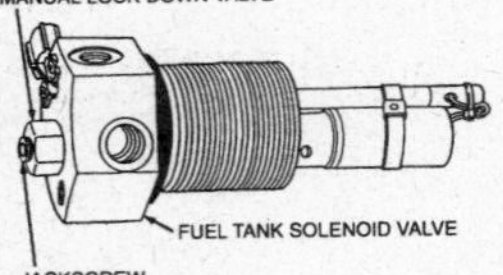 • **Is pressure 0 kPa (0 psi)?**	Yes ▶ No ▶	GO to **A21**. GO to **A17**.
A17	CHECK CIRCUIT 787 (PK/BK)		
	• Open manual bleed valve on Rotunda Fuel Filter Neck Venting Kit 134-00117 or equivalent and vent system pressure to 0 kPa (0 psi). • Close bleed valve on Rotunda Fuel Filter Neck Venting Kit 134-00117 or equivalent. • Remove upper fuel tank rack assembly vapor vent box as described. • Using an ohmmeter, measure resistance of Circuit 787 (PK/BK) between upper tank assembly 8-pin harness connector Pin 6 and fuel tank No. 2 solenoid valve connector, and between upper tank assembly 8-pin harness connector Pin 5 and fuel tank No. 1 solenoid valve connector. • **Is resistance 5 ohms or less for each circuit?**	Yes ▶ No ▶	GO to **A18**. SERVICE suspect circuit for open. RESTORE vehicle. RETEST system.
A18	CHECK CIRCUIT 57 (BK)		
	• Using an ohmmeter, measure resistance of Circuit 57 (BK) between fuel tank No. 1 and No. 2 solenoid valve connectors and upper tank assembly 8-pin harness connector. • **Is resistance 5 ohms or less?**	Yes ▶ No ▶	GO to **A19**. SERVICE Circuit 57 (BK) for open. GO to **A19**.

FM1029900302070X

Fig. 4 Pinpoint Test A: Fuel Tank Solenoid Valve Diagnosis (Part 7 of 9). 1997–98 Crown Victoria

	Test Step	Result ▶	Action to Take
A19	CHECK FUEL TANK NO. 2 SOLENOID VALVE OPERATION		
	NOTE: Battery must be fully charged to perform solenoid diagnostics • Make sure manual bleed valve is closed on Rotunda Fuel Filter Neck Venting Kit 134-00117 or equivalent. • Install upper fuel tank assembly without vent box installed, make all fuel line and electrical connections as described. • Tighten fuel tank No. 1 solenoid valve manual lock down jackscrew to 7-9 N·m (62-79 lb-in). • Open fuel tank No. 2 solenoid valve manual lock down. • Connect Rotunda Electrical Harness for Venting Tanks 134-00120 or equivalent to harness 8-pin connector. • Connect fuel tank No. 2 solenoid valve connector. • Make sure fuel tank No. 1 solenoid valve connector is disconnected. • Connect NGS or equivalent to data link connector. • Select PCM. • Select ACTIVE COMMAND MODES. • Select OUTPUT TEST MODE. • Hold Rotunda Electrical Harness for Venting Tanks 134-00120 or equivalent to tank No. 2 position. • NOTE: This procedure will supply power to the fuel tank solenoid valve for approximately 30-60 seconds. If time expires, cycle START/STOP button on NGS to restore power. Push START button. • Read system pressure on Rotunda Fuel Filter Neck Venting Kit 134-00117 or equivalent gauge. • Release Rotunda Electrical Harness for Venting Tanks 134-00120 or equivalent switch. • Press STOP button. • **Is pressure 0 kPa (0 psi) when triggered ON?**	Yes ▶ No ▶	MARK fuel tank No. 2 solenoid valve "Does Not Operate." Solenoid will be replaced after completing diagnostics. GO to **A20**. MARK fuel tank No. 2 solenoid valve "Good" and GO to **A20**.
A20	CHECK FUEL TANK NO. 1 SOLENOID VALVE OPERATION		
	• Open manual bleed valve on Rotunda Fuel Filter Neck Venting Kit 134-00117 or equivalent and vent system pressure to 0 kPa (0 psi). • Close manual bleed valve on Rotunda Fuel Filter Neck Venting Kit 134-00117 or equivalent. • Disconnect fuel tank No. 2 solenoid valve connector. • Connect fuel tank No. 1 solenoid valve connector. • Tighten fuel tank No. 1 solenoid valve manual lock down jackscrew to 7-9 N·m (62-79 lb-in). • Connect NGS or equivalent to data link connector. • Select PCM. • Select ACTIVE COMMAND MODES. • Select OUTPUT TEST MODE. • Hold Rotunda Electrical Harness for Venting Tanks 134-00120 or equivalent to tank No. 1 position. • NOTE: This procedure will supply power to the fuel tank solenoid valve for approximately 30-60 seconds. If time expires, cycle START/STOP button on NGS to restore power. • Push START button. • Read system pressure on Rotunda Fuel Filter Neck Venting Kit 134-00117 or equivalent gauge. • Release Rotunda Electrical Harness for Venting Tanks 134-00120 or equivalent switch. • Press STOP button. • **Is pressure 0 kPa (0 psi) when triggered ON?**	Yes ▶ No ▶	MARK fuel tank No. 1 solenoid valve "Does Not Operate." Solenoid will be replaced after completing diagnostics. GO to **A21**. MARK fuel tank No. 1 solenoid "Good" and GO to **A21**.

FM1029900302080X

Fig. 4 Pinpoint Test A: Fuel Tank Solenoid Valve Diagnosis (Part 8 of 9). 1997–98 Crown Victoria

3. Install Rotunda engine lifting brackets No. 014-00340, or equivalent.
4. Install Rotunda three bar engine support No. 014-00750, or equivalent, to engine lifting brackets.
5. Raise and support vehicle.
6. Remove engine support insulator through bolts, **Fig. 6.**
7. Remove accessory and oil cooler line retaining clips from front engine support insulators.
8. Remove front anti-lock brake wire harness from body and front sub frame retainers.
9. Remove steering coupling pinch bolt, then separate steering coupling from lower steering column shaft.
10. Support both front suspension lower arms and remove front suspension lower arm strut through bolt.
11. Separate front suspension lower arm struts from front suspension lower arms.
12. Slowly lower front suspension lower arms until hanging freely.
13. Support front sub frame with suitable jackstands.
14. Remove eight front sub frame retaining bolts.
15. Slowly lower front sub frame to gain access to front engine support insulators.
16. Remove bolts retaining front engine support insulators.
17. Reverse procedure to install.

CROWN VICTORIA & GRAND MARQUIS

1997–98

1. Remove air cleaner outlet tube.
2. Drain engine coolant into suitable container.
3. Remove cooling fan blade and fan shroud.
4. Relieve system fuel pressure as outlined under " Precautions."
5. Remove upper radiator hose.
6. Remove windshield wiper motor and mounting bracket.
7. Using a suitable A/C recovery station, evacuate A/C system as outlined in "System Evacuation" under " Air Conditioning."
8. Disconnect A/C manifold and tube at A/C compressor and remove bolt retaining A/C manifold and tube assembly to right hand coil bracket.
9. Remove engine harness connector from wiring bracket on power brake booster.
10. Disconnect transmission harness connector.
11. Disconnect heater hose then remove upper stud bolt and lower bolt retaining water hose to right side cylinder head.
12. Remove heater blower motor switch resistor.
13. Remove upper bolt retaining right hand front engine mount insulator to front engine mount insulator support.
14. Disconnect vacuum hoses from EGR control valve and EGR valve to exhaust manifold tube.
15. Remove EGR control valve.
16. Disconnect both heated oxygen sensors.
17. Raise and support vehicle.
18. Remove two through bolts from left hand front engine support insulator and one through bolt from right hand front engine support insulator, **Fig. 7.**
19. Remove EGR valve to exhaust manifold tube line nut from right hand exhaust manifold and remove EGR valve to exhaust manifold tube.
20. Disconnect exhaust system from exhaust manifolds.
21. Lower exhaust system and wire to cross member to hold in position.
22. Position a suitable jack and wood block under oil pan rearward of oil pan drain plug.
23. Raise engine approximately 4 inches.
24. Install a wood block under oil pan and lower engine onto wood block.
25. Remove three retaining bolts from both front engine support insulators and remove insulators from vehicle.
26. Reverse procedure to install, tighten all bolts and nuts to specification.

1999–2000

1. For right hand engine mount, remove starter.

Test Step		Result ▶	Action to Take
A21	CHECK FUEL TANK NO. 3 SOLENOID VALVE FOR STUCK OPEN CONDITION		
	• Disconnect Rotunda Electrical Harness for Venting Tanks 134-00120 or equivalent. • Tighten fuel tank No. 1 solenoid valve manual lock down jackscrew to 7-9 N-m (62-79 lb-in). • Open manual bleed valve on Rotunda Fuel Filter Neck Venting Kit 134-00117 or equivalent and vent system pressure to 0 kPa (0 psi). • Close manual bleed valve on Rotunda Fuel Filter Neck Venting Kit 134-00117 or equivalent. • Open fuel tank No. 3 solenoid valve manual lock down jackscrew. • Read system pressure. • **Is pressure 0 kPa (0 psi)?**	Yes ▶ No ▶	GO to **A22**. MARK fuel tank No. 3 solenoid valve as "Stuck Open." Solenoid will be replaced after completing diagnostics. GO to **A23**.
A22	CHECK FUEL TANK NO. 3 SOLENOID VALVE OPERATION		
	• Connect fuel tank No. 3 solenoid connector. • Connect Rotunda New Generation Star (NGS) Tester 007-00500 or equivalent to data link connector. • Select PCM. • Select ACTIVE COMMAND MODES. • Select OUTPUT TEST MODE. • NOTE: This procedure will supply power to the fuel tank solenoid valve for approximately 30-60 seconds. If time expires, cycle START/ STOP button on New Generation Star (NGS) Tester to restore power. • Push START button. • Read system pressure on Rotunda Fuel Filter Neck Venting Kit 134-00117 or equivalent gauge. • Push STOP button. • **Did pressure read 0 kPa (0 psi) when triggered ON?**	Yes ▶ No ▶	MARK fuel tank No. 3 solenoid valve "Stuck Closed." Solenoid will be replaced after completing diagnostics. GO to **A23**. GO to **A23**.
A23	GHECK FUEL TANK NO. 4 SOLENOID VALVE STUCK OPEN CONDITION		
	• Open manual bleed valve on Rotunda Fuel Filter Neck Venting Kit 134-00117 or equivalent and vent system pressure to 0 kPa (0 psi). • Close manual bleed valve on Rotunda Fuel Filter Neck Venting Kit 134-00117 or equivalent. • Tighten fuel tank No. 1 solenoid valve manual lock down jackscrew to 7-9 N-m (62-79 lb-in). • Open fuel tank No. 4 solenoid valve manual lock down jackscrew. • Read system pressure. • **Is pressure 0 kPa (0 psi)?**	Yes ▶ No ▶	GO to **A24**. MARK fuel tank No. 4 solenoid valve as "Stuck Open." REPLACE all solenoids marked "Stuck Closed." "Stuck Open" or "Does Not Operate." RESTORE vehicle. RETEST system.
A24	CHECK FUEL TANK NO. 4 SOLENOID VALVE OPERATION		
	• Disconnect fuel tank No. 3 solenoid valve connector. • Connect fuel tank No. 4 solenoid valve connector. • Connect NGS or equivalent to data link connector. • Select PCM. • Select ACTIVE COMMAND MODES. • Select OUTPUT TEST MODE. • NOTE: This procedure will supply power to the fuel tank solenoid valve for approximately 30-60 seconds. If time expires, cycle START/ STOP button on NGS to restore power. • Push START button. • Read system pressure on Rotunda Fuel Filter Neck Venting Kit 134-00117 or equivalent gauge. • Push STOP button. • **Did pressure read 0 kPa (0 psi) when triggered ON?**	Yes ▶ No ▶	MARK fuel tank No. 4 solenoid valve "Stuck Closed." REPLACE all solenoids marked "Stuck Open," "Stuck Closed" or "Does Not Operate." RESTORE vehicle. RETEST system. MARK fuel tank No. 4 solenoid valve as "Good." REPLACE all solenoids marked "Stuck Closed," "Stuck Open," or "Does Not Operate." RESTORE vehicle. RETEST system.

FM1029900302090X

Fig. 4 Pinpoint Test A: Fuel Tank Solenoid Valve Diagnosis (Part 9 of 9). 1997–98 Crown Victoria

TEST CONDITIONS	TEST DETAILS/RESULTS/ACTIONS
A1 CHECK FUEL SYSTEM SOLENOID OPERATION	
NOTE: The battery must be fully charged to perform solenoid diagnostics.	
NOTE: Whenever connecting the vent tool make sure the bleed valve on the tool is closed.	
1 	2 Connect the grounding cable, the venting hose assembly and the Fuel Filler Neck Venting Kit to the vent stack and the fuel fill valve.
3  Tank No. 3 Solenoid Connector C416. Tank No. 4 Solenoid Connector C417. 8-Pin Upper Tank Rack Harness Connector C421.	4 Open the manual back flow valve on the fuel filler valve. 5 Open the bleed valve on the vent tool for 60 seconds. 6 Close the manual bleed valve on the vent tool. 7 Observe the system pressure on the Fuel Filler Neck Venting Kit Gauge. • Is the pressure 0 kPa (0 psi)? → **Yes** System pressure is correct. However, all four solenoid valves must be checked for being "stuck closed." GO to **A2**. → **No** GO to **A15**.

FM1029900303010X

Fig. 5 Pinpoint Test A: Fuel Tank Solenoid Valve Diagnosis (Part 1 of 20). 1999 Crown Victoria & Grand Marquis

2. For left hand engine mount, remove oil dipstick tube.
3. Support vehicle engine with a suitable engine support device
4. Remove three bolts from each mount, then the mount(s).
5. Reverse procedure to install.

ENGINE

REPLACE

COUGAR & THUNDERBIRD

1. Drain coolant into a suitable container, then remove air cleaner outlet tube and engine air cleaner.
2. Evacuate A/C system as outlined in "System Evacuation " under "Air Conditioning, " then remove fan blade and fan shroud.
3. Relieve fuel system pressure as described under " Precautions" and disconnect fuel lines.
4. Disconnect 42-pin connector and 8-pin connector and secure clear of engine.
5. Disconnect accelerator cable and speed control actuator with a screwdriver.
6. Disconnect throttle valve control actuating cable.
7. Disconnect electrical connector and vacuum hose from canister purge solenoid.
8. Disconnect power supply from power distribution box and starter relay.
9. Disconnect vacuum supply hose from throttle body adapter vacuum port.
10. Disconnect transmission oil cooler tubes from transmission oil cooler, then disconnect upper radiator hose from outlet tube.
11. Disconnect heater supply and return hoses.
12. Disconnect A/C compressor inlet and outlet hoses from A/C compressor using spring coupling disconnect tool No. T81P-19623-G1 and T81P-19623-G2, or equivalents.
13. Disconnect engine to frame wire and body ground strap from dash panel.
14. Raise and support vehicle and remove front wheels.
15. Disconnect right and left front anti-lock sensor and brackets wiring connectors.
16. Remove right and left front disc brake caliper bolts. Remove front disc brake calipers and secure to vehicle with wire. **Do not allow calipers to suspend from brake hoses.**
17. Disconnect right and left front suspension upper arms from front wheel spindles.
18. Disconnect front spring and shocks from front suspension lower arms.
19. Drain engine oil into suitable container, then disconnect dual converter Y pipe from exhaust manifolds and resonator.
20. Disconnect transmission shift cable and bracket.
21. Mark relationship of driveshaft centering socket yoke to rear axle universal joint flange.
22. Remove four bolts connecting driveshaft centering socket yoke to rear axle universal joint flange. Support rear axle assembly with suitable jack stand.
23. Remove two nut and bolt assemblies retaining the front of the rear axle assembly to the rear sub-frame.
24. Loosen rear differential bracket to body bolts and lower from vehicle.
25. Slide driveshaft rearward until it is clear of extension housing, then remove lower radiator hose from radiator inlet tube.
26. Loosen spring clamps and remove power steering hoses from power steering oil cooler. Disconnect wiring bulkhead connector.
27. Support front sub-frame using Rotunda Powertrain Lift Tool No. 014-00765 and Adapter tool No. 014-00341, or equivalents.
28. Remove rear engine support insulator retaining bolts, then disconnect steering coupling at pinch bolt joint.
29. Remove eight front sub-frame bolts.
30. Lower engine and transmission from vehicle.
31. Disconnect power steering pressure

TEST CONDITIONS	TEST DETAILS/RESULTS/ACTIONS
A2 CHECK FUEL TANK NO. 4 SOLENOID VALVE	
NOTE: Make sure the manual lock-down jackscrew on fuel tank No. 4 solenoid valve is open. **NOTE:** This procedure will supply power to the fuel tank solenoid valve for approximately 30-60 seconds. If time expires, cycle the start/stop button on the NGS Tester to restore power.	
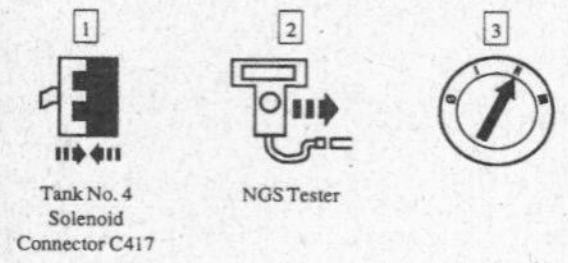	4 Select the proper output test mode on the NGS Tester and press the start button. 5 Observe the system pressure on the Fuel Filler Neck Venting Kit Gauge. 6 Press the stop button on the NGS Tester. • Was the pressure on the gauge 0 kPa (0 psi) when triggered on? → **Yes** GO to **A3**. → **No** Mark No. 4 solenoid valve "good." GO to **A5**.

FM1029900303020X

Fig. 5 Pinpoint Test A: Fuel Tank Solenoid Valve Diagnosis (Part 2 of 20). 1999 Crown Victoria & Grand Marquis

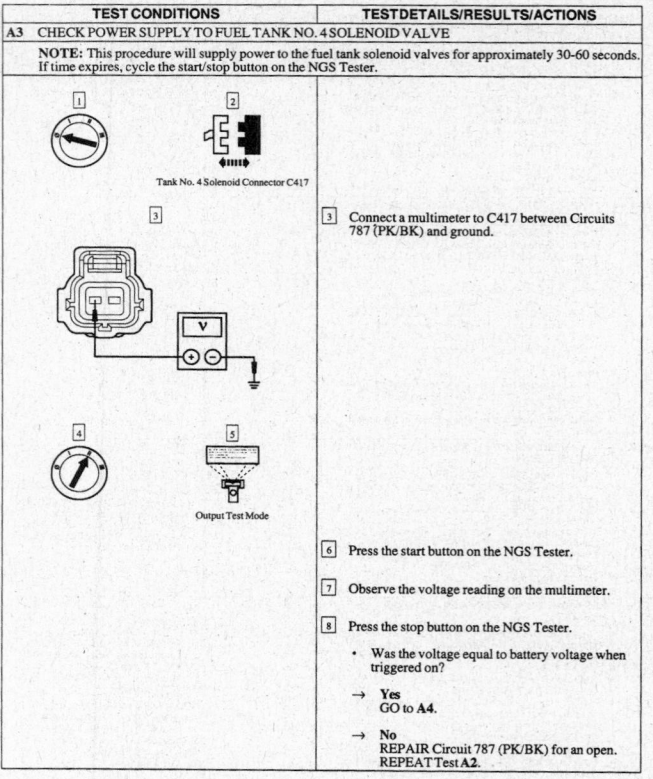

TEST CONDITIONS	TEST DETAILS/RESULTS/ACTIONS
A3 CHECK POWER SUPPLY TO FUEL TANK NO. 4 SOLENOID VALVE	
NOTE: This procedure will supply power to the fuel tank solenoid valves for approximately 30-60 seconds. If time expires, cycle the start/stop button on the NGS Tester.	
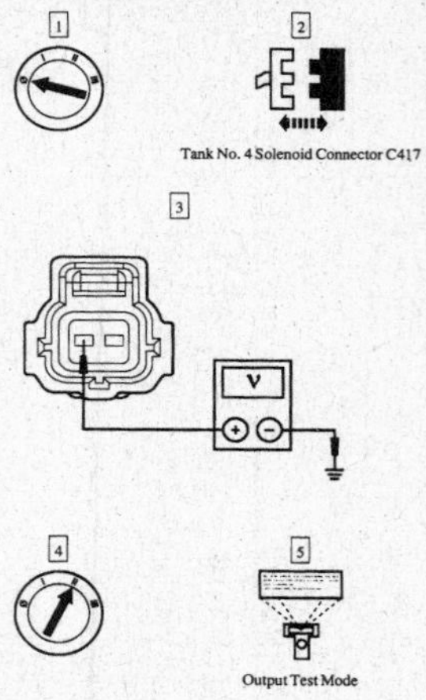	3 Connect a multimeter to C417 between Circuits 787 (PK/BK) and ground. 6 Press the start button on the NGS Tester. 7 Observe the voltage reading on the multimeter. 8 Press the stop button on the NGS Tester. • Was the voltage equal to battery voltage when triggered on? → **Yes** GO to **A4**. → **No** REPAIR Circuit 787 (PK/BK) for an open. REPEAT Test **A2**.

FM1029900303030X

Fig. 5 Pinpoint Test A: Fuel Tank Solenoid Valve Diagnosis (Part 3 of 20). 1999 Crown Victoria & Grand Marquis

and return hoses from power steering pump.
32. Remove engine wire harness retainers from front sub-frame.
33. Remove left and right front engine support insulator through bolts.
34. Attach engine lifting eyes from Rotunda Engine Lift Bracket Set No. 014-00334, or equivalent, on sides of left and right cylinder heads.
35. Connect Rotunda Floor Crane tool No. 077-00043, or equivalent, to Engine Lift Brackets.
36. Raise engine and transmission assembly and carefully separate engine from front sub frame.
37. Remove starter motor, then the transmission oil cooler tubes.
38. Remove retaining nut from transmission line stud to cylinder block.
39. Remove transmission housing cover from cylinder block to access torque converter retaining nuts. Rotate crankshaft until each nut is accessible and remove nuts.
40. Lower engine and transmission assembly, then disconnect transmission wire harness connectors at transmission.
41. Remove six bolts retaining transmission to engine. Separate engine from transmission.
42. Reverse procedure to install, noting the following:
    a. Tighten to specifications.
    b. Align paint marks on flywheel and torque converter when connecting engine to transmission.
    c. Fill and bleed cooling system.
    d. Evacuate and recharge A/C system.
    e. Fill engine with new engine oil.
    f. Start engine and check for coolant, oil and fuel leaks.

CROWN VICTORIA & GRAND MARQUIS

1997–98

1. Mark position of hood hinges and remove hood.
2. Drain coolant into a suitable container and recover refrigerant as outlined in "System Evacuation" under "Air Conditioning"
3. Relieve fuel system pressure as described under "Precautions," then disconnect fuel lines.
4. Remove engine cooling fan, shroud and radiator, then remove wiper module and bracket.
5. Remove air inlet tube and 42-pin electrical harness connector from bracket at brake vacuum booster, **Fig. 8.**
6. Disconnect 42-pin connector and transmission harness electrical connector, then position connectors aside.
7. Disconnect accelerator, speed control cables and throttle valve cable.
8. Disconnect purge solenoid electrical connector and vacuum hose.
9. Disconnect power distribution and starter relay power supply.
10. Disconnect vacuum hose from throttle body port.
11. Disconnect heater hoses, then the alternator electrical harness at fender apron and junction box.
12. Using tool No. T81P-19623-G1, G2, or equivalent, remove A/C compressor inlet and outlet attaching hoses, **Fig. 9.**
13. Disconnect EVO sensor electrical connector from power steering pump.
14. Disconnect body ground strap at dash panel, then raise and support vehicle.
15. Drain engine oil into suitable container.
16. Disconnect exhaust pipes at manifolds, then lower exhaust system and suspend with wire from crossmember.
17. Remove transmission line bracket attaching nut, then remove engine to transmission knee braces attaching bolts and stud, **Fig. 10.**
18. Remove starter motor, then disconnect power steering pump from engine and position aside.
19. Remove plug to access torque converter attaching nuts, then rotate crankshaft to remove nuts (Four required).
20. Remove six engine to transmission attaching bolts.
21. Remove engine mount through bolts.
22. Lower vehicle and support transmission with suitable jack.
23. Install engine lift brackets, **Fig. 11,** then connect suitable lift equipment.
24. Carefully raise engine and separate from transmission, then remove engine from engine compartment.
25. Reverse procedure to install. Tighten to bolts and nuts specifications.

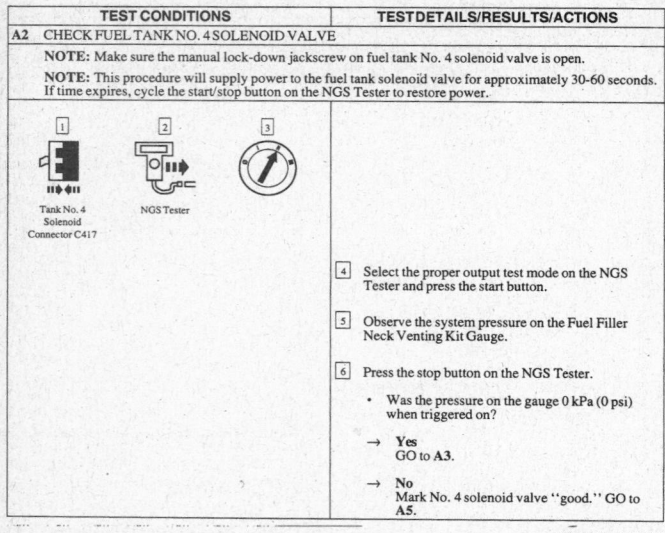

TEST CONDITIONS	TEST DETAILS/RESULTS/ACTIONS
A4 CHECK FUEL TANK NO. 4 SOLENOID VALVE CIRCUIT 57 (BK) FOR AN OPEN	
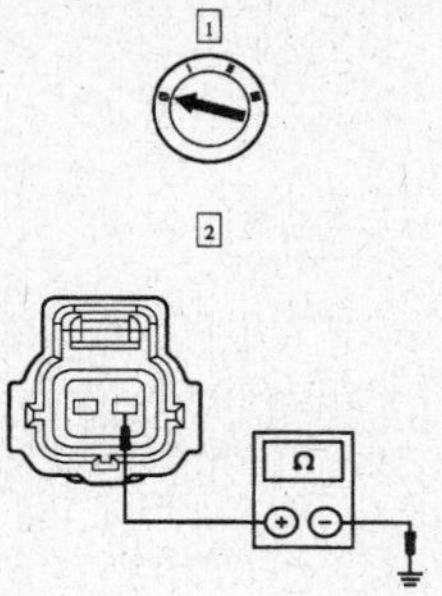	3 Measure the resistance between C417, Circuit 57 (BK) and ground. • Is resistance less than 5 ohms? → **Yes** Mark fuel tank No. 4 solenoid valve "stuck closed." A new solenoid valve will be installed after completing diagnostics. GO to **A5**. → **No** REPAIR Circuit 57 (BK) for an open. REPEAT Test **A2**.

FM1029900303040X

Fig. 5 Pinpoint Test A: Fuel Tank Solenoid Valve Diagnosis (Part 4 of 20). 1999 Crown Victoria & Grand Marquis

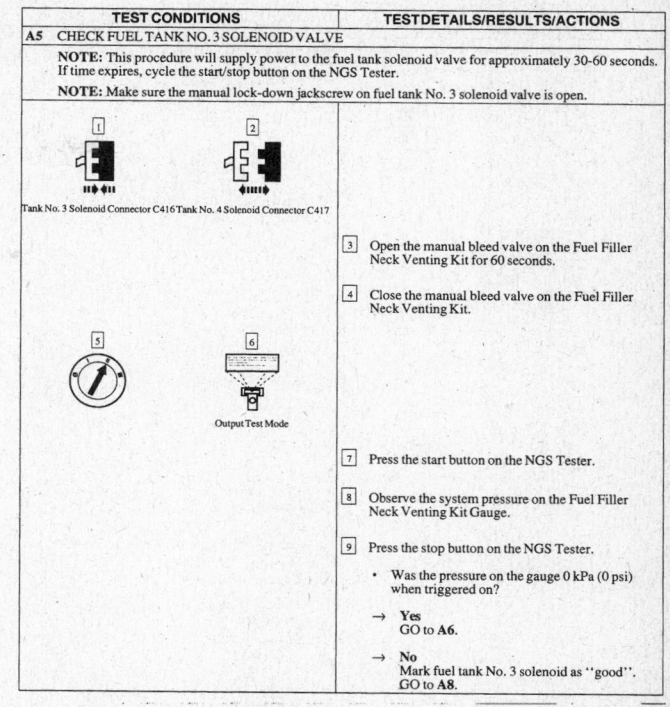

TEST CONDITIONS	TEST DETAILS/RESULTS/ACTIONS
A5 CHECK FUEL TANK NO. 3 SOLENOID VALVE	
NOTE: This procedure will supply power to the fuel tank solenoid valve for approximately 30-60 seconds. If time expires, cycle the start/stop button on the NGS Tester. **NOTE:** Make sure the manual lock-down jackscrew on fuel tank No. 3 solenoid valve is open.	
	3 Open the manual bleed valve on the Fuel Filler Neck Venting Kit for 60 seconds. 4 Close the manual bleed valve on the Fuel Filler Neck Venting Kit.
	7 Press the start button on the NGS Tester. 8 Observe the system pressure on the Fuel Filler Neck Venting Kit Gauge. 9 Press the stop button on the NGS Tester. • Was the pressure on the gauge 0 kPa (0 psi) when triggered on? → **Yes** GO to **A6**. → **No** Mark fuel tank No. 3 solenoid as "good". GO to **A8**.

FM1029900303050X

Fig. 5 Pinpoint Test A: Fuel Tank Solenoid Valve Diagnosis (Part 5 of 20). 1999 Crown Victoria & Grand Marquis

1999-2000

1. Remove hood.
2. Evacuate A/C system using a suitable A/C recovery station as outlined in "System Evacuation" under " Air Conditioning.".
3. Remove air cleaner outlet tube.
4. Relieve fuel pressure as outlined in "Precautions, " then disconnect fuel lines.
5. Remove wiper arm and pivot shaft.
6. Drain engine coolant into suitable container.
7. Disconnect lower radiator hose from oil filter adapter.
8. **On models equipped with oil cooler,** disconnect two coolant hoses, then remove oil cooler and secure to front of engine.
9. **On all models,** remove battery.
10. Disconnect hoses from transmission fluid cooler and power steering cooler.
11. Remove radiator upper sight shield
12. Reposition clamp and disconnect upper radiator hose from water hose connection. Secure hose to radiator assembly.
13. Disconnect electrical connector from fan motor and position out of way.
14. Remove nuts and separate lines from A/C condenser core.
15. Remove bolts and radiator support brackets, then the radiator.
16. Disconnect engine bulkhead connectors, **Fig. 12.**
17. Disconnect accelerator cable and speed control actuator cable.
18. **On models equipped with gasoline engines,** remove accelerator cable and speed control actuator cable from clips and position out of way.
19. **On all models,** disconnect main vacuum supply hose.
20. Remove bolt, **Fig. 13.**
21. Raise and support vehicle, then remove starter motor.
22. Support exhaust system, then remove exhaust system nuts.
23. Remove torque converter inspection cover.
24. Remove torque converter nut access plug, **Fig. 14.**
25. Remove bolt from bracket assembly, **Fig. 15.**
26. Remove nut and ground wire, **Fig. 16.**
27. Remove five bolts and one stud, **Fig. 17.**
28. **On models equipped with gasoline engine,**
    a. Remove evaporative emission canister purge valve, **Fig. 18.**
    b. Position clamps out of way and remove heater hoses.
    c. Remove nut and disconnect electrical connectors on right hand inner fender, **Fig. 19.**
29. **On models equipped with natural gas engine,**
    a. Disconnect electrical connectors, **Fig. 20.**
    b. Remove cover, then the nut and wiring, **Fig. 21.**
30. **On all models,** remove bolt and body ground, **Fig. 22.**
31. Disconnect A/C cycling switch electrical connector, then remove nut, **Fig. 23.**
32. Disconnect air conditioning lines.
33. Disconnect and unplug right hand heated oxygen sensor connector.
34. Disconnect left heated oxygen sensor and separate transmission harness from rear of left hand cylinder head.
35. Disconnect power steering pressure hose.
36. Remove bolt from bracket, **Fig. 24.**
37. Raise and support vehicle.
38. Remove left hand bolts, **Fig. 25.**
39. Remove right hand bolt, **Fig. 26.**
40. Lower vehicle.
41. Install suitable engine lifting equipment.
42. Support transmission.
43. Remove engine assembly from vehicle.
44. Reverse procedure to install, tighten all fasteners to specification.

INTAKE MANIFOLD

REPLACE

COUGAR & THUNDERBIRD

1. Drain coolant into a suitable container.
2. Relieve fuel system pressure as described under " Precautions."
3. Remove air cleaner outlet tube, then release drive belt tensioner and remove drive belt.
4. Remove ignition wires from spark plugs.
5. Disconnect ignition wire and brackets from camshaft cover studs.
6. Disconnect both ignition coils and camshaft position sensor.

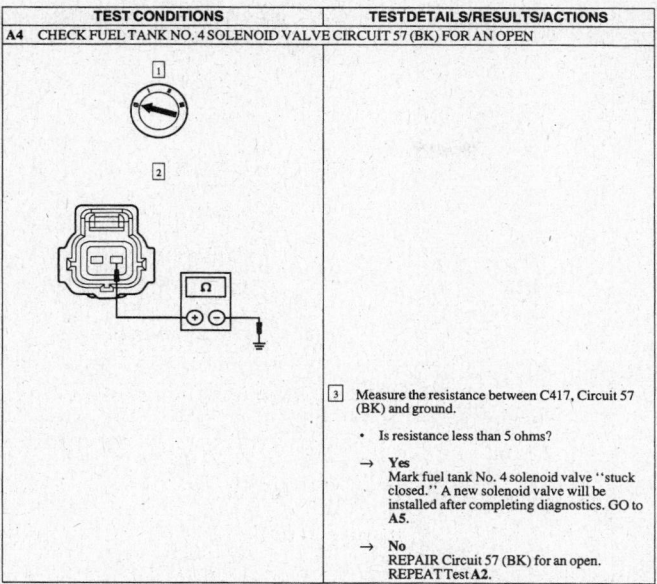

TEST CONDITIONS	TEST DETAILS/RESULTS/ACTIONS
A6 CHECK POWER SUPPLY TO FUEL TANK NO. 3 SOLENOID VALVE	
NOTE: This procedure will supply power to the fuel tank solenoid valves for approximately 30-60 seconds. If time expires, cycle the start/stop button on the NGS Tester.	
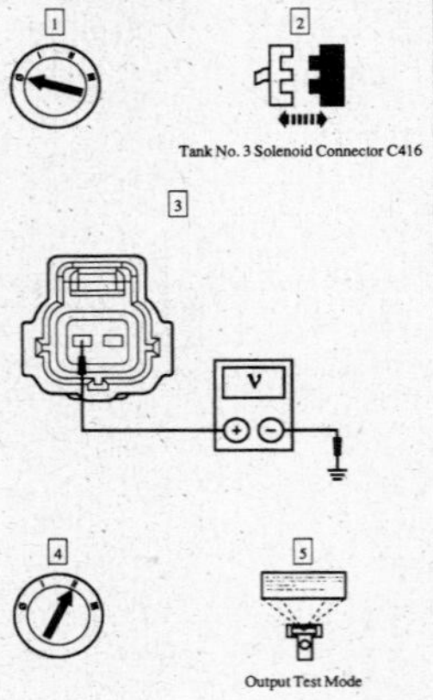	3 Connect a multimeter to C416 between Circuits 787 (PK/BK) and ground. 6 Press the start button on the NGS Tester. 7 Observe the voltage reading on the multimeter. 8 Press the stop button on the NGS Tester. • Was the voltage equal to battery voltage when triggered on? → **Yes** GO to **A7**. → **No** REPAIR Circuit 787 (PK/BK) for an open. REPEAT Test **A5**.

FM1029900303060X

Fig. 5 Pinpoint Test A: Fuel Tank Solenoid Valve Diagnosis (Part 6 of 20). 1999 Crown Victoria & Grand Marquis

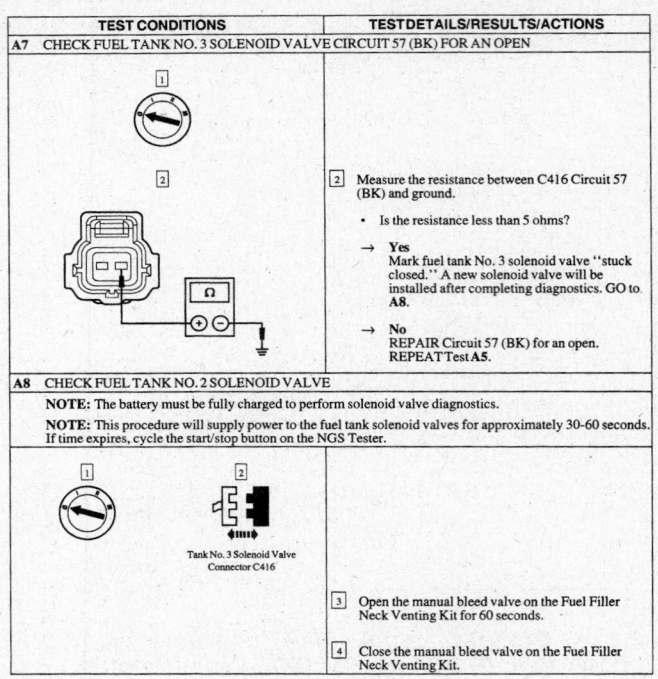

TEST CONDITIONS	TEST DETAILS/RESULTS/ACTIONS
A7 CHECK FUEL TANK NO. 3 SOLENOID VALVE CIRCUIT 57 (BK) FOR AN OPEN	
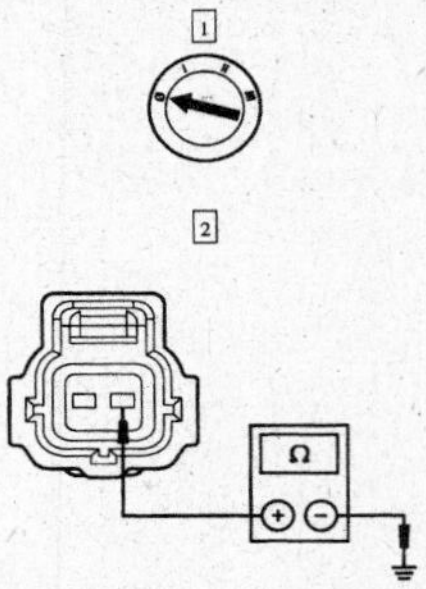	2 Measure the resistance between C416 Circuit 57 (BK) and ground. • Is the resistance less than 5 ohms? → **Yes** Mark fuel tank No. 3 solenoid valve "stuck closed." A new solenoid valve will be installed after completing diagnostics. GO to **A8**. → **No** REPAIR Circuit 57 (BK) for an open. REPEAT Test **A5**.
A8 CHECK FUEL TANK NO. 2 SOLENOID VALVE	
NOTE: The battery must be fully charged to perform solenoid valve diagnostics. **NOTE:** This procedure will supply power to the fuel tank solenoid valves for approximately 30-60 seconds. If time expires, cycle the start/stop button on the NGS Tester.	
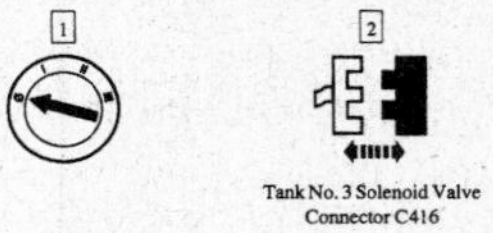	3 Open the manual bleed valve on the Fuel Filler Neck Venting Kit for 60 seconds. 4 Close the manual bleed valve on the Fuel Filler Neck Venting Kit.

FM1029900303070X

Fig. 5 Pinpoint Test A: Fuel Tank Solenoid Valve Diagnosis (Part 7 of 20). 1999 Crown Victoria & Grand Marquis

7. Remove four bolts retaining ignition coil to ignition coil brackets.
8. Disconnect alternator wiring harness from junction block at front fender apron and from alternator.
9. Remove two bolts retaining alternator mounting bracket to intake manifold.
10. Remove two bolts retaining alternator to cylinder block, then remove alternator.
11. Raise and support vehicle.
12. Disconnect oil pressure sender and EVO harness sensor and reposition wiring for clearance.
13. Disconnect EGR valve to exhaust manifold tube from right exhaust manifold.
14. Lower vehicle, then disconnect accelerator cable and speed control actuator from throttle body.
15. Remove accelerator cable bracket from intake manifold and position clear of area.
16. Disconnect throttle valve control actuating cable from throttle body.
17. Disconnect vacuum hose from throttle body adapter vacuum port.
18. Disconnect heater supply hose.
19. Remove two bolts retaining thermostat housing to intake manifold and position upper radiator hose and thermostat housing clear of manifold.
20. Remove nine bolts retaining intake manifold to cylinder heads, then remove intake manifold and gaskets, **Fig. 27.**
21. Reverse procedure to install, noting the following:
    a. Ensure alignment tabs on intake manifold gasket are aligned with holes in cylinder head.
    b. Install and tighten nine intake manifold retaining bolts in sequence, **Fig. 28** to specifications.
    c. Replace O-ring on thermostat housing.
    d. Tighten to specifications.
    e. Fill and bleed cooling system.

CROWN VICTORIA & GRAND MARQUIS

1997–98

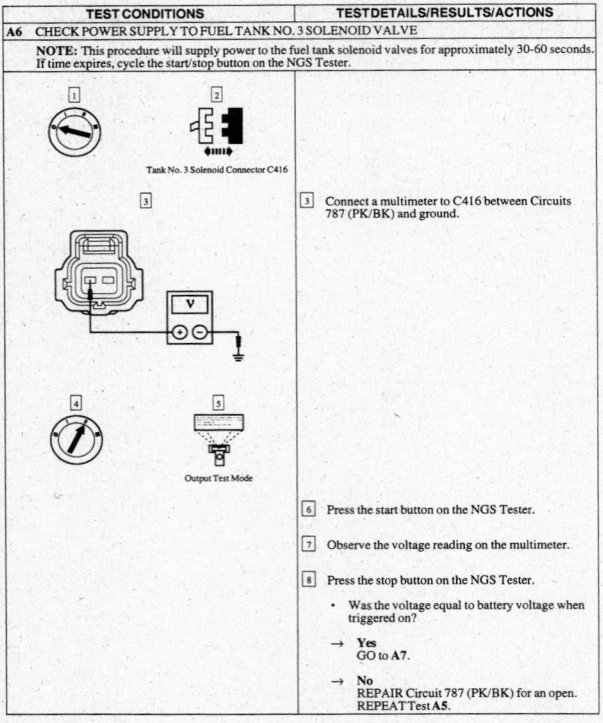

1. Drain coolant into a suitable container.
2. Remove air cleaner outlet tube.
3. Relieve fuel system fuel pressure as described under "Precautions."
4. Remove wiper governor and air inlet tube.
5. Release belt tensioner and remove accessory drive belt.
6. Raise and support vehicle.
7. Disconnect fuel charging wiring from crankshaft position sensor and A/C clutch.
8. Remove oil bypass filter.
9. Disconnect fuel charging wiring from oil pressure sensor, oil filter adapter bracket and power steering pump and move wiring out of the way.
10. Disconnect EGR valve to exhaust manifold tube from righthand exhaust manifold.
11. Disconnect EGR back pressure transducer hoses from EGR valve to exhaust manifold tube.
12. Disconnect fuel charging wring from heated oxygen sensors.
13. Lower vehicle.
14. **On 1997 models,** disconnect ignition wire set and retainers from valve cover studs and alternator bracket, then all ignition wires from both ignition coils.
15. **On 1998 models,** disconnect fuel charging wiring from eight ignition coils.
16. **On all models,** disconnect alternator wiring from power distribution box at front fender apron and alternator.
17. Remove alternator and bracket.
18. Remove positive crankcase ventilation valve from valve cover.
19. Disconnect vacuum hose from throttle body adapter vacuum port.
20. **On natural gas engines,** disconnect fuel pressure regulator coolant hoses from heater water hoses.
21. **On all models,** remove heater water hoses.
22. Disconnect engine control sensor extension wire from 42 pin connector and 8 pin transmission connector located at power brake booster.
23. **On gasoline engines,** disconnect engine control sensor extension wire from EVR sensor, idle air control valve, EGR transducer, throttle position sensor, ignition coils and fuel injectors.
24. **On all models,** remove fuel charging wiring retainers from valve cover stud bolts.
25. Remove fuel charging wiring and

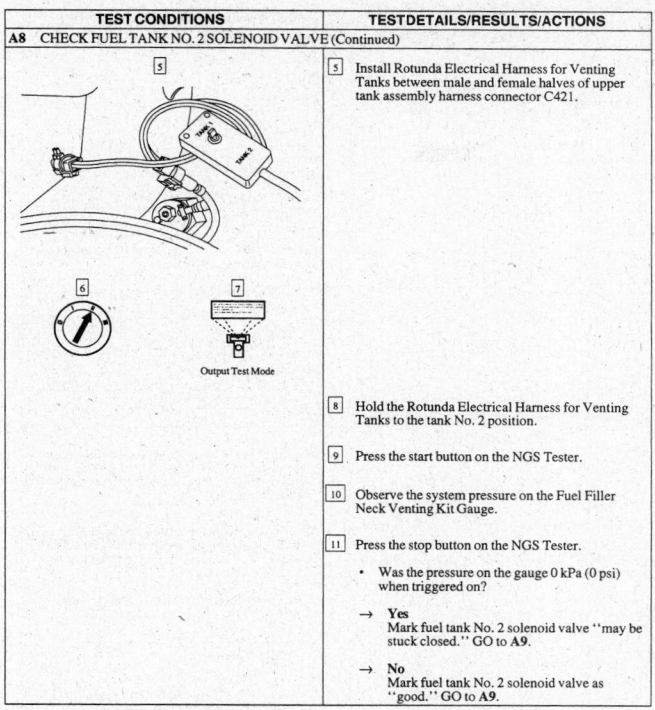

TEST CONDITIONS	TEST DETAILS/RESULTS/ACTIONS
A8 CHECK FUEL TANK NO. 2 SOLENOID VALVE (Continued)	
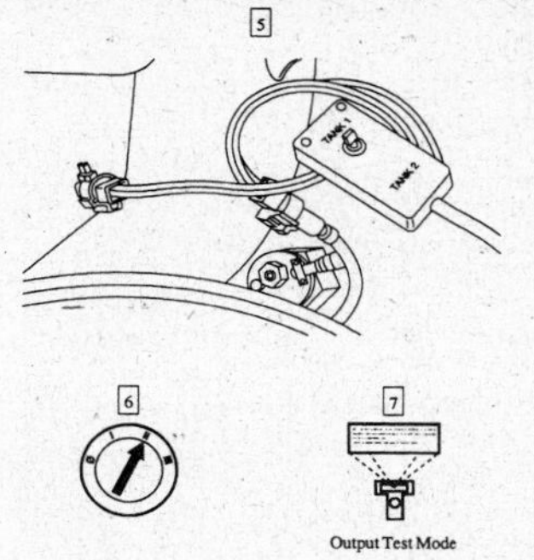	5 Install Rotunda Electrical Harness for Venting Tanks between male and female halves of upper tank assembly harness connector C421. 8 Hold the Rotunda Electrical Harness for Venting Tanks to the tank No. 2 position. 9 Press the start button on the NGS Tester. 10 Observe the system pressure on the Fuel Filler Neck Venting Kit Gauge. 11 Press the stop button on the NGS Tester. • Was the pressure on the gauge 0 kPa (0 psi) when triggered on? → **Yes** Mark fuel tank No. 2 solenoid valve "may be stuck closed." GO to **A9**. → **No** Mark fuel tank No. 2 solenoid valve as "good." GO to **A9**.

FM1029900303080X

Fig. 5 Pinpoint Test A: Fuel Tank Solenoid Valve Diagnosis (Part 8 of 20). 1999 Crown Victoria & Grand Marquis

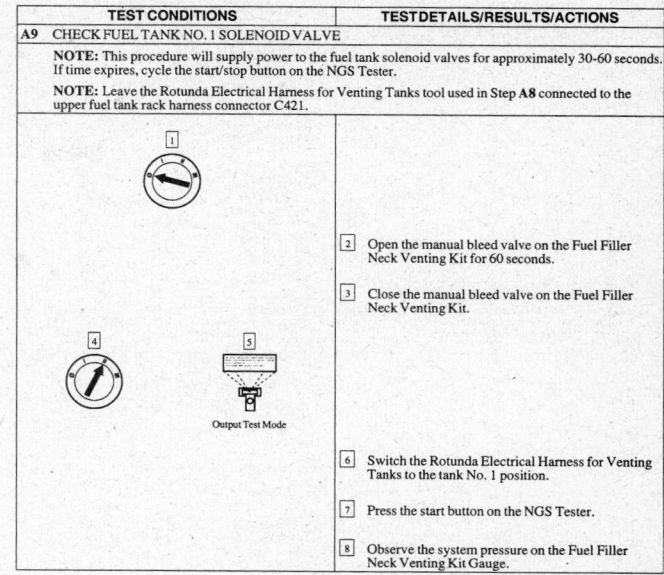

TEST CONDITIONS	TEST DETAILS/RESULTS/ACTIONS
A9 CHECK FUEL TANK NO. 1 SOLENOID VALVE	
NOTE: This procedure will supply power to the fuel tank solenoid valves for approximately 30-60 seconds. If time expires, cycle the start/stop button on the NGS Tester. **NOTE:** Leave the Rotunda Electrical Harness for Venting Tanks tool used in Step **A8** connected to the upper fuel tank rack harness connector C421.	
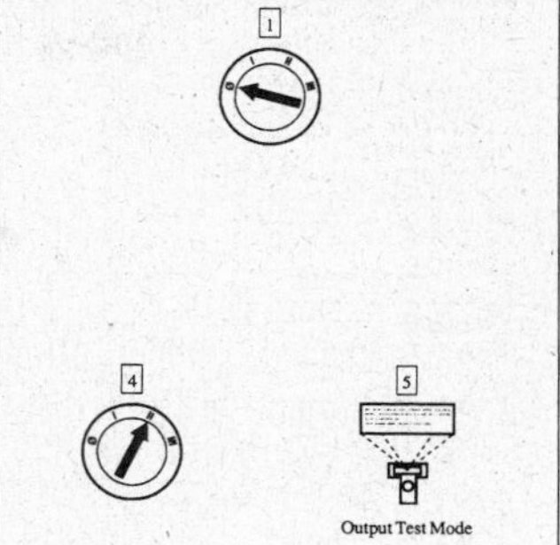	2 Open the manual bleed valve on the Fuel Filler Neck Venting Kit for 60 seconds. 3 Close the manual bleed valve on the Fuel Filler Neck Venting Kit. 6 Switch the Rotunda Electrical Harness for Venting Tanks to the tank No. 1 position. 7 Press the start button on the NGS Tester. 8 Observe the system pressure on the Fuel Filler Neck Venting Kit Gauge.

FM1029900303090X

Fig. 5 Pinpoint Test A: Fuel Tank Solenoid Valve Diagnosis (Part 9 of 20). 1999 Crown Victoria & Grand Marquis

transmission wiring from bracket on rear of lefthand cylinder head.

26. Disconnect accelerator cable and speed control actuator cable using a screwdriver.
27. **On gasoline engines,** proceed as follows:
    a. Remove two bolts and intake manifold shield, then disconnect main emission vacuum control connector from fuel injection supply manifold and evaporative emission valve.
    b. Disconnect EGR valve to exhaust manifold tube from EGR valve and remove EGR valve to exhaust manifold tube.
    c. Remove accelerator cable bracket stud bolt.
    d. Remove five retaining bolts from throttle body adapter to intake manifold.
28. **On all models,** remove to bolts retaining water hose connection to intake manifold. Position water hose connection and upper radiator hose out of way.
29. **On natural gas engines,** throttle body adapter, accelerator cable bracket, EGR valve, idle air control valve and EGR valve to exhaust manifold tube can remain attached to intake manifold.
30. **On all models,** fuel charging wiring, fuel injection supply manifold and fuel injector nozzle tip can remain attached to intake manifold on both engines.
31. Remove nine bolts retaining intake manifold to cylinder heads, then intake and gaskets.
32. Reverse procedure to install, noting the following:
    a. Clean cylinder head and intake manifold surfaces.
    b. Install new intake manifold gaskets.
    c. Tighten manifold bolts to specification, in sequence shown, **Fig. 29.**

1999–2000

Natural Gas Vehicle

1. Remove wiper arm & pivot shaft.
2. Remove air cleaner outlet tube.
3. Relieve fuel pressure as outlined in "Precautions"
4. Disconnect fuel charging wiring electrical connectors from ignition coils and fuel injectors.
5. Disconnect fuel charging electrical connectors from fuel pressure sensor, fuel pump temperature sensor and engine coolant temperature sensor.
6. Remove isolation valve wiring lead from upper alternator support bracket and disconnect connector.
7. Disconnect alternator battery cable.
8. Remove power distribution box access cover, then remove nut and wiring.
9. Disconnect fuel charging wiring electrical connectors from the following components:
    a. Inner fender splash shield connectors.
    b. A/C pressure transducer.
    c. Cylinder head temperature sensor jumper.
    d. Camshaft position sensor.
    e. Alternator.
    f. Throttle position sensor.
    g. Radio ignition interference capacitor.
    h. EGR vacuum regulator solenoid.
    i. Differential pressure feedback EGR.
    j. Idle air control valve.
10. Disconnect throttle cable and speed control actuator cable from throttle body.
11. Remove cable retaining bracket bolt and position cables and bracket out of way.
12. Remove fuel charging wiring retaining bolts, then position harness out of way.
13. Disconnect fuel lines and hoses from differential pressure feedback EGR and vacuum line from EGR valve.
14. Disconnect main chassis vacuum line.
15. Disconnect crankcase vent tube at two locations and remove from vehicle.
16. Disconnect vacuum lines from throttle body adapter and EGR vacuum regulator solenoid.
17. Disconnect EGR tube from EGR valve.
18. Remove bolts from isolation valve, then remove fuel injection supply manifold and fuel injectors as an assembly.
19. Disconnect heater hose from intake manifold.
20. Disconnect upper radiator hose from water outlet adapter.
21. Remove all eight ignition coils.
22. Remove upper alternator support bracket.
23. Remove water outlet adapter, thermostat and O-ring.
24. Remove bolts, then the intake manifold.
25. Remove intake manifold gaskets and clean all surfaces.

TEST CONDITIONS	TEST DETAILS/RESULTS/ACTIONS
A9 CHECK FUEL TANK NO. 1 SOLENOID VALVE (Continued)	
	[9] Press the stop button on the NGS Tester. • Was the pressure on the gauge 0 kPa (0 psi) when triggered on? → **Yes** Fuel tank No. 1 solenoid valve "may be stuck closed." GO to **A10.** → **No** Mark fuel tank No. 1 solenoid valve "good." To complete diagnostics, install a new solenoid valve if the solenoid valve is marked "stuck closed." If fuel tank No. 2 solenoid valve was marked "may be stuck closed," GO to **A10** . If all solenoid valves were marked "good," diagnostics are complete. RESTORE the vehicle and test the system for normal operation.
A10 CHECK UPPER TANK RACK CIRCUIT 57 (BK)	
NOTE: At this point in the diagnostics it is necessary to access the upper fuel tank rack harness connections. Due to packaging considerations, it will be necessary to remove the upper tank rack assembly to remove the upper tank rack vent box.	
[1] 	[2] Disconnect and remove the Rotunda Electrical Harness for Venting Tanks from upper tank rack assembly harness connector C421. [3] Open the manual bleed valve on the Fuel Filter Neck Venting Kit and vent system pressure to 0 kPa (0 psi). [4] Close the manual bleed valve on the Fuel Filter Neck Venting Kit. [5] Remove the upper fuel tank rack assembly. [6] Remove the upper fuel tank rack assembly vent box.

FM1029900303100X

Fig. 5 Pinpoint Test A: Fuel Tank Solenoid Valve Diagnosis (Part 10 of 20). 1999 Crown Victoria & Grand Marquis

TEST CONDITIONS	TEST DETAILS/RESULTS/ACTIONS
A10 CHECK UPPER TANK RACK CIRCUIT 57 (BK) (Continued)	
[7]  Tank No. 1 Solenoid Valve Connector C414 [8]  Tank No. 2 Solenoid Valve Connector C415	[9] With the upper fuel tank rack assembly removed, measure the resistance from both fuel tank No. 1 solenoid valve connector C414, Circuit 57 (BK) and fuel tank No. 2 solenoid connector C415, Circuit 57 (BK) to the upper tank rack assembly harness 8-pin connector C421 pin 1. • Is the resistance less than 5 ohms on both circuits? → **Yes** GO to **A11**. → **No** REPAIR Circuit 57 (BK) for an open. GO to **A11**.
A11 CHECK UPPER TANK RACK CIRCUIT 787 (PK/BK)	
	[1] Measure the resistance between the upper tank rack assembly 8-pin harness connector C421 pin 6 and fuel tank No. 2 solenoid valve connector C415 Circuit 787 (PK/BK). [2] Measure the resistance between the upper tank rack assembly 8-pin harness connector C421 pin 5 and fuel tank No. 1 solenoid valve connector C414, Circuit 787 (PK/BK). • Is the resistance less than 5 ohms on both circuits? → **Yes** GO to **A12**. → **No** REPAIR Circuit 787 (PK/BK) for an open. INSTALL the complete upper tank rack assembly (including the vent box) in the vehicle. REPEAT Test **A8**.

FM1029900303110X

Fig. 5 Pinpoint Test A: Fuel Tank Solenoid Valve Diagnosis (Part 11 of 20). 1999 Crown Victoria & Grand Marquis

26. Reverse procedure to install, noting the following:
    a. Use new intake manifold gaskets.
    b. Tighten bolts in sequence, **Fig. 29,** to specification.

Gasoline Vehicle

1. Drain engine coolant into suitable container.
2. Remove air cleaner outlet tube.
3. Relieve fuel pressure as outlined in "Precautions."
4. Remove wiper arm and pivot shaft.
5. Remove drive belt.
6. Raise and support vehicle.
7. Disconnect electrical connectors at crankshaft position sensor and A/C compressor.
8. Remove oil filter.
9. Disconnect oil pressure sensor electrical connector and power steering switch electrical connector.
10. Disconnect EGR valve from manifold.
11. Disconnect two differential pressure feedback hoses.
12. Disconnect right hand heated oxygen sensor electrical connector.
13. Disconnect fuel charging wiring electrical connectors from ignition coils and fuel injectors.
14. Disconnect accelerator cable and speed control actuator cable.
15. Remove cables from EGR tube heat shield and position out of way.
16. Remove EGR tube heat shield.
17. Disconnect evaporative emissions return tube, main chassis vacuum supply line and EGR valve vacuum supply.
18. Disconnect PCV tube assembly at two locations and remove.
19. Disconnect electrical connector from EGR vacuum regulator.
20. Disconnect vacuum line from evaporative emission canister purge valve.
21. Disconnect alternator cable and position out of way.
22. Remove upper mounting bracket and electrical connector from alternator.
23. Remove upper radiator and heater hose.
24. Disconnect electrical connector from idle air control valve and throttle position sensor.
25. Disconnect EGR tube from EGR valve.
26. Remove left hand oxygen sensor and transmission electrical connectors from wiring bracket, then remove bracket.
27. Remove throttle body.
28. Separate fuel charging wiring pushpin connector from crash bracket, remove bolt and stud, then the crash bracket.
29. Disconnect vacuum lines and remove vacuum harness.
30. Remove fuel injection supply manifold and fuel injectors as an assembly.
31. Remove all eight ignition coils.
32. Remove water outlet adapter, then the thermostat and gasket.
33. Remove intake manifold and gaskets, clean gasket sealing surfaces.
34. Reverse procedure to install, noting the following:
    a. Install new gaskets.
    b. Install intake manifold and hand tighten bolts at locations shown, **Fig. 30.**
    c. Install ignition coils and tighten bolts to specification.
    d. Install fuel injection supply manifold and tighten studs to specification.
    e. Install crash bracket loosely.
    f. Install thermostat and water outlet adapter loosely with bolts.
    g. Tighten intake manifold bolts to specification in sequence, **Fig. 31.**

EXHAUST MANIFOLD

REPLACE

COUGAR & THUNDERBIRD

1. On lefthand exhaust manifold, remove bolt retaining oil level indicator tube.
2. Raise and support vehicle, then disconnect both heated oxygen sensors.
3. Remove EGR valve to exhaust manifold tube line nut from right exhaust manifold and remove EGR valve.
4. Disconnect three-way catalytic converter from exhaust manifolds.
5. Lower catalytic converter and wire to crossmember in positions shown in **Fig. 32.**
6. On left exhaust manifold, disconnect steering shaft and position clear of area. Remove eight bolts retaining exhaust manifold.

TEST CONDITIONS	TESTDETAILS/RESULTS/ACTIONS
A12 CHECK UPPER FUEL TANK RACK ASSEMBLY MANUAL LOCK-DOWNS	
	1 With the upper fuel tank rack assembly still removed, check the fuel tank No. 1 and No. 2 solenoid valves manual lock-downs. • Are the manual lock-downs open? → **Yes** INSTALL new upper fuel tank rack assembly solenoids if marked "may be stuck closed." INSTALL the complete upper tank rack assembly (including vent box) in the vehicle. REPEAT Test **A8**. → **No** INSTALL the upper tank rack assembly without the vent box. Make all fuel line connections. GO to **A13**.
A13 CHECK FUEL TANK NO. 2 SOLENOID VALVE MANUAL LOCK-DOWN	
NOTE: Make sure the bleed valve on the Fuel Filler Neck Venting Kit is closed before proceeding with this test.	
	1 Open fuel tank No. 2 solenoid valve manual lock-down jackscrew. 2 Open the bleed valve on the Fuel Filler Neck Venting Kit for 60 seconds. 3 Close the bleed valve on the Fuel Filler Neck Venting Kit. 4 Observe the system pressure on the Fuel Filler Neck Venting Kit Gauge. • Is the pressure on the gauge 0 kPa (0 psi)? → **Yes** Mark fuel tank No. 2 solenoid valve "good." GO to **A14**. → **No** Mark fuel tank No. 2 solenoid valve "stuck open." GO to **A14**.
A14 CHECK FUEL TANK NO. 1 SOLENOID VALVE MANUAL LOCK-DOWN	
	1 Tighten the manual lock-down jackscrew on fuel tank No. 2 solenoid valve to 9 Nm (79 lb/in). 2 Open fuel tank No. 1 solenoid valve manual lock-down jackscrew.

FM1029900303120X

Fig. 5 Pinpoint Test A: Fuel Tank Solenoid Valve Diagnosis (Part 12 of 20). 1999 Crown Victoria & Grand Marquis

TEST CONDITIONS	TESTDETAILS/RESULTS/ACTIONS
A14 CHECK FUEL TANK NO. 1 SOLENOID VALVE MANUAL LOCK-DOWN (Continued)	
	3 Open the bleed valve on the Fuel Filler Neck Venting Kit for 60 seconds. 4 Close the bleed valve on the Fuel Filler Neck Venting Kit. 5 Observe the system pressure on the Fuel Filler Neck Venting Kit Gauge. • Is the system pressure on the Fuel Filler Neck Venting Kit Gauge 0 kPa (0 psi)? → **Yes** Mark fuel tank No. 1 solenoid valve "good." GO to **A8** to retest the upper tank rack. → **No** MARK fuel tank No. 1 solenoid valve "stuck open." INSTALL new upper fuel tank rack assembly solenoid valves if marked "stuck open." RESTORE the vehicle. TEST the system for normal operation.
A15 CHECK ALL SOLENOID CIRCUITS 787 (PK/BK) FOR A SHORT TO B+	
1  2 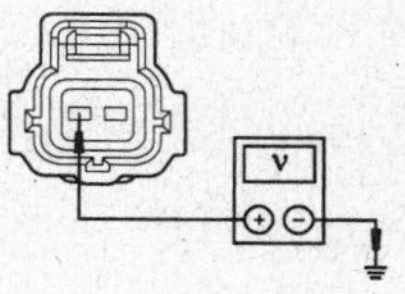 	2 Measure the voltage at fuel tank No. 3 (C416) and No. 4 (C417) solenoid connectors Circuit 787 (PK/BK) and ground. Also measure the voltage at the upper fuel tank rack assembly harness connector C421 (male side of connector, pins 5 and 6) Circuits 787 (PK/BK) and ground. • Is battery voltage present on any connector 787 (PK/BK) circuit? → **Yes** REPAIR Circuit 787 (PK/BK) for a short to B+. REPEAT Test **A1**. → **No** GO to **A16**.

FM1029900303130X

Fig. 5 Pinpoint Test A: Fuel Tank Solenoid Valve Diagnosis (Part 13 of 20). 1999 Crown Victoria & Grand Marquis

7. On right exhaust manifold, remove eight bolts retaining exhaust manifold to cylinder head, then remove manifold.
8. Reverse procedure to install, noting the following:
   a. Tighten exhaust manifold retaining nuts in sequence shown in **Fig. 33** to specifications.
   b. Loosen line nut at EGR valve prior to installing assembly into vehicle. This will allow enough movement to align EGR valve retaining bolts.
   c. Ensure exhaust system clears No. 3 crossmember. Adjust as necessary.
   d. Tighten all components to specifications.

CROWN VICTORIA & GRAND MARQUIS

1997-98

1. Remove air cleaner outlet tube and drain coolant into a suitable container.
2. Remove cooling fan and shroud, then relieve fuel system pressure as described under "Precautions."
3. Disconnect fuel lines and remove upper radiator hose.
4. Remove wiper governor and support bracket.
5. Recover A/C refrigerant as outlined in "Air Conditioning " section, then disconnect A/C compressor outlet hose at compressor and remove bolt retaining hose assembly to front cover stud bolt.
6. Disconnect 42-pin electrical connector and transmission harness connector.
7. Disconnect heater water hose, then remove nut retaining ground strap to righthand cylinder head.
8. **On natural gas models,** remove upper stud bolt and lower bolt retaining heater water hose to righthand cylinder head and move out of the way.
9. **On all models,** remove heater blower motor switch resistor.
10. Remove bolt retaining righthand front engine support insulator to front sub frame.
11. Disconnect both heated oxygen sensors.
12. Raise and support vehicle.
13. Remove oil bypass filter.
14. Two through bolts are required for lefthand front engine support insulator and one through bolt is required for righthand front engine support insulator.
15. Remove EGR valve to exhaust manifold tube nut from righthand exhaust manifold.
16. Disconnect three way catalytic converter from righthand and lefthand exhaust manifold.
17. Lower exhaust and secure to crossmember.
18. For lefthand exhaust manifold, remove front engine support insulator from cylinder block and eight nuts retaining exhaust manifold.
19. Remove lefthand exhaust manifold and two exhaust manifold gaskets.
20. Position a screw type jackstand and a block of wood under oil pan, rearward of oil drain hold.
21. Raise engine approximately 4 inches.
22. For righthand exhaust manifold, remove eight nuts retaining exhaust manifold to cylinder head and retaining studs and exhaust manifold and gasket.
23. Reverse procedure to install, noting the following:
   a. Position manifold to cylinder head and tighten to specifications, in sequence shown in **Fig. 33.**
   b. Tighten to specifications.

1999-2000

1. Raise and support vehicle.
2. Disconnect oxygen sensor connectors.
3. Remove exhaust manifold to catalytic converter nuts, then disconnect converters at exhaust inlet pipes.
4. Remove catalytic converters from vehicle.
5. Disconnect EGR tube at exhaust manifold connector.
6. Remove nuts, then the exhaust manifolds and gaskets.
7. Reverse procedure to install, tighten manifold nuts to specification in sequence, **Figs. 34 and 35.**

TEST CONDITIONS	TESTDETAILS/RESULTS/ACTIONS
A16 ISOLATE UPPER AND LOWER TANK RACK ASSEMBLIES	
	1 Tighten the manual lock-down jackscrew on fuel tank No. 3 and No. 4 solenoid valves to 9 Nm (79 lb/in). 2 Open the manual bleed valve on the Fuel Filler Neck Venting Kit for 60 seconds. 3 Close the manual bleed valve on the Fuel Filler Neck Venting Kit. 4 Observe the system pressure on the Fuel Filler Neck Venting Kit Gauge. • Is the pressure on the gauge 0 kPa (0 psi)? → **Yes** GO to **A21**. → **No** GO to **A17**.
A17 CHECK FUEL TANK NO. 1 CIRCUIT 787 (PK/BK)	
NOTE: At this point in the diagnostics it is necessary to access the upper fuel tank rack harness connectors. Due to packaging considerations, it will be necessary to remove the upper tank rack assembly to remove the upper tank rack vent box.	
1 	2 Make sure the manual lock-downs on fuel tank No. 3 and No. 4 are still closed from Step **A16**. 3 Open the manual bleed valve on the Fuel Filler Neck Venting Kit and vent the system pressure to 0 kPa (0 psi). 4 Close the manual bleed valve on the Fuel Filler Neck Venting Kit. 5 Remove the upper tank rack assembly.

FM1029900303140X

Fig. 5 Pinpoint Test A: Fuel Tank Solenoid Valve Diagnosis (Part 14 of 20). 1999 Crown Victoria & Grand Marquis

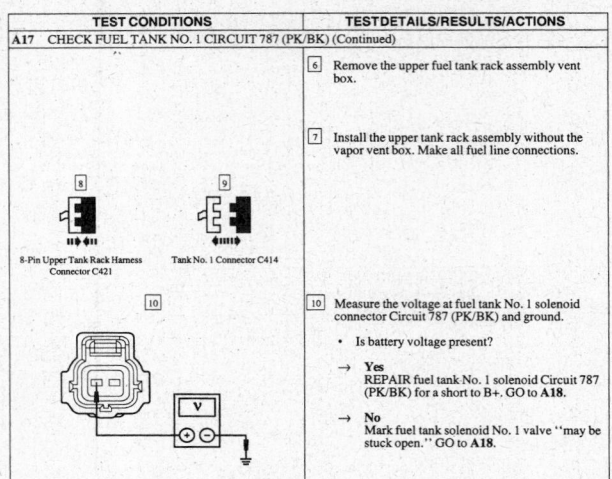

TEST CONDITIONS	TESTDETAILS/RESULTS/ACTIONS
A17 CHECK FUEL TANK NO. 1 CIRCUIT 787 (PK/BK) (Continued)	
	6 Remove the upper fuel tank rack assembly vent box. 7 Install the upper tank rack assembly without the vapor vent box. Make all fuel line connections.
8 9  8-Pin Upper Tank Rack Harness Connector C421 / Tank No. 1 Connector C414	
10 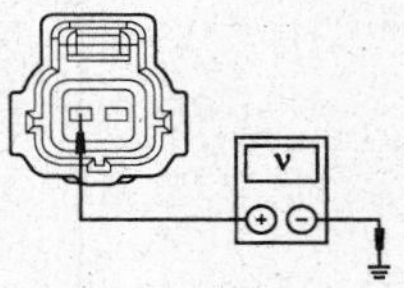	10 Measure the voltage at fuel tank No. 1 solenoid connector Circuit 787 (PK/BK) and ground. • Is battery voltage present? → **Yes** REPAIR fuel tank No. 1 solenoid Circuit 787 (PK/BK) for a short to B+. GO to **A18**. → **No** Mark fuel tank solenoid No. 1 valve "may be stuck open." GO to **A18**.

FM1029900303150X

Fig. 5 Pinpoint Test A: Fuel Tank Solenoid Valve Diagnosis (Part 15 of 20). 1999 Crown Victoria & Grand Marquis

CYLINDER HEAD

REPLACE

COUGAR & THUNDERBIRD

REMOVAL

Cylinder head must not be set on head face. If valves are open, damage will occur.

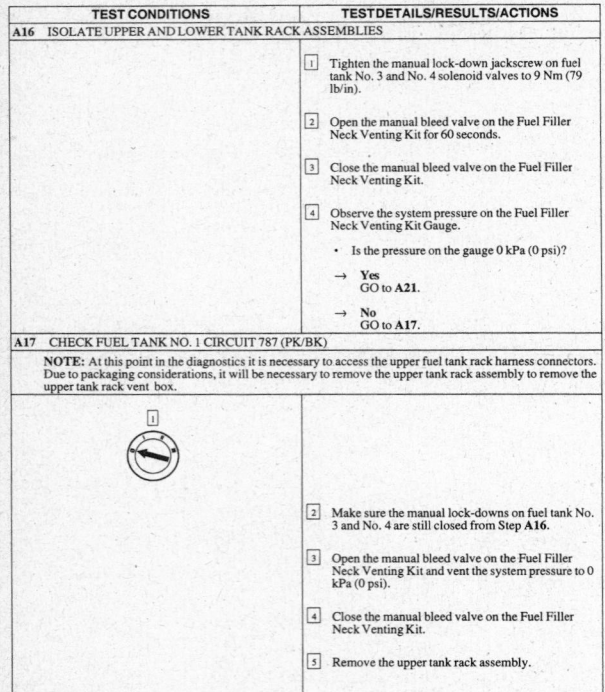

1. Drain coolant into a suitable container and remove fan blade and fan shroud.
2. Relieve fuel system pressure as described under "Precautions."
3. Remove air cleaner outlet tube and the windshield wiper governor.
4. Release drive belt tensioner and remove drive belt. **Do not pull on ignition wires.**
5. Disconnect ignition wires from spark plugs.
6. Disconnect ignition wire and brackets from camshaft cover studs.
7. Disconnect fuel charging wires from both ignition coils and camshaft position sensor.
8. Remove bolts retaining power steering oil reservoir to the left ignition coil bracket and position clear of area.
9. Remove three nuts retaining right ignition coil bracket to engine front cover.
10. Remove left ignition coil and ignition wires as an assembly.
11. Remove four nuts retaining left ignition coil bracket to engine front cover.
12. Slide ignition coil brackets and ignition wire bracket assembly off mounting studs and remove from vehicle.
13. Remove water pump pulley.
14. Disconnect alternator wiring harness from junction block, front fender apron and alternator.
15. Remove two bolts retaining alternator mounting bracket to intake manifold.
16. Remove two bolts retaining alternator to cylinder block and remove alternator.
17. Disconnect and remove positive crankcase ventilation valve from camshaft cover.
18. Disconnect 42-pin engine harness connector and 8-pin connector leading to mass airflow sensor.
19. Remove nut retaining A/C liquid line to right strut tower.
20. Lift A/C liquid line and feed the 42-pin connector under the A/C liquid line. Position the 42-pin connector clear of area.
21. Disconnect crankshaft position sensor, A/C clutch and canister purge solenoid connectors.
22. Raise and support vehicle, then remove bolts retaining power steering pump to cylinder block and engine front cover. **The front lower bolt on the power steering pump will not come all the way out.**
23. Secure power steering pump clear of area with suitable wire.
24. Remove four bolts retaining oil pan to front engine cover.
25. Remove crankshaft pulley bolt and crankshaft pulley retaining washer from crankshaft.
26. Install crankshaft damper remover tool No. T58P-6316-D, or equivalent, on crankshaft pulley and pull crankshaft pulley from crankshaft.
27. Disconnect EVO sensor and oil pressure sender.
28. Disconnect EGR valve to exhaust manifold tube from right exhaust manifold.
29. Disconnect three-way catalytic converter from right and left exhaust manifolds.
30. Lower exhaust and secure with wire to crossmember in positions shown, **Fig. 32.**
31. Remove bolt retaining starter wiring harness to rear of right cylinder head.
32. Remove bolts and stud bolts retaining right valve cover to cylinder head and remove valve cover.
33. Disconnect accelerator cable and speed control actuator.
34. Remove accelerator cable bracket from intake manifold and position clear of area.
35. Remove bolts and stud bolts retaining left valve cover to cylinder head and remove valve cover.
36. Disconnect throttle valve control actuating cable from throttle body.
37. Disconnect vacuum hose from throttle body adapter vacuum port.
38. Disconnect both heated oxygen sensors, then disconnect heater water hose.
39. Remove two bolts retaining thermostat housing to intake manifold and position upper radiator hose and thermostat housing out of the way.
40. Remove nine bolts retaining intake manifold to cylinder heads and remove intake manifold.
41. Remove intake manifold gaskets, then remove seven stud bolts and four bolts retaining engine front cover to engine and remove engine front cover.
42. Remove timing chains as described under "Timing Chains, Gears, Tensioners & Guides, Replace."
43. Remove ten bolts retaining left cylinder

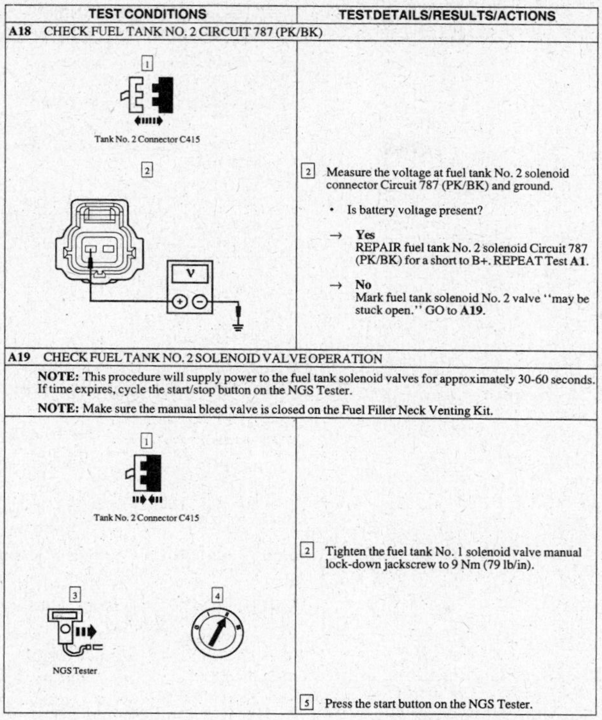

TEST CONDITIONS	TEST DETAILS/RESULTS/ACTIONS
A18 CHECK FUEL TANK NO. 2 CIRCUIT 787 (PK/BK)	
1 Tank No. 2 Connector C415	
2	2 Measure the voltage at fuel tank No. 2 solenoid connector Circuit 787 (PK/BK) and ground. • Is battery voltage present? → **Yes** REPAIR fuel tank No. 2 solenoid Circuit 787 (PK/BK) for a short to B+. REPEAT Test **A1**. → **No** Mark fuel tank solenoid No. 2 valve "may be stuck open." GO to **A19**.
A19 CHECK FUEL TANK NO. 2 SOLENOID VALVE OPERATION	
NOTE: This procedure will supply power to the fuel tank solenoid valves for approximately 30-60 seconds. If time expires, cycle the start/stop button on the NGS Tester. **NOTE:** Make sure the manual bleed valve is closed on the Fuel Filler Neck Venting Kit.	
1 Tank No. 2 Connector C415	
3 NGS Tester 4	2 Tighten the fuel tank No. 1 solenoid valve manual lock-down jackscrew to 9 Nm (79 lb/in).
	5 Press the start button on the NGS Tester.

FM1029900303160X

Fig. 5 Pinpoint Test A: Fuel Tank Solenoid Valve Diagnosis (Part 16 of 20). 1999 Crown Victoria & Grand Marquis

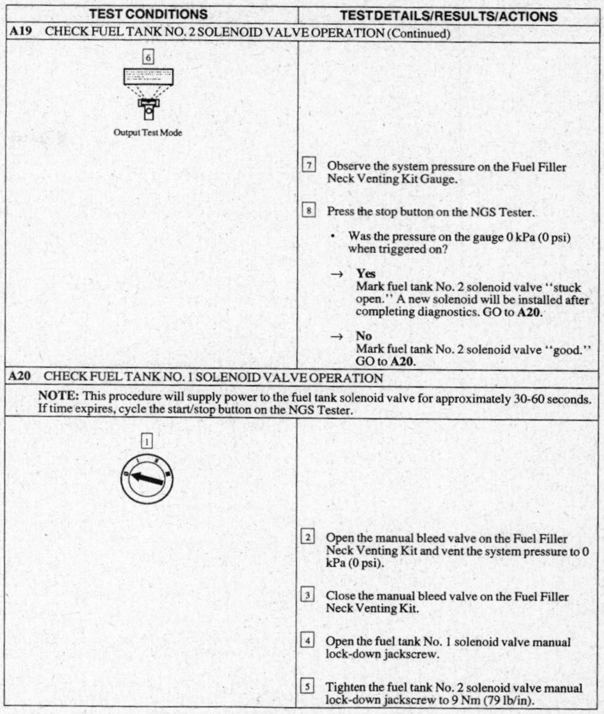

TEST CONDITIONS	TEST DETAILS/RESULTS/ACTIONS
A19 CHECK FUEL TANK NO. 2 SOLENOID VALVE OPERATION (Continued)	
6 Output Test Mode	
	7 Observe the system pressure on the Fuel Filler Neck Venting Kit Gauge.
	8 Press the stop button on the NGS Tester. • Was the pressure on the gauge 0 kPa (0 psi) when triggered on? → **Yes** Mark fuel tank No. 2 solenoid valve "stuck open." A new solenoid will be installed after completing diagnostics. GO to **A20**. → **No** Mark fuel tank No. 2 solenoid valve "good." GO to **A20**.
A20 CHECK FUEL TANK NO. 1 SOLENOID VALVE OPERATION	
NOTE: This procedure will supply power to the fuel tank solenoid valve for approximately 30-60 seconds. If time expires, cycle the start/stop button on the NGS Tester.	
1	2 Open the manual bleed valve on the Fuel Filler Neck Venting Kit and vent the system pressure to 0 kPa (0 psi).
	3 Close the manual bleed valve on the Fuel Filler Neck Venting Kit.
	4 Open the fuel tank No. 1 solenoid valve manual lock-down jackscrew.
	5 Tighten the fuel tank No. 2 solenoid valve manual lock-down jackscrew to 9 Nm (79 lb/in).

FM1029900303170X

Fig. 5 Pinpoint Test A: Fuel Tank Solenoid Valve Diagnosis (Part 17 of 20). 1999 Crown Victoria & Grand Marquis

head to cylinder block, noting the following:
   a. The lower rear bolt cannot be removed due to interference with the power brake booster.
   b. Use a rubber band or similar item to retain the bolt away from the cylinder block as shown in **Fig. 36.**
44. Remove left cylinder head.
45. Remove ground strap, one stud and one bolt retaining water heater hose to right cylinder head.
46. Remove ten bolts retaining the right cylinder head to the cylinder block, noting the following:
   a. The lower rear bolt cannot be removed due to interference with the A/C evaporator housing.
   b. Use a rubber band or similar item to hold bolt away from cylinder block as shown in **Fig. 37.**
47. Remove right cylinder head.
48. Clean cylinder head, intake manifold, camshaft cover and cylinder block sealing surfaces.
49. Inspect head face surface for scratches near coolant passage and combustion chamber.

INSTALLATION

1. **Cylinder head bolts must be replaced with new bolts.** They are torque-to-yield designed and cannot be reused.
2. Rotate crankshaft to a stable position where valves do not extend below cylinder head face.
3. Position new head gasket on cylinder block. Install lower rear cylinder head bolts and retain in position with rubber bands as described during removal procedure.
4. Position left cylinder head on cylinder block. Apply clean engine oil to all head bolt spot-faces.
5. Remove rubber band from lower rear bolt and install nine remaining bolts hand tight.
6. Tighten left cylinder head bolts as follows:
   a. **Torque** bolts in sequence, **Fig. 38,** to 28–31 ft. lbs.
   b. Rotate all bolts in same sequence 85–95.°
   c. Loosen head bolts a minimum of one full turn.
   d. **Torque** head bolts again to 28–31 ft. lbs. in sequence.
   e. Rotate head bolts in sequence 85–95.°
   f. Rotate head bolts again in sequence another 85–95.°
7. Position right cylinder head on cylinder block dowels. Apply clean engine oil to all head bolt spot-faces.
8. Remove rubber band from lower rear bolt and install nine remaining bolts hand tight.
9. Tighten right cylinder head bolts as follows:
   a. **Torque** bolts in sequence, **Fig. 39,** to 28–31 ft. lbs.
   b. Rotate all bolts in same sequence 85–95.°
   c. Loosen head bolts a minimum of one full turn.
   d. **Torque** head bolts again in sequence to 28–31 ft. lbs.
   e. Rotate head bolts in sequence 85–95.°
   f. Rotate head bolts in sequence an additional 85–95.°
10. Position heater water hose on cylinder head and install two bolts.
11. Rotate camshafts using flats matched at center of camshaft until both are in time and install Cam Positioning tool No. T92P-6256-A, or equivalent, on flats of camshaft. This will prevent camshafts from rotating.
12. Position crankshaft at No. 1 TDC by rotating crankshaft 45.° **Crankshaft must only be rotated in clockwise direction and only as far as TDC.**
13. Install timing chains as described under "Timing Chains, Gears, Tensioners & Guides, Replace."
14. Reverse remainder of removal procedure to complete cylinder head installation, noting the following:
   a. Tighten to specifications.
   b. Tighten intake manifold bolts to specifications in sequence shown in **Fig. 28.**
   c. Apply silicone gasket and sealant

TEST CONDITIONS	TEST DETAILS/RESULTS/ACTIONS
A20 CHECK FUEL TANK NO. 1 SOLENOID VALVE OPERATION (Continued)	
6 7 8 9 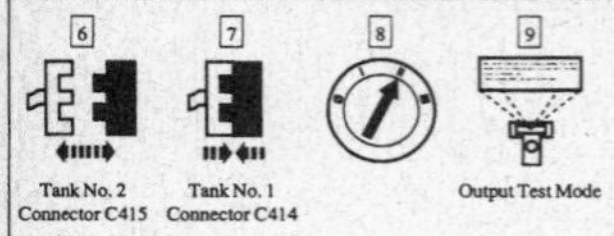	10 Press the start button on the NGS Tester. 11 Observe the system pressure on the Fuel Filler Neck Venting Kit Gauge. 12 Press the stop button on the NGS Tester. • Was the pressure on the gauge 0 kPa (0 psi) when triggered on? → **Yes** Mark fuel tank No. 1 solenoid valve "stuck open." INSTALL new upper tank rack assembly valves if marked "stuck open." RESTORE the vehicle and repeat Test **A1**. → **No** Mark fuel tank No. 1 solenoid valve "good." RESTORE the vehicle. TEST the system for normal operation.
A21 CHECK FUEL TANK NO. 3 SOLENOID VALVE FOR STUCK OPEN CONDITION	
1 	2 Open the manual lock-down jackscrew on fuel tank No. 3 solenoid valve. 3 Make sure the manual lock-down jackscrew on fuel tank No. 4 solenoid valve is still closed from Step **A16**. 4 Open the manual bleed valve on the Fuel Filler Neck Venting Kit for 60 seconds. 5 Close the manual bleed valve on the Fuel Filler Neck Venting Kit.

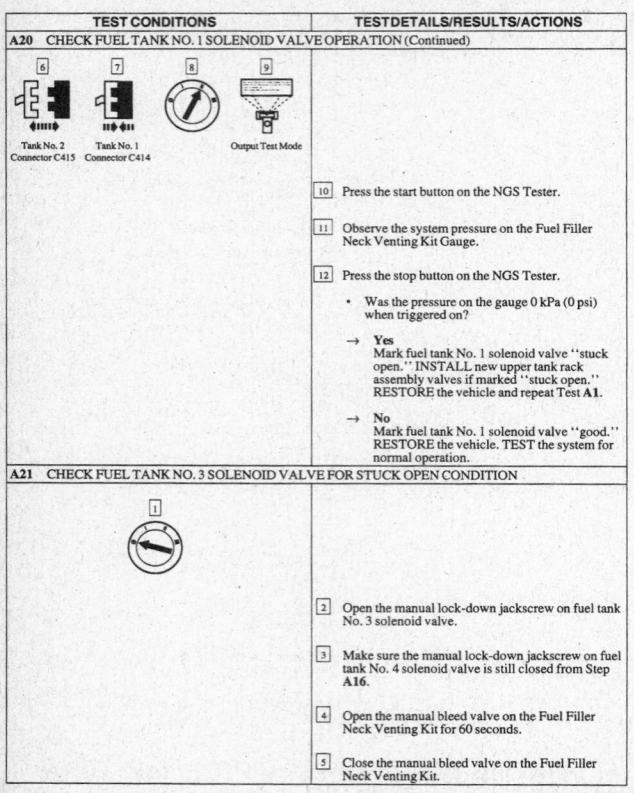

FM1029900303180X

Fig. 5 Pinpoint Test A: Fuel Tank Solenoid Valve Diagnosis (Part 18 of 20). 1999 Crown Victoria & Grand Marquis

TEST CONDITIONS	TEST DETAILS/RESULTS/ACTIONS
A21 CHECK FUEL TANK NO. 3 SOLENOID VALVE FOR STUCK OPEN CONDITION (Continued)	
	6 Observe the system pressure on the Fuel Filler Neck Venting Kit Gauge. • Is the pressure on the gauge 0 kPa (0 psi)? → **Yes** Mark fuel tank No. 3 solenoid valve "good." GO to **A22**. → **No** Mark fuel tank No. 3 solenoid valve "stuck open." A new solenoid valve will be installed when diagnostics are complete. GO to **A22**.
A22 CHECK FUEL TANK NO. 4 SOLENOID FOR STUCK OPEN CONDITION	
1 	2 Close the manual lock-down jackscrew fuel tank No. 3 solenoid valve to 9 Nm (79 lb/in). 3 Open the manual bleed valve on the Fuel Filler Neck Venting Kit and vent the system pressure to 0 kPa (0 psi). 4 Close the manual bleed valve on the Fuel Filler Neck Venting Kit. 5 Open the manual lock-down jackscrew on fuel tank No. 4 solenoid valve. 6 Open the manual bleed valve on the Fuel Filler Neck Venting Kit for 60 seconds. 7 Close the manual bleed valve on the Fuel Filler Neck Venting Kit.

FM1029900303190X

Fig. 5 Pinpoint Test A: Fuel Tank Solenoid Valve Diagnosis (Part 19 of 20). 1999 Crown Victoria & Grand Marquis

part No. F1AZ-19562-A, or equivalent, at both places where the engine front cover meets the cylinder head.

d. Ensure exhaust system clears the No. 3 crossmember. Adjust as necessary.
e. Apply silicone gasket and sealant part No. F1AZ-19562-A, or equivalent, in keyway of crankshaft pulley as shown in **Fig. 40.**

CROWN VICTORIA & GRAND MARQUIS

1997–98

1. Remove intake manifold.
2. Raise and support vehicle.
3. The front lower bolt on power steering pump will not come all the way out. Remove bolts retaining power steering pump to engine. Position power steering pump out of the way.
4. Remove crankshaft pulley, then four oil pan to engine front cover retaining bolts.
5. Disconnect three way catalytic converters from right and lefthand exhaust manifolds.
6. Lower exhaust system and secure to crossmember with wire.
7. Remove retainer for starter motor wiring harness from rear of cylinder head.
8. Lower vehicle.
9. Remove power steering reservoir and bracket.
10. Remove water pump pulley, then disconnect positive battery cable at power distribution box and harness.
11. Remove pushpin from positive battery cable on back of cylinder head. Position out of the way.
12. Remove righthand valve cover retaining bolts, stud bolts and cover.
13. Remove A/C high pressure line retaining nut from front cover assembly stud bolt.
14. Remove eight stud bolts and seven bolts retaining front cover to cylinder block, then the front cover.
15. Remove timing chain as described under "Timing Chain, Replace."
16. Remove bolts attaching left cylinder head.
17. Lower rear bolt cannot be removed due to interference with brake vacuum booster. Use a rubber band or similar item to hold bolt away from engine, **Fig. 36.**
18. Remove left cylinder head.
19. Remove ground strap retaining heater return line to right cylinder head.
20. **On gasoline engines,** remove two EVR retaining and sensor.
21. **On all models,** remove two stud bolts or one stud bolt and one bolt retaining heater tube to righthand cylinder head.
22. Remove bolts attaching right cylinder head. **The lower rear bolt cannot be removed due to interference with evaporator housing.** Use a rubber band or similar item to hold bolt away from engine as shown, **Fig. 36.**
23. Remove right cylinder head.
24. Reverse procedure to install, noting the following:
    a. Rotate crankshaft counterclockwise 45.° This ensures that all pistons are below top of engine block deck face.
    b. **Torque** head bolts in sequence, **Figs. 38 and 39,** to 28–31 ft. lbs.
    c. Rotate all bolts in same sequence 85–95.°
    d. Loosen head bolts a minimum of one full turn.
    e. **Torque** head bolts again in sequence to 28–31 ft. lbs.
    f. Rotate head bolts in sequence 85–95.°
    g. Rotate head bolts in sequence an additional 85–95°
    h. Rotate crankshaft clockwise 45.° This will position crankshaft at TDC No. 1. **Crankshaft must only be rotated in clockwise direction and only as far as TDC.**
    i. Tighten remaining components to specifications.

1999–2000

Right Side

1. Remove intake manifold as outlined in "Intake Manifold, Replace"
2. Remove valve cover as outlined in "Camshaft Cover, Replace."
3. Remove engine front cover as outlined in "Front Cover, Replace."
4. Remove spark plugs.
5. Remove A/C evaporator housing.

6. Position clamp out of the way and remove coolant hose.
7. Remove nut and cylinder head ground strap.
8. Disconnect EGR transducer.
9. Remove ground strap stud.
10. Remove water bypass tube, inspect O-rings and replace as necessary.
11. Remove timing chains as outlined in "Timing Chains, Gears, Tensioners & Guides."
12. Remove right hand and left hand timing chain guides.
13. Remove any remaining hardware or wiring from cylinder head.
14. Raise and support vehicle.
15. Disconnect left and right exhaust manifolds.
16. Lower vehicle.
17. Loosen right side cylinder head bolts in three one turn passes in sequence, **Fig. 39.**
18. Remove cylinder head and gasket.
19. Clean gasket sealing surfaces and bolt holes.
20. Reverse procedure to install, noting the following:
    a. Install new gasket.
    b. Install bolts and tighten in sequence in six steps.
    c. Step 1: **Torque** bolts in sequence, **Fig. 39,** to 28–31 ft. lbs.
    d. Step 2: Tighten an additional 85–95.°
    e. Step 3: Loosen bolts a minimum of one full turn (360°).
    f. Step 4: **Torque** bolts in sequence, to 28–31 ft. lbs.
    g. Step 5: Tighten an additional 85-95.°
    h. Step 6: Tighten an additional 85-95.°

Left Side

1. Remove intake manifold as outlined in "Intake Manifold, Replace"
2. Remove timing chains as outlined in "Timing Chains, Gears, Tensioners & Guides, Replace"
3. Remove left side exhaust manifold.
4. Disconnect radio ignition interference capacitor and remove engine control sensor wiring.
5. Remove oil dipstick tube, inspect O-rings and replace as necessary.
6. Remove left hand timing chain guide.
7. No. 8 cylinder head bolt cannot be completely removed, it will be necessary to support No. 8 cylinder head bolt with rubber band or tape to keep bolt from interfering with removal, **Fig. 36.**
8. Loosen cylinder head bolts in three one turn passes in sequence, **Fig. 38.**
9. Remove cylinder head and gasket.
10. Reverse procedure to install, noting the following:
    a. Install new gasket.
    b. Install bolts and tighten in sequence in six steps.
    c. Step 1: **Torque** bolts in sequence, **Fig. 38,** to 28–31 ft. lbs.
    d. Step 2: Tighten an additional 85–95.°
    e. Step 3: Loosen bolts a minimum of one full turn (360°).
    f. Step 4: **Torque** bolts in sequence, to 28–31 ft. lbs.
    g. Step 5: Tighten an additional 85–95.°
    h. Step 6: Tighten an additional 85–95.°

TEST CONDITIONS	TEST DETAILS/RESULTS/ACTIONS
A22 CHECK FUEL TANK NO. 4 SOLENOID FOR STUCK OPEN CONDITION (Continued)	
	[8] Observe the system pressure on the Fuel Filler Neck Venting Kit Gauge. • Is the pressure on the gauge 0 kPa (0 psi)? → **Yes** Mark fuel tank No. 4 solenoid valve "good." If No. 3 solenoid valve was marked "stuck open," INSTALL a new solenoid valve at this time. RESTORE the vehicle. Test the system for normal operation. → **No** Fuel tank No. 4 solenoid valve is stuck open. INSTALL a new fuel tank No. 4 solenoid valve. INSTALL new solenoid valves for all other solenoid valves marked "stuck open." RESTORE the vehicle. TEST the system for normal operation.

FM1029900303200X

Fig. 5 Pinpoint Test A: Fuel Tank Solenoid Valve Diagnosis (Part 20 of 20). 1999 Crown Victoria & Grand Marquis

VALVE LIFT SPECIFICATIONS

Year	Intake, Inch	Exhaust, Inch
1997–2000	.472	.472

VALVE ARRANGEMENT

FRONT TO REAR

Right Bank..................I-E-I-E-I-E-I-E
Left Bank....................E-I-E-I-E-I-E-I

CAMSHAFT LOBE LIFT SPECIFICATIONS

Year	Intake, Inch	R. Exhaust, Inch	L. Exhaust, Inch
1997–2000	.2591	.2593	.2597

VALVE ADJUSTMENT

These engines are equipped with hydraulic valve lash adjusters, the intake and exhaust valves cannot be adjusted.

ROCKER ARMS/ ROLLER FOLLOWER

REPLACE

1. Remove camshaft covers as described under "Camshaft Cover, Replace."
2. Position piston of cylinder at bottom of stroke and camshaft lobe at base circle.
3. Install valve spring spacer tool No. T91P-6565-AH, or equivalent, between spring coils to prevent valve seal damage. **If spacer is not installed, retainer will hit valve stem seal and damage seal.**
4. Install Valve Spring Compressor tool No. T91P-6565-AH, or equivalent, under camshaft and on top of valve spring retainer, **Fig. 41.**
5. Compress valve spring and remove rocker arm.
6. Remove valve spring compressor and spacer.
7. Repeat steps 2 through 6 for remaining cylinders as required.
8. Reverse procedure to install. Apply clean engine oil to valve stem and tip, rocker arm roller contact surfaces and valve tappet.

VALVE TAPPET

REPLACE

1. Remove rocker arms as outlined previously.
2. Remove valve tappets from cylinder heads.
3. Clean and inspect valve tappets.
4. Reverse procedure to install, noting the following:
    a. Apply clean engine oil to valve stem and tip, rocker arm roller contact surfaces and valve tappets and cylinder head valve tappet bore.
    b. Valve tappets must have no more than .039 inches of plunger travel prior to installation.

VALVE SPRING & VALVE STEM OIL SEAL

REPLACE

REMOVAL

If, during this procedure, air pressure has forced the piston to the bottom of the cylinder, any loss of air pressure will allow the valve to fall into the cylinder. A rubber band, tape or string wrapped around the end of the valve stem will prevent this and still allow enough travel to check the valve for binding and excess guide to valve stem clearance.

1. Remove camshaft covers as described under "Camshaft Cover, Replace."
2. Remove rocker arms/roller followers as described under " Rocker Arms/ Roller Follower, Replace."

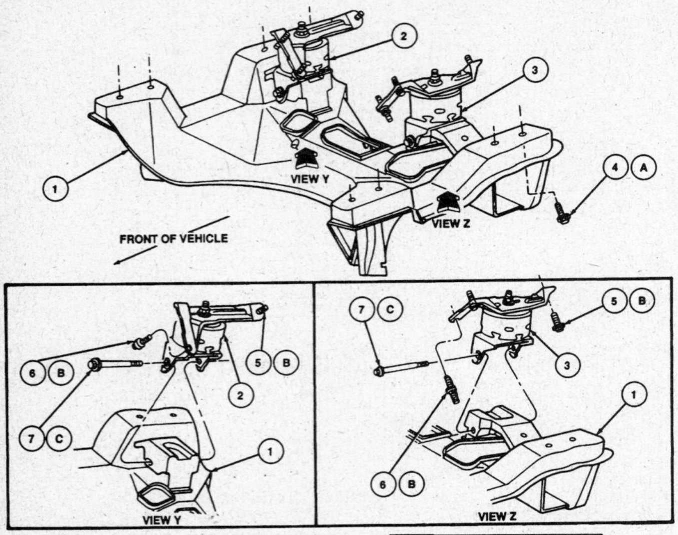

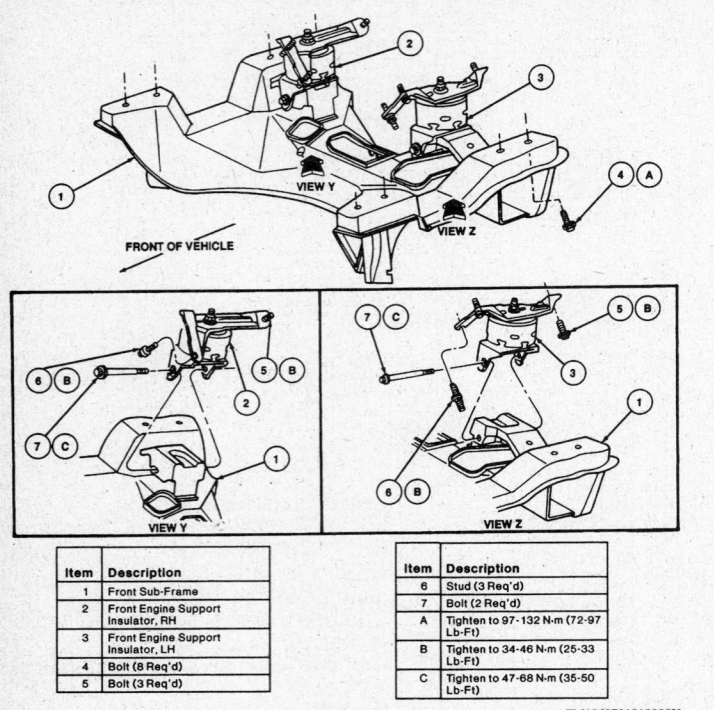

Item	Description
1	Front Sub-Frame
2	Front Engine Support Insulator, RH
3	Front Engine Support Insulator, LH
4	Bolt (8 Req'd)
5	Bolt (3 Req'd)

Item	Description
6	Stud (3 Req'd)
7	Bolt (2 Req'd)
A	Tighten to 97-132 N·m (72-97 Lb-Ft)
B	Tighten to 34-46 N·m (25-33 Lb-Ft)
C	Tighten to 47-68 N·m (35-50 Lb-Ft)

FM1069701018000X

Fig. 6 Engine mount replacement. Cougar & Thunderbird

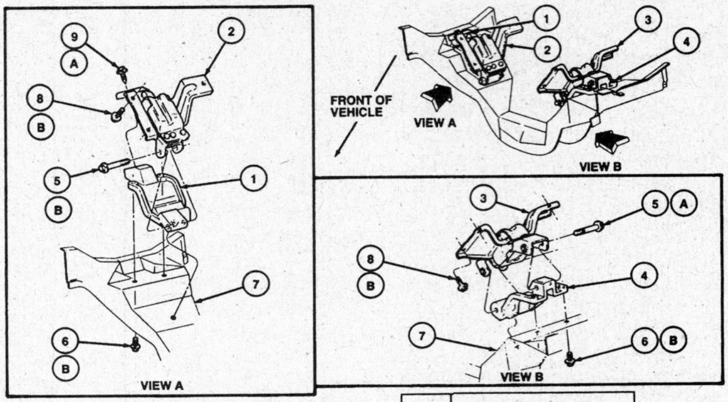

Item	Description
1	Front Engine Mount Insulator Support, RH
2	Front Engine Support Insulator
3	Front Engine Support Insulator
4	Front Engine Mount Insulator Support, LH

Item	Description
5	Bolt (3 Req'd)
6	Bolt (6 Req'd)
7	Crossmember
8	Bolt (6 Req'd)
9	Bolt
A	Tighten to 47-63 N·m (35-46 Lb-Ft)
B	Tighten to 60-81 N·m (45-59 Lb-Ft)

FM1069701019000X

Fig. 7 Engine mount replacement. 1997–98 Crown Victoria & Grand Marquis

3. Remove spark plug, then position piston at top of stroke with both valves closed.
4. Install suitable air line with adapter in spark plug opening, then apply air pressure. Failure of air pressure to hold valves closed is an indication of valve or valve seat damage that may require cylinder head removal.
5. Install Valve Spring Spacer tool No. T91P-6565-AH, or equivalent, between valve spring coils.
6. Using Valve Spring Compressor tool No. T91P-6565-A, or equivalent, compress valve spring.
7. Remove valve spring retainer keys, valve spring retainer and valve spring.
8. Use suitable locking pliers, remove valve stem seal.
9. Repeat steps as required until all seals are removed.

INSTALLATION

1. **Piston must be at Top Dead Center (TDC) of cylinder being serviced.**
2. Remove air pressure, then inspect valve stem for damage. Rotate valve and check valve stem tip eccentric movement during rotation.
3. Position valve up and down through normal travel and check stem for binding. **If valve has been damaged. It will be necessary to remove cylinder head for service.**
4. If valve condition is good, apply engine oil to valve stem and hold valve closed, then apply air pressure in cylinder.
5. Using Valve Stem Seal Replacer tool No. T91P-6571-A, or equivalent, install valve stem seal.
6. Position valve spring and retainer over valve stem.
7. Install Valve Spring Spacer tool No. T91P-6565-AH, or equivalent, between spring coils.
8. Using Valve Spring Compressor tool No. T91P-6565-A, or equivalent, compress valve spring and install valve spring retainer key.
9. Turn off air supply, then remove adapter from spark plug opening.
10. Install spark plug, then roller follower and camshaft cover.
11. Start engine and check for leaks.

CAMSHAFT COVER

REPLACE

CROWN VICTORIA & GRAND MARQUIS

1997–98

Right Side

1. Disconnect positive battery cable at power distribution box.
2. Remove retaining bolt from positive battery cable bracket located on rear of righthand cylinder head. Position bracket out of the way.
3. Disconnect fuel charging wiring from crankshaft position sensor, A/C clutch, ignition coils and radio ignition interference capacitor. Position harness out of the way.
4. Disconnect vent hose from evaporative emission canister purge valve.
5. Remove PCV valve and position aside.
6. Remove camshaft cover attaching bolts, then remove camshaft cover.
7. Reverse procedure to install. Tighten to specifications.

Left Side

1. Remove air outlet tube.
2. Relieve fuel pressure as outlined under "Precautions, " then disconnect fuel lines.
3. Raise and support vehicle.
4. Remove oil bypass filter.
5. Disconnect fuel charging wiring from power steering pump, oil pressure sensor and oil filter adapter bracket.
6. Lower vehicle.
7. Disconnect fuel charging wiring from camshaft position sensor and valve cover studs.
8. Remove windshield wiper governor.
9. **On 1997 models,** disconnect spark plug ignition wires. **Do not remove wires.** Remove ignition wire brackets, then position wires aside.
10. **On 1998 models,** disconnect ignition coils.
11. **On all models,** disconnect 42 pin connector and transmission harness connector from fuel charging wiring at power brake booster.
12. Remove camshaft cover attaching bolts, then remove camshaft cover.
13. Reverse procedure to install. Tighten to specifications.

1999–2000

Right Side

1. Raise and support vehicle.
2. Disconnect crankshaft position sensor (CKP sensor) and A/C compressor electrical connectors.
3. Lower the vehicle and disconnect A/C cycling switch connector.

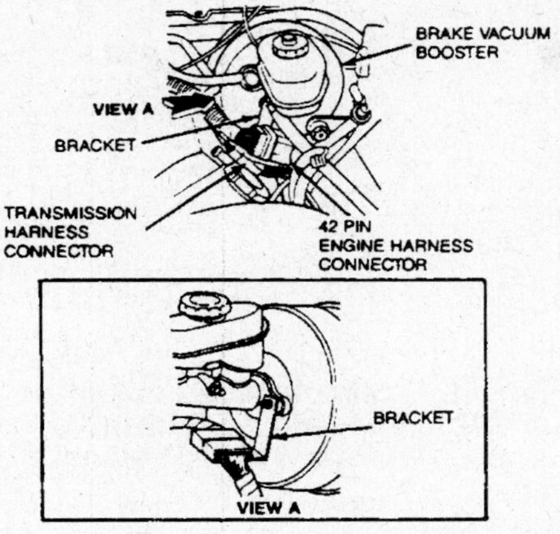

FM1069100128000X

Fig. 8 Engine & transmission harness connectors. 1997–98 Crown Victoria & Grand Marquis

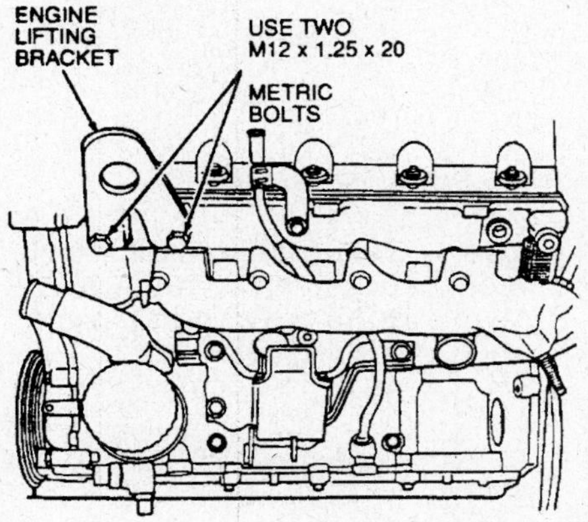

FM1069100131000X

Fig. 11 Engine lift bracket installation. 1997–98 Crown Victoria & Grand Marquis

4. Relieve fuel pressure as outlined under "Precautions, " then disconnect fuel lines.
5. Disconnect ignition coils and fuel injector connectors.
6. Disconnect the fuel injector electrical connectors.
7. Remove positive crankcase ventilation (PCV) tube and position out of the way.
8. Remove evaporative emission (EVAP) canister purge valve.
9. Reposition hold-down clamp and remove the hose from the bypass tube.
10. Disconnect harness retainers from valve cover and position harness out of the way.
11. Remove studs, bolts and cam cover.
12. Reverse procedure to install, noting the following:
    a. Apply sealant in the locations shown, **Fig. 42.** Use Silicone Gasket and Sealant F7AZ-19554-EA, or equivalent.
    b. Tighten bolts in sequence, **Fig. 43.**

Left Side

1. Raise and support vehicle.
2. Remove oil bypass filter.
3. Disconnect power steering pressure

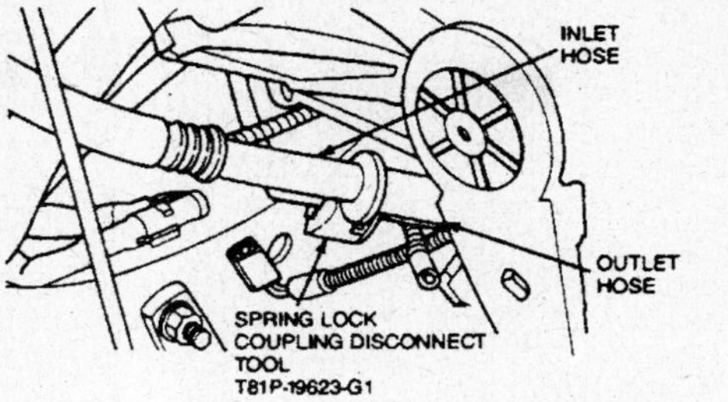

FM1069100129000X

Fig. 9 A/C compressor lines removal. 1997–98 Crown Victoria & Grand Marquis

(PSP) switch and oil pressure sensor connectors.

4. Lower the vehicle.
5. Disconnect cylinder head temperature sensor jumper wire connector.
6. Remove bolt and two studs and position bracket out of the way.
7. Disconnect camshaft position (CMP) sensor connector.
8. Disconnect alternator connector and fuel charging wiring connectors from the coils and the fuel injectors.
9. Disconnect idle air control (IAC) valve and throttle position (TP) sensor connector.
10. Disconnect forty-two pin connector, sixteen-pin connector and transmission connector.
11. Remove six bolts and five studs, then cam cover.
12. Reverse procedure to install, noting the following:
    a. Apply sealant in the locations shown, **Fig. 42.** Use Silicone Gasket and Sealant F7AZ-19554-EA, or equivalent.
    b. Refill and check the engine oil level.
13. Tighten bolts in sequence, **Fig. 44.**

FRONT COVER

REPLACE

1997–98

The cam covers must be removed prior to engine front cover or engine damage and or leakage may occur upon reassembly.

1. Remove drive belt, then water pump pulley.
2. Raise and support vehicle.
3. The front lower bolt on power steering pump will not come all the way out. Remove bolts retaining power steering pump to cylinder block and engine front cover.
4. Wire power steering pump out of the way.
5. Remove four oil pan to engine front cover bolts.
6. Remove crankshaft pulley bolt and crankshaft pulley retaining washer from crankshaft.
7. Install Crankshaft Damper Remover tool No. T58P-6316-D, or equivalent, on crankshaft pulley and pull crankshaft pulley from crankshaft.
8. Lower vehicle.

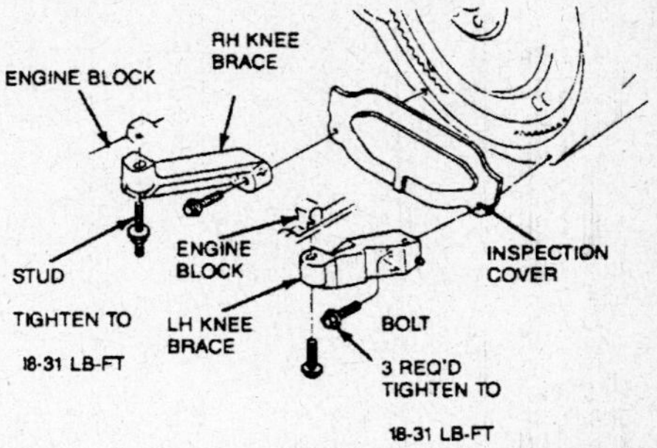

FM1069100130000X

Fig. 10 Transmission line bracket assembly removal. 1997–98 Crown Victoria & Grand Marquis

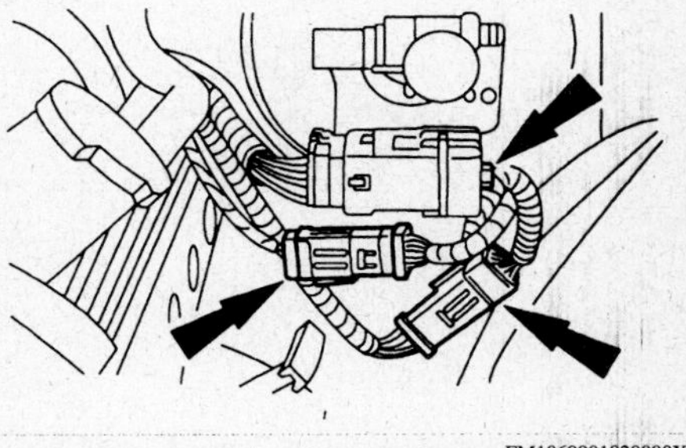

FM1069901020000X

Fig. 12 Engine bulkhead connectors. 1999–2000 Crown Victoria & Grand Marquis

9. Remove nuts retaining air conditioner high pressure line to righthand cover stud.
10. Remove both valve covers.
11. Disconnect fuel charging wiring from camshaft position sensor.
12. Position power steering hoses out of the way.
13. Remove two nuts and one bolt retaining power steering reservoir bracket.
14. Remove bolt retaining belt idler pulley, then pulley.
15. Disconnect fuel charging wiring from crankshaft position sensor, then remove crankshaft position sensor.
16. **On 1997 models,** remove left and right coil bracket attaching nuts, then pull bracket and ignition wires from mounting studs and position aside.
17. **On all models,** remove eight stud bolts and seven bolts retaining front cover to engine.
18. Remove front cover.
19. Reverse procedure to install, noting the following:
    a. Apply silicone gasket and sealant E3AZ-19562-A, or equivalent, in damper keyway. Ensure crankshaft key and keyway are aligned, using Crankshaft Damper Replacer T47P-6316-B, or equivalent, install crankshaft damper.
    b. Tighten bolts in sequence, **Fig. 45** to specifications.
    c. **Torque** four oil pan to engine front cover bolts in two steps in sequence, **Fig. 46,** first to 15 ft. lbs, then an additional 60.°

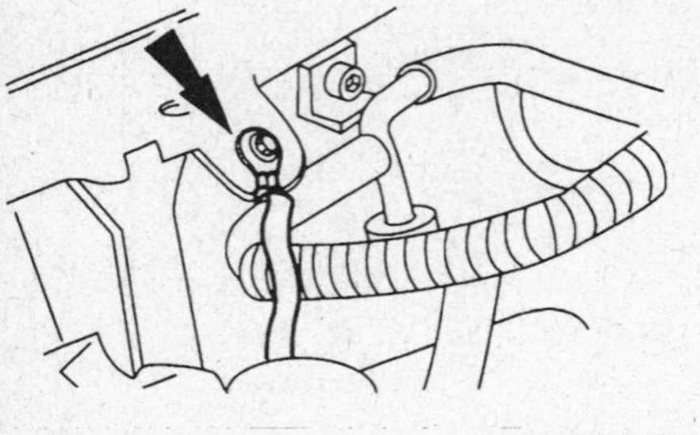

FM1069901021000X

Fig. 13 Ground wire retaining bolt. 1999–2000 Crown Victoria & Grand Marquis

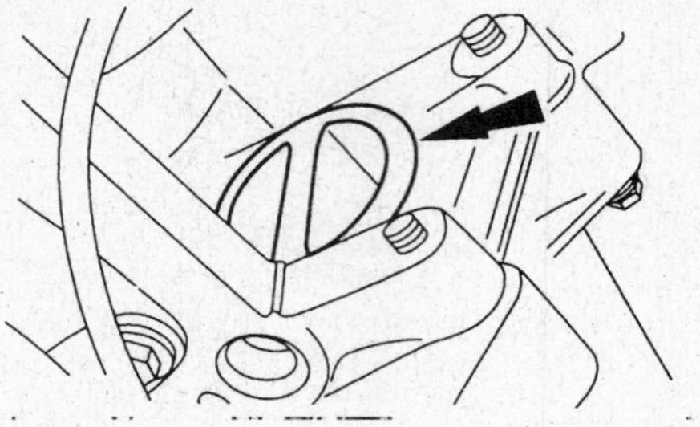

FM1069901022000X

Fig. 14 Torque converter nut access plug. 1999–2000 Crown Victoria & Grand Marquis

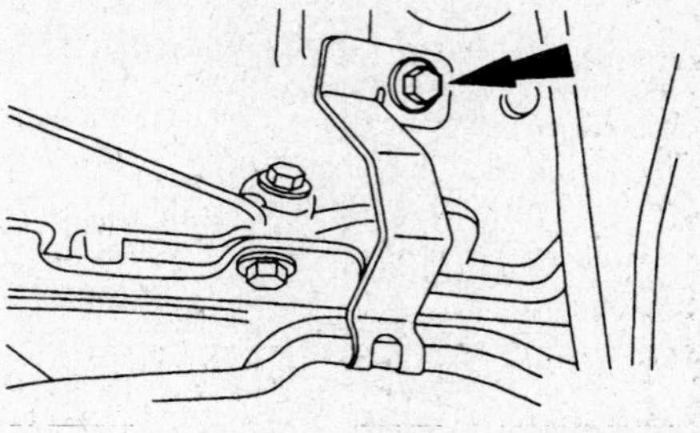

FM1069901023000X

Fig. 15 Transmission cooler line bracket assembly. 1999–2000 Crown Victoria & Grand Marquis

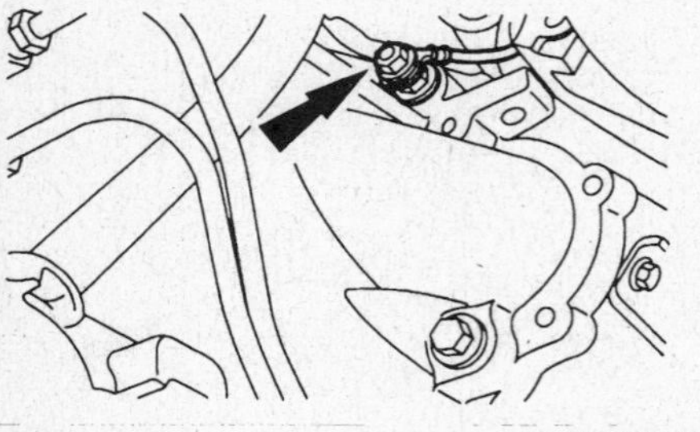

FM1069901024000X

Fig. 16 Starter nut & ground wire. 1999–2000 Crown Victoria & Grand Marquis

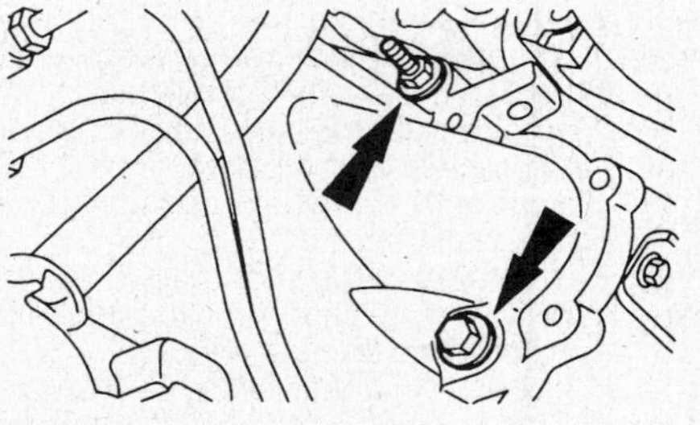

FM1069901025000X

Fig. 17 Starter bolts & stud. 1999–2000 Crown Victoria & Grand Marquis

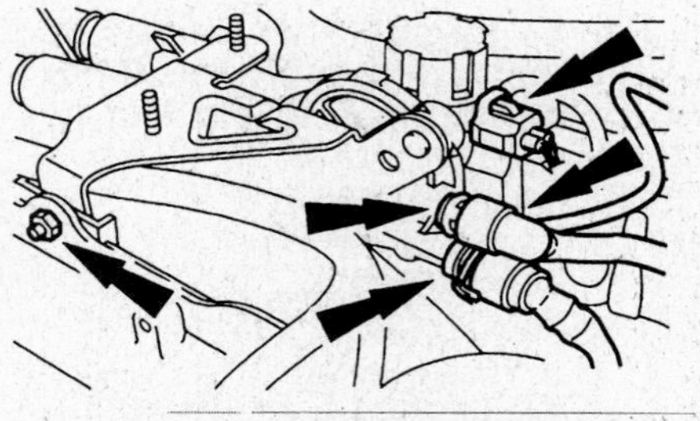

FM1069901026000X

Fig. 18 Evaporative emission canister purge valve. 1999–2000 Crown Victoria & Grand Marquis

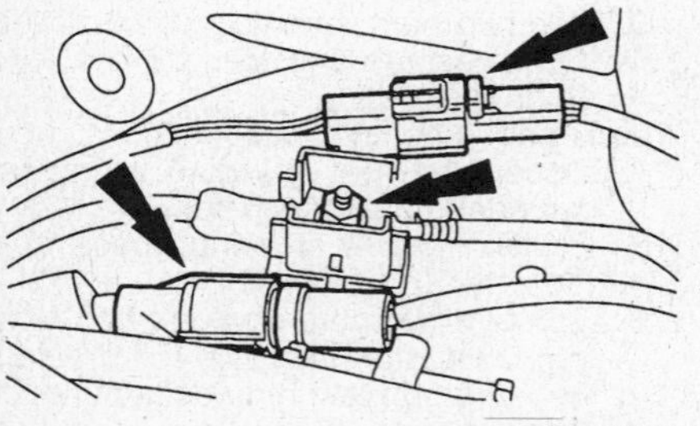

FM1069901027000X

Fig. 19 Electrical connectors, right inner fender. 1999–2000 Crown Victoria & Grand Marquis

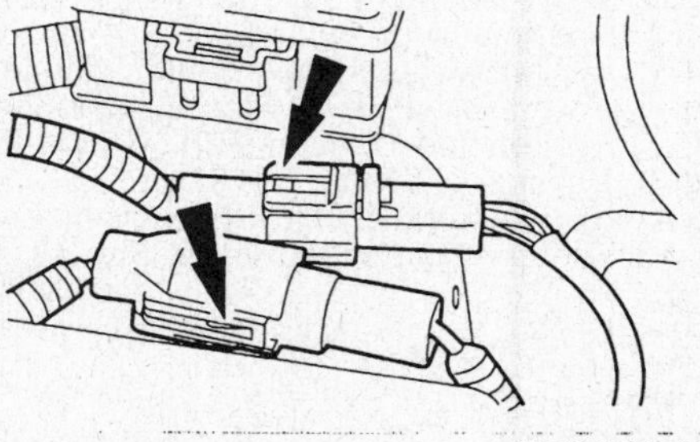

FM1069901028000X

Fig. 20 Electrical connectors. 1999–2000 Crown Victoria & Grand Marquis w/natural gas engine

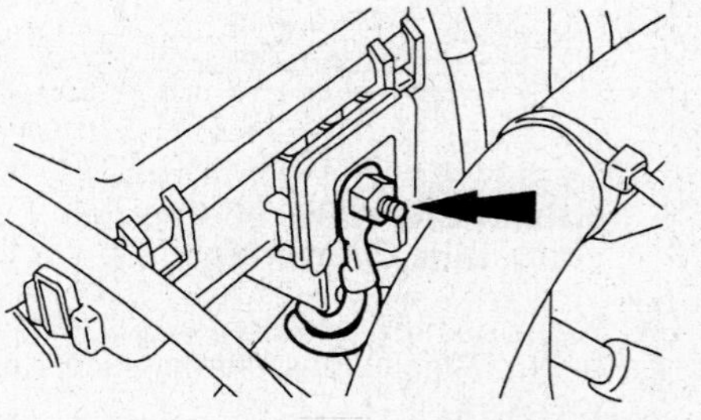

FM1069901029000X

Fig. 21 Cover, nut & wiring removal. 1999–2000 Crown Victoria & Grand Marquis w/natural gas engine

1999-2000

1. Remove both cam covers and water pump.
2. Raise and support vehicle.
3. Remove power steering bolts and position pump aside.
4. Remove oil pan drain plug and drain engine oil into suitable container.
5. Remove oil pan to front cover bolts.
6. Remove crankshaft front seal.
7. Remove belt idler pulley.
8. Remove front cover bolts and stud bolts.
9. Remove engine front cover from front cover to cylinder block dowel.
10. Reverse procedure to install, noting the following:
    a. If the engine front cover is not secured within four minutes, the sealant must be removed and sealing area cleaned with Metal Surface Cleaner F4AZ-19A536-RA , or equivalent. Allow to dry until there is no sign of wetness, or for four minutes, whichever is longer. Failure to follow this procedure can cause future oil leakage. Apply silicone along the cylinder head-to-block surface and the oil pan-to-cylinder block surface.
    b. Use Silicone Gasket and Sealant F7AZ-19554-EA, or equivalent.
    c. Ensure crankshaft key and keyway are aligned, using Crankshaft Damper Replacer T74P-6316-B, or equivalent, install crankshaft pulley.

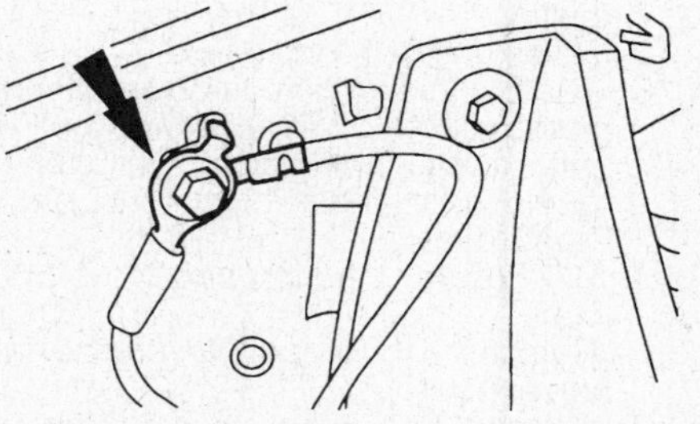

FM1069901030000X

Fig. 22 Body ground wires. 1999–2000 Crown Victoria & Grand Marquis

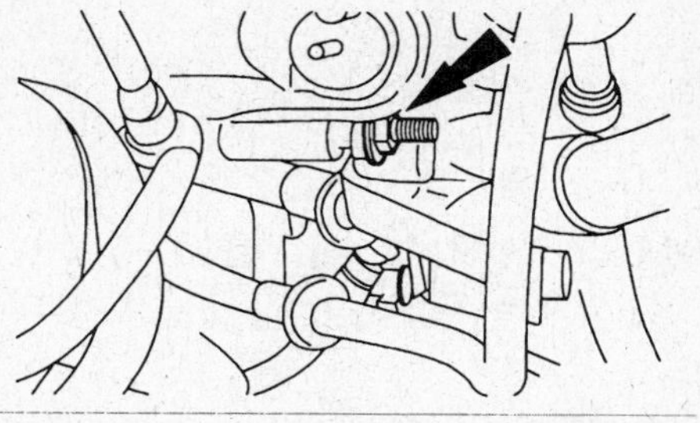

Fig. 23 A/C line bracket. 1999–2000 Crown Victoria & Grand Marquis

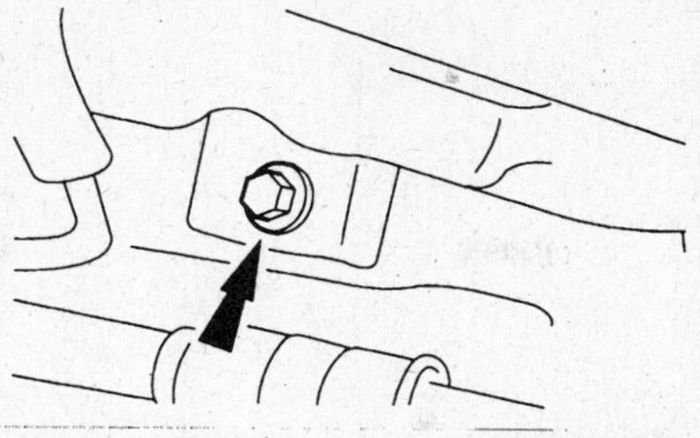

Fig. 24 Bolt removal. 1999–2000 Crown Victoria & Grand Marquis

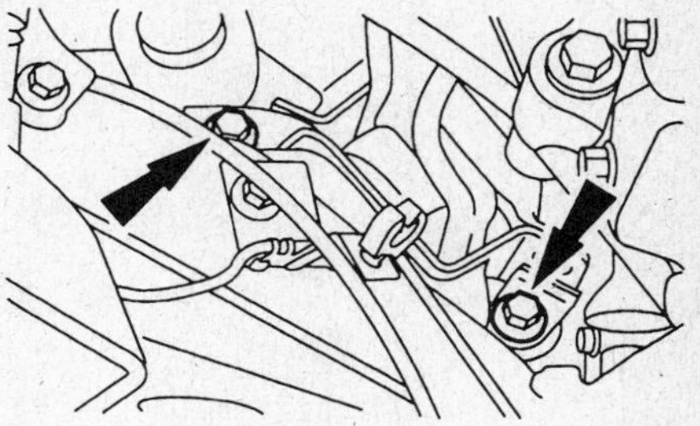

Fig. 25 Left hand engine insulator through bolts. 1999–2000 Crown Victoria & Grand Marquis

d. **Torque** bolts 1 through 7 in sequence, **Fig. 47,** to 15–22 ft. lbs., then bolts 6 through 15 to 29–40 ft. lbs.

e. **Torque** four oil pan to engine front cover bolts in two steps in sequence, **Fig. 48,** first to 15 ft. lbs, then an additional 60.°

FRONT COVER SEAL

REPLACE

1. Release belt tensioner and remove serpentine drive belt.
2. Raise and support vehicle, then remove crankshaft damper attaching bolt and washer.
3. Using crankshaft damper removal tool No. T58P-6316-D, or equivalent, remove crankshaft damper.
4. Using front cover seal removal tool No. T74P-6700-A, or equivalent, remove front cover seal.
5. Reverse procedure to install, noting the following:
   a. Install front cover seal using replacement tool No. T88T-6701-A, or equivalent.
   b. Apply silicone gasket and sealant part No. F6AZ-19562-AA, or equivalent, in damper keyway. Ensure crankshaft key and keyway are aligned, using Crankshaft Damper Replacer tool No. T74P-6316-B, or equivalent, install crankshaft damper.
   c. **Torque** bolt to 66 ft. lbs.
   d. Loosen one complete turn.
   e. **Torque** to 35–39 ft. lbs., then tighten an additional 85–95.°

CAMSHAFT

REPLACE

1. Remove cooling fan and shroud.
2. Relieve fuel system pressure as described under " Precautions."
3. Remove camshaft covers as described under "Camshaft Cover, Replace."
4. Remove front cover as described under "Front Cover, Replace."
5. Remove timing chains as described under "Timing Chains, Gears, Tensioners & Guides, Replace."
6. Rotate crankshaft counterclockwise 45.° Ensure pistons are below top of engine deck face. **Crankshaft must be in position prior to rotating camshafts or piston and/or valve damage may result.**

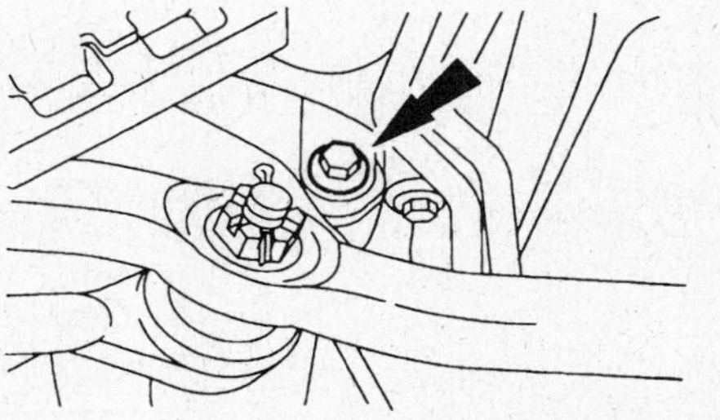

Fig. 26 Right hand engine insulator through bolt. 1999–2000 Crown Victoria & Grand Marquis

7. Install Valve Spring Compressor tool No. T91P-6565-A, or equivalent, under camshaft and on valve spring retainer.
8. Install Valve Spring Spacer tool No. T91P-6565-AH, or equivalent, between spring coils and camshaft to prevent damage.
9. Camshaft must be at base circle before compressing valve spring, then rotate camshaft, as required, until roller followers are removed.
10. Compress valve spring, then remove roller follower.
11. Repeat steps 7 through 10 until all roller followers are removed.
12. Remove camshaft cap cluster assembly attaching bolt, **Fig. 49.**
13. Tap upward on camshaft cap, **Fig. 50,** then carefully remove camshaft cap and camshaft.
14. Reverse procedure to install. Tighten camshaft cap cluster to specifications, **Fig. 49.**

PISTON & ROD ASSEMBLY

If old pistons are serviceable, ensure they are installed on original rods from which they were removed. Check side clearance between connecting rods and crankshaft journal. Correct clearance is .00059–.01772 inch.

1. Assemble pistons, pins, bearings, caps, nuts and bolts in original positions.
2. Install pistons with notch to front of engine.
3. Alternatively tighten connecting rod caps to specifications.
4. After installation, rotate crankshaft to ensure smooth operation.

CRANKSHAFT REAR OIL SEAL

REPLACE

1. Using a suitable jack, lower transmission and support.
2. Remove flywheel.
3. Remove crankshaft oil slinger using Rear Crankshaft Slinger Remover tool No. T95P-6701-AH and Slide Hammer T50T-100-A, or equivalents.
4. Remove crankshaft rear oil seal using Rear Crankshaft Seal Remover tool No. T95P-6701-EH and Slide Hammer T50T-100-A, or equivalents.
5. If required, remove crankshaft rear oil seal retainer.
6. Reverse procedure to install, noting the following:
   a. Do not use metal scrapers, wire brushes, power abrasive discs or other abrasive means to clean the sealing surfaces. These tools cause scratches and gouges which make leak paths. Use a plastic scraping tool to remove all traces of old sealant.
   b. Clean sealing surfaces with Metal Surface Cleaner F4AZ-19A536-RA, or equivalent. Allow to dry until there is no sign of wetness, or four minutes, whichever is longer, failure to follow this procedure can cause future oil leakage.
   c. Use Silicone Gasket and Sealant F7AZ-19554-EA, or equivalent.

TIMING CHAINS, GEARS, TENSIONERS & GUIDES

REPLACE

REMOVAL

Do not rotate the crankshaft and/or

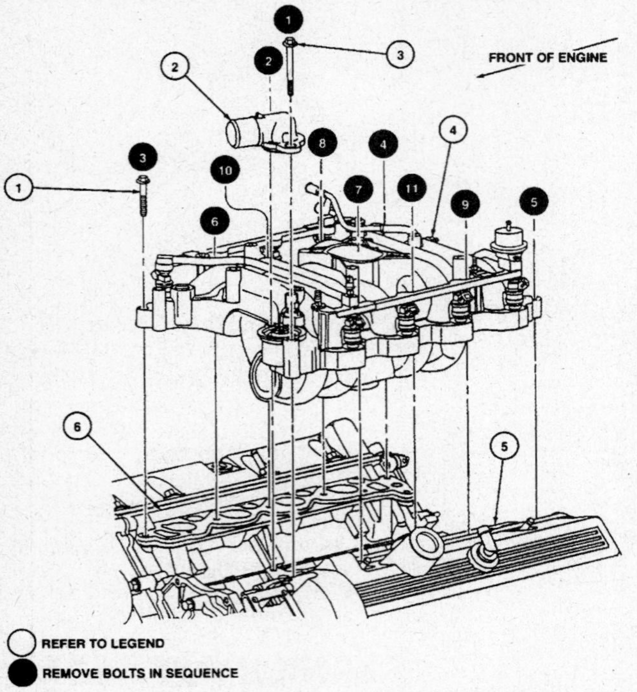

Item	Description
1	Bolt (8 Req'd)
2	Water Hose Connection
3	Bolt (2 Req'd)

Item	Description
4	Intake Manifold
5	Cylinder Head, LH
6	Cylinder Head, RH

FM1059800162000X

Fig. 27 Intake manifold bolt removal sequence. Cougar & Thunderbird

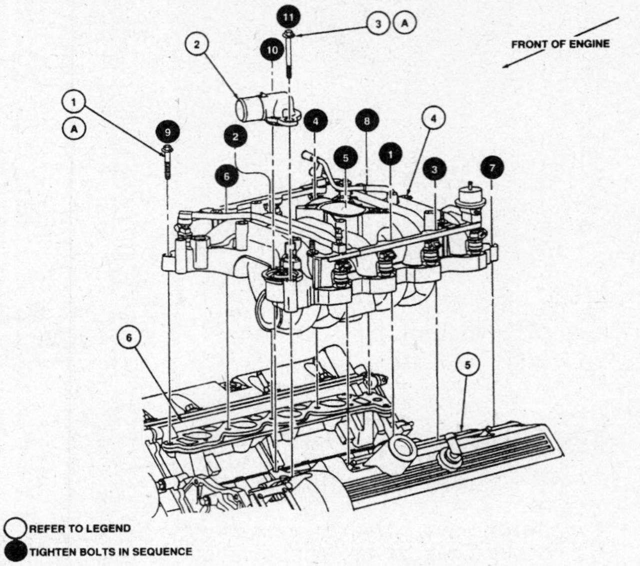

Item	Description
1	Bolt (8 Req'd)
2	Water Hose Connection
3	Bolt (2 Req'd)

Item	Description
4	Intake Manifold
5	Cylinder Head, LH
6	Cylinder Head, RH
A	Tighten to 20-30 N-m (15-22 Lb-Ft)

FM1059800163000X

Fig. 28 Intake manifold tightening sequence. Cougar & Thunderbird

camshaft with the timing chains removed and the cylinder heads installed. Rotation of camshaft or crankshaft may result in valve and/or piston damage.

If engine has jumped time, cylinder heads must be removed to repair damage to valves and/or pistons.

1. Remove all necessary components to access timing chains.
2. Remove crankshaft position sensor tooth wheel and rotate engine to No. 1 cylinder TDC.
3. To prevent accidental rotation of camshafts, install cam positioning tools No. T92P-6256-A, or equivalents, to flats on camshafts as shown, **Fig. 51.**
4. Remove two bolts retaining right tensioner to cylinder head and remove tensioner.
5. Remove right tensioner arm, then two bolts securing right chain guide to cylinder head and chain guide.
6. Remove right camshaft sprocket retaining bolt, washer, gear and spacer, if necessary.
7. Remove two bolts securing left tensioner to cylinder head and remove tensioner.
8. Remove left tensioner arm, then the bolts securing left chain guide to cylinder head. Remove chain guide.
9. Remove left chain from camshaft gears.
10. Remove left camshaft gear.
11. Remove left camshaft sprocket retaining bolt, washer, gear and spacer, if necessary.
12. **Do not rotate crankshaft and/or camshaft while timing chains are removed.**

INSTALLATION

If engine has jumped time, ensure all repairs to engine components and/or valve train are completed. Then rotate engine counterclockwise 45.° This will position all pistons below top of deck face. Install cylinder heads.

1. Install Cam positioning tools No. T92P-6256-A, or equivalent, to prevent camshafts from rotating.
2. Install timing chain guides (both sides), then bolts and tighten to specifications.
3. Position left and right camshaft spacers and gears on camshaft, if removed.
4. Install washer and camshaft gear retaining bolt. Do not tighten at this time.
5. Install left crankshaft gear. Ensure tapered portion of gear faces away from engine block.
6. If copper links of timing chain are not visible, split chain in half and mark two opposing links as shown, **Fig. 52.**
7. Install left timing chain on camshaft gear. Ensure copper link is aligned with timing mark of camshaft gear. **Fig. 53.**
8. Install left timing chain on crankshaft gear. Ensure copper link is aligned with timing mark on crankshaft gear.
9. Install right crankshaft gear. Ensure tapered portion of gear faces toward engine block.
10. Install right timing chain on camshaft gear. Ensure copper link is aligned with timing mark of camshaft gear.
11. Install right timing chain on crankshaft gear. Ensure copper link is aligned with crankshaft gear.
12. Lubricate tensioner arm contact surfaces with engine oil and install right and left tensioner arms on dowels. **Fig. 54.**
13. Install right and left timing chain tensioners. Tighten to specifications. **Do not remove lockpins until timing chain guides are installed.**
14. Install chain guides. Tighten to specifications.
15. Remove lockpins from timing chain tensioners and ensure all timing marks are aligned.
16. Remove cam positioning tools and install all components removed during removal procedure. Tighten to specifications.

OIL PAN

REPLACE

1997–98

1. Remove air inlet tube and drain cooling system.
2. Drain engine coolant into a suitable container, then remove cooling fan and shroud.
3. Relieve fuel system pressure as described under " Precautions," then disconnect fuel lines.
4. Remove upper radiator hose, wiper module and support bracket.

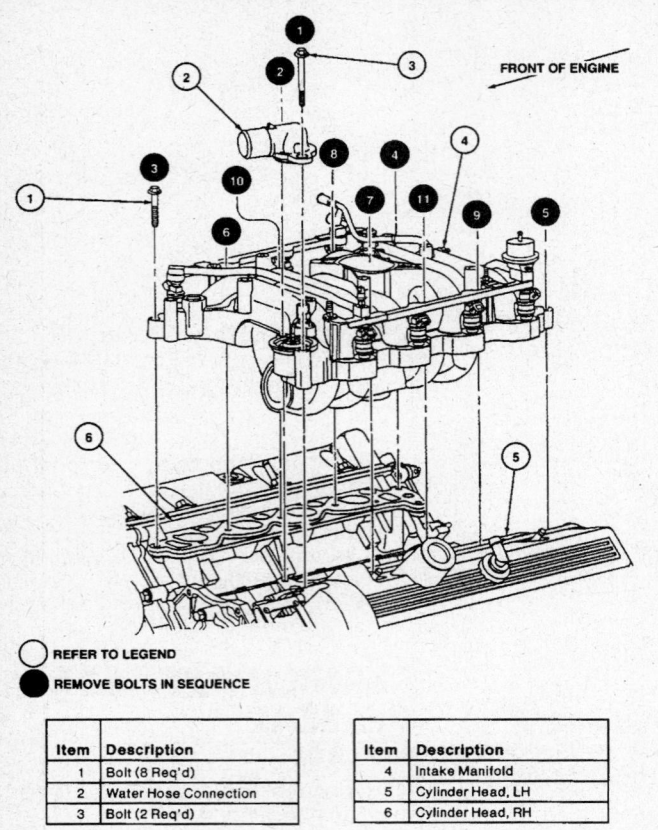

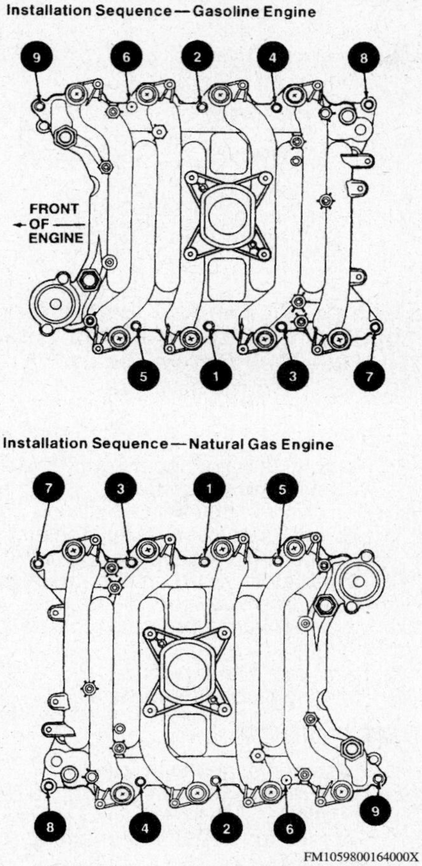

Fig. 29 Intake manifold tightening sequence. Natural gas engine & 1997–98 w/gasoline engine

5. Evacuate A/C system as outlined in "System Evacuation " under "Air Conditioning ," then disconnect A/C compressor outlet hose. Remove bolt securing hose assembly to right coil bracket.
6. Disconnect engine electrical harness 42-pin connector from bracket on brake vacuum booster.
7. Remove right cylinder head ground strap attaching nut, then remove upper stud and lower bolt securing heater hose to cylinder head.
8. Remove blower motor resistor.
9. Raise and support vehicle.
10. Drain engine oil into a suitable container, then reinstall oil pan drain plug with new gasket.
11. Remove right engine mount to lower engine bracket attaching bolt.
12. Disconnect exhaust system from manifolds.
13. Lower exhaust and secure to crossmember with wire.
14. Position a suitable jack and block of wood below oil pan, rearward of drain plug.
15. Raise engine approximately four inches, then insert two wood blocks, approximately 2.5–2.75 inches thick, under each engine mount.
16. Lower engine onto wood blocks and remove jack from below oil pan.
17. Loosen 16 retaining bolts and remove oil pan. **It may be necessary to loosen, without removing, the two nuts on rear transmission mount and raise extension housing of transmission slightly to remove oil pan.**
18. Reverse procedure to install. Tighten bolts in sequence, **Fig. 55** to specifications.

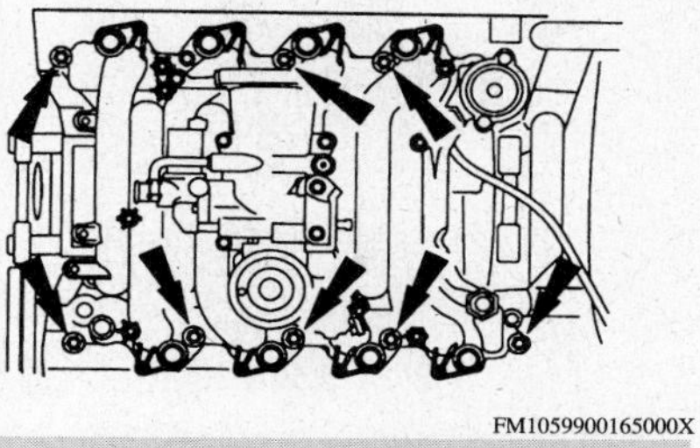

Fig. 30 Intake manifold initial tightening sequence. 1999–2000 Crown Victoria & Grand Marquis w/gasoline engine

1999–2000

1. Remove air cleaner outlet tube.
2. Remove wiper arm and pivot shaft assembly.
3. Remove drive belt, fan motor and shroud assembly.
4. Relieve fuel system pressure as described under " Precautions," then disconnect fuel lines.
5. Remove exhaust gas recirculation (EGR) tube.
6. Remove alternator and blower motor speed control.
7. Remove righthand engine mount bolt.
8. Raise and support vehicle.
9. Remove two lefthand engine mount bolts.
10. Remove four nuts and support the exhaust.
11. Remove bolt for transmission line support bracket.
12. Loosen nuts for transmission mount.
13. Lower the vehicle.
14. The right motor mount has a second bolt accessed from the top. Remove mount bolt.
15. Raise engine with a suitable floor crane and support engine.
16. Raise and support vehicle.
17. Remove the oil pan bolts, then position oil pan aside and remove bolts from oil pickup tube.
18. Remove bolt from oil pickup tube bracket.
19. Remove O-ring and inspect.
20. Remove oil pan and gasket from vehicle through the front.
21. Reverse procedure to install. Tighten oil pan bolts in sequence, **Fig. 56** to specification.

OIL PUMP

REPLACE

1. Remove camshaft covers, front cover and oil pan as previously described.
2. Remove timing chains as described under "Timing Chains, Gears, Tensioners & Guides, Replace."
3. Remove oil pump mounting bolts, then remove oil pump, **Fig. 57.**
4. Reverse procedure to install, noting the following:
   a. Align oil pump inner rotor with flat of crankshaft.
   b. **Torque** oil pump attaching bolts to 72–108 inch lbs.

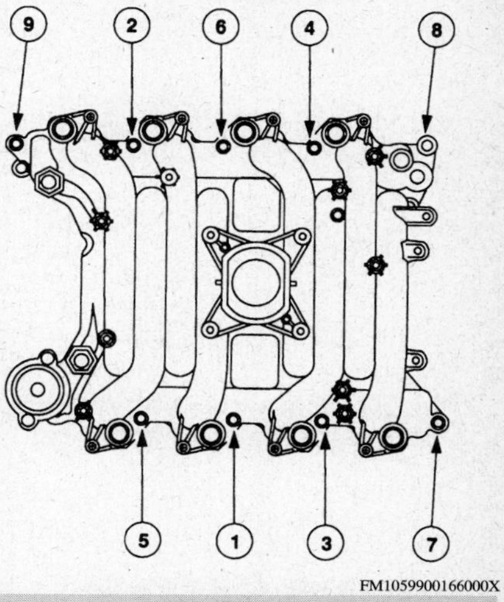

Fig. 31 Intake manifold bolt tightening sequence. 1999–2000 Crown Victoria & Grand Marquis w/gasoline engine

BELT TENSION DATA

Automatic belt tensioners are spring loaded devices which set and maintain drive belt tension. The drive belt should not require tension adjustment for the life of belt. Automatic tensioners have belt wear indicator marks. If indicator mark is not between indicator lines, belt is worn or an incorrect belt is installed.

SERPENTINE DRIVE BELT

BELT ROUTING

Refer to **Figs. 58 and 59** for drive belt routing.

ADJUSTMENT

Automatic belt tensioners are spring loaded devices which set and maintain the drive belt tension. The drive belt should not require tension adjustment.

REPLACEMENT

1. Rotate tensioner away from belt using a breaker bar installed in ½ inch square hole in tensioner arm.
2. Lift old belt over alternator pulley flange and remove.
3. When installing, position new belt over pulleys. Ensure all V-grooves make proper contact with pulley.

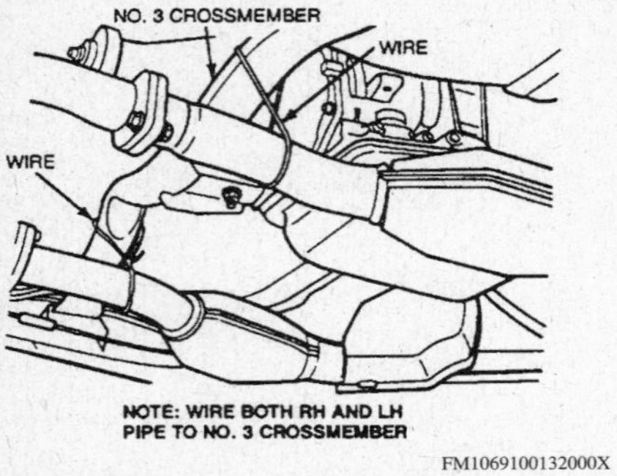

Fig. 32 Catalytic converter to crossmember attachment

4. Ensure belt is properly installed on each pulley.

COOLING SYSTEM BLEED

1. Place heater temperature switch in maximum heat position.
2. Start engine and allow to idle. While engine is idling, feel for hot air at A/C vents.
3. If air discharge remains cool and engine coolant temperature gauge does not move, engine coolant level is low in engine and must be filled.
4. Stop engine, allow to cool and fill cooling system.
5. Start engine and allow to idle until normal operating temperature is reached. Hot air should discharge from A/C vents. Engine coolant temperature gauge should maintain a stabilized reading in the middle of the NORMAL range and the upper radiator hose should feel hot to the touch.
6. Shut engine off and allow to cool.
7. Check engine for coolant leaks.
8. Check engine coolant level in overflow bottle and fill as necessary.

THERMOSTAT

REPLACE

1. Drain coolant into suitable container until level is below upper radiator hose and thermostat housing.
2. **On 1999–2000 models,** remove engine appearance cover.
3. **On all models,** disconnect upper radiator hose at thermostat housing, then remove two thermostat housing retaining bolts.
4. Remove O-ring seal and thermostat from intake manifold. Inspect O-ring for damage and replace if necessary.
5. Reverse procedure to install. Tighten bolts to specifications.

WATER PUMP

REPLACE

1. Drain coolant into a suitable container.
2. **On Cougar and Thunderbird models,** remove engine cooling fan and shroud.
3. **On all models,** loosen water pump

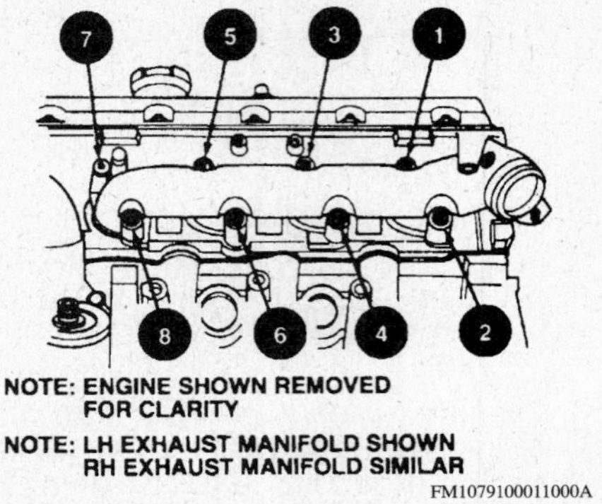

Fig. 33 Exhaust manifold tightening sequence

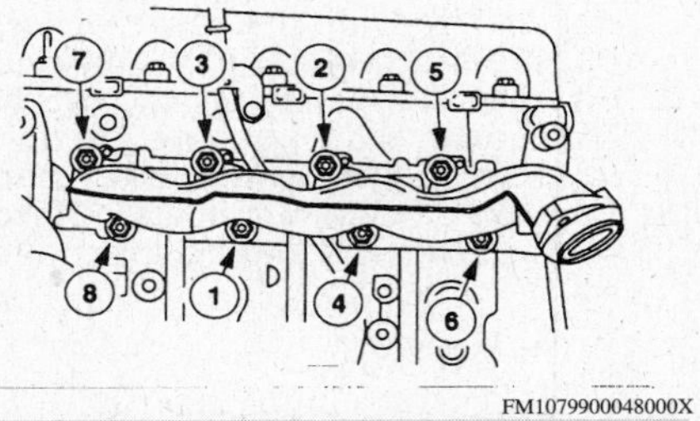

Fig. 35 Exhaust manifold tightening sequence, left side. 1999–2000 Crown Victoria & Grand Marquis

mounting bolts, then release belt tensioner and remove accessory drive belt.

4. Remove water pump pulley mounting bolts, then remove water pump pulley.
5. Loosen mounting bolts and remove water pump.
6. Reverse procedure to install. Replace O-ring and tighten to specifications.

RADIATOR

REPLACE

COUGAR & THUNDERBIRD

1. Drain coolant into a suitable container.
2. Disconnect upper, lower and overflow hose from radiator.
3. Disconnect automatic transmission fluid cooler inlet and outlet lines from radiator.
4. Remove cooling fan motor, fan blade and fan shroud assembly.
5. Remove radiator upper support attaching bolts, then lift radiator from the vehicle.
6. Reverse procedure to install.

CROWN VICTORIA & GRAND MARQUIS

1997–98

1. Drain engine coolant into a suitable container.
2. Remove fan shroud.
3. Disconnect upper, lower and overflow hoses from radiator.

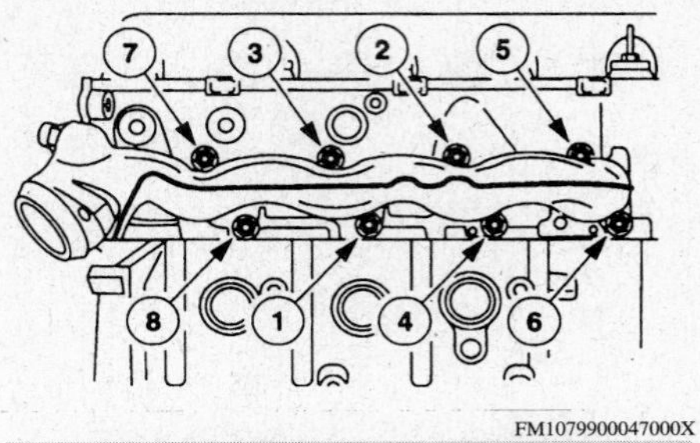

Fig. 34 Exhaust manifold tightening sequence, right side. 1999–2000 Crown Victoria & Grand Marquis

4. Remove radiator upper support retaining bolts and supports.
5. Remove two attaching bolts on each side of radiator, connecting radiator, oil cooler and A/C condenser core.
6. Tilt radiator toward engine, then lift oil cooler and A/C condenser core dislodging from radiator end tanks retaining tabs.
7. Remove radiator pull up.
8. Reverse procedure to install.

1999–2000

1. Raise and support vehicle.
2. Drain engine coolant into a suitable container.
3. Remove fan blade, motor and shroud assembly.
4. Release three hold downs and remove radiator sight shield.
5. Remove upper and lower radiator hoses from radiator.
6. Remove radiator support bolts and supports.
7. Remove bolts and position A/C condenser core and transmission oil cooler away from the radiator.
8. Remove radiator from vehicle.
9. Reverse procedure to install.

FUEL PUMP

REPLACE

COUGAR & THUNDERBIRD

1. Relieve fuel system pressure as described under " Precautions."
2. Raise and support vehicle.
3. Drain fuel from fuel tank, then remove the exhaust system as required for access. **The plastic fuel tube connections are on top of the fuel tank and are inaccessible. The fuel tank must be lowered to gain access to the connections.**
4. Disconnect fuel hoses and tubes, then disconnect one end of the vapor crossover hose at the rear over the driveshaft.
5. Disconnect fuel tank to filler pipe hose.
6. Place a safety support under the fuel tank, then remove bolts from the fuel tank support straps. Use caution to not deform the fuel tank, fuel tank support or fuel tank support straps.
7. Lower the fuel tank and disconnect the

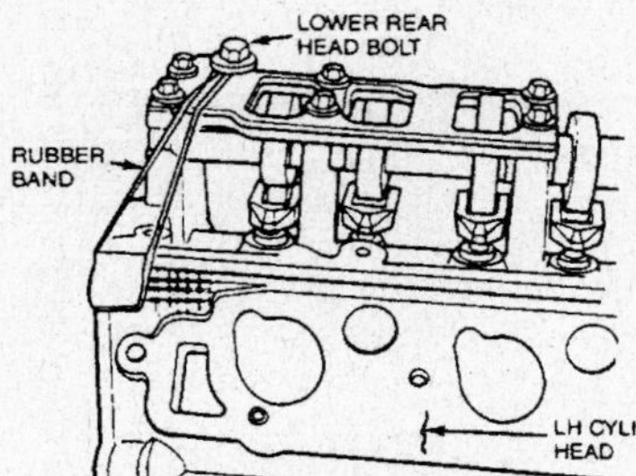

Fig. 36 Lefthand lower rear head bolt removal

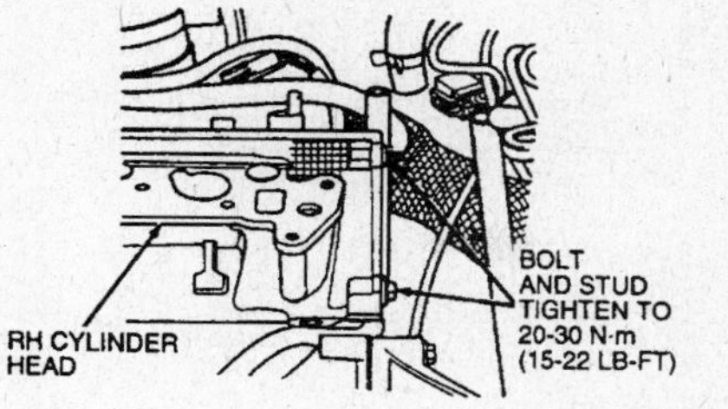

Fig. 37 Right cylinder head removal

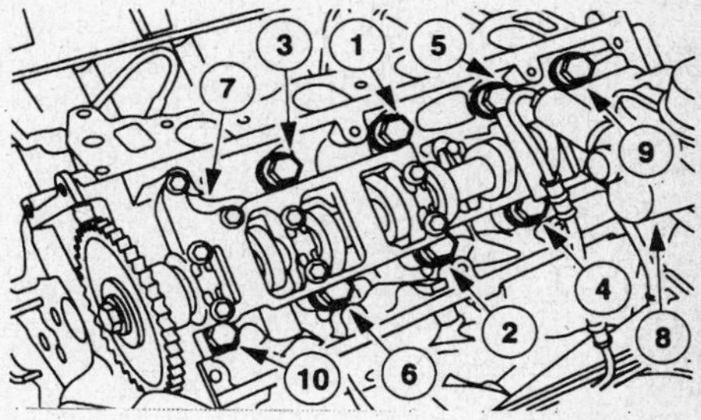

Fig. 38 Cylinder head bolt tightening sequence, left side

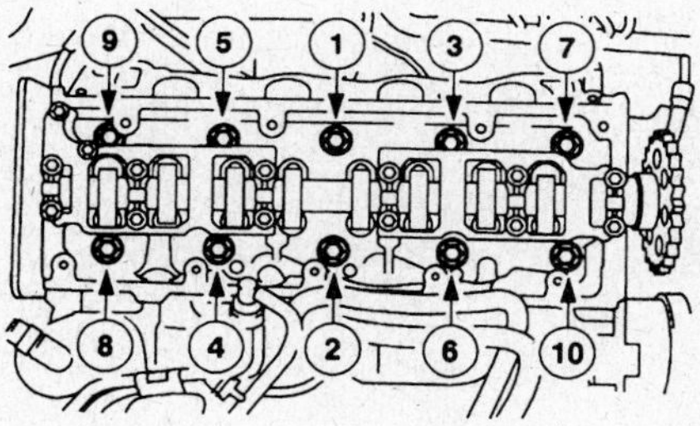

Fig. 39 Cylinder head bolt tightening sequence, right side

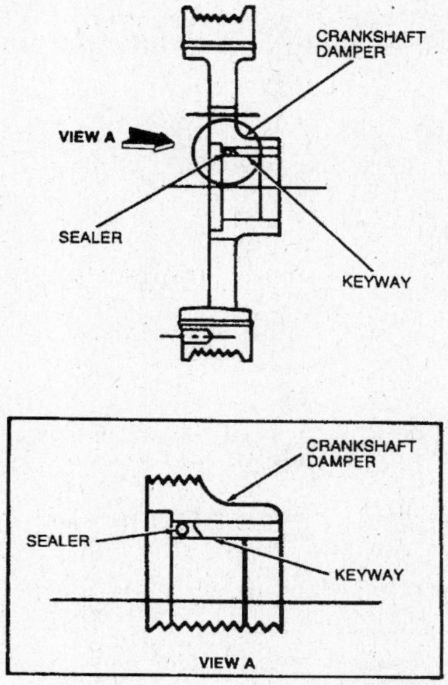

Fig. 40 Crankshaft pulley keyway silicone gasket sealant application locations

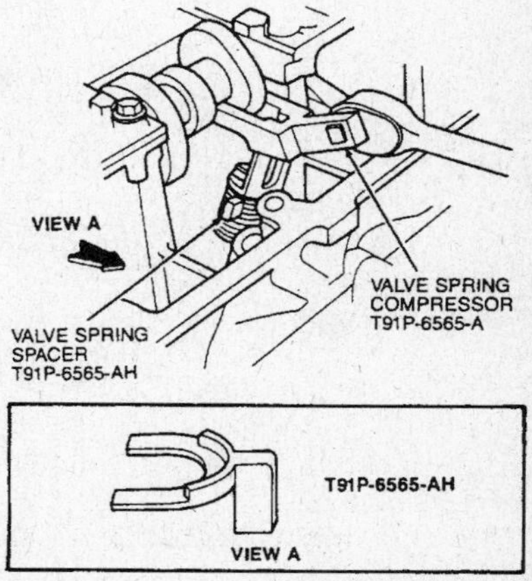

Fig. 41 Valve spring compression

fuel lines and electrical connector from the fuel gauge sender, if required.

8. Remove any dirt that has accumulated around the fuel pump retaining flange so it will not enter the fuel tank during fuel pump removal and installation.
9. Turn fuel pump locking retainer ring counterclockwise using fuel tank sender wrench tool No. D84P-9275-A, or equivalent, and remove fuel pump locking retainer ring.
10. Remove fuel pump assembly and the seal ring.
11. Reverse procedure to install, noting the following:
    a. Apply a light coating of Premium Long-Life Grease part No. XG-1 or XG-1-K, or equivalent, on new fuel pump sealing ring to secure in position during installation.
    b. Ensure all locking tabs are under tabs before tightening locking ring.
    c. Tighten to specifications.

CROWN VICTORIA & GRAND MARQUIS

1. Relieve fuel system pressure as described under "Precautions."
2. Drain fuel tank, then raise and support vehicle.
3. **On 1998–2000 models,** remove fuel tank, then disconnect pressure transducer connector on top rear corner of the fuel tank.
4. **On all models,** remove any dirt that has accumulated around fuel pump module so it will not enter fuel tank during removal and installation.
5. Remove six bolts from around perimeter of fuel pump module.
6. Remove fuel pump module.
7. Reverse procedure to install, noting the following:
    a. Tighten to specifications.
    b. Using Fuel Pressure Gauge tool No. T80L-9974-B, or equivalent, on fuel charging assembly Schraeder valve, turn ignition from Off to On position for 3 seconds. Repeat OFF to ON switching 5 to 10 times until pressure gauge shows at least 35 psi.

FUEL FILTER

REPLACE

COUGAR & THUNDERBIRD

1. Relieve fuel system pressure as described under "Precautions"
2. Raise and support vehicle.
3. Remove push connect fittings at both ends of the fuel filter and base. Install new retainer clips in each push connect fitting.
4. Remove fuel filter and base from bracket by loosening worm gear clamp. Note direction of the flow arrow as installed in the bracket to ensure proper replacement.
5. Reverse procedure to install. Tighten to specifications.

CROWN VICTORIA & GRAND MARQUIS

1. Turn engine off and relieve fuel system pressure as described under "Precautions."
2. Raise and support vehicle.
3. Remove push connect fittings at both ends of the filter. Install new retainer clips in each push connect fitting.
4. Remove fuel filter and retainer from metal bracket by removing two retainer bolts.
5. Remove filter from retainer. Note direction of flow arrow points to open end of retainer.
6. Remove rubber insulator rings from filter.
7. Reverse procedure to install, noting the following:
    a. Replace insulator if filter moves freely after installation of retainer.
    b. **On 1997–98 models, torque** fuel filter clamp to 72–108 inch lbs.
    c. **On 1999–2000 models, torque** fuel filter clamp to 18–26 inch lbs.
    d. **On all models,** start engine and inspect for fuel leaks.

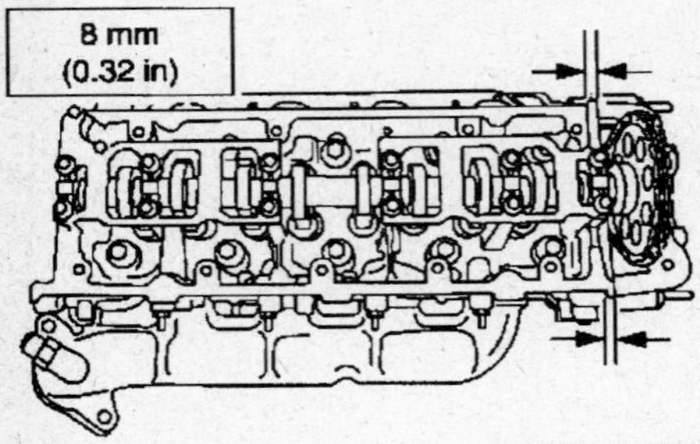

FM1069900847000X

Fig. 42 Sealant application locations. 1999–2000 Crown Victoria & Grand Marquis

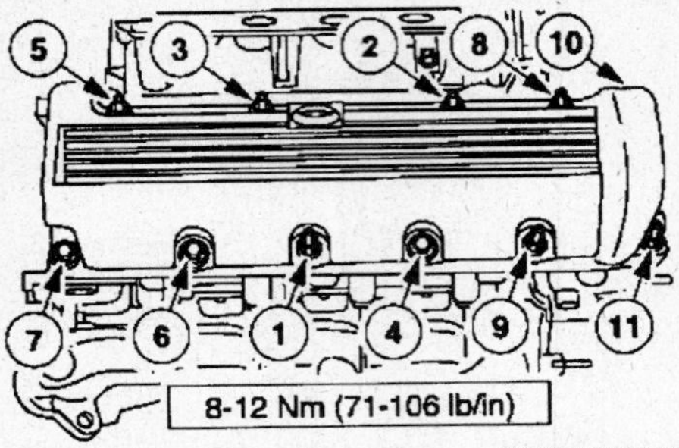

FM1069900848000X

Fig. 43 Righthand cam cover tightening sequence. 1999–2000 Crown Victoria & Grand Marquis

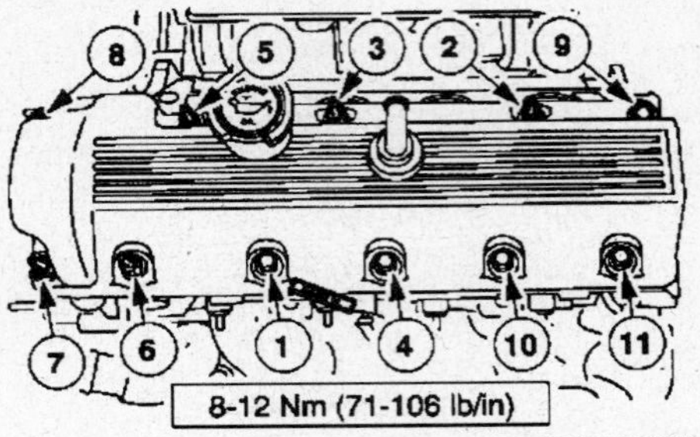

FM1069900849000X

Fig. 44 Lefthand cam cover bolt tightening sequence. 1999–2000 Crown Victoria & Grand Marquis

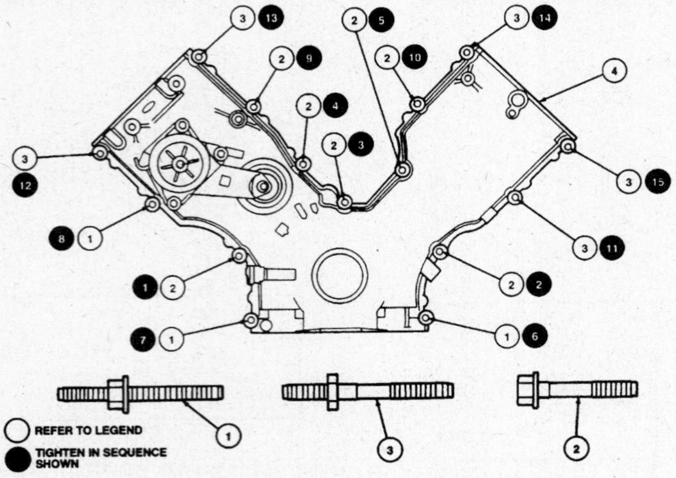

Item	Description
1	Stud Bolt (3 Req'd)
2	Bolt (7 Req'd)

Item	Description
3	Stud Bolt (5 Req'd)
4	Engine Front Cover

FM1069800850000X

Fig. 45 Front cover tightening sequence. 1997–98

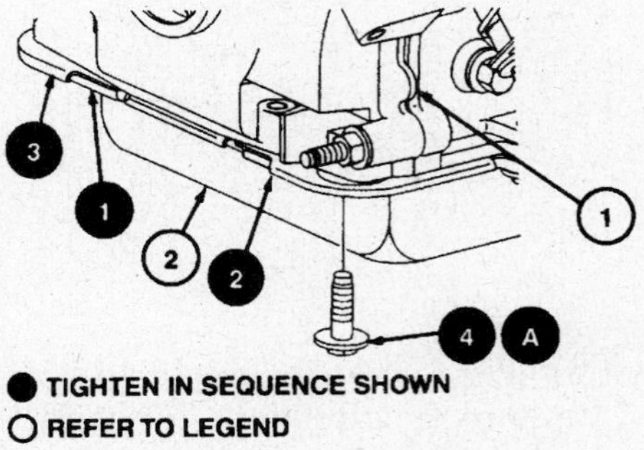

Item	Description
1	Engine Front Cover
2	Oil Pan
3	Bolt (4 Req'd)
4	Tighten in sequence in two steps: 1 Tighten to 20 N·m (14 Lb-Ft). 2 Tighten an additional 60 degrees.

FM1069800851000X

Fig. 46 Oil pan to front cover bolt tightening sequence. 1997–98

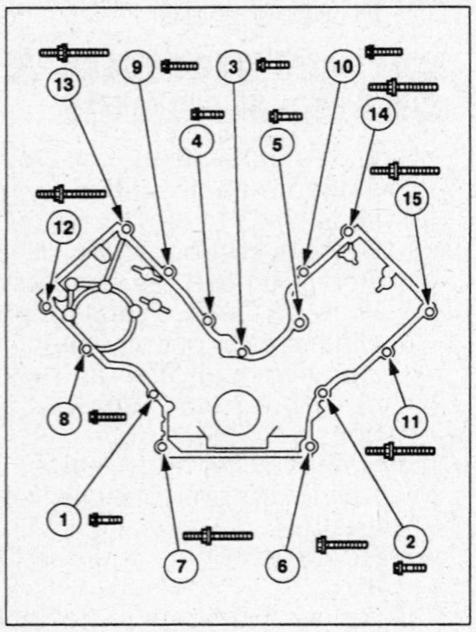

Item	Description
1	Bolt, Hex Flange Head Pilot, M8 x 1.25 x 53
2	Bolt, Hex Flange Head Pilot, M8 x 1.25 x 53
3	Bolt, Hex Flange Head Pilot, M8 x 1.25 x 53

Item	Description
4	Bolt, Hex Flange Head Pilot, M8 x 1.25 x 53
5	Bolts, Hex Flange Head Pilot, M8 x 1.25 x 53
6	Bolt, Hex-Head Pilot, M10 x 1.5 x 1.5 x 103.1
7	Stud, Hex-Head Pilot, M10 x 1.5 x 1.5 x 103.1
8	Screw and Washer, Hex Pilot, M10 x 1.5 x 57.5
9	Screw and Washer, Hex Pilot, M10 x 1.5 x 57.5
10	Screw and Washer, Hex Pilot, M10 x 1.5 x 57.5
11	Stud and Washer, Hex Head Pilot, M10 x 1.5 x M8 x 1.25 x 109.6
12	Stud and Washer, Hex Head Pilot, M10 x 1.5 x M8 x 1.25 x 109.6
13	Stud and Washer, Hex Head Pilot, M10 x 1.5 x M8 x 1.25 x 109.6
14	Stud and Washer, Hex Head Pilot, M10 x 1.5 x M8 x 1.25 x 109.6
15	Stud and Washer, Hex Head Pilot, M10 x 1.5 x M8 x 1.25 x 109.6

FM1069901038000X

Fig. 47 Front cover tightening sequence. 1999–2000

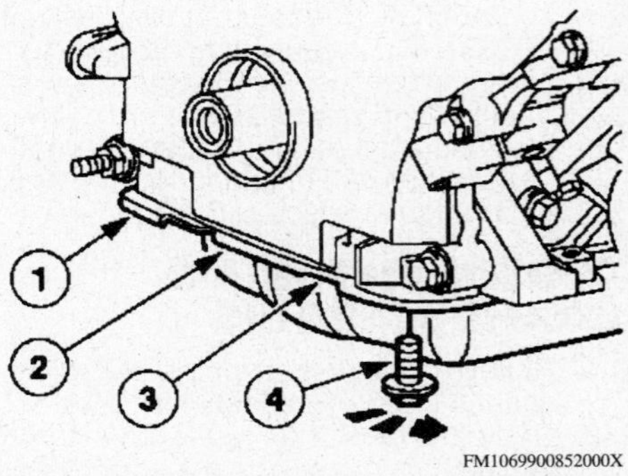

FM1069900852000X

Fig. 48 Oil pan to front cover bolt tightening sequence. 1999–2000

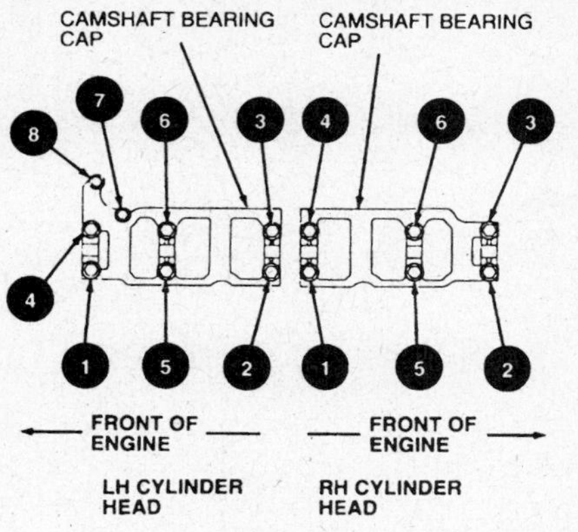

Fig. 49 Camshaft cap cluster tightening sequence

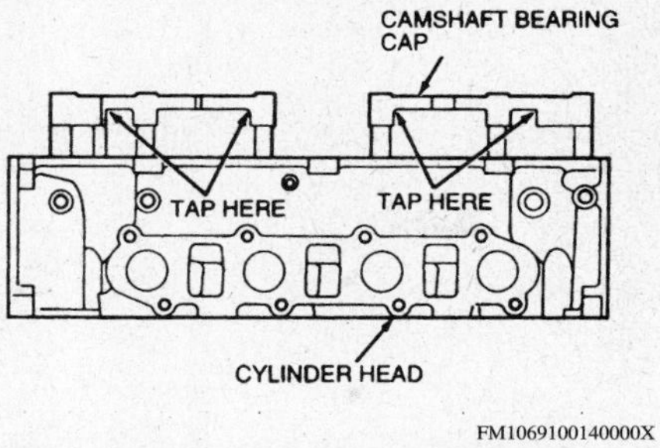

Fig. 50 Camshaft replacement

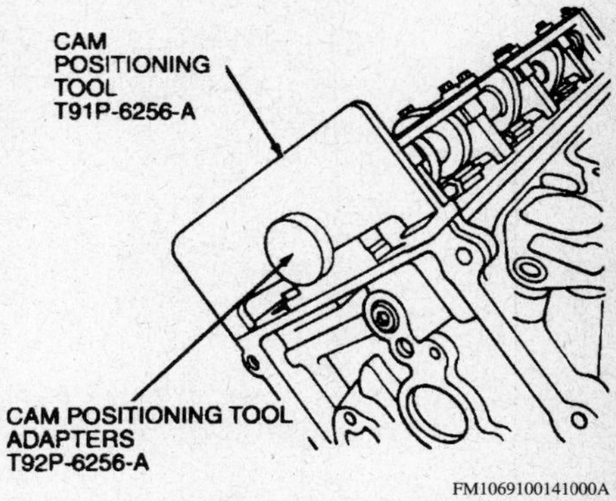

Fig. 51 Camshaft positioning tool

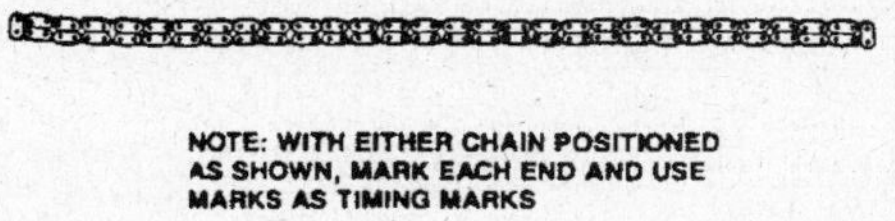

NOTE: WITH EITHER CHAIN POSITIONED AS SHOWN, MARK EACH END AND USE MARKS AS TIMING MARKS
FM1069100142000X

Fig. 52 Timing chain marks

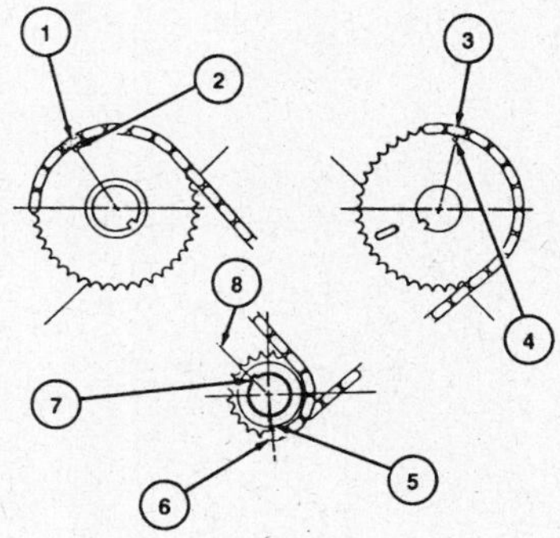

Item	Part Number	Description
1	—	RH Camshaft Timing Chain Mark
2	—	RH Camshaft Sprocket Mark
3	—	LH Camshaft Timing Chain Mark
4	—	RH Camshaft Sprocket Mark
5	—	Crankshaft Sprocket Mark
6	—	Crankshaft Timing Chain Mark
7	6306	Crankshaft Sprocket
8	—	Crankshaft Keyway Center Line

FM1069100143000X

Fig. 53 Lefthand timing chain installation

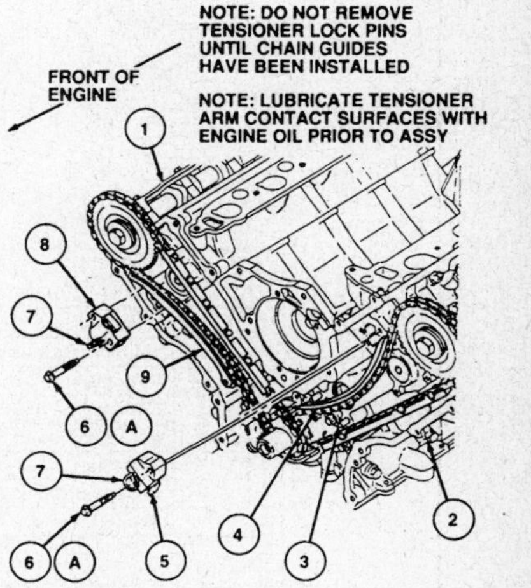

Item	Part Number	Description
1	6049	Cylinder Head (RH)
2	6049	Cylinder Head (LH)
3	N806007	Dowel
4	6L253	Timing Chain Tensioner Arm (LH)
5	6L266	Timing Chain Tensioner (LH)
6	N606543-S2	Bolt (2 Req'd)
7	—	Lock Pin (Part of 6L266)
8	6L266	Timing Chain Tensioner (RH)
9	6L253	Timing Chain Tensioner Arm (RH)
A	—	Tighten to 20-30 N·m (15-22 Lb-Ft)

FM1069100144000X

Fig. 54 Tensioner arm installation

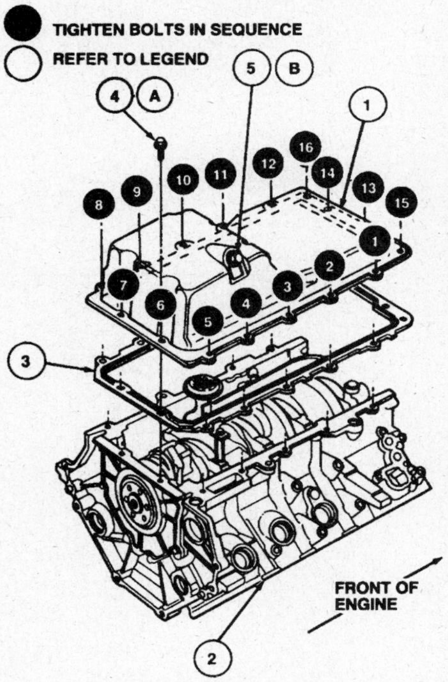

Item	Description
1	Oil Pan
2	Cylinder Blocks
3	Oil Pan Gasket
4	Bolt (16 Req'd)
5	Oil Pan Drain Plug
A	Tighten to 20 N·m (15 Lb-Ft Then an Additional 60 Degrees)
B	Tighten to 11-16 N·m (9-11 Lb-Ft)

FM1069800853000X

Fig. 55 Oil pan tighten sequence. 1997–98

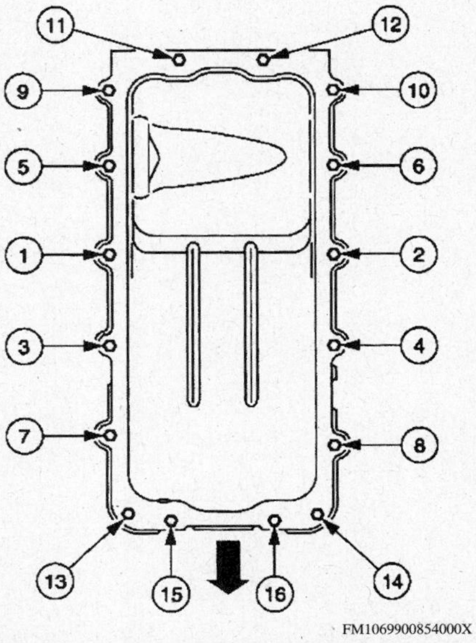

Fig. 56 Oil pan tighten sequence. 1999–2000

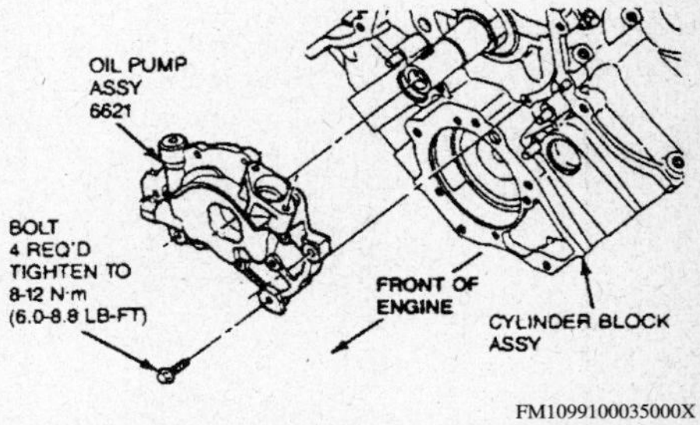

Fig. 57 Oil pump assembly

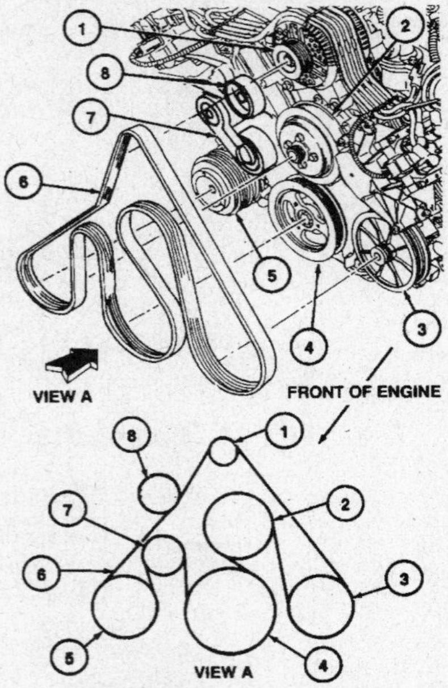

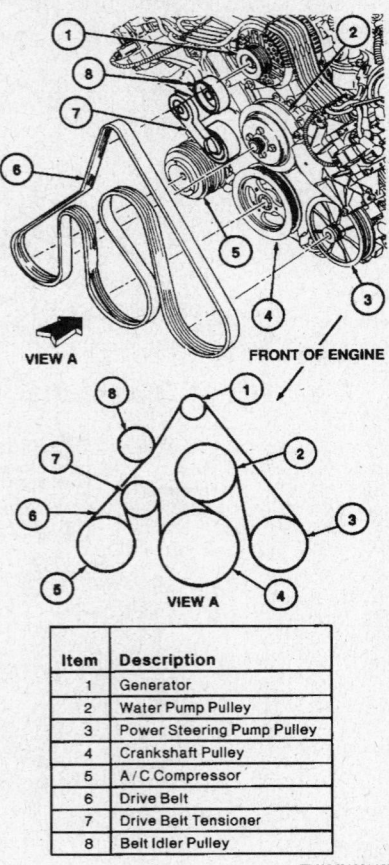

Item	Description
1	Generator
2	Water Pump Pulley
3	Power Steering Pump Pulley
4	Crankshaft Pulley
5	A / C Compressor
6	Drive Belt
7	Drive Belt Tensioner
8	Belt Idler Pulley

FM1069100145000A

Fig. 58 Serpentine drive belt routing. 1997–99

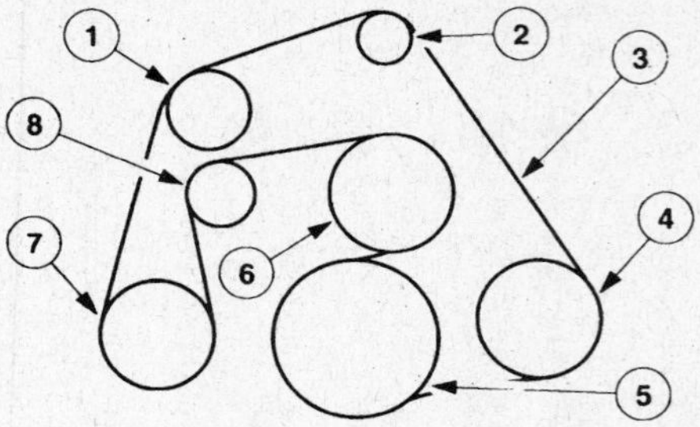

Item	Description
1	Belt idler pulley
2	Generator pulley
3	Drive belt
4	Power steering pump pulley
5	Crankshaft pulley
6	Water pump pulley
7	A/C clutch pulley
8	Drive belt tensioner pulley

FM1069901042000X

Fig. 59 Serpentine drive belt routing. 2000

TIGHTENING SPECIFICATIONS

COUGAR & THUNDERBIRD

Year	Component	Torque/ Ft. Lbs.
1997	Alternator Mounting Bolts	15–22
	Camshaft Sprocket Bolt	82–95
	Connecting Rod Bolt	30-33
	Crankshaft Pulley Bolt	⑤
	Cylinder Head Bolts	②
	ECT Sensor	12–16
	EGR Valve To Exhaust Manifold Tube To Connector	26–33
	EGR Valve To Intake Manifold	15–22
	Engine To Transmission Bolts	41–50
	Exhaust Manifold Bolts	14–16
	Flywheel To Crankshaft Bolt	54–64
	Front Cover	15–22
	Front Engine Support Insulator Through Bolts	15–22
	Front Sub-Frame To Body Bolts	70–96
	Front Suspension Lower Arms To Spring & Shock Bolt	118–162
	Front Suspension Upper Arms To Front Wheel Spindles	51–67
	Fuel Filter Worm Gear Clamp	16–24①
	IAC Valve Bolts	72–108①
	Intake Manifold Bolts	15–22
	Main Bearing Cap Adjusting Screw	⑥
	Main Bearing Cap Side Bolts	④
	Oil Cooler Tube Bracket To Transmission Case	15–22
	Oil Filter Adapter Bolt	15–22
	Oil Pan Bolts	15
	Oil Pan Drain Plug	9–11
	Oxygen Sensors	28–33
	Power Steering Pump Bolts	15–22
	Rear Axle Assembly To Rear Sub-Frame	72–89
	Rear Axle Differential Insulator Nuts	75–94
	Rear Axle Universal Joint Flange	70–95
	Rear Engine Support Insulator Retaining Bolts	15–22
	Spark Plugs	80–177①
	Thermostat Housing Bolts	15–22
	Throttle Body & Adapter Bolts	73–100
	Torque Converter Retaining Nuts	22–25
	Transmission Case To Cylinder Block	18–31
	Valve Cover Bolts	70–106①
	Water Pump Pulley	15–22

① — Inch lbs.
② — Refer to "Cylinder Head, Replace."
③ — Tighten an additional 90–120.°
④ — Tighten in two steps, first to 7 ft. lbs., then to 14–16 ft. lbs.
⑤ — Tighten in four steps, first to 67 ft. lbs., second loosen one full turn, third tighten to 37 ft. lbs., then fourth tighten an additional 90.°
⑥ — Tighten in two steps, first to 44 inch lbs., second to 6–8 ft. lbs.
⑦ — Tighten an additional 60.°

CROWN VICTORIA & GRAND MARQUIS

Year	Component	Torque/ Ft. Lbs.
1997–2000	A/C Compressor Mounting Bolts	15–22
	Alternator To Cylinder Block	15–22
	Camshaft Bearing Caps	71–107⑤
	Camshaft Gear Bolt	82–95
	Connecting Rod Bolt	③
	Front Cover Bolt	15–22
	Cylinder Head Bolt	①
	Damper To Crankshaft Bolt	④
	ECT Sensor	12–17
	EGR Tube Connector	33–48
	EGR Valve Line Nut	26–33
	EGR Valve To Intake Manifold	15–22
	Engine Mount Attaching Bolts	45–59
	Engine Mount Through Bolts	15–22
	Engine To Transmission Bolts	30–44
	Engine To Transmission Braces	18–31
	Exhaust Manifold	14–16
	Exhaust Pipe To Exhaust Manifold	20–30
	Flywheel Bolts	54–64
	Front Cover	⑥
	Fuel Rail Retaining Bolts	71–106
	Fuel Tank Strap	22–30
	HEGO Sensors	27–33
	Intake Manifold	15–22
	Main Bearing Cap	22-25
	Oil Filter Adapter	15–22
	Oil Inlet Tube To Main Bearing Cap	15–22
	Oil Inlet Tube To Oil Pump Bolt	72–106⑤
	Oil Pan Drain Plug	98–143⑤
	Oil Pan To Cylinder Block	15–22
	Oil Pump To Cylinder Block	72–107⑤
	Power Steering Pump To Engine	15–22
	Rear Engine Mount Nuts	35–47
	Rear Engine Mount To Crossmember Bolts	51–67
	Rear Oil Seal Retainer	71–106⑤
	Spark Plug	⑦
	Thermostat Mounting Bolts	15–22
	Throttle Body & Adapter Assembly	71–106⑤
	Timing Chain Guides	71-106⑤
	Timing Chain Tensioner Bolts	15–22
	Torque Converter Nuts	22–25
	Water Pump Mounting Bolts	15–22
	Water Pump Pulley Bolts	15–22

① — Refer to "Cylinder Head, Replace."
② — Tighten an additional 85–95.°
③ — On 1997–98 models, torque nuts in three steps: First step, torque to 15–18 ft. lbs.; second step, torque to 30–33 ft. lbs; last step tighten an additional 90–120.° On 1999–2000 models, torque to 30–33 ft. lbs, then tighten an additional 90–120.°
④ — Tighten in four steps, first to 66 ft. lbs., second loosen one full turn, third tighten to 35–39 ft. lbs and fourth tighten an additional 90.°
⑤ — Inch lbs.
⑥ — 1997–98 models, torque bolts to 15–22 ft. lbs.; 1999–2000 models, torque bolts 1 through 7 to 15–22 ft. lbs, torque bolts 6 through 15 to 29–40 ft. lbs.
⑦ — 1997–98 models, torque to 7–15 ft. lbs.; 1999–2000 models, torque to 15 ft. lbs.

Rear Axle & Suspension

NOTE: On Air Bag Equipped Models, Refer To " Air Bag System Precautions" Located In The Front Of This Manual For System Disarming & Arming Procedures.

NOTE: Refer To "Computer Relearn Procedures " Located In The Front Of This Manual For Computer Relearn Procedures.

INDEX

PRECAUTIONS

AIR BAG SYSTEMS

Refer to "Air Bag System Precautions" in the front of this manual for system disarming and arming procedures.

AIR SUSPENSION PRESSURE RELIEF

Before servicing any air suspension components, disconnect power to system by turning air suspension switch OFF or by disconnecting battery ground cable.

Do not remove an air spring under any circumstances when there is pressure in the air spring. Do not remove any component supporting an air spring without either exhausting the air or providing support for air spring.

BATTERY GROUND CABLE

Prior to service, disconnect battery ground cable and isolate as required.

DESCRIPTION

CROWN VICTORIA & GRAND MARQUIS

The gear set, **Fig. 1,** consist of a ring gear and an overhung drive pinion which is supported by two opposed tapered roller bearings. Pinion bearing preload is maintained by a collapsible spacer on the pinion shaft and adjusted by the pinion nut. The differential case is a one piece design with two openings to allow assembly of internal components and lubricant flow. The pinion shaft is retained with a threaded bolt assembled to the case. The differential case is mounted in the carrier between two opposed tapered roller bearings. The bearings are retained in the carrier by removable bearing caps. Differential bearing preload and ring gear backlash are adjusted by the use of shims located between the differential bearing cups and the carrier housing. Axle shafts are held in the housing by C-locks positioned in a slot on the axle shaft splined end, **Fig. 2.**

COUGAR & THUNDERBIRD

This system shown in **Figs. 3 and 4,** employs constant velocity (CV) joints at both its inboard (differential) and outboard (wheel) ends for vehicle operating smoothness. The CV joints are connected by an interconnecting shaft which is splined at both ends and retained in the inboard and outboard CV joints by circlips.

The inboard CV joint stub shaft is splined and held in the differential side gear by circlip. The outboard CV joint stub shaft is pressed into the hub and secured with a free-spinning locknut. The CV joints are lube-for-life with a special CV joint grease and require no periodic lubrication. The CV boots should be periodically inspected and replaced immediately when damage or grease leakage is evident.

Halfshaft removal from the differential is accomplished by applying a load to the back face of the inboard CV joint assembly to overcome the circlip. The outboard joint end must be pressed from the hub.

The inboard tripod CV joints can be disassembled and serviced. Other then the CV boot, the outboard CV joint is serviced only as an assembly with the shaft.

REAR AXLE

REPLACE

CROWN VICTORIA & GRAND MARQUIS

1. Turn air suspension switch to Off position.
2. Raise and support vehicle and position safety stands below rear frame crossmember.
3. Mark driveshaft flange and pinion flange for correct alignment during installation. Remove four driveshaft retainer bolts and disconnect driveshaft.
4. Remove rear wheels, rear disc brake calipers and brake discs, then wire the caliper out of the way.
5. Remove rear disc rotor and parking brake rear cable and conduit from the parking brake cable equalizer. Reroute parking brake rear cable and conduit out of the way.
6. Remove anti-lock brake sensors Reroute anti-lock brake sensor wiring.
7. Remove rear stabilizer bar from rear stabilizer bar link and bushing.
8. Remove rear stabilizer bar bracket bolts, rear stabilizer bar brackets and the rear stabilizer bar.
9. If equipped with rear air springs, remove height sensor.
10. **On 1998–2000 models,** take care not to damage threads on the bellcrank stud and separate the Watts linkage from the rear axle housing. Remove retainer nut from the bellcrank stud.
11. **On all models,** use additional support straps to secure the rear axle to the jack and support rear axle housing with a suitable jack.

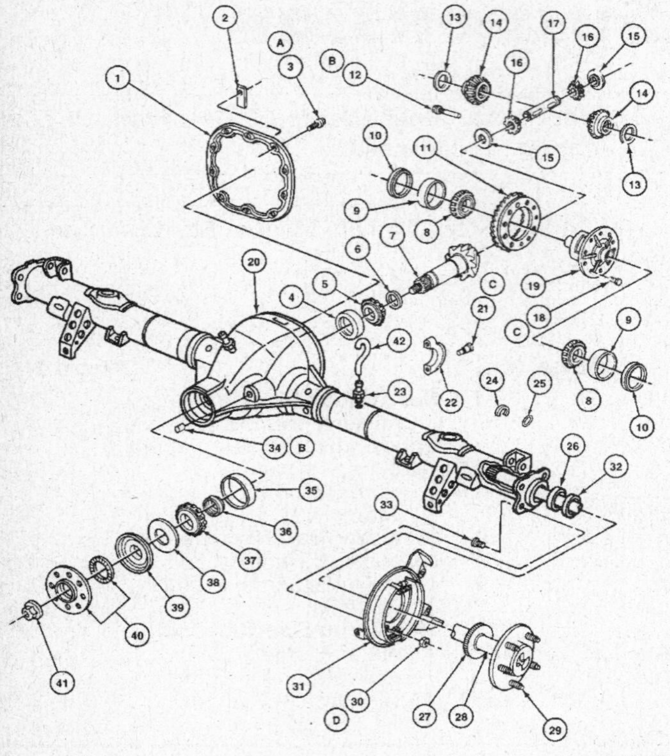

FM3039800316010X

Fig. 1 Exploded view of rear axle (Part 1 of 2). Crown Victoria & Grand Marquis

Item	Description
1	Axle Housing Cover
2	Identification Tag
3	Axle Housing Cover Bolt
4	Rear Axle Pinion Bearing Cup
5	Differential Pinion Bearing (Rear)
6	Drive Pinion Bearing Adjustment Shim
7	Drive Pinion (Part of 4209)
8	Differential Bearing (RH)
9	Differential Bearing Cup
10	Differential Bearing Shim
11	Ring Gear (Part of 4209)
12	Differential Pinion Shaft Lock Pin
13	Differential Side Gear Thrust Washer
14	Differential Side Gear
15	Differential Pinion Thrust Washer
16	Differential Pinion Gear
17	Differential Pinion Shaft
18	Rear Axle Differential Gear Case Bolt
19	Differential Case
20	Rear Axle Housing
21	Bolt
22	Differential Bearing Cap (Part of 4010)
23	Rear Axle Housing Vent
24	U-Washer

Item	Description
25	Rear Axle Shaft O-Ring
26	Rear Wheel Bearing
27	Rear Brake Anti-Lock Sensor Indicator
28	Axle Shaft
29	Lug Bolt
30	Nut
31	Rear Wheel Disc Brake Adapter
32	Inner Wheel Bearing Oil Seal
33	Bolt
34	Fill Plug
35	Differential Drive Pinion Bearing Cup
36	Differential Drive Pinion Collapsible Spacer
37	Differential Pinion Bearing (Front)
38	Rear Axle Drive Pinion Shaft Oil Slinger
39	Rear Axle Drive Pinion Seal
40	Rear Axle Universal Joint Flange
41	Drive Pinion Nut
42	Formed Vent Hose
A	Tighten to 38-52 N·m (28-38 Lb-Ft)
B	Tighten to 20-40 N·m (15-30 Lb-Ft)
C	Tighten to 95-115 N·m (70-84 Lb-Ft)
D	Tighten to 27-40 N·m (20-30 Lb-Ft)

FM3039800316020X

Fig. 1 Exploded view of rear axle (Part 2 of 2). Crown Victoria & Grand Marquis

12. Remove shock absorber lower retainer nuts and shock absorbers from retainer brackets.
13. Remove lower control arm retainer and upper control arm retainer nuts and bolts.
14. Unseat air springs and lower rear axle from vehicle.
15. Reverse procedure to install. Tighten to specifications.

COUGAR & THUNDERBIRD

1. Remove right hand wheel cover, then loosen lug nuts.
2. Raise vehicle on a frame contact type hoist.
3. Remove wheel and tire assembly.
4. Remove right and left hand brake sensors.
5. Remove rear suspension arm and bushing bolt. Wire upper suspension arm to top of rear shock absorber so it does not interfere with or damage CV joint boot when halfshaft is removed.
6. Using a paint marker, mark position of rear suspension arm and bushing in relation to rear wheel knuckle with bushings in relaxed position.
7. Install Front Hub Remover/Replacer tool Nos. T81P-1104-C with Metric Hub Remover Adapters T83P-1104-BH on Hub Adapter T86P-1104-A1, or equivalents, to righthand wheel studs. Turn wrench counterclockwise until halfshafts is free in rear hub.
8. Remove rear suspension arm and bushing retaining bolts.
9. Remove rear wheel knuckle assembly from driveshaft and joint assembly.

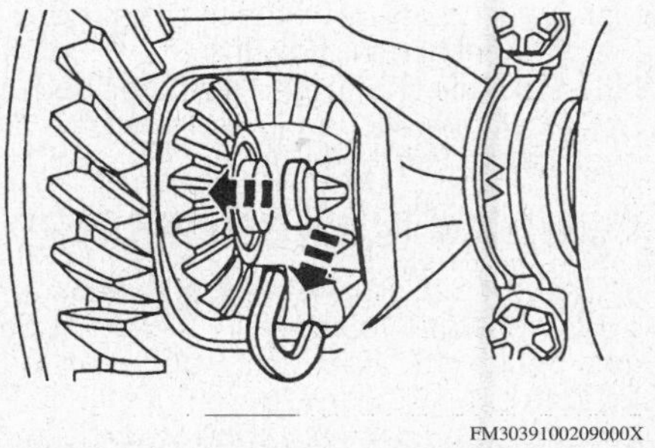

FM3039100209000X

Fig. 2 Axle shaft C-lock. Crown Victoria & Grand Marquis

10. Carefully rest halfshaft on rear suspension arm and bushing and wire rear wheel knuckle to top of rear shock absorber.
11. Inboard CV joint stud shaft pilot bearing housing seal must be replaced whenever halfshaft is removed. Remove righthand halfshaft from rear axle housing using CV Joint Remover tool No. T89P-3514-A, or equivalent.
12. Remove halfshaft from vehicle. Install Differential Plug T89P-4850-B, or equivalent, into rear axle housing to prevent lubricant loss.
13. Mark driveshaft centering socket yoke in relation to rear axle universal joint flange. Remove driveshaft retaining bolts.
14. Slide driveshaft forward and rest on driveshaft center bridge support reinforcement.
15. With transmission jack supporting rear axle housing, remove axle differential rear insulator to crossmember retaining nuts.
16. Remove rear axle differential rear insulator from axle housing cover.
17. Remove axle front retaining bolts, nuts, bushings and washers.
18. **Do not damage CV joint boot.** Inboard CV joint stub shaft pilot bearing housing seal must be replaced whenever a halfshaft (CV joint) has been removed from rear axle housing.
19. Remove lefthand halfshaft (inboard CV joint) from rear axle housing using CV Joint Remover tool No. T89P-3514-A, or equivalent. Push tool inward (toward rear axle housing).
20. Partially lower rear axle housing. While lowering rear axle housing, move to right and disengage rear axle housing from lefthand inboard CV joint stub shaft.
21. Install Differential Plug tool No. T89P-4850-B, or equivalent, in lefthand side of rear axle housing and lower rear axle housing from vehicle.
22. Reverse procedure to install, noting the following:
    a. **New hub retainer nut, CV joint stub shaft circlips and differential seals must be installed.**
    b. Tighten to specifications.

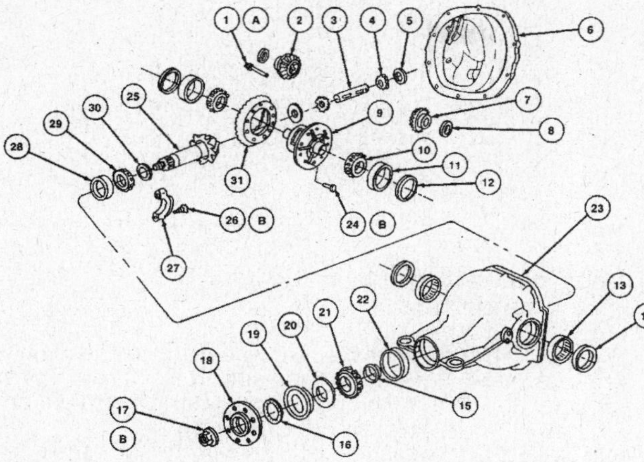

Item	Description
1	Differential Pinion Shaft Lock Pin
2	Differential Side Gear
3	Differential Pinion Shaft
4	Differential Pinion Gear
5	Differential Pinion Thrust Washer
6	Axle Housing Cover
7	Differential Side Gear
8	Differential Side Gear Thrust Washer
9	Differential Case
10	Differential Bearing
11	Differential Bearing Cup
12	Differential Bearing Shim
13	Pilot Bearing
14	Inboard Cv Joint Stub Shaft Pilot Bearing Housing Seal
15	Differential Drive Pinion Collapsible Spacer

Item	Description
16	Drive Pinion Oil Seal Deflector
17	Drive Pinion Nut
18	Rear Axle Universal Joint Flange
19	Rear Axle Drive Pinion Seal
20	Rear Axle Drive Pinion Shaft Oil Slinger
21	Differential Pinion Bearing , Front
22	Differential Drive Pinion Bearing Cup
23	Rear Axle Housing
24	Rear Axle Differential Gear Case Bolt
25	Pinion Gear (Part of 4209)
26	Bolt
27	Differential Bearing Cap (Part of 40 10)
28	Rear Axle Pinion Bearing Cup

FM3039700317010X

Fig. 3 Exploded view of rear axle assembly (Part 1 of 2). Cougar & Thunderbird

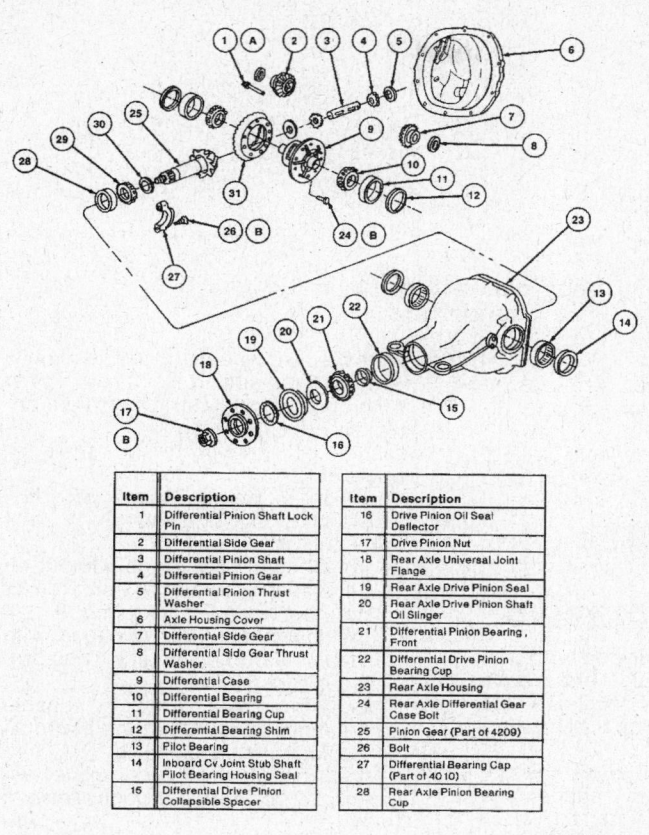

Item	Description
29	Differential Pinion Bearing , Rear
30	Drive Pinion Bearing Adjustment Shim

Item	Description
31	Ring Gear (Part of 4209)
A	Tighten to 20-41 N-m (15-30 Lb-Ft)
B	Tighten to 95-115 N-m (70-84 Lb-Ft)

FM3039700317020X

Fig. 3 Exploded view of rear axle assembly (Part 2 of 2). Cougar & Thunderbird

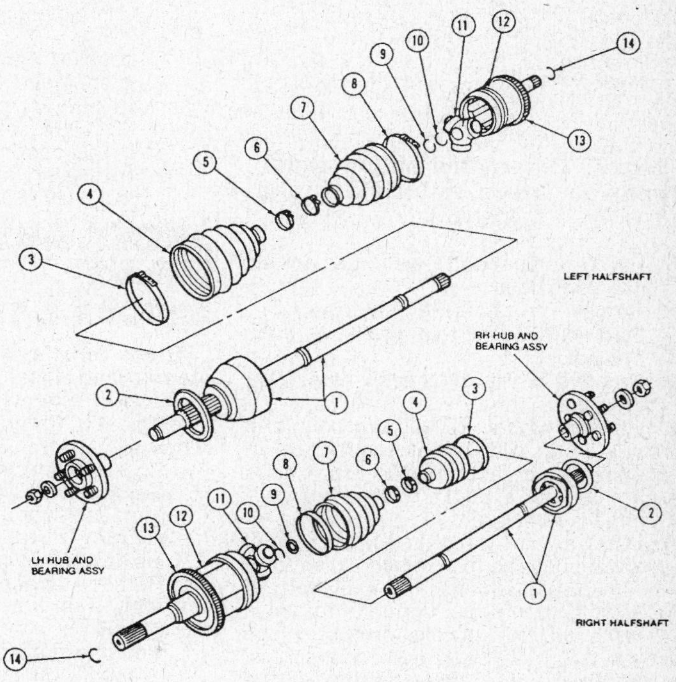

ITEM	DESCRIPTION
1.	OUTBOARD CV JOINT/INTERCONNECTING SHAFT ASSY
2.	DUST SEAL
3.	BOOT CLAMP (LARGE OUTBOARD)
4.	BOOT (OUTBOARD)
5.	BOOT CLAMP (SMALL OUTBOARD)
6.	BOOT CLAMP (SMALL INBOARD)
7.	BOOT (INBOARD)
8.	BOOT CLAMP (LARGE INBOARD)
9.	STOP RING
10.	CIRCLIP
11.	TRIPOD ASSY
12.	INBOARD JOINT OUTER RACE
13.	SENSOR RING (ANTI-SKID)
14.	CIRCLIP

FM3039100210000X

Fig. 4 Rear wheel drive halfshaft system. Cougar & Thunderbird

REAR AXLE SHAFT

REPLACE

CROWN VICTORIA & GRAND MARQUIS

Removal

1. Turn air suspension switch OFF.
2. Raise and support vehicle. Remove rear wheel and tire assembly.
3. Remove disc brake calipers and rotors and rear anti-lock brake sensor.
4. Drain rear axle fluid into suitable container, by removing cover.
5. Remove differential pinion shaft lock bolt and differential pinion shaft. **Fig. 5.**
6. Push flanged end of axle shafts toward center of vehicle and remove C-lock from button end of axle shaft. **Fig. 2.**
7. Remove axle shaft from housing, use caution not to damage oil seal and ABS sensor ring.

Installation

1. Ensure O-ring is present on spline end of axle shaft.
2. Carefully slide axle shaft into axle housing. Use extreme caution to not damage bearing seal or ABS sensor ring.
3. Start splines into side gear and push firmly until button end of axle shaft can be seen in differential case.
4. Install C-lock on button end of axle shaft splines. Push shaft outboard until splines engage and the C-lock seats in counterbore of differential side gear.
5. Position differential pinion shaft through case and pinion gears, aligning hole in shaft with lock bolt hose. Apply rear axle lubricant E0AZ-19554-BA, or equivalent, to pinion shaft lock bolt. Tighten to specifications.
6. Install cover and tighten to specifications.
7. Install ABS speed sensor, rotors and calipers. Tighten to specifications.

REAR HALFSHAFT

REPLACE

COUGAR & THUNDERBIRD

Do not begin this removal procedure unless following parts are available; new hub retainer nut; new inboard CV joint stub shaft circlip and new differential oil seal. Once removed, these parts must not be reused during assembly. Their torque holding ability is diminished during removal.

1. Remove wheel cover/hub cover and hub retainer nut, then loosen wheel nuts.
2. Raise and support vehicle on a frame contact hoist.
3. Remove rear wheel and tire assembly.
4. Remove anti-lock brake sensors.
5. Pull back on parking brake release lever and at same time pull on cable. This will slacken cable so cable end can be removed from brake caliper attachment.

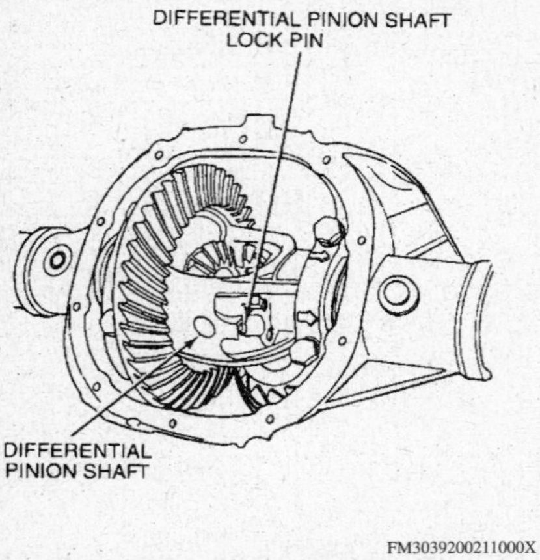

Fig. 5 Differential pinion shaft removal. Crown Victoria & Grand Marquis

6. Remove upper and lower brake caliper attaching bolts.
7. Remove caliper assembly from rotor, then wire caliper to brake junction bracket.
8. Remove brake rotor push nuts, then the rotor.
9. Remove upper control arm bolts and nuts, then wire upper control arm to upper shock absorber so that it does not damage CV joint boots when halfshaft is removed.
10. Using a paint marker, mark position of lower control arm in relation to knuckle with lower bushings in their relaxed position. When upper control arm bolt is removed from knuckle, lower bushings will return to their relaxed positions. **Failure to mark this position will result in bushing wind-up on assembly and incorrect ride height, causing misalignment and premature tire wear.**
11. Install hub remover T81P-1104-C, or equivalent, to hub studs as shown in **Fig. 6.**
12. Turn wrench counterclockwise until halfshaft is free in hub.
13. Remove lower control arm attaching bolts.
14. Remove knuckle assembly while supporting outboard CV joint and boot. Carefully rest halfshaft on lower control arm.
15. Insert CV joint removal tool No. T89P-3514-A, or equivalent, between differential housing and CV joint. Push tool outward until CV joint becomes free from differential side gear. **Extreme care must be taken to prevent damage to the differential oil seal, differential housing, sensor ring and/or CV joint and boot.**
16. Remove halfshaft from vehicle, then plug differential housing to prevent loss of lubricant.
17. Reverse procedure to install, noting the following:
    a. Install new differential oil seal and circlip on inboard CV joint.
    b. Align reference marks on lower control arm to marks on knuckle/bushing assembly.
    c. If equipped with rear disc brakes, **torque** caliper retaining bolts to 80–100 ft. lbs.
    d. If equipped with anti-lock brakes, **torque** brake sensor retaining bolts to 14–20 ft. lbs.

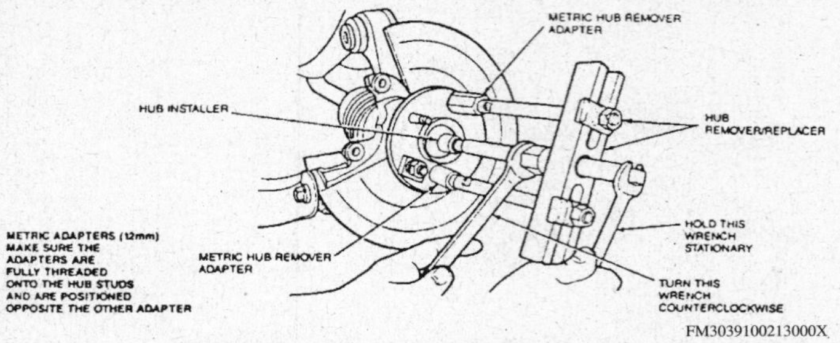

Fig. 6 Mounting hub removal tool. Cougar & Thunderbird

SHOCK ABSORBER

REPLACE

COUGAR & THUNDERBIRD

These vehicles are equipped with gas pressurized rear shock absorbers which will extend unassisted. Do not apply heat or flame to shock tube during removal.

1. Position vehicle on drive-on hoist or alignment pit, so that rear suspension arms are supported during removal.
2. Remove all upper attaching parts from inside of luggage compartment.
3. Remove attaching bolt and at lower arm, then remove shock absorber, **Fig. 7.**
4. Reverse procedure to install. Tighten to specifications.

CROWN VICTORIA & GRAND MARQUIS

1. Turn air suspension switch OFF.
2. Raise and support vehicle.
3. Release air pressure from air springs.
4. To assist in removing upper attachment on shock absorbers using a plastic dust tube, place an open end wrench on hex stamped into dust tube's metal cap. For shock absorbers with a steel dust tube, grasp tube to prevent stud rotation when loosening retaining nut.
5. Remove shock absorber retaining nut, washer and insulator assembly from stud on upper side of frame.
6. Compress shock absorber to clear hole in frame and remove inner insulator and washer from upper retaining stud.
7. Remove self-locking nut and disconnect shock absorber lower stud from mounting bracket on rear axle tube.
8. Reverse procedure to install. Tighten to specifications.

COIL SPRING

REPLACE

COUGAR & THUNDERBIRD

1. Raise and support vehicle.
2. Remove rear wheel and tire assembly.
3. Remove rear stabilizer bar link nuts at both ends of stabilizer bar. Rotate bar up and out of the way.
4. Disconnect parking brake cable at brake caliper.
5. Install three Spring Cages, tool No. 086-00031, or equivalent, to rear springs as follows:
    a. Install one spring cage without an adjuster link to inboard side or innermost bend of spring, **Fig. 8.**
    b. Install two more spring cages, with adjusters, at 120° angles to the previously installed cage.
6. Place a transmission jack or suitable stand under lower rear control arm as far outboard as possible.
7. Support rear knuckle and caliper assembly by wiring upper control arm to body.
8. Remove lower shock absorber mounting bolt and nut.
9. Mark position of toe adjustment cam to subframe for reference. Loosen both inboard pivot bolts on lower control arm. **Control arm must not be lowered until pivot bolts are loose. Do not attempt to remove plastic cap on front of pivot nut.**
10. Remove two bolts and nuts attaching lower control arm to knuckle, **Fig. 9.**
11. Lower control arm by lowering jack. Ensure spring cages properly seat on spring as control arm is dropped.
12. Remove jack, pull control arm down fully by hand and remove rear spring with cages in place.
13. Using coil spring compressor tool No. D78P-5310-A, or equivalent, compress spring and remove spring cages.
14. Remove upper and lower spring insulators from spring.
15. Reverse procedure to install, compress spring to approximately 10.5 inches overall length prior to installation.

CROWN VICTORIA & GRAND MARQUIS

1997–98

1. Raise rear of vehicle and support at frame. Support rear axle with a suitable jack.
2. Remove rear stabilizer bar.
3. Disconnect lower studs of two shock absorbers from mounting brackets on rear axle assembly.
4. Unsnap parking brake rear cable and

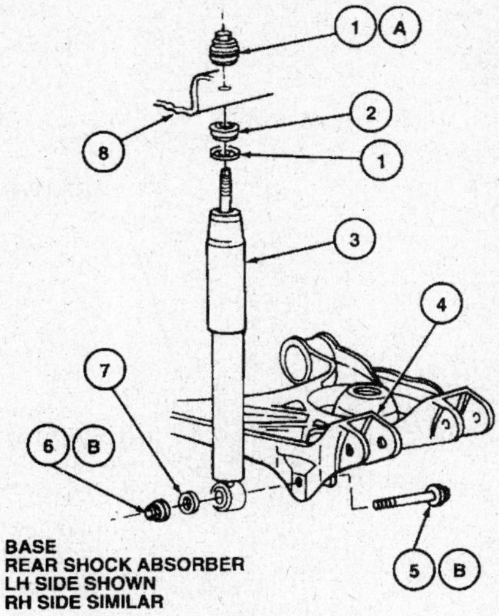

Item	Description
1	Washer (2 Req'd)
2	Insulator
3	Rear Shock Absorber
4	Rear Suspension Arm and Bushing, Lower
5	Bolt
6	Nut
7	Washer
8	Body
A	Tighten to 37-54 N·m (28-39 Lb-Ft) (All Except Shock Damping)
B	Tighten to 128-172 N·m (95-126 Lb-Ft)

FM2039100011000X

Fig. 7 Shock absorber replacement. Cougar & Thunderbird

conduit from upper arm retainer before lowering rear axle housing.

5. Lower hoist and axle housing until rear springs are released.
6. Remove rear spring and rear spring center mounting insulators from vehicle.
7. Reverse procedure to install. Install an insulator between upper seat and spring, if necessary. Tighten to specifications.

1999-2000

1. Mark rear shock absorber relative to protective sleeve with vehicle in a static, level ground position (curb height).
2. Raise and support vehicle on a hoist.
3. Remove both wheel and tire assemblies.
4. Remove nuts and bushings, then rotate stabilizer bar off links.
5. Support rear axle.
6. All vehicles are equipped with gas pressurized shock absorbers which will extend unassisted. Do not apply heat or flame to the shock absorbers during removal or component servicing. Failure to follow these instructions can result in personal injury. Remove nuts and disconnect the shock absorbers from axle. Discard the nuts.
7. Carefully lower axle and remove springs and spring insulators.
8. Reverse procedure to install. Tighten bolts to specifications.

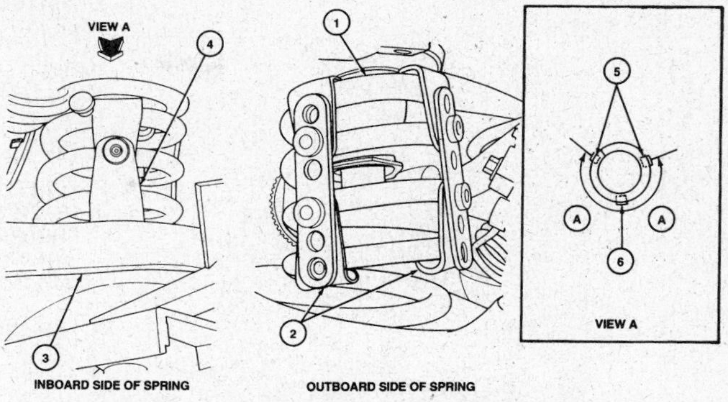

Item	Description
1	Rear Spring
2	Rotunda Spring Cages (With Adjusters)
3	Rear Suspension Arm and Bushing

Item	Description
4	Rotunda Spring Cages (Without Adjusters)
5	Spring Cages
6	Inboard Side of Spring
A	Approximately 120 Degrees

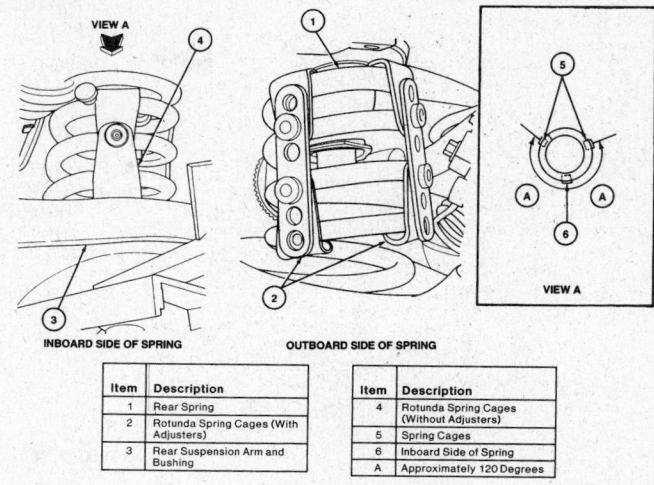

FM2039100013000X

Fig. 8 Mounting spring cages. Cougar & Thunderbird

AIR SPRING

REPLACE

CROWN VICTORIA & GRAND MARQUIS

1997-98

1. Turn the air suspension switch OFF, then raise and support vehicle.
2. Remove heat shield as required, then rear air spring retainer.
3. Remove air spring solenoid valve.
4. Remove spring piston to axle spring seat as follows:
   a. Insert Air Spring Remover T90P-5310-A, or equivalent, between axle tube and spring seat on forward side of axle.
   b. Position tool so that its flat end rests on air spring piston knob. Push downward, forcing piston and retainer clip off axle spring seat.
5. Remove spring.
6. Reverse procedure to install.

1999-2000

1. Turn the air suspension switch OFF, then raise and support vehicle.
2. Remove rear air spring retainer.
3. Lift bottom of air spring off rear axle.
4. Disconnect electrical connector. Push on red air line retaining ring and disconnect air line. Remove air spring.
5. Reverse procedure to install.

CONTROL ARM

REPLACE

COUGAR & THUNDERBIRD

Lower Arm

1. Remove coil spring as described in "Coil Spring, Replace."
2. **To prevent damage, do not attempt to remove plastic cap on front pivot nut.** Remove inner control arm pivot bolts and nuts, then the arm assembly.
3. Remove suspension compensator link from suspension arm and bushing.
4. Reverse procedure to install. Tighten to specifications.

Upper Arm

1. Raise and support vehicle.
2. Remove rear wheel and tire assembly.
3. Support knuckle and hub assembly so that it cannot swing outward.
4. Remove inner and outer pivot bolts and nuts at upper control arm, then the upper control arm.
5. Reverse procedure to install, noting that inner pivot bolt used for camber adjustment has a specially shaped washer under bolt head. Ensure fasteners are used in correct locations. Set camber adjustment as described in "Wheel Alignment." Tighten to specifications.

CROWN VICTORIA & GRAND MARQUIS

Lower Arm

1. Turn air suspension switch OFF.
2. Mark rear suspension shock tube relative to protective sleeve with vehicle on level ground.
3. Raise and support vehicle.
4. Remove wheel and tire assembly.
5. Release air pressure from rear air springs.
6. Support rear axle assembly.
7. Remove and discard rear suspension lower arm pivot bolt and nut from axle bracket.
8. Remove and discard rear suspension lower arm pivot bolt and nut from the frame bracket. Remove rear suspension lower arm.
9. Reverse procedure to install, noting the following:
   a. The rear suspension lower arm bolts must be tightened with vehicle

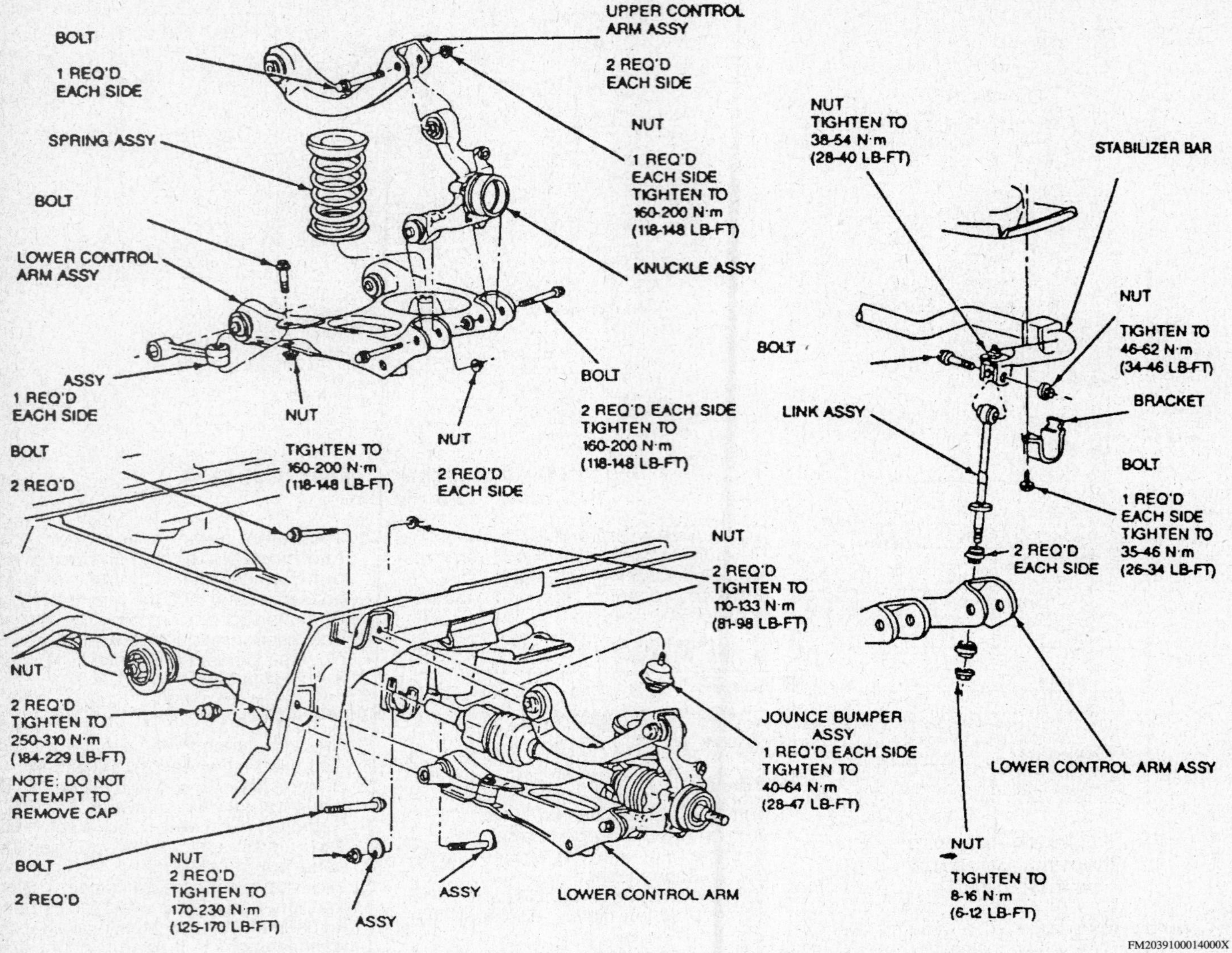

Fig. 9 Exploded view of rear suspension. Cougar & Thunderbird

at curb height.

b. The rear suspension lower arms are interchangeable from side to side with "OUTBOARD" stamped on the side of the arm for positioning during installation.
c. Position rear suspension lower arm to the frame bracket and install a new pivot bolt and nut. Insert the bolt so the nut faces inboard. Do not tighten at this time.
d. Raise axle assembly to the position that compresses the shock absorber to the previously established alignment mark (curb height).
e. Tighten rear suspension lower arm to the frame bracket pivot bolt to specifications.

Upper Arm

1. Turn air suspension switch OFF.
2. Mark rear suspension shock absorber relative to protective sleeve with vehicle in a static, level ground position (curb height).
3. Raise and support vehicle.
4. Support rear axle assembly.
5. Release air pressure from air springs.
6. Do not use excessive force when removing the pivot bolt and flag nut on right upper suspension arm to axle bracket. Damage to the brake line can occur. Remove and discard rear suspension upper arm pivot bolt and nut from axle bracket.
7. Remove and discard rear suspension upper arm pivot bolt and nut from the frame bracket.
8. Remove rear suspension upper arm.
9. Reverse procedure to install, noting the following:
   a. The rear suspension upper arm bolts must be tightened with the vehicle at curb height.
   b. The rear suspension upper arms are interchangeable from side to side with "FRONT" and "OUTBOARD" stamped on the side of the arms for positioning during installation.
   c. Position rear suspension upper arm to the frame bracket and install a new pivot bolt and nut. Insert the bolt so the nut faces inboard. Do not tighten at this time.
   d. Raise axle assembly to position that compresses the shock absorber to the previously established alignment mark (curb height).
   e. Tighten bolts to specifications.

Lateral Arm & Watts Link Pivot Assembly

1. Turn air suspension switch OFF.
2. Mark rear suspension shock absorber relative to protective sleeve with vehicle in a static, level ground position (curb height).
3. Raise and support vehicle.
4. Support rear axle.
5. Release air pressure from air springs.
6. Disconnect height sensor from mounting bracket.
7. Remove and discard both lateral arm assembly pivot bolts and nuts.
8. The Watts link pivot stud is coated with a dry adhesive and must be replaced whenever pivot nut or stud is loosened

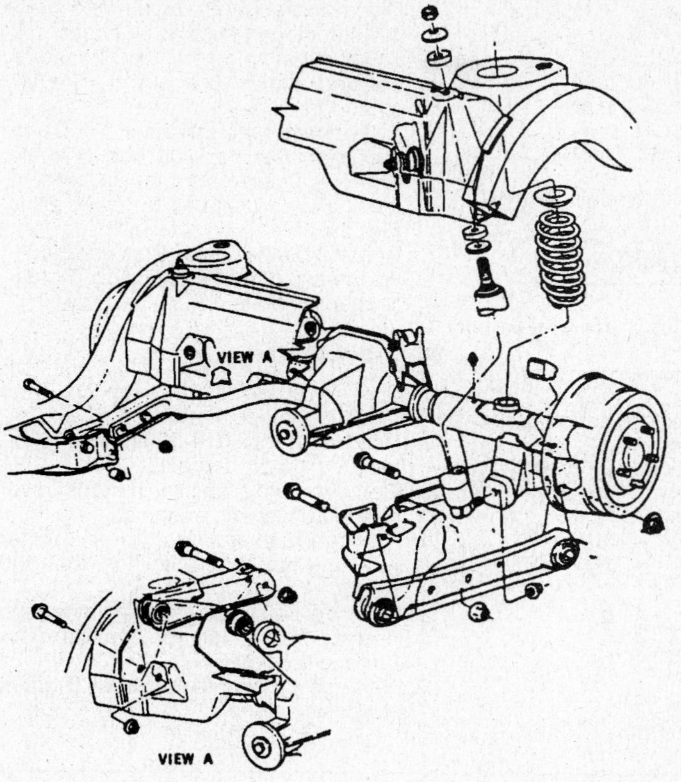

FM2039100012000X

Fig. 10 Exploded view of rear suspension. 1997 Crown Victoria & Grand Marquis

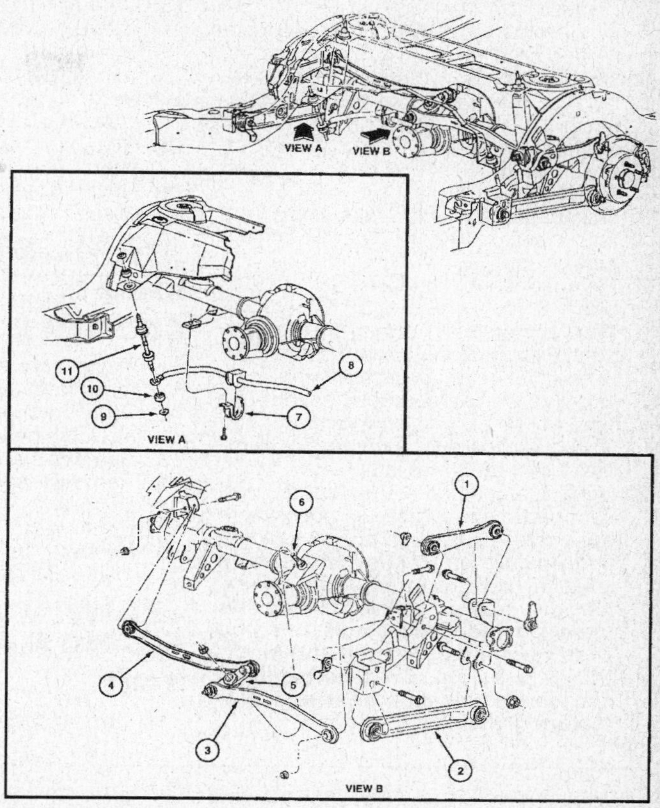

FM2039800059010X

Fig. 11 Exploded view of rear suspension (Part 1 of 2). 1998–2000 Crown Victoria & Grand Marquis

Item	Description
1	Rear Suspension Upper Arm
2	Rear Suspension Lower Arm
3	Lateral Arm, LH (Part of 4264)
4	Lateral Arm, RH (Part of 4264)
5	Watts Link Pivot (Part of 4264)

Item	Description
6	Watts Link Pivot Stud
7	Stabilizer Bar Bracket
8	Stabilizer Bar and Isolator Assy
9	Stabilizer Bar Link Retaining Nut
10	Stabilizer Bar Bushing
11	Stabilizer Bar Link

FM2039800059020X

Fig. 11 Exploded view of rear suspension (Part 2 of 2). 1998–2000 Crown Victoria & Grand Marquis

or removed with a new Watts link pivot nut and stud service kit.

9. If the Watts link pivot stud on axle assembly loosens while removing pivot nut, continue to loosen pivot stud until you can insert an open end wrench to hold pivot stud. While holding pivot stud, remove & discard pivot nut.
10. Lower axle until Watts link is free of pivot stud. Remove lateral arm assembly.
11. Remove and discard Watts link pivot stud.
12. Reverse procedure to install, noting the following:
    a. Install a new Watts link pivot stud.
    b. The rear suspension lateral arm pivot bolts and Watts link pivot nut must be tightened with vehicle at curb height.
    c. Install lateral arm assembly on pivot stud making sure flange of right arm faces front of vehicle.
    d. Raise axle until lateral arm assembly aligns with frame brackets and install new pivot bolts and nuts. Do not tighten at this time.
    e. Raise axle assembly to position that compresses shock absorber to previously established alignment mark (curb height). Tighten bolts to specification.

KNUCKLE

REPLACE

COUGAR & THUNDERBIRD

Do not begin this procedure unless a new hub retainer nut is available. Once removed, this part cannot be reused during assembly. Its torque holding and/or retention capability is greatly diminished during removal.

1. Remove wheel cover/hub cover from wheel and tire assembly, then loosen wheel nuts.
2. Remove and discard hub nut and washer.
3. Raise and support vehicle, then remove wheel and tire assembly.
4. Using needle nose pliers, slide parking brake cable adjustment clip downward until front parking brake cable and conduit is free.
5. **On models with disc brakes,** proceed as follows:
    a. Remove parking brake cable from caliper.
    b. Remove upper and lower caliper attaching bolts and remove caliper

assembly from rotor.
c. Carefully wire caliper to brake junction bracket.
6. **On all models,** with push on nuts removed, remove brake rotor or drum assembly.
7. Remove three bolts retaining splash shield to knuckle and remove splash shield.
8. Disconnect parking brake cable and disconnect brake line from wheel cylinder.
9. Remove upper control arm nut and bolt.
10. Wire upper control arm to body to prevent damage to CV boots when knuckle and hub assembly is removed.
11. Install hub remover/replacer tool No. T81P-1104-C, or equivalent, to hub studs. Turn wrench counterclockwise until halfshaft is free in hub.
12. Using a paint marker, mark position of control arm in relation to knuckle with bushings in a relaxed position. When upper control arm bolt is removed from knuckle, lower arm bushings will return to a relaxed position. **Failure to mark position will cause bushing wind up upon assembly and incorrect ride height. These conditions can cause misalignment and premature tire wear.**
13. Note approximate angle of knuckle in relaxed position by measuring distance from upper bushing to any convenient point on vehicle body.
14. Remove lower control arm to knuckle attaching bolts and nuts.
15. Remove knuckle assembly from halfshaft.
16. Reverse procedure to install. Tighten to specifications.

STABILIZER BAR

REPLACE

COUGAR & THUNDERBIRD

1. Raise and support vehicle, then remove both rear wheels.
2. Remove both stabilizer bar link upper retaining bolts and nuts.
3. Remove stabilizer bar bracket bolts.
4. Remove rear muffler hanger retaining nuts.
5. Remove stabilizer bar from vehicle.
6. Reverse procedure to install. Tighten to specifications.

CROWN VICTORIA & GRAND MARQUIS

1997

1. Turn air suspension switch Off.
2. Raise and support vehicle and place jackstands under frame side rails.
3. Lower hoist and rear axle assembly housing until shock absorbers are fully extended.
4. Disconnect rear stabilizer bars from rear stabilizer bar link and bushing. Remove bolts, nuts and spacers attaching stabilizer bar to lower arms, **Fig. 10.**
5. Remove stabilizer bar from vehicle.
6. Reverse procedure to install. Tighten to specifications.

1998–2000

1. Turn air suspension switch Off, then raise and support vehicle.
2. Use Hi-Lift Jack 014-00942, or equivalent, to support rear axle.
3. Remove both stabilizer bar link lower retaining nuts and bushings, **Fig. 11.**
4. Remove both stabilizer bar link upper retaining nuts and bushings, then the links.
5. Remove both stabilizer bar mounting bracket bolts, then remove stabilizer bar and brackets.
6. Reverse procedure to install. Tighten to specifications.

TIGHTENING SPECIFICATIONS

COUGAR & THUNDERBIRD

Year	Component	Torque/ Ft. Lbs.
1997	ABS Sensor Bolt	14–20
	Axle Hub Nut	188–254
	Caliper Locating Pins, Rear Disc Brakes	73–97
	Driveshaft Companion Flange Bolts	70–95
	Lower Control Arm To Knuckle	84–112
	Lower Control Arm To Subframe (Front)	166–202
	Lower Control Arm To Subframe (Rear)	142–191
	Lower Control Arm To Toe Compensator Link Nut	110–148
	Pinion Nut	140
	Shock Absorber To Lower Control Arm	95–126
	Shock Absorber Upper Mount	28–39
	Stabilizer Bar Link To Lower Control Arm	96–108①
	Stabilizer Bar Bracket To Sub Frame Bolt	26–34
	Stabilizer Link To Stabilizer Bar	34–46
	Upper Control Arm To Knuckle	110–148
	Upper Control Arm To Subframe	51–67
	Wheel Lug Nut	85–104

① — Inch lbs.

CROWN VICTORIA & GRAND MARQUIS

Year	Component	Torque/ Ft. Lbs.
1997–2000	Caliper Locating Pin Retainer	21–26
	Driveshaft Flange Bolts	70–95
	Height Sensor Mounting Bracket To Lateral Arm Nut	9–12
	Lateral Arm To Frame Bracket Bolt	65–88
	Lateral Arm To Watts Link Pivot Nut	60–77
	Lower Arm To Axle & Frame	95–127
	Lower Arm To Frame	120–150
	Pinion Shaft Lock Bolt	15–29
	Rear Cover Bolts	25–34
	Shock Absorber To Axle Bracket	57–75
	Shock Absorber Upper Mount Nut	26–34
	Stabilizer Bar Bracket Bolt To Axle	16–21
	Stabilizer Link To Stabilizer Bar Nuts	19
	Stabilizer Link Nut To Stabilizer Bar	13–16
	Upper Arm To Axle	65–88
	Upper Arm To Frame	95–127
	Watts Link Pivot Nut	158–212
	Watts Link Pivot Stud	189–211
	Wheel Lug Nuts	80–106

Front Suspension & Steering

NOTE: On Air Bag Equipped Models, Refer To " Air Bag System Precautions" Located In The Front Of This Manual For System Disarming & Arming Procedures.

NOTE: Refer To "Computer Relearn Procedures " Located In The Front Of This Manual For Computer Relearn Procedures.

INDEX

PRECAUTIONS

AIR BAG SYSTEMS

Refer to "Air Bag System Precautions" in the front of this manual for system disarming and arming procedures.

BATTERY GROUND CABLE

Prior to service, disconnect battery ground cable and isolate as required.

WHEEL BEARING

ADJUST

These models are equipped with sealed bearing units which do not require adjustment or maintenance. If the bearing is found to be defective, then the hub and bearing must be replaced as an assembly.

WHEEL BEARING

REPLACE

1. Raise and support front of vehicle, then remove wheel and tire assembly.
2. Remove grease cap from hub.
3. Remove disc brake caliper with brake hose attached. Suspend caliper from suspension with wire. Do not allow caliper to hang from brake hose.
4. Remove brake rotor.
5. Remove hub nut, then remove hub and bearing assembly, **Fig. 1.** If difficulty is encountered in hub removal, use hub removal tool No. T81P-1104-C, or equivalent.

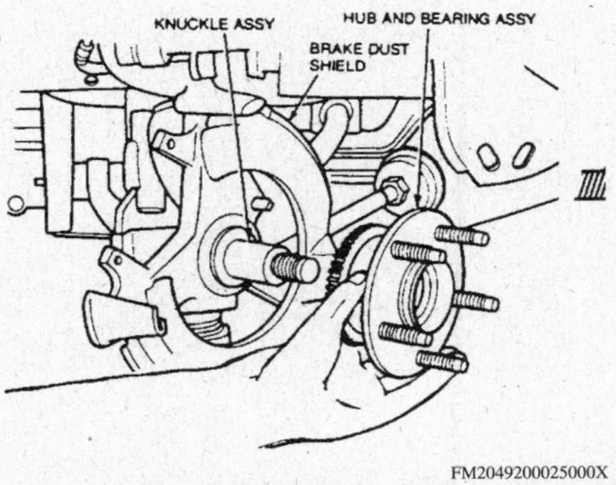

Fig. 1 Hub & wheel bearing assembly

6. Reverse procedure to install. Use a new hub nut and tighten to specifications.

BALL JOINT INSPECTION

LOWER

1. Raise and support vehicle until wheel is clear of floor.
2. Support front suspension lower arm so there is no load on front suspension lower arm ball joint.
3. Try to rock wheel top to bottom, if any wobble is felt, look for movement between front suspension lower arm and front wheel spindle.
4. If front suspension lower arm ball joint appears tight, check front wheel bearing. Any movement present indicates front suspension lower arm ball joint wear.

UPPER

1. Raise and support vehicle.
2. Support front suspension lower arm with jackstands so there is no load on upper ball joint.
3. Rock wheel top to bottom. While wheel is being moved, observe the upper ball joint at front wheel spindle. Any movement between upper ball joint and front wheel spindle indicates upper ball joint wear.

BALL JOINT

REPLACE

COUGAR & THUNDERBIRD

Lower Ball

1. Remove lower control arm as described under "Control Arm, Replace."
2. Remove and discard ball joint boot seal, then position lower control arm in a vise.
3. Press ball joint from lower control arm using removal tools No. D89P-3010-A, D84P-3395-A4 and T74P-4635-C, or equivalent, **Fig. 2.**
4. Reverse procedure to install. Do not remove protective cover from ball joint until after it has been installed. Press ball joint into lower control arm until fully seated. After installing lower control arm, check and adjust wheel alignment as necessary. Tighten to specifications.

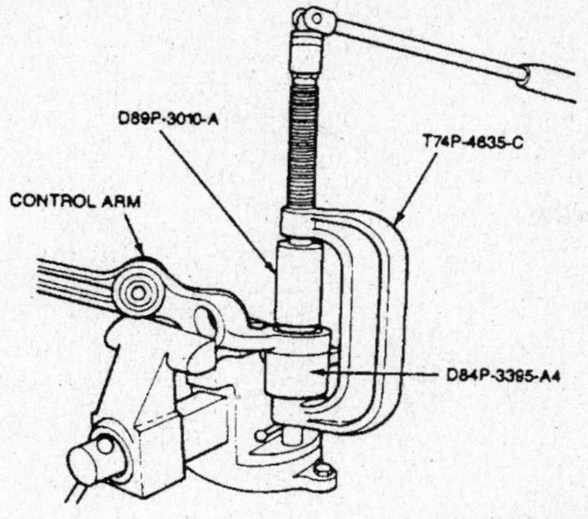

Fig. 2 Lower ball joint replacement. Cougar & Thunderbird

Upper

The upper ball joint and upper control arm must be replaced as an assembly. Refer to "Control Arm, Replace."

CROWN VICTORIA & GRAND MARQUIS

Lower

1. Raise and support vehicle.
2. Remove front wheel spindle as outlined.
3. Remove and discard joint boot seal.
4. Press out arm bushing joint using U-Joint tool Nos. T74P-4635-C, Ball Joint Remover D89P-3010-A, or equivalent, and Receiving Cup D84P-3395-A4, or equivalent, **Fig. 3.**
5. Reverse procedure to install, noting the following:
   a. When installing a new front suspension arm bushing joint, the protective cover must be left in place during installation to protect ball joint seal. It may be necessary to cut off end of the cover to allow it to pass through receiving cup.
   b. Install ball joint with Ball Joint Replacer D89P-3010-B, Receiving Cup tool D84P-3395-A4 and U-joint Tool T74P-4635-C, or equivalents, **Fig. 4.**
   c. Inspect wheel alignment.

Upper

1. Raise and support front of vehicle. Remove wheel assembly.
2. Position jack below lower control arm at ball joint.
3. Remove retaining nut and punch bolt from upper ball joint stud.
4. Mark position of alignment cams.
5. Remove ball joint retaining nuts.
6. Remove ball joint and spread slot with pry bar to separate ball joint stud from spindle.
7. Reverse procedure to install. Tighten to specifications.

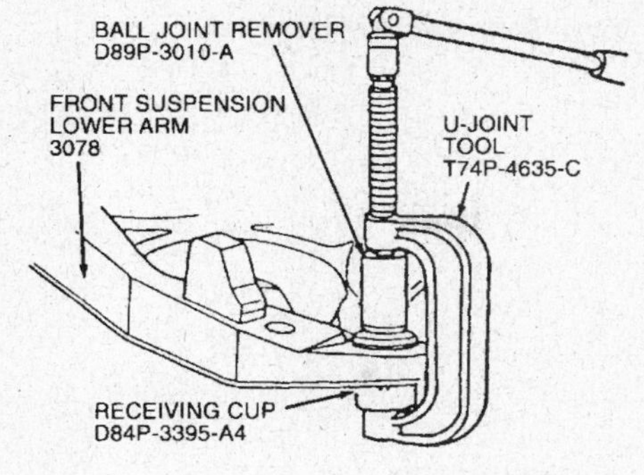

Fig. 3 Lower ball joint removal. Crown Victoria & Grand Marquis

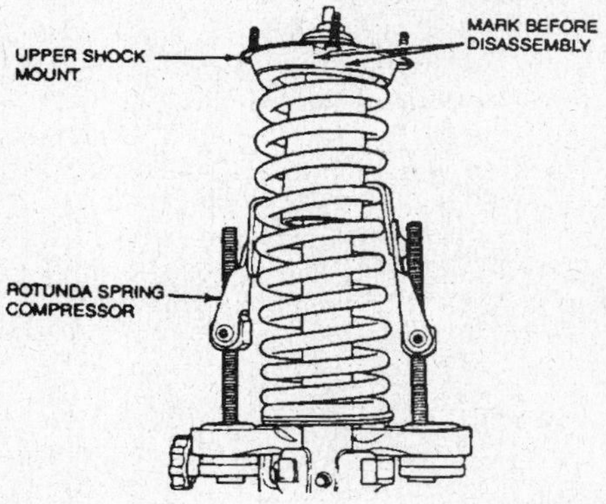

Fig. 5 Upper mount to spring alignment mark placement. Cougar & Thunderbird

COIL SPRING

REPLACE

COUGAR & THUNDERBIRD

The upper shock mount cannot be rotated when the shock and spring are assembled. Mark position of upper mount to coil spring with chalk, paint or grease pencil, prior to disassembly, Fig. 5. If upper mount is not properly positioned during assembly it will not install in vehicle. If installing new coil spring or upper mount transfer reference marks from removed parts to new parts.

1. Remove coil spring and shock strut assembly from vehicle as described under "Strut, Replace."
2. Position shock assembly in spring compressor tool No. 086-00029, or equivalent.
3. Compress spring and remove upper mount.
4. Release spring compressor to remove coil spring.
5. Position shock and coil assembly in spring compressor tool No. 086-00029, or equivalent, and compress spring to install upper mount.
6. Install upper mount aligning reference marks.
7. Install nut and tighten to specification.
8. Release spring compressor, ensuring coil spring is properly seated.
9. Install coil spring and shock strut assembly from vehicle as described under "Strut, Replace."
10. Tighten to specifications.

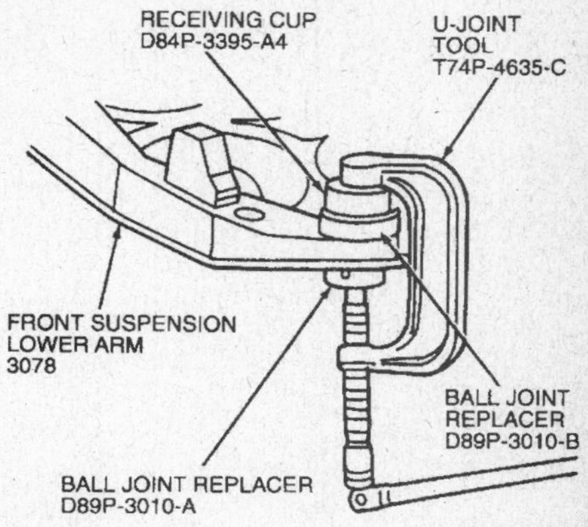

Fig. 4 Lower ball joint installation. Crown Victoria & Grand Marquis

CROWN VICTORIA & GRAND MARQUIS

1. Raise and support vehicle. Remove wheel assembly.
2. Remove two bolts retaining front shock absorber to front suspension lower arm.
3. Remove upper nut, retainer and grommet from front shock absorber, then front shock absorber.
4. **On 1997–98 models,** remove steering center link from pitman arm, then support vehicle with safety stands under jacking pads and lower hoist.
5. **On all models,** using Coil Spring Compressor D78P-5310-A, or equivalent, install one plate with pivot ball seat facing downward into coils of front coil spring. Rotate plate so it is flush with upper surface of front suspension lower arm.
6. Install other plate with pivot ball seat facing upward into coils of front coil spring. Insert upper ball joint nut through coils of front coil spring so nut rests in upper plate. This pin can only be inserted one way into upper ball nut because of a stepped hole design.
7. Insert compression rod into opening in the front suspension lower arm, through upper and lower plate and upper ball nut. Insert securing pin through upper ball nut and compression rod, **Fig. 6.**
8. With upper ball nut secured, turn upper plate so it walks up coil until it contacts upper front spring insulator. Then back off one half turn.
9. Install lower ball nut and thrust washer on compression rod and screw on forcing nut, **Fig. 7.**
10. Tighten forcing nut until front coil spring is compressed enough so it is free in its front spring insulator.
11. Remove two front lower arm pivot bolts, disengage lower arm from crossmember and remove coil spring.

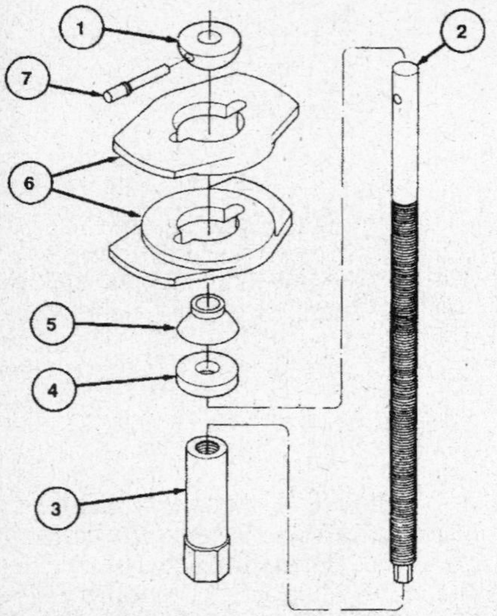

Item	Description
1	Upper Ball (Part of 204-D001 (D78P-5310-A))
2	Compression Rod (Part of 204-D001 (D78P-5310-A))
3	Forcing Nut (Part of 204-D001 (D78P-5310-A))
4	Thrust Washer (Part of 204-D001 (D78P-5310-A))
5	Lower Ball Nut (Part of 204-D001 (D78P-5310-A))
6	Plate (Part of 204-D001 (D78P-5310-A))
7	Pin (Part of 204-D001 (D78P-5310-A))

FM2029700148000X

Fig. 6 Compression rod assembly. Crown Victoria & Grand Marquis

Spring Compressor Installation

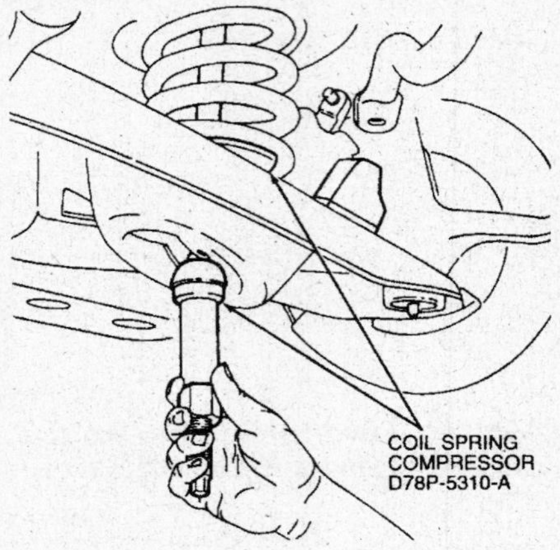

Spring Compressor Location

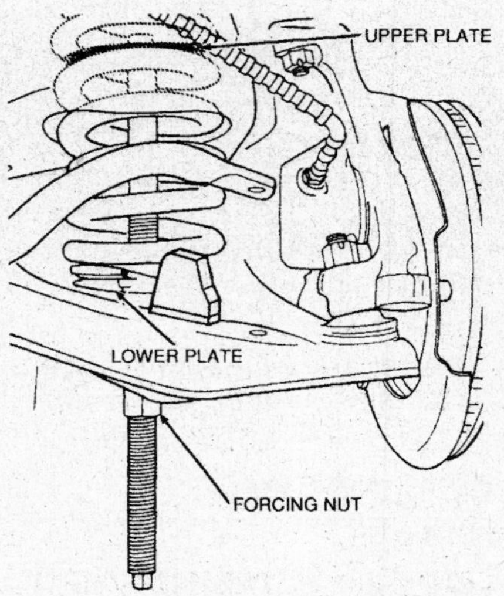

FM2029700149000X

Fig. 7 Spring compressor installation. Crown Victoria & Grand Marquis

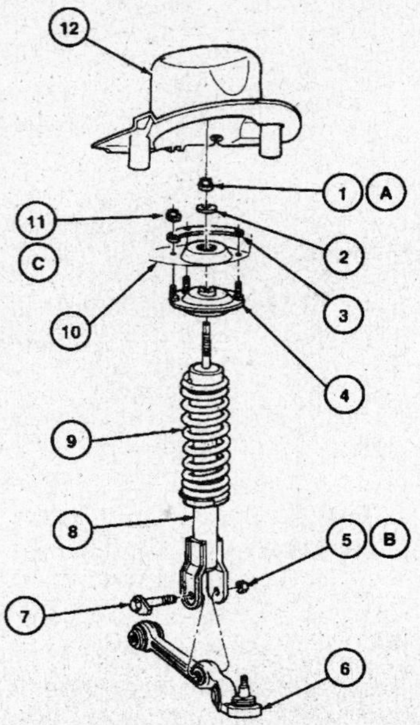

Item	Part Number	Description
1	N805377-S100	Nut (2 Req'd)
2	18041	Washer (2 Req'd)
3	18T003	Shock Absorber Housing Seal (2 Req'd)
4	18183	Front Shock Absorber Mounting Bracket (2 Req'd)
5	N805476-S160	Nut (2 Req'd)
6	3079	Front Suspension Lower Arm
7	N806798-S56	Bolt (2 Req'd)
8	18124	Front Shock Absorber
9	5310	Front Coil Spring (2 Req'd)
10	—	Body (Ref)
11	N801310-S100	Nut (6 Req'd)
12	18A179	Front Shock Absorber Strut Cover Cup
A	—	Tighten to 50-71 N·m (37-52 Lb-Ft)
B	—	Tighten to 170-230 N·m (125-170 Lb-Ft)
C	—	Tighten to 22-31 N·m (17-22 Lb-Ft)

FM2029100042000A

Fig. 8 Strut & coil spring replacement. Cougar & Thunderbird

12. If a new front coil spring is to be installed proceed as follows:
    a. Mark position of upper and lower plates on front coil spring with chalk.
    b. With an assistant, compress a new front coil spring for installation. Measure compressed length and amount of curvature of old front coil spring.
13. Loosen forcing nut to relieve spring tension and remove tools from front coil spring.
14. Reverse procedure to install. Tighten to specifications.

STRUT

REPLACE

COUGAR & THUNDERBIRD

Removal

1. Remove plastic cover at upper shock mount.
2. Remove three upper mounting nuts and collar plate from studs in engine compartment.
3. Raise and support vehicle, then remove tire and wheel assemblies.
4. Remove lower shock mounting bolt and nut, **Fig. 8.**
5. Separate link from spindle using joint separator tool No. D88L-3006-A or equivalent.
6. Support lower control arm assembly with transmission jack.
7. Raise control arm and spindle with jack until stabilizer link can be completely separated from spindle. Position link out of the way.
8. Remove spindle to upper control arm attaching nut and bolt. Discard nut and bolt.
9. Lower jack to separate spindle from upper control arm. Do not allow spindle to hang free, support with wire or other means.
10. Remove support from lower control arm and remove shock and coil spring assembly.
11. Reverse procedure to install. Tighten to specifications.

SHOCK ABSORBER

REPLACE

CROWN VICTORIA & GRAND MARQUIS

1. Remove upper shock absorber nut.
2. Raise vehicle and install safety stands.
3. Remove two screws from lower end of shock absorber, then remove shock absorber.
4. Reverse procedure to install.

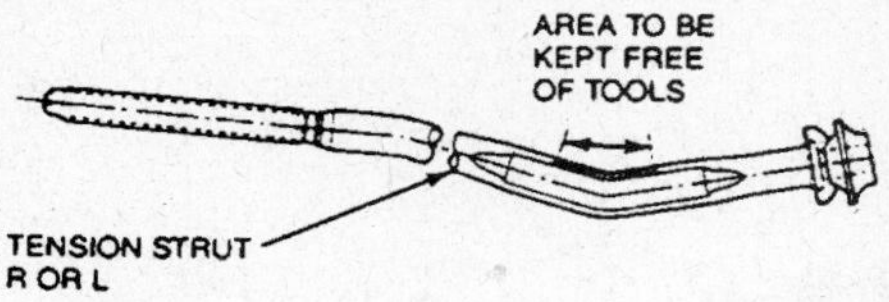

FM2029100046000X

Fig. 9 Tension strut. Cougar & Thunderbird

CONTROL ARM

REPLACE

COUGAR & THUNDERBIRD

LOWER

1. Raise and support vehicle.
2. Remove tire and wheel assembly.
3. Loosen lower ball joint nut three or four turns.
4. Rap spindle to separate ball joint. Leave nut attached.
5. Support spindle by wire to prevent excessive sagging of upper control arm.
6. Mark position of camber adjustment cam.
7. Remove nut attaching tension strut to control arm. Hold strut by flats with wrench while turning nut. **Do not hold strut or damage surface in area shown in Fig. 9, damage to tension strut may result.**
8. Remove lower shock bolt and nut.
9. Remove pivot (camber) bolt and nut.
10. Remove nut at lower ball joint and remove control arm, **Fig. 10.**
11. Reverse procedure to install, after installation check front end alignment and adjust as necessary. Tighten to specifications.

UPPER

1. Raise and support vehicle.
2. Remove tire and wheel assembly.
3. Remove and discard upper spindle to ball joint bolt and nut. Slightly spread spindle at slot and remove ball joint.
4. Lower vehicle, then break off flags on upper control arm pivot bolt heads.
5. Remove upper control arm bolts, then upper control arm, **Fig. 10.**
6. Reverse procedure to install. Tighten to specifications.

CROWN VICTORIA & GRAND MARQUIS

1997–98

Lower

1. Raise and support front of vehicle, then remove front wheels.
2. Remove brake caliper, rotor, dust shield and ABS sensor, if equipped.
3. Remove jounce bumper, if equipped.
4. Remove shock absorber.
5. Disconnect steering sector shaft arm drag link from steering gear sector shaft arm.
6. Loosen lower ball joint stud nut one or two turns.
7. Tap front wheel spindle sharply, near lower stud, with a hammer to loosen stud in front wheel spindle.
8. Place a floor jack under front suspen-

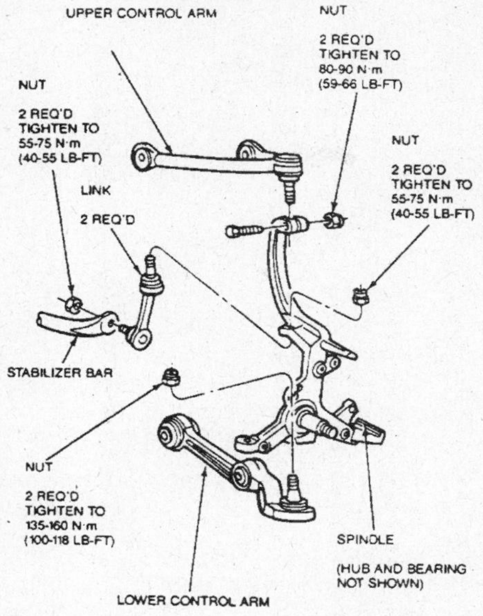

FM2029100045000X

Fig. 10 Control arms & steering knuckle. Cougar & Thunderbird

Item	Description
5	Front Suspension Bumper
6	Bolt (4 Req'd)
7	Nut (4 Req'd)
A	Tighten to 148-201 N·m (109-148 Lb-Ft)
B	Tighten to 34-47 N·m (26-34 Lb-Ft)

FM2029700150020X

Fig. 11 Lower arm removal (Part 2 of 2). 1997–98 Crown Victoria & Grand Marquis

sion lower arm.

9. Compress ball joint with tool, then tap spindle, near lower stud, to loosen stud in spindle.
10. Remove ball joint press tool, then position a suitable jack under lower control arm.
11. Install suitable coil spring compression tool, then remove coil spring.
12. Remove ball joint nut, then the lower control arm assembly, **Fig. 11.**
13. Reverse procedure to install, noting the following:
    a. Tighten to specifications.
    b. Ensure coil spring is properly aligned, **Fig. 11.**
    c. Check and adjust wheel alignment.

Upper

1. Raise and support front of vehicle, then remove front wheels.
2. Remove upper ball joint attaching nut cotter pin, then loosen upper ball joint nut one or two turns. **Do not remove nut from stud at this time.**
3. Install ball joint press tool T57P-3006-B, or equivalent, between upper and

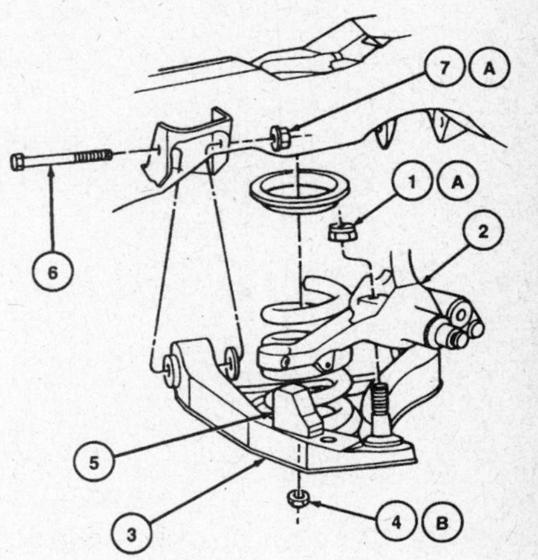

Item	Description
1	Nut (2 Req'd)
2	Front Wheel Spindle
3	Front Suspension Lower Arm
4	Nut (2 Req'd)

FM2029700150010X

Fig. 11 Lower arm removal (Part 1 of 2). 1997–98 Crown Victoria & Grand Marquis

lower ball joint studs.

4. Compress ball joint with tool, then tap spindle, near upper stud, to loosen stud in spindle.
5. Remove ball joint press tool, then position a suitable jack under lower control arm.
6. Remove upper control arm attaching bolts, then the upper control arm assembly.
7. Reverse procedure to install. Tighten to specifications and check wheel alignment.

1999–2000

Lower

1. Raise and support vehicle.
2. Remove wheel and tire assembly.
3. Remove cotter pin and nut from tie rod end.
4. Using tie rod end removal tool No. 211–001, or equivalent, remove tie rod end from front wheel spindle.
5. Remove coil spring as outlined in "Coil Spring, Replace"
6. Remove and discard lower ball joint nut.
7. Using pitman arm puller tool No. 211–003, or equivalent, remove ball joint from steering knuckle.
8. Remove lower control arm.
9. Reverse procedure to install.

Upper

1. Raise and support vehicle.
2. Remove wheel and tire assembly.
3. Place a suitable jack under front suspension lower arm and lower vehicle until lower arm begins to move.
4. Attach a piece of safety wire to front wheel spindle and secure spindle to vehicle frame.

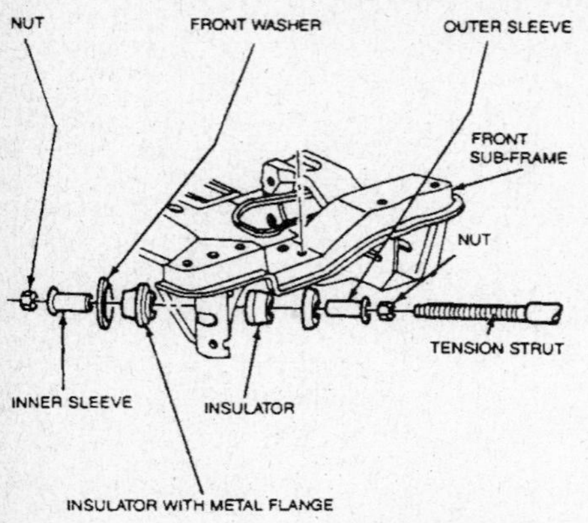

Fig. 12 Tension strut installation. Cougar & Thunderbird

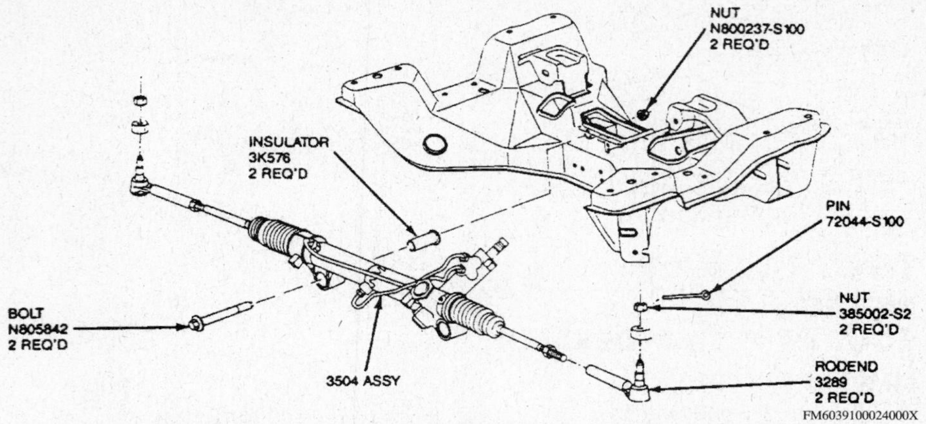

Fig. 13 Power rack & pinion steering gear installation. Cougar & Thunderbird

5. Remove upper steering knuckle bolt and nut to release upper ball joint from knuckle.
6. Remove upper control arm mounting bolts and nuts, then the control arm.
7. Reverse procedure to install, then inspect wheel alignment.

STABILIZER BAR

REPLACE

COUGAR & THUNDERBIRD

Link Assembly

1. Raise and support vehicle.
2. Remove nuts from stabilizer bar link. **Use care to avoid damaging ball joint seal. If seal is damaged, replace complete stabilizer bar link assembly.**
3. Separate link studs from front wheel spindle and front stabilizer bar using Ball Joint Remover D88L-3006-A, or equivalent.
4. Reverse procedure to install.

Mounting Bracket Insulator

1. Remove front sub frame.
2. Remove air cleaner outlet tube.
3. Remove stabilizer bar bracket bolts and stabilizer bar brackets.
4. Remove drive belt and raise and support vehicle.
5. Remove front tire and wheel assemblies.
6. Remove cotter pins and castellated nuts at tie rod ends.
7. Separate tie rod ends from front wheel spindles using Tie Rod End Remover TOOL-3290-D, or equivalent.
8. Remove transmission oil cooler line clip.
9. **Use care to avoid damaging ball joint seal. If seal is damaged, replace complete stabilizer bar link assembly.**
10. Remove stabilizer bar to lower stabilizer bar link retaining nuts.
11. Remove stabilizer bar link from stabilizer bar using Ball Joint Remover D88L-3006-A, or equivalent.
12. Remove stabilizer bar through right wheel opening.
13. Remove lower suspension arm stabilizer bar insulators from front stabilizer bar.
14. Reverse procedure to install

CROWN VICTORIA & GRAND MARQUIS

1. Raise and support vehicle.
2. Remove nuts from stabilizer bar link.
3. Remove four stabilizer bar brackets retaining nuts, then lower arm stabilizer bar insulator from stabilizer bar.
4. **On 1997–98 models,** pry locking tab away from frame and slide stud out. Tap stud with a hammer if necessary.
5. **On all models,** remove stabilizer bar from vehicle.
6. Reverse procedure to install. Tighten to specifications.

SPINDLE ASSEMBLY

REPLACE

COUGAR & THUNDERBIRD

1. Raise and support vehicle.
2. Remove tire and wheel assembly.
3. Remove brake caliper and rotor.
4. Remove hub and bearing assembly.
5. Remove anti-lock brake sensor and position out of the way.
6. Remove tie rod end cotter pin and loosen castellated nut. Separate tie rod end from spindle using tie rod end remover tool No. 3290-D, or equivalent.
7. Remove stabilizer bar link at spindle using joint separator tool No. D88L-3006-A, or equivalent.
8. Separate lower ball joint from spindle. Loosen nut and rap spindle with hammer. Remove nut.
9. Remove and discard upper spindle to upper control arm bolt and nut. Spread slot slightly and remove spindle from control arm and vehicle.
10. Reverse procedure to install. Tighten to specifications.

TENSION STRUT

REPLACE

COUGAR & THUNDERBIRD

Removal

1. Raise and support vehicle.
2. Remove tire and wheel assembly.
3. Hold tension strut on flats with wrench. Remove front sub-frame attaching nut and insulator. **Do not hold strut or damage surface in area shown in Fig. 9, damage to tension strut may result.**
4. Mark position, or note number of visible threads at tension strut rear sub-frame nut.
5. Back off tension strut rear sub-frame nut.
6. Remove tension strut to lower control arm attaching nut.
7. Remove lower shock bolt and nut.
8. Remove brake hose bracket to body attaching bolt.
9. Remove ABS sensor attaching bolt and position sensor out of the way.
10. Pry lower control arm rearward and remove tension strut.

Installation

1. If front tension strut insulators were removed, de-burr insulator sleeves before reassembly. If new sleeves are used, inner sleeve must be shorter than outer sleeve. Cut up to 1/4 inch off inner sleeve if necessary, **Fig. 12.**
2. Install tension strut retaining nut all the way down on threads. Install with nylon insert facing forward.
3. Install outer sleeve and rear washer. Word "REAR" must face outward.
4. Install rear insulator (without metal flange) with large end toward sub-frame.
5. Install tension strut in sub-frame.
6. Install front insulator, with the word "FRONT" toward front of vehicle and metal flange toward sub-frame.
7. Install front washer, with the words "THIS SIDE OUT" toward front of vehicle.

8. Install inner sleeve, loosely install front nut.
9. Install front washer and insulator on rear of tension strut, cup to face away from insulator.
10. Install tension strut into lower control arm.
11. Install rear insulator with small end toward control arm.
12. Install washer and cup facing rear of vehicle.
13. Return torsion strut to sub-frame nut to original position.
14. Install lower shock bolt and nut.
15. Holding tension strut with wrench, tighten strut to sub-frame to specification.
16. Tighten tension strut to lower control arm attaching nut to specification.
17. Install brake hose bracket, tighten to specifications.
18. Install ABS sensor, tighten to specifications.
19. Install tire and wheel assembly, inspect front wheel alignment.

POWER STEERING GEAR

REPLACE

COUGAR & THUNDERBIRD

1. Raise and support vehicle. Remove both front wheel and tire assemblies.
2. Remove cotter pins at outer tie rod ends and remove castellated nuts at each end. Discard cotter pins.
3. Separate tie rod ends from spindles, using tie rod end removal tool No. 3290-D, or equivalent.
4. Disconnect and plug power steering return line hose.
5. Disconnect power steering pressure line at intermediate fitting and position out of the way.
6. Remove steering shaft retaining bolt.
7. Remove rack to sub-frame bolts and nuts, access nuts through hole in front crossmember, **Fig. 13.**
8. Lower rack as necessary, to remove pressure line inlet tube. Remove and discard plastic seal on inlet tube.
9. Cut tie strap securing pressure line to each tube.
10. Remove steering rack from vehicle.
11. Reverse procedure to install. Tighten to specifications.

CROWN VICTORIA & GRAND MARQUIS

1. Remove stone shield, if equipped.
2. Disconnect pressure and return lines from steering gear. Plug lines and ports in gear to prevent entry of dirt.
3. Remove clamp bolt that secures flex coupling to steering gear and to column.
4. Raise car and remove sector shaft nut.
5. Use Pitman Arm Puller T64P-3590-F, or equivalent, to remove pitman arm.
6. Support steering gear, then remove attaching bolts.
7. Work steering gear free of flex coupling and remove it from car.
8. Reverse procedure to install. Tighten to specifications.

POWER STEERING PUMP

REPLACE

COUGAR & THUNDERBIRD

1. Disconnect return hose from power steering pump reservoir and allow fluid to drain into a suitable container.
2. Disconnect pressure hose from pump fitting, then remove pump mounting bracket and disconnect drive belt from pulley.
3. **On models with fixed pump system,** remove pulley.
4. **On all models,** remove power steering pump.
5. Reverse procedure to install. Tighten to specifications.
6. **Do not overtighten pressure hose fitting.** Swivel and/or endplay of the fitting is normal and does not indicate a loose fitting.

CROWN VICTORIA & GRAND MARQUIS

1. Disconnect power steering pump return line and allow power steering pump fluid to drain into a suitable container.
2. Disconnect power steering pump pressure hose from pump fitting.
3. Disconnect drive belt from power steering pump pulley, remove pulley, then remove pump.
4. Reverse procedure to install. Tighten to specifications.
5. **Do not overtighten pressure hose fitting.** Swivel and/or endplay of the fitting is normal and does not indicate a loose fitting.

TIGHTENING SPECIFICATIONS

COUGAR & THUNDERBIRD

Year	Component	Torque/ Ft. Lbs
1997	ABS Sensor Bolt	40–60①
	Axle Nut	189–254
	Brake Caliper Torx Bolts	25
	Brake Hose Retaining Bolt	9–11
	Driveshaft Nut	189–254
	Hose Fittings At Gear	20–25
	Hub Nut	189–254
	Lower Control Arm To Shock	118–162
	Lower Control Arm To Spindle (Ball Joint)	80–120
	Lower Control Arm To Sub-Frame	92–125
	Lower Control Arm To Tension Strut	90–120
	Pressure Hose Fitting At Pump	10–15
	Pump Mounting Bracket	30–45
	Shock To Upper Mount	37–45
	Stabilizer Bar Bracket	40–55
	Stabilizer Bar Link To Spindle	40–55
	Stabilizer Bar Link To Stabilizer Bar	40–55
	Steering Flex Coupling Nut	20–30
	Steering Gear To Crossmember	100–144
	Tension Strut To Sub-frame	90–120
	Tie Rod Ball Socket To Rack	55–65
	Tie Rod End To Jam Nut	35–50
	Tie Rod End To Spindle	39–54
	Upper Control Arm To Body	55–90
	Upper Control Arm To Spindle (Ball Joint)	50–65
	Upper Shock Mount To Body	16–23
	Wheel Hub Nut	189–254
	Wheel Lug Nuts	85–106

① — Inch Lbs.

CROWN VICTORIA & GRAND MARQUIS

Year	Component	Torque/ Ft. Lbs
1997–2000	Axle Nut	189–254
	Ball Joint To Lower Spindle	107–129
	Ball Joint To Upper Spindle	56–76
	Brake Caliper Torx Bolts	24
	Flex Coupling to Gear Input Shaft Bolt	20–30
	Lower Arm To Crossmember	110–148
	Lower Arm To Frame	110–148
	Pinch Bolt & Nut	56–76
	Pitman Arm Nut	35–46
	Pressure Hose To Gear	16–25
	Quick Connect Tube Nut	35–45
	Return Hose To Gear	26–34
	Shock Absorber Top Stud Nut	25–33
	Shock Absorber Lower Bolts	10–12
	Stabilizer Bar Link To Spindle	20–25
	Stabilizer Link To Bar	34–46
	Steering Gear To Side Rail Mounting Bolts	50–65
	Steering Pump To Engine	15–22
	Tie Rod End To Spindle	35–46
	Upper Ball Joint To Upper Arm	107–129
	Wheel Lug Nuts	85–104

Wheel Alignment

INDEX

PRELIMINARY INSPECTION

1. Ensure all tires are inflated to proper pressure.
2. Inspect tire for wear patterns that may indicate improper wheel alignment, tire imbalance or damage due to bulges or separation.
3. Inspect suspension for modifications such as trailer towing equipment or heavy duty handling components.
4. Inspect vehicle for signs of overloading or sagging; ensure luggage compartment does not contain heavy objects.
5. Road test vehicle to isolate area of concern.

FRONT WHEEL ALIGNMENT

COUGAR & THUNDERBIRD

Caster

Caster is adjusted by moving the tension strut relative to the front sub-frame. Loosen nuts securing strut to sub-frame and adjust caster by running the nuts in appropriate direction until desired setting is achieved. The setting should be locked by holding adjusting nut and **torquing** locknut to 104–118 ft. lbs.

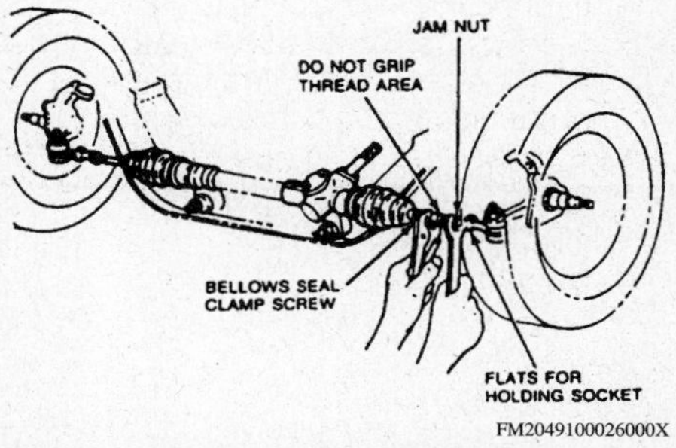

Fig. 1 Toe-in adjustment. Cougar & Thunderbird

Camber

Camber is adjusted by rotating a cam bolt at lower control arm inner pivot. Loosen nut securing adjustment and adjust by rotating bolt head. Lock adjustment by holding bolt and **torque** nut to 125 ft. lbs.

Toe-In

1. Check to see that steering shaft and steering wheel marks are in alignment and in the top position.
2. Loosen clamp screw on tie rod bellows and free the seal on the rod to prevent twisting of bellows, **Fig. 1.**
3. Place opened end wrench on flats of tie rod socket to prevent socket from turning, then loosen tie rod jam nuts.
4. Use suitable pliers to turn tie rod inner end to correct the adjustment to specifications. Do not use pliers on tie rod threads. Turning to reduce number of threads showing will increase toe-in. Turning in opposite direction will reduce toe-in.
5. **Torque** tie rod jam nuts to 43–49 ft. lbs.

CROWN VICTORIA & GRAND MARQUIS

Caster & Camber

Adjusting cams are provided for caster and camber adjustment, **Fig. 2.**

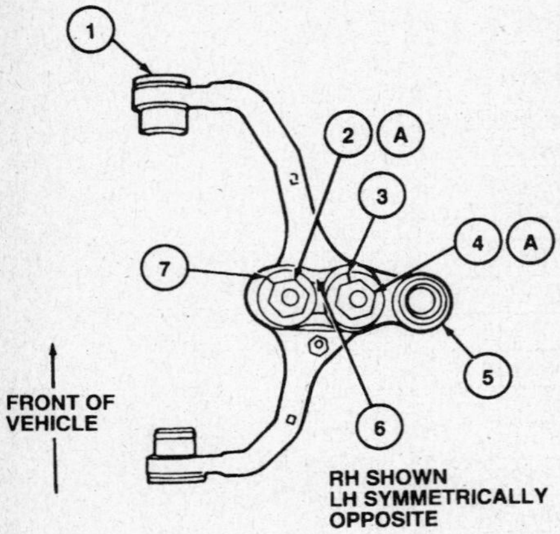

Item	Description
1	Front Suspension Lower Arm
2	Camber Adjust
3	Reference Mark
4	Caster Adjust
5	Front Suspension Upper Ball Joint
6	RH Identification on Forging

FM2049700059010X

Fig. 2 Caster & camber adjustment (Part 1 of 2). Crown Victoria & Grand Marquis

1. Check caster and camber and record readings.
2. A vehicle within the minimum to maximum tolerances may require alignment adjustment to the nominal setting (zero) because side to side setting is out of specification and must be corrected.
3. If adjustment is required, loosen two nuts on top of adjusting cams.
4. Turn hex cams as required to obtain desired valve.
5. After proper caster and camber settings have been set, hold each cam and tighten nuts to 109–148 ft. lbs.
6. Check toe in and steering wheel spoke position and adjust both (as required) at the same time.

Item	Description
7	Reference Mark
A	Turn Adjusting Cams Clockwise to Increase and Counterclockwise to Decrease

FM2049700059020X

Fig. 2 Caster & camber adjustment (Part 2 of 2). Crown Victoria & Grand Marquis

Toe & Steering Wheel Spoke Position

After adjusting caster and camber, check steering wheel spoke position with front wheels in straight ahead position. If spokes are not in their normal position, they can be properly adjusted while toe is being adjusted.

1. Loosen two clamp bolts on each front wheel spindle tie rod adjusting sleeve, **Fig. 3.**
2. Adjust toe. If steering wheel spokes are in normal position, lengthen or shorten both rods equally to obtain correct toe.
3. If steering wheel spokes are not correct, make necessary rod adjustments to obtain correct toe and steering wheel alignment.
4. When toe and steering wheel position are both correct, lubricate clamp, bolts and nuts. **Torque** clamp bolts on both connecting rod sleeves to 20–22 ft. lbs.
5. Sleeve position should not be changed when clamp bolts are tightened for proper clamp bolt orientation.

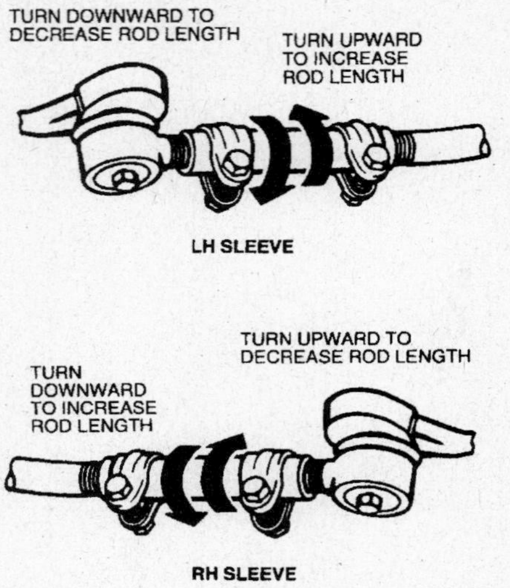

FM2049700060000X

Fig. 3 Toe adjustment. Crown Victoria & Grand Marquis

REAR WHEEL ALIGNMENT

COUGAR & THUNDERBIRD

Camber

Camber is adjusted by rotating a cam bolt at upper control arm inner pivot. Loosen nut securing adjustment and adjust by rotating head of bolt. Lock adjustment by holding bolt and **torque** nut to 98 ft. lbs.

Toe-In

The recommended adjustment sequence for rear alignment is to set toe then camber. Toe should be rechecked before final tightening.

Toe is adjusted by rotating a cam bolt at lower arm inner pivot. Loosen nut securing adjustment and adjust by rotating bolt head. Lock adjustment by holding bolt and **torque** nut to 170 ft. lbs.

ESCORT, TRACER & ZX2

NOTE: Refer To Rear Of This Manual For Vehicle Manufacturer's Special Service Tool Suppliers.

INDEX OF SERVICE OPERATIONS

Specifications

GENERAL ENGINE SPECIFICATIONS

Year	Engine Liter	Engine VIN Code②	Fuel System	Bore & Stroke, Inches	Compression Ratio	Net H.P. @ RPM	Maximum Torque Ft. Lbs. @ RPM	Normal Oil Pressure, psi
1997–2000	2.0L SOHC	P	SEFI	3.34 x 3.46	9.2	110 @ 5000	125 @ 3750	35–65
	2.0L DOHC	3	SEFI	3.34 x 3.46	10.0	130 @ 5750	127 @ 4250	54–80①

EFI — Electronic Fuel Injection
SEFI — Sequential Electronic Fuel Injection
① — Engine hot @ 4000 RPM.
② — Eighth digit of Vehicle Identification Number (VIN) denotes engine code.

TUNE UP SPECIFICATIONS

Engine (VIN Code)①	Spark Plug Gap, Inch	Ignition Timing, °BTDC: Firing Order Fig.④	Ignition Timing, °BTDC: Man. Trans.	Ignition Timing, °BTDC: Auto. Trans.	Ignition Timing, °BTDC: Timing Mark Fig.	Curb Idle Speed③: Man. Trans.	Curb Idle Speed③: Auto. Trans.	Fast Idle Speed: Man. Trans.	Fast Idle Speed: Auto Trans.	Fuel Pump Pressure, psi	Valve Clearance, Inch
1997–2000											
2.0L/P SOHC	.054	③	10	10	⑦	⑥	⑥	⑥	⑥	35–45	⑧
2.0L/3 DOHC	.54	③	②	②	⑦	⑥	⑥	⑥	⑥	35–45	⑤

BTDC — Before Top Dead Center.
N — Neutral
① — The eighth digit of the Vehicle Identification Number (VIN) denotes engine code.
② — Computer controlled, non-adjustable.
③ — Firing order, 1-3-4-2. Refer to **Fig. A** for spark plug wire connections @ ignition coil pack.
④ — Before disconnecting wires from distributor cap, determine location of No. 1 wire in cap, as distributor position may have been altered from that shown @ the end of this chart.
⑤ — Intake, .0043–.0071 inch; exhaust, .016–.0134 inch.
⑥ — Idle speed controlled by an automatic idle speed control.
⑦ — Equipped with a crankshaft position sensor. Timing is not adjustable.
⑧ — Equipped with hydraulic lash adjusters.

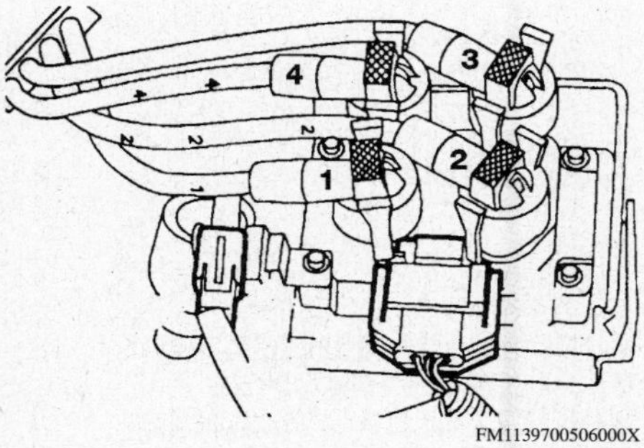

Fig. A

FRONT WHEEL ALIGNMENT SPECIFICATIONS

Year	Model	Caster Angle, Degrees		Camber Angle, Degrees		Total Toe, Inch	Steering Axis Inclination, Deg.	Maximum Steering Angle, Deg.		Ball Joint Wear
		Limits	Desired	Limits	Desired			Inner	Outer	
1997–2000	Escort & Tracer	+1.8 to +3.8	+2.8	-1.63 to +.36	-.63	0 to +.16	0 to +.4	—	—	①
1998–2000	ZX2	+1.55 to +3.15	+2.3	-.35 to +1.15	+.4	0 to +.16	0 to +.4	—	—	①

① — Refer to "Ball Joint Inspection" under "Front Suspension & Steering."

REAR WHEEL ALIGNMENT SPECIFICATIONS

Year	Model	Camber Angle, Degrees		Total Toe, Inch	Thrust Angle, Deg.
		Limits	Desired		
1997–2000	Escort & Tracer	-1.68 to +.98	-.68	-.1 to +.5	—
1998–2000	ZX2	-2.22 to -.11	-1.11	-.1 to +.5	—

FLUID CAPACITIES & COOLING SYSTEM DATA

Year	Engine Liter/ VIN④	Coolant Capacity, Qts.		Radiator Cap Relief Pressure, Lbs.	Thermo. Opening Temp.	Fuel Tank Gals.	Engine Oil Refill Qts.①	Transaxle Oil	
		Manual Transaxle	Automatic Transaxle					Manual Transaxle Pints	Auto. Transaxle Qts.②
1997–98	2.0L/P	5.8	7.9	16	188–195	12.7	4.0	—	5.7③
	2.0L/3	7.0	7.5	16	197	12.8	4.5	⑤	5.7③
1999–2000	2.0L/P	5.8	7.9	20	188–195	26	4.0	—	5.7③
	2.0L/3	7.0	7.5	20	197	26	4.5	⑤	5.7③

① — Includes filter.
② — Approximate. Make final inspection w/dipstick.
③ — Without converter drained.
④ — The eighth digit of the Vehicle Identification Number (VIN) denotes engine code.
⑤ — Remove vehicle speed sensor from Transaxle. Add specified fluid and use speed sensor to check level. Full mark is at point between top & bottom of vehicle speed sensor gear.

LUBRICANT DATA

Year	Lubricant Type			
	Transaxle		Power Steering	Brake System
	Manual	Automatic		
1997–2000	75W-90 GL-4	Mercon	Mercon	DOT 3

Electrical

NOTE: On Air Bag Equipped Models, Refer To " Air Bag System Precautions" Located In The Front Of This Manual For System Disarming & Arming Procedures.

NOTE: Refer To "Computer Relearn Procedures" Located In The Front Of This Manual For Computer Relearn Procedures.

INDEX

PRECAUTIONS

BATTERY GROUND CABLE

Prior to service, disconnect battery ground cable and isolate as required.

AIR BAG SYSTEMS

Refer to "Air Bag System Precautions" in the front of this manual for system disarming and arming procedures.

FUSE PANEL & FLASHER LOCATION

These vehicles use two fuse panels. The passenger compartment fuse panel is located below the instrument panel, to the left of the steering wheel. The engine compartment fuse panel is located on the left side of the engine compartment.

The flasher unit is located at the relay panel behind the lefthand side of the instrument panel.

FUEL PUMP RELAY LOCATION

Fuel pump output is controlled by the Constant Control Relay Module (CCRM), located in the front lefthand corner of the engine compartment.

RELAY CENTER LOCATION

The relay panel is located behind the left-hand side of the instrument panel, above the I/P fuse panel.

STARTER

REPLACE

2.0L SOHC ENGINE

1. Remove air duct from throttle body to resonance chamber.
2. Remove starter motor upper mount bolts, then raise and support vehicle.
3. Disconnect "S" terminal connector from starter solenoid. When disconnecting connector from "S" terminal, grasp connector and depress plastic tab to remove.
4. Remove "B" terminal attaching nut and disconnect cable from terminal.
5. Remove starter motor lower mounting bolt, then the starter motor.
6. Reverse procedure to install. **Torque** upper and lower mounting bolts to 18–20 ft. lbs. and " B" terminal attaching nut to 7–12 ft. lbs.

2.0L DOHC ENGINE

1. Remove air cleaner outlet tube, then raise and support vehicle.
2. Remove lower starter bolt, then lower vehicle.
3. Remove remaining two bolts, then raise and support vehicle.
4. Remove starter motor from block mounting surface, then the connector retaining nut.
5. Remove starter from vehicle.
6. Reverse procedure to install. **Torque** connector nut to 5 ft. lbs. and mounting bolts to 15–20 ft. lbs.

COIL PACK

REPLACE

1. Disconnect ignition coil electrical connector.
2. Disconnect spark plug wires from ignition coil by squeezing locking tabs to release coil boot retainers.
3. Remove four ignition coil retaining bolts and noise filter condenser.
4. Save noise filter condenser for installation with new ignition coil.
5. Reverse procedure to install. **Torque** bolts to 40–60 inch lbs.

IGNITION LOCK

REPLACE

1. Remove steering wheel as described under "Steering Wheel, Replace."
2. Remove combination switch as described under "Multi-Function Switch, Replace."
3. Disconnect ignition switch electrical connectors.
4. Remove ignition/shifter interlock cable

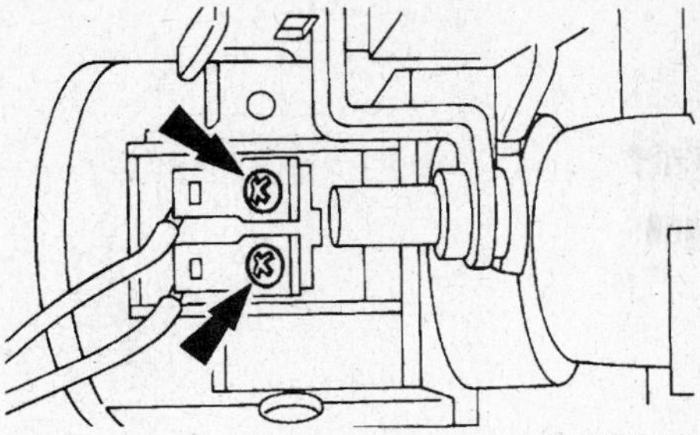

Fig. 1 Ignition key reminder switch screws

mounting bracket bolt and position bracket and cable aside.
5. Groove head of ignition switch lock cylinder bracket bolts with hammer and chisel.
6. Remove ignition switch lock cylinder bracket bolts, ignition switch lock cylinder and bracket. Discard bolts.
7. Reverse procedure to install. Tighten lock cylinder bracket bolts until bolt heads break off.

IGNITION SWITCH

REPLACE

1. Remove upper and lower steering column shrouds.
2. Disconnect ignition switch electrical connector.
3. Remove ignition switch electrical connector cover screws.
4. Remove ignition key reminder switch screws, **Fig. 1.**
5. Remove ignition switch, **Fig. 2.**
6. Reverse procedure to install.

HEADLAMP SWITCH

REPLACE

The headlamp, fog lights and turn signal switches are serviced with the multi-function switch as a unit. Refer to "Multi-Function Switch, Replace" for procedure.

FOG LAMP SWITCH

REPLACE

The headlamp, fog lamp and turn signal switches are serviced with the multi-function switch. Refer to "Multi-Function Switch, Replace" for procedure.

STOP LIGHT SWITCH

REPLACE

1. Disconnect stop lamp switch electrical connector.
2. Remove stop lamp locknut, then the stop lamp switch.
3. Reverse procedure to install, adjust stop lamp switch by turning the switch until it contacts the brake pedal, then turn an additional half turn.

MULTI-FUNCTION SWITCH

REPLACE

1. Remove four retaining screws from steering column lower cover, then remove lower cover.
2. Remove steering column upper cover, then disconnect three multi-function switch electrical connectors.
3. Remove multi-function switch retaining screw, then pull electrical connectors from retaining brackets and remove switch.
4. Reverse procedure to install.

TURN SIGNAL SWITCH

REPLACE

The headlamp, fog lights and turn signal switches are serviced with the multi-function switch as a unit. Refer to "Multi-Function Switch, Replace" for procedure.

DIMMER SWITCH

REPLACE

ESCORT & TRACER

1. Detach hood release cable from left lower dash trim panel, then remove four retaining screws and left lower dash trim panel.
2. Disconnect electrical connector from dimmer switch, then squeeze two lock tabs and remove dimmer switch through front of trim panel.
3. Reverse procedure to install.

ZX2

1. Remove instrument panel upper finish panel insert, then the hood latch release handle retaining nut.
2. Remove instrument panel steering column cover attaching screw, then the cover.
3. Disconnect light switch rheostat resistor electrical connector.
4. Depress locking tabs and remove light switch from instrument panel steering column cover.
5. Reverse procedure to install.

STEERING WHEEL

REPLACE

1. Ensure front wheels are in straight-ahead position.
2. Disconnect battery ground cable, then wait at least one minute for back-up power supply to deplete.
3. Remove two driver side air bag module bolts from rear of steering wheel.
4. Pull driver side air bag module up and away from steering wheel and disconnect air bag module electrical connector from air bag sliding contact.
5. Remove air bag module.
6. Remove steering wheel bolt.
7. Using steering wheel puller tool, remove steering wheel.
8. Reverse procedure to install. **Torque** steering wheel mounting bolt to 34–46 ft. lbs.

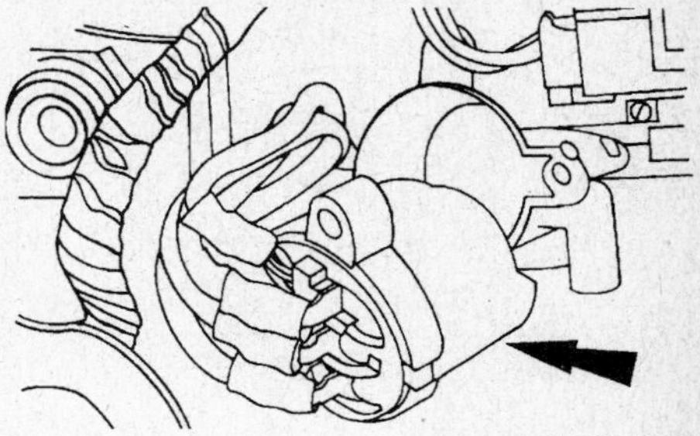

Fig. 2 Ignition switch removal

INSTRUMENT CLUSTER

REPLACE

ESCORT & TRACER

1. If equipped with tilt steering wheel, tilt steering wheel downward.
2. Remove hood latch release handle bolt.
3. Remove five retaining screws and the instrument panel finish panel, **Fig. 3.**
4. Remove four instrument cluster mounting screws, then pull cluster from instrument panel and disconnect electrical connectors at back of instrument cluster.
5. Reverse procedure to install.

ZX2

1. Remove instrument panel upper finish panel insert, then hood latch release handle attaching nut.
2. Remove instrument panel steering column cover attaching screw, then the cover.
3. Disconnect light switch rheostat resistor electrical connector.
4. Remove instrument panel upper finish panel attaching screws, then the panel.
5. Disconnect power mirrors switch electrical connector.
6. Remove four instrument cluster retaining screws, then disconnect three electrical connectors.
7. Remove instrument cluster from vehicle.
8. Reverse procedure to install.

RADIO

REPLACE

1. Set temperature control switch to Cold position.
2. Disconnect heater temperature cable.
3. Using radio removal tool No. T87P-19061-A, or equivalent, pull out Integrated Control Panel (ICP), **Fig. 4.**
4. Disconnect radio antenna lead, then the radio electrical connectors.
5. Remove radio from instrument panel.
6. Reverse procedure to install.

WIPER MOTOR

REPLACE

FRONT

1. Make sure windshield wiper motor is in the Off position and wiper pivot arms

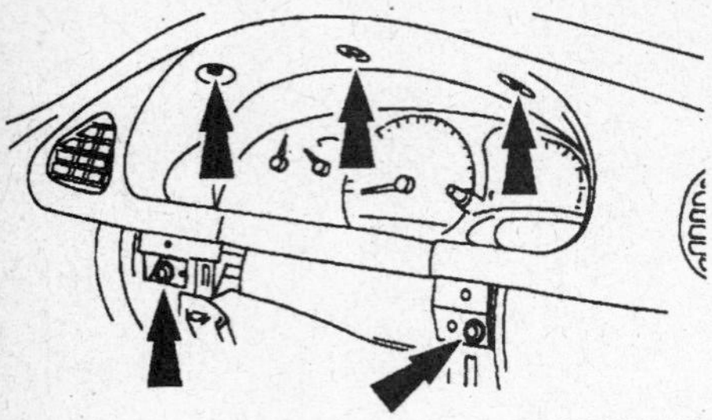

Fig. 3 I/P finish panel removal. Escort & Tracer

are parked in the highest position on the windshield.
2. Raise and support hood, then remove five center cowl top vent grille retainers and screws.
3. Remove two outer cowl top vent grille retainers and screws.
4. Lift clip up and off windshield wiper mounting arm and pivot shaft.
5. Slide windshield wiper mounting arm and pivot shaft off windshield wiper motor.
6. Disconnect windshield wiper motor electrical connector, then remove wiper motor bolts and wiper motor.
7. Reverse procedure to install. **Torque** wiper motor mounting bolts to 5–7 ft. lbs.

REAR

1. Lift wiper arm attaching nut cover and remove nut, then pull wiper arm from pivot shaft.
2. Remove shaft seal from outer bushing attaching nut, then remove outer bushing attaching nut and outer bushing.
3. Remove liftgate trim panel as follows:
   a. Remove three push-in retainers and hi-mount stop lamp cover.
   b. Remove liftgate seaming welt from along trim panel, then disengage 10 retaining clips and remove trim panel.
   c. Remove cargo area lamp.
4. Disconnect wiper motor electrical connector, then remove three wiper motor mounting bolts and wiper motor.
5. Reverse procedure to install noting the following:
   a. **Torque** wiper motor mounting bolts to 5–7 ft. lbs. and outer bushing attaching nut to 35–52 inch lbs.
   b. Turn wiper switch to the ON position and allow pivot shaft to move through three or four cycles, then turn wiper switch off.
   c. Position wiper arm on pivot shaft so tip of blade is .79–.98 inch from rear window molding.
   d. **Torque** wiper arm attaching nut to 5–7 ft. lbs.

WIPER SWITCH

REPLACE

The windshield wiper switch is serviced with the multi-function switch as a unit. Refer to "Multi-Function Switch, Replace" for procedure.

WIPER TRANSMISSION

REPLACE

ESCORT & TRACER

1. With hood closed, remove seven screw covers from cowl grille screws.
2. Remove seven cowl grille screws, the cowl grille.
3. Pry up four baffle retaining clips, then remove baffle trim piece.
4. Remove two retaining screws from each pivot shaft, then the pivot shaft and wiper linkage assembly.
5. Reverse procedure to install. **Torque** pivot shaft retaining screws to 5–7 ft. lbs.

ZX2

1. Remove windshield wiper pivot arms, then raise and support hood.
2. Remove five center cowl top vent grille retainers and screws, then the two outer cowl top vent grille retainers, screws and washers.
3. Remove pushpins from left and right air distribution flange baffles.
4. Remove windshield wiper mounting arm and pivot shaft retaining clip, then slide arm and shaft off windshield wiper motor.
5. Remove windshield wiper mounting arm and pivot shaft attaching screws, then pull arm and pivot shaft out through right air distribution flange baffle opening.
6. Reverse procedure to install. **Torque** pivot shaft retaining screws to 5–7 ft. lbs.

BLOWER MOTOR

REPLACE

ESCORT & TRACER

1. Remove trim panel below glove compartment.
2. Remove wiring bracket and bolt, then disconnect blower motor electrical connector.
3. Remove three blower motor attaching bolts, then blower motor.
4. Remove blower wheel retaining clip, then blower wheel from blower motor.
5. Reverse procedure to install.

ZX2

1. Remove three blower motor retaining screws, then the blower motor.
2. Disconnect blower motor electrical connector.
3. Remove blower motor wheel retainer and blower wheel.
4. Reverse procedure to install. **Torque** blower motor retaining screws to 21–23 inch lbs.

HEATER CORE

REPLACE

ESCORT & TRACER

1. Disconnect heater hoses at bulkhead.
2. Disconnect mode selector and temperature control cables from cams and retaining clips.
3. Loosen heater to blower clamp, then remove three heater unit mounting nuts, **Fig. 5.**
4. Remove instrument panel refer to "Dash Panel Service ."
5. Disconnect antenna lead from retaining clip, then remove heater unit.
6. Remove insulator, then four brace capscrews and brace.
7. Disconnect vacuum control motor vacuum connector.
8. Remove windshield defroster nozzle connectors.
9. Loosen A/C evaporator outlet duct clamp screw.
10. Remove lower heater core housing retaining nut.
11. Remove upper heater core housing retaining nuts and the heater core housing.
12. Remove heater dash panel seal.
13. Remove screws and the heater core cover.
14. Remove heater core from heater unit, **Fig. 6.**
15. Reverse procedure to install.

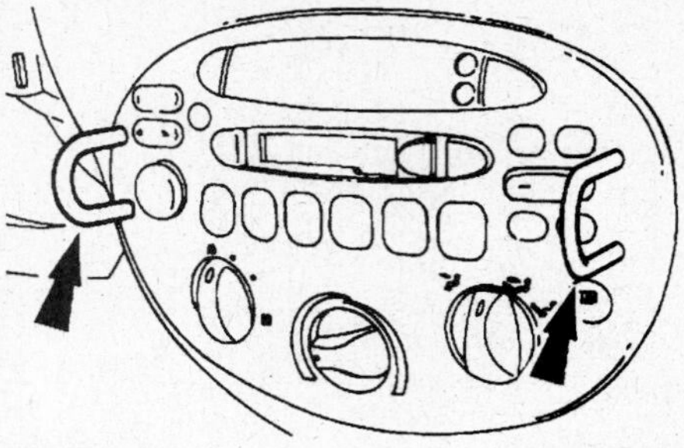

Fig. 4 Radio removal

ZX2

1. Drain engine coolant into a suitable container.
2. Remove air cleaner outlet tube, then disconnect heater hoses from heater core.
3. Remove instrument panel as outlined under "Dash Panel Service" section.
4. Disconnect antenna lead from heater core housing, then the vacuum control motor vacuum connector.
5. Disconnect vacuum lines from A/C evaporator housing retainer.
6. Remove windshield defroster nozzle pushpins and attaching screws.
7. Loosen A/C evaporator outlet duct clamp screw, then remove lower heater core housing retaining nut.
8. Remove upper heater core housing retaining nuts and heater core housing.
9. Remove heater dash panel seal, then the screws and heater core cover.
10. Remove heater core.
11. Reverse procedure to install.

EVAPORATOR CORE

REPLACE

ESCORT & TRACER

Do not disassemble A/C evaporator

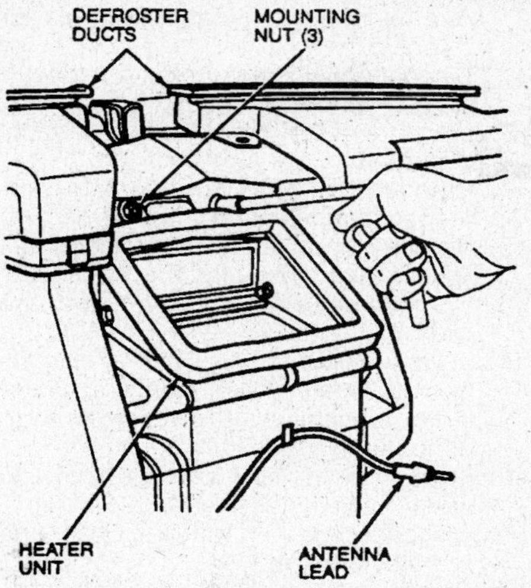

Fig. 5 Heater unit removal. Escort & Tracer

housing. If the evaporator core must be replaced, replace the entire A/C evaporator as a unit.

1. Recover refrigerant as outlined in the "Air Conditioning " section.
2. Disconnect A/C vacuum line from evaporator housing.
3. Disconnect rear condenser to evaporator tube spring lock coupling.
4. Disconnect accumulator/drier spring lock coupling.
5. Remove instrument panel as described in "Dash Panel Service."
6. Loosen A/C evaporator outlet duct clamp bolt.
7. Disconnect A/C blower motor electrical connector.
8. Disconnect vacuum control motor vacuum connector.
9. Disconnect vacuum lines from A/C evaporator housing retainer.
10. Remove four A/C evaporator housing retaining nuts and the evaporator housing.
11. Reverse procedure to install.

ZX2

1. Recover refrigerant as outlined in the "Air Conditioning " section.
2. Disconnect A/C vacuum line, then remove spring lock coupling from rear condenser to evaporator line.
3. Remove suction line support clip retaining nuts.
4. Disconnect suction line spring lock coupling.
5. Remove instrument panel as described in "Dash Panel Service."
6. Remove righthand windshield defroster nozzle pushpins and screws, then the defroster nozzle.
7. Loosen A/C evaporator outlet duct clamp bolt, then disconnect A/C blower motor electrical connector.
8. Disconnect vacuum control motor vacuum connector, then the vacuum lines from A/C evaporator housing retainer.
9. Remove nuts and A/C evaporator housing, then disconnect vacuum line.
10. Remove screws and A/C vacuum reservoir tank and bracket.
11. Remove two inlet duct door vacuum control motor retaining nuts.
12. Remove push nut and vacuum control motor, then the air inlet duct attaching screws.
13. Remove blower motor and heater blower motor switch resistor.
14. Remove evaporator tube and drain tube dash panel seals.
15. Remove evaporator core.
16. Reverse procedure to install.

Heater Core

Removal

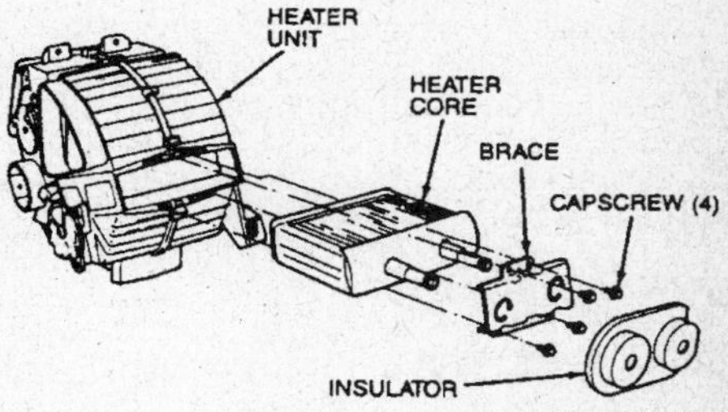

Fig. 6 Heater core removal. Escort & Tracer

2.0L SOHC Engine

NOTE: On Air Bag Equipped Models, Refer To "Air Bag System Precautions" Located In The Front Of This Manual For System Disarming & Arming Procedures.

NOTE: Refer To "Computer Relearn Procedures" Located In The Front Of This Manual For Computer Relearn Procedures.

INDEX

PRECAUTIONS

AIR BAG SYSTEMS

Refer to "Air Bag System Precautions" in the front of this manual for system disarming and arming procedures.

BATTERY GROUND CABLE

Prior to service, disconnect battery ground cable and isolate as required.

FUEL SYSTEM PRESSURE RELIEF

Remove the schrader valve cap, **Fig. 1**, at the end of the fuel injection supply manifold and attach fuel pressure gauge No. T80L-9974-B. Open the pressure gauge manual valve to relieve fuel system pressure.

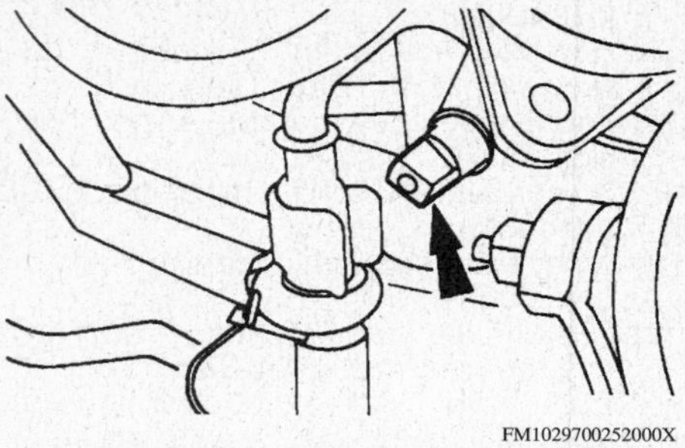

Fig. 1 Schrader valve cap location

COMPRESSION PRESSURE

1. Run engine to warm to normal operating temperature.
2. Turn ignition switch to Off position, then remove spark plugs.
3. Place Transaxle in Park position (A/T) or Neutral position (M/T) and apply parking brake.
4. Block throttle plate in wide open position.
5. Install compression gauge into spark plug hole.
6. Install auxiliary starter switch in starting circuit.
7. Crank engine, using auxiliary starter switch, a minimum of five compression strokes and record highest reading. Note the number of compression strokes required to obtain highest reading.
8. Repeat test on each cylinder, cranking engine approximately the same number of compression strokes.
9. Compression pressure are within specification if the lowest reading cylinder is within 75% of the highest reading.

ENGINE

REPLACE

REMOVAL

1. Relieve fuel system pressure as described under " Precautions."
2. Remove hood.
3. Recover refrigerant as outlined in the "Air Conditioning " section.
4. Remove battery and battery tray.
5. Remove air cleaner outlet tube.
6. Disconnect vacuum hoses from Exhaust Gas Recirculation (EGR) valve (A), brake booster (B), throttle body (C), fuel pressure regulator (D) and intake manifold (E), **Fig. 2.**
7. Disconnect two vacuum lines (A), remove two bolts (B) and position vacuum tree (C) aside, **Fig. 3.**
8. Disconnect speed control cable (if equipped), accelerator cable and throttle valve control actuating cable from throttle control lever.
9. Disconnect shift cable from bracket and set aside.
10. Disconnect two main engine/fuel charging wiring connectors.
11. Disconnect Constant Control Relay Module (CCRM) electrical connector and remove the CCRM and bracket.
12. Disconnect EGR backpressure transducer electrical connector, two vacuum hoses and remove the transducer.
13. Disconnect transmission range sensor electrical connector, transaxle solenoid connector, then remove two bolts, CCRM and bracket.
14. Disconnect EGR backpressure transducer electrical connector, two vacuum hoses and the transducer.
15. Disconnect transmission range sensor electrical connector, transaxle solenoid electrical connector and turbine speed connector.
16. Disconnect vehicle speed sensor electrical connector.
17. Disconnect upstream Heated Oxygen Sensor (HO2S) electrical connector mounted on cooling fan shroud.
18. Disconnect downstream HO2S electrical connector.
19. Remove screw and position ground strap aside.
20. Disconnect engine cooling fan electrical connector.
21. Remove three bolts and position power steering pressure hose aside.
22. Use disconnect tool No. D87L-9280-B (½ inch), or equivalent, to disconnect fuel return line from fuel injection supply manifold.
23. Remove exhaust manifold heat shield.
24. Remove four exhaust manifold to catalytic converter nuts.
25. Remove upper starter bolt and position bracket aside.
26. Disconnect transaxle fluid cooler lines from transaxle.
27. Remove A/C line bracket bolt.
28. Disconnect A/C manifold and tube spring lock coupling at accumulator/drier.
29. Disconnect A/C manifold and tube spring lock coupling at condenser.
30. Remove accessory drive belt, auto tensioner and accessory drive belt tensioner (models equipped with A/C).
31. Drain fluid from power steering reservoir.
32. Position drain pan under power steering reservoir and disconnect power steering lines.
33. Raise and support vehicle.
34. Remove lug nuts and front wheel and tire assemblies.
35. Remove lefthand splash shield.
36. Remove righthand splash shield.
37. Drain engine coolant and engine oil.
38. Remove four bolts and crossmember.
39. Remove catalytic converter bolts and the catalytic converter.
40. Remove front wheel driveshafts and joints.
41. Disconnect S-terminal wire and the B-terminal nut and cable from starter solenoid.
42. Disconnect oil pressure switch electrical connector.
43. Disconnect A/C compressor electrical connector.
44. Remove four bolts and the A/C compressor and manifold lines.
45. Remove hose clamp and disconnect lower radiator hose from radiator.
46. Remove camshaft pulley bolt and the pulley.
47. Lower vehicle.
48. Loosen heater hose clamp at water outlet connection and disconnect heater hose.
49. Loosen heater hose clamp at bulkhead and remove heater hose.
50. Disconnect upper radiator hose and remove radiator.
51. Disconnect generator electrical connectors.
52. Disconnect battery positive cable from alternator.
53. Attach engine lifting bracket tool No. T70P-6000, or equivalent, on left rear side of cylinder head.
54. Install three-bar engine support tool No. D88L-6000-A, or equivalent, as shown in **Fig. 4.**
55. Raise and support vehicle.
56. Remove transaxle support crossmember.
57. Lower vehicle.
58. Remove four nuts and transaxle mount.
59. Remove righthand engine support insulator through bolt.
60. Attach suitable lifting eye on transaxle and use for balance, if necessary.
61. Attach suitable lifting device and remove engine and transaxle assembly.
62. Separate transaxle from engine.
63. Mount engine on stand and remove lifting device.

INSTALLATION

1. Assemble engine to transaxle and lower assembly into engine compartment.
2. Install righthand engine support insulator through bolt.
3. Remove universal lifting eye from transaxle, if necessary.
4. Install four motor mount nuts.
5. Install three-bar engine support tool No. D88L-6000-A, or equivalent, as shown in **Fig. 4.**
6. Raise and support vehicle.
7. Install transaxle mounts and support crossmember.
8. Remove engine lifting bracket tool No. T70P-6000 from cylinder head.
9. Route generator and starter motor wiring harness behind engine.
10. Connect generator electrical connectors.
11. Install radiator assembly and connect upper radiator hose.
12. Install heater hose at bulkhead.
13. Install heater hose at water outlet connection.
14. Raise and support vehicle.

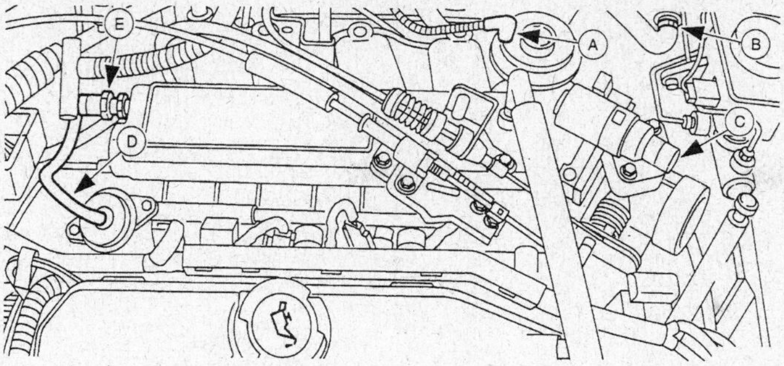

FM1069700594000X

Fig. 2 Vacuum hose locations

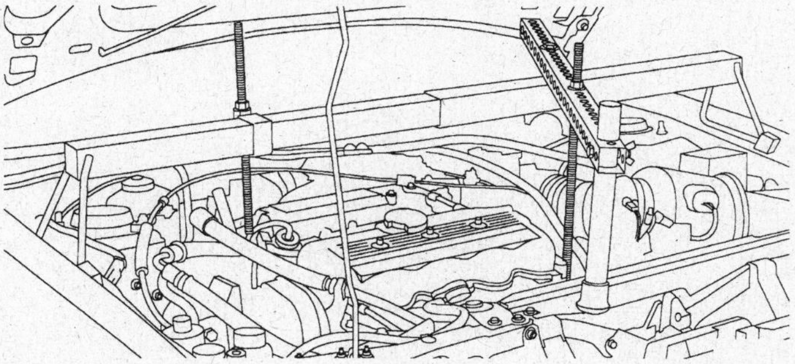

FM1069700593000X

Fig. 4 Engine support tool installation

15. Install crankshaft pulley.
16. Install lower radiator hose and clamp.
17. Install A/C compressor and manifold lines.
18. Connect A/C compressor manifold connector.
19. Connect oil pressure switch electrical connector.
20. Connect starter motor S-terminal wire and B-terminal cable and nut.
21. Install front wheel driveshafts and joints.
22. Position catalytic converter and install new gasket between converter and muffler inlet pipe and resonator.
23. Install two catalytic converter to muffler inlet pipe and resonator bolts and nuts.
24. Install two catalytic converter bracket bolts.
25. Install crossmember.
26. Install righthand splash shield.
27. Install lefthand splash shield.
28. Install front wheel and tire assemblies.
29. Lower vehicle.
30. Connect power steering reservoir pump hose and power steering pressure hose.
31. Install automatic tensioner, accessory drive belt and accessory drive belt idler.
32. Connect A/C line at accumulator/drier and condenser.
33. Install A/C line bracket bolt.
34. Connect transaxle cooler lines to transaxle.
35. Install starter motor bolt.
36. Install four exhaust manifold to catalytic converter nuts.
37. Install exhaust manifold heat shield.
38. Connect fuel supply line to fuel injection supply manifold.
39. Connect fuel return line to fuel injection supply manifold.
40. Install power steering pressure hose and brackets.
41. Install ground strap to generator bracket.
42. Connect engine cooling fan electrical connector.
43. Connect downstream Heated Oxygen Sensor (HO2S) electrical connector.
44. Connect upstream HO2S electrical connector.
45. Connect vehicle speed sensor electrical connector.
46. Connect transmission range sensor electrical connector, transaxle solenoid electrical connector and turbine speed sensor electrical connector.
47. Install EGR backpressure transducer and connect electrical connector and two pressure hoses.
48. Install Constant Control Relay Module (CCRM) and bracket and connect CCRM electrical connector.
49. Connect two main engine/fuel charging wiring electrical connectors.
50. Install shift cable and clip.
51. Install speed control cable, accelerator cable and throttle valve control actuating cable to throttle control lever.
52. Install vacuum tree and two vacuum lines.
53. Connect vacuum hoses to EGR valve (A), brake booster (B), throttle body (C), fuel pressure regulator (D) and intake manifold (E), **Fig. 2.**
54. Install air cleaner outlet tube.
55. Install battery tray and battery.
56. Recharge A/C system then refill cooling system as outlined under "Cooling System, Bleed."
57. Fill engine with oil to proper level.
58. Install hood.

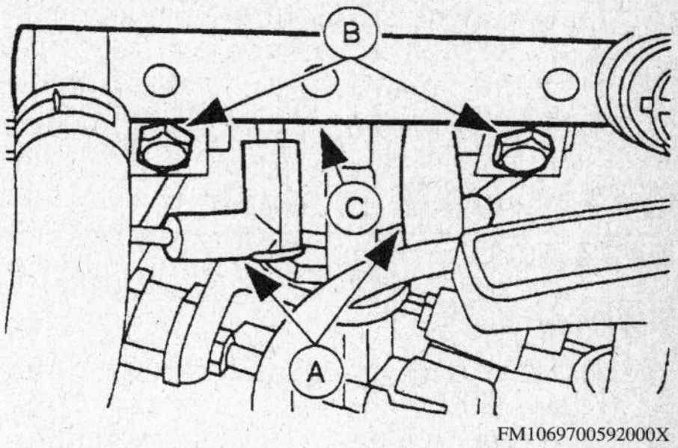

FM1069700592000X

Fig. 3 Vacuum tree

INTAKE MANIFOLD

REPLACE

1. Relieve fuel system pressure as outlined under " Precautions."
2. Drain engine coolant into a suitable container, then remove air cleaner outlet tube.
3. Disconnect vacuum hoses from EGR valve (A), positive crankcase ventilation valve (B), throttle body (C), fuel pressure regulator (D) and intake manifold (E), **Fig. 2.**
4. Disconnect speed control cable.
5. Remove two speed control cable bracket bolts and position bracket and cables aside.
6. Disconnect idle air control valve and throttle position sensor electrical connectors, **Fig. 5.**
7. Remove oil level indicator tube bracket bolt from intake manifold.
8. Disconnect EGR manifold tube located below EGR valve.
9. Raise and support vehicle.
10. Remove oil level indicator tube from engine block.
11. Remove lower intake manifold nuts.
12. Lower vehicle.
13. Remove upper intake manifold nuts, intake manifold and gasket.
14. Reverse procedure to install, noting the following:
    a. Tighten to specifications.
    b. Fill radiator and bleed cooling system as outlined under " Cooling System Bleed."

EXHAUST MANIFOLD

REPLACE

1. Relieve fuel system pressure as outlined under " Precautions."
2. Remove drive belt.
3. Disconnect upstream HO2S electrical connector mounted on top of cooling fan shroud.
4. Remove exhaust manifold shield.
5. Remove two exhaust gas recirculation (EGR) tube to exhaust manifold nuts and studs, **Fig. 5.**
6. Remove three power steering pressure hose bracket bolts and position bracket aside.
7. Loosen lower alternator mounting bolt and remove upper bolt, then pivot alternator forward.
8. Remove exhaust manifold to catalytic converter attaching nuts.
9. Remove eight exhaust manifold

mounting nuts, then carefully remove exhaust manifold and gasket.
10. Reverse procedure to install. Tighten to specifications.

CYLINDER HEAD

REPLACE

REMOVAL

1. Relieve fuel pressure as described under "Precautions."
2. Remove timing belt as described under "Timing Belt, Replace."
3. Remove air cleaner intake tube and outlet half of engine air cleaner.
4. Disconnect vacuum hoses from Exhaust Gas Recirculation (EGR) valve (A), brake booster (B), throttle body (C), fuel pressure regulator (D) and intake manifold (E), **Fig. 2.**
5. Disconnect speed control cable, accelerator cable and throttle valve control actuating cable from throttle control lever.
6. Remove two speed control cable bracket bolts and position bracket and cables aside.
7. Disconnect two fuel charging wiring electrical connectors.
8. Disconnect crankshaft position sensor electrical connector.
9. Disconnect upstream heated oxygen sensor electrical connector mounted on cooling fan shroud.
10. Using disconnect tool No. D87L-9280-A, or equivalent, disconnect fuel supply line and fuel return line from fuel injection supply manifold.
11. Remove power steering pressure hose bracket and position hose aside.
12. Loosen alternator lower bolt, remove alternator upper bolt and tilt alternator forward.
13. Remove oil level indicator tube bracket bolt from intake manifold.
14. Disconnect EGR tube from EGR valve.
15. Disconnect EGR tube from exhaust manifold.
16. Remove exhaust manifold shield.
17. Remove exhaust manifold to catalytic converter nuts.
18. Raise and support vehicle.
19. Drain engine coolant into a suitable container.
20. Remove righthand splash shield.
21. Remove oil level indicator tube from cylinder block.
22. Disconnect A/C compressor electrical connector.
23. Remove A/C compressor mounting bolts and suspend compressor with wire.
24. Loosen lower four bolts and one nut securing front engine accessory drive bracket about 4 turns. Do not remove.
25. Lower vehicle.
26. Remove uppermost front engine accessory drive bracket to cylinder head bolt.
27. Remove A/C line bracket to front engine accessory drive bracket bolt.
28. Remove valve cover.
29. Disconnect upper radiator hose from thermostat housing water hose connection.

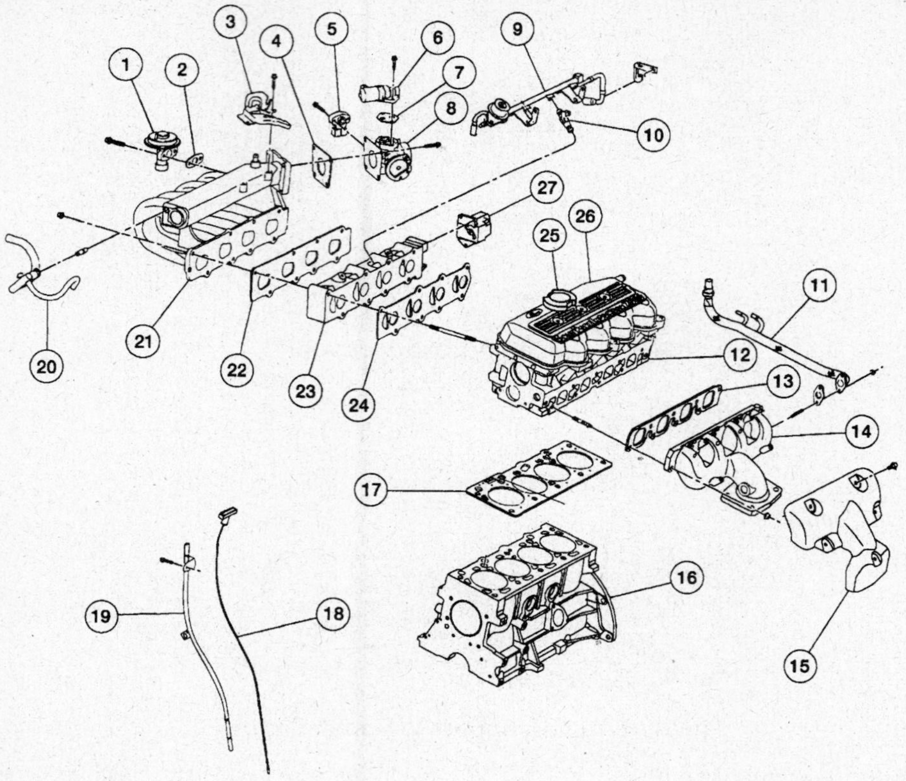

Item	Description
1	EGR Valve
2	EGR Valve Gasket
3	Accelerator Cable Bracket
4	Throttle Body Gasket
5	Throttle Position Sensor
6	Idle Air Control Valve
7	Idle Air Control Gasket

Item	Description
8	Throttle Body
9	Fuel Injection Supply Manifold
10	Fuel Injector
11	EGR Valve to Exhaust Manifold Tube
12	Cylinder Head
13	Exhaust Manifold Gasket

FM1069700595010X

Fig. 5 Intake & exhaust manifold replacement (Part 1 of 2)

Item	Description
14	Exhaust Manifold
15	Exhaust Manifold Shield
16	Cylinder Block
17	Head Gasket
18	Oil Level Dipstick
19	Oil Level Indicator Tube
20	Intake Manifold Tube

Item	Description
21	Intake Manifold
22	Intake Manifold Upper Gasket
23	Intake Manifold Runner Control (IMRC)
24	Intake Manifold Gasket
25	Oil Filler Cap
26	Valve Cover
27	IMRC Actuator

FM1069700595020X

Fig. 5 Intake & exhaust manifold replacement (Part 2 of 2)

30. Disconnect heater hose from thermostat housing.
31. Remove cylinder head bolts, cylinder head and gasket.

INSTALLATION

1. Clean all old gasket material from mating surface, then install new cylinder head gasket and cylinder head.
2. Lubricate cylinder head bolts and install as follows:
   a. **Torque** bolts to 30–44 ft. lbs. in sequence shown, **Fig. 6.**
   b. Back off bolts ½ turn.
   c. **Retorque** bolts in same sequence to 30–44 ft. lbs.

   d. Turn bolts, in same tightening sequence, an additional 180° in two steps of 90° each.
3. Install uppermost front engine accessory drive bracket bolt.
4. Install A/C line bracket on front engine accessory drive bracket.
5. Install new valve cover and gasket.
6. Raise and support vehicle.
7. Tighten four front engine accessory drive bracket bolts and one nut.
8. Remove wire support and install A/C compressor and four bolts.
9. Close radiator drain plug.
10. Install righthand splash shield assembly.
11. Install oil level indicator tube.
12. Lower vehicle.
13. Install heater hose and upper radiator hose.
14. Install timing belt as described under "Timing Belt, Replace."
15. Install alternator.
16. Install power steering pressure hose to front engine accessory drive bracket.
17. Connect crankshaft position sensor electrical connector.
18. Connect two main engine/fuel charging wiring electrical connectors.
19. Install oil level indicator tube bolt and tighten to specifications.
20. Install EGR manifold tube at EGR valve.
21. Install EGR valve manifold tube to exhaust manifold.
22. Connect fuel supply line to fuel injection supply manifold.
23. Connect fuel return line to fuel injection supply manifold.
24. Install new gasket and four exhaust manifold to catalytic converter nuts.
25. Install exhaust manifold heat shield.
26. Install speed control cable bracket.
27. Connect speed control cable, accelerator cable and throttle valve control actuating cable to the throttle control lever.
28. Install vacuum hoses.
29. Install outlet half of engine air cleaner and air cleaner intake tube.
30. Fill radiator and bleed cooling system as outlined under " Cooling System Bleed."

VALVE ADJUSTMENT

This engine uses hydraulic valve lash adjusters. Valve clearance is adjusted automatically.

TIMING BELT

REPLACE

REMOVAL

1. Remove drive belt and drive belt tensioner.
2. Remove three engine front cover attaching nuts, three attaching bolts, then the front cover.
3. Raise and support vehicle, then remove righthand wheel and tire assembly.
4. Remove righthand splash shield.
5. Remove crankshaft pulley attaching bolt, then the pulley.

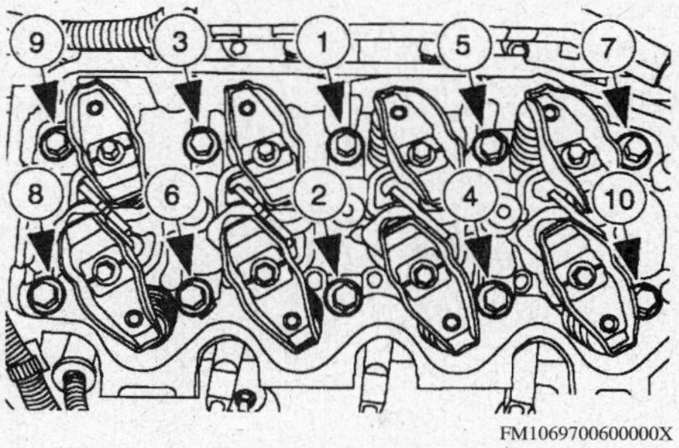

Fig. 6 Cylinder head bolt tightening sequence

6. Align timing marks as shown in **Fig. 7**
7. Loosen timing belt tensioner bolt.
8. Using an 8 mm Allen wrench, turn timing belt counterclockwise ¼ turn.
9. Insert ⅛ inch drill bit to lock timing belt tensioner in place.
10. Remove timing belt.

INSTALLATION

1. Install timing belt in a counterclockwise direction, over the crankshaft pulley, over the camshaft pulley, under the timing belt tensioner, then over the water pump sprocket. **During installation, maintain the belt span between the crankshaft and camshaft sprockets.**
2. Remove ⅛ inch drill bit holding timing belt tensioner in position.
3. Allow tensioner to tension timing belt, then tighten tensioner bolt to specification.
4. Rotate crankshaft two turns in normal direction of rotation.
5. Ensure crankshaft and camshaft timing marks are aligned, **Fig. 7.** If timing mark are not aligned, timing belt must be removed and reinstalled.
6. Install engine front cover, then the crankshaft pulley.
7. Install splash shield, then the wheel and tire assembly.
8. Lower vehicle, then install accessory drive belt tensioner and drive belt.

CAMSHAFT

REPLACE

1. Remove engine air cleaner.
2. Remove three bolts, valve cover and gasket.
3. Remove camshaft front seal.
4. Remove ignition coil as described under "Electrical " section.
5. Remove ignition coil bracket, **Fig. 8.**
6. Remove eight valve tappets.
7. Remove two bolts and camshaft thrust plate.
8. Remove and discard cup plug from rear of cylinder head.
9. Remove camshaft from rear of cylinder head.
10. Reverse procedure to install.

OIL PAN

REPLACE

1. Remove catalytic converter.
2. Remove oil pan drain plug and drain oil from engine.
3. Remove two oil pan to transaxle bolts and catalytic converter to oil pan bracket.
4. Remove ten oil pan bolts, then the oil pan and oil pan gasket. Discard gasket.
5. Clean and inspect mounting faces of both oil pan and cylinder block.
6. Apply suitable liquid gasket and install oil pan. **Torque** bolts in sequence, **Fig. 9,** to 15–22 ft. lbs.
7. Install catalytic converter to oil pan bracket.
8. Install catalytic converter.
9. Install oil pan drain plug. Tighten to specifications.
10. Lower vehicle.
11. Fill engine with oil to proper level.
12. Start engine and check for leaks.

OIL PUMP

REPLACE

1. Remove timing belt as outlined under "Timing Belt, Replace."
2. Remove oil pan.
3. Disconnect crankshaft position sensor electrical connector.
4. Remove two bolts and the oil pump screen cover and tube. Discard gasket.
5. Remove oil pump and gasket.
6. Reverse procedure to install. Tighten to specifications.

BELT TENSION DATA

No manual drive belt tension adjustments are necessary. The drive belt tensioner automatically adjusts belt tension.

SERPENTINE DRIVE BELT

Refer to **Figs. 10 and 11** for serpentine drive belt routing.

COOLING SYSTEM BLEED

After filling cooling system, run engine for approximately 12 minutes with radiator pressure cap off, then top off radiator. Secure cap, then and with engine running, fill coolant reservoir to FULL HOT mark with coolant.

THERMOSTAT

REPLACE

1. Remove air cleaner outlet tube.
2. Raise and support vehicle.
3. Remove two lefthand splash shield bolts.
4. Drain radiator.
5. Lower vehicle.
6. Disconnect coolant temperature indicator sender unit and engine coolant temperature sensor electrical connectors.
7. Disconnect upper radiator hose and heater coolant hose from thermostat housing.

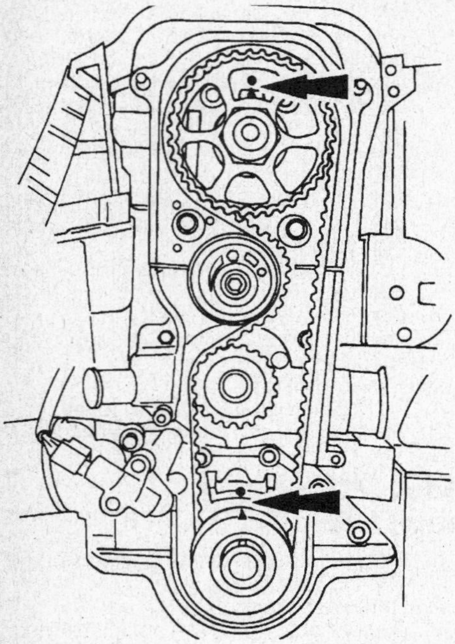

FM1069700595000X

Fig. 7 Timing mark alignment

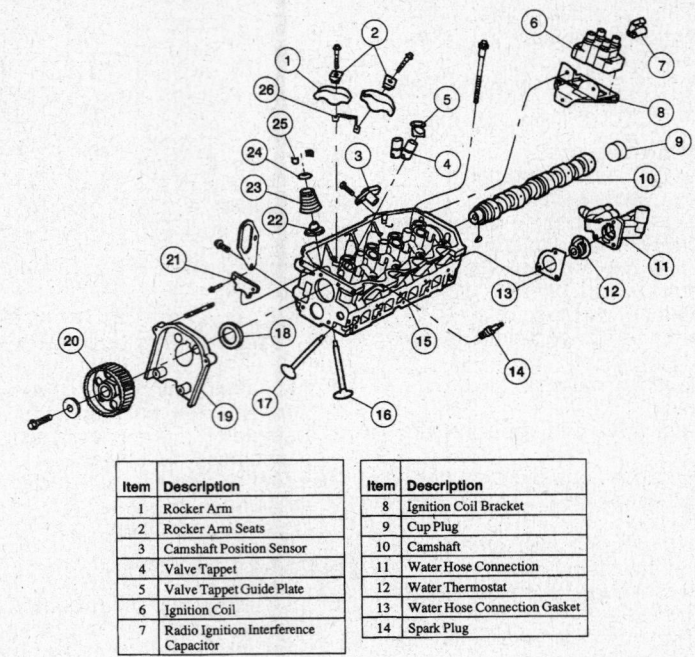

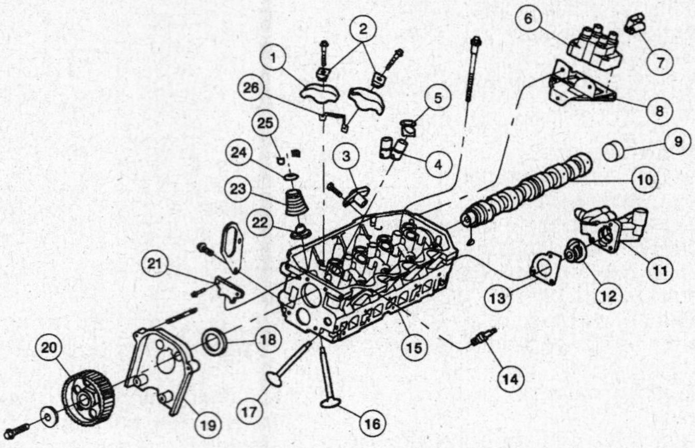

Item	Description
1	Rocker Arm
2	Rocker Arm Seats
3	Camshaft Position Sensor
4	Valve Tappet
5	Valve Tappet Guide Plate
6	Ignition Coil
7	Radio Ignition Interference Capacitor

Item	Description
8	Ignition Coil Bracket
9	Cup Plug
10	Camshaft
11	Water Hose Connection
12	Water Thermostat
13	Water Hose Connection Gasket
14	Spark Plug

FM1069700598010X

Fig. 8 Exploded view of cylinder head (Part 1 of 2)

Item	Description
15	Cylinder Head
16	Intake Valve
17	Exhaust Valve
18	Camshaft Front Seal
19	Engine Front Cover
20	Camshaft Sprocket

Item	Description
21	Camshaft Thrust Plate
22	Valve Stem Seal
23	Valve Spring
24	Valve Spring Retainer
25	Valve Spring Retainer Key
26	Valve Tappet Guide Plate Retainer

FM1069700598020X

Fig. 8 Exploded view of cylinder head (Part 2 of 2)

8. Remove thermostat housing bolts, thermostat housing and the thermostat.
9. Reverse procedure to install. Tighten thermostat housing bolts to specifications.

RADIATOR

REPLACE

1. Remove fan motor, blade and shroud assembly.
2. Raise and support vehicle.
3. Remove lefthand splash shield bolts and the lefthand splash shield.
4. Drain coolant from radiator.
5. Disconnect lower radiator hose and lower oil cooler outlet tube.
6. Remove two oil cooler tube bracket bolts.
7. Lower vehicle.
8. Disconnect upper radiator hose.
9. Remove radiator cap and disconnect overflow hose.
10. Disconnect upper oil cooler inlet tube.
11. Remove four radiator support bracket bolts and the radiator.
12. Reverse procedure to install. Fill cooling system and bleed as outlined under "Cooling System, Bleed."

WATER PUMP

REPLACE

1. Drain engine coolant into a suitable container.
2. Remove timing belt as described under "Timing Belt, Replace."
3. Remove timing belt tensioner bolt and timing belt tensioner.
4. Remove lower radiator hose from water pump.
5. Lower vehicle.
6. Disconnect heater hose from water pump.
7. Remove three bolts (A), one stud (B) and the water pump (C), **Fig. 12.**
8. Reverse procedure to install. Tighten to specifications.

FUEL PUMP

REPLACE

1. Relieve fuel system pressure as described under " Precautions."
2. Remove rear seat cushion, then locate fuel pump access cover and disconnect fuel pump electrical connector.
3. Remove four fuel pump access cover screws then the access cover plate.
4. Remove fuel line clips and disconnect fuel lines from top of fuel pump.
5. Remove fuel pump locking retainer ring then the fuel pump.
6. Reverse procedure to install.

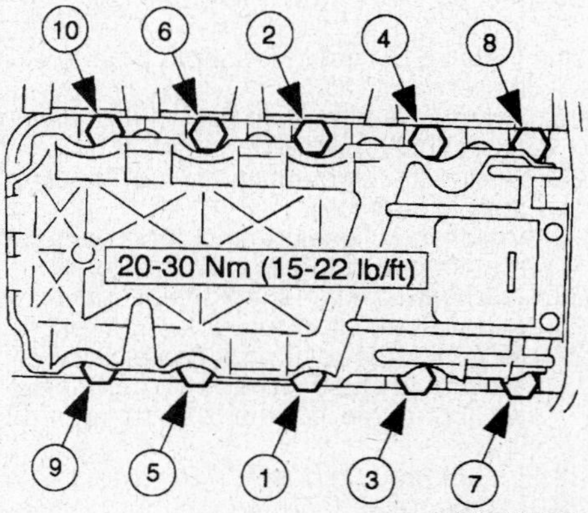

FM1099700077000X

Fig. 9 Oil pan bolt tightening sequence

FUEL FILTER

REPLACE

1. Release fuel system pressure as described under " Precautions."
2. Place suitable container under fuel filter.
3. Loosen fuel filter bracket clamp.
4. Remove fuel line clips.
5. Disconnect fuel tubes and remove fuel filter, **Fig. 13.**
6. Reverse procedure to install.

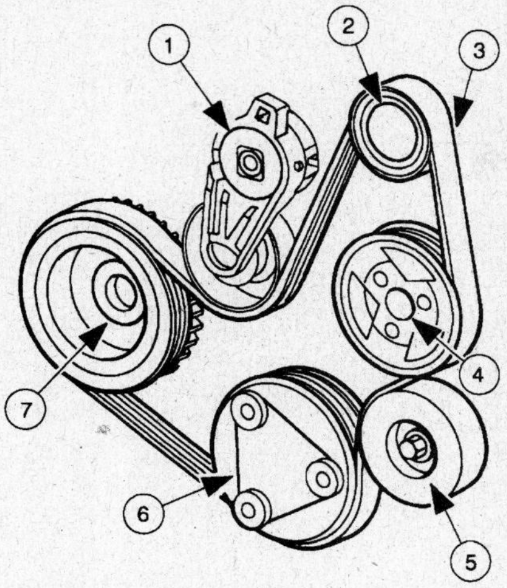

Item	Part Number	Description
1	6B209	Drive Belt Tensioner
2	10346	Generator
3	8620	Drive Belt
4	3A733	Power Steering Pump Pulley
5	6C348	Accessory Drive Belt Routing Pulley
6	19703	A/C Compressor
7	6A312	Crankshaft Pulley

FM1069700596000X

Fig. 10 Drive belt routing. Models with A/C

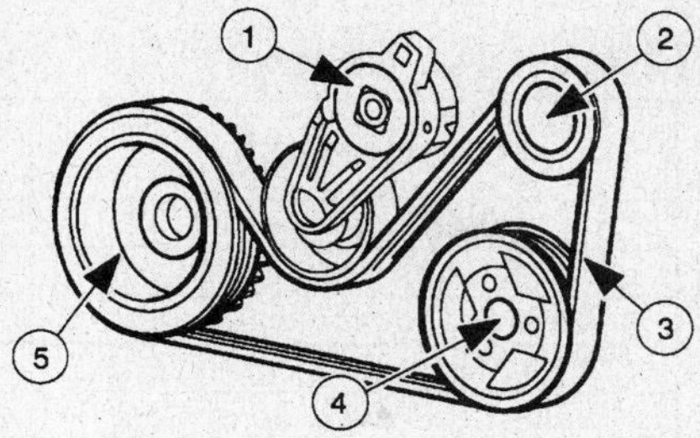

Item	Part Number	Description
1	6B209	Drive Belt Tensioner
2	10346	Generator
3	8620	Drive Belt
4	3A733	Power Steering Pump Pulley
5	6A312	Crankshaft Pulley

FM1069700597000X

Fig. 11 Drive belt routing. Models less A/C

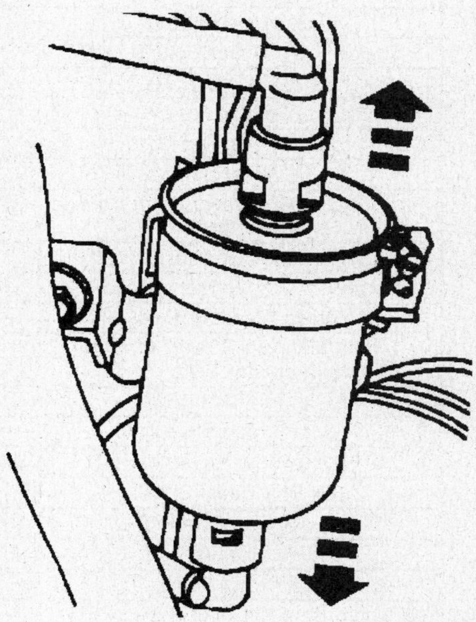

Fig. 13 Fuel filter replacement

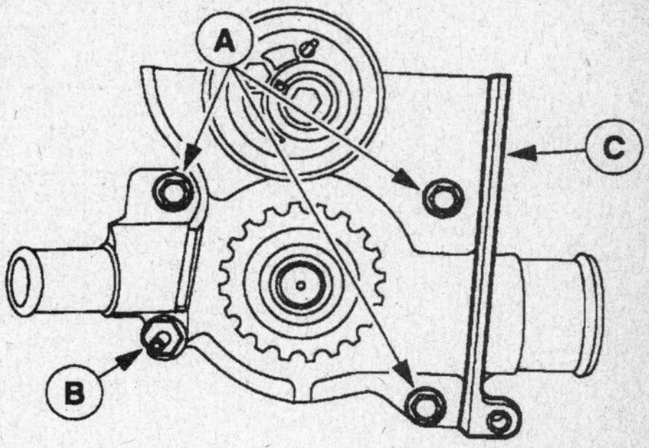

Fig. 12 Water pump replacement

TIGHTENING SPECIFICATIONS

Year	Component	Torque/Ft. Lbs.
1997– 2000	A/C Compressor Bolts	15–22
	A/C Line Bracket Bolt	15–18
	Alternator Lower Mounting Bolt	15–22
	Alternator Upper Mounting Bolt	30–40
	Camshaft Position Sensor Bolt	15–22
	Camshaft Sprocket Bolt	70–85
	Camshaft Thrust Plate Bolts	6–10
	Catalytic Converter Bracket Bolts	15–20
	Catalytic Converter To Exhaust Mounting Nuts	26–34
	Catalytic Converter To Oil Pan Bracket Bolts	30–40
	Connecting Rod Cap Nuts	26–30
	Constant Control Relay Module	6–8
	Crankshaft Main Bearing Cap Bolts	66–79
	Crankshaft Pulley Bolt	81–96
	Cylinder Head Bolts	②
	EGR Manifold Tube	15–20
	Engine Front Cover Bolts & Nuts	6–8
	Engine Mounting Bracket Bolts	31–42
	Exhaust Manifold Heat Shield	45–61①
	Exhaust Manifold Nuts	15–18
	Flywheel Bolts	54–67
	Front Engine Accessory Drive Bracket Bolts/Nut	30–40
	Ignition Coil Bracket Bolts	6–8
	Ignition Coil Mounting Bolts	40–61①
	Intake Manifold Nuts	15–22
	Intake Manifold Runner Control Actuator Bolts	6–8
	LH Splash Shield Bolts	69–98①
	Motor Mount Nuts	50–69
	Oil Level Indicator Tube Bolt	6–8
	Oil Pan Baffle Bolts	15–22
	Oil Pan Bolts	15–22
	Oil Pan Drain Plug	15–22
	Oil Pump Bolts	8–12
	Oil Pump Screen Cover & Tube Bolts	6–8
	Oil Pressure Sensor Switch	8–12
	Power Steering Pressure Hose Bracket	64–87①
	Power Steering Pump Bolts	30–41
	Power Steering Pump Pulley Bolts	15–22
	RH Engine Support Insulator Through Bolt	50–69
	RH Splash Shield	6–8.
	Rocker Arm Bolts	17–22
	Speed Control Cable Bracket Bolts	64–87①
	Starter Mounting Bolt	18–20
	Timing Belt Tensioner Bolt	15–22
	Thermostat Housing	8–12
	Valve Cover Bolts	6–8
	Water Outlet Connection Bolts	8–11
	Water Pump Bolts	15–22

① — Inch Lbs.
② — Refer to “Cylinder Head, Replace” for tightening sequence.

2.0L DOHC Engine

NOTE: For procedures not outlined in this section, refer to "Contour, Mystique & 1999–2000 Cougar."

NOTE: On Air Bag Equipped Models, Refer To " Air Bag System Precautions" Located In The Front Of This Manual For System Disarming & Arming Procedures.

NOTE: Refer To "Computer Relearn" Located In The Front Of This Manual For Computer Relearn Procedures.

INDEX

PRECAUTIONS

AIR BAG SYSTEMS

Refer to "Air Bag System Precautions" in the front of this manual for system disarming and arming procedures.

BATTERY GROUND CABLE

Prior to service, disconnect battery ground cable and isolate as required.

FUEL SYSTEM PRESSURE RELIEF

Remove the schrader valve cap from the end of the fuel injection supply manifold, **Fig. 1.** Attach fuel pressure gauge No. T80L-9974-B, or equivalent, to the schrader valve cap opening. Open the pressure gauge manual valve to relieve fuel system pressure.

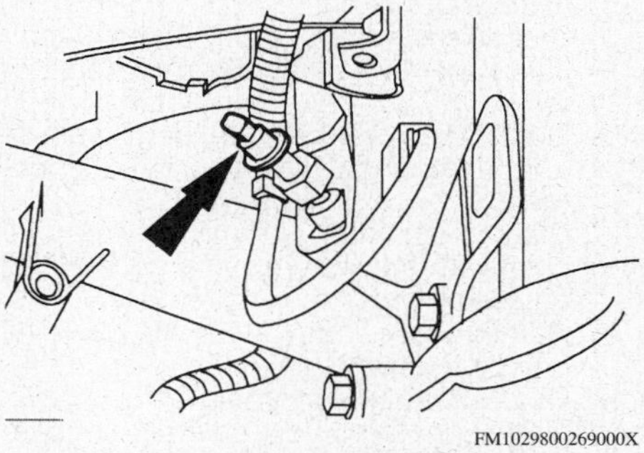

Fig. 1 Schrader valve cap location

COMPRESSION PRESSURE

Compression pressure should be checked at normal operating temperature with spark plugs removed and throttle plate wide open. Cylinder compression pressure is considered within specification if lowest reading cylinder is within 75 percent of highest reading.

ENGINE

REPLACE

1. Remove hood, then release fuel system pressure as described under "Precautions."
2. Remove battery and battery tray.
3. Remove air cleaner assembly.
4. Remove throttle return spring and constant control relay module bracket as an assembly.
5. Disconnect heated oxygen sensor, then drain engine coolant into a suitable container.
6. Recover refrigerant as outlined in the "Air Conditioning " section.
7. Remove catalytic converter, then the splash shield.
8. Disconnect starter motor wiring, then remove accessory drive belt.
9. Remove A/C compressor, then disconnect lower radiator hose and heater hose.
10. Disconnect power steering pressure line.
11. **On models equipped with automatic transaxle,** remove torque converter inspection cover and converter nuts.
12. **On all models,** remove front roll restrictor nuts and restrictor.
13. Remove axle shafts as outlined under "Front Wheel Drive Axles," then disconnect transaxle cooler lines.
14. **On models equipped with automatic transaxle,** remove transaxle cooler line bolts and transaxle cooler lines, then disconnect transaxle shift cable.
15. **On models equipped with manual transaxle,** disconnect transaxle control rod and support.
16. **On all models,** disconnect fuel charging wiring from transaxle internal wiring harness connector, turbine shaft speed sensor, transaxle range sensor and heated oxygen sensor connectors.
17. Remove radiator, fan shroud and fan motor as an assembly.
18. Disconnect accelerator cable and speed control actuator cable.
19. Disconnect power steering return hose, then remove radiator coolant recovery reservoir.
20. Disconnect generator wiring and vacuum lines.
21. Disconnect fuel charging wiring harness connectors, then the heater water hoses, vehicle speed sensor and the ground strap.
22. Disconnect fuel line, then support engine with suitable lifting device.
23. Remove remaining engine mount nuts and bolts.
24. Remove engine and transaxle as an assembly with engine lifting brackets T70P-6000 or equivalent, and engine lift.
25. Reverse procedure to install, noting the following:

a. Install axle shafts as outlined under "Front Wheel Drive Axles."
b. Fill engine oil to specification and fill and bleed cooling system as outlined under "Cooling System Bleed."
c. Charge A/C system as outlined under "Air Conditioning."

INTAKE MANIFOLD

REPLACE

1. Release fuel system pressure as described under "Precautions."
2. Remove air cleaner outlet tube, then disconnect throttle position sensor wiring.
3. Remove throttle body from intake manifold.
4. Raise and support vehicle, then drain engine coolant into a suitable container.
5. Remove heater line bolt, then lower the vehicle.
6. Disconnect heater hoses from heater core.
7. Disconnect main engine control sensor wiring and remove connectors from mounting bracket.
8. Disconnect vacuum supply hoses from intake manifold.
9. Disconnect crankcase ventilation hose from valve cover, then remove fuel charging wiring and drive belt.
10. Remove generator mounting bolt and position generator aside.
11. Disconnect fuel line, then remove intake manifold attaching bolts and nuts.
12. Reverse procedure to install.

EXHAUST MANIFOLD

REPLACE

1. Disconnect fan motor wiring, then remove fan shroud.
2. Raise and support vehicle, then disconnect heated oxygen sensor wiring connector.
3. Remove catalytic converter from exhaust manifold, then lower vehicle.
4. Remove oil level indicator tube bracket bolt, then exhaust manifold heat shield.
5. Remove exhaust manifold attaching bolts and studs.
6. Reverse procedure to install.

FUEL INJECTION SUPPLY MANIFOLD

REPLACE

1. Ensure ignition switch is in the Off position, then relieve fuel pressure as outlined under "Precautions."
2. Disconnect spring lock coupling with tool Nos. D87L-9280–A or D87L-9280–B, or equivalent.
3. Remove air cleaner outlet tube, then the throttle body.
4. Disconnect fuel injector electrical connectors.
5. Disconnect fuel pressure sensor vacuum line and electrical connector.
6. Disconnect fuel temperature sensor wiring connector, then remove fuel charging wiring and position aside.
7. Remove fuel injection supply manifold bolts, then the supply line.
8. Reverse procedure to install. Lubricate injector O-rings with clean engine oil.

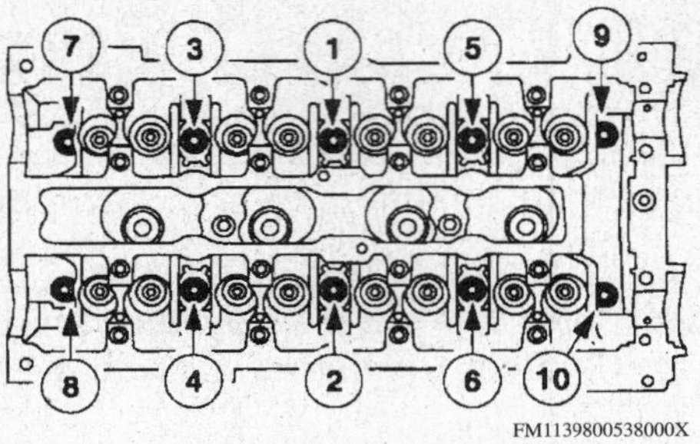

Fig. 2 Cylinder head tightening sequence

CYLINDER HEAD

REPLACE

1. Relieve fuel system as outlined under "Precautions."
2. Remove air cleaner outlet tube, then the timing belt as outlined under "Timing Belt, Replace."
3. Disconnect vacuum hoses from PCV valve, throttle body, intake manifold and fuel pressure sensor.
4. Disconnect speed control cable and accelerator cable from control lever.
5. Disconnect fuel charging wiring electrical connectors at main engine connector.
6. Disconnect crankshaft position sensor and heated oxygen sensor connectors.
7. Disconnect fuel line, then remove power steering pump and bracket as an assembly.
8. Remove generator, then the oil level indicator tube.
9. Raise and support vehicle, then drain engine coolant into a suitable container.
10. Remove splash shield bolts and shield, then disconnect A/C compressor electrical connector.
11. Remove A/C compressor and position aside.
12. Lower vehicle, then disconnect spark plug wires and remove plugs.
13. Remove valve cover, then disconnect upper radiator hose from thermostat housing.
14. Disconnect heater water hose from thermostat housing, then remove camshafts, ignition coil and bracket.
15. Remove water thermostat housing, then the cylinder head.
16. Remove cylinder head gasket and discard.
17. Reverse procedure to install, noting the following:
    a. Install new head gasket on cylinder block.
    b. Using sequence shown in **Fig. 2**, **torque** cylinder head bolts in three steps. First step to 12–18 ft. lbs.; second step to 26–33 ft. lbs.; third step an additional 90.°

VALVE COVER

REPLACE

1. Disconnect crankcase ventilation hose from fitting on valve cover.
2. Disconnect oil control solenoid electrical connector, then remove appearance cover.
3. Position accelerator cable and speed control cable aside.
4. Remove spark plug wires, then the upper timing belt cover.
5. Remove valve cover bolts, then the cover.
6. Reverse procedure to install.

TIMING BELT COVER

REPLACE

1. Remove upper timing belt cover bolts and cover.
2. Loosen water pump pulley bolts, then remove drive belt.
3. Remove idler pulley, then the water pump pulley bolts and pulley.
4. Raise and support vehicle, then remove middle timing belt cover bolts and cover.
5. Remove crankshaft pulley, then the lower timing belt cover bolts and cover.
6. Reverse procedure to install.

TIMING BELT

REPLACE

Avoid turning camshaft or crankshaft when the timing belt has been removed. If movement is required, use extreme caution to avoid valve damage from piston contact.

1. Remove spark plugs, then rotate crankshaft so No. 1 cylinder is at Top Dead Center (TDC), **Fig. 3.**
2. Remove bolt and install crankshaft TDC timing peg T97P-6000–A, or equivalent, **Fig. 4.**
3. Remove timing belt upper cover.
4. Raise and support vehicle.
5. Remove splash shield, then loosen water pump pulley bolts.
6. Remove center timing belt cover and crankshaft pulley.
7. Remove timing belt lower cover.
8. Lower vehicle, then remove accessory drive belt.
9. Remove accessory drive belt idler pulley.
10. Remove water pump pulley.
11. Disconnect PCV hose from valve cover.
12. Disconnect oil control solenoid electrical connector.
13. Remove appearance cover.
14. Position accelerator control and speed control cables aside.
15. Remove ignition wire and bracket.
16. Remove valve cover.
17. Align camshafts using alignment tool No. T94P-6256-CH or equivalent. It may be necessary to rotate exhaust camshaft clockwise to install alignment tool, **Fig. 3.**
18. Loosen timing belt tensioner pulley bolt.

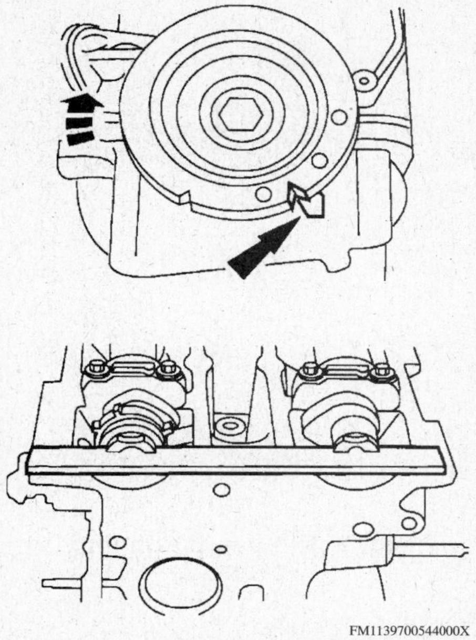

Fig. 3 Crankshaft & camshaft timing mark alignment

19. Release belt tension by disconnecting tensioner tab from timing cover backplate.
20. Remove timing belt from camshaft and crankshaft sprockets.
21. Reverse procedure to install noting the following:
    a. Rotate crankshaft clockwise against TDC timing peg.
    b. Engage timing belt tensioner tab into upper timing cover backplate.
    c. Install new timing belt keeping belt against crankshaft and exhaust camshaft sprockets.
    d. Using a suitable 6 mm hex head wrench, adjust tensioner until index marks align. Tighten tensioner bolt to specifications.
    e. Remove TDC peg and camshaft alignment tool.

TIMING

ADJUST

1. Ensure correct notch on crankshaft pulley is indexed to lower cylinder block. Position crankshaft just before top dead center.
2. Remove bolt and install TDC timing peg, **Fig. 4.**
3. Rotate crankshaft clockwise against peg.
4. Install camshaft alignment timing tool T94P-6256-CH, or equivalent, on back of camshafts. Exhaust camshaft may have to be rotated clockwise to install alignment tool.
5. Install intake timing sprocket and loosely install bolt.
6. Rotate oil control bushing one full turn and inspect for binding. Position bushing with single hole in the 12 o'clock position.
7. Install a new exhaust sprocket O-ring into exhaust sprocket, then the exhaust camshaft sprocket. Ensure tab on sprocket engages hole positioned at 12 o'clock in oil control solenoid bushing, then loosely install bolt.
8. Loosely install timing belt tensioner.
9. Install timing belt, then engage timing belt tensioner tab into upper timing cover backplate.
10. Using a 6 mm Allen wrench, adjust timing belt tensioner until index marks are aligned, then tighten bolt to specifications.
11. Camshaft must be held stationary with an open end wrench. Do not use alignment tool to hold camshaft in position or damage to the camshaft may occur.
12. **Torque** intake camshaft sprocket bolt to 48–53 ft. lbs.
13. **Torque** exhaust camshaft sprocket in two steps: first to 50 ft. lbs., then remove TDC peg and camshaft alignment tool and **torque** bolt to 85–92 ft. lbs.
14. Ensure correct notch in crankshaft pulley is indexed to lower cylinder block, then position crankshaft just before top dead center.
15. Remove bolt and install TDC timing peg, then rotate crankshaft clockwise against peg.
16. Exhaust camshaft may need to be rotated clockwise to install alignment tool. If tool will not align and install in the camshaft, repeat procedure.
17. Remove alignment tool and TDC timing peg and install bolt.

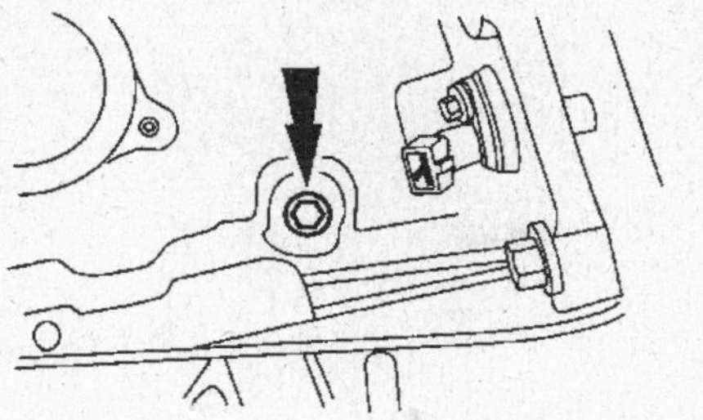

Fig. 4 Crankshaft TDC timing peg tool installation location

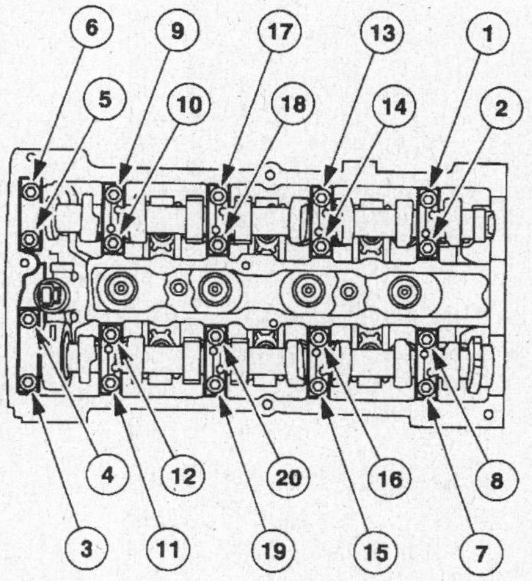

Fig. 6 Camshaft loosening sequence

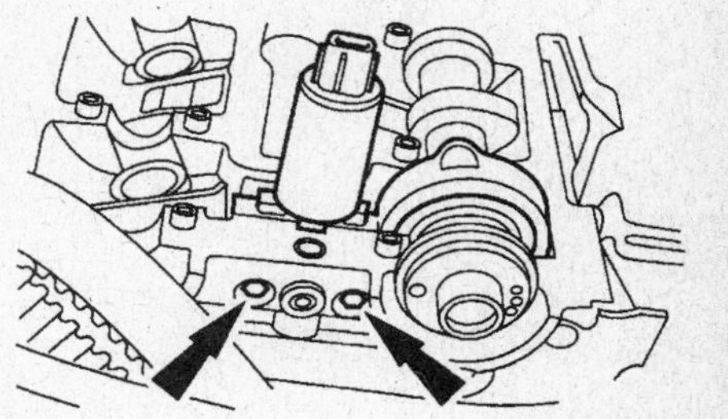

Fig. 5 Oil control solenoid flange removal

CAMSHAFT

REPLACE

REMOVAL

1. Remove timing belt as outlined under "Timing Belt, Replace," then the valve cover and camshaft sprockets.
2. Remove oil control solenoid flange bolts and flange, **Fig. 5.**
3. Remove camshaft journal caps in sequence, **Fig. 6.**
4. Remove camshafts, then the oil control sensor and bushing.
5. Inspect camshafts for wear.

INSTALLATION

1. Verify valve clearance as outlined under "Valve Clearance Specifications."
2. Install oil control solenoid bushing and flange on exhaust camshaft, **Fig. 7.**
3. **Front camshaft journal cap must be installed and bolts tightened to specification within four minutes of sealer application or oil leaks may occur.**
4. Coat sealing surface of front camshaft journal cap with gasket maker E2AZ-19562-B, or equivalent.
5. Position camshaft, then lubricate camshaft bearing surfaces with Engine Assembly Lubricant D9AZ-19579-D or equivalent.
6. Install camshaft, then apply a thin coat of silicone gasket and sealant F6AZ-19562-AA, or equivalent, to sealing surface of front camshaft bearing cap.
7. Install camshaft journal caps, then using sequence shown in **Fig. 8,** tighten cap bolts to specifications.
8. Inspect oil control solenoid flange O-rings, replace if necessary.
9. Install oil control solenoid flange bolts.
10. Rotate camshafts one full turn and inspect for binding.
11. Install camshaft sprockets.
12. Install timing belt as outlined under "Timing Belt, Replace."
13. Install valve cover as outlined under "Valve Cover, Replace."

CRANKSHAFT SEAL

REPLACE

1. Remove timing belt as outlined under "Timing Belt, Replace."

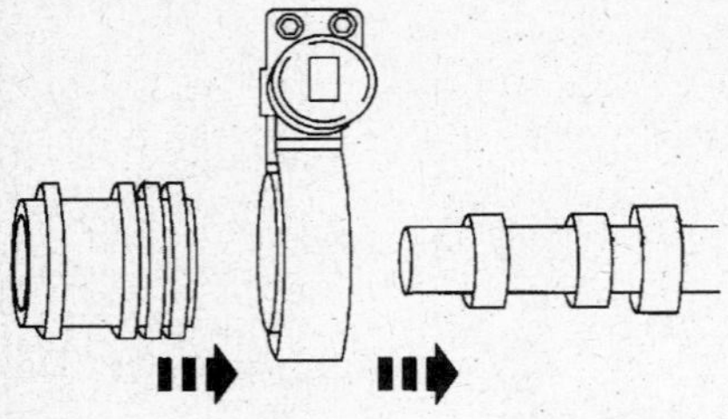

FM1029800272000X

Fig. 7 Oil control solenoid bushing & flange installation

2. Remove crankshaft sprocket and timing belt guide washer.
3. Use care to avoid damaging crankshaft surface, then using seal remover T92C-6700-CH, or equivalent, remove front seal from oil pump.
4. Reverse procedure to install. Use oil pump replacer T81P-6700-A, or equivalent to install seal.

CRANKSHAFT REAR OIL SEAL

REPLACE

1. **On models equipped with automatic transaxle,** remove transaxle as outlined in "Automatic Transaxle/ Transmission" section.
2. **On models equipped with manual transaxle,** remove transaxle, then clutch pressure plate and clutch disc as outlined in "Clutch & Manual Transaxle."
3. **On all models,** use care to avoid damaging cranking sealing surface, then using Seal Remover T92C-6700-CH, or equivalent, remove seal.
4. Inspect crankshaft rear oil seal area, then coat seal and seal area with engine oil.
5. Ensure edges of crankshaft rear oil seal are not rolled over, then using crankshaft rear seal pilot tool No. T88P-6701-B2 and crankshaft rear seal replacer tool No. T88P-6701-B1, or equivalents, install rear oil seal.

OIL PAN

REPLACE

1. Raise and support vehicle, then drain engine oil into a suitable container.
2. Remove catalytic convertor.
3. Remove seventeen oil pan bolts evenly, then the oil pan.
4. Reverse procedure to install, noting the following:
   a. Clean and inspect mounting faces of oil pan and cylinder block.
   b. Apply .1 inch continuous bead of silicone gasket and sealant F6AZ-19562-AA, or equivalent, to oil pan. **Install oil pan within four minutes after sealer has been applied.**
   c. Using sequence shown in **Fig. 9, torque** oil pan bolts to 15–22 ft. lbs.

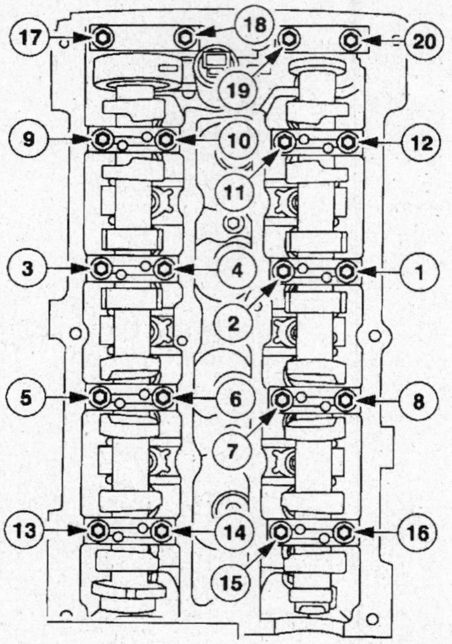

FM1029800273000X

Fig. 8 Camshaft tightening sequence

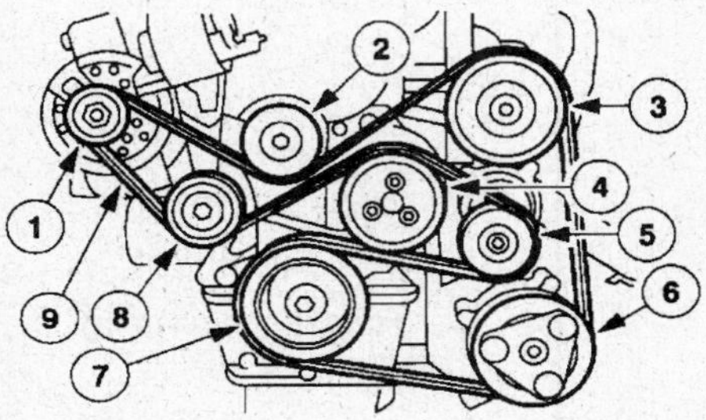

Item	Description
1	Generator
2	Drive Belt Idler Pulley
3	Power Steering Pump Pulley
4	Water Pump Pulley
5	Drive Belt Tensioner
6	A/C Compressor
7	Crankshaft
8	Drive Belt Idler Pulley
9	Accessory Drive Belt

FM1139800548000X

Fig. 10 Serpentine drive belt routing

OIL PUMP SERVICE

OIL PUMP SCREEN COVER & TUBE

1. Remove oil pan as outlined under "Oil Pan, Replace."
2. Remove oil pump screen bolts and discard oil pump inlet tube.
3. Reverse procedure to install.

BELT TENSION DATA

Automatic drive belt tensioners are

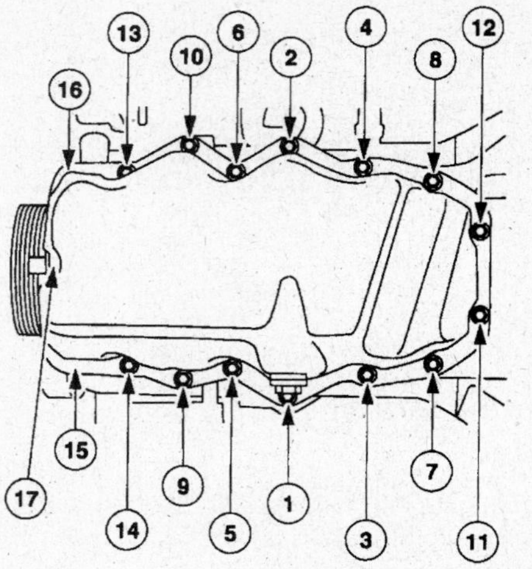

FM1029800274000X

Fig. 9 Oil pan tightening sequence

spring loaded devices which set and maintain drive belt tension. The drive belt should not require tension adjustment for the life to the belt. Automatic drive belt tensioners have drive belt wear indicator marks. If the indicator mark is not approximately in the middle between MIN and MAX tabs on the engine front cover, the drive belt is worn or an incorrect drive belt is installed.

SERPENTINE DRIVE BELT

Refer to **Fig. 10** for serpentine drive belt routing.

COOLING SYSTEM BLEED

1. Select maximum heater temperature and blower motor speed settings. Position control to discharge air through the vents.
2. Start engine and allow to idle. While engine is idling, feel for hot air at the vents.
3. If air discharge remains cool and engine coolant temperature gauge does not move, engine coolant level is low and must be filled. Stop engine, allow to cool and fill coolant.
4. Start engine and allow to idle until normal operating temperature is reached. Hot air should blow from vents and the engine temperature gauge should maintain a stabilized reading in the NORMAL range and the upper radiator hose should feel hot to the touch.

THERMOSTAT

REPLACE

1. Drain engine coolant to a point below thermostat.
2. Disconnect camshaft position sensor, then remove bolts and move housing and hose to one side.
3. Remove thermostat and seal from housing.

4. Inspect seal and thermostat.
5. Reverse procedure to install.

RADIATOR

REPLACE

1. Raise and support vehicle, then drain radiator into a suitable container.
2. Remove righthand splash shield, then disconnect lower radiator hose and if equipped lower oil cooler outlet tube.
3. Lower vehicle, remove upper radiator hose from radiator, then, if equipped the upper oil cooler inlet tube.
4. Disconnect connector at fan motor, then remove radiator cap and overflow hose.
5. Remove bolts and nuts for A/C condenser core from brackets at top of radiator.
6. Remove radiator and shroud arm from the vehicle, then the fan motor shroud assembly from radiator.
7. Reverse procedure to install.

WATER PUMP

REPLACE

1. Raise and support vehicle, then drain radiator into a suitable container.
2. Remove splash shield bolts and shield.
3. Loosen water pump pulley attaching bolts, then remove drive belt.
4. Remove A/C compressor bolts and position compressor aside.
5. Remove water pump from middle timing belt cover.
6. Reverse procedure to install.

FUEL PUMP

REPLACE

1. Relieve fuel pressure as outlined under "Precautions."
2. Remove rear seat cushion, then disconnect two fuel delivery module connectors.
3. Remove four access cover attaching screws, then the access cover.
4. Disconnect fuel delivery module connector, then remove fuel clip and pull fuel line off.
5. Using fuel tank locking wrench tool No. D90P-9275-A, or equivalent, remove locking retainer ring.
6. Remove fuel pump from fuel tank.
7. Reverse procedure to install.

FUEL FILTER

REPLACE

1. Relieve fuel pressure as outlined under "Precautions."
2. Place a suitable container below fuel filter, then loosen fuel filter bracket clamp bolt.
3. Remove fuel line clips and disconnect fuel lines.
4. Remove filter from bracket.
5. Reverse procedure to install.

TIGHTENING SPECIFICATIONS

Year	Component	Torque/Ft. Lbs.
1997–2000	A/C Compressor Bolts	15–22
	A/C Line Bracket Bolt	15–18
	Accelerator & Speed Control Bracket Bolts	72–84(1)
	Alternator Bolt	34
	Appearance Cover	48–84(1)
	Camshaft Position Sensor Bolt	48–84(1)
	Catalytic Converter Bracket Bolts	15–20
	Catalytic Converter To Exhaust Mounting Nuts	30–40
	Catalytic Converter To Oil Pan Bracket Bolts	30–40
	Constant Control Relay Module	72–96(1)
	Crankshaft Pulley Bolt	81–89
	Cylinder Head Bolts	(2)
	Exhaust Camshaft Sprocket Bolt	88
	Exhaust Camshaft Sprocket Plug	26–30
	Exhaust Manifold Heat Shield	72–96(1)
	Exhaust Manifold Nuts	11–12
	Flywheel Bolts	54–67
	Front Roll Restrictor Nuts	48–65
	Front Roll Restrictor Bolts	50–69
	Front Engine Support Isolator Bolt	50–69
	Ignition Coil Bracket Bolts	14–16
	Ignition Coil Mounting Bolts	40–61(1)
	Intake Camshaft Sprocket Bolt	48–53
	Intake Manifold Nuts	12–15
	Motor Mount Nuts	50–69
	Oil Control Solenoid Flange Bolt	72–96(1)
	Oil Level Indicator Tube Bolt	72–96(1)
	Oil Pan Bolts	(3)
	Oil Pan Drain Plug	29–41
	Oil Pump Bolts	84–108(1)

Continued

TIGHTENING SPECIFICATIONS—Continued

Year	Component	Torque/Ft. Lbs.
1997-2000	Oil Pump Screen Cover & Tube Bolts	72–96①
	Oil Pressure Sensor Switch	19
	Power Steering Pump Bolts	30–41
	Rear Engine Support Isolator Nuts & Bolts	50–69
	Rear Roll Restrictor Nuts	28–38
	Splash Shield Bolts	72–96①
	Timing Belt Tensioner Bolt	18
	Valve Cover Bolts	60–72①
	Water Pump Bolts	16

① — Inch Lbs.
② — Refer to “Cylinder Head, Replace” for tightening procedure.
③ — Refer to “Oil Pan, Replace” for tightening procedure.

Clutch & Manual Transaxle

INDEX

ADJUSTMENTS

CLUTCH

The Escort and Tracer use a hydraulic clutch control system. This system consists of a fluid reservoir, master cylinder, pressure line and slave cylinder. The clutch master cylinder is mounted on the bulkhead near the brake master cylinder. This hydraulic system utilizes brake fluid from the brake master cylinder reservoir. This system has no provisions for adjustment.

CLUTCH PEDAL

To determine if the pedal height requires adjustment, measure the distance from the bulkhead to the upper center of pedal pad. The distance should be 8.35–8.54 inches. Use the following procedure if adjustment is required.

1. Disconnect clutch switch electrical connector.
2. Loosen clutch switch locknut.
3. Turn clutch switch until correct height is achieved.
4. **Torque** locknut to 10–13 ft. lbs.
5. Connect electrical connector.

CLUTCH PEDAL FREEPLAY

To determine if the pedal freeplay requires adjustment, depress clutch pedal by hand until clutch resistance is felt. Measure the distance between upper pedal height and where the resistance is felt. Freeplay should be .22–.59. Use the following procedure if adjustment is necessary.

1. Loosen clutch pedal pushrod locknut.
2. Turn pushrod until pedal freeplay is within specification.
3. Check that disengagement height is correct when the pedal is fully depressed. Minimum disengagement height is 1.6 inches.
4. **Torque** pushrod locknut to 9–12 ft. lbs.

HYDRAULIC SYSTEM SERVICE

CLUTCH SLAVE CYLINDER, REPLACE

1. Disconnect pressure line from slave cylinder, then plug line to prevent leakage.
2. Remove slave cylinder retaining bolts, then cylinder.
3. Reverse procedure to install. **Torque** slave cylinder retaining bolts to 12–17 ft. lbs.

HYDRAULIC CLUTCH BLEED

The clutch hydraulic system must be bled whenever the pressure line is disconnected.

The fluid in the reservoir must be maintained at the ¾ level or higher during air bleeding.

1. Remove bleeder cap from slave cylinder and attach vinyl hose to bleeder screw, place other end of hose in container.
2. Slowly pump clutch pedal several times.
3. With clutch pedal depressed, loosen bleeder screw to release trapped air.
4. Tighten bleeder screw.
5. Repeat steps 2 through 4 until no air bubbles appear in fluid.

CLUTCH MASTER CYLINDER, REPLACE

Escort & Tracer

1. Remove battery and battery tray assembly.
2. Disconnect clutch pressure line from master cylinder.
3. Using needle nose vise grips, or equivalent. clamp off brake fluid feed line to clutch master cylinder.
4. Disengage clamp, then remove brake fluid feed hose from clutch master cylinder.
5. From inside vehicle, remove master cylinder retaining nut.
6. From inside engine compartment, remove master cylinder retaining nut, then master cylinder.
7. Align clutch pedal pushrod, then install master cylinder. **Torque** retaining nuts to 14–19 ft. lbs.
8. Connect master cylinder pressure line, then **torque** pressure line retaining nut

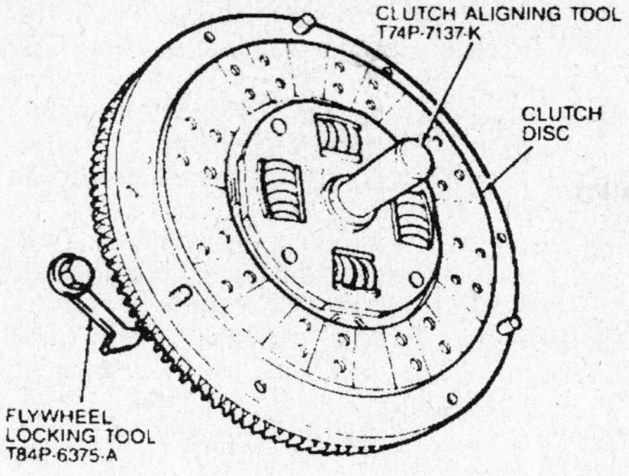

FM5049100047000X

Fig. 1 Clutch disc installation. Escort & Tracer

to 10–16 ft. lbs.

9. Install hose and clamp assembly, then battery and tray.
10. Bleed air from system.

ZX2

1. Disconnect clutch master cylinder hose from clutch master cylinder and plug it to prevent excess fluid loss.
2. Disconnect lower clutch slave cylinder tube from clutch master cylinder.
3. Remove clutch master cylinder nut from inside passenger compartment.
4. Remove clutch master cylinder nut and clutch master cylinder from engine compartment.
5. Reverse procedure to install.

CLUTCH

REPLACE

ESCORT & TRACER

1. Remove transaxle as described under "Transaxle, Replace."
2. Install flywheel locking tool Nos. T84P-6375-A and T74P-7137-K, or equivalents, into a transaxle mounting hole on engine block, then engage tooth of locking tool into flywheel ring gear.
3. Loosen pressure plate cover attaching bolts evenly to avoid distorting cover. If same pressure plate and cover are to be installed, mark cover and flywheel so pressure plate can be installed in its original position.
4. Remove pressure plate and clutch disc from flywheel.
5. Reverse procedure to install, noting the following:
   a. Clean splines on clutch disc and transaxle input shaft, then apply a small amount of Clutch Grease part No. C1AZ-19590-B, or equivalent, to clutch disc and input shaft splines. **Avoid getting grease on clutch face.**
   b. Position clutch disc plate onto flywheel as shown in **Fig. 1.**
   c. Ensure three dowel pins on flywheel are aligned with dowel pins on pressure plate.
   d. Finger tighten cover attaching bolts, then align clutch disc using tool No. T74P-7137-K, or equivalent.

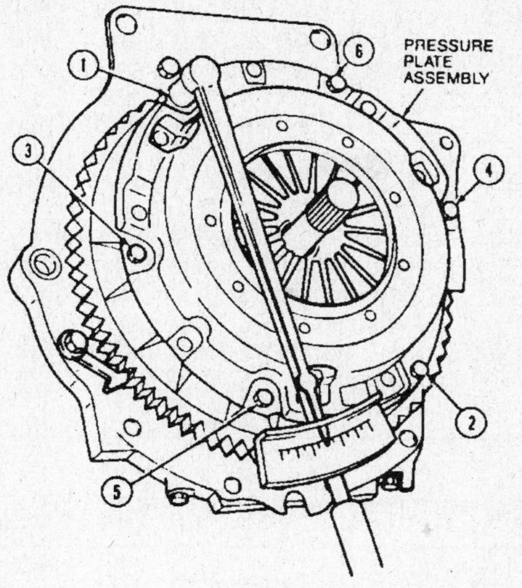

FM5049100048000X

Fig. 2 Pressure plate tightening sequence

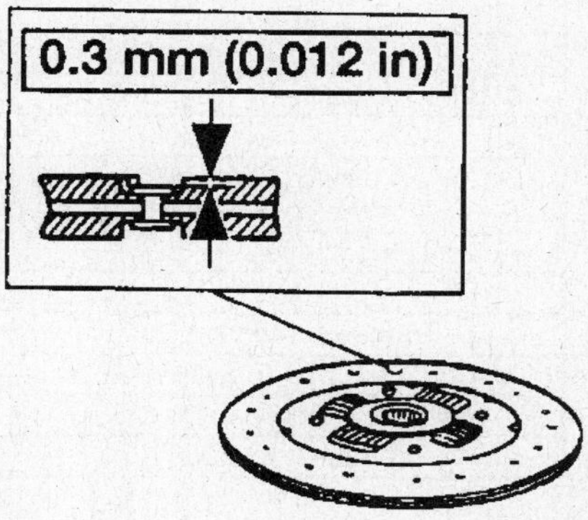

FM5049800101000X

Fig. 4 Clutch disc inspection. ZX2

   e. Evenly **torque** bolts to 13–20 ft. lbs. in sequence shown, **Fig. 2.**
   f. Remove alignment tool, then install transaxle then bleed clutch as outlined under "Hydraulic System Service."

ZX2

1. Remove transaxle as described under "Transaxle, Replace."
2. Use dial indicator and dial indicator bracket to inspect clutch pressure plate diaphragm fingers, **Fig. 3.** Rotate pressure plate to inspect diaphragm fingers runout.
3. Install flywheel holding tool T74P-6375-A and clutch aligner tool T74P-7137-K, or equivalents.
4. Remove clutch pressure plate bolts evenly to prevent pressure plate damage, if parts are to be reused, mark position of clutch pressure plate and flywheel.
5. Use a slide caliper and measure the depth to rivet heads. Replace clutch disc if any rivet head measurement is not within specification, **Fig. 4.**
6. If clutch disc is saturated with oil, inspect rear engine crankshaft seal for leakage.

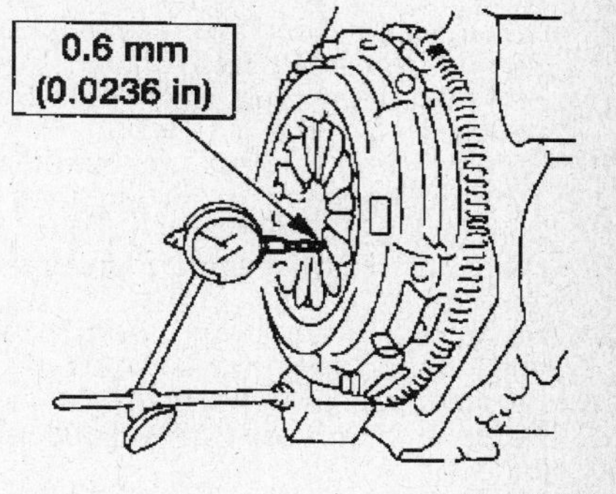

FM5049800100000X

Fig. 3 Clutch pressure plate diaphragm fingers inspection. ZX2

7. Use an emery cloth to remove minor imperfections in the clutch disc lining surface. Inspect clutch disc for oil or grease saturation, worn or loose facings, warpage or loose rivets at hub, loose or broken torsion dampening springs and wear or rust on splines. Replace clutch disc if any of these conditions are present.
8. Inspect clutch disc run out. Replace clutch disc if runout is not within .0276 inch.
9. Inspect clutch release fork for cracks, distortion, excessive wear on release bearing contact surface and damaged tines.
10. Use clutch aligner and position clutch disc on flywheel.
11. Position clutch pressure plate on flywheel, then install pressure plate bolts, then using sequence shown in **Fig. 2, torque** bolts to 17–32 ft. lbs. in several steps.
12. Remove alignment tool, then install transaxle and bleed clutch hydraulic system as outlined under "Hydraulic System Service."

TRANSAXLE

REPLACE

1. Remove battery and battery tray.
2. Remove air cleaner outlet tube.
3. Remove engine air cleaner
4. Disconnect Constant Control Relay Module (CCRM) electrical connector.
5. Remove CCRM bracket bolt and nut.
6. Remove CCRM bracket as an assembly.
7. Disconnect clutch slave cylinder tube from hydraulic clutch hose, then plug hose.
8. Disconnect back-up lamp electrical connector.
9. Remove electrical connector support bracket.
10. Disconnect vehicle speed sensor electrical connector.
11. Install three-bar engine support tool No. D88L-6000-A, or equivalent.
12. Remove three lefthand engine support insulator mounting bracket nuts.
13. Remove two upper transaxle to engine bolts.

14. Raise and support vehicle.
15. Remove wheel and tire assembly.
16. Remove lefthand splash shield.
17. Remove drain plug and drain transaxle.
18. Remove front engine crossmember bolts and front engine crossmember.
19. Disconnect A/C line from retainer located on front of engine support crossmember.
20. Remove engine support crossmember and lefthand engine mount nuts.
21. Remove transaxle mount nuts.
22. Remove front wheel driveshaft and joints.
23. Install two transaxle plugs (part No. T88C-7025-AH, or equivalent) into transaxle and hold differential side gears.
24. Remove gearshift stabilizer bar and support nut.
25. Remove stabilizer bar and support from transaxle.
26. Remove transaxle gearshift rod nut.
27. Remove transaxle gearshift bolt, then the gearshift rod and the clevis from input shift shaft.
28. Remove starter as described in "Electrical" section.
29. Disconnect lower clutch slave cylinder tube and plug to prevent excess fluid loss.
30. Remove two clutch slave cylinder nuts then the clutch slave cylinder.
31. Remove two lower transaxle to engine bolts.
32. Position transaxle jack, tool No. 014-00210, or equivalent, under transaxle and secure transaxle to jack.
33. Remove middle transaxle to engine bolts, then carefully lower transaxle out of vehicle.
34. Reverse procedure to install.

TIGHTENING SPECIFICATIONS

Year	Component	Torque/Ft. Lbs.
ESCORT & TRACER		
1997– 2000	Back-Up Lamp Switch	15–21
	Front Transaxle Support Insulator Bolts	12–17
	Lower Transaxle To Engine Bolts	27–38
	Middle Transaxle To Engine Bolts	27–38
	Shift Rail Guide Bolt	7–12
	Transaxle Case To Flywheel Housing Bolts	14–19
	Transaxle Drain Plug	29–40
	Transaxle Gearshift Rod Nut	12–17
	Transaxle Mount Nuts	28–38
	Upper Transaxle To Engine Bolts	47–66
	Vehicle Speed Sensor Bolt	72–108①
	Wheel Lug Nuts	66–87
ZX2		
1998– 2000	Back-Up Lamp Switch	14–18
	Clutch Slave Cylinder Nuts	12–17
	Engine Isolator Through Bolts	50–68
	Engine Isolator Nuts	28–37
	Engine Support Crossmember Bolts	47–65
	Front Engine Crossmember	48–65
	Left Engine Support Insulator Nuts	50–68
	Left Support Insulator Nuts & Bolts	32–44
	Left Support Insulator To Transaxle Nuts	50–68
	Lower Rear Support Insulator bolts	50–68
	Lower Transaxle To Engine Bolts	28–38
	Middle Transaxle To Engine Bolts	28–38
	Shift Rail Guide Bolt	7–12
	Transaxle Case To Flywheel Housing Bolts	14–19
	Transaxle Drain Plug	29–40
	Transaxle Gearshift Rod Nut	12–17
	Upper Transaxle To Engine Bolts	28–38
	Vehicle Speed Sensor (VSS) Bolt	72–96①

① — Inch lbs.

Rear Suspension

INDEX

DESCRIPTION

The rear suspension uses double-acting, oil filled shock/strut assemblies with straight wound coil springs. the rear wheels and brake drums/rotors are supported by a sealed roller bearing mounted on a spindle. A staked nut is used to retain the bearing and hub in position on the spindle. The staked nut cannot be reused. **Rear lateral links base part No. 5A995 are available in a solid (left side) and adjustable (right side) type. Both types are interchangeable side-to-side. When replacement of the solid link is necessary, an adjustable link should be installed.**

WHEEL BEARING

ADJUST

1. Raise and support vehicle, then remove rear wheel.
2. **On models with disc brakes,** remove brake caliper and rotor.
3. **On models with drum brakes,** remove brake drum.
4. **On all models,** position a dial indicator to wheel hub.
5. Push and pull wheel hub by hand and measure wheel bearing play.
6. If wheel bearing play exceeds .002 inch, check and adjust locknut torque or replace wheel bearing if necessary.

REAR WHEEL SPINDLE

REPLACE

DISC BRAKES

1. Raise and support vehicle, then remove rear wheel.
2. Remove cap from rear wheel hub, then remove brake caliper and rotor.
3. Remove nut securing rear wheel hub to rear wheel spindle and hub, then bolts securing brake dust shield.
4. **On models equipped with anti-lock brakes,** remove ABS sensor bracket bolt.
5. **On all models,** remove nuts and bolts securing rear shock/strut assembly to rear wheel spindle.
6. Remove bolt and washer securing rear trailing arm to rear wheel spindle.
7. Remove rear stabilizer bar as described under "Stabilizer Bar, Replace."
8. Remove nuts and bolts securing front and rear lateral links to rear wheel spindle, then remove spindle.

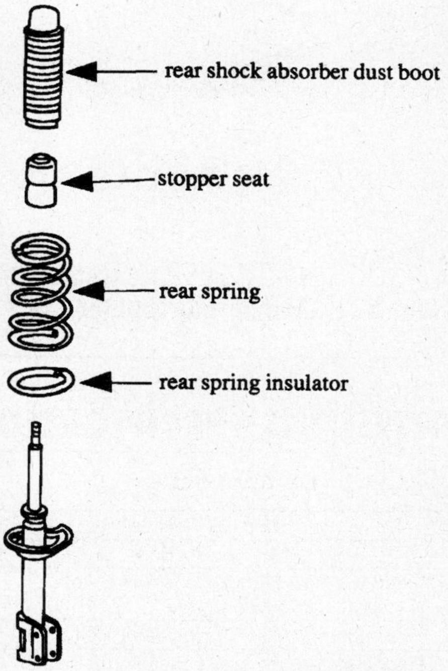

FM2029700113000X

Fig. 1 Coil spring replacement

9. Reverse procedure to install. Tighten nuts and bolts to specification.

DRUM BRAKES

1. Raise and support vehicle, then remove rear wheel.
2. Remove cap from rear wheel hub, then remove rear brake drum.
3. Remove nut securing rear wheel hub to rear wheel spindle, then the hub from the spindle.
4. Remove drum brake backing plate from spindle.
5. Remove nuts and bolts securing rear shock/strut assembly to rear wheel spindle.
6. Remove bolt and washer securing rear trailing arm to rear wheel spindle.
7. Remove rear stabilizer bar as described under "Stabilizer Bar, Replace."
8. Remove nuts and bolts securing front and rear lateral links to rear wheel spindle, then remove spindle.
9. Reverse procedure to install. Tighten nuts and bolts to specification.

STRUT

REPLACE

1. **On sedan and ZX2 models,** remove rear seat trim and the package tray trim panel.
2. **On wagon models,** remove quarter trim panel.
3. **On all models,** remove two upper shock strut nuts.
4. Raise and support vehicle.
5. Slide brake hose clip off.
6. Remove ABS sensor bracket bolt, if equipped.
7. Remove two lower strut assembly nuts and bolts, then the strut assembly.
8. Reverse procedure to install.

COIL SPRING

REPLACE

1. Secure spring and shock assembly in bench vise and use spring compressor tool No. 164-R3556, or equivalent, to compress rear spring and relieve tension on piston rod nut.
2. Remove shock absorber top mounting cover.
3. Remove piston rod nut and retainer.
4. Remove rear strut insulator.
5. Separate rear shock absorber dust boot and stopper seat, **Fig. 1.**
6. Remove rear spring and rear spring insulator.
7. Reverse procedure to install. Tighten shock absorber insulator bolt to specification.

STABILIZER BAR

REPLACE

1. Raise and support vehicle.
2. Remove rear stabilizer bar end nut (1), end bolt (2) and retainer (3), **Fig. 2.**
3. Remove two upper rear stabilizer bar end bushings (4).
4. Remove rear stabilizer bar end retainer spacer (5).
5. Remove two lower rear stabilizer bar end bushings (6) and retainer (7).
6. Remove four stabilizer bar bracket bolts and the stabilizer bar.
7. Reverse procedure to install. Tighten to specifications.

LATERAL LINKS & TRAILING LINK

REPLACE

1. Raise and support vehicle, then remove rear wheel.
2. Remove rear stabilizer bar as described under "Stabilizer Bar, Replace."
3. Remove cap covering front and rear lateral link pivot bolts, then position a floor jack stand under rear suspension crossmember.
4. Remove bolts securing rear suspension crossmember to vehicle frame, then lower floor jack stand to allow rear suspension crossmember to be lowered from vehicle frame.
5. Remove front and rear lateral link pivot nut, washer and bolt from the crossmember, then remove front and rear lateral links from crossmember.
6. Remove bolt, washers and nut securing front and rear lateral links to rear wheel spindle, then remove front and rear lateral links.
7. Remove nuts securing parking brake cable and cable bracket to trailing link.
8. Remove trailing link bolts and washers from vehicle frame and rear wheel spindle, then remove rear trailing link.
9. Reverse procedure to install. Tighten nuts and bolts to specification.

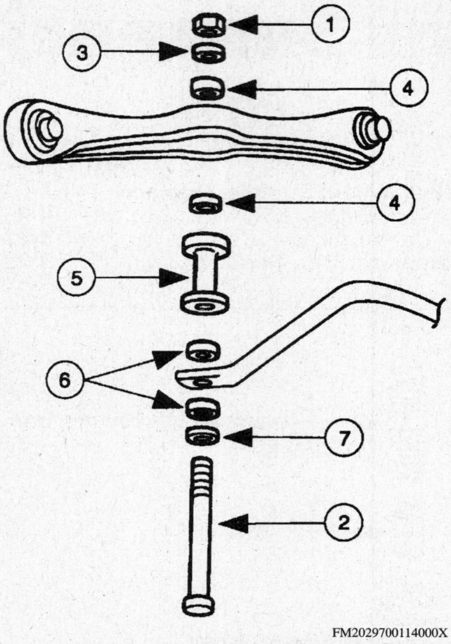

Fig. 2 Stabilizer bar replacement

TIGHTENING SPECIFICATIONS

Year	Component	Torque/Ft. Lbs.
1997–2000	Lower Shock Strut Nuts	76–100
	Rear ABS Sensor Bolt	14–18
	Rear Brake Anti-Lock Sensor Bracket Bolts	14–18
	Rear Shock Absorber Insulator Bolt	41–49
	Rear Suspension Arm & Bushing Bolt	50–70
	Rear Suspension Arm & Bushing Nut	64–86
	Rear Suspension Trailing Link Bolt	69–94
	Rear Wheel Disc Brake Shield Bolts	34–49
	Stabilizer Bar Bracket Bolts	32–43

Front Suspension & Steering

INDEX

DESCRIPTION

The front suspension is a McPherson strut design with cast steering knuckles. The shock absorber strut assembly includes a mounting block, a thrust bearing, an upper spring seat, a rubber spring seat, a bound stopper and coil spring mounted to the shock strut.

The front wheels and brake rotors are supported by a sealed roller bearing mounted in the steering knuckle. A snap ring holds the bearing in the knuckle. The halfshaft is secured to the front hub assembly with a staked nut. The staked nut cannot be reused.

WHEEL BEARING

REPLACE

1. Remove front wheel knuckle as outlined under "Steering Knuckle, Replace."
2. Remove and discard inner wheel bearing oil seal.
3. Using bearing puller attachment tool No. 205-D064 (D84L-1123-A) or equivalent, press wheel hub from the front wheel knuckle.
4. Remove retainer ring from the front wheel knuckle.
5. Use bearing pulling attachment to press front wheel bearing from front wheel knuckle.
6. Reverse procedure to install.

STEERING KNUCKLE

REPLACE

1. Raise and support vehicle.
2. Remove wheel and tire assembly.
3. Remove brake caliper bolts and secure caliper with wire, **Fig. 1**.
4. Remove front rotor.
5. Carefully raise staked portion of front axle wheel hub retainer, then remove retainer.
6. Remove cotter pin and tie rod end nut from tie rod end.
7. Use tie rod end separator tool No. T85M-3395-A, or equivalent, to separate tie rod end nut from front wheel knuckle.
8. Remove ABS sensor.
9. Remove ball joint nut and through bolt.
10. Separate front suspension lower arm ball joint from front wheel knuckle.
11. Remove two strut mounting bolts from front wheel knuckle.
12. Separate strut assembly from front wheel knuckle and remove knuckle.
13. Reverse procedure to install.

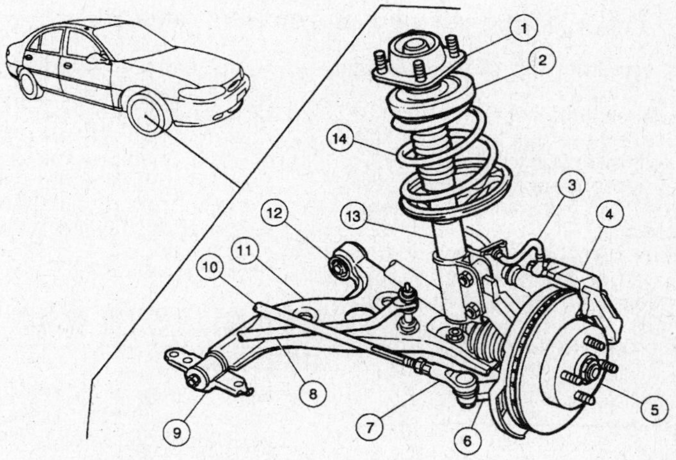

Item	Description
1	Front Shock Absorber Upper Mounting Bracket
2	Upper Spring Seat (Part of 18198)
3	Front Brake Hose
4	Disc Brake Caliper
5	Front Disc Brake Rotor
6	Front Wheel Knuckle
7	Tie Rod End
8	Front Stabilizer Bar
9	Front Suspension Lower Arm Mounting Bolt Bushing (Rear)
10	Front Wheel Spindle Tie Rod
11	Front Suspension Lower Arm
12	Front Suspension Lower Arm Mounting Bolt Bushing (Front)
13	Front Shock Absorber
14	Front Coil Spring

FM20297001150000X

Fig. 1 Front suspension components

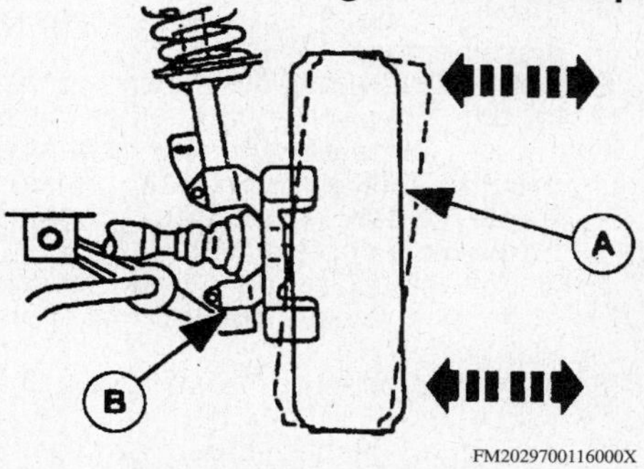

FM20297001160000X

Fig. 2 Ball joint inspection

BALL JOINT INSPECTION

1. Raise and support vehicle.
2. Grasp lower edge of tire (A) and move wheel in and out from pivot center line (B), **Fig. 2.**
3. Ball joint should be replaced if excessive movement is felt (more than 1⁄32 inch).

BALL JOINT

REPLACE

1. Raise and support vehicle.
2. Remove wheel and tire assembly.
3. Remove ball joint nut and through bolt.
4. Separate front suspension lower arm ball joint from front wheel knuckle.
5. Remove two ball joint nuts and front suspension lower arm ball joint.
6. Reverse procedure to install.

COIL SPRING

REPLACE

1. Remove front shock/strut assembly as described under " Strut, Replace."

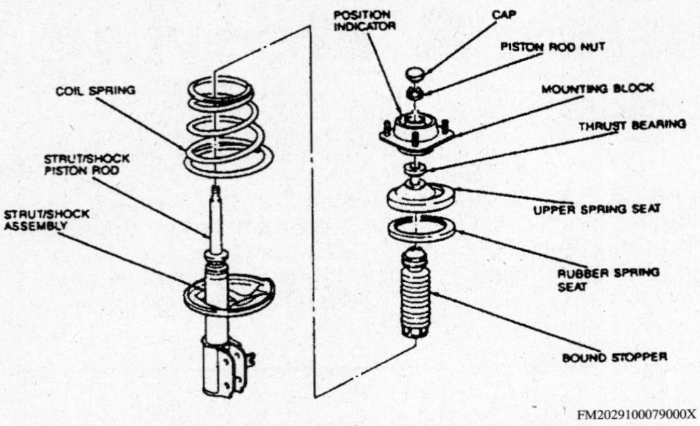

Fig. 3 Exploded view of front strut assembly

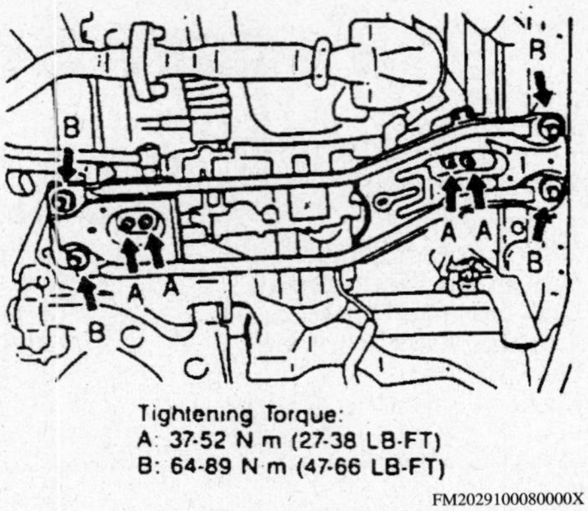

Fig. 4 Crossmember bolt tightening sequence

2. Remove cap from top of shock/strut assembly.
3. Secure shock/strut assembly mounting block in a vise, then turn piston rod nut one full revolution to loosen.
4. Install an appropriate spring compressor onto shock/strut spring, then compress spring.
5. Remove nut, mounting block, thrust bearing, upper spring seat, rubber spring seat, coil spring and bound stopper **Fig. 3.**
6. Reverse procedure to install.

STRUT

REPLACE

1. Raise and support vehicle, then remove front wheel.
2. Remove clip securing flexible brake hose to shock/strut assembly.
3. Remove two nuts and bolts securing shock/strut assembly to steering knuckle.
4. Remove upper mounting block nuts on strut tower, then remove shock/strut assembly.
5. Reverse procedure to install noting the following:
   a. Position shock/strut assembly into wheel housing, ensure that direction indicator on mounting block faces inboard.
   b. Tighten upper mounting block to strut tower nuts to and shock/strut assembly bolts to specification.

CONTROL ARM

REPLACE

1. Raise and support vehicle, then remove stabilizer bar nuts, washers, bushings, sleeves and bolts.
2. Remove lower control arm front bushing bolt and washer, then remove bolts securing lower control arm rear bushing retaining strap.
3. Remove nut and bolt securing lower ball joint to steering knuckle, then separate steering knuckle from lower ball joint.
4. Remove lower control arm.
5. Reverse procedure to install noting the following:
   a. Tighten lower control arm pivot bolt nut, ball joint retaining bolt and nut, lower control arm rear bushing retaining strap bolts and lower control arm front pivot bolt to specification.
   b. Install stabilizer bar bolts, sleeves, bushings, washers and nuts and tighten so that .67–.75 inch of thread is showing.

STABILIZER BAR

REPLACE

1. Support engine with three bar engine support tool No. D88L-6000-A, or equivalent, then raise and support vehicle.
2. Remove front wheels, then remove nuts securing steering gear mounting brackets.
3. Position steering gear slightly forward, then remove stabilizer bar nuts, washers, bushings, sleeves and bolts from lower control arm.
4. Remove rear crossmember nuts from rear transaxle mount and vehicle frame.
5. Loosen front crossmember bolts and nuts from front transaxle mount and vehicle frame, then lower rear end of crossmember.
6. Remove nuts and bolts securing chassis frame to vehicle frame, then lower chassis frame. **Engine and transaxle mounts will support the chassis frame when unbolting chassis frame from vehicle frame.**
7. Unbolt stabilizer bar from chassis frame and remove stabilizer bar from vehicle.
8. Reverse procedure to install noting the following:
   a. Tighten stabilizer bar to chassis frame bolts to specification.
   b. Tighten chassis frame to vehicle frame bolts to specification.
   c. Tighten crossmember to vehicle frame and transaxle mounts as shown in **Fig. 4.**
   d. Install stabilizer bar bolts, sleeves, bushings, washers and nuts and tighten so that .67–.75 inch of thread is showing.
   e. Tighten steering gear bracket nuts to specification.

POWER STEERING GEAR

REPLACE

1. Turn ignition switch to ACC position.
2. Remove five nuts, then the steering column tube boot.
3. Remove steering column input shaft coupling to steering gear input shaft and control bolt.
4. Raise and support vehicle.
5. Remove front wheel assemblies.
6. Remove and discard cotter pin from tie rod end nut.
7. Remove tie rod end nut, then use tie rod end separator tool No. T85M-3395-A, or equivalent, to separate tie rod from wheel knuckle, **Fig. 5.**
8. Remove righthand splash shield.
9. Remove crossmember.
10. Disconnect power steering return hose and plug the line.
11. Remove strap attaching hoses to steering gear housing.
12. **On models with manual transaxle, proceed as follows:**
    a. Disconnect transmission gearshift rod and clevis from transaxle.
    b. remove extension bar nut and disconnect gearshift lever stabilizer bar and support from transaxle.
13. **On all models,** remove steering gear mounting brackets.
14. Remove two nuts from each bracket.
15. Remove two steering gear mounting brackets.
16. Remove pushpin and position righthand boot shield aside.
17. Remove steering gear assembly from righthand side of vehicle.
18. Reverse procedure to install.

POWER STEERING PUMP

REPLACE

2.0L SOHC ENGINE

1. Remove power steering pump reservoir.
2. Remove power steering pump pulley.
3. Raise and support vehicle.
4. Remove six bolts and righthand splash shield.

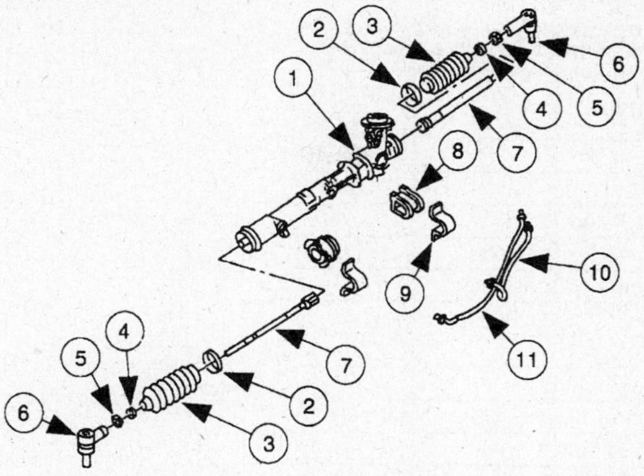

Item	Description
1	Steering Gear
2	Inner Front Suspension Steering Ball Stud Dust Seal (Part of 3332)
3	Front Suspension Steering Ball Stud Dust Seal
4	Outer Front Suspension Steering Ball Stud Dust Seal (Part of 3332)
5	Tie Rod End Jam Nut (Part of 3A130)

Item	Description
6	Tie Rod End
7	Front Wheel Spindle Tie Rod
8	Steering Gear Insulator
9	Steering Gear Mounting Bracket
10	Power Steering Left Turn Pressure Hose
11	Power Steering Right Turn Pressure Hose

FM6029700218000X

Fig. 5 Power steering gear components

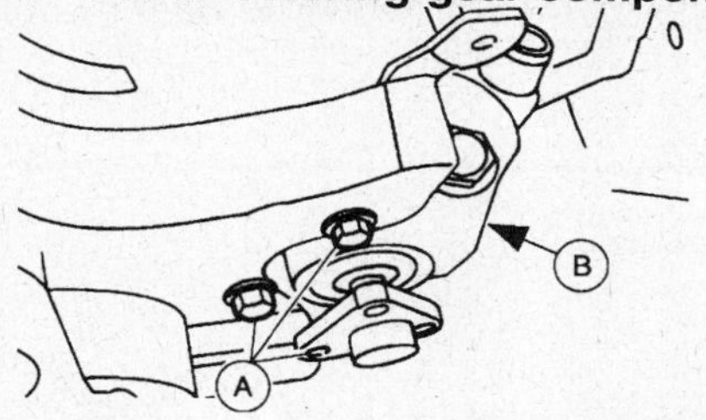

FM6029700217000X

Fig. 6 Power steering pump replacement. 2.0L SOHC engine

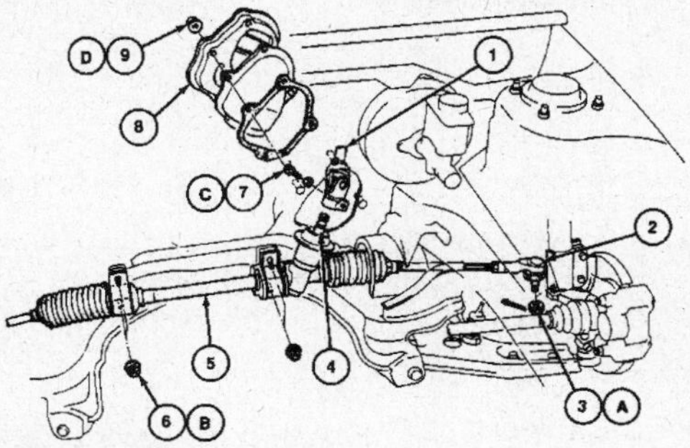

Item	Description
1	Steering Column Intermediate Shaft Coupling
2	Tie Rod End
3	Tie Rod End Nut
4	Steering Gear Input Worm Gear and Rack
5	Steering Gear
6	Steering Gear Mounting Bracket Nut (2 Req'd)
7	Steering Column Gear Input Shaft Coupling-to-Steering Gear Input Worm Gear and Rack Bolt

Item	Description
8	Steering Column Tube Boot
9	Steering Column Tube Boot Nut (5 Req'd)
A	Tighten to 34-46 N·m (25-34 Lb-Ft)
B	Tighten to 37-52 N·m (27-38 Lb-Ft)
C	Tighten to 45 N·m (33 Lb-Ft)
D	Tighten to 4 N·m (35 Lb-In)

FM6039100026000X

Fig. 7 Exploded view of manual steering gear

5. Disconnect power steering pressure hose.
6. Lower vehicle.
7. Loosen clamp and disconnect power steering reservoir to pump hose.
8. Remove power steering pump mounting bolts (A) and the pump (B), **Fig. 6.**
9. Reverse procedure to install.

2.0L DOHC ENGINE

1. Disconnect radiator overflow tube and position aside.
2. Remove A/C hose clamp bolt, then unclip speed control cable from A/C hose bracket.
3. Remove A/C hose bracket, then raise and support vehicle.
4. Remove lower right splash shield bolts and shield.
5. Turn belt tensioner bolt clockwise and remove accessory drive belt.
6. Disconnect power steering pressure hose from power steering pump, then lower vehicle.
7. Remove power steering hose brackets, then disconnect heated oxygen sensor connector.
8. Remove engine block ground bracket, then disconnect power steering return hose from power steering pump.
9. Raise and support vehicle, then remove power steering pressure hose from vehicle.
10. Lower vehicle, then remove four pump bolts and pump.
11. Discard power steering pump heat shield.
12. Reverse procedure to install. Install new power steering pump heat shield.

MANUAL STEERING GEAR

REPLACE

1. From inside of vehicle, remove nuts securing set plate, remove set plate, **Fig. 7.**
2. Remove intermediate shaft to pinion shaft bolt from inside of vehicle.
3. Raise and support vehicle, then remove front wheels.
4. Remove cotter pins and nuts securing tie rod ends to steering knuckles.
5. Separate tie rod end from steering knuckle using tie rod end separator tool No. T85M-3395-A, or equivalent.
6. **On vehicles equipped with manual transaxle,** disconnect extension bar.
7. **On all vehicles,** remove nuts securing steering gear brackets to bulkhead, then remove the brackets.
8. Remove steering gear from vehicle.
9. Reverse procedure to install noting the following:
   a. Tighten steering gear bracket nuts, extension bar nut, tie rod end nut and intermediate shaft to pinion shaft bolt to specification.

TIGHTENING SPECIFICATIONS

Year	Component	Torque/Ft. Lbs.
1997–2000	Crossmember Bolts	69–97
	Front Wheel Spindle Tie Rod	40–50
	Power Steering Pump Bolts	①
	Power Steering Pump Pulley Bolts	15–22
	Pressure Hose To Steering Gear Fitting	40–54
	Return Hose To Steering Gear Fitting	20–25
	RH Splash Shield	72–96②
	Shock/Strut Assembly Bolts	69–93
	Steering Gear Mounting Bracket Nuts	28–38
	Tie Rod End Jam Nut	25–37
	Tie Rod End Nut	25–33
	Upper Mounting Block to Strut Tower	22–30
	Wheel Lug Nuts	65–87

① — 2.0L SOHC engine, 30–41 ft. lbs.; DOHC engines 15–22 ft. lbs.
② — Inch lbs.

Wheel Alignment

INDEX

PRELIMINARY INSPECTION

1. Inspect tires for proper inflation and similar tread wear.
2. Inspect hub and bearing for excessive wear, repair as required.
3. Inspect ball joints.
4. Inspect tie rod ends for excessive looseness.
5. Check wheel and tire runout.
6. Inspect vehicle ride height.
7. Inspect rack and pinion for looseness at frame.
8. Ensure proper strut operation.
9. Check suspension and steering components for damage, replace as required.

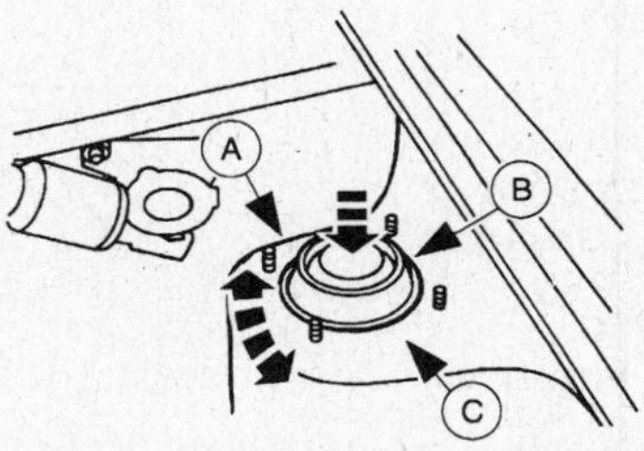

Direction Indicator	Difference From Standard Position	
	Camber Angle	Caster Angle
A	7/30 Degrees	7/30 Degrees
B	29/60 Degrees	0 Degrees
C	7/30 Degrees	7/30 Degrees

Fig. 1 Camber adjustment

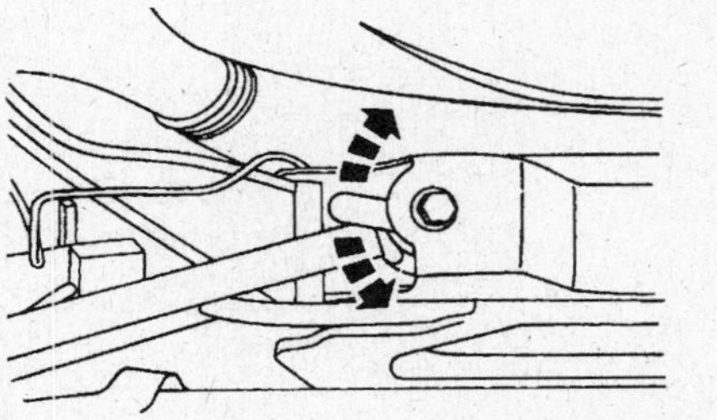

Fig. 2 Rear toe adjustment

FRONT WHEEL ALIGNMENT

CAMBER

1. Raise and support front of vehicle.
2. From inside engine compartment, remove mounting block nuts located on top of strut tower.
3. Push mounting block downward and turn to desired position, **Fig. 1.**
4. Install mounting block nuts, then **torque** to 22–30 ft. lbs.

TOE

1. Loosen left and right tie rod locknuts.
2. Release clips at small ends of steering gear boots.
3. Turn tie rods equally until desired toe-in setting is reached. Left and right tie rods are both righthand threads. One turn of the tie rod (both sides) makes a toe-in change of about .24 inch.
4. **Torque** tie rod locknuts to 25–29 ft. lbs.

REAR WHEEL ALIGNMENT

TOE

1. Loosen rear suspension arm and bushing bolt.
2. Turn adjusting cam until toe is within specifications, **Fig. 2.**
3. **Torque** rear suspension arm and bushing bolt to 63–86 ft. lbs.

CONTINENTAL, MARK VIII & TOWN CAR

NOTE: Refer To Rear Of This Manual For Vehicle Manufacturer's Special Service Tool Suppliers.

INDEX OF SERVICE OPERATIONS

Specifications

GENERAL ENGINE SPECIFICATIONS

Year	Engine Liter	Engine VIN Code②	Fuel System	Bore & Stroke	Compression Ratio	Net HP @ RPM③	Maximum Torque, Ft. Lbs. @ RPM	Normal Oil Pressure, psi
1997	4.6L SOHC	W	SFI	3.55 x 3.54	9.0	210 @ 4250	275 @ 3250	20–45
	4.6L DOHC	V	SFI	3.55 x 3.54	9.85	①	⑥	20–45
1998	4.6L SOHC	W	SFI	3.55 x 3.54	9.0	④	⑤	20–45
	4.6L DOHC	V	SFI	3.55 x 3.54	9.85	①	⑥	20–45
1999–2000	4.6L SOHC	W	SFI	3.55 x 3.54	9.0	⑦	⑧	20–45
	4.6L DOHC	V	SFI	3.55 x 3.54	9.85	275 @ 5750	275 @ 4750	20–45

SFI — Sequential Fuel Injection
SOHC — Single Overhead Cam
DOHC — Dual Overhead Cam
① — Continental, 260 @ 5750; Mark VIII standard equipment, 280 @ 5500; Mark VIII LSC, 290 @ 5750.
② — The eighth digit of the VIN denotes engine code.
③ — Ratings are net (as installed in vehicle).
④ — Single exhaust, 200 @ 4500; dual exhaust, 220 @ 4500.
⑤ — Single exhaust, 265 @ 3500; dual exhaust, 275 @ 3500.
⑥ — Continental, 265 @ 4750; Mark VIII standard equipment, 285 @ 4500; Mark VIII LSC, 295 @ 4500.
⑦ — Single exhaust, 205 @ 4250; dual exhaust, 220 @ 4500.
⑧ — Single exhaust, 280 @ 3000; dual exhaust, 290 @ 3500.

TUNE UP SPECIFICATIONS

Year & Engine/ Liter	Spark Plug Gap, Inch	Ignition Timing, °BTDC Firing Order, Fig.④	Ignition Timing, °BTDC Degrees	Ignition Timing, °BTDC Timing Mark, Fig.	Curb Idle Speed, RPM	Fast Idle Speed, RPM	Fuel Pump Pressure, psi	Valve Clearance③
1997								
4.6L SOHC	.054	A	10②	⑤	⑥	⑥	35–40①	.80–.120
4.6L DOHC⑦	.054	B	10②	⑤	⑥	⑥	35–40①	.80–.120
4.6L DOHC⑧	.054	⑨	10②	⑤	⑥	⑥	35–40①	.80–.120
1998–2000								
4.6L	.054	⑨	10②	⑤	⑥	⑥	35–40①	.80–.120

BTDC — Before Top Dead Center
DOHC — Dual Overhead Cam
SOHC — Single Overhead Cam
① — Wrap shop towel around fuel diagnostic valve to prevent fuel spillage. Connect a suitable fuel pressure gauge to fuel diagnostic valve. Energize fuel pump & note fuel pressure gauge reading.
② — Non-adjustable.
③ — With cylinder at top dead center, hold steady pressure on lifter until fully collapsed to check clearance.
④ — Before disconnecting wires from distributor cap, determine location of No. 1 wire in cap, as distributor position may have been altered from that shown at the end of this chart.
⑤ — Equipped w/crankshaft sensor.
⑥ — Idle speeds are controlled by the automatic idle control.
⑦ — Continental.
⑧ — Mark VIII.
⑨ — PCM controls eight separate ignition coils, each coil is mounted directly above its respective spark plug.

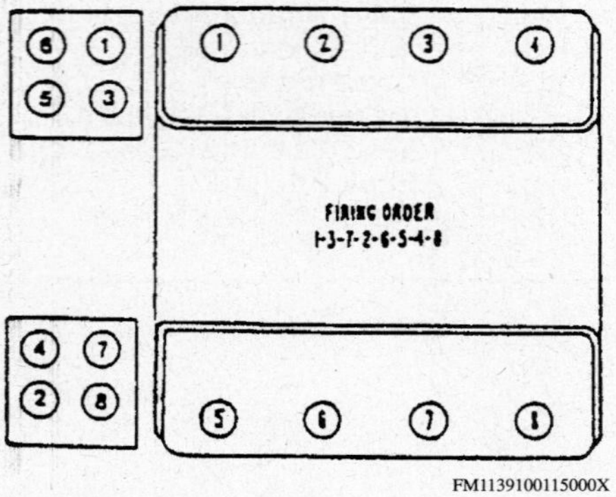

Fig. A

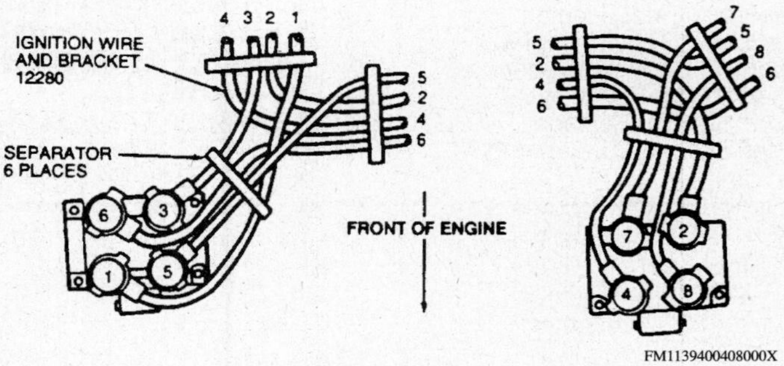

Fig. B

FRONT WHEEL ALIGNMENT SPECIFICATIONS

Year	Model	Caster Angle, Degrees		Camber Angle, Degrees				Toe-In, Inch	Toe Out On Turns, Degrees		Ball Joint Wear, Inch
		Limits	Desired	Limits		Desired			Outer Wheel	Inner Wheel	
				Left	Right	Left	Right				
1997–98	Mark VIII	+4.75 to +6.25	+5.5	-1.25 to +.25	-1.25 to +.25	-.5	-.5	②	19.73	20	⑤
1997–2000	Conti-nental	+3.50 to +5.50	+4.5	–1.30 to +.100	–1.70 to +.100	–.7	–.7	①	18.21	20	④
	Town Car	+5.25 to +6.75	+6.0	-1.25 to +.25	-1.25 to +.25	-.5	-.5	③	18.51	20	⑥

① — Total toe -.20 degrees.
② — Total toe, +.25 degrees.
③ — Total toe out, -.125
④ — No horizontal movement is allowed.
⑤ — Any radial play is unacceptable and ball joint should be measured between control arm and spindle using a dial gauge.
⑥ — Upper ball joint, .015 inch lateral play measured between upper control arm and spindle using a dial gauge; lower ball joint, no lateral movement is allowable.

REAR WHEEL ALIGNMENT SPECIFICATIONS

Model	Camber Angle, Degrees				Toe-In, Degrees
	Limits		Desired		
	Left	Right	Left	Right	
Continental	–1.20 to –.20	–1.20 to –.20	–.70	–.70	①
Mark VIII	–1.00 to .00	–1.00 to .00	–.50	–.50	②

① — Total toe, +.20 degrees.
② — Total toe, +.12 degrees.

FLUID CAPACITIES & COOLING SYSTEM DATA

Year	Engine	Coolant Capacity, Qts.	Radiator Cap Relief Pressure, psi	Thermo. Opening Temp., Dreg. F	Fuel Tank, Gal.	Engine Oil Refill, Qts.②	Auto. Trans., Qts.②	Rear Axle Oil, Pints④
1997–2000	4.6L DOHC	16	16	196	18	6①	14.0	3.0
	4.6L SOHC	14	16	196	③	5①	13.6	3.75

① — With filter change.
② — Approximate. Make final check w/dipstick.
③ — 18–20 gal. depending on vehicle options.
④ — Differential w/tractional, add 4 oz. friction modifier.

LUBRICANT DATA

Year	Lubricant Type			
	Automatic Transmission/ Transvalue	Rear Axle	Power Steering	Brake System
1997	Emerson	①	②	DOT 3
1998–2000	Emerson V	①	②	DOT 3

① — Use ESP-M2C154-A (XY-80W90-QL), or equivalent, plus four ounces of EST-M2C118-A (C8AZ-19B546-A) friction modifier, or equivalent, for tractional axles.
② — Automatic trans. fluid or power steering fluid E6AZ-19582-AA.

Electrical

NOTE: Refer To "Air Bag System Precautions" Located In The Front Of This Manual For System Disarming & Arming Procedures.

NOTE: Refer To "Computer Relearn Procedures" Located In The Front Of This Manual For computer Relearn Procedures.

NOTE: Prior To Performing Any Service Operations Listed In This Section, Consult The "Technical Service Bulletins " Section For Related Information.

INDEX

PRECAUTIONS

AIR BAG SYSTEM

Refer to "Air Bag System Precautions" in the front of this manual for system disarming and arming procedures.

BATTERY GROUND CABLE

Prior to service, disconnect battery ground cable and isolate as required.

FUSE PANEL & FLASHER LOCATION

CONTINENTAL

The fuse panel is located under the instrument panel to the left side of the steering column.

The turn signal and hazard flashers are located in and part of lighting control module found under left side of instrument panel.

MARK VIII

The instrument panel fuse panel is located under the instrument panel to the left side of the steering column.

The engine compartment fuse box found on left side of the engine compartment, next to the coolant bottle.

The turn signal and hazard flashers are located behind the right side of the instrument panel, right of the radio.

TOWN CAR

1997

The instrument panel fuse panel is located under the instrument panel to the left side of the steering column.

The engine compartment fuse panel is located at the front right side of the engine compartment, forward of the wheel well.

The turn signal and hazard flashers are part of the lighting control module, located below the left side of the instrument panel.

1998-2000

The instrument panel fuse panel is located behind the leftward side of the instrument panel, left of the steering column.

The engine compartment power distribution box is located on the rear leftward side of the engine compartment.

The turn signal and hazard flashers are part of the lighting control module, located behind the center of the instrument panel.

RELAY CENTER LOCATION

CONTINENTAL

The relay center, known as the Constant Control Relay Module (CCRM), is located on the radiator support in the lower front center of the engine compartment. The relay center contains the following relays, fuel pump, A/C fan, PCM power and the A/C control relay.

MARK VIII

The relay center, known as the Variable Control Relay Module (VCRM), is located in the lower front center of engine compartment, on the radiator support. The relay center contains the following relays, low speed fuel pump, A/C fan, PCM power and the A/C control relay.

TOWN CAR

The relay center is located on top of the left wheel well in engine compartment.

FUEL PUMP RELAY LOCATION

CONTINENTAL

The fuel pump relay, is part of the CCRM. The fuel pump control module is located at the front right side of the luggage compartment.

MARK VIII

The low speed fuel pump relay is part of the VCRM. The high speed fuel pump relay is located in the engine compartment fuse box.

TOWN CAR

1997

The fuel pump relay is located in the relay center.

1998–2000

The fuel pump relay is located in the power distribution box.

STARTER

REPLACE

When servicing starter or performing any maintenance in the area of starter, note the heavy gauge input lead connected to the starter solenoid is hot at all times. Ensure protective cap is installed over terminal and is replaced after service. When battery has been disconnected and reconnected, some abnormal drive symptoms may occur while the EEC processor relearns its adaptive strategy. The vehicle may need to be driven 10 miles or more to relearn strategy.

1. Raise and support vehicle.
2. **On Continental models,** remove lower air deflector.
3. **On all models,** disconnect starter cable and push-on connector at starter solenoid. **When disconnecting hard shell connector at S terminal, pull plastic shell straight out, do not pull on wire.**
4. Remove starter mounting bolts and the starter. It may be necessary to turn wheels to left or right to gain clearance for removal.
5. Reverse procedure to install, noting the following:
   a. **Torque** starter cable to starter terminal to 84–108 inch lbs.

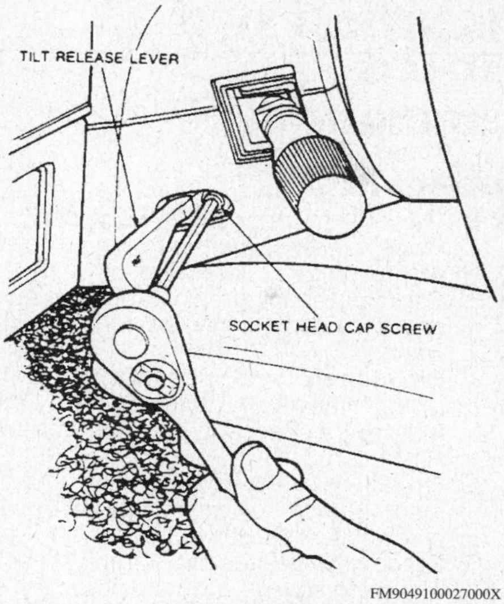

Fig. 1 Tilt release lever removal. Continental

   b. **Torque** lower air deflector shield to 6–12 ft. lbs.
   c. **Torque** starter mounting bolts 15–19 ft. lbs.
   d. Replace red solenoid cap.

COIL PACK

REPLACE

MARK VIII & 1998–2000 CONTINENTAL & TOWN CAR

The PCM controls the eight separate ignition coils, each coil is mounted directly above its respective spark plug.

1. Remove air cleaner outlet tube.
2. Remove right and leftward spark plug/ignition coil covers.
3. Pull ignition coil wire from spark plug.
4. Disconnect connector from ignition coil.
5. Remove ignition coil from spark plug.
6. Inspect coil for cracks, dirt and carbon fouling.
7. Reverse procedure to install. **Torque** spark plug/ignition coil covers to 72–108 inch lbs.

1997 CONTINENTAL & TOWN CAR

1. **On Continental models,** disconnect wiring from IAT sensor and remove crankcase ventilation tube from air cleaner outlet tube.
2. **On all models,** disconnect radio ignition interference capacitor at wiring connector.
3. Disconnect secondary ignition wires by squeezing locking tabs and pulling upward.
4. Remove four coil mounting screws, then the ignition coils along with the radio ignition interference capacitor.
5. Reverse procedure to install, noting the following:
   a. Apply silicone brake caliper grease and dielectric compound to all ignition wire boots.
   b. **Torque** coil fasteners to 45–61 inch lbs.

IGNITION LOCK

REPLACE

FUNCTIONAL LOCK

CONTINENTAL & MARK VIII

1. Turn lock cylinder key to Run position.
2. Using a ⅛ inch drift, depress lock cylinder retaining pin through access hole and remove lock cylinder, **Note position of bearing retainer prior to removal.**
3. Remove blue plastic bearing retainer by inserting suitable screwdriver with a 90° bend on its tip between bearing retainer and bearing, then prying upward.
4. Insert tip of screwdriver into double-d slot of bearing, then rotate 90°. Remove bearing.
5. Remove lock drive gear. Note position of lock drive gear relative to rack teeth.
6. Reverse procedure to install. Noting the following:
   a. Position of steering column lock gear is correct if last tooth on drive gear steering column lock gear is meshed with the last tooth on rack.
   b. Position steering column upper bearing retainer in lock cylinder housing and rotate double-d slot 90 degrees.
   c. Press blue plastic steering column upper bearing retainer into lock cylinder housing, ensure original position.
   d. Line up flats of steering column lock gear with flats of washer by pulling down on the steering column lock cam.
   e. Install ignition switch assembly.
   f. Check for proper start in park and neutral, no start in drive and reverse and locked in lock position.

TOWN CAR

1997

1. Turn lock cylinder key to Run position.
2. Place a ⅛ inch punch in hole in trim shroud under lock cylinder.
3. Depress retaining pin with punch and remove lock cylinder by pulling outward.
4. Install lock cylinder by turning it to Run position and depressing retaining pin. Ensure cylinder is fully seated and aligned with interlocking washer prior to turning key Off.
5. Rotate lock cylinder with key to ensure proper operation.

1998–2000

1. Turn ignition lock cylinder to Run position.
2. Press ignition switch lock cylinder release pin while pulling on lock cylinder.
3. Reverse procedure to install.

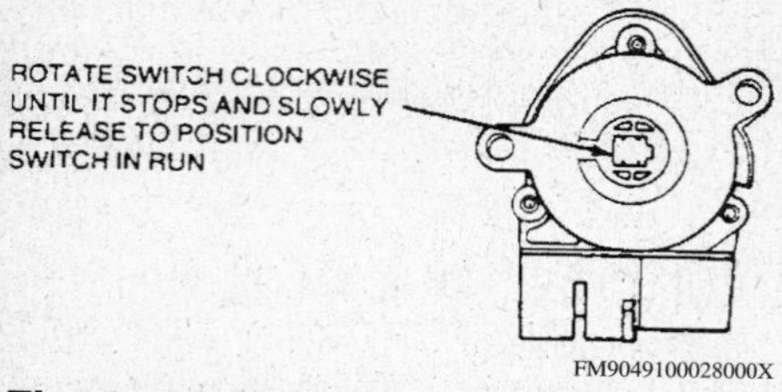

Fig. 2 Ignition switch adjustment. Continental

NON-FUNCTIONAL LOCK

CONTINENTAL & MARK VIII & 1997 TOWN CAR

Removal

1. Remove steering wheel.
2. Disconnect key warning switch electrical connector.
3. **On models equipped with ignition switch cap,** use channel–lock or vise–grip type pliers to twist cap from lock cylinder.
4. **On all models,** using a 1/8 inch drill bit, drill out retaining pin. **Do not drill deeper than 1/2 inch.**
5. Place a chisel at base of ignition lock cylinder cap, then strike chisel with sharp blows to break cap away from cylinder.
6. Using a 3/8 inch drill bit, drill down middle of ignition lock key slot 1 3/4 inches until lock cylinder breaks loose from breakaway base of lock cylinder.
7. Remove lock cylinder and drill shavings from lock cylinder housing.
8. Remove retainer, washer, ignition switch and actuator, then clean all drill shavings from casting.
9. Inspect lock cylinder housing; if any damage is present, replace housing.

Installation

1. Install actuator and ignition switch.
2. Install trim and electrical parts.
3. Install new ignition lock cylinder.
4. Install steering wheel.
5. Ensure lock operates properly.

1998–2000 TOWN CAR

1. Remove steering wheel, then twist cap from ignition switch lock cylinder.
2. Drill out lock cylinder retaining pin with a 1/8 inch drill bit.
3. Drill down middle of ignition key slot with a 3/8 inch drill bit until ignition switch lock cylinder breaks loose.
4. Remove ignition switch lock cylinder, then the bearing retainer from steering column.
5. Remove steering column lock housing bearing and steering column lock gear from steering column.
6. Reverse procedure to install. Clean all drill shavings from steering column.

IGNITION SWITCH

REPLACE

CONTINENTAL

REMOVAL

1. Turn lock cylinder key to Run position.
2. Place a 1/8 inch punch in hole in trim shroud under lock cylinder.
3. Depress retaining pin with punch and remove lock cylinder by pulling outward.
4. **On models equipped with tilt column,** remove tilt release lever by removing one socket head capscrew, **Fig. 1.**
5. **On all models,** remove four instrument panel lower cover retaining screws, then the lower cover.
6. Remove three steering column shroud mounting screws, then the shroud.
7. Remove four steering column to support bracket mounting bolts, then lower column.
8. Remove three screws from diverter plate, then the diverter plate from column.
9. Disconnect ignition switch electrical connector.
10. Remove two tamper resistant Torx screws mounting ignition switch, then the switch.

INSTALLATION

1. Ensure ignition switch is in the Run position by rotating switch fully clockwise to start position and releasing slowly, **Fig. 2.**
2. Install ignition switch and cover assembly, then two Torx mounting screws. **Torque** screws to 30–48 inch lbs.
3. Connect ignition switch electrical connector.
4. Position diverter plate on column and install three mounting screws. **Torque** screw to 30–48 inch lbs.
5. Align steering column mounting holes with support bracket, install four nuts and **torque** to 15–25 ft. lbs.
6. Install steering column shrouds.
7. Install instrument panel lower cover.
8. **On models with tilt column,** install tilt release lever, then capscrew and **torque** to 72–96 inch lbs. Check operation of tilt column through its entire range and ensure there is no interference with instrument panel.
9. **On all models,** connect battery ground cable.
10. Check column functions as follows:
    a. With shift lever in Park position and ignition lock cylinder in Lock position, ensure steering wheel locks.
    b. With shift lever in Drive position and ignition lock cylinder in run position, rotate lock cylinder toward Lock position until it stops, ensure engine electrical is Off and steering wheel does not lock.
    c. Rotate ignition lock cylinder counterclockwise and check for accessory power.
    d. Place shift lever in Park position, then rotate ignition lock cylinder clockwise to the Start position and ensure starter is energized.

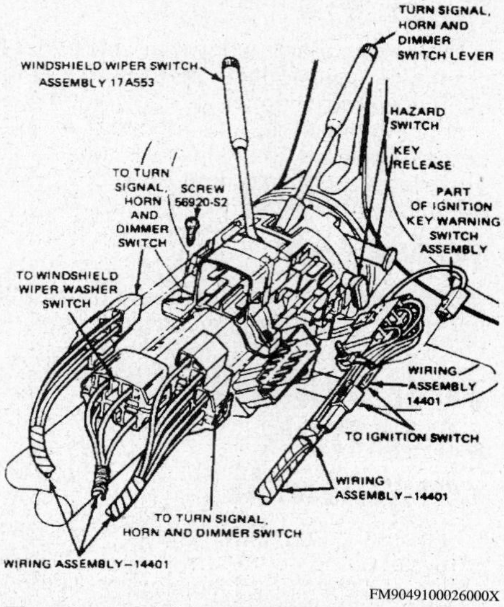

Fig. 3 Ignition switch installation. 1997 Mark VIII

MARK VIII

1997

Removal

1. Remove steering column shroud.
2. Remove column lock lever.
3. Disconnect ignition switch electrical connector.
4. Rotate ignition key lock cylinder to the Run position.
5. Remove two ignition switch mounting bolts.
6. Disengage ignition switch from actuator pin.
7. Remove ignition switch.

Installation

1. Adjust ignition switch by sliding carrier to Run position.
2. Ensure ignition key lock cylinder is in Run position.
3. Install ignition switch pin into actuator hole in column.
4. Install switch mounting screws and **torque** to 50–70 inch lbs.
5. Connect ignition switch electrical connector, **Fig. 3.**
6. Connect battery ground cable.
7. Check ignition switch for proper operation.
8. Install steering column shrouds.
9. Install lock lever.

1998

1. Remove ignition switch lock cylinder. Refer to " Ignition Lock, Replace."
2. Remove bolts and instrument panel steering column cover.

3. Position ignition switch cylinder bracket aside by disconnecting electrical connectors and removing bolts.
4. Disconnect ignition/shifter interlock cable.
5. Remove ignition switch cylinder bracket.
6. Remove ignition switch.
7. Reverse procedure to install.

TOWN CAR

1997

Refer to "1997" under "Mark VIII" for replacement procedure.

1998–2000

1. Remove lefthand instrument panel sound insulator pushpins, then disconnect insulator panel courtesy lamp electrical connector.
2. Remove sound insulator from instrument panel.
3. Remove lower steering column opening cover mounting screws, then the steering column opening cover.
4. Remove instrument panel steering column opening cover reinforcement.
5. Loosen ignition switch electrical connector mounting bolt, then disconnect electrical connector.
6. Ensure ignition switch is in the Off position.
7. Remove ignition switch mounting bolts, then the switch.
8. Reverse procedure to install, noting the following:
   a. **Torque** ignition switch mounting bolts to 47–64 inch lbs.
   b. **Torque** electrical connector mounting bolt to 7–10 inch lbs.
   c. **Torque** steering column reinforcement mounting bolts to 31–45 inch lbs.

NEUTRAL SAFETY SWITCH

REPLACE

CONTINENTAL

The Transmission Range (TR) sensor is located on the outside of the transmission. The TR sensor completes the start circuit in Park or Neutral and the backup lamp circuit in reverse. The sensor also opens and closes a set of four switches that are monitored by the Powertrain Control Module (PCM) to determine the position of the manual lever (PRND21).

1. Place gearshift lever in Neutral, then remove engine air cleaner.
2. Disconnect TR sensor electrical connector.
3. Remove manual control lever to manual shaft mounting nut, then the manual control lever from transaxle.
4. Remove TR sensor mounting bolts, then the sensor.
5. Reverse procedure to install, adjusting sensor as follows:
   a. Install TR sensor mounting bolts loosely.
   b. Ensure manual shift lever is in the Neutral position.

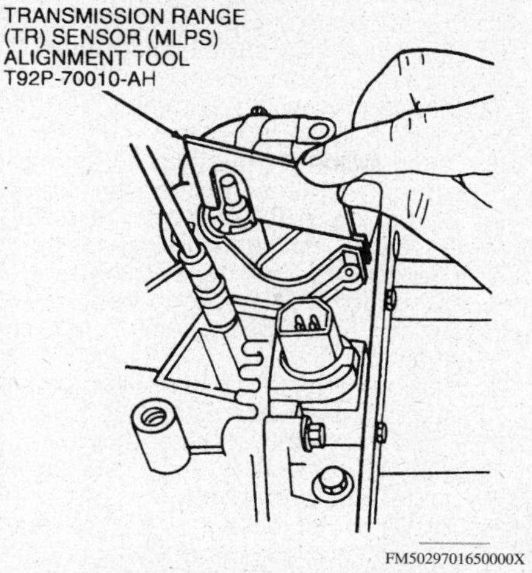

Fig. 4 TR sensor alignment. Continental

   c. Align TR sensor with TR sensor alignment tool No. T92P-70010-AH, or equivalent, **Fig. 4.**
   d. **Torque** mounting bolts to 7–12 ft. lbs.

MARK VIII & TOWN CAR

The Transmission Range (TR) sensor is located on the outside of the transmission. The TR sensor completes the start circuit in Park or Neutral and the backup lamp circuit in reverse. The sensor also opens and closes a set of four switches that are monitored by the Powertrain Control Module (PCM) to determine the position of the manual lever (PRND21).

1. Turn air suspension switch off, then raise and support vehicle.
2. Disconnect TR sensor electrical connector.
3. Disconnect transmission shift linkage.
4. Remove TR sensor mounting bolts, then the sensor.
5. Reverse procedure to install, adjusting sensor as follows:
   a. Install TR sensor mounting bolts loosely.
   b. Ensure manual shift lever is in the Neutral position.
   c. Align TR sensor slots with TR sensor alignment tool No. T97L-70010-A, or equivalent, **Fig. 5.**
   d. **Torque** mounting bolts to 60–84 inch lbs.

HEADLAMP SWITCH

REPLACE

CONTINENTAL

1. Remove screws mounting bottom of instrument panel cover.
2. Remove screws mounting lighting control module to instrument panel.
3. Pull lighting control module from instrument panel, then disconnect wiring connectors.
4. Reverse procedure to install.

MARK VIII

1. Remove headlamp switch knob by pulling it off.
2. Remove lamp switch knob applique by pulling at lefthand end to unsnap it from the finish panel and twist out bulb socket.
3. Remove two screws mounting lefthand end of finish panel to the instrument panel.
4. Remove two screws at top of cluster opening mounting finish panel to the instrument panel.
5. Remove upper steering column cover by pulling up on forward edge to unsnap four snap-in tabs.
6. Pull lefthand end of finish panel rearward far enough to disconnect two wiring connectors.
7. Remove two screws mounting switch to center finish panel.
8. Reverse procedure to install.

TOWN CAR

1997

1. Insert suitable hooked tool into headlight switch knob slot and remove spring tension on knob, then pull off.
2. Remove headlamp auto dimmer switch knob, if equipped.
3. Remove righthand and lefthand moldings from instrument panel by pulling away from instrument panel and snapping out of retainers.
4. Remove 12 finish panel mounting screws.
5. Remove finish panel, then the headlamp switch bracket mounting screws and bracket.
6. Remove switch to bracket mounting nut, then disconnect electrical connector and remove switch.
7. Reverse procedure to install.

1998–2000

1. Pull radio out from instrument cluster finish panel with radio removal tool No. T87P-19061-A, or equivalent.
2. Disconnect radio electrical connectors and antenna cable, then remove radio.
3. Remove instrument cluster finish panel mounting screws and pull cluster finish panel rearward.
4. Disconnect clock, headlamp switch and dimmer switch electrical connectors.
5. Remove instrument cluster finish panel and position aside.
6. Remove headlamp switch mounting screws, then the headlamp switch.
7. Reverse procedure to install.

STOP LIGHT SWITCH

REPLACE

CONTINENTAL & MARK VIII & 1997 TOWN CAR

1. Disconnect wires at switch connector.
2. Remove hair pin retainer, then slide switch, pushrod and nylon washers and bushing away from brake pedal and remove switch, **Fig. 6.**
3. Reverse procedure to install.

1998–2000 TOWN CAR

1. Remove lower insulator panel from lefthand side of instrument panel.

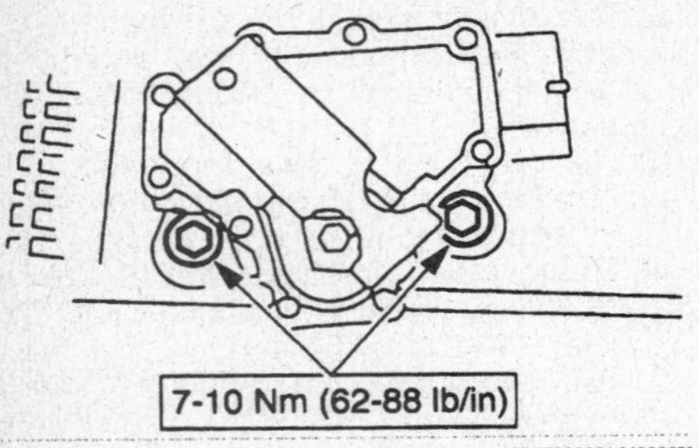

FM5029801649000X

Fig. 5 TR sensor alignment. Mark VIII & Town Car

2. Disconnect Brake Pedal Position (BPP) switch electrical connector.
3. Remove cotter pin, sleeve and BPP switch.
4. Reverse procedure to install.

MULTI-FUNCTION SWITCH

REPLACE

1. Place tilt column to lowest position and remove tilt lever.
2. Remove ignition lock cylinder.
3. Remove shroud mounting screws, then the upper and lower shroud.
4. Remove wiring harness retainer, then disconnect electrical connectors.
5. Remove multi-function switch to steering column mounting screws, then the multi-function switch.
6. Reverse procedure to install.

STEERING WHEEL

REPLACE

1. Center front wheels to straight ahead position.
2. Disconnect back-up power supply and remove air bag module as outlined in "Passive Restraints."
3. Disconnect speed control wire harness from steering wheel.
4. Remove steering wheel mounting bolt.
5. Using steering wheel puller tool No. T67L-3600-A, or equivalent, remove steering wheel.
6. Reverse procedure to install, noting the following:
   a. Ensure air bag wire is not pinched.
   b. Install new steering wheel bolt and **torque** to 23–33 ft. lbs.

INSTRUMENT CLUSTER

REPLACE

CONTINENTAL

1. Position vehicle on a flat surface to prevent movement when gear shift selector is out of position.
2. Turn ignition switch to unlock shift lever, then move lever down from front of electronic instrument cluster (EIC).
3. Tilt steering column down, then remove right and left finish molding by pulling upward to unsnap clips.
4. Disconnect electrical connectors.
5. Remove five Torx screws below cluster that retain applique.
6. Unsnap applique along top, then pull applique away from panel.
7. Disconnect switch assembly electrical connectors.
8. Remove three mounting screws from bottom of steering column shroud.
9. Lift up top section of shroud and remove clip on left side near steering wheel. Separate upper section of shroud from side section near ignition switch. Slip upper section off shift lever.
10. Remove four Torx screws mounting cluster to instrument panel.
11. Place a soft cloth on steering column to prevent scratching front surface of cluster when removed.
12. Tilt top of cluster slightly toward rear of vehicle, then disconnect two snaps beneath cluster mounting PRNDL assembly.
13. Unplug three connectors behind cluster. **Connectors have locking tabs that must be pressed in to unplug connection.**
14. Loosen two clips mounting PRNDL assembly to cluster, then position aside.
15. Push bottom of cluster into instrument panel, then tilt top of cluster toward rear of vehicle and remove cluster.
16. Reverse procedure to install.

MARK VIII

1. Remove instrument panel finish panel.
2. Remove four cluster to finish panel mounting screws. Do not remove screws securing lens and mask to backplate.
3. Rotate cluster face down and disconnect instrument cluster connector.
4. Slide cluster to right of instrument panel opening and unhook instrument panel harness from hook on back of instrument cluster.
5. Remove cluster assembly from panel.
6. Reverse procedure to install.

TOWN CAR

1997

Analog Cluster

1. Remove cluster trim cover mounting screws, then the trim cover.
2. Remove lower steering cover mounting screws, then the lower steering cover.
3. Remove lower half of steering column shroud.
4. Remove transmission indicator bracket mounting screw, then disconnect cable loop and bracket pin from steering column. Also remove column bracket from column.
5. Remove cluster mounting screws, then disconnect electrical feed plug from connector and remove cluster assembly.
6. Remove mounting screws from lens and mask assembly.
7. Remove temperature and fuel gauge from cluster.
8. Remove PRNDL mounting screws from speedometer.

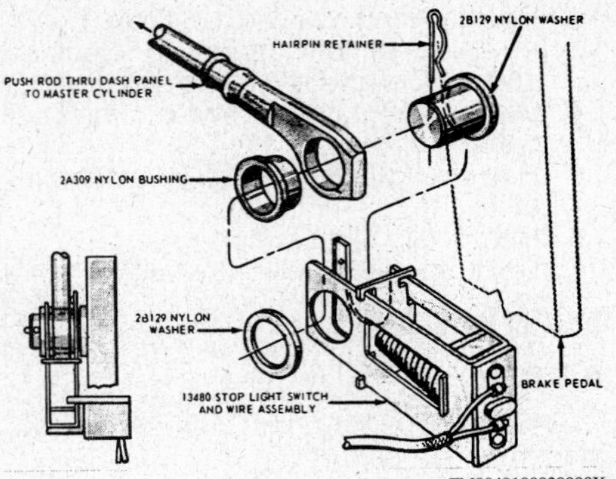

FM9049100029000X

Fig. 6 Stop light switch. Continental & Mark VIII & 1997 Town Car

9. Remove speedometer.

Digital Cluster

1. Unsnap center molding on righthand and lefthand sides of instrument panel.
2. Remove steering column cover and shroud.
3. Remove knobs from auto dim and auto lamp, if equipped.
4. Remove 13 instrument panel mounting screws, then pull panel out.
5. Move shift lever to 1 position for easier access.
6. Disconnect electrical connectors from warning module, switch module and center panel switches, if equipped.
7. Remove instrument panel.
8. Disconnect electrical connector from front of cluster.
9. Disconnect PRNDL assembly from cluster, by carefully bending bottom tab down and pulling assembly forward.
10. Pull cluster out and disconnect electrical connector.
11. Remove instrument cluster.
12. Reverse procedure to install.

1998–2000

1. Pull radio out from instrument cluster finish panel with radio removal tool No. T87P-19061-A, or equivalent.
2. Disconnect radio electrical connectors and antenna cable, then remove radio.
3. Remove instrument cluster finish panel mounting screws and pull cluster finish panel rearward.
4. Disconnect clock, headlamp switch and dimmer switch electrical connectors.
5. Remove instrument cluster finish panel and position aside.
6. Remove lower steering column cover mounting bolts.
7. Position parking brake release aside.
8. Remove lower steering column cover from instrument panel.
9. Remove steering column reinforcement mounting bolts, then the lower steering column reinforcement from instrument panel.
10. Disconnect transmission range indicator cable.
11. Remove transmission range indicator

cable bracket mounting bolt, then position cable aside.
12. Remove instrument cluster mounting screws and pull cluster rearward.
13. Disconnect cluster electrical connectors, then remove cluster from instrument panel.
14. Reverse procedure to install.

RADIO

REPLACE

When installing radio, adjust antenna trimmer for peak performance.

1. Install radio removal tool No. T87P-19061-A, or equivalent, into radio face plate, push tool in approximately one inch to release retaining clips.
2. Apply a light spreading force on tools and slowly pull radio from instrument panel.
3. Disconnect wiring connectors and antenna cable.
4. Reverse procedure to install.

WIPER MOTOR

REPLACE

CONTINENTAL

1. Disconnect power lead electrical connector from wiper motor.
2. Remove lefthand windshield wiper arm.
3. Remove linkage retaining clip from arm on motor by lifting locking tab up and pulling clip away from pin.
4. Remove motor and bracket assembly mounting bolts, then the motor.
5. Reverse procedure to install. **Torque** motor mounting bolts to 60–84 inch lbs.

MARK VIII

1. Turn ignition switch to Run position. Turn on windshield wipers and cycle to mid-wipe position, then turn off ignition.
2. Remove left and righthand wiper arms.
3. Remove cowl top to hood seal.
4. Remove left and righthand cowl vent screens.
5. Remove four mounting screws and washers, then the cowl top extension.
6. Disconnect two wiring connectors from motor.
7. Remove mounting bolts and washer assemblies from wiper module.
8. Lift module slightly to disengage support bracket from dash panel mounting stud. Move module sideways about 2 inches toward passenger side and remove module from vehicle.
9. Disconnect linkage drive arm from motor crankpin after removing clip.
10. Remove wiper motor's three mounting screws and remove motor from module.
11. Reverse procedure to install. **Before installing blade and arm assemblies to pivot shafts, cycle motor and turn off wiper switch to ensure wiper linkage is in park position.**

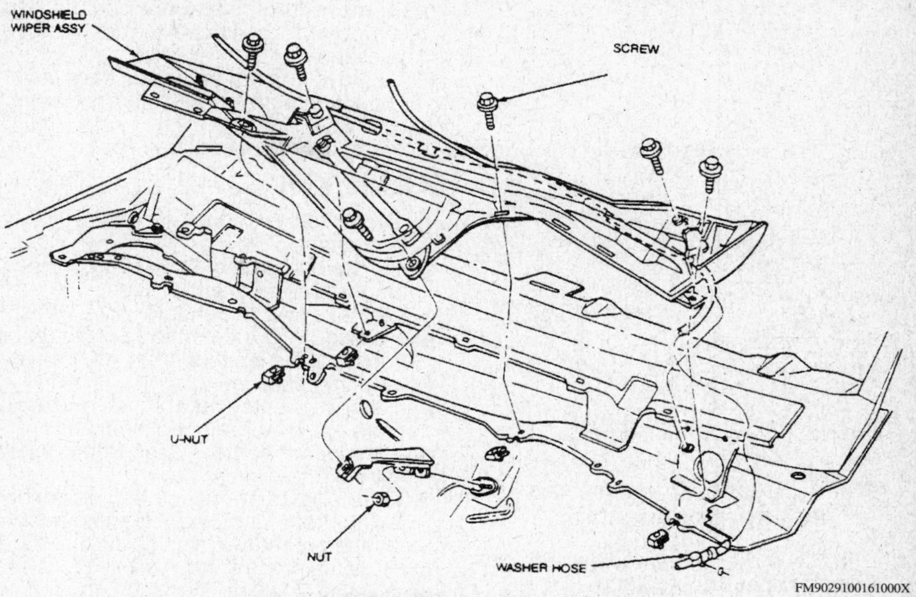

Fig. 7 Windshield wiper assembly. 1997 Town Car

TOWN CAR

1997

1. Remove rear hood seal, then the wiper arm assemblies.
2. Remove cowl vent screens and disconnect washer hoses from jets.
3. Disconnect electrical connectors from wiper motor.
4. Remove wiper assembly mounting screws, then lift assembly out of cowl, **Fig. 7.**
5. Unsnap and remove wiper linkage cover.
6. Remove linkage retaining clip from motor operating arm.
7. Remove motor mounting screws, then the motor.
8. Reverse procedure to install.

1998–2000

1. Remove windshield wiper pivot arm mounting nuts.
2. Remove wiper pivot arms from pivot shafts.
3. Remove cowl top vent panels.
4. Remove wiper mounting arm and pivot shaft assembly mounting nuts and bolt.
5. Position wiper mounting arm and pivot shaft assembly aside and disconnect electrical connector.
6. Remove wiper motor output shaft bolt.
7. Remove wiper motor mounting bolts, then the wiper motor.
8. Reverse procedure to install, noting the following:
   a. **Torque** wiper motor mounting bolts to 72–84 inch lbs.
   b. **Torque** wiper motor output shaft bolt to 10–12 ft. lbs.

WIPER SWITCH

REPLACE

Refer to "Multi-Function Switch, Replace" for replacement procedure.

BLOWER MOTOR

REPLACE

CONTINENTAL

1. Remove release retainers and lower glove compartment door.
2. Remove recirc duct support bracket mounting screw.
3. Remove electrical connector mounting screw, then disconnect three connectors from bracket and remove bracket.
4. Remove vacuum connection to recirc door vacuum motor, then disconnect aspirator hoses from muffler.
5. Remove six recirculation duct mounting screws.
6. Remove recirc duct from evaporator assembly from between instrument panel and evaporator case.
7. Disconnect blower motor electrical lead.
8. Remove blower motor wheel assembly mounting nut, then remove wheel.
9. Remove four blower motor mounting screws, then remove the motor from evaporator case.
10. Reverse procedure to install.

MARK VIII

1. Lower glove compartment door to gain access to rear of evaporator case.
2. Disconnect blower motor electrical connector.
3. Remove A/C evaporator air control venturi and in-vehicle temperature sensor aspirator hose.

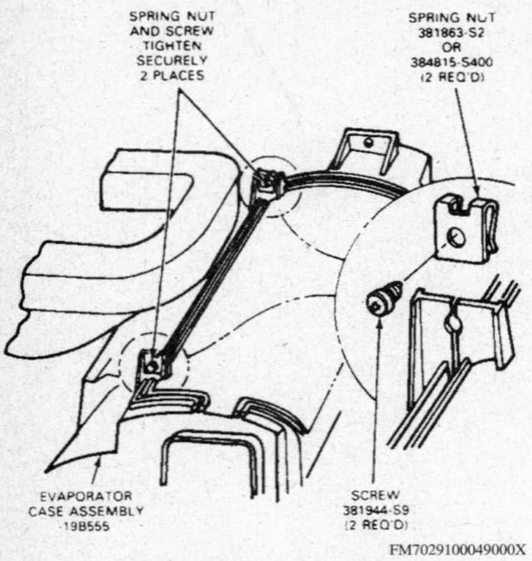

Fig. 8 Evaporator case tab drilling. Continental

4. Remove pulse width modulator (blower motor speed controller).
5. Remove screw and pull blower motor assembly out of blower motor housing.
6. Pull push nut off blower motor shaft and remove blower wheel from shaft.
7. Reverse procedure to install.

TOWN CAR

1997

1. Disconnect blower motor lead from wiring harness, then remove blower motor cooling tube from blower motor.
2. Remove four blower motor mounting screws.
3. Rotate motor and wheel assembly slightly to the right so bottom edge of mounting plate follows contour of wheelwell splash panel, then lift the motor and wheel assembly up and out of housing.
4. Reverse procedure to install.

1998–2000

1. Remove windshield washer fluid reservoir mounting nut, then position reservoir aside.
2. Remove righthand fender apron mounting screws and position apron aside.
3. Disengage wire harness connector from retainer, then disconnect blower motor electrical connector.
4. Disconnect rubber hose from blower motor.
5. Remove blower motor mounting screws, then the blower motor.
6. Reverse procedure to install.

HEATER CORE

REPLACE

CONTINENTAL

1. Remove instrument panel as outlined under "Dash Panel Service."
2. Remove evaporator case assembly.
3. Remove vacuum source from heater core tube.
4. Remove seal from heater core tubes.
5. Remove three blend door actuator to evaporator case screws, then remove actuator.
6. Remove four heater core access cover mounting screws, then remove cover and seal.
7. Remove heater core and seal.

MARK VIII

1. Drain radiator coolant into suitable container.
2. Remove instrument panel as outlined under "Dash Panel Service."
3. Remove seal from heater core tubes.
4. Remove A/C electronic door actuator motor, three screws, from A/C evaporator housing.
5. Remove heater core cover and seal from A/C evaporator housing.
6. Disconnect heater hoses from heater tubes.
7. Carefully pull evaporator assembly away from dash panel and remove evaporator case from vehicle.
8. Reverse procedure to install.

TOWN CAR

1997

1. Remove heater outlet floor duct.
2. Remove instrument panel as outlined in "Dash Panel Service."
3. Disconnect heater hose from heater core tubes, then plug heater hoses and core tubes.
4. Remove one nut mounting upper lefthand corner of evaporator case to dash panel.
5. Disconnect two vacuum supply hoses from vacuum source, then push vacuum hoses and grommet into passenger compartment.
6. Disconnect wiring harness from A/C electronic blend door actuator.
7. Disconnect white vacuum hose from heater and A/C air inlet duct door vacuum control motor.
8. Remove two nuts along lower flange of plenum chamber.
9. Disconnect A/C electronic blend door actuator and electronic module connectors located on the side of the heater air plenum chamber.
10. Remove heater air plenum chamber by pulling rearward.
11. Remove four heater core cover mounting screws, then the cover from plenum.
12. Remove heater core and seal assembly from plenum assembly.
13. Reverse procedure to install.

1998–2000

1. Position driver seat as far back as possible, then remove seat track covers.
2. Remove mounting bolts from front of seat.
3. Move seat forward as far as possible and remove seat track covers.
4. Remove mounting nuts from rear of seat.
5. Disconnect seat electrical connectors, then remove driver seat from vehicle.
6. Position passenger front seat as far back as possible, then remove seat track covers.

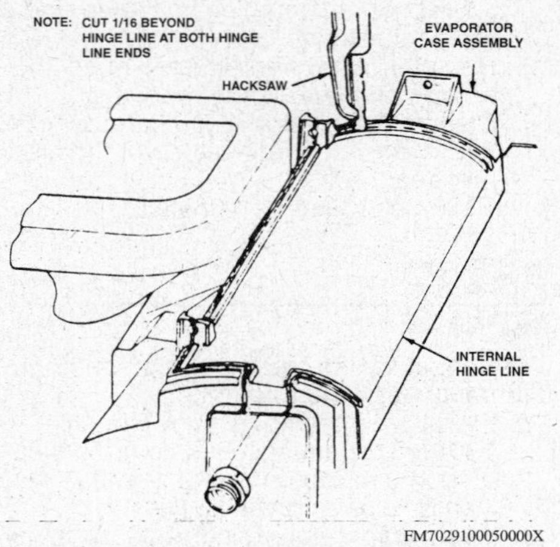

Fig. 9 Cutting evaporator case. Continental

7. Remove mounting bolts from front of seat.
8. Move seat forward as far as possible and remove seat track covers.
9. Remove mounting nuts from rear of seat.
10. Disconnect seat electrical connectors, then remove passenger front seat from vehicle.
11. Remove front center seat.
12. Remove carpet from front floor.
13. Remove rear seat airflow duct pushpin, then the rear seat airflow duct.
14. Remove instrument panel as outlined in "Dash Panel Service."
15. Drain coolant from radiator until level is below heater core.
16. Remove windshield wiper mounting arm and pivot shaft as outlined previously.
17. Remove cowl top extension mounting nut.
18. Disconnect wiper motor electrical connector, then remove cowl top extension.
19. Disconnect vacuum hoses and electrical connector from evaporative emissions canister purge valve.
20. Remove evaporative emissions canister purge valve mounting nuts, then the valve.
21. Disconnect heater water hoses from heater core.
22. Remove plenum chamber mounting nut from cowl.
23. Remove windshield washer fluid reservoir mounting nut, then position reservoir aside.
24. Remove righthand fender apron mounting screws, then position apron aside.
25. Remove A/C evaporative core housing mounting nut and bolt.
26. Disconnect vacuum hoses and electrical connectors from plenum chamber.
27. Remove mounting nuts from plenum chamber lower flange.
28. Remove mounting nut from plenum chamber upper flange, then the plenum chamber from instrument panel carrier.
29. Remove heater core cover mounting screws.

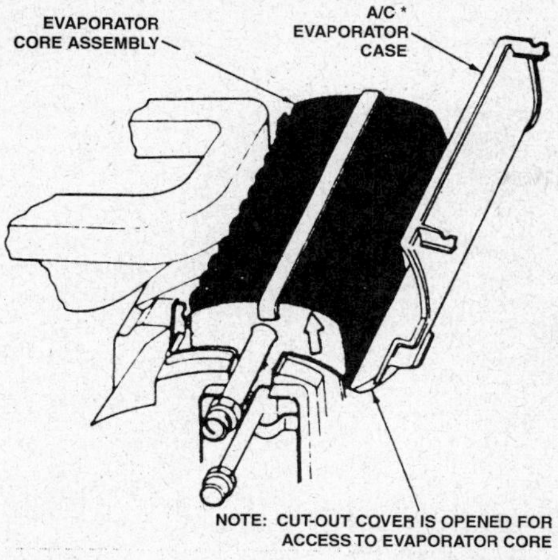

Fig. 10 Evaporator case from core removal. Continental

30. Remove heater core cover and seal from plenum chamber.
31. Remove heater core from plenum chamber.
32. Reverse procedure to install.

EVAPORATOR CORE

REPLACE

CONTINENTAL

1. Remove evaporator case as outlined under "Heater Core, Replace."
2. Disconnect and remove vacuum harness.
3. Remove six screws mounting recirculation duct, then remove duct.
4. Remove two screws from air inlet duct and remove duct from evaporator case.
5. Remove support bracket, then screws holding electronic connector bracket to recirculation duct.
6. Remove blend door actuator and cold engine lockout switch.
7. Remove molded seal from evaporator core tubes.
8. Drill a 3⁄16 inch hole in both upright tabs on top of evaporator case, **Fig. 8.**
9. Using a hot knife or small saw blade, cut top of evaporator case between raised outline, **Fig. 9.**
10. Fold cutout cover back from opening and lift evaporator core from case, **Fig. 10.**
11. Reverse procedure to install, noting the following:
    a. Transfer four foam core seals to new evaporator core.
    b. Install caulking cord No. D9AZ-19560-A, or equivalent, to seal evaporator case against leakage along cut line.

MARK VIII

1. Remove instrument panel.
2. Remove seal from heater core tubes, **Fig. 11.**
3. Remove blend door actuator to evaporator case mounting screws.
4. Remove actuator from case.
5. Remove access cover and seal from evaporator case.
6. Partially drain coolant from radiator and disconnect heater hoses from heater core.
7. Pull heater core and seals from evaporator case.
8. Reverse procedure to install. Fill radiator with specified coolant and check system operation.

TOWN CAR

1997

1. Remove evaporator case as outlined under "Heater Core, Replace."
2. Remove dash panel seal, then the heat shield from bottom of evaporator case.
3. Remove six screws mounting two halves of case together.
4. Separate two halves of evaporator case, then remove evaporator core and mounting bracket.
5. Disconnect the suction accumulator/drier inlet from evaporator core outlet tube, **Fig. 12.**
6. Reverse procedure to install, noting the following:
    a. Install new O-rings to accumulator/drier.
    b. Apply caulking cord No. D9AZ-19560-A, or equivalent, to case flange and around evaporator core tubes.
    c. Install a new heat shield on bottom of evaporator case assembly with staples.

1998–2000

1. Recover refrigerant as outlined in "Air Conditioning" section.
2. Remove righthand cowl vent screen mounting screws, then the vent screen.
3. Disconnect vacuum hoses and electrical connector from evaporative emissions canister purge valve.
4. Remove evaporative emissions canister purge valve mounting nuts, then the valve.
5. Remove windshield washer fluid reservoir mounting nut, then position reservoir aside.
6. Disengage four wire harness retainers from top of righthand fender apron.
7. Remove righthand fender apron mounting screws, then the fender apron.
8. Disconnect A/C cycling switch electrical connector.
9. Disconnect blower motor electrical connector, then disengage wire harness from retainer.
10. Disconnect evaporator to compressor suction line from suction accumulator/drier.
11. Disconnect suction accumulator/drier from A/C evaporator core.
12. Remove A/C accumulator/drier mounting bracket clamp screw, then the accumulator/drier from vehicle.
13. Disconnect condenser to evaporator tube from evaporator.
14. Remove righthand sound insulator pushpins, then the sound insulator from instrument panel.
15. Remove in-car temperature sensor hose and elbow from evaporator housing.
16. Remove mounting nuts from top and bottom of evaporator housing.
17. Remove blower motor mounting screw and nut.
18. Remove evaporator housing mounting screws.
19. Separate housing and remove blower motor from A/C evaporator core.
20. Remove A/C evaporator core screw, then the evaporator core from housing.
21. Remove bracket from A/C evaporator core.
22. Reverse procedure to install.

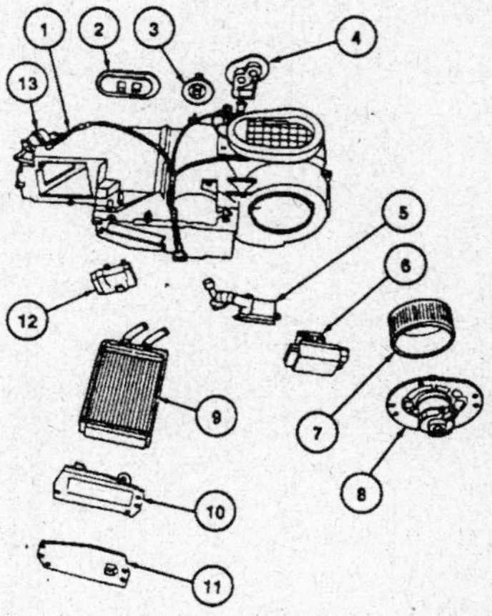

Item		Description
1		A/C Evaporator Housing
2		Heater Dash Panel Seal
3		A/C Evaporator Drain Tube Seal
4		A/C Evaporator Drain Tube Seal
5		A/C Evaporator Air Control Venturi
6		Pulse Width Modulator Assy (Blower Motor Speed Controller)
7		Blower Motor Wheel
8		A/C Blower Motor
9		Heater Core
10		Heater Core Cover Seal
11		Heater Core Cover
12		A/C Electronic Door Actuator Motor
13		Vacuum Control Motor

FM7029100053000A

Fig. 11 Exploded view of evaporator case. Mark VIII

TECHNICAL SERVICE BULLETINS

INSTRUMENT CLUSTER WARNING LIGHTS LIT DIMLY

Continental

On some of these models the instrument cluster warning light(s) may be dimly lit.

This condition may be caused by the ignition switch. To correct this condition, replace ignition switch.

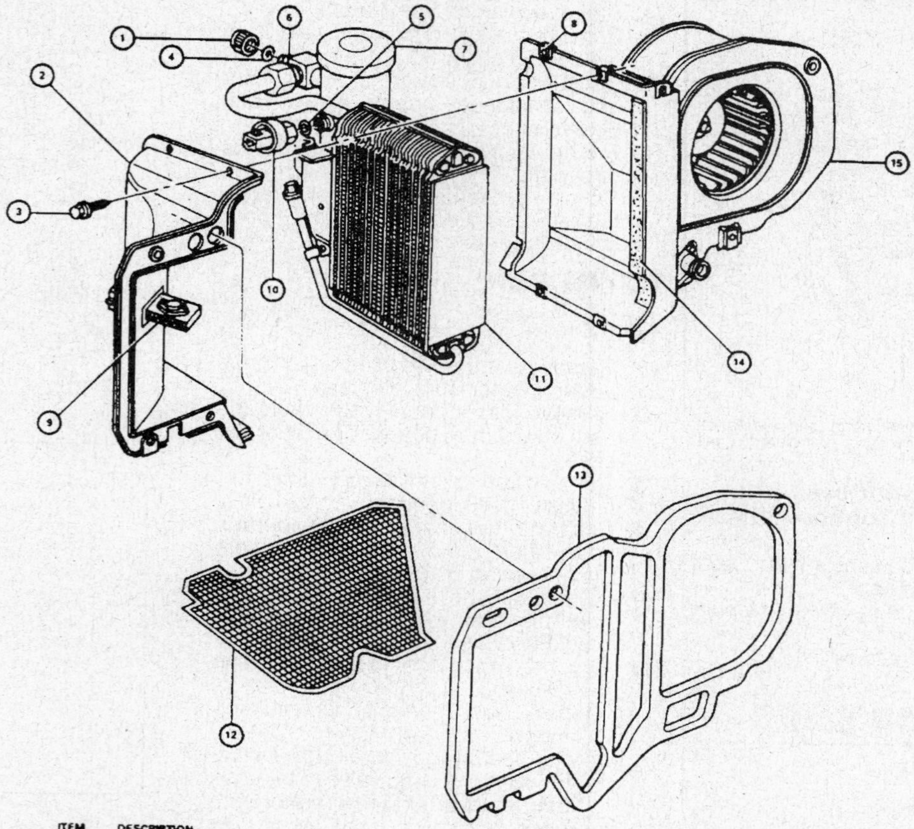

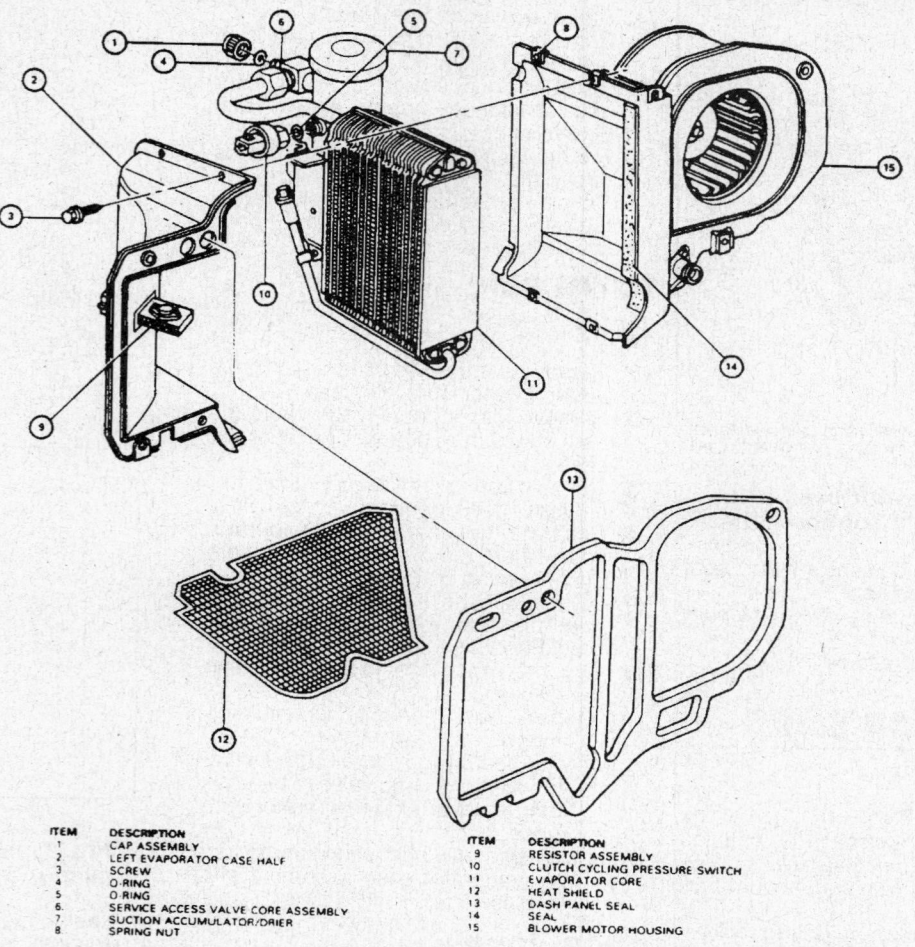

ITEM	DESCRIPTION
1	CAP ASSEMBLY
2	LEFT EVAPORATOR CASE HALF
3	SCREW
4	O-RING
5	O-RING
6.	SERVICE ACCESS VALVE CORE ASSEMBLY
7	SUCTION ACCUMULATOR/DRIER
8	SPRING NUT
9	RESISTOR ASSEMBLY
10	CLUTCH CYCLING PRESSURE SWITCH
11	EVAPORATOR CORE
12	HEAT SHIELD
13	DASH PANEL SEAL
14	SEAL
15	BLOWER MOTOR HOUSING

FM7029100052000X

Fig. 12 Exploded view of evaporator case. 1997 Town Car

4.6L Engine

NOTE: Refer To " Air Bag System Precautions " Located In The Front Of This Manual For System Disarming & Arming Procedures.

INDEX

PRECAUTIONS

AIR BAG SYSTEMS

Refer to "Air Bag System Precautions" in the front of this manual for system disarming and arming procedures.

BATTERY GROUND CABLE

Prior to service, disconnect battery ground cable and isolate as required.

FUEL SYSTEM PRESSURE RELIEF

Fuel supply lines will remain pressurized after the engine is shutoff. Pressure must be relieved prior to any fuel system servicing. Relieve fuel system pressure as follows:

1. Remove fuel tank cap.
2. Attach fuel pressure gauge tool No. T80L-9974-B, or equivalent, to pressure relief valve righthand rear fuel rail
3. Place outlet hose of tool in suitable container.
4. Open valve of tool to relieve pressure.

COMPRESSION PRESSURE

Cylinder compression pressure should range between 134 psi (being the lowest maximum pressure) and 250 psi (being the highest maximum pressure) at an engine cranking speed of 180 RPM minimum. The compression in each cylinder should fall within the specified compression pressure range with no more than a 75% variance in compression.

ENGINE MOUNT

REPLACE

CONTINENTAL

ENGINE MOUNT

1. Turn off air suspension. Switch is located in trunk under flap of compartment trim.
2. Raise and support vehicle
3. Position a suitable jack and wood block under engine.
4. Remove nut mounting mounts to subframe.
5. Raise engine only sufficiently to allow mount removal. **Do not raise engine excessively or separation of inner CV joints may occur. If necessary remove driveshafts as outlined under " Front Wheel Drive Axles."**
6. Remove bolts mounting mount to engine support bracket, then remove mount.
7. Reverse procedures to install. Tighten to specifications.

TRANSAXLE MOUNT

1. Turn off air suspension, switch is located in trunk under flap of compartment trim.
2. Raise and support vehicle, then remove left front wheel assembly.
3. Place a suitable transmission jack under transaxle.
4. Raise jack sufficiently to take load off transaxle mount.
5. Remove nut and bolts mounting mount to subframe and transaxle.
6. Raise transaxle only sufficiently to allow mount removal. **Do not raise transaxle excessively or separation of inner CV joints may occur. If necessary remove driveshafts as outlined under "Front Wheel Drive Axles."**
7. Remove bolts mounting support bracket to transaxle.
8. Remove mount by rotating counterclockwise.
9. Reverse procedures to install. Tighten to specifications.

MARK VIII

ENGINE MOUNTS

All self locking or Loctite coated type fasteners must be replaced with new

self locking fasteners. All residual locking compound must be removed from tapped holes before new bolts are installed.

Removal

1. Remove engine appearance cover, then air cleaner outlet tube.
2. Install suitable lifting eyes to engine, then install suitable engine support frame and lift engine sufficiently to relieve tension on mounts. **Do not lift engine too high as lines and wiring may be damaged.**
3. Raise and support vehicle, then remove front wheel assemblies.
4. Remove motor mount though bolts
5. Prepare subframe for lowering by disconnecting all engine wiring and equipment clipped or attached.
6. Mark steering shaft coupling for later alignment, then disconnect at pinch bolt.
7. Support front suspension lower control arms with suitable jacks.
8. Disconnect lower control arms from shock strut, then lower jacks to allow control arms to hang freely.
9. Place suitable jacks under subframe, positioned to allow subframe to be lowered and motor mounts to be accessed.
10. Remove subframe mounting bolts, then lower subframe.
11. Remove mounting bolts of mount(s) to be replaced, then mount.

Installation

1. Place new motor mount(s) into position and loosely install engine to motor mount mounting bolts.
2. Position sub frame to body with jacks, loosely install bolts, then align subframe as follows:
   a. With subframe in loose contact with body, place two alignment pins made from a suitable ¾ inch OD diameter tubing or pipe through holes in subframe and into holes in body.
   b. Tighten one bolt in each corner of subframe, remove alignment pins.
   c. Tighten subframe mounting bolts to specification, then tighten motor mount bolts to specification
3. Using suitable jacks, position lower control arms into shock struts, then install lower shock strut bolts and tighten to specification.
4. Align and install steering coupling, then tighten pinch bolt to specification.
5. Attach all wiring lines and hoses to subframe using suitable clips and fasteners.
6. Install motor mount to subframe through bolts, then tighten to specification.
7. Install wheel assemblies, lower vehicle, then tighten lug bolts to specification.
8. Remove engine support frame and lifting eyes.
9. Install air cleaner outlet tube, engine appearance cover and battery ground cable.

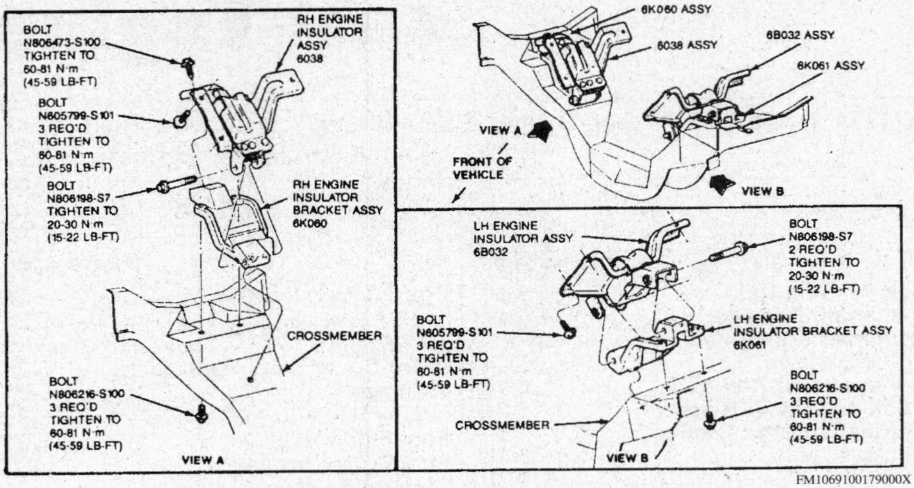

Fig. 1 Front engine mounts. 1997 Town Car

10. Check and adjust front wheel alignment.

TRANSMISSION MOUNT

1. Raise and support vehicle.
2. Support transmission using a suitable jack.
3. Remove and/or lower exhaust components as necessary to allow removal of transmission crossmember.
4. Remove bolts mounting mount to transmission and crossmember.
5. Remove bolts mounting crossmember to body, then remove crossmember and mount
6. Reverse procedure to install. Tighten to specifications.

TOWN CAR

1997

Front Mount

1. Disconnect ground and positive battery cables.
2. Remove air inlet tube.
3. Drain cooling system into a suitable container, then remove cooling fan and shroud.
4. Relieve fuel system pressure as outlined under " Precautions."
5. Remove upper radiator hose.
6. Remove wiper module and support bracket.
7. Recover A/C system as outlined under "Air Conditioning. "
8. Disconnect A/C compressor outlet hose, then remove hose assembly to righthand coil bracket mounting bolt.
9. Remove engine electrical harness 42-pin connector from bracket on brake vacuum booster.
10. Disconnect engine electrical connector, then disconnect transmission harness electrical connector.
11. Disconnect throttle valve cable at throttle body.
12. Disconnect heater outlet hose.
13. Remove heater outlet hose assembly to righthand cylinder head upper mounting stud, then loosen lower bolt and position aside.
14. Remove blower motor resistor.
15. Remove righthand engine mount to lower engine bracket mounting bolt.
16. Disconnect EGR valve vacuum hoses and tube.
17. Remove EGR valve to intake manifold mounting bolts.
18. Disconnect heated exhaust gas oxygen (H2OS) sensors.
19. Raise and support vehicle.
20. Remove righthand front engine mount two through bolts, then remove lefthand front engine mount through bolt, **Fig. 1.**
21. Remove EGR tube line mounting nut at righthand exhaust manifold, then remove EGR valve assembly.
22. Disconnect exhaust pipes at exhaust manifolds, then lower and support exhaust at crossmember.
23. Position suitable jack and wood block under oil pan, rearward of drain plug, then raise engine approximately four inches.
24. Install wood block under oil pan, then lower engine onto wood block.
25. Remove engine mount mounting bolts.
26. Reverse procedure to install, noting the following:
   a. Tighten mounting bolts to specifications.
   b. Refer to **Fig. 1** for engine mount tightening specifications.

Rear Mount

1. Raise and support vehicle, then using suitable jack and wood block support transmission.
2. Remove rear mount to crossmember mounting bolts.
3. Remove mount to transmission mounting bolt, **Fig. 2.**
4. Raise transmission with suitable jack, then remove mount assembly.
5. Reverse procedure to install. Refer to **Fig. 2** for rear engine mount tightening specifications.

1998–2000

Righthand Mount

1. Remove starter motor as outlined in "Electrical" section.

2. Using a suitable lifting device, support engine.
3. Remove three righthand engine mount mounting bolts.
4. Remove righthand engine mount.
5. Reverse procedure to install.

Lefthand Mount

1. Remove oil level indicator tube.
2. Using a suitable lifting device, support engine.
3. Remove three righthand engine mount mounting bolts.
4. Remove righthand engine mount.
5. Reverse procedure to install.

ENGINE

REPLACE

CONTINENTAL

The engine is removed in unit with transaxle and subframe. Ensure suitable powertrain lifting equipment is available. Vehicle must be supported on a suitable frame contact lift.

1. Mark steering shaft coupling for later alignment, then disconnect at pinch bolt.
2. Remove engine appearance cover, then air cleaner outlet tube.
3. Drain cooling system into a suitable container.
4. Recover A/C system as outlined under "Air Conditioning."
5. Relieve fuel system pressure as outlined under " Precautions," then disconnect fuel lines.
6. Mark for later assembly, then disconnect and position aside the following components accessible through hood opening:
   a. Control sensor wiring from powertrain control module (PCM).
   b. Engine control sensor wiring near power brake booster.
   c. Control sensor wiring from mass air flow (MAF) sensor and evaporative emission canister purge (EVAP) valve.
   d. All vacuum hoses.
   e. Throttle and cruise control cable, shields and brackets.
   f. Shift cable and control wiring from transaxle.
   g. Transaxle cooler lines from transaxle.
   h. Heater and coolant hoses from engine.
   i. Power steering return hose from reservoir, drain reservoir into a suitable container.
   j. Alternator wiring.
   k. Any additional wiring, cabling and hosing connecting powertrain to chassis.
7. Raise and support vehicle, then remove front wheel assemblies.
8. Mark for later assembly, disconnect and position aside the following components accessible from under vehicle:
   a. Right and left ride height sensor links.

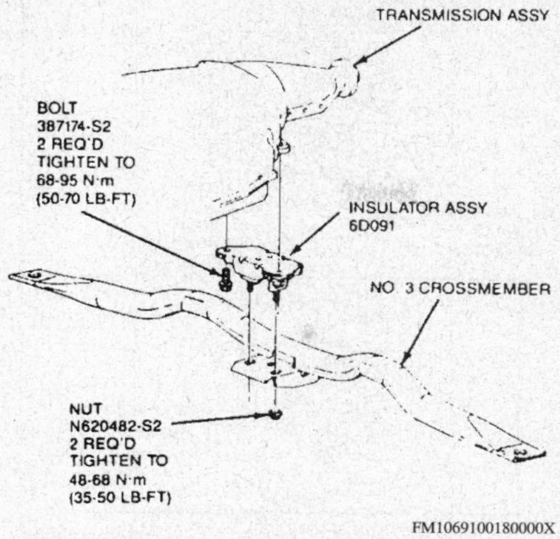

Fig. 2 Rear engine mount. 1997 Town Car

   b. Right and left stabilizer bar links from stabilizer bar.
   c. Right and left lower control arms at ball joint.
   d. Right and left tie rod ends at knuckle.
   e. Right and left axle nuts, then remove driveshafts from hubs.
   f. Radiator lower splash shield.
   g. Drain engine oil into a suitable container.
   h. Exhaust system components as necessary for clearance.
   i. Hoses and lines from power steering, transmission and radiator. Drain fluids into suitable containers.
   j. Starter wiring.
   k. A/C lines from compressor.
   l. Any additional wiring, cabling and hosing connecting powertrain to chassis.
9. Support powertrain/subframe assembly with suitable engine lifting equipment.
10. Remove subframe mounting bolts, then lower powertrain/subframe assembly from vehicle, place on stable supports.
11. Remove engine and transaxle from powertrain/subframe assembly as follows:
   a. Attach suitable lifting eyes to engine.
   b. Disconnect any additional wiring, cabling and hosing connecting engine to transaxle and subframe.
   c. Connect suitable lifting equipment to lifting eyes.
   d. Lift assembly sufficiently to relieve pressure on motor and transaxle mounts, then remove mount to subframe bolts.
   e. Lift assembly from subframe, then place on stable supports.
   f. Remove engine to transaxle and torque converter bolts, separate engine from transaxle.
   g. Place engine into suitable work bench, then remove remaining components to allow engine replacement.
12. Reverse procedure to install. Tighten to specifications, then inspect front end alignment.

MARK VIII

1997

1. Disconnect both battery cables, then mark hood hinge positions for installation alignment.
2. Remove hood.
3. Remove engine appearance cover.
4. Remove IAT sensor electrical connector.
5. Remove air cleaner outlet tube and resonator.
6. Remove hood, drain cooling system.
7. Remove wiper module and bracket.
8. Recover A/C system.
9. Remove engine cooling fan, shroud and radiator.
10. Relieve fuel system pressure as outlined under " Precautions." then disconnect fuel lines.
11. Disconnect 42-pin connector and transmission harness electrical connector, at left fender well, then position connectors aside.
12. Remove power distribution box and harness, then disconnect B+ wiring connector at distribution box.
13. Disconnect electrical connectors at EVAP canister purge valves.
14. Disconnect accelerator cable, speed control actuator from throttle body and cable brackets.
15. Disconnect canister purge vacuum line at throttle body.
16. Disconnect chassis supply vacuum line at cowl.
17. Disconnect heater inlet and outlet tubes at rear of righthand cylinder head.
18. Disconnect upper radiator hose at bypass tube and overflow hose at recovery reservoir.
19. Remove pressure and return hoses at power steering pump, then remove pump.
20. Remove upper cooling inlet hose from radiator.
21. Install engine lifting tool No. 014-00340, or equivalent.
22. Disconnect A/C refrigerant hoses at compressor. Refer to " Air Conditioning" section for procedure and precautions.
23. Raise vehicle and suitably support.
24. Remove front wheels.
25. Disconnect righthand and lefthand ride height sensor electrical connectors.
26. Remove right and left front brake calipers and suitably support.
27. Disconnect right and left front suspension upper control arms from steering knuckle.
28. Drain engine oil.
29. Remove converter Y pipe from lefthand and righthand exhaust manifolds.
30. Disconnect ground strap from right front fender.
31. Disconnect power steering pressure hose at steering gear.
32. Remove lower radiator hose.
33. Remove right and left strut at front suspension lower control arms.

34. Disconnect engine control sensor wiring and gear selector linkage.
35. Disconnect lower oil cooler tube from radiator.
36. Remove driveshaft mounting bolts at pinion flange.
37. Loosen rear differential bracket body bolts and lower.
38. Remove driveshaft.
39. Remove battery positive cable, then disconnect low oil sensor connector and wiring from oil pan.
40. Remove starter.
41. Support powertrain frame using powertrain lift tool No. 014-0765 and adapter tool No. 014-000341, or equivalents.
42. Remove rear engine support insulator, then disconnect steering coupling pinch bolt.
43. Remove powertrain frame mounting bolts, then lower engine and transmission from vehicle.
44. Reverse procedure to install, noting the following;
    a. Refill and check, engine oil, transmission fluid, power steering fluid, and engine coolant.
    b. Recharge A/C system as described in the "Air Conditioning" section.
    c. Check front end alignment.

1998

1. Remove battery and air cleaner outlet tube.
2. Drain engine cooling system into a suitable container.
3. Remove windshield wiper.
4. Recover A/C system refrigerant as outlined under "Air Conditioning."
5. Disconnect secondary air injection valve inlet tube from secondary air injection pump outlet hose.
6. Remove fan motor.
7. Relieve fuel system pressure as outlined under "Precautions."
8. Disconnect 42-pin connector at rear of lefthand valve cover.
9. Position power distribution box out of way.
10. Disconnect generator wires from power distribution box.
11. Disconnect headlamp dash panel junction wire and generator wire connectors.
12. Remove accelerator and cruise control cables.
13. Disconnect evaporative emission hose at upper intake manifold.
14. Disconnect chassis vacuum supply hose.
15. Disconnect heater water hose and heater water hose behind righthand cylinder head.
16. Remove generator mounting bracket.
17. Remove upper radiator hose and water bypass hose from water outlet tube.
18. Disconnect radiator overflow hose.
19. Remove power steering pressure line from bracket, then the pressure and return hoses.
20. Disconnect transmission cooling tubes and lower radiator hose from radiator.
21. Remove A/C compressor lines.
22. Raise and support vehicle, then remove front tires.

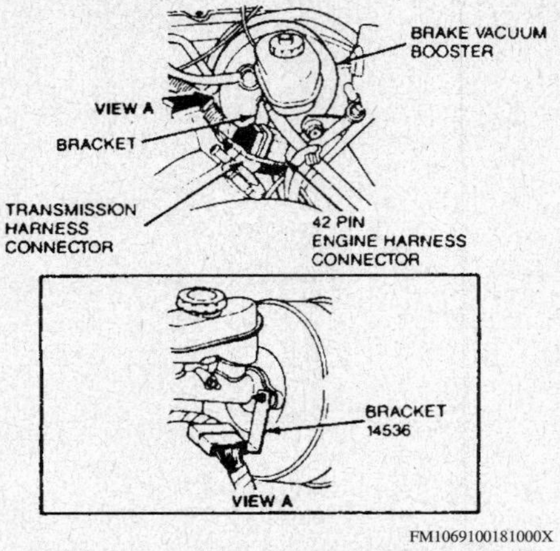

Fig. 3 Engine & transmission harness connectors. 1997 Town Car

23. Disconnect right and lefthand air suspension height sensor connectors.
24. Remove stabilizer bar link from front stabilizer bar.
25. Disconnect right and left tie rod ends.
26. Disconnect right and left lower front wheel spindles.
27. Disconnect right and left front spring and shock from front suspension lower arm strut.
28. Remove dual converter Y pipe, then the starter motor.
29. Remove steering coupling at pinch bolt joint.
30. Remove ground strap from righthand fender apron.
31. Mark rear driveshaft yoke and axle flange so they may be installed in original positions.
32. Remove four bolts from rear axle universal joint flange to driveshaft centering socket yoke.
33. Disconnect nuts and position rear driveshaft aside.
34. Remove lefthand front shock absorber strut cover cup.
35. Disconnect neutral switch wiring connectors near lefthand fender wall.
36. Remove power brake booster hose from lower intake manifold.
37. Disconnect vacuum hoses near lefthand fender wall.
38. Disconnect fuel lines from fuel rail.
39. Remove shift cable and bracket.
40. Position a suitable powertrain lift and transmission support bracket under engine.
41. Remove crossmember.
42. Lower engine.
43. Disconnect transmission lines.
44. Remove transmission dipstick tube bolt from cylinder head.
45. Remove torque converter bolts.
46. Remove transmission housing bolts.
47. Remove flywheel bolts.
48. Remove engine rear plate.
49. Reverse procedure to install, tighten all fasteners to specification.

TOWN CAR

1997

1. Disconnect both battery cables, then mark hood hinge positions for installation alignment.
2. Remove hood, drain cooling system and recover A/C system refrigerant as outlined under "Air Conditioning."
3. Relieve fuel system pressure as outlined under " Precautions," then disconnect fuel lines.
4. Remove engine cooling fan, shroud and radiator.
5. Remove wiper module and bracket.
6. Remove air inlet tube.
7. Remove 42-pin electrical harness connector from bracket at brake vacuum booster, **Fig. 3.**
8. Disconnect 42-pin connector and transmission harness electrical connector, then position connectors aside.
9. Using suitable tool, disconnect accelerator and speed control cables.
10. Disconnect throttle valve cable.
11. Disconnect purge solenoid electrical connector and vacuum hose.
12. Disconnect power distribution and starter relay power supply.
13. Disconnect throttle body elbow vacuum port supply hose.
14. Disconnect heater inlet and return hoses.
15. Disconnect alternator electrical harness at fender apron and junction box.
16. Using tool No. T81P-19623-G1, G2, or equivalent, remove A/C compressor inlet and outlet mounting hoses, **Fig. 4.**
17. Disconnect EVO sensor electrical connector.
18. Disconnect body ground strap at dash panel.
19. Raise and support vehicle, then drain engine oil.
20. Disconnect exhaust pipes at exhaust manifolds, then lower and support exhaust at crossmember.
21. Remove transmission line bracket mounting nut, then remove engine to transmission knee braces mounting bolts and stud, **Fig. 5.**
22. Remove starter assembly.
23. Remove power steering pump mounting nuts and position pump aside.
24. Remove engine block plug to gain access to torque converter mounting nuts, then rotate crankshaft to remove mounting nuts.
25. Remove engine to transmission mounting bolts.
26. Remove righthand front engine mount two through bolts, then remove lefthand front engine mount through bolt.
27. Lower vehicle, using suitable jack, support transmission.
28. Install engine lift brackets, **Fig. 6,** then connect suitable lift equipment.
29. Carefully raise engine and separate from transmission, then remove engine.
30. Reverse procedure to install, noting the following:
    a. Refer to **Fig. 1,** for engine mount

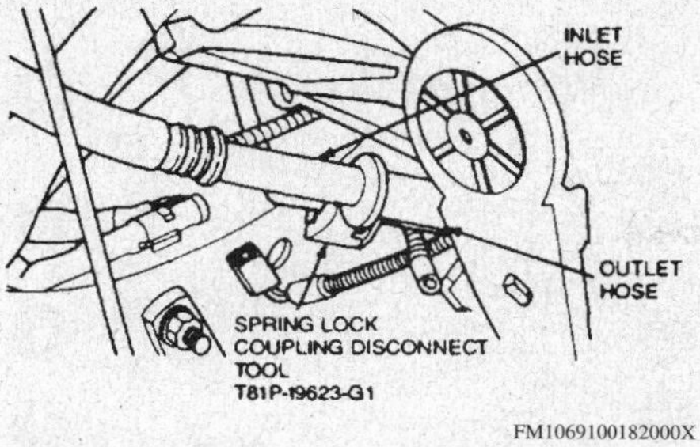

Fig. 4 A/C compressor lines. 1997 Town Car

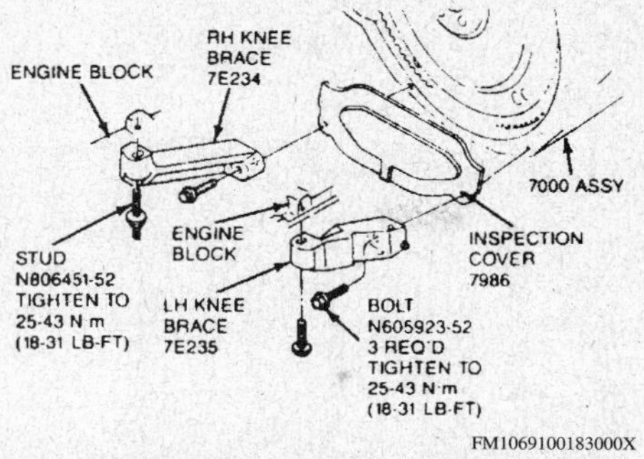

Fig. 5 Transmission line bracket assembly. 1997 Town Car

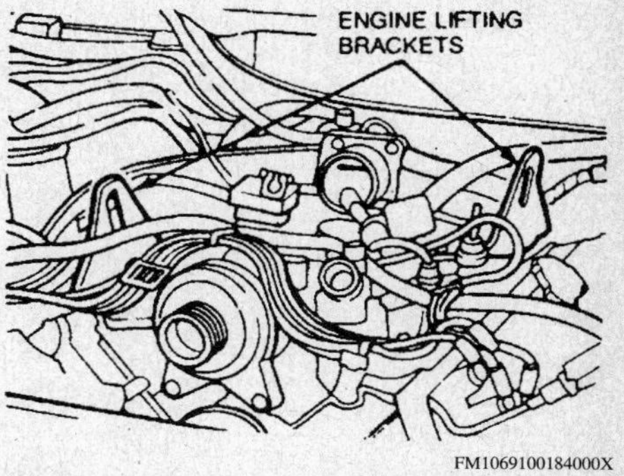

Fig. 6 Engine lift brackets. 1997 Town Car

tightening specifications.

b. Refer to **Fig. 5**, for transmission brace tightening specifications.

1998–2000

1. Mark hood hinge positions for installation alignment, then remove hood.
2. Recover A/C refrigerant as outlined in "Air Conditioning " section.
3. Relieve fuel pressure as outlined under "Precautions. "
4. Remove windshield wiper governor.
5. Raise and support vehicle.
6. Drain engine coolant, then disconnect lower radiator hose.
7. Lower vehicle and disconnect degas bottle supply hose.
8. Remove battery.
9. Disconnect hoses from transmission fluid cooler and power steering fluid cooler.
10. Remove radiator upper sight shield, then the engine appearance cover.
11. Remove upper radiator hose.
12. Disconnect cooling fan motor electrical connector.
13. Disconnect A/C condenser lines.
14. Remove radiator support brackets, then the radiator.
15. Loosen two air inlet duct clamp screws, then disconnect air inlet duct.
16. Remove air cleaner outlet tube mounting nut, then the air cleaner outlet tube.
17. Disconnect engine bulkhead connectors.
18. Disconnect accelerator and speed control actuator cables.
19. Remove accelerator and speed control actuator cables from retaining clips and position aside.
20. Disconnect main vacuum supply hose.
21. Remove engine ground mounting bolt from cowl.
22. Remove starter motor as outlined in "Electrical" section.
23. Remove exhaust pipe to exhaust manifold mounting nuts, then support exhaust.
24. Remove fuel line support bracket mounting bolt.
25. Remove engine ground wire mounting nut from transmission housing.
26. Remove transmission housing to engine mounting bolts and stud.
27. Disconnect vacuum hoses and electrical connector from evaporative emissions canister purge valve.
28. Remove evaporative emissions canister purge valve mounting nuts, then the valve.
29. Disconnect heater hoses from heater core.
30. Remove connector bracket mounting nut, then disconnect electrical connectors on top of righthand fender apron.
31. Disconnect A/C cycling switch electrical connector.
32. Remove nut, then disconnect A/C lines from compressor.
33. Disconnect fuel lines from fuel rail.
34. Disconnect right and left oxygen sensor electrical connectors.
35. Disconnect power steering pressure hose.
36. Disconnect lower radiator hose from oil filter adapter.
37. Raise and support vehicle, then remove left and right engine mount mounting bolts.
38. Disconnect two coolant hoses and remove oil cooler.
39. Lower vehicle and install suitable engine lifting device.
40. Support transmission and remove engine from vehicle.
41. Reverse procedure to install. Tighten all fasteners to specifications.

INTAKE MANIFOLD

REPLACE

TOWN CAR & 1997 CONTINENTAL

1. Drain cooling system into a suitable container.
2. **On Continental models,** remove engine appearance cover, air cleaner outlet tube and air intake resonator.
3. **On all models,** relieve fuel system fuel pressure as outlined under "Precautions."
4. Remove wiper module and air inlet tube.
5. Release belt tensioner and remove accessory drive belt.
6. Disconnect ignition plug wires from spark plugs. **Do not pull on wire(s).**
7. Disconnect ignition wire brackets from Valve cover studs.
8. Disconnect both ignition coils, CID sensor and ignition wires from both coils.
9. Remove ignition wire tray and ignition wire assembly.
10. Disconnect alternator wiring harness from junction block, fender apron and alternator.
11. **On Continental models,** disconnect upper radiator hose and water bypass tube to the thermostat hose at the water bypass tube.
12. **On all models,** disconnect electrical connectors at ECT and engine temperature sending unit at bottom of coolant bypass tube.
13. Remove coolant bypass tube
14. Remove alternator and mounting bracket.
15. **On Continental models,** disconnect accelerator cable and speed control actuator from throttle body.
16. **On all models,** disconnect the following vacuum lines:
    a. Chassis vacuum supply hose.
    b. Fuel pressure regulator vacuum harness.
    c. Righthand and lefthand intake manifold runner controls (IMRC).
    d. Intake manifold connection.
    e. Crankcase vent.
    f. Throttle body.
    g. PCV
17. Disconnect and remove upper engine wiring harness from intake manifold.
18. Disconnect eight fuel injector connectors.
19. Remove EGR valve.
20. Disconnect IAC and TPS electrical connectors.
21. Loosen and remove 20 intake manifold to cylinder head mounting bolts and studs in sequence, **Fig. 7.**
22. Remove intake manifold.
23. **On Town Car models,** raise and support vehicle.
24. **On all models,** disconnect oil sending unit and EVO sensor, then position aside.
25. Disconnect EGR tube from right exhaust manifold, then lower vehicle.
26. Disconnect 42-pin connector, A/C compressor, HDR sensor and canister purge solenoid.
27. Remove PCV valve from valve cover, then disconnect canister purge vent hose from PCV valve.
28. Disconnect accelerator and speed control cables from throttle body, then remove accelerator cable bracket from intake manifold and position aside.
29. Disconnect throttle valve cable from throttle body.
30. Disconnect vacuum hose from throttle body adapter port.
31. Disconnect both HEGO sensors and

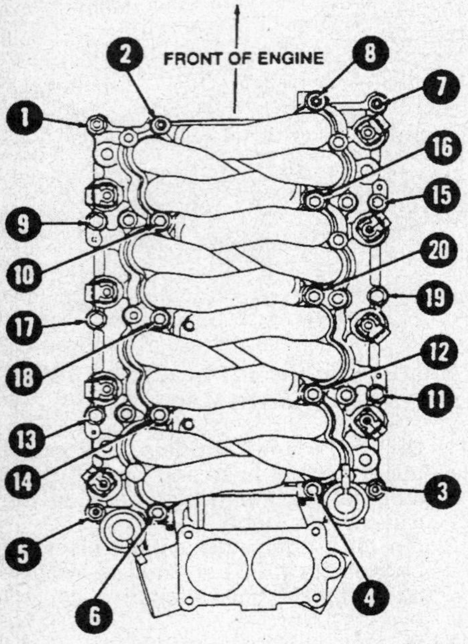

Fig. 7 Intake manifold bolt removal sequence. 1997 Continental

heater supply hose.

32. Remove thermostat housing, then disconnect upper hose and position aside.
33. Remove bolts mounting intake manifold, then the intake manifold and gaskets.
34. Reverse procedure to install, noting the following:
    a. Clean cylinder head and intake manifold surfaces.
    b. Install new intake manifold gaskets.
    c. **On Town Car models, torque** manifold mounting bolts to 72–108 inch lbs. in sequence, **Fig. 8.**
    d. **On Continental models, torque** intake manifold runner control (IMRC) bolts, to 15–22 ft. lbs., in sequence, **Figs. 9 & 10.**

MARK VIII

Upper, Lower & Intake Manifold Runner Control (IMRC)

1. Drain cooling system into a suitable container.
2. Remove water bypass tube.
3. Remove generator.
4. Disconnect accelerator and cruise control cables.
5. Disconnect evaporative emission hose from upper intake manifold.
6. Disconnect throttle position sensor connector.
7. Disconnect crankcase ventilation hose from intake manifold.
8. Disconnect idler air control valve connector.
9. Loosen EGR tube nut from EGR valve.
10. Disconnect EGR valve vacuum hose.
11. Remove bolts and remove upper intake manifold.
12. Remove fuel injection supply manifold.

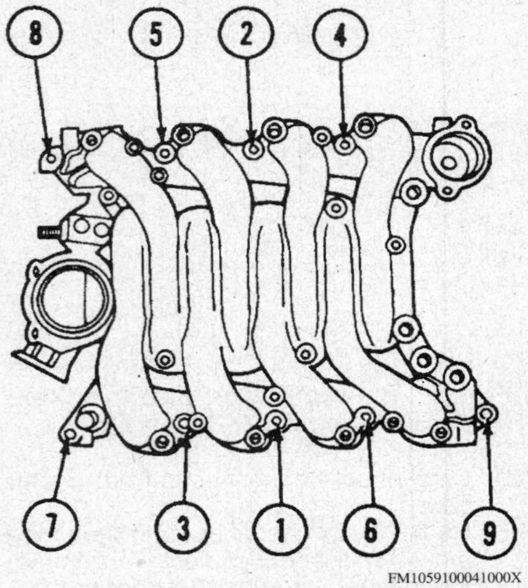

Fig. 8 Intake manifold tightening sequence. Town Car

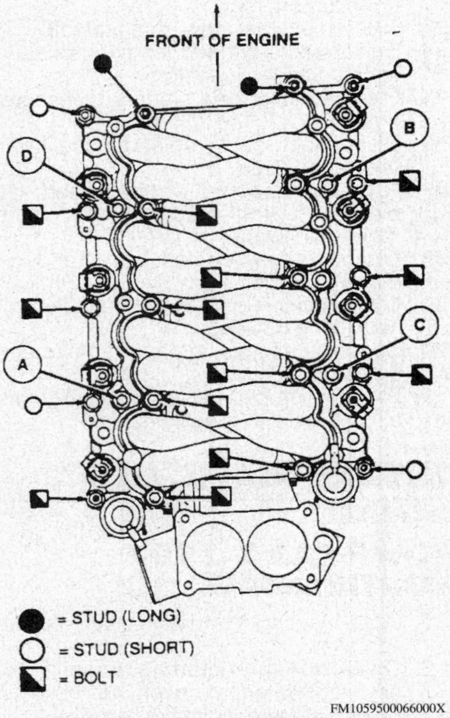

Fig. 10 Intake manifold runner control (IMRC) tightening sequence. 1997 Continental

13. Remove bolts and remove lower intake manifold.
14. Disconnect right and left intake manifold runner control cable.
15. Remove intake manifold runner control and upper and lower gaskets. **Ensure new lower IMRC gaskets are used during installation.**
16. Reverse procedure to install noting the following:
    a. **Torque** lower intake manifold outer bolts to 72–84 inch lbs. then an additional 85–95°, **Fig. 11.**
    b. **Torque** remaining lower intake

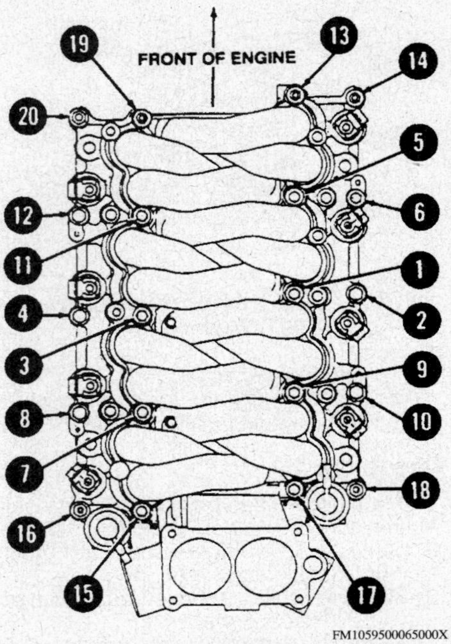

Fig. 9 Intake manifold tightening sequence. 1997 Continental

manifold bolts to 15–22 ft. lbs. in sequence, **Fig. 12.**

1998–2000 CONTINENTAL

1. Drain engine cooling system into a suitable container.
2. Remove air cleaner outlet tube.
3. Relive fuel system pressure as outlined under "Precautions. "
4. Disconnect fuel line.
5. Disconnect alternator wiring harness, then remove mounting bracket.
6. Remove water bypass tube.
7. Disconnect accelerator cable and speed control actuator cable from throttle body.
8. Remove accelerator cable bracket and position out of way.
9. Disconnect chassis vacuum supply tube.
10. Disconnect crankcase ventilation tube.
11. Disconnect vacuum lines at fuel injection supply manifold.
12. Disconnect intake manifold runner control actuator cables.
13. Disconnect main emissions hose.
14. Disconnect heater hose.
15. Disconnect engine control wiring from:
    a. Idle air control valve.
    b. Throttle position sensor.
    c. Fuel temperature sensor.
    d. Fuel injectors.
16. Disconnect EGR to exhaust manifold tube and EGR vacuum line.
17. Disconnect fuel injection supply manifold.
18. Loosen bolts and studs in three even steps in sequence, **Fig. 13,** and remove.
19. Remove intake manifold.
20. Remove intake manifold runner controls.

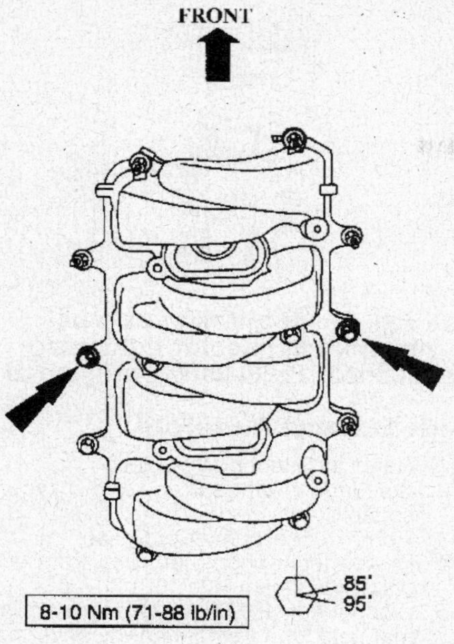

FM1059800141000X

Fig. 11 Lower intake outer bolt location. Mark VIII

21. Remove and discard runner gaskets and intake manifold gaskets.
22. Remove EGR valve, idle air control valve and throttle body.
23. Clean all sealing surfaces.
24. Reverse procedure to install noting the following:
    a. Tighten idle air control valve and EGR valve to specifications.
    b. **Torque** intake manifold bolts 5, 7, 9 and 11, **Fig. 13,** to 9–11 ft. lbs.
    c. **Torque** remaining bolts to 13–16 ft. lbs.
    d. Tighten all bolts an additional 85–95° in sequence.
    e. **Torque** bolts in **Fig. 14** to 72–84 inch lbs. then tighten an additional 85–95°.

INTAKE MANIFOLD RUNNER CONTROL (IMRC)

REPLACE

Remove intake manifold runner control as outlined under " Intake Manifold, Replace."

EXHAUST MANIFOLD

REPLACE

CONTINENTAL

1997

Right Exhaust Manifold

1. Turn suspension switch off, then disconnect battery ground cable.
2. Raise and support vehicle.
3. Disconnect heated oxygen sensors (HO_2S), then remove dual converter Y pipe.

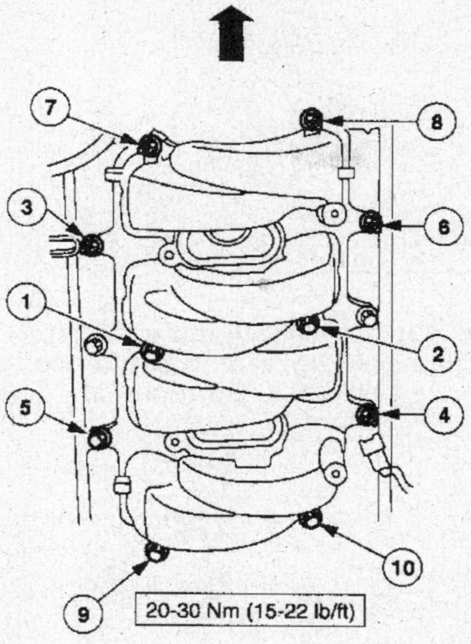

FM1059800142000X

Fig. 12 Lower intake tightening sequence. Mark VIII

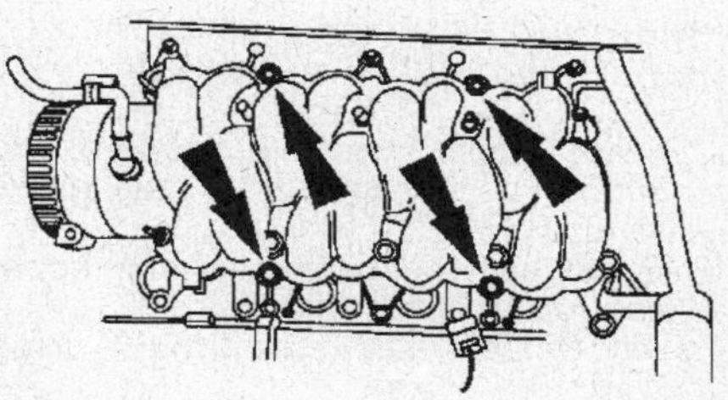

FM1059800148000X

Fig. 14 Manifold bolt location. 1998–2000 Continental

4. If necessary, remove HO_2S from exhaust manifold extension connector to access bolts, then remove bolts and exhaust manifold extension connector.
5. Disconnect EGR valve tube from manifold using a suitable 22 mm crowfoot wrench. **It may be necessary to completely remove tube to allow clearance for manifold removal.**
6. Disconnect secondary air injection tube from exhaust manifold.
7. Remove nuts from exhaust manifold, then remove manifold and gasket through righthand wheel well. Discard manifold gasket.
8. Reverse procedure to install. Tighten to specifications in sequence, **Fig. 15.**

Left Exhaust Manifold

1. Turn suspension switch off, then disconnect battery ground cable.
2. Raise and support vehicle.
3. Remove engine lower splash shield.
4. Disconnect Heated Oxygen Sensors (HO_2S), then remove dual converter Y pipe.
5. Disconnect secondary air injection tube from exhaust manifold.
6. Remove nuts from exhaust manifold, then remove manifold and gasket. Discard manifold gasket.
7. Reverse procedure to install. Tighten to specifications in sequence, **Fig. 15.**

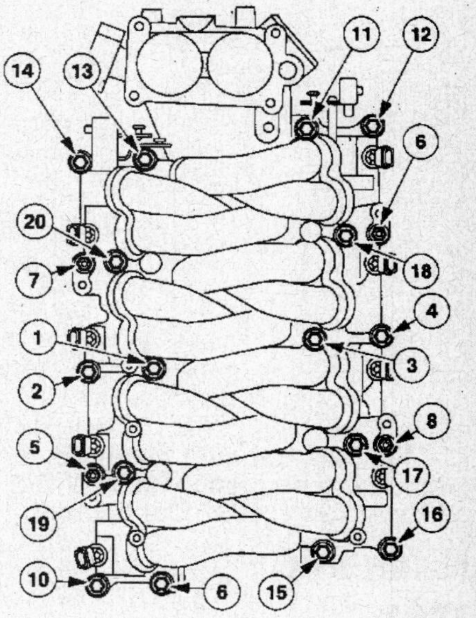

FM1059800147000X

Fig. 13 Intake manifold loosing & tightening sequence. 1998–2000 Continental

1998–2000

Right Exhaust Manifold

1. Raise and support vehicle.
2. Remove right front wheel and tire assembly.
3. Remove radiator air deflector.
4. Remove duel converter Y pipe.
5. Remove four bolts to exhaust manifold connector, then the gasket.
6. Disconnect EGR valve tube from exhaust manifold.
7. Remove engine support insulator strut.
8. Remove exhaust manifold.
9. Reverse procedure to install noting the following:
    a. Tighten exhaust manifold nuts to specifications in sequence, **Fig. 16.**
    b. **Torque** exhaust manifold connector bolts to 13–17 ft. lbs. in sequence, **Fig. 17,** then **torque** to 31–39 ft. lbs. in sequence.

Left Exhaust Manifold

1. Recover A/C system refrigerant as outlined under " Air Conditioning."
2. Raise and support vehicle.
3. Remove radiator air deflector.
4. Remove duel converter Y pipe.
5. Disconnect A/C suction discharge manifold from A/C compressor.
6. Remove Manifold.
7. Reverse procedure to install, tighten exhaust manifold nuts to specifications in sequence, **Fig. 18.**

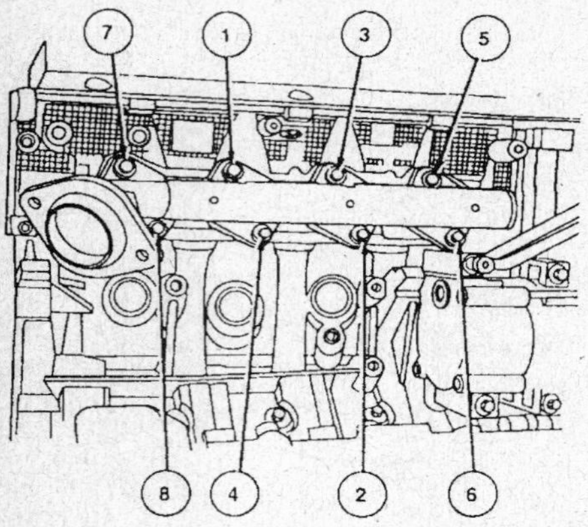

FM1079100013000X

Fig. 15 Exhaust manifold tightening sequence. Mark VIII & Town Car & 1997 Continental

MARK VIII

1997

Right Exhaust Manifold

1. Remove engine cover.
2. Disconnect air intake temperature sensor (IAT) connector and crankcase vent tube from air cleaner outlet tube.
3. Loosen air cleaner outlet to throttle body bolt.
4. Loosen clamp on engine air cleaner outlet tube assembly to engine air cleaner. Disconnect tube.
5. Remove mounting bolt from support bracket clamp on righthand cam cover to engine air cleaner outlet tube assembly.
6. Remove air cleaner and resonator assembly.
7. Disconnect righthand oxygen sensor.
8. Remove four manifold to cylinder head mounting bolts from upper side of exhaust manifold.
9. Raise and support vehicle.
10. Disconnect exhaust pipe from lefthand catalyst.
11. Disconnect catalyst from exhaust manifold and remove catalyst.
12. Reverse procedure to install. Tighten righthand exhaust manifold to cylinder head bolts to specifications in sequence, **Fig. 15.**

Left Exhaust Manifold

1. Turn off air suspension switch in cargo compartment.
2. Disconnect battery ground cable.
3. Disconnect oxygen sensor.
4. Install engine support tripod onto engine compartment and attach to engine.
5. Raise and support vehicle.
6. Remove front wheel and tire assemblies.
7. Disconnect EGR tube at lefthand catalyst.
8. Disconnect lefthand exhaust pipe at catalyst and right catalyst at exhaust manifold.
9. Disconnect left and righthand ride height sensor wiring connectors and remove right and lefthand side brake caliper bolts. Remove calipers and support to vehicle using mechanic's wire.
10. Disconnect right and lefthand upper control arms from spindles.
11. Disconnect steering shaft couple at rag joint.
12. Remove fastener mounting power steering lines to subframe.
13. Support subframe with engine jack.
14. Remove two motor mount through bolts.
15. Remove left and right lower strut to control arm bolts and nuts.
16. Remove eight subframe bolts, then lower subframe.
17. Remove lefthand manifold mounting bolts, then the manifold.
18. Remove and discard front and rear exhaust manifold gaskets.
19. Reverse procedure to install, noting the following
    a. Install new front and rear exhaust manifold gaskets.
    b. Tighten lefthand exhaust manifold to cylinder head bolts to specifications in sequence, **Fig. 15.**

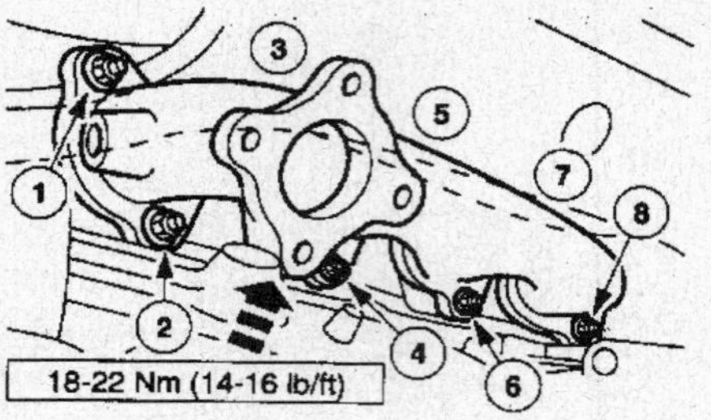

FM1059800143000X

Fig. 16 Righthand exhaust manifold tightening sequence. 1998–2000 Continental

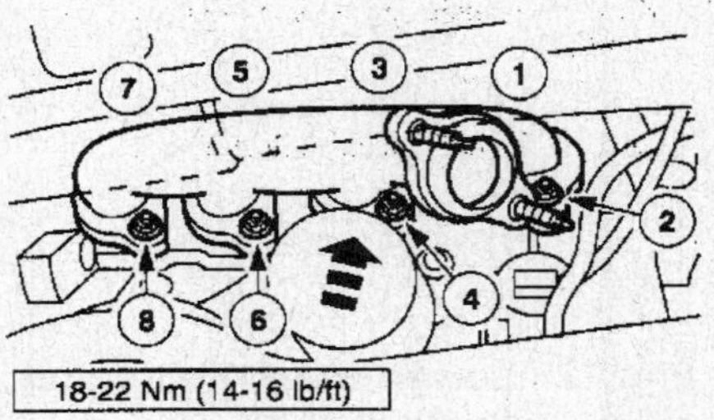

FM1059800145000X

Fig. 18 Lefthand exhaust manifold tightening sequence. 1998–2000 Continental

1998

Right Exhaust Manifold

1. Disconnect righthand heated oxygen sensors.
2. Remove duel converter Y pipe.
3. Disconnect exhaust air tube from exhaust manifold.
4. Remove nuts, then the exhaust manifold.
5. Reverse procedure to install, tighten exhaust manifold nuts to specifications in sequence, **Fig. 19.**

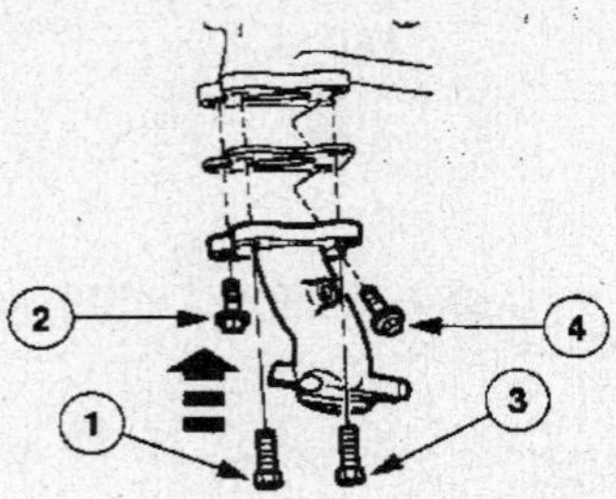

FM1059800144000X

Fig. 17 Righthand exhaust manifold connector tightening sequence. 1998–2000 Continental

Left Exhaust Manifold

1. Raise and support vehicle.
2. Disconnect lefthand heated oxygen sensors.
3. Remove duel converter Y pipe.
4. Disconnect exhaust air tube from exhaust manifold.
5. Disconnect EGR valve to exhaust manifold tube from lefthand converter.
6. Remove nuts, then the manifold.
7. Reverse procedure to install, tighten manifold nuts to specifications in sequence, **Fig. 19.**

TOWN CAR

1997

1. Remove air inlet tube.
2. Drain cooling system, then remove cooling fan and shroud.
3. Relieve fuel system fuel pressure as outlined in " Precautions."
4. Remove upper radiator hose.
5. Remove wiper module and support bracket, then discharge refrigerant from system.
6. Disconnect A/C compressor outlet hose at compressor, then remove bolt mounting hose assembly to right coil bracket.
7. Remove 42-pin engine harness connector from mounting bracket on brake vacuum booster.
8. Disconnect 42-pin connector and transmission harness connector, **Fig. 20.**
9. Remove oil dipstick tube, on left exhaust manifold, then disconnect throttle valve cable from throttle body.
10. Disconnect heater outlet hose, then remove ground strap to right cylinder head.
11. Remove upper stud, then loosen lower bolt mounting heater outlet hose to right cylinder head and position aside.
12. Remove blower motor resistor.
13. Remove right engine insulator, then disconnect vacuum hoses from EGR valve and EGR tube.
14. Remove EGR valve assembly mounting bolts, then disconnect HEGO sensor.
15. Raise and support vehicle.
16. Remove two through bolts for left engine insulator and one through bolt for the right.
17. Remove EGR tube line nut from right manifold, then remove EGR assembly.

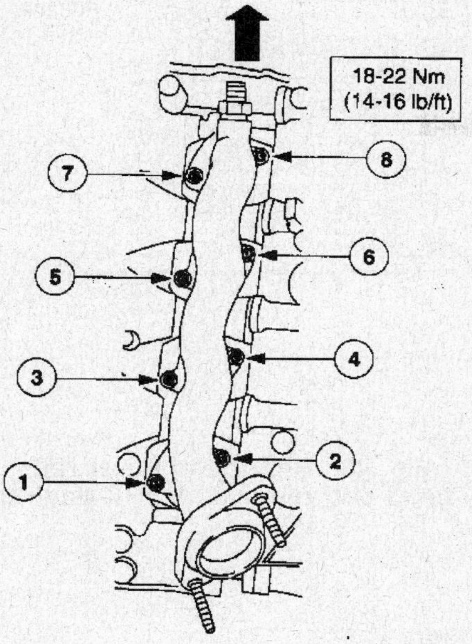

FM1059800146000X

Fig. 19 Exhaust manifold tightening sequence. 1998 Mark VIII

18. Disconnect exhaust from right and left manifolds, then suspend with wire.
19. Position a suitable jack and block of wood under oil pan, then raise engine approximately four inches.
20. If removing left manifold, remove engine insulator from cylinder block, then remove mounting bolts and manifold.
21. If removing right manifold, remove mounting bolts and manifold.
22. Reverse procedure to install. Tighten manifold bolts to specification in sequence, **Fig. 15.**

1998–2000

1. Raise and support vehicle.
2. Remove exhaust pipe to exhaust manifold mounting nuts, then support exhaust.
3. Disconnect EGR valve to exhaust tube from righthand side manifold.
4. Remove exhaust manifold to cylinder head mounting bolts.
5. Reverse procedure to install. Tighten manifold bolts to specifications in sequence, **Fig. 15.**

CYLINDER HEAD

REPLACE

SOHC ENGINE

1. Drain cooling system, then remove cooling fan and shroud.
2. Relieve fuel system fuel pressure. **Refer to "Precautions" in this section.**
3. Remove air inlet tube and wiper module.
4. Release belt tensioner, then remove accessory drive belt.
5. Disconnect ignition wires from spark plugs. **Do not pull on ignition wire(s).**
6. Disconnect ignition wire brackets from valve cover studs.
7. Remove bolt mounting A/C high pressure line to right coil bracket.
8. Disconnect both ignition coils and CID sensor.
9. Remove right and left coil bracket to front cover mounting nuts.
10. Slide ignition coil brackets and ignition wire assembly off mounting studs, then remove from vehicle.
11. Remove water pump pulley, then disconnect alternator wiring harness from junction block, fender apron and alternator.
12. Remove alternator and mounting bracket.
13. Disconnect positive battery cable at power distribution box, then remove mounting bolt from positive battery cable bracket located on right side of cylinder head.
14. Disconnect vent hose from canister purge solenoid, then place positive battery cable aside.
15. Disconnect canister purge solenoid vent hose from PCV valve, then remove PCV valve from valve cover.
16. Remove 42-pin engine harness connector from mounting bracket on brake vacuum booster, then disconnect and position aside.
17. Disconnect HDR sensor, A/C compressor clutch and canister purge solenoid electrical connectors.
18. Raise and support vehicle.
19. Remove bolts mounting power steering pump to engine block and cylinder front cover. **Front lower bolt on power steering will not come all the way out.**
20. Remove bolts mounting oil pan to front cover.
21. Remove crankshaft damper mounting bolt and washer from crankshaft.
22. Install crankshaft damper remover tool No. T58P-6316-D, or equivalent, on damper, then pull damper from crankshaft.
23. Disconnect EVO sensor and oil sending unit and position aside.
24. Disconnect EGR tube from right exhaust manifold.
25. Disconnect exhaust for right and left manifolds, then suspend with wire.
26. Remove bolt mounting starter wiring harness to rear of right cylinder head, then lower vehicle.
27. Remove right and left valve cover to cylinder head.
28. Disconnect accelerator and speed control cables.
29. Remove accelerator bracket from intake manifold and position aside.
30. Disconnect throttle valve cable from throttle body, then the vacuum hose from throttle body elbow port.
31. Disconnect both HEGO sensor and heater supply hose.
32. Remove thermostat housing, then disconnect upper hose and position aside.
33. Remove bolts mounting intake manifold, then the intake manifold and gaskets, **Fig. 21.**
34. Remove timing chain as outlined under "Timing Chain, Replace."

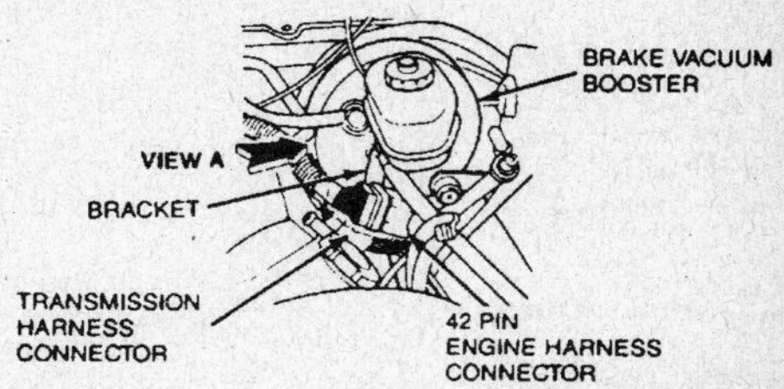

FM1069100185000X

Fig. 20 Engine & transmission harness connectors. 1997 Town Car

35. Remove bolts mounting left cylinder head. **The lower rear bolt cannot be removed due to interference with the brake vacuum booster. Use a rubber band or similar item to hold bolt away from engine, Fig. 22.**
36. Remove left cylinder head.
37. Remove ground strap mounting heater return line to right cylinder head.
38. Remove bolts mounting EVR sensor, then the sensor.
39. Remove bolts mounting right cylinder head. **The lower rear bolt cannot be removed due to interference with the evaporator housing. Use a rubber band or similar item to hold bolt away from engine, Fig. 23.**
40. Remove right cylinder head.
41. Reverse procedure to install, noting the following:
    a. Rotate crankshaft counterclockwise 45° to ensure all pistons are below top of engine block deck face.
    b. **Torque** cylinder head bolts to 28–31 ft. lbs., in sequence, **Fig. 24.**
    c. Tighten bolts an additional 85–95° in sequence.
    d. Loosen all bolts a minimum of 360°.
    e. **Torque** bolts to 28–31 ft. lbs. in sequence.
    f. Tighten bolts an additional 85–95°.
    g. Tighten bolts another 85–95°.
    h. Rotate crankshaft clockwise 45°. This will position crankshaft at TDC No. 1. **Crankshaft must only be rotated in the clockwise direction and only as far as TDC.**

DOHC ENGINE

1. Remove engine from vehicle as outlined under "Engine, Replace."
2. Remove valve covers as outlined under "Valve Cover, Replace."
3. Remove engine front cover as outlined under "Front Cover, Replace."
4. Remove intake manifold as outlined under "Intake Manifold, Replace."
5. Remove crankshaft position sensor pulse wheel.
6. Remove rocker arms as outlined under "Hydraulic Lifters, Replace."
7. Remove exhaust manifolds as outlined under "Exhaust Manifold, Replace."
8. Rotate engine to TDC of No. 1 cylinder, **Fig. 25.**
9. Install camshaft positioning tool No. T93P-6256-A, or equivalent, to camshafts, **Fig. 26.**

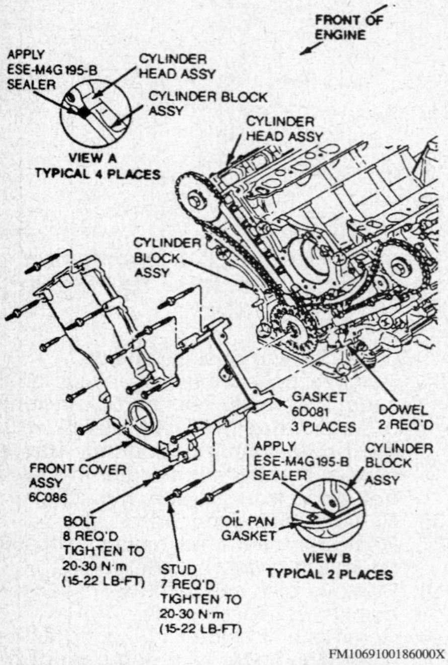

Fig. 21 Front cover removal. SOHC engine

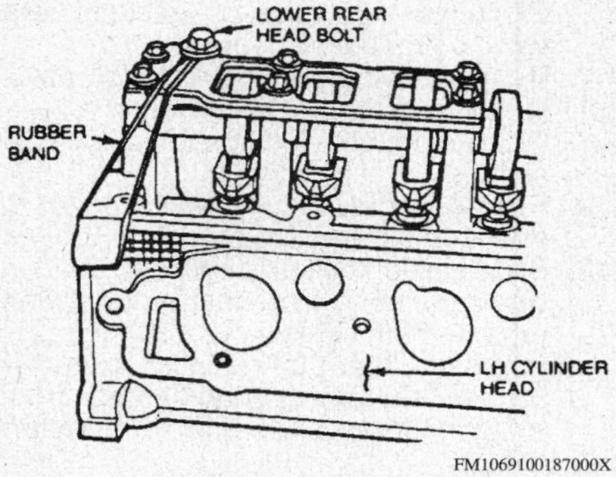

Fig. 22 Lefthand lower rear head bolt removal. SOHC engine

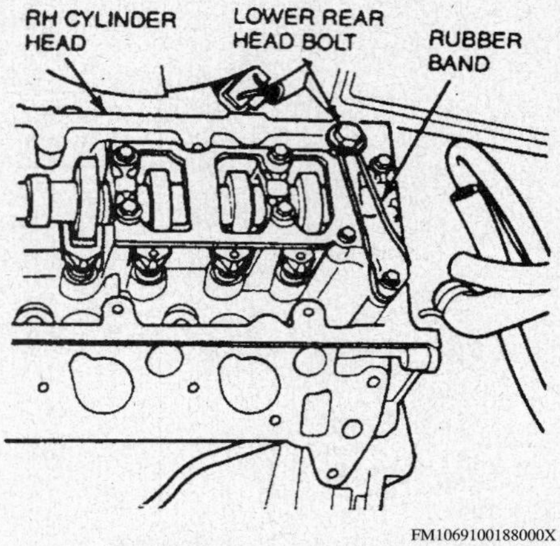

Fig. 23 Righthand lower rear head bolt removal. SOHC engine

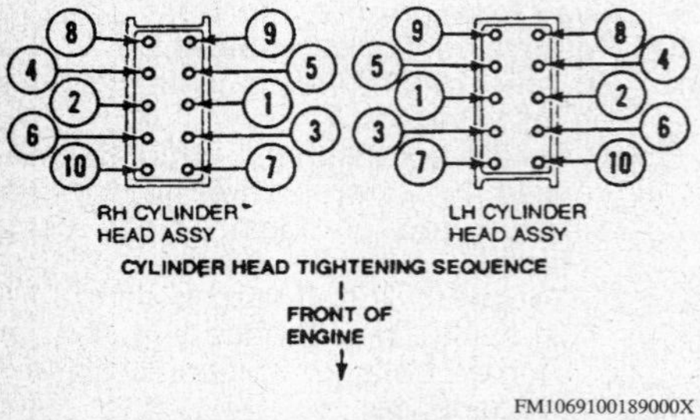

Fig. 24 Cylinder head tightening sequence. SOHC engine

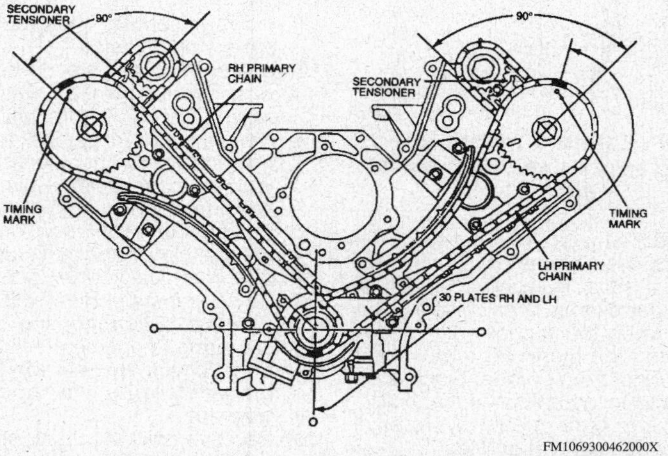

Fig. 25 Setting engine to TDC of No. 1 cylinder. DOHC engine

10. Remove primary timing chain as outlined under "Timing Chain, Replace." **Do not remove camshaft sprocket and secondary timing chain at this time.**
11. Remove heater hose tube from right cylinder head.
12. Loosen cylinder head bolts in sequence, **Fig. 27.**
13. Remove and discard cylinder head bolts.
14. Remove cylinder head and gaskets, discard gaskets.
15. If head casting is to be replaced, remove secondary timing chain and sprockets as outlined under outlined under "Timing Chain, Replace," then remove camshafts as outlined under " Camshaft, Replace."
16. Reverse procedure to install, noting the following:
    a. **Use new cylinder head bolts and gaskets.**
    b. Lightly oil new cylinder head bolts with clean motor oil.
    c. **Torque** cylinder head bolts to 27–32 ft. lbs., in sequence, **Fig. 24.**
    d. Tighten bolts an additional 85–95° in sequence.
    e. Tighten bolts an additional 85–95° in sequence.

VALVE COVER

REPLACE

1997

RIGHT SIDE

1. Remove positive battery cable bracket to cylinder head mounting bolt.
2. Disconnect high data rate (HDR) sensor, A/C compressor clutch and canister purge solenoid electrical connectors, then position aside.
3. Disconnect purge solenoid vent hose, then position positive battery cable aside.
4. Disconnect spark plug ignition wires. **Do not remove wires.**
5. Remove ignition wire brackets, then position wires aside.
6. Remove PCV valve and position aside.
7. Remove valve cover mounting bolts, then remove valve cover.
8. Reverse procedure to install. Tighten valve cover bolts to specifications.

LEFT SIDE

1. Remove air inlet tube.
2. Relieve fuel pressure as outlined under "Precautions, " then disconnect fuel lines.
3. Raise and support vehicle.
4. Disconnect EVO sensor and oil pressure sending unit electrical connectors, then position electrical harness aside.
5. Lower vehicle, remove 42-pin electrical harness connector from bracket at brake vacuum booster, **Fig. 3,** then disconnect and position aside.
6. Remove windshield wiper module.
7. Disconnect spark plug ignition wires. **Do not remove wires.**
8. Remove ignition wire brackets, then position wires aside.
9. Remove valve cover mounting bolts, then remove valve cover.
10. Reverse procedure to install. Tighten valve cover bolts to specifications.

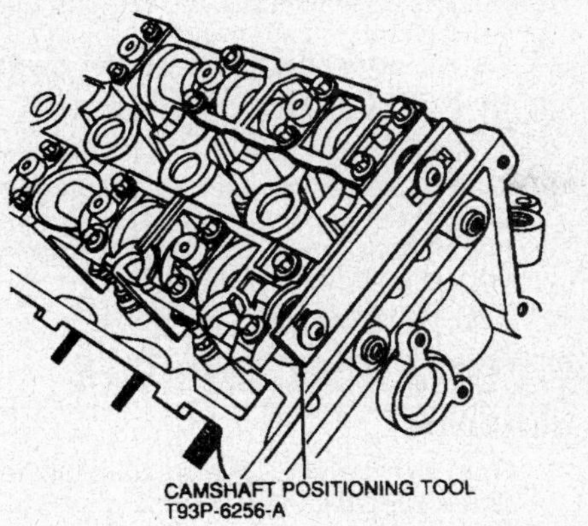

FM1069300463000X

Fig. 26 Camshaft positioning tool installation DOHC engine

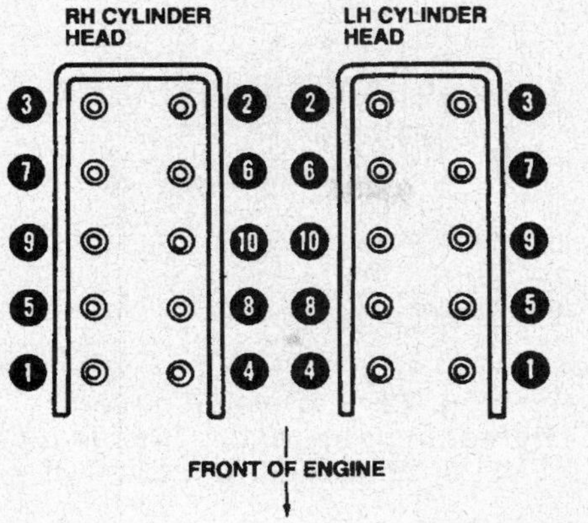

FM1069300464000X

Fig. 27 Cylinder head bolt loosening sequence. DOHC engine

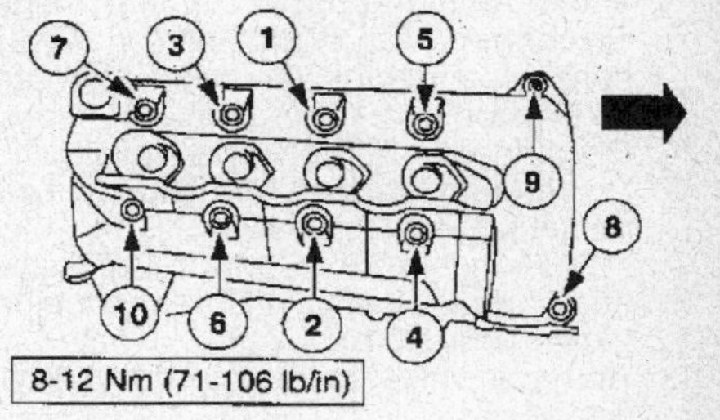

FM1059800149000X

Fig. 28 Righthand valve cover tightening sequence. Mark VIII & 1998–2000 Continental

1998–2000

CONTINENTAL

Right Side

1. Drain cooling system into a suitable container.
2. Remove water bypass tube.
3. Relieve fuel system pressure as outlined under " Precautions."
4. Disconnect fuel tube.
5. Disconnect heater hose.
6. Remove PCV valve from righthand valve cover.
7. Remove main chassis vacuum supply tube.
8. Disconnect powertrain control module grounds.
9. Disconnect engine control sensor wiring from powertrain control module.
10. Remove bolts and ignition coil cover.
11. Disconnect engine control sensor wiring from ignition coils.
12. Remove nuts and position engine control sensor wiring out of way.
13. Remove four ignition coils.
14. Remove cross vehicle support arm.
15. Remove eight bolts and two studs from valve cover, then the valve cover.
16. Reverse procedure to install noting the following:
    a. Ensure sealing surfaces are clean and dry before assembly of valve cover.
    b. Install new spark plug bore O-ring seals.
    c. Apply Silicone Gasket and Sealant F6AZ-19562-AA, or equivalent, in two places where engine front cover meets cylinder head. **Valve cover bolts and studs must be installed and tightened to specifications within four minutes of sealant application.**
    d. Tighten valve cover bolts to specifications in sequence, **Fig. 28.**

Left Side

1. Drain cooling system into a suitable container.
2. Remove water bypass hose, then the crankcase ventilation tube from lefthand valve cover.
3. Remove ignition coil cover from lefthand valve cover, then the ignition coils.
4. Remove two nuts and position fuel charging wiring out of way.
5. Disconnect air suspension relay.
6. Remove bolts and position air suspension relay out of way.
7. Remove valve cover bolts and studs, then the valve cover.
8. Reverse procedure to install noting the following:
    a. Ensure sealing surfaces are clean and dry before assembly of valve cover.
    b. Install new spark plug bore O-ring seals.
    c. Apply Silicone Gasket and Sealant F6AZ-19562-AA, or equivalent, in two places where engine front cover meets cylinder head. **Valve cover bolts and studs must be installed and tightened to specifications within four minutes of sealant application.**
    d. Tighten valve cover bolts to specifications in sequence, **Fig. 29.**

MARK VIII

Right Side

1. Remove ignition coils from right cylinder head.
2. Remove upper intake manifold assembly as outlined under " Intake Manifold, Replace."
3. Remove crankcase ventilation tube from valve cover.
4. Remove valve cover bolts, then the valve cover.
5. Reverse procedure to install noting the following:
    a. Ensure sealing surfaces are clean and dry before assembly of valve cover.
    b. Install new spark plug bore O-ring seals.
    c. Apply Silicone Gasket and Sealant F6AZ-19562-AA, or equivalent, in two places where engine front cover meets cylinder head. **Valve cover bolts and studs must be installed and tightened to specifications within four minutes of sealant application.**
    d. Tighten valve cover bolts to specifications in sequence, **Fig. 28.**

Left Side

1. Remove windshield wiper module assembly.
2. Remove nuts and position EGR vacuum regulator control out of way.
3. Remove positive crankcase ventilation valve from valve cover and position aside.
4. Remove ignition coils from left cylinder head.
5. Remove bolts and position master cylinder aside.
6. Remove front shock absorber strut cover cup.
7. Disconnect vacuum harness from E.A.S. solenoid near left fender wall.
8. Position power distribution box and bracket aside.
9. Disconnect fuel injector wiring and position aside.
10. Disconnect 42-pin connector at rear of left valve cover.
11. Disconnect engine wiring from fender apron.
12. Remove bolts, then the valve cover.
13. Reverse procedure to install noting the following:
    a. Ensure sealing surfaces are clean and dry before assembly of valve cover.
    b. Install new spark plug bore O-ring seals.
    c. Apply Silicone Gasket and Sealant F6AZ-19562-AA, or equivalent, in two places where engine front cover meets cylinder head. **Valve cover bolts and studs must be installed and tightened to specifications within four minutes of sealant application.**
    d. Tighten valve cover bolts to specifications in sequence, **Fig. 29.**

TOWN CAR

Left Side

1. Raise and support vehicle.
2. Remove oil bypass filter.
3. Disconnect power steering and oil pressure switch connectors.
4. Lower vehicle and disconnect purge canister connector.
5. Remove power steering bracket bolts

and stud, then position bracket aside.
6. Disconnect Camshaft Position (CMP) sensor connector, then the alternator connector.
7. Disconnect coils from spark plugs.
8. Disconnect fuel injector electrical connectors.
9. Disconnect Idle Air Control (IAC) valve and Throttle Position (TP) sensor electrical connectors.
10. Remove valve cover mounting bolts and studs.
11. Reverse procedure to install.

Right Side

1. Raise and support vehicle.
2. Disconnect Crankshaft Position (CKP) sensor and A/C compressor electrical connectors.
3. Lower vehicle and disconnect A/C cycling switch.
4. Disconnect fuel lines.
5. Disconnect ignition coils from each spark plug.
6. Disconnect fuel injector connectors.
7. Remove crankcase ventilation tube and the evaporative emission canister purge valve.
8. Remove wiring harness hold-down clamp, then separate harness from valve cover.
9. Remove valve cover mounting bolts and studs.
10. Reverse procedure to install.

VALVE ARRANGEMENT

FRONT TO REAR

Town Car

Right Side ....I-E-I-E-I-E-I-E
Left Side
E-I-E-I-E-I-E-I

Continental & Mark VIII

Right Side .S-P-E-E-S-P-E-E-S-P-E-E-S-P-E-E①
Left Side ...E-E-P-S-E-E-P-S-E-E-P-S-E-E-P-S

①–S=Secondary-Intake; P=Primary-Intake; E=Exhaust.

CAMSHAFT LOBE LIFT SPECIFICATIONS

Intake & Exhaust.................. .2549

VALVE CLEARANCE SPECIFICATIONS

Valve lift should measure .020–.069 inch at intake valves and .046–.095 inch at exhaust valves with hydraulic lifter completely collapsed.

VALVE ADJUSTMENT

This engine has automatic hydraulic lifters. No valve adjustment is required.

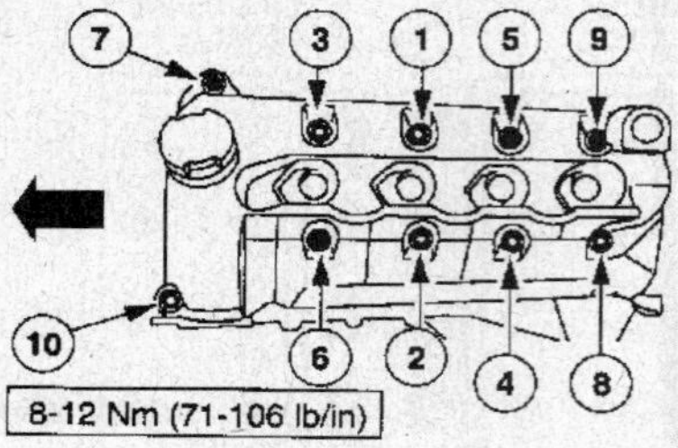

Fig. 29 Left valve cover tightening sequence. 1998 Mark VIII & 1998–2000 Continental

VALVE SPRING & VALVE STEM OIL SEAL

REPLACE

REMOVAL

If, during this procedure, air pressure has forced the piston to the bottom of the cylinder, any loss of air pressure will allow the valve to fall into the cylinder. A rubber band, tape or string wrapped around the end of the valve stem will prevent this and still allow enough travel to check the valve for binding and excess guide to valve stem clearance.

1. Remove valve covers as outlined under "Valve Cover, Replace."
2. Remove roller followers as outlined under "Hydraulic Lifters, Replace."
3. Remove spark plug, then position piston at top of stroke with both valves closed.
4. Install suitable air line with adapter in spark plug opening, then apply air pressure. Failure of air pressure to hold the valves closed is an indication of valve or valve seat damage that may require cylinder head removal.
5. Install .40 inch shim between spring coils.
6. Using Valve Spring Compressor tool No. T91P-6565-A, or equivalent, compress valve spring.
7. Remove keepers, retainer and valve spring.
8. Use suitable locking pliers, remove valve stem seal.
9. Repeat previous steps, as required.

INSTALLATION

1. **Piston must be at Top Dead Center (TDC) of cylinder being serviced.**
2. Remove air pressure, then inspect valve stem for damage. Rotate valve and check valve stem tip eccentric movement during rotation.
3. Position valve up and down through normal travel and check the stem for binding. **If the valve has been damaged. It will be necessary to remove cylinder head for service.**
4. If valve condition is good, apply engine oil to valve stem and hold valve closed, then apply air pressure in cylinder.
5. Using Valve Stem Seal Replacer tool No. T88T-6571-A, or equivalent, install valve stem seal.
6. Position valve spring and retainer over valve stem.
7. Install .40 inch shim between spring coils.
8. Compress valve spring, then install keepers.
9. Turn off air supply, then remove adapter from spark plug opening.
10. Install spark plug, then roller follower and valve cover.
11. Start engine and check for leaks.

HYDRAULIC LIFTERS

REPLACE

1. Remove valve covers as outlined under "Valve Cover, Replace."
2. Position piston of cylinder at bottom of stroke and camshaft lobe at base circle.
3. Install .40 inch shim between spring coils to prevent damage.
4. Install Valve Spring Compressor tool No. T91P-6565-A, or equivalent, under camshaft and on valve spring retainer, **Fig. 30.**
5. Compress valve spring, then remove roller follower.
6. Remove valve spring compressor and shim.
7. Remove hydraulic lifter, as required.
8. Repeat previously steps, as required.
9. Reverse procedure to install, noting the following:
   a. Valve lash adjuster must have no more than 1.5 mm of plunger travel prior to installation.
   b. When installing roller follower, piston must be at bottom of stroke and camshaft at base circle.

FRONT COVER

REPLACE

1997

1. Remove engine cooling fan and shroud.
2. Loosen water pump pulley mounting bolts, then remove serpentine drive belt.
3. Remove water pump pulley mounting bolts, then remove pulley.
4. Raise and support vehicle.
5. Remove power steering pump mounting bolts. **Front lower power steering pump bolt will not come out.**
6. Support power steering pump and position aside.
7. Remove oil pan to front cover mounting bolts.
8. Remove crankshaft damper mounting bolt and washer.
9. Using crankshaft damper remover tool No. T58P-6316-D, or equivalent, remove crankshaft damper.
10. Lower vehicle.
11. Remove A/C high pressure line to righthand coil bracket mounting bolt.
12. Remove valve covers front mounting bolts, then loosen remaining cover bolts.
13. Using plastic wedges or suitable tool, prop up valve covers.
14. Disconnect ignition coils and Crankshaft Identification (CID) sensor.

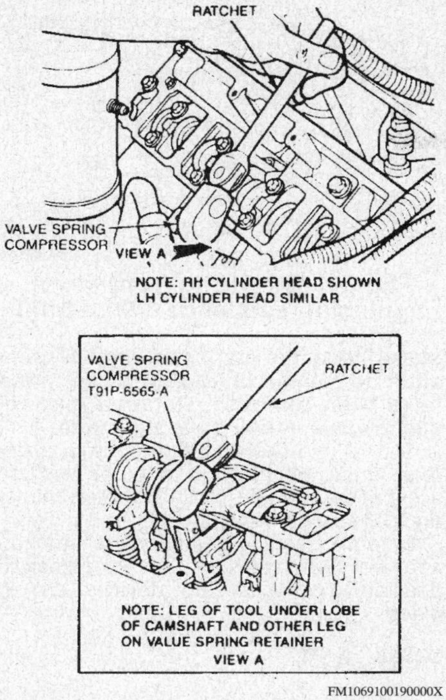

Fig. 30 Valve spring compressor

15. Remove righthand coil bracket mounting nuts, then position power steering hose aside.
16. Remove lefthand coil bracket mounting nuts, then pull bracket and ignition wires from mounting studs and position aside.
17. Remove front cover mounting bolts and studs, **Fig. 31,** then the front cover.
18. Reverse procedure to install, noting the following:
    a. Refer to **Fig. 31** for front cover tightening specifications.
    b. Tighten mounting bolts to specifications.
    c. Apply silicone gasket and sealant E3AZ-19562-A, or equivalent, in damper keyway. Ensure crankshaft key and keyway are aligned, using Crankshaft Damper Replacer T47P-6316-B, or equivalent, install crankshaft damper.

1998–2000

Removal

1. Drain cooling system into a suitable container.
2. Remove water outlet tube and water bypass tube hoses.
3. Remove air cleaner outlet tube.
4. Remove fan assembly, then the drive belt.
5. Remove water pump pulley, then the hoses from secondary air injection diverter valve.
6. Remove bolt from secondary air injection manifold tube.
7. Disconnect secondary air injection manifold tube from diverter valve.
8. Remove nuts, then the secondary air injection diverter valve.
9. Disconnect power steering pump connector.
10. Remove bolts from battery to starter relay cable and bracket.
11. Drain engine oil into a suitable container.
12. Remove bolts from oil pan to engine front cover.
13. Disconnect camshaft sensor connector.
14. Remove power steering pump and power steering pump reservoir.
15. Remove crankshaft pulley bolt.
16. Remove crankshaft pulley using crankshaft damper remover tool No. TP58P-6316-D, or equivalent.
17. Remove left and right valve covers as outlined under " Valve Cover, Replace."
18. Remove serpentine belt idler pulley and tensioner.
19. Disconnect crankshaft position sensor connector.
20. Remove bolts, then the engine front cover.

Installation

1. Apply Silicone Gasket Sealant F6AZ-19562-AA, or equivalent, along head to block surface and block to oil pan (six places), **Fig. 32.**
2. Install engine front cover on dowel pins on front of cylinder block.
3. Loosely install bolts and studs to front cover.
4. Tighten front cover bolts to specifications in sequence, **Fig. 33.**
5. Tighten oil pan bolts to specifications in sequence, **Fig. 34,** then an additional 60°.
6. Install belt idler pulley, install bolt and tighten to specifications.
7. Install drive belt tensioner and tighten to specifications.
8. Install crankshaft pulley as follows:
    a. Apply silicone gasket and sealant F6AZ-19562-AA, or equivalent, to woodruff key slot on crankshaft pulley.
    b. Install crankshaft pulley using crankshaft damper replacer tool No. T74P-6316-D, or equivalent.
    c. Install and **torque** crankshaft bolt to 66 ft. lbs.
    d. Loosen crankshaft bolt at least 360°.
    e. **Torque** crankshaft bolt to 35–39 ft. lbs.
    f. Tighten crankshaft bolt an additional 85–90°.
9. Install water pump pulley.
10. Install right and left valve covers as outlined under " Valve Cover, Replace."
11. Connect crankshaft position sensor connector.
12. Install power steering pump and power steering pump reservoir.
13. Connect camshaft sensor connector.
14. Install oil pan drain plug.
15. Install bolts from battery to starter relay cable and bracket.
16. Connect power steering pump connector.
17. Install secondary air injection diverter valve.

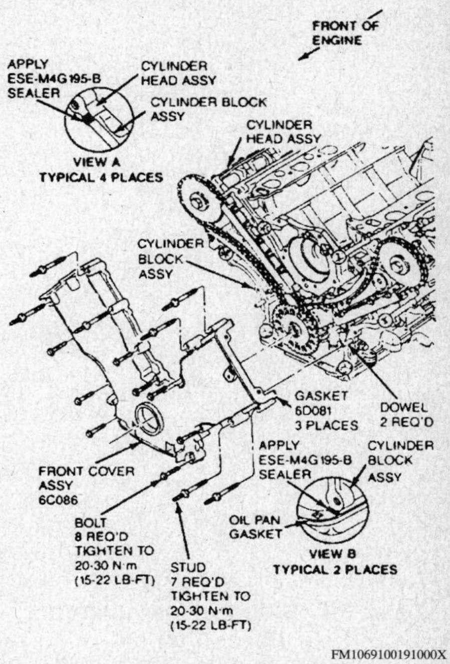

Fig. 31 Front engine cover assembly. 1997

18. Connect secondary air injection manifold tube to diverter valve.
19. Install bolt to secondary injection manifold tube.
20. Connect hoses and vacuum line to secondary air injection diverter valve.
21. Install drive belt, fan assembly, air cleaner outlet tube, water outlet tube and water bypass tube hoses.
22. Connect battery ground cable.
23. Fill engine with oil to specification.
24. Fill engine cooling system to specification.

FRONT COVER SEAL

REPLACE

CONTINENTAL

1. Remove drive belt.
2. Disconnect upper motor mount.
3. Raise and support vehicle.
4. Remove right front wheel and tire assembly.
5. Remove right inner fender.
6. Support engine, transaxle and front sub frame with a suitable powertrain lift and universal powertrain removal bracket.
7. Remove front subframe brackets.
8. Partially lower engine transaxle and front subframe as an assembly.
9. Remove crankshaft pulley using crankshaft damper remover tool No. TP58P-6316-D, or equivalent.
10. Using front cover seal remover tool No. T74P-6700-A, or equivalent, remove front cover seal.
11. Reverse procedure to install noting the following:
    a. Lubricate engine front cover seal and front cover with clean engine oil.

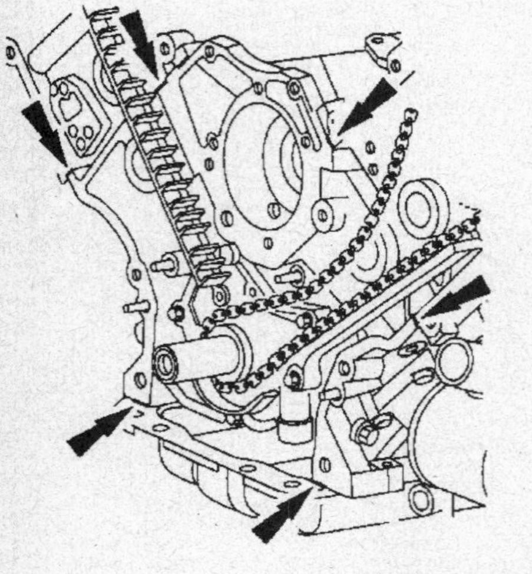

FM1069800792000X

Fig. 32 Silicone installation. 1998–2000

b. Use crankshaft seal replacer tool No. T88T-6701-A, or equivalent to install oil seal.
c. Apply silicone gasket and sealant F6AZ-19562-AA, or equivalent, to woodruff key slot on crankshaft pulley.
d. Install crankshaft pulley using crankshaft damper replacer tool No. T74P-6316-D, or equivalent.
e. Install and **torque** crankshaft bolt to 66 ft. lbs.
f. Loosen crankshaft bolt at least 360°.
g. **Torque** crankshaft bolt to 35–39 ft. lbs.
h. Tighten crankshaft bolt an additional 85–90°.

MARK VIII & TOWN CAR

1997

1. Release belt tensioner, then remove serpentine drive belt.
2. Raise and support vehicle.
3. Remove crankshaft damper mounting bolt and washer.
4. Using crankshaft damper remover tool No. T58P-6316-D, or equivalent, remove crankshaft damper.
5. Using front cover seal remover tool No. T74P-6700-A, or equivalent, remove front cover seal.
6. Reverse procedure to install, noting the following:
   a. Using front cover seal replacer tool No. T88T-6701-A1, A2, or equivalent, install front cover seal.
   b. Apply silicone gasket and sealant E3AZ-19562-A, or equivalent, in damper keyway. Ensure crankshaft key and keyway are aligned, using Crankshaft Damper Replacer T47P-6316-B, or equivalent, install crankshaft.

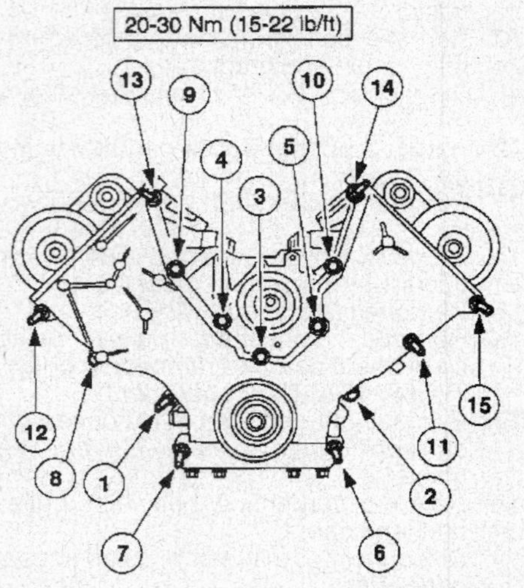

FM1069800793000X

Fig. 33 Front cover tightening sequence. 1998–2000

1998–2000

1. Disconnect diverter valve hoses.
2. Disconnect tube from both exhaust manifolds and diverter valve.
3. Remove nuts from bracket and remove secondary air injection diverter valve.
4. Remove serpentine drive belt.
5. Remove crankshaft pulley bolt.
6. Remove crankshaft pulley using crankshaft damper remover tool No. TP58P-6316-D, or equivalent.
7. Using front cover seal remover tool No. T74P-6700-A, or equivalent, remove front cover seal.
8. Reverse procedure to install noting the following:
   a. Lubricate engine front cover seal and front cover with clean engine oil.
   b. Use crankshaft seal replacer tool No. T88T-6701-A, or equivalent to install oil seal.
   c. Apply silicone gasket and sealant F6AZ-19562-AA, or equivalent, to woodruff key slot on crankshaft pulley.
   d. Install crankshaft pulley using crankshaft damper replacer tool No. T74P-6316-D, or equivalent.
   e. Install and **torque** crankshaft bolt to 66 ft. lbs.
   f. Loosen crankshaft bolt at least 360°.
   g. **Torque** crankshaft bolt to 35–39 ft. lbs.
   h. Tighten crankshaft bolt an additional 85–90°.

TIMING CHAIN

REPLACE

These engines have an interference fit design. If engine has jumped time, damage will result to cylinder, valve and piston assemblies.

At no time, when the timing chains are removed and the cylinder heads are installed, may the crankshaft and/or camshaft be rotated unless all rocker arms have been removed. Rotation may result in valve and/or piston damage.

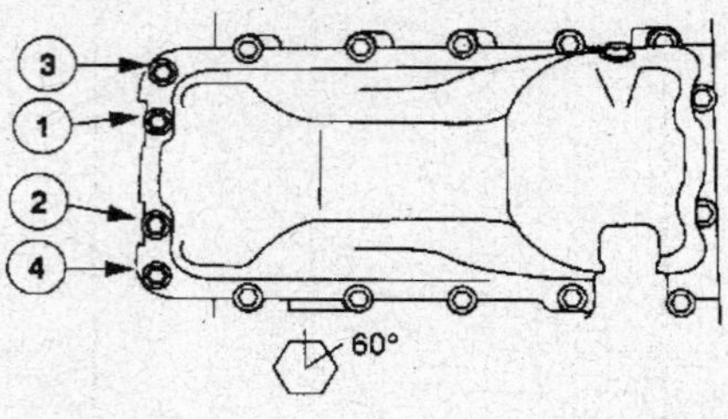

FM1069800794000X

Fig. 34 Oil pan to front cover tightening sequence. 1998–2000

SOHC and DOHC engines have a primary timing chain. DOHC engines also use a secondary timing chain between intake and exhaust camshafts.

Before loosening or tightening camshaft sprocket nuts and bolts, ensure camshaft positioning and locking devices are in place.

PRIMARY

Removal

1. **On Continental models,** remove engine as outlined under "Engine, Replace."
2. **On all models,** remove valve covers as outlined under "Valve Cover, Replace."
3. Remove rocker arms as outlined under "Hydraulic Lifters, Replace."
4. Remove front engine cover as outlined under "Front Engine Cover, Replace."
5. **On models equipped with SOHC engine,** remove oil pan.
6. **On all models,** remove crankshaft position pulse wheel, then rotate engine to No. 1 TDC, **Figs. 25 and 35.**
7. **On models equipped with SOHC engine,** install cam positioning tool No. T91P-6256-A, or equivalent, on camshaft flats, **Fig. 36.**
8. **On models equipped with DOHC engine,** install camshaft positioning tool No. T93P-6256-A, **Fig. 26.** and camshaft holding tool No. T93P-6256-AH, or equivalents, **Fig. 37,** to camshafts.
9. **On all models,** remove righthand tensioner mounting bolts, then remove tensioner and arm.
10. Remove righthand chain guide mounting bolts, then remove chain guide. **Note length of bolts for installation.**
11. Remove righthand timing chain, then remove righthand crankshaft sprocket. **Note position of sprocket for installation.**
12. Remove righthand camshaft gear mounting bolt, washer, gear and spacer (spacer used only on SOHC engines), if required.
13. Remove lefthand tensioner mounting bolts, then remove tensioner and arm.
14. Remove lefthand chain guide mounting bolts, then remove chain guide. **Note length of bolts for later installation.**

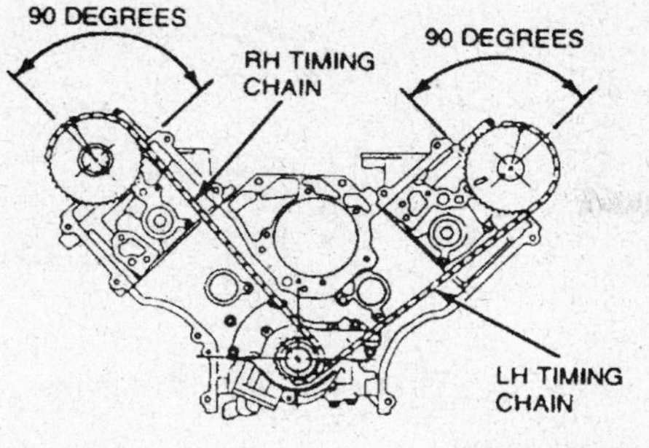

Fig. 35 Engine rotation to TDC. SOHC engine

15. Remove lefthand timing chain, then remove lefthand crankshaft sprocket. **Note position of gear for later installation.**
16. Remove lefthand camshaft gear mounting bolt, washer, sprocket and spacer (spacer used only on SOHC engines), if required.

Installation

If engine has jumped time, ensure all repairs to engine components and/or valve train are completed. During timing chain installation ensure all rocker arm have been remove, if cam or crank should turn with rockers installed engine damage will result.

1. Rotate engine until keyway is 45° counterclockwise from vertical.
2. **On models equipped with DOHC engines,** ensure secondary timing chain and tensioner are correctly installed.
3. **On SOHC engines,** install cam positioning tool No. T91P-6256-A, or equivalent, on camshaft flats, **Fig. 36.**
4. **On models equipped with DOHC engines,** install camshaft positioning tool No. T93P-6256-A, **Fig. 26,** and camshaft holding tool No. T93P-6256-AH, or equivalents, **Fig. 37,** to camshafts.
5. **On all models,** if removed, install primary timing chain cam sprockets onto camshaft, tighten nuts finger tight at this time
6. Install lefthand timing chain onto camshaft sprocket, ensure one of the colored links of timing chain is aligned with timing marks of camshaft sprocket, **Fig. 38.**
7. Install left timing chain onto crankshaft sprocket. Ensure one of the colored links of timing chain is aligned with timing marks of crankshaft sprocket. Ensure tapered boss of crankshaft sprocket is facing away from engine block, **Fig. 39.**
8. Bleed timing chain tensioner as outlined under " Timing Chain Tensioner, Bleed."
9. Install left chain rail, tensioner and arm. Tighten to specifications.
10. Using a suitable C-clamp across both timing chain rails, remove all slack from timing chain, then release timing chain tensioner.
11. Repeat above procedures for right timing chain, note that crank shaft sprocket tapered boss faces towards engine

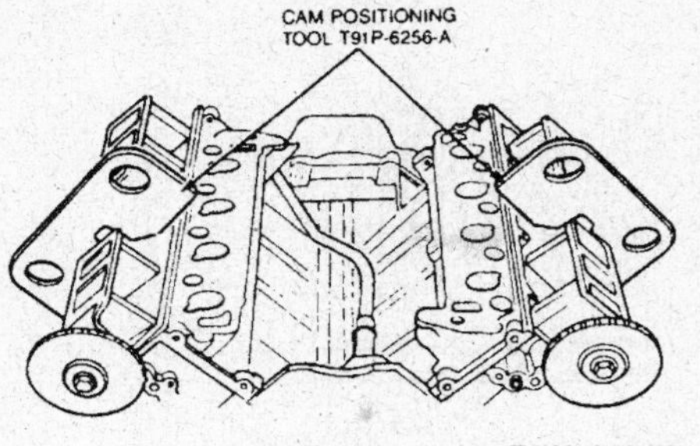

Fig. 36 Camshaft positioning tool. SOHC engine

block, **Fig. 39.**

12. Tighten camshaft sprocket nuts to specification.
13. Install crankshaft position pulse wheel.
14. **On models equipped with SOHC engines,** install oil pan.
15. **On all models,** install front engine cover as outlined under "Front Engine Cover, Replace."
16. Install rocker arms as outlined under "Hydraulic Lifters, Replace."
17. Install valve covers as outlined under "Valve Cover, Replace."
18. **On Continental models,** install engine as outlined under "Engine, Replace."

SECONDARY

Ensure camshaft locking tools are in place before loosening or tightening cam sprocket bolts. Engine damage will result if tools are not properly installed.

1. Remove primary timing chain as outlined above.
2. Compress and lock spring loaded secondary timing chain tensioner.
3. Remove mounting bolt from intake camshafts. **Note position of all spacers sprockets and washers for later assembly.**
4. Remove secondary timing chain and sprockets.
5. Remove bolts mounting secondary timing chain tensioner to head, then remove tensioner.
6. Reverse procedure to install. Tighten to specifications.

TIMING CHAIN TENSIONER BLEED

1. Position timing chain tensioner in suitable soft-jawed vise.
2. Using suitable tool, position ratchet lock mechanism from ratchet stem, then slowly compress tensioner plunger by rotating vise handle. **Tensioner must be compressed slowly or internal seal damage may result.**
3. When tensioner plunger bottoms in tensioner bore, continue holding ratchet lock mechanism, then push ratchet mechanism down until flush with tensioner face.
4. While holding ratchet stem flush to tensioner face, release ratchet lock mechanism, then install paper clip or

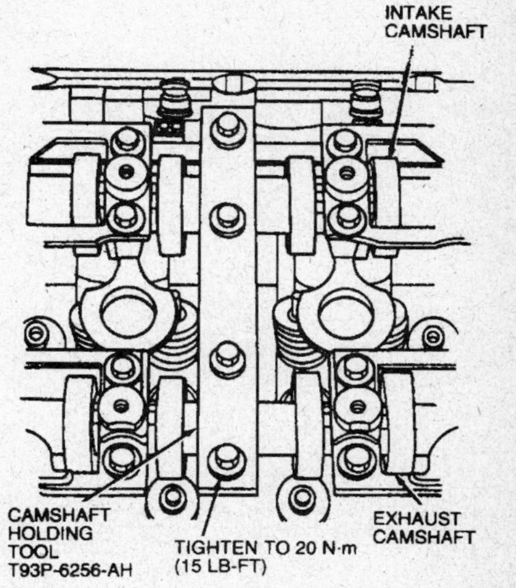

Fig. 37 Camshaft holding tool. DOHC engine

suitable tool to lock tensioner in collapsed position, **Fig. 40.**

5. **Do not remove paper clip or suitable tool until timing chain, tensioner arm, tensioner and timing chain guide are installed on engine.**

CAMSHAFT

REPLACE

1. Remove timing chains as outlined under "Timing Chain, Replace."
2. Rotate crankshaft key counterclockwise 45° from vertical. Ensure pistons are below top of engine deck face. **Crankshaft must be in position prior to rotating camshafts or piston and/or valve damage may result if all rocker arms have not been removed.**
3. Remove camshaft cap cluster assembly mounting bolts, **Figs. 41 and 42.**
4. **On models equipped with SOHC engine,** tap upward on camshaft cap, **Fig. 43,** then carefully remove camshaft cap and camshaft.
5. **On models equipped with DOHC engines,** remove first the exhaust then the intake camshaft cap cluster, tap upward on camshaft cap, **Fig. 43,** then carefully remove camshaft cap and camshaft.
6. **On all models,** reverse procedure to install, noting the following:
   a. Refer to **Figs. 41 and 42** for camshaft cap cluster bolt tightening sequence.
   b. Tighten mounting nuts and bolts to specifications.

PISTON & ROD ASSEMBLY

If the old pistons are serviceable, make certain that they are installed on the rods from which they were removed. Check side

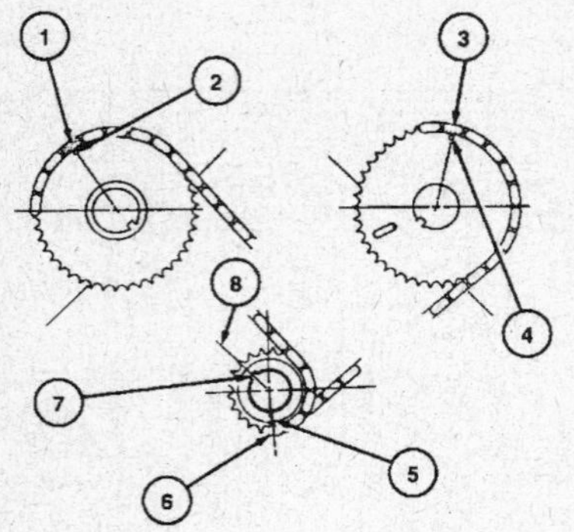

Item	Description
1	RH Camshaft Timing Chain Mark
2	RH Camshaft Sprocket Mark
3	LH Camshaft Timing Chain Mark
4	RH Camshaft Sprocket Mark
5	Crankshaft Sprocket Mark
6	Crankshaft Timing Chain Mark
7	Crankshaft Sprocket
8	Crankshaft Keyway Center Line

FM1069300467000X

Fig. 38 Crankshaft to camshaft timing

clearance between connecting rods and crankshaft journal. Clearance should be .015–.040 inch.

MAIN & ROD BEARINGS

Main bearing vertical bolts and rod bolts used in these engines are of the "Torque To Yield" type and can not be reused. Ensure replacement bolts are available before servicing main or rod bearings.

DOHC ENGINE

Refer to **Figs. 44 and 45** for main bearing cap removal and tightening sequences, noting the following:

1. Seat bearing caps using a brass hammer.
2. **Torque** vertical main bearing bolts 1–20 to 72–108 inch lbs.
3. **Torque** vertical main bearing bolts 1–10 to 16–21 ft. lbs., and main bearing bolts 11–20 to 17–32 ft. lbs.
4. Rotate vertical main bearing bolts 1–20 an additional 85–90°.
5. **Torque** main bearing cap adjusting screws 21–30 in sequence to 44 inch lbs., then in sequence to 90 inch lbs.
6. **Torque** main bearing cap side bolts 31–40 to 84 inch lbs., then in sequence to 14–17 ft. lbs.

SOHC ENGINE

Refer to **Fig. 46** for main bearing cap removal and tightening sequence. **Torque** bolts to 22–25 ft. lbs., then tighten each bolt an additional 85–90°.

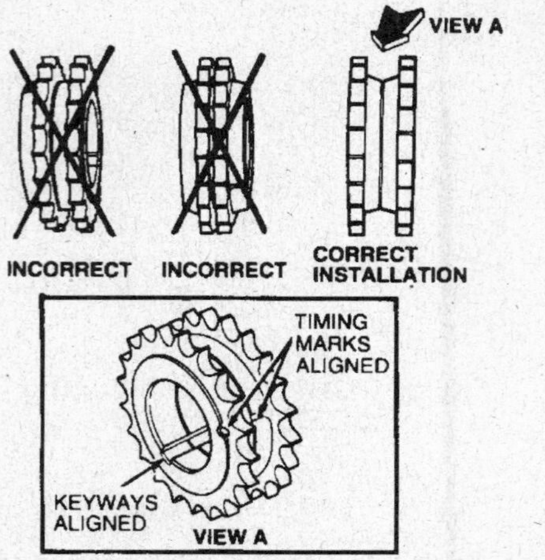

FM1069300466000X

Fig. 39 Crankshaft sprocket position

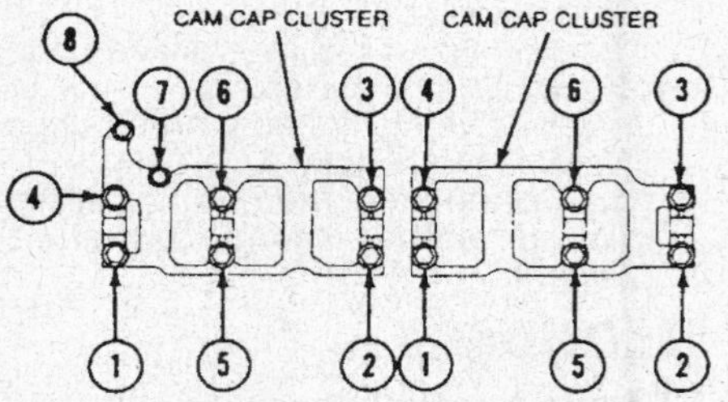

FM1069100194000X

Fig. 41 Camshaft cap cluster assembly. SOHC engine

CRANKSHAFT REAR OIL SEAL

REPLACE

1997

If oil pan gasket is damaged while removing crankshaft rear oil seal retainer, replace oil pan gasket as outlined.

1. Remove transmission or transaxle as outlined in " Automatic Transmission/ Transaxles" section.
2. Remove flexplate assembly.
3. Remove rear oil seal retainer mounting bolts, **Fig. 47.**
4. With oil seal retainer properly supported on a clean work surface, drive seal out of retainer using a suitable punch.
5. Clean all mating surfaces, then apply a suitable silicone sealer to engine block mating surface.
6. Install seal retainer to engine, tighten retainer bolts to specifications in sequence, **Fig. 48.**
7. Install new seal into retainer using installation tool No. T82L-6701-A and adapter tool No. T91P-6701-A, or equivalents.
8. Install transmission/transaxle.

1998–2000

1. Remove transmission as outlined in "Automatic Transmission/Transaxles " section.
2. Remove flywheel.

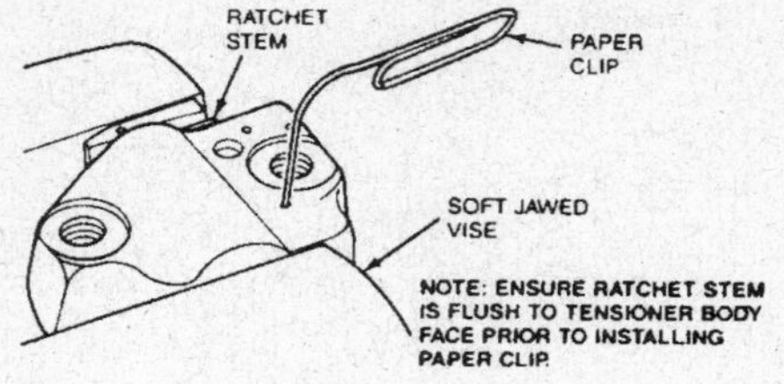

FM1069100198000X

Fig. 40 Timing chain tensioner bleed

3. Using rear crankshaft slinger remover tool No. T-95P-6701-AH, or equivalent, and a suitable slide hammer, remove crankshaft oil slinger.
4. Remove crankshaft rear oil seal using rear crankshaft seal remover tool No. T95P-6701-BH, or equivalent, and a suitable slide hammer.
5. Reverse procedure to install, noting the following:
   a. Use crankshaft seal replacer tool No. T-95P-6701-AH and rear crankshaft seal adapter tool No. T-95P-6701-DH, or equivalents, to install rear oil seal.
   b. With rear crankshaft seal adapter still installed, use rear crankshaft slinger replacer and rear crankshaft seal replacer to install crankshaft oil slinger.

OIL PAN

REPLACE

CONTINENTAL

1997

1. Turn suspension switch off, then disconnect battery ground cable.
2. Remove oil dip stick, then raise and support vehicle.
3. Drain engine oil into a suitable container.
4. Remove dual converter Y pipe.
5. Disconnect wiring connectors to allow pan removal.
6. Disconnect power steering line from front engine cover, then position aside for clearance.
7. Remove oil pan mounting bolts, then pan and gasket. Discard oil pan gasket.
8. Reverse procedure to install, noting the following:
   a. Ensure all mating surfaces are clean and free of scratches and gouges.
   b. Apply a small amount of a suitable silicone sealer at joint of block and front cover and rear seal retainer.
   c. Tighten pan bolts to specification in sequence, **Fig. 49.**

1998–2000

1. Drain engine oil into a suitable container.
2. Remove duel converter Y pipe.
3. Disconnect sensor wiring from low oil level sensor and oil pan rail.
4. Remove 16 bolts, then the oil pan.

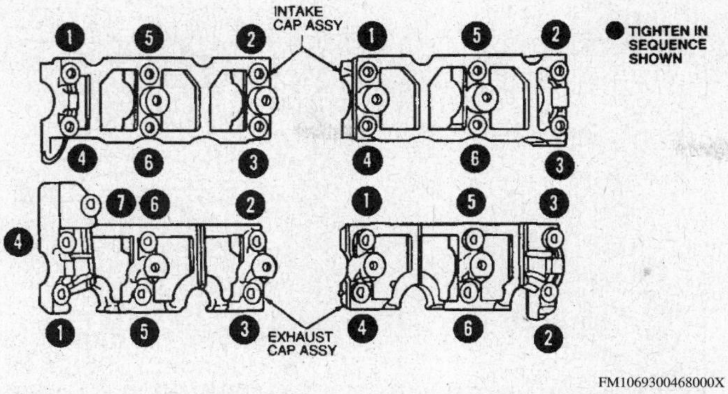

Fig. 42 Camshaft cap cluster assembly. DOHC engine

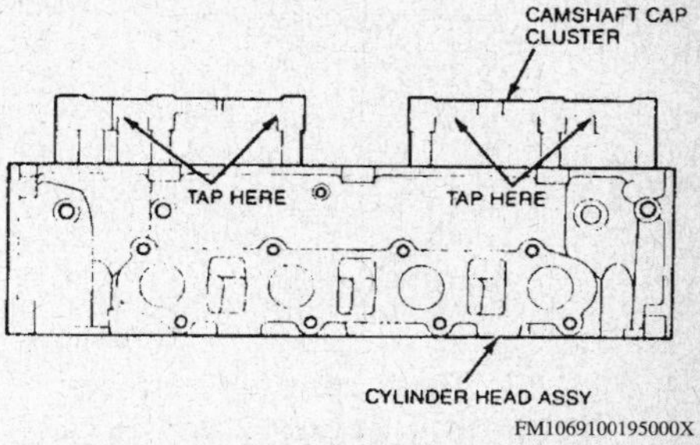

Fig. 43 Camshaft cap cluster removal. SOHC engine

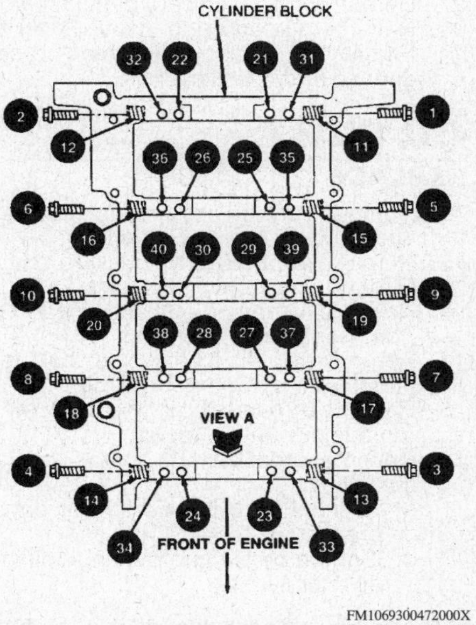

Fig. 44 Main bearing cap removal sequence. DOHC engine

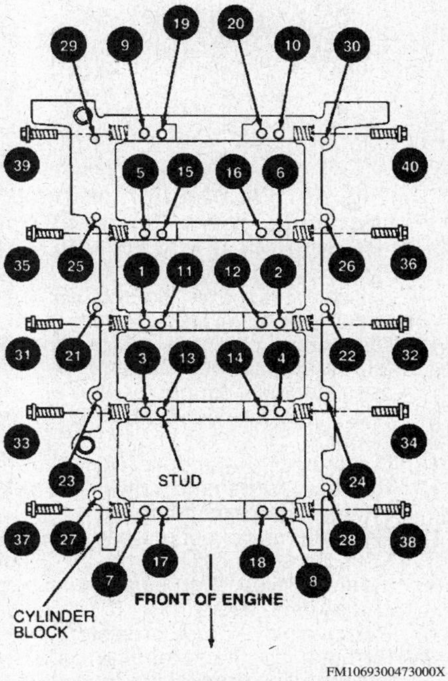

Fig. 45 Main bearing cap tightening sequence. DOHC engine

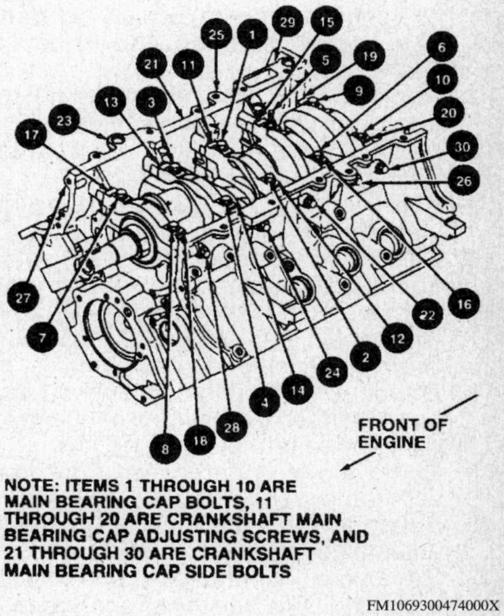

FRONT OF ENGINE
NOTE: ITEMS 1 THROUGH 10 ARE MAIN BEARING CAP BOLTS, 11 THROUGH 20 ARE CRANKSHAFT MAIN BEARING CAP ADJUSTING SCREWS, AND 21 THROUGH 30 ARE CRANKSHAFT MAIN BEARING CAP SIDE BOLTS
FM1069300474000X

Fig. 46 Main bearing cap tightening sequence. SOHC engine

5. Reverse procedure to install noting the following:
   a. Tighten oil pan bolts to specifications in sequence, **Fig. 50,** then in sequence an additional 60°.
   b. Fill engine with clean oil to specification.

MARK VIII

1997

1. Remove engine appearance cover, then air cleaner outlet tube.
2. Install suitable lifting eyes to engine, then install suitable engine support frame and lift engine sufficiently to relieve tension on mounts. **Do not lift engine too high as lines and wiring may be damaged.**
3. Raise and support vehicle, then remove front wheel assemblies.
4. Remove motor mount though bolts
5. Prepare subframe for lowering by disconnecting all engine wiring and equipment clipped or attached.
6. Mark steering shaft coupling for later

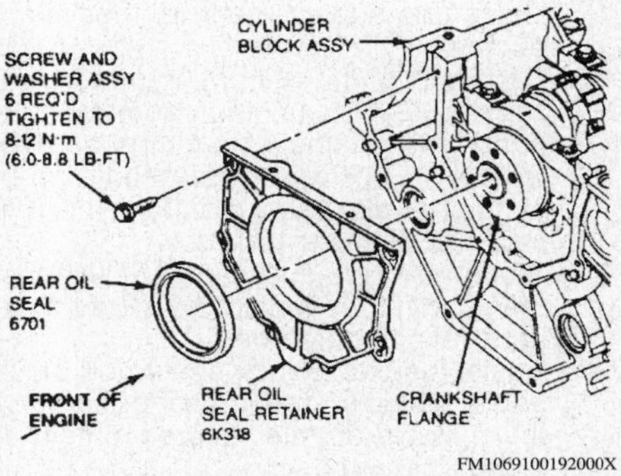

Fig. 47 Crankshaft rear oil seal. 1997

alignment, then disconnect at pinch bolt.

7. Support front suspension lower control arms with suitable jacks.
8. Disconnect lower control arms from shock strut, then lower jacks to allow control arms to hang freely.
9. Place suitable jack under subframe, positioned to allow subframe to be lowered and motor mounts to be accessed.
10. Remove subframe mounting bolts, then lower subframe.
11. Remove oil pan mounting bolts, then oil pan. Discard gaskets.
12. Reverse procedure to install, noting the following:
    a. Ensure all mating surfaces are clean and free of scratches and gouges.
    b. Apply a small amount of a suitable silicone sealer at joint of block and front cover and rear seal retainer.
    c. Tighten pan bolts to specification in sequence, **Fig. 49.**

1998

1. Drain engine oil into a suitable container.
2. Install engine lifting set tool No. 014-00340, or equivalent on engine.
3. Install three bar engine support tool No. D88L-6000-A, or equivalent, to engine lifting set.
4. Raise and support vehicle.

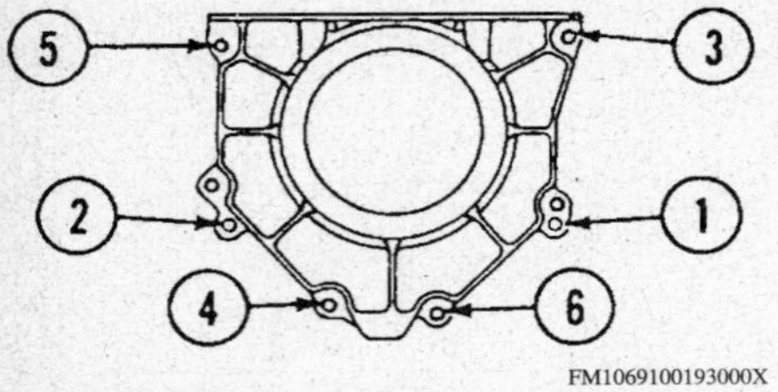

FM1069100193000X

Fig. 48 Rear oil seal retainer tightening sequence. 1997

5. Remove bolts from front engine support insulators.
6. Raise and support engine with three bar engine support. **Ensue no damage occurs to lines and hoses at rear of engine.**
7. Remove front tires, then the tie rod ends from front wheel spindles.
8. Remove front suspension lower arm from front wheel spindles.
9. Remove stabilizer bar link from front stabilizer bar.
10. Disconnect front air spring and shock from front suspension lower arm strut.
11. Remove front fender splash shield.
12. Disconnect anti-lock brake sensor.
13. Drain power steering fluid.
14. Disconnect steering coupling at pinch bolt joint, then the power steering pressure and return hoses.
15. Remove wiring harnesses from front sub frame.
16. Support front sub-frame with suitable adjustable jacks at four points.
17. Remove eight front sub-frame to body mounting bolts and lower sub frame.
18. Disconnect sensor wiring from low oil level sensor and oil pan rail.
19. Remove oil pan bolts, then the oil pan.
20. Remove bolts from oil pump screen and cover, then the oil pump screen cover and tube.
21. Remove oil pan gasket.
22. Reverse procedure to install noting the following:
    a. Tighten oil pump screen and cover bolts to specifications shown in **Fig. 51.**
    b. **Torque** oil pan bolts to specifications in sequence, **Fig. 50,** then tighten in sequence an additional 60°.
    c. Fill engine with clean oil to specification.

TOWN CAR

1. Disconnect ground and positive battery cables.
2. Remove air inlet tube.
3. Drain cooling system, then remove cooling fan and shroud.
4. Relieve fuel system pressure as outlined under " Precautions," then disconnect fuel lines.
5. Remove upper radiator hose.
6. Remove wiper module and support bracket.
7. Discharge A/C system.
8. Disconnect A/C compressor outlet hose, then remove hose assembly to righthand coil bracket mounting bolt.
9. Remove engine electrical harness 42-

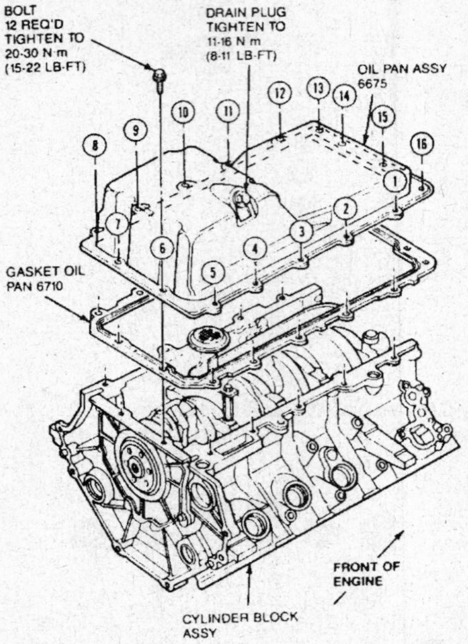

FM1099100040000X

Fig. 49 Oil pan tightening sequence. Town Car & 1997 Continental & Mark VIII

pin connector from bracket on brake vacuum booster.

10. Disconnect engine electrical connector, then disconnect transmission harness electrical connector.
11. Disconnect throttle valve cable at throttle body.
12. Disconnect heater outlet hose.
13. Remove righthand cylinder head grounds strap mounting nut.
14. Remove heater outlet hose assembly to righthand cylinder head upper mounting stud, then loosen lower bolt and position aside.
15. Remove blower motor resistor.
16. Remove righthand engine mount to lower engine bracket mounting bolt.
17. Disconnect EGR valve vacuum hoses and tube.
18. Remove EGR valve to intake manifold mounting bolts.
19. Raise and support vehicle, then drain engine oil.
20. Remove righthand front engine mount two through bolts, then remove lefthand front engine mount through bolt.
21. Remove EGR tube line mounting nut at righthand exhaust manifold, then remove EGR valve assembly.
22. Disconnect exhaust pipes at exhaust manifolds, then lower and support exhaust at crossmember.
23. Position suitable jack and wood block under oil pan, rearward of drain plug, then raise engine approximately 4 inches.
24. Install two wood blocks approximately 2.5–2.75 inches thick under each engine mount.
25. Lower engine to wood blocks, then remove jack.
26. Remove oil pan mounting bolts. It may be necessary to loosen rear transmission mount mounting nuts and with

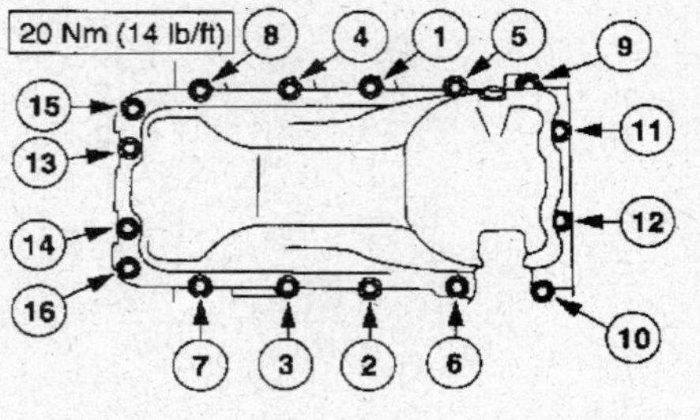

FM1069800796000X

Fig. 50 Oil pan tightening sequence. 1998 Mark VIII & 1998–2000 Continental

suitable jack, then raise extension housing slightly to remove oil pan.

27. Remove oil pan, discard pan gasket.
28. Reverse procedure to install. Refer to **Fig. 49** for oil pan bolt tightening sequence and specifications.

OIL PUMP

REPLACE

1. Remove valve covers as outlined under "Valve Cover, Replace."
2. Remove front cover as outlined under "Front Engine Cover, Replace."
3. Remove oil pan as outlined under "Oil Pan, Replace. "
4. Remove timing chains as outlined under "Timing Chain, Replace."
5. Remove oil pump mounting bolts, then remove oil pump, **Fig. 52.**
6. Reverse procedure to install, noting the following:
    a. Align oil pump inner rotor with flat of crankshaft.
    b. Tighten oil pump mounting bolts to specifications.

BELT TENSION DATA

Automatic belt tensioners are spring loaded devices which set and maintain the drive belt tension. The drive belt should not require tension adjustment for the life of the belt. Automatic tensioners have belt wear indicator marks. If the indicator mark is not between the indicator lines, the belt is worn or an incorrect belt is installed.

SERPENTINE DRIVE BELT

BELT ROUTING

Refer to **Figs. 53 and 54** for drive belt routing.

BELT REPLACEMENT

1. Rotate tensioner away from belt using a breaker bar installed in ½ inch square hole in tensioner arm.
2. Lift old belt over alternator pulley flange and remove.
3. When installing new belt over pulleys. Ensure all V-grooves make proper contact with pulley.
4. Ensure belt is properly installed on each pulley.

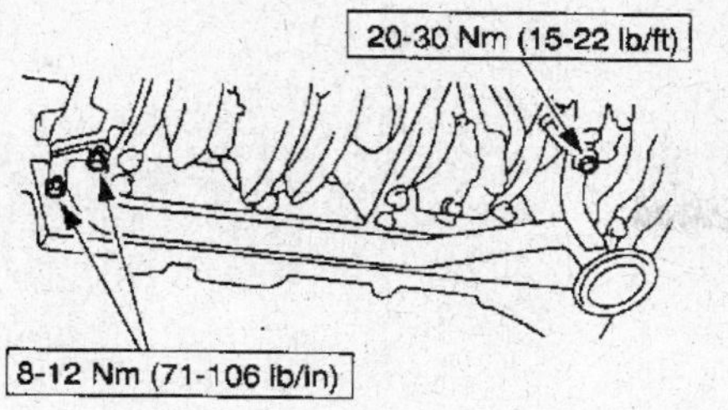

Fig. 51 Oil pump screen & cover bolts torque specifications. 1998 Mark VIII

COOLING SYSTEM BLEED

A pressurized reservoir system is used which constantly separates the air from the cooling system. When the thermostat is open, coolant flows through a small hose from the top of the radiator outlet tank to the reservoir. The reservoir separates any entrapped air from the coolant and replenishes the system through the lower hose. The reservoir serves as the location for service fill, coolant expansion during warm up, system pressurization from the pressure cap and air separation during operation. The reservoir is designed to have approximately ½–1 liter of air when cold to allow for coolant expansion.

Add coolant to the minimum level on the reservoir.

THERMOSTAT

REPLACE

DOHC ENGINE

1. Drain coolant level below upper radiator hose and thermostat housing.
2. Disconnect lower radiator, coolant recovery and engine return hoses at thermostat housing, **Fig. 55,** then remove two thermostat housing mounting bolts.
3. Remove O-ring seal and thermostat from thermostat housing. Inspect O-ring for damage and replace if necessary.
4. Reverse procedure to install. Tighten to specifications.

SOHC ENGINE

1. Drain coolant level below upper radiator hose and thermostat housing.
2. Disconnect upper radiator hose at thermostat housing, then remove two thermostat housing mounting bolts.
3. Remove O-ring seal and thermostat from intake manifold. Inspect O-ring for damage and replace if necessary.
4. Reverse procedure to install. Tighten to specifications.

WATER PUMP

REPLACE

1. Drain cooling system, then remove engine cooling fan and shroud.

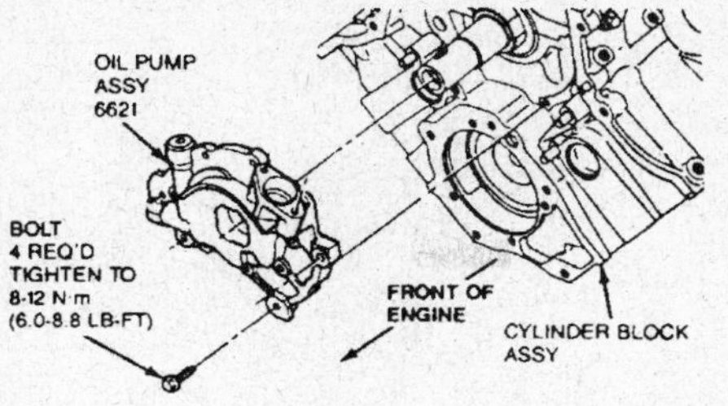

Fig. 52 Oil pump assembly

2. Release belt tensioner, then remove accessory drive belt, **Fig. 56.**
3. Remove water pump pulley mounting bolts, then remove water pump pulley.
4. Remove water pump mounting bolts, then remove water pump.
5. Reverse procedure to install. Tighten mounting bolts to specifications.

RADIATOR

REPLACE

1. Drain engine coolant, then disconnect de-aireation hose and both radiator hoses.
2. Disconnect automatic transmission fluid inlet and outlet lines. Note, when removing transmission cooler lines, use a back-up wrench to hold fitting.
3. **On models equipped with fan shroud,** proceed as follows:
   a. Remove upper shroud mounting bolts at radiator support.
   b. Remove upper A/C condenser core to radiator mounting bolts.
   c. Lift fan shroud enough to disengage lower retaining clips and lay shroud over fan.
4. **On all models,** remove radiator upper support mounting bolts, then supports.
5. Reverse procedure to install, noting the following:
   a. Operate engine, check automatic transmission, radiator and coolant recovery tank for proper fluid level.

FUEL PUMP

REPLACE

1. Relieve fuel system pressure as outlined under " Precautions."
2. Using suitable tool, drain fuel tank at fuel filler neck.
3. Raise and support vehicle.
4. Disconnect fuel supply and return line fittings and vent line.
5. Disconnect fuel pump and sender electrical connectors.
6. Remove fuel tank mounting support straps, then carefully lower fuel tank assembly. Ensure dirt does not enter

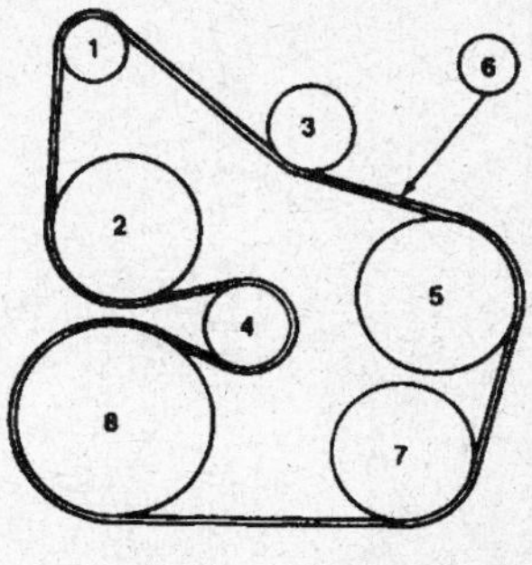

Item		Description
1		Generator
2		Water Pump Pulley
3		Belt Idler Pulley
4		Drive Belt Tensioner
5		Power Steering Pump
6		Drive Belt
7		A/C Compressor
8		Crankshaft Pulley

FM1069300469000X

Fig. 53 Drive belt routing. Continental

tank or fuel system.

7. Using fuel tank sender wrench No. D74P-9275-A, or equivalent, turn fuel pump locking ring counterclockwise, then remove locking ring.
8. Remove fuel pump assembly, then remove and discard seal ring.
9. Reverse procedure to install, noting the following:
   a. Once fuel pump is installed, using fuel pressure gauge tool No. T80L-9974-B, or equivalent, on the fuel charging assembly Schraeder valve, turn ignition from OFF to ON position for 3 seconds. Repeat OFF to ON switching 5–10 times until pressure gauge shows at least 35 psi.

FUEL FILTER

REPLACE

1. Turn engine off and relieve fuel system pressure as outlined under "Precautions."
2. Raise and support vehicle.
3. Remove push connect fittings at both ends of fuel filter. Install new retainer clips in each push connect fitting.
4. Remove fuel filter and retainer from metal bracket by removing two retainer bolts.
5. Remove filer from retainer. Note direction of flow arrow.
6. Remove rubber insulator rings from filter.
7. Reverse procedure to install, noting the following:
   a. Replace insulator(s) if filter moves freely after retainer installation.
   b. **Torque** mounting bolts to 27–44 inch lbs.
   c. Start engine and inspect for leaks.

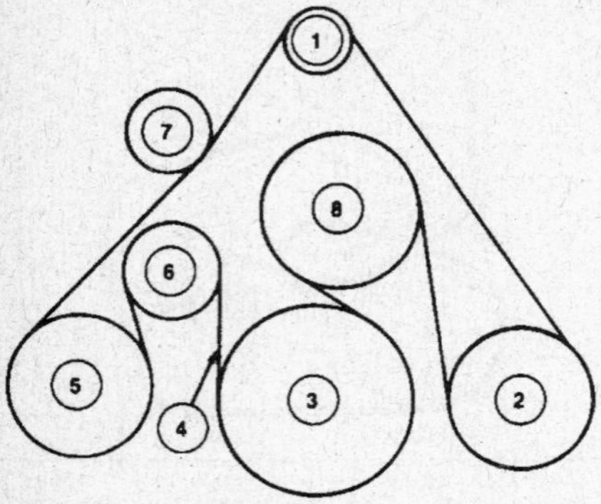

Item		Description
1		Generator
2		Power Steering Pump
3		Crankshaft Pulley
4		Drive Belt
5		A / C Compressor
6		Drive Belt Tensioner
7		Belt Idler Pulley
8		Water Pump

FM1069300470000X

Fig. 54 Drive belt routing. Mark VIII & Town Car

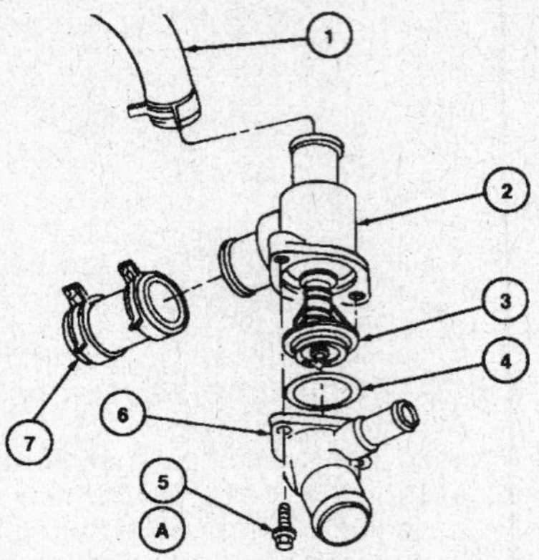

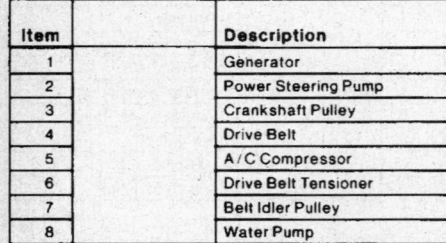

Item		Description
1		Water Bypass Hose
2		Lower Water Thermostat Housing
3		Water Thermostat
4		O-Ring Seal
5		Bolt (2 Req'd)
6		Upper Water Thermostat Housing
7		Engine Return Hose
A		Tighten to 20-30 N·m (15-22 Lb-Ft)

FM1069300471000X

Fig. 55 Thermostat housing. DOHC engine

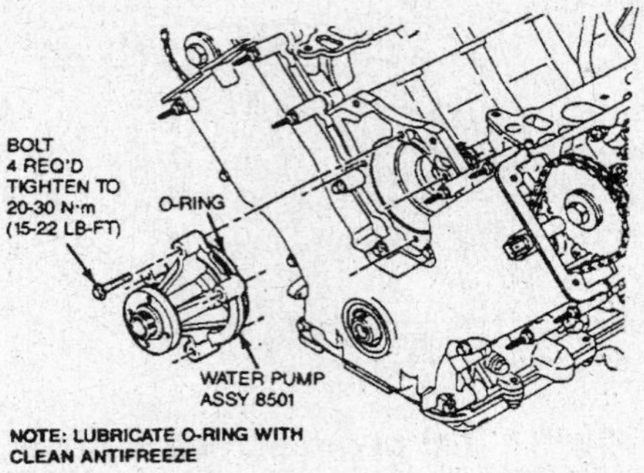

FM1089100059000X

Fig. 56 Water pump replacement

TIGHTENING SPECIFICATIONS

Year	Component	Torque/Ft. Lbs.
DOHC ENGINE		
1997–2000	Alternator Brackets To Cylinder Block	15–22
	Belt Idler Pulley	15–22
	Belt Tensioner	15–22
	Camshaft	81–95
	Camshaft Cover	72–108⑥
	Camshaft Sprocket	81–95
	Crankshaft Damper	114–121
	Crankshaft Pulley	⑧
	Connecting Rod	18–24④
	Cylinder Front Cover	15–22
	Cylinder Head	③
	Drive Belt Tensioner	15–22
	EGR Valve & Tube Assembly To Exhaust Manifold Line	26–33
	EGR Valve To Intake Manifold	15–22
	EGR Tube Connector	30–33
	EGR Valve To Exhaust Manifold Tube	26–33
	Engine Insulators	15–22
	Engine To Transmission	30–44
	Exhaust Manifold Studs	96–108⑥
	Exhaust Manifold To Cylinder Head	15–22
	Exhaust Pipe To Exhaust Manifold	20–30
	Flywheel	54–64
	Front Engine Cover	15–22
	Front Engine Mount	45–59

Continued

TIGHTENING SPECIFICATIONS—Continued

Year	Component	Torque/Ft. Lbs.
DOHC ENGINE		
1997-2000	Front Engine Mount Through Bolts	15–22
	Fuel Filer	27–44⑥
	Heater Outlet Hose	15–22
	Idle Air Control	14
	IMRC Bolts To Intake	⑦
	Intake Manifold To Cylinder Head	53–64
	Lower Control Arm To Strut	118–162
	Low Oil Level Sensor	15–22
	Main Bearing	⑤
	Oil Inlet Tube To Main Bearing Cap	15–22
	Oil Filter Adapter	15–22
	Oil Inlet Tube To Oil Pump	72–108⑥
	Oil Pan Drain Plug	8–12
	Oil Pan To Cylinder Block	14
	Oil Pump To Cylinder Block	72–108⑥
	Oxygen Sensor	27–33
	Power Steering Pump To Engine	15–22
	Power Steering Pump Reservoir	72–96⑥
	Powertrain Frame	73–100
	Pulley To Crankshaft	②
	Rear Axle Assembly To Rear Subframe	72–89
	Rear Engine Mount, Bolt	50–70
	Rear Engine Mount, Nut	35–50
	Rear Engine Support	15–22
	Spark Plug	84–96⑥
	Thermostat Housing	15–22
	Throttle Body	72–108⑥
	Torque Converter	22–25
	Upper Control Arm To Steering Knuckle	50–68
	Upper Manifold	15–22
	Valve Cover	72–108⑥
	Water Bypass Tube	72–96⑥
	Water Pump To Cylinder Block	15–22
	Water Pump To Pulley	15–22
SOHC ENGINE		
1997–2000	Accelerator Cable Bracket	72–96⑥
	Alternator To Cylinder Block	15–22
	Camshaft	81–95
	Camshaft Cover	72–108⑥
	Connecting Rod	29–34①
	Crankshaft Damper	114–121
	Crankshaft Pulley	⑧
	Cylinder Front Cover	15–22
	Cylinder Head	③
	Damper To Crankshaft	114–121
	Engine To Transmission	30–44
	EGR Valve To Intake Manifold	15–22
	Exhaust Manifold To Cylinder Head	15–22
	Exhaust Pipe To Exhaust Manifold	20–30
	Front Engine Mount	45–59

Continued

TIGHTENING SPECIFICATIONS—Continued

Year	Component	Torque/Ft. Lbs.
DOHC ENGINE		
1997-2000	Front Engine Mount Through Bolts	15–22
	Fuel Filter	27–44⑥
	Intake Manifold To Cylinder Head	53–64
	Main Bearing Cap Adjusting	⑤
	Main Bearing Cap Side	⑤
	Main Bearing Cap Vertical	⑤
	Oil Inlet Tube To Main Bearing Cap	15–22
	Oil Inlet Tube To Oil Pump	72–106⑥
	Oil Pan Drain Plug	8–12
	Oil Pan To Cylinder Block	14
	Oil Pump To Cylinder Block	72–108⑥
	Rear Engine Mount, Bolt	50–70
	Rear Engine Mount, Nut	35–50
	Spark Plug	84–96⑥
	Thermostat Housing	15–22
	Torque Converter	15–22
	Valve Cover	72–108⑥
	Water Pump To Cylinder Block	15–22
	Water Pump To Pulley	15–22

①— Tighten an additional 90–120°.
②— Refer to "Front Cover Seal, Replace." for tightening specifications and sequence.
③— Refer to "Cylinder Head, Replace" for tightening specifications and sequence.
④— Tighten an additional 85–90°.
⑤— Refer to "Main & Rod Bearings" for tightening specifications and sequence.
⑥— Inch lbs.
⑦— Refer to "Intake Manifold, Replace" for tightening specifications and sequence.
⑧— Refer to "Front Cover, Replace" for tightening specifications and sequence.

Rear Axle & Suspension

NOTE: Prior To Performing Any Service Operations Listed In This Section, Consult The "Technical Service Bulletins " Section For Related Information.

INDEX

DESCRIPTION

CONTINENTAL

The Continental utilizes a fully independent rear suspension consisting of McPherson struts with integral air springs and dual-damping shock absorbers, counterbalancing torsion springs and a height sensor.

The air suspension and dual damping functions are controlled by a microcomputer based module which receives inputs for vehicle speed, door switch position, damping actuator feedback, steering wheel turning rate and angle, engine vacuum, throttle position, brake actuation, ignition switching, and vehicle ride height. The dual-damping function automatically switches from a soft to firm ride when the driving situation (hard cornering, acceleration or braking, etc.) dictates the need for increased damping effect.

The rear struts, **Fig. 1,** use a dual path mount which separates the strut and air spring mounting surfaces, to help provide for maximum isolation. The counterbalancing torsion springs, fitted between the strut and lower control arm, produce an outward force on the strut that tends to offset the binding forces induced by the rear wheels. The rotary design Hall effect type height sensor, **Fig. 2,** permits multiple height positions to be defined, resulting in specialized leveling during all types of driving and load characteristics.

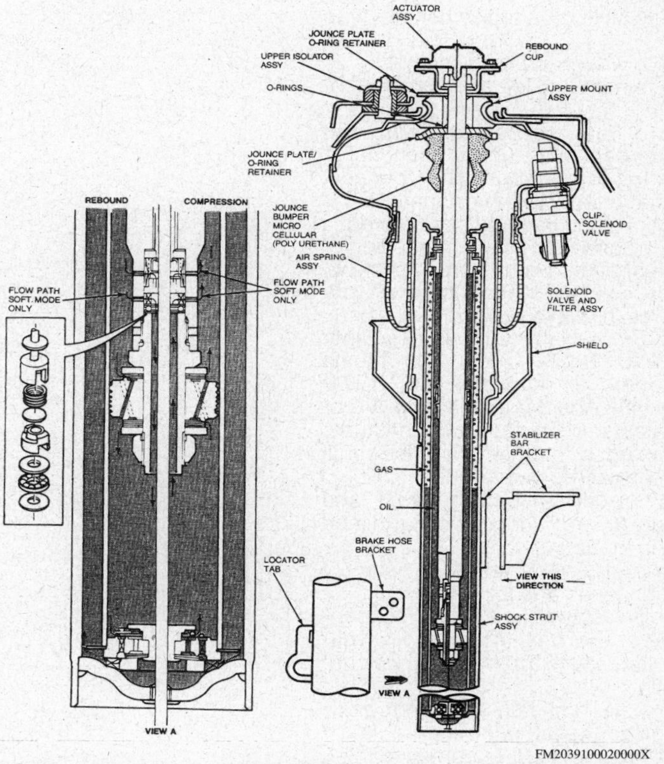

Fig. 1 Cross-sectional view of rear strut assembly. Continental

MARK VIII

This system employs constant velocity (CV) joints at both its inboard (differential) and outboard (wheel) ends for vehicle operating smoothness, **Figs. 3 and 4.** The CV joints are connected by an interconnecting shaft which is splined at both ends and retained in the inboard and outboard CV joints by circlips.

The inboard CV joint stub shaft is splined and held in the differential side gear by circlip. The outboard CV joint stub shaft is pressed into the hub and secured with a free-spinning locknut. The CV joints are lube-for-life with a special CV joint grease and require no periodic lubrication. The CV boots should be periodically inspected and replaced immediately when damage or grease leakage is evident.

Halfshaft removal from the differential is accomplished by applying a load to the back face of the inboard CV joint assembly to overcome the circlip. The outboard joint end must be pressed from the hub.

The inboard tripod CV joints can be disassembled and serviced. Other then the CV boot, the outboard CV joint is serviced only as an assembly with the shaft.

TOWN CAR

The gear set, **Fig. 5,** consist of a ring gear and an overhung drive pinion which is supported by two opposed tapered roller bearings. Pinion bearing preload is maintained by a collapsible spacer on the pinion shaft and adjusted by the pinion nut. The differential case is a one piece design with two openings to allow assembly of internal components and lubricant flow. The pinion shaft is retained with a threaded bolt assembled to the case. The differential case is mounted in the carrier between two opposed tapered roller bearings. The bearings are retained in the carrier by removable bearing caps. Differential bearing preload and ring gear backlash are adjusted by the use of shims located between the differential bearing cups and the carrier housing. Axle shafts are held in the housing by C-locks positioned in a slot on the axle shaft splined end, **Fig. 6.**

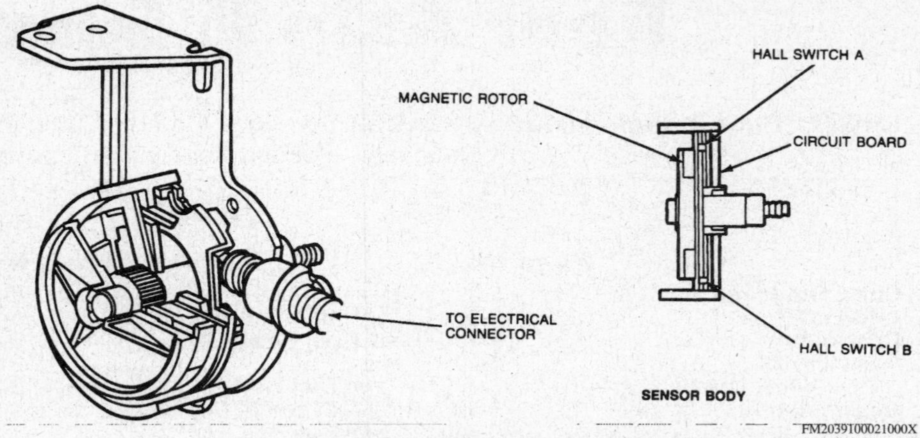

FM2039100021000X

Fig. 2 Rotary height sensor. Continental

REAR AXLE

REPLACE

MARK VIII

1. Remove right hand wheel cover, then loosen lug nuts.
2. Raise vehicle on a frame contact type hoist.
3. Remove wheel and tire assembly.
4. Remove right and left hand brake sensors.
5. Remove rear suspension arm and bushing bolt. Wire upper suspension arm to top of rear shock absorber so it does not interfere with or damage CV joint boot when halfshaft is removed.
6. Using a paint marker, mark position of rear suspension arm and bushing in relation to rear wheel knuckle with bushings in relaxed position.
7. Install Front Hub Remover/Replacer tool Nos. T81P-1104-C with Metric Hub Remover Adapters T83P-1104-BH on Hub Adapter T86P-1104-A1, or equivalents, to righthand wheel studs. Turn wrench counterclockwise until halfshafts is free in rear hub.
8. Remove rear suspension arm and bushing to rear suspension arm and bushing mounting bolts.
9. Remove rear wheel knuckle assembly from driveshaft and joint assembly.
10. Carefully rest halfshaft on rear suspension arm and bushing and wire rear wheel knuckle to top of rear shock absorber.
11. Inboard CV joint stud shaft pilot bearing housing seal must be replaced whenever halfshaft is removed. Remove righthand halfshaft from rear axle housing using CV Joint Remover tool No. T89P-3514-A, or equivalent.
12. Remove halfshaft from vehicle. Install Differential Plug T89P-4850-B, or equivalent, into rear axle housing to prevent lubricant loss.
13. Mark driveshaft centering socket yoke in relation to rear axle universal joint flange. Remove driveshaft mounting bolts.
14. Slide driveshaft forward and rest on driveshaft center bridge support reinforcement.
15. With transmission jack supporting rear

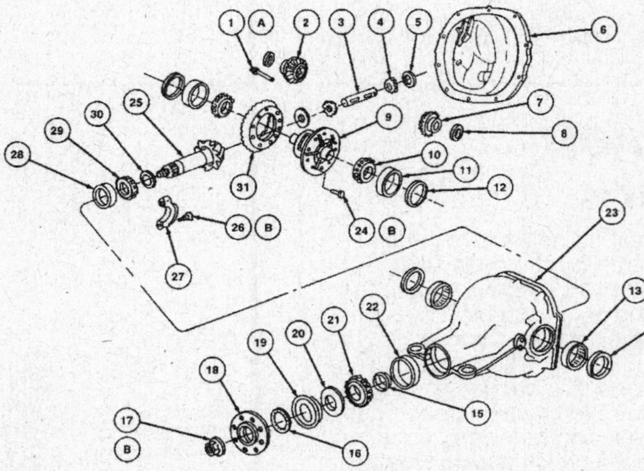

Item	Description
1	Differential Pinion Shaft Lock Pin
2	Differential Side Gear
3	Differential Pinion Shaft
4	Differential Pinion Gear
5	Differential Pinion Thrust Washer
6	Axle Housing Cover
7	Differential Side Gear
8	Differential Side Gear Thrust Washer
9	Differential Case
10	Differential Bearing
11	Differential Bearing Cup
12	Differential Bearing Shim
13	Pilot Bearing
14	Inboard Cv Joint Stub Shaft Pilot Bearing Housing Seal
15	Differential Drive Pinion Collapsible Spacer

Item	Description
16	Drive Pinion Oil Seal Deflector
17	Drive Pinion Nut
18	Rear Axle Universal Joint Flange
19	Rear Axle Drive Pinion Seal
20	Rear Axle Drive Pinion Shaft Oil Slinger
21	Differential Pinion Bearing , Front
22	Differential Drive Pinion Bearing Cup
23	Rear Axle Housing
24	Rear Axle Differential Gear Case Bolt
25	Pinion Gear (Part of 4209)
26	Bolt
27	Differential Bearing Cap (Part of 40 10)
28	Rear Axle Pinion Bearing Cup

FM3039700317010X

Fig. 3 Exploded view of rear axle assembly (Part 1 of 2). Mark VIII

Item	Description
29	Differential Pinion Bearing , Rear
30	Drive Pinion Bearing Adjustment Shim

Item	Description
31	Ring Gear (Part of 4209)
A	Tighten to 20-41 N·m (15-30 Lb-Ft)
B	Tighten to 95-115 N·m (70-84 Lb-Ft)

FM3039700317020X

Fig. 3 Exploded view of rear axle assembly (Part 2 of 2). Mark VIII

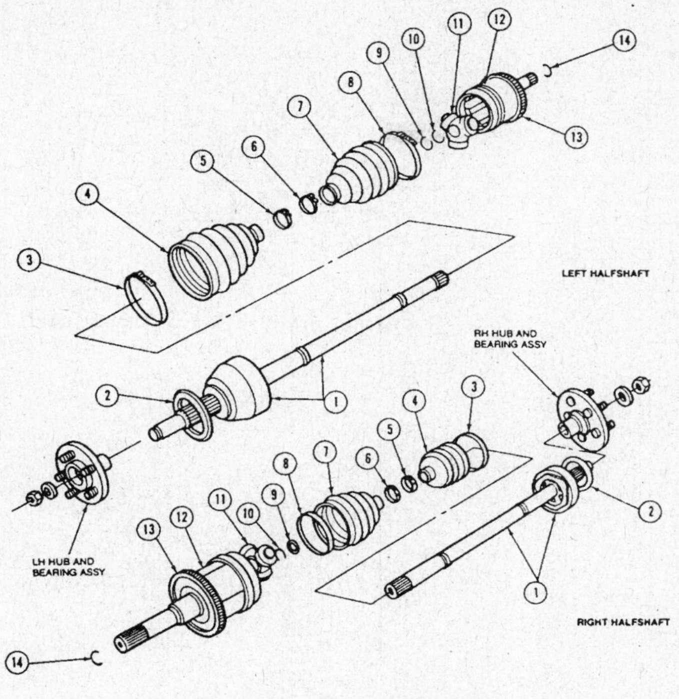

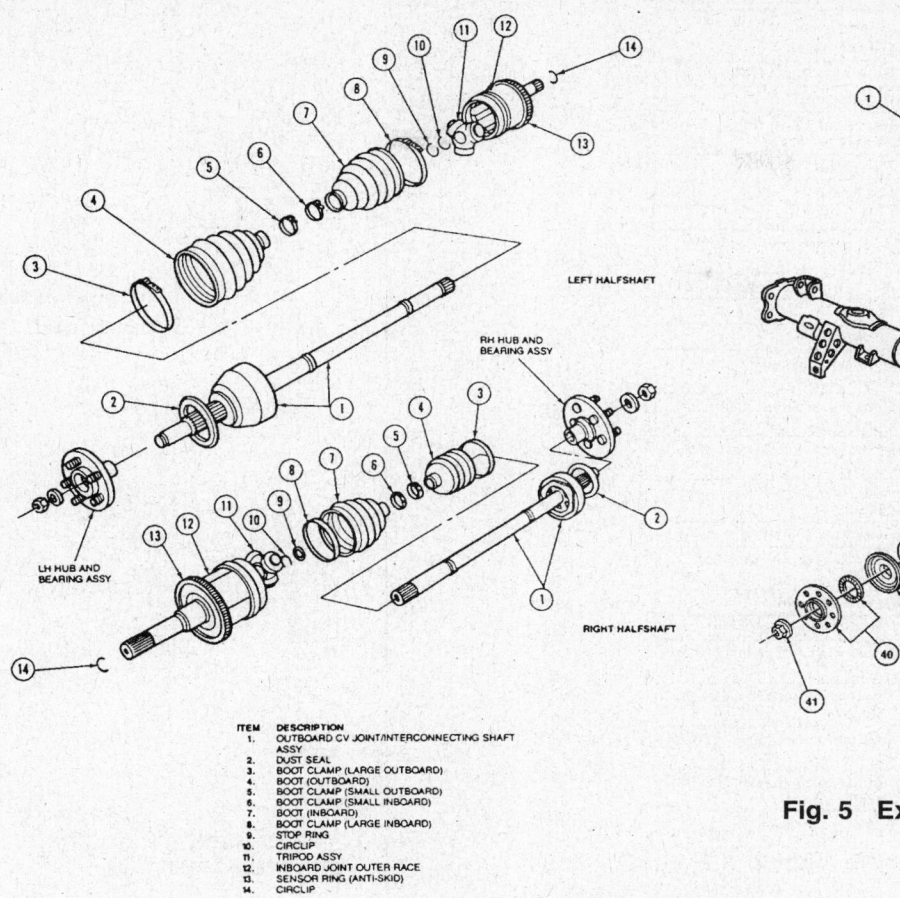

ITEM	DESCRIPTION
1.	OUTBOARD CV JOINT/INTERCONNECTING SHAFT ASSY
2.	DUST SEAL
3.	BOOT CLAMP (LARGE OUTBOARD)
4.	BOOT (OUTBOARD)
5.	BOOT CLAMP (SMALL OUTBOARD)
6.	BOOT CLAMP (SMALL INBOARD)
7.	BOOT (INBOARD)
8.	BOOT CLAMP (LARGE INBOARD)
9.	STOP RING
10.	CIRCLIP
11.	TRIPOD ASSY
12.	INBOARD JOINT OUTER RACE
13.	SENSOR RING (ANTI-SKID)
14.	CIRCLIP

FM3039100210000X

Fig. 4 Rear wheel drive halfshaft system. Mark VIII

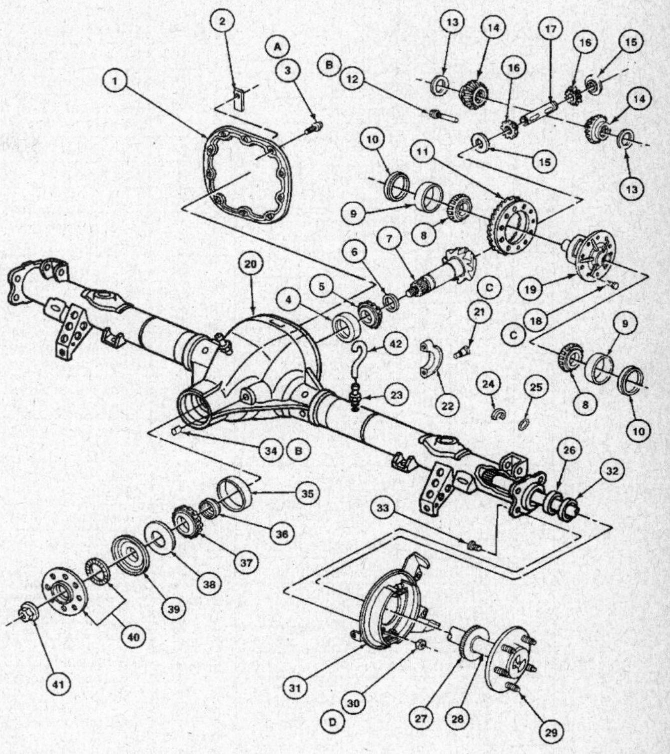

FM3039800316010X

Fig. 5 Exploded view of rear axle (Part 1 of 2). Town Car

axle housing, remove axle differential rear insulator to crossmember mounting nuts.
16. Remove rear axle differential rear insulator from axle housing cover.
17. Remove axle front mounting bolts, nuts, bushings and washers.
18. **Do no damage CV joint boot.** Inboard CV joint stub shaft pilot bearing housing seal must be replaced whenever a halfshaft (CV joint) has been removed from rear axle housing.
19. Remove lefthand halfshaft (inboard CV joint) from rear axle housing using CV Joint Remover tool No. T89P-3514-A, or equivalent. Push tool inward (toward rear axle housing).
20. Partially lower rear axle housing. While lowering rear axle housing, move to right and disengage rear axle housing from lefthand inboard CV joint stub shaft.
21. Install Differential Plug tool No. T89P-4850-B, or equivalent, in lefthand side of rear axle housing and lower rear axle housing from vehicle.
22. Reverse procedure to install, noting the following:
    a. **New hub retainer nut, CV joint stub shaft circlips and differential seals must be installed.**
    b. Tighten to specifications.

TOWN CAR

1. Turn switch air suspension Off.
2. Raise vehicle and position safety stands below rear frame crossmember.
3. Mark driveshaft flange and pinion flange for correct alignment during installation. Remove four driveshaft retainer bolts and disconnect driveshaft.
4. Remove rear wheels, rear disc brake calipers, brake discs and wire the caliper out of the way.
5. Remove rear disc rotor and parking brake rear cable and conduit from the parking brake cable equalizer. Reroute parking brake rear cable and conduit out of the way.
6. Remove anti-lock brake sensors Reroute anti-lock brake sensor wiring.
7. Remove rear stabilizer bar from rear stabilizer bar link and bushing.
8. Remove rear stabilizer bar bracket bolts, rear stabilizer bar brackets and the rear stabilizer bar.
9. If equipped with rear air springs, remove height sensor.
10. **On 1998–2000 models,** take care not to damage threads on the bellcrank stud and separate the Watts linkage from the rear axle housing. Remove retainer nut from the bellcrank stud.
11. **On all models,** use additional support straps to secure the rear axle to the jack and support rear axle housing with a suitable jack.
12. Remove shock absorber lower retainer nuts and shock absorbers from retainer brackets.
13. Remove lower control arm retainer and upper control arm retainer nuts and bolts.
14. Unseat air springs and lower rear axle from vehicle.
15. Reverse procedure to install. Tighten to specifications.

REAR AXLE SHAFT

REPLACE

TOWN CAR

Removal

1. Turn air suspension switch OFF.
2. Raise and support vehicle. Remove rear wheel and tire assembly.
3. Remove disc brake calipers and rotors.
4. Drain rear axle fluid by removing cover.
5. Remove differential pinion shaft lock bolt and differential pinion shaft, **Fig. 7.**
6. Push flanged end of axle shafts toward center of vehicle and remove C-lock from button end of axle shaft, **Fig. 6.**
7. Remove axle shaft from housing, use caution not to damage oil seal and ABS sensor ring.

Item	Description
1	Axle Housing Cover
2	Identification Tag
3	Axle Housing Cover Bolt
4	Rear Axle Pinion Bearing Cup
5	Differential Pinion Bearing (Rear)
6	Drive Pinion Bearing Adjustment Shim
7	Drive Pinion (Part of 4209)
8	Differential Bearing (RH)
9	Differential Bearing Cup
10	Differential Bearing Shim
11	Ring Gear (Part of 4209)
12	Differential Pinion Shaft Lock Pin
13	Differential Side Gear Thrust Washer
14	Differential Side Gear
15	Differential Pinion Thrust Washer
16	Differential Pinion Gear
17	Differential Pinion Shaft
18	Rear Axle Differential Gear Case Bolt
19	Differential Case
20	Rear Axle Housing
21	Bolt
22	Differential Bearing Cap (Part of 4010)
23	Rear Axle Housing Vent
24	U-Washer
25	Rear Axle Shaft O-Ring
26	Rear Wheel Bearing
27	Rear Brake Anti-Lock Sensor Indicator
28	Axle Shaft
29	Lug Bolt
30	Nut
31	Rear Wheel Disc Brake Adapter
32	Inner Wheel Bearing Oil Seal
33	Bolt
34	Fill Plug
35	Differential Drive Pinion Bearing Cup
36	Differential Drive Pinion Collapsible Spacer
37	Differential Pinion Bearing (Front)
38	Rear Axle Drive Pinion Shaft Oil Slinger
39	Rear Axle Drive Pinion Seal
40	Rear Axle Universal Joint Flange
41	Drive Pinion Nut
42	Formed Vent Hose
A	Tighten to 38-52 N·m (28-38 Lb-Ft)
B	Tighten to 20-40 N·m (15-30 Lb-Ft)
C	Tighten to 95-115 N·m (70-84 Lb-Ft)
D	Tighten to 27-40 N·m (20-30 Lb-Ft)

FM3039800316020X

Fig. 5 Exploded view of rear axle (Part 2 of 2). Town Car

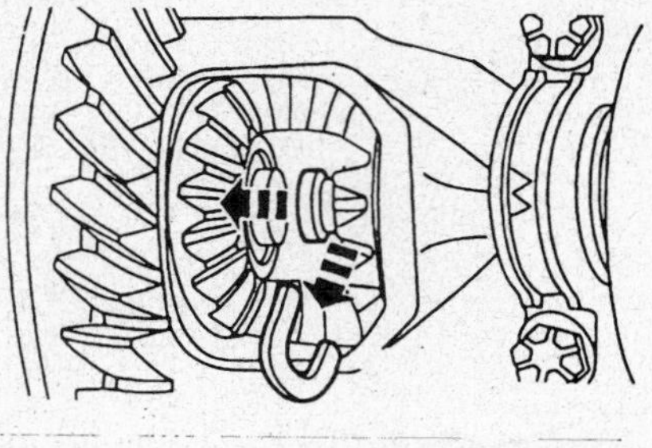

FM3039100209000X

Fig. 6 Axle shaft C-lock. Town Car

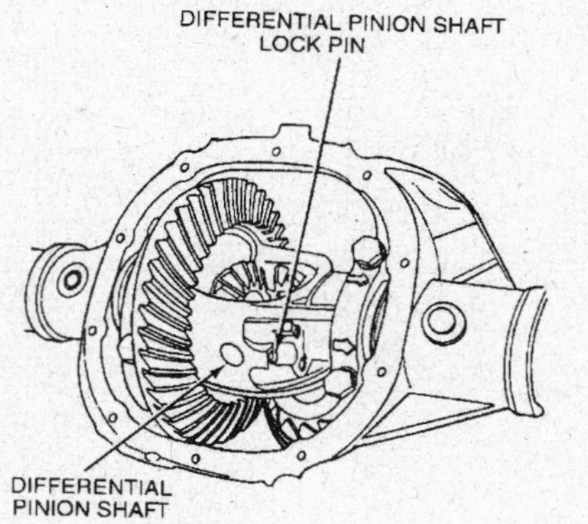

FM3039200211000X

Fig. 7 Differential pinion shaft removal. Town Car

Installation

1. Ensure O-ring is present on spline end of axle shaft.
2. Carefully slide axle shaft into axle housing. Use extreme caution to not damage bearing seal or ABS sensor ring.
3. Start splines into side gear and push firmly until button end of axle shaft can be seen in differential case.
4. Install C-lock on button end of axle shaft splines. Push shaft outboard until splines engage and the C-lock seats in counterbore of differential side gear.
5. Position differential pinion shaft through case and pinion gears, aligning hole in shaft with lock bolt hose. Apply rear axle lubricant E0AZ-19554-BA, or equivalent, to pinion shaft lock bolt. Tighten to specifications.
6. Install cover and tighten to specifications.
7. Install ABS speed sensor, rotors and calipers. Tighten to specifications.

REAR HALFSHAFT

REPLACE

MARK VIII

Do not begin this removal procedure unless following parts are available; new hub retainer nut; new inboard CV joint stub shaft circlip and new differential oil seal. Once removed, these parts must not be reused during assembly. Their torque holding ability is diminished during removal.

1. Remove wheel cover/hub cover and remove hub retainer nut, then loosen wheel nuts.
2. Raise and support vehicle on a frame contact hoist.
3. Remove rear wheel and tire assembly.
4. Remove anti-lock brake sensors.
5. Pull back on parking brake release lever and at same time pull on cable. This will slacken cable so cable end can be removed from brake caliper attachment.
6. Remove upper and lower brake caliper mounting bolts.
7. Remove caliper assembly from rotor, then carefully wire caliper to brake junction bracket.
8. Remove brake rotor push nuts and remove rotor.
9. Remove upper control arm bolts and nuts, then wire upper control arm to upper shock absorber so that it does not damage CV joint boots when halfshaft is removed.
10. Using a paint marker, mark position of lower control arm in relation to knuckle with lower bushings in their relaxed position. When upper control arm bolt is removed from knuckle, lower bushings will return to their relaxed positions. **Failure to mark this position will result in bushing wind-up on assembly and incorrect ride height, causing misalignment and premature tire wear.**
11. Install hub remover T81P-1104-C, or equivalent, to hub studs, **Fig. 8.**
12. Turn wrench counterclockwise until halfshaft is free in hub.
13. Remove lower control arm mounting bolts.
14. Remove knuckle assembly while supporting outboard CV joint and boot. Carefully rest halfshaft on lower control arm.
15. Insert CV joint removal tool No. T89P-3514-A, or equivalent, between differential housing and CV joint. Push tool outward until CV joint becomes free from differential side gear. **Extreme care must be taken to prevent damage to the differential oil seal, differential housing, sensor ring and/or CV joint and boot.**
16. Remove halfshaft from vehicle, then plug differential housing to prevent loss of lubricant.
17. Reverse procedure to install, noting the following:
    a. Install new differential oil seal and circlip on inboard CV joint.
    b. Ensure to align reference marks on lower control arm to marks on knuckle/bushing assembly.
    c. **On models equipped with rear disc brakes,** tighten caliper mounting bolts to specifications.
    d. **On models equipped with anti-lock brakes,** tighten brake sensor mounting bolts to specifications.

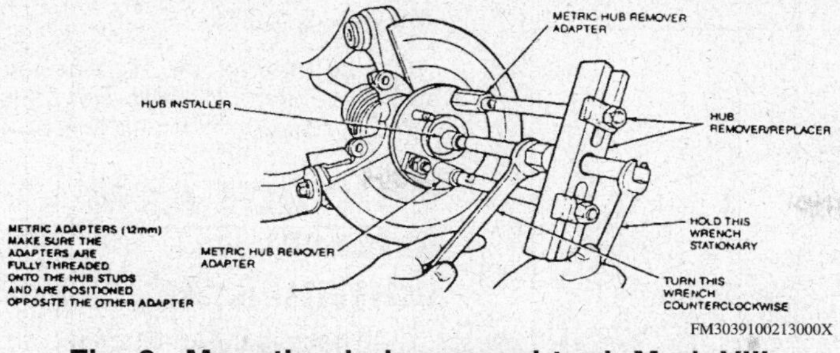

Fig. 8 Mounting hub removal tool. Mark VIII

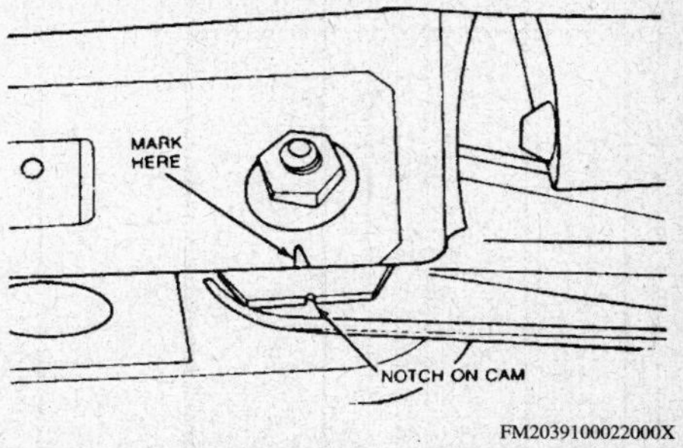

Fig. 9 Marking toe adjustment cam. Continental

PROPELLER SHAFT

REPLACE

MARK VIII

1997

To maintain proper drive line balance, mark the driveshaft, universal joints, slip yoke and companion flange before removing the shaft assembly so it can be reinstalled in its original position.

1. Remove companion flange to drive pinion flange mounting bolts.
2. Pull driveshaft rearward until slip yoke clears transmission extension housing.
3. Reverse procedure to install.

1998

1. Lower fuel tank. Refer to "Fuel Pump, Replace" in the "4.6L Engine" section.
2. Remove mounting bolts and sub frame center support member.
3. Remove sub frame crossmember.
4. Place an index mark on rear axle universal joint flange and driveshaft centering socket yoke.
5. Separate driveshaft centering socket yoke from rear axle universal joint flange.
6. Remove driveshaft.
7. Reverse procedure to install.

TOWN CAR

To maintain proper drive line balance, mark the driveshaft, universal joints, slip yoke and companion flange before removing the shaft assembly so it can be reinstalled in its original position.

1. Remove companion flange to drive pinion flange mounting bolts.
2. Pull driveshaft rearward until slip yoke clears transmission extension housing.
3. Reverse procedure to install.

STRUT

REPLACE

CONTINENTAL

1. Place the air suspension switch in the Off position before performing any work, or whenever raising the rear suspension.
2. Position suitable jack or hoist under vehicle, then raise just enough to contact body.
3. Disconnect air suspension electrical wiring and all related parts that will interfere with strut removal.
4. Loosen, but do not remove, the strut to inner body mounting nuts.
5. Raise and support vehicle, then remove wheel and tire assembly.
6. Remove brake hose to strut bracket mounting clip, then position hose aside.
7. If applicable, remove stabilizer bar mounting hardware and insulators, then separate stabilizer bar from link.
8. If applicable, remove tension strut to spindle mounting nut, washer and insulator, then move spindle rearward until it can be separated from tension strut.
9. Mark position of notch on toe adjustment cam, **Fig. 9.**
10. Remove strut to spindle pinch bolt, then using a pry bar or other suitable tool, separate pinch joint as necessary to allow for strut removal.
11. Disengage strut from pinch joint, then lower vehicle as necessary to allow removal of upper mounting nuts.
12. Remove strut from vehicle.
13. Reverse procedure to install.

TENSION STRUT

REPLACE

CONTINENTAL

1. If necessary, disconnect air suspension electrical wiring and all related parts that will interfere with tension strut removal.
2. Raise vehicle on frame contact hoist using lift pads located rearward of front wheels and forward of rear wheels. Raise hoist only enough to contact body.
3. Loosen, but do not remove, the upper strut to inner body mounting nuts, then raise and support vehicle.
4. Remove wheel and tire assembly.
5. Remove tension strut to spindle and tension strut to body mounting nuts.
6. While moving spindle rearward, remove tension strut from vehicle.
7. Reverse procedure to install, using new washers and bushings.

SHOCK ABSORBER

REPLACE

MARK VIII

Turn air suspension switch off before replacing shock absorber.

1. Open luggage compartment to gain access to upper shock absorber attachment.
2. Remove rubber cap from shock absorber stud, then remove nut, washer and insulator.
3. Raise vehicle and support rear axle.
4. Remove lower shock absorber protective cover, then remove cross bolt and nut from lower shock absorber mounting bracket.
5. From underneath vehicle, compress shock absorber to clear hole in upper shock tower, then remove shock absorber. **These models are equipped with gas pressurized shock absorbers which extend unassisted during removal. Do not apply heat or flame to the shock absorber tube during removal.**
6. Reverse procedure to install. Tighten mounting bolts to specifications.

TOWN CAR

Turn air suspension switch off before raising vehicle.

1. Raise and support vehicle.
2. Support rear axle with suitable jack.
3. Release air pressure from air springs.
4. Remove shock absorber upper mounting nut, washer and insulator, **Figs. 10 and 11.**
5. Remove self-locking mounting nut from lower shock absorber stud, discard nut.
6. Remove shock absorber.
7. Reverse procedure to install.

COIL SPRING

REPLACE

TOWN CAR

1997

1. Raise rear of vehicle and support at frame side sills. Support rear axle with a suitable jack.
2. Disconnect shock absorbers and stabilizer bar from axle housing, **Fig. 10.**
3. Disconnect righthand parking brake cable from righthand upper arm retainer.
4. Lower the axle housing until coil springs are released.
5. Remove springs and insulators, **Fig. 10.**
6. Reverse procedure to install.

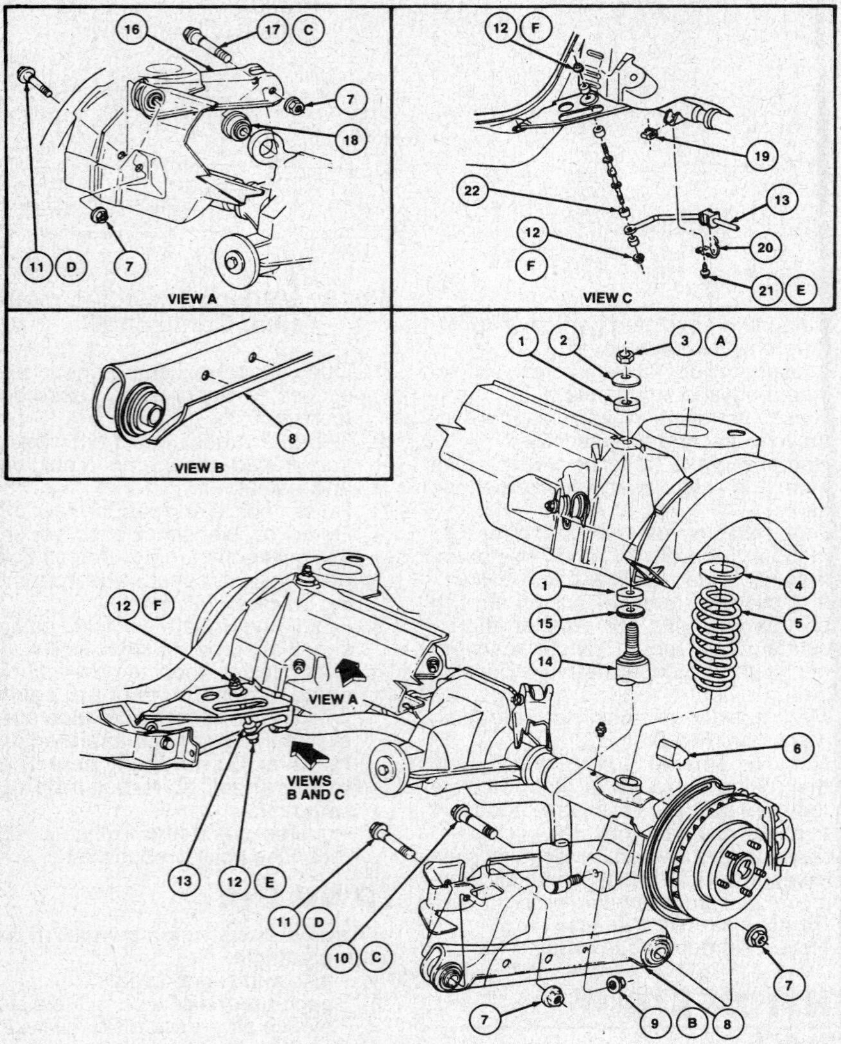

Item	Description
1	Grommet (2 Req'd)
2	Washer (2 Req'd)
3A	Nut (2 Req'd)
4	Insulator (2 Req'd)
5	Coil Spring (2 Req'd)
6	Bumper (2 Req'd)
7	Nut (2 Req'd)
8	Lower Arm Assy (2 Req'd)
9B	Nut (2 Req'd)
10C	Bolt (2 Req'd)
11D	Bolt (2 Req'd)
12F	Nut (4 Req'd)
13	Stabilizer Bar Assy
14	Shock Assy (2 Req'd)
15	Washer (2 Req'd)
16	Upper Arm and Bushing Assy

Item	Description
17C	Bolt (2 Req'd)
18	Bushing (2 Req'd)
19	Bolt (2 Req'd)
20	Bracket (2 Req'd)
21E	Screw (2 Req'd)
22	Bushing (8 Req'd)
A	Tighten to 21.2-28.8 N·m (16-21 Lb-Ft)
B	Tighten to 76.5-103.5 N·m (56.4-76.3 Lb-Ft)
C	Tighten to 140-180 N·m (103-132 Lb-Ft)
D	Tighten to 162-203 N·m (119-149 Lb-Ft)
E	Tighten to 21-29 N·m (16-21 Lb-Ft)
F	Tighten to 17-23 N·m (13-17 Lb-Ft)

FM2039600061000X

Fig. 10 Rear suspension components. 1997 Town Car

1998–2000

These models are equipped with an air spring, refer to " Active Suspension Systems" for air spring replacement.

CONTROL ARM

REPLACE

CONTINENTAL

1. If necessary, disconnect air suspension electrical wiring and all related parts that will interfere with control arm removal.
2. Raise and support vehicle.
3. Mark position of notch on toe adjustment cam, **Fig. 9.**
4. Remove control arm to spindle mounting bolt, nut, and washer.
5. Remove control arm to body mounting bolt and nut, then the control arm.
6. Reverse procedure to install. Inspect rear wheel alignment and adjust as necessary.

MARK VIII & TOWN CAR

Lower

1. Turn air suspension switch to off position, then raise and support vehicle and remove wheel assembly.
2. Vent air springs to atmosphere by removing air spring solenoid.
3. Remove two air spring to lower control arm mounting bolts, then the air spring from lower arm.
4. Remove control arm to frame and control arm to axle bracket pivot bolts and nuts.
5. Remove lower control arm.
6. Reverse procedure to install.

Upper

Always replace control arm in pairs. If one arm requires replacement, replace the same arm on the opposite side of the vehicle.

1. Turn air suspension switch off.
2. Raise and support vehicle, then disconnect rear height sensor from side arm. Note position of sensor adjustment bracket to aid in reassembly.
3. Remove upper arm to axle and upper arm to frame bracket pivot bolts and nuts.
4. Remove upper control arm.
5. Reverse procedure to install.

STABILIZER BAR

REPLACE

CONTINENTAL

1. If necessary, disconnect air suspension electrical wiring and all related parts that will interfere with stabilizer bar removal.
2. Raise and support vehicle.
3. Remove stabilizer bar to link mounting nuts, washers and insulators.
4. Remove U-bracket mounting bolts, then the stabilizer bar.
5. Reverse procedure to install, using new mounting parts.

MARK VIII & TOWN CAR

1. Turn air suspension switch off, then raise and support vehicle.
2. Remove both rear wheel and tire assemblies.
3. Disconnect emergency brake cables from stabilizer bar.
4. Remove both stabilizer bar link upper mounting nuts and insulators.
5. Remove links from stabilizer bar eyelets by pushing bar ends up and rotating out of the way.
6. Remove both stabilizer bar bracket bolts.
7. Remove brackets from T-slots in subframe.
8. Remove rear muffler hanger mounting nuts.
9. Remove stabilizer bar from vehicle.
10. Reverse procedure to install.

LATERAL LINK

REPLACE

1998–2000 TOWN CAR

1. Turn air suspension switch off.
2. Raise and support vehicle.
3. Support rear axle with a suitable jack.
4. Release air pressure from air spring, then disconnect height sensor from mounting bracket.
5. Remove and discard both lateral arm assembly pivot bolts and nuts to frame brackets, **Fig. 11.**
6. Remove and discard Watts link pivot nut.
7. Lower axle until Watts link is free of pivot stud.
8. Remove lateral arm assembly.
9. Remove and discard Watts link pivot stud.
10. Reverse procedure to install.

TECHNICAL SERVICE BULLETINS

WHINING NOISE HEARD FROM AXLE AT 50–65 MPH

1997 Town Car

On these models a whining noise my be heard from the axle while driving at 50–65 mph during acceleration, deceleration or cruise.

This condition may be caused by the axle transmitting the noise through the driveshaft and frame to the interior of the vehicle. To correct this condition proceed as follows:

1. Set tire pressure to specification. Tire pressure specification is listed on a label on passenger side rear door opening.
2. Inspect tires for uneven wear and installation of non-standard tires (i.e., snow tires). **Uneven tire wear or aggressive tread patterns can create noises similar to axle noise.**

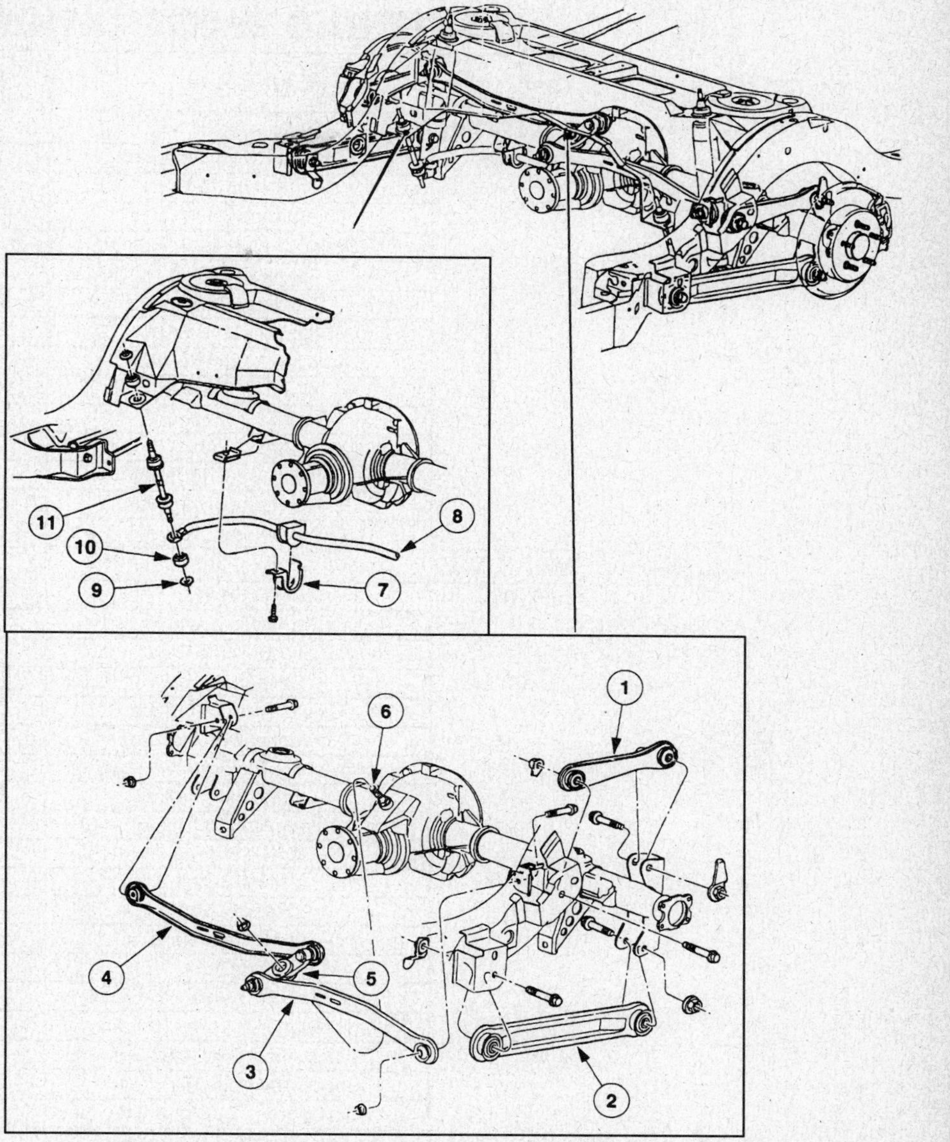

Item	Description
1	Rear Suspension Upper Arm
2	Rear Suspension Lower Arm
3	Lateral Arm, LH
4	Lateral Arm, RH
5	Watts Link Pivot

Item	Description
6	Watts Link Pivot Stud
7	Stabilizer Bar Bracket
8	Stabilizer Bar and Isolator Assy
9	Stabilizer Bar Link Retaining Nut
10	Stabilizer Bar Bushing
11	Stabilizer Bar Link

FM2039800062000X

Fig. 11 Rear suspension components. 1998–2000 Town Car

3. Drive vehicle until driveline is at operating temperature.
4. Evaluate for axle noise with overdrive cancel switch On (transmission must be in third gear). Perform a series of gentle accelerations, decelerations and cruises.
5. If axle noise is present, install frame brace kit (F7AZ-4B410-AA) to No. 4 frame crossmember. Refer to instruction sheet included with kit.
6. Verify effectiveness of repair.

TIGHTENING SPECIFICATIONS

Year	Component	Torque/Ft. Lbs.
CONTINENTAL		
1997–2000	Arm Inner Pivot Retainer	45–65
	Control Arm To Body	45–65
	Control Arm To Spindle	42–57
	Spring Clamp To Spindle	10–15
	Spring To Stud	10–15
	Stabilizer Bar Link	60–84②
	Stabilizer U-Bracket	25–37
	Strut Top Mount To Body	19–26
	Strut To Spindle	51–70
	Strut To Top Mount	35–50
	Stud To Arm	17–24
	Tension Strut To Body	35–50
	Tension Strut To Spindle	35–50
	Wheel Lug Nuts	85–104
MARK VIII		
1997–98	ABS Sensor	14–20
	Air Spring To Lower Arm	25–35
	Brake Backing Plate	20–40
	Caliper Mount	80–100
	Clevis Bracket To Axle	55–70
	Differential Bearing Cap	70–85
	Differential Pinion Shaft Lock	15–30
	Lower Arm To Axle	90–100
	Lower Arm To Frame	80–105
	Oil Filler Plug	15–30
	Pivot Bolts	100
	Rear Cover	①
	Rear Muffler Hanger	17–24
	Ring Gear	70–85
	Sensor Lower Bracket To Frame	84–120②
	Sensor Upper Bracket To Frame	10–12
	Shock Absorber Cross Bolt	59
	Shock Absorber To Frame	17–27
	Shock Absorber To Clevis Bracket	45–60
	Shock Absorber Upper Mount	24–26
	Stabilizer Bar Bracket To Subframe	25–34
	Stabilizer Bar To Axle	13–20
	Stabilizer Bar To Body	13–18
	Upper Arm To Axle	70–100
	Upper Arm To Frame	80–105
	Wheel Lug	85–104

Continued

TIGHTENING SPECIFICATIONS—Continued

Year	Component	Torque/Ft. Lbs.
TOWN CAR		
1997	Air Spring To Lower Arm	25–35
	Brake Backing Plate	20–40
	Clevis Bracket To Axle	55–70
	Differential Bearing Cap	70–85
	Differential Pinion Shaft Lock	15–30
	Lower Arm To Axle	90–100
	Lower Arm To Frame	80–105
	Oil Filler Plug	15–30
	Pivot Bolts	100
	Rear Cover	①
	Rear Muffler Hanger	17–24
	Ring Gear	70–85
	Sensor Lower Bracket To Frame	84–120②
	Sensor Upper Bracket To Frame	10–12
	Shock Absorber To Clevis Bracket	45–60
	Shock Absorber To Frame	17–27
	Stabilizer Bar Bracket To Subframe	25–34
	Stabilizer Bar To Axle	13–20
	Stabilizer Bar To Body	13–18
	Upper Arm To Axle	70–100
	Upper Arm To Frame	80–105
	Wheel Lug	85–104
1998–2000	Height Sensor Mounting Bracket To Lateral Arm	9–12
	Lateral Arm To Frame Bracket	65–88
	Lateral Arm To Watts Link Pivot	60–77
	Lower Suspension Arm To Axle Bracket	95–127
	Lower Suspension Arm To Frame Bracket	95–127
	Shock Absorber To Axle Bracket	57–75
	Shock Absorber To Upper Mount Nut	26–34
	Stabilizer Bar Bracket To Axle	16–21
	Stabilizer Link Nut To Stabilizer Bar	13–16
	Stabilizer Link Upper Nut To Frame	13–16
	Upper Suspension Arm To Axle Bracket	65–88
	Upper Suspension Arm To Frame Bracket	95–127
	Watts Link Pivot	158–212
	Watts Link Pivot Stud	189–211
	Wheel Lug	85–105

① — Torque plastic cover, 15–20 ft. lbs.; metal cover, 25–35 ft. lbs.

② — Inch lbs.

Front Suspension & Steering

NOTE: On Air Bag Equipped Models, Refer To " Air Bag System Precautions" Located In The Front Of This Manual For System Disarming & Arming Procedures.

INDEX

PRECAUTIONS

AIR BAG SYSTEMS

Refer to "Air Bag System Precautions" in the front of this manual for system disarming and arming procedures.

AIR SUSPENSION SYSTEM

Always place the air suspension switch in the Off position before performing any work, or whenever raising the front suspension.

WHEEL BEARING

ADJUST

MARK VIII & TOWN CAR

On these models the wheel bearings are preset and cannot be adjusted.

WHEEL BEARING

REPLACE

MARK VIII & TOWN CAR

1. Raise and support front of vehicle, then remove wheel and tire assembly.
2. Remove grease cap from hub.
3. Remove brake caliper and suspend from chassis with wire. Do not allow caliper to hang from brake hose.
4. Remove push clips, if equipped, then remove brake rotor, **Fig. 1.**
5. Remove hub nut, then remove hub and bearing assembly. If difficulty is encountered, use front hub remover tool No. T81P-1104-C, or equivalent, to remove hub and bearing assembly.
6. Reverse procedure to install. A new hub and bearing mounting nut should be installed. Tighten hub bearing nut to specifications.

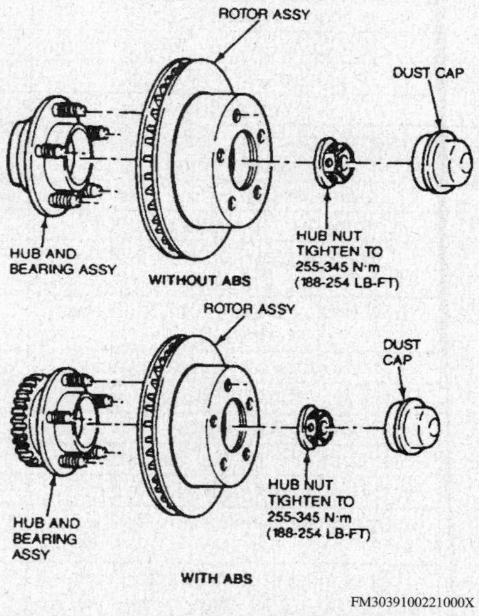

Fig. 1 Hub & bearing assembly. Mark VIII & Town Car

BALL JOINT INSPECTION

UPPER

Town Car

1. Raise car on floor jacks placed beneath lower control arms.
2. Grasp lower edge of tire and move wheel in and out.
3. As wheel is being moved in and out, observe upper end of spindle and upper arm.
4. Any movement between upper end of spindle and upper arm indicates ball joint wear and loss of preload. If such movement is observed, replace upper ball joint. **During the foregoing check, the lower ball joint will be unloaded and may move. Disregard all such movement of the lower joint. Also, do not mistake loose wheel bearings for a worn ball joint.**

LOWER

Mark VIII

1. Raise and support vehicle under subframe.
2. Attach dial indicator at ball joint to be checked so as to measure lateral movement between the spindle and the arm. Either upper or lower ball joint may be checked in this manner.
3. Hold tire at top and bottom and slowly move tire in and out. Note reading on dial indicator. If reading exceeds .015 inch, replace ball joint.

Town Car

These models are equipped with lower ball joint wear indicators. To check ball joint for wear, support vehicle in normal driving position with both ball joints loaded. Observe the checking surface of the ball joint. If the checking surface is inside the cover, replace the ball joint.

BALL JOINT

REPLACE

MARK VIII

These ball joints are not serviceable. If they require replacement, the control arm and ball joint must be replaced as an assembly. Tighten ball joint stud to specifications

TOWN CAR

1. Raise and support vehicle, then remove wheel and tire assembly. Position jack stands under both sides of

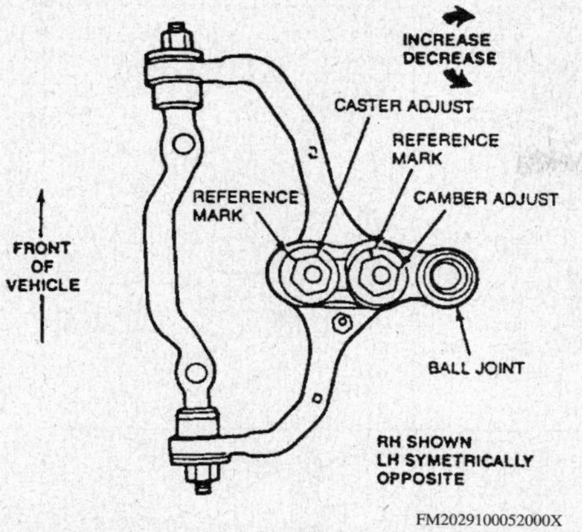

Fig. 2 Upper control assembly. Town Car

frame just to the rear of lower control arm.
2. Position a suitable jack under lower control arm.
3. Remove nut from upper ball joint to steering knuckle pinch bolt, then tap out pinch bolt.
4. Mark positions of caster and camber adjusting cams for use during installation, **Fig. 2.**
5. Remove two bolts mounting ball joint to upper control arm.
6. Using a suitable pry bar, spread slot to release ball joint from steering knuckle and remove.
7. Reverse procedure to install. Align caster and camber marks made during removal. After completing installation, check front wheel alignment.

COIL SPRING

REPLACE

CONTINENTAL

Refer to "Strut, Replace" for coil spring replacement procedure.

TOWN CAR

1. Raise and support vehicle.
2. Remove wheel and tire assembly.
3. Disconnect stabilizer bar link from lower control arm.
4. Remove shock absorber.
5. Remove steering center link from Pitman arm.
6. Compress coil spring with a suitable spring compressor.
7. Remove two lower control arm pivot bolts and disengage arm from crossmember.
8. Remove spring from vehicle.
9. Reverse procedure to install. Tighten stabilizer bar to lower control arm nuts and lower control arm to crossmember bolts to specifications.

STRUT

REPLACE

CONTINENTAL

1. Remove hub nut and loosen the upper strut mounting nuts, **Fig. 3.**

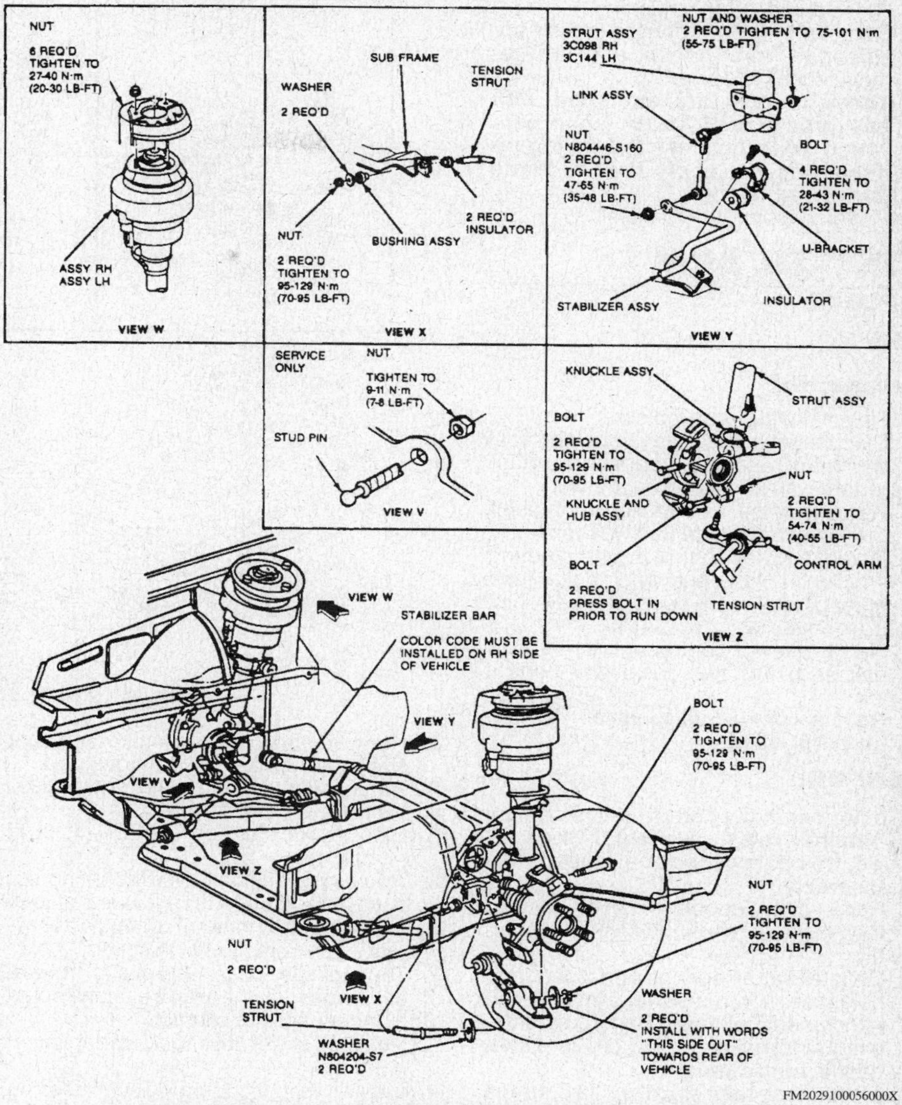

Fig. 3 Front suspension components. Continental

2. Raise and support vehicle. **Do not lift vehicle from lower control arm.**
3. Disconnect air suspension electrical wiring and all related parts that will interfere with strut removal.
4. Remove wheel and tire assembly.
5. Remove brake caliper and suspend with wire, then disconnect tie rod end.
6. Remove stabilizer bar link nut, then remove link from strut.
7. Remove lower control arm to steering knuckle pinch nut and bolt, then spread joint as necessary and disengage control arm from knuckle.
8. Using a suitable hub installation/removal tool, press axle from hub/rotor assembly. Wire axle shaft as necessary to maintain level position. **Do not permit axle shaft to move outward during disengagement from hub, since damage to CV joints could result.**
9. Remove strut to steering knuckle pinch bolt, then spread joint and remove steering knuckle and hub assembly.
10. Remove strut upper mounting nuts, then remove strut from vehicle.
11. Reverse procedure to install. Tighten to specifications.

SHOCK ABSORBER

REPLACE

MARK VIII

These models are equipped with gas pressurized shock absorbers which extend unassisted during removal. Do not apply heat or flame during removal.

1. Raise and support vehicle.
2. Remove shock actuator.
3. Remove upper shock mount to body nuts from inside luggage compartment.
4. Remove bolt and nut at lower arm, then remove shock absorber.
5. Reverse procedure to install.

TOWN CAR

1. Remove nut, washer and bushing from upper end of shock absorber.

2. Raise and support vehicle.
3. Remove screws mounting shock absorber to lower control arm and remove shock absorber.
4. **These models are equipped with gas pressurized shock absorbers which extend unassisted during removal. Do not apply heat or flame during removal.**
5. Reverse procedure to install.

CONTROL ARM

REPLACE

LOWER

Continental

1. Raise and support vehicle.
2. Disconnect air suspension electrical wiring and all related parts that will interfere with control arm removal.
3. Remove wheel and tire assembly, then the tension strut nut and washer.
4. Remove lower control arm to steering knuckle pinch nut and bolt, then spread joint and separate ball joint from knuckle.
5. Remove lower control arm inner pivot bolt and nut, then the lower control arm.
6. Reverse procedure to install. Tighten to specifications.

Mark VIII

Do not begin procedure unless a new hub retainer nut is available. Once removed, this part cannot be reused during assembly.

1. Raise and support front of vehicle, then remove rear knuckle/hub assembly.
2. Deflate rear air springs and disengage height sensor from lower arm ball stud attachment (lefthand only). Ensure the integral lower air spring clip is disengaged from lower arm.
3. Disconnect rear stabilizer bar straps from emergency brake cables (both sides).
4. Remove rear stabilizer bar link nuts at their lower arm attachment ends.
5. Remove link bushings and push link ends up and out of lower arm, then rotate bar and link assembly out of the way.
6. Mark toe adjustment cam-to-subframe position. Loosen both pivot attachment nuts at lower arm to subframe positions but do not remove bolts.
7. Remove shock absorber to lower control arm bolt.
8. Remove inner pivot bolts and nuts.
9. Remove lower control arm from vehicle.
10. Reverse procedure to install, noting the following:
    a. Tighten lower control arm to toe compensating link nut to specification.
    b. Ensure air spring assembly is fully seated and the spring is not kinked.

Town Car

1. Raise and support front of vehicle, then remove front wheels.

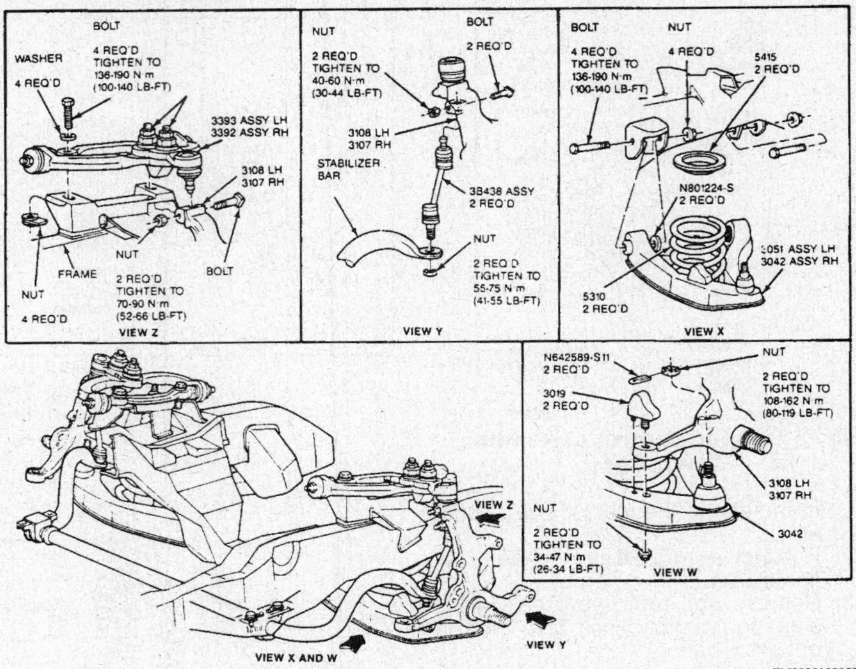

Fig. 4 Front suspension. Town Car

2. Remove brake caliper, rotor, dust shield and ABS sensor, if equipped.
3. Remove jounce bumper, if equipped.
4. Remove shock absorber.
5. Disconnect steering center link from pitman arm.
6. Remove lower ball joint mounting nut cotter pin, then loosen lower ball joint nut one or two times, **Fig. 4.** Do not remove nut from stud at this time.
7. Tap spindle boss sharply to relieve stud pressure, then tap near lower stud to loosen stud in spindle.
8. Position a suitable jack under lower control arm.
9. Install suitable coil spring compression tool, then remove coil spring.
10. Remove ball joint nut, then the lower control arm assembly.
11. Reverse procedure to install, noting the following:
    a. Tighten ball joint mounting nut specifications.
    b. Ensure coil spring is properly aligned, **Fig. 4.**
    c. Tighten control arm to crossmember mounting bolts and nuts to specifications.
    d. Check wheel alignment.

UPPER

Mark VIII

1. Raise and support vehicle.
2. Remove wheel and tire assembly, **Fig. 5.**
3. Support knuckle and hub assembly.
4. Support knuckle and hub assembly so it cannot swing outward.
5. Remove inner and outer pivot bolts and nuts at upper control arm.
6. Reverse procedure to install. Tighten inner pivot nut to specification.

Town Car

1. Raise and support vehicle, then remove wheel and tire assembly. Position jack stands under both side of frame just to the rear of lower control arm.
2. Position a suitable jack under lower control arm.
3. Remove nut from upper ball joint to steering knuckle pinch bolt, then tap out pinch bolt.
4. Mark positions of caster and camber adjusting cams for use during installation, **Fig. 2.**
5. Using a suitable pry bar, spread slot to release ball joint from steering knuckle.
6. Remove upper control arm mounting bolts, then remove upper arm assembly, **Fig. 4.**
7. Reverse procedure to install. Align caster and camber marks made during removal. After completing installation, check front end alignment.

STABILIZER BAR

REPLACE

CONTINENTAL

1. Raise and support vehicle.
2. Remove stabilizer bar link to strut and link to bar mounting nuts.
3. Remove stabilizer bar mounting brackets, then the stabilizer bar. It may be necessary to move steering gear from subframe and lower rear of subframe to gain access to mounting brackets.
4. Reverse procedure to install. Tighten to specifications.

MARK VIII

1. Turn air suspension switch off, then raise and support vehicle.

2. Remove both rear wheel and tire assemblies.
3. Disconnect emergency brake cables from stabilizer bar.
4. Remove both stabilizer bar link upper mounting nuts and insulators.
5. Remove links from stabilizer bar eyelets by pushing bar ends up and rotating out of the way.
6. Remove both stabilizer bar bracket bolts.
7. Remove brackets from T-slots in subframe.
8. Remove rear muffler hanger mounting nuts.
9. Remove stabilizer bar from vehicle.
10. Reverse procedure to install.

TOWN CAR

1. Raise and support vehicle.
2. Remove stabilizer bar mounting clamps, then the stabilizer bar mounting bolts from each stabilizer link.
3. Remove stabilizer bar assembly, **Fig. 4.**
4. Reverse procedure to install.

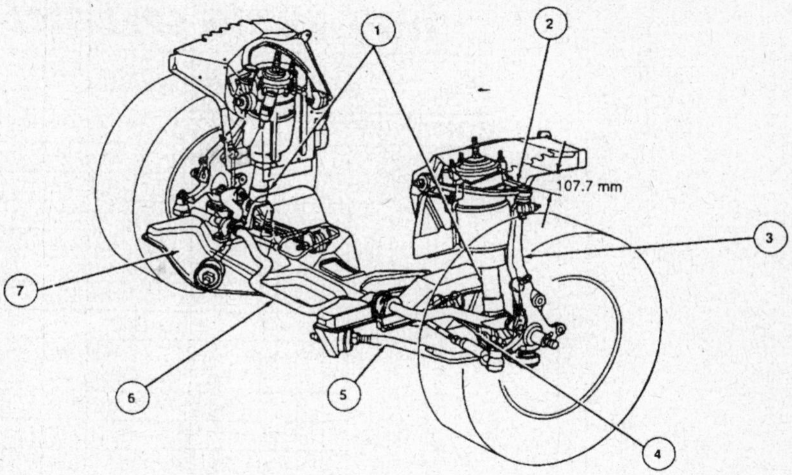

Item	Description	Item	Description
1	Spring / Shock Assy	4	Lower Control Arm
2	Upper Control Arm	5	Tension Strut (2 Req'd)
3	Spindle	6	Stabilizer Bar
		7	Front Subframe Assy

FM2029100054000X

Fig. 5 Front Suspension. Mark VIII

POWER STEERING GEAR

REPLACE

CONTINENTAL

1. Remove steering column boot attachments, then the intermediate shaft mounting bolts and shaft.
2. Remove secondary steering column boot from inside of passenger compartment.
3. Raise and support vehicle.
4. Remove tie rod ends from spindle, then gear to subframe mounting bolts.
5. Remove both height sensor attachments, then both rear subframe to body mounting bolts.
6. Remove exhaust pipe to catalytic converter.
7. Carefully lower subframe assembly approximately four inches.
8. Remove heat shield band and fold down shield.
9. Rotate gear to clear bolts from subframe and pull left to allow room for line fitting removal.
10. Remove line fittings, then drain using a suitable pan.
11. Remove lefthand sway bar link, then gear assembly through lefthand wheel housing.
12. Reverse procedure to install.

TOWN CAR

1. Remove stone shield, if equipped.
2. Disconnect pressure and return lines from steering gear. Plug lines and ports in gear to prevent entry of dirt.
3. Remove two bolts that secure flex coupling to steering gear and to column.
4. Raise car and remove sector shaft nut.
5. Use a puller to remove pitman arm.
6. Support steering gear, then remove mounting bolts.
7. Work steering gear free of flex coupling and remove it from car.
8. Reverse procedure to install.

MARK VIII

1. Raise and support vehicle, then remove front wheel and tire assemblies.
2. Remove cotter pins at outer tie rod ends and castellated nuts at each end. Discard cotter pins.
3. Separate tie rod end studs from spindles using tie rod end remover, 3290-D, or equivalent.
4. Place suitable container under vehicle, then disconnect and plug power steering return line hose.
5. Disconnect power steering pressure line at intermediate fitting.
6. Remove steering shaft mounting bolt.
7. Remove rack to subframe bolts and nuts.
8. Lower rack as necessary to remove pressure line inlet tube. Remove and discard plastic seal on inlet tube.
9. Cut tie strap securing pressure line to each tube.
10. Remove steering rack from vehicle.
11. Reverse procedure to install. Tighten steering rack mounting bolts and steering shaft mounting bolt to specifications.

POWER STEERING PUMP

REPLACE

CONTINENTAL

1. Loosen tensioner assembly and rotate tensioner pulley clockwise.
2. Remove belt from alternator and power steering pulley.
3. Remove three bolts mounting pump to bracket and remove pump.
4. Reverse procedure to install.

MARK VIII

1. Disconnect fluid return hose from reservoir and drain power steering fluid into a container.
2. Remove pressure hose from pump fitting. Do not remove fitting from pump.
3. Disconnect belt from pulley. If necessary, remove pulley from pump installing pulley removal tool No. T75L-3733-A, or equivalent, so small diameter threads engage in pump shaft. While holding small hex head, rotate tool nut to remove pulley. Do not apply in and out pressure on pump shaft as this will damage the internal thrust areas.
4. Remove pump.
5. If pulley was removed, install tool and while holding small hex head, turn tool nut clockwise to install pulley. Pulley must be flush within .010 inch of the end of the pump. Do not apply in and out pressure on shaft. Remove tool.

TOWN CAR

1. Disconnect power steering pump return line and allow power steering pump fluid to drain into a suitable container.
2. Disconnect power steering pump pressure hose from pump fitting.
3. Disconnect drive belt from power steering pump pulley, remove pulley, then remove pump.
4. Reverse procedure to install. **Torque** pump to mounting bracket bolts to 30–45 ft. lbs. **On Ford model CII power steering pump, torque** pressure hose to pump fitting to 10–15 ft. lbs. Endplay on this fitting is normal and does not indicate a loose fitting.

TIGHTENING SPECIFICATIONS

Year	Component	Torque/Ft. Lbs.
CONTINENTAL		
1997–2000	Control Arm To Knuckle	40–55
	Control Arm To Sub-Frame	70–95
	Front Bolts To Support Bracket	30–41
	Intermediate Shaft To Steering Column	15–25
	Outlet Fitting To Valve Cover	25–34
	Pivot Bolt	45–57
	Pressure Hose Tube Nut To Pump Pressure Fitting	20–25
	Pump To Bracket	30–45
	Return Hose To Pump Hose Clamp	8–24
	Stabilizer Bar Bracket To Sub-Frame	21–32
	Stabilizer Bar Link Assembly To Bar	35–48
	Stabilizer Bar Link Assembly To Strut	55–75
	Strut To Knuckle	70–95
	Strut Top Mount To Body	22–32
	Strut To Top Mount	35–50
	Support Bracket To Cylinder Head	15–22
	Tension Strut To Control Arm	70–95
	Tension Strut To Sub Frame	70–95
	Tie Rod Ball Socket Assembly To Rack	55–65
	Tie Rod End To Spindle Nut	35–47
	Tie Rod End To Steering Knuckle	23–25
	Wheel Lug	85–104
MARK VIII		
1997–98	Air Compressor To Bracket	30–40①
	Ball Joint To Spindle	100–120
	Compressor Bracket To Frame	30–40①
	Front Bolts To Support Bracket	30–45
	Hub Bearing	189–254
	Inner Pivot Nut	50–68
	Lower Arm To No. 2 Crossmember	110–150
	Lower Control Arm To Toe Compensating Link	83–113
	Pinion Bearing Plug	40–60
	Pinion Bearing Locknut	30–40
	Pivot Bolt	30–45
	Pressure Hose Fitting To Pump	10–15
	Pump Bracket To Rear Support	18–24
	Pump To Bracket	30–45
	Rear Support To Engine Head	30–45
	Return Hose To Pump	12–24①
	Sensor Lower Attachment To Arm	8–12
	Sensor Upper Attachment To Frame	26–34
	Shock Strut Upper Mount	55–92
	Shock Upper Mount To Body	62–75
	Spindle To Shock Strut	140–200
	Stabilizer Bar Mounting Clamp	40–55
	Stabilizer Bar To Lower Arm	9–12
	Steering Gear To No. 2 Crossmember	90–100
	Steering Rack	100–144
	Steering Shaft	20–30
	Support Bracket To Engine	30–45

Continued

TIGHTENING SPECIFICATIONS—Continued

Year	Component	Torque/Ft. Lbs.
MARK VIII		
1999-98	Support Bracket To Water Pump	30–45
	Tie Rod Ball Socket Assembly To Rack	55–65
	Tie Rod End To Jam Nut	35–50
	Tie Rod End To Spindle	35–47
	Wheel Lug	85–104
TOWN CAR		
1997–2000	Air Compressor To Bracket	30–40①
	Ball Joint To Spindle	100–120
	Compressor Bracket To Frame	30–40①
	Front Bolts To Support Bracket	30–45
	Hub Bearing	189–254
	Inner Pivot Nut	50–68
	Lower Arm To No. 2 Crossmember	110–150
	Lower Control Arm To Toe Compensating Link	83–113
	Pinion Bearing Locknut	30–40
	Pinion Bearing Plug	40–60
	Pivot Bolt	30–45
	Pressure Hose Fitting To Pump	10–15
	Pump Bracket To Rear Support	18–24
	Pump To Bracket	30–45②
	Rear Support To Engine Head	30–45
	Return Hose To Pump	12–24①
	Sensor Lower Attachment To Arm	8–12
	Sensor Upper Attachment To Frame	26–34
	Shock Upper Mount To Body	62–75
	Shock Strut Upper Mount	55–92
	Spindle To Shock Strut	140–200
	Stabilizer Bar Mounting Clamp	40–55
	Stabilizer Bar To Lower Arm	9–12
	Steering Gear To No. 2 Crossmember	90–100
	Steering Rack	100–144
	Steering Shaft	20–30
	Support Bracket To Engine	30–45
	Support Bracket To Water Pump	30–45
	Tie Rod Ball Socket Assembly To Rack	55–65
	Tie Rod End To Jam	35–50
	Tie Rod End To Spindle	35–47
	Wheel Lug	85–104

① — Inch lbs.

② — On Ford model CII power steering pump, 10–15 ft. lbs.

Wheel Alignment

INDEX

PRELIMINARY INSPECTION

Prior to performing the front wheel alignment, a preliminary inspection should be made to determine the condition of the vehicle's suspension components. The following checks and procedures should be made prior to performing front wheel alignment:

1. Vehicle must be leveled by performing the air suspension system test.
2. Inflate tires to specified pressure (cold).
3. Check vehicle ride height.
4. Inspect all suspension and steering components for looseness.
5. Check existing caster, camber, and toe settings prior to alignment.
6. Check all suspension fasteners for proper tightness.
7. Alignment equipment must be capable of four wheel alignment.
8. Alignment rack must be leveled to 1/16 of an inch, side to side and front to rear and be equipped with wheel runout compensation.

Do not attempt to adjust alignment by heating or bending.

FRONT WHEEL ALIGNMENT

MARK VIII & TOWN CAR

Caster and camber can be adjusted by loosening the bolts that attach the upper suspension arm to the shaft at the frame side rail, and moving the arm assembly in or out in the elongated bolt holes. Since any movement of the arm affects both caster and camber, both factors should be balanced against one another when making the adjustment.

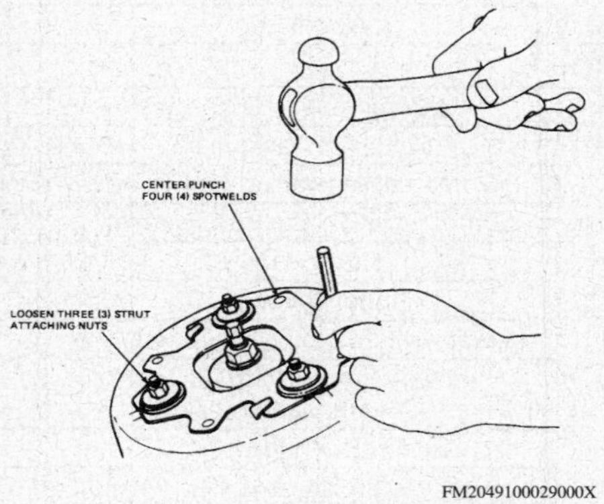

Fig. 1 Caster & camber adjustment tools. Mark VIII & Town Car

Caster

1. To adjust caster, install adjusting tool, **Fig. 1.**
2. Loosen both upper arm inner shaft mounting bolts and move either front or rear of the shaft in or out as necessary to increase or decrease caster angle. Then tighten bolt to retain adjustment.

Camber

1. Loosen both upper arm inner mounting bolts and move both front and rear ends of shaft inward or outward as necessary to increase or decrease camber angle.
2. Tighten bolts and recheck caster and readjust if necessary.

Toe-In

Position the front wheels in their straight-ahead position. Then turn both tie rod adjusting sleeves an equal amount until the desired toe-in setting is obtained.

CONTINENTAL

Toe-In

To adjust toe-in, lock steering wheel in straight ahead position using suitable steering wheel holder. Loosen, then slide off small outer clamps from steering boot to prevent boot from twisting during adjustment procedure. Loosen tie rod adjusting and jam nuts, then adjust length of left and right tie rods until each wheel has 1/2 the desired total toe specification. After adjustment is completed, tighten jam nuts, reinstall outer clamps and remove steering wheel holder.

REAR WHEEL ALIGNMENT

CONTINENTAL

Camber

Camber is factory set and cannot be adjusted.

Toe-In

Toe-In is adjusted by rotating the cams located inside the rear inner lower control arm bushings.

VEHICLE RIDE HEIGHT

Refer to the "Active Suspension Systems" section for ride height adjustment procedures.

LS

NOTE: Refer To The Rear Of This Manual For Manufacturer's Special Service Tool Suppliers.

INDEX OF SERVICE OPERATIONS

Specifications

GENERAL ENGINE SPECIFICATIONS

Year	Engine		Fuel System	Bore x Stroke, Inches	Comp. Ratio	Net HP @ RPM	Maximum Torque, Ft. Lbs. @ RPM	Normal Oil Pressure, psi
	Liter	VIN Code①						
2000	3.0L	S	SFI	3.50 x 3.13	10.5	210 @ 6500	205 @ 4750	—
	3.9L	A	SFI	3.38 x 3.35	10.5	252 @ 6100	267 @ 4300	—

①— The eighth digit of the VIN denotes engine code.

TUNE UP SPECIFICATIONS

Year	Engine/VIN①	Spark Plug Gap	Firing Order	Curb Idle Speed	Fuel Pump Pressure, psi	Valve Clearance, Inch	
						Intake	Exhaust
2000	3.0L/S	.051–.057	1-4-2-5-3-6	②	30–65	.0069–.0089	.0128–.0148
	3.9L/A	.039–.034	1-5-4-2-6-3-7-8	②	30–65	.0043–.0071	.0106–.0134

①— The eighth digit of the VIN denotes engine code.

②— Idle speed is electronically controlled and is non-adjustable.

FRONT WHEEL ALIGNMENT SPECIFICATIONS

Year	Caster Angle, Degrees				Camber Angle, Degrees				Toe-In, Degrees	Ball Joint Wear, Inch①
	Limits	Desired	Split		Limits	Desired	Split			
			Limits	Desired			Limits	Desired		
2000	+7.79 to +8.79	+8.29	-.7 to +.7	0	-.65 to +.35	-.15	-.7 to +.7	0	-.09 to +.41	1/32

①— Radial play.

REAR WHEEL ALIGNMENT SPECIFICATIONS

Year	Camber, Degrees		Toe-In, Degrees				Ball Joint Wear, Inch①
	Limits	Desired	Limits	Desired	Split Limits	Split Desired	
2000	-1.75 to -.25	-1.75 to -.25	-.13 to +.37	+.12	-.01 to +.49	+.24	1/32

① — Radial play.

FLUID CAPACITIES & COOLING SYSTEM DATA

Year	Engine/ VIN③	Coolant Capacity, Qts.		Radiator Cap Relief Pressure, Lbs.	Thermo. Opening Temp.	Fuel Tank, Gals.	Engine Oil Refill, Qts.	Rear Axle, Pts.④	Transmission Oil	
		Less A/C	With A/C						Man. Trans., Pts.	Auto. Trans., Qts.
2000	3.0L/S	10.6	10.6	16	①	18	—	3	②	11.9
	3.9L/A	11.3	11.3	16	①	18	—	3	—	11.9

① — Thermostat begins to open at 192–199°F and is fully open at 219°F.

② — Fill transmission to .02 inch below lower edge of fill plug bore.

③ — The eighth digit of the VIN denotes engine code.

④ — Fill 1/8–3/16 inch from bottom of filler hole.

LUBRICANT DATA

Year	Lubricant Type					
	Transmission Manual	Transmission Automatic	Rear Axle	Power Steering	Brake System	Hydraulic Clutch Fluid
2000	—	Mercon V XT-5-Q-M	①	②	DOT 3	DOT 3

① — Use 75W-140 synthetic rear axle lubricant F1TZ–19580–B, or equivalent, meeting Ford specification WSL–M2C192–A.

② — Use Motorcraft Mercon multi-purpose ATF transmission fluid XT-2-QDX, or equivalent, meeting Ford specification Mercon.

Electrical

NOTE: On Air Bag Equipped Models, Refer To "Air Bag System Precautions" Located In The Front Of This Manual For System Disarming & Arming Procedures.

NOTE: Refer To "Computer Relearn Procedures " Located In The Front Of This Manual For Computer Relearn Procedures.

INDEX

PRECAUTIONS

AIR BAG SYSTEMS

Refer to "Air Bag System Precautions" in the front of this manual for system disarming and arming procedures.

BATTERY GROUND CABLE

Prior to service, disconnect battery ground cable and isolate as required.

ELECTROSTATIC DISCHARGE

Electronic modules are sensitive to electrical charges. Ensure modules are not exposed to these charges or damage may result.

MODULE CONFIGURATION

Newly released modules will require configuration after being installed on the vehicle. All configurable modules will be packaged in a kit which contains a warning label and multi-language sheet which lists requirements to configure the modules.

There are two types of configuration data. The first type is used by the module so that it can interact with the vehicle correctly. The second type is customer preference driven. These are items that the customer may or may not want to have enabled. To program customer driven preferences, a Ford service function card (FSF) and the New Generation Star Tester (NGS), tool No. 007-00500, or equivalents must be used to toggle preferences on or off.

The New Generation Star Tester (NGS), tool No. 007-00500, or equivalent, must be used to retrieve configuration data from the old module before it is removed from the vehicle. This information will be transferred into the new module so that the new module will contain the same settings as the old module.

The following modules require configuration when being replaced; ABS control module, ABS control module with traction control, interactive vehicle dynamic (IVD) module, instrument cluster, instrument cluster with message center, rear electronic module (REM), front electronic module (FEM), driver door module (DDM), dual automatic temperature control (DATC) module, remote emergency satellite cellular unit (RESCU) module, and the steering column lock module (SCLM) when PCM is replaced on manual transmission equipped models. If configuring PCM, the NGS tester flash cable tool No. 007-00531, or equivalent, must be used.

To perform the configuration process, proceed as follows:

1. Connect New Generation Star Tester tool No. 007-00500 with Ford service function (FSF) card to vehicle DLC.
2. Follow scan tool instructions to upload configuration data.
3. Install new module. **NGS will not retain configuration data for more than 24 hours.**
4. Download stored configuration information to new module using FSF card and NGS tester.
5. If unable to carry out configuration process, proceed as follows:
   a. Inspect for signs of electrical damage.
   b. If NGS does not communicate with vehicle, ensure program card is correctly installed, vehicle connections are secure and that ignition switch is in run position.
   c. If NGS still does not communicate with vehicle, diagnose module communications network concern.

FUSE PANEL & FLASHER LOCATION

BATTERY JUNCTION BOX

The battery junction box is located under the luggage compartment floor lining.

CENTRAL JUNCTION BOX

The central junction box is located under the righthand side of the instrument panel.

INTERIOR AUXILIARY JUNCTION BOX

The interior auxiliary junction box is located in the lefthand footwell. This junction

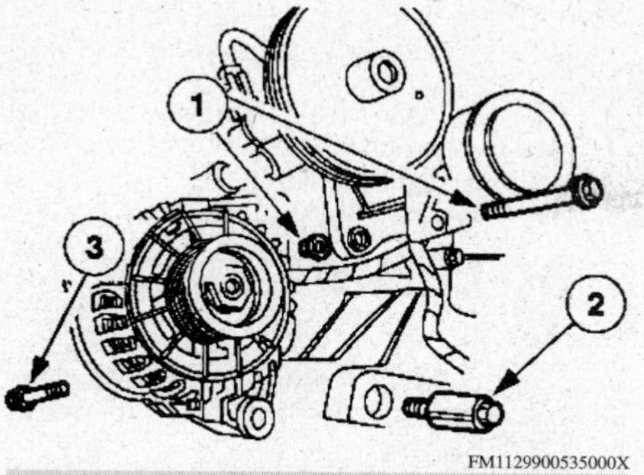

Fig. 1 Alternator tightening sequence. 3.9L engine

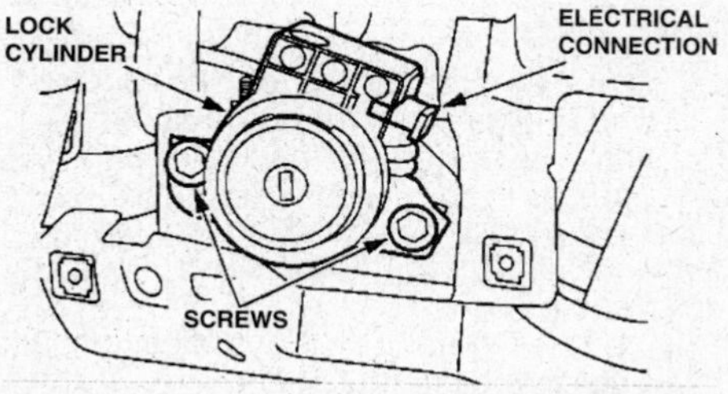

Fig. 4 Ignition switch lock cylinder assembly removal

box contains a power junction stud and the DLC.

UNDERHOOD AUXILIARY JUNCTION BOX

The underhood auxiliary junction box is located in the engine compartment on the righthand side.

TRAILER TOW AUXILIARY JUNCTION BOX

The trailer tow auxiliary junction box is located in the luggage compartment along the rear end of the vehicle.

FLASHER

The flashing function is controlled by the front electronic module. The module is located at the lefthand "A" pillar.

FUEL PUMP RELAY LOCATION

The fuel pump relay is located under the luggage compartment floor lining in the battery junction box.

STARTER

REPLACE

1. Raise and support vehicle.
2. Remove ground strap from starter mounting stud.
3. Remove starter cable cover from starter, then the starter cables.
4. Remove starter attaching bolts, then the starter.

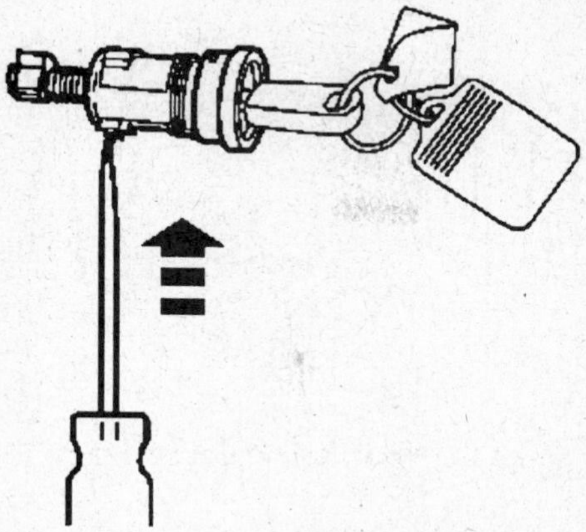

Fig. 2 Ignition lock cylinder removal

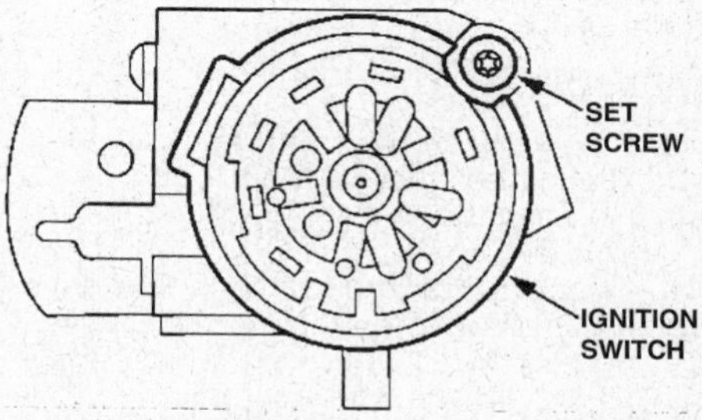

Fig. 5 Ignition switch removal

5. Reverse procedure to install. **Torque** starter attaching bolts to 18 ft. lbs.

ALTERNATOR

REPLACE

3.0L ENGINE

1. Remove accessory drive belt.
2. Raise and support vehicle.
3. Remove lower splash shield.
4. Support alternator, then remove attaching bolts.
5. Disconnect alternator electrical connections and remove alternator.
6. Reverse procedure to install noting the following:
   a. **Torque** alternator electrical connectors to 71 inch lbs.
   b. **Torque** alternator mounting bolts to 33 ft. lbs.

3.9L ENGINE

1. Remove air intake tube as follows:
   a. Remove engine appearance cover.
   b. Disconnect IAT sensor, breather hose and idle air control valve inlet tube.
   c. Remove air intake tube support nut and washer.
   d. Loosen tube clamps and remove tube.
2. Remove accessory drive belt.
3. Raise and support vehicle, then remove front lower splash shield.

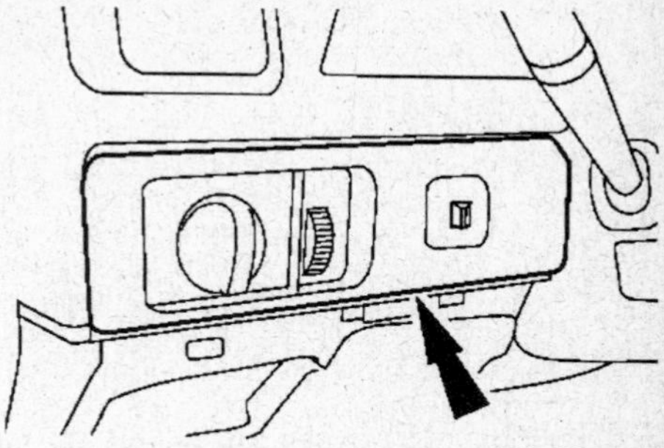

Fig. 3 Outer instrument panel finish panel removal

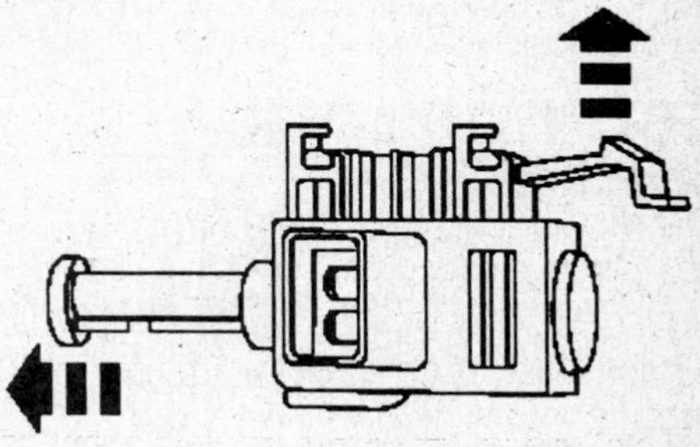

Fig. 6 Clutch pedal position switch

4. Support alternator, then remove attaching bolts.
5. Turn alternator as necessary, then remove positive cable from alternator.
6. Lower alternator and disconnect electrical connector.
7. Rotate alternator as necessary, then remove.
8. Reverse procedure to install noting the following:
   a. **Torque** alternator electrical connector to 71 inch lbs.
   b. **Torque** alternator attaching bolts to 15 ft. lbs. in sequence shown in **Fig. 1.**
   c. Tighten alternator attaching bolts in sequence an additional 90.°

IGNITION COIL

REPLACE

These engines use a coil on plug ignition system with an individual coil mounted on top of each spark plug.

3.0L ENGINE

1. Remove engine appearance cover.
2. If replacing righthand ignition coils, remove upper intake manifold as outlined under "Intake Manifold, Replace."
3. Disconnect coil electrical connector.
4. Remove coil attaching bolts, then the ignition coil.
5. Reverse procedure to install noting the following:
   a. Ensure coils are seated and boot is not damaged. If boot is damaged, coil must be replaced.

b. **Torque** coil attaching bolts to 53 inch lbs.

3.9L ENGINE

1. Remove engine appearance cover.
2. Remove air intake tube as follows:
   a. Remove engine appearance cover.
   b. Disconnect IAT sensor, breather hose and idle air control valve inlet tube.
   c. Remove air intake tube support nut and washer.
   d. Loosen tube clamps and remove tube.
3. Remove ignition coil cover.
4. Disconnect coil electrical connectors.
5. Remove coil attaching bolts, then the ignition coils.
6. Reverse procedure to install. **Torque** attaching bolts to 44 inch lbs.

IGNITION LOCK

REPLACE

1. Remove steering column lower cover.
2. Remove hood release handle attaching bolts, then the release handle assembly.
3. Remove lower dash heater duct from below steering column.
4. Remove steering column opening cover reinforcement.
5. Place ignition switch in run position.
6. Using a suitable screwdriver, depress ignition switch lock cylinder tab, **Fig. 2.**
7. Remove ignition switch lock cylinder.
8. Reverse procedure to install. Verify proper lock cylinder operation.

IGNITION SWITCH

REPLACE

1. Remove instrument cluster finish panel as follows:
   a. Adjust steering column to full tilt down and full extended position.
   b. Remove lower steering column cover, then the outer instrument panel finish panel, **Fig. 3.**
   c. Remove inner instrument panel finish panel.
   d. Remove instrument cluster finish panel attaching screws, then disconnect in-car air temperature sensor.
   e. Remove instrument cluster finish panel.
2. Disconnect ignition switch electrical connector and remove ignition switch lock cylinder attaching screws.
3. Remove ignition switch lock cylinder assembly, **Fig. 4.**
4. Ensure ignition switch is in off position.
5. Remove ignition switch set screw, then the ignition switch, **Fig. 5.**
6. Reverse procedure to install.

CLUTCH START SWITCH

REPLACE

1. Disconnect clutch pedal position switch electrical connector.
2. Lift switch retaining tag, then remove switch, **Fig. 6.**
3. Reverse procedure to install.

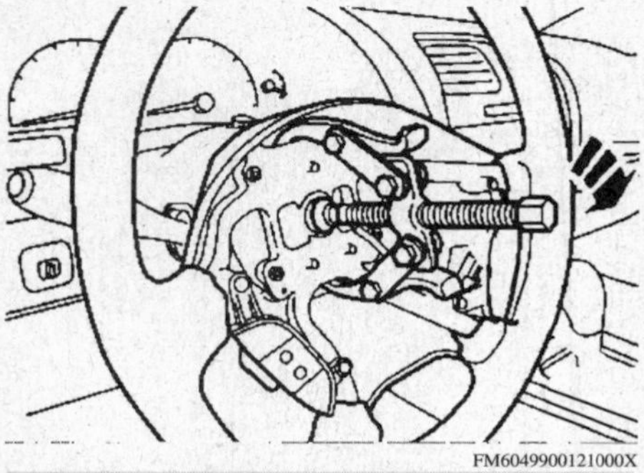

Fig. 7 Steering wheel removal

NEUTRAL SAFETY SWITCH

REPLACE

REMOVAL

1. Raise and support vehicle.
2. Remove exhaust system.
3. Remove body brace, then the heat shield.
4. Check and record front and rear driveshaft driveline angles as outlined under "Rear Axle & Suspension," "Driveline Angle Measurement."
5. Remove driveshaft as outlined under "Rear Axle & Suspension."
6. Support transmission with a suitable transmission jack. Ensure transmission is properly secured to jack using a safety chain.
7. Remove transmission mount, then lower transmission to gain access to neutral safety switch (digital TR sensor).
8. Disconnect shift cable.
9. Disconnect TR sensor electrical connector, then remove sensor.

INSTALLATION

1. Place TR sensor flush against boss on transmission case, then loosely install sensor attaching bolts.
2. Place manual lever in neutral position.
3. Align TR sensor using sensor alignment tool No. T97L-70010-A, or equivalent.
4. **Torque** sensor screws evenly to 89 inch lbs.
5. Reconnect TR sensor electrical connector.
6. Connect shift cable, then install rear mount.
7. Adjust shift cable as outlined under "Automatic Transmissions/ Transaxles."
8. Install driveshaft as outlined under "Rear Axle & Suspension."
9. Install exhaust system.

HEADLAMP SWITCH

REPLACE

1. Remove lower instrument panel steering column cover.
2. Remove outer instrument panel finish panel located to left of steering column.
3. Release four retaining clips, then remove headlamp switch from outer instrument panel finish panel.
4. Reverse procedure to install.

STOP LIGHT SWITCH

REPLACE

1. Remove instrument panel insulator.
2. Disconnect and remove brake pedal position switch.
3. Reverse procedure to install.

MULTI-FUNCTION SWITCH

REPLACE

1. Remove steering wheel as outlined under "Steering Wheel, Replace."
2. Remove upper and lower steering column shrouds.
3. Apply two strips of masking tape across air bag sliding contact to prevent rotation.
4. Depress three clips and position air bag sliding contact aside.
5. Disconnect multi-function switch electrical connector, then remove switch.
6. Reverse procedure to install.

STEERING WHEEL

REPLACE

1. Ensure front wheels are in straight ahead position.
2. Remove driver's air bag module as outlined under "Air Bag Systems."
3. Remove horn switch.
4. Loosen steering wheel attaching bolt.
5. Using differential bearing cone removal tool No. T77F-4220-B1, or equivalent, loosen steering wheel, **Fig. 7.**
6. Remove steering wheel puller, then the steering wheel attaching bolt and steering wheel. Discard steering wheel attaching bolt.
7. Reverse procedure to install. Install new steering wheel attaching bolt and **torque** to 30 ft. lbs.

INSTRUMENT CLUSTER

REPLACE

Prior to removal of instrument cluster, module configuration must be retrieved. Refer to "Module Configuration" for procedure.

1. Remove instrument cluster finish panel as follows:
   a. Adjust steering column to full tilt down and full extended position.
   b. Remove lower steering column cover, then the outer instrument panel finish panel, **Fig. 3.**
   c. Remove inner instrument panel finish panel.
   d. Remove instrument cluster finish panel attaching screws, then disconnect in-car air temperature sensor.
   e. Remove instrument cluster finish panel.

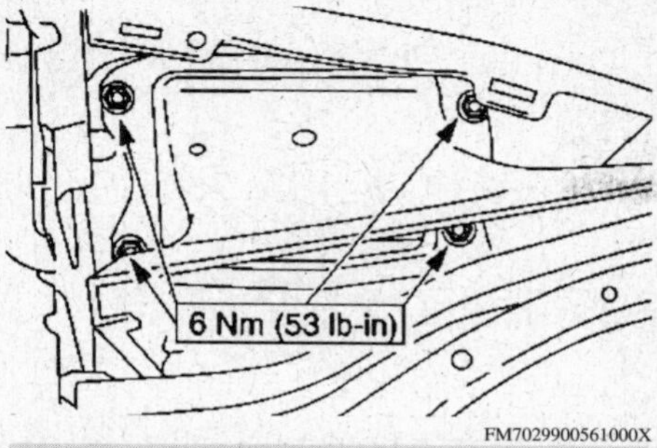

Fig. 8 Cabin air filter housing bolt locations

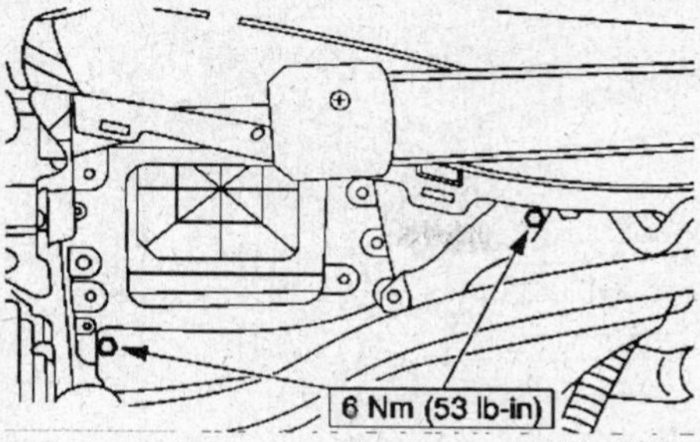

Fig. 9 Plenum panel removal

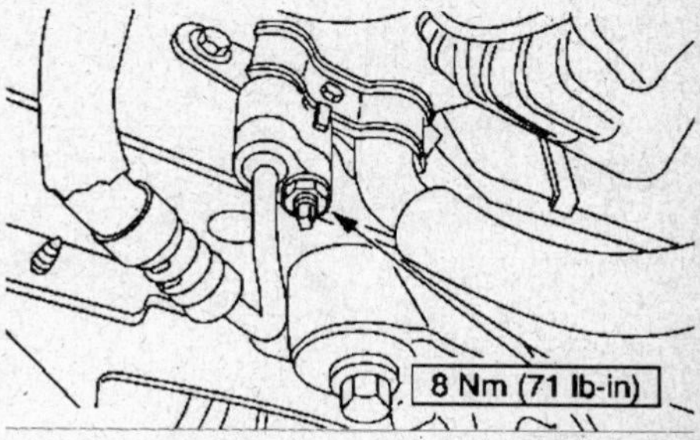

Fig. 10 Peanut fitting location

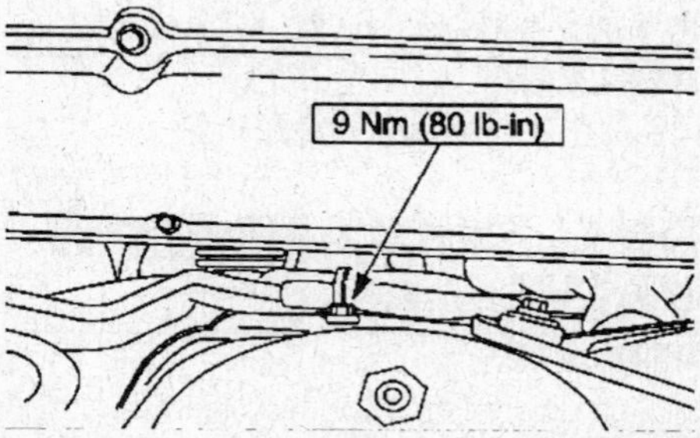

Fig. 11 A/C line bracket location (Part 1 of 2)

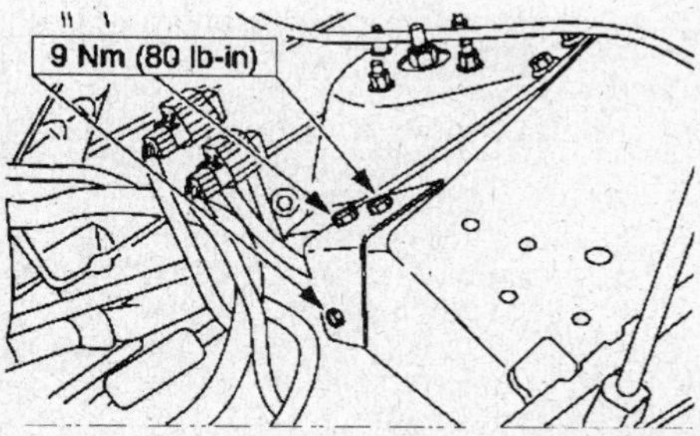

Fig. 11 A/C line bracket location (Part 2 of 2)

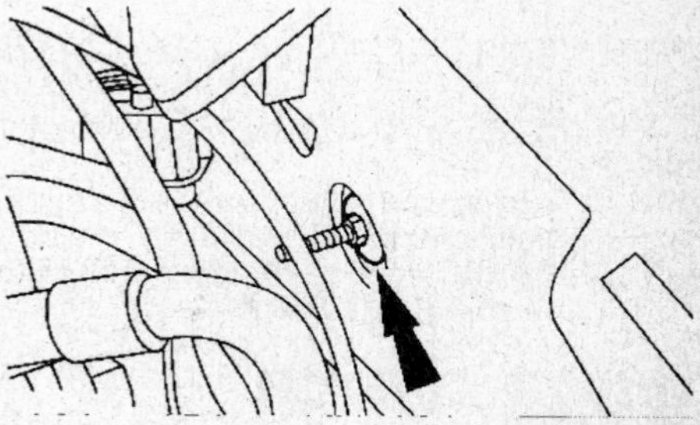

Fig. 12 Engine compartment evaporator housing bolt location (Part 1 of 3)

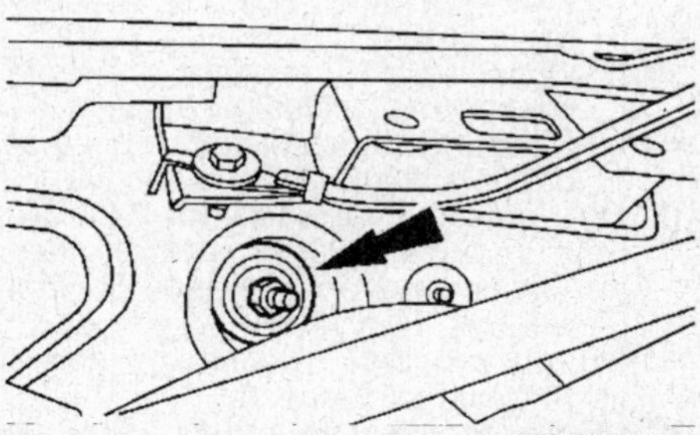

Fig. 12 Engine compartment evaporator housing bolt location (Part 2 of 3)

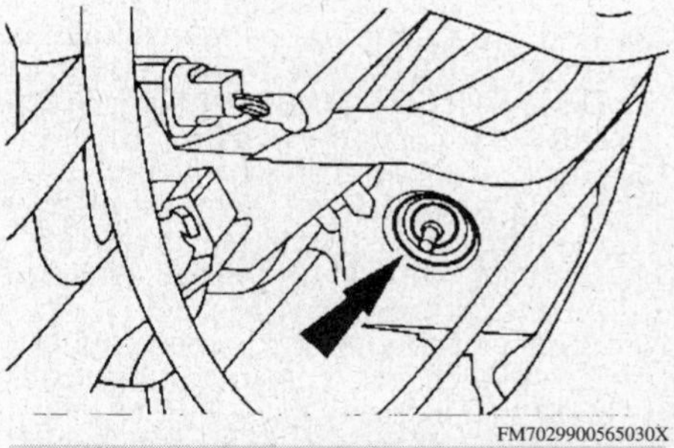

Fig. 12 Engine compartment evaporator housing bolt location (Part 3 of 3)

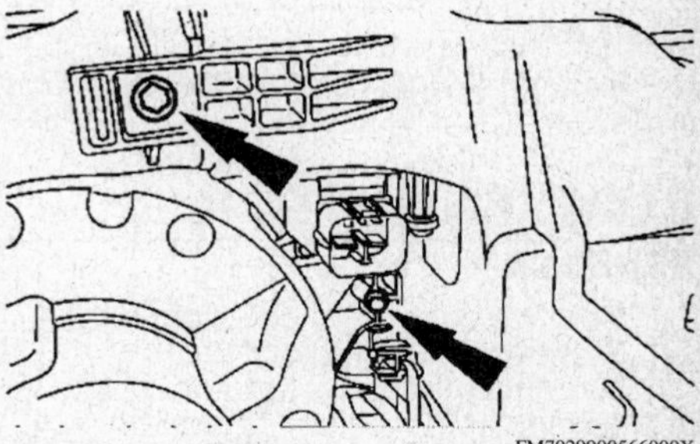

Fig. 13 Evaporator housing to air inlet housing screw location

2. Remove hood release handle.
3. Remove instrument panel steering column cover.
4. Remove floor heat duct.
5. Remove steering column reinforcement.
6. Loosen steering column attaching bolts and lower steering column.
7. Place a suitable cloth over upper steering column cover to prevent damage to instrument cluster lens.
8. Remove instrument cluster attaching bolts, then the instrument cluster.
9. Reverse procedure to install. Download module configuration from NGS tester into new module.

RADIO

REPLACE

1. Remove A/C register finish panel.
2. Remove ash tray finish panel.
3. Remove audio/climate control assembly attaching bolts.
4. Disconnect electrical connectors and antenna cable.
5. Remove audio/climate control unit.
6. Separate audio unit from audio/climate control assembly.
7. Reverse procedure to install.

WIPER MOTOR

REPLACE

1. Remove wiper arms.
2. Remove cowl vent screen as follows:
   a. Remove two part pin retainers and separate velcro attachment of rubber hinge cover to rear outboard corner of cowl vent screen.
   b. Lift cowl vent screen to release clips.
   c. Remove cowl vent screen.
3. Remove strut tower support brace.
4. Remove coolant overflow bottle and position aside.
5. Remove wiper mounting arm and pivot shaft bolts.
6. Disconnect drain boot from windshield wiper mounting arm and pivot shaft assembly.
7. Position windshield wiper mounting arm and pivot shaft assembly aside, then loosen upper windshield wiper motor bolt.
8. Rotate wiper output arm to 6 o'clock position.
9. Remove lower wiper motor bolts.
10. Rotate bottom of wiper mounting arm and pivot shaft assembly upward.
11. Remove windshield wiper mounting arm and pivot shaft assembly.
12. Remove remaining wiper motor attaching bolts, then the wiper motor.
13. Reverse procedure to install noting the following:

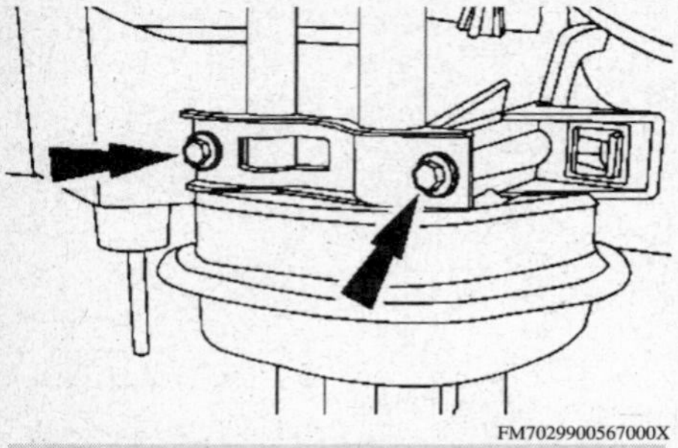

Fig. 14 Heater core cover screw location

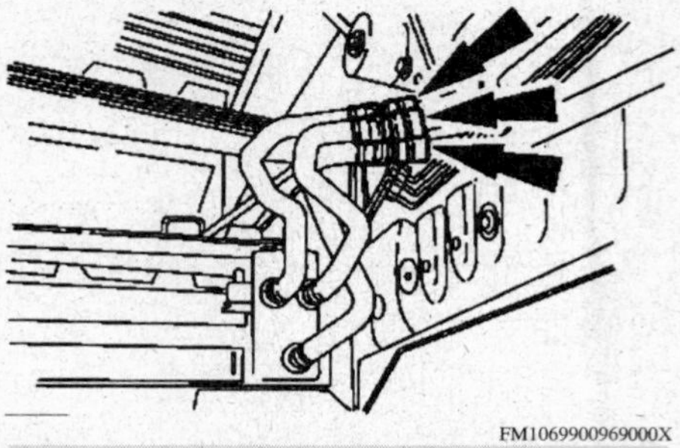

Fig. 15 Dual coolant flow valve

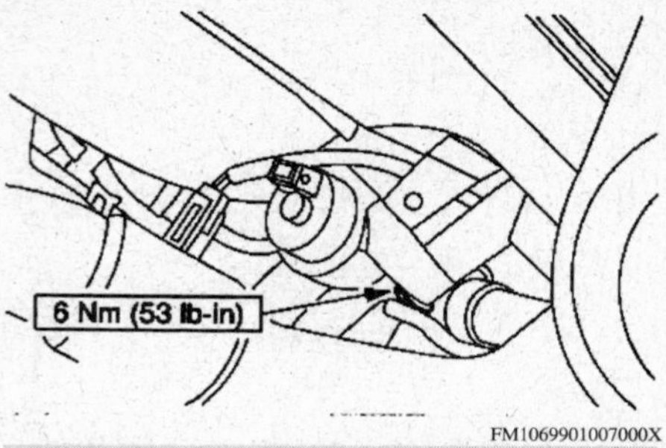

Fig. 16 Auxiliary coolant pump removal

a. **Torque** wiper pivot arm nuts to 18 ft. lbs.
b. **Torque** strut support brace bolts to 15 ft. lbs.
c. **Torque** mounting arm and pivot shaft bolts to 9 ft. lbs.
d. **Torque** wiper motor crank bolt and attaching bolts to 9 ft. lbs.

WIPER SWITCH

REPLACE

Refer to "Multi-Function Switch, Replace" for procedure.

WIPER TRANSMISSION

REPLACE

Refer to "Wiper Motor, Replace" for procedure.

BLOWER MOTOR

REPLACE

1. Remove passenger side floor duct.
2. Remove blower motor cover.
3. Disconnect blower motor electrical connector.
4. Remove blower motor.
5. Reverse procedure to install.

CABIN AIR FILTER

REPLACE

1. Remove righthand cowl cover.
2. Push on righthand corner of filter to release clip.
3. Release lefthand clip and remove cabin air filter.
4. Reverse procedure to install.

HEATER CORE

REPLACE

1. Recover A/C refrigerant as outlined under "Air Conditioning."
2. Disconnect heater hose assembly from heater core.
3. Remove cabin air filter plenum as follows:
   a. Remove cabin air filter as outlined under "Cabin Air Filter, Replace."
   b. Remove strut tower support brace.
   c. Remove filter housing attaching bolts, **Fig. 8.**
   d. Remove plenum panel attaching bolts, then the plenum panel, **Fig. 9.**
4. Disconnect coolant recovery line.
5. Remove forward heater hose mounting bolt at righthand shock tower.
6. Raise and support vehicle.
7. Remove rear heater hose mounting bolt from body side and position heater hose assembly aside.
8. Disconnect spring lock coupling using spring lock coupling tool T84L–19623–B, or equivalent.
9. Remove nut and disconnect peanut fitting, **Fig. 10.**
10. Remove peanut fitting bracket bolt.
11. Remove A/C line bracket bolts, **Fig. 11.**
12. Remove thermostatic expansion valve manifold and tube assembly.
13. Remove instrument panel as outlined under "Dash Panel Service."
14. Disconnect electrical connector at top of evaporator core housing.
15. Remove cowl top attaching bolt.
16. Remove evaporator housing attachment bolt.
17. Remove the following nuts located in engine compartment, **Fig. 12.**
18. Remove evaporator core housing.
19. Remove evaporator core housing to air inlet housing screws, **Fig. 13.**
20. Disengage clip and separate evaporator core housing from air inlet housing.
21. Remove housing gasket.
22. Remove nine screws, then disengage clip and separate evaporator core housing from air inlet housing.
23. Disconnect bypass door connector and position harness aside.
24. Remove screws as shown in **Fig. 14.**
25. Remove heater core.
26. Reverse procedure to install noting the following:
   a. Lubricate A/C O-ring seal using PAG refrigerant oil YN–12–C, F7AZ–19589–DA, or equivalent, meeting Ford specification WSH–M1C231–B.
   b. **Torque** A/C peanut fitting to 71 inch lbs.
   c. **Torque** expansion valve fitting to 15 ft. lbs.
   d. **Torque** evaporator housing to engine compartment nuts and cowl top attachment bolt to 62 inch lbs.
   e. **Torque** evaporator housing bolt to 44 inch lbs.
   f. Ensure heater hoses are correctly connected to heater core.

EVAPORATOR CORE

REPLACE

Refer to "Heater Core, Replace" for procedure.

DUAL COOLANT FLOW VALVE

REPLACE

1. Drain cooling system as follows:
   a. Ensure engine is cold.
   b. Wrap a suitable shop towel around pressure relief cap, then remove cap.
   c. **Ensure coolant does not come into contact with accessory drive belt.**
   d. Open radiator draincock and drain coolant into a suitable container.
   e. Disconnect coolant return hose at oil cooler if equipped.
2. **On models equipped with 3.9L engine,** remove auxiliary coolant pump as outlined under "Auxiliary Coolant Flow Pump, Replace."
3. **On all models,** disconnect coolant valve electrical connector.
4. Place identification marks on dual coolant flow valve for installation reference, **Fig. 15.**
5. Raise and support vehicle.
6. Remove coolant valve mounting nut and bolt.
7. Raise valve and disconnect coolant supply and return lines.
8. Remove coolant flow valve.
9. Reverse procedure to install.

AUXILIARY COOLANT FLOW PUMP

REPLACE

1. Drain cooling system as follows:
   a. Ensure engine is cold.
   b. Wrap a suitable shop towel around pressure relief cap, then remove cap.
   c. **Ensure coolant does not come into contact with accessory drive belt.**
   d. Open radiator draincock and drain coolant into a suitable container.
   e. Disconnect coolant return hose at oil cooler if equipped.

2. Disconnect auxiliary coolant pump electrical connector.
3. Remove coolant pump to fan shroud attaching bolts, **Fig. 16.**
4. Disconnect coolant pump hoses, then remove pump.
5. Reverse procedure to install. **Torque** auxiliary coolant pump attaching bolts to 53 inch lbs.

3.0L Engine

NOTE: On Air Bag Equipped Models, Refer To "Air Bag System Precautions" Located In The Front Of This Manual For System Disarming & Arming Procedures.

NOTE: Refer To "Computer Relearn Procedures " Located In The Front Of This Manual For Computer Relearn Procedures.

INDEX

PRECAUTIONS

AIR BAG SYSTEMS

Refer to "Air Bag System Precautions" in the front of this manual for system disarming and arming procedures.

BATTERY GROUND CABLE

Prior to service, disconnect battery ground cable and isolate as required.

FUEL SYSTEM PRESSURE RELIEF

1. Remove schrader valve cap and install fuel pressure gauge tool No. T80L-9974-B, or equivalent, to schrader valve.
2. Slowly open manual valve on pressure gauge and drain fuel into a suitable container.

QUICK DISCONNECT HOSES

R-CLIP

When working with R-clip type connections, **Fig. 1,** do not use tools to disconnect. Use of tools may deform clip components and could cause leaks.

To disconnect, bend shipping tab downward, **Fig. 1.** Spread R-clip and push clip into fitting. Separate fitting from tube.

To install, first inspect fitting and tube for damage and ensure connections are clean. Apply a light coat of clean 5W-30 motor oil to male end of tube. Insert R-clip into fitting. Align tube and fitting, then insert tube into fitting and push together until a click is heard. Pull on connection to ensure it is fully engaged.

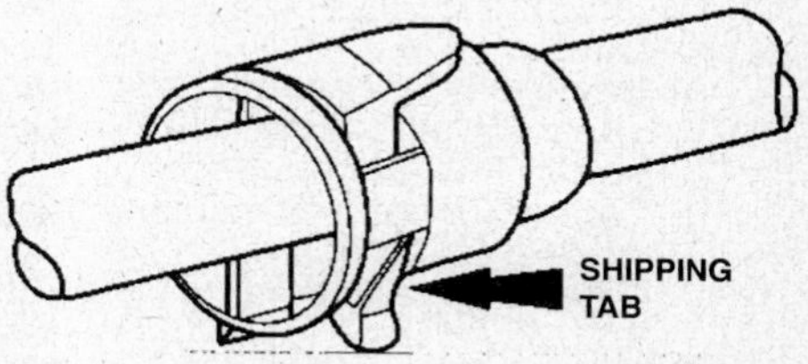

Fig. 1 R-clip connection

SPRING LOCK

When working with spring lock type connections, **Fig. 2,** spring lock tool set No. T84L-19623-B, or equivalent, must be used to disconnect fittings. When connecting spring lock type fittings, inspect and clean both coupling ends. Lubricate fuel line O-ring seals with clean 5W-30 motor oil. When connection is made, pull on line to ensure it is fully engaged.

VAPOR TUBE

To disconnect vapor tube connections, squeeze fitting (1) and disconnect vapor tube from fitting (2), **Fig. 3.** To connect, ensure fittings are clean and free from damage. Push tube onto fitting until it snaps into place. Pull on connection to verify fitting is secure.

COMPRESSION PRESSURE

Before performing compression test, ensure the following conditions are met:

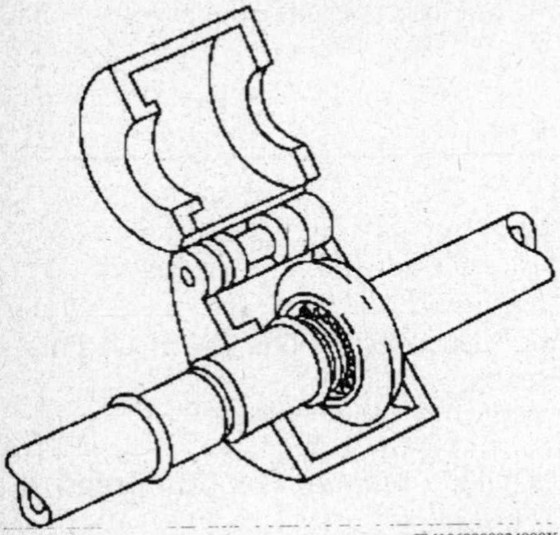
FM1069900924000X

Fig. 2 Spring lock connection

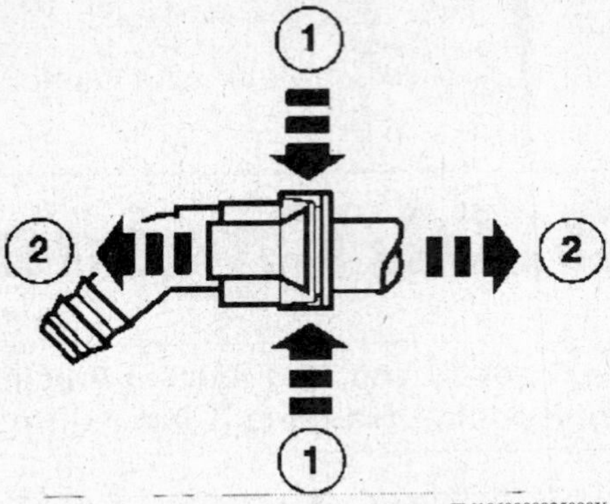

FM1069900925000X

Fig. 3 Vapor tube connection

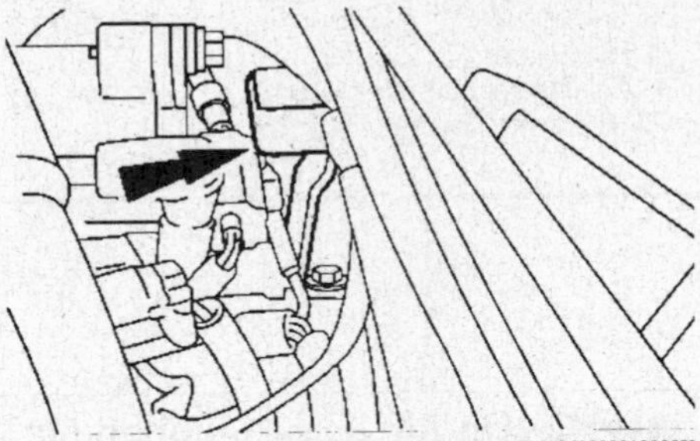
FM1069900913000X

Fig. 4 Wire harness bracket removal

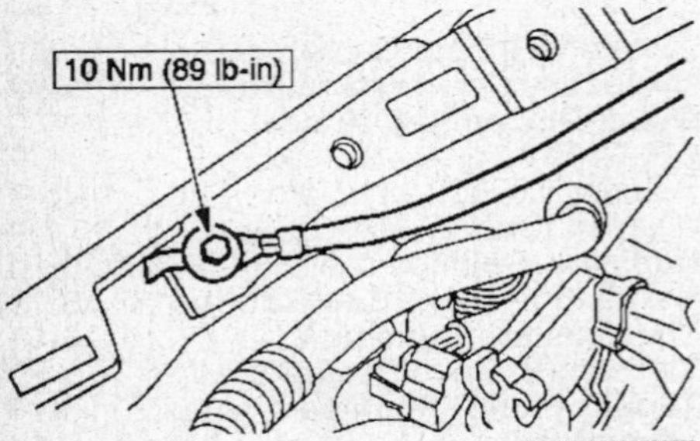

FM1069900915000X

Fig. 5 Ground strap location

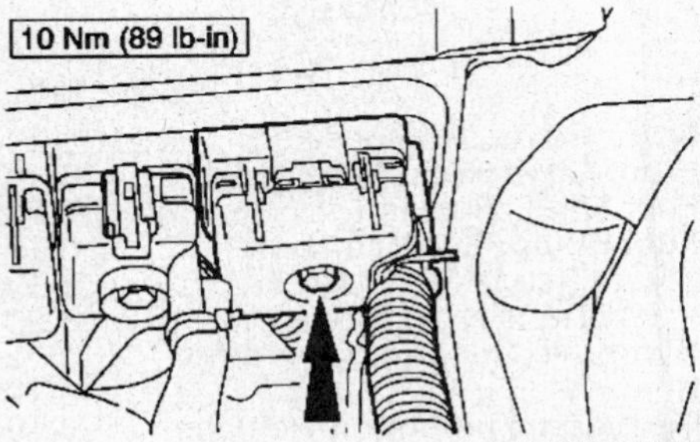

FM1069900916000X

Fig. 6 Main engine harness connector

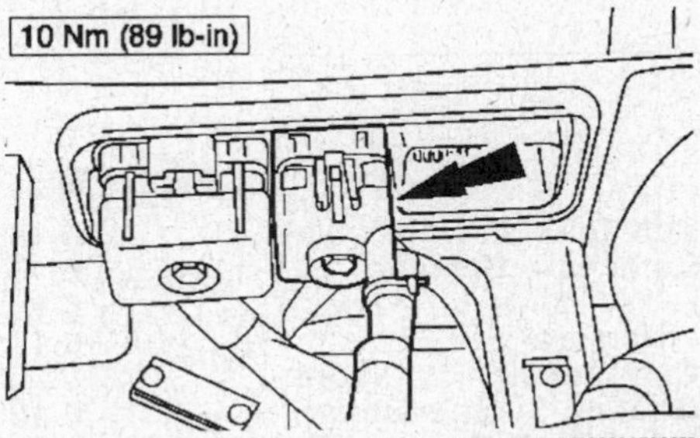

FM1069900917000X

Fig. 7 Main transmission harness connector

crankcase oil is of correct viscosity and at correct level, ensure battery is fully charged and engine is at normal operating temperature.

1. Turn ignition switch to off position.
2. Remove all spark plugs.
3. Set throttle plates to wide open position.
4. Install a suitable compression gauge in No. 1 cylinder.
5. Install an auxiliary starter switch in starting circuit.
6. With ignition switch off, use auxiliary starter switch to crank engine a minimum of five compression strokes.
7. Note number of compression strokes necessary to reach highest reading and record highest reading.
8. Repeat test on each cylinder, cranking engine same number of compression strokes.
9. Indicated compression pressures are considered within specifications if lowest reading cylinder is within 75 percent of highest reading.

ENGINE MOUNT

REPLACE

1. Remove cowl vent screen as outlined under "Wiper Motor, Replace."
2. Remove strut brace.
3. Remove wire harness bracket, **Fig. 4.**
4. Disconnect intake manifold tuning valve electrical connector.
5. Remove intake manifold tuning valve attaching bolts, then the valve.
6. Remove cabin air filter plenum as outlined under "Heater Core, Replace."
7. Remove engine mount upper nut.
8. Raise and support vehicle.
9. Remove engine mount lower nut.
10. Raise engine and remove mount.
11. Reverse procedure to install noting the following:
    a. **Ensure intake manifold tuning valve is fully seated into intake before installing bolts.**
    b. **Torque** intake manifold tuning valve to 89 inch lbs.
    c. **Torque** upper mount nut to 30 ft. lbs.
    d. **Torque** lower mount nut to 46 ft. lbs.

ENGINE

REPLACE

When carrying out operations which involve the removal and installation of the driveshaft, always check the joint angles and make the necessary adjustments as outlined under "Rear Axle & Suspension," "Driveline Angle Measurement."

1. Disconnect IAT sensor electrical connector.
2. Disconnect aspirator and PCV hose from air cleaner outlet tube.
3. Remove air cleaner outlet tube.
4. Remove engine appearance cover.
5. Drain cooling system as follows:
    a. Ensure engine is cold.
    b. Wrap a suitable shop towel around pressure relief cap, then remove cap.
    c. **Ensure coolant does not come into contact with accessory drive belt.**
    d. Open radiator draincock and drain coolant into a suitable container.
    e. **On models equipped with oil cooler,** disconnect coolant return hose at oil cooler.
6. **On all models,** recover A/C refrigerant as outlined under "Air Conditioning."
7. Remove upper radiator sight shield, then the upper radiator support brackets.
8. Disconnect A/C pressure switch connector.
9. Remove power steering reservoir bolts and position reservoir aside.
10. Disconnect fuel lines.
11. Disconnect brake aspirator vacuum hose, then remove right and left cowl trim panels.
12. Unclip chassis vacuum lines from support bracket, then disconnect lines.
13. Remove strut brace support.
14. Remove cabin air filter plenum as outlined under "Heater Core, Replace."
15. Disconnect main vacuum hose from rear of intake manifold.
16. Disconnect throttle and speed control cables and unclip from bracket.
17. Remove ground strap bolt, **Fig. 5.**
18. Disconnect main engine wiring harness and transmission harness connectors, **Figs. 6 and 7.**

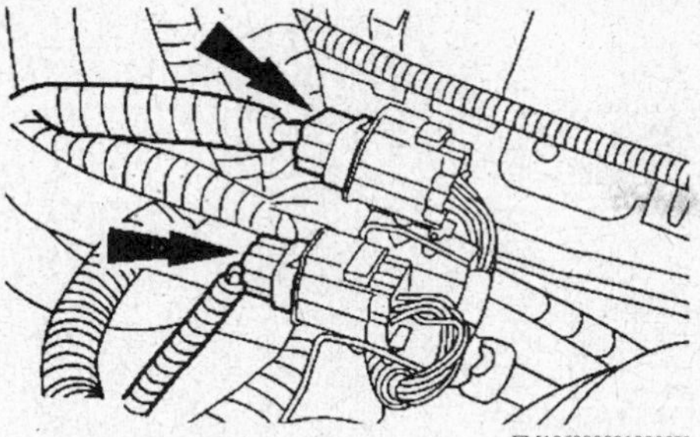

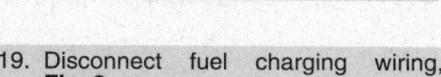

Fig. 8 Fuel charging wiring connectors

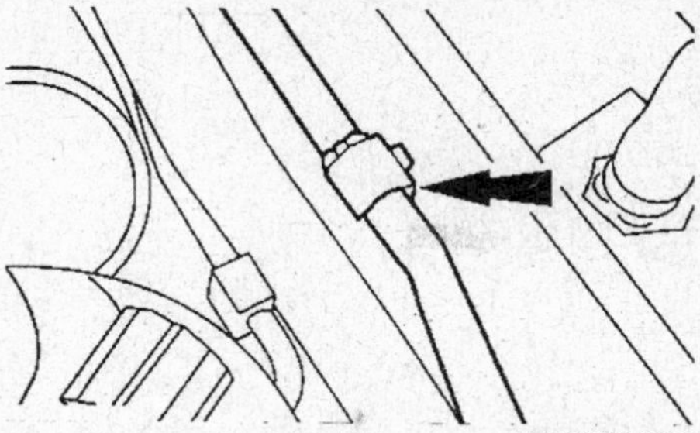

Fig. 9 Frame line location

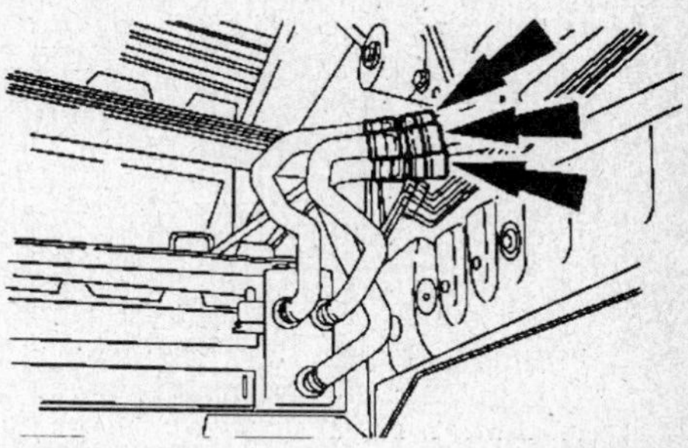

Fig. 10 Dual coolant flow valve

19. Disconnect fuel charging wiring, **Fig. 8.**
20. Disconnect wiring harness retainer from bracket.
21. Remove A/C line mounting bracket.
22. Remove hydraulic cooling fan reservoir and position aside.
23. Unclip line from frame as shown in **Fig. 9.**
24. Raise and support vehicle.
25. Drain engine oil.
26. Remove right and left splash shields.
27. Remove A/C manifold bolt, then position manifold aside.
28. Place reference marks on dual coolant flow valve coolant lines for installation reference.
29. Disconnect coolant hoses from dual coolant flow valve using quick disconnect tool No. T85T-18539-AH, or equivalent, **Fig. 10.**
30. Remove exhaust system and heat shields.
31. Remove driveshaft as outlined under "Rear Axle & Suspension."
32. Disconnect shift cable at transmission.
33. Remove shift cable bracket bolt.
34. Remove front tires.
35. Disconnect right and left front ABS sensors.
36. Remove front calipers as outlined under "Disc Brakes " and position aside.
37. Disconnect stabilizer link lower mounts and upper ball joints.
38. Remove lower strut mount bolts.
39. Disconnect starter wiring harness at starter.
40. Disconnect power steering pressure electrical connectors.
41. Remove steering shaft clamp bolt.
42. Remove torque converter nuts.
43. Disconnect hose as shown in **Fig. 11.**
44. Support rear of vehicle using suitable safety stands.
45. Support engine, transmission, front and center crossmembers and cooling system with a suitable powertrain lift and transmission support bracket.
46. Remove four transmission crossmember bolts.
47. Remove four front and four center crossmember bolts.
48. Lower engine and transmission assembly from vehicle.
49. Install two engine lifting brackets tool No. 303-050, or equivalent, to engine.
50. Using a suitable engine lift and spreader bar, support engine and transmission in front subframe.

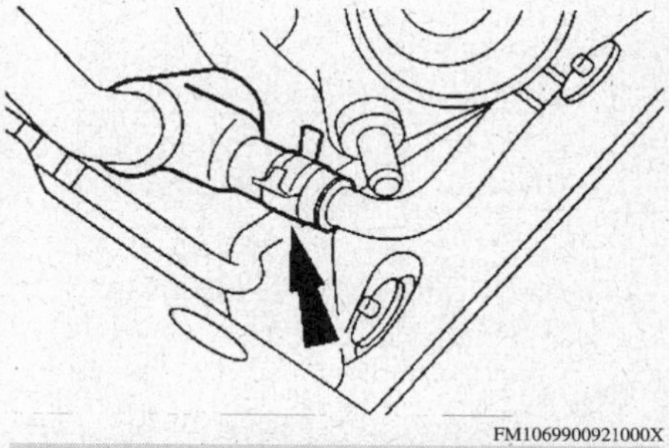

Fig. 11 Hose disconnect location

51. Disconnect two wire harness retainers and position harness aside.
52. Remove starter, then the oxygen sensor bracket.
53. Remove upper then lower transmission to engine attaching bolts.
54. Remove right and left engine mount upper attaching nuts.
55. Remove accessory drive belt.
56. Disconnect power steering pump electrical connector.
57. Remove power steering pump and position aside.
58. Disconnect hydraulic cooling fan pump electrical connector.
59. Remove hydraulic cooling fan pump and position aside.
60. Disconnect upper radiator hose.
61. **On models equipped with automatic transmission,** disconnect cooler line bracket from oil pan.
62. Remove transmission cooler lines from transmission and plug fittings.
63. **On models equipped with oil cooler,** disconnect oil cooler hoses.
64. **On all models,** remove remaining transmission to engine attaching bolts and separate transmission from engine.
65. **On models equipped with manual transmission,** remove clutch assembly.
66. **On all models,** remove flywheel.
67. Unclip right and left wire harness retainers.
68. Remove rear separator plate assembly.
69. Mount engine to a suitable workstand, then remove lifting equipment.
70. Reverse procedure to install.

INTAKE MANIFOLD

REPLACE

UPPER INTAKE MANIFOLD

1. Drain cooling system as follows:
   a. Ensure engine is cold.
   b. Wrap a suitable shop towel around pressure relief cap, then remove cap.
   c. **Ensure coolant does not come into contact with accessory drive belt.**
   d. Open radiator draincock and drain coolant into a suitable container.
   e. **On models equipped with oil cooler,** disconnect coolant return hose at oil cooler.
2. Remove air cleaner outlet tube.
3. Disconnect TP sensor and IAC electrical connectors.
4. Disconnect speed control and accelerator cables and position aside.
5. Disconnect coolant hoses, PCV hose and vapor purge hose from throttle body.
6. Disconnect EGR vacuum hose, then the EGR tube.
7. Remove cowl vent screen.
8. Remove vacuum hoses and cruise control cables from mounting brackets.
9. Disconnect differential pressure feedback EGR electrical connector.
10. Remove differential pressure feedback EGR transducer and position aside.
11. Remove fuel pressure sensor shield.
12. Disconnect vacuum hose from rear of intake manifold.
13. Disconnect intake manifold tuning valve electrical connector.
14. Disconnect exhaust vacuum regulator electrical connector and vacuum line.
15. Remove upper intake support bolt.
16. Remove upper intake attaching bolts, then the upper intake manifold. Inspect gaskets and discard as necessary.
17. Reverse procedure to install. Tighten manifold to specifications in sequence as shown in **Fig. 12.**

LOWER INTAKE MANIFOLD

1. Remove upper intake manifold as outlined under "Upper Intake Manifold."
2. Disconnect fuel lines.
3. Remove fuel line bracket bolt.

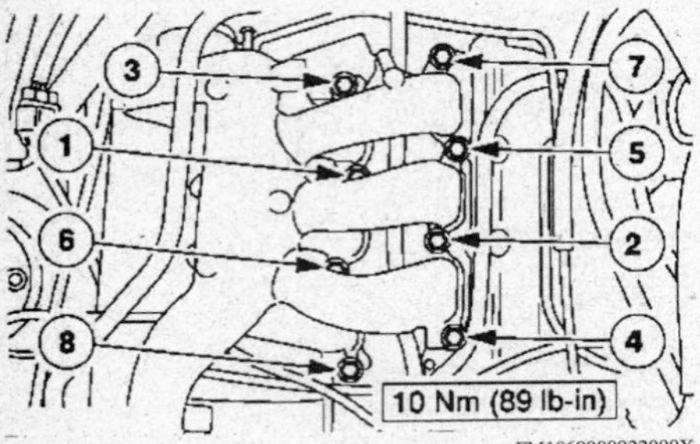

Fig. 12 Upper intake manifold tightening sequence

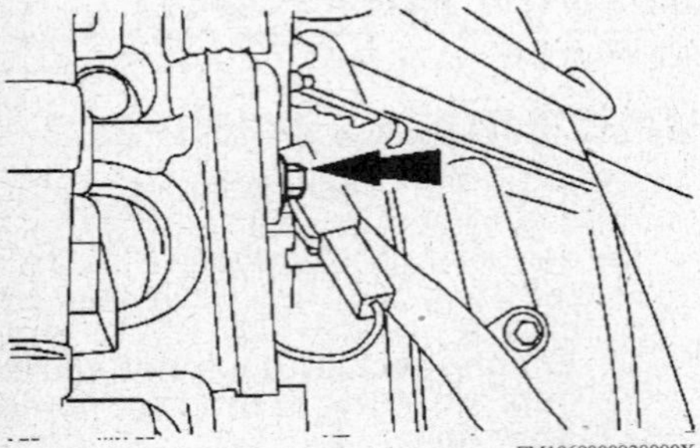

Fig. 15 Lefthand noise suppressor bolt location

4. Disconnect fuel pressure sensor vacuum line, then the fuel charging wiring harness connector.
5. Disconnect crankcase ventilation tube and position aside.
6. Remove lower intake manifold attaching bolts, then the manifold. **Fuel injection supply manifold and lower intake manifold must be removed as an assembly.**
7. Reverse procedure to install noting the following:
   a. Inspect fuel injector O-rings and replace as necessary.
   b. Inspect lower intake manifold gaskets and replace as necessary.
   c. Tighten to specifications.

EXHAUST MANIFOLD

REPLACE

LEFTHAND

1. Remove heat shield if equipped.
2. Remove three upper nuts on manifold.
3. Remove secondary air tube from exhaust manifold if equipped.
4. Remove dual converter Y-pipe.
5. Remove three lower nuts and exhaust manifold.
6. Reverse procedure to install. Install new gasket and tighten to specifications in sequence as shown in **Fig. 13.**

RIGHTHAND

1. Remove heat shield.
2. Remove secondary air tube from exhaust manifold if equipped.
3. Remove dual Y-pipe.

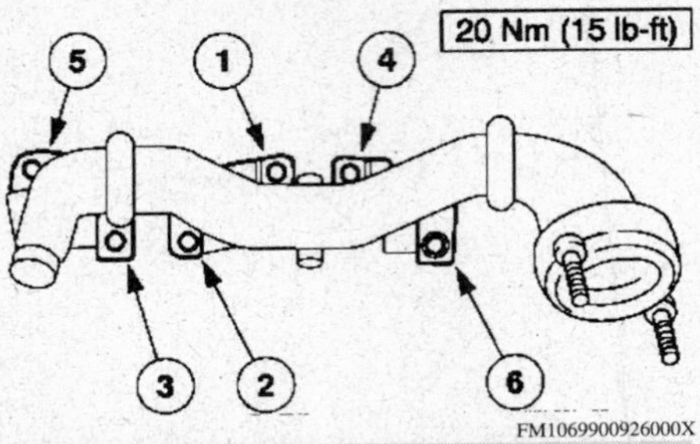

Fig. 13 Exhaust manifold tightening sequence

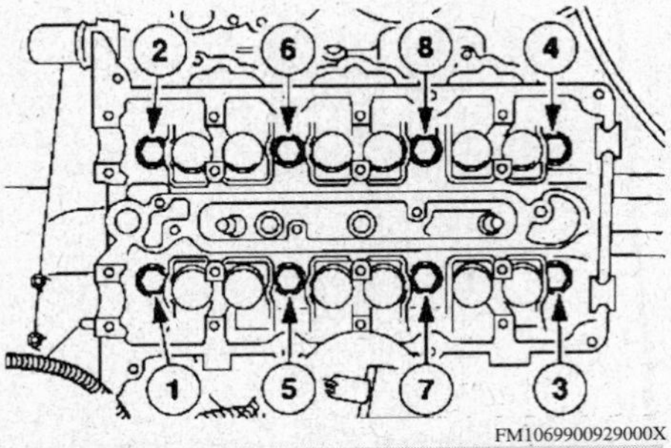

Fig. 16 Cylinder head bolt removal sequence

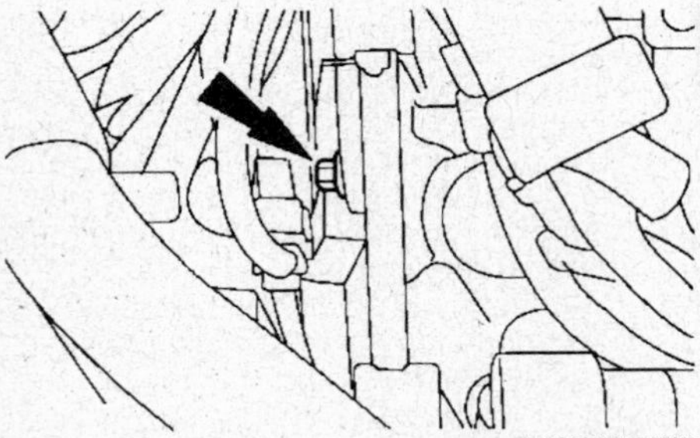

Fig. 18 Righthand noise suppressor bolt location

4. Disconnect EGR valve to exhaust manifold tube.
5. Remove manifold attaching nuts, then the manifold.
6. Reverse procedure to install. Install new gasket and tighten to specifications as shown in **Fig. 13.**

CYLINDER HEAD

REPLACE

When cleaning cylinder head surfaces, do not use metal scrapers, wires brushes, power abrasive discs or other abrasive methods to clean sealing surfaces. Use only a plastic scraping tool to remove all traces of gasket material.

Cylinder head bolts are of torque-to-yield style and must be replaced when removed.

Lefthand and righthand cylinder head gaskets are not interchangeable.

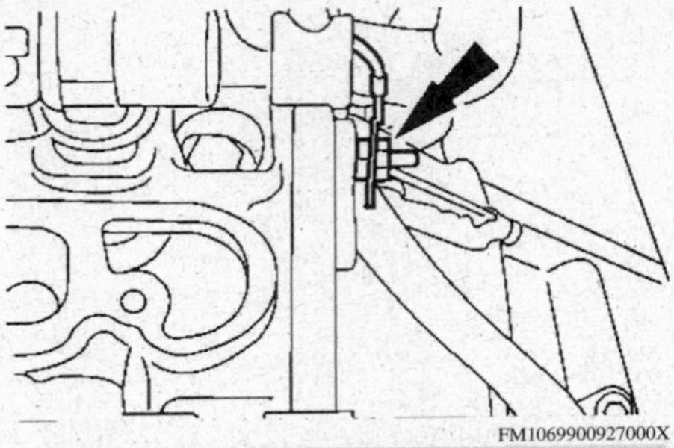

Fig. 14 Lefthand cylinder head ground strap location

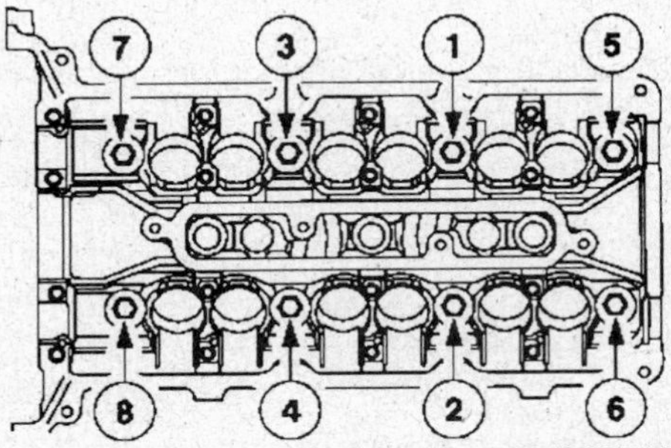

Fig. 17 Cylinder head tightening sequence

LEFTHAND

1. Remove camshafts as outlined under "Camshaft, Replace."
2. Remove exhaust manifold as outlined under "Exhaust Manifold, Replace."
3. Remove lower intake manifold as outlined under "Intake Manifold, Replace."
4. Remove cylinder head ground strap, stud and bolt, **Fig. 14.**
5. Remove noise suppressor bolt, **Fig. 15.**
6. Disconnect coolant outlet hose from thermostat housing.
7. Remove thermostat housing.
8. Remove oil level indicator tube stud bolt.
9. Remove cylinder head bolts in sequence, **Fig. 16.**
10. Reverse procedure to install. Tighten in sequence as shown in **Fig. 17** as follows:
    a. First step, 22 ft. lbs.
    b. Second step, rotate all bolts 90.°
    c. Third step, loosen all bolts 360.°
    d. Fourth step, 22 ft. lbs.
    e. Fifth step, rotate additional 90.°
    f. Sixth step, rotate additional 90.°

RIGHTHAND

1. Remove camshafts as outlined under "Camshaft, Replace."
2. Remove exhaust manifold as outlined under "Exhaust Manifold, Replace."
3. Remove lower intake manifold as outlined under "Intake Manifold, Replace."
4. Remove noise suppressor bolt, **Fig. 18.**

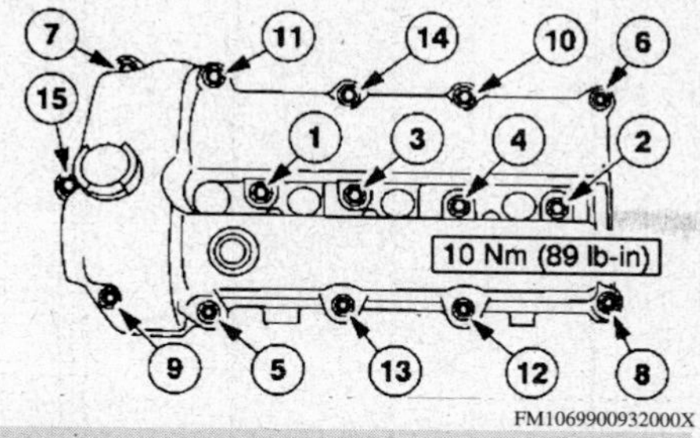

Fig. 19 Valve cover tightening sequence

5. Disconnect outlet hose from thermostat housing.
6. Remove thermostat housing.
7. Remove cylinder head bolts in sequence, **Fig. 16.**
8. Reverse procedure to install. Tighten in sequence as shown in **Fig. 17** as follows:
   a. First step, 22 ft. lbs.
   b. Second step, rotate additional bolts 90.°
   c. Third step, loosen all bolts 360.°
   d. Fourth step, 22 ft. lbs.
   e. Fifth step, rotate additional 90.°
   f. Sixth step, rotate additional 90.°

VALVE COVER

REPLACE

LEFTHAND

1. Remove lefthand ignition coils as outlined under "Ignition Coil, Replace."
2. Remove cylinder head temperature sensor.
3. Remove vacuum hoses from appearance cover support bracket.
4. Remove appearance cover support bracket.
5. Disconnect PCV tube and position aside.
6. Remove ignition coil harness from retainers.
7. Remove studs, bolts and valve cover.
8. Reverse procedure to install. Apply a .2 inch bead of silicone gasket sealant part No. F7AZ-19554-EA, or equivalent, to front cover joints. Tighten to specifications in sequence as shown in **Fig. 19.**

RIGHTHAND

1. Remove upper intake manifold as outlined under "Intake Manifold, Replace."
2. Disconnect PCV tube and position aside.
3. Remove righthand ignition coils as outlined under "Ignition Coil, Replace."
4. Remove wiring harness retainer from stud.
5. Remove upper intake manifold support bracket and position aside.
6. Remove wiring harness bracket nuts and position aside.
7. Remove valve cover attaching bolts and studs, then the valve cover.
8. Reverse procedure to install. Apply a .2 inch bead of silicone gasket sealant part No. F7AZ-19554-EA, or equivalent, to front cover joints. Tighten to specifications in sequence as shown in **Fig. 19.**

VALVE ARRANGEMENT

Inner ....I-I-I-I-I-I
Outer ....E-E-E-E-E-E

VALVE ADJUSTMENT

Rotating the engine in a counterclockwise direction will cause engine damage.

When marking shims, the only approved method is using a permanent marker. Scratches or paint on shim will cause incorrect lash adjustment and severe engine damage.

When measuring valve lash, ensure camshaft lobes are 180° away from each valve tappet.

1. Remove right and left valve covers as outlined under "Valve Cover, Replace."
2. Rotate engine clockwise to position camshaft lobe away from shim surface, **Fig. 20.**
3. Using feeler gauge set tool No. D81L-4201-A, or equivalent, measure clearance between camshaft and shim surface, **Fig. 20.** Refer to "Tune Up Specifications " for correct valve clearance.
4. Use a suitable marker to mark position of timing chain in relation to camshaft sprockets to ensure timing remains correct.
5. Place alignment marks on camshaft caps for installation reference. Caps should be marked for location and orientation.
6. Remove camshaft thrust cap and rear camshaft cap from camshaft that requires adjustment.
7. Install camshaft lift tools, tool No. 303-659, or equivalents and hand tighten. Taller tool should be installed in place of rear camshaft cap to allow camshaft to be lifted for shim removal.
8. Remove center camshaft caps.
9. Mark location of each shim.
10. Use a rubber tipped air gun and compressed air to remove shims that require adjustment.
11. Measure and record thickness of each shim to correspond with valve clearance.
12. To calculate required shim thickness, use the following formula: original shim thickness + measured clearance – desired clearance = required shim thickness.
13. When correct shim thickness has been calculated, reverse procedure to install noting the following:
    a. Apply a coat of clean 5W-30 motor oil to replacement shims and install shims.
    b. Apply a coat of clean 5W-30 motor oil to camshaft journals and bearing caps.
    c. Rotate crankshaft in clockwise direction to rotate camshafts two full revolutions. Recheck valve clearance and timing.

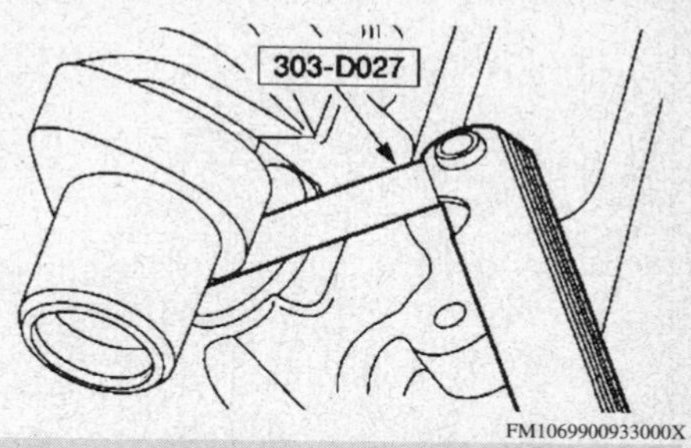

Fig. 20 Valve lash measurement

CRANKSHAFT DAMPER

REPLACE

1. Remove accessory drive belt.
2. Remove secondary air valve, bracket and tube if equipped.
3. Raise and support vehicle.
4. Remove front center splash panel.
5. Remove crankshaft pulley bolt and washer.
6. Using damper removal tool No. 303-D121, or equivalent, remove crankshaft damper. **Ensure removal tool grabs inside of damper or damage will occur.**
7. Reverse procedure to install noting the following:
   a. Ensure all damper and crankshaft surfaces are clean.
   b. Apply silicone gasket and sealant part No. F7AZ-19554-EA, or equivalent, to end of keyway slot.
   c. Lubricate outside sealing surface of crankshaft pulley with clean 5W-30 motor oil.
   d. Using damper installer tool No. T74P-6316-B, or equivalent, install damper and **torque** as follows; first step, 89 ft. lbs.; second step loosen 360°; third step 37 ft. lbs.; fourth step, tighten additional 90.°

FRONT COVER

REPLACE

1. Remove right and left valve covers as outlined under "Valve Cover, Replace."
2. Using three bar engine support kit tool No. 303-F072, or equivalent, support engine.
3. Raise and support vehicle.
4. Remove splash shields.
5. Drain cooling system as follows:
   a. Ensure engine is cold.
   b. Wrap a suitable shop towel around pressure relief cap, then remove cap.
   c. **Ensure coolant does not come into contact with accessory drive belt.**
   d. Open radiator draincock and drain coolant into a suitable container.
   e. **On models equipped with oil cooler,** disconnect coolant return hose at oil cooler.
6. **On all models,** disconnect upper water pump hose, then the upper and lower radiator hoses.

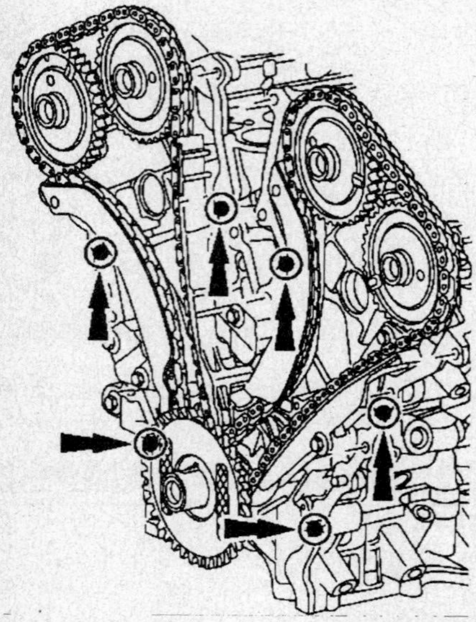

Fig. 21 Front cover sealant application points

7. Disconnect and remove radiator hose assembly.
8. Disconnect lower water pump hose.
9. Remove accessory drive belt.
10. Remove water pump as outlined under "Water Pump, Replace."
11. Remove oil pan as outlined under "Oil Pan, Replace. "
12. Remove power steering pump as outlined under "Front Suspension & Steering."
13. Remove hydraulic cooling fan pump as outlined under "Hydraulic Cooling Fan Pump, Replace"
14. Remove idler pulley, then the belt tensioner.
15. Remove crankshaft damper as outlined under "Crankshaft Damper, Replace."
16. Remove crankshaft front oil seal using seal removal tool No. T92C-6700-CH, or equivalent.
17. Remove front cover attaching bolts, then the front cover.
18. Reverse procedure to install noting the following:
    a. Apply a .24 inch diameter dot of silicone gasket and sealant part No. F7AZ-19554-EA, or equivalent, as shown in **Fig. 21.** Ensure front cover is installed within 6 minutes of sealer application.
    b. Install front cover and tighten to specifications in sequence as shown in **Fig. 22.**
    c. Install front crankshaft seal using seal installer tool No. T88T-6701-1, or equivalent.

FRONT COVER SEAL

REPLACE

1. Remove crankshaft damper as outlined under "Crankshaft Damper, Replace."

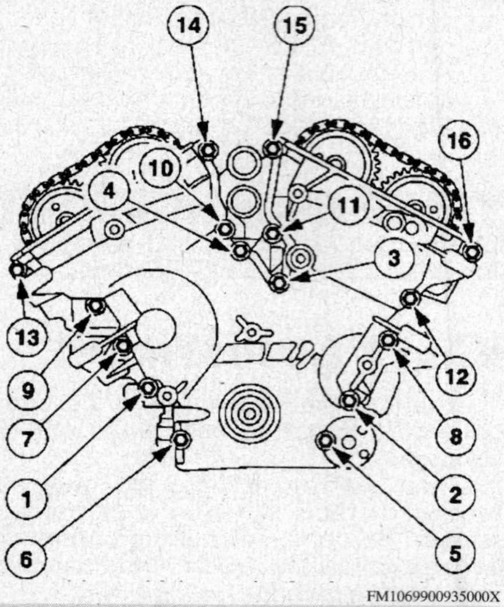

Fig. 22 Front cover tightening sequence

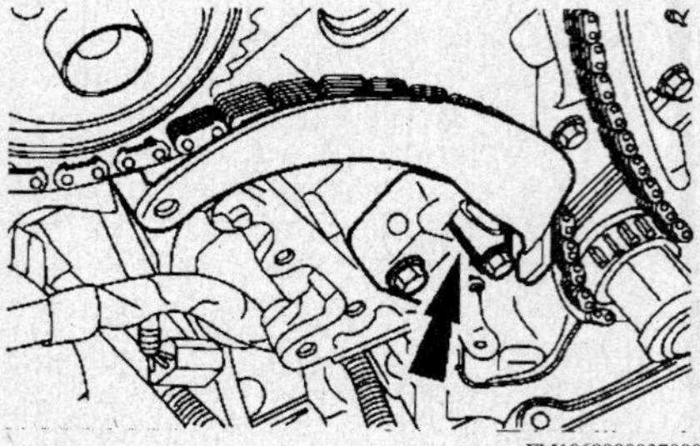

Fig. 24 Timing chain tensioner retension

2. Using seal remover tool No. T92C-6700-CH, or equivalent, remove front cover seal.
3. Reverse procedure to install noting the following:
    a. Lubricate inside diameter of seal using clean 5W-30 motor oil.
    b. Using seal installer tool No. T88T-6701-A, or equivalent, install front cover seal.

TIMING CHAIN

REPLACE

Rotating the engine in a counterclockwise direction will cause engine damage.

REMOVAL

1. Remove front cover as outlined under "Front Cover, Replace."
2. Remove ignition pulse ring.
3. Reinstall crankshaft damper bolt and washer.
4. Rotate crankshaft clockwise until keyway is positioned in 9 o'clock position, **Fig. 23.**
5. If timing chain tensioner and chain are to be reused, place identification

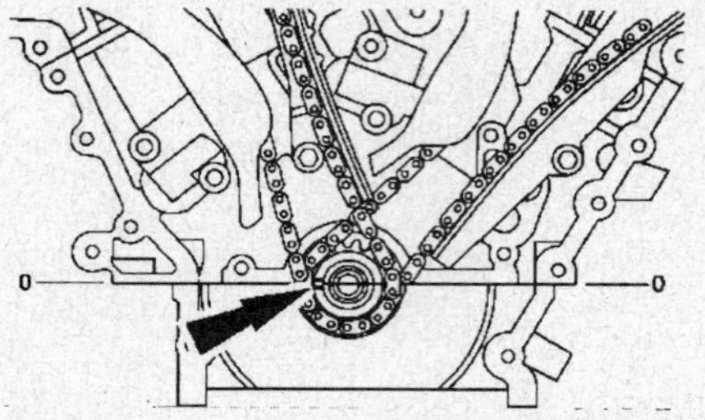

Fig. 23 Crankshaft keyway alignment

marks on them for installation reference. Do not interchange right and left timing components.
6. Place a suitable paper clip into righthand timing chain tensioner before removing bolts, **Fig. 24.**
7. Remove righthand timing chain tensioner and arm.
8. Remove righthand timing chain, then the chain guide.
9. Install a suitable paper clip into lefthand timing chain tensioner.
10. Remove lefthand timing chain tensioner and arm, then the timing chain and guide.

INSTALLATION

Ensure crankshaft keyway remains in 9 o'clock position until cams are properly positioned or valve damage will occur.

1. Verify crankshaft keyway is in 9 o'clock position, **Fig. 23.**
2. Rotate right and left camshafts to locate them to neutral positions, **Fig. 25.**
3. Place lefthand chain tensioner into a suitable soft-jawed vise.
4. Hold tensioner ratchet lock mechanism away from ratchet stem using a suitable pick, **Fig. 26.**
5. **During tensioner compression, do not release ratchet stem until tensioner piston is fully bottomed in bore or stem will become damaged.** Slowly compress chain tensioner.
6. Retain lefthand tensioner piston using a suitable paper clip, **Fig. 27.**
7. Rotate crankshaft clockwise to 11 o'clock position.
8. Remove crankshaft damper bolt and washer.
9. Install lefthand timing chain guide and tighten to specifications. Ensure short bolt is installed into upper hole and long bolt into lower hole.
10. Install lefthand timing chain. Align gold timing chain index link with marks on camshaft and crankshaft sprockets, **Fig. 28.**
11. Install left timing chain tensioner and tighten to specifications. Ensure tensioner piston is fully engaged in tensioner arm.
12. Remove paper clip from left tensioner and install crankshaft damper bolt and washer.

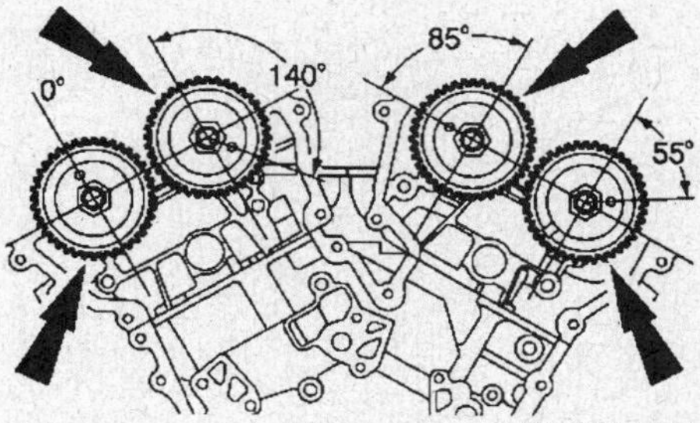

Fig. 25 Camshaft neutral positions

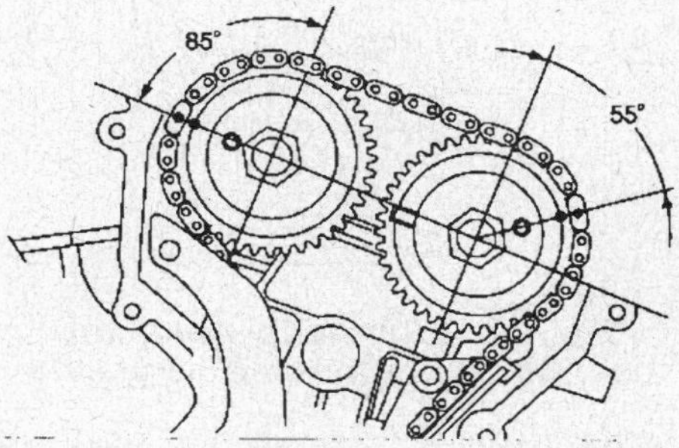

Fig. 28 Primary lefthand timing chain alignment mark inspection

13. Rotate crankshaft clockwise until keyway is positioned between 2 o'clock and 3 o'clock position.
14. Verify gold timing chain index links on lefthand timing chain are still aligned with timing index marks on crankshaft and camshaft sprockets, **Fig. 29.**
15. Place righthand chain tensioner into a suitable soft-jawed vise.
16. Hold tensioner ratchet lock mechanism away from ratchet stem using a suitable pick, **Fig. 26.**
17. **During tensioner compression, do not release ratchet stem until tensioner piston is fully bottomed in bore or stem will become damaged.** Slowly compress chain tensioner.
18. Retain righthand tensioner piston using a suitable paper clip, **Fig. 27.**
19. Install righthand timing chain guide and tighten to specifications.
20. Install righthand timing chain. Align gold chain index marks with camshaft and crankshaft alignment marks, **Fig. 30.**
21. Install right timing chain tensioner and tighten to specifications.
22. Remove paper clip from righthand tensioner.
23. Verify gold timing index links on righthand timing chain are still aligned with timing index marks on camshaft and crankshaft sprockets, **Fig. 31.**
24. Remove crankshaft damper bolt and washer.
25. Install ignition pulse ring.
26. Install front cover as outlined under "Front Cover, Replace."

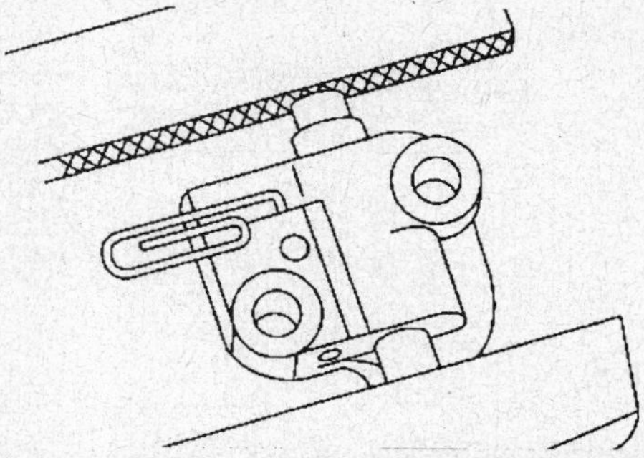

Fig. 26 Timing chain tensioner ratchet lock access hole

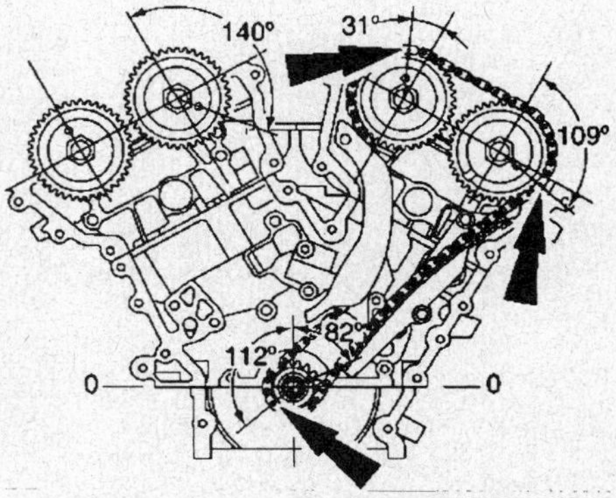

Fig. 29 Secondary lefthand timing chain alignment mark inspection

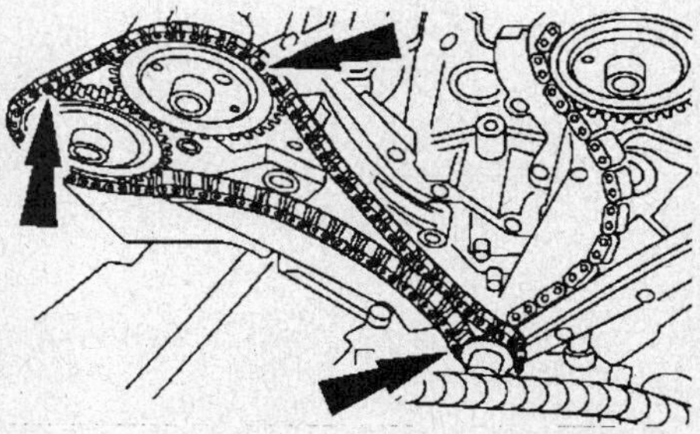

Fig. 31 Secondary righthand timing chain alignment mark inspection

CAMSHAFT

REPLACE

When removing camshafts, camshaft journal thrust caps must be removed prior to loosening other camshaft journal cap bolts.

When installing camshafts, camshaft bearing caps must be installed prior to installing thrust caps.

Camshaft journal caps and cylinder

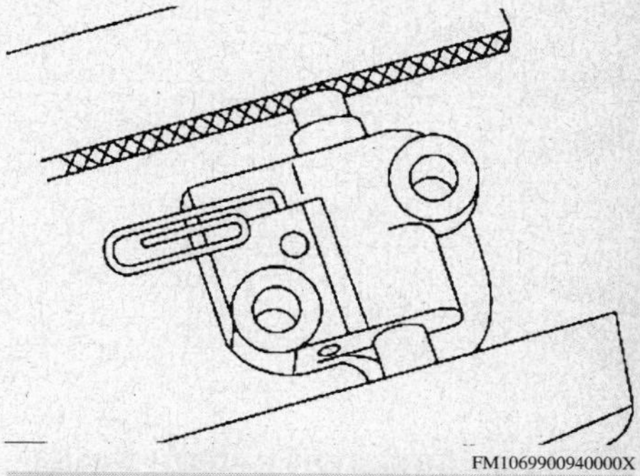

Fig. 27 Timing chain tensioner piston retension

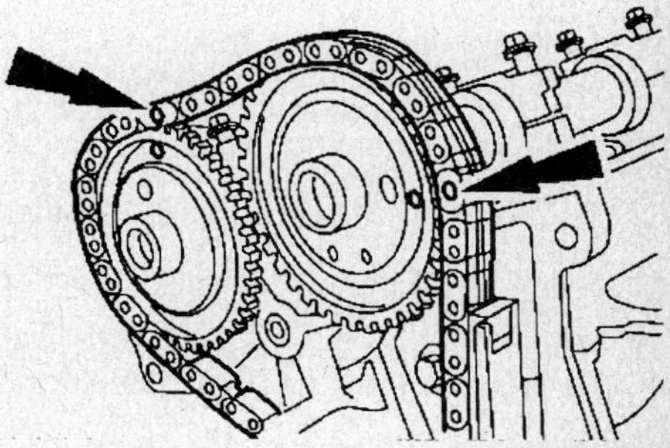

Fig. 30 Primary righthand timing chain alignment mark inspection

heads are numbered to ensure they are assembled in their original positions.

REMOVAL

1. Remove upper intake manifold as outlined under "Intake Manifold, Replace."
2. Remove front cover as outlined under "Front Cover, Replace."
3. Remove timing chains as outlined under "Timing Chain, Replace."
4. Remove camshaft journal thrust caps, **Fig. 32.**
5. Remove remaining camshaft journal caps, then the camshafts.

INSTALLATION

1. Ensure all bearing caps are installed to original positions.
2. Lubricate camshafts and all bearing surfaces with clean 5W-30 motor oil.
3. Install camshaft bearing caps. Do not tighten bolts at this time.
4. Install camshaft thrust caps. Do not tighten bolts at this time.
5. Tighten camshaft bearing caps to specifications in sequence as shown in **Figs. 33 and 34.**
6. If new camshafts were installed, adjust valve lash as outlined under "Valve Adjustment."
7. **Verify crankshaft keyway is in the 9 o'clock position before rotating**

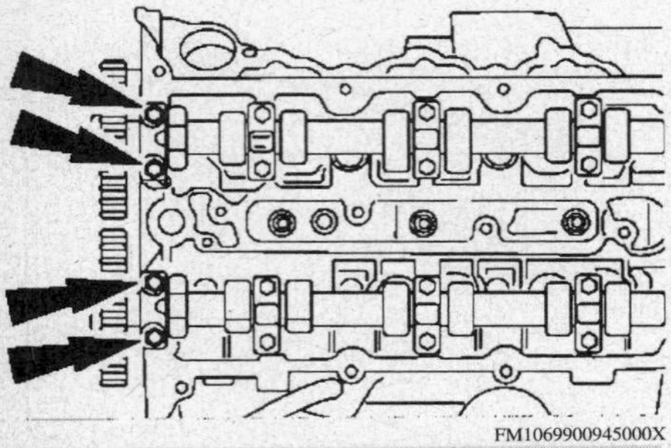

Fig. 32 Camshaft journal thrust cap location

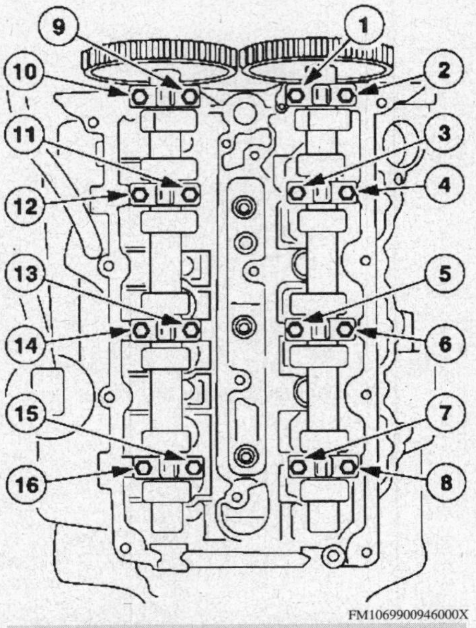

Fig. 33 Lefthand camshaft bearing cap tightening sequence

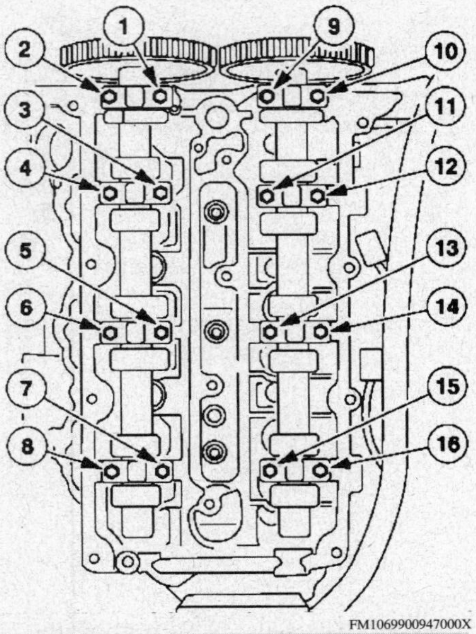

Fig. 34 Righthand camshaft bearing cap tightening sequence

camshafts or engine damage will result.

8. Rotate camshafts to ensure they are not binding. If binding occurs, ensure bearing caps are in original positions. Loosen all bearing caps in reverse order and retighten.
9. Install timing chains as outlined under "Timing Chain, Replace."
10. Install front cover as outlined under "Front Cover, Replace."
11. Install upper intake manifold as outlined under "Intake Manifold, Replace."

PISTON & ROD ASSEMBLY

When removing pistons and connecting rods, place reference marks on all parts involved for installation reference.

Connecting rod bearing caps are cracked and split from connecting rods during the manufacturing process. When assembling parts, ensure all mating surfaces are clean and ensure identification marks on cap and rod are aligned.

Connecting rod bolts are of torque-to-yield design and must be replaced when removed.

Connecting rod bolts are of torque-to-yield design and must be replaced once taken apart. When installing pistons, ensure arrow on piston is facing toward front of engine. For connecting rod bolt tightening specifications refer to "Tightening Specifications."

MAIN BEARINGS

When cleaning gasket surfaces, do not use metal scrapers, wires brushes, power abrasive discs or other abrasive methods to clean sealing surfaces. Use only a plastic scraping tool to remove all traces of gasket material.

Lower cylinder block bolts and studs are of torque-to-yield design and must be replaced when removed.

To select and install main bearings, proceed as follows:

1. Read code on crankshaft flange (1), and code on engine block rear face (2), **Fig. 35.**
2. First 2 numbers after asterisk make up code for main No. 1 and next two numbers for main No. 2. The first 2 numbers after second asterisk make up code for main No. 3 and last two numbers for main No. 4. Refer to **Fig. 36** for bearing grade selection chart.

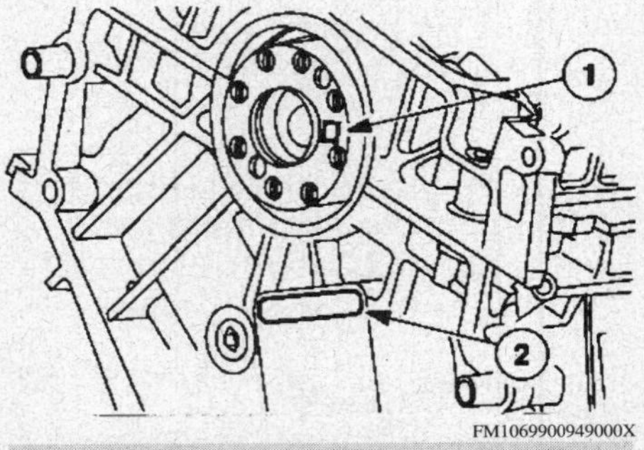

Fig. 35 Cylinder block and crankshaft bearing reference marks

3. As an example, if block code is *0609*0711* and crankshaft code is *8480*8082*, main No. 1 will use grade 1 bearings as determined by intersection of 06 block column and 84 crankshaft row, **Fig. 36.** Using these codes as an example, main Nos. 2, 3 and 4 will use grade 2.
4. Install upper main bearing and upper thrust bearing to cylinder block in proper locations.
5. Lubricate bearings using clean 5W-30 motor oil, then install crankshaft to cylinder block.
6. Install lower main bearings and lower thrust bearing into lower cylinder block in proper locations.
7. Ensure all gasket surfaces are clean using Ford Metal Surface Cleaner part No. F4AZ-19A536-RA, or equivalent. Allow to dry until there is no sign of wetness present.
8. Apply a .12 inch bead of silicone gasket sealant part No. F7AZ-19554-EA, or equivalent, to lower cylinder block. End bead of gasket material .24 inch from rear crankshaft seal bore on both sides, **Fig. 37.** Bolts and studs must be tightened within four minutes of applying sealant.
9. Install lower cylinder block studs (1) and bolts (2), **Fig. 38.**
10. Install new bolts and studs and **torque** in sequence, **Fig. 39,** as follows:
    a. Bolts 1–8, 18 ft. lbs.
    b. Bolts 9–16, 30 ft. lbs.
    c. Bolts 1–16, additional 90.°
    d. Bolts 17–22, 18 ft. lbs.
11. Remove excess sealer from front cover and rear seal bore inner diameter areas.
12. Rotate crankshaft in clockwise direction to verify free rotation.

CRANKSHAFT REAR OIL SEAL

REPLACE

1. **On models equipped with automatic transmissions,** remove transmission as outlined under "Automatic Transmission/Transaxle."
2. **On models equipped with manual transmissions,** remove transmission as outlined under "Clutch & Manual Tranmission."
3. **On all models,** remove flywheel.
4. Using seal removal tool No. T95P-6701-EH and slide hammer tool No. 307-005, or equivalents, remove rear crankshaft seal.
5. Lubricate outer lips and inner seal of new crankshaft rear seal with clean 5W-30 motor oil.
6. Using seal installer tool No. T82L-6701-A and rear adapter bolts tool No. T91P-6701-A, or equivalents, install rear oil seal.

BLOCK CODE (columns) / **CRANKSHAFT CODE** (rows)

	98	99	00	01	02	03	04	05	06	07	08	09	10	11	12	13	14	15	16	17	18	19	20	21
91	1	1	1	1	1	1	1	1	1	1	1	1	1	1	1	1	1	2	2	2	2	2	2	2
90	1	1	1	1	1	1	1	1	1	1	1	1	1	1	1	1	2	2	2	2	2	2	2	2
89	1	1	1	1	1	1	1	1	1	1	1	1	1	1	1	2	2	2	2	2	2	2	2	2
88	1	1	1	1	1	1	1	1	1	1	1	1	1	1	2	2	2	2	2	2	2	2	2	2
87	1	1	1	1	1	1	1	1	1	1	1	1	1	2	2	2	2	2	2	2	2	2	2	2
86	1	1	1	1	1	1	1	1	1	1	1	1	2	2	2	2	2	2	2	2	2	2	2	2
85	1	1	1	1	1	1	1	1	1	1	1	2	2	2	2	2	2	2	2	2	2	2	2	2
84	1	1	1	1	1	1	1	1	1	1	2	2	2	2	2	2	2	2	2	2	2	2	2	3
83	1	1	1	1	1	1	1	1	1	2	2	2	2	2	2	2	2	2	2	2	2	2	3	3
82	1	1	1	1	1	1	1	1	2	2	2	2	2	2	2	2	2	2	2	2	2	3	3	3
81	1	1	1	1	1	1	1	2	2	2	2	2	2	2	2	2	2	2	2	2	3	3	3	3
80	1	1	1	1	1	1	2	2	2	2	2	2	2	2	2	2	2	2	2	3	3	3	3	3
79	1	1	1	1	1	2	2	2	2	2	2	2	2	2	2	2	2	2	3	3	3	3	3	3
78	1	1	1	1	2	2	2	2	2	2	2	2	2	2	2	2	2	3	3	3	3	3	3	3
77	1	1	1	2	2	2	2	2	2	2	2	2	2	2	2	2	3	3	3	3	3	3	3	3
76	1	1	2	2	2	2	2	2	2	2	2	2	2	2	2	3	3	3	3	3	3	3	3	3
75	1	2	2	2	2	2	2	2	2	2	2	2	2	2	3	3	3	3	3	3	3	3	3	3
74	2	2	2	2	2	2	2	2	2	2	2	2	2	3	3	3	3	3	3	3	3	3	3	3
73	2	2	2	2	2	2	2	2	2	2	2	2	3	3	3	3	3	3	3	3	3	3	3	3
72	2	2	2	2	2	2	2	2	2	2	2	3	3	3	3	3	3	3	3	3	3	3	3	3
71	2	2	2	2	2	2	2	2	2	2	3	3	3	3	3	3	3	3	3	3	3	3	3	3
70	2	2	2	2	2	2	2	2	2	3	3	3	3	3	3	3	3	3	3	3	3	3	3	3
69	2	2	2	2	2	2	2	2	3	3	3	3	3	3	3	3	3	3	3	3	3	3	3	3
68	2	2	2	2	2	2	2	3	3	3	3	3	3	3	3	3	3	3	3	3	3	3	3	3

FM1069900948000X

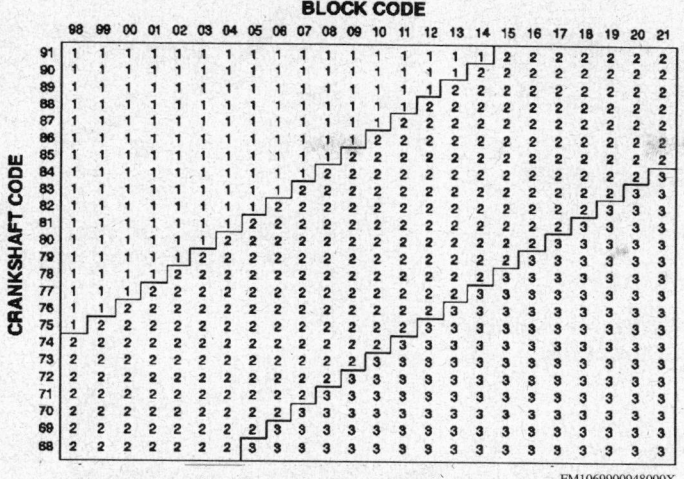

Fig. 36 Bearing grade selection chart

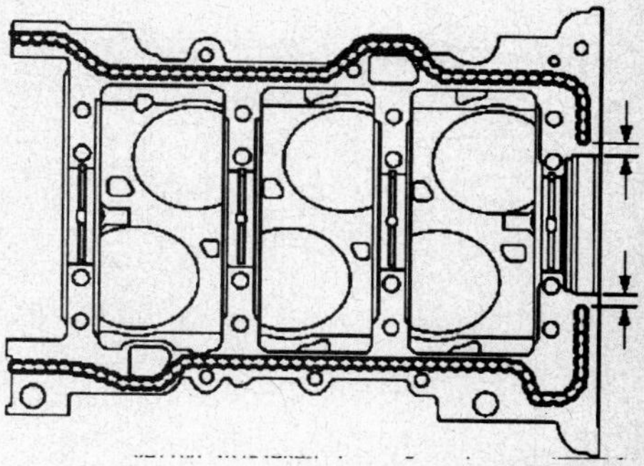

FM1069900950000X

Fig. 37 Lower cylinder block sealant application

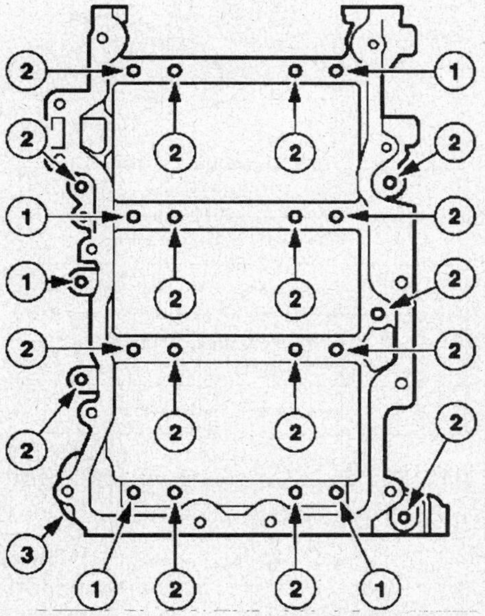

Fig. 38 Lower cylinder block bolt identification

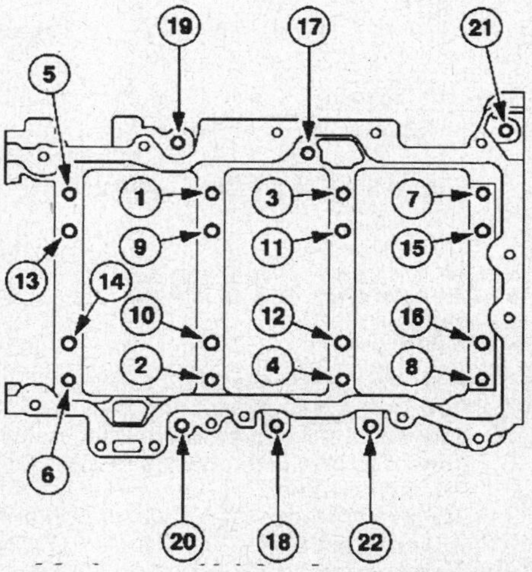

Fig. 39 Lower cylinder block tightening sequence

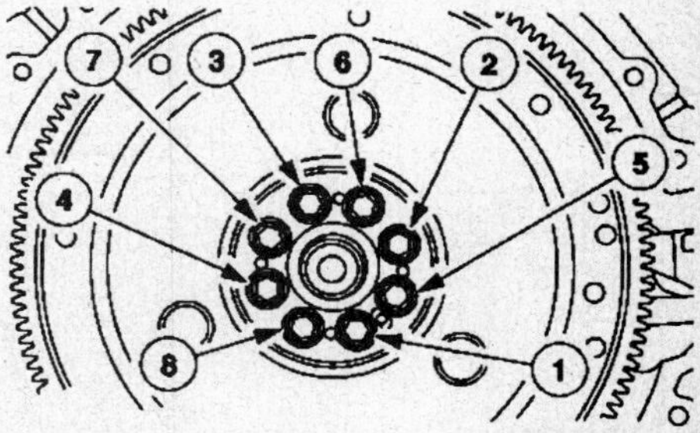

Fig. 40 Flywheel tightening sequence

7. Install flywheel with elongated hole over crankshaft dowel.
8. Install flywheel bolts and tighten to specifications in sequence, **Fig. 40.**
9. **On models equipped with automatic transmissions,** install transmission as outlined under "Automatic Transmission/Transaxle."
10. **On models equipped with manual transmissions,** install transmission as outlined under "Clutch & Manual Tranmission."

OIL PAN

REPLACE

1. Install three bar engine support kit tool No. 303-F072, or equivalent, to support engine.
2. Raise and support vehicle.
3. Drain engine oil.
4. Remove alternator as outlined under "Alternator, Replace."
5. Remove A/C compressor mounting bolts, then support compressor using suitable mechanics wire.
6. Remove electronic thermactor air bracket bolts if equipped.
7. Remove power steering line from oil pan stud if equipped.
8. Remove steering gear attaching nuts and support steering gear.
9. Remove right and left control arm through bolts, then the right and left motor mount nuts.
10. Remove left and right subframe bolts, **Figs. 41 and 42.**
11. Remove transmission cooler line bracket nut.
12. Remove transmission to oil pan bolts.
13. Remove oil pan attaching bolts.
14. Pry subframe downward and remove oil pan.
15. Reverse procedure to install noting the following:
    a. Install new gasket to oil pan.
    b. Apply a .4 inch dot of silicone gasket sealant part No. F7AZ-19554-EA or equivalent, to oil pan as shown in **Fig. 43.** Oil pan must be installed and bolts tightened within six minutes of sealant application.
    c. Install oil pan and tighten to specification as shown in **Fig. 44.**
    d. Ensure vehicle suspension alignment is within specifications.

OIL PUMP

REPLACE

1. Remove timing chains as outlined under "Timing Chain, Replace."
2. Remove oil pan as outlined under "Oil Pan, Replace."
3. Remove oil pump screen tube.
4. Remove oil pump attaching bolts, then the oil pump, **Fig. 45.**
5. Reverse procedure to install. Tighten to specifications.

OIL COOLER

REPLACE

1. Drain cooling system as follows:
    a. Ensure engine is cold.
    b. Wrap a suitable shop towel around pressure relief cap, then remove cap.

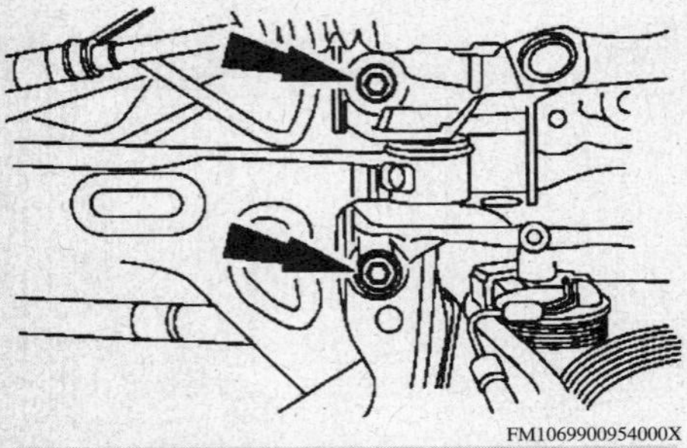

FM1069900954000X

Fig. 41 Lefthand subframe bolt location

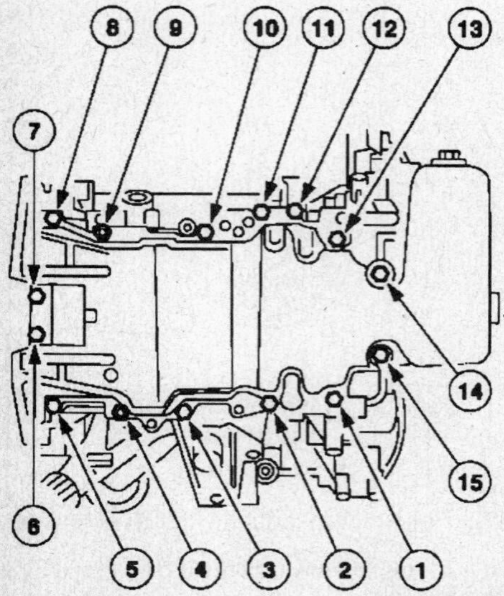

FM1069900957000X

Fig. 44 Oil pan tightening sequence

c. **Ensure coolant does not come into contact with accessory drive belt.**
d. Open radiator draincock and drain coolant into a suitable container.
e. Disconnect coolant hoses at oil cooler.

2. Remove oil cooler attaching bolt, then the oil cooler.
3. Reverse procedure to install noting the following:
   a. Position oil cooler and gasket, then install attaching bolt. Rotate cooler clockwise until locating pin hits the stop.
   b. Tighten to specifications.

BELT TENSION DATA

Vehicle is equipped with an automatic belt tensioner. Belt tension is not adjustable. Refer to **Fig. 46** to inspect tensioner.

SERPENTINE DRIVE BELT ROUTING

Refer to **Fig. 47** for serpentine drive belt routing.

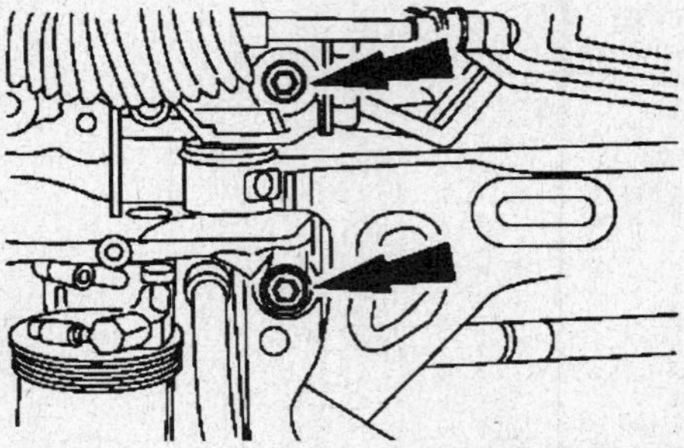

FM1069900955000X

Fig. 42 Righthand subframe bolt location

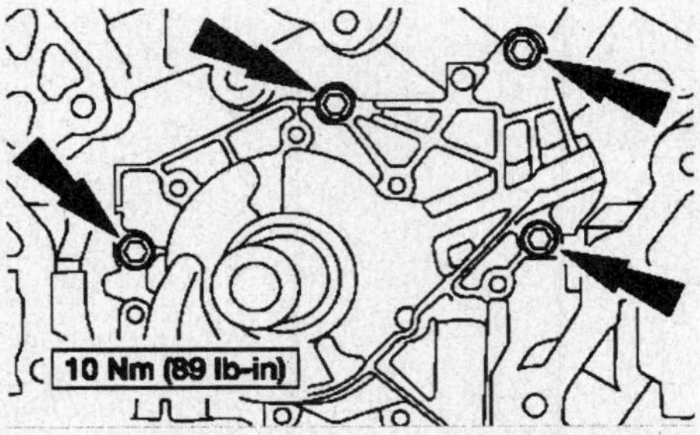

FM1069900958000X

Fig. 45 Oil pump removal

COOLING SYSTEM BLEED

1. Open engine air bleed, **Fig. 48.**
2. Open heater air bleed, **Fig. 49.**
3. Add coolant to overflow bottle. Allow system to equalize until no more coolant can be added.
4. Close engine air bleed when coolant begins to escape.
5. Install cap to overflow bottle.
6. Start and run engine with heater air bleed open. Turn heater to MAX position.
7. Close heater air bleed when a steady stream of coolant flows from it at idle.
8. Allow engine to idle for 5 minutes, then add coolant to overflow bottle as needed to maintain cold fill MAX mark.
9. Reopen heater air bleed to release any trapped air and close again.
10. Operate engine at 1500 RPM for 3–5 minutes or until hot air comes from heater.
11. Return to idle and verify hot air is still coming from heater.
12. Turn engine off and allow to cool. After engine has cooled, add coolant to overflow bottle to bring level to MAX cold fill mark.

THERMOSTAT

REPLACE

1. Drain cooling system as follows:
   a. Ensure engine is cold.
   b. Wrap a suitable shop towel around pressure relief cap, then remove cap.

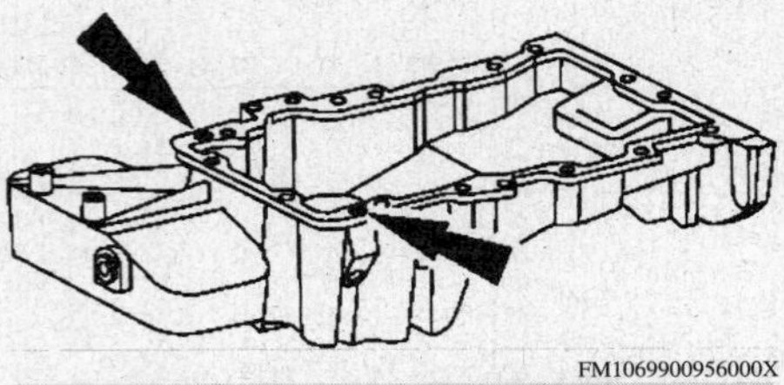

FM1069900956000X

Fig. 43 Oil pan sealant application points

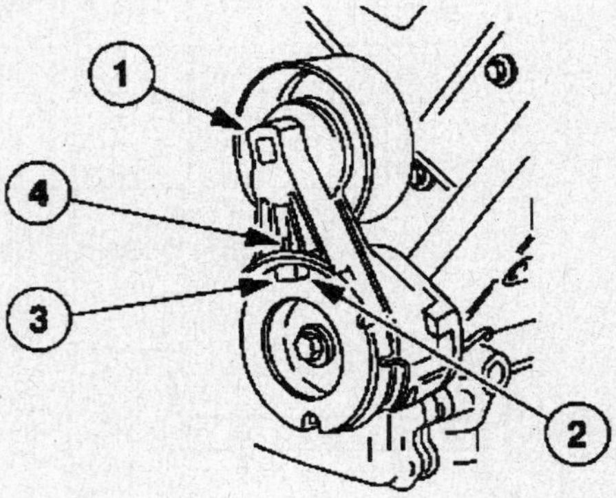

Item	Description
1	Belt tension relief point
2	Unacceptable belt wear range
3	Acceptable belt installation and wear range
4	Belt length indicator

FM1069900959000X

Fig. 46 Belt tensioner inspection

c. **Ensure coolant does not come into contact with accessory drive belt.**
d. Open radiator draincock and drain coolant into a suitable container.
e. Disconnect coolant hoses at oil cooler if equipped.

2. Remove air cleaner outlet tube.
3. Disconnect hoses from thermostat housing, **Fig. 50.**
4. Remove thermostat housing, then the thermostat and seal.
5. Reverse procedure to install.

WATER PUMP

REPLACE

1. Drain cooling system as follows:
   a. Ensure engine is cold.
   b. Wrap a suitable shop towel around pressure relief cap, then remove cap.
   c. **Ensure coolant does not come into contact with accessory drive belt.**
   d. Open radiator draincock and drain coolant into a suitable container.

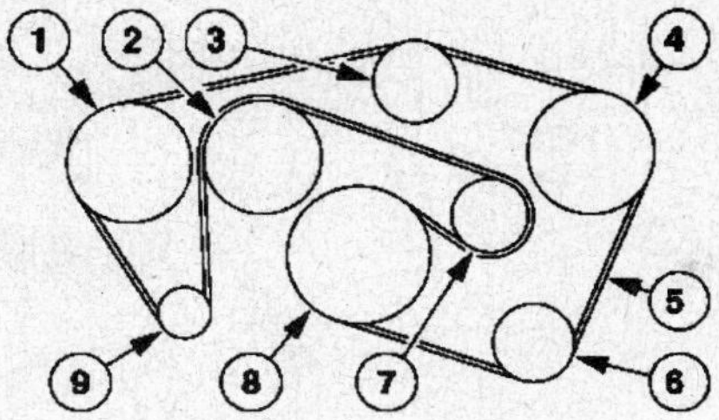

Item	Description
1	Hydraulic fan pump pulley
2	Water pump pulley
3	Belt idler pulley
4	Power steering pump pulley
5	Drive belt
6	A/C clutch pulley
7	Drive belt tensioner
8	Crankshaft vibration damper
9	Generator pulley

FM1069900960000X

Fig. 47 Serpentine drive belt routing

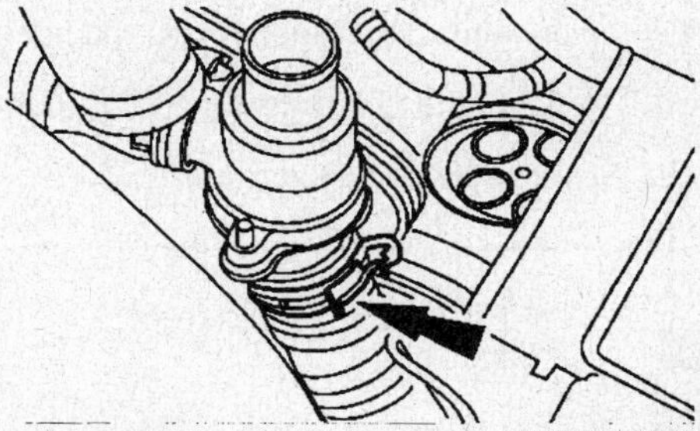

FM1069900964000X

Fig. 50 Thermostat housing location

   e. Disconnect coolant hoses at oil cooler if equipped.
2. Remove air cleaner outlet tube.
3. Disconnect engine vent hose, **Fig. 48.**
4. Disconnect upper and lower radiator hoses, then the heater supply and water pump hoses.
5. Remove water crossover assembly.
6. Disconnect water inlet hose from coolant outlet tube.
7. Disconnect and remove water inlet hose from pump.
8. Remove accessory drive belt.
9. Remove water pump attaching bolts and studs, then the water pump. Record location of water pump studs for installation reference.
10. Reverse procedure to install.

RADIATOR

REPLACE

1. Drain cooling system as follows:
   a. Ensure engine is cold.

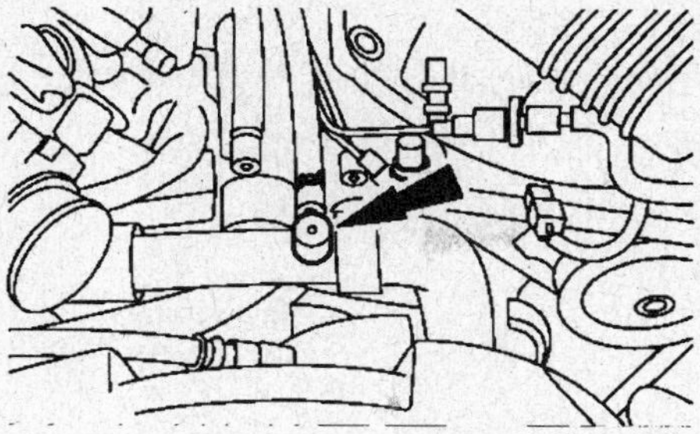

FM1069900962000X

Fig. 48 Engine air bleed location

   b. Wrap a suitable shop towel around pressure relief cap, then remove cap.
   c. **Ensure coolant does not come into contact with accessory drive belt.**
   d. Open radiator draincock and drain coolant into a suitable container.
   e. Disconnect coolant hoses at oil cooler if equipped.
2. Remove upper radiator sight shield.
3. Remove air cleaner outlet tube.
4. Remove radiator support brackets, then the upper radiator hose.
5. Remove receiver drier attaching bolt and position receiver drier aside.
6. Disconnect high pressure cooling fan line, then the return hose.
7. Separate return hose from fan shroud and position aside.
8. Remove fan shroud.
9. Support A/C condenser using suitable mechanics wire.
10. Raise and support vehicle.
11. Remove right and left splash shields, then the radiator air deflector.
12. Disconnect lower radiator hose.
13. Remove condenser to radiator attaching bolts.
14. Remove condenser support brackets, then the radiator through bottom of vehicle.
15. Reverse procedure to install.

HYDRAULIC FAN MOTOR

REPLACE

Refer to "Radiator, Replace" for procedure.

HYDRAULIC COOLING FAN PUMP

REPLACE

1. Remove accessory drive belt.
2. Remove lower cooling fan pump bolt.
3. Disconnect hose and allow to drain, **Fig. 51.**
4. Disconnect cooling fan pump electrical connector.
5. Remove high pressure line bracket.
6. Disconnect high pressure line.
7. Remove two upper pump bolts, then the cooling fan pump.

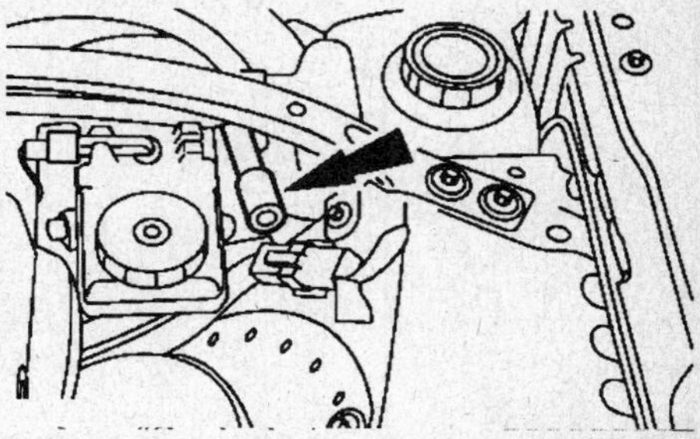

FM1069900963000X

Fig. 49 Heater air bleed location

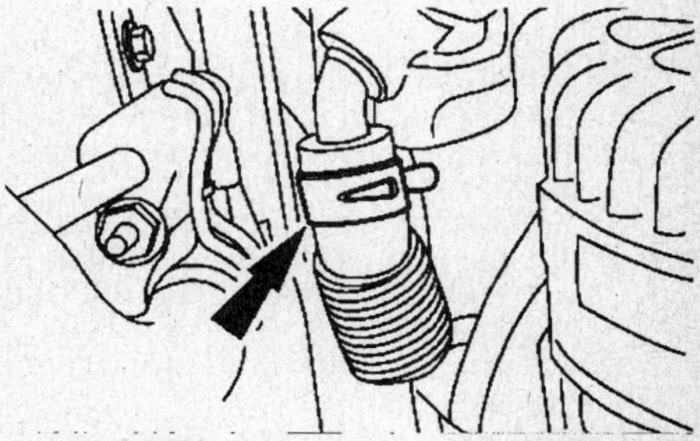

FM1069900961000X

Fig. 51 Hose location

8. Reverse procedure to install.

FUEL PUMP

REPLACE

The fuel system contains two pumps. One is the "fuel delivery module" which provides fuel pressure to the engine. The second pump is a "jet pump" or "transfer" pump which maintains fuel levels in both sides of the fuel tank.

The jet pump is located on the lefthand side of the fuel tank and contains a fuel level sensor and a check valve which maintains system pressure after the pump is shut off.

The fuel delivery module is located on the righthand side of the fuel tank and contains a fuel level sensor and an inlet screen on the bottom of the pump.

To disconnect fuel lines from pumps, press down on fuel line connector while pressing release tabs. Pull straight up to remove.

Whenever fuel pumps are removed, new fuel pump gaskets must be installed.

FUEL DELIVERY MODULE

1. Relieve fuel pressure as outlined under "Precautions."
2. Drain fuel tank as follows:
   a. Release rear seat mini-buckle.
   b. Depress two seat cushion latches, then remove rear seat cushion and insulation.
   c. Remove fuel pump access covers. Ensure all fuel pump connectors are fully seated.
   d. Remove black connector elbow on transfer pump, **Fig. 52.**

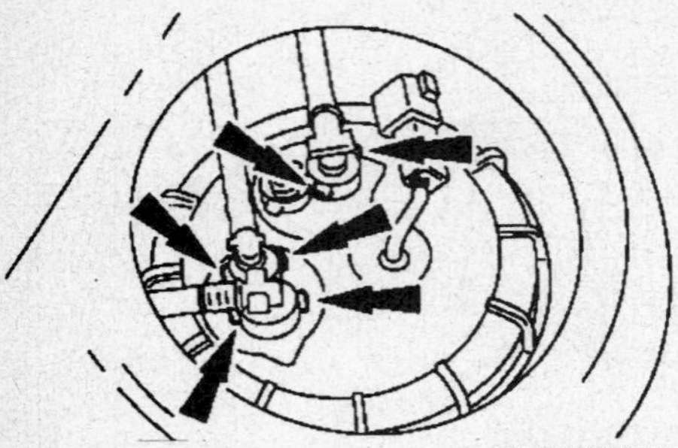

FM1069900965000X

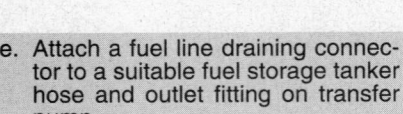

Fig. 52 Transfer pump fuel line connections

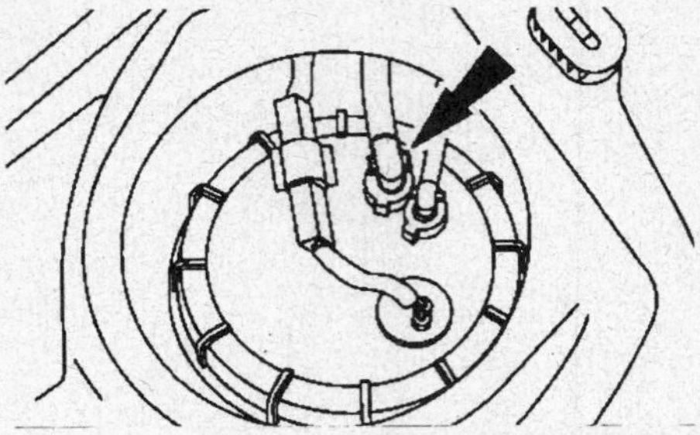

FM1069900966000X

Fig. 53 Fuel delivery module fuel line connections

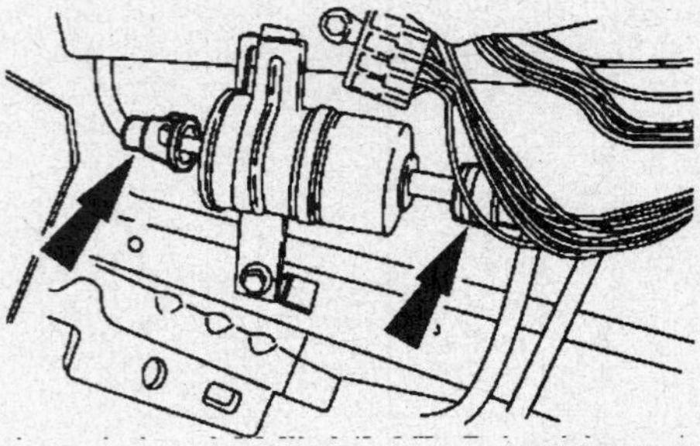

FM1069900967000X

Fig. 54 Fuel filter location

e. Attach a fuel line draining connector to a suitable fuel storage tanker hose and outlet fitting on transfer pump.
f. Siphon fuel until tank side is empty.
g. Attach fuel draining connector to fuel delivery module, **Fig. 53,** and repeat steps d, e and f.

3. Disconnect remaining fuel line from fuel delivery module.
4. Disconnect fuel delivery module electrical connector.
5. Loosen fuel pump lockring using fuel sender wrench tool No. 310-069, or equivalent.
6. Remove fuel delivery module lockring.
7. Position pump flange clear of pump opening, then press lock tabs and release pump from tank mounting flange. Lift straight up and out of retainer cup and tilt while in tank to drain fuel from reservoir. Straighten and lift straight up and out of tank. Drain excess fuel into a suitable container.
8. Reverse procedure to install.

JET (TRANSFER) PUMP

1. Relieve fuel pressure as outlined under "Precautions."
2. Drain fuel tank as outlined under "Fuel Delivery Module."
3. Ensure fuel line connectors are fully seated prior to pressing release tabs.
4. Disconnect fuel lines from transfer pump.
5. Disconnect electrical connector from transfer pump.
6. Loosen transfer pump lockring using fuel sender wrench tool No. 310-069, or equivalent.
7. Remove lockring, then the transfer pump.
8. Reverse procedure to install.

FUEL FILTER

REPLACE

1. Relieve fuel pressure as outlined under "Precautions."
2. Raise and support vehicle.
3. Remove left front wheel.
4. Remove splash shield fasteners.
5. Disconnect fuel line R-clip fittings, **Fig. 54.**
6. Remove fuel filter attaching bolt, then the filter.
7. Reverse procedure to install.

TIGHTENING SPECIFICATIONS

Year	Component	Torque, Ft. Lbs.
2000	A/C Compressor	18
	Alternator	35
	Belt Tensioner	35
	Camshaft Bearing Caps	89①
	CKP Sensor	89①
	CMP Sensor	89①
	Connecting Rod	②
	Coolant Inlet Tube	18
	Coolant Outlet Tube	18
	Crankshaft Damper	③
	Cylinder Head	④
	Dipstick Tube	89①
	EGR Tube To EGR Valve	30
	Engine Appearance Cover Bracket	53
	Engine Mount Lower Nut	46
	Engine Mount Upper Nut	46
	Exhaust Manifold Heat Shield	89①
	Exhaust Manifold To Cylinder Head	15
	Exhaust Pipe To Exhaust Manifold	30
	Flywheel	59
	Front Brake Caliper	76
	Front Cover	18
	Front & Center Crossmember Bolts	76
	Front Intake Manifold Support Nut	89①

Continued

TIGHTENING SPECIFICATIONS—Continued

Year	Component	Torque, Ft. Lbs.
2000	Hydraulic Cooling Fan Pump	18
	Hydraulic Cooling Fan Reservoir	108①
	Idler Pulley	18
	Lower Control Arm Through Bolt	129
	Lower Cylinder Block	⑤
	Lower Intake Manifold To Cylinder Head	89①
	Lower Stabilizer Link Nut	41
	Lower Strut Mount Bolts	129
	Main Bearing Cap	⑤
	Oil Cooler	42
	Oil Pan	18
	Oil Pan To Transmission Bolts	35
	Oil Pump	89①
	Oil Pump Screen	89①
	Power Steering Pump	18
	Power Steering Reservoir	108①
	Radiator Support Brackets	89①
	Starter Motor	18
	Steering Gear Nuts	76
	Steering Shaft Clamp Bolt	18
	Subframe	77
	Thermostat Housing	96①
	Timing Chain Guide	18
	Timing Chain Tensioner	18
	Torque Converter Nuts	23–28
	Transmission Crossmember	41
	Transmission Cooler Lines	15
	Transmission To Engine Bolts	35
	Transmission To Oil Pan Bolts	35
	Upper Ball Joint	66
	Upper Intake Manifold Support Bracket Bolt	89①
	Upper Intake Manifold Support Bracket Nut	53①
	Upper Intake Manifold To Lower Intake Manifold	89①
	Valve Cover	89①
	Water Pump	18
	Wheel Lug Nuts	100

① — Inch lbs.

② — Tighten using new bolts in 3 steps as follows: 1st step, 17 ft. lbs.; second step, 32 ft. lbs.; 3rd step, additional 90.°

③ — Refer to "Crankshaft Damper, Replace."

④ — Refer to "Cylinder Head, Replace."

⑤ — Refer to "Main Bearings."

3.9L Engine

NOTE: On Air Bag Equipped Models, Refer To " Air Bag System Precautions" Located In The Front Of This Manual For System Disarming & Arming Procedures.

NOTE: Refer To "Computer Relearn Procedures " Located In The Front Of This Manual For Computer Relearn Procedures.

INDEX

PRECAUTIONS

AIR BAG SYSTEMS

Refer to "Air Bag System Precautions" in the front of this manual for system disarming and arming procedures.

BATTERY GROUND CABLE

Prior to service, disconnect battery ground cable and isolate as required.

FUEL SYSTEM PRESSURE RELIEF

1. Remove schrader valve cap and install fuel pressure gauge tool No. T80L-9974-B, or equivalent, to schrader valve.
2. Slowly open manual valve on pressure gauge and drain fuel into a suitable container.

QUICK DISCONNECT HOSES

R-CLIP

When working with R-clip type connections, **Fig. 1,** do not use tools to disconnect. Use of tools may deform clip components and could cause leaks.

To disconnect, bend shipping tab downward, **Fig. 1.** Spread R-clip and push clip into fitting. Separate fitting from tube.

To install, first inspect fitting and tube for damage and ensure connections are clean.

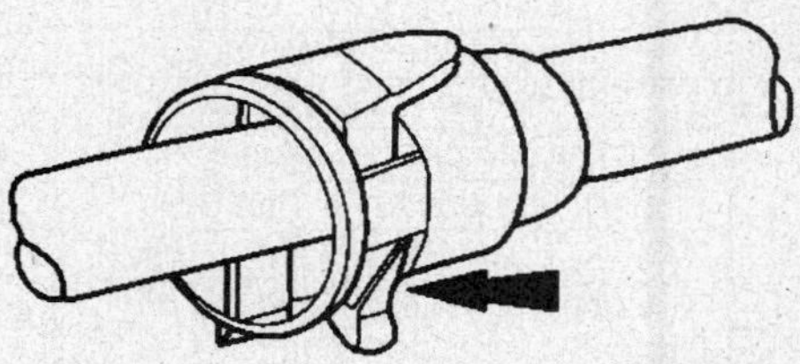

FM1069900970000X

Fig. 1 R-clip connection

Apply a light coat of clean 5W-30 motor oil to male end of tube. Insert R-clip into fitting. Align tube and fitting, then insert tube into fitting and push together until a click is heard. Pull on connection to ensure it is fully engaged.

SPRING LOCK

When working with spring lock type connections, **Fig. 2,** spring lock tool set No. T84L-19623-B or equivalent, must be used to disconnect fittings. When connecting spring lock type fittings, inspect and clean both coupling ends. Lubricate fuel line O-ring seals with clean 5W-30 motor oil. When connection is made, pull on line to ensure it is fully engaged.

VAPOR TUBE

To disconnect vapor tube connections, squeeze fitting (1) and disconnect vapor tube from fitting (2), **Fig. 3.** To connect, ensure fittings are clean and free from damage. Push tube onto fitting until it snaps into place. Pull on connection to verify fitting is secure.

COMPRESSION PRESSURE

Before performing compression test, ensure the following conditions are met: crankcase oil is of correct viscosity and at correct level, ensure battery is fully charged and engine is at normal operating temperature.

1. Turn ignition switch to off position.
2. Remove all spark plugs.
3. Set throttle plates to wide open position.
4. Install a suitable compression gauge in No. 1 cylinder.
5. Install an auxiliary starter switch in starting circuit.
6. With ignition switch off, use auxiliary starter switch to crank engine a minimum of five compression strokes.
7. Note number of compression strokes necessary to reach highest reading and record highest reading.
8. Repeat test on each cylinder, cranking engine same number of compression strokes.
9. Indicated compression pressures are considered within specifications if lowest reading cylinder is within 75 percent of highest reading.

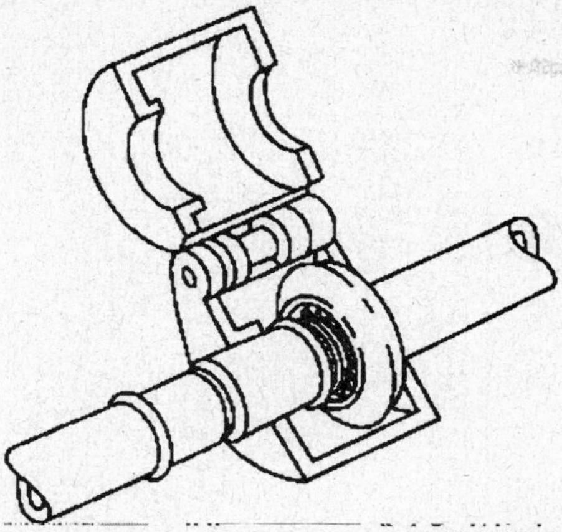

FM1069900971000X

Fig. 2 Spring lock connection

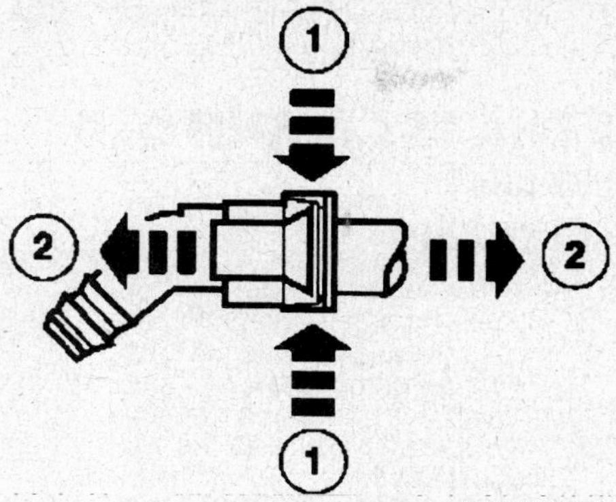

FM1069900972000X

Fig. 3 Vapor tube connection

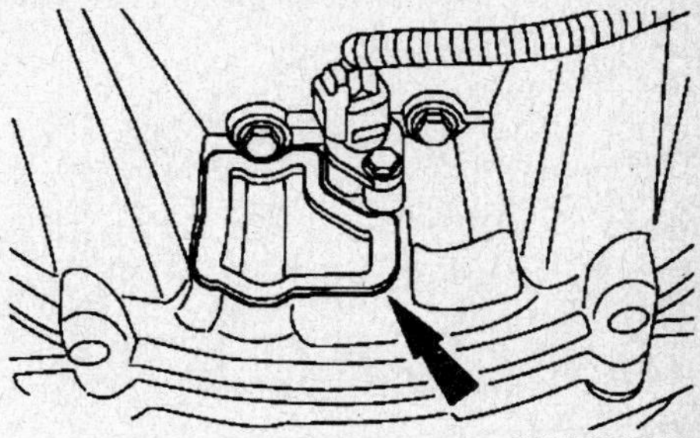

FM1069900973000X

Fig. 4 Flywheel inspection cover

ENGINE MOUNT

REPLACE

1. Using engine lifting eye kit tool No. D81L-6001-D and three bar engine support kit tool No. D88L-6000-A, or equivalents, support engine.
2. Raise and support vehicle.
3. Remove upper and lower engine mount nuts.
4. Remove engine mount and bracket.
5. Reverse procedure to install.

ENGINE

REPLACE

When carrying out operations which involve the removal and installation of the driveshaft, always check the joint angles and make the necessary adjustments as outlined under " Rear Axle & Suspension," "Driveline Angle Measurement. "

1. Remove air cleaner and outlet tube.
2. Remove engine appearance cover.
3. Drain cooling system as follows:
   a. Ensure engine is cold.
   b. Wrap a suitable shop towel around pressure relief cap, then remove cap.
   c. **Ensure coolant does not come into contact with accessory drive belt.**
   d. Open radiator draincock and drain coolant into a suitable container.
   e. **On models equipped with oil cooler,** disconnect coolant return hose at oil cooler.
4. **On all models,** remove upper radiator sight shield.
5. Remove upper radiator support brackets.
6. Recover refrigerant as outlined under "Air Conditioning. "
7. Disconnect A/C pressure switch.
8. Release power steering line from frame rail.
9. Remove power steering reservoir and position aside.
10. Disconnect fuel lines.
11. Disconnect evaporative canister purge hose, then the main vacuum supply hose.
12. Remove cowl panels.
13. Remove cowl panel support bracket.
14. Disconnect throttle and speed control cables.
15. Disconnect ground strap.
16. Remove cabin air filter and plenum as outlined under " Heater Core, Replace."
17. Disconnect powertrain bulkhead connectors from righthand strut tower and position aside.
18. Remove cowl to engine insulation panel.
19. Disconnect remaining bulkhead connectors.
20. Place reference marks on heater hoses for installation reference.
21. Disconnect four heater hoses at water control valve.
22. Remove hydraulic cooling fan reservoir and position aside.
23. Disconnect water valve electrical connector.
24. Raise and support vehicle.
25. Remove front wheels.
26. Remove front anti-lock brake sensors.
27. Remove front calipers as outlined under "Disc Brakes " and position aside.
28. Remove two sway bar link lower bolts.
29. Hold ball joint external hex, then remove upper ball joint nuts.
30. Separate upper ball joints from spindles.
31. Remove lower strut mount bolts.
32. Remove center splash panel, then the right and left splash shields.
33. Disconnect A/C high pressure line.
34. Disconnect low pressure A/C quick disconnect coupler.
35. Remove exhaust system.
36. Remove driveshaft as outlined under "Rear Axle & Suspension."
37. Disconnect shift cable if equipped.
38. Remove shift cable bracket bolt if equipped.
39. Disconnect hydraulic cooling fan lines from righthand frame rail.
40. Disconnect power steering lines from lefthand frame rail.
41. Remove steering gear electrical connectors.
42. Disconnect steering coupling.
43. Disconnect starter motor electrical connections, then the alternator electrical connector.
44. Remove flywheel inspection cover, **Fig. 4.**
45. Place reference marks on torque converter stud, nut and adapter plate for installation reference.
46. Remove eight torque converter nuts from flywheel spacer.
47. **On models equipped with engine block heater,** disconnect engine block heater plug at grille opening.
48. **On all models,** support rear of vehicle using suitable safety stands.
49. Support engine transmission, front suspension, front and center crossmemebers and cooling system using a suitable powertrain lift and transmission support bracket. Disconnect transmission support system as necessary.
50. Remove four front and four center support bolts, **Fig. 5.**
51. Lower entire powertrain assembly from vehicle.
52. Disconnect engine block heater if equipped.
53. Disconnect A/C manifold hose from compressor.
54. Disconnect power steering pump reservoir return hose and hydraulic cooling fan reservoir return hose. Drain fluid into a suitable container.
55. Remove lower radiator hose bolts.
56. Disconnect radiator hoses, then the heater hoses.
57. Remove transmission cooler line bracket nut.
58. Disconnect transmission cooler lines, then the power steering pressure line.
59. Remove power steering line bracket.
60. Install engine lifting eye kit tool No. D81L-6001-D, or equivalent, to engine.
61. Remove six lower transmission bolts.
62. Install spreader bar tool No. D93P-6001-A3, or equivalent, to engine lifting eyes.
63. Attach a suitable engine crane to spreader bar and support engine and transmission.
64. Remove engine mount upper nuts.
65. Remove engine and transmission from subframe and place on floor.
66. Remove wiring harness attaching nuts, then the remaining transmission to engine attaching bolts.
67. Separate engine from transmission, then mount engine to a suitable stand.
68. Reverse procedure to install.

Fig. 5 Front & center support bolt location

INTAKE MANIFOLD

REPLACE

When cleaning cylinder head surfaces, do not use metal scrapers, wires brushes, power abrasive discs or other abrasive methods to clean sealing surfaces. Use only a plastic scraping tool to remove all traces of gasket material.

1. Remove air cleaner outlet tube.
2. Drain cooling system as follows:
   a. Ensure engine is cold.
   b. Wrap a suitable shop towel around pressure relief cap, then remove cap.
   c. **Ensure coolant does not come into contact with accessory drive belt.**
   d. Open radiator draincock and drain coolant into a suitable container.
   e. Disconnect coolant return hose at oil cooler if equipped.
3. Remove wiper motor and arm assembly as outlined under " Wiper Motor, Replace."
4. Remove engine compartment brace.
5. Disconnect accelerator and speed control cables.
6. Disconnect main vacuum hose and vacuum harness.
7. Disconnect EGR vacuum line.
8. Disconnect EGR valve to exhaust manifold tube.
9. Disconnect camshaft position sensor, then the evaporative emission canister purge valve line.
10. Remove fuel pressure sensor connector.
11. Disconnect inline vacuum connector to fuel pressure sensor.
12. Relieve fuel pressure as outlined under "Precautions."
13. Disconnect fuel line, then the knock sensor and cylinder head temperature sensor connectors from bracket.
14. Raise wiring harness, then disconnect lefthand fuel injector connectors.
15. Disconnect idle air control, TP sensor and crankcase ventilation tube.
16. Disconnect coolant hoses from throttle body.
17. Raise wiring harness and disconnect righthand fuel injectors.
18. Remove manifold attaching bolts in sequence as shown in **Fig. 6.**
19. Reverse procedure to install. Tighten to specifications in sequence as shown in **Fig. 6.**

EXHAUST MANIFOLD

REPLACE

LEFTHAND

1. Remove dipstick tube.
2. Raise and support vehicle.
3. Remove exhaust catalyst pipe
4. Remove eight exhaust manifold attaching bolts, then the manifold.
5. Reverse procedure to install. Tighten to specifications.

RIGHTHAND

1. Raise and support vehicle.
2. Disconnect exhaust catalyst from manifold.
3. Disconnect starter motor electrical connections.
4. Disconnect EGR tube from exhaust manifold.
5. Remove eight exhaust manifold attaching bolts.
6. Reverse procedure to install. Tighten to specifications.

CYLINDER HEAD

REPLACE

When cleaning cylinder head surfaces, do not use metal scrapers, wires brushes, power abrasive discs or other abrasive methods to clean sealing surfaces. Use only a plastic scraping tool to remove all traces of gasket material.

Cylinder head bolts should be replaced when removed.

When marking shims, the only approved method is using a permanent marker. Scratches or paint on shim will cause incorrect lash adjustment and severe engine damage.

1. Remove intake manifold as outlined under "Intake Manifold, Replace."
2. Remove engine sound insulator.
3. Remove camshafts as outlined under "Camshaft, Replace."
4. Place reference marks on bucket and shim tappets for installation reference and remove as necessary.
5. Remove water crossover tube.
6. Disconnect cylinder head temperature sensor, then the camshaft position sensor.
7. Raise and support vehicle.
8. Disconnect exhaust system from exhaust manifolds.
9. Disconnect EGR tube from exhaust manifold, then lower vehicle.
10. Remove right and left front cylinder head bolts, **Fig. 7.**
11. Remove righthand cylinder head bolts in sequence as shown in **Fig. 8.**
12. Remove righthand cylinder head and gasket.
13. Remove lefthand cylinder head bolts in sequence as shown in **Fig. 9. Bolt (2), Fig. 9, cannot be fully removed. Retain bolt (2) above decking surface using a rubber band when removing cylinder head.**

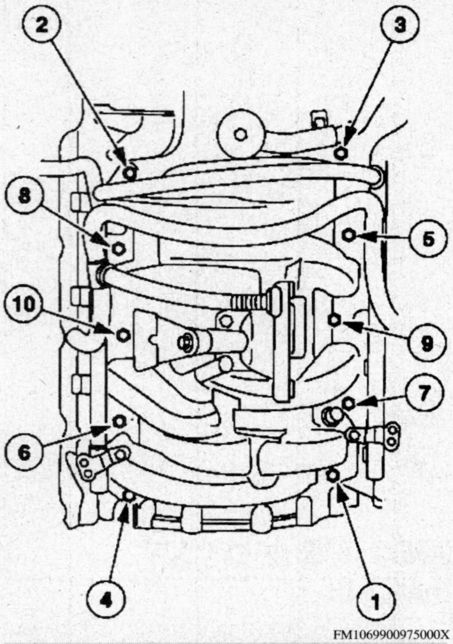

Fig. 6 Intake manifold loosening & tightening sequence

14. Remove lefthand cylinder head and gasket.
15. Reverse procedure to install noting the following:
    a. Install cylinder heads and tighten in sequence, **Figs. 10 and 11** as follows: first step, finger tighten; second step, 15 ft. lbs.; third step, 26 ft. lbs.; fourth step, 33 ft. lbs.; fifth step, additional 90°; sixth step, additional 90.°
    b. **Torque** front cylinder head bolts to 15 ft. lbs., then an additional 90.°

VALVE COVER

REPLACE

LEFTHAND

1. Remove engine appearance cover.
2. Remove air cleaner housing.
3. Disconnect crankcase ventilation tube.
4. Relieve fuel system pressure as outlined under " Precautions."
5. Disconnect fuel line.
6. Disconnect evaporative emission canister purge valve hose, then the air assist tube.
7. Remove vapor management valve appearance cover and disconnect hose.
8. Position evaporative emission canister purge valve, engine vacuum regulator, and bracket aside.
9. Position engine wiring harness up, then remove ignition coil cover and ignition coils.
10. Disconnect three front and one rear wiring harness retainers.
11. Remove fuel line bracket bolt.
12. Remove reservoir attaching bolts and position aside as necessary.
13. Remove oil level indicator tube.

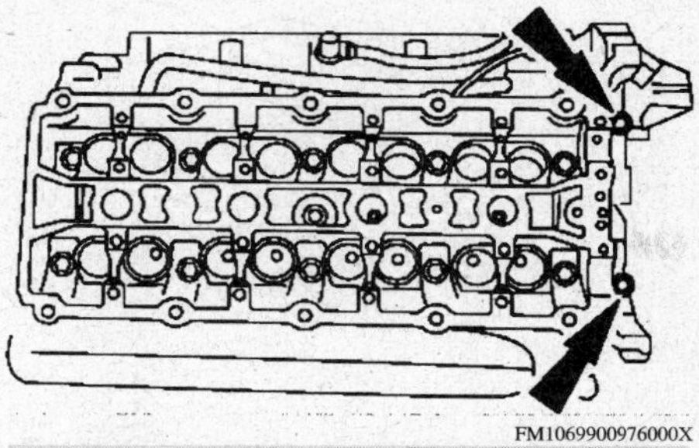

Fig. 7 Front cylinder head bolt location

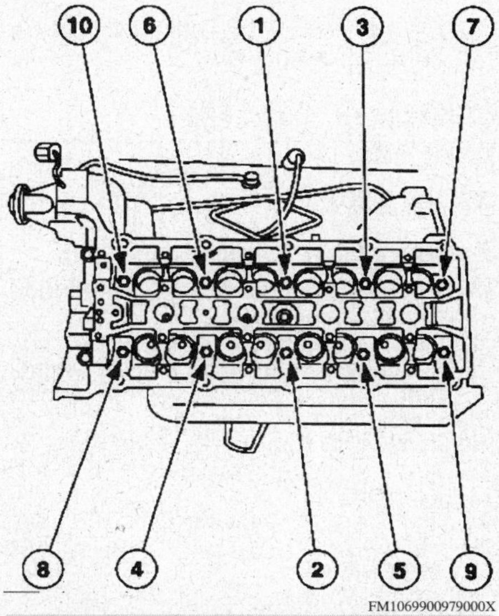

Fig. 10 Lefthand cylinder head tightening sequence

14. Remove brake line bracket, then the lefthand valve cover using sequence shown in **Fig. 12.**
15. Reverse procedure to install noting the following:
    a. Apply a .12 inch bead of silicone gasket and sealant part No. F7AZ-19554-EA or equivalent, at cylinder head to front cover joints, **Fig. 13.**
    b. Tighten to specifications in sequence as shown in **Fig. 12.**

RIGHTHAND

1. Remove air cleaner outlet tube.
2. Remove hydraulic cooling fan reservoir and position aside.
3. Disconnect crankcase ventilation hose.
4. Disconnect wiring harness brackets and position aside as necessary.
5. Remove ignition coil cover, then disconnect ignition coils.
6. Raise engine wiring harness and disconnect fuel injectors.
7. Disconnect three front and one rear wiring harness retainer, then remove ignition coils.
8. Remove right valve cover in sequence as shown in **Fig. 14.**

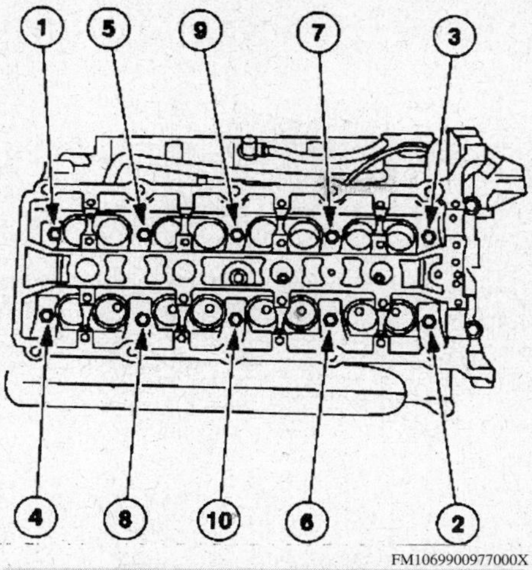

Fig. 8 Righthand cylinder head removal sequence

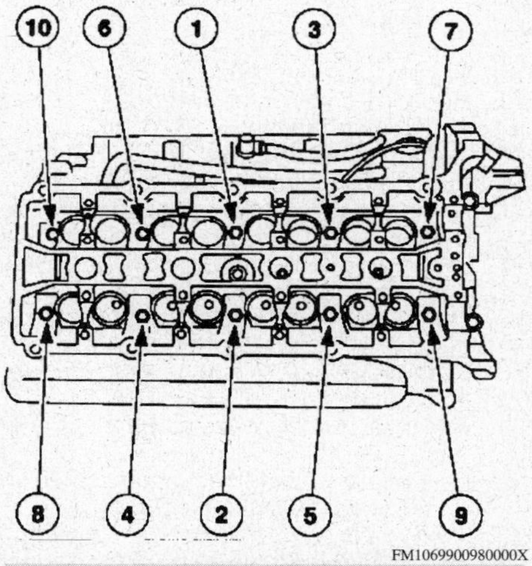

Fig. 11 Righthand cylinder head tightening sequence

9. Reverse procedure to install noting the following:
    a. Apply silicone gasket and sealant part No. F7AZ-19554-EA, or equivalent, to cylinder head and front cover joints, **Fig. 13.**
    b. Tighten to specifications in sequence as shown in **Fig. 14.**

VALVE ARRANGEMENT

Inner..............................I-I-I-I-I-I-I-I
Outer..................E-E-E-E-E-E-E-E

VALVE ADJUSTMENT

1. Remove valve covers as outlined under "Valve Cover, Replace."
2. Remove spark plugs.
3. When measuring valve clearance, ensure camshaft is on base circle, **Fig. 15.**
4. Using a suitable feeler gauge, measure and record all valve clearances.

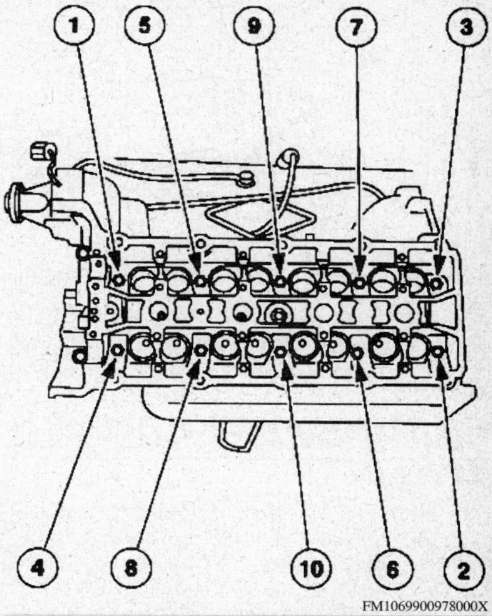

Fig. 9 Lefthand cylinder head removal sequence

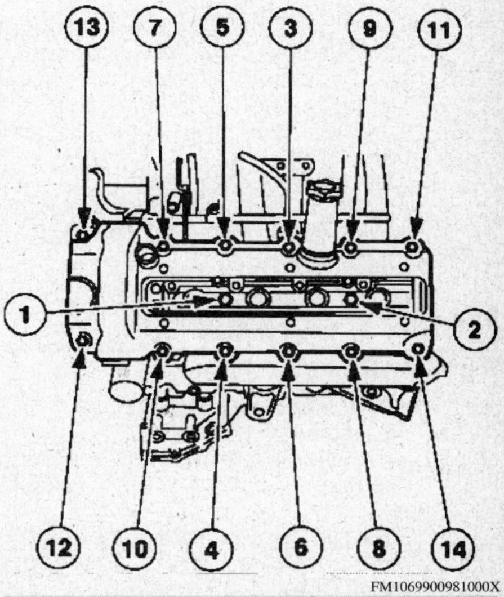

Fig. 12 Lefthand valve cover loosening & tightening sequence

Refer to "Specifications" for valve clearance specifications.

5. If adjustment is necessary, remove camshafts as outlined under "Camshaft, Replace."
6. Remove shims from bucket tappet. Shims are marked for thickness (example, 2.22 mm will read 222 on shim.)
7. Select shims using the following formula: required shim thickness = measured clearance plus base shim thickness minus most desirable clearance. Desirable clearance is .006 inch for intake and .012 inch for exhaust.
8. Reverse procedure to install. Measure new valve clearance and ensure it is within specifications.

Fig. 13 Valve cover sealant application points

CRANKSHAFT DAMPER

REPLACE

1. Remove hydraulic cooling fan as outlined under "Radiator, Replace."
2. Remove accessory drive belt.
3. Remove crankshaft pulley attaching bolt.
4. Remove crankshaft damper using damper remover tool No. T58P-6316-D, or equivalent.
5. Reverse procedure to install noting the following:
   a. Apply silicone gasket and sealant part No. F7AZ-19554-EA, or equivalent, to damper keyway.
   b. Using damper installation tool No. T74P-6316-B, or equivalent, install damper.
   c. Tighten damper bolt as follows: first step, 59 ft. lbs.; second step, loosen bolt 2 turns; third step, 37 ft. lbs.; fourth step 90.°

FRONT COVER

REPLACE

1. Drain cooling system as follows:
   a. Ensure engine is cold.
   b. Wrap a suitable shop towel around pressure relief cap, then remove cap.
   c. **Ensure coolant does not come into contact with accessory drive belt.**
   d. Open radiator draincock and drain coolant into a suitable container.
   e. **On models equipped with oil cooler,** disconnect coolant return hose at oil cooler.
2. Remove valve covers as outlined under "Valve Cover, Replace."
3. Remove cooling fan as outlined under "Radiator, Replace."
4. Loosen water pump bolts.
5. Remove accessory drive belts.
6. Remove water pump pulley, then cover alternator.
7. Remove lower radiator hose bolts.
8. Disconnect upper radiator hose from water crossover.
9. Disconnect heater hose.
10. Remove idler pulleys.
11. Remove crankshaft damper as outlined under "Crankshaft Damper, Replace."
12. Recover freon as outlined under "Air Conditioning."
13. Raise and support vehicle.

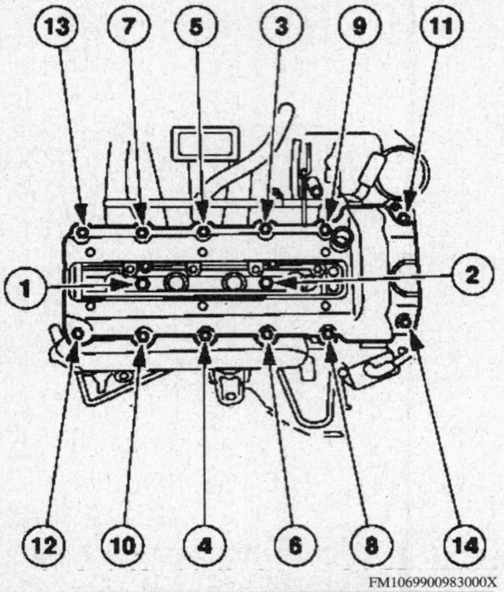

Fig. 14 Righthand valve cover loosening & tightening sequence

14. Remove splash shields.
15. Remove power steering hose bracket and position aside.
16. Remove A/C compressor manifold from compressor.
17. Disconnect compressor electrical connector.
18. Remove A/C compressor attaching bolts, then the compressor.
19. Drain power steering reservoir, then disconnect reservoir hose.
20. Remove power steering pump and position aside.
21. Remove power steering pump bracket.
22. Remove alternator as outlined under "Electrical," "Alternator, Replace."
23. Drain hydraulic cooling fan reservoir and disconnect hydraulic fan pump reservoir hose.
24. Remove hydraulic cooling fan pump, then the pump bracket.
25. Remove front cover bolts in sequence as shown in **Fig. 16.** Using a plastic scraper, clean gasket surfaces.
26. Reverse procedure to install noting the following:
   a. Inspect front cover gaskets and replace as necessary.
   b. Apply a .12 inch wide bead of silicone gasket and sealant part No. F7AZ-19554-EA or equivalent, to eight points as shown in **Fig. 17.**
   c. Install front cover and tighten in sequence shown in **Fig. 18** as follows: first step, 44 inch lbs.; second step, 89 inch lbs.

FRONT COVER SEAL

REPLACE

1. Remove crankshaft damper as outlined under "Crankshaft Damper, Replace."
2. Using seal removal tool No. 303-409, or equivalent, remove front seal
3. Reverse procedure to install. Install

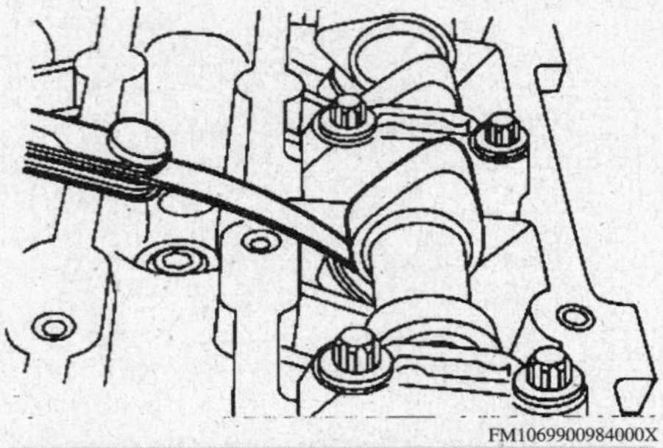

Fig. 15 Valve clearance measurement

new seal using seal installer tool No. 303-646, or equivalent.

TIMING CHAIN

REPLACE

PRIMARY

Removal

1. Remove front cover as outlined under "Front Cover, Replace."
2. Raise and support vehicle.
3. Remove crankshaft position sensor, then the torque converter access cover.
4. Turn crankshaft to 45° ATDC and ensure crankshaft keyway is at 6 o'clock position.
5. Install crankshaft positioning tool No. 303-645, or equivalent, to ignition pulse wheel.
6. Lower vehicle, then install camshaft locking tool No. 303-530, or equivalent, to righthand cylinder head.
7. Loosen outer camshaft bolt, **Fig. 19.**
8. Loosen camshaft damper bolt and slide camshaft sprockets forward on bolts, **Fig. 20.**
9. Remove righthand timing chain tensioner and blanking plate.
10. Remove tensioner arm, then the timing chain guide.
11. Remove righthand primary timing chain and crankshaft sprocket as an assembly.
12. Remove camshaft locking tool from righthand cylinder head.
13. Install camshaft locking tool to lefthand cylinder head.
14. Loosen outer camshaft bolt, **Fig. 21.**
15. Loosen lefthand camshaft damper bolt and slide camshaft sprockets forward on bolts, **Fig. 22.**
16. Remove lefthand timing chain tensioner and blanking plate, then the tensioner arm.
17. Remove lefthand timing chain guide.
18. Remove left timing chain and crankshaft gear as an assembly.

Installation

1. Insert a suitable wire into timing chain tensioner and dislodge check ball, **Fig. 23.**
2. Compress tensioner using finger pressure, then remove wire.
3. If timing mark on left timing chain

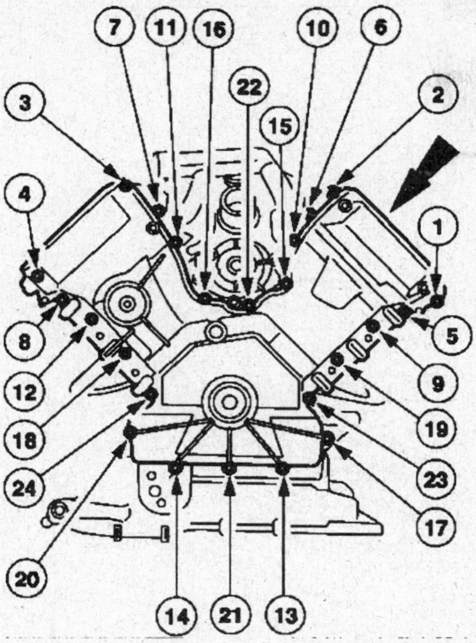

Fig. 16 Front cover removal sequence

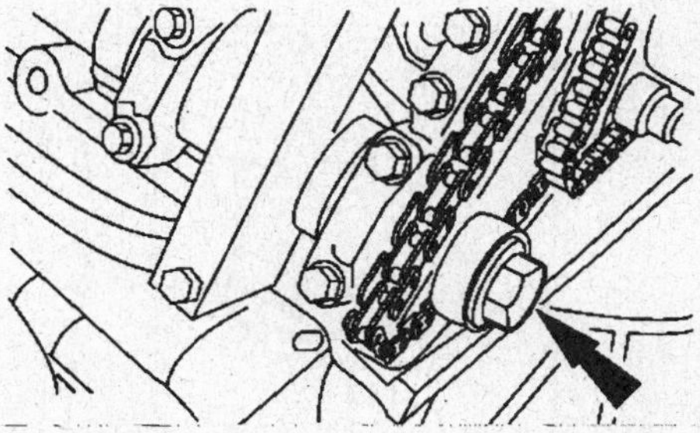

Fig. 19 Righthand outer camshaft bolt

crankshaft gear is facing toward rear of engine, install right timing chain crankshaft gear with mark facing forward. If timing mark on left timing chain crankshaft gear is facing toward front of engine, install right timing chain crankshaft gear with mark facing toward rear of engine.

4. Ensure camshaft holding tool is installed on left cylinder head.
5. Position timing chain over left intake camshaft sprocket.
6. Position crankshaft gear into timing chain.
7. Position timing chain and crankshaft gear over crankshaft as an assembly.
8. Install left timing chain guide and tensioner arm.
9. Position left blanking plate as shown in **Fig. 24. If blanking plate is not positioned as shown, oil galley will not seal resulting in low oil pressure and engine damage.**
10. Install left timing chain tensioner and blanking plate.
11. Install a suitable tie strap to take up timing chain slack, **Fig. 25.**

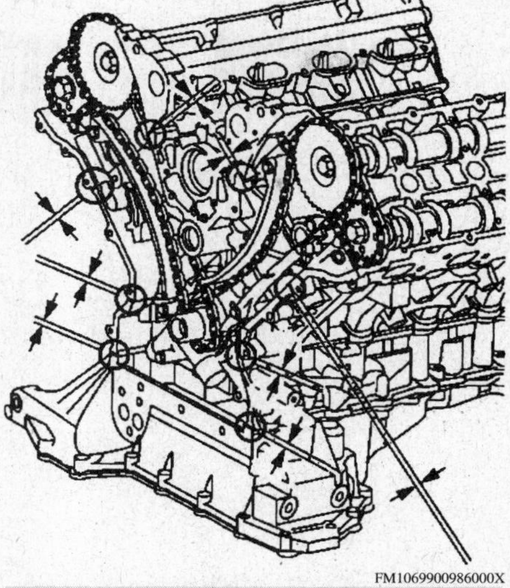

Fig. 17 Front cover sealant application points

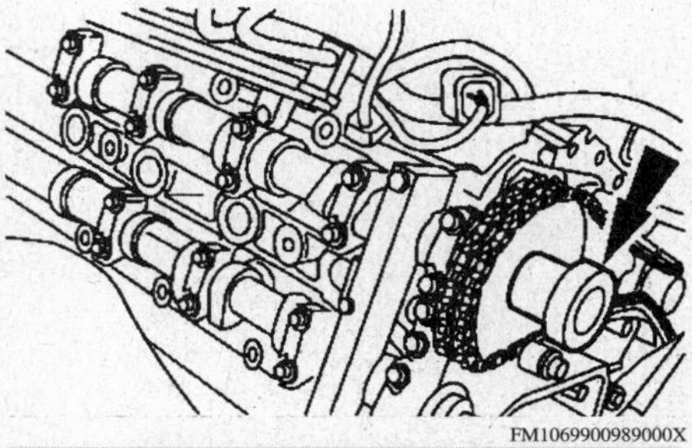

Fig. 20 Righthand camshaft damper bolt

12. Using timing chain tensioning tool No. 303-532, or equivalent, apply tension to left exhaust camshaft sprocket and tighten camshaft sprocket bolts as follows: first step, 15 ft. lbs.; second step, tighten additional 90.°
13. Install camshaft holding tool to right cylinder head. It may be necessary to adjust camshafts to install holding tool.
14. Position timing chain over right intake camshaft sprocket.
15. Place crankshaft gear into timing chain.
16. Install timing chain and crankshaft gear over crankshaft as an assembly.
17. Install right chain guide and tensioner arm.
18. Position right blanking plate as shown in **Fig. 26. If blanking plate is not positioned as shown, oil galley will not seal resulting in low oil pressure and engine damage.**
19. Install right timing chain tensioner and blanking plate.
20. Install a suitable tie strap to take up timing chain slack, **Fig. 25.**
21. Exhaust camshaft sprocket bolt must be fully tightened before tightening intake camshaft sprocket bolt.
22. Using timing chain tensioning tool No.

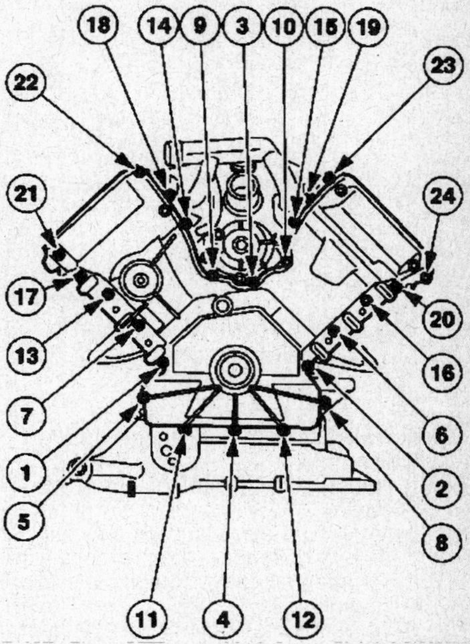

Fig. 18 Front cover tightening sequence

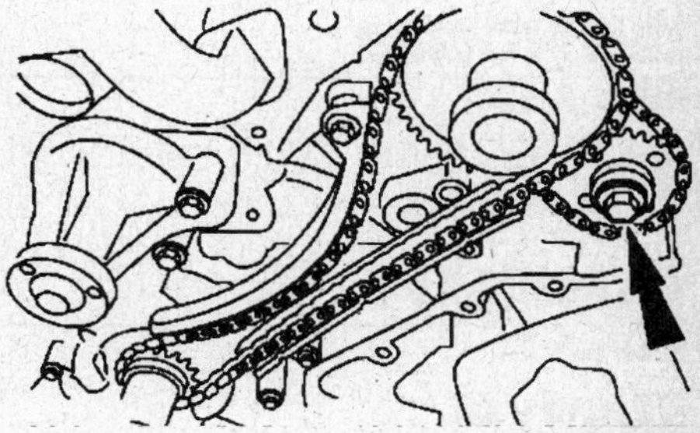

Fig. 21 Lefthand outer camshaft bolt

303-532, or equivalent, apply tension to right exhaust camshaft sprocket and tighten sprocket bolts as follows: first step, 15 ft. lbs.; second step, tighten an additional 90.°

23. Remove camshaft locking tool and tie straps.
24. Raise and support vehicle.
25. Remove crankshaft locking tool.
26. Install crankshaft position sensor and torque converter cover.
27. Lower vehicle.
28. Install front cover as outlined under "Front Cover, Replace."

SECONDARY

1. Remove primary timing chains as outlined under " Primary."
2. Remove exhaust camshaft sprocket bolt, then the intake camshaft sprocket bolt.
3. Remove sprockets, damper and chain as an assembly.
4. Remove secondary timing chain tensioner.

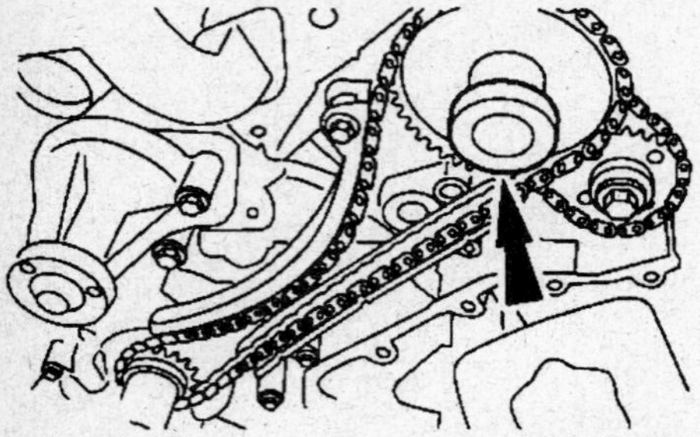

FM1069900991000X

Fig. 22 Lefthand camshaft damper bolt

5. Reverse procedure to install noting the following:
   a. Insert a wire into tensioner check valve.
   b. Apply hand pressure until tensioner is fully collapsed, then remove wire.
   c. Tighten all nuts and bolts to specifications.
   d. When installing secondary timing chains, ensure camshaft holding tool No. 303-530, or equivalent, is in place.

TIMING CHAIN TENSIONER

REPLACE

Refer to "Timing Chain, Replace" for procedure.

CAMSHAFT

REPLACE

REMOVAL

1. Remove primary and secondary timing chains as outlined under " Timing Chain, Replace."
2. Remove camshaft locking tool.
3. Place reference marks on all camshaft bearing caps and record locations for installation reference.
4. Remove right and left camshaft bearing caps, then the camshafts. Place reference marks on shims and bucket tappets and record all locations for installation reference. **A permanent marker is the only approved method of marking shims and bucket tappets. Scratches or paint on shims will result in incorrect lash adjustments and engine damage.**

INSTALLATION

1. Apply clean 5W-30 motor oil to all camshaft journals, camshaft caps and camshaft lobes.
2. Install left and right cylinder head camshafts and tighten in sequence, **Figs. 27 and 28,** as follows:
   a. Hand tighten.
   b. **Torque** to 53 inch lbs.
   c. Tighten an additional 90.°
3. If any valvetrain components were replaced, perform valve lash adjustment as outlined under "Valve Adjustment."

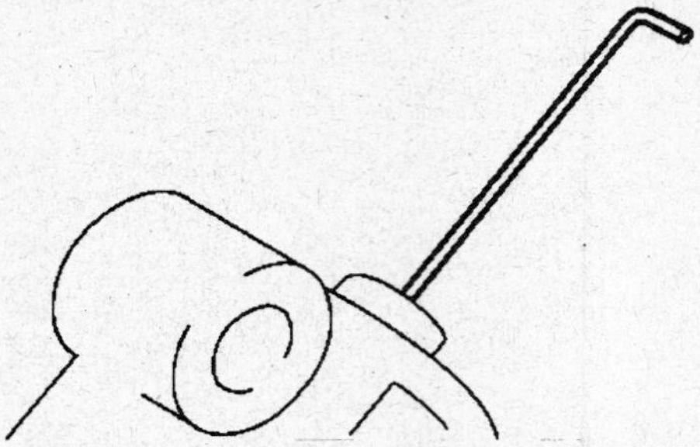

FM1069900992000X

Fig. 23 Timing chain tensioner reset

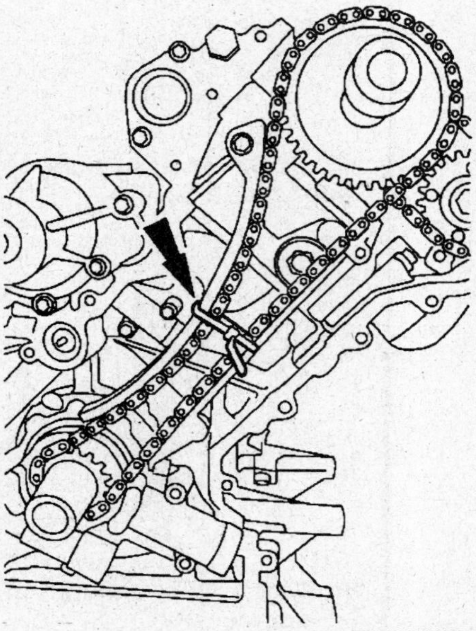

FM1069900994000X

Fig. 25 Timing chain installation

4. Install camshaft locking tool No. 303-530, or equivalent, to left cylinder head.
5. Install primary and secondary timing chains as outlined under "Timing Chain, Replace."

CRANKSHAFT REAR OIL SEAL

REPLACE

1. Raise and support vehicle.
2. Remove transmission as outlined under "Automatic Transmissions/ Transaxles," then remove flywheel.
3. Remove rear crankshaft oil seal using screw tool No. T95T-5310-AR2 and seal remover/installer tool No. 303-647, or equivalents.
4. Reverse procedure to install noting the following:
   a. Lubricate outer lips and inner seal of new oil seal before installation.
   b. Install new seal using seal remover/ installer tool No. 303-647, or equivalent.

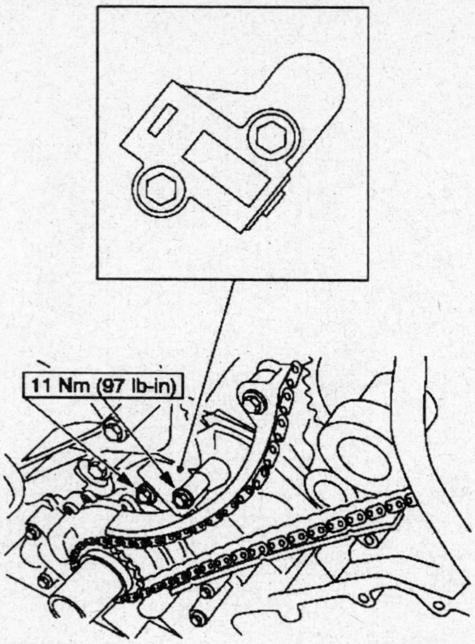

FM1069900993000X

Fig. 24 Lefthand blanking plate installation

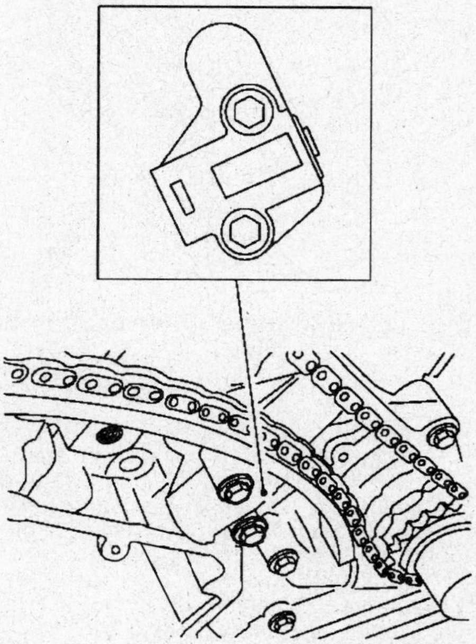

FM1069900995000X

Fig. 26 Righthand blanking plate installation

   c. Tighten flywheel to specifications in sequence, **Fig. 29.**

OIL PAN

REPLACE

1. Raise and support vehicle.
2. Drain engine oil.
3. Remove oil pan attaching bolts, then the oil pan.
4. Reverse procedure to install noting the following:

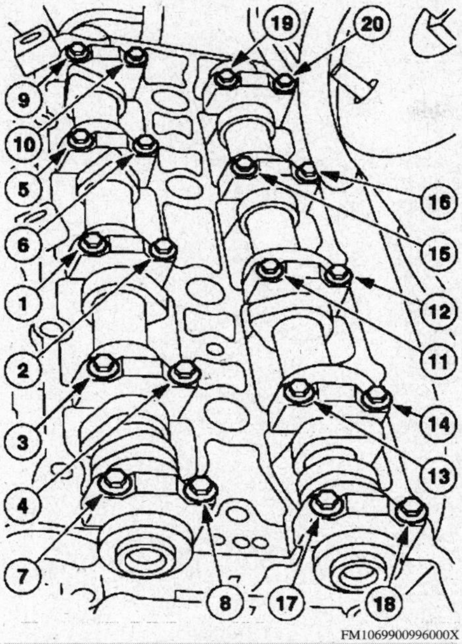

Fig. 27 Left cylinder head camshaft tightening sequence

a. Inspect oil pan gasket and replace as necessary.
b. Tighten to specifications in sequence, **Fig. 30.**

OIL PUMP

REPLACE

1. Remove primary timing chains as outlined under " Timing Chain, Replace."
2. Remove oil pump attaching bolts, then the oil pump.
3. Reverse procedure to install. Tighten to specifications.

OIL COOLER

REPLACE

1. Drain cooling system as follows:
   a. Ensure engine is cold.
   b. Wrap a suitable shop towel around pressure relief cap, then remove cap.
   c. **Ensure coolant does not come into contact with accessory drive belt.**
   d. Open radiator draincock and drain coolant into a suitable container.
   e. Disconnect coolant return hose at oil cooler.
2. Remove center air deflector, then the oil filter.
3. Disconnect oil cooler coolant hoses.
4. Remove oil cooler attaching bolts, then the oil cooler.
5. Reverse procedure to install. Tighten to specifications.

BELT TENSION DATA

Vehicle is equipped with an automatic belt tensioner. Belt tension is not adjustable. Refer to **Fig. 31** to inspect tensioner.

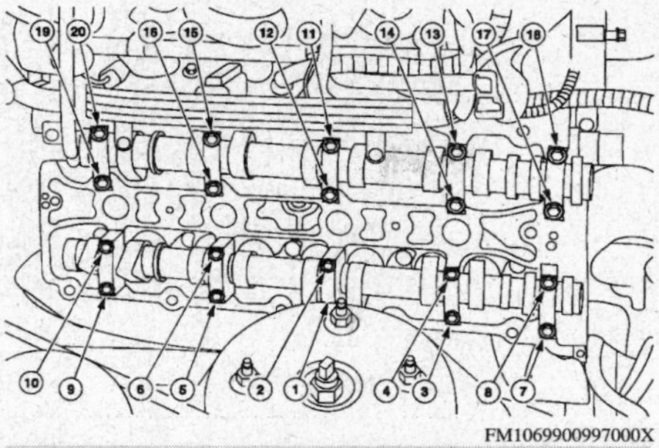

Fig. 28 Right cylinder head camshaft tightening sequence

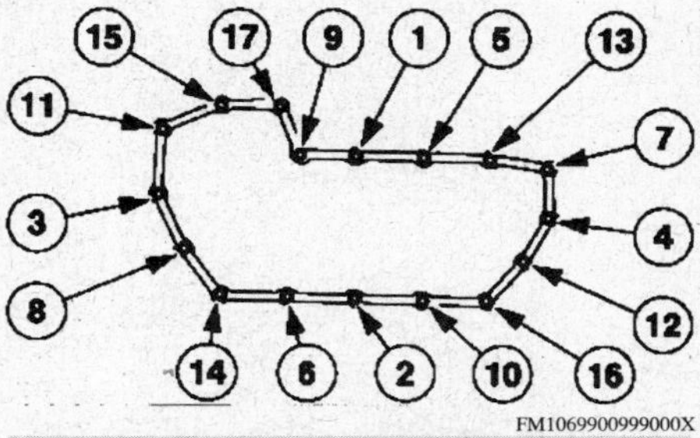

Fig. 30 Oil pan tightening sequence

SERPENTINE DRIVE BELT ROUTING

Refer to **Fig. 32** for serpentine drive belt routing.

COOLING SYSTEM BLEED

1. Remove engine fill cap, **Fig. 33.**
2. Open heater air bleed, **Fig. 34.**
3. Add coolant to overflow bottle allowing system to equalize until no more coolant can be added.
4. Install overflow bottle cap.
5. Add as much coolant as possible to engine fill cap opening. Ensure coolant does not come in contact with accessory drive belt.
6. Install engine fill cap.
7. Start engine and turn heater to Max position.
8. Close heater bleed when a steady stream of coolant is present.
9. Allow engine to idle for five minutes adding coolant to overflow bottle as needed to maintain cold fill Max mark.
10. Re-open heater air bleed to release any trapped air and close again.
11. Operate engine at 2000 RPM for 3–5 minutes or until hot air comes from heater.
12. Return engine to idle and verify hot air is still coming from heater.
13. Turn engine off and allow to cool.
14. Add coolant to overflow bottle to bring level to cold fill Max level.

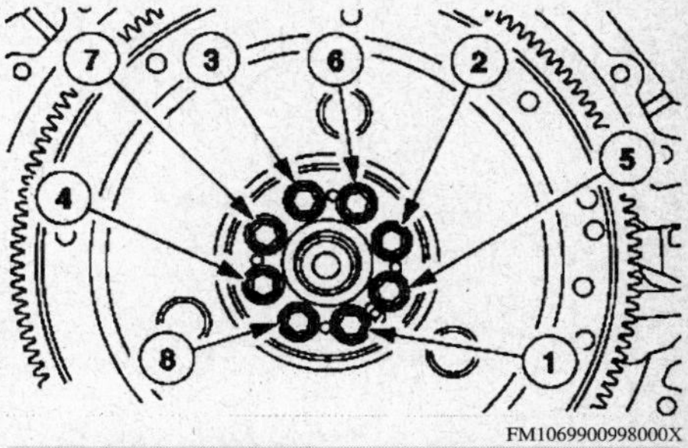

Fig. 29 Flywheel tightening sequence

THERMOSTAT

REPLACE

1. Drain cooling system as follows:
   a. Ensure engine is cold.
   b. Wrap a suitable shop towel around pressure relief cap, then remove cap.
   c. **Ensure coolant does not come into contact with accessory drive belt.**
   d. Open radiator draincock and drain coolant into a suitable container.
   e. **On models equipped with oil cooler,** disconnect coolant return hose at oil cooler.
2. **On all models,** remove air cleaner outlet tube.
3. Remove coolant tube from front of engine, **Fig. 35.**
4. Remove coolant tube bracket studs.
5. Disconnect lower radiator hose from thermostat housing.
6. Remove thermostat housing cover, **Fig. 36,** then the thermostat.
7. Reverse procedure to install. Tighten to specifications.

WATER PUMP

REPLACE

1. Drain cooling system as follows:
   a. Ensure engine is cold.
   b. Wrap a suitable shop towel around pressure relief cap, then remove cap.
   c. **Ensure coolant does not come into contact with accessory drive belt.**
   d. Open radiator draincock and drain coolant into a suitable container.
   e. **On models equipped with oil cooler,** disconnect coolant return hose at oil cooler.
2. **On all models,** loosen water pump pulley bolts.
3. Remove accessory drive belt.
4. Remove water pump pulley bolts, then the pulley.
5. Remove water pump attaching bolts, then the water pump. Inspect water pump O-ring seal and replace as necessary.
6. Reverse procedure to install noting the following:
   a. Lubricate water pump O-ring using

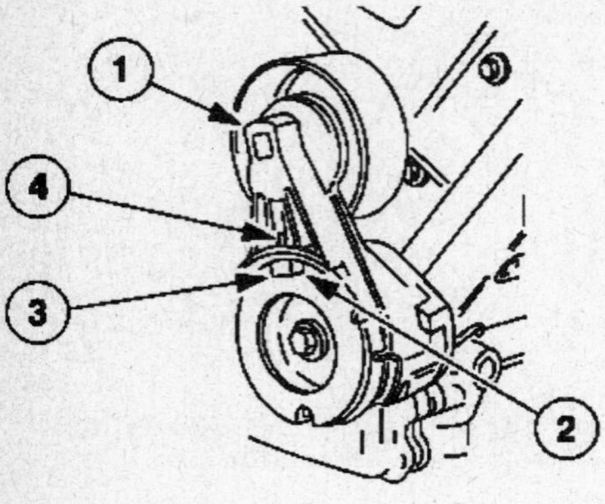

Item	Description
1	Belt tension relief point
2	Unacceptable belt wear range
3	Acceptable belt installation and wear range
4	Belt length indicator

FM1069901000000X

Fig. 31 Belt tensioner inspection

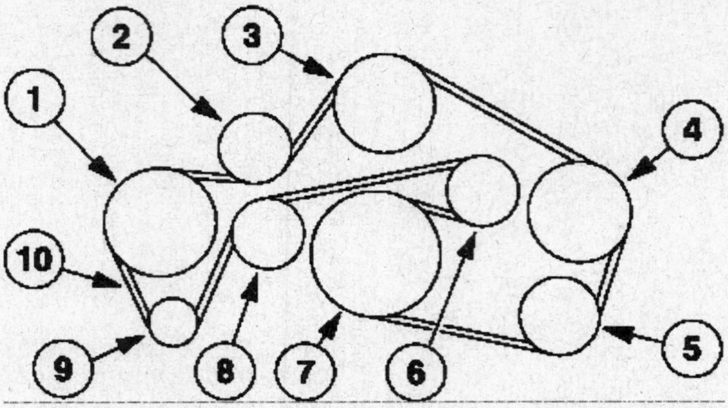

FM1069901001010X

Fig. 32 Serpentine drive belt routing (Part 1 of 2)

Item	Description
1	Hydraulic fan pump pulley
2	Belt idler pulley—unflanged
3	Water pump pulley
4	Power steering pump pulley
5	A/C clutch pulley
6	Drive belt tensioner
7	Crankshaft vibration damper
8	Belt idler pulley—flanged
9	Generator pulley
10	Drive belt

FM1069901001020X

Fig. 32 Serpentine drive belt routing (Part 2 of 2)

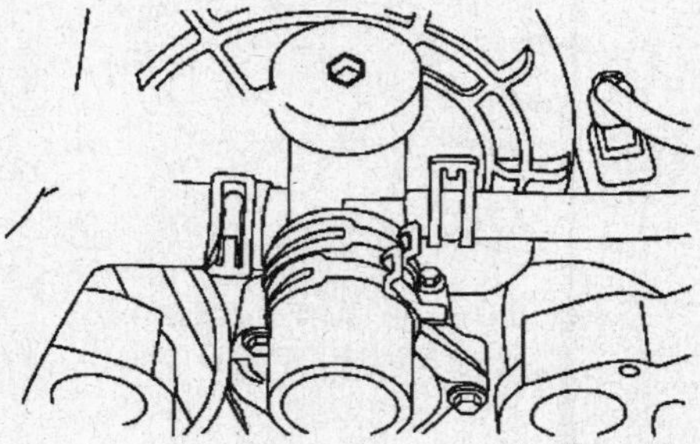

FM1069901002000X

Fig. 33 Engine fill cap location

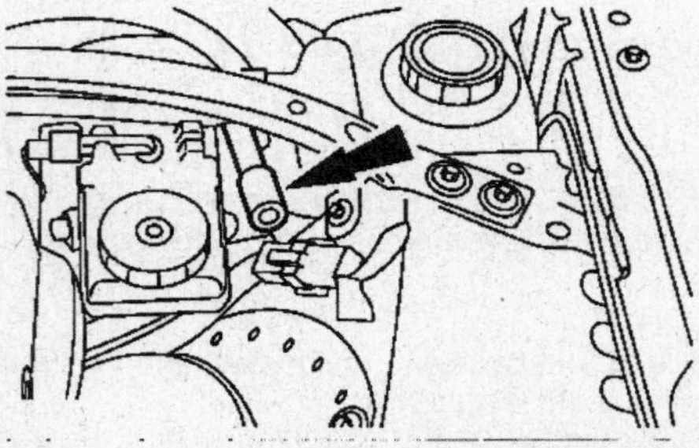

FM1069901003000X

Fig. 34 Heater air bleed location

premium engine coolant part No. E2FZ-19549-AA, or equivalent.
b. Tighten all nuts and bolts to specifications.
c. Bleed cooling system.

RADIATOR

REPLACE

1. Drain cooling system as follows:
   a. Ensure engine is cold.
   b. Wrap a suitable shop towel around pressure relief cap, then remove cap.
   c. **Ensure coolant does not come into contact with accessory drive belt.**
   d. Open radiator draincock and drain coolant into a suitable container.
   e. Disconnect coolant hoses at oil cooler if equipped.
2. Remove upper radiator sight shield.
3. Remove air cleaner outlet tube.
4. Remove radiator support brackets, then the upper radiator hose.
5. Remove receiver drier attaching bolt and position receiver drier aside.
6. Remove electric water pump bolt and position aside, **Fig. 37.**
7. Disconnect high pressure cooling fan line, then the return hose.
8. Separate return hose from fan shroud and position aside.
9. Remove fan shroud.
10. Support A/C condenser using suitable mechanics wire.
11. Raise and support vehicle.
12. Remove right and left splash shields, then the radiator air deflector.
13. Disconnect lower radiator hose.
14. Remove condenser to radiator attaching bolts.
15. Remove condenser support brackets, then the radiator through bottom of vehicle.
16. Reverse procedure to install.

HYDRAULIC FAN MOTOR

REPLACE

Refer to "Radiator, Replace" for procedure.

HYDRAULIC COOLING FAN PUMP

REPLACE

1. Remove alternator as outlined under "Alternator, Replace" in the "Electrical" section.
2. Disconnect hose as shown in **Fig. 38** and drain fluid into suitable container.
3. Disconnect fan pump electrical connector.
4. Remove high pressure line bracket and disconnect high pressure line.
5. Remove cooling fan pump attaching bolts, then the cooling fan.
6. Reverse procedure to install. Tighten to specifications.

FUEL PUMP

REPLACE

The fuel system contains two pumps. One is the " fuel delivery module" which

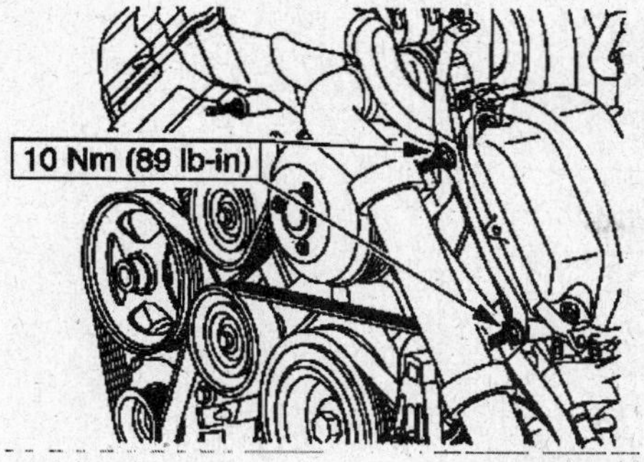

FM1069901004000X

Fig. 35 Coolant tube removal

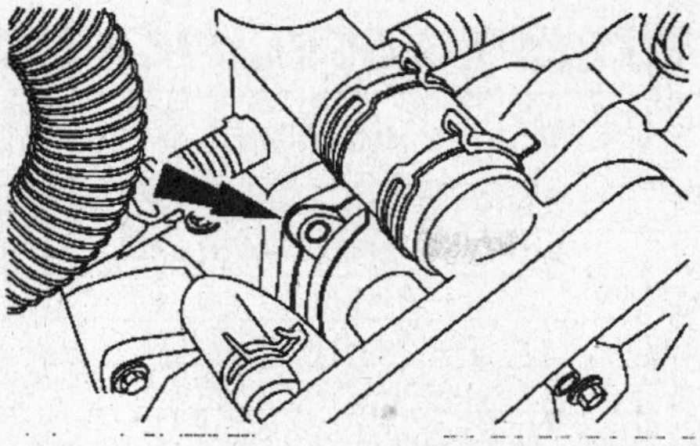

FM1069901005000X

Fig. 36 Thermostat housing cover removal

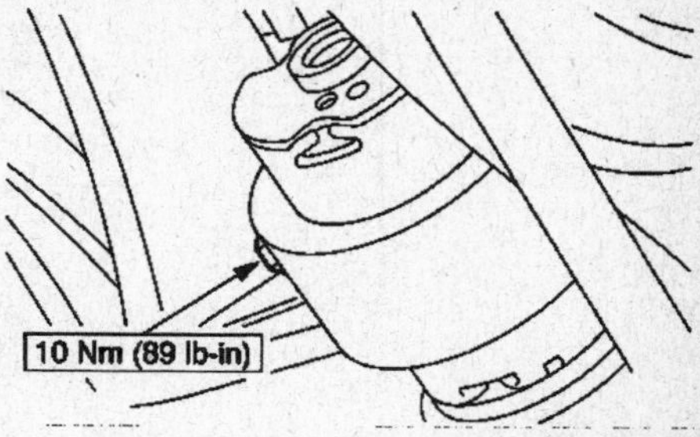

FM1069901006000X

Fig. 37 Electric water pump location

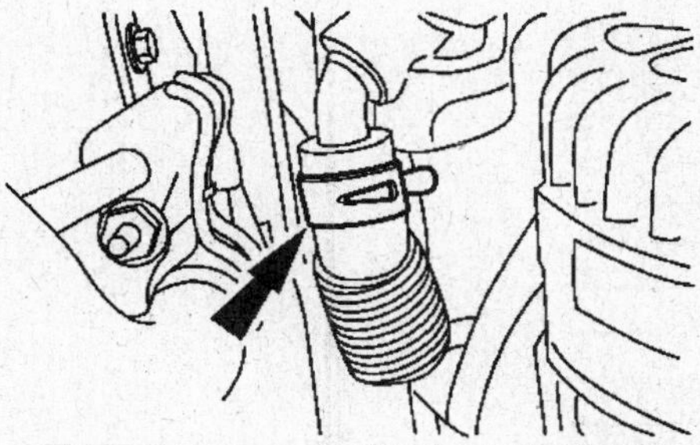

FM1069901008000X

Fig. 38 Fan pump hose location

FM1069901009000X

Fig. 39 Transfer pump fuel line connections

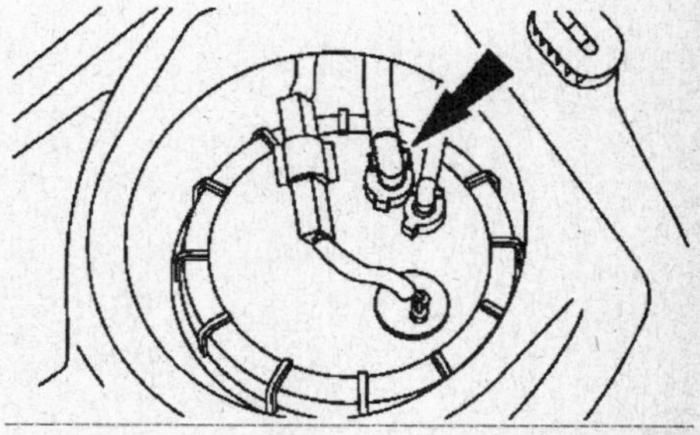

FM1069901010000X

Fig. 40 Fuel delivery module fuel line connections

provides fuel pressure to the engine. The second pump is a "jet pump" or " transfer" pump which maintains fuel levels in both sides of the fuel tank.

The jet pump is located on the lefthand side of the fuel tank and contains a fuel level sensor and a check valve which maintains system pressure after the pump is shut off.

The fuel delivery module is located on the righthand side of the fuel tank and contains a fuel level sensor and an inlet screen on the bottom of the pump.

To disconnect fuel lines from pumps, press down on fuel line connector while pressing release tabs. Pull straight up to remove.

Whenever fuel pumps are removed, new fuel pump gaskets must be installed.

FUEL DELIVERY MODULE

1. Relieve fuel pressure as outlined under "Precautions. "
2. Drain fuel tank as follows:
   a. Release rear seat mini-buckle.
   b. Depress two seat cushion latches, then remove rear seat cushion and insulation.
   c. Remove fuel pump access covers.
   d. Ensure all fuel pump connections are fully seated.
   e. Remove black connector elbow on transfer pump, **Fig. 39.**
   f. Attach a fuel line draining connector to a suitable fuel storage tanker hose and outlet fitting on transfer pump.

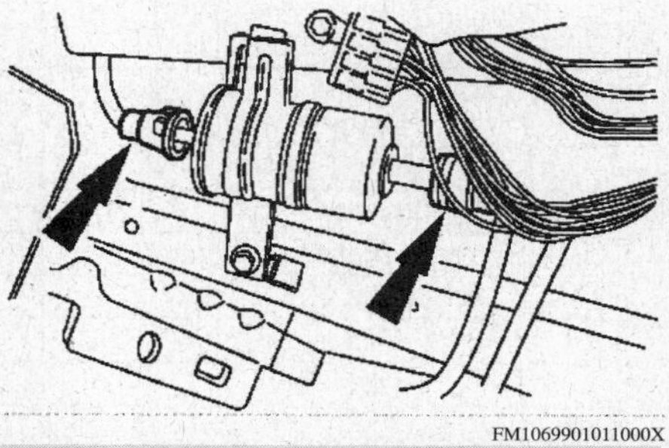

FM1069901011000X

Fig. 41 Fuel filter location

   g. Siphon fuel until tank side is empty.
   h. Attach fuel draining connector to fuel delivery module, **Fig. 40,** and repeat steps e, f and g.
3. Disconnect remaining fuel line from fuel delivery module.
4. Disconnect fuel delivery module electrical connector.
5. Loosen fuel pump lockring using fuel sender wrench tool No. 310-069, or equivalent.
6. Remove fuel delivery module lockring.
7. Position pump flange clear of pump opening, then press lock tabs and release pump from tank mounting flange. Lift straight up and out of retainer cup and tilt while in tank to drain fuel from reservoir. Straighten and lift straight up and out of tank. Drain excess fuel into a suitable container.
8. Reverse procedure to install.

JET (TRANSFER) PUMP

1. Relieve fuel pressure as outlined under "Precautions. "
2. Drain fuel tank as outlined under "Fuel Delivery Module."
3. Ensure fuel line connectors are fully seated prior to pressing release tabs.
4. Disconnect fuel lines from transfer pump.
5. Disconnect electrical connector from transfer pump.
6. Loosen transfer pump lockring using fuel sender wrench tool No. 310-069, or equivalent.
7. Remove lockring, then the transfer pump.
8. Reverse procedure to install.

FUEL FILTER

REPLACE

1. Relieve fuel pressure as outlined under "Precautions. "
2. Raise and support vehicle.
3. Remove left front wheel.
4. Remove splash shield fasteners.
5. Disconnect fuel line R-clip fittings, **Fig. 41.**
6. Remove fuel filter attaching bolt, then the filter.
7. Reverse procedure to install.

TIGHTENING SPECIFICATIONS

Year	Component	Torque, Ft. Lbs.
2000	A/C Compressor	18
	A/C Manifold To Compressor	15
	Alternator	⑤
	Belt Tensioner	37
	Camshaft Bearing Caps	⑩
	Camshaft Sprockets	15⑦
	Condenser To Radiator Bolts	89①
	Cowl Panel Support Bracket	80①
	Crankshaft Damper	③
	Crankshaft Position Sensor	89①
	Cylinder Head	②
	EGR Tube To EGR Valve	30
	EGR Tube To Exhaust Manifold	30
	Electric Water Pump Attaching Bolt	89①
	Engine Mount Bracket To Cylinder Block	34
	Engine Mount Upper & Lower Nuts	30
	Exhaust Catalyst To Exhaust Manifold	30
	Exhaust Manifold To Cylinder Head	18
	Flywheel	⑧
	Front Cover	④
	Front & Center Support Bolts	76
	Hydraulic Cooling Fan Pump	18
	Hydraulic Cooling Fan Pump Bracket	18
	Hydraulic Cooling Fan Reservoir Lower Bolt	106①
	Hydraulic Cooling Fan Reservoir Upper Bolt	53①
	Idler Pulley	18
	Intake Manifold	15
	Lower Strut Mount Bolts	129
	Lower Sway Bar Link	41
	Oil Cooler	43
	Oil Pan	⑨
	Oil Pump	53①⑦
	Power Steering Pressure Line	89①
	Power Steering Pump Bracket	18
	Power Steering Pump To Bracket	18
	Power Steering Reservoir Lower Bolt	106①
	Power Steering Reservoir Upper Bolt	53①
	Primary Timing Chain Guide	97①
	Primary Timing Chain Tensioner	97①
	Receiver/Drier Bracket	8
	Secondary Timing Chain Tensioner	97①
	Steering Coupling	26
	Thermostat Housing	80①
	Torque Converter To Flywheel	28
	Transmission Cooler Lines	89①
	Transmission To Engine Bolts	35
	Upper Ball Joint Nuts	66
	Upper Radiator Support Brackets	89①
	Valve Cover	89①
	Water Pump	71①⑦
	Water Pump Pulley	89①⑥
	Wheel Lug Nuts	100

① — Inch lbs.
② — Refer to "Cylinder Head, Replace."

③ — Refer to "Crankshaft Damper, Replace."
④ — Refer to "Front Cover, Replace."
⑤ — Refer to "Alternator, Replace" in "Electrical" section.
⑥ — Tighten an additional 45.°
⑦ — Tighten an additional 90.°
⑧ — Tighten in sequence using two steps as follows: 1st step, 11 ft. lbs.; 2nd step, 81 ft. lbs.
⑨ — Tighten in sequence using two steps as follows: 1st step, 44 inch lbs.; 2nd step, 9 ft. lbs.
⑩ — Refer to "Camshaft, Replace."

Clutch & Manual Transmission

NOTE: On Air Bag Equipped Models, Refer To " Air Bag System Precautions" Located In The Front Of This Manual For System Disarming & Arming Procedures.

NOTE: Refer To "Computer Relearn Procedures " Located In The Front Of This Manual For Computer Relearn Procedures.

INDEX

PRECAUTIONS

AIR BAG SYSTEMS

Refer to "Air Bag System Precautions" in the front of this manual for system disarming and arming procedures.

BATTERY GROUND CABLE

Prior to service, disconnect battery ground cable and isolate as required.

DESCRIPTION

The clutch system consists of a flywheel, clutch disc, pressure plate, master cylinder, clutch release hub and bearing.

The clutch master cylinder transmits fluid pressure to the slave cylinder which moves the clutch release hub and bearing.

The clutch master cylinder uses brake fluid and shares a common reservoir with brake master cylinder.

MAINTENANCE

FLUID CHECK

Fluid level should be within .02 inch below lower edge of fill plug bore, **Fig. 1.**

FLUID CHANGE

1. Raise and support vehicle.
2. Remove fill plug, **Fig. 1.**
3. Remove drain plug and drain fluid into a suitable container, **Fig. 2.**
4. Install drain plug and tighten to specifications.
5. Fill transmission as outlined under "Fluid Check. "

ADJUSTMENTS

The hydraulic clutch system adjusts automatically to compensate for clutch disc wear. The clutch linkage is not adjustable.

HYDRAULIC SYSTEM SERVICE

CLUTCH SYSTEM BLEED

1. Raise and support vehicle.
2. Remove dust cover, then the bleeder screw cover.
3. Attach a bleed jar to bleed nipple and open bleeder screw 1 turn.
4. Depress clutch pedal repeatedly until emerging fluid is free of bubbles. Ensure fluid reservoir is full during bleed procedure.
5. After bleeding, tighten bleeder screw and depress clutch pedal 10 times and verify proper clutch operation.
6. Ensure fluid level is between Min and Max marks.

CLUTCH MASTER CYLINDER

1. Disconnect footwell lamp electrical connector.
2. Remove clutch pedal position switch bracket bolts and position bracket aside.
3. Remove snap ring and disconnect clutch master cylinder pushrod.
4. Remove snap ring from hydraulic line, then disconnect line from elbow.
5. Remove clutch master cylinder attaching nuts, then the master cylinder, **Fig. 3.**
6. Reverse procedure to install. Tighten to specifications and bleed clutch hydraulic system.

SLAVE CYLINDER

1. Remove transmission as outlined under "Transmission, Replace."
2. Remove hydraulic tube connector, **Fig. 4.**
3. Remove slave cylinder attaching bolts, then the slave cylinder.
4. Reverse procedure to install. Tighten to specifications and bleed clutch hydraulic system.

HYDRAULIC TUBES

1. Remove snap ring and tube from clutch master cylinder connector.
2. Disconnect clutch slave cylinder hydraulic line.
3. Remove hydraulic tube bracket nut.
4. Remove hydraulic tube and bracket.
5. Reverse procedure to install. Tighten to specifications, install new O-ring to slave cylinder port and bleed clutch hydraulic system.

CLUTCH

REPLACE

When carrying out operations which involve the removal and installation of the driveshaft, always check the joint angles and make the necessary adjustments as outlined under " Rear Axle & Suspension," "Driveline Angle Measurement. "

1. Remove transmission as outlined under "Transmission, Replace."
2. Support clutch plate using clutch alignment tool No. T74P-7137-K, or equivalent.

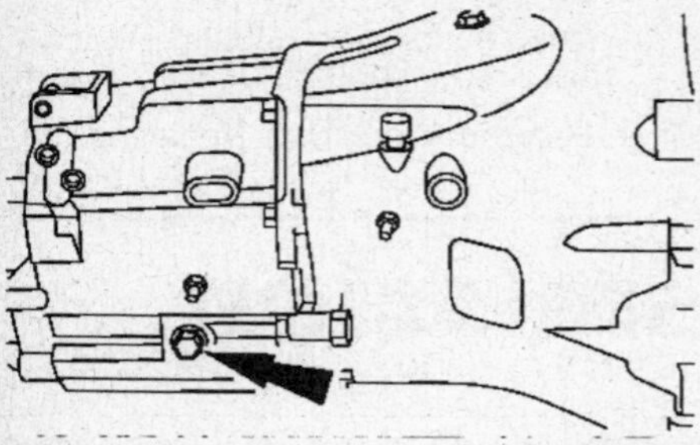
FM5039900671000X

Fig. 1 Transmission fill plug

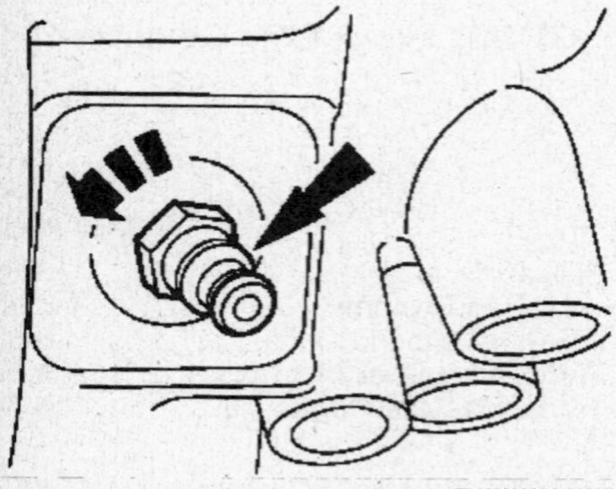
FM5039900670000X

Fig. 4 Hydraulic tube connector

3. Remove pressure plate attaching bolts in a uniform sequence.
4. Remove clutch disc and pressure plate.
5. Reverse procedure to install noting the following:
   a. Align clutch disc using clutch alignment tool No. T74P-7137-K, or equivalent.
   b. Tighten pressure plate to specifications using a diagonal sequence.

PILOT BEARING

REPLACE

When carrying out operations which involve the removal and installation of the driveshaft, always check the joint angles and make the necessary adjustments as outlined under " Rear Axle & Suspension," "Driveline Angle Measurement. "

1. Remove transmission as outlined under "Transmission, Replace."
2. Remove clutch as outlined under "Clutch, Replace. "
3. Using slide hammer tool No. T58L-101-B, or equivalent, remove pilot bearing from crankshaft.

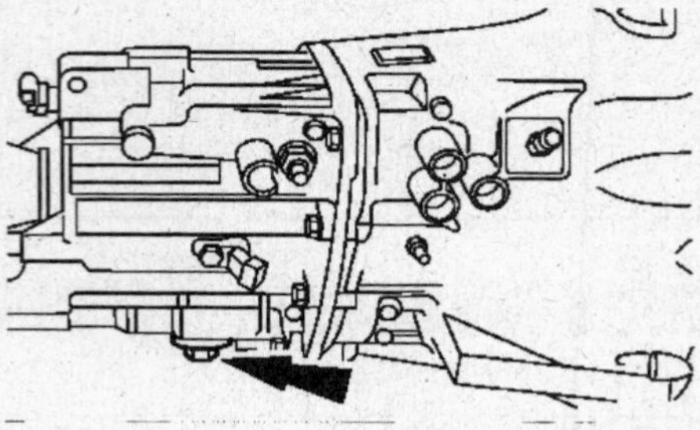
FM5039900672000X

Fig. 2 Transmission drain plug

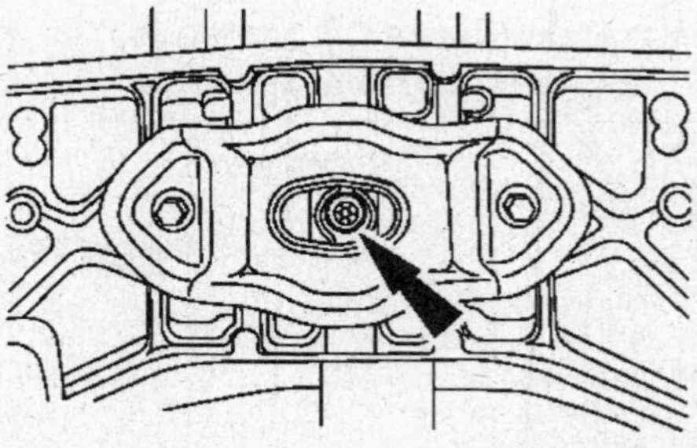
FM5039900673000X

Fig. 5 Support insulator removal

4. Reverse procedure to install. Install pilot bearing using installer tool No. T85T-7137-A, or equivalent.

TRANSMISSION

REPLACE

When carrying out operations which involve the removal and installation of the driveshaft, always check the joint angles and make the necessary adjustments as outlined under " Rear Axle & Suspension," "Driveline Angle Measurement. "

1. Raise and support vehicle.
2. Remove selector rod locating pin and disconnect selector rod.
3. Remove intermediate muffler.
4. Remove center heat shield.
5. Place reference marks on transmission flange, driveshaft flexible coupling, flange bolts, nuts, washers and balance add on nuts if equipped for installation reference.
6. Support front section of driveshaft. **Do not loosen flexible coupling or remove from driveshaft.**
7. Loosen driveshaft yoke locknut and move driveshaft front section toward center bearing.

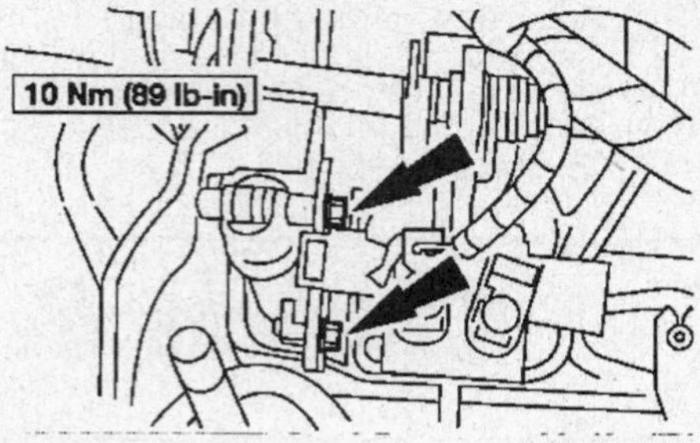

FM5039900669000X

Fig. 3 Clutch master cylinder removal

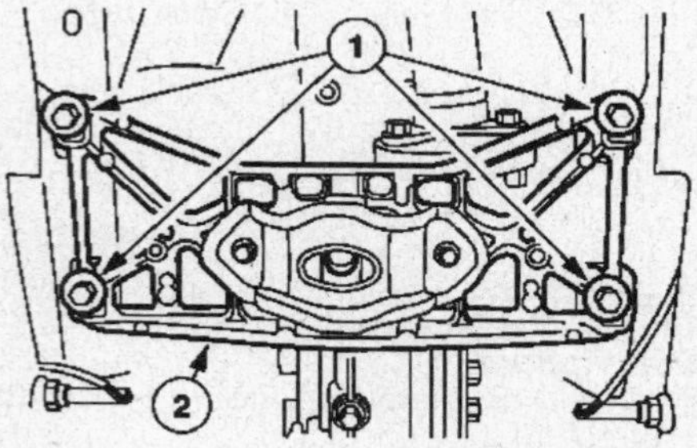

FM5039900674000X

Fig. 6 Transmission support removal

8. Disconnect right and left catalyst monitor sensor.
9. Remove wiring harness from top of transmission.
10. Disconnect VSS and reverse light switch.
11. Remove wiring harness from transmission.
12. Place a suitable transmission jack under transmission and secure transmission to jack.
13. Remove support insulator, **Fig. 5.**
14. Remove transmission support, **Fig. 6.**
15. Remove slave cylinder supply tube retaining clip, then the tube.
16. Plug slave cylinder tube to prevent fluid loss.
17. Remove transmission to engine attaching bolts.
18. Disconnect starter motor ground cable and remove starter wiring harness.
19. Remove starter motor, then the transmission.
20. Reverse procedure to install noting the following:
    a. Tighten all nuts and bolts to specifications.
    b. Install new O-ring to slave cylinder tube.
    c. Bleed clutch hydraulic system.

TIGHTENING SPECIFICATIONS

Year	Component	Torque, Ft. Lbs.
2000	Clutch Hydraulic Tube Bracket	89①
	Clutch Master Cylinder	89①
	Driveshaft Yoke Locknuts	66
	Pressure Plate To Flywheel	17
	Slave Cylinder	16
	Starter Motor	18
	Support Insulator	30
	Transmission Drain Plug	37
	Transmission Fill Plug	37
	Transmission Flex Coupling Balance Nuts	18
	Transmission Flex Coupling Nuts	63
	Transmission To Engine Bolts	35

① — Inch lbs.

Rear Axle & Suspension

NOTE: On Air Bag Equipped Models, Refer To " Air Bag System Precautions" Located In The Front Of This Manual For System Disarming & Arming Procedures.

NOTE: Refer To "Computer Relearn Procedures " Located In The Front Of This Manual For Computer Relearn Procedures.

INDEX

PRECAUTIONS

AIR BAG SYSTEMS

Refer to "Air Bag System Precautions" in the front of this manual for system disarming and arming procedures.

BATTERY GROUND CABLE

Prior to service, disconnect battery ground cable and isolate as required.

DESCRIPTION

The rear axle is an integral-type housing hypoid gear design, **Fig. 1.** The ring and pinion consists of an eight inch ring gear and an overhung drive pinion which is supported by two opposed tapered roller bearings. Pinion preload is maintained by a drive pinion collapsible spacer on the pinion shaft and is adjusted by the pinion nut. Differential bearing preload and ring gear backlash are adjusted by differential bearing shims located between differential bearing cup and rear axle housing.

Halfshafts are held in the differential case by a driveshaft bearing retainer circlip which engages a step in the differential side gear.

The suspension is an independent design featuring upper and lower control arms, shock absorber and spring assembly, adjustable toe links, stabilizer bar and wheel knuckles. Refer to **Fig. 2** for rear suspension components.

When servicing suspension components, always use new appropriate nuts and bolts when removed.

When carrying out operations which involve the removal and installation of the driveshaft, always check the joint angles and make the necessary adjustments as outlined under " Driveline Angle Measurement."

REAR AXLE

REPLACE

1. Remove halfshafts as outlined under "Rear Halfshaft, Replace."
2. Remove exhaust system and heat shield as necessary.
3. Place reference marks on pinion

flange, flex coupling and driveshaft to pinion flange bolts, nuts, washers and weighted washers for installation reference.
4. Support driveshaft, then remove driveshaft to pinion flange bolts and nuts. **Do not remove flex coupling on driveshaft flange.**
5. Loosen driveshaft yoke adjuster nut using driveshaft coupler wrenches, tool No. 205-474, or equivalents.
6. Remove center bearing mounting bolts and shims. Mark position of shims for installation reference.
7. Slide rear driveshaft to full forward position and tighten adjuster nut.
8. Position a suitable jack under axle housing and secure axle to jack.
9. Remove three axle mounting nuts, **Fig. 3.**
10. Lower axle housing from vehicle.
11. Reverse procedure to install. Tighten to specifications.

STUB SHAFT BEARING & SEAL

REPLACE

1. Remove halfshaft as outlined under "Rear Halfshaft, Replace."
2. Using bearing cup remover tool No. T77F-1102-A and slide hammer tool No. T50T–100–A, or equivalents, remove stub shaft bearing housing seal and bearing.
3. Lubricate new bearing with SAE 75W-140 synthetic rear axle lubricant F1TZ-19580–B, or equivalent.
4. Install bearing into rear axle housing bore using bearing replacer tool No. T89P-1244-A and handle tool No. T80T-4000-W, or equivalents.
5. Lubricate lip of seal with premium long life grease XG-1-C, or equivalent.
6. Install seal using seal replacer tool No. T89P-4850-A and handle tool No. T80T-4000-W, or equivalents.
7. Install halfshaft as outlined under "Rear Halfshaft, Replace."

PINION FLANGE & SEAL

REPLACE

REMOVAL

1. Raise and support vehicle, then remove rear wheels.
2. Remove rear brake calipers and position aside as outlined under "Disc Brakes."
3. Disconnect propeller shaft as outlined under "Propeller Shaft, Replace."
4. Record torque necessary to maintain rotation of pinion gear using a suitable inch lb. torque wrench.
5. Install flange holding tool No. 205-478, or equivalent. Install cotter pin as shown in **Fig. 4.**
6. Using a suitable breaker bar, remove and discard pinion nut.
7. Place a reference mark on pinion flange in relation to drive pinion stem for installation reference, **Fig. 5.**
8. Using flange removal tool No. 307-408, or equivalent, remove flange from axle.
9. Remove pinion seal.

INSTALLATION

1. Lubricate new seal using premium long life grease XG–1–C, or equivalent.
2. Install seal using seal installer tool No. T79P-4676-A, or equivalent.
3. Lubricate pinion flange spines using SAE 75W-140 synthetic rear axle lubricant F1TZ–19580–B, or equivalent.
4. Polish pinion flange seal journal using suitable crocus cloth if necessary.
5. Align pinion flange with drive pinion shaft.
6. Install flange using holding tool No. 205-478 and pinion flange installer tool No. 205-479, or equivalents. Ensure cotter pin is installed as shown in **Fig. 4.**
7. Install a new pinion nut.
8. Using flange holding tool, hold pinion flange while tightening new pinion nut. Nut should be tightened until proper preload is reached. Refer to "Tightening Specifications" for proper pinion preload. **If necessary to reduce preload, a new collapsible spacer and pinion nut must be installed.**

REAR HALFSHAFT

REPLACE

Halfshaft assemblies are not repairable. If wear or damage is present, replace entire halfshaft assembly. When servicing halfshafts, ensure excessive angle is not applied to CV joints and that joints are not pulled apart or separated.

The halfshafts on models equipped with 3.9L engine are larger in diameter and are not interchangeable with halfshafts from 3.0L models.

1. Raise and support vehicle.
2. Remove rear tires.
3. Remove and discard axle wheel hub nut.
4. Remove rear brake rotors as outlined under "Disc Brakes."
5. Remove ABS sensors as outlined under "Anti-Lock Brakes."
6. Remove lower knuckle attaching bolt.
7. Press CV joint from hub using hub remover/replacer tool No. T81P-1104-C, hub remover adapter tool No. T86P-1104-A1 and hub remover adapter tool No. T83P-1104-BH, or equivalents.
8. Raise and support knuckle, then remove CV joint from hub.
9. Separate CV joint from differential side gear using halfshaft removal tool No. 205-472, or equivalent. Ensure crown of tool forks face away from axle housing.
10. Remove halfshaft from axle housing.
11. Install differential plug tool No. T89P-4850-B, or equivalent, to differential.
12. Reverse procedure to install noting the following:
    a. Install new axleshaft circlip.
    b. Before installing halfshaft to differential housing, install seal protector tool No. 205-461. Slide CV joint into housing until splines are past seal, then remove seal protector. Ensure halfshaft is fully seated to differential.
    c. Install new wheel hub nut.
    d. Tighten to specifications.

DRIVELINE ANGLE MEASUREMENT

1. Park vehicle on a level surface.
2. Remove exhaust heat shield attaching bolts and slide shield as far forward as possible to expose driveshaft to axle coupling.
3. Rotate driveshaft several times by hand to neutralize center support bearing and flex couplings.
4. Place pinion angle level gauge tool No. T86P-4602-A, or equivalent, on left frame rail with special tool facing passenger side, **Fig. 6.**
5. Zero angle gauge tool using thumbscrew.
6. Mark location where special tool was zeroed. **When measuring driveline angle, bolts should not be removed from flange.**
7. Measure transmission angle "A," **Fig. 7,** as follows:
    a. Remove one nut from flex coupling to transmission flange.
    b. Install driveline adapter tool No. 205-449, or equivalent, to front of flex coupling and tighten nut. Ensure adapter contacts flex coupling bolt sleeve to obtain accurate reading.
    c. Place pinion angle gauge in angle adapter with angle gauge facing passenger side and record reading.
8. Measure front driveshaft angle "B," **Fig. 7,** as follows:
    a. Remove one nut from flex coupling to front driveshaft connection.
    b. Install driveline adapter tool No. 205-449, or equivalent, to front of flex coupling and tighten nut. Ensure adapter contacts flex coupling bolt sleeve to obtain accurate reading.
    c. Place pinion angle gauge in angle adapter with angle gauge facing passenger side and record reading.
9. Measure rear driveshaft angle "C," **Fig. 7,** as follows:
    a. Remove one nut from flex coupling to rear driveshaft connection.
    b. Install driveline adapter tool No. 205-449, or equivalent, to front of flex coupling and tighten nut. Ensure adapter contacts flex coupling bolt sleeve to obtain accurate reading.
    c. Place pinion angle gauge in angle adapter with angle gauge facing passenger side and record reading.
10. Measure differential pinion angle "D," **Fig. 7,** as follows:
    a. Remove one nut from flex coupling to pinion flange connection.
    b. Install driveline adapter tool No. 205-449, or equivalent, to front of

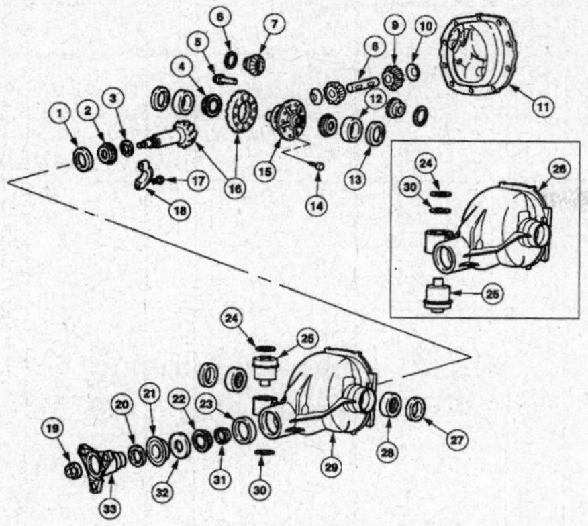

Item	Description
1	Rear axle pinion bearing cup
2	Pinion bearing
3	Drive pinion bearing adjustment shim
4	Differential bearing
5	Differential pinion shaft lock bolt
6	Differential side gear thrust washer
7	Differential side gear
8	Differential pinion shaft
9	Differential pinion gear
10	Differential pinion thrust washer
11	Differential housing cover
12	Differential bearing cup
13	Differential bearing shim
14	Rear axle ring gear case bolt
15	Differential case

FM2039900064010X

Fig. 1 Exploded view of rear axle (Part 1 of 2)

flex coupling and tighten nut. Ensure adapter contacts flex coupling bolt sleeve to obtain accurate reading.

c. Place pinion angle gauge in angle adapter with angle gauge facing passenger side and record reading.

11. Calculate angles of joints 1, 2 and 3 as follows, referring to **Fig. 7,** for driveline angle specifications:
    a. A-B=Joint 1.
    b. B-C=Joint 2.
    c. C-D=Joint 3.
12. If adjustment is necessary, install appropriate center support bearing adjusting washers. Ensure left and right washers are of equal thickness.
13. Refer to **Fig. 8** for washer selection chart.

PROPELLER SHAFT

REPLACE

1. Raise and support vehicle.
2. Remove muffler and extension pipe, then the body brace.
3. Remove heat shield.
4. Inspect and record driveline angles as outlined under " Driveline Angle Measurement."
5. Place reference marks on bolts, washers, nuts and flex coupling to transmission flange and pinion flange for installation reference.

16	Ring gear and pinion
17	Bolt
18	Differential bearing cap (part of 4010)
19	Pinion nut
20	Drive pinion oil seal deflector
21	Rear axle drive pinion seal
22	Pinion bearing
23	Differential drive pinion bearing cup
24	Front mount shim
25	Rear axle differential front lower insulator
26	Rear axle housing (aluminum)
27	Inboard CV joint stub shaft pilot bearing housing seal
28	Inboard CV joint stub shaft pilot bearing housing
29	Rear axle housing (nodular iron)
30	Rear axle differential front lower insulator cap
31	Differential drive pinion collapsible spacer
32	Rear axle drive pinion shaft oil slinger
33	Rear axle pinion flange

FM2039900064020X

Fig. 1 Exploded view of rear axle (Part 2 of 2)

6. Remove driveshaft to axle flange attaching nuts. **Do not remove flex coupling to driveshaft attaching bolts, Fig. 9.**
7. Using driveshaft coupler wrenches, tool No. 205-474, or equivalents, loosen driveshaft length adjustment nut.

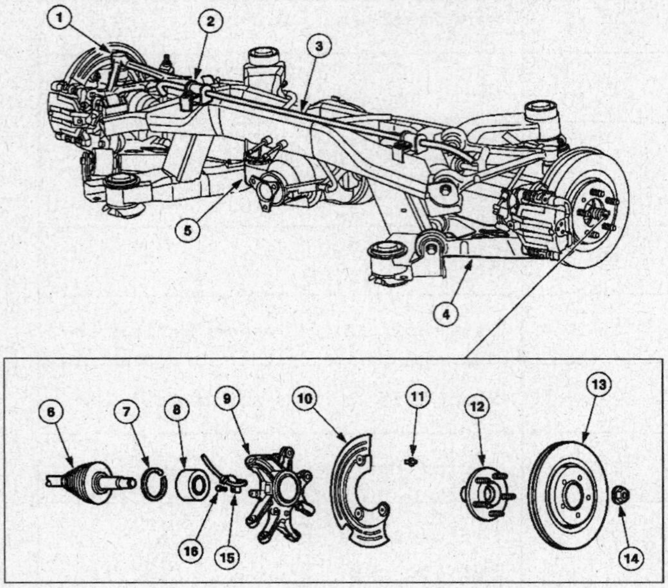

Item	Description
1	Upper arm
2	Stabilizer bar link
3	Stabilizer bar retaining bracket
4	Stabilizer bar
5	Lower arm
6	Axle shaft
7	Snap ring
8	Wheel hub bearing
9	Knuckle
10	Rear brake disc shield
11	Rivet

FM2039900065010X

Fig. 2 Rear suspension components (Part 1 of 2)

12	Hub
13	Rear brake disc
14	Hub retainer
15	ABS sensor
16	Screw

FM2039900065020X

Fig. 2 Rear suspension components (Part 2 of 2)

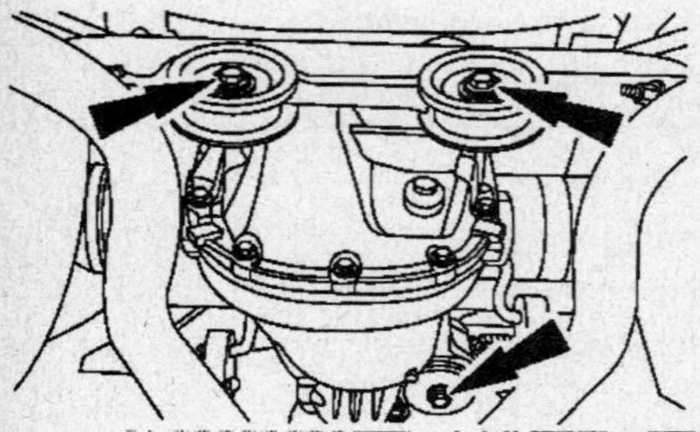

FM2039900066000X

Fig. 3 Axle mounting nuts

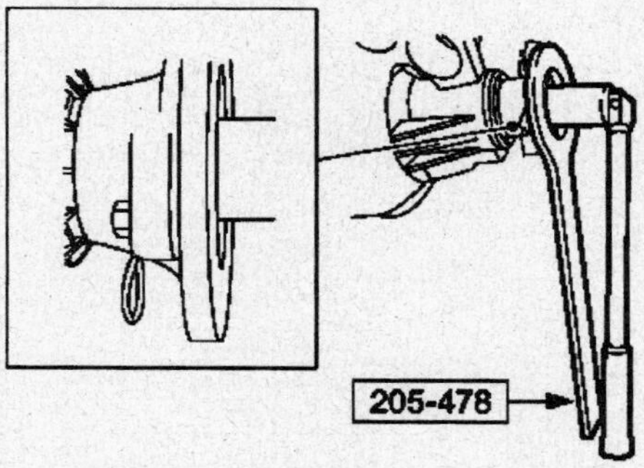

FM2039900075000X

Fig. 4 Flange holding tool installation

8. Remove transmission flange to driveshaft attaching nuts. **Do not remove flex coupling to driveshaft attaching bolts.**
9. Slide front shaft assembly rearward, then handtighten adjustment nut to prevent separation of front and rear shafts.
10. Remove center bearing support brace nuts, then the driveshaft assembly.
11. Reverse procedure to install noting the following:
    a. Add one gram of premium long life grease XG-1-C, or equivalent, to both alignment bushing cavities.
    b. Apply Threadlock 262 E2FZ–19554–B, or equivalent, to driveshaft to flange nuts and bolts.
    c. Tighten to specifications.

U-JOINT

REPLACE

The single center U-joint is of a lubed for life design that requires no periodic lubrication. This u-joint is staked to the yoke and is not removable.

PROPELLER SHAFT CENTER BEARING

REPLACE

1. Remove propeller shaft as outlined under “Propeller Shaft, Replace.”
2. Place alignment marks on driveshaft assemblies for installation reference.
3. Loosen adjustment nut and separate front and rear shaft assemblies.
4. Place propeller shaft in a suitable vise and clamp at driveshaft weld yoke.
5. Using 2 jaw puller tool No. D80L-1002-L and bearing puller tool No. D84L-1123-A, or equivalents, remove retaining ring and center bearing and bracket assembly.
6. Reverse procedure to install. Using driveshaft alignment bushing remover tube tool No. 205-D073, or equivalent, and a suitable hammer, install center bearing and retaining ring to driveshaft.

PROPELLER SHAFT ALIGNMENT BUSHING

REMOVAL

1. Remove propeller shaft as outlined under “Propeller Shaft, Replace.”
2. Place alignment marks on front and rear driveshaft assemblies for installation reference.
3. Loosen length adjustment nut and separate front and rear shaft assemblies.
4. Remove flex coupling nuts, then the bolts and flex coupling.
5. Place driveshaft end yoke into a suitable vise.
6. Using blind hole puller set tool No. D80L-100A, driveshaft alignment bushing remover tube tool No. 205-D073 and handle tool No. T80T-4000-W, or equivalents, remove alignment

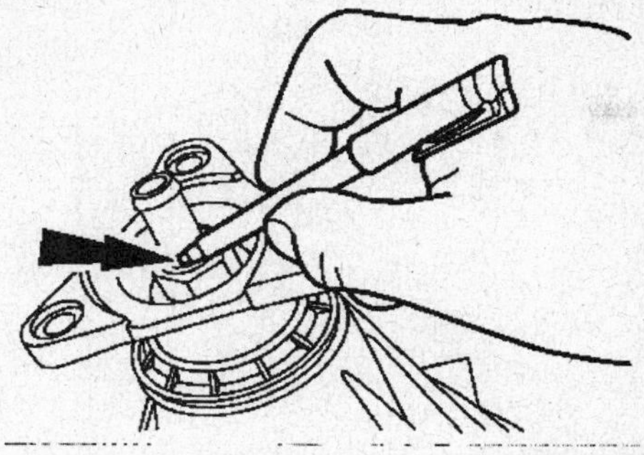

FM2039900076000X

Fig. 5 Pinion flange marks

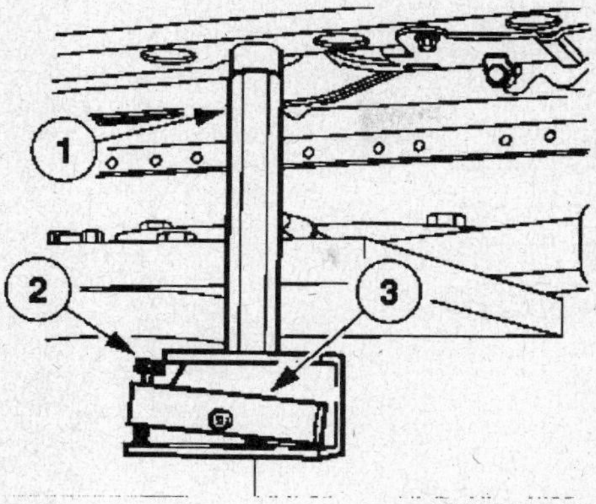

FM3039900334000X

Fig. 6 Pinion angle gauge setup

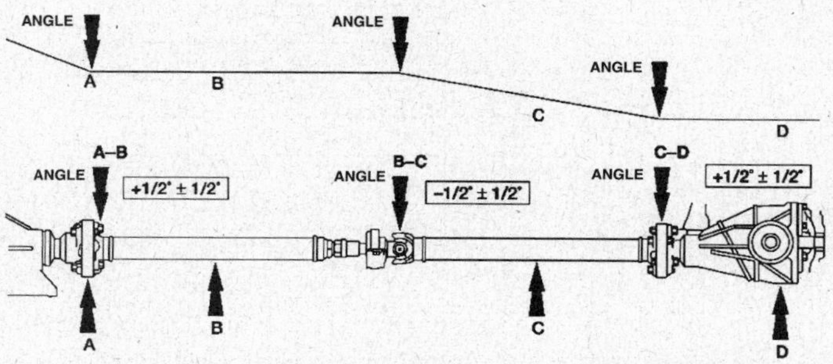

FM3039900335000X

Fig. 7 Driveline angle inspection points

bushing inner core, **Fig. 10.**

7. Using removal tools, remove bushing shell, **Fig. 11.**

INSTALLATION

There are six bushings in each flex coupling. Three bushing protrude from each side of coupling. Arrows on the side of coupling point toward protruding end of bushing. When installing flex coupling, protruding end of bushing must seat in driveshaft flange counterbore or damage will occur to coupling during operation.

1. Align bushing with propeller shaft, then install using handle tool No. T80T-4000-W and alignment bearing installer tool No. 205-D074, or equivalents.
2. Install flex coupling as follows:
   a. Position protruding end of bushing against driveshaft flange, **Fig. 12.**
   b. Apply Threadlock 262 E2FZ–19554–B, or equivalent, to flex coupling bolts and nuts, then install. Ensure bolt heads seat against driveshaft flange and nuts against flex coupling. Bolt heads are serrated and must be held in place while nut is tightened to specifications.
3. Align reference marks of front and rear propeller shafts, then assemble both shafts. Finger tighten nut to prevent separation of shaft assembly.
4. Add one gram of premium long life grease XG–1–C, or equivalent, to both alignment bushing cavities before installing propeller shaft.
5. Install propeller shaft as outlined under "Propeller shaft, Replace."

HUB & BEARING

REPLACE

1. Remove knuckle as outlined under "Knuckle, Replace. "
2. Using a .22 inch drill bit, drill out dust shield rivets. If larger bit is needed, it should not exceed .24 inch.
3. Remove dust shield.
4. Place knuckle in a suitable press. Ensure knuckle is level and is supported as close to bearing bore as possible. Knuckle extremities should not be used for support.
5. Remove hub from knuckle using a suitable press, step plate adapter set tool No. D80L-630-A and bearing puller tool No. T71P-4621-B, or equivalents. When hub is pressed from bearing, bearing inner race will also be removed. **Do not install race back into bearing.**
6. Remove bearing retaining snap ring.
7. Support knuckle in press as close to bearing bore as possible.
8. Remove bearing from knuckle using appropriate step plate adapter.
9. If hub will be reused, remove inner bearing race from hub using a suitable press and bearing puller tool No. T71P-4621-B, or equivalent.
10. Reverse procedure to install noting the following:
    a. Attach dust shield using aluminum rivets.
    b. When installing hub to bearing, ensure bearing inner race is properly supported.

BALL JOINT INSPECTION

1. Raise and support vehicle.
2. Inspect wheel bearings as outlined under "Wheel Bearing Inspection."
3. Position a suitable safety stand under lower suspension arm.
4. Grasp tire at top and bottom and attempt to move inward and outward.
5. If movement is more than 1⁄32 inch replace control arm.

WHEEL BEARING INSPECTION

1. Raise and support vehicle.
2. Ensure brake pads are retracted enough to allow free movement of tire.
3. Grasp tire at top and bottom and move wheel inward and outward while lifting weight of tire off bearing.
4. If tire is loose on spindle or does not rotate freely, install new hub and bearing as necessary.

STRUT

REPLACE

When working with strut, do not apply heat during removal or service.

1. Open luggage compartment.
2. Remove carpet, then the spare tire and trim covers to access strut upper attaching bolts.
3. Remove four strut upper attaching nuts and discard, **Fig. 13.**
4. Raise and support vehicle.
5. Remove strut lower attaching bolt and nut and discard.
6. Remove strut assembly from vehicle.
7. Reverse procedure to install. Tighten to specifications.

STRUT SERVICE

DISASSEMBLE

When working with strut, do not apply heat during removal or service.

If reusing components, place alignment marks on all parts for installation reference.

1. Remove strut as outlined under "Strut, Replace."
2. Place strut into a suitable vise, **Fig. 14.**
3. Compress spring using a suitable spring compressor.
4. Remove center nut while holding shock absorber rod, **Fig. 15.**
5. Remove upper mount and dust boot.
6. Uncompress spring and remove from strut.

ASSEMBLE

1. Inspect all strut components for damage or wear. If spring paint is damaged, a new spring should be installed.
2. Compress spring using a suitable spring compressor.

Part Number	Thickness, Inch
W704775	.079
W704776	.118
W704777	.157
W704778	.020
W704779	.240
W704780	.280

Fig. 8 Driveshaft washer selection

3. Position upper mount and dust boot on spring. Ensure all parts are properly aligned.
4. Install new upper strut mount nut and tighten to specifications.
5. Remove strut from spring compressor and vise.
6. Install strut as outlined under "Strut, Replace."

CONTROL ARM

REPLACE

LOWER

Removal

If lower arm bushings require service, entire lower control arm must be replaced.

1. With vehicle at a static level position, remove hub cap and measure distance from center of hub to lip of fender, **Fig. 16.**
2. Raise and support vehicle.
3. Remove rear wheels.
4. Remove rear brake rotor as outlined under "Disc Brakes."
5. Remove lower strut to control arm attaching bolt and nut, then discard.
6. Remove lower stabilizer link to control arm attaching nut and discard.
7. Remove lower knuckle to control arm attaching nut and bolt, then discard.
8. Remove lower arm to subframe attaching bolts and nuts and discard.
9. Remove lower control arm.

Installation

Do not tighten lower arm to subframe or knuckle bolts and nuts until curb height is at correct level.

1. Connect lower arm to subframe using new bolts and nuts.
2. Install knuckle to lower arm using new bolt and nut.
3. Connect stabilizer bar link to lower suspension arm using new nut and tighten to specifications.
4. Install strut to lower control arm using new nut and bolt and tighten to specifications.
5. Position a suitable jackstand under lower arm and raise suspension until measurement between center of hub and lip of fender is as recorded during removal procedure.
6. Tighten lower arm attaching nuts to specifications and remove jackstand.
7. Install rear rotors as outlined under "Disc Brakes."
8. Install wheels, then lower vehicle.

UPPER

Removal

If upper arm bushings and ball joints require service, entire upper control arm must be replaced.

1. With vehicle at a static level position, remove hub cap and measure distance from center of hub to lip of fender, **Fig. 16.**
2. Raise and support vehicle.
3. Remove rear wheels.
4. Unclip ABS sensor wire retainer from suspension arm.
5. Disconnect and remove ABS sensor and position aside.
6. Remove and discard upper ball joint to knuckle nut and separate knuckle from ball joint.
7. Remove upper arm to subframe nuts and bolts and discard.
8. Remove upper suspension arm.

Installation

Do not tighten upper arm to subframe or knuckle nuts and bolts until suspension is at proper curb height.

1. Install upper arm to subframe using new nuts and bolts.

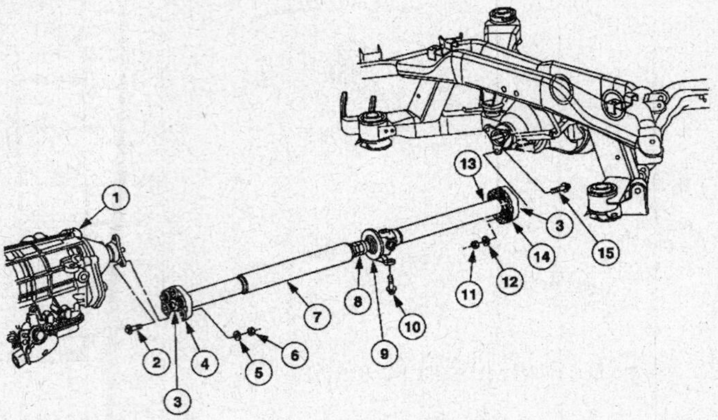

Item	Description
1	Transmission
2	Bolt
3	Alignment bushing
4	Flex coupling
5	Washer
6	Nut
7	Shaft assembly, front
8	Nut, length adjustment
9	Center bearing and bracket assembly
10	Bolt
11	Nut
12	Washer
13	Shaft assembly, rear
14	Flex coupling
15	Bolt

FM2039900077000X

Fig. 9 Driveshaft components

2. Install upper arm to knuckle using new nut.
3. Clip ABS sensor wire to upper suspension arm.
4. Position a suitable jack under suspension lower arm.
5. Raise suspension until measurement between center of hub and lip of fender is as recorded during removal procedure.
6. Tighten upper arm to subframe and knuckle attaching nuts to specifications.
7. Lower suspension and remove jack.
8. Install wheels and lower vehicle.

TOE LINK

REPLACE

1. Raise and support vehicle.
2. Remove rear wheels.
3. Disconnect toe link from knuckle, **Fig. 17.**
4. Remove toe link from subframe, then the toe link.
5. Reverse procedure to install. Tighten to specifications using new toe link attaching nuts and ensure wheel alignment is within specifications.

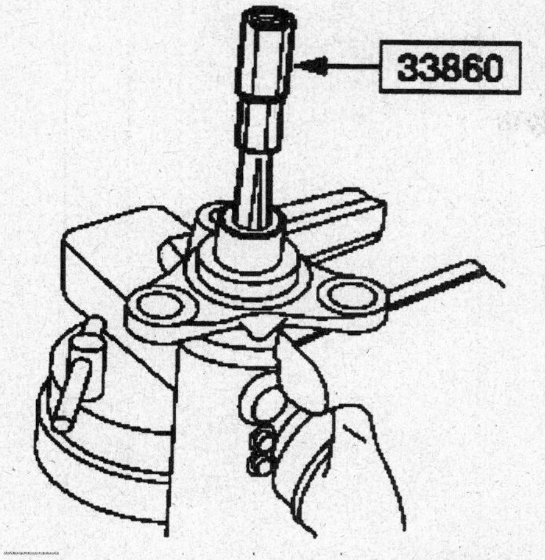

FM2039900067010X

Fig. 10 Propeller shaft bushing inner core removal (Part 1 of 4)

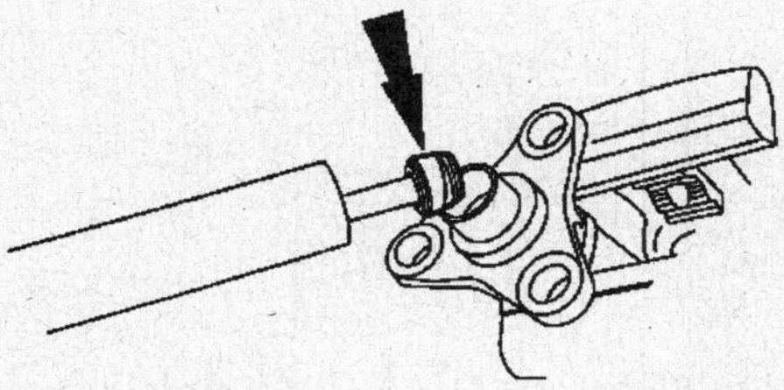

FM2039900067040X

Fig. 10 Propeller shaft bushing inner core removal (Part 4 of 4)

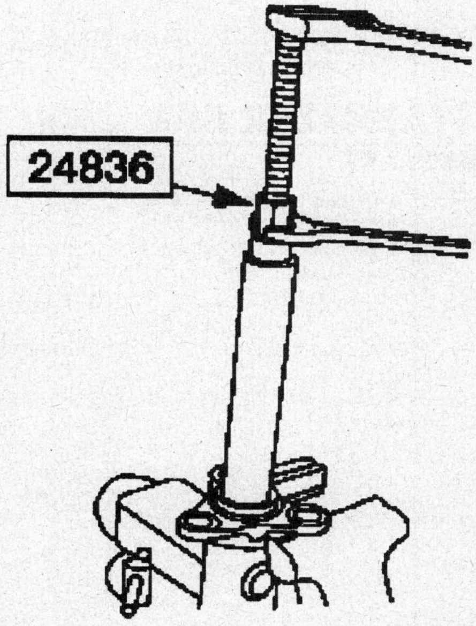

FM2039900068030X

Fig. 11 Propeller shaft bushing shell removal (Part 3 of 4)

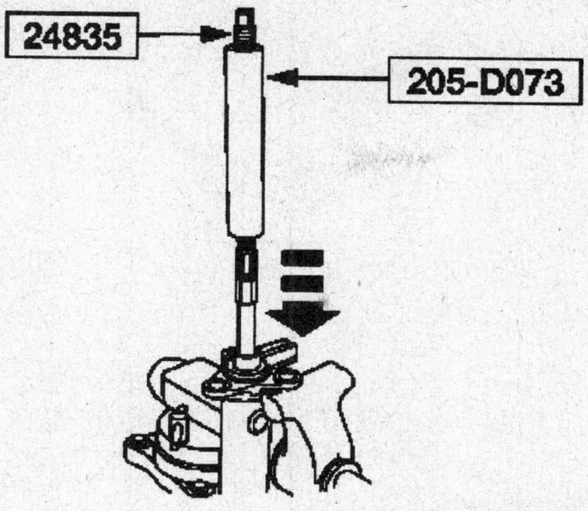

FM2039900067020X

Fig. 10 Propeller shaft bushing inner core removal (Part 2 of 4)

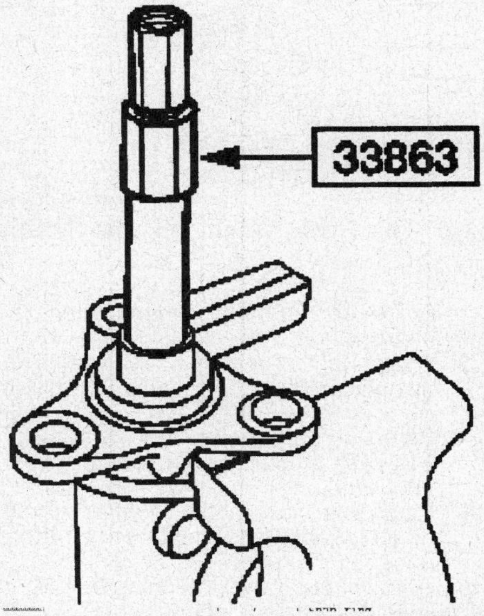

FM2039900068010X

Fig. 11 Propeller shaft bushing shell removal (Part 1 of 4)

KNUCKLE

REPLACE

1. With vehicle at a static level position, remove hub cap and measure distance from center of hub to lip of fender, **Fig. 16.**
2. Raise and support vehicle, then remove rear wheels.
3. Remove and discard hub nut.
4. Remove rear rotors as outlined under "Disc Brakes."
5. Disconnect toe link from knuckle.
6. Remove ABS sensor and position aside.
7. Disconnect lower suspension arm from knuckle.

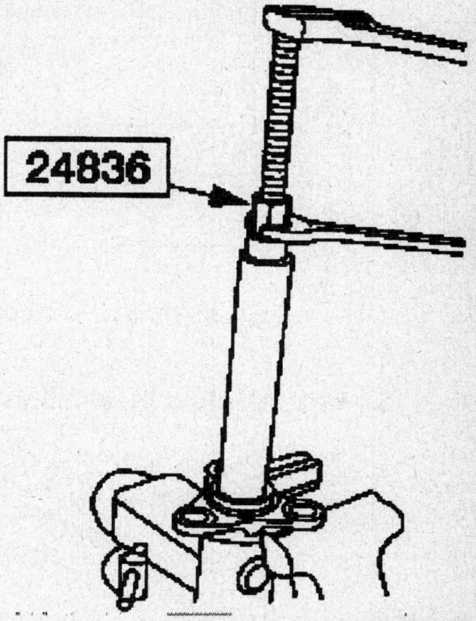

FM2039900067030X

Fig. 10 Propeller shaft bushing inner core removal (Part 3 of 4)

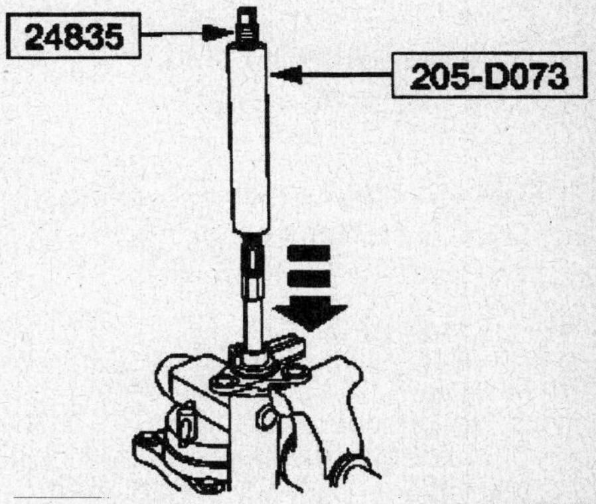

FM2039900068020X

Fig. 11 Propeller shaft bushing shell removal (Part 2 of 4)

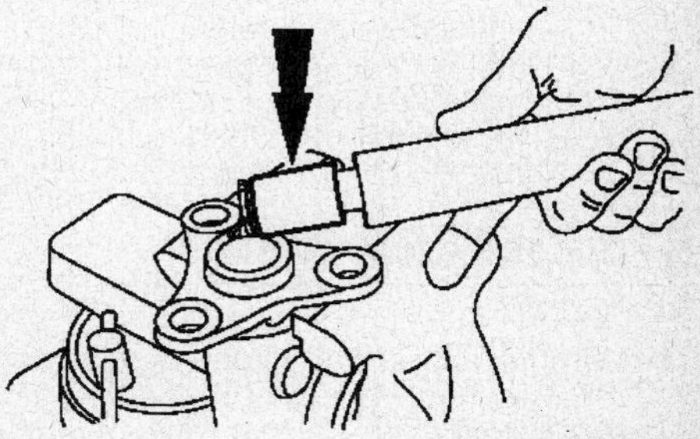

FM2039900068040X

Fig. 11 Propeller shaft bushing shell removal (Part 4 of 4)

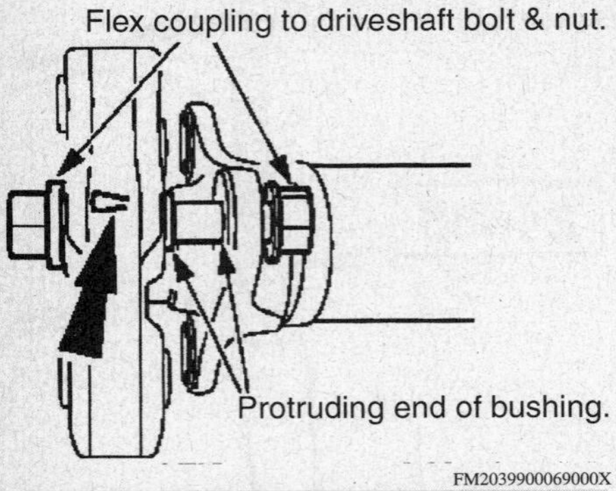

Fig. 12 Flex coupling installation

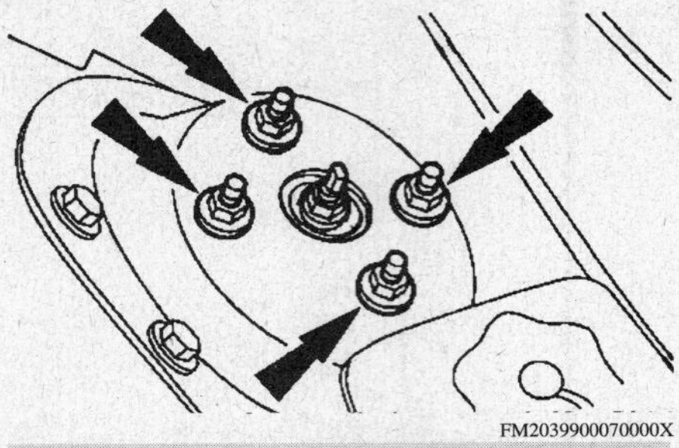

Fig. 13 Strut upper attaching nuts

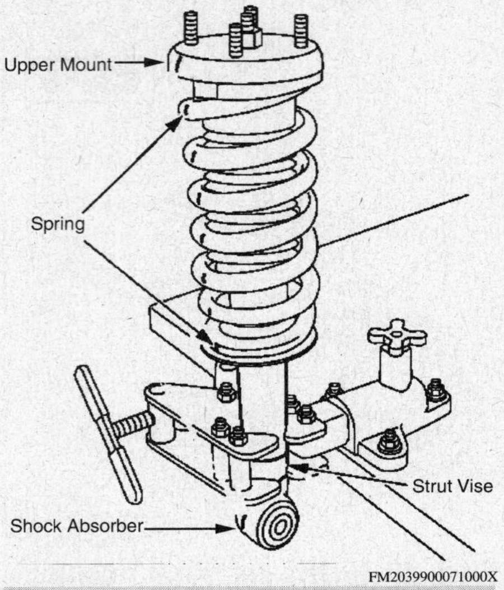

Fig. 14 Rear strut components

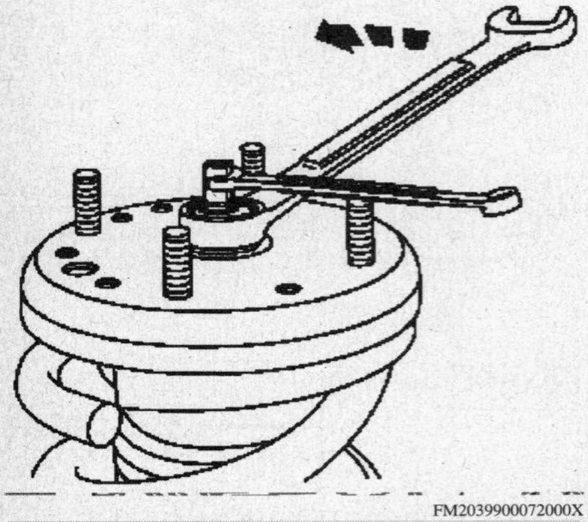

Fig. 15 Rear strut center nut removal

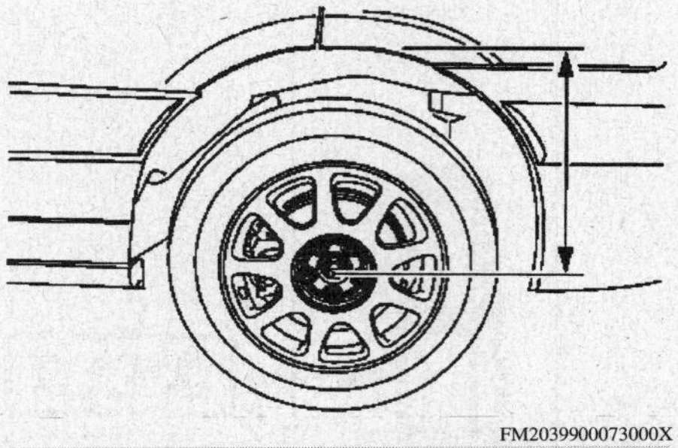

Fig. 16 Curb height measurement

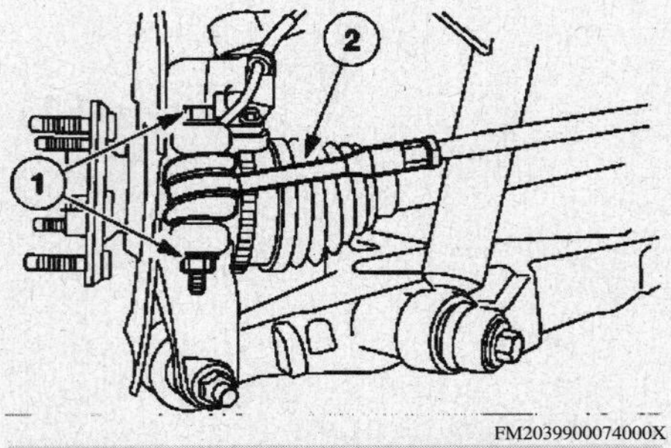

Fig. 17 Toe link removal

8. Support axleshaft.
9. Remove axleshaft from hub using hub remover/replacer tool No. T81P-1104-C, hub remover adapter tool No. T86P-1104-A and hub remover adapters tool No. T83P-1104-BH, or equivalents.
10. Remove upper ball joint from knuckle, then remove knuckle.
11. Reverse procedure to install noting the following:
    a. Ensure suspension is at proper curb height before tightening knuckle attaching bolts.
    b. When servicing suspension components, always use new appropriate nuts and bolts when removed.
    c. Tighten to specifications.

STABILIZER BAR

REPLACE

1. With vehicle at a static level position, remove hub cap and measure distance from center of hub to lip of fender, **Fig. 16.**
2. Raise and support vehicle, then remove wheels.
3. Disconnect propeller shaft from axle as outlined under " Propeller Shaft, Replace."
4. Place Rotunda powertrain lift tool No. 014-00765, or equivalent, under rear subframe.
5. Place reference marks on all subframe attaching bolts for installation reference.
6. Remove subframe attaching bolts and lower subframe 8 inches.
7. Remove stabilizer link caps from right and left stabilizer links.
8. Disconnect right and left stabilizer links from stabilizer bar.
9. Remove stabilizer bar brackets and bushings.
10. Secure right and left knuckles to subframe using suitable mechanics wire.
11. Disconnect right and left upper control arms from subframe.
12. Remove stabilizer bar.
13. Reverse procedure to install noting the following:
    a. Ensure suspension is at proper curb height before tightening knuckle attaching bolts.
    b. When servicing suspension components, always use new appropriate nuts and bolts when removed.
    c. Tighten to specifications.

STABILIZER BAR LINK

REPLACE

1. Raise and support vehicle, then remove rear wheels.
2. Disconnect stabilizer bar link from suspension lower arm.
3. Remove protective cap from stabilizer bar link.
4. Remove stabilizer link from stabilizer bar.
5. Reverse procedure to install noting the following:
    a. When servicing suspension components, always use new appropriate nuts and bolts when removed.
    b. Tighten to specifications.

TIGHTENING SPECIFICATIONS

Year	Component	Torque, Ft. Lbs.
2000	Anti-Lock Brake Sensor Bolt	89①
	Axle Fill Plug	25
	Center Bearing Bolts	32
	Driveshaft Length Adjustment Nut	58
	Flex Coupling To Driveshaft Nuts	60
	Front Differential Mounting Bolts	52
	Hub Nut	221
	Lower Arm & Bushing To Knuckle Pivot Bolt Nut	111
	Lower Arm & Bushing To Subframe Pivot Bolt & Nut	111
	Pinion Nut	②
	Rear Differential Mounting Bolts	76
	Shock & Spring Assembly To Lower Arm	98
	Stabilizer Bar Bracket Bolts	41
	Stabilizer Bar Link Nuts	35
	Subframe To Body Bolts	76
	Toe Link Nuts	41
	Upper Arm & Bushing To Subframe Pivot Bolt Nut	66
	Upper Ball Joint Nut	66
	Upper Shock Absorber Rod To Upper Shock Mount Nut	37
	Upper Shock Absorber Mount To Body Nuts	21
	Yoke Adjuster Nut	66
	Wheel Lug Nuts	100

① — Inch lbs.

② — Tighten until proper preload specification is achieved as follows: used bearings, 8–10 inch lbs.; new bearings, 16–28 inch lbs.

Front Suspension & Steering

NOTE: On Air Bag Equipped Models, Refer To " Air Bag System Precautions" Located In The Front Of This Manual For System Disarming & Arming Procedures.

NOTE: Refer To "Computer Relearn Procedures " Located In The Front Of This Manual For Computer Relearn Procedures.

INDEX

PRECAUTIONS

AIR BAG SYSTEMS

Refer to "Air Bag System Precautions" in the front of this manual for system disarming and arming procedures.

BATTERY GROUND CABLE

Prior to service, disconnect battery ground cable and isolate as required.

DESCRIPTION

The front suspension is an aluminum short-arm-long-arm that features struts, stabilizer bar and stabilizer bar links, **Fig. 1. When servicing suspension components, always use new appropriate nuts and bolts when removed.**

HUB & BEARING

REPLACE

1. Raise and support vehicle.
2. Remove front wheels.
3. Remove brake rotor as outlined under "Disc Brakes."
4. Remove inner fender splash shield and position aside.
5. Disconnect ABS wheel speed sensor and separate from wire retainers. **Do not remove ABS sensor from hub unless new sensor and wire are being installed.**
6. Remove wheel hub and bearing attaching bolts and discard, **Fig. 2.**
7. Remove wheel hub and bearing from knuckle. **Do not use a slide hammer or strike back of wheel hub and bearing to remove. Hub and bearing should slide out from knuckle.**
8. Reverse procedure to install noting the following:
   a. Ensure knuckle bore is clean enough to allow hub and bearing to be seated by hand.
   b. Apply Motorcraft high temperature nickel anti-seize lubricant F6AZ–9L494–AA, or equivalent, to bearing carrier and wheel knuckle
   c. Install new suspension attaching bolts and nuts, then tighten to specifications.

BALL JOINT INSPECTION

1. Raise and support vehicle.
2. Inspect wheel bearings as outlined under "Wheel Bearing Inspection."
3. Position a suitable safety stand under lower suspension arm.
4. Grasp tire at top and bottom and attempt to move inward and outward.
5. If movement is more than 1⁄32 inch on upper or lower ball joint, replace control arm.

WHEEL BEARING INSPECTION

1. Raise and support vehicle.
2. Ensure brake pads are retracted enough to allow free movement of tire.
3. Grasp tire at top and bottom and move wheel inward and outward while lifting weight of tire off bearing.
4. If tire is loose on spindle or does not rotate freely, install new hub and bearing as necessary.

STRUT

REPLACE

Do not use heat to remove strut attaching bolts.

1. Raise and support vehicle, then remove front wheels.
2. Disconnect stabilizer bar link from control arm and discard nut.
3. Remove and discard strut to lower control arm attaching bolt.
4. Remove strut to body attaching bolts, **Fig. 3. Do not remove strut center nut.**
5. Reverse procedure to install. Install new suspension attaching bolts and nuts and tighten to specifications.

COIL SPRING & STRUT SERVICE

Do not use heat to remove strut attaching bolts.

1. Remove strut as outlined under "Strut, Replace."
2. Mount strut in a suitable vise, **Fig. 4.**
3. Place reference marks on all strut components for installation reference.
4. Compress spring using a suitable spring compressor.
5. Hold shock absorber center rod and remove center nut from strut.
6. Remove upper mount and dust boot.
7. Uncompress spring and remove from spring compressor.
8. Reverse procedure to install noting the following:
   a. Inspect spring, upper and lower spring seats, mount and insulator for damage and replace as necessary. If spring coating is damaged,

replace spring.
b. Install new strut attaching nuts and bolts and tighten to specifications.

CONTROL ARM

REPLACE

LOWER

Removal

1. Ensure ignition switch is off in unlocked position.
2. Raise and support vehicle, then remove wheels.
3. Remove splash shields as necessary.
4. Disconnect stabilizer bar link from lower control arm and discard nut.
5. Disconnect strut from lower control arm and discard nut and bolt.
6. Disconnect lower control arm from steering knuckle and discard nut.
7. Remove front lower control arm bolt and nut and discard.
8. Remove two nuts and bolts (1), loosen nut and bolt (2) and rotate steering gear rack (3) to access lower control arm rear bolt, **Fig. 5.**
9. Remove and discard rear lower control arm nut and bolt.

Installation

1. Position lower control arm and install new caster adjustment cam bolt and nut, **Fig. 6.** Install bolt with cam lobe down ensuring cam is seated between cam guides on No. 1 crossmember. Nut should not be fully tightened until wheel alignment is performed.
2. Install new camber adjustment cam bolt and nut, **Fig. 7.** Install bolt with cam lobe down ensuring cam is seated in groove of No. 2 crossmember. Nut should not be fully tightened until wheel alignment is performed.
3. Connect lower ball joint to control arm using a new nut. Ensure tapered washer is installed on ball joint.
4. Connect stabilizer link and strut to lower arm using new bolt and nuts.
5. Install splash shields if previously removed.
6. Tighten bolts and nuts loosened when repositioning steering gear.
7. Install wheels, then lower vehicle and ensure wheel alignment is within specifications.

LEFT UPPER

1. Remove hub cap.
2. Measure and record distance from lip of fender to center of wheel hub, **Fig. 8.**
3. Remove air cleaner.
4. Remove upper control arm nut and discard, **Fig. 9.**
5. Raise and support vehicle, then remove front wheel.
6. Remove strut as outlined under "Strut, Replace."
7. Secure knuckle to body using suitable mechanics wire.
8. Disconnect upper control arm from steering knuckle and discard nut.
9. Remove control arm from body and discard nuts and bolts.
10. Reverse procedure to install noting the following:
    a. Ensure suspension is at proper curb height before tightening control arm attaching bolts.
    b. When servicing suspension components, always use new appropriate nuts and bolts when removed.
    c. Tighten to specifications.

RIGHT UPPER

1. Remove hub cap.
2. Measure and record distance from lip of fender to center of wheel hub, **Fig. 8.**
3. Remove and discard nut from engine compartment, **Fig. 10.**
4. Disconnect wiring harness and brackets as necessary to access control arm attaching bolts and nuts.
5. Remove upper control arm attaching nut and discard.
6. Remove strut as outlined under "Strut, Replace."
7. Secure knuckle to body using suitable mechanics wire.
8. Disconnect upper ball joint from steering knuckle and discard nut.
9. Remove upper arm attaching bolts and nuts, then the upper arm. Discard attaching bolts and nuts.
10. Reverse procedure to install noting the following:
    a. Ensure suspension is at proper curb height before tightening control arm attaching bolts.
    b. When servicing suspension components, always use new appropriate nuts and bolts when removed.
    c. Tighten to specifications.

STEERING KNUCKLE

REPLACE

1. Remove wheel hub and bearing as outlined under " Hub & Bearing, Replace."
2. Disconnect tie rod, upper control arm and lower control arm from steering knuckle and discard nuts.
3. Remove steering knuckle from vehicle.
4. Reverse procedure to install noting the following:
    a. Support steering knuckle using a suitable jackstand during installation.
    b. When servicing suspension components, always use new appropriate nuts and bolts when removed.
    c. Tighten to specifications.

STABILIZER BAR

REPLACE

1. Remove air cleaner.
2. Remove stabilizer bracket bolt as shown in **Fig. 11.**
3. Raise and support vehicle, then remove front wheels.
4. Remove right, left and center splash shields.
5. Disconnect stabilizer bar link from control arm and stabilizer bar and discard nuts.
6. Disconnect strut from left lower control arm and discard bolt and nut.
7. Disconnect lower control arm from left steering knuckle and discard nut.
8. Remove heater water valve bracket and position valve aside.
9. Remove stabilizer bar brackets and bushings. Right front bolt should be removed first.
10. Remove stabilizer bar through left wheel well.
11. Reverse procedure to install noting the following:
    a. When servicing suspension components, always use new appropriate nuts and bolts when removed.
    b. Tighten to specifications.

TIE ROD

REPLACE

Refer to "Power Steering" section for inner and outer tie rod replacement procedures.

POWER STEERING GEAR

REPLACE

1. Raise and support vehicle, then remove front wheels.
2. Disconnect tie rod ends from steering knuckles and discard nuts.
3. Disconnect power steering gear electrical connector.
4. Loosen steering shaft bolt.
5. Remove pinch bolt and disconnect intermediate shaft.
6. Remove power steering hose bracket.
7. Disconnect power steering hoses from steering gear. Plug hose ends at gear.
8. Remove steering gear attaching nuts, bolts and gear. Discard attaching nuts and bolts.
9. Reverse procedure to install noting the following:
    a. Install new seal to power steering lines using teflon seal replacer set tool No. D90P-3517-A, or equivalent.
    b. When servicing suspension components, always use new appropriate nuts and bolts when removed.
    c. Tighten to specifications.
    d. Fill system and inspect for leaks. Ensure wheel alignment is within specifications.

POWER STEERING PUMP

REPLACE

3.0L ENGINE

1. Remove engine appearance cover.
2. Remove air cleaner and outlet tube.
3. Remove accessory drive belt.
4. Disconnect power steering reservoir to pump hose and drain fluid into a suitable container.

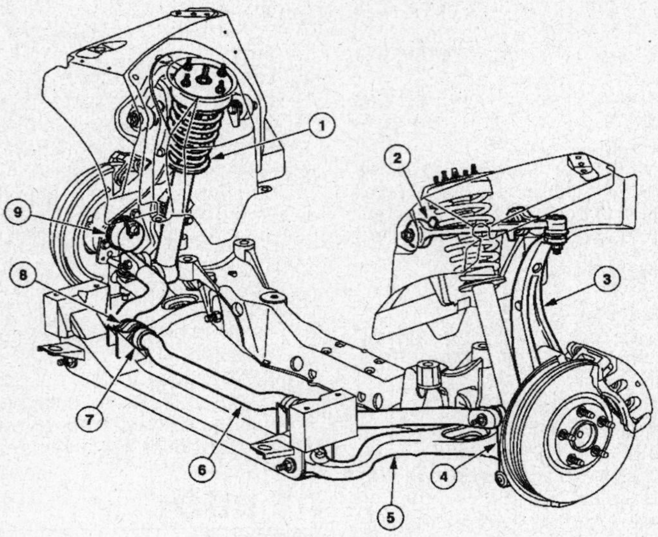

Item	Description
1	Shock absorber and spring assy
2	Upper arm and bushing
3	Wheel knuckle
4	Stabilizer bar link
5	Lower arm and bushing
6	Stabilizer bar
7	Stabilizer bar bushing
8	Stabilizer bar bracket
9	Wheel hub and bearing

FM2029900148000X

Fig. 1 Front suspension components

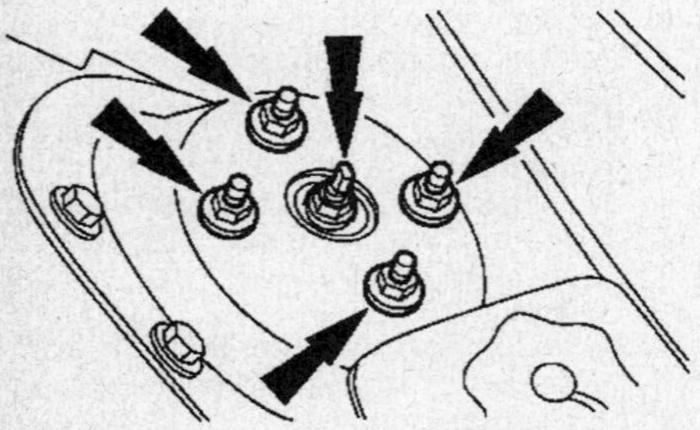

FM2029900150000X

Fig. 3 Strut to body attaching bolts

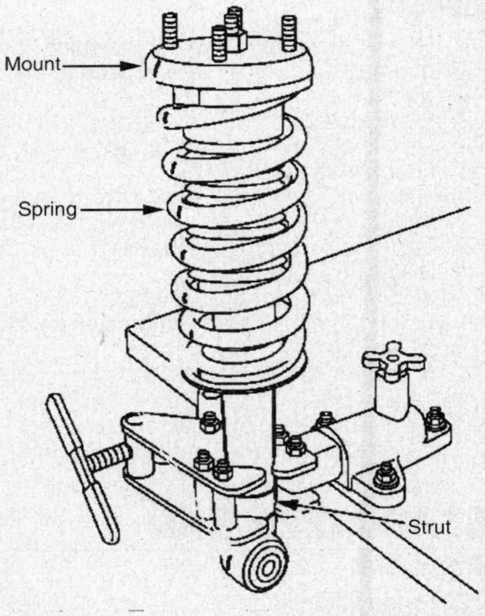

FM2029900151000X

Fig. 4 Front strut components

5. Raise and support vehicle, then remove front wheels.
6. Remove lower power steering pump shield, **Fig. 12.**
7. Remove power steering hose bracket bolt, then disconnect hose from pump.
8. Remove pump attaching bolts, then the pump.
9. Reverse procedure to install noting the following:
   a. Install new O-rings to power steering hoses using telfon seal replacer set tool No. D90P-3517-A, or equivalent.
   b. Tighten upper pump attaching bolts after lower bolts are installed.
   c. Fill power steering system and inspect for leaks.

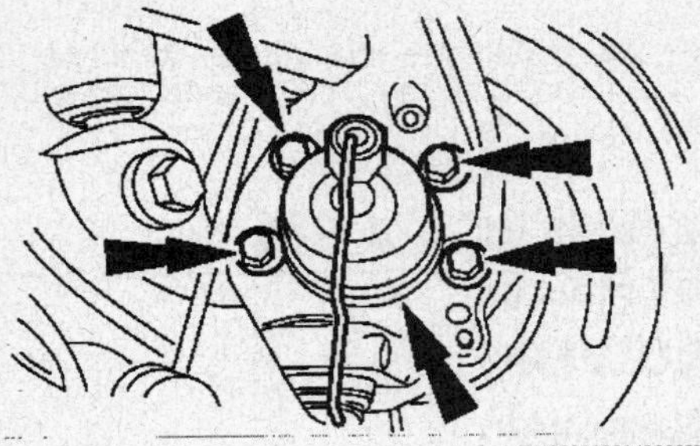

FM2029900149000X

Fig. 2 Wheel hub & bearing removal

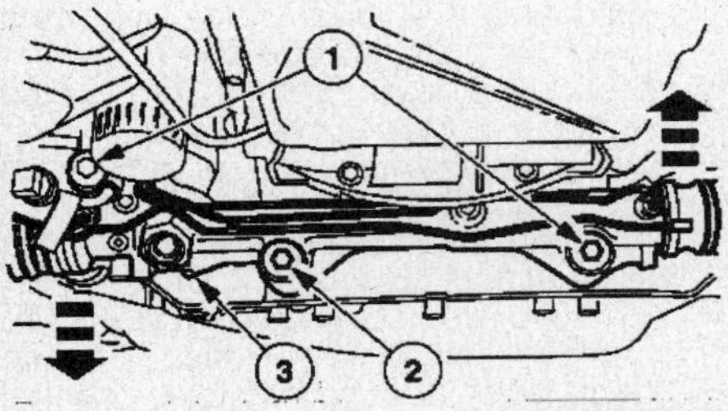

FM2029900152000X

Fig. 5 Lower control arm rear bolt access

3.9L ENGINE

1. Remove engine appearance cover.
2. Remove air cleaner and outlet tube.
3. Remove coolant tube attaching bolts, **Fig. 13.**
4. Remove accessory drive belt.
5. Disconnect power steering reservoir to pump hose and drain fluid into suitable container.
6. Remove power steering reservoir attaching bolts and position reservoir aside.
7. Raise and support vehicle, then remove front wheels.
8. Remove power steering pump shields, **Fig. 12.**
9. Remove pump line bracket bolt, **Fig. 14.**
10. Disconnect power steering pump electrical connector and wire retainer.
11. Remove A/C compressor attaching bolts and position compressor aside.
12. Disconnect power steering pressure hose from pump.
13. Remove pump attaching bolts, **Fig. 15.**
14. Lower vehicle, then remove remaining pump attaching bolts and pump.
15. Reverse procedure to install noting the following:
    a. Install new O-ring seals to power steering lines using teflon seal replacer set tool No. D90P-3517-A, or equivalent.

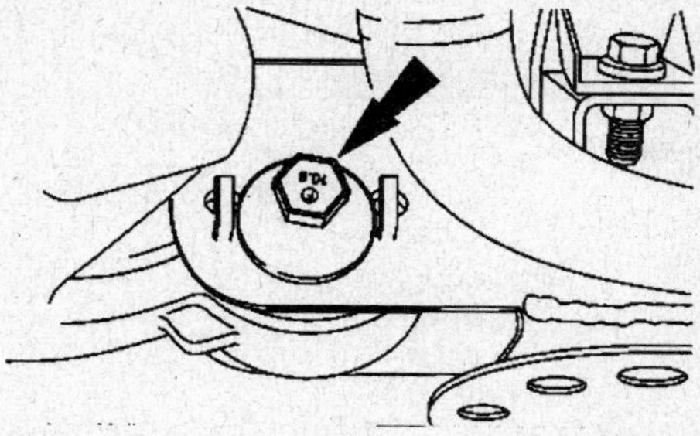

Fig. 6 Caster adjustment bolt installation

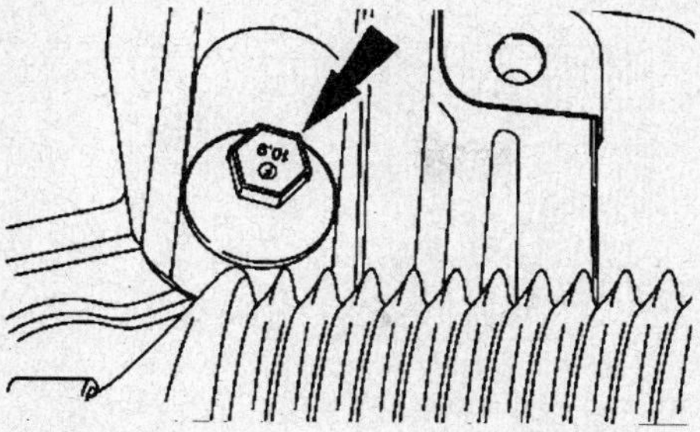

Fig. 7 Camber adjustment bolt installation

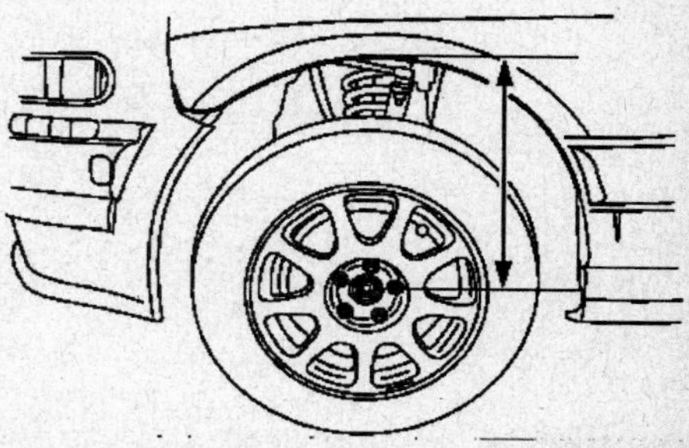

Fig. 8 Curb height measurement

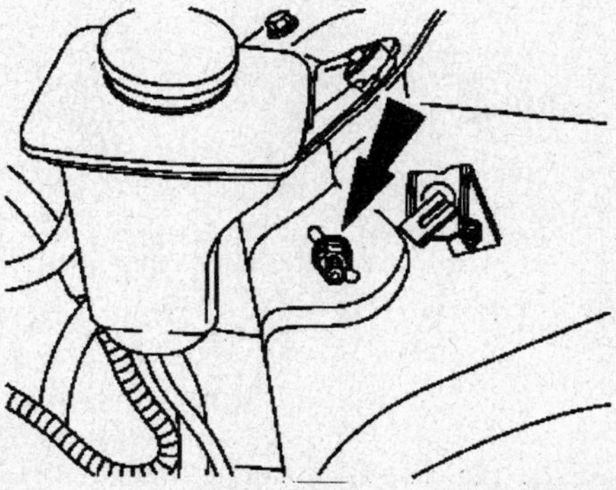

Fig. 9 Upper control arm attaching nut location

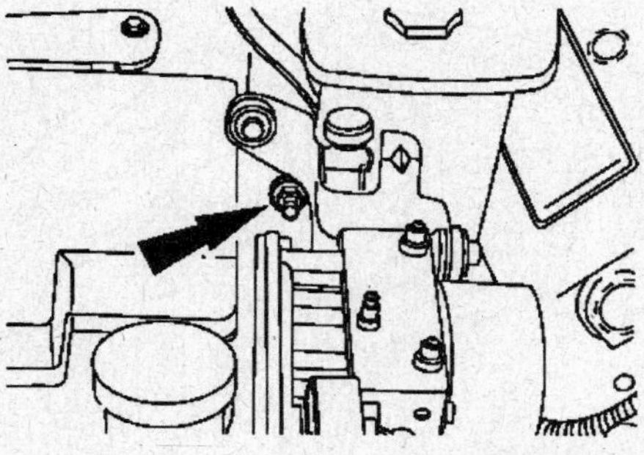

Fig. 10 Engine compartment nut location

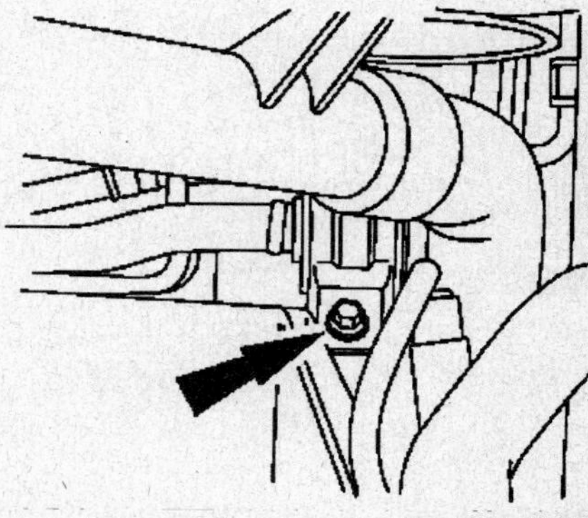

Fig. 11 Stabilizer bracket bolt removal

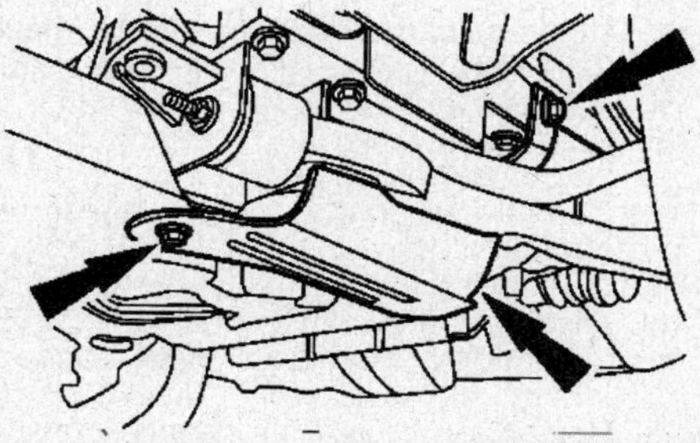

Fig. 12 Power steering pump shield (Part 1 of 2)

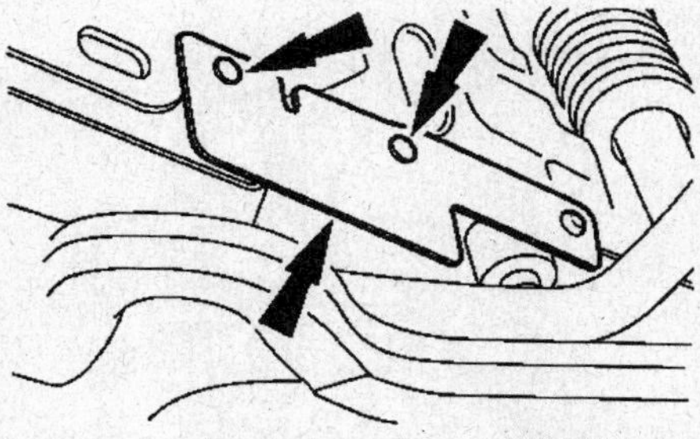

Fig. 12 Power steering pump shield (Part 2 of 2)

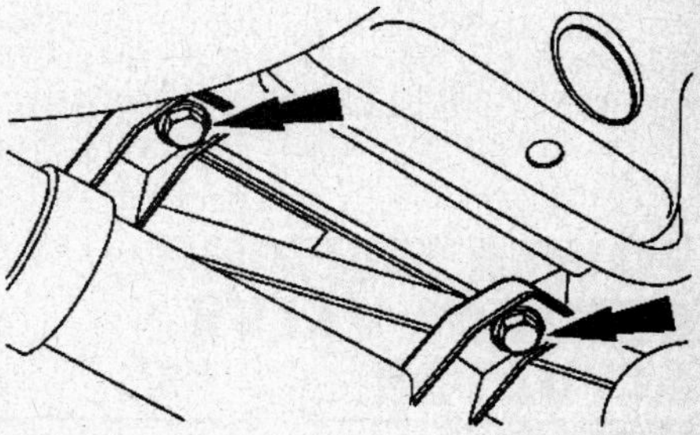

Fig. 13 Coolant tube bolt location

   b. Upper bolts should only be tightened after lower bolts are installed.
   c. Tighten to specifications.

POWER STEERING SYSTEM BLEED

1. Ensure power steering reservoir is filled to proper level.
2. Install vacuum tester tool No. 014-R1054, or equivalent, to reservoir, **Fig. 16.**
3. Start engine and allow to idle.
4. Apply maximum vacuum for at least 3 minutes at idle. Maintain vacuum with vacuum pump.
5. Remove vacuum tester.
6. Add Motorcraft Mercon multi-purpose ATF transmission fluid XT–2–QDX, or equivalent, fluid to bring reservoir to proper level.
7. Attach vacuum tester to reservoir and apply maximum vacuum. Cycle steering wheel from stop to stop every 30 seconds for 5 minutes. **Do not hold steering wheel against stops for more than 5 seconds.**
8. Remove vacuum tester and install reservoir cap.
9. Ensure fluid is at proper level and inspect system for leaks.
10. Repeat procedure as necessary.

POWER STEERING FLUID COOLER

REPLACE

1. Recover refrigerant as outlined under"Air Conditioning. "
2. Remove right, left and center splash shields.
3. **On models equipped with 3.9L engine,** disconnect air intake tube and position aside.
4. **On all models,** disconnect A/C lines from condenser.
5. Support condenser, then remove condenser attaching bolts and condenser.
6. Remove and discard fluid cooler

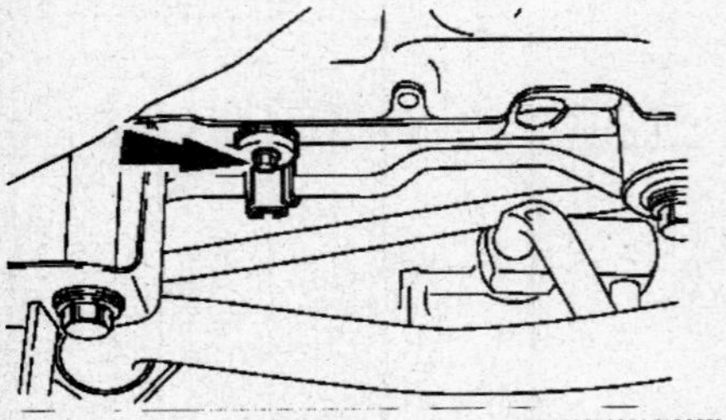

Fig. 14 Power steering line bracket

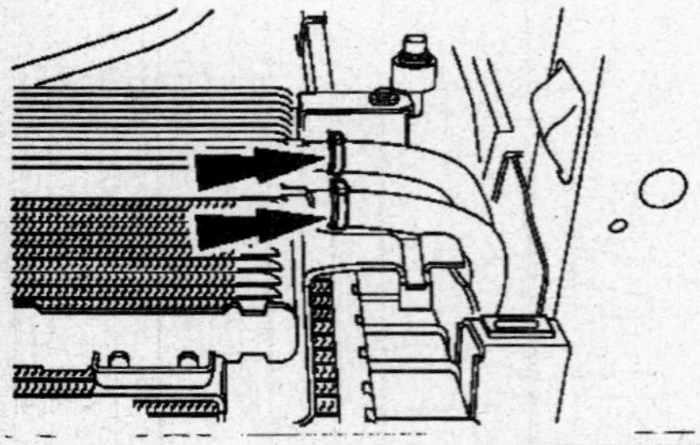

Fig. 17 Power steering fluid cooler

clamps, **Fig. 17.**

7. Disconnect fluid cooler hoses and drain into a suitable container.
8. Remove cooler attaching bolts, then the cooler.
9. Reverse procedure to install. Tighten fluid cooler clamps using CV boot clamp tool No. T95P-3514-A, or equivalent. Refill and purge air from system.

POWER STEERING CONTROL VALVE ACTUATOR

REPLACE

1. Raise and support vehicle.
2. Disconnect steering control valve electrical connector.
3. Remove power steering hose bracket and position aside.
4. Disconnect and plug power steering hoses.
5. Remove control valve actuator, **Fig. 18.**
6. Reverse procedure to install noting the following:
   a. Install new O-rings to power steering lines using teflon seal replacer set tool No. D90P-3517-A, or equivalent.
   b. Tighten to specifications.

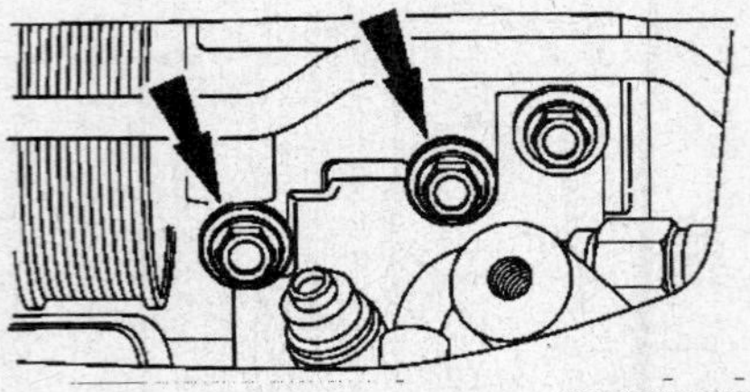

Fig. 15 Power steering pump bolts

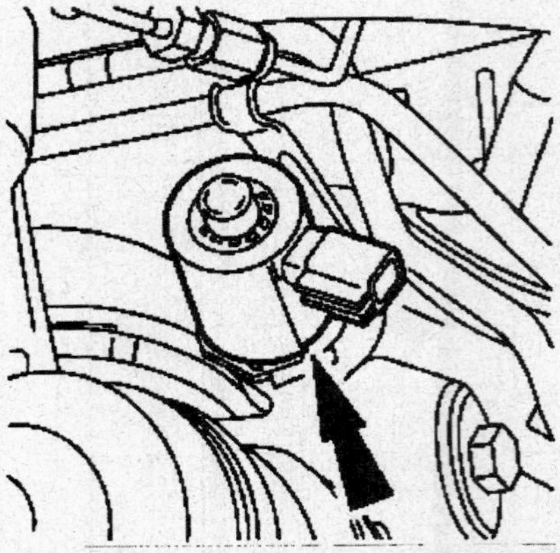

Fig. 18 Power steering control valve actuator

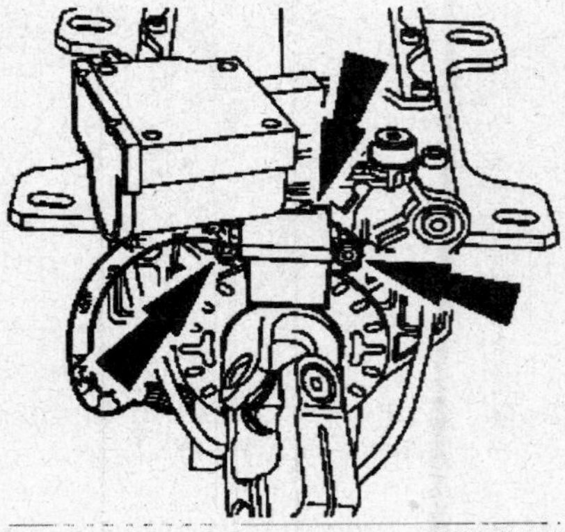

Fig. 19 Steering wheel rotation sensor removal (Part 2 of 2)

STEERING WHEEL ROTATION SENSOR

REPLACE

1. Center steering wheel ensuring wheels are in straight ahead position.
2. Remove driver air bag module as outlined under " Passive Restraint Systems."
3. Remove lower steering column opening finish panel, then the hood release assembly.
4. Remove lefthand lower heater duct.
5. Pull carpet away from console tunnel and remove bracket bolts.
6. Remove steering column opening reinforcement.
7. Disconnect steering wheel rotation sensor, then the electric tilt/ telescoping motor electrical connectors.
8. Disconnect lower steering column electrical connectors.
9. Secure steering column shaft and steering column using suitable mechanics wire. **Ensure steering column and shaft do not rotate.**
10. Remove and discard steering column shaft pinch bolt and disconnect shaft.
11. Support steering column, then remove and discard column lock nuts.
12. Lower steering column, then remove sensor attaching screws and sensor, **Fig. 19.**
13. Reverse procedure to install. Install new steering column lock nuts and pinch bolt and tighten to specifications.

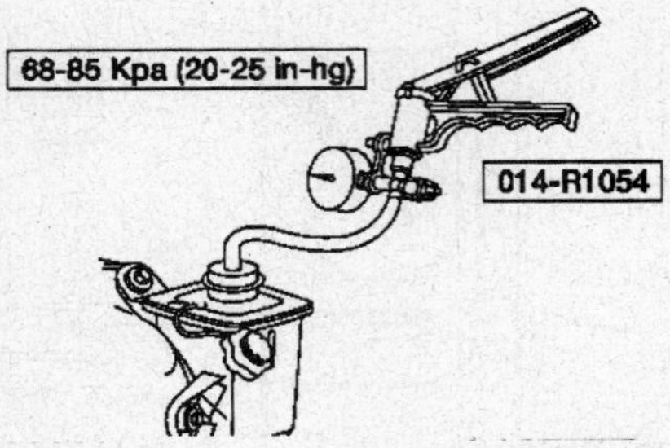

Fig. 16 Power steering vacuum bleed

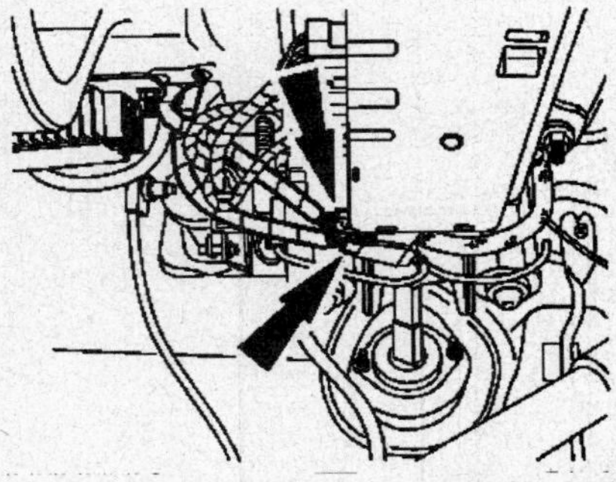

Fig. 19 Steering wheel rotation sensor removal (Part 1 of 2)

TIGHTENING SPECIFICATIONS

Year	Component	Torque, Ft. Lbs.
2000	A/C Compressor	18
	Control Valve Actuator	22
	Engine Control Wiring Bracket	44①
	Heater Water Valve Bracket	44①
	Hub & Bearing To Knuckle	66
	Intermediate Shaft Bolt	18
	Intermediate Shaft To Gear Pinch Bolt	26
	Lower Arm To Frame	129
	Lower Arm To Knuckle	111
	Power Steering Cooler To Radiator	89①
	Power Steering Hose Brackets	89①
	Power Steering Pressure Hose	23
	Power Steering Return Hose To Gear	23
	Power Steering Pump	18
	Power Steering Reservoir Lower Bolt	9
	Power Steering Reservoir Upper Bolt	53①
	Radiator Tube To Engine	89①
	Stabilizer Bar Bracket	41
	Stabilizer Bar Link	41
	Steering Column Lock Nuts	30
	Steering Column Opening Reinforcement Bolts	15
	Steering Column Shaft To Intermediate Shaft Pinch Bolt	26
	Steering Gear Lock Nuts	76
	Steering Sensor Mounting Bolts	27①
	Strut To Body	21
	Strut To Lower Arm	129
	Tie Rod End To Knuckle	74
	Upper Control Arm To Body	35
	Upper Control Arm To Knuckle	66
	Upper Strut Rod To Upper Mount	37
	Wheel Lug Nuts	100

① — Inch lbs.

Wheel Alignment

INDEX

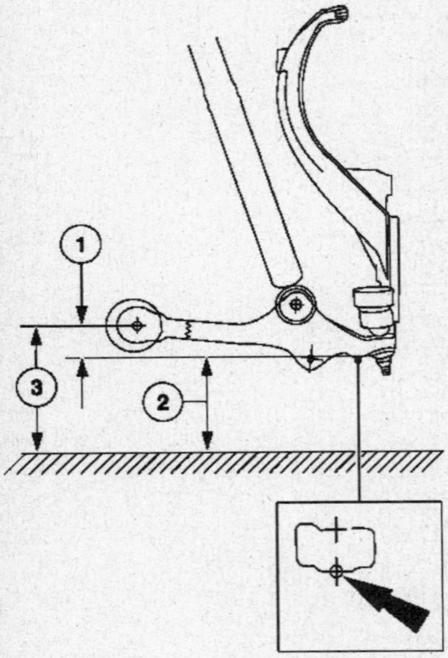

Item	Description
1	Ride height = B-A
2	Measurement A
3	Measurement B

FM2049900063000X

Fig. 1 Front ride height measurement

PRELIMINARY INSPECTION

1. Inspect all suspension and steering components for looseness and wear and correct as necessary.
2. Inspect tires for similar tread and proper air pressure.
3. Ensure vehicle ride height is within specifications.

RIDE HEIGHT

Refer to **Figs. 1 and 2** for ride height measurement. Front ride height should be 2.1–2.7 inches and rear ride height should be .7–1.3 inches.

FRONT WHEEL ALIGNMENT

CASTER & CAMBER

If vehicle is equipped with hex head bolts in lower control arm, new cam bolts and lock nuts must be installed before adjusting

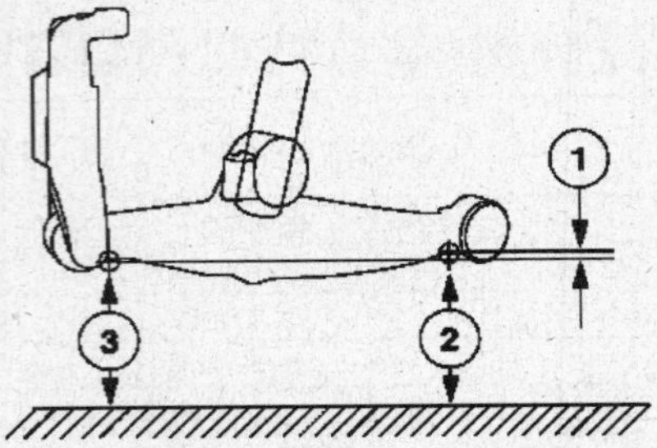

Item	Description
1	Ride height = A-B
2	Measurement A
3	Measurement B

FM2049900064000X

Fig. 2 Rear ride height measurement

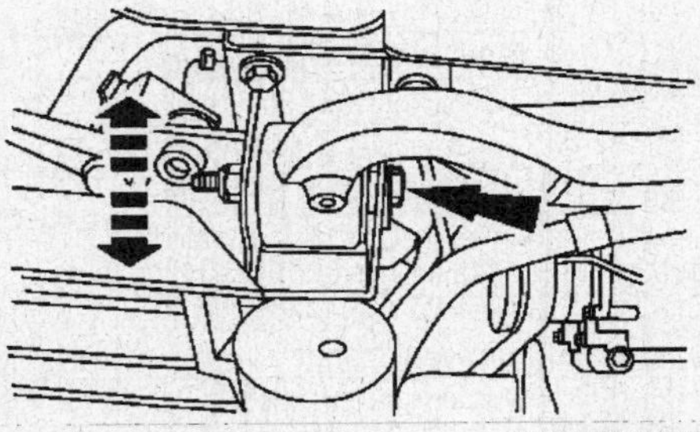

FM2049900061000X

Fig. 4 Caster adjustment bolt

suspension. If new bolts are to be installed, refer to "Control Arm, Replace" under "Front Suspension & Steering."

1. In order to turn camber and caster cams, loosen lower control arm attaching nuts, **Figs. 3 and 4.**
2. Rotate caster adjustment bolt until caster is within specifications.
3. Rotate camber adjustment bolt while supporting lower control arm by hand until camber is within specifications. Adjustments to camber may affect toe setting. Toe and camber may need to be adjusted at the same time. Refer to "Toe" to adjust toe settings.
4. Tighten lower control arms to specifications and recheck alignment. Readjust as necessary.

TOE

1. Start engine and center steering wheel.
2. Turn engine off and hold steering wheel in straight ahead position by attaching a rigid link from steering wheel to brake pedal.
3. Remove tie rod boot clamps, then loosen jam nuts, **Fig. 5.**
4. Clean and lubricate nuts and tie rod threads.
5. Rotate inner tie rod link to adjust to. Do not allow bellows to twist when tie rod is rotated.
6. Ensure toe is within specifications and tighten jam nuts.
7. Recheck alignment settings and adjust as necessary.

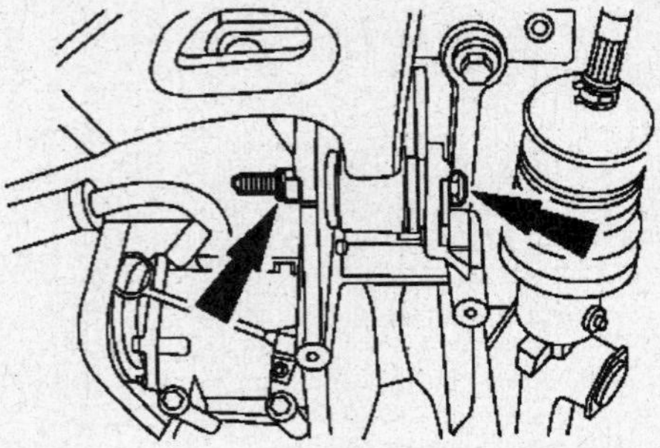

FM2049900060000X

Fig. 3 Camber adjustment bolt

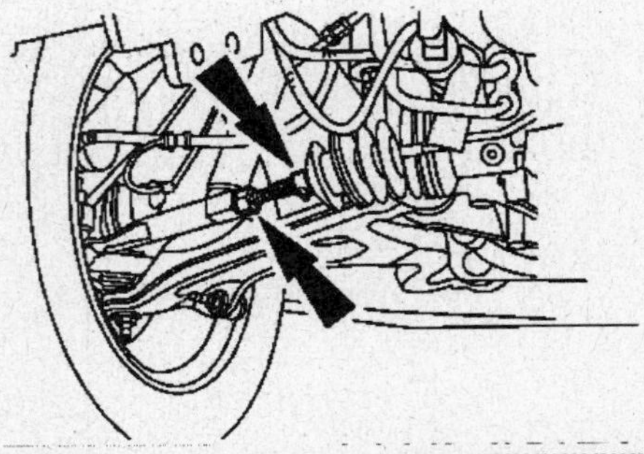

FM2049900062000X

Fig. 5 Tie rod adjustment

REAR WHEEL ALIGNMENT

CASTER & CAMBER

Caster and camber are not adjustable on the rear suspension.

TOE

1. Clean toe link threads and nut.
2. Loosen toe link jam nut and turn toe link until alignment is within specifications.
3. Tighten jam nut.
4. Ensure alignment is within specifications.

MUSTANG

NOTE: Refer To The Rear Of This Manual For Vehicle Manufacturer's Special Service Tool Suppliers.

INDEX OF SERVICE OPERATIONS

Specifications

GENERAL ENGINE SPECIFICATIONS

Year	Engine Liter (VIN Code)①	Fuel System	Bore & Stroke	Compression Ratio	Net H.P. @ RPM②	Maximum Torque Ft. Lbs. @ RPM	Normal Oil Pressure, psi
1997	3.8L (4)	SEFI	3.81 × 3.39	9.0	150 @ 4000	215 @ 2750	40–60③
	4.6L DOHC (V)	SEFI	3.55 × 3.54	9.5	305 @ 5800	300 @ 4800	20–45④
	4.6L SOHC (W)	SEFI	3.55 × 3.54	9.0	215 @ 4400	285 @ 3500	20–45④
1998	3.8L (4)	SEFI	3.81 × 3.39	9.0	150 @ 4000	215 @ 2750	40–60③
	4.6L DOHC (V)	SEFI	3.55 × 3.54	9.5	305 @ 5800	300 @ 4800	20–45④
	4.6L SOHC (W)	SEFI	3.55 × 3.54	9.0	225 @ 4750	290 @ 3500	20–45④
1999	3.8L (4)	SEFI	3.81 × 3.39	9.1	190 @ 5250	225 @ 3000	40–125③
	4.6L (V) DOHC	SEFI	3.81 × 3.39	9.0	260 @ 5250	300 @ 4000	20–45④
	4.6L (X) SOHC	SEFI	3.55 × 3.54	9.1	250 @ 4750	290 @ 3500	20–45④
2000	3.8L (4)	SEFI	3.81 × 3.39	—	—	—	40–125③
	4.6L (V) DOHC	SEFI	3.55 × 3.54	—	—	—	20–45④
	4.6L (X) SOHC	SEFI	3.55 × 3.54	—	—	—	20–45④

DOHC — Double overhead cam four valve per cylinder

SEFI — Sequential Multi-Port Electronic Fuel Injection

SOHC — Single overhead cam two valve per cylinder

① — Eighth digit denotes engine code.

② — Net rating as installed in vehicle.

③ — Engine hot @ 2500 RPM.

④ — Engine hot @ 1500 RPM.

TUNE UP SPECIFICATIONS

Year & Engine	Spark Plug Gap	Ignition Timing BTDC				Curb Idle Speed		Fast Idle Speed		Fuel Pump Pressure, psi	Valve Lash, Inch
		Firing Order Fig.	Man. Trans.	Auto. Trans.	Mark Fig.	Man. Trans.	Auto Trans.	Man. Trans.	Auto. Trans.		
1997											
3.8L	.054	A②	10⑥	10⑥	⑦	⑤	⑤	⑤	⑤	30–45⑧	④
4.6L	.054	③	10⑥	10⑥	⑦	⑤	⑤	⑤	⑤	30–45⑧	④
1998											
3.8L	.054	A②	10⑥	10⑥	⑦	⑤	⑤	⑤	⑤	30–45①	④
4.6L	.054	③	10⑥	10⑥	⑦	⑤	⑤	⑤	⑤	30–45①	④
1999–2000											
3.8L	.054	A②	10⑥	10⑥	⑦	⑤	⑤	⑤	⑤	35–55①	④
4.6L	.054	③	10⑥	10⑥	⑦	⑤	⑤	⑤	⑤	35–55①	④

BTDC — Before Top Dead Center

D — Drive

① — Wrap shop towel around fitting to prevent fuel spillage, then connect suitable fuel pressure gauge to fuel diagnostic valve on fuel rail assembly. Gradually open fuel pressure gauge test valve to relieve fuel system pressure & drain fuel into a suitable container. Close fuel pressure gauge test valve. Turn ignition On. Access output test mode on scan tool & operate fuel pump to obtain maximum fuel pressure. Fuel pump will operate for approximately 8 seconds. Inspect fuel pressure gauge reading.

② — Cylinder numbering front to rear, righthand bank, 1, 2, 3 ; lefthand bank, 4, 5, 6. Firing order 1–4–2–5–3–6.

③ — Cylinder numbering front to rear: righthand bank 1, 2, 3, 4; lefthand bank 5, 6, 7, 8. Firing order 1-3-7-2-6-5-4-8. Refer to **Fig. B** for ignition coil tower terminal numbering.

④ — Equipped w/hydraulic valve tappets.

⑤ — Idle speed controlled by an automatic idle speed control.

⑥ — Non-adjustable. Do not attempt to inspect base timing. False readings will be received.

⑦ — Equipped w/crankshaft position sensor.

⑧ — Wrap shop towel around fuel diagnostic valve to prevent fuel spillage. Connect suitable fuel pressure gauge to fuel diagnostic valve. Turn ignition On to energize fuel pump, then inspect pressure gauge reading.

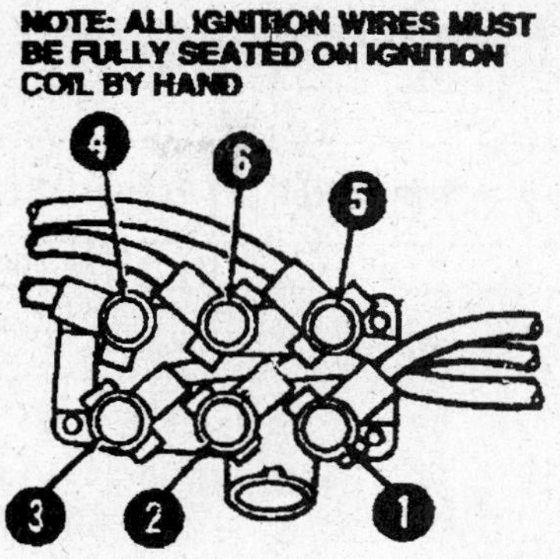

FM1138800242000X

Fig. A

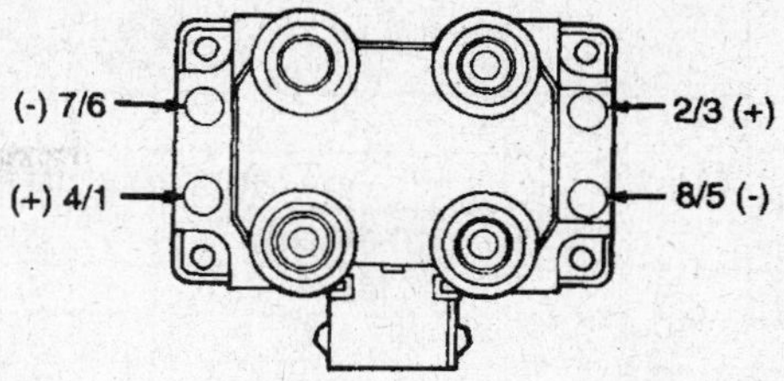

FM1139600469000X

Fig. B

FRONT WHEEL ALIGNMENT SPECIFICATIONS

Caster Angle, Degrees①		Camber Angle, Degrees		Total Toe, Inch②		Toe Out On Turns, Degrees	
Limits	Desired	Limits	Desired	Limits	Desired	Outer Wheel	Inner Wheel
1997–98							
+2.45 to +3.95	+3.2	−1.35 to +.15	−.6	0 to +.50	+.25	19.84	20
1999–2000							
+2.45 to +3.95	+3.2	−1.25 to +.25	−.5	0 to +.50	+.25	—	—

① — Difference side to side, lefthand minus righthand should not exceed .75°.

② — Toe-In (+). Toe-Out (–).

FLUID CAPACITIES & COOLING SYSTEM DATA

Year	Engine (VIN①)	Cooling Capacity, Qts.		Radiator Cap Relief Pressure, Lbs.	Thermo. Opening Temp. Deg. F	Fuel Tank Gals.	Engine Oil Refill Qts.	Transmission Oil		Rear Axle Oil Pints
		Less A/C	With A/C					Man. Trans. Pints	Auto. Trans. Qts.③	
1997	3.8L (4)	11.8	11.8	16	196	15.4	4②	④	13.9	⑥
	4.6L (W)	14.1	14.1	16	192	15.4	4②	④	12.8	⑥
	4.6L (V)	14.1	14.1	16	192	15.4	5②	④	12.8	⑥
1998	3.8L (4)	11.8	11.8	16	193	15.7	4②	④	13.9	⑥
	4.6L (X)	14.1	14.1	16	188	15.7	⑤	④	12.8	⑥
	4.6L (V)	14.1	14.1	16	188	15.7	6	④	12.8	⑥
1999	3.8L (4)	11.8	11.8	16	196	15.5	5⑦	④	13.9	⑥
	4.6L (V)	14.1	14.1	16	196	15.5	5⑦	④	12.8	⑥
	4.6L (X)	14.1	14.1	16	196	15.5	5⑦	④	12.8	⑥
2000	3.8L (4)	19.2	19.2	16	196	15.7	—	—	13.9	⑧
	4.6L (V)	19.2	19.2	16	196	15.7	—	—	12.8	⑧
	4.6L (X)	19.2	19.2	16	196	15.7	—	—	12.8	⑧

① — Eighth digit of Vehicle Identification Number (VIN) denotes engine code.

② — Add 1 qt. w/filter change.

③ — Approximate. Make final inspection w/dipstick.

④ — T45 transmission, 6.6 pts.; w/T50 transmission, 5.6 pts.

⑤ — W/oil cooler 6.675 ± .125 qts.; less oil cooler 6.425 ± .125 qts.

⑥ — 7.5 inch ring gear, 3.25 pts.; 8.8 inch ring gear, 3.75 pts.

⑦ — Includes filter.

⑧ — 7.5 inch ring gear, 3.25 pts.; 8.8 inch ring gear less Independent Rear Suspension (IRS), 3.75 pts.; 8.8 inch ring gear w/IRS, 2.75 pts.

LUBRICANT DATA

Year	Model	Lubricant Type				
		Transmission		Rear Axle	Power Steering	Brake System
		Automatic	Manual			
1997–98	All	Mercon	Mercon	①	Mercon	DOT 3
1999	All	Mercon V	Mercon	①	Mercon V	DOT 3
2000	All	Mercon V	Mercon	①	Mercon XT-2-QDX	DOT 3

① — XY-80W90-QL gear lubricant. On models equipped w/Traction-Lok axle, add 4 ounces of friction modifier.

Electrical

NOTE: On Air Bag Equipped Models, Refer To " Air Bag System Precautions" Located In The Front Of This Manual For System Disarming & Arming Procedures.

NOTE: Refer To "Computer Relearn Procedures " Located In The Front Of This Manual For Computer Relearn Procedures.

INDEX

PRECAUTIONS

AIR BAG SYSTEMS

Refer to "Air Bag System Precautions" in front of this manual for system disarming and arming procedures.

BATTERY GROUND CABLE

Prior to service, disconnect battery ground cable and isolate as required.

FUSE PANEL & FLASHER LOCATION

1997-98

The fuse panel is located on lefthand side of steering column, under instrument panel.

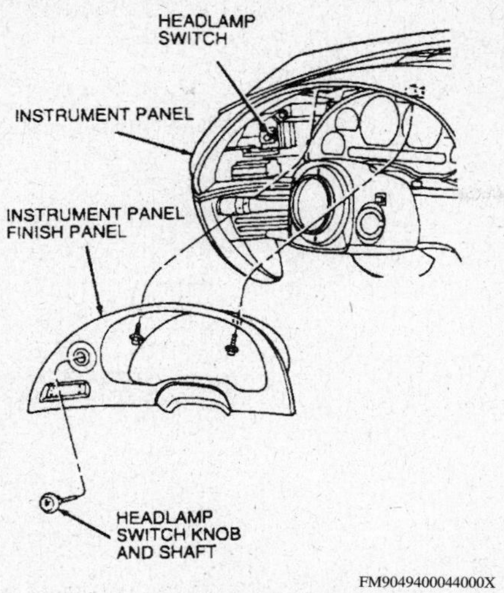

Fig. 1 Headlamp switch replacement. 1997–98

A power distribution center containing engine fuses and relays for horn, starter and fog lamps is located in lefthand side of engine compartment, behind radiator.

The combination turn signal and emergency warning indicator flasher is attached by a bracket to lower lefthand instrument panel reinforcement, above fuse holder.

1999–2000

The fuse panel is located below and to the lefthand side of the steering column near the brake pedal. To access these fuses, carefully remove the panel cover.

There is also a power distribution and relay box located in the engine compartment, adjacent to the battery.

RELAY CENTER LOCATION

1997–98

The relay panel is located in the righthand front corner of the engine compartment, mounted to the upper radiator support.

1999–2000

On these models a relay and power distribution box is located under the hood. Always ensure its cover is intact when filling fluid reservoirs or servicing the battery.

FUEL PUMP RELAY LOCATION

1997–98

The fuel pump relay is part of the Constant Control Relay Module (CCRM), located on a bracket behind the engine coolant reservoir.

1999–2000

The fuel pump relay is located in the underhood relay and power distribution box.

STARTER

REPLACE

1997–98

1. Raise and support front of vehicle.
2. Disconnect "S" terminal connector. **Pull on connector only.**
3. Disconnect starter cable from starter.
4. Remove starter motor bolts, then starter.
5. Reverse procedure to install, noting the following:
   a. **Torque** starter bolts to 15–19 ft. lbs.
   b. **Torque** starter cable nut to 6.7–10.3 ft. lbs.

1999–2000

1. Raise and safely support vehicle.
2. **On models equipped with 3.8L engine,** remove ground cable nut.
3. **On models equipped with 4.6L engine,** disconnect HO2S electrical connector, remove bracket nuts and bracket.
4. **On all models,** remove solenoid protective cap and wiring nuts, then position wiring aside.
5. Remove starter motor mounting bolts, then the starter.
6. Reverse procedure to install, noting the following:
   a. **Torque** starter mounting bolts to 17 ft. lbs.
   b. **Torque** solenoid "B" terminal nut to 9 ft. lbs.
   c. **Torque** solenoid terminal nut to 53 inch lbs.
   d. **On models equipped with 3.8L engine, torque** ground cable nut to 17 ft. lbs.
   e. **On models equipped with 4.6L engine, torque** HO2S bracket nut to 18 ft. lbs.

ALTERNATOR

REPLACE

1997–98

1. Disconnect wire harness attachments to alternator and voltage regulator.
2. Disengage alternator drive belt from pulley.
3. **On models equipped with 4.6L engine,** remove retaining bolts and alternator mounting bracket.
4. **On all models,** remove mounting bolts and alternator.
5. Reverse procedures to install noting the following:
   a. **On models equipped with 4.6L engine, torque** mounting bolts 15–22 ft. lbs.
   b. **On models equipped with 3.8L engine, torque** upper bolt 16–21 ft. lbs. and lower bolt 30–40 ft. lbs.
   c. **On all models, torque** output terminal nut 60–84 inch. lbs.

1999–2000

1. Remove serpentine drive belt from alternator pulley, but leave belt in place to ease installation.
2. **On models equipped with 4.6L** **SOHC engine,** remove alternator upper bracket, then press tab to release alternator electrical connector. **Do not pull on tab. Press it carefully.**
3. **On all models,** disconnect alternator electrical connections.
4. Remove alternator mounting bolts, then the alternator.
5. Reverse procedure to install, noting the following:
   a. **On models equipped with 3.8L engine, torque** alternator lower mounting bolt to 35 ft. lbs., upper bolt to 18 ft. lbs. and battery positive cable nut to solenoid to 72 inch lbs.
   b. **On models equipped with 4.6L engines, torque** alternator lower mounting bolts to 18 ft. lbs., upper bolts to 89 inch lbs. and battery positive cable nut to solenoid to 72 inch lbs.
   c. **On all models,** inspect serpentine drive belt and replace if required.

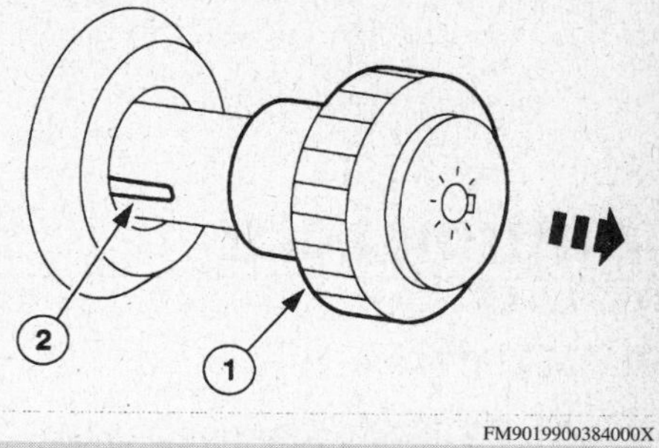

Fig. 2 Headlamp switch knob removal. 1999–2000

IGNITION COIL PACK

REPLACE

1997–98

1. Disconnect fuel charging wiring connectors and radio ignition interference capacitor.
2. Squeeze locking tabs to release boot retainers and remove ignition wires by twisting while pulling.
3. Remove coil mounting screws and coil.
4. Reverse procedure to install and **torque** mounting screws to 44–61 inch lbs.

1999–2000

1. Disconnect electrical connectors as required.
2. Tag spark plug wires, then squeeze their locking tabs, disconnect and position them aside.
3. Note radio ignition interference capacitor location, remove coil mounting bolts, then the coil.
4. Reverse procedure to install, noting the following:
   a. Ensure radio ignition interference capacitor is located under proper coil mounting bolt.
   b. **Torque** coil mounting bolts to 53 inch lbs.

c. Apply silicone brake caliper grease and dielectric compound part No. D7AZ-19A331-A, or an equivalent meeting Ford specification ESE-M1C171-A to inside of each wire coil boot.

IGNITION LOCK

REPLACE

FUNCTIONAL

1. Turn ignition to Run.
2. Insert a suitable drift punch in hole in upper steering column shroud under ignition switch.
3. Depress retaining pin while pulling out on ignition switch to remove it from steering column lock cylinder housing.
4. Reverse procedure to install. Ensure lock cylinder operates properly.

NON-FUNCTIONAL

1. Remove steering wheel as outlined under "Steering Wheel, Replace."
2. Using locking type pliers or suitable equivalent, twist ignition switch lock cylinder cap until it separates from ignition switch lock cylinder.
3. Working through access hole in lower steering column shroud, use a small pilot punch to center punch retaining pin, then drill out with a 1/8 inch diameter drill.
4. Using a 3/8 inch diameter bit, drill down middle of key slot approximately 1 3/4 inches until lock cylinder breaks loose from breakaway base.
5. Remove ignition switch lock cylinder.
6. Closely note positions of column lock gear, bearing and retainer, then remove bearing retainer, steering column lock housing bearing, ignition switch lock cylinder and steering column lock gear.
7. Reverse procedures to install, noting the following:
   a. **Carefully inspect steering column lock cylinder housing for damage. If damaged, steering column lock cylinder housing must be replaced.**
   b. Ensure all components are properly aligned and oriented as noted during removal.
   c. Coat lock gear and housing with ignition lock grease part No. F0AZ-19584-A, or an equivalent meeting Ford specification ESA-M1C232-A.

IGNITION SWITCH

REPLACE

1997–98

Removal

1. Disconnect ignition switch electrical connector.
2. Rotate ignition switch lock cylinder to Run position.
3. Remove two ignition switch retaining screws, then disengage from the actuator pin.

Installation

1. Adjust ignition switch by sliding carrier to switch Run position. **A new replacement ignition switch assembly should already be set in Run position as received.**
2. Install ignition switch onto actuator pin.
3. Install retaining screws, **torque** to 60–84 inch lbs.
4. Connect electrical connector to ignition switch.
5. Inspect ignition switch for proper operation.

1999–2000

1. Remove steering column lower cover mounting screws, then the cover.
2. Remove instrument panel reinforcement mounting screws, then the reinforcement.
3. Loosen ignition switch electrical connector retaining bolt, then disconnect the connector.
4. Ensure ignition is Off.
5. Remove ignition switch mounting screws, then the switch.
6. Reverse procedure to install, noting the following:
   a. **Torque** ignition switch mounting screws to 53 inch lbs.
   b. **Torque** instrument panel reinforcement mounting screws to 80.5 inch lbs.
   c. **Torque** steering column lower cover mounting screws to 80.5 inch lbs.

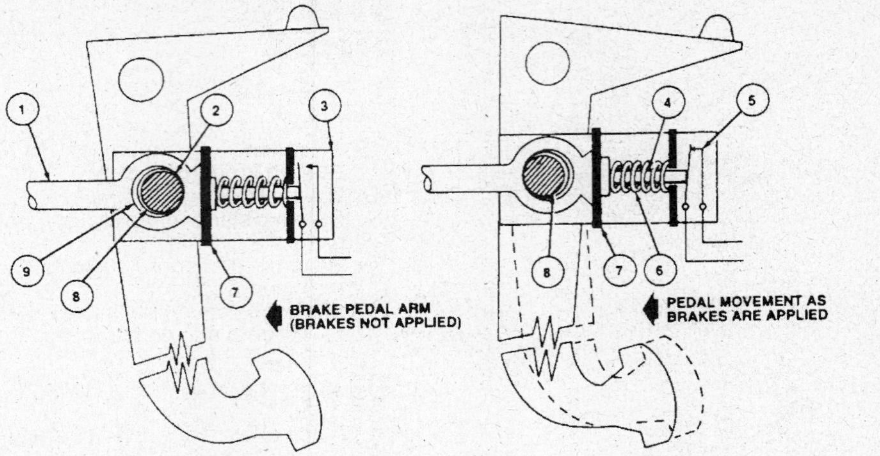

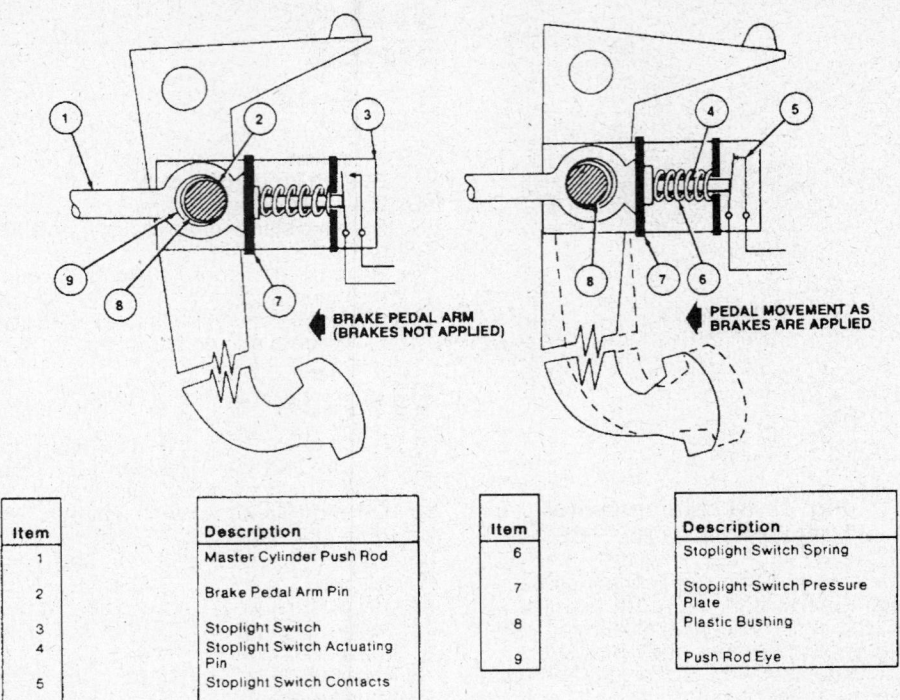

Item	Description
1	Master Cylinder Push Rod
2	Brake Pedal Arm Pin
3	Stoplight Switch
4	Stoplight Switch Actuating Pin
5	Stoplight Switch Contacts

Item	Description
6	Stoplight Switch Spring
7	Stoplight Switch Pressure Plate
8	Plastic Bushing
9	Push Rod Eye

FM9049400043000X

Fig. 3 Stop lamp switch replacement. 1997–98

CLUTCH START SWITCH

REPLACE

1997–98

The starter/clutch interlock switch is designed to prevent starting engine unless clutch pedal is fully depressed. Switch is connected between ignition switch and starter motor relay coil and maintains an open circuit with clutch pedal in up position (clutch engaged).

The switch is designed to automatically self-adjust first time clutch pedal is pressed to floor. Self-adjuster consists of a two-piece clip snapped together over a serrated rod. When plunger or rod is extended, clip bottoms out on serrations to a position determined by clutch pedal travel. In this way, switch is set to close starter circuit when clutch is pressed all way to floor (clutch disengaged). To replace clutch interlock switch, proceed as follows:

1. Disconnect harness connector from clutch pedal position switch.
2. Disconnect locating tab lock, then rotate switch approximately 90° clockwise.
3. Remove switch lock plate, then pry switch off clutch pushrod by hand.
4. Reverse procedure to install. An audible click will be heard when clutch

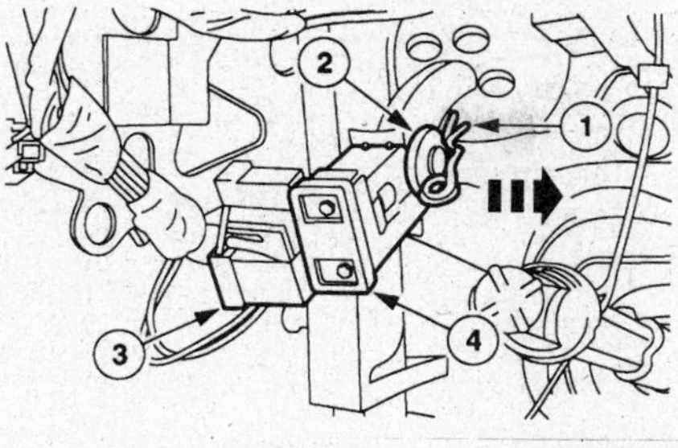

FM9019900385000X

Fig. 4 Stop lamp switch replacement. 1999–2000

pedal position switch is mounted properly onto clutch pushrod.

1999–2000

1. Disconnect clutch pedal position switch electrical connector.
2. Note switch's positioning, then remove mounting bolt and the switch.
3. Reverse procedure to install. Tighten mounting bolt securely and inspect for proper operation.

NEUTRAL SAFETY SWITCH

REPLACE

1997–98

1. Place manual control lever in Neutral position.
2. Raise and support vehicle, then disconnect electrical harness from Transmission Range (TR) sensor.
3. Remove two TR sensor bolts, then sensor.
4. Ensure manual control lever is in Neutral position.
5. Install TR sensor, then, loosely, sensor bolts.
6. Align TR sensor slots using transmission range sensor alignment (MLPS alignment) tool No. T92P-70010-AH, or equivalent.
7. **Torque** sensor bolts to 84–108 inch lbs., then remove tool.
8. Connect electrical harness to TR sensor, then lower the vehicle.
9. Connect battery ground cable, then inspect for proper operation with parking brake control engaged. Engine should start only in Park or Neutral.

1999–2000

On these models the neutral safety switch is incorporated into the digital transmission range (TR) sensor.

1. Apply parking brake, then place transmission in Neutral position.
2. Raise and safely support vehicle.
3. Disconnect TR sensor electrical connector.
4. Disconnect range selector cable.
5. Remove TR sensor mounting bolts, then the sensor.
6. Reverse procedure to install, noting the following:

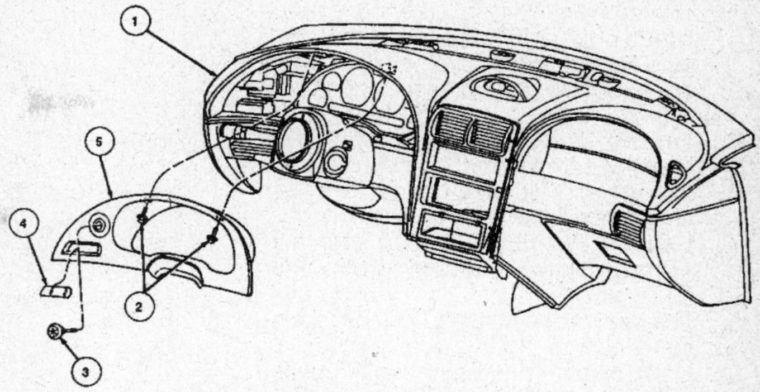

Item	Description
1	Instrument Panel
2	Screw and Washer Assy (2 Req'd)
3	Light Switch Knob
4	Instrument Panel Control Opening Cover
5	Instrument Panel Finish Panel

FM1049700013000X

Fig. 5 Instrument cluster bezel removal. 1997–98

a. Install TR sensor into position, then loosely snug mounting bolts.
b. Ensure shift lever shaft is in Neutral position.
c. Using TR sensor alignment tool No. T97L-70010-A, or equivalent, align sensor slots.
d. **Torque** sensor mounting bolts to 62–89 inch lbs.
e. Ensure starter cranks only in Park or Neutral position.

HEADLAMP SWITCH

REPLACE

1997–98

1. Pull headlamp switch to full On position.
2. Reaching through opening in instrument panel, depress shaft release button on headlamp switch and remove headlamp switch knob and shaft, **Fig. 1.**
3. Remove cluster instrument panel finish panel as follows:
   a. Remove two screws above instrument cluster, then pull instrument panel finish panel to unsnap clip above lefthand register.
   b. Pull panel to unsnap three clips on righthand side vertical/horizontal edge, then remove panel.
4. Remove headlamp switch nut and pull switch through opening in instrument cluster.
5. Disconnect wiring to headlamp switch and remove headlamp switch.
6. Reverse procedure to install.

1999–2000

1. Pull headlamp switch to full On position.
2. Insert a suitable thin tool into knob slot (2), **Fig. 2,** then pull and remove the knob (1).
3. Remove instrument cluster finish retaining panel screws, then the panel.
4. Remove headlamp switch mounting screws, then the switch.
5. Disconnect headlamp switch electrical connector.
6. Reverse procedure to install.

STOP LIGHT SWITCH

REPLACE

1997–98

1. Disconnect wires at connector.
2. Remove hairpin retainer, then slide switch, pushrod and nylon washers and bushing away from pedal and remove switch, **Fig. 3.**
3. Position stop lamp switch so U-shaped side is nearest brake pedal and directly over/under pin.
4. Slide stoplamp switch up/down, trapping master cylinder pushrod and blade bushing between stoplamp switch side plates.
5. Push stoplamp switch and pushrod assembly firmly toward brake pedal arm, then assemble outside white plastic washer to pin and install hairpin retainer to trap whole assembly.
6. Assemble wire harness connector to stop lamp switch and install wires in retaining clip. **Stop lamp switch wire harness must have sufficient length to travel with switch during full stroke of brake pedal. If wire length is insufficient, reroute harness or service as required.**
7. Inspect stop lamp switch for proper operation.

1999–2000

1. Remove stop lamp switch linkage clip (1) and retainer (2), **Fig. 4.**
2. Disconnect switch electrical connector (3), then remove the switch (4).
3. Reverse procedure to install. Inspect stop lamp switch for proper operation.

MULTI-FUNCTION SWITCH

REPLACE

1997–98

1. Place a 1/8 diameter wire pin or suitable

equivalent in hole in steering column shroud under ignition switch lock cylinder, then depress retaining pin while pulling out on ignition switch lock cylinder.

2. Remove four steering column shroud retaining screws, then the shrouds.
3. Disconnect electrical connectors from multi-function switch.
4. Remove two multi-function switch to steering column retaining screws, then the switch.
5. Reverse procedures to install noting the following:
   a. **Torque** multi-function switch screws to 19–25 inch lbs.
   b. **Torque** steering column shroud retaining screws to 6–8 inch lbs.

1999–2000

1. Remove ignition lock cylinder as outlined under " Ignition Lock, Replace."
2. Remove tilt wheel handle.
3. Remove steering column upper and lower shroud retaining screws, then the shrouds.
4. Remove multi-function switch mounting screws.
5. Disconnect multi-function switch electrical connectors, then remove the switch.
6. Reverse procedure to install. **Torque** multi-function switch mounting screws to 18–26 inch lbs.

STEERING WHEEL

REPLACE

1997–98

1. Center front wheels to straight-ahead position.
2. Remove two cover caps from steering wheel back cover to access driver side air bag module bolts.
3. Lift module off steering wheel and disconnect electrical connector, then remove module from steering wheel.
4. Disconnect horn and speed control wire harness from steering wheel.
5. Remove and discard steering wheel bolt.
6. Using steering wheel remover tool No. T67L-3600-A, or equivalent, remove steering wheel from steering column and route air bag sliding contact assembly wire harness through steering wheel as steering wheel is lifted off steering column. **Be sure control assembly wire harness does not get caught on steering wheel when lifting wheel off steering column, to avoid damage to control assembly wire harness.**
7. Reverse procedure to install, noting the following:
   a. **Ensure air bag sliding contact wire is not pinched or air bag monitor will detect a fault condition.**
   b. Route air bag sliding contact assembly wire harness through steering wheel opening at three o'clock position.
   c. Position steering wheel on steering column. Steering wheel and steering column gear input shaft coupling alignment marks should be aligned.
   d. **Torque** steering wheel bolt to 22–33 ft. lbs.
   e. **Torque** air bag module bolts to 36–47 inch lbs.

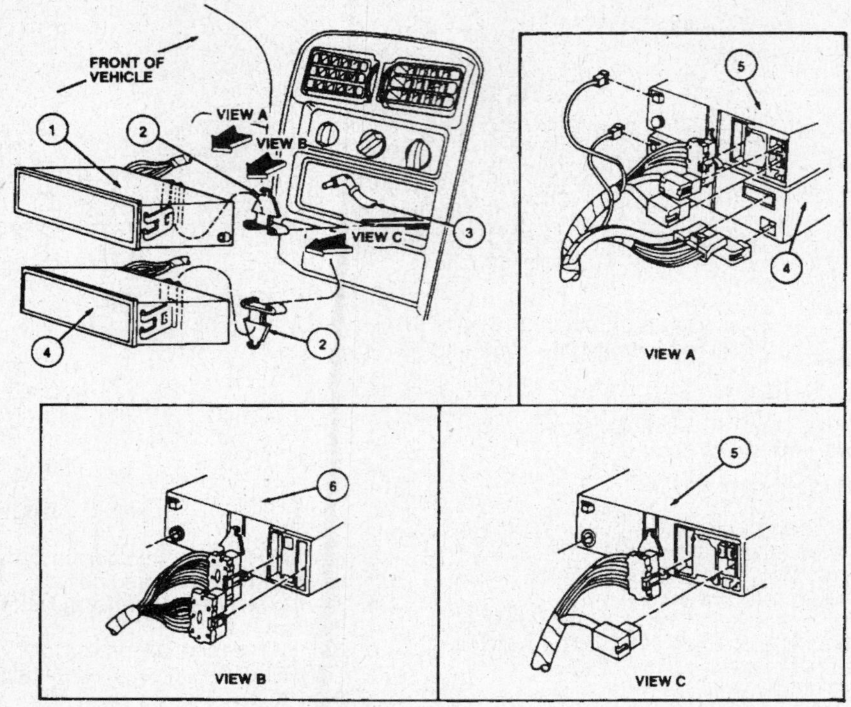

Item	Description
1	ESR Radio Chassis, ESC Radio Chassis and PAC Radio Chassis
2	Radio Chassis Support
3	Radio Antenna Lead In Cable
4	Digital Audio Compact Disc Player
5	ESC Radio Chassis, PAC Radio Chassis
6	ESR Radio Chassis

FM9039400008000X

Fig. 6 Radio removal. 1997–98

1999–2000

1. Ensure front wheels are in straight-ahead position.
2. Disconnect and isolate battery ground cable.
3. Remove round plugs on sides of steering wheel to access driver's air bag module mounting bolts.
4. Disconnect air bag module electrical connectors, then carefully remove module and store on a bench with pad side facing upward.
5. Remove and discard steering wheel to column retaining bolt.
6. Using a suitable puller tool, remove steering wheel.
7. Reverse procedure to install, noting the following:
   a. Install a new steering wheel retaining bolt and **torque** to 23–32 ft. lbs.
   b. **Torque** driver's air bag module mounting bolts to 80.5 inch lbs.
   c. From a safe location away from air bag modules, turn ignition On and ensure air bag indicator lamp lights for approximately 6 seconds, then turns off.

INSTRUMENT CLUSTER

REPLACE

1997–98

1. Remove headlamp switch knob as outlined under "Headlamp Switch, Replace."
2. Remove two upper screws from instrument cluster bezel (Instrument panel finish panel), then instrument cluster bezel, **Fig. 5.**
3. Remove four screws from instrument cluster panel, then pull instrument cluster away from instrument panel.
4. Disconnect two cluster printed circuit connectors from instrument cluster back plate, then remove cluster. **Do not remove gauge pointer if gauges are being removed from cluster assembly. Magnetic gauges cannot be calibrated again.**
5. Reverse procedure to install.

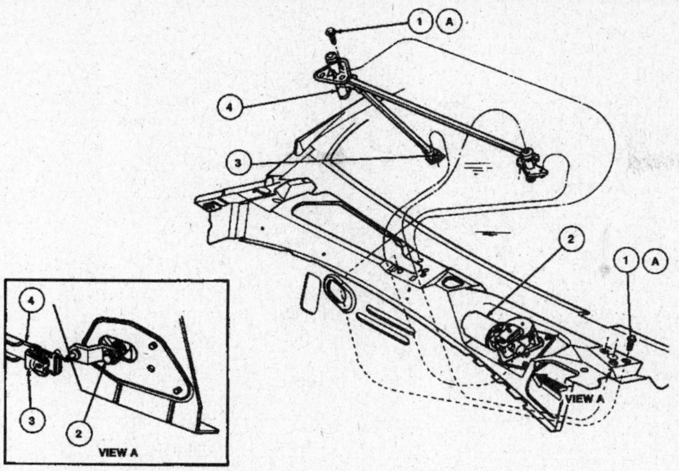

Item	Description
1	Screw and Washer (8 Req'd)
2	Windshield Wiper Motor
3	Windshield Wiper Linkage Clip
4	Windshield Wiper Mounting Arm and Pivot Shaft
A	Tighten to 13-17 N-m (10-12 Lb-Ft)

FM1049700011000X

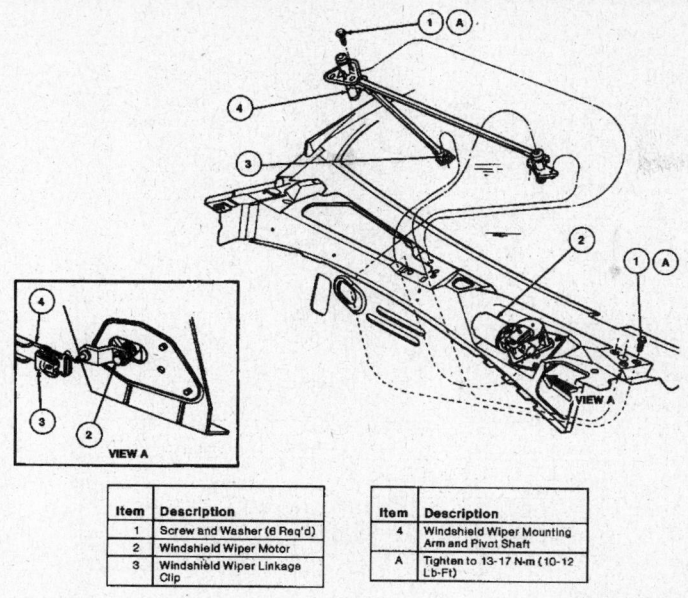

Fig. 7 Exploded view of wiper transmission. 1997–98

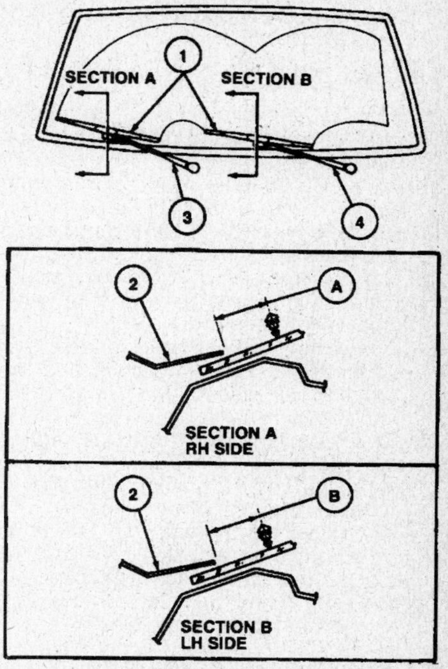

Item	Description
1	Windshield Wiper Blade
2	Cowl Vent Screen
3	Windshield Wiper Pivot Arm (RH)
4	Windshield Wiper Pivot Arm (LH)
A	55-81 mm (2.16-3.18 inches)
B	56-80 mm (2.20-3.14 inches)

FM1049700012000X

Fig. 8 Windshield wiper blade dimensions. 1997–98

1999–2000

1. Remove headlamp switch knob as outlined under "Headlamp Switch, Replace."
2. Remove instrument cluster finish retaining panel screws, then the panel.
3. Remove instrument cluster mounting screws, then carefully pull cluster out to access and disconnect electrical connector.
4. Carefully remove instrument cluster from vehicle.
5. Reverse procedure to install. Ensure all instruments and lamps operate properly.

RADIO

REPLACE

1997–98

1. Insert radio removing tools No. T87P-19061, or equivalent, into face plate approximately one inch.
2. Using light pressure, spread radio face plate removal tools to release clips, **Fig. 6.**
3. Remove radio, then disconnect antenna and electrical connectors.
4. Remove stereo tape cartridge container or digital audio compact disc player.

1999–2000

1. Insert radio removal tool No. T87P-19061-A, or equivalent into face plate, **but do not use excessive force.**
2. Carefully pull radio out of instrument panel.
3. Disconnect radio electrical connectors and antenna lead-in cable.
4. Reverse procedure to install.

WIPER MOTOR

REPLACE

The internal permanent magnets used in the windshield wiper motor are of a ceramic material. Care must be exercised in handling the motor to avoid damaging the magnets. The motor must not be struck or tapped with a hammer or other object.

1. Turn windshield wipers on. When blades reach full upright travel on glass, turn ignition Off.
2. Disconnect and isolate battery ground cable.
3. Remove windshield wiper pivot arms and blades.
4. Carefully remove cowl top vent grille.
5. Disconnect wiper motor adapter and connecting linkage clip from motor arm.
6. Remove linkage drive arm from windshield wiper motor.
7. Disconnect wiper motor electrical connector, then remove motor to cowl mounting fasteners.
8. Remove wiper motor.
9. Reverse procedures to install, noting the following:
   a. **On 1997–98 models, torque** wiper motor retaining screws to 10–12 ft. lbs.
   b. **On 1999–2000 models, torque** wiper motor retaining screws to 11 ft. lbs.
   c. **On all models,** cycle wipers back to park position, then install arms and blades.

WIPER SWITCH

REPLACE

The wiper switch is part of the multi-function switch. For replacement procedure, refer to "Multi-Function Switch, Replace."

WIPER TRANSMISSION

REPLACE

1997–98

1. Turn windshield wipers on. When blades reach full upright travel on glass, turn ignition Off.
2. Remove windshield wiper pivot arm and wiper blade from wiper mounting arm and pivot shaft, **Fig. 7**
3. Remove cowl top vent grille, then the wiper adapter and connecting arm clip retaining windshield wiper mounting arm and pivot shaft to motor output arm.
4. Remove windshield wiper mounting arm and pivot shaft retaining screws, then guide wiper mounting arm and pivot shafts from righthand side of cowl chamber.
5. Reverse procedure to install noting the following:
   a. Ensure wiper motor is in park position before installing pivot arm and wiper blade.
   b. Set windshield wiper blade to specified dimensions, **Fig. 8.**
   c. **Torque** windshield wiper mounting

arm and pivot shaft screws 10–12 ft. lbs.

1999–2000

1. Turn windshield wipers on. When blades reach full upright travel on glass, turn ignition Off.
2. Disconnect and isolate battery ground cable.
3. Remove windshield wiper pivot arms and blades.
4. Carefully remove cowl top vent grille.
5. Remove linkage drive arm from windshield wiper motor.
6. Lower the hood, then remove wiper transmission mounting bolts and the transmission assembly through right-hand cowl chamber opening.
7. Reverse procedure to install, noting the following:
   a. Install retaining clip onto end of wiper transmission linkage.
   b. **Torque** transmission mounting bolts to 11 ft. lbs.
   c. Connect battery ground cable.
   d. Cycle wipers back to park position, then install arms and blades.

BLOWER MOTOR

REPLACE

1997–98

1. Disconnect jumper wire harness from main harness electrical connector, then the jumper wire harness from blower motor switch resistor.
2. Remove three blower motor mounting screws, then pull blower motor out of A/C evaporator housing.
3. Remove heater blower motor cover and stiffener plate.
4. Disconnect jumper wire harness from blower motor.
5. Reverse procedure to install. Install gasket material to new A/C blower motor.

1999–2000

1. Disconnect jumper wire harness from main harness electrical connector.
2. Disconnect main harness at blower motor resistor.
3. Remove blower motor mounting screws.
4. Separate cover from motor, then the motor from the housing.
5. Disconnect jumper harness at blower motor.
6. Carefully remove blower motor from vehicle.
7. Reverse procedure to install.

HEATER CORE

REPLACE

1997–98

1. Remove evaporator case as outlined under "Evaporator Case, Replace."
2. Disconnect vacuum harness from A/C evaporating and position aside.
3. Remove four heater core access cover screws, then cover from heater case.
4. Remove heater dash panel seal from heater inlet and outlet tubes, then pull heater core out of heater case.
5. Reverse procedure to install.

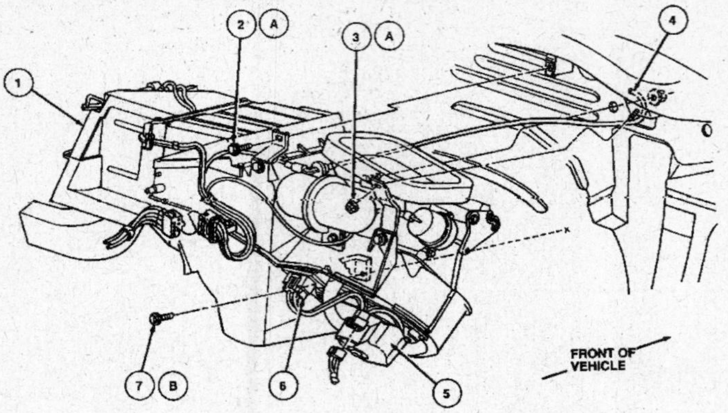

Item	Description
1	A/C Evaporator Housing
2	Screw
3	Nut
4	To Vacuum Source
5	Blower Motor

Item	Description
6	Heater Blower Motor Switch Resistor
7	Screw
A	Tighten to 10.2-13.6 N-m (91-122 Lb-In)
B	Tighten to 1.6-2.2 N-m (15-19 Lb-In)

FM1049700014000X

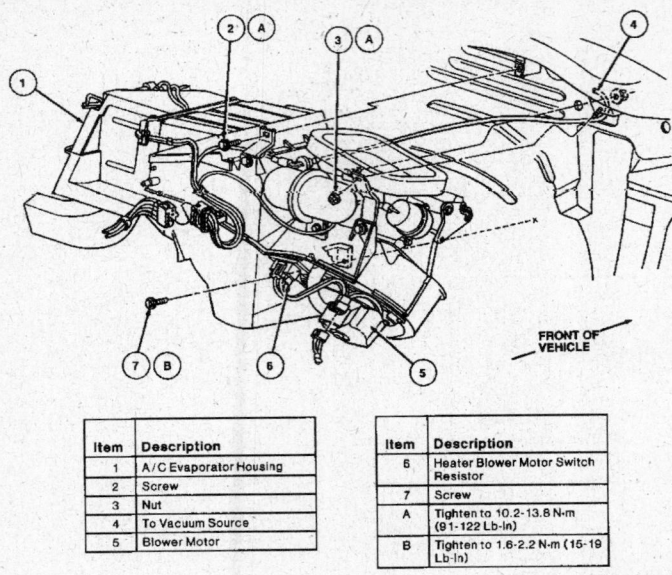

Fig. 9 Evaporator housing & components. 1997–98

1999–2000

1. Remove evaporator core housing as outlined under " Evaporator Core, Replace."
2. Remove foam sealing strip.
3. Remove heater core cover screws, then the cover.
4. Remove heater core.
5. Reverse procedure to install.

EVAPORATOR CASE

REPLACE

1997–98

1. Remove instrument panel as outlined under "Instrument Panel, Replace."
2. Place suitable container under heater water hose connections.
3. Disconnect heater water hoses from heater core tubes.
4. Disconnect vacuum supply hose (black) from vacuum source in engine compartment.
5. Recover A/C system as outlined under "Air Conditioning. "
6. Remove nut retaining A/C evaporator housing to cowl panel.
7. Working from inside vehicle, remove one screw attaching bottom of evaporator housing to cowl panel.
8. Remove A/C evaporator case support bracket to cowl top panel retaining screw, then the mounting bracket to cowl top panel retaining screw, **Fig. 9.**
9. Disconnect wire harness connector at blower motor.
10. Carefully pull evaporator housing away from cowl panel and remove from vehicle.
11. Reverse procedures to install noting the following:
    a. **Torque** evaporator housing to cowl top bracket nut and screw to 84–120 inch lbs.
    b. **Torque** bottom housing to cowl panel screw to 15–19 in lbs.
    c. **Torque** evaporator housing to cowl panel retaining nut to 59–83 in lbs.

EVAPORATOR CORE

REPLACE

1997–98

Whenever an A/C evaporator core is replaced, it is necessary to replace suction accumulator/drier.

Before an A/C evaporator core is replaced, it must be leak tested in vehicle as outlined in "Air Conditioning."

If it is necessary to replace an evaporator core, new core is serviced with a service replacement A/C evaporator housing which has new core. All vacuum control motors, heater core, vacuum reservoir tank and bracket, blower motor, vacuum lines and air ducts from old evaporator housing must be transferred to new evaporator housing, **Fig. 10.**

1. Remove evaporator core case as outlined under "Evaporator Case, Replace."
2. Remove heater core as outline under "Heater Core, Replace."
3. Remove A/C recirculating air duct as follows:
   a. Remove three retaining screws, then the vacuum line from vacuum control motor.
   b. Remove recirculating air duct.
4. Remove A/C vacuum reservoir tank and bracket.
5. Remove vacuum hose harness from attachment points.
6. Remove heater air damper door vacuum control motor as follows:
   a. Remove vacuum control motor arm from A/C damper door cam.
   b. Disconnect vacuum hose harness from control motor.

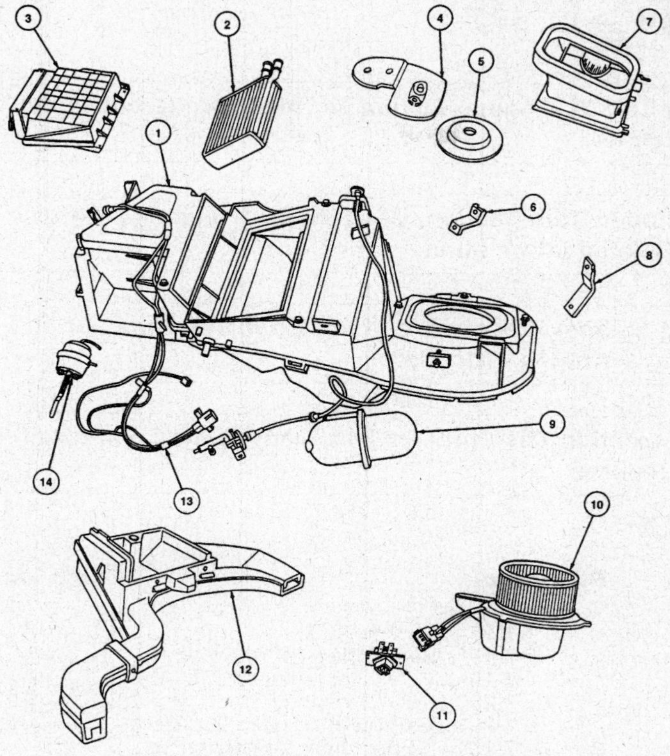

Item	Description
1	A/C Evaporator Housing
2	Heater Core
3	Heater Core Cover

Item	Description
4	Heater Dash Panel Seal
5	A/C Evaporator Drain Tube Seal

FM7029600245010X

Fig. 10 Evaporator core replacement (Part 1 of 2). 1997–98

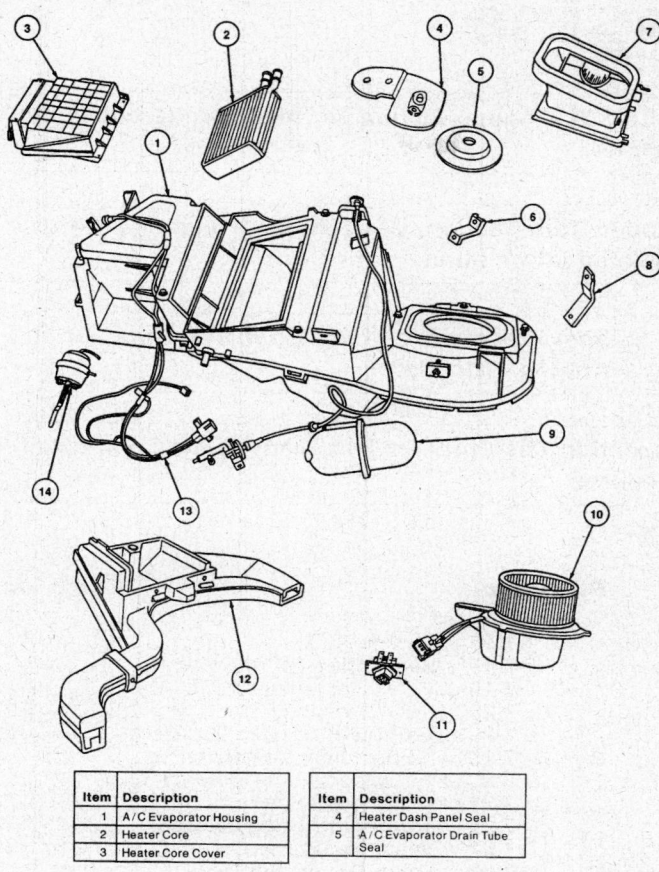

Item	Description
6	A/C Evaporator Case Mounting Bracket
7	A/C Recirculating Air Duct
8	A/C Evaporator Case Support Bracket
9	A/C Vacuum Reservoir Tank and Bracket

Item	Description
10	Blower Motor
11	Heater Blower Motor Switch Resistor
12	Heater Outlet Floor Duct
13	Vacuum Hose Harness
14	Vacuum Control Motor

FM7029600245020X

Fig. 10 Evaporator core replacement (Part 2 of 2). 1997–98

c. Remove two vacuum motor retaining screws, then the motor.

7. Remove heater blower motor switch resistor as follows:
   a. Disconnect jumper wire harness from heater blower motor switch resistor.
   b. Remove two heater blower motor switch resistor to evaporator housing retaining screws, then the resistor.
8. Remove blower motor as outlined under "Blower Motor, Replace."
9. Remove retaining screws and heater outlet floor duct.
10. Remove A/C evaporator case support bracket to evaporator housing retaining screw, then the support bracket.
11. Remove A/C evaporator case mounting bracket to evaporator housing retaining screw, then the mounting bracket.
12. Remove A/C evaporator drain tube seal from evaporator housing.
13. Reverse procedures to install.

1999–2000

1. Recover refrigerant charge using approved equipment and methods.
2. Drain coolant into an approved container.
3. Remove instrument panel as outlined under "Instrument Panel, Replace."
4. Place suitable container under heater water hose connections.
5. Disconnect heater hoses at underhood core fittings.
6. Disconnect vacuum connector near firewall.
7. Remove A/C accumulator assembly.
8. Disconnect A/C liquid line.
9. Remove evaporator core housing nuts and screws at firewall.
10. Remove evaporator core housing bolts from inside passenger compartment.
11. Carefully remove evaporator core housing from vehicle.
12. Reverse procedure to install. **Torque** evaporator core housing bolts inside passenger compartment to 71 inch lbs.

3.8L Engine

NOTE: For Procedures Not Found In This Section, Refer To 3.8L Engine Section In The "Thunderbird & 1997 Cougar" Chapter.

NOTE: Prior To Performing Any Service Operations Listed In This Section, Consult The "Technical Service Bulletins " Section For Related Information.

NOTE: On Air Bag Equipped Models, Refer To " Air Bag System Precautions" Located In The Front Of This Manual For System Disarming & Arming Procedures.

NOTE: Refer To "Computer Relearn Procedures " Located In The Front Of This Manual For Computer Relearn Procedures.

INDEX

PRECAUTIONS

AIR BAG SYSTEMS

Refer to "Air Bag System Precautions" in the front of this manual for system disarming and arming procedures.

BATTERY GROUND CABLE

Prior to service, disconnect battery ground cable and isolate as required.

FUEL SYSTEM PRESSURE RELIEF

Fuel supply tubes will remain pressurized for long periods of time after engine shutdown. This pressure must be relieved before beginning fuel system service or personal injury and vehicle damage may occur. A valve is provided on the fuel injection supply manifold for this purpose.

1. Remove engine air cleaner.
2. Connect EFI/CFI fuel pressure gauge tool No. T80L-9974-B, or equivalent to fuel pressure relief valve on fuel injection supply manifold.
3. Open manual valve on fuel pressure gauge tool to relieve fuel system pressure.

COMPRESSION PRESSURE

When inspecting cylinder compression, lowest cylinder must be within 75% of highest cylinder. Perform compression test with engine at normal operating temperature, spark plugs and air cleaner removed and the throttle propped wide open.

ENGINE

REPLACE

1997–98

Removal

1. Drain engine cooling system into an approved container.
2. Disconnect underhood lamp wiring connector.
3. Mark position of hood hinge, then remove hood.
4. Disconnect alternator to voltage regulator wiring assembly, then remove radiator upper sight shield.
5. Release drive belt tensioner and remove drive belt.
6. Remove air cleaner outlet tube as follows:
   a. Disconnect wire harness from intake air temperature sensor, then crankcase ventilation tube from air cleaner outlet tube.
   b. Loosen air cleaner tube clamps on outlet tube, then disconnect outlet tube from throttle body.
   c. Disconnect outlet tube from mass airflow sensor, then remove tube.
7. Disconnect electric fan motor.
8. Disconnect constant control relay module at wiring connector, then remove radiator coolant recovery reservoir.
9. Remove radiator electric motor, fan blade and fan shroud as an assembly as outlined in "Electrical" section.
10. Remove upper radiator hose.
11. **On models equipped with automatic transmission,** disconnect transmission oil cooler inlet and outlet tubes.
12. **On all models,** disconnect heater inlet and heater return tube hoses.

13. Disconnect lower radiator hose at water pump, then remove radiator bolts and radiator.
14. Disconnect power steering pressure hose, then remove power steering pump and bracket and position aside.
15. Remove mass airflow sensor, then disconnect power steering pressure switch at wiring connector.
16. **On models equipped with air conditioning,** proceed as follows:
    a. Disconnect A/C clutch from fuel charging wiring.
    b. Recover A/C system refrigerant as outlined under "Air Conditioning."
    c. Disconnect A/C compressor lines. Cap or plug open lines.
    d. Remove A/C compressor bolts, then compressor.
17. **On all models,** remove wiring shield, then disconnect accelerator cable and speed control actuator from throttle body.
18. Remove accelerator cable bracket and position aside with cables.
19. Relieve fuel system pressure as outlined under "Precautions."
20. Disconnect fuel supply hose, then fuel return hose.
21. Disconnect fuel charging wiring from engine control sensor wiring at 40-pin connector.
22. Disconnect main vacuum source hose, then the direct ignition control module at wiring connector.
23. Disconnect fuel vapor hose.
24. **On models equipped with air conditioning,** remove A/C compressor mounting bracket with drive belt tensioner attached.
25. **On all models,** raise and support vehicle, then position drain pan beneath engine oil pan.
26. Drain engine oil, then remove oil bypass filter and move drain pan away from vehicle.
27. Disconnect heated oxygen sensors.
28. Remove dual converter and pipe.
29. Remove inspection plug from engine rear plate.
30. **On models equipped with automatic transmission,** remove torque converter bolts.
31. **On all models,** remove engine to transmission bolts.
32. **On models equipped with automatic transmission,** remove transmission oil cooler line retainers from righthand front engine support insulator.
33. **On all models,** remove front engine support insulator to crossmember nuts.
34. Remove starter motor as outlined in "Electrical" section.
35. Remove ground cable, then starter motor wire harness retainers on both lefthand and righthand sides.
36. Partially lower vehicle, then position floor jack under transmission.
37. Position suitable engine lifting equipment, then remove engine assembly from vehicle and place on work stand.

Installation

Lightly oil all bolt and stud threads before installation, except those specifying special sealant.

1. Install suitable engine lifting equipment and remove engine assembly from work stand.
2. Position engine in engine compartment, then install two engine to transmission bolts.
3. Lower engine onto front engine support insulators, then remove lifting equipment. **Seat lefthand side front engine support insulator locating pin before righthand side front engine support insulator.**
4. Remove floor jack from under transmission, then tighten two engine to transmission bolts.
5. Raise and support vehicle, then install remaining engine to transmission bolts and tighten all engine to transmission bolts to specifications.
6. **On models equipped with automatic transmission,** install torque converter bolts and tighten to specifications.
7. **On all models,** install inspection plug to engine rear plate and front engine support insulator nuts then tighten insulator nuts to specifications.
8. Install starter motor as outlined under "Electrical."
9. **On models equipped with automatic transmission,** install transmission oil cooler line bracket.
10. **On all models,** install dual converter and pipe.
11. Connect heated oxygen sensor.
12. Install oil bypass filter, then lower vehicle.
13. **On models equipped with air conditioning,** install A/C compressor mounting bracket with drive belt tensioner attached.
14. **On all models,** connect fuel vapor hose.
15. Install radiator coolant recovery reservoir, then connect constant control relay module at wiring connector.
16. Connect main vacuum source hose, then fuel charging wiring to engine control sensor wiring at 40-pin connector.
17. Connect ignition control module at wiring connector.
18. Remove plugs from fuel supply and return lines, then connect lines.
19. Install accelerator cable bracket, then connect accelerator cable and speed control actuator to throttle body.
20. Install wiring shield.
21. **On models equipped with air conditioning,** proceed as follows:
    a. Install A/C compressor and bolts, then tighten to specifications.
    b. Remove caps or plugs on A/C compressor lines, then connect lines to compressor.
    c. Connect A/C clutch to fuel charging wiring.
22. **On all models,** connect power steering pressure switch at wiring connector, then install mass airflow sensor.
23. Install power steering pump and bracket, then connect power steering hoses.
24. Install radiator, then connect lower radiator hose to water pump.
25. Install heater inlet and heater return tube hoses.
26. **On models equipped with automatic transmission,** install transmission cooler lines.
27. **On all models,** install upper radiator hose.
28. Install radiator electric motor, fan blade and fan shroud as an assembly as outlined under "Electrical."
29. Connect electric fan motor to engine control sensor wiring.
30. Install radiator coolant recovery reservoir, then connect constant control relay module at wiring connector.
31. Position drive belt, then install radiator upper sight shield.
32. Install air cleaner outlet tube to throttle body as follows:
    a. Position air cleaner outlet tube to vehicle, then connect air cleaner outlet tube to mass air flow sensor.
    b. Connect air cleaner outlet tube to throttle body and install tube clamps to tube. **Torque** clamps 21–28 inch lbs.
    c. Connect crankcase ventilation tube to air cleaner outlet tube.
    d. Connect wire harness to intake air temperature sensor.
33. Install hood to original marked position.
34. Connect underhood lamp wiring, then battery ground cable.
35. Refill crankcase to proper level with specified engine oil.
36. Refill engine cooling system.
37. **On models equipped with air conditioning,** drain, evacuate, pressure test and recharge A/C system as outlined under "Air Conditioning."
38. **On all models,** start engine and inspect for leaks.

1999–2000

1. Recover A/C refrigerant charge using approved methods and equipment.
2. Drain coolant into an approved container.
3. Relieve fuel system pressure as outlined under "Precautions."
4. Disconnect hood ground strap and underhood lamp electrical connector.
5. Mark hood hinge to hood positions, then remove hinge bolts and the hood.
6. Disconnect vacuum hose near firewall.
7. Disconnect battery positive cable at alternator and the alternator electrical connectors.
8. Place a suitable container under the power steering pump, then disconnect the fluid lines at the pump.
9. Disconnect lower radiator hose at water pump.
10. Disconnect upper radiator hose at coolant outlet.
11. Remove coolant reservoir.
12. Disconnect accelerator cable.
13. Remove accelerator cable bracket mounting bolts, then position the bracket aside.
14. Remove air cleaner assembly and outlet tube.
15. Disconnect A/C manifold and tube.
16. Disconnect A/C compressor electrical connector.

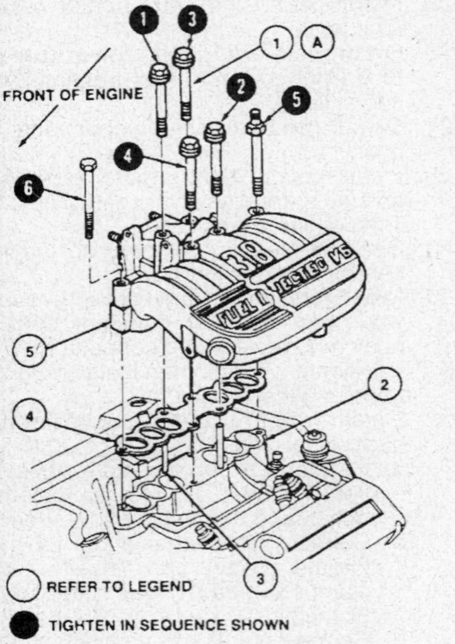

Item	Description
1A	Bolt (6 Req'd)
2	Lower Intake Manifold
3	Locating Pins (2 Req'd)
4	Intake Manifold Upper Gasket
5	Upper Intake Manifold
A	Tighten in sequence in three steps: • 10 N·m (8 Lb-Ft) • 20 N·m (15 Lb-Ft) • 32 N·m (24 Lb-Ft)

FM1059400060000X

Fig. 1 Upper intake manifold bolt tightening sequence. 1997–98

17. Using fuel line disconnection set tool No. T90T-9550-S, or equivalent, disconnect fuel supply line.
18. Disconnect vacuum hose at righthand rear corner of engine compartment.
19. Place suitable container under heater hose connections.
20. Disconnect heater hoses at underhood core fittings.
21. Disconnect 42-pin electrical connector at righthand rear corner of engine compartment, then position wiring harness aside.
22. Disconnect vacuum tube and connector at rear of TBI unit.
23. Disconnect EVAP return tube.
24. Raise and safely support vehicle on a suitable hoist.
25. Remove starter motor as outlined in "Electrical" section.
26. Remove exhaust Y-pipe as follows:
    a. Disconnect electrical connectors at righthand and lefthand O2 sensors.
    b. Remove dual converter assembly mounting nuts.
    c. Remove righthand and lefthand exhaust manifold flange nuts.
    d. Remove Y-pipe assembly from vehicle.
27. Remove engine ground strap attaching nut to disconnect the strap.
28. Drain engine oil into an approved container.
29. **On models equipped with automatic transmission,** remove inspection cover and the four torque converter to flexplate nuts. Discard the nuts.
30. **On all models,** remove bellhousing upper and lower bolts.
31. **On models equipped with automatic transmission,** remove transmission fluid filler tube.
32. **On all models,** remove righthand and lefthand engine mount nuts.
33. Lower the vehicle.
34. Support transmission using a suitable floor jack and block of wood.
35. Install engine lifting brackets tool No. D94L-6001-A, or equivalent.
36. Connect spreader bar tool No. D93L-6001-A3, or equivalent to brackets.
37. Using a suitable crane or skyhook, carefully lift engine up and out of engine compartment, then mount on a suitable stand.
38. Reverse procedure to install, noting the following:
    a. **On models equipped with automatic transmission,** install four new torque converter to flexplate nuts.
    b. **On all models,** tighten all fasteners to specifications.
    c. Install oil pan drain plug and close radiator petcock.
    d. Start engine and bring to operating temperature then inspect for and correct any fluid leakage.

INTAKE MANIFOLD

REPLACE

1997–98

Upper

1. Remove air cleaner outlet tube as follows:
    a. Disconnect wire harness from intake air temperature sensor, then crankcase ventilation tube from air cleaner outlet tube.
    b. Loosen air cleaner tube clamps on outlet tube, then disconnect outlet tube from throttle body.
    c. Disconnect outlet tube from mass airflow sensor, then remove tube.
2. Disconnect accelerator cable at throttle body, then speed control actuator.
3. Remove accelerator cable bracket bolts and position cable aside.
4. Disconnect vacuum lines at intake manifold, then all required electrical connectors.
5. Disconnect one crankcase ventilation tube at upper intake manifold and one at PCV valve.
6. Remove throttle body if required, then EGR valve from upper intake manifold.
7. Remove nut and bolt retaining engine support and wiring retainer bracket at lefthand front of intake manifold, then set aside with ignition wires.
8. Note and record their locations, re-

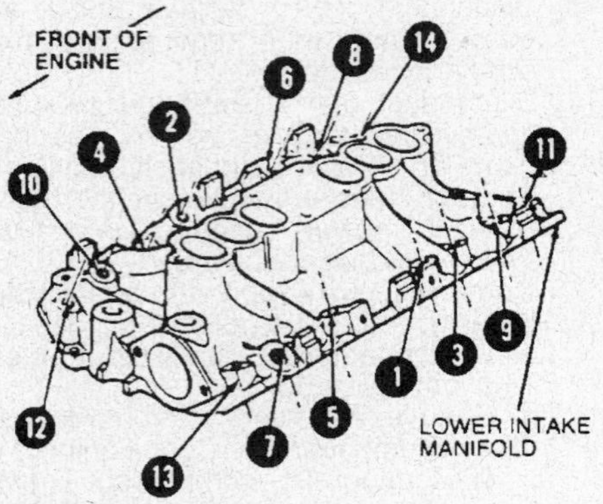

TIGHTEN IN NUMERICAL SEQUENCE IN STEPS AS FOLLOWS:
STEP 1 — 11 N·m (8 LB-FT)
STEP 2 — 20 N·m (15 LB-FT)

FM1059400061000X

Fig. 2 Lower intake manifold bolt tightening sequence. 1997–98

move upper intake manifold bolts/studs, then upper intake manifold and gasket.

9. Reverse procedure to install. **Torque** upper intake manifold bolts in sequence, **Fig. 1,** first to 96 inch lbs.; second, to 15 ft. lbs. and finally to 24 ft. lbs.

Lower

1. Drain engine cooling system.
2. Remove upper intake manifold as previously described.
3. Remove fuel injector and fuel injection supply manifold.
4. Remove heater water outlet hose.
5. Remove lower intake manifold bolts/studs, then lower intake manifold. **Intake manifold is sealed at each end with RTV type sealer. To break seal, it may be necessary to pry on front of manifold with screwdriver blade. If it is necessary to pry on intake manifold, use care to prevent damage to machined surfaces.**
6. Remove and discard intake manifold gasket and end seals.
7. If lower intake manifold is to be disassembled, proceed as follows:
    a. Remove water outlet connection and water thermostat, then engine coolant temperature sensor. Water bypass tube is pressed in and is not serviceable.
    b. Remove heater elbow.
    c. Remove all vacuum and electrical fittings.
8. Reverse procedure to install, noting the following:
    a. Lightly oil all bolt and stud threads before installation.
    b. When using silicone rubber sealer, assembly must occur within 15 minutes after sealer application. After this time, sealer may start to set and its effectiveness may be reduced.
    c. Ensure lower intake manifold, cylinder head and cylinder block mating surfaces are clean and free of old gasket and sealing material. Clean

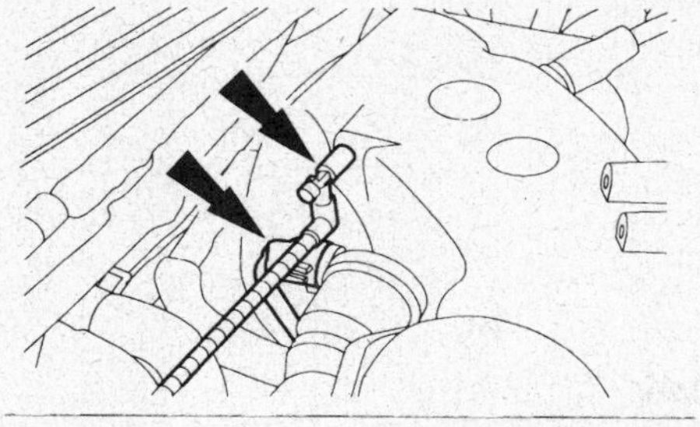

Fig. 3 Vacuum tube at upper intake manifold. 1999–2000

with suitable solvent.

d. **If intake manifold was disassembled,** apply coat of pipe sealant with Teflon part No. D8AZ-19554-A, or equivalent, to all vacuum fittings, heater elbows and electrical fittings.

e. Install lower intake manifold bolts and stud bolt in original locations.

f. **Torque** lower intake manifold bolts and stud bolt in sequence, **Fig. 2,** first to 96 inch lbs., then to 15 ft. lbs.

g. Fill cooling system, then start engine and inspect for leaks.

1999–2000

Upper

1. Remove air cleaner outlet tube.
2. Disconnect vacuum tube, **Fig. 3,** and the Idle Air Control (IAC) solenoid.
3. Disconnect Throttle Position (TP) sensor and EVAP return tube.
4. Disconnect accelerator cable from TBI unit and position aside.
5. Remove solenoid bracket bolts, **Fig. 4.**
6. Disconnect PCV tube and all vacuum tubes as required.
7. Remove ignition coil mounting bolts, then position the coil aside.
8. Note and record their locations, then remove upper intake manifold mounting bolts.
9. Remove upper intake manifold, then discard the gasket.
10. Reverse procedure to install, noting the following:
    a. Install a new upper to lower intake manifold gasket.
    b. Ensure all manifold mounting bolts are in their proper locations as noted during removal.
    c. **Torque** manifold mounting bolts in sequence outlined in **Fig. 5** in three steps: first, to 53 inch lbs.; second, to 71 inch lbs.; finally, rotate them an additional 90°.

Lower

1. Drain coolant into an approved container.
2. Remove upper intake manifold as outlined above.
3. Relieve fuel system pressure as outlined under "Precautions."
4. Disconnect fuel pressure sensor electrical connector.

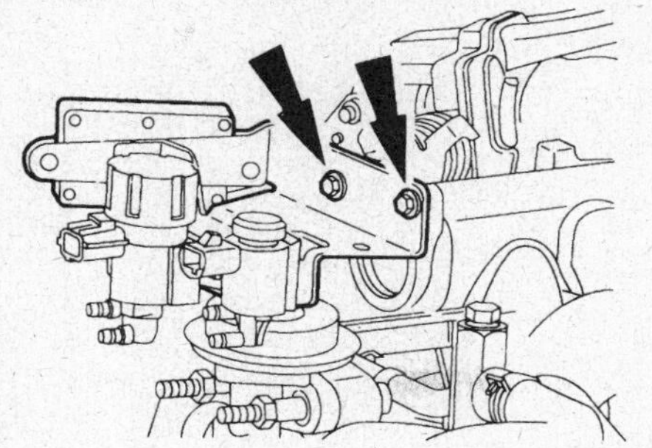

Fig. 4 Solenoid bracket bolts. 1999–2000

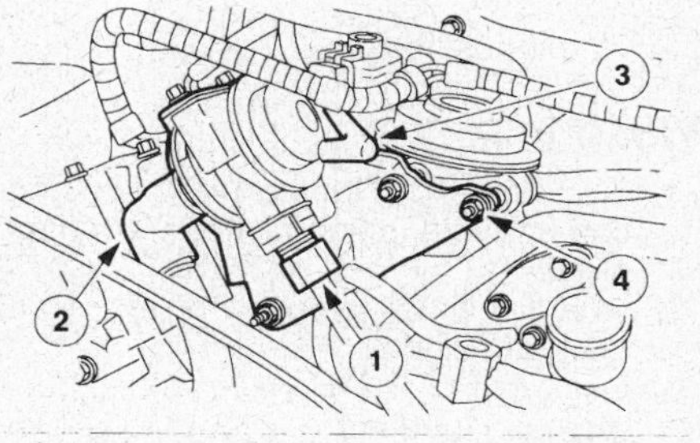

Fig. 6 Exhaust air supply valve assembly. 1999–2000

5. Disconnect fuel injection supply manifold.
6. Disconnect engine wiring harness and position it aside.
7. Disconnect heater hose at rear of engine.
8. Position spark plug wire loom aside, then remove stud bolt.
9. Disconnect EGR valve vacuum tube.
10. **On models equipped with exhaust air supply valve assembly, Fig. 6,** proceed as follows:
    a. Loosen tube nut (1).
    b. Disconnect air tube (2).
    c. Disconnect vacuum tube (3).
    d. Remove nuts (4), then the valve assembly.
11. **On all models,** loosen EGR hex tube nut and disconnect the tube.
12. Disconnect radiator upper hose and bypass hose.
13. Disconnect all required electrical connectors.
14. Remove bypass tube bolt.
15. Remove fuel injection supply manifold attaching bolts, then the supply manifold and injectors as an assembly.
16. Note and record their locations, then remove lower intake manifold mounting bolts. Eight are short, six are long.
17. Carefully remove lower intake manifold. Discard the gaskets and end seals.
18. Reverse procedure to install, noting the following:
    a. Apply beads of silicone gasket sealant part No. F7AZ-19554-EA, or an equivalent meeting Ford

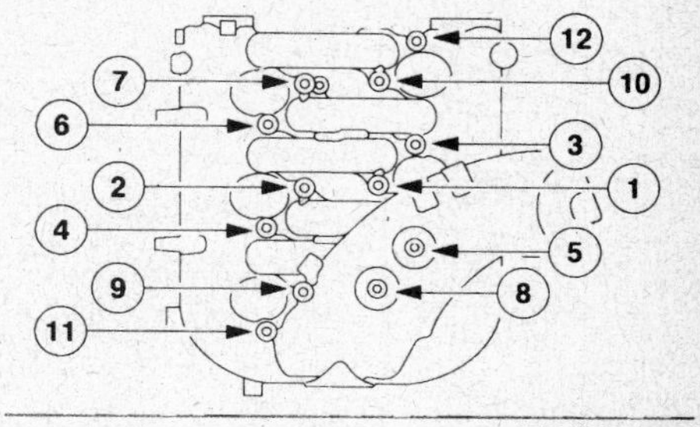

Fig. 5 Upper intake manifold bolt tightening sequence. 1999–2000

specification WSE-M4G323-A4 to end seal mounting points as illustrated in **Fig. 7.**

b. Apply beads of sealant to lower intake manifold mounting locations as illustrated in **Fig. 8.**

c. Install lower intake manifold within 4 minutes of sealant application.

d. Ensure all manifold mounting bolts are in their proper locations as noted during removal.

e. **Torque** manifold mounting bolts in sequence outlined in **Fig. 9** in two steps: first, to 44 inch lbs.; second, to 89 inch lbs.

f. Close radiator petcock, then fill cooling system.

g. Start engine and bring to operating temperature then inspect for and correct any fluid leakage.

EXHAUST MANIFOLD

REPLACE

1997–98

Lefthand

1. Remove oil level indicator tube support bracket.
2. Disconnect heated oxygen sensor from fuel charging wiring, then ignition wires from spark plugs.
3. Raise and support vehicle.
4. Remove exhaust manifold to converter and pipe nuts, then lower vehicle.
5. Remove exhaust manifold bolts, then lefthand exhaust manifold and gasket, **Fig. 10.**
6. If installing new manifold, remove oxygen sensor.
7. Reverse procedure to install, noting the following:
    a. Lightly oil all bolt and stud threads before installation, except those specifying special sealant.
    b. Clean manifold, cylinder head and dual converter and Y-pipe mating surfaces.
    c. Coat heated oxygen sensor threads with high temperature anti-seize compound. **Do not allow anti-seize compound to enter sensor flutes. Possible damage to heated oxygen sensor may occur.**
    d. Position exhaust manifold and exhaust manifold gasket on cylinder

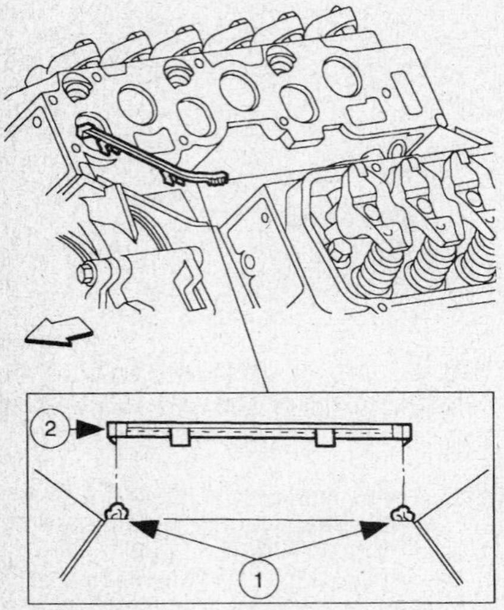

FM1059900171000X

Fig. 7 Lower intake manifold end seals (1-sealant beads, 2-end seals). 1999–2000

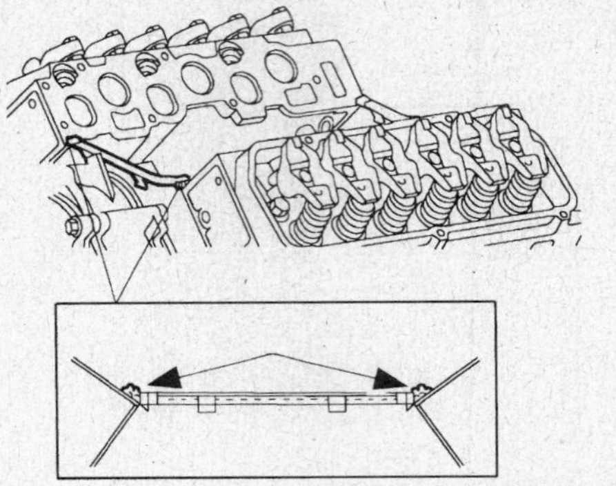

FM1059900172000X

Fig. 8 Lower intake manifold sealant bead locations. 1999–2000

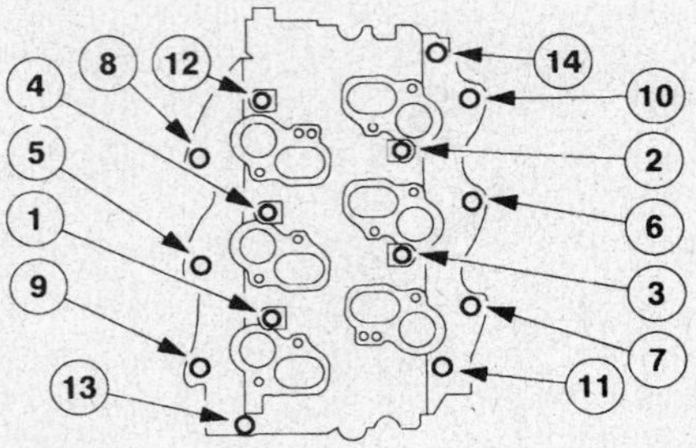

FM1059900173000X

Fig. 9 Lower intake manifold bolt tightening sequence. 1999–2000

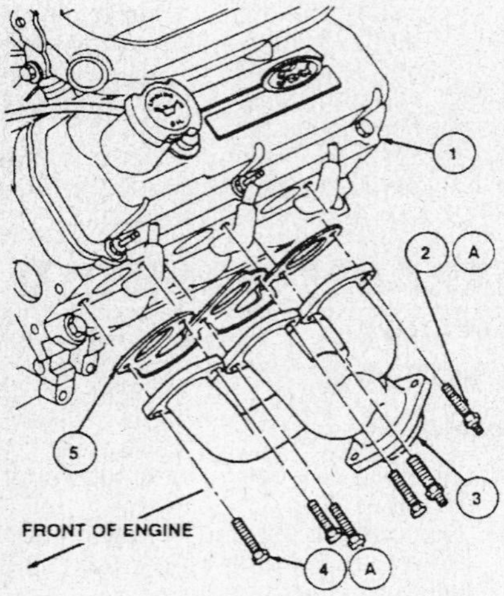

Item	Description
1	Cylinder Head
2A	Stud (3 Req'd)
3	LH Exhaust Manifold
4A	Bolt (3 Req'd)
5	Exhaust Manifold Gasket
A	Tighten to 20-33 N-m (15-22 Lb-Ft)

FM1059400062000X

Fig. 10 Lefthand exhaust manifold replacement. 1997–98

head, then install pilot bolt (lower front bolt hole on No. 5 cylinder). Slight warpage in exhaust manifold may cause misalignment between bolt holes in cylinder head and exhaust manifold. Elongate holes in exhaust manifold as required to correct misalignment. Do not elongate pilot hole.

e. Tighten bolts and nuts to specifications. Start engine and inspect for exhaust leaks.

Righthand

1. Disconnect coil ignition wire from ignition coil and ignition wires from spark plugs.
2. Remove spark plugs, then raise and support vehicle.
3. Disconnect EGR valve to exhaust manifold tube from exhaust manifold.
4. **On models equipped with automatic transmission,** remove transmission fluid level indicator tube.
5. **On all models,** remove heater inlet tube and hose.
6. Remove exhaust manifold to dual converter Y-pipe nuts, then lower vehicle.
7. Remove exhaust manifold bolts, then manifold and gasket, **Fig. 11.**
8. If installing new manifold, remove heated oxygen sensor.
9. Reverse procedure to install, noting the following:
   a. Lightly oil all bolt and stud threads before installation, except those specifying special sealant.
   b. Clean righthand exhaust manifold, cylinder head and dual converter and Y-pipe mating surfaces.
   c. Coat heated oxygen sensor threads with high temperature antiseize compound. **Do not allow anti-seize compound to enter sensor flutes. Possible damage to heated oxygen sensor may occur.**
   d. Position exhaust manifold and exhaust manifold gasket on cylinder head and start two bolts. Slight warpage in exhaust manifold may cause misalignment between bolt holes in cylinder head and exhaust manifold. Elongate holes in exhaust manifold as required to correct misalignment. Do not elongate pilot hole.
   e. Tighten bolts and nuts to specifications. Start engine and inspect for exhaust leaks.
   f. Inspect transmission fluid level.

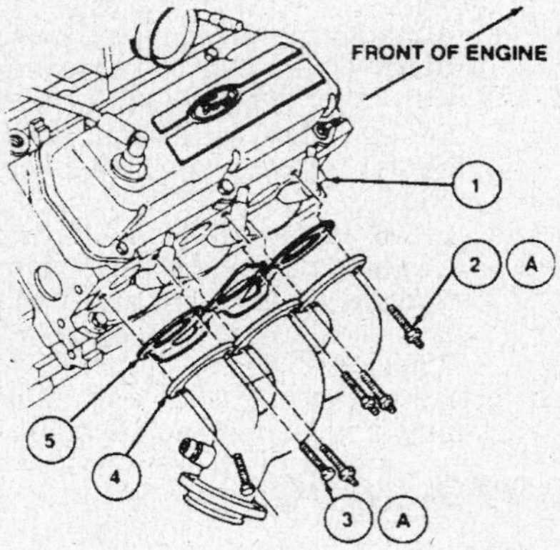

Item	Description
1	Cylinder Head
2A	Stud (4 Req'd)
3A	Bolt (2 Req'd)
4	RH Exhaust Manifold
5	Exhaust Manifold Gasket
A	Tighten to 30-36 N-m (22-46 Lb-Ft)

FM1059400063000X

Fig. 11 Righthand exhaust manifold replacement. 1997–98

1999-2000

Lefthand

1. Raise and safely support vehicle on a hoist.
2. Remove lefthand manifold flange nuts, then lower the vehicle.
3. Remove engine oil dipstick tube.
4. **On models equipped with exhaust air supply valve,** loosen tube nut at front of exhaust manifold.
5. **On all models,** remove exhaust manifold to cylinder head mounting nuts, then the manifold. Discard the gasket.
6. Reverse procedure to install, noting the following:
   a. Install a new exhaust manifold gasket.
   b. Tighten manifold mounting bolts in sequence outlined in **Fig. 12.**
   c. Tighten all other fasteners to specifications.
   d. Start engine and correct any exhaust leaks.

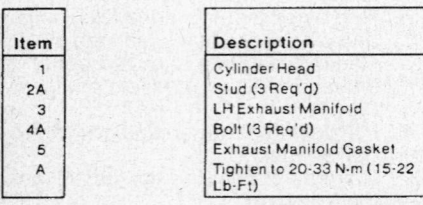

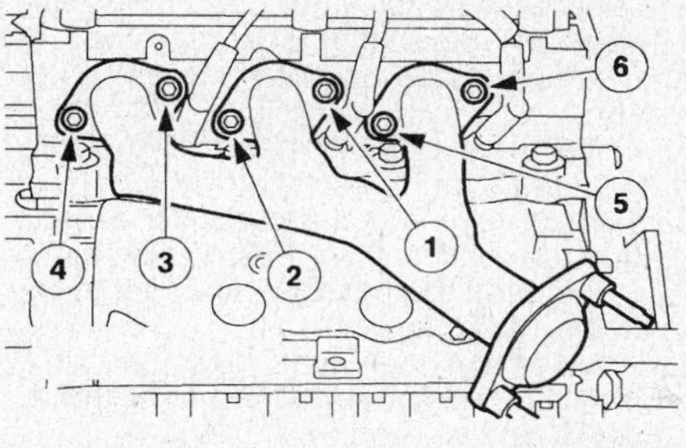

FM1079900049000X

Fig. 12 LH exhaust manifold bolt tightening sequence. 1999–2000

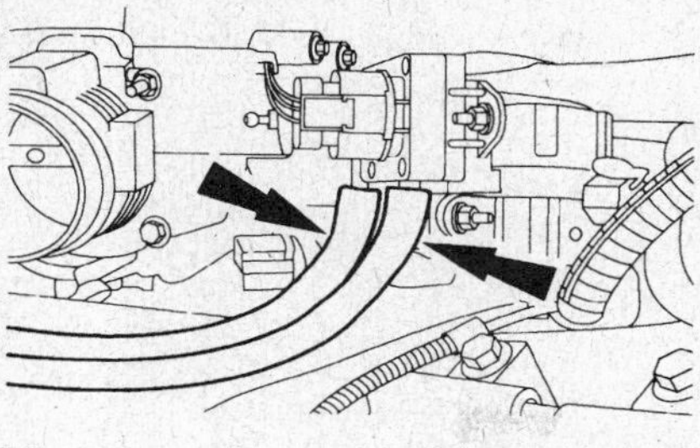

FM1059900174000X

Fig. 13 Two hoses at TBI unit. 1999–2000

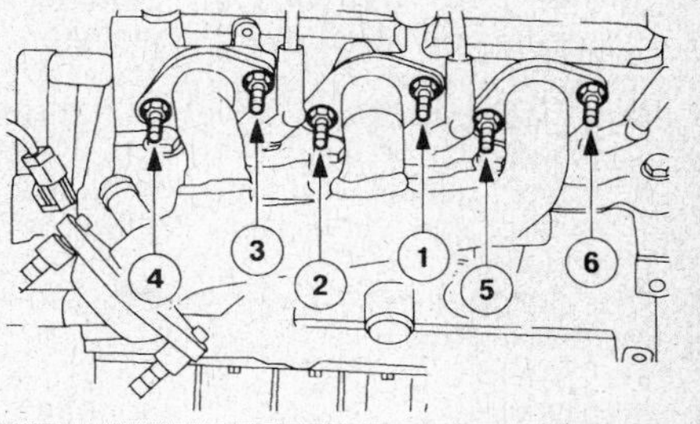

FM1079900050000X

Fig. 14 RH exhaust manifold bolt tightening sequence. 1999–2000

Righthand

1. Remove air cleaner outlet tube.
2. Disconnect two hoses at TBI unit, **Fig. 13.**
3. **On models equipped with exhaust air supply valve assembly, Fig. 6,** proceed as follows:
   a. Loosen tube nut (1).
   b. Disconnect air tube (2).
   c. Disconnect vacuum tube (3).
   d. Remove nuts (4), then the valve assembly.
4. **On all models,** loosen EGR hex tube nut, disconnect required vacuum lines and remove the tube.
5. Raise and safely support vehicle on a hoist.
6. Remove righthand manifold flange nuts, then lower the vehicle.
7. **On models equipped with exhaust air supply valve assembly,** loosen tube nut at front of righthand exhaust manifold.
8. **On all models,** remove manifold to cylinder head mounting nuts, then the manifold. Discard the gasket.
9. Reverse procedure to install, noting the following:
   a. Install a new exhaust manifold gasket.
   b. Tighten manifold mounting bolts in sequence outlined in **Fig. 14.**
   c. Tighten all other fasteners to specifications.
   d. Start engine and correct any exhaust leaks.

CYLINDER HEAD

REPLACE

1997–98

Removal

1. Drain engine cooling system.
2. Remove air cleaner outlet tube from throttle body as follows:
   a. Disconnect wire harness from intake air temperature sensor, then crankcase ventilation tube from air cleaner outlet tube.
   b. Loosen air cleaner tube clamps on outlet tube, then disconnect outlet tube from throttle body.
   c. Disconnect outlet tube from mass airflow sensor, then remove tube.
3. Loosen drive belt tensioner, then remove drive belts.
4. **On lefthand cylinder head,** proceed as follows:
   a. Remove oil filler cap.
   b. Remove power steering pump front mounting bracket bolts.
   c. Remove alternator, then belt idler pulley.
   d. Remove power steering pump/alternator bracket bolts, then place pump/bracket assembly aside, with hoses connected, in position to prevent fluid leakage.
5. **On righthand cylinder head,** proceed as follows:
   a. Remove drive belt.
   b. **On models equipped with air conditioning,** remove A/C mounting bracket bolts, then place A/C compressor aside with hoses connected.
   c. **On models less air conditioning,** remove A/C idler pulley.
   d. **On all models,** remove positive crankcase ventilation valve.
6. **On both cylinder heads,** remove upper intake manifold as outlined under "Intake Manifold, Replace. "
7. Remove valve cover as outlined under "Valve Cover, Replace."
8. Remove fuel injection supply manifold.
9. Remove lower intake manifold as outlined under " Intake Manifold, Replace."
10. Remove exhaust manifolds as outlined under "Exhaust Manifold, Replace."
11. Loosen rocker arm fulcrum bolts enough to allow rocker arm to be lifted off pushrod, then rotate to one side.
12. Remove pushrods, then identify their positions. They should be installed in their original positions during assembly.
13. Remove cylinder head bolts, then the heads. Discard bolts.
14. Remove and discard old head gaskets.

Installation

Always use new cylinder head bolts to ensure a leakproof assembly. Torque retention with used bolts could vary, which might result in coolant or compression leakage at cylinder head mating surface area.

1. Prepare cylinder head components as follows:
   a. Lightly oil all bolts and stud bolt threads before installation, except those specifying special sealant.
   b. Clean cylinder head, intake manifold, rocker arm cover and head gasket surfaces. If cylinder head was removed for head gasket replacement, inspect flatness of cylinder head and cylinder block gasket surfaces.
2. Position new head gasket(s) onto cylinder block using dowels for alignment, then position cylinder heads onto cylinder block.
3. **Torque** new cylinder head bolts in sequence, **Fig. 15,** first to 15 ft. lbs., next to 29 ft. lbs. and finally to 36 ft. lbs., then proceed as follows:
   a. Back off cylinder head bolts, one at a time, two to three revolutions. **Do not loosen all bolts at same time. Only work on one bolt at a time.**
   b. **Torque** long bolts, in sequence, **Fig. 15,** to 29–37 ft. lbs., then rotate an additional 180°. **Torque** short bolts, in sequence, **Fig. 15,** to 15–22 ft. lbs., then rotate an additional 180°.
4. Dip each pushrod end in engine assembly lubricant D9AZ-19579-D, or equivalent.
5. Install pushrods in their original positions, then lubricate all rocker arms with engine assembly lubricant D9AZ-19579-D, or equivalent.
6. Install rocker arms.
7. Install exhaust manifolds as outlined under "Exhaust Manifold, Replace."
8. Install lower intake manifold as outlined under " Intake Manifold, Replace."
9. Install fuel injection supply manifold.
10. Position rocker arm and new valve cover on cylinder head and install bolts. Note location of ignition wire routing clip stud bolts. Tighten rocker arm bolts to specifications.
11. Install upper intake manifold as outlined under " Intake Manifold, Replace."
12. Install spark plugs and tighten to specifications, then connect ignition wires to spark plugs.
13. **On lefthand cylinder head,** proceed as follows:
    a. Install oil filler cap.

b. Install alternator/power steering pump mounting bracket, then alternator.
c. Install accessory drive belt tensioner.
d. Install power steering pump and support bracket, then tighten to specifications.
14. **On righthand cylinder head,** proceed as follows:
a. Install PCV valve.
b. Install A/C compressor mounting and supporting brackets, then compressor, if equipped.
15. **On both cylinder heads,** install drive belt and tighten as outlined under "Serpentine Drive Belt."
16. Connect battery ground cable.
17. Install air cleaner outlet tube as follows:
a. Install outlet tube, then connect tube to mass airflow sensor.
b. Connect outlet tube to throttle body, then tighten air cleaner tube clamps on outlet tube.
c. Connect crankcase ventilation tube to air cleaner outlet tube, then wire harness to intake air temperature sensor.
18. Fill engine cooling system with specified coolant. **This engine has aluminum cylinder heads and requires a special corrosion inhibited coolant formulation to avoid cooling system damage.**
19. Start engine and inspect for coolant, fuel and oil leaks.

1999–2000

Removal

1. Drain coolant into an approved container.
2. Remove appropriate exhaust manifold as outlined under " Exhaust Manifold, Replace."
3. Remove lower intake manifold as outlined under "Intake Manifold, Replace."
4. **On lefthand cylinder head,** proceed as follows:
a. Tag their locations, then position spark plug wires aside.
b. Disconnect PCV valve.
c. Remove ignition coil mounting bolts, then position coil aside.
d. Remove lefthand valve cover. Discard the gasket.
5. **On righthand cylinder head,** proceed as follows:
a. Disconnect crankcase ventilation hose.
b. Disconnect transducer vacuum hoses.
c. **On models equipped with exhaust air supply valve assembly, Fig. 6,** loosen tube nut (1), disconnect air tube (2) and vacuum tube (3), remove nuts (4), then the valve assembly.
d. **On all models,** disconnect and remove EGR tube.
e. Tag their locations, then position spark plug wires aside.
f. Remove air cleaner outlet tube.

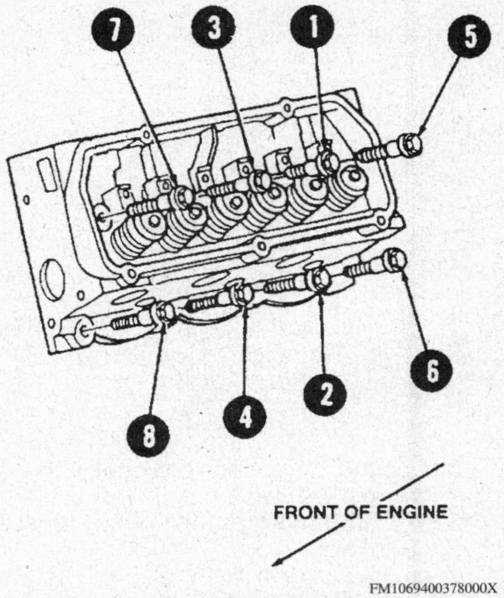

Fig. 15 Cylinder head bolt tightening sequence. 1997–98

g. Disconnect throttle and speed control cables.
h. Remove TBI unit mounting nuts and bolts, then the TBI unit. Discard the gasket.
i. Remove righthand valve cover. Discard the gasket.
6. **On both cylinder heads,** keeping them in order, remove rocker arm retaining bolts, rocker arms and pushrods.
7. Remove serpentine belt.
8. **On lefthand cylinder head,** proceed as follows:
a. Using pulley remover tool No. T69L-10300-B, or equivalent, remove power steering pump pulley.
b. Remove mounting brackets for power steering pump and alternator.
9. **On righthand cylinder head,** proceed as follows:
a. Recover A/C refrigerant charge using approved methods and equipment.
b. Disconnect A/C manifold and tube assembly.
c. Disconnect A/C compressor clutch electrical connector.
d. Remove A/C compressor mounting bracket.
10. **On both cylinder heads,** remove exhaust manifold mounting studs.
11. Note and record locations of long and short cylinder head bolts, then remove and discard them.
12. Carefully remove the cylinder heads.

Installation

Always use new cylinder head bolts to ensure a leakproof assembly. Torque retention with used bolts could vary, which might result in coolant or compression leakage at cylinder head mating surface area.

1. Ensure all gasket surfaces are clean and flat.
2. Install new head gaskets with small hole to front of engine, **Fig. 16.**
3. Lubricate new cylinder head bolts with clean 5W-30 engine oil.
4. Carefully place cylinder head in position.
5. Install new cylinder head long bolts, then the short ones.
6. **Torque** cylinder head bolts in sequence outlined in **Fig. 17** in three steps: first, to 15 ft. lbs.; second, to 30 ft. lbs.; third, to 37 ft. lbs.
7. Back off cylinder head bolts one at a time. **Do not loosen all bolts at once. Work on one bolt at a time.**
8. **Torque** short bolts in sequence to 18 ft. lbs., then rotate an additional 180°.
9. **Torque** long bolts in sequence to 33 ft. lbs., then rotate an additional 180°.
10. **Torque** rocker arm bolts in two steps: first, to 44 inch lbs.; second, to 26 ft. lbs.
11. Continue installation process by reversing remaining removal procedures.
12. Install TBI unit with a new mounting gasket. **Torque** nuts and bolts to 80.5 inch lbs., then rotate an additional 85–90°.
13. Start engine and bring it to operating temperature, then inspect for and correct any fluid leaks.

VALVE COVER

REPLACE

1997–98

1. Disconnect ignition wires from spark plugs, then ignition wire routing clips from valve cover bolt studs.
2. **On lefthand valve cover,** remove oil filler cap, then crankcase ventilation hose.
3. **On righthand valve cover,** remove positive crankcase ventilation valve.
4. **On both valve covers,** remove valve cover screws, then cover and gasket.
5. Reverse procedure to install, noting the following:
a. Lightly oil bolt and stud threads before installation. Using solvent, clean cylinder head and valve cover sealing surfaces to remove all gasket material and dirt.
b. Tighten valve cover bolts to specifications.

1999–2000

1. Tag spark plug wires, then position them aside.
2. **On lefthand valve cover,** proceed as follows:
a. Disconnect PCV valve.
b. Remove ignition coil mounting bolts.
c. Position coil aside.
3. **On righthand valve cover,** proceed as follows:
a. Disconnect crankcase ventilation hose.
b. Disconnect transducer vacuum hoses.
c. **On models equipped with exhaust air supply valve assembly, Fig. 6,** loosen tube nut (1), disconnect air tube (2) and vacuum tube

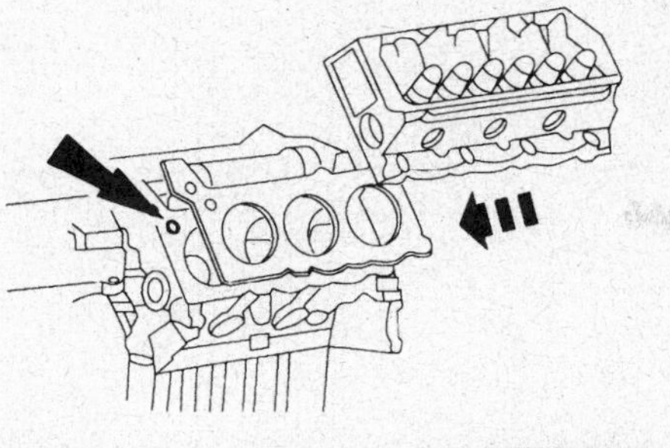

Fig. 16 Cylinder head gasket orientation. 1999–2000

(3), remove nuts (4), then the valve assembly.

d. **On all models,** disconnect and remove EGR tube.
e. Tag their locations, then position spark plug wires aside.
f. Remove air cleaner outlet tube.
g. Disconnect throttle and speed control cables.
h. Remove TBI unit mounting nuts and bolts, then the TBI unit. Discard the gasket.

4. **On both valve covers,** remove cover, then discard the gasket.
5. Reverse procedure to install. Tighten all fasteners to specifications.

VALVE ADJUSTMENT

This engine is equipped with hydraulic valve lash adjusters. No adjustment is required.

FRONT COVER

REPLACE

1997-98

1. Drain engine cooling system, then remove air cleaner and outlet tube.
2. Remove cooling fan motor, fan blade and fan shroud assembly.
3. Remove drive belt and water pump pulley, then the power steering pump bracket retaining bolts and lay pump aside.
4. **On models with A/C,** remove compressor front support bracket leaving A/C compressor in place.
5. **On all models,** remove heater water outlet tube retaining bolts, then the tube and O-ring from water pump.
6. Disconnect upper radiator hose at water hose connection, then the fuel charging wiring from the Camshaft Position (CMP) sensor.
7. Remove hold down clamp and lift CMP sensor and housing out of front cover.
8. Raise and support vehicle.
9. Remove crankshaft pulley and vibration damper using crankshaft damper remover tool No. T58P-6316-D, or equivalent and vibration damper remover adapter tool No. T82L-6316-B, or equivalent. **Crankshaft vibration damper and pulley are initially balanced as a unit so if vibration damper and pulley have to be separated, mark them so they maybe assembled in same position.**
10. Remove oil bypass filter, then disconnect lower radiator hose at water pump.
11. Remove oil pan as outlined under "Oil Pan, Replace. "
12. Lower the vehicle, then remove front cover retaining bolts.
13. Remove front cover and water pump as an assembly.
14. Remove front cover gasket if required, Crankshaft Position (CKP) sensor shield, CKP sensor and oil pump.
15. Reverse procedures to install, noting the following:
    a. **On models with engines built through May 1, 1997,** install front cover gasket part No. YF2Z-6020-AA. Refer to " Technical Service Bulletins" in this engine section for additional information.
    b. **On all models,** tighten all fasteners to specifications.
    c. Start engine and bring to operating temperature, then inspect for and correct any fluid leaks.

1999-2000

1. Drain coolant into an approved container.
2. Remove serpentine belt.
3. Raise and support vehicle on a hoist.
4. Rotate crankshaft pulley in engine's normal running direction until No. 1 piston reaches TDC mark.
5. Remove crankshaft pulley bolt.
6. Using crankshaft pulley remover tool Nos. T58P-6316-D and T82L-6316-B, or equivalents, remove pulley.
7. Remove water pump pulley bolts, then the pulley.
8. Remove power steering pump and bracket with hoses intact. Position pump aside.
9. Loosen nut and disconnect EGR valve tube.
10. Disconnect upper radiator and bypass hoses above front cover.
11. Remove CMP sensor electrical connector and mounting bolts, then the sensor.
12. Remove heater water outlet tube.
13. Ensure No. 1 piston is still at TDC.
14. Remove camshaft synchronizer assembly mounting bolt and washer, then the sensor. **Oil pump intermediate shaft should be removed with synchronizer.**
15. Disconnect radiator lower hose at water pump.
16. Disconnect CKP sensor.
17. Remove engine front wiring harness pin-style retainer.
18. **Be sure to record locations, types and sizes of all front cover fasteners. Pay attention to the hidden cap screw, Fig. 18.** The cover will be damaged if this is overlooked during removal.
19. Carefully slide front cover off its alignment dowels, then discard the gasket.
20. Reverse procedure to install, noting the following:
    a. Ensure all gasket surfaces are clean and flat.

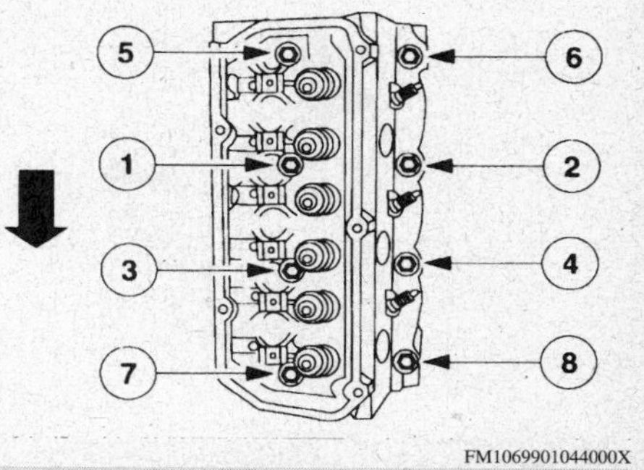

Fig. 17 Cylinder head bolt tightening sequence. 1999–2000

b. **Before installing front cover gasket,** apply a small portion of silicone gasket sealant part No. F7AZ-19554-EA, or equivalent to locations illustrated in **Fig. 19.**
c. Install new front cover gasket.
d. **After installing front cover gasket,** apply silicone gasket sealant to top of oil pan surface as illustrated in **Fig. 20.**
e. Ensure all front cover mounting bolts are in their proper locations as noted before removal.
f. **Torque** bolts in sequence outlined in **Fig. 21** to 18 ft. lbs., then rotate them an additional 90°. **Bolt No. 12 is not included in staged tightening.**
g. Coat camshaft synchronizer gear with clean 10W-30 engine oil.
h. Install synchro positioning tool No. 303-630, or equivalent by rotating tool until it engages synchronizer housing notch and armature.
i. Install synchronizer housing assembly so tool's arrow is 54° from engine centerline, **Fig. 22.**
j. Install camshaft synchronizer assembly attaching bolt.
k. Tighten all fasteners to specifications.
l. Start engine and bring to operating temperature, then inspect for and correct any leaks.

OIL PAN

REPLACE

1997-98

1. Remove air cleaner outlet as follows:
    a. Disconnect wire harness from intake air temperature sensor, then crankcase ventilation tube from air cleaner outlet tube.
    b. Loosen air cleaner tube clamps on outlet tube, then disconnect outlet tube from throttle body.
    c. Disconnect outlet tube from mass airflow sensor, then remove tube.
2. Remove two radiator upper sight shield bolts and position shield aside.
3. Remove hood weather seal.
4. Remove windshield wipers as outlined under "Electrical. "

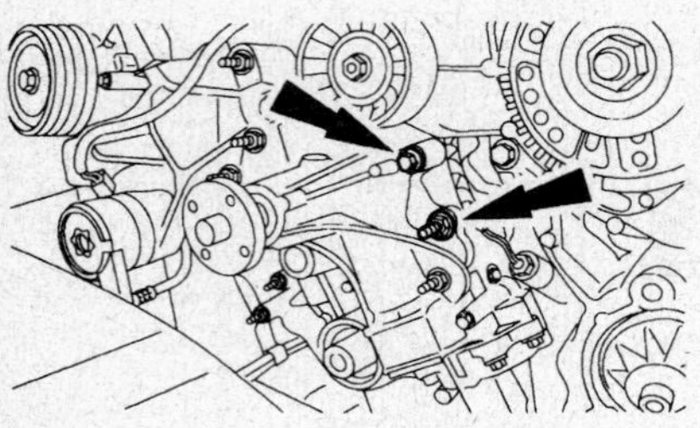

FM1069901045000X

Fig. 18 Front cover capscrew location. 1999–2000

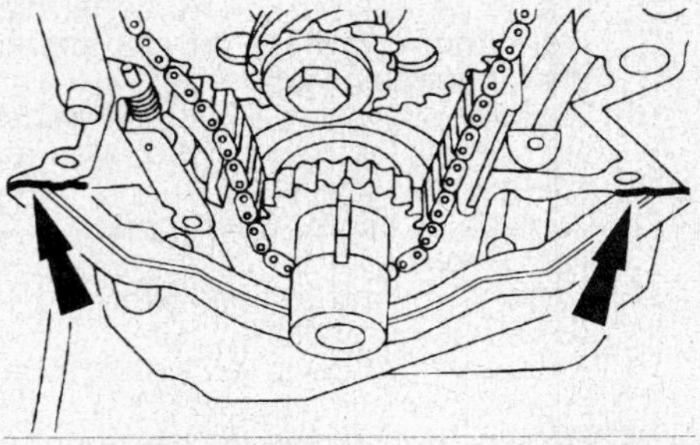

FM1069901046000X

Fig. 19 Sealant application before gasket installation. 1999–2000

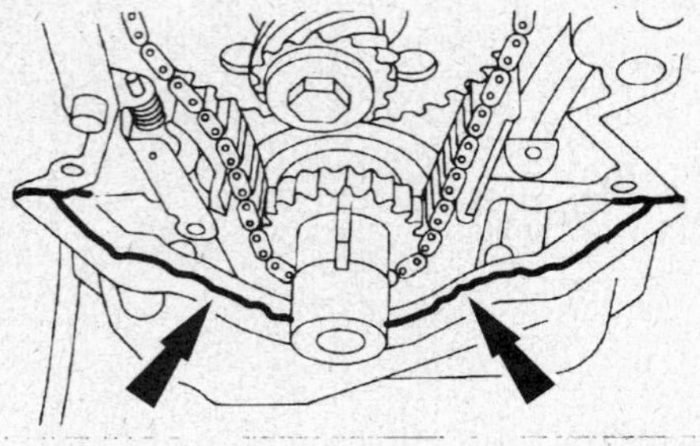

FM1069901047000X

Fig. 20 Sealant application after gasket installation. 1999–2000

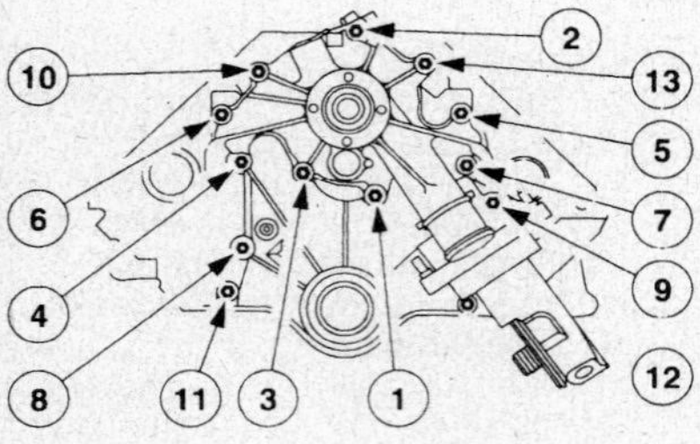

FM1069901048000X

Fig. 21 Front cover bolt tightening sequence. 1999–2000

5. Remove lefthand cowl vent screen and wiper module.
6. Install suitable engine support, then raise and support vehicle.
7. Remove front engine support insulator through bolts, then partially lower vehicle.
8. Raise engine with engine support, then raise and support vehicle.
9. Remove starter motor as outlined under "Electrical."
10. Position drain pan under vehicle, then drain engine oil.
11. Remove oil bypass filter, then starter motor wire and ground strap.
12. **On models equipped with automatic transmission,** remove automatic transmission oil cooler lines.
13. **On all models,** remove oil pan to bellhousing bolts and bolts at crankshaft position sensor lower shield.
14. Remove remaining oil pan bolts.
15. Remove steering shaft pinch bolt, then separate steering shaft.
16. Position transmission jack under front subframe, then remove six rearward bolts on front subframe and loosen two forward front subframe bolts.
17. Remove lower shock absorber to front suspension lower arm bolts and nuts.
18. Lower front subframe.
19. Remove oil pan, then empty any residual oil from pan.
20. Remove oil pump screen cover and tube bolts and support bracket nut.
21. Remove oil pump screen cover and tube, then discard oil pump inlet tube gasket.
22. Reverse procedure to install, noting the following:
    a. When using silicone rubber (RTV) sealer, assembly must occur within 15 minutes after sealer application. After this time, sealer may start to set and its sealing effectiveness may be reduced.
    b. Apply silicone gasket and sealant F1AZ019652-A, or equivalent to oil pan.
    c. Seat lefthand side locating pin before righthand side locating pin.
    d. Tighten bolts to specifications and in sequence, **Fig. 23.**
    e. Refill engine oil, then start engine and inspect for leaks.

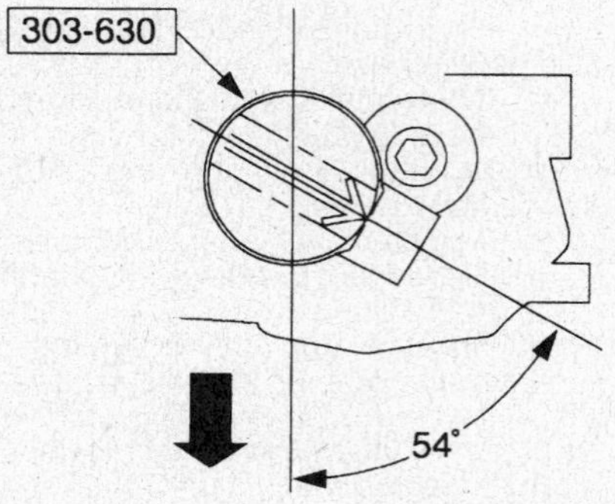

FM1069901049000X

Fig. 22 Camshaft synchronizer assembly installation. 1999–2000

1999–2000

1. Remove air cleaner outlet tube.
2. Remove radiator upper sight shield.
3. Remove coolant reservoir.
4. Install engine lift bracket tool set No. D94L-6001-A, or equivalent.
5. Install engine support tool No. 303-F072, or equivalent, then raise and support vehicle on a hoist.
6. Remove lefthand and righthand engine mount nuts, then lower the vehicle.
7. Raise engine with engine support, then raise and support vehicle on the hoist.
8. Position approved drain pan under vehicle, then drain engine oil.
9. Remove starter motor as outlined under "Electrical."
10. Position wiring harness bracket aside.
11. Remove bellhousing lower bolts.
12. Remove oil pan bolts.
13. Position suitable jack under front subframe, then remove four lower and two upper bolts on front subframe.
14. Loosen two forward front subframe bolts.
15. Carefully lower the front subframe.
16. Remove oil pan, then empty any residual oil from it.
17. Reverse procedure to install, noting the following:
    a. **When using silicone rubber (RTV) sealer, assembly must occur within 15 minutes after sealer application. After this time, sealer may start to set and its sealing effectiveness may be reduced.**
    b. Apply silicone gasket sealant F7AZ-19554-EA, or equivalent to oil pan and block sealing surfaces as illustrated, **Fig. 24.**
    c. Move oil pan into position and loosely install its bolts.
    d. Tighten bolts to specifications in sequence outlined in **Fig. 25.**
    e. Install oil pan drain plug, then fill engine with oil.
    f. Start engine and inspect for leaks.

OIL PUMP

REPLACE

1997–98

1. Remove oil bypass filter if required.
2. Remove oil pump and filter body to front cover bolts, then oil pump and filter body from front cover.
3. Inspect O-ring for distortion and wear. Replace if required.
4. Reverse procedure to install. Tighten front cover bolts to specifications.

1999–2000

1. Raise and safely support vehicle on a hoist.
2. Drain engine oil into an approved container.
3. Remove engine oil filter.
4. Remove oil pump cover and filter pad housing bolts, then the housing.
5. Separate oil pump drive and driven gears from the cover assembly. Discard the O-ring.
6. Using straightedge and feeler gauge, measure across oil pump cover and

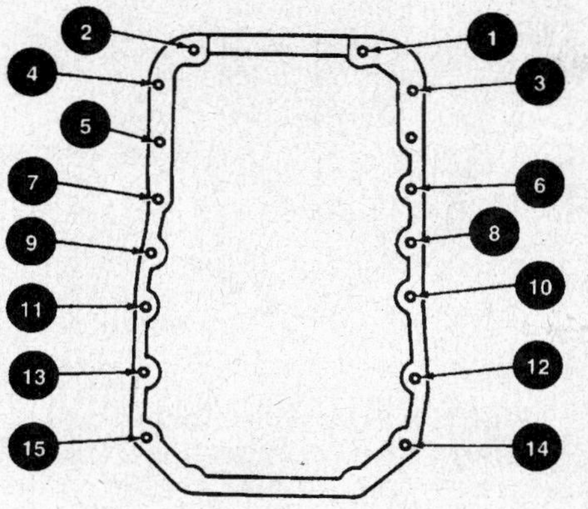

FM1099600078000X

Fig. 23 Oil pan bolt tightening sequence. 1997–98

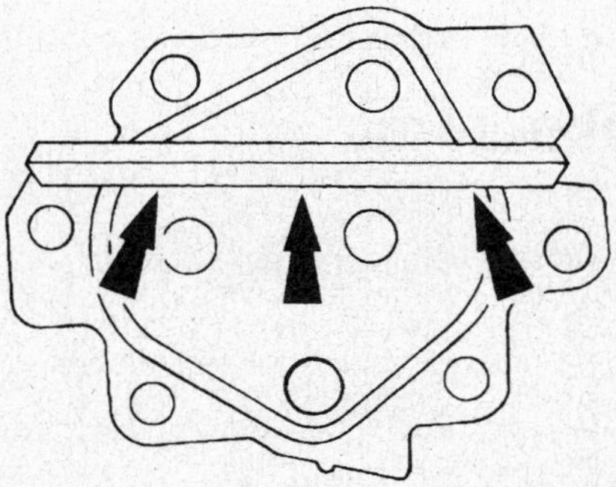

FM1099900084000X

Fig. 26 Oil pump cover & front cover surface inspections. 1999–2000

front cover mounting surfaces and determine wear or warpage, **Fig. 26.** If surface is warped more than .0016 inch, replace oil pump cover or front cover.

7. Remove front cover as outlined under "Front Cover, Replace."
8. Flip cover over and remove plug over oil pump pressure relief valve, **Fig. 27.**
9. Remove pressure relief valve ball and spring, **Fig. 28.**
10. Clean all components in suitable solvent.
11. Reverse procedure to install, noting the following:
    a. Lubricate oil pump components with clean 5W-30 engine oil.
    b. Assemble pressure relief valve ball and spring with a new plug.
    c. Tighten all fasteners to specifications.
    d. Start engine and bring to operating temperature, then inspect for and correct any leaks.

OIL PUMP SERVICE

1997–98

1. Remove oil pump as outlined under "Oil Pump, Replace."
2. Lift pump gears out of pocket in oil

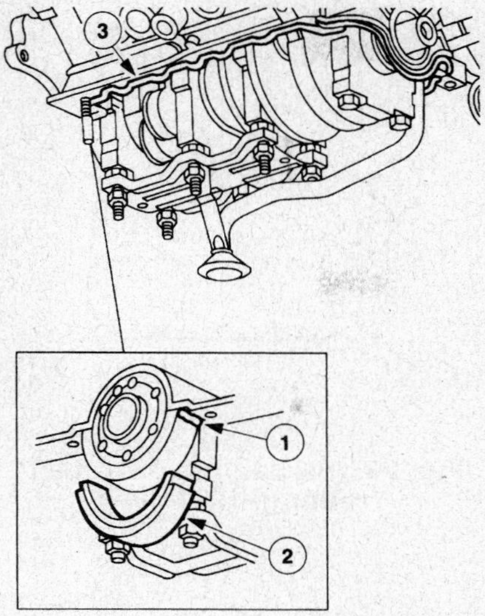

FM1099900082000X

Fig. 24 Oil pan sealant locations. 1999–2000

pump and filter body, then remove oil pump body seal and discard.

3. Clean front cover and oil pump and filter body sealing surfaces.
4. Using straightedge and feeler gauge, measure across front cover mounting surface for wear or warpage.
5. If surface is out of flat by more than .0016 inch, replace front cover as outlined under "Front Cover, Replace."
6. Lightly pack gear pockets with petroleum jelly or coat all gear surfaces with engine assembly lubricant D9AZ-19579-D. **Do not use chassis lubricants. Failure to properly coat oil pump gears may result in pump failing to prime when engine is started.**
7. Install gears in oil pump and filter body pocket. Ensure petroleum jelly fills all voids between gears and pockets.
8. Position oil pump body seal and install oil pump and filter body to front cover using alignment dowels on front cover.
9. Tighten oil pump and filter body bolts to specifications.

1999–2000

Refer to "Oil Pump, Replace" for procedure.

OIL PRESSURE RELIEF VALVE

1997–98

1. After drilling hole through valve plug, remove plug with slide hammer or by prying.
2. Remove spring and pressure relief valve from bore.
3. Thoroughly clean pressure relief valve bore and pressure relief valve to remove any metal chips which may have entered bore during drilling.
4. Inspect pressure relief valve and valve bore for wear, scoring or galling. If inspection determines part(s) to be un-

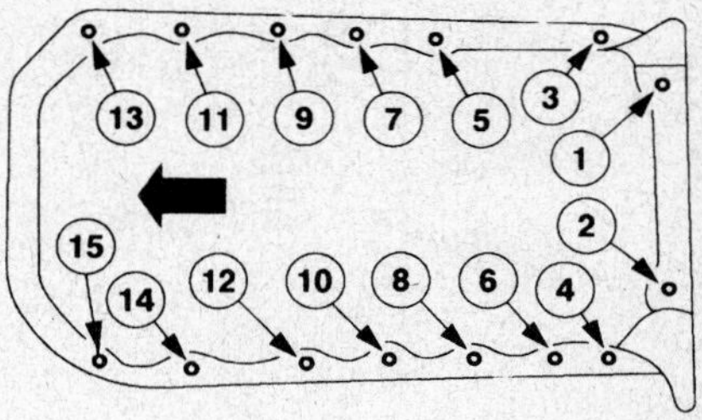

FM1099900083000X

Fig. 25 Oil pan bolt tightening sequence. 1999–2000

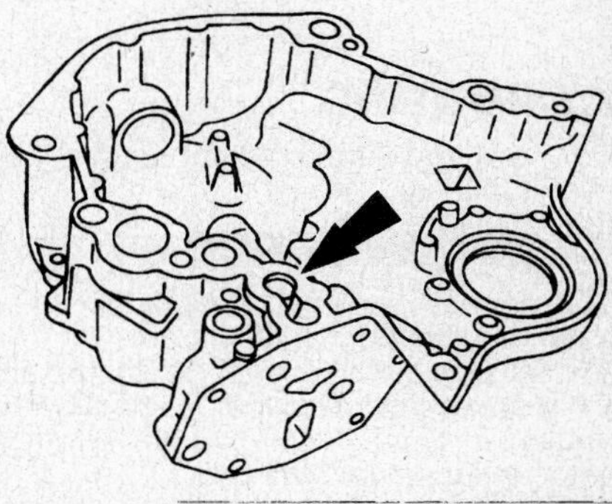

FM1099900085000X

Fig. 27 Oil pump pressure relief valve removal. 1999–2000

serviceable, replace pressure relief valve and/or oil pump and filter body.

5. Measure clearance between pressure relief valve and bore. Valve should slip into bore without side play or binding.
6. Inspect spring for signs of fatigue or collapse.
7. Lubricate pressure relief valve with engine oil and install in bore. End with smaller diameter goes in first.
8. Position spring in bore, then install new plug. Plug can be tapped into bore using plastic tipped hammer. Ensure plug is .01 inch below machined surface.

1999–2000

Refer to "Oil Pump, Replace" for procedure.

SERPENTINE DRIVE BELT

Conditions requiring belt replacement are excessive wear, rib chunk-out, severe glazing and frayed cords. Replace any belt exhibiting any one of these conditions. Cracks on rib side of a belt are considered acceptable.

If the belt has chunks missing from its ribs, it should be replaced. If two or more adjacent ribs have lost sections ½ inch or longer, or if missing chunks are creating a noise or vibration condition, replace the belt.

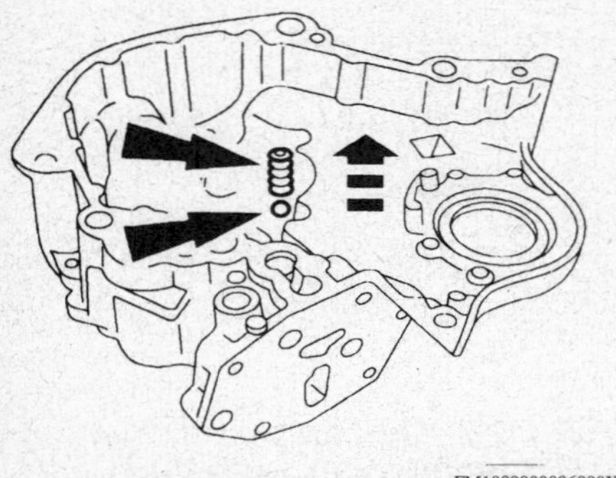

Fig. 28 Oil pressure relief valve ball & spring. 1999–2000

BELT ROUTING

Refer to **Figs. 29 and 30** for serpentine drive belt routing.

BELT REPLACEMENT

1. Lift or rotate automatic tensioner.
2. Remove belt(s).
3. Install new belt over pulleys. Ensure all V-grooves make proper contact with pulley.
4. Rotate tensioner over belt.

COOLING SYSTEM BLEED

1. Remove vent plug, **Fig. 31,** before filling radiator. After radiator has filled, install the plug and **torque** to 108 inch lbs.
2. Fill radiator completely full, then install radiator cap.
3. Fill coolant reservoir and degas bottle to full cold mark.
4. Set heater control to full hot, high fan and set controls so air vents from dash vents.
5. Start and operate engine until fully warmed up while observing water temperature gauge:
   a. If system is functioning properly, temperature will indicate normal and hot air will be felt at dash outlets.
   b. If system is not functioning properly, temperature gauge will not read and/or no hot air will be felt at dash vents.
6. If system is not functioning properly, allow engine to cool then repeat procedure.
7. If system is functioning properly, allow engine to cool, then fill coolant reservoir to full cold mark if required.

WATER PUMP

REPLACE

1997–98

1. Drain engine cooling system.
2. Remove radiator electric motor, fan blade and fan shroud as an assembly as outlined in "Electrical" section.

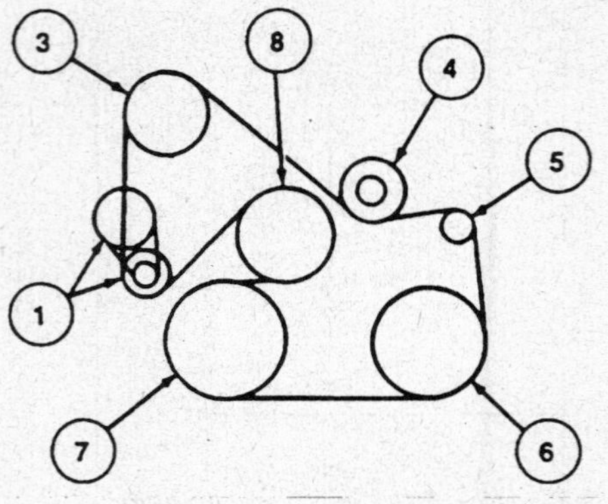

Fig. 29 Serpentine drive belt routing. 1997–98

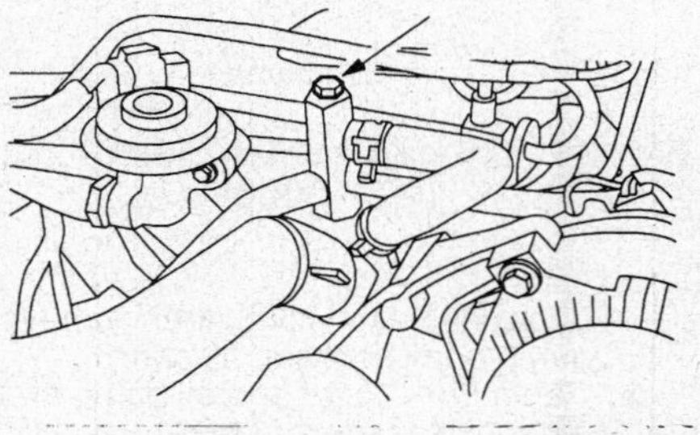

Fig. 31 Cooling system vent plug

3. Rotate drive belt tensioner, then remove drive belt.
4. Remove water pump pulley bolts, then pulley.
5. Remove power steering pump pulley and water pump to power steering pump brace.
6. Remove heater water outlet tube bolts and heater water outlet tube from water pump.
7. Disconnect lower radiator hose from water pump.
8. Remove water pump bolts, stud bolts and nuts, then water pump. Discard old water pump housing gasket. **If using prying device to assist in water pump removal, be careful not to damage mating surfaces.**
9. Reverse procedure to install, noting the following:
   a. Lightly oil all bolt and stud threads before installation, except those specifying special sealant.
   b. Apply gasket and trim adhesive No. D7AZ-19B508-B, or equivalent, to water pump housing gasket to hold in position.
   c. Coat threads of No. 1 water pump bolt with pipe sealant with Teflon D8AZ-19554-A, or equivalent, before installing.
   d. Fill engine cooling system with specified coolant. **This engine has aluminum cylinder heads and requires special corrosion inhibiting coolant formula to avoid cooling system damage.**

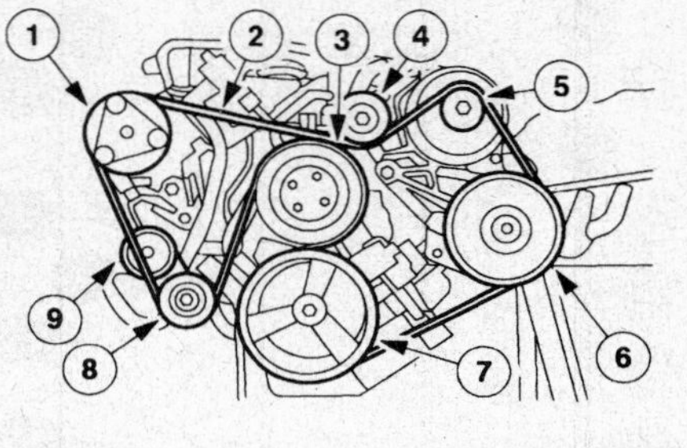

Fig. 30 Serpentine drive belt routing (1-A/C compressor, 2-belt, 3-water pump, 4-idler, 5-alternator, 6-PS pump, 7-crankshaft, 8-tensioner pulley, 9-tensioner). 1999–2000

   e. Start engine and inspect for coolant leaks.

1999–2000

1. Drain coolant into an approved container.
2. Loosen water pump pulley bolts.
3. Remove serpentine belt.
4. Using pulley remover tool No. T69L-10300-B, or equivalent, remove power steering pump pulley.
5. Remove water pump pulley bolts, then the pulley.
6. Remove power steering pump mounting bolts, then position pump aside with hoses intact.
7. Remove power steering pump mounting bracket attaching bolts, then the bracket.
8. Disconnect radiator lower hose at water pump.
9. Remove power steering fluid reservoir mounting bolts, then position the reservoir aside with hoses intact.
10. Disconnect CMP sensor electrical connector.
11. Remove CMP sensor mounting bolt, then the sensor.
12. Remove water pump stud, bolts and nuts, then carefully pull pump away from front cover.
13. Reverse procedure to install, noting the following:
    a. Clean and inspect all gasket mounting surfaces.
    b. Install a new water pump gasket, then mount pump into position. Tighten fasteners in sequence outlined in **Fig. 32.**

RADIATOR

REPLACE

1997–98

1. **On models equipped with automatic transmission,** disconnect automatic transmission fluid cooler inlet and outlet lines from radiator using disconnect tool No. T82L-9500-AH, or equivalent.
2. **On all models,** drain cooling system,

then disconnect radiator upper and lower hoses and overflow hose from radiator.
3. Remove two upper shroud bolts at radiator support, then lift fan shroud enough to disengage lower clips and lay shroud back over fan.
4. Remove radiator upper support bolts, then support.
5. Lift radiator from vehicle.
6. **On models equipped with automatic transmission,** if installing new radiator, transfer oil cooler line connectors to new radiator using pipe sealant with suitable oil resistant sealer.
7. **On all models,** position radiator assembly into vehicle, then install upper supports and bolts.
8. **On models equipped with automatic transmission,** connect oil cooler lines.
9. **On all models,** install radiator electric motor, fan blade and fan shroud as an assembly by inserting two lower legs to radiator support with two bolts.
10. Install radiator support upper brackets and bolts, then tighten to specifications.
11. Connect radiator upper, lower and overflow hoses, noting the following:
    a. Close petcock, then position hose clamps at least 2 inches from each end of hose.
    b. Slide hose on connections.
    c. Tighten clamp to specifications. **Ensure clamps are beyond bead and place in center of clamping surface of connections. New hose clamps must be installed inside hose alignment marks.**
12. Fill radiator with specified antifreeze and water mixture.
13. Operate engine and inspect for leaks at hose connections and at automatic transmission fluid cooler lines. **To avoid possible personal injury or vehicle damage, do not operate engine with hood open until fan blade has been first examined for cracks and separation.**
14. Inspect automatic transmission, radiator and coolant recovery reservoir fluid levels.

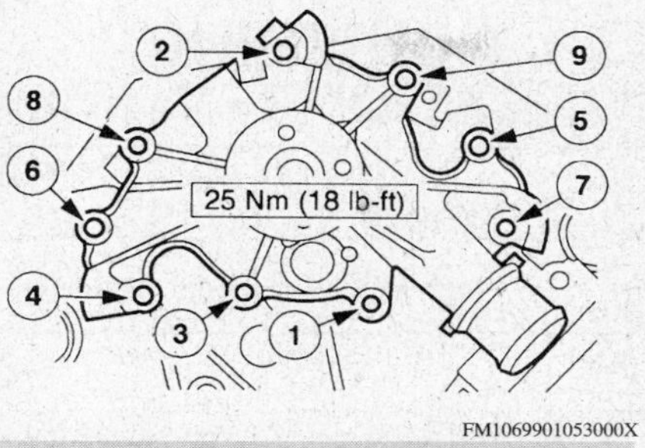

Fig. 32 Water pump fastener tightening sequence. 1999–2000

1999–2000

1. Drain coolant from radiator and degas bottle into an approved container.
2. Disconnect cooling fan motor electrical connector, then separate fan harness from shroud.
3. Remove fan shroud lefthand and righthand mounting bolts.
4. Remove cooling fan, motor and shroud as an assembly.
5. Remove radiator sight shield.
6. Disconnect radiator upper hose at radiator.
7. **On models equipped with automatic transmission,** remove lower and upper cooler tube fittings.
8. **On all models,** raise and safely support vehicle on a hoist.
9. Disconnect radiator lower hose at radiator, then lower the vehicle.
10. Remove radiator supports, then carefully lift radiator out of vehicle.
11. Reverse procedure to install, noting the following:
    a. Tighten all fasteners to specifications.
    b. Close radiator petcock, then fill cooling system.
    c. Start engine and bring to operating temperature, then inspect for and correct any leaks.

TECHNICAL SERVICE BULLETINS

ENGINE OIL CONTAMINATED w/COOLANT, UNDETERMINED COOLANT LOSS

1996–98

On these models, coolant may leak into the engine oiling system at the intake manifold gaskets or front cover gasket.

To correct this condition, install revised front cover and intake gaskets.

On engines built through May 1, 1997, install front cover gasket part No. YF2Z-6020-AA.

On engines built through April 24, 1998, install intake gasket kit part No. F6ZZ-9433-AA. **Ensure side gasket bead material is blue. Do not install gaskets with any other bead color.**

When installing the lower intake manifold, hand-tighten the center bolts to ease installation of the remaining bolts. The new gaskets have a slightly thicker side gasket bead material.

TIGHTENING SPECIFICATIONS

Component	Torque/Ft. Lbs.
1997–98	
A/C Compressor Bolts	30–45
Connecting Rod Nuts	⑦
Crankcase Ventilation Tube Mounting Bracket To Lower Intake Manifold Stud	15–22
Cylinder Head Bolts	⑥
Dual Converter & Pipe To Exhaust Manifold Nuts	16–23
EGR Valve To Exhaust Manifold Bolt	25–35
Engine Front Cover Bolts	15–22
Engine Support & Wiring Bracket Bolt & Nut	15–22
Engine Support Insulator Nuts	72–98
Engine Support Insulator Through Bolts	35–50
Engine To Transmission Bolts	⑤
Exhaust Manifold Bolts	23–26
Fuel Injection Supply Manifold Screws	72–84①
Heated Oxygen Sensor	28–33
Heater Water Outlet Tube To Water Pump Bolts	71–105.5①
Ignition Wire Routing Clip Stud Bolts	71–102①

Continued

TIGHTENING SPECIFICATIONS—Continued

Component	Torque/Ft. Lbs.
1997–98	
Lower Intake Manifold Bolts	③
Lower Shock Absorber To Front Suspension Lower Arm Bolts	103–144
Main Bearing Cap Bolts Or Stud	81–89
Oil Level Indicator Tube Support Bracket Nut	15–22
Oil Pan Bolts	79–105.5①
Oil Pump & Filter Body Bolts	④
Oil Pump Intermediate Shaft Clamp	15–22
Oil Pump Screen Cover & Tube Bolts	15–22
Oil Pump Screen Cover & Tube Bracket Nut	30–40
Radiator Bolts	71–92.5①
Radiator Hose Clamps	20–30①
Rocker Arm Bolts	84–108①
Spark Plugs	7–15
Steering Shaft Pinch Bolt	30–42
Throttle Body Nuts	②
Torque Converter Bolts	20–34
Upper Intake Manifold Bolts	③
Water Outlet Connection Bolts	15–22
Water Pump Bolts	15–22
Water Pump Nuts	53–71①
Water Pump Pulley Bolts	12–18
Water Pump Stud Bolts	15–22
1999–2000	
A/C Compressor Bracket Head Stud Bolt	18
A/C Compressor Bracket Bolts & Nuts	35
A/T Fluid Cooler Line Fittings At Radiator	22
Alternator Mount Bracket	18
Alternator Positive Cable Nut	89①
Bulkhead 42-Pin Electrical Connector Bolt	89①
Camshaft Synchronizer Drive Gear To Cam	33
Camshaft Synchronizer To Front Cover Bolt	18
Camshaft Thrust Plate To Block Bolts	108①
CMP Sensor Bolt	27①
Connecting Rod Cap Bolts	⑧
Coolant Reservoir To Head Stud Bolts	89①
Coolant Reservoir To Bracket Bolts	44①
Crankshaft Main Bearing Bolts	37⑨
Crankshaft Pulley Bolt	118
Cylinder Head Bolts	⑥
EGR Transducer Bracket To Intake Manifold	89①
EGR Tube To Exhaust Manifold Nut	30
Engine Mount Ground Strap To Motor Mount	20
Engine Mount To Bracket Bolts & Nuts	52
Engine Mount To Subframe Nuts	85
Engine To Transmission Bolts	30
Exhaust Air Supply Tube	22
Exhaust Air Supply Valve Nuts	89①
Exhaust Manifold Nuts	24
Exhaust Manifold Studs	72①
Fan Shroud To Radiator Bolts	80.5①
Flywheel To Crankshaft Bolts	59
Front Cover To Block Bolts	18
Front Subframe To Body Bolts	66

Continued

TIGHTENING SPECIFICATIONS—Continued

Component	Torque/Ft. Lbs.
1999–2000	
Front Subframe To Tower Bolts	85
Fuel Supply Manifold Bolts	89①
Hood Ground Strap To Hinge Bolt	108①
Ignition Coil To Intake Manifold	53①
Lower Intake Manifold To Head Bolts	③
Oil Dipstick Tube To Head Bolt	89①
Oil Pan Baffle Nuts	35
Oil Pan Drain Plug	19
Oil Pan To Block Bolts	⑩
Oil Pan To Bellhousing Bolts	33
Oil Pickup Tube To Baffle Nut	35
Oil Pickup Tube To Block Bolts	18
Oil Pump Cover To Front Cover Bolts	18
PS Pressure Tube To Pump Nut	30
PS Pump Bolts	18
PS Pump Bracket Nuts	72①
PS Pump Bracket To Water Pump Bolts & Nuts	15
Radiator Support Bolts	22
Rocker Arm Pivot To Head Bolts	⑥
Steering Column Pinch Bolt	35
Throttle Cable Bracket Bolts	89①
Timing Chain Tensioner Bolts	108①
Upper To Lower Intake Manifold Bolts	③
Valve Cover Mounting Bolts & Studs	89①
Valve Lifter Guide Plate Bolts	108①
Water Outlet Tube To Front Water Pump Bolt	89①
Water Outlet Tube To Intake Stud	89①
Water Pump Pulley Bolts	18
Wire Harness & Bracket To Motor Mount Nuts	20

① — Inch lbs.

② — Cross-torque to 15–22 ft. lbs.

③ — Refer to "Intake Manifold, Replace."

④ — M8 bolts, 18–22 ft. lbs.; M6 bolts, 72–96 inch lbs.

⑤ — Automatic transmission, 40–50 ft. lbs.; manual transmission, 28–38 ft. lbs.

⑥ — Refer to "Cylinder Head, Replace."

⑦ — Torque to 15–18 ft. lbs., then 30–33 ft. lbs., then advance each nut an additional 90–120°.

⑧ — Torque in three steps: first, to 18 ft. lbs.; second, to 33 ft. lbs.; third, rotate an additional 105°.

⑨ — Tighten an additional 120°.

⑩ — Refer to "Oil Pan, Replace."

4.6L Engine

NOTE: For Procedures Not Found In This Section, Refer To 4.6L Engine Section In The Lincoln Chapter.

NOTE: On Air Bag Equipped Models, Refer To " Air Bag System Precautions" Located In The Front Of This Manual For System Disarming & Arming Procedures.

NOTE: Refer To "Computer Relearn Procedures " Located In The Front Of This Manual For Computer Relearn Procedures.

INDEX

PRECAUTIONS

AIR BAG SYSTEMS

Refer to "Air Bag System Precautions" in front of this manual for system disarming and arming procedures.

BATTERY GROUND CABLE

Prior to service, disconnect battery ground cable and isolate as required.

FUEL SYSTEM PRESSURE RELIEF

Fuel supply tubes will remain pressurized for long periods of time after engine shutdown. This pressure must be relieved before beginning fuel system service or personal injury or damage to vehicle may occur. A valve is provided on fuel injection supply manifold for this purpose.

1. Connect EFI/CFI fuel pressure gauge tool No. T80L-9974-B, or equivalent, to fuel pressure relief valve on fuel injection supply manifold.
2. Place outlet hose of tool into a suitable fuel container.
3. Open manual valve on fuel pressure gauge tool to relieve fuel system pressure.

COMPRESSION PRESSURE

When inspecting cylinder compression, lowest cylinder must be within 75% of highest cylinder. Perform compression test with engine at normal operating temperature, spark plugs and air cleaner removed and the throttle propped wide open.

ENGINE MOUNT

REPLACE

1997–98

Whenever self locking bolts and nuts are removed they must be discarded and replaced with new components.

1. Raise and support vehicle.
2. Support engine using a suitable jack with wood block placed under engine.
3. Remove nuts retaining engine support to crossmember.
4. Raise engine, using jack, until engine support is free of crossmember.
5. Remove stud bolts and bolts retaining engine support to block, then remove engine support.
6. Reverse procedure to install. Tighten bolts to specifications.

1999–2000

1. Install lift bracket tool No. D93P-6001-A3, or equivalent.
2. Install engine support tool No. 303-290-A, or equivalent.
3. Remove starter motor as outlined in "Electrical" section.
4. Remove engine mount nuts, then lower the vehicle.
5. Raise engine using the support tool.
6. Raise vehicle, then remove engine mount.
7. Reverse procedure to install. Tighten fasteners to specifications.

ENGINE

REPLACE

1997–98

1. Mark hood bolt locations, then remove hood.
2. Remove engine compartment braces.
3. Remove air cleaner outlet, then recover A/C refrigerant. Cap all A/C fittings.
4. Drain cooling system into a suitable container, then remove coolant recovery reservoir.
5. Remove cooling fan motor and shroud, then disconnect upper radiator hose at water bypass tube.
6. **On models equipped with DOHC engine,** disconnect connector from secondary air injection diverter valve vacuum regulator control, then disconnect secondary air injection pump

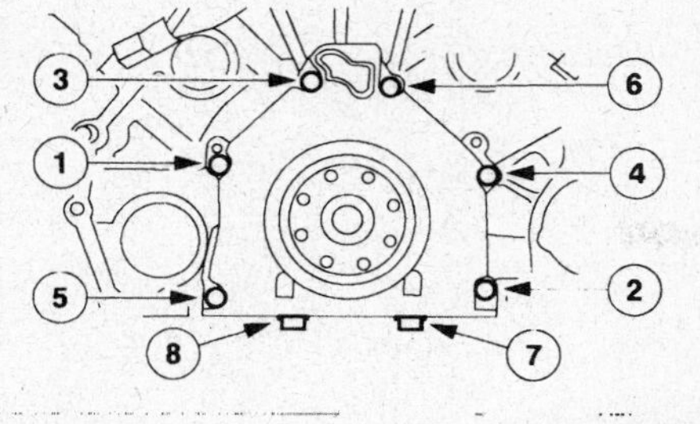

FM1069901054000X

Fig. 1 Rear main seal retainer plate bolt tightening sequence. 1999–2000 SOHC engine

hose from diverter valve.

7. **On all models,** relieve fuel system pressure as outlined under “Precautions,” then disconnect fuel lines from fuel supply manifold.
8. Disconnect 42-pin connector and other engine wiring from firewall. Disconnect accelerator cable and speed control cable from engine.
9. Disconnect canister purge and chassis vacuum hoses from engine.
10. Disconnect alternator wiring from alternator, then engine wiring connectors at power distribution box.
11. **On models equipped with automatic transmission,** disconnect transmission cooler lines.
12. **On all models,** remove power steering return hose and pressure hose from pump and drain into a suitable container.
13. Disconnect return line hose from power steering reservoir, then remove reservoir.
14. Connect a suitable lifting eye to rear of righthand cylinder head.
15. Raise and support vehicle, then disconnect A/C lines from compressor. Cap all A/C lines and fittings.
16. Drain engine oil into a suitable container.
17. Remove dual converter Y-pipe, then the lower radiator hose from vehicle.
18. Remove starter as outlined under “Starter, Replace ” in “Electrical” section.
19. Remove transmission as outlined under appropriate transmission section.
20. Disconnect heater hoses from tubes at rear of righthand cylinder head.
21. Remove nuts from righthand and lefthand engine support through bolts.
22. Lower vehicle.
23. Connect a suitable lifting eye to front of lefthand cylinder head, then connect suitable lifting equipment to lifting eyes.
24. Remove engine from vehicle, place on a stable surface to remove clutch and pressure plate, if equipped.
25. Mount engine to a suitable work stand.
26. Reverse procedure to install, noting the following:
    a. Tighten bolts to specifications.
    b. Fill and bleed power steering as outlined under “ Power Steering” section.
    c. Fill and bleed cooling system as outlined under “ Cooling System Bleed.”
    d. Evacuate and charge A/C system.

1999–2000

SOHC ENGINE

Removal

1. Drain coolant into an approved container.
2. Recover A/C refrigerant charge using approved methods and equipment.
3. Mark hinge locations, then disconnect ground strap and underhood lamp electrical connector and remove hood.
4. Remove battery.
5. Remove air cleaner and outlet tube.
6. Remove degas bottle.
7. Relieve fuel system pressure.
8. Disconnect fuel lines as required.
9. Disconnect radiator upper hose at water outlet.
10. Disconnect throttle and speed control cables, then the return spring.
11. Remove throttle and speed control cable bracket mounting bolts, then position them all aside.
12. Disconnect HVAC vacuum supply hoses.
13. Place a suitable drain pan below heater hose firewall fittings, then disconnect the hoses.
14. Remove bulkhead multi-pin electrical connector attaching bolt, then disconnect the connector.
15. Separate wiring harness at three firewall locations.
16. Disconnect all required electrical connectors at TBI unit.
17. Remove safety clip from manifold suction tube, then disconnect the tube.
18. Disconnect A/C pressure cycling switch electrical connector.
19. Separate the liquid tube from A/C condenser.
20. Disconnect power steering hose from fluid reservoir.
21. Disconnect all engine to body or frame ground wires.
22. Disconnect fusible link and electrical connector near battery tray.
23. Disconnect ground connector near washer fluid reservoir.
24. Slide underhood power distribution box access cover up, then remove nut and battery cables.
25. Separate degas sensor electrical connector from battery tray.
26. Raise and safely support vehicle on a hoist.
27. Disconnect HO2S electrical connectors.
28. Remove exhaust pipe to manifold flange nuts.
29. Remove starter as outlined in “Electrical” section.
30. Remove nine bellhousing to engine bolts.
31. Disconnect engine to body lower ground strap.
32. Remove serpentine belt.

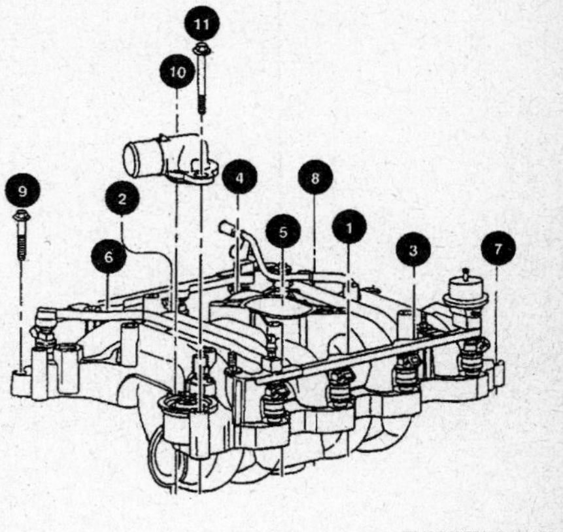

FM1059600101000X

Fig. 2 Intake manifold tightening sequence. 1997–98 SOHC engine

33. Position a suitable drain pan below power steering pump.
34. Disconnect power steering fluid lines at pump.
35. Using power steering pump pulley remover tool No. T69L-10300-B, or equivalent, remove power steering pump pulley.
36. Remove mounting bolts as required, then the power steering pump.
37. Lower the vehicle.
38. Remove safety clip from receiver-dryer suction tube, then disconnect the tube.
39. Remove safety clip from evaporator core line, then disconnect the line.
40. Disconnect A/C line at rear of condenser.
41. Remove two nuts at righthand exhaust manifold.
42. Raise and safely support vehicle on a hoist.
43. Remove six remaining righthand exhaust manifold nuts. **The manifold will not be removed just yet.**
44. Lower the vehicle.
45. Remove alternator as outlined in “Electrical” section.
46. Install engine lifting bracket tool No. 303-639, or equivalent.
47. Using a suitable crane or skyhook, raise engine to access and remove righthand exhaust manifold from bottom of engine compartment.
48. Install engine lifting brackets tool No. 303-D074, or equivalent.
49. Support transmission with a suitable floor jack and a block of wood.
50. Connect spreader bar tool No. D93P-6001-A3, or equivalent to crane or skyhook.
51. Connect spreader bar to lifting brackets.
52. Raise engine slightly to access and disconnect transmission wiring pin at support bracket.
53. Carefully lift engine up and out of engine compartment.
54. If engine will be mounted on a stand, proceed as follows:
    a. Remove flywheel mounting bolts, then the flywheel.

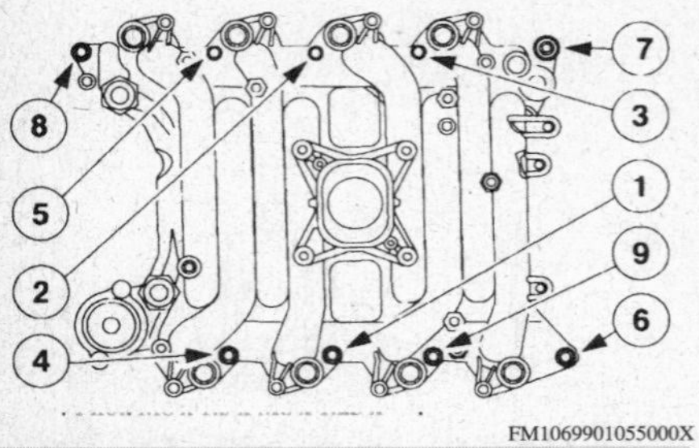

Fig. 3 Intake manifold bolt tightening sequence. 1999–2000 SOHC engine

   b. Remove separator plate.
   c. Using slide hammer tool No. T50T-100-A and rear oil slinger remover tool No. T95P-6701-AH, or equivalents, remove slinger.
   d. Using the slide hammer and rear seal remover tool No. T95P-6701-EH, or equivalent, remove rear seal.
   e. Remove rear seal retainer plate.
   f. Mount engine on stand.

Installation

1. If engine was mounted on a stand, proceed as follows:
   a. Apply a .16 inch bead of silicone gasket sealant part No. F6AZ-19562-A, or equivalent around rear oil seal retainer sealing surface. **Allow to dry until wetness disappears or four minutes, whichever is longer. If not secured within four minutes, remove sealant and clean sealing area with a suitable metal surface cleaner.**
   b. Install retainer plate. Tighten bolts in sequence outlined in **Fig. 1.**
   c. Lubricate a new rear main seal with clean 5W-30 engine oil.
   d. Using rear main seal installer tool No. T95P-6701-BH and adapter tool No. T95P-6701-DH, or equivalents, install rear seal.
   e. Using slinger replacer tool No. T95P-6701-CH, or equivalent, install oil slinger.
   f. Install separator plate.
   g. Install flywheel. **Torque** bolts 54–64 ft. lbs.
2. Using a suitable crane or skyhook, lower engine into vehicle.
3. Remove engine lefthand and righthand lifting tools.
4. Install engine lifting bracket tool No. 303-639, or equivalent.
5. Raise engine to install righthand exhaust manifold and a new gasket through bottom of engine compartment. Tighten nuts to specifications.
6. Lower engine completely into vehicle, then remove lift bracket tool.
7. Install alternator. Tighten fasteners to specifications.
8. Raise and safely support vehicle on hoist.
9. Install power steering pump, noting the following:
   a. **On models equipped with CII style pump,** install pulley using tool No. T65P-3A733-C, or equivalent.
   b. **On models equipped with CIII style pump,** install pulley using tool No. T91P-3A733-A, or equivalent.
10. **On all models,** install engine lower ground strap to body. **Torque** bolts to 18 ft. lbs.
11. Install bellhousing to engine bolts. Tighten to specifications.
12. Install starter motor. Tighten fasteners to specifications.
13. Connect HO2S electrical connectors while exhaust pipe is being moved into proper position. Tighten flange nuts to specifications.
14. Install new A/C fitting O-rings lubricated with clean PAG oil.
15. Continue with installation by reversing remaining removal procedures.
16. Start engine and bring to operating temperature, then inspect for and correct any fluid leaks.

DOHC ENGINE

Removal

1. Drain coolant into an approved container.
2. Recover A/C refrigerant charge using approved methods and equipment.
3. Remove air cleaner and outlet tube.
4. Relieve fuel system pressure.
5. Disconnect fuel lines as required.
6. Remove radiator upper hose.
7. Disconnect throttle and speed control cables, then the return spring.
8. Remove throttle and speed control cable bracket mounting bolts, then position them all aside.
9. Disconnect EVAP emissions return line.
10. Disconnect 16-pin and 42-pin electrical connectors.
11. Separate wiring harness at three firewall locations.
12. Disconnect all required electrical connectors at TBI unit.
13. Disconnect HVAC vacuum supply hoses.
14. Place a suitable drain pan below heater hose firewall fittings, then disconnect the hoses.
15. Remove wiring support bracket nuts, then the bracket.
16. Disconnect electrical connectors near underhood power distribution box.
17. Slide underhood power distribution box access cover up, then remove nut and battery cables.
18. Disconnect low coolant sensor electrical connector.
19. Disconnect coolant hose at bypass tube.
20. Remove transmission shift lever knob.
21. Remove console panel shifter plate. Lift the boot over the lever.
22. Remove shift lever mounting bolts, then the lever.
23. Remove inner boot mounting screws, then the boot.
24. Remove four shifter assembly mounting bolts, then the shifter assembly.
25. Raise and safely support vehicle on a hoist.
26. Remove front wheels and tires.

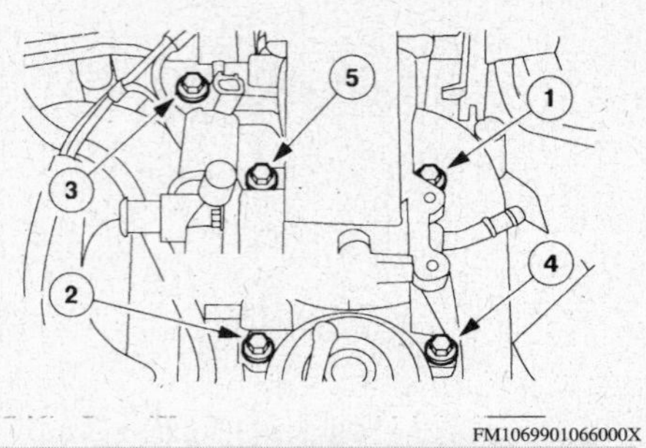

Fig. 4 TBI unit bolt tightening sequence. 1999–2000 SOHC engine

27. Disconnect front wheel speed sensor electrical connectors.
28. Remove front brake caliper mounting bolts, then position calipers aside with suitable wire or rope.
29. Remove three-way catalytic converter mounting fasteners, then the converter.
30. Disconnect A/C compressor inlet and outlet lines.
31. Position A/C muffler assembly aside.
32. Remove starter motor as outlined in "Electrical" section.
33. Position wiring harness at front of engine aside.
34. Disconnect engine oil pressure sensor electrical connector.
35. Remove engine power ground cable nut, then the cable.
36. Disconnect hose from engine oil filter adapter.
37. Remove radiator lower hose.
38. Disconnect clutch cable at transmission.
39. Disconnect power steering high pressure line.
40. Disconnect lower power steering line from fluid cooler.
41. Disconnect hose at power steering fluid reservoir.
42. Remove bolt and anti-rotation clip at power steering pump.
43. Disconnect high pressure line fitting at power steering pump.
44. Separate steering shaft from steering gear. Discard the bolt.
45. Remove pin-style retainers, then position lefthand and righthand splash shields aside.
46. Remove stabilizer bar clamp nuts.
47. Remove inspection cover attaching bolts, then the cover.
48. Remove exhaust air supply valve tube nuts at exhaust manifolds.
49. Position universal powertrain lift and extension.
50. Scribe crossmember alignment marks as required to aid in installation.
51. Remove crossmember to body and frame bolts.
52. Carefully remove powertrain assembly from vehicle.
53. Install engine righthand lifting bracket tool No. D93P-6001-A1, or equivalent.
54. Install engine lefthand lifting bracket

tool No. D93P-6002-A2, or equivalent.
55. Install suitable engine lifting crank or skyhook.
56. Remove motor mount nuts.
57. Disconnect transmission wiring.
58. Remove transmission to engine bolts.
59. Raise and separate engine from front A-frame assembly.

Installation

1. Position engine onto subframe.
2. Install clutch assembly.
3. Connect engine to transmission. Tighten bellhousing bolts to specifications.
4. Connect transmission wiring.
5. Install engine mount to subframe nuts. Tighten to specifications.
6. Remove engine lifting equipment and brackets.
7. Raise powertrain up into vehicle. Ensure shifter clears floor tunnel opening.
8. Install subframe to body bolts. Tighten to specifications.
9. Remove powertrain lift and extension bar.
10. Install inspection cover.
11. Install sway bar clamp nuts.
12. Install splash shields.
13. Connect steering shaft to gear. **Install a new bolt. Torque** bolt to 37 ft. lbs.
14. Connect power steering hoses and lines.
15. Connect clutch cable at transmission.
16. Install radiator lower hose.
17. Connect hose to oil filter adapter.
18. Install engine ground cable.
19. Connect engine oil pressure sender electrical connector.
20. Position engine front wiring harness, then install three nuts.
21. Install starter motor.
22. Move A/C muffler assembly into proper position.
23. Install new A/C fitting O-rings lubricated with clean PAG oil.
24. Continue with installation by reversing remaining removal procedures.
25. Start engine and bring to operating temperature, then inspect for and correct any fluid leaks.

INTAKE MANIFOLD

REPLACE

SOHC Engine

1997-98

1. Drain engine cooling system into a suitable container, then relieve fuel system pressure as outlined under "Precautions."
2. Remove air cleaner outlet tube.
3. Remove serpentine belt as outlined under "Serpentine Drive Belt."
4. Disconnect ignition wires at spark plugs, then remove ignition wires and guides from valve cover studs.
5. Disconnect electrical connectors from ignition coils and camshaft position sensor.
6. Remove ignition coils, then disconnect alternator wiring connectors.
7. Remove alternator to intake manifold mounting brackets, then the alternator from engine.

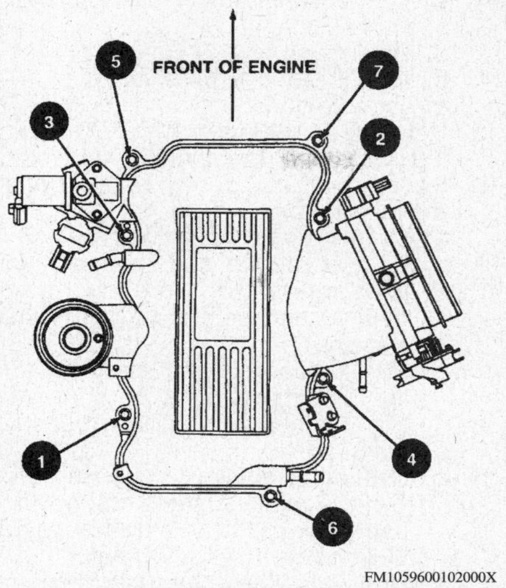

Fig. 5 Upper intake manifold tightening sequence. 1997–98 DOHC engine

8. Raise and support vehicle.
9. Disconnect wiring connectors from engine oil pressure sensor and power steering variable orifice pressure sensor, then position wiring aside.
10. Disconnect EGR tube from righthand exhaust manifold, then lower the vehicle.
11. Disconnect accelerator and speed control cables and brackets, then position and secure aside.
12. Disconnect vacuum hose from throttle body.
13. Disconnect heater water hose from intake manifold.
14. Remove bolts from thermostat housing, then position and secure hose and housing aside.
15. Remove nine remaining intake manifold bolts, then intake manifold.
16. Reverse procedure to install, noting the following:
    a. Tighten bolts to specifications.
    b. Ensure mating surfaces of manifold and heads are clean and free of burrs and gouges.
    c. Ensure alignment tabs of new intake gaskets are aligned with holes in cylinder head.
    d. Install and lightly tighten manifold bolts one through nine in sequence, **Fig. 2,** then tighten bolts to specifications in sequence.
    e. Position new O-ring seal for thermostat housing, then install housing and tighten bolts to specifications.
    f. Fill and bleed cooling system as outlined under " Cooling System Bleed."

1999-2000

1. Drain coolant into an approved container.
2. Remove air cleaner outlet tube.
3. Relieve fuel system pressure as outlined under " Precautions."
4. Disconnect fuel lines as required.
5. Remove radiator upper hose.
6. Disconnect accelerator and speed control cables, then the return spring.
7. Remove accelerator and speed control cable bracket bolts, then position cables aside.
8. Remove breather tube at valve cover.
9. Disconnect EVAP emissions return line.
10. Disconnect differential pressure feedback EGR electrical connector.
11. Disconnect hoses from differential pressure feedback EGR transducer.
12. Disconnect EGR vacuum regulator solenoid electrical connector and vacuum supply.
13. Remove EGR vacuum regulator solenoid bracket from intake manifold.
14. Disconnect EGR tube from EGR valve.
15. Remove PCV valve and hose as a unit.
16. Disconnect EGR valve vacuum lines.
17. Disconnect IAC valve electrical connector.
18. Disconnect main vacuum supply from TBI unit base adapter.
19. Disconnect TPS electrical connector.
20. Remove TBI unit and adapter mounting bolts, then the TBI unit and adapter as an assembly. Discard the gasket if it is damaged.
21. Disconnect fuel pressure sensor electrical connector and fuel charging ground wire.
22. Disconnect all eight ignition coil and fuel injector electrical connectors.
23. Disconnect HVAC vacuum supply lines, then remove the HVAC harness.
24. Remove four fuel supply manifold mounting studs.
25. Remove injectors and supply manifold as a unit.
26. Remove ignition coil mounting bolts, then the coils.
27. Remove alternator as outlined in "Electrical" section.
28. Disconnect heater hose at rear of intake manifold.
29. Unclip engine wiring harness at manifold, then position it aside.
30. Disconnect coolant temperature sender electrical connector.
31. Remove thermostat housing, thermostat and O-ring. Discard O-ring if it is damaged.
32. Remove intake manifold mounting bolts in sequence illustrated in **Fig. 3. The gaskets can be used again if they are not damaged.**
33. Reverse procedure to install, noting the following:
    a. Clean and inspect all gasket sealing surfaces.
    b. Replace any gaskets and O-rings if they appear in doubtful condition.
    c. Tighten intake manifold mounting bolts in sequence illustrated in **Fig. 3.**
    d. **Torque** TBI unit mounting bolts to 89 inch lbs. in sequence illustrated in **Fig. 4.**
    e. Ensure all electrical connectors, vacuum lines and hoses are securely connected.
    f. Close radiator petcock, then fill and bleed cooling system as outlined under "Cooling System Bleed."
    g. Start engine and bring to operating

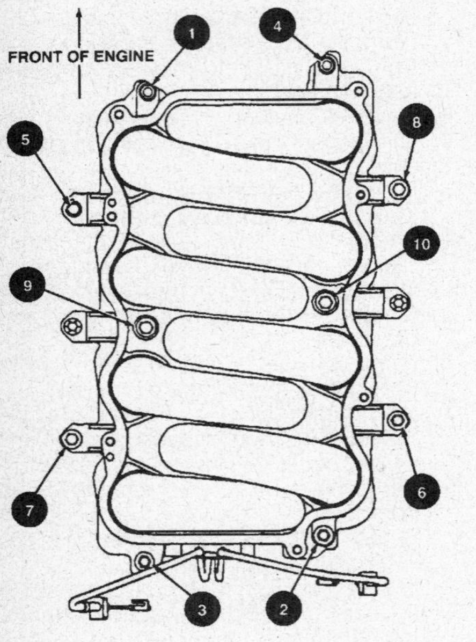

Fig. 6 Lower intake manifold loosening sequence. 1997–98 DOHC engine

temperature, then inspect for and correct any leaks.

DOHC Engine

1997–98

UPPER

1. Turn ignition and wipers on, then turn ignition Off when wipers reach mid cycle (straight up).
2. Remove wiper module.
3. Drain engine cooling system into a suitable container, then relieve fuel system pressure as outlined under "Precautions."
4. Remove air cleaner outlet tube.
5. Remove engine drive belt as outlined under "Serpentine Drive Belt."
6. Remove ignition wire covers from valve covers.
7. Disconnect ignition wires at spark plugs and coils. **Do not pull on wires. Pull on caps only.**
8. Remove ignition wires and guides from engine.
9. Disconnect wiring connectors from alternator and mounting bracket.
10. Remove alternator to intake manifold mounting brackets.
11. Disconnect and remove water bypass tube.
12. Mark and disconnect all wiring connectors to upper intake manifold components.
13. Remove alternator from engine.
14. Disconnect accelerator and speed control cables and brackets.
15. Mark and disconnect all vacuum hose connections to intake manifold components.
16. Disconnect PCV hose, then remove idle air control valve inlet tube.
17. Disconnect and remove as required for bolt access:
    a. EGR valve.
    b. Idle Air Control (IAC) valve.
    c. Throttle body.
18. Remove upper intake manifold retaining bolts, then upper intake manifold.
19. Reverse procedure to install, noting the following:
    a. Tighten bolts to specifications.
    b. Ensure mating surfaces of manifolds are clean and free of burrs and gouges and seal is properly positioned.
    c. Install upper intake manifold and lightly tighten bolts in sequence **Fig. 5,** then tighten to specifications.
    d. Lubricate coolant bypass tube O-rings with a suitable rubber lubricant. **Use extreme care not to cut O-rings during installation.**
    e. Use a suitable ohmmeter to ensure a good ground for temperature sender mounted on coolant bypass tube.
    f. Fill and bleed cooling system as outlined under "Cooling System Bleed."
    g. **Do not allow engine coolant to come into contact with serpentine belt and pulleys. if required, remove belt and flush with clean water.**

LOWER

Removal

1. Remove upper intake manifold as outlined under "Intake Manifold, Replace."
2. Disconnect connectors from fuel manifold and fuel injectors, then disconnect wiring harness and mounting clips.
3. Loosen then remove intake manifold bolts and stud bolts in sequence outlined in **Fig. 6.**
4. Disconnect wiring from IMRC controller while lifting intake manifold assembly from engine.
5. Remove fuel manifolds with injectors from intake manifold.
6. Remove righthand and lefthand lower intake manifolds with IMRC from intake manifold. Discard all gaskets and load limit spacers.

Installation

1. Ensure all mating surfaces are clean and free of old adhesive, burrs and gouges.
2. Remove protective backing from adhesive surface of gaskets for lower intake manifolds with IMRC, then position gaskets onto both lower manifolds with IMRC. Ensure tapered pins of lower manifolds properly align with IMRC.
3. Install both lower manifolds with IMRC to intake manifold. **Tighten bolts only finger tight at this time.**
4. Install fuel injectors and fuel supply manifold to intake manifold.
5. Place new intake manifold gaskets into position on cylinder head, ensuring proper location of gasket alignment pins.
6. Guide manifold assembly into position while connecting IMRC wiring.
7. Install bolts 7 through 10, **Fig. 7. Do not tighten bolts at this time.**
8. Install remaining bolts and stud bolts, then hand tighten them.
9. Tighten bolts and stud bolts to specifications in sequence, **Fig. 7.**
10. **Torque** lower intake manifold with IMRC to intake manifold bolts to 71–105.5 inch lbs.
11. Connect IMRC cables and levers.
12. Connect fuel manifold and fuel injector wiring connectors, then install retaining clips.
13. Install upper intake manifold as outlined under "Upper Intake Manifold."

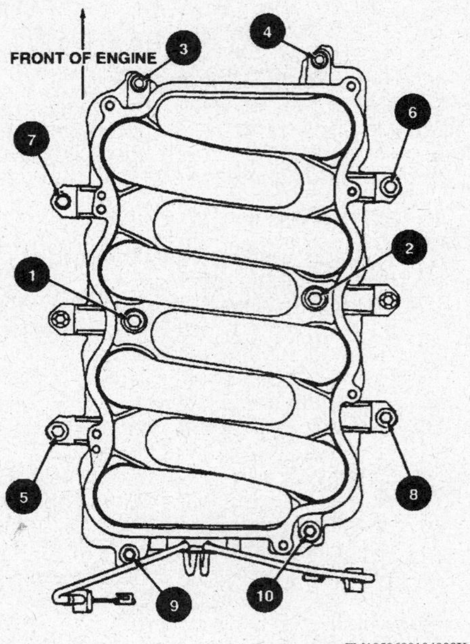

Fig. 7 Lower intake manifold tightening sequence. 1997–98 DOHC engine

1999–2000

UPPER

1. Remove air cleaner outlet tube.
2. Disconnect accelerator and speed control cables, then the return spring.
3. Remove accelerator and speed control cable bracket bolts, then position cables aside.
4. Disconnect TPS electrical connector.
5. Disconnect EVAP emissions return hose.
6. Disconnect IAC control valve electrical connector.
7. Disconnect differential pressure feedback EGR.
8. Disconnect main vacuum supply and EGR vacuum lines.
9. Disconnect differential pressure feedback EGR hoses.
10. Disconnect EGR valve to exhaust tube from EGR valve.
11. Disconnect EGR vacuum regulator solenoid vacuum lines and electrical connector.

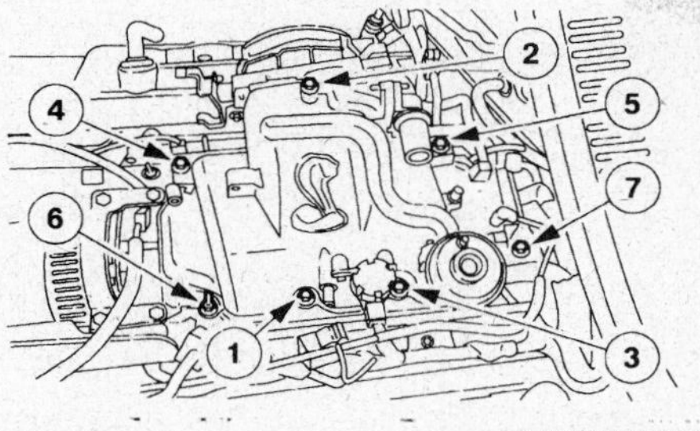

FM1069901056000X

Fig. 8 Upper intake manifold bolt tightening sequence. 1999–2000 DOHC engine

12. Remove PCV valve and tube as a unit.
13. Remove upper intake manifold attaching bolts in sequence illustrated in **Fig. 8.**
14. Carefully remove upper intake manifold from vehicle. Discard the gasket.
15. Reverse procedure to install, noting the following:
    a. Clean and inspect all gasket sealing surfaces.
    b. Install a new upper to lower intake gasket.
    c. Position upper intake manifold, then tighten bolts in sequence outlined in **Fig. 8.**

LOWER

1. Remove upper intake manifold as outlined in this section.
2. Relieve fuel system pressure as outlined in "Precautions."
3. Remove coolant bypass tube.
4. Remove alternator as outlined in "Electrical" section.
5. Disconnect fuel pressure sensor electrical connector and vacuum line.
6. Disconnect all fuel injector electrical connectors.
7. Separate fuel charging wiring from three injection supply manifold studs.
8. Remove lower intake manifold mounting bolts and studs in sequence illustrated in **Fig. 9.**
9. Carefully remove lower intake manifold from vehicle. Discard the gaskets.
10. Reverse procedure to install, noting the following:
    a. Clean and inspect all gasket surfaces.
    b. Install new manifold mounting gaskets.
    c. Position lower intake manifold, then tighten fasteners in sequence illustrated in **Fig. 9.**

EXHAUST MANIFOLD

REPLACE

1997–98

SOHC ENGINE

1. When removing lefthand exhaust manifold, remove bolt for oil dipstick tube.
2. Raise and support vehicle.

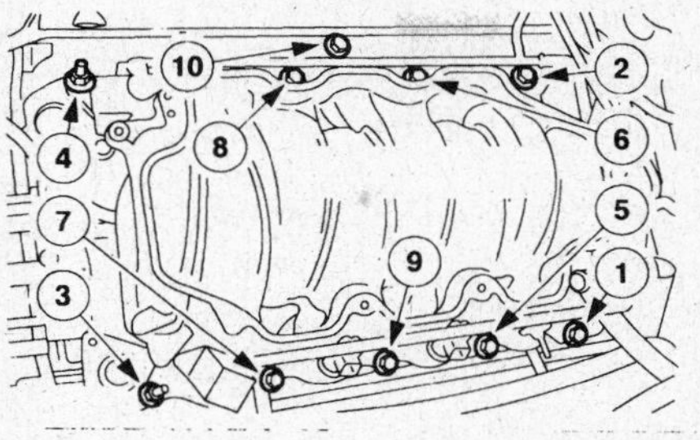

FM1069901057000X

Fig. 9 Lower intake manifold fastener tightening sequence. 1999–2000 DOHC engine

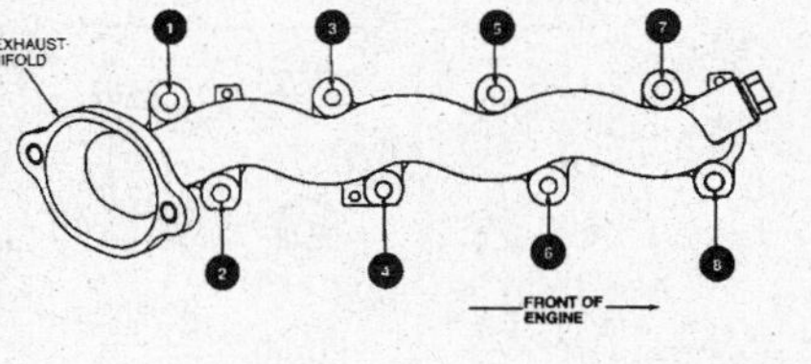

FM1079600019000X

Fig. 11 Righthand exhaust manifold tightening sequence. 1997–98 DOHC engine

3. Disconnect wire connectors to heated oxygen sensors.
4. When removing lefthand exhaust manifold, remove EGR tube from manifold.
5. Disconnect dual converter Y-pipe from exhaust manifolds, then support pipe from subframe with suitable wire.
6. When removing lefthand exhaust manifold, disconnect steering shaft and position aside.
7. When removing lefthand exhaust manifold, remove lefthand motor mount bracket from engine if required for clearance.
8. Remove exhaust manifold retaining nuts, then manifold, discarding gaskets.
9. Reverse procedure to install, noting the following:
    a. Tighten bolts to specifications.
    b. Ensure mating surfaces of manifold and head are clean and free of burrs and gouges.
    c. Ensure alignment of new intake gaskets with holes in cylinder head.
    d. Install and lightly tighten manifold bolts in sequence, **Fig. 10,** then tighten to specifications.

DOHC ENGINE

Righthand Side

1. Remove air cleaner outlet tube.
2. Disconnect secondary air injection tube.
3. Remove upper mounting nuts from exhaust manifold.
4. Raise and support vehicle.
5. Remove dual converter Y-pipe.
6. Remove lower exhaust manifold mounting nuts, then the manifold. Discard gaskets.

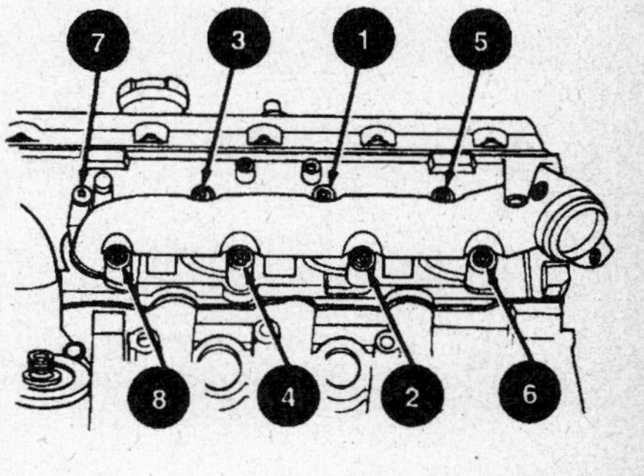

FM1079600021000X

Fig. 10 Exhaust manifold tightening sequence. 1997–98 SOHC engine

7. Reverse procedure to install, noting the following:
    a. Ensure mating surfaces are clean and free of burrs and gouges.
    b. Tighten bolts to specifications.
    c. Tighten exhaust manifold bolts to specifications in sequence, **Fig. 11.**

Lefthand Side

1. Install suitable lifting hooks to engine.
2. Install a suitable engine support frame.
3. Raise engine to release pressure on motor mounts.
4. Raise and support vehicle, then remove front wheels assemblies.
5. Remove EGR and secondary air injection tubes from lefthand exhaust manifold.
6. Remove dual converter Y-pipe.
7. Disconnect righthand and lefthand ball joints and tie rod ends from hub and spindle assemblies.
8. Disconnect steering coupling at pinch bolt.
9. Support subframe with suitable adjustable jacks.
10. Remove motor mount and subframe bolts, then lower subframe to allow clearance for manifold removal.
11. Remove exhaust manifold mounting bolts, then manifold, discarding gaskets.
12. Reverse procedure to install, noting the following:
    a. Tighten bolts to specifications.
    b. Ensure mating surfaces of manifold and head are clean and free of burrs and gouges.
    c. Ensure alignment of new intake gaskets with holes in cylinder head.
    d. Install and lightly tighten manifold bolts in sequence, **Fig. 12,** then tighten bolts in sequence to specifications.

1999–2000

1. Raise and safely support vehicle on a hoist.
2. Disconnect exhaust pipe HO2S electrical connectors.
3. **If removing lefthand manifold on models equipped with DOHC engine,** disconnect EGR tube at manifold.
4. **On all models,** remove exhaust pipe

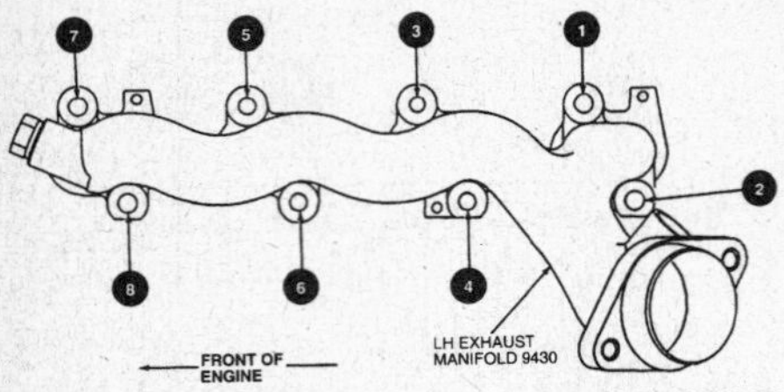

Fig. 12 Lefthand exhaust manifold tightening sequence. 1997–98 DOHC engine

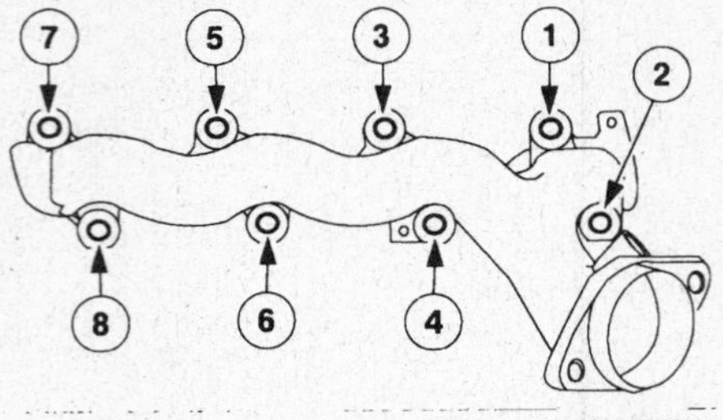

Fig. 13 Lefthand exhaust manifold nut tightening sequence. 1999–2000

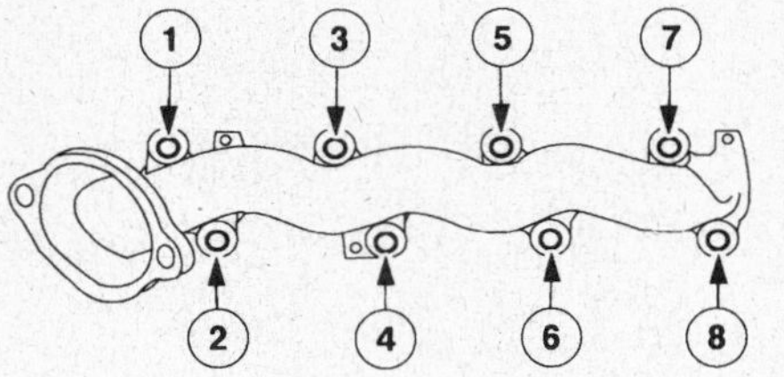

Fig. 14 Righthand exhaust manifold nut tightening sequence. 1999–2000

flange to manifold bolts.

5. Remove manifold to cylinder head nuts, then the manifold and gasket. Discard the gasket.
6. Reverse procedure to install, noting the following:
   a. Always install new manifold to head gaskets.
   b. Tighten manifold attaching nuts in sequences illustrated in **Figs. 13 and 14.**
   c. Start engine and inspect for exhaust leaks.

VALVE COVER

REPLACE

1997–98

SOHC ENGINE

Righthand

1. Remove air cleaner outlet tube, then disconnect the 42- and 8-pin connectors leading to mass airflow and intake air temperature sensors.
2. Remove nut retaining A/C line to righthand front fender apron, then lift the A/C line and feed 42-pin connector under A/C line and position aside.
3. Relieve fuel system pressure as outlined under " Precautions," then disconnect fuel lines.
4. Disconnect ignition wires from spark plugs. **Do not pull on ignition wires as wire may separate from connector.**
5. Remove ignition wires and ignition wire separators from valve cover studs and position aside.
6. Remove Positive Crankcase Ventilation (PCV) valve from crankcase ventilation grommet.
7. Remove bolts and stud bolts, then the valve cover.
8. Reverse procedures to install noting the following:
   a. Use silicone gasket and sealant F6AZ-19562-AA, or equivalent meeting specification WSE-M4G323-A6.
   b. Tighten valve cover bolts to specification and in sequence, **Fig. 15.**

Lefthand

1. Remove air cleaner outlet tube.
2. Disconnect speed control actuator cable from throttle body and position aside.
3. Disconnect engine control sensor extension wire from electronic variable orifice and oil pressure sensors, then position aside.
4. Disconnect ignition wires from spark plugs. **Do not pull on ignition wires as they may separate from connector.**
5. Remove ignition wires and separators from studs.
6. Remove bolts and stud bolts, then the valve cover.
7. Reverse procedure to install noting the following:
   a. Use silicone gasket and sealant F6AZ-19562-AA, or equivalent meeting specification WSE-M4G323-A6.
   b. Tighten valve cover bolts to specifications in sequence, **Fig. 15.**

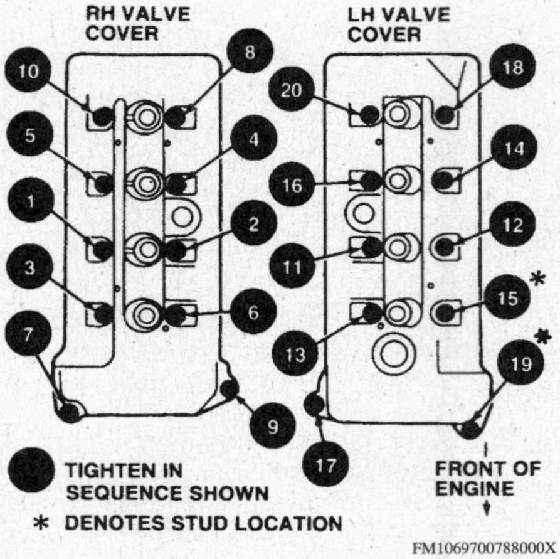

Fig. 15 Valve cover tightening sequence. 1997–98

DOHC ENGINE

Righthand

1. Remove engine compartment brace, then the air cleaner outlet tube.
2. Remove four ignition wire cover retaining screws, then the cover.
3. Disconnect ignition wires from spark plugs. **Do not pull on ignition wires as they may separate from connector.**
4. Remove retaining bolts, then the valve cover.
5. Reverse procedures to install noting the following:
   a. Use silicone gasket and sealant F6AZ-19562-AA, or equivalent meeting specification WSE-M4G323-A6.
   b. Tighten valve cover bolts to specifications in sequence, **Fig. 15.**

Lefthand

1. Remove engine compartment brace, then the windshield wiper module assembly.
2. Remove PCV valve from crankcase ventilation grommet, then the oil level indicator tube retaining nut from valve cover.
3. Remove four lefthand ignition wire cover retaining nuts, then the cover.
4. Disconnect ignition wires from spark plugs. **Do not pull on ignition wires as they may separate from connectors.**
5. Remove bolts and stud bolts, then the valve cover. **With valve cover removed, ensure spark plug bore to valve cover seals are in place on spark plug bore towers.**
6. Reverse procedures to install noting the following:
   a. Use silicone gasket and sealant F6AZ-19562-AA, or equivalent meeting specification WSE-M4G323-A6.
   b. Tighten valve cover bolts to specifications in sequence, **Fig. 15.**

1999–2000

SOHC ENGINE

Lefthand

1. Remove oil dipstick tube bracket bolt, then position the tube aside.
2. Disconnect breather tube at valve cover grommet.
3. Unhook engine wiring harness at valve cover retaining clips.
4. Remove valve cover bolts and studs, then the cover.
5. Reverse procedure to install, noting the following:
   a. Using a plastic scraper, clean away all traces of sealant.
   b. Apply a .32 inch bead of silicone gasket sealant part No. F7AZ-19554-EA, or equivalent to valve cover sealing surfaces. **Do not allow more than four minutes to elapse.**

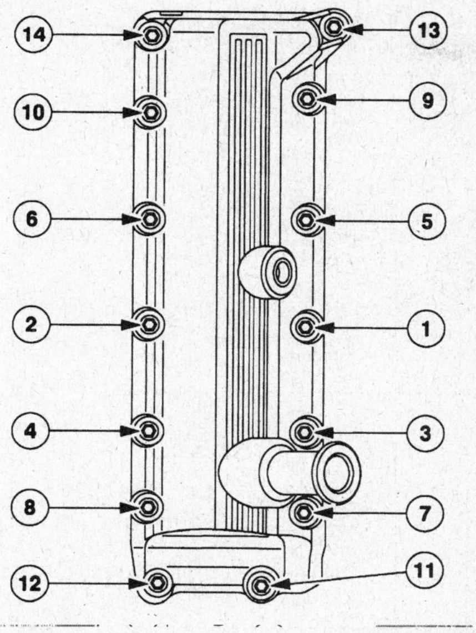

Fig. 16 Valve cover bolt tightening sequence. 1999–2000 SOHC engine

c. Tighten valve cover bolts and studs in sequence illustrated in **Fig. 16.**

Righthand

1. Remove air cleaner outlet tube.
2. Relieve fuel system pressure as outlined under " Precautions."
3. Disconnect fuel lines as required.
4. Unhook engine wiring harness at valve cover retaining clips.
5. Disconnect PCV valve and hose at valve cover grommet, then position them aside.
6. Remove valve cover bolts and studs, then the cover.
7. Reverse procedure to install, noting the following:
   a. Using a plastic scraper, clean away all traces of sealant.
   b. Apply a .32 inch bead of silicone gasket sealant part No. F7AZ-19554-EA, or equivalent to valve cover sealing surfaces. **Do not allow more than four minutes to elapse.**
   c. Tighten valve cover bolts and studs in sequence illustrated in **Fig. 16.**

DOHC ENGINE

Lefthand

1. Remove brake hydro-booster as follows:
   a. Turn engine off, then depress brake pedal several times. This discharges accumulator.
   b. Disconnect brake fluid level sensor electrical connector.
   c. Position a suitable drain pan, then disconnect brake fluid lines on lower side of master cylinder.
   d. Position a suitable drain pan, then disconnect power steering fluid return line hose.
   e. Disconnect power steering pressure lines at hydro-booster. Discard Teflon seals.
   f. Remove self-locking pin in hydro-booster linkage.
   g. Remove stop lamp switch and hydro-booster pushrod from brake pedal pin.
   h. Remove hydro-booster mounting nuts at firewall.
   i. Remove brake hydro-booster unit from vehicle.
2. Disconnect clutch cable at clutch pedal, then position aside.
3. Remove lefthand bank ignition coils.
4. Remove valve cover attaching fasteners, then the cover.
5. Reverse procedure to install, noting the following:
   a. Using a plastic scraper, clean away all traces of sealant.
   b. Apply a .32 inch bead of silicone gasket sealant part No. F7AZ-19554-EA, or equivalent to valve cover sealing surfaces. **Do not allow more than four minutes to elapse.**
   c. Tighten valve cover bolts and studs in sequence illustrated in **Fig. 17.**
   d. Install new power steering pressure line Teflon seals.
   e. Tighten all fasteners to specifications.
   f. Bleed brake and power steering fluid systems.

Righthand

1. Remove righthand bank ignition coils.
2. Relieve fuel system pressure as outlined under " Precautions."
3. Disconnect fuel lines as required.
4. Disconnect EVAP emissions return tube.
5. Remove valve cover attaching fasteners, then the cover.
6. Reverse procedure to install, noting the following:
   a. Using a plastic scraper, clean away all traces of sealant.
   b. Apply a .32 inch bead of silicone gasket sealant part No. F7AZ-19554-EA, or equivalent to valve cover sealing surfaces. **Do not allow more than four minutes to elapse.**
   c. Tighten valve cover bolts and studs in sequence illustrated in **Fig. 18.**
   d. Tighten all fasteners to specifications.

FRONT COVER

REPLACE

1997–98

SOHC Engine

1. Remove valve covers as outlined under "Valve Cover, Replace."
2. Remove oil pan as outlined "Oil Pan, Replace."
3. Remove cooling fan motor, fan blade, then the fan shroud.
4. Loosen water pump pulley bolts, then remove drive belt.

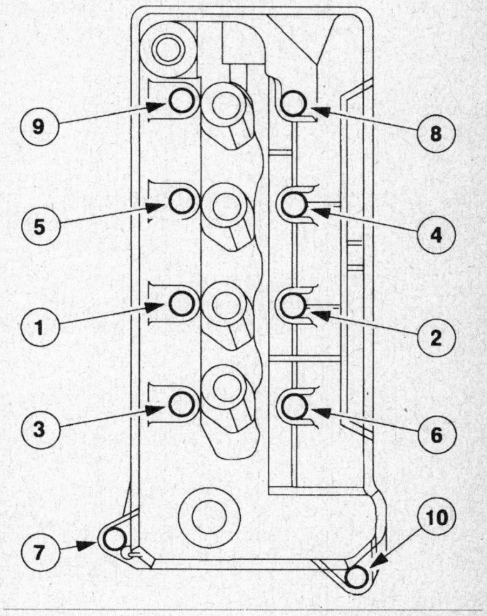

Fig. 17 Lefthand valve cover bolt tightening sequence. 1999–2000 DOHC engine

5. Remove water pump pulley, then raise and support vehicle.
6. Remove power steering pump to cylinder blocks and engine front cover retaining bolts. **Front lower bolt on power steering pump will not come all the way out.**
7. Remove crankshaft pulley bolt and retaining washer from crankshaft.
8. Remove crankshaft pulley using puller tool No. T58P-6316-D, or equivalent.
9. Lower vehicle and remove power steering oil reservoir to lefthand coil bracket retaining bolts, then position reservoir aside.
10. Disconnect fuel charging wiring from both ignition coils and CMP sensor.
11. Remove three righthand ignition coil bracket to front cover retaining bolts, then the lefthand ignition coil from bracket and position aside.
12. Remove three lefthand ignition coil bracket to front cover retaining bolts.
13. Slide righthand ignition coil bracket and wires off mounting studs and lay assembly on top of engine.
14. Remove belt idler pulley retaining bolts, then the pulley.
15. Disconnect fuel charging wiring from CKP sensor .
16. Remove nine stud bolts and six bolts retaining front cover to engine, then the front cover.
17. Reverse procedure to install, noting the following:
    a. Apply a .31–.47 inch bead of silicone gasket sealant F6AZ-19562-AA, or equivalent meeting specification WSE-M4G323-A6 to points illustrated in **Fig. 19.**
    b. Tighten bolts to specifications.

DOHC Engine

1. Remove strut tower support brace,

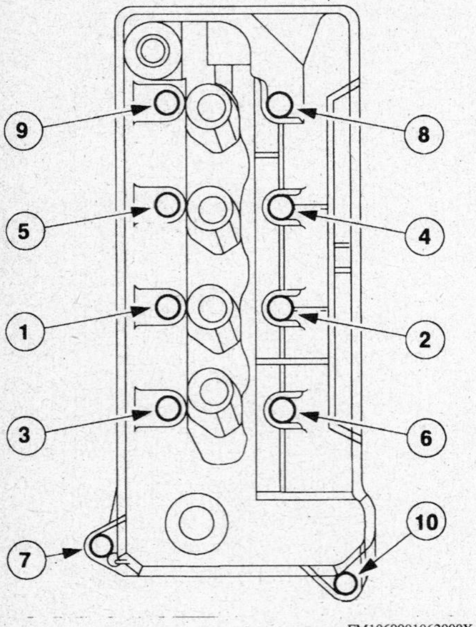

FM1069901062000X

Fig. 18 Righthand valve cover bolt tightening sequence. 1999–2000 DOHC engine

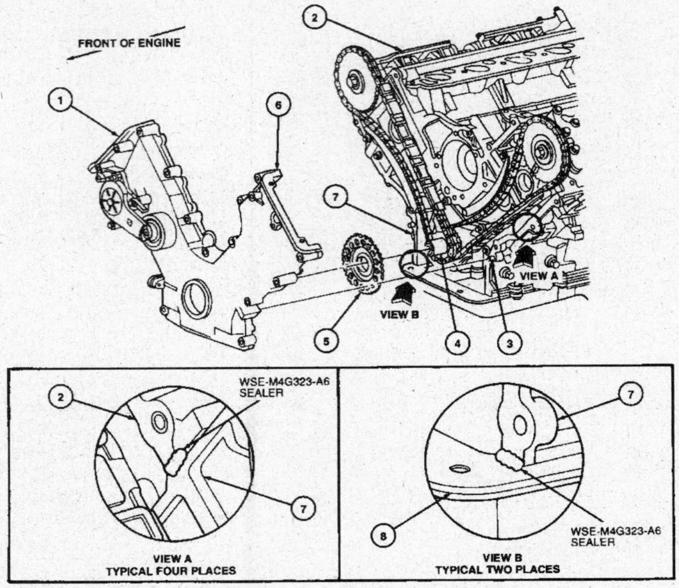

Item	Description
1	Engine Front Cover
2	Cylinder Head
3	Dowel (2 Req'd)
4	Crankshaft

Item	Description
5	Crankshaft Position Sensor Pulse Wheel
6	Engine Front Cover Gasket
7	Cylinder Blocks
8	Oil Pan Gasket

FM1069700790000X

Fig. 19 Sealant points. 1997–98 SOHC engine

then the air cleaner outlet tube.

2. Drain engine cooling system and remove water bypass tube to water thermostat housing hose and upper radiator hose at water bypass tube.
3. Remove cooling fan motor, fan shroud and fan blade assembly.
4. Remove engine control sensor wiring support bracket retaining bolt from lefthand center of front cover.
5. Remove strap retaining fuel charging wiring to front cover.
6. Remove drive belt, then loosen water pump pulley bolts.
7. Remove water pump pulley and lower water pump to cylinder block retaining bolt.
8. Remove bolts and stud bolt retaining power steering pump reservoir to lefthand ignition coil bracket.
9. Raise and support vehicle.
10. Remove power steering pressure hose to pump bracket retaining bolt.
11. Remove power steering pump to cylinder blocks and front cover retaining bolts. **Front lower bolt on power steering pump will not come all the way out.**
12. Position power steering pump and reservoir out of way.
13. Remove four oil pan to front cover retaining bolts, then the crankshaft pulley retaining bolt and washer.
14. Remove crankshaft pulley from crankshaft using remover tool No. T58P-6316-D, or equivalent.
15. Lower vehicle and remove valve covers as outlined under " Valve Cover, Replace."
16. Disconnect fuel charging wiring from both ignition coils and CMP sensor.
17. Remove three righthand ignition coil bracket to front cover retaining bolts.
18. Remove three nuts and one bolt retaining lefthand ignition coil bracket to front cover.
19. Slide both ignition coil brackets and wires off mounting studs.
20. Remove belt idler pulley retaining bolt, then the pulley.
21. Remove nine stud bolts and six bolts retaining front cover to engine, then four oil pan to front cover bolts.
22. Remove front cover.
23. Reverse procedures to install noting the following:
    a. Apply an 8–12 mm bead of silicone gasket sealant F6AZ-19562-AA, or equivalent meeting specification WSE-M4G323-A6 to points illustrated in **Fig. 20.**
    b. Tighten bolts to specifications.

1999–2000

SOHC Engine

1. Remove RFI capacitor mounting nuts, then position capacitor aside.
2. Remove valve covers as outlined under "Valve Cover, Replace."
3. Drain coolant from radiator and degas bottle into an approved container.
4. Disconnect cooling fan motor electrical connector, then separate fan harness from shroud.
5. Remove fan shroud lefthand and righthand mounting bolts.
6. Remove cooling fan, motor and shroud as an assembly.
7. Remove serpentine belt.
8. Remove water pump pulley bolts, then the pulley.
9. Remove A/C muffler assembly mounting nut, then position assembly aside.
10. Raise and safely support vehicle on a hoist.
11. Drain engine oil into an approved container.
12. Position power steering pump aside.
13. Disconnect CKP sensor electrical connector.
14. Remove battery cable support nuts at front of engine.
15. Remove crankshaft pulley bolt.
16. Using puller tool No. T58P-6316-D, or equivalent, remove crankshaft pulley.
17. Using seal remover tool No. T74P-6700-A, or equivalent, remove crankshaft front seal.
18. Remove oil pan to front cover bolts.
19. Lower the vehicle.
20. Position a suitable drain pan below power steering fluid reservoir, then remove the reservoir.
21. Disconnect CMP electrical connector.
22. Remove serpentine belt idler pulley.
23. Mark their locations, remove front cover attaching bolts and studs, then the cover. Discard the gaskets.
24. Reverse procedure to install, noting the following:
    a. Apply silicone gasket sealer part No. F7AZ-19554-EA, or equivalent in locations illustrated in **Fig. 21.**
    b. Ensure all fasteners return to their original locations, **Fig. 22.**
    c. **Torque** oil pan to front cover bolts in three steps: first, to 18 inch lbs.; second, to 15 ft. lbs; finally, rotate them an additional 60°.
    d. Using installer and aligner tool No. T88T-6701-A, or equivalent, install a new crankshaft pulley oil seal.
    e. Apply silicone gasket sealer to

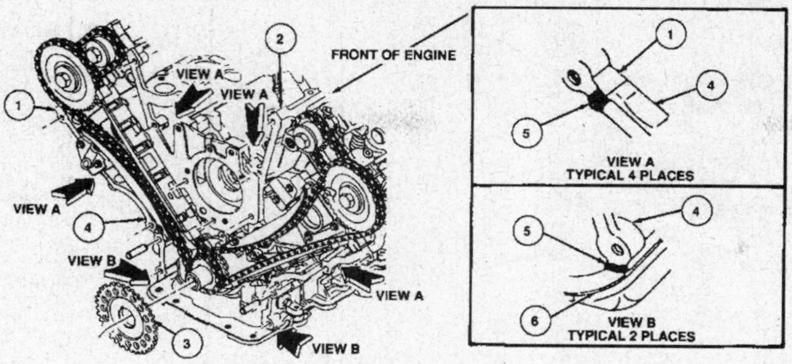

Item	Description
1	Cylinder Head, RH
2	Cylinder Head, LH
3	Ignition Pulse Crankshaft Sensor Ring

Item	Description
4	Cylinder Blocks
5	Sealer
6	Oil Pan Gasket

FM1069700789000X

Fig. 20 Sealant points. 1997–98 DOHC engine

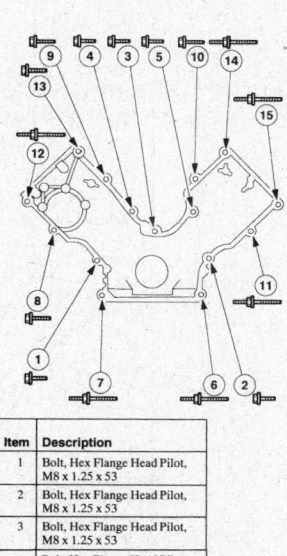

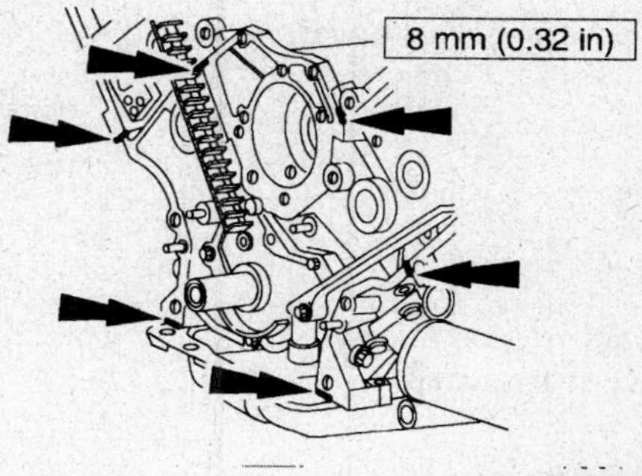

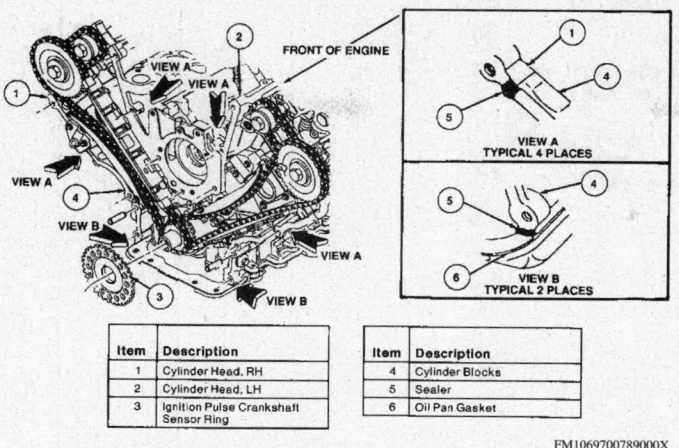

FM1069901063000X

Fig. 21 Front cover sealant application locations. 1999–2000

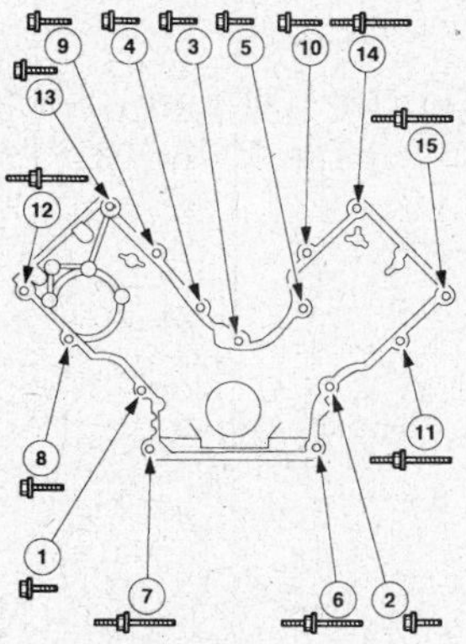

Item	Description
1	Bolt, Hex Flange Head Pilot, M8 x 1.25 x 53
2	Bolt, Hex Flange Head Pilot, M8 x 1.25 x 53
3	Bolt, Hex Flange Head Pilot, M8 x 1.25 x 53
4	Bolt, Hex Flange Head Pilot, M8 x 1.25 x 53
5	Bolt, Hex Flange Head Pilot, M8 x 1.25 x 53
6	Stud, Hex-Head Pilot, M10 x 1.5 x 1.5 x 103.1
7	Stud, Hex-Head Pilot, M10 x 1.5 x 1.5 x 103.1
8	Screw and Washer, Hex Pilot, M10 x 1.5 x 57.5
9	Screw and Washer, Hex Pilot, M10 x 1.5 x 57.5
10	Screw and Washer, Hex Pilot, M10 x 1.5 x 57.5
11	Stud and Washer, Hex-Head Pilot, M10 x 1.5 x M8 x 1.25 x 109.6
12	Stud and Washer, Hex-Head Pilot, M10 x 1.5 x M8 x 1.25 x 109.6
13	Stud and Washer, Hex-Head Pilot, M10 x 1.5 x M8 x 1.25 x 109.6
14	Stud and Washer, Hex-Head Pilot, M10 x 1.5 x M8 x 1.25 x 109.6
15	Stud and Washer, Hex-Head Pilot, M10 x 1.5 x M8 x 1.25 x 109.6

FM1069901064000X

Fig. 22 Front cover fastener locations. 1999–2000 SOHC engine

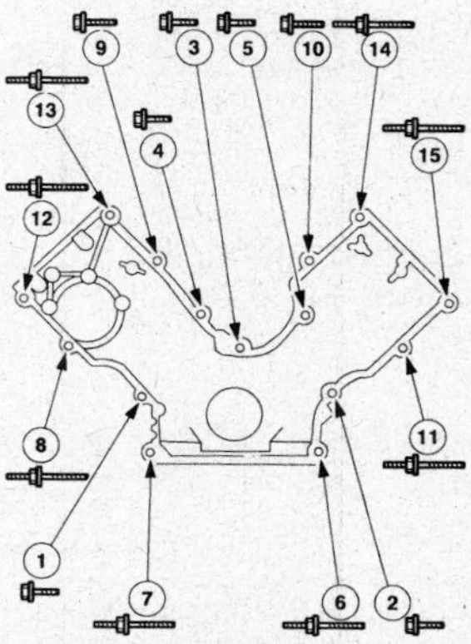

Item	Description
1	Bolt, Hex Flange Head Pilot, M8 x 1.25 x 53
2	Bolt, Hex Flange Head Pilot, M8 x 1.25 x 53
3	Bolt, Hex Flange Head Pilot, M8 x 1.25 x 53
4	Bolt, Hex Flange Head Pilot, M8 x 1.25 x 53
5	Bolt, Hex Flange Head Pilot, M8 x 1.25 x 53
6	Stud, Hex-Head Pilot, M8 x 1.5 x 1.5 x 103.1
7	Stud, Hex-Head Pilot, M8 x 1.5 x 1.5 x 103.1
8	Stud, Hex Pilot, M8 x 1.5 x 57.5
9	Screw and Washer, Hex Pilot, M8 x 1.5 x 57.5
10	Screw and Washer, Hex Pilot, M8 x 1.5 x 57.5
11	Stud and Washer, Hex-Head Pilot, M8 x 1.5 x M8 x 1.25 x 91.0
12	Stud and Washer, Hex-Head Pilot, M8 x 1.5 x M8 x 1.25 x 91.0
13	Stud and Washer, Hex-Head Pilot, M8 x 1.5 x M8 x 1.25 x 91.0
14	Stud and Washer, Hex-Head Pilot, M8 x 1.5 x M8 x 1.25 x 91.0
15	Stud and Washer, Hex-Head Pilot, M8 x 1.5 x M8 x 1.25 x 91.0

FM1069901065000X

Fig. 23 Front cover fastener locations. 1999–2000 4.6L DOHC engine

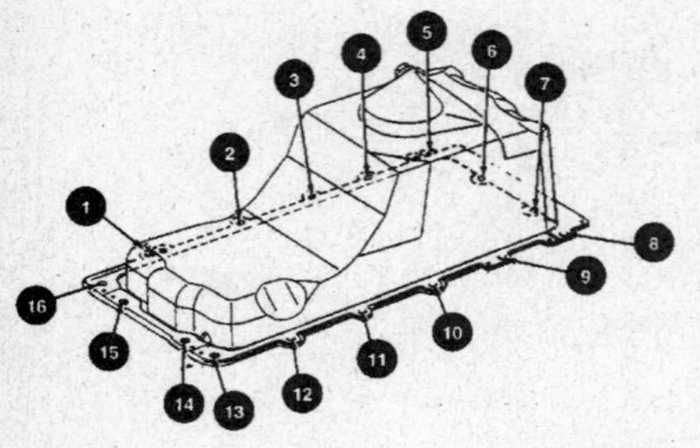

FM1069600461000X

Fig. 24 Oil pan bolt tightening sequence. 1997–98 DOHC engine

crankshaft pulley keyway slot. **Do not allow more than four minutes to elapse.**

f. Using installer tool No. T74P-6316-B, or equivalent, install crankshaft pulley.

g. **Torque** crankshaft pulley bolt to 66 ft. lbs., then loosen one full turn. **Torque** to 37 ft. lbs., then rotate an additional 90°.

h. Tighten remaining fasteners to specifications.

i. Start engine and bring to operating temperature, then inspect for and correct any leaks.

DOHC Engine

1. Remove valve covers as outlined under “Valve Cover, Replace.”
2. Drain coolant from radiator and degas bottle into an approved container.
3. Disconnect cooling fan motor electrical connector, then separate fan harness from shroud.
4. Remove fan shroud lefthand and righthand mounting bolts.
5. Remove cooling fan, motor and shroud as an assembly.
6. Remove water pump pulley bolts, then the pulley.
7. Raise and safely support vehicle on a hoist.
8. Drain engine oil into an approved container.
9. Remove crankshaft pulley bolt.
10. Using puller tool No. T58P-6316-D, or equivalent, remove crankshaft pulley.
11. Remove A/C muffler assembly mounting nut, then position assembly aside.
12. Remove power steering pump mounting bolts, then position pump aside.
13. Disconnect CKP sensor electrical connector.
14. Remove front oil pan to front cover bolts.
15. Using seal remover tool No. T74P-6700-A, or equivalent, remove crankshaft front oil seal.
16. Lower the vehicle.
17. Disconnect CMP sensor electrical connector.
18. Remove serpentine belt idler pulley.
19. Mark their locations, remove front cover attaching bolts and studs, then the cover. Discard the gaskets.
20. Reverse procedure to install, noting the following:

a. Apply silicone gasket sealer part

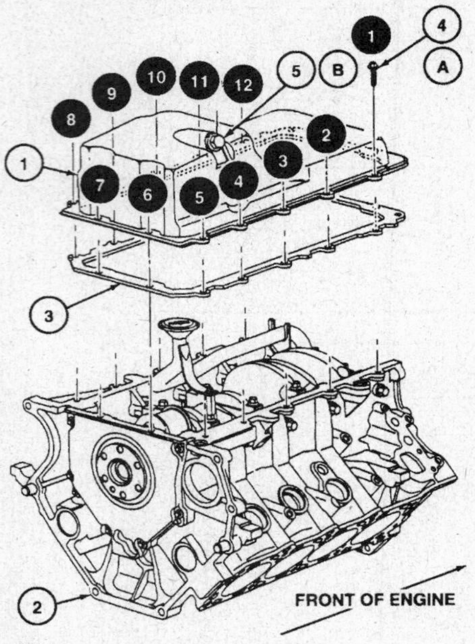

TIGHTEN BOLTS IN SEQUENCE

REFER TO LEGEND

Item	Description
1	Oil Pan
2	Cylinder Blocks
3	Oil Pan Gasket
4	Bolt
5	Drain Plug (Part of 6675)
A	Tighten to 20 N·m (15 Lb-Ft) Then Rotate 60 Degrees
B	Tighten to 11-16 N·m (9-11 Lb-Ft)

FM1099600079000X

Fig. 25 Oil pan bolt tightening sequence. 1997–98 SOHC engine

No. F7AZ-19554-EA, or equivalent in locations illustrated in **Fig. 21.**

b. Ensure all fasteners return to their original locations, **Fig. 23.**

c. **Torque** oil pan to front cover bolts in three steps: first, to 18 inch lbs.; second, to 15 ft. lbs; finally, rotate them an additional 60°.

d. Using installer and aligner tool No. T88T-6701-A, or equivalent, install a new crankshaft pulley oil seal.

e. Apply silicone gasket sealer to crankshaft pulley keyway slot. **Do not allow more than four minutes to elapse.**

f. Using installer tool No. T74P-6316-B, or equivalent, install crankshaft pulley.

g. **Torque** crankshaft pulley bolt to 66 ft. lbs., then loosen one full turn. **Torque** to 37 ft. lbs., then rotate an additional 85–95°.

h. Tighten remaining fasteners to specifications.

i. Start engine and bring to operating temperature, then inspect for and

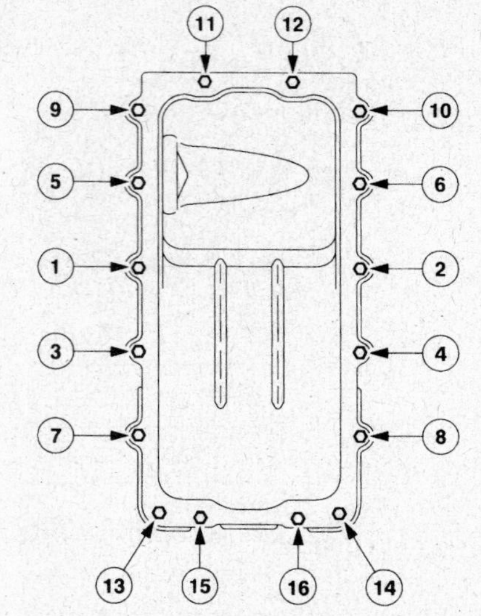

FM1099900087000X

Fig. 26 Oil pan bolt tightening sequence. 1999–2000

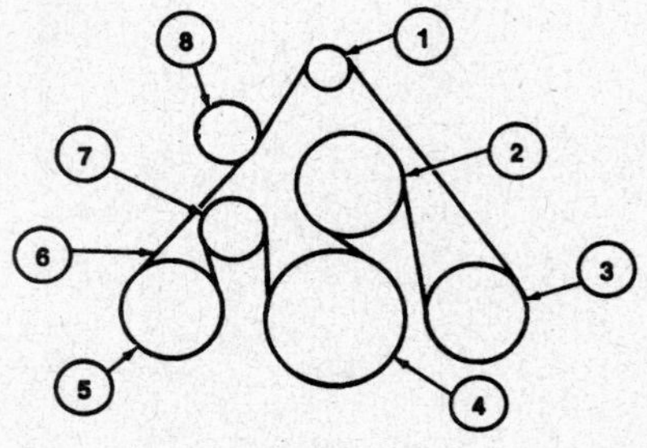

1 Alternator
2 Water pump pulley
3 Power steering pulley
4 Crankshaft pulley
5 A/C compressor
6 Drive belt
7 Drive belt tensioner
8 Belt idler pulley

FM1069600460000X

Fig. 27 Serpentine belt routing. 1997–98

correct any leaks.

OIL PAN

REPLACE

1997-98

DOHC Engine

1. Remove engine dipstick.
2. Install suitable lifting eyes to engine, then install suitable engine lifting frame and raise engine to release pressure on motor mounts.
3. Raise and support vehicle, then remove front wheel assemblies.
4. Disconnect lefthand and righthand tie rod ends and ball joints from hub and spindles.
5. Disconnect steering coupling at pinch bolt joint, then remove engine mount nuts.
6. Support subframe with suitable adjustable jacks

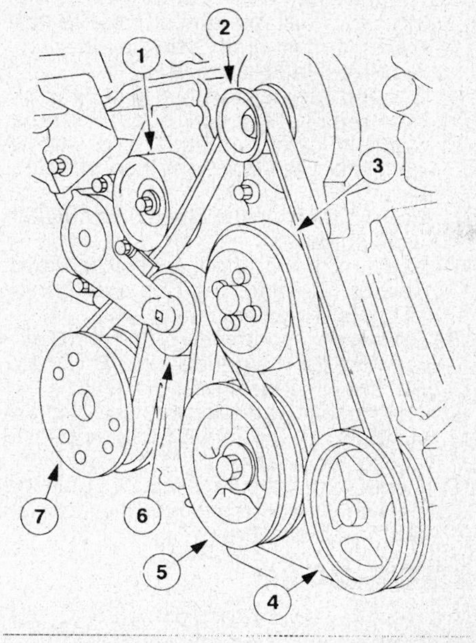

Fig. 28 Serpentine belt routing (1-idler, 2-alternator, 3-water pump, 4-PS pump, 5-crankshaft, 6-tensioner, 7-A/C compressor). 1999 & 2000 early production

7. Remove front strut to spindle bolts, then separate strut and spindle.
8. Remove subframe to body bolts, then lower subframe sufficiently to allow oil pan removal.
9. Disconnect wiring connectors to oil pan sensors.
10. Remove bolts from oil pan, then remove oil pan and gasket, discard gasket.
11. Reverse procedure to install, noting the following:
    a. Tighten bolts to specifications.
    b. Apply suitable silicone sealer to areas where block meets front and rear engine covers.
    c. Tighten oil pan bolts to specifications in sequence, **Fig. 24.**

SOHC Engine

1. Remove engine compartment brace from front fender aprons and dash panel.
2. Raise and support vehicle, then drain engine oil.
3. Remove retaining bolts and front subframe crossmember reinforcement, then the motor mount to front subframe crossover nuts.
4. Remove transmission housing cover, then use suitable safety stand to raise engine approximately four inches and position suitable wood block under crankshaft pulley.
5. Install 2 ½ –2 ¾ inch wood blocks under each front engine support insulator, then remove oil pan retaining bolts.
6. Remove oil pan. **It may be necessary to adjust engine height several times for sufficient removal clearance.**
7. Reverse procedure to install and **torque** oil pan bolts to 14 ft. lbs., in sequence, **Fig. 25,** then rotate an additional 60°.

1999-2000

SOHC Engine

1. Remove air cleaner outlet tube.
2. Remove radiator sight shield.
3. Install engine lifting bracket tool No. D93P-6001-A2, or equivalent to lefthand front corner of engine.
4. Install engine support tool No. 303-290-A, or equivalent.
5. Raise and safely support vehicle on a hoist.
6. Drain engine oil into an approved container.
7. Remove lefthand and righthand engine mount nuts.
8. Lower the vehicle.
9. Raise engine by using the support tool.
10. Raise and safely support vehicle.
11. Using compressor tool No. D78P-5310-A, or equivalent, compress front coil springs.
12. Position a suitable jack stand under subframe.
13. Remove four engine mount bolts.
14. Loosen, but do not completely remove, the front subframe bolts.
15. Lower the front subframe.
16. Remove oil pan mounting bolts, then the pan. **If the gasket is in good condition it may be used again.**
17. Reverse procedure to install, noting the following:
    a. Use a plastic scraper to remove all traces of gasket material and sealant.
    b. Clean and inspect all gasket surfaces.
    c. Apply silicone gasket sealant part No. F7AZ-19554-EA, or equivalent to rear oil seal retainer to block sealing surface, and at the front cover to block mating surface. **Do not allow more than four minutes to elapse before installing oil pan.**
    d. Move oil pan into position and loosely install its bolts.
    e. **Torque** bolts in sequence illustrated in **Fig. 26** in three steps: first, to 18 inch lbs.; second, to 15 ft. lbs.; finally, rotate an additional 60°.
    f. Start engine and bring to operating temperature, then inspect and correct any leaks.

DOHC Engine

1. Remove air cleaner outlet tube.
2. Remove radiator sight shield.
3. Install engine lifting bracket tool No. D93P-6001-A2, or equivalent.
4. Support engine using engine support kit tool No. 303-F072, or equivalent.
5. Raise and safely support vehicle on a hoist.
6. Remove lefthand and righthand engine mount nuts.
7. Lower the vehicle.
8. Raise engine by using the support tool.

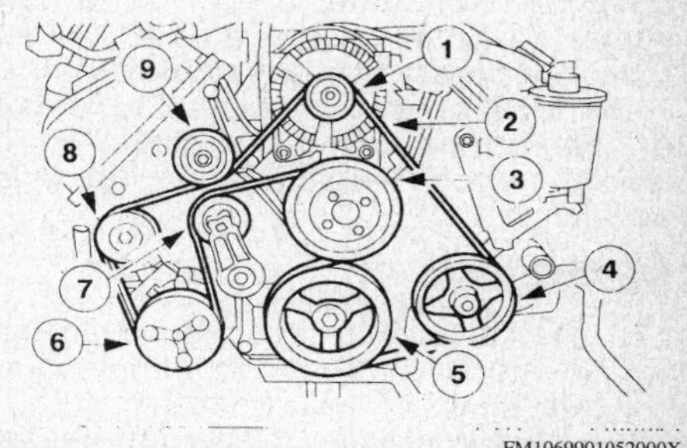

Fig. 29 Serpentine belt routing (1-alternator, 2-belt, 3-water pump, 4-PS pump, 5-crankshaft, 6-A/C compressor, 7-tensioner, 8 & 9-idler pulleys). 2000 late production

9. Raise and safely support vehicle.
10. Drain engine oil into an approved container.
11. Using compressor tool No. D78P-5310-A, or equivalent, compress front coil springs.
12. Position a suitable jack stand under subframe.
13. Remove four subframe side bolts.
14. Loosen, but do not completely remove, the front subframe bolts.
15. Lower the front subframe.
16. Remove oil pan mounting bolts, then the pan. **If the gasket is in good condition it may be used again.**
17. Reverse procedure to install, noting the following:
    a. Use a plastic scraper to remove all traces of gasket material and sealant.
    b. Clean and inspect all gasket surfaces.
    c. Apply silicone gasket sealant part No. F7AZ-19554-EA, or equivalent to rear oil seal retainer to block sealing surface, and at the front cover to block mating surface. **Do not allow more than four minutes to elapse before installing oil pan.**
    d. Move oil pan into position and loosely install its bolts.
    e. **Torque** bolts in sequence illustrated in **Fig. 26** in three steps: first, to 18 inch lbs.; second, to 15 ft. lbs.; finally, rotate an additional 60°.
    f. Start engine and bring to operating temperature, then inspect and correct any leaks.

BELT TENSION DATA

These models are equipped with an automatic drive belt tensioner. No adjustment or maintenance is required.

SERPENTINE DRIVE BELT

Always use square drive tool in hole in tensioner to move tensioner. Never pry on tensioner pulley. When releasing

drive belt tensioner, never allow tensioner to snap back. Damage to tensioner or personal injury could result.

Do not allow engine coolant to remain on serpentine belt or pulleys. If required, remove belt and flush with clean water.

REMOVAL

1. Insert a suitable square drive tool into square hole in tensioner arm, then rotate tensioner away from belt.
2. Lift belt from pulley, then slowly release tensioner.
3. Remove belt from vehicle.

INSTALLATION

1. Route belt as shown in **Figs. 27 through 29** Ensure belt is properly seated in pulley grooves.
2. Insert a suitable square drive tool into square hole in tensioner arm, then rotate tensioner away from belt.
3. Position belt under tensioner, then slowly release tensioner onto belt.

COOLING SYSTEM BLEED

1. Fill radiator completely full, then install radiator cap.
2. Fill coolant reservoir and degas bottle to full cold mark.
3. Set heater control to full hot, high fan and set controls so air vents from dash vents.
4. Start and operate engine until fully warmed up while observing water temperature gauge:
   a. If system is functioning properly, temperature will indicate normal and hot air will be felt at dash outlets.
   b. If system is not functioning properly, temperature gauge will not read and/or no hot air will be felt at dash vents.
5. If system is not functioning properly, allow engine to cool then repeat procedure.
6. If system is functioning properly, allow engine to cool, then fill coolant reservoir to full cold mark if required.

WATER PUMP

REPLACE

1. Drain engine coolant into a suitable container.
2. Loosen bolts retaining water pump pulley to water pump.
3. Remove serpentine belt as outlined under "Serpentine Drive Belt."
4. Remove water pump retaining bolts, then the pump and gasket. Discard the gasket.
5. Reverse procedure to install. Tighten bolts to specifications.

RADIATOR

REPLACE

1997-98

1. Disconnect transmission cooler lines using quick disconnect tool No. T82L-9500-AH, or equivalent.
2. Drain cooling system, then disconnect hoses from radiator.
3. Remove cooling fan and shroud as an assembly.
4. Remove coolant reservoir and bracket.
5. Remove upper radiator support bracket, then radiator.
6. Reverse procedure to install, noting the following:
   a. Ensure coolant hoses and clamps are properly positioned and tightened.
   b. Bleed cooling system as outlined under "Cooling System Bleed."

1999-2000

1. Drain coolant from radiator and degas bottle into an approved container.
2. Disconnect cooling fan motor electrical connector, then separate fan harness from shroud.
3. Remove fan shroud lefthand and righthand mounting bolts.
4. Remove cooling fan, motor and shroud as an assembly.
5. Remove radiator sight shield.
6. Disconnect radiator upper hose at radiator.
7. **On models equipped with automatic transmission,** remove lower and upper cooler tube fittings.
8. **On all models,** raise and safely support vehicle on a hoist.
9. Disconnect radiator lower hose at radiator, then lower the vehicle.
10. Remove radiator supports, then carefully lift radiator out of vehicle.
11. Reverse procedure to install, noting the following:
    a. Tighten all fasteners to specifications.
    b. Close radiator petcock, then fill and bleed cooling system as outlined under "Cooling System Bleed."
    c. Start engine and bring to operating temperature, then inspect for and correct any leaks.

FUEL PUMP

REPLACE

1997-98

1. Relieve fuel system pressure as outlined under " Precautions."
2. Remove fuel from fuel tank by pumping into a suitable fuel storage tanker.
3. Raise and support vehicle, then remove fuel tank filler line.
4. Support fuel tank with a suitable jack, then remove fuel tank support straps.
5. Partially lower fuel tank, then disconnect fuel lines and electrical connectors.
6. Lower fuel tank and place on a suitable work surface.
7. Clean area around fuel pump/level sensor retaining ring to prevent entry of contaminants into tank.
8. Remove fuel pump/level sensor retaining ring using wrench tool No. D84P-9275-A, or equivalent.
9. Note location and position of alignment notches, then remove fuel pump/level sensor from tank.
10. Reverse procedure to install. Lubricate new sealing O-ring to hold it in position during installation.

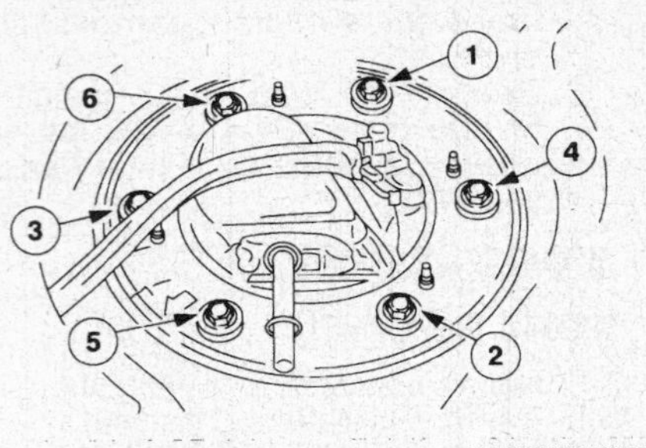

Fig. 30 Fuel tank sender unit bolt tightening sequence. 1999–2000

1999-2000

1. Relieve fuel system pressure as outlined under " Precautions."
2. Using draining tool No. 310-F013 and storage tanker tool No. 164-R3202, or equivalents, drain all fuel from fuel tank.
3. Raise and safely support vehicle on a hoist.
4. Remove filler pipe attaching bolt, then disconnect pipe hose connections to tank.
5. Disconnect fuel tank electrical connector.
6. Disconnect vapor tube fitting at lefthand front side of tank.
7. Place a suitable jack stand under tank.
8. Remove front two bolts from fuel tank support straps, then position the lefthand strap aside.
9. Remove righthand support strap rear bolt, then the strap.
10. Partially lower the tank, then disconnect fuel lines as follows:
    a. **On 3/8 inch fuel lines,** use spring lock coupler tool No. D87L-9280-A, or equivalent.
    b. **On 1/2 inch fuel lines,** use spring lock coupler tool No. D87L-9280-B, or equivalent.
11. Cut pipe-to-tank grommet's outer edge to ease filler pipe removal, then carefully remove grommet from tank. **This grommet must be removed before separating the tank from the filler pipe or the filler tube check valve will be damaged.**
12. Carefully lower and remove tank, then move to a suitable bench.
13. Clean all dirt and debris away from area around fuel sender unit mounting flange.
14. Note sender unit orientation, then remove mounting bolts.
15. **Use caution when removing sender unit to avoid damaging filter, float arm, tubing and wiring.** Pull sender unit up until locking tabs are accessible.
16. Reach through opening and squeeze locking tabs together, then remove sender unit from tank.

17. Reverse procedure to install, noting the following:
    a. Clean all dirt and debris away from area around fuel sender unit mounting flange.
    b. Align sender unit with fuel tank retainer as noted during removal.
    c. Install mounting bolts finger tight, then tighten to specifications in sequence illustrated in **Fig. 30.**
    d. Lubricate filler pipe check valve area and a new tank-to-filler pipe grommet with Serfactant (Merpol) meeting specification ESE-M99B144-B, or equivalent.

FUEL FILTER

REPLACE

1. Relieve fuel system pressure as outlined under " Precautions."
2. Raise and support vehicle.
3. Remove push connector fittings from fuel filter ends as follows:
    a. **On ⅜ inch fuel lines,** use spring lock coupler tool No. D87L-9280-A, or equivalent.
    b. **On ½ inch fuel lines,** use spring lock coupler tool No. D87L-9280-B, or equivalent.
4. Loosen worm gear clamp, then remove filter from bracket. Note flow arrow as installed to ensure proper direction of fuel flow through filter.
5. Reverse procedure to install. Always use new retainer clips in each fitting.

TIGHTENING SPECIFICATIONS

Component	Torque/Ft. Lbs.
1997–98	
Accelerator Cable Brackets	69.5–105.5①
Alternator Mounting To Block	15–22
Ball Joint To Spindle Nut	109–149
Clutch Pressure To Flywheel	19–24
Cylinder Head	③
Drive Belt Tensioner and Idler Pulley	15–22
Front Strut To Spindle	141–191
Fuel Injection Supply Manifold	69.5–105.5①
EGR Tube Connector	33–48
EGR Vacuum Regulator	45–60①
EGR Valve To Exhaust Tube Nuts	30–33
EGR Valve To Manifold	15–22
Engine Lifting Eyes	30–37
Engine Support To Crossmember	94–126
Engine Support To Engine (Small Bolts)	25–33
Engine Support To Engine (Large Bolts)	44–60
Exhaust Manifold To Head	13–16
Idle Air Control Valve Bolt	69.5–105.5①
Ignition Coil To Engine	15–22
Ignition Wire Cover	45–60①
Intake Manifold To Lower Intake Manifold	71–89①
Intake Manifold To Cylinder Head	15–22
Low Oil Sensor	20–30
Oil Cooler To Oil Filter Adapter	59–74
Oil Pan Bolts (DOHC)	15–22
Oil Pan Bolts (SOHC)	②
Oil Pan Drain Plug	8–12
Stabilizer Bar Link	11–16
Sub Frame To Body	70–96
Throttle Body To Intake	71–105.6①
Tie Rod To Spindle	35–47
Upper Intake Manifold To Intake Manifold	71–105.5①
Valve Cover	72–108①
Water Pump Pulley Bolts	15–22
Water Pump To Block	15–22
Wheel Lug Nut	85–105
1999–2000	
A/C Compressor Bolts	18
A/C Muffler Nut	15
Alternator Mounting Bracket Retainers	89①
Battery Cable To Alternator Nut	89①
Battery Cable Support Brackets	15

Continued

TIGHTENING SPECIFICATIONS—Continued

Component	Torque/Ft. Lbs.
1999–2000	
Clutch Pressure Plate Bolts	26
CKP Sensor Bolt	89①
CMP Sensor Bolt	89①
Crankshaft Pulley To Crankshaft Bolt	④
Crankshaft Rear Seal Retainer Bolts	89①
Cylinder Head Bolts	③
ECT Sensor	15
EGR Sensor Bracket	72–108①
EGR Vacuum Regulator Solenoid Bracket	89①
EGR Valve Tube To EGR Valve Nut	26
EGR Valve Tube To Exhaust Manifold	30
Engine Mount Nuts	111
Engine Mount To Block Bolts	52
Exhaust Manifold Nuts	15
Exhaust Manifold Stud To Cylinder Head (SOHC)	7–10
Exhaust Manifold Stud To Cylinder Head (DOHC)	18
Front Brake Caliper Bolts	23
Front Cover Bolts	④
Fuel Rail Studs	89①
Fuel Tank Sender Unit Bolts	89①
Heater Hose Fitting Studs To Manifold (DOHC)	18
IAC Valve	89①
Ignition Coil Bolts	53①
Ignition Coil Cover Bolts	89①
Intake Manifold Bolts To Cylinder Head	18
Oil Dipstick Tube Bolt	89①
Oil Filter (SOHC)	11
Oil Filter (DOHC)	37
Oil Filter Adapter Bolts	18
Oil Filter Adapter Insert	43
Oil Pan Drain Plug	19
Oil Pan Mounting Bolts	②
Oil Pump Screen Cover & Tube To Main Cap Stud Spacer Bolt	18
Oil Pump Screen Cover & Tube To Pump Bolt	89①
Oil Pump To Block Bolt	89①
Power Steering Pump To Block Bolts	18
RFI Capacitor Nut	89①
Serpentine Belt Idler Pulley	18
Serpentine Belt Tensioner Bolts	18
Spark Plugs	13
Subframe Bolts	85
TBI Unit Bolts	⑤
Throttle Cable Bracket Bolts	89①
Torque Converter Nuts	18
Transmission Shift Lever Bolts	27
Transmission Shift Lever Inner Boot Bolts	89①
Transmission Shift Lever Plate To Transmission Bolts	13
Valve Cover Bolts & Studs	89①
Water Bypass Tube	30
Water Bypass Tube Bracket Bolt	18
Water Outlet Adapter	18
Water Pump Pulley Bolts	18
Water Pump To Block Bolts	18

Continued

TIGHTENING SPECIFICATIONS—Continued

Component	Torque/Ft. Lbs.
1999–2000	
Wheel Lug Nuts	95

① — Inch pounds.
② — Refer to "Oil Pan, Replace" for tightening procedures.
③ — Refer to "Cylinder Head, Replace" for tightening procedures.
④ — Refer to "Front Cover, Replace" for tightening procedures.
⑤ — Refer to "Intake Manifold, Replace" for tightening procedures.

Clutch & Manual Transmission

NOTE: On Air Bag Equipped Models, Refer To " Air Bag System Precautions" Located In The Front Of This Manual For System Disarming & Arming Procedures.

NOTE: Refer To "Computer Relearn Procedures " Located In The Front Of This Manual For Computer Relearn Procedures.

INDEX

PRECAUTIONS

AIR BAG SYSTEMS

Refer to "Air Bag System Precautions" in front of this manual for system disarming and arming procedures.

BATTERY GROUND CABLE

Prior to service, disconnect battery ground cable and isolate as required.

ADJUSTMENTS

CLUTCH PEDAL

1997-98

A self-adjusting type clutch mechanism is used. Adjust mechanism consists of a spring-loaded ratchet quadrant attached to clutch cable. To adjust clutch pedal, grasp clutch pedal and pull upward, then slowly depress clutch pedal. If a click is heard during procedure, an adjustment was required and has been accomplished. This procedure should be performed at least every 5000 miles.

1999-2000

On these models a self-adjusting type clutch mechanism is used. It automatically adjusts itself to compensate for clutch plate wear. No periodic attention is required, although if the brake or clutch pedal are being replaced their bushings should be lubricated with a light film of clean engine oil.

CLUTCH PEDAL POSITION (CPP) SWITCH

The clutch pedal position switch is self-adjusting. Press the clutch pedal to the floor to reset.

CLUTCH

REPLACE

1997-98

The clutch pedal must be lifted to disengage adjusting mechanism during clutch release lever cable installation. Failure to do so will result in damage to the self-adjuster mechanism.

Under no circumstances should a prying instrument such as a screwdriver or a pry bar be used to install or remove the clutch release lever cable from the clutch and brake pedal pivot shaft.

Refer to **Fig. 1** during clutch replacement.

Removal

1. Lift clutch pedal to upper most position to disengage clutch and brake pedal pivot shaft.
2. Push clutch and brake pedal pivot shaft forward and unhook clutch release lever cable from clutch and brake pedal pivot shaft and allow it to slowly swing rearward.
3. Raise and support vehicle.
4. Remove clutch release lever dust shield.
5. Disconnect clutch release lever cable from clutch release shaft.
6. Remove retaining clip, then clutch release lever cable from flywheel housing.
7. Remove starter motor from flywheel housing, then engine rear plate to front lower flywheel housing bolts.
8. Remove transmission as outlined under "Transmission, Replace."
9. Remove flywheel housing back just far enough to clear clutch pressure plate, then remove housing.
10. Remove clutch release shaft from flywheel housing by pulling it through window in flywheel housing until retainer spring disengages from pivot.

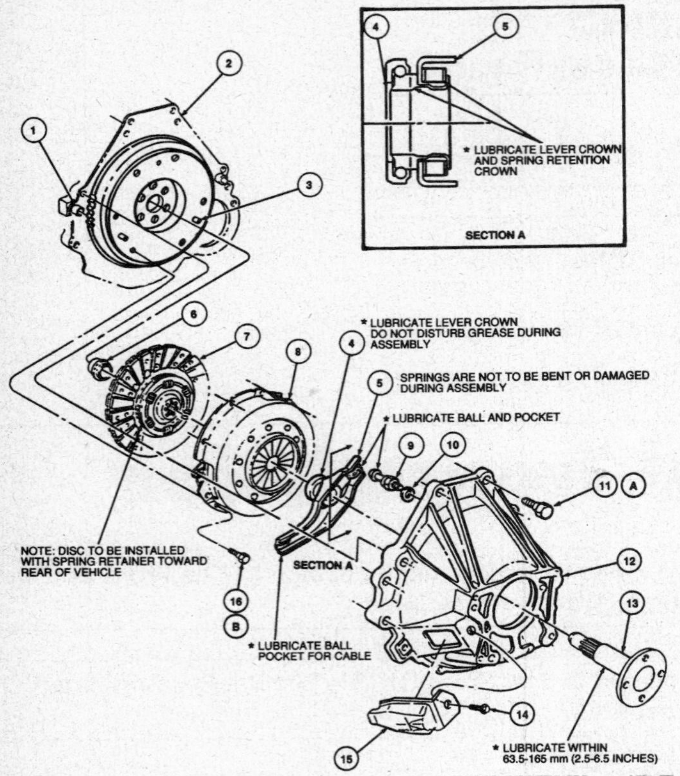

FM5049400071010X

Fig. 1 Clutch disc & pressure plate replacement (Part 1 of 2). 1997–98

Item	Description
1	Flywheel Housing to Block Dowel (2 Req'd)
2	Rear Face of Block and Flywheel (Part of 6010)
3	Flywheel-To-Clutch Pressure Plate Dowel (3 Req'd)
4	Clutch Release Hub and Bearing
5	Clutch Release Lever
6	Pilot Bearing (Install with Seal Toward Rear of Vehicle)
7	Clutch Disc
8	Clutch Pressure Plate
9	Clutch Release Lever Stud
10	Washer
11	Bolt (6 Req'd) (3.8L) Bolt (6 Req'd) (4.6L)

Item	Description
12	Flywheel Housing
13	Main Drive Gear Bearing Retainer
14	Bolt
15	Clutch Release Lever Dust Shield (Installed After Cable Assy)
16	Screw and Washer Assy (6 Req'd) (3.8L) Screw and Washer Assy (6 Req'd) (4.6L)

FM5049400071020X

Fig. 1 Clutch disc & pressure plate replacement (Part 2 of 2). 1997–98

11. Remove clutch release hub and bearing from clutch release shaft.
12. Loosen six clutch pressure plate bolts evenly to release spring tension gradually and avoid distorting clutch pressure plate. If same clutch pressure plate is to be installed, mark plate and flywheel so pressure plate can be installed in its original position.
13. Remove clutch pressure plate and clutch disc from flywheel.

Installation

1. Position clutch disc and pressure plate assembly on flywheel, noting following:
   a. Three flywheel housing to block dowels on flywheel must be properly aligned with clutch pressure plate. Bent, damaged or missing dowels must be replaced.
   b. Start threading clutch pressure plate bolts into place but do not tighten.
   c. Avoid touching clutch disc face, dropping components or contaminating them with oil or grease.
   d. Align clutch disc using suitable alignment tool inserted in pilot bearing.
   e. To avoid clutch pressure plate distortion, alternately tighten bolts a few turns at a time, until they are all tight, then tighten to specifications.
2. Install transmission to flywheel housing.
3. Install engine rear plate to flywheel front lower housing bolts, then connect clutch release cable to flywheel housing and connect retaining clip.
4. Connect clutch release lever cable to clutch release shaft, then install clutch release lever dust shield.
5. Install starter motor as outlined in "Electrical" section.
6. Lower vehicle, then install clutch release lever cable as follows:
   a. Lift clutch pedal to disengage clutch and brake pedal pivot shaft.
   b. Push clutch and brake pedal pivot shaft forward and hook end of clutch release lever cable over rear of clutch and brake pedal pivot shaft.
7. Cycle clutch pedal several times to adjust clutch release lever cable.

1999–2000

Removal

Refer to **Figs. 2 and 3** when servicing the clutch components.

1. Remove transmission as outlined under appropriate "Transmission, Replace" procedure in this section.
2. Mark pressure plate and flywheel to ease installation.
3. **Loosen pressure plate to flywheel bolts evenly,** then remove them completely.
4. Remove pressure plate and disc.

Installation

1. Clean flywheel with an alcohol based-solvent to remove all traces of oil film. **Do not use a petroleum based solvent.**
2. Using clutch alignment tool No. T74P-7137-K, or equivalent, align clutch disc to flywheel.
3. Install pressure plate using alignment tool and alignment marks made during removal.
4. **On models equipped with 3.8L engine, torque** pressure plate to flywheel bolts to 24 ft. lbs. in sequence illustrated in **Fig. 4.**
5. **On models equipped with 4.6L SOHC engine, torque** pressure plate to flywheel bolts to 16 ft. lbs. in sequence illustrated in **Fig. 4.**
6. **On models equipped with 4.6L DOHC engine, torque** pressure plate to flywheel bolts to 33 ft. lbs. in sequence illustrated in **Fig. 4,** then rotate them an additional 60°.
7. **On all models,** remove alignment tool.
8. Install transmission.

TRANSMISSION

REPLACE

1997–98

T50D Transmission

1. Working inside vehicle, remove gearshift lever boot and console panel gear shift plate.
2. Remove two gearshift lever retaining bolts, then the lever and isolator from transmission stub shaft.
3. Raise and safely support vehicle on a hoist, then mark driveshaft for installation reference.
4. Disconnect driveshaft from rear axle universal joint flange, then slide driveshaft off transmission output and fifth gear drive shaft and install extension housing seal replacer tool No. T61L-7657-A, or equivalent, into extension housing to prevent lubricant leakage.

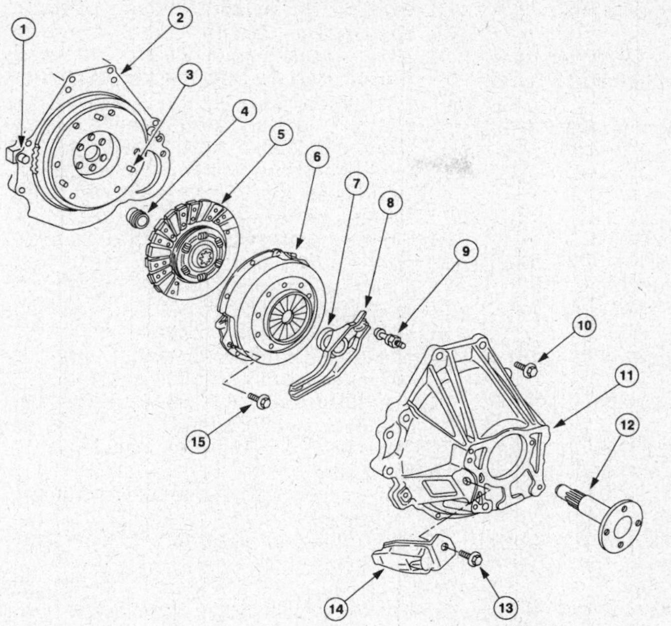

Fig. 2 Exploded view of clutch assembly (1-dowel, 2-engine block, 3-dowel, 4-pilot bearing, 5-clutch disc, 6-pressure plate, 7-release bearing, 8-release fork, 9-stud, 10-bolt, 11-bellhousing, 12-main drive gear bearing retainer, 13-bolt, 14-dust boot, 15-screw & washer assembly). 1999–2000 w/3.8L engine

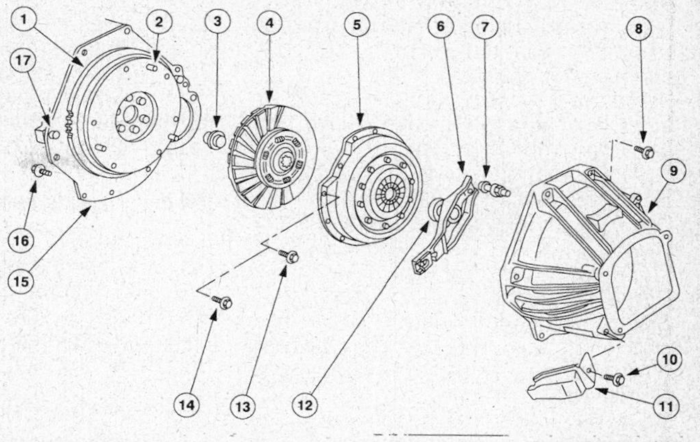

Fig. 3 Exploded view of clutch assembly (1-flywheel, 2-dowel, 3-pilot bearing, 4-clutch disc, 5-pressure plate, 6-release fork, 7-stud, 8-bolt, 9-bellhousing, 10-bolt, 11-dust boot, 12-release bearing, 13 & 14-bolts, 15-engine block, 16-bolt, 17-dowel). 1999–2000 w/4.6L engine

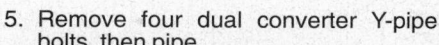

5. Remove four dual converter Y-pipe bolts, then pipe.
6. Remove two rear transmission support to rear engine support nuts, then bolts.
7. Support engine and transmission with transmission jack.
8. Remove two rear engine support bolt nuts.
9. Remove rear engine support bolts, then raise jack slightly and remove rear engine support.
10. Disconnect wiring harness from back-up lamp switch.
11. Remove speedometer cable bolt, then speedometer drive gear from transmission.
12. Remove four transmission to flywheel housing bolts.
13. Move transmission and jack rearward until transmission input shaft clears flywheel housing. If required, lower engine enough to obtain clearance for transmission removal.
14. Reverse procedure to install, noting the following:
    a. Ensure transmission and flywheel housing mounting surfaces are free of dirt, paint and burrs.
    b. Fill transmission with specified transmission fluid. Apply pipe sealant with Teflon D8AZ-19554-A, or equivalent, to transmission case plug in a clockwise direction prior to installation.
    c. Tighten bolts to specifications.
    d. Lower vehicle, then inspect shift and crossover motion for full shift engagement and smooth crossover operation.

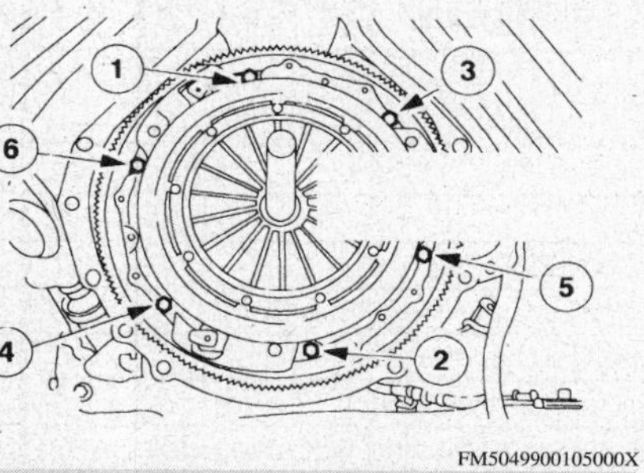

Fig. 4 Pressure plate to flywheel bolt tightening sequence. 1999–2000

T45 Transmission

1. Working inside vehicle, remove gearshift lever boot, then the console panel gear shift plate.
2. Remove two gearshift lever retaining bolts, then the lever and isolator from transmission stub shaft.
3. Raise and support vehicle.
4. Remove driveshaft from rear axle and slide out of transmission output shaft. Mark driveshaft so that it may be installed in same position.
5. Install extension housing seal replacer tool No. T96P-7127-A, or equivalent into extension housing to prevent fluid loss.
6. Remove eight dual converter H-pipe retaining bolts, then the H-pipe.
7. Remove retaining bolt and clutch release lever dust shield, then disconnect clutch cable.
8. Remove two rear transmission support to transmission support crossmember retaining nuts, then support engine and transmission with a suitable jack.
9. Remove two nuts from rear engine support bolts, then raise jack slightly and remove transmission support crossmember.
10. Disconnect wiring harness from back-up lamp switch, then the electrical connector from speedometer sensor on extension housing.
11. Disconnect battery cable and ignition wire from starter motor.
12. Remove three starter motor retaining bolts, then the starter.
13. Support cylinder blocks and balancer.
14. Remove seven clutch housing to cylinder block retaining bolts.
15. Move transmission and jack rearward until input shaft clears clutch pressure plate. If required, lower engine to obtain clearance for transmission removal.
16. Reverse procedures to install. Tighten bolts to specifications.

1999–2000

T50D Transmission

1. Lift up on clutch pedal, then secure it in place.
2. Remove shift lever knob.
3. Remove console panel gearshift plate, then lift boot up and over the lever.
4. Remove shift lever retaining bolts, then the lever.
5. Raise and safely support vehicle on a hoist.
6. Disconnect HO2S electrical connectors.
7. Remove lefthand and righthand exhaust pipe to manifold and muffler nuts.

8. Remove dual converter Y-pipe.
9. Mark driveshaft at companion flange and pinion flange, then at the slip yoke and transmission tail shaft.
10. Disconnect back-up lamp switch electrical connector, then the wiring harness from the transmission.
11. Remove starter motor as outlined in "Electrical" section.
12. Disconnect OSS sensor electrical connector, then the wiring harness from the transmission.
13. Remove clutch release lever cover.
14. Disconnect clutch release cable from clutch release fork. **Do not depress clutch pedal while transmission is removed.**
15. Remove clutch cable retainer, then disconnect cable at transmission.
16. If transmission will be disassembled, drain lubricant into an approved container.
17. Support transmission with a suitable jack.
18. Remove crossmember mounting bolts, then the crossmember.
19. Remove inspection cover.
20. Lower the transmission, then remove upper bellhousing bolts.
21. Carefully lower the transmission and remove from vehicle.
22. Reverse procedure to install, noting the following:
    a. Align driveshaft marks made during removal.
    b. Tighten all fasteners to specifications.
    c. Ensure all electrical connectors and transmission drain plug are securely in place.
    d. Inspect transmission lubricant level and fill as required.

T45 Transmission

1. Remove shift lever knob.
2. Remove console panel gearshift plate, then lift boot up and over the lever.
3. Remove shift lever retaining bolts, then the lever.
4. Raise and safely support vehicle on a hoist.
5. Disconnect HO2S electrical connectors.
6. Remove lefthand and righthand exhaust pipe to manifold and muffler nuts.
7. Remove dual converter H-pipe.
8. Mark driveshaft at companion flange and pinion flange, then at the slip yoke and transmission tail shaft.
9. Disconnect back-up lamp switch electrical connector, then the wiring harness from the transmission.
10. Remove starter motor as outlined in "Electrical" section.
11. Disconnect Output Shaft Speed (OSS) sensor electrical connector, then the wiring harness from the transmission.
12. Remove clutch release lever cover.
13. Disconnect clutch release cable from clutch release fork. **Do not depress clutch pedal while transmission is removed.**
14. Remove clutch cable retainer, then disconnect cable at transmission.
15. If transmission will be disassembled, drain lubricant into an approved container.
16. Support transmission with a suitable jack.
17. Remove crossmember mounting bolts, then the crossmember.
18. Remove inspection cover.
19. Lower the transmission, then remove upper bellhousing bolts.
20. Carefully lower the transmission and remove from vehicle.
21. Reverse procedure to install, noting the following:
    a. Align driveshaft marks made during removal.
    b. Tighten all fasteners to specifications.
    c. Ensure all electrical connectors and transmission drain plug are securely in place.
    d. Inspect transmission lubricant level and fill as required. Apply Teflon pipe sealant part No. D8AZ-19554-A, or equivalent to filler plug threads.

TIGHTENING SPECIFICATIONS

Component	Torque/Ft. Lbs.
1997–98	
Driveshaft Nuts	70–95
Dual Converter H- Or Y-Pipe	20–30
Flywheel Housing To Case Retaining Bolts (T45)	15–25
Flywheel housing To Cylinder Block Bolts	28–38
Gearshift Lever To Transmission	20–25
Transmission Extension Housing Retaining Bolts (T45)	15–25
Transmission Extension Housing Retaining Bolts (T50)	45–64
Transmission To Flywheel Housing Retaining Bolts (T50)	45–64
Transmission Extension Housing Support Retaining Nut	25–35
Transmission Support Bolts	35–50
1999–2000	
Back-Up Lamp Switch	27
Bellhousing To Block Bolts	55
Bellhousing To Case Bolts (T45)	20
Case Cover To Case Bolts (T50D)	108②
Companion To Pinion Flanges	83
Crossmember To Frame Bolts	30
Crossmember To Transmission Support Bolts	43
Drain Plug	17
Dual Converter Pipe To Manifold Nuts	30
Dual Converter Pipe To Muffler Bolts	26

Continued

TIGHTENING SPECIFICATIONS—Continued

Component	Torque/Ft. Lbs.
1999–2000	
Filler Plug	13
HO2S Bracket Nut (4.6L)	18
Inner Shift Boot To Floor Pan	89②
Inspection Cover Bolts	20
OSS Sensor Bolt	89②
Pressure Plate To Flywheel Bolts	①
Shift Lever To Extension Housing	13
Shift Lever To Stub Shaft	27
Starter Ground Cable Nut (3.8L)	17
Starter Mounting Bolts	17
Starter Solenoid "B" Terminal Nut	108②
Starter Solenoid Terminal Nut	53②
Tailshaft Housing To Case	40

①— Refer to "Clutch, Replace" for tightening procedure.
②— Inch lbs.

Rear Axle & Suspension

INDEX

DESCRIPTION

EXCEPT 1999–2000 COBRA

This rear axle, **Fig. 1** is an integral design hypoid with center line of pinion set below center line of ring gear. Semi-floating axle shafts are retained in housing by ball bearings and bearing retainers at axle ends.

Differential is mounted on two opposed tapered roller bearings which are retained in housing by removable caps. Differential bearing preload and drive gear backlash is adjusted by nuts located behind each differential bearing cup.

Drive pinion assembly is mounted on two opposed tapered roller bearings. Pinion bearing preload is adjusted by a collapsible spacer on pinion shaft. Pinion and ring gear tooth contact is adjusted by shims between rear bearing cone and pinion gear.

1999–2000 COBRA

On these models the hypoid type axle, **Fig. 2,** has an 8.8 inch ring gear and a one piece differential case. Two opposed pinion bearings support the drive pinion gear in the differential housing. Two pinion gears engage the differential side gears with their halfshaft splines.

REAR AXLE

REPLACE

EXCEPT 1999–2000 COBRA

1. Raise and support vehicle, then position safety stands under rear frame crossmember.
2. Drain lubricant from axle by removing axle housing cover.
3. Remove wheels, rear disc brake calipers and rear disc brake rotors as outlined under "Disc Brakes."
4. Remove differential pinion shaft lock pin from differential pinion shaft, then the pinion shaft.
5. Carefully remove rear brake anti-lock sensor. **Damage to rear brake anti-lock sensor may occur if sensor is not removed before axle shaft.**
6. Push axle shafts inward to remove rear axle shaft U-washers, then remove axle shafts.
7. Remove brake junction block to axle housing cover bolt, then brake hose support bracket from clips and position aside.
8. Disconnect driveshaft at rear axle universal joint flange and wire it to underbody. Mark driveshaft centering socket yoke and rear axle universal joint flange.
9. Support rear axle housing with jackstands or hoist, then disengage rear brake hose from rear brake hose to rear axle housing clips.
10. Disconnect rear axle housing vent from rear axle housing. Some rear axle housing vents may be secured to rear axle housing through brake junction block. At assembly apply threadlock

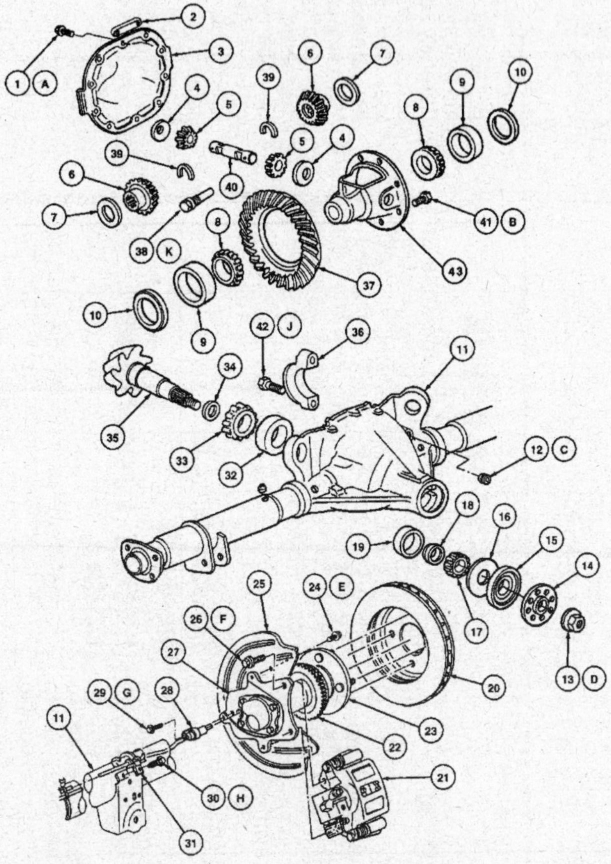

Fig. 1 Exploded view of integral rear axle (Part 1 of 2). Less Traction-Lok or 1999–2000 Cobra

Item		Description
1		Bolt
2		Rear Axle Brake Line Clip
3		Axle Housing Cover
4		Differential Pinion Thrust Washer
5		Differential Pinion Gear
6		Differential Side Gear
7		Differential Side Gear Thrust Washer
8		Differential Bearing
9		Differential Bearing Cup
10		Differential Bearing Shim
11		Rear Axle Housing
12		Filler Plug
13		Pinion Nut
14		Rear Axle Universal Joint Flange
15		Rear Axle Drive Pinion Seal
16		Rear Axle Drive Pinion Shaft Oil Slinger
17		Differential Pinion Bearing
18		Differential Drive Pinion Collapsible Spacer
19		Differential Drive Pinion Bearing Cup
20		Rear Disc Brake Rotor
21		Rear Disc Brake Caliper
22		Rear Brake Anti-Lock Sensor Indicator
23		Axle Shaft Flange (Part of 4234)
24		Bolt (3 Req'd)
25		Rear Wheel Disc Brake Shield
26		Caliper Anchor Bolt
27		Left Hand Rear Disc Brake Adapter
		Right Hand Rear Disc Brake Adapter

Item		Description
28		Rear Brake Anti-Lock Sensor
29		Bolt
30		Bolt
31		Clip
32		Rear Axle Pinion Bearing Cup
33		Differential Pinion Bearing
34		Drive Pinion Bearing Adjustment Shim
35		Drive Pinion (Part of 4209)
36		Bearing Cap (Part of 4010)
37		Ring Gear (Part of 4209)
38		Differential Pinion Shaft Lock Pin
39		U-Washer
40		Differential Pinion Shaft
41		Rear Axle Differential Gear Case Bolt
42		Bolt (Part of 4010)
43		Differential Case
A		Tighten to 24-38 N·m (18-28 Lb-Ft)
B		Tighten to 95-115 N·m (70-85 Lb-Ft)
C		Tighten to 20-41 N·m (15-30 Lb-Ft)
D		Tighten to 190 N·m (140 Lb-Ft)
E		Tighten to 8-12 N·m (6-9 Lb-Ft)
F		Tighten to 87-119 N·m (64-87.7 Lb-Ft)
G		Tighten to 5-7 N·m (40-60 Lb-In)
H		Tighten to 10-14 N·m (7-10 Lb-Ft)
J		Tighten to 102-122 N·m (75-90 Lb-Ft)
K		Tighten to 20-41 N·m (15-30 Lb-Ft)

FM3039400270020X

Fig. 1 Exploded view of integral rear axle (Part 2 of 2). Less Traction-Lok or 1999–2000 Cobra

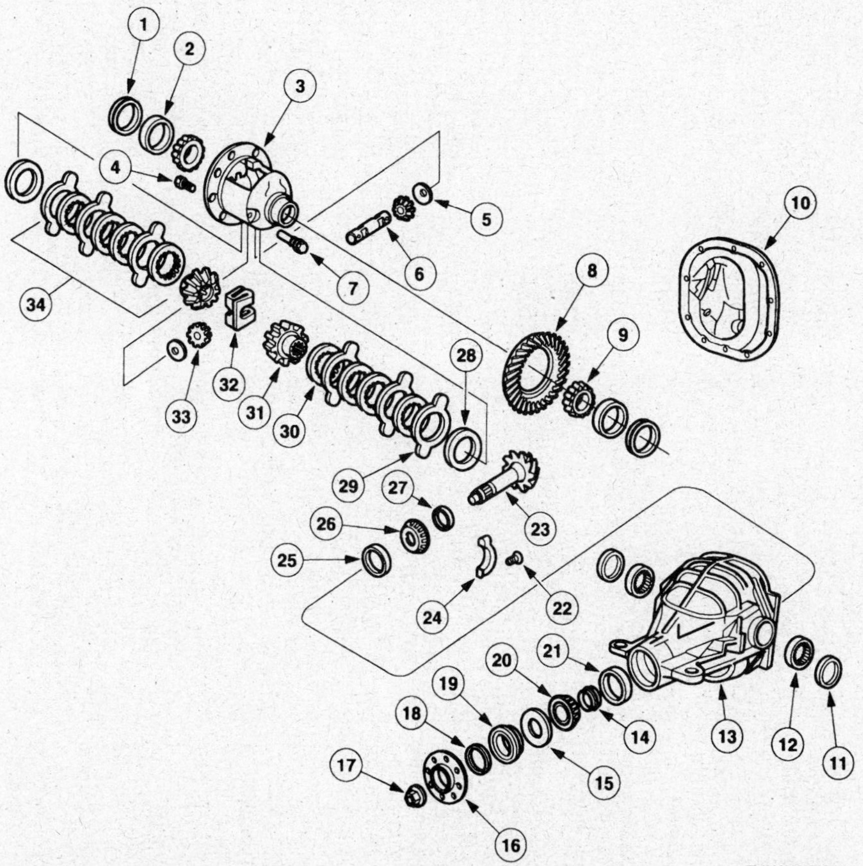

FM3039900337010X

Fig. 2 Exploded view of rear axle (Part 1 of 2). 1999–2000 Cobra

Item	Description
1	Differential bearing shim
2	Differential bearing cup
3	Differential case
4	Differential ring gear case bolt
5	Differential pinion thrust washer
6	Differential pinion shaft
7	Differential pinion shaft lock bolt
8	Differential ring gear
9	Differential bearing
10	Differential housing cover
11	Inboard CV joint stub shaft pilot bearing housing seal
12	Inboard CV joint stub shaft pilot bearing
13	Differential housing
14	Differential drive pinion collapsible spacer
15	Rear axle drive pinion shaft oil slinger
16	Rear axle pinion flange

Item	Description
17	Pinion nut
18	Drive pinion oil seal deflector
19	Rear axle drive pinion seal
20	Pinion bearing
21	Differential drive pinion bearing cup
22	Bolt
23	Drive pinion gear
24	Differential bearing cap
25	Rear axle pinion bearing cup
26	Pinion bearing
27	Drive pinion bearing adjustment shim
28	Rear axle differential clutch shim
29	Clutch plate
30	Clutch disc
31	Differential side gear
32	Differential clutch spring
33	Differential pinion gear
34	Differential clutch pack

FM3039900337020X

Fig. 2 Exploded view of rear axle (Part 2 of 2). 1999–2000 Cobra

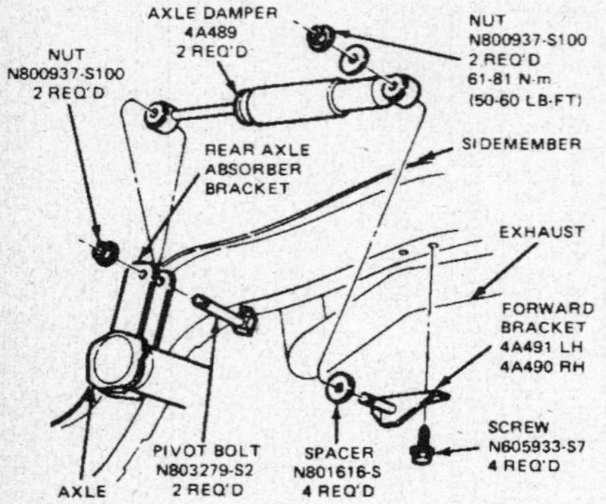

FM2039100027000X

Fig. 3 Axle damper assembly

and sealer E0AZ-19554-AA, or equivalent, to thread to ensure retention.

11. Disconnect lower shock absorber studs from rear shock absorber lower mounting bracket on rear axle housing, then remove rear suspension arm and bushing nuts and bolts from axle housing rear bracket mountings.
12. Lower rear axle housing assembly until rear springs are released, then lift out rear springs.
13. Remove rear suspension lower arm to rear axle housing nuts and bolts, then disconnect both rear suspension lower arms from rear axle housing.
14. Lower rear axle housing and remove it from vehicle.
15. Reverse procedure to install, noting the following:
    a. Installing rear wheel bearing or inner wheel bearing oil seal without proper tool may result in an early rear wheel bearing or inner wheel bearing oil seal failure. If inner wheel bearing oil seal becomes cocked in bore during installation, remove it and install a new one.
    b. Differential pinion shaft lock pin must be tightened to specification using stud and bearing mount tool No. E0AZ-19554-BA, or equivalent.
    c. Ensure machined surfaces on both axle housing cover and rear axle housing are clean before installing new silicone sealant. Inside of axle must be covered when cleaning machined surface to prevent axle contamination. Tighten axle housing cover bolt in crosswise pattern to ensure uniform draw on axle housing cover.

1999–2000 COBRA

1. Park vehicle at curb height and on level ground.
2. Mark rear shock absorber positions relative to their upper sleeves.
3. Raise and safely support vehicle.
4. Remove rear wheels and tires.
5. Remove exhaust system.
6. Note transverse bar fastener orientation at this time.
7. Remove pinion nose crossmember mounting nuts, then the crossmember.

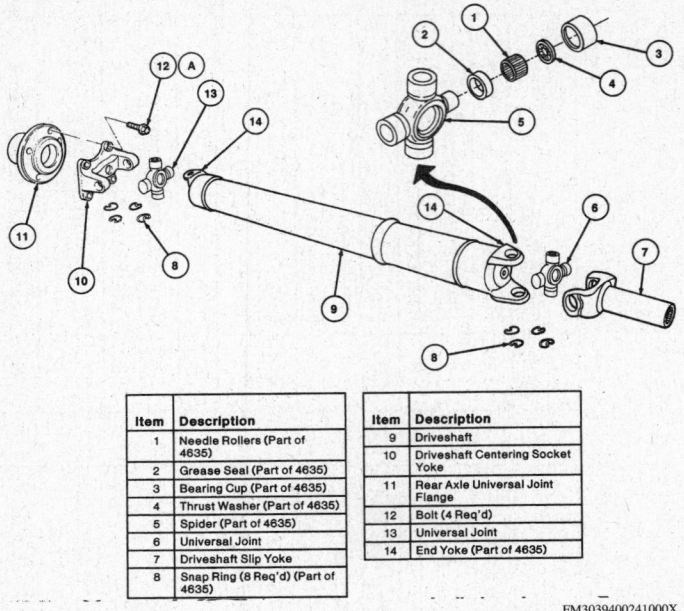

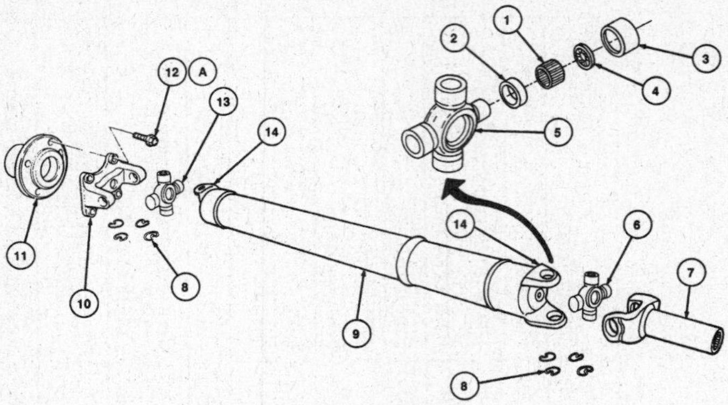

Item	Description
1	Needle Rollers (Part of 4635)
2	Grease Seal (Part of 4635)
3	Bearing Cup (Part of 4635)
4	Thrust Washer (Part of 4635)
5	Spider (Part of 4635)
6	Universal Joint
7	Driveshaft Slip Yoke
8	Snap Ring (8 Req'd) (Part of 4635)

Item	Description
9	Driveshaft
10	Driveshaft Centering Socket Yoke
11	Rear Axle Universal Joint Flange
12	Bolt (4 Req'd)
13	Universal Joint
14	End Yoke (Part of 4635)

FM3039400241000X

Fig. 4 Driveshaft & universal joint components. w/single Cardan type U-joint

8. Mark driveshaft companion flange to pinion flange orientation.
9. Remove and discard companion flange to pinion flange bolts, then position the driveshaft aside with suitable wire or rope.
10. Disconnect parking brake cables and conduits from parking brake lever and calipers.
11. Separate the parking brake cables and conduits from knuckles.
12. Remove rear brake rotors.
13. Remove rear brake calipers and support brackets from knuckles as assemblies. Position calipers aside with suitable wire or rope.
14. Remove rear brake anti-lock sensors and position them aside.
15. Support lower suspension arm and bushing with a suitable jack stand.
16. Remove and discard lower suspension arm nuts and bolts.
17. Remove and discard toe link cotter pins and nuts.
18. Using separator tool No. T64P-3590-F, or equivalent, disconnect toe links from knuckles.
19. Mark cam bolt orientations relative to upper control arms and bushings.
20. Remove and discard lower control arm bushing nuts and bolts.
21. Disconnect knuckles from lower control arms.
22. Mark new upper control arm cam bolts in same position as old ones for future reference.
23. Remove and discard upper control arm bushing nuts and bolts.
24. Disconnect knuckles from upper control arms.
25. Using halfshaft removal tool No. 205-475, or equivalent, exert just enough pressure to overcome the circlip, then separate CV joint from side gear. **Ensure tool fork crowns face away from differential housing. Position the tool properly between CV joint and housing to avoid damaging differential seal.**
26. Install seal protector tool No. 205-461, or equivalent.
27. Carefully remove halfshaft and knuckle assemblies from vehicle.
28. Install differential plug tool No. T89P-4850-B, or equivalent into housing bores.
29. Support differential housing with a suitable transmission jack.
30. Remove differential to frame mounting bolts, then carefully lower the axle assembly from the vehicle. Avoid damaging vent hose.
31. Reverse procedure to install, noting the following:
    a. Inspect differential mounting bushings and replace as required. Remove by hand only.
    b. Ensure all orientation marks made during removal are properly aligned.
    c. Install seal protector tool No. 205-461, or equivalent before install halfshafts.
    d. Ensure inboard CV joints cannot be pulled out of differential side gears. If this is possible, their circlips have not seated properly. Push in on joints until circlips are fully engaged.
    e. Ensure transverse bar is in place and bolt passes through it. **Do not tighten until vehicle is back on ground and shock absorber marks are aligned as noted during removal.**
    f. Install new cam bolts and nuts at control arms and bushings. **Do not tighten them until vehicle is back**

on ground and shock absorber marks are aligned as noted during removal.

g. Apply high temperature nickel anti-seize lubricant part No. F6AZ-9L494-AA, or equivalent to rear brake anti-lock sensors at their axle housing contact points.
h. Tighten all fasteners to specifications.
i. Inspect wheel alignment and adjust as required.

REAR AXLE SHAFT

REPLACE

EXCEPT 1999–2000 COBRA

1. Raise and support vehicle, then remove rear wheel and tire assembly.
2. Remove brake drum as outlined under "Drum Brakes " section or rear disc brake calipers and rear disc brake rotors as outlined under "Disc Brakes."
3. Clean all dirt from carrier cover area with wire brush and/or cloth.
4. Remove axle housing cover and drain lubricant from axle.
5. Remove differential pinion shaft lock pin and differential pinion shaft.
6. Carefully remove rear brake anti-lock sensor.
7. Push flanged end of axle shaft toward center of vehicle, then remove C-lock from button end of axle shaft assembly.
8. Remove axle shaft from housing. Do not damage oil seal.
9. Reverse procedure to install.

1999–2000 COBRA

Refer to "Rear Axle, Replace" for this procedure.

AXLE DAMPER

REPLACE

1. Raise vehicle and support rear axle.
2. Remove rear wheel, then axle damper front retaining pivot bolt, **Fig. 3.**
3. Remove axle damper rear retaining nut, then the driveline vibration damper and washers.
4. Reverse procedure to install.

PROPELLER SHAFT

REPLACE

EXCEPT 1999–2000 COBRA

1. To maintain balance, mark relationship of rear driveshaft yoke and drive pinion flange of axle if alignment marks are not visible.
2. Disconnect rear U-joint from companion flange, **Fig. 4.** Wrap tape around loose bearing caps to prevent them from falling off spider. Pull driveshaft toward rear of vehicle until slip yoke clears transmission extension housing and seal. Install suitable plug into extension housing to prevent lubricant leakage.
3. Lubricate slip yoke splines with suitable grease, then remove plug from transmission extension.
4. Inspect housing seal for damage and replace if required.
5. Align slip yoke index mark with transmission output shaft mark and install driveshaft assembly. Do not allow slip yoke assembly to bottom on output shaft with excessive force.
6. Install driveshaft so index mark on rear flange is aligned with index mark on axle companion flange to ensure original driveline balance. When installing new driveshaft assembly, align factory made yellow paint mark at rear of driveshaft tube with factory made yellow paint mark on axle companion flange.
7. **Torque** flange bolts 70–95 ft. lbs.

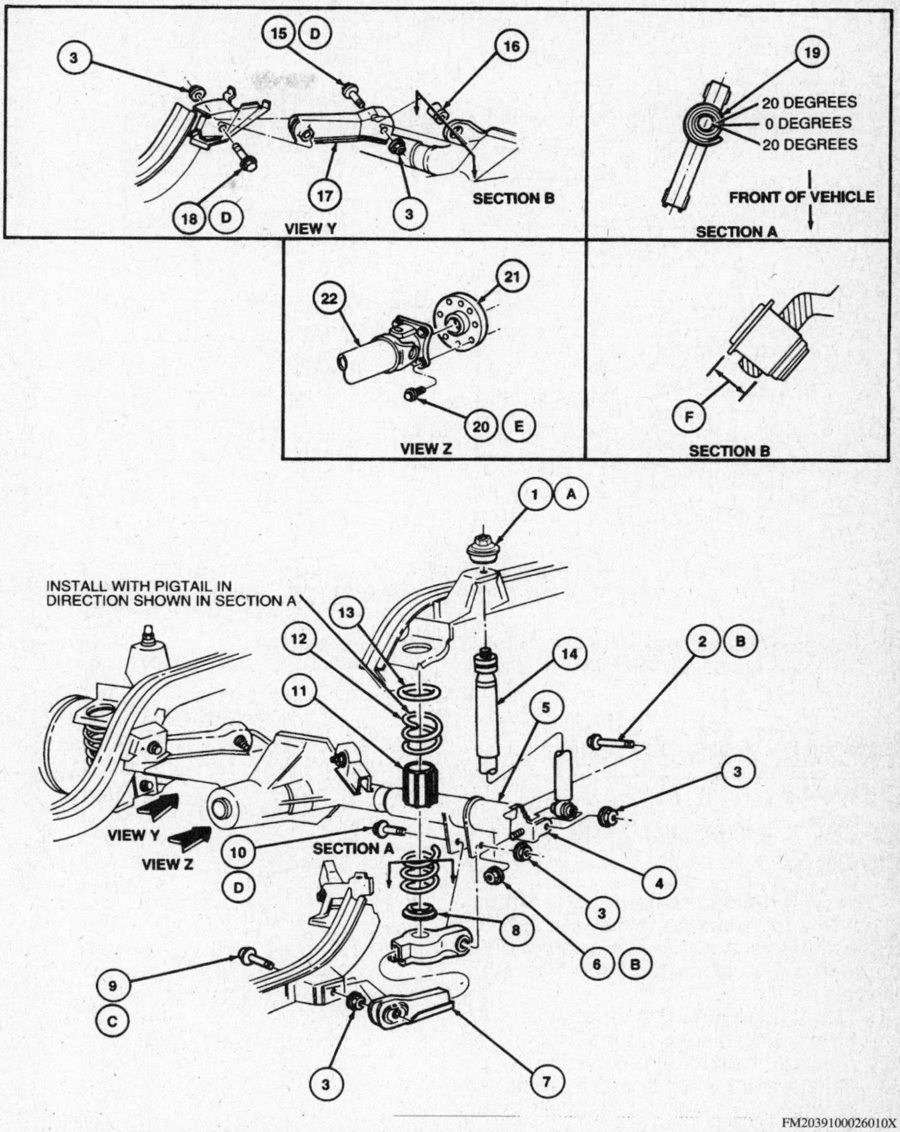

Fig. 5 Exploded view of rear suspension (Part 1 of 2). Except 1999–2000 Cobra

1999–2000 COBRA

1. Raise and safely support vehicle.
2. Remove exhaust hangers from rubber mounts.
3. Remove two attaching nuts on left-hand side exhaust flange.
4. Lower the muffler pipe to clear the flange, then move muffler assembly forward to disconnect third exhaust hanger.
5. Mark driveshaft companion flange to pinion flange orientation.
6. Mark driveshaft yoke to transmission tailshaft orientation.
7. Remove and discard companion flange to pinion flange bolts.
8. Lower the rear end of driveshaft until it clears axle housing.
9. Carefully pull driveshaft rearward out of transmission.

Item	Description
1	Nut, Insulator Assy (Part of 18198)
2	Bolt (2 Req'd)
3	Nut (2 Req'd)
4	Rear Shock Absorber Lower Mounting Bracket (2 Req'd)
5	Axle
6	Nut (2 Req'd)
7	Rear Suspension Lower Arm (2 Req'd)
8	Rear Spring Insulator (2 Req'd)
9	Bolt (2 Req'd)
10	Bolt
11	Rear Spring Damper (2 Req'd)
12	Rear Spring (2 Req'd)
13	Rear Spring Insulator (2 Req'd)
14	Rear Shock Absorber (2 Req'd)
15	Bolt (2 Req'd)
16	Rear Suspension Arm Bushing (2 Req'd)
17	Rear Suspension Arm and Bushing (2 Req'd)
18	Bolt (2 Req'd)
19	Pigtail
20	Bolt (4 Req'd)
21	Rear Axle Universal Joint Flange
22	Driveshaft
A	Tighten to 34-46 N·m (25-34 Lb-Ft)
B	Tighten to 76-103 N·m (57-75 Lb-Ft)
C	Tighten to 98-132 N·m (71-79 Lb-Ft)
D	Tighten to 98-132 N·m (71-79 Lb-Ft)
E	Tighten to 56-77 N·m (41-56 Lb-Ft)
F	Install to 35.5-36.5 mm (1.39-1.43 In)

FM2039100026020X

Fig. 5 Exploded view of rear suspension (Part 2 of 2). Except 1999–2000 Cobra

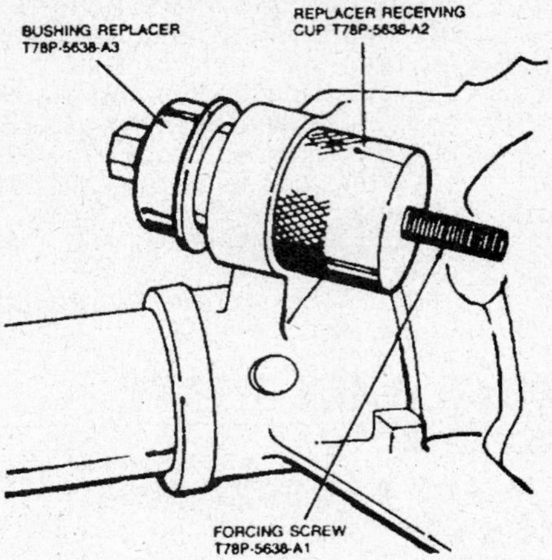

Fig. 6 Upper control arm axle bracket bushing installation. Except 1999–2000 Cobra

10. Reverse procedure to install. Tighten all fasteners to specifications.

SHOCK ABSORBER

REPLACE

EXCEPT 1999–2000 COBRA

These vehicles are equipped with gas pressurized shock absorbers which will extend unassisted. Do not apply heat or flame to shock absorber tube during removal.

1. Open luggage compartment, then, from inside luggage compartment, remove rubber cap, if equipped.
2. Remove nut, washer and insulator assembly from shock absorber upper stud.
3. Raise and support vehicle, then support rear axle.
4. Remove nut, washer and insulator assembly from shock absorber lower stud.
5. From underside of vehicle, compress shock absorber to clear it from hole in upper shock tower.
6. Remove shock absorber.
7. Reverse procedure to install. Tighten bolts to specifications.

1999–2000 COBRA

These vehicles are equipped with gas pressurized shock absorbers which will extend unassisted. Do not apply heat or flame to shock absorber tube during removal.

1. Open the luggage compartment, then position carpet aside.
2. Remove and discard shock absorber retaining nut, washer and insulator assembly.
3. Raise and safely support vehicle.
4. Remove and discard shock absorber lower mounting bolt and nut.

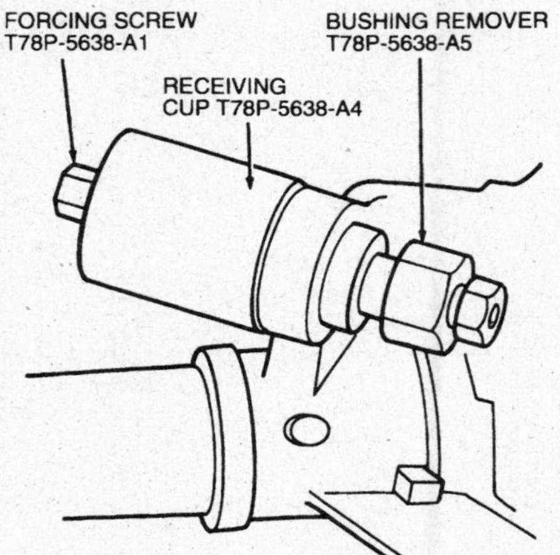

Fig. 7 Upper control arm axle bracket bushing removal. Except 1999–2000 Cobra

5. Remove shock absorber from vehicle, then the insulator and washer from the absorber.
6. Reverse procedure to install, noting the following:
   a. Install a new lower insulator and washer onto shock absorber.
   b. **Ensure hardened washer sits between lower control arm and bushing and the absorber.**
   c. Install a new upper insulator, washer and nut.
   d. Tighten all fasteners to specifications.

COIL SPRING

REPLACE

EXCEPT 1999–2000 COBRA

1. Raise rear of vehicle and support at rear body crossmember.
2. Remove stabilizer bar, if equipped, **Fig. 5.**
3. Lower axle housing until shock absorbers are fully extended. **Axle housing must be supported with suitable jack.**
4. Position suitable jack under lower control arm rear pivot bolt to support control arm, then remove pivot bolt.
5. Carefully lower control arm until spring tension is relieved, then remove coil spring and insulator.
6. Reverse procedure to install. Tighten lower control arm pivot bolt to specifications, with suspension at curb height.

1999–2000 COBRA

1. Raise and safely support vehicle on a hoist.
2. Support No. 1 crossmember with a suitable jack stand.
3. Remove rear tires and wheels.
4. Remove both mufflers.
5. Remove driveshaft as outlined under "Propeller Shaft, Replace" in this section.
6. Disconnect parking brake cables and conduits at parking brake levers, rear brake calipers and rear knuckles.
7. Remove parking brake cable brackets at coil spring seats.
8. Remove rear brake line to axle mounting bolts, then position lines aside.
9. Remove rear wheel speed sensor mounting bolts, then the sensors.
10. Unhook ABS sensor wiring harness at subframe.
11. Support lower control arms and bushings with suitable jack stands.
12. Discard shock absorber lower mounting nuts and bolts.
13. Lower the lower control arms and bushings, then remove jack stands.
14. Using powertrain lift tool No. 014-00765, or equivalent, safely support rear subframe.
15. Remove and discard subframe front mounting nuts.
16. Remove and discard subframe rear

mounting nuts and bolts.
17. Carefully lower the subframe, allowing it to pivot on its front bolts.
18. Remove springs and insulators.
19. Reverse procedure to install, noting the following:
    a. Install a new lower insulator and washer onto shock absorber.
    b. **Ensure hardened washer sits between lower control arm and bushing and the absorber.**
    c. Tighten all fasteners to specifications.
    d. Bleed brake fluid system.
    e. Inspect wheel alignment and adjust as required.

CONTROL ARM

REPLACE

EXCEPT 1999–2000 COBRA

Upper

1. Raise rear of vehicle and support at rear body crossmember.
2. Remove upper control arm rear and front pivot bolts, then the control arm.
3. If control arm axle bracket bushings are to be replaced, refer to **Figs. 6 and 7.**
4. Position upper control arm into side rail bracket, then install front pivot bolt. Do not tighten bolt at this time.
5. Raise rear axle until upper control arm rear pivot bolt hole is aligned with hole in axle housing, then install rear pivot bolt. Do not tighten bolt at this time.
6. Position suspension at curb height. Tighten front pivot bolt to specifications.

Lower

1. Raise and support vehicle, then support body at rear crossmember.
2. Lower hoist until rear shock absorbers are fully extended, then place transmission jack under lower arm to axle pivot bolt. **Rear axle housing must be supported by hoist, transmission jack or jackstands.**
3. Remove and discard lower control arm front pivot bolt and nut, **Fig. 5.**
4. Remove control arm.
5. Reverse procedure to install. Tighten front and rear pivot bolts to specifications.

1999–2000 COBRA

Upper

1. Park vehicle at curb height and on level ground.
2. Mark rear shock absorber positions relative to their upper sleeves.
3. Raise and safely support vehicle.
4. Remove rear wheels and tires.
5. Remove rear brake rotor.
6. Remove coil springs as outlined under "Coil Spring, Replace" in this section.
7. Raise subframe into position, then remove and discard its front bolts.

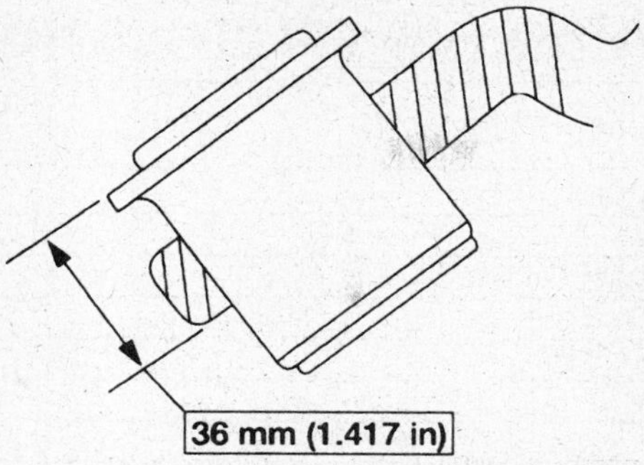

Fig. 8 Upper control arm bushing installation. 1999–2000 Cobra

8. Mark cam bolt position orientation relative to upper control arm and bushing.
9. Mark new upper control arm cam bolt in same position as old one for future reference.
10. Remove and discard upper control arm bushing nut and bolt.
11. Disconnect knuckle from upper control arm.
12. Remove upper control arm nut and bolt, then the arm. Discard nut and bolt.
13. Reverse procedure to install, noting the following:
    a. Install new cam bolts and nuts at control arms and bushings. **Do not tighten until vehicle is back on ground and shock absorber marks are aligned as noted during removal.**
    b. Tighten all fasteners to specifications.
    c. Inspect wheel alignment and adjust as required.

Lower

1. Park vehicle at curb height and on level ground.
2. Mark rear shock absorber positions relative to their upper sleeves.
3. Note transverse bar fastener orientation at this time.
4. Remove coil springs as outlined under "Coil Spring, Replace" in this section.
5. Disconnect lower control arm from knuckle. Discard nut and bolt.
6. Disconnect lower control arm from subframe. Discard nuts and bolts.
7. Reverse procedure to install, noting the following:
    a. Install lower control arm with new fasteners. **Do not tighten until vehicle is back on ground and shock absorber marks are aligned as noted during removal.**
    b. Note transverse bar fastener orientation at this time.
    c. Ensure transverse bar is in place and bolt passes through it. **Do not tighten until vehicle is back on ground and shock absorber marks are aligned as noted during removal.**
    d. Tighten all fasteners to specifications.
    e. Inspect wheel alignment and adjust as required.

CONTROL ARM BUSHING

REPLACE

EXCEPT 1999–2000 COBRA

1. Remove control arm as outlined under "Control Arm, Replace."
2. Place bushing remover and installer set tool No. T78P-5638-A, or equivalent, as shown, **Fig. 7,** and remove bushing.
3. Using installer tool, install bushing into control arm bushing ear of rear axle housing, **Fig. 6.**
4. Install control arm as outlined under "Control Arm, Replace."

1999–2000 COBRA

1. Remove upper control arm as outlined under "Control Arm, Replace."
2. Using appropriate components from bushing remover and installer set tool No. T79P-5638-A, or equivalent, carefully remove bushing.
3. Reverse procedure to install, noting the following:
    a. Using appropriate components from bushing remover and installer set tool No. T79P-5638-A, or equivalent, install the new bushing.
    b. Using a properly calibrated micrometer, ensure bushing is properly installed as illustrated in **Fig. 8.**
    c. Inspect wheel alignment and adjust as required.

STABILIZER BAR

REPLACE

EXCEPT 1999–2000 COBRA

1. Raise and support rear of vehicle.
2. Remove four bolts attaching stabilizer bar to brackets on lower control arms.
3. Remove stabilizer bar from vehicle.
4. Reverse procedure to install.

1999–2000 COBRA

1. Remove rear coil springs as outlined under "Coil Spring, Replace" in this section.
2. Raise subframe into position, then remove and discard its front bolts.
3. Lower the subframe out of vehicle.
4. Remove stabilizer link and nuts. Discard the nuts.
5. Remove stabilizer bar brackets and bolts. Discard the bolts.
6. Remove stabilizer bar and bushings.
7. Reverse procedure to install. Tighten all fasteners to specifications.

TIGHTENING SPECIFICATIONS

Component	Torque/Ft. Lbs.
1997–98	
Axle Damper	57–75
Bumper Bracket Retaining	8–11
Bumper To Bracket	12–20
Clevis Bracket To Axle	57–75
J-Nut	30–39
Lower Arm To Axle	98–132
Lower Arm To Frame	98–132
Rear Axle U-Joint Flange Bolts	70–95
Shock Absorber Lower Attachment	57–75
Shock Absorber To Clevis Bracket	57–75
Shock Absorber Upper Attachment	25–33
U-Joint Flange Bolt	41–56
Upper Arm To Axle	98–132
Wheel Lug Nuts	85–105
1999–2000 EXCEPT COBRA	
Axle Damper Bracket To Frame Bolts	59
Axle Damper Front Bolt	66
Axle Damper Rear Nut	66
Bracket Assembly To Differential Housing Bolts	35
Differential Pinion Shaft Lock Pin	15–30
Lower Control Arm To Axle Bolts	111
Lower Control Arm To Body Bolts	111
Parking Brake Cable Bracket	41
Pinion Bumper Mount To Body Bolts	10
Shock Absorber Clevis Bracket To Axle Nuts	80
Shock Absorber To Body Nuts	30
Shock Absorber To Lower Arm & Bushing Bolts	59
Stabilizer Bar To Lower Arm Bolt	41
Upper Control Arm To Axle Bolts	66
Upper Control Arm To Frame Bolts	76
Wheel Lug Nuts	95
1999–2000 COBRA	
ABS Sensor Bolts	17
Axle Shaft To Hub Retainer	240
Brake Fluid Line To Caliper Bolts	30
Brake Rotor Dust Shield To Knuckle Bolts	89①
Differential Front Lower Insulator Nut & Bolt	52
Differential Rear Insulator Bolt	76
Differential Rear Insulator To Axle Housing Bolts	76
Driveshaft To Companion Flange Bolts	83
Lower Control Arm & Bushing To Knuckle Nuts	85
Lower Control Arm & Bushing To Subframe Bolts	184
Lubricant Filler Plug	25
Pinion Nose Crossmember Nuts	184
Parking Brake Cable Bracket To Lower Arm & Bushing Bolts	11
Shock Absorber To Body Nuts	30
Shock Absorber To Lower Arm & Bushing Bolts	98
Stabilizer Bar Bracket Bolts	41
Stabilizer Bar Link Nuts	35
Subframe Rear Bracket To Body Bolts	59
Subframe To Body Bolts	76
Subframe To Rear Bracket Bolts	76
Toe Link To Knuckle Nuts	35
Toe Link To Subframe Nuts	35

Continued

TIGHTENING SPECIFICATIONS—Continued

Component	Torque/Ft. Lbs.
1999–2000 COBRA	
Upper Control Arm & Bushing To Knuckle Nuts	66
Upper Control Arm & Bushing To Subframe Nuts	66
Wheel Hub Retainer	251
Wheel Lug Nuts	95

① — Inch lbs.

Front Suspension & Steering

INDEX

DESCRIPTION

The front suspension, **Fig. 1,** is of a modified McPherson strut design using shock struts and coil springs. The springs are mounted between the lower control arm and a crossmember spring pocket.

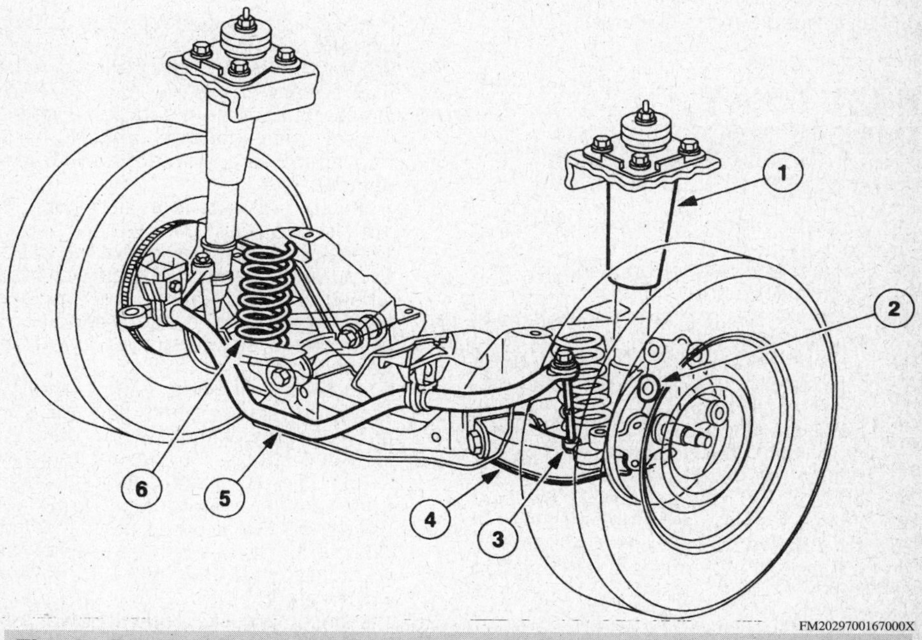

Fig. 1 Front suspension assembly (1-strut, 2-spindle, 3-stabilizer bar link, 4-lower control arm, 5-stabilizer bar, 6-spring)

WHEEL BEARING

ADJUST

Wheel bearings are not adjustable.

WHEEL BEARING

REPLACE

The wheel bearing and wheel hub must be replaced as an assembly.

1. Raise and support vehicle, then remove wheel and tire assembly.
2. Remove and discard front hub cap grease seal from wheel hub.
3. Remove two front disc brake caliper assembly bolts, then the caliper assembly. **Do not let front disc brake caliper assembly hang by front brake hose. Suspend it with suitable wire or rope.**
4. Remove front disc brake rotor. Discard the factory push-on nuts.
5. Remove and discard front axle wheel hub retainer.
6. Remove wheel hub and bearing. If assembly cannot be removed by hand, use front hub remover/replacer tool No. T81P-1104-C, or equivalent.
7. Reverse procedure to install, noting the following:
   a. Install a new wheel hub retainer and hub cap grease seal.
   b. Tighten all fasteners to specifications.

FRONT WHEEL SPINDLE

REPLACE

1. Raise and support vehicle.
2. Remove front wheel and tire assembly, then the front brake anti-lock sensor from front wheel spindle.
3. Remove disc brake caliper, rotor and dust shield.
4. Remove wheel hub, then the front stabilizer bar from lower arm assembly.
5. Remove tie rod end from wheel spindle using tie rod end remover tool No.

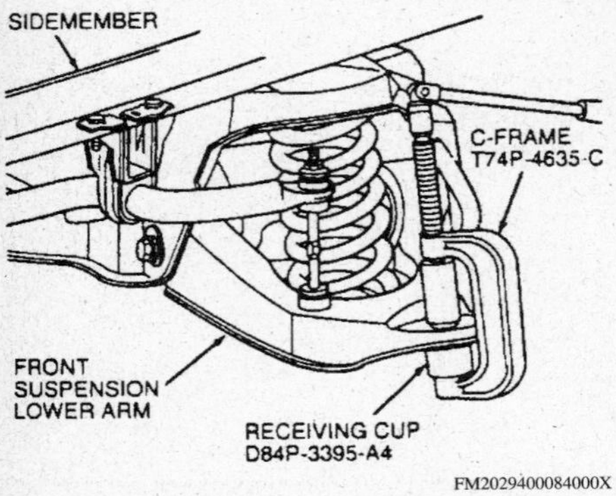

Fig. 2 Control arm ball joint removal. 1997–98

3290-D, or equivalent. **To prevent damage to front suspension lower arm do not remove nut from ball joint stud at this time.**

6. Loosen ball joint nut one or two turns, then tap spindle boss sharply to relieve stud pressure.
7. Place floor jack under front suspension lower arm, then compress front coil spring as outlined under "Coil Spring, Replace."
8. Remove stud nut, then the front anti-lock sensor bracket.
9. Remove two front wheel spindle to front shock absorber retaining bolts, then the wheel spindle.
10. Reverse procedures to install. Tighten all fasteners to specifications.

BALL JOINT INSPECTION

1997–99

1. Raise and safely support front of vehicle.
2. Ensure front wheel hub and bearing assemblies are in good condition.
3. Place suitable jack stands under lower control arms.
4. Position suitable dial indicator to measure lateral movement between spindle and ball joint.
5. Grasp tire at top and bottom and slowly move inward and outward, noting dial indicator reading.
6. **On 1997–98 models,** replace ball joint if movement exceeds .015 inch.
7. **On 1999 models,** replace lower control arm if movement exceeds .031 inch.

2000

1. Raise and safely support front of vehicle.
2. Ensure front wheel hub and bearing assemblies are in good condition.
3. Place suitable jack stands under appropriate control arm.
4. Observe relative movement between lower spindle arm and ball joint while an assistant pushes and pulls bottom of tire.
5. Replace ball joint if radial movement exceeds 1⁄32 inch.

BALL JOINT

REPLACE

1997–98

1. Raise vehicle on hoist.
2. Remove front wheel spindle as outlined under "Front Wheel Spindle, Replace."
3. Remove and discard joint boot seal.
4. Press out front suspension arm bushing joint using U-joint tool No. T74P-4635-C, or equivalent and ball joint remover tool No. D84P-3395-A4, or equivalent, **Fig. 2**
5. When installing new front ball joint, protective cover must be left in place during installation to protect ball joint seal. It may be necessary to cut off end of cover to allow it to pass through receiving cup.
6. Install ball joint with ball joint replacer tool No. D89P-3010-B, cup tool No. D84P-3395-A4 and C-frame tool No. T74P-4635C, or equivalents, **Fig. 3.**
7. Install lower control arm as outlined under "Control Arm, Replace."

1999–2000

On these models the ball joint and lower control arm must be replaced as a unit.

COIL SPRING

REPLACE

1. Park vehicle at curb height and on level ground.
2. Mark front strut positions relative to their upper sleeves.
3. Raise and support vehicle, allowing front suspension lower arms to hang free, then remove wheel and tire assembly.
4. Remove brake caliper, then wire or rope it out of way.
5. Use tie rod end remover tool No. 3290-D, or equivalent to disconnect front wheel spindle connecting rod or end assembly from front wheel spindle.
6. Disconnect stabilizer bar link from lower control arm.
7. Remove steering gear retaining bolts if required, then position gear so suspension arm bolt may be removed.
8. Use coil spring compressor tool No. D78P-5310-A, or equivalent, to install plate between coils near front coil spring toe. Mark upper plate location on coils for installation. **Be careful not to nick spring coils when installing upper plate.**
9. Install compression rod into lower arm spring pocket hole, through coil spring and into upper plate, then install lower plate, lower ball nut, thrust washer and bear, and forcing nut onto compression rod.
10. Tighten forcing nut on compressor tool until drag is felt, then remove suspension arm-to-crossmember nuts and bolts. Compressor tool may have to be adjusted to ease bolt removal.
11. Loosen compression rod forcing nut until tension is relieved, then remove forcing nut.

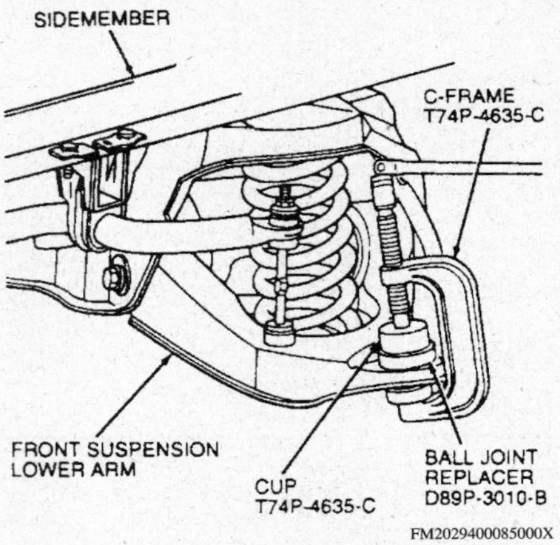

Fig. 3 Control arm ball joint installation. 1997–98

12. Remove compression rod and coil spring.
13. Reverse procedure to install, noting the following:
    a. Ensure lower spring end is positioned between two holes in lower control arm spring pocket.
    b. Tighten stabilizer bar and steering gear to No. 2 crossmember to specifications.
    c. Tighten tie rod to steering spindle to specifications.

STRUT

REPLACE

1. Place ignition in unlocked position to permit free movement of front wheels as required.
2. Raise and safely support vehicle on a hoist.
3. Remove appropriate front wheel and tire.
4. Remove disc brake caliper, then position aside with suitable wire or rope.
5. Remove ABS wheel speed sensor mounting bolt, then the sensor.
6. Disconnect ABS sensor wiring harness at bracket.
7. Support lower control arm with suitable jack stand.
8. Remove two strut to front wheel spindle retaining nuts.
9. Carefully lower the lower control arm and remove jack stand.
10. Lower the vehicle, then remove strut upper mounting nuts and bolts. Discard nuts.
11. Remove strut from vehicle.
12. Reverse procedures to install. Tighten bolts to specifications.

CONTROL ARM

REPLACE

1. Park vehicle at curb height and on level ground.
2. Mark front strut positions relative to their upper sleeves.
3. Raise and support vehicle, allowing front suspension lower arms to hang free.
4. Remove wheel and tire assembly.

5. If required to obtain more working room, remove front disc brake caliper, then position it aside with suitable wire or rope.
6. Remove front disc brake rotor and front disc brake rotor shield as outlined under "Disc Brakes."
7. Disconnect front wheel spindle connecting rod or end assembly from front wheel spindle using tie rod end remover tool No. 3290-D, or equivalent.
8. Remove steering gear bolts and position gear so front suspension lower arm bolt is accessible.
9. Disconnect front stabilizer link from front suspension lower arm.
10. Loosen ball joint nut one or two turns, then tap spindle boss sharply to relieve stud pressure. **Do not remove ball joint nut at this time.**
11. Use spring compressor tool No. D78P-5310-A, or equivalent, to install plate between coils near top of front coil spring. Mark location of plate on coils for installation and use care not to nick spring coils when installing upper plate.
12. Install compression rod into front suspension lower arm spring pocket hole, through front coil spring, into upper plate.
13. Install lower plate, lower ball nut, thrust washer and bearing and forcing nut onto compression rod, then tighten forcing nut until drag on nut is felt.
14. Remove and discard ball joint stud nut, then the entire front shock absorber and front wheel spindle assembly. Wire aside to obtain working room.
15. Remove and discard front suspension lower arm to crossmember nuts and bolts. Compressor tool forcing nut may need to be tightened or loosened for easy bolt removal.
16. Loosen compression rod forcing nut until spring tension is relieved, then remove forcing nut, front suspension lower arm and front coil spring.
17. Reverse procedure to install, noting the following:
    a. Ensure spring end is positioned between two holes in front suspension lower arm pocket.
    b. Tighten all fasteners to specifications.
    c. Inspect wheel alignment and adjust as required.

STABILIZER BAR

REPLACE

1. Raise and support vehicle.
2. Disconnect stabilizer bar from each link, then remove insulator clamps, insulators and stabilizer bar from vehicle.
3. Reverse procedure to install. Tighten clamp to side rail bolts and stabilizer bar to link nuts to specifications.

STABILIZER BAR BUSHING

REPLACE

Refer to "Stabilizer Bar, Replace," for stabilizer bar bushing replacement procedure.

POWER STEERING GEAR

REPLACE

1997–98

1. Turn ignition On.
2. Place front wheels in straight-ahead position.
3. Raise and support vehicle, then position drain pan to catch fluid from power steering lines.
4. Remove front wheels and tires as required.
5. Remove flexible coupling to power steering gear input shaft and control bolt.
6. Remove two front wheel spindle connecting end cotter pins and nuts, then separate studs from spindle arms using tie rod end remover tool No. 3290-D, or equivalent.
7. Remove two steering gear to No. 2 front crossmember nuts, insulator washers and bolts.
8. Remove front rubber insulators, then position steering gear to allow access to hydraulic lines.
9. Disconnect hydraulic lines, then remove steering gear.
10. Reverse procedure to install, noting the following:
    a. **Hydraulic lines are designed to swivel when properly tightened. Do not attempt to eliminate looseness by overtightening fittings, or plastic seals may be damaged.**
    b. Ensure all rubber insulators are pushed completely inside steering gear housing before installing bolts.
    c. Fill power steering system with specified steering fluid.
    d. If front wheel spindle connecting rod or ends were loosened, inspect and adjust front end alignment.

1999–2000

1. Place front wheels in straight-ahead position, but do not lock steering column.
2. Raise and safely support vehicle, then remove front wheels and tires.
3. Remove tie rod end to spindle nut. discard cotter pin.
4. Using tie rod end separator tool No. 3290-D, or equivalent, separate tie rod end from spindle.
5. Rotate steering column intermediate shaft as required, then remove and discard pinch bolt.
6. Lower the vehicle.
7. Place front wheels in straight-ahead position, then lock steering column. **Do not rotate steering wheel when lower column shaft is disconnected or air bag clockspring will be damaged.**
8. Disconnect intermediate shaft coupling.
9. Remove steering gear mounting nuts, washers and bolts. Position gear forward.
10. Position drain pan to catch fluid from power steering lines.
11. Disconnect power steering hoses, then remove and discard O-rings. Plug all open ports to prevent leakage and contamination.
12. Carefully remove steering gear from vehicle.
13. Reverse procedure to install, noting the following:
    a. Install new O-rings using seal replacement tool set No. D90P-3517-A, or equivalent.
    b. Always install a new shaft coupling pinch bolt.
    c. Tighten all fasteners to specifications.
    d. Fill and bleed power steering fluid system.

POWER STEERING PUMP

REPLACE

1997–98

1. Disconnect return hose from power steering pump reservoir and allow fluid to drain into suitable container.
2. Disconnect pressure hose from power steering pump fitting, then remove pump mounting bracket and disconnect drive belt from pulley.
3. Remove belt from pulley, then pulley.
4. Remove power steering pump.
5. Reverse procedure to install, noting the following:
6. Tighten pump to mounting bracket bolts and pressure hose to pump tube nut to specifications.
7. **Endplay of pressure hose to pump fitting is normal and does not indicate a loose fitting. Do not overtighten.**

1999–2000

Type CII

1. Remove serpentine drive belt.
2. Position drain pan to catch fluid from power steering lines.
3. Disconnect power steering hose, then remove and discard O-ring. Plug open ports to prevent leakage and contamination.
4. Using removal tool No. T69L-10300-B, or equivalent, remove pump pulley.
5. Remove all power steering mounting bolts, then the pump.
6. Reverse procedure to install, noting the following:
    a. Using installer tool No. T65P-3A733-C, or equivalent, install pump pulley.

b. Install new O-ring using seal replacement tool set No. D90P-3517-A, or equivalent.
c. Tighten all fasteners to specifications.
d. Fill and bleed power steering fluid system.

Type CIII

1. Remove serpentine drive belt.
2. Raise and safely support vehicle.
3. Using removal tool No. T69L-10300-B, or equivalent, remove pump pulley.
4. Remove accessible mounting bolt and bracket.
5. Position drain pan to catch fluid from power steering lines.
6. Disconnect power steering hoses, then remove and discard O-rings. Plug open ports to prevent leakage and contamination.
7. Remove remaining power steering mounting bolts, then the pump.
8. Reverse procedure to install, noting the following:
   a. Inspect pump pulley for paint marks in hub web area. **If two paint marks are visible, discard that pulley and install a new one.** If there is only one mark on no mark at all, use a suitable paint pencil to mark web area and that pulley is ready to install.
   b. Using installer tool No. T91P-3A733-A, or equivalent, install pump pulley.
   c. Install new O-ring using seal replacement tool set No. D90P-3517-A, or equivalent.
   d. Tighten all fasteners to specifications.
   e. Fill and bleed power steering fluid system.

TIGHTENING SPECIFICATIONS

Component	Torque/Ft. Lbs.
1997–98	
Ball Joint To Spindle	109–149
Front Axle Wheel Hub Retainer	221–295
Front Suspension Lower Arm To No. 2 Crossmember	141–191
Shock Absorber To Wheel Spindle	141–191
Stabilizer Bar Link	11–16
Stabilizer Bar Mounting Clamp To Bracket	44–59
Steering Gear To Crossmember	90–99
Strut Lower Mounting To Spindle	141–199
Strut To Upper Mounting Bracket Nut	55–92
Strut Upper Mount To Body	25–34
Tie Rod End To Spindle	35–47
Wheel Lug Nuts	85–105
1999–2000	
ABS Sensor Bolt	53①
ABS Sensor Wire Bracket Nuts	21
Ball Joint To Spindle Nuts	129
Lower Control Arm To Body Nuts	148
Stabilizer Bar Bracket Nuts	52
Stabilizer Bar Link Nuts	14
Steering Gear To Crossmember Nuts	52
Strut To Spindle Nuts	148
Strut Upper Mount To Body Nuts & Bolts	30
Strut Upper Nut	74
Tie Rod To Spindle Nuts	41
Wheel Hub & Bearing Retainer Nut	258
Wheel Lug Nuts	95

① — Inch lbs.

Wheel Alignment

INDEX

PRELIMINARY INSPECTION

1. Inspect tires for proper inflation and similar tread wear.
2. Inspect hub and bearing for excessive wear. Replace as required.
3. Inspect ball joints.
4. Inspect tie rod ends for excessive looseness.
5. Measure wheel and tire runout.
6. Inspect rack and pinion for looseness at frame.
7. Ensure proper strut operation.
8. Inspect suspension and steering components for damage. Replace as required.
9. Inspect vehicle ride height.

FRONT WHEEL ALIGNMENT

BASIC INSPECTION

Inspect front wheel alignment under following curb load conditions:

1. Spare tire, wheel, jack and jack handle in proper positions.
2. Front seats in rearmost positions.
3. All other loading and aftermarket equipment removed.
4. All tires inflated to specified cold pressure.
5. All excessive mud, dirt and road deposit accumulation removed from chassis and underbody.

CASTER

Caster angle is preset during production and not adjustable. **However, if caster is still not within specifications by 0.6° after all other sources have been inspected and corrected as required, perpendicular slot cutting is allowed at the tops of the strut towers. Each millimeter of adjustment will yield approximately 0.12° in caster change. Do not cut any slots longer than 0.2 inch in any direction.**

CAMBER

1. Remove pop rivet from camber plate.
2. Loosen two strut mount to body apron nuts and one strut mount to body apron bolt.
3. Move top of shock strut as needed to bring camber angle within specifications, then tighten nuts. **It is not necessary to replace pop rivet.**

TOE-IN

1. Determine if steering shaft and steering wheel marks are in alignment and in top position.
2. Loosen clamp screw on tie rod bellows and free seal on rod to prevent bellows from twisting.
3. Loosen tie rod jam nut.
4. Use suitable pliers to turn tie rod inner end to correct adjustment to specifications. Do not use pliers on tie rod threads. Turning to reduce number of threads showing will increase toe-in. Turning in opposite direction will reduce toe-in. Tighten nut to specifications.

REAR WHEEL ALIGNMENT

1999–2000 COBRA

On these models the independent rear suspension alignment is adjustable for camber and toe. After performing preliminary inspections as outlined in this section, proceed as follows:

1. Loosen upper control arm pivot nuts.
2. Rotate bolts and cams until camber is within range. Tighten nuts to specifications.
3. Loosen toe control jam nuts, then rotate toe link until toe is within range. Tighten nuts to specifications.

PROBE

NOTE: Refer To Rear Of This Manual For Vehicle Manufacturer's Special Service Tool Suppliers.

INDEX OF SERVICE OPERATIONS

Specifications

GENERAL ENGINE SPECIFICATIONS

Engine Liter (VIN Code)②	Fuel System	Bore & Stroke	Compression Ratio	Net H.P. @ RPM	Maximum Torque Ft. Lbs. @ RPM	Normal Oil Pressure psi
2.0L (A)	EFI	3.27 x 3.62	9.0	118 @ 5500	127 @ 4500	57–71③
2.5L (B)	EFI	3.33 x 2.92	9.2	164 @ 6000	160 @ 4800	①

① — 49–71psi w/engine warm & operating @ 3000 RPM; 28 psi w/engine warm & operating @ 1000 RPM.

② — Eighth digit denotes engine code.

③ — With engine warm & operating @ 3000 RPM.

TUNE UP SPECIFICATIONS

Engine (VIN Code①)	Spark Plug Gap	Ignition Timing BTDC				Curb Idle Speed		Fast Idle Speed		Fuel Pump Pressure, psi.	Valve Clearance, Inch
		Firing Order Fig.	Man. Trans.	Auto. Trans.	Mark Fig.	Man. Trans.	Auto. Trans.	Man. Trans.	Auto Trans.		
2.0L (A)	.041	②	10⑥	10⑥	E	700	700N	⑤	⑤	37–46④	⑦
2.5L (B)	.041	③	10⑧	10⑧	B	650	650N	⑤	⑤	39–45④	⑦

BTDC — Before Top Dead Center

N — Neutral

① — Eighth digit denotes engine code.

② — Firing order, 1-3-4-2. Refer to **Fig. A** for spark plug wire connections at distributor cap.

③ — Firing order, 1-2-3-4-5-6. Refer to **Fig. C** for spark plug wire connections at distributor cap.

④ — Wrap shop towel around fitting to prevent fuel spillage, then connect suitable fuel pressure gauge to fuel diagnostic valve on fuel rail assembly. Place ignition switch in On position & check fuel pressure gauge reading.

⑤ — Computer controlled, non-adjustable.

⑥ — Remove shorting bar from double wire spout connector.

⑦ — Equipped w/hydraulic lash adjusters.

⑧ — Ground Data Link Connector (DLC) STI (Ten) terminal, refer to **Fig. D.**

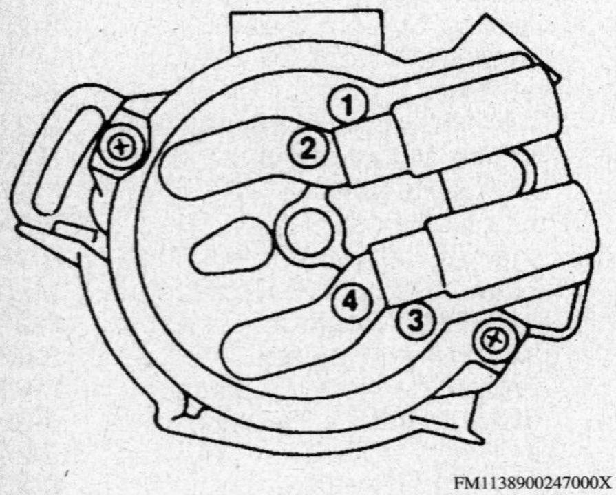

FM1138900247000X

Fig. A

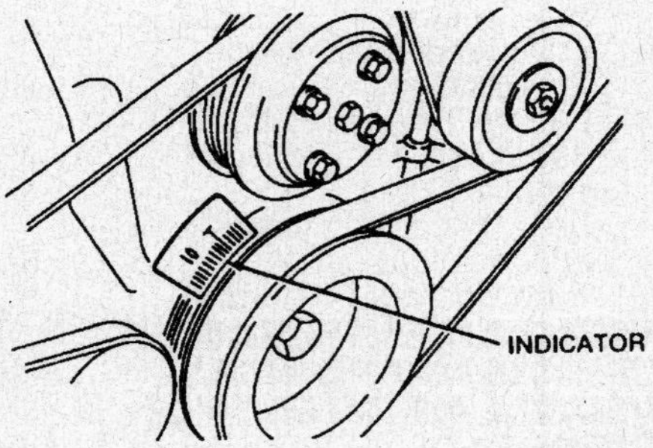

FM1138900248000X

Fig. B

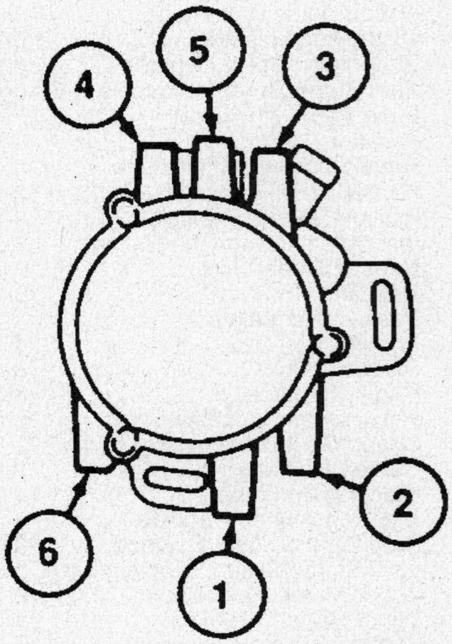

FM1138900249000X

Fig. C

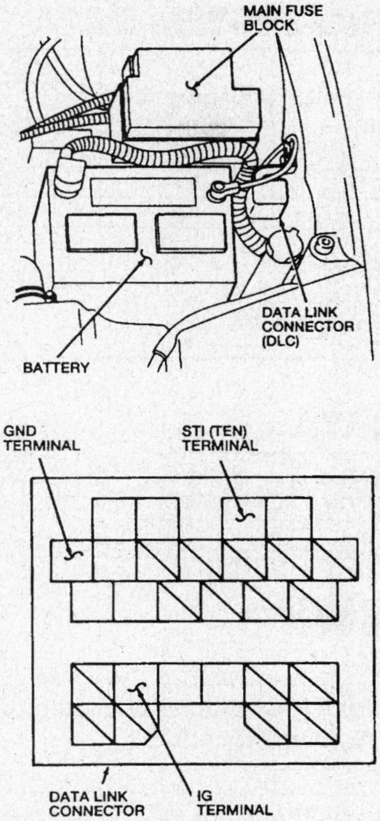

Fig. D

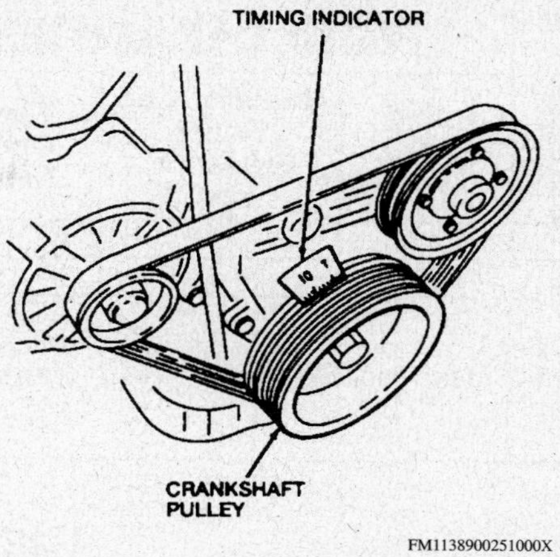

Fig. E

FRONT WHEEL ALIGNMENT SPECIFICATIONS

Model	Caster Angle, Degrees		Camber Angle, Degrees		Toe, Inch①		King Pin Incli-nation, Degrees	Steering Angle, Degrees		Ball Joint Wear
	Limits	Desired	Limits	Desired	Limits	Desired		Inner Wheel	Outer Wheel	
2.0L	$+1\frac{53}{60}$ to $+3\frac{53}{60}$	$+2\frac{53}{60}$	$-1\frac{1}{5}$ to $-\frac{1}{5}$	$-\frac{7}{10}$	+.08 to +.16	+.12	$15\frac{5}{12}$	37	32	②
2.5L	$+1\frac{9}{10}$ to $+3\frac{9}{10}$	$+2\frac{9}{10}$	$-1\frac{2}{5}$ to $-\frac{2}{5}$	$-\frac{9}{10}$	+.08 to +.16	+.12	$15\frac{11}{15}$	37	32	②

① — Toe-In (+). Toe-Out (-).

② — Refer to "Ball Joint Inspection" under "Front Suspension & Steering."

REAR WHEEL ALIGNMENT SPECIFICATIONS

Model	Camber Angle, Degrees		Total Toe, Inch①		Thrust Angle, Degrees	
	Limits	Desired	Limits	Desired	Limits	Desired
2.0L	$-1\frac{7}{10}$ to $+\frac{3}{10}$	$-\frac{7}{10}$	+.08 to +.16	+.12	$-\frac{1}{10}$ to $+\frac{1}{10}$	0
2.5L	$-1\frac{9}{10}$ to $+\frac{1}{10}$	$-\frac{9}{10}$	+.08 to +.16	+.12	$-\frac{1}{10}$ to $+\frac{1}{10}$	0

① — Toe-In (+). Toe-Out (-).

FLUID CAPACITIES & COOLING SYSTEM DATA

Engine	Cooling Capacity, Qts.	Radiator Cap Relief Pressure, Lbs.	Thermo. Opening Temp., °F	Fuel Tank, Gals.	Engine Oil Refill, Qts.①	Transaxle Oil, Qts.	
						5 Speed	Auto. Trans. Qts.②
2.0L	7.4	16	180	15.5	3.7	2.9	③
2.5L	7.9	13	180	15.5	4.2	2.9	③

① — Includes filter.
② — Approximate. Make final check w/dipstick.
③ — With 4EAT transaxle, 9.3 qts.; w/CD4E transaxle, 6.0 qts.

LUBRICANT DATA

Transaxle		Power Steering	Brake System
Manual	Automatic		
GL-4	Mercon	Mercon	DOT 3

Electrical

NOTE: On Air Bag Equipped Models, Refer To " Air Bag System Precautions" Located In The Front Of This Manual For System Disarming & Arming Procedures.

NOTE: Refer to "Computer Relearn Procedures " Located In The Front Of This Manual For Computer Relearn Procedures.

INDEX

PRECAUTIONS

AIR BAG SYSTEMS

Refer to "Air Bag System Precautions" in front of this manual for system disarming and arming procedures.

BATTERY GROUND CABLE

Prior to service, disconnect battery ground cable and isolate as required.

FUSE PANEL & FLASHER LOCATION

The main fuse panel is located on left-hand side of engine compartment, near strut tower. The interior fuse panel is located behind lefthand side kick panel.

The flasher relay box is located below the instrument cluster, near the lefthand kick panel.

FUEL PUMP RELAY LOCATION

Fuel pump relay is located in the engine compartment fuse box, located at the left-hand side of engine compartment.

RELAY CENTER LOCATION

Relay center is located on the left front inner fender in the engine compartment near the battery, **Fig. 1.**

STARTER

REPLACE

2.0L ENGINE

When servicing starter or performing any maintenance in area of starter, note heavy gauge input lead connected to starter solenoid is Hot at all times.

1. Remove air cleaner assembly, then air cleaner duct.
2. Remove upper starter motor retaining bolts.
3. Raise and support vehicle, then remove intake manifold support bracket retaining bolts and bracket.
4. Disconnect wiring from starter assembly.
5. Remove lower starter motor retaining bolt, then starter motor from vehicle.
6. Reverse procedure to install, noting the following:
   a. Install upper starter motor retaining bolts first.
   b. **Torque** starter motor retaining bolts to 23–34 ft. lbs.
   c. **Torque** starter solenoid B-terminal nut to 6.5–10 ft. lbs.
   d. **Torque** intake manifold support bracket retaining bolts to 28–38 ft. lbs.

2.5L ENGINE

Manual Transaxle

When servicing starter or performing any maintenance in area of starter, note heavy gauge input lead connected to starter solenoid is Hot at all times.

1. Remove fresh air duct and air cleaner assembly.
2. Disconnect wiring electrical connections from starter motor assembly.
3. Remove three starter motor retaining bolts, then starter motor assembly.
4. Reverse procedure to install, noting the following:
   a. **Torque** starter motor retaining bolts to 24–33 ft. lbs.
   b. **Torque** starter solenoid B-terminal nut to 12–16 ft. lbs.

Automatic Transaxle

When servicing starter or performing any maintenance in area of starter, note heavy gauge input lead connected to starter solenoid is Hot at all times.

1. Remove fresh air duct and air cleaner assembly.
2. Using screwdriver, or equivalent, disconnect shift cable from selector lever by prying cable from lever.
3. Squeeze lock tabs on shift cable, then remove shift cable from cable bracket.
4. Mark positions of wiring harness connectors, then disconnect engine wiring harness from following components:
   a. Knock sensor.
   b. Throttle position sensor.
   c. Two fuel rail connectors.
   d. Distributor.
   e. Manual lever position (MLP) switch.
   f. Automatic transaxle.
   g. Two wire harness connectors.
5. Position engine wiring harness aside.
6. Remove two selector cable bracket mounting bolts, then bracket.
7. Remove starter motor support bracket, then disconnect starter motor electrical connectors.
8. Remove three starter motor retaining bolts, then starter motor from vehicle.
9. Reverse procedure to install, noting the following:
   a. **Torque** starter motor retaining bolts to 24–33 ft. lbs.
   b. **Torque** starter solenoid B-terminal nut to 12–16 ft. lbs.
   c. **Torque** selector cable bracket mounting bolts to 5–7 ft. lbs.

The Location of the Starter Relay, Main Relay, Circuit (Fuel Pump) Relay, Turn Signal Lamp Relay, Horn Relay, Daytime Running Lamp (DRL) Relay (Canada Only), A/C Relay, Headlamp Relay, and Fog Lamp Relay

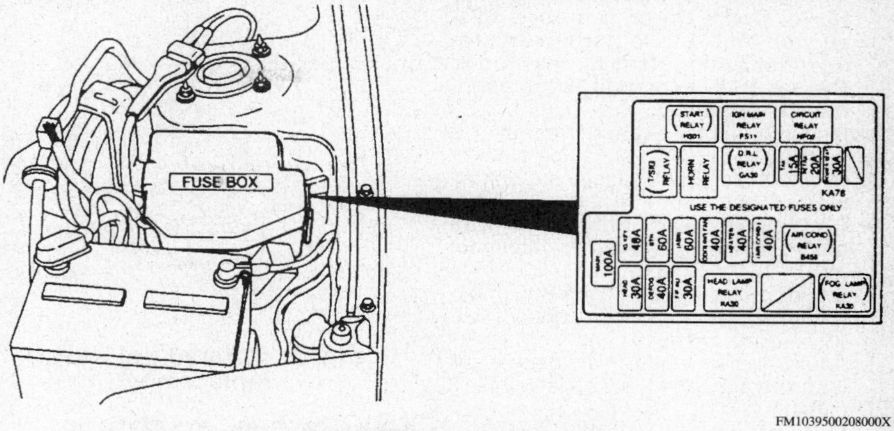

Fig. 1 Relay center location

ALTERNATOR

REPLACE

2.0L ENGINE

1. Remove alternator upper mounting bolt.
2. Loosen alternator adjusting arm, then remove drive belt.
3. Raise and support vehicle, then remove bolts and crossmember.
4. Disconnect alternator electrical connectors.
5. Remove lower alternator mounting bolt, then the alternator.
6. Reverse procedure to install, noting the following:
   a. Adjust drive belt tension to specifications.
   b. **Torque** lower bolt to 27–38 ft. lbs.
   c. **Torque** upper bolt to 8–10 ft. lbs.
   d. **Torque** crossmember bolts to 69–96 ft. lbs.

2.5L ENGINE

1. Disconnect alternator wiring.
2. Loosen drive belt tensioner center nut and adjusting bolt, then remove upper alternator mounting bolt.
3. Raise and support vehicle.
4. Remove right wheel splash guard screws and splash guard.
5. Remove drive belt from alternator.
6. **On models with A/C,** remove compressor attaching bolts and position aside. **It is not necessary to disconnect A/C compressor refrigerant lines.**
7. **On all models,** loosen alternator lower mounting bolt.
8. Push alternator so it lifts out of saddle mount, then roll down and lift until lower bolt clears slot.
9. Remove alternator.
10. Reverse procedure to install, noting the following:
    a. Adjust drive belt to specifications.
    b. **Torque** lower bolt to 28–38 ft. lbs.
    c. **Torque** upper bolt to 14–18 ft. lbs.
    d. **Torque** A/C mounting bolts to 18–26 ft. lbs.

DISTRIBUTOR

REPLACE

2.0L ENGINE

Removal

1. **On vehicles equipped with automatic transaxle,** disconnect coil electrical connector.
2. **On all models,** disconnect distributor electrical connector.
3. Remove two distributor cap retaining screws, then position cap and wires aside.
4. Rotate engine until No. 1 piston is at Top Dead Center (TDC) on compression stroke. **It may be necessary to remove No. 1 spark plug to confirm compression stroke.**
5. Remove two distributor hold-down bolts, then distributor from vehicle.

Installation

1. Match alignment marks (dots) on distributor shaft and distributor housing.

2. Apply clean engine oil to O-ring on distributor.
3. Install distributor. **Ensure rotor points to No. 1 wire tower. If rotor is misaligned, pull distributor out and rotate distributor shaft to next tooth. Repeat this step until rotor alignment is correct.**
4. Install distributor cap and two retaining screws.
5. Connect distributor electrical connector.
6. **On vehicles with automatic transaxle,** connect coil electrical connector.
7. **On all models,** hand tighten distributor hold-down bolts, then connect battery ground cable.
8. Adjust ignition timing as necessary, then **torque** hold-down bolts to 14–18 ft. lbs.

2.5L ENGINE

1. Disconnect Volume Air Flow (VAF) meter electrical connector from lefthand side of air cleaner assembly.
2. Remove Fuel Pressure Regulator Control (FPRC) solenoid retaining screw from righthand side of air cleaner assembly, then position solenoid aside.
3. Remove air cleaner fresh air duct, then air cleaner assembly from vehicle.
4. Mark position of spark plug wires for installation reference, then disconnect spark plug wires from distributor cap as shown in "Tune-Up Specifications."
5. Disconnect two distributor electrical connectors from top of distributor.
6. Remove distributor hold-down bolts, then distributor assembly from vehicle.
7. Reverse procedure to install, noting the following:
   a. One of tangs on distributor shaft is larger than other. This ensures only one installation position.
   b. Hand tighten distributor hold-down bolts.
   c. **Torque** air cleaner assembly nuts and bolts to 14–18 ft. lbs.
   d. **Torque** fresh air duct nuts and three bolts to 6–7 ft. lbs.
   e. Check and adjust engine timing.
   f. **Torque** distributor hold-down bolts to 19–25 ft. lbs.

COIL PACK

REPLACE

2.0L ENGINE

1. Twist and pull ignition coil to distributor high tension wiring from coil pack terminal.
2. Remove connector cover and disconnect connector from coil.
3. Remove mounting nut and coil pack.
4. Reverse procedure to install. **Torque** mounting nut to 6–7 ft. lbs.

2.5L ENGINE

Coil is part of distributor, refer to "Distributor, Replace."

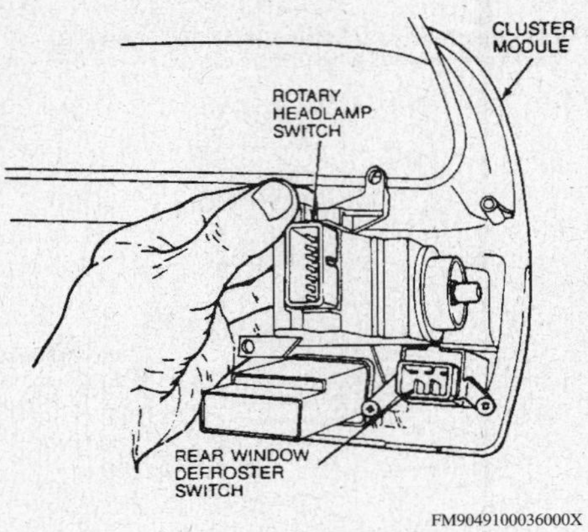

Fig. 2 Rotary light switch replacement

IGNITION SWITCH

REPLACE

It is not necessary to remove steering wheel to remove ignition switch.

1. Remove four lower steering column panel screws, then separate upper and lower steering column panels.
2. Remove lock cylinder illumination bulb from lower steering column panel.
3. Remove upper and lower steering column panels.
4. Disconnect ignition switch electrical connector.
5. Remove ignition switch retaining screw, then ignition switch assembly from vehicle.
6. Reverse procedure to install.

CLUTCH START SWITCH

REPLACE

Switch assembly is located on lefthand side of clutch pedal support bracket.

1. Remove two switch retaining nuts, then pull switch downward to gain access to electrical connector.
2. Disconnect connector from switch, then remove switch.
3. Reverse procedure to install.

NEUTRAL SAFETY SWITCH

REPLACE

1. Remove air cleaner assembly.
2. Using a screwdriver, or equivalent, pry shift cable from transaxle shift lever.
3. Disconnect neutral position switch electrical connector.
4. Remove switch retaining bolts, then remove switch.
5. Reverse procedure to install, noting the following:
   a. Align neutral mark on top of switch (center line) with flats of switch shaft.
   b. **Torque** switch retaining bolts to 6–7 ft. lbs.

HEADLAMP SWITCH

REPLACE

1. Remove turn signal switch as described in this section.
2. Pull rotary switch knob from switch stem.
3. Remove light switch attaching screws, then the switch, **Fig. 2.**
4. Reverse procedure to install.

STOP LIGHT SWITCH

REPLACE

1. Remove lower steering column trim.
2. Disconnect brake switch electrical connector.
3. Remove brake switch by pulling it straight out from brake pedal.
4. Reverse procedure to install. Ensure switch is correctly installed by pushing switch in until it bottoms out against brake pedal.

COMBINATION SWITCH

REPLACE

1. Remove steering wheel as described under "Steering Wheel, Replace."
2. Remove four lower steering column panel retaining screws.
3. Separate upper and lower steering column panels, then remove lock cylinder illumination bulb from lower panel.
4. Remove upper and lower steering column panels.
5. Apply two strips of tape across clockspring and housing to prevent accidental rotation.
6. Remove three clockspring retaining screws, then lift clockspring off steering column.
7. Remove clockspring ground screw, then disconnect electrical connector.
8. Remove clockspring assembly from steering column.
9. Remove cancel cam and spring from steering shaft, then three combination switch retaining screws.
10. Disconnect combination switch electrical connectors.
11. Slide combination switch off steering column shaft.
12. Reverse procedure to install.

TURN SIGNAL SWITCH

REPLACE

Refer to "Combination Switch, Replace" procedure for turn signal switch replacement.

STEERING WHEEL

REPLACE

1. Center front wheels to straight ahead position.
2. Disconnect speed control electrical connector, if equipped.
3. Make an alignment mark on steering wheel and steering shaft for correct alignment during assembly.
4. Remove steering wheel retaining nut. **Do not attempt to remove steering wheel by hitting steering shaft with a hammer. Steering shaft will collapse, causing steering wheel to bind.**

5. Install steering wheel puller tool No. T67L-3600-A, or equivalent, to steering wheel.
6. Remove steering wheel assembly from column, routing wire harness through steering wheel as steering wheel is lifted off shaft.
7. Apply two strips of tape across clockspring and housing to prevent accidental rotation. If clockspring rotates, adjust as follows:
   a. Turn clockspring clockwise until it stops. **Do not apply excessive force to clockspring.**
   b. Rotate clockspring counterclockwise 2.75 turns.
   c. Align marks on clockspring and housing.
8. Reverse procedure to install. **Torque** steering wheel retaining nut to 29–36 ft. lbs.

INSTRUMENT CLUSTER

REPLACE

1. Loosen hood release handle mounting nut.
2. Remove lower instrument panel cover screw.
3. Remove courtesy lamp from lower instrument panel cover by turning bulb ¼ turn counterclockwise, then pulling bulb straight out.
4. Remove lower instrument panel cover, then five instrument cluster bezel screws.
5. Disconnect resistor panel lamp dimmer switch electrical connector.
6. Remove instrument cluster bezel.
7. Remove two upper steering column retaining bolts and lower steering column.
8. Remove four instrument cluster retaining screws.
9. Disconnect instrument cluster from electrical connectors, then remove cluster from vehicle.
10. Reverse procedure to install.

RADIO

REPLACE

COMPACT DISC RADIO (CDR) & GRAPHIC EQUALIZER (GEQ)

1. Remove two armrest compartment retaining screws, then armrest compartment, if equipped.
2. **On manual transaxle models,** unscrew shifter knob.
3. **On automatic transaxle models,** remove emergency override key switch cover from top of floor console.
4. **On all models,** engage parking brake, then gently pull up on upper half of floor console to separate it from lower half.
5. Disconnect cigar lighter and cigar lighter element electrical connectors.
6. Remove ashtray illumination bulb from upper half of console.
7. Remove two dash panel control console bezel screws.
8. Remove four equalizer retaining screws, then the equalizer, if necessary.
9. Insert radio removal tools No. T87P-19061-A, or equivalent, into face plate holes until tension of tools locking into place can be felt.
10. Flex outward on both sides of radio simultaneously, then pull radio outward using tools as handles.
11. Disconnect electrical connectors and antenna lead-in cable from back of radio.
12. Reverse procedure to install.

SUB-WOOFER AMPLIFIER

Sub-woofer amplifier is located behind lefthand quarter trim panel, near B-pillar.

1. Remove package tray.
2. Remove trunk end screws, then trunk end trim.
3. Remove lefthand lower trunk side trim as follows:
   a. Remove three push tabs.
   b. Remove two screws.
4. Remove lefthand quarter trim panel.
5. Remove sub-woofer amplifier assembly as follows:
   a. Remove two amplifier attaching nuts.
   b. Disconnect electrical connector.
   c. Remove sub-woofer amplifier assembly.
6. Reverse procedure to install. **Torque** sub-woofer amplifier assembly attaching nuts to 5 ft. lbs.

PREMIUM SOUND AMPLIFIER

Premium sound amplifier is located behind righthand quarter trim panel, near B-pillar.

1. Remove package tray.
2. Remove trunk end screws, then trunk end trim.
3. Remove righthand lower trunk side trim as follows:
   a. Remove three push tabs.
   b. Remove two screws.
4. Remove righthand quarter trim panel.
5. Remove premium sound amplifier assembly as follows:
   a. Remove three amplifier attaching nuts.
   b. Disconnect two amplifier electrical connectors.
   c. Remove premium sound amplifier assembly.
6. Reverse procedure to install. **Torque** amplifier attaching nuts to 5 ft. lbs.

WIPER MOTOR

REPLACE

FRONT

1. Remove wiper arm retaining nut covers, then retaining nuts.
2. Remove wiper arm assemblies from vehicle.
3. Remove lower windshield molding.
4. Disconnect wiper linkage from wiper motor output arm.
5. Remove wiring harness mounting bracket from wiper motor mounting bracket.
6. Remove four wiper motor mounting bracket retaining bolts, then disconnect wiper motor ground.
7. Disconnect wiper motor electrical connector, then remove wiper motor assembly from vehicle.
8. Reverse procedure to install, noting the following:
   a. Driver side wiper arm is marked D. Passenger wiper arm is marked PL.
   b. **Torque** wiper motor mounting bracket retaining bolts to 5–7 ft. lbs.
   c. **Torque** wiper arm retaining nuts to 7–10 ft. lbs.

REAR

1. Remove wiper arm and blade assembly.
2. Remove wiper motor shaft support nut cover, then support nut.
3. Remove liftgate side trim, then liftgate lower trim
4. Disconnect wiper motor electrical connector.
5. Remove three wiper motor retaining bolts, then disconnect ground wire.
6. Remove wiper motor assembly from vehicle.
7. Reverse procedure to install, noting the following:
   a. **Torque** wiper motor retaining bolts to 5–7 ft. lbs.
   b. **Torque** wiper motor shaft support nut to 2–4 ft. lbs.

WIPER SWITCH

REPLACE

FRONT

Refer to "Combination Switch, Replace" procedure for windshield wiper switch replacement.

REAR

1. Remove two armrest retaining screws, then armrest, if equipped.
2. **On models with manual transaxle,** unscrew shifter knob.
3. **On models with automatic transaxle,** remove emergency override key switch cover from top of floor console.
4. **On all models,** engage parking brake, then gently pull up on upper half of floor console to separate it from lower half.
5. Disconnect cigar lighter and cigar lighter element electrical connectors from wiring harness.
6. Remove ashtray illumination bulb from upper half of console.
7. Remove two dash panel control console bezel screws, then bezel.
8. Disconnect wiper switch electrical connector, then squeeze attaching tabs of switch assembly to remove wiper switch from control bezel.
9. Reverse procedure to install.

WIPER TRANSMISSION

REPLACE

FRONT

1. Remove wiper arm and blade assemblies.
2. Remove lower molding, then wiper linkage cover.
3. Pull wiper linkage from wiper motor output arm.
4. Remove pivot shaft retaining caps.
5. Remove pivot shafts and linkage.
6. Reverse procedure to install.

BLOWER MOTOR

REPLACE

1. Remove two hush panel retaining screws from below instrument panel.
2. Disconnect courtesy lamp electrical connector, then remove hush panel.
3. Disconnect blower motor electrical connector, then remove three blower motor retaining screws.
4. Remove blower motor assembly.
5. Reverse procedure to install.

HEATER CORE

REPLACE

1. Partially drain engine cooling system, then disconnect heater hoses at bulkhead in engine compartment.
2. Remove instrument cluster as described under "Instrument Cluster, Replace."
3. Remove instrument panel as outlined under "Dash Panel, Replace."
4. Loosen upper left evaporator/blower unit nut to allow for removal of heater unit.
5. Remove three heater unit retaining screws, then heater unit from vehicle.
6. Remove four brace screws, then the brace from heater unit.
7. Remove heater core from heater unit.
8. Reverse procedure to install.

EVAPORATOR CORE

REPLACE

1. Recover A/C refrigerant as outlined in "Air Conditioning " section.
2. Disconnect high and low pressure lines from bulkhead, then vacuum line.
3. Remove instrument cluster as described under "Instrument Cluster, Replace."
4. Remove instrument panel as outlined under "Dash Panel Service."
5. Disconnect blower motor electrical connector, then the resistor electrical connector.
6. Remove evaporator/blower case brace retaining nuts and bolts, then the brace.
7. Remove three nuts and one bolt retaining evaporator/blower case to bulkhead.
8. Remove evaporator/blower case from vehicle.
9. Remove five evaporator/blower case screws, then separate evaporator/blower case halves.
10. Remove evaporator core from case.
11. Reverse procedure to install.

2.0L Engine

NOTE: Refer To " Air Bag System Precautions " Located In The Front Of This Manual For System Disarming & Arming Procedures.

NOTE: Prior To Performing Any Service Operations Listed In This Section, Consult The "Technical Service Bulletins " Section For Related Information.

NOTE: Refer to "Computer Relearn Procedures " Located In The Front Of This Manual For Computer Relearn Procedures.

INDEX

PRECAUTIONS

AIR BAG SYSTEMS

Refer to "Air Bag System Precautions" in front of this manual for system disarming and arming procedures.

FUEL SYSTEM PRESSURE RELIEF

1. Start engine, then remove fuel pump relay from fuse box, **Fig. 1.**
2. After engine stalls, turn ignition off.
3. Install fuel pump relay.
4. When disconnecting fuel lines, use rag as protection from fuel spray. **Plug hoses after they are disconnected.**

BATTERY GROUND CABLE

Prior to service, disconnect battery ground cable and isolate as required.

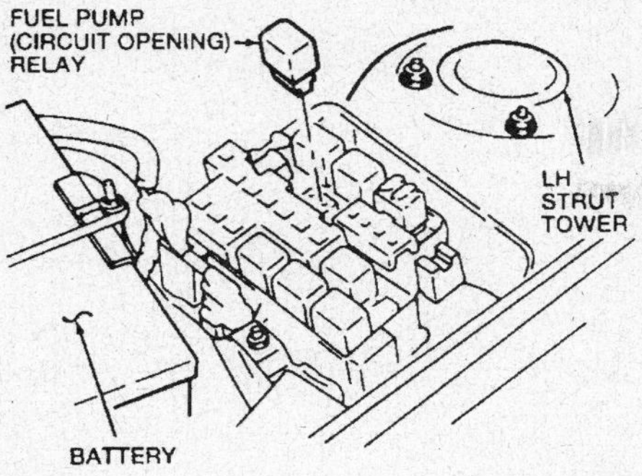

FM1029100148000X

Fig. 1 Fuel pump relay removal

ENGINE SEALANT & GASKET MATERIAL

Exhaust gas sensors (EGO) can be contaminated by high volatility type silicones. This type of silicone can be found in sealants and gasket material. When volatile silicones migrate and come in contact with EGO, contamination can occur rendering EGO defective.

When performing service on engine, use only low volatility type silicone sealant. Replace EGO if contaminated. **Do not use conventional silicone rubber sealants when low volatility silicone sealant is specified.**

Use Ford part number F1AZ-19662-A Low Volatility RTV sealant, or equivalent where specified.

COMPRESSION PRESSURE

Compression pressure check should be performed with engine at normal operating temperature with spark plugs removed, distributor connector disconnected and throttle wide open. Compression pressure should be 179 psi with a minimum of 142 psi.

ENGINE MOUNT

REPLACE

Refer to **Fig. 2** when replacing engine mounts.

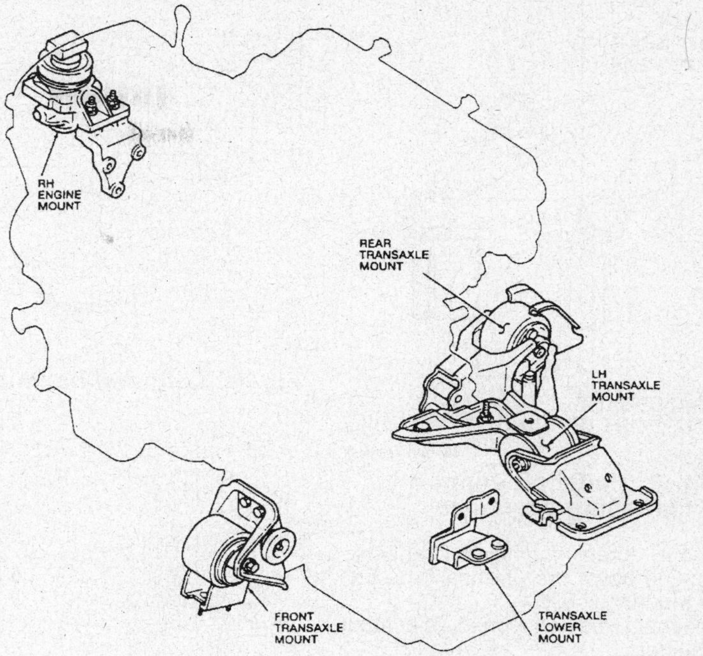

FM1069100266000X

Fig. 2 Engine mount locations

ENGINE

REPLACE

AUTOMATIC TRANSAXLE

1. Relieve fuel system pressure as described under " Precautions."
2. Remove battery and battery tray from vehicle.
3. Disconnect engine compartment lamp electrical connector, then carefully remove hood assembly.
4. Drain engine oil and cooling system.
5. Remove air intake system.
6. Remove A/C compressor mounting bolts if equipped, and position compressor aside. Support compressor assembly with wire.
7. Disconnect fuel lines from fuel rail assembly and position aside. **Plug disconnected fuel lines to prevent any fuel leakage. Label fuel lines for installation reference.**
8. Disconnect all engine wiring connectors and position aside. **Label connectors for installation reference.**
9. Remove power steering pump belt shield, then loosen power steering pump adjustment bolt.
10. Loosen power steering pump lock bolt and through bolt, then remove power steering belt.
11. Remove power steering hose hold-down bracket mounting bolts and brackets from cylinder head cover.
12. Remove power steering belt adjuster, then disconnect power steering pressure switch connector.
13. Remove power steering pump through bolt and position pump aside.
14. Loosen alternator adjusting bolt, then remove alternator upper mounting bolt and alternator belt.
15. Remove both radiator hoses.
16. Disconnect speed control vacuum line from back righthand side of intake manifold, if necessary.
17. Disconnect vacuum line connecting carbon canister to metal EGR vacuum line.
18. Disconnect EGR temperature sensor connector, if necessary.
19. Disconnect accelerator cable, then brake booster vacuum line from back lefthand side of intake manifold.
20. Disconnect heater hoses and remove starter motor upper mounting bolts.
21. Raise and support vehicle, then remove splash shield bolts and splash shields.
22. Disconnect starter motor electrical connector, then remove starter motor.
23. Remove intake manifold support bracket.
24. Remove halfshaft support bearing attaching bolts.
25. Disconnect oil pressure sensor connector.
26. Remove torque converter to flexplate attaching nuts.

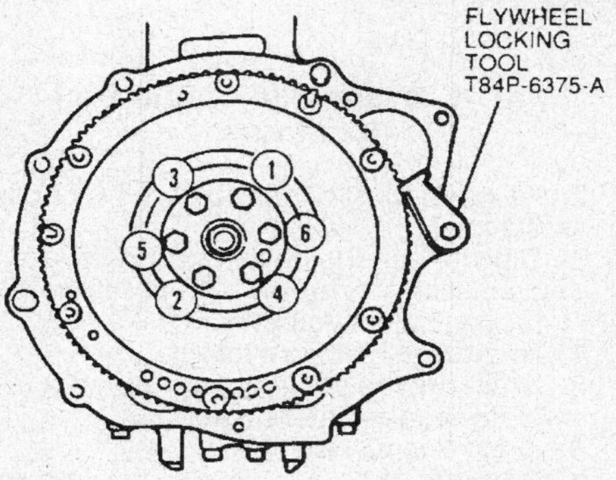

FM1069100267000X

Fig. 3 Flex plate tightening sequence

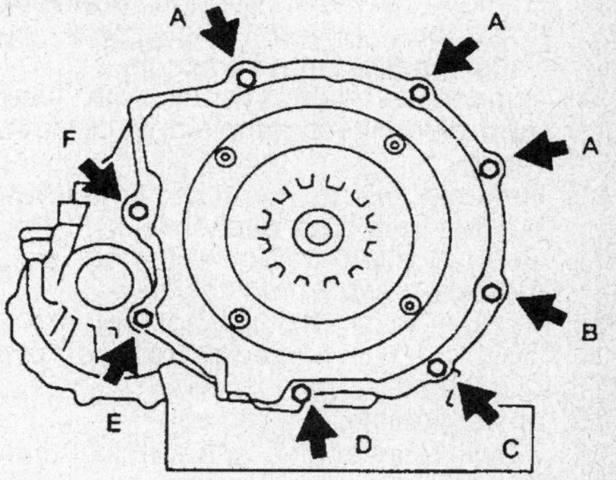

FM1069100268000X

Fig. 4 Transaxle to engine bolt locations. Automatic transaxle

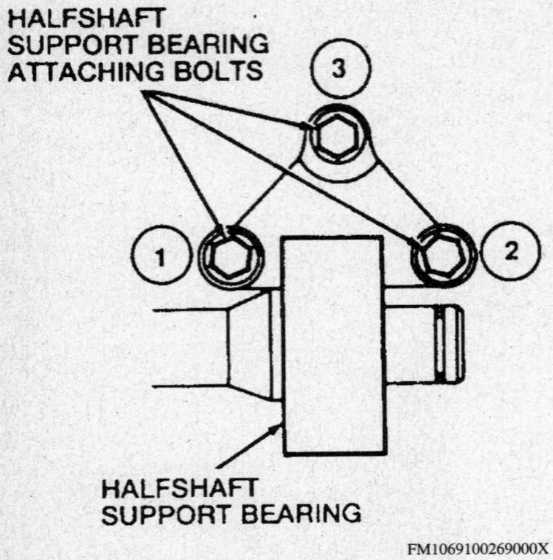

Fig. 5 Halfshaft support tightening sequence

27. Remove three engine to transaxle mounting bolts, then transaxle to engine mounting bolts.
28. Disconnect oxygen sensor electrical connector.
29. Remove converter inlet pipe to catalytic converter attaching nuts.
30. Remove exhaust support attaching bolts, then converter inlet pipe to exhaust manifold attaching nuts.
31. Support exhaust system with wire, then disconnect remaining alternator wiring.
32. Remove wiring harness hold-down bracket from back of alternator.
33. Remove alternator lower through bolt, then alternator from vehicle.
34. Using crankshaft pulley holder tool No. T92C-6316-AH, or equivalent, remove crankshaft pulley.
35. Lower vehicle.
36. Slowly raise engine with a jack and remove righthand engine mount.
37. Attach an engine hoist to lifting eyes on engine, then remove remaining transaxle to engine mounting bolts.
38. Remove engine from vehicle.
39. Reverse procedure to install, noting the following:
    a. Install flywheel locking tool No. T84P-6375-A, or equivalent, then using sequence shown in **Fig. 3** tighten flex plate mounting bolts in two or three steps to specifications.
    b. Refer to **Fig. 4,** then tighten transaxle to engine mounting bolts as follows; **torque** bolts marked "A" to 50–73 ft. lbs., **torque** bolts marked "B" to 50–73 ft. lbs., **torque** bolts marked "C" to 28–38 ft. lbs., **torque** bolts marked "D" to 14–18 ft. lbs., **torque** bolts marked "E" to 28–38 ft. lbs., **torque** bolts marked "F" to 50–73 ft. lbs.
    c. Using sequence shown in **Fig. 5,** tighten halfshaft support bearing attaching bolts to specifications.

MANUAL TRANSAXLE

1. Relieve fuel system pressure as described under " Precautions."

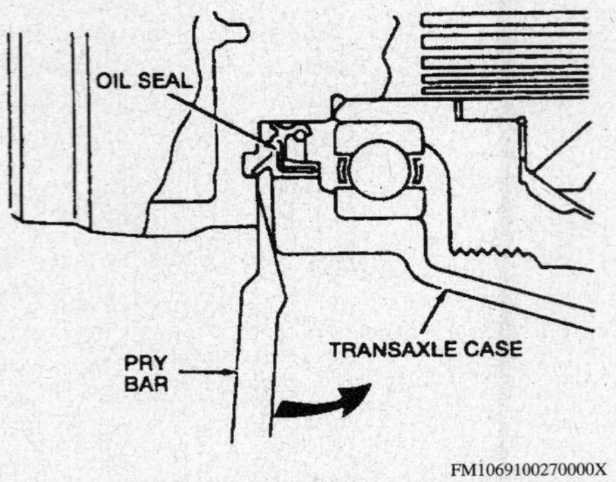

Fig. 6 Lefthand halfshaft removal

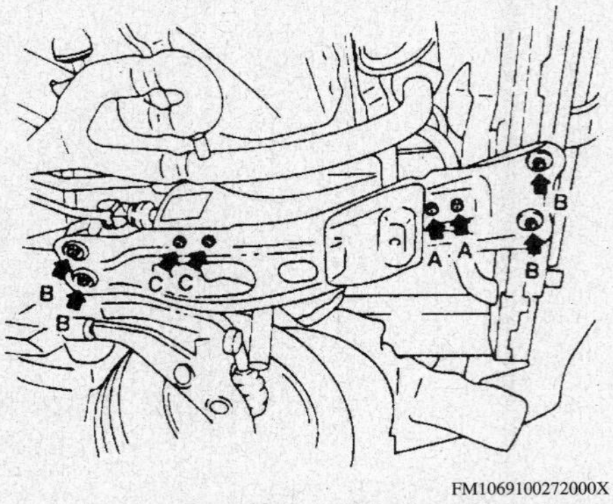

Fig. 8 Transaxle cradle bolt locations

2. Remove battery and battery tray from vehicle.
3. Disconnect engine compartment lamp electrical connector, then carefully remove and set aside hood assembly.
4. Remove air intake system.
5. Drain engine coolant, then remove radiator and radiator hoses.
6. Drain engine oil.
7. Remove A/C compressor mounting bolts, if equipped, and position compressor aside. Support compressor assembly with wire.
8. Disconnect fuel lines from fuel rail assembly and position aside. **Plug disconnected fuel lines to prevent any fuel leakage. Label fuel lines for installation reference.**
9. Disconnect all engine wiring connectors and position aside. **Label connectors for installation reference.**
10. Remove power steering pump belt shield, then loosen power steering pump adjustment bolt.
11. Loosen power steering pump lock bolt and through bolt, then remove power steering belt.
12. Remove power steering hose hold-down bracket mounting bolts and brackets from cylinder head cover.
13. Remove power steering belt adjuster, then disconnect power steering pressure switch connector.
14. Remove power steering pump through bolt and position pump aside.
15. Loosen alternator adjusting bolt, then remove alternator upper mounting bolt and alternator belt.
16. Drain engine coolant and remove both

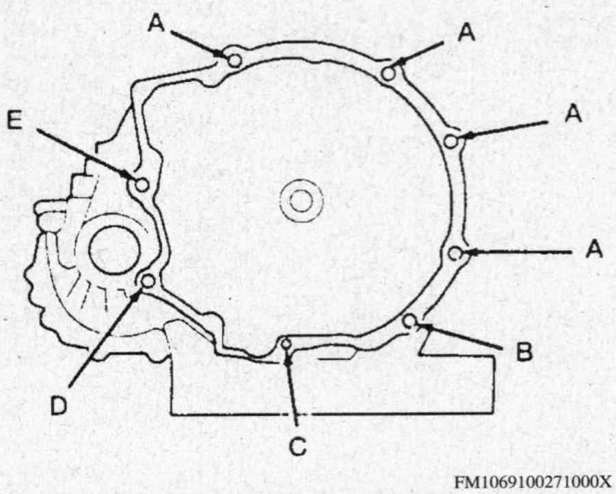

Fig. 7 Transaxle to engine bolt locations. Manual transaxle

radiator hoses.
17. Disconnect speed control vacuum line from back righthand side of intake manifold, if necessary.
18. Disconnect vacuum line connecting carbon canister to metal EGR vacuum line.
19. Disconnect EGR temperature sensor connector, if equipped.
20. Disconnect accelerator cable, then brake booster vacuum line from back lefthand side of intake manifold.
21. Disconnect heater hoses and remove starter motor upper attaching bolts.
22. Disconnect speed control actuator electrical connector.
23. Remove two speed control actuator attaching nuts and set actuator aside.
24. Remove two fuel filter mounting bracket bolts and set fuel filter and bracket aside.
25. Remove ignition control module.
26. Remove ground wire bracket mounted between transaxle and rear transaxle mount.
27. Remove rear transaxle mount through bolt, then transaxle ground located at top rear of transaxle.
28. Disconnect Brake On/Off (BOO) switch and Vehicle Speed Sensor (VSS) connectors from rear of transaxle.
29. Remove slave cylinder line fitting from slave cylinder. **Plug metal line to prevent fluid leakage.**
30. Pull spring clips from slave cylinder line mounting brackets, then remove rubber line from metal line.
31. Disconnect Park/Neutral Position (PNP) switch from front of transaxle.
32. Raise and support vehicle, then remove front wheels and splash shields.
33. Remove six transverse member attaching bolts, then transverse member.
34. Remove six transaxle cradle nuts and two bolts, then transaxle cradle.
35. Remove two transaxle lower mount bolts and transaxle lower mount.
36. Remove halfshafts as follows:
    a. Using hammer and chisel, carefully raise staked portion of halfshaft attaching nut.
    b. Apply brakes, then remove halfshaft attaching nut. **Discard nut after removal, never reuse nut.**

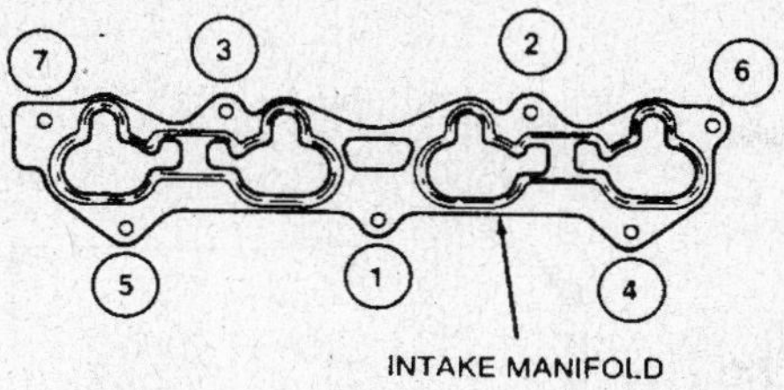

FM1059100053000X

Fig. 9 Intake manifold tightening sequence

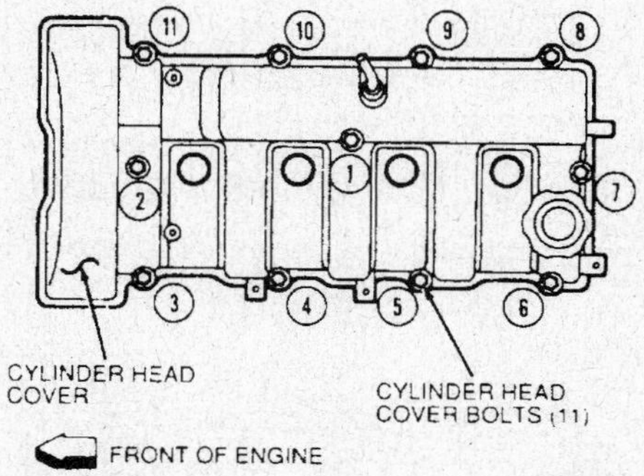

FM1069100275000X

Fig. 12 Cylinder head cover bolt loosening sequence

c. Remove righthand stabilizer control link from lower control arm attaching bracket.
d. Remove righthand side ball joint clamp bolt, then pry lower control arm from ball joint clamp.
e. Separate righthand side halfshaft from wheel hub. If halfshaft splines bind, use jaw puller tool No. D80L-1002-L, or equivalent. **Never strike halfshaft with any object.**
f. Using an angled pry bar, or equivalent, remove lefthand halfshaft by prying between constant velocity joint outer race and transaxle housing, **Fig. 6.** Carefully tap pry bar end to unseat circlip on sidegear end of halfshaft.
g. Remove three halfshaft support bearing attaching bolts.
h. Separate righthand halfshaft assembly from differential by carefully prying halfshaft from transaxle.
i. Support halfshaft assemblies and slide out of transaxle.
j. Using transaxle plug set T88C-7025-AH, or equivalent, plug transaxle openings to prevent leakage.

37. Remove intake manifold support bracket.
38. Remove rear transaxle mount bolts, then mount.
39. Disconnect starter motor electrical connector, then remove starter motor.
40. Disconnect oil pressure sensor and oxygen sensor electrical connectors.
41. Remove converter inlet pipe to catalytic converter attaching nuts.
42. Remove exhaust support attaching bolts, then converter inlet pipe to exhaust manifold attaching nuts.
43. Support exhaust system with wire.
44. Remove extension bar nut and washer, then disengage bar from transaxle.

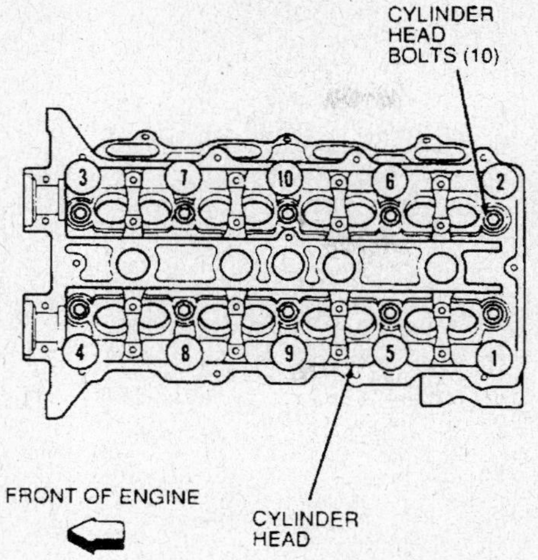

FM1069100273000X

Fig. 10 Cylinder head bolt loosening sequence

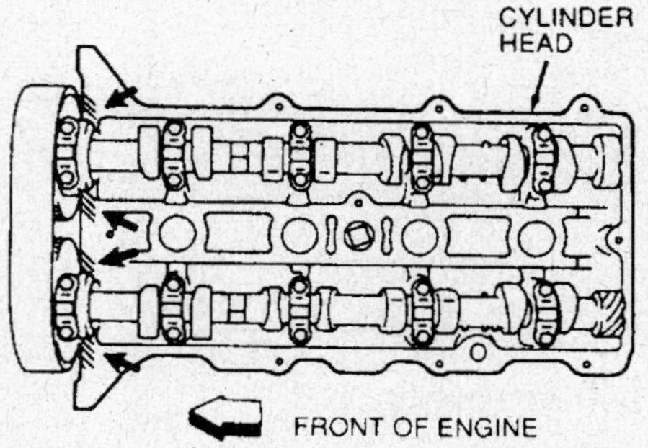

FM1069100276000X

Fig. 13 Cylinder head sealant application

45. Remove transaxle shift linkage through bolt and nut, then disengage shift linkage from transaxle.
46. Remove wiring harness hold-down bracket from back of alternator, then alternator lower through bolt.
47. Disconnect remaining alternator wiring and remove alternator.
48. Using crankshaft pulley holder tool No. T92C-6316-AH, or equivalent, remove crankshaft pulley attaching bolt.
49. Remove crankshaft pulley and guide plate.
50. Lower vehicle, then slightly raise engine with a jack and remove righthand engine mount.
51. Attach an engine hoist to lifting eyes on engine, then remove lefthand transaxle mount nuts and bolts.
52. Remove lefthand transaxle mount through bolt, then the mount.
53. Remove engine and transaxle assembly from vehicle.
54. Remove transaxle to engine mounting bolts and separate engine from transaxle.
55. Remove clutch and flywheel.
56. Remove crankshaft rear cover plate bolt and plate.
57. Reverse procedure to install, noting the following:
    a. Refer to **Fig. 7,** then tighten transaxle to engine mounting bolts as follows; **torque** bolts marked "A" to 66–86 ft. lbs., **torque** bolts marked "B" to 28–38 ft. lbs., **torque** bolts marked "C" to 14–18 ft. lbs., **torque** bolts marked "D" to 28–38 ft. lbs., **torque** bolts marked "E" to 66–86 ft. lbs.
    b. Refer to **Fig. 8, torque** then tighten transaxle cradle nuts as follows; **torque** bolts marked "A" 55–77 ft. lbs., **torque** bolts marked "B" 50–68 ft. lbs., **torque** bolts marked " C" 32–44 ft. lbs.

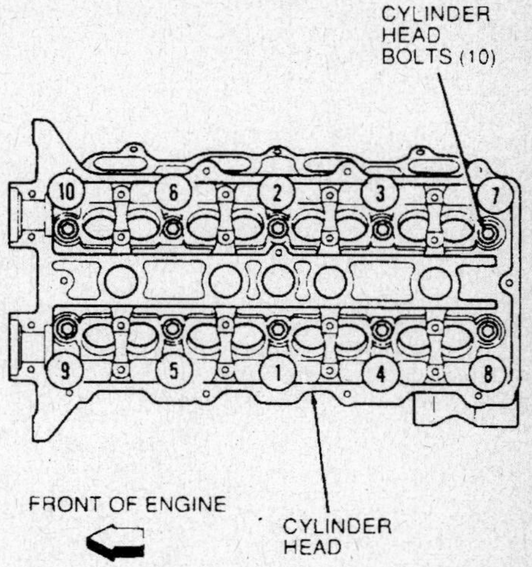

FM1069100274000X

Fig. 11 Cylinder head bolt tightening sequence

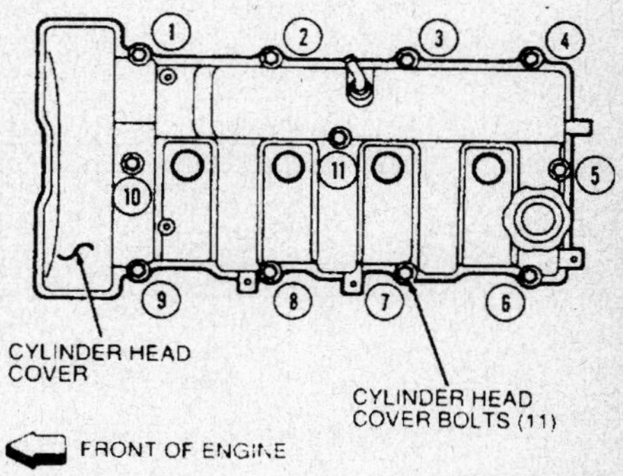

FM1069100277000X

Fig. 14 Cylinder head cover bolt tightening sequence

INTAKE MANIFOLD

REPLACE

1. Remove air intake system and fuel line mounting bracket.
2. Disconnect throttle cable.
3. Disconnect coolant line from idle air bypass air valve.
4. Disconnect coolant and vacuum lines from throttle body. **Mark vacuum lines for installation reference.**
5. Disconnect throttle position sensor connector.
6. **On models with automatic transaxle,** disconnect idle switch connector.
7. **On all models,** disconnect brake

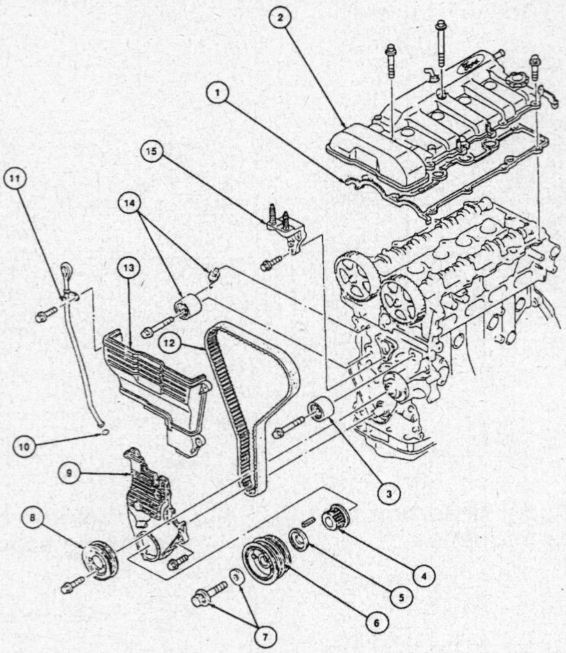

Item	Description
1	Cylinder Head Cover Gasket
2	Cylinder Head Cover
3	Idler
4	Crankshaft Sprocket
5	Guide Plate
6	Crankshaft Pulley

Item	Description
7	Crankshaft Pulley Bolt and Washer
8	Water Pump Pulley
9	Timing Belt Lower Cover
10	Engine Oil Dipstick O-Ring
11	Engine Oil Dipstick
12	Timing Belt
13	Timing Belt Upper Cover

FM1069100278000X

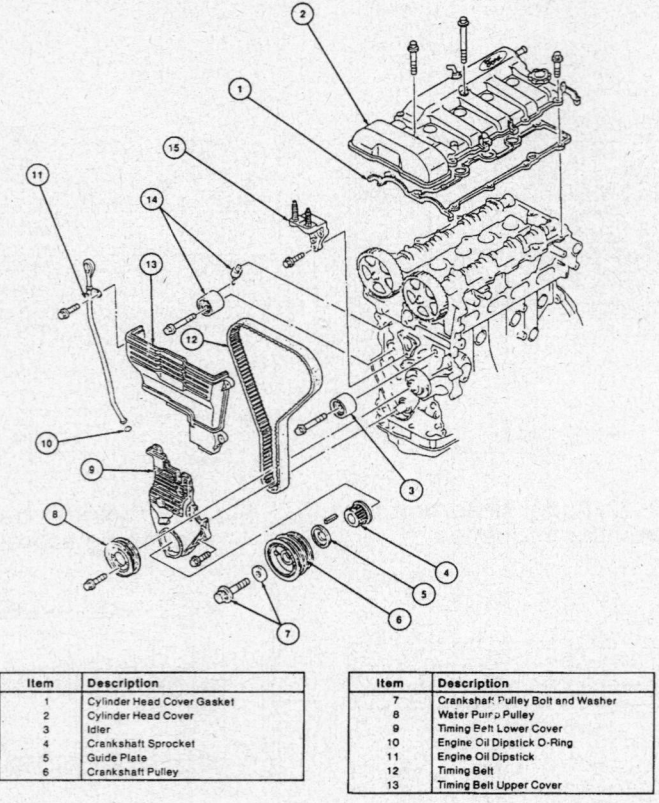

Fig. 15 Timing belt assembly

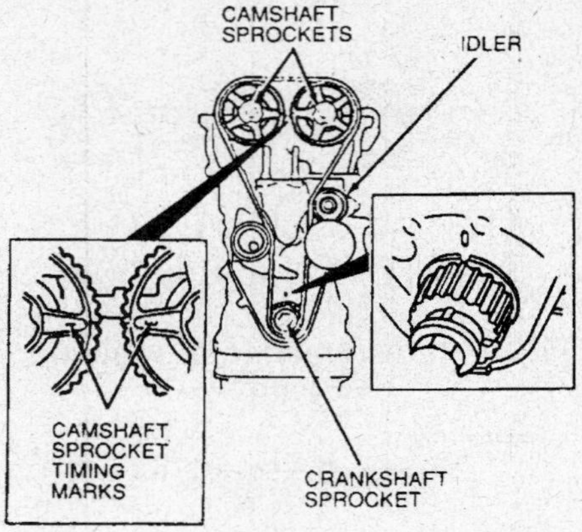

FM1069100279000X

Fig. 16 Timing mark alignment

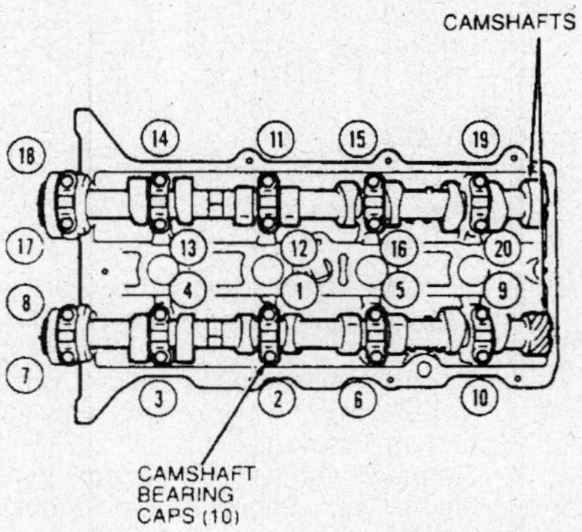

FM1069100282000X

Fig. 19 Camshaft bearing cap tightening sequence

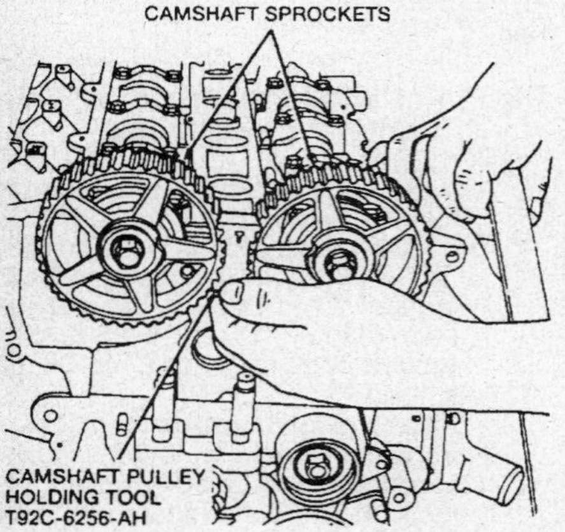

FM1069100280000X

Fig. 17 Camshaft pulley holding tool positioning

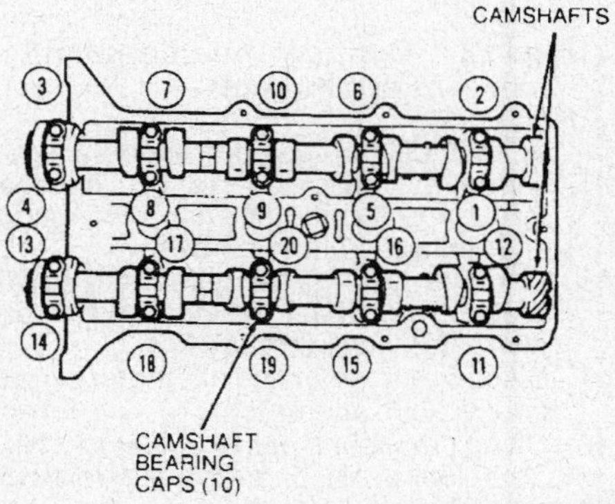

FM1069100281000X

Fig. 18 Camshaft bearing cap loosening sequence

booster vacuum line from back left-hand side of intake manifold.
8. Disconnect EGR temperature sensor connector, if equipped.
9. Disconnect speed control vacuum line from back righthand side of intake manifold.
10. Disconnect EGR solenoid connectors.
11. Remove PCV valve from cylinder head cover.
12. Raise and support vehicle.
13. Remove intake manifold support bracket, then EGR pipe from intake manifold.
14. Lower vehicle and remove intake manifold attaching bolts and nuts.
15. Remove intake manifold and discard gasket.
16. Reverse procedure to install. Refer to **Fig. 9** for manifold tightening sequence, then tighten bolts and nuts to specifications.

EXHAUST MANIFOLD

REPLACE

1. Remove seven exhaust manifold heat shield bolts, then heat shield.
2. Disconnect oxygen sensor connector, then using EGO sensor wrench tool No. T79P-9472-A, or equivalent, remove sensor.
3. Raise and support vehicle.
4. Support exhaust system with wire, then remove three converter inlet pipe to exhaust manifold attaching nuts. Discard nuts.
5. Remove EGR pipe from back of exhaust manifold.
6. Lower vehicle.
7. Remove exhaust manifold mounting nuts, bolts and gasket. Discard nuts and manifold gasket.
8. Reverse procedure to install. Tighten nuts and bolts to specifications.

CYLINDER HEAD

REPLACE

1. Drain cooling system, then remove air intake system.
2. Remove power steering hose hold-down bracket bolts from cylinder head cover.
3. Remove power steering pump belt shield, then loosen adjusting bolt.
4. Loosen lock bolt and power steering pump through bolt.
5. Remove power steering belt.
6. Loosen alternator adjusting bolt, then loosen alternator upper mounting bolt.
7. Raise and support vehicle, then remove righthand splash shield.
8. Loosen lower alternator through bolt,

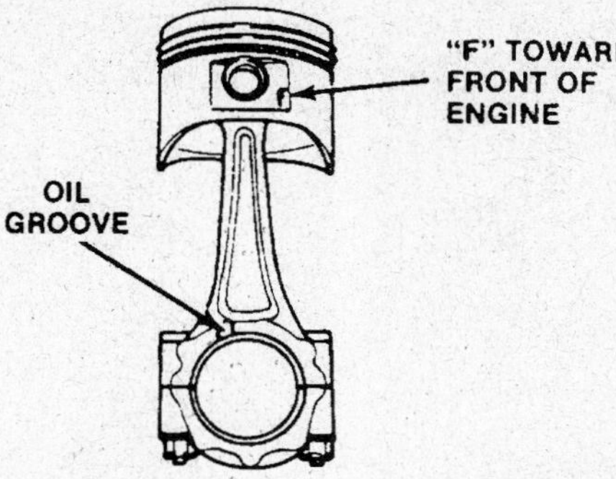

FM1069100284000X

Fig. 20 Piston & rod assembly

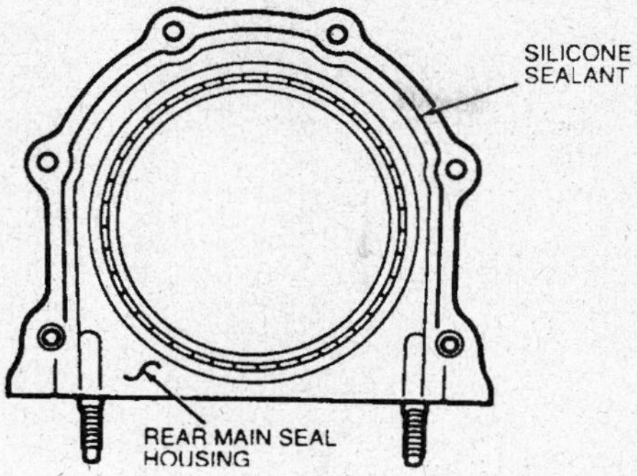

FM1069100283000X

Fig. 21 Rear main seal housing sealant application

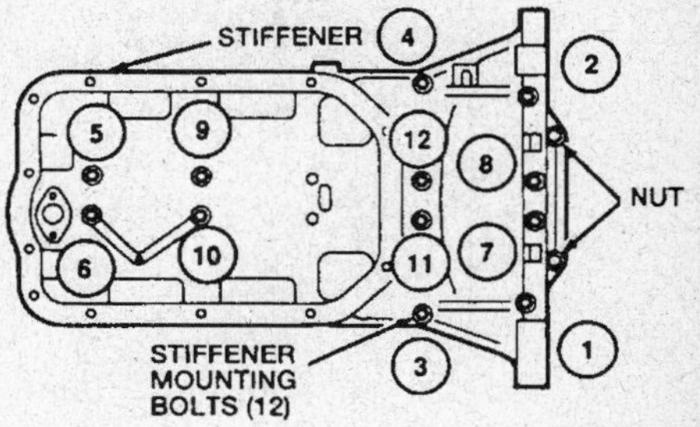

FM1069100285000X

Fig. 22 Stiffener bolt loosening sequence

Drive Belt	New N (lb)	Used N (lb)	Limit N (lb)
GENERATOR	740-830 (170-180)	500-680 (110-150)	390 (88)
P/S, P/S + A/C	590-780 (140-170)	500-680 (110-150)	390 (88)

FM1069100288000X

Fig. 25 Belt tension specifications

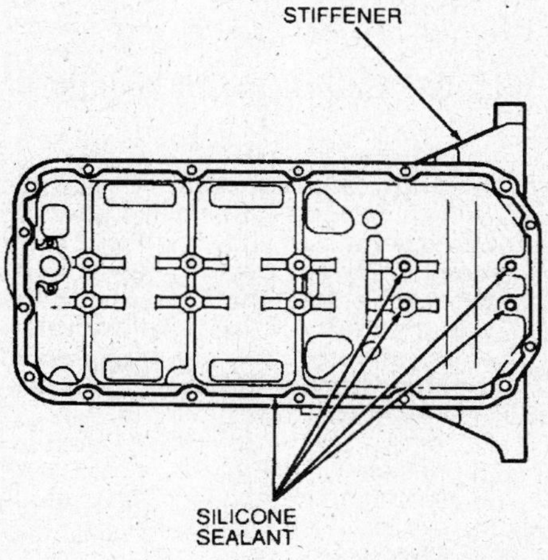

FM1069100286000X

Fig. 23 Stiffener sealant application

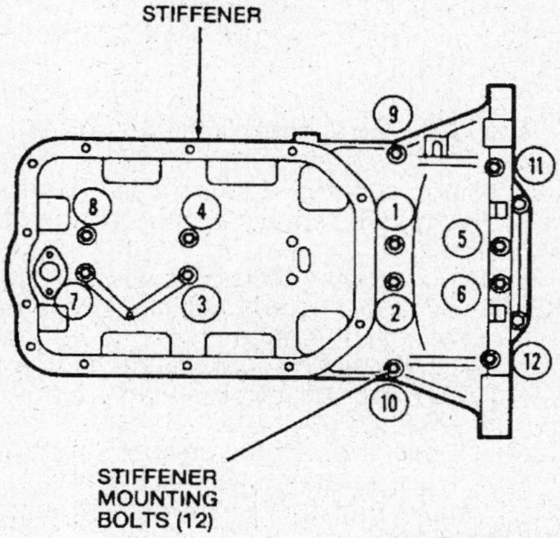

FM1069100287000X

Fig. 24 Stiffener bolt tightening sequence

lower vehicle and remove alternator belt.

9. Remove power steering pump through bolt and lock bolt, then position pump aside.
10. Remove alternator bracket nut and bolt, then position bracket aside.
11. Remove exhaust manifold as described under "Exhaust Manifold, Replace."
12. Carefully remove cylinder head cover as described under " Valve Cover, Replace."
13. Remove timing belt as described under "Timing Belt, Replace."
14. Disconnect distributor/coil connectors, then all connectors at coolant temperature sensor housing.
15. Remove coolant temperature sensor housing from cylinder head and discard gasket.
16. Remove two distributor cap attaching screws, then distributor cap. Position cap and wires aside.
17. Rotate engine until No. 1 piston is at TDC on compression stroke.
18. Remove two distributor hold-down bolts, then the distributor.
19. Remove camshafts as described under "Camshaft, Replace. "
20. Remove cylinder head bolts in sequence shown in **Fig. 10.** Discard bolts.
21. Remove cylinder head and gasket from engine, then discard gasket.
22. Reverse procedure to install, noting the following:
    a. Ensure cylinder head and cylinder block mating surfaces are clean.
    b. **Do not reuse cylinder head bolts.**
    c. Using tightening sequence shown in **Fig. 11, torque** cylinder head bolts in two steps to 13–16 ft. lbs. After initial tightening, apply a paint mark to cylinder head bolts, then tighten bolts an additional 85–95° in sequence. Finally tighten all bolts an additional 85–95.°
    d. Ensure timing marks are aligned on distributor shaft and distributor housing.

VALVE COVER

REPLACE

1. Remove power steering hose hold-down brackets.
2. Disconnect spark plug wires and wire clips. **Mark wires for installation reference.**
3. Disconnect breather tube from cover, then PCV valve.
4. Using bolt loosening sequence shown in **Fig. 12,** remove cylinder head cover bolts in two steps.
5. Carefully pry cylinder head cover from cylinder head.
6. Remove cylinder head cover gasket, then discard.
7. Reverse procedure to install, noting the following:
    a. Apply a coat of silicone sealant to new cylinder head cover gasket.
    b. Apply silicone sealant to cylinder head as shown in **Fig. 13.**
    c. Refer to **Fig. 14** for bolt tightening sequence, then tighten cylinder head cover bolts in two steps to specifications

CAMSHAFT LOBE LIFT SPECIFICATIONS

Intake: ....1.6859–1.6918 inches
Exhaust: ....1.7003–1.7062 inches

VALVE CLEARANCE SPECIFICATIONS

Hydraulic valve lash adjusters provide automatic lash adjustment which maintains a zero inch clearance between camshaft lobes and valve stems.

VALVE ADJUSTMENT

This engine uses hydraulic valve lifters. No adjustment is required.

HYDRAULIC LASH ADJUSTERS

REPLACE

1. Remove camshaft as outlined in "Camshaft, Replace. "
2. Number and remove hydraulic lash adjusters (HLA).
3. Reverse procedure to install, noting the following:

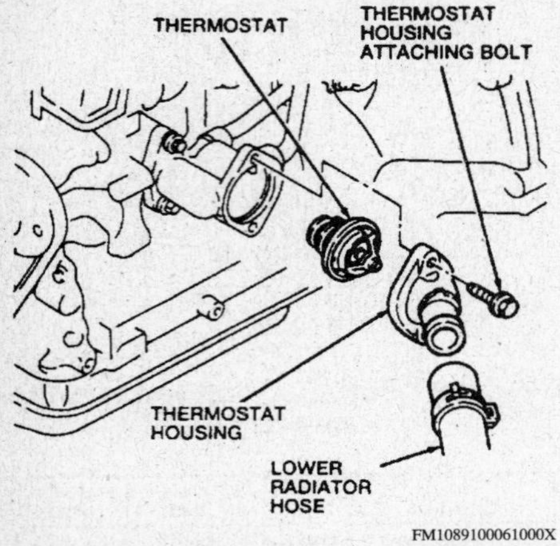

Fig. 26 Thermostat replacement

a. If reusing original adjusters, ensure they are installed in original positions.
b. Coat HLA friction surfaces with clean engine oil.

FRONT COVER SEAL

REPLACE

1. Drain cooling system, then remove air intake system.
2. Remove power steering hose hold-down bracket bolts from cylinder head cover.
3. Remove power steering pump belt shield, then loosen adjusting bolt.
4. Loosen lock bolt and power steering pump through bolt.
5. Remove power steering belt.
6. Loosen alternator adjusting bolt, then alternator upper mounting bolt.
7. Raise and support vehicle, then remove splash shields.
8. Loosen lower alternator through bolt, lower vehicle and remove alternator belt.
9. Using crankshaft pulley holder tool No. T92C-6316-AH, or equivalent, remove crankshaft pulley attaching bolt.
10. Remove crankshaft pulley, sprocket and guide plate.
11. Using seal remover tool No. T92C-6700, or equivalent, remove front oil seal.
12. Reverse procedure to install.

TIMING BELT

REPLACE

Refer to **Fig. 15,** when performing following procedure.

1. Remove valve cover as described under "Valve Cover, Replace."
2. Remove power steering pump belt shield, then loosen adjusting bolt.
3. Loosen lock bolt and power steering pump through bolt, then remove power steering belt.
4. Loosen alternator adjusting bolt and alternator upper mounting bolt, then remove alternator belt.
5. Support engine using three bar engine support tool No. 014-00750, or equivalent.

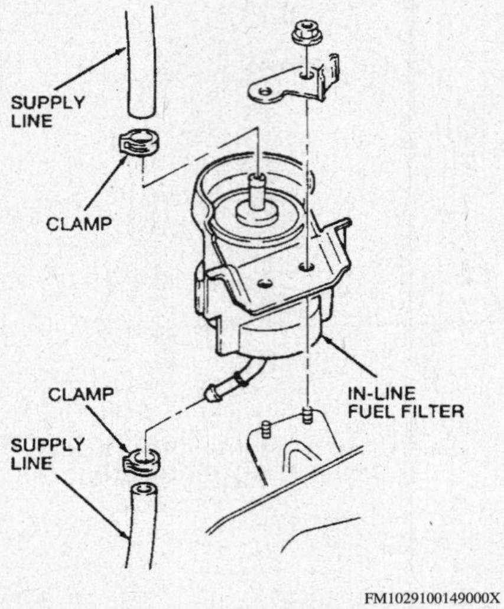

Fig. 27 Fuel filter replacement

6. Using suitable jack, raise engine slightly and remove righthand engine mount.
7. Remove timing belt upper cover.
8. Raise and support vehicle, then remove splash shields.
9. Using crankshaft pulley holder tool No. T92C-6316-AH, or equivalent, remove crankshaft pulley attaching bolt.
10. Remove crankshaft pulley, sprocket and guide plate.
11. Remove timing belt lower cover bolts, then the cover.
12. Temporarily install crankshaft pulley attaching bolt.
13. Turn crankshaft until timing mark on crankshaft sprocket lines up with timing mark on oil pump and camshaft sprocket timing marks (E and I) line up as shown in **Fig. 16.**
14. Lower vehicle and insert camshaft pulley holding tool No. T92C-6256-AH, or equivalent, **Fig. 17.**
15. Use an Allen wrench to turn timing belt tensioner and remove timing belt tensioner spring from hook pin.
16. Remove timing belt. **If reusing old timing belt, mark direction of belt for installation reference.**
17. Reverse procedure to install, noting the following
    a. Ensure all timing marks are aligned as shown in **Fig. 16.**
    b. Tighten to specifications.

CAMSHAFT

REPLACE

1. Remove valve cover as described under "Valve Cover, Replace."
2. Remove power steering pump belt shield, then loosen adjusting bolt.
3. Loosen lock bolt and power steering pump through bolt, then remove power steering belt.
4. Loosen alternator adjusting bolt and alternator upper mounting bolt, then remove alternator belt.
5. Remove timing belt as described under "Timing Belt, Replace."

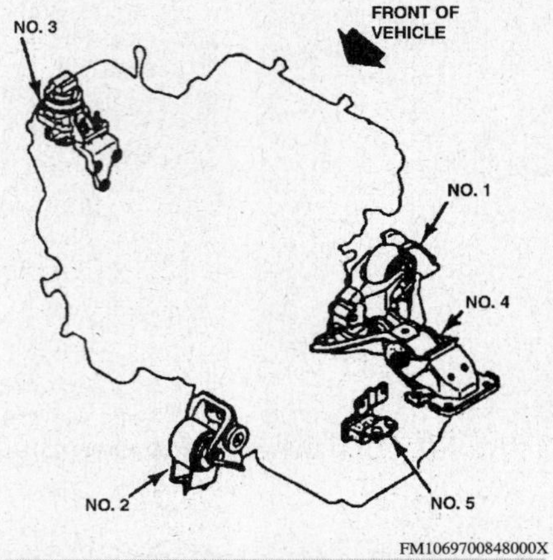

Fig. 28 Engine mount location

6. Holding camshaft with a suitable wrench, remove camshaft sprockets.
7. Using sequence shown in **Fig. 18,** remove camshaft bearing cap bolts in two steps. **Camshaft bearing caps are marked for installation reference, ensure caps are installed in their correct position.**
8. Remove camshafts.
9. Reverse procedure to install. Using sequence shown in **Fig. 19,** tighten camshaft bearing cap bolts in three steps as follows:
    a. **Torque** to 35 inch lbs.
    b. **Torque** to 6 ft. lbs.
    c. **Torque** to 8–11 ft. lbs.

PISTON & ROD ASSEMBLY

Refer to **Fig. 20** for piston and rod assembly installation direction.

CRANKSHAFT REAR OIL SEAL

REPLACE

1. Remove transaxle as described under "Engine, Replace."
2. Remove flywheel or flex plate as described under "Engine, Replace."
3. Remove rear main seal housing to stiffener attaching nuts.
4. Remove six rear main seal housing to block attaching bolts, then seal housing from block.
5. Using seal removal tool No. T92C-6700-CH, or equivalent, remove seal from housing.
6. Reverse procedure to install, noting the following:
    a. Apply a bead of silicone sealant to rear main seal housing as shown in **Fig. 21.**
    b. Tighten to specifications.

OIL PAN

REPLACE

1. Raise and support vehicle.
2. Remove righthand splash shield, then drain oil from engine.

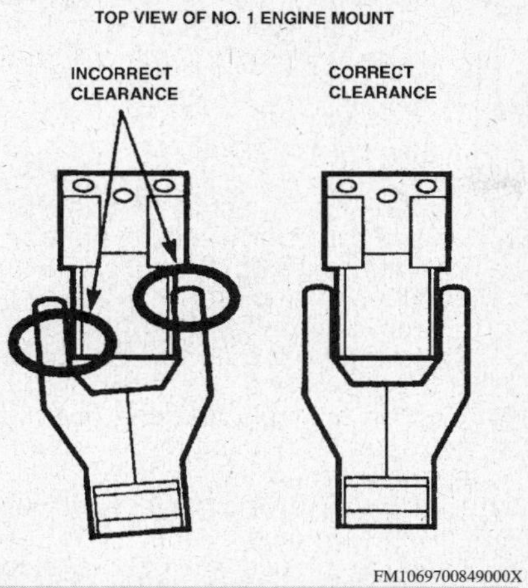

Fig. 29 Engine mount clearance inspection

3. Disconnect oxygen sensor connector, then support exhaust system using a screw type jack.
4. Remove converter inlet pipe to exhaust manifold attaching nuts and position pipe aside.
5. Remove oil pan mounting bolts and carefully pry pan from stiffener.
6. Reverse procedure to install, applying a continuous bead of sealant around oil pan. Tighten to specifications.

OIL PUMP

REPLACE

1. Remove power steering pump belt shield, then loosen adjusting bolt.
2. Loosen lock bolt and power steering pump through bolt, then remove power steering belt.
3. Loosen alternator adjusting bolt, then loosen alternator upper mounting bolt and remove alternator belt.
4. Raise and support vehicle, then remove righthand splash shield.
5. Using crankshaft pulley holder tool No. T92C-6316-AH, or equivalent, remove crankshaft pulley attaching bolt.
6. Remove crankshaft pulley, sprocket and guide plate.
7. Remove A/C compressor and position aside, then compressor mounting bracket.
8. Remove oil pan as described under "Oil Pan, Replace."
9. Remove oil pickup tube and discard gasket.
10. Remove rear main seal housing to stiffener attaching bolts.
11. Remove stiffener mounting bolts in two steps using sequence shown in **Fig. 22.**
12. Remove seven oil pump attaching bolts, then pump.
13. Reverse procedure to install, noting the following:
    a. Apply a bead of silicone sealer to pump as shown in **Fig. 23.**
    b. Tighten stiffener mounting bolts in sequence shown in **Fig. 24,** to specifications.

BELT TENSION DATA

Refer to **Fig. 25** for correct belt tension.

COOLING SYSTEM BLEED

This engine does not require a specific bleed procedure. After filling cooling system, run engine to operating temperature with radiator/pressure cap off. Air will automatically bleed through cap opening.

THERMOSTAT

REPLACE

1. Drain cooling system, then remove lower radiator hose from thermostat housing, **Fig. 26.**
2. Remove two thermostat housing attaching bolts, then housing.
3. Remove thermostat from housing.
4. Reverse procedure to install. Tighten to specifications.

WATER PUMP

REPLACE

1. Drain cooling system.
2. Remove power steering pump belt shield, then loosen adjusting bolt.
3. Loosen lock bolt and power steering pump through bolt, then remove power steering belt.
4. Loosen alternator adjusting bolt, then loosen alternator upper mounting bolt and remove alternator belt.
5. Remove valve cover as described under "Valve Cover, Replace."
6. Raise and support vehicle.
7. Using water pump pulley tool No. T92C-6312-AH, or equivalent, remove water pump pulley.
8. Remove splash shields, then timing belt as described under " Timing Belt, Replace."
9. Remove five water pump attaching bolts, then water pump.
10. Reverse procedure to install. Tighten to specifications.

RADIATOR

REPLACE

Allow radiator to cool prior to beginning procedure. Slowly remove radiator cap to release system pressure. **Caution must be used as system contains scalding hot fluid which when under pressure can blow out of radiator fill neck, causing personal injury.**

1. Slowly remove radiator cap, then open drain valve at bottom of radiator and drain system.
2. Remove fresh air duct.
3. Remove upper and lower radiator hoses.
4. Disconnect overflow hose.

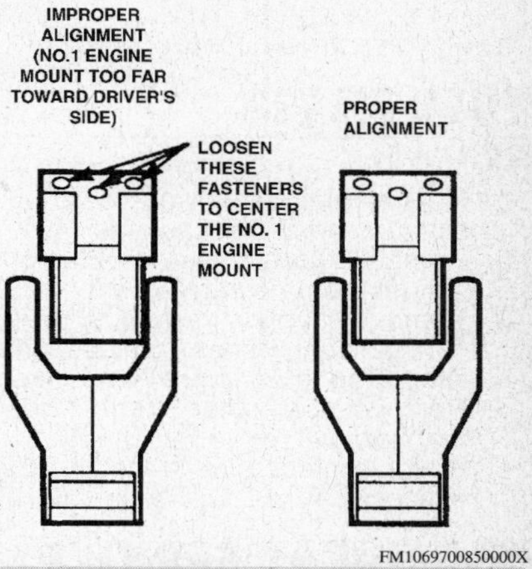

Fig. 30 Engine mount alignment

5. Disconnect cooling fan motor electrical connector.
6. **On models equipped with automatic transaxle,** disconnect transaxle oil cooler lines at radiator and plug hose ends to prevent leakage.
7. **On all models,** remove radiator mounting brackets.
8. Remove radiator and cooling fan assembly from vehicle.
9. Reverse procedure to install, noting the following:
    a. Tighten radiator mounting bracket bolts specifications.
    b. Check and fill cooling system and transaxle fluid levels.
    c. Operate engine until normal engine coolant temperature is reached and check for leaks.

FUEL PUMP

REPLACE

1. Relieve fuel system pressure as described under " Precautions."
2. Drain fuel from fuel tank, then raise and support vehicle.
3. Loosen filler neck hose clamp and remove hose.
4. Loosen overflow hose clamp and remove hose.
5. Loosen fuel supply and return line clamps, then remove hoses.
6. Loosen two fuel tank vapor line clamps and remove hoses.
7. Disconnect fuel pump sender electrical connector from body harness mating connector.
8. Remove four attaching nuts on exhaust heat shield.
9. Remove one attaching nut on fuel tank shield.
10. Support fuel tank and remove center fuel tank strap.
11. Remove righthand fuel tank strap, then fuel tank shield.
12. Remove lefthand fuel tank strap, then the tank.
13. Using a hammer and chisel, remove fuel pump lock ring.

14. Remove fuel pump assembly from tank.
15. Reverse procedure to install.

FUEL FILTER

REPLACE

1. Relieve fuel system pressure as described under " Precautions."
2. Remove two fuel filter mounting nuts on fuel filter bracket, **Fig. 27.**
3. Remove supply line clamps, then disconnect supply lines from both ends of filter. **Plug lines to prevent leakage.**
4. Remove fuel filter from mounting bracket.
5. Reverse procedure to install. Tighten to specifications.

TECHNICAL SERVICE BULLETINS

BUZZ, VIBRATION OR CLICKING NOISE

A buzz/vibration in reverse gear at idle or a clicking noise accompanied by a vibration while turning right or left during acceleration may be heard and/or felt. This condition could be confused with a drive axle or internal transaxle concern. This may be caused by misalignment of the No. 1 engine mount.

Inspect engine mounts and realign the powertrain if necessary. Realigning the powertrain should reduce the possibility of noise and vibration. Proceed to the following repair procedure.

1. Ensure all engine mount bolts are tightened to specification.
2. Ensure proper torque is applied to bracket bolts and bolts that go through rubber bushing. **Ensure bolts are not seized. A seized bolt may appear to be properly torqued.**
3. Check alignment of engine mounts, **Figs. 28 and 29.**
4. If No. 1 engine mount is not aligned correctly, use a three bar engine support tool No. 014–00750, or equivalent, and support engine and transmission assembly.
5. Remove battery, ignition coil, air cleaner and air cleaner ducts.
6. Loosen bolts that go through rubber bushing in order of Nos. 3, 4, 1 and 2.
7. **Torque** two No. 5 mount nuts 50–68 ft. lbs.
8. Recheck clearance between No. 1 engine mount and bracket from top of vehicle.
9. Ensure No. 1 engine mount is centered. If mount is not centered, proceed to next step. If mount is centered, proceed to step 15.
10. Remove two wiring harness to bulkhead retaining nuts located above No. 1 engine mount.
11. Loosen two nuts and one bolt that retain No. 1 engine mount to engine mounting member.
12. Using a suitable pry bar, reposition No. 1 engine mount so there is equal distance from each side of bracket to No. 1 mount, **Fig. 30.**
13. While holding No. 1 mount in place, **torque** two nuts and one bolt 50-68 ft. lbs.
14. Install wiring harness to bulkhead.
15. Install battery, ignition coil, air cleaner and air cleaner ducts.

TIGHTENING SPECIFICATIONS

Year	Component	Torque/ Ft. Lbs.
1997	A/C Compressor Mounting Bolts	18–26
	A/C Compressor Mounting Bracket	27–38
	Alternator Bracket	14–19
	Alternator Lower Through Bolt	27–38
	Alternator Upper Mounting Bolt	14–18
	Automatic Transaxle To Engine	50–73
	Battery Tray Mounting Bolt	72–84①
	Camshaft Bearing Cap Bolts	⑤
	Camshaft Sprocket	36–45
	Coolant Return Pipe Mounting Bracket	14–19
	Coolant Temperature Sensor Housing	14–19
	Connecting Rod Bearing Cap Bolts	③
	Converter Inlet Pipe To Exhaust Manifold	27–38
	Crankshaft Pulley Attaching Bolt	116–123
	Crankshaft Rear Cover	72–84①
	Cylinder Head Bolts	②
	Cylinder Head Cover	52–69①
	Distributor	14–19
	EGR Pipe To Exhaust Manifold	24–34
	Engine Lifting Eye Attaching Bolts	27–38
	Engine Mount Bracket Attaching Bolt	32–45
	Engine Mount Attaching Nuts	54–75
	Engine Mount Through Bolts	63–86
	Exhaust Manifold Bolts	12–17
	Exhaust Manifold Heat Shield	72–84①
	Exhaust Manifold Nuts	14–21
	Exhaust Support Attaching Bolt	27–38
	Extension Bar Nut	28–38
	Fan Shroud	72–84①
	Flex Plate	70–75
	Flywheel	70–75

Continued

TIGHTENING SPECIFICATIONS—Continued

Year	Component	Torque/ Ft. Lbs.
1997	Fuel Filter Bracket	72–96①
	Fuel Rail Supply Line Fitting	18–25
	Halfshaft Support Bearing Attaching Bolt	32–45
	Idler Bolt	27–38
	Intake Manifold	14–19
	Intake Manifold Support Bracket	27–38
	LH Transaxle Mount Nuts	50–68
	LH Transaxle Mount Through Bolt	63–86
	Main Bearing Cap Bolts	④
	Oil Drain Plug	22–30
	Oil Pan Mounting Bolts	14–19
	Oil Pickup Tube Mounting Bolts	72–84①
	Oil Pressure Sensor	9–12
	Oil Pump Attaching Bolts	14–19
	Oil Strainer	72–84①
	Oxygen Sensor	22–36
	Power Steering Hose Bracket-To-Pump Bolt	23–34
	Power Steering Hose Hold-Down Bracket Mounting Bolt	72–84①
	Power Steering Pump Belt Shield Attaching Bolts	60–84①
	Power Steering Pump Lock Bolt	23–34
	Power Steering Pump Through Bolt	32–45
	Radiator Mounting	14-18
	Rear Main Seal Housing To Block	72–84①
	Rear Main Seal Housing To Stiffener Attaching Nuts	72–84①
	Rear Transaxle Mount Bolts	50–68
	Splash Shield Bolts	72–84①
	Starter	23–34
	Stiffener Mounting Bolts	14–19
	Thermostat Housing	14–19
	Timing Belt Tensioner Bolt	27–38
	Timing Cover Bolts	72–84①
	Transaxle Cradle Nuts	⑥
	Transaxle Lower Mount Bolts	50–68
	Transaxle Shift Linkage Through Bolt	14–18
	Transaxle To Engine Block	⑥
	Transverse Member Bolts	68–96
	Water Bypass Pipe Mounting Bolt	14–19
	Water Pump Attaching Bolts	14–19
	Water Pump Pulley Attaching Bolts	72–84①
	Wheel Lug Nuts	65–86

①— Inch lbs.
②— Refer to "Cylinder Head, Replace."
③— 16–19 ft. lbs., then tighten an additional 85–95.°
④— 13–16 ft. lbs.; then tighten an additional 90.°
⑤— Refer to "Camshaft, Replace."
⑥— Refer to "Manual Transaxle" under "Engine, Replace."

2.5L Engine

NOTE: Refer To " Air Bag System Precautions " Located In The Front Of This Manual For System Disarming & Arming Procedures.

NOTE: Refer to "Computer Relearn Procedures " Located In The Front Of This Manual For Computer Relearn Procedures.

INDEX

PRECAUTIONS

AIR BAG SYSTEMS

Refer to "Air Bag System Precautions" in front of this manual for system disarming and arming procedures.

FUEL SYSTEM PRESSURE RELIEF

1. Start engine, then remove fuel pump relay from fuse box.
2. After engine stalls, turn ignition off and replace fuel pump relay.

BATTERY GROUND CABLE

Prior to service, disconnect battery ground cable and isolate as required.

ENGINE SEALANT & GASKET MATERIAL

Exhaust gas sensors (EGO) can be contaminated by high volatility type silicones. This type of silicone can be found in sealants and gasket material. When volatile silicones migrate and come in contact with EGO, contamination can occur rendering EGO defective.

When performing service on engine use only low volatility type silicone sealant. Replace EGO if contaminated. **Do not use conventional silicone rubber sealants when low volatility silicone sealant is specified.**

Use Ford part number F1AZ-19662-A Low Volatility RTV sealant, or equivalent where specified.

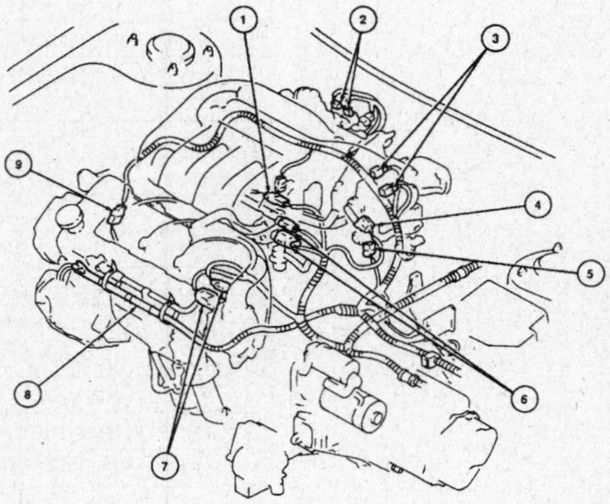

Item	Description
1	Knock Sensor
2	Variable Resonance Induction System (VRIS) Solenoids
3	EGR Control and Vent Solenoids
4	Throttle Position (TP) Sensor
5	Idle Air Control Bypass Air (IAC BPA)
6	Injector
7	Distributor
8	A/C and Generator Wiring Harness
9	Crankshaft Position (CKP) Sensor

FM1069100298000X

Fig. 1 Engine electrical connectors

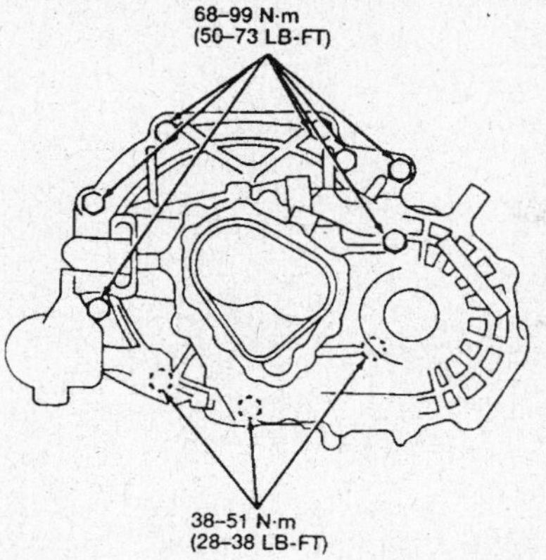

FM1069100299000X

Fig. 2 Transaxle to engine mounting bolts. Manual transaxle

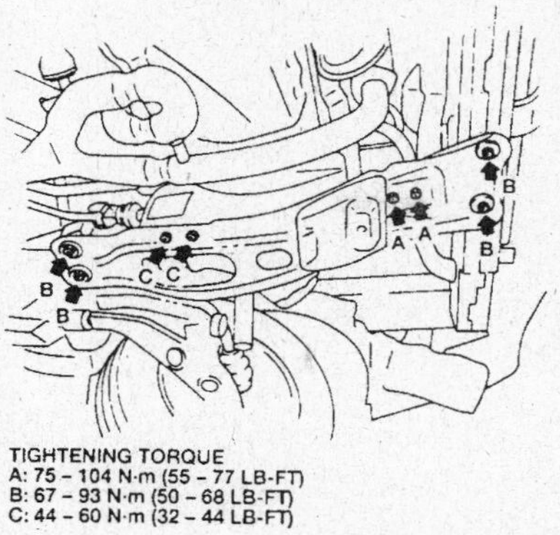

FM1069100300000X

Fig. 3 Manual transaxle cradle mounting

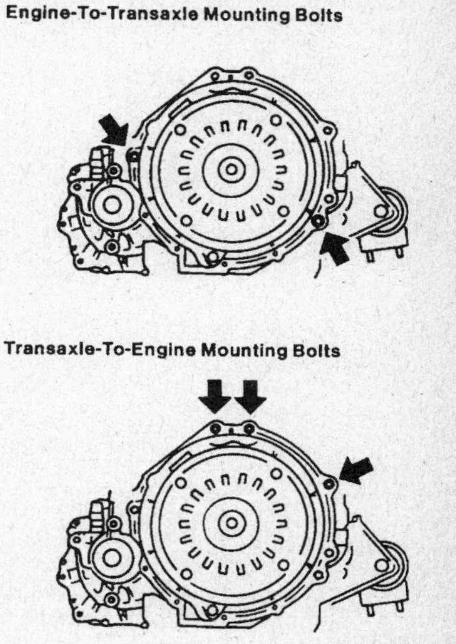

FM1069100301000X

Fig. 4 Transaxle to engine mounting. Models w/automatic transaxle

COMPRESSION PRESSURE

Compression pressure check should be performed with engine at normal operating temperature with spark plugs removed, distributor and ignition coil connectors disconnected and throttle wide open. Compression pressure should be 203 psi with a minimum of 142 psi.

ENGINE MOUNT

REPLACE

Refer to "Engine, Replace" procedure for engine mount replacement.

ENGINE

REPLACE

REMOVAL

1. Relieve fuel system pressure as described under " Precautions."
2. Remove battery and battery tray.
3. Remove fresh air duct and air cleaner assembly.
4. Raise and support vehicle.
5. Remove front tires and lower splash shields.
6. Remove six transverse member mounting bolts, then the transverse member.
7. Remove transaxle cradle attaching bolts and nuts, then the cradle.
8. Disconnect electrical connector from front oxygen sensor.
9. Remove three nuts from lefthand converter inlet pipe, then disconnect electrical connector from rear oxygen sensor.
10. Remove three nuts from rear exhaust manifold-to-converter inlet pipe flange.
11. **On models with manual transaxle,** proceed as follows:
    a. Remove nut and washer, then the extension bar from transaxle.
    b. Remove transaxle shift linkage through-bolt and nut, then disconnect linkage from transaxle.
12. **On all models,** disconnect A/C and oil pressure switch electrical connectors.
13. **On models with manual transaxle,** proceed as follows:
    a. Remove slave cylinder hydraulic line from cylinder, then the spring clips from line.
    b. Remove halfshafts as described in "Front Wheel Drive Axles" section.
    c. Remove rear transaxle mount.
14. **On all models,** loosen center locknut on power steering/water pump belt tensioner, then loosen tensioner adjusting bolt and remove belt.
15. Working through pump pulley, remove three steering pump mounting bolts.
16. Separate steering pump from rear bracket, then position pump aside.
17. Remove A/C compressor from mounting bracket and position aside. **Leave refrigerant lines connected, but do not allow compressor to hang by them.**
18. Lower vehicle.
19. **On models with manual transaxle,** separate power steering hose bracket from steering pump, loosen generator and A/C belt tensioner locknut and adjusting bolt, then remove belt.
20. **On all models,** drain cooling system.
21. Disconnect coolant overflow hose from engine coolant overflow reservoir, then remove outlet (upper) hose from engine coolant elbow and disconnect radiator cooling fan connector.
22. Remove inlet (lower) hose from thermostat housing, then the two radiator hold-down bolts.
23. Remove radiator and cooling fans.
24. Disconnect generator electrical connections. Label for installation reference.
25. Disconnect engine electrical and vacuum connections, **Fig. 1.** Label for installation reference.
26. Disconnect heater hoses from engine block, then fuel supply line from fuel rails.
27. Disconnect accelerator cable from throttle body, then with fuel lines connected, remove fuel filter and position aside.
28. Attach lifting cables to engine eye hooks and lift engine to tighten cables.
29. Remove left side transaxle mount nuts and through-bolt.
30. Remove both front transaxle mount nuts.
31. Remove two nuts and through bolt from righthand side engine mount, then the mount.
32. Remove engine and transaxle from vehicle. If necessary, separate engine from transaxle.

INSTALLATION

Manual Transaxle

1. Tighten engine to transaxle attaching bolts to specifications as shown in **Fig. 2.**
2. Lower engine and transaxle into engine compartment.
3. Install rear transaxle mount and tighten three nuts to specifications.
4. Install front and lefthand side transaxle mounts, then tighten mount nuts to specifications.
5. Install righthand engine mount and tighten nuts and through bolt to specifications.
6. Remove lift chains from engine eye hooks, then raise and support vehicle.
7. Install power steering pump and tighten mounting bolts to specifications.
8. Install drive belt over power steering and water pump pulleys, then tighten belt tensioner and center nut.
9. Install A/C compressor, tightening its mounting bolts to specifications, then position drive belt on A/C, crankshaft and generator pulleys. Tighten belt tensioner and center nut.
10. Align extension bar and tighten nut to specifications, then install transaxle shift linkage and tighten bolt to specifications.
11. Install halfshafts as described in "Front Wheel Drive Axle" section.
12. Install transaxle cradle, then the attaching nuts and bolts as shown in **Fig. 3.** Tighten to specifications.

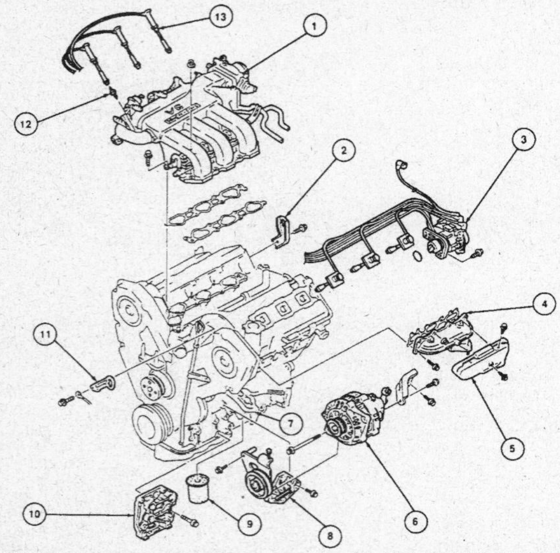

Item	Description
1	Throttle Body Assembly
2	Rear Engine Lifting Eye
3	Distributor and Spark Plug Wires
4	Front (LH) Exhaust Manifold
5	Front (LH) Exhaust Manifold Insulator
6	Generator
7	Oil Cooler Assembly
8	Bracket and Tensioner
9	Oil Filter
10	A / C Compressor Bracket
11	Front Engine Lifting Eye
12	Spark Plugs
13	Spark Plug Wires

FM1059100055000X

Fig. 5 Intake manifold

13. Install converter inlet pipes. Tighten nuts to specification.
14. Install transverse member. Tighten mounting bolts to specification.
15. Install splash shields and wheels, then lower vehicle.
16. Install power steering hose bracket retaining bolt at top of pump.
17. Connect electrical connectors and vacuum hoses, then install battery tray.
18. Connect throttle cable to throttle body, then the slave cylinder line to slave cylinder.
19. Install slave cylinder line into two spring clips on bracket.
20. Install radiator and cooling fan assembly, then the radiator hoses.
21. Install battery tray and battery, then bleed clutch system.
22. Refill fluids, then check engine operation. Check for fluid loss.

Automatic Transaxle

1. Tighten engine to transaxle attaching bolts to specification as shown in **Fig. 4,** then lower engine and transaxle into vehicle.
2. Install righthand engine mount and tighten bolts and nuts to specification.
3. Tighten lefthand transaxle mount through-bolt to specification.
4. Remove lifting device, then raise and support vehicle.
5. Install front and rear transaxle mount through-bolts and tighten to specification.
6. Lower vehicle, then align cooling fan relay bracket and install two bolts.
7. Connect shift cable to Manual Lever Position (MLP) switch and install spring clip.
8. Install fuel filter, then connect throttle cable to throttle body.
9. Using a new copper crush washer, install fuel rail supply line and tighten line fitting to specifications.
10. Attach heater hoses to thermostat housing, then reconnect all disconnected electrical and vacuum connections.
11. Install radiator and cooling fan assembly, then the radiator hoses.
12. Install A/C compressor. Tighten bolts to specifications.
13. Tighten power steering hose bracket-to-pump bolt to specifications.
14. Working through pump pulley, install three steering pump bolts and tighten to specifications.
15. Install power steering/water pump belt, then raise and support vehicle and install halfshafts.
16. Connect converter inlet pipes to exhaust manifolds and tighten attaching nuts to specifications.
17. Install transverse member and tighten bolts to specification.
18. Install front splash shields and wheels, then lower vehicle.
19. Install generator/A/C belt and air cleaner case.
20. Install battery tray and battery, then refill fluids and check engine operation. Check for fluid loss.

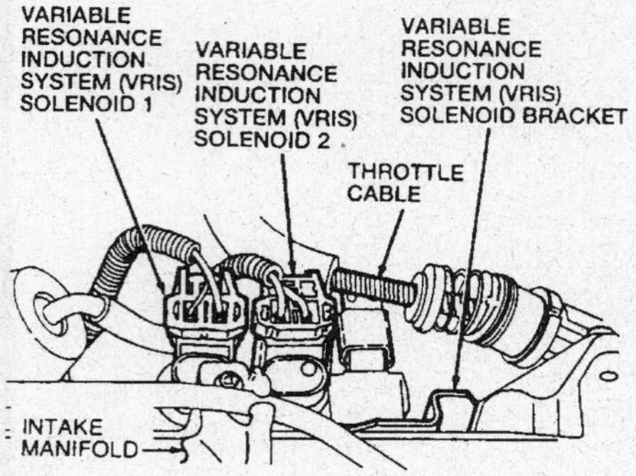

FM1069100302000X

Fig. 6 VRIS bracket removal

INTAKE MANIFOLD

REPLACE

Refer to **Fig. 5** when replacing intake manifold.

1. Relieve fuel system pressure as outlined under " Precautions."
2. Drain cooling system.
3. Disconnect vacuum hoses and electrical connectors from air cleaner assembly, then remove the assembly.
4. Disconnect knock sensor electrical connector, then remove the sensor bracket from intake manifold.
5. Remove crankshaft position sensor bracket from righthand side of intake manifold.
6. Remove rear spark plug wires, then the Variable Resource Induction System (VRIS) solenoid electrical connector bracket from rear of intake manifold, **Fig. 6.**
7. Disconnect PCV valve vacuum hose from intake manifold, then the throttle position sensor and fuel rail electrical connectors.
8. Disconnect throttle cable from throttle body, then remove vacuum hose from fuel vapor canister.
9. Disconnect fuel supply line at fuel rails and discard copper crush washers, then remove vacuum and fuel lines from fuel pressure regulator.
10. Remove EGR breather tube, then the intake manifold bolts and nuts in two or three steps.
11. Reverse procedure to install, noting the following:
    a. Use two new copper crush washers when installing fuel rail supply line.
    b. Use new intake manifold gaskets.
    c. Tighten all bolts and nuts to specifications.

EXHAUST MANIFOLD

REPLACE

1. Raise and support vehicle.
2. Disconnect two oxygen sensor connectors, then remove three nuts at each exhaust manifold and lower exhaust system.
3. Remove three exhaust manifold insulator bolts, then the insulator.

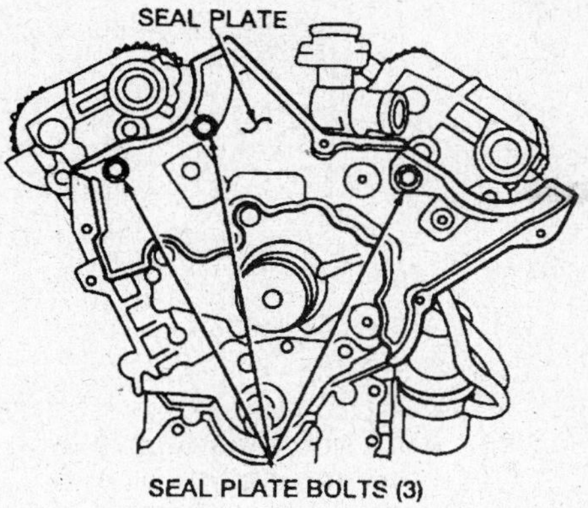

Fig. 7 Seal plate bolt removal

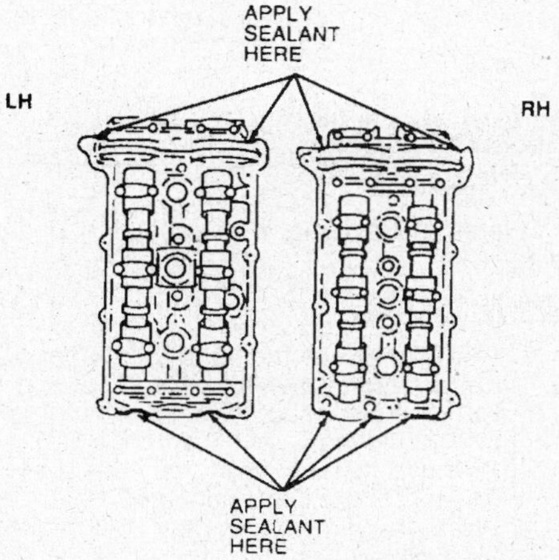

Fig. 10 Cylinder head sealant application

4. Remove manifold retaining nuts and attaching bolts.
5. Reverse procedure to install, noting the following:
   a. Use a new gasket.
   b. Tighten exhaust manifold insulator bolts, then manifold nuts and bolts to specifications.

CYLINDER HEAD

REPLACE

1. Drain cooling system, then remove timing belt covers and timing belt as described under "Timing Belt, Replace."
2. Remove intake manifold as described under "Intake Manifold, Replace."
3. Remove valve covers as described under "Valve Cover, Replace."
4. Remove camshafts as described under "Camshaft, Replace. "
5. Remove three seal plate bolts, then the seal plate, **Fig. 7.**
6. Remove coolant elbow, then raise and support vehicle.
7. Disconnect oxygen sensor connectors and lower catalytic converter inlet pipes, then lower vehicle.
8. Remove hydraulic lash adjusters from cylinder head and mark them for installation reference. **Adjuster failure may result if reused adjusters are not returned to bores from which they were removed.** Store adjusters intended for reuse upside-down in an oil-filled container.

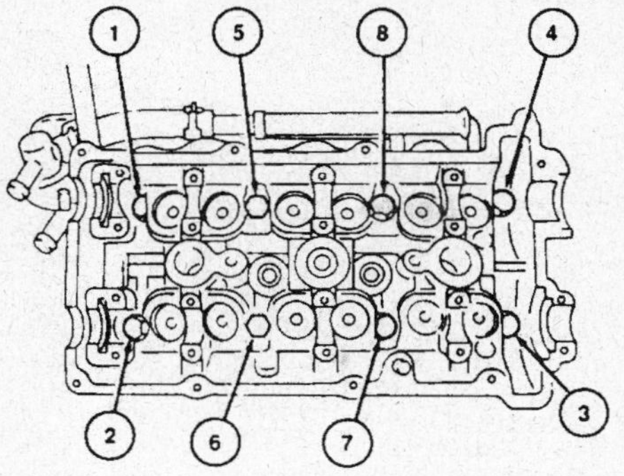

Fig. 8 Cylinder head bolt removal

9. Using sequence shown in **Fig. 8,** remove cylinder head bolts in two or three steps and discard bolts.
10. Remove cylinder head and discard gasket.
11. Reverse procedure to install, noting the following:
    a. Because left and right head gaskets are not interchangeable, ensure gasket identifying mark faces up when gasket is installed.
    b. Clean engine oil should be applied to lash adjuster friction surfaces.
    c. Adjusters to be reused must return to their original bores.
    d. Apply clean engine oil to threads of new cylinder head bolts.
    e. Using sequence shown in **Fig. 9, torque** cylinder head bolts in four steps; first step to 10 ft. lbs., second step to 17–19 ft. lbs., third step an additional 85–95°, fourth step another 85–95.°

VALVE COVER

REPLACE

1. Remove intake manifold as described under "Intake Manifold, Replace."
2. Remove upper timing belt cover bolts.
3. Remove cylinder head cover bolts, then ventilation pipe from front cover.
4. Remove cylinder head cover and any remaining sealant or gasket material.
5. Reverse procedure to install, noting the following:
   a. Apply silicone sealant to areas shown in **Fig. 10.**
   b. Using sequence shown in **Fig. 11,** tighten cover bolts in two steps to specifications.
   c. Tighten upper timing belt cover bolts to specifications.

VALVE ARRANGEMENT

Intake valves are situated on inboard side of each cylinder head and Exhaust on outboard side.

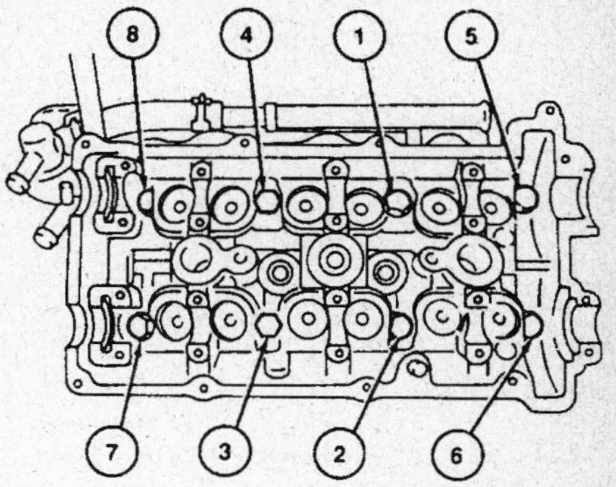

Fig. 9 Cylinder head bolt tightening sequence

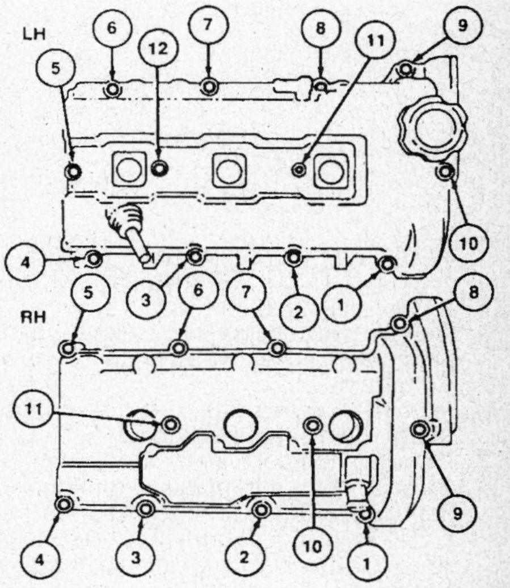

Fig. 11 Cylinder head cover bolt tightening sequence

CAMSHAFT LOBE LIFT SPECIFICATIONS

Standard: ....1.7145 inches
Wear limit: ....1.7067 inches

VALVE CLEARANCE SPECIFICATIONS

Hydraulic valve lash adjusters provide automatic lash adjustment which maintains a zero inch clearance between camshaft lobes and valve stems.

VALVE ADJUSTMENT

Because this engine uses hydraulic lash adjusters, adjustment is not necessary.

HYDRAULIC LIFTERS

REPLACE

1. Remove valve covers as outlined under "Valve Cover, Replace."

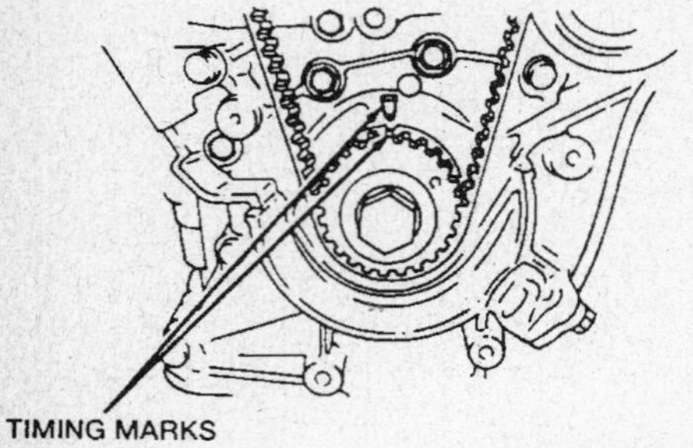

Fig. 12 Crankshaft timing belt gear to TDC alignment

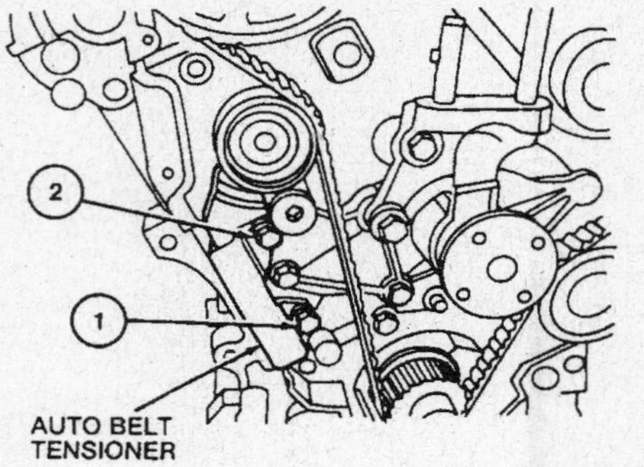

Fig. 13 Auto belt tensioner bolt removal

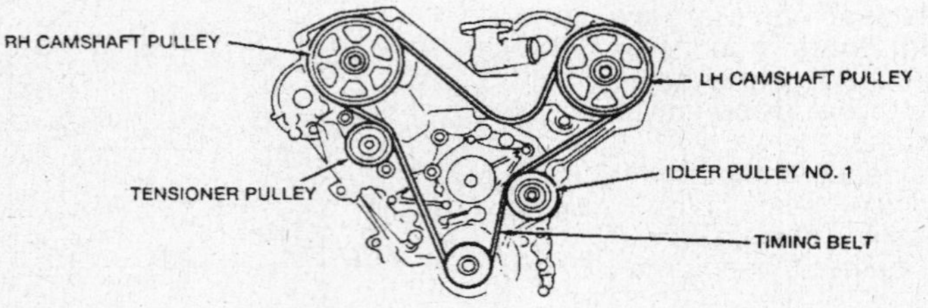

Fig. 15 Timing belt routing

2. Remove accessory drive belts, then timing belt as described under "Timing Belt, Replace."
3. Remove camshafts as described under "Camshaft, Replace. "
4. Remove hydraulic lash adjusters from cylinder head and, if any are to be reused, mark those for installation reference. **Adjuster failure may result if reused adjusters are not returned to bores from which they were removed.**
5. Reverse procedure to install. **Coat friction surfaces with clean engine oil.**

TIMING BELT

REPLACE

1. Disconnect engine coolant temperature sensor and crankshaft position sensor electrical connectors.
2. Remove accessory drive belts.
3. Loosen right front wheel lug nuts, then raise and support front of vehicle.
4. Remove right front wheel and tire assembly, then the splash shield.
5. Remove belt idler bracket lower bolt.
6. Using a suitable crankshaft pulley holding tool, hold crankshaft pulley in position and loosen crankshaft pulley retaining bolt.
7. Remove crankshaft pulley bolt, then the pulley.
8. Remove three lower timing belt cover attaching bolts.
9. Using a suitable water pump pulley holding tool, hold pulley in position and loosen pulley retaining bolts.
10. Remove water pump pulley.
11. Using a suitable strap wrench, hold power steering pump pulley in position and loosen power steering pump pulley retaining bolt.
12. Remove power steering pump pulley.
13. Remove belt idler bracket upper bolt, then the idler bracket.
14. Remove oil dipstick tube attaching bolt, then the dipstick tube.
15. Remove upper timing cover attaching bolts, then the timing belt covers.
16. Support engine using a suitable jack.
17. Remove righthand engine mount attaching nuts.
18. Remove righthand engine mount through bolt, then the mount.
19. Align crankshaft timing belt gear to TDC as shown in **Fig. 12** by turning crankshaft in direction of normal rotation.
20. Remove two auto belt tensioner bolts in order shown in **Fig. 13.**
21. If timing belt is going to be reused, place a directional mark on belt that indicates direction of rotation, then remove belt.
22. Reverse procedure to install, noting the following:
    a. Compress auto belt tensioner until hole in piston is aligned with second hole in case. Insert a .06 inch diameter wire or pin through second hole to keep piston compressed, **Fig. 14.**
    b. Align camshafts to TDC.
    c. Turn crankshaft counterclockwise until timing gear is offset from TDC by one tooth, then install timing belt, **Fig. 15.**
    d. Turn crankshaft clockwise until crankshaft timing mark is again at TDC. Turning crankshaft should place all belt slack at or near tensioner.
    e. Install tensioner and tighten mounting bolts to specifications, then remove pin.
    f. Turn crankshaft two complete revolutions to ensure timing is still correct.

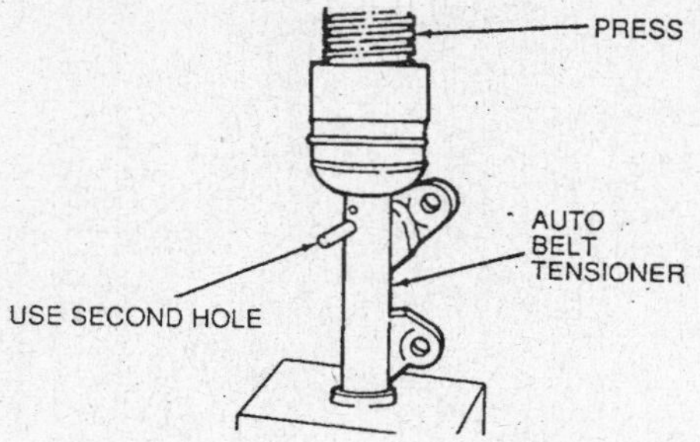

Fig. 14 Auto belt tensioner piston compressing

CAMSHAFT

REPLACE

Refer to **Fig. 16** when replacing camshaft.

REMOVAL

1. Remove intake manifold as described under "Intake Manifold, Replace."
2. Remove valve covers as described under "Valve Cover, Replace."
3. Remove timing belt as described under "Timing Belt, Replace."
4. Remove camshaft pulley lock bolts, then the pulleys.
5. Turn camshafts until knock pins are aligned with marks on camshaft caps, **Fig. 17.** This will reduce pressure on hydraulic lash adjusters. **Do not remove camshaft when lobes are depressing any adjusters, as damage to camshaft or thrust journal support may result.**
6. **Camshaft caps are identified on righthand bank (rear) by numbers and on lefthand bank (front) by letters.** Loosen lefthand (front) camshaft cap bolts in five or six steps as shown in **Fig. 18.**
7. After removing left (front) camshaft caps, remove remaining camshaft cap bolts in sequence shown in **Fig. 19.**
8. Remove camshaft caps and camshafts, then oil seals from camshafts. **To avoid damaging cylinder head thrust bearing support, remove thrust caps last.**

INSTALLATION

1. Install new oil seals on camshafts, then apply clean engine oil to camshaft journals and supports.
2. Install camshafts so gear marks align.
3. Apply a light coat of sealant to areas shown in **Fig. 20. Do not allow sealant to contact camshafts.**
4. Install thrust caps and tighten bolts until they are fully seated against cylinder head.
5. Install remaining camshaft caps, noting the following:

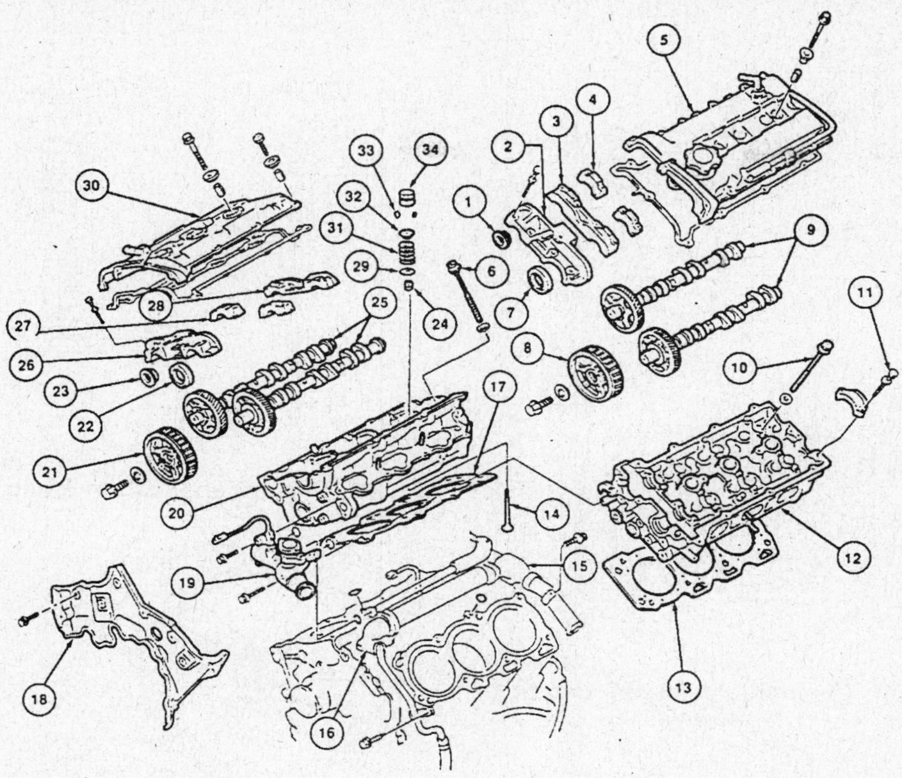

Item	Description
1	Blind Cap, Front (LH)
2	End Cap, Front (LH)
3	Thrust Cap, Front (LH)
4	Camshaft Caps, Front (LH)
5	Cylinder Head Cover, Front (LH)
6	Cylinder Head Bolt, Rear (RH)
7	Oil Seal, Front (LH)
8	Camshaft Pulley, Front (LH)
9	Camshafts, Front (LH)
10	Cylinder Head Bolt, Front (LH)
11	Camshaft Distributor Cap
12	Cylinder Head, Front (LH)
13	Cylinder Head Gasket, Front (LH)
14	Valve
15	Thermostat Housing
16	Coolant Elbow
17	Cylinder Head Gasket, Rear (RH)
18	Seal Plate
19	Coolant Elbow
20	Cylinder Head, Rear (RH)
21	Camshaft Pulley, Rear (RH)
22	Oil Seal, Rear (RH)
23	Blind Cap, Rear (RH)
24	Valve Guide
25	Camshafts, Rear (RH)
26	End Cap, Rear (RH)
27	Camshaft Caps, Rear (RH)
28	Thrust Cap, Rear (RH)
29	Lower Valve Seat
30	Cylinder Head Cover, Rear (RH)
31	Valve Spring
32	Upper Valve Seat
33	Valve Keeper
34	Hydraulic Lash Adjuster (HLA)

FM1069100312000X

Fig. 16 Camshafts replacement

a. Right (rear) bank caps are numbered and left (front) are lettered.
b. Tighten camshaft cap bolts to specifications in five equal steps, following sequence shown in **Fig. 21.**

6. Holding camshafts in place with a suitable wrench, install camshaft pulley and pulley lock bolts, then tighten lock bolts to specifications.
7. Install timing belt, cylinder head covers

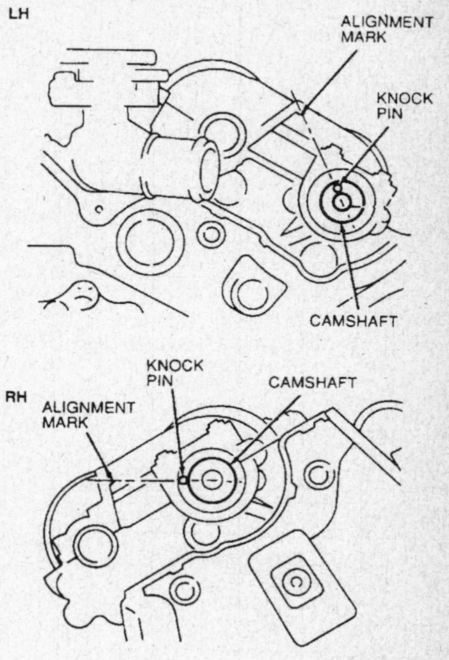

FM1069100313000X

Fig. 17 Camshaft knock pin & cap mark alignment

and intake manifold.

CRANKSHAFT REAR OIL SEAL

REPLACE

REMOVAL

Automatic Transaxle

1. Remove transaxle.
2. Use holding tool No. T74P-6375-A, or equivalent, hold flexplate in position.
3. Remove flexplate attaching bolts using sequence shown in **Fig. 22. Mark bolts for installation reference.**
4. Remove backing plate, flexplate and adapter.
5. Using seal remover tool No. T92C-6700-CH, or equivalent, remove rear main seal.

Manual Transaxle

1. Remove transaxle, then secure flywheel by installing holding tool No. T74P-6375-A, or equivalent.
2. Loosen pressure plate bolts in two or three steps, then remove bolts and pressure plate.
3. Remove flywheel attaching bolts using sequence shown in **Fig. 23.**
4. Using seal remover tool No. T92C-6700-CH, or equivalent, remove rear main seal.

INSTALLATION

Automatic Transaxle

1. Apply clean engine oil to outer lips of rear main seal.
2. Position seal on crankshaft seal replacer tool No. T92C-6701-BH, or equivalent.

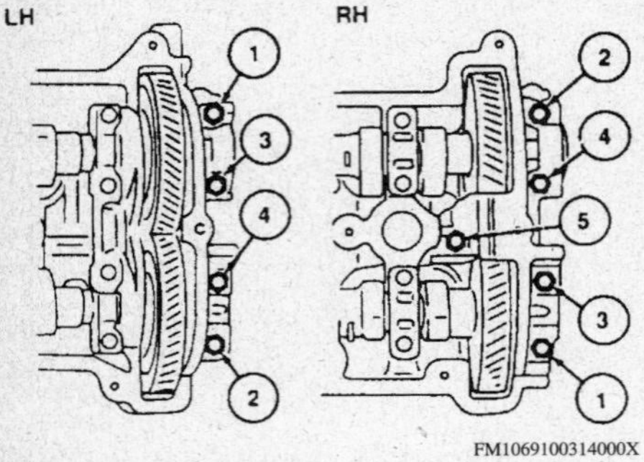

Fig. 18 Front camshaft cap bolt removal

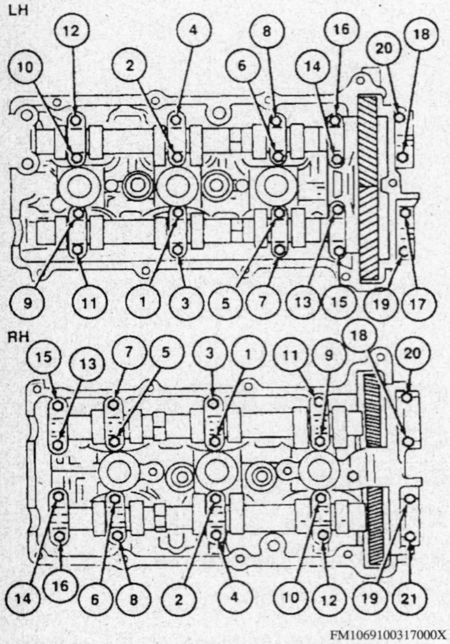

Fig. 21 Camshaft cap bolt tightening sequence

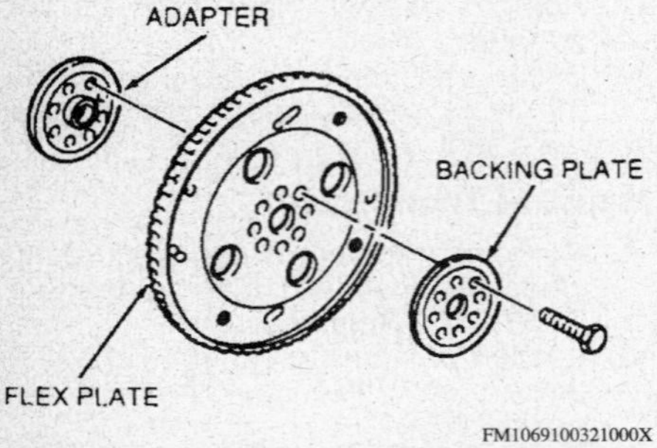

Fig. 24 Flexplate bolt tightening sequence

3. Install seal.
4. Align flexplate as follows:
   a. Align adapter, flexplate and backing plate, then loosely install flexplate bolts.
   b. Install holding tool No. T74P-6375-A, or equivalent, then using sequence shown in **Fig. 24,** tighten flexplate bolts to specifications.

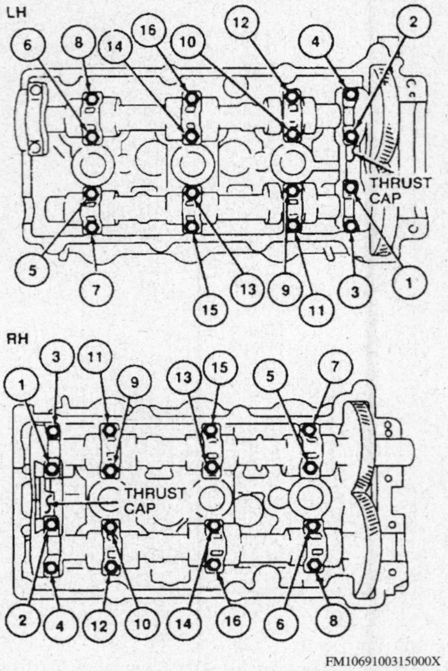

Fig. 19 Inside camshaft cap bolt removal

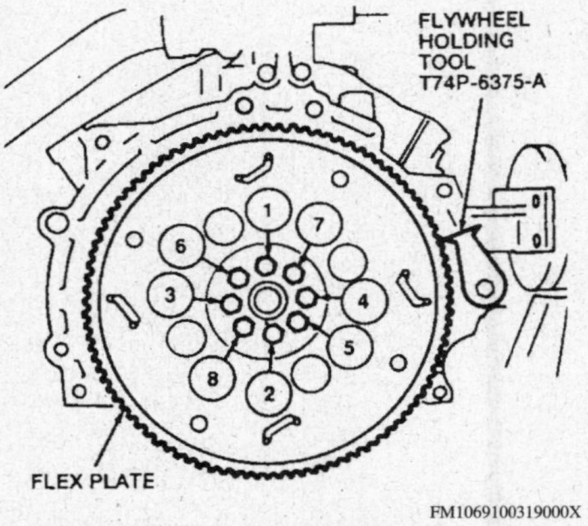

Fig. 22 Flexplate bolt removal sequence

5. Install transaxle and check for leaks.

Manual Transaxle

1. Apply clean engine oil to outer lips of rear main seal.
2. Position seal on crankshaft seal replacer tool No. T92C-6701-BH, or equivalent.
3. Install seal.
4. Align flywheel as follows:
   a. align flywheel to crankshaft, then loosely install flywheel bolts.
   b. Install holding tool No. T74P-6375-A, or equivalent, then using sequence shown in **Fig. 25,** tighten flywheel bolts in two passes to specification.
   c. Using clutch aligning tool No. T74P-7137-K, or equivalent, install clutch disc and pressure plate.
5. Install transaxle and check for leaks.

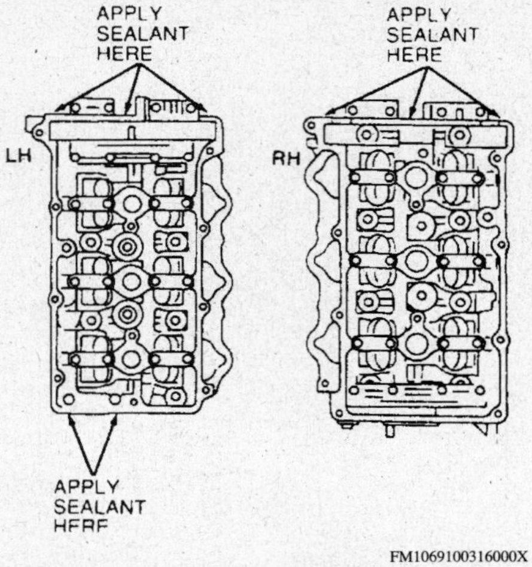

Fig. 20 Sealant application areas

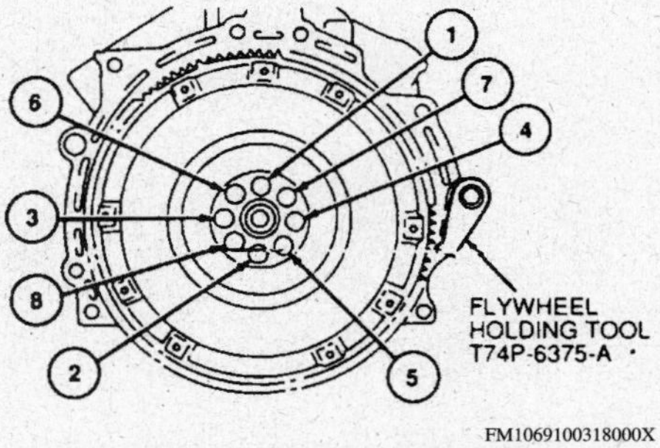

Fig. 23 Flywheel bolt removal sequence

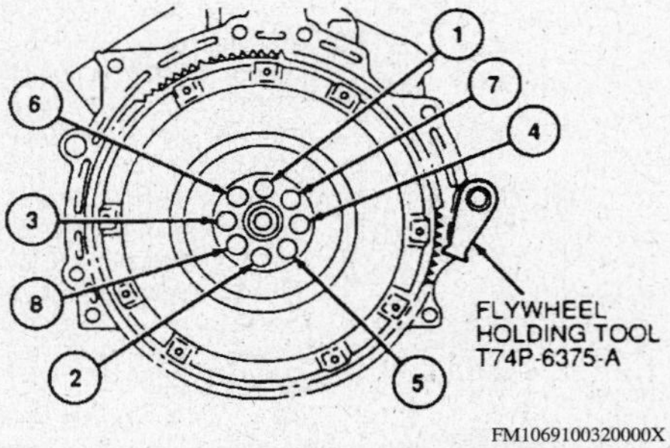

Fig. 25 Flywheel bolt tightening sequence

OIL PAN

REPLACE

1. Drain engine oil, then disconnect both oxygen sensor connectors and lower exhaust system to gain access to oil pan bolts.
2. Remove oil pan bolts, then the oil pan.
3. Remove any remaining sealant from mating surfaces. **Failure to fully remove old sealant may cause engine block to crack.**
4. Reverse procedure to install, noting the following:
   a. Apply a continuous bead of sealant inside bolt holes and overlap ends.
   b. Install pan within five minutes of applying sealant.

c. Tighten bolts to specifications.

OIL PUMP

REPLACE

REMOVAL

1. Remove timing belt as described under "Timing Belt, Replace."
2. Remove oil pan as described under "Oil Pan, Replace."
3. Recover A/C refrigerant as outlined in "Air Conditioning" section.
4. Remove A/C compressor and mounting bracket.
5. Remove power steering pump and tensioner.
6. Using crankshaft damper tool No. T74P-6316-A, or equivalent, remove crankshaft timing gear from crankshaft.
7. Remove nine oil pump attaching bolts, then two oil strainer to oil pump bolts.
8. Remove oil pump and housing from engine block.
9. Remove O-ring, then any sealant from oil pump mating surfaces.
10. Using a press and front seals tool No. T74P-6150-A, or equivalent, remove oil seal from oil pump housing.

INSTALLATION

1. Using a press and front seals tool No. T74P-6150-A, or equivalent, install a new oil seal.
2. Fit oil pump with a new O-ring.
3. Apply a continuous bead of silicone sealant to mating surface of oil pump. **Prevent sealant from entering oil hole.** Install pump within five minutes of sealant application, then tighten pump retaining bolts to specifications.
4. Install crankshaft timing gear and key.
5. Install power steering pump and tensioner. Tighten to specifications.
6. Attach A/C compressor bracket to engine block and tighten to specifications.
7. Attach A/C compressor to its mounting bracket and tighten to specifications.
8. Install oil strainer to oil pump and tighten bolts to specifications, then install oil pan as described under "Oil Pan, Replace."
9. Install timing belt as described under "Timing Belt, Replace."
10. Evacuate and recharge A/C system.

BELT TENSION DATA

Refer to **Fig. 26** for drive belt tension and torque specifications.

SERPENTINE DRIVE BELT

1. Loosen tensioner locknut.
2. Loosen tensioner adjusting bolt until there is enough slack to remove belt.
3. Reverse procedure to install.

Drive Belt Tension	New N (lb)	Used N (lb)	Limit N (lb)
Generator	690-880 (160-190)	500-680 (110-150)	440 (99)
Generator + A/C	690-880 (160-190)	500-680 (110-150)	440 (99)
P/S	550-680 (130-150)	400-530 (88-120)	340 (77)

FM1069100322000A

Fig. 26 Drive belt tension

COOLING SYSTEM BLEED

These engines do not require a specific bleed procedure. After filling cooling system, run engine to operating temperature with radiator/pressure cap off. Air will then be automatically bled through cap opening.

THERMOSTAT

REPLACE

1. Drain cooling system, then remove fresh air duct and air cleaner assembly.
2. Disconnect lower radiator hose at coolant inlet pipe.
3. Remove coolant inlet pipe, then thermostat housing. **Discard O-ring seal.**
4. Remove thermostat from housing.
5. Reverse procedure to install. Use a new thermostat housing O-ring seal.

WATER PUMP

REPLACE

1. Drain cooling system, then remove timing belt as described under "Timing Belt, Replace."
2. Using water pump pulley tool No. T92C-6312-AH, or equivalent, remove four water pump pulley bolts, then the pulley.
3. Remove five water pump mounting bolts, then the pump.
4. Reverse procedure to install, noting the following:
   a. Use a new water pump O-ring seal.
   b. Tighten all bolts to specifications.

RADIATOR

REPLACE

Allow radiator to cool prior to beginning following procedure. Slowly remove radiator cap to release system pressure. **Caution must be used as system contains scalding hot fluid which when under pressure can blow out of radiator fill neck, causing personal injury.**

1. Slowly remove radiator cap, then open drain valve at bottom of radiator and drain system.
2. Remove fresh air duct.
3. Remove upper and lower radiator hoses.
4. Remove radiator overflow hose.
5. Remove coolant expansion tank.
6. Disconnect cooling fan motor and A/C condenser cooling fan motor electrical connectors.
7. **On models equipped with automatic transaxle,** disconnect transaxle oil cooler lines at radiator and plug hose ends to prevent leakage.
8. **On all models,** remove radiator mounting brackets.
9. Move air bag electrical wiring harness to allow clearance for radiator removal.
10. Remove radiator, engine cooling fan, and A/C cooling fan from vehicle as an assembly.
11. Reverse procedure to install, noting the following:
    a. Tighten radiator mounting bracket bolts to specifications.
    b. Check and fill cooling system and transaxle fluid levels.
    c. Tighten fan shroud bolts to specifications.
    d. Operate engine until normal engine coolant temperature is reached and check for leaks.

FUEL PUMP

REPLACE

1. Relieve fuel system pressure as described under " Precautions."
2. Drain fuel from fuel tank, then raise and support vehicle.
3. Loosen filler neck hose clamp and remove hose.
4. Loosen overflow hose clamp and remove hose.
5. Loosen fuel supply and return line clamps, then remove hoses.
6. Loosen two fuel tank vapor line clamps and remove hoses.
7. Disconnect fuel pump sender electrical connector.
8. Remove four attaching nuts on exhaust heat shield.
9. Remove fuel tank shield attaching nut.
10. Support fuel tank and remove center fuel tank strap.
11. Remove righthand fuel tank strap, then fuel tank shield.
12. Remove lefthand fuel tank strap, then the tank.
13. Using a hammer and chisel, remove fuel pump lock ring.
14. Remove fuel pump assembly from tank.
15. Reverse procedure to install.

FUEL FILTER

REPLACE

1. Relieve fuel system pressure as described under " Precautions."
2. Remove two fuel filter mounting nuts on fuel filter bracket.
3. Remove supply line clamps, then disconnect supply lines from both ends of filter. **Plug lines to prevent leakage.**
4. Remove fuel filter mounting bracket.
5. Reverse procedure to install.

TIGHTENING SPECIFICATIONS

Year	Component	Torque/Ft. Lbs.
1997	A/C Compressor Mounting Bolts	28–38
	A/C Compressor Mounting Bracket	28–38
	Alternator Bolts	27–38
	Battery Tray Mounting Bolt	72–84①
	Camshaft Bearing Cap Bolts	8–10
	Camshaft Pulley Lockbolts	90–103
	Coolant Elbow Bolts	14–18
	Converter Inlet Pipes	30–41
	Crankshaft Pulley Bolt	116–122
	Cylinder Head	②
	Cylinder Head Cover	72–84①
	Engine Mount Attaching Nuts	54–77
	Engine Mount Bracket Attaching Bolt	32–45
	Engine Mount (RH) Through Bolts	50–68
	Engine Mount (LH) Through Bolts	63–86
	Exhaust Manifold Bolts	14–18
	Exhaust Manifold Nuts	14–18
	Extension Bar Nut	22–33
	Flex Plate	45–50
	Flywheel	45–49
	Front Engine Lifting Eye Attaching Bolts	14–18
	Front Engine Mount Nuts	55–75
	Front Engine Mount Through Bolt	63–86
	Fuel Filter Bracket	72–96①
	Oil Drain Plug	22–30
	Oil Pan Mounting Bolts, Long	72–84①
	Oil Pan Mounting Bolts, Short	14–18
	Oil Pressure Switch	9–13
	Oil Pump Attaching Bolts	14–18
	Power Steering Pump Belt Tensioner Lower Bolt	14–18①
	Power Steering Pump Belt Tensioner Upper Bolt	24–33①
	Power Steering Pump Rear Bracket Bolt	24–33
	Rear Engine Lifting Eye Attaching Bolts	27–38
	Rear Engine Mount Nuts	50–68
	Rear Engine Mount Through Bolt	63–86
	Splash Shield Bolts	72–84①
	Tensioner Locknut	24–34
	Thermostat Housing	14–18
	Timing Cover Bolts	72–84①
	Transaxle Cradle Nuts	③
	Transaxle Mount Nuts (Automatic Trans.)	50–68
	Transaxle Mount Nuts (Manual Trans.)	32–44
	Transaxle Mount Through Bolt	63–86
	Transaxle Shift Linkage Through Bolt	12–16
	Transaxle To Engine Block	③
	Transverse Member Bolts	69–93
	Water Pipe Mounting Bolt	14–18
	Water Pump Attaching Bolts	14–18
	Water Pump Pulley Attaching Bolts	72–84①
	Wheel Lug Nuts	66–86

① — Inch lbs.

② — Refer to "Cylinder Head, Replace."

③ — Refer to "Manual Transaxle" under "Engine, Replace."

Clutch & Manual Transaxle

NOTE: Refer To " Air Bag System Precautions " Located In The Front Of This Manual For System Disarming & Arming Procedures.

NOTE: Refer to "Computer Relearn Procedures " Located In The Front Of This Manual For Computer Relearn Procedures.

INDEX

PRECAUTIONS

AIR BAG SYSTEMS

Refer to "Air Bag System Precautions" in the front of this manual for system disarming and arming procedures.

BATTERY GROUND CABLE

Prior to service, disconnect battery ground cable and isolate as required.

ADJUSTMENTS

CLUTCH PEDAL HEIGHT

1. Measure distance from bulkhead to upper center of pedal pad, **Fig. 1.**
2. Distance should be 7.32–8.31 inches.
3. If adjustment is required, remove lower dash panel, then the air ducts.
4. Loosen locknut, then turn stopper bolt until pedal height is within specifications.
5. After adjustment, tighten locknut to specifications, then install air ducts and lower dash panel.
6. Depress clutch pedal repeatedly, then measure pedal height. Readjust as necessary.

CLUTCH PEDAL FREEPLAY

1. Measure clutch pedal freeplay distance, **Fig. 1.** Freeplay should measure .04–.19 inch.
2. If adjustment is required, remove lower dash panel, then the air ducts.
3. Loosen locknut, then turn pushrod until pedal freeplay is within specifications.
4. Measure distance from floor to center of pedal pad when pedal is fully depressed. Distance should be 2.64 inches.
5. Tighten locknut to specifications.
6. Install air ducts, then the lower dash panel.

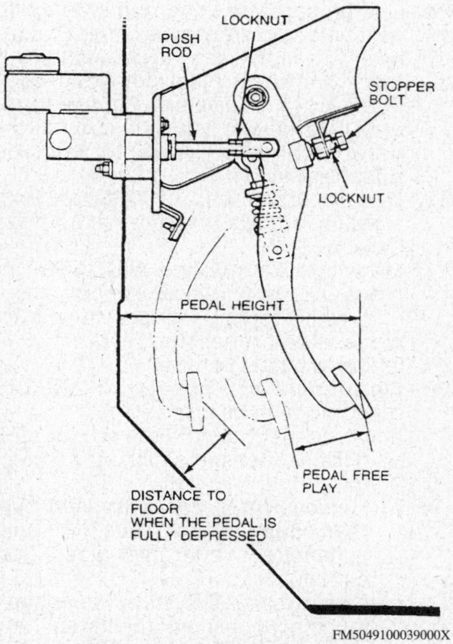

Fig. 1 Clutch adjustment

HYDRAULIC SYSTEM SERVICE

SLAVE CYLINDER, REPLACE

1. Disconnect pressure line from slave cylinder, then plug line to prevent leakage. **Avoid twisting pressure line during removal.**
2. Remove slave cylinder attaching bolts, then the slave cylinder.
3. Reverse procedure to install. Tighten bolts to specifications.

CLUTCH BLEED

Clutch hydraulic system must be bled whenever pressure line is disconnected.

Fluid in reservoir must be maintained at ¾ level or higher during air bleeding.

1. Remove bleeder cap from slave cylinder and attach vinyl hose to bleeder screw, then place other end of hose in clear container partially filled with hydraulic fluid.
2. Slowly pump clutch pedal several times.
3. With clutch pedal depressed, loosen bleeder screw to release trapped air.
4. Tighten bleeder screw. **Pedal must remain depressed until bleeder screw has been tightened.**
5. Repeat previous three steps until no air bubbles appear in fluid.

CLUTCH MASTER CYLINDER

1. Disconnect reservoir hose from clutch master cylinder, then plug hose.
2. Disconnect pressure line from clutch master cylinder. **Avoid twisting line during removal.**
3. Working from passenger compartment, remove clutch master cylinder upper retaining nut.
4. Working from engine compartment, remove clutch master cylinder lower retaining nut.
5. Carefully pull clutch master cylinder and gasket from bulkhead.
6. Reverse procedure to install, noting the following:
   a. Install new gasket.
   b. Tighten clutch master cylinder retaining nuts to specifications.
   c. Tighten pressure line flare fitting to specifications.
   d. Bleed air from system.

CLUTCH

REPLACE

1. Remove transaxle from vehicle.
2. Install flywheel lock tool No. T74P-6375-A, or equivalent, into transaxle mounting hole on engine, then engage tooth of locking tool into flywheel ring gear.
3. Remove bolts attaching pressure plate assembly to flywheel, then pressure plate assembly, **Fig. 2.**
4. Remove clutch disc and aligning tool.

5. Reverse procedure to install. Tighten to specifications.

TRANSAXLE

REPLACE

1. Remove air cleaner assembly and fresh air duct.
2. Remove battery and battery tray, then transaxle ground strap bolts and straps.
3. Disconnect vehicle speed sensor (VSS) electrical connector from top RH rear corner of transaxle.
4. Disconnect Park/Neutral Position (PNP) switch electrical connector from lower front of transaxle.
5. Disconnect back-up lamp switch electrical connector from rear of transaxle.
6. Disconnect two spring clips from clutch slave cylinder line. It is not necessary to disconnect clutch slave cylinder line from slave cylinder.
7. Remove two slave cylinder attaching bolts and position slave cylinder aside.
8. Install engine support tool No. 014–00750, or equivalent, then remove upper transaxle to engine attaching bolts.
9. Remove two upper starter motor bolts. It is not necessary to disconnect fuel lines from fuel filter.
10. Remove two fuel filter attaching nuts and position fuel filter aside.
11. Remove two nuts and through bolt from lefthand transaxle mount.
12. Raise and support vehicle.
13. **On models equipped with 2.0L engine,** remove intake manifold support bracket bolts, then the bracket.
14. **On all models,** disconnect S-terminal wire nut.
15. Remove B-terminal wire nut, then disconnect B-terminal wire.
16. Remove lower starter motor bolt, then the starter.
17. Drain transaxle fluid into suitable container, then discard drain plug washer.
18. Remove front tire and wheel assemblies.
19. Unstake halfshaft attaching nuts, then remove and discard halfshaft attaching nuts.
20. Remove lower splash shields.
21. Remove six transverse member bolts, then lower transverse member from vehicle.
22. Remove bolt and nut from lefthand lower ball joint. Pry lower arm down to separate ball joint from knuckle.
23. Pull lower edge of spindle outward to separate it from end of halfshaft.
24. Use prybar to remove end of lefthand halfshaft from transaxle case. Pry between transaxle case and halfshaft.
25. Install transaxle plug tool No. T-88C-7025-AH, or equivalent. **Failure to install transaxle plugs may allow differential side gears to become misaligned.**
26. Remove other end of halfshaft from steering knuckle and remove from vehicle.
27. **On models equipped with ABS,** remove clips from wheel speed sensor and wheel speed sensor nuts from wheel speed sensor harness mount on lefthand side of vehicle.
28. **On models equipped with 2.5L engine,** proceed as follows:
    a. Disconnect both Heated Oxygen (HO2S) Sensor electrical connectors.
    b. Remove three converter inlet pipe to exhaust manifold nuts from both exhaust converter inlet pipes. Discard nuts.
    c. Lower exhaust system far enough to gain access to righthand halfshaft support bearing.
29. **On all models,** remove three halfshaft support bearing bolts.
30. **On models equipped with ABS,** remove clips from wheel speed sensor and wheel speed sensor nuts from wheel speed sensor harness mount on lefthand side of vehicle.
31. **On all models,** remove nut and bolt from righthand lower ball joint.
32. Pry lower arm down to separate ball joint from knuckle.
33. Pull lower edge of spindle outward to separate it from halfshaft. **Failure to install transaxle plugs may allow differential side gears to become misaligned.**
34. Pull righthand halfshaft from transaxle case and install transaxle plug tool No. T88C-7025-AH, or equivalent.
35. Remove six nuts and two bolts from transaxle cradle.
36. Disconnect transaxle shift linkage and extension bar from transaxle.
37. Remove three rear transaxle mount to transaxle bolts. Support transaxle with transmission jack.
38. Remove three rear transaxle mount bolts and rear transaxle mount.
39. Remove lower transaxle to engine attaching bolts, then separate transaxle from engine and lower transaxle from vehicle.
40. Reverse procedure to install, noting the following:
    a. Apply a thin coating of clutch grease, or equivalent to the spline of input shaft.
    b. Install a new washer on transaxle drain plug.
    c. Install new halfshaft retaining nuts.

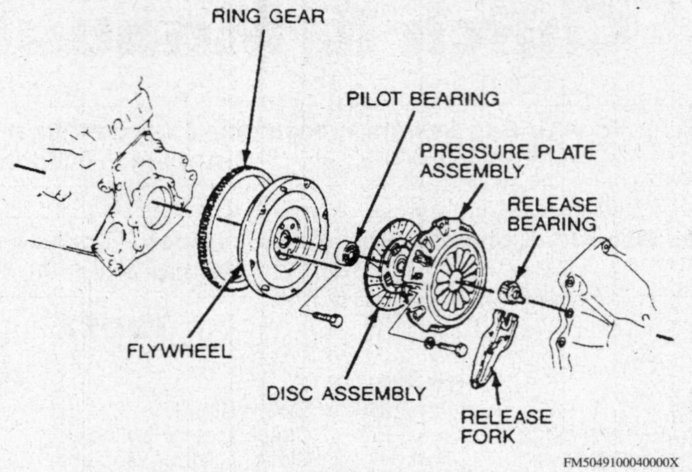

Fig. 2 Clutch assembly

TIGHTENING SPECIFICATIONS

Year	Component	Torque/ Ft. Lbs.
1997	Back-Up Lamp Switch	15–21
	Clutch Master Cylinder Nuts	14–18
	Clutch Pedal Adjusting Locknut	10–13
	Converter Inlet Pipe To Exhaust Manifold	30–41
	Extension Bar Nut	28–38
	Halfshaft Nuts	174–235③
	Halfshaft Support Bearing Bolts	32–45
	Intake Manifold Bracket Bolts	27–38
	Lefthand Transaxle Mount Nuts	32–44
	Lefthand Transaxle Mount Through Bolt	63–86
	Lower Engine To Transaxle Mounting Bolts	28–38
	Neutral Position Switch	15–21
	Oil Level Plug	29–43
	Pinch Bolt (Lower Ball Joint)	26–41
	Pressure Line Flare Fitting	10–15
	Pressure Plate	13–18
	Rear Transaxle Mount To Transaxle Bolts	50–68
	Shift Rod Bolt	8–10
	Slave Cylinder	12–16
	Splash Shield Bolts	72–96①
	Starter Motor Bolts	28–38
	Transaxle Cradle Nuts & Bolts	50–77
	Transaxle Shift Linkage Nut	14–18
	Transverse Member Bolts	69–96
	Upper Engine To Transaxle Mounting Bolts①	66–86
	Upper Engine To Transaxle Mounting Bolts②	50–73
	Wheel Lug Nuts	65–87

① — 2.0L Engine.

② — 2.5L Engine.

③ — Nut must be staked after tightening.

Rear Axle & Suspension

INDEX

DESCRIPTION

Rear suspension, **Fig. 1,** is fully independent and utilizes McPherson struts at each rear wheel. If vehicle is equipped with programmed ride control system, rear strut towers locate programmed ride control actuators and strut assemblies. A forged rear spindle bolts to shock absorber, double rear lateral links and a single trailing arm.

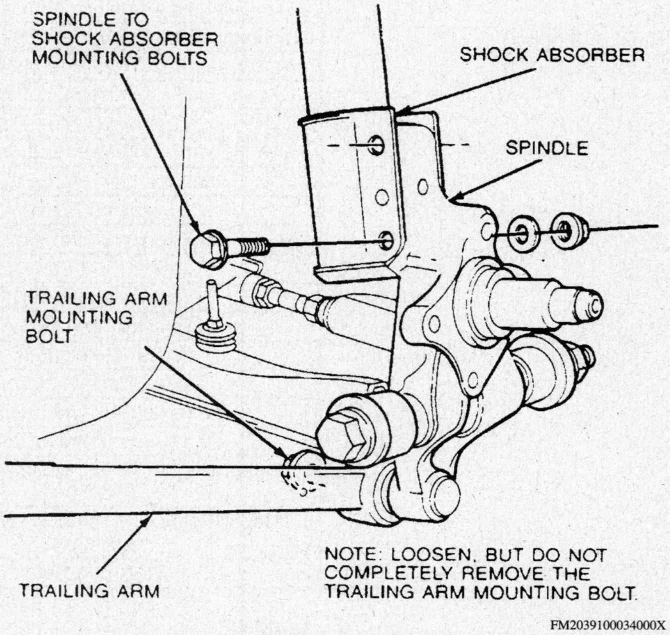

Fig. 1 Rear suspension components

HUB & BEARING

REPLACE

Hub and wheel bearing must be replaced as an assembly.

1. Raise and support vehicle.
2. Remove rear wheel, then carefully raise staked portion of spindle locknut.
3. Remove and discard spindle locknut. **Retaining nut must not be reused. When loosening locknut, lock hub by applying service brakes.**
4. Remove brake drum or disc brake caliper and rotor.
5. Remove hub/wheel bearing assembly from vehicle.
6. Reverse procedure to install, noting the following:
   a. Tighten new spindle locknut to specifications.
   b. Stake spindle locknut at spindle indentation.

WHEEL BEARING

ADJUST

1. Raise and support vehicle, then remove rear wheel.
2. **On models equipped with disc brakes,** remove rear disc brake caliper assembly.
3. **On all models,** install wheel lug nuts, then position dial indicator tool No. 4201-C, or equivalent, against center of wheel hub.
4. Push and pull brake drum or rotor by hand, measuring wheel bearing endplay.
5. If bearing endplay exceeds .002 inch, check and adjust spindle retaining nut torque. Replace hub/wheel bearing if necessary.

STRUT

REPLACE

1. Raise and support vehicle, then remove rear wheels.
2. **On models equipped with anti-lock brakes,** remove speed sensor routing bracket.
3. **On all models,** remove brake line U-clip from strut assembly.
4. Remove two spindle to strut retaining bolts.
5. Remove trunk side panel to gain access to strut assembly.
6. Remove three upper strut retaining nuts, then strut assembly.
7. Reverse procedure to install. Tighten retaining nuts and bolts to specification.

REAR CROSSMEMBER

REPLACE

1. Raise and support vehicle.
2. Remove spindle through bolts.
3. Remove stabilizer bar as described under "Stabilizer Bar, Replace."
4. Remove lateral link as described under "Rear Lateral Link, Replace."
5. Remove four rear crossmember to frame retaining bolts, then the rear crossmember.
6. Remove front lateral link.
7. Reverse procedure to install. Tighten all bolts to specifications.

TRAILING ARM

REPLACE

1. Raise and support vehicle.
2. Disconnect parking brake cable bracket from trailing arm.
3. Remove trailing arm to spindle bolt.
4. Remove trailing arm to frame bolt, then trailing arm from vehicle.
5. Reverse procedure to install. Tighten all bolts to specifications.

STABILIZER BAR

REPLACE

1. Raise and support vehicle.
2. Remove two stabilizer bar to stabilizer control link retaining nuts.
3. Remove two stabilizer bracket retaining nuts and bolts, then the stabilizer bar from vehicle.
4. Reverse procedure to install, noting the following:
   a. Apply rubber grease to inside surface of stabilizer bar bushings.
   b. Align bushing with installation mark on stabilizer bar during installation.
   c. Tighten all bolts to specifications.

LATERAL LINK

REPLACE

FRONT

1. Raise and support vehicle.
2. Remove spindle through bolt, then position a suitable jack beneath rear crossmember.
3. Remove four crossmember to frame retaining bolts.
4. Lower rear crossmember assembly to gain access to front lateral link to rear crossmember retaining bolt.
5. Remove access hole cap, then the front lateral link to rear crossmember retaining bolt.
6. Remove front lateral link from vehicle.
7. Reverse procedure to install, noting the following:
   a. Tighten all bolts to specifications.
   b. Check wheel alignment.

REAR

1. Raise and support vehicle.
2. Remove spindle through bolt.
3. Remove stabilizer control link as described under " Stabilizer Bar, Replace."
4. **Before removing adjusting cam bolt, scribe a mark on cam plate and crossmember for reference during installation.** Remove adjusting cam bolt.
5. Remove rear lateral link from vehicle.
6. Reverse procedure to install, noting the following:
   a. Tighten all bolts to specifications.
   b. Check wheel alignment.

TIGHTENING SPECIFICATIONS

Year	Component	Torque/ Ft. Lbs.
1997	Adjusting Cam Bolt	58–86
	Front Lateral Link To Rear Crossmember Bolt	58–86
	Rear Crossmember To Frame Bolts	27–40
	Rear Lateral Link To Stabilizer Control Link Nuts	27–40
	Speed Sensor Retaining Bolt	36–60①
	Spindle Locknut	130–174
	Spindle Through Bolt	64–86
	Spindle To Strut Mounting Bolts	69–87
	Stabilizer Bar To Stabilizer Control Link Nuts	27–40
	Stabilizer Bracket Bolts	27–40
	Stabilizer Bracket Nuts	27–40
	Trailing Arm To Frame Bolt	58–86
	Trailing Arm To Spindle Bolt	64–86
	Upper Strut Retaining Nuts	34–46
	Wheel Bearing Locknut	130–174
	Wheel Lug Nuts	65–87

① — Inch lbs.

Front Suspension & Steering

INDEX

DESCRIPTION

Front suspension consists of McPherson struts and a single wishbone lower control arm. Upper end of coil spring rides in a heavy rubber spring seat. A forged steering knuckle is bolted to shock absorber.

Wide stance control arms are supported by rubber bushings at each end. Body lean on turns is controlled by a hollow stabilizer bar that connects both lower control arms. Front hub and rotor assemblies are supported by one piece roller bearings mounted in steering knuckle. Wheel bearing is pressed into steering knuckle. Hub assembly is pressed into wheel bearing assembly.

WHEEL HUB & STEERING KNUCKLE

REPLACE

1. Raise and support vehicle.
2. Remove tire and wheel assembly.
3. Carefully raise staked portion of halfshaft attaching nut using a small cape chisel, **Fig. 1.**
4. Remove halfshaft attaching nut. When loosening nut, lock hub in position by having a helper lock brakes. **Discard nut, it should not be reused.**
5. Remove stabilizer bar link bolts.
6. Separate tie rod end from steering knuckle, **Fig. 2.**
7. Remove caliper, then anchor bracket assembly. Suspend caliper from coil spring. **Do not allow to hang from brake line.**
8. Remove brake rotor, **Fig. 3.**
9. **On models equipped with anti-lock brakes,** proceed as follows:
   a. Remove two wheel speed sensor retaining bolts, then the speed sensor.
   b. Remove wheel speed sensor routing bracket.
10. **On all models,** use tie rod end tool No. 3290-D, or equivalent, to separate tie rod end from steering knuckle arm.
11. Remove lower ball joint clamp bolt, then separate ball joint from steering knuckle.
12. Remove steering knuckle to strut attaching bolts.
13. Slide front hub/steering knuckle assembly from strut bracket and halfshaft, **Fig. 3. Use caution not to damage grease seals. If hub binds on halfshaft splines, lightly tap end of halfshaft with a plastic hammer. If halfshaft splines become rusted to hub, use a two-jawed puller or a hub puller to separate.**
14. Reverse procedure to install. Tighten to specifications, then stake nut, **Fig. 4.** Tighten tie rod ending attaching nut to specifications.

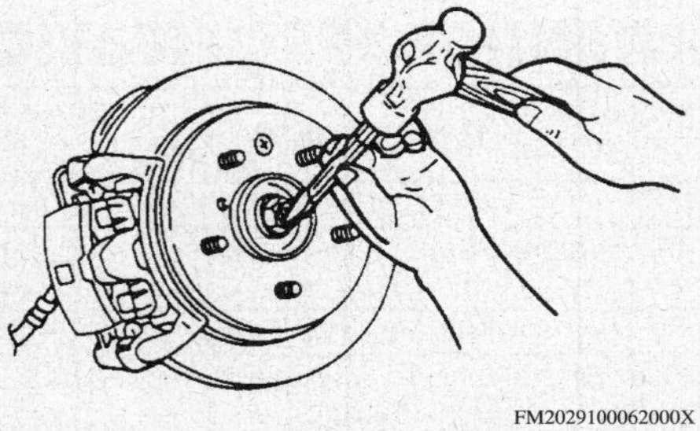

Fig. 1 Halfshaft attaching nut stake removal

BALL JOINT INSPECTION

Check for ball joint wear by raising vehicle until wheel is off ground. Support suspension arm so there is no load on suspension strut. Attempt to rock wheel top-to-bottom. If any wobble is felt, look for movement between suspension lower arm and wheel knuckle. Any movement indicates ball joint wear.

BALL JOINT

REPLACE

BALL JOINT SERVICE

Ball joints on this vehicle are not serviceable parts. Only dust boots are replaceable.

1. Remove lower control arm as outlined in this section.
2. Place control arm in a vise.
3. Remove dust boot with a chisel, **Fig. 5. Use caution not to damage ball joint.**
4. Liberally coat inside of new dust boot with lubricant C1AZ-19590-B, or equivalent.
5. Install dust boot with dust boot tool No. T88C-5493-AH, or equivalent, **Fig. 6.**
6. Install lower control arm.

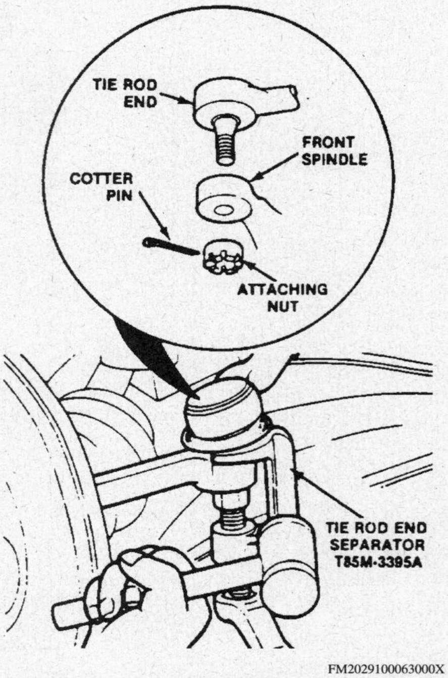

Fig. 2 Separating tie rod end from steering knuckle

COIL SPRING

REPLACE

1. Raise and support vehicle, then remove front wheels.
2. **On models equipped with anti-lock brakes,** remove wheel speed sensor routing bracket.
3. **On all models,** remove brake line U-clip from strut housing.
4. Remove two steering knuckle to strut mounting bolts.
5. Remove four upper strut retaining nuts, then the strut assembly from vehicle.
6. Secure strut assembly in McPherson strut spring compressor tool No. D85P-7178-A, or equivalent.
7. Compress coil spring, then remove strut retaining nut.
8. Remove strut assembly from spring compressor.
9. Release spring compressor, then remove coil spring, upper rubber spring seat, upper spring seat, thrust bearing

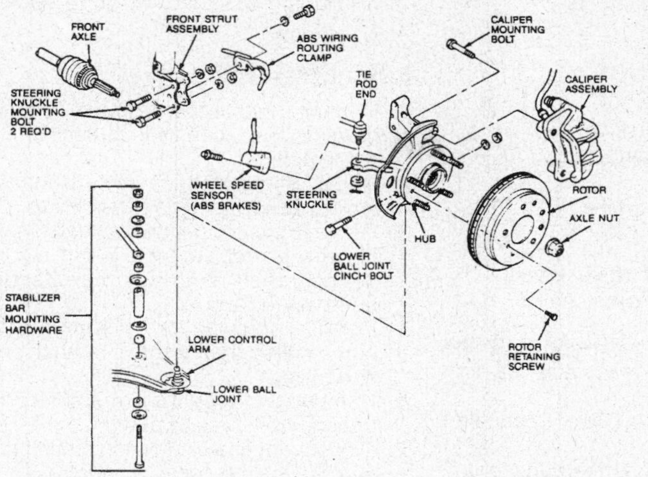

FM2029100064000X

Fig. 3 Steering knuckle, hub & rotor installation

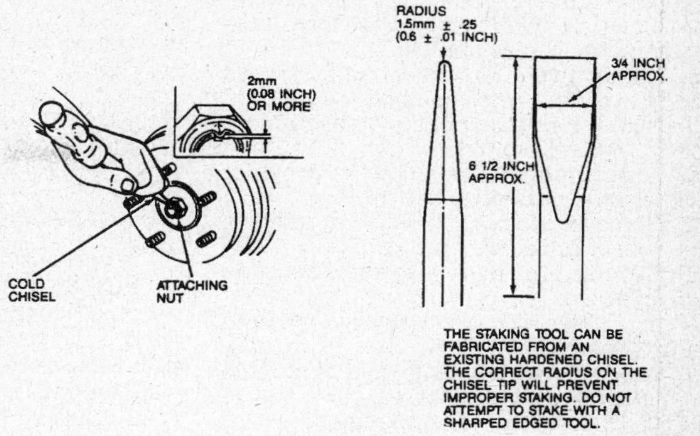

FM2029100065000X

Fig. 4 Staking halfshaft attaching nut

and strut mounting block.
10. Install strut mounting block, thrust bearing, upper spring seat, upper rubber spring seat and coil spring in spring compressor. **Face direction indicator on strut mounting block toward rear outboard position during reassembly.**
11. Compress coil spring. **Ensure lower coil of spring is seated on step of lower seat.**
12. Position new strut in compressed coil spring.
13. Install strut retaining nut. Tighten nut to specification.
14. Release spring compressor, then remove strut assembly.
15. Reverse procedures to install, noting the following:
    a. Tighten all bolts to specifications.
    b. Check front wheel alignment.

STRUT

REPLACE

Refer to "Coil Spring, Replace" for procedure.

CONTROL ARM

REPLACE

LOWER

1. Raise and support vehicle, then remove front wheels.
2. Remove lower ball joint pinch bolt.
3. Remove stabilizer control link to lower control arm retaining nut.
4. Separate ball joint stud from steering knuckle.
5. Remove two lower control arm bushing retaining bolts.
6. Remove lower control arm from vehicle.
7. Position new control arm against vehicle underbody.
8. Install lower control arm rear bushing bolt and tighten to specifications.
9. Install lower control arm front bushing bolt and tighten to specifications.
10. Install ball joint stud into steering knuckle.
11. Install ball joint pinch bolt and tighten to specifications.
12. Install stabilizer control link to lower control arm nut and tighten to specifications.
13. Install front wheels and tighten wheel lugs to specifications.

STABILIZER BAR

REPLACE

1. Raise and support vehicle, then remove front wheel.
2. Remove six transverse member retaining bolts, then transverse member.
3. Remove two bolts and six nuts from transaxle cradle, then cradle.
4. Disconnect heated oxygen sensor electrical connectors.
5. Disconnect converter inlet pipe(s) at exhaust manifold(s) and position aside.
6. **On models equipped with manual transaxle,** remove extension bar nut, then transaxle shift linkage bolt.
7. **On all models,** position a jack under front crossmember, then remove four bolts and two nuts retaining crossmember to body.
8. Remove stabilizer bar to stabilizer control link retaining nuts, then four stabilizer bar bracket bolts.
9. Lower front crossmember to allow for removal of stabilizer bar.
10. Remove stabilizer bar from right side of vehicle.
11. Reverse procedure to install, noting the following:
    a. Tighten all bolts to specifications.
    b. Apply rubber grease to inside surfaces of stabilizer bushings.
    c. Align bushing with installation mark on stabilizer bar.

POWER STEERING GEAR

REPLACE

1. Install three bar engine support tool

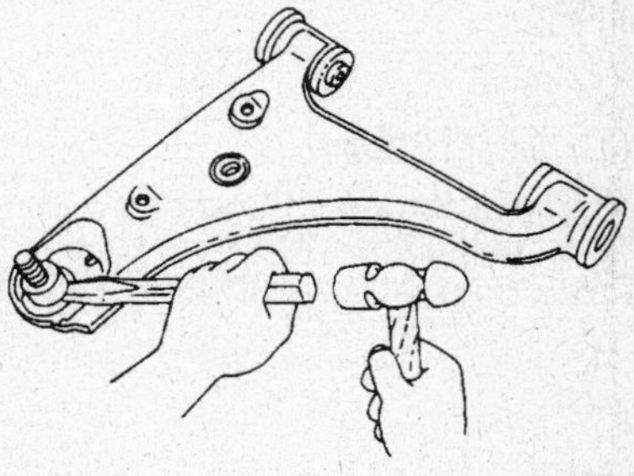

FM2029100066000X

Fig. 5 Ball joint dust boot removal

No. D88L-6000-A, or equivalent.
2. Raise and support vehicle, then remove front wheels.
3. Using tie rod end tool No. 3290-D, or equivalent, separate tie rod ends from left and right steering knuckles.
4. Remove left and right lower splash shields.
5. Remove six transverse member retaining bolts, then transverse member.
6. Remove two bolts and six retaining nuts from transaxle cradle, then the cradle.
7. **On models equipped with 2.5L engine,** disconnect two heated oxygen sensor electrical connectors.
8. **On models equipped with 2.5L engine,** remove converter inlet pipes from exhaust manifolds, then position aside.
9. **On all models,** using two line wrenches, disconnect high pressure line from steering gear. Plug open lines.
10. Disconnect return line from steering gear, then plug line.
11. Remove ground wire bracket from rear engine mount.
12. Remove three rear engine mount to transaxle retaining bolts.
13. Remove rear motor mount through bolt, then the rear engine mount.
14. Remove two steering gear mounting brackets.
15. Remove steering intermediate shaft to pinion shaft pinch bolt.
16. **On models equipped with manual transaxles,** remove extension bar retaining nut and position bar aside.
17. **On all models,** position transmission

jack under front crossmember, then remove six bolts and two retaining nuts from front crossmember.

18. Remove vent tube attached to driver's side of front crossmember.
19. Remove stabilizer bar to stabilizer control link retaining nuts.
20. Lower front crossmember to allow for removal of steering gear.
21. Remove steering gear from driver's side of vehicle.
22. Reverse procedure to install, noting the following:
    a. Tighten all components to specifications.
    b. Fill power steering fluid to correct level and check for leaks.
    c. Check front wheel alignment.

POWER STEERING PUMP

REPLACE

2.0L ENGINE

1. Remove two power steering pump belt shield retaining bolts, then shield.
2. Remove pump adjustment bolt, then pump retaining bolt.
3. Remove power steering pump drive belt.

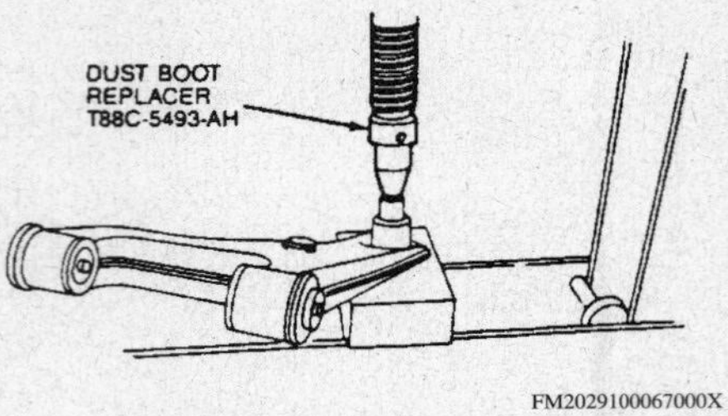

Fig. 6 Ball joint dust boot installation

4. Insert a screwdriver through hole in pump pulley, then remove retaining nut and pulley.
5. Remove two supply line manifold bolts.
6. Remove high pressure line banjo bolt, then disconnect pump pressure switch electrical connector.
7. Remove power steering pump through bolt, then the pump assembly.
8. If necessary, remove power steering pump brackets.
9. Reverse procedure to install, noting the following:
    a. Install new banjo bolt crush washers.
    b. Tighten all components to specifications.

2.5L ENGINE

1. Remove high pressure line hold-down bracket bolt, then high pressure line banjo bolt.
2. Raise and support vehicle, then remove passenger side front wheel.
3. Remove passenger side splash shield.
4. Loosen power steering pump adjusting bolt, then remove power steering pump drive belt.
5. Insert a screwdriver through hole in pump pulley, then remove retaining nut and pulley.
6. Remove two supply line manifold bolts from power steering pump.
7. Disconnect power steering pump pressure switch electrical connector.
8. Remove four power steering pump bracket to engine block retaining bolts.
9. Remove power steering pump from vehicle.
10. Reverse procedure to install, noting the following:
    a. Install new banjo bolt crush washers.
    b. Tighten all components to specifications.

TIGHTENING SPECIFICATIONS

Year	Component	Torque/ Ft. Lbs.
1997	Ball Joint Clamp Bolt	25–42
	Extension Bar Nut	28–38
	Front Crossmember	68–96
	Halfshaft Attaching Nut	174–235
	Intermediate Shaft to Pinion Shaft Bolt	13–20
	Lower Control Arm Front Bushing Bolt	58–78
	Lower Control Arm Rear Bushing Bolts	69–96
	Lower Control Arm Rear Bushing Nut	66–86
	Power Steering Pump Through Bolt (2.0L)	32–45
	Power Steering Pump To Engine Block (2.5L)	23–34
	Pulley Nut	36–43
	Rear Engine Mount Through Bolt	63–86
	Rear Engine Mount To Transaxle Bolts	50–68
	Speed Sensor Retaining Bolts	12–17
	Stabilizer Bar To Stabilizer Control Link Nuts	27–40
	Stabilizer Control Link To Lower Control Arm Nut	27–40
	Steering Gear Mounting Bracket Bolts	27–40
	Steering Knuckle To Strut	68–86
	Strut Retaining Nut	66–86
	Supply Line Manifold Bolts	10–13
	Tie Rod End	22–33
	Transaxle Cradle Nuts & Bolts	50–77
	Transaxle Shift Linkage Bolt	14–18
	Transverse Member Bolts	68–96
	Wheel Lug Nuts	65–87

Wheel Alignment

INDEX

PRELIMINARY INSPECTION

Before measuring and setting front wheel alignment, rest front wheels on turn plates.

Before setting rear toe, rest rear wheels on slider plates or turn plates. Before setting any alignment angle, jounce vehicle three times at each end to establish trim height.

Special adapters are available for using a magnetic hub gauge at rear wheels. Depending on type of equipment used, these may not be necessary. Hub gauge will snap into place on brake drum after hub cap and bearing cap are removed. Magnetic mounting toe gauges may also be installed in same manner.

Always perform wheel alignment on a level alignment rack. Do not attempt to check or adjust front wheel alignment without first inspecting front end components.

Check all factors of front wheel alignment except turning angle before making any adjustments. Check turning angle only after camber and toe have been adjusted to specification. Check front wheel alignment under following curb load conditions:

1. Establish standing curb height.
2. Remove heavy weights from trunk.
3. Ensure all tires are inflated to specification (cold).
4. Ensure fuel tank, oil reservoir and radiator are filled to specification. If necessary, add six pounds of weight to trunk for each gallon of gasoline missing from tank.
5. Place front seats in full rear position.
6. Check rear toe adjustment.
7. Always road test vehicle after adjusting alignment. If vehicle still pulls, switch front tires. If vehicle still pulls in same direction, recheck alignment and rear tracking. If vehicle pulls in opposite direction, rotate tires, then road test again.

FRONT WHEEL ALIGNMENT

Always adjust rear toe before setting front alignment angles.

CASTER

Front caster adjustment is not a separate procedure on this vehicle. Front caster should fall within specification when front camber is adjusted. If caster does not fall within specification, check control arms, stabilizers and bushings. If these components are satisfactory, check vehicle body for distortion at suspension mounting points.

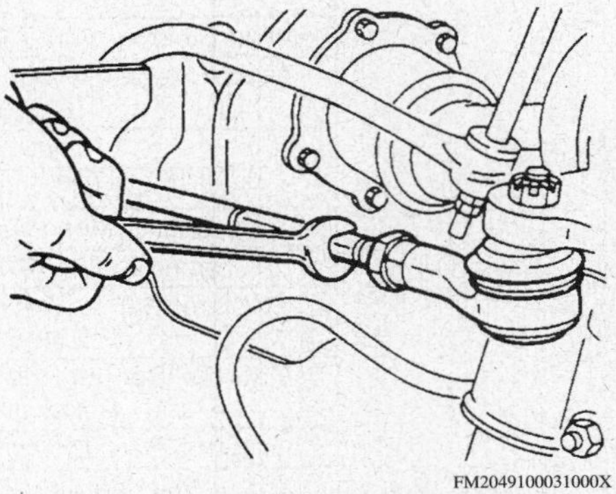

Fig. 1 Front toe-in adjustment

CAMBER

1. Raise vehicle and support at body so that front suspension is unloaded.
2. Remove tire and wheel assembly.
3. Remove upper strut attaching nuts.
4. Lower strut, then rotate strut mounting block until camber is within specification.
5. Reinstall strut in strut tower.
6. **Torque** strut attaching nuts to 34–46 ft. lbs., then recheck camber adjustment.

TOE-IN

1. Loosen jam nuts at tie rod ends, then release clips at small ends of steering gear boots. **Ensure boots are free on tie rod ends so that they will not be twisted when tie rods are turned.**
2. Turn tie rods into or out of tie rod ends an equal amount on each side, **Fig. 1.** To increase toe-in, turn right tie rod toward front of vehicle, and turn left tie rod toward rear of vehicle. To decrease toe-in, turn tie rods in opposite direction. One turn of each side tie rod changes toe-in by approximately .28 inch.
3. Check front tracking. **Always set tracking immediately after setting toe.** Set tracking by using rear wheels as a reference point. Follow equipment manufacturer's instructions to check tracking. Angle of each front wheel in relationship to rear wheels must be same.
4. Ensure toe-in is still within specifications, then **torque** jam nuts to 51–72 ft. lbs.
5. Ensure steering gear boot ends are correctly positioned on appropriate sections of tie rods, then install boot clips.
6. Measure turning angle by placing front wheels on a turning-radius gauge and fully turning wheels to left, then right.

REAR WHEEL ALIGNMENT

TOE-IN

1. Loosen cam nut on rear lateral link.
2. Turning adjusting cam bolt one graduation mark changes toe-in about .13 inch. **Turning left cam bolt counterclockwise increases toe-in, turning cam bolt clockwise increases toe-out. Turning right cam bolt clockwise increases toe-in, turning cam bolt counterclockwise increases toe-out.**
3. Adjust toe-in to correct setting.
4. **Torque** cam nut to 58–86 ft. lbs.

SABLE & TAURUS

NOTE: Refer To The Rear Of This Manual For Vehicle Manufacturer's Special Service Tools.

INDEX OF SERVICE OPERATIONS

Specifications

GENERAL ENGINE SPECIFICATIONS

Liter/VIN Code②	Fuel System	Bore & Stroke	Comp. Ratio	Net H.P. @ RPM	Maximum Torque/Ft. Lbs. @ RPM	Normal Oil Pressure, psi
1997–99						
3.0L/S	SFI	3.50 x 3.13	—	200 @ 5750	200 @ 4500	45.0④
3.0L/U	SFI	3.50 x 3.14	—	145 @ 5250	170 @ 3250	40.0–60.0①
3.0L/1	SFI	3.50 x 3.14	—	145 @ 5250	170 @ 3250	40.0–60.0①
3.0L/2	SFI	3.50 x 3.14	—	145 @ 5250	170 @ 3250	40.0–60.0①
3.4L/N	SFI	3.25 x 3.13	—	235 @ 6100	230 @ 4800	20.0–45.0③

SFI — Sequential Fuel Injection
① — At 2500 RPM w/engine at operating temperature.
② — The eighth digit of the VIN denotes engine code.
③ — At 1500 RPM w/engine at operating temperature.
④ — With engine at operating temperature.

TUNE UP SPECIFICATIONS

Liter/VIN Code①	Spark Plug Gap	Ignition Timing, °BTDC				Curb Idle Speed, RPM		Fast Idle Speed, RPM		Fuel Pump Pressure, psi	Valve Clearance
		Firing Order Fig. ②	Man. Trans.	Auto. Trans.	Mark Fig.	Man. Trans.	Auto. Trans.	Man. Trans.	Auto. Trans.		
1997											
3.0L/S	.054	B	—	10⑦	⑧	—	④	—	④	35–45⑨	—
3.0L/U	.044	A	—	10⑦	⑧	—	④	—	④	35–45⑨	—
3.0L/1	.044	A	—	10⑦	⑧	—	④	—	④	35–45⑨	—
3.0L/2	.044	A	—	10⑦	⑧	—	④	—	④	35–45⑨	—
3.4L/N	.044	③	—	10⑦	⑧	—	④	—	④	35–45⑨	⑤
1998–99											
3.0L/S	.054	B	—	10⑦	⑧	—	④	—	④	35–45⑨	⑥
3.0L/U	.044	A	—	10⑦	⑧	—	④	—	④	35–45⑨	⑥
3.0L/1	.044	A	—	10⑦	⑧	—	④	—	④	35–45⑨	⑥
3.0L/2	.044	A	—	10⑦	⑧	—	④	—	④	35–45⑨	⑥
3.4L/N	.044	③	—	10⑦	⑧	—	④	—	④	35–45⑨	⑤

BTDC — Before Top Dead Center
D — Drive
① — The eighth digit of the VIN denotes engine code.
② — Before disconnecting wires from distributor cap or coil, determine location of wire, as position may have been altered from that mounting at end of this chart.
③ — Cylinder numbering front to rear: righthand bank, 1, 2, 3, 4; lefthand bank, 5, 6, 7, 8. Firing order: 1-5-4-2-6-3-7-8.
④ — Idle speed is controlled by an automatic idle control system.
⑤ — Intake, .006–.010 inch @ room temperature; exhaust, .010–.014 inch @ room temperature.
⑥ — Equipped w/hydraulic valve lifters; no provision for adjustment.
⑦ — Non-adjustable.
⑧ — Equipped w/crankshaft position sensor.
⑨ — Engine running.

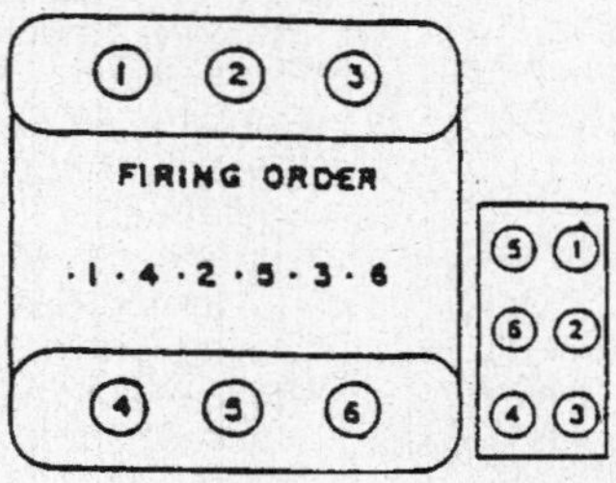

FM1139300273000X

Fig. A

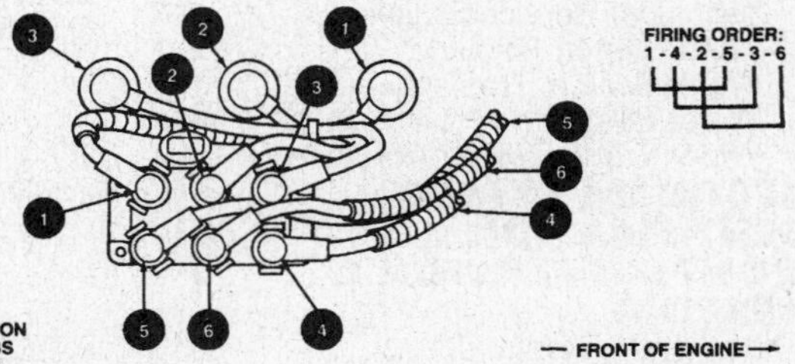

FM1139600507000X

Fig. B

FRONT WHEEL ALIGNMENT SPECIFICATIONS

Model	Caster Angle, Degrees		Camber Angle, Degrees				Total Toe, Degrees①		Ball Joint Wear
			Limits		Desired				
	Limits	Desired	Left	Right	Left	Right	Limits	Desired	
1997–99									
All	+2.8 to +4.8	+3.8	-1.1 to +.1	-1.1 to +.1	-.5	-.5	-.45 to +.05	-.20	②

① — Turning angle at outside wheel on turns w/inner wheel @ 20° is 18.25.°

② — Refer to "Ball Joint Inspection" in "Front Suspension & Steering" section.

REAR WHEEL ALIGNMENT SPECIFICATIONS

Model	Camber Angle, Degrees①		Total Toe-In, Degrees	
	Limits	Desired	Limits	Desired
1997–99				
All	-1.3 to -.1	-.6	-.13 to +.37	+.12

① — Not adjustable.

FLUID CAPACITIES & COOLING SYSTEM DATA

Model	Engine Liter/VIN④	Coolant Capacity, Qts.	Radiator Cap Relief Pressure, Lbs.	Thermo. Opening Temp. °F	Fuel Tank Gals.	Engine Oil Refill, Qts.②	Transaxle Capacity	
							Manual Trans., Pts.	Auto. Trans., Qts.①
1997								
All	3.0L/U, 1 & 2	11.6	16	197	③	4.5	—	⑥
	3.0L/S	10.5	16	197	③	5.8	—	⑥
SHO	3.4L/N	10.8	16	197	③	6.7	—	⑥
1998–99								
All	3.0L/U, 1 & 2	11.6	16	197	⑤	4.5	—	⑥
	3.0L/S	10.5	16	197	16.0	5.8	—	⑥
SHO	3.4L/N	10.8	16	197	16.0	6.7	—	⑥

① — Approximate; make final inspection w/dipstick.

② — Includes filter.

③ — Standard tank, 16 gals.; optional tank, 18 gals.

④ — The eighth digit of the VIN denotes engine code.

⑤ — Standard tank, 16.0 gals.; Flex Fuel tank, 18 gals.

⑥ — Models w/AX4S transaxle, 12.25 qts.; models w/AX4N transaxle, 13.50 qts.

LUBRICANT DATA

Year	Transaxle		Power Steering	Brake System
	Manual	Automatic		
1997	—	Mercon	①	DOT 3
1998–99	—	Mercon V	②	DOT 3

① — Premium power steering fluid part No. E6AZ-19582-AA, or equivalent.

② — Motorcraft MERCON Multi-Purpose ATF part No. XT-2-QDX, or equivalent.

Electrical

NOTE: On Air Bag Equipped Models, Refer To " Air Bag System Precautions" Located In The Front Of This Manual For System Disarming & Arming Procedures.

NOTE: Prior To Performing Any Service Operations Listed In This Section, Consult The "Technical Service Bulletins " Section For Related Information.

INDEX

PRECAUTIONS

AIR BAG SYSTEMS

Refer to "Air Bag System Precautions" in the front of this manual for system disarming and arming procedures.

BATTERY GROUND CABLE

Prior to service, disconnect battery ground cable and isolate as required.

FUSE PANEL & FLASHER LOCATION

The fuse panel is located under the instrument cluster or instrument panel, left of the steering column. The combination turn signal/hazard flasher is located behind on the lefthand side instrument panel reinforcement above the fuse panel.

RELAY CENTER LOCATION

The relay panel/power distribution center is located at the front center of the engine compartment, attached to the radiator support. This panel contains the PCM relay, low fan control relay, high fan control relay and A/C WAC relay.

FUEL PUMP RELAY LOCATION

The fuel pump relay is located at the front center of the engine compartment, in the power distribution center.

STARTER

REPLACE

When servicing the starter motor, note that the heavy gauge input lead connected to the starter solenoid is hot at all times. Ensure the protective cap is installed over the terminal and is replaced after service.

1. Raise and support vehicle.
2. Disconnect engine control sensor wiring and starter battery cable from starter solenoid. **When disconnecting hard-shell connector of engine control sensor wiring at S-terminal, grasp plastic shell and pull straight off. Do not pull on wire. Replace any part of connector that is damaged during removal.**
3. Remove upper and lower starter mounting bolts, then the starter motor.
4. Reverse procedure to install. **Torque** upper and lower mounting bolts to 16–21 ft. lbs. and starter battery cable to solenoid nut to 84–120 inch lbs.

ALTERNATOR

REPLACE

3.0L ENGINE

VIN S Engine

1. Remove accessory drive belt from alternator.
2. Remove nut, then position engine control sensor wiring and hose bracket out of the way.
3. Loosen alternator pulley nut, then Remove inboard upper alternator bolt.
4. Loosen outboard upper alternator bolt.
5. Disconnect electrical harness connector and output terminal wiring.
6. Raise and support vehicle, then remove wheel and tire assembly.
7. Remove alternator splash shield, then outboard upper alternator bolt.
8. Remove lower alternator bolt.
9. Remove alternator pulley nut, then the alternator.
10. Reverse procedure to install, noting the following:
    a. **Torque** alternator mounting bolts to 15–22 ft. lbs.
    b. **Torque** alternator output nut to 80–106 inch lbs.
    c. **Torque** alternator pulley nut to 60–100 ft. lbs.

VIN U, 1 & 2 Engines

The alternator is not internally serviceable.

1. Disconnect the electrical connectors from the integral alternator/voltage regulator.
2. Loosen the generator pivot bolt, then remove the mounting brace bolt from the alternator.
3. Disengage the accessory drive belt from the alternator pulley.
4. Remove generator brace.
5. Remove the generator pivot bolt, then the alternator/voltage regulator.
6. Reverse procedure to install, noting the following:
    a. **Torque** mounting nut and mounting

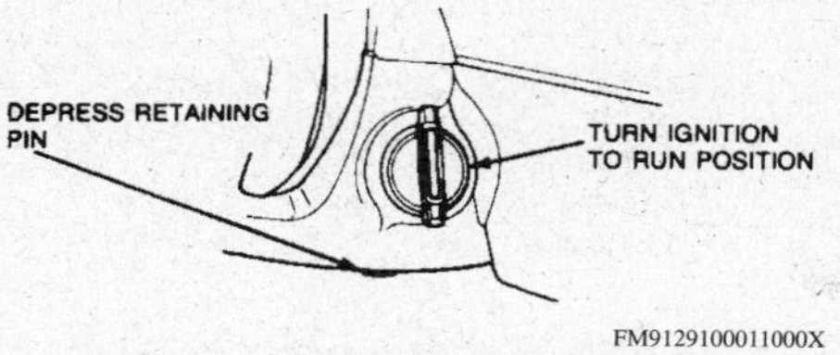

FM9129100011000X

Fig. 1 Ignition lock cylinder removal

brace bolt to 15–22 ft. lbs. and alternator brace bolts to 72–96 inch lbs.
   b. **Torque** pivot bolt to 30–40 ft. lbs.
   c. **Torque** alternator output nut (B+) to 60–84 inch lbs.

3.4L ENGINE

1. Remove right side cowl vent screen.
2. Raise and support vehicle, then remove right front wheel assembly.
3. Remove right tie-rod, then accessory drive belt from alternator.
4. Disconnect electrical harness connector and output terminal wiring.
5. Remove nut and position engine control sensor wiring out of the way.
6. Remove one bolt and two stud bolts, then the alternator from vehicle.
7. Reverse procedure to install, noting the following:
   a. **Torque** alternator mounting bolt and stud bolts to 15–22 ft. lbs.
   b. **Torque** engine control sensor wiring mounting nut to 11–14 ft. lbs.
   c. **Torque** alternator output nut to 80–106 inch lbs.

IGNITION LOCK

REPLACE

1. Place ignition switch in Run position and, working through steering column lower shroud, **Fig. 1,** depress lock cylinder retaining pin with suitable ⅛ inch drill or drift punch.
2. Pull ignition lock cylinder from housing.
3. Rotate replacement lock cylinder to Run position and, while depressing retaining pin, insert lock cylinder into housing. To ensure proper installation, rotate ignition switch through travel.

IGNITION SWITCH

REPLACE

1. Remove lower instrument panel steering column cover, **Fig. 2.**
2. Turn ignition lock to Run position.
3. Disconnect ignition switch electrical connector.
4. Remove mounting screws and ignition switch.
5. Reverse procedure to install, noting the following:
   a. Ensure ignition lock is in Run position when installing ignition switch.
   b. **Torque** ignition switch mounting screws to 50–69 inch lbs.
   c. Inspect ignition switch for proper function, including Start and Accessory positions.

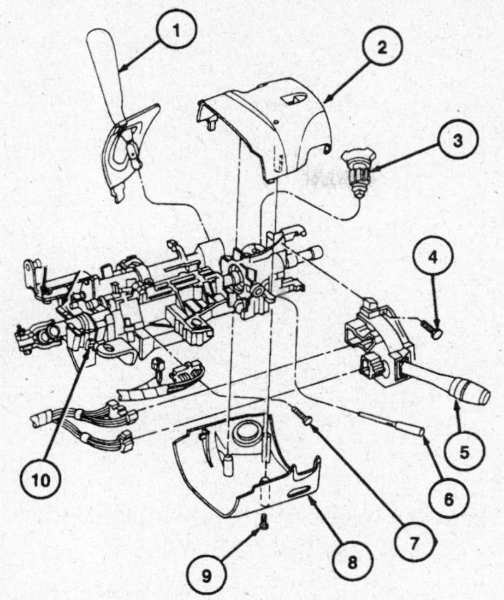

Item	Description
1	Gearshift Lever
2	Upper Steering Column Shroud
3	Ignition Lock Assy
4	Screw (2 Req'd)
5	Multi-Function Switch
6	Tilt Steering Column Lock Lever
7	Screw
8	Steering Column Shroud
9	Screw (3 Req'd)
10	Ignition Switch

FM9129600018000X

Fig. 2 Ignition switch removal

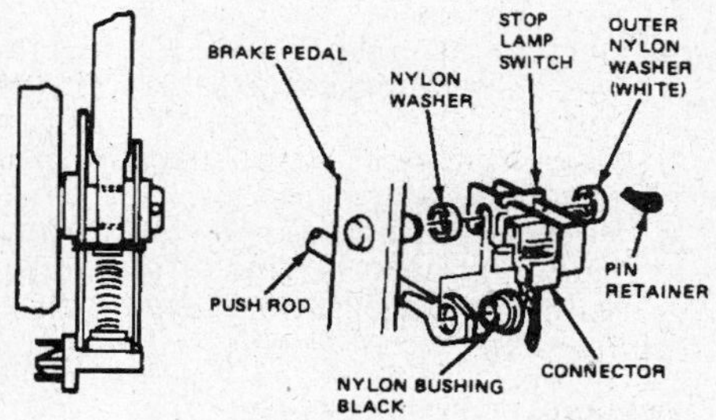

FM9049100033000X

Fig. 4 Stop lamp switch installation

CLUTCH START SWITCH

REPLACE

REMOVAL

1. Remove panel above clutch pedal and disconnect starter/clutch interlock switch wiring.
2. Remove mounting screw, hairpin clip and starter/clutch interlock switch.
3. Depress barb at end of rod and pull rod from clutch pedal.

INSTALLATION

1. Install switch with self-adjusting clip about one inch from end of rod. **During installation of switch, clutch pedal must be fully up, otherwise switch may become misadjusted.**
2. Insert eyelet end of rod over clutch pedal pin and install hairpin clip, **Fig. 3.**
3. Align switch mounting hole with mounting bracket hole, install and tighten mounting screw.
4. Adjust starter/clutch interlock switch by pressing clutch pedal to floor.
5. Connect wiring connector and install panel above clutch pedal.

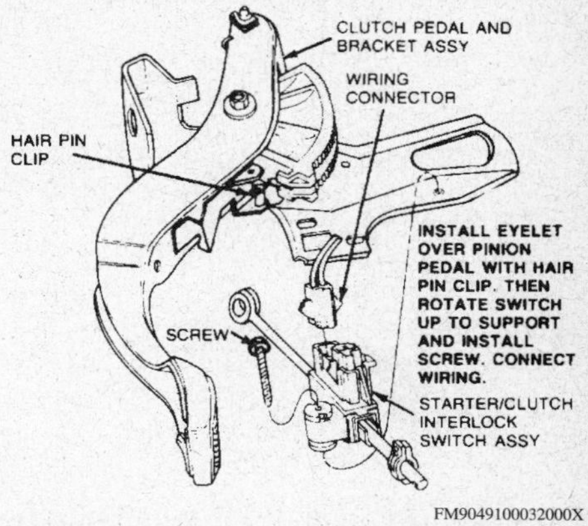

FM9049100032000X

Fig. 3 Starter/clutch interlock switch replacement

NEUTRAL SAFETY SWITCH

REPLACE

Neutral safety switch functions are incorporated into the transaxle range sensor. The following procedure covers range sensor replacement.

1. Place manual control lever in Neutral position.
2. Remove engine air cleaner and air cleaner outlet tube.
3. Disconnect transmission range sensor electrical connector.
4. Remove manual control lever from transaxle.
5. Remove mounting bolts and transmission range sensor.
6. Reverse procedure to install, noting the following:
   a. Ensure manual control lever is in Neutral position.
   b. Install transmission range sensor and mounting bolts loosely.
   c. Align position sensor using manual lever position sensor alignment tool No. T92P-70010-AH, or equivalent.
   d. **Torque** sensor mounting bolts to 84–108 inch lbs.
   e. **Torque** manual lever mounting bolts to 8–11 ft. lbs.

HEADLAMP SWITCH

REPLACE

1. Pry headlamp switch housing from instrument panel.
2. Depress release button on headlamp switch and pull away from instrument panel.
3. Disconnect headlamp switch electrical connectors and remove switch.

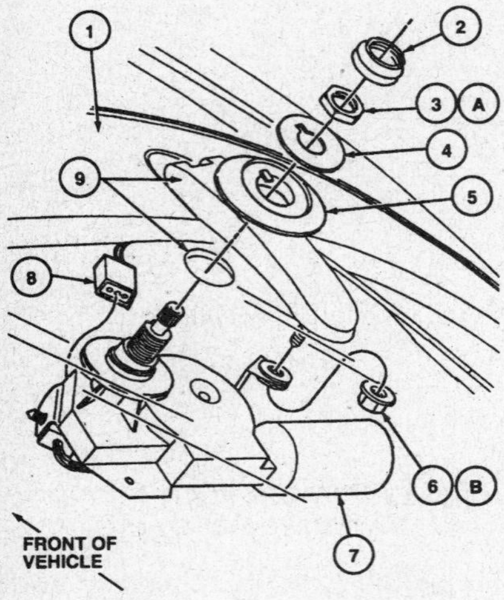

Item	Description
1	Liftgate
2	Windshield Wiper Output Arm Cover
3	Nut
4	Washer
5	Bezel
6	Nut and Washer
7	Windshield Wiper Motor
8	Rear Window Wiper / Washer Wire
9	Liftgate Window
A	Tighten to 15-20 N·m (11-15 Lb-Ft)
B	Tighten to 5-7 N·m (44-62 Lb-In)

FM9029600401000X

Fig. 5 Rear wiper motor removal

4. Reverse procedure to install.

STOP LIGHT SWITCH

REPLACE

1. Lift stop lamp switch harness wiring connector locking tab and remove connector.
2. Remove hairpin retainer and white nylon washer, and slide switch and pushrod assembly away from brake pedal. Remove switch by sliding up and/or down. **Since switch side plate nearest switch is slotted, it is not necessary to remove master cylinder pushrod, black bushing or one white bushing nearest brake pedal from brake pedal pin, Fig. 4.**
3. Position switch so U-shaped side is nearest brake pedal and directly over brake pedal pin. **The black bushing must be in position in pushrod eyelet with washer face on side away from pedal arm.**
4. Slide switch up and down as necessary to trap black plastic bushing and pushrod between two switch side plates, and push switch and pushrod assembly towards brake pedal arm.
5. Install white nylon washer on pedal pin and hairpin retainer. **Do not substitute other types of pin retainers. Replace only with production type hairpin retainer.**
6. Connect wire harness connector to switch and inspect brake lamps for proper operation. Brake lamps should illuminate with less than six pounds of force applied at brake pedal pad.

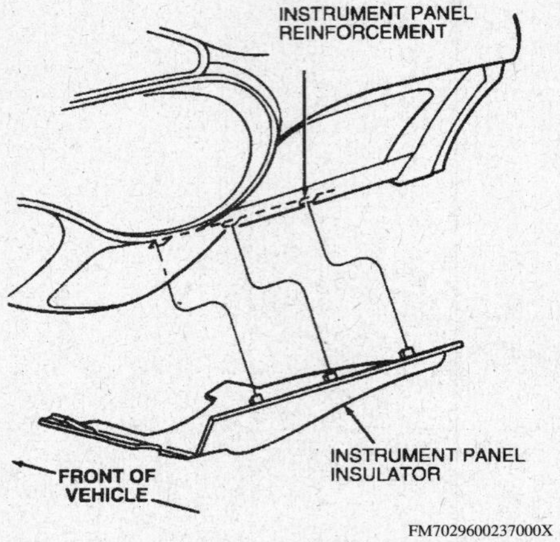

FM7029600237000X

Fig. 6 Instrument panel insulator panel removal

MULTI-FUNCTION SWITCH

REPLACE

1. **On models with tilt steering column,** move column to lowest position, and remove tilt lever and key release lever.
2. **On all models,** remove ignition lock as outlined under "Ignition Lock, Replace."
3. Remove upper and lower steering column shrouds.
4. Remove multi-function switch mounting screws and disengage switch from casting.
5. Disconnect electrical connectors, then remove switch.
6. Reverse procedure to install. **Torque** multi-function switch mounting screws to 18–27 inch lbs. and tilt lever mounting screw to 6–8 inch lbs.

STEERING WHEEL

REPLACE

1. Center front wheels to straight-ahead position.
2. Disconnect speed control wire harness from steering wheel.
3. Remove driver's air bag module and store on bench with pad side facing upward.
4. Remove and discard steering wheel mounting bolt.
5. Using steering wheel puller tool No. T67L-3600-A, or equivalent, remove steering wheel. Route contact assembly wire harness through steering wheel as wheel is lifted off shaft.
6. Reverse procedure to install, noting the following:
   a. Ensure front wheels are in straight-ahead position.
   b. Route contact assembly wire harness through steering column opening at three o'clock position.
   c. Align steering shaft alignment marks.
   d. **Torque** new steering wheel mounting bolt to 26–34 ft. lbs.

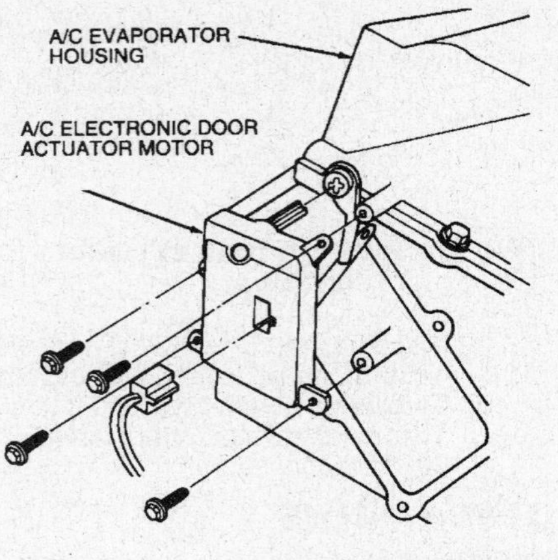

FM7029600238000X

Fig. 7 A/C electronic door actuator motor removal

INSTRUMENT CLUSTER

REPLACE

ANALOG INSTRUMENTATION

Column Shift

1. Remove ignition switch lock cylinder as outlined under " Ignition Lock, Replace."
2. Remove upper and lower steering column shrouds.
3. Remove instrument panel steering column cover from instrument panel.
4. Remove integrated control panel from instrument panel.
5. Tilt steering wheel to its lowest possible position.
6. Remove finish panel from instrument panel.
7. Detach PRNDL cable loop from column shift selector tube.
8. Remove adjustment nut from PRNDL cable, then cable from bracket.
9. Remove mounting screws and pull cluster toward steering wheel.
10. Reach behind instrument cluster and disconnect three electrical connectors.
11. Remove cluster assembly from instrument panel.
12. Reverse procedure to install.

Floor Shift

1. Remove ignition switch lock cylinder as outlined under " Ignition Lock, Replace."
2. Remove upper and lower steering column shrouds.
3. Remove mounting screws and finish panel from instrument panel.
4. Tilt steering wheel to its lowest possible position.
5. Remove four instrument cluster

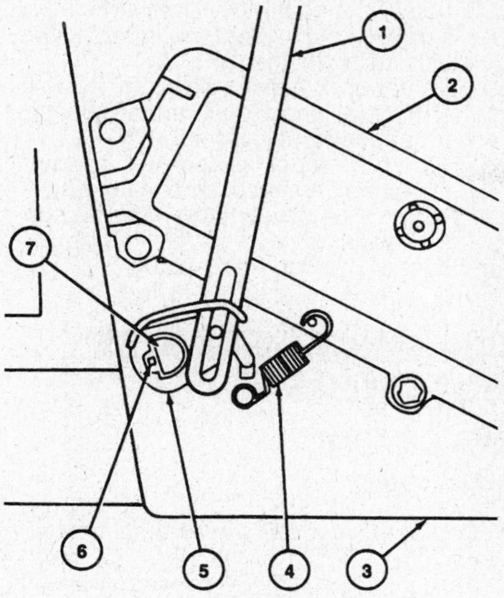

Item	Description
1	Metal Link
2	Heater Core Cover
3	A/C Evaporator Housing
4	Spring
5	Lever
6	Locking Ramp (Part of Secondary A/C Air Temperature Control Door Shaft)
7	Secondary A/C Air Temperature Control Door Shaft

FM7029600239000X

Fig. 8 Spring & metal link removal

mounting screws and pull top of cluster toward steering wheel.
6. Reach behind instrument cluster and disconnect three electrical connectors.
7. Remove cluster.
8. Reverse procedure to install.

ELECTRONIC

1. Remove lower trim panels.
2. Remove steering column cover and PRNDL cable to cluster mounting screws.
3. Pull cluster trim panel rearward, disconnect switch module and remove trim panel.
4. Remove mounting screws and pull cluster bottom rearward.
5. Reach behind and underneath cluster, and disconnect electrical connectors.
6. Pull cluster bottom rearward to remove.
7. Reverse procedure to install.

RADIO

REPLACE

1. Install radio removal tool No. T87P-19061-A, or equivalent, to radio face plate and push tool inward about 1–1½ inches to release radio clips. **Do not push tool with excessive force or radio damage may result.**
2. Apply light even force on tool and pull radio from instrument panel.
3. **On models with automatic temperature control,** disconnect sensor hose and elbow.
4. **On all models,** disconnect radio electrical connectors and antenna lead.
5. Reverse procedure to install.

WIPER MOTOR

REPLACE

FRONT

On these models, the wiper mounting arm and pivot shafts are connected together with non-removable plastic ball joints. Except for the wiper motor, the entire wiper transmission assembly is non-serviceable.

1. Remove wiper arm mounting nuts from pivot shafts. **Note normal park positions of wiper arms and blades.**
2. Turn ignition On and wiper switch to LO. When arms and blades to move to a straight up-and-down position, turn ignition Off.
3. Remove wiper arms from pivot shafts.
4. Turn eight plastic cowl vent screen nuts ¼ turn counterclockwise.
5. Remove six clips mounting vent screen to inner panels.
6. Remove screws mounting wiper assembly to cowl and assembly.
7. Reverse procedure to install, noting the following:
   a. Turn ignition switch to On position and wiper control switch to Low or High.
   b. Turn wiper control switch to Off position after wipers have cycled once or twice. This will allow them to park properly and will prevent damage.
   c. **Torque** wiper assembly screws to 84–120 inch lbs.
   d. Install wiper arms and blades in their previously noted park positions.
   e. **Torque** pivot arm nuts to 22–29 ft. lbs.

REAR

1. Open liftgate and remove window wiper motor cover, **Fig. 5.**
2. Disconnect rear window wiper/washer electrical connector.
3. Unscrew and remove windshield wiper output arm cover.
4. Remove outside mounting nut, washer and bezel.
5. Remove wiper motor to liftgate window hinge mounting nut.
6. Remove wiper motor from liftgate.
7. Reverse procedure to install.

WIPER SWITCH

REPLACE

FRONT

The windshield wiper switch is an integral part of the multi-function switch. Refer to "Multi-Function Switch, Replace" for replacement procedures.

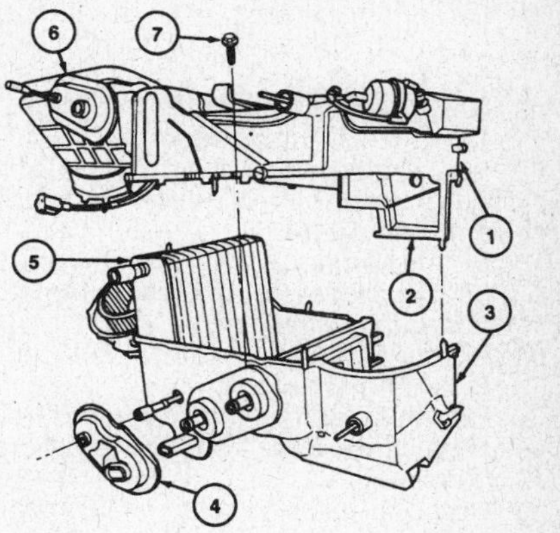

Item	Description
1	A/C Evaporator Housing Upper Half
2	Heater Air Damper Door
3	A/C Evaporator Housing Lower Half
4	Foam Seal (Evaporator Core Inlet)
5	A/C Evaporator Core
6	Foam Seal (Evaporator Core Outlet)
7	Screw (17 Req'd)

FM7029600240000X

Fig. 9 Evaporator removal

REAR

1. Pull rear wiper/washer switch straight out of instrument panel.
2. Disconnect electrical connector and remove switch.
3. Reverse procedure to install.

WIPER TRANSMISSION

REPLACE

The wiper mounting arm and pivot shafts are connected by non-removable plastic ball joints. Except for the wiper motor, the wiper transmission is non-serviceable. Refer to "Wiper Motor, Replace" for procedures.

BLOWER MOTOR

REPLACE

1. Pull instrument panel insulator from lower righthand side instrument panel reinforcement, **Fig. 6.**
2. Disconnect blower motor electrical connector.
3. Remove mounting screws and blower motor from A/C evaporator housing.
4. Reverse procedure to install.

HEATER CORE

REPLACE

1. Drain coolant into a suitable container.
2. Remove instrument panel as outlined in "Dash Panels."
3. Disconnect heater hoses from heater core and plug heater core tubes.
4. Remove four A/C electronic door actuator motor to A/C evaporator housing mounting screws, **Fig. 7.**

5. Disengage spring from heater core cover and remove spring from lever, **Fig. 8.**
6. Gently depress locking ramp and remove lever from secondary A/C air temperature control door end. **Do not bend any part of lever. It is brittle and will break.**
7. Rotate primary A/C air temperature door shaft downward, swing metal link and remove from pin.
8. Remove three heater core cover mounting screws.
9. Remove heater core cover and heater core cover seal from A/C evaporator housing.
10. Remove heater core and seal from A/C evaporator housing by pushing on heater core tubes.
11. Reverse procedure to install.

EVAPORATOR CORE

REPLACE

Whenever an evaporator core is replaced, the suction accumulator/dryer must also be replaced.

1. Drain coolant into a suitable container.
2. Recover A/C system as outlined under "Air Conditioning."
3. Disconnect heater hoses from heater core and plug heater core tubes.
4. Disconnect vacuum supply hose from in-line vacuum check valve in engine compartment.
5. Disconnect liquid line and accumulator from evaporator core at dash panel. Cap refrigerant lines and evaporator core to prevent entrance of dirt and excess moisture.
6. Remove instrument panel as outlined in "Dash Panels."
7. Remove mounting screw and evaporator case to instrument panel shake brace.
8. Remove two screws holding floor register and floor ducts to bottom of evaporator case.
9. Remove three evaporator housing to dash panel mounting nuts, located in engine compartment.
10. Remove support bracket to cowl top panel mounting screws.
11. Remove evaporator housing to Powertrain Control Module (PCM) mounting bracket mounting nut.
12. Carefully pull evaporator housing assembly away from dash panel and remove. **Whenever evaporator case is removed it will be necessary to replace suction accumulator/dryer.**
13. Remove foam seals from evaporator core tubes.
14. Remove A/C electronic door actuator motor to evaporator housing mounting screws, **Fig. 7.**
15. Disengage spring from heater core cover and remove spring from lever, **Fig. 8.**
16. Gently depress locking ramp and remove lever from secondary A/C air temperature control door end. **Do not bend any part of lever. It is brittle and will break.**
17. Rotate primary A/C air temperature control door shaft downward, swing metal link and remove from pin.
18. Remove screws from around evaporator housing flange joint.
19. Using suitable side cutters, or equivalent, cut all snap loops around evaporator housing flange joint.
20. Separate upper evaporator housing from lower evaporator housing, **Fig. 9.**
21. Remove evaporator from lower evaporator housing.
22. Reverse procedure to install.

TECHNICAL SERVICE BULLETINS

NO CRANK

1997–98

On these models, the starter may not crank.

This condition may be caused by an excessive current drain discharging the battery. To correct this condition, proceed as follows:

1. Isolate excessive drain by removing fuses.
2. If drain cannot be isolate, measure current drain. Current drain for VIN U, 1 and 2 engines should be 16 mAmps, and for VIN N and S engines, 20.5 mAmps.
3. If current drain is with specifications, inspect Anti-Lock Brake System (ABS) module connector C1507 for water entry or corrosion signs and repair as necessary.

3.0L Engine

NOTE: On Air Bag Equipped Models, Refer To " Air Bag System Precautions" Located In The Front Of This Manual For System Disarming & Arming Procedures.

NOTE: Prior To Performing Any Service Operations Listed In This Section, Consult The "Technical Service Bulletins " Section For Related Information.

INDEX

PRECAUTIONS

AIR BAG SYSTEMS

Refer to "Air Bag System Precautions" in the front of this manual for system disarming and arming procedures.

FLEXIBLE FUEL MODELS

Flexible Fuel (FF) vehicles use unique methanol-compatible components. Certain gasoline-only components may appear identical to these FF vehicle components. Under no circumstances should these components be interchanged.

FUEL SYSTEM PRESSURE RELIEF

When releasing fuel pressure on flexible fuel vehicles, use methanol resistant gloves and eye protection. Avoid prolonged skin contact with liquid or breathing of vapors.

If methanol fuel should be spilled on paint, flush immediately with cold water. **Do not wipe, or paint damage may occur.**

Fuel supply lines will remain pressurized for long periods of time after engine shutdown. This pressure must be relieved before any service is attempted. A valve is provided on the fuel rail assembly for this purpose.

1. Remove air cleaner assembly.
2. Connect pressure gauge tool No. T80L-9974-A or T80L-9974-B, or equivalent, onto fuel rail assembly fuel valve.
3. Open manual valve on pressure gauge tool.
4. To pressurize fuel system, proceed as follows:
   a. Install pressure gauge tool onto fuel rail pressure fitting.
   b. Turn ignition On for three seconds, 5–10 times until pressure gauge indicates 13 psi.

BATTERY GROUND CABLE

Prior to service, disconnect battery ground cable and isolate as required.

COMPRESSION PRESSURE

When inspecting cylinder compression, the lowest cylinder must be within 75 percent of the highest cylinder. Perform compression inspection with engine at normal operating temperature, spark plugs removed and throttle wide open.

ENGINE MOUNT

REPLACE

LEFTHAND & RIGHTHAND FRONT ENGINE SUPPORT INSULATORS

1. Raise and support vehicle.
2. Place jack and wood block in suitable place under engine block.
3. Remove lefthand and righthand front engine support insulator to subframe mounting nuts, **Figs. 1 and 2.**
4. Raise jack assembly enough to remove load from lefthand and righthand engine support insulators.
5. Remove bolts from lefthand and righthand engine support insulators, then the insulators from subframe.
6. Reverse procedure to install.

ENGINE & TRANSAXLE SUPPORT INSULATOR

1. Raise and support vehicle. Remove lefthand front tire and wheel assembly.
2. Support transaxle assembly with suitable transmission jack.
3. Remove engine and transaxle support insulator to rear engine and transaxle bracket mounting nut, **Fig. 3.**
4. Remove two engine and transaxle support insulator to subframe through bolts.
5. Raise transaxle assembly enough to remove load from engine and transaxle support insulator and remove support insulator from subframe.
6. Reverse procedure to install.

ENGINE

REPLACE

1. Disconnect steering coupling at pinch bolt joint inside passenger compartment.
2. **On VIN S engine,** remove cowl extension and wiper arm.
3. **On all models,** disconnect engine control sensor wiring from intake air temperature sensor.
4. Disconnect crankcase ventilation tube and aspirator hose from air cleaner outlet tube.
5. Remove air cleaner outlet tube.
6. Drain engine coolant and recover A/C system.
7. Relieve fuel system pressure as outlined under "Precautions."
8. Disconnect fuel tubes from fuel injection supply manifold.
9. Disconnect chassis vacuum supply hose and evaporative emission hose from upper intake manifold, and position hoses out of way.
10. Remove electrical ground straps from dash panel.
11. Disconnect engine control sensor wiring from Powertrain Control Module (PCM) and position wiring out of way.
12. Remove connectors for engine control sensor wiring from mounting bracket on power brake booster and disconnect sensor wiring at two connectors.
13. Disconnect engine control sensor wiring from MAF sensor and evaporative emission canister purge valve.
14. Remove shield, and disconnect accelerator cable and speed control actuator cable from throttle body. Position cable aside.
15. Remove accelerator bracket from throttle body.
16. Remove transmission range sensor and manual control lever to transaxle manual lever shaft mounting nut.
17. Remove connectors for engine control sensor from mounting bracket on top of transaxle and disconnect wiring at two connectors.
18. Disconnect wiring connectors from secondary air injection pump relay located on mounting bracket on top of transaxle.
19. Disconnect fluid cooler inlet tube from transaxle.
20. Disconnect heater hoses from water pump and water hose connection.
21. Disconnect upper radiator hose and de-gas tube from water hose connection.
22. Remove power steering return hose from power steering oil reservoir and drain.
23. Disconnect alternator wiring harness from alternator and remove wiring harness mounting clip from alternator mounting bracket.
24. Disconnect A/C compressor lines from A/C compressor.
25. Slightly raise and support vehicle. Remove tire and wheel assemblies.
26. Remove righthand and lefthand stabilizer bar links from stabilizer bar.
27. Separate righthand and lefthand front suspension lower control arm ball joints from wheel knuckles.
28. Separate lefthand and righthand tie rod ends from front wheel knuckle.
29. Remove lefthand and righthand halfshafts from front wheel knuckles as outlined in "Front Drive Axles."
30. Raise and support vehicle.

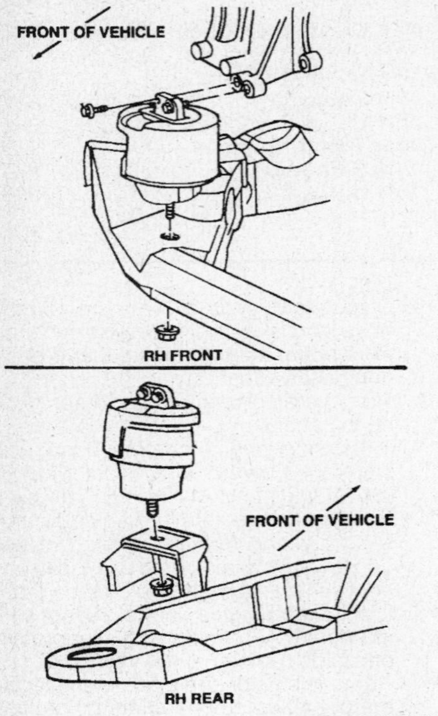

Fig. 1 Engine mounts. VIN U, 1 & 2 engines

31. Remove splash shield from radiator support and drain engine oil into a suitable container.
32. **On VIN S engine,** remove heated oxygen sensors from converter Y-pipe.
33. **On all models,** remove dual converter Y-pipe.
34. Disconnect power steering pressure hose from power steering/transaxle fluid cooler connection and position hose out of way.
35. Disconnect lower radiator hose from radiator and radiator overflow hose.
36. Disconnect starter motor electrical connectors and remove starter motor.
37. Disconnect lower fluid cooler tube from transaxle.
38. Support front subframe, engine and transaxle assembly using Rotunda powertrain lift tool No. 014-00765 and universal powertrain removal bracket tool No. 014-00766, or equivalents.
39. Remove four front subframe mounting bolts, and lower engine, transaxle and front subframe.
40. Disconnect power steering hose from power steering pump.
41. Install engine lifting brackets tool No. T70P-6000, or equivalent.
42. Connect Rotunda separator bar tool No. 014-00793, or equivalent, to lifting brackets.
43. Remove engine and transaxle mounts as outlined under " Engine Mount, Replace."
44. Lift engine and transaxle from front subframe.
45. **On VIN S engine,** remove flywheel to torque converter mounting nuts.
46. **On all models,** lower engine and transaxle and support transaxle on a level surface.

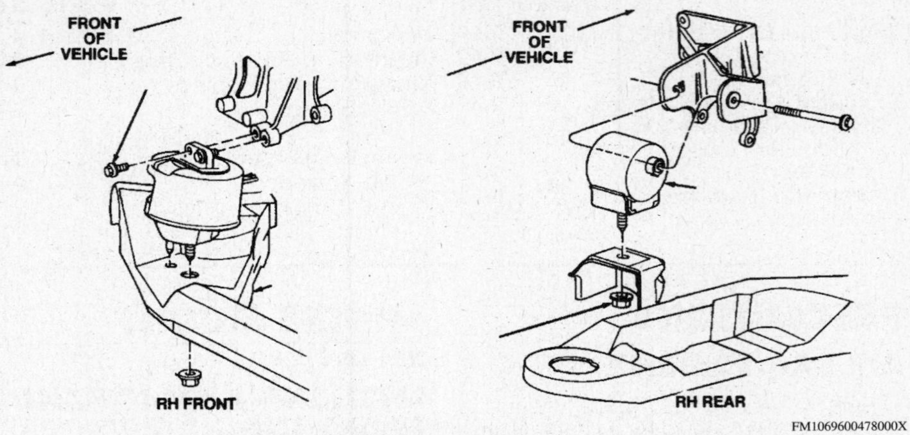

Fig. 2 Engine mounts. VIN S engine

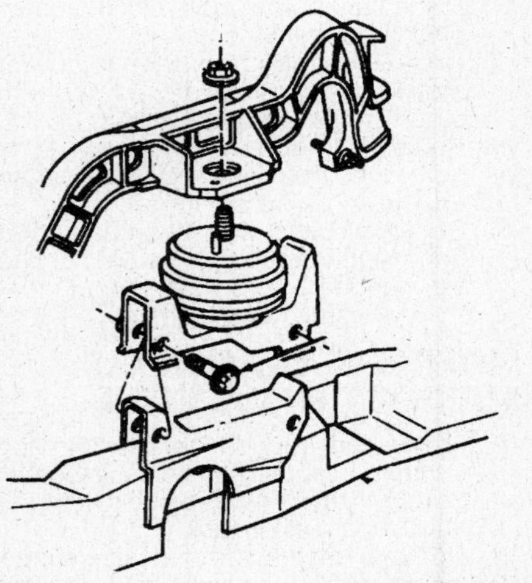

Fig. 3 Engine & transaxle mount

47. Remove transaxle to cylinder block bolts and separate engine from transaxle.
48. Reverse procedure to install.

INTAKE MANIFOLD

REPLACE

UPPER INTAKE MANIFOLD

VIN U, 1 & 2 Engines

1. Remove air cleaner outlet tube.
2. Remove accelerator cable shield from accelerator cable bracket.
3. Remove accelerator retracting spring and disconnect accelerator cable and speed control actuator cable from throttle lever.
4. Remove accelerator bracket mounting bolts from side of throttle body and position bracket out of way.
5. Remove fuel pressure regulator vacuum hose.
6. Completely loosen EGR valve to exhaust manifold tube nut at EGR valve.
7. Disconnect EGR backpressure transducer hoses from EGR valve to exhaust manifold tube.
8. Remove crankcase ventilation hose, aspirator vacuum supply hose and evaporative emission return tube from fittings underneath upper intake manifold.
9. Disconnect engine control sensor wiring connections to idle air control valve, throttle position sensor, EGR backpressure transducer and EGR vacuum regulator solenoid.
10. Drain engine coolant and disconnect de-gas tube from radiator coolant recovery reservoir and lower intake manifold fitting.
11. Remove upper alternator brace mounting nuts and bolts, then brace.
12. Remove engine control sensor wiring bracket from throttle body mounting stud bolt and position wiring out of way.
13. Remove intake manifold support from throttle body and righthand cylinder head.
14. Loosen and remove upper intake manifold mounting bolts and stud bolts. **Note their locations for proper installation.**
15. Lift and remove upper intake manifold from lower intake manifold.
16. Reverse procedure to install, noting the following:
    a. Lightly oil all bolt and stud bolt threads prior to installation.
    b. Clean and inspect all sealing surfaces of intake manifold and throttle body.

VIN S Engine

1. Remove air cleaner outlet tube.
2. Remove accelerator cable shield from accelerator cable bracket.
3. Remove accelerator retracting spring and disconnect accelerator cable and speed control actuator cable from throttle lever.
4. Remove accelerator spring, cable bracket and throttle body.
5. Disconnect engine control sensor wiring from throttle position sensor and idle air control valve.
6. Remove evaporative emission hose from upper intake manifold.
7. Remove crankcase vent connector

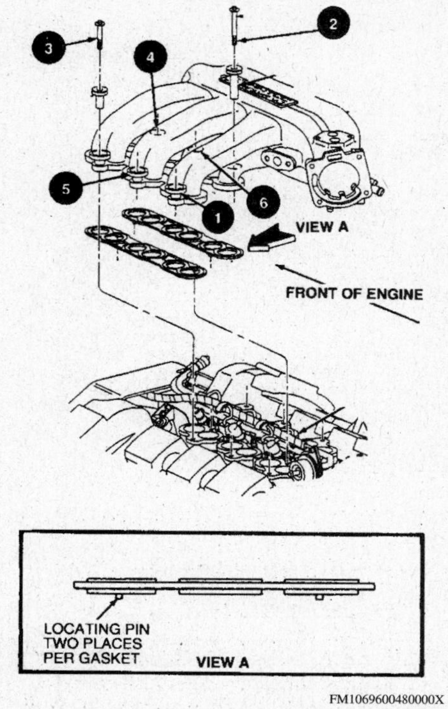

Fig. 4 Upper intake manifold bolt removal sequence. VIN S engine

and hose from upper intake manifold to PCV valve.

8. Disconnect main emission vacuum control connector from upper intake manifold and secondary air injection diverter valve.
9. Remove EGR valve, secondary air diverter valve bracket and position bracket out of way.
10. Remove upper intake manifold mounting bolts in sequence, **Fig. 4.**
11. Remove manifold gaskets and discard.
12. Reverse procedure to install, noting the following:
    a. Always use new manifold gaskets.
    b. **Torque** upper intake manifold bolts to 96–108 inch lbs. in sequence. **Fig. 5.**

LOWER INTAKE MANIFOLD

VIN U, 1 & 2 Engines

1. Remove upper intake manifold as outlined under " Upper Intake Manifold."
2. Relieve fuel system pressure as outlined under " Precautions."
3. Disconnect fuel lines as follows:
    a. Remove clip from spring lock coupling.
    b. Position fuel line disconnect tool No. D87L-9280-A or No. D87L-9280-B, or equivalent, onto coupling, **Fig. 6.**
    c. Push disconnect tool into cage opening to release female fitting from garter spring.
    d. Pull male and female fittings apart, and remove disconnect tool from coupling.
    e. Inspect coupling for missing or damaged O-rings. If either O-ring is damaged, both O-rings have to be replaced.
4. Remove vacuum lines. **Mark vacuum lines for installation.**
5. Disconnect engine control sensor wiring from camshaft position sensor, ignition coil and water temperature sending unit.
6. Disconnect engine control sensor wiring retainers from valve cover stud bolts.
7. Carefully disconnect all fuel injector connectors and position sensor wiring out of way.
8. Remove ignition wires from spark plugs, then the harness retainers from valve cover stud bolts.
9. Remove camshaft position sensor.
10. Remove ignition coil from rear of left-hand cylinder head.
11. Remove valve covers as outlined under "Valve Cover, Replace."
12. Loosen cylinder No. 3 intake valve rocker arm seat mounting bolt and rotate rocker arm off of push rod and away from top of valve stem, and remove push rod.
13. Remove lower intake manifold Torx bolts, and using a pry bar, break seal between lower intake manifold and cylinder block.
14. Remove lower intake manifold, fuel injection supply manifold and fuel injectors as an assembly.
15. Reverse procedure to install, noting the following:
    a. Lightly oil bolts and studs prior to installation.
    b. Clean all mating surfaces. When scraping old gasket material lay a clean cloth in valve lifter valley to catch gasket material.
    c. Apply a drop of silicone rubber part No. D6AZ-19562-AA, or equivalent, to intersection of cylinder block and cylinder head, **Fig. 7.**
    d. Install front and rear intake manifold seals, **Fig. 7.**
    e. **Torque** bolts to 15–22 ft. lbs., then to 20–24 ft. lbs.
    f. Prior to installing camshaft position sensor coat entire surface of sensor with engine assembly lubricant part No. D9AZ-19579-D, or equivalent.
    g. Apply clean engine oil to No. 3 intake valve, push rod and rocker arm.
    h. Prior to tightening rocker arm, rotate crankshaft to position camshaft lobe straight down and away from valve lifter.

VIN S Engine

1. Remove upper intake manifold as outlined under " Upper Intake Manifold."
2. Relieve fuel system pressure as outlined under " Precautions."
3. Disconnect fuel lines as follows:
    a. Remove clip from spring lock coupling.

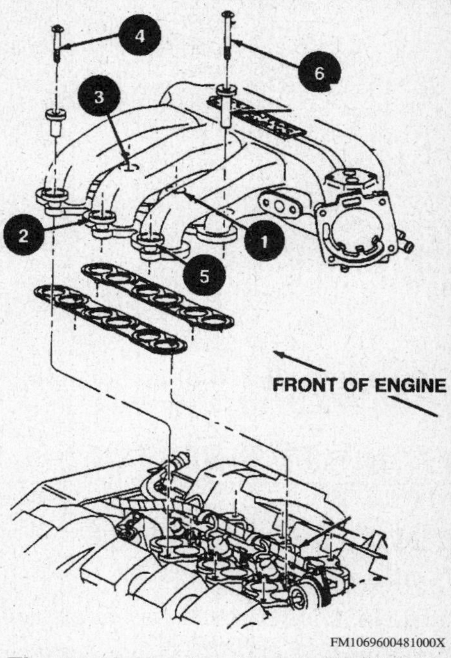

Fig. 5 Upper intake manifold bolt tightening sequence. VIN S engine

    b. Position fuel line disconnect tool No. D87L-9280-A or No. D87L-9280-B, or equivalent, onto coupling, **Fig. 6.**
    c. Push disconnect tool into cage opening to release female fitting from garter spring.
    d. Pull male and female fittings apart, and remove disconnect tool from coupling.
    e. Inspect coupling for missing or damaged O-rings. If either O-ring is damaged, both O-rings have to be replaced.
4. Remove vacuum lines. **Mark vacuum lines for installation.**
5. Disconnect intake manifold runner actuator control cable from lower intake manifold lever and bracket. **Do not loosen or bend intake manifold runner control actuator cable retainer bracket. Bracket alignment is important and potential actuator damage may occur.**
6. Disconnect ignition wires from lefthand cylinder head (cylinder Nos. 4, 5 and 6) and position wires out of way.
7. Remove fuel injection supply manifold and fuel injectors from lower intake manifold.
8. Remove lower intake manifold mounting bolts in sequence, **Fig. 8.**
9. Remove intake manifold and gaskets from cylinder head, discard gaskets.
10. Reverse procedure to install, noting the following:
    a. Always use new gaskets.
    b. **Torque** lower intake manifold bolts to 96–108 inch lbs. in sequence-,**Fig. 9.**
    c. Inspect intake manifold runner control plate operation.

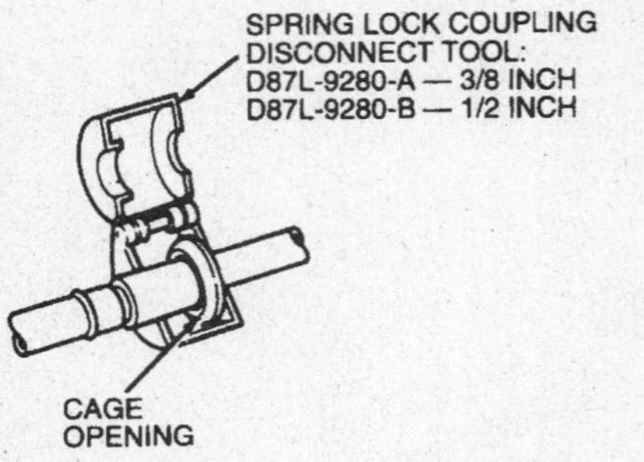

FM1069600482000X

Fig. 6 Fuel line tool installation. VIN U, 1 & 2 engines

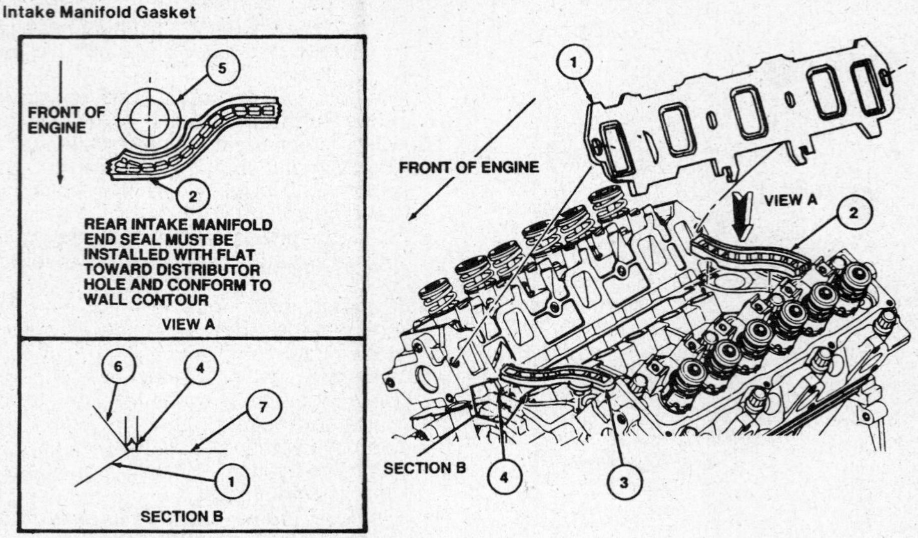

Item	Description
1	Intake Manifold Gasket (2 Req'd)
2	End Seal
3	End Seal
4	Silicone Rubber (4 Places)

Item	Description
5	Distributor Hole
6	Cylinder Head (2 Req'd)
7	Cylinder Block

FM1069600483000X

Fig. 7 Lower intake manifold. VIN U, 1 & 2 engines

EXHAUST MANIFOLD

REPLACE

VIN U, 1 & 2 ENGINES

Lefthand Side

1. Relieve fuel system pressure as outlined under " Precautions."
2. Remove dipstick tube support bracket and exhaust pipe to manifold mounting nuts.
3. Remove engine control sensor wiring from oil level indicator tube bracket.
4. Remove oil level dipstick and dipstick tube.
5. Remove Y-pipe mounting nuts.
6. Remove exhaust manifold to cylinder head mounting bolts and manifold.
7. Reverse procedure to install. Lightly lubricate nuts and bolts with engine oil, and tighten to specifications.

Righthand Side

1. Relieve fuel system pressure as outlined under " Precautions."
2. Remove EGR backpressure transducer hoses from EGR valve to exhaust manifold tube.
3. Using suitable back-up wrench on EGR tube lower adapter, remove EGR tube from exhaust manifold.
4. Remove mounting nuts and heat shield.
5. Remove coolant bypass tube.
6. Remove exhaust pipe to manifold mounting nuts.
7. Remove exhaust manifold to cylinder head mounting bolts and manifold.
8. Reverse procedure to install, noting the following:
   a. Lightly lubricate nuts and bolts with engine oil.
   b. Tighten manifold mounting bolts to specifications.
   c. Tighten exhaust pipe to manifold mounting nuts to specifications.
   d. Tighten EGR tube to specifications.

VIN S ENGINE

Lefthand Side

1. Raise and support vehicle.
2. Remove dual converter Y-pipe.
3. Remove secondary air injection manifold tube from exhaust manifold.
4. Remove lower exhaust manifold mounting nuts.
5. Remove lefthand exhaust manifold and gasket from cylinder head, discard gasket.
6. Reverse procedure to install.

Righthand Side

1. Remove upper intake manifold as outlined under " Intake Manifold, Replace."
2. Remove ignition coil from righthand valve cover.
3. Remove EGR valve to exhaust manifold tube.
4. Remove secondary air injection manifold tube.
5. Raise and support vehicle, and remove dual converter Y-pipe.
6. Remove lower exhaust manifold mounting nuts and lower vehicle.
7. Remove upper exhaust manifold mounting nuts.
8. Remove righthand exhaust manifold and gasket from cylinder head, discard gasket.
9. Reverse procedure to install.

CYLINDER HEAD

REPLACE

VIN U, 1 & 2 ENGINES

1. Relieve fuel system pressure as outlined under " Precautions."
2. Rotate crankshaft to 0° TDC of compression stroke.
3. Drain cooling system.
4. Remove air cleaner outlet tube.
5. Remove upper and lower intake manifolds as outlined under " Intake Manifold, Replace."
6. Using a ½ inch drive breaker bar inserted into the automatic belt tensioner, rotate and relax tension on serpentine belt, and remove belt. Remove generator if lefthand side cylinder head is being removed.
7. Remove mounting bolts, power steering pump and bracket as an assembly with hoses attached. Position pump and bracket assembly aside in an upright position to prevent leakage of fluid.
8. If lefthand side cylinder head is being removed, remove coil bracket and dipstick tube. If righthand side cylinder head is being removed, remove ground strap and throttle cable support bracket.
9. Remove exhaust manifolds, then the PCV valve and valve covers.
10. Loosen remaining rocker arm fulcrum bolts enough to allow rocker arms to be swung aside and pushrods removed. Keep pushrods in order so they can be installed in original positions.
11. Remove cylinder head mounting bolts, then the cylinder head and gasket. Discard gaskets and bolts.
12. Reverse procedure to install, noting the following:
    a. Lightly oil new cylinder head bolts threads prior to installation.
    b. Replace any damaged gasket alignment dowels.
    c. **On 1997–98 models, torque** cylinder head bolts to 52–66 ft. lbs., in sequence, **Fig. 10,** then loosen bolts in sequence one full turn.

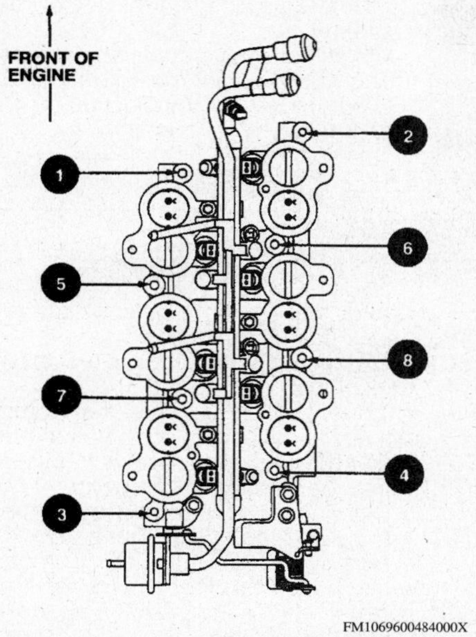

Fig. 8 Lower intake manifold bolt removal sequence. VIN S engine

d. **Torque** cylinder head bolts, to 34–40 ft. lbs., then to 63–73 ft. lbs. in sequence.
e. **On 1999 models, torque** cylinder head bolts to 35–39 ft. lbs. in sequence, **Fig. 10,** then loosen bolts in sequence one full turn.
f. **Torque** cylinder head bolts to 20–24 ft. lbs. in sequence.
g. Tighten cylinder head bolts 85–95° in sequence shown, then final tighten an additional 85–95.°
h. **On all models,** prior to installation, lubricate rocker arm assemblies and dip each pushrod end in oil conditioner part No. D9AZ-19579-C, or other suitable heavy engine oil.
i. Starting with engine at TDC compression No. 1 cylinder, rotate crankshaft one full turn clockwise, and install No. 2 and No. 5 exhaust, and No. 1 and No. 4 intake push rod and rocker arm assembly.
j. **Torque** rocker arm bolts to 6–11 ft. lbs., then to 20–28 ft. lbs.
k. Rotate crankshaft ⅓ turn clockwise, and install remaining push rod and rocker arm assemblies.
l. **Torque** rocker arm bolts to 6–11 ft. lbs., then to 20–28 ft. lbs.
m. Ensure all rocker arm bolts are fully seated to their shoulder after tightening.
n. If any valve train components were replaced or intermixed, inspect valve clearance as outlined under "Valve Clearance Specifications. "

VIN S ENGINE

1. Remove engine as outlined under "Engine, Replace. "
2. Remove upper and lower intake manifolds as outlined under " Intake Manifold, Replace."
3. Remove engine control sensor wiring mounting nuts and bolts.
4. Remove mounting nut, crankcase ventilation tube from oil separator and water bypass tube stud bolt.
5. Remove radiator and heater hoses from water bypass tube.
6. Remove water bypass tube from cylinder head.
7. Remove power steering pump from engine front cover.
8. Remove A/C compressor mounting bracket from water pump brace.
9. Remove mounting brackets and A/C compressor
10. Remove alternator.
11. Remove water pump to engine front cover mounting bolts.
12. Install flywheel holding tool No. T74P-6375-A, or equivalent, to cylinder block and engage flywheel.
13. Remove crankshaft accessory drive pulley and bracket assembly from engine front cover. **Crankshaft drive pulley shaft has lefthand thread.**
14. Remove crankshaft pulley retainer bolt and washer from crankshaft.
15. Using front damper puller tool No. T58P-6316-D, or equivalent, remove crankshaft pulley from crankshaft.
16. Remove flywheel holding tool from cylinder block.
17. Remove ignition coil from righthand valve cover.
18. Remove valve cover retainer bolts and studs for both lefthand and righthand valve covers.
19. Remove valve covers from cylinder heads.
20. Remove spark plugs.
21. Remove oil level dipstick, dipstick tube and O-ring from lefthand cylinder head and cylinder block.
22. Remove lefthand and righthand exhaust manifolds and gaskets from cylinder heads.
23. Drain engine oil, and remove oil pan and gasket from cylinder block.
24. Remove drive belt tensioner from righthand side of engine front cover.
25. Remove camshaft and crankshaft position sensors from front cover.
26. Remove front cover mounting bolts in sequence, **Fig. 11.**
27. Remove engine front cover and gasket, discard gasket.
28. Remove crankshaft position sensor pulse ring from crankshaft.
29. Rotate crankshaft clockwise to position crankshaft keyway to 11 o'clock location. **Rotating crankshaft in a counterclockwise direction may make timing chain bind and cause engine damage.**
30. Ensure alignment arrows on camshafts are aligned. If arrows are not aligned, rotate crankshaft clockwise one complete revolution.
31. Rotate crankshaft so keyway is in three o'clock position. This will position righthand cylinder head camshafts to neutral position (base circle).
32. Remove mounting bolts and righthand timing chain tensioner.
33. Remove cylinder head camshaft journal thrust cap bolts and thrust caps from righthand cylinder head. **Cylinder head camshaft journal caps and cylinder heads are numbered to ensure they are assembled in their original positions. Do not mix with camshaft journals from another head.**

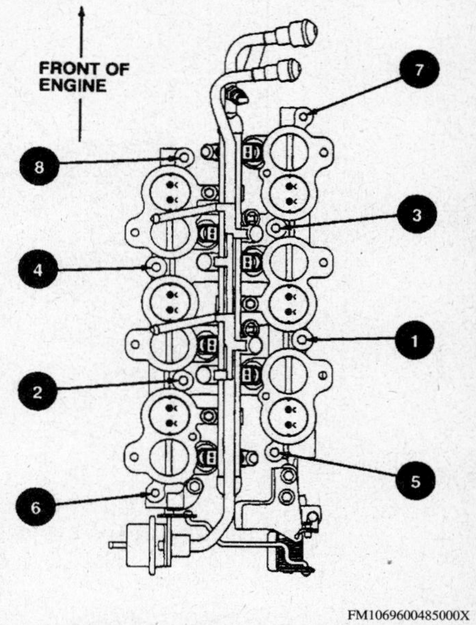

Fig. 9 Lower intake manifold bolt tightening sequence. VIN S engine

34. Loosen remaining righthand cylinder head camshaft journal cap bolts in sequence, **Fig. 12.**
35. Remove righthand timing chain tensioner arm and righthand timing chain. **Mark position of tensioner arm and timing chain guide for installation.**
36. Remove righthand timing chain guide and crankshaft sprocket.
37. Remove righthand cylinder head camshaft journal caps and bolts, camshafts, rocker arms and valve lifters. **Mark position of rocker arms and valve lifters for installation.**
38. Rotate crankshaft clockwise two revolutions and position crankshaft keyway to 11 o'clock location. This will position crankshaft to neutral position (base circle).
39. Ensure alignment arrows on camshafts are aligned. If arrows are not aligned, rotate crankshaft clockwise one complete revolution.
40. Remove mounting bolts and lefthand timing chain tensioner.
41. Remove cylinder head camshaft journal thrust cap bolts and thrust caps from lefthand cylinder head. **Cylinder head camshaft journal caps and cylinder heads are numbered to ensure they are assembled in their original positions. Do not mix with camshaft journals from another head.**
42. Loosen remaining lefthand cylinder head camshaft journal cap bolts in sequence, **Fig. 12.**
43. Remove lefthand timing chain tensioner arm and lefthand timing chain. **Mark position of tensioner arm and**

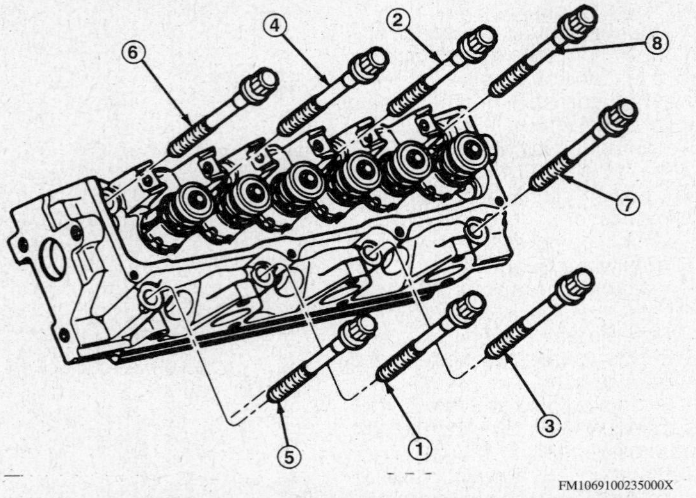

Fig. 10 Cylinder head bolt tightening sequence. VIN U, 1 & 2 engines

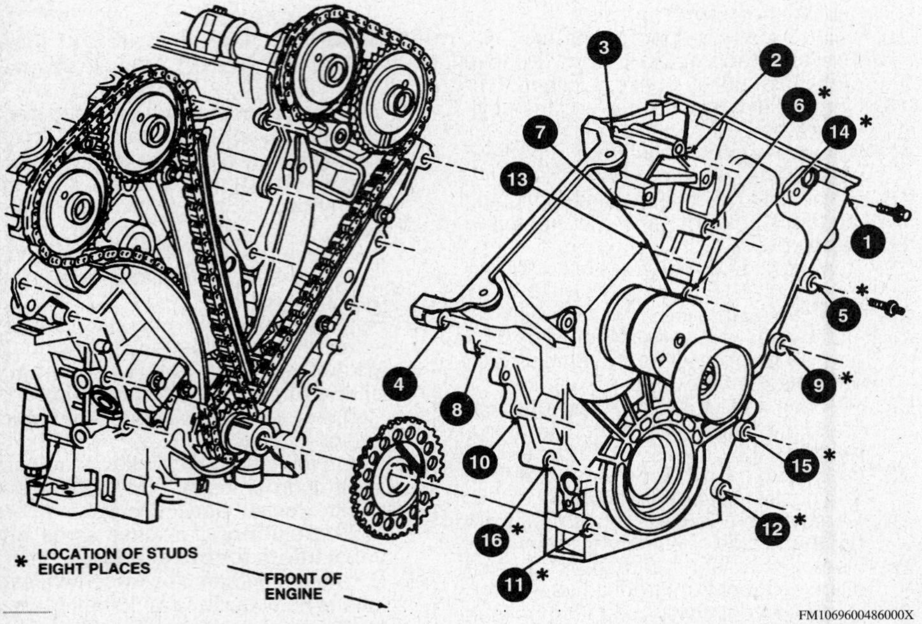

Fig. 11 Front cover bolt removal sequence. VIN S engine

timing chain guide for installation.

44. Remove lefthand timing chain guide and crankshaft sprocket.
45. Remove lefthand cylinder head camshaft journal caps and bolts, camshafts, rocker arms and valve lifters. **Mark position of rocker arms and valve lifters for installation.**
46. Remove EGR backpressure transducer mounting bracket and EGR backpressure transducer from righthand cylinder head.
47. Remove cylinder head mounting bolts and washers in sequence, **Fig. 13.**
48. Remove cylinder head and gasket from cylinder block.
49. Reverse procedure to install, noting the following:
    a. Place timing chain tensioners in a soft jawed vise, and slowly compress tensioner piston and bleed oil from tensioner, **Fig. 14.**
    b. Use new gasket and cylinder head bolts. **Cylinder head bolts must not be used again. These bolts are torque-to-yield designed and engine damage could result.**
    c. **Torque** cylinder head bolts to 28–31 ft. lbs. in sequence, **Fig. 15,** then tighten 85–95.°
    d. Loosen cylinder head bolts one full turn.
    e. **Torque** to 28–31 ft. lbs. and tighten 85–95.°
    f. Finally, tighten cylinder head bolts and additional 85–95.°
    g. Ensure timing chains are installed properly as outlined under "Timing Chain, Replace."
    h. Apply 7⁄16 inch bead of black silicone rubber part No. F4AZ-19562-B, or equivalent, in six locations on cylinder block, **Fig. 16.** Install front cover within six minutes of applying sealant.
    i. When installing crankshaft damper, apply black silicone rubber part No. F4AZ-19562-B to inside diameter of crankshaft damper keyway.

VALVE COVER

REPLACE

VIN U, 1 & 2 ENGINES

1. Relieve fuel system pressure as outlined under " Precautions."
2. Disconnect spark plug wires from spark plugs.
3. Remove spark plug wire separators from valve cover mounting bolt studs.
4. If lefthand side valve cover is being removed, performing the following:
    a. Disconnect crankcase breather hose and remove oil filler cap.
    b. Remove fuel injector harness standoffs from inboard rocker arm cover studs and position harness out of way.
5. If righthand side rocker arm cover is removed, proceed as follows:
    a. Remove upper intake manifold as outlined under " Intake Manifold, Replace."
    b. Disconnect EGR tube and heater hoses.
    c. Remove PCV valve and move fuel injector harness out of way.
6. Remove rocker arm cover mounting bolts and cover.
7. Reverse procedure to install, noting the following:
    a. Lightly oil bolt and stud threads prior to installation.
    b. Apply bead of RTV sealant at cylinder head to intake manifold rail step.
    c. Tighten rocker arm cover mounting bolts and EGR tube to specifications.

VIN S ENGINE

Righthand

1. Remove upper intake manifold as outlined under " Intake Manifold, Replace."
2. Remove ignition wires from ignition coil and spark plugs.
3. Remove ignition coil.
4. Remove crankcase ventilation tube from righthand valve cover.
5. Remove engine control sensor wiring and evaporative emission hose mounting nuts and stud bolts from righthand valve cover. Position emission hose out of way.
6. Remove mounting bolts, valve cover and gaskets.
7. Reverse procedure to install, noting the following:
    a. Apply a 5⁄16 inch bead of black silicone rubber part No. F4AZ-19562-B, or equivalent, at two places on valve cover sealing surfaces where engine front cover and cylinder head contact.
    b. Install new gasket.

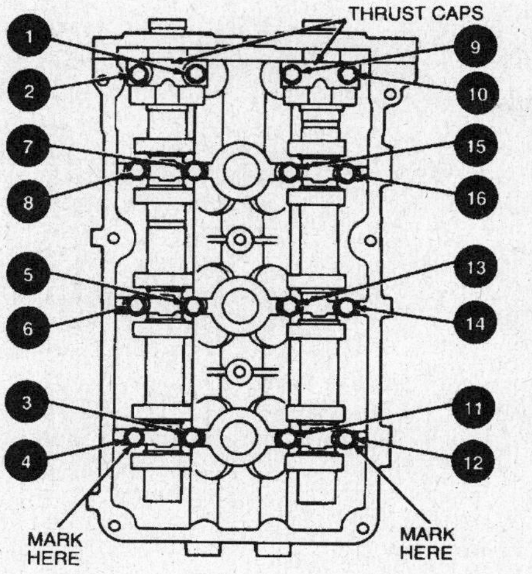

FM1069600487000X

Fig. 12 Camshaft journal cap bolt removal sequence. VIN S engine

c. Install valve cover within six minutes of applying sealer.

Lefthand

1. Remove crankcase ventilation tube from lefthand valve cover.
2. Remove engine control sensor wiring mounting nuts and stud bolts from valve cover. Position sensor wiring out of way.
3. Remove ignition wires from spark plugs and valve cover.
4. Remove mounting bolts, stud bolts and valve cover.
5. Reverse procedure to install, noting the following:
   a. Apply a 5⁄16 inch bead of black silicone rubber part No. F4AZ-19562-B, or equivalent, at two places on valve cover sealing surfaces where engine front cover and cylinder head contact, **Fig. 17.**
   b. Install new gasket.
   c. Install valve cover within six minutes of applying sealer.

VALVE ARRANGEMENT

VIN U, 1 & 2 ENGINES

Front To Rear

Righthand Side .... I-E-I-E-I-E
Lefthand Side .... E-I-E-I-E-I

CAMSHAFT LOBE LIFT SPECIFICATIONS

VIN U, 1 & 2 ENGINES

Exhaust .... .260 inch
Intake .... .260 inch

VIN S ENGINE

Exhaust .... .188 inch
Intake .... .188 inch

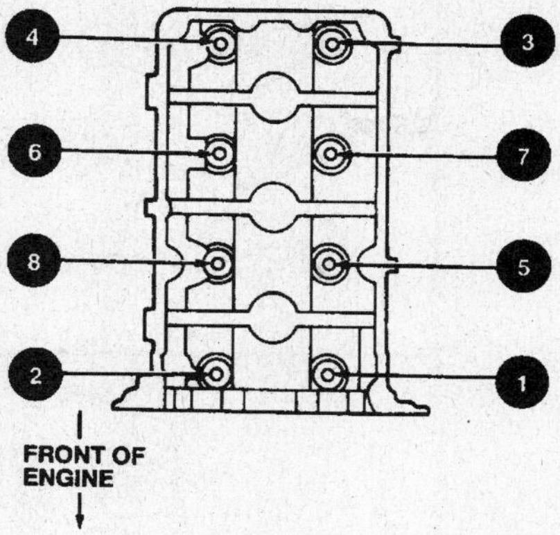

FM1069600488000X

Fig. 13 Cylinder head bolt removal sequence. VIN S engine

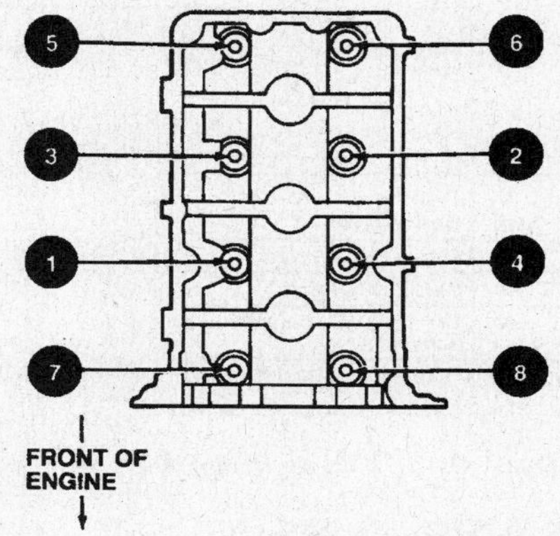

FM1069600490000X

Fig. 15 Cylinder head bolt tightening sequence. VIN S engine

VALVE CLEARANCE SPECIFICATIONS

VIN U, 1 & 2 ENGINES

If any valve train component is replaced or if valve train components become intermixed, valve clearance will have to be inspected on those valves.

1. Using a suitable pry bar, apply pressure to push rod side of rocker arm until hydraulic lifter has bled down and bottomed out.
2. Ensure clearance between valve stem and rocker arm is .085 and .185 inch.

VALVE ADJUSTMENT

Hydraulic valve lifters are used in this engine. No adjustment is required.

HYDRAULIC LIFTERS

REPLACE

VIN U, 1 & 2 ENGINES

Before replacing a hydraulic valve lifter for noisy operation, ensure the noise is not

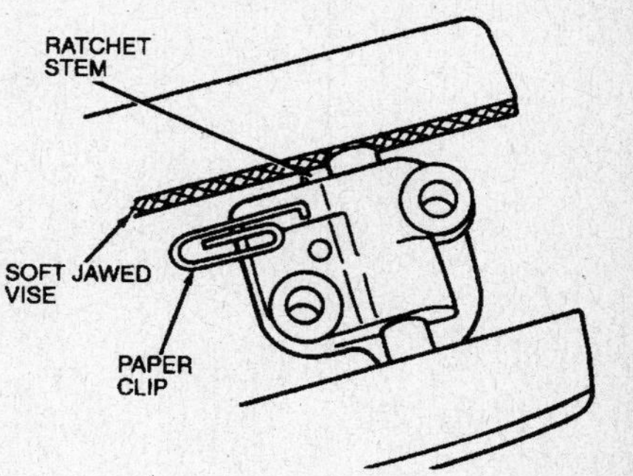

FM1069600489000X

Fig. 14 Timing chain tensioner. VIN S engine

caused by improper rocker arm to stem clearance, worn rocker arms, pushrods or valve tips.

1. Set engine to TDC compression No. 1 cylinder.
2. Remove intake manifold as outlined under "Intake Manifold, Replace."
3. Loosen remaining rocker arm fulcrum mounting bolts enough to swing rocker arm aside to allow pushrods to be removed and remove pushrods. Keep pushrods in order so they can be returned to original positions.
4. Remove bolts from roller lifter guide retainer plate, **Fig. 18,** and lift retainer plate from engine.
5. Remove roller lifter guide from lifter pair by lifting straight up.
6. **If lifters are stuck in their bores by excessive varnish or gum buildup, use a suitable claw type puller to remove roller lifters with a rocking and twisting motion.**
7. Place roller lifter lifters in a rack so they can be installed in original positions.
8. Reverse procedure to install, noting the following:
   a. Ensure word UP and/or button is facing upward when installing roller lifter guide plates.
   b. Lubricate lifters, lifter bores, rocker arms and pushrods with oil conditioner part No. D9AZ-19579-A, or suitable heavy engine oil.
   c. Starting with engine at TDC compression No. 1 cylinder, rotate crankshaft one full turn clockwise, and install No. 2 and No. 5 exhaust, and No. 1 and No. 4 intake push rod, and rocker arm assembly.
   d. **Torque** rocker arm bolts to 6–11 ft. lbs., then to 20–28 ft. lbs.
   e. Rotate crankshaft 1⁄3 turn clockwise, and install remaining push rod and rocker arm assemblies.
   f. **Torque** rocker arm bolts to 6–11 ft. lbs., then to 20–28 ft. lbs.
   g. Ensure all rocker arm bolts are fully seated to their shoulder after tightening.
   h. If any valve train components were replaced or intermixed, inspect valve clearance as outlined under "Valve Clearance Specifications."

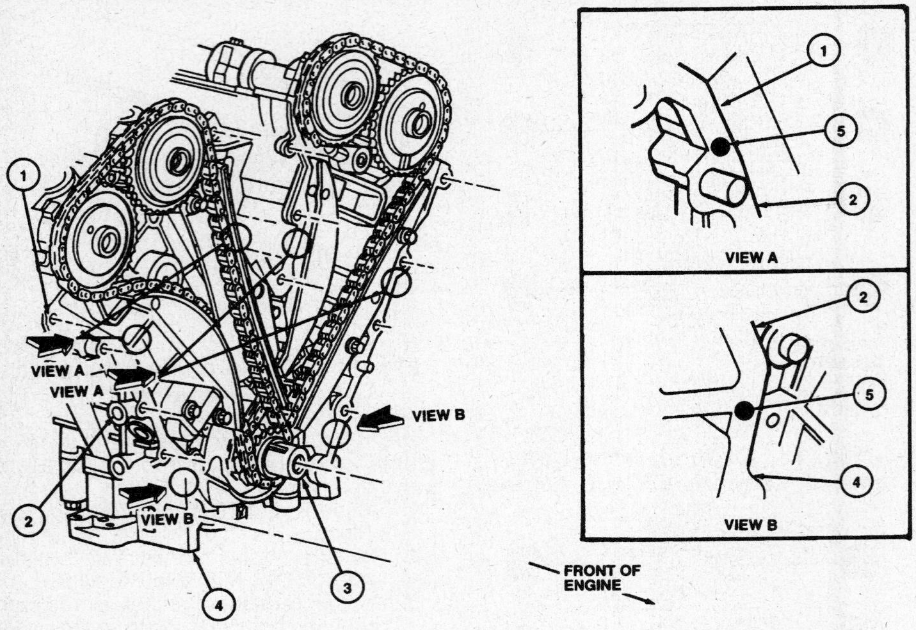

Item	Description
1	RH Cylinder Head
2	Upper Cylinder Block
3	Crankshaft
4	Lower Cylinder Block
5	Black Silicone Rubber

Item	Description
6	Engine Front Cover
7	Stud Bolt (8 Req'd)
8	Crankshaft Position Sensor Pulse Ring
A	Tighten to 20-30 N·m (15-22 Lb-Ft)

FM1069600491000X

Fig. 16 Front cover sealer locations. VIN S engine

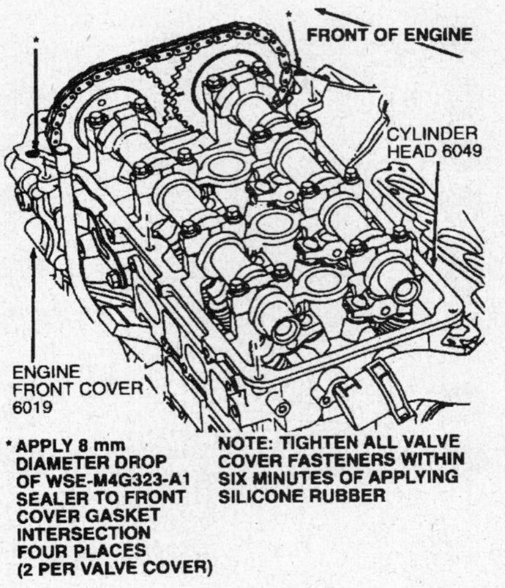

FM1069600492000X

Fig. 17 Valve cover sealer locations. VIN S engine

FRONT COVER

REPLACE

VIN U, 1 & 2 ENGINES

1. Relieve fuel system pressure as outlined under " Precautions."
2. Loosen four water pump pulley bolts with drive belt in place.
3. Using a ½ inch drive breaker bar inserted into serpentine belt auto tensioner, rotate tensioner to relieve tension until belt may be removed, and remove belt.
4. Drain cooling system, and remove lower radiator hose and heater hose from water pump.
5. Remove crankshaft pulley and damper as outlined under " Front Cover Seal, Replace."
6. Drain and remove oil pan as outlined under "Oil Pan, Replace."
7. Remove timing cover to block mounting bolts. Timing cover and water pump may be removed as an assembly by not removing bolts Nos. 11–15, **Fig. 19.**
8. After cover is pulled away from block, remove water pump pulley and bolts.
9. Inspect timing chain deflection for excessive wear.
10. Reverse procedure to install, noting the following:
    a. Carefully clean all gasket material from timing cover and cylinder block. **The aluminum timing cover gouges easily. Use care when scraping gasket.**
    b. Inspect timing cover crankshaft seal, replace if necessary.
    c. Before installing bolt Nos. 1, 2 and 3, apply pipe sealant No. D6AZ-19558-A, or equivalent.
    d. Tighten front cover bolts in sequence, **Fig. 19.**
    e. **Torque** bolts 1–10 to 15–22 ft. lbs., then bolts 11–15 to 96–108 inch lbs.

VIN S ENGINE

1. Remove engine as outlined under "Engine, Replace."
2. Remove crankcase ventilation tube mounting nut, tube from oil separator and water bypass tube stud bolt.
3. Remove power steering pump from engine front cover.
4. Remove A/C compressor mounting bracket from water pump brace.
5. Remove mounting brackets and A/C compressor
6. Remove alternator.
7. Remove water pump to engine front cover mounting bolts.
8. Install flywheel holding tool No. T74P-6375-A, or equivalent, to cylinder block and engage flywheel.
9. Remove crankshaft accessory drive pulley and bracket assembly from engine front cover. **Crankshaft drive pulley shaft has a lefthand thread.**
10. Remove crankshaft pulley retainer bolt and washer from crankshaft.
11. Using front damper puller tool No. T58P-6316-D, or equivalent, remove crankshaft pulley from crankshaft.
12. Remove flywheel holding tool from cylinder block.
13. Drain engine oil, and remove oil pan and gasket from cylinder block.
14. Remove drive belt tensioner from righthand side of engine front cover.
15. Remove camshaft and crankshaft position sensors from front cover.
16. Remove front cover mounting bolts and studs in sequence, **Fig. 11.**
17. Remove engine front cover and gasket, discard gasket.
18. Reverse procedure to install, noting the following:
    a. Apply 7⁄16 inch bead of black silicone rubber part No. F4AZ-19562-B, or equivalent, in six locations on cylinder block, **Fig. 16.** Install front cover within six minutes of applying sealant.
    b. **Torque** front cover bolts to 15–22 ft. lbs. in sequence, **Fig. 20.**
    c. When installing crankshaft damper, apply black silicone rubber part No. F4AZ-19562-B, or equivalent, to inside diameter of crankshaft damper keyway.

FRONT COVER SEAL

REPLACE

VIN U, 1 & 2 ENGINES

1. Loosen accessory drive belts and remove righthand front wheel.
2. Remove four crankshaft pulley to damper mounting bolts, and remove accessory drive belt and pulley.
3. Remove vibration damper mounting bolt, and using suitable puller, vibration damper.
4. Using flat bladed screwdriver or other suitable tool, pry seal from front timing cover. **Use caution not to damage front cover or crankshaft.**
5. Lubricate replacement seal lip with

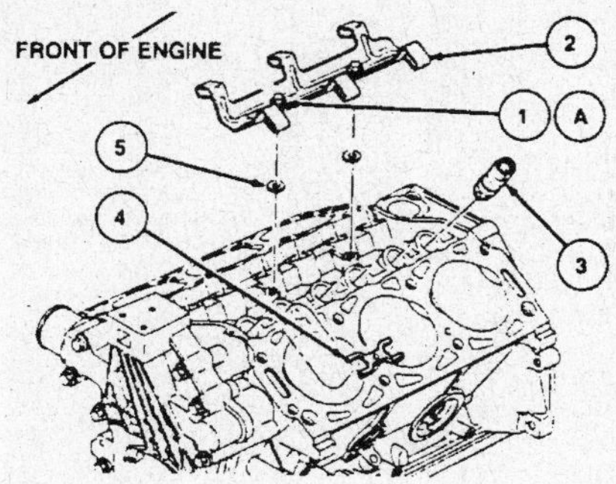

Item		Description
1A		Bolt (2 Req'd) (Part of 6K654)
2		Tappet Guide Plate and Retainer
3		Valve Tappet (12 Req'd)
4		Valve Tappet Guide Plate (6 Req'd)
5		Washer (2 Req'd) (Part of 6K564)
A		Tighten to 10-14 N·m (8-10 Lb-Ft)

FM1069500392000X

Fig. 18 Roller lifter removal. VIN U, 1 & 2 engines

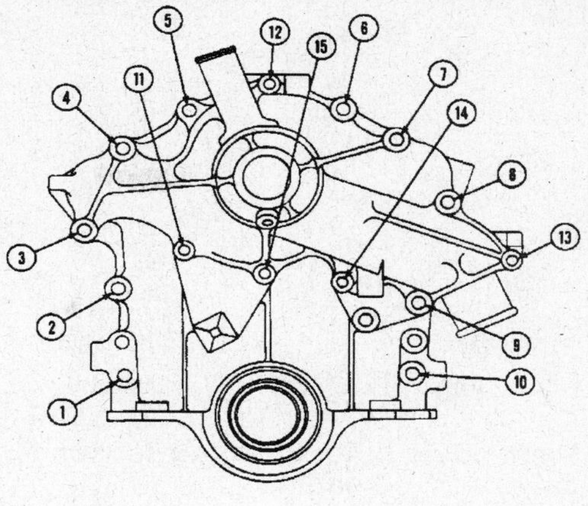

FASTENER AND HOLE NO.	FASTENERS		
	PART NO.	SIZE	FASTENER APPLICATION
1	N804113-S8	M8 x 1.25 x 43.5	F/C TO BLOCK
2	N804113-S100	M8 x 1.25 x 43.5	F/C TO BLOCK
3	N804811-S100	M8 x 1.25 x 70	W/P & F/C TO BLOCK
4	N804811-S8	M8 x 1.25 x 70	W/P & F/C TO BLOCK
5	N605909-S8	M8 x 1.25 x 42	F/C TO BLOCK
6	N804811-S8	M8 x 1.25 x 70	W/P & F/C TO BLOCK
7	N804811-S8	M8 x 1.25 x 70	W/P & F/C TO BLOCK
8	N804811-S8	M8 x 1.25 x 70	W/P & F/C TO BLOCK
9	N804811-S8	M8 x 1.25 x 70	W/P & F/C TO BLOCK
10	N605909-S8	M8 x 1.25 x 42	F/C TO BLOCK
11	N804168-S8	M6 x 1 x 25	W/P TO F/C
12	N804168-S8	M6 x 1 x 25	W/P TO F/C
13	N804168-S8	M6 x 1 x 25	W/P TO F/C
14	N804168-S8	M6 x 1 x 25	W/P TO F/C
15	N804168-S8	M6 x 1 x 25	W/P TO F/C

W/P — Water Pump Assy
F/C — Front Cover Assy
T/P — Timing Pointer

FM1069100236000X

Fig. 19 Timing cover & water pump removal. VIN U, 1 & 2 engines

clean engine oil and install seal with suitable seal installer.

6. Lubricate inner hub surface of vibration damper with clean engine oil and apply RTV sealant to keyway of inner hub surface of vibration damper.
7. Install vibration damper and tighten mounting bolt to specifications.
8. Install crankshaft pulley and tighten bolts to specifications.
9. Install accessory drive belts and righthand front wheel.
10. Start engine and inspect for oil leaks.

TIMING CHAIN

REPLACE

VIN U, 1 & 2 ENGINES

1. Remove front engine cover as outlined under "Front Cover, Replace"
2. Rotate crankshaft until No. 1 piston is at TDC and timing marks are aligned, **Fig. 21.**
3. Remove camshaft sprocket mounting bolt and washer.
4. Inspect timing chain deflection for excessive wear.
5. Slide sprockets and timing chain forward and remove as an assembly.
6. Reverse procedure to install, noting the following:
   a. Slide timing chain and sprockets on with timing marks aligned, **Fig. 22.**
   b. The camshaft bolt is a special oil transferring part. **Do not replace with a standard bolt.**
   c. Tighten to specifications.

VIN S ENGINE

1. Remove engine as outlined under "Engine, Replace."
2. Remove front cover as outlined under "Front Cover, Replace."
3. Remove crankshaft position sensor pulse ring from crankshaft.
4. Rotate crankshaft clockwise to position crankshaft keyway to 11 o'clock location. **Rotating crankshaft in a counterclockwise direction may cause timing chain to bind and cause engine damage.**
5. Ensure alignment arrows on righthand camshafts are aligned. If arrows are not aligned, rotate crankshaft clockwise one complete revolution.
6. Rotate crankshaft so keyway is in three o'clock position. This will position righthand cylinder head camshafts to neutral position (base circle).
7. Remove mounting bolts and righthand timing chain tensioner.
8. Remove righthand timing chain tensioner arm and righthand timing chain. **Mark position of tensioner arm and timing chain guide for installation reference.**
9. Remove righthand timing chain guide and crankshaft sprocket.
10. Rotate crankshaft clockwise two revolutions and position crankshaft keyway to 11 o'clock location. This will position crankshaft to neutral position (base circle).
11. Ensure alignment arrows on lefthand camshafts are aligned. If arrows are not aligned, rotate crankshaft clockwise one complete revolution.
12. Remove lefthand timing chain tensioner mounting bolts and lefthand timing chain tensioner.
13. Remove lefthand timing chain tensioner arm and lefthand timing chain. **Mark position of tensioner arm and timing chain guide for installation reference.**
14. Remove lefthand timing chain guide and crankshaft sprocket.
15. Reverse procedure to install, noting the following:
    a. Place timing chain tensioners in a soft jawed vise.
    b. Slowly compress tensioner piston and bleed oil from tensioner, **Fig. 14.**
    c. Ensure timing marks on sprockets and timing chain links are aligned, **Fig. 23.**
    d. Install front cover as outlined under "Front Cover, Replace."

CAMSHAFT

REPLACE

VIN U, 1 & 2 ENGINES

1. Remove engine and mount in suitable work stand.
2. Remove front cover and timing chain as outlined under " Timing Chain, Replace."
3. Remove intake manifolds and hydraulic valve lifters as outlined under "Hydraulic Valve Lifters, Replace."
4. Remove camshaft thrust plate and carefully pull camshaft from cylinder block. Use caution to avoid damaging bearings, journals and lobes.

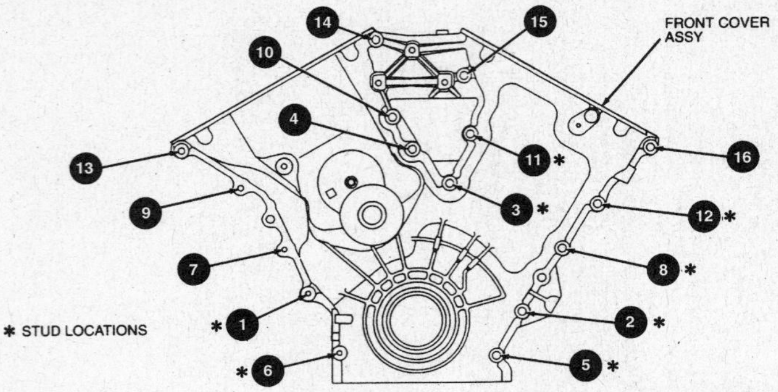

FM1069600493000X

Fig. 20 Front cover bolt tightening sequence. VIN S engine

5. Reverse procedure to install, noting the following:
   a. Tighten camshaft thrust plate mounting screws to specifications.
   b. Lubricate lifters, lifter bores, rocker arms and pushrods with oil conditioner part No. D9AZ-19579-A, or suitable heavy engine oil.

VIN S ENGINE

Refer to "Cylinder Head, Replace" for camshaft removal and installation procedure.

PISTON & ROD ASSEMBLY

Assemble the rod to the piston with the notch on the piston dome on the same side as the button on the connecting rod identification marks. Assemble piston and rod assembly in engine with notch in dome facing front of engine, **Fig. 24.**

After installation, inspect connecting rod big end side clearance. Clearance should be .006–.014 inch.

MAIN & ROD BEARINGS

Main bearings are available in standard sizes and undersizes of .001 and .002 inch.

CRANKSHAFT REAR OIL SEAL

REPLACE

1. Remove transaxle and flywheel.
2. Remove rear cover plate.
3. Using a suitable tool, punch a hole into seal metal surface between lip and block. Using slide hammer tool No. T77L-9533-B, or equivalent, remove seal.
4. Coat crankshaft seal area and seal lip with engine oil, and using tool No. T82L-6701-A, or equivalent, install seal.
5. Install rear cover plate and two dowels.
6. Install flywheel and tighten bolts to specifications.

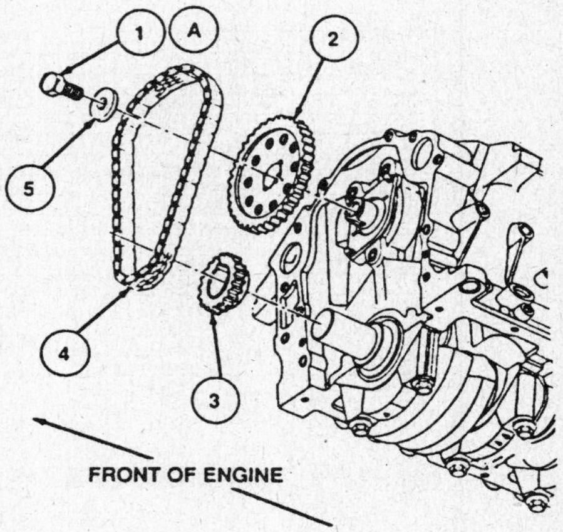

Item	Description
1A	Bolt
2	Camshaft Sprocket
3	Crankshaft Sprocket
4	Timing Chain Lubricate With Oil
5	Washer-Cam Sprocket
A	Tighten to 50-70 N·m (37-51 Lb-Ft)

FM1069100238000X

Fig. 22 Timing chain installation. VIN U, 1 & 2 engines

OIL PAN

REPLACE

VIN U, 1 & 2 ENGINES

This procedure has been revised by a Technical Service Bulletin.

1. Relieve fuel system pressure as outlined under " Precautions."
2. Remove oil dipstick.
3. Raise and support vehicle.
4. **On models with low oil level sensor,** remove retainer clip at sensor and disconnect sensor electrical connector.
5. **On all models,** drain crankcase.
6. Remove starter motor and disconnect Exhaust Gas Oxygen (EGO) sensor electrical connector.
7. Remove Y-pipe and catalytic converter assembly.

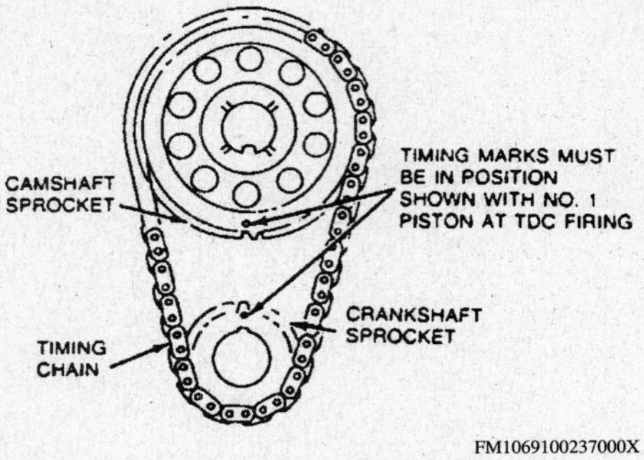

FM1069100237000X

Fig. 21 Timing chain alignment. VIN U, 1 & 2 engines

8. Remove lower engine/flywheel dust cover from converter/flywheel housing.
9. Remove oil pan to cylinder block and front cover mounting screws, **Fig. 25,** and oil pan and gasket.
10. Reverse procedure to install, noting the following:
    a. Carefully remove all traces of old RTV sealant from oil pan and engine block.
    b. Install oil pan gasket applying Weatherstrip & Rubber Adhesive No. E8Z-19552-A, or equivalent, to gasket surface that mates with engine block.
    c. Apply Weatherstrip & Rubber Adhesive No. E8Z-19552-A, or equivalent, to entire engine block sealing surface including front cover and rear main bearing cap. Do not apply sealant to front cover-to-block and rear bearing cap-to-block parting lines.
    d. Seal parting lines with bead of Silicone Gasket Sealant No. F7AZ-195540-EA, or equivalent.
    e. Install oil pan by carefully aligning bolt holes.
    f. Tighten four corner bolts to specifications, then tighten remaining bolts to specifications, back to front.
    g. Ensure all bolts are tighten to specifications.
    h. Finish installing oil pan.
    i. Start engine and allow to reach operating temperature (cooling fan should cycle at least once.)
    j. Stop engine and tighten oil pan bolts to specifications.
    k. Inspect oil pan gasket for extreme shifting out of place.

VIN S ENGINE

This procedure has been revised by a Technical Service Bulletin.

1. Raise and support vehicle.
2. Remove dual converter Y-pipe and drain engine oil.
3. Remove oil pan mounting bolts from transaxle housing.
4. Remove access plug from engine rear plate.
5. Remove transaxle support bracket from oil pan and transaxle.
6. Remove oil pan mounting bolts and

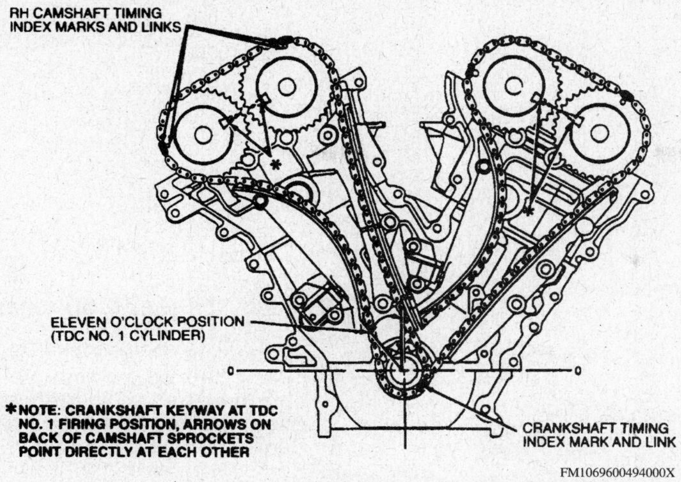

Fig. 23 Timing mark alignment. VIN S engine

stud bolts in sequence, **Fig. 26.**

7. Remove oil pan and oil pan gasket.
8. Reverse procedure to install, noting the following:
   a. Carefully remove all traces of old RTV sealant from oil pan and engine block.
   b. Install oil pan gasket applying Weatherstrip & Rubber Adhesive No. E8Z-19552-A, or equivalent, to gasket surface that mates with engine block.
   c. Apply Weatherstrip & Rubber Adhesive No. E8Z-19552-A, or equivalent, to entire engine block sealing surface including front cover and rear main bearing cap. Do not apply sealant to front cover-to-block and rear bearing cap-to-block parting lines.
   d. Seal parting lines with bead of Silicone Gasket Sealant No. F7AZ-195540-EA, or equivalent.
   e. Install oil pan by carefully aligning bolt holes.
   f. Tighten four corner bolts to specifications, then tighten remaining bolts to specifications, back to front.
   g. Ensure all bolts are tighten to specifications.
   h. Finish installing oil pan.
   i. Start engine and allow to reach operating temperature (cooling fan should cycle at least once.)
   j. Stop engine and tighten oil pan bolts to specifications.
   k. Inspect oil pan gasket for extreme shifting out of place.

OIL PUMP

REPLACE

VIN U, 1 & 2 ENGINES

1. Remove oil pan as outlined under "Oil Pan, Replace."
2. Remove oil pump mounting bolts, **Fig. 27.**
3. Remove oil pump and intermediate shaft.
4. If necessary, pull intermediate shaft from oil pump.
5. Reverse procedure to install. When installing intermediate shaft into replacement pump, ensure shaft retainer clicks into position.

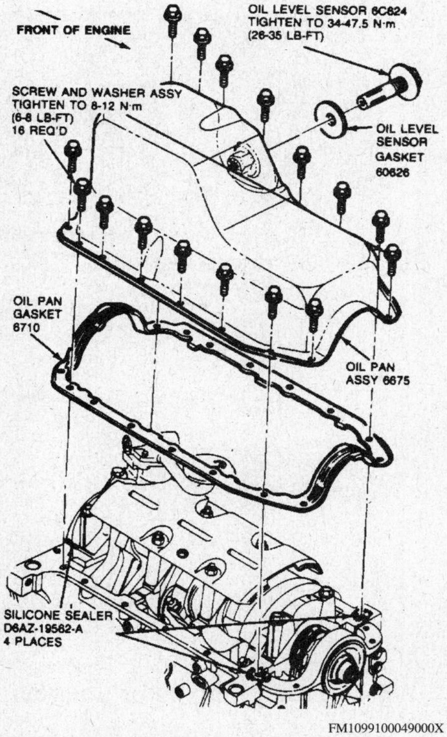

Fig. 25 Oil pan. VIN U, 1 & 2 engines

VIN S ENGINE

1. Remove timing chains as outlined under "Timing Chain, Replace."
2. Remove mounting bolts and oil pump from crankshaft.
3. Reverse procedure to install.

OIL PUMP SERVICE

VIN U, 1 & 2 ENGINES

1. Wash all parts in suitable solvent and dry with compressed air.

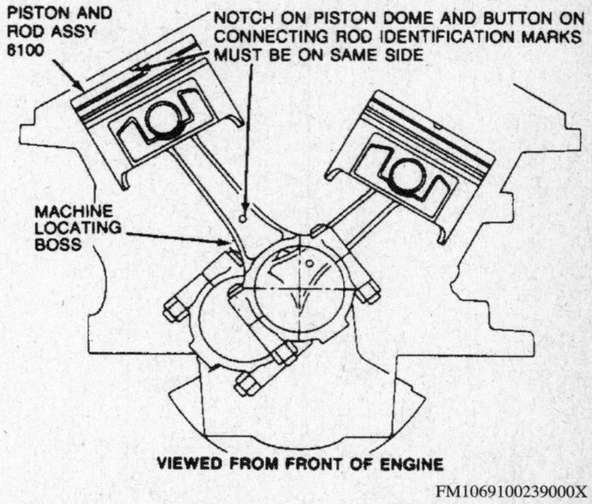

Fig. 24 Piston & rod assembly

2. Ensure all dirt and particles are removed.
3. Inspect inner pump housing for wear or damage.
4. Inspect pump cover mating surface for wear. Scuff marks are normal. If surface is worn or grooved, replace pump assembly.
5. Inspect rotor for nicks, burrs or score marks, and remove imperfections with suitable oil stone.
6. Using suitable feeler gauge, measure inner tip to outer rotor tip clearance, **Fig. 28.** Clearance should be .0024–.0071 inch.
7. Install suitable straightedge and measure rotor endplay, **Fig. 29.** Clearance should be .0012–.0035 inch.
8. If any clearance does not meet specifications, replace oil pump assembly.

BELT TENSION DATA

Belt	New, Lbs.	Used, Lbs.
5-Rib	140–160	110–130
6-Rib	①	①

① — Automatic tensioner.

SERPENTINE DRIVE BELT

BELT ROUTING

Refer to **Figs. 30 and 31** for serpentine drive belt routing.

BELT, REPLACE

1. **On VIN U, 1 & 2 engines,** rotate drive belt tensioner in a clockwise direction.
2. **On VIN S engine,** rotate drive belt tensioner in a counterclockwise direction.
3. **On all models,** remove serpentine drive belt.
4. Reverse procedure to install. Ensure spring keeper releases.

COOLING SYSTEM BLEED

1. Select maximum blower motor and heater temperature settings. Set controls to discharge air through instrument panel A/C vents.

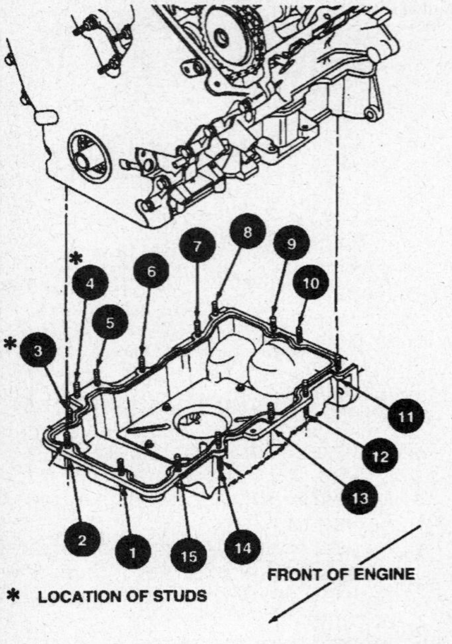

FM1069600495000X

Fig. 26 Oil pan bolt removal sequence. VIN S engine

2. Start engine, and allow it to idle. Feel for hot air at A/C vents.
3. **If air discharge remains cool and engine coolant temperature gauge does not move, coolant level is low and must be filled. Stop engine, allow to cool. Add coolant to bring level to top of Cold Fill mark on de-gas bottle.**
4. Start engine and allow to idle until operating temperature is reached. Hot air should now blow through A/C vents, temperature gauge should rest in NORMAL range, and upper radiator hose should feel hot to touch.
5. Stop engine, allow to cool and inspect for leaks.
6. **When engine coolant level indicator flashes,** approximately one to 1 ½ quarts of coolant may now be added to de-gas bottle after proper refill.

THERMOSTAT

REPLACE

REMOVAL

1. Drain cooling system below level of upper radiator hose.
2. Remove upper radiator hose and thermostat housing mounting bolts.
3. Remove housing and thermostat as an assembly, discarding old gasket. Clean sealing surfaces with gasket scraper. Ensure not to gouge aluminum surfaces as these gouges may form leaks.

INSTALLATION

1. Install thermostat into housing, ensuring jiggle valve is up in relation to housing.
2. Position gasket onto housing using

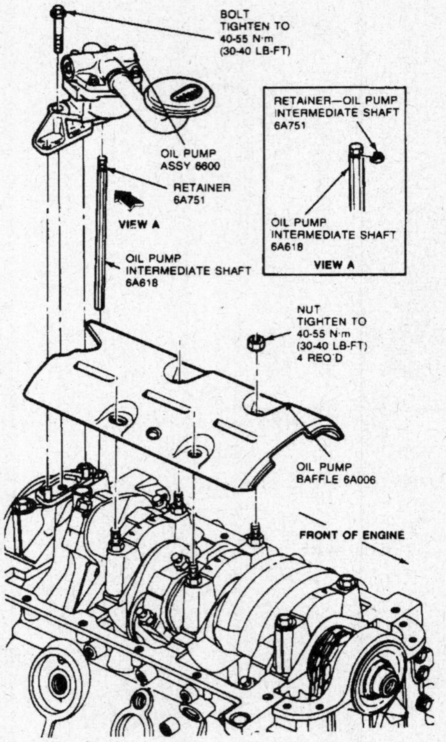

FM1099100050000X

Fig. 27 Oil pump removal. VIN U, 1 & 2 engines

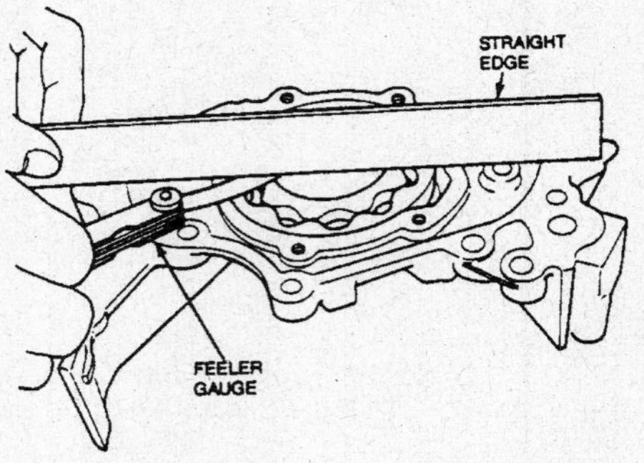

FM1099100052000X

Fig. 29 Oil pump rotor endplay

bolts as holding device, and install housing assembly and mounting bolts.
3. Install upper radiator hose.
4. Fill and bleed cooling system with recommended amount and mixture as outlined under "Cooling System Bleed."
5. Start engine and inspect for leaks.

WATER PUMP

REPLACE

VIN U, 1 & 2 ENGINES

1. Drain cooling system.
2. Disconnect heater hose from water pump.
3. With drive belt still tight, loosen water pump pulley to pump hub mounting bolts.
4. Remove drive belt as outlined under

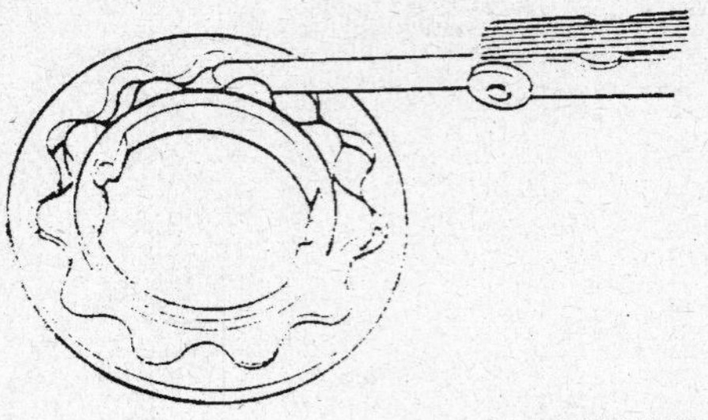

FM1099100051000X

Fig. 28 Oil pump tip clearance

"Serpentine Drive Belt." **The pump pulley cannot be removed at this time because of insufficient clearance between body and pump.**
5. Remove drive belt tensioner.
6. Remove water pump mounting bolts, **Fig. 19,** and lift water pump and pulley assembly up and out of vehicle. Remove pulley.
7. Lightly lubricate all bolts and stud threads with oil.
8. Position pulley on replacement pump and install pump/pulley assembly. Tighten mounting bolts to specifications as outlined under " Front Cover, Replace," in sequence, **Fig. 19.**
9. Install water pump pulley to pump hub mounting bolts and tighten to specifications.
10. Reverse procedure to install.

VIN S ENGINE

1. Drain engine cooling system.
2. Remove drive belt as outlined under "Serpentine Drive Belt."
3. Remove radiator and heater hoses from water pump.
4. Remove mounting bolts and water pump.
5. Reverse procedure to install.

RADIATOR

REPLACE

1. Remove air cleaner assembly, battery and battery tray.
2. Raise and support vehicle.
3. Drain cooling system.
4. Remove lower radiator hose shield and disconnect lower radiator hose.
5. Disconnect lower transmission oil cooler tube from radiator.
6. Remove two lower radiator mounts.
7. Lower vehicle and remove two headlamp assembly to upper support mounting bolts.
8. Loosen pinch bolts and remove headlamp assembly.
9. Remove two front bumper cover to front fender mounting screws.
10. Raise and support vehicle. Remove tire and wheel assemblies.
11. Remove lower radiator air deflector to lower radiator mounting screws.
12. Remove mounting screws and air deflector.
13. Remove lefthand and righthand splash shield to lower radiator air deflector mounting screws.
14. Remove lefthand and righthand splash shield top center mounting screws.

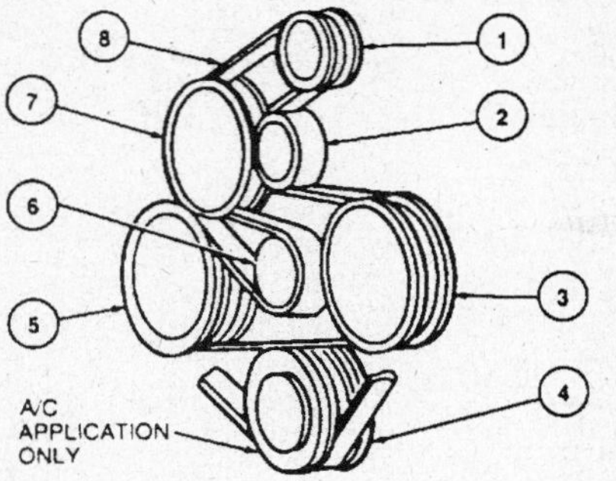

Item		Description
1		Generator
2		Drive Belt Tensioner
3		Power Steering Pump
4		A/C Compressor
5		Crankshaft Pulley
6		Idler Pulley
7		Water Pump
8		Drive Belt

FM1069500393000X

Fig. 30 Serpentine belt routing. VIN U, 1 & 2 engines

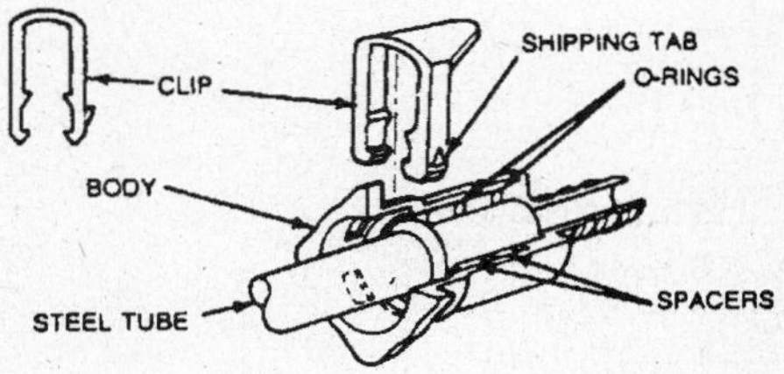

FM1029100142000X

Fig. 32 Push connect fitting removal

15. Remove lefthand and righthand splash shield push pins.
16. Remove remaining mounting screws and splash shields.
17. Remove two bumper cover to front fenders side mounting nuts.
18. Remove front bumper cover to radiator support mounting screws.
19. Disconnect parking/turn signal and side marker lamp electrical connectors.
20. Remove front bumper cover.
21. Lower vehicle, remove hood latch support mounting bolts and position support aside.
22. Disconnect radiator upper hose and coolant overflow hose from radiator.
23. Remove power distribution box and harness from radiator support and position aside.
24. Remove A/C ambient air temperature sensor and wiring from upper radiator support.
25. Remove front air bag sensor and bracket from upper radiator support.
26. **On models with engine block heaters,** remove wiring from upper radiator support.
27. **On all models,** remove upper radiator support to front fender mounting bolts.
28. Remove remaining upper radiator support mounting bolts and upper radiator support.
29. Remove engine sensor control wiring mounting screws and position wiring aside.
30. Disconnect cooling fan electrical connectors.
31. Remove nut from power steering/transmission cooler bracket.
32. Remove A/C condenser core mounting bolts and stud bolt.
33. Position A/C condenser core forward and support with suitable mechanics wire.
34. Disconnect upper transmission oil cooler tube from radiator and remove both lower radiator brackets.
35. Tilt radiator forward and lift from vehicle.
36. Reverse procedure to install.

FUEL PUMP

REPLACE

1. Relieve fuel system pressure as outlined under "Precautions."
2. **On flexible fuel models,** remove fuel from tank as follows:
   a. Remove foam and rubber protective cover from special quick disconnect fitting on fuel drain tube found on righthand side of fuel tank.
   b. Attach adapter hose tool No. 034-00020, or equivalent, to suitable fuel storage tank.
   c. Pump out fuel from tank.
3. **On non-flexible fuel models,** remove fuel from fuel tank by pumping fuel out of fuel filler neck using a suitable fuel storage tanker.
4. **On all models,** raise and support vehicle.
5. Disconnect and remove fuel filler neck.
6. Support fuel tank and remove tank support straps.
7. Lower fuel tank partially and remove fuel lines, electrical connectors and vent lines from tank.
8. Remove tank and place on suitable workbench.
9. Turn fuel pump locking ring counterclockwise and remove locking ring.
10. Remove fuel pump, bracket and gasket assembly.
11. Reverse procedure to install.

FUEL FILTER

REPLACE

1. Relieve fuel system pressure as outlined under "Precautions."
2. Twist push connect fittings at each end of filter until they move freely on tube.
3. Bend and break shipping tab from hairpin clip, and spread two clip legs approximately 1/8 inch, **Fig. 32.**
4. Remove clip from tube and fitting by pulling gently on triangular end.
5. Separate fitting and hose assembly from fuel filter.
6. Install retainer clips in each connect fitting.
7. Loosen worm gear mounting clip and

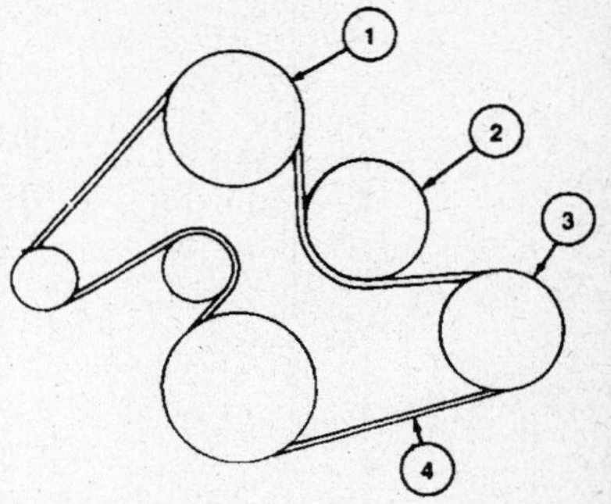

Item	Part Number	Description
1	3A674	Power Steering Pump
2	8501	Water Pump
3	19703	A/C Compressor
4	8620	Drive Belt

FM1069600497000X

Fig. 31 Serpentine belt routing. VIN S engine

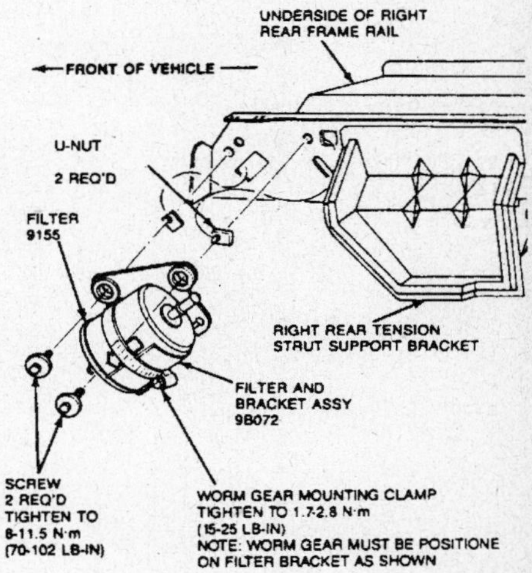

FM1029100143000X

Fig. 33 Fuel filter replacement

remove filter from bracket, **Fig. 33.**

8. Reverse procedure to install.

TECHNICAL SERVICE BULLETINS

INCREASED STEERING EFFORT OR ALTERNATOR LAMP ON IN WET WEATHER

1997 Models w/VIN S Engine

On these built through Aug. 1, 1997, steering effort may increase, alternator lamp may be on, or Front End Accessory Drive (FEAD) belt may slip in wet weather or the crankshaft pulley may be damaged or broken.

This condition may be caused by the FEAD belt. To correct this condition, replace the FEAD belt (part No. F5DZ-8620-EA).

TIGHTENING SPECIFICATIONS

Year	Component	Torque/ Ft. Lbs.
VIN U, 1 & 2 ENGINES		
1997–99	A/C Compressor Mounting	35
	Alternator Brace To Upper Intake Manifold	9–14
	Alternator To Bracket	27
	Alternator To Cylinder Head	35
	Camshaft Position Sensor Housing mounting	18
	Camshaft Sprocket To Camshaft	37–51
	Camshaft Thrust Plate	84⑥
	Coil & Bracket To Cylinder Head	30–40
	Connecting Rod	23–28
	Crankshaft Damper To Crankshaft	93–121
	Crankshaft Position Sensor	45–61⑥
	Crankshaft Pulley To Damper	30–44
	Cylinder Head	①
	De-gas Tube To Upper Intake Manifold	72–108⑥
	EGR Tube To EGR Valve & Exhaust Manifold	26–47
	EGR Tube Retainer To Exhaust Manifold	30–34
	EGR Valve To Upper Intake Manifold	15–22
	Engine Front Cover, Bolts 1–10	15–22
	Engine Front Cover, Bolts 11–15	72–108⑥
	Engine To Transaxle/Torque Converter Assembly	30–44
	Exhaust Manifold	15–18
	Flywheel To Crankshaft	54–64
	Front Subframe To Body	57–76
	Fuel Injection Supply Manifold To Intake Manifold	72–108⑥
	Ignition Coil Bracket	30–40
	Intake Manifold Support To RH Cylinder Head	30–40
	Intake Manifold Support To Throttle Body	72–108⑥
	Intake Manifold To Cylinder Head	15–22⑤
	Main Bearing Cap	56–62
	Oil Filter Insert To Cylinder Block	20–29
	Oil Galley & Cooling Jacket Plugs	14
	Oil Level Indicator Tube To Exhaust Manifold	12–14
	Oil Pan Drain Plug	9–11
	Oil Pan To Cylinder Block	84–120⑥
	Oil Pressure Sensor	12–16
	Oil Pump To Cylinder Block	30–40
	Power Steering Pump To Cylinder Block	30–40
	RH Exhaust Manifold Heat Shield	72–108⑥
	Spark Plug	7–15
	Throttle Cable Bracket	13
	Torque Converter	20–33
	Transmission Range Sensor	12–16
	Upper Intake Manifold To Lower Intake Manifold	15–22
	Valve Tappet Guide Plate To Cylinder Block	84–120⑥
	Water Bypass Tube	15–22
	Water Outlet Connection To Intake Manifold	84–120⑥
	Water Pump Pulley To Hub	15–22
	Water Pump To Front Cover (No. 4–9)	15–22
	Water Pump To Front Cover (No. 11–15)	72–108⑥
	Wiring Retainer Bracket	15–22
	Y-Pipe To Exhaust Manifold	25–34

Continued

TIGHTENING SPECIFICATIONS—Continued

Year	Component	Torque/ Ft. Lbs.
VIN S ENGINE		
1997–99	A/C Compressor	15–22
	Accelerator Bracket To Throttle Body	8–12
	Accessory Drive Crankshaft Pulley Bracket	15–22
	Accessory Drive Crankshaft Pulley To Damper	70–77
	Alternator	15–22
	Battery Ground Cable To Engine	15–22
	Camshaft Position Sensor	72–108⑥
	Connecting Rod	29–33③
	Crankcase Ventilation Tube	44–62⑥
	Crankshaft Damper To Crankshaft	②
	Crankshaft Position Sensor	72–108⑥
	Cylinder Head	①
	Cylinder Head Camshaft Journal Cap	72–108⑥
	Drive Belt Idler Pulley	15–22
	EGR Vacuum Regulator Solenoid	44–61⑥
	EGR Valve	15–22
	Engine To Transaxle	25–33
	Exhaust Manifold	13–16
	Flywheel To Crankshaft	54–64
	Front Axle Wheel Hub Retainer	170–202
	Front Subframe To Body	57–75
	Front Wheel Knuckles To Suspension Lower Arms	67–80
	Idle Air Control Valve	72–108⑥
	Ignition Coil	72⑥
	Lower Intake Manifold	72–108⑥
	Oil Filter Mounting Insert To Cylinder Block	20–29
	Oil Pan Baffle	15–22
	Oil Pan Drain Plug	16–22
	Oil Pan To Cylinder Block	15–22
	Oil Pan To Transaxle	25–33
	Oil Pressure Sensor	9–12
	Oil Pump Screen Cover & Tube	15–22
	Oil Pump To Cylinder Block	72–108⑥
	Oil Separator	72–108⑥
	Oxygen Sensor	26–34
	Power Steering Pump	72–108⑥
	Powertrain Control Module	32
	RH Engine Support Insulator	75–102
	Secondary Air Injection Diverter Valve Bracket	72–108⑥
	Shift Cable Bracket	15–19
	Shift Rod To Transaxle	17
	Spark Plugs	7–15
	Stabilizer Bar To Transaxle	30–40
	Starter Motor	15–22
	Steering Shaft & Joint Bolt	18
	Thermostat Housing	72–108⑥
	Throttle Body	72–108⑥
	Tie Rod End Stud	35–46
	Timing Chain Guide	15–22
	Timing Chain Tensioner	15–22
	Torque Converter To Flywheel	20–34

Continued

TIGHTENING SPECIFICATIONS—Continued

Year	Component	Torque/ Ft. Lbs.
VIN S ENGINE		
1997-99	Transaxle Support Bracket	15–22
	Transmission Oil Cooler Line	18–22
	Transmission Range Sensor	12–16
	Upper Front Engine Support Insulator	50–70
	Upper Intake Manifold	72–108⑥
	Valve Cover	72–108⑥
	Water Bypass Tube	72–108⑥
	Water Pump	15–22④
	Water Pump To Housing	16–18
	Wheel Lug	95

① — Refer to "Cylinder Head, Replace."
② — Torque to 89 ft. lbs., then loosen one full turn. Torque 27–32 ft. lbs., then tighten an additional 85–95.°
③ — Tighten an additional 90–120.°
④ — Tighten an additional 85–95.°
⑤ — Final torque to 20–24 ft. lbs.
⑥ — Inch lbs.

3.4L Engine

NOTE: On Air Bag Equipped Models, Refer To " Air Bag System Precautions" Located In Front Of This Manual For System Disarming & Arming Procedures.

INDEX

PRECAUTIONS

AIR BAG SYSTEMS

Refer to "Air Bag System Precautions" in the front of this manual for system disarming and arming procedures.

FUEL SYSTEM PRESSURE RELIEF

Fuel supply lines will remain pressurized for long periods of time after engine shutdown. This pressure must be relieved before any service is attempted. A valve is provided on the fuel injection supply manifold for this purpose. To relieve system pressure, proceed as follows:

1. Remove fuel tank filler cap.
2. Remove air cleaner assembly.
3. Connect pressure gauge tool No. T80L-9974-B, or equivalent, to fuel pressure relief valve.
4. Open manual valve on gauge to relieve pressure.

BATTERY GROUND CABLE

Prior to service, disconnect battery ground cable and isolate as required.

COMPRESSION PRESSURE

When inspecting cylinder compression, the lowest cylinder must be within 75 percent of the highest cylinder. Perform compression inspection with engine at normal

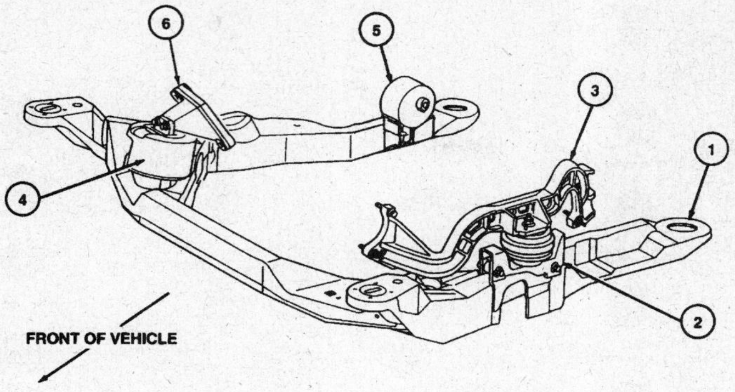

Item	Description
1	Front Sub-Frame
2	Engine and Transmission Support Insulator
3	Rear Engine Support Bracket

Item	Description
4	Front Engine Support Insulator, LH
5	Front Engine Support Insulator, RH
6	Front Engine Support Bracket

FM1069600599000X

Fig. 1 Engine & transaxle mounts

operating temperature, spark plugs removed and throttle wide open.

ENGINE MOUNT

REPLACE

FRONT

Removal

1. Raise and support vehicle.
2. Place jack and wooden block in suitable location under engine block.
3. Remove nuts mounting lefthand and righthand front engine support insulators to subframe, **Fig. 1.**
4. Raise engine enough to unload insulators.
5. Remove remaining bolts from lefthand insulator and front support insulator.
6. Remove through bolt from righthand front support insulator and insulator from front engine support mounting bracket.

Installation

1. Attach lefthand front support insulator with two bolts. Tighten to specifications.
2. Attach righthand front support insulator to case rear bracket with one through bolt. Tighten to specifications.
3. Lower engine down onto subframe. **Prevent front engine support bracket from rotating when tightening to avoid noise, vibration and harshness conditions.**
4. Install lefthand and righthand insulator to subframe mounting nuts. Tighten to specifications.

REAR

Refer to the "3.0L (VIN S, U, 1 & 2) Engines" section for procedures.

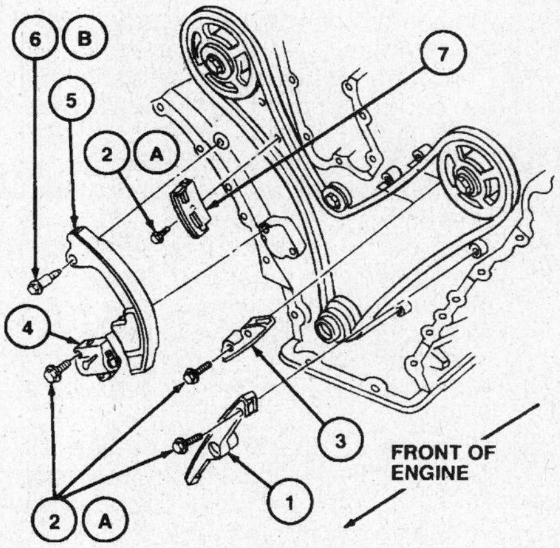

Item	Description
1	Timing Chain Guide
2	Timing Chain / Belt Tensioner Bolt (6 Req'd)
3	Timing Chain Guide, LH
4	Timing Chain Tensioner
5	Timing Chain Tensioner Arm
6	Timing Chain Tensioner Pivot Bolt
7	Timing Chain Guide
A	Tighten to 18-27 N·m (14-19 Lb-Ft)
B	Tighten to 34-53 N·m (25-39 Lb-Ft)

FM1069700602000X

Fig. 3 Timing chain guide & tensioner

ENGINE

REPLACE

1. Remove battery and tray.
2. Remove oil filler cap and engine appearance cover.
3. Disconnect engine control sensor wiring from engine air/fuel ratio control

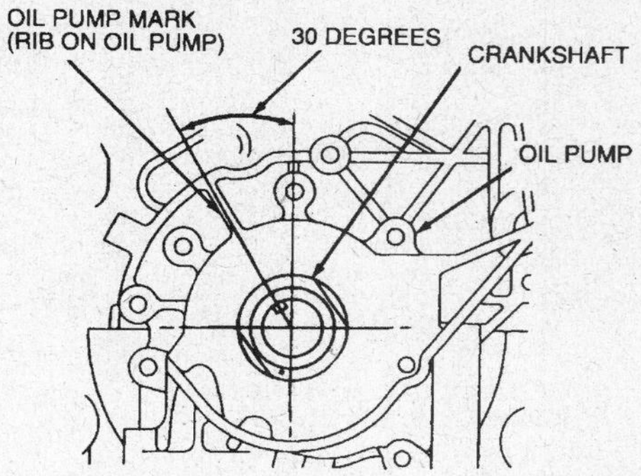

FM1069700601000X

Fig. 2 Crankshaft & oil pump timing mark alignment

bracket and mass air flow sensor.

4. Disconnect air cleaner outlet tube from throttle body.
5. Release air cleaner cover.
6. Disconnect crankcase ventilation hose from air cleaner outlet tube.
7. Remove air cleaner and outlet tube as an assembly.
8. Remove windshield wiper module.
9. Remove main vacuum connector mounting nuts and supply hose from connector.
10. Remove wiper motor connector and grommet from cowl top extension and remove extension.
11. Remove accelerator cable splash shield.
12. Disconnect speed control and accelerator cables from throttle body.
13. Remove speed control and accelerator cable mounting bolts, and position cables aside.
14. Disconnect main engine control harness connector and transaxle range sensor connector.
15. Position transaxle shift cable and bracket aside.
16. Remove power steering reservoir cap.
17. Drain engine coolant and oil into suitable containers.
18. Raise and support vehicle.
19. Disconnect power steering return hose from lefthand end of steering fluid cooler, allowing fluid to drain into a suitable container.
20. Disconnect upper fluid cooler tube from lefthand end of transaxle fluid cooler, allow fluid to drain into a suitable container.
21. Disconnect upper fluid cooler tube from lefthand rubber line.
22. Lower vehicle to ground.
23. Disconnect heater water hose at heater water tubes.
24. Disconnect canister purge valve vacuum hose.
25. Disconnect main vacuum hose at intake manifold.
26. Disconnect engine control sensor wiring from powertrain control module bracket.
27. Remove engine ground strap bolt and position strap aside.
28. Disconnect engine control sensor wiring from canister purge valve solenoid.
29. Relieve fuel pressure as outlined under "Precautions."

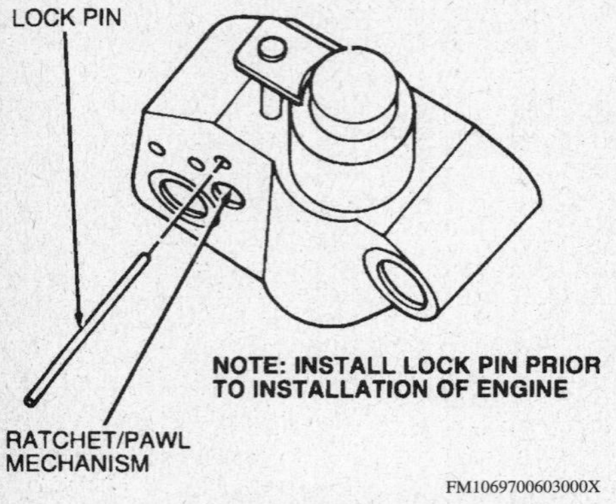

Fig. 4 Tensioner lock pin installation

30. Disconnect fuel supply and return tubes from fuel injection supply manifold.
31. Disconnect power steering pump to reservoir hose at pump.
32. Disconnect de-gas tubes from radiator recovery reservoir.
33. Recover A/C as outlined under "Air Conditioning."
34. Disconnect engine control sensor wiring connector from A/C pressure cutoff switch.
35. Loosen A/C manifold to compressor mounting bolt.
36. Disconnect A/C pressure cutoff switch from compressor and position aside.
37. Disconnect upper radiator hose at water pump.
38. Disconnect lower radiator hose at water pump and position aside.
39. Disconnect battery to starter relay cable, remove mounting nut and move cable aside.
40. Remove front wheels.
41. Disconnect catalyst monitor sensors and heated oxygen sensor.
42. Remove dual three-way converter and pipe.
43. Disconnect battery cable at alternator.
44. Disconnect ride level sensors at front suspension lower arm.
45. Remove stabilizer bar link to front suspension mounting nuts.
46. Disconnect tie rod end from knuckle.
47. Remove wheel hub mounting nuts.
48. Disconnect ball joints from suspension lower arm.
49. Position knuckle and shock absorber assemblies aside.
50. Secure drive axle shafts to subframe.
51. Remove four flexplate to torque converter nuts.
52. Remove lower four transaxle to engine block bolts.
53. Remove steering column pinch bolt from intermediate shaft coupling and separate coupling from steering gear.
54. Support front subframe, engine, and transaxle assembly with Rotunda powertrain lift tool No. 014-00765 and universal powertrain removal bracket tool No. 014-00766, or equivalents.
55. Remove subframe mounting bolts.
56. Lower engine, transaxle and subframe.
57. Disconnect engine control sensor wiring connector from secondary air injection pump.
58. Disconnect engine control sensor wiring connector from transaxle and transaxle speed sensor.
59. Disconnect engine control sensor wiring connector from power steering pressure switch.
60. Remove power steering lefthand turn pressure hose mounting nut at power steering pump and move hose aside.
61. Remove four upper engine block to transaxle bolts.
62. Remove righthand front drive axle assembly.
63. Remove righthand front engine support insulator bracket mounting bolts.
64. Remove lefthand front upper engine support insulator to bracket bolts.
65. Lift engine from transaxle.
66. Reverse procedure to install. Tighten all fasteners to specifications.

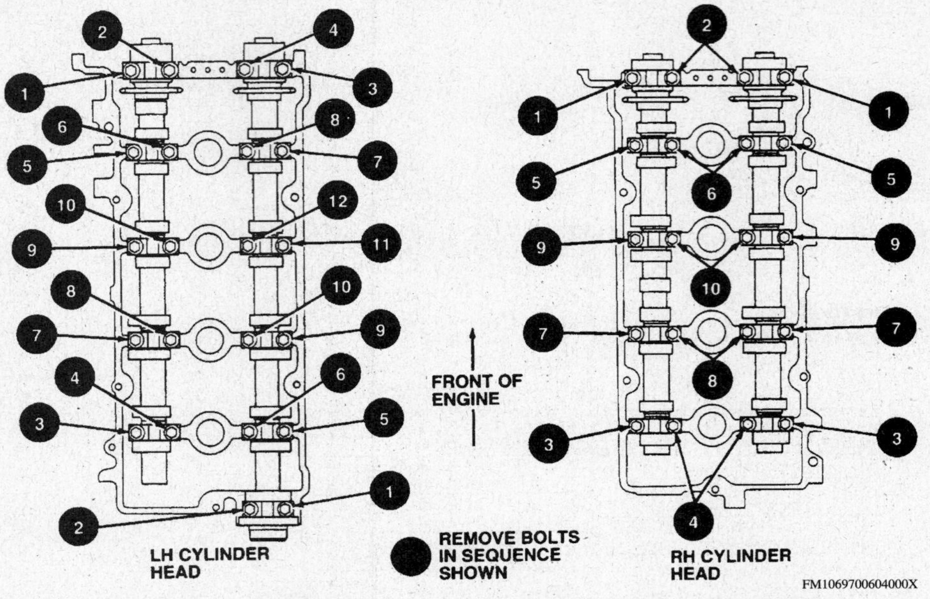

Fig. 5 Camshaft journal cap bolt loosening sequence

INTAKE MANIFOLD

REPLACE

UPPER

1. Relieve fuel system pressure as outlined under "Precautions."
2. Remove engine appearance cover.
3. Remove righthand half of cowl vent screen.
4. Remove throttle body.
5. Disconnect main emission vacuum supply hose from surge tank fitting and EGR valve, and position hose aside.
6. Disconnect vacuum tube from manifold vacuum union.
7. Remove transducer mounting bracket from surge tank and position bracket aside.
8. Remove manifold supports from surge tank and cylinder head.
9. Remove EGR valve.
10. Remove mounting bolts and tank stays from front and rear of surge tank.
11. Remove radio ignition capacitor bracket and position capacitor aside.
12. **Remove intake manifold mounting bolts in an alternating sequence.**
13. Reverse procedure to install. Tighten manifold mounting bolts in an alternating sequence to specifications.

LOWER

1. Remove upper intake manifold as outlined under "Upper Intake Manifold."
2. Disconnect fuel injection supply and return lines from supply manifold.
3. Disconnect intake manifold runner control deactivation cable.
4. Remove deactivation cable from bracket and position aside.
5. Disconnect engine control sensor wiring from injectors and wiring retainers, and move wiring out of way.
6. Remove supply manifold and injectors from lower intake manifold.
7. Remove manifold to cylinder head bolts in an alternating sequence and manifold.
8. Reverse procedure to install, noting the following:
   a. Ensure intake manifold runner control plate operates properly.
   b. Tighten manifold mounting bolts in an alternating sequence to specifications.

EXHAUST MANIFOLD

REPLACE

LEFTHAND SIDE

1. Raise and support vehicle.
2. Remove dual converter Y-pipe and lower exhaust manifold mounting nuts.
3. Lower vehicle, and remove secondary air injection manifold tube and heat shield from manifold.
4. Remove oil dipstick tube mounting bolt.

5. Remove upper manifold mounting nuts.
6. Remove manifold and gasket.
7. Reverse procedure to install. Tighten fasteners to specifications.

RIGHTHAND SIDE

1. Remove secondary air injection manifold tube from manifold.
2. Remove three bolts from heat shield.
3. Raise and support vehicle.
4. Remove EGR valve to manifold tube from manifold.
5. Disconnect EGR valve to manifold tube from EGR transducer.
6. Remove dual converter Y-pipe and lower manifold mounting nuts.
7. Lower vehicle and remove manifold heat shield.
8. Remove upper manifold mounting nuts.
9. Remove manifold and gasket.
10. Reverse procedure to install. Tighten all fasteners to specifications.

CYLINDER HEAD

REPLACE

1. Remove engine as outlined under "Engine, Replace, " and mount on suitable stand.
2. Remove accessory drive belt.
3. Remove A/C compressor, alternator and alternator bracket.
4. Remove water pump drive belt.
5. Remove water pump drive pulley from lefthand intake camshaft.
6. Disconnect main emission vacuum supply hose from surge tank fitting, air injection diverter valve and EGR valve.
7. Disconnect engine control sensor wiring from EGR backpressure transducer, EGR vacuum regulator solenoid and secondary vacuum valve.
8. Remove transducer mounting bolts from surge tank.
9. Disconnect EGR pressure sensor valve hoses from EGR valve to exhaust manifold tube and remove transducer mounting bracket.
10. Remove EGR valve to exhaust manifold tube from EGR valve and exhaust manifold.
11. Remove intake manifold supports from surge tank and cylinder head, and surge tank.
12. Disconnect engine control sensor wiring connections from idle air control valve and throttle position sensor.
13. Remove water bypass hose from throttle body.
14. Remove idle air control valve and gasket, and throttle body from engine air inlet connector.
15. Remove upper intake manifold.
16. Disconnect engine control sensor wiring from the following components:
    a. Water temperature sending units.
    b. Ignition coils.
    c. Radio ignition capacitor.
    d. Fuel injectors.
    e. Camshaft and crankshaft position sensors.
    f. Oil pressure sending unit.

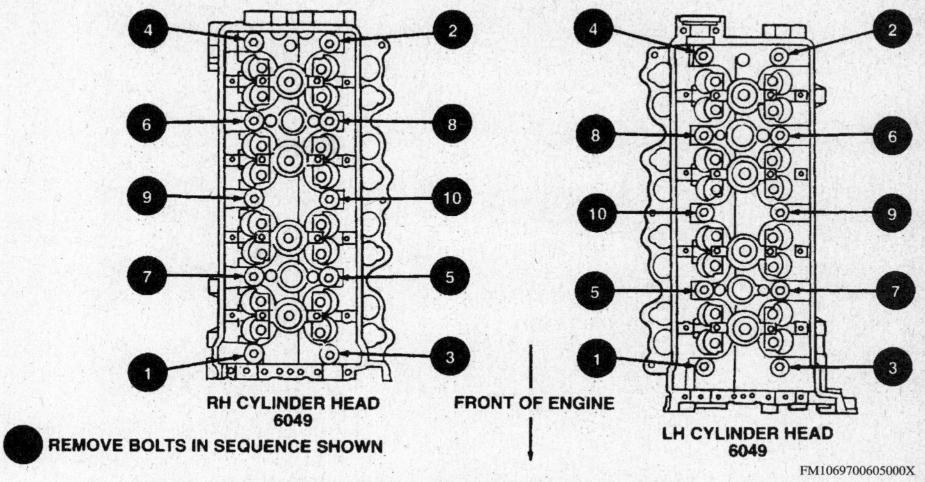

Fig. 6 Cylinder head bolt loosening sequence

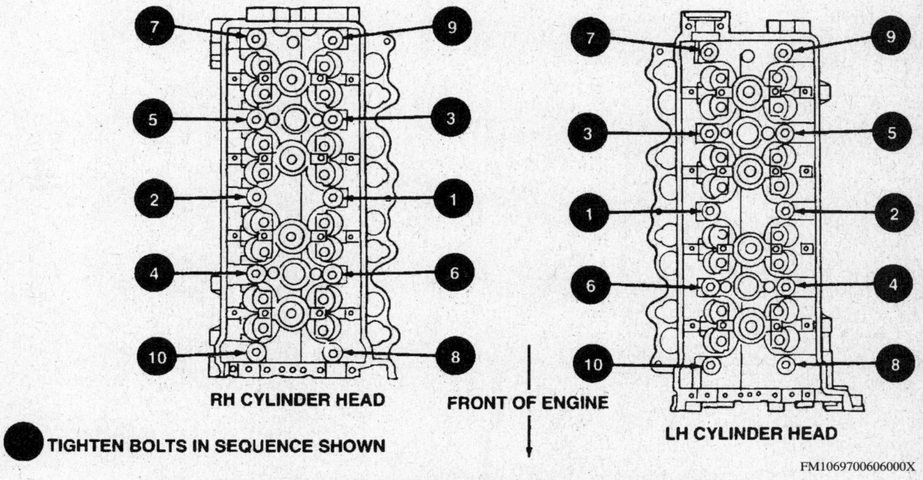

Fig. 7 Cylinder head bolt tightening sequence

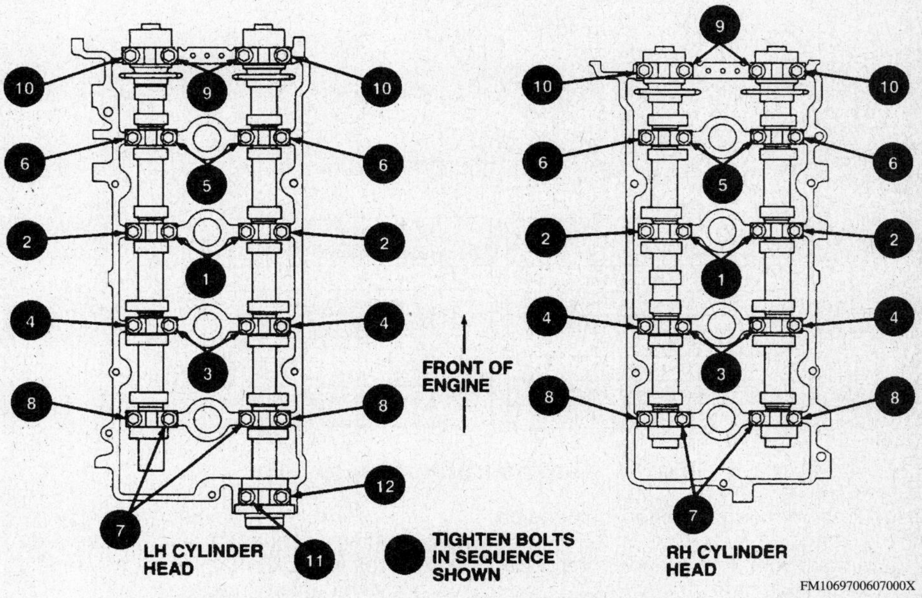

Fig. 8 Camshaft journal cap bolt tightening sequence

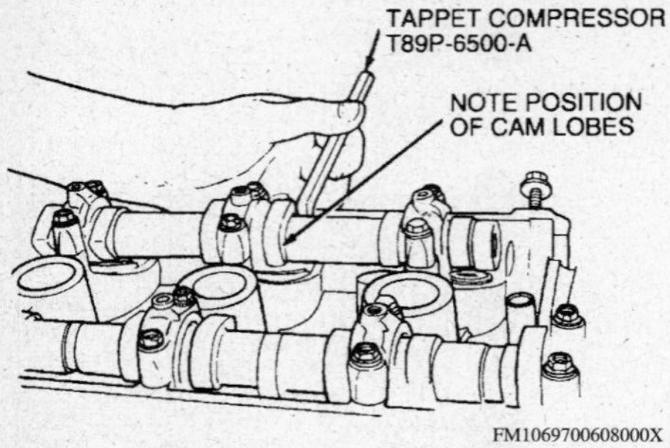

Fig. 9 Valve lifter depression

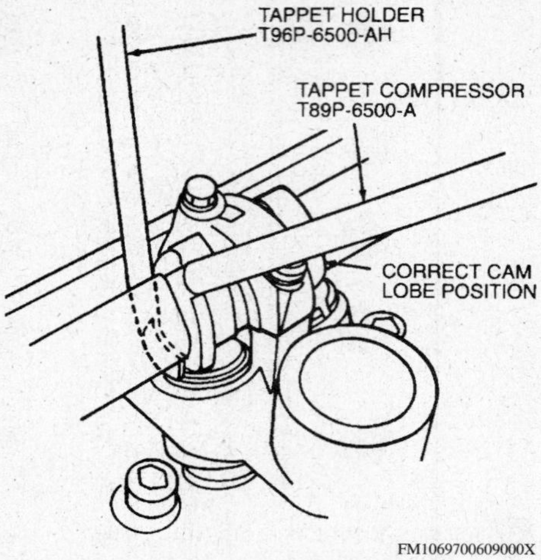

Fig. 10 Lifter holder tool insertion

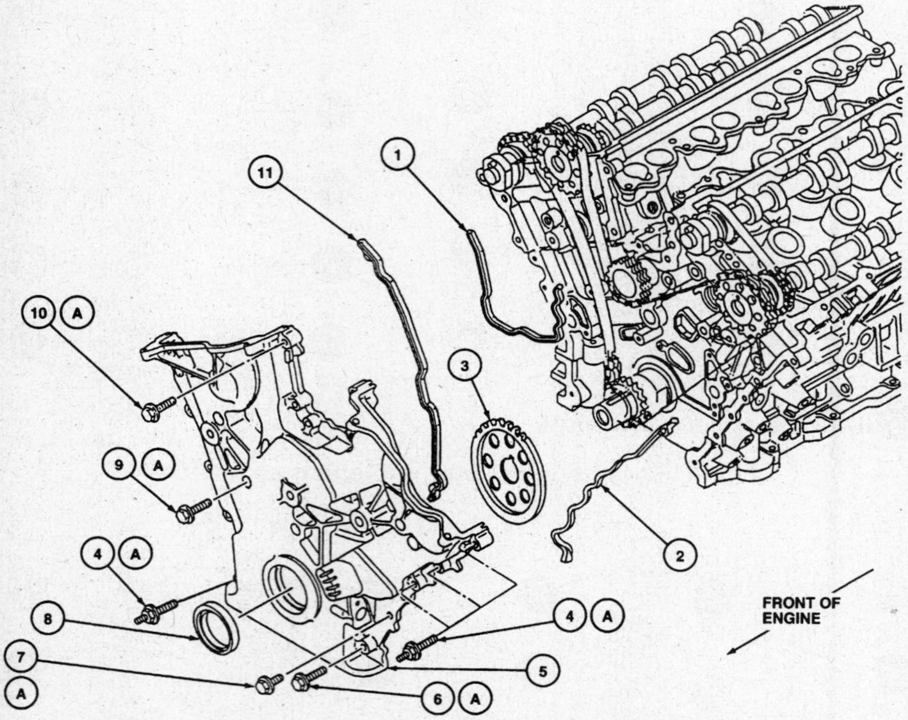

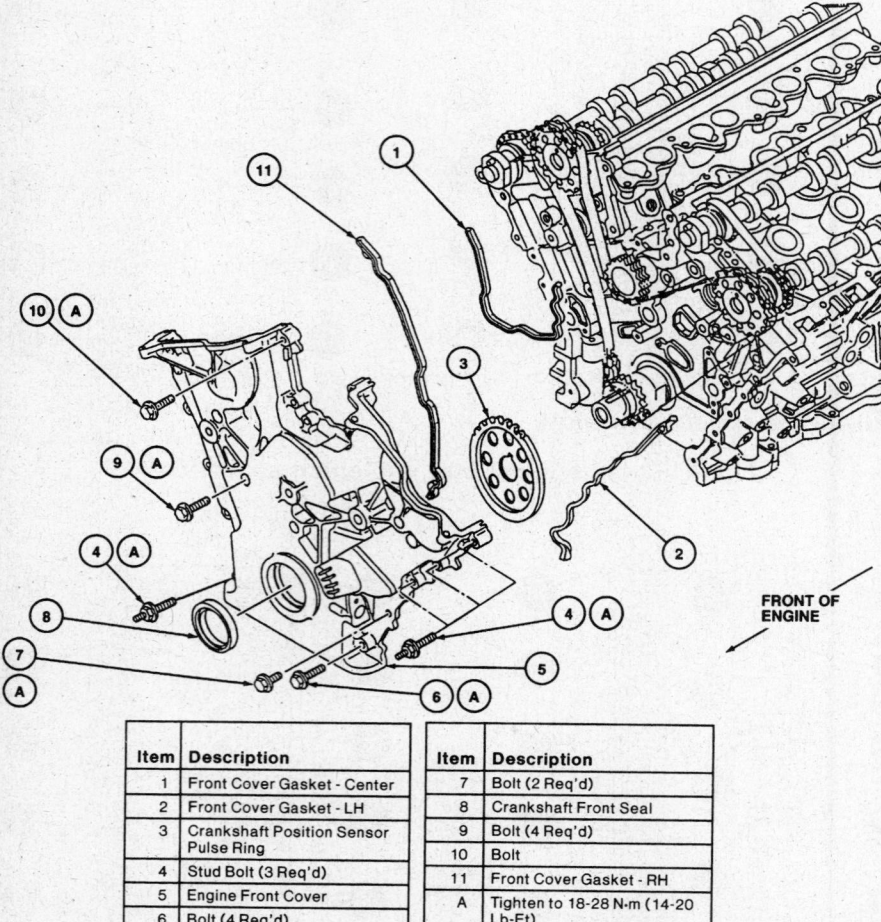

Item	Description
1	Front Cover Gasket - Center
2	Front Cover Gasket - LH
3	Crankshaft Position Sensor Pulse Ring
4	Stud Bolt (3 Req'd)
5	Engine Front Cover
6	Bolt (4 Req'd)

Item	Description
7	Bolt (2 Req'd)
8	Crankshaft Front Seal
9	Bolt (4 Req'd)
10	Bolt
11	Front Cover Gasket - RH
A	Tighten to 18-28 N·m (14-20 Lb-Ft)

FM1069700620000X

Fig. 11 Engine front cover removal

g. Engine control sensor extension wiring.
h. Intake manifold runner control deactivation motor.

17. Remove engine control sensor wiring from engine assembly.
18. Remove exhaust air supply tube from exhaust manifolds and secondary air injection diverter valve.
19. Remove secondary air injection diverter valve from exhaust air supply valve mounting bracket.
20. Remove exhaust manifolds.
21. Remove lower intake manifolds.
22. Remove upper radiator hose from water crossover.
23. Remove water crossover from right-hand cylinder head.
24. Remove oil cooler to water pump hoses at water pump.
25. Remove water pump.
26. Remove valve covers.
27. Remove spark plugs.
28. Remove power steering pump pulley, pump, and pump support.
29. Remove crankshaft pulley using steering wheel puller tool No. T67L-3600-A, or equivalent.
30. Remove camshaft and crankshaft position sensors.
31. Remove crankshaft front seal from engine front cover using locknut pin remover tool No. T78P-3504-N, or equivalent.
32. Remove engine front cover.
33. Remove crankshaft position sensor pulse ring from crankshaft.
34. Rotate crankshaft to place number one piston at top dead center by aligning crankshaft keyway groove with oil pump mark, **Fig. 2.**
35. Ensure camshaft sprocket timing marks are on top, and if not, rotate crankshaft one complete revolution.
36. Remove timing chain guides, tensioner arm and tensioner, **Fig. 3.**
37. Using a small screwdriver, release tensioner ratchet/pawl mechanism through tensioner access hole.
38. Compress tensioner rack and piston into tensioner housing by inserting a small wire into top of piston, and gently unseat oil check ball. **Compress tensioner by hand and leave in a compressed state for installation purposes.**
39. While tensioner is compressed, insert a .060 inch drill bit or wire into small hole above ratchet. This engages lock groove in rack of tensioner, **Fig. 4.**
40. Remove balance shaft driven gear and sprocket key from dynamic balance shaft.
41. Remove balance shaft thrust plate from engine block.
42. Thread balance shaft replacer tool No. T96P-6A333-AH, or equivalent, into balance shaft.
43. Thread impact slide hammer tool No. T50T-100-A, or equivalent, into replacer, and pull shaft and front bearing out.
44. Thread impact slide hammer into replacer and insert remover through inside diameter of rear bearing, and pull rear bearing out.
45. Remove timing chain sprocket tensioners from cylinder heads.
46. **Note camshaft journal caps and cylinder head numbering. This will ensure caps are returned to their original locations.**
47. **Remove camshaft journal thrust caps first.**
48. Loosen remaining journal cap bolts in sequence, **Fig. 5.**
49. Remove camshafts.
50. Remove timing chain crankshaft sprocket.
51. Remove cylinder head mounting bolts and washers in sequence, **Fig. 6.**

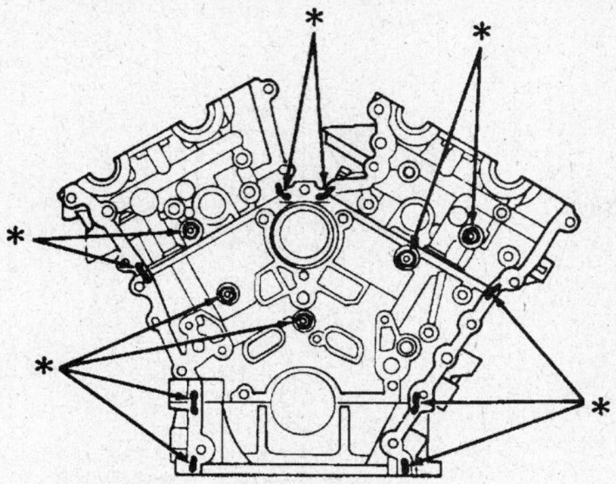

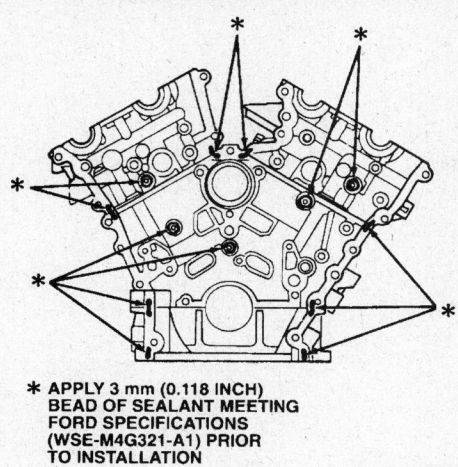

* APPLY 3 mm (0.118 INCH) BEAD OF SEALANT MEETING FORD SPECIFICATIONS (WSE-M4G321-A1) PRIOR TO INSTALLATION

FM1069700611000X

Fig. 12 Engine front cover sealer locations

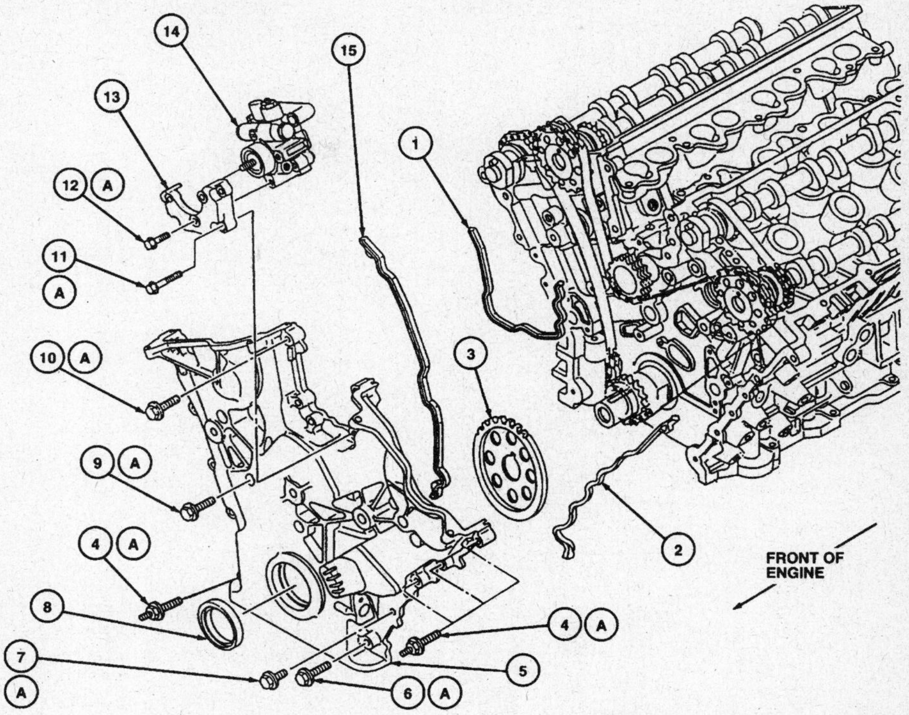

Item	Description
1	Front Cover Gasket—Center
2	Front Cover Gasket—LH
3	Crankshaft Shutter
4	Stud Bolt (4 Req'd)
5	Engine Front Cover
6	Bolt (4 Req'd)
7	Bolt (2 Req'd)
8	Crankshaft Front Seal
9	Bolt (4 Req'd)

Item	Description
10	Bolt (1 Req'd)
11	Bolt (4 Req'd)
12	Bolt (3 Req'd)
13	Power Steering Pump Support
14	Power Steering Pump
15	Front Cover Gasket—RH
A	Tighten to 18-28 N·m (14-20 Lb-Ft)

FM1069700621000X

Fig. 13 Engine front cover installation

52. Reverse procedure to install, noting the following:
    a. Install new torque-to-yield cylinder head bolts.
    b. **Torque** cylinder head bolts to 20–23 ft. lbs. in sequence, **Fig. 7,** then tighten an additional 85–95.°
    c. **Ensure No. 1 piston is at top dead center, Fig. 2.**
    d. Apply a .08–.11 inch bead of silicone gasket and sealant part No. F6AZ-19562-AA, or equivalent, to lefthand cylinder head intake camshaft journal cap.
    e. Install camshaft journal caps in their original locations and loosely install mounting bolts.
    f. **Torque** journal cap bolts to 60–108 inch lbs. in sequence, **Fig. 8,** then to 12–15 ft. lbs.

VALVE COVER

REPLACE

1. Remove engine appearance cover.
2. Remove righthand half of cowl vent screen.
3. Disconnect main emission vacuum supply hose from surge tank fitting, air injection diverter valve and EGR valve.
4. Disconnect vacuum tube from intake manifold vacuum union.
5. Disconnect EGR valve to exhaust manifold tube from bottom of EGR valve.
6. Position power steering lefthand turn pressure hose aside.
7. Position transducer mounting bracket aside.
8. Remove surge tank.
9. Remove ignition coils.
10. Remove radio ignition capacitor mounting nut.
11. Disconnect crankcase ventilation tube from valve cover.
12. Position engine control sensor wiring aside.
13. Remove valve cover bolts and cover.
14. Reverse procedure to install, noting the following:
    a. Clean cover sealing surfaces with a shop towel and metal surface cleaner part No. F4AZ-19A536-RA, or equivalent.
    b. Apply a .31 inch diameter bead of silicone rubber sealer part No. F4AZ-19562-B, or equivalent, on cover sealing surfaces where engine front cover and cylinder heads contact.
    c. The old gasket may be used again if it is not damaged.
    d. Position cover on cylinder head within six minutes of sealer application.

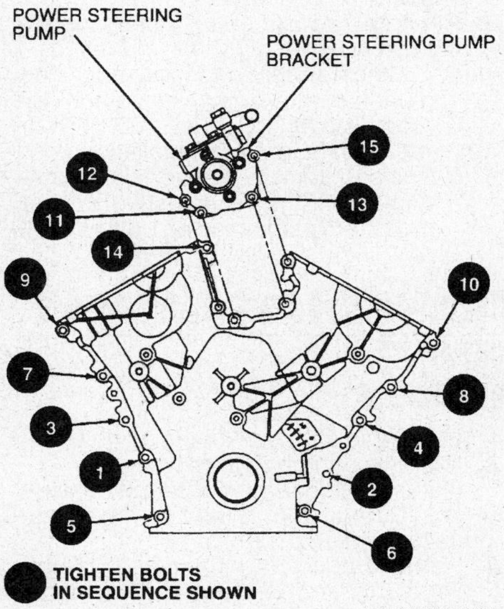

FM1069700612000X

Fig. 14 Engine front cover bolt tightening sequence

CAMSHAFT LOBE LIFT SPECIFICATIONS

Exhaust .... .335 inch
Intake............................... .323 inch

VALVE CLEARANCE SPECIFICATIONS

To inspect valve clearances, proceed as follows:

1. **Camshaft lobes must be directed 90° or more away from valve lifters.**
2. Insert feeler gauge at 90° angle to camshaft.

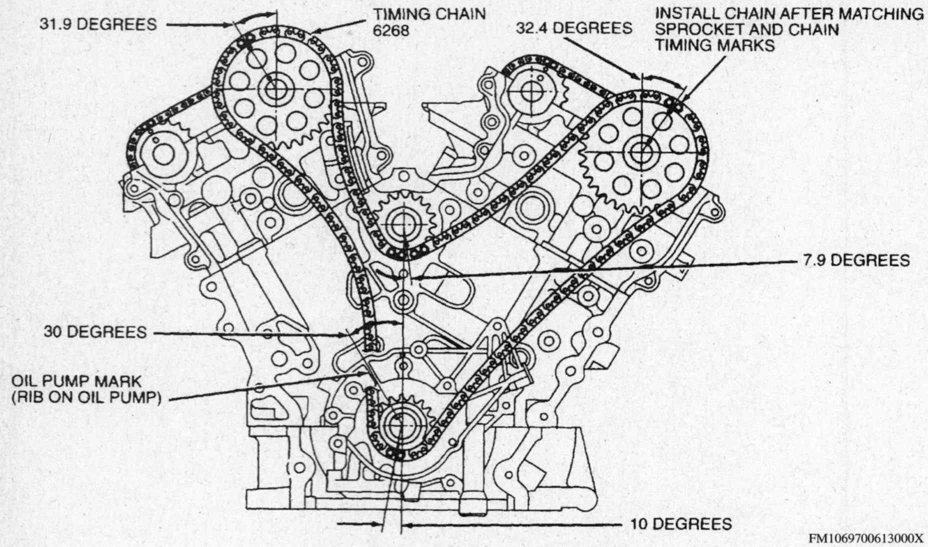

Fig. 15 Timing mark alignment

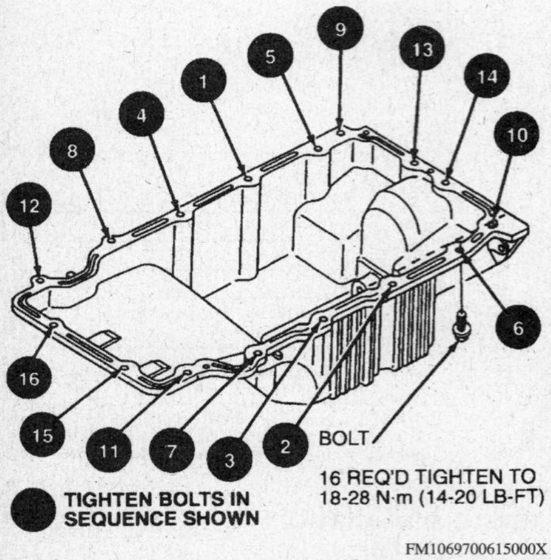

Fig. 17 Oil pan bolt tightening sequence

3. Ensure intake valve clearance at room temperature is .006–.010 inch.
4. Ensure exhaust valve clearance at room temperature is .010--.014 inch.

VALVE ADJUSTMENT

Because hydraulic valve lifters are used in this engine, no periodic valve adjustment is required. However, should any valve train components be replaced or intermixed, clearances on those valves must be inspected and corrected. To adjust valve clearances, proceed as follows:

1. Insert lifter compressor tool No. T89P-6500-A, or equivalent, under camshaft next to lobe and rotate down to depress bucket valve lifter, **Fig. 9.**
2. Insert lifter holder tool No. T96P-6500-AH, or equivalent, and remove compressor tool, **Fig. 10.**
3. Direct a jet of compressed air toward hole in face of valve adjusting spacer to lift spacer off lifter. **Wear eye protection during this procedure.**
4. Determine size of adjusting spacer by numbers on bottom face of spacer or by measuring with micrometer. Install spacer that will provide needed clearance.
5. Install new spacer with numbers facing down.
6. Repeat procedure for each valve by rotating crankshaft as needed.
7. After all valves have been inspected, ensure spacers are fully seated in their lifters.

HYDRAULIC LIFTERS

REPLACE

1. Remove camshafts as outlined under "Cylinder Head, Replace."
2. Remove lifters and valve adjusting spacers.
3. Reverse procedure to install, noting the following:
   a. Lubricate lifters and valve adjusting spacers with engine assembly lubricant part No. D9AZ-19579-D, or equivalent, prior to installation.
   b. Install lifters in their original locations, with valve adjusting spacer numbered sides facing down.

CRANKSHAFT DAMPER

REPLACE

REMOVAL

1. Raise and support vehicle on hoist.
2. Remove righthand front wheel.
3. Remove forward righthand splash shield from front fender apron to access crankshaft damper.
4. Remove accessory drive belt as outlined under "Separated Accessory Drive System."
5. Remove damper bolt and washer from crankshaft.
6. Remove damper from crankshaft using steering wheel puller tool No. T67L-3600-A, or equivalent.

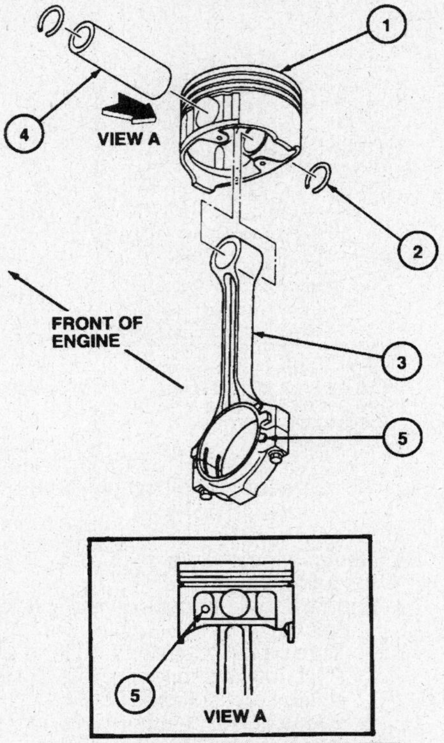

Item	Description
1	Piston, Pin and Ring
2	Piston Pin Retainer (2 Req'd)
3	Connecting Rod
4	Piston Pin
5	Front Mark

FM1069700614000X

Fig. 16 Piston & rod assembly

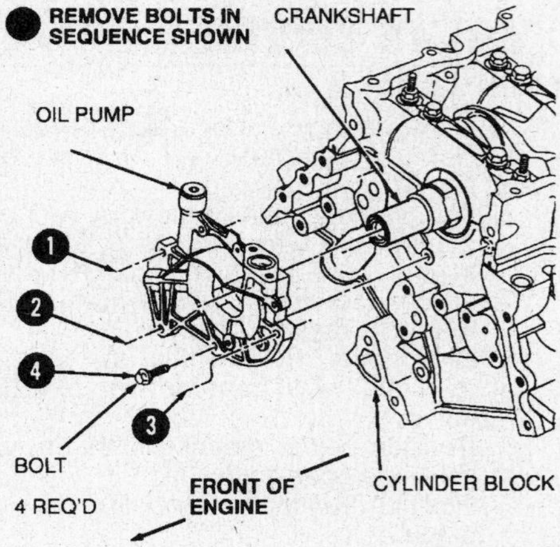

Fig. 18 Oil pump bolt removal sequence

INSTALLATION

1. Clean sealing surfaces with metal surface cleaner part No. F4AZ-19A536-RA, or equivalent.
2. Apply black silicone rubber part No. F4AZ-19562-B, or equivalent, to front

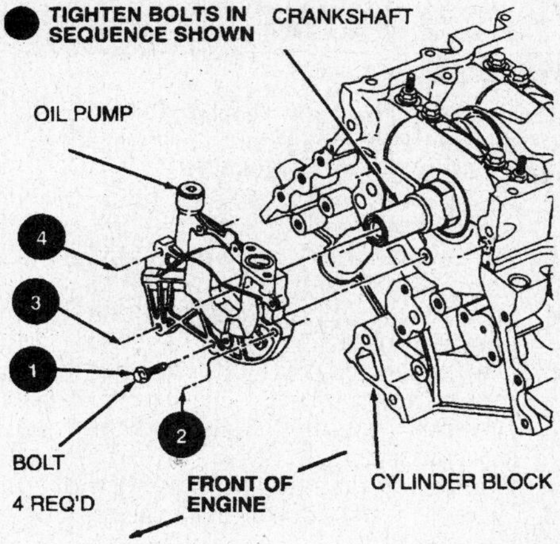

FM1069700617000X

Fig. 19 Oil pump bolt tightening sequence

of crankshaft on inside diameter surface of damper at keyway.
3. Install damper using vibration damper and seal replacer tool No. T82L-6316-A, or equivalent, and crankshaft damper bolt washer.
4. Install mounting bolt and tighten as follows:
   a. **Torque** bolt to 78–99 ft. lbs.
   b. Loosen bolt at least one full turn.
   c. **Torque** bolt to 35–39 ft. lbs.
   d. Rotate bolt an additional 85–95.°
5. Install drive belt and splash shield.

FRONT COVER

REPLACE

1. Remove front cover assembly, **Fig. 11.**
2. Clean cover to engine block and cylinder head sealing surfaces with metal surface cleaner part No. F4AZ-19A536-RA, or equivalent.
3. Apply a .118 inch bead of black silicone rubber part No. F4AZ-19562-B, or equivalent, in eight gasket surface joints and five mounting bosses on engine block, **Fig. 12.**
4. Install front cover with bolts and stud bolts in proper locations, **Fig. 13.**
5. Tighten bolts in sequence, **Fig. 14.**

FRONT COVER SEAL

REPLACE

1. Remove engine front cover as outlined under "Front Cover, Replace."
2. Remove crankshaft front seal using locknut pin remover tool No. T78P-3504-N, or equivalent.
3. Reverse procedure to install, noting the following:
   a. Install new seal using vibration damper and seal replacer tool No. T82L-6316-A, or equivalent.

TIMING CHAIN

REPLACE

1. Remove engine front cover as outlined under"Front Cover, Replace."
2. Rotate crankshaft to place number one piston at top dead center by aligning

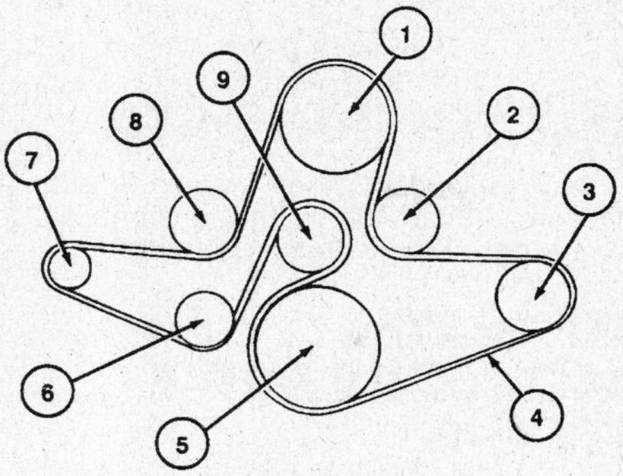

Item	Description
1	Power Steering Pump Pulley
2	Idler Pulley (RH)
3	A/C Compressor
4	Drive Belt

FM1069700618000X

Fig. 20 Accessory drive belt routing

crankshaft keyway groove with oil pump mark, **Fig. 2.**
3. Ensure camshaft sprocket timing marks are on top, and if not, rotate crankshaft one complete revolution.
4. Using a small screwdriver, release tensioner ratchet/pawl mechanism through tensioner access hole.
5. Compress tensioner rack and piston into tensioner housing by inserting a small wire into top of piston, and gently unseat oil check ball. **Compress tensioner by hand, and leave in a compressed state for future installation.**
6. While tensioner is compressed, insert a .060 inch drill bit or wire into small hole above ratchet. This engages lock groove in rack of tensioner, **Fig. 4.**
7. Remove timing chain.
8. Reverse procedure to install, noting following:
   a. Ensure number one cylinder piston is in top dead center position.
   b. Timing chain and sprocket marks must be properly aligned, **Fig. 15.**

CAMSHAFT

REPLACE

Refer to "Cylinder Head, Replace" for camshaft removal and installation procedure.

PISTON & ROD ASSEMBLY

Assemble piston with its front mark, **Fig. 16,** aligned with the connecting rod's front mark. These markings must also face the front of the engine on installation.

Torque new torque-to-yield connecting rod cap bolts in several alternating passes to 30–33 ft. lbs., then rotate an additional 90–120.° After installation, ensure big end side clearance is .006–.012 inch. Maximum service limit is .0137 inch.

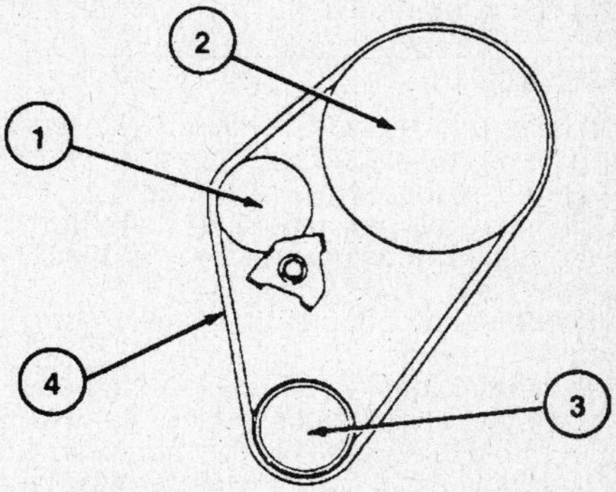

Item	Description
1	Drive Belt Tensioner
2	Crankshaft Pulley
3	Water Pump
4	Drive Belt

FM1069700619000X

Fig. 21 Water pump drive belt routing

MAIN & ROD BEARINGS

Main bearings are available in standard sizes and undersizes of .001 and .002 inch.

CRANKSHAFT REAR OIL SEAL

REPLACE

REMOVAL

This engine uses a one-piece crankshaft rear seal, which must be replaced with the same type. The complete seal is replaceable without removing the crankshaft.

1. Remove transaxle assembly as outlined in "Automatic Transmissions/Transaxles" chapter.
2. Remove flexplate.
3. Position seal remover tool No. T95P-6701-EH, or equivalent, on end of crankshaft, and rotate tool clockwise to thread remover into seal lip until tight.
4. Install impact slide hammer tool No. T50T-100-A, or equivalent, into remover and pull seal from engine block.

INSTALLATION

1. Clean and inspect all sealing surfaces.
2. Lubricate crankshaft flange and oil seal bore with engine assembly lubricant part No. D9AZ-19579-D, or equivalent.
3. Install new seal using seal replacer tool No. T82L-6701-A, and adapter tool No. T91P-6701-A, or equivalents.
4. Tighten bolts in an alternating sequence to evenly seat seal. Ensure seal is flush to rear of block or does not protrude more than .020 inch.

OIL PAN

REPLACE

1. Raise and support vehicle. Drain engine oil into a suitable container.
2. Remove dual converter Y-pipe.
3. Remove oil pan mounting bolts from transaxle housing and engine block, then pan.
4. Reverse procedure to install, noting the following:
   a. After cleaning all sealing surfaces with metal surface cleaner part No. F4AZ-19A536-RA, or equivalent, apply a .16 inch thickness bead of black silicone rubber part No. F4AZ-19562-B, or equivalent, to surfaces where pan, front cover and block meet.
   b. Tighten oil pan bolts to specifications in sequence, **Fig. 17.**
   c. Tighten oil drain plug to specifications.

OIL PUMP

REPLACE

1. Remove timing chain as outlined under "Timing Chain, Replace."
2. Remove oil pump screen cover and tube from pump.
3. Remove mounting nuts and oil pan baffle from lower engine block mounting studs.
4. Remove oil pump mounting bolts in sequence, **Fig. 18.**
5. Carefully remove pump from block.
6. Reverse procedure to install, noting following:
   a. Rotate oil pump inner rotor to align with flat on crankshaft.
   b. Carefully install pump onto crankshaft until seated against engine block.
   c. Tighten pump mounting bolts to specifications in sequence, **Fig. 19.**

OIL PUMP SERVICE

This type of oil pump has no serviceable internal components. If any component does not meet specifications, the entire pump must be replaced.

1. Wash all parts in suitable solvent and dry with compressed air.
2. Ensure all dirt and particles are removed.
3. Inspect inner pump housing for wear or damage.
4. Inspect pump cover mating surface for wear. Scuff marks are normal. If surface is worn or grooved, replace pump assembly.
5. Inspect rotor for nicks, burrs or score marks, and remove imperfections with suitable oil stone.
6. Using a suitable feeler gauge, measure inner tip to outer rotor tip clearance. Clearance should be .0024–.0071 inch.
7. Using a suitable straightedge and feeler gauge, measure rotor endplay. Endplay should be .0012–.0035 inch.
8. If any clearance does not meet specifications, replace oil pump assembly.

BELT TENSION DATA

On these models, belt tension is automatically maintained by the tensioner assembly and no adjustment is required.

SEPARATED ACCESSORY DRIVE SYSTEM

BELT ROUTING

Refer to **Figs. 20 and 21** for drive belt routing.

BELT REPLACEMENT

Accessory Drive Belt

1. Raise and support vehicle.
2. Use a 3/8 inch ratchet on lifting lug to rotate tensioner counterclockwise and engage spring keeper.
3. Remove belt from tensioner.
4. Lower vehicle and remove belt.
5. Reverse procedure to install, noting the following:
   a. Install belt over all pulleys except tensioner.
   b. Raise and support vehicle.
   c. Rotate tensioner and install belt. Ensure V-grooves make proper contact with pulleys and spring keeper has released.

Water Pump Drive Belt

1. Rotate belt tensioner clockwise by hand and remove belt from tensioner.
2. Remove belt from water pump pulley.
3. Reverse procedure to install. Ensure V-grooves make proper contact with pulleys.

COOLING SYSTEM BLEED

1. Select maximum blower motor and heater temperature settings. Set controls to discharge air through instrument panel A/C vents.
2. Start engine and allow it to idle. Feel for hot air at A/C vents.
3. **If air discharge remains cool and engine coolant temperature gauge does not move, coolant level is low and must be corrected. Stop engine and allow it to cool. Add coolant to bring level to top of Cold Fill mark on de-gas bottle.**
4. Start engine and allow it to idle until operating temperature is reached. Hot air should now blow through A/C vents, temperature gauge should rest in Normal range and upper radiator hose should feel hot to touch.
5. Stop engine, allow it to cool and inspect for leaks.
6. When engine coolant level indicator flashes, approximately 1–1½ quarts of coolant may now be added to de-gas bottle after proper refill.

THERMOSTAT

REPLACE

1. Raise and support vehicle. Drain coolant into a suitable container until level is below that of thermostat.
2. Disconnect lower radiator hose from thermostat housing.
3. Remove battery, power distribution box and battery tray.
4. Disconnect upper radiator hose and position aside.
5. Disconnect lower radiator hose at thermostat housing.
6. Remove mounting bolts and thermostat housing.
7. Remove O-ring seal and thermostat.
8. Reverse procedure to install, noting the following:
   a. Tighten thermostat housing bolts in an alternating sequence to specifications.
   b. Fill de-gas bottle until coolant reaches minimum cold fill level.

WATER PUMP

REPLACE

1. Raise and support vehicle. Drain coolant into a suitable container.
2. Remove engine appearance cover.
3. Remove battery and battery tray.
4. Remove drive belt from water pump and pump pulley.
5. Disconnect throttle body supply and return hoses, heater core return hose and oil cooler hose from water pump.
6. Remove thermostat from water pump housing.
7. Remove bolts and collar mounting water pump housing from lefthand cylinder head.
8. Disconnect water inlet and outlet hoses from water pump, and remove water pump.
9. Remove mounting bolt and belt idler pulley from pump housing.
10. Reverse procedure to install, noting the following:
    a. Tighten all fasteners to specifications.
    b. Fill de-gas bottle until coolant reaches minimum cold fill level.

RADIATOR

REPLACE

1. Remove battery and tray.
2. Remove engine appearance cover.
3. Raise and support vehicle. Drain coolant into a suitable container.
4. Remove lower radiator hose shield.
5. Disconnect lower radiator hose at radiator.
6. Disconnect lower transaxle cooler tube from radiator using fuel line disconnect tool No. T90T-9550-S, or equivalent.
7. Remove two lower radiator mounts.
8. Remove front bumper cover.
9. Lower vehicle, remove hood latch support bolts and position support aside.
10. Disconnect upper radiator hose and overflow hose at radiator.

11. Remove power distribution box, harness and bracket, and position box and harness aside.
12. Remove upper radiator support.
13. Remove engine control sensor wiring mounting screws and position wiring aside.
14. Disconnect engine cooling fans from sensor wiring.
15. Remove one nut from power steering/transaxle cooler bracket.
16. Remove three bolts and one stud nut from A/C condenser core.
17. Position condenser core forward and secure it with mechanic's wire.
18. Disconnect upper transaxle oil cooler tube from radiator using fuel line disconnect tool No. T90T-9550-S, or equivalent.
19. Remove both lower radiator brackets.
20. Lower radiator two inches.
21. Tilt radiator forward and lift it clear of vehicle.
22. Reverse procedure to install, noting the following:
    a. Tighten both lower radiator brackets and hood latch support assembly bolts to specifications.
    b. Fill de-gas bottle until coolant reaches minimum cold fill level.

FUEL PUMP

REPLACE

REMOVAL

On these models, the fuel pump is incorporated into the fuel tank sending unit and must be replaced as a complete assembly.

1. Relieve fuel system pressure as outlined under " Precautions."
2. Raise and support vehicle.
3. Drain fuel tank through filler pipe.
4. Remove vent hose clamps at metal lines and hoses.
5. Using fuel line disconnect tool No. T90T-9550-S, or equivalent, disconnect rear fuel supply and vapor tubes at push-connect fittings for fuel filter and base, and fuel tube retainer behind fuel filter and base.
6. Disconnect tank electrical connector at lefthand side of filter and base.
7. Disconnect push-connect fitting at upper righthand rear corner of tank.
8. Place a safety stand under tank and remove bolts at rear of safety straps, allowing straps to swing out of way.
9. **On flexible fuel vehicles,** remove plastic shield and fuel tank as an assembly.
10. **On all models,** lower tank safely to ground.
11. Place tank on workbench and clean any accumulated dirt around fuel pump module mounting flange.
12. Turn retainer ring counterclockwise using fuel tank sender wrench tool No. T74P-9275-A, or equivalent, and remove ring.
13. Pull module sender plate up out of tank until locking tabs are accessible.
14. Squeeze locking tabs together and remove module from tank.

INSTALLATION

1. Apply a light coating of premium long-life grease part No. XG-1-C, or an equivalent, meeting Ford specification ESA-M1C75-BA, on a new O-ring seal to hold in place during assembly.
2. Install O-ring into groove.
3. Install fuel module carefully into tank so that filter, hoses and float rod do not bind. When module is engaged, a distinct click will sound, and two outside locking tabs will engage into retainer.
4. Install tank into vehicle, add at least 10 gallons of fuel and inspect for leaks.
5. Install MFI fuel pressure gauge tool No. T80L-9974-B, or equivalent, as outlined in "Fuel System Pressure Relief" procedure under "Precautions."
6. Turn ignition to Run position for three seconds at least five to ten times until gauge reads at least 30 psi.

FUEL FILTER

REPLACE

1. Relieve fuel system pressure as outlined under " Precautions."
2. Twist push connect fittings at each end of filter until they move freely on tube.
3. Bend and break shipping tab from hairpin clip, and spread two clip legs approximately 1/8 inch.
4. Remove clip from tube and fitting by pulling gently on triangular end.
5. Separate fitting and hose assembly from fuel filter.
6. Install retainer clips in each connect fitting.
7. Loosen worm gear mounting clip and remove filter from bracket.
8. Reverse procedure to install.

TIGHTENING SPECIFICATIONS

Year	Component	Torque/ Ft. Lbs.
1997–99	Access Drive Tensioner Assembly To Alternator Bracket	23–28
	A/C Compressor Mounting	17–27
	Alternator Bracket To Cylinder Block	28–41
	Alternator Bracket To Cylinder Head	17–27
	Alternator To Bracket	28–41
	Balance Shaft Sprocket Balancer	34–42
	Camshaft Bearing Caps To Cylinder Head	①
	Camshaft Position Sensor To Cylinder Head	72–108④
	Camshaft Timing Sprocket To Camshaft	48–70
	Connecting Rod Cap	②
	Crankshaft Damper	③
	Crankshaft Position Sensor	72–108④
	Cylinder Block Bearing Holder	16–22
	Cylinder Head	①
	Cylinder Head Water Jacket Plug	53–63
	Engine Front Cover	14–20

Continued

TIGHTENING SPECIFICATIONS—Continued

Year	Component	Torque/ Ft. Lbs.
1997-99	Engine Front Cover To Idler Pulley	27–38
	Engine Mount Insulator To Subframe	57–75
	Engine Mount Lefthand Front Support Insulator	44–59
	Engine Mount Righthand Front Support Insulator	39–53
	Engine To Transaxle	25–33
	EGR Tube To EGR Valve	19–25
	EGR Tube To Exhaust Manifold	19–25
	EGR Valve mounting	12–16
	Exhaust Manifold Shield	12–16
	Exhaust Manifold Stud	11–19
	Flexplate To Crankshaft	55–61
	Front Axle Wheel Hub Retainer	170–202
	Front Subframe To Body	57–76
	Hood Latch Support	18–25
	Intake Manifold	14–20
	Knuckle To Lower Control Arm	50–67
	Lower Intake Manifold To Cylinder Head	14–20
	Oil Cooler To Cooler Adapter	30–36
	Oil Drain Plug	15–25
	Oil Pan	14–20
	Oil Pump	7–10
	Radiator Lower Bracket	72–108④
	Secondary Air Injection Tube To Manifold	30–33
	Stabilizer Link To Bar	30–40
	Thermostat Housing	72–108④
	Tie Rod End	35–46
	Timing Chain Tensioner Arm To Righthand Cylinder Head	25–39
	Torque Converter	20–33
	Valve Cover Bolts & Stud	72–108④
	Water Outlet To Cylinder Block	72–108④
	Water Pump	14–20
	Water Pump Belt Idler Pulley	7–12
	Water Pump Drive Pulley To Intake Camshaft	7–12
	Y-Pipe To Exhaust Manifold	25–33

①— Refer to “Cylinder Head, Replace.”

②— Refer to “Piston & Rod Assembly.”

③— Refer to “Crankshaft Damper, Replace.”

④— Inch lbs.

Rear Suspension

INDEX

DESCRIPTION

SEDAN

These models utilize an independent rear suspension. Each side consists of a McPherson strut, an upper mount and washers, two parallel lower control arms, a tension strut, a spindle and a stabilizer bar mounted on the strut.

The top of the McPherson strut is attached to the inner body side panel, while the lower end of the strut is attached to the spindle with a pinch clamp and bolt. The parallel lower control arms attach to the underbody with nuts and bolts. The tension strut attaches to the lower part of the spindle and to the underbody, **Fig. 1.**

WAGON

These models also utilize an independent rear suspension. Each side consists of an upper and lower control arm, a shock absorber, a two-piece spindle tension control strut and a coil spring.

The top of the shock absorber is attached to the body side panel by a rubber insulated top mount assembly and to the lower control arms by two nuts. The upper control arm attaches to the crossmember and the upper part of the spindle. The lower control arm attaches to the underbody and lower part of the spindle. The coil spring operates against the lower control arm and is located inboard of the shock absorber, **Fig. 2.**

WHEEL BEARING

ADJUST

The rear wheel bearings are of a sealed cartridge design and are not adjustable.

REAR WHEEL SPINDLE

REPLACE

SEDAN

Removal

1. Raise and support vehicle. Remove tire and wheel assembly. **Do not raise vehicle by tension strut or strut may be damaged.**
2. **On models with rear disc brakes,** proceed as follows:
   a. Remove brake caliper and adapter, and hang them out of way.
   b. Brake rotor and wheel hub.
   c. Remove brake shield and anti-lock sensor.
3. **On models with rear drum brakes,** proceed as follows:
   a. Remove brake drum and brake hose to strut mounting clip.
   b. Remove mounting bolts and brake backing plate. Wire plate out of way.
4. **On all models,** remove control arm to spindle mounting bolts, washers and nuts, tension strut nut, washer and bushing.
5. Remove spindle to strut pinch bolt and spindle.

Installation

1. Position replacement spindle onto tension strut and onto shock strut.
2. Install new strut to spindle pinch bolt. Do not tighten at this time.
3. Install tension strut bushing, washer and new nut. Do not tighten at this time.
4. Install new control arm to spindle mounting bolts.
5. Using suitable jack, raise lower control arm to normal curb height.
6. Tighten spindle to strut bolt, tension strut nut and control arm to spindle mounting nuts to specifications.
7. **On models with rear disc brakes,** install brake caliper, adapter, brake rotor, wheel hub, brake shield and anti-lock sensor.
8. **On models with rear drum brakes,** install brake backing plate, brake hose to strut mounting clip, and brake drum.

WAGON

Removal

1. Raise and support vehicle. Remove tire and wheel assembly. **If vehicle is raised on frame contact hoist, position suitable jack under lower control arm to raise arm to normal curb height.**
2. **On models with rear disc brakes,** proceed as follows:
   a. Remove brake caliper and adapter, and hang out of way.
   b. Remove brake rotor and wheel hub.
   c. Remove brake shield and anti-lock sensor.
3. **On models with rear drum brakes,** remove brake drum, wheel bearings and brake backing plate.
4. **On all models,** remove upper control arms to crossmember mounting nuts and bolts.
5. Remove bolt, one washer, adjusting cam and nut mounting spindle to lower control arm.
6. Remove spindle and upper control arm as an assembly, then upper control arm to spindle mounting nut and spindle.

Installation

1. Install upper control arms to spindle using a new nut. Do not tighten at this time.
2. Position spindle and upper control arm assembly on lower control arm. Install new nut and washer, existing adjusting cam and new nut. Do not tighten at this time.
3. Position front and rear upper control arms to body bracket, and install new nuts and bolts. Do not tighten at this time.
4. Ensure lower control arm is at normal curb height.
5. Tighten upper control arms to body bracket mounting bolts, upper control arms to spindle mounting nut and spindle to lower control arm mounting nut to specifications.

STRUT

REPLACE

SEDAN

1. Position suitable jack or hoist under vehicle, and raise just enough to contact body. **Do not raise vehicle by tension strut, or strut may be damaged.**
2. Working in trunk, loosen, but do not remove, three strut to inner body mounting nuts.
3. Raise and support vehicle. Remove tire and wheel assembly.

4. Remove brake differential valve to control arm mounting bolt.
5. Using suitable wire, suspend control arm to body to ensure proper support after strut removal.
6. Remove brake hose to shock strut bracket mounting clip and position hose aside.
7. If equipped with stabilizer bar, remove U-bracket from body, stabilizer bar mounting nut, washer and insulator. Separate stabilizer bar from link.
8. Remove tension strut to spindle mounting nut, washer and insulator, and move spindle rearward enough to separate it from tension strut.
9. Remove strut to spindle pinch bolt, and using a pry bar or other suitable tool, separate pinch joint as necessary to allow for strut removal.
10. Remove strut from pinch joint and lower vehicle as necessary to allow removal of three strut to inner body mounting bolts loosened previously. Remove strut. **During strut removal, use care not to stretch rear brake hose or kink steel brake line.**
11. Reverse procedure to install, using new mounting parts. Tighten to specifications, in following order: stabilizer link to strut, strut pinch bolt, tension strut to spindle, stabilizer link to stabilizer bar, stabilizer bar U-bracket and strut top mount.

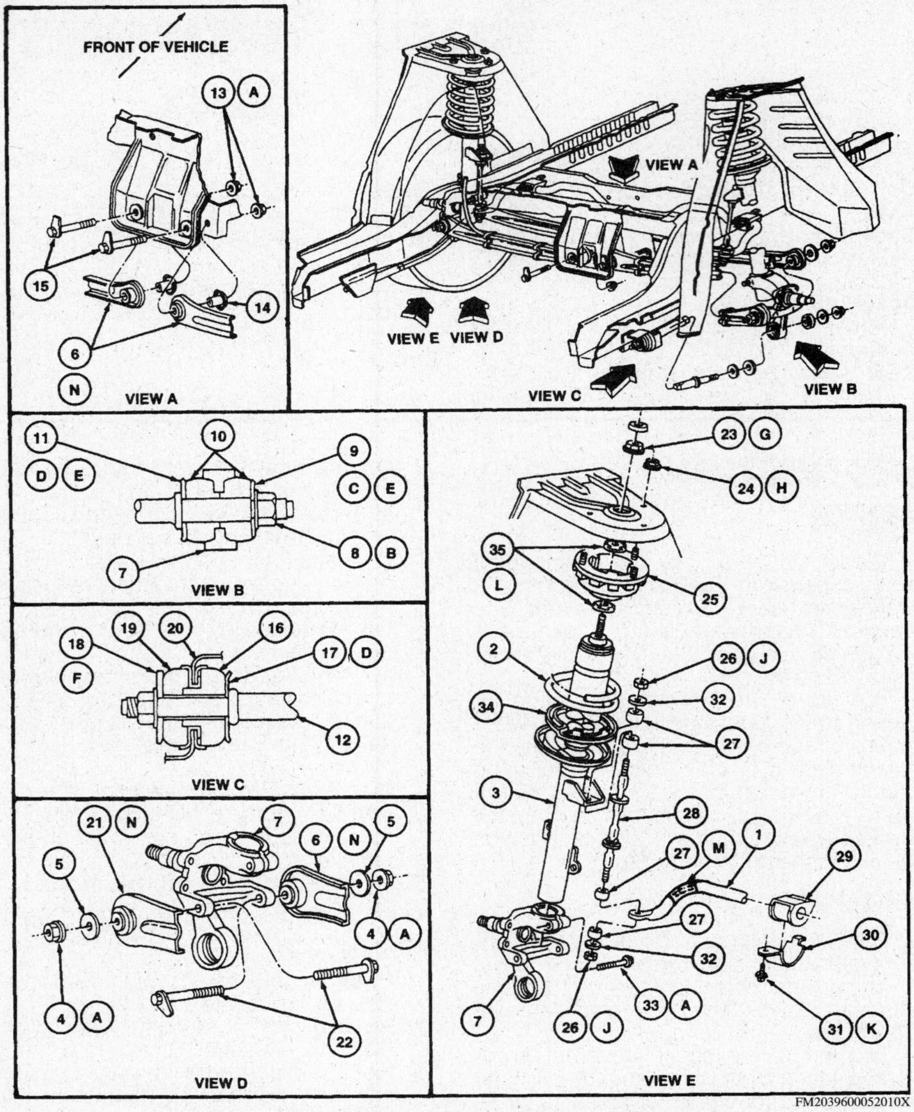

Fig. 1 Rear suspension (Part 1 of 2). Sedan

STRUT SERVICE

SEDAN

1. Remove strut assembly as outlined under "Strut, Replace."
2. Remove mounting nut, washer, insulator and link from strut.
3. Mark location of insulator to top mount. Place strut, spring and upper mount assembly in suitable spring compressor, and compress spring.
4. While preventing strut shaft from turning with a 10 mm six-point deep well socket on top of shaft, remove mounting nut with oxygen sensor wrench tool No. T94P-9472-A, or equivalent. **If strut is to be used again, do not use vise grips or pliers to hold strut shaft as damage will result.**
5. Carefully loosen spring compressor tool, and remove top mount bracket assembly, spring insulator and spring, **Fig. 3.**
6. Reverse procedure to install, noting following:
   a. When installing spring on strut, ensure spring is properly located in upper and lower spring seats, **Fig. 4.**
   b. When tightening strut nut, prevent strut shaft from turning.

TENSION STRUT

REPLACE

SEDAN

1. Raise vehicle on frame contact hoist using lift pads located rearward of front wheels and forward of rear wheels. Raise hoist only enough to contact body.
2. Working inside trunk, loosen, but do not remove, three strut to inner body mounting nuts.
3. Raise vehicle, and remove tire and wheel assembly.
4. Remove and discard tension strut to spindle mounting nut.
5. Remove and discard tension strut to body mounting nut.
6. While moving spindle rearward, remove tension strut.
7. Install new inner washers and bushings on both ends of tension strut, **Fig. 5.**
8. Install tension strut end into body bracket, outer bushing, washers and nut. Do not tighten nut at this time.
9. While moving spindle rearward, install tension strut in spindle, outer bushing, washer and nut.
10. Ensure bushings are properly seated in mountings, **Fig. 5.**
11. Support spindle with suitable jack stand, and working inside trunk, remove three strut to inner body mounting nuts. Install new nuts and tighten to specifications.
12. Remove jack stand, and install tire and wheel assembly.
13. Lower vehicle.

WAGON

Removal

1. Raise vehicle on frame contact hoist.
2. Remove wheel and tension strut to lower control arm mounting nut and bolt.
3. Remove tension strut to body bracket mounting nut and bolt, and tension strut.

Installation

1. Insert front end of replacement torsion strut in body bracket, and install new mounting nut and bolt. Do not tighten at this time.

2. Position rear end of torsion strut in lower control arm and install new mounting nut and bolt.
3. Tighten torsion strut to body bracket mounting nut and bolt to specifications.
4. Install wheel and tire assembly.

SHOCK ABSORBER

REPLACE

WAGON

1. Raise and support rear of vehicle. Remove tire and wheel assembly. **If a frame contact hoist is used, support lower control arm with floor jack. If a twin post lift is used, support body with floor jacks on lifting pads forward of tension strut body bracket.**
2. Loosen shock absorber to lower control arm mounting nuts. Do not remove nuts at this time.
3. Lower vehicle and remove rear compartment access panels.
4. Remove shock absorber top mounting nut, washer and insulator.
5. Raise and support vehicle.
6. Remove absorber to lower control arm mounting nuts and absorber. **The shock absorbers are gas filled and will require an effort to collapse for removal.**
7. If absorbers are to be used again, do not grip their shafts with pliers or vise grips, as this will damage shafts' surface finish and result in fluid leaks.
8. Reverse procedure to install. **Use a new bushing repair kit on top of absorber.** Tighten all fasteners to specifications.

COIL SPRING

REPLACE

WAGON

Removal

1. Raise vehicle on frame contact hoist, and using suitable floor jack, raise lower control arm to normal curb height.
2. Remove tire and wheel assembly.
3. Remove brake hose bracket from body.
4. Remove shock absorber.
5. Install spring cage tool No. 164-R3555, or equivalent, on spring.
6. Remove and discard upper ball joint nut, and separate joint from spindle.
7. Slowly lower rear suspension arm and bushing, and remove spring and its insulators.

Installation

1. Install lower spring insulator on control arm. Ensure insulator is seated properly.
2. Position upper insulator on spring and install spring on lower control arm. Ensure spring is properly seated.
3. Slowly raise suspension arm and bushing, and guide upper insulator onto upper spring seat on underbody.
4. Position upper ball joint into suspension arm and bushing.
5. Install shock absorber, stabilizer bar and bracket.
6. Remove spring cage tool.
7. Install brake hose bracket to body.
8. Install tire and wheel assembly.
9. Lower vehicle and inspect rear wheel alignment.

Item	Description
1	Rear Stabilizer Bar
2	Rear Spring
3	Shock Absorber
4	Nut (4 Req'd)
5	Washer (4 Req'd)
6	Rear Lower Suspension Arm (2 Req'd)
7	Rear Wheel Spindle
8	Nut (4 Req'd)
9	Washer (2 Req'd)
10	Rear Suspension Tie Rod Bushing (4 Req'd)
11	Washer (2 Req'd)
12	Rear Suspension Tension Strut (2 Req'd)
13	Nut (4 Req'd)
14	Rear Suspension Arm Adjusting Cam Kit (4 Req'd)
15	Bolt (4 Req'd)
16	Rear Strut Body End Bushing Inner (2 Req'd)
17	Washer (2 Req'd)
18	Washer (2 Req'd)
19	Bushing - Outer (2 Req'd)
20	Body
21	Forward Lower Suspension Arm (2 Req'd)
22	Bolt (4 Req'd)
23	Nut (2 Req'd)
24	Nut (6 Req'd)
25	Rear Shock Absorber Bracket (2 Req'd)
26	Nut (4 Req'd)
27	Lower Suspension Arm Stabilizer Bar Insulator (8 Req'd)
28	Rear Stabilizer Bar Link (2 Req'd)

Item	Description
29	Lower Suspension Arm Stabilizer Bar Insulator (2 Req'd)
30	Stabilizer Bar Bracket (2 Req'd)
31	Bolt (2 Req'd)
32	Washer (4 Req'd)
33	Bolt (2 Req'd)
34	Rear Spring Center Mounting Insulator (Part of 18080)
35	Washer (2 Req'd)
A	Tighten to 68-92 N-m (50-68 Lb-Ft)
B	Tighten to 47-63 N-m (35-46 Lb-Ft)
C	Stamped Rear
D	Stamped This Side Out
E	Assemble N802855-S36 and N801335-S36 As Shown
F	Assemble 5B536 and 5B537 As Shown
G	Tighten to 53-71 N-m (39-53 Lb-Ft)
H	Tighten to 25-34 N-m (19-26 Lb-Ft)
J	Tighten to 7-9 N-m (62-79 Lb-In)
K	Tighten to 34-46 N-m (25-33 Lb-Ft)
L	Dished-Side Down
M	Color Code Must Be Installed on RH Side Of Vehicle
N	Arm Assemblies Must Be Installed As Shown. Trim Flange To Be Rearward On Front Arms And Left Rear Arm. Trim Flange To Be Forward On Right Rear Arm All Arms Are Stamped Bottom On Lower Surface

FM2039600052020X

Fig. 1 Rear suspension (Part 2 of 2). Sedan

CONTROL ARM

REPLACE

LOWER

SEDAN

Removal

1. Raise and support vehicle, **but not by tension strut and bushing.**
2. Disconnect brake proportioning valve from lefthand side front control arm, parking brake cable and conduit from control arms.
3. Remove control arm to spindle mounting bolt, nut and washer.
4. Remove control arm to body bracket mounting bolt and nut, then control arm.

Installation

1. Position control arm (and cam, where required, **Fig. 6,**) at body bracket, and install new nut and bolt. Do not tighten at this time. **When installing control arms, offset must face up (the arms are stamped "bottom " on lower edge). flange edge of righthand side rear arm stamping must face front of vehicle. Other three must face rear of vehicle. During installation, note that control arms have two adjustment cams that fit inside bushings at control arm to body attachment. Cam is installed from rear on lefthand arm and from front on righthand arm, Fig. 6.**
2. Position outer end of arm at spindle, and install new bolt, washer and nut. Tighten nut to specifications.
3. Tighten control arm to body bracket mounting nut to specifications.
4. Attach parking brake cables and brake proportioning valve to control arms.
5. Lower vehicle, inspect rear toe and adjust as necessary.

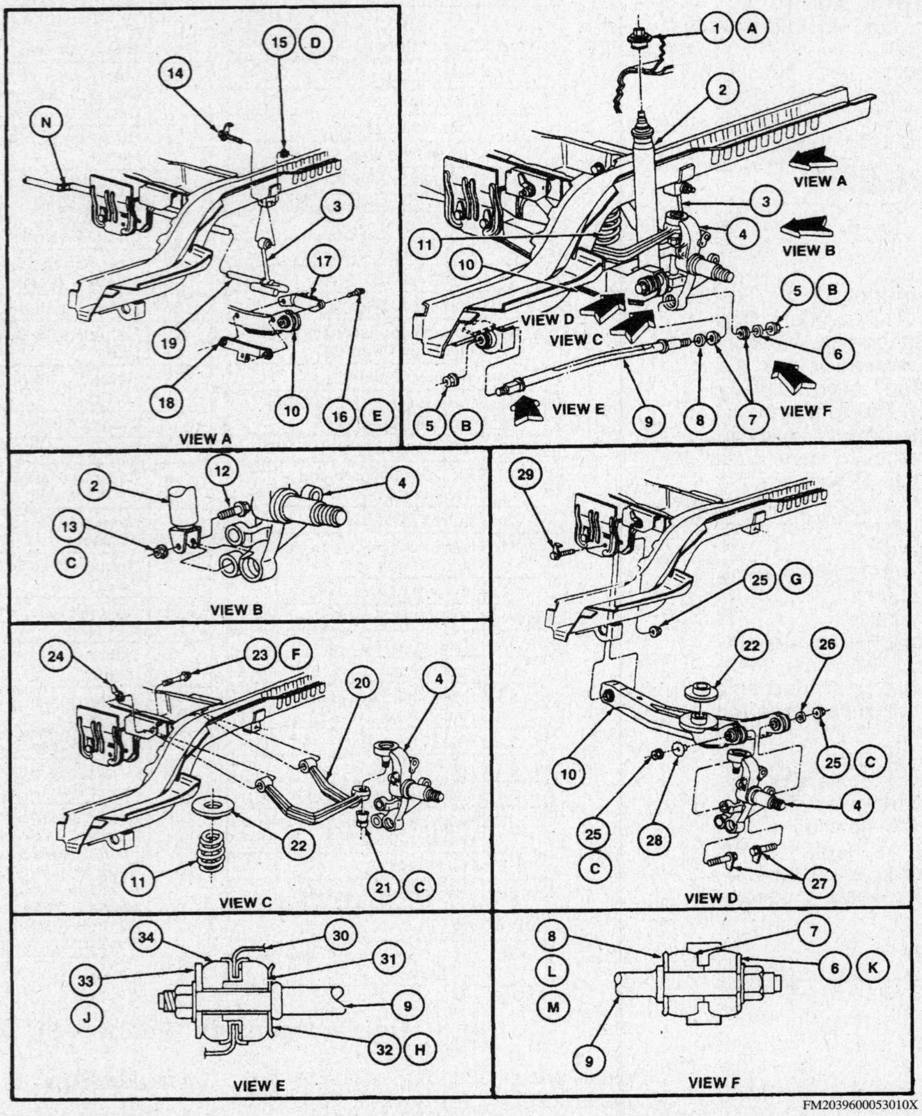

Fig. 2 Rear suspension (Part 1 of 2). Wagon

Item	Description
1	Upper Shock Absorber Nut (2 Req'd)
2	Shock Absorber (2 Req'd)
3	Rear Stabilizer Bar Link and Bushing
4	Rear Wheel Spindle
5	Nut (4 Req'd)
6	Washer (2 Req'd)
7	Rear Suspension Tie Rod Bushing (4 Req'd)
8	Washer (2 Req'd)
9	Rear Suspension Tension Strut and Bushing (2 Req'd)
10	Rear Suspension Arm and Bushing
11	Rear Spring (2 Req'd)
12	Bolt (2 Req'd)
13	Nut (2 Req'd)
14	Bolt (2 Req'd)
15	Nut (2 Req'd)
16	Bolt (4 Req'd)
17	Stabilizer Bar Bracket
18	Nut and Retainer Assembly (2 Req'd)
19	Rear Stabilizer Bar
20	Rear Suspension Arm and Bushing
21	Nut (2 Req'd)
22	Rear Spring Insulators (4 Req'd)
23	Bolt (4 Req'd)
24	Nut (4 Req'd)
25	Nut (2 Req'd)

Item	Description
26	Washer (2 Req'd)
27	Bolt (4 Req'd)
28	Rear Suspension Arm Adjusting Cam Kit (2 Req'd)
29	Bolt (2 Req'd)
30	Body
31	Rear Strut Body End Bushing Inner (2 Req'd)
32	Washer (2 Req'd)
33	Sleeve (2 Req'd)
34	Bushing Outer(2 Req'd)
A	Tighten to 25-34 N·m (19-25 Lb-Ft)
B	Tighten to 47-63 N·m (35-46 Lb-Ft)
C	Tighten to 68-92 N·m (50-67 Lb-Ft)
D	Tighten to 60-80 N·m (45-59 Lb-Ft)
E	Tighten to 19-26 N·m (14-19 Lb-Ft)
F	Tighten to 98-132 N·m (73-97 Lb-Ft)
G	Tighten to 54-71 N·m (40-52 Lb-Ft)
H	Stamped "This Side Out"
J	Assemble 5B536 and 5B537 As Shown
K	Stamped "Rear"
L	Stamped "This Side Out"
M	Assemble N802855-S36 and N801335-S36 As Shown
N	Color Code Must Be Installed On

FM2039600053020X

Fig. 2 Rear suspension (Part 2 of 2). Wagon

WAGON

Removal

1. Raise and support rear of vehicle. Remove tire and wheel assembly.
2. Remove rear spring as outlined under "Coil Spring, Replace."
3. Remove lower control arm to body bracket mounting bolt and control arm.

Installation

1. Position lower control arm in body bracket, and install new nut and bolt with bolt head toward front of vehicle. Do not tighten at this time.
2. Install rear spring as outlined under "Coil Spring, Replace."
3. Using suitable jack, support lower control arm at normal curb height and tighten control arm to body bracket mounting bolt to specifications.
4. Tighten lower control arm to spindle mounting bolt to specifications.
5. Install tire and wheel assembly, and lower vehicle.

UPPER

WAGON

Removal

1. Raise vehicle on frame contact hoist, and using suitable floor jack, raise lower control arm to normal curb height.
2. Remove wheel and tire assembly, then brake hose bracket from body.
3. Loosen spindle to upper control arms mounting nut.
4. Loosen spindle to lower control arm mounting nut.
5. Remove and discard upper ball joint nut, and separate joint from spindle.
6. Remove upper control arms to body brackets mounting nuts and bolts. Ensure spindle does not fall outward.
7. Carefully tilt upper part of spindle outward until upper control arms are clear of body brackets. Wire spindle in this position.
8. Remove spindle to upper control arms mounting nut and upper control arms.

Installation

1. Install upper control arms on spindle and install new nut. Do not tighten at this time.
2. Position upper control arms in body brackets, and install new nuts and bolts. Tighten to specifications. Remove wire from spindle.
3. Tighten control arms to spindle mounting nuts to specifications.
4. Install brake hose bracket on body, and tire and wheel assembly.
5. Remove floor jack and lower vehicle.
6. Inspect rear wheel alignment and adjust as necessary.

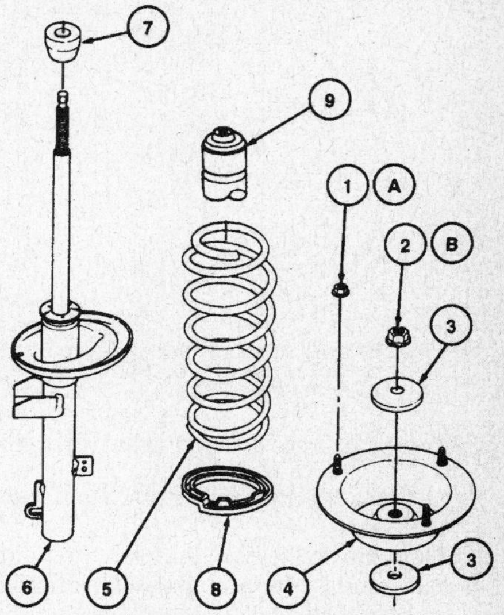

Item	Description
1	Nut (3 Req'd)
2	Nut
3	Washer (2 Req'd)
4	Rear Shock Absorber Bracket
5	Rear Spring
6	Shock Absorber
7	Rear Shock Absorber Jounce Bumper (Part of 18080)
8	Rear Spring Center Mounting insulator (Part of 18080)
9	Dust Boot (Part of 18080)
A	Tighten to 25-34 N·m (19-25 Lb-Ft)
B	Tighten to 53-71 N·m (39-53 Lb-Ft)

FM2039600054000X

Fig. 3 Rear strut & spring components

STABILIZER BAR

REPLACE

SEDAN

1. Raise and support vehicle, **but not by tension strut and bushing.**
2. Remove stabilizer bar to link mounting nuts, washers and insulators from both sides.
3. Remove U-bracket mounting bolts and stabilizer bar.
4. Remove link to strut mounting nuts, washers and insulators.
5. Inspect mounting parts for damage and replace as necessary.
6. Reverse procedure to install. Use new mounting parts, and tighten all fasteners to specifications.

WAGON

1. Raise and support vehicle.
2. Place jackstands under rear suspension arm and bushings so bar links and bushings are neutralized.
3. Remove U-bracket mounting nuts and bolts from either side, and slide

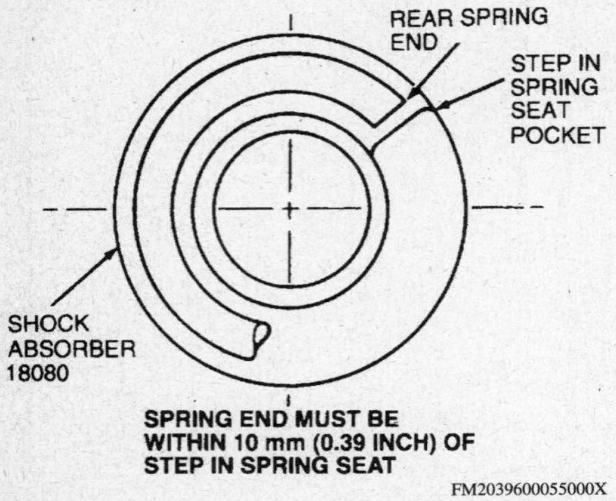

Fig. 4 Spring & seat positioning

U-brackets and insulators from stabilizer bar.

4. Remove link to body bracket mounting nuts and bolts, and stabilizer and link assemblies.
5. Slide link assemblies from stabilizer bar.
6. Inspect all components for damage and replace as necessary.

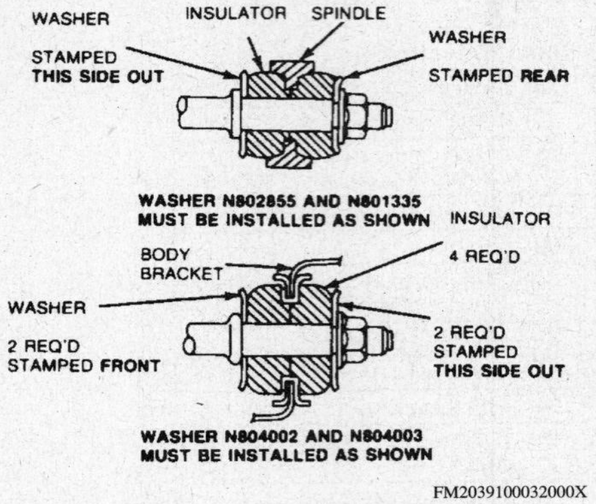

Fig. 5 Tension strut bushing installation. Sedan

7. Reverse procedure to install. Use new mounting parts, and tighten all fasteners to specifications.

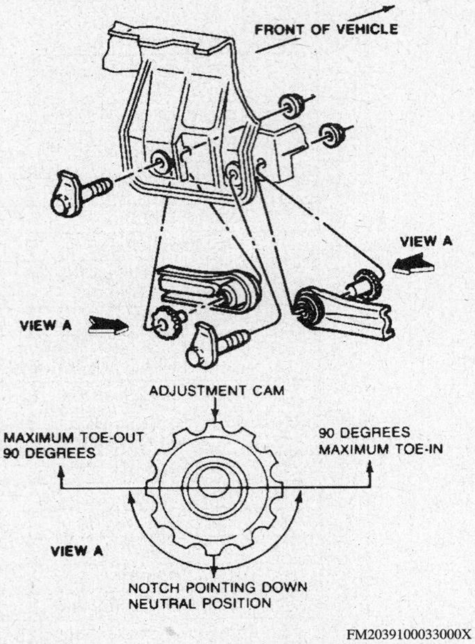

Fig. 6 Lower control arm bushing & cam installation. Sedan

TIGHTENING SPECIFICATIONS

Year	Component	Torque/ Ft. Lbs.
SEDAN		
1997–99	Brake Hose Bracket	9–12
	Control Arm To Body	73–97
	Control Arm To Spindle	50–67
	Stabilizer Bar Link To Stabilizer Bar	60–84①
	Stabilizer Bar Link To Strut	60–84①
	Stabilizer U-Bracket To Body	25–34
	Strut Rod Nut	39–53
	Strut Top Mount To Body	19–26
	Strut To Spindle	50–67
	Strut To Top Mount	35–50
	Tension Strut To Body	35–50
	Tension Strut To Spindle	35–50
	Wheel Bearing	188–254
	Wheel Lug	85–105
WAGON		
1997–99	Brake Hose Bracket	9–12
	Lower Control Arm To Body	40–52
	Shock Absorber To Body	19–27
	Shock Absorber To Lower Suspension Arm	12–20
	Shock Absorber To Lower Suspension Spindle	50–67
	Spindle To Lower Control Arm	50–67
	Stabilizer Bar U-Bracket To Lower Suspension Arm	20–30
	Stabilizer Link Assembly To Body	44–59
	Tension Strut To Body	35–46
	Tension Strut To Spindle	35–46
	Upper Ball Joint	50–68
	Upper Control Arms To Body	70–95
	Upper Control Arms To Spindle	150–190
	Upper Suspension Arm To Spindle	40–55
	Wheel Bearing	188–254
	Wheel Lug	85–105

① — Inch lbs.

Front Suspension & Steering

NOTE: Prior To Performing Any Service Operations Listed In This Section, Consult The "Technical Service Bulletins " Section For Related Information.

INDEX

DESCRIPTION

This suspension is of the gas filled McPherson strut type, **Fig. 1.** The strut top mount consists of a rubber insulated bearing and seat and coil spring insulator. The top mount is attached to the body side apron by three bolts. The lower part of the strut is mounted in the steering knuckle and is retained by a pinch bolt. A forged lower control arm is attached to the subframe and to the steering knuckle. A tension strut is connected to the lower control arm and to the forward part of the subframe.

WHEEL BEARING

REPLACE

1. Turn ignition switch to OFF position and place steering column in unlocked position.
2. Remove wheel hub retainer nut, raise and support vehicle.
3. Remove cotter pin and nut from tie rod end stud. Discard cotter pin and nut.
4. Using tie rod end remover tool No. 3290-D, and tie rod adapter tool No. T81P-3504-W, or equivalents, remove tie rod end from front wheel knuckle. **Do not use power tools to remove nut. Avoid damaging rod boot seal.**
5. Remove stabilizer bar link from front wheel knuckle.
6. Remove disc brake caliper and wire aside.
7. Remove anti-lock brake sensor.
8. Remove and discard lower ball joint nut.
9. Using Rotunda spring compressor tool No. 164-R-3571, or equivalent, compress front coil spring until lower ball joint clears front suspension lower arm.
10. Using suitable special service tools, push front axle from hub.
11. Remove and discard three hub and bearing retainer bolts from front wheel knuckle.
12. **Wheel hub is not pressed into front wheel knuckle. Do not use a slide hammer to remove a stuck wheel hub. Do not strike back of inner bearing race.**
13. If bearing carrier is corroded to front wheel knuckle, apply a rust penetrant part No. D7AZ-19A501-AA, or equivalent, to inboard and outboard wheel hub/knuckle mating surface and allow to soak. Using a suitable pry bar, pry wheel hub from knuckle assembly.
14. Reverse procedure to install, noting the following:
    a. If wheel hub is damaged or if any endplay is detectable, replace wheel hub.
    b. Remove any foreign material from knuckle bearing bore.
    c. Lightly lubricate mating surfaces of bearing and front wheel knuckle.

BALL JOINT INSPECTION

1. Raise vehicle until wheels fall to a full down position.
2. Grasp lower edge of tire and move wheel assembly in and out.
3. As wheel is being moved, observe lower end of knuckle and lower control arm. Any movement would indicate abnormal ball joint wear.
4. If movement is observed, replace lower control arm assembly.

BALL JOINT

REPLACE

The ball joint must be replaced with the control arm as an assembly.

STRUT

REPLACE

1. Place ignition switch in Off position and ensure steering wheel is not locked.
2. Remove hub nut and loosen three strut mounting nuts.
3. Raise and support vehicle. **Do not raise vehicle with lower control arm.**
4. **On SHO models,** disconnect height sensor wiring connector.
5. **On all models,** remove wheel and tire assembly.
6. Remove brake caliper and wire it aside.
7. Remove brake rotor and tie rod end. **Do not use power tools to remove tie rod nut. Avoid damaging boot seal.**
8. Remove nut and stabilizer bar link from strut.
9. Remove lower control arm to steering knuckle pinch nut and bolt, and slightly spread joint and remove lower control arm.
10. Using suitable hub remover/installer, press axle from hub. Wire axle shaft to body to maintain level position. **Do not allow axle shaft to move outward. Overextension of constant velocity (CV) joint could result in separation of internal parts, which could cause CV joint failure.**
11. Remove strut to steering knuckle pinch bolt, spread joint slightly, and remove steering knuckle and hub assembly.
12. Remove mounting nuts and strut assembly.
13. Reverse procedure to install. Tighten all fasteners to specifications in following order: strut to steering knuckle pinch bolt, lower control arm to steering knuckle pinch bolt, stabilizer bar assembly to strut, tie rod end mounting nut, and strut mounting nuts. With vehicle on ground, tighten hub nut to specifications.

COIL SPRING & STRUT SERVICE

1. Compress strut spring with Rotunda coil spring compressor tool No. 164-R3571, or equivalent.
2. Using a 10 mm box wrench, restrain strut shaft, and remove strut mounting nut with suitable 21 mm crowfoot socket. **Do not allow strut shaft to rotate.**
3. Loosen compressor tool, remove strut top mount bracket assembly, bearing and seat assembly, and spring, **Fig. 2.**
4. Reverse procedure to install.

CONTROL ARM

REPLACE

1. Turn ignition switch to OFF position and place steering column in unlocked position.
2. Raise and support vehicle.

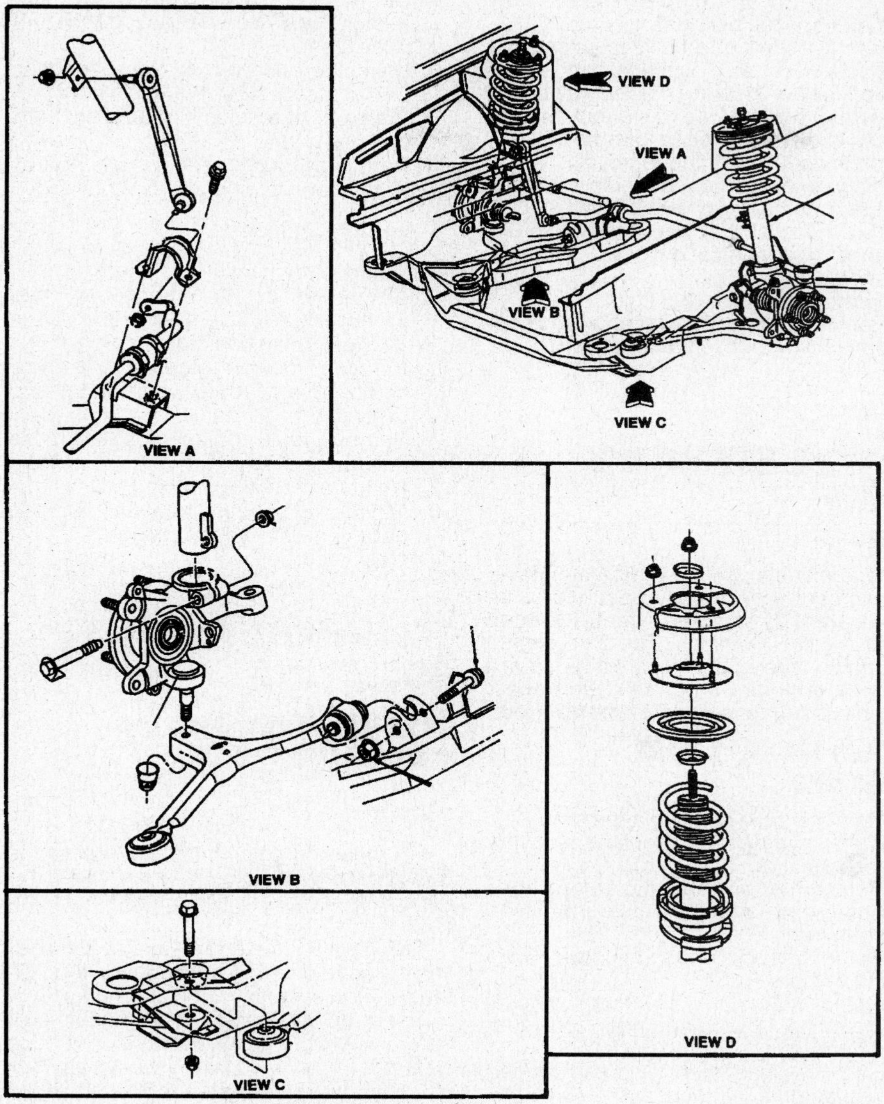

FM2029600112000X

Fig. 1 Front suspension assembly

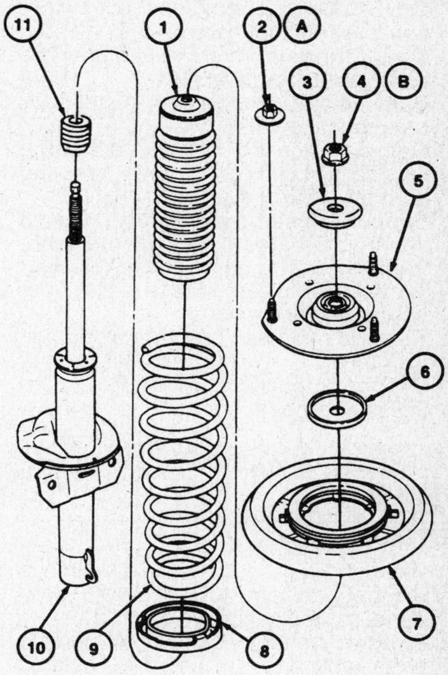

Item	Description
1	Dust Boot
2	Nut (3 Req'd)
3	Washer
4	Nut
5	Front Shock Absorber Mounting Bracket
6	Washer
7	Front Suspension Bearing and Seal
8	Front Spring Insulator
9	Front Coil Spring
10	Front Spring and Shock
11	Jounce Bumper
A	Tighten to 30-40 N·m (23-29 Lb-Ft)
B	Tighten to 53-72 N·m (40-53 Lb-Ft)

FM2029500087000X

Fig. 2 McPherson strut assembly

3. **On SHO models,** disconnect height sensor wiring connector.
4. **On all models,** remove and discard lower ball joint nut.
5. Using ball joint remover tool No. T96P-3010-A and tie rod end remover tool No. T81P-3504-W, or equivalents, separate ball joint from knuckle.
6. Using Rotunda spring compressor tool No. 164-R-3571, or equivalent, compress front coil spring until lower ball joint clears front suspension lower arm.
7. Remove forward lower suspension arm mounting nut and bolt.
8. Remove rear lower suspension arm mounting nut and bolt, and suspension arm from the vehicle.
9. Reverse procedure to install.

STEERING KNUCKLE

REPLACE

1. Place ignition switch in Off position and ensure steering wheel is unlocked.
2. Remove hub nut and loosen three strut mounting nuts.
3. Raise and support vehicle. **Do not raise vehicle with lower control arm.**
4. Remove wheel and tire assembly.
5. **On SHO models,** disconnect height sensor wiring connector.
6. **On all models,** remove brake caliper and wire it aside.
7. Remove brake rotor and tie rod end.
8. Remove nut and stabilizer bar link from strut.
9. Remove lower control arm to steering knuckle pinch nut and bolt, and slightly spread joint and remove lower control arm.
10. Using suitable hub remover/installer, press axle from hub. Wire axle shaft to body to maintain level position. **Do not allow axle shaft to move outward. Overextension of constant velocity (CV) joint could result in separation of internal parts, which could cause CV joint failure.**
11. Remove rotor splash shield.
12. Remove strut to steering knuckle pinch bolt, spread joint slightly, and remove steering knuckle and hub assembly.
13. Reverse procedure to install, noting the following:
    a. Tighten all fastener to specifications in following order: strut to steering knuckle pinch bolt, lower control arm to steering knuckle pinch bolt, stabilizer bar assembly to strut, tie rod end mounting nut, and strut mounting nuts.
    b. With vehicle on ground, tighten hub nut to specifications.

STABILIZER BAR

REPLACE

1. Raise and support vehicle on a hoist, and place safety stands behind front subframe.

2. **On SHO models,** disconnect height sensor wiring connector.
3. **On all models,** remove stabilizer bar link to strut mounting nuts.
4. Remove stabilizer bar link to stabilizer bar mounting nuts.
5. Remove steering gear to subframe mounting bolts and move steering gear off subframe.
6. Support subframe with a second set of safety stands and remove rear subframe mounting bolts. Lower rear part of subframe to gain access to stabilizer bar mounting brackets.
7. Remove mounting brackets and stabilizer bar.
8. Reverse procedure to install. Tighten all fasteners to specifications.

POWER STEERING GEAR

REPLACE

1. Working inside of vehicle, remove steering column tube boot to cowl panel mounting screws.
2. Remove steering column intermediate shaft coupling to steering column lower yoke mounting bolt.
3. Position steering column tube boot out of way and remove steering column intermediate shaft coupling to power steering rack pinch bolt.
4. Remove steering column intermediate shaft coupling.
5. Raise and support vehicle on a twin post hoist. Remove front tire and wheel assemblies.
6. Disconnect exhaust system at dual converter Y-pipe attachment and remove dual converter Y-pipe.
7. Support vehicle with jackstands under rear edge of front subframe.
8. Remove tie rod cotter pins and nuts, and separate tie rod end from wheel knuckles.
9. Remove tie rod from front wheel spindle tie rod. Mark position of jam nut to maintain alignment.
10. Remove nuts from steering gear to front subframe bolts.
11. Remove rear subframe to body mounting bolts.
12. Lower front twin post carefully until rear subframe separates from body, approximately four inches.
13. Remove heat shield push-pin retainers from power steering hose bracket.
14. Remove steering shaft U-joint shield.
15. Remove screw and power steering lefthand turn pressure hose from power steering hose bracket.
16. Remove mounting screws and power steering hose bracket.
17. Remove lefthand stabilizer bar link and disconnect VAPS electrical connectors from power steering auxiliary actuator.
18. Rotate power steering short rack to clear bolts from front subframe and pull left to ease line fitting removal.
19. Place drain pan under vehicle and remove hydraulic power steering pressure hose and power steering return hose from fittings on power steering short rack.
20. Remove stabilizer bar links.
21. Remove power steering short rack assembly through lefthand wheelwell.
22. Reverse procedure to install.

POWER STEERING PUMP

REPLACE

These models use three different power steering pumps. Type CII appears on 3.0L (VIN U, 1 and 2) engines. Type CIII is used on 3.0L (VIN S) engines. The 3.4L engine uses pump type ZUA. **All three types are replaced only as complete assemblies. They have no serviceable components.**

3.0L VIN U, 1 & 2 ENGINES

1. Remove drive belt and alternator.
2. Drain and remove coolant recovery reservoir.
3. Remove power steering return hose from pump and drain fluid into clean container.
4. Remove idler pulley from power steering pump support.
5. Remove power steering bracket mounting bolt from under tensioner mounting.
6. Remove power steering pump support with pump still attached.
7. Remove pulley using pump pulley remover tool No. T69L-10300-B, or equivalent.
8. Reverse procedure to install. Tighten all fasteners to specifications.

3.0L VIN S ENGINE

1. Drain and remove coolant recovery reservoir.
2. Remove drive belt.
3. Remove power steering reservoir pump hose from between pump and reservoir. Drain fluid into clean container.
4. Remove pulley using pump pulley remover tool No. T69L-10300-B, or equivalent.
5. Disconnect power steering lefthand turn pressure hose from pump.
6. Remove three pump mounting bolts and pump.
7. Reverse procedure to install. Tighten all fasteners to specifications.

3.4L ENGINE

1. Remove drive belt.
2. Disconnect power steering lefthand turn pressure hose from pump. Drain fluid into clean container.
3. Remove power steering reservoir pump hose from between pump and reservoir.
4. Remove three pump mounting bolts and pump.
5. Remove mounting nut and pulley.
6. Reverse procedure to install. Tighten all fasteners to specifications.

TECHNICAL SERVICE BULLETINS

STEERING GRUNT OR GROAN

1997

On these models, there may be grunts and groans when the steering wheel returns to its center position during a full right-hand turn.

This may be caused by the steering gear valve sleeve creating a resonance through the steering system.

To correct this condition on models built before July 11, 1996, install a revised hose (part No. F7DZ-3A713-AA) as follows:

1. Remove power steering return hose from steering rack.
2. Remove other end of power steering hose from power steering filter. Be careful not to damage filter.
3. Install new hose with clamp included in package.
4. Fill power steering system with Mercon Multi-Purpose ATF part No. XT-2-QDX, or equivalent.

To correct this condition on models built after July 10, 1996, or on models that the preceding has already be done, replace the power steering gear short assembly (part No. F7DZ-3L547-AA).

TIGHTENING SPECIFICATIONS

Year	Component	Torque/ Ft. Lbs.
1997–99	Control Arm Pivot Bolt	72–97
	Control Arm To Subframe	72–97
	Hub Nut	170–202
	Stabilizer Bar Bracket To Subframe	22–39
	Stabilizer Bar Link Assembly To Stabilizer Bar	35–48
	Stabilizer Bar Link Assembly To Shock Strut	57–75
	Steering Gear mounting Nuts	85–100
	Strut Top Mount To Body	30–40
	Strut To Top Mount	39–53
	Strut To Knuckle	72–97
	Tension Strut To Control Arm	70–95
	Tension Strut To Subframe	70–95
	Tie Rod End To Steering Knuckle	35–46
	Wheel Lug	85–105
1997–98	Control Arm To Knuckle	50–67
	Power Steering High Pressure Hose	25–30
	Power Steering Return Hose	25–30

Wheel Alignment

NOTE: Prior To Performing Any Service Operations Listed In This Section, Consult The "Technical Service Bulletins " Section For Related Information.

INDEX

FRONT WHEEL ALIGNMENT

CASTER & CAMBER

Caster is not adjustable. If inspection shows caster to not be within specifications, inspect vehicle for suspension component damage, deteriorated bushings or distorted body mounting points.

1. Loosen subframe to body mounting bolts.
2. Install a ¾ inch outside diameter pipe or similar tool into lefthand front subframe and body alignment holes, **Fig. 1.**
3. Align lefthand front subframe and body alignment holes, and slightly tighten lefthand front subframe mounting bolt.
4. Repeat previous alignment steps on righthand front alignment holes and inspect lefthand front alignment again.
5. Tighten subframe mounting bolts to specifications.
6. Center punch spot welds on both strut alignment plates and loosen strut mounting nuts, **Fig. 2.**
7. Using Rotunda Spot-Eze, or equivalent, remove spot welds. **Do not drill deeper than thickness of alignment plates.**
8. Remove strut mounting nuts and alignment plates.
9. Remove burrs from strut towers and alignment plates, and paint all exposed metal on strut towers and alignment plates.
10. Install alignment plates and loosely install strut mounting nuts.
11. Align front end and tighten strut mounting nuts to specifications.
12. Drill three ⅛ inch holes as indicated in **Fig. 3,** through alignment plates and strut towers, and paint exposed metal. **Do not drill deeper than ⅜ inch into strut tower.**
13. Install three ⅛ inch diameter pop rivets with a grip range of ¼ inch into alignment plate/strut tower.

TOE-IN

1. Lock steering wheel in straight ahead position using suitable steering wheel holder.

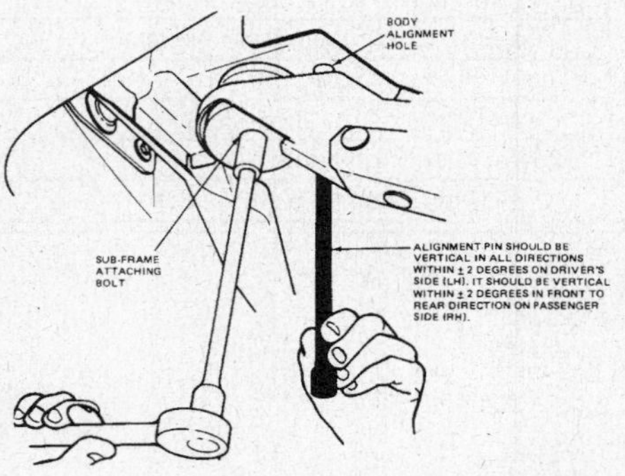

FM2049100028000X

Fig. 1 Front suspension alignment

2. Loosen and slide off small outer clamps from steering boot to prevent boot from twisting during adjustment procedure.
3. Loosen tie rod adjusting, and adjust lefthand and righthand tie rods until each wheel has half the desired total toe specification.
4. Tighten tie rod adjusting nuts and install clamps.
5. Remove steering wheel holding tool.

REAR WHEEL ALIGNMENT

CASTER & CAMBER

The caster and camber angles are factory set and cannot be adjusted. However, rear camber adjustment kit part No. E7DZ-5K751-B, or an equivalent, may be installed to allow for adjustment.

TOE-IN

On sedan models, toe-in is adjusted by rotating the cams located inside the rear inner lower control arm bushings.

On wagon models, toe-in is adjusted by rotating the cams located inside the outer lower control arm bushings.

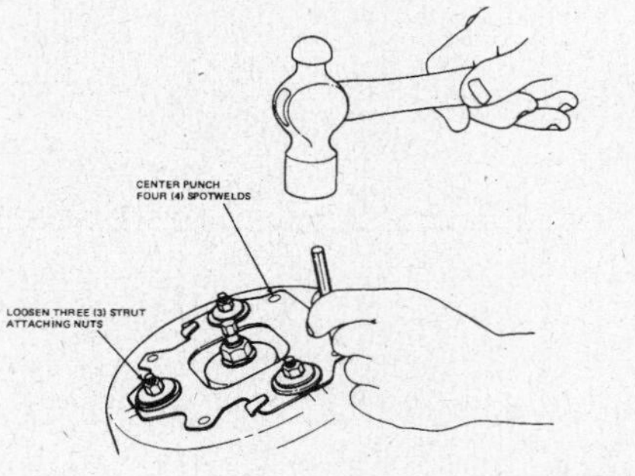

FM2049100029000X

Fig. 2 Alignment plate loosening

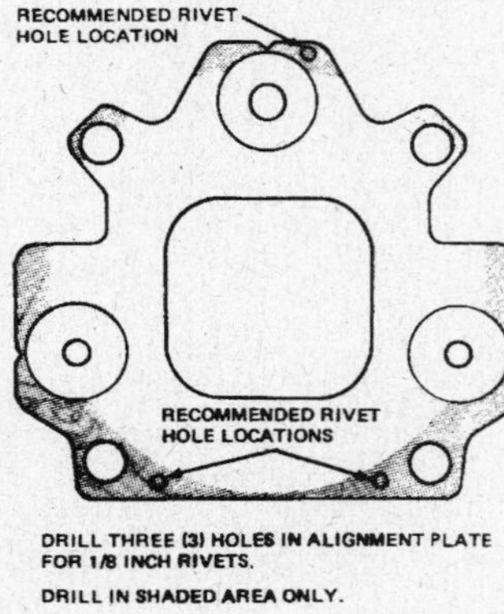

FM2049100030000X

Fig. 3 Rivet hole location

TECHNICAL SERVICE BULLETINS

PREMATURE REAR TIRE WEAR

1997

On these models, the rear tires may wear prematurely on their inner edges. This may be caused by incorrect camber and toe settings.

To correct this condition, install an adjustable rear camber kit (part No. E7DZ-5K751-B). Follow kit instructions.

FOCUS

NOTE: Refer To The Rear Of This Manual For Manufacturer's Special Service Tool Suppliers.

INDEX OF SERVICE OPERATIONS

Specifications

GENERAL ENGINE SPECIFICATIONS

Year	Engine		Fuel System	Bore x Stroke, Inches	Comp. Ratio	Net HP @ RPM	Maximum Torque, Ft. Lbs. @ RPM	Oil Pressure, psi
	Liter	VIN Code①						
2000	2.0L (DOHC)	3	SFI	3.39 x 3.52	9.6:1	130	135	②
	2.0L (SOHC)	P	SFI	3.39 x 3.52	9.35:1	110	125	③

SFI–Sequential Electronic Fuel Injection.
① — The eighth digit of the VIN denotes engine code.
② — Pressure at normal operating temperature should be 19–36 psi @ 800–850 RPM and 54–80 psi @ 4000 RPM.
③ — Pressure at normal operating temperature should be 35–65 psi @ 2000 RPM.

TUNE UP SPECIFICATIONS

Year	Engine/ VIN①	Spark Plug Gap, Inch	Firing Order, Fig.	Curb Idle Speed	Fuel Pump Pressure, psi	Valve Clearance, Inch	
						Intake	Exhaust
2000	2.0L (DOHC)/3	.054	1–3–4–2	②	35–55③	.004–.007	.010–.013
	2.0L (SOHC)/P	.054	1–3–4–2	②	35–55③	—	—

① — The eighth digit of the VIN denotes engine code.
② — Idle speed is electronically controlled and is non adjustable.
③ — Key on, engine off.

FRONT WHEEL ALIGNMENT SPECIFICATIONS

Year	Caster Angle, Degrees		Camber Angle, Degrees		Toe-In, Degrees
	Limits	Desired	Limits	Desired	
2000①	+1.93 to +3.93	+2.93	-1.85 to +.6	-.6	-.17 to +.17
2000②	+1.44 to +3.5	+2.47	-1.87 to +.63	-.62	-.17 to +.17

① — Except wagon.
② — Wagon.

REAR WHEEL ALIGNMENT SPECIFICATIONS

Year	Camber, Degrees		Toe-In, Degrees	
	Limits	Desired	Limits	Desired
2000①	-2.18 to +.27	-.93	+.3 to +.7	+.5
2000②	-1.86 to +.64	-.61	+.14 to +.54	+.34

① — Except Wagon.
② — Wagon.

FLUID CAPACITIES & COOLING SYSTEM DATA

Year	Engine/VIN①	Coolant Capacity, Qts.	Radiator Cap Relief Pressure, Lbs.	Thermo. Opening Temp.	Fuel Tank, Gals.	Engine Oil Refill, Qts.②	Transmission Fluid Man. Trans., Qts.	Transmission Fluid Auto. Trans., Qts.
2000	2.0L (DOHC)/3	5.2–6.1	20	197°F	13.2	4.5	2	7
	2.0L (SOHC)/P	—	20	190°F	13.2	4	2.4	7

① — The eighth digit of the VIN denotes engine code.

② — Including oil filter.

LUBRICANT DATA

Year	Lubricant Type					
	Transmission			Power Steering	Brake System	Hydraulic Clutch Fluid
	Manual		Automatic			
	iB5	MTX 75				
2000	①	②	Mercon V XT-5-QM	③	DOT 3	DOT 4

① — Transaxle fluid meeting Ford specification WSD-M2C200–C.

② — Transaxle fluid meeting Ford specification ESD-M2C186–A.

③ — Power steering fluid meeting Ford specification WSA-M2C195–A.

Electrical

NOTE: On Air Bag Equipped Models, Refer To " Precautions" Located In This Section For System Disarming & Arming Procedures.

INDEX

PRECAUTIONS

AIR BAG SYSTEMS

Disarming

1. Disconnect battery ground cable.
2. Wait at least one minute for RCM back-up power supply to deplete stored energy.
3. Remove driver air bag module as described under "Air Bag Module."
4. Install driver air bag simulator tool No. 418-037, or equivalent, to air bag connector harness side.
5. Remove glove compartment.
6. Disconnect passenger side air bag connector.
7. Install passenger air bag simulator tool No. 418-138, or equivalent, to passenger air bag connector harness side.
8. Disconnect side air bag module under driver's seat.
9. Install side air bag simulator tool No. 418-139, or equivalent, to side air bag connector harness side.
10. Disconnect side air bag module under passenger's seat.
11. Install side air bag simulator tool No. 418-139, or equivalent, to side air bag connector harness side.
12. Access side safety belt retractor pretensioner in driver's side B-pillar.
13. Disconnect side pretensioner electrical connector.
14. Install pretensioner simulator tool No. 418-139, or equivalent, to vehicle harness.
15. Access side safety belt retractor pretensioner in passenger's side B-pillar.
16. Disconnect side pretensioner electrical connector.
17. Install pretensioner simulator tool No.

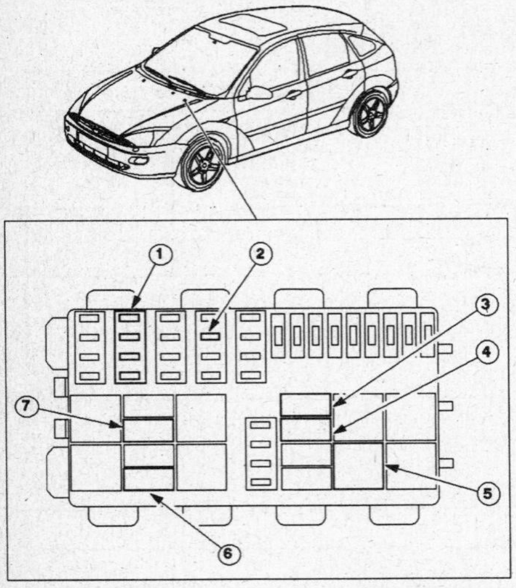

FM9049900301010X

Fig. 1 Central junction box (Part 1 of 2)

418-139, or equivalent, to vehicle harness.
18. Connect battery ground cable.

Arming

1. Disconnect battery ground cable.
2. Wait at least one minute for RCM backup power supply to deplete stored energy.
3. Remove pretensioner simulator tool No. 418-139, or equivalent, from passenger's side of vehicle harness.
4. Connect passenger's side pretensioner electrical connector.
5. Remove pretensioner simulator tool No. 418-139, or equivalent, from driver's side of vehicle harness.
6. Connect driver's side pretensioner electrical connector.
7. Remove side air bag simulator tool from passenger's side air bag connector harness.
8. Connect side air bag module under passenger's seat.
9. Remove side air bag simulator tool from driver's side air bag connector harness.
10. Connect side air bag module under driver's seat.
11. Remove air bag simulator tool from passenger's air bag connector harness side.
12. Install glove compartment.
13. Remove air bag simulator tool from driver's air bag connector harness side.
14. Install driver air bag module as described under "Air Bag Module."
15. Connect battery ground cable.
16. Turn ignition switch to Run position.
17. Air bag indicator lamp should light continuously for approximately six seconds, then turn off.
18. If lamp fails to light, remains lit continuously or flashes, there is an air bag SRS fault and diagnosis will be necessary. **Flashing may not occur until approximately 30 seconds after ignition switch has turned to Run position.**

BATTERY GROUND CABLE

Prior to service, disconnect battery ground cable and isolate as required.

ELECTROSTATIC DISCHARGE

Electronic modules are sensitive to electrical charges. Ensure modules are not exposed to these charges or damage may result.

FUSE PANEL & FLASHER LOCATION

The central junction box is located in the lefthand side footwell, **Fig. 1.**

The fuse box is located under the lefthand side of instrument panel, **Fig. 2.**

FUEL PUMP RELAY LOCATION

The fuel pump relay is located in the battery junction box in the engine compartment, **Fig. 3.**

STARTER

REPLACE

2.0L DOHC ENGINE

1. Raise and support vehicle.
2. Disconnect starter motor electrical connector.
3. Remove mounting bolts and starter motor.
4. Reverse procedure to install, noting the following:
   a. **Torque** mounting bolts to 26 ft. lbs.
   b. **Torque** electrical connector nut to 106 inch lbs.

2.0L SOHC ENGINE

1. Remove air cleaner outlet tube.
2. Remove starter motor mounting bolts.
3. Raise and support vehicle.
4. Disconnect starter motor electrical connector.
5. Remove starter motor.
6. Reverse procedure to install, noting the following:
   a. **Torque** mounting bolts to 26 ft. lbs.
   b. **Torque** electrical connector nut to 106 inch lbs.

ALTERNATOR

REPLACE

2.0L DOHC ENGINE

1. Remove drive belt.
2. Remove cover and disconnect electrical connectors.
3. Remove mounting bolt and secure coolant expansion tank to one side.
4. Secure power steering reservoir to one side.
5. Remove mounting bolt and secure engine wiring loom bracket to one side.
6. Disconnect ground cable.
7. Remove mounting nuts and secure evaporative emission canister purge valve to one side.
8. Remove righthand mounting bolt and fully loosen lefthand bolt. Lefthand bolt cannot be remove at this time.
9. Remove alternator.
10. Reverse procedure to install, noting the following:
    a. **Torque** mounting bolts to 18 ft. lbs.
    b. **Torque** electrical connector nut to 71 inch lbs.

2.0L SOHC ENGINE

1. Remove drive belt.
2. Remove power steering pipe support brackets.
3. Remove exhaust manifold heat shield.
4. Raise and support vehicle.
5. Disconnect alternator electrical connectors.
6. Remove mounting bolts and alternator.
7. Reverse procedure to install, nothing the following:
   a. **Torque** mounting bolts to 35 ft. lbs.
   b. **Torque** electrical connector nut to 71 inch lbs.

Item	Description
1	Fuse F16 (10 A) for dipped beam, left
2	Fuse F17 (10 A) for dipped beam, right
3	Fuse F26 (10 A) main beam, left
4	Fuse F27 (10 A) main beam, right
5	Fuse F22 (15 A) - Dipped beam /daytime running lights
6	Main beam relay
7	Dipped beam relay
8	Headlamp washer system relay
9	Brake light relay
10	Daytime running lights relay

FM9049900301020X

Fig. 1 Central junction box (Part 2 of 2)

IGNITION COIL

REPLACE

2.0L DOHC ENGINE

1. Disconnect spark plug wires from ignition coil.
2. Disconnect ignition coil electrical connector.
3. Remove mounting bolts and ignition coil.
4. Reverse procedure to install. **Torque** mounting bolts to 53 inch lbs.

2.0L SOHC ENGINE

1. Disconnect spark plug wires from ignition coil.

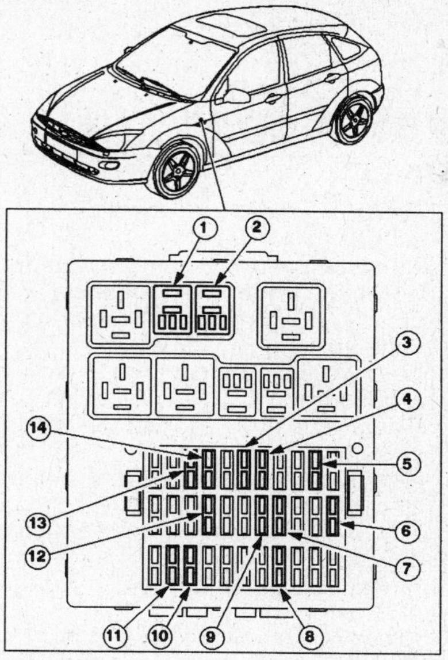

FM9049900302010X

Fig. 2 Fuse box (Part 1 of 2)

2. Disconnect ignition coil electrical and capacitor connector.
3. Remove mounting bolts, ignition coil, capacitor and bracket.
4. Remove mounting bolts, then the ignition coil and capacitor from bracket.
5. Reverse procedure to install. **Torque** mounting bolts to 88 inch lbs.

IGNITION LOCK

REPLACE

1. Remove mounting screws, fastener and instrument panel lower panel.
2. Disconnect steering column upper shroud using a suitable thin bladed screwdriver to release clip on each side.
3. Remove audio control switch using a suitable thin bladed screwdriver to release locking tang and disconnecting electrical connector.
4. Release locking lever, then remove mounting screws and steering column lower shroud.
5. Disconnect electrical connector, then remove mounting screw and passive anti-theft system transceiver.
6. Insert and turn ignition key to accessory position No. 1.
7. Depress detent using a suitable thin bladed screwdriver.
8. Remove lock cylinder.
9. Reverse procedure to install.

IGNITION SWITCH

REPLACE

1. Remove mounting screws, fastener and instrument panel lower panel.
2. Disconnect steering column upper shroud using a suitable thin bladed screwdriver to release clip on each side.
3. Release locking lever, then remove mounting screws and steering column lower shroud.
4. Release clips and remove ignition switch.
5. Reverse procedure to install.

NEUTRAL SAFETY SWITCH

REPLACE

1. Disconnect Transmission Range (TR) sensor electrical connector and selector lever cable.
2. Remove manual control lever. **Shift lever must be held while loosening manual shaft lever.**
3. Remove mounting bolts and TR sensor.
4. Reverse procedure to install, noting the following:
   a. Align TR sensor with alignment tool No. 307-415, or equivalent.
   b. **Torque** mounting bolts to 88 inch lbs.

HEADLAMP SWITCH

REPLACE

1. Remove driver's side lower footwell trim.
2. Remove mounting screws and disconnect lamp switch bezel.
3. Remove mounting screws, disconnect electrical connectors and remove lamp switch.
4. Reverse procedure to install.

AIR BAG MODULE

REPLACE

DRIVER'S

1. Disarm air bag system as described under "Precautions."
2. Turn steering wheel to access and remove mounting bolts.
3. Disconnect electrical connector from air bag module and sliding contact.
4. Remove air bag module.
5. Disconnect contact plate left and right-hand electrical connectors.
6. Reverse procedure to install. **Torque** mounting bolts to 44 inch lbs.

STEERING WHEEL

REPLACE

1. Remove air bag module as previously described.
2. Ensure steering wheel is centered.
3. Remove ignition key to lock steering in position.
4. Disconnect speed control electrical connector.
5. Remove mounting bolt and steering wheel.
6. Reverse procedure to install, noting the following:
   a. Ensure air bag sliding contact is centralized.
   b. **Torque** mounting bolt to 37 ft. lbs.
   c. Turn steering wheel counterclockwise to check location.

Item	Description
1	Rear wiper relay
2	Windscreen wiper relay
3	Fuse F35 (7,5 A) - Interior lights
4	Fuse F36 (7,5 A) - Interior lights
5	Fuse F39 (10A) - reversing lights
8	Fuse F59 (7,5 A) - Direction indicators, electronic module
9	Fuse F47 (7,5A) - left-hand side lights
10	Fuse F54 (15 A) - Brake light
11	Fuse F53 (10A) - reversing lights
12	Fuse F44 (20 A) - Fog lamps
13	Fuse F32 (10 A) for instrument cluster illumination
14	Fuse F33 (15 A) - Hazard warning lights switch

FM9049900302020X

Fig. 2 Fuse box (Part 2 of 2)

STEERING COLUMN

REPLACE

1. Disarm air bag module as described under "Precautions."
2. Center steering wheel, then remove key to lock steering in position.
3. Remove mounting screws and fasteners, then disconnect instrument panel lower panel.
4. Disconnect hood release cable and data link electrical connector.
5. Remove instrument panel lower panel.
6. Remove steering column upper shroud under suitable thin bladed screwdriver to release clips.
7. Release steering column locking lever, then remove mounting screws and steering column lower shroud.
8. Disconnect passive anti-theft system transceiver, wiper/washer switch and air bag sliding contact/speed control electrical connectors.
9. Disconnect ignition switch and turn signal/flash-to-pass switch electrical connectors.
10. Release locating pin and wiring harness, then disconnect wiring harness from steering column.
11. Remove mounting bolt and disconnect steering column pinion shaft extension.
12. Remove mounting nuts, Torx bolt and steering column.
13. Reverse procedure to install, noting the following:
    a. **Torque** mounting bolt and nuts to 115 inch lbs.
    b. **Torque** steering column pinion

shaft extension mounting bolt to 21 ft. lbs.
c. **Torque** hood release cable nut to 15 ft. lbs.

INSTRUMENT CLUSTER

REPLACE

1. Disconnect instrument cluster bezel.
2. Disconnect luggage compartment release switch electrical connector and remove instrument cluster bezel.
3. Remove instrument cluster mounting screws.
4. Release locking tang and disconnect electrical connector.
5. Remove instrument cluster. **Instrument cluster must be kept upright to avoid allowing leaking silicone liquid to leak from gauges.**
6. Reverse procedure to install.

RADIO

REPLACE

1. Install radio remover tools No. T87P-19061-A, or equivalent, into locating holes until they click into place.
2. Pull tools gently left and right until locking tangs release.
3. Slide radio out of instrument panel.
4. Disconnect electrical connectors and remove radio.
5. Reverse procedure to install.

WIPER MOTOR

REPLACE

FRONT

1. Ensure wiper motor is in park position.
2. Lift plastic caps and loosen wiper arm mounting nuts approximately two turns.
3. Lift and release wiper arms from taper, then move to one side.
4. Remove mounting nuts and wiper arms.
5. Remove caps, mounting bolts and air cowl grille.
6. Remove wiper motor protective cap and disconnect electrical connector.
7. Remove mounting bolts, wiper motor and linkage.
8. Mark lever position in relation to assembly plate for installation alignment.
9. Remove mounting nut, bolts and wiper motor from plate and lever.
10. Reverse procedure to install, noting the following:
    a. Ensure wiper motor is in park position.
    b. **Torque** wiper motor mounting bolts to 71 inch lbs.
    c. **Torque** linkage bolt to 15 ft. lbs.
    d. Fit guide pins before fitting mounting bolts when installing wiper linkage.
    e. Ensure wiper blades do not touch air cowl griller or molding.
    f. Check wiper operation.

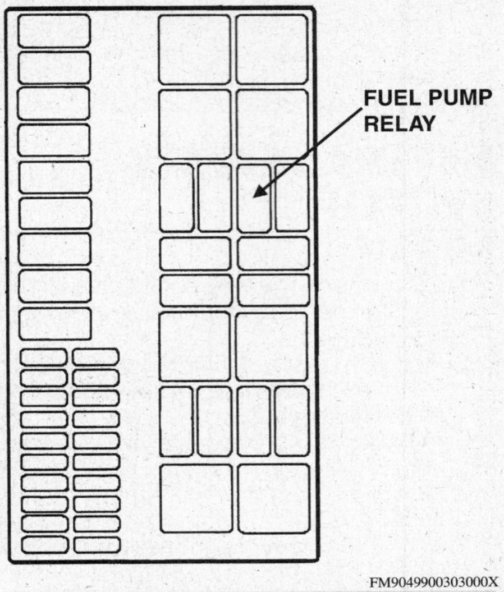

Fig. 3 Battery junction box

REAR

1. Ensure wiper motor is in park position.
2. Lift plastic caps and loosen wiper arm mounting nuts approximately two turns.
3. Lift and release wiper arms from taper, then move to one side.
4. Remove mounting nuts and wiper arms.
5. Remove two mounting bolts and 10 clips, then the cover.
6. Disconnect wiper motor electrical connector and ground lead.
7. Remove mounting bolts and wiper motor from bracket.
    a. Ensure wiper motor is in park position.
    b. **Torque** wiper motor mounting bolts to 71 inch lbs.
    c. Check wiper operation.

BLOWER MOTOR

REPLACE

1. Remove passenger side footwell lower trim.
2. Disconnect floor level ventilation hose.
3. Disconnect electrical connect.
4. Remove mounting screws and blower motor.
5. Reverse procedure to install.

CABIN AIR FILTER

REPLACE

1. Position wipers vertically.
2. Remove caps, mounting screws and passenger side of air cowl grille.
3. Open flap and remove filter.
4. Reverse procedure to install, noting the following:
    a. Ensure filter is installed in correct direction flow.
    b. Clean grille rubber edging between wiper motor and filter housing.
    c. Ensure air cowl grille gasket is seated correctly.

HEATER CORE

REPLACE

1. Remove radio as previously described.
2. Recover air conditioning refrigerant as described under "Air Conditioning."
3. Drain cooling system into suitable container.
4. Remove steering column as previously described.
5. Remove instrument cluster as previously described.
6. Remove floor console front mounting screws.
7. Remove center console rear cup holder insert.
8. Remove center console mounting nuts.
9. Remove park brake shroud from handle and disconnect from center console.
10. Raise parking brake control lever fully.
11. **On models equipped with manual transaxle,** place gearshift lever in neutral position.
12. **On all models,** remove center console.
13. Remove radio as previously described.
14. Remove mounting bolts and glove compartment.
15. Remove passenger air bag module.
16. Remove mounting screws, then disconnect clips, bezel and climate control/radio bezel.
17. Disconnect electrical connectors and cables, then remove climate control/radio bezel.
18. Remove mounting screws and heater core housing assembly panel.
19. Install mounting bolt finger tight and remove instrument panel mounting clips using suitable fork lever with pad.
20. Remove instrument panel side mounting bolts.
21. Remove mounting bolts and glove compartment catch.
22. Remove instrument panel mounting bolts.
23. Disconnect defroster tubes, cable clips and instrument panel.
24. Remove instrument panel.
25. Disconnect heat exchanger coolant hoses.
26. Disconnect evaporator refrigerant lines using fluid pipe remover tool No. T83P-19623-C, or equivalent.
27. Remove cap and cross vehicle beam mounting bolt.
28. Disconnect and remove ventilation hoses from cross vehicle beam righthand side.
29. Remove mounting screws and disconnect wiring harness from cross vehicle beam righthand side.
30. Disconnect and remove ventilation hoses from cross vehicle beam lefthand side.

31. Disconnect central junction box from cross vehicle beam.
32. Disconnect wiring harness from cross vehicle beam lefthand side.
33. Remove ventilation hose and disconnect wiring harness from cross vehicle beam center.
34. Remove mounting bolts and brackets, then the cross vehicle beam.
35. Remove rear footwell ventilation hoses.
36. Disconnect wiring harness from heater housing.
37. Remove mounting nuts and housing. Two of the four nuts are in the engine compartment.
38. Disconnect floor level ventilation hose.
39. Remove mounting bolts and seven retaining tangs, then separate housing parts.
40. Remove heat exchanger.
41. Remove mounting bolts and four retaining tangs, then separate heater/blower housing parts.
42. Remove nine retaining tangs and separate blower/recirculated air housing parts.
43. Remove five retaining tangs and separate air recirculating housing.
44. Remove air deflector.
45. Remove 11 retaining tangs and separate heater/evaporator housing.
46. Reverse procedure to install, noting the following.
    a. **Torque** passenger compartment mounting nuts to 80 inch lbs.
    b. **Torque** engine compartment mounting nuts to 62 inch lbs.
    c. **Torque** cross vehicle beam bracket mounting bolts to 12 ft. lbs.
    d. **Torque** cross vehicle beam mounting screws to 15 ft. lbs.
    e. Install new O-rings lubricated with suitable refrigerant oil.
    f. Fill air conditioning system with suitable refrigerant.
    g. Fill cooling system with suitable coolant.

EVAPORATOR CORE

REPLACE

Refer to" Heater Core, Replace" for evaporator core replacement.

2.0L DOHC Engine

NOTE: On Air Bag Equipped Models, Refer To "Electrical" Section Of This Chapter For System Disarming & Arming Procedures.

INDEX

PRECAUTIONS

AIR BAG SYSTEMS

Refer to "Electrical" section of this chapter for system disarming and arming procedures.

BATTERY GROUND CABLE

Prior to service, disconnect battery ground cable and isolate as required.

FUEL SYSTEM PRESSURE RELIEF

1. Remove fuel pump fuse.
2. Start and run engine until it stalls.
3. Crank engine for approximately five seconds to ensure fuel supply manifold pressure has been relieved.
4. Install fuel pump fuse.

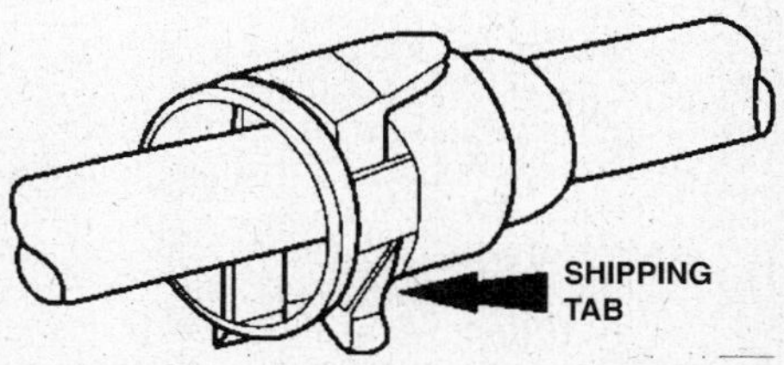

Fig. 1 R-clip connection

QUICK DISCONNECT HOSES

RA-CLIP

When working with R-clip type connections, **Fig. 1,** do not use tools to disconnect. Use of tools may deform clip components and could cause leaks.

To disconnect, bend shipping tab downward, **Fig. 1.** Spread R-clip and push clip into fitting. Separate fitting from tube.

To install, first inspect fitting and tube for damage and ensure connections are clean. Apply a light coat of clean 5W–30 motor oil to male end of tube. Insert R-clip into fitting. Align tube and fitting, then insert tube into fitting and push together until a click is heard. Pull on connection to ensure it is fully engaged.

SPRING LOCK

When working with spring lock type connections, **Fig. 2,** spring lock tool set No. T84L–19623–B, or equivalent, must be used to disconnect fittings. When connecting spring lock type fittings, inspect and clean both coupling ends. Lubricate fuel

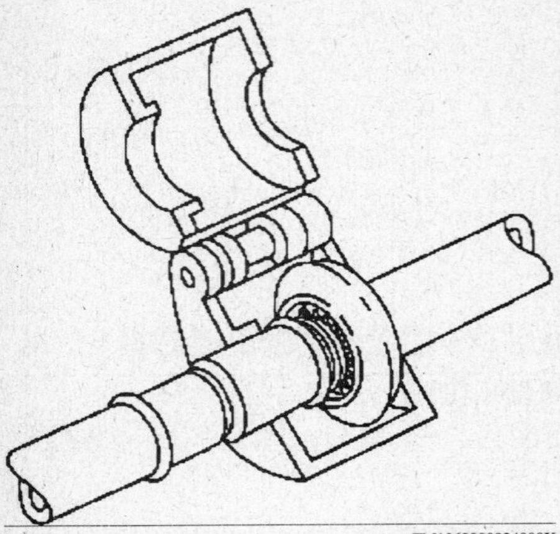

FM1069900924000X

Fig. 2 Spring lock connection

line O-ring seals with clean 5W–30 motor oil. When connection is made, pull on line to ensure it is fully engaged.

VAPOR TUBE

To disconnect vapor tube connections, squeeze fitting (1) and disconnect vapor tube from fitting (2), **Fig. 3.** To connect, ensure fittings are clean and free from damage. Push tube onto fitting until it snaps into place. Pull on connection to verify fitting is secure.

COMPRESSION PRESSURE

Before performing compression test, ensure the following conditions are met: crankcase oil is of correct viscosity and at correct level, ensure battery is fully charged and engine is at normal operating temperature.

1. Turn ignition switch to off position.
2. Remove all spark plugs.
3. Set throttle plates to wide open position.
4. Install a suitable compression gauge in No. 1 cylinder.
5. Install an auxiliary starter switch in starting circuit.
6. With ignition switch off, use auxiliary starter switch to crank engine a minimum of five compression strokes.
7. Note number of compression strokes necessary to reach highest reading and record highest reading.
8. Repeat test on each cylinder, cranking engine same number of compression strokes.
9. Indicated compression pressures are considered within specifications if lowest reading cylinder is within 75 percent of highest reading.

ENGINE

REPLACE

1. Ensure engine is cool, then open coolant expansion tank.
2. Remove battery, then the battery tray and ground cable.
3. Disconnect MAF sensor and PCV hose from air cleaner housing.
4. Remove air cleaner housing.
5. Disconnect all body ground cables as required.
6. Remove air cleaner intake hose from core support.
7. Drain engine coolant into a suitable container.
8. Loosen right and left suspension strut center nuts five turns. Use a suitable allen key to prevent strut piston rod from turning.
9. Loosen right and left front wheel nuts.
10. **On models equipped with manual transaxle,** move shift lever to neutral position, then remove shift lever cover and attach gearshift alignment tool No. T97P–7025–A, or equivalent, to gearshift lever.
11. **On all models,** disconnect speed control and accelerator cables.
12. Disconnect the following connectors:
    a. Ignition coil.
    b. Radio interference filter.
    c. Heated oxygen sensor.
    d. Cooling fan.
    e. Fuel injector wiring.
    f. Alternator and engine harness.
13. **On models equipped with manual transaxle,** disconnect reverse lamp switch, then the high pressure line from clutch slave cylinder.
14. **On all models,** disconnect vehicle speed sensor and CKP sensor.
15. Remove air deflector and cooling fan.
16. Disconnect engine vacuum hoses.
17. Relieve fuel pressure as outlined under "Precautions. "
18. Disconnect fuel lines, then the heater hoses.
19. **On models equipped with automatic transaxle,** proceed as follows:
    a. Disconnect selector lever cable from transaxle.
    b. Remove selector cable bracket.
    c. Mark location of transaxle cooling lines, then remove.
20. **On models equipped with manual transaxle,** proceed as follows:
    a. Disconnect shift cable from gear lever.
    b. Pretension the abutment collars by turning counterclockwise and remove cable assembly from bracket.
    c. Disconnect selector cable from selector lever.
    d. Pretension abutment collars by turning counterclockwise and remove cable assembly from bracket.
    e. Release adjustment mechanism by pressing inward.
21. **On all models,** raise and support vehicle.
22. Remove drive belt cover.
23. Disconnect power steering pressure switch, then remove accessory drive belt.
24. **On models equipped with A/C** remove compressor from mounting bracket, then attach to radiator crossmember.
25. **On all models,** disconnect coolant hose, then remove power steering pump attaching bolts.

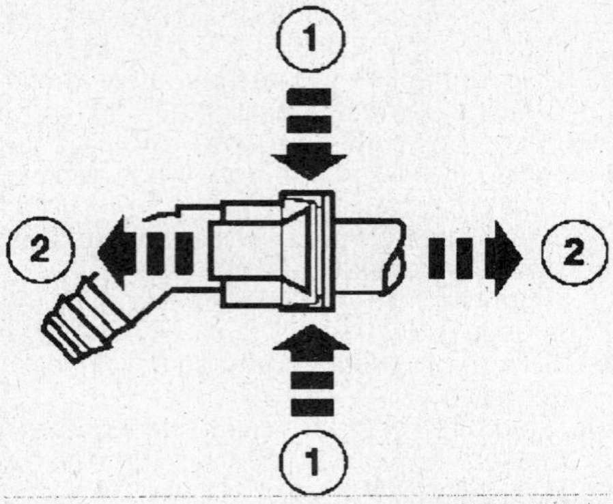

FM1069900925000X

Fig. 3 Vapor tube connection

26. Lower vehicle, then disconnect power steering high pressure line.
27. Remove power steering pump, then the coolant expansion tank and position aside.
28. Remove power steering reservoir and position aside.
29. Raise and support vehicle.
30. Remove flexible exhaust pipe.
31. Remove engine roll restrictor.
32. Remove front wheels.
33. Remove lower ball joint attaching bolts, then disconnect lower ball joint from steering knuckle.
34. Disconnect intermediate shaft bearing cap and discard nuts and bearing cap. **Ensure inner joint is not bent more than 18° and outer joint is not bent more than 45°.**
35. Pull intermediate shaft with front halfshaft from transmission and support using suitable mechanics wire.
36. Remove lefthand driveshaft from transaxle and support using suitable mechanics wire.
37. Install differential plug tool No. 205–164, or equivalent, to both sides of differential.
38. Place assembly table with wooden blocks under vehicle, then lower vehicle until engine and transmission assembly is on assembly stand.
39. Secure engine and transmission assembly to assembly stand using a suitable safety strap.
40. Remove rear engine mount, then the front engine mount.
41. Raise and support vehicle.
42. Install engine lift brackets tool No. T70P–6000 and spreader bar tool No. D93P–6001–A3, or equivalents to engine.
43. Attaching a suitable lifting crane to spreader bar.
44. Remove starter motor and ground cable.
45. Remove engine to transmission attaching bolts, then separate engine from transmission.
46. Reverse procedure to install noting the following:
    a. When installing front driveshafts, use new snap rings, center bearing caps and bolts. Right halfshaft

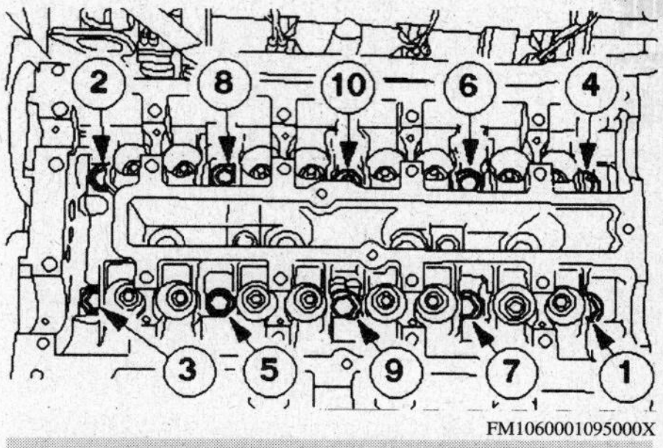

Fig. 4 Cylinder head bolt loosening sequence

should be installed first, then the left.

b. **On models equipped with manual transaxle,** bleed hydraulic clutch system.

c. **On all models,** fill all fluids to proper level and inspect for leaks.

INTAKE MANIFOLD

REPLACE

1. Relieve fuel system pressure as outlined under " Precautions."
2. Disconnect MAF sensor electrical connector, crankcase ventilation hose and air intake hose from air cleaner housing.
3. Remove air cleaner housing from engine compartment.
4. Disconnect accelerator cable and speed control cable from throttle body.
5. Remove EGR valve and EGR pipe bracket.
6. Disconnect vacuum hoses from throttle body.
7. Disconnect fuel injector and Camshaft Position (CMP) sensor electrical connectors.
8. Remove fuel line from throttle body.
9. Remove intake manifold studs from front of engine.
10. Remove intake manifold attaching bolts and nuts, then the intake manifold.
11. Reverse procedure to install. Tighten bolts, nuts and studs to specification.

EXHAUST MANIFOLD

REPLACE

1. Raise and support vehicle.
2. Remove exhaust manifold bracket, then disconnect heated oxygen sensor electrical connectors.
3. Lower vehicle and remove heat shield from side of engine.
4. Remove air cleaner housing and air inlet hose.
5. Remove catalytic converter to exhaust manifold attaching bolts.
6. Remove exhaust manifold to cylinder head attaching bolts, then the exhaust manifold.
7. Reverse procedure to install.

CYLINDER HEAD

REPLACE

When cleaning cylinder head surfaces, do not use metal scrapers, wires brushes, power abrasive discs or other abrasive methods to clean sealing surfaces. Use only a plastic scraping tool to remove all traces of gasket material.

Cylinder head bolts are of torque-to-yield style and must be replaced when removed.

1. Raise and support vehicle, then drain cooling system.
2. Disconnect brake booster pipe from intake manifold, then the oil pressure switch connector.
3. Lower vehicle and remove intake manifold as outlined under " Intake Manifold, Replace."
4. Remove exhaust manifold heat shield, then the catalytic converter to exhaust manifold attaching bolts.
5. Remove thermostat housing attaching bolts, then the thermostat housing.
6. Remove power steering pipe bracket and oil level indicator tube.
7. Remove timing belt as outlined under "Timing Belt, Replace."
8. Remove camshafts as outlined under "Camshaft, Replace. "
9. Remove power steering pump from its bracket and position aside.
10. Remove alternator from bracket and position aside.
11. Remove upper bolt from alternator bracket.
12. Remove cylinder head attaching bolts in sequence, **Fig. 4.**
13. Remove cylinder head.
14. Reverse procedure to install, noting the following:
    a. Ensure sealing surface and bolt holes are clean.
    b. Using sequence shown in **Fig. 5,** tighten cylinder head bolts in three steps. First step, **torque** bolts to 15 ft. lbs.; second step, **torque** bolts to 29.5 ft. lbs.; third step, tighten bolts an additional 90.°

VALVE COVER

REPLACE

1. Remove air inlet hose from throttle body and air cleaner housing.
2. Remove timing belt upper cover attaching bolts, then the upper cover.
3. Disconnect spark plug connectors and the crankcase ventilation hose.
4. Remove valve cover attaching bolts, then the valve cover.
5. Reverse procedure to install.

VALVE CLEARANCE SPECIFICATIONS

Valve	Clearance, Inches
Intake	.004–.007
Exhaust	.010–.013

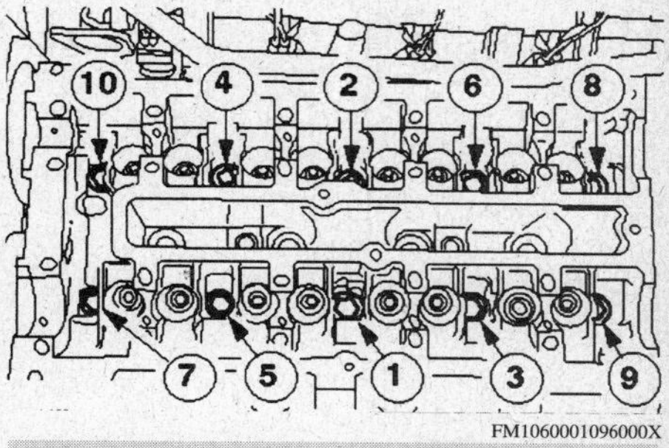

Fig. 5 Cylinder head bolt tightening sequence

VALVE ADJUSTMENT

1. Remove valve cover as outlined under "Valve Cover, Replace."
2. Turn crankshaft to TDC on No. 1 cylinder.
3. Measure valve clearance on No. 1 cylinder, using a suitable feeler gauge.
4. Rotate engine 180°, then measure valve clearance on No. 3 cylinder.
5. Rotate engine 180°, then measure valve clearance on No. 4 cylinder.
6. Rotate engine 180°, then measure valve clearance on No. 2 cylinder.
7. If valve adjustment is necessary, remove camshafts as outlined under "Camshaft, Replace."
8. Each tappet is marked with a number that indicates its thickness in millimeters.
9. To determine correct size tappet needed add tappet size to measured clearance.
10. Select and install a tappet that will bring clearance within specifications, refer to "Valve Clearance Specifications."
11. Install camshafts as outlined under "Camshaft, Replace. "

CRANKSHAFT DAMPER

REPLACE

1. Raise and support vehicle.
2. Remove serpentine drive belt as outlined under " Serpentine Drive Belt."
3. Remove crankshaft pulley/vibration damper.
4. Reverse procedure to install.

TIMING BELT

REPLACE

REMOVAL

1. Raise and support vehicle.
2. Remove serpentine drive belt as outlined under " Serpentine Drive Belt."
3. Remove crankshaft pulley/vibration damper.
4. Remove lower timing belt cover.
5. Lower vehicle, then remove coolant expansion tank and position aside.
6. Remove power steering fluid reservoir and position aside.
7. Position a suitable jack with a wooden

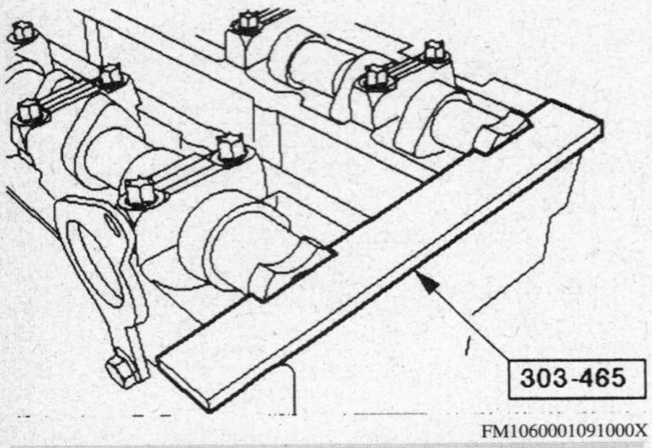

Fig. 6 Camshaft alignment

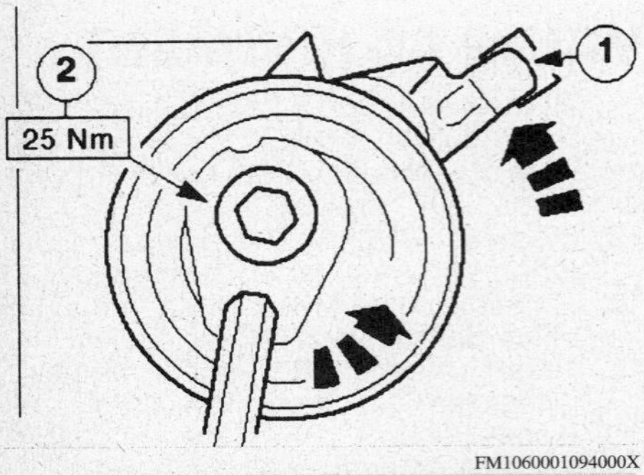

Fig. 9 Timing belt tensioner alignment

block under the oil pan, then raise engine enough to remove load from front engine mount.
8. Mark position of front engine mount for installation reference, then remove engine mount.
9. Remove timing belt upper cover attaching bolts. **Do not remove upper cover at this time.**
10. Remove timing belt center cover and front engine mounting bracket.
11. Remove timing belt upper cover.
12. Disconnect spark plug wire connectors, then the PCV hose.
13. Remove cylinder head cover, then the spark plugs.
14. Turn crankshaft until cylinder No. 1 is at TDC.
15. Loosen timing belt tensioner attaching bolt by turning clockwise, then turn bolt four turns and unhook timing belt tensioner.
16. Remove timing belt.
17. To prevent camshaft pulley from turning, attach camshaft pulley remover tool No. T74P-6256-B, or equivalent, to camshaft pulley.
18. Loosen camshaft pulley attaching bolts.

INSTALLATION

1. Turn camshafts to ignition position on No. 1 cylinder, then insert camshaft alignment plate tool No. 303–465, or equivalent, **Fig. 6.**
2. Position crankshaft to TDC on No. 1 cylinder, **Fig. 7.**
3. Remove blanking plug and install crankshaft TDC timing peg tool No.

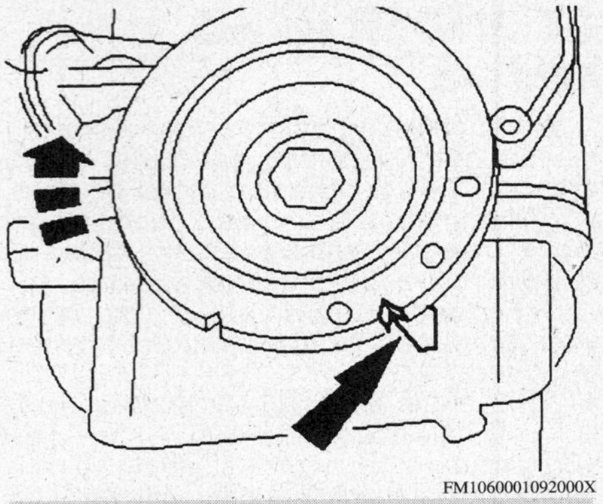

Fig. 7 Crankshaft timing mark alignment

T97-P6000-A, or equivalent, **Fig. 8.**
4. Starting from crankshaft timing pulley and working counterclockwise, install timing belt. Pull belt tight while installing.
5. Hook belt tensioner into pressed steel cover. Loosely install tensioner bolt.
6. Tension belt by turning tensioner counterclockwise until arrow points at mark, **Fig. 9.**
7. To prevent camshaft pulley from turning, attach camshaft pulley remover tool No. T74P-6256-B, or equivalent, to camshaft pulley.
8. Tighten camshaft pulley attaching bolts to specifications.
9. Remove crankshaft TDC timing peg and camshaft alignment plate tools.
10. Turn crankshaft two complete revolutions in normal direction of rotation, then check for correct valve timing as follows:
    a. Install crankshaft TDC timing peg tool No. T97-P6000-A, or equivalent, ensure crankshaft is touching tool.
    b. Insert camshaft alignment plate tool No. 303–465, or equivalent, if necessary, loosen pulleys to correct camshaft alignment.
    c. Remove crankshaft TDC timing peg and camshaft alignment plate tools.
11. Install blanking plug and tighten to specifications.
12. Install cylinder head cover and spark plugs.
13. Coat inside of spark plug connectors with suitable silicone sealant, then connect to spark plugs.
14. Place center and upper timing belt covers into position.
15. Install center cover and front engine mounting bracket attaching bolts and tighten to specification.
16. Ensure upper timing belt cover and gasket are properly aligned, then install upper cover attaching bolts and tighten to specification.
17. Install front engine mount, power steering reservoir and coolant expansion tank.
18. Remove jack and wooden block from under oil pan.

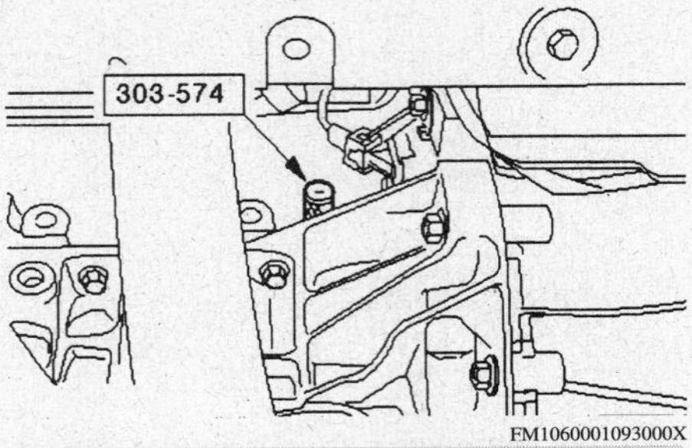

Fig. 8 Crankshaft TDC timing peg installation

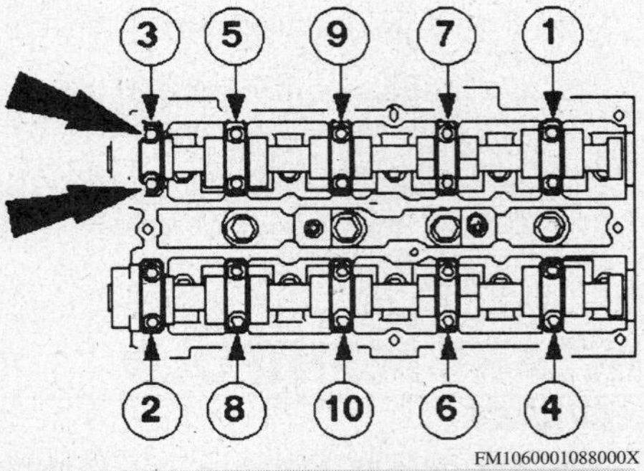

Fig. 10 Camshaft bearing cap bolt loosening sequence

19. Raise and support vehicle, then install lower timing belt cover.
20. Install crankshaft pulley.
21. Install serpentine belt and drive belt cover.
22. Lower vehicle.

CAMSHAFT

REPLACE

REMOVAL

1. Remove intake manifold as outlined under "Intake Manifold, Replace."
2. Remove timing belt as outlined under "Timing Belt, Replace."
3. To prevent camshaft pulley from turning, attach camshaft pulley remover tool No. T74P-6256-B, or equivalent, to camshaft pulley.
4. Remove camshaft pulley retaining bolt, then the camshaft pulley.
5. Using loosening sequence shown in **Fig. 10,** remove camshaft bearing cap attaching bolts in several steps.
6. Remove oil seals and camshafts.

INSTALLATION

1. Camshaft bearing caps have identification numbers stamped on the outer face. Apply a suitable sealant to bearing caps marked " 0" and "5" as shown in **Fig. 11.**
2. Turn crankshaft to approximately 60° BTDC on No. 1 cylinder.
3. Lubricate camshafts and bearing caps

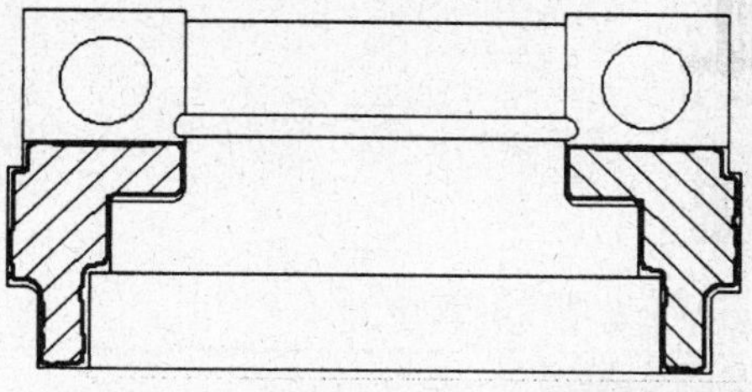

FM1060001089000X

Fig. 11 Camshaft bearing cap sealant application

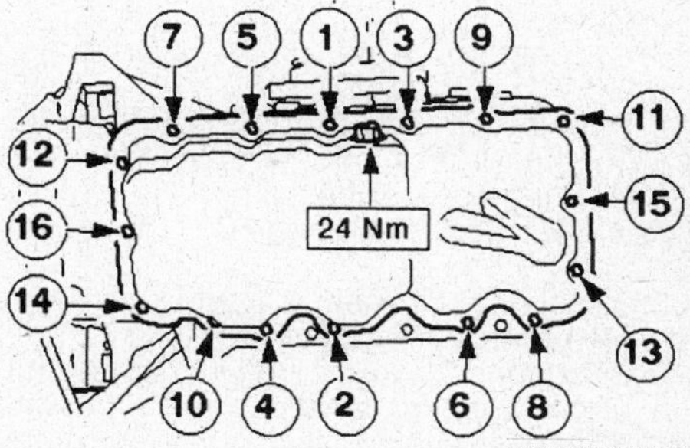

FM1060001098000X

Fig. 14 Oil pan bolt tightening sequence

with clean engine oil, then place camshafts into position so that none of the cams are at full lift.

4. Install and tighten camshaft bearing cap bolts as follows:
   a. Using tightening sequence shown in **Fig. 12,** install and tighten camshaft bearing cap bolts evenly ½ turn at a time.
   b. **Torque** bolts to 88 inch lbs. in sequence
   c. **Torque** bolts to 14 ft. lbs. in sequence.
5. Lubricate camshaft and new camshaft oil seal lip with clean engine oil, then install oil seal.
6. Install camshaft timing pulleys. **Do not tighten pulley bolts fully at this time. Pulleys must be able to turn freely on the camshafts.**
7. Install timing belt as outlined under "Timing Belt, Replace."
8. Install intake manifold as outlined under "Intake Manifold, Replace."
9. Install valve cover as outlined under "Valve Cover, Replace."

CRANKSHAFT SEAL

REPLACE

1. Remove crankshaft timing belt as outlined under " Timing Belt, Replace."
2. Pull off crankshaft pulley hub.
3. Remove timing belt thrust washer. Note position of thrust washer for installation reference.
4. Remove crankshaft front oil seal using oil seal remover tool No. 303-49, or equivalent.
5. Reverse procedure to install. Lubricate new oil seal with clean engine oil.

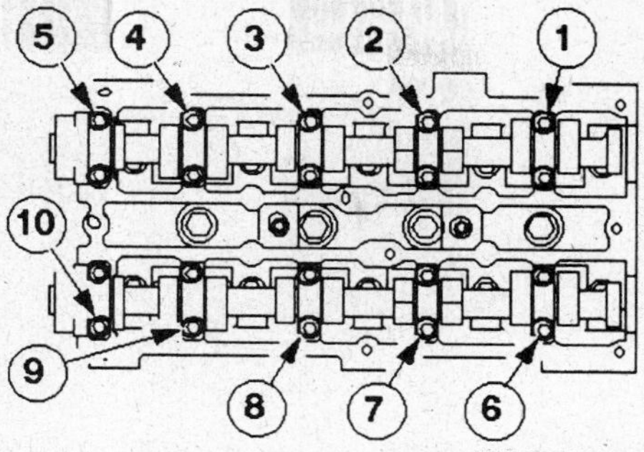

FM1060001090000X

Fig. 12 Camshaft bearing cap bolt tightening sequence

CRANKSHAFT REAR OIL SEAL

REPLACE

1. Remove engine assembly as outlined under "Engine, Replace."
2. Remove transaxle to engine attaching bolts, then separate transaxle from engine.
3. **On models with manual transaxle,** attach flywheel locking device tool No. T74P-6375-A, or equivalent, to flywheel, then remove clutch pressure plate, clutch disk and flywheel.
4. **On models with automatic transaxle,** attach flywheel locking device tool No. T74P-6375-A, or equivalent, to driveplate, then remove driveplate attaching bolts and the driveplate.
5. **On all models,** remove crankshaft rear seal using seal remover tool No. T92C-6700-CH, or equivalent.
6. Reverse procedure to install.

OIL PAN

REPLACE

1. Raise and support vehicle, then drain engine oil.
2. Remove oil pan attaching bolts.
3. Separate oil pan from lower crankcase with a suitable sharp tool.
4. Reverse procedure to install, noting the following:
   a. Install ten M6 X 20 studs into dead end bores shown in **Fig. 13. Always use studs. Sealer in dead end bores may cause damage to ladder frame.**
   b. Apply suitable sealant to oil pan mating surface. Install oil pan within ten minutes of applying sealant.
   c. Using sequence shown in **Fig. 14,** tighten oil pan bolts in two steps: first step, **torque** bolts to 53 inch lbs.; second step, **torque** bolts to 89 inch lbs.

SERPENTINE DRIVE BELT

ROUTING

Refer to **Figs. 15 and 16** for serpentine belt routing.

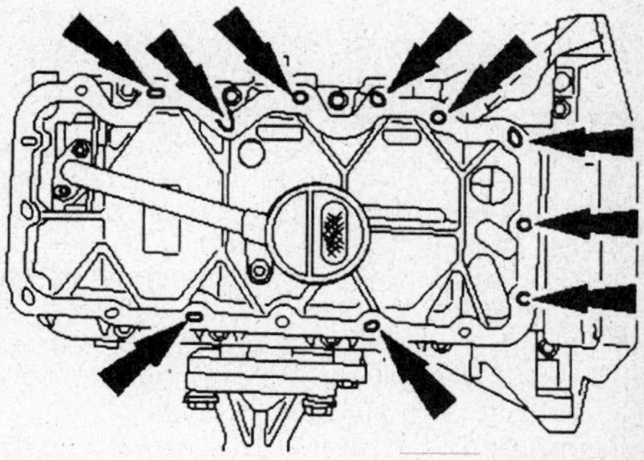

FM1060001097000X

Fig. 13 Lower crankcase dead end bore stud installation

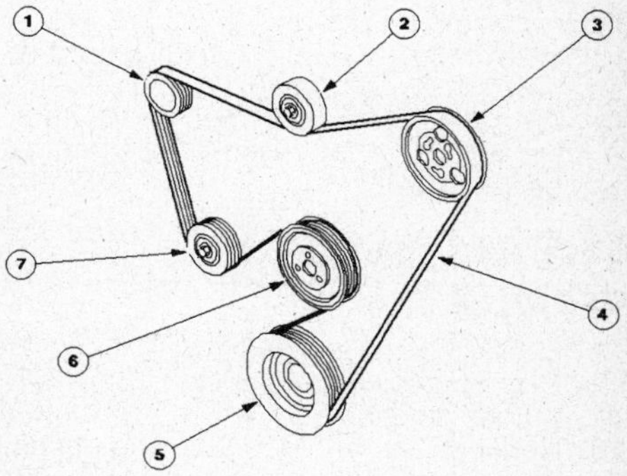

Item	Description
1	Generator pulley
2	Belt idler pulley
3	Power steering pump pulley
4	Accesory drive belt
5	Crankshaft pulley
6	Water pump pulley
7	Belt tensioner

FM1060001106000X

Fig. 15 Serpentine drive belt routing. Less A/C

REPLACE

1. Raise and support vehicle.
2. Remove splash shield.
3. Rotate belt tensioner counterclockwise, then remove belt.
4. Reverse procedure to install.

COOLING SYSTEM BLEED

When releasing system pressure, cover the expansion tank cap with a thick cloth to prevent the possibility of scalding.

When draining the engine coolant or changing coolant system components, do not allow coolant to come into contact with the timing belt or accessory drive belt. Contamination of belts may result in premature failure.

1. Relieve cooling system pressure by

turning expansion tank cap 1/4 turn, remove cap when pressure has been released.
2. Raise and support vehicle.
3. Drain coolant into suitable container.
4. Close radiator drain valve when all coolant has been drained from system.
5. Lower vehicle.
6. Disconnect heater supply hose from engine.
7. Using a suitable funnel, fill cooling system through the supply hose until coolant starts to trickle from engine.
8. Reconnect heater supply hose.
9. Set heater temperature control to HOT position and heater blower motor switch to OFF position. Ensure A/C is switched OFF.
10. Refill coolant expansion tank to MAX mark.
11. Install expansion tank cap.
12. Warm engine up at 2750 RPM for two fan cycles.
13. Allow engine to cool, then check coolant level and top up to MAX mark as necessary

THERMOSTAT

REPLACE

1. Drain engine cooling system.
2. Disconnect coolant hoses from thermostat housing.
3. Remove thermostat housing bolts, then the housing.
4. Remove thermostat and gasket.
5. Reverse procedure to install.

WATER PUMP

REPLACE

1. Drain engine cooling system.
2. Loosen water pump pulley attaching bolts.
3. Remove drive belt as outlined under "Serpentine Drive Belt."
4. Remove water pump pulley.
5. Remove timing belt as outlined under "Timing Belt, Replace."
6. Remove timing belt idler pulley.
7. Disconnect water pump hose.
8. Remove water pump lower and lower bolts, then the water pump.
9. Remove and discard water pump sealing ring.

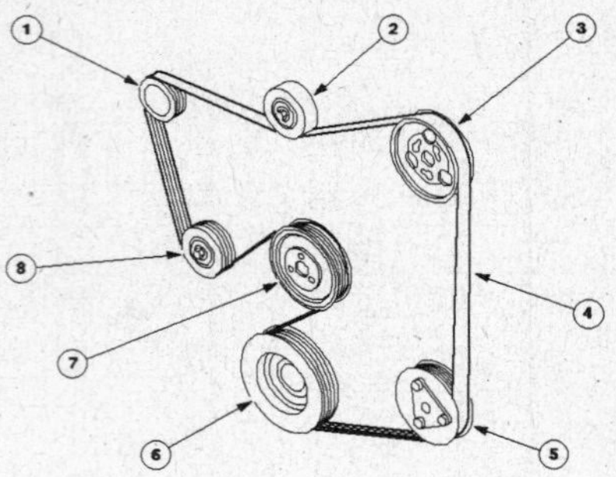

Item	Description
1	Generator pulley
2	Belt idler pulley
3	Power steering pump pulley
4	Accessory drive belt
5	A/C compressor pulley
6	Crankshaft pulley
7	Water pump pulley
8	Belt tensioner

FM1060001107000X

Fig. 16 Serpentine drive belt routing. With A/C

10. Reverse procedure to install.

RADIATOR

REPLACE

1. Remove cooling fan motor and shroud.
2. Drain coolant into suitable container.
3. Raise and support vehicle.
4. Remove 4-pin type retainers from radiator air deflector.
5. Lower vehicle, then disconnect upper radiator hose.
6. Raise and support vehicle.
7. **On models equipped with A/C,** support condenser and transaxle fluid cooler.
8. **On all models,** disconnect lower radiator hoses.
9. Disconnect horn electrical connector.
10. Remove radiator support bracket bolts, then bracket.
11. Remove radiator from vehicle.
12. Reverse procedure to install, noting the following:
    a. **Torque** radiator bracket bolts to 19 ft. lbs.
    b. Fill, then bleed coolant system as outlined under " Coolant System, Bleed."

FUEL PUMP

REPLACE

1. Relieve fuel pressure as outlined under "Precautions. "
2. Drain fuel tank into a suitable container.
3. Disconnect exhaust pipe from rear hanger.
4. Disconnect center muffler from hanger.
5. Disconnect exhaust pipe from remaining hangers, then position aside.
6. Remove heat shield.
7. Disconnect fuel tank vent and filler pipes.
8. Disconnect inline fuel coupling as outlined under " Precautions."
9. Disconnect evaporative emission pipe, then the rollover valve connector.
10. Place a suitable jack under fuel tank, then remove fuel tank support strap bolt.
11. Partially lower tank and disconnect fuel pump electrical connector.
12. Disconnect fuel pressure sensor electrical connector.
13. Remove fuel tank from vehicle.
14. Remove fuel pump module from fuel tank using fuel tank sender unit wrench tool No. 310-069, or equivalent.
15. Reverse procedure to install.

FUEL FILTER

REPLACE

1. Relieve fuel system pressure as outlined under " Precautions."
2. Raise and support vehicle.
3. Disconnect evaporative emission pipe.
4. Remove fuel filter outlet pipe, then disconnect fuel filter inlet pipe.
5. Remove fuel filter and bracket pipe.
6. Separate fuel filter from bracket.
7. Reverse procedure to install.

TIGHTENING SPECIFICATIONS

Year	Component	Torque, Ft. Lbs.
2000	Alternator Bracket To Cylinder Block	48
	Alternator To Bracket	18
	Camshaft Bearing Cap	③
	Camshaft Pulleys	50
	Catalytic Converter To Exhaust Manifold	35
	Catalytic Converter To Exhaust Pipe	35
	ClutchPressure Plate	21
	Connecting Rod Bearing Cap	⑥
	Crankcase Ventilation Pipe Bracket	17
	Crankshaft Belt Pulley	85
	Cylinder Block Oil Gallery Blanking Plugs	17
		②
	Drive Belt Idler Pulley	30
	Driveplate	83
	EGR Pipe to Ignition Coil Bracket	53①
	EGR Valve	18
	Engine Roll Restrictor To Subframe	35
	Engine Roll Restrictor To Transaxle	35
	Exhaust Manifold Heat Shield	89①
	Exhaust Manifold Nuts	12
	Exhaust Manifold Studs	44①
	Flywheel	83
	Front Engine Lifting Eye	35
	Front Engine Mounting To Engine	59
	Fuel Pump Module	59
	Fuel Rail	89①
	Idler Pulley	17
	Ignition Coil Bracket To	15
	Intake Manifold Bolts & Nuts	13
	Intake Manifold Studs	44①
	Lower Crankcase to Cylinder Block	16
	Main Bearing Bolts	⑤
	Oil Drain Plug	18
	Oil Intake Pipe To Oil Pump	89①
	Oil Pan	④
	Oil Pressure Switch	20
	Oil Pump	96①
	Power Steering Pump To Bracket	18
	Rear Crankshaft Oil Seal Carrier	13
	Rear Engine Lifting Eye	35
	Rear Engine Mounting To Body	35
	Spark Plugs	11
	Starter Motor To Transmission	26
	Thermostat Housing	15
	Timing Belt Cover (Upper)	89①
	Timing Belt Tensioner	18
	Transaxle Oil Drain Plug	33
	Valve Cover	62①
	Water Pump Pulley	18
	Wheel Lug Nuts	63

① — Inch lbs.
② — Refer to ", Replace" for tightening procedure.
③ — Refer to "Camshaft, Replace" for tightening procedure.
④ — Refer to "Oil Pan, Replace" for tightening procedure.
⑤ — First step, torque to 18 ft. lbs.; second step, an additional 60.°
⑥ — First step, torque to 26 ft. lbs.; second step, an additional 90.°

2.0L SOHC Engine

NOTE: On Air Bag Equipped Models, Refer To " Electrical" Section Of This Chapter For System Disarming & Arming Procedures.

INDEX

PRECAUTIONS

AIR BAG SYSTEMS

Refer to "Electrical" section of this chapter for system disarming and arming procedures.

BATTERY GROUND CABLE

Prior to service, disconnect battery ground cable and isolate as required.

FUEL SYSTEM PRESSURE RELIEF

1. Remove fuel pump fuse.
2. Start engine and allow to idle until engine stalls.
3. Crank engine for approximately five seconds to make sure fuel supply manifold pressure has been relieved.
4. Install fuel pump fuse into battery junction box.

QUICK DISCONNECT HOSES

R-CLIP

When working with R-clip type connections, **Fig. 1**, do not use tools to disconnect. Use of tools may deform clip components and could cause leaks.

To disconnect, bend shipping tab downward, **Fig. 1.** Spread R-clip and push clip into fitting. Separate fitting from tube.

To install, first inspect fitting and tube for damage and ensure connections are clean. Apply a light coat of clean 5W–30 motor oil to male end of tube. Insert R-clip into fitting. Align tube and fitting, then insert tube into fitting and push together until a click is heard. Pull on connection to ensure it is fully engaged.

SPRING LOCK

When working with spring lock type connections, **Fig. 2,** spring lock tool set No.

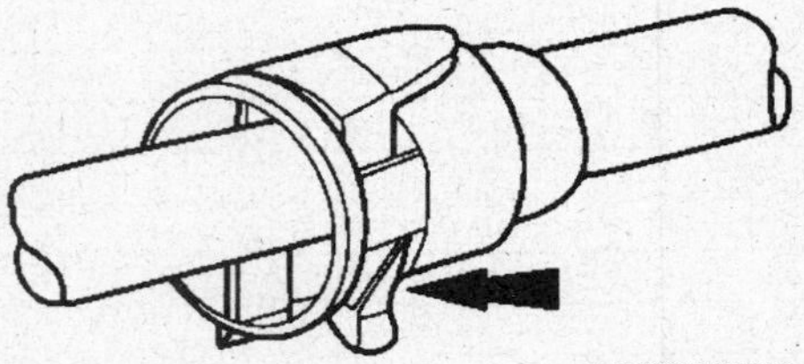

Fig. 1 R-clip connection

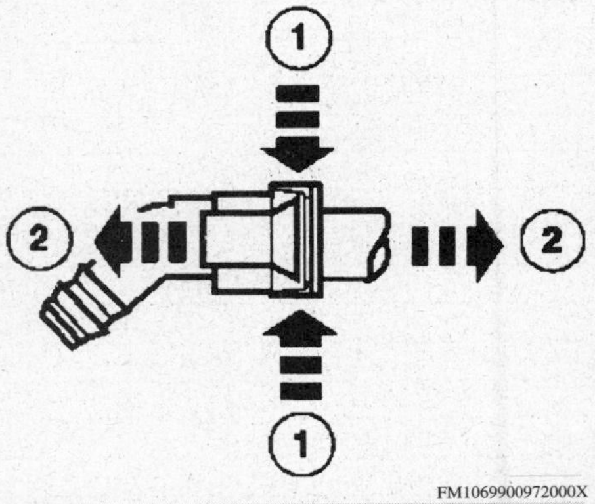

Fig. 3 Vapor tube connection

T84L–19623–B or equivalent, must be used to disconnect fittings. When connecting spring lock type fittings, inspect and clean both coupling ends. Lubricate fuel line O-ring seals with clean 5W–30 motor oil. When connection is made, pull on line to ensure it is fully engaged.

VAPOR TUBE

To disconnect vapor tube connections, squeeze fitting (1) and disconnect vapor tube from fitting (2), **Fig. 3.** To connect, ensure fittings are clean and free from damage. Push tube onto fitting until it snaps into

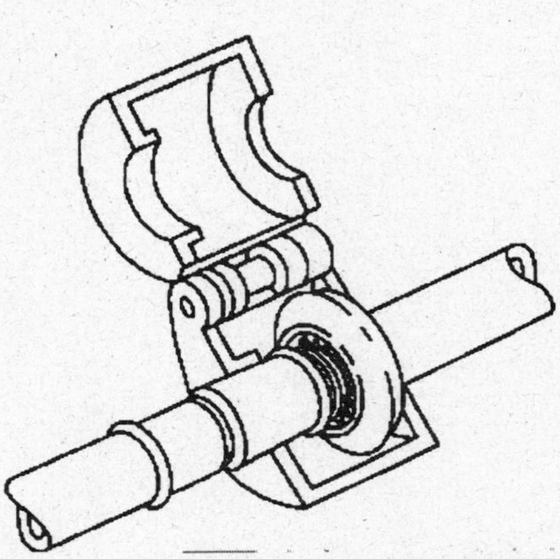

Fig. 2 Spring lock connection

place. Pull on connection to verify fitting is secure.

COMPRESSION PRESSURE

Before performing compression test, ensure the following conditions are met: crankcase oil is of correct viscosity and at correct level, ensure battery is fully charged and engine is at normal operating temperature.

1. Turn ignition switch to OFF position.
2. Remove all spark plugs.
3. Set throttle plates to wide open position.
4. Install a suitable compression gauge in No. 1 cylinder.
5. Install an auxiliary starter switch in starting circuit.
6. With ignition switch off, use auxiliary starter switch to crank engine a minimum of five compression strokes.

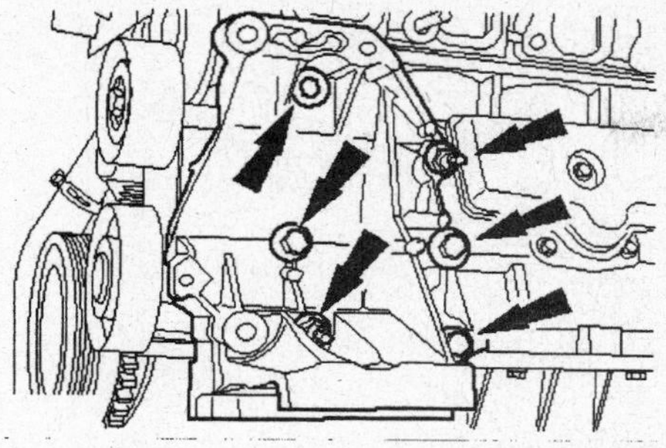

FM1060001072000X

Fig. 4 Alternator bracket

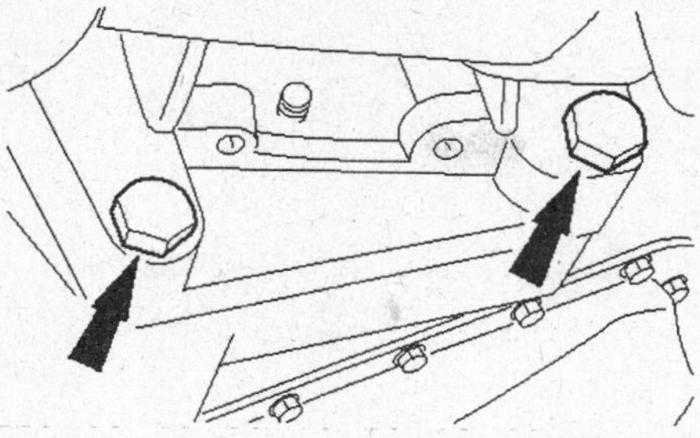

FM1060001073000X

Fig. 5 Transaxle lower flange bolts

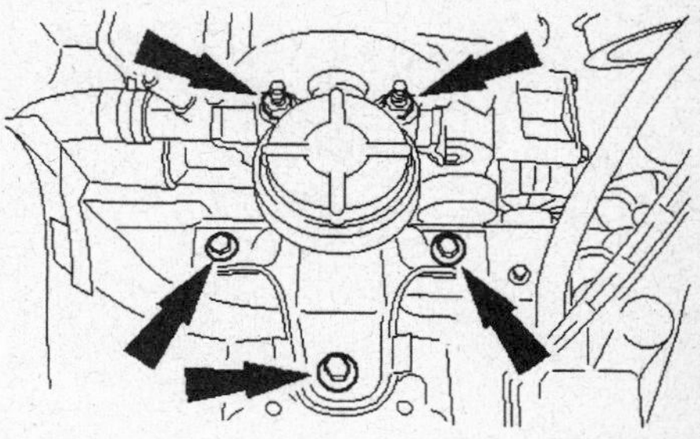

FM1060001074000X

Fig. 6 Engine front mounting

7. Note number of compression strokes necessary to reach highest reading and record highest reading.
8. Repeat test on each cylinder, cranking engine same number of compression strokes.
9. Indicated compression pressures are considered within specifications if lowest reading cylinder is within 75 percent of highest reading.

ENGINE

REPLACE

AUTOMATIC TRANSAXLE

1. Open coolant expansion tank.
2. Disconnect ground lead from battery tray assembly, then remove tray.
3. Disconnect ground cable from chassis.
4. Drain coolant into suitable container.
5. Using a suitable Allen wrench to prevent strut piston rod from turning, loosen strut nuts by five turns on both sides.
6. Disconnect mass air flow sensor electrical connector, intake air hose, then remove air cleaner housing from rubber bushing.
7. Remove air cleaner intake pipe, accelerator cable and speed control cable.
8. Disconnect electrical connectors from power steering pump pressure switch, alternator and heated oxygen sensor.
9. Disconnect both powertrain control module connectors.
10. Remove vacuum hoses from EVAP, Brake Servo, Delta Pressure Feedback Electronic System Sensor and EGR valve.
11. Disconnect vacuum hoses from intake manifold.
12. Relieve fuel pressure as outlined under "Precautions."
13. Disconnect fuel hose and drain excess fuel into suitable container.
14. Disconnect coolant hose from intake manifold.
15. Remove coolant hoses from water pump and coolant pipe, then disconnect coolant expansion tank and set aside.
16. Remove PAS reservoir and lay to one side.
17. Remove radiator fan assembly.
18. Remove upper starter motor bolts.
19. Remove accessory drive belt.
20. Remove power steering high pressure pipe, then remove power steering pump and position to one side.
21. Remove alternator and alternator bracket, **Fig. 4.**
22. Disconnect both lower suspension arms.
23. Disconnect oxygen sensor electrical connectors, then remove drive belt cover.
24. **On models equipped with air conditioning,** remove A/C compressor and tie to radiator cross member.
25. **On all models,** disconnect exhaust pipe.
26. Remove torque converter cover bolts, then disconnect torque converter from engine drive plate.
27. Remove transaxle lower flange bolts, **Fig. 5.**
28. Disconnect righthand front drive halfshaft from intermediate shaft.
29. Remove lefthand front drive halfshaft from tripod housing.
30. Remove intermediate shaft and secure out of way with cable tie.
31. Disconnect starter motor electrical connectors, then remove starter motor.
32. Remove crankshaft pulley, righthand engine support insulator and lefthand and righthand transaxle flange bolts.
33. Disconnect fuel line, drain excess fuel into suitable container.
34. Attach suitable engine lifting device, then raise engine slightly to relieve pressure on support insulators.
35. Remove engine front mounting, **Fig. 6.**
36. Disconnect crankshaft position sensor electrical connector.
37. Remove upper transaxle flange bolts, then separate engine from transaxle.
38. Remove engine assembly from top of vehicle.
39. Use torque converter holding tool No. 307-346, or equivalent, to hold torque converter in transaxle assembly.
40. Reverse procedure to install.

MANUAL TRANSMISSION

1. Open coolant expansion tank.
2. Remove battery ground cable from battery tray assembly, then remove tray from vehicle.
3. Disconnect ground cable from vehicle chassis.
4. Drain coolant into suitable container.
5. Using a suitable allen wrench to prevent strut piston rods from turning, loosen both strut nut approximately five turns.
6. Disconnect mass air flow sensor electrical connector, remove air intake hose, then remove air cleaner housing from rubber bushing.
7. Remove air cleaner air intake pipe.
8. Remove accelerator and speed control cables and lay to one side.
9. Disconnect electrical connectors from power steering pressure switch, alternator and heated oxygen sensor.
10. Disconnect both powertrain control modules.
11. Disconnect vehicle speed sensor and reverse lamp switch electrical connectors.
12. Remove high pressure pipe from clutch slave cylinder.
13. Remove vacuum hoses from EVAP, brake servo, Delta Pressure Feedback Electronic System Sensor and EGR valve.
14. Remove any remaining vacuum hoses from intake manifold.
15. Disconnect fuel line and drain excess fuel into suitable container.
16. Remove coolant hoses from intake manifold, water pump and coolant pipes.
17. Remove coolant expansion tank and position to one side.
18. Remove accessory drive belt.
19. Remove power steering high pressure pipe, then remove power steering pump and position to one side.
20. Remove PA reservoir and position to one side.
21. Remove radiator fan, catalytic converter, flexible exhaust pipe and drive belt cover.
22. Remove shift cable and selector cable cover, then the cables.
23. **On models equipped with air conditioning,** remove air conditioning compressor and secure it to radiator crossmember.
24. **On all models,** remove righthand engine support insulator, **Fig. 7.**
25. Remove both lower suspension arms.
26. Remove righthand front drive halfshaft from intermediate shaft. **Inner joint must not be bent at more than 18°, outer joint must not be bent at more than 45°.**
27. Remove lefthand front drive halfshaft from tripod housing.

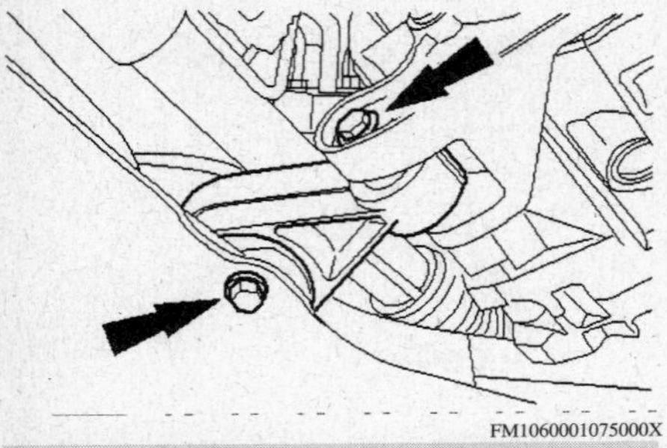

Fig. 7 Right hand engine support insulator

28. Position engine assembly stand with wooden blocks on it under vehicle.
29. Carefully lower vehicle until engine and transaxle assembly is on engine stand.
30. Remove engine rear mount, **Fig. 8.**
31. Remove front engine mount, **Fig. 6.**
32. Secure engine and transaxle assembly with restraining strap to assembly table.
33. Carefully raise vehicle, then pull assembly stand forward with engine and transaxle assembly.
34. Use a suitable lifting device to separate engine from transaxle.
35. Reverse procedure to install.

INTAKE MANIFOLD

REPLACE

1. Raise and support vehicle.
2. Remove intake manifold bracket, **Fig. 9.**
3. Disconnect electrical connector of mass air flow sensor, remove intake hose, then remove air cleaner housing from rubber bushing.
4. Unhook accelerator and speed control cables, pull off plastic clips and position cables to one side.
5. Remove vacuum hoses from EVAP system, brake servo, Delta Pressure Feedback Electronic System Sensor and EGR valve.
6. Disconnect and remove EGR valve.
7. Clamp coolant hoses to prevent leakage and remove from intake manifold.
8. Disconnect throttle position sensor and idle air control valve.
9. Remove oil level indicator tube.
10. Remove any remaining vacuum hoses or electrical connectors from intake manifold.
11. Remove intake manifold mounting bolts, then the manifold.
12. Reverse procedure to install, noting the following:
    a. Replace intake manifold gasket.
    b. Install intake manifold bolts and tighten to specification.

EXHAUST MANIFOLD

REPLACE

1. Remove air cleaner housing from rubber bushing.
2. Disconnect heated oxygen sensor electrical connector.

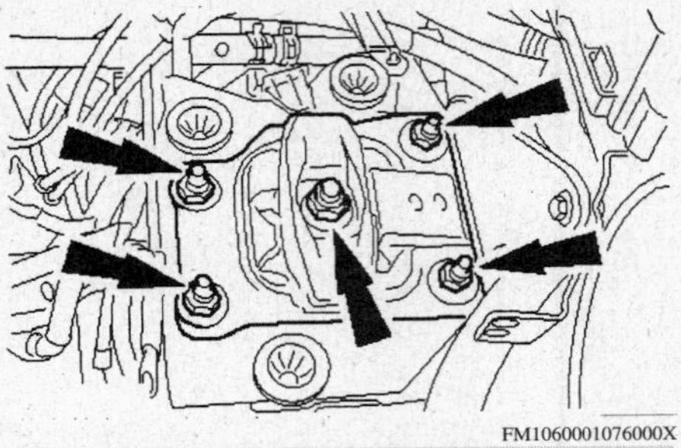

Fig. 8 Rear engine mount

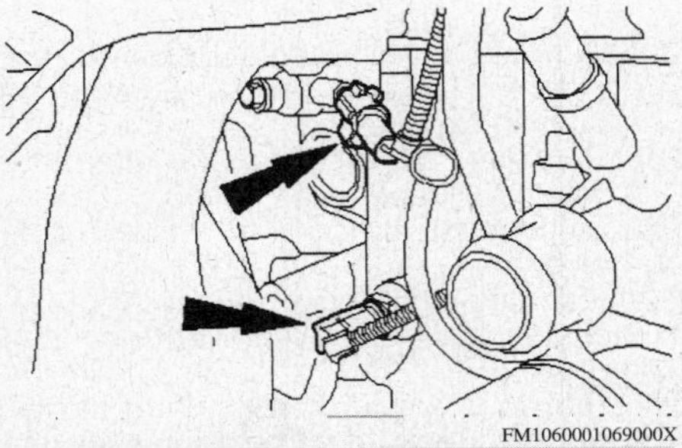

Fig. 10 Knock sensor & oil pressure switch connectors

3. Remove exhaust manifold heat shield.
4. Remove EGR tube at exhaust manifold, then loosen tube nut approximately three turns at valve.
5. Remove catalytic converter.
6. Remove exhaust manifold attaching nuts, then the manifold.
7. Reverse procedure to install.

CYLINDER HEAD

REPLACE

When cleaning cylinder head surfaces, do not use metal scrapers, wires brushes, power abrasive discs or other abrasive methods to clean sealing surfaces. Use only a plastic scraping tool to remove all traces of gasket material.

Cylinder head bolts are of torque-to-yield style and must be replaced when removed.

1. Disconnect mass air flow sensor, detach intake air hose, then remove air cleaner housing from rubber bushing.
2. Detach battery ground cable from battery tray, then remove battery tray.
3. Unhook accelerator and speed control cables, pull off plastic clips and position cables to one side.
4. Disconnect both powertrain control module connectors.
5. Disconnect heated oxygen sensor electrical connector.
6. Detach vacuum hoses from EVAP, brake servo, Delta Pressure Feedback Electronic System Sensor and EGR valve.
7. Remove oil level indicator tube.
8. Drain coolant into suitable container and remove coolant hoses from thermostat housing.

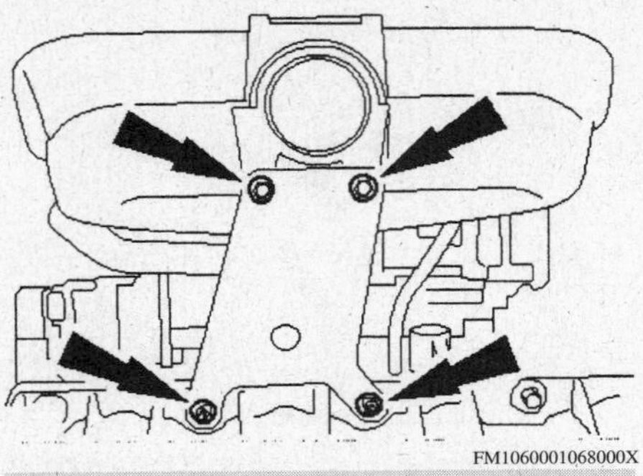

Fig. 9 Intake manifold bracket

9. Disconnect fuel line, drain excess fuel into suitable container.
10. Raise and support vehicle.
11. Disconnect knock sensor and oil pressure sensor electrical connectors, **Fig. 10.**
12. Remove intake manifold bracket.
13. Disconnect and remove catalyst monitor sensor electrical connector.
14. Lower vehicle.
15. Remove exhaust manifold heat shield.
16. Remove catalytic converter from exhaust manifold.
17. Remove timing belt as outlined in "Timing Belt, Replace."
18. Disconnect crankshaft position sensor electrical connector.
19. Loosen cylinder head bolts in sequence, **Fig. 11,** then remove cylinder head.
20. Reverse procedure to install, noting the following:
    a. Lubricate cylinder head bolts with Super Premium 5W 30 SAE X0–5W 30–QSP, or equivalent, meeting Ford specification WSS-M2C153–G prior to installation.
    b. Install cylinder head and **torque** cylinder head bolts in sequence, **Fig. 12,** to 37 ft. lbs.
    c. Back all bolts off one half turn (180°).
    d. **Torque** all bolts in sequence to 37 ft. lbs.
    e. Rotate all bolts in sequence, 90°.
    f. Rotate all bolts a final time, in sequence, 90°.

CAMSHAFT OIL SEAL

REPLACE

1. Remove timing belt as outlined under "Timing Belt, Replace."
2. Using wrench tool No. 303-098, or equivalent, remove camshaft sprocket.
3. Using seal remover tool No. 303-409, or equivalent, remove and discard camshaft oil seal.
4. Reverse procedure to install, noting the following:
    a. Lubricate new camshaft seal and camshaft running face with clean 5W-30 engine oil.
    b. Using seal installer tool No. 303-160, or equivalent, install new seal. Draw seal into place with timing belt sprocket bolt.

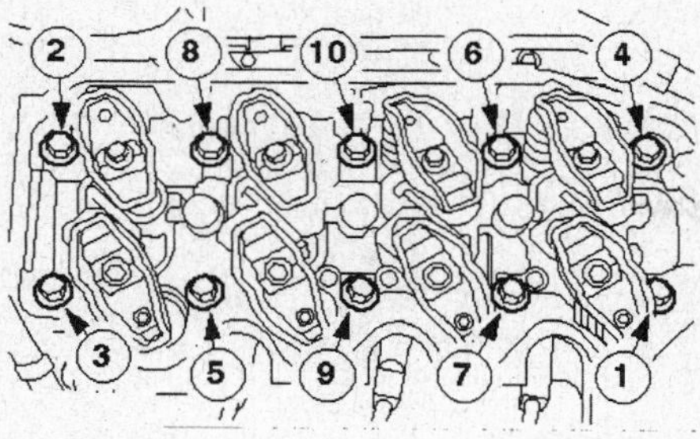

Fig. 11 Cylinder head bolt loosening sequence

c. Use wrench tool No. 303-098, or equivalent, to hold sprocket in place while tightening bolt.
d. Tighten all fasteners to specifications.
e. Start engine, then inspect for and correct any leakage.

VALVE ADJUSTMENT

Valve clearance is hydraulically controlled and is not adjustable.

TIMING BELT

REPLACE

1. Remove coolant reservoir mounting bolt, then position reservoir aside.
2. Disconnect power steering fluid reservoir and position aside.
3. Using a suitable 3/8 inch drive breaker bar, rotate serpentine belt tensioner to relieve tension, then remove the belt.
4. Raise and support vehicle.
5. Remove timing belt upper cover.
6. Remove crankshaft pulley retaining bolt, then the pulley.
7. Lower the vehicle.
8. Disconnect spark plug wires at the plugs.
9. Remove spark plug wire separators at valve cover.
10. Remove spark plugs.
11. Support engine using a suitable floor jack and a wooden block under oil pan.
12. Slowly raise engine until tension is relieved from its front mount.
13. Remove engine front mount.
14. Remove timing belt cover.
15. Remove engine front mount bracket.
16. Rotate engine in normal rotation direction until timing marks are properly aligned, **Fig. 13.**
17. Using a suitable 8MM hex wrench, rotate timing belt tensioner counterclockwise 1/4 turn, then insert a 1/8 inch drill bit to lock tensioner in place.
18. Remove timing belt.
19. Reverse procedure to install, noting the following:
   a. Route the new timing belt over pulleys in a counterclockwise direction, starting at crankshaft. Keep tension on belt span from crankshaft to camshaft while routing belt over camshaft.
   b. Remove drill bit from tensioner.

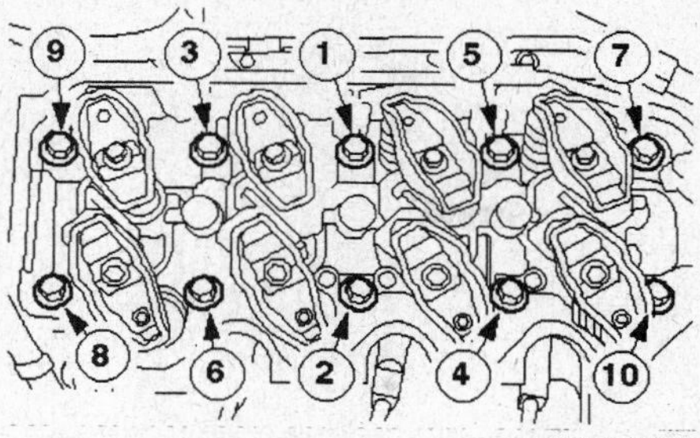

Fig. 12 Cylinder head bolt tightening sequence

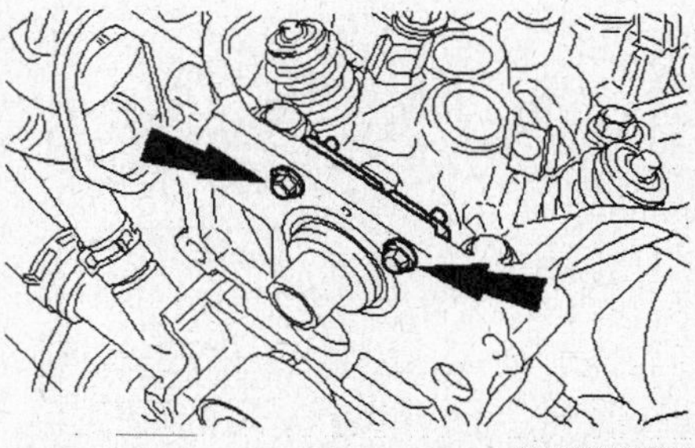

Fig. 14 Camshaft thrust plate

   c. Rotate crankshaft at least two turns clockwise to position No. 1 piston at TDC.
   d. Ensure timing marks are properly aligned, **Fig. 13.** Repeat previous steps if marks are not aligned as illustrated.
   e. Tighten all fasteners to specifications.

CAMSHAFT

REPLACE

1. Disconnect battery ground cable from battery tray, then remove tray from vehicle.
2. Disconnect mass air flow sensor and air cleaner outlet pipe, then remove air cleaner assembly from rubber bushing.
3. Remove air cleaner intake pipe.
4. Disconnect and remove ignition coil.
5. Disconnect PCV hoses.
6. Remove valve cover and rocker arms.
7. Remove valve tappet guide plate retainers, valve guide tappet plates, then the valve tappets. Keep tappets in order for reassembly.
8. Remove timing belt as outlined under "Timing Belt, Replace."
9. Remove camshaft oil seal.
10. Support engine with a suitable engine lifting device.
11. Remove rear engine mount, **Fig. 8.**
12. Remove camshaft thrust plate, **Fig. 14.**
13. Remove and discard blanking plug from rear of cylinder head.
14. Remove camshaft from rear of cylinder head.
15. Reverse procedure to install, noting the following:

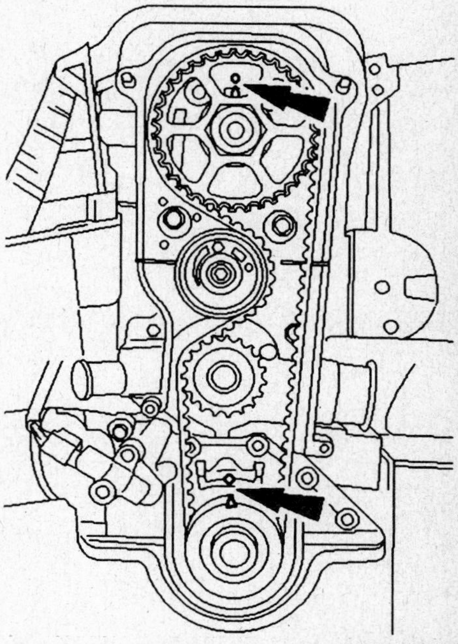

Fig. 13 Timing mark alignment

   a. Coat cylinder head bore with Super Premium 5W30 SAE motor oil, or equivalent, meeting Ford specification prior to camshaft installation.
   b. Install camshaft through rear of cylinder head.
   c. Tighten all fasteners to specification.

CRANKSHAFT FRONT OIL SEAL

REPLACE

1. Remove timing belt as outlined under "Timing Belt, Replace."
2. Support engine using a suitable floor jack and a wooden block under oil pan.
3. Install engine support tool Nos. 303-290, 303-050, 303-290-01 and 303-290-03, or their equivalents.
4. Remove floor jack.
5. Raise and support vehicle.
6. Remove crankshaft timing belt pulley.
7. Using seal remover tool No. 303-409, or equivalent, remove and discard crankshaft seal.
8. Reverse procedure to install, noting the following:
   a. Lubricate new crankshaft seal and the crankshaft surface with clean 5W-30 engine oil.
   b. Using seal installer tool No. 303-164, or equivalent, install crankshaft front seal.
   c. Start engine, then inspect for and correct any leakage.

CRANKSHAFT REAR OIL SEAL

REPLACE

1. Remove transaxle assembly.
2. Remove flywheel.

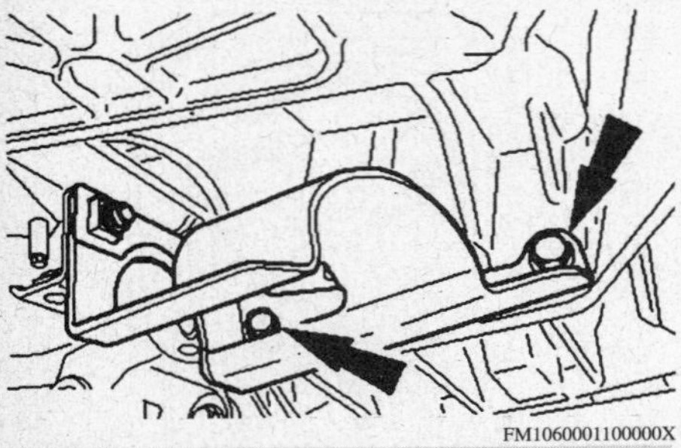

Fig. 15 Bolt & bracket locations

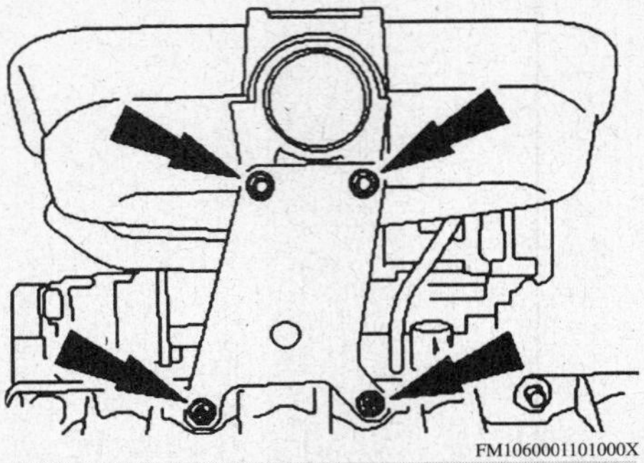

Fig. 16 Intake manifold bracket removal

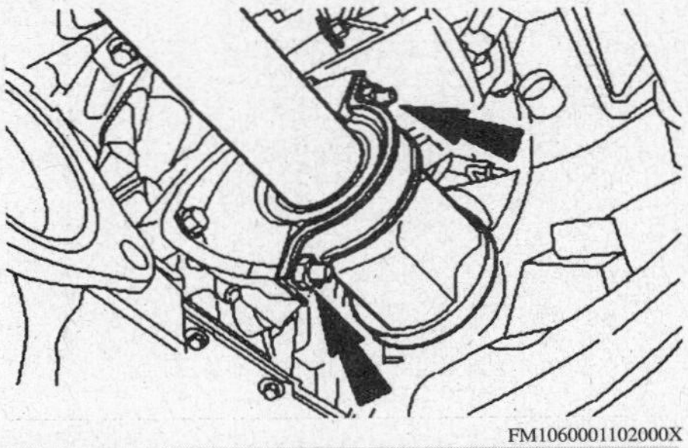

Fig. 17 Axle shaft bracket clamp removal

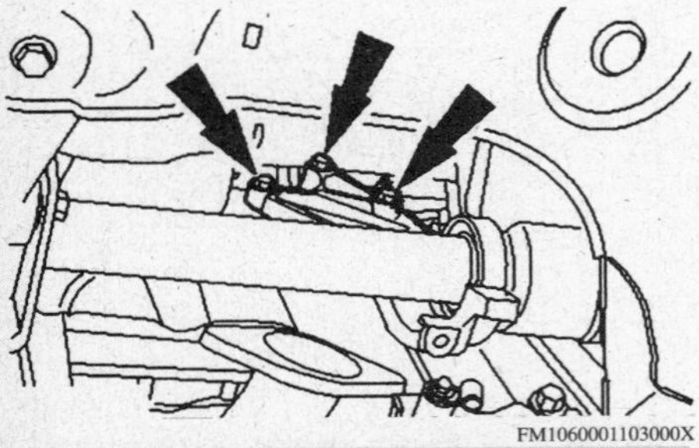

Fig. 18 Axle shaft bracket removal

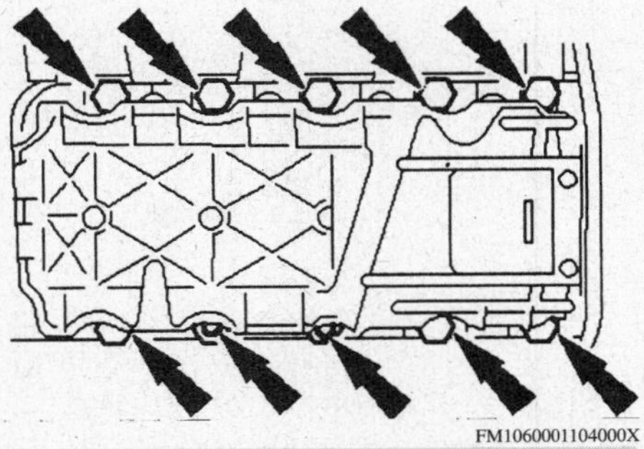

Fig. 19 Oil pan stud bolt locations

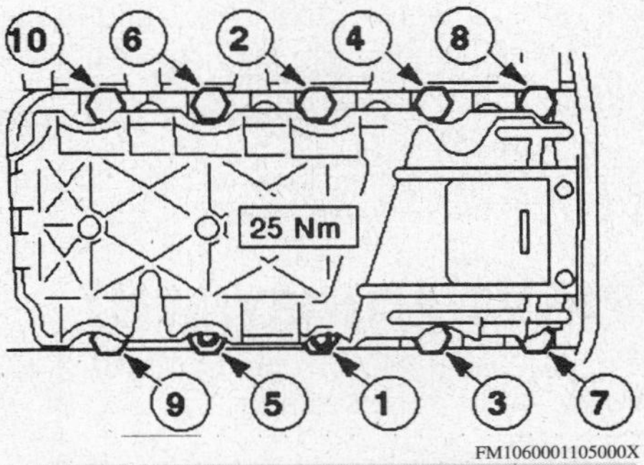

Fig. 20 Oil pan fastener tightening sequence

3. Using seal removal tool No. 303–409, or equivalent, carefully pry out seal.
4. Inspect rear seal area of crankshaft for damage or excessive wear.
5. Reverse procedure to install.

OIL PAN

REPLACE

1. Remove three-way catalytic converter.
2. Remove bolts and two brackets, **Fig. 15.**
3. Remove intake manifold bracket bolts and the bracket, **Fig. 16.**
4. Remove axle shaft bracket clamp bolts and the clamp, **Fig. 17.**
5. Remove axle shaft bracket bolts and the bracket, **Fig. 18.**
6. Remove coolant tube bolt.
7. Drain engine oil into an approved container.
8. Note locations of oil pan stud bolts, **Fig. 19.**
9. Remove oil pan attaching fasteners, then the oil pan. Discard the gasket.
10. Reverse procedure to install, noting the following:
    a. **Do not use abrasive grinding discs when removing gasket material. Use plastic scrapers. Avoid gouging or scratching aluminum sealing surfaces.**
    b. Use a suitable solvent to clean gasket sealing surfaces.
    c. Apply a .12 inch wide bead of silicone gasket sealant meeting Ford specification WSE-M4G323-A6, or equivalent, at oil pump to block joints and crankshaft rear seal retainer to block joints. **Oil pan must be installed within 10 minutes of sealant application.**
    d. Ensure press-fit tabs fully engage in oil pan gasket channel.
    e. Tighten oil pan fasteners to specifications in sequence outlined in **Fig. 20.**
    f. Fill engine with proper engine oil.
    g. Start engine, then inspect for and correct any leakage.

SERPENTINE DRIVE BELT TENSIONER

REPLACE

1. Raise and support vehicle.
2. Remove serpentine belt splash shield.
3. Using a suitable ⅜ inch drive breaker bar, rotate tensioner clockwise, then remove belt.
4. Remove power steering pipe to exhaust manifold bracket nuts, then position pipe aside.
5. Remove exhaust manifold heat shield fasteners, then the shield.
6. Remove serpentine drive belt tensioner mounting fasteners, then the tensioner.
7. Reverse procedure to install. Tighten all fasteners to specifications.

OIL PUMP

REPLACE

1. Remove timing belt as outlined in "Timing Belt, Replace."
2. Install suitable engine support fixture.
3. Remove crankshaft timing belt pulley, oil pan and crankshaft position sensor.
4. Remove two bolts, then the oil pump screen cover and tube. Discard gasket
5. Remove oil pump bolts, **Fig. 21,** then the oil pump. Discard gasket, remove oil pump seal.
6. Reverse procedure to install.

SERPENTINE DRIVE BELT ROUTING

Refer to **Figs. 22 and 23,** for serpentine accessory drive belt routing.

COOLING SYSTEM BLEED

When releasing system pressure, cover the expansion tank cap with a thick cloth to prevent the possibility of scalding.

When draining the engine coolant or changing coolant system components, do not allow coolant to come into contact with the timing belt or accessory drive belt. Contamination of belts may result in premature failure.

1. Relieve cooling system pressure by turning expansion tank cap a quarter of a turn, remove cap when pressure has been released.
2. Raise and support vehicle.
3. Drain coolant into suitable container.
4. Close radiator drain valve when all coolant has been drained from system.
5. Lower vehicle.
6. Disconnect heater supply hose from engine.

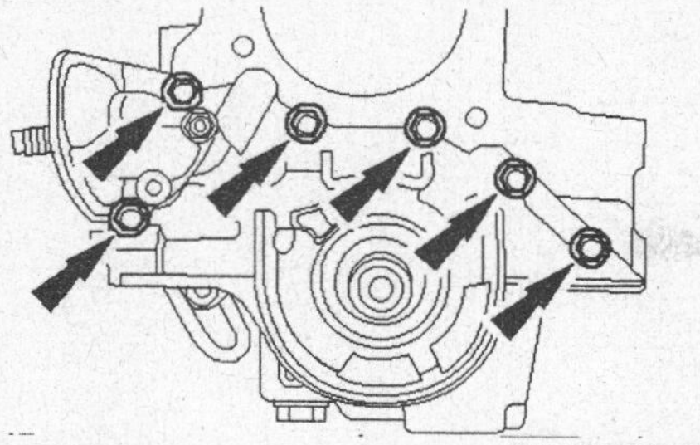

FM1060001077000X

Fig. 21 Oil pump replacement

7. Using a suitable funnel, fill cooling system through the supply hose until coolant starts to trickle from engine.
8. Reconnect heater supply hose.
9. Set heater temperature control to HOT position and heater blower motor switch to OFF position. Ensure A/C is switched OFF.
10. Refill coolant expansion tank to MAX mark.
11. Install expansion tank cap.
12. Warm engine up at 2750 RPM for two fan cycles.
13. Allow engine to cool, then check coolant level and top up to MAX mark as necessary

THERMOSTAT

REPLACE

1. Drain coolant into an approved container.
2. Remove thermostat housing bolts, then the housing.
3. Remove thermostat.
4. Remove and discard O-ring seals.
5. Reverse procedure to install, noting the following:
   a. Install new thermostat with new O-ring seals.
   b. Tighten thermostat housing bolts to specifications.
   c. Fill and bleed cooling system as outlined under " Cooling System Bleed."
   d. Inspect for and correct any leakage.

WATER PUMP

REPLACE

1. Drain cooling system into suitable container.
2. Remove timing belt and timing belt tensioner as outlined in " Timing Belt, Replace."
3. Disconnect coolant hoses.
4. Remove water pump.
5. Reverse procedure to install.

RADIATOR

REPLACE

1. Raise and support vehicle.
2. Remove cooling fan motor and shroud.
3. Drain coolant into suitable container.

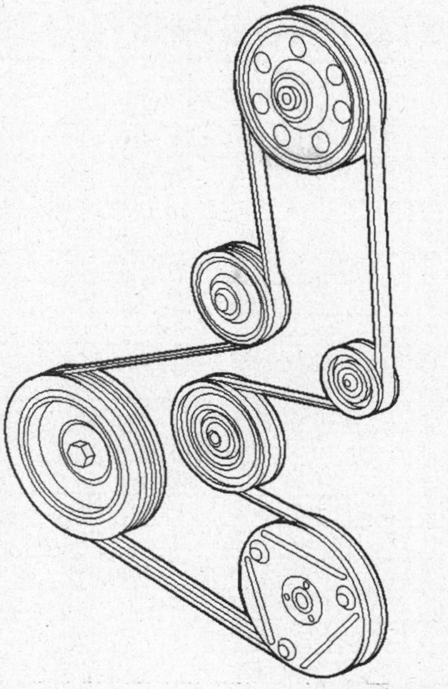

FM1060001079000X

Fig. 22 Serpentine belt routing. With A/C

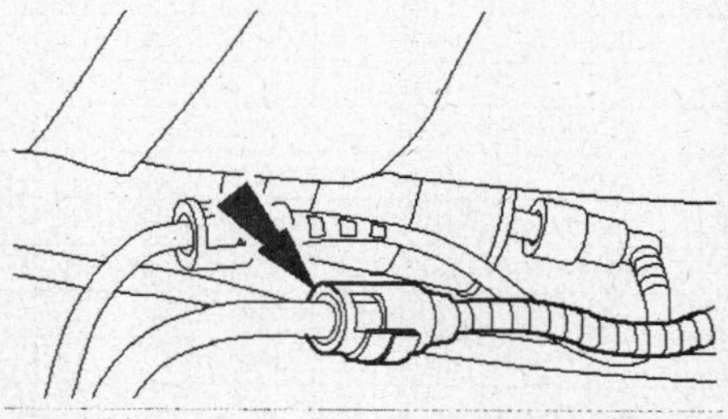

FM1060001083000X

Fig. 24 Evaporative emission pipe

4. Remove four pin type retainers from radiator air deflector.
5. Lower vehicle.
6. Disconnect upper radiator hose.
7. Raise and support vehicle.
8. **On models equipped with air conditioning,** support condenser and transaxle cooler.
9. **On all models,** disconnect upper coolant hose, radiator lower coolant hoses and horn electrical connectors.
10. Remove radiator support bracket bolts, then the bracket.
11. Remove radiator from vehicle.
12. Reverse procedure to instal.

FUEL PUMP

REPLACE

1. Relieve fuel pressure as outlined in "Precautions. "
2. Drain fuel tank into suitable container.
3. Disconnect exhaust pipe from hanger insulators.

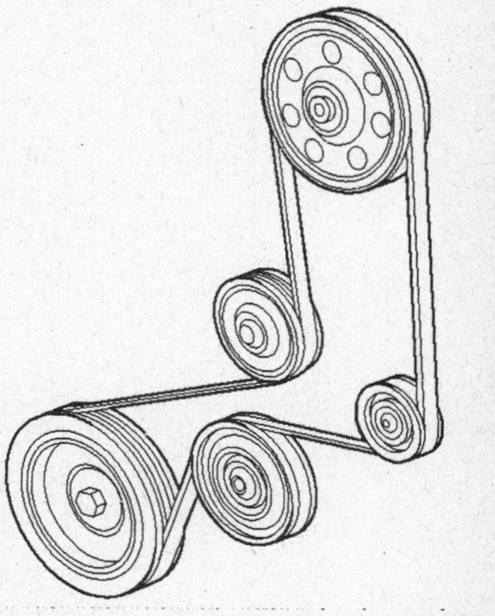

FM1060001080000X

Fig. 23 Serpentine belt routing. Less A/C

4. Disconnect center muffler from exhaust insulator.
5. Disconnect exhaust pipe and secure to frame with wire.
6. Remove heat shield.
7. Make a note of position of fuel vent and filler pipe retaining clamps and clip for installation reference.
8. Disconnect fuel tank vent and filer pipes.
9. Disconnect inline fuel coupling.
10. Disconnect evaporative emission pipe and rollover valve.
11. Place a suitable jack or lifting device under fuel tank.
12. Remove fuel tank support strap bolt, then partially lower fuel tank.
13. Disconnect fuel pump electrical connector and fuel tank pressure sensor electrical connector, then lower tank from vehicle.
14. Disconnect fuel supply line from fuel pump module.
15. Using fuel tank sender wrench No. 310–069, or equivalent, remove lock-ring.
16. Rotate fuel pump module counter-clockwise and lift from tank.
17. Reverse procedure to install.

FUEL FILTER

REPLACE

1. Relieve fuel pressure as outlined in "Precautions. "
2. Raise and support vehicle.
3. Disconnect evaporative emission pipe, **Fig. 24.**
4. Remove fuel filter outlet pipe.
5. Disconnect fuel filter inlet pipe.
6. Remove fuel filter and bracket, then remove fuel filter from bracket.
7. Reverse procedure to install.

TIGHTENING SPECIFICATIONS

Year	Component	Torque/ Ft. Lbs.
2000	A/C Compressor Bolts	18
	Accessory Drive Bracket Bolts & Nuts	35
	Alternator Mounting Bolts (Lower & Upper)	35
	Battery Tray	18
	Camshaft Position Sensor	18
	Camshaft Pulley Bolt	77
	Camshaft Thrust Plate Bolts	89②
	Catalytic Converter To Exhaust Manifold Bolts	30
	Crankshaft Position Sensor	53②
	Crankshaft Pulley	89
	Cylinder Head Bolts	①
	EGR Manifold Tube To Exhaust Manifold	53②
	EGR Valve To EGR Manifold Tube	18
	EGR Valve To Intake Manifold	53②
	Engine Oil Drain Plug	18
	Engine Roll Restrictor To Subframe	35
	Engine Roll Restrictor To Transaxle	35
	Exhaust Manifold Nuts	20
	Flexible Exhaust Pipe	35
	Front Engine Mounting To Body	35
	Front Engine Mounting To Engine	59
	Intake Manifold Bracket Nuts & Bolts	89②
	Intake Manifold Nuts	③
	Intermediate Shaft Bracket	35
	Knock Sensor	10
	Lefthand Transaxle Flange Bolts	35
	Lower Ball Joint To Spindle Carrier	35
	Lower Transaxle Flange Bolts	35
	Oil Intake Pipe To Oil Pump	89②
	Oil Pan Baffle	18
	Oil Pan To Crankcase	18
	Oil Pump	10
	Oil Pump Tube	89②
	Power Steering Pump	17
	Rear Crankshaft Oil Seal Retainer	18
	Rear Engine Mounting (Nut On Transaxle Mounting Bracket)	98
	Rear Engine Mounting To Body	35
	Rocker Arms	18
	Starter Motor To Transaxle	26
	Thermostat Housing	10
	Timing Belt Cover (Lower)	89②
	Timing Belt Cover (Upper)	35
	Timing Belt Tensioner	18
	Upper Transaxle Flange Bolts	35
	Valve Cover Bolts	80②
	Water Pump	18
	Wheel Lug Nuts	63

① — Refer to procedure outlined in "Cylinder Head, Replace"

② — Inch Lbs.

③ — 89 Inch Lbs. plus 180°.

Clutch & Manual Transaxle

NOTE: On Air Bag Equipped Models, Refer To " Electrical" Section Of This Chapter For System Disarming & Arming Procedures.

INDEX

PRECAUTIONS

AIR BAG SYSTEMS

Refer to "Electrical" section of this chapter for system disarming and arming procedures.

BATTERY GROUND CABLE

Prior to service, disconnect battery ground cable and isolate as required.

DESCRIPTION

This model is equipped with a hydraulic clutch system with both the iB5 and MTX75 transaxles.

ADJUSTMENTS

SHIFT LINKAGE

iB5 Transaxle

1. Shift transaxle into neutral, then remove gearshift lever cover.
2. Insert 3 mm drill bit **Fig. 1,** then raise and support vehicle.
3. Open shift and selector cable cover.
4. Unlock selector cable by depressing colored insert, then move selector to center position **Fig. 2.**
5. Move gearshift lever to righthand or lefthand stop position to engage 3rd or 4th gear, then lock selector cable **Fig. 3.**
6. Close shift and selector cable cover, then lower vehicle.
7. Remove drill bit, then install shift lever cover.

HYDRAULIC SYSTEM SERVICE

CLUTCH SYSTEM BLEED

iB5 Transaxle

1. Disconnect MAF sensor electrical connector then remove air intake pipe.
2. Drain brake fluid reservoir to MIN mark using suitable suction device.
3. Fill reservoir of vacuum pump tool No. 416–D002, or equivalent, with Super DOT 4 brake fluid to approximately 100 ml.
4. Install vacuum pump, **reservoir must be below bleed nipple.**
5. Open bleed nipple and pump approximately 80 ml of brake fluid into clutch control system.
6. Tighten bleeder screw, then remove vacuum pump.
7. Bleed clutch control system by depressing clutch pedal 4–5 times ensuring full travel is reached.
8. Install air intake pipe, then connect MAF sensor.
9. Check brake fluid level and fill with Super DOT 4 brake fluid if level is below MIN mark.
10. Start engine and carefully engage reverse after 2 seconds, if abnormal noises are heard depress clutch pedal 4–5 times ensuring full travel is reached. If abnormal noises are still heard, repeat steps 1–9.

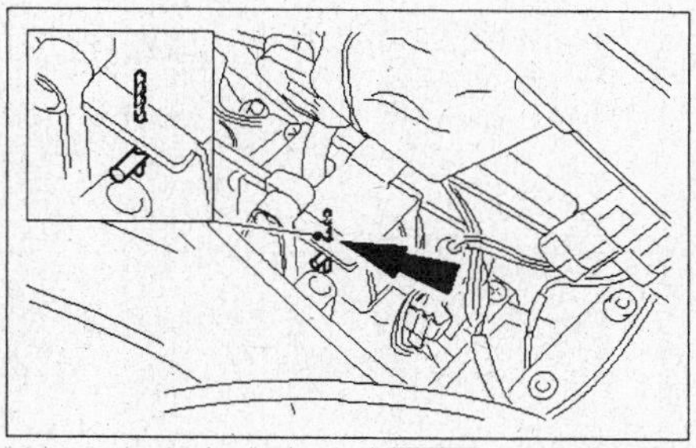

FM5049900106000X

Fig. 1 3m drill bit placement

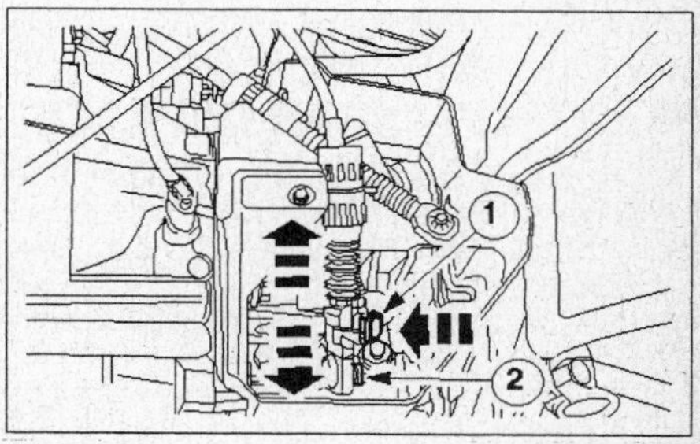

FM5049900107000X

Fig. 2 Shift linkage adjustment

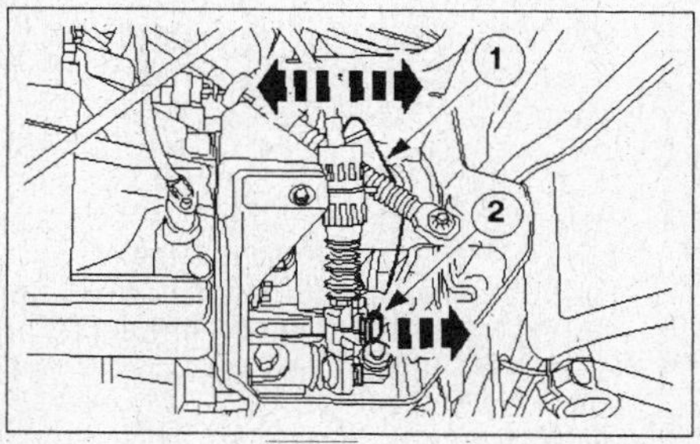

FM5049900108000X

Fig. 3 3rd or 4th gear adjustment

MTX75 Transaxle

1. Fill brake fluid reservoir to top edge with Super DOT 4 brake fluid.
2. Remove protective cap from bleed nipple, then install a suitable transparent hose.
3. Place hose in a suitable container, then depress clutch pedal slowly several times and hold at bottom of its travel.
4. Open bleed nipple until brake fluid flows through bleed hose, then tighten bleed nipple.
5. Release clutch pedal and repeat steps 3 and 4 until brake fluid which flows into container is clear and free of bubbles.
6. Install protective cap, then depress clutch pedal ten times and check its operation.
7. Fill brake fluid reservoir with Super DOT 4 brake fluid if level is below MIN mark.

CLUTCH MASTER CYLINDER

1. Drain brake fluid reservoir.
2. Disconnect MAF sensor, then remove air cleaner assembly.
3. Remove central junction box.
4. Remove lines from clutch master cylinder.
5. Remove lower instrument panel cover, then footwell insulation panel.
6. Remove clutch master cylinder clip and mounting bolts

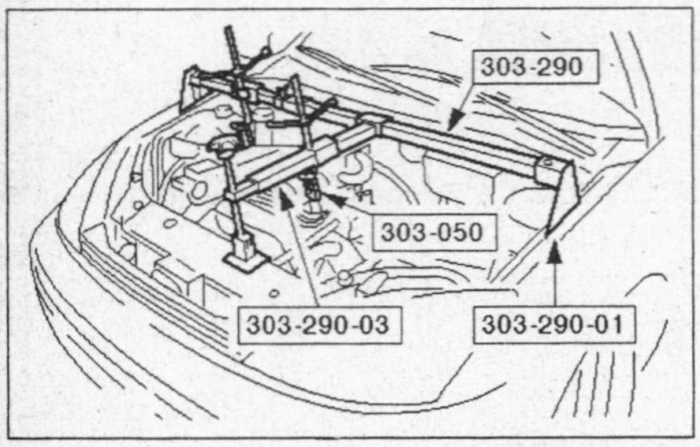

FM5049900109000X

Fig. 4 Engine support fixture

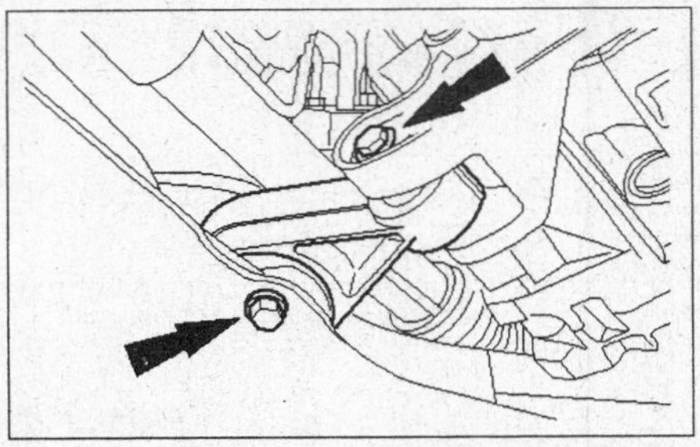

FM5049900110000X

Fig. 5 Roll restrictor

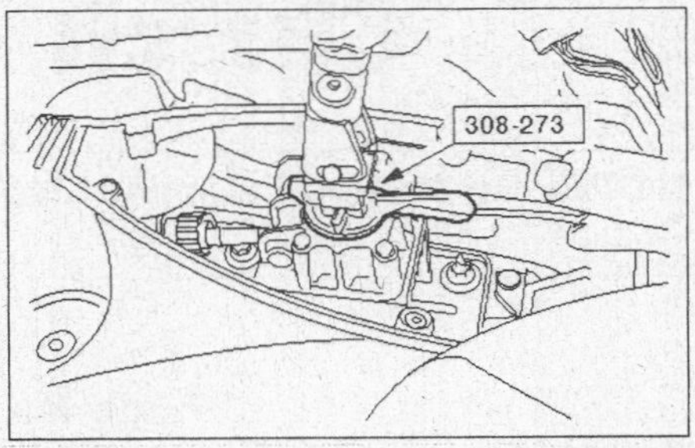

FM5049900111000X

Fig. 6 Gearshift lever aligner tool

7. Remove clutch master cylinder from pedal mount, then pull piston rod from clutch pedal.
8. Reverse procedure to install, bleed clutch system as outlined under "Clutch System Bleed."

SLAVE CYLINDER REPLACE

1. Remove Transaxle as outlined under "Transmission, Replace."
2. Remove slave cylinder bolts, then slave cylinder.
3. Reverse procedure to install noting the following:
   a. **On MTX75 transaxles,** use new slave cylinder and seal ring.
   b. **On all transaxles,** bleed clutch system as outlined under "Clutch System Bleed."

CLUTCH

REPLACE

1. Remove transaxle as outlined under "Transaxle, Replace."
2. Remove pressure plate bolts evenly loosening a maximum of two turns working in a diagonal pattern.
3. Remove pressure plate and clutch disc.
4. Reverse procedure to install noting the following:
   a. Use clutch disc alignment tool No. 308–020, or equivalent, to center clutch disc to locating pins on flywheel.
   b. Using new bolts, tighten bolts a maximum of two turns working in a diagonal pattern to specifications.
   c. Ensure input shaft of transaxle aligns squarely into hub of clutch disc.

TRANSAXLE

REPLACE

IB5 TRANSAXLE

1. Remove battery, then battery tray.
2. Using an allen key to prevent piston rod from rotating, loosen left and right strut nuts five turns.
3. Disconnect MAF sensor, then remove air cleaner assembly and intake pipe.
4. Remove high pressure line from clutch slave cylinder.
5. Disconnect vacuum hoses, VSS connector and reverse light switch connector.

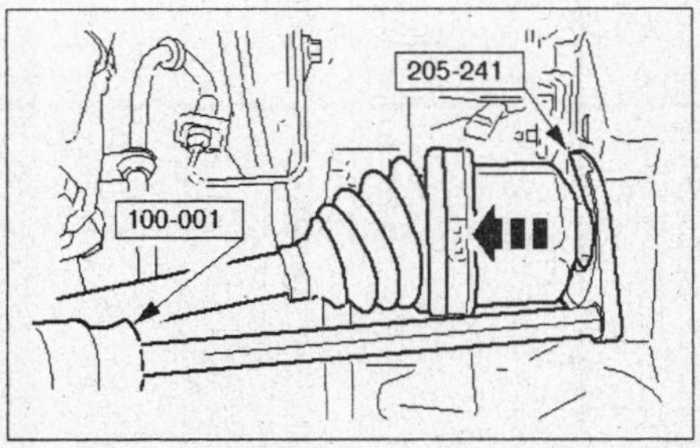

FM5049900112000X

Fig. 7 Lefthand driveshaft removal

6. Install engine support fixture tool Nos. 303–050, 303–290, 303–290–01 and 303–290–03, or equivalents **Fig. 4.**
7. Remove rear engine mount, then mounting bracket.
8. Using engine support, lower engine/transaxle.
9. Raise and support vehicle. then open cover on shift and selector cable.
10. Remove shift and selector cable end fittings from shift and selector lever.
11. Remove shift and selector cable from bracket by turning lower part of abutment clockwise and upper part counter clockwise.
12. Remove right and left lower suspension arm ball joints.
13. Remove righthand halfshaft intermediate bearing mounting bracket.
14. Remove righthand and lefthand halfshafts and secure, **ensure inner joints do not bend more than 18° and outer joints more than 45°.**
15. Disconnect front exhaust pipe and detach from rubber insulators, then remove roll resistor **Fig. 5.**
16. Using engine support lower engine/transaxle as far as possible.
17. Remove drive belt cover, then lower flange bolts.
18. Using suitable wooden block, tilt engine/transaxle forward.
19. Remove starter motor flange bolt, then position starter motor aside.
20. Support transaxle using suitable transaxle jack, then remove flange bolts and lower transaxle.
21. Reverse procedure to install tightening to specifications.

MTX75 TRANSAXLE

1. Remove battery, then battery tray.
2. Disconnect MAF sensor, crankcase ventilation hose and intake hose, then remove air cleaner assembly.
3. Disconnect ground lead.
4. Using an Allen key to prevent piston rod from rotating, loosen right and left strut nuts five turns.
5. Shift transaxle into neutral and remove gearshift lever cover, then install gearshift lever aligner tool No. 308–273, or equivalent, **Fig. 6.**
6. Remove intake tube, then air cleaner intake with resonator.
7. Remove shift cable from gear lever, then turn abutment collar counter clockwise and remove cable from bracket.
8. Remove selector cable from selector lever, then turn abutment collar counter clockwise and remove cable from bracket.
9. Raise and support vehicle, then remove flexible exhaust pipe.
10. Remove roll restrictor **Fig. 5.**
11. Remove righthand and lefthand suspension arms.
12. Loosen righthand driveshaft together with intermediate shaft.
13. Remove intermediate shaft bearing cap and discard cap and nuts.
14. Remove intermediate shaft from transaxle together with driveshaft and secure, **ensure inner joint does not bend more than 18° and outer joint more than 45°.**
15. Using driveshaft removal tool Nos. 100–001 and 205–241 or equivalent, **Fig. 7,** loosen driveshaft from transaxle.
16. Remove lefthand driveshaft from transaxle and secure, **ensure inner joint does not bend more than 18° and outer joint more than 45°.** Plug transaxle opening.
17. Remove drive belt cover, then lower vehicle.
18. Remove clutch slave cylinder high pressure line, then secure using suitable ties.
19. Disconnect reverse light switch connector.
20. Install engine support fixture tool Nos. 303–290A, 303–290–01, 303–290–02

and 303–290–03A, or equivalents **Fig. 8.**
21. Remove rear engine mount.
22. Using engine support lower engine/transaxle assembly slightly.
23. Remove rear engine mount bracket, then two upper flange bolts.
24. Remove starter motor bolts, then position and secure starter motor aside.
25. Raise and support vehicle, then disconnect VSS connector.
26. Push engine/transaxle assembly forward, then install suitable wooden block between engine and subframe.
27. Support transaxle using suitable transaxle jack, then remove lower flange bolts.
28. Lower transaxle from vehicle.
29. Reverse procedure to install tightening to specifications.

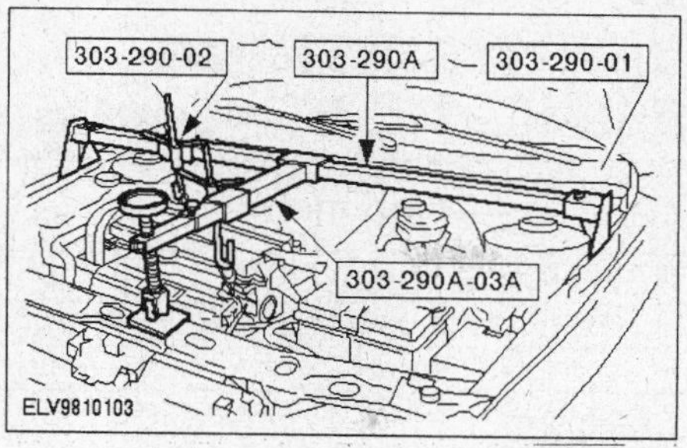

FM5049900113000X

Fig. 8 Engine support fixture

TIGHTENING SPECIFICATIONS

Year	Component	Torque, Ft. Lbs.
IB5 TRANSAXLE		
2000	Battery Box	18
	Bleed Nipple	89①
	Clutch Slave Cylinder	89①
	Engine Roll Restrictor To Engine	35
	Engine Roll Restrictor To Subframe	35
	Flange Bolts Transaxle To Engine	35
	Front Exhaust Pipe	35
	Gearshift Cable Bracket	15
	Gearshift Cable Cover	44①
	Lower Suspension Arm To Spindle Carrier	35
	Pressure Plate	21
	Rear Engine Mount	35
	Rear Engine Mount Bracket	59
	Rear Engine Mount Strut	89①
	Reverse Lamp Switch	13
	Selector Finger	13
	Selector Gate	16
	Selector Lever To Selector Shaft	18
	Slave Cylinder High Pressure Line Bracket	21
	Suspension Strut Nut Top	35
	Transaxle Fluid Filler Plug	26
	Transaxle Housing	17
	Transaxle Housing Final Cover	10

Continued

TIGHTENING SPECIFICATIONS—Continued

Year	Component	Torque, Ft. Lbs.
MTX75 TRANSAXLE		
2000	Ball Joint To Selector Lever Shaft	11
	Bleed Nipple	10
	Catalytic Convertor To Exhaust	35
	Clutch Slave Cylinder To Transaxle	89①
	Flange Bolts	35
	Gearshift Lever To Gearshift Lever Shaft	22
	Gearshift Lever To Selector Shaft	30
	Lower Suspension Arm Ball Joint To Spindle Carrier	35
	Pressure Plate	21
	Rear Engine Mount Bracket To Transaxle	59
	Rear Engine Mount Central Nut	98
	Rear Engine Mount Four Nuts	35
	Reverse Gear Idler Shaft Mount	25
	Reverse Light Actuating Pin	18
	Reverse Light Switch	89①
	Righthand Halfshaft Center Bearing To Bracket	18
	Roll Restrictor To Subframe	35
	Roll Restrictor To Transaxle	35
	Selector Gate To Housing	89①
	Selector Finger To Selector Shaft	21
	Starter Motor To Transaxle Housing	26
	Suspension Strut Nut	35
	Transaxle End Housing To Clutch End Hosing Section	24
	Transaxle Fluid Drain Plug	33
	Transaxle Fluid Fill Plug	33

① — Inch lbs.

Rear Suspension

NOTE: On Air Bag Equipped Models, Refer To "Electrical" Section Of This Chapter For System Disarming & Arming Procedures.

INDEX

PRECAUTIONS

AIR BAG SYSTEMS

Refer to "Electrical" section of this chapter for system disarming and arming procedures.

BATTERY GROUND CABLE

Prior to service, disconnect battery ground cable and isolate as required.

DESCRIPTION

Refer to **Figs. 1 and 2,** when removing rear suspension components.

HUB & BEARING

REPLACE

1. Raise and support vehicle, then remove wheel.
2. Remove dust cap, if dust cap is damaged on removal a new dust cap must be used on installation.
3. Remove hub retaining nut **Fig. 3.**
4. Remove hub assembly.
5. Remove and discard ABS sensor ring.
6. Remove circlip, then using a suitable drift, press out the bearing **Fig. 4.**
7. Reverse procedures to install. Tighten new retainer and wheel lug nuts to specifications.

WHEEL BEARING INSPECTION

1. Raise and support vehicle and check loose bearing by rocking wheels at top and bottom.
2. Spin wheel quickly by hand and make sure wheel turns smoothly without noise.
3. Position Dial Indicator Gauge Bracket Tool No. 100–D004 and Dial Indicator Gauge Tool No. 100–D005, or equivalent, against wheel hub, then push and pull wheel hub.**Fig. 5.**
4. Push and pull wheel by hand in an axial direction and measure end play.
5. If end play exceeds specifications, check and adjust rear axle wheel hub retainer, replace bearing as necessary.

REAR WHEEL SPINDLE

REPLACE

1. Release parking brake adjustment.
2. Loosen wheel nuts, raise and support vehicle, then remove wheel.
3. **On models with anti-lock brakes,** detach wheel speed sensor **Fig. 6.**
4. **On all models,** remove dust cap, if dust cap is damaged during removal, replace with new cap **Fig. 7.**
5. Remove hub retaining nut, then brake drum. CAUTION: Use a socket to remove hub retaining nut to prevent damage. Ensure ABS ring is not knocked or damaged and is kept free from metallic fragments when removing brake drum.
6. Remove wheel spindle **Fig. 8.**
7. Reverse procedures to install noting the following:
   a. Tighten parking brake adjustment.
   b. CAUTION: Use a socket to install hub retaining nut to prevent damage. Ensure ABS ring is not knocked or damaged and is kept free from metallic fragments when installing brake drum.

SHOCK ABSORBER

REPLACE

1. **On 3–door models,** remove luggage compartment interior trim panel, then remove shock absorber top mounting nut **Fig. 9.**
2. **On all models,** raise and support vehicle.
3. Remove lower shock absorber bolt.
4. Remove upper shock absorber bolt, then remove shock absorber **Figs. 10 and 11.**
5. Reverse procedure to install noting the following:
   a. Final tightening of suspension components must be performed with vehicle weight on road wheels.
   b. Tighten lower mounting bolt to specifications.

CONTROL ARM

REPLACE

REAR LOWER ARM

1. Loosen wheel nuts, then raise and support vehicle.
2. Set suspension to design height.
3. Remove rear wheel.
4. Remove stabilizer bar link from lower arm.
5. Using suitable coil spring compressor, remove rear lower arm **Fig. 12.**
6. Reverse procedure to install lower arm.

FRONT LOWER ARM

1. Set suspension to design height.
2. Remove mounting bolts, then remove front lower arm **Fig. 13.**
3. Reverse procedures to install.

UPPER ARM

1. Loosen wheel nuts, then set suspension to design height.
2. Remove wheel and outer bolt **Fig. 14.**
3. Remove inner bolt, then remove upper arm **Fig. 15.**
4. Reverse procedures to install.

COIL SPRING

Refer to "Control Arm, Replace" when removing coil spring.

TIE-BAR

REPLACE

1. Remove brake backing plate.
2. Detach parking brake sleeve, then detach parking brake cable **Fig. 16.**
3. Detach cable guide, then pull cable and guide through tie-bar.
4. Detach rear brake flex hose, disconnecting pipe at union **Fig. 17.**
5. Set suspension to design height.
6. Remove shock absorber lower bolt, front lower arm outer bolt, then remove.

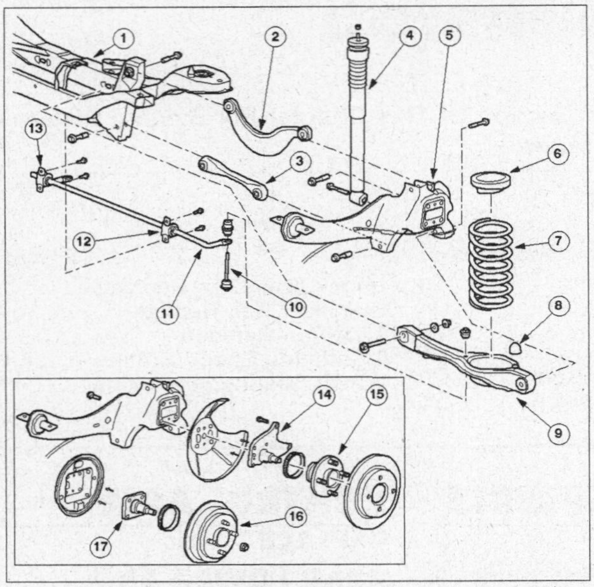

Item	Description
1	Crossmember
2	Upper arm
3	Front lower arm
4	Shock absorber assembly
5	Tie-bar and knuckle
6	Spring pad
7	Spring
8	Bump stop
9	Rear lower arm
10	Stabilizer bar link
11	Stabilizer bar
12	Stabilizer bar bushing
13	Stabilizer bar bushing clamp
14	Wheel spindle (disc brakes)
15	Wheel hub (disc brakes)
16	Drum and hub assembly (drum brakes)
17	Wheel spindle (drum brakes)

FM2039900095000X

Fig. 1 Rear suspension. Except Wagon

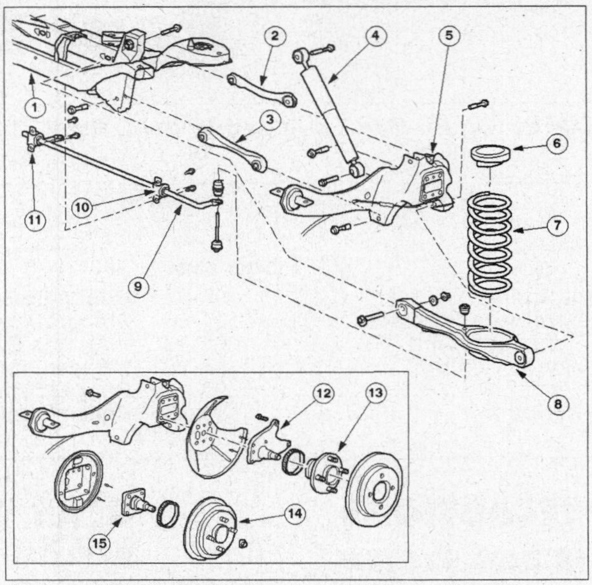

Item	Description
1	Crossmember
2	Upper arm
3	Front lower arm
4	Shock absorber
5	Tie-bar and knuckle
6	Spring pad
7	Spring
8	Rear lower arm
9	Stabilizer bar
10	Stabilizer bar bushing
11	Stabilizer bar bushing clamp
12	Wheel spindle (disc brakes)
13	Wheel hub (disc brakes)
14	Drum and hub assembly (drum brakes)
15	Wheel spindle (drum brakes)

FM2039900096000X

Fig. 2 Rear suspension. Wagon

7. Using suitable coil spring compressor, remove rear lower arm bolts **Fig. 18.**
8. Remove spring.
9. Detach and remove upper arm.
10. Remove tie-bar front mounting bolts, then tie-bar.
11. Reverse procedures to install noting the following:
    a. Bleed brake system.
    b. Check rear wheel alignment.

REAR CROSSMEMBER

REPLACE

1. Raise and support vehicle.
2. Remove stabilizer bar as described under "Stabilizer Bar, Replace."
3. Remove rear lower arms, front lower arms and upper arms as described under "Control Arm, Replace." Ensure wheel knuckles are supported before removing arms.
4. Support exhaust system, then remove exhaust system bracket.
5. **On 3–door models,** disconnect EVAP emission canister vent solenoid electrical connector **Fig. 19.**
6. Remove vent pipes, then emission canister **Fig. 20.**
7. **On all models,** support rear crossmember with suitable jack, then remove three retaining bolts from either side **Fig. 21.**
8. Lower and remove crossmember.
9. Reverse procedures to install noting the following:
    a. Do not lower suspension from design height.
    b. Check rear wheel alignment.

STABILIZER BAR

REPLACE

1. Set suspension to design height.
2. Detach stabilizer bar link from rear lower arms **Fig. 22.**
3. Remove stabilizer bar from both sides **Fig. 23.**
4. Reverse procedures to install noting the following:
    a. Verify bushing nipple is on the left-hand side when installing onto stabilizer bar in either side **Fig. 24.**
    b. Apply water to clamp to assist installation.

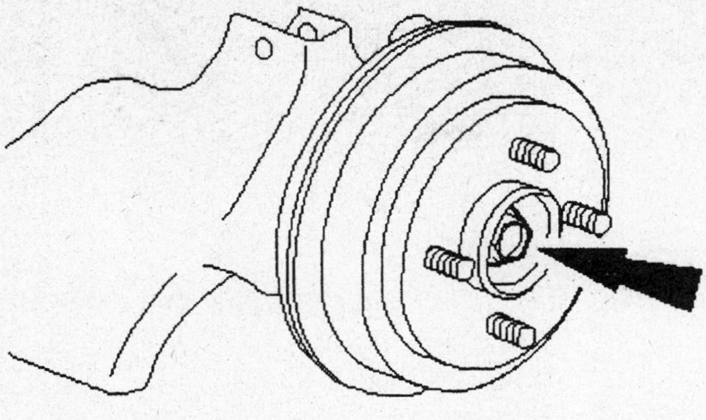

FM2039900097000X

Fig. 3 Hub nut removal

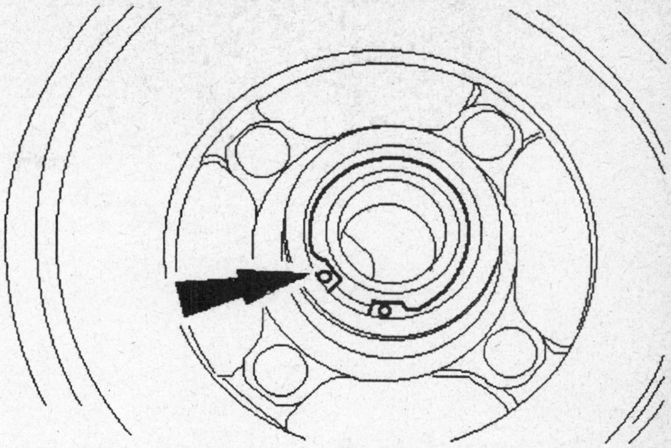

FM2039900098000X

Fig. 4 Circlip removal

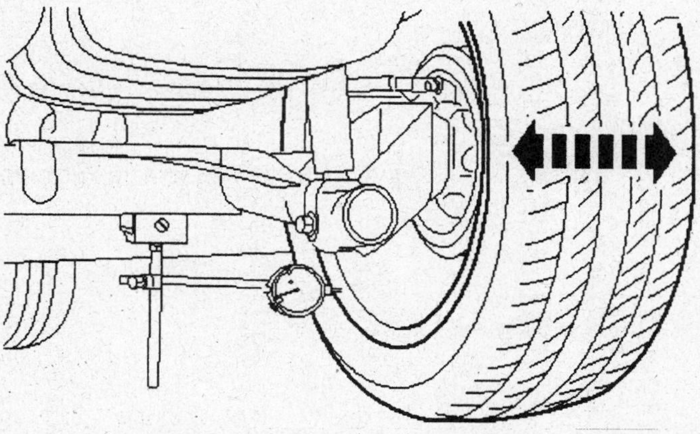

FM2039900099000X

Fig. 5 Wheel bearing inspection

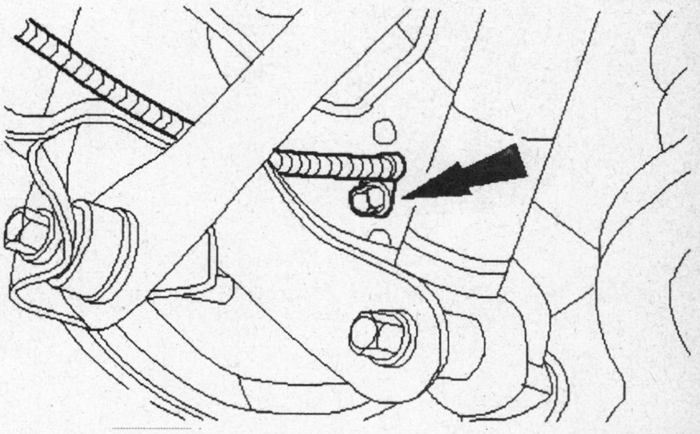

FM2039900100000X

Fig. 6 Wheel speed sensor removal

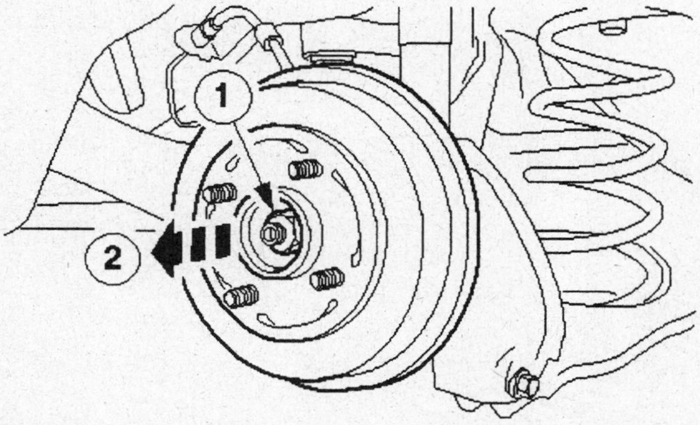

FM2039900101000X

Fig. 7 Hub nut & cap removal

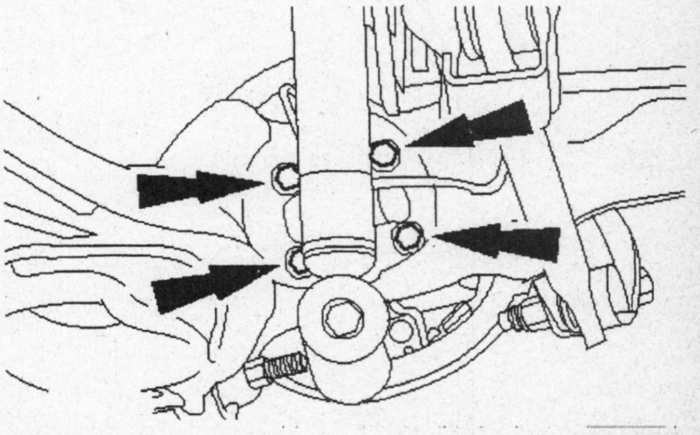

FM2039900102000X

Fig. 8 Spindle removal

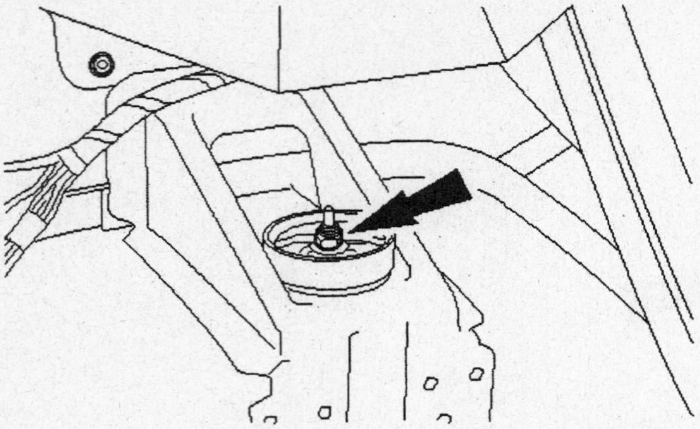

FM2039900103000X

Fig. 9 Shock absorber removal (3-door)

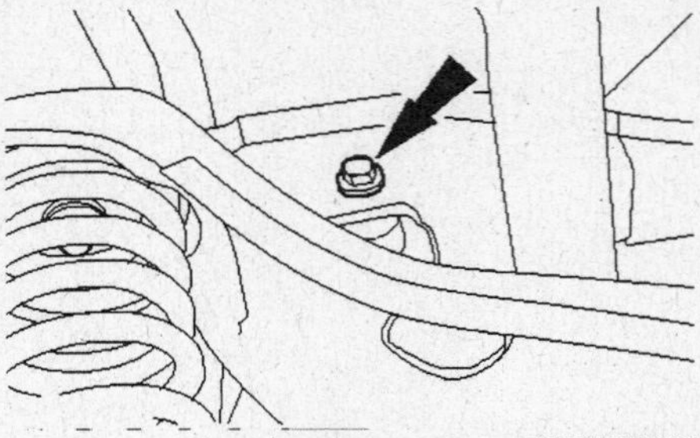

FM2039900104000X

Fig. 10 Upper bolt removal

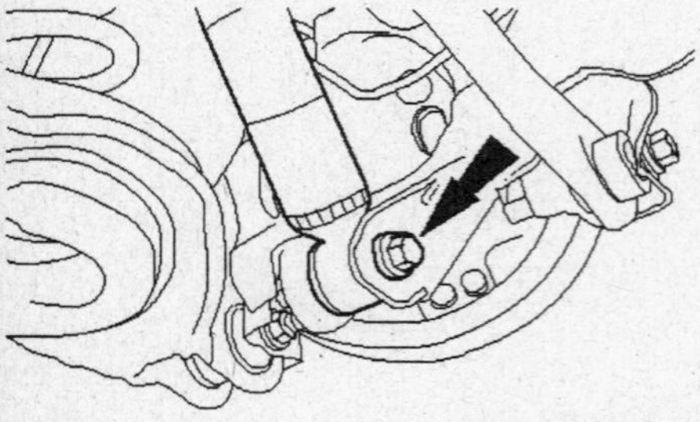

FM2039900105000X

Fig. 11 Lower bolt & shock removal

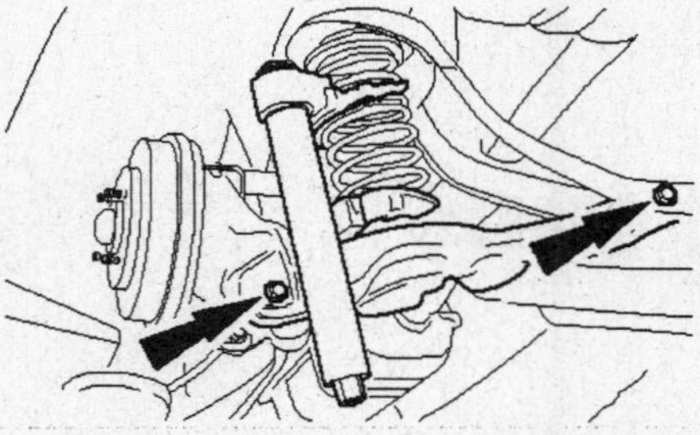

FM2039900106000X

Fig. 12 Rear lower arm removal

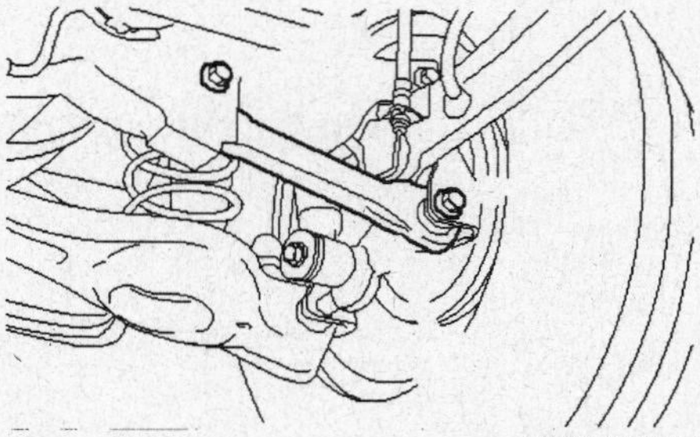

FM2039900107000X

Fig. 13 Front lower arm removal

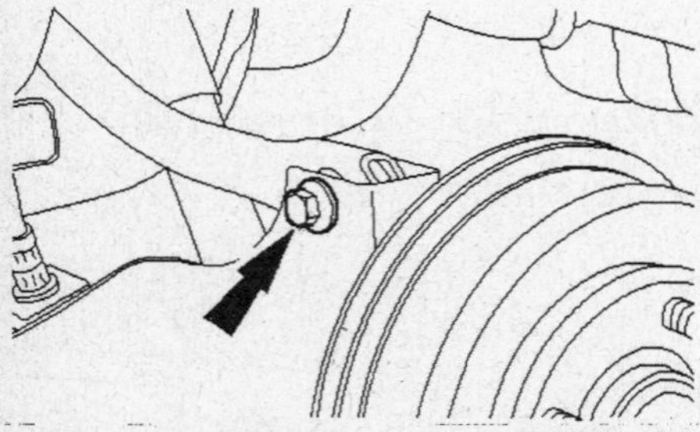

FM2039900108000X

Fig. 14 Upper arm bolt removal

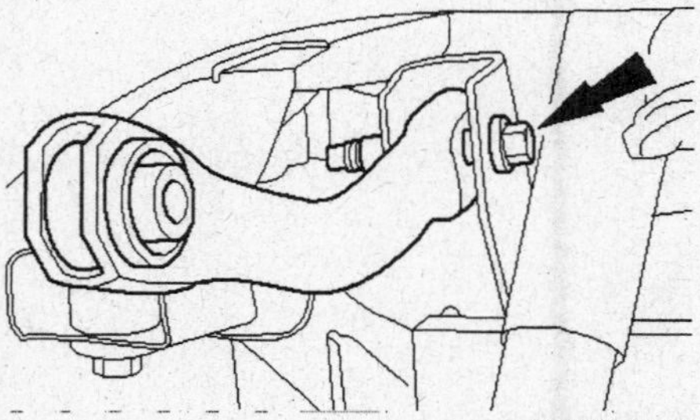

FM2039900109000X

Fig. 15 Upper arm removal

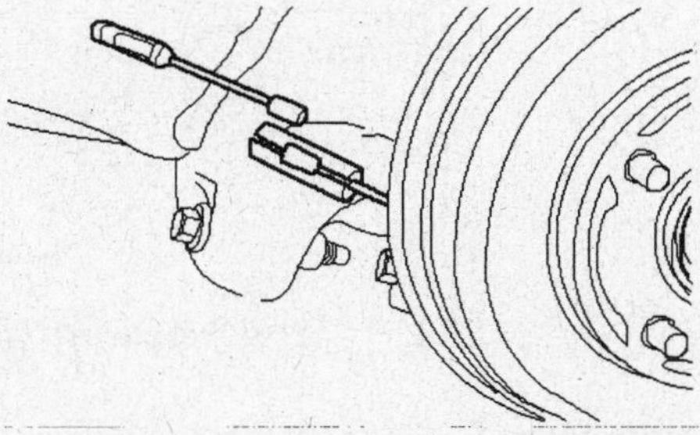

FM2039900110000X

Fig. 16 Parking brake cable removal

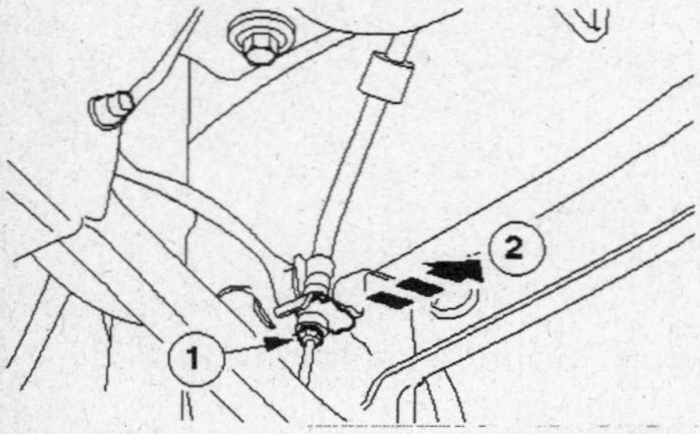

FM2039900111000X

Fig. 17 Brake pipe union removal

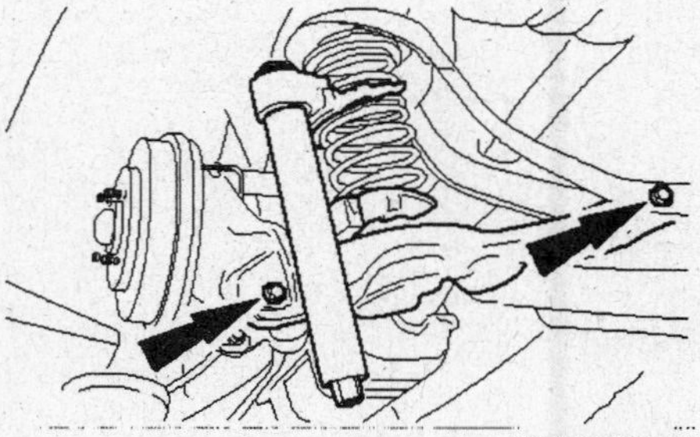

FM2039900112000X

Fig. 18 Spring & lower arm bolt removal

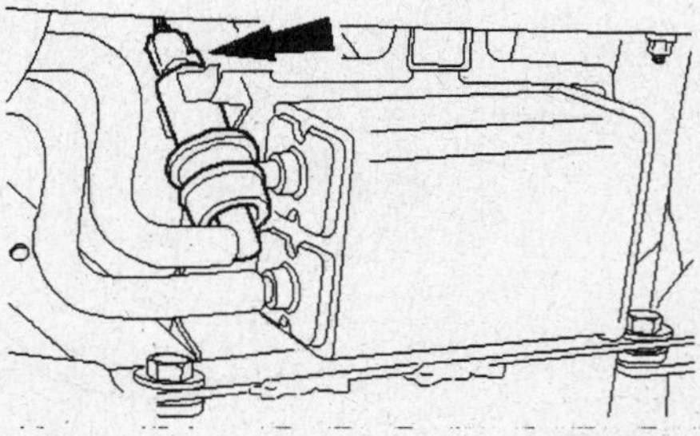

FM2039900113000X

Fig. 19 EVAP emission canister connector removal

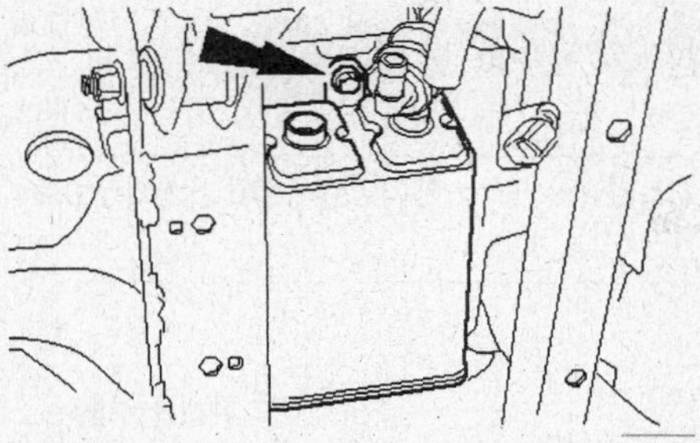

FM2039900114000X

Fig. 20 EVAP canister removal

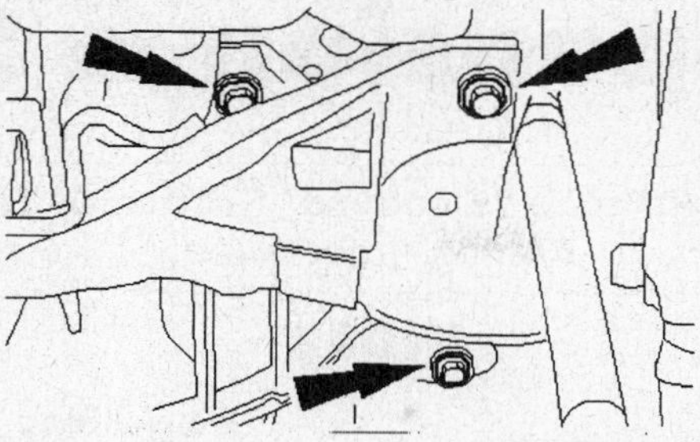

FM2039900115000X

Fig. 21 Crossmember removal

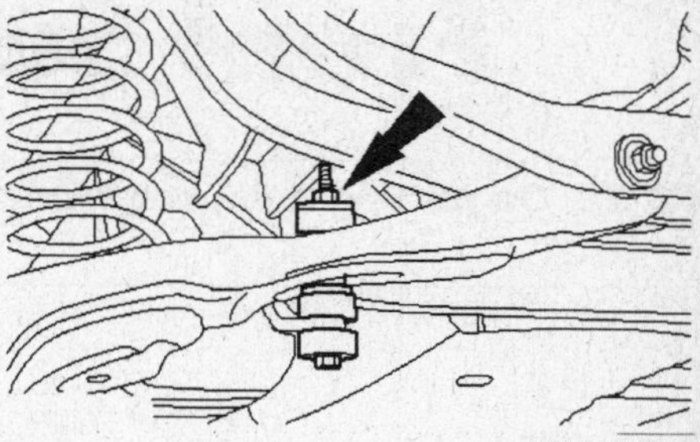

FM2039900116000X

Fig. 22 Stabilizer bar link removal

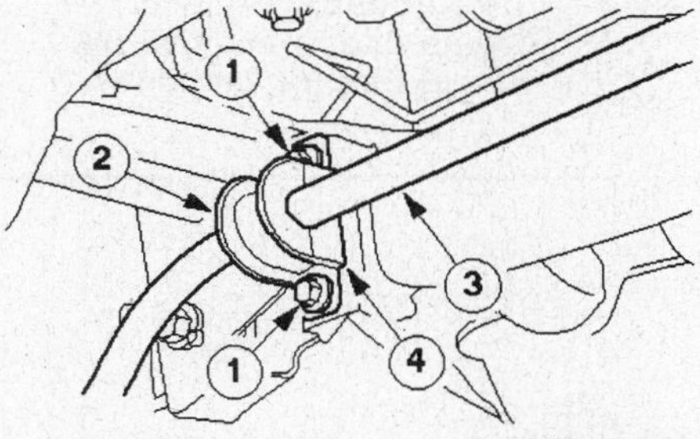

FM2039900117000X

Fig. 23 Stabilizer bar removal

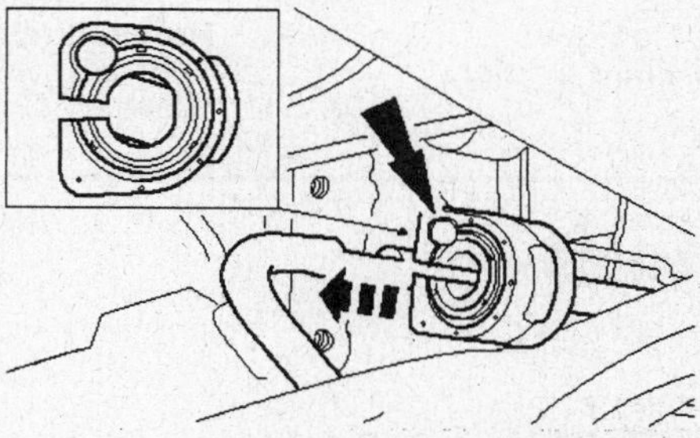

FM2039900118000X

Fig. 24 Stabilizer bushing

TIGHTENING SPECIFICATIONS

Year	Component	Torque, Ft. Lbs
2000	Crossmember Retaining Bolt	85
	EVAP Canister Bolt	84①
	Front Lower Arm Bolt	85
	Inside Rear Lower Arm Bolt	84①
	Lower Arm Bolt	85
	Lower Shock Bolt	85
	Lug Nut	94
	Outside Rear Lower Arm Bolt	85
	Spindle Bolt	49
	Stabilizer Bar Link	11
	Stabilizer Bracket Bolt	35
	Tie Bar Mounting Bolt	85
	Top Shock Mounting Bolt	13
	Upper Arm Bolt	85
	Upper Shock Bolt	85
	Wheel Hub Nut	173
	Wheel Speed Sensor	84①

① — Inch lbs.

Front Suspension & Steering

NOTE: On Air Bag Equipped Models, Refer To "Electrical" Section Of This Chapter For System Disarming & Arming Procedures.

INDEX

PRECAUTIONS

AIR BAG SYSTEMS

Refer to "Electrical" section of this chapter for system disarming and arming procedures.

BATTERY GROUND CABLE

Prior to service, disconnect battery ground cable and isolate as required.

DESCRIPTION

Refer to **Fig. 1** for exploded view of front suspension.

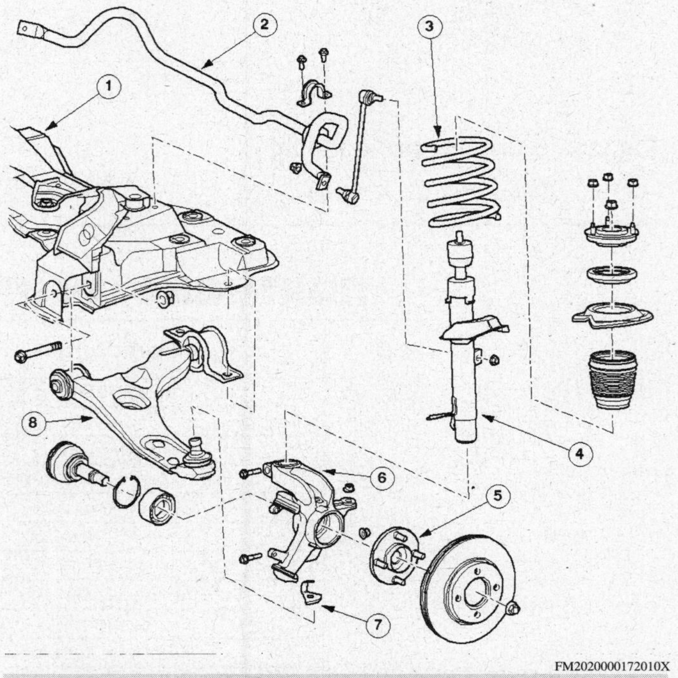

Fig. 1 Exploded view of front suspension (Part 1 of 2)

HUB & BEARING

REPLACE

1. Remove knuckle as outlined under "Steering Knuckle, Replace."
2. Using bearing puller No. 205–D064, or equivalent, and suitable drift, remove wheel hub and outer bearing race, **Fig. 2.**
3. Remove bearing circlip.
4. Using suitable drift, remove inner bearing.
5. Using bearing cup installer No. 205–139, or equivalent, and suitable drift, install new bearing.
6. Install bearing circlip.
7. Install wheel hub.
8. Install knuckle.

WHEEL BEARING INSPECTION

The wheel bearing cannot be adjusted. Replacement is required if inspection fails.

1. Road test vehicle on smooth road. Make several right and left turns.
2. Replace left bearing if noise is heard on right turns.
3. Replace right bearing if noise is heard on left turns.
4. If noise is heard on right and left turns, inspect side that is louder first.
5. Inspect bearing as follows:
   a. Raise and support vehicle. rock wheels at top and bottom to check for bearing looseness.
   b. Spin wheel quickly by hand. Ensure wheel turns smoothly without noise from bearing.
   c. Remove wheel and tire assembly, then brake caliper anchor plate.
   d. Position dial indicator gauge bracket and gauge Nos. 100–D004 & 100–D005, or equivalent, against wheel hub, then push and pull wheel hub.
   e. Measure end play.
   f. Replace bearing if end play exists.

BALL JOINT

REPLACE

Refer to "Control Arm, Replace" when servicing the ball joint.

STRUT

REPLACE

1. Raise and support vehicle, then remove wheel and tire assembly.
2. Remove knuckle as outlined under "Steering Knuckle, Replace."

Item	Description
1	Crossmember
2	Stabilizer bar
3	Spring
4	Strut
5	Wheel hub
6	Wheel knuckle
7	Lower arm ball joint heat shield
8	Lower arm

FM2020000172020X

Fig. 1 Exploded view of front suspension (Part 2 of 2)

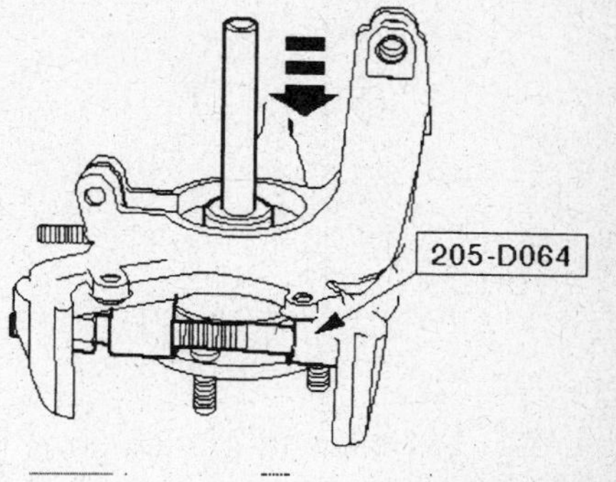

FM2020000168000X

Fig. 2 Hub & outer race removal

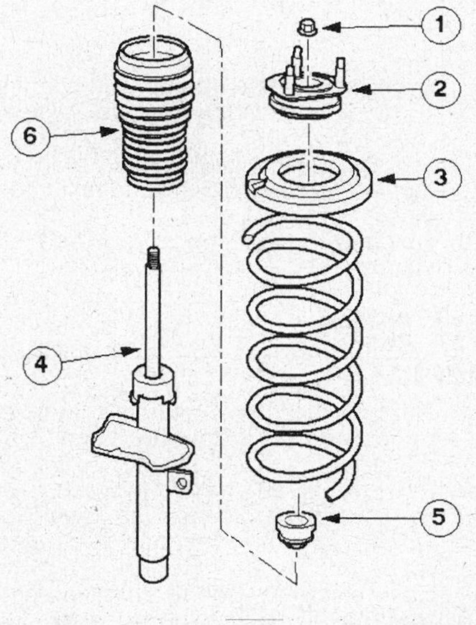

FM2020000180000X

Fig. 3 Strut & spring service

3. Remove strut tower nuts, then strut and spring assembly from vehicle.
4. Reverse procedure to install.

COIL SPRING & STRUT SERVICE

1. Using suitable coil spring compressor, compress spring.
2. Use suitable allen key to prevent piston rod rotation, then remove thrust bearing nut.
3. Disassemble strut and spring assembly as shown, **Fig. 3.**
4. Reverse procedure to assemble.

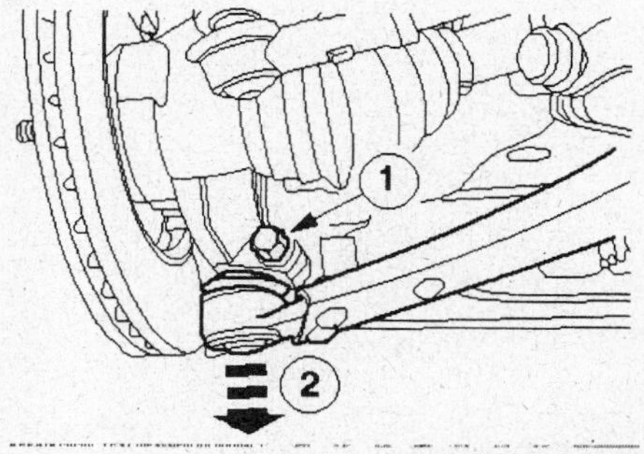

FM2020000169000X

Fig. 4 Ball joint removal

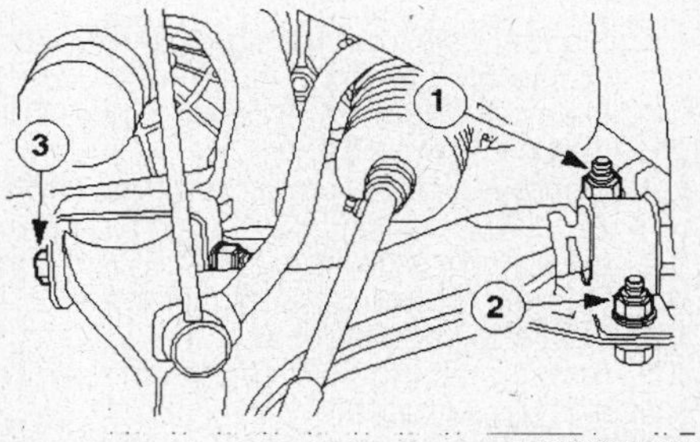

FM2020000171000X

Fig. 6 Lower arm tightening sequence

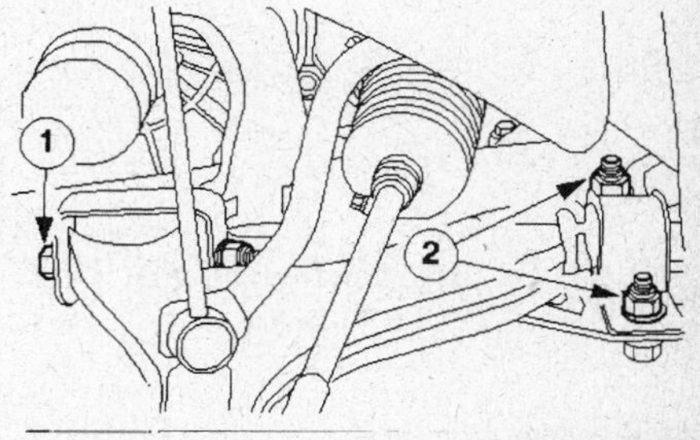

FM2020000170000X

Fig. 5 Lower arm removal

CONTROL ARM

REPLACE

1. Raise and support vehicle, then remove wheel and tire assembly.
2. Remove ball joint bolt, then ball joint from knuckle, **Fig. 4.**
3. Remove lower arm bolts, **Fig. 5.**
4. Remove lower arm from vehicle.
5. Install lower arm. New nuts, bolts and washers must be used.
6. Referring to **Fig. 6,** tighten bolts and nuts as follows:
   a. **Torque** nut 1 to 74 ft. lbs.
   b. Tighten nut 1 an additional 60°.
   c. **Torque** nut 2 to 89 ft. lbs.
   d. **Torque** bolt 3 to 89 ft. lbs.
   e. Tighten bolt 3 an additional 90°. Ensure bolt 3 torque is 125–170 ft. lbs.

STEERING KNUCKLE

REPLACE

1. Loosen strut tower nuts at least 5 turns.
2. Raise and support vehicle, then remove wheel and tire assembly.
3. Disconnect brake hose from support bracket.
4. Disconnect wheel speed sensor, then remove and secure brake caliper.
5. Remove brake rotor.
6. Remove tie rod end using tie rod end remover No. 211–001, or equivalent.
7. Remove ball joint from knuckle.
8. Remove hub retaining nut, then using suitable puller, separate wheel hub from half shaft.
9. Remove knuckle pinch bolt from strut.
10. Remove knuckle from strut, then vehicle.
11. Reverse procedure to install. Refer to **Fig. 7** when installing halfshaft.

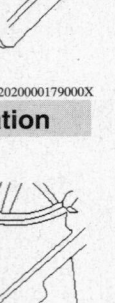

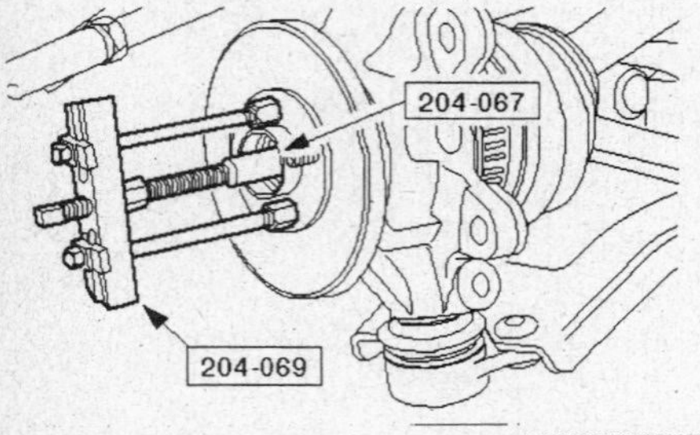

Fig. 7 Halfshaft installation

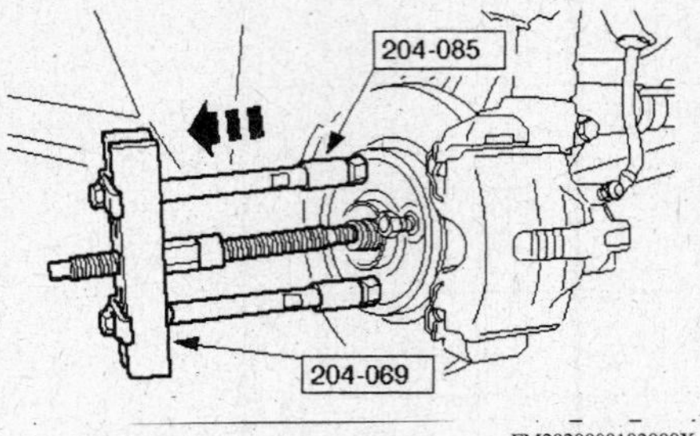

Fig. 8 Halfshaft separation

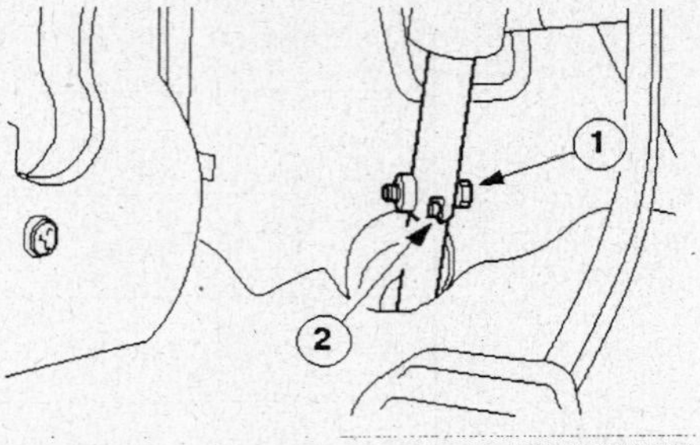

Fig. 9 Column shaft removal

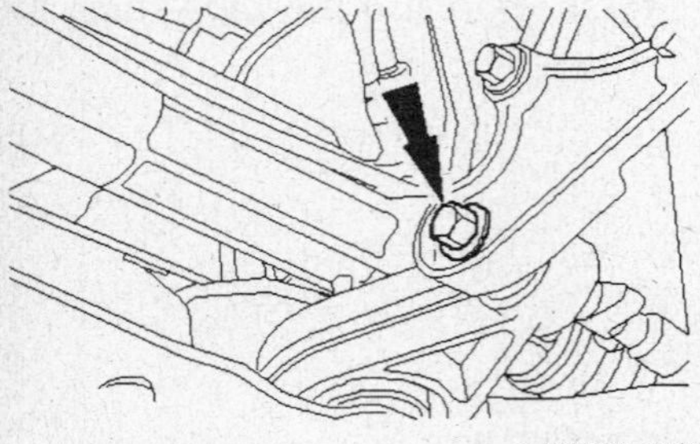

Fig. 10 Support insulator bolt removal

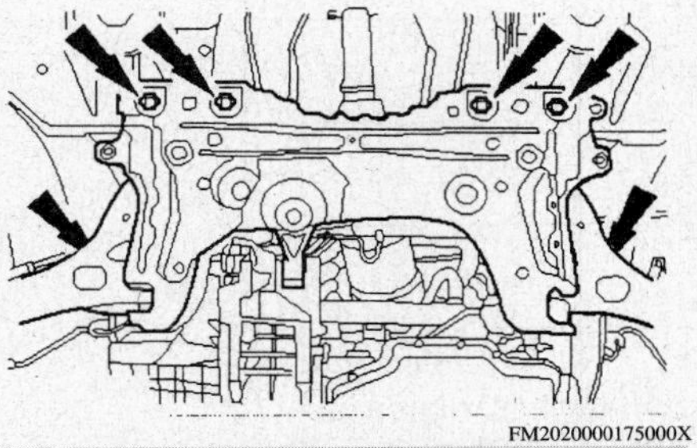

Fig. 11 Crossmember removal

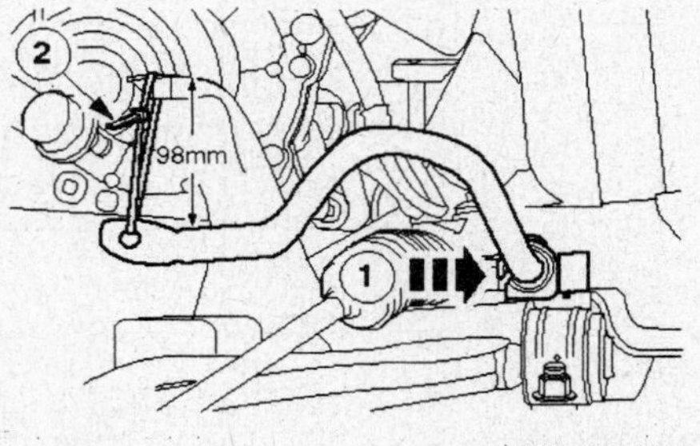

Fig. 12 Stabilizer bar design height setting

HALFSHAFT

REPLACE

1. Loosen strut lock nut 5 rotations. Use allen key to prevent piston from rotating.
2. Raise and support vehicle, then remove wheel and tire assembly.
3. Disconnect ball joint from knuckle.
4. Remove hub nut.
5. Using puller No. 204–069 and stud extension tool No. 204–085, or equivalents, **Fig. 8,** separate halfshaft from wheel hub.
6. **On right side,** remove intermediate shaft bearing mounting nuts.
7. **On either side,** remove halfshaft from transaxle using puller No. 205–241 and handle No. 100–001, or equivalents.
8. Allow fluid to drain into suitable container.
9. Reverse procedure to install. Ensure halfshaft is fully seated into transaxle.

STABILIZER BAR

REPLACE

1. Center steering wheel , then lock in position.
2. Disconnect steering column shaft from pinion extension, **Fig. 9.**
3. Raise and support vehicle, then remove wheel and tire assemblies.
4. Remove tie rod end nuts, then using tie rod end remover No. 211–001, or equivalent, detach tie rod ends from knuckles.
5. Disconnect stabilizer bar links.
6. Remove ball joints from knuckles.

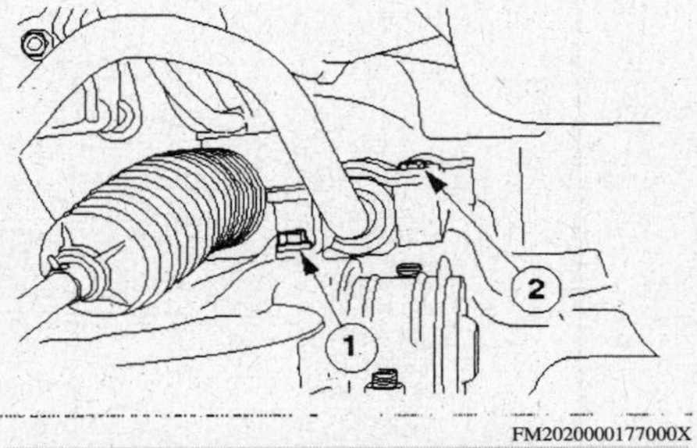

Fig. 13 Clamp tightening sequence

7. Remove support insulator to transaxle center bolt, **Fig. 10.**
8. Using suitable transmission jack, support crossmember.
9. Remove six crossmember bolts, **Fig. 11.**
10. Lower crossmember.
11. Remove clamp bolts and clamps.
12. Remove stabilizer bar.
13. Install bushings onto stabilizer bar. **Do not use lubricant.**
14. Set and support stabilizer bar to design height, **Fig. 12.**
15. Install clamps and clamp bolts.
16. Referring to **Fig. 13,** tighten bolts in sequence as follows:
    a. **Torque** bolts to 37 ft. lbs.
    b. **Torque** bolts to 52 ft. lbs.
17. Remove stabilizer supports.
18. Using alignment tool No. 502–002, or equivalent, align crossmember as follows:
    a. Insert guide pins through alignment holes, **Fig. 14.**
    b. Slide locking plates into grooves and tighten guide pin sleeve.
    c. Raise crossmember, engaging guide pins into chassis aligning holes.
19. Install crossmember bolts, then remove transmission jack and alignment pins.
20. Reverse remaining procedure to install.

TIE ROD

REPLACE

1. Remove steering gear as outlined under "Power Steering Gear, Replace."
2. Remove tie rod end and locknut.
3. Remove boot from steering gear.
4. Rotate pinion to expose rack gear teeth.
5. Secure steering gear in suitable vise.
6. Remove tie rod using suitable pipe wrench, **Fig. 15.**
7. Remove all traces of thread locking compound.
8. Reverse procedure to install. Apply thread locking compound to inner threads of new tie rod.

TIE ROD END

REPLACE

1. Raise and support vehicle, then remove wheel and tire assembly.
2. Loosen tie rod end lock nut, then remove retaining nut.
3. Using tie rod end remover No. 211–001, or equivalent, release tie rod end from knuckle.
4. Note number of turns required to remove tie rod end.

5. Remove tie rod end and lock nut.
6. Reverse procedure to install. Inspect toe adjustment after installation.

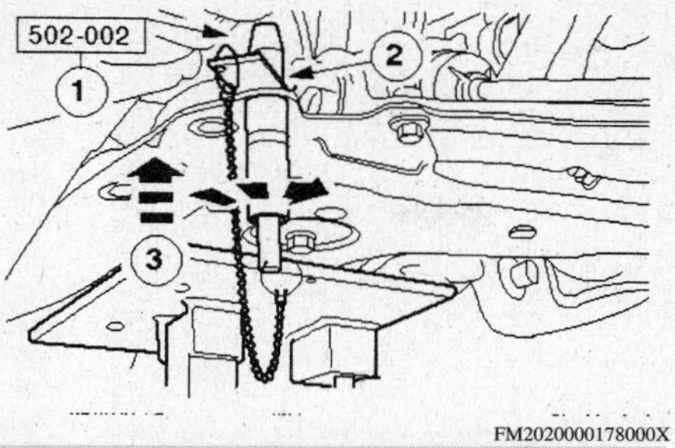

Fig. 14 Crossmember alignment

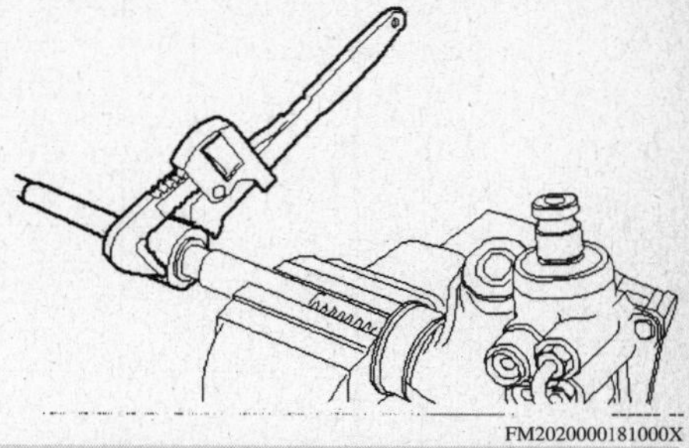

Fig. 15 Tie rod removal

POWER STEERING GEAR

REPLACE

Refer to **Fig. 16** for power steering system components.

1. Center steering wheel, then lock into position.
2. Remove instrument panel lower cover.
3. Disconnect steering column shaft from pinion extension.
4. Raise and support vehicle, then remove front wheel and tire assemblies.
5. Using tie rod end removal tool No. 211–001, or equivalent, remove tie rod ends from knuckles.
6. Disconnect stabilizer bar links from struts.
7. Using coupling tool No. 310–041, or equivalent, disconnect fluid cooler hose and allow fluid to drain into suitable container.
8. Remove support insulator to transaxle center bolt, **Fig. 17.**
9. Remove steering gear heat shield.
10. Disconnect hose support clamp, then remove power steering hoses from steering gear. Allow fluid to drain into suitable container.
11. Using suitable transmission jack, support crossmember.
12. Remove 6 crossmember bolts, **Fig. 18.**
13. Lower crossmember.
14. Remove steering column coupling shaft and floor seal.
15. Move floor seal upwards.
16. Remove bolts, then steering gear.
17. Inspect and replace O-rings as required.
18. Install steering column coupling shaft and floor seal.
19. Using alignment tool No. 502–002, or equivalent, align crossmember as follows:
    a. Insert guide pins through alignment holes, **Fig. 19.**
    b. Slide locking plates into grooves and tighten guide pin sleeve.
    c. Raise crossmember, engaging guide pins into chassis aligning holes.
20. Install crossmember bolts, then remove alignment pins.
21. Reverse remaining procedure to complete installation. Fill and bleed power steering system as outlined under “Power Steering System, Bleed.”

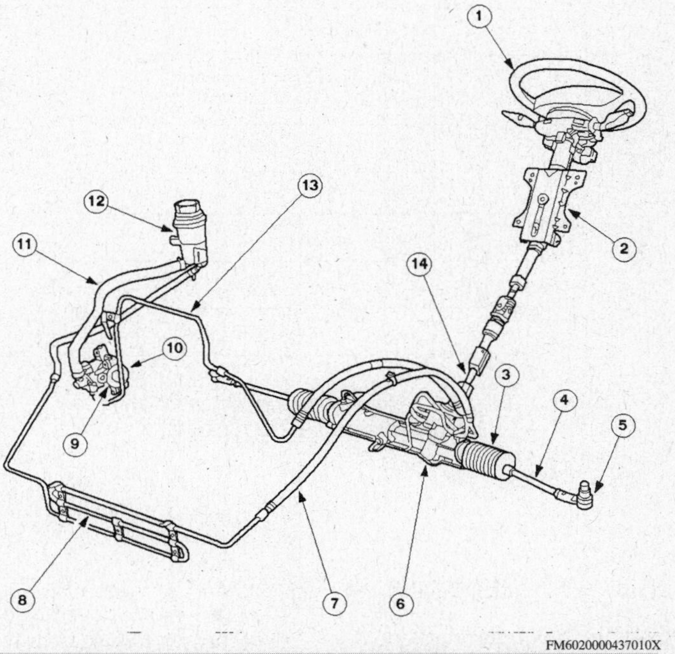

Fig. 16 Power steering system components (Part 1 of 2)

POWER STEERING PUMP

REPLACE

1. Remove accessory drive belt, then raise and support vehicle.
2. Using coupling tool No. 310–041, or equivalent, disconnect fluid cooler hose and allow fluid to drain into suitable container.
3. Lower vehicle, then detach pressure line support brackets.
4. Detach speed control cable as required.
5. Disconnect PSP switch electrical connector.
6. Cover alternator to prevent fluid contamination, then disconnect low pressure hose.
7. Disconnect pressure line union, then allow fluid to drain into suitable container.
8. Remove four pump bolts, then pump from vehicle.
9. Remove PSP switch and pressure hose union from pump.
10. Reverse procedure to install, noting the following:
    a. Using installer No. 211–D027, or equivalent, install new O-ring seal onto pressure line.
    b. Fill and bleed system as outlined under “Power Steering System, Bleed.”

POWER STEERING PUMP PULLEY

REPLACE

1. Remove accessory drive belt.
2. Using remover No. 211–185, or equivalent, remove power steering pump pulley. Ensure pulley is flush with end of pump shaft.
3. Reverse procedure to install.

POWER STEERING SYSTEM BLEED

1. Fill power steering fluid reservoir to MAX mark with fresh power steering fluid.
2. Start engine and slowly turn wheel from lock to lock once. Ensure fluid level does not fall below MIN mark as air could enter system.

Item	Description
1	Steering wheel
2	Steering column
3	Boot
4	Tie-rod
5	Tie-rod end
6	Steering gear
7	Steering gear to fluid cooler hose
8	Fluid cooler
9	Power steering pressure (PSP) switch
10	Power steering pump
11	Fluid supply hose
12	Fluid reservoir
13	Pump to steering gear hose
14	Steering column shaft coupling

FM6020000437020X

Fig. 16 Power steering system components (Part 2 of 2)

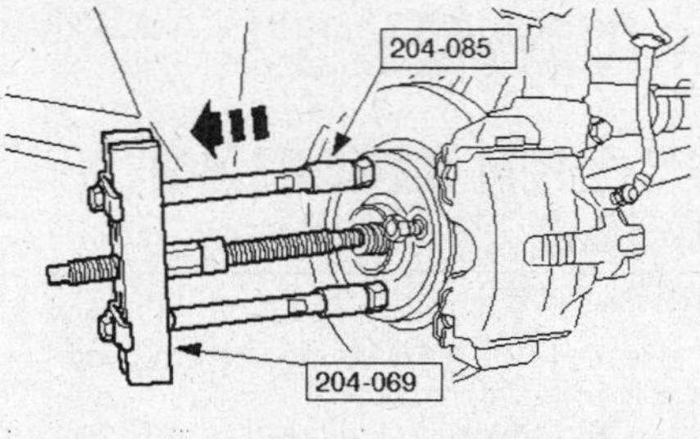

Fig. 17 Support bolt removal

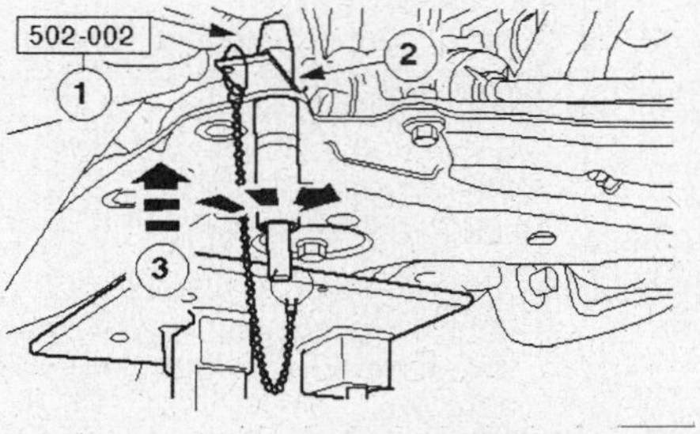

Fig. 19 Crossmember alignment

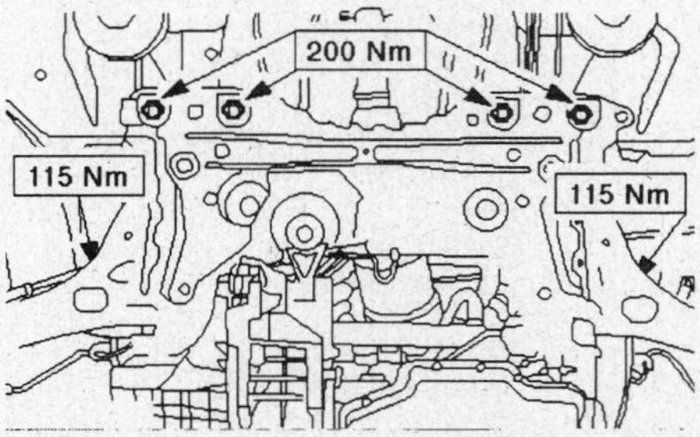

Fig. 18 Crossmember mounting bolts

3. Stop engine and inspect system for leaks.
4. Check and fill reservoir as required.
5. Using vacuum tool No. 416–D002, or equivalent, maintain a vacuum of 15 in.-Hg. If vacuum decreases more than 2 in.-Hg in 5 minutes, check for leaks.
6. Start engine and turn wheel from lock to lock once, then turn to the right just off the lock stop.
7. Stop engine and apply a vacuum of 15 in.-Hg. Maintain vacuum for 5 minutes until air is evacuated from the system.
8. Release vacuum, then repeat steps 6 and 7, turning wheel to the left, just off the stop lock.
9. Remove vacuum tool and fill reservoir as required.
10. Start engine and turn wheel from lock to lock. If excessive noise is apparent, repeat procedure.
11. If noise level is still unacceptable, allow vehicle to stand overnight and repeat procedure.

POWER STEERING FLUID COOLER

REPLACE

1. Disconnect coolant expansion tank and position aside.
2. Remove hose from power steering fluid reservoir and allow fluid to drain into suitable container.
3. Detach hose from bracket, then raise and support vehicle.
4. Remove radiator splash shield.
5. Using coupling tool No. 310–041, or equivalent, disconnect fluid cooler hose and allow fluid to drain into suitable container.
6. Remove fluid cooler from vehicle.
7. Reverse procedure to install. Fill and bleed power steering system as outlined under "Power Steering System, Bleed."

TIGHTENING SPECIFICATIONS

Year	Component	Torque, Ft. Lbs.
2000	Caliper To Knuckle Bolts	21
	Column Shaft to Pinion Bolt	26
	Crossmember Front Bolts	85
	Crossmember Rear Bolts	148
	Fluid Cooler Bolts	44①
	Hose Clamps	17
	Hub Nut	233
	Knuckle to Strut Pinch Bolt	66
	Lower Arm to Knuckle Pinch Bolt	37
	Pressure Line To Pump Union	48
	Pressure Line Support Bracket	②
	Pump Bolts	17
	PSP Switch	15
	Speed Sensor Bolt	80①
	Stabilizer Bar Link Nuts	37
	Steering Gear Bolts	59
	Steering Gear Heat Shield	53①
	Strut Mounting Nuts	18
	Strut Thrust Bearing Nut	35
	Support Insulator Center Bolt	37
	Tie Rod End Retaining Nuts	35
	Wheel Lug Nuts	63

① — Inch lbs.
② — DOHC engine, 18 ft. lbs. SOHC engine, 44 inch lbs.

Wheel Alignment

INDEX

PRELIMINARY INSPECTION

This procedure should be performed on a suitable flat surface in accordance with the equipment manufacturer's directions.

1. Inspect all suspension components for damage or wear and replace as required.
2. Inflate all tires to specifications.
3. Ensure vehicle is at curb weight.
4. The spare tire, jack and all vehicle tools must be in their proper locations.
5. Remove all luggage and additional items from vehicle.
6. Jounce vehicle to bring suspension to normal design height setting.

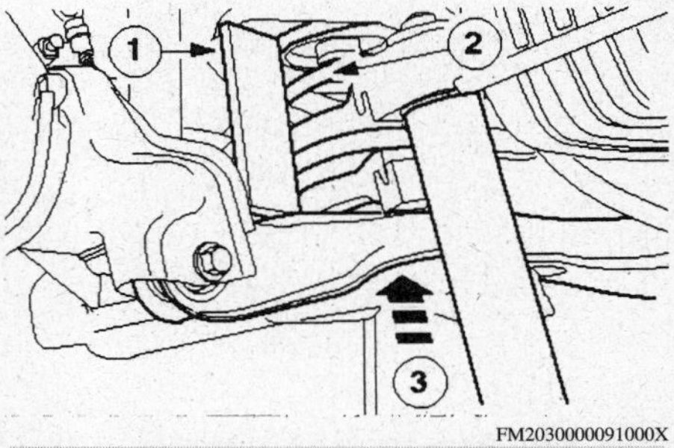

Fig. 1 Suspension design height setting

SUSPENSION DESIGN HEIGHT SETTING

The final suspension tightening procedures must be done only at the design height setting.

1. Raise and safely support vehicle.
2. **On sedan models,** proceed as follows:
   a. Fabricate a .787 inch wide by 4.45 inch long spacer.
   b. Compress suspension coil spring (2) using a suitable coil spring compressor until rear lower arm (3) contacts spacer (1), **Fig. 1,** then position spacer as illustrated and raise rear lower control arm.
   c. Remove jounce bumper (1), **Fig. 2,** then install spacer (2) between rear

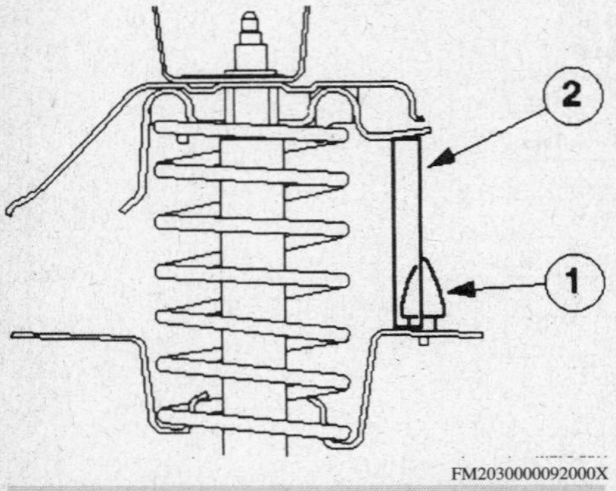

Fig. 2 Spacer installation. Sedan

lower arm and crossmember, ensuring it is in a vertical plane.

3. **On wagon models,** proceed as follows:
   a. Fabricate a .787 inch wide by 6.18 inch long spacer.
   b. Compress suspension using a suitable coil spring compressor until rear lower arm contacts spacer, **Fig. 1,** then position spacer as illustrated and raise rear lower control arm.
   c. Install spacer between rear lower arm and crossmember, ensuring it is in a vertical plane, **Fig. 3.**

FRONT WHEEL ALIGNMENT

CASTER & CAMBER

On these models, caster and camber are not adjustable.

TOE

1. Perform "Preliminary Inspection" as outlined in this section.
2. Inspect toe setting using suitable equipment.
3. Center the steering wheel, then lock it in position and remove ignition key.
4. Loosen both tie rod end locknuts.
5. Remove tie rod boot outer clamps.
6. Rotate each tie rod in equal clockwise or counterclockwise amounts to adjust toe setting.
7. **Torque** tie rod end locknuts to 46 ft. lbs.
8. Install boot outer clamps.
9. Inspect toe setting again and adjust if required.

REAR WHEEL ALIGNMENT

CASTER & CAMBER

On these models, caster and camber are not adjustable.

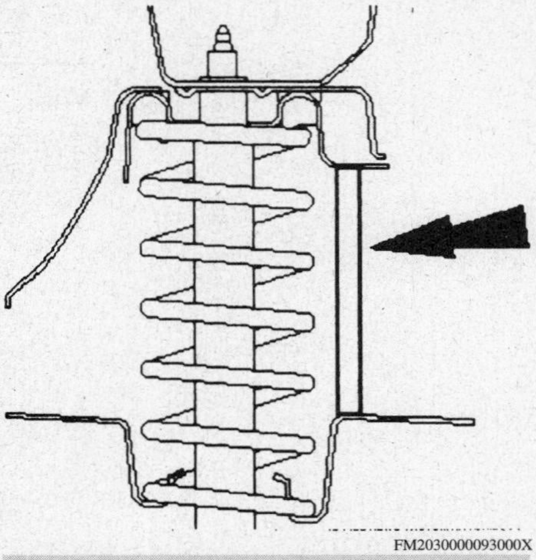

Fig. 3 Spacer installation. Wagon

TOE

1. Perform "Preliminary Inspection" as outlined in this section.
2. Inspect toe setting using suitable equipment.
3. Loosen rear lower arm cam bolt nut.
4. Rotate bolt and eccentric until proper toe setting is reached.
5. **Torque** cam bolt nut to 85 ft. lbs.
6. Inspect toe setting again and adjust if required.

AIR CONDITIONING

TABLE OF CONTENTS

System Testing

NOTE: On Air Bag Equipped Models, Refer To "Air Bag System Precautions" Located In The Front Of This Manual For System Disarming & Arming Procedures.

INDEX

PRECAUTIONS

BATTERY GROUND CABLE

Prior to service, disconnect battery ground cable and isolate as required.

SAFETY

Protective goggles should be worn when opening any refrigerant lines. A bottle of sterile mineral oil and a quantity of weak boric acid solution must always be kept nearby when servicing air conditioning system. **If liquid coolant does touch eyes, immediately use a few drops of sterile mineral oil to wash them out, then wash eyes clean with weak boric acid solution. Seek a doctor's aid immediately even though irritation may have ceased.**

Freon refrigerant used in vehicle A/C systems will usually be in a vapor state when being handled in a repair shop. But if a portion of liquid coolant should come in contact with hands or face, note that its temperature momentarily will be at least 22° below zero.

When checking a system for leaks with a torch type leak detector, do not breathe vapors coming from flame. Do not recover refrigerant in area of a live flame. A poisonous phosgene gas is produced when refrigerant is burned. While small amount of this gas produced by a leak detector is not harmful unless inhaled directly at flame.

Never allow temperature of refrigerant drums to exceed 125°F. Resultant increase in temperature will cause a corresponding increase in pressure which may cause safety plug to release or drum to burst.

If it is necessary to heat a drum of refrigerant when charging a system, drum should be placed in water that is no hotter than 125°F. Never use a blowtorch, or other open flame. If possible, a pressure release mechanism should be attached before drum is heated.

CLEANLINESS

Air conditioning systems are extremely sensitive to moisture and dirt. Importance of clean working conditions is extremely important, as smallest particle of foreign matter in an air conditioning system will contaminate refrigerant, causing rust, ice or damage to compressor. For this reason, all replacement parts are sold in vacuum sealed containers and should not be opened until they are to be installed in system. If, for any reason, a part has been removed from its container for any length of time, part must be completely flushed remove any dust or moisture that may have accumulated during storage. In cases of collision repairs where system has been open for any length of time, entire system must be purged completely and a new receiver-drier must be installed because element of existing unit will have become saturated and unable to remove any moisture from system once system is recharged.

When making gauge connections, purge gauge lines first by cracking charging valve and allowing a small amount of refrigerant to flow through lines, then connect lines immediately.

Cleanliness is especially important when servicing compressors because of very close tolerances used in these units. Consequently, repairs to compressor itself should not be attempted unless all proper tools are at hand and a virtually spotless work area is provided.

GENERAL SERVICE

Use care when disconnecting or connecting refrigerant lines; always use a back-up wrench and be careful not to overtighten any connection. Overtightening may result in a line or flare seat distortion and a system leak.

When making pressure checks on systems having service valves, be sure valve is in intermediate position. If turned in too far, hose connection will be closed, a position used for isolating compressor. When closing gauge port, do not overtighten valve or damage to seat will result.

After disconnecting gauge lines, check valve areas to be sure service valves are correctly seated and Schraeder valves, if used, are not leaking.

DESCRIPTION

Major components of R-134a air conditioning systems are similar to those used previously on R-12 fixed orifice tube type systems. R-12 and R-134a components are similar in design and function. As a result, all diagnosis and testing procedures for R-12 components can be used for R-134a system components. However, it should be noted that R-134a system components can only be replaced with other R-134a components. R-134a components cannot be replaced with components used with R-12 systems. Same rule applies for R-12 components, they cannot be replaced with R-134a components.

To identify which type of air conditioning system a particular vehicle has, visually inspect system for identification tags located on major components. R-134a system components have yellow R-134a NON-CFC tags. These systems can also be identified by a gold colored air conditioning compressor clutch and green colored O-rings used throughout system.

EXERCISE SYSTEM

An important fact most car owners ignore is that A/C system must be used periodically. Car manufacturers caution that when air conditioner is not used regularly, particularly during cold months, it should be turned on for a few minutes once every two or three weeks while engine is running. This keeps system in good operating condition.

Checking out system for effects of disuse before onset of summer is one of most important aspects of A/C system servicing.

First clean out condenser core, mounted in most cases at front of vehicle's radiator. All obstructions, such as leaves, bugs, and dirt, must be removed, as they will reduce heat transfer and impair efficiency of system. Make sure space between condenser and radiator also is free of foreign matter.

Ensure evaporator water drain is open. Evaporator cools and dehumidifies air before it enters car.

PERFORMANCE TEST

R-134a systems require use of special service equipment designed specifically for R-134a systems. R-12 servicing equipment cannot be used on R-134a systems.

EXCEPT ASPIRE, ESCORT, PROBE, TRACER & ZX2

Refrigerant system problems are diagnosed by checking refrigerant pressures and clutch cycle rate and times. Compare pressures and cycle time to charts shown in **Fig. 1.** Conditional requirements for refrigerant system tests must be satisfied to obtain accurate pressure readings. If findings do not fall between lines on respective charts, refer to **Fig. 2** to determine specific cause of improper readings.

After necessary repairs have been performed, take pressure readings while meeting conditional requirements to ensure problem has been corrected.

Visual inspection of system may determine problems with refrigerant system. By making a visual inspection, some of following problems can be diagnosed: obstructed air passages, broken belts, disconnected or broken wires, loose or broken mounting brackets and refrigerant leaks.

A refrigerant leak will usually appear as an oily residue at leakage point in system.

IMPORTANT — TEST REQUIREMENTS

The following test conditions must be established to obtain accurate pressure readings:

- Run engine at 1500 rpm for 10 minutes.
- Operate A/C system on max A/C (recirculating air).
- Run blower at max speed.
- Stabilize in car temperature @ 70°F to 80°F (21°C to 22°C).

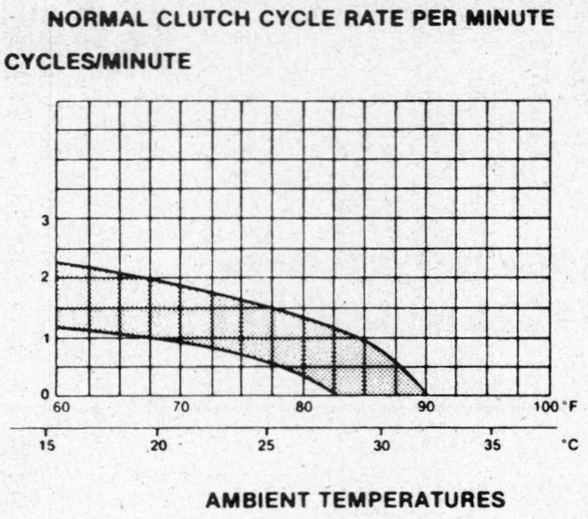

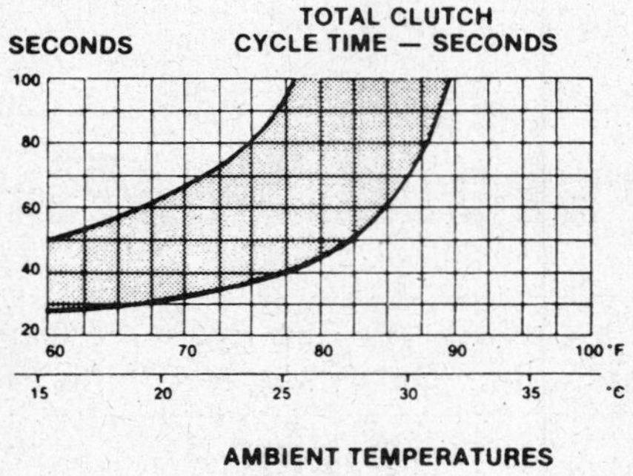

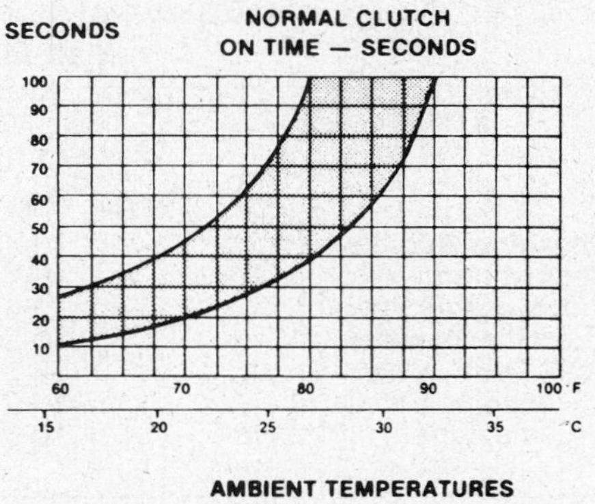

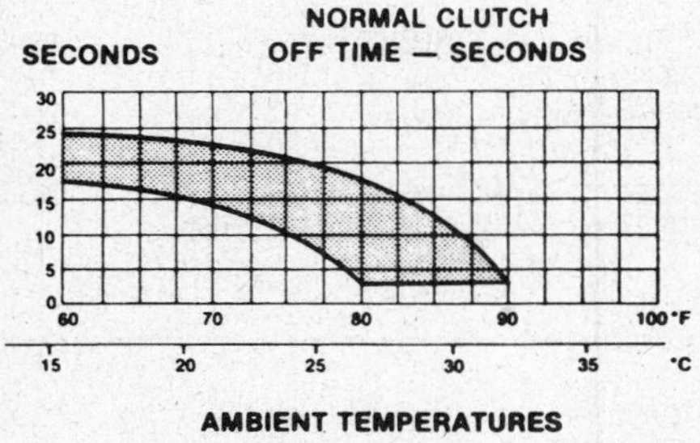

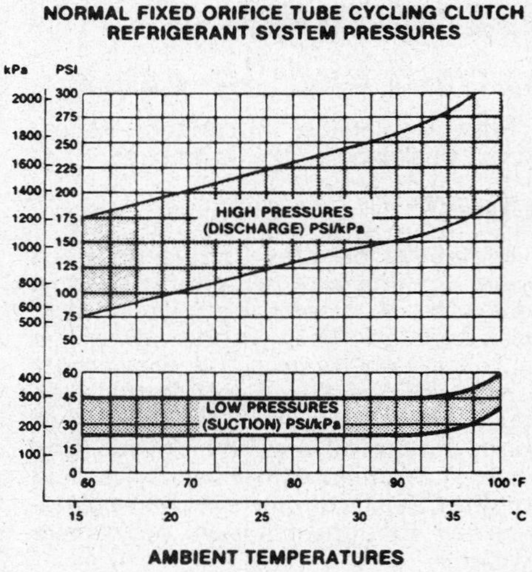

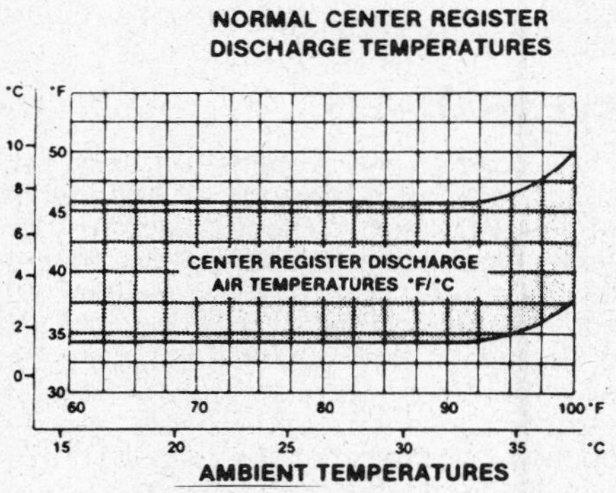

FM7029100026000X

Fig. 1 Refrigerant pressure & temperature charts. Except Aspire, Escort, Probe, Tracer & ZX2

ASPIRE

1. Connect manifold gauge set to system.
2. Start engine and turn A/C system on.
3. As soon as system is stabilized, record high and low pressures as indicated by manifold gauges.
4. Low side pressure should be 20–41 psi, and high side pressure should be 185–263 psi.
5. As low side pressure drops, high side pressure should rise. As low side pressure rises, high side pressure should drop.
6. Record center duct temperature.
7. Determine and record ambient temperature
8. Compare test readings with charts shown in **Fig. 3.**

ESCORT, TRACER & ZX2

1. Connect manifold gauge set to system.
2. Start engine and turn on A/C system.
3. As soon as system is stabilized, record

high and low pressures as shown by manifold gauges.
4. Low side pressure should be 35–50 psi. High side pressure should be 178–235 psi. As low pressure drops, high pressure should rise.
5. When clutch disengages, low side pressure should rise and high side pressure should drop.
6. Determine A/C clutch cycle rate per minute (one cycle is A/C clutch On time plus Off time).
7. Record A/C Off time in seconds.
8. Record A/C On time in seconds.
9. Record center duct temperature.
10. Determine and record ambient temperature.
11. Compare test readings with applicable chart, **Fig. 1.**

PROBE

1. Connect manifold gauge set to system.
2. Start engine and turn on A/C system.
3. As soon as system is stabilized, record high and low pressures as shown by manifold gauges.
4. High side pressure should read 178-235 psi. As low pressure drops, high pressure should rise.
5. When clutch disengages, low side pressure should rise and high side pressure should drop.
6. Determine A/C clutch cycle rate per minute (1 cycle is A/C clutch On time plus Off time).
7. Record A/C Off time in seconds.
8. Record A/C On time in seconds.
9. Record center duct temperature.
10. Determine and record ambient temperature.
11. Compare test readings with applicable chart, **Fig. 1.**

NOTE: System test requirements must be met to obtain accurate test readings for evaluation. Refer to the normal refrigerant system pressure/temperature and the normal clutch cycle ratio and times charts.

High (Discharge) Pressure	Low (Suction) Pressure	Clutch Cycle Time			Component — Causes
		Rate	On	Off	
High	High	Continuous Run			Condenser — Inadequate Airflow
High	Normal to High				Engine Overheating
Normal to High	Normal				Air in Refrigerant Refrigerant Overcharge (a) Humidity or Ambient Temp Very High (b)
Normal	High				Fixed Orifice Tube — Missing O Rings Leaking/Missing
Normal	High	Slow	Long	Long	Clutch Cycling Switch — High Cut In
Normal	Normal	Slow or No Cycle	Long or Continuous	Normal or No Cycle	Moisture in Refrigerant System Excessive Refrigerant Oil
		Fast	Short	Short	Clutch Cycling Switch — Low Cut In or High Cut Out
Normal	Low	Slow	Long	Long	Clutch Cycling Switch — Low Cut Out
Normal to Low	High	Continuous Run			Compressor — Low Performance
Normal to Low	Normal to High				A/C Suction Line — Partially Restricted or Plugged (c)
Normal to Low	Normal	Fast	Short	Normal	Evaporator — Restricted Airflow
			Short to Very Short	Normal to Long	Condenser fixed orifice Tube or A/C Liquid Line — Partically Restricted or Plugged
			Short to Very Short	Short to Very Short	Low Refrigerant Charge
			Short to Very Short	Long	Evaporator Core — Partially Restricted or Plugged
Normal to Low	Low	Continuous Run			A/C Suction Line — Partially Restricted or Plugged (d) Clutch Cycling Switch — Sticking Closed
Low	Normal	Very Fast	Very Short	Very Short	Clutch Cycling Switch — Cycling Range Too Close
Erratic Operation or Compressor Not Running		—	—	—	Clutch Cycling Switch — Dirty Contacts or Sticking Open Poor Connection at A/C Clutch Connector or Clutch Cycling Switch Connector A/C Electrical Circuit Erratic
Additional Possible Cause Components Associated with Inadequate Compressor Operation					
• Compressor Drive Belt — Loose • Compressor Clutch — Slipping • Clutch Coil Open — Shorted or Loose Mounting • Control Assembly Switch — Dirty Contacts or Sticking Open • Clutch Wiring Circuit — High Resistance Open or Blown Fuse					
Additional Possible Cause Components Associated with a Damaged Compressor					
• Compressor Clutch — Seized • Clutch Cycling Switch — Sticking Closed • Suction Accumulator Drier — Refrigerant Oil Bleed Hole Plugged • Refrigerant Leaks					

(a) Compressor may make noise on initial run. This is slugging condition caused by excessive liquid refrigerant.
(b) Compressor clutch may not cycle in ambient temperatures above 80°F depending on humidity conditions.
(c) Low pressure reading will be normal to high if pressure is taken at accumulator and if restriction is downstream of service access valve.
(d) Low pressure reading will be low if pressure is taken near the compressor and restriction is upstream of service access valve.

FM7029100028000X

Fig. 2 Refrigerant system pressure evaluation chart. Except Aspire, Escort, Probe, Tracer & ZX2

LEAK TEST

R-134a systems require use of special service equipment designed specifically for R-134a systems. R-12 servicing equipment cannot be used on R-134a systems.

Testing refrigerant system for leaks is one of most important phases of troubleshooting. One or more of methods outlined will prove useful in detecting leaks or checking connections if service work is performed. Before beginning any leak test, attach a manifold gauge set and note pressure. If little or no pressure is indicated, a partial charge must be installed. Check all connections, compressor head gasket, oil filler plug and compressor shaft seal for leaks.

ELECTRONIC DETECTORS

There are a number of electronic leak detectors available to perform leak tests. Refer to operating instructions for unit being used and observe these general procedures:

1. Move detector probe one inch per second in areas of suspected leaks.
2. Position probe below test point, as refrigerant gas is heavier than air.
3. Be sure to check service access gauge port valve fittings, particularly when valve caps are missing, as dirt accumulations can destroy sealing area of valve core when manifold gauge set is attached. Replace missing valve caps after cleaning valve core area. **Valve caps should only be finger tightened. Using pliers to tighten valve caps may distort sealing surface of valve.**
4. Check for leaks in manifold gauge set and hoses, as well as rest of system.

FLAME-TYPE (HALIDE) DETECTORS

When using flame-type detectors, avoid inhaling fumes produced by burning refrigerant. Do not use this type detector where concentrations of combustible or explosive gases, dusts or vapors may exist.

1. Adjust detector flame as low as possible to obtain maximum sensitivity. Be sure copper element is cherry red and not burned away. Flame will be almost colorless.
2. Slowly move detector along areas of suspected leaks. A slight leak will cause flame to change to a bright yellow-green color. A significant leak will be indicated by a brilliant blue flame. Position detector under areas being tested as refrigerant gas is heavier than air. **Presence of dust in pickup hose may cause a change in color of flame. If not recognized, a false diagnosis could be made. Store leak detector in a clean place and ensure hose is free of dust before leak testing.**
3. Check for leaks in manifold gauge set and hoses, as well as rest of system.
4. Use a small fan to ventilate areas where leak detector indicates refrigerant constantly. These areas are contaminated with refrigerant and must be ventilated before leak can be pinpointed.

FLUID LEAK DETECTORS

Apply leak detector solution around joints to be tested. A cluster of bubbles will form immediately if there is a leak. A white foam that forms after a short while will indicate an extremely small leak. In some confined areas such as sections of evaporator and condenser, electronic leak detectors will be more useful.

TRACER DYE

R-134a fluorescent tracer dye has been added to the A/C systems of new vehicles. Leak checking can be performed with an ultraviolet lamp and is an acceptable alternative to using an electronic leak detector. The fluorescent lifespan of the leak tracer dye is 500 hours of A/C system use, after which another injection of dye is required. A/C system pressure must be above 80 psi for the operation. Scan all components, fittings and lines of the A/C system with Rotunda Ultraviolet Lamp 164–R0721, or equivalent, the exact location of the leak or leaks can be pinpointed by the bright yellow-green glow of the tracer dye. Since more than one leak may exist in the system, always inspect each component.

After the leak is serviced, the traces of dye can be removed from the previously leaking areas by using any general purpose oil solvent. Verify the service by operation the A/C system for a short while and reinspecting the system with the UV lamp. Rotunda Fluoro-Lite for R-134a/PAG A/C Systems 164–R3712, or equivalent, may be introduced into the A/C system using Rotunda R-134a Fluorescent Tracer Dye Injector 164–R2610, or equivalent. Inject the dye while charging the system and check for leaks as follows:

1. Adjust quick disconnect valve on dye injector to maximum counterclockwise (closed) position.
2. Remove plug from end of dye injector reservoir and fill reservoir with ¼ ounces of Rotunda Fluoro-Lite for R-134a/PAG A/C Systems 164-R3712, or equivalent.
3. Replace plug, then tighten securely.
4. Attach low-side quick disconnect from either the manifold gauge set or the charging station to the plug on the dye injector.
5. Install dye injector quick disconnect valve to high-pressure service port on vehicle.
6. Adjust all quick disconnect valves to maximum clockwise (open) position.
7. Charge vehicle with required amount of refrigerant , then flow of refrigerant through dye injector will inject dye into vehicle system.
8. When vehicle charging is complete, close dye injector and high-side quick disconnect valves and remove quick disconnects from vehicle.
9. Recover refrigerant from dye injector and close low-side quick disconnect valve.
10. Remove dye injector from low-side quick disconnect valve. The dye injector should only be connected to charging/recovery station when dye is to be injected. The dye injector has a one-way check valve that will prevent system refrigerant recovery and evacuation.
11. Using Rotunda Ultraviolet Lamp 164–R0721 or equivalent, check system for leaks.

DISCHARGING SYSTEM

R-134a systems require use of special service equipment designed specifically for R-134a systems. R-12 servicing equipment cannot be used on R-134a systems.

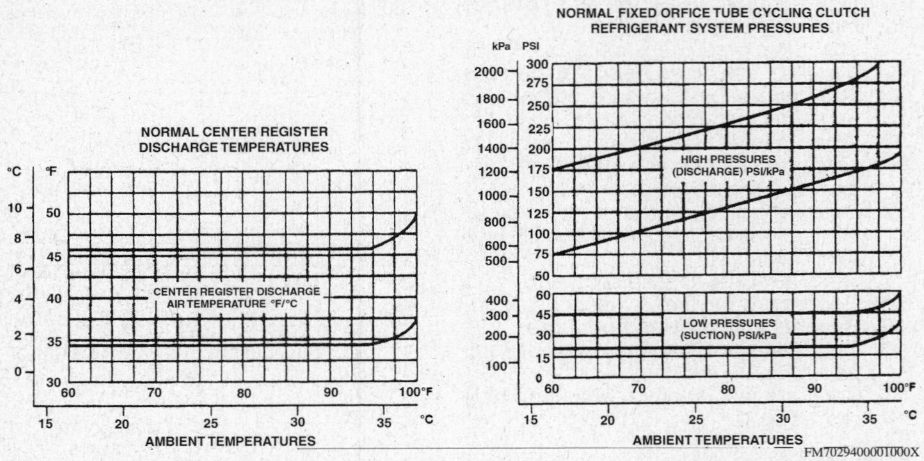

Fig. 3 Refrigerant pressure & temperature charts. Aspire

R-12 recovery stations cannot be used on R-134a systems. A separate recovery station must be used on R-134a systems. Refrigerants are not compatible and will contaminate R-12 recovery station.

Use of refrigerant recovery and recycling stations allows recovery and reuse of refrigerant after contaminants and moisture have been removed.

When using a recovery or recycling station, follow manufacturer's operating instructions, noting following:

1. **Use extreme caution and observe all safety and service precautions related to use of refrigerants.**
2. Connect refrigerant recycling station hose(s) to vehicle A/C service port(s) and recovery station inlet fitting. Hoses used should have shutoff devices or check valves within 12 inches of hose ends to minimize introduction of air into recycling station and to minimize amount of refrigerant released when hose(s) is disconnected.
3. Turn recycling station On to start recovery process. Allow recycling station to pump refrigerant from A/C system until station pressure gauge indicates vacuum.
4. After vehicle A/C system has been evacuated, close station inlet valve, if equipped.
5. Turn station Off. On some stations pump will automatically be turned Off by a low pressure switch.
6. Allow vehicle A/C system to remain closed for approximately two minutes. Observe vacuum level indicated on gauge. If pressure does not rise, disconnect recycling station hose(s).
7. If system pressure rises, repeat steps 3 through 6 until vacuum level remains stable for two minutes.
8. Service A/C system as necessary, then evacuate and recharge A/C system.

SYSTEM EVACUATION

R-134a systems require use of special service equipment designed specifically for R-134a systems. R-12 servicing equipment cannot be used on R-134a systems.

Vacuum pumps suitable for removing air and moisture from A/C systems are commercially available. A specification for system pump down used here is 28–29½ inches vacuum. This reading can be attained at or near sea level only. For each 1000 feet of altitude, reading will be one inch of vacuum less than standard specification given. For example, at 5000 feet elevation, only 23–24½ inches of vacuum can be obtained. **System must be completely discharged before it can be evacuated. Damage to vacuum pump will result if pressurized refrigerant is allowed to enter pump assembly.**

1. Connect vacuum pump to gauge manifold. With gauges connected into system, remove cap from vacuum hose connector. Install center hose from gauge manifold to vacuum pump connector. Mid position high and low side compressor service valve (if used). Open high and low side gauge manifold hand valves.
2. Operate vacuum pump a minimum of 30 minutes for air and moisture removal. Watch compound gauge to see that system pumps down into a vacuum. System will reach 28–29½ inches Hg vacuum in a maximum of five minutes. If system does not pump down, check all connections and leak test if necessary.
3. Close gauge manifold hand valves and shutoff vacuum pump.
4. Check ability of system to hold vacuum. Watch compound gauge to see that gauge does not rise at a faster rate than one inch vacuum every four or five minutes. If compound gauge rises at too rapid a rate, install partial charge and leak test. Then discharge system as outlined above.
5. If system holds vacuum, charge system with refrigerant.

CHARGING SYSTEM

R-134a systems require use of special service equipment designed specifically for R-134a systems. R-12 servicing equipment cannot be used on R-134a systems.

Refer to "A/C Specifications" for refrigerant capacities.

When charging from small cans, do not open manifold gauge set high pressure (discharge) gauge valve, as this can cause containers to explode.

1. Connect manifold gauge set **Fig. 4**, then set valves closed to center hose, disconnect vacuum pump from manifold gauge set.
2. Connect center hose of manifold gauge set to refrigerant supply.
3. Purge air from center hose by loosening hose at manifold gauge set and open refrigerant drum valve. When refrigerant escapes from hose, tighten center hose connection at manifold gauge set.
4. On vehicles so equipped, disconnect wire harness connector at clutch cycling pressure switch. Install jumper wire across terminals of connector.
5. On all models, open manifold gauge set low side valve and allow refrigerant to enter system. Refrigerant can must be kept upright if vehicle low pressure service gauge port is not on suction accumulator/drier or suction accumulator fitting.

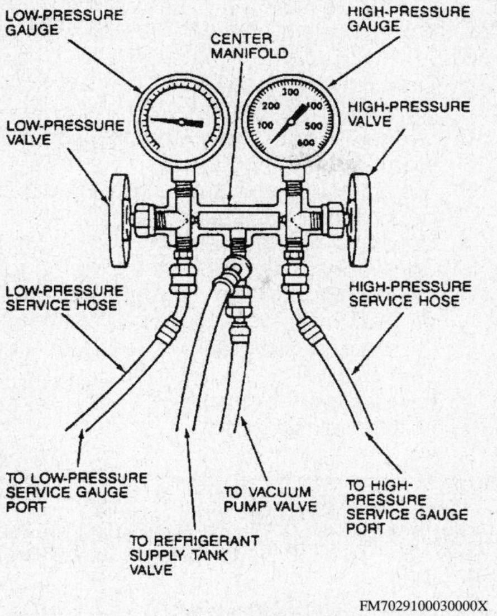

Fig. 4 Refrigerant system service connections

6. When system stops drawing refrigerant in, start engine and set control lever to A/C position and blower switch to Hi position to draw remaining refrigerant into system.
7. When specified weight of refrigerant is in system, close gauge set low pressure valve and refrigerant supply valve.
8. On vehicles so equipped, remove jumper wire from clutch cycling pressure switch connector and connect connector to pressure switch.
9. On all models, operate system until pressures stabilize to check operation and system pressures. During high ambient temperatures, a high volume fan may be necessary to blow air through radiator and condenser to cool engine and prevent excessive refrigerant system pressures.
10. When charging is complete and system operating pressures are normal, disconnect manifold gauge set from vehicle and install protective caps on service gauge port valves.

System Service

NOTE: On Air Bag Equipped Models, Refer To " Air Bag System Precautions" Located In The Front Of This Manual For System Disarming & Arming Procedures.

INDEX

OIL CHARGE

Refrigerant oil required for R-134a air conditioning systems is a polyalkylene glycol (PAG) oil. Ford specification part No. WSH-M1C231-B, or equivalent. This type of refrigerant oil is designed specifically for R-134a systems and is not suitable for use in R-12 systems. Never use an R-134a refrigerant oil in R-12 systems. Never use R-12 refrigerant oil YN-9 in R-134a systems.

FORD FS-10 SWASH PLATE 10 CYLINDER COMPRESSOR

A new service replacement compressor contains 7 oz. of refrigerant oil.

1. Drain and measure oil from old compressor.
2. Drain oil from new compressor into clean measuring device.
3. If 3–5 oz. were drained from old compressor, add equal amount plus 1 oz. of new oil to new compressor.
4. If more than 5 oz. were drained from old compressor, add equal amount of new oil to new compressor.
5. If less then 3 oz. was drained from old compressor, add 3 oz. to new compressor.
6. When other air conditioning system components are replaced, add the following quantities of refrigerant oil:
   a. Accumulator, same amount drained from old accumulator plus 2 oz.
   b. Evaporator core, 3 oz.
   c. Condenser, 1 oz.
7. Add 2 oz. of new oil after replacing other system components such as hoses, evaporator core orifice, cycling switch, compressor pressure relief valve and pressure cutoff switch, or following minor repairs such O-ring, port, compressor shaft seal and hose leaks.

FORD VS-90

Refer to "Ford FS-10 Swash Plate 10 Cylinder Compressor."

NIPPONDENSO 10P15 SERIES COMPRESSORS

A new service replacement compressor contains 8 oz. of refrigerant oil.

1. Drain and measure oil from old compressor.
2. Drain oil from new compressor into clean measuring device.
3. If 3–5 oz. were drained from old compressor, install equal amount plus 1 oz. of new oil to new compressor.
4. If more than 5 oz. were drained from old compressor, install equal amount of new oil to new compressor.
5. If less then 3 oz. was removed from old compressor, install 3 oz. in new compressor.
6. When other air conditioning system components are replaced, add the following quantities of refrigerant oil:
   a. Accumulator, same amount drained from old accumulator plus 2 oz.
   b. Evaporator core, 3 oz.
   c. Condenser, 1 oz.

7. Replacement of other components such as valves or hoses does not require any additional refrigerant oil. However, if a hose bursts with a fully charged system, an additional 2 oz. is recommended and accumulator should be replaced.

PANASONIC COMPRESSOR

When replacing system components, add or drain the following quantities of refrigerant oil: compressor, drain 1.7 oz.; condenser, add one oz.; receiver-drier, add amount drained from old drier plus .34 oz.

On Aspire models, a new service replacement compressor contains 5.91 oz. of refrigerant oil.

On Probe models, a new service replacement compressor contains 6.78 oz. of refrigerant oil.

1. Drain and measure oil from old compressor.
2. Drain oil from new compressor into clean measuring device.
3. Install equal amount plus .676 oz. of new oil to compressor.
4. When other air conditioning system components are replaced, add the following quantities of refrigerant oil:
   a. Accumulator, same amount drained from old accumulator plus 1 oz.
   b. Evaporator core, 3 oz.
   c. Condenser, 1 oz.
5. **On Aspire models,** replacement of other components such as hoses does not require any additional refrigerant oil.
6. **On Probe models,** add 2 oz. of new oil following minor repairs such as O-ring, port, compressor shaft seal and hose leaks.

OIL LEVEL CHECK

Oil level of these compressors should be checked whenever refrigerant has been lost due to leakage or through normal system servicing.

Specifications

INDEX

A/C SPECIFICATIONS

Year	Compressor Model	Refrigerant		Refrigerant Oil		Compressor Clutch Air Gap, Inch
		Type	Capacity, Lbs.	Viscosity	Total System Capacity, Oz. ①	
ASPIRE						
1997	Panasonic	R-134a	1.56	②	5.9	.016–.024
CONTINENTAL						
1997–2000	Ford FS-10	R-134a	2.13	②	7	.014–.033
CONTOUR						
1997–2000	Ford FS-10	R-134a	1.63	②	7	.014–.033
COUGAR						
1997	Ford FS-10	R-134a	2.25	②	7	.014–.033
1999–2000	Ford FS-10	R-134a	③	②	④	.014–.033
CROWN VICTORIA						
1997–2000	Ford FS-10	R-134a	2.13	②	7	.014–.033
ESCORT						
1997	Ford FS-10	R-134a	1.75	②	7	.018–.033
1998–2000	Ford FS-10	R-134a	1.75	②	7	.014–.033
GRAND MARQUIS						
1997–2000	Ford FS-10	R-134a	2.13	②	7	.014–.033
LS						
2000	Ford VS-90	R-134a	1.75	②	7	.014–.033
MARK VIII						
1997–98	Ford FS-10	R-134a	2.13	②	7	.014–.033
MUSTANG						
1997–2000	Ford FS-10	R-134a	2.13	②	7	.014–.033
MYSTIQUE						
1997–2000	Ford FS-10	R-134a	1.63	②	7	.014–.033
PROBE						
1997	Panasonic	R-134a	1.75	②	6.8	.016–.019

Continued

A/C SPECIFICATIONS—Continued

Year	Compressor Model	Refrigerant		Refrigerant Oil		Compressor Clutch Air Gap, Inch
		Type	Capacity, Lbs.	Viscosity	Total System Capacity, Oz. ①	
SABLE						
1997–99	Ford FS-10	R-134a	2.13	②	7	.014–.033
TAURUS						
1997–99	Ford FS-10	R-134a	2.13	②	7	.014–.033
TAURUS SHO						
1997–99	Sanden	R-134a	2.13	②	7	.016–.027
THUNDERBIRD						
1997	Ford FS-10	R-134a	2.25	②	7	.014–.033
TOWN CAR						
1997–2000	Ford FS-10	R-134a	2.13	②	7	.014–.033
TRACER						
1997	Ford FS-10	R-134a	1.75	②	7	.018–.033
1998–99	Ford FS-10	R-134a	1.75	②	7	.014–.033
ZX2						
1997	Ford FS-10	R-134a	1.75	②	7	.018–.033
1998–2000	Ford FS-10	R-134a	1.75	②	7	.014–.033

① — Oil level inches cannot be checked.

② — Motorcraft YN-12b PAG (Polyalkaline Glycol), or equivalent.

③ — See label on vehicle.

④ — Transfer the oil from the accumulator/dehydrator being renewed to a measuring cylinder.

Fill the new accumulator/dehydrator with the same quantity of fresh oil plus 90 ml.

CHARGING VALVE LOCATION

Model	High Pressure Fitting	Low Pressure Fitting
Aspire	High Pressure Line From Compressor	Low Pressure Line From Compressor
Continental	High Pressure Line From Compressor	Accumulator
Cougar	High Pressure Line From Compressor	Low Pressure Line From Compressor
Contour	High Pressure Line From Compressor	Low Pressure Line From Compressor
Crown Victoria	High Pressure Line From Compressor	Accumulator
Escort	High Pressure Line From Compressor	Low Pressure Line From Compressor
Grand Marquis	High Pressure Line From Compressor	Accumulator
LS	High Pressure Line From Compressor	Accumulator
Mark VIII	High Pressure Line From Compressor	Low Pressure Line From Compressor
Mystique	High Pressure Line From Compressor	Low Pressure Line From Compressor
Probe	High Pressure Line From Compressor	Low Pressure Line From Compressor
Sable	High Pressure Line From Compressor	Accumulator
Taurus	High Pressure Line From Compressor	Accumulator
Thunderbird	High Pressure Line From Compressor	Low Pressure Line From Compressor
Town Car	High Pressure Line From Compressor	Accumulator
Tracer	High Pressure Line From Compressor	Low Pressure Line From Compressor
ZX2	High Pressure Line From Compressor	Low Pressure Line From Compressor

BELT TENSION

Engine	New, Lbs.	Used, Lbs.
1.3L	110–132	95–110
2.0L④	①	①
2.0L⑤	140–170	110–150
2.5L④	①	①
2.5L⑤	160–190	110–150
3.0L	②	③
3.0L⑥	②	③
3.4L SHO	①	①
3.8L	①	①
3.9L	①	①
4.6L	①	①

① — Drive belt tension is not adjustable. Drive belt tensioner automatically adjusts tensioner.
② — 5-rib belt, 140–160 lbs.; 6-rib belt, belt tension is not adjustable; drive belt tensioner automatically adjusts tensioner.
③ — 5-rib belt, 110–130 lbs.; 6-rib belt, belt tension is not adjustable; drive belt tensioner automatically adjusts tensioner.
④ — Contour, Escort, Mystique, Tracer, ZX2 & 1999 Cougar.
⑤ — Probe.
⑥ — LS.

COOLING FANS

NOTE: On Air Bag Equipped Models, Refer To "Air Bag System Precautions" Located In The Front Of This Manual For System Disarming & Arming Procedures.

TABLE OF CONTENTS

Variable Speed Fans

INDEX

PRECAUTIONS

AIR BAG SYSTEMS

Refer to "Air Bag System Precautions" in the front of this manual for system disarming and arming procedures.

BATTERY GROUND CABLE

Prior to service, disconnect battery ground cable and isolate as required.

DESCRIPTION

The fan drive clutch is a fluid coupling containing silicone oil. Fan speed is regulated by the torque-carrying capacity of the silicone oil.

Two types of fan drive clutches are in use. On one type, **Fig. 1,** a bimetallic strip and control piston on the front of the fluid coupling regulates the amount of silicone oil entering the coupling. The bimetallic strip bows outward with an increase in surrounding temperature and allows a piston to move outward. The piston opens a valve regulating flow of silicone oil into the coupling from a reserve chamber. The oil is returned to a reserve chamber through a bleed hole when the valve is closed.

On the other type of fan drive clutch, **Fig. 2,** a heat-sensitive, bimetal spring connected to an opening plate controls the oil flow. Both units cause fan speed to increase with a rise in temperature and to decrease as temperature goes down.

On some models, a Flex-Fan is used instead of a fan drive clutch. Flexible blades vary volume of air being drawn through radiator, automatically increasing pitch at low engine speeds.

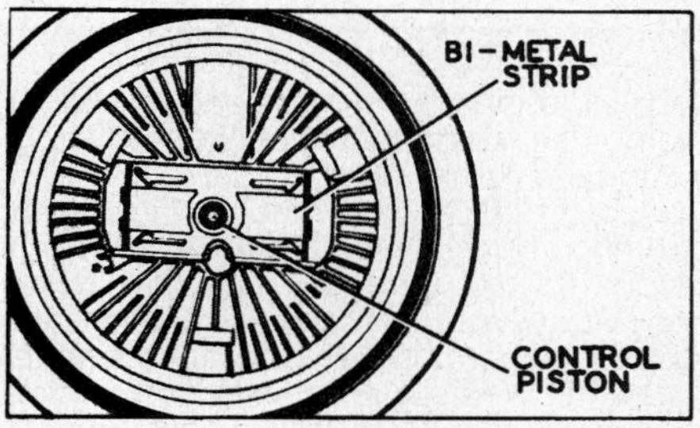

FM1089100013000X

Fig. 1 Variable-speed fan w/flat bimetal thermostatic spring

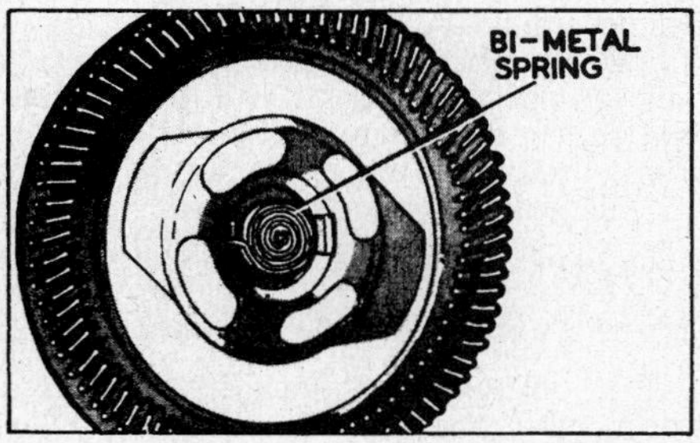

FM1089100014000X

Fig. 2 Variable-speed fan w/coiled bimetal thermostatic spring

SYSTEM DIAGNOSIS & TESTING

FAN DRIVE CLUTCH TEST

Do not operate engine until fan has been first checked for possible cracks and separations.

Run engine at a fast idle speed (1000 RPM) until normal operating temperature is reached. Unit must be operated for at least five minutes immediately before being tested.

Stop the engine and, using a glove or a cloth to protect hand, immediately check effort required to turn fan. If considerable effort is required, the coupling is operating satisfactorily. If very little effort is required to turn the fan, coupling is not operating properly and should be replaced.

If the clutch fan is a coiled bimetallic spring type, it may be tested while vehicle is being driven. Disconnect the bimetallic spring and rotate 90° counterclockwise to disable the temperature-controlled freewheeling feature of the clutch. If this cures overheating condition, replace clutch fan.

COMPONENT SERVICE

To prevent silicone fluid from draining into fan drive bearing, do not store or place drive unit on bench with rear of shaft pointing downward.

Remove the unit from water pump and remove assembly from car.

Variable speed fan with flat bimetal thermostatic spring may be partially disassembled for inspection and cleaning. Remove screws holding assembly together and separate fan from drive clutch. Next remove metal strip on front by pushing one end of it toward fan clutch body so it clears mounting bracket. Then push strip to side so its opposite end will spring out of place. Remove small control piston underneath it.

Check piston for free movement of coupling device. If piston sticks, clean it with emery cloth. If bimetal strip is damaged, replace entire unit. Strips are not interchangeable.

When reassembling, install control piston so projection on end will contact metal strip, then install metal strip. After reassembly, clean clutch drive with a cloth soaked in solvent. Avoid dipping clutch assembly in any type of liquid. Install assembly in reverse order of removal.

Coil spring type fan clutch cannot be disassembled, serviced or repaired. If it does not function properly it must be replaced with a new unit.

Electric Cooling Fans

NOTE: On Air Bag Equipped Models, Refer To "Air Bag System Precautions" Located In The Front Of This Manual For System Disarming & Arming Procedures.

NOTE: Wire Color Code Identification And Symbol Identification Located At The Front Of This Manual Can Be Used As An Aid When Using Wiring Circuits Found In This Section.

INDEX

PRECAUTIONS

AIR BAG SYSTEMS

Refer to "Air Bag System Precautions" in the front of this manual for system disarming and arming procedures.

BATTERY GROUND CABLE

Prior to service, disconnect battery ground cable and isolate as required.

DESCRIPTION

ASPIRE

The cooling fan system consists of an electro-mechanical fan, a temperature switch and a temperature relay.

The temperature switch, located in the thermostat housing, senses engine coolant temperature. The relay, located in the left hand front corner of the engine compartment between the battery and the headlamp, provides the ground path to complete the circuit.

When the coolant temperature is below approximately 194°F, the temperature switch is closed. When the temperature is above approximately 207°F, the temperature switch is opened, allowing the relay contacts to close, completing the ground circuit and activating the cooling fan.

Vehicles equipped with air conditioning (A/C) have an added relay, allowing bypassing of the engine temperature portion of the circuit, and enabling fan activation any time the A/C system is in use.

CONTINENTAL

The electric drive cooling fan system consists of a fan and a two-speed electric motor. The fan motor will only run when ignition switch is in Run position.

Cooling fan is controlled during engine operation by the Integrated Relay Control Module (IRCM) and EEC module. These controls activate the fan at low speed when engine temperature reaches approximately 215°F, or when A/C is on and vehicle does not provide enough air flow. Fan will continue to run until engine temperature drops to approximately 210°F.

Cooling fan will run at high speed when fan has been operating at low speed, but engine temperature is still above 230°F, or during idle when engine temperature has reached approximately 236°F. Cooling fan will begin to operate at low speed when engine temperature drops to approximately 224°F. Cooling fan does not cycle with A/C.

CONTOUR & MYSTIQUE & 1999–2000 COUGAR

The cooling fan system consists of a fan blade with a two-speed cooling fan motor. Vehicles with the 2.0L engine have a single cooling fan motor and fan blade system, vehicles with the 2.5L engine have dual cooling fan motors and fan blades.

The cooling fan motors operate only when the ignition switch is in the Run position, preventing cooling fan motor operation after the ignition switch is turned to the Off position.

CROWN VICTORIA, GRAND MARQUIS & TOWN CAR

Auxiliary cooling fan motor runs continuously when air conditioning is on and does not cycle on/off with A/C clutch. Fan will shut off at speeds above 45 mph when coolant temperature is less than 220°F. Auxiliary cooling fan will also operate when temperatures are above 220°F even with A/C off.

ESCORT, TRACER & ZX2

The cooling fan is controlled by a Constant Control Relay Module (CCRM), Powertrain Control Module (PCM) and Engine Coolant Temperature (ECT) sensor. The fan comes on when engine temperature is at 221°F and when the air conditioning is turned on.

MARK VIII

Variable Control Relay Module (VCRM) is used to control engine cooling fan operation speed and A/C clutch operation in addition to other non-A/C functions. VCRM control fan operation when required will increase and decrease fan speed as necessary depending on refrigerant system high side pressure. VCRM also can turn the A/C clutch circuit off if high side pressure exceeds 425 psi.

The VCRM stops fan control operation at vehicle speeds in excess of approximately 45 mph. Fan operation will resume when vehicle speed drops to approximately 42 mph. Fan control will not shut off when AC high side pressure is above 300 psi. In event of an ACP sensor failure, fan control will continue to operate.

MUSTANG

This system consists of a dual-speed fan, which operates only when ignition switch is in the run position. Cooling fan is controlled during vehicle operation by the Constant Control Relay Module (CCRM) and Powertrain Control Module (PCM). Cooling fan operates when coolant temperature reaches 221°F, or with air conditioning on and vehicle speed below 43 mph. Fan will continue to run until coolant temperature drops to 200°F, or vehicle speed reaches at least 48 mph.

PROBE

Cooling fan incorporates a two-speed electric motor. The engine coolant temperature sensor (ECT) measures coolant temperature at water outlet connection and sends a signal to the PCM which activates the cooling fan.

On 2.0L engine models, low cooling fan control relay is activated at 207°F, or below that temperature when air conditioning system is operating. High cooling fan control relay is activated at 226°F or when ECT sensor fails.

On 2.5L engine models, low cooling fan motor is activated at 212°F, with high cooling fan motor activated at 226°F.

SABLE & TAURUS

Electric cooling fan system consists of two electrical fans, CCRM, PCM, A/C cycling switch and A/C clutch coil circuit. The cooling fan motors operate only when ignition switch is in the RUN position, preventing cooling fan from operating after the ignition switch is turned Off. **The electric cooling fan may come on at any time without warning with ignition switch in the RUN position, even if the motor is not running.**

THUNDERBIRD & 1997 COUGAR

Electric drive cooling fan system consists of a fan and a two-speed electric motor. Fan motor will only run when ignition switch is in Run position.

Cooling fan is controlled during engine operation by the Constant Control Relay Module (CCRM) and Powertrain Control Module (PCM). These controls activate the fan at low speed when engine temperature reaches approximately 222°F, or when A/C is on and vehicle does not provide enough air flow. Fan will continue to run until engine temperature drops to approximately 214°F.

Cooling fan will run at high speed when fan has been operating at low speed, but engine temperature is still above 228°F, and stops running when engine temperature drops to approximately 224°F. Cooling fan does not cycle with A/C.

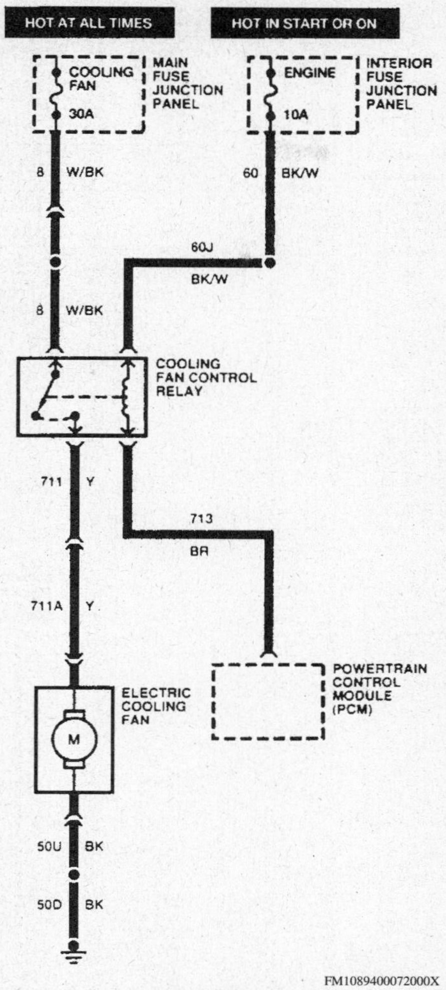

Fig. 1 Cooling fan wiring diagram. Aspire

SYSTEM DIAGNOSIS & TESTING

Cooling fan systems used on models not listed in this section are controlled by the Powertrain Control Module. Refer to **MOTOR's "Domestic Engine Performance & Driveability Manual"** for Powertrain Control (EEC) diagnostic procedures and testing on these models.

Perform visual inspection prior to performing any diagnosis and testing procedures.

1. Check coolant level and condition.
2. Check condition of radiator, thermostat and hoses.
3. Check for fan blade interference.
4. Check for proper mounting of fan motor.
5. Check for proper fan blade attachment to motor.
6. Check for blown fuses.
7. Check wiring harnesses for damaged wires and poor or corroded connectors.
8. Ensure battery is fully charged.

WIRING DIAGRAMS

Refer to **Figs. 1 through 18** for wiring diagrams.

DIAGNOSTIC TESTS

ASPIRE

Refer to **Fig. 19** for symptom chart and **Figs. 20 through 23** for diagnostic charts.

CONTINENTAL, MARK VIII & THUNDERBIRD & 1997 COUGAR

Refer to **Fig. 24** for symptom chart and **Figs. 25 through 28** for diagnostic charts.

CONTOUR & MYSTIQUE & 1999-2000 COUGAR

Refer to **Fig. 29** for symptom chart and **Figs. 30 through 33** for diagnostic charts.

CROWN VICTORIA, GRAND MARQUIS & TOWN CAR

Refer to **Fig. 34** for symptom chart and **Figs. 35 through 38** for diagnostic charts.

ESCORT, TRACER & ZX2

Refer to **Fig. 39** for symptom chart and **Figs. 40 through 43** for diagnostic charts.

MUSTANG

1997-98

Refer to "Continental, Mark VIII & Thunderbird & 1997 Cougar."

1999-2000

Refer to **Fig. 44** for symptom chart and **Figs. 45 through 48** for diagnostic charts.

PROBE

2.0L Engine

Refer to **Fig. 49** for symptom chart and **Figs. 50 and 51** for diagnostic charts.

2.5L Engine

Refer to **Fig. 52** for symptom chart and **Figs. 53 through 57** for diagnostic charts.

SABLE & TAURUS

Refer to **Fig. 58** for symptom chart and **Figs. 59 through 61** for diagnostic charts.

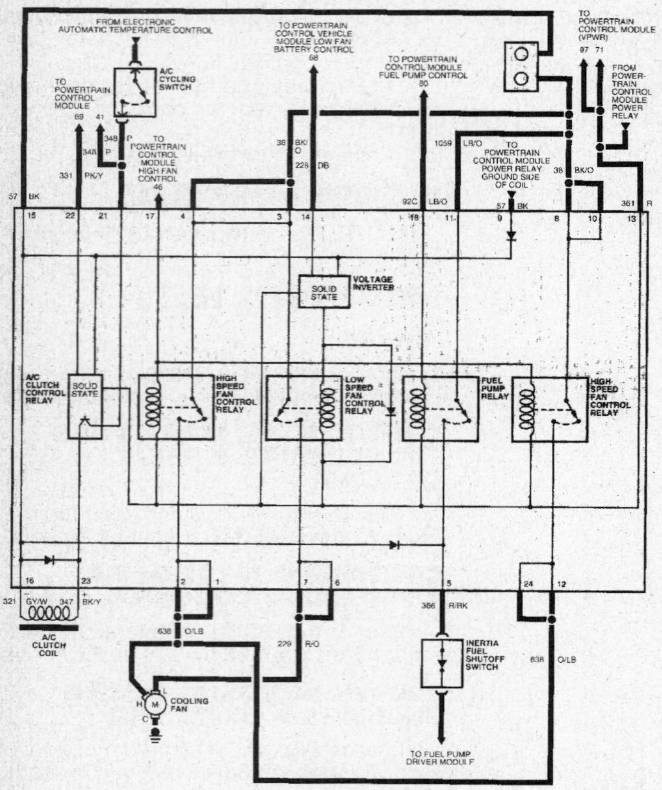

FM1089500102000X

Fig. 2 Cooling fan wiring diagram. Continental

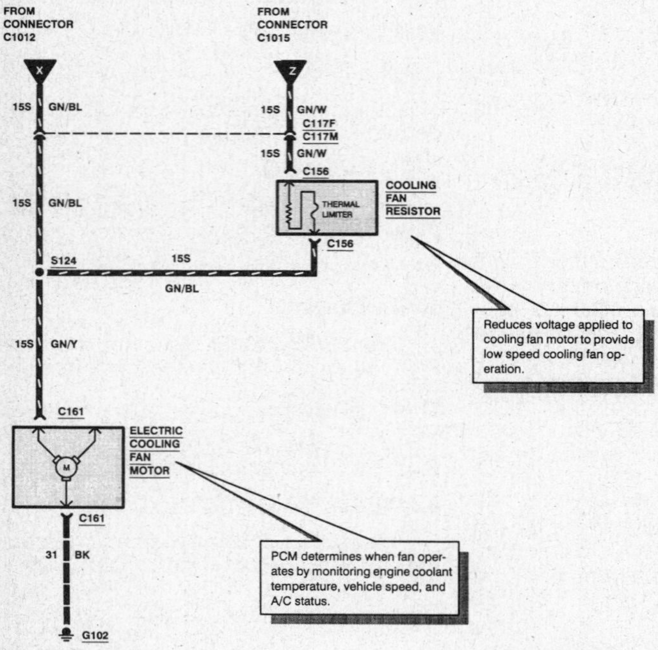

FM1089500106020A

Fig. 3 Cooling fan wiring diagram (Part 2 of 2). 1997 Contour & Mystique w/2.0L engine

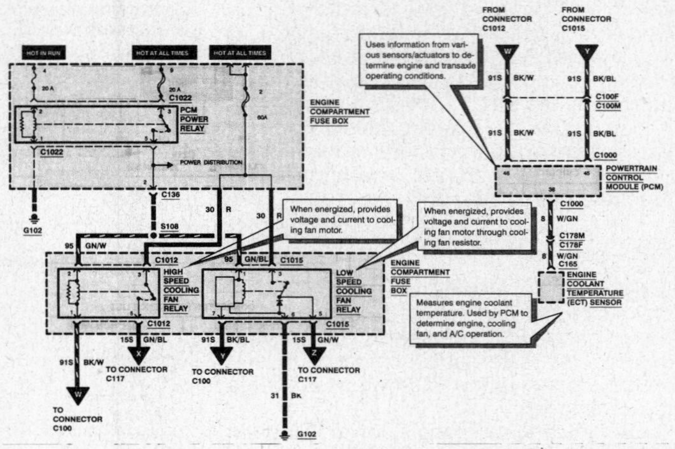

FM1089500106010A

Fig. 3 Cooling fan wiring diagram (Part 1 of 2). 1997 Contour & Mystique

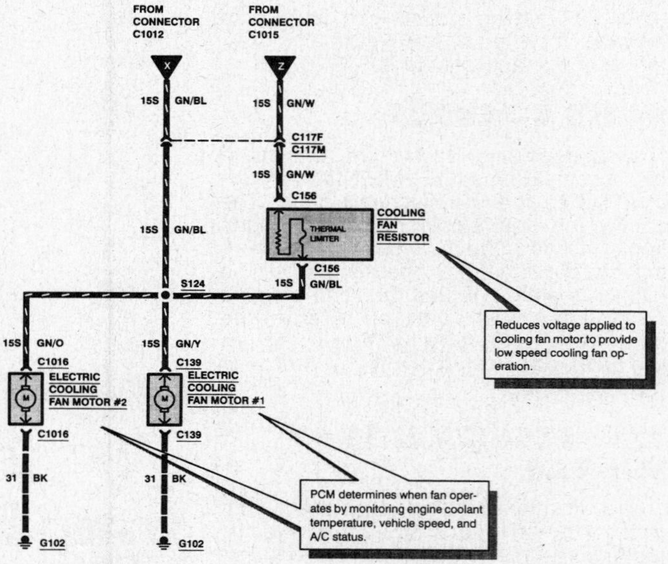

FM1089500106030A

Fig. 3 Cooling fan wiring diagram (Part 2 of 2). 1997 Contour & Mystique w/2.5L engine

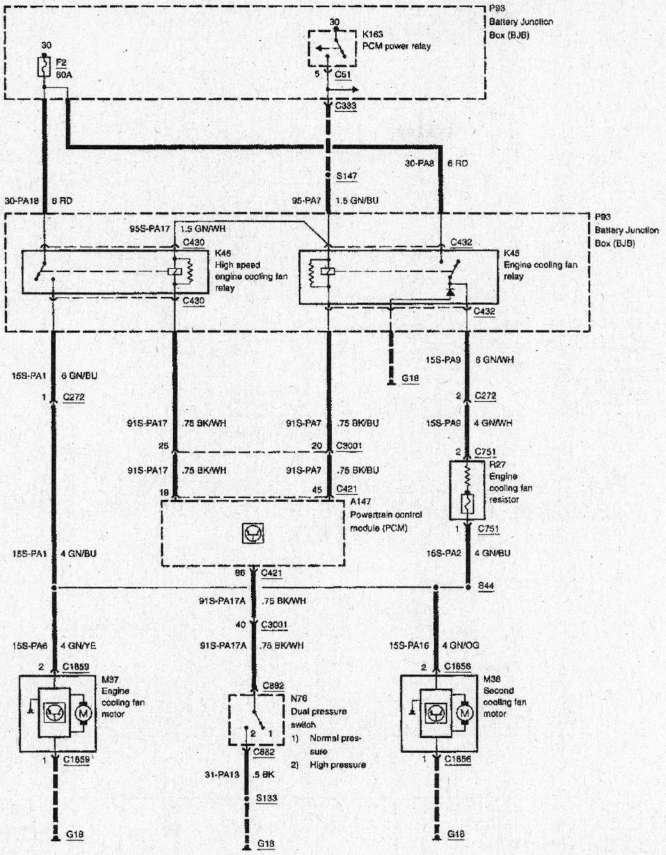

FM1089800173000X

Fig. 4 Cooling fan wiring diagram. 1998–2000 Contour, Mystique & 1999–2000 Cougar

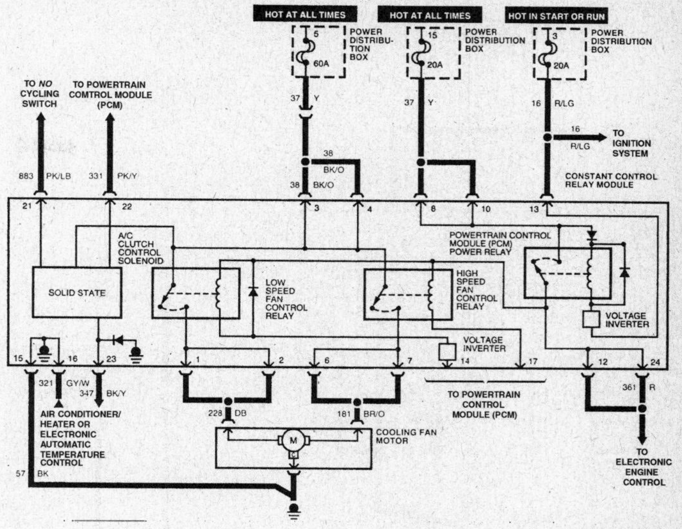

FM1089400078000A

Fig. 5 Cooling fan wiring diagram. Thunderbird & 1997 Cougar

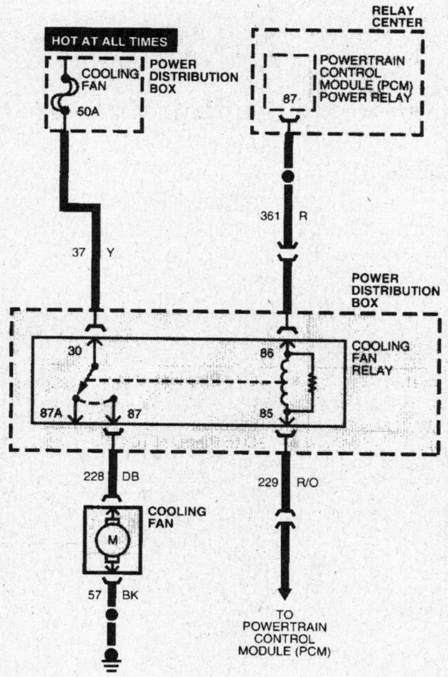

FM1089500109000X

Fig. 6 Cooling fan wiring diagram. 1997 Crown Victoria & Grand Marquis

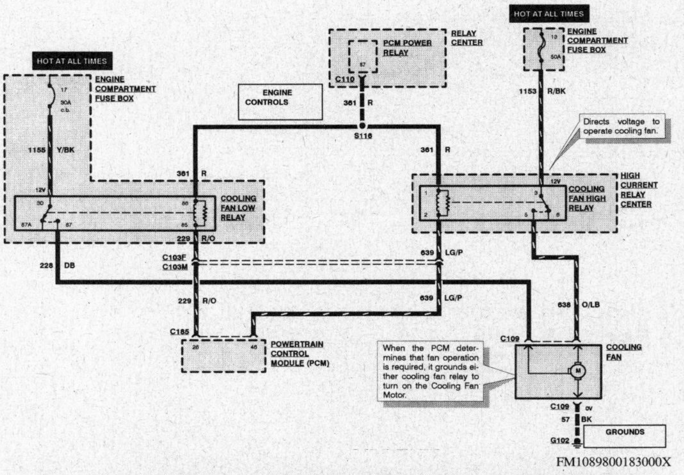

FM1089800183000X

Fig. 7 Cooling fan wiring diagram. 1998–2000 Crown Victoria & Grand Marquis.

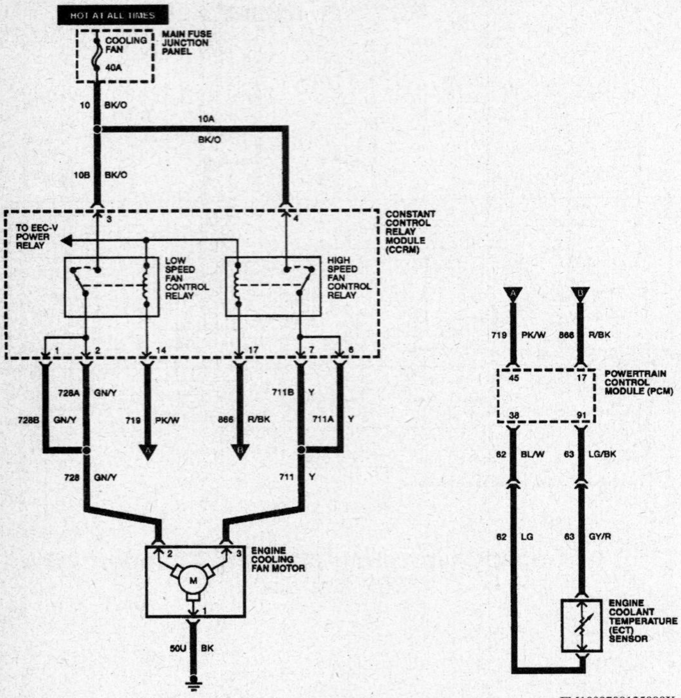

FM1089700125000X

Fig. 8 Cooling fan wiring diagram. 1997 Escort & Tracer

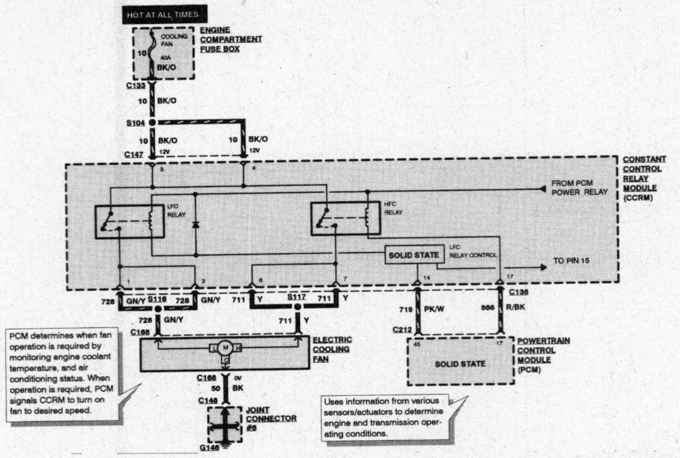

FM1089800184010X

Fig. 9 Cooling fan wiring diagram (Part 1 of 2). 1998–2000 Escort & 1998–99 Tracer & 1998–2000 ZX2

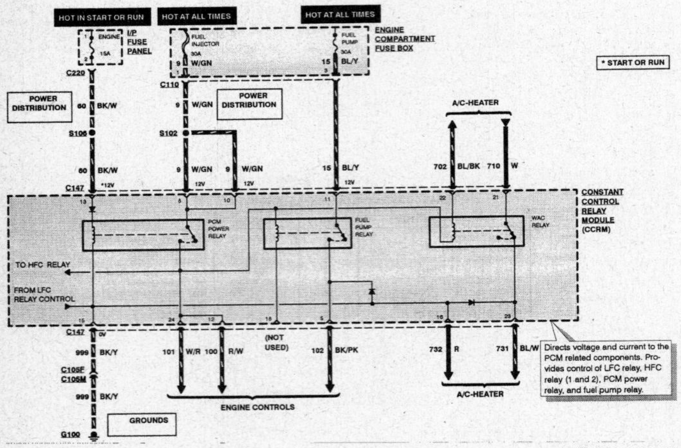

FM1089800184020X

Fig. 9 Cooling fan wiring diagram (Part 2 of 2). 1998–2000 Escort & 1998–99 Tracer & 1998–2000 ZX2

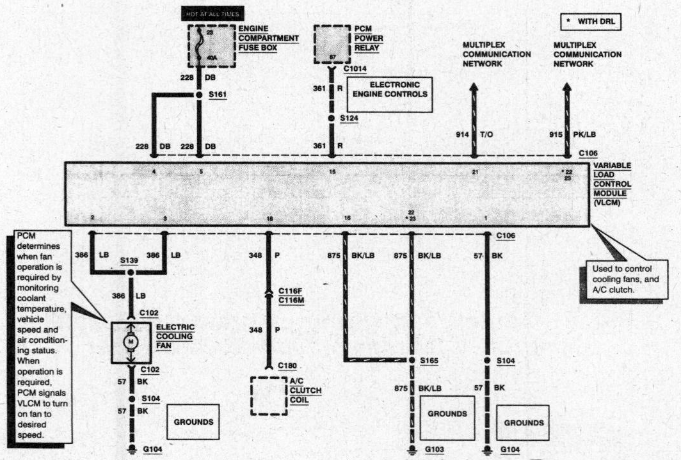

FM1089700174000X

Fig. 10 Cooling fan wiring diagram. Mark VIII

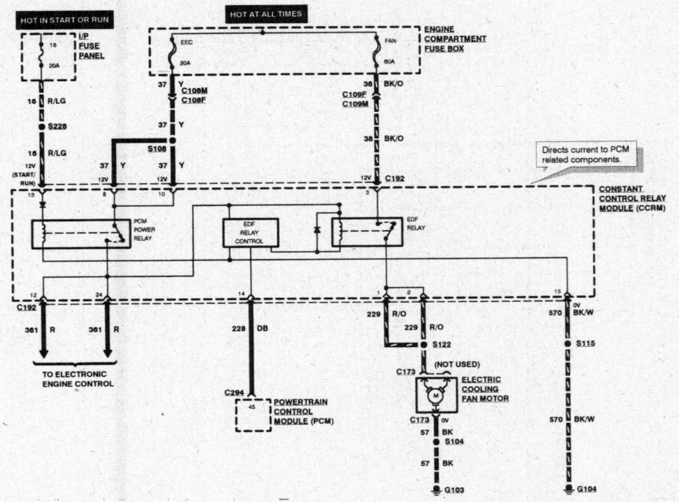

FM7019600059000A

Fig. 11 Cooling fan wiring circuit. 1997–98 Mustang w/3.8L engine

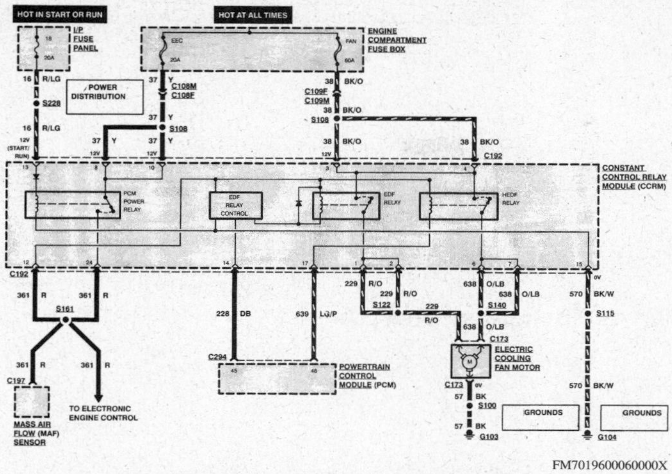

Fig. 12 Cooling fan wiring circuit. 1997–98 Mustang w/4.6L engine

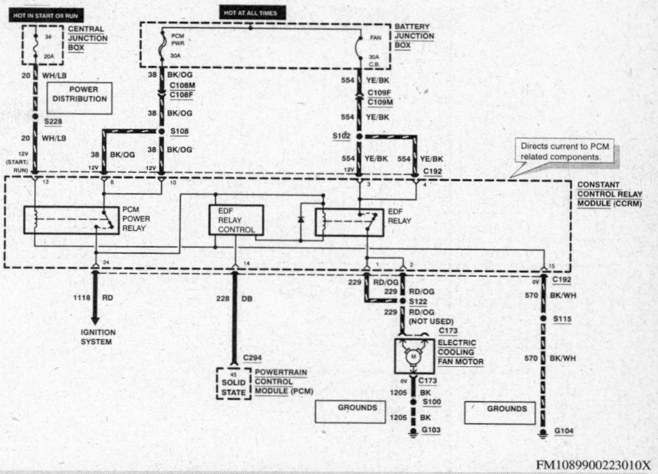

Fig. 13 Cooling fan wiring circuit. 1999–2000 Mustang w/3.8L engine

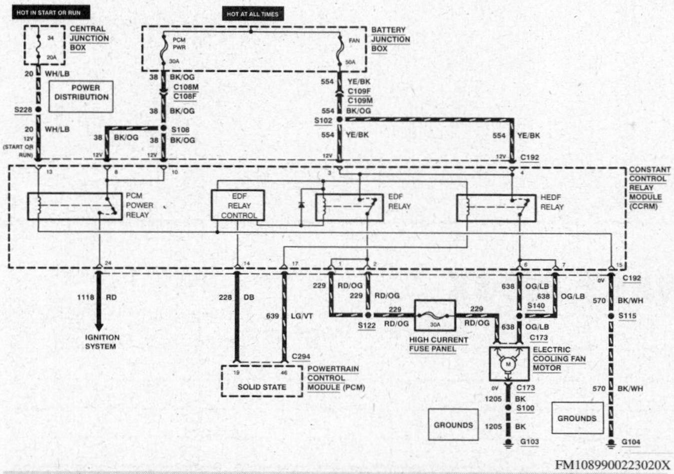

Fig. 14 Cooling fan wiring circuit. 1999–2000 Mustang w/4.6L engine

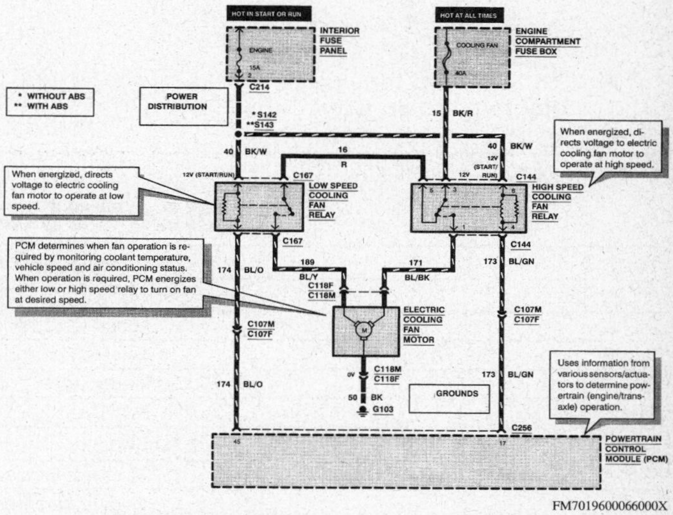

Fig. 15 Cooling fan wiring circuit. Probe w/2.0L engine

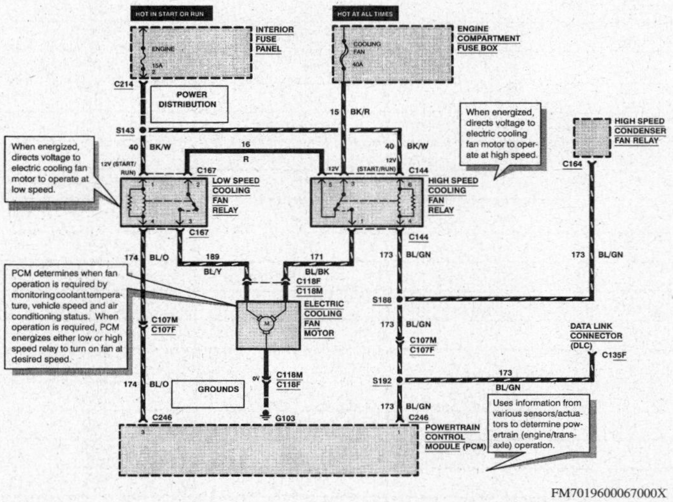

Fig. 16 Cooling fan wiring circuit. Probe w/2.5L engine

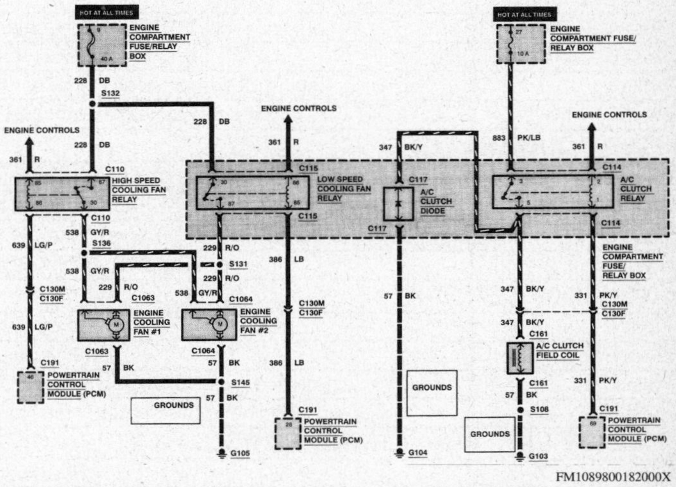

Fig. 17 Cooling fan wiring diagram. 1997–99 Sable & Taurus

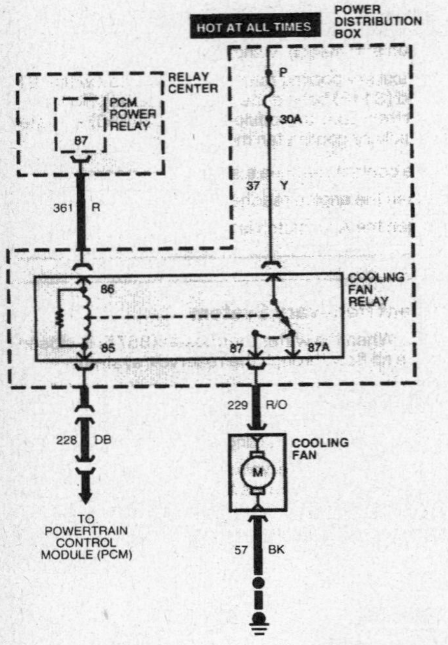

FM1089500108000X

Fig. 18 Cooling fan wiring diagram. Town Car

Condition	Possible Source	Action
• Loss of Coolant	• External leaks. • Internal leaks.	• GO to Pinpoint Test A1.
• Engine Overheats	• Water thermostat. • Low coolant. • Circuit. • Fuses. • Fan control relay. • Engine cooling fan motor. • Radiator.	• GO to Pinpoint Test B1.
• Engine Does Not Reach Normal Operating Temperature	• Water thermostat.	• Water Thermostat Component Test.
• Cooling Fan Operates Continuously	• Circuit. • Fan control relay. • Engine coolant temperature sensor (ECT sensor).	• GO to Pinpoint Test D1. •
• Block Heater Does Not Operate Properly	• Block heater. • Block heater wiring.	• GO to Pinpoint Test C1.

FM1089600133000X

Fig. 19 Symptom Chart. Aspire

DIAGNOSTIC CHART INDEX

Test	Description	Page No.	Fig. No.
ASPIRE			
Test A	Loss Of Coolant	11-9	20
Test B	Engine Overheats	11-10	21
Test C	Engine Block Heater Does Not Operate Properly	11-10	22
Test D	Cooling Fan Operates Continuously	11-10	23
CONTINENTAL, MARK VIII & THUNDERBIRD			
Test A	Loss of Coolant	11-10	25
Test B	Engine Overheats	11-11	26
Test C	Engine Does Not Reach Normal Operating Temperature	11-11	27
Test D	Block Heater Does Not Operate Properly	11-11	28
CONTOUR & MYSTIQUE			
Test A	Loss Of Coolant	11-11	30
Test B	Engine Overheats	11-11	31
Test C	Engine Does Not Reach Normal Operating Temperature	11-12	32
Test D	Engine Block Heater Does Not Operate Properly	11-12	33
1997 COUGAR			
Test A	Loss of Coolant	11-10	25
Test B	Engine Overheats	11-11	26
Test C	Engine Does Not Reach Normal Operating Temperature	11-11	27
Test D	Block Heater Does Not Operate Properly	11-11	28
1999–2000 COUGAR			
Test A	Loss Of Coolant	11-11	30
Test B	Engine Overheats	11-11	31
Test C	Engine Does Not Reach Normal Operating Temperature	11-12	32
Test D	Engine Block Heater Does Not Operate Properly	11-12	33
CROWN VICTORIA, GRAND MARQUIS & TOWN CAR			
Test A	Loss Of Coolant	11-12	35
Test B	Engine Overheats	11-12	36

Continued

DIAGNOSTIC CHART INDEX—Continued

Test Step		Result	Action to Take
A1	VISUAL INSPECTION		
	• Key OFF. • Visual check for evidence of coolant leakage at: — All hoses and hose connections. — Radiator seams, radiator core and radiator draincock. — All block core plugs and drain plugs. — Edges of all cooling system gaskets. — Transmission fluid cooler fittings. — Vehicle heating system components. — Water pump. • **Is there evidence of coolant leakage?**	Yes ▶ No ▶	SERVICE the component in question. GO to **A2**.
A2	INTERNAL INSPECTION		
	• Visual check for white smoke from the exhaust system while the engine is running. • Examine engine oil for evidence of coolant at the oil level dipstick. • Examine coolant for evidence of engine oil or transmission fluid. • **Is oil or fluid evident in coolant, or coolant evident in oil or fluid?**	Yes ▶ No ▶	LOCATE and repair source of contamination.

FM1089600134000X

Fig. 20 Test A: Loss Of Coolant. Aspire

Test Step	Result	Action to Take
B1 CHECK COOLANT LEVEL		
• Verify the coolant level is at the FULL mark on the radiator coolant recovery reservoir. • Verify the coolant level is at the top of the filler tube (after removing the radiator cap). • **Is the coolant level OK?**	Yes No	GO to **B2**. GO to Pinpoint Test A1.
B2 CHECK COOLING FAN OPERATION		
• Key OFF. • Disconnect the engine coolant temperature sensor C103. • Key ON. • **Does the engine cooling fan motor run?**	Yes No	Test Thermostat engine coolant temperature sensor. GO to **B3**.
B3 CHECK FUSES		
• Key OFF. • Check the 10A ENGINE fuse located in the interior fuse junction panel and the 30A COOLING FAN fuse located in the main fuse junction panel. • **Are the fuses OK?**	Yes No	GO to **B9**. GO to **B4**.
B4 CHECK SYSTEM		
• Key OFF. • Replace the blown fuse(s). • Key ON. • **Do(es) the fuse(s) fail again?**	Yes No	GO to **B5**. GO to **B6**.
B5 CHECK FOR SHORT(S) TO GROUND		
• Key OFF. • Remove the 30A COOLING FAN fuse and/or 10A ENGINE fuse. • Disconnect the fan control relay C133. • Measure the resistance of the "BK/W" wire between the bottom terminal of the 10A ENGINE fuse holder and ground. • Measure the resistance of the "BK/R" wire between the left terminal of the 30A COOLING FAN fuse holder and ground. • **Are the resistances less than 5 ohms?**	Yes No	SERVICE the wire(s) in question. REPLACE the 10A ENGINE fuse and/or the 30A COOLING FAN fuse. GO to **B9**.
B6 CHECK ENGINE COOLING FAN MOTOR		
• Key OFF. • Disconnect the engine cooling fan motor C135. • Measure the resistance between engine cooling fan motor terminals C135-1 and C135-2. • **Is the resistance less than 50 ohms?**	Yes No	GO to **B7**. REPLACE the engine cooling fan motor.
B7 CHECK ENGINE COOLING FAN MOTOR GROUND		
• Measure the resistance between engine cooling fan motor pin C135-2 (BK) and ground. • **Is the resistance less than 5 ohms?**	Yes No	GO to **B8**. SERVICE the "BK" wire for open.
B8 CHECK COOLING FAN MOTOR POWER SUPPLY		
• Jumper terminal C135-1 (Y) to the battery positive terminal. • Jumper terminal C135-2 (BK) to the battery negative terminal. • **Does the engine cooling fan motor operate?**	Yes No	SERVICE the "Y" wire for open. Diagnose circuit as necessary.

FM1089600135010X

Fig. 21 Test B: Engine Overheats (Part 1 of 2). Aspire

Test Step	Result	Action to Take
C1 CHECK BLOCK HEATER		
• Install a new block heater. • **Does the block heater operate properly now?**	Yes No	REPLACE the block heater. REPLACE the block heater wiring.

FM1089600136000X

Fig. 22 Test C: Engine Block Heater Does Not Operate Properly. Aspire

Condition	Possible Source	Action
• Loss of Coolant	• Damaged radiator. • Damaged water pump. • Loose/damaged radiator hoses. • Loose/damaged heater hoses. • Damaged heater core. • Damaged engine gaskets. • Damaged engine oil cooler. • Damaged radiator coolant recovery reservoir or degas bottle.	• GO to Pinpoint Test A.
• Engine Overheats	• Damaged water thermostat. • Damaged water pump. • Internal engine coolant leak. • Cooling fan inoperative. • Plugged radiator. • Plugged heater core.	• GO to Pinpoint Test B.
• Engine Does Not Reach Normal Operating Temperature	• Damaged water thermostat. • Cooling fan. • Low engine coolant.	• GO to Pinpoint Test C.
• Block Heater Does Not Operate Properly	• Block heater power cable. • Block heater.	• GO to Pinpoint Test D.
• Cooling Fan Runs Continuously	• Circuit. • Constant control relay module (CCRM). • Powertrain control module. • Engine coolant temperature sensor.	• **Diagnose circuit as necessary.**
• Cooling Fan Runs, No Low Speed	• Circuit. • Constant control relay module (CCRM). • Powertrain control module. • Cooling fan motor.	• **Diagnose circuit as necessary.**
• Cooling Fan Runs, No High Speed	• Circuit. • Constant control relay module (CCRM). • Powertrain control module. • Cooling fan motor.	• **Diagnose circuit as necessary.**

FM1089600156000X

Fig. 24 Symptom Chart. Continental, Mark VIII & Thunderbird & 1997–98 Mustang & 1997 Cougar

Test Step	Result	Action to Take
B9 CHECK FAN CONTROL RELAY		
• Key OFF • Disconnect the fan control relay C133. • Jumper terminal C133-1 and terminal C133-2 on the fan control relay to the battery positive terminal. • Measure the voltage between terminal C133-4 on the fan control relay and the battery negative terminal. • Jumper terminal C133-3 on the fan control relay to the battery negative terminal. • Measure the voltage between terminal C133-4 on the fan control relay and the battery negative terminal. • **Is the voltage greater than 10 volts with terminal C133-3 jumper to the battery negative terminal, and less than 1 volt with terminal C133-3 not connected to the battery negative terminal?**	Yes No	GO to **B10**. REPLACE the fan control relay.
B10 CHECK POWER SUPPLY TO FAN CONTROL RELAY		
• Key ON. • Measure the voltage between the fan control relay pin C133-1 (BK/W) and ground. • Measure the voltage between the fan control relay pin C133-2 (W/BK) and ground. • **Are the voltages greater than 10 volts?**	Yes No	GO to **B6**. SERVICE the wire(s) in question for opens.

FM1089600135020X

Fig. 21 Test B: Engine Overheats (Part 2 of 2). Aspire

Test Step	Result	Action to Take
D1 CHECK FAN CONTROL RELAY		
• Key OFF. • Disconnect the fan control relay C133. • Jumper terminals C133-1 and C133-2 on the fan control relay to the battery positive terminal. • Measure the voltage between terminal C133-4 on the fan control relay and the battery negative terminal. • Jumper terminal C133-3 on the fan control relay to the battery negative terminal. • Measure the voltage between terminal C133-4 on the fan control relay and the battery negative terminal. • **Is the voltage greater than 10 volts with terminal C133-3 jumper to the battery positive terminal, and less than 1 volt with terminal C133-3 not connected to the battery negative terminal?**	Yes No	Diagnose circuit as necessary. REPLACE the fan control relay.

FM1089600137000X

Fig. 23 Test D: Cooling Fan Operates Continuously. Aspire

Test Step	Result	Action to Take
A1 CHECK ENGINE COOLANT LEVEL		
NOTE: If engine is hot, allow engine to cool down before proceeding. • Check engine coolant level at radiator and radiator coolant recovery reservoir or degas bottle. • **Is engine coolant level OK?**	Yes No	GO to **A2**. REFILL. GO to **A2**.
A2 CHECK FOR VISIBLE LEAKAGE		
NOTE: Engine coolant has an added dye color that makes the coolant an excellent leak detector. Check entire cooling system for visible leakage. • **Is there visible leakage?**	Yes No	SERVICE. RETEST system. GO to **A3**.
A3 CHECK PRESSURE RELIEF CAP		
• Using Rotunda Radiator/Heater Core Pressure Tester 014-R1072 or equivalent, test radiator cap. • **Did pressure relief cap test OK?**	Yes No	GO to **A4**. REPLACE damaged pressure relief cap. RETEST system.

FM1089600157010X

Fig. 25 Test A: Loss of Coolant (Part 1 of 2). Continental, Mark VIII & Thunderbird & 1997–98 Mustang & 1997 Cougar

Test Step	Result	Action to Take
A4 CHECK COOLANT FOR INTERNAL LEAKAGE		
• Inspect coolant in radiator and radiator coolant recovery reservoir or degas bottle for signs of transmission fluid or engine oil. • **Is oil evident in coolant?**	Yes No	Locate & Repair source of contamination. GO to **A5**.
A5 CHECK ENGINE AND TRANSMISSION FOR COOLANT		
• Remove oil level dipsticks from engine and transmission. • Carefully inspect oil level dipsticks for evidence of coolant. • **Is coolant evident?**	Yes No	Locate & Repair source of contamination. GO to **A6**.
A6 PRESSURE TEST COOLING SYSTEM		
• Using Rotunda Radiator/Heater Core Pressure Tester 014-R1072 or equivalent, pressurize cooling system NOTE: Check inside vehicle for possible heater core leakage. • Check for any signs of visible leakage. • **Is there leakage?**	Yes No	SERVICE as required. SERVICE heater core leakage RETEST system. Cooling system is operational at this time. RETEST system.

FM1089600157020X

Fig. 25 Test A: Loss of Coolant (Part 2 of 2). Continental, Mark VIII & Thunderbird & 1997–98 Mustang & 1997 Cougar

Test Step		Result	Action to Take
B1	CHECK ENGINE COOLANT LEVEL		
	NOTE: If engine is hot, allow engine to cool down before proceeding. • Remove pressure relief cap and check engine coolant level at radiator and radiator coolant recovery reservoir or degas bottle. • **Is engine coolant level OK?**	Yes No	GO to **B2**. REFILL. GO to Pinpoint Test A.
B2	CHECK COOLANT CONDITION		
	• Check coolant for contaminants such as rust or corrosion. Also check for fluid discoloration. • **Is coolant condition OK?**	Yes No	GO to **B3**. FLUSH system as described. RETEST system.
B3	CHECK FOR AIR FLOW OBSTRUCTION		
	• Inspect A/C condenser core and radiator for obstructions such as leaves or bugs. • **Is there any obstruction?**	Yes No	REMOVE obstruction and CLEAN A/C condenser core and radiator RETEST system. GO to **B4**.
B4	CHECK HEATER CORE OPERATION		
	• Install pressure relief cap. • As engine starts to warm up, feel the inlet and outlet heater water hoses. They should feel the same after three or four minutes. • **Is outlet heater water hose the same temperature as the inlet heater water hose?**	Yes No	GO to **B5**. TURN engine OFF before it overheats. SERVICE heater core RETEST system.
B5	CHECK WATER THERMOSTAT OPERATION		
	• Allow engine to run for 10 minutes. • Feel the inlet and outlet heater water hoses and the underside of the upper radiator hose. • **Are the upper radiator hose and heater water hoses cold?**	Yes No	REPLACE water thermostat RETEST system. LEAVE engine running. GO to **B6**.
B6	CHECK COOLING FAN		
	• Check temperature gauge at instrument cluster. Allow engine to RUN until high side of normal range is attained. • Check for cooling fan operation. • **Did cooling fan operate OK?**	Yes No	Diagnose engine operation. Diagnose climate control.

FM1089600158000X

Fig. 26 Test B: Engine Overheats. Continental, Mark VIII & Thunderbird & 1997–98 Mustang & 1997 Cougar

Test Step		Result	Action to Take
D1	CHECK POWER CABLE OPEN		
	• Check resistance of Circuits 1, 2 and 3 in power cable using Rotunda 73 Digital Multimeter 105-R0051 or equivalent. • **Is resistance less than 5 ohms?**	Yes No	GO to **D2**. REPLACE power cable. RETEST system.
	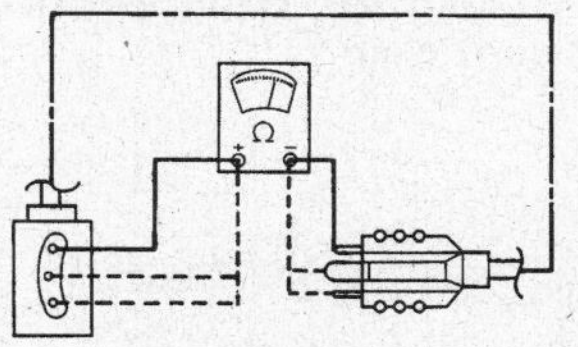		
D2	CHECK POWER CABLE SHORT		
	• Check resistance of Circuits 1, 2 and 3 in power cable using Rotunda 73 Digital Multimeter 105-R0051 or equivalent. • **Is resistance more than 10 K ohms?**	Yes No	REPLACE block heater. RETEST system. REPLACE power cable. RETEST system.
	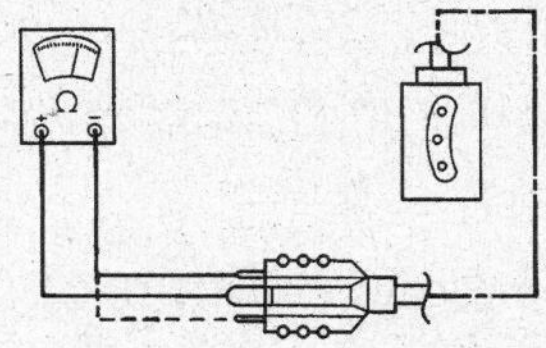		

FM1089600160000X

Fig. 28 Test D: Block Heater Does Not Operate Properly. Continental, Mark VIII & Thunderbird & 1997–98 Mustang & 1997 Cougar

Condition	Possible Source	Action
• Engine Overheats	• Damaged water thermostat. • Damaged water pump. • Internal engine coolant leak. • Cooling fan inoperative. • Plugged radiator. • Plugged heater core.	• GO to Pinpoint Test B.
• Engine Does Not Reach Normal Operating Temperature	• Damaged water thermostat. • Cooling fan. • Low engine coolant.	• GO to Pinpoint Test C.
• Engine Block Heater Does Not Operate Properly	• Block heater power cable. • Block heater.	• GO to Pinpoint Test D.
• Low Speed Fan Inoperative	• Low speed relay. • Cooling fan resistor. • Powertrain control module.	• Diagnose circuit as necessary.
• High Speed Fan Inoperative	• High speed relay. • A/C pressure cut-off switch. • Powertrain control module.	• Diagnose circuit as necessary.

FM1089600147020X

Fig. 29 Symptom Chart (Part 2 of 2). Contour & Mystique & 1999–2000 Cougar

Test Step		Result	Action to Take
C1	CHECK ENGINE TEMPERATURE		
	• Start engine and allow to RUN for 10 minutes. • Feel inlet and outlet heater water hoses and underside of upper radiator hose. • **Are upper radiator hose and heater water hoses cold?**	Yes No	REPLACE water thermostat RETEST system. Diagnose instrument cluster.

FM1089600159000X

Fig. 27 Test C: Engine Does Not Reach Normal Operating Temperature. Continental, Mark VIII & Thunderbird & 1997–98 Mustang & 1997 Cougar

Condition	Possible Source	Action
• Loss of Coolant	• Damaged radiator. • Damaged water pump. • Loose/damaged radiator hoses. • Loose/damaged heater hoses. • Damaged heater core. • Damaged engine gaskets. • Damaged radiator coolant recovery reservoir.	• GO to Pinpoint Test A.

FM1089600147010X

Fig. 29 Symptom Chart (Part 1 of 2). Contour & Mystique & 1999–2000 Cougar

Test Step		Result	Action to Take
A1	CHECK ENGINE COOLANT LEVEL		
	NOTE: If engine is hot, allow engine to cool down before proceeding. • Check engine coolant level at radiator coolant recovery reservoir. • **Is engine coolant level OK?**	Yes No	System OK. REFILL. GO to **A2**.
A2	CHECK FOR VISIBLE LEAKAGE		
	• Engine coolant has an added dye color that makes the coolant an excellent leak detector. • Check entire cooling system for visible leakage. • **Is there visible leakage?**	Yes No	SERVICE. RETEST system. GO to **A3**.
A3	CHECK PRESSURE RELIEF CAP		
	• Using Rotunda Radiator/Heater Core Pressure Tester 014-R1052 or equivalent, test pressure relief cap. • **Did pressure relief cap test OK?**	Yes No	GO to **A4**. REPLACE damaged pressure relief cap. RETEST system.
A4	CHECK COOLANT FOR INTERNAL LEAKAGE		
	• Inspect coolant in radiator coolant recovery reservoir for signs of transmission fluid or engine oil. • **Is oil evident in coolant?**	Yes No	Locate & Repair source of contamination. GO to **A5**.
A5	CHECK ENGINE AND TRANSAXLE FOR COOLANT		
	• Remove oil level dipsticks from engine and transaxle. • Carefully inspect oil level dipsticks for evidence of coolant. • **Is coolant evident?**	Yes No	Locate & Repair source of contamination. GO to **A6**.
A6	PRESSURE TEST COOLING SYSTEM		
	• Using Rotunda Radiator/Heater Core Pressure Tester 014-R1052 or equivalent, pressurize cooling system. • Check for any signs of visible leakage. • NOTE: Check inside vehicle for possible heater core leakage. • **Is there leakage?**	Yes No	SERVICE. RETEST system. Cooling system is operational at this time. RETEST system.

FM1089600148000X

Fig. 30 Test A: Loss Of Coolant. Contour & Mystique & 1999–2000 Cougar

Test Step		Result	Action to Take
B1	CHECK ENGINE COOLANT LEVEL		
	NOTE: If engine is hot, allow engine to cool down before proceeding. • Check engine coolant level at radiator coolant recovery reservoir. • **Is engine coolant level OK?**	Yes No	GO to **B2**. REFILL. GO to Pinpoint Test A.
B2	CHECK COOLANT CONDITION		
	• Check coolant for contaminants such as rust or corrosion. Also check for discolorization. • Check with hydrometer for protection level between -34 to -43°C (-30 to -45°F). • **Is coolant condition OK?**	Yes No	GO to **B3**. FLUSH system. RETEST system.
B3	CHECK FOR AIR FLOW OBSTRUCTION		
	• Inspect A/C condenser core and radiator for obstructions such as leaves or bugs. • **Is there any obstruction?**	Yes No	REMOVE obstruction and CLEAN A/C condenser core and radiator. RETEST system. GO to **B4**.
B4	CHECK HEATER CORE OPERATION		
	• Install pressure relief cap. • Start engine and allow to run. • As engine starts to warm up, feel the inlet and outlet heater water hoses. They should be the same temperature after three or four minutes. • **Is outlet heater water hose the same temperature as the inlet heater water hose?**	Yes No	GO to **B5**. TURN engine OFF before it overheats. SERVICE heater core. RETEST system.
B5	CHECK WATER THERMOSTAT OPERATION		
	• Allow engine to run for 10 minutes. • Feel the inlet and outlet heater water hoses and the underside of the upper radiator hose. • **Are the upper radiator hose and heater water hoses cold?**	Yes No	REPLACE water thermostat. RETEST system. LEAVE engine RUNNING. GO to **B6**.
B6	CHECK COOLING FAN(S)		
	• Check engine coolant temperature gauge at instrument cluster. Allow engine to RUN until high side of normal range is attained. • Check for cooling fan operation. • **Did cooling fan(s) operate OK?**	Yes No	Diagnose engine operation. Diagnose climate control.

FM1089600149000X

Fig. 31 Test B: Engine Overheats. Contour & Mystique & 1999–2000 Cougar

	Test Step	Result	Action to Take
C1	CHECK ENGINE TEMPERATURE		
	• Start engine and allow to RUN for 15 minutes. • Feel inlet and outlet heater water hoses and underside of upper radiator hose. • **Are upper radiator hose and heater water hoses cold?**	Yes ▶ No ▶	TEST water thermostat. RETEST system. Engine coolant temperature gauge testing procedure.

FM1089600150000X

Fig. 32 Test C: Engine Does Not Reach Normal Operating Temperature. Contour & Mystique & 1999–2000 Cougar

	Test Step	Result	Action to Take
D3	CHECK HEATER SHORT TO GROUND		
	• Measure resistance from terminal 1 of power cable to engine block. • Measure resistance from terminal 3 of power cable to engine block. • **Does resistance equal 1,000,000 ohms or more?**	Yes ▶ No ▶	GO to **D4.** REPLACE block heater. RESTORE vehicle. RETEST system.
D4	CHECK HEATER ELEMENT RESISTANCE		
	• Measure resistance from terminal 1 of power cable to terminal 3 of power cable. • **Does resistance measure between 30 ohms and 40 ohms?**	Yes ▶ No ▶	SERVICE AC power source. Block heater OK. REPLACE block heater. Heater element either open or shorted.

FM1089600151020X

Fig. 33 Test D: Engine Block Heater Does Not Operate Properly (Part 2 of 2). Contour & Mystique & 1999–2000 Cougar

	Test Step	Result	Action to Take
A1	CHECK ENGINE COOLANT LEVEL		
	NOTE: If engine is hot, allow engine to cool down before proceeding. • Check engine coolant level at degas bottle. • **Is coolant level OK?**	Yes ▶ No ▶	GO to **A2.** REFILL. GO to **A7.**
A2	CHECK FOR VISIBLE LEAKAGE		
	• Engine coolant has an added dye color that makes the coolant an excellent leak detector. • Check entire cooling system for visible leakage. • **Is there visible leakage?**	Yes ▶ No ▶	SERVICE. RETEST system. GO to **A3.**
A3	CHECK PRESSURE RELIEF CAP		
	• Using Rotunda Radiator/Heater Core Pressure Tester 014-R1069 or equivalent, test pressure relief cap. • **Did pressure relief cap test OK?**	Yes ▶ No ▶	GO to **A4.** REPLACE damaged pressure relief cap. RETEST system.
A4	CHECK COOLANT FOR INTERNAL LEAKAGE		
	• Inspect coolant in degas bottle for signs of transmission fluid or engine oil. • **Is oil evident in coolant?**	Yes ▶ No ▶	Locate & Repair source of contamination. GO to **A5.**

FM1089600162010X

Fig. 35 Test A: Loss Of Coolant (Part 1 of 2). Crown Victoria, Grand Marquis & Town Car

	Test Step	Result	Action to Take
A5	CHECK ENGINE AND TRANSMISSION FOR COOLANT		
	• Remove oil level dipsticks from engine and transmission. • Carefully inspect oil level dipsticks for evidence of coolant. • **Is coolant evident?**	Yes ▶ No ▶	If coolant is in engine oil, CHECK for leak in engine head gasket or cracked engine block. If coolant is in transmission fluid, SERVICE for transmission fluid leakage. GO to **A6.**
A6	PRESSURE TEST COOLING SYSTEM		
	• Using Rotunda Radiator/Heater Core Pressure Tester 014-R1069 or equivalent, pressurize cooling system • Check for any signs of visible leakage. NOTE: Check inside vehicle for possible heater core leakage. • **Is there leakage?**	Yes ▶ No ▶	SERVICE. RETEST system. GO to **A7.**
A7	CHECK COOLANT RECOVERY		
	• Allow engine to cool. Remove pressure relief cap and inspect cap for foreign material between sealing gasket and diaphragm. • **Is cap OK?**	Yes ▶ No ▶	GO to **A8.** SERVICE
A8	CHECK DEGAS HOSE		
	• Remove degas hose. • Inspect hose for obstruction, cracks or cuts. • **Is hose condition OK?**	Yes ▶ No ▶	GO to **A9.** SERVICE degas hose as required. RESTORE vehicle.
A9	CHECK DEGAS BOTTLE		
	• Replenish coolant in degas bottle to FULL COLD level as described. • Inspect degas bottle for leaks. • **Is there leakage at degas bottle?**	Yes ▶ No ▶	REPLACE degas bottle. RESTORE vehicle. Pressure Test, Component Tests. SERVICE as required.

FM1089600162020X

Fig. 35 Test A: Loss Of Coolant (Part 2 of 2). Crown Victoria, Grand Marquis & Town Car

	Test Step	Result	Action to Take
D1	CHECK ENGINE BLOCK HEATER POWER CABLE		
	• Check continuity of Circuits 1, 2 and 3 in engine block heater power cable using Rotunda Digital Volt Ohmmeter 014-00407 or equivalent. • **Is there continuity in Circuits 1, 2 and 3?**	Yes ▶ No ▶	GO to **D2.** REPLACE block heater power cable. RETEST system.
D2	CHECK GROUND		
	• Install power cable to block heater. • Measure resistance from ground terminal of power cable, Pin 2, to engine block. • **Does resistance equal 1 ohm or less?**	Yes ▶ No ▶	GO to **D3.** REPLACE block heater. RESTORE vehicle. RETEST system.

FM1089600151010X

Fig. 33 Test D: Engine Block Heater Does Not Operate Properly (Part 1 of 2). Contour & Mystique & 1999–2000 Cougar

Condition	Possible Source	Action
• Loss of Coolant	• Damaged radiator. • Loose/damaged radiator hoses. • Loose/damaged heater hoses. • Damaged heater core. • Damaged engine gaskets. • Damaged degas bottle. • Damaged fluid cooler (police/trailer tow only).	• GO to Pinpoint Test A.
• Engine Overheats	• Damaged water thermostat. • Damaged water pump. • Internal engine coolant leak. • Cooling fan inoperative. • Plugged radiator, interior or exterior. • Plugged heater core. • Electro-Drive cooling fan operating in reverse.	• GO to Pinpoint Test B.
• Engine Does Not Reach Normal Operating Temperature	• Damaged water thermostat. • Cooling fans.	• GO to Pinpoint Test C.
• Block Heater Does Not Operate Properly	• Block heater. • Block heater power cable.	• GO to Pinpoint Test D.
• Auxiliary Electric Cooling Fan Runs Continuously	• Circuit. • Powertrain control module. • Engine coolant temperature sensor.	• Diagnose circuit as necessary.

FM1089600161000X

Fig. 34 Symptom Chart. Crown Victoria, Grand Marquis & Town Car

	Test Step	Result	Action to Take
B1	CHECK ENGINE COOLANT LEVEL		
	NOTE: If engine is hot, allow engine to cool down before proceeding. • Remove pressure relief cap and check engine coolant level at degas bottle. • **Is engine coolant level OK?**	Yes ▶ No ▶	GO to **B2.** REFILL. GO to Pinpoint Test A.
B2	CHECK COOLANT CONDITION		
	• Check coolant for contaminants such as rust or corrosion. Also check for color discoloration. • **Is coolant condition OK?**	Yes ▶ No ▶	GO to **B3.** FLUSH system. RETEST system.
B3	CHECK FOR AIR FLOW OBSTRUCTION		
	• Inspect A/C condenser core and radiator for obstructions such as leaves or bugs. • **Is there any obstruction?**	Yes ▶ No ▶	REMOVE obstruction and CLEAN A/C condenser core and radiator RETEST system. GO to **B4.**

FM1089600163010X

Fig. 36 Test B: Engine Overheats (Part 1 of 2). Crown Victoria, Grand Marquis & Town Car

Test Step		Result	Action to Take
B4	CHECK HEATER CORE OPERATION		
	• Install pressure relief cap. • Start engine and allow to run. • As engine starts to warm up, feel the inlet and outlet heater water hoses. They should feel the same after three or four minutes. • **Is outlet heater water hose the same temperature as the inlet heater water hose?**	Yes No	GO to **B5**. TURN engine OFF before it overheats. SERVICE heater core RETEST system.
B5	CHECK WATER THERMOSTAT OPERATION		
	• Allow engine to run for 10 minutes. • Feel the inlet and outlet heater water hoses and the underside of the upper radiator hose. • **Are the upper radiator hose and heater water hoses cold?**	Yes No	REPLACE water thermostat RETEST system. LEAVE engine RUNNING. GO to **B6**.
B6	CHECK COOLING FAN CLUTCH		
	• Check for proper cooling fan clutch operation. • **Is cooling fan clutch operating correctly?**	Yes No	GO to **B7**. REPLACE fan clutch. RETEST system.
B7	CHECK AUXILIARY ELECTRIC COOLING FAN		
	• Connect Rotunda New Generation Star (NGS) Tester 007-00500 or equivalent to vehicle. • Key on, engine off. • Output Test Mode accessed on tester. • Command cooling fan on. • **Does auxiliary electric cooling fan come on rotating in the proper direction?**	Yes No	Diagnose engine operation. GO to **B8**.
B8	CHECK FOR POWER AND GROUND TO AUXILIARY ELECTRIC COOLING FAN		
	• Still in output test mode (OTM) with cooling fan commanded ON. • Measure voltage at Circuit 228 (DB) and ground at the cooling fan vehicle harness connector. • **Is voltage greater than 10.5 volts?**	Yes No	Turn ignition switch OFF. CHECK Circuit 229 (DB) and ground Circuit 57 (BK) are not reversed to the fan motor. If circuits are OK, REPLACE cooling fan. RESTORE vehicle. RETEST system. REMAIN in Output Test Mode (OTM). GO to **B9**.
B9	CHECK GROUND CIRCUIT TO AUXILIARY ELECTRIC COOLING FAN		
	• Still in output test mode (OTM) with cooling fan commanded ON. • Cooling fan disconnected. • Measure voltage between the battery negative terminal and Circuit 228 (DB) at the cooling fan vehicle harness connector. • **Is voltage now greater than 10.5 volts?**	Yes No	TURN ignition switch OFF. SERVICE open ground Circuit 57 (BK) to cooling fan. RECONNECT cooling fan. RESTORE vehicle. RETEST system. TURN ignition switch OFF. GO to **B10**.
B10	CHECK FOR B+ TO AUXILIARY ELECTRIC COOLING FAN RELAY		
	• Turn ignition switch OFF. • Disconnect cooling fan relay. • Measure voltage between the B+ Circuit 37 (Y) at the cooling fan relay and the battery negative post. • **Is voltage greater than 10.5 volts?**	Yes No	GO to **B11**. SERVICE open B+ circuit to cooling fan relay. RESTORE vehicle. RETEST system.
B11	CHECK POWER-TO-FAN CIRCUIT CONTINUITY		
	• Turn ignition switch OFF. • Cooling fan disconnected. • Cooling fan relay disconnected. • Measure resistance between the cooling fan relay power Circuit 37 (Y) and fan power Circuit 228 (DB) vehicle harness connector. • **Is resistance less than 5.0 ohms?**	Yes No	REPLACE cooling fan relay. RESTORE vehicle. RETEST system. SERVICE open in Circuit 228 (DB) between cooling fan relay and cooling fan connector. RESTORE vehicle. RETEST system.

FM1089600163020X

Fig. 36 Test B: Engine Overheats (Part 2 of 2). Crown Victoria, Grand Marquis & Town Car

Test Step		Result	Action to Take
D1	CHECK POWER CABLE OPEN		
	• Check resistance of Circuits 1, 2 and 3 in power cable using Rotunda 73 Digital Multimeter 105-R0051 or equivalent. • **Is resistance less than 5.0 ohms?** 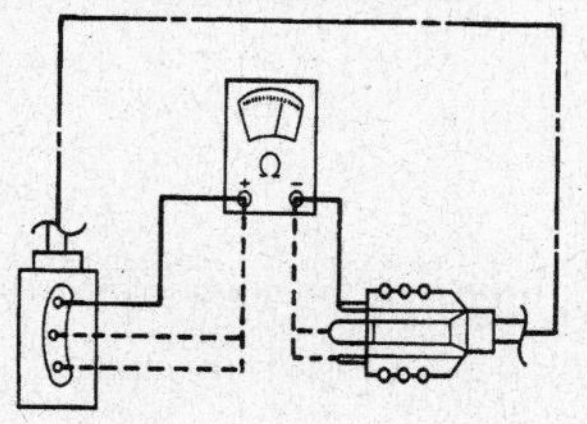	Yes No	GO to **D2**. REPLACE power cable. RETEST system.
D2	CHECK POWER CABLE FOR SHORT		
	• Check resistance of Circuits 1,2 and 3 in power cable using Rotunda 73 Digital Multimeter 105-R0051 or equivalent. • **Is resistance more than 10 k ohms?** 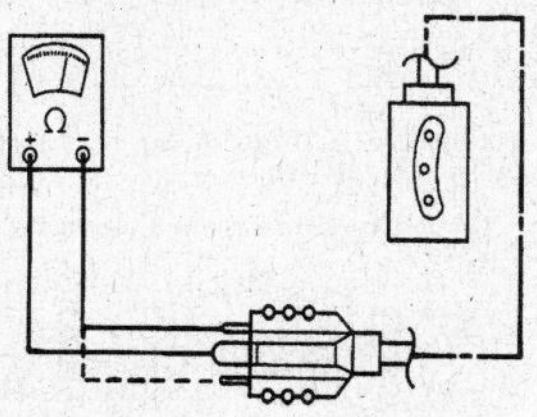	Yes No	REPLACE block heater. RETEST system. REPLACE power cable. RETEST system.

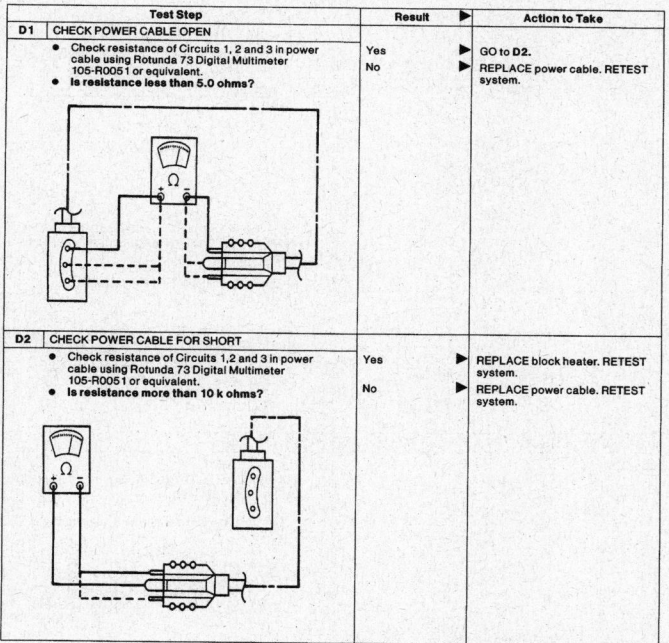

FM1089600165000X

Fig. 38 Test D: Block Heater Does Not Operate Properly. Crown Victoria, Grand Marquis & Town Car

Test Step		Result	Action to Take
C1	CHECK ENGINE TEMPERATURE		
	• Start engine and allow to run for 15 minutes. • Feel inlet and outlet heater water hoses and underside of upper radiator hose. • **Are upper radiator hose and heater water hoses cold?**	Yes No	REPLACE water thermostat RETEST system. Diagnose instrument cluster.

FM1089600164000X

Fig. 37 Test C: Engine Does Not Reach Normal Operating Temperature. Crown Victoria, Grand Marquis & Town Car

Condition	Possible Source	Action
• Loss of Coolant	• Hoses and hose connections. • Radiator. • Water pump. • Heater core. • Gaskets. • Engine casting cracks. • Engine block core plugs.	• GO to Pinpoint Test A.
• Engine Overheats	• Engine coolant weak, contaminated or low. • Thermostat. • Fuse. • Constant control relay module. • Circuit. • Fan motor. • Engine coolant temperature sensor. • Powertrain control module.	• GO to Pinpoint Test B.
• Engine Does Not Reach Normal Operating Temperature	• Thermostat.	• REPLACE the thermostat.
• Engine Block Heater Does Not Operate Properly	• Power cord. • Engine block heater.	• REPLACE the power cord. • REPLACE the engine block heater.
• Engine Cooling Fan Operates Continuously	• Constant control relay module. • Circuit. • Powertrain control module.	• Diagnose circuit as necessary.
• Engine Cooling Fan Low Speed Inoperative	• Constant control relay module. • Circuit. • Powertrain control module. • Fan motor.	• Diagnose circuit as necessary.
• Engine Cooling Fan High Speed Inoperative	• Constant control relay module. • Circuit. • Powertrain control module. • Fan motor.	• Diagnose circuit as necessary.

FM1089600130000X

Fig. 39 Symptom Chart. Escort, Tracer & ZX2

TEST CONDITIONS	TEST DETAILS/RESULTS/ACTIONS
A1 VISUAL INSPECTION	
1 	2 Visually inspect for evidence of coolant leakage. • Is (are) there any visible coolant leak(s)? → **Yes** REPAIR the component(s) in question. REFER to the appropriate section. → **No** PERFORM the Pressure Test.

FM1089600131000X

Fig. 40 Test A: Loss Of Coolant. Escort, Tracer & ZX2

TEST CONDITIONS	TEST DETAILS/RESULTS/ACTIONS
B1 CHECK COOLANT	
	1 Inspect the coolant level and quality. • Is the coolant OK? → **Yes** GO to **B2**. → **No** If coolant is weak or contaminated, FLUSH and REPLACE as necessary. If the coolant is low, REFILL the system and PERFORM the Pressure Test.

FM1089600132010X

Fig. 41 Test B: Engine Overheats (Part 1 of 2). Escort, Tracer & ZX2

TEST CONDITIONS	TEST DETAILS/RESULTS/ACTIONS
B2 CHECK THERMOSTAT	
	1 Perform the thermostat operation component test • Is the thermostat OK? → **Yes** → **No** REPLACE the thermostat.

FM1089600132020X

Fig. 41 Test B: Engine Overheats (Part 2 of 2). Escort, Tracer & ZX2

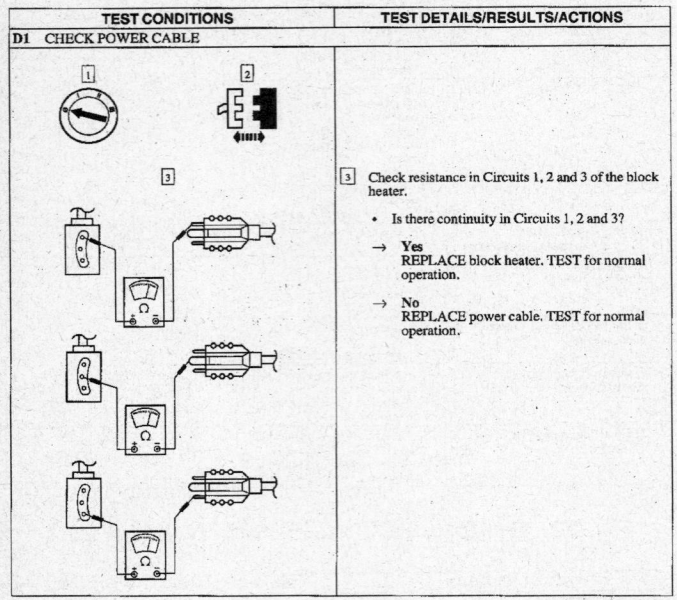

TEST CONDITIONS	TEST DETAILS/RESULTS/ACTIONS
D1 CHECK POWER CABLE	
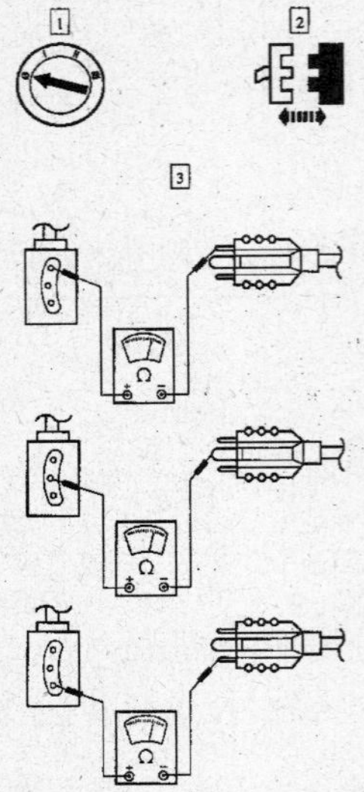	3 Check resistance in Circuits 1, 2 and 3 of the block heater. • Is there continuity in Circuits 1, 2 and 3? → **Yes** REPLACE block heater. TEST for normal operation. → **No** REPLACE power cable. TEST for normal operation.

FM1089700176000X

Fig. 43 Test D: Block Heater Does Not Operate Properly. Escort, Tracer & ZX2

TEST CONDITIONS	TEST DETAILS/RESULTS/ACTIONS
A1 CHECK THE ENGINE COOLANT LEVEL	
Note: Allow the engine to cool before checking the engine coolant level.	
1 	2 Visually check the engine coolant level at the degas bottle or coolant expansion tank. • Is the engine coolant level within specification? → **Yes** GO to **A2**. → **No** REFILL the engine coolant as necessary. GO to **A6**.

FM1089900204010X

Fig. 45 Test A: Loss Of Coolant (Part 1 of 4). 1999–2000 Mustang

TEST CONDITIONS	TEST DETAILS/RESULTS/ACTIONS
C1 CHECK ENGINE TEMPERATURE	
1 	1 **Test Thermostat** • Is the thermostat OK? → **Yes** REFER to the Symptom Chart in this section. → **No** REPLACE the water thermostat. TEST for normal operation.

FM1089700175000X

Fig. 42 Test C: Engine Does Not Reach Normal Operating Temperature. Escort, Tracer & ZX2

Condition	Possible Source	Action
• Loss of coolant	• Radiator. • Water pump seal. • Radiator hoses. • Heater hoses. • Heater core. • Engine gaskets. • Degas bottle or coolant expansion tank.	• GO to Pinpoint Test A.
• The engine overheats	• Water thermostat. • Water pump. • Internal engine coolant leak. • Radiator. • Heater core. • Cooling fan. • Pressure relief cap or radiator cap.	• GO to Pinpoint Test B.
• The engine does not reach normal operating temperature	• Water thermostat.	• GO to Pinpoint Test C.
• The block heater does not operate correctly	• Block heater power cable. • Block heater.	• GO to Pinpoint Test D.

FM1089900203000X

Fig. 44 Symptom Chart. 1999–2000 Mustang

TEST CONDITIONS	TEST DETAILS/RESULTS/ACTIONS
A2 CHECK THE PRESSURE RELIEF CAP	
	1 Carry out the Cap—3.8L or Cap—4.6L test • Is pressure relief cap/radiator cap OK? → **Yes** GO to **A3**. → **No** INSTALL a new pressure relief cap/radiator cap. TEST the system for normal operation.
A3 CHECK THE ENGINE COOLANT FOR INTERNAL LEAK	
1 	2 Inspect the engine coolant in degas bottle/coolant expansion tank for signs of transmission fluid or engine oil. • Is oil or transmission fluid evident in the coolant? → **Yes** If engine oil is evident If transmission fluid is evident, REPAIR or INSTALL a new radiator as necessary. → **No** GO to **A4**.
A4 CHECK THE ENGINE AND THE TRANSMISSION FOR COOLANT	
	1 Remove the oil level dipstick from the engine and the transmission. • Is coolant evident in the oil or transmission fluid? → **Yes** If coolant is in engine If coolant is in transmission, REPAIR or INSTALL a new radiator as necessary. → **No** GO to **A5**.

FM1089900204020X

Fig. 45 Test A: Loss Of Coolant (Part 2 of 4). 1999–2000 Mustang

TEST CONDITIONS	TEST DETAILS/RESULTS/ACTIONS
A5 PRESSURE TEST THE ENGINE COOLING SYSTEM	
	1 Pressure test the engine cooling system; go to Component Tests in this section. • Does the engine cooling system leak? → **Yes** REPAIR or install new components. TEST the system for normal operation. → **No** The cooling system is operational. RETURN to the Symptom Chart.
A6 CHECK THE COOLANT RECOVERY SYSTEM	
	1 **WARNING: Never remove the pressure relief cap/radiator cap under any conditions while the engine is operating. Failure to follow these instructions could result in damage to the cooling system or engine and/or personal injury. To avoid having scalding hot coolant or steam blow out of the cooling system, use extreme care when removing the pressure relief cap from a hot degas bottle or the radiator cap from the radiator. Wait until the engine has cooled, then wrap a thick cloth around the pressure relief cap and turn it slowly one turn (counterclockwise) or with a thick cloth around the radiator cap turn the radiator cap (counterclockwise) slowly to the first pressure stop, step back while the pressure is released from the cooling system. When certain all the pressure has been released, remove the pressure relief cap/radiator cap (still with a cloth).** Allow the engine to cool. 2 Remove the pressure relief cap/radiator cap. 3 Inspect the pressure relief cap/radiator cap for foreign material between the sealing gasket and the diaphragm. • Is the pressure relief cap/radiator cap OK? → **Yes** GO to **A7**. → **No** CLEAN the pressure relief cap/radiator cap or INSTALL a new cap. TEST the system for normal operation. GO to **A1**.

FM1089900204030X

Fig. 45 Test A: Loss Of Coolant (Part 3 of 4). 1999–2000 Mustang

TEST CONDITIONS	TEST DETAILS/RESULTS/ACTIONS
A7 CHECK THE DEGAS BOTTLE/COOLANT EXPANSION TANK	
	1 **Note:** The engine must be cool when coolant is added to the degas bottle/coolant expansion tank. Add coolant to the degas bottle/coolant expansion tank until the fluid is between the coolant fill level marks. • Does the degas bottle/coolant expansion tank leak? → **Yes** INSTALL a new degas bottle/coolant expansion tank. TEST the system for normal operation. → **No** CARRY out the cooling system pressure test; REPAIR as necessary. TEST the system for normal operation.

FM1089900204040X

Fig. 45 Test A: Loss Of Coolant (Part 4 of 4). 1999–2000 Mustang

TEST CONDITIONS	TEST DETAILS/RESULTS/ACTIONS
B1 CHECK THE ENGINE COOLANT LEVEL	
Note: If the engine is hot, allow the engine to cool before proceeding.	
1 	1 **WARNING: Never remove the pressure relief cap/radiator cap under any conditions while the engine is operating. Failure to follow these instructions could result in damage to the cooling system or engine and/or personal injury. To avoid having scalding hot coolant or steam blow out of the cooling system, use extreme care when removing the pressure relief cap from a hot degas bottle or the radiator cap from the radiator. Wait until the engine has cooled, then wrap a thick cloth around the pressure relief cap and turn it slowly one turn (counterclockwise) or with a thick cloth around the radiator cap turn the radiator cap (counterclockwise) slowly to the first pressure stop. Step back while the pressure is released from the cooling system. When certain all the pressure has been released, remove the pressure relief cap/radiator cap (still with a cloth).** 2 Check the engine coolant level at the degas bottle/coolant expansion tank. • Is the engine coolant OK? → **Yes** GO to **B2**. → **No** REFILL the engine coolant at the degas bottle/coolant expansion tank. GO to Pinpoint Test A.
B2 CHECK THE COOLANT CONDITION	
	1 Check the coolant for contaminants such as rust, corrosion, or discoloration. • Is the coolant condition OK? → **Yes** GO to **B3**. → **No** FLUSH the engine cooling system; TEST the system for normal operation.

FM1089900205010X

Fig. 46 Test B: Engine Overheats (Part 1 of 3). 1999–2000 Mustang

TEST CONDITIONS	TEST DETAILS/RESULTS/ACTIONS
B3 CHECK FOR AN AIRFLOW OBSTRUCTION	
	1 Inspect the A/C condenser core and radiator for obstructions such as leaves or dirt. • Is there an obstruction? → **Yes** REMOVE the obstruction. CLEAN the A/C condenser core and radiator. TEST the system for normal operation. → **No** GO to **B4**.
B4 CHECK THE HEATER CORE OPERATION	
2 	1 Install the pressure relief cap/radiator cap. 3 As the engine starts to heat up, feel the inlet and outlet heater water hoses. They should feel approximately the same after three or four minutes. • Is the outlet heater water hose approximately the same temperature as the inlet heater water hose? → **Yes** GO to **B5**. → **No** TURN the engine off. REPAIR or INSTALL a new heater core. TEST the system for normal operation.
B5 CHECK THE WATER THERMOSTAT OPERATION	
1 	1 Start the engine and allow the engine to run for ten minutes.

FM1089900205020X

Fig. 46 Test B: Engine Overheats (Part 2 of 3). 1999–2000 Mustang

TEST CONDITIONS	TEST DETAILS/RESULTS/ACTIONS
B5 CHECK THE WATER THERMOSTAT OPERATION (Continued)	
	2 Feel the inlet and outlet heater water hoses and the underside of the upper radiator hose. • Are the upper radiator hose and the heater water hoses cold? → **Yes** INSTALL a new water thermostat; TEST the system for normal operation. → **No** GO to **B6**.
B6 CHECK THE COOLING FAN OPERATION	
1 	1 Carry out the cooling fan component tests; go to Component Tests. • Is the cooling fan operation OK? → **Yes** For diagnosis and testing of the engine, REFER to Section 303-00. → **No** INSTALL a new fan component determined; TEST the system for normal operation.

FM1089900205030X

Fig. 46 Test B: Engine Overheats (Part 3 of 3). 1999–2000 Mustang

TEST CONDITIONS	TEST DETAILS/RESULTS/ACTIONS
C1 CHECK THE ENGINE TEMPERATURE (Continued)	
2 	2 Feel the inlet and heater water hoses and the underside of the upper radiator hose. • Are the upper radiator hose and the heater water hoses cold? → **Yes** INSTALL a new water thermostat; TEST the system for normal operation. → **No** For diagnosis and testing of the engine coolant temperature gauge

FM1089900206020X

Fig. 47 Test C: Engine Does Not Reach Normal Operating Temperature (Part 2 of 2). 1999–2000 Mustang

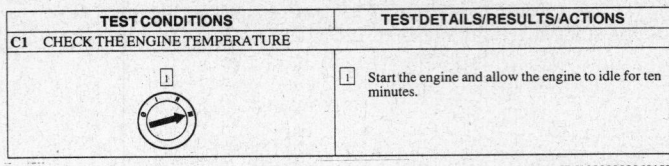

TEST CONDITIONS	TEST DETAILS/RESULTS/ACTIONS
C1 CHECK THE ENGINE TEMPERATURE	
1 	1 Start the engine and allow the engine to idle for ten minutes.

FM1089900206010X

Fig. 47 Test C: Engine Does Not Reach Normal Operating Temperature (Part 1 of 2). 1999–2000 Mustang

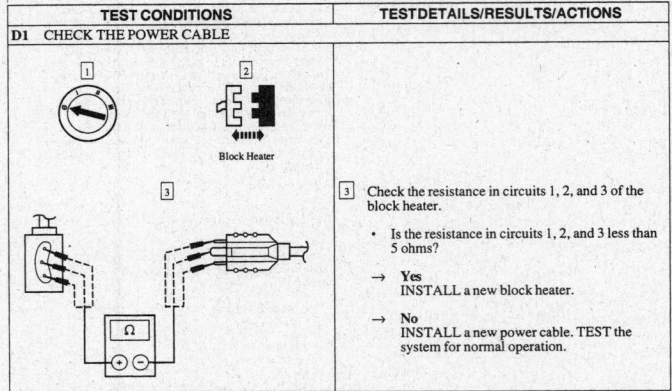

TEST CONDITIONS	TEST DETAILS/RESULTS/ACTIONS
D1 CHECK THE POWER CABLE	
1  2  3 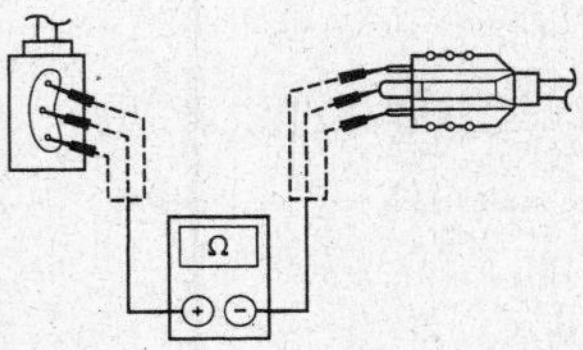	3 Check the resistance in circuits 1, 2, and 3 of the block heater. • Is the resistance in circuits 1, 2, and 3 less than 5 ohms? → **Yes** INSTALL a new block heater. → **No** INSTALL a new power cable. TEST the system for normal operation.

FM1089900207000X

Fig. 48 Test D: Block Heater Does Not Operate Correctly. 1999–2000 Mustang

Condition	Possible Source	Action
• Loss of Coolant	• Hoses and hose connections. • Radiator. • Water pump. • Heater core. • Gaskets.	• GO to Pinpoint Test A1.
• Engine Overheats	• Low coolant level. • Malfunctioning water thermostat. • Circuit. • Fan control relays. • Engine cooling fan motor.	• GO to Pinpoint Test B1.
• Engine Does Not Reach Normal Operating Temperature	• Water thermostat.	• Test Thermostat
• Engine Block Heater Does Not Operate Properly (Canadian Vehicles Only)	• Engine block heater.	• REPLACE the engine block heater.
• Cooling Fan Operates Continuously	• Circuit. • Fan control relays. • Engine cooling fan motor. • Engine coolant temperature sensor (ECT Sensor).	• Diagnose circuit as necessary.
• Cooling Fan Runs, No Low Speed	• Circuit. • Fan control relays. • Engine cooling fan motor.	• Diagnose circuit as necessary.
• Cooling Fan Runs, No High Speed	• Circuit. • High fan control relay. • Engine cooling fan motor.	• Diagnose circuit as necessary.

FM1089600138000X

Fig. 49 Symptom Chart. Probe w/2.0L engine

Test Step		Result		Action to Take
A1	VISUAL INSPECTION			
	• Key OFF. • Visually check for evidence of coolant leakage at: — All hoses and hose connection. — Radiator seams, radiator core and radiator draincock. — All engine block core plugs and drain plugs. — Edges of all cooling system gaskets. — Transmission oil cooler fittings. — Heater core. — Water pump. • Examine oil dipstick for evidence of coolant in engine oil. • Check radiator for evidence of oil in coolant (leakage at transmission oil cooler). • **Is there evidence of coolant leakage?**	Yes	▶	SERVICE the component.
		No	▶	PERFORM Pressure Test

FM1089600139000X

Fig. 50 Test A: Loss Of Coolant. Probe w/2.0L engine

Test Step		Result		Action to Take
B1	CHECK COOLANT LEVEL			
	• Verify the coolant level is at the F mark on the radiator overflow container dipstick. • **Is the coolant level at the F mark?**	Yes	▶	GO to **B2**.
		No	▶	CHECK for coolant leaks.
B2	CHECK FOR DIAGNOSTIC TROUBLE CODES			
	• Perform the Quick Test procedure • **Are any diagnostic trouble codes present?**	Yes	▶	REPAIR as necessary.
		No	▶	GO to **B3**.
B3	CHECK THERMOSTAT			
	• Test Thermostat • **Is the water thermostat OK?**	Yes	▶	PERFORM the Radiator Cap Pressure Test
		No	▶	REPLACE the water thermostat.

FM1089600140000X

Fig. 51 Test B: Engine Overheats. Probe w/2.0L engine

Condition	Possible Source	Action
• Loss of Coolant	• Hoses and hose connections. • Radiator. • Water pump. • Vehicle heating system. • Gaskets.	• GO to Pinpoint Test A1.
• Engine Overheats	• Water thermostat. • Radiator cap.	• GO to Pinpoint Test B1.
• Engine Does Not Reach Normal Operating Temperature	• Water thermostat.	• PERFORM the Water Temperature component test
• Engine Block Heater Does Not Operate Properly (Canadian Vehicles Only)	• Engine block heater.	• REPLACE the engine block heater.
• Cooling Fan Operates Continuously	• Circuit. • High fan control relay and low fan control relay. • Engine cooling fan motor. • A/C pressure cut-off switch. • Engine coolant temperature sensor (ECT sensor).	• GO to Pinpoint Test C1.
• Cooling Fan Runs, No Low Speed	• Circuit. • High fan control relay and low fan control relay. • Engine cooling fan motor.	• GO to Pinpoint Test D1.
• Cooling Fan Runs, No High Speed	• Circuit. • High fan control relay. • Engine cooling fan motor.	• GO to Pinpoint Test E1.

FM1089600141000X

Fig. 52 Symptom Chart. Probe w/2.5L engine

Test Step		Result		Action to Take
A1	VISUAL INSPECTION			
	• Key OFF. • Visually check for evidence of coolant leakage at: — All hoses and hose connections. — Radiator seams, radiator core, and radiator draincock. — All engine block core plugs and drain plugs. — Edges of all cooling system gaskets. — Transmission oil cooler fittings. — Vehicle heating system components. — Water pump. • Examine oil dipstick for evidence of coolant in engine oil. • Check radiator for evidence of oil in coolant (leakage at transmission oil cooler). • **Is there evidence of coolant leakage?**	Yes	▶	SERVICE the component.
		No	▶	PERFORM the Pressure Test

FM1089600142000X

Fig. 53 Test A: Loss Of Coolant. Probe w/2.5L engine

Test Step		Result		Action to Take
B1	CHECK COOLANT LEVEL			
	• Verify that the coolant level is at the F mark on the radiator overflow container cap dipstick. • Verify that the coolant level is at the top of the filler tube (after removing the radiator cap). • **Is the coolant level OK?**	Yes	▶	GO to **B2**.
		No	▶	CHECK for coolant loss. If necessary, perform the Pressure Test
B2	CHECK COOLING FAN OPERATION			
	• Start the engine. • Bring engine up to operating temperature. • **Does the engine cooling fan run?**	Yes	▶	Test Thermostat
		No	▶	GO to **B3**.
B3	CHECK FUSES			
	• Key OFF. • Check the 15A ENGINE fuse located in the interior fuse junction panel and the 40A COOLING FAN fuse located in the main fuse junction panel. • **Are the fuses OK?**	Yes	▶	GO to **B6**.
		No	▶	GO to **B4**.
B4	CHECK SYSTEM			
	• Key OFF. • Replace the blown fuse(s). • Key ON. • **Do(es) the fuse(s) fail again?**	Yes	▶	GO to **B5**.
		No	▶	GO to **B6**.
B5	CHECK FOR SHORT(S) TO GROUND			
	• Key OFF. • Remove the 40A COOLING FAN fuse. • Disconnect the interior fuse junction panel C214. • Remove the low and high fan control relays. • Measure the resistance between the interior fuse junction panel C214-2, "BK/W," and ground. • Measure the resistance between the left terminal of the 40A COOLING FAN fuse holder and ground. • **Are the resistances less than 5 ohms?**	Yes	▶	SERVICE the wire(s) in question.
		No	▶	RECONNECT the interior fuse junction panel connector (C1). REPLACE the 15A ENGINE fuse and/or the 40A COOLING FAN fuse. GO to **B6**.
B6	CHECK ENGINE COOLING FAN MOTOR			
	• Key OFF. • Disconnect the engine cooling fan motor C118. • Apply 12 volts to the engine cooling fan motor (fan side) C118, "BL/Y" wire terminal or the "BL/BK" wire terminal. • Apply ground to the engine cooling fan motor (fan side) C118, "BK" wire terminal. • **Does the engine cooling fan motor operate?**	Yes	▶	GO to **B7**.
		No	▶	REPLACE the engine cooling fan motor.
B7	CHECK ENGINE COOLING FAN MOTOR GROUND			
	• Key OFF. • Disconnect the engine cooling fan motor C118. • Measure the resistance between the engine cooling fan motor C118, "BK," and ground. • **Is the resistance less than 5 ohms?**	Yes	▶	GO to **B8**.
		No	▶	SERVICE the "BK" wire for open.
B8	CHECK LOW FAN CONTROL RELAY			
	• Key OFF. • Remove the low fan control relay. • Apply 12 volts to the low fan control relay C167, terminals 1 and 2. • Measure the voltage at the low fan control relay C167, terminal 3. • Apply ground to the low fan control relay C167, terminal 4. • Measure the voltage at the low fan control relay C167, terminal 3. • **Is the voltage greater than 10 volts with ground applied, and less than 1 volt with ground not applied?**	Yes	▶	GO to **B9**.
		No	▶	REPLACE the low fan control relay.

FM1089600143010X

Fig. 54 Test B: Engine Overheats. (Part 1 of 2). Probe w/2.5L engine

Test Step		Result		Action to Take
B9	CHECK HIGH FAN CONTROL RELAY			
	• Key OFF. • Remove the high fan control relay. • Apply 12 volts to the high fan control relay C144, terminals 2 and 5. • Measure the voltage at the high fan control relay C144, terminal 4. • Apply ground to the high fan control relay C144, terminal 3. • Measure the voltage at the high fan control relay C144, terminal 1. • **Is the voltage greater than 10 volts at high fan control relay C144, terminal 4 with ground not applied, and greater than 10 volts at the high fan control relay C144, terminal 1 with ground applied?**	Yes	▶	GO to **B10**.
		No	▶	REPLACE the high fan control relay.
B10	CHECK POWER SUPPLY TO FAN CONTROL RELAYS			
	• Key OFF. • Remove the low fan control relay and the high fan control relay. • Key ON. • Measure the voltage at the low fan control relay C167-1, "BK/W," and the high fan control relay C144-5, "BK/W." • Measure the voltage at the high fan control relay C144-2, "BK/R." • **Are the voltages greater than 10 volts?**	Yes	▶	Diagnose circuit as necessary.
		No	▶	SERVICE the wire(s) in question for opens.

FM1089600143020X

Fig. 54 Test B: Engine Overheats. (Part 2 of 2). Probe w/2.5L engine

Test Step		Result		Action to Take
C1	CHECK LOW FAN CONTROL RELAY			
	• Key OFF. • Remove the low fan control relay. • Apply 12 volts to the low fan control relay C167, terminals 1 and 2. • Measure the voltage at the low fan control relay C167, terminal 3. • Apply ground to the low fan control relay C167, terminal 4. • Measure the voltage at the low fan control relay C167, terminal 3. • **Is the voltage greater than 10 volts with ground applied, and less than 1 volt with ground not applied?**	Yes	▶	GO to **C2**.
		No	▶	REPLACE the low fan control relay.
C2	CHECK HIGH FAN CONTROL RELAY			
	• Key OFF. • Remove the high fan control relay. • Apply 12 volts on the high fan control relay C144, terminals 2 and 5. • Measure the voltage at the high fan control relay C144, terminal 4. • Apply ground to the high fan control relay C144, terminal 3. • Measure the voltage at the high fan control relay C144, terminal 1. • **Is the voltage greater than 10 volts on the "R" wire terminal with ground not applied, and greater than 10 volts on the "BL/BK" wire terminal with ground applied?**	Yes	▶	Diagnose circuit as necessary.
		No	▶	REPLACE the high fan control relay.

FM1089600144000X

Fig. 55 Test C: Cooling Fan Operates Continuously. Probe w/2.5L engine

	Test Step	Result	Action to Take
D1	CHECK ELECTRIC FAN LOW OPERATION		
	• Key OFF. • Disconnect the engine cooling fan motor C118. • Apply 12 volts to the at the engine cooling fan motor C118, "BL/Y" wire terminal (fan side). • Apply ground to the engine cooling fan motor C118, "BK" wire terminal (fan side). • **Does the low speed of the engine cooling fan motor operate properly?**	Yes No	GO to **D2**. REPLACE the engine cooling fan motor.
D2	CHECK LOW FAN CONTROL RELAY		
	• Key OFF. • Remove the low fan control relay. • Apply 12 volts to low fan control relay C167, terminals 1 and 2. • Measure the voltage at the low fan control relay C167, terminal 3. • Apply ground to the low fan control relay C167, terminal 4. • Measure the voltage at the low fan control relay C167, terminal 3. • **Is the voltage greater than 10 volts with ground applied, and less than 1 volt with ground not applied?**	Yes No	GO to **D3**. REPLACE the low fan control relay.
D3	CHECK HIGH FAN CONTROL RELAY		
	• Key OFF. • Remove the high fan control relay. • Apply 12 volts to high fan control relay C144, terminals 2 and 5. • Measure the voltage at the high fan control relay C144, terminal 4. • Apply ground to the high fan control relay C144, terminal 3. • Measure the voltage at the high fan control relay C144, terminal 1. • **Is the voltage greater than 10 volts at the high fan control relay C144 terminal 4, with ground not applied, and greater than 10 volts on terminal 1 with ground applied?**	Yes No	GO to **D4**. REPLACE the high fan control relay.
D4	CHECK POWER SUPPLY TO LOW FAN CONTROL RELAY		
	• Key OFF. • Remove the low fan control relay. • Key ON. • Measure the voltage at the low fan control relay C167-1, "BK/W." • **Is the voltage greater than 10 volts?**	Yes No	GO to **D5**. SERVICE the "BK/W" wire.
D5	CHECK ENGINE COOLING FAN MOTOR GROUND		
	• Key OFF. • Disconnect the engine cooling fan motor C118. • Measure the resistance between the engine cooling fan motor C118, "BK" and ground. • **Is the resistance less than 5 ohms?**	Yes No	GO to **D6**. SERVICE the "BK" wire.

FM1089600145010X

Fig. 56 Test D: Cooling Fan Runs, No Low Speed (Part 1 of 2). Probe w/2.5L engine

	Test Step	Result	Action to Take
E1	CHECK ENGINE COOLING FAN MOTOR HIGH OPERATION		
	• Key OFF. • Disconnect the engine cooling fan motor C118. • Apply 12 volts to the engine cooling fan motor C118, "BL/BK" wire terminal (fan side). • Apply ground to the engine cooling fan motor C118, "BK," wire terminal (fan side). • **Does the high speed of the engine cooling fan motor operate properly?**	Yes No	GO to **E2**. REPLACE the engine cooling fan motor.
E2	CHECK HIGH FAN CONTROL RELAY		
	• Key OFF. • Remove the high fan control relay. • Apply 12 volts to the high fan control relay C144, terminals 2 and 5. • Measure the voltage at the high fan control relay C144, terminal 4. • Apply ground to the high fan control relay C144, terminal 3. • Measure the voltage at the high fan control relay C144, terminal 1. • **Is the voltage greater than 10 volts at the high fan control relay C144, terminal 4 with ground not applied, and greater than 10 volts at the high fan control relay C144, terminal 1 with ground applied?**	Yes No	GO to **E3**. REPLACE the high fan control relay.
E3	CHECK POWER SUPPLY TO HIGH FAN CONTROL RELAY		
	• Key OFF. • Remove the high fan control relay. • Key ON. • Measure the voltage at the high fan control relay C144-2, "BK/R" and C144-5, "BK/W." • **Are the voltages greater than 10 volts?**	Yes No	SERVICE the "BL/BK" wire between the engine cooling fan motor and the high fan control relay. SERVICE the wire(s) in question.

FM1089600146000X

Fig. 57 Test E: Cooling Fan Runs, No High Speed. Probe w/2.5L engine

	Test Step	Result	Action to Take
D6	CHECK WIRE BETWEEN LOW FAN CONTROL RELAY AND HIGH FAN CONTROL RELAY		
	• Key OFF. • Remove the low fan control relay and the high fan control relay. • Measure the resistance between the low fan control relay C167-2, "R," and the high fan control relay C144, "R." • Measure the resistance between the low fan control relay C167-2, "R," and ground. • **Is the resistance less than 5 ohms between the low fan control relay and the high fan control relay, and greater than 10,000 ohms between the low fan control relay and ground?**	Yes No	SERVICE the "BL/Y" wire between the engine cooling fan motor and the low fan control relay. SERVICE the "R" wire.

FM1089600145020X

Fig. 56 Test D: Cooling Fan Runs, No Low Speed (Part 2 of 2). Probe w/2.5L engine

Condition	Possible Source	Action
• Loss of Coolant	• Damaged radiator. • Damaged water pump. • Loose/damaged radiator hoses. • Loose/damaged heater water hoses. • Loose/damaged degas bottle supply hose (engine and radiator). • Loose/damaged coolant reservoir pressure relief cap. • Damaged heater core. • Damaged engine gaskets/O-rings. • Damaged/incorrectly installed thermostat O-ring. • Damaged cylinder head. • Damaged cylinder block.	• GO to Pinpoint Test A.
• Engine Overheats	• Low coolant level. • Incorrect coolant mixture. • Loose/damaged degas bottle pressure relief cap. • Damaged water thermostat. • Damaged water pump. • Internal engine coolant leak. • Cooling fan inoperative. • Plugged radiator. • Plugged heater core. • Collapsed lower radiator hose. • Plugged internal engine coolant passage.	• GO to Pinpoint Test B.
• Engine Does Not Reach Normal Operating Temperature	• Damaged water thermostat. • Cooling fan. • Low engine coolant.	• Diagnose circuit as necessary.
• Engine Block Heater Does Not Operate Properly	• Block heater power cable. • Block heater.	• GO to Pinpoint Test C.
• Cooling Fan Runs Continuously	• Circuit. • Constant control relay module (CCRM). • Powertrain control module. • Engine coolant temperature sensor.	• Diagnose circuit as necessary.
• Cooling Fan Runs, No Low Speed	• Circuit. • Constant control relay module (CCRM). • Fan dropping resistor damaged. • Powertrain control module. • Cooling fan motor.	• Diagnose circuit as necessary.
• Cooling Fan Runs, No High Speed	• Circuit. • Constant control relay module (CCRM). • Powertrain control module. • Cooling fan motor.	• Diagnose circuit as necessary.

FM1089600152000X

Fig. 58 Symptom Chart. 1997–99 Sable & Taurus

	Test Step	Result	Action to Take
A1	CHECK ENGINE COOLANT LEVEL		
	NOTE: If engine is hot, allow engine to cool down before proceeding. • Check engine coolant level at degas bottle. • **Is engine coolant level OK?**	Yes No	GO to **A2**. REFILL. GO to **A7**.

FM1089600153010X

Fig. 59 Test A: Loss Of Coolant (Part 1 of 2). 1997–99 Sable & Taurus

	Test Step	Result		Action to Take
A2	CHECK FOR VISIBLE LEAKAGE			
	• Engine coolant has an added dye color that makes the coolant an excellent leak detector. • Check entire cooling system for visible leakage. • **Is there visible leakage?**	Yes	▶	SERVICE. RETEST system.
		No	▶	GO to **A3.**
A3	CHECK PRESSURE RELIEF CAP			
	• Using Rotunda Radiator/Heater Core Pressure Tester 014-R1072 or equivalent, test pressure relief cap. • **Did pressure relief cap test OK?**	Yes	▶	GO to **A4.**
		No	▶	REPLACE damaged radiator cap. RETEST system.
A4	CHECK COOLANT FOR INTERNAL LEAKAGE			
	• Inspect coolant in degas bottle for signs of transmission fluid or engine oil. • **Is oil evident in coolant?**	Yes	▶	Locate & Repair source of contamination.
		No	▶	GO to **A5.**
A5	CHECK ENGINE AND TRANSAXLE FOR COOLANT			
	• Remove oil level dipstick from engine and transaxle. • Carefully inspect oil level dipstick for evidence of coolant. • **Is coolant evident?**	Yes	▶	Locate & Repair source of contamination.
		No	▶	GO to **A6.**
A6	PRESSURE TEST COOLING SYSTEM			
	• Using Rotunda Radiator/Heater Core Pressure Tester 014-R1072 or equivalent, pressurize cooling system. • Check for any signs of visible leakage. NOTE: Check inside vehicle for possible heater core leakage. • **Is there leakage?**	Yes	▶	RETEST system.
		No	▶	Cooling system is operational at this time. RETEST system.
A7	CHECK COOLANT RECOVERY			
	• Allow engine to cool. Remove pressure relief cap, inspect cap for foreign material between sealing gasket and diaphragm. • **Is cap OK?**	Yes	▶	GO to **A8.**
		No	▶	SERVICE.
A8	CHECK RADIATOR OVERFLOW HOSE			
	• Remove radiator overflow hose. • Inspect hose for obstructions, cracks or cuts. • **Is hose condition OK?**	Yes	▶	GO to **A9.**
		No	▶	SERVICE radiator overflow hose as required.
A9	CHECK RESERVOIR			
	• Replenish coolant in degas bottle to top of cold fill range. • Inspect reservoir for leaks. • **Is there leakage at reservoir?**	Yes	▶	REPLACE degas bottle.
		No	▶	REFER to Pressure Test. SERVICE as required.

FM1089600153020X

Fig. 59 Test A: Loss Of Coolant (Part 2 of 2). 1997–99 Sable & Taurus

	Test Step	Result		Action to Take
B2	CHECK COOLANT CONDITION			
	• Check coolant for contaminants such as rust or corrosion. Also check for fluid discoloration. • Check coolant concentration for proper 50/50 mixture. • **Is coolant condition OK?**	Yes	▶	GO to **B3.**
		No	▶	FLUSH system RETEST system.
B3	CHECK FOR AIR FLOW OBSTRUCTION			
	• Inspect A/C condenser core and radiator for obstructions such as leaves or bugs. • **Is there any obstruction?**	Yes	▶	REMOVE obstruction and CLEAN A/C condenser core and radiator RETEST system.
		No	▶	GO to **B4.**
B4	CHECK HEATER CORE OPERATION			
	• Install pressure relief cap. • Start engine and allow to run. • As engine starts to warm up, feel the inlet and outlet heater water hoses. They should feel the same after three or four minutes. • **Is outlet heater water hose the same temperature as the inlet heater water hose?**	Yes	▶	GO to **B5.**
		No	▶	TURN engine OFF before it overheats. SERVICE heater core. RETEST system.
B5	CHECK WATER THERMOSTAT OPERATION			
	• Allow engine to run for 10 minutes. • Feel the inlet and outlet heater water hoses and the underside of the upper radiator hose. • **Are the upper radiator hose and heater water hoses cold?**	Yes	▶	REPLACE water thermostat RETEST system.
		No	▶	LEAVE engine RUNNING. GO to **B6.**
B6	CHECK COOLING FAN			
	• Check temperature gauge at instrument cluster. Allow engine to RUN until high side of normal range is attained. • Check for cooling fan operation. • **Did cooling fan operate OK?**	Yes	▶	Diagnose engine operation.
		No	▶	Diagnose circuit as necessary.

FM1089600154020X

Fig. 60 Test B: Engine Overheats (Part 2 of 2). 1997–99 Sable & Taurus

	Test Step	Result		Action to Take
B1	CHECK ENGINE COOLANT LEVEL			
	NOTE: If engine is hot, allow engine to cool down before proceeding. • Remove pressure relief cap and check engine coolant level at pressure relief cap and degas bottle. • **Is engine coolant level OK?**	Yes	▶	GO to **B2.**
		No	▶	REFILL as described. GO to Pinpoint Test A.

FM1089600154010X

Fig. 60 Test B: Engine Overheats (Part 1 of 2). 1997–99 Sable & Taurus

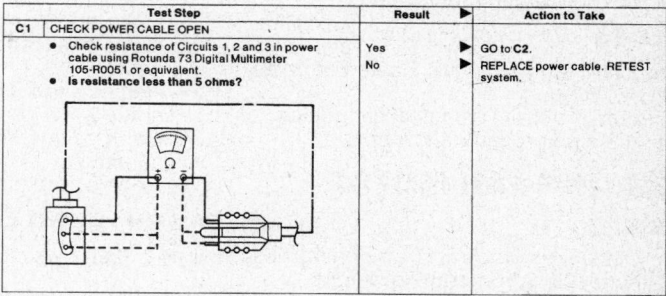

	Test Step	Result		Action to Take
C1	CHECK POWER CABLE OPEN			
	• Check resistance of Circuits 1, 2 and 3 in power cable using Rotunda 73 Digital Multimeter 105-R0051 or equivalent. • **Is resistance less than 5 ohms?**	Yes	▶	GO to **C2.**
		No	▶	REPLACE power cable. RETEST system.

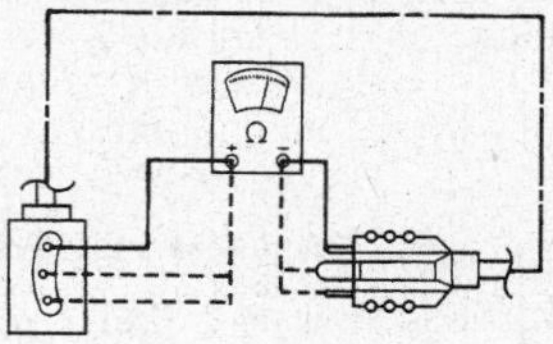

FM1089600155010X

Fig. 61 Test C: Block Heater Does Not Operate Properly (Part 1 of 2). 1997–99 Sable & Taurus

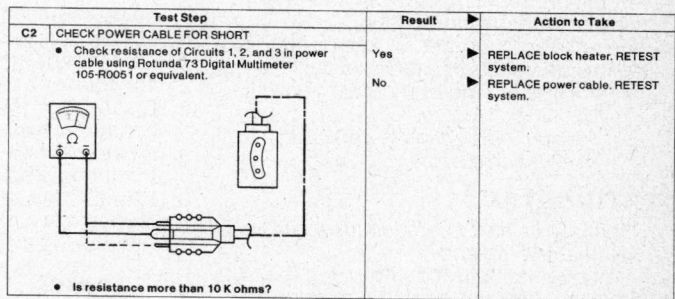

	Test Step	Result		Action to Take
C2	CHECK POWER CABLE FOR SHORT			
	• Check resistance of Circuits 1, 2, and 3 in power cable using Rotunda 73 Digital Multimeter 105-R0051 or equivalent. • **Is resistance more than 10 K ohms?**	Yes	▶	REPLACE block heater. RETEST system.
		No	▶	REPLACE power cable. RETEST system.

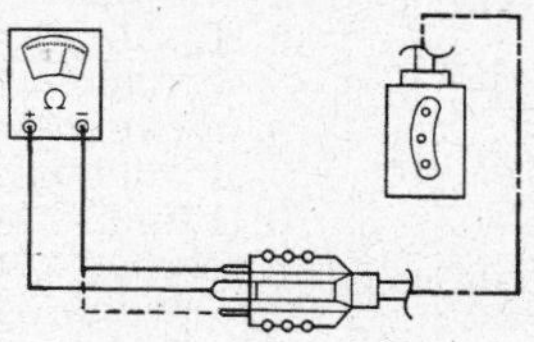

FM1089600155020X

Fig. 61 Test C: Block Heater Does Not Operate Properly (Part 2 of 2). 1997–99 Sable & Taurus

COMPONENT REPLACEMENT

CCRM/IRCM

CONTINENTAL

Refer to "Cooling Fan Motor."

MUSTANG

1997

1. Remove radiator upper sight shield, then disconnect headlamp dash panel junction wire from constant control relay module (CCRM).
2. Remove radiator coolant recovery reservoir retainer bolt.
3. Remove CCRM bracket retainers and bracket from radiator support.
4. Remove CCRM mounting screws and engine control sensor wiring from bracket.
5. Reverse procedure to install. **Torque** CCRM bracket mounting bolts to 72–96 inch lbs.

1998–2000

1. **On models equipped with 3.8L engine,** remove right inner fender splash shield.
2. **On all models,** disconnect CCRM and remove CCRM mounting nuts.
3. Reverse procedure to install, noting the following:
   a. **On models equipped with 3.8L engine, torque** CCRM mounting nuts to 12–17 inch lbs.
   b. **On models equipped with 4.6L engine, torque** CCRM mounting nuts to 36 inch lbs.

SABLE & TAURUS

1. Disconnect engine control sensor wiring from module connector
2. Release clips and module from battery tray.
3. Reverse procedure to install. **Torque** engine control sensor connector to 12–18 inch lbs.

THUNDERBIRD & 1997 COUGAR

1. Remove radiator sight shield.
2. Disconnect electrical connector, then remove integrated relay control assembly from radiator support.
3. Reverse procedure to install.

COOLING FAN RELAY

ASPIRE

Cooling fan relay is located in left hand side of engine compartment, near battery.

1. Remove screw from top of relay.
2. Remove protective boot.
3. Disconnect electrical connector.
4. Reverse procedure to install.

CONTOUR & MYSTIQUE

1. Locate fan control relay in engine compartment power distribution box, then remove relay.
2. Reverse procedure to install.

PROBE

Cooling fan relays are located on radiator cowl support.

1. Pull relay from electrical connector.
2. Reverse procedure to install.

COOLING FAN MOTOR

ASPIRE

1. Disconnect cooling fan wiring harness connectors from routing clamps.
2. Remove four screws mounting fan and shroud to radiator, then the fan and shroud.
3. Remove fan mounting nut and washer, then the fan from motor shaft.
4. Remove mounting screws, then separate fan motor from shroud.
5. Reverse procedure to install, noting following for Probe models only:
   a. **Torque** fan motor mounting bolts to 16–19 inch lbs.
   b. **Torque** shroud mounting bolts to 72–96 inch lbs.

CONTINENTAL

1. Remove radiators as described under "Radiator, Replace."
2. Remove fan shroud mounting bolts, cooling fan motor/blade/shroud assembly.
3. Remove fan blade mounting clips and blades.
4. Remove motor mounting screws and motors.
5. If necessary, remove Constant Control Relay Module (CCRM).
6. Reverse procedure to install. **Torque** CCRM mounting screws to 40–56 inch lbs. and shroud mounting bolts to 24–48 ft. lbs.

CONTOUR & MYSTIQUE

1997-98

1. Disconnect wiring connectors and mounting clips.
2. Remove cooling fan ground cable from RH front fender apron.
3. Remove shroud screws and position for access to fan motor.
4. Remove cooling fan motor.
5. Reverse procedure to install.

1999-2000 w/2.0L Engine

1. Remove battery, then raise and support vehicle.
2. Remove lower radiator splash shield.
3. Remove air conditioning accumulator bolts and place to one side.
4. Disconnect fan resistor connector.
5. Lower vehicle.
6. Disconnect fan motor connectors and remove wiring harness from fan shroud.
7. Remove motors, fans, and shroud assembly.
8. Reverse procedure to install.

1999-2000 w/2.5L Engine

1. Drain cooling system into a suitable container.
2. Remove steel coolant pipe connecting bottom hose to water pump hose.
3. Disconnect hoses and remove pipe.
4. Raise and support vehicle.
5. Disconnect fan resistor and motor connectors.
6. Remove fan wiring harness from fan shroud.
7. Remove motor, fan and shroud assembly.
8. Reverse procedure to install.

1999-2000 COUGAR

2.0L Engine

1. Raise and support vehicle.
2. Remove lower radiator splash shield.
3. Disconnect fan motor connector.
4. Disconnect fan resistor connector and wiring harness.
5. Remove air conditioning accumulator bolts and place to one side.
6. Lower vehicle.
7. Disconnect air conditioning compressor connector.
8. Disconnect heated oxygen sensor connector and wiring harness.
9. Disconnect air conditioning tube from mounting bracket.
10. Remove fan shroud nut, then the fan shroud.
11. Reverse procedure to install.

2.5L Engine

1. Drain coolant into suitable container.
2. Remove radiator.
3. Raise and support vehicle.
4. Disconnect cooling fan connector and wiring harness.
5. Disconnect all remaining electrical connectors and remaining harnesses.
6. Remove fan assembly.
7. Reverse procedure to install.

CROWN VICTORIA, GRAND MARQUIS & TOWN CAR

1997-98

1. Disconnect cooling fan motor wiring connector.
2. Remove fan shroud.
3. Remove radiator upper sight shield.
4. Loosen fan shroud from radiator mounting and remove lower radiator hose from supports on fan shroud.
5. Lift shroud out of vehicle.
6. Remove cooling fan motor assembly from fan shroud.
7. Reverse procedure to install noting following:
   a. **Torque** cooling fan motor mounting screws to 27–53 inch lbs.
   b. **Torque** fan shroud mounting screws to 24–48 inch lbs.

1999-2000

Caution: Do not mix standard (green) coolant with Extended Life (orange) coolant.

1. Drain coolant from degas bottle.
2. Disconnect degas bottle supply and overflow hoses.
3. Remove mounting bolt, then the degas bottle.
4. Disconnect fan motor connector.
5. Remove two bolts, then the fan blade, fan motor and fan shroud assembly.
6. Reverse procedure to install.

ESCORT, TRACER & ZX2

Fan motor, blade and shroud are not serviced separately.

1. Remove air cleaner outlet tube.
2. Disconnect fan motor electrical connector, then upstream heated oxygen sensor electrical connector.
3. Remove three shroud bolts, then fan blade and shroud as assembly.
4. Reverse procedure to install.

MARK VIII

1. Loosen fan shroud from radiator, then remove lower hose from shroud.
2. Lift fan motor assembly and shroud out from vehicle, then disconnect fan motor electrical connector.
3. Remove four mounting bolts, then separate fan from shroud.
4. Reverse procedure to install.

MUSTANG

1997-98

1. Remove fan wiring harness from routing clips.
2. Disconnect wiring harness from fan motor connector (pull up on single lock finger to separate connector).
3. Remove shroud mounting screws, then the fan assembly.
4. Remove mounting clip from end of motor shaft, then the fan. A small metal burr may be present on motor after mounting clip is removed. Removal of burr may be necessary prior to fan removal.
5. Remove fan motor to shroud mounting nuts, then the fan motor.
6. Reverse procedure to install. **Torque** motor to shroud nuts to 48–62 inch lbs. and shroud to radiator screws to 72–96 inch lbs.

1999-2000

1. Remove degas bottle or coolant expansion tank.
2. Disconnect electrical connector and separate fan harness from shroud.
3. Remove mounting bolts, fan, motor and shroud.
4. Reverse procedure to install. **Torque** mounting bolts to 89 inch lbs.

PROBE

1. Drain cooling system and remove fresh air duct.
2. **On models equipped with 2.0L engine,** remove upper and lower radiator hoses.
3. **On models equipped with 2.5L engine,** proceed as follows:
   a. Remove expansion tank upper radiator hose, then disconnect tube from expansion tank.

b. Remove expansion tank lower radiator hose from radiator.
4. **On all models,** remove overflow tube from expansion tank, then remove tank and disconnect fan electrical connectors.
5. **On models equipped with 2.5L engine,** remove upper and lower radiator hoses.
6. **On models equipped with automatic transaxle,** disconnect transaxle oil cooler hoses.
7. **On all models,** remove radiator mounting brackets and radiator.
8. Remove four fan shroud bolts, then the shroud.
9. Remove cooling fan mounting clip, then the fan from fan motor.
10. Remove three fan motor bolts.
11. Reverse procedure to install. **Torque** fan motor bolts to 16–19 inch lbs. and radiator mounting bolts to 14-18 ft. lbs.

SABLE & TAURUS

1997–98

1. Disconnect cooling fan motor wiring connector.
2. Remove cooling fan motor from shroud.
3. Reverse procedure to install. **Torque** fan mounting bolts to 71–106 inch lbs.

1999

Do not mix Standard (green) Coolant with Extended Life Coolant (orange). If mixing occurs, drain engine cooling system and refill with originally equipped coolant type. If this contamination occurs, the service change interval on Extended Life Coolant will be reduced from 6 years/150,000 miles to 3 years/30,000 miles.

1. Remove engine air cleaner assembly.
2. Remove battery and battery tray.
3. Using a suitable AC recovery station, recover AC refrigerant from system.
4. Raise and support vehicle.
5. Drain engine coolant into suitable container.
6. Remove four bolts mounting lower radiator hose shield, then the hose shield.
7. Disconnect lower radiator hose from radiator.
8. Disconnect A/C evaporator muffler and hoses from A/C condenser core.
9. Disconnect lower transmission oil cooler tube from radiator using tool No. No. 310-S039 (3/8 inch fuel line disconnect tool), or equivalent.
10. Remove two screws from the lower transmission oil cooler tube and allow transmission oil cooler tube to hang.
11. Remove both transmission oil cooler tubes from left end of power steering/transmission oil cooler.
12. Remove lower radiator mounts.
13. Lower vehicle.
14. Remove four bolts hood latch support and position hood latch support aside.
15. Remove front bumper cover.
16. Remove upper radiator support.
17. Disconnect radiator overflow hose from radiator.
18. Remove power distribution box and harness and bracket and position power distribution box and harness aside.
19. Disconnect fan motor from engine control sensor wiring.
20. Remove six screws mounting engine control sensor wiring and position engine control sensor wiring aside.
21. Disconnect power steering fluid cooler from power steering pump.
22. Support fan blade and fan shroud assembly.
23. Remove four bolts from cooling fan motor, fan blade and fan shroud assembly brackets to sub-frame.
24. Lift cooling fan motor, fan blade and fan shroud assembly out of vehicle.
25. Reverse procedure to install.

THUNDERBIRD & 1997 COUGAR

1. Disconnect fan motor wiring connector.
2. Remove male terminal connector mounting clip from shroud mounting tab.
3. Remove overflow hose from shroud, then two upper shroud to radiator support mounting bolts.
4. Lift cooling fan motor past radiator.
5. Reverse procedure to install.

Hydraulic Cooling Fans

NOTE: On Air Bag Equipped Models, Refer To "Air Bag System Precautions" Located In The Front Of This Manual For System Disarming & Arming Procedures.

NOTE: Wire Color Code Identification And Symbol Identification Located At The Front Of This Manual Can Be Used As An Aid When Using Wiring Circuits Found In This Section.

INDEX

PRECAUTIONS

AIR BAG SYSTEMS

Refer to "Air Bag System Precautions" in the front of this manual for system disarming and arming procedures.

BATTERY GROUND CABLE

Prior to service, disconnect battery ground cable and isolate as required.

DESCRIPTION

The hydraulic cooling fan is controlled by the Powertrain Control Module (PCM) via the hydraulic fan solenoid. The fan motor operates only when the engine is running.

The cooling fan operates at 2200–2400 RPM. Operating pressure is 900 psi, with a maximum pressure of 1200 psi. The fans operating flow rate is 3.75–4.25 gallons per minute.

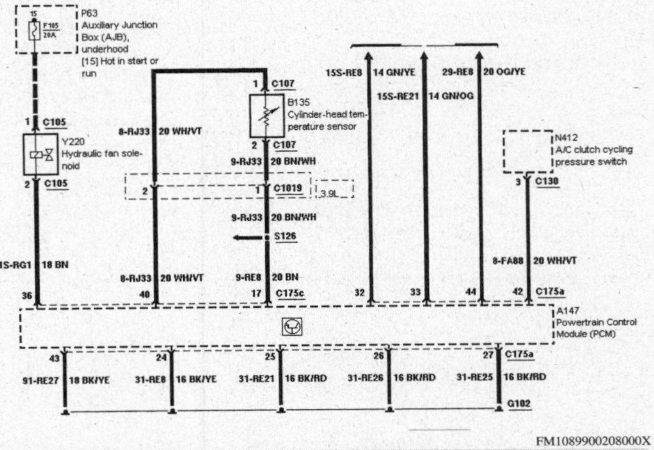

Fig. 1 Wiring diagram. LS

SYSTEM DIAGNOSIS & TESTING

The hydraulic cooling fan system is controlled by the Powertrain Control Module. Refer to **MOTOR's "Domestic Engine Performance & Driveability Manual"** for powertrain control diagnostic procedures and testing.

Perform visual inspection prior to performing any diagnosis and testing procedures. Inspect the following:

1. Leaks.
2. Restricted airflow through condenser/radiator.
3. Damaged hoses.
4. Loose/damaged hose clamps.
5. Damaged water gasket.
6. Damaged head gaskets.
7. Damaged water pump.
8. Damaged radiator.
9. Damaged degas bottle.
10. Damaged heater core.
11. Hydraulic cooling fan system:
    a. Fluid level.
    b. Hydraulic line or joint leaks.
    c. Kinked hydraulic lines.
12. Damaged cylinder head temperature sensor.
13. Damaged wiring.
14. Hydraulic cooling fan pump solenoid/solenoid wiring.

WIRING DIAGRAMS

Refer to **Fig. 1** for wiring diagram.

DIAGNOSTIC TESTS

Refer to **Fig. 2** for symptom chart and to **Figs. 3 through 6** for diagnostic charts.

COMPONENT REPLACEMENT

COOLING FAN MOTOR

1. Drain engine cooling system into suitable container.
2. Remove upper radiator sight shield.
3. Remove air cleaner outlet tube.
4. Remove mounting bolts and radiator support brackets, **Fig. 7.**
5. Remove upper radiator hose.
6. Remove mounting bolt and position receiver drier out of way.
7. **On models equipped with 3.9L engine,** remove mounting bolt and position electric water pump out of way, **Fig. 8.**
8. **On all models,** disconnect high pressure cooling fan line, **Fig. 9.**
9. Disconnect return hose, **Fig. 10.**
10. Separate return hose from fan shroud and position out of way, **Fig. 11.**
11. Remove mounting bolts and fan shroud assembly, **Fig. 12.**
12. Support A/C condenser with suitable mechanics wire.
13. Raise and support vehicle.
14. Remove mounting screws, then right and lefthand splash shields.
15. Remove radiator air deflector.
16. Disconnect lower radiator hose.
17. Remove radiator condenser mounting bolts.
18. Remove mounting bolts and condenser support brackets.
19. Remove radiator from vehicle bottom.

Condition	Possible Source	Action
Loss Of Engine Coolant	Auxiliary Water Pump (3.9L Engine Only)	Go To Pinpoint Test A
	Degas Bottle	
	Engine Gaskets	
	Heater Control Valve	
	Heater Core	
	Heater Hoses	
	Oil Cooler	
	PCV Heater System	
	Radiator	
	Radiator Hoses	
	Thermostat Housing Assembly	
	Throttle Body Adapter Heating (3.9L Engine)	
	Water Pump Seal	
Engine Overheats	Airlock In The System	Go To Pinpoint Test B
	Cooling Fan	
	Heater Core	
	Internal Engine Coolant Leak	
	Pressure Relief Cap	
	Radiator	
	Radiator airflow Obstruction	
	Water Pump	
	Water Thermostat	
Engine Does Not Reach Normal Operating Temperature	Water Thermostat	Go To Pinpoint Test C
Block Heater Does Not Operate Correctly	Block Heater	Go To Pinpoint Test D
	Block Heater Power Cable	
Noisy Cooling Fan Operation	Blocked Reservoir Screen	REFILL Fluid To Specified Level. INSTALL A New Line. CHECK For Leaks And Retest. RETEST And CHECK For Leaks.
	Hydraulic Motor	
	Hydraulic Pump	
	Incorrect Fluid Level	
	Kinked Or Leaking Line	

Fig. 2 Symptom Chart. LS

20. Reverse procedure to install, noting the following:
    a. **Torque** radiator condenser mounting bolts to 89 inch lbs.
    b. **Torque** lower radiator hose clamp to 10 ft. lbs.
    c. **Torque** cooling fan high pressure line mounting bolt to 15 ft. lbs.
    d. **Torque** cooling fan high pressure line bracket mounting bolt to 71 inch lbs.
    e. **Torque** electric water pump mounting bolt to 89 inch lbs.
    f. **Torque** receiver drier mounting bolt 96 inch lbs.
    g. **Torque** upper radiator support mounting bolts to 89 inch lbs.

A1 CHECK THE ENGINE COOLANT LEVEL

Note:
Allow the engine to cool before checking the engine coolant level.

1

2 Visually check the engine coolant level at the degas bottle.

- **Is the engine coolant level within specification?**

→ **Yes**

Go to «A2».

→ **No**

REFILL the engine coolant as necessary. Go to «A6».

FM1089900209010X

Fig. 3 Test A: Loss Of Coolant (Part 1 of 6)

A2	DEGAS BOTTLE PRESSURE RELIEF CAP

1 ⚠ WARNING:
Never remove the pressure relief cap under any conditions while the engine is operating. Failure to follow these instructions could result in damage to the cooling system or engine and/or personal injury. To avoid having scalding hot coolant or steam blow out of the cooling system, use extreme care when removing the pressure relief cap from a hot degas bottle. Wait until the engine has cooled, then wrap a thick cloth around the pressure relief cap and turn it slowly one turn (counterclockwise). Step back while the pressure is released from the cooling system. When certain all the pressure has been released, remove the pressure relief cap (still with a cloth).

Allow the engine to cool.

2 Remove the pressure relief cap.

3 Inspect the pressure relief cap for foreign material between the sealing gasket and the diaphragm.

- **Is the pressure relief cap OK?**

→ **Yes**

REFER to Component Tests.

→ **No**

CLEAN or INSTALL a new pressure relief cap. TEST the system for normal operation. Go to «A1».

FM1089900209020X

Fig. 3 Test A: Loss Of Coolant (Part 2 of 6)

A4	CHECK THE ENGINE FOR COOLANT

1 Remove the oil level indicator from the engine.

- **Is coolant evident in the oil?**

→ **Yes**

If coolant is in the engine, inspect engine.

→ **No**

Go to «A5».

FM1089900209040X

Fig. 3 Test A: Loss Of Coolant (Part 4 of 6)

B1	CHECK THE ENGINE COOLANT LEVEL

Note:
If the engine is hot, allow the engine to cool before proceeding.

1

⚠ WARNING:
Never remove the pressure relief cap under any conditions while the engine is operating. Failure to follow these instructions could result in damage to the cooling system or engine and/or personal injury. To avoid having scalding hot coolant or steam blow out of the cooling system, use extreme care when removing the pressure relief cap from a hot degas bottle. Wait until the engine has cooled, then wrap a thick cloth around the pressure relief cap and turn it slowly one turn (counterclockwise). Step back while the pressure is released from the cooling system. When certain all the pressure has been released, remove the pressure relief cap (still with a cloth).

2 Check the engine coolant level at the degas bottle.

- **Is the engine coolant OK?**

→ **Yes**

Go to «B2».

→ **No**

REFILL the engine coolant at the degas bottle. GO to «Pinpoint Test A».

FM1089900210010X

Fig. 4 Test B: Engine Overheats (Part 1 of 6)

A3	CHECK THE ENGINE COOLANT FOR INTERNAL LEAK

1

2 Inspect the engine coolant in the degas bottle for signs of engine oil.

- **Is oil evident in the coolant?**

→ **Yes**

If engine oil is evident, inspect engine.

→ **No**

Go to «A4».

FM1089900209030X

Fig. 3 Test A: Loss Of Coolant (Part 3 of 6)

A5	PRESSURE TEST THE ENGINE COOLING SYSTEM

1 Pressure test the engine cooling system

- **Does the engine cooling system leak?**

→ **Yes**

REPAIR or INSTALL new components. TEST the system for normal operation.

→ **No**

The cooling system is operational. RETURN to the Symptom Chart.

FM1089900209050X

Fig. 3 Test A: Loss Of Coolant (Part 5 of 6)

A6	CHECK THE DEGAS BOTTLE

1 **Note:**
The engine must be cool when coolant is added to the degas bottle.

Add coolant to the degas bottle until fluid is between the coolant fill level marks.

- **Does the degas bottle leak?**

→ **Yes**

INSTALL a new degas bottle. TEST the system for normal operation.

→ **No**

CARRY OUT the cooling system pressure test.
REPAIR as necessary. TEST the system for normal operation.

FM1089900209060X

Fig. 3 Test A: Loss Of Coolant (Part 6 of 6)

B2	CHECK THE COOLANT CONDITION

1 Check the coolant for contaminants such as rust, corrosion, or discoloration.

- **Is the coolant condition OK?**

→ **Yes**

Go to «B3».

→ **No**

FLUSH the engine cooling system; REFER to «Flushing—Engine and Radiator» in this section. TEST the system for normal operation.

FM1089900210020X

Fig. 4 Test B: Engine Overheats (Part 2 of 6)

B3 CHECK FOR AN AIRFLOW OBSTRUCTION

1 Inspect the A/C condenser core and radiator for obstructions such as leaves or dirt.

- **Is there an obstruction?**

➔ **Yes**

REMOVE the obstruction. CLEAN the A/C condenser core and radiator. TEST the system for normal operation.

➔ **No**

Go to «B4».

FM1089900210030X

Fig. 4 Test B: Engine Overheats (Part 3 of 6)

B4 CHECK THE HEATER CORE OPERATION

1 Install the pressure relief cap.

2

3 As the engine starts to heat up, feel the inlet and outlet heater water hoses. They should feel approximately the same after three or four minutes.

- **Is the outlet heater water hose approximately the same temperature as the inlet heater water hose?**

➔ **Yes**

Go to «B5».

➔ **No**

TURN the engine off. REPAIR or INSTALL a new heater core.
TEST the system for normal operation.

FM1089900210040X

Fig. 4 Test B: Engine Overheats (Part 4 of 6)

B5 CHECK THE WATER THERMOSTAT OPERATION

1

Start the engine and allow the engine to run for 10 minutes.

2

3 Feel the upper and lower radiator hoses.

- **Are the upper and lower radiator hoses cold?**

➔ **Yes**

INSTALL a new water thermostat. TEST the system for normal operation.

➔ **No**

Go to «B6».

FM1089900210050X

Fig. 4 Test B: Engine Overheats (Part 5 of 6)

B6 CHECK THE COOLING FAN OPERATION

1

Carry out the cooling fan component tests

- **Is the cooling fan operation OK?**

➔ **Yes**

Refer to MOTOR's "AUTO ENGINE PERFORMANCE AND DRIVEABILITY MANUAL."

➔ **No**

INSTALL a new fan component as necessary. TEST the system for normal operation.

FM1089900210060X

Fig. 4 Test B: Engine Overheats (Part 6 of 6)

C1 CHECK THE ENGINE TEMPERATURE

1

Start the engine and allow the engine to idle for 10 minutes.

2

Feel the upper and lower radiator hoses.

- **Are the upper and lower radiator hoses cold?**

➔ **Yes**

INSTALL a new water thermostat. TEST the system for normal operation.

➔ **No**

Diagnose and test the engine coolant temperature gauge.

FM1089900211000X

Fig. 5 Test C: Check Engine Temperature

D1 CHECK THE POWER CABLE

1

2

Block Heater

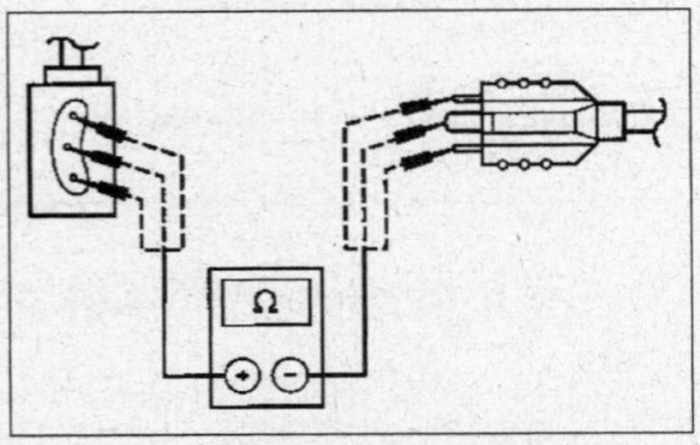

3

Check the resistance in circuits 1, 2, and 3 of the block heater.

- **Are the resistances in circuits 1, 2, and 3 less than 5 ohms?**

→ **Yes**

INSTALL a new block heater. TEST the system for normal operation.

→ **No**

INSTALL a new power cable. TEST the system for normal operation.

FM1089900212000X

Fig. 6 Test D: Check Power Cable

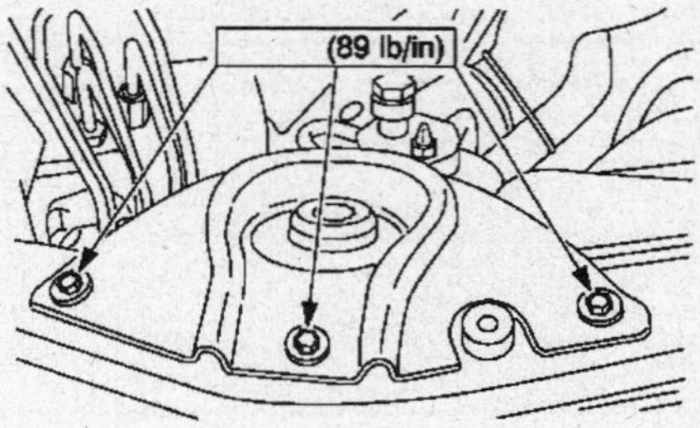

FM1089900213000X

Fig. 7 Radiator support brackets replacement. LS

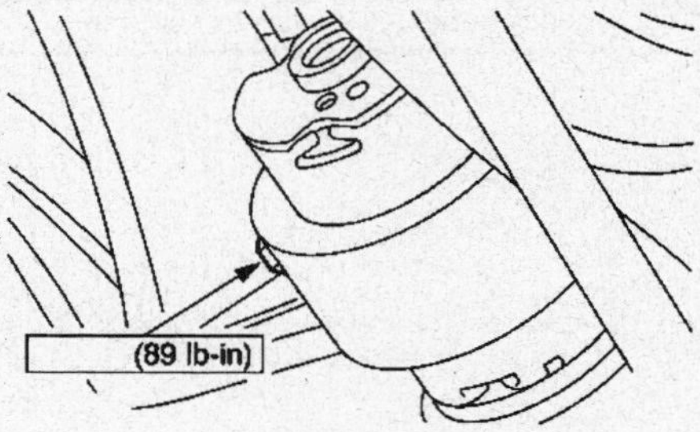

FM1089900214000X

Fig. 8 Electric water pump replacement. LS equipped w/3.9L engine

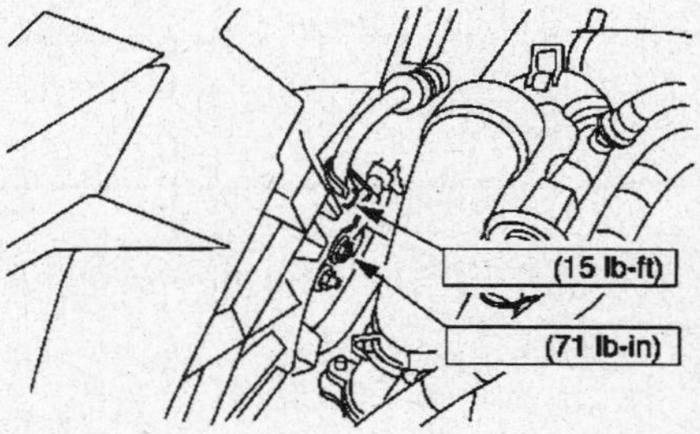

FM1089900215000X

Fig. 9 Cooling fan high pressure line replacement. LS

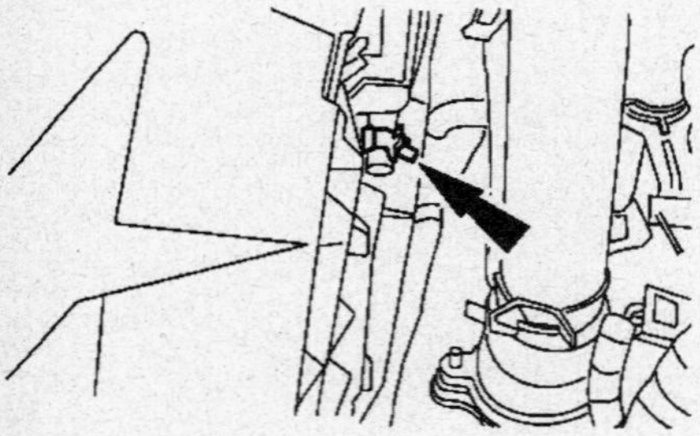

FM1089900216000X

Fig. 10 Return line replacement. LS

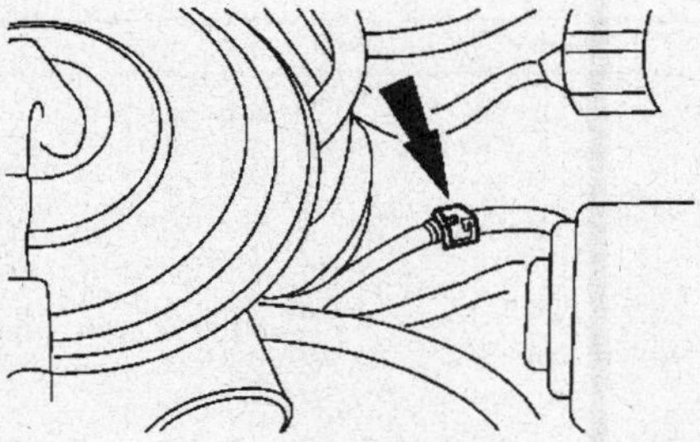

FM1089900217000X

Fig. 11 Fan shroud return line separation. LS

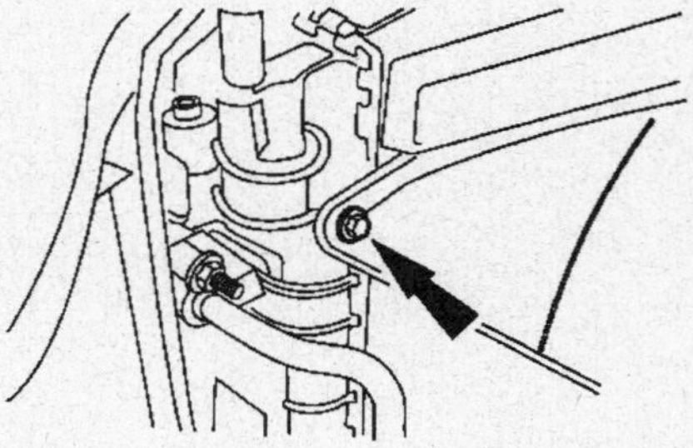

FM1089900218000X

Fig. 12 Fan shroud mounting bolts replacement. LS

STARTER MOTORS

TABLE OF CONTENTS

Ford Motorcraft Starters

INDEX

APPLICATION CHART

Model	Year
Continental	1997–2000
Contour	1997–2000
Cougar	1997
	1999–2000
Crown Victoria	1997–2000
Escort	1997–99
Grand Marquis	1997–2000
LS	2000
Mark VIII	1997–98
Mustang	1997–2000
Mystique	1997–2000
Sable	1997–99
Taurus	1997–99
Thunderbird	1997
Town Car	1997–2000
Tracer	1997–99
ZX2	1998–2000

GENERAL INFORMATION

SOLENOID SWITCHES

The solenoid switch on a cranking motor not only closes the circuit between the battery and the cranking motor but also shifts the drive pinion into mesh with the engine flywheel ring gear. This is done by means of a linkage between the solenoid switch plunger and the shift lever on the cranking motor.

There are two windings in the solenoid; a pull-in winding and a hold-in winding. Both windings are energized when the external control switch is closed. They produce a magnetic field which pulls the plunger in so that the drive pinion is shifted into mesh, and the main contacts in the solenoid switch are closed to connect the battery directly to the cranking motor. Closing the main switch contacts shorts out the pull-in winding since this winding is connected across the main contacts. The magnetism produced by the hold-in winding is sufficient to hold the plunger in, and shorting out the pull-in winding reduces drain on the battery. When the control switch is opened, it disconnects the hold-in winding from the battery. When the hold-in winding is disconnected from the battery, the shift lever spring withdraws the plunger from the solenoid, opening the solenoid switch contacts and at the same time withdrawing the drive pinion from mesh. Proper operation of the switch depends on maintaining a definite balance between the magnetic strength of the pull-in and hold-in windings.

This balance is established in the design by the size of the wire and the number of turns specified. An open circuit in the hold-in winding or attempts to crank with a discharged battery will cause the switch to chatter.

STARTER MOTOR SERVICE

To obtain full performance data on a starting motor or to determine the cause of abnormal operation, the starting motor should be submitted to a no-load and torque test. These tests are best performed with the starter mounted on a starter bench tester.

From a practical standpoint, however, a simple torque test may be made quickly with the starter in the car. Ensure the battery is fully charged and that the starter circuit wires and terminals are in good condition, then operate the starter to see if the engine turns over normally. If it does not, the torque developed is below standard and the starter should be removed for further checking.

DESCRIPTION

FORD MOTORCRAFT STARTER w/GEAR REDUCED PERMANENT MAGNET

This type of starter motor, **Fig. 1,** has the starter solenoid mounted on the starter housing. The starter relay connects battery power to the starter solenoid, causing it to energize. On models equipped with manual transmission, a clutch switch in the starter control circuit prevents operation unless the clutch pedal is depressed. On models equipped with automatic transmission, a neutral safety switch in the starter control circuit prevents operation of the starter unless the selector lever is in the Neutral or Park position.

When the starter solenoid is energized, a magnetic field is created in the solenoid windings. The plunger core is drawn to the solenoid coil and a lever connected to the drive assembly engages the drive pinion gear into the flywheel ring gear. When the plunger is all the way in, its contact disc closes the circuit between the battery and the motor feed terminals. This sends current to the motor and the drive pinion gear cranks the flywheel to start the engine. When the current flows to the engine, the solenoid pull-in coil is bypassed and the hold-in coil keeps the drive pinion gear engaged with the flywheel until the ignition switch is released from the On position.

TROUBLESHOOTING

When trouble develops in the starting motor circuit and the starter cranks the engine slowly or not at all, several preliminary checks can be made to determine whether the problem is the battery, starter, wiring or

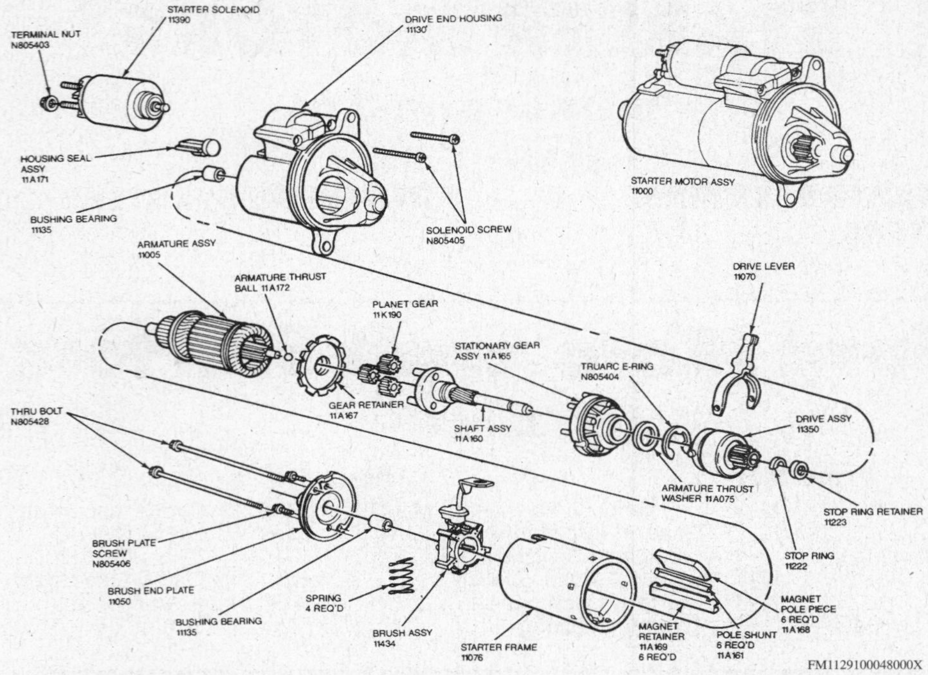

Fig. 1 Ford Motorcraft gear reduced permanent magnet starter motor

elsewhere. Many conditions besides defects in the starter itself can result in poor cranking performance.

To make a quick check of the starter system, turn on the headlights. They should operate normally. If they do not, the battery may be run down.

If the battery is in a charged condition so that lights operate normally, operate the starting motor. Any one of three things will happen to the lights: (1) They will go out, (2) dim considerably or (3) stay bright without any cranking action taking place.

LIGHTS GO OUT

If the lights go out as the starter switch is closed, it indicates that there is a poor connection between the battery and starting motor. This poor connection will most often be found at the battery terminals. Correction is made by removing the cable clamps from the terminals, cleaning the terminals and clamps, replacing the clamps and tightening them securely. A coating of corrosion inhibitor or petroleum jelly may be applied to the clamps and terminals to slow the formation of corrosion.

LIGHTS DIM

If the lights dim considerably as the starter switch is closed and the starter operates slowly or not at all, the battery may be run down, or there may be some mechanical condition in the engine or starting motor that is throwing a heavy burden on the starting motor. This imposes a high discharge rate on the battery which causes noticeable dimming of the lights.

Check the battery state of charge. If it is charged, the trouble probably lies in either the engine or starting motor. In the engine, tight bearings or pistons or heavy oil place an added burden on the starting motor. Low temperatures also hamper starting motor performance since it thickens engine oil and makes the engine considerably harder to crank and start. Also, a battery is less efficient at low temperatures.

In the starting motor, a bent armature, loose pole shoe screws or worn bearings may allow the armature to drag. This will reduce cranking performance and increase current draw. More serious internal damage is sometimes found. Thrown armature windings or commutator bars, which sometimes occur on overrunning clutch drive starting motors, are usually caused by excessive overrunning after starting. This is the result of such conditions as the driver keeping the starting switch closed too long after the engine has started, the driver opening the throttle too wide in starting, or improper fast idle adjustment. Any of these subject the overrunning clutch to extra strain so it tends to seize, spinning the armature at high speed with resulting armature damage. Another cause may be engine backfire during cranking which may result from ignition timing being too far advanced. To avoid such failures, the driver should pause a few seconds after a false start to ensure the engine has come completely to rest before another start is attempted. In addition, the ignition timing should be checked if engine backfiring has caused the trouble.

LIGHTS STAY BRIGHT, NO CRANKING ACTION

This condition indicates an open circuit at some point, either in the starter itself, the starter switch or control circuit. The solenoid control circuit can be eliminated momentarily by placing a heavy jumper lead across the solenoid main terminals to see if the starter will operate. This connects the starter directly to the battery and if it operates, it indicates that the control circuit is not functioning normally. The wiring and control units must be checked to locate the trouble.

If the starter does not operate with the jumper attached, it will probably have to be removed from the engine so it can be examined in detail.

CIRCUIT INSPECTION

Excessive resistance in the circuit between the battery and starter will reduce cranking performance. The resistance can be checked by using a voltmeter to measure voltage drop in the circuits while the starter is operated. There are three checks to be made:

1. Voltage drop between vehicle frame and grounded battery terminal post (not cable clamp).
2. Voltage drop between vehicle frame and starting motor field frame.
3. Voltage drop between insulated battery terminal post and starting motor terminal stud (or the battery terminal stud of the solenoid).

Each of these should show no more than one-tenth (.1) volt drop when the starting motor is cranking the engine. Do not use the starter for more than 30 seconds at a time to avoid overheating.

If excessive voltage drop is found in any of these circuits, make correction by disconnecting the cables, cleaning the connections carefully, and then reconnecting

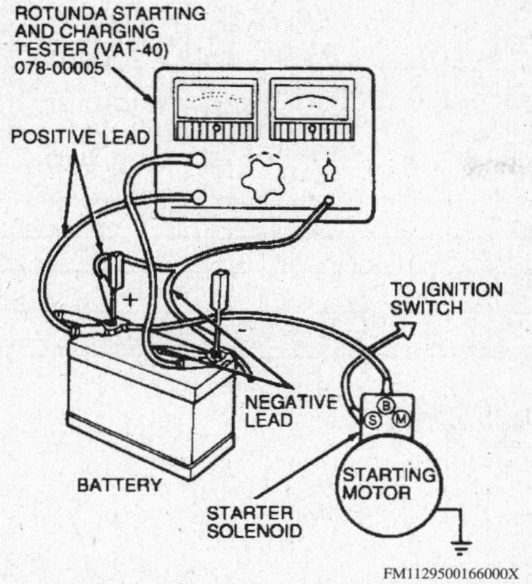

Fig. 2 Gear reduced permanent magnet starter cranking circuit test connections

the cables firmly in place. A coating of petroleum jelly on the battery cables and terminal clamps will slow corrosion.

On some models, extra long battery cables may be required due to the location of the battery and starter. This may result in somewhat higher voltage drop than the above recommended .1 volt. The only means of determining the normal voltage drop in such cases is to check several of these vehicles. Then when the voltage drop is well above the normal figure for all cars checked, abnormal resistance will be indicated and correction can be made.

STARTER DRIVE TROUBLE

Starter drive troubles are easy to diagnose and they usually cannot be confused with ordinary starter difficulties. If the starter does not turn over at all or if it drags, look for trouble in the starter or electrical supply system. Concentrate on the starter drive or ring gear if the starter is noisy, if it turns but does not engage the engine, or if the starter won't disengage after the engine is started. After the starter is removed, the trouble can usually be located quickly.

Worn or chipped ring gear or starter pinion are the usual causes of noisy operation. Before replacing either or both of these parts try to find out what caused the damage. With the Bendix type drive, incomplete engagement of the pinion with the ring gear is a common cause of tooth damage. The wrong pinion clearance on starter drives of the overrunning clutch type leads to poor meshing of the pinion and ring gear and too rapid tooth wear.

A less common cause of noise with either type of drive is a bent starter armature shaft. When this shaft is bent, the pinion gear alternately binds and then only partly meshes with the ring gear. Most manufacturers specify a maximum of .003 inch radial runout on the armature shaft.

Clutch Drive Failure

The overrunning clutch type drive seldom becomes so worn that it fails to engage since it is directly activated by a fork and lever. The only thing that is likely to happen is that, once engaged, it will not turn the engine because the clutch itself is worn out. A much more frequent difficulty and one that rapidly wears ring gear and teeth is partial engagement. Proper meshing of the pinion is controlled by the end clearance between the pinion gear and the starter housing or pinion stop, if used.

On some starters, the solenoids are completely enclosed in the starter housing and the pinion clearance is not adjustable. If the clearance is not correct, the starter must be disassembled and checked for excessive wear of solenoid linkage, shift lever mechanism, or improper assembly of parts.

Failure of the overrunning clutch drive to disengage is usually caused by binding between the armature shaft and the drive. If the drive, particularly the clutch, shows signs of overheating it indicates that it is not disengaging immediately after the engine starts. If the clutch is forced to overrun too long, it overheats and turns a bluish color. For the cause of the binding, look for rust or gum between the armature shaft and the drive, or for burred splines. Excess oil on the drive will lead to gumming, and inadequate air circulation in the flywheel housing will cause rust.

Overrunning clutch drives cannot be overhauled in the field so they must be replaced. In cleaning, never soak them in a solvent because the solvent may enter the clutch and dissolve the sealed-in lubricant. Wipe them off lightly with kerosene and lubricate them sparingly with Lubriplate No. 777, or equivalent.

Bendix Drive Failure

When a Bendix type drive doesn't engage the cause usually is one of three things: either the drive spring is broken, one of the drive spring bolts has sheared off, or the screw shaft threads won't allow the pinion to travel toward the flywheel. In the first two cases, remove the drive by unscrewing the setscrew under the last coil of the drive spring and replace the broken parts. Gummed or rusty screw shaft threads are fairly common causes of Bendix drive failure and are easily cleaned with a little kerosene or steel wool, depending on the trouble. Here again, as in the case of overrunning clutch drives, use light oil sparingly, and be sure the flywheel housing has adequate ventilation. There is usually a breather hole in the bottom of the flywheel housing which should be open.

The failure of a Bendix drive to disengage or to mesh properly is most often caused by gummed or rusty screw shaft threads. When this is not true, look for mechanical failure within the drive itself.

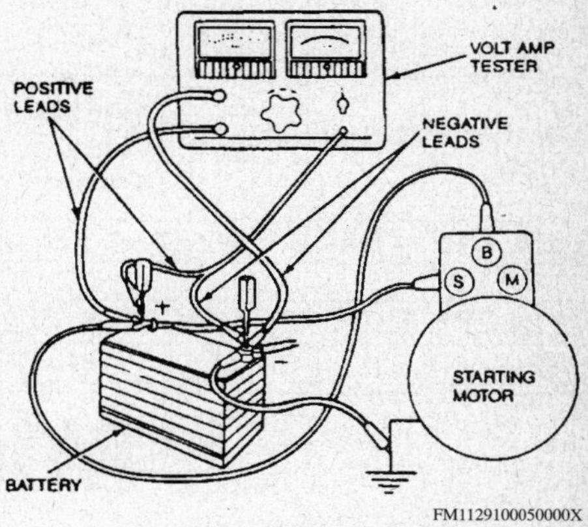

Fig. 3 Starter no load test connection. Gear reduced permanent magnet starter motor

DIAGNOSIS & TESTING

FORD MOTORCRAFT STARTER w/GEAR REDUCED PERMANENT MAGNET

Starter Load Test

1. Connect test equipment as shown in **Fig. 2.** Ensure no current is flowing through ammeter and heavy duty carbon pile rheostat portion of circuit.
2. Disconnect push-on S-connector at starter relay, then connect remote control starter switch between positive battery terminal and S terminal.
3. Using remote starter, crank engine with ignition in the Off position, then determine exact reading on voltmeter.
4. Stop cranking engine, then reduce resistance of carbon pile until voltmeter indicates same reading as obtained with starter cranking the engine. Ammeter should indicate 140–200 amps.

Starter No-Load Test

1. Connect test equipment as shown in **Fig. 3.** Ensure current is not flowing through ammeter and starter is securely mounted in vise.
2. Disconnect starter from battery, then reduce resistance of rheostat until voltmeter indicates reading obtained while starter was running.
3. Ammeter should indicate starter no load current draw. Refer to "Starter Specifications."
4. If current exceeds specifications, check for rubbing armature, bent starter shaft, binding starter bearings or electrical shorts in armature or starter brush assembly.

STARTER SPECIFICATIONS

Starter Frame Dia., Inch	Brush Spring Tension, Ounces	No Load, Amps	Max Load, Amps	Normal Load Current Draw, Amps	Normal Engine Cranking, RPM	Minimum Stall, Ft. Lbs. @ 5 Volts
ESCORT, TRACER & ZX2						
3.0	64	60–80	800	130–190	200–250	10
EXCEPT ESCORT, TRACER & ZX2						
3.0	64	60–80	800	130–220	140–220	11

Mitsubishi Starters

INDEX

APPLICATION CHART

Model	Year
Probe w/2.5L①	1997
Aspire	1997

① — Automatic Transmission.

GENERAL INFORMATION

Refer to "Ford Motorcraft Starters" for general information.

DESCRIPTION

The starter system has a low current and high current electrical circuit. The low current is the control circuit. It includes ignition switch, starter solenoid, neutral safety switch or clutch switch. The high current connects starter to the battery positive terminal. This circuit uses heavy gauge cables because of high current flow required to operate the starter motor, **Figs. 1 and 2.**

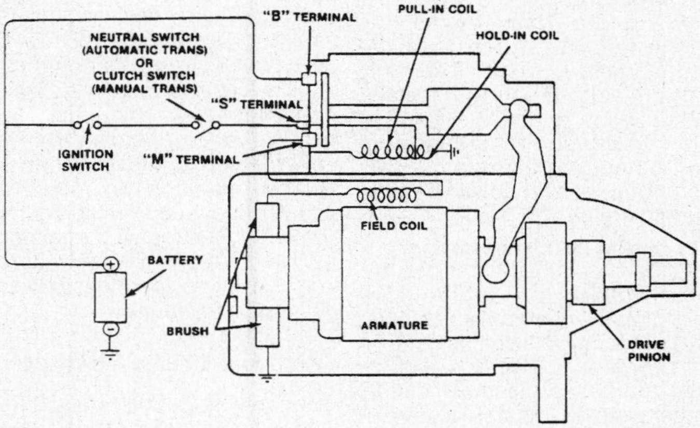

Fig. 1 Mitsubishi starter motor

TROUBLESHOOTING

Refer to "Ford Motorcraft Starters" for troubleshooting information.

ENGINE CRANKS SLOWLY

1. Undercharged battery.
2. Loose connections or corroded battery cables.
3. Starter motor.

ENGINE WILL NOT CRANK

1. Undercharged battery.
2. Ignition switch.
3. Clutch pedal position switch or manual lever position switch.
4. Loose or corroded cable connections.
5. Worn or damaged ignition circuit grounds.
6. Starter motor.
7. Starter solenoid.

ENGINE WILL NOT CRANK/ STARTER MOTOR SPINS

1. Starter motor.
2. Flywheel ring gear.

ENGINE STARTS w/CLUTCH ENGAGED

1. Starter clutch pedal position switch.
2. Manual lever position switch

DIAGNOSIS & TESTING

PINION DEPTH ADJUSTMENT

Aspire

1. Connect one 12 volt battery as shown in **Fig. 3.**
2. Disconnect field coil connector from M terminal.
3. With battery connected, solenoid should released pinion gear.
4. With pinion extended, measure gap between pinion gear and collar. Pinion clearance should be .020–.080 inch,
5. If clearance is not within limits, check for improper installation or worn parts and replace as necessary. Clearance may be adjusted by adding or removing shims between solenoid and the drive end housing as necessary. **If test must be repeated, allow solenoid to cool.**

Probe

1. Disconnect M terminal wire.
2. Connect positive battery lead to starter solenoid S-terminal. **Do not apply battery voltage for more than 10 seconds.**
3. Connect negative battery lead to

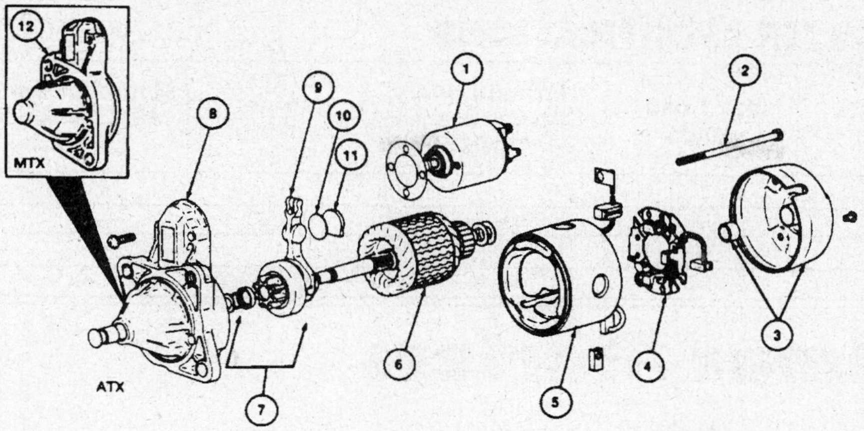

Item		Description
1		Starter Solenoid
2		Thru Bolt
3		Brush End Plate and Bushing
4		Brush Holder
5		Starter Field Coil
6		Starter Motor Armature

Item		Description
7		Starter Drive
8		Drive End Housing (ATX)
9		Drive Lever and Pin
10		Drive Lever and Pin Plate
11		Drive Lever and Pin Seal
12		Drive End Housing (MTX)

FM1129400082000X

Fig. 2 Exploded view of starter motor assembly

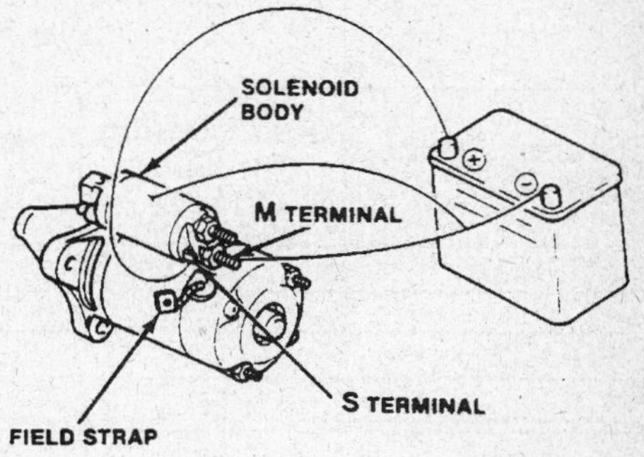

FM1129100052000X

Fig. 3 Pinion depth adjustment

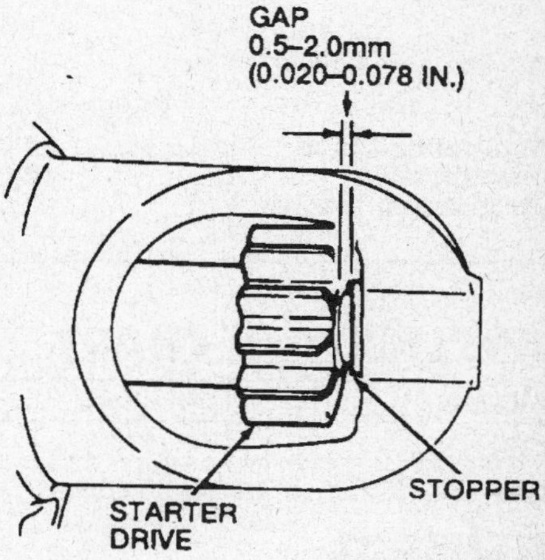

FM1129400081000X

Fig. 4 Starter drive pinion gap measurement. Probe

clean, rust-free portion of the starter field coil.

4. Measure clearance between starter drive and stopper, **Fig. 4.** Starter drive pinion gap should measure .020–.078 inch.
5. If starter pinion gap is not within specifications, increase or decrease number of washers between magnetic switch and starter field coil.

NO LOAD TEST

1. Connect test equipment as shown in **Fig. 5.**
2. Connect remote starter switch and ensure starter turns smoothly.
3. **On Aspire models,** voltmeter should read no less than 11.5 volts and ammeter should read no more than 60 amps.
4. **On Probe models,** voltmeter should read no less than 11 volts and ammeter should read no more than 70 amps.
5. **On all models,** if voltage is low or amperage is high, check battery or repair starter as necessary.

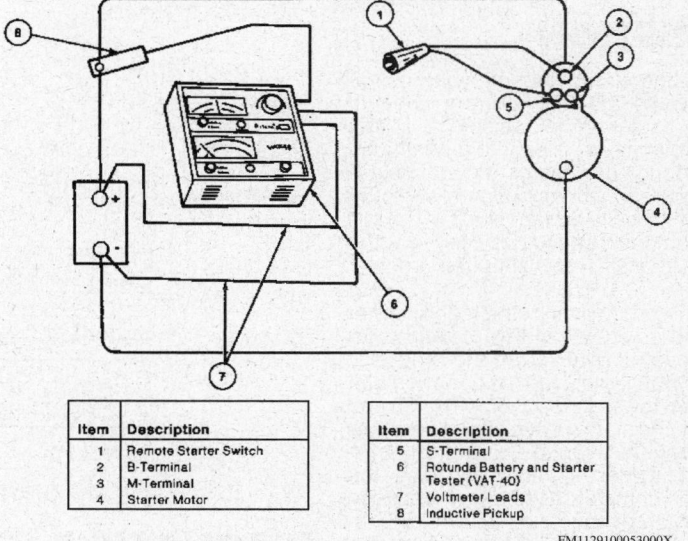

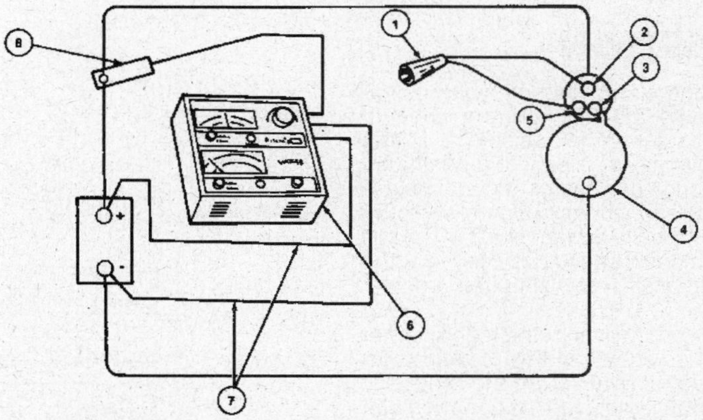

Item	Description
1	Remote Starter Switch
2	B-Terminal
3	M-Terminal
4	Starter Motor

Item	Description
5	S-Terminal
6	Rotunda Battery and Starter Tester (VAT-40)
7	Voltmeter Leads
8	Inductive Pickup

FM1129100053000X

Fig. 5 Starter load test connection

STARTER SPECIFICATIONS

Starter Frame Dia., Inch	Brush Spring Tension, Ounces	No Load, Amps	Max Load, Amps	Normal Load Current Draw, Amps	Normal Engine Cranking, RPM	Minimum Stall, Ft. Lbs. @ 5 Volts
ASPIRE						
4.0	32–69	60	800	150–250	180–250	10
PROBE						
3.0	64	70	800	130–190	200–250	10

Melmac Starters

INDEX

APPLICATION CHART

Model	Year
Probe①	1997

① — 2.0L & 2.5L w/manual transaxle.

GENERAL INFORMATION

Refer to "Ford Motorcraft Starters" for general information.

DESCRIPTION

The starting circuit uses heavy duty cables to handle the high current used to crank the engine. The resistance in the starting circuit must be kept to a minimum, allowing enough current for adequate starter motor operation. Loose or corroded connections or partially broken wires will result in slow cranking speeds may prevent the starter motor from cranking the engine, **Fig. 1.**

The armature is connected to the starter drive pinion as shown in **Fig. 2.** As the armature moves forward from the magnetic field of the pull-in coil, the starter drive pinion is moved toward the flywheel. At the end of its travel, the starter drive pinion engages with the flywheel. Once the starter drive pinion and flywheel are fully engaged, the contact disc completes the circuit between the B and M terminals and the armature rotates. A hold-in coil is energized by the S-terminal, to supply the additional magnetic force required to keep the contact disc engaged as the starter draws current and the system voltage drops.

TROUBLESHOOTING

Refer to "Ford Motorcraft Starters" for troubleshooting information.

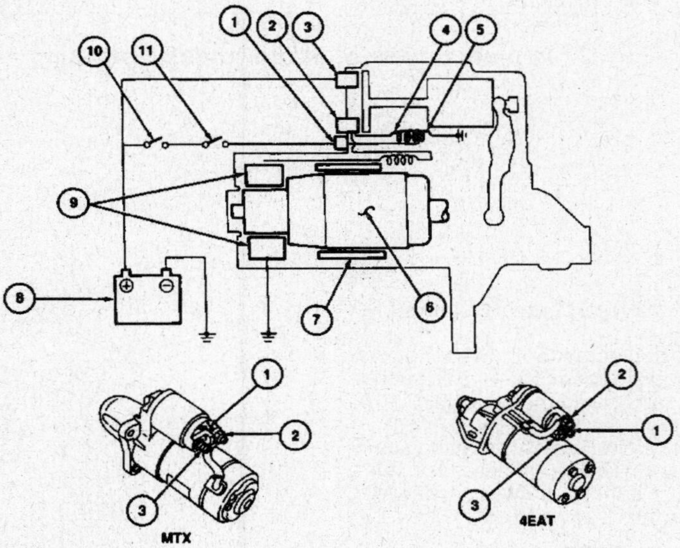

Item	Description
1	S-Terminal
2	M-Terminal
3	B-Terminal
4	Pull In Coil
5	Hold In Coil
6	Starter Motor Armature

Item	Description
7	Magnet
8	Battery
9	Brush Set
10	Ignition Switch
11	Transmission Range (TR) Switch (4EAT) or Starter Clutch Pedal Position (SCPP) Switch (MTX)

FM1129500165000X

Fig. 1 Starting system & starter internal wiring

DIAGNOSIS & TESTING

DIAGNOSTIC PINPOINT TEST

Probe

Refer to **Fig. 3** to diagnose starter motor problems by symptom, then refer to pinpoint tests, **Figs. 4 through 6,** for corrective action.

NO LOAD TEST

1. Remove starter motor, then connect a fully charged battery and test equipment as shown in, **Fig. 7.**
2. Engage remote starter switch.
3. The starter motor should eject the pinion and run smoothly. If the starter does not run smoothly, repair or replace as necessary.
4. While the starter motor is running,

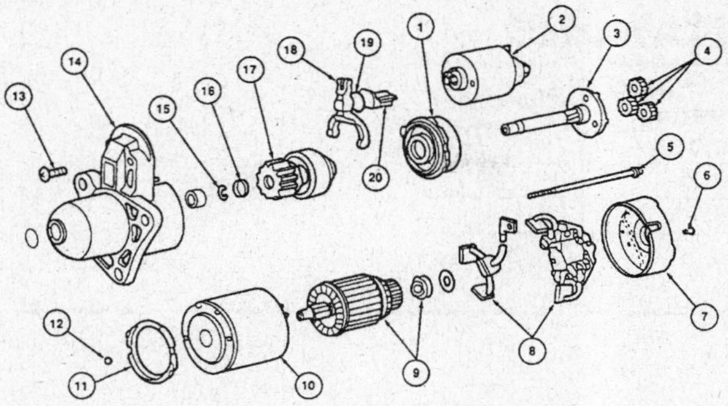

Item	Description	Item	Description
1	Stationary Gear	11	Seal
2	Starter Solenoid	12	Ball Bearing Spacer
3	Output Shaft	13	Solenoid Screw
4	Planetary Gears (3)	14	Drive End Housing
5	Through Bolt	15	Stop Ring
6	Brush Assembly Screw	16	Stop Ring Retainer
7	Rear Cover	17	Pinion Drive Assembly
8	Brush Assembly	18	Drive Lever
9	Armature Assembly	19	Drive Lever Disk
10	Starter End Frame	20	Drive Lever Disk Stop

FM1129100054000X

Fig. 2 Exploded view of starter motor assembly

Test Step		Result	▶	Action to Take
B1	CHECK BATTERY CONNECTIONS			
	• Inspect the battery terminals for loose or corroded connections. • **Are the battery terminals clean and tight?**	Yes No	▶ ▶	GO to **B2**. CLEAN and TIGHTEN battery connections.
B2	CHECK BATTERY			
	• Check the battery. • **Is the battery OK?**	Yes No	▶ ▶	GO to **B3**. CHARGE or REPLACE the battery.

FM1129500163010X

Fig. 5 Test B: Engine does not crank (Part 1 of 2). Probe

Test Step		Result	▶	Action to Take
C1	CHECK STARTER MOTOR MOUNTING			
	• Inspect the starter motor mounting. • Check the starter motor mounting bolts for looseness. • **Is the starter motor mounted properly?**	Yes No	▶ ▶	GO to **C2**. REMOUNT or REPLACE the starter motor.
C2	CHECK STARTER DRIVE ENGAGEMENT			
	• Remove the starter motor. • Inspect the starter drive and flywheel for damage. • **Is the starter drive and flywheel OK?**	Yes No	▶ ▶	PERFORM the Motor Pinion Test in this section. REPLACE as necessary.

FM1129500164000X

Fig. 6 Test C: Unusual starter noise. Probe

Condition	Possible Source	Action
• Engine Cranks Slowly	• Loose or corroded battery cable connections. • Undercharged battery. • Loose or corroded starter motor connections. • Malfunctioning starter motor.	• GO to Pinpoint Test A1.
• Engine Does Not Crank	• Loose or corroded battery cable connections. • Loose or corroded starter motor connectors. • Undercharged battery. • Damaged transmission range (TR) switch. • Damaged starter clutch pedal position (SCPP) switch. • Faulty ignition circuit grounds. • Malfunctioning starter motor. • Malfunctioning ignition switch.	• GO to Pinpoint Test B1.
• Unusual Starter Noise	• Starter motor improperly mounted. • Malfunctioning starter motor. • Improper starter drive engagement to flywheel.	• GO to Pinpoint Test C1.

FM1129500161000X

Fig. 3 Starter motor diagnostic symptom chart. Probe

Test Step		Result	▶	Action to Take
A1	CHECK BATTERY CONNECTIONS			
	• Inspect the battery terminals for loose or corroded connections. • **Are the battery terminals clean and tight?**	Yes No	▶ ▶	GO to **A2**. CLEAN and TIGHTEN battery cable connections.
A2	CHECK BATTERY			
	• Check the battery. • **Is the battery OK?**	Yes No	▶ ▶	GO to **A3**. CHARGE or REPLACE battery.
A3	CHECK STARTER MOTOR CONNECTIONS			
	• Inspect the starter motor terminals for loose or corroded connections. • **Are the starter motor terminal connections clean and tight?**	Yes No	▶ ▶	PERFORM the component tests in this section. CLEAN and TIGHTEN starter motor connections.

FM1129500162000X

Fig. 4 Test A: Engine cranks slowly. Probe

Test Step		Result	▶	Action to Take
B3	CHECK POWER SUPPLY TO STARTER MOTOR			
	• Key OFF. • Disconnect starter motor C176. • Depress the clutch pedal on manual transaxle vehicles. • Key in START position. • Measure the voltage on the "BK/R" wire at starter motor C176. • **Is the voltage greater than 10 volts?**	Yes No	▶ ▶	GO to **B4**. diagnose transmission range (TR) switch circuit.
B4	CHECK STARTER MOTOR GROUND CIRCUIT			
	• Perform the Starter Motor Ground Circuit test • **Is the starter motor ground circuit OK?**	Yes No	▶ ▶	REMOVE the starter motor and PERFORM the component tests in this section. REPAIR or REPLACE the battery ground cable and/or engine ground cable as necessary.

FM1129500163020X

Fig. 5 Test B: Engine does not crank (Part 2 of 2). Probe

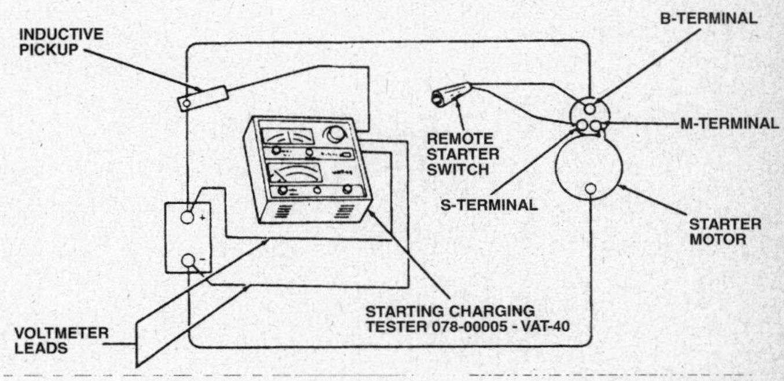

FM1129100055000X

Fig. 7 Starter motor no-load test electrical connections

check the voltmeter and ammeter readings.

5. The voltage reading should be greater than 11 volts and ammeter should read no more than 70 amps.
6. If voltage or amperage is not as specified, replace the starter motor.

STARTER MOTOR PINION TEST

1. Remove starter motor from vehicle.
2. Place starter motor in bench vise and secure it.
3. Using a fully charged battery, connect the negative lead of the battery to the case of the starter motor. **Do not leave the positive lead from the battery connected to the starter for more than ten seconds.**
4. Touch the positive lead from the battery to the S-terminal, then ensure pinion ejects.
5. If the pinion does not eject, repair or replace starter motor as necessary.
6. Remove positive lead from starter motor. Pinion should return to its original position.
7. If the pinion does not return to original position, repair or replace starter motor.

STARTER SPECIFICATIONS

Year	Engine	Brush Spring Tension, Ounces	No Load, Amps
1997	2.5L①	58–78	90
	2.5L②	58–78	70

① — Manual trans.
② — Automatic trans.

ALTERNATORS

NOTE: NOTE: On Air Bag Equipped Models, Refer To " Air Bag System Precautions" Located In The Front Of This Manual For System Disarming & Arming Procedures.

NOTE: Refer To "Computer Relearn Procedure " Located In The Front Of This Manual For Computer Relearn Procedures.

TABLE OF CONTENTS

Ford Motorcraft Alternator

NOTE: "Electrical Symbol & Wire Color Code Identification" Located In The Front Of This Manual May Be Used As An Aid When Using Wiring Circuits Found In This Section.

INDEX

APPLICATION CHART

Model	Year
Continental	1997–2000
Contour	1997–99
Cougar	1997
	1999
Crown Victoria	1997–2000
Escort	1997–99
Grand Marquis	1997–2000
LS	2000
Mustang	1997–2000
Mystique	1997–99
Sable	1997–99

Continued

APPLICATION CHART—Continued

Model	Year
Taurus	1997–99
Thunderbird	1997
Town Car	1997–99
Tracer	1997–99
ZX2	1998–99

PRECAUTIONS

AIR BAG SYSTEMS

Refer to "Air Bag System Precautions" in the front of this manual for system disarming and arming procedures.

BATTERY GROUND CABLE

Prior to service, disconnect battery ground cable and isolate as required.

GENERAL

1. Ensure battery polarity is correct when servicing units. Reversed battery polarity will damage rectifiers and regulators.
2. If booster battery is used for starting, ensure polarity is correct.
3. When a fast charger is used to charge a vehicle battery, vehicle battery cables should be disconnected unless fast charger is equipped with a special alternator protector, in which case vehicle battery cables need not be disconnected. Also fast charger should never be used to start a vehicle as damage to rectifiers will result.
4. Unless system includes a load relay or field relay, grounding alternator output terminal will damage alternator and/or circuits. This is true even when system is not in operation since a circuit breaker is not used and battery voltage is applied to the alternator output terminal at all times. The field or load relay acts as a circuit breaker in that it is controlled by ignition switch.
5. Before starting any on vehicle tests of alternator or regulator, battery should be checked and circuit inspected for faulty wiring or insulation, loose or corroded connections and poor ground circuits.
6. Ensure alternator belt tension is tight enough to prevent slipping under load.
7. To prevent damage to the system, ignition switch should be off and battery ground cable disconnected before making any test connections .
8. Vehicle battery must be fully charged or a fully charged battery may be installed for test purposes.

DESCRIPTION

The electrical charging system is a negative ground system consisting of an integral alternator/voltage regulator (IGR), charge indicator, storage battery and necessary wiring and cables.

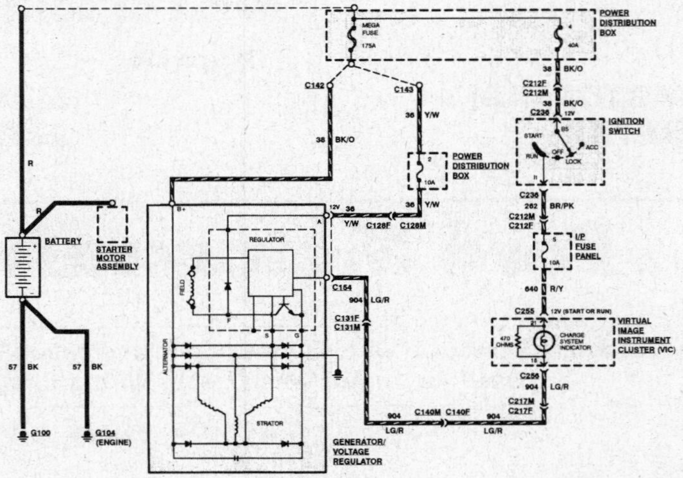

FM1129800313000X

Fig. 1 Wiring diagram. Continental

The "I" circuit, or ignition circuit is used to turn on the alternator regulator. This circuit is powered up with the ignition switch in the Run position. The circuit also turns the indicator lamp on if there is a fault in the charging system.

The "A" circuit, or the battery sense circuit, is used to sense battery voltage. This circuit also supplies power to the alternator stator and coil. With the system functioning normally, alternator output current is determined by voltage at the "A" circuit (battery sense voltage). "A" circuit voltage is compared to a set voltage inside the regulator to maintain the correct alternator output. The set voltage will vary with temperature and is typically higher in the winter than in the summer, allowing for better battery recharge in the winter and reducing the chance of overcharging the battery in the summer.

The "S" circuit, or stator and coil circuit, is used to feedback a voltage signal from the alternator to the regulator. This voltage is typically one-half battery voltage and is used by the regulator to turn off the indicator.

If an ammeter is used in the charging system, the regulator 1 terminal and the alternator stator terminal are not used. When the ignition switch is turned ON, the field relay closes and electrical current passes through regulator A terminal and is metered to the alternator field. When the engine is started, the alternator field rotates causing the alternator to operate.

Closing the ignition switch energizes the warning lamp or ammeter and turns on the regulator output stage. The alternator receives maximum field current and is ready to generate an output voltage. As the alternator rotor speed increases, the output and stator terminal voltages increase from zero to the system regulation level determined by the regulator setting. When the ignition switch is turned off, the solid state relay circuit turns the output stage off, interrupting the current flow through the regulator so there is not a current drain on the battery.

DIAGNOSIS & TESTING

Wiring Diagrams

CONTINENTAL

Refer to **Fig. 1** for charging system wiring diagram.

CONTOUR & MYSTIQUE

Refer to **Figs. 2 and 3** for charging system wiring diagrams.

COUGAR & THUNDERBIRD

Refer to **Figs. 4 and 5** for charging system wiring diagrams.

CROWN VICTORIA & GRAND MARQUIS

Refer to **Fig. 6** for charging system wiring diagram.

ESCORT, TRACER & ZX2

Refer to **Fig. 7** for charging system wiring diagram.

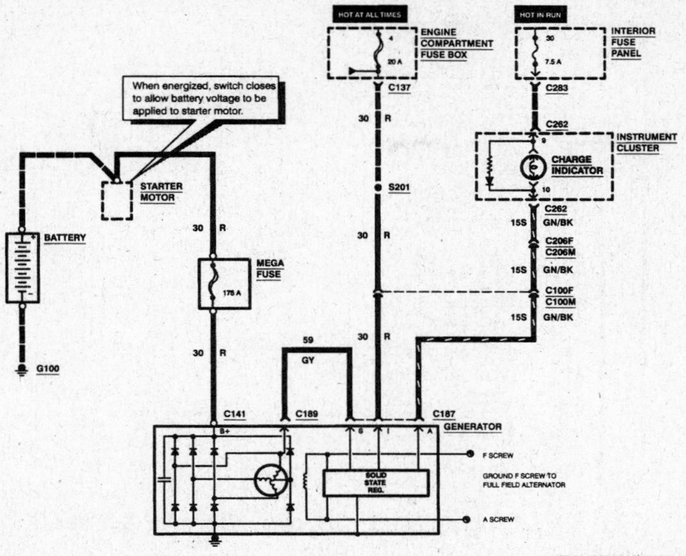

FM1129700307000X

Fig. 2 Wiring diagram. 1997 Contour & Mystique

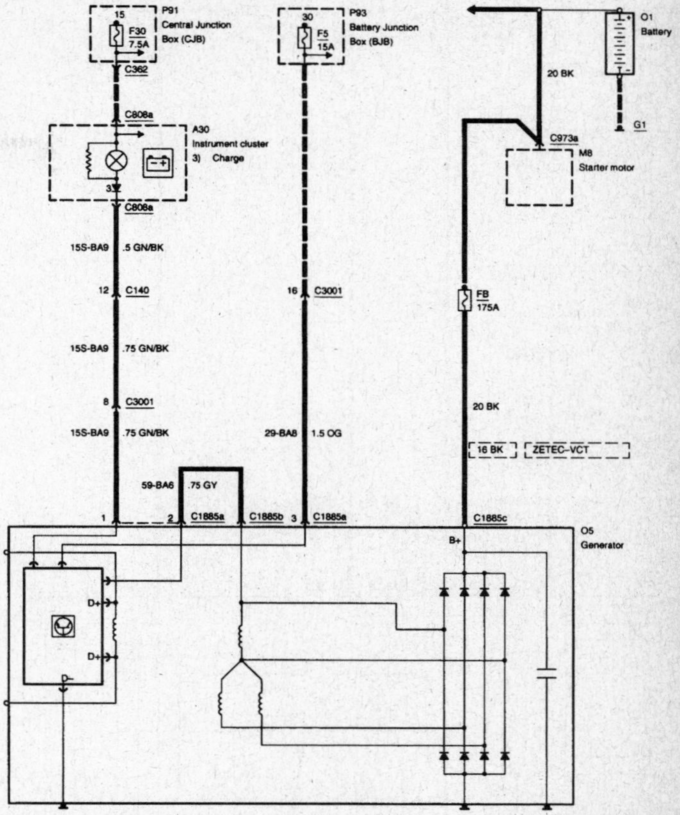

FM1129800308000X

Fig. 3 Wiring diagram. 1998–2000 Contour & Mystique

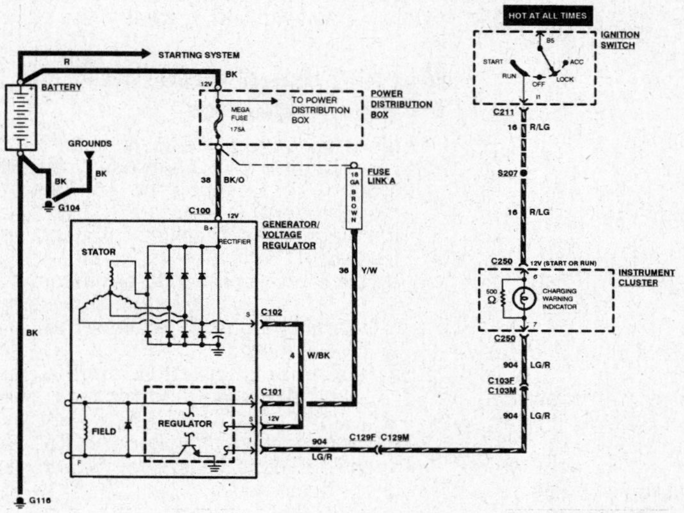

FM1129700316000X

Fig. 4 Wiring diagram. 1997 Cougar & Thunderbird

LS

Refer to **Fig. 8** for charging system wiring diagram.

MUSTANG

Refer to **Figs. 9 and 10** for charging system wiring diagrams.

SABLE & TAURUS

Refer to **Figs. 11 and 12** for charging system wiring diagrams.

TOWN CAR

Refer to **Figs. 13 and 14** for charging system wiring diagrams.

Diagnostic Tests

CONTINENTAL

Refer to **Figs. 15 and 16** for symptom charts and **Figs. 17 through 36** for diagnostic tests.

CONTOUR & MYSTIQUE

Refer to **Figs. 37 and 38** for symptom charts and **Figs. 39 through 54** for diagnostic tests.

THUNDERBIRD & 1997 COUGAR

Refer to **Fig. 55** for symptom chart and **Figs. 56 through 63** for diagnostic tests.

1999–2000 COUGAR

DIAGNOSIS BY SYMPTOM

Charging System Warning Indicator Is On, Intermittent Or Flickers w/Engine Running

1. Possible sources are as follows:
   a. Accessory drive belt.
   b. Fuse No. 7 (20A).
   c. Wiring circuit.
   d. Alternator.

   Refer to "Pinpoint test A."

Charging System Warning Indicator Is Off w/Ignition Switch In Run Position & Engine Off

1. Possible sources are as follows:
   a. Bulb.
   b. Circuit.
   c. Alternator.

Radio Interference

1. Possible sources are as follows:
   a. Circuit.
   b. Alternator.

   Refer to "Pinpoint Test B: Ratio Interference."

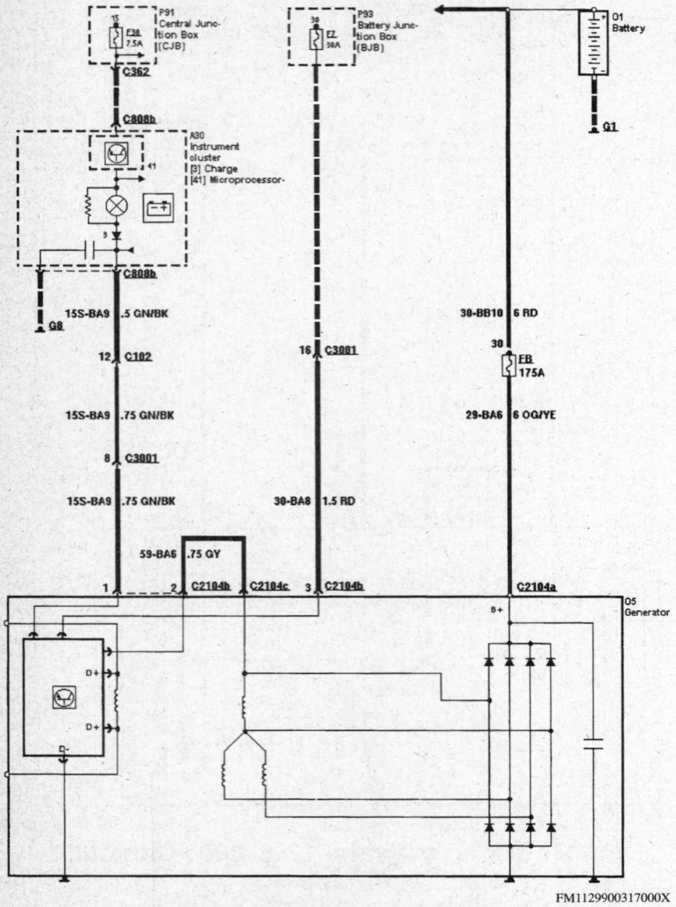

Fig. 5 Wiring diagram. 1999–2000 Cougar

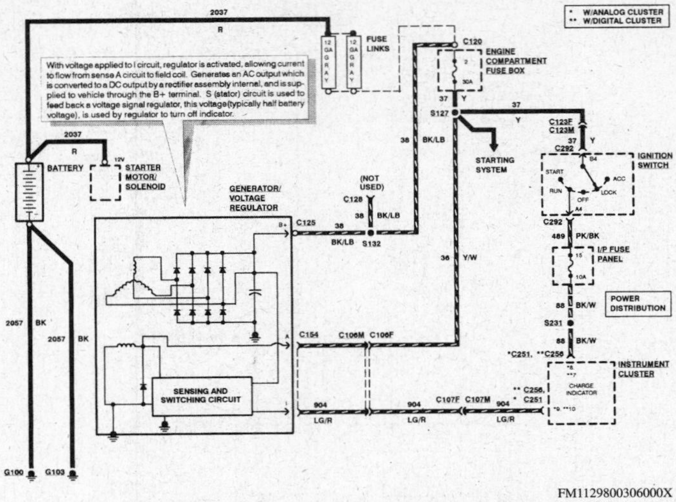

Fig. 6 Wiring diagram. Crown Victoria & Grand Marquis

System Overcharges

1. Possible sources are as follows:
   a. Alternator.

PINPOINT TEST A: CHARGING SYSTEM WARNING INDICATOR IS ON w/ENGINE RUNNING

Test A1: Check Battery

1. Check battery capacity.
2. If battery capacity is not at normal operating range, replace battery.
3. Recheck system.

Test A2: Check Charging System

1. Perform load test as described in this section.
2. If alternator output is not as specified, refer to " Test A3: Check For A Good Ground."

Test A3: Check For A Good Ground

1. Measure voltage between alternator case and battery negative terminal.
2. If voltage is less than .5 volts, refer to "Test A4: Check Battery Cable."
3. If voltage is more than .5 volts, clean and tighten alternator mounting bolts, engine to body ground strap and battery round cable.
4. Recheck system for normal operation.
5. If voltage is still not as specified, replace battery ground cable.

Test A4: Check Battery Cable

1. Measure voltage between alternator B+ terminal and battery positive terminal. Voltage should be less than .5 volts.
2. If voltage is as specified, refer to "Test A5: Check Battery Feed To The Alternator."
3. If voltage is not as specified, clean and tighten battery positive cable connections.
4. Recheck system operation. If voltage is still not as specified, replace battery positive cable.

Test A5: Check Battery Feed To The Alternator

1. Measure voltage between alternator B+ terminal and ground. Battery voltage should be present.
2. If voltage is as specified, refer to "Test A6: Check Power To The Voltage Regulator."
3. If voltage is not as specified, inspect fuseable link FB 175A.
4. Recheck system operation. If voltage is not as specified, repair battery positive cable.

Test A6: Check Power To Voltage Regulator

1. Measure voltage between alternator connector pin No. 3 harness side and ground. There should be 10 volts or more present.
2. If voltage is as specified, proceed as follows:
   a. **On models with 2.5L engine,** refer to "Test A7: Charging System Warning Indicator Is On w/The Engine Running."
   b. **On models with 2.0L engine,** replace alternator and recheck system.
3. **On all models,** if voltage is not as specified, inspect fuse No. F7 and recheck system.

Check Output Feedback To Regulator

1. Measure resistance between alternator connector pin No. 2 harness side and pin No. 1 harness side. Resistance should be less than 5 ohms.
2. If resistance is as specified, replace alternator and recheck system.
3. If resistance is not as specified, repair circuit and recheck system.

PINPOINT TEST B: RADIO INTERFERENCE

Test B1: Isolate The Alternator

1. Remove accessory drive belt.
2. Run engine for a few seconds with radio turned on.
3. If radio interference is still present, inspect audio entertainment system for malfunctions.
4. If radio interference is not present, clean and tighten battery clamps and

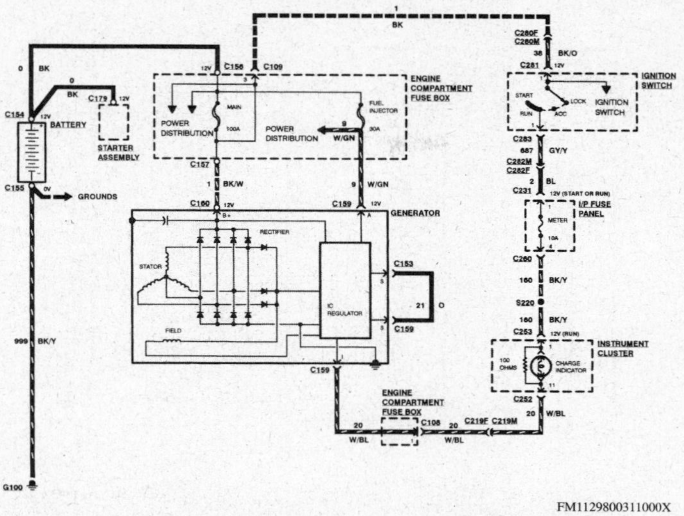

Fig. 7 Wiring diagram. Escort, Tracer & ZX2

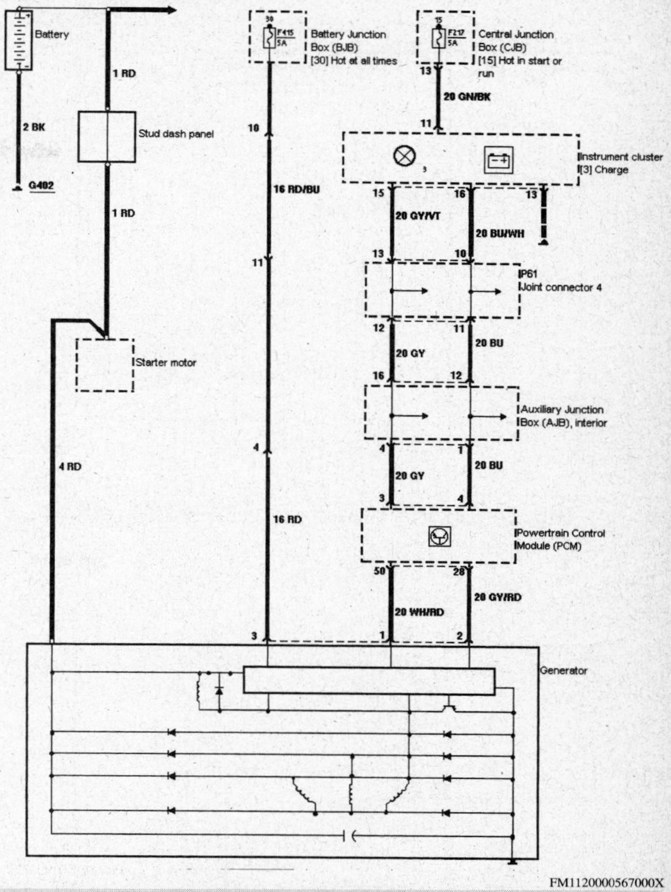

Fig. 8 Wiring diagram. LS

alternator mounting bolts.

5. If interference is still present, replace alternator.

CROWN VICTORIA & GRAND MARQUIS

Refer to **Figs. 64 and 65** for symptom chart and **Figs. 66 through 81** for diagnostic tests.

ESCORT & TRACER

Refer to **Fig. 82** for symptom chart and **Figs. 83 through 89** for diagnostic tests.

LS

Refer to **Fig. 90** for symptom chart and **Figs. 91 through 95** for diagnostic tests.

MUSTANG

Refer to **Figs. 96 through 98** for symptom charts and **Figs. 99 through 121** for diagnostic tests.

SABLE & TAURUS

Refer to **Fig. 122** for symptom chart and **Figs. 123 through 130** for diagnostic tests.

TOWN CAR

Refer to **Figs. 131 and 132** for symptom charts and **Figs. 133 through 152** for diagnostic tests.

No-Load Test

1997–99 CONTINENTAL, CONTOUR, COUGAR, ESCORT, MYSTIQUE, THUNDERBIRD, TOWN CAR, TRACER, ZX2 & 1999–2000 CROWN VICTORIA, GRAND MARQUIS & MUSTANG

1. Connect voltmeter leads across battery terminals.
2. Read and record voltage. This value is the base voltage.
3. Start engine and monitor engine speed.
4. Run engine at 1500 RPM with no electrical load.
5. Read voltage, noting the following:
   a. Voltage should be 14.1–15.1 volts.
   b. If voltage increase is less than 2.5 volts over base voltage, refer to "Load Test" in this section.
   c. If there is no voltage increase or voltage increase is greater than 2.5 volts, refer to "Diagnostic Tests" in this section.

CONTINENTAL, SABLE, TAURUS & TOWN CAR

To check charging system, use Rotunda alternator tester tool No. 010–00725, or equivalent.

1. Switch Rotunda alternator tester to voltmeter function.
2. Connect voltmeter positive lead to alternator B+ terminal and negative lead to ground.
3. Turn all electrical accessories.
4. With engine running at 2000 RPM, check alternator output voltage. Voltage should be between 13 and 15 volts. If voltage is not as specified, refer to "Diagnostic Tests" in this section.

Load Test

1997 CONTINENTAL & TOWN CAR, 1997–99 CONTOUR, COUGAR, ESCORT, MYSTIQUE, THUNDERBIRD, TRACER & 1999–2000 CROWN VICTORIA, GRAND MARQUIS & MUSTANG

1. Connect leads of voltmeter across battery terminals.
2. Read and record voltage. This value is the base voltage.
3. With engine running, turn on air conditioner if equipped, turn blower motor to high speed and set headlamps to high beam position.
4. Increase engine speed to approximately 2000 RPM, noting the following:
   a. Voltage should increase a minimum of .5 volts above base voltage.
   b. If voltage does not increase, refer to "Diagnostic Tests" in this section.
   c. If voltage increases as specified, charging system is operating normally.

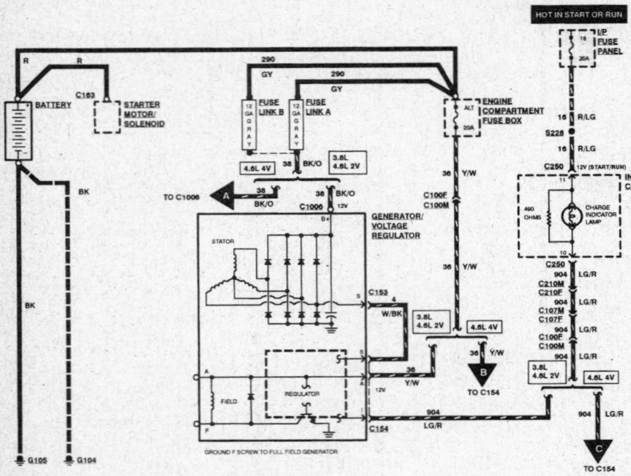

FM1129800312000X

Fig. 9 Wiring diagram. 1997–98 Mustang

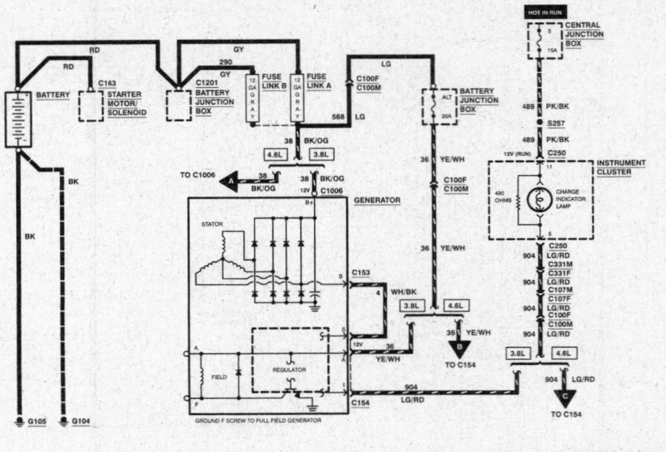

FM1129900540000X

Fig. 10 Wiring diagram. 1999–2000 Mustang

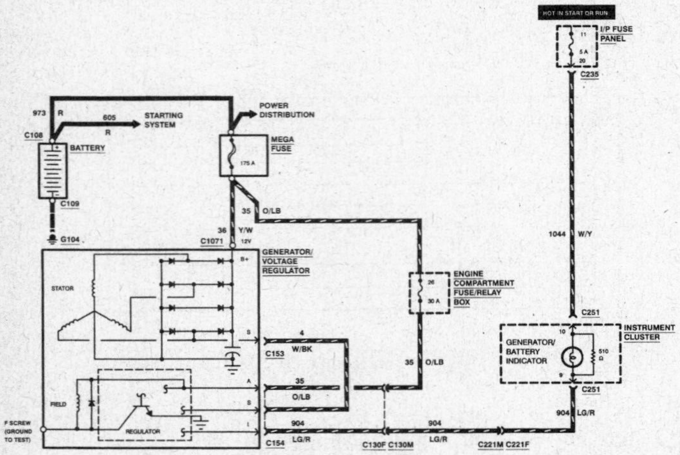

FM1129800309000X

Fig. 11 Wiring diagram. Sable & Taurus w/3.0L SOHC engine

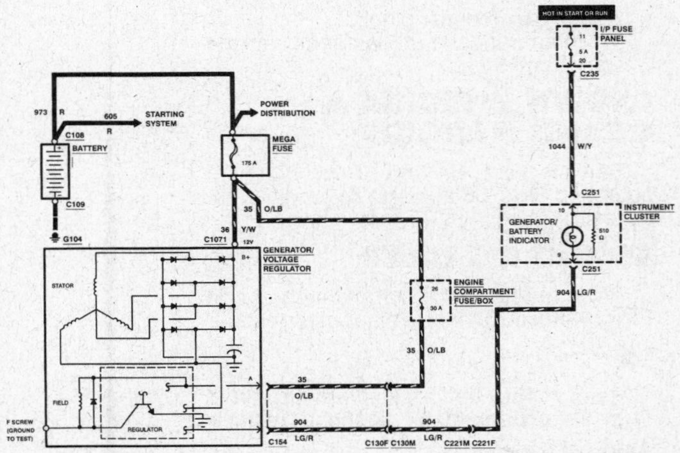

FM1129800310000X

Fig. 12 Wiring diagram. Sable & Taurus w/3.0L & 3.4L DOHC engines

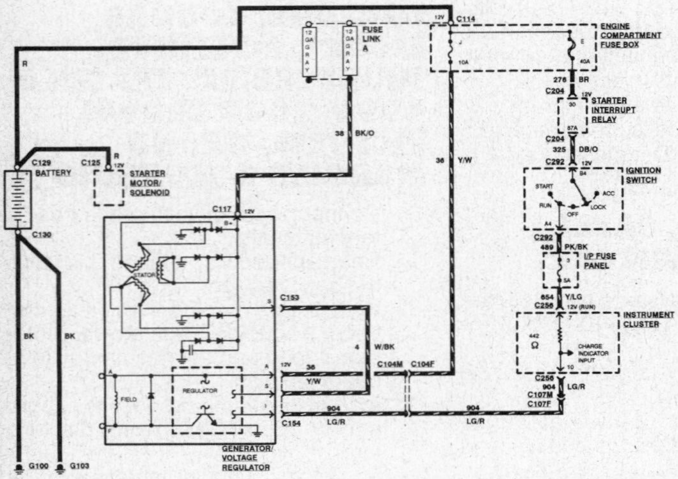

FM1129700314000X

Fig. 13 Wiring diagram. 1997 Town Car

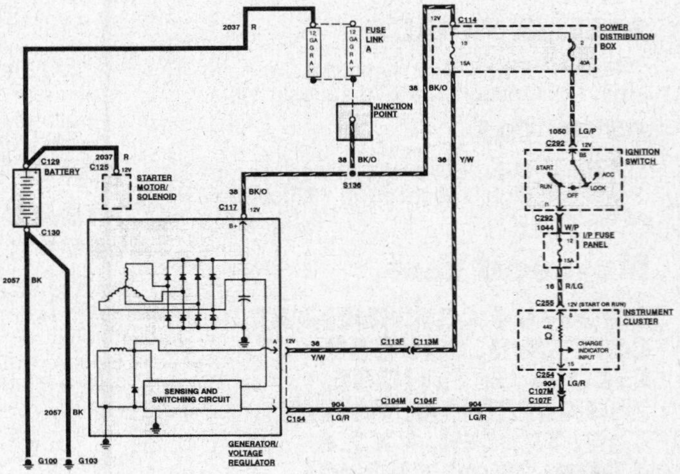

FM1129800315000X

Fig. 14 Wiring diagram. 1998–2000 Town Car

1998–2000 CONTINENTAL & 1998–2000 SABLE, TAURUS & TOWN CAR

To check charging system, use Rotunda alternator tester tool No. 010–00725, or equivalent.

1. Turn off all lamps and electrical components.
2. Place transmission in Neutral position, then apply parking brake.
3. Switch alternator tester to ammeter function.
4. Connect positive and negative leads of tester to battery.
5. Connect current probe to alternator B+ output lead.
6. With engine running at 2000 RPM, adjust tester load bank to determine output of alternator, noting the following:
   a. **On Sable, Taurus and 1998 Continental,** alternator output should be greater than 87 amps at 2000 RPM.
   b. **On 1998 Town Car,** alternator output should be greater than 107 amps at 2000 RPM.
   c. **On all models,** if alternator output is not as specified, refer to "Diagnostic Tests" in this section.

Drain Test

Check for current drains on battery in excess of 50 milliamps with all the electrical accessories off and the vehicle at rest. This test can be performed three ways.

CLAMP ON DC AMMETER TEST

1. Connect a 12–volt test lamp in series with battery positive terminal. If test lamp glows then a drain exists.
2. Use a clamp-on current probe to battery positive or negative terminal. Ensure probe is properly calibrated to prevent false readings.
3. Connect an in-line ammeter between battery positive or negative post and its respective cable.
4. Turn ignition switch to Off position. Ensure all electrical loads are off.
5. Ensure engine compartment lamp operates properly, then disconnect lamp.
6. Clamp meter clip securely around positive or negative battery cable. **Do not start vehicle with clip on cable.**
7. Record current reading, noting the following:
   a. Current reading should be less than .05 amp.
   b. If current reading exceeds .05 amps, it indicates a constant drain which could cause a discharged battery.
   c. Possible sources of current drain are vehicle lamps such as engine compartment lamp, glove compartment lamp or luggage compartment lamp.
8. If drain is not caused by vehicle lamps, remove fuses one at a time until cause of drain is located.
9. If drain is still undetermined, disconnect leads at starter relay one at a time to find problem circuit.

INLINE MULTIMETER TEST

This test will require a digital volt amp-ohmmeter with an appropriate ampere scale.

1. Place ignition switch in Off position. Ensure there are no electrical loads on.
2. Ensure engine compartment lamp operates properly, then disconnect lamp.
3. Check battery voltage. If voltage is less than 11.5 volts, charge battery to above 11.5 volts.
4. Connect one ammeter lead to battery ground terminal and other lead to disconnected battery ground cable.
5. **Do not crank engine with ammeter connected.** Set ammeter to DC amperage scale, noting the following:
   a. Current reading should be less than .05 amp.
   b. If reading is between .2 and .9 amp, a drain may be present.
   c. Possible sources of current drain are vehicle lamps such as engine compartment lamp, glove compartment lamp or luggage compartment lamp.
6. If drain is not caused by vehicle lamps, remove fuses one at a time until cause of drain is located.
7. If drain is still undetermined, disconnect leads at starter relay one at a time to find problem circuit.

BATTERY CABLE DISCONNECTED TEST

1. Connect a 12–volt test lamp in series with battery positive terminal. If test lamp glows a drain exists.
2. Use a clamp-on current probe to battery positive or negative terminal. Ensure probe is properly calibrated to prevent false readings.
3. Connect an in-line ammeter between battery positive or negative post and its respective cable.
4. Without starting engine, turn ignition switch to Run position for a few seconds, then to the Off position.
5. Wait one minute for illuminated entry lamps to turn off, if equipped.
6. Connect ammeter and read amperage, noting the following:
   a. Current reading should be less than .05 amp.
   b. If reading exceeds .05 amp after a few minutes and drain did not show up in previous tests, drain is most likely caused by a faulty electronic component.
7. Remove fuses and disconnect starter leads one at a time to locate problem circuit.

DIAGNOSTIC CHART INDEX

Test	Description	Page No.	Fig. No.
1997 CONTINENTAL			
—	Symptom Chart	13-10	15
Test A	System Does Not Charge	13-11	17
Test B	System Overcharges	13-11	18
Test C	Indicator Lamp Stays On, Engine Running	13-11	19
Test D	Indicator Lamp Stays On, Ignition Switch Off	13-11	20
Test E	Indicator Lamp Does Not Come On	13-11	21
Test F	Indicator Lamp Flickers/Intermittent	13-12	22
Test G	Alternator Is Noisy	13-12	23
Test H	Radio Interference	13-12	24
1998–2000 CONTINENTAL			
—	Symptom Chart	13-10	16
Test A	Warning Indicator Is On, Engine Running	13-12	25
Test B	Warning Indicator Is Off w/Ignition Switch In Run Position & Engine Off	13-12	26
Test C	Warning Indicator Is On w/ Engine Running & Battery Voltage Increases	13-13	27

Continued

DIAGNOSTIC CHART INDEX—Continued

Continued

DIAGNOSTIC CHART INDEX—Continued

Continued

DIAGNOSTIC CHART INDEX—Continued

Condition	Possible Source	Action
• System Does Not Charge	• Ignition switch off battery drain. • Circuitry. • Generator. • Battery. • Battery connections. • Drive belt.	• GO to Pinpoint Test A.
• System Overcharges (Battery Boils Over)	• Circuitry. • Poor ground. • Generator.	• GO to Pinpoint Test B.
• Indicator Lamp Stays ON, Engine Running	• Circuitry. • Generator.	• GO to Pinpoint Test C.
• Indicator Lamp Stays ON, Ignition Switch OFF	• Circuitry. • Instrument cluster.	• GO to Pinpoint Test D.
• Indicator Lamp Does Not Come On	• Burned out lamp. • Poor ground. • Circuitry. • Generator.	• GO to Pinpoint Test E.
• Indicator Lamp Flickers / Intermittent	• Loose connection to generator, voltage regulator or power distribution box. • Circuitry. • Loose brush holder screw. • Generator.	• GO to Pinpoint Test F.
• Generator Noisy	• Accessory drive belt. • Accessory brackets. • Bent pulley. • Generator. • Other accessories.	• GO to Pinpoint Test G.
• Radio Interference	• Generator. • Other components.	• GO to Pinpoint Test H.

FM1129700235000X

Fig. 15 Symptom chart. 1997 Continental

Condition	Possible Source	Action
• The Charging System Warning Indicator is ON with the Engine Running (The Battery Voltage Does Not Increase)	• A Circuit 35 (O/LB). • A Circuit in-line mini-fuse. • B+ Circuit 36 (Y/W). • B+ mega fuse. • I Circuit 904 (LG/R) • Voltage regulator. • Generator	• GO to Pinpoint Test A.
• The Charging System Warning Indicator is OFF with the Ignition Switch in the RUN Position and the Engine OFF (Battery Voltage Does Not Increase)	• Voltage regulator connector. • I Circuit 904 (LG/R). • Fuse 19 (10A). • Voltage regulator. • Loose or damaged generator. • Harness connector.	• GO to Pinpoint Test B.
• The Charging System Warning Indicator is ON with the Engine Running and the Battery Voltage Increases	• Generator. • Voltage regulator.	• GO to Pinpoint Test C.

FM1129800244010X

Fig. 16 Symptom chart (Part 1 of 2). 1998–2000 Continental

Condition	Possible Source	Action
• The Charging System Warning Indicator is OFF with the Ignition Switch in the RUN Position and the Engine OFF (Battery Voltage Increases)	• Charging system warning indicator lamp bulb. • Instrument cluster. • Generator. • Voltage regulator.	• GO to Pinpoint Test D.
• The Charging System Warning Indicator Operates Correctly but the Battery Voltage Does Not Increase	• B+ Circuit 36 (Y/W). • B+ mega fuse. • Loose or damaged harness connector. • Battery cables. • Generator. • Voltage regulator.	• GO to Pinpoint Test E.
• The Battery is Dead or Will Not Stay Charged or Low Battery or Generator Voltage	• Corroded terminal(s). • Loose connection(s). • High key-off load. • Generator. • Voltage regulator.	• GO to Pinpoint Test F.
• The Charging System Warning Indicator Flickers/Is Intermittent	• Loose connection(s). • In-line mini-fuse A Circuit loose. • Fuse 19 (10A) I Circuit loose. • Generator. • Voltage regulator.	• GO to Pinpoint Test G.
• The System Overcharges (Battery Voltage Greater Than 15.5 Volts)	• A Circuit 35 (O/LB). • Generator (low output). • Voltage regulator. • I Circuit 904 (LG/R).	• GO to Pinpoint Test H.
• Battery Leakage or Damage	• A Circuit 35 (O/LB). • Generator. • Voltage regulator. • Battery.	• GO to Pinpoint Test J.
• The Voltage Gauge Reads High or Low	• Generator (low output) • Voltage regulator. • Voltage gauge. • Instrument cluster/wiring.	• GO to Pinpoint Test K.
• The Generator is Noisy	• Loose bolts/brackets. • Drive belt. • Generator/Pulley.	• GO to Pinpoint Test L.
• Radio Interference	• Generator. • Wiring/routing. • In-vehicle entertainment system.	• GO to Pinpoint Test M.

FM1129800244020X

Fig. 16 Symptom chart (Part 2 of 2). 1998–2000 Continental

Test Step		Result	Action to Take
A5	CHECK FOR KEY-OFF DRAIN		
	• Perform Battery Drain Testing. • **Is current drain less than 50 mA?**	Yes No	GO to **A6**. Find cause of ignition switch off battery drain.
A6	CHECK BATTERY		
	• Perform the Battery Capacity Test. • **Is the battery capacity OK?**	Yes No	GO to **A7**. REPLACE battery.
A7	CHECK FOR OPEN B+ CIRCUIT		
	• Measure voltage at B+ terminal on back of generator. • **Is voltage at B+ terminal equal to battery voltage?**	Yes No	GO to **A8**. SERVICE open in B+ Circuit.
A8	CHECK FOR OPEN A CIRCUIT		
	• Measure voltage at A Circuit on voltage regulator. • **Is voltage at A Circuit equal to battery voltage?**	Yes No	GO to **A9**. CHECK Fuse 21 (10A) in Circuit 36 (Y/W) and REPLACE if required. If OK, SERVICE open in Circuit 36 (Y/W).
A9	CHECK FOR OPEN I CIRCUIT		
	• Turn ignition switch to RUN position. • NOTE: Voltage regulator must be connected to wiring harness for this test. Measure voltage at connector C154 I-terminal, Circuit 904 (LG/R). • **Is voltage greater than 1 V?**	Yes No	GO to **A10**. SERVICE open or high resistance in Circuit 904 (LG/R).
A10	CHECK VOLTAGE DROP IN A CIRCUIT		
	• Measure voltage drop between A Circuit on voltage regulator and positive (+) battery post. • **Is voltage drop less than 0.25 V?**	Yes No	GO to **A11**. SERVICE excess voltage drop in Circuit 36 (Y/W). CHECK Fuse 21 (10A) and connectors in Circuit 36 (Y/W). SERVICE as required.
A11	CHECK VOLTAGE DROP IN B+ CIRCUIT		
	• Turn ignition switch to RUN position. • Turn headlamps on and set blower on HIGH. • With engine running at 2000 rpm, measure voltage drop between B+ terminal on back of generator and positive (+) battery post. • **Is voltage drop less than 0.5 V?**	Yes No	REPLACE generator. SERVICE excess voltage drop in B+ Circuit 38 (BK/O). CHECK fuse in B+ Circuit 38 (BK/O) and the connections between the battery and power distribution box.

FM1129700236020X

Fig. 17 Test A: System Does Not Charge (Part 2 of 2). 1997 Continental

Test Step		Result	Action to Take
A1	CHECK DRIVE BELT TENSIONER		
	• Perform drive belt tensioner check procedure. • **Is the drive belt adjusted properly?**	Yes No	GO to **A2**. REPLACE drive belt.
A2	CHECK BATTERY CONNECTIONS		
	• Inspect the battery cables for loose or corroded connections. • Inspect battery for corrosion. • **Are the battery cables clean, tight and free from corrosion?**	Yes No	GO to **A3**. SERVICE battery and cables as necessary. RESTORE vehicle. RETEST system.
A3	LOOSE BATTERY POST		
	• Check for loose battery posts. • **Are posts OK?**	Yes No	GO to **A4**. REPLACE battery.
A4	CRACKED BATTERY COVER		
	• Remove battery hold down clamps and shields. • Check for broken/cracked case or battery cover. • **Are case and cover OK?**	Yes No	GO to **A5**. REPLACE battery.

FM1129700236010X

Fig. 17 Test A: System Does Not Charge (Part 1 of 2). 1997 Continental

Test Step		Result	Action to Take
B1	CHECK VOLTAGE DROP IN A CIRCUIT		
	• Turn ignition switch to RUN. • Measure voltage between A Circuit on voltage regulator and positive (+) battery post. • **Is voltage drop less than 0.25 V?**	Yes No	GO to **B2**. SERVICE excess voltage drop in Circuit 36 (Y/W). CHECK Fuse 21 (10A) and connectors in Circuit 36 (Y/W) and SERVICE as required.
B2	CHECK VOLTAGE DROP IN I CIRCUIT		
	• NOTE: Voltage regulator must be connected to wiring harness for this test. • Measure voltage at connector C154 I-terminal, Circuit 904 (LG/R). • **Is voltage greater than 1 V?**	Yes No	GO to **B3**. SERVICE high resistance in Circuit 904 (LG/R).
B3	CHECK FOR POOR GROUNDS		
	• Check for poor ground connections between voltage regulator and generator, generator and engine, or engine and battery. • **Are all ground connections clean and tight?**	Yes No	REPLACE generator. CLEAN or SERVICE grounds as required.

FM1129700237000X

Fig. 18 Test B: System Overcharges. 1997 Continental

Test Step		Result	Action to Take
C1	CHECK FOR OPEN A CIRCUIT		
	• Measure voltage at A Circuit on voltage regulator. • **Is voltage at A Circuit equal to battery voltage?**	Yes No	GO to **C2**. CHECK Fuse 21 (10A) in Circuit 36 (Y/W) and REPLACE if required. If OK, SERVICE open in Circuit 36 (Y/W).
C2	CHECK FOR SHORTED I CIRCUIT		
	• Remove voltage regulator connector C154. • Turn ignition switch to RUN. • **Is indicator lamp on?**	Yes No	SERVICE short to ground in Circuit 904 (LG/R). GO to **C3**.
C3	CHECK GENERATOR OUTPUT VOLTAGE		
	• Measure voltage at the B+ terminal on back of generator with engine running at 2000 rpm and all accessories turned OFF. • **Is voltage greater than 15.5 V?**	Yes No	GO to Pinpoint Test D to find cause of high output voltage. REPLACE generator.

FM1129700238000X

Fig. 19 Test C: Indicator Lamp Stays On, Engine Running. 1997 Continental

Test Step		Result	Action to Take
D1	CHECK LAMP CIRCUIT WIRING		
	• Turn ignition switch OFF. • Remove voltage regulator connector C154. • Measure voltage at connector C154 I-terminal, Circuit 904 (LG/R). • **Is voltage equal to B+?**	Yes No	SERVICE Circuit 640 (R/Y). Circuit should be hot in RUN only. SERVICE instrument cluster.

FM1129700239000X

Fig. 20 Test D: Indicator Lamp Stays On, Ignition Switch Off. 1997 Continental

Test Step		Result	Action to Take
E1	CHECK INSTRUMENT CLUSTER OPERATION		
	• Turn ignition switch to RUN. • **Are all other warning lamps and instrument cluster lit for a short time?**	Yes No	GO to **E2**. SERVICE instrument cluster.
E2	CHECK FOR OPEN I CIRCUIT		
	• Disconnect voltage regulator connector C154. • Turn ignition switch to RUN. • Measure voltage at wiring harness I-terminal, Circuit 904 (LG/R). • **Is voltage equal to B+?**	Yes No	GO to **E3**. SERVICE open in Circuit 904 (LG/R).
E3	CHECK FOR BURNED OUT BULB		
	• Connect C154 I-terminal, Circuit 904 (LG/R) to ground with a jumper wire. • **Is indicator lamp on?**	Yes No	REMOVE jumper wire. GO to **E4**. REPLACE lamp or SERVICE high resistance in lamp socket or Circuit 904 (LG/R).
E4	CHECK FOR POOR GROUNDS		
	• Check for poor ground connections between voltage regulator and generator, generator and engine, or engine and battery. • **Are all ground connections clean and tight?**	Yes No	REPLACE generator. CLEAN or SERVICE grounds as required.

FM1129700240000X

Fig. 21 Test E: Indicator Lamp Does Not Come On. 1997 Continental

Test Step		Result	Action to Take
F1	CHECK FOR LOOSE CONNECTIONS		
	• Check these connections for corrosion, loose or bent pins, or loose eyelets: — Voltage regulator connector C154. — Generator B+ eyelet. — Power distribution box eyelets. — Battery cables. • **Are all connections clean and tight?**	Yes No	GO to **F2**. CLEAN or SERVICE connections as required.
F2	CHECK FOR LOOSE A CIRCUIT FUSE		
	• Turn ignition switch to RUN. • Check Fuse 21 (10A) in power distribution box for a loose connection by wiggling fuse with engine running. • **Does indicator lamp flicker?**	Yes No	SERVICE loose fuse connection. GO to **F3**.
F3	CHECK A CIRCUIT CONNECTIONS		
	• With engine running, connect A Circuit on voltage regulator to positive (+) battery post using a jumper wire. • **Does indicator lamp flicker?**	Yes No	REPLACE generator. SERVICE poor connection in Circuit 36 (Y/W).

FM1129700241000X

Fig. 22 Test F: Indicator Lamp Flickers/Intermittent. 1997 Continental

TEST CONDITIONS	TEST DETAILS/RESULTS/ACTIONS
A1 CHECK A CIRCUIT FUSE 20 (15A)	
	2 Check the A circuit Fuse 20 (15A) in the Power Distribution Box. • Is the fuse OK? → **Yes** GO to **A2**. → **No** REPLACE Fuse 20 (15A). Test the system for normal operation.
A2 CHECK THE DRIVE BELT TENSION	
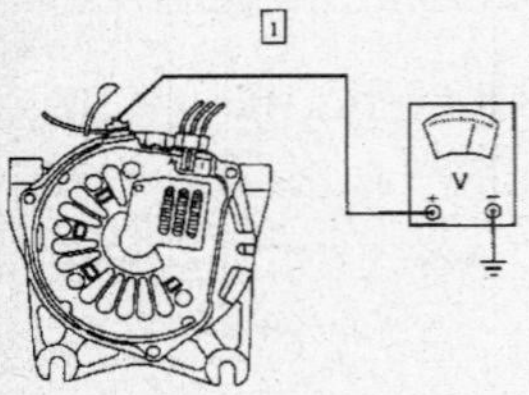	1 Measure the voltage between the B+ terminal at the generator circuit 38 (BK/O). • Is the voltage equal to battery positive voltage (B+)? → **Yes** GO to **A3**. → **No** REPAIR Circuit 38 (BK/O). TEST the system for normal operation.

FM1129800245010X

Fig. 25 Test A: Warning Indicator Is On, Engine Running (Part 1 of 3). 1998–2000 Continental

TEST CONDITIONS	TEST DETAILS/RESULTS/ACTIONS
A4 CHECK I CIRCUIT 904 (LG/R) FOR AN OPEN	
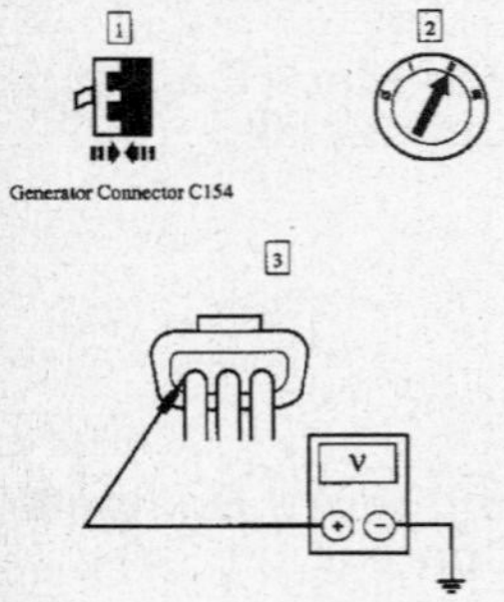	3 **NOTE:** The voltage regulator must be connected to the wiring harness for this test. Measure the voltage between the voltage regulator I-terminal, Circuit 904 (LG/R) and ground. • Is the voltage greater than 1 volt? → **Yes** GO to **A5**. → **No** REPAIR Circuit 904 (LG/R) as necessary. TEST the system for normal operation.
A5 CHECK GENERATOR OUTPUT	
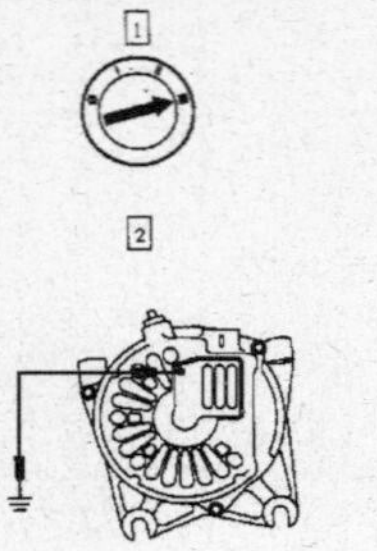	2 With the engine running, ground the F pin on the generator/regulator. • Does the battery voltage increase and the charging system warning indicator turn off? → **Yes** REPLACE the generator. TEST the system for normal operation. → **No** REPLACE the generator. TEST the system for normal operation.

FM1129800245030X

Fig. 25 Test A: Warning Indicator Is On, Engine Running (Part 3 of 3). 1998–2000 Continental

Test Step		Result	Action to Take
G1	CHECK FOR ACCESSORY DRIVE BELT NOISE		
	• Check drive belt to make sure that it is installed properly and is not damaged. • **Is drive belt OK?**	Yes No	GO to **G2**. SERVICE accessory drive belt as required.
G2	CHECK GENERATOR MOUNTING		
	• Check the generator and generator mounting bracket for loose bolts or misalignment condition. • **Is generator mounted correctly?**	Yes No	If noise is still present, REPLACE generator. INSTALL generator to specifications.

FM1129700242000X

Fig. 23 Test G: Alternator Is Noisy. 1997 Continental

Test Step		Result	Action to Take
H1	CHECK RADIO INTERFERENCE WITH REGULATOR DISCONNECTED		
	• Turn ignition switch to RUN. • Tune radio to a station where interference is present. • Disconnect voltage regulator connector C154. • **Is interference present with connector disconnected?**	Yes No	LOCATE cause of the radio interference. REPLACE generator.

FM1129700243000X

Fig. 24 Test H: Radio Interference. 1997 Continental

TEST CONDITIONS	TEST DETAILS/RESULTS/ACTIONS
A3 CHECK CIRCUIT 36 (Y/W)	
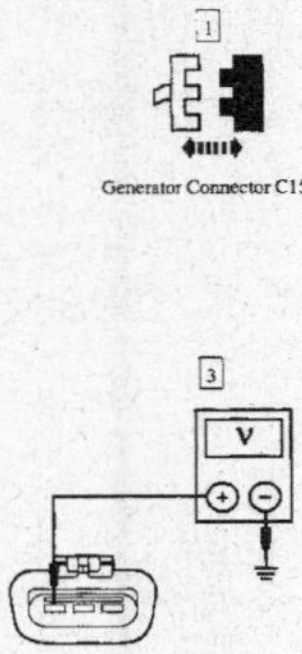	2 Measure the voltage between the voltage regulator connector C154 Pin A, Circuit 36 (Y/W) and ground. • Is the voltage equal to battery positive voltage (B+)? → **Yes** GO to **A4**. → **No** REPAIR Circuit 36 (Y/W). TEST the system for normal operation.

FM1129800245020X

Fig. 25 Test A: Warning Indicator Is On, Engine Running (Part 2 of 3). 1998–2000 Continental

TEST CONDITIONS	TEST DETAILS/RESULTS/ACTIONS
B1 CHECK GENERATOR CONNECTOR C154	
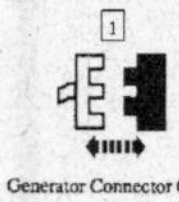	2 Check the generator connector C154 for bent or damaged pins. • Is the connector OK? → **Yes** GO to **B2**. → **No** REPAIR connector C154 as necessary. TEST the system for normal operation.
B2 CHECK GENERATOR GROUNDS	
	1 Check all ground connections between the generator, voltage regulator, and battery. • Are the ground connections OK? → **Yes** GO to **B3**. → **No** REPAIR connections as necessary. TEST the system for normal operation.

FM1129800246010X

Fig. 26 Test B: Warning Indicator Is Off w/Ignition Switch In Run Position & Engine Off (Part 1 of 2). 1998–2000 Continental

TEST CONDITIONS	TEST DETAILS/RESULTS/ACTIONS
B3 CHECK VOLTAGE AT I CIRCUIT 904 (LG/R)	
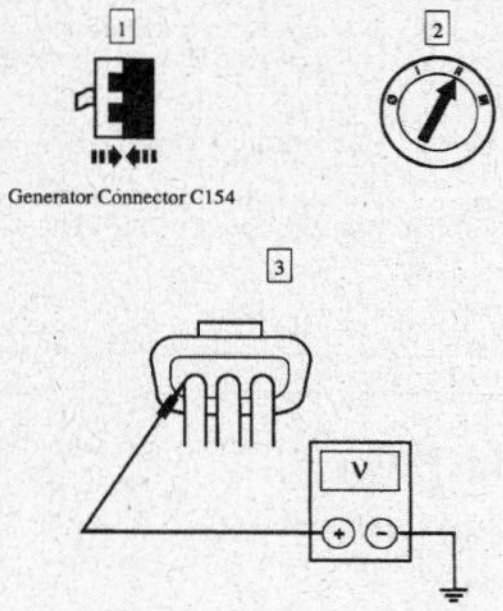	4 **NOTE:** The generator connector C154 must be connected to the generator for this test. Measure the voltage between the generator I terminal, Circuit 904 (LG/R) and ground. • Is the voltage greater than 1 volt? → **Yes** REPLACE the **Alternator** → **No** REPAIR Circuit 904 (LG/R) for open circuit. TEST the system for normal operation.

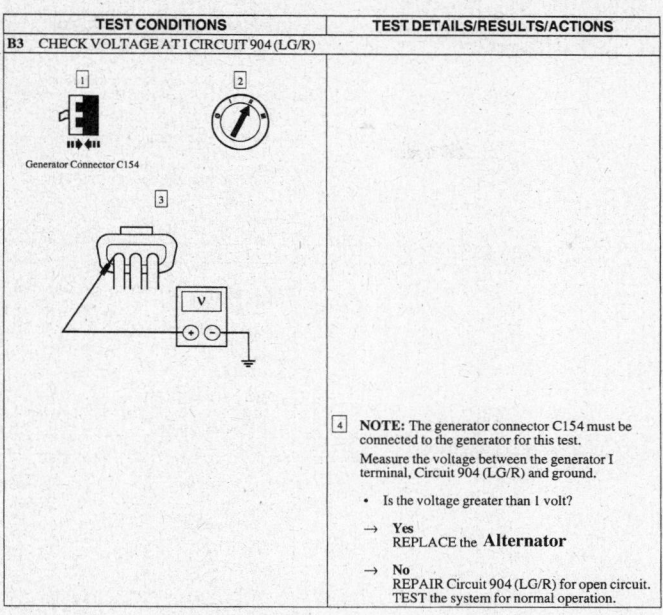

FM1129800246020X

Fig. 26 Test B: Warning Indicator Is Off w/Ignition Switch In Run Position & Engine Off (Part 2 of 2). 1998–2000 Continental

TEST CONDITIONS	TEST DETAILS/RESULTS/ACTIONS
C3 CHECK WARNING INDICATOR OPERATION	
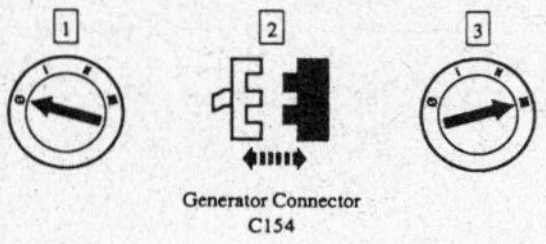	4 With the engine running at idle, check the Warning Indicator. • Is the warning indicator on? → **Yes** REPAIR connector C154, I Circuit 904 (LG/R) as necessary. TEST the system for normal operation. → **No** GO to Pinpoint Test D.

FM1129800247020X

Fig. 27 Test C: Warning Indicator Is On w/Engine Running & Battery Voltage Increases (Part 2 of 2). 1998–2000 Continental

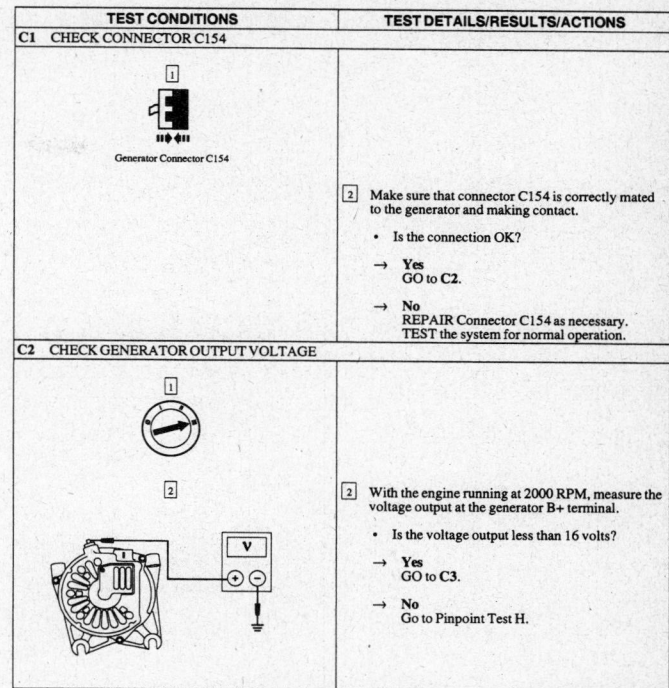

TEST CONDITIONS	TEST DETAILS/RESULTS/ACTIONS
C1 CHECK CONNECTOR C154	
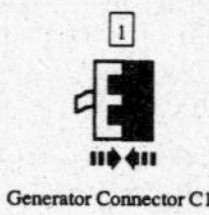	2 Make sure that connector C154 is correctly mated to the generator and making contact. • Is the connection OK? → **Yes** GO to **C2**. → **No** REPAIR Connector C154 as necessary. TEST the system for normal operation.
C2 CHECK GENERATOR OUTPUT VOLTAGE	
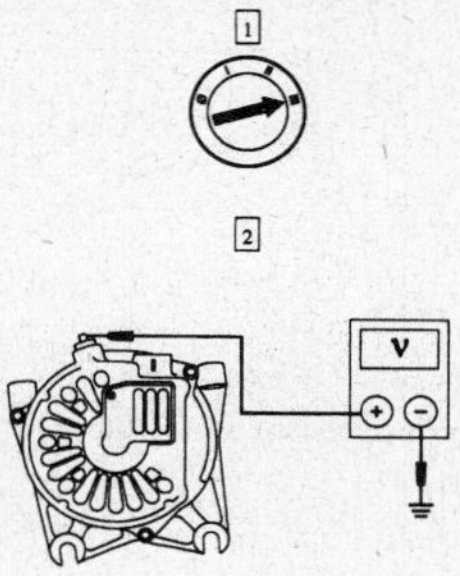	2 With the engine running at 2000 RPM, measure the voltage output at the generator B+ terminal. • Is the voltage output less than 16 volts? → **Yes** GO to **C3**. → **No** Go to Pinpoint Test H.

FM1129800247010X

Fig. 27 Test C: Warning Indicator Is On w/Engine Running & Battery Voltage Increases (Part 1 of 2). 1998–2000 Continental

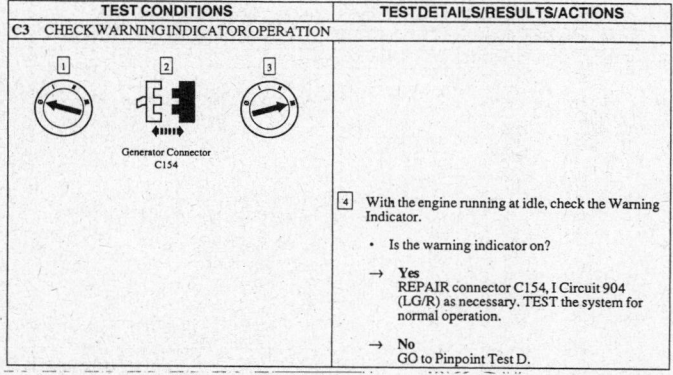

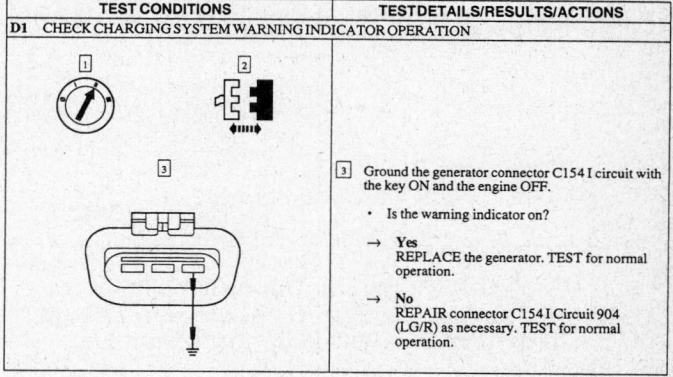

TEST CONDITIONS	TEST DETAILS/RESULTS/ACTIONS
D1 CHECK CHARGING SYSTEM WARNING INDICATOR OPERATION	
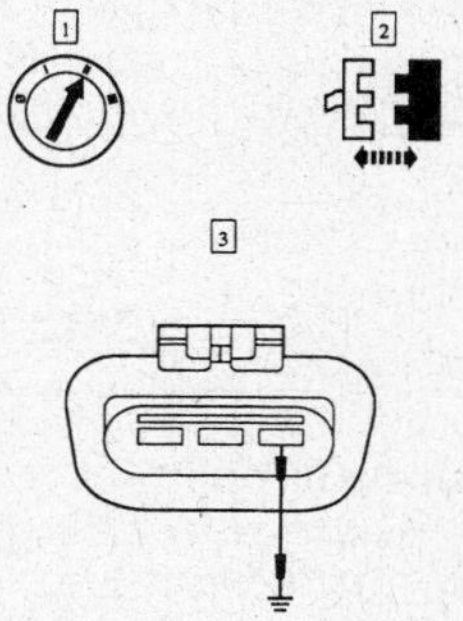	3 Ground the generator connector C154 I circuit with the key ON and the engine OFF. • Is the warning indicator on? → **Yes** REPLACE the generator. TEST for normal operation. → **No** REPAIR connector C154 I Circuit 904 (LG/R) as necessary. TEST for normal operation.

FM1129800248000X

Fig. 28 Test D: Warning Indicator Is Off w/Ignition Switch In Run Position & Engine Off. 1998–2000 Continental

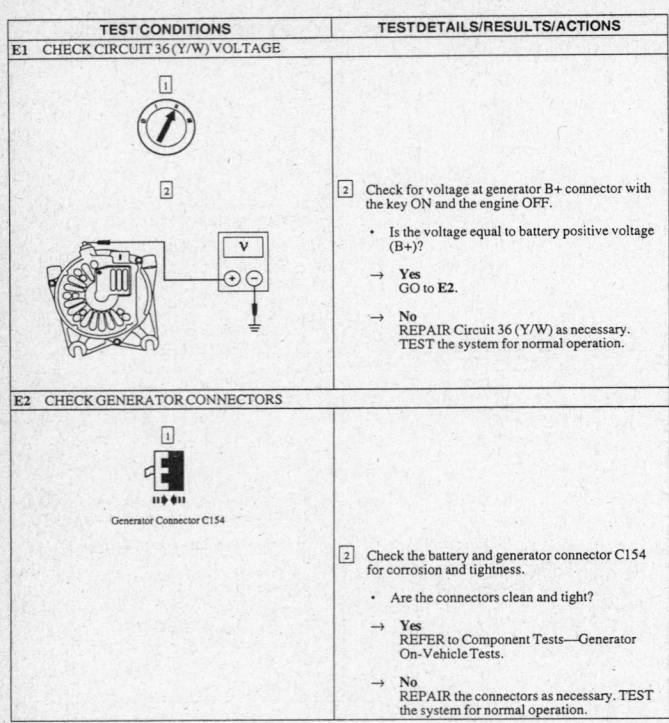

TEST CONDITIONS	TEST DETAILS/RESULTS/ACTIONS
E1 CHECK CIRCUIT 36 (Y/W) VOLTAGE	
1 	
2 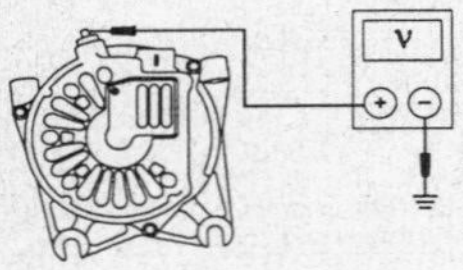	2 Check for voltage at generator B+ connector with the key ON and the engine OFF. • Is the voltage equal to battery positive voltage (B+)? → **Yes** GO to **E2**. → **No** REPAIR Circuit 36 (Y/W) as necessary. TEST the system for normal operation.
E2 CHECK GENERATOR CONNECTORS	
1  Generator Connector C154	
	2 Check the battery and generator connector C154 for corrosion and tightness. • Are the connectors clean and tight? → **Yes** REFER to Component Tests—Generator On-Vehicle Tests. → **No** REPAIR the connectors as necessary. TEST the system for normal operation.

FM1129800249000X

Fig. 29 Test E: Warning Indicator Operates Correctly But Battery Voltage Does Not Increase. 1998–2000 Continental

TEST CONDITIONS	TEST DETAILS/RESULTS/ACTIONS
F4 CHECK OTHER SYSTEMS FOR DRAINS	
	1 Check for drains from electronic modules. • Are electronic modules OK? → **Yes** RECHARGE the battery. TEST the system for normal operation. → **No** REPLACE the defective module as necessary. TEST the system for normal operation.

FM1129800250020X

Fig. 30 Test F: Battery Is Dead Or Will Not Stay Charged Or Low Battery Or Alternator Voltage (Part 2 of 2). 1998–2000 Continental

TEST CONDITIONS	TEST DETAILS/RESULTS/ACTIONS
F1 CHECK BATTERY DRAIN	
	1 Make sure that all interior lights and switches are off and all doors are closed. Perform battery drain test. • Is the drain greater than 0.5 amps? → **Yes** Go to Component Tests, Battery—Drain Testing. → **No** GO to **F2**.
F2 CHECK GENERATOR OUTPUT	
	1 Check generator output. (Refer to Component Test, Alternator On-Vehicle Tests. • Is the generator OK? → **Yes** GO to **F3**. → **No** REPLACE the generator. TEST the system for normal operation.
F3 CHECK BATTERY CONDITION	
	1 Check the battery capacity. • Is the battery OK? → **Yes** GO to **F4**. → **No** REPLACE the battery. TEST the system for normal operation.

FM1129800250010X

Fig. 30 Test F: Battery Is Dead Or Will Not Stay Charged Or Low Battery Or Alternator Voltage (Part 1 of 2). 1998–2000 Continental

TEST CONDITIONS	TEST DETAILS/RESULTS/ACTIONS
G1 CHECK POWER TO CIRCUITS 36 (Y/W) AND 904 (LG/R)	
1  2  Fuse 20 (15A) 3  Fuse 5 (10A)	
	4 Check Fuse 5 (10A) and the Fuse 20 (15A). • Are the fuses OK? → **Yes** GO to **G2**. → **No** REPAIR as necessary. TEST the system for normal operation.

FM1129800251010X

Fig. 31 Test G: Warning Indicator Flickers/ Intermittent (Part 1 of 2). 1998–2000 Continental

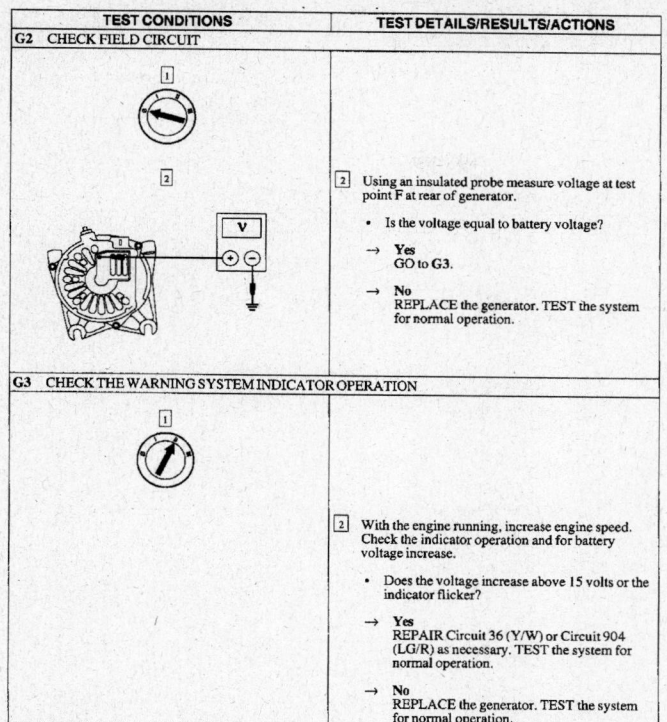

TEST CONDITIONS	TEST DETAILS/RESULTS/ACTIONS
G2 CHECK FIELD CIRCUIT	
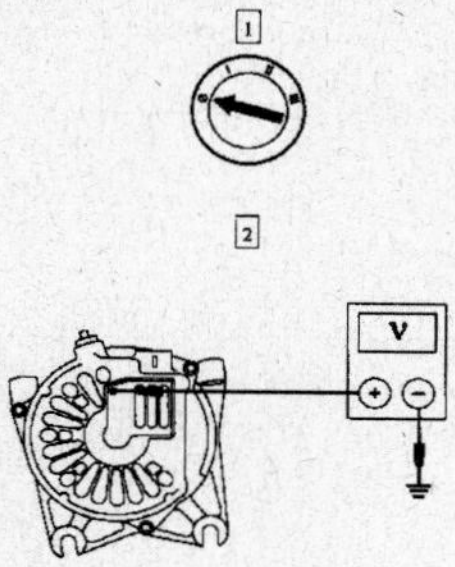	2 Using an insulated probe measure voltage at test point F at rear of generator. • Is the voltage equal to battery voltage? → **Yes** GO to **G3**. → **No** REPLACE the generator. TEST the system for normal operation.
G3 CHECK THE WARNING SYSTEM INDICATOR OPERATION	
	2 With the engine running, increase engine speed. Check the indicator operation and for battery voltage increase. • Does the voltage increase above 15 volts or the indicator flicker? → **Yes** REPAIR Circuit 36 (Y/W) or Circuit 904 (LG/R) as necessary. TEST the system for normal operation. → **No** REPLACE the generator. TEST the system for normal operation.

FM1129800251020X

Fig. 31 Test G: Warning Indicator Flickers/ Intermittent (Part 2 of 2). 1998–2000 Continental

TEST CONDITIONS	TEST DETAILS/RESULTS/ACTIONS
H2 CHECK BATTERY VOLTAGE	
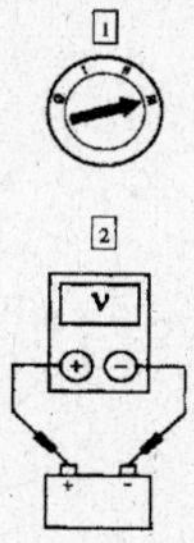	3 With the engine running turn off all accessories. Increase the engine speed and monitor the voltage at the battery. • Does battery voltage remain less than 15 volts? → **Yes** GO to **H3**. → **No** GO to **H5**.

FM1129800252020X

Fig. 32 Test H: System Overcharges, Battery Voltage Greater Than 15.5 Volts (Part 2 of 4). 1998–2000 Continental

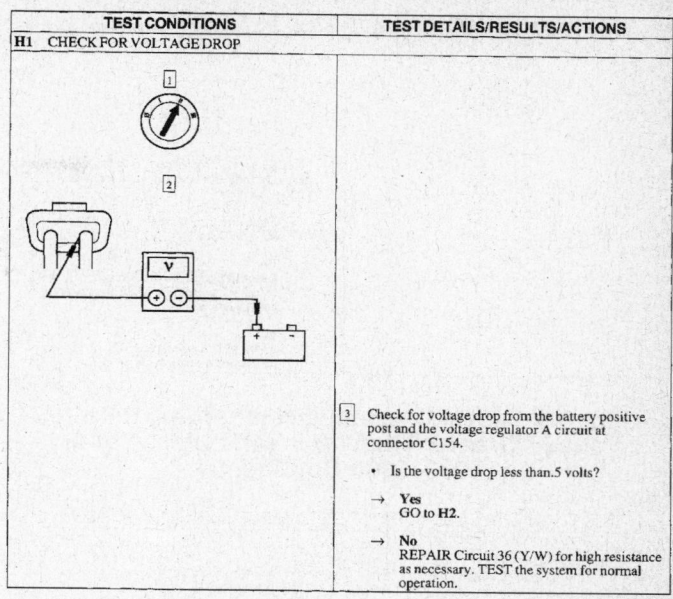

TEST CONDITIONS	TEST DETAILS/RESULTS/ACTIONS
H1 CHECK FOR VOLTAGE DROP	
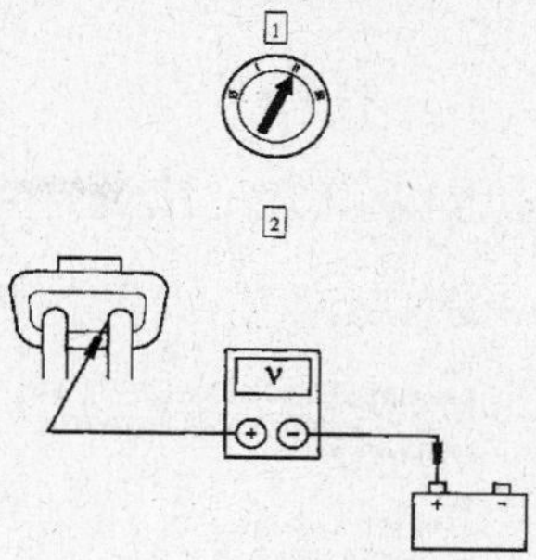	3 Check for voltage drop from the battery positive post and the voltage regulator A circuit at connector C154. • Is the voltage drop less than.5 volts? → **Yes** GO to **H2**. → **No** REPAIR Circuit 36 (Y/W) for high resistance as necessary. TEST the system for normal operation.

FM1129800252010X

Fig. 32 Test H: System Overcharges, Battery Voltage Greater Than 15.5 Volts (Part 1 of 4). 1998–2000 Continental

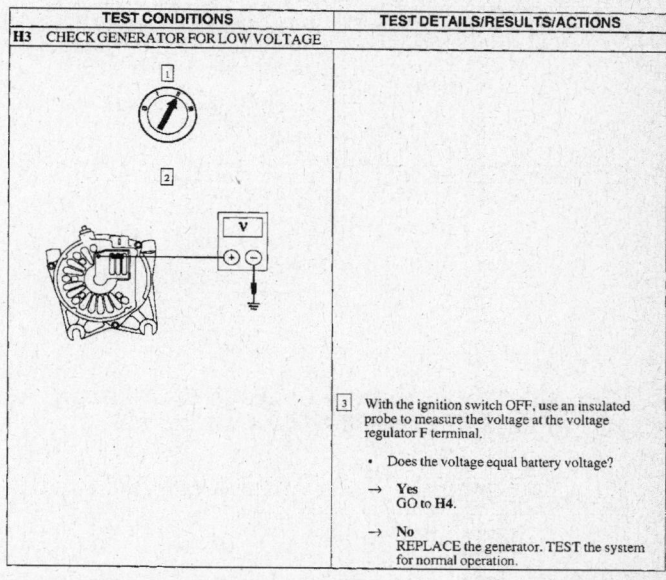

TEST CONDITIONS	TEST DETAILS/RESULTS/ACTIONS
H3 CHECK GENERATOR FOR LOW VOLTAGE	
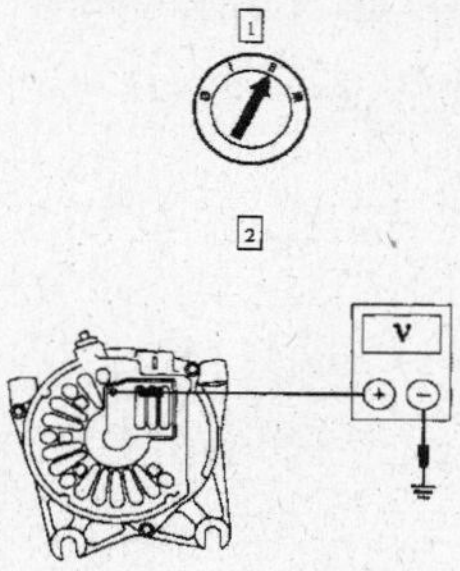	3 With the ignition switch OFF, use an insulated probe to measure the voltage at the voltage regulator F terminal. • Does the voltage equal battery voltage? → **Yes** GO to **H4**. → **No** REPLACE the generator. TEST the system for normal operation.

FM1129800252030X

Fig. 32 Test H: System Overcharges, Battery Voltage Greater Than 15.5 Volts (Part 3 of 4). 1998–2000 Continental

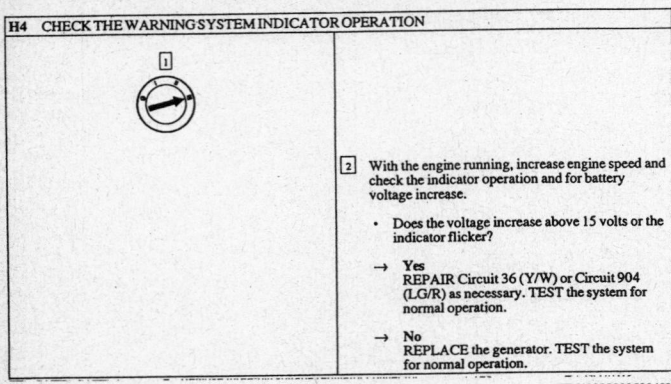

TEST CONDITIONS	TEST DETAILS/RESULTS/ACTIONS
H4 CHECK THE WARNING SYSTEM INDICATOR OPERATION	
1 	2 With the engine running, increase engine speed and check the indicator operation and for battery voltage increase. • Does the voltage increase above 15 volts or the indicator flicker? → **Yes** REPAIR Circuit 36 (Y/W) or Circuit 904 (LG/R) as necessary. TEST the system for normal operation. → **No** REPLACE the generator. TEST the system for normal operation.

FM1129800252040X

Fig. 32 Test H: System Overcharges, Battery Voltage Greater Than 15.5 Volts (Part 4 of 4). 1998–2000 Continental

TEST CONDITIONS	TEST DETAILS/RESULTS/ACTIONS
J3 CHECK BATTERY MOUNTING	
	1 Make sure the battery is properly mounted and level in the battery tray. • Is the battery properly mounted? → **Yes** GO to **J4**. → **No** REPAIR as necessary. TEST the system for normal operation.
J4 CHECK FOR BATTERY CONTACT	
	1 Make sure that there are no fasteners or other parts contacting the battery case causing excess pressure. • Is there anything contacting the battery case? → **Yes** REPAIR as necessary. TEST the system for normal operation. → **No** GO to **J5**.
J5 CHECK BATTERY CASE FOR DAMAGE	
	1 Check the battery case for defects such as cracks or poor seals. • Is the battery OK? → **Yes** System is OK. Test the system for normal operation. → **No** REPLACE the battery. TEST the system for normal operation.

FM1129800253020X

Fig. 33 Test J: Battery Leakage Or Damage (Part 2 of 2). 1998–2000 Continental

TEST CONDITIONS	TEST DETAILS/RESULTS/ACTIONS
K1 CHECK BATTERY VOLTAGE	
1  2 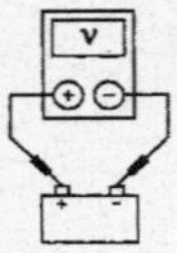	3 With the engine running turn off all accessories. Increase the engine speed and monitor the voltage at the battery. • Is the battery voltage more than 15 volts? → **Yes** Go to Pinpoint Test H. → **No** GO to **K2**.

FM1129800254010X

Fig. 34 Test K: Voltage Gauge Reads High Or Low (Part 1 of 2). 1998–2000 Continental

TEST CONDITIONS	TEST DETAILS/RESULTS/ACTIONS
J1 CHECK FOR ACID LEAKAGE DAMAGE	
	1 Check for Acid damage to vehicle harness and to the body. • REPAIR damaged areas as necessary. → **Yes** REPAIR damaged areas as necessary. → **No** GO to **J2**.
J2 CHECK CHARGING SYSTEM FOR OVERCHARGING	
1  2 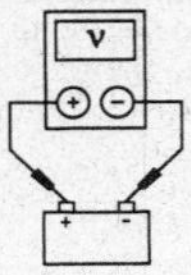	3 With the engine running turn off all accessories. Increase the engine speed and monitor the voltage at the battery. • Does battery voltage increase more than 15 volts? → **Yes** Go to Pinpoint Test H. → **No** GO to **J3**.

FM1129800253010X

Fig. 33 Test J: Battery Leakage Or Damage (Part 1 of 2). 1998–2000 Continental

TEST CONDITIONS	TEST DETAILS/RESULTS/ACTIONS
K2 CHECK VOLTAGE GAUGE OPERATION	
1 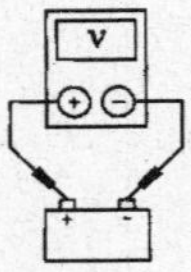	2 With the engine running monitor the voltage gauge reading and the battery voltage. • Are the voltage readings consistent? → **Yes** System is operating normally. → **No** Inspect instrument cluster.

FM1129800254020X

Fig. 34 Test K: Voltage Gauge Reads High Or Low (Part 2 of 2). 1998–2000 Continental

TEST CONDITIONS	TEST DETAILS/RESULTS/ACTIONS
L1 CHECK FOR ACCESSORY DRIVE NOISE	
	1 Check the drive belt to make sure it is properly installed and aligned. • Is the drive belt OK? → **Yes** GO to L2. → **No** REPAIR the accessory drive belt as required. RETEST the system.

FM1129800255010X

Fig. 35 Test L: Alternator Is Noisy (Part 1 of 2). 1998–2000 Continental

TEST CONDITIONS	TEST DETAILS/RESULTS/ACTIONS
L2 CHECK THE GENERATOR MOUNTING	
	1 Check the generator and generator mounting brackets for loose bolts or misalignment. • Is the generator mounted correctly? → **Yes** REPLACE the generator. RETEST the system. → **No** INSTALL the generator to specifications. RETEST the system.

FM1129800255020X

Fig. 35 Test L: Alternator Is Noisy (Part 2 of 2). 1998–2000 Continental

TEST CONDITIONS	TEST DETAILS/RESULTS/ACTIONS
M1 CHECK FOR RADIO INTERFERENCE	
1 	
	2 Tune the radio to a station where the interference is present.
3  Generator Connector C154	• Is the interference present with the generator Connector C154 removed? → **Yes** LOCATE the cause of the radio interference. RETEST the system. → **No** REPLACE the generator. RETEST the system.

FM1129800256000X

Fig. 36 Test M: Radio Interference. 1998–2000 Continental

Condition	Possible Source	Action
• System Overcharges (Battery Boils Over)	• Voltage drop in 'A', Circuit 30 (R). • Voltage drop in 'I', Circuit 15S (GN/BK). • Poor ground. • Voltage regulator. • Generator.	• GO to Pinpoint Test A.
• Indicator Lamp Stays ON, Engine Running	• Open 'A', Circuit 30 (R). • Shorted 'I', Circuit 15S (GN/BK). • Open/high resistance in 'S', Circuit 59 (GY). • Voltage regulator. • Generator.	• GO to Pinpoint Test B.
• Indicator Lamp Stays ON, Ignition Switch OFF	• Lamp, Circuit 14 (P) shorted to B+. • Improper lamp circuit wiring. • Instrument cluster.	• GO to Pinpoint Test C.
• Indicator Lamp Does Not Come ON	• Open/high resistance in 'I', Circuit 15S (GN/BK). • Burned out lamp. • Poor ground. • 'S', Circuit 59 (GY) shorted to B+. • Voltage regulator. • Generator.	• GO to Pinpoint Test D.
• Indicator Lamp Flickers/Intermittent	• Loose connection to generator, voltage regulator, or power distribution box. • Loose or poor connection in Circuit 14 (P) or 14 (P/Y). • Loose brush holder screw. • Voltage regulator. • Generator.	• GO to Pinpoint Test E.
• Generator Noisy	• Accessory drive belt. • Accessory brackets. • Bent pulley. • Generator. • Other accessories.	• GO to Pinpoint Test F.
• Radio Interference	• Voltage regulator. • Generator. • Other components.	• GO to Pinpoint Test G.
• Battery Does Not Hold a Charge	• Ignition switch OFF battery drain. • Open/voltage drop in 'B+', Circuit 30 (R). • Open/voltage drop in 'A', Circuit 30 (R). • Open/high resistance in 'I', Circuit 15S (GN/BK). • Voltage regulator. • Generator.	• GO to Pinpoint Test H.

FM1129700257000X

Fig. 37 Symptom chart. 1997 Contour & Mystique

Condition	Possible Sources	Action
• The System Does Not Charge	• Circuitry. • Voltage regulator. • Generator.	• GO to Pinpoint Test A.
• The System Overcharges	• Voltage regulator. • Circuitry. • Generator.	• GO to Pinpoint Test B.
• The Charging System Warning Indicator Stays On	• Circuitry. • Voltage regulator. • Generator. • Instrument cluster.	• GO to Pinpoint Test C.

FM1129800297010X

Fig. 38 Symptom chart (Part 1 of 2). 1998–2000 Contour & Mystique

Condition	Possible Sources	Action
• The Charging System Warning Indicator Is Inoperative	• Circuitry. • Lamp. • Voltage regulator. • Generator.	• GO to Pinpoint Test D.
• The Charging System Warning Indicator Flickers / Is Intermittent	• Circuitry. • Voltage regulator. • Generator.	• GO to Pinpoint Test E.
• The Generator Is Noisy	• Accessory drive belt. • Accessory brackets. • Pulley. • Generator.	• GO to Pinpoint Test F.
• Radio Interference	• Voltage regulator. • Generator.	• GO to Pinpoint Test G.
• The Battery Does Not Hold A Charge	• Battery. • Voltage regulator. • Generator.	• GO to Pinpoint Test H.

FM1129800297020X

Fig. 38 Symptom chart (Part 2 of 2). 1998–2000 Contour & Mystique

Test Step	Result ▶	Action to Take
A1 CHECK VOLTAGE DROP IN 'A' CIRCUIT		
• Turn ignition switch to RUN position. • Measure voltage between test point 'A' on voltage regulator and positive (+) battery post. • **Is voltage drop less than 0.25 V?**	Yes ▶ No ▶	GO to **A2**. SERVICE excess voltage drop in Circuit 30 (R). CHECK fuse and connectors in Circuit 30 (R) and SERVICE as required.
A2 CHECK VOLTAGE DROP IN 'I' CIRCUIT		
• NOTE: Voltage regulator must be connected to wiring harness for this test. Back probe generator connector C187 to measure voltage at wiring harness 'I' terminal, Circuit 15S (GN/BK). • **Is voltage greater than 1 V?**	Yes ▶ No ▶	GO to **A3**. SERVICE high resistance in Circuit 15S (GN/BK).
A3 CHECK FOR POOR GROUNDS		
• Check for poor ground connections between voltage regulator and generator, generator and engine, or engine and battery. • **Are all ground connections clean and tight?**	Yes ▶ No ▶	GO to **A4**. CLEAN or SERVICE grounds as required.
A4 CHECK FOR FIELD CIRCUIT DRAIN		
• Turn ignition switch to OFF position. • Measure voltage at test point 'F' on voltage regulator. • **Is voltage at test point 'F' equal to battery voltage?** 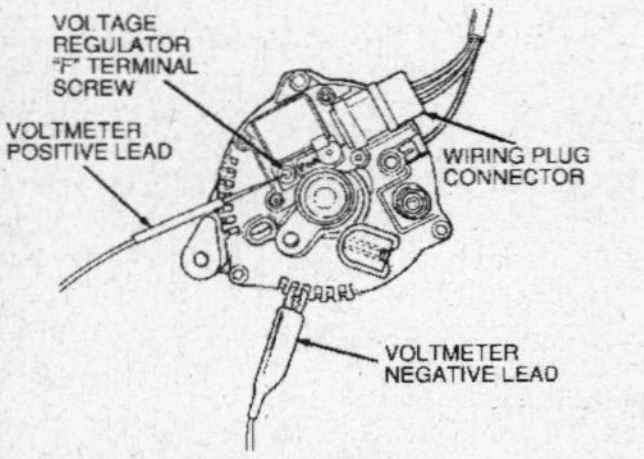	Yes ▶ No ▶	Generator is OK. REPLACE voltage regulator. GO to **A5**.
A5 CHECK FOR GROUNDED SLIP RING		
• Remove generator from vehicle. • Remove voltage regulator. • Measure resistance from each generator slip ring to the generator housing. • **Is resistance from either slip ring to housing less than 200 ohms?**	Yes ▶ No ▶	If grease or dirt has accumulated near slip rings, CLEAN slip rings and RECHECK resistance. If still less than 200 ohms, REPLACE generator. REPLACE voltage regulator.

FM1129700258000X

Fig. 39 Test A: System Overcharges. 1997 Contour & Mystique

Test Step	Result ▶	Action to Take
C1 CHECK LAMP CIRCUIT WIRING		
• Turn ignition switch to OFF position. • Remove three-pin voltage regulator connector C187. • Measure voltage at wiring harness 'I' terminal, Circuit 15S (GN/BK). • **Is voltage greater than 10 V?**	Yes ▶ No ▶	SERVICE instrument cluster. SERVICE Circuit 15S (GN/BK). Circuit should be HOT in RUN position only.

FM1129700259000X

Fig. 41 Test C: Indicator Lamp Stays On, Ignition Switch Off. 1997 Contour & Mystique

Test Step	Result ▶	Action to Take
D1 CHECK FOR OPEN 'I' CIRCUIT		
• Remove three-pin voltage regulator connector C187. • Turn ignition switch to RUN position. • Measure voltage at wiring harness 'I' terminal, Circuit 15S (GN/BK). • **Is voltage greater than 10 V?**	Yes ▶ No ▶	GO to **D2**. SERVICE open in Circuit 15S (GN/BK).
D2 CHECK FOR BURNED OUT BULB		
• Connect wiring harness 'I' terminal, Circuit 15S (GN/BK) to ground with a jumper wire. • **Is indicator lamp on?**	Yes ▶ No ▶	REMOVE jumper wire. GO to **D3**. REPLACE lamp or SERVICE high resistance in lamp socket or Circuit 15S (GN/BK).
D3 CHECK FOR POOR GROUNDS		
• Check for poor ground connections between voltage regulator and generator, generator and engine, or engine and battery. • **Are all ground connections clean and tight?**	Yes ▶ No ▶	GO to **D4**. CLEAN or SERVICE grounds as required.
D4 CHECK 'S' CIRCUIT WIRING		
• Ignition switch in RUN. • Remove one-pin 'S' connector C189 from generator. • Measure voltage at wiring harness 'S' terminal, Circuit 59 (GY). • **Is voltage greater than 10 V?**	Yes ▶ No ▶	SERVICE Circuit 59 (GY). Circuit should be HOT only when engine is running. GO to **D5**.
D5 CHECK FOR SHORTED RECTIFIER		
• Ignition switch in RUN. • Measure voltage at 'S' terminal on the back of generator. • **Is voltage greater than 1 V?**	Yes ▶ No ▶	If lamp is on with one-pin 'S' connector removed, REPLACE generator. REPLACE voltage regulator.

FM1129700260000X

Fig. 42 Test D: Indicator Lamp Does Not Come On. 1997 Contour & Mystique

Test Step	Result ▶	Action to Take
B1 CHECK FOR OPEN 'A' CIRCUIT		
• Measure voltage at test point 'A' on the voltage regulator. • **Is voltage at test point 'A' equal to battery voltage?** 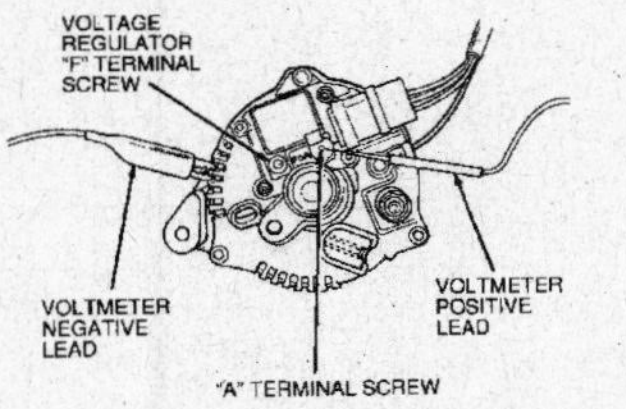	Yes ▶ No ▶	GO to **B2**. SERVICE open in Circuit 30 (R).
B2 CHECK FOR SHORTED 'I' CIRCUIT		
• Remove three-pin voltage regulator connector C187. • Turn ignition switch to RUN position. • **Is indicator lamp on?**	Yes ▶ No ▶	SERVICE short to ground in Circuit 15S (GN/BK). GO to **B3**.
B3 CHECK 'S' CIRCUIT FUNCTION		
• Install voltage regulator connector. • Remove one-pin 'S' connector C189. • Connect wiring harness 'S' terminal, Circuit 59 (GY) to positive (+) battery post using a jumper wire. • **Is indicator lamp on?**	Yes ▶ No ▶	REMOVE jumper wire. GO to **B4**. REMOVE jumper wire. GO to **B5**.
B4 CHECK FOR OPEN 'S' CIRCUIT		
• Remove three-pin voltage regulator connector C189. • Measure wiring resistance between the one-pin 'S' connector and 'S' (center) pin of voltage regulator connector. • **Is resistance greater than 5 ohms?**	Yes ▶ No ▶	SERVICE open or excess resistance in Circuit 59 (GY). CHECK for loose or bent pin in voltage regulator or connector. If OK, REPLACE voltage regulator.
B5 CHECK STATOR OUTPUT VOLTAGE		
• Reconnect voltage regulator connector. • Start engine. • Measure voltage at 'S' terminal on the back of the generator. • **Is voltage at least half of battery voltage?**	Yes ▶ No ▶	GO to **B6**. GO to Pinpoint Test H to find cause of low generator output.
B6 CHECK GENERATOR OUTPUT VOLTAGE		
• Measure voltage at B+ terminal on the back of generator with engine running at 2000 rpm and all accessories turned OFF. • **Is voltage greater than 15.5 V?**	Yes ▶ No ▶	REPLACE voltage regulator. TURN ignition switch OFF. TEST 175 amp maxi fuse for continuity. REPLACE as required. If 175 amp maxi fuse is continuous, GO to Pinpoint Test A to find cause of high output voltage.

FM1129700321000X

Fig. 40 Test B: Indicator Lamp Stays On, Engine Running. 1997 Contour & Mystique

Test Step	Result ▶	Action to Take
E1 CHECK FOR LOOSE CONNECTIONS		
• Check these connections for corrosion, loose or bent pins, or loose eyelets: — Three-pin voltage regulator connector C189. — One-pin 'S' connector C189. — Generator 'B+' eyelet. — Power distribution box eyelets. — Battery cables. • **Are all connections clean and tight?**	Yes ▶ No ▶	GO to **E2**. CLEAN or SERVICE connections as required.
E2 CHECK FOR FIELD CIRCUIT DRAIN		
• Turn ignition switch to OFF position. • Measure voltage at test point 'F' on the voltage regulator. • **Is voltage at test point 'F' equal to battery voltage?**	Yes ▶ No ▶	GO to **E3**. GO to **E5**.

FM1129700261010X

Fig. 43 Test E: Indicator Lamp Flickers/Intermittent (Part 1 of 2). 1997 Contour & Mystique

Test Step		Result	Action to Take
E3	CHECK FOR LOOSE 'A' CIRCUIT FUSE		
	• Start engine. • Check fuse IGN (20A) in power distribution box for a loose connection by wiggling fuse with engine running. • **Does indicator lamp flicker?**	Yes	SERVICE loose fuse connection.
		No	GO to **E4**.
E4	CHECK 'A' CIRCUIT CONNECTIONS		
	• With engine running, connect test point 'A' on the voltage regulator to the positive (+) battery post using a jumper wire. • **Does indicator lamp flicker?**	Yes	REPLACE voltage regulator. If concern still exists, REPLACE generator.
		No	SERVICE poor connection in Circuit 30 (R).
E5	CHECK BRUSH HOLDER SCREWS		
	• Remove generator from vehicle. • Check the brush holder screws, located on voltage regulator (test points 'F' and 'A'). • **Are the brush holder screws tight?**	Yes	GO to **E6**.
		No	Torque screws to 2.8-4.0 N·m (25-35 lb-in).
E6	CHECK FOR GROUNDED SLIP RING		
	• Remove voltage regulator. • Measure resistance from each generator slip ring to generator housing. • **Is resistance from either slip ring to housing less than 200 ohms?**	Yes	If grease or dirt has accumulated near slip rings, CLEAN slip rings and RECHECK resistance. If still less than 200 ohms, REPLACE generator.
		No	REPLACE voltage regulator.

FM1129700261020X

Fig. 43 Test E: Indicator Lamp Flickers/Intermittent (Part 2 of 2). 1997 Contour & Mystique

Test Step		Result	Action to Take
G1	VERIFY RADIO INTERFERENCE		
	• Start engine. • Tune radio to a station where interference is present. • Remove three-pin voltage regulator connector C187. • **Is interference present with connector removed?**	Yes	Locate cause of radio interference.
		No	REPLACE generator.

FM1129700263000X

Fig. 45 Test G: Radio Interference. 1997 Contour & Mystique

Test Step		Result	Action to Take
H1	CHECK BATTERY CAPACITY		
	• Perform battery capacity testing. • **Is battery capacity OK?**	Yes	GO to **H2**.
		No	REPLACE battery. GO to **H2**.
H2	CHECK FOR KEY-OFF DRAIN		
	• Turn ignition switch to OFF position. • Turn off all lamps and accessories and close doors. • Disconnect negative battery cable. • Connect an ammeter between battery ground (-) cable and negative battery post. • **Is current drain less than 100 mA?**	Yes	GO to **H3**.
		No	LOCATE cause of ignition switch OFF battery drain.
H3	CHECK FOR OPEN 'B+' CIRCUIT		
	• Measure voltage at 'B+' terminal on back of generator, Circuit 30 (R). • **Is voltage at 'B+' terminal equal to battery voltage?**	Yes	GO to **H4**.
		No	SERVICE open in Circuit 30 (R).
H4	CHECK FOR OPEN 'A' CIRCUIT		
	• Measure voltage at test point 'A' on voltage regulator. • **Is voltage at test point 'A' equal to battery voltage?**	Yes	GO to **H5**.
		No	SERVICE open in Circuit 30 (R).
H5	CHECK FOR OPEN FIELD CIRCUIT		
	• Turn ignition switch to RUN. • Measure voltage at test point 'F' on voltage regulator. • **Is voltage at test point 'F' equal to battery voltage?**	Yes	GO to **H6**.
		No	GO to **H12**.
H6	CHECK FOR OPEN 'I' CIRCUIT		
	• Turn ignition switch to RUN position. • NOTE: Voltage regulator must be connected to wiring harness for this test. Measure voltage at wiring harness 'I' terminal, Circuit 15S (GN/BK). • **Is voltage greater than 1 V?**	Yes	GO to **H7**.
		No	SERVICE open or high resistance in Circuit 15 (GN/BK).
H7	CHECK VOLTAGE DROP IN 'A' CIRCUIT		
	• Measure voltage drop between test point 'A' on voltage regulator and positive (+) battery post. • **Is voltage drop less than 0.25 V?**	Yes	GO to **H8**.
		No	SERVICE excess resistance in Circuit 30 (R). CHECK connectors in Circuit 30 (R) and SERVICE as required.
H8	CHECK FIELD TURN-ON		
	• Measure voltage at test point 'F' on voltage regulator. • **Is voltage at test point 'F' less than 2 V?**	Yes	GO to **H9**.
		No	GO to **H12**.
H9	CHECK FOR SHORTED RECTIFIER		
	• Remove one-pin 'S' connector C189 from generator. • Measure voltage between the 'S' terminal on back of generator and ground. • Measure voltage between the positive (+) battery terminal and the 'S' terminal on the back of the generator. • **Is either voltage reading greater than 1 V?**	Yes	REPLACE generator.
		No	GO to **H10**.
H10	CHECK VOLTAGE DROP IN 'B+' CIRCUIT		
	• Install 'S' connector C189. • Start engine. (Jump start engine if necessary.) • Turn headlights ON and blower on HIGH. • With engine running at 2000 rpm, measure voltage drop between the 'B+' terminal on back of generator and the positive (+) battery post. • **Is voltage drop less than 0.5 V?**	Yes	GO to **H11**.
		No	SERVICE excess voltage drop in Circuit 30 (R). CHECK connections between the battery and power distribution box.

FM1129700264010X

Fig. 46 Test H: Battery Does Not Hold A Charge (Part 1 of 2). 1997 Contour & Mystique

Test Step		Result	Action to Take
F1	CHECK FOR ACCESSORY DRIVE NOISE		
	• Check drive belt to make sure it is installed properly and is not damaged. • Check accessory mounting brackets for loose bolts or misalignment condition. • Check for a bent pulley. • **Is accessory drive OK?**	Yes	GO to **F2**.
		No	SERVICE accessory drive as required.
F2	CHECK GENERATOR MOUNTING		
	• Check generator and generator mounting brackets for loose bolts or misalignment condition. • **Is generator mounted correctly?**	Yes	GO to **F3**.
		No	INSTALL generator to specification.
F3	CHECK GENERATOR PULLEY		
	• Check generator pulley for damage (bent) or a misalignment condition. • **Is pulley OK?**	Yes	If noise is still present REPLACE generator.
		No	REPLACE generator pulley.

FM1129700262000X

Fig. 44 Test F: Alternator Is Noisy. 1997 Contour & Mystique

Test Step		Result	Action to Take
H11	CHECK FOR OPEN STATOR PHASE		
	• Connect test point 'F' on voltage regulator to negative (-) battery post using a jumper wire. • Perform the Load Test as described under Generator On-Vehicle Tests. • **Is generator output greater than the minimum output specified?**	Yes	REPLACE voltage regulator.
		No	REPLACE generator.
H12	CHECK FOR OPEN / SHORTED FIELD		
	• Remove generator from vehicle. • Remove voltage regulator. • Measure resistance between generator slip rings. • **Is resistance greater than 10 ohms or less than 1 ohm?**	Yes	REPLACE generator.
		No	CHECK for worn brushes (less than 8 mm (1/3 inch) long) or open brush leads and REPLACE if required. If OK, REPLACE voltage regulator.

FM1129700264020X

Fig. 46 Test H: Battery Does Not Hold A Charge (Part 2 of 2). 1997 Contour & Mystique

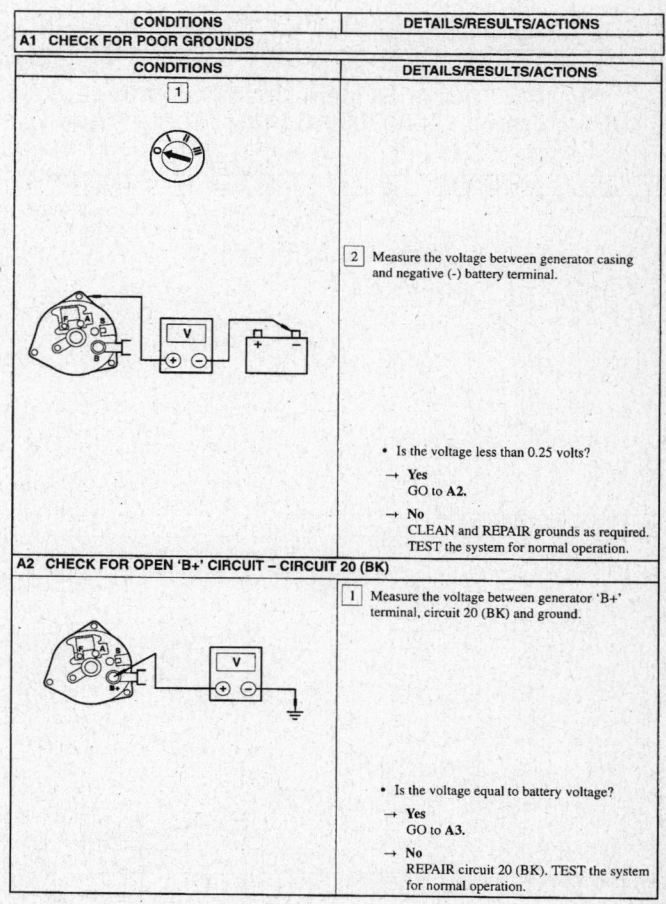

CONDITIONS	DETAILS/RESULTS/ACTIONS
A1 CHECK FOR POOR GROUNDS	
CONDITIONS	**DETAILS/RESULTS/ACTIONS**
1 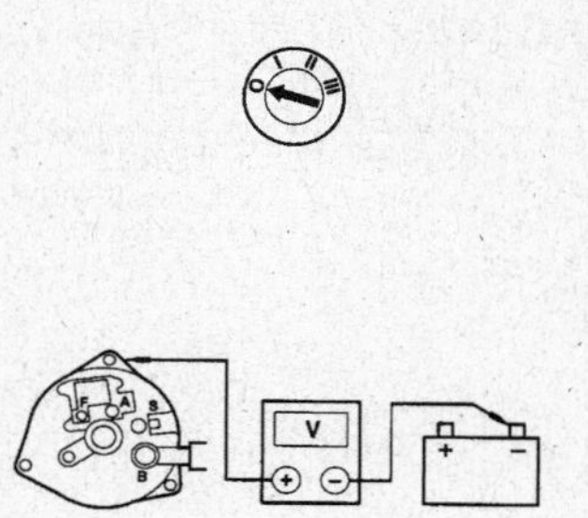	2 Measure the voltage between generator casing and negative (-) battery terminal. • Is the voltage less than 0.25 volts? → **Yes** GO to **A2**. → **No** CLEAN and REPAIR grounds as required. TEST the system for normal operation.
A2 CHECK FOR OPEN 'B+' CIRCUIT – CIRCUIT 20 (BK)	
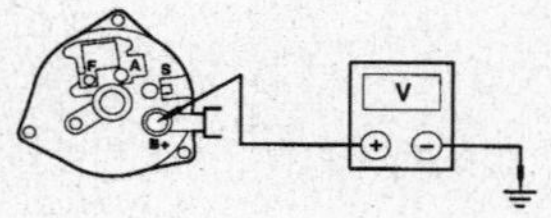	1 Measure the voltage between generator 'B+' terminal, circuit 20 (BK) and ground. • Is the voltage equal to battery voltage? → **Yes** GO to **A3**. → **No** REPAIR circuit 20 (BK). TEST the system for normal operation.

FM1129800298010X

Fig. 47 Test A: System Does Not Charge (Part 1 of 6). 1998–2000 Contour & Mystique

CONDITIONS	DETAILS/RESULTS/ACTIONS
A3 CHECK FOR OPEN 'A' CIRCUIT	
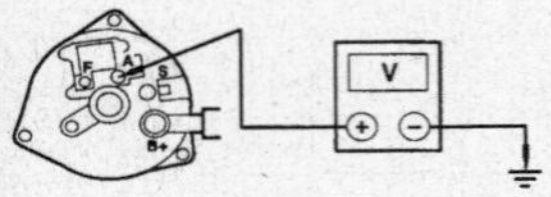	1 Measure the voltage between voltage regulator test point 'A', and ground. • Is the voltage equal to battery voltage? → **Yes** GO to **A4.** → **No** REPAIR circuit 20 (BK). TEST the system for normal operation.
A4 CHECK FOR OPEN FIELD CIRCUIT	
1 	
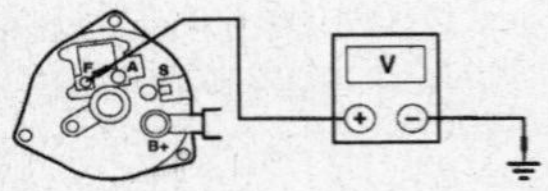	2 Measure the voltage between voltage regulator test point 'F', and ground.

FM1129800298020X

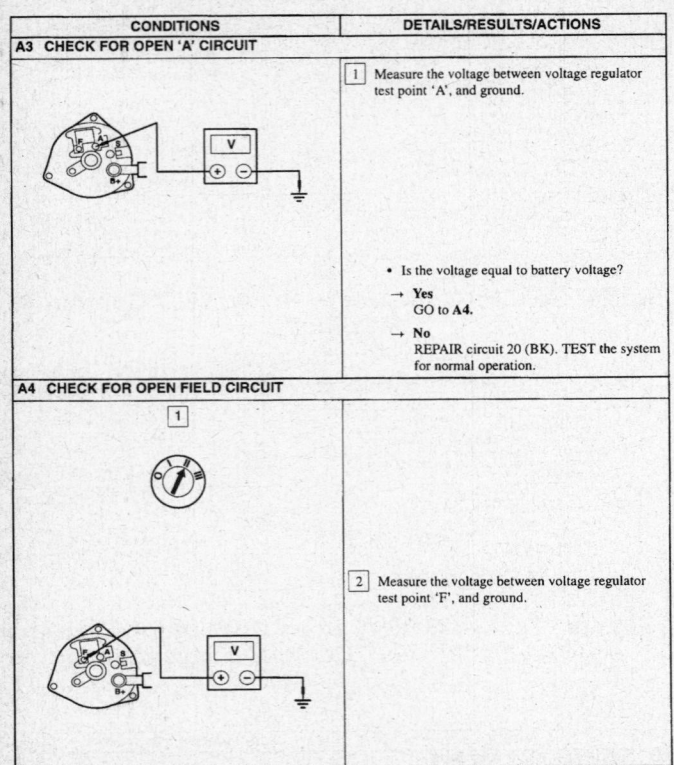

Fig. 47 Test A: System Does Not Charge (Part 2 of 6). 1998–2000 Contour & Mystique

CONDITIONS	DETAILS/RESULTS/ACTIONS
	• Is the voltage equal to battery voltage? → **Yes** GO to **A5.** → **No** REPLACE the generator. TEST the system for normal operation.
A5 CHECK CIRCUIT 15S-BA9 (GN/BK)	
NOTE: The voltage regulator must be connected this test.	
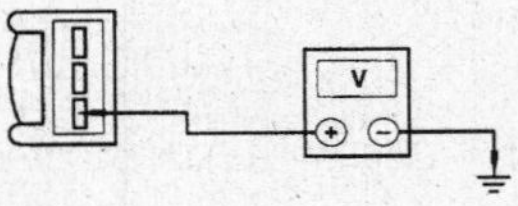	1 Measure the voltage between the rear voltage regulator C1885a-1, circuit 15S-BA9 (GN/BK), and ground. • Is the voltage greater than 1 volt? → **Yes** GO to **A6.** → **No** REPAIR circuit 15S-BA9 (GN/BK). TEST the system for normal operation.
A6 CHECK VOLTAGE DROP IN 'A' CIRCUIT	
1 	

FM1129800298030X

Fig. 47 Test A: System Does Not Charge (Part 3 of 6). 1998–2000 Contour & Mystique

CONDITIONS	DETAILS/RESULTS/ACTIONS
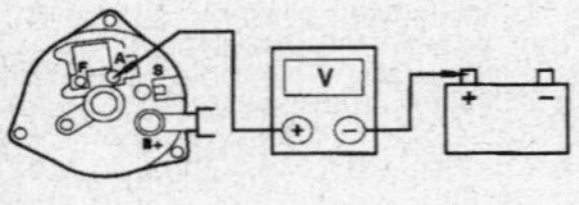	2 Measure the voltage between voltage regulator test point 'A', and the positive (+) battery terminals. • Is the voltage less than 0.25 volt? → **Yes** GO to **A7.** → **No** REPAIR circuit 20 (BK). TEST the system for normal operation.
A7 CHECK FIELD TURN ON	
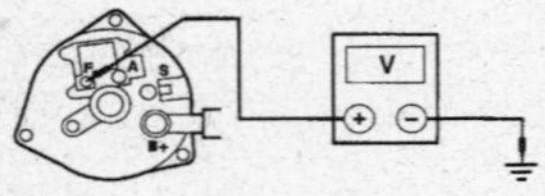	1 Measure the voltage between voltage regulator test point 'F', and ground. • Is the voltage less than 2 volts? → **Yes** GO to **A8.** → **No** REPLACE the generator. TEST the system for normal operation.
A8 CHECK FOR SHORTED RECTIFIER	

FM1129800298040X

Fig. 47 Test A: System Does Not Charge (Part 4 of 6). 1998–2000 Contour & Mystique

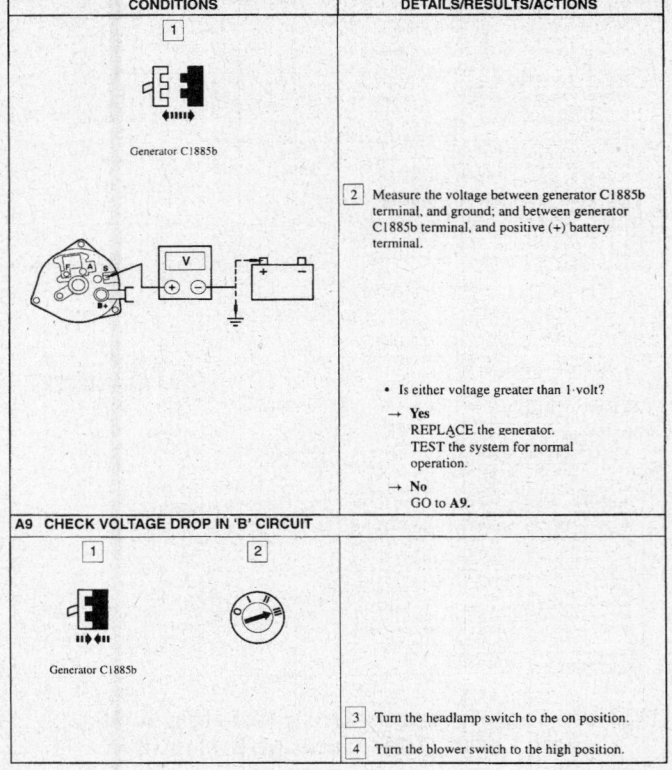

CONDITIONS	DETAILS/RESULTS/ACTIONS
1  Generator C1885b	
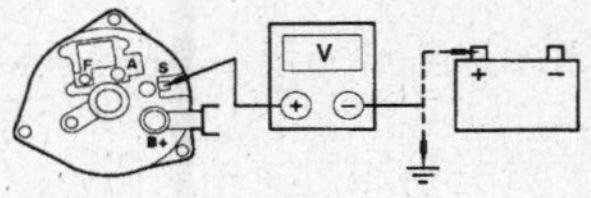	2 Measure the voltage between generator C1885b terminal, and ground; and between generator C1885b terminal, and positive (+) battery terminal. • Is either voltage greater than 1 volt? → **Yes** REPLACE the generator. TEST the system for normal operation. → **No** GO to **A9.**
A9 CHECK VOLTAGE DROP IN 'B' CIRCUIT	
1  Generator C1885b 2 	3 Turn the headlamp switch to the on position. 4 Turn the blower switch to the high position.

FM1129800298050X

Fig. 47 Test A: System Does Not Charge (Part 5 of 6). 1998–2000 Contour & Mystique

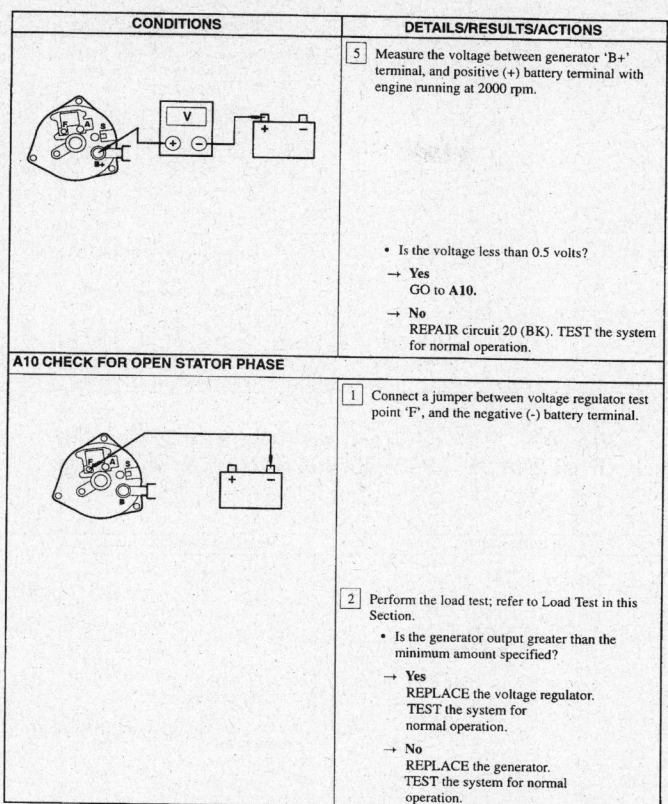

CONDITIONS	DETAILS/RESULTS/ACTIONS
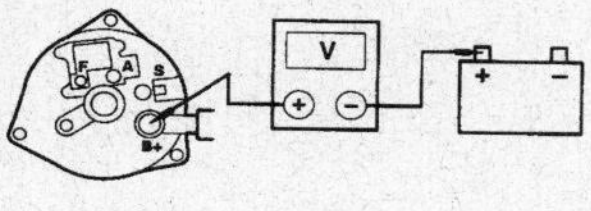	5 Measure the voltage between generator 'B+' terminal, and positive (+) battery terminal with engine running at 2000 rpm. • Is the voltage less than 0.5 volts? → **Yes** GO to **A10.** → **No** REPAIR circuit 20 (BK). TEST the system for normal operation.
A10 CHECK FOR OPEN STATOR PHASE	
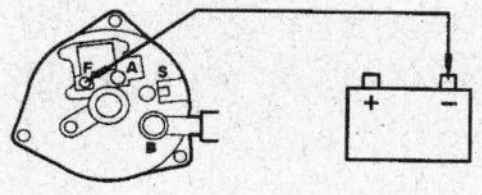	1 Connect a jumper between voltage regulator test point 'F', and the negative (-) battery terminal.
	2 Perform the load test; refer to Load Test in this Section. • Is the generator output greater than the minimum amount specified? → **Yes** REPLACE the voltage regulator. TEST the system for normal operation. → **No** REPLACE the generator. TEST the system for normal operation.

FM1129800298060X

Fig. 47 Test A: System Does Not Charge (Part 6 of 6). 1998–2000 Contour & Mystique

CONDITIONS	DETAILS/RESULTS/ACTIONS
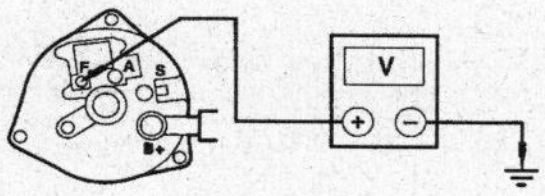	4 Measure the voltage between voltage regulator test point 'F', and ground. • Is the voltage equal to the battery voltage? → **Yes** REPLACE the voltage regulator. TEST the system for normal operation. → **No** REPAIR circuit 20 (BK). TEST the system for normal operation.

FM1129800299020X

Fig. 48 Test B: System Overcharges (Part 2 of 2). 1998–2000 Contour & Mystique

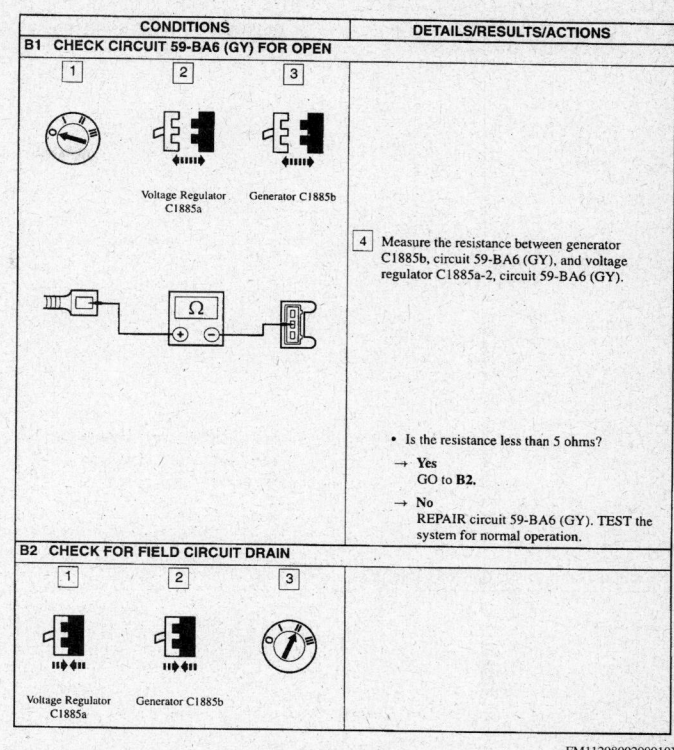

CONDITIONS	DETAILS/RESULTS/ACTIONS
B1 CHECK CIRCUIT 59-BA6 (GY) FOR OPEN	
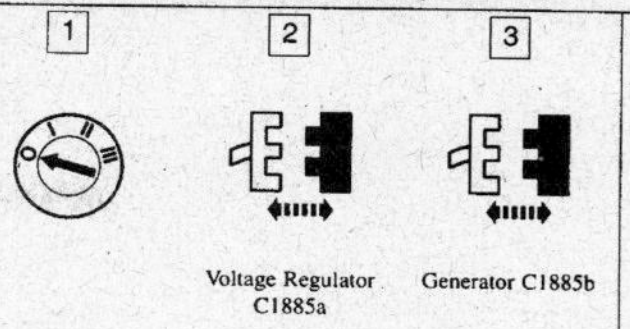	
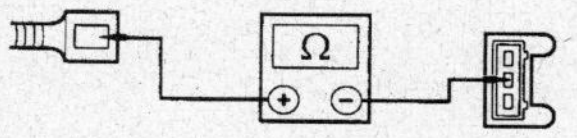	4 Measure the resistance between generator C1885b, circuit 59-BA6 (GY), and voltage regulator C1885a-2, circuit 59-BA6 (GY). • Is the resistance less than 5 ohms? → **Yes** GO to **B2.** → **No** REPAIR circuit 59-BA6 (GY). TEST the system for normal operation.
B2 CHECK FOR FIELD CIRCUIT DRAIN	
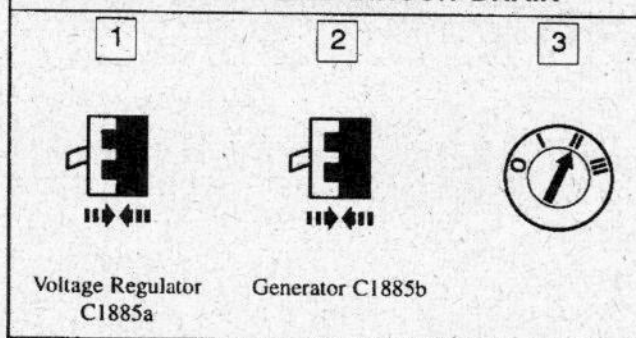	

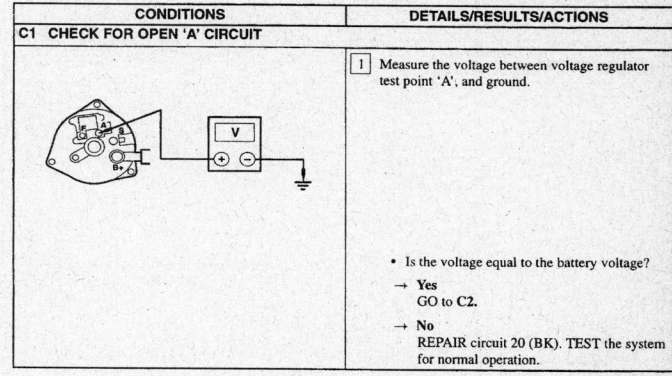

FM1129800299010X

Fig. 48 Test B: System Overcharges (Part 1 of 2). 1998–2000 Contour & Mystique

CONDITIONS	DETAILS/RESULTS/ACTIONS
C1 CHECK FOR OPEN 'A' CIRCUIT	
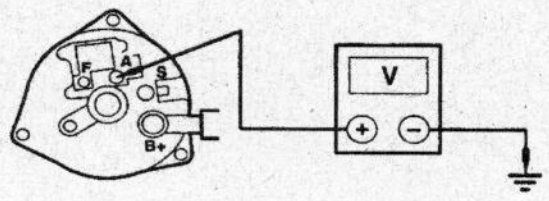	1 Measure the voltage between voltage regulator test point 'A', and ground. • Is the voltage equal to the battery voltage? → **Yes** GO to **C2.** → **No** REPAIR circuit 20 (BK). TEST the system for normal operation.

FM1129800300010X

Fig. 49 Test C: Warning Indicator Stays On (Part 1 of 3). 1998–2000 Contour & Mystique

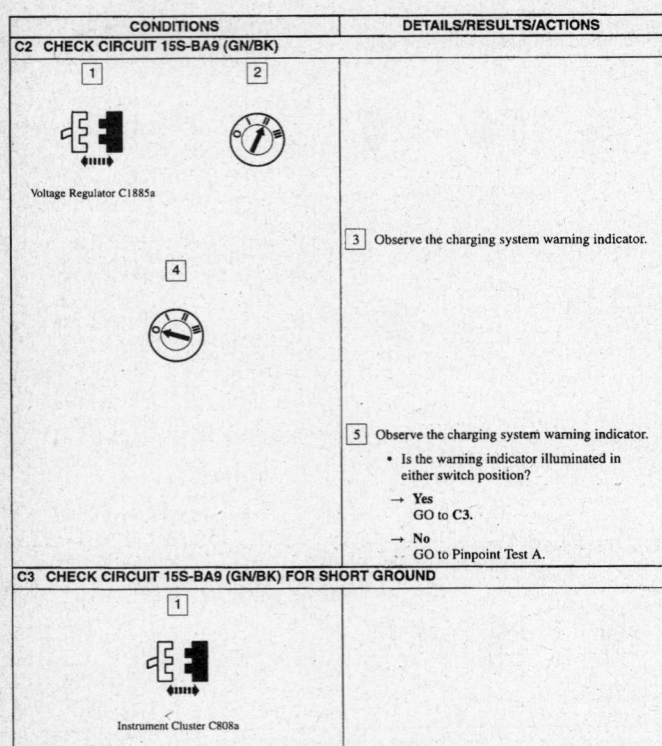

CONDITIONS	DETAILS/RESULTS/ACTIONS
C2 CHECK CIRCUIT 15S-BA9 (GN/BK)	
1  Voltage Regulator C1885a	
2 	
	3 Observe the charging system warning indicator.
4 	
	5 Observe the charging system warning indicator. • Is the warning indicator illuminated in either switch position? → **Yes** GO to **C3.** → **No** GO to Pinpoint Test A.
C3 CHECK CIRCUIT 15S-BA9 (GN/BK) FOR SHORT GROUND	
1  Instrument Cluster C808a	

FM1129800300020X

Fig. 49 Test C: Warning Indicator Stays On (Part 2 of 3). 1998–2000 Contour & Mystique

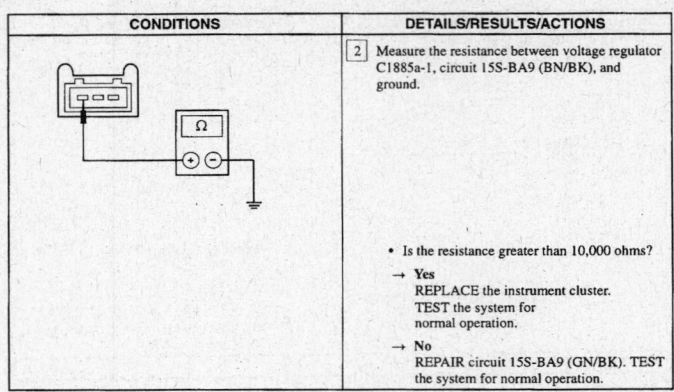

CONDITIONS	DETAILS/RESULTS/ACTIONS
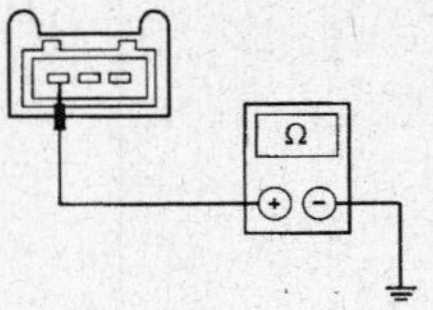	2 Measure the resistance between voltage regulator C1885a-1, circuit 15S-BA9 (BN/BK), and ground. • Is the resistance greater than 10,000 ohms? → **Yes** REPLACE the instrument cluster. TEST the system for normal operation. → **No** REPAIR circuit 15S-BA9 (GN/BK). TEST the system for normal operation.

FM1129800300030X

Fig. 49 Test C: Warning Indicator Stays On (Part 3 of 3). 1998–2000 Contour & Mystique

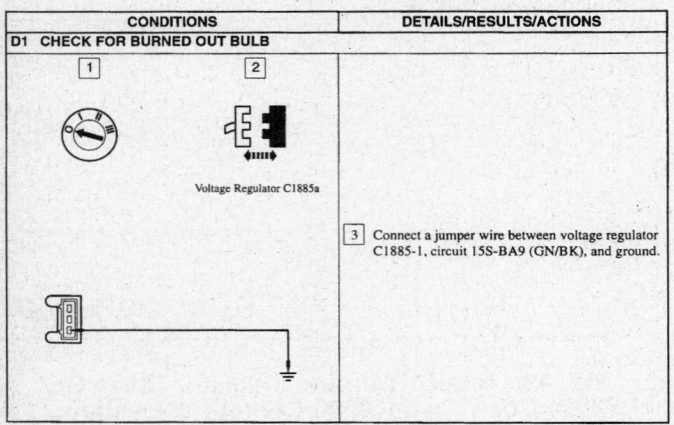

CONDITIONS	DETAILS/RESULTS/ACTIONS
D1 CHECK FOR BURNED OUT BULB	
1 	
2  Voltage Regulator C1885a	
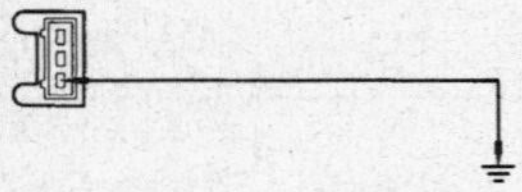	3 Connect a jumper wire between voltage regulator C1885-1, circuit 15S-BA9 (GN/BK), and ground.

FM1129800301010X

Fig. 50 Test D: Warning Indicator Is Inoperative (Part 1 of 4). 1998–2000 Contour & Mystique

CONDITIONS	DETAILS/RESULTS/ACTIONS
4 	• Does the charging system warning indicator illuminate? → **Yes** GO to **D2.** → **No** GO to **D5.**
D2 CHECK GENERATOR GROUND	
1 	
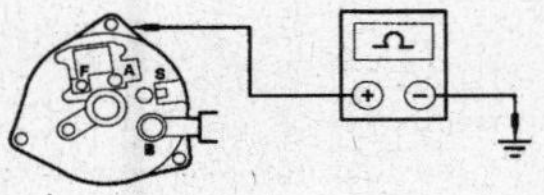	2 Measure the resistance between the generator casing and ground. • Is the resistance less than 5 ohms? → **Yes** GO to **D3.** → **No** CLEAN and REPAIR grounds as necessary. TEST the system for normal operation.

FM1129800301020X

Fig. 50 Test D: Warning Indicator Is Inoperative (Part 2 of 4). 1998–2000 Contour & Mystique

CONDITIONS	DETAILS/RESULTS/ACTIONS
D3 CHECK CIRCUIT 59-BA6 (GY) FOR SHORT TO BATTERY	
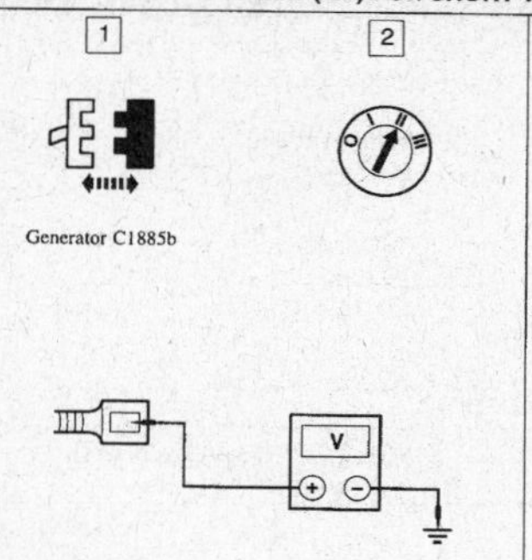	3 Measure the voltage between generator C1885b, circuit 59-BA6 (GY), and ground. • Is any voltage indicated? → **Yes** REPAIR circuit 59-BA6 (GY). TEST the system for normal operation. → **No** GO to **D4.**
D4 CHECK FOR SHORTED RECTIFIER	
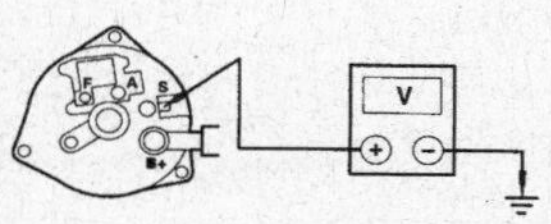	1 Measure the voltage between generator C1885b terminal, and ground.

FM1129800301030X

Fig. 50 Test D: Warning Indicator Is Inoperative (Part 3 of 4). 1998–2000 Contour & Mystique

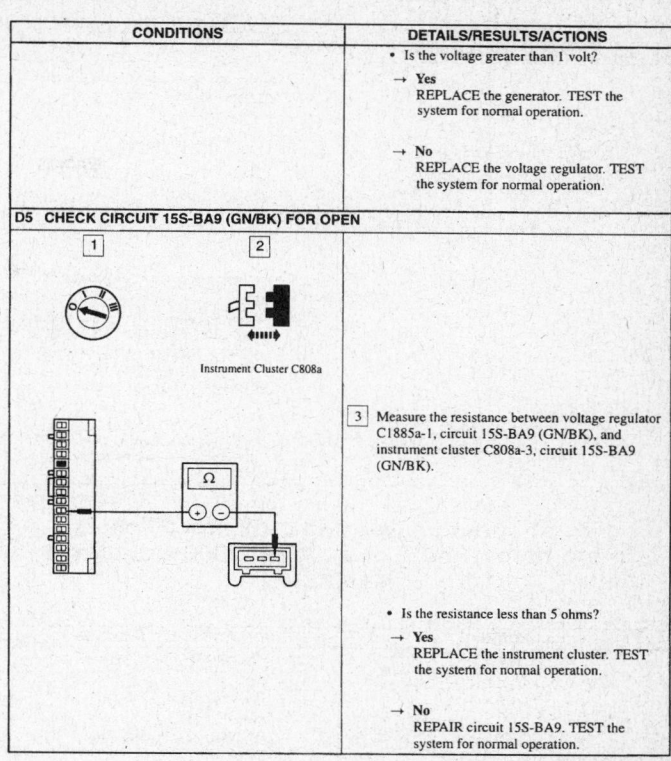

CONDITIONS	DETAILS/RESULTS/ACTIONS
	• Is the voltage greater than 1 volt? → **Yes** REPLACE the generator. TEST the system for normal operation. → **No** REPLACE the voltage regulator. TEST the system for normal operation.
D5 CHECK CIRCUIT 15S-BA9 (GN/BK) FOR OPEN	
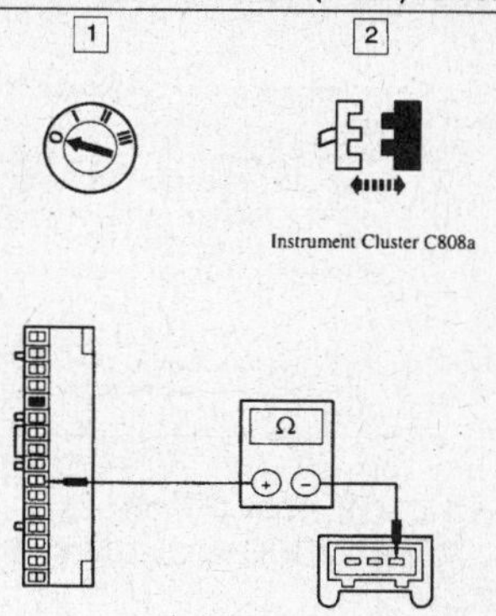	3 Measure the resistance between voltage regulator C1885a-1, circuit 15S-BA9 (GN/BK), and instrument cluster C808a-3, circuit 15S-BA9 (GN/BK). • Is the resistance less than 5 ohms? → **Yes** REPLACE the instrument cluster. TEST the system for normal operation. → **No** REPAIR circuit 15S-BA9. TEST the system for normal operation.

FM1129800301040X

Fig. 50 Test D: Warning Indicator Is Inoperative (Part 4 of 4). 1998–2000 Contour & Mystique

CONDITIONS	DETAILS/RESULTS/ACTIONS
E1 CHECK FOR FIELD CIRCUIT DRAIN	
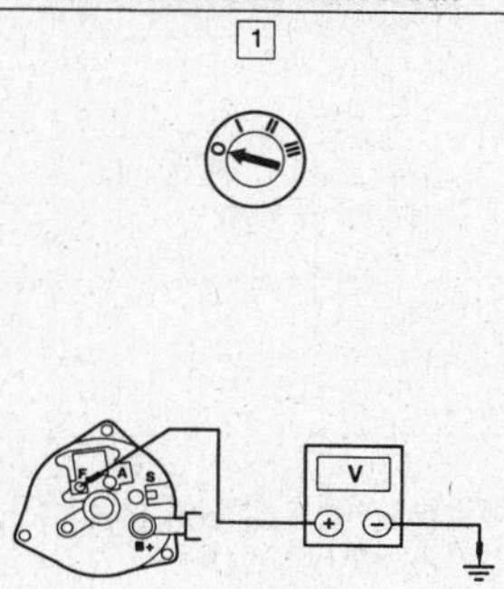	2 Measure the voltage between voltage regulator test point 'F', and ground. • Is the voltage equal to battery voltage? → **Yes** GO to **E2.** → **No** GO to **E3.**
E2 CHECK 'A' CIRCUIT CONNECTIONS	
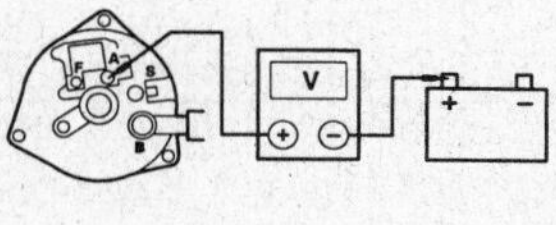	1 With the engine running connect a jump wire between test point 'A' on the voltage regulator and the positive (+) battery post.

FM1129800302010X

Fig. 51 Test E: Warning Indicator Flickers/ Intermittent (Part 1 of 3). 1998–2000 Contour & Mystique

CONDITIONS	DETAILS/RESULTS/ACTIONS
	• Does the charging system warning indicator flicker? → **Yes** REPLACE the voltage regulator. TEST the system for normal operation. If concern still exits, REPLACE the generator. TEST the system for normal operation. → **No** REPAIR circuit 20 (BK) TEST the system for normal operation.
E3 CHECK FOR LOOSE BRUSH HOLDER SCREWS	
	1 Remove the generator. 2 Check the brush holder screws located on voltage regulator test points 'A' and 'F'. • Are the brush holder screws tight? → **Yes** GO to **E4.** → **No** TIGHTEN the screws to 3.0 Nm. TEST the system for normal operation.

FM1129800302020X

Fig. 51 Test E: Warning Indicator Flickers/ Intermittent (Part 2 of 3). 1998–2000 Contour & Mystique

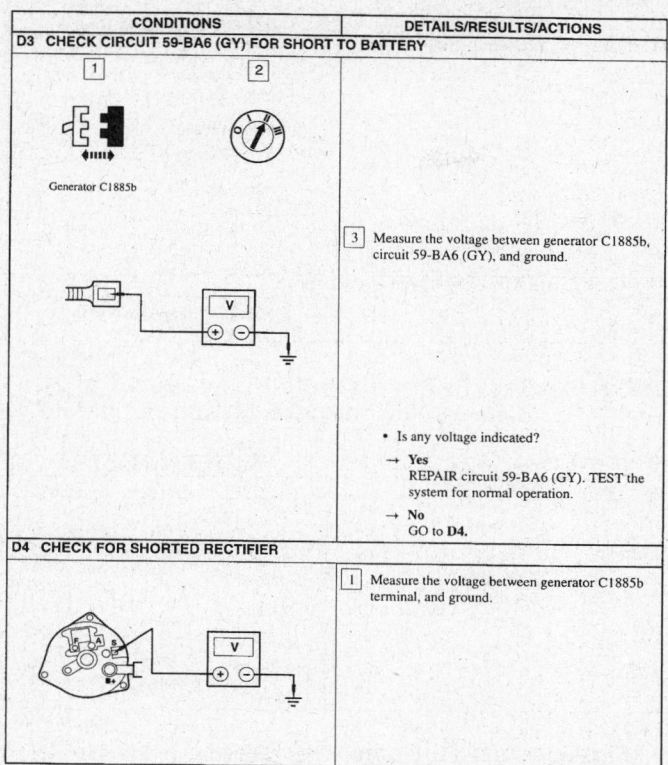

CONDITIONS	DETAILS/RESULTS/ACTIONS
E4 CHECK THE SLIP RINGS FOR SHORT TO GROUND	
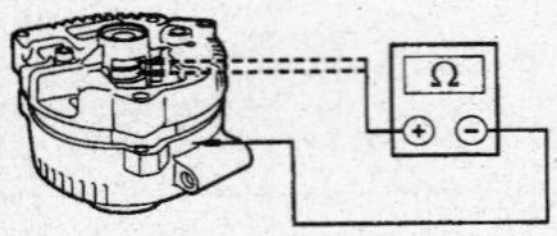	1 Measure the resistance between each generator slip ring and the generator casing. • Are the resistances less than 200 ohms? → **Yes** If grease or dirt has accumulated near slip rings, CLEAN the slip ring and CHECK resistance. If still less than 200 ohms REPLACE the generator. TEST the system for normal operation. → **No** REPLACE the voltage regulator. TEST the system for normal operation.

FM1129800302030X

Fig. 51 Test E: Warning Indicator Flickers/ Intermittent (Part 3 of 3). 1998–2000 Contour & Mystique

CONDITIONS	DETAILS/RESULTS/ACTIONS
	• Is the generator installed properly? → **Yes** GO to **F3.** → **No** INSTALL the generator correctly. TEST the system for normal operation.
F3 CHECK GENERATOR PULLEY	
	1 Check the generator pulley for damage and correct alignment. • Is the generator pulley OK? → **Yes** REPLACE the generator. TEST the ection system for normal operation. → **No** REPLACE the generator pulley. TEST the system for normal operation.

FM1129800303020X

Fig. 52 Test F: Alternator Is Noisy (Part 2 of 2). 1998–2000 Contour & Mystique

CONDITIONS	DETAILS/RESULTS/ACTIONS
H1 CHECK BATTERY CAPACITY	
	1 Perform battery capacity test. • Is the battery capacity OK? → **Yes** GO to **H2.** → **No** REPLACE the battery. TEST the system for normal operation.
H2 CHECK FOR KEY-OFF CURRENT DRAIN	
	1 Perform the battery drain component test. • Is the current drain OK? → **Yes** GO to **H3.** → **No** RETURN to the component tests to find the cause of key-off battery drain. TEST the system for normal operation.

FM1129800305010X

Fig. 54 Test H: Battery Does Not Hold A Charge (Part 1 of 2). 1998–2000 Contour & Mystique

CONDITIONS	DETAILS/RESULTS/ACTIONS
F1 CHECK FOR ACCESSORY DRIVE NOISE	
	1 Check the accessory drive for the following: – Correct drive belt installation. – Damaged pulley. • Is the accessory drive OK? → **Yes** GO to **F2.** → **No** REPAIR as required. TEST the system for normal operation.
F2 CHECK GENERATOR FOR PROPER INSTALLATION	
	1 Check generator and mounting brackets for proper alignment and installation.

FM1129800303010X

Fig. 52 Test F: Alternator Is Noisy (Part 1 of 2). 1998–2000 Contour & Mystique

CONDITIONS	DETAILS/RESULTS/ACTIONS
G1 VERIFY RADIO INTERFERENCE	
1 	2 Tune the radio to a station where interference is present.

FM1129800304010X

Fig. 53 Test G: Radio Interference (Part 1 of 2). 1998–2000 Contour & Mystique

CONDITIONS	DETAILS/RESULTS/ACTIONS
3 4 5 	• Is interference present with the voltage regulator disconnected? → **Yes** INSPECT audio entertainment system. → **No** REPLACE the generator. TEST the system for normal operation.

FM1129800304020X

Fig. 53 Test G: Radio Interference (Part 2 of 2). 1998–2000 Contour & Mystique

CONDITIONS	DETAILS/RESULTS/ACTIONS
H3 CHECK THE GENERATOR	
	1 Perform the generator base voltage and no-load test. • Is the generator output voltage within the specified range? → **Yes** REPLACE the battery. TEST the system for normal operation. → **No** GO to Pinpoint Test A.

FM1129800305020X

Fig. 54 Test H: Battery Does Not Hold A Charge (Part 2 of 2). 1998–2000 Contour & Mystique

Condition	Possible Source	Action
• System Does Not Charge	• Circuitry. • Voltage regulator. • Generator. • Battery. • Battery connections. • Drive belt.	• GO to Pinpoint Test A.
• System Overcharges (Battery Boils Over)	• Circuitry. • Poor ground. • Voltage regulator. • Generator.	• GO to Pinpoint Test B.
• Indicator Lamp Stays ON, Engine Running	• Circuitry. • Voltage regulator. • Generator.	• GO to Pinpoint Test C.
• Indicator Lamp Stays ON, Ignition Switch OFF	• Circuitry. • Instrument cluster.	• GO to Pinpoint Test D.
• Indicator Lamp Does Not Come On	• Circuitry. • Burned out lamp. • Poor ground. • Voltage regulator. • Generator.	• GO to Pinpoint Test E.
• Indicator Lamp Flickers / Intermittent	• Loose connection to generator or power distribution box. • Circuitry. • Loose brush holder screw. • Voltage regulator. • Generator.	• GO to Pinpoint Test F.
• Generator Noisy	• Accessory drive belt. • Accessory brackets. • Bent pulley. • Generator. • Other accessories.	• GO to Pinpoint Test G.
• Radio Interference	• Voltage regulator. • Generator. • Other components.	• GO to Pinpoint Test H.

FM1129700200000X

Fig. 55 Symptom chart. Thunderbird & 1997 Cougar

Test Step		Result ▶	Action to Take
A5	CHECK BATTERY		
	• Perform the Battery Capacity Testing. • **Is the battery capacity OK?**	Yes ▶ No ▶	GO to **A6.** REPLACE battery.
A6	CHECK FOR KEY-OFF DRAIN		
	• Perform Battery Drain Testing as described. • **Is current drain less than 50 mA?**	Yes ▶ No ▶	GO to **A7.** GO to Drain Testing in Component Tests to find cause of ignition switch-OFF battery drain.
A7	CHECK FOR OPEN B+ CIRCUIT		
	• Measure voltage at B+ terminal on back of generator, Circuit 38 (BK/O). • **Is voltage at B+ terminal equal to battery voltage?**	Yes ▶ No ▶	GO to **A8.** SERVICE open in Circuit 38 (BK/O).
A8	CHECK FOR OPEN A CIRCUIT		
	• Measure voltage at terminal A on the voltage regulator. • **Is voltage equal to battery voltage?**	Yes ▶ No ▶	GO to **A9.** CHECK Fuse 11 (15A) in Circuit 36 (Y/W) and REPLACE if required. If OK, SERVICE open in Circuit 36 (Y/W).
A9	CHECK FOR OPEN I CIRCUIT		
	• Turn ignition switch to RUN. • NOTE: voltage regulator must be connected to wiring harness for this test. Measure voltage at connector C101 I terminal, Circuit 904 (LG/R). • **Is voltage greater than 1 V?**	Yes ▶ No ▶	GO to **A10.** SERVICE open or high resistance in Circuit 904 (LG/R).
A10	CHECK VOLTAGE DROP IN A CIRCUIT		
	• Measure voltage drop between test point A on voltage regulator and positive (+) battery post. • **Is voltage drop less than 0.25 V?**	Yes ▶ No ▶	GO to **A11.** SERVICE excess voltage drop in Circuit 36 (Y/W). CHECK Fusible link (18GA) (15A) and connectors in Circuit 36 (Y/W). SERVICE as required.
A11	CHECK FOR SHORTED RECTIFIER		
	• Remove one-pin S connector C102 from generator. • Measure voltage between the S terminal on back of generator and ground. • Measure voltage between positive (+) battery terminal and S terminal on back of generator. • **Is either voltage reading greater than 1 V?**	Yes ▶ No ▶	REPLACE generator. RECONNECT one-pin S connector. GO to **A12.**
A12	CHECK VOLTAGE DROP IN B+ CIRCUIT		
	• Turn ignition switch to RUN. • Turn headlamps ON and set blower on HIGH. • With engine running at 2000 rpm, measure voltage drop between the B+ terminal on back of generator and positive (+) battery post. • **Is voltage drop less than 0.5 V?**	Yes ▶ No ▶	GO to **A13.** SERVICE excess voltage drop in Circuit 38 (BK/O). CHECK Mega Fuse (175A) in Circuit 38 (BK/O) and the connections between battery and power distribution box.
A13	CHECK FOR OPEN/SHORTED FIELD		
	• Remove generator from vehicle. • Remove voltage regulator. • Measure resistance between the generator slip rings. • **Is resistance greater than 10 ohms OR less than 1 ohm?**	Yes ▶ No ▶	REPLACE generator. REPLACE voltage regulator. RETEST system.

FM1129700201020X

Fig. 56 Test A: System Does Not Charge (Part 2 of 2). Thunderbird & 1997 Cougar

Test Step		Result ▶	Action to Take
A1	CHECK BATTERY CONNECTIONS		
	• Inspect battery cables for loose or corroded connections. • Inspect battery for corrosion. • **Are battery cables clean, tight and free from corrosion?**	Yes ▶ No ▶	GO to **A2.** SERVICE battery and cables as necessary. RESTORE vehicle. RETEST system.
A2	CHECK DRIVE BELT TENSION		
	• Perform drive belt adjustment procedure. • **Is the drive belt adjusted properly?**	Yes ▶ No ▶	GO to **A3.** ADJUST or REPLACE drive belt.
A3	LOOSE BATTERY POST		
	• Check for loose battery posts. • **Are posts OK?**	Yes ▶ No ▶	GO to **A4.** REPLACE battery.
A4	CRACKED BATTERY COVER		
	• Remove battery hold-down clamps and shields. • Check for broken/cracked case or battery cover. • **Are case and cover OK?**	Yes ▶ No ▶	GO to **A5.** REPLACE battery.

FM1129700201010X

Fig. 56 Test A: System Does Not Charge (Part 1 of 2). Thunderbird & 1997 Cougar

Test Step		Result ▶	Action to Take
B1	CHECK VOLTAGE DROP IN A CIRCUIT		
	• Turn ignition switch to RUN position. • Measure voltage between terminal A on the voltage regulator connector C101 and positive (+) battery post. • **Is voltage drop less than 0.25 V?**	Yes ▶ No ▶	GO to **B2.** SERVICE excess voltage drop in Circuit 36 (Y/W). CHECK Fuse 11 (15A) and connectors in Circuit 36 (Y/W) and SERVICE as required.
B2	CHECK VOLTAGE DROP IN I CIRCUIT		
	• NOTE: Voltage regulator must be connected to wiring harness for this test. Measure voltage at connector C101 I terminal, Circuit 904 (LG/R). • **Is voltage drop less than 1 V?**	Yes ▶ No ▶	GO to **B3.** SERVICE high resistance in Circuit 904 (LG/R).
B3	CHECK FOR POOR GROUNDS		
	• Check for poor ground connections between voltage regulator and generator, battery and engine, or engine and battery. • **Are all ground connections clean and tight?**	Yes ▶ No ▶	GO to **B4.** CLEAN or SERVICE grounds as required.
B4	CHECK FOR GROUNDED SLIP RING		
	• Remove generator from vehicle. • Remove voltage regulator. • Measure resistance from each generator slip ring to generator housing. • **Is resistance from either slip ring to housing less than 200 ohms?**	Yes ▶ No ▶	If grease or dirt has accumulated near slip rings, CLEAN slip rings and RECHECK resistance. If still less than 200 ohms, REPLACE generator. REPLACE voltage regulator.

FM1129700202000X

Fig. 57 Test B: System Overcharges. Thunderbird & 1997 Cougar

Test Step		Result ▶	Action to Take
C1	CHECK FOR OPEN A CIRCUIT		
	• Measure voltage at test point A on the voltage regulator. • **Is voltage at test point A equal to battery voltage?**	Yes ▶ No ▶	GO to **C2.** CHECK Fuse 22 (15A) in Circuit 36 (Y/W) and REPLACE if required. If OK, SERVICE open in Circuit 36 (Y/W).
C2	CHECK FOR SHORTED I CIRCUIT		
	• Disconnect three-pin voltage regulator connector C101. • Turn ignition switch to RUN. • **Is indicator lamp on?**	Yes ▶ No ▶	SERVICE short to ground in Circuit 904 (LG/R). GO to **C3.**
C3	CHECK S CIRCUIT FUNCTION		
	• Install voltage regulator connector. • Disconnect one-pin S connector C102. • Connect wiring harness S terminal, Circuit 4 (W/BK) to positive (+) battery post using a jumper wire. • **Is indicator lamp on?**	Yes ▶ No ▶	REMOVE jumper wire. GO to **C4.** REMOVE jumper wire. GO to **C5.**
C4	CHECK FOR OPEN S CIRCUIT		
	• Remove three-pin voltage regulator connector C101. • Measure wiring resistance between one-pin S connector C102 and S (center) pin of voltage regulator connector. • **Is resistance greater than 1 ohm?**	Yes ▶ No ▶	SERVICE open or excess resistance in Circuit 4 (W/BK). CHECK for loose or bent pin in voltage regulator or connector. If OK, REPLACE voltage regulator.
C5	CHECK STATOR OUTPUT VOLTAGE		
	• Turn ignition switch to RUN position. • Measure voltage at S terminal on back of generator. • **Is voltage at least 1/2 of battery voltage?**	Yes ▶ No ▶	GO to **C6.** GO to Pinpoint Test A to find the cause of low generator output.
C6	CHECK GENERATOR OUTPUT VOLTAGE		
	• Measure voltage at B+ terminal on the back of generator with engine running at 2000 rpm and all accessories turned OFF. • **Is voltage greater than 15.5 V?**	Yes ▶ No ▶	GO to Pinpoint Test B to find the cause of high output voltage. REPLACE voltage regulator.

FM1129700203000X

Fig. 58 Test C: Indicator Lamp Stays On, Engine Running. Thunderbird & 1997 Cougar

Test Step		Result ▶	Action to Take
D1	CHECK LAMP CIRCUIT WIRING		
	• Turn ignition switch to OFF position. • Remove three-pin voltage regulator connector C101. • Measure voltage at C101 I-terminal, Circuit 904 (LG/R). • **Is voltage greater than 0 V?**	Yes ▶ No ▶	SERVICE Circuit 16 (R/LG). Circuit should be HOT in ignition switch in RUN only. SERVICE instrument cluster.

FM1129700204000X

Fig. 59 Test D: Indicator Lamp Stays On, Ignition Switch Off. Thunderbird & 1997 Cougar

Test Step		Result	Action to Take
E1	CHECK FOR OPEN I CIRCUIT		
	• Disconnect three-pin voltage regulator connector C101. • Turn ignition switch to RUN position. • Measure voltage at wiring harness I-terminal, Circuit 904 (LG/R). • **Is voltage equal to B+?**	Yes No	▶ GO to **E2.** ▶ SERVICE open in Circuit 904 (LG/R).
E2	CHECK FOR BURNED OUT BULB		
	• Connect connector C101 I terminal, Circuit 904 (LG/R) to ground with a jumper wire. • **Is indicator lamp on?**	Yes No	▶ REMOVE jumper wire. GO to **E3.** ▶ REPLACE lamp or SERVICE high resistance in lamp socket or Circuit 904 (LG/R).
E3	CHECK FOR POOR GROUNDS		
	• Check for poor ground connections between voltage regulator and generator, battery and engine, or engine and battery. • **Are all ground connections clean and tight?**	Yes No	▶ GO to **E4.** ▶ CLEAN or SERVICE grounds as required.
E4	CHECK S CIRCUIT WIRING		
	• Remove one-pin S connector C102 from generator. • Measure voltage at wiring harness S terminal, Circuit 4 (W/BK). • **Is voltage greater than 0 V?**	Yes No	▶ SERVICE Circuit 4 (W/BK). Circuit should be HOT only when engine is running. ▶ GO to **E5.**
E5	CHECK FOR SHORTED RECTIFIER		
	• Measure voltage at the S-terminal on the back of the generator. • **Is voltage greater than 1 V?**	Yes No	▶ If lamp is on with connector C102 removed, REPLACE generator. ▶ REPLACE voltage regulator.

FM1129700205000X

Fig. 60 Test E: Indicator Lamp Does Not Come On. Thunderbird & 1997 Cougar

Test Step		Result	Action to Take
G1	CHECK FOR ACCESSORY DRIVE NOISE		
	• Check the drive belt to make sure that it is installed properly and is not damaged. • **Is drive belt OK?**	Yes No	▶ GO to **G2.** ▶ SERVICE accessory drive belt as required.
G2	CHECK GENERATOR MOUNTING		
	• Check generator and generator mounting bracket for loose bolts or misalignment condition. • **Is generator mounted correctly?**	Yes No	▶ GO to **G3.** ▶ INSTALL generator to specifications.
G3	CHECK GENERATOR PULLEY		
	• Check generator pulley for damage (bent) or a misalignment condition. • **Is pulley OK?**	Yes No	▶ If noise is still present, REPLACE generator. ▶ REPLACE generator pulley.

FM1129700207000X

Fig. 62 Test G: Alternator Is Noisy. Thunderbird & 1997 Cougar

Condition	Possible Source	Action
• System Does Not Charge	• Ignition switch OFF battery drain. • Circuitry. • Voltage regulator. • Generator. • Battery. • Battery connections. • Drive belt.	• GO to Pinpoint Test A.
• System Overcharges (Battery Boils Over)	• Circuitry. • Poor ground. • Voltage regulator. • Generator.	• GO to Pinpoint Test B.
• Indicator Lamp Stays ON, Engine Running	• Circuitry. • Voltage regulator. • Generator.	• GO to Pinpoint Test C.
• Indicator Lamp Stays ON, Ignition Switch OFF	• Circuitry. • Improper lamp circuit wiring. • Instrument cluster.	• GO to Pinpoint Test D.
• Indicator Lamp Does Not Come On	• Burned out lamp. • Circuitry. • Poor ground. • Voltage regulator. • Generator.	• GO to Pinpoint Test E.
• Indicator Lamp Flickers/Intermittent	• Loose connection to generator, voltage regulator or power distribution box. • Circuitry. • Loose brush holder screw. • Voltage regulator. • Generator.	• GO to Pinpoint Test F.
• Generator Noisy	• Accessory drive belt. • Accessory brackets. • Bent pulley. • Generator. • Other accessories.	• GO to Pinpoint Test G.
• Radio Interference	• Voltage regulator. • Generator. • Other components.	• GO to Pinpoint Test H.

FM1129800266000X

Fig. 64 Symptom chart. 1997–99 Crown Victoria & Grand Marquis

Test Step		Result	Action to Take
F1	CHECK FOR LOOSE CONNECTIONS		
	• Check these connections for corrosion, loose or bent pins, or loose eyelets: — three-pin voltage regulator connector C101 — one-pin S connector C102 — generator B+ eyelet — power distribution box eyelets — battery cables • **Are all connections clean and tight?**	Yes No	▶ GO to **F2.** ▶ CLEAN or SERVICE connections as required.
F2	CHECK FOR FIELD CIRCUIT DRAIN		
	• Turn ignition switch OFF. • Measure voltage at test point F on the voltage regulator. • **Is voltage at test point F equal to battery voltage?**	Yes No	▶ GO to **F3.** ▶ GO to **F5.**
F3	CHECK FOR LOOSE A CIRCUIT FUSE		
	• Start engine. • Check fusible link (18GA) in power distribution box for a loose connection by wiggling fuse with the engine running. • **Does indicator lamp flicker?**	Yes No	▶ SERVICE loose fuse connection. ▶ GO to **F4.**
F4	CHECK A CIRCUIT CONNECTIONS		
	• With engine running, connect voltage regulator terminal A at 3-pin connector C101 to positive (+) battery post using a jumper wire. • **Does indicator lamp flicker?**	Yes No	▶ REPLACE voltage regulator. If concern still exists, REPLACE generator. ▶ SERVICE poor connection in Circuit 36 (Y/W).
F5	CHECK BRUSH HOLDER SCREWS		
	• Remove generator from vehicle. • Check the brush holder screws, located on voltage regulator. • **Are the brush holder screws tight?**	Yes No	▶ GO to **F6.** ▶ Torque screws to 2.8-4.0 N-m (25-35 lb-in).
F6	CHECK FOR GROUNDED SLIP RING		
	• Remove voltage regulator. • Measure resistance from each generator slip ring to the generator housing. • **Is resistance from either slip ring to housing less than 200 ohms?**	Yes No	▶ If grease or dirt has accumulated near the slip rings, CLEAN the slip rings and RECHECK resistance. If still less than 200 ohms, REPLACE generator. ▶ REPLACE voltage regulator.

FM1129700206000X

Fig. 61 Test F: Indicator lamp Flickers/Intermittent. Thunderbird & 1997 Cougar

Test Step		Result	Action to Take
H1	VERIFY RADIO INTERFERENCE		
	• Start engine. • Tune radio to a station where interference is present. • Remove three-pin voltage regulator connector C101. • **Is interference present with connector removed?**	Yes No	▶ Locate the cause of the radio interference. ▶ REPLACE generator.

FM1129700208000X

Fig. 63 Test H: Radio Interference. Thunderbird & 1997 Cougar

Condition	Possible Source	Action
• Battery is discharged or voltage is low	• Corroded terminal(s). • Loose connection(s). • High key-off current drain(s). • Battery. • Generator.	• GO to Pinpoint Test A.
• The charging system warning indicator is on with the engine running (the system voltage does not increase)	• Circuitry. • Voltage regulator. • Generator.	• GO to Pinpoint Test B.
• The system overcharges (battery voltage greater than 15.5 volts)	• Circuitry. • Voltage regulator. • Generator.	• GO to Pinpoint Test C.
• The charging system warning indicator is on with the engine running and the system increases voltage	• Circuitry. • Instrument cluster. • Voltage regulator. • Generator.	• GO to Pinpoint Test D.
• The charging system warning indicator is off with the ignition switch in the RUN position and the engine off	• Bulb. • Circuitry. • Instrument cluster. • Voltage regulator. • Generator.	• GO to Pinpoint Test E.
• The charging system warning indicator flickers or is intermittent	• Corroded terminal(s). • Fuse(s). • Circuitry. • Voltage regulator. • Generator.	• GO to Pinpoint Test F.
• The generator is noisy	• Bolts or brackets. • Drive belt. • Generator or pulley.	• GO to Pinpoint Test G.
• Radio interference	• Generator. • Circuitry. • In-vehicle entertainment system.	• GO to Pinpoint Test H.

FM1120000541000X

Fig. 65 Symptom chart. 2000 Crown Victoria & Grand Marquis

Test Step		Result	Action to Take
A1	CHECK BATTERY CONNECTIONS		
	• Inspect battery cables for loose or corroded connections. • Inspect battery for corrosion. • **Are battery cables clean, tight and free from corrosion?**	Yes ▶ No ▶	GO to **A2**. SERVICE battery and cables as necessary. RESTORE vehicle. RETEST system.
A2	CHECK DRIVE BELT TENSION		
	• Perform drive belt adjustment procedure. • **Is the drive belt adjusted properly?**	Yes ▶ No ▶	GO to **A3**. ADJUST or REPLACE drive belt.
A3	LOOSE BATTERY POST		
	• Check for loose battery posts. • **Are posts OK?**	Yes ▶ No ▶	GO to **A4**. REPLACE battery.
A4	CRACKED BATTERY COVER		
	• Remove battery hold down clamps and shields. • Check for broken / cracked case or battery cover. • **Are case and cover OK?**	Yes ▶ No ▶	GO to **A5**. REPLACE battery.

FM1129800267010X

Fig. 66 Test A: System Does Not Charge (Part 1 of 2). 1997–99 Crown Victoria & Grand Marquis

Test Step		Result	Action to Take
B1	CHECK VOLTAGE DROP IN A CIRCUIT		
	• Turn ignition switch to RUN position. • Measure voltage between test point A on voltage regulator connector C154 and positive (+) battery post. • **Is voltage drop less than 0.25 V?**	Yes ▶ No ▶	GO to **B2**. SERVICE excess voltage drop in Circuit 36 (Y / W). CHECK power distribution box Fuse STR / ALT (30A) and connectors in Circuit 36 (Y / W). SERVICE as required.
B2	CHECK VOLTAGE DROP IN I CIRCUIT		
	NOTE: Voltage regulator must be connected to wiring harness for this test. • Measure voltage at wiring harness I terminal connector C154, Circuit 904 (LG / R). • **Is voltage greater than 1 V?**	Yes ▶ No ▶	GO to **B3**. SERVICE high resistance in Circuit 904 (LG / R).
B3	CHECK FOR POOR GROUNDS		
	• Check for poor ground connections between voltage regulator and generator, battery and engine, or engine and battery. • **Are all ground connections clean and tight?**	Yes ▶ No ▶	GO to **B4**. CLEAN or SERVICE grounds as required.
B4	CHECK FOR GROUNDED SLIP RING		
	• Remove generator from vehicle. • Remove voltage regulator. • Measure resistance from each generator slip ring to the generator housing. • **Is resistance from either slip ring to housing less than 200 ohms?**	Yes ▶ No ▶	If grease or dirt has accumulated near slip rings, CLEAN slip rings and RECHECK resistance. If still less than 200 ohms, REPLACE generator. REPLACE voltage regulator.

FM1129800268000X

Fig. 67 Test B: System Overcharges. 1997–99 Crown Victoria & Grand Marquis

Test Step		Result	Action to Take
C1	CHECK FOR OPEN A CIRCUIT		
	• Measure voltage at test point A on the voltage regulator. • **Is voltage at test point A equal to battery voltage?**	Yes ▶ No ▶	GO to **C2**. CHECK power distribution box Fuse STR / ALT (30A) in Circuit 36 (Y / W) and REPLACE if required. If OK, SERVICE open in Circuit 36 (Y / W).
C2	CHECK FOR SHORTED I CIRCUIT		
	• Remove three-pin voltage regulator connector C154. • Turn ignition switch to RUN position. • **Is indicator lamp on?**	Yes ▶ No ▶	SERVICE short to ground in Circuit 904 (LG / R). GO to **C3**.
C3	CHECK S CIRCUIT FUNCTION		
	• Install voltage regulator connector C154. • Remove one-pin S connector C153. • Connect wiring harness S terminal, Circuit 4 (W / BK) to positive (+) battery post using a jumper wire. • **Is indicator lamp on?**	Yes ▶ No ▶	REMOVE jumper wire. GO to **C4**. REMOVE jumper wire. GO to **C5**.
C4	CHECK FOR OPEN S CIRCUIT		
	• Remove three-pin voltage regulator connector C154. • Measure wiring resistance between the one-pin S connector and the S (center) pin of the voltage regulator connector. • **Is resistance greater than 1 ohm?**	Yes ▶ No ▶	SERVICE open or excess resistance in Circuit 4 (W / BK). CHECK for loose or bent pin in voltage regulator or connector. If OK, REPLACE voltage regulator.
C5	CHECK STATOR OUTPUT VOLTAGE		
	• Start engine. • Measure voltage at S terminal on back of generator. • **Is voltage at least 1 / 2 of battery voltage?**	Yes ▶ No ▶	GO to **C6**. GO to Pinpoint Test A to find the cause of low generator output.
C6	CHECK GENERATOR OUTPUT VOLTAGE		
	• Measure voltage at the B+ terminal on back of generator with engine running at 2000 rpm and all accessories turned OFF. • **Is voltage greater than 15.5 V?**	Yes ▶ No ▶	GO to Pinpoint Test B to find cause of high output voltage. REPLACE voltage regulator.

FM1129800269000X

Fig. 68 Test C: Indicator Lamp Stays On, Engine Running. 1997–99 Crown Victoria & Grand Marquis

Test Step		Result	Action to Take
A5	CHECK BATTERY		
	• Perform Battery Capacity Testing. • **Is the battery capacity OK?**	Yes ▶ No ▶	GO to **A6**. REPLACE battery.
A6	CHECK FOR KEY-OFF DRAIN		
	• Perform Battery Drain Testing as described. • **Is current drain less than 50 mA (or test lamp off)?**	Yes ▶ No ▶	GO to **A7**. GO to Drain Testing in Component Tests to find cause of ignition switch-OFF battery drain.
A7	CHECK FOR OPEN B+ CIRCUIT		
	• Measure voltage at B+ terminal on back of generator, Circuit 38 (BK / O). • **Is voltage at B+ terminal equal to battery voltage?**	Yes ▶ No ▶	GO to **A8**. SERVICE open in Circuit 38 (BK / O).
A8	CHECK FOR OPEN A CIRCUIT		
	• Measure voltage at test point A on voltage regulator. • **Is voltage at test point A equal to battery voltage?**	Yes ▶ No ▶	GO to **A9**. CHECK power distribution box Fuse STR / ALT (30A) in Circuit 36 (Y / W) and REPLACE if required. If OK, SERVICE open in Circuit 36 (Y / W).
A9	CHECK FOR OPEN I CIRCUIT		
	NOTE: Voltage regulator must be connected to wiring harness for this test. • Turn ignition switch to RUN position. • Measure voltage at wiring harness I terminal, Circuit 904 (LG / R) at connector C154. • **Is voltage greater than 1 V?**	Yes ▶ No ▶	GO to **A10**. SERVICE open or high resistance in Circuit 904 (LG / R).
A10	CHECK VOLTAGE DROP IN A CIRCUIT		
	• Measure voltage drop between test point A on the voltage regulator and positive (+) battery post. • **Is voltage drop less than 0.25 V?**	Yes ▶ No ▶	GO to **A11**. SERVICE excess voltage drop in Circuit 36 (Y / W). CHECK fuse and connectors in Circuit 36 (Y / W) and SERVICE as required.
A11	CHECK FOR SHORTED RECTIFIER		
	• Remove one-pin S connector C153 from generator. • Measure voltage between the S terminal on back of generator and ground. • Measure voltage between positive (+) battery terminal and S terminal on back of generator. • **Is either voltage reading greater than 1 V?**	Yes ▶ No ▶	REPLACE generator. GO to **A12**.
A12	CHECK VOLTAGE DROP IN B+ CIRCUIT		
	• Install S connector C153. • Turn ignition switch to RUN. • Turn headlamps ON and set blower on HIGH. • With engine running at 2000 rpm, measure voltage drop between B+ terminal on back of generator and positive (+) battery post. • **Is voltage drop less than 0.5 V?**	Yes ▶ No ▶	GO to **A13**. SERVICE excess voltage drop in Circuit 38 (BK / O). CHECK fuse link in Circuit 38 and connections between battery and power distribution box.
A13	CHECK FOR OPEN / SHORTED FIELD		
	• Remove generator from vehicle. • Remove voltage regulator. • Measure resistance between the generator slip rings. • **Is resistance greater than 10 ohms OR less than 1 ohm?**	Yes ▶ No ▶	REPLACE generator. REPLACE voltage regulator. RETEST system.

FM1129800267020X

Fig. 66 Test A: System Does Not Charge (Part 2 of 2). 1997–99 Crown Victoria & Grand Marquis

Test Step		Result	Action to Take
D1	CHECK LAMP CIRCUIT WIRING		
	• Turn ignition switch to OFF position. • Remove three-pin voltage regulator connector C154. • Measure voltage at wiring harness I terminal, Circuit 904 (LG / R). • **Is voltage greater than 0 V?**	Yes ▶ No ▶	SERVICE Circuit 904 (LG / R). Circuit should be HOT in RUN position only. SERVICE instrument cluster.

FM1129800270000X

Fig. 69 Test D: Indicator Lamp Stays On, Ignition Switch Off. 1997–99 Crown Victoria & Grand Marquis

Test Step		Result	Action to Take
E1	CHECK FOR OPEN I CIRCUIT		
	• Remove three-pin voltage regulator connectorC154. • Turn ignition switch to RUN position. • Measure voltage at wiring harness I terminal, Circuit 904 (LG/R). • **Is voltage equal to B+?**	Yes	GO to **E2.**
		No	SERVICE open in Circuit 904 (LG/R).
E2	CHECK FOR BURNED OUT BULB		
	• Connect wiring harness I terminal, Circuit 904 (LG/R) to ground with a jumper wire. • **Is indicator lamp on?**	Yes	REMOVE jumper wire. GO to **E3.**
		No	REPLACE lamp or SERVICE high resistance in lamp socket or Circuit 904 (LG/R).
E3	CHECK FOR POOR GROUNDS		
	• Check for poor ground connections between voltage regulator and generator, battery and engine, or engine and battery. • **Are all ground connections clean and tight?**	Yes	GO to **E4.**
		No	CLEAN or SERVICE grounds as required.
E4	CHECK S CIRCUIT WIRING		
	• Remove one-pin S connector C153 from generator. • Measure voltage at wiring harness S terminal, Circuit 4 (W/BK). • **Is voltage greater than 0 V?**	Yes	SERVICE Circuit 4 (W/BK). Circuit should be HOT only when engine is running.
		No	GO to **E5.**
E5	CHECK FOR SHORTED RECTIFIER		
	• Measure voltage at the S terminal on the back of generator. • **Is voltage greater than 1 V?**	Yes	If lamp is on with one-pin S connector removed, REPLACE generator.
		No	REPLACE voltage regulator.

FM1129800271000X

Fig. 70 Test E: Indicator Lamp Does Not Come On. 1997–99 Crown Victoria & Grand Marquis

Test Step		Result	Action to Take
G1	CHECK FOR ACCESSORY DRIVE NOISE		
	• Check drive belt to make sure that it is installed properly and is not damaged. • **Is drive belt OK?**	Yes	GO to **G2.**
		No	and SERVICE accessory drive belt as required.
G2	CHECK GENERATOR MOUNTING		
	• Check generator and generator mounting bracket for loose bolts or misalignment condition. • **Is generator mounted correctly?**	Yes	GO to **G3.**
		No	INSTALL generator to specification.
G3	CHECK GENERATOR PULLEY		
	• Check generator pulley for damage (bent) or a misalignment condition. • **Is pulley OK?**	Yes	If noise is still present REPLACE generator.
		No	REPLACE generator pulley.

FM1129800273000X

Fig. 72 Test G: Alternator Is Noisy. 1997–99 Crown Victoria & Grand Marquis

TEST CONDITIONS	TEST DETAILS/RESULTS/ACTIONS
A1 CHECK BATTERY CONDITION	
	[1] Carry out the Battery — Condition Test to determine if the battery can hold a charge and is OK for use. • Is the battery OK? → **Yes** GO to **A2**. → **No** INSTALL a new battery. TEST the system for normal operation.
A2 CHECK FOR GENERATOR OUTPUT	
	[1] Carry out the On-Vehicle Generator Load/No-Load Tests. • Is the generator OK? → **Yes** GO to **A3**. → **No** GO to Pinpoint Test B.
A3 CHECK FOR CURRENT DRAINS	
	[1] Carry out the Battery — Drain Test. • Are there any excessive current drains? → **Yes** REPAIR as necessary. TEST the system for normal operation. → **No** GO to **A4**.

FM1120000542010X

Fig. 74 Test A: Battery Discharged or Voltage Low (Part 1 of 2). 2000 Crown Victoria & Grand Marquis

Test Step		Result	Action to Take
F1	CHECK FOR LOOSE CONNECTIONS		
	• Check these connections for corrosion, loose or bent pins, or loose eyelets: — Three-pin voltage regulator connector C154. — One-pin S connector C153. — Generator B+ eyelet. — Power distribution box eyelets. — Battery cables. • **Are all connections clean and tight?**	Yes	GO to **F2.**
		No	CLEAN or SERVICE connections as required.
F2	CHECK FOR LOOSE A CIRCUIT FUSE		
	• Turn ignition switch to RUN. • Check power distribution box Fuse STR/ALT (30A) for a loose connection by wiggling fuse with engine running. • **Does indicator lamp flicker?**	Yes	SERVICE loose fuse connection.
		No	GO to **F3.**
F3	CHECK A CIRCUIT CONNECTIONS		
	• With engine running, connect test point A on voltage regulator to the positive (+) battery post using a jumper wire. • **Does indicator lamp flicker?**	Yes	GO to **F4.**
		No	SERVICE poor connection in Circuit 36 (Y/W).
F4	CHECK BRUSH HOLDER SCREWS		
	• Remove generator from vehicle. • Check brush holder screws, located on voltage regulator. • **Are the brush holder screws tight?**	Yes	GO to **F5.**
		No	TIGHTEN screws.
F5	CHECK FOR GROUNDED SLIP RING		
	• Remove voltage regulator. • Measure resistance from each generator slip ring to generator housing. • **Is resistance from either slip ring to housing less than 200 ohms?**	Yes	If grease or dirt has accumulated near slip rings, CLEAN slip rings and RECHECK resistance. If still less than 200 ohms, REPLACE generator.
		No	REPLACE voltage regulator.

FM1129800272000X

Fig. 71 Test F: Indicator Lamp Flickers/Intermittent. 1997–99 Crown Victoria & Grand Marquis

Test Step		Result	Action to Take
H1	VERIFY RADIO INTERFERENCE		
	• Start engine. • Tune radio to a station where interference is present. • Remove three-pin voltage regulator connectorC154. • **Is interference present with connector removed?**	Yes	LOCATE cause of the radio interference.
		No	REPLACE generator.

FM1129800274000X

Fig. 73 Test H: Radio Interference. 1997–99 Crown Victoria & Grand Marquis

TEST CONDITIONS	TEST DETAILS/RESULTS/ACTIONS
A4 CHECK FOR CURRENT DRAINS WHICH SHUT OFF WHEN THE BATTERY IS DISCONNECTED	
	[1] Carry out the Battery — Electronic Drains Which Shut Off When the Battery Cable is Disconnected Test. • Are there any current drains which shut off when the battery is disconnected? → **Yes** REPAIR as necessary. TEST the system for normal operation. → **No** GO to Pinpoint Test B.

FM1120000542020X

Fig. 74 Test A: Battery Discharged or Voltage Low (Part 2 of 2). 2000 Crown Victoria & Grand Marquis

TEST CONDITIONS	TEST DETAILS/RESULTS/ACTIONS
B1 CHECK GENERATOR B+ CIRCUIT 38 (BK/OG)	
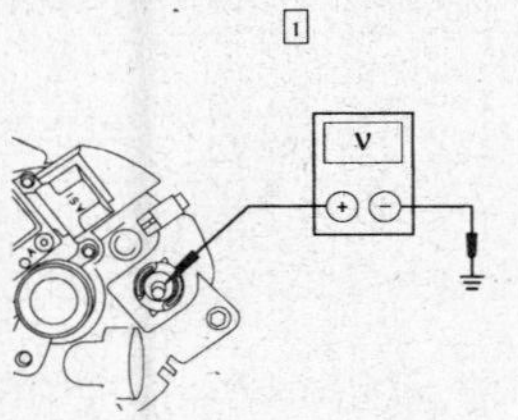	[1] Measure the voltage between generator B+ terminal, circuit 38 (BK/OG), component side and ground. • Is the voltage equal to battery positive voltage (B+)? → **Yes** GO to **B2**. → **No** REPAIR the circuit. TEST the system for normal operation.

FM1120000543010X

Fig. 75 Test B: Indicator Stays On, Engine Running (Part 1 of 3). 2000 Crown Victoria & Grand Marquis

TEST CONDITIONS	TESTDETAILS/RESULTS/ACTIONS
B2 CHECK GENERATOR GROUND A CIRCUIT 36 (YE/WH)	
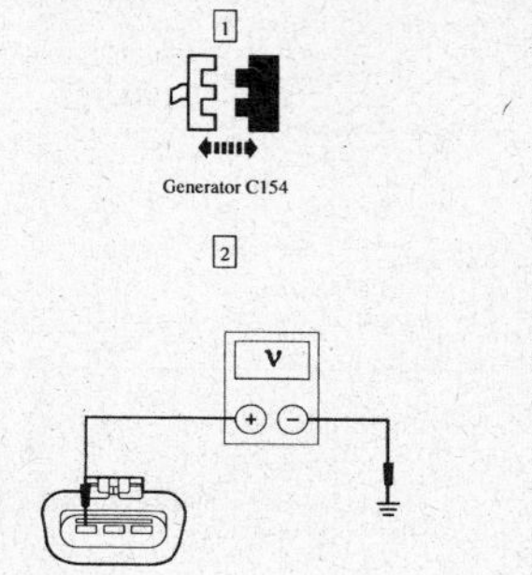	2 Measure the voltage between generator C154 pin A, circuit 36 (YE/WH), harness side and ground. • Is the voltage equal to battery positive voltage (B+)? → **Yes** GO to **B3**. → **No** REPAIR the circuit. TEST the system for normal operation.
B3 CHECK I CIRCUIT 904 (LG/RD) FOR AN OPEN	
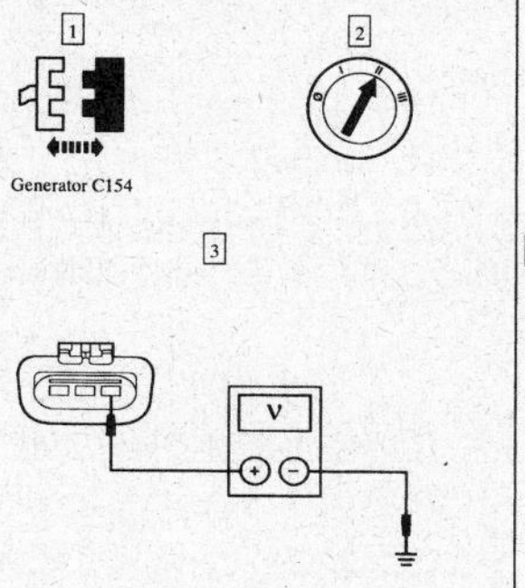	3 With the ignition switch in the RUN position and the engine off, measure the voltage between generator C154 pin I, circuit 904 (LG/RD), harness side and ground. • Is the voltage equal to battery positive voltage (B+)? → **Yes** GO to **B4** → **No** REPAIR the circuit. TEST the system for normal operation.

FM1120000543020X

Fig. 75 Test B: Indicator Stays On, Engine Running (Part 2 of 3). 2000 Crown Victoria & Grand Marquis

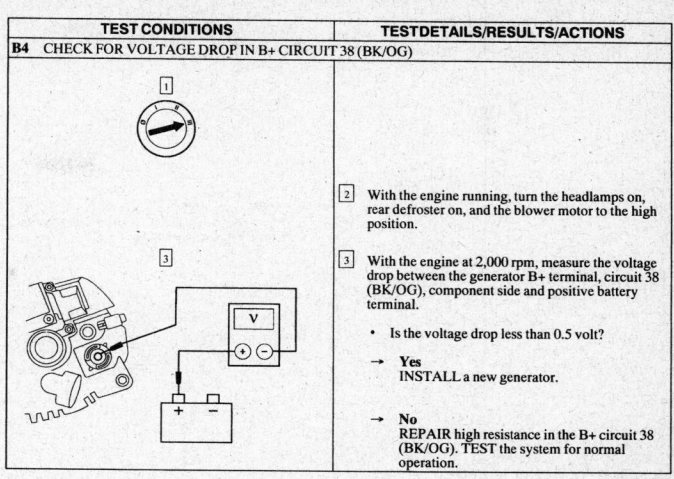

TEST CONDITIONS	TESTDETAILS/RESULTS/ACTIONS
C1 CHECK FOR VOLTAGE DROP IN A CIRCUIT 36 (YE/WH)	
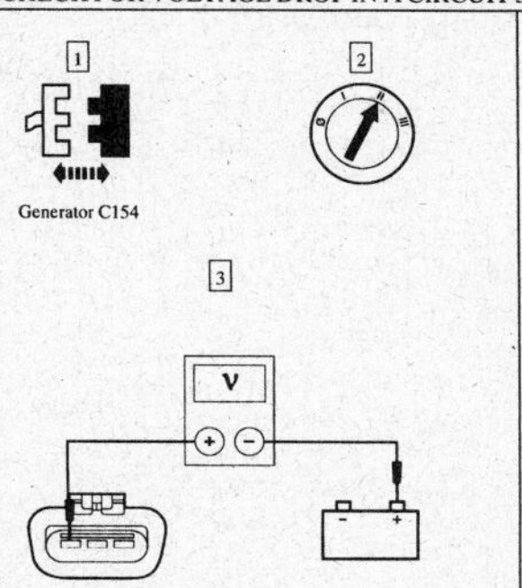	3 Measure the voltage drop between generator C154 pin A, circuit 36 (YE/WH), harness side and positive battery terminal. • Is the voltage drop less than 0.5 volt? → **Yes** GO to **C2**. → **No** REPAIR the high resistance in A circuit 36 (YE/WH). TEST the system for normal operation.
C2 CHECK GENERATOR AND BATTERY GROUND CONNECTIONS	
	2 Check the ground connections between the generator and the engine, and the battery and the engine. • Are all ground connections clean and tight? → **Yes** INSTALL a new generator. TEST the system for normal operation. → **No** REPAIR ground connections as necessary. Test the system for normal operation.

FM1120000544000X

Fig. 76 Test C: System Overcharges. 2000 Crown Victoria & Grand Marquis

TEST CONDITIONS	TESTDETAILS/RESULTS/ACTIONS
B4 CHECK FOR VOLTAGE DROP IN B+ CIRCUIT 38 (BK/OG)	
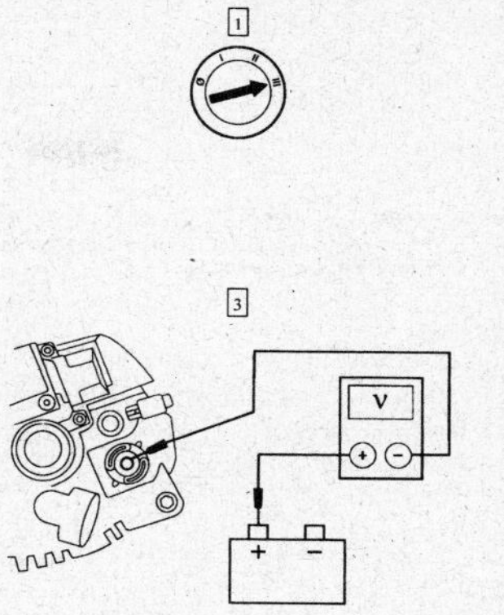	2 With the engine running, turn the headlamps on, rear defroster on, and the blower motor to the high position. 3 With the engine at 2,000 rpm, measure the voltage drop between the generator B+ terminal, circuit 38 (BK/OG), component side and positive battery terminal. • Is the voltage drop less than 0.5 volt? → **Yes** INSTALL a new generator. → **No** REPAIR high resistance in the B+ circuit 38 (BK/OG). TEST the system for normal operation.

FM1120000543030X

Fig. 75 Test B: Indicator Stays On, Engine Running (Part 3 of 3). 2000 Crown Victoria & Grand Marquis

TEST CONDITIONS	TESTDETAILS/RESULTS/ACTIONS
D1 CHECK I CIRCUIT 904 (LG/RD) FOR SHORT TO GROUND	
	2 With the ignition switch in the RUN position, check the charging system warning indicator. • Is the charging system warning indicator illuminated? → **Yes** REPAIR generator I circuit 904 (LG/RD) for a short to ground. TEST the system for normal operation. → **No** INSTALL a new generator. TEST the system for normal operation.

FM1120000545000X

Fig. 77 Test D: Indicator Stays On, Engine Running. 2000 Crown Victoria & Grand Marquis

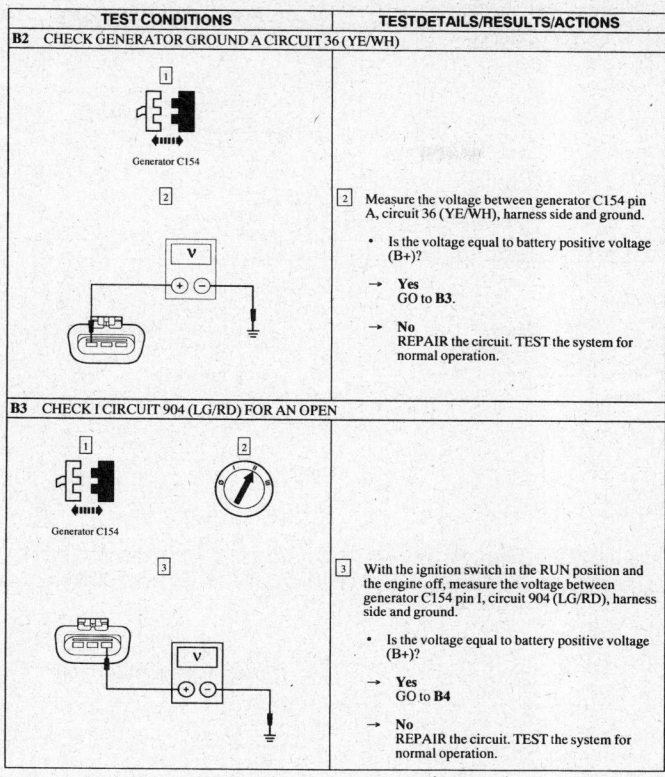

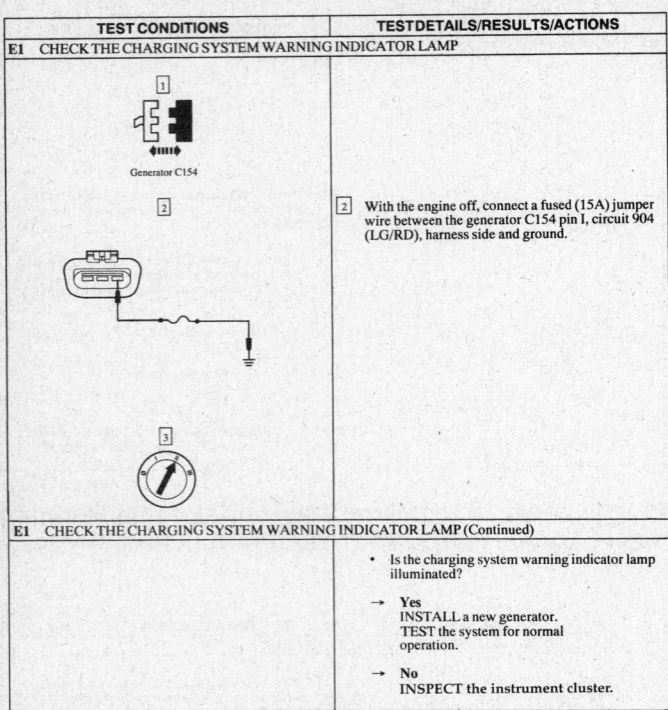

TEST CONDITIONS	TESTDETAILS/RESULTS/ACTIONS
E1 CHECK THE CHARGING SYSTEM WARNING INDICATOR LAMP	
[1]  Generator C154	
[2] 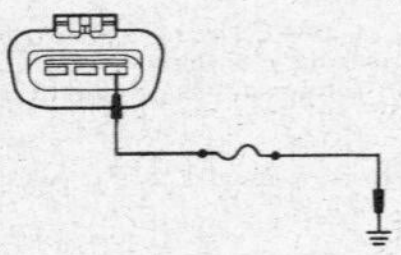	[2] With the engine off, connect a fused (15A) jumper wire between the generator C154 pin I, circuit 904 (LG/RD), harness side and ground.
[3] 	
E1 CHECK THE CHARGING SYSTEM WARNING INDICATOR LAMP (Continued)	
	• Is the charging system warning indicator lamp illuminated? → **Yes** INSTALL a new generator. TEST the system for normal operation. → **No** INSPECT the instrument cluster.

FM1120000546000X

Fig. 78 Test E: Indicator Off, Key On. 2000 Crown Victoria & Grand Marquis

TEST CONDITIONS	TESTDETAILS/RESULTS/ACTIONS
F3 CHECK A CIRCUIT 36 (YE/WH) CONNECTIONS	
[1] 	
[2] 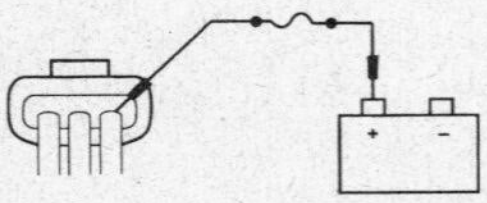	[2] Connect a fused (15A) jumper wire between generator C154, pin A, circuit 36 (YE/WH), harness side and the positive battery terminal.
[3] 	[3] With the engine running note the charging system warning indicator operation. • Does the charging system warning indicator flicker? → **Yes** INSTALL a new generator. TEST the system for normal operation. → **No** REPAIR loose connection(s) in circuits. TEST the system for normal operation.

FM1120000547020X

Fig. 79 Test F: Indicator Flickers or Intermittent (Part 2 of 2). 2000 Crown Victoria & Grand Marquis

TEST CONDITIONS	TESTDETAILS/RESULTS/ACTIONS
F1 CHECK FOR LOOSE CONNECTIONS	
	[1] Check all generator, battery, and power distribution connections for looseness, corrosion, loose or bent terminals, or loose eyelets. • Are all connections clean and tight? → **Yes** GO to **F2**. → **No** REPAIR as necessary. TEST the system for normal operation.
F2 CHECK FUSE CONNECTIONS	
[1] 	[1] With the engine running, check BJB fuse 2 (30A) in A circuit 36 (YE/WH) and the CJB fuse 15 (10A) in I circuit 904 (LG/RD) for looseness by wiggling the fuse and noting the charging system warning indicator lamp operation. • Does the charging system warning indicator flicker? → **Yes** REPAIR loose fuse connection(s) as necessary. TEST the system for normal operation. → **No** GO to **F3**.

FM1120000547010X

Fig. 79 Test F: Indicator Flickers or Intermittent (Part 1 of 2). 2000 Crown Victoria & Grand Marquis

TEST CONDITIONS	TESTDETAILS/RESULTS/ACTIONS
G1 CHECK FOR ACCESSORY DRIVE NOISE	
	[1] Check the accessory drive belt for damage and correct installation. Check the accessory mounting brackets and generator pulley for looseness or misalignment. • Is the accessory drive OK? → **Yes** GO to **G2**. → **No** REPAIR as necessary. TEST the system for normal operation.
G2 CHECK GENERATOR MOUNTING	
	[1] Check the generator mounting for loose bolts or misalignment. • Is the generator mounted correctly? → **Yes** GO to **G3**. → **No** REPAIR as necessary. TEST the system for normal operation.
G3 CHECK GENERATOR FOR ELECTRICAL NOISE	
[1]  Generator C154 [2] 	[3] With the engine running, turn the headlamps on, rear defroster on, and the blower motor to the high position. • Is the noise still present? → **Yes** GO to **G4**. → **No** INSTALL a new generator. TEST the system for normal operation.

FM1120000548010X

Fig. 80 Test G: Alternator Is Noisy (Part 1 of 2). 2000 Crown Victoria & Grand Marquis

TEST CONDITIONS	TEST DETAILS/RESULTS/ACTIONS
G4 CHECK GENERATOR FOR MECHANICAL NOISE	
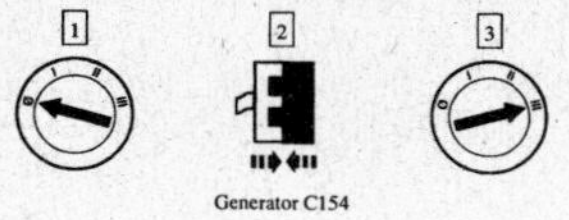	4 Turn all accessories OFF. With the engine running, use a stethoscope or equivalent listening device to probe the generator for unusual mechanical noise. • Is the generator the noise source? → **Yes** INSTALL a new generator. TEST the system for normal operation. → **No** INSPECT for source of engine noise.

FM1120000548020X

Fig. 80 Test G: Alternator Is Noisy (Part 2 of 2). 2000 Crown Victoria & Grand Marquis

TEST CONDITIONS	TEST DETAILS/RESULTS/ACTIONS
H1 VERIFY GENERATOR IS SOURCE OF RADIO INTERFERENCE	
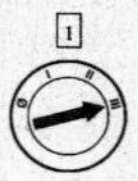	1 With the engine running, tune the radio to a station where the interference is present.
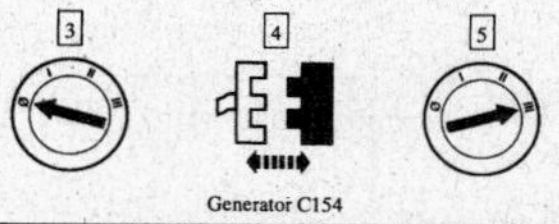	2 Tune the radio to a station where the interference is present.
H1 VERIFY GENERATOR IS SOURCE OF RADIO INTERFERENCE (Continued)	
	• Is the interference present with the generator disconnected? → **Yes** INSPECT the in-vehicle entertainment system. → **No** INSTALL a new generator. TEST the system for normal operation.

FM1120000549000X

Fig. 81 Test H: Radio Interference. 2000 Crown Victoria & Grand Marquis

Condition	Possible Source	Action
• The System Overcharges	• Voltage drop in circuit A. • Generator. • Regulator.	• GO to Pinpoint Test A.
• The Charging System Warning Indicator Stays On	• Open A circuit. • Shorted I circuit. • Open/high resistance S circuit. • Regulator. • Generator.	• GO to Pinpoint Test B.
• The Charging System Warning Indicator Is Inoperative	• Circuitry. • Instrument cluster.	• INSPECT Instrument Cluster & Panel Lighting.
• The Charging System Warning Indicator Flickers/Is Intermittent	• Circuitry. • Generator.	• GO to Pinpoint Test C.
• Generator Is Noisy	• Drive belt. • Generator. • Related components.	• GO to Pinpoint Test D.

FM1129800227010X

Fig. 82 Symptom chart (Part 1 of 2). Escort, Tracer & ZX2

Condition	Possible Source	Action
• Radio Interference	• Generator. • Regulator. • Other components.	• GO to Pinpoint Test E.
• The Battery Does Not Hold a Charge	• Battery drain. • Circuitry. • Regulator. • Generator. • Battery.	• GO to Pinpoint Test F.
• The System Does Not Charge	• Drive Belt. • Generator. • Circuitry.	• GO to Pinpoint Test G.

FM1129800227020X

Fig. 82 Symptom chart (Part 2 of 2). Escort, Tracer & ZX2

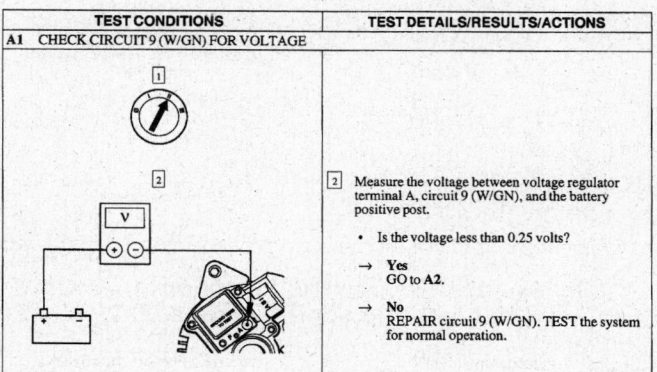

TEST CONDITIONS	TEST DETAILS/RESULTS/ACTIONS
A1 CHECK CIRCUIT 9 (W/GN) FOR VOLTAGE	
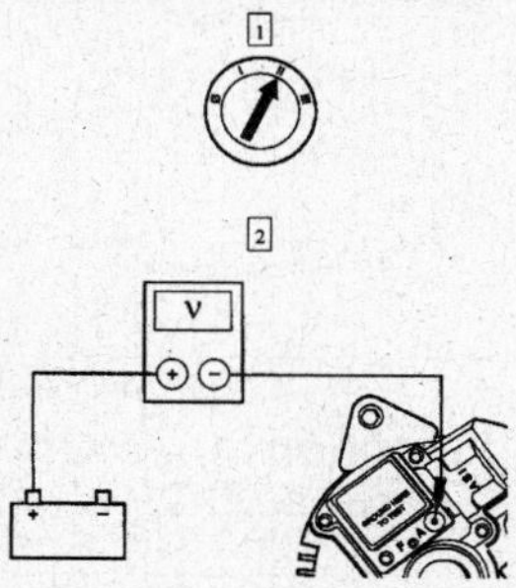	2 Measure the voltage between voltage regulator terminal A, circuit 9 (W/GN), and the battery positive post. • Is the voltage less than 0.25 volts? → **Yes** GO to **A2**. → **No** REPAIR circuit 9 (W/GN). TEST the system for normal operation.

FM1129800228010X

Fig. 83 Test A: System Overcharges (Part 1 of 2). Escort, Tracer & ZX2

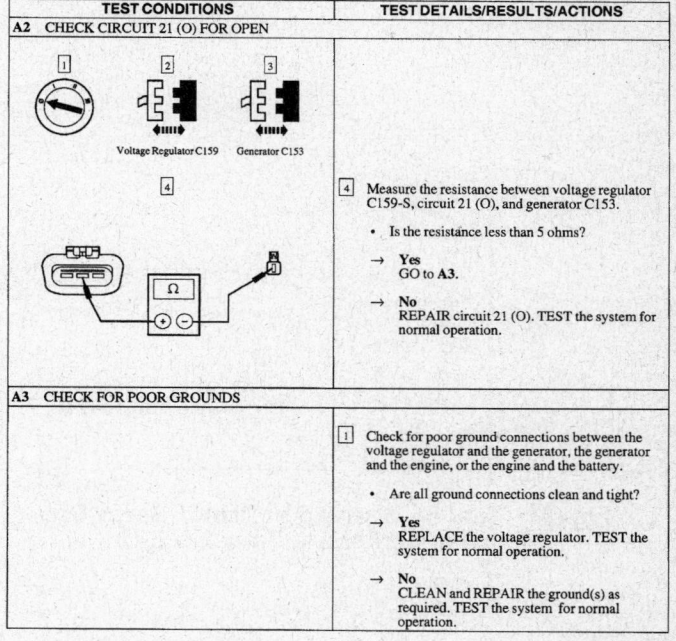

TEST CONDITIONS	TEST DETAILS/RESULTS/ACTIONS
A2 CHECK CIRCUIT 21 (O) FOR OPEN	
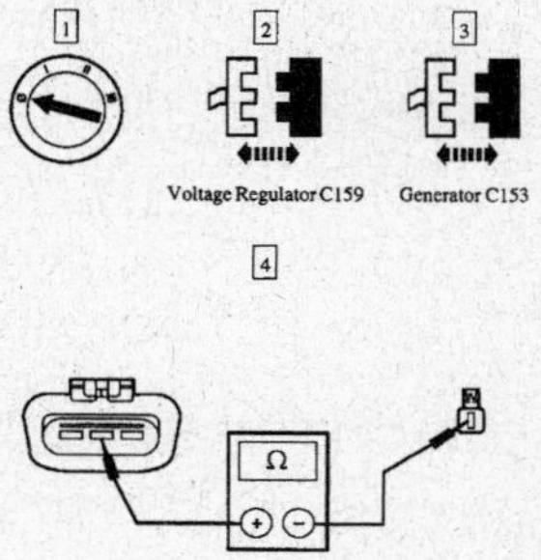	4 Measure the resistance between voltage regulator C159-S, circuit 21 (O), and generator C153. • Is the resistance less than 5 ohms? → **Yes** GO to **A3**. → **No** REPAIR circuit 21 (O). TEST the system for normal operation.
A3 CHECK FOR POOR GROUNDS	
	1 Check for poor ground connections between the voltage regulator and the generator, the generator and the engine, or the engine and the battery. • Are all ground connections clean and tight? → **Yes** REPLACE the voltage regulator. TEST the system for normal operation. → **No** CLEAN and REPAIR the ground(s) as required. TEST the system for normal operation.

FM1129800228020X

Fig. 83 Test A: System Overcharges (Part 2 of 2). Escort, Tracer & ZX2

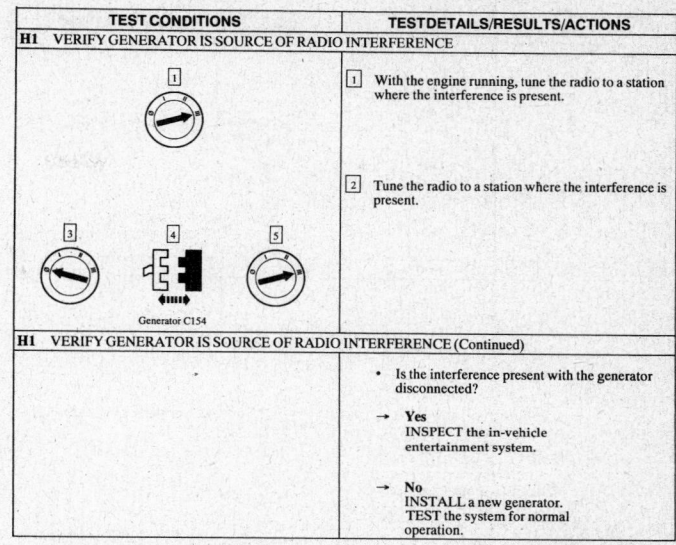

TEST CONDITIONS	TEST DETAILS/RESULTS/ACTIONS
B1 CHECK SYSTEM VOLTAGE	
	1 Perform No-Load Test in this section. • Is the system voltage below the specified range (undercharging)? → **Yes** GO to **B2**. → **No** REPAIR circuit 20 (W/BL) for short to ground. TEST the system for normal operation.
B2 CHECK CIRCUIT 9 (W/GN) FOR OPEN	
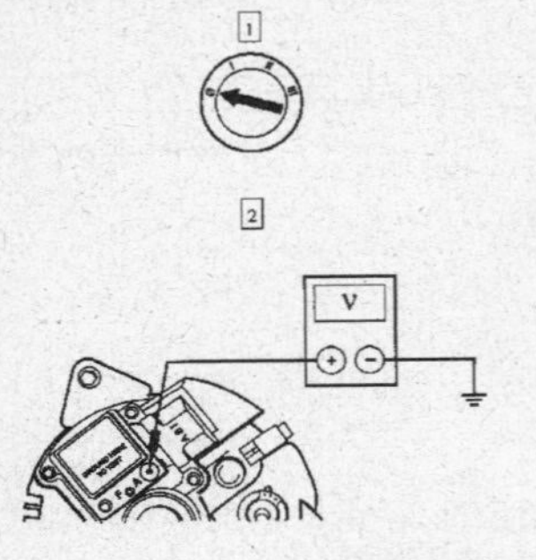	2 Measure the voltage between voltage regulator terminal A and ground. • Is the voltage equal to battery voltage? → **Yes** GO to **B3**. → **No** REPAIR circuit 9 (W/GN). TEST the system for normal operation.

FM1129800229010X

Fig. 84 Test B: Warning Indicator Stays On (Part 1 of 4). Escort, Tracer & ZX2

TEST CONDITIONS	TEST DETAILS/RESULTS/ACTIONS
B3 CHECK CIRCUIT 20 (W/BL) FOR OPEN	
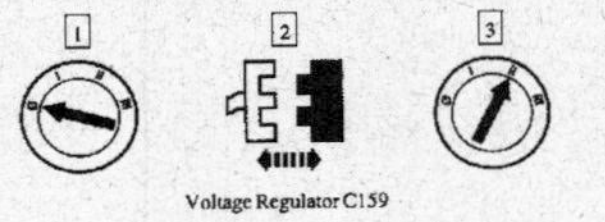	• Is the warning indicator lamp on? → **Yes** REPAIR circuit 20 (W/BL). TEST the system for normal operation. → **No** GO to **B4**.
B4 VERIFY CIRCUIT 21 (O) OPERATES	
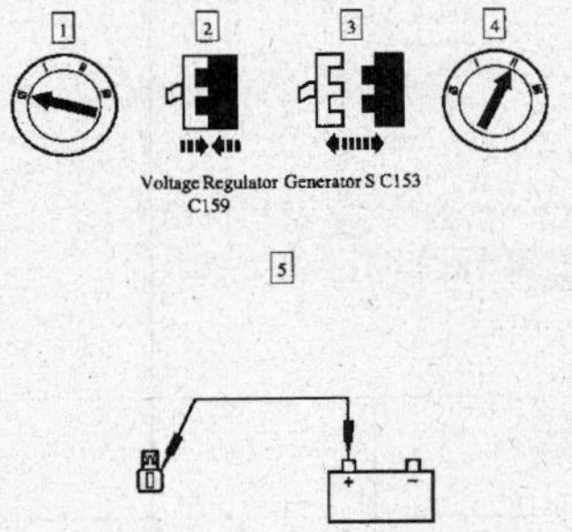	5 Install a jumper wire between generator S terminal C153 and the positive battery post. • Is the warning indicator lamp on? → **Yes** REMOVE jumper; GO to **B5**. → **No** REMOVE jumper; GO to **B6**.

FM1129800229020X

Fig. 84 Test B: Warning Indicator Stays On (Part 2 of 4). Escort, Tracer & ZX2

TEST CONDITIONS	TEST DETAILS/RESULTS/ACTIONS
B5 CHECK CIRCUIT 21 (O) FOR OPEN	
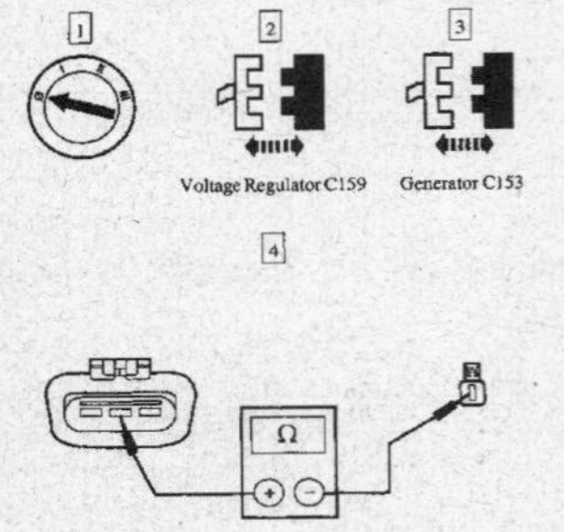	4 Measure the resistance between voltage regulator C159-S, circuit 21 (O), and generator C153. • Is the resistance less than 5 ohms? → **Yes** REPLACE the voltage regulator. TEST the system for normal operation. → **No** REPAIR circuit 21 (O). TEST the system for normal operation.
B6 CHECK STATOR OUTPUT VOLTAGE	
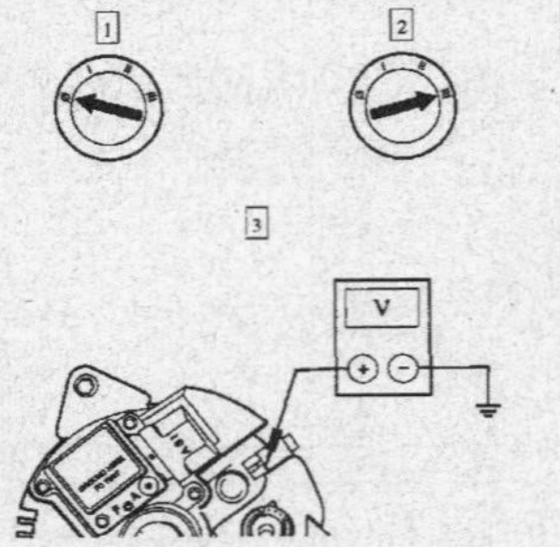	3 Measure the voltage between generator S terminal and ground. • Is the voltage at least 50% of the battery voltage? → **Yes** GO to **B7**. → **No** GO to Symptom Chart and RECHECK condition.

FM1129800229030X

Fig. 84 Test B: Warning Indicator Stays On (Part 3 of 4). Escort, Tracer & ZX2

TEST CONDITIONS	TEST DETAILS/RESULTS/ACTIONS
B7 CHECK GENERATOR OUTPUT VOLTAGE	
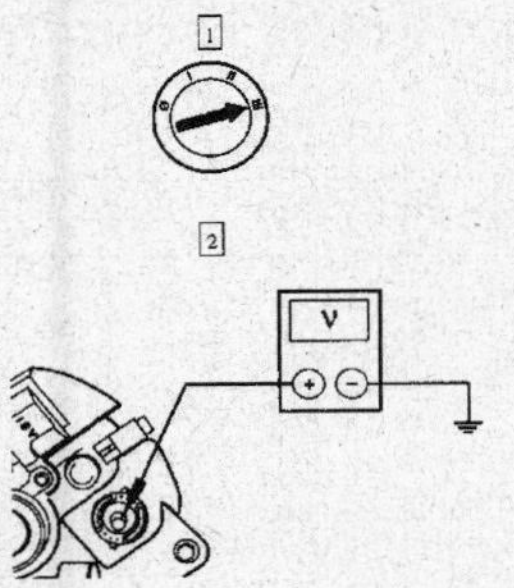	2 Measure the voltage between generator B+ terminal and ground with the engine running at 1500 rpm and all accessories off. • Is the voltage 14.1 volts or greater? → **Yes** GO to Pinpoint Test A. → **No** REPLACE the voltage regulator. TEST the system for normal operation.

FM1129800229040X

Fig. 84 Test B: Warning Indicator Stays On (Part 4 of 4). Escort, Tracer & ZX2

TEST CONDITIONS	TEST DETAILS/RESULTS/ACTIONS
C1 CHECK FOR LOOSE CONNECTIONS	
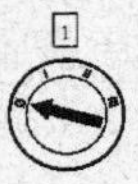	2 Check the following connections for corrosion, loose or bent pins and/or terminals, or loose eyelets: — Voltage regulator connector. — Generator S terminal connector. — Generator B+ eyelet. — Power distribution box eyelets. — Battery cables. • Are all connections clean and tight? → **Yes** GO to **C2**. → **No** REPAIR or CLEAN connections as required. TEST the system for normal operation.

FM1129800230010X

Fig. 85 Test C: Warning Indicator Flickers/ Intermittent (Part 1 of 2). Escort, Tracer & ZX2

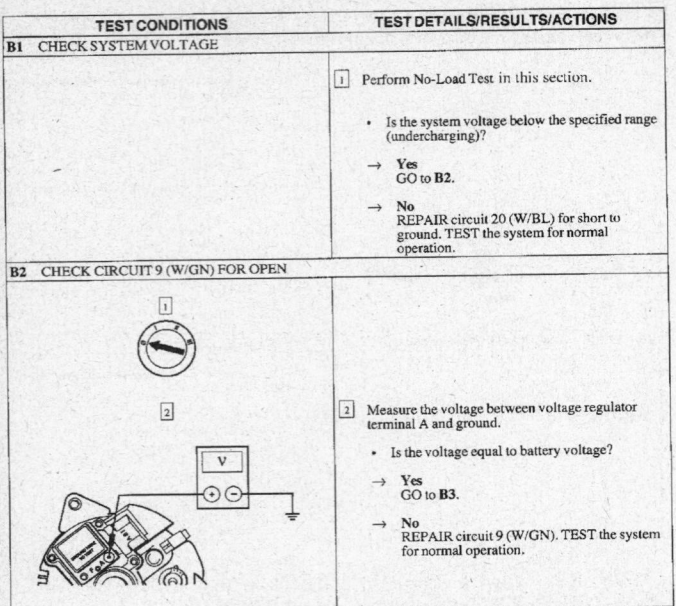

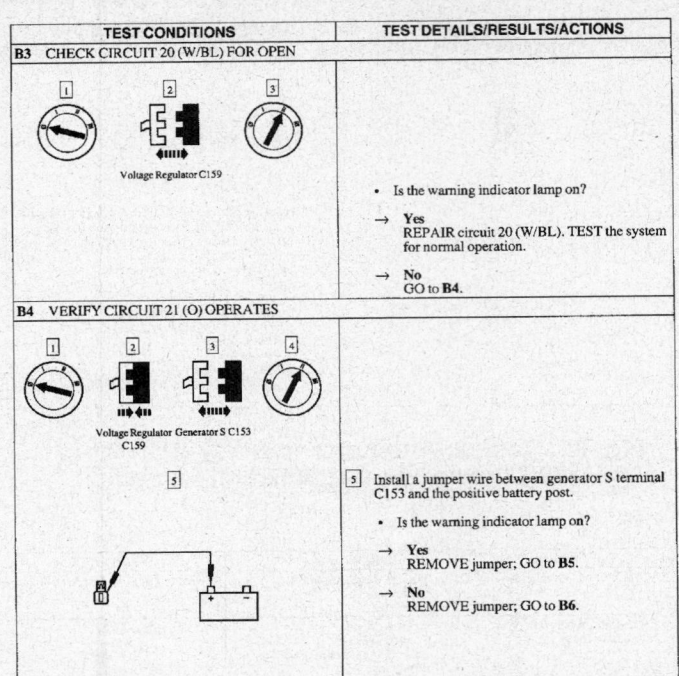

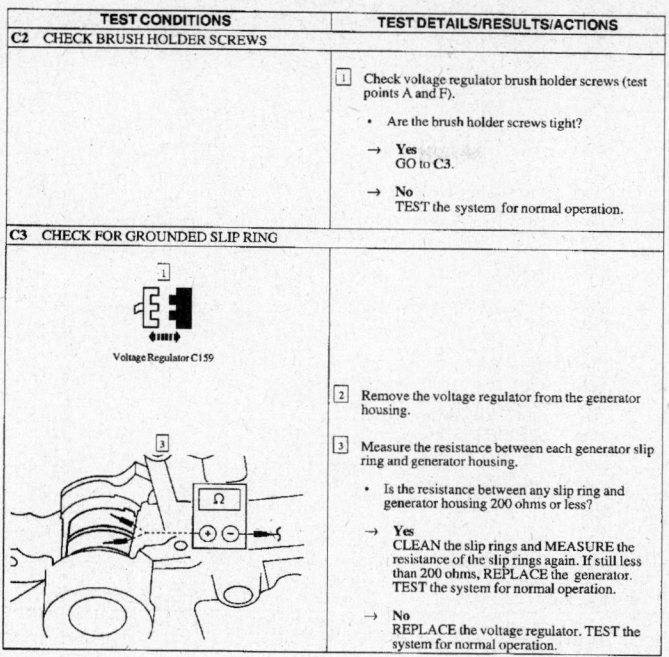

TEST CONDITIONS	TEST DETAILS/RESULTS/ACTIONS
C2 CHECK BRUSH HOLDER SCREWS	
	1 Check voltage regulator brush holder screws (test points A and F). • Are the brush holder screws tight? → **Yes** GO to **C3**. → **No** TEST the system for normal operation.
C3 CHECK FOR GROUNDED SLIP RING	
1  Voltage Regulator C159 3 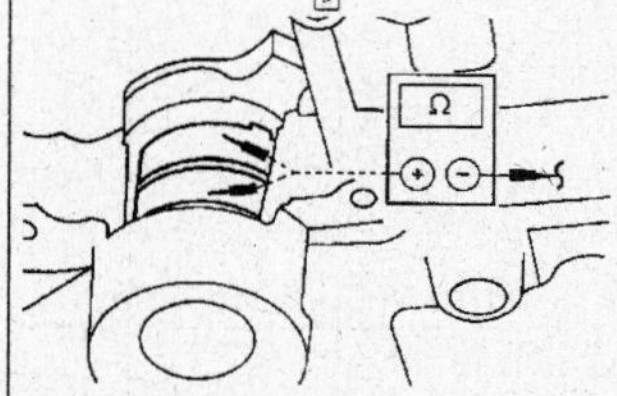	2 Remove the voltage regulator from the generator housing. 3 Measure the resistance between each generator slip ring and generator housing. • Is the resistance between any slip ring and generator housing 200 ohms or less? → **Yes** CLEAN the slip rings and MEASURE the resistance of the slip rings again. If still less than 200 ohms, REPLACE the generator. TEST the system for normal operation. → **No** REPLACE the voltage regulator. TEST the system for normal operation.

FM1129800230020X

Fig. 85 Test C: Warning Indicator Flickers/ Intermittent (Part 2 of 2). Escort, Tracer & ZX2

TEST CONDITIONS	TEST DETAILS/RESULTS/ACTIONS
D1 CHECK FOR ACCESSORY DRIVE NOISE (Continued)	
	3 Check for a bent pulley. • Is the accessory drive belt system OK? → **Yes** GO to **D2**. → **No** Inspect accessory drive system and repair as necessary.
D2 SUBSTITUTE KNOWN GOOD GENERATOR	
1  2  Generator 4 	3 Install a known good generator. • Is the noise present with a known good generator? → **Yes** INSTALL original generator and CHECK other accessories to FIND the cause of the noise. → **No** REPLACE the generator. TEST the system for normal operation.

FM1129800231020X

Fig. 86 Test D: Alternator Is Noisy (Part 2 of 2). Escort, Tracer & ZX2

TEST CONDITIONS	TEST DETAILS/RESULTS/ACTIONS
D1 CHECK FOR ACCESSORY DRIVE NOISE	
	1 Check the drive belt for damage and verify correct installation 2 Check the accessory mounting brackets for loose bolts or misalignment.

FM1129800231010X

Fig. 86 Test D: Alternator Is Noisy (Part 1 of 2). Escort, Tracer & ZX2

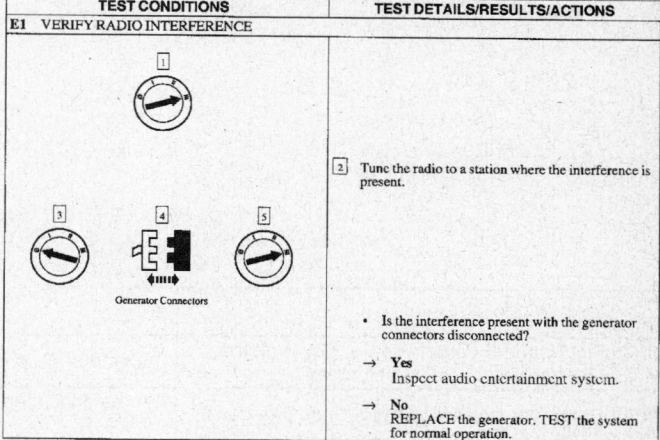

TEST CONDITIONS	TEST DETAILS/RESULTS/ACTIONS
E1 VERIFY RADIO INTERFERENCE	
1  3  4  Generator Connectors 5 	2 Tune the radio to a station where the interference is present. • Is the interference present with the generator connectors disconnected? → **Yes** Inspect audio entertainment system. → **No** REPLACE the generator. TEST the system for normal operation.

FM1129800232000X

Fig. 87 Test E: Radio Interference. Escort, Tracer & ZX2

TEST CONDITIONS	TEST DETAILS/RESULTS/ACTIONS
F1 CHECK BATTERY	
1 	2 Inspect condition of battery. • Is the battery OK? → **Yes** GO to **F2**. → **No** REPLACE the battery. TEST the system for normal operation.

FM1129800233010X

Fig. 88 Test F: Battery Does Not Hold A Charge (Part 1 of 2). Escort, Tracer & ZX2

TEST CONDITIONS	TEST DETAILS/RESULTS/ACTIONS
F2 CHECK FOR KEY-OFF DRAIN	
	1 Perform the Drain Testing. • Is the drain less than 0.05 amps? → **Yes** GO to Pinpoint Test G. → **No** REPAIR the system in question. TEST the system for normal operation.

FM1129800233020X

Fig. 88 Test F: Battery Does Not Hold A Charge (Part 2 of 2). Escort, Tracer & ZX2

TEST CONDITIONS	TEST DETAILS/RESULTS/ACTIONS
G1 CHECK DRIVE BELT TENSION	
	[1] Inspect the drive belt tension • Is the drive belt tension correct? → **Yes** GO to **G2**. → **No** REPLACE the drive belt or drive belt tensioner. TEST the system for normal operation.
G2 CHECK SYSTEM VOLTAGE	
	[1] Perform No-Load Test. • Is the system voltage below the specified range (undercharging)? → **Yes** GO to Pinpoint Test B. → **No** Perform Drain Testing in this section. REPAIR the system in question. TEST the system for normal operation.

FM1129800234000X

Fig. 89 Test G: System Does Not Charge. Escort, Tracer & ZX2

Condition	Possible Source	Actions To Take
Charging System Failure. High or Low Voltage, Indicator Illuminated, Engine Running	Alternator, Fuses, B+ Circuit 30-BA6 (RD), Circuit 30-BA25 (RD)	Go to Test A.
Dead Battery or Battery Will Not Stay Charged	Alternator, Battery, Fuses, B+ Circuit 30-BA6, Indicator Lamp Bulb, Harness Connector or Terminals	Go to Test B
Indicator Lamp Inoperative, Key On Engine Off	Alternator, Indicator Lamp Bulb, PCM, Circuit 30-BA25 (RD)	Go to Test C.
	Instrument Cluster	Repair as Required
Alternator is Noisy	Loose Bolts or Brackets, Drive belt, Alternator or Pulley	Go to Test D
Radio Interference	Alternator, Wiring, Routing, Vehicle Entertainment System	Go to Test E

Fig. 90 Symptom chart. LS

A1 CHECK SYSTEM VOLTAGE

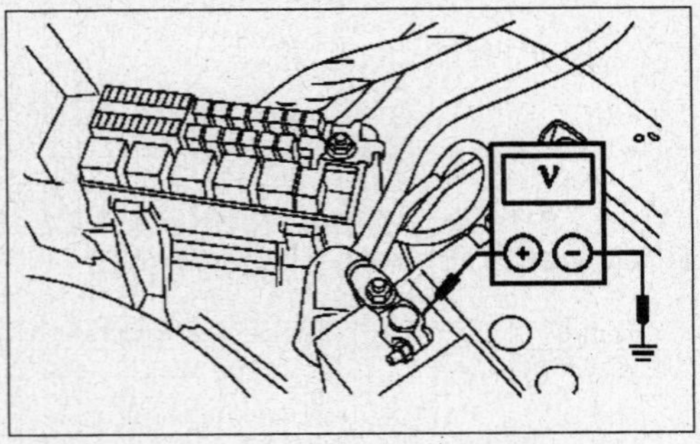

1

With the engine running, measure the voltage at the battery.

- **Is the battery voltage between 13 and 15 volts?**

➔ **Yes**

Go to «A3».

➔ **No**

Go to «A2».

FM1120000568010X

Fig. 91 Test A: Charging System Failure (Part 1 of 8). LS

A2 CHECK THE ACCESSORY DRIVE BELT

1

2 Inspect the accessory drive belt for condition and tension.

- **Is the accessory drive belt OK?**

➔ **Yes**

Go to «A3».

➔ **No**

INSTALL a new drive belt.

FM1120000568020X

Fig. 91 Test A: Charging System Failure (Part 2 of 8). LS

A3 CHECK GENERATOR CONNECTIONS

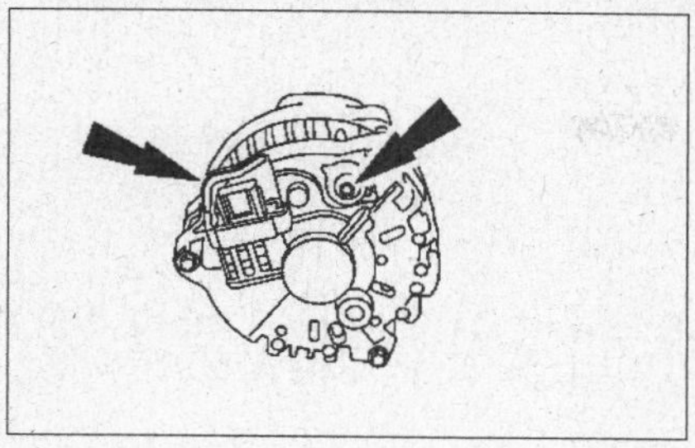

1

2 *Generator C102*

3 Check generator/regulator C102, circuit 30-BA25, generator B+ terminal C199, circuit 30-BA6, and generator mounting bolts for corrosion and tightness.

- **Are the generator connections clean and tight?**

→ **Yes**

Go to «A4».

→ **No**

REPAIR as necessary. TEST the system for normal operation.

FM1120000568030X

Fig. 91 Test A: Charging System Failure (Part 3 of 8). LS

A4 CHECK THE BATTERY CABLES/CONNECTIONS FOR TIGHTNESS

1 Check all battery cable/connections/clamps for corrosion and tightness. (Max voltage drop is 0.8 volt.)

- **Are the battery connections clean and tight?**

→ **Yes**

Go to «A5».

→ **No**

REPAIR as necessary. TEST the system for normal operation.

FM1120000568040X

Fig. 91 Test A: Charging System Failure (Part 4 of 8). LS

A5 CHECK THE BATTERY CONDITION

1 Check the battery condition.

- **Is the battery OK?**

→ **Yes**

Go to «A6».

→ **No**

INSTALL a new battery; TEST the system for normal operation.

FM1120000568050X

Fig. 91 Test A: Charging System Failure (Part 5 of 8). LS

A6 CHECK THE GENERATOR B+ TERMINAL VOLTAGE

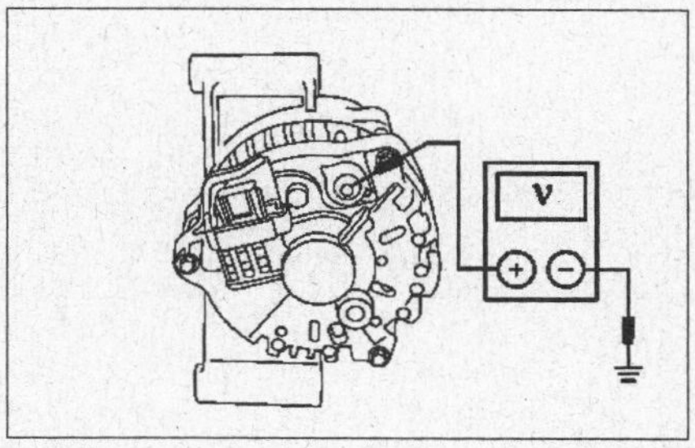

1

Measure the voltage between the generator B+ terminal, circuit 30-BA6 (RD), harness side and ground.

- **Is the voltage equivalent to battery B+ voltage?**

→ **Yes**

Go to «A7».

→ **No**

REPAIR circuit 30-BA6 (RD). TEST the system for normal operation.

FM1120000568060X

Fig. 91 Test A: Charging System Failure (Part 6 of 8). LS

A7 CHECK GENERATOR CIRCUIT 30–BA25

1 *Generator C102*

2

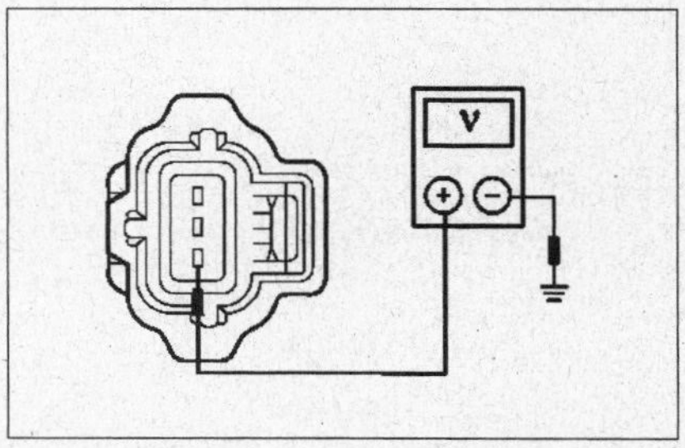

3

Measure the voltage between the generator C102 A sense, circuit 30-BA25 (RD), harness side and ground.

- **Is the voltage equivalent to battery voltage?**

→ **Yes**

Go to «A8».

→ **No**

REPAIR circuit 30-BA25 (RD) as necessary. TEST the system for normal operation.

FM1120000568070X

Fig. 91 Test A: Charging System Failure (Part 7 of 8). LS

A8	CHECK THE GENERATOR OUTPUT

1 Check the generator output. Utilizing the SABRE Premium Battery and Electrical Tester or equivalent tool, carry out Component Tests, Generator On-Vehicle tests in this section.

- **Is the generator OK?**

➔ **Yes**

REFER to **MOTOR's** "Domestic Engine Performance & Driveability Manual."

➔ **No**

INSTALL a new generator; TEST the system for normal operation.

FM1120000568080X

Fig. 91 Test A: Charging System Failure (Part 8 of 8). LS

B2	CHECK FOR DRAINS ON THE BATTERY

1

2 Carry out the battery drain test.

- **Do any drains greater than 50 milliamps exist?**

➔ **Yes**

REPAIR as necessary. TEST the system for normal operation.

➔ **No**

Go to «B3».

FM1120000569020X

Fig. 92 Test B: Dead Battery or Battery Will Not Hold Charge (Part 2 of 3). LS

C1	CHECK GENERATOR CONNECTOR C102

1 *Generator C102*

2 *Generator C102*

Check generator C102 for bent or damaged pins. Make sure the connector is mated correctly and making contact.

- **Is the connector OK?**

➔ **Yes**

Go to «C2».

➔ **No**

REPAIR connector C102 as necessary. TEST the system for normal operation.

FM1120000570010X

Fig. 93 Test C: Indicator Lamp Inoperative, Key On Engine Off (Part 1 of 2). LS

B1	CHECK THE BATTERY CONDITION

1 Check the battery capacity.

- **Is the battery OK?**

➔ **Yes**

Go to «B2».

➔ **No**

INSTALL a new battery; TEST the system for normal operation.

FM1120000569010X

Fig. 92 Test B: Dead Battery or Battery Will Not Hold Charge (Part 1 of 3). LS

B3	CHECK THE GENERATOR OUTPUT

1 Check the generator output.

- **Is the generator OK?**

➔ **Yes**

INSPECT ALTERNATOR WIRING HARNESS & CONNECTORS

➔ **No**

INSTALL a new generator; TEST the system for normal operation.

FM1120000569030X

Fig. 92 Test B: Dead Battery or Battery Will Not Hold Charge (Part 3 of 3). LS

C2	CHECK THE WARNING INDICATOR OPERATION

1

2 *Generator C102*

3

4

With the engine running and generator C102 disconnected, wait 30 seconds and observe the warning indicator operation.

- **Is the warning indicator off?**

➔ **Yes**

CHECK the warning indicator bulb.

➔ **No**

INSPECT AS REQUIRED

FM1120000570020X

Fig. 93 Test C: Indicator Lamp Inoperative, Key On Engine Off (Part 2 of 2). LS

D1	CHECK FOR ACCESSORY DRIVE NOISE

1. Check the drive belt for damage and verify installation.
2. Check all accessory mountings for loose bolts or misalignment.
3. Check for a bent generator pulley.
4. Check all accessories for a bent, misaligned or loose pulley.
5. With a mechanic's stethoscope or other suitable listening device, probe the generator, other accessories/idler pulley(s), and tensioners, to determine which component is generating the noise.

- **Is the generator noisy?**

➔ **Yes**

INSTALL a new generator; TEST the system for normal operation.

➔ **No**

INSPECT the accessory drive system.

FM1120000571000X

Fig. 94 Test D: Alternator Noisy. LS

E1	VERIFY THERE IS RADIO INTERFERENCE

1. Start and run the engine.
2. Tune the radio to a station where interference is present.

- **Is the interference present with the generator disconnected?**

➔ **Yes**

INSPECT the in-vehicle entertainment system.

➔ **No**

INSTALL a new generator; TEST the system for normal operation.

FM1120000572000X

Fig. 95 Test E: Radio Interference. LS

Condition	Possible Source	Action
• System Does Not Charge	• Circuitry. • Voltage regulator. • Generator. • Battery. • Battery connections. • Drive belt.	• GO to Pinpoint Test A.
• System Overcharges (Battery Boils Over)	• Circuitry. • Poor ground. • Voltage regulator. • Generator.	• GO to Pinpoint Test B.
• Indicator Lamp Stays ON, Engine Running	• Circuitry. • Voltage regulator. • Generator.	• GO to Pinpoint Test C.
• Indicator Lamp Stays ON, Ignition Switch OFF	• Circuitry. • Improper lamp circuit wiring. • Instrument cluster.	• GO to Pinpoint Test D.
• Indicator Lamp Does Not Come On	• Circuitry. • Burned out lamp. • Poor ground. • Voltage regulator. • Generator.	• GO to Pinpoint Test E.
• Indicator Lamp Flickers/Intermittent	• Loose connection to generator, voltage regulator or power distribution box. • Circuitry. • Loose brush holder screw. • Voltage regulator. • Generator.	• GO to Pinpoint Test F.
• Generator Noisy	• Accessory drive belt. • Accessory brackets. • Bent pulley. • Generator. • Other accessories.	• GO to Pinpoint Test G.
• Radio Interference	• Voltage regulator. • Generator. • Other components.	• GO to Pinpoint Test H.

FM1129700209000X

Fig. 96 Symptom chart. 1997–98 Mustang

Condition	Possible Source	Action
• The battery is not being charged by generator	• Voltage regulator connector. • Charging system warning indicator lamp bulb. • Voltage regulator. • Generator. • Connections.	• GO to Pinpoint Test A.
• Battery overcharging (voltage is greater than 15.5 volts)	• S Circuit 4 (WH/BK). • Generator. • Voltage regulator.	• GO to Pinpoint Test B.
• The charging system warning indicator is on with the engine running (system is charging)	• I Circuit 904 (LG/RD). • Instrument cluster. • S Circuit 4 (WH/BK). • Generator. • Voltage regulator.	• GO to Pinpoint Test C.
• The charging system indicator lamp does not come on	• I Circuit 904 (LG/RD). • Connections. • Battery cables. • Generator. • Voltage regulator. • Instrument panel. • Indicator lamp.	• GO to Pinpoint Test D.
• The charging system warning indicator flickers or is intermittent	• Connections. • I Circuit fuse loose CJB Fuse 5 (15A). • A Circuit fuse loose. • Generator. • Voltage regulator.	• GO to Pinpoint Test E.
• The generator is noisy	• Bolts or brackets. • Drive belt. • Generator or pulley.	• GO to Pinpoint Test F.

FM1120000550010X

Fig. 97 Symptom chart (Part 1 of 2). 1999–2000 Mustang w/3.8L engine

Condition	Possible Source	Action
• Radio interference	• Generator. • Wiring or routing. • In-vehicle entertainment system.	• GO to Pinpoint Test G.
• The voltage gauge (if equipped) is inaccurate	• Generator. • Voltage regulator. • Voltage gauge. • Instrument cluster. • Wiring.	• Repair as required.
• Battery is discharged or voltage is low	• Corroded terminal(s). • Loose connection(s). • High key-off current drains. • Battery. • Generator.	• GO to Pinpoint Test O.

FM1120000550020X

Fig. 97 Symptom chart (Part 2 of 2). 1999–2000 Mustang w/3.8L engine

Condition	Possible Source	Action
• The battery is not being charged by the generator	• Fuse links. • I Circuit 904 (LG/RD). • I Circuit fuse (20A). • Generator. • Charging system warning indicator lamp bulb. • Harness connector.	• GO to Pinpoint Test H.
• Battery overcharging (voltage greater than 15.5 volts)	• Generator.	• GO to Pinpoint Test I.
• The charging system warning indicator lamp is on with the engine running (system is charging)	• I Circuit 904 (LG/RD). • Instrument cluster. • Generator.	• GO to Pinpoint Test J.
• The charging system warning indicator lamp does not come on	• Lamp bulb. • Instrument cluster. • I Circuit 904 (LG/RD). • Harness connector. • Generator.	• GO to Pinpoint Test K.

FM1120000551010X

Fig. 98 Symptom chart (Part 1 of 2). 1999–2000 Mustang w/4.6L engine

Condition	Possible Source	Action
• The charging system warning indicator lamp flickers or is intermittent	• Corroded terminals. • Connections. • Fuses. • Generator.	• GO to Pinpoint Test L.
• The generator is noisy	• Bolts or brackets. • Drive belt. • Generator or pulley.	• GO to Pinpoint Test M.
• Radio interference	• Harness routing. • In-vehicle entertainment system. • A Circuit 36 (YE/WH). • Generator.	• GO to Pinpoint Test N.
• Voltage gauge (if equipped) is inaccurate.	• Generator. • Voltage regulator. • Voltage gauges. • Instrument cluster. • Wiring.	• REPAIR as required.
• Battery is discharged or voltage is low	• Corroded terminal(s). • Loose connection(s). • High key-off current drains. • Battery. • Generator.	• GO to Pinpoint Test O.

FM1120000551020X

Fig. 98 Symptom chart (Part 2 of 2). 1999–2000 Mustang w/4.6L engine

	Test Step	Result	Action to Take
A5	CHECK BATTERY		
	• Perform Battery Capacity Testing. • **Is the battery OK?**	Yes No	▶ GO to **A6**. ▶ REPLACE battery.
A6	CHECK FOR KEY-OFF DRAIN		
	• Perform Battery Drain Testing as described. • **Is current drain less than 50 mA (or test lamp off)?**	Yes No	▶ GO to **A7**. ▶ GO to Drain Testing to find cause of ignition switch-OFF battery drain.
A7	CHECK FOR OPEN B+ CIRCUIT		
	• Measure voltage at B+ terminal at generator connector C1006. • **Is voltage at B+ terminal equal to battery voltage?**	Yes No	▶ GO to **A8**. ▶ SERVICE open in Circuit 38 (BK/O).
A8	CHECK FOR OPEN A CIRCUIT		
	• Measure voltage at A circuit on the voltage regulator connector C154. • **Is voltage at A circuit equal to battery voltage?**	Yes No	▶ GO to **A9** on 3.8L and 4.6L (2V). GO to **A10** for 4.6L (4V). ▶ CHECK power distribution box Fuse ALT (20A) in Circuit 36 (Y/W) and REPLACE if required. If OK, SERVICE open in Circuit 36 (Y/W).
A9	CHECK FOR OPEN FIELD CIRCUIT		
	• Measure voltage at test point F on voltage regulator. • **Is voltage at test point F equal to battery voltage?**	Yes No	▶ GO to **A10**. ▶ GO to **A16**.
A10	CHECK FOR OPEN I CIRCUIT		
	• Turn ignition switch to RUN position. • NOTE: Voltage regulator must be connected to wiring harness for this test. Measure voltage at wiring harness I terminal of connector C154, Circuit 904 (LG/R). • **Is voltage greater than 1 V?**	Yes No	▶ GO to **A11**. ▶ SERVICE open or high resistance in Circuit 904 (LG/R).
A11	CHECK VOLTAGE DROP IN A CIRCUIT		
	• Measure voltage drop between A Circuit on voltage regulator and positive (+) battery post. • **Is voltage drop less than 0.25 V?**	Yes No	▶ GO to **A12** on 3.8L and 4.6L (2V). On 4.6L (4V), GO to **A14**. ▶ SERVICE excess voltage drop in Circuit 36 (Y/W). CHECK fuse and connectors in Circuit 36 (Y/W) and SERVICE as required.
A12	CHECK FIELD TURN-ON		
	• Measure voltage at test point F on voltage regulator. • **Is voltage at test point F less than 2 V?**	Yes No	▶ GO to **A13**. ▶ GO to **A16**.
A13	CHECK FOR SHORTED RECTIFIER		
	• Remove one-pin S connector C153 from generator. • Measure voltage between S terminal on back of generator and ground. • Measure voltage between positive (+) battery terminal and S terminal on back of generator. • **Is either voltage reading greater than 1 V?**	Yes No	▶ REPLACE generator. ▶ GO to **A14**.
A14	CHECK VOLTAGE DROP IN B+ CIRCUIT		
	• Turn ignition switch to RUN position. • Turn headlamps ON and set blower on HIGH. • With engine running at 2000 rpm, measure voltage drop between the B+ terminal on back of generator and positive (+) battery post. • **Is voltage drop less than 0.5 V?**	Yes No	▶ GO to **A15** on 3.8L and 4.6L (2V). On 4.6L (4V), REPLACE generator. ▶ SERVICE excess voltage drop in Circuit 38 (BK/O). CHECK fuse link in Circuit 38 (BK/O) and the connections between the battery and power distribution box.

FM1129700210020X

Fig. 99 Test A: System Does Not Charge (Part 2 of 3). 1997–98 Mustang

	Test Step	Result	Action to Take
A1	CHECK BATTERY CONNECTIONS		
	• Inspect battery cables for loose or corroded connections. • Inspect battery for corrosion. • **Are battery cables clean, tight and free from corrosion?**	Yes No	▶ GO to **A2**. ▶ CLEAN and TIGHTEN battery cables.
A2	CHECK DRIVE BELT TENSION		
	• Perform drive belt adjustment procedure. • **Is the drive belt adjusted properly?**	Yes No	▶ GO to **A3**. ▶ ADJUST or REPLACE drive belt.
A3	LOOSE BATTERY POST		
	• Check for loose battery posts. • **Are posts OK?**	Yes No	▶ GO to **A4**. ▶ REPLACE battery.
A4	CRACKED BATTERY COVER		
	• Remove battery hold down clamps and shields. • Check for broken/cracked case or battery cover. • **Are case and cover OK?**	Yes No	▶ GO to **A5**. ▶ REPLACE battery.

FM1129700210010X

Fig. 99 Test A: System Does Not Charge (Part 1 of 3). 1997–98 Mustang

	Test Step	Result	Action to Take
A15	CHECK FOR OPEN STATOR PHASE		
	• Connect test point F on the voltage regulator to negative (-) battery post using a jumper wire. • Perform Generator Load Test as described. • **Is generator output current greater than minimum output specified?**	Yes No	▶ REPLACE voltage regulator. ▶ REPLACE generator.
A16	CHECK FOR OPEN/SHORTED FIELD		
	• Remove generator from vehicle. • Remove voltage regulator. • Measure resistance between generator slip rings. • **Is resistance greater than 10 ohms OR less than 1 ohm?**	Yes No	▶ REPLACE generator. ▶ REPLACE voltage regulator. RETEST system.

FM1129700210030X

Fig. 99 Test A: System Does Not Charge (Part 3 of 3). 1997–98 Mustang

	Test Step	Result	Action to Take
B1	CHECK VOLTAGE DROP IN A CIRCUIT		
	• Turn ignition switch to ON. • Measure voltage between A circuit on voltage regulator and positive (+) battery post. • **Is voltage drop less than 0.25 V?**	Yes No	▶ GO to **B2**. ▶ SERVICE excess voltage drop in Circuit 36 (Y/W). CHECK power distribution box Fuse ALT (20A) and connectors in Circuit 36 (Y/W) and SERVICE as required.
B2	CHECK VOLTAGE DROP IN I CIRCUIT		
	• NOTE: Voltage regulator must be connected to wiring harness for this test. Measure voltage at wiring harness I terminal connector C154, Circuit 904 (LG/R). • **Is voltage greater than 1 V?**	Yes No	▶ GO to **B3**. ▶ SERVICE high resistance in Circuit 904 (LG/R).
B3	CHECK FOR POOR GROUNDS		
	• Check for poor ground connections between voltage regulator and generator, generator and engine, or engine and battery. • **Are all ground connections clean and tight?**	Yes No	▶ GO to **B4** on 3.8L and 4.6L (2V). REPLACE generator on 4.6L (4V). ▶ CLEAN or SERVICE grounds as required.
B4	CHECK FOR FIELD CIRCUIT DRAIN		
	• Turn ignition switch to OFF position. • Measure voltage at test point F on voltage regulator. • **Is voltage at test point F equal to battery voltage?**	Yes No	▶ Generator is OK. REPLACE voltage regulator. ▶ GO to **B5**.
B5	CHECK FOR GROUNDED SLIP RING		
	• Remove generator from vehicle. • Remove voltage regulator. • Measure resistance from each generator slip ring to the generator housing. • **Is resistance from either slip ring to housing less than 200 ohms?**	Yes No	▶ If grease or dirt has accumulated near slip rings, CLEAN slip rings and RECHECK resistance. If still less than 200 ohms, REPLACE generator. ▶ REPLACE voltage regulator.

FM1129700211000X

Fig. 100 Test B: System Overcharges. 1997–98 Mustang

	Test Step	Result	Action to Take
C1	CHECK FOR OPEN A CIRCUIT		
	• Measure voltage at A circuit on voltage regulator. • **Is voltage at A circuit equal to battery voltage?**	Yes	GO to **C2.**
		No	CHECK fuse in Circuit 36 (Y/W) and REPLACE if required. If OK, SERVICE open in Circuit 36 (Y/W).
C2	CHECK FOR SHORTED I CIRCUIT		
	• Remove voltage regulator connector C154. • Turn ignition switch to RUN. • **Is indicator lamp on?**	Yes	SERVICE short to ground in Circuit 904 (LG/R).
		No	GO to **C3** on 3.8L and 4.6L (2V). GO to **C6** on 4.6L (4V).
C3	CHECK S CIRCUIT FUNCTION		
	• Install voltage regulator connector C154. • Remove one-pin S connector. • Connect wiring harness S terminal, Circuit 4 (W/BK) to positive (+) battery post using a jumper wire. • **Is indicator lamp on?**	Yes	REMOVE jumper wire. GO to **C4.**
		No	REMOVE jumper wire. GO to **C5.**
C4	CHECK FOR OPEN S CIRCUIT		
	• Remove three-pin voltage regulator connector C154. • Measure wiring resistance between one-pin S connector C153and S (center) pin of voltage regulator connector. • **Is resistance greater than 1 ohm?**	Yes	SERVICE open or excess resistance in Circuit 4 (W/BK).
		No	CHECK for loose or bent pin in voltage regulator or connector. If OK, REPLACE voltage regulator.
C5	CHECK STATOR OUTPUT VOLTAGE		
	• Turn ignition switch to RUN. • Measure voltage at S terminal on back of generator. • **Is voltage at least 1/2 of battery voltage?**	Yes	GO to **C6.**
		No	GO to Pinpoint Test A to find the cause of low generator output.
C6	CHECK GENERATOR OUTPUT VOLTAGE		
	• Measure voltage at B+ terminal at connector C1006 on the back of generator with engine running at 2000 rpm and all accessories turned OFF. • **Is voltage greater than 15.5 V?**	Yes	GO to Pinpoint Test B to find the cause of high output voltage.
		No	REPLACE voltage regulator on 3.8L and 4.6L (2V). REPLACE generator on 4.6L (4V).

FM1129700212000X

Fig. 101 Test C: Indicator Lamp Stays On, Engine Running. 1997–98 Mustang

	Test Step	Result	Action to Take
E4	CHECK S CIRCUIT WIRING		
	• Remove one-pin S connector from generator C153. • Measure voltage at wiring harness S terminal, Circuit 4 (W/BK). • **Is voltage greater than zero V?**	Yes	SERVICE Circuit 4 (W/BK). Circuit should be HOT only when engine is running.
		No	GO to **E5.**
E5	CHECK FOR SHORTED RECTIFIER		
	• Measure voltage at the S terminal on the back of generator. • **Is voltage greater than 1 V?**	Yes	If lamp is on with one-pin S connector removed, REPLACE generator.
		No	REPLACE voltage regulator.

FM1129700214020X

Fig. 103 Test E: Indicator Lamp Does Not Come On (Part 2 of 2). 1997–98 Mustang

	Test Step	Result	Action to Take
G1	CHECK FOR ACCESSORY DRIVE NOISE		
	• Check the drive belt to make sure that it is installed properly and is not damaged. • **Is drive belt OK?**	Yes	GO to **G2.**
		No	SERVICE accessory drive belt as required.
G2	CHECK GENERATOR MOUNTING		
	• Check generator and generator mounting bracket for loose bolts or misalignment condition. • **Is generator mounted correctly?**	Yes	GO to **G3.**
		No	INSTALL generator to specification.
G3	CHECK GENERATOR PULLEY		
	• Check generator pulley for damage (bent) or a misalignment condition. • **Is pulley OK?**	Yes	REPLACE generator.
		No	REPLACE generator pulley.

FM1129700216000X

Fig. 105 Test G: Alternator Is Noisy. 1997–98 Mustang

	Test Step	Result	Action to Take
D1	CHECK LAMP CIRCUIT WIRING		
	• Turn ignition switch to OFF position. • Disconnect voltage regulator connector C154. • Measure voltage at wiring harness I terminal, Circuit 904 (LG/R). • **Is voltage greater than zero V?**	Yes	SERVICE Circuit 16 (R/LG). Circuit should be HOT in ignition switch START or RUN only.
		No	SERVICE instrument cluster.

FM1129700213000X

Fig. 102 Test D: Indicator Lamps Stay On, Ignition Switch Off. 1997–98 Mustang

	Test Step	Result	Action to Take
E1	CHECK FOR OPEN I CIRCUIT		
	• Remove voltage regulator connector C154. • Turn ignition switch to RUN. • Measure voltage at wiring harness I terminal, Circuit 904 (LG/R). • **Is voltage equal to B+?**	Yes	GO to **E2.**
		No	SERVICE open in Circuit 904 (LG/R).
E2	CHECK FOR BURNED OUT BULB		
	• Connect wiring harness I terminal, Circuit 904 (LG/R) to ground with a jumper wire. • **Is indicator lamp on?**	Yes	REMOVE jumper wire. GO to **E3.**
		No	REPLACE lamp or SERVICE high resistance in lamp socket or Circuit 904 (LG/R).
E3	CHECK FOR POOR GROUNDS		
	• Check for poor ground connections between voltage regulator and generator, generator and engine, or engine and battery. • **Are all ground connections clean and tight?**	Yes	GO to **E4** on 3.8L and 4.6L (2V). REPLACE generator on 4.6L (2V).
		No	CLEAN or SERVICE grounds as required.

FM1129700214010X

Fig. 103 Test E: Indicator Lamp Does Not Come On (Part 1 of 2). 1997–98 Mustang

	Test Step	Result	Action to Take
F1	CHECK FOR LOOSE CONNECTIONS		
	• Check these connections for corrosion, loose or bent pins, or loose eyelets: — voltage regulator connector C154 — one-pin S connector C153 3.8L and 4.6L (2V) only — generator B+ eyelet — power distribution box eyelets — battery cables • **Are all connections clean and tight?**	Yes	GO to **F2** on 3.8L and 4.6L (2V). GO to **F3** on 4.6L (2V).
		No	CLEAN or SERVICE connections as required.
F2	CHECK FOR FIELD CIRCUIT DRAIN		
	• Turn ignition switch to OFF position. • Measure voltage at test point F on voltage regulator. • **Is voltage at test point F equal to battery voltage?**	Yes	GO to **F3.**
		No	GO to **F5.**
F3	CHECK FOR LOOSE A CIRCUIT FUSE		
	• Turn ignition switch to RUN. • Check the power distribution box ALT Fuse (20A) for a loose connection by wiggling fuse with engine running. • **Does indicator lamp flicker?**	Yes	SERVICE loose fuse connection.
		No	GO to **F4.**
F4	CHECK A CIRCUIT CONNECTIONS		
	• With engine running, connect A circuit on voltage regulator to positive (+) battery post using a jumper wire. • **Does indicator lamp flicker?**	Yes	REPLACE voltage regulator. If concern still exists, REPLACE generator on 3.8L and 4.6L (2V). REPLACE generator on 4.6L (2V).
		No	SERVICE poor connection in Circuit 36 (Y/W).
F5	CHECK BRUSH HOLDER SCREWS		
	• Remove generator from vehicle. • Check the brush holder screws, located on the voltage regulator (test points F and A). • **Are the brush holder screws tight?**	Yes	GO to **F6.**
		No	TIGHTEN screws to 2.8-4.0 N·m (25-35 lb-in).
F6	CHECK FOR GROUNDED SLIP RING		
	• Remove voltage regulator. • Measure resistance from each generator slip ring to the generator housing. • **Is resistance from either slip ring to housing less than 200 ohms?**	Yes	If grease or dirt has accumulated near slip rings, CLEAN slip rings and RECHECK resistance. If still less than 200 ohms, REPLACE generator.
		No	REPLACE voltage regulator.

FM1129700215000X

Fig. 104 Test F: Indicator Lamp Flickers/ Intermittent. 1997–98 Mustang

	Test Step	Result	Action to Take
H1	VERIFY RADIO INTERFERENCE		
	• Turn ignition switch to RUN position. • Tune radio to a station where interference is present. • Remove voltage regulator connector C154. • **Is interference present with connector removed?**	Yes	Locate cause of radio interference.
		No	REPLACE generator.

FM1129700217000X

Fig. 106 Test H: Radio Interference. 1997–98 Mustang

TEST CONDITIONS	TEST DETAILS/RESULTS/ACTIONS
A1 CHECK GENERATOR B+ CIRCUIT 38 (BK/OG) VOLTAGE	
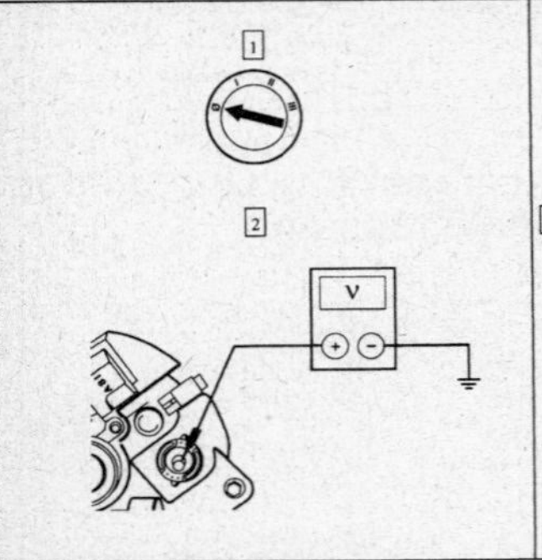	2 Measure the voltage between the generator B+ Circuit 38 (BK/OG) terminal and ground. • Is the voltage equal to battery positive voltage (B+)? → **Yes** GO to **A2**. → **No** REPAIR circuit. TEST the system for normal operation.
A2 CHECK A CIRCUIT 36 (YE/WH)	
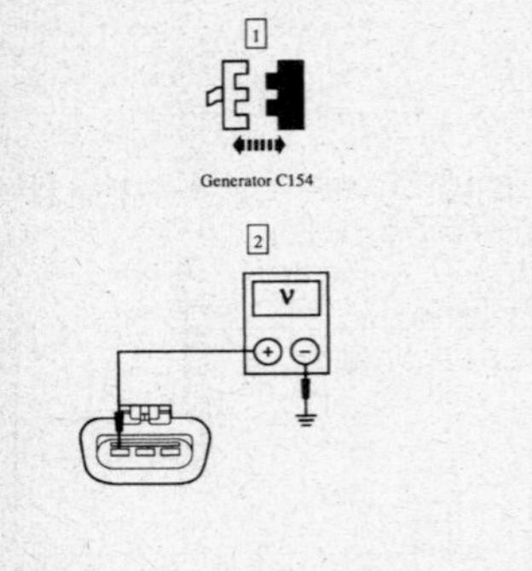	2 Measure the voltage between the generator C154 Pin A, Circuit 36 (YE/WH) harness side and ground. • Is the voltage equal to battery positive voltage (B+)? → **Yes** GO to **A3**. → **No** REPAIR circuit. TEST the system for normal operation.

FM1120000552010X

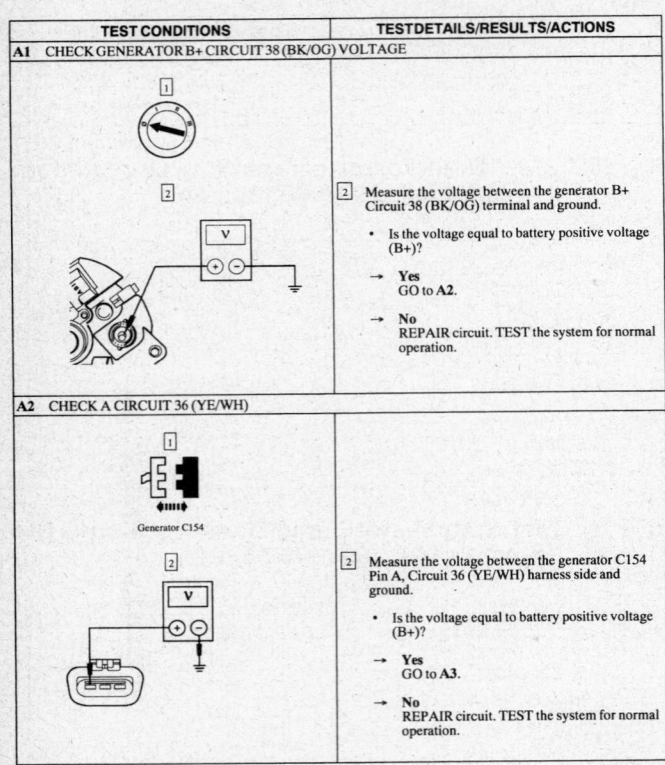

Fig. 107 Test A: System Does Not Charge (Part 1 of 3). 1999–2000 Mustang w/3.8L Engine

TEST CONDITIONS	TEST DETAILS/RESULTS/ACTIONS
A3 CHECK I CIRCUIT 904 (LG/RD)	
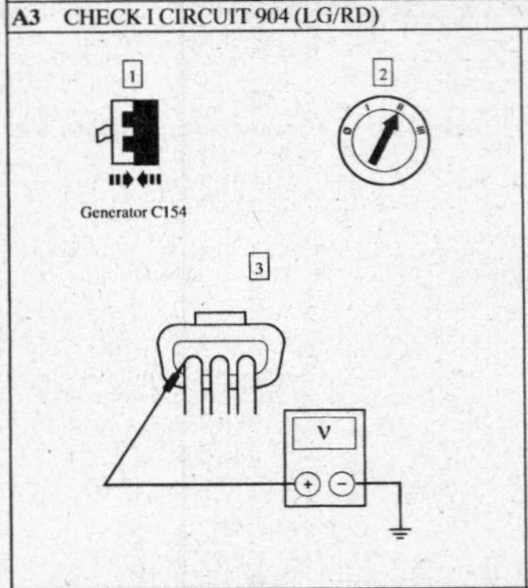	3 With the key ON, engine OFF, measure the voltage by backprobing between generator C154 Pin I, Circuit 904 (LG/RD) harness side and ground. • Is the voltage equal to battery B+? → **Yes** GO to **A4**. → **No** REPAIR circuit. TEST the system for normal operation.
A4 CHECK FOR VOLTAGE DROP IN B+ CIRCUIT 38 (BK/OG)	
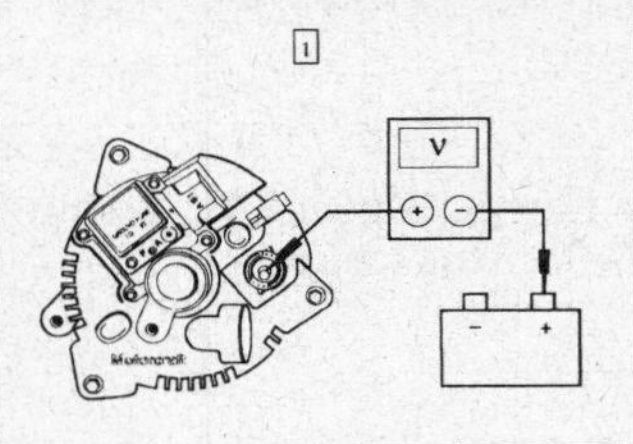	1 Measure the voltage drop between the B+ terminal on the generator and the battery positive post. • Is the voltage drop less than 0.5 volt? → **Yes** GO to **A5**. → **No** REPAIR high resistance in the B+ circuit. TEST the system for normal operation.

FM1120000552020X

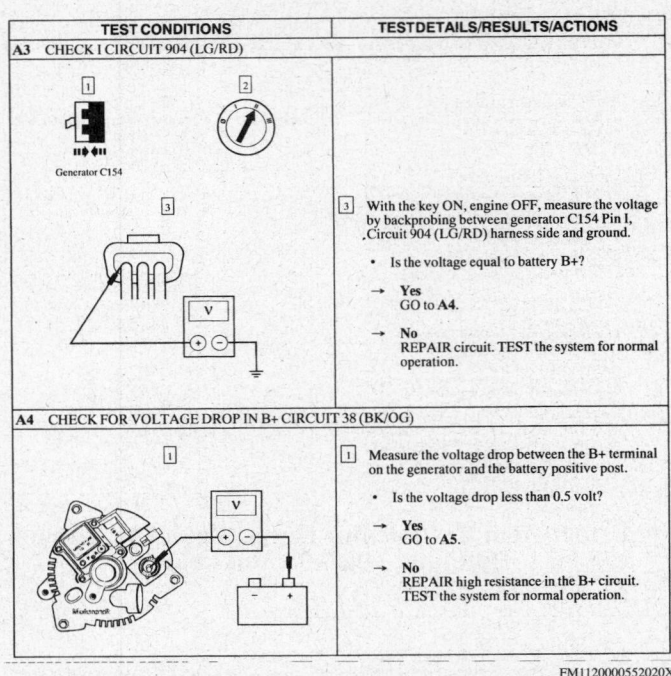

Fig. 107 Test A: System Does Not Charge (Part 2 of 3). 1999–2000 Mustang w/3.8L Engine

TEST CONDITIONS	TEST DETAILS/RESULTS/ACTIONS
A5 CHECK THE GENERATOR OUTPUT	
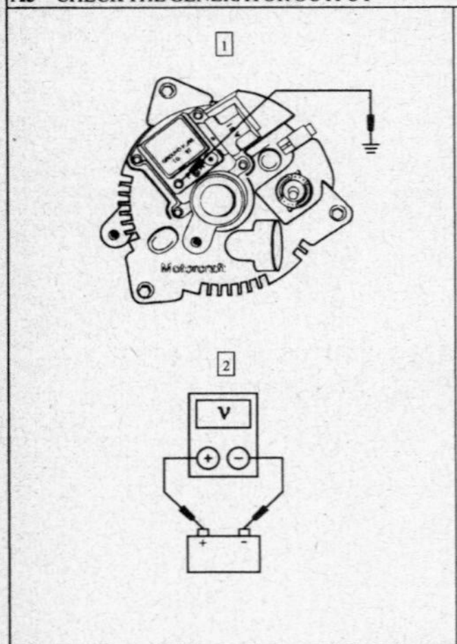	1 With the engine running, connect a jumper wire between the F terminal on the voltage regulator and ground. 2 Measure the voltage between the two battery terminals. • Does the battery voltage increase? → **Yes** INSTALL a new voltage regulator TEST the system for normal operation. → **No** INSTALL a new generator TEST the system for normal operation.

FM1120000552030X

Fig. 107 Test A: System Does Not Charge (Part 3 of 3). 1999–2000 Mustang w/3.8L Engine

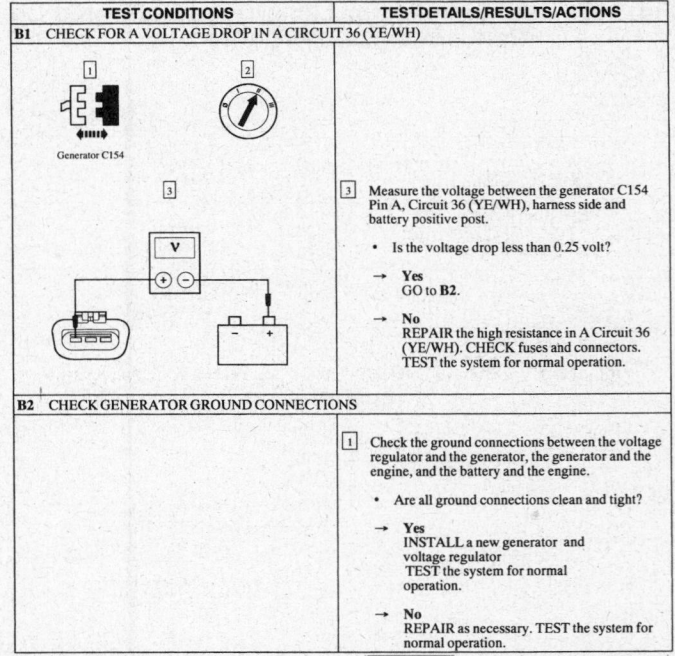

TEST CONDITIONS	TEST DETAILS/RESULTS/ACTIONS
B1 CHECK FOR A VOLTAGE DROP IN A CIRCUIT 36 (YE/WH)	
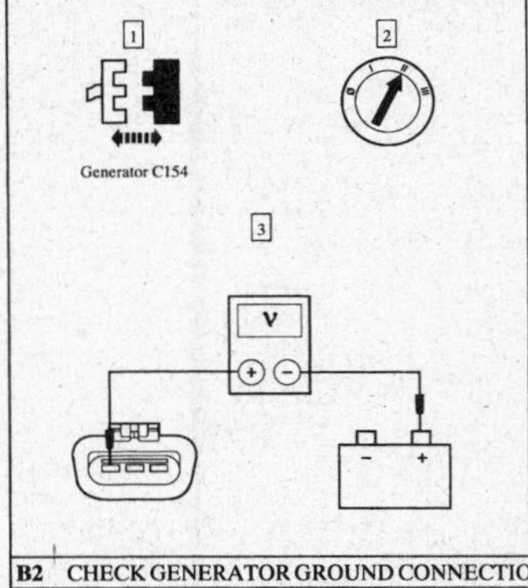	3 Measure the voltage between the generator C154 Pin A, Circuit 36 (YE/WH), harness side and battery positive post. • Is the voltage drop less than 0.25 volt? → **Yes** GO to **B2**. → **No** REPAIR the high resistance in A Circuit 36 (YE/WH). CHECK fuses and connectors. TEST the system for normal operation.
B2 CHECK GENERATOR GROUND CONNECTIONS	
	1 Check the ground connections between the voltage regulator and the generator, the generator and the engine, and the battery and the engine. • Are all ground connections clean and tight? → **Yes** INSTALL a new generator and voltage regulator TEST the system for normal operation. → **No** REPAIR as necessary. TEST the system for normal operation.

FM1120000553000X

Fig. 108 Test B: System Overcharging. 1999–2000 Mustang w/3.8L Engine

TEST CONDITIONS	TEST DETAILS/RESULTS/ACTIONS
C1 CHECK I CIRCUIT 904 (LG/RD) FOR SHORT TO GROUND	
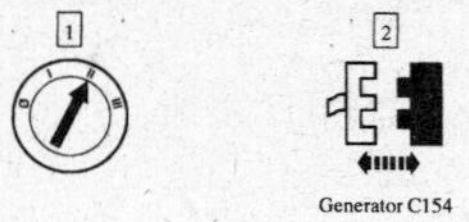	3 Turn the key ON, engine OFF. • Is the charging system warning indicator lamp on? → **Yes** REPAIR the short to ground in I Circuit 904 (LG/RD). TEST the system for normal operation. → **No** GO to **C2**.
C2 INSPECT GENERATOR S C153	
	1 Inspect generator C153 to make sure it is correctly mated to the generator and making contact with the S terminal. • Is the generator C153 OK? → **Yes** GO to **C3**. → **No** REPAIR as necessary. TEST the system for normal operation.

FM1120000554010X

Fig. 109 Test C: Indicator Lamp Remains Illuminated w/Engine Running (Part 1 of 2). 1999–2000 Mustang w/3.8L Engine

TEST CONDITIONS	TEST DETAILS/RESULTS/ACTIONS
C3 CHECK GENERATOR FOR LOW VOLTAGE	
 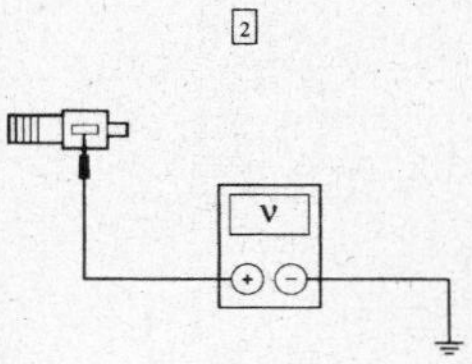	2 With the engine running at 2,000 rpm, measure the voltage between generator C153, Circuit 4 (WH/BK), harness side and ground. • Is the voltage greater than 5 volts? → **Yes** INSTALL a new voltage regulator TEST the system for normal operation. → **No** INSTALL a new generator TEST the system for normal operation.

FM1120000554020X

Fig. 109 Test C: Indicator Lamp Remains Illuminated w/Engine Running (Part 2 of 2). 1999–2000 Mustang w/3.8L Engine

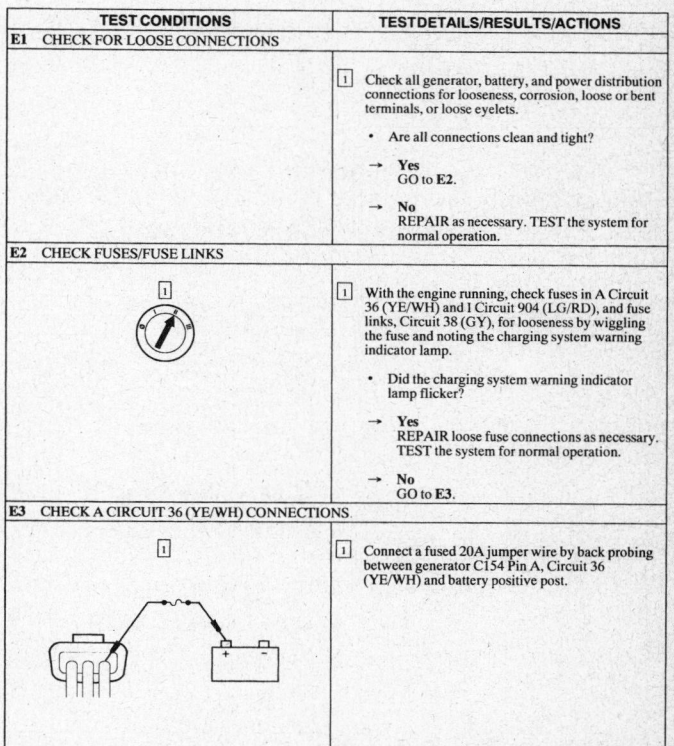

TEST CONDITIONS	TEST DETAILS/RESULTS/ACTIONS
D1 CHECK CHARGING SYSTEM WARNING INDICATOR LAMP	
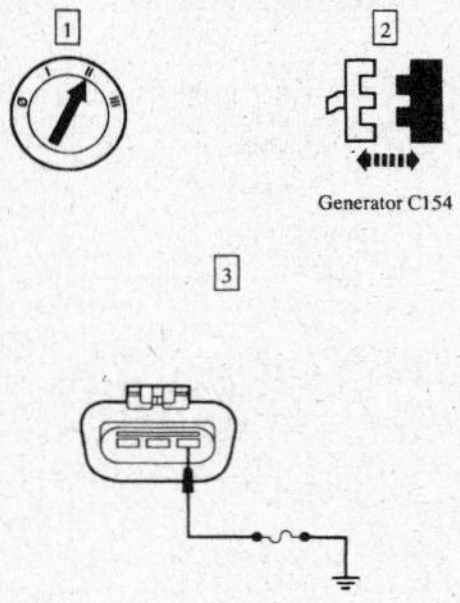	3 With the engine OFF, connect a fused 15A jumper wire between generator C154 Pin I, Circuit 904 (LG/RD), harness side and ground. • Is the charging system warning indicator lamp on? → **Yes** INSTALL a new voltage regulator TEST the system for normal operation. → **No** INSPECT lamp as required.

FM1120000555000X

Fig. 110 Test D: Indicator Lamp Does Not Illuminate. 1999–2000 Mustang w/3.8L Engine

TEST CONDITIONS	TEST DETAILS/RESULTS/ACTIONS
E1 CHECK FOR LOOSE CONNECTIONS	
	1 Check all generator, battery, and power distribution connections for looseness, corrosion, loose or bent terminals, or loose eyelets. • Are all connections clean and tight? → **Yes** GO to **E2**. → **No** REPAIR as necessary. TEST the system for normal operation.
E2 CHECK FUSES/FUSE LINKS	
	1 With the engine running, check fuses in A Circuit 36 (YE/WH) and I Circuit 904 (LG/RD), and fuse links, Circuit 38 (GY), for looseness by wiggling the fuse and noting the charging system warning indicator lamp. • Did the charging system warning indicator lamp flicker? → **Yes** REPAIR loose fuse connections as necessary. TEST the system for normal operation. → **No** GO to **E3**.
E3 CHECK A CIRCUIT 36 (YE/WH) CONNECTIONS	
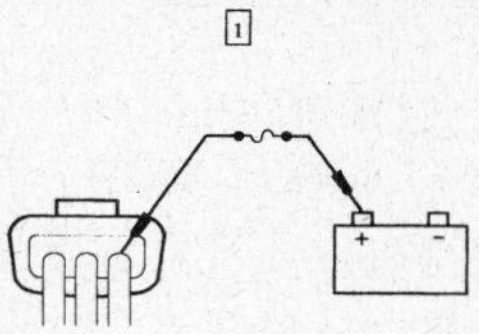	1 Connect a fused 20A jumper wire by back probing between generator C154 Pin A, Circuit 36 (YE/WH) and battery positive post.

FM1120000556010X

Fig. 111 Test E: Indicator Lamp Flickers Or Intermittently Illuminates (Part 1 of 3). 1999–2000 Mustang w/3.8L Engine

TEST CONDITIONS	TESTDETAILS/RESULTS/ACTIONS
E3 CHECK A CIRCUIT 36 (YE/WH) CONNECTIONS (Continued)	
2 	2 With the engine running, check the charging system warning indicator lamp. • Does the charging system warning indicator lamp flicker? → **Yes** GO to **E4**. → **No** REPAIR loose connections in circuits. TEST the system for normal operation.
E4 INSPECT GENERATOR S C153	
	1 Check the generator S connector C153 to make sure it is correctly mated to the generator and making good contact with the S terminal on the generator. • Is generator C153 (S connector) OK? → **Yes** GO to **E5**. → **No** REPAIR as necessary. TEST the system for normal operation.
E5 CHECK GENERATOR BRUSHES	
	1 Remove the generator from the vehicle.
2 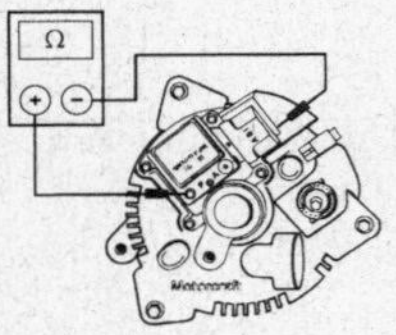	2 Measure the resistance between the A and F terminals on the voltage regulator. • Is the resistance less than 5 ohms? → **Yes** INSTALL a new generator TEST the system for normal operation. → **No** GO to **E6**.

FM1120000556020X

Fig. 111 Test E: Indicator Lamp Flickers Or Intermittently Illuminates (Part 2 of 3). 1999–2000 Mustang w/3.8L Engine

TEST CONDITIONS	TESTDETAILS/RESULTS/ACTIONS
F1 CHECK FOR ACCESSORY DRIVE NOISE	
	1 Check the accessory drive belt for damage and correct installation. Check the accessory mounting brackets and generator pulley for looseness or misalignment. • Is the accessory drive OK? → **Yes** GO to **F2**. → **No** REPAIR as necessary. TEST the system for normal operation.
F2 CHECK GENERATOR MOUNTING	
	1 Check the generator mounting for loose bolts or misalignment. • Is the generator mounted correctly? → **Yes** GO to **F3**. → **No** REPAIR as necessary. TEST the system for normal operation.
F3 CHECK GENERATOR FOR ELECTRICAL NOISE	
1 2  Generator C154	3 With the engine running, turn the headlights ON, rear defroster ON, and the blower motor to HI. • Is the noise still present? → **Yes** GO to **F4**. → **No** INSTALL a new generator (10346). TEST the system for normal operation.

FM1120000557010X

Fig. 112 Test F: Alternator Noisy (Part 1 of 2). 1999–2000 Mustang w/3.8L Engine

TEST CONDITIONS	TESTDETAILS/RESULTS/ACTIONS
E6 CHECK FOR A GROUNDED SLIP RING	
1 	1 Remove the voltage regulator from the generator.
2 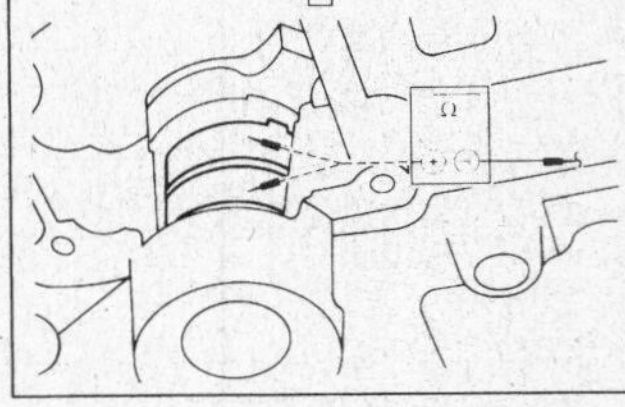	2 Measure the resistance between both generator slip rings and ground. • Is the resistance greater than 1K ohms? → **Yes** INSTALL a new generator TEST the system for normal operation. → **No** INSTALL a new voltage regulator TEST the system for normal operation.

FM1120000556030X

Fig. 111 Test E: Indicator Lamp Flickers Or Intermittently Illuminates (Part 3 of 3). 1999–2000 Mustang w/3.8L Engine

TEST CONDITIONS	TESTDETAILS/RESULTS/ACTIONS
F4 CHECK GENERATOR FOR MECHANICAL NOISE	
1  Generator C154	2 Turn all accessories OFF. With the engine running, use a stethoscope or equivalent listening device to probe the generator for unusual mechanical noise. • Is the generator the noise source? → **Yes** INSTALL a new generator TEST the system for normal operation. → **No** diagnose the source of engine noise.

FM1120000557020X

Fig. 112 Test F: Alternator Noisy (Part 2 of 2). 1999–2000 Mustang w/3.8L Engine

TEST CONDITIONS	TESTDETAILS/RESULTS/ACTIONS
G1 VERIFY GENERATOR IS SOURCE OF RADIO INTERFERENCE	
1 	1 Start and run the engine. 2 Tune the radio to a station where the interference is present.
3 4 5  Generator C154	
	• Is the interference present with the generator disconnected? → **Yes** INSPECT the in-vehicle entertainment system. → **No** INSTALL a new generator (10346). TEST the system for normal operation.

FM1120000558000X

Fig. 113 Test G: Radio Interference. 1999–2000 Mustang w/3.8L Engine

TEST CONDITIONS	TESTDETAILS/RESULTS/ACTIONS
H1 CHECK GENERATOR B+ CIRCUIT 38 (BK/OG) VOLTAGE	
1 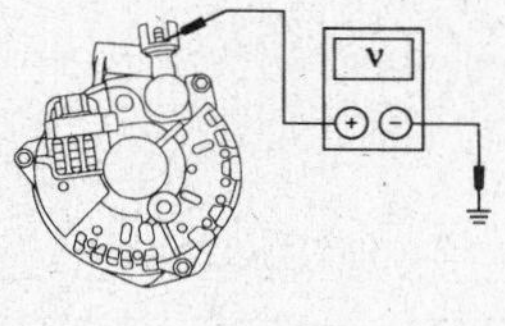	1 Measure the voltage between the generator B+ terminal, harness side and ground. • Is the voltage equal to battery positive voltage (B+)? → **Yes** GO to **H2**. → **No** REPAIR generator B+ circuit as necessary. TEST the system for normal operation.
H2 CHECK A CIRCUIT 36 (YE/WH)	
1  Generator C154 2 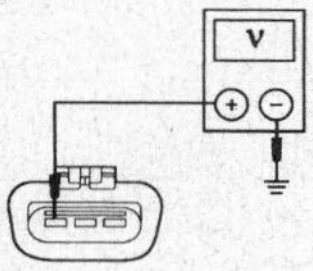	2 Measure the voltage between the generator C154 pin A, circuit 36 (YE/WH) harness side, and ground. • Is the voltage equal to battery positive voltage (B+)? → **Yes** GO to **H3**. → **No** REPAIR circuit. TEST the system for normal operation.

FM1120000559010X

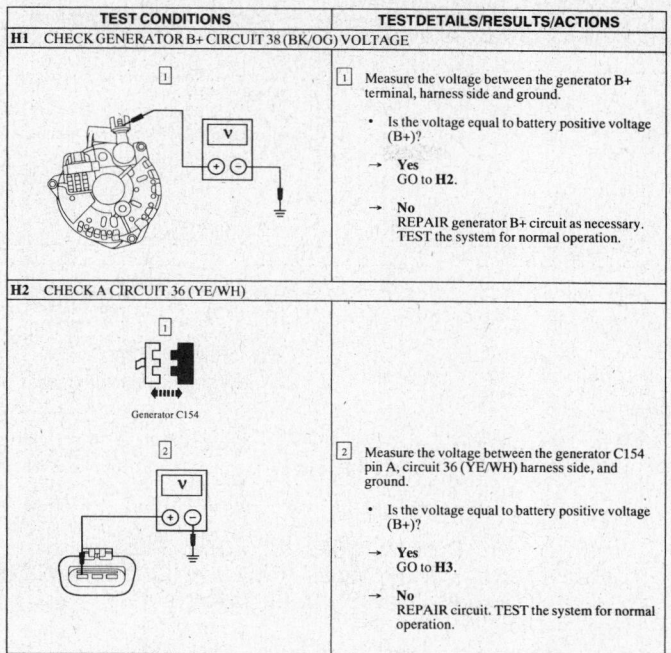

Fig. 114 Test H: System Does Not Charge (Part 1 of 2). 1999–2000 Mustang w/4.6L Engine

TEST CONDITIONS	TESTDETAILS/RESULTS/ACTIONS
H3 CHECK I CIRCUIT 904 (LG/RD)	
1  Generator C154 2  3 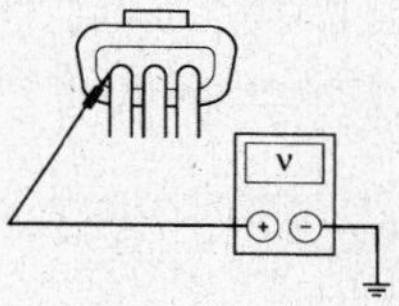	3 **Note:** The generator (GEN) must be connected to the wiring harness for this test. • Measure the voltage between generator C154 pin I, circuit 904 (LG/RD), harness side and ground. • Is the voltage equal to B+? → **Yes** GO to **H4**. → **No** REPAIR circuit. TEST the system for normal operation.
H4 CHECK FOR VOLTAGE DROP IN THE B+ CIRCUIT	
1  2 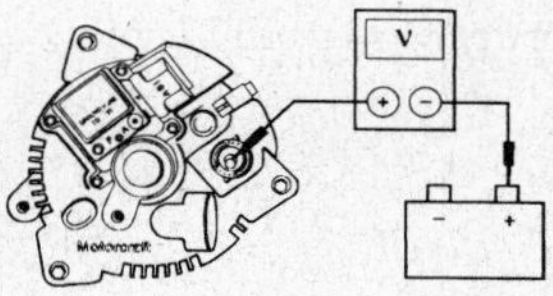	2 With the engine running, headlights ON, defroster ON, blower on HI, measure the voltage drop between the B+ terminal on generator and the battery positive post. • Is the voltage drop less than .5 volt? → **Yes** INSTALL a new generator TEST the system for normal operation. → **No** REPAIR the high resistance in the B+ circuit as necessary. TEST the system for normal operation.

FM1120000559020X

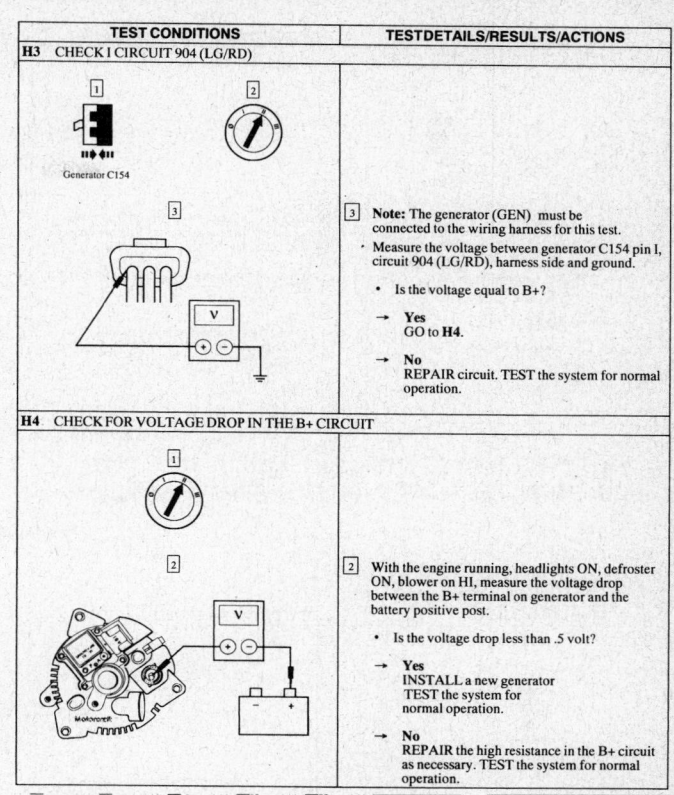

Fig. 114 Test H: System Does Not Charge (Part 2 of 2). 1999–2000 Mustang w/4.6L Engine

TEST CONDITIONS	TESTDETAILS/RESULTS/ACTIONS
I1 CHECK FOR A VOLTAGE DROP IN A CIRCUIT 36 (YE/WH)	
1  Generator C154 2 	3 With the key ON, engine OFF, measure the voltage between generator C154, pin A, circuit 36 (YE/WH), harness side and battery positive post. • Is the voltage drop less than 0.25 volt? → **Yes** GO to **I2**. → **No** REPAIR circuit. TEST the system for normal operation.
I2 CHECK GROUND CONNECTIONS	
	1 Check ground connections between the generator and the engine, and the battery and the engine. • Are all ground connections clean and tight? → **Yes** INSTALL a new generator TEST the system for normal operation. → **No** REPAIR as necessary. TEST the system for normal operation.

FM1120000560000X

Fig. 115 Test I: System Overcharging. 1999–2000 Mustang w/4.6L Engine

TEST CONDITIONS	TESTDETAILS/RESULTS/ACTIONS
J1 CHECK FOR SHORTED I CIRCUIT	
1  2  Generator C154	• Is the charging system warning indicator lamp on? → **Yes** REPAIR generator I circuit 904 (LG/RD) for a short to ground as necessary. TEST the system for normal operation. → **No** INSTALL a new generator TEST the system for normal operation.

FM1120000561000X

Fig. 116 Test J: Indicator Lamp Illuminates, Engine Running. 1999–2000 Mustang w/4.6L Engine

TEST CONDITIONS	TESTDETAILS/RESULTS/ACTIONS
K1 CHECK CHARGING SYSTEM INDICATOR LAMP	
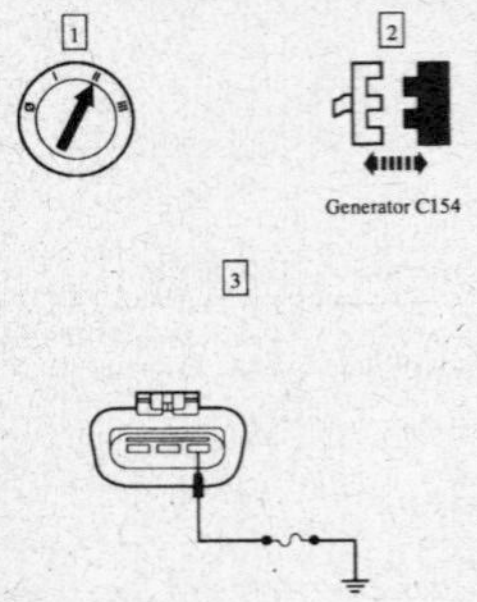	3 With the key ON and the engine OFF, connect a jumper wire between generator C154 pin I, circuit 904 (LG/RD), harness side and ground. • Is the charging system warning indicator lamp on? → **Yes** INSTALL a new generator (10346). TEST the system for normal operation. → **No**

FM1120000562000X

Fig. 117 Test K: Indicator Lamp Does Not Illuminate. 1999–2000 Mustang w/4.6L Engine

TEST CONDITIONS	TESTDETAILS/RESULTS/ACTIONS
L3 CHECK A CIRCUIT 36 (YE/WH) CONNECTIONS	
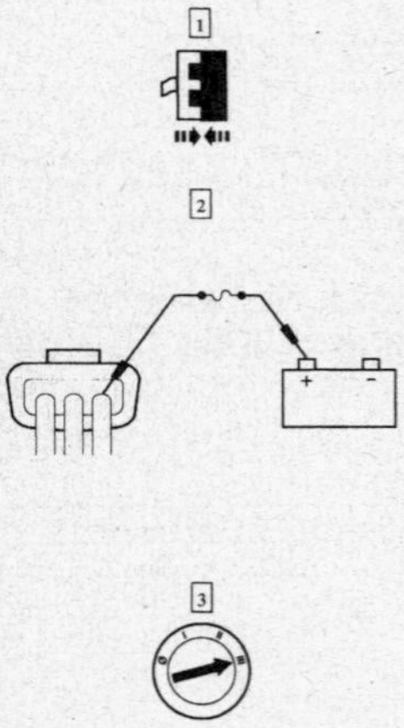	2 Connect a jumper wire between the generator C154, pin A, circuit 36 (YE/WH), harness side and battery positive post. 3 Start and run the engine. • Does the charging system warning indicator lamp flicker? → **Yes** INSTALL a new generator TEST the system for normal operation. → **No** REPAIR loose connections in circuits. TEST the system for normal operation.

FM1120000563020X

Fig. 118 Test L: Indicator Lamp Flickers or Intermittently Illuminates (Part 2 of 2). 1999–2000 Mustang w/4.6L Engine

TEST CONDITIONS	TESTDETAILS/RESULTS/ACTIONS
L1 CHECK FOR LOOSE CONNECTIONS	
	1 Check all generator, battery, and power distribution connections for looseness, corrosion, loose or bent terminals, or loose eyelets. • Are all connections clean and tight? → **Yes** GO to **L2**. → **No** TEST the system for normal operation.
L2 CHECK FUSES AND FUSE LINKS	
	1 With the engine running, check the fuses for A circuit 36 (YE/WH) and I circuit 904 (LG/RD), and circuit 38 (GY) fuse links for looseness by wiggling the fuse/fuse link and noting the charging system warning indicator lamp operation. • Did the charging system warning indicator lamp flicker? → **Yes** REPAIR loose fuse connections as necessary. TEST the system for normal operation. → **No** GO to **L3**.

FM1120000563010X

Fig. 118 Test L: Indicator Lamp Flickers or Intermittently Illuminates (Part 1 of 2). 1999–2000 Mustang w/4.6L Engine

TEST CONDITIONS	TESTDETAILS/RESULTS/ACTIONS
M1 CHECK FOR ACCESSORY DRIVE NOISE	
	1 Check the accessory drive (serpentine) belt for damage and to verify correct installation. Check the accessory mounting brackets for loose bolts or misalignment. Check for a bent generator pulley. • Is the accessory drive OK? → **Yes** GO to **M2**. → **No** continue diagnosis and testing of the accessory drive system or REPAIR as necessary. TEST the system for normal operation.
M2 CHECK GENERATOR MOUNTING	
	1 Check the generator mounting for loose bolts or misalignment. • Is the generator mounted correctly? → **Yes** GO to **M3**. → **No** REPAIR as necessary. TEST the system for normal operation.
M3 CHECK GENERATOR FOR ELECTRICAL NOISE	
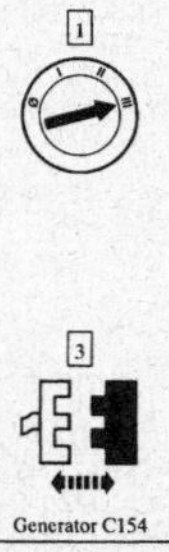	2 With the engine running, turn the headlights ON, rear defroster ON, and blower motor to HI.

FM1120000564010X

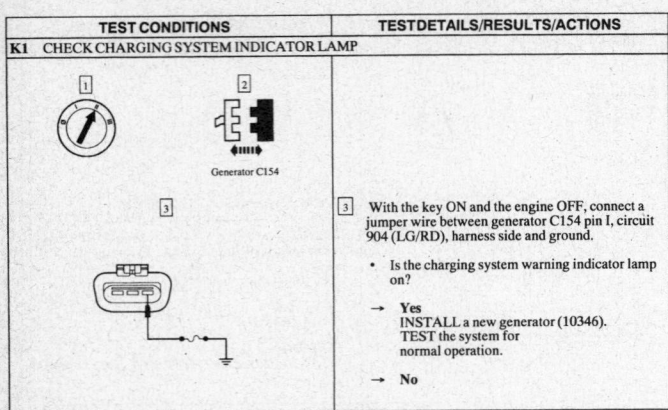

Fig. 119 Test M: Alternator is Noisy (Part 1 of 2). 1999–2000 Mustang w/4.6L Engine

TEST CONDITIONS	TESTDETAILS/RESULTS/ACTIONS
M3 CHECK GENERATOR FOR ELECTRICAL NOISE (Continued)	
	• Is the noise still present with the generator disconnected? → **Yes** GO to **M4**. → **No** INSTALL a new generator TEST the system for normal operation.
M4 CHECK GENERATOR FOR MECHANICAL NOISE	
1  Generator C154	2 Turn all accessories OFF. With the engine running, use a stethoscope or other listening device, to listen to the generator for unusual mechanical noise. • Is the generator the noise source? → **Yes** INSTALL a new generator TEST the system for normal operation. → **No** diagnose the source of engine noise.

FM1120000564020X

Fig. 119 Test M: Alternator is Noisy (Part 2 of 2). 1999–2000 Mustang w/4.6L Engine

TEST CONDITIONS	TESTDETAILS/RESULTS/ACTIONS
O1 CHECK BATTERY CONDITION	
	1 Carry out the Battery — Condition Test to determine if the battery can hold a charge and is OK for use. • Is the battery OK? → **Yes** GO to **O2**. → **No** INSTALL a new battery. TEST the system for normal operation.
O2 CHECK FOR GENERATOR OUTPUT	
	1 Carry out the On-Vehicle Generator Load/No-Load Test. • Is the generator OK? → **Yes** GO to **O3**. → **No** GO to Pinpoint Test B.
O3 CHECK FOR CURRENT DRAINS	
	1 Carry out the Battery — Drain Test. • Are there any excessive current drains? → **Yes** REPAIR as necessary. TEST the system for normal operation. → **No** GO to **O4**.

FM1120000566010X

Fig. 121 Test O: Battery Discharged or Voltage Low (Part 1 of 2). 1999–2000 Mustang w/4.6L Engine

TEST CONDITIONS	TESTDETAILS/RESULTS/ACTIONS
N1 VERIFY GENERATOR FOR SOURCE OF RADIO INTERFERENCE	
	1 With the engine running, tune the radio to station where interference is present and disconnect generator C154. • Is radio interference still present with the generator C154 disconnected? → **Yes** diagnose the cause of the radio interference. → **No** INSTALL a new generator TEST the system for normal operation.

FM1120000565000X

Fig. 120 Test N: Radio Interference. 1999–2000 Mustang w/4.6L Engine

TEST CONDITIONS	TESTDETAILS/RESULTS/ACTIONS
O4 CHECK FOR CURRENT DRAINS WHICH SHUT OFF WHEN THE BATTERY IS DISCONNECTED	
	1 Carry out the Battery — Electronic Drains Which Shut Off When the Battery Cable is Disconnected Test. • Are there any current drains which shut off when the battery is disconnected? → **Yes** REPAIR as necessary. TEST the system for normal operation. → **No** If 3G generator, GO to Pinpoint Test A. If 4G or 6G generator, GO to Pinpoint Test H.

FM1120000566020X

Fig. 121 Test O: Battery Discharged or Voltage Low (Part 2 of 2). 1999–2000 Mustang w/4.6L Engine

Condition	Possible Source	Action
• System Does Not Charge	• Ignition switch OFF battery drain. • Circuitry. • Voltage regulator. • Generator. • Battery. • Battery connections. • Drive belt.	• GO to Pinpoint Test A.
• System Overcharges (Battery Boils Over)	• Circuitry. • Poor ground. • Voltage regulator. • Generator.	• GO to Pinpoint Test B.
• Indicator Lamp Stays On, Engine Running	• Circuitry. • Voltage regulator. • Generator.	• GO to Pinpoint Test C.
• Indicator Lamp Stays On, Ignition Switch OFF	• Circuitry. • Improper lamp circuit wiring. • Instrument cluster.	• GO to Pinpoint Test D.

FM1129800218010X

Fig. 122 Symptom chart (Part 1 of 2). Sable & Taurus

Condition	Possible Source	Action
• Indicator Lamp Does Not Come On	• Circuitry. • Burned out indicator bulb. • Poor ground. • Voltage regulator. • Generator.	• GO to Pinpoint Test E.
• Indicator Lamp Flickers / Intermittent	• Loose connection to generator, voltage regulator or power distribution box. • Circuitry. • Loose brush holder screw. • Voltage regulator. • Generator.	• GO to Pinpoint Test F.
• Generator Noisy	• Accessory drive belt. • Accessory brackets. • Bent pulley. • Generator. • Other accessories.	• GO to Pinpoint Test G.
• Radio Interference	• Voltage regulator. • Generator. • Other components.	• GO to Pinpoint Test H.

FM1129800218020X

Fig. 122 Symptom chart (Part 2 of 2). Sable & Taurus

Test Step		Result	Action to Take
A1	CHECK DRIVE BELT TENSIONER		
	• Check the automatic drive belt tensioner. • **Is the drive belt adjusted properly?**	Yes ▶ No ▶	GO to **A2**. REPLACE the drive belt.
A2	CHECK BATTERY CONNECTIONS		
	• Inspect the battery cables for loose or corroded connections. • Inspect battery for corrosion. • **Are the battery cables clean, tight and free from corrosion?**	Yes ▶ No ▶	GO to **A3**. SERVICE battery and cables as necessary. RESTORE vehicle. RETEST system.
A3	LOOSE BATTERY POST		
	• Check for loose battery posts. • **Are posts OK?**	Yes ▶ No ▶	GO to **A4**. REPLACE battery. RETEST system.
A4	CRACKED BATTERY COVER		
	• Remove battery hold down clamps and shields. • Check for broken/cracked case or battery cover. • **Are case and cover OK?**	Yes ▶ No ▶	GO to **A5**. REPLACE battery.
A5	CHECK FOR KEY-OFF DRAIN		
	• Perform battery Drain Testing as described. • **Is current drain less than 50 mA (or test lamp off)?**	Yes ▶ No ▶	GO to **A6**. SERVICE the cause of ignition switch OFF battery drain. RETEST system.
A6	CHECK BATTERY		
	• Perform the battery Capacity Testing as described in Component Tests. • **Is the battery capacity OK?**	Yes ▶ No ▶	GO to **A7**. REPLACE battery. RETEST system.
A7	CHECK FOR OPEN B+ CIRCUIT		
	• Measure voltage at B+ terminal on the back of the generator. • **Is voltage at B+ terminal equal to battery voltage?**	Yes ▶ No ▶	GO to **A8**. SERVICE open in B+ Circuit. RETEST system.

FM1129800219010X

Fig. 123 Test A: System Does Not Charge (Part 1 of 2). Sable & Taurus

Test Step		Result	Action to Take
A8	CHECK FOR OPEN A CIRCUIT		
	• Measure voltage at A circuit on the voltage regulator. • **Is voltage at test point A equal to battery voltage?**	Yes ▶ No ▶	GO to **A9**. CHECK Alternator Fuse (30A) in Circuit 35 (O/LB) and REPLACE if required. If OK, SERVICE open in Circuit 35 (O/LB). RETEST system.
A9	CHECK FOR OPEN I CIRCUIT		
	NOTE: Voltage regulator must be connected to wiring harness for this test. • Turn ignition switch to RUN position. • Measure voltage at connector C154 I terminal, Circuit 904 (LG/R). • **Is voltage greater than 1 V?**	Yes ▶ No ▶	GO to **A10**. SERVICE open or high resistance in Circuit 904 (LG/R). RETEST system.
A10	CHECK VOLTAGE DROP IN A CIRCUIT		
	• Measure voltage drop between test point A on the voltage regulator and the positive (+) battery post. • **Is voltage drop less than 0.25 V?**	Yes ▶ No ▶	GO to **A11**. SERVICE excess voltage drop in Circuit 35 (O/LB). CHECK Alternator Fuse (30A) and connectors in Circuit 35 (O/LB) and SERVICE as required. RETEST system.
A11	CHECK VOLTAGE DROP IN B+ CIRCUIT		
	• Start engine. • Turn headlamps on and set blower on HIGH. • With engine running at 2000 rpm, measure voltage drop between the B+ terminal on the back of the generator and the positive (+) battery post. • **Is voltage drop less than 0.5 V?**	Yes ▶ No ▶	GO to **A12**. SERVICE excess voltage drop in B+ Circuit. CHECK the connections between the battery and power distribution box. RETEST system.
A12	CHECK FOR OPEN/SHORTED FIELD		
	• Remove generator from vehicle. • Remove voltage regulator. • Measure resistance between the generator slip rings. • **Is resistance greater than 10 ohms OR less than 1 ohm?**	Yes ▶ No ▶	REPLACE generator. RETEST system. REPLACE voltage regulator. RETEST system.

FM1129800219020X

Fig. 123 Test A: System Does Not Charge (Part 2 of 2). Sable & Taurus

Test Step		Result	Action to Take
B1	CHECK VOLTAGE DROP IN A CIRCUIT		
	• Turn ignition switch to RUN. • Measure voltage between A terminal on the voltage regulator and the positive (+) battery post. • **Is voltage drop less than 0.25 V?**	Yes ▶ No ▶	GO to **B2**. SERVICE excess voltage drop in Circuit 35 (O/LB). CHECK Alternator Fuse (30A) and connectors in Circuit 35 (O/LB) and SERVICE as required. RETEST system.
B2	CHECK VOLTAGE DROP IN I CIRCUIT		
	• NOTE: Voltage regulator must be connected to wiring harness for this test. Measure voltage at connector C154 I terminal, Circuit 904 (LG/R). • **Is voltage greater than 1 V?**	Yes ▶ No ▶	GO to **B3**. SERVICE high resistance in Circuit 904 (LG/R). RETEST system.
B3	CHECK FOR POOR GROUNDS		
	• Check for poor ground connections between voltage regulator and generator, generator and engine, or engine and battery. • **Are all ground connections clean and tight?**	Yes ▶ No ▶	REPLACE generator. RETEST system. CLEAN or SERVICE grounds as required. RETEST system.

FM1129800220000X

Fig. 124 Test B: System Overcharges. Sable & Taurus

Test Step		Result	Action to Take
C1	CHECK FOR OPEN A CIRCUIT		
	• Measure voltage at terminal A on the voltage regulator. • **Is voltage at test point A equal to battery voltage?**	Yes ▶ No ▶	GO to **C2**. CHECK Alternator Fuse (30A) in Circuit 35 (O/LB) and REPLACE if required. If OK, SERVICE open in Circuit 35 (O/LB). RETEST system.
C2	CHECK FOR SHORTED I CIRCUIT		
	• Disconnect voltage regulator connector C154. • Turn ignition switch to RUN position. • **Is indicator lamp on?**	Yes ▶ No ▶	SERVICE short to ground in Circuit 904 (LG/R). RETEST system. GO to **C3**.
C3	CHECK GENERATOR OUTPUT VOLTAGE		
	• Measure voltage at the B+ terminal on the back of the generator with the engine running at 2000 rpm and all accessories turned OFF. • **Is voltage greater than 15.5 V?**	Yes ▶ No ▶	GO to Pinpoint Test B to find the cause of high output voltage. RETEST system. REPLACE voltage regulator. RETEST system.

FM1129800221000X

Fig. 125 Test C: Indicator Lamp Stays On, Engine Running. Sable & Taurus

Test Step		Result	Action to Take
D1	CHECK LAMP CIRCUIT WIRING		
	• Turn ignition switch to OFF position. • Disconnect voltage regulator connector C154. • Measure voltage at C154 I terminal, Circuit 904 (LG/R). • **Is voltage greater than zero V?**	Yes ▶ No ▶	SERVICE Circuit 1044 (W/Y). Circuit should be HOT in RUN or START position only. RETEST system. SERVICE instrument cluster. RETEST system.

FM1129800222000X

Fig. 126 Test D: Indicator Lamp Stays On, Ignition Switch Off. Sable & Taurus

Test Step		Result	Action to Take
E1	CHECK INSTRUMENT CLUSTER OPERATION		
	• Turn ignition switch to RUN. • **Are all other warning lamps and instrument cluster lit for a short time?**	Yes ▶ No ▶	GO to **E2**. SERVICE instrument cluster.
E2	CHECK FOR OPEN I CIRCUIT		
	• Disconnect voltage regulator connector C154. • Turn ignition switch to RUN. • Measure voltage at C154 I terminal, Circuit 904 (LG/R). • **Is voltage equal to B+?**	Yes ▶ No ▶	GO to **E3**. SERVICE open in Circuit 904 (LG/R). RETEST system.
E3	CHECK FOR BURNED OUT BULB		
	• Connect C154 I-terminal, Circuit 904 (LG/R) to ground with a jumper wire. • **Is indicator lamp on?**	Yes ▶ No ▶	REMOVE jumper wire. GO to **E4**. REPLACE lamp or SERVICE high resistance in lamp socket or Circuit 904 (LG/R). RETEST system.
E4	CHECK FOR POOR GROUNDS		
	• Check for poor ground connections between voltage regulator and generator, generator and engine, or engine and battery. • **Are all ground connections clean and tight?**	Yes ▶ No ▶	REPLACE generator. CLEAN or SERVICE grounds as required. RETEST system.

FM1129800223000X

Fig. 127 Test E: Indicator Lamp Does Not Come On. Sable & Taurus

Test Step		Result	Action to Take
F1	CHECK FOR LOOSE CONNECTIONS		
	• Check these connections for corrosion, loose or bent pins, or loose eyelets: — Voltage regulator connector C154. — One-pin S connector C153 (3.0L (2V) only). — Generator B+ eyelet. — Power distribution box eyelets. — Battery cables. • **Are all connections clean and tight?**	Yes ▶ No ▶	GO to **F2**. CLEAN or SERVICE connections as required. RETEST system.
F2	CHECK FOR LOOSE A CIRCUIT FUSE		
	• Start engine. • Check the Alternator Fuse (30A) in the power distribution box for a loose connection by wiggling the fuse with the engine running. • **Does indicator lamp flicker?**	Yes ▶ No ▶	SERVICE loose fuse connection. RETEST system. GO to **F3**.
F3	CHECK A CIRCUIT CONNECTIONS		
	• With engine running, connect Circuit A on the voltage regulator to the positive (+) battery post using a jumper wire. • **Does indicator lamp flicker?**	Yes ▶ No ▶	REPLACE voltage regulator, if concern still exists REPLACE generator. RETEST system. SERVICE poor connection in Circuit 35 (O/LB). RETEST system.

FM1129800224000X

Fig. 128 Test F: Indicator Lamp Flickers/ Intermittent. Sable & Taurus

Test Step		Result	Action to Take
G1	CHECK FOR ACCESSORY DRIVE BELT NOISE		
	• Check the drive belt to make sure that it is installed properly and is not damaged. • **Is drive belt OK?**	Yes ▶ No ▶	GO to **G2**. SERVICE accessory drive belt as required. RETEST system.
G2	CHECK GENERATOR MOUNTING		
	• Check the generator and generator mounting bracket for loose bolts or misalignment condition. • **Is generator mounted correctly?**	Yes ▶ No ▶	If noise is still present, REPLACE generator. RETEST system. INSTALL generator to specifications. RETEST system.

FM1129800225000X

Fig. 129 Test G: Alternator Is Noisy. Sable & Taurus

Test Step		Result	Action to Take
H1	CHECK RADIO INTERFERENCE WITH REGULATOR DISCONNECTED		
	• Start engine. • Tune radio to a station where interference is present. • Remove voltage regulator connector C154. • **Is interference present with connector removed?**	Yes ▶ No ▶	Locate cause of radio interference. REPLACE generator. RETEST system.

FM1129800226000X

Fig. 130 Test H: Radio Interference. Sable & Taurus

Condition	Possible Source	Action
• The Charging System Warning Indicator is ON with the Engine Running (The Battery Voltage Does Not Increase)	• A Circuit. • A Circuit in-line mini-fuse. • B+ Circuit 38 (B/O). • B+ fuse links. • I Circuit 904 (LG/R) • Generator	• GO to Pinpoint Test A.
• The Charging System Warning Indicator is OFF with the Ignition Switch in RUN and the Engine OFF (Battery Voltage Does Not Increase When the Engine is Running).	• Voltage regulator connector. • I Circuit 904 (LG/R). • I Circuit fuse(s). • Charging system warning indicator lamp bulb. • Loose or damaged generator. • Harness connector.	• GO to Pinpoint Test B.
• The Charging System Warning Indicator is ON with the Engine Running and the Battery Voltage Increases	• Generator.	• GO to Pinpoint Test C.
• The Charging System Warning Indicator is OFF with the Ignition Switch in RUN and the Engine OFF (Battery Voltage Increases When the Engine is Running).	• Charging system warning indicator lamp bulb. • Instrument cluster. • Generator.	• GO to Pinpoint Test D.

FM1129800284010X

Fig. 132 Symptom chart (Part 1 of 2). 1998–99 Town Car

Condition	Possible Source	Action
• The Charging System Warning Indicator Operates Correctly but the Battery Voltage Does Not Increase	• B+ Circuit 38 (B/O). • B+ fuse links. • Loose or damaged harness connector. • Battery cables. • Generator. • Voltage regulator.	• GO to Pinpoint Test E.
• The Battery is Dead or Will Not Stay Charged or Low Battery or Generator Voltage	• Corroded terminal(s). • Loose connection(s). • High key-off load. • Generator.	• GO to Pinpoint Test F.
• The Charging System Warning Indicator Flickers or Is Intermittent	• Loose connection(s). • In-line mini-fuse A Circuit loose. • I Circuit fuse(s). • Generator.	• GO to Pinpoint Test G.
• The System Overcharges (Battery Voltage Greater Than 15.5 Volts)	• A Circuit. • Generator. • I Circuit.	• GO to Pinpoint Test H.
• Battery Leakage or Damage	• A Circuit. • Generator. • Battery.	• GO to Pinpoint Test J.
• The Voltage Gauge Reads High or Low	• Generator. • Voltage gauge. • Instrument cluster/wiring.	• GO to Pinpoint Test K.
• The Generator is Noisy	• Loose bolts/brackets. • Drive belt. • Generator/Pulley.	• GO to Pinpoint Test L.
• Radio Interference	• Generator. • Wiring/routing. • In-vehicle entertainment system.	• GO to Pinpoint Test M.

FM1129800284020X

Fig. 132 Symptom chart (Part 2 of 2). 1998–2000 Town Car

Test Step		Result	Action to Take
A1	CHECK BATTERY CONNECTIONS		
	• Inspect battery cables for loose or corroded connections. • Inspect battery for corrosion. • **Are battery cables clean, tight and free from corrosion?**	Yes ▶ No ▶	GO to **A2**. SERVICE battery and cables as necessary. RESTORE vehicle. RETEST system.
A2	CHECK DRIVE BELT TENSION		
	• Perform drive belt adjustment procedure. • **Is the drive belt adjusted properly?**	Yes ▶ No ▶	GO to **A3**. ADJUST or REPLACE drive belt.
A3	LOOSE BATTERY POST		
	• Check for loose battery posts. • **Are posts OK?**	Yes ▶ No ▶	GO to **A4**. REPLACE battery.

FM1129700276010X

Fig. 133 Test A: System Does Not Charge (Part 1 of 2). 1997 Town Car

Condition	Possible Source	Action
• System Does Not Charge	• Ignition switch OFF battery drain. • Circuitry. • Voltage regulator. • Generator. • Battery. • Battery connections. • Drive belt.	• GO to Pinpoint Test A.
• System Overcharges (Battery Boils Over)	• Circuitry. • Poor ground. • Voltage regulator. • Generator.	• GO to Pinpoint Test B.
• Indicator Lamp Stays ON, Engine Running	• Circuitry. • Voltage regulator. • Generator.	• GO to Pinpoint Test C.
• Indicator Lamp Stays ON, Ignition Switch OFF	• Circuitry. • Improper lamp circuit wiring. • Instrument cluster.	• GO to Pinpoint Test D.
• Indicator Lamp Does Not Come On	• Circuitry. • Burned out lamp. • Poor ground. • Voltage regulator. • Generator.	• GO to Pinpoint Test E.
• Indicator Lamp Flickers / Intermittent	• Loose connection to generator, voltage regulator or power distribution box. • Circuitry. • Loose brush holder screw. • Voltage regulator. • Generator.	• GO to Pinpoint Test F.
• Generator Noisy	• Accessory drive belt. • Accessory brackets. • Bent pulley. • Generator. • Other accessories.	• GO to Pinpoint Test G.
• Radio Interference	• Voltage regulator. • Generator. • Other components.	• GO to Pinpoint Test H.

FM1129700275000X

Fig. 131 Symptom chart. 1997 Town Car

Test Step		Result	Action to Take
A4	CRACKED BATTERY COVER		
	• Remove battery hold down clamps and shields. • Check for broken/cracked case or battery cover. • **Are case and cover OK?**	Yes ▶ No ▶	GO to **A5**. REPLACE battery.
A5	CHECK BATTERY		
	• Perform Battery Capacity Testing as described. • **Is the battery capacity OK?**	Yes ▶ No ▶	GO to **A6**. REPLACE battery.
A6	CHECK FOR KEY-OFF DRAIN		
	• Perform Battery Drain Testing as described. • **Is current drain less than 50 mA?**	Yes ▶ No ▶	GO to **A7**. LOCATE cause of ignition switch-OFF battery drain.
A7	CHECK FOR OPEN B+ CIRCUIT		
	• Measure voltage at B+ terminal on back of generator, Circuit 38 (BK/O). • **Is voltage at B+ terminal equal to battery voltage?**	Yes ▶ No ▶	GO to **A8**. SERVICE open in Circuit 38 (BK/O).
A8	CHECK FOR OPEN A CIRCUIT		
	• Measure voltage at terminal A on voltage regulator. • **Is voltage equal to battery voltage?**	Yes ▶ No ▶	GO to **A9**. CHECK Fuse J (10A) in Circuit 36 (Y/W) and REPLACE if required. If OK, SERVICE open in Circuit 36 (Y/W).
A9	CHECK FOR OPEN I CIRCUIT		
	NOTE: Voltage regulator must be connected to wiring harness for this test. • Disconnect connector C154. • Turn ignition switch to RUN position. • Measure voltage at wiring connector Pin C154 I-terminal, Circuit 904 (LG/R). • **Is voltage greater than 1 V?**	Yes ▶ No ▶	GO to **A10**. SERVICE open or high resistance in Circuit 904 (LG/R).
A10	CHECK VOLTAGE DROP IN A CIRCUIT		
	• Measure voltage drop between terminal A on the voltage regulator and positive (+) battery post. • **Is voltage drop less than 0.25 V?**	Yes ▶ No ▶	GO to **A11**. SERVICE excess voltage drop in Circuit 36 (Y/W). CHECK Fuse J (10A) and connectors in Circuit 36. SERVICE as required.
A11	CHECK FOR SHORTED RECTIFIER		
	• Disconnect connector C153 from generator. • Measure voltage between the S-terminal on back of generator and ground. • Measure voltage between positive (+) battery terminal and S terminal on back of generator. • **Is either voltage reading greater than 1 V?**	Yes ▶ No ▶	REPLACE generator. GO to **A12**.
A12	CHECK VOLTAGE DROP IN B+ CIRCUIT		
	• Connect connector C153. • Turn ignition switch to RUN. • Turn headlamps ON and set blower on HIGH. • With engine running at 2000 rpm, measure voltage drop between B+ terminal on back of generator and positive (+) battery post. • **Is voltage drop less than 0.5 V?**	Yes ▶ No ▶	GO to **A13**. SERVICE excess voltage drop in Circuit 38 (BK/O). CHECK fuse link in Circuit 38 and connections between battery and power distribution box.
A13	CHECK FOR OPEN/SHORTED FIELD		
	• Remove generator from vehicle. • Remove voltage regulator. • Measure resistance between the generator slip rings. • **Is resistance greater than 10 ohms OR less than 1 ohm?**	Yes ▶ No ▶	REPLACE generator. REPLACE voltage regulator. RETEST system.

FM1129700276020X

Fig. 133 Test A: System Does Not Charge (Part 2 of 2). 1997 Town Car

	Test Step	Result	Action to Take
B1	CHECK VOLTAGE DROP IN A CIRCUIT		
	• Turn ignition switch to RUN position. • Measure voltage between terminal A on voltage regulator and positive (+) battery post. • **Is voltage drop less than 0.25 V?**	Yes ▶	GO to **B2.**
		No ▶	SERVICE excess voltage drop in Circuit 36 (Y/W). CHECK Fuse J (10A) and connectors in Circuit 36 (Y/W). SERVICE as required.
B2	CHECK VOLTAGE DROP IN I CIRCUIT		
	NOTE: Voltage regulator must be connected to wiring harness for this test. • Measure voltage at connector C154 I-terminal, Circuit 904 (LG/R). • **Is voltage greater than 1 V?**	Yes ▶	GO to **B3.**
		No ▶	SERVICE high resistance in Circuit 904 (LG/R).
B3	CHECK FOR POOR GROUNDS		
	• Check for poor ground connections between voltage regulator and generator, battery and engine, or engine and battery. • **Are all ground connections clean and tight?**	Yes ▶	GO to **B4.**
		No ▶	CLEAN or SERVICE grounds as required.
B4	CHECK FOR GROUNDED SLIP RING		
	• Remove generator from vehicle. • Remove voltage regulator. • Measure resistance from each generator slip ring to the generator housing. • **Is resistance from either slip ring to housing less than 200 ohms?**	Yes ▶	If grease or dirt has accumulated near slip rings, CLEAN slip rings and RECHECK resistance. If still less than 200 ohms, REPLACE generator.
		No ▶	REPLACE voltage regulator.

FM1129700277000X

Fig. 134 Test B: System Overcharges. 1997 Town Car

	Test Step	Result	Action to Take
D1	CHECK LAMP CIRCUIT WIRING		
	• Turn ignition switch OFF. • Disconnect voltage regulator connector C154. • Measure voltage at C154 I-terminal, Circuit 904 (LG/R). • **Is voltage greater than zero V?**	Yes ▶	SERVICE Circuit 904 (LG/R). Circuit should be HOT in RUN only.
		No ▶	SERVICE instrument cluster.

FM1129700279000X

Fig. 136 Test D: Indicator Lamp Stays On, Ignition Switch Off. 1997 Town Car

	Test Step	Result	Action to Take
F1	CHECK FOR LOOSE CONNECTIONS		
	• Check these connections for corrosion, loose or bent pins, or loose eyelets: — Three-pin voltage regulator connector C154. — One-pin S connector C153. — Generator B+ eyelet. — Power distribution box eyelets. — Battery cables. • **Are all connections clean and tight?**	Yes ▶	GO to **F2.**
		No ▶	CLEAN or SERVICE connections as required.
F2	CHECK FOR LOOSE A CIRCUIT FUSE		
	• Turn ignition switch to RUN. • Check Fuse J (10A) in power distribution box for a loose connection by wiggling fuse with engine running. • **Does indicator lamp flicker?**	Yes ▶	SERVICE loose fuse connection.
		No ▶	GO to **F3.**
F3	CHECK A CIRCUIT CONNECTIONS		
	• With engine running, connect Terminal A on voltage regulator to the positive (+) battery post using a jumper wire. • **Does indicator lamp flicker?**	Yes ▶	GO to **F4.**
		No ▶	SERVICE poor connection in Circuit 36 (Y/W).
F4	CHECK BRUSH HOLDER SCREWS		
	• Remove generator from vehicle. • Check brush holder screws, located on voltage regulator. • **Are the brush holder screws tight?**	Yes ▶	GO to **F5.**
		No ▶	TIGHTEN screws to specification.
F5	CHECK FOR GROUNDED SLIP RING		
	• Remove voltage regulator. • Measure resistance from each generator slip ring to generator housing. • **Is resistance from either slip ring to housing less than 200 ohms?**	Yes ▶	If grease or dirt has accumulated near slip rings, CLEAN slip rings and RECHECK resistance. If still less than 200 ohms, REPLACE generator.
		No ▶	REPLACE voltage regulator.

FM1129700281000X

Fig. 138 Test F: Indicator Lamp Flickers/ Intermittent. 1997 Town Car

	Test Step	Result	Action to Take
C1	CHECK FOR OPEN A CIRCUIT		
	• Measure voltage at terminal A on the voltage regulator. • **Is voltage at test point A equal to battery voltage?**	Yes ▶	GO to **C2.**
		No ▶	CHECK Fuse J (10A) in Circuit 36 (Y/W) and REPLACE if required. If OK, SERVICE open in Circuit 36 (Y/W).
C2	CHECK FOR SHORTED I CIRCUIT		
	• Disconnect three-pin voltage regulator connector C154. • Turn ignition switch to RUN. • **Is indicator lamp on?**	Yes ▶	SERVICE short to ground in Circuit 904 (LG/R).
		No ▶	GO to **C3.**
C3	CHECK S CIRCUIT FUNCTION		
	• Connect voltage regulator connector C154. • Disconnect connector C153. • Connect wiring harness S-terminal, Circuit 4 (W/BK) to positive (+) battery post using a jumper wire. • **Is indicator lamp on?**	Yes ▶	REMOVE jumper wire. GO to **C4.**
		No ▶	REMOVE jumper wire. GO to **C5.**
C4	CHECK FOR OPEN S CIRCUIT		
	• Disconnect voltage regulator connector C154. • Measure wiring resistance between the connector C153 and the S-terminal of the voltage regulator connector C154. • **Is resistance greater than 1 ohm?**	Yes ▶	SERVICE open or excess resistance in Circuit 4 (W/BK).
		No ▶	CHECK for loose or bent pin in voltage regulator or connector. If OK, REPLACE voltage regulator.
C5	CHECK STATOR OUTPUT VOLTAGE		
	• Start engine. • Measure voltage at S-terminal on back of generator. • **Is voltage at least 1/2 of battery voltage?**	Yes ▶	GO to **C6.**
		No ▶	GO to Pinpoint Test A to find the cause of low generator output.
C6	CHECK GENERATOR OUTPUT VOLTAGE		
	• Measure voltage at the B+ terminal on back of generator with engine running at 2000 rpm and all accessories turned OFF. • **Is voltage greater than 15.5 V?**	Yes ▶	GO to Pinpoint Test B to find cause of high output voltage.
		No ▶	REPLACE voltage regulator.

FM1129700278000X

Fig. 135 Test C: Indicator Lamp Stays On, Engine Running. 1997 Town Car

	Test Step	Result	Action to Take
E1	CHECK FOR OPEN I CIRCUIT		
	• Disconnect voltage regulator connector C154. • Turn ignition switch to RUN. • Measure voltage at C154 I-terminal, Circuit 904 (LG/R). • **Is voltage equal to B+?**	Yes ▶	GO to **E2.**
		No ▶	SERVICE open in Circuit 904 (LG/R).
E2	CHECK FOR BURNED OUT BULB		
	• Connect C154 I-terminal, Circuit 904 (LG/R) to ground with a jumper wire. • **Is indicator lamp on?**	Yes ▶	REMOVE jumper wire. GO to **E3.**
		No ▶	REPLACE lamp or SERVICE high resistance in lamp socket or Circuit 904 (LG/R).
E3	CHECK FOR POOR GROUNDS		
	• Check for poor ground connections between voltage regulator and generator, battery and engine, or engine and battery. • **Are all ground connections clean and tight?**	Yes ▶	GO to **E4.**
		No ▶	CLEAN or SERVICE grounds as required.
E4	CHECK S CIRCUIT WIRING		
	• Disconnect S connector C153 from generator. • Measure voltage at C153 S-terminal, Circuit 4 (W/BK). • **Is voltage greater than 0 V?**	Yes ▶	SERVICE Circuit 4 (W/BK). Circuit should be HOT only when engine is running.
		No ▶	GO to **E5.**
E5	CHECK FOR SHORTED RECTIFIER		
	• Measure voltage at the S-terminal on the back of generator. • **Is voltage greater than 1 V?**	Yes ▶	If lamp is on with connector C153 disconnected, REPLACE generator.
		No ▶	REPLACE voltage regulator.

FM1129700280000X

Fig. 137 Test E: Indicator Lamp Does Not Come On. 1997 Town Car

	Test Step	Result	Action to Take
G1	CHECK FOR ACCESSORY DRIVE NOISE		
	• Check drive belt to make sure it is installed properly and is not damaged. • **Is drive belt OK?**	Yes ▶	GO to **G2.**
		No ▶	SERVICE accessory drive belt as required.
G2	CHECK GENERATOR MOUNTING		
	• Check generator and generator mounting bracket for loose bolts or misalignment condition. • **Is generator mounted correctly?**	Yes ▶	GO to **G3.**
		No ▶	INSTALL generator to specification.
G3	CHECK GENERATOR PULLEY		
	• Check generator pulley for damage (bent) or a misalignment condition. • **Is pulley OK?**	Yes ▶	If noise is still present REPLACE generator.
		No ▶	REPLACE generator pulley.

FM1129700282000X

Fig. 139 Test G: Alternator Is Noisy. 1997 Town Car

	Test Step	Result	Action to Take
H1	VERIFY RADIO INTERFERENCE		
	• Start engine. • Tune radio to a station where interference is present. • Remove three-pin voltage regulator connector C154. • **Is interference present with connector removed?**	Yes ▶	**LOCATE** cause of the radio interference.
		No ▶	REPLACE generator.

FM1129700283000X

Fig. 140 Test H: Radio Interference. 1997 Town Car

TEST CONDITIONS	TEST DETAILS/RESULTS/ACTIONS
A1 CHECK A CIRCUIT GENERATOR (10A) MINI FUSE	
1 2 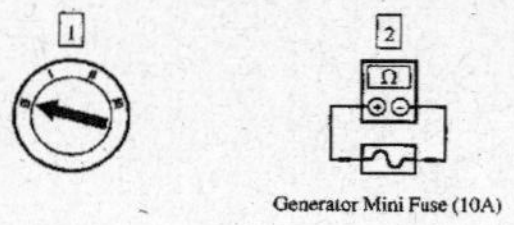	2 Check the generator (10A) A Circuit Mini Fuse in the power distribution box. • Is the fuse OK? → **Yes** GO to **A2**. → **No** REPLACE the Generator Mini Fuse (10A). TEST the system for normal operation.
A2 CHECK GENERATOR OUTPUT CIRCUIT	
1 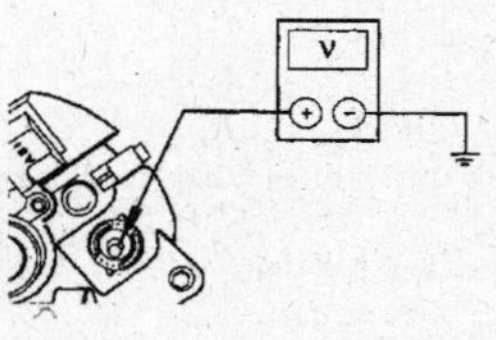	1 Measure the voltage at the B+ terminal of the generator, Circuit 38 (BK/O). • Is the voltage equal to battery positive voltage (B+)? → **Yes** GO to **A3**. → **No** REPAIR generator output Circuit 38 (BK/O) or fusible links Circuit 290 (GY). TEST the system for normal operation.

FM1129800285010X

Fig. 141 Test A: Warning Indicator Is On w/Engine Running, Battery Voltage Does Not Increase (Part 1 of 3). 1998–2000 Town Car

TEST CONDITIONS	TEST DETAILS/RESULTS/ACTIONS
A3 CHECK GENERATOR A CIRCUIT	
1 2 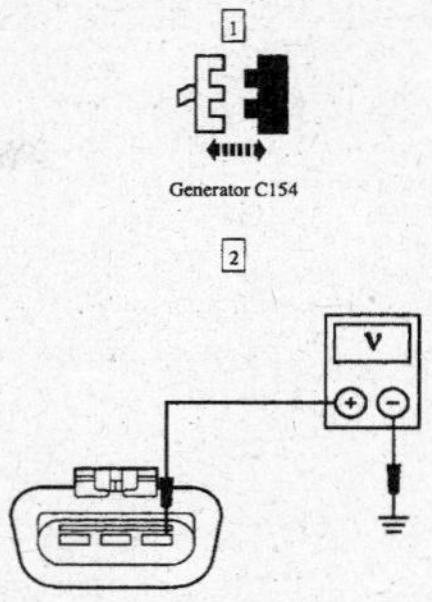	2 Measure the voltage at voltage regulator Connector C154 Pin C, Circuit 36 (Y/W). • Is the voltage equal to battery positive voltage (B+)? → **Yes** GO to **A4**. → **No** REPAIR Circuit 36 (Y/W). TEST the system for normal operation.
A4 CHECK GENERATOR I CIRCUIT FOR AN OPEN	
1 2 3 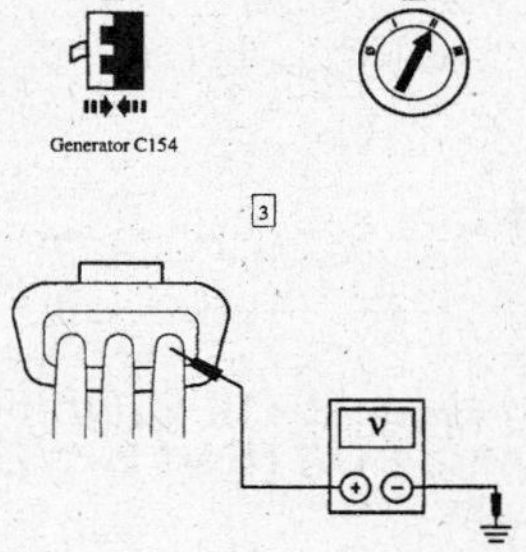	3 **NOTE:** The generator must be connected to the wiring harness for this test. With the engine running, measure the voltage between the generator I-terminal, Circuit 904 (LG/R). • Is the voltage greater than 1 volt? → **Yes** GO to **A5**. → **No** REPAIR Circuit 904 (LG/R) as necessary. TEST the system for normal operation.

FM1129800285020X

Fig. 141 Test A: Warning Indicator Is On w/Engine Running, Battery Voltage Does Not Increase (Part 2 of 3). 1998–2000 Town Car

TEST CONDITIONS	TEST DETAILS/RESULTS/ACTIONS
A5 CHECK THE GENERATOR OUTPUT	
1 2 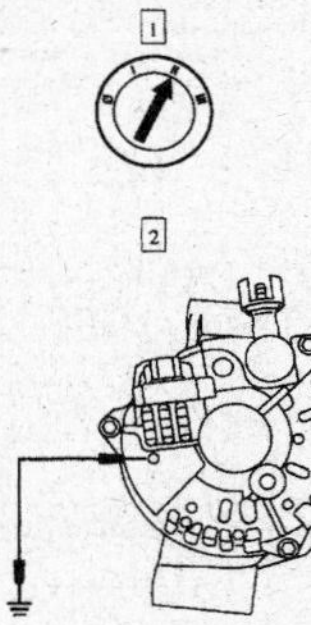	2 With the engine running, ground Test Point F on the generator. • Does the battery voltage increase and the charging system warning indicator turn off? → **Yes** REPLACE THE generator. TEST the system for normal operation. → **No** REPLACE THE generator. TEST the system for normal operation.

FM1129800285030X

Fig. 141 Test A: Warning Indicator Is On w/Engine Running, Battery Voltage Does Not Increase (Part 3 of 3). 1998–2000 Town Car

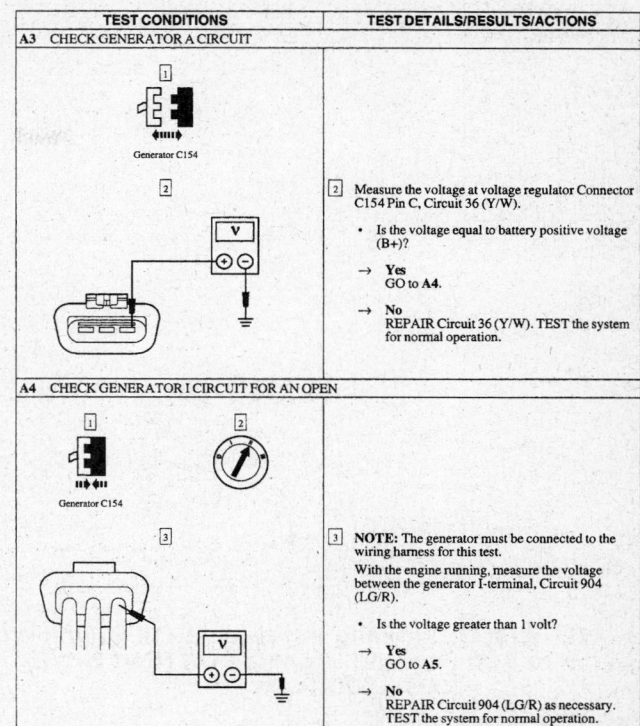

TEST CONDITIONS	TEST DETAILS/RESULTS/ACTIONS
B1 CHECK GENERATOR CONNECTOR C154	
1 	2 Check generator Connector C154 for bent or damaged pins. • Is the connector OK? → **Yes** GO to **B2**. → **No** REPAIR Connector C154 as necessary. TEST the system for normal operation.

FM1129800286010X

Fig. 142 Test B: Warning Indicator Is Off w/Ignition Switch In Run Position & Engine Off (Part 1 of 2). 1998–2000 Town Car

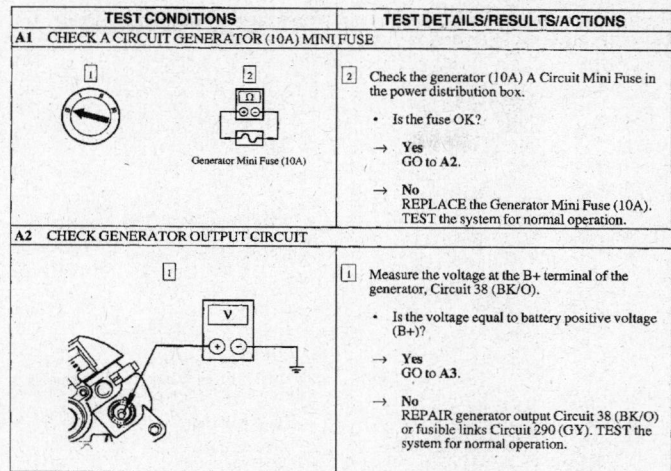

TEST CONDITIONS	TEST DETAILS/RESULTS/ACTIONS
B2 CHECK THE GENERATOR GROUNDS	
	1 Check all the ground connections between the generator and the battery. • Are all the ground connections OK? → **Yes** GO to **B3**. → **No** REPAIR the connections as necessary. TEST the system for normal operation.
B3 CHECK THE VOLTAGE AT THE GENERATOR I CIRCUIT	
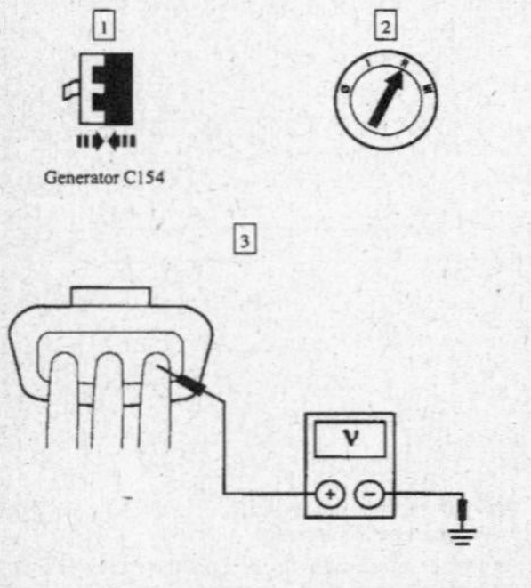	3 **NOTE:** The generator Connector C154 must be connected to the generator test. With engine running, measure the voltage at the generator I terminal, Circuit 904 (LG/R). • Is the voltage greater than 1 volt? → **Yes** REPLACE the generator. → **No** REPAIR Circuit 904 (LG/R) for an open circuit. TEST the system for normal operation.

FM1129800286020X

Fig. 142 Test B: Warning Indicator Is Off w/Ignition Switch In Run Position & Engine Off (Part 2 of 2). 1998–2000 Town Car

TEST CONDITIONS	TEST DETAILS/RESULTS/ACTIONS
D1 CHECK THE CHARGING SYSTEM WARNING INDICATOR OPERATION	
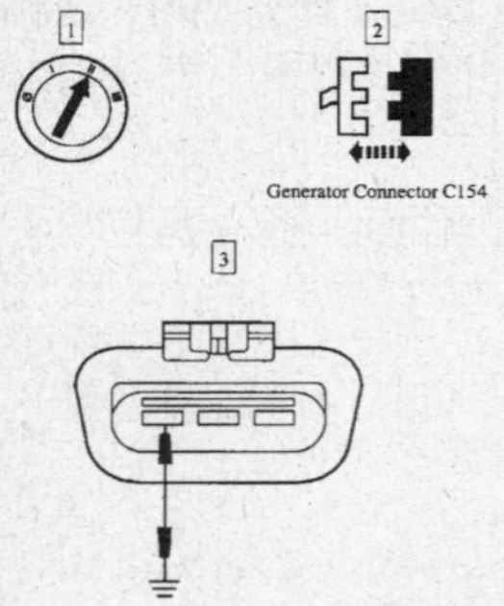	3 Ground the generator Connector C154 I Circuit with the key ON and the engine OFF. • Is the warning indicator on? → **Yes** REPLACE the generator. TEST the system for normal operation. → **No** REPAIR Connector C154, I Circuit 904 (LG/R) as necessary. TEST the system for normal operation.

FM1129800288000X

Fig. 144 Test D: Warning Indicator Off w/Ignition Switch In Run Position & Engine Off. 1998–2000 Town Car

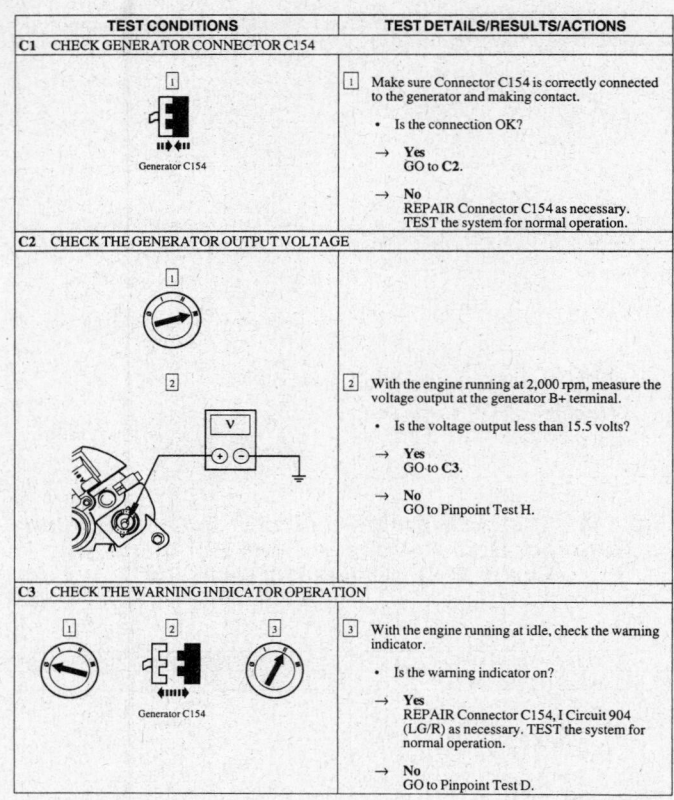

TEST CONDITIONS	TEST DETAILS/RESULTS/ACTIONS
C1 CHECK GENERATOR CONNECTOR C154	
	1 Make sure Connector C154 is correctly connected to the generator and making contact. • Is the connection OK? → **Yes** GO to **C2**. → **No** REPAIR Connector C154 as necessary. TEST the system for normal operation.
C2 CHECK THE GENERATOR OUTPUT VOLTAGE	
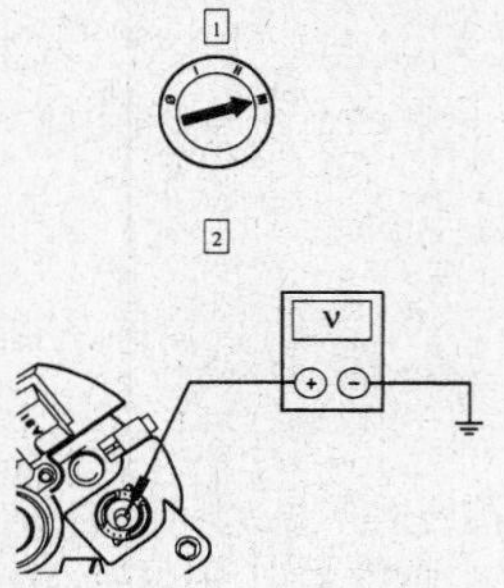	2 With the engine running at 2,000 rpm, measure the voltage output at the generator B+ terminal. • Is the voltage output less than 15.5 volts? → **Yes** GO to **C3**. → **No** GO to Pinpoint Test H.
C3 CHECK THE WARNING INDICATOR OPERATION	
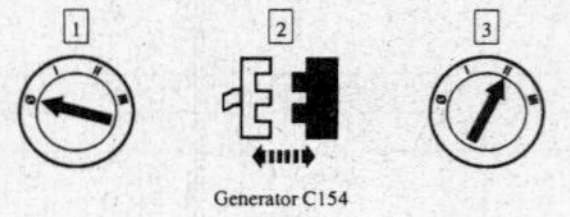	3 With the engine running at idle, check the warning indicator. • Is the warning indicator on? → **Yes** REPAIR Connector C154, I Circuit 904 (LG/R) as necessary. TEST the system for normal operation. → **No** GO to Pinpoint Test D.

FM1129800287000X

Fig. 143 Test C: Warning Indicator Is On w/Engine Running & Battery Voltage Increase. 1998–2000 Town Car

TEST CONDITIONS	TEST DETAILS/RESULTS/ACTIONS
E1 CHECK THE GENERATOR OUTPUT (B+ TERMINAL) VOLTAGE	
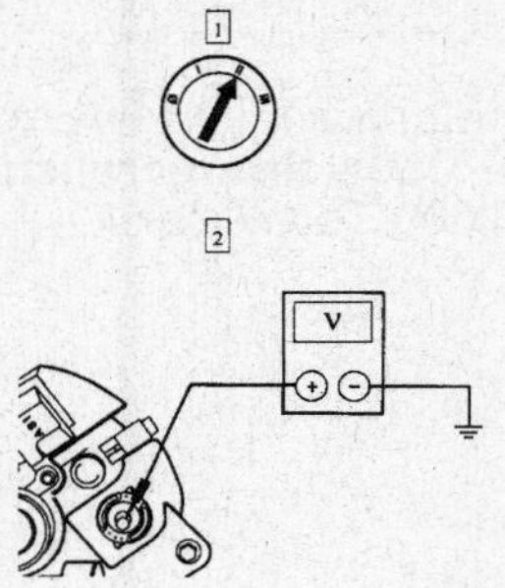	2 Check for voltage at the generator B+ Connector with the key ON and the engine OFF. • Is the voltage equal to battery positive voltage B+? → **Yes** GO to **E2**. → **No** REPAIR the generator output circuit as necessary. TEST the system for normal operation.

FM1129800289010X

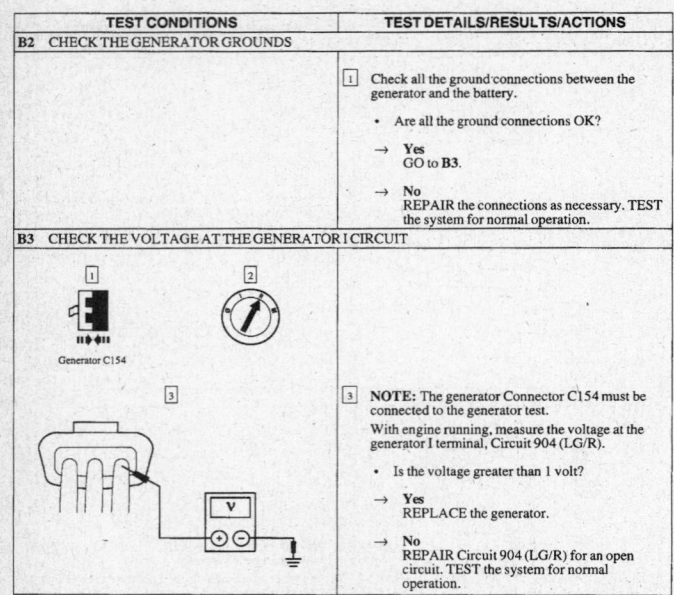

Fig. 145 Test E: Warning Indicator Operates Correctly But Battery Voltage Does Not Increase (Part 1 of 2). 1998–2000 Town Car

TEST CONDITIONS	TEST DETAILS/RESULTS/ACTIONS
E2 CHECK THE GENERATOR CONNECTORS	
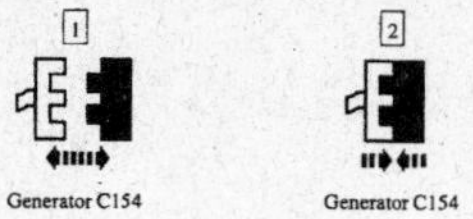	3 Check the battery connections and generator Connector C154 for corrosion and tightness. • Are the connectors clean and tight? → **Yes** REFER to Lead and No Lead Tests in this section. → **No** REPAIR the connectors as necessary. TEST the system for normal operation.

FM1129800289020X

Fig. 145 Test E: Warning Indicator Operates Correctly But Battery Voltage Does Not Increase (Part 2 of 2). 1998–2000 Town Car

TEST CONDITIONS	TEST DETAILS/RESULTS/ACTIONS
F1 CHECK FOR DRAINS ON THE BATTERY	
	2 Make sure all the interior lights and switches are off and all doors are closed. Perform the Battery Drain Test; refer to Component Tests, Battery—Drain Testing in this section. • Is the drain greater than .05 amps? → **Yes** Go to Component Tests—Battery—Drain Testing. → **No** GO to **F2**.

FM1129800290010X

Fig. 146 Test F: Battery Is Dead Or Will Not Stay Charged Or Low Battery Or Alternator Voltage (Part 1 of 2). 1998–2000 Town Car

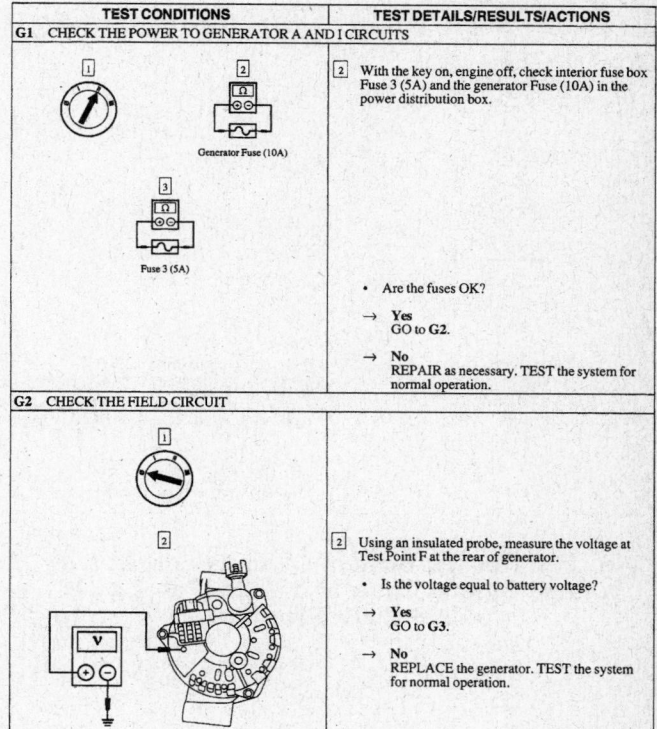

TEST CONDITIONS	TEST DETAILS/RESULTS/ACTIONS
F2 CHECK THE GENERATOR OUTPUT	
	1 Check the generator output; refer to Component Tests, Alternator On-Vehicle Tests in this section. • Is the generator OK? → **Yes** GO to **F3**. → **No** REPLACE the generator. TEST the system for normal operation.
F3 CHECK THE BATTERY CONDITION	
	1 Check the battery capacity • Is the battery OK? → **Yes** GO to **F4**. → **No** REPLACE the battery. TEST the system for normal operation.
F4 CHECK OTHER SYSTEMS FOR DRAINS	
	1 Check for drains from the electronic modules; refer to Component Test, Battery—Electronic Drains Which Shut Off When the Battery Cable is Disconnected in this section. • Are all the electronic modules OK? → **Yes** RECHARGE the battery. TEST the system for normal operation. → **No** REPLACE the damaged module as necessary. TEST the system for normal operation.

FM1129800290020X

Fig. 146 Test F: Battery Is Dead Or Will Not Stay Charged Or Low Battery Or Alternator Voltage (Part 2 of 2). 1998–2000 Town Car

TEST CONDITIONS	TEST DETAILS/RESULTS/ACTIONS
G1 CHECK THE POWER TO GENERATOR A AND I CIRCUITS	
 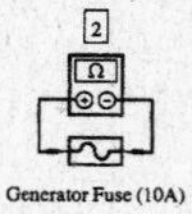 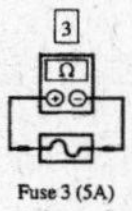	2 With the key on, engine off, check interior fuse box Fuse 3 (5A) and the generator Fuse (10A) in the power distribution box. • Are the fuses OK? → **Yes** GO to **G2**. → **No** REPAIR as necessary. TEST the system for normal operation.
G2 CHECK THE FIELD CIRCUIT	
 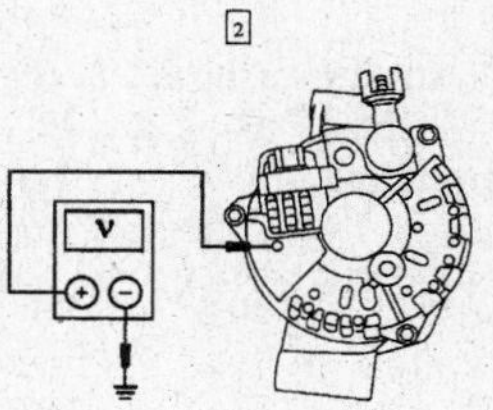	2 Using an insulated probe, measure the voltage at Test Point F at the rear of generator. • Is the voltage equal to battery voltage? → **Yes** GO to **G3**. → **No** REPLACE the generator. TEST the system for normal operation.

FM1129800291010X

Fig. 147 Test G: Warning Indicator Flickers Or Is Intermittent (Part 1 of 2). 1998–2000 Town Car

TEST CONDITIONS	TEST DETAILS/RESULTS/ACTIONS
G3 CHECK THE SYSTEM WARNING INDICATOR OPERATION	
1 	2 With the engine running, increase engine speed to 2000 rpm and check the indicator operation for battery voltage increase. • Does the voltage reading increase above 15.5 volts or the warning indicator flicker? → **Yes** REPLACE the generator. TEST the system for normal operation. → **No** REPAIR Circuit 36 (Y/W) or Circuit 904 (LG/R) as necessary. TEST the system for normal operation.

FM1129800291020X

Fig. 147 Test G: Warning Indicator Flickers Or Is Intermittent (Part 2 of 2). 1998–2000 Town Car

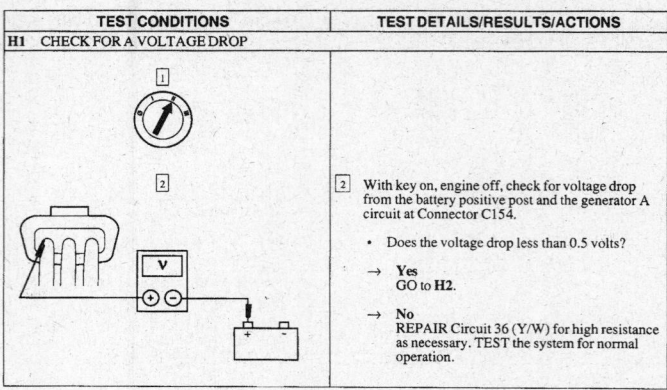

TEST CONDITIONS	TEST DETAILS/RESULTS/ACTIONS
H1 CHECK FOR A VOLTAGE DROP	
1, 2 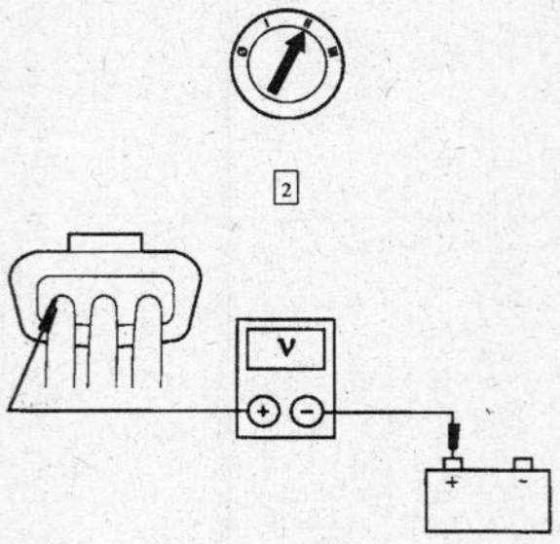	2 With key on, engine off, check for voltage drop from the battery positive post and the generator A circuit at Connector C154. • Does the voltage drop less than 0.5 volts? → **Yes** GO to **H2**. → **No** REPAIR Circuit 36 (Y/W) for high resistance as necessary. TEST the system for normal operation.

FM1129800292010X

Fig. 148 Test H: System Overcharges, Battery Voltage Greater Than 15.5 Volts (Part 1 of 4). 1998–2000 Town Car

TEST CONDITIONS	TEST DETAILS/RESULTS/ACTIONS
H2 CHECK THE BATTERY VOLTAGE	
1, 2 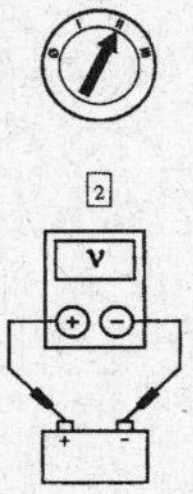	3 With the engine running, turn off all the accessories. Increase the engine speed and monitor the voltage at the battery. • Does battery voltage remain less than 15 volts? → **Yes** GO to **H3**. → **No** GO to **H5**.

FM1129800292020X

Fig. 148 Test H: System Overcharges, Battery Voltage Greater Than 15.5 Volts (Part 2 of 4). 1998–2000 Town Car

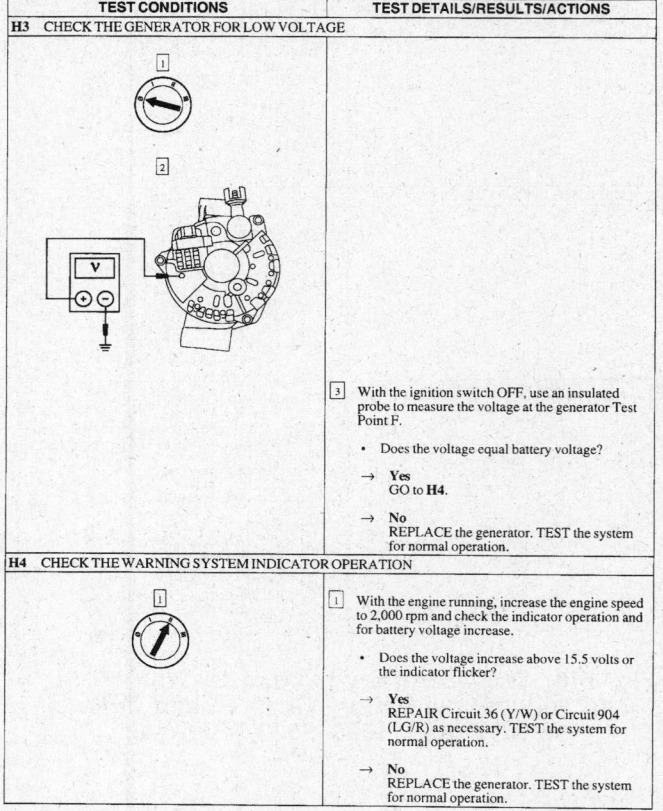

TEST CONDITIONS	TEST DETAILS/RESULTS/ACTIONS
H3 CHECK THE GENERATOR FOR LOW VOLTAGE	
1, 2 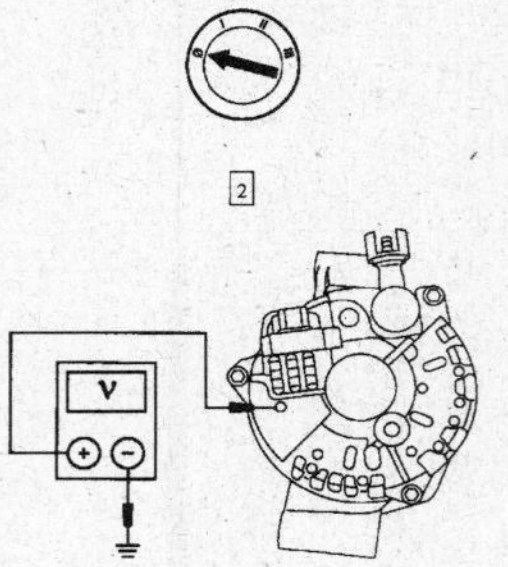	3 With the ignition switch OFF, use an insulated probe to measure the voltage at the generator Test Point F. • Does the voltage equal battery voltage? → **Yes** GO to **H4**. → **No** REPLACE the generator. TEST the system for normal operation.
H4 CHECK THE WARNING SYSTEM INDICATOR OPERATION	
1 	1 With the engine running, increase the engine speed to 2,000 rpm and check the indicator operation and for battery voltage increase. • Does the voltage increase above 15.5 volts or the indicator flicker? → **Yes** REPAIR Circuit 36 (Y/W) or Circuit 904 (LG/R) as necessary. TEST the system for normal operation. → **No** REPLACE the generator. TEST the system for normal operation.

FM1129800292030X

Fig. 148 Test H: System Overcharges, Battery Voltage Greater Than 15.5 Volts (Part 3 of 4). 1998–2000 Town Car

TEST CONDITIONS	TEST DETAILS/RESULTS/ACTIONS
H5 CHECK THE VOLTAGE REGULATOR OPERATION	
1 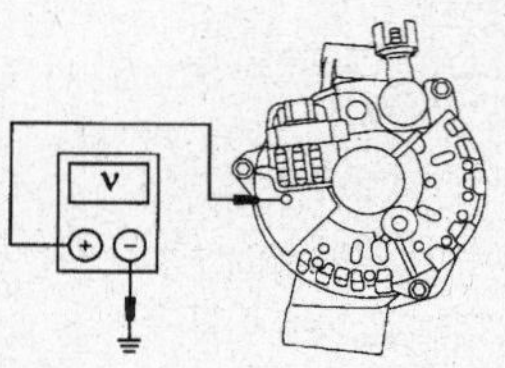	1 With the engine running, use an insulated probe to monitor the voltage at Test Point F while increasing the engine speed. • Does the voltage reading at Pin F increase with higher engine speed? → **Yes** REPLACE the generator. TEST the system for normal operation. → **No** REPLACE the generator. TEST the system for normal operation.

FM1129800292040X

Fig. 148 Test H: System Overcharges, Battery Voltage Greater Than 15.5 Volts (Part 4 of 4). 1998–2000 Town Car

TEST CONDITIONS	TEST DETAILS/RESULTS/ACTIONS
J2 CHECK THE CHARGING SYSTEM FOR OVERCHARGING (Continued)	
2 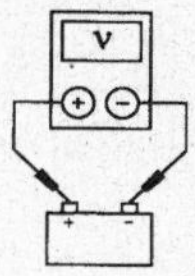	• Does battery voltage increase more than 15.5 volts? → **Yes** GO to Pinpoint Test H. → **No** GO to **J3**.
J3 CHECK THE BATTERY MOUNTING	
	1 Make sure the battery is properly mounted and level in the battery tray. • Is the battery properly mounted? → **Yes** GO to **J4**. → **No** REPAIR as necessary. TEST the system for normal operation.
J4 CHECK FOR BATTERY CONTACT	
	1 Make sure there are no fasteners or other parts contacting the battery case causing excess pressure. • Is there anything contacting the battery case? → **Yes** REPAIR as necessary. TEST the system for normal operation. → **No** GO to **J5**.

FM1129800293020X

Fig. 149 Test J: Battery Leakage Or Damage (Part 2 of 3). 1998–2000 Town Car

TEST CONDITIONS	TEST DETAILS/RESULTS/ACTIONS
J1 CHECK FOR ACID LEAKAGE DAMAGE	
	1 Check for acid damage to the vehicle harnesses and to the body. • Is there acid damage? → **Yes** REPAIR the damaged areas as necessary. → **No** GO to **J2**.
J2 CHECK THE CHARGING SYSTEM FOR OVERCHARGING	
1 	1 With the engine running, turn off all the accessories. Increase the engine speed and monitor the voltage at the battery.

FM1129800293010X

Fig. 149 Test J: Battery Leakage Or Damage (Part 1 of 3). 1998–2000 Town Car

TEST CONDITIONS	TEST DETAILS/RESULTS/ACTIONS
J5 CHECK THE BATTERY CASE FOR DAMAGE	
	1 Check the battery case for defects such as cracks or poor seals. • Is the battery OK? → **Yes** The system is OK. TEST the system for normal operation. → **No** REPLACE the battery. TEST the system for normal operation.

FM1129800293030X

Fig. 149 Test J: Battery Leakage Or Damage (Part 3 of 3). 1998–2000 Town Car

TEST CONDITIONS	TEST DETAILS/RESULTS/ACTIONS
K1 CHECK BATTERY VOLTAGE	
1  2 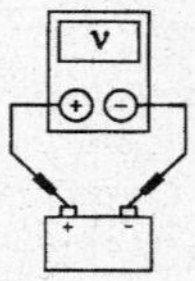	2 With the engine running, turn off all the accessories. Increase the engine speed to 2,000 rpm and monitor the voltage at the battery. • Is the battery voltage more than 15.5 or less than 13 volts? → **Yes** GO to Pinpoint Test H for readings higher than 15.5 volts. GO to Pinpoint Test F for readings less than 13 volts. → **No** GO to **K2**.

FM1129800294010X

Fig. 150 Test K: Voltage Gauge Reads High Or Low (Part 1 of 2). 1998–2000 Town Car

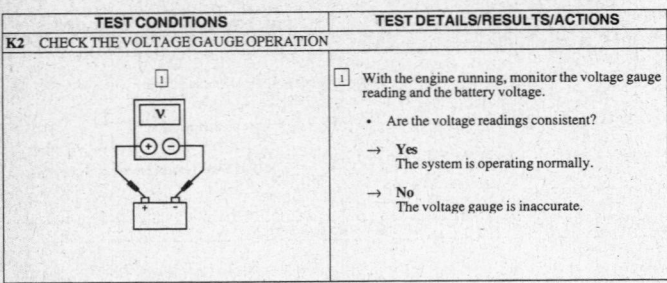

TEST CONDITIONS	TEST DETAILS/RESULTS/ACTIONS
K2 CHECK THE VOLTAGE GAUGE OPERATION	
1 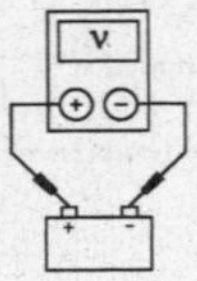	1 With the engine running, monitor the voltage gauge reading and the battery voltage. • Are the voltage readings consistent? → **Yes** The system is operating normally. → **No** The voltage gauge is inaccurate.

FM1129800294020X

Fig. 150 Test K: Voltage Gauge Reads High Or Low (Part 2 of 2). 1998–2000 Town Car

TEST CONDITIONS	TEST DETAILS/RESULTS/ACTIONS
M1 VERIFY THERE IS RADIO INTERFERENCE	
1 	1 Start and run the engine.
	2 Tune the radio to a station where the interference is present.
3 	3 Turn the engine off.
4 	4 Disconnect the generator Connector C176.
5 	5 Start and run the engine. • Is the interference present with the generator disconnected? → **Yes** INSPECT the in-vehicle entertainment system. → **No** GO to **M2**.
M2 SUBSTITUTE A KNOWN GOOD GENERATOR	
1 	1 Turn the engine off. 2 Install a known good generator.

FM1129800296010X

Fig. 152 Test M: Radio Interference (Part 1 of 2). 1998–2000 Town Car

TEST CONDITIONS	TEST DETAILS/RESULTS/ACTIONS
L1 CHECK FOR ACCESSORY DRIVE NOISE	
	1 Check the drive belt for damage and verify installation 2 Check the accessory mounting brackets for loose bolts or misalignment. 3 Check for a bent generator pulley. 4 Check other accessories for a bent, misaligned or loose pulley. • Is the accessory drive OK? → **Yes** REPLACE the generator. TEST the system for normal operation. → **No** INSPECT the accessory drive system.

FM1129800295000X

Fig. 151 Test L: Alternator Is Noisy. 1998–2000 Town Car

TEST CONDITIONS	TEST DETAILS/RESULTS/ACTIONS
M2 SUBSTITUTE A KNOWN GOOD GENERATOR (Continued)	
3 	3 Start and run the engine. • Is there radio interference with a known good generator? → **Yes** INSTALL the original generator and INSPECT the in-vehicle entertainment system. → **No** REPLACE the generator. TEST the system for normal operation.

FM1129800296020X

Fig. 152 Test M: Radio Interference (Part 2 of 2). 1998–2000 Town Car

ALTERNATOR SPECIFICATIONS

Model	Year	Model	Amp Rating
Continental	1997	F5OU-AA	130
	1998–2000	F8OU-CA	130
Contour	1997–99	—	130
Cougar	1997	③	130
	1999–2000	—	—
Crown Victoria	1997–2000	F6AU	130
Escort	1997–2000	F5OU-AA	75
Grand Marquis	1997–2000	F6AU	130
LS	2000	④	105
Mustang	1997–2000	②	130
Mystique	1997–2000	—	130

Continued

ALTERNATOR SPECIFICATIONS—Continued

Model	Year	Model	Amp Rating
Sable	1997	①	130
	1998–2000	F6DU-F	130
Taurus	1997	①	130
	1998–2000	F6DU-F	130
Thunderbird	1997	③	130
Town Car	1997	F6AU	130
	1998–2000	F6LU-CA	
Tracer	1997–99	F5OU-AA	130
ZX2	1998–2000	F1DU-A	95

① — 3.0L SOHC engine, F1DU-A; /3.0L & 3.4L DOHC engines, F5OU-AA.
② — 3.8L & 4.6L SOHC engines, F6AU; 4.6L DOHC engine, F6ZU-BC.
③ — 3.8L engine, F4SU-A; 4.6L engine, F62U-A.
④ — 3.0L engine, XR8U-AC. 3.9L engine, XR8U-CD.

Mando, Melco & Melmac Alternators

INDEX

APPLICATION CHART

Model	Year	Alternator
Aspire	1997	Mando
Mark VIII	1997–98	Melco
Probe	1997	Melmac

PRECAUTIONS

AIR BAG SYSTEMS

Refer to "Air Bag System Precautions" in the front of this manual for system disarming and arming procedures.

BATTERY GROUND CABLE

Prior to service, disconnect battery ground cable and isolate as required.

GENERAL

1. Ensure battery polarity is correct when servicing units. Reversed battery polarity will damage rectifiers and regulators.
2. If booster battery is used for starting, ensure polarity is correct.

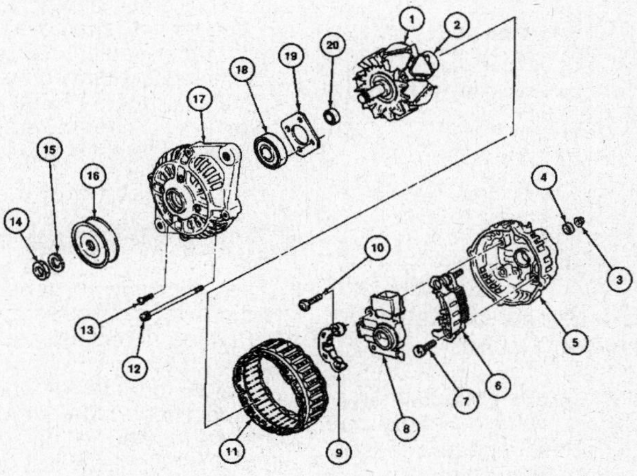

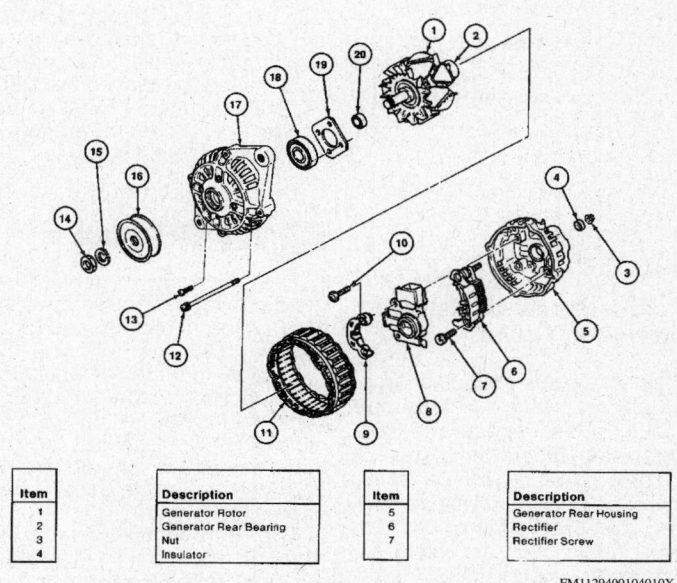

Item	Description	Item	Description
1	Generator Rotor	5	Generator Rear Housing
2	Generator Rear Bearing	6	Rectifier
3	Nut	7	Rectifier Screw
4	Insulator		

FM1129400104010X

Fig. 1 Exploded view of Mando alternator (Part 1 of 2). Aspire

Item	Description	Item	Description
8	Generator Regulator	14	Generator Pulley Nut
9	Shield	15	Lockwasher
10	Generator Regulator Screws (2)	16	Generator Pulley
11	Stator and Coil	17	Generator Front Housing
12	Generator Front Housing Capscrews (4)	18	Generator Front Bearing
13	Bearing Retainer Screws (4) (Part of 10A396)	19	Bearing Retainer
		20	Generator Fan / Pulley Spacer

FM1129400104020X

Fig. 1 Exploded view of Mando alternator (Part 2 of 2). Aspire

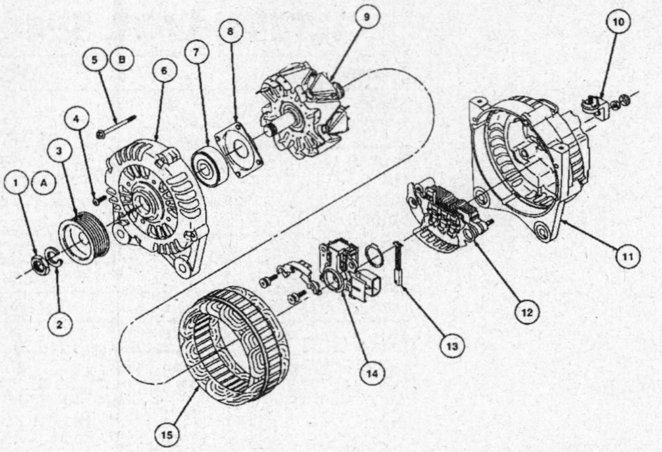

Item	Description	Item	Description
1A	Nut	10	Generator Stator Terminal
2	Washer	11	Generator Rear Housing and Bearing
3	Generator Pulley	12	Rectifier
4	Front Bearing Retainer Screw (4 Req'd)	13	Generator Brush and Terminal Holder (2 Req'd)
5B	Through Bolt	14	Generator Regulator
6	Generator Front Housing	15	Stator and Coil
7	Generator Front Bearing	A	Tighten to 82-135 N-m (60-100 Lb-Ft)
8	Front Bearing Retainer	B	Tighten to 4.0 6.7 N-m (35-59 Lb-In)
9	Generator Rotor		

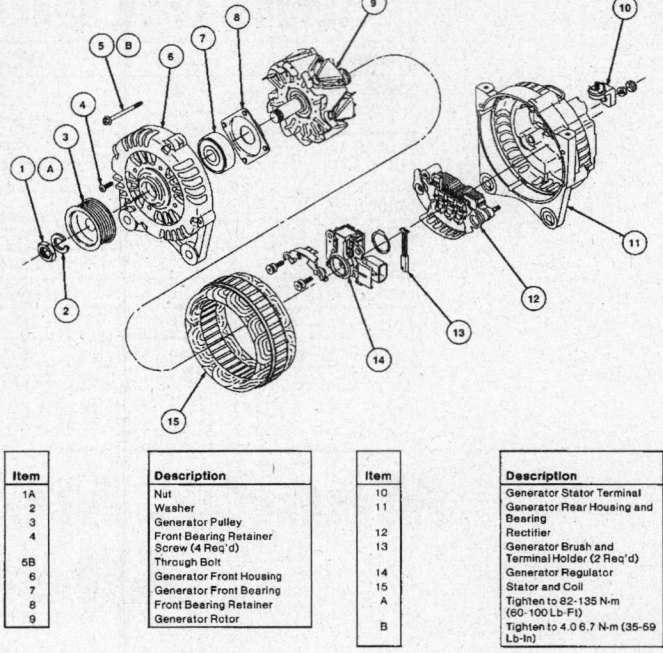

FM1129300105000X

Fig. 2 Exploded view of Melco alternator. Mark VIII

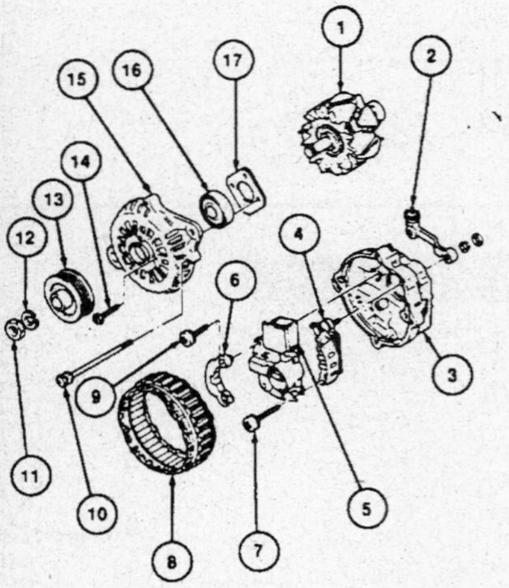

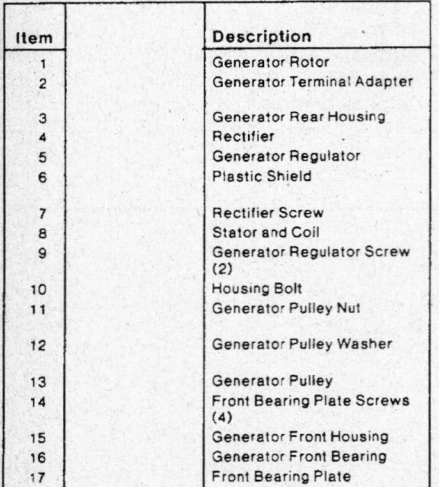

Item	Description
1	Generator Rotor
2	Generator Terminal Adapter
3	Generator Rear Housing
4	Rectifier
5	Generator Regulator
6	Plastic Shield
7	Rectifier Screw
8	Stator and Coil
9	Generator Regulator Screw (2)
10	Housing Bolt
11	Generator Pulley Nut
12	Generator Pulley Washer
13	Generator Pulley
14	Front Bearing Plate Screws (4)
15	Generator Front Housing
16	Generator Front Bearing
17	Front Bearing Plate

FM1129400097000X

Fig. 3 Exploded view of Melmac alternator. Probe

2. When a fast charger is used to charge a vehicle battery, vehicle battery cables should be disconnected unless fast charger is equipped with a special alternator protector, in which case vehicle battery cables need not be disconnected. Also fast charger should never be used to start a vehicle as damage to rectifiers will result.
3. Unless system includes a load relay or field relay, grounding alternator output terminal will damage alternator and/or circuits. This is true even when system is not in operation since a circuit breaker is not used and battery voltage is applied to the alternator output terminal at all times. The field or load relay acts as a circuit breaker in that it is controlled by ignition switch.
4. Before starting any on vehicle tests of alternator or regulator, battery should be checked and circuit inspected for faulty wiring or insulation, loose or corroded connections and poor ground circuits.
5. Ensure alternator belt tension is tight enough to prevent slipping under load.
6. To prevent damage to the system, ignition switch should be off and battery ground cable disconnected before making any test connections .
7. Vehicle battery must be fully charged or a fully charged battery may be installed for test purposes.

DESCRIPTION

The charging system is a negative ground system consisting of an alternator with a integral rectifier and regulator, **Figs. 1 through 3.**

The "B" terminal is connected internally to the rectifier bridge output. Externally, the cable connected to the " B" terminal supplies Direct Current (DC) output to the electrical system to charge the battery and operate the vehicle accessories while the engine is running.

The "L" terminal is connected internally (through a network of integrated circuits) to the field coil. When the ignition switch is turned on, the field coil is energized to "turn on " regulator power transistor.

The "S" terminal is connected internally to the voltage regulator sensing circuit. Externally, the "S " terminal is connected to the ignition side of the ignition switch. The "S" circuit is used to tell the voltage regulator how much alternator output is required.

The Integrated Circuit (IC) electronic voltage regulator is part of the rotor, brush, and brush holder assembly. There is no voltage adjustment. The IC regulator automatically reduces regulated voltage when ambient temperature increases, so that battery charging voltage is maintained at the correct level.

DIAGNOSIS & TESTING

Wiring Diagrams

ASPIRE

Refer to **Fig. 4** for charging system wiring diagram.

MARK VIII

Refer to **Fig. 5** for charging system wiring diagram.

PROBE

Refer to **Fig. 6** for charging system wiring diagram.

Diagnostic Tests

ASPIRE

Refer to **Fig. 7** for symptom chart and **Figs. 8 through 14** for diagnostic tests.

MARK VIII

Refer to **Fig. 15** for symptom chart and **Figs. 16 through 27** for diagnostic tests.

PROBE

Refer to **Fig. 28** for symptom chart and **Figs. 29 through 34** for diagnostic tests.

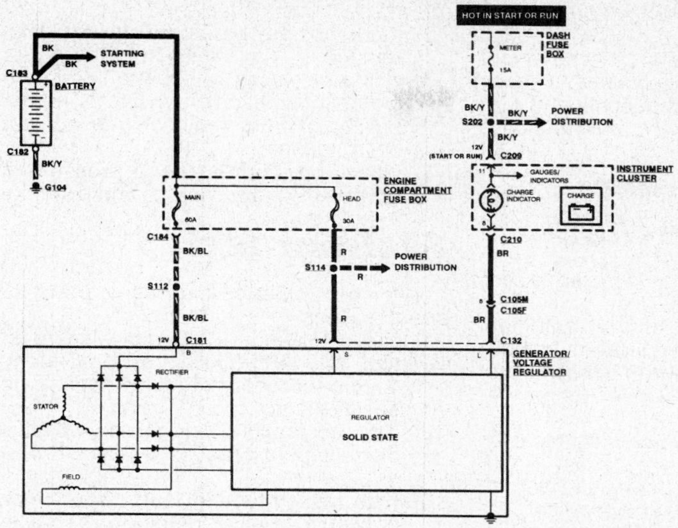

FM1129700318000X

Fig. 4 Wiring diagram. Aspire

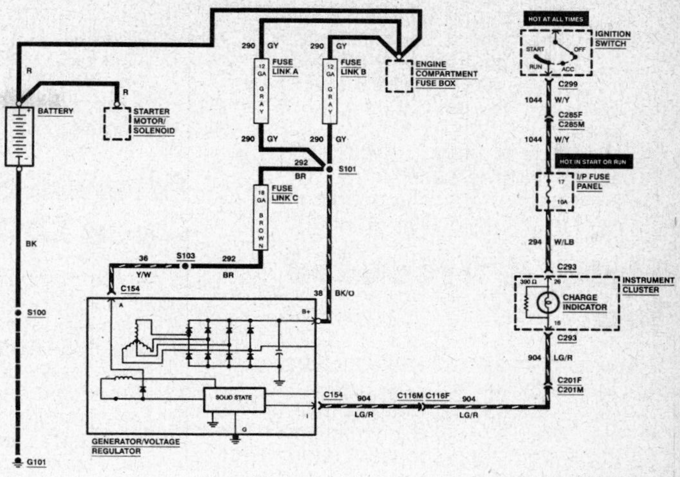

FM1129700320000X

Fig. 5 Wiring diagram. Mark VIII

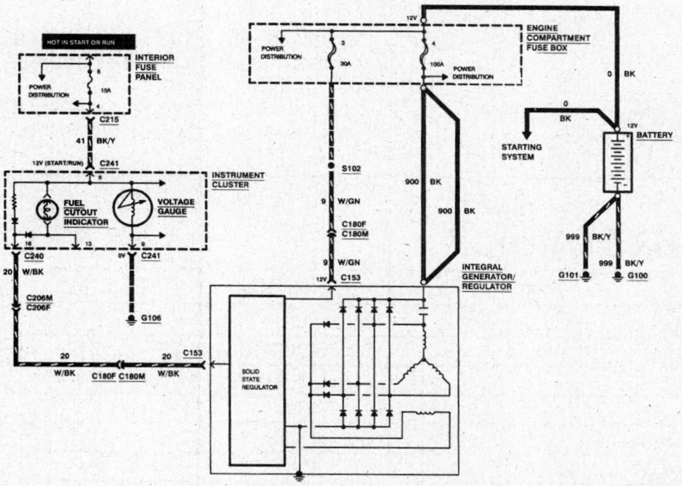

FM1129700319000X

Fig. 6 Wiring diagram. Probe

Condition	Possible Source	Action
• System Does Not Charge	• Loose or worn drive belt. • Loose or corroded battery connections. • Battery. • Generator. • Circuit.	• GO to Pinpoint Test A1.
• System Overcharges (Battery Boils Over)	• Generator.	• GO to Pinpoint Test B1.
• Indicator Lamp Stays On, Engine Running	• Charging system indicator circuit.	• GO to Pinpoint Test C1.
• Indicator Lamp Does Not Come On	• Charging system indicator circuit. • Battery. • Generator.	• GO to Pinpoint Test D1.
• Indicator Lamp Flickers / Intermittent	• Loose connections. • Generator belt slipping. • Generator.	• GO to Pinpoint Test E1.
• Generator Noisy	• Loose or worn drive belt. • Bent generator pulley. • Generator.	• GO to Pinpoint Test F1.
• Battery Does Not Hold a Charge	• Loose or worn drive belt. • Loose or corroded battery cables. • Battery. • Generator.	• GO to Pinpoint Test G1.

FM1129400106000A

Fig. 7 Diagnostic symptom chart. Aspire

No-Load Test

Prior to testing, turn headlamps on for 10–15 seconds to remove battery surface charge. Wait until voltage stabilizes before performing test.

1. Connect Rotunda 88 Digital Multimeter tool No. 105-00053, or equivalent.
2. Connect Rotunda 73 Digital Multimeter tool No. 105-00051, or equivalent, across battery terminals and record base voltage.
3. Start engine and run at 1500 RPM with no electrical load.
4. Voltage should be 14.1–14.7 volts.
5. If voltage increases, but voltage increase is less than 2.5 volts, perform "Load Test."
6. If voltage does not increase, or increases more than 2.5 volts, perform "Output Test."

Load Test

1. With engine running, turn headlamps on and blower motor to high. If equipped, turn on air conditioning.
2. Increase engine speed to 2000 RPM.
3. Voltage should increase at least .5 volts above base voltage.
4. If voltage does not increase as specified, perform " Output Test."

Output Test

VAT-40 TESTER

1. Connect Rotunda VAT-40 tool No. 078-00005, or equivalent, leads to vehicle and turn all accessories off.
2. Turn ignition switch to On position and read discharge rate on ammeter.
3. Start engine and run at 1500–2000 RPM.
4. Slowly increase load control knob of Rotunda VAT-40 until highest amp reading is obtained, then turn load control knob off.
5. Add discharge rate to highest amp reading for total alternator output.
6. Alternator is functioning properly if total alternator output is more than specified, **Fig. 35.**
7. If amperage is below specifications, refer to "Voltage Test."

ARBST TESTER

1. Switch Alternator, Regulator, Battery and Starter Tester (ARBST) tool No. 010-00725, or equivalent, to ammeter function, then connect positive and negative leads to battery.
2. Connect current probe to alternator "B+" output lead.
3. With engine running at 2000 RPM, adjust ARBST load bank to determine alternator output.
4. Alternator is functioning properly if total alternator output is more than specified, **Fig. 35.**
5. If amperage is below specifications, refer to "Voltage Test."

Voltage Test

1. With ignition switch in On position and engine off, ensure alternator wiring connector terminal, **Figs. 36 and 37,** voltages are as follows:
   a. "B"-terminal, battery voltage.
   b. "L"-terminal, approximately one volt.
   c. "S"-terminal, battery voltage.
2. Start engine and run at curb idle RPM, then ensure alternator wiring connector terminal voltages are as follows:

a. "B"-terminal, 14.1–14.7 volts.
b. "L"-terminal, 13.0–14.0 volts.
c. "S"-terminal, 14.1–14.7 volts.

3. If voltage is as specified, inspect wiring harness between battery and "B" terminal.
4. If voltage is below specifications, inspect wiring harness.
5. If wiring harness is in good condition, refer to " Stator & Coil Grounded Test."

Stator & Grounded Test

Alternator must be disassembled to conduct this tests.

1. Use Rotunda 73 Digital Multimeter tool No. 105-00051, or equivalent, to check three stator and coil leads, and stator and coil core continuity.
2. If there is continuity, replace stator and coil.

Stator & Coil Open Test

Alternator must be disassembled to conduct this test.

1. Inspect stator and coil laminations for overheating.
2. If burn spots are evident, replace stator and coil.
3. Use Rotunda 73 Digital Multimeter tool No. 105-00051, or equivalent, to check stator and coil leads for continuity.
4. If there is no continuity, replace stator.

Alternator Rotor Open Or Short Test

Alternator must be disassembled to conduct this test.

1. Use Rotunda 73 Digital Multimeter tool No. 105-00051, or equivalent, to measure resistance between two slip rings.
2. If resistance is not 3.5–4.5 ohms, replace rotor.
3. Check for continuity between each slip ring and rotor core.
4. If there is continuity, replace rotor.
5. Check slip ring color and condition.
6. If rings are dark, clean them with fine sandpaper.
7. If rings are grooved, refinish them on a lathe.

Brush Test

Alternator must be disassembled to inspect brushes.

1. Inspect bushes for wear.
2. If brushes are worn down to wear line, replace.
3. Using a suitable spring pressure gauge, push each brush into its' holder until tip of brush projects .079 inch out of its' holder.
4. Check brush pressure. If pressure is not 5.6–15.5 oz., replace brush spring.

Rectifier Test

Alternator must be disassembled to inspect rectifier.

1. Using Rotunda 73 Digital Multimeter tool No. 105-00051, or equivalent, check for continuity between diode positive leads and heat sink.
2. If no continuity exists for any positive diode lead to heat sink, replace rectifier.
3. Reverse ohmmeter leads and check continuity between diode negative leads and heat sink.
4. If continuity exists from any negative diode lead to heat sink, replace rectifier.
5. Check diode trio (smaller diodes between main diode leads) for continuity in both directions.
6. If any diode does not show continuity in one direction only, replace diode trio.

DIAGNOSTIC CHART INDEX

Test	Description	Page No.	Fig. No.
ASPIRE			
—	Diagnostic Symptom Chart	13-57	7
Test A	System Does Not Charge	13-59	8
Test B	System Overcharges	13-59	9
Test C	Indicator Lamp Stays On, Engine Running	13-59	10
Test D	Indicator Lamp Does Not Come On	13-60	11
Test E	Indicator Lamp Flickers/Intermittent	13-60	12
Test F	Alternator Noisy	13-60	13
Test G	Battery Does Not Hold Charge	13-60	14
MARK VIII			
—	Diagnostic Symptom Chart	13-60	15
Test A	Charging System Warning Indicator Is On w/The Engine Running (Battery Voltage Does Not Increase)	13-60	16
Test B	Charging System Warning Indicator Is Off w/Ignition Switch In Run Position & Engine Off (Battery Voltage Does Not Increase)	13-61	17
Test C	Charging System Warning Indicator Is On w/Engine Running & Battery Voltage Increases	13-62	18
Test D	Charging System Warning Indicator Is Off w/Ignition Switch In The Run Position & Engine Off (Battery Voltage Increases)	13-62	19
Test E	Charging System Warning indicator Operates Correctly But Battery Voltage Does Not Increase	13-63	20
Test F	Battery Dead Or Will Not Stay Charged Or Low Battery Or Generator Voltage	13-63	21
Test G	Charging System Warning Indicator Flickers	13-63	22
Test H	System Overcharges (Battery Voltage Greater Than 15.5 Volts)	13-64	23
Test J	Battery Leakage Or Damage	13-64	24
Test K	Voltage Gauge Reads High Or Low	13-65	25
Test L	Generator Is Noisy	13-65	26
Test M	Radio Interference	13-65	27
PROBE			
—	Diagnostic Symptom Chart	13-65	28

Continued

DIAGNOSTIC CHART INDEX—Continued

Test Step		Result ▶	Action to Take
A1	CHECK BATTERY CONNECTIONS		
	• Inspect the battery cables for loose or corroded connections. • **Are the battery cables clean and tight?**	Yes ▶ No ▶	GO to **A2**. CLEAN and TIGHTEN the battery cables.
A2	CHECK DRIVE BELT TENSION		
	• Perform the drive belt adjustment procedure • **Is the drive belt adjusted properly?**	Yes ▶ No ▶	GO to **A3**. ADJUST or REPLACE the drive belt.
A3	CHECK WIRE BETWEEN GENERATOR AND MAIN FUSE JUNCTION PANEL		
	• Key OFF. • Disconnect generator connector. • Disconnect 80A main fuse. • Measure resistance of "BK/BL" wire between generator connector and main fuse junction panel. • Measure resistance of "BK/BL" wire between generator connector and ground. • **Is the resistance of "BK/BL" wire 5 ohms or less when measured between generator connector and main junction fuse panel, and 10,000 ohms or greater when measured between generator connector and ground?**	Yes ▶ No ▶	GO to **A4**. SERVICE the wire in question.
A4	CHECK WIRE BETWEEN MAIN FUSE JUNCTION PANEL AND BATTERY POSITIVE TERMINAL CONNECTOR		
	• Key OFF. • Disconnect 80A main fuse. • Disconnect battery positive terminal connector. • Measure the resistance of the "BK" wire between the battery positive terminal connector and the main fuse junction panel. • Measure the resistance of the "BK" wire between the main fuse junction panel and ground. • **Is the resistance of the "BK" wire 5 ohms or less when measured between the main fuse junction panel and the battery positive terminal connector, and 10,000 ohms or greater when measured between the main fuse junction panel and ground?**	Yes ▶ No ▶	GO to **A5**. SERVICE the wire in question.
A5	CHECK FOR OPEN "S" CIRCUIT		
	• Key OFF. • Disconnect generator connector. • Measure voltage at wiring harness "S" terminal, circuit 7A (R). • **Is the voltage at "S" terminal equal to battery voltage?**	Yes ▶ No ▶	GO to **A6**. CHECK 30A HEAD fuse and REPLACE if necessary. If OK, REPAIR open in Circuit 7A (R).
A6	CHECK BATTERY		
	• Perform the Battery component tests • Is the battery OK?	Yes ▶ No ▶	PERFORM the Generator component tests REPLACE the battery.

FM1129400108010A

Fig. 8 Test A: System Does Not Charge. Aspire

Test Step		Result ▶	Action to Take
B1	CHECK FOR OPEN "S" CIRCUIT		
	• Key OFF. • Disconnect generator connector. • Measure voltage at wiring harness "S" terminal circuit, 7A (R). • **Is the voltage at "S" terminal equal to battery voltage?**	Yes ▶ No ▶	GO to **B2**. CHECK 30A HEAD fuse and REPLACE if necessary. If OK, REPAIR open in circuit 7A (R).

FM1129400109000A

Fig. 9 Test B: System Overcharges (Part 1 of 2). Aspire

Test Step		Result ▶	Action to Take
B2	CHECK GENERATOR		
	• Perform the Generator component tests • **Is the generator OK?**	Yes ▶ No ▶	Charging system OK. RETURN to the Symptom Chart. REPAIR or REPLACE the generator.

FM1129400109020X

Fig. 9 Test B: System Overcharges (Part 2 of 2). Aspire

Test Step		Result ▶	Action to Take
C1	CHECK WIRE BETWEEN INSTRUMENT CLUSTER AND INTERIOR FUSE JUNCTION PANEL		
	• Key OFF. • Disconnect instrument cluster connector C1. • Disconnect 15A METER fuse at interior fuse junction panel. • Measure the resistance of the "BK/Y" wire between instrument cluster connector C1 and the interior fuse junction panel. • Measure the resistance of the "BK/Y" wire between instrument cluster connector C1 and ground. • **Is the resistance of the "BK/Y" wire 5 ohms or less when measured between instrument cluster connector C1 and interior fuse junction panel, and 10,000 ohms or greater between instrument cluster connector C1 and ground?**	Yes ▶ No ▶	GO to **C3**. SERVICE the "BK/Y" wire.
C2	CHECK WIRE BETWEEN INSTRUMENT CLUSTER AND GENERATOR		
	• Key OFF. • Disconnect instrument cluster connector C2. • Disconnect the generator connector. • Measure the resistance of the "BR" wire between instrument cluster connector C2 and the generator connector. • Measure the resistance of the "BR" wire between instrument cluster connector C2 and ground. • **Is the resistance less than 5 ohms between instrument cluster connector C2 and the generator, and greater than 10,000 ohms between the instrument cluster connector C2 and ground?**	Yes ▶ No ▶	GO to **C3**. SERVICE the "BR" wire.
C3	CHECK FOR OPEN "S" CIRCUIT		
	• Key OFF. • Disconnect generator connector. • Measure voltage at wiring harness "S" terminal, circuit 7A (R). • **Is the voltage at "S" terminal equal to battery voltage?**	Yes ▶ No ▶	GO to **C4**. CHECK 30A HEAD fuse and REPLACE if necessary. If OK, REPAIR open in circuit 7A (R).
C4	CHECK DRIVE BELT TENSION		
	• Perform the drive belt adjustment procedure • **Is the drive belt adjusted properly?**	Yes ▶ No ▶	GO to **C2**. ADJUST or REPLACE the drive belt.
C5	CHECK GENERATOR		
	• Perform the Generator component tests • **Is the generator OK?**	Yes ▶ No ▶	GO to **D1**. REPAIR or REPLACE the generator.

FM1129400110000A

Fig. 10 Test C: Indicator Lamp Stays On, Engine Running. Aspire

Test Step		Result ▶	Action to Take
D1	CHECK WIRE BETWEEN INSTRUMENT CLUSTER AND GENERATOR		
	• Key OFF. • Disconnect the generator connector. • Key ON. • Ground the "BR" wire on the generator connector. • **Does the charging system indicator illuminate?**	Yes ▶ No ▶	service the generator. GO to **D2**.
D2	CHECK CHARGING SYSTEM INDICATOR MINIATURE BULB		
	• Key OFF. • Remove the charging system indicator miniature bulb. • Check the continuity between the terminals of the charging system indicator miniature bulb. • **Does continuity exist?**	Yes ▶ No ▶	GO to **D3**. REPLACE the charging system indicator miniature bulb.
D3	CHECK WIRE BETWEEN INSTRUMENT CLUSTER AND GENERATOR		
	• Key OFF. • Locate and disconnect the black instrument cluster connector C2. • Disconnect the generator connector. • Measure the resistance of the "BR" wire between the black instrument cluster connector C2 and the generator connector. • Measure the resistance of the "BR" wire between the black instrument cluster connector C2 and ground. • **Is the resistance less than 5 ohms between the instrument cluster and the generator, and greater than 10,000 ohms between the instrument cluster and ground?**	Yes ▶ No ▶	REPLACE the instrument cluster printed circuit. SERVICE the "BR" wire.

FM1129400111000A

Fig. 11 Test D: Indicator Lamp Does Not Come On. Aspire

Test Step		Result ▶	Action to Take
F1	CHECK DRIVE BELT TENSION		
	• Perform the drive belt adjustment procedure • **Is the drive belt adjusted properly?**	Yes ▶ No ▶	GO to **F2**. ADJUST or REPLACE the drive belt.
F2	CHECK GENERATOR PULLEY		
	• Remove the drive belt. • Check the generator pulley for damage. • **Is the generator pulley OK?**	Yes ▶ No ▶	INSPECT the generator bearings. REPLACE the generator pulley.

FM1129600129000X

Fig. 13 Test F: Alternator Noisy. Aspire

Condition	Possible Source	Action
• The Charging System Warning Indicator is ON with the Engine Running (The Battery Voltage Does Not Increase)	• A Circuit 35 (O/LB). • A Circuit in-line mini-fuse. • B+ Circuit 36 (Y/W). • B+ mega fuse. • I Circuit 904 (LG/R). • Voltage regulator. • Generator.	• GO to Pinpoint Test A.
• The Charging System Warning Indicator is OFF with the Ignition Switch in the RUN Position and the Engine OFF (Battery Voltage Does Not Increase)	• Voltage regulator connector. • I Circuit 905 (LG/R). • Fuse 19 (10A). • Voltage regulator. • Loose or damaged generator. • Harness connector.	• GO to Pinpoint Test B.
• The Charging System Warning Indicator Stays ON with the Engine Running and the Battery Voltage Increases	• Generator. • Voltage regulator.	• GO to Pinpoint Test C.
• The Charging System Warning Indicator is OFF with the Ignition Switch in the RUN Position and the Engine OFF (Battery Voltage Increases)	• Charging system warning indicator lamp bulb. • Instrument cluster. • Generator. • Voltage regulator.	• GO to Pinpoint Test D.

FM1129700167010X

Fig. 15 Diagnostic symptom chart (Part 1 of 2). Mark VIII

Test Step		Result ▶	Action to Take
E1	CHECK FOR LOOSE CONNECTIONS		
	• Check these connections for corrosion, loose or bent pins, or loose eyelets: — 'L' and 'S' connector — Generator 'B' eyelet — Battery cables • **Are all connections clean and tight?**	Yes ▶ No ▶	GO to **E2**. CLEAN or SERVICE connections as required.
E2	CHECK FOR LOOSE GENERATOR BELT		
	• Check generator drive belt when engine is cold, or has been stopped for at least 30 minutes. — The drive belt deflection should measure 8-9mm (0.31-0.35 inch) for a new belt, or 9-10mm (0.35-0.39 inch) for a used belt. • **Is the generator drive belt adjusted correctly?**	Yes ▶ No ▶	GO to **D1**. PERFORM the Alternator Belt Adjustment Procedure

FM1129400112000A

Fig. 12 Test E: Indicator Lamp Flickers/Intermittent. Aspire

Test Step		Result ▶	Action to Take
G1	CHECK BATTERY CONNECTIONS		
	• Check the battery cables for loose or corroded connections. • **Are the battery cables clean and tight?**	Yes ▶ No ▶	GO to **G2**. CLEAN and TIGHTEN the battery cables.
G2	CHECK DRIVE BELT TENSION		
	• Perform the drive belt adjustment procedure • **Is the drive belt adjusted properly?**	Yes ▶ No ▶	PERFORM the Battery component tests ADJUST or REPLACE the drive belt.

FM1129600130000X

Fig. 14 Test G: Battery Does Not Hold Charge. Aspire

Condition	Possible Source	Action
• The Charging System Warning Indicator Operates Correctly but the Battery Voltage Does Not Increase	• B+ Circuit 36 (Y/W). • B+ mega fuse. • Loose or damaged harness connector. • Battery cables. • Generator. • Voltage regulator.	• GO to Pinpoint Test E.
• The Battery is Dead or Will Not Stay Charged or Low Battery or Generator Voltage	• Corroded terminal(s). • Loose connection(s). • High key-off load. • Generator. • Voltage regulator.	• GO to Pinpoint Test F.
• The Charging System Warning Indicator Flickers/Is Intermittent	• Loose connection(s). • In-line mini-fuse A Circuit loose. • Fuse 19 (10A) I Circuit loose. • Generator. • Voltage regulator.	• GO to Pinpoint Test G.
• The System Overcharges (Battery Voltage Greater Than 15.5 Volts)	• A Circuit 35 (O/LB). • Generator (low output). • Voltage regulator. • I Circuit 904 (LG/R).	• GO to Pinpoint Test H.
• Battery Leakage or Damage	• A Circuit 35 (O/LB). • Voltage regulator. • Voltage gauge. • Instrument cluster/wiring.	• GO to Pinpoint Test J.
• The Voltage Gauge Reads High or Low	• Generator (low output). • Voltage regulator. • Voltage gauge. • Instrument cluster/wiring.	• GO to Pinpoint Test K.
• The Generator is Noisy	• Loose bolts/brackets. • Drive belt. • Generator/Pulley.	• GO to Pinpoint Test L.
• Radio Interference	• Generator. • Wiring/routing.. • In-vehicle entertainment system.	• GO to Pinpoint Test M.

FM1129700167020X

Fig. 15 Diagnostic symptom chart (Part 2 of 2). Mark VIII

TEST CONDITIONS	TEST DETAILS/RESULTS/ACTIONS
A1 CHECK A CIRCUIT FUSE LINK (18GA)	
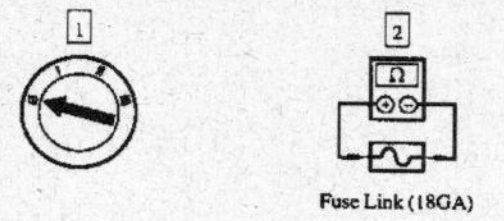	2 Check the A circuit Fuse 20 (15A) in the Power Distribution Box. • Is the fuse OK? → **Yes** GO to **A2**. → **No** REPLACE the Fuse Link (18GA). TEST the system for normal operation.
A2 CHECK CIRCUIT 38 (BK/O)	
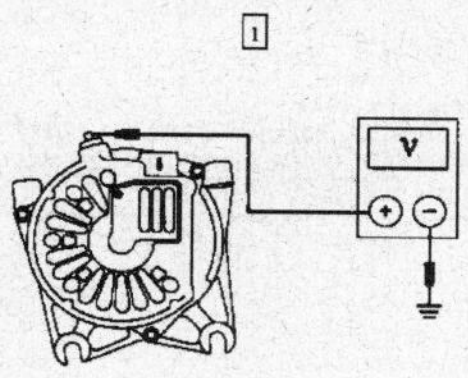	1 Measure the voltage between the B+ terminal at the generator Circuit 38 (BK/O) and ground. • Is the voltage equal to battery positive voltage (B+)? → **Yes** GO to **A3**. → **No** REPAIR Circuit 38 (BK/O). TEST the system for normal operation.

FM1129700168010X

Fig. 16 Test A: Charging System Warning Indicator Is On w/The Engine Running (Battery Voltage Does Not Increase, Part 1 of 3). Mark VIII

TEST CONDITIONS	TEST DETAILS/RESULTS/ACTIONS
A3 CHECK CIRCUIT 36 (Y/W)	
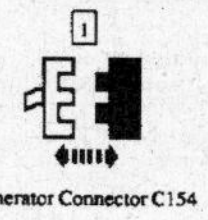	
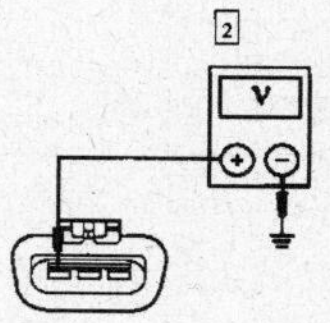	2 Measure the voltage between the voltage regulator connector C154 Pin A, Circuit 36 (Y/W) and ground. • Is the voltage equal to battery positive voltage (B+)? → **Yes** GO to **A4**. → **No** REPAIR Circuit 36 (Y/W). TEST the system for normal operation.
A4 CHECK I CIRCUIT 904 (LG/R) FOR AN OPEN	

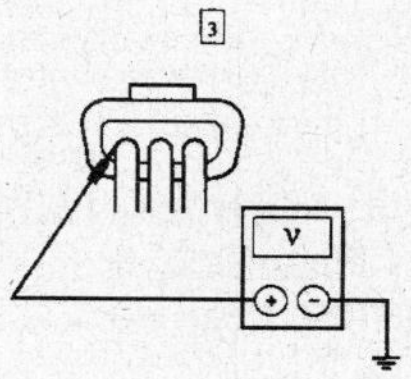	3 **NOTE:** The voltage regulator must be connected to the wiring harness for this test. Measure the voltage between the voltage regulator I-terminal, Circuit 904 (LG/R) and ground. • Is the voltage greater than 1 volt? → **Yes** GO to **A5**. → **No** REPAIR Circuit 904 (LG/R) as necessary. TEST the system for normal operation.

FM1129700168020X

Fig. 16 Test A: Charging System Warning Indicator Is On w/The Engine Running (Battery Voltage Does Not Increase, Part 2 of 3). Mark VIII

TEST CONDITIONS	TEST DETAILS/RESULTS/ACTIONS
A5 CHECK GENERATOR OUTPUT	

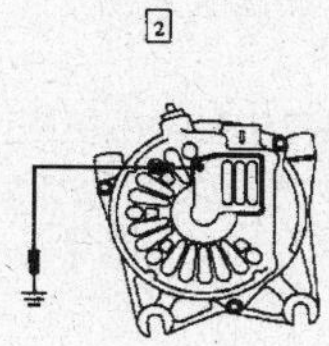	2 With the engine running, ground the F pin on the generator/regulator. • Does the battery voltage increase and the charging system warning indicator turn off? → **Yes** REPLACE the generator. TEST the system for normal operation. → **No** REPLACE the generator. TEST the system for normal operation.

FM1129700168030X

Fig. 16 Test A: Charging System Warning Indicator Is On w/The Engine Running (Battery Voltage Does Not Increase, Part 3 of 3). Mark VIII

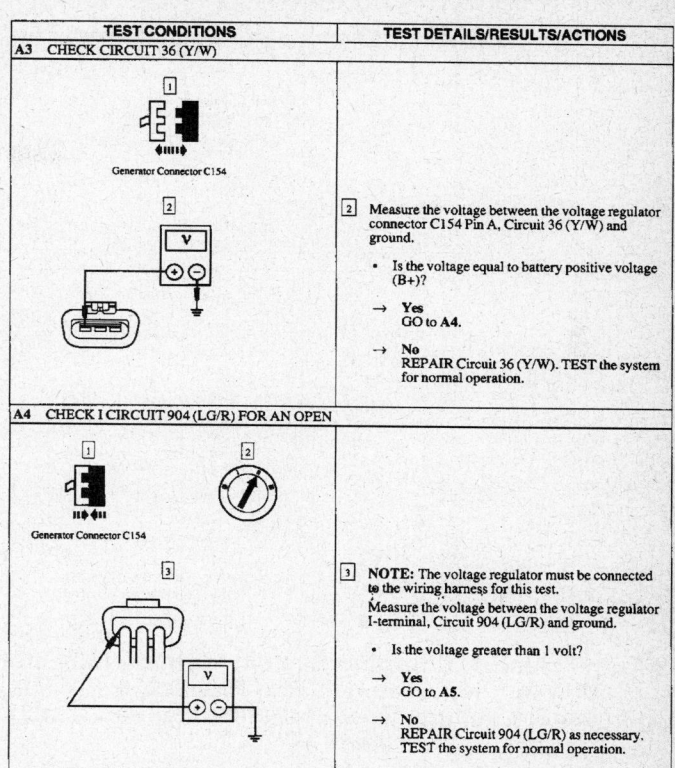

TEST CONDITIONS	TEST DETAILS/RESULTS/ACTIONS
B1 CHECK GENERATOR CONNECTOR C154	
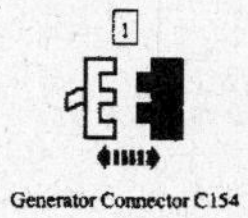	2 Check generator connector C154 for bent, or damaged pins. • Is the connector OK? → **Yes** GO to **B2**. → **No** REPAIR connector C154 as necessary. TEST the system for normal operation.

FM1129700169010X

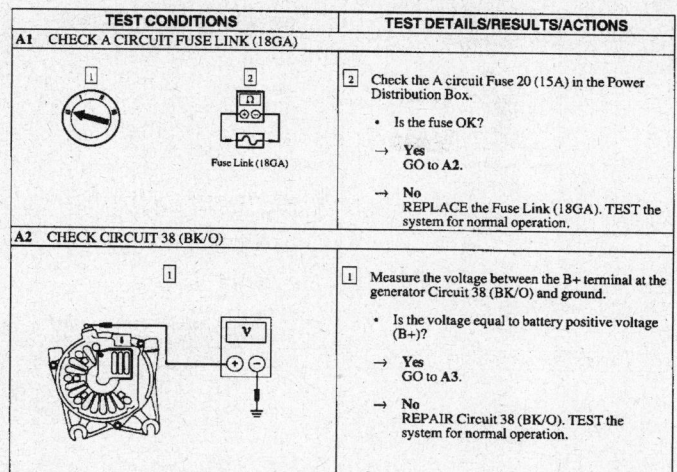

Fig. 17 Test B: Charging System Warning Indicator Is Off w/Ignition Switch In Run Position & Engine Off (Battery Voltage Does Not Increase, Part 1 of 2). Mark VIII

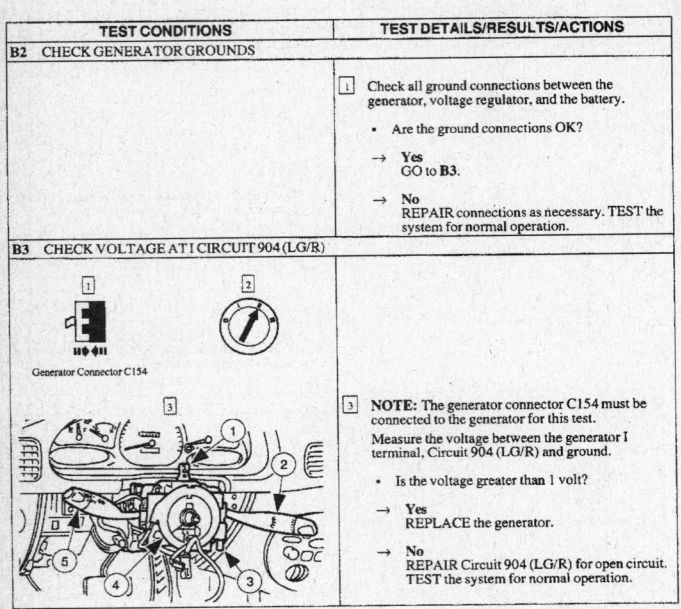

TEST CONDITIONS	TEST DETAILS/RESULTS/ACTIONS
B2 CHECK GENERATOR GROUNDS	
	1 Check all ground connections between the generator, voltage regulator, and the battery. • Are the ground connections OK? → **Yes** GO to **B3**. → **No** REPAIR connections as necessary. TEST the system for normal operation.
B3 CHECK VOLTAGE AT I CIRCUIT 904 (LG/R)	
1  2  3 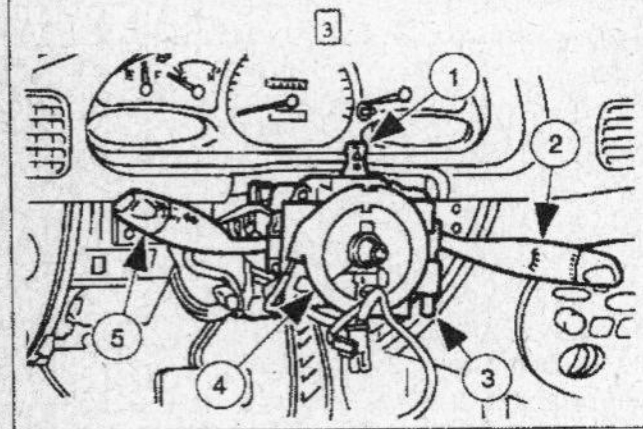	3 **NOTE:** The generator connector C154 must be connected to the generator for this test. Measure the voltage between the generator I terminal, Circuit 904 (LG/R) and ground. • Is the voltage greater than 1 volt? → **Yes** REPLACE the generator. → **No** REPAIR Circuit 904 (LG/R) for open circuit. TEST the system for normal operation.

FM1129700169020X

Fig. 17 Test B: Charging System Warning Indicator Is Off w/Ignition Switch In Run Position & Engine Off (Battery Voltage Does Not Increase, Part 2 of 2). Mark VIII

TEST CONDITIONS	TEST DETAILS/RESULTS/ACTIONS
C3 CHECK WARNING INDICATOR OPERATION	
1 2 3 	4 With the engine running at idle, check the Warning Indicator. • Is the Warning Indicator on? → **Yes** REPAIR connector C154, I circuit 904 (LG/R) as necessary. TEST the system for normal operation. → **No** GO to Pinpoint Test D.

FM1129700170020X

Fig. 18 Test C: Charging System Warning Indicator Is On w/Engine Running & Battery Voltage Increases (Part 2 of 2). Mark VIII

TEST CONDITIONS	TEST DETAILS/RESULTS/ACTIONS
C1 CHECK CONNECTOR C154	
1 	2 Make sure the connector C154 is correctly mated to the generator and making contact. • Is the connection OK? → **Yes** GO to **C2**. → **No** REPAIR Connector C154 as necessary. TEST the system for normal operation.
C2 CHECK GENERATOR OUTPUT VOLTAGE	
1  2 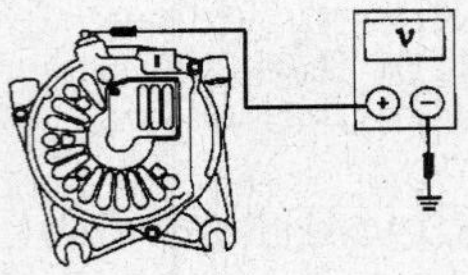	2 With the engine running at 2000 RPM, measure the voltage output at the generator B+ terminal. • Is the voltage output less than 16 volts? → **Yes** GO to **C3**. → **No** GO to Pinpoint Test H.

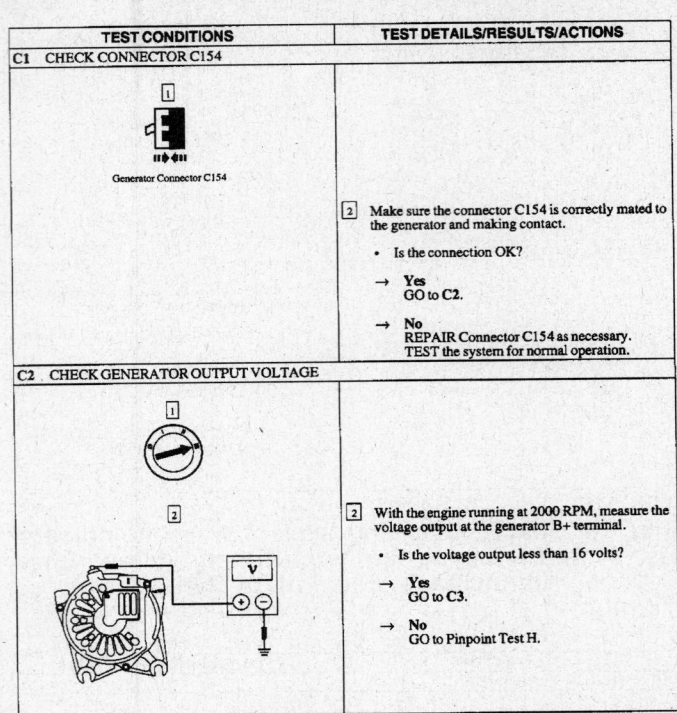

FM1129700170010X

Fig. 18 Test C: Charging System Warning Indicator Is On w/Engine Running & Battery Voltage Increases (Part 1 of 2). Mark VIII

TEST CONDITIONS	TEST DETAILS/RESULTS/ACTIONS
D1 CHECK CHARGING SYSTEM WARNING INDICATOR OPERATION	
1 2  3 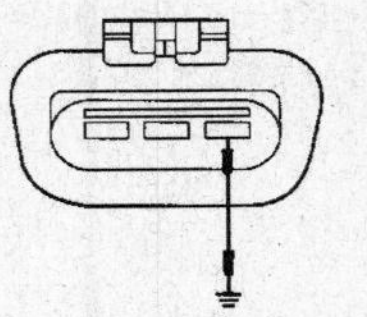	3 Ground the generator connector C154 I circuit with the key ON and the engine OFF. • Is the warning indicator on? → **Yes** REPLACE the generator. TEST the system for normal operation. → **No** REPAIR connector C154 I circuit 904 (LG/R) as necessary. TEST the system for normal operation.

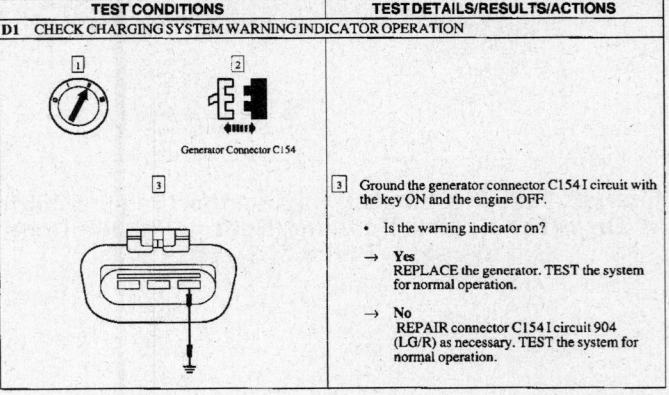

FM1129700171000X

Fig. 19 Test D: Charging System Warning Indicator Is Off w/Ignition Switch In The Run Position & Engine Off (Battery Voltage Increases). Mark VIII

TEST CONDITIONS	TEST DETAILS/RESULTS/ACTIONS
E1 CHECK CIRCUIT 38 (BK/O) VOLTAGE	
1 	
2 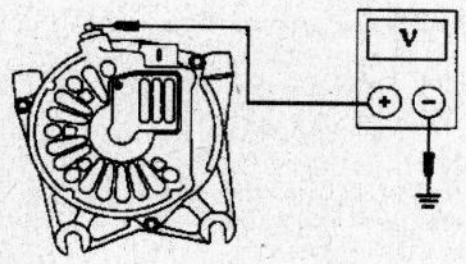	2 Check for voltage at generator B+ connector with the key ON and the engine OFF. • Is the voltage equal to battery positive voltage (B+)? → **Yes** GO to **E2**. → **No** SERVICE Circuit 38 (BK/O) as necessary. TEST the system for normal operation.
E2 CHECK GENERATOR CONNECTORS	
1  Generator Connector C154	
	2 Check the battery and generator connector C154 for corrosion and tightness. • Are the connectors clean and tight? → **Yes** Diagnose system. → **No** SERVICE the connectors as necessary. TEST the system for normal operation.

FM1129700172000X

Fig. 20 Test E: Charging System Warning indicator Operates Correctly But Battery Voltage Does Not Increase. Mark VIII

TEST CONDITIONS	TEST DETAILS/RESULTS/ACTIONS
F4 CHECK OTHER SYSTEMS FOR DRAINS	
	1 Check for drains from electronic modules. • Are electronic modules OK? → **Yes** RECHARGE the battery. TEST the system for normal operation. → **No** REPLACE the defective module as necessary. TEST the system for normal operation.

FM1129700173020X

Fig. 21 Test F: Battery Dead Or Will Not Stay Charged Or Low Battery Or Generator Voltage (Part 2 of 2). Mark VIII

TEST CONDITIONS	TEST DETAILS/RESULTS/ACTIONS
F1 CHECK BATTERY DRAIN	
1 	
	2 Make sure that all interior lights and switches are off and all doors are closed. Perform battery drain test • Is the drain greater than 0.5 amps? → **Yes** GO to Component Tests—Battery—Drain Testing → **No** GO to **F2**.
F2 CHECK GENERATOR OUTPUT	
	1 Check generator output. • Is the generator OK? → **Yes** GO to **F3**. → **No** REPLACE the generator. TEST the system for normal operation.
F3 CHECK BATTERY CONDITION	
	1 Check the battery capacity. • Is the battery OK? → **Yes** GO to **F4**. → **No** REPLACE the battery. TEST the system for normal operation.

FM1129700173010X

Fig. 21 Test F: Battery Dead Or Will Not Stay Charged Or Low Battery Or Generator Voltage (Part 1 of 2). Mark VIII

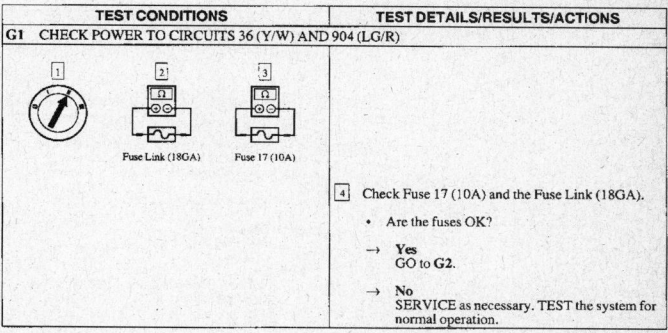

TEST CONDITIONS	TEST DETAILS/RESULTS/ACTIONS
G1 CHECK POWER TO CIRCUITS 36 (Y/W) AND 904 (LG/R)	
1  2  Fuse Link (18GA) 3 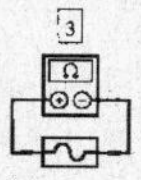 Fuse 17 (10A)	
	4 Check Fuse 17 (10A) and the Fuse Link (18GA). • Are the fuses OK? → **Yes** GO to **G2**. → **No** SERVICE as necessary. TEST the system for normal operation.

FM1129700174010X

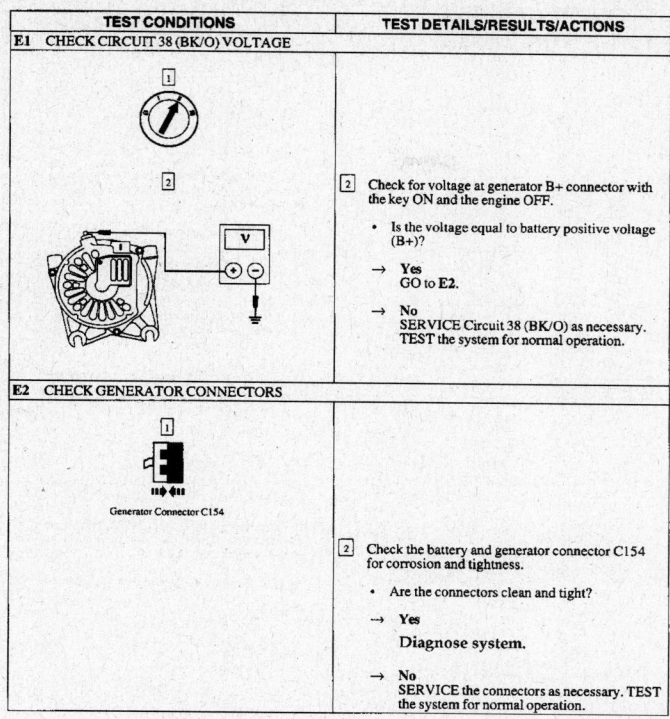

Fig. 22 Test G: Charging System Warning Indicator Flickers (Part 1 of 2). Mark VIII

TEST CONDITIONS	TEST DETAILS/RESULTS/ACTIONS
G2 CHECK FIELD CIRCUIT	
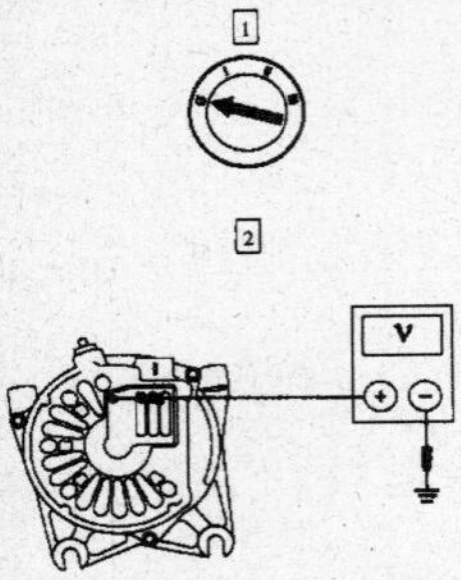	2 Using an insulated probe measure voltage at test point F at rear of generator. • Is the voltage equal to battery voltage? → **Yes** GO to **G3**. → **No** REPLACE generator. TEST the system for normal operation.
G3 CHECK THE WARNING SYSTEM INDICATOR OPERATION	
	2 With the engine running, increase engine speed. Check the indicator operation and for battery voltage increase. • Does the voltage increase above 15 volts or the indicator flicker? → **Yes** SERVICE Circuit 36 (Y/W) or Circuit 904 (LG/R) as necessary. TEST the system for normal operation. → **No** REPLACE the generator. TEST the system for normal operation.

FM1129700174020X

Fig. 22 Test G: Charging System Warning Indicator Flickers (Part 2 of 2). Mark VIII

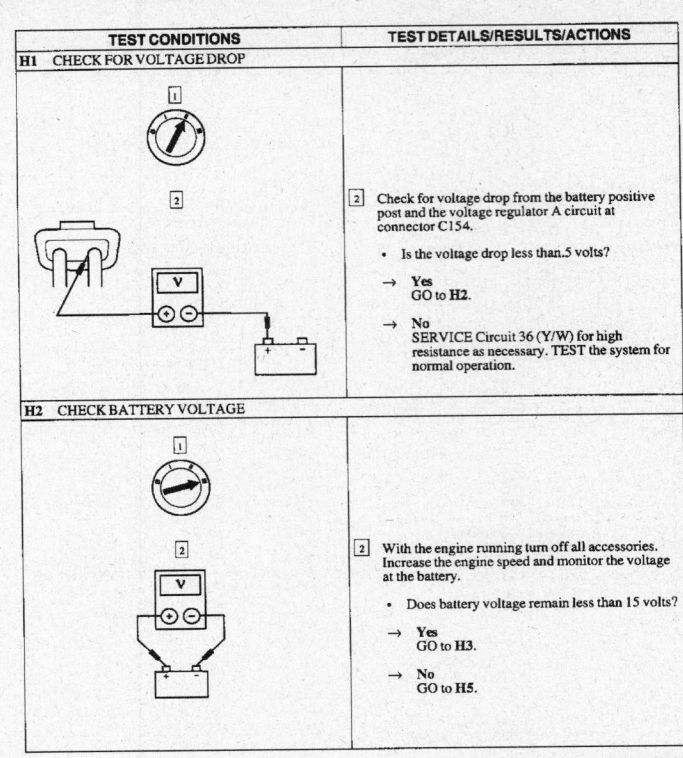

TEST CONDITIONS	TEST DETAILS/RESULTS/ACTIONS
H3 CHECK GENERATOR FOR LOW VOLTAGE	
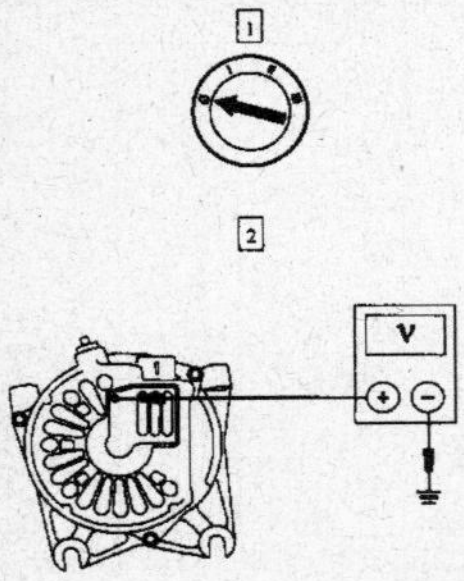	2 With the ignition switch OFF, use an insulated probe to measure the voltage at the voltage regulator F terminal. • Does the voltage equal battery voltage? → **Yes** GO to **H4**. → **No** REPLACE the generator. TEST the system for normal operation.
H4 CHECK THE WARNING SYSTEM INDICATOR OPERATION	
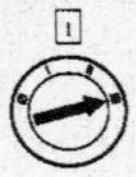	2 With the engine running, increase engine speed and check the indicator operation and for battery voltage increase. • Does the voltage increase above 15 volts or the indicator flicker? → **Yes** SERVICE Circuit 36 (Y/W) or Circuit 904 (LG/R) as necessary. TEST the system for normal operation. → **No** REPLACE the generator. TEST the system for normal operation.

FM1129700175020X

Fig. 23 Test H: System Overcharges (Battery Voltage Greater Than 15.5 Volts, Part 2 of 3). Mark VIII

TEST CONDITIONS	TEST DETAILS/RESULTS/ACTIONS
H1 CHECK FOR VOLTAGE DROP	
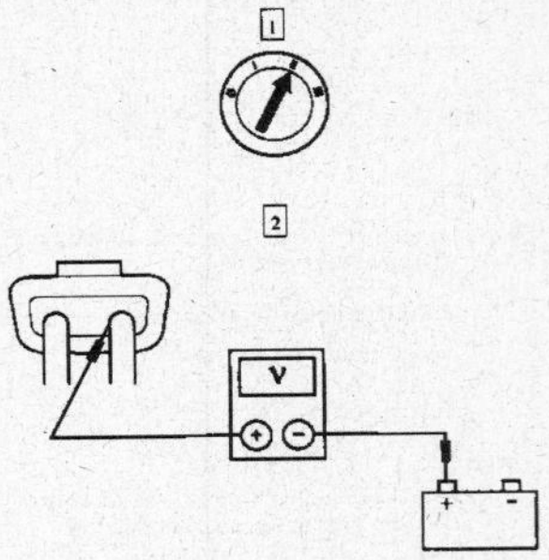	2 Check for voltage drop from the battery positive post and the voltage regulator A circuit at connector C154. • Is the voltage drop less than .5 volts? → **Yes** GO to **H2**. → **No** SERVICE Circuit 36 (Y/W) for high resistance as necessary. TEST the system for normal operation.
H2 CHECK BATTERY VOLTAGE	
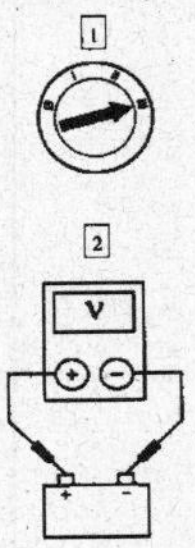	2 With the engine running turn off all accessories. Increase the engine speed and monitor the voltage at the battery. • Does battery voltage remain less than 15 volts? → **Yes** GO to **H3**. → **No** GO to **H5**.

FM1129700175010X

Fig. 23 Test H: System Overcharges (Battery Voltage Greater Than 15.5 Volts, Part 1 of 3). Mark VIII

TEST CONDITIONS	TEST DETAILS/RESULTS/ACTIONS
H5 CHECK VOLTAGE REGULATOR OPERATION	
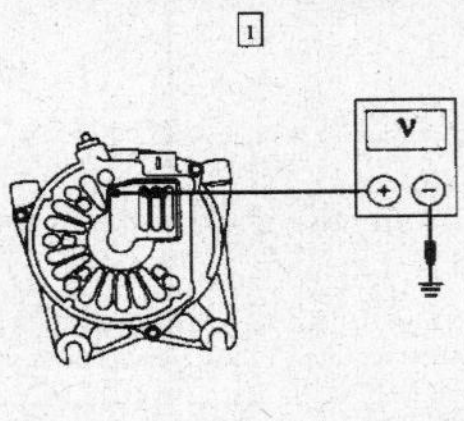	1 With the engine running use an insulated probe to monitor the voltage at the F pin while increasing the engine speed. • Does the voltage at pin F increase with higher engine speed? → **Yes** REPLACE the voltage regulator. TEST the system for normal operation. → **No** REPLACE the generator. TEST the system for normal operation.

FM1129700175030X

Fig. 23 Test H: System Overcharges (Battery Voltage Greater Than 15.5 Volts, Part 3 of 3). Mark VIII

TEST CONDITIONS	TEST DETAILS/RESULTS/ACTIONS
J1 CHECK FOR ACID LEAKAGE DAMAGE	
	1 Check for acid damage to vehicle harnesses and to the body. • Is there acid damage? → **Yes** SERVICE damaged areas as necessary. → **No** GO to **J2**.

FM1129700176010X

Fig. 24 Test J: Battery Leakage Or Damage (Part 1 of 3). Mark VIII

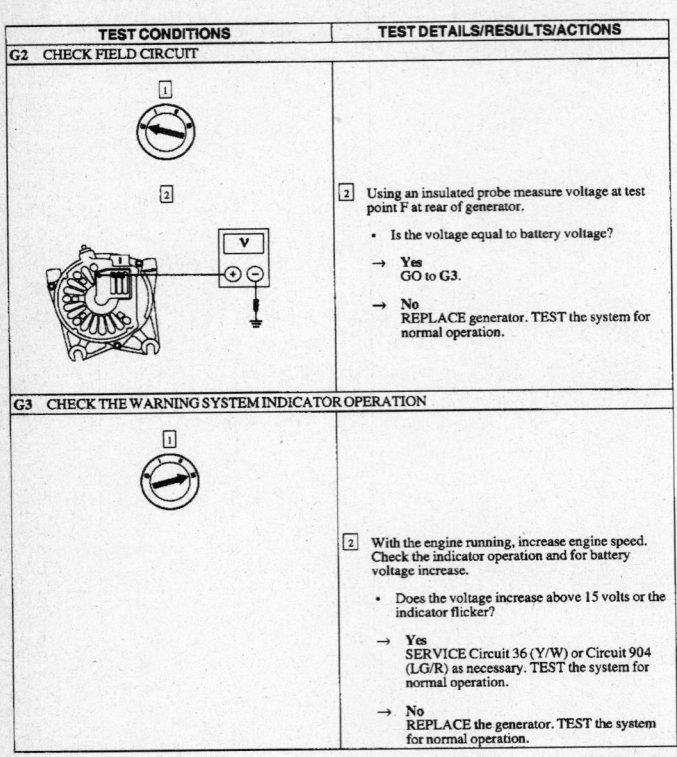

TEST CONDITIONS	TEST DETAILS/RESULTS/ACTIONS
J2 CHECK CHARGING SYSTEM FOR OVERCHARGING	
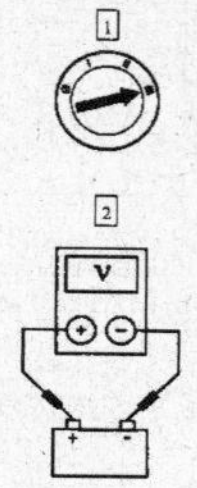	2 With the engine running turn off all accessories. Increase the engine speed and monitor the voltage at the battery. • Does battery voltage increase more than 15 volts? → **Yes** GO to Pinpoint Test H. → **No** GO to **J3**.
J3 CHECK BATTERY MOUNTING	
	1 Make sure the battery is properly mounted and level in the battery tray. • Is the battery properly mounted? → **Yes** GO to **J4**. → **No** SERVICE as necessary. TEST the system for normal operation.
J4 CHECK FOR BATTERY CONTACT	
	1 Make sure that there are no fasteners or other parts contacting the battery case causing excess pressure. • Is there anything contacting the battery case? → **Yes** SERVICE as necessary. TEST the system for normal operation. → **No** GO to **J5**.

FM1129700176020X

Fig. 24 Test J: Battery Leakage Or Damage (Part 2 of 3). Mark VIII

TEST CONDITIONS	TEST DETAILS/RESULTS/ACTIONS
K1 CHECK BATTERY VOLTAGE	
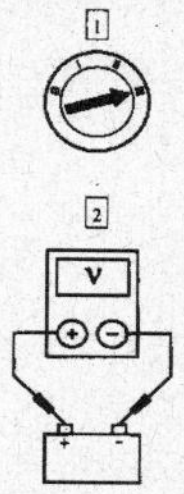	2 With the engine running turn off all accessories. Increase the engine speed and monitor the voltage at the battery. • Is the battery voltage more than 15 volts? → **Yes** GO to Pinpoint Test H. → **No** GO to **K2**.

FM1129700177010X

Fig. 25 Test K: Voltage Gauge Reads High Or Low (Part 1 of 2). Mark VIII

TEST CONDITIONS	TEST DETAILS/RESULTS/ACTIONS
M1 CHECK FOR RADIO INTERFERENCE	
	2 Tune the radio to a station where the interference is present. • Is the interference present with the generator connector C154 disconnected? → **Yes** find the cause of the radio interference. TEST the system for normal operation. → **No** REPLACE the generator. TEST the system for normal operation.

FM1129700179000X

Fig. 27 Test M: Radio Interference. Mark VIII

TEST CONDITIONS	TEST DETAILS/RESULTS/ACTIONS
J5 CHECK BATTERY CASE FOR DAMAGE	
	1 Check the battery case for defects such as cracks, or poor seals. • Is the battery OK? → **Yes** System is OK. TEST the system for normal operation. → **No** REPLACE the battery. TEST the system for normal operation.

FM1129700176030X

Fig. 24 Test J: Battery Leakage Or Damage (Part 3 of 3). Mark VIII

TEST CONDITIONS	TEST DETAILS/RESULTS/ACTIONS
K2 CHECK VOLTAGE GAUGE OPERATION	
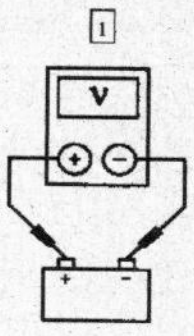	1 With the engine running monitor the voltage gauge reading and the battery voltage. • Are the voltage readings consistent? → **Yes** System is operating normally. → **No** Diagnose instrument cluster.

FM1129700177020X

Fig. 25 Test K: Voltage Gauge Reads High Or Low (Part 2 of 2). Mark VIII

TEST CONDITIONS	TEST DETAILS/RESULTS/ACTIONS
L1 CHECK FOR ACCESSORY DRIVE NOISE	
	1 Check the drive belt to make sure it is properly installed and aligned. • Is the drive belt OK? → **Yes** GO to **L2**. → **No** SERVICE the accessory drive system as required. TEST the system for normal operation.
L2 CHECK THE GENERATOR MOUNTING	
	1 Check the generator and the generator mounting brackets for loose bolts or misalignment. • Is the generator mounted correctly? → **Yes** REPLACE the generator. TEST the system for normal operation. → **No** INSTALL the generator to specifications. TEST the system for normal operation.

FM1129700178000X

Fig. 26 Test L: Generator Is Noisy. Mark VIII

Condition	Possible Source	Action
• System Does Not Charge	• Loose or worn drive belt. • Corroded battery connections. • Battery. • Generator.	• GO to Pinpoint Test A1.
• System Overcharges (Battery Boils Over)	• Generator.	• GO to Pinpoint Test B1.
• Voltage Gauge Reads High	• Generator. • Battery voltage gauge.	• GO to Pinpoint Test C1.
• Voltage Gauge Reads Low	• Loose or worn drive belt. • Loose or corroded battery cables. • Battery. • Generator. • Battery voltage gauge.	• GO to Pinpoint Test D1.
• Generator Noisy	• Loose or worn drive belt. • Bent generator pulley. • Generator.	• GO to Pinpoint Test E1.
• Radio Interference	• Circuit. • FM limitation. • Antenna. • Noise suppression equipment. • Ignition system. • Generator.	• REFER to "Radio Interference" in FORD Motorcraft Alternator section.

FM1129400098000A

Fig. 28 Diagnostic symptom chart (Part 1 of 2). Probe

Condition	Possible Source	Action
• Battery Does Not Hold a Charge	• Loose or worn drive belt. • Damaged battery cables. • Battery. • Generator.	• GO to Pinpoint Test F1.

FM1129400098020X

Fig. 28 Diagnostic symptom chart (Part 2 of 2). Probe

Test Step		Result	Action to Take
B1	CHECK GENERATOR		
	• Perform the Generator component tests • Is the generator OK?	Yes	▶ Charging system OK. RETURN to the Symptom Chart.
		No	▶ REPAIR or REPLACE the generator.

FM1129400100000A

Fig. 30 Test B: System Overcharges. Probe

Test Step		Result	Action to Take
D1	CHECK BATTERY CONNECTIONS		
	• Inspect the battery cables for loose or corroded connections. • **Are the battery cables clean and tight?**	Yes	▶ GO to **D2**.
		No	▶ CLEAN or TIGHTEN the battery cables.
D2	CHECK DRIVE BELT TENSION		
	• Perform the drive belt adjustment • **Is the drive belt adjusted properly?**	Yes	▶ GO to **D3**.
		No	▶ ADJUST or REPLACE the drive belt.
D3	CHECK BATTERY		
	• Perform the Battery component tests • **Is the battery OK?**	Yes	▶ GO to **D4**.
		No	▶ REPLACE the battery.

FM1129400102010A

Fig. 32 Test D: Voltage Gauge Reads Low (Part 1 of 2). Probe

Test Step		Result	Action to Take
E1	CHECK DRIVE BELT TENSION		
	• Perform the drive belt adjustment procedure • **Is the drive belt adjusted properly?**	Yes	▶ GO to **E2**.
		No	▶ ADJUST or REPLACE the drive belt.
E2	CHECK GENERATOR PULLEY		
	• Remove the generator drive belt. • Inspect the generator pulley for damage. • **Is the generator pulley OK?**	Yes	▶ PERFORM the Alternator Bench Test
		No	▶ REPLACE the generator pulley.

FM1129400103000A

Fig. 33 Test E: Alternator Noisy. Probe

Year	Amp Rating	Min. Amps @ 2000
ASPIRE		
1997	60	54
MARK VIII		
1997–98	130	87
PROBE		
1997	80①	72
	90②	81

① — 2.0L engine.
② — 2.5L engine.

Fig. 35 Total alternator output specifications

Test Step		Result	Action to Take
A1	CHECK BATTERY CONNECTIONS		
	• Inspect the battery cables for loose or corroded connections. • **Are the battery cables clean and tight?**	Yes	▶ GO to **A2**.
		No	▶ CLEAN or TIGHTEN the battery cables.
A2	CHECK DRIVE BELT TENSION		
	• Perform the drive belt adjustment procedure • **Is the drive belt adjusted properly?**	Yes	▶ GO to **A3**.
		No	▶ ADJUST or REPLACE the drive belt.
A3	CHECK BATTERY		
	• Perform the Battery component tests in this section. • **Is the battery OK?**	Yes	▶ PERFORM the Alternator component tests
		No	▶ REPLACE the battery.

FM1129400099000A

Fig. 29 Test A: System Does Not Charge. Probe

Test Step		Result	Action to Take
C1	CHECK GENERATOR		
	• Perform the Generator component tests • **Is the generator OK?**	Yes	▶ diagnose the battery voltage gauge.
		No	▶ REPAIR or REPLACE the generator.

FM1129400101000A

Fig. 31 Test C: Voltage Gauge Reads High. Probe

Test Step		Result	Action to Take
D4	CHECK GENERATOR		
	• Perform the Generator component tests • **Is the generator OK?**	Yes	▶ diagnose the battery voltage gauge.
		No	▶ REPAIR or REPLACE the generator.

FM1129400102020A

Fig. 32 Test D: Voltage Gauge Reads Low (Part 2 of 2). Probe

Test Step		Result	Action to Take
F1	CHECK BATTERY CONNECTIONS		
	• Inspect the battery cables for loose or corroded connections. • **Are the battery cables clean and tight?**	Yes	▶ GO to **F2**.
		No	▶ CLEAN or TIGHTEN the battery cables.
F2	CHECK DRIVE BELT TENSION		
	• Perform the drive belt adjustment procedure • **Is the drive belt adjusted properly?**	Yes	▶ PERFORM the Battery component tests
		No	▶ ADJUST or REPLACE the drive belt.

FM1129600131000X

Fig. 34 Test F: Battery Does Not Hold Charge. Probe

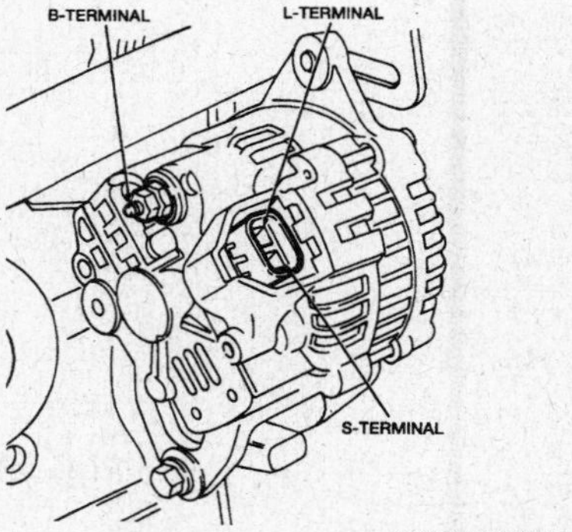

FM1129400126000X

Fig. 36 Mando alternator terminals. Aspire

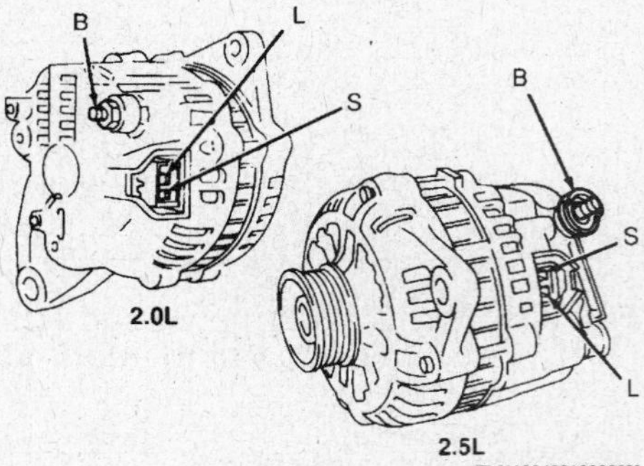

FM1129400128000X

Fig. 37 Melmac alternator terminals. Probe

ALTERNATOR SPECIFICATIONS

Model	Year	Model	Amp Rating
Aspire	1997	—	60
Mark VIII	1997–98	F6LU-CA	130
Probe	1997	—	80①
	1997	—	90②

① — 2.0L engine.
② — 2.5L engine.

STEERING COLUMNS

NOTE: On Models Equipped With Air Bags, Refer To "Air Bag System Precautions" Located In The Front Of This Manual For System Disarming & Arming Procedures.

NOTE: Refer To "Computer Relearn Procedure " Located In The Front Of This Manual For Computer Relearn Procedures.

NOTE: Models Equipped With "Automatic Ride Control System" Utilize A Steering Sensor Located On The Steering Column Assembly. For Replacement Of Sensor, Refer To " Automatic Ride Control System" In The "Active Suspension " Section.

INDEX

PRECAUTIONS

AIR BAG SYSTEMS

Refer to "Air Bag System Precautions" in the front of this manual for system disarming and arming procedures.

BATTERY GROUND CABLE

Prior to service, disconnect battery ground cable and isolate as required. Allow one minute for back-up power supply to be depleted.

DESCRIPTION

The steering column used on vehicles equipped with air bags is of a modular construction and features easy to service electrical switches. The washer/wiper switch and the combination turn signal/hazard/horn/flash to pass/dimmer switch are attached with self-tapping screws.

These vehicles are equipped with either a brush type slip ring or a clockspring type slip ring. Removal and installation procedures for the two types are the same except where noted.

Fasteners used on steering column components must be replaced after removal. The fasteners are coated with an epoxy adhesive, and are not reusable.

Whenever the steering column is removed from the vehicle, or is separated from the steering gear, the steering column must be in locked position to prevent the steering wheel from being rotated accidentally and damaging the air bag slip ring.

The Lincoln LS model is equipped with the power tilt/telescopic steering column which is of modular construction that features easy to service electrical switches.

The power tilt/telescopic steering columns are equipped with an electric tilt and telescopic mechanism, that allows the steering wheel angle and length to be adjusted to suit the driver.

Vehicles equipped with the memory package, steering wheel position is stored in memory the same way as driver seat position and retrieved as a personality feature. The steering column is controlled by the instrument cluster module.

STEERING COLUMN

REPLACE

ASPIRE

1. Remove steering wheel, then the turn signal and windshield wiper switch and ignition switch as described in "Electrical" section.
2. Remove lower steering column shaft lower bolt.
3. Remove two lower, then the two upper steering column mounting bracket bolts.
4. Once free, lower upper end of steering column as necessary to access steering column gear input shaft coupling at lower end, **Fig. 1.**
5. Mark juncture of steering column gear input shaft coupling and lower steering column shaft to ensure proper alignment during assembly.
6. Remove steering column.
7. Reverse procedure to install, noting the following:
   a. Ensure steering column gear input shaft coupling is not upside down.
   b. Align index marks between lower steering column shaft and steering column gear input shaft coupling.

CONTINENTAL

1. Ensure wheels are in straight ahead position.
2. Remove steering wheel as described in "Electrical " section of "Lincoln" chapter.
3. Remove instrument panel lower trim cover, then the air bag sliding contact as described under "Passive Restraint Systems"chapter.
4. Remove tilt wheel handle and shank by unscrewing it from column and removing four screws.
5. Rotate ignition switch lock cylinder to run position, then press lock cylinder retaining pin through access hole and remove lock cylinder.
6. Remove four upper and lower steering column shrouds.
7. Remove instrument panel reinforcement brace.
8. Disconnect shift cable and bracket from steering column, then the transmission shift cable loop from shift tube hook.
9. Remove two multi-function switch retaining screws and lay switch aside.
10. Remove ignition switch retaining screw, then disconnect wiring from switch.
11. Remove two front steering column

nuts, then the steering column impact absorber.
12. Remove pinch bolt from steering column lower yoke.
13. While supporting column assembly, remove two rear column assembly retaining nuts, then lower column and disconnect parking brake release vacuum hose extensions at parking brake release switch or remove vacuum release assembly.
14. Disconnect shift cable and bracket from selector lever pivot.
15. Remove shift cable and bracket from lower column mounting.
16. Remove two shift lock actuator retaining screws, then the shift lock actuator.
17. Reverse procedure to install. Tighten to specification.

CONTOUR & MYSTIQUE

Do not remove steering wheel and driver side air bag module as an assembly unless the column is locked or the steering column gear input shaft coupling is secured to keep it from turning. This will avoid damage to the air bag sliding contact assembly.

1. Park vehicle with wheels in straight ahead position.
2. Remove steering column opening finish panel.
3. Remove upper and lower steering column shrouds.
4. Remove pinch bolt at lower steering column shaft and disengage shaft from steering gear.
5. Disconnect wiring harness connectors from steering column switches.
6. Remove four bolts, then lower the steering column and remove from vehicle.
7. Reverse procedure to install.

CROWN VICTORIA, GRAND MARQUIS & TOWN CAR

Refer to **Figs. 2 and 3,** when performing the following procedure.

1. Ensure front wheels are in straight ahead position.
2. Remove air bag sliding contact.
3. Disconnect multi-function electrical connectors.
4. Remove two screws, then the multi-function switch.
5. Remove instrument panel reinforcement brace.
6. Disconnect ignition switch electrical connector.
7. Disconnect brake shift interlock solenoid connector.
8. Remove passive anti-theft system (PATS) sensor ring.
9. Disconnect, then remove shift cable and bracket from steering column.
10. Remove and discard lower steering column shaft pinch bolt.
11. Disconnect lower steering column shaft from steering column lower yoke.
12. Remove four steering column mounting nuts, then lower steering column to floor.
13. Disconnect parking brake release vacuum hose extension from parking brake release switch.

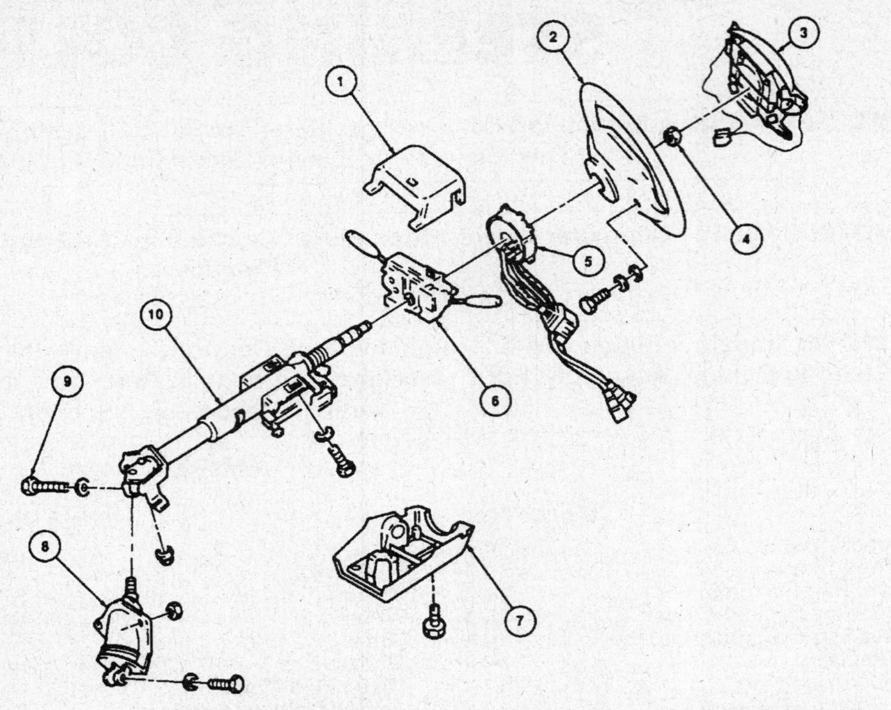

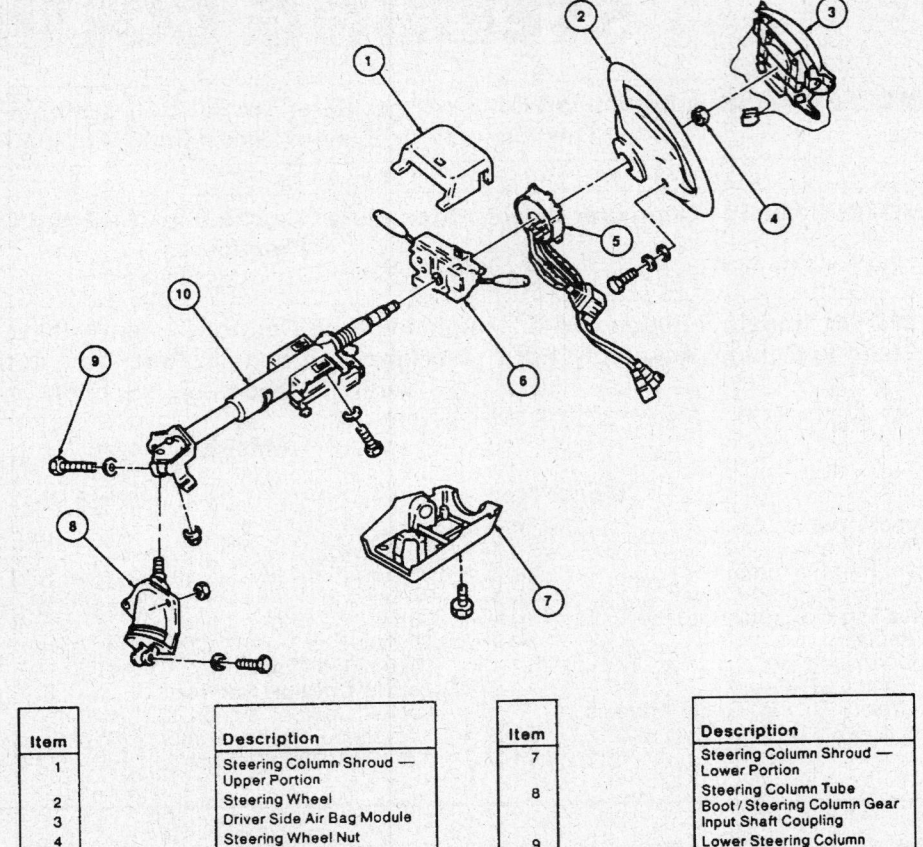

Item	Description	Item	Description
1	Steering Column Shroud — Upper Portion	7	Steering Column Shroud — Lower Portion
2	Steering Wheel	8	Steering Column Tube Boot / Steering Column Gear Input Shaft Coupling
3	Driver Side Air Bag Module	9	Lower Steering Column Shaft Bolt
4	Steering Wheel Nut	10	Steering Column
5	Air Bag Sliding Contact		
6	Turn Signal and Windshield Wiper Switch		

FM6049400065000X

Fig. 1 Exploded view of steering column. Aspire

14. Disconnect and position shift cable and bracket out of way.
15. Remove steering column from vehicle.
16. Reverse procedure to install. Tighten hardware to specification.

ESCORT, TRACER & ZX2

Refer to **Fig. 4,** when performing the following procedure.

1997

1. Remove steering wheel as described in "Electrical" section
2. Remove screws, then the upper and lower steering column shrouds.
3. Remove bolt, then the instrument panel steering column cover.
4. Remove combination switch assembly, then two bolts and lower steering column.
5. Remove nuts, then the slotted column tube boot and inner steering column tube boot.
6. Remove steering column input shaft coupling to steering gear input shaft and control bolt.
7. Remove steering column support bracket nuts.
8. Remove steering column.
9. Reverse procedure to install. Tighten to specification.

1998–2000

1. Remove steering wheel as described in "Electrical" section
2. Remove screws, then the upper and lower steering column shrouds.
3. Loosen nut, then remove hood latch control handle and cable. Position aside.
4. Remove screws, then release instrument panel steering column cover.
5. Disconnect headlamp switch electrical connector, then remove instrument panel steering column cover.
6. Disconnect steering column electrical connectors, then remove retainer plate.
7. Remove bolts, then lower steering column tube.
8. Remove steering column input shaft coupling to steering gear input shaft pinch bolt.
9. Remove steering column support bracket nuts, then the steering column.
10. Reverse procedure to install. Tighten to specification.

LS

Refer to **Fig. 5,** when performing the following procedure.

1. Ensure wheels are in straight ahead position.
2. Remove driver side air bag module

and air bag sliding contact as outlined in "Passive Restraint Systems" section.
3. Remove steering wheel as described in "Electrical " section of "Lincoln" chapter.
4. Remove steering column shaft pinch bolt, then discard bolt and separate intermediate shaft from steering column yoke.
5. Disconnect electrical connectors from electronic steering sensor, then the steering column release motor.
6. **On models equipped with automatic transmission,** while supporting steering column remove and discard lock nuts.
7. **On models equipped with manual transmission,** while supporting steering column remove and discard lock nuts. Lower steering column, then disconnect lock actuator electrical connector.
8. **On all models,** remove steering column from vehicle.
9. Reverse procedure to install. Tighten nuts and bolts to specifications.

MARK VIII

1. Remove driver side air bag module and air bag sliding contact as outlined in "Passive Restraint Systems" section.
2. Remove steering wheel as described in "Electrical " section of "Lincoln" chapter.
3. Remove two lower instrument panel insulator retaining screws, then the courtesy light and place lower instrument panel insulator out of way.
4. Remove two steering column cover retaining screws, then position steering column cover aside.
5. Remove four instrument panel reinforcement to instrument panel retaining bolts and position reinforcement aside.
6. Remove A/C duct, then disconnect three electrical connectors at junction box.
7. Disconnect electrical connector at bottom of steering column.
8. Remove pinch bolt from steering column lower yoke.
9. Slide intermediate shaft into lower steering shaft.
10. While supporting steering column, remove four steering column retaining nuts.
11. Remove steering column from vehicle.
12. Reverse procedures to install. Tighten to specification.

MUSTANG

1. Remove steering wheel as described in "Electrical " section of "Mustang" chapter.
2. Remove steering column lower yoke to lower steering column shaft retaining bolt.
3. Remove ignition switch lock cylinder as described in " Electrical" section of "Mustang" chapter.
4. Remove steering column opening cover and reinforcement, then the instrument panel cross brace.

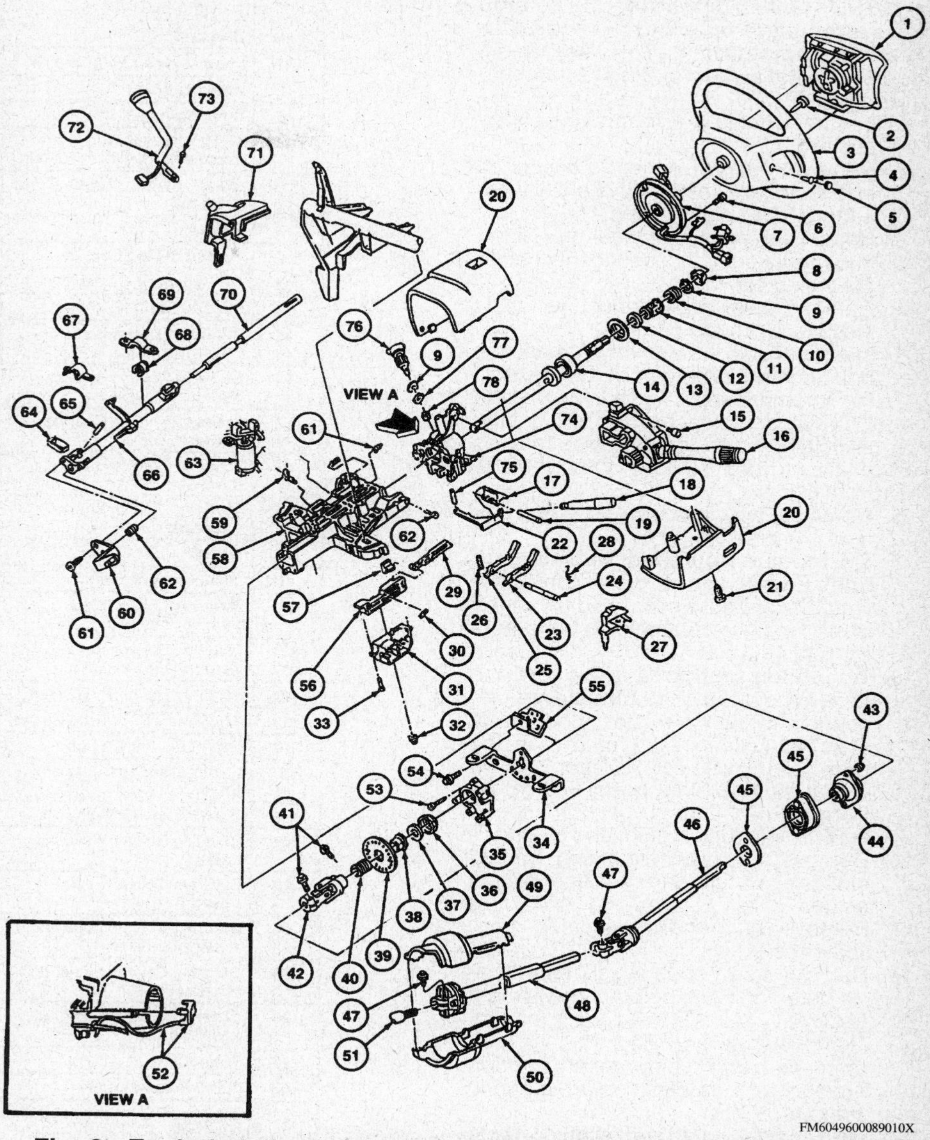

Fig. 2 Exploded view of steering column (Part 1 of 2). 1997 Crown Victoria, Grand Marquis & Town Car

5. Remove upper and lower steering column shrouds.
6. Disconnect electrical connectors from ignition switch and key warning buzzer.
7. Remove multi-function switch retaining screws and position aside.
8. Remove two nuts retaining steering shaft tube boot to dash panel.
9. Remove four steering column to instrument panel retaining nuts, then lower column to clear four mounting bolts.
10. **On models equipped with automatic transmission,** remove ignition/shifter interlock cable.
11. **On all models,** remove steering column.
12. Reverse procedures to install. Tighten to specification.

PROBE

1. Ensure wheels are in straight ahead position.
2. Remove steering wheel and multi-function switch as described in "Electrical" section of "Ford Probe " chapter.
3. Remove hood latch control handle and cable from lower side panel.
4. Disconnect right hand foot interior lamp electrical connector, then remove instrument panel lower side panel retaining screw.
5. Remove instrument panel lower side panel, then disconnect all necessary electrical connectors.
6. Disconnect ignition/shifter interlock cable.
7. Remove lower steering column shaft bolt, then the two upper column bracket bolts.
8. Reverse procedures to install. Tighten to specification.

SABLE & TAURUS

Do not remove steering wheel or air bag module as an assembly unless the

column is locked or the steering column gear input shaft coupling is secured to keep it from turning. This will avoid damage to the air bag sliding contact assembly.

1. Ensure wheels are in straight ahead position.
2. Remove steering wheel as described in "Electrical " section of "Ford Taurus & Mercury Sable" chapter.
3. Remove bolt retaining steering column intermediate shaft coupling to steering column lower yoke.
4. Remove lower instrument panel steering column cover.
5. Insert suitable scratch awl into access hole located in bottom of lower steering column shroud. Push in on ignition lock cylinder release pin, rotate ignition switch lock cylinder clockwise to RUN position, then remove lock cylinder from column.
6. Remove upper and lower steering column shrouds.
7. **On models equipped with column shift,** unsnap and slide shift control selector lever boot toward end of control lever. Remove control lever by removing retaining pin.
8. **On models equipped with overdrive lock out switch on column lever,** disconnect wiring connector at bottom of steering column and remove wiring from column with control lever.
9. **On all models,** disconnect wiring connectors for ignition switch, horn, speed control, interlock switch, and air bag.
10. Remove screws retaining multi-function switch and position switch aside.
11. Remove shift indicator cable from shifter tube.
12. Remove screw securing shifter indicator retainer from column adjustment cable.
13. Remove nuts securing steering column to instrument panel support bracket and carefully lower steering column.
14. **On models equipped with console shift,** remove interlock cable and actuator, **Fig. 6.**
15. **On all models,** remove steering column from vehicle.
16. Reverse procedure to install. Adjust shift indicator cable as necessary.

Item	Description
1	Driver Side Air Bag Module
2	Steering Wheel Bolt
3	Steering Wheel
4	Air Bag Module Retaining Screws (2 Req'd)
5	Steering Wheel Spoke Cover (2 Req'd)
6	Screw
7	Air Bag Sliding Contact
8	Turn Indicator Cancel Cam
9	Bearing Retainer
10	Steering Column Upper Bearing Spring
11	Steering Column Bearing Sleeve (Upper)
12	Steering Column Bearing (Upper)(Small)
13	Steering Column Bearing (Large)
14	Steering Column Shaft Assembly
15	Screw
16	Multi-Function Switch
15	Steering Column Lock Cylinder Housing
16	Steering Column Lock Actuator Lever Pin
17	Steering Column Lock Cam
18	Tilt Wheel Handle and Shank
19	Pin—Lock Cam Pivot
20	Lower Steering Column Cover
21	Shroud Retaining Screws
22	Steering Column Release Lever
23	Steering Column Lock RH Lever
24	Steering Column Lock Actuator Lever Pin
25	Steering Column Lock Left Hand Lever
26	Steering Column Locking Lever Spring
27	Wiring Shield
28	Tilt Release Spring
29	Steering Column Lock Lever Actuator
30	Steering Column Lock Spring (Shaft)
31	Ignition Switch
32	Lower Column Mounting Nuts
33	Screw
34	Steering Column Mounting Bracket
35	Steering Column Lower Bearing Retainer
36	Steering Column Bearing Sleeve
37	Steering Column Bearing (Lower)
38	Steering Column Bearing Tolerance Ring (Lower)
39	Suspension Height Sensor Control Ring
40	Steering Column Upper Bearing Spring
41	Bolt—Flange Yoke
42	Steering Column Lower Yoke
43	Nut (2 Req'd)
44	Steering Column Tube Boot
45	Steering Column Insulator Collar
46	Lower Steering Column Shaft (Upper)
47	Bolt
48	Lower Steering Column Shaft (Lower)
49	Steering Shaft U-Joint Shield (Upper)
50	Steering Shaft U-Joint Shield (Lower)
51	Input Shaft (Part of 3504)
52	Ignition Key Warning Switch Terminal and Wire
53	Screw (4 Req'd)
54	Screw
55	Wire Connector Bracket
56	Steering Column Lock Lever Actuator (Lower)
57	Steering Column Lock Pawl
58	Steering Actuator Housing
59	Steering Column Lock Actuator Cover
60	Transmission Selector Lever Arm and Support
61	Screw
62	Gearshift Selector Tube Spring
63	Shift Lock Actuator
64	Gearshift Lever
65	Gearshift Lever Pin
66	Transmission Column Shift Selector Tube
67	Insert Plate
68	Bushing
69	Cap
70	Plunger
71	Seal
72	Gearshift Lever
73	Gearshift Lever Pin

FM6049600089020X

Fig. 2 Exploded view of steering column (Part 2 of 2). 1997 Crown Victoria, Grand Marquis & Town Car

THUNDERBIRD & 1997 COUGAR

All steering column tube components are assembled with fasteners. They are designed with a thread locking system to prevent loosening due to vibrations associated with normal vehicle operation.

1. Ensure vehicle front wheels are in straight ahead position.
2. Remove steering wheel as described in "Electrical " section.
3. Remove instrument panel righthand and lefthand lower moldings.
4. Remove instrument panel lower trim cover, then the air bag sliding contact.
5. Remove tilt steering column lock lever by unscrewing it from steering column tube.
6. Rotate ignition switch to RUN position, then press ignition switch retaining pin through access hole with ⅛ inch drift and remove switch.
7. Remove four lower steering column shroud screws, then the upper and lower steering column shrouds.
8. Remove instrument panel reinforcement.
9. Remove multi-function switch screws, then position aside.
10. Remove pinch bolt from steering column lower yoke, then while supporting

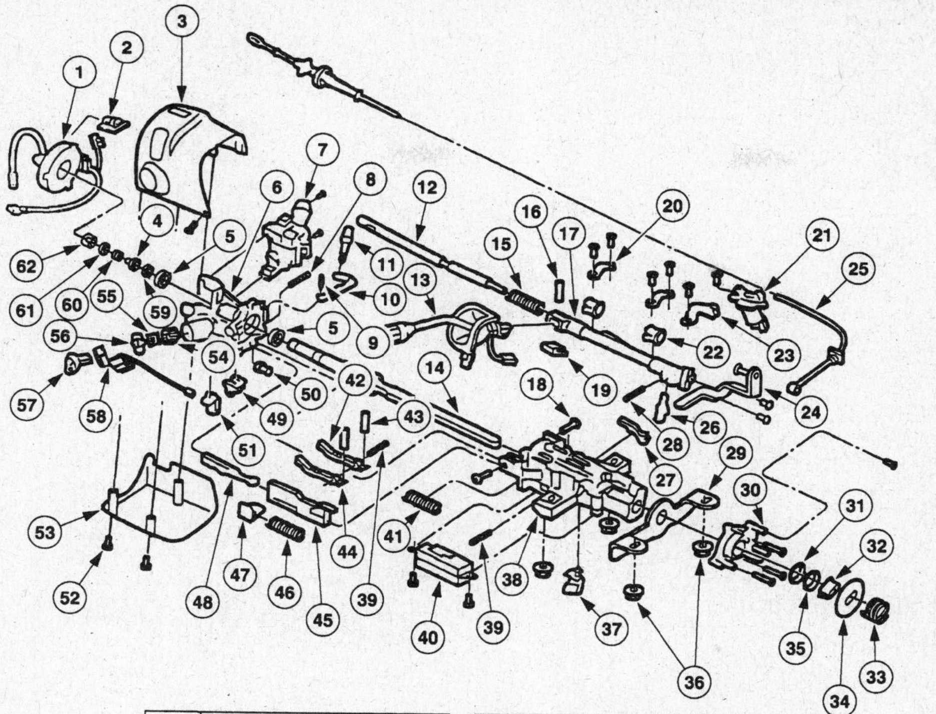

Item	Description
1	Air Bag Sliding Contact
2	Cellular Phone Voice Activated-Microphone
3	Steering Column Shroud
4	Steering Column Bearing Sleeve

Item	Description
5	Steering Column Bearing
6	Steering Column Lock Cylinder Housing
7	Multi-Function Switch
8	Pin

FM6049900124010X

Fig. 3 Exploded view of steering column (Part 1 of 3). 1998-2000 Crown Victoria, Grand Marquis & Town Car

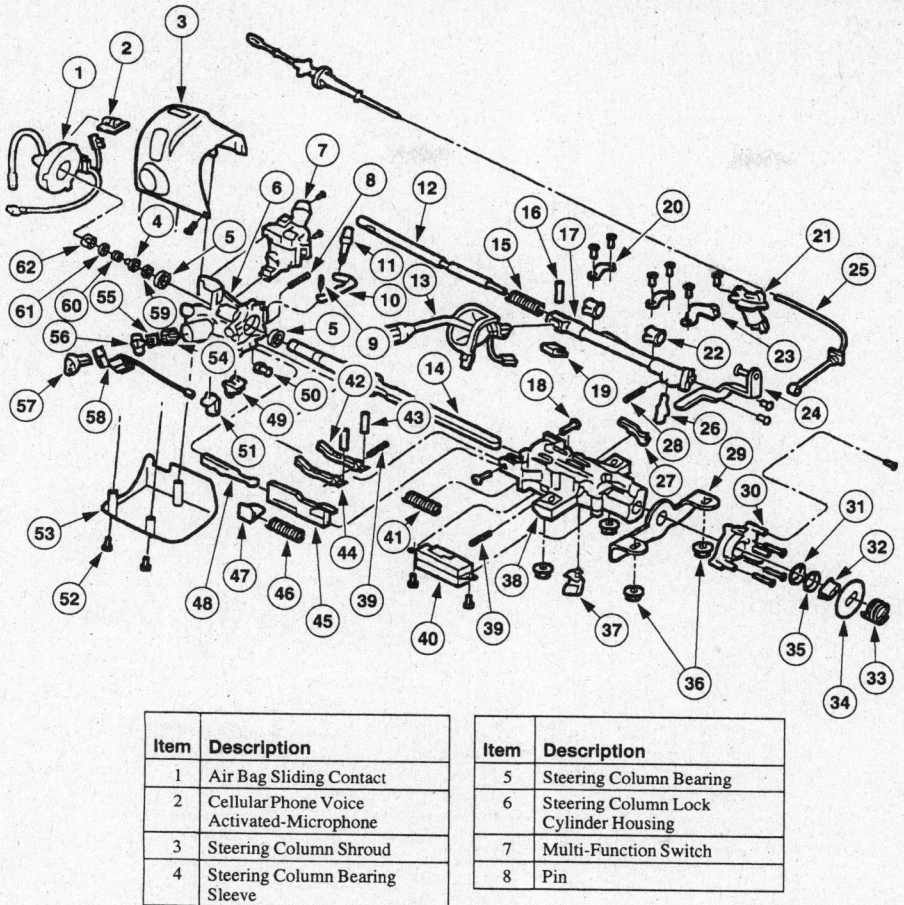

Item	Description
9	Steering Column Release Lever Pin
10	Steering Column Release Lever
11	Tilt Wheel Handle and Shank
12	Column Shift Selector Lever Plunger
13	Gearshift Lever
14	Steering Column Shaft
15	Transmission Control Selector Lever Plunger Spring
16	Gearshift Lever Pin
17	Transmission Column Shift Selector Tube
18	Tilt Column Pivot Screw
19	Transmission Control Selector Lever Spring Clip
20	Gearshift Tube Bushing Clamp
21	Brake Shift Interlock Solenoid
22	Gearshift Lever Socket Bushing
23	Transmission Shift Selector Position Insert
24	Transmission Selector Lever Arm and Support
25	Shift Cable and Bracket
26	Gearshift Lever
27	Steering Column Lock Pawl
28	Gearshift Lever Pin
29	Steering Column Instrument Panel Bracket
30	Steering Column Lower Bearing Retainer
31	Steering Column Bearing Sleeve
32	Steering Column Bearing Tolerance Ring
33	Steering Column Bearing Spring
34	Suspension Height Sensor Control Ring

Item	Description
35	Steering Column Bearing
36	Steering Column Retaining Nuts
37	Wiring Harness Retainer
38	Steering Actuator Housing
39	Steering Column Lock Lever Pin
40	Ignition Switch
41	Steering Column Position Spring
42	Steering Column Lock Lever
43	Steering Column Position Lock Spring
44	Steering Column Locking Lever
45	Steering Column Lock Lever Actuator
46	Steering Column Lock Spring
47	Steering Column Lock Pawl
48	Steering Column Lock Actuator
49	Steering Column Lock Cam
50	Steering Column Tilt Flange Bumper
51	Wiring Harness Retainer
52	Shroud Screws
53	Steering Column Shroud
54	Steering Column Lock Gear
55	Steering Column Lock Housing Bearing
56	Bearing Retainer
57	Ignition Switch Lock Cylinder
58	Passive Anti-Theft System (PATS) Sensor Ring
59	Steering Column Bearing Tolerance Ring
60	Steering Column Upper Bearing Spring
61	Bearing Retainer
62	Turn Indicator Cancel Cam

FM6049900124020X

Fig. 3 Exploded view of steering column (Part 2 of 3). 1998-2000 Crown Victoria, Grand Marquis & Town Car

steering column tube assembly, remove nuts.

11. Remove ignition/shifter interlock cable retaining screws and cable end assembly, then the steering column tube from vehicle.
12. Reverse procedure to install. Tighten to specification.

1999-2000 COUGAR

1. Remove driver side instrument panel lower cover.
2. Center and lock steering wheel.
3. Remove steering column upper and lower shrouds.
4. Disconnect flexible coupling from steering shaft.
5. Disconnect electrical connectors from steering column.
6. Cut cable tie, then disconnect air bag control module connector.
7. Unclip wiring harnesses, unbolt steering column, then slide outwards to disengage retaining tab.
8. Reverse procedure to install. Tighten to specification.

STEERING COLUMN SERVICE

ASPIRE, CONTOUR, ESCORT, MYSTIQUE, PROBE, TRACER, ZX2 & 1999-2000 COUGAR

The steering column is serviced as a unit. If service other than the air bag clockspring, combination switch or ignition switch assembly is required, steering column must be replaced.

1996

CONTINENTAL

1. Remove steering wheel as described in "Electrical " section of the "Lincoln" chapter.
2. Remove air bag sliding contact as described in " Passive Restraint Systems" section.
3. Remove turn indicator cancel cam by pushing up with flat bladed screwdriver or equivalent. **Note direction of flush surface.**
4. Remove ignition switch, then the snap ring retaining bearing retainer and steering column upper bearing spring, **Fig. 7.**
5. Remove bearing retainer and steering column upper bearing spring.
6. Remove steering column bearing tolerance ring.
7. **On models equipped with column shift,** remove seven transmission column shift selector tube to steering column retaining bolts.
8. **On all models,** remove shift lock actuator.
9. Using a suitable drift and hammer, tap steering column lock actuator lever pin loose, then remove with pliers.
10. Remove plastic bearing retainer from lock cylinder bore, then the steering column lock housing bearing.
11. Remove ignition lock gear.
12. Remove steering column lower yoke, steering column upper bearing spring, suspension height sensor control ring and steering column bearing tolerance ring from lower end of steering column.
13. Remove two pivot bolts. **Use caution as steering column position spring will release when bolts are removed.**

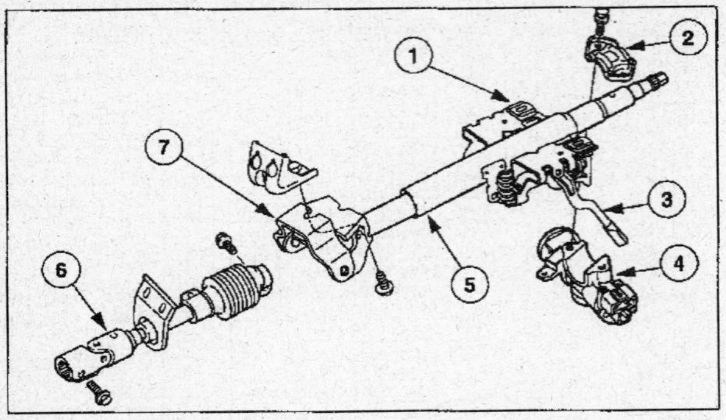

Item	Description
1	Steering Column Upper Mounting Bracket
2	Ignition Switch Lock Cylinder Bracket
3	Tilt Lever (If Equipped)
4	Lock Cylinder

Item	Description
5	Steering Column
6	Steering Column Intermediate Shaft Coupling
7	Steering Column Support Bracket

FM6049700096000X

Fig. 4 Exploded view of steering column. Escort, Tracer & ZX2

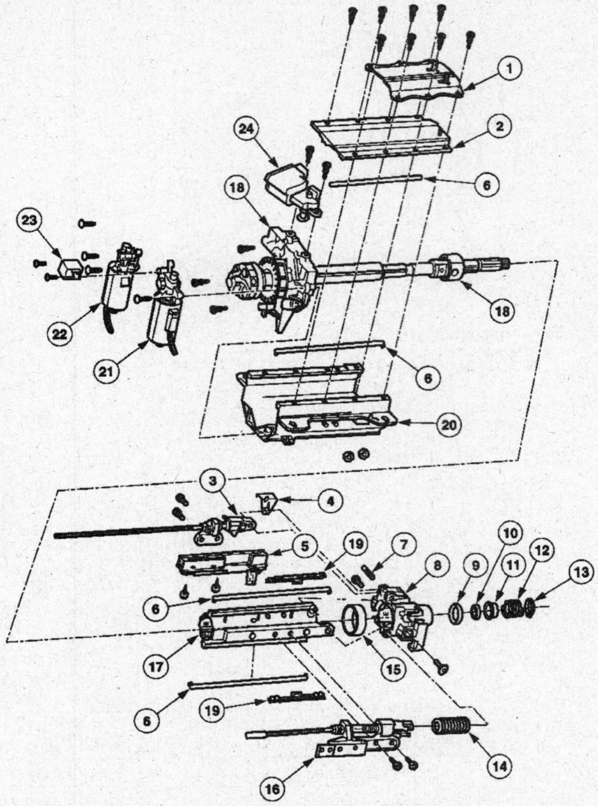

Item	Part Number	Description
1	3F790	Steering column outer housing plate
2	3F789	Steering column outer housing
3	3F797	Steering column actuator assembly (tilt)

FM60499001220I0X

Fig. 5 Exploded view of steering column (Part 1 of 2). LS

14. Remove ignition lock cylinder housing from column assembly and pull steering shaft out from top.
15. Remove steering column lock lever actuator, then the lower steering column tube bearing retainer and mounting bracket.
16. Remove tilt position lever arm pivot pin using a drift or suitable equivalent.
17. Remove steering column locking lever and position lock spring.
18. Reverse procedure to assemble. Tighten to specification.

1998-2000

Refer to "Crown Victoria, Grand Marquis & Town Car" for steering column service

CROWN VICTORIA, GRAND MARQUIS & TOWN CAR

1997

1. Remove steering wheel as described in "Electrical " section of the "Crown Victoria, Grand Marquis, Thunderbird & 1997 Cougar" and "Lincoln" chapters.
2. Remove steering column as described under "Steering Column Replace."
3. Remove steering column lower yoke, upper bearing spring, suspension height sensor control ring and bearing tolerance ring.
4. Using a suitable flat-bladed screwdriver, remove turn indicator cancel cam, **Fig. 2.**
5. Remove ignition switch assembly, then the bearing retainer and steering column upper bearing spring.
6. Remove steel steering column bearing tolerance ring and bearing sleeve.
7. Remove gearshift lever and shift lock actuator.
8. Remove shift cable and bracket.
9. Using a suitable drift and hammer, remove tilt position lever pivot pin, steering column locking lever, lock left hand lever, and locking lever springs, **Fig. 8.**
10. Remove plastic bearing retainer and metal steering column lock housing bearing from ignition switch lock cylinder bore.
11. Remove steering column lock gear, note position of lock gear to actuator lock.
12. Remove two steering column lock cylinder housing pivot bolts, **Fig. 9. Use caution because steering column position spring will release when bolts are removed.**
13. Remove steering column lock cylinder housing.
14. Remove steering gear input worm gear and rack from steering column.
15. Remove steering column lock lever actuator and steering actuator housing, then the column bearing and lower bearing retainer.
16. Reverse procedure to assemble. Tighten to specification.

1998-2000

Refer to **Figs. 3 and10** when performing the following procedure.

1. Remove steering column as described under "Steering Column Replace."
2. **Carefully note position of steering column lock gear, bearing and retainer prior to removal.**
3. Remove bearing retainer, then the lock housing bearing and lock gear.
4. Disconnect electrical connector, then remove screws and shock absorber electronic steering sensor.
5. Remove steering column lower bearing spring and sensor ring.
6. Remove steering column bearing tolerance ring from column shaft.
7. Remove bolts, then ignition switch.
8. Remove two lock cylinder housing pivot screws.
9. **Steering column position spring is under tension and may come out with great force.**

4	3A517	Steering column connector link
5	14A605	Steering column potentiometer assembly
6	3B628	Steering column track
7	3D545	Steering column release pin
8	3511	Steering column tube flange
9	3517	Steering column tube bearing assembly
10	3L539	Steering column upper bearing tolerance ring
11	3518	Steering column bearing sleeve
12	3520	Steering column upper bearing spring
13	97663	Steering column upper bearing retainer
14	3D655	Steering column position spring
15	3517	Steering column tube bearing assembly
16	3F797	Steering column actuator assembly (telescopic)
17	3F791	Steering column inner housing
18	3524	Steering column upper shaft assembly
19	3F795	Steering column inner track bearing retainer assembly
20	3B718	Steering column support assembly
21	3D538	Steering column release motor assembly (telescopic)
22	3D538	Steering column release motor assembly (tilt)
23	18B015	Steering wheel absorber electronic steering sensor
24	3K772	Steering wheel lock actuator (manual transmission only)

FM6049900122020X

Fig. 5 Exploded view of steering column (Part 2 of 2). LS

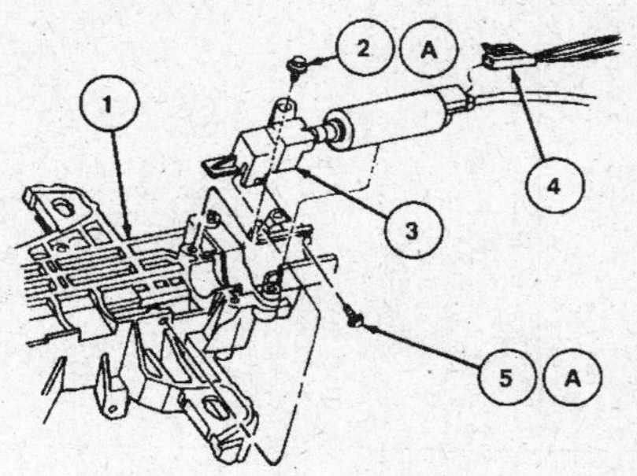

Item	Description
1	Steering Actuator Housing
2	Screw
3	Ignition / Shifter Interlock Cable
4	Electrical Connector (Part of 14401)
5	Screw
A	Tighten to 1.5-2 N·m (13-18 Lb-In)

FM6049500084000X

Fig. 6 Interlock cable & actuator. Sable & Taurus

10. Pry up on steering column locking levers using a shop fabricated tool, remove column position spring.
11. Remove turn signal cancel cam, then the snap ring.
12. Remove steering column upper bearing spring, then the bearing sleeve.
13. Slide steering column shaft in toward steering column lock cylinder housing, then out.
14. Slide steering column bearing tolerance ring off steering column shaft.
15. Using a suitable punch, remove column bearing from steering column lock cylinder housing.
16. Remove screws, then the parking brake release switch.
17. Remove bolts, then the brake shift interlock solenoid.
18. Remove bolts, then clamps and shift tube.
19. Remove bolts, then the transmission selector lever arm and support.
20. Remove gearshift selector tube spring, then drive out gearshift lever pin from shift tube.
21. Remove gearshift lever, then the column shift selector lever plunger. If lever plunger is bent, install a new one.
22. Remove two gearshift lever socket bushings, then the transmission control selector lever spring clip.
23. Drive out steering column lock lever pin, then remove steering column lock pawl.
24. Remove lower steering column bearing and sleeve.
25. Remove bolts, then the steering column lower bearing retainer.
26. Remove upper and lower steering column actuators.
27. Reverse procedure to assemble. Tighten to specifications.

CONTOUR & MYSTIQUE

On these models, the steering column must be replaced in all cases where the air bag has been deployed.

1. Remove air bag module retaining screws from back of steering wheel, then module.
2. Disconnect wiring harness connectors for air bag module and speed control.
3. Remove steering wheel retaining bolt.
4. Remove steering wheel. Use caution to not damage air bag sliding contact harness during removal.
5. Apply tape across air bag sliding contact assembly stator and rotor to prevent accidental rotation.
6. Remove lock cylinder, ignition switch, and combination switch as described in "Electrical" section of "Contour & Mystique" chapter.
7. Remove lower steering shaft bearing retainer, **Fig. 11.**
8. Remove lower steering shaft.
9. Reverse procedure to install. Tighten hardware to specification.

LS

Disassembly

Refer to **Fig. 5,** when performing the following procedure.

1. Remove steering column as described under "Steering Column Replace."
2. Place steering column in a vise.
3. **On models equipped with manual transmission,** using a suitable drill with ⅜ inch drill bit remove heads of shear bolts.
4. Remove steering wheel lock actuator, ensure not to damage actuator.
5. Using locking pliers, remove shear bolts from steering column upper shaft assembly.
6. **On all models,** remove electronic steering sensor.

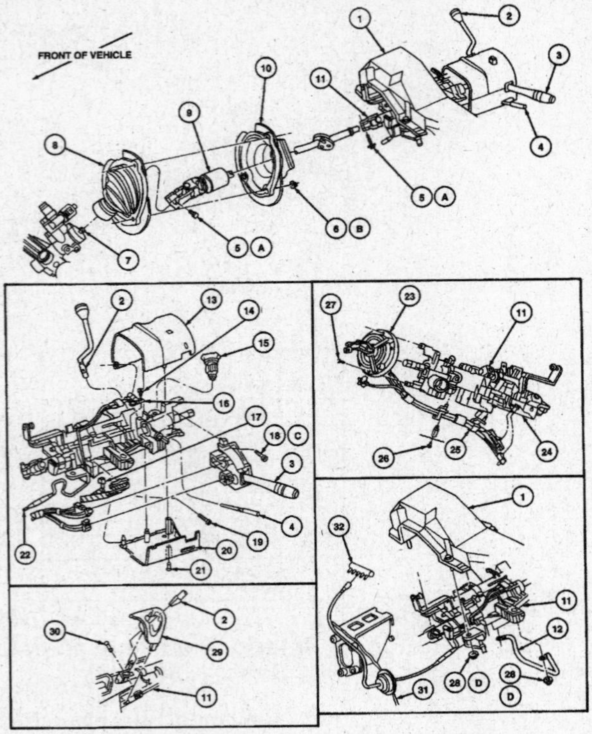

Item	Description
1	Instrument Panel Beam (Part of 04320)
2	Gearshift Lever
3	Multi-Function Switch
4	Tilt Wheel Handle and Shank
5	Bolt (2 Req'd)
6	Nut (3 Req'd)
7	Power Steering Short Rack
8	Steering Column Boot Assy, Primary
9	Steering Column Intermediate Shaft Coupling
10	Steering Column Boot Assy, Secondary
11	Steering Column
12	Steering Column Absorber
13	Steering Column Shroud, Upper
14	Screw (2 Req'd)
15	Ignition Lock Cylinder
16	Parking Brake Release Switch
17	To Shift Lock Actuator
18	Screw (2 Req'd)

Item	Description
19	Screw (Part of 14401)
20	Steering Column Shroud
21	Screw (4 Req'd)
22	Parking Brake Release Vacuum Hose
23	Air Bag Sliding Contact
24	Wire Connector Bracket
25	Wiring Harness Retainer
26	Screw
27	Screw (3 Req'd)
28	Nut (4 Req'd)
29	Steering Column Opening Weather Seal
30	Gearshift Lever Pin
31	Dash Panel
32	Vacuum Manifold

FM6049500100000X

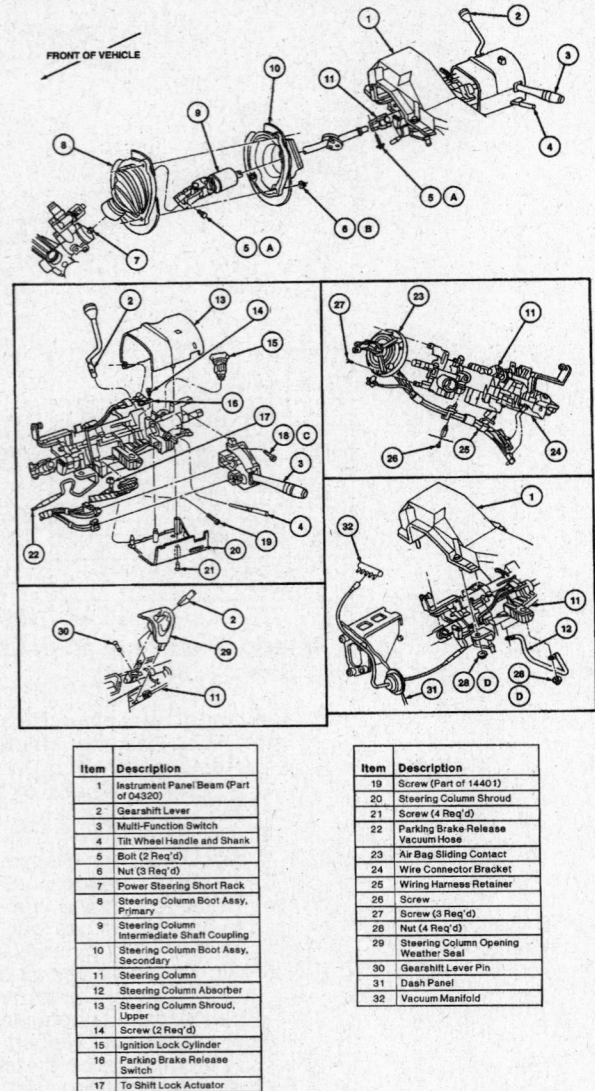

Fig. 7 Exploded view of steering column. 1997 Continental

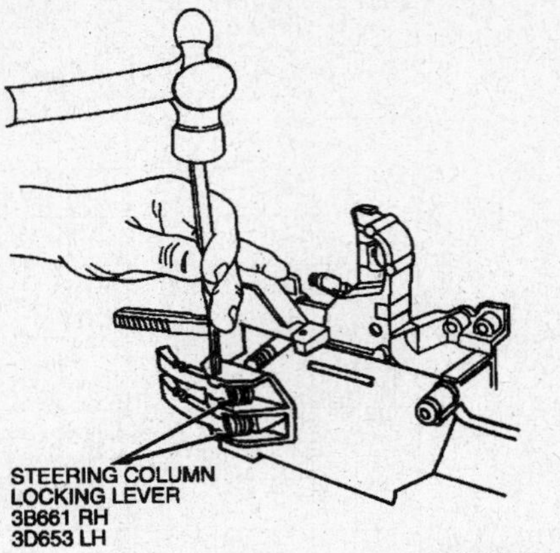

FM6049500099000X

Fig. 8 Locking lever removal

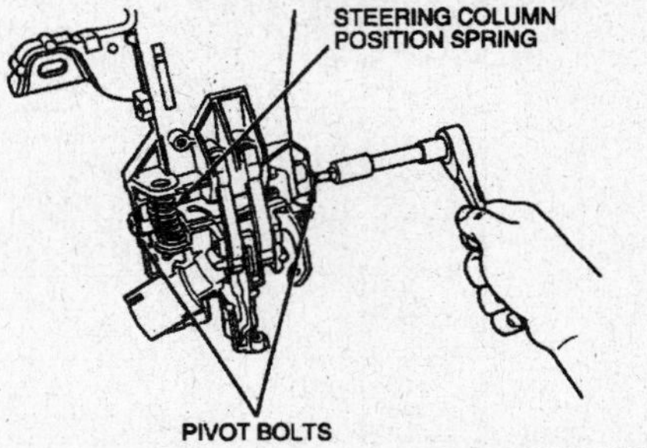

FM6049500098000X

Fig. 9 Pivot bolt removal

7. **Do not telescope steering column manually or by any means except for those described in this procedure. Failure to do so can result in damage to steering column potentiometer and actuator assembly. Ensure overtravel of potentiometer does not occur while operating it with a battery charger, to avoid damage and electrical failures.**
8. Disconnect steering column release motor (telescopic) electrical connector (21).
9. Using a suitable 1 amp 12 volts battery charger connected to release motor (telescopic) electrical terminals, then telescope column out until it is fully extended.
10. Connect steering column release motor (telescopic) electrical connector.
11. If steering column release motor is damaged or inoperable, a new one must be installed before telescoping steering column.
12. Do not disconnect harness electrical connectors from steering column release motor assemblies.
13. Remove screws, then the steering column release motor assemblies.
14. Remove retaining bolts, then the steering column outer housing cover plate (1), outer housing (2) and column track (6).
15. Remove steering column connector link (4).
16. Install spring compressor tool No. 211-201 (T97P-3D655-A) or equivalent on steering column position spring, hand tighten.
17. Remove spring retaining bolts. Using special tool, release spring tension, then remove spring and tool.
18. Separate front and rear halves of steering column upper shaft assembly and column inner housing.
19. Note: steering column upper shaft assembly sensor ring and coupler are serviced as an assembly.
20. Remove rear half of steering column upper shaft assembly from steering column support assembly.
21. **Curl strap on steering column actuator assembly (16) must not be bent or altered under any circumstance.**
22. Remove steering column actuator assembly (telescopic). If curl strap is damaged, a new actuator assembly (telescopic) must be installed.
23. Remove column track from column support assembly, then the potentiometer assembly.
24. Remove steering column release pin, then place inner housing assembly in a vise.
25. Remove steering column actuator assembly (tilt), then inner track bearing retainer assemblies and column tracks.
26. Remove steering column tube flange, then the column upper bearing retainer.
27. Remove column upper bearing spring, then the column bearing sleeve.
28. Using a flat blade screwdriver, spread out steering column upper bearing tolerance ring and slide it out of column upper shaft assembly.
29. Remove front half of steering column upper shaft assembly.
30. Using suitable brass drifts, drive out small and large steering column tube bearing assemblies.

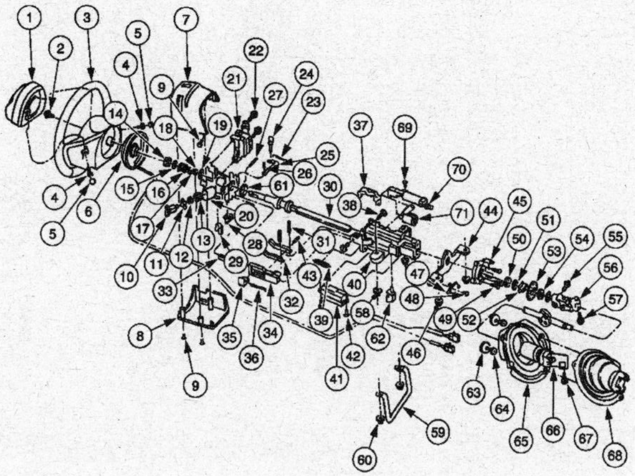

Item	Part Number	Description
1	043B13	Driver Air Bag Module
2	N804385-S100	Steering Wheel Bolt
3	3600	Steering Wheel
4	N808324-S424	Air Bag Module Retaining Screws
5	3L518	Steering Wheel Spoke Cover
6	14A664	Air Bag Sliding Contact – Assy
7	3530	Steering Column Shroud – (Upper)
8	3530	Steering Column Shroud – (Lower)
9	55929	Shroud Retaining Screws
10	11582	Ignition Switch Lock Cylinder
11	3C610	Bearing Retainer
12	3E700	Steering Column Lock Housing Bearing
13	3E717	Steering Column Lock Gear
14	13318	Turn Indicator Cancel Cam
15	3C610	Snap Ring
16	3520	Steering Column Upper Bearing Spring
17	3518	Steering Column Bearing Sleeve

FM6049900123010X

Fig. 10 Exploded view of steering column (Part 1 of 3). 1998–2000 Continental

18	3L539	Steering Column Bearing Tolerance Ring
19	3517	Steering Column Bearing – (Small)
20	3511	Steering Column Lock Cylinder Housing
21	13K359	Multi-Function Switch
22	390345-S36	Screws
23	3D655	Steering Column Position Spring
24	3F609	Tilt Wheel Handle and Shank
25	3D544	Steering Column Release Lever
26	N805857	Steering Column Lock Actuator Lever Pin
27	N806157	Pin-Lock Cam Pivot
28	3E695	Steering Column Lock Cam
29	14A163	Wiring Harness Retainer – (Upper)
30	3524	Steering Shaft Assy
31	3B664	Steering Column Locking Lever Spring
32	3B661 (RH), 3D653 (LH)	Steering Column Locking Lever
33	3E715	Steering Column Lock Lever Actuator – (Upper)
34	3E715	Steering Column Lock Lever Actuator – (Lower)
35	3E691	Steering Column Lock Pawl – (Shaft)
36	3E696	Steering Column Lock Spring – (Shaft)
37	14A099	Wiring Shield
38	N806582	Tilt Pivot Screws
39	3D655	Steering Column Position Spring
40	3F723	Steering Actuator Housing
41	11572	Ignition Switch
42	N805858	Screws
43	3F530	Steering Column Lock Actuator Lever Pin
44	3668	Steering Column Lower Mounting Bracket
45	3D681	Steering Column Lower Bearing Retainer
46	N806423-S56	Column Mounting Nuts
47	14A206	Wire Connector Bracket
48	N804409	Screw
49	N805859	Lower Bearing Housing Retaining Screws
50	3518	Steering Column Bearing Sleeve – (Lower)
51	3517	Steering Column Bearing – (Lower)
52	3L539	Steering Column Bearing Tolerance Ring
53	3C131	Suspension Height Sensor Control Ring

FM6049900123020X

Fig. 10 Exploded view of steering column (Part 2 of 3). 1998–2000 Continental

Assembly

1. Using suitable bearing installer tools, install large and small steering column tube bearing assemblies.
2. Slide steering shaft into tilt housing, then install steering column upper bearing tolerance ring.
3. Install column bearing sleeve, then the upper bearing spring.
4. Install steering column upper bearing retainer, then the tube flange with bolts.
5. Position steering column actuator assembly (tilt), then install bolts.
6. Install steering column release pin, then the potentiometer assembly with screws.
7. Install steering column actuator assembly (telescopic) with retaining nuts.
8. Install steering column track on column support assembly. Apply Premium Long-Life Grease part No. XG-1-C or equivalent to bearing surface of steering column track.
9. **Staging of steering column inner track bearing assemblies is very critical. They must be installed against rear column inner housing track bearing assembly retaining end. Inner housing must be installed in fully extended (out) position. Failure to do so will result in damage to steering column.**
10. Attach steering column tracks and inner track bearing assemblies on steering column inner housing.
11. Apply Premium Long-Life Grease part No. XG-1-C or equivalent to column track bearing assemblies and bearing surface of steering column tracks.
12. Install rear half of steering column upper shaft assembly into steering column support assembly with bolts.
13. Join front and rear halves of steering column upper shaft assembly and steering column inner housing in column support housing.
14. Position steering column spring.
15. Using compressor tool No. 211-201 (T97P-3D655-A,) compress spring until actuator assembly (telescopic) bolt holes align. Install bolts and remove special tool.
16. Install steering column connector link, then column track on outer housing. Apply grease to bearing surface of steering column track.
17. Ensure steering column inner track bearing retainer assemblies are correctly staged.
18. Install steering column outer housing, then the housing cover plate and hand tighten loosely.
19. Check that steering column inner track bearings are correctly staged, correct as required.
20. Apply Threadlock 262, E2FZ-19554-B or equivalent to bolt threads and tighten bolts to specification.
21. Install steering column release motor assemblies with screws.
22. Disconnect steering column release motor (telescopic) electrical connector.

54	3520	Steering Column Upper Bearing Spring
55	N803942-S100	Bolt — Flange Yoke
56	3N725	Steering Column Lower Yoke
57	N803942	Bolt
58	N806423-S56	Upper Column Mounting Nuts
59	3E644	Steering Column Absorber
60	N801555	Nuts
61	3517	Steering Column Bearing — (Large)
62	14A163	Wiring Harness Retainer — (Lower)
63	N804326	Nut (2 Req'd)
64	N804795-S2	Nut (3 Req'd)
65	3513	Steering Column Opening Weather Seal
66	3A525	Steering Column Intermediate Shaft Coupling
67	N806349-S100	Bolt
68	3513	Steering Column Opening Weather Seal — (Secondary)
69	N806038-S2	Screw
70	3F719	Ignition/Shifter Interlock Cable
71	7H178	Bracket

FM6049900123030X

Fig. 10 Exploded view of steering column (Part 3 of 3). 1998–2000 Continental

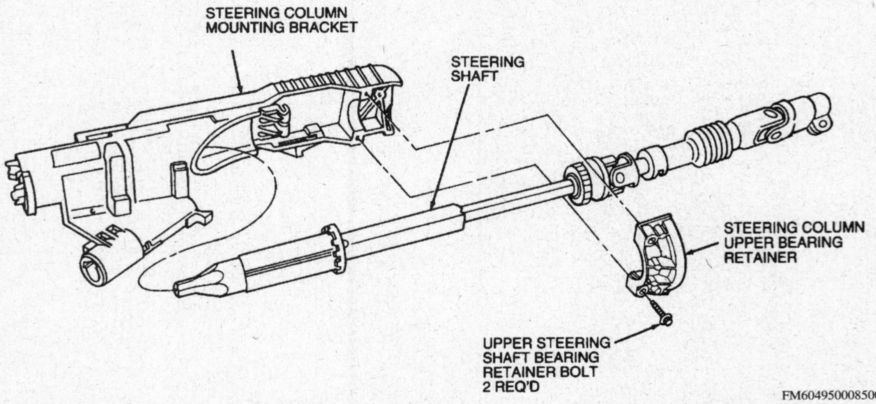

Fig. 11 Lower steering shaft removal. Contour & Mystique

23. Using a suitable 1 amp 12 volt battery charger connected to electrical terminals of motor, test column for normal operation.
24. Connect steering column release motor (telescopic) electrical connector.
25. Disconnect steering column release motor (tilt) electrical connector.
26. Using a suitable 1 amp 12 volt battery charger connected to electrical terminals of motor, test column for normal operation.
27. Connect steering column release motor (tilt) electrical connector.
28. Install electronic steering sensor with screws.
29. **On models equipped with manual transmission,** install steering wheel lock actuator and new shear bolts.

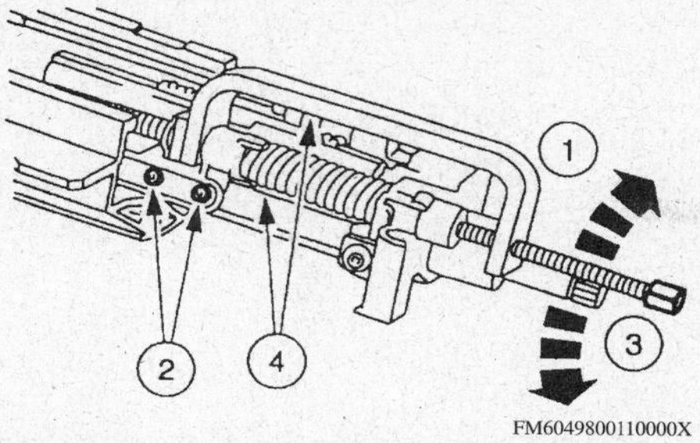

Fig. 12 Tilt spring removal. Mark VIII

30. **On all models,** remove steering column from vise.
31. Install steering column to vehicle as described under " Steering Column Replace."

MARK VIII

1. Remove shock absorber electronic steering sensor.
2. Remove tilt and telescope motors, then the housing cover.
3. Remove potentiometer link.
4. Install tilt spring compressor tool No. T97P-3D655-A, or equivalent, **Fig. 12.**
5. Remove telescoping actuator retaining bolts.
6. Slowly turn tilt spring compressor bolt counterclockwise to release spring tension.
7. Remove tilt spring compressor and tilt spring.
8. Separate front and rear halves of steering column shaft. **Scribe mark on steering shaft tube to show location of steering shaft flat.**
9. Remove potentiometer, then the telescope actuator.
10. Separate front steering shaft assembly from support housing.
11. Remove tilt actuator pivot pin and retaining bolts, then the tilt actuator.
12. Remove tilt pivot bolts.
13. Remove retaining ring, then press out rear steering shaft.
14. Using a suitable brass drift, or equivalent, drive out steering column small and large rear bearings.
15. Reverse procedure to assemble.

MUSTANG

Disassemble

1. Remove steering column tube as described under " Steering Column, Replace."
2. Remove steering column lower yoke, steering column upper bearing spring, suspension height sensor control ring and steering column upper bearing tolerance ring, **Fig. 13.**
3. Remove turn indicator cancel cam, pushing up with flat-bladed screwdriver. Note direction of flush surface.
4. Remove ignition switch, then the steering column bearing retainer and spring.
5. Remove steel steering column upper bearing tolerance ring and steering column tube bearing sleeve, then the plastic steering column upper bearing retainer from ignition switch bore.
6. Remove metal steering column lock housing bearing from ignition switch bore, then the steering column lock gear.
7. Remove two pivot bolts, then the lock cylinder housing. **Use caution. Steering column position spring will release when bolts are removed.**
8. Remove steering gear input worm gear and rack from steering column tube assembly
9. Remove steering column lock lever actuator and steering actuator housing.
10. Remove lower steering column tube bearing and steering column lower bearing retainer.
11. Use drift to remove tilt position lever, then remove steering column lock left hand lever and steering column locking lever springs.

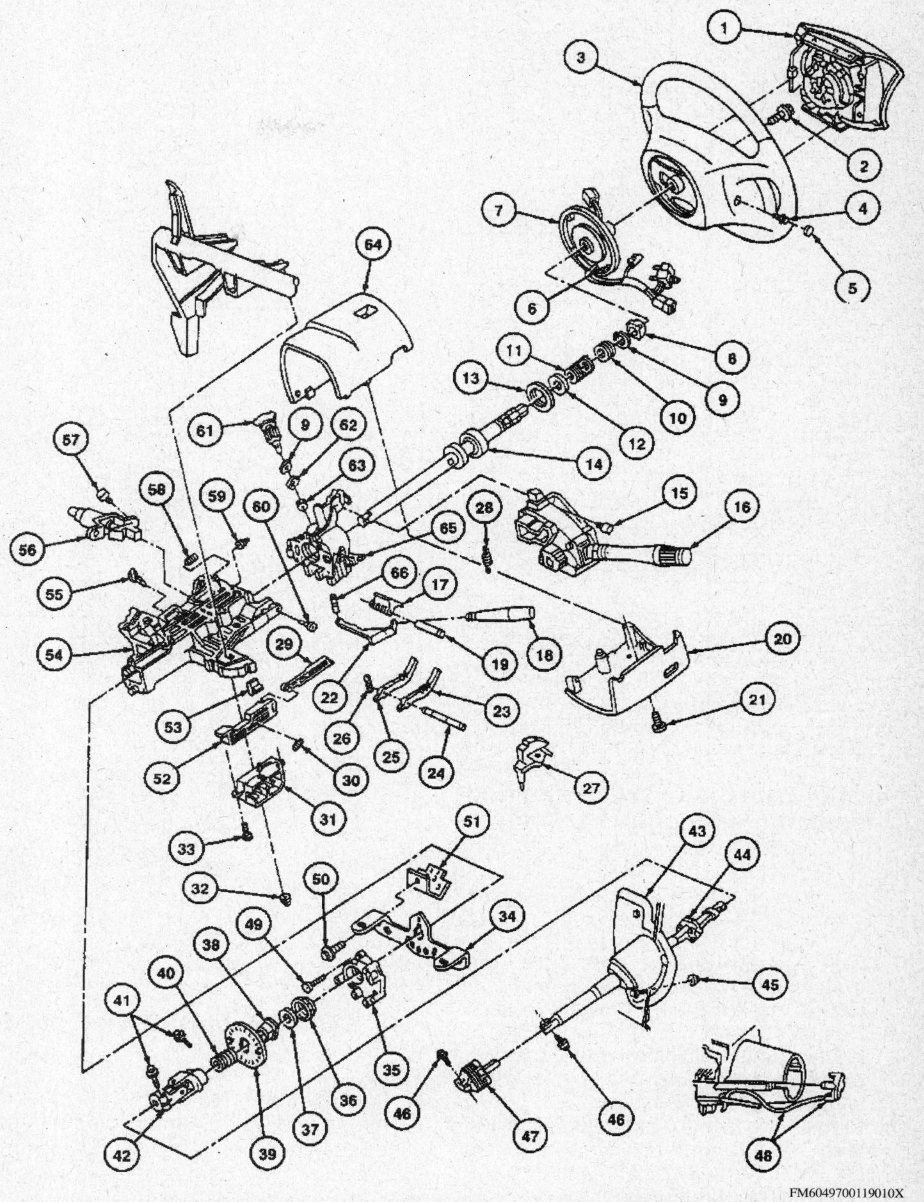

Fig. 13 Exploded view of steering column (Part 1 of 2). Mustang

Assemble

1. Install steering gear input worm gear and rack into steering actuator housing.
2. Install lower steering column tube bearing and steering column instrument panel clamp. Tighten to specifications.
3. Install suspension height sensor control ring, steering column upper bearing tolerance ring, steering column upper bearing spring and steering column lower yoke to steering gear input worm gear and rack. Tighten to specifications.
4. Position steering column lock lever actuator, steering actuator housing in

Item	Description
1	Driver Air Bag Module
2	Steering Wheel Bolt
3	Steering Wheel
4	Air Bag Module Retaining Screws (2 Req'd)
5	Steering Wheel Spoke Cover (2 Req'd)
6	Locking Tabs
7	Air Bag Sliding Contact
8	Turn Indicator Cancel Cam
9	Snap Ring
10	Steering Column Upper Bearing Spring
11	Steering Column Bearing Sleeve (Upper)
12	Steering Column Bearing (Upper)(Small)
13	Steering Column Bearing (Large)
14	Steering Shaft Assy
15	Screw
16	Multi-Function Switch
17	Steering Column Lock Cam
18	Tilt Wheel Handle and Shank
19	Pin - Lock Cam Pivot
20	Steering Column Shroud (Lower)
21	Shroud Retaining Screws
22	Steering Column Release Lever
23	Steering Column Lock RH Lever
24	Steering Column Lock Actuator Lever Pin
25	Steering Column Lock Left Hand Lever
26	Steering Column Locking Lever Spring
27	Wiring Shield
28	Steering Column Position Spring
29	Steering Column Lock Lever Actuator
30	Steering Column Lock Spring (Shaft)
31	Ignition Switch
32	Lower Column Mounting Nuts
33	Screw
34	Steering Column Mounting Bracket

Item	Description
35	Steering Column Lower Bearing Retainer
36	Steering Column Bearing Sleeve
37	Steering Column Bearing (Lower)
38	Steering Column Bearing Tolerance Ring (Lower)
39	Suspension Height Sensor Control Ring
40	Steering Column Upper Bearing Spring
41	Bolt - Flange Yoke
42	Steering Column Lower Yoke
43	Steering Column Tube Boot
44	Lower Steering Column Shaft
45	Nut
46	Bolt
47	Steering Column Intermediate Shaft Coupling
48	Ignition Key Warning Switch Terminal and Wire
49	Lower Bearing Housing Retaining Screw
50	Screw
51	Wire Connector Bracket
52	Steering Column Lock Lever Actuator (Lower)
53	Steering Column Lock Pawl
54	Steering Actuator Housing
55	Steering Column Lock Actuator Cover
56	Ignition / Shifter Interlock Cable
57	Screw
58	Steering Column Position Spring
59	Steering Column Tilt Flange Bumper
60	Tilt Pivot Screws
61	Ignition Switch Lock Cylinder
62	Steering Column Lock Housing Bearing
63	Steering Column Lock Gear
64	Steering Column Shroud (Upper)
65	Steering Column Lock Cylinder Housing
66	Steering Column Lock Actuator Lever Pin

FM6049700119020X

Fig. 13 Exploded view of steering column (Part 2 of 2). Mustang

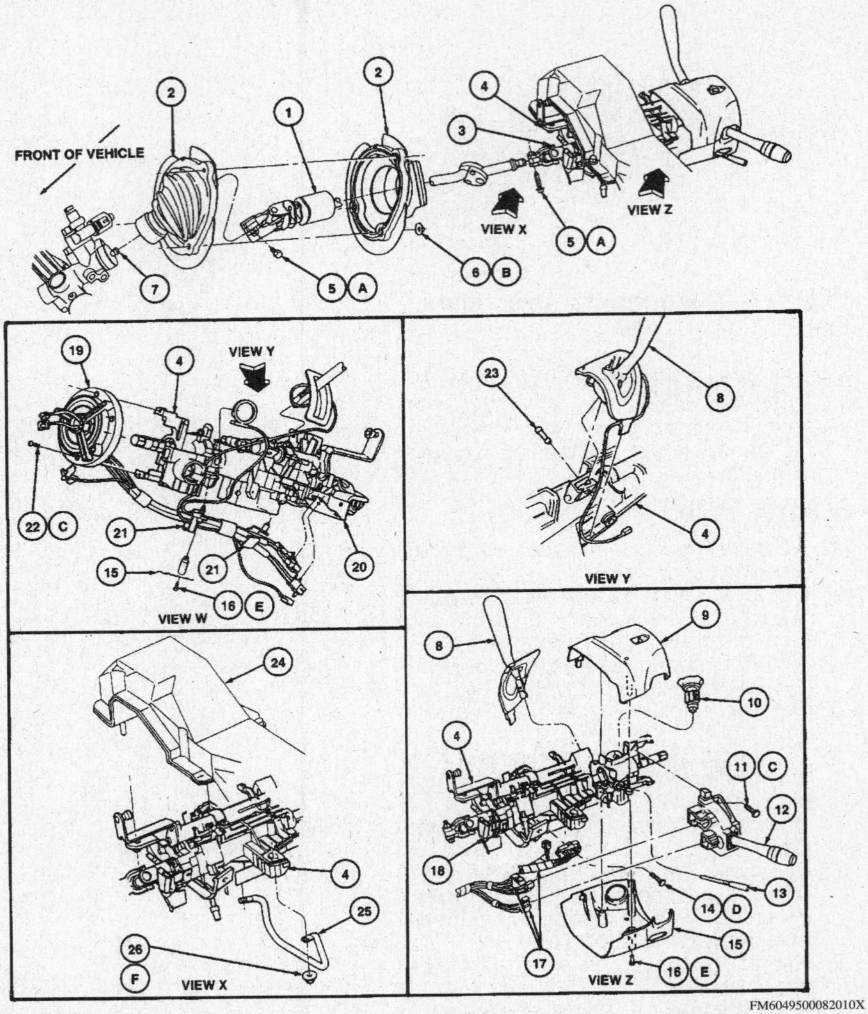

FM6049500082010X

Fig. 14 Exploded view of steering column (Part 1 of 2). Sable & Taurus w/column shift

Item	Description
1	Steering Column Intermediate Shaft Coupling
2	Steering Column Opening Weather Seal (2 Req'd)
3	Steering Column Lower Yoke
4	Steering Column Tube
5	Bolt (2 Req'd)
6	Nut (3 Req'd)
7	Steering Gear
8	Steering Column Intermediate Shaft Coupling
9	Steering Column Shroud
10	Ignition Switch Lock Cylinder
11	Bolt (2 Req'd)
12	Multi-Function Switch
13	Tilt Wheel Handle and Shank
14	Screw (Part of 14401)
15	Steering Column Shroud
16	Screw (3 Req'd)
17	Main Wiring
18	Steering Column Lower Bearing Retainer

Item	Description
19	Air Bag Sliding Contact
20	Wire Connector Bracket
21	Wiring Harness Retainer (2 Req'd)
22	Screw (3 Req'd)
23	Gearshift Lever Pin
24	Part of Instrument Panel Brace
25	Steering Column Absorber
26	Nut (4 Req'd)
A	Tighten to 22-28 N-m (16-21 Lb-Ft)
B	Tighten to 5-6 N-m (40-56 Lb-In)
C	Tighten to 2-3 N-m (19-25 Lb-In)
D	Tighten to 0.9-1.3 N-m (8-10 Lb-In)
E	Tighten to 0.7-1.0 N-m (6-8 Lb-In)
F	Tighten to 13-17 N-m (10-12 Lb-Ft)

FM6049500082020X

Fig. 14 Exploded view of steering column (Part 2 of 2). Sable & Taurus w/column shift

lock cylinder housing, then spray actuators with multi-purpose grease part No. DOAZ-19584-AA, or equivalent.

5. Position actuator cam in lock cylinder housing and install cam pivot pin with small hammer. Tap pin in until flush with lock cylinder housing.
6. Install one steering column locking lever spring and righthand steering column locking lever with steering column lock actuator lever pin.
7. Tap steering column lock actuator lever pin into place while driving out drift.
8. Support steering actuator housing in vise and drive steering column lock actuator lever pin flush with steering actuator housing.
9. Place two nuts or spacers to hold steering column lock lefthand lever/righthand steering column locking lever away from steering actuator housing.
10. Lube pivot bolts with multi-purpose grease part No. DOAZ-19584-AA, or equivalent, then position steering column position spring on lock cylinder housing and install lock cylinder housing and pivot bolts. Tighten pivot bolts to specifications.
11. Install steel steering column upper bearing tolerance ring and steering column tube bearing sleeve over steering column.
12. Install steering column upper bearing spring and new steering column upper bearing retainer on top side of steering column upper bearing spring using ¾ inch by ⅔ inch PVC pipe.
13. Install turn indicator cancel cam, flush surface facing up.
14. Install ignition switch, then align pin from ignition switch with slot in lock/column assembly and position slot in lock/column assembly with index mark on casting. Tighten screws to specifications.
15. Install steering column lock gear, then coat lock gear with multi-purpose grease part No. DOAZ-19584-AA, or equivalent.
16. Install metal steering column lock housing bearing, then coat lock gear with multi-purpose grease part No. DOAZ-19584-AA, or equivalent.
17. Install steering column upper bearing retainer.
18. Install steering column tube as described under " Steering Column, Replace."

SABLE & TAURUS

1. Remove steering column as described under "Steering Column, Replace."
2. Remove steering column lower yoke, bearing spring, suspension height

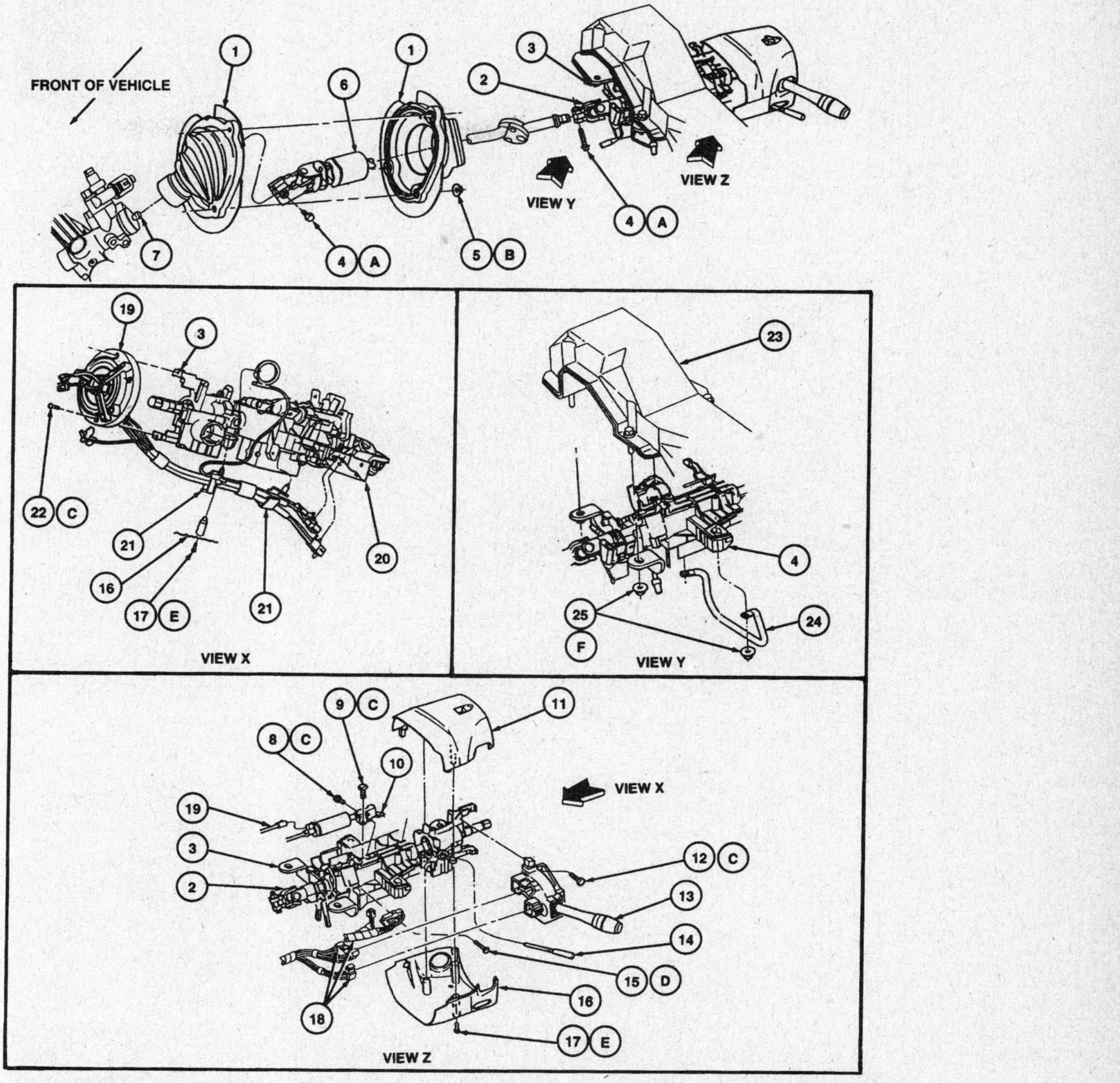

FM6049500083010X

Fig. 15 Exploded view of steering column (Part 1 of 2). Sable & Taurus w/floor shift

sensor control ring and steering column bearing tolerance ring.

3. Remove turn indicator cancel cam by pushing up with flat bladed screwdriver, or suitable equivalent. **Note direction of flush surface.**
4. Remove two ignition switch retaining bolts, then the ignition switch assembly, **Figs. 14 and 15.**
5. Remove bearing retainer and steering column upper bearing spring.
6. Remove steel steering column bearing tolerance ring and bearing sleeve.
7. Remove plastic bearing retainer from ignition switch lock cylinder bore, then the metal steering column lock housing bearing.
8. Remove steering column lock gear, then two tilt pivot bolts, **Fig. 9. Use caution as steering column position spring will release when bolts are removed.**
9. Remove steering column lock cylinder housing, then the steering shaft assembly from steering column.

Item	Description
1	Steering Column Opening Weather Seal (2 Req'd)
2	Steering Column Lower Yoke
3	Steering Column Tube
4	Bolt (2 Req'd)
5	Nut (3 Req'd)
6	Steering Column Intermediate Shaft Coupling
7	Steering Gear
8	Bolt (1 Req'd)
9	Bolt (1 Req'd)
10	Ignition / Shifter Interlock Cable
11	Steering Column Shroud
12	Bolt (2 Req'd)
13	Multi-Function Switch
14	Tilt Wheel Handle and Shank
15	Screw (Part of 14401)
16	Steering Column Shroud
17	Screw (3 Req'd)

Item	Description
18	Main Wiring
19	Air Bag Sliding Contact
20	Wire Connector Bracket
21	Wiring Harness Retainer (2 Req'd)
22	Screw (3 Req'd)
23	Part of Instrument Panel Bace
24	Steering Column Absorber
25	Nut (4 Req'd)
A	Tighten to 22-28 N·m (16-21 Lb-Ft)
B	Tighten to 5-6 N·m (40-56 Lb-In)
C	Tighten to 2-3 N·m (1925 Lb-In)
D	Tighten to 0.9-1.3 N·m (8-11 Lb-In)
E	Tighten to 0.7-1.0 N·m (6-8 Lb-In)
F	Tighten to 13-17 N·m (10-12 Lb-Ft)

FM6049500083020X

Fig. 15 Exploded view of steering column (Part 2 of 2). Sable & Taurus w/floor shift

10. **On models equipped with column shift,** proceed as follows:
    a. remove shift lock actuator and transmission shift selector insert.
    b. Remove four transmission column shift selector tube retaining screws.
    c. Remove pin retaining steering column lock pawl from steering actuator housing and remove lock pawl.
11. **On all models,** remove steering column lock lever actuator from steering actuator housing.
12. Remove three screws retaining steering column lower bearing retainer, then the bearing from lower bearing retainer.
13. Remove steering column mounting bracket, then the lock actuator lever pin.
14. Remove steering column locking lever, lock left hand lever and locking lever springs, **Fig. 8.**
15. Reverse procedure to assemble.

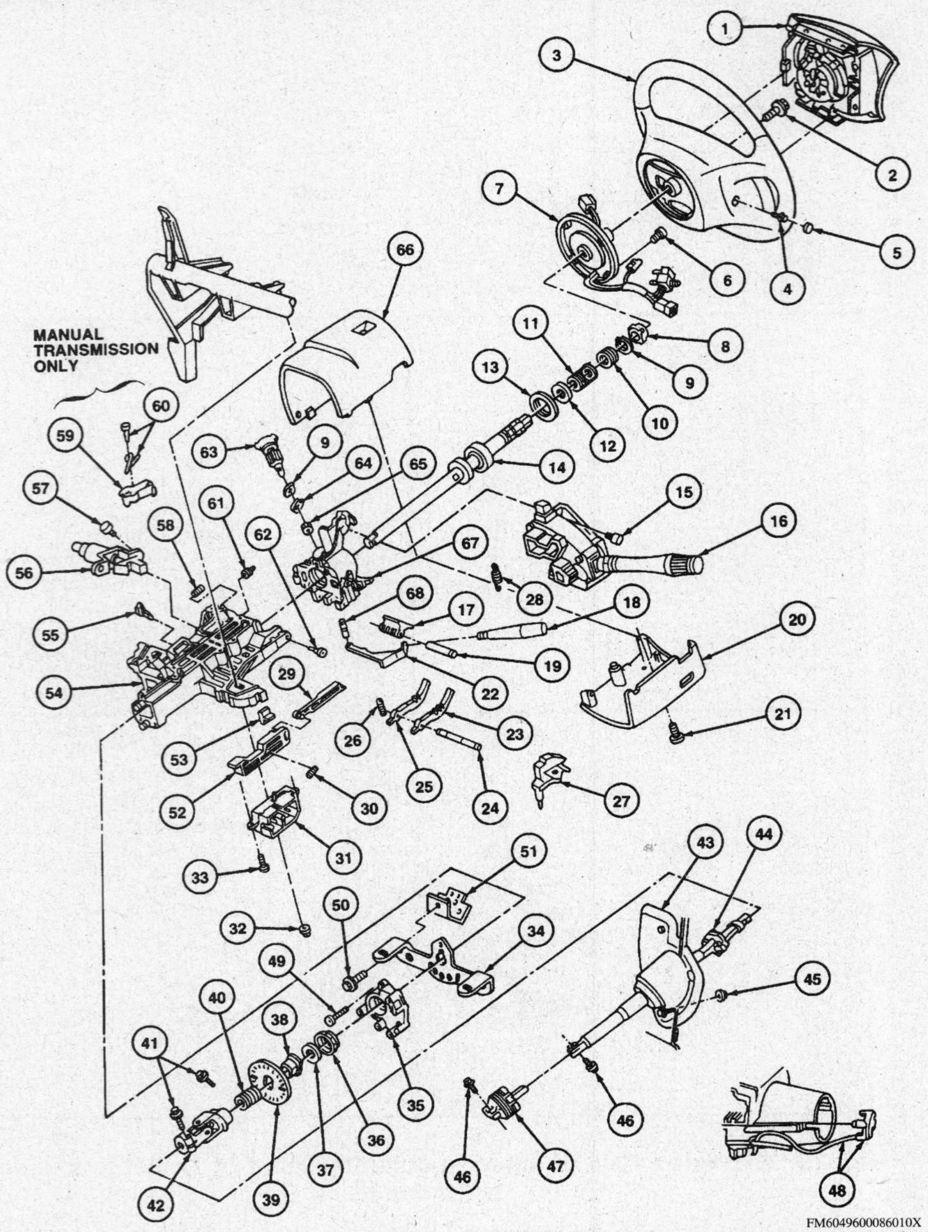

Fig. 16 Exploded view of steering column (Part 1 of 2). Thunderbird & 1997 Cougar

Tighten to specification.

THUNDERBIRD & 1997 COUGAR

1. Remove steering wheel as described in "Electrical " section of the "Crown Victoria, Grand Marquis, Thunderbird & 1997 Cougar" chapter.
2. Remove steering column lower yoke, upper bearing spring, suspension height sensor control ring and bearing tolerance ring.
3. Using a suitable flat-bladed screwdriver, remove turn indicator cancel cam, **Fig. 16.**
4. Remove ignition switch assembly, then the bearing retainer and steering column upper bearing spring.
5. Remove steel steering column bearing tolerance ring and bearing sleeve.
6. Remove plastic bearing retainer and metal steering column lock housing bearing from ignition switch lock cylinder bore.
7. Remove steering column lock gear noting position of lock gear to actuator lock.
8. Remove two steering column lock cylinder housing pivot bolts, **Fig. 9. Use caution because steering column position spring will release when bolts are removed.**
9. Remove steering column shaft assembly from steering column.
10. Remove steering column lock lever actuator and steering actuator housing, then the column bearing and lower bearing retainer.
11. Using a suitable drift and hammer, remove tilt position lever pivot pin, steering column locking lever, lock left hand lever, and locking lever springs, **Fig. 8.**
12. Reverse procedure to assemble. Tighten hardware to specification.

Item	Description	Item	Description
1	Driver Side Air Bag Module	36	Steering Column Bearing Sleeve
2	Steering Wheel Bolt	37	Steering Column Bearing (Lower)
3	Steering Wheel	38	Steering Column Bearing Tolerance Ring (Lower)
4	Air Bag Module Retaining Screws (2 Req'd)	39	Suspension Height Sensor Control Ring
5	Steering Wheel Spoke Cover (2 Req'd)	40	Steering Column Upper Bearing Spring
6	Screw	41	Bolt - Flange Yoke
7	Air Bag Sliding Contact	42	Steering Column Lower Yoke
8	Turn Indicator Cancel Cam	43	Steering Column Tube Boot
9	Bearing Retainer	44	Lower Steering Column Shaft
10	Steering Column Upper Bearing Spring	45	Nut
11	Steering Column Bearing Sleeve (Upper)	46	Bolt
12	Steering Column Bearing (Upper)(Small)	47	Steering Column Intermediate Shaft Coupling
13	Steering Column Bearing (Large)	48	Ignition Key Warning Switch Terminal and Wire
14	Steering Column Shaft Assy	49	Lower Bearing Housing Retaining Screw
15	Screw	50	Screw
16	Multi-Function Switch	51	Wire Connector Bracket
17	Steering Column Lock Cam	52	Steering Column Lock Lever Actuator (Lower)
18	Tilt Wheel Handle and Shank	53	Steering Column Lock Pawl
19	Pin - Lock Cam Pivot	54	Steering Actuator Housing
20	Lower Steering Column Cover	55	Steering Column Lock Actuator Cover
21	Shroud Retaining Screws	56	Ignition / Shifter Interlock Cable
22	Steering Column Release Lever	57	Screw
23	Steering Column Lock RH Lever	58	Steering Column Position Spring
24	Steering Column Lock Actuator Lever Pin	59	Key Release Lever (Manual Transmission Only)
25	Steering Column Lock Left Hand Lever	60	Steering Column Lock Actuator Lever Pin (Manual Transmission Only)
26	Steering Column Locking Lever Spring	61	Steering Column Tilt Flange Bumper
27	Wiring Shield	62	Tilt Pivot Screws
28	Tilt Release Spring	63	Ignition Switch Lock Cylinder
29	Steering Column Lock Lever Actuator	64	Steering Column Lock Housing Bearing
30	Steering Column Lock Spring (Shaft)	65	Steering Column Lock Gear
31	Ignition Switch	66	Upper Steering Column Cover
32	Lower Column Mounting Nuts	67	Steering Column Lock Cylinder Housing
33	Screw	68	Steering Column Lock Actuator Lever Pin
34	Steering Column Mounting Bracket		
35	Steering Column Lower Bearing Retainer		

FM6049600086020X

Fig. 16 Exploded view of steering column (Part 2 of 2). Thunderbird & 1997 Cougar

TIGHTENING SPECIFICATIONS

Model	Component	Torque/ Ft. Lbs.
Aspire	Air Bag Sliding Contact Screws	18-26①
	Lower Steering Column Mounting Bracket Nuts	13-20
	Lower Steering Column Shaft Lower Bolt	13-20
	Lower Steering Column Shaft Upper Bolt	13-20
	Steering Column Gear Input Shaft Bolt	13-20
	Steering Gear Bolts	27-38
	Steering Wheel Nut	29-36
	Upper Steering Column Mounting Bracket Bolts	12-17
Continental	Air Bag Contact Assembly Screws	18-26
	Air Bag Module Nuts	36-47
Contour & Mystique	Air Bag Contact Assembly Screws	18-26
	Air Bag Module Nuts	36-47
	Air Bag Module Screws	8-10
	Lower Yoke To Steering Shaft	19-25
	Steering Actuator Housing Pivot Bolts	14-19
	Steering Wheel Bolt	37
1997 Cougar	Air Bag Module Screws	7-10
	Air Bag Sliding Contact Screws	18-26①
	Clockspring Assembly Screw	18-26①
	Column Lower Mounting Bracket Bolt	60-96①
	Ignition Switch Screw	60-96①
	Instrument Panel Reinforcement Brace Bolts	25-38
	Interlock Cable Screws	12-17①
	Intermediate Shaft To Flex Coupling Bolt	30-42
	Intermediate Shaft To U-Joint Bolt	30-42
	Lock Housing Pivot Bolt	14-20
	Lower Column Bearing Bolt	60-96①
	Lower Yoke to Lower Column Shaft Bolt	19-25
	Multi-Function Switch Screws	18-26①
	Shift Control Tube Screw	60-96①
	Steering Column Boot	43-60
	Steering Column Mounting Nut	9-14
	Steering Shaft Yoke Coupling Screw	31-41
	Steering Wheel to Column Shaft Bolt	23-35
	Tilt Lever	28-44①
1999-2000 Cougar	Air Bag Module Screws	44①
	Flexible Coupling To Steering Column Pinch Bolt	18
	Flexible Coupling To Steering Gear Pinch Bolt	14
	Lower Bearing Retainer Collar	17
	Steering Column Mounting Bolts	18
	Steering Wheel To Column Shaft Bolt	37
Crown Victoria, Grand Marquis & Town Car	Air Bag Clockspring Assembly Screws	18-26①
	Air Bag Module Nuts	36–48①
	Lower Steering Column Shaft Bolt	19-25
	Steering Column Support Bracket Nuts	9-14
	U-Joint Pinch Bolt	26-41

Continued

TIGHTENING SPECIFICATIONS—Continued

Model	Component	Torque/ Ft. Lbs.
Escort & Tracer	Driver Side Air Bag Module Bolts	72–96①
	Ignition/Shifter Interlock Cable Mounting Bracket Bolt	35-53①
	Intermediate Shaft To Pinion Shaft Bolt	30-37
	Steering Column Gear Input Shaft Coupling To Intermediate Shaft Bolt	30-37
	Steering Column Shaft To Steering Column Gear Input Shaft Coupling Bolt	30-37
	Steering Column Support Bracket Nuts	84-108①
	Steering Column Upper Mounting Bracket Bolts	7-10
	Steering Wheel Bolt	34-46
LS	Steering Shaft Pinch Bolt	22
	Steering Column Mounting Nut	13
	Steering Column Upper Shaft Assembly Mounting Bolts	10
	Steering Column Actuator Assembly Telescopic Retaining Bolt	11
	Steering Column Actuator Assembly Telescopic Retaining Nut	13
	Steering Column Actuator Assembly Tilt Retaining Bolt	11
	Steering Column Actuator Assembly Tilt Retaining Nut	13
	Steering Column Outer Housing Cover Plate Mounting Bolts	10
	Steering Column Tube Flange Pivot Bolts	17
	Steering Wheel Lock Actuator Mounting bolts	108①
Mark VIII	Air Bag Sliding Contact Screws	35-44①
	Clockspring Screws	35-44①
	Instrument Panel Reinforcement Brace	25-38
	Interlock Assembly Screws	12-17①
	Lower Steering Column Shaft Bolt	29-41
	Multi-Function Switch Screws	18-26①
	Steering Gear Input Worm Gear and Rack	23-33
	Steering Column Pivot Bolts	14-19
	Telescope Actuator Retaining Nuts	7-10
	Tilt Actuator Retaining Bolts	10-13
Mustang	Multi-Function Switch Screws	18-26①
	Cross Bar Beam To Column Collar Nuts	22-30
	Ignition/Shifter Interlock Cable Screws	10-13①
	Ignition Switch Screws	60-96①
	Lock Cylinder Housing Pivot Bolts	14-20
	Lower Steering Column Tube Bearing & Steering Column Instrument Panel Clamp Screws	60-96①
	Steering Column Gear Input Shaft Coupling To Steering Column Bolt	30-40
	Steering Column Lower Shaft & U-Joint Assembly To Steering Gear Input Shaft Flange	20-37
	Steering Column Lower Yoke Bolt	31-42
Probe	Clockspring Screws	18-26①
	Intermediate Shaft Bolt	13-20
	Lower Column Bracket Nut	12-17
	Steering Wheel Nut	29-36
	Upper Column Bracket Bolts	12-17

Continued

TIGHTENING SPECIFICATIONS—Continued

Model	Component	Torque/ Ft. Lbs.
Sable & Taurus	Air Bag Sliding Contact	18-26①
	Air Bag Module Screws	89-124①
	Ignition Switch	44-61①
	Interlock Cable Retaining Screw	13-18
	Lower Shroud	6-8①
	Main Wiring Harness Screw	8-11①
	Steering Column Gear Input Shaft Coupling To Column Shaft Bolt	16-21
	Steering Column Lower Yoke To Steering Gear And Rack Bolt	16-21
	Steering Column Mounting Bracket Screws	60-96①
	Steering Column Mounting Nuts	10-12
	Steering Column Tube Boot Nuts	40-56①
	Steering Column Tube Flange Pivot Bolts	13-19
	Steering Wheel Nut	25-34
Thunderbird	Air Bag Module Screws	7-10
	Air Bag Sliding Contact Screws	18-26①
	Clockspring Assembly Screw	18-26①
	Column Lower Mounting Bracket bolt	60-96①
	Ignition Switch Screw	60-96①
	Instrument Panel Reinforcement Brace Bolts	25-38
	Interlock Cable Screws	12-17①
	Intermediate Shaft To Flex Coupling Bolt	30-42
	Intermediate Shaft To U-Joint Bolt	30-42
	Lock Housing Pivot Bolt	14-20
	Lower Column Bearing Bolt	60-96①
	Lower Yoke To Lower Column Shaft Bolt	19-25
	Multi-Function Switch Screws	18-26①
	Shift Control Tube Screw	60-96①
	Steering Column Boot	43-60
	Steering Column Mounting Nut	9-14
	Steering Shaft Yoke Coupling Screw	31-41
	Steering Wheel To Column Shaft Bolt	23-35
	Tilt Lever	28-44①

① — Inch lbs.

MANUAL STEERING GEARS
Aspire

NOTE: On Air Bag Equipped Models, Refer To "Air Bag System Precautions" Located In The Front Of This Manual For System Disarming & Arming Procedures.

NOTE: Refer To "Computer Relearn Procedure" Located In The Front Of This Manual For Computer Relearn Procedures.

INDEX

PRECAUTIONS

AIR BAG SYSTEMS

Refer to "Air Bag System Precautions" in the front of this manual for system disarming and arming procedures.

BATTERY GROUND CABLE

Prior to service, disconnect battery ground cable and isolate as required.

TROUBLESHOOTING

STEERING FEELS HEAVY w/VEHICLE RAISED

1. Poor lubrication, foreign material in mechanism, damaged or binding ball joint.
2. Improper steering gear preload.
3. Faulty steering gear.
4. Faulty steering shaft joint.
5. Worn or cracked steering gear bushings.
6. Faulty suspension component.

STEERING WHEEL PULLS

1. Faulty steering linkage.
2. Faulty wheel or tire.
3. Faulty brake system.
4. Faulty suspension component.
5. Uneven tire wear.
6. Tire inflation incorrect.
7. Fatigued front coil springs.

INSTABILITY WHEN DRIVING

1. Worn or damaged steering joints.
2. Improper steering gear preload.
3. Damaged steering linkage.
4. Damaged wheel or tire.
5. Faulty suspension component.

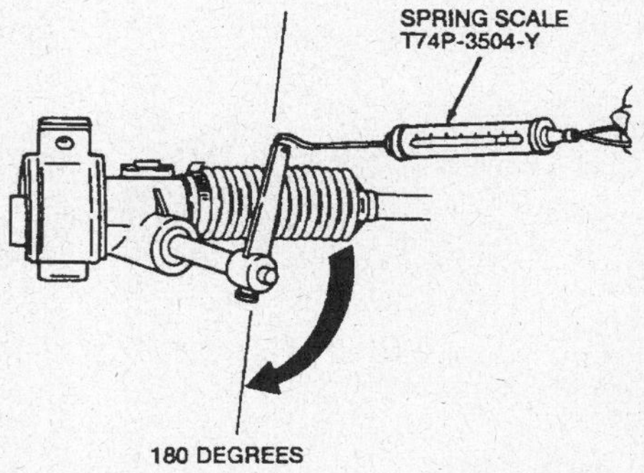

Fig. 1 Rack preload/support yoke adjustment

UNSTABLE STEERING

1. Faulty steering gear.
2. Faulty steering joints.
3. Faulty steering linkage.

EXCESSIVE STEERING WHEEL PLAY

1. Worn steering gear.
2. Worn or damaged steering joints.
3. Loose steering gear mounting bolts.

POOR STEERING WHEEL RETURN

1. Damaged or binding steering joints.
2. Improper steering gear preload.
3. Faulty wheel or tire.
4. Faulty suspension component.

STEERING WHEEL VIBRATES

1. Damaged steering linkage.
2. Loose steering gear mounting bolts.
3. Damaged or binding steering joints.
4. Worn or faulty front wheel bearing.
5. Faulty wheel or tire.
6. Faulty suspension component.

ABNORMAL NOISE

1. Loose steering gear mounting bolt.
2. Faulty steering gear.
3. Obstruction near steering column.
4. Loose steering linkage.
5. Worn steering joints.

EXCESSIVE STEERING EFFORT

1. Tire under inflation.
2. Excessive uneven tire wear.
3. Insufficient lubrication or steering gear housing bellows damage, allowing entry of foreign matter.
4. Abnormal wear, damage or seizure of front wheel spindle connecting rod or end.
5. Steering gear damage.
6. Steering column gear input shaft coupling binding.
7. Front suspension lower arm ball joint friction excessive.
8. Steering gear preload incorrect.
9. Steering gear insulator worn or damaged.
10. No lubricant in steering gear housing.

ADJUSTMENTS

RACK PRELOAD/SUPPORT YOKE

1. Remove steering gear.
2. Loosen yoke plug, then **torque** yoke plug to 22-30 inch lbs.
3. Use spring scale tool No. T74P-3504-Y, or equivalent, to measure force needed to turn steering wheel input

worm gear 180° from steering gear rack center position, **Fig. 1.**

4. Adjust steering gear input worm gear to position where most turning force was needed.
5. **Torque** yoke plug to 48 inch lbs., then back it off 5-35.°
6. Install yoke locking nut, **Fig. 2,** and **torque** to 29-36 ft. lbs.
7. Install steering gear.

STEERING GEAR SERVICE

DISASSEMBLE

1. Remove mount brackets and rubber mounts, then position steering gear in suitable soft jaw vise.
2. Mark position of tie rod ends in relation to tie rods, then remove tie rod ends and boots.
3. Disengage tab washers from ball joints using suitable tool, extend rack from either side of housing, then remove tie rods from rack.
4. Remove rack preload adjusting screw and jam nut from yoke cover, **Fig. 3.**
5. Remove cover and yoke spring from housing, then the spacer and yoke.
6. Carefully pry pinion oil seal from housing, then remove seal spacer, snap ring and pinion and bearing assembly.
7. Remove rack from pinion side of housing. **If rack is removed through right side (bushing end) of housing, damage to bushing may result.**
8. If pinion lower bearing is to be replaced, remove it at this time using suitable slide hammer type puller.
9. Press the three rack support bushing lock tabs inward, then remove bushing from right side of housing using puller mentioned in previous step.

INSPECTION

1. Inspect rack and pinion gear teeth for abnormal wear, and steering gear housing for cracks or damage. Replace components as necessary.
2. Position rack in V blocks, then check runout in center portion of rack using suitable dial indicator. If runout exceeds .0039 inch, replace rack and pinion gear.
3. Rotate pinion bearings and check for looseness or rough operation. If upper bearing requires replacement, replace bearing and pinion gear as an assembly.
4. Check fit of rack support bushing on rack for looseness or abnormal wear. Replace bushing as necessary.
5. Check tie rod ball joints and tie rod ends for free flexing without excessive looseness. Replace joints and tie rod ends as required.
6. Check tie rods for bending and boots for cuts, nicks or abrasions. Replace parts as necessary.

ASSEMBLE

1. Lubricate rack and pinion teeth, pinion bearings, housing, pinion oil seal lips, rack support yoke and bushing and

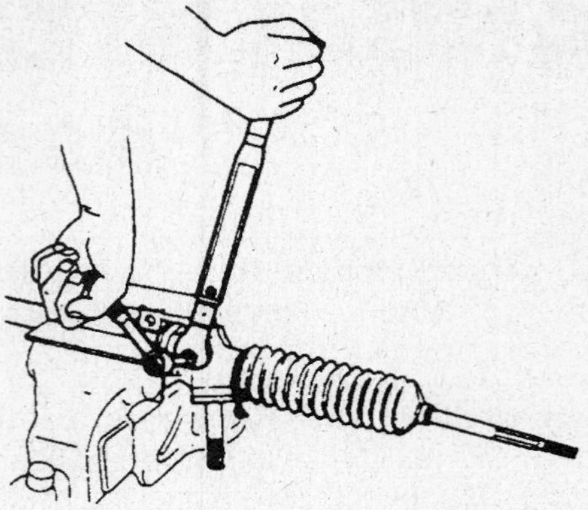

FM6039400029000X

Fig. 2 Yoke locknut installation

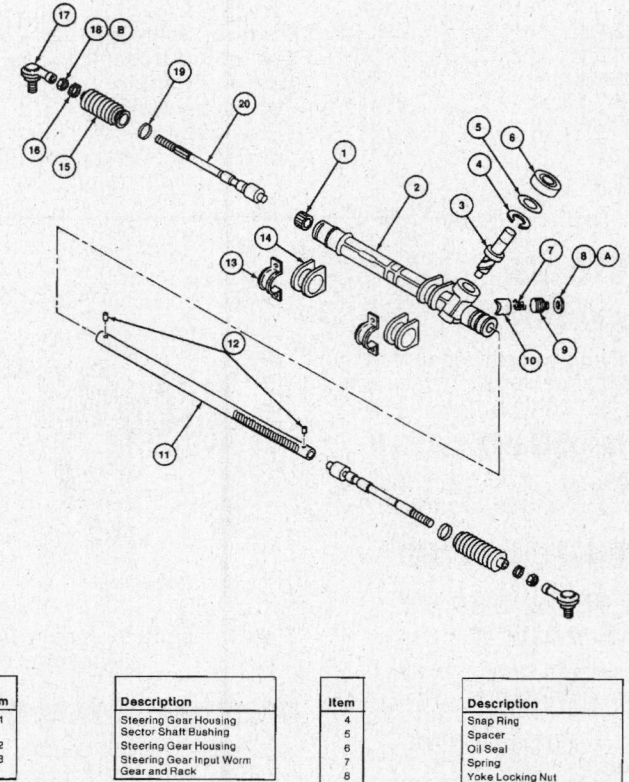

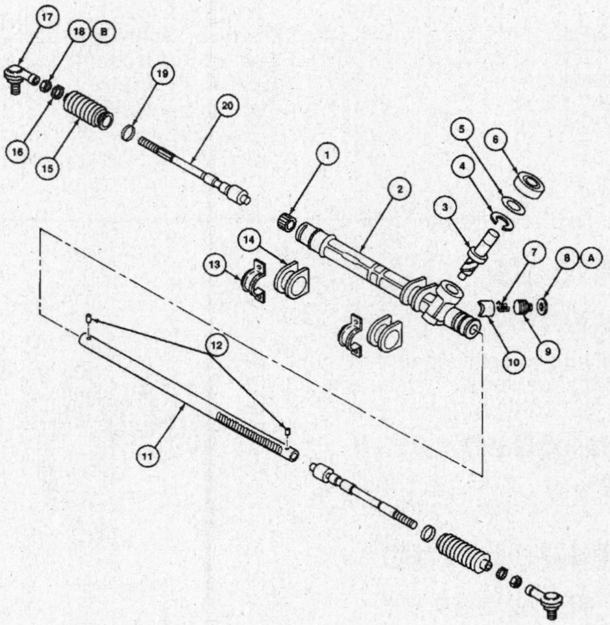

Item	Description	Item	Description
1	Steering Gear Housing Sector Shaft Bushing	4	Snap Ring
2	Steering Gear Housing	5	Spacer
3	Steering Gear Input Worm Gear and Rack	6	Oil Seal
		7	Spring
		8	Yoke Locking Nut

FM6039500031010X

Fig. 3 Exploded view of steering gear assembly (Part 1 of 2)

Item	Description	Item	Description
9	Yoke Plug	17	Tie Rod End (2 Req'd)
10	Support Yoke	18	Tie Rod End Jam Nut (2 Req'd)
11	Steering Gear Sector Shaft	19	Front Suspension Steering Ball Stud Dust Seal Wire (2 Req'd)
12	Lock Pin (2 Req'd)	20	Front Wheel Spindle Tie Rod (2 Req'd)
13	Steering Gear Mounting Bracket (2 Req'd)	A	Tighten to 39-49 N·m (29-36 Lb-Ft)
14	Steering Gear Insulator (2 Req'd)	B	Tighten to 34-50 N·m (25-36 Lb-Ft)
15	Front Suspension Steering Ball Stud Dust Seal (2 Req'd)		
16	Front Suspension Steering Ball Stud Dust Seal Clamp (2 Req'd)		

FM6039500031020X

Fig. 3 Exploded view of steering gear assembly (Part 2 of 2)

rack using lithium-based greased. **Ensure rack vent holes remain open and are not clogged with grease after lubrication.**

2. Install rack support bushing into right end of housing, engaging lock tabs with housing slots.
3. If lower pinion bearing requires replacement, install it at this time into housing using suitable bushing installer.
4. Install rack through left side of housing. Ensure rack teeth face pinion bore. When properly positioned, left side of rack should extend approximately 2.4 inches from end of housing, **Fig. 4.**
5. Install pinion and upper bearing assembly into housing. When bearing is fully seated, pinion notch for steering column universal joint clamp bolt should face forward 35-55° as seen from top end of pinion shaft when rack is centered, **Fig. 4.**

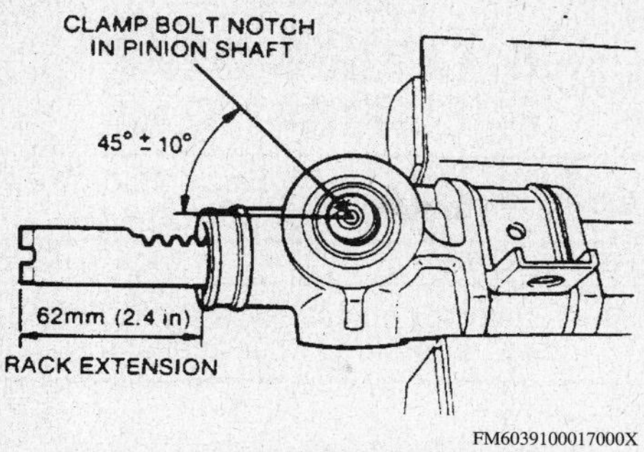

Fig. 4 Rack & pinion/bearing assembly installation

6. Install pinion bearing snap ring with beveled side facing upward, then the seal spacer tabbed side down. Ensure tab is positioned in snap ring gap.
7. Wrap pinion shaft teeth with suitable tape to prevent damage to oil seal lip, then drive seal into housing using suitable tool.
8. Place new ball joint tab washers on rack ends, then install tie rods onto rack and tighten to specifications.
9. Using a suitable punch, stake tab washer lips into notches on rack, then bend washer tabs against flats on ball joints.
10. Install boots and tie rod ends.
11. Install rack support yoke, spacer and yoke spring into housing. Ensure spacer is positioned with raised center facing outward.
12. Apply sealant to yoke cover threads, then install cover and tighten to specifications.
13. Check and adjust rack yoke preload adjustment as outlined under "Adjustments."

STEERING GEAR SPECIFICATIONS

Gear Type	Rack Preload, Inch Lbs.
Rack & Pinion	①

① — Refer to "Adjustments" in this section for preload specifications.

TIGHTENING SPECIFICATIONS

Component	Torque/Ft. Lbs.
Front Wheel Spindle Tie Rods	8-10
Steering Column Gear Input Shaft Coupling Bolt	13–20
Steering Gear Bolts	27–38
Tie Rod End Jam Nut	25-36
Tie Rod End Nut	31-41
Wheel Hub Bolts	65–87
Yoke Locking Nut	29–36

POWER STEERING

TABLE OF CONTENTS

Power Steering Pressure Specifications

Year	Vehicle	Engine	Minimum Flow①②	Minimum Relief Pressure, psi	Maximum Relief Pressure, psi	Pump Model③	Maximum Free Flow @ 1500 RPM①
1997	Aspire	1.3L	–	1067	1138	–	–
	Continental	4.6L	1.7	1300	1480	HBD-AX & 3A674	2.7
	Contour	2.0L	.9	1050	1230	HBD-AE	2.6
		2.5L	1.25	1050	1380	HBD-AE	2.6
	Cougar	3.8L④	.95	1200	1380	HBC-JW	2.6
		4.6L⑦	1.14	1200	1380	HBD-AN	2.7⑥
	Crown Victoria	4.6L	1.4	1200	1380	CIII	3.2⑤
	Escort	2.0L	1.15	1117	1247	CIII	2.4
	Grand Marquis	4.6L	1.4	1200	1380	CIII	3.2⑤
	Mark VIII	4.6L	1.4	1200	1380	HBD-AN	2.7
	Mustang	3.8L	.9	1050	1230	HBC-KC	–
		4.6L	1.25	1200	1380	HBD-CA	–
	Mystique	2.0L	.9	1050	1230	HBD-AE	2.6
		2.5L	1.25	1050	1380	HBD-AE	2.6
	Probe	2.0L	–	1210	1270	–	–
		2.5L	–	1210	1270	–	–
	Sable	3.0L (2V)	.9	1300	1480	HBC-LC	2.3
		3.0L (4V)	.9	1300	1480	HBC-BM	2.3
	Taurus	3.0L (2V)	.9	1300	1480	HBC-LC	2.3
		3.0L (4V)	.9	1300	1480	HBC-BM	2.3
		3.4L	2.0	1470	1590	ZUA	2.6
	Thunderbird	3.8L④	.95	1200	1380	HBC-JW	2.6
		4.6L⑦	1.14	1200	1380	HBD-AN	2.7⑥
	Tracer	2.0L	1.15	1117	1247	CIII	2.4
	Town Car	4.6L	1.4	1200	1380	CIII	3.2⑤
1998	Continental	4.6L	1.7	1300	1480	HBD-AX & 3A674	2.7
	Contour	2.0L & 2.5L	1.15	—	1380	HBD-AE	2.4
	Crown Victoria	4.6L	1.4	1200	1380	CIII	3.2⑤
	Escort	2.0L	1.15	1117	1247	CIII	2.4
	Grand Marquis	4.6L	1.4	1200	1380	CIII	3.2⑤
	Mark VIII	4.6L	1.4	1200	1380	HBD-AN	2.7
	Mustang	3.8L	.9	1050	1230	HBC-KC	–
		4.6L	1.25	1200	1380	HBD-CA	–
	Mystique	2.0L & 2.5L	1.15	—	1380	HBD-AE	2.4
	Sable	3.0L (2V)	.9	1300	1480	HBC-LC	2.3
		3.0L (4V)	.9	1300	1480	HBC-BM	2.3
	Taurus	3.0L (2V)	.9	1300	1480	HBC-LC	2.3
		3.0L (4V)	.9	1300	1480	HBC-BM	2.3
		3.4L	2.0	1470	1590	ZUA	2.6
	Town Car	4.6L	1.4	1200	1380	CIII	3.2⑤
	Tracer	2.0L	1.15	1117	1247	CIII	2.4
	ZX2	2.0L	1.15	1117	1247	CIII	2.4

Continued

Year	Vehicle	Engine	Minimum Flow①②	Minimum Relief Pressure, psi	Maximum Relief Pressure, psi	Pump Model③	Maximum Free Flow @ 1500 RPM①
1999	Continental	4.6L	1.7	1300	1480	HBD-AX & 3A674	2.7
	Contour	2.0L & 2.5L	1.15	—	1380	HBD-AE	2.4
	Cougar	2.0L & 2.5L	1.13	1200	1380	HBD-AE	2.4⑤
	Crown Victoria	4.6L	1.4	1200	1380	CIII	3.2⑤
	Escort	2.0L	1.15	1117	1247	CIII	2.4
	Grand Marquis	4.6L	1.4	1200	1380	CIII	3.2⑤
	Mustang	3.8L	.9	1050	1230	C11	2.6
		4.6L	1.25	1200	1380	C111	2.6
	Mystique	2.0L & 2.5L	1.15	—	1380	HBD-AE	2.4
	Sable	3.0L (2V)	.9	1300	1480	HBC-LC	2.3
		3.0L (4V)	.9	1300	1480	HBC-BM	2.3
	Taurus	3.0L (2V)	.9	1300	1480	HBC-LC	2.3
		3.0L (4V)	.9	1300	1480	HBC-BM	2.3
		3.4L	2.0	1470	1590	ZUA	2.6
	Town Car	4.6L	1.4	1200	1380	CIII	3.2⑤
	Tracer	2.0L	1.15	1117	1247	CIII	2.4
	ZX2	2.0L	1.15	1117	1247	CIII	2.4
2000	Continental	4.6L	1.7	1300	1480	HBD-AX & 3A674	2.7
	Crown Victoria	4.6L	1.4	1200	1380	CIII	3.2⑤
	Grand Marquis	4.6L	1.4	1200	1380	CIII	3.2⑤
	LS	3.0L	1.4	1400	1530	3A674	2.4
		3.9L	1.4	1400	1530	3A674	2.4
	Mustang	3.8L	.9	1050	1230	CII	2.6
		4.6L	1.25	1200	1380	CIII	2.6

① — Gallons per minute.
② — Flow is dependent on pump model, engine RPM & pulley ratio. Engine idle speed must be within specifications when checking minimum flow.
③ — Power steering pump identification tag is located on the reservoir body.
④ — Base model.
⑤ — At 2500 RPM.
⑥ — Measured w/vehicle not moving.
⑦ — EVO variable assist.

Power Steering Pump Application Chart

Year	Model	Type	Page No.
1997	Aspire	4	16-10
	Continental	2	16-6
	Contour	5	16-12
	Cougar w/3.8L	2	16-6
	Cougar w/4.6L	5	16-12
	Crown Victoria	5	16-12
	Escort/Tracer	2	16-6
	Grand Marquis	5	16-12
	Mark VIII	5	16-12
	Mustang w/3.8L	2	16-6
	Mustang w/4.6L	5	16-12
	Mystique	5	16-12
	Probe	3	16-10
	Sable w/3.0L (2V)	2	16-6
	Sable w/3.0L (4V)	5	16-12
	Taurus w/3.0L (2V)	2	16-6
	Taurus w/3.0L (4V)	5	16-12
	Taurus SHO	1	16-6
	Thunderbird w/3.8L	2	16-6
	Thunderbird w/4.6L	5	16-12
1998	Continental	2	16-6
	Contour	5	16-12
	Crown Victoria	5	16-12
	Escort	5	16-12
	Grand Marquis	5	16-12
	Mark VIII	5	16-12
	Mustang w/3.8L	2	16-6
	Mustang w/4.6L	5	16-12
	Mystique	5	16-12
	Sable w/3.0L (2V)	2	16-6
	Sable w/3.0L (4V)	5	16-12
	Taurus w/3.0L (2V)	2	16-6
	Taurus w/3.0L (4V)	5	16-12
	Taurus SHO	1	16-6
	Town Car	5	16-12
	Tracer	5	16-12
	ZX2	5	16-12
1999	Continental	2	16-6
	Contour	5	16-12
	Cougar	5	16-12
	Crown Victoria	5	16-12
	Escort	5	16-12
	Grand Marquis	5	16-12
	Mustang w/3.8L	2	16-6
	Mustang w/4.6L	5	16-12
	Mystique	5	16-12
	Sable w/3.0L (2V)	2	16-6
	Sable w/3.0 (4V)	5	16-12
	Taurus w/3.0L (2V)	2	16-6
	Taurus w/3.0 (4V)	5	16-12
	Taurus SHO 3.4L	1	16-6
	Tracer	5	16-12
	Town Car	5	16-12

Continued

Year	Model	Type	Page No.
1999	ZX2	5	16-12
2000	Continental	2	16-6
	Crown Victoria	5	16-12
	Grand Marquis	5	16-12
	LS	2	16-6
	Mustang w/3.8L	2	16-6
	Mustang w/4.6L	5	16-12

Power Steering Gear Application Chart

Year	Model	Type	Page No.
1997	Aspire	4	16-25
	Continental	2①	16-14
	Contour	2	16-14
	Cougar	2①	16-14
	Crown Victoria	3①	16-21
	Escort	2	16-14
	Grand Marquis	3①	16-21
	Mark VIII	2①	16-14
	Mustang	2	16-14
	Mystique	2	16-14
	Probe	1	16-12
	Sable	2①	16-14
	Taurus	2①	16-14
	Thunderbird	2①	16-14
	Tracer	2	16-14
	Town Car	3①	16-21
1998	Continental	2①	16-14
	Contour	2	16-14
	Crown Victoria	3	16-21
	Escort	2	16-14
	Grand Marquis	3	16-21
	Mark VIII	2①	16-14
	Mustang	2	16-14
	Mystique	2	16-14
	Sable	2①	16-14
	Taurus	2①	16-14
	Tracer	2	16-14
	Town Car	3	16-21
	ZX2	2	16-14
1999	Continental	2①	16-14
	Contour	2	16-14
	Cougar	2	16-14
	Crown Victoria	3	16-21
	Escort	2	16-14
	Grand Marquis	3	16-21
	Mustang	2	16-14
	Mystique	2	16-14
	Sable	2①	16-14
	Taurus	2①	16-14
	Town Car	3	16-21
	Tracer	2	16-14
	ZX2	2	16-14

Continued

Year	Model	Type	Page No.
2000	Continental	2①	16-14
	Crown Victoria	3	16-21
	Grand Marquis	3	16-21
	LS	2	16-14
	Mustang	2	16-14

① — Refer to "Power Steering Assist Systems."

Power Steering Assist System Application Chart

Year	Model	Type	Page No.
1997–99	Cougar	1	16-28
	Crown Victoria	1	16-28
	Grand Marquis	1	16-28
	Mark VIII	1	16-28
	Sable	2	16-58
	Taurus	2	16-58
	Thunderbird	1	16-28
	Town Car	1	16-28
2000	Crown Victoria	1	16-28
	Grand Marquis	1	16-28

Type 1-ZUA Vane-Type Pump

NOTE: These Pumps Are Not Serviceable. If Service Is Necessary, Pump Must Be Replaced.

Type 2-Ford Model CII Slipper-Type Pump

INDEX

PRECAUTIONS

AIR BAG SYSTEMS

Refer to "Air Bag System Precautions" in the front of this manual for system disarming and arming procedures.

BATTERY GROUND CABLE

Prior to service, disconnect battery ground cable and isolate as required.

DESCRIPTION

The Ford model CII power steering pump is a belt driven 10-slipper type pump incorporating a fiberglass filled nylon reservoir. The reservoir is attached to the rear side of the aluminum pump housing assembly. The pump body is encased within the housing and reservoir assembly. The pump design incorporates a pump pressure fitting which allows the pump pressure line to swivel. A pressure sensitive identification tag is attached to the reservoir body. This tag indicates the basic model number and the suffix.

TROUBLESHOOTING

POWER STEERING PUMP LEAKS

1. Excessive fluid fill.

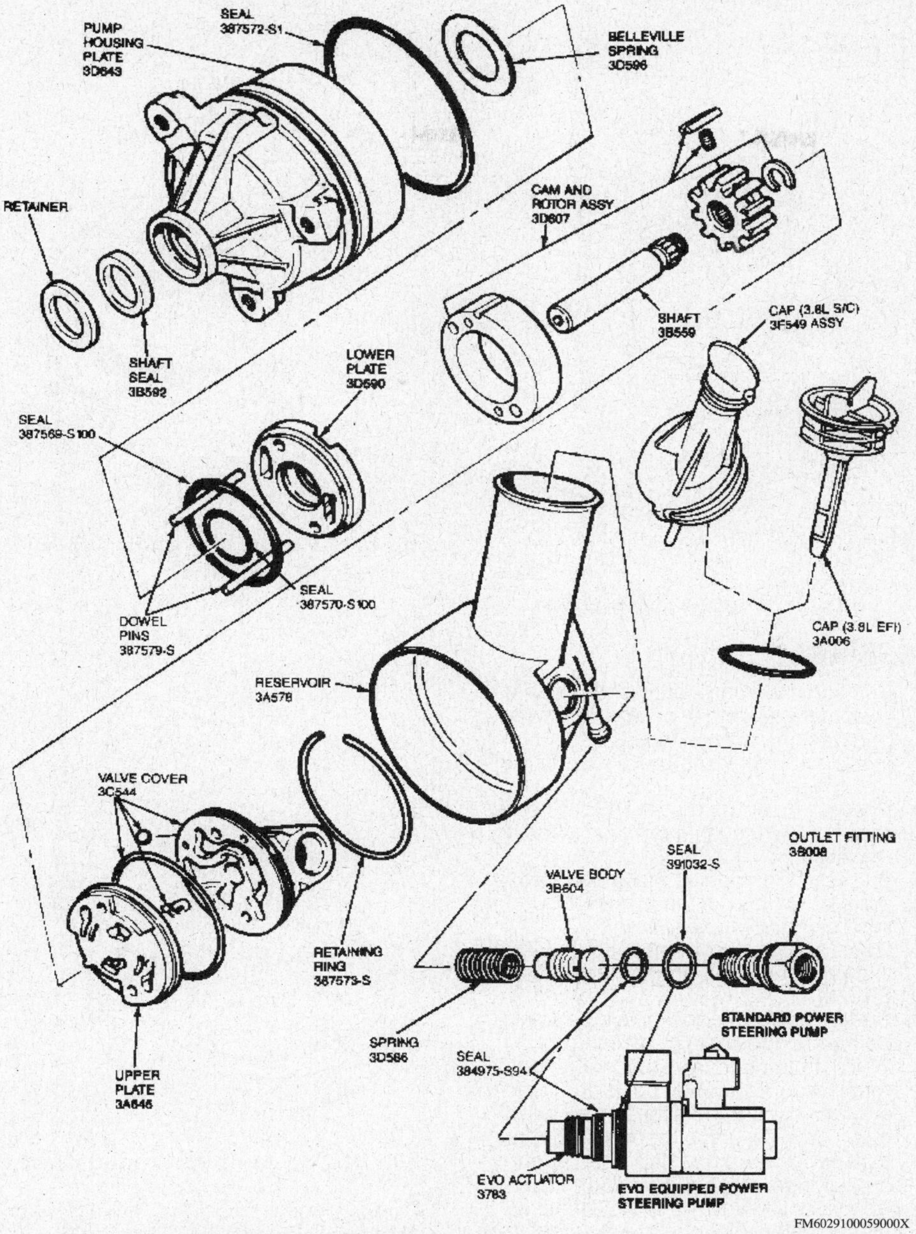

Fig. 1 Exploded view of Ford Model CII power steering pump

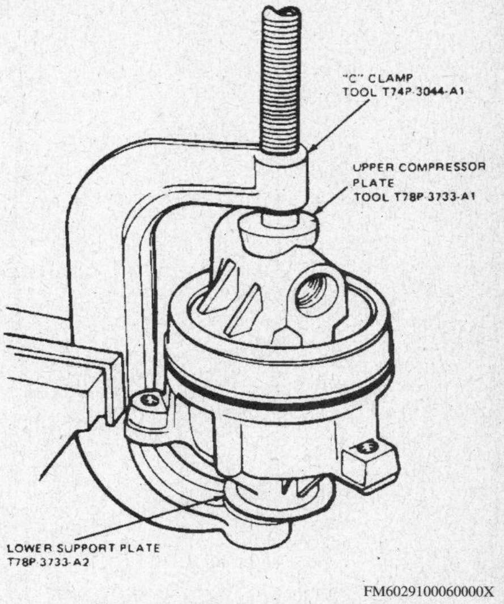

Fig. 2 Positioning pump in C-clamp

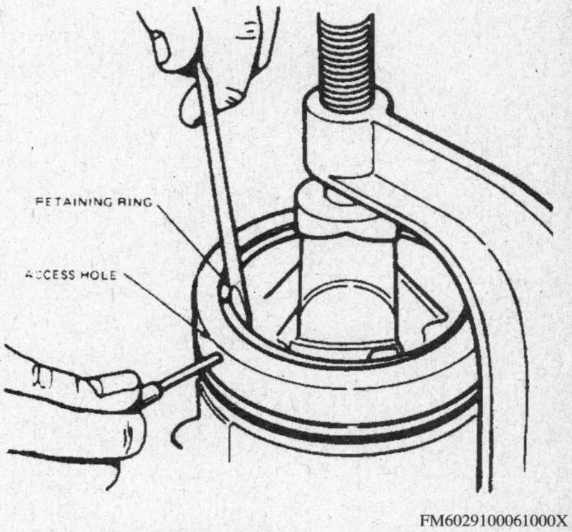

Fig. 3 Valve cover retaining ring removal

2. Dipstick missing, loose, damaged or missing O-ring.
3. Broken or cracked fluid reservoir.
4. Loose or damaged hose fittings.
5. Shaft seal not pressed flush with housing surface.
6. Shaft seal damage.
7. Rotor shaft damage, helical grooving or OD has an axial scratch.
8. Shaft bushing worn.
9. Plugged drainback hole.
10. Damaged or missing reservoir O-ring.
11. Damaged or missing outlet fitting O-rings.
12. Excessive pump assembly bracket vibration.
13. Plate and bushing reservoir seal groove damage, metal chips or foreign material in seal groove.
14. Faulty outlet fitting.

POWER STEERING PUMP NOISE, MOAN OR WHINE

1. Fluid aeration.
2. Low fluid.
3. Hose grounded.
4. Steering column grounded.
5. Valve cover O-ring or baffle missing or damaged.
6. Interference between components in pumping elements.
7. Loose or poor bracket alignment.
8. Cam contour damaged.

COMPONENT SERVICE

DISASSEMBLE

1. Remove pulley from pump, **Fig. 1.**
2. Remove outlet fitting, flow control valve and flow control valve spring from pump, then remove reservoir.
3. Place a suitable C-clamp in a vise.
4. Position lower support plate tool No. T78P-3733-A2, or equivalent, over pump rotor shaft.
5. Install upper compressor plate tool No. T78P-3733-A1, or equivalent, into upper portion of C-clamp.
6. While holding Compressor tool, place

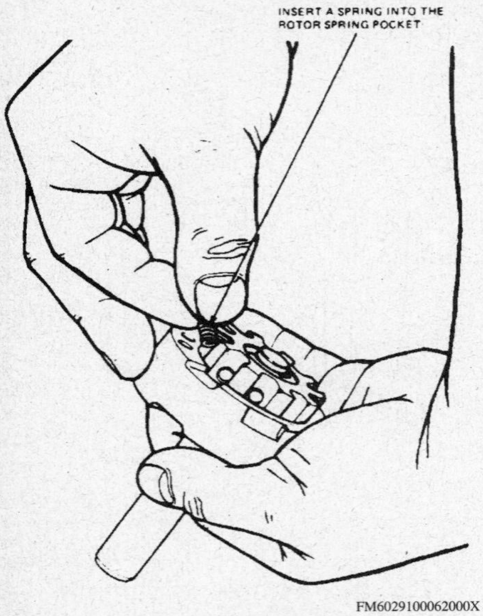
INSERT A SPRING INTO THE
ROTOR SPRING POCKET
FM6029100062000X

Fig. 4 Slipper springs installation

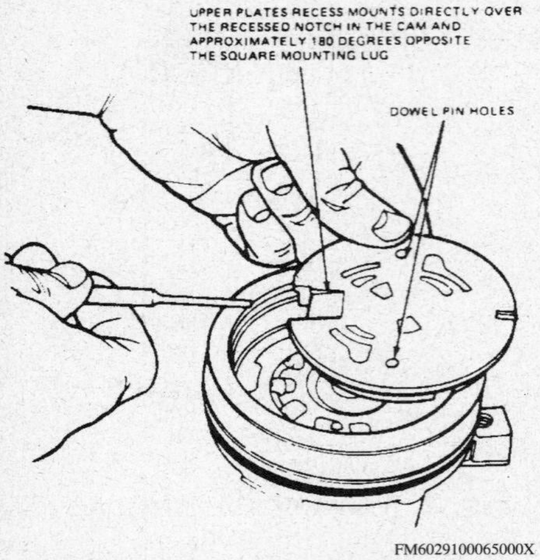
UPPER PLATES RECESS MOUNTS DIRECTLY OVER
THE RECESSED NOTCH IN THE CAM AND
APPROXIMATELY 180 DEGREES OPPOSITE
THE SQUARE MOUNTING LUG
DOWEL PIN HOLES
FM6029100065000X

Fig. 7 Upper pressure plate installation

pump assembly into C-clamp with rotor shaft facing downward, **Fig. 2.**

7. Tighten C-clamp until a slight bottoming of valve cover is observed.
8. Through small hole located on side of pump housing, insert a suitable drift and push inward on valve cover snap ring. While pushing inward on snap ring, place a screwdriver under snap ring edge and remove ring from housing, **Fig. 3.**
9. Loosen C-clamp and remove lower support plate tool No. T78P-3733-A2, or equivalent, then remove pump assembly.
10. Remove pump valve cover and O-ring.
11. Remove rotor shaft, upper plate, cam and rotor assembly and two dowel pins.
12. Remove lower plate and spring, by tapping housing on a flat surface.
13. Using a suitable screwdriver, remove rotor shaft seal.

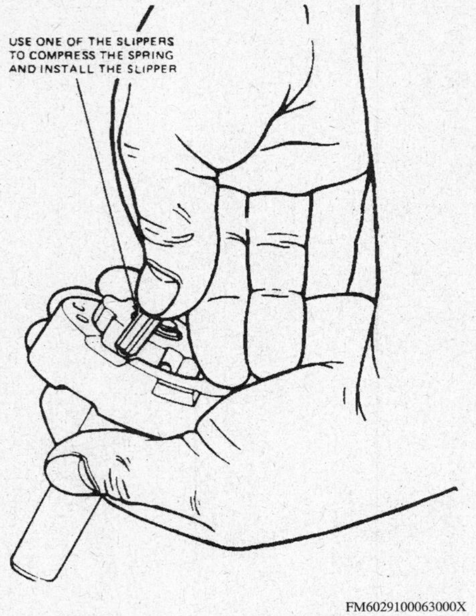
USE ONE OF THE SLIPPERS
TO COMPRESS THE SPRING
AND INSTALL THE SLIPPER
FM6029100063000X

Fig. 5 Slipper installation

ASSEMBLE

1. Position rotor on rotor shaft splines with triangle detent on rotor counterbore facing upward, **Fig. 1.**
2. Install snap ring into groove on end of rotor shaft.
3. Position insert cam over rotor. Ensure recessed notch on insert cam is facing upward.
4. With rotor extended upward approximately half out of cam, insert spring into rotor pocket, **Fig. 4.**
5. Use a slipper to compress spring, then install slipper with groove facing cam, **Fig. 5.**
6. Perform steps 4 and 5 on slipper cavity beneath opposite inlet recess.
7. While holding cam stationary, index rotor left or right one space and install another spring and slipper until all ten rotor cavities have been filled. Use care when turning rotor that springs and slippers remain in position.
8. Apply Loctite No. 242 or 271 adhesive, or equivalent, to outside diameter of seal and Locquic NF or T primer, or equivalent, to seal bore in housing. Install rotor shaft seal using seal driver tool No. T78P-3733-A3, or equivalent. Using a plastic mallet, drive seal into bore until properly seated.
9. Position pump plate on flat surface with pulley side facing downward.
10. Install two dowel pins and spring into housing. **Spring must be inserted with dished surface facing upward.**
11. Lubricate inner and outer O-ring seals with power steering fluid, then install seals on lower pressure plate.
12. Install lower pressure plate into housing and over dowel pin with O-ring seals facing toward front of pump. Position assembly on C-clamp. Place seal driver tool No. T78P-3733-A3, or equivalent, into rotor shaft hole and press on lower plate lightly until it bot-

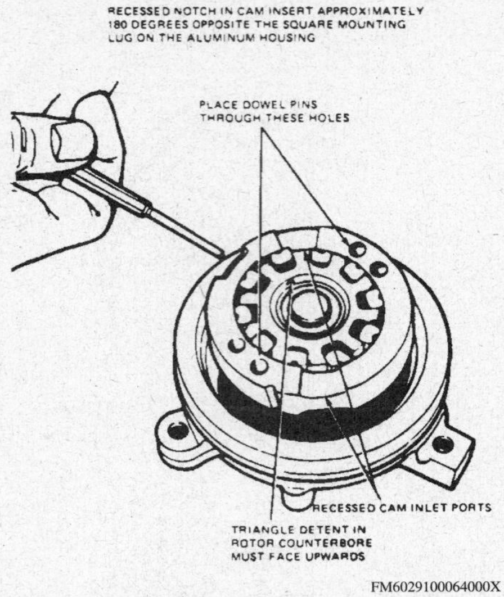
RECESSED NOTCH IN CAM INSERT APPROXIMATELY
180 DEGREES OPPOSITE THE SQUARE MOUNTING
LUG ON THE ALUMINUM HOUSING
PLACE DOWEL PINS
THROUGH THESE HOLES
RECESSED CAM INLET PORTS
TRIANGLE DETENT IN
ROTOR COUNTERBORE
MUST FACE UPWARDS
FM6029100064000X

Fig. 6 Assembling cam, slippers & rotor

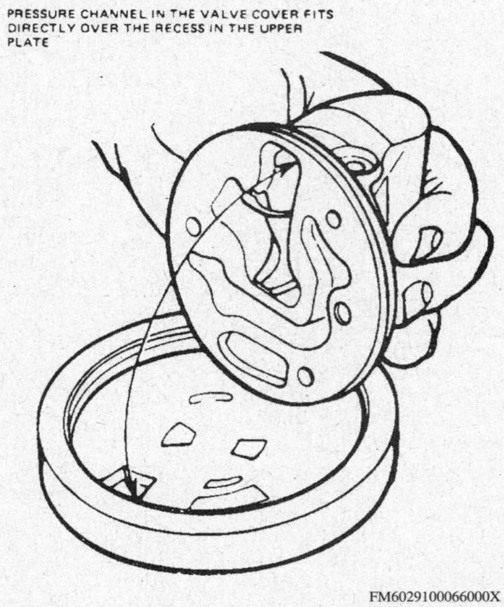
PRESSURE CHANNEL IN THE VALVE COVER FITS
DIRECTLY OVER THE RECESS IN THE UPPER
PLATE
FM6029100066000X

Fig. 8 Valve cover installation

toms in pump housing. This will seat the outer O-ring seal.

13. Install cam, rotor and slippers and rotor shaft assembly into pump housing over dowel pins. When installing assembly into pump housing, stepped holes must be used for dowel pins and notch in cam insert must be toward reservoir and approximately 180° opposite square mounting lug on housing, **Fig. 6.**
14. Position upper pressure plate over dowel pins with recess directly over recessed notch on cam insert and approximately 180° opposite square mounting lug, **Fig. 7.**
15. Lubricate O-ring seal with power steering fluid, then position O-ring on valve cover. Ensure plastic baffle is securely in position on valve cover. A coat of petroleum jelly may be used to hold baffle in position.

16. Insert valve cover over dowel pins. Ensure outlet fitting hole in valve cover is aligned with square mounting lug on housing, **Fig. 8.**
17. Place assembly in C-clamp and compress valve cover into pump housing until snap ring groove on housing is exposed.
18. Install valve cover snap ring in pump housing. Ensure snap ring ends are near access hole in pump housing.
19. Remove pump assembly from C-clamp.
20. Lubricate O-ring seal with power steering fluid, then place seal on pump housing.
21. Install reservoir on pump housing.
22. Install flow control valve and spring into valve cover.
23. Lubricate O-ring seals with power steering fluid, then place seals on outlet fitting.
24. Install outlet fitting on valve cover. Tighten outlet fitting to specifications. Use care not to cock flow control valve when installing. Do not force valve forward otherwise damage to housing may result.

TIGHTENING SPECIFICATIONS

THUNDERBIRD & 1997 COUGAR

Year	Component	Torque/Ft. Lbs.
1997	Front Bolts To Support Bracket	30–45
	Outlet Fitting	25–34
	Pivot Bolt	30–45
	Pump To Bracket	30–45
	Pump Bracket To Rear Support	18–24
	Quick Connect Power Steering Fitting	20–25
	Rear Support To Engine Head	30–45
	Return Hose To Pump (Hose Clamp)	12–24①
	Support Bracket To Engine	30–45
	Support Bracket To Water Pump Housing	30–45

① — Inch lbs.

MUSTANG

Year	Component	Torque/Ft. Lbs.
1997-98	Front Bolts To Support Bracket	30–45
	Outlet Fitting To Reservoir & Valve Cover	25–34
	Pivot Bolt	30–45
	Pressure Hose Tube Nut To Pump Pressure Fitting	10–25
	Pump To Bracket	30–45
	Pump Bracket To Rear Support	①
	Rear Support To Engine Head	30–45
	Return Hose To Pump (Hose Clamp)	12–24②
	Support Bracket To Engine	30–45
	Support Bracket To Water Pump Housing	30–45
1999-2000	Power Steering Pump Mounting Bolts	38
	Pressure Line Fitting At Pump	30

① — Less A/C, 30–45 ft. lbs., with A/C, 18–24 ft. lbs.
② — Inch lbs.

SABLE & TAURUS

Year	Component	Torque/Ft. Lbs.
1997–99	Hose Bracket	84-96①
	Pressure Hose Fitting	24–30
	Return Hose Fitting	24–30
	Support Bracket	17–24

① — Inch lbs.

Type 3-Mazda Vane-Type Pump

NOTE: These Pumps Are Not Serviceable. If Service Is Necessary, Pump Must Be Replaced.

Type 4-Aspire Vane-Type Pump

INDEX

PRECAUTIONS

AIR BAG SYSTEMS

Refer to "Air Bag System Precautions" in the front of this manual for system disarming and arming procedures.

BATTERY GROUND CABLE

Prior to service, disconnect battery ground cable and isolate as required.

DESCRIPTION

The power steering pump generates hydraulic pressure to reduce the effort required to turn the steering wheel.

The power steering pump is mounted on the front of the engine. The pump has a vane-type deign, and is driven by the crankshaft through a drive belt and pulley. Fluid is drawn into the pump from the reservoir when the engine is running. the fluid is pressurized by the rotation of the rotor and vanes, then sent to the steering gear.

Fluid pressure is monitored and regulated by a Power Steering Pressure Switch (PSP Switch) and a control valve located in the power steering pump.

TROUBLESHOOTING

HEAVY STEERING WHEEL MOVEMENT

1. Loose or damaged belt.
2. Low fluid level or air in fluid.
3. Twisted or crimped hose or pipe.
4. Fluid leakage.
5. Low hydraulic pressure.
6. Insufficient tire pressure.
7. Improperly adjusted wheel alignment.
8. Faulty ball joint linkage.
9. Binding steering shaft.

POOR STEERING WHEEL RETURN

1. Incorrect tire pressure.
2. Improperly adjusted wheel alignment.
3. Faulty ball joint linkage.

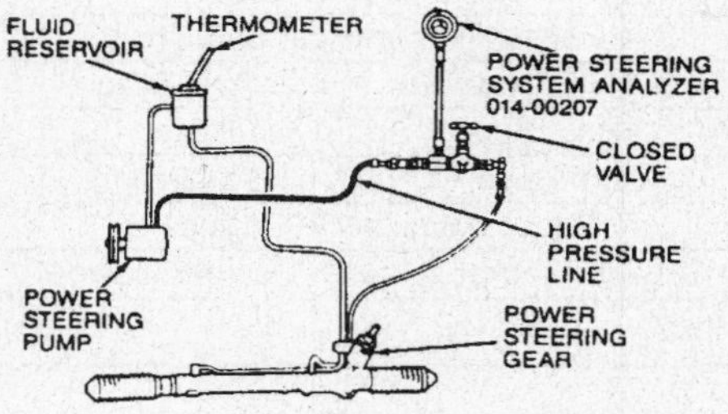

Fig. 1 Pressure test connections

4. Restricted, over tightened or bent steering shaft.

UNEVEN STEERING EFFORT

1. Loose belt.
2. Loose steering shaft bolt(s).
3. Rough steering linkage operation.
4. Faulty steering gear.

STEERING WHEEL PULLS

1. Incorrect tire pressure.
2. Improper preload adjustment.
3. Faulty wheel bearing.
4. Improperly adjusted wheel alignment.
5. Faulty steering gear.

FLUID LEAKAGE

1. Hose coupling.
2. Damaged or clogged hose.
3. Faulty reservoir tank.
4. Faulty steering pump.
5. Faulty steering gear.

ABNORMAL NOISE

1. Loose power steering pump.
2. Loose steering gear.
3. Loose pump bracket.
4. Loose pump pulley nut.
5. Improperly adjusted belt.
6. Faulty steering gear.
7. Faulty steering pump.
8. Obstruction near steering column or pressure hose.
9. Fluid aeration.
10. Loose steering linkage.

DIAGNOSIS & TESTING

POWER STEERING PRESSURE TEST

During the following procedure, power steering pressure may exceed 1200 psi. Ensure proper tool alignment prior to performing test. Exercise extreme caution or damage and/or personal injury may result.

1. Disconnect power steering pump pressure hose where it connects to tubing. Install power steering system analyzer tool No. 014-00207 and adapter tool No. 014-00454, or equivalents, **torque** fitting to 29–36 ft. lbs., **Fig. 1.**
2. Position thermometer in power steering pump reservoir. **Ensure gauge valve is open to allow normal system function. Do not hold steering wheel against a stop for more than 10 seconds at a time.**
3. Start engine, then slowly turn steering wheel from lock to lock ten times to bleed system.
4. If required, turn steering wheel fully left and right several times to raise fluid temperature to 122–140°F (50–60°C). **Gauge valve must be briefly closed to read operating pressures. Do not leave valve closed for more than 15 seconds.**
5. To measure pump output pressure, close gauge set valve, then increase engine speed to 1000–1500 RPM, read pressure, then open valve. Operating pressure should be 1067–1138 psi, if pressure is low, repair or replace pump.
6. To measure pressure at gear, open valve, then increase engine speed to 1000–1500 RPM, turn steering wheel fully left and right, read pressure. Operating pressure should be 1067–1138 psi, if pressure is low, repair or replace steering gear.
7. Remove gauge set and adapter, connect high pressure hose and **torque** fitting to 29–36 ft. lbs.
8. Remove thermometer, then start engine, slowly turn steering wheel lock to

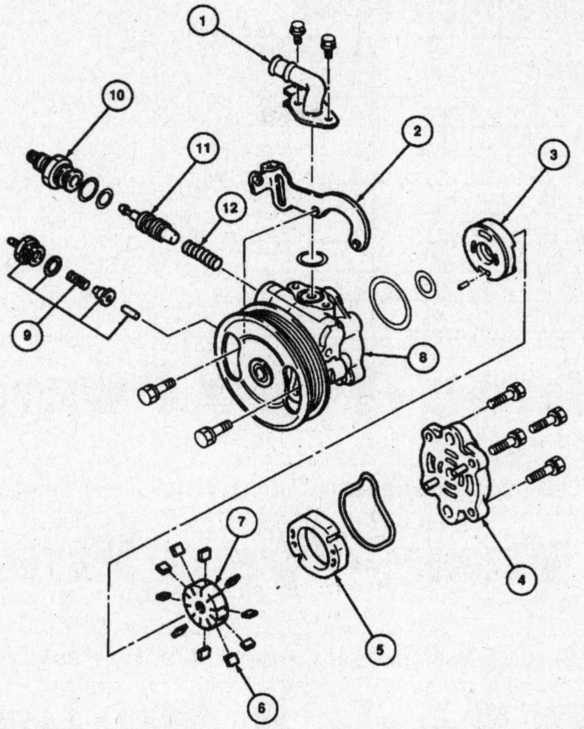

Item	Description
1	Supply Tube
2	Power Steering Pump Support
3	Side Plate
4	Rear Body
5	Cam Ring
6	Vanes

Item	Description
7	Rotor
8	Front Body
9	Power Steering Pressure Switch
10	Power Steering Pump Valve Outlet Fitting
11	Valve
12	Spring

FM6029400197000X

Fig. 2 Exploded view of power steering pump. Aspire

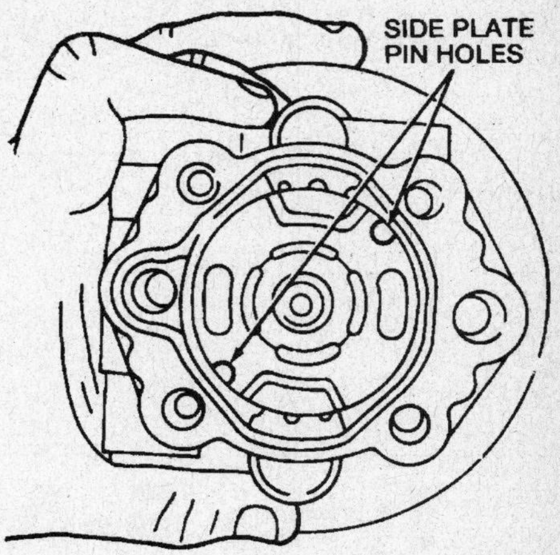

FM6029400198000X

Fig. 3 Side plate alignment

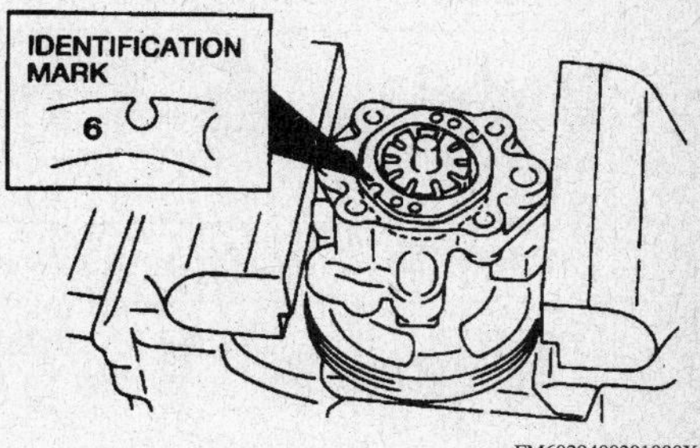

FM6029400201000X

Fig. 6 Cam ring installation. Aspire

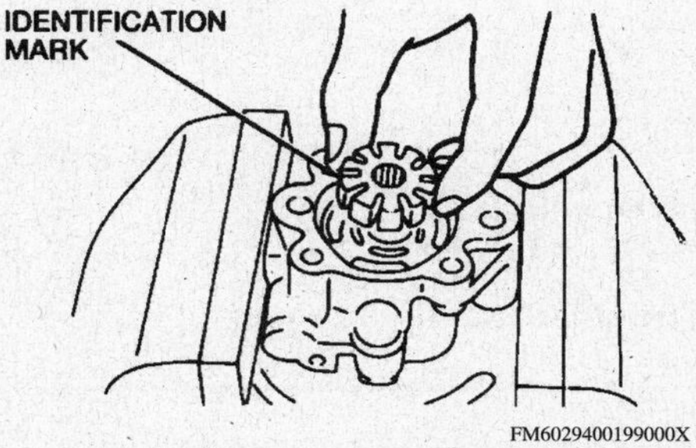

FM6029400199000X

Fig. 4 Rotor installation

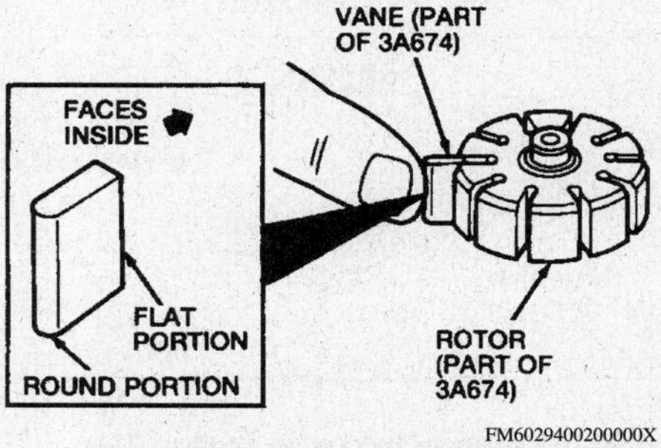

FM6029400200000X

Fig. 5 Vane installation

lock ten times to bleed system.

COMPONENT SERVICE

OVERHAUL

1. Remove air cleaner and intake tube.
2. Disconnect wiring connector from power steering pressure (PSP) switch.
3. Disconnect and plug power steering reservoir pump hose.
4. Disconnect and plug power steering pressure hose.
5. Loosen, but do not remove pump bolts.
6. Loosen drive belt adjusting bolt and drive belt tensioner shaft, then remove drive belt.
7. Remove power steering pump.
8. Secure pump in vise with protective jaws. Pulley should be on top in horizontal position.
9. Remove pump support bolts and support, **Fig. 2.**
10. Remove supply tube bolts and tubes.
11. Remove supply O-ring.
12. Remove pressure switch (PSP), O-ring, spring, seat and plunger.
13. Remove valve outlet fitting, then O-ring from fitting.
14. Remove valve and spring from valve bore.
15. Reposition pump in vise to remove four rear body bolts, then lift off rear body cover.
16. Remove rear body O-ring, cam ring, rotor and vanes.
17. Remove side plate and O-rings
18. Reverse procedure to install, noting:
    a. Replace O-rings with new parts.
    b. Align side plate, **Fig. 3,** to ease installation.
    c. Install rotor with identification mark facing upward, **Fig. 4.**
    d. Install vanes with round portion facing outward from rotor, **Fig. 5.**
    e. Install cam ring with identification mark facing downward, **Fig. 6.**
    f. Tighten to specification.

TIGHTENING SPECIFICATIONS

Year	Component	Torque/Ft. Lbs.
1997	High Pressure Line To Pump Fitting	29–43
	Pressure Hose Nut	12–17
	Pressure Switch (PSP)	18–22
	Pump Rear Body Bolts	13–16
	Pump Supply Tube Bolts	5–6
	Pump Valve Outlet Fitting	36–51
	Pump Through Bolt Nut	27–38
	Pump Support Bolts	22–29

Type 5-Atsugi Vane-Type Pump

NOTE: These Pumps Are Not Serviceable. If Service Is Necessary, Pump Must Be Replaced.

Type 6-Ford CIII Vane-Type Pump

NOTE: These Pumps Are Not Serviceable. If Service Is Necessary, Pump Must Be Replaced.

Type 1–TRW SSD Rack & Pinion Steering Gear

NOTE: On Air Bag Equipped Models, Refer To " Air Bag System Precautions" Located In The Front Of This Manual For System Disarming & Arming Procedures.

NOTE: Refer To "Computer Relearn Procedures " Located In The Front Of This Manual For Computer Relearn Procedures.

INDEX

PRECAUTIONS

AIR BAG SYSTEMS

Refer to "Air Bag System Precautions" in the front of this manual for system disarming and arming procedures.

BATTERY GROUND CABLE

Prior to service, disconnect battery ground cable and isolate as required.

DESCRIPTION

This power rack and pinion steering gear is a hydraulic assisted unit.

TROUBLESHOOTING

Refer to **Fig. 1,** for troubleshooting procedures.

DIAGNOSIS & TESTING

POWER STEERING PRESSURE TEST

1. Raise and support vehicle, then remove crossmember.
2. Disconnect power steering pressure line between pump and gear, allowing fluid in line to drain.
3. Attach Rotunda power steering system analyzer No. 014-00207 with adapter No. 014-00454, or equivalents, between pressure hose connection as shown in **Fig. 2. Torque** fittings to 29–36 ft. lbs.
4. Place a thermometer in pump reservoir. **Ensure valve on analyzer is OPEN to allow system to function normally. Do not hold steering wheel against stops for more than fifteen seconds at a time.**
5. Bleed system as follows:
   a. Check fluid level in reservoir and add fluid if necessary.
   b. Turn ignition switch to On position, engine not running, then turn steering wheel fully left and right ten times.

Condition	Possible Source	Action
• Steering Wheel Movement Is Hard / Difficult	• Insufficient tire pressure. • Low fluid level, or air in fluid. • Loose or damaged drive belt. • Crimped or twisted hose(s). • Crimped pipe(s). • Low hydraulic pressure. • Improperly adjusted wheel alignment. • Steering column lower yoke does not operate smoothly. • Steering column is contacting another component.	• ADJUST tire pressure. • ADD fluid, or BLEED air. CHECK for leaks in system. • INSPECT the power steering drive belt tension. • INSPECT hose(s). • INSPECT pipe(s). • PERFORM the Pump Flow and Pressure Tests • ADJUST wheel alignment. • PERFORM the Turning Effort Check in this section. • INSPECT steering column. REPAIR as necessary.

FM6029100160010A

Fig. 1 Troubleshooting chart (Part 1 of 2)

Condition	Possible Source	Action
• Poor Steering Wheel Return	• Incorrect tire pressure. • Improperly adjusted wheel alignment. • Steering column lower yoke does not operate smoothly. • Input shaft and control is over tight, restricted or bent.	• ADJUST tire pressure. • ADJUST wheel alignment. • PERFORM the Turning Effort Check in this section. • INSPECT input shaft and control. REPAIR as necessary.
• Required Steering Effort Is Uneven	• Loose power steering drive belt. • Steering column is restricted, loose installation bolt(s). • Steering column lower yoke does not operate smoothly. • Malfunction of steering gear.	• INSPECT the power steering drive belt tension. • INSPECT steering column. REPAIR as necessary. • PERFORM the Turning Effort Check in this section. • REPLACE steering gear.
• Steering Wheel Pulls to One Side	• Incorrect tire size or tire pressure. • Improper preload adjustment, or wear of front wheel bearing. • Improperly adjusted wheel alignment. • Malfunction of steering gear.	• REPLACE tires or ADJUST tire pressure. • INSPECT front wheel bearing. • ADJUST wheel alignment. • REPLACE steering gear.
• Fluid Leakage	• Problem at hose coupling. • Damaged or clogged hose. • Damaged power steering pump reservoir. • Overflow. • Malfunction of power steering pump. • Malfunction of steering gear.	• REPAIR or REPLACE hose coupling. • REPLACE hose. • REPLACE power steering pump auxiliary reservoir. • BLEED air, or ADJUST fluid level. • REPLACE power steering pump. • REPLACE steering gear.
• Abnormal Noise	• Power steering drive belt either loose or too tight. • Air in system. • Loose power steering pump pulley nut. • Loose power steering pump support. • Loose power steering pump. • Loose steering gear. • Malfunction of power steering pump. • Malfunction of steering gear. • Play or looseness of steering column lower yoke.	• INSPECT the power steering drive belt tension. ADJUST power steering drive belt. • BLEED air. • TIGHTEN power steering pump pulley nut. • TIGHTEN power steering pump support. • TIGHTEN power steering pump. • TIGHTEN steering gear. • REPLACE power steering pump. • REPLACE steering gear. • TIGHTEN, ADJUST, or REPLACE steering column lower yoke.

FM6029100160020A

Fig. 1 Troubleshooting chart (Part 2 of 2)

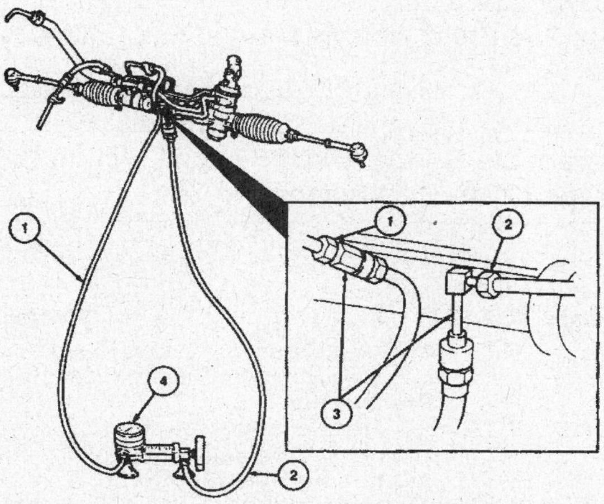

Item	Description
1	Fluid Flow from the Power Steering Pump
2	Fluid Flow to the Steering Gear
3	Power Steering Analyzer Fittings
4	Power Steering Analyzer

FM6029100161000A

Fig. 2 Connecting Rotunda power steering system analyzer

c. Recheck fluid level, add fluid if necessary.

d. Repeat steps b and c until fluid level stabilizes, then start engine and allow to idle.

e. Turn steering wheel fully left and right ten times, then verify that fluid is not foamy.

f. If air is still present in system, repeat steps b through e. **If foam is still present after repeating steps, check system for air leaks.**

g. If fluid level has decreased, add fluid and repeat step e until fluid level stabilizes.

6. Leave engine running, then if necessary, turn steering wheel fully left and right several times to raise fluid temperature to 122–140°F.
7. Close valve on analyzer briefly and increase engine speed to 1000–1500 RPM, then read pump output pressure. Pressure should be 1210–1270 psi. **Valve on analyzer must be briefly closed to read operating pressures. Do not leave valve closed for longer than 15 seconds.**
8. If pressure is too low, repair or replace pump. If pressure is too high, check for a crimped pipe and repair or replace as necessary, or replace pump.
9. Open valve on analyzer and increase engine speed to 1000–1500 RPM, then turn steering wheel all way to left or right and read pressure generated at steering gear. Pressure should be 1210–1270 psi.
10. If pressure is not within specifications, repair or replace steering gear.
11. Turn ignition to Off position, then remove analyzer and adapter.
12. Reconnect high pressure hose and tighten connection to specification, then bleed system as described in step 5.

POWER STEERING SYSTEM SERVICE

Adjustments

RACK YOKE PRELOAD

1. Remove steering gear from vehicle, then secure gear in a soft-jawed vise.
2. Measure pinion preload using pinion torque adapter No. T90-3504-JH, or equivalent. Torque at neutral position ± 90 degrees, should be 9–12 inch lbs. At any other position, torque should be 15 inch lbs.
3. If preload is not within specifications, loosen adjusting cover locknut, apply thread locking compound to exposed threads of adjusting cover, **torque** adjusting cover to 87 inch lbs. using yoke plug adapter No. T81P-3504-U, or equivalent, then loosen it. **Torque** cover again to 39–48 inch lbs., then loosen 20 degrees.
4. Install adjusting cover locknut and **torque** to 36–43 ft. lbs. using yoke locknut wrench No. T88C-3504-KH, or equivalent, while holding adjusting cover. **Do not allow adjusting cover to turn.**

Component Service

STEERING GEAR

With exception of power steering right turn pressure hose, power steering left turn pressure hose, power steering return hose, power steering pressure hose, tie rod end, front wheel spindle tie rod and front suspension steering ball stud dust seal, the steering gear is serviced as an assembly.

Type 2–Ford Integral Rack & Pinion Steering Gear

NOTE: On Air Bag Equipped Models, Refer To " Air Bag System Precautions" Located In The Front Of This Manual For System Disarming & Arming Procedures.

NOTE: Refer To "Computer Relearn Procedures " Located In The Front Of This Manual For Computer Relearn Procedures.

NOTE: Also Refer To "Type 1–Ford Variable Assist Electronic Variable Orifice (EVO) System" For Mark VIII, Thunderbird & 1997 Cougar, Models Equipped With EVO System.

INDEX

PRECAUTIONS

AIR BAG SYSTEMS

Refer to "Air Bag System Precautions" in the front of this manual for system disarming and arming procedures.

BATTERY GROUND CABLE

Prior to service, disconnect battery ground cable and isolate as required.

DESCRIPTION

These power rack and pinion steering gears, **Figs. 1 through 3.** are hydraulic-mechanical units, using an integral piston and rack to provide power assisted steering control. Internal valve controls pump flow and pressure as required during operation. The unit consists of a rotary hydraulic control valve connected to the input shaft and a boost cylinder integral with the rack.

OPERATION

The rotary control valve utilizes the relative rotational position of the input shaft and valve sleeve to control fluid flow. As the steering wheel is turned, the resistance of the wheels and weight of the vehicle cause a torsion bar to deflect, **Figs. 1 through 3.** This torsion bar deflection changes position of rotary valve and sleeve ports, thereby directing fluid under pressure to the proper end of the power cylinder. The pressure differential acting on the piston attached to the rack, provides the power assist.

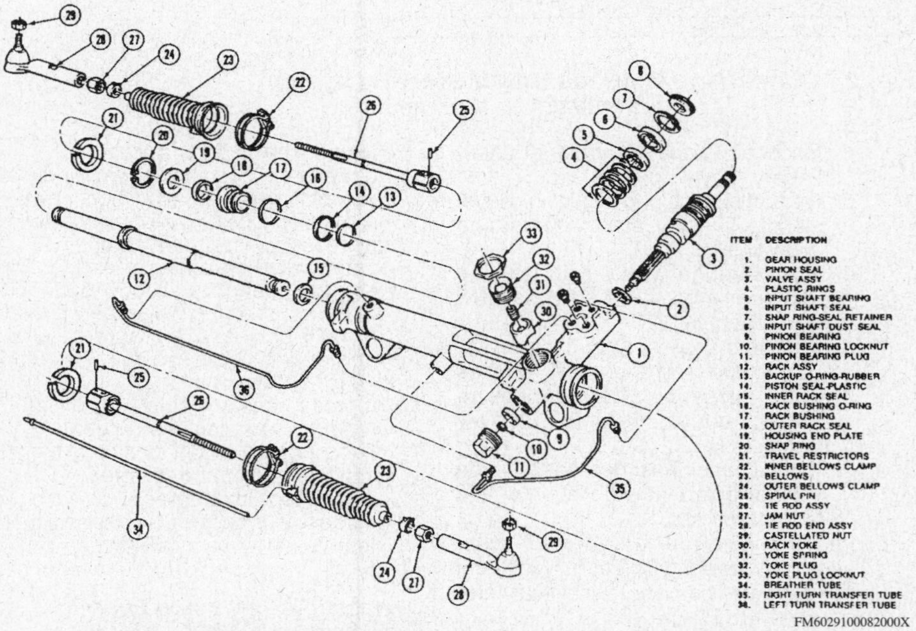

Fig. 1 Exploded view of steering gear. Mark VIII, Mustang, Thunderbird & 1997 Cougar

The control valve is forced back to a centered position by the torsion bar when steering effort is removed. Pressure is then equalized on each side of the piston and the front wheels tend to return to a straight ahead position.

TROUBLESHOOTING

Refer to **Fig. 4,** for troubleshooting procedure.

DIAGNOSIS & TESTING

POWER STEERING PRESSURE TEST

During the following procedure, power steering system pressure may exceed 1200 psi. Ensure proper tool fit prior to performing test. Exercise extreme caution or damage or personal injury may result.

1. Prior to performing pump flow and pressure tests, ensure following conditions exist:
   a. Proper pump reservoir fluid level.
   b. Correct tire air pressure.
   c. Proper pump belt tension.
   d. Correct model and vehicle pump application.
   e. Correct size pulleys on pump and engine.
   f. Ensure system is not damaged or leaking, repair as required.
2. The following test equipment is required:
   a. Engine tachometer.
   b. Thermometer: 0–300°F (17.8–148.9°C).
   c. **On all models except SHO,** power steering system analyzer tool No. 014-00207, or equivalent.
   d. **On all models,** set of adapter fittings.
3. The test procedure used in conjunction with the power steering system analyzer can be used to determine:
   a. System backpressure.
   b. Pump flow.
   c. Steering gear internal leakage.
   d. Pump relief pressure.
4. The readouts from step 3 can be used to determine which of the following conditions or components may be faulty:
   a. Hose or fitting restriction.
   b. Sticking gear valve.
   c. Insufficient pump capacity.
   d. Sticking relief valve.
   e. Suspension system binding.
5. Disconnect pump high pressure line, then connect suitable analyzer hose adapter, **Figs. 5 through 8.**
6. **On all models except SHO,** thread other analyzer adapter to pump.
7. **On all models,** connect analyzer hose to adapters, tighten both connections to 15 ft. lbs. maximum.
8. If required, add power steering fluid, start engine and allow to run about two minutes. Ensure idle is set to specifications.
9. With engine at idle, record the following:
   a. Flow, gallons per minute at 167–177°F (76–80°C).
   b. Pressure, psi at 167–177°F (76–80°C), at idle with gate fully open.
   c. If gallon per minute flow is below specifications, pump may require service, however continue test, check flow and relief pressure.
   d. If pressure is above 150 psi check hoses for restrictions.
10. Partially close gate valve to build up 740 psi, observe and record flow at 167–177°F (76–80°C):

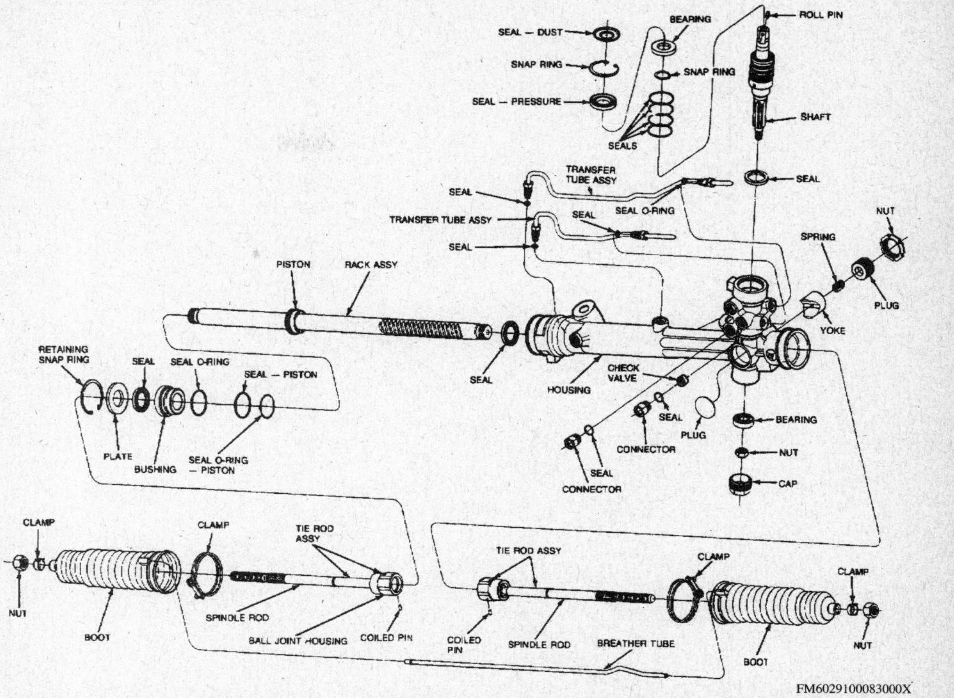

Fig. 2 Exploded view of steering gear. Continental, Sable & Taurus

   a. **On all models except SHO,** if flow drops lower than .9 gallons per minute, disassemble pump and replace cam pack, if pressure plates are cracked or worn, replace.
11. **On all models,** completely close and partially open gate valve three times. **Do not allow valve to remain closed for more then five seconds.** Observe and record pressure.
12. **On all models except SHO,** if pressure is lower than specifications, replace pump flow control valve.
13. If pressure is above specifications, pump flow control valve should be removed and cleaned or replaced.
14. **On all models,** increase engine speed to about 1500 RPM, observe and record flow.
15. **On all models except SHO,** if flow exceeds maximum free flow per minute, pump flow control valve should be removed and cleaned or replaced.
16. **On all models,** check idle speed, with engine at idle, turn steering wheel to left and right stops, record pressure and flow at stops.
17. Pressure at both stops should be about the same as maximum pump output pressure, flow should drop below .5 gallons per minute.
18. If pressure is not within specification, excessive internal leakage is indicated, remove and disassemble steering gear, replace worn or damaged parts and inspect rack piston and valve seals for damage.
19. While watching pressure gauge, turn steering wheel slightly in both directions and quickly release wheel, gauge needle should move from normal backpressure and snap back as the wheel is released. If needle returns slowly or sticks, the steering gear rotary valve is sticking.
20. Remove and disassemble steering as described under " Disassemble," then flush power steering hoses and pump before gear installation.
21. If problem still exists, check ball joint and linkage.
22. Disconnect and remove analyzer, then connect lines.

POWER STEERING SYSTEM SERVICE

Power Steering System Bleed

1. Air trapped in power steering system may be removed with power steering pump air evacuator assembly vacuum tester No. 021-00014, or equivalent.
2. **Do not use engine vacuum to purge power steering system.**
3. Remove reservoir cap.
4. Check and fill reservoir to cold fill mark with suitable fluid.
5. Disconnect ignition coil wire, then raise and support front wheels.
6. Crank engine with starter motor, then check fluid level. **Do not turn steering wheel.**
7. If fluid level has dropped, fill reservoir to cold fill mark, crank engine with starter motor while turning steering wheel lock to lock, then check fluid level.
8. Install air evacuator rubber stopper tightly to pump reservoir, then connect coil wire.
9. With engine at idle, apply 15 inch Hg maximum vacuum to pump reservoir

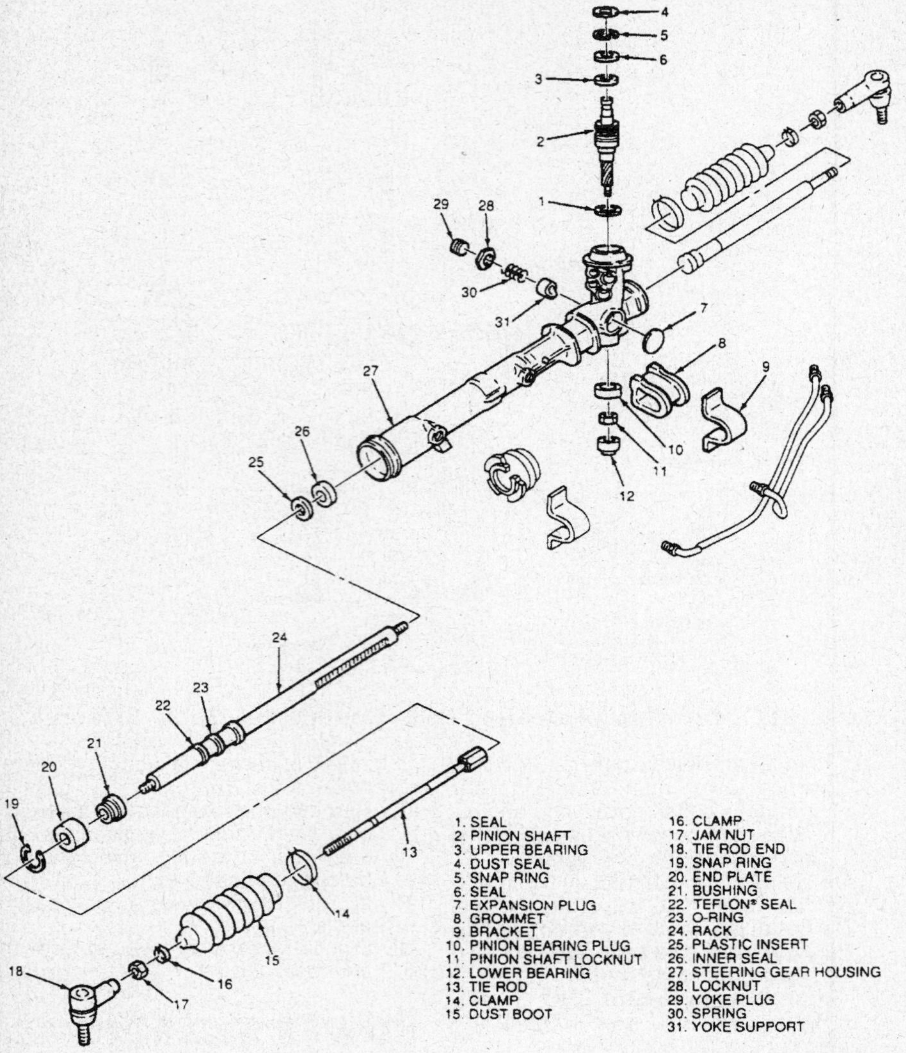

FM6029100084000X

Fig. 3 Exploded view of steering gear. Escort & Tracer

CONDITION	POSSIBLE SOURCE	ACTION
• Wander — Vehicle wander is a condition where the vehicle wanders side to side on the roadway when it is driven straight ahead while the steering wheel is held in a firm position. Evaluation should be conducted on a level road (little road crown).	• Improper wheel alignment.	• Set alignment to specification.
	• Loose outer tie rod ends.	• Replace outer tie rod end assemblies.
	• Inner tie rod ball housing loose or worn.	• Replace inner tie rod assemblies.
	• Gear assembly mounting loose.	• Tighten mounting bolts to specification.
	• Loose suspension struts or ball joints.	• Adjust or replace as required.
	• Column intermediate shaft connecting bolts loose.	• Tighten bolts to specification.
	• Loose wheel bearings.	• Service as required.
	• Column intermediate shaft joints loose or worn.	• Replace intermediate shaft.
• Feedback — (Rattle, chuckle, knocking noises in the steering gear). Feedback is a condition where roughness is felt in the steering wheel by the driver when the vehicle is driven over rough pavement.	• Column U-joints loose.	• Replace if bad.
	• Loose outer tie rod ends.	• Replace outer tie rod end assemblies.
	• Loose/worn inner tie rod ball.	• Replace inner tie rod assemblies.
	• Gear assembly mounting loose.	• Tighten mounting bolts to specification.
	• Loose pinion bearing cap.	• Tighten cap to specification.
	• Loose pinion bearing locknut.	• Tighten locknut to specification.
	• Piston disengaged or loose on rack.	• Replace rack assembly.
	• Steering gear yoke worn.	• Replace yoke assembly.
	• Column intermediate shaft connecting bolts loose.	• Tighten bolts to specification.
	• Loose suspension struts on ball joints.	• Adjust or replace as necessary.

FM6029100087010X

Fig. 4 Troubleshooting (Part 1 of 3)

for a minimum of three minutes, as air purges from system, vacuum will decrease, maintain adequate vacuum.

10. Release vacuum, then remove vacuum source, if fluid level has dropped, fill to cold fill mark.
11. With engine at idle, apply 15 inch Hg maximum vacuum to pump reservoir, turn steering wheel from lock to lock ever 30 seconds for about five minutes. **Do not hold steering wheel on stops when turning.** Maintain adequate vacuum.
12. Release vacuum, then remove vacuum equipment add power steering fluid if required, install cap.
13. Start engine, turn steering wheel, check connections for oil leaks.
14. If severe aeration is indicated, repeat steps 7 through 13.

Power Steering System Flush

1. Disconnect power steering return hose.
2. Place return line in suitable container, then plug reservoir return line at reservoir.
3. Fill reservoir using Motorcraft Dexron II part No. ESW-M2C33-F, or equivalent.
4. Disconnect coil wire, then raise and support front wheels.
5. While adding about two quarts of fluid, turn ignition to start position (using ignition key), then crank engine with starter and turn steering wheel right to left.
6. When all the fluid is added, turn ignition off, and connect coil wire.
7. Remove reservoir return line plug, then connect line to reservoir.
8. Fill reservoir to specified level.
9. Lower vehicle, then start engine, slowly turn steering wheel several times lock to lock, then recheck fluid level, add as required.

Adjustments

STEERING GEAR

CONTINENTAL, MARK VIII, MUSTANG, SABLE, TAURUS, THUNDERBIRD & 1997 COUGAR

Rack yoke bearing preload is the only service adjustment required. This adjustment is performed with the steering gear removed from the vehicle. Refer to the individual car chapters for steering gear removal.

1. Clean exterior of steering gear, then install two long bolts and washers through bushings and attach to bench fixture tool No. T57L-500-B, or equivalent.
2. Do not remove external pressure lines unless damaged or leaking. Drain power steering fluid by rotating input shaft from lock to lock two times using pinion shaft torque adapter tool No. T74P-3504-R, or equivalent. Cover ports on valve housing with a clean

CONDITION	POSSIBLE SOURCE	ACTION
• Poor Returnability — Sticky Feel — Poor returnability is noticed when the steering fails to return to center following a turn without manual effort from the driver. In addition, when the driver returns the steering to center, it may have a sticky or catchy feel	• Misaligned steering column or column flange rubbing steering wheel and/or flange.	• Align column.
	• Check rotational torque of intermediate shaft joints.	• If binding, replace intermediate shaft.
	• Improper wheel alignment.	• Set to specification.
	• Tight inner tie rod ball joints.	• Replace inner tie rod as required.
	• Binding in valve assembly	• Replace input shaft valve assembly.
	• Bent or damaged rack.	• Replace rack assembly.
	• Bent or damaged sub-frame.	• Replace as necessary.
	• Column bearing binding.	• Replace bearing.
	• Tight suspension struts or lower control arm ball joints.	• Adjust or replace as required.
	• Contamination in system.	• Flush power steering system.
	• Deformed engine mounts.	• Replace as required.
• Heavy Steering Efforts (Poor or loss of assist) — A heavy effort and poor assist condition is recognized by the driver while turning corners and especially while parking. A road test will verify this condition	• Leakage/loss of fluid.	• external leakage service.
	• Low pump fluid.	• Fill as necessary.
	• Pump external leakage.	• Service
	• Improper drive belt tension.	• Readjust belt tension.
	• Hose or cooler external leakage.	• Replace as necessary.
	• Improper engine idle speed.	• Readjust idle.
	• Pulley loose or warped.	• Replace pulley.
	• Pump/flow pressure not to specification.	
	• Hose/cooler line restrictions.	• Clear or replace as required.
	• Valve plastic ring cut or twisted.	• Replace ring.
	• Damaged/worn plastic piston ring.	• Replace ring.
	• Loose/missing rubber backup piston O-ring.	• Replace/install O-ring.
	• Loose rack piston.	• Replace rack assembly.
	• Gear assembly oil passages restricted.	• Clear/service as required.
	• Bent/damaged rack assembly.	• Replace rack assembly.

FM6029100087020X

Fig. 4 Troubleshooting (Part 2 of 3)

POWER STEERING SYSTEM TESTING

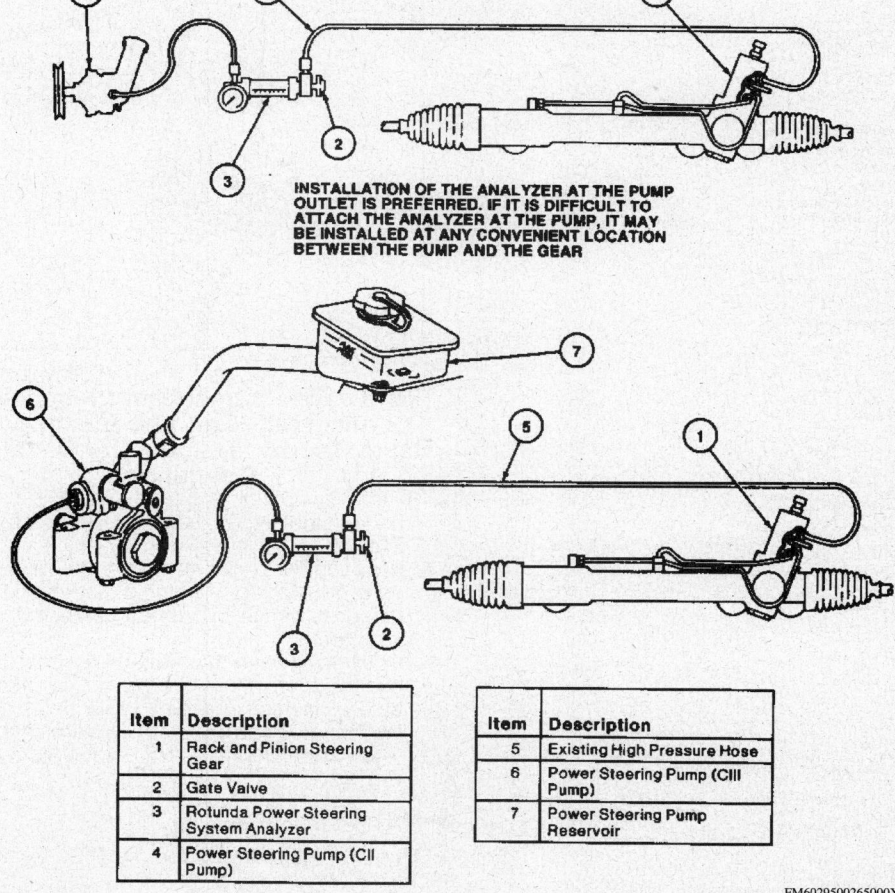

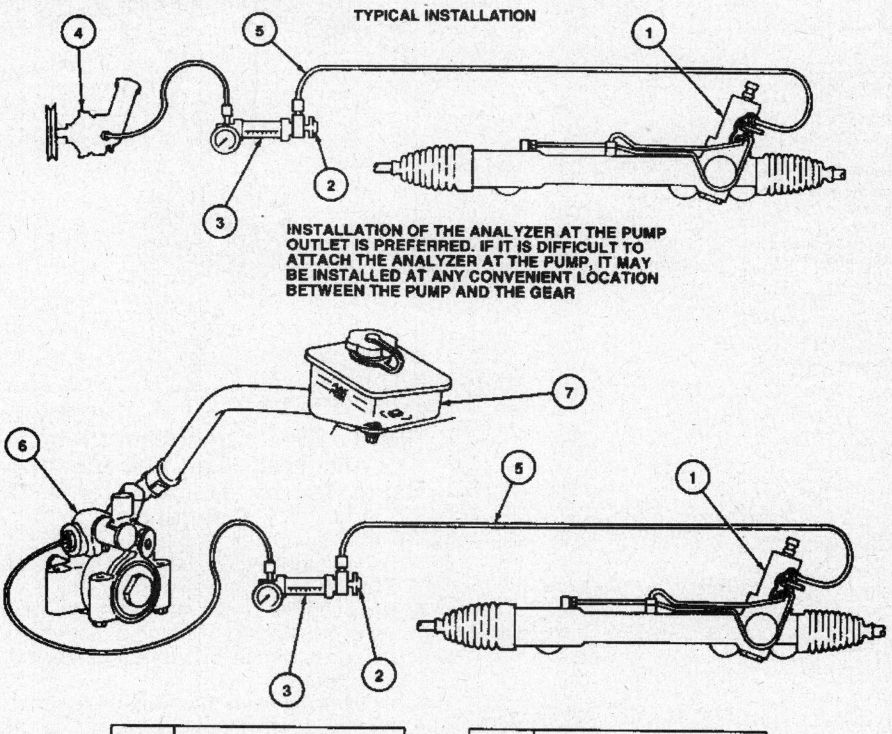
TYPICAL INSTALLATION
4
5
1
2
3
INSTALLATION OF THE ANALYZER AT THE PUMP OUTLET IS PREFERRED. IF IT IS DIFFICULT TO ATTACH THE ANALYZER AT THE PUMP, IT MAY BE INSTALLED AT ANY CONVENIENT LOCATION BETWEEN THE PUMP AND THE GEAR
7
6
5
1
3
2

Item	Description
1	Rack and Pinion Steering Gear
2	Gate Valve
3	Rotunda Power Steering System Analyzer
4	Power Steering Pump (CII Pump)

Item	Description
5	Existing High Pressure Hose
6	Power Steering Pump (CIII Pump)
7	Power Steering Pump Reservoir

FM6029500265000X

Fig. 5 Pressure test connections. Mark VIII, Mustang, Thunderbird & 1997 Cougar

CONDITION	POSSIBLE SOURCE	ACTION
• Hissing Sound There is some noise in all power steering systems. One of the most common is a hissing sound most evident at standstill parking. There is no relationship between this noise and the performance of the steering gear. **CAUTION: Do not hold steering wheel at full lock more than five seconds, as damage to power steering pump may result.**	• Hiss may be expected when the steering wheel is at the end of travel or when turning at standstill.	• Hiss is a normal characteristic of rotary steering gears and in no way affects steering. Do not replace the rack assembly unless the hiss is extremely objectionable. A replacement rack will also exhibit a slight noise and is not always a cure for the condition. Investigate for a grounded column or a loose boot at the dash panel. Any metal-to-metal contact will transmit valve hiss into the passenger compartment through the steering column. Verify clearance between flexible coupling components. Ensure steering column shaft and gear are aligned so flexible coupling rotates in a flat plane and is not distorted as shaft rotates.

FM6029100087030X

Fig. 4 Troubleshooting (Part 3 of 3)

shop cloth while draining gear.

3. Position an inch lb. torque wrench and pinion shaft adapter tool No. T74P-3504-R, or equivalent, on input shaft splines.
4. Loosen yoke plug locknut using pinion housing yoke locknut wrench tool No. T78P-3504-H, or equivalent, then loosen yoke plug using a ¾ inch socket wrench, **Fig. 9.**
5. Clean yoke plug threads, then with rack at center of travel, **torque** yoke plug to 40–50 inch lbs.
6. Back off yoke plug approximately ⅛ turn until **torque** required to rotate input shaft is 7–18 inch lbs.
7. While holding yoke plug in position, tighten locknut to specifications. Using pinion housing yoke locknut wrench tool No. T78P-3504-H, or equivalent. Recheck input shaft rotating torque after tightening locknut.
8. If the external pressure lines were removed in step two, they must be replaced with new pressure lines. Remove the copper seals from the pressure ports previous to installation of new lines.
9. Remove steering gear from holding fixture, then install external pressure lines. Tighten pump to gear and return line fittings and valve and power cylinder (gear housing) fittings to specifications.

Component Service

CONTINENTAL, MARK VIII, MUSTANG, SABLE, TAURUS, THUNDERBIRD & 1997 COUGAR

TIE ROD ENDS, BELLOWS & BALL JOINT SOCKETS

Disassemble

1. Install two long bolts and washers through bushings and attach gear to holding fixture tool No. T57L-500–B, or equivalent.
2. Loosen jam nuts on outer ends of tie rods, then remove tie rod ends and jam nuts.
3. Remove four clamps attaching bellows to tie rods and gear housing.
4. Drain power steering fluid, then remove bellows with breather tube. Use care not to damage bellows.

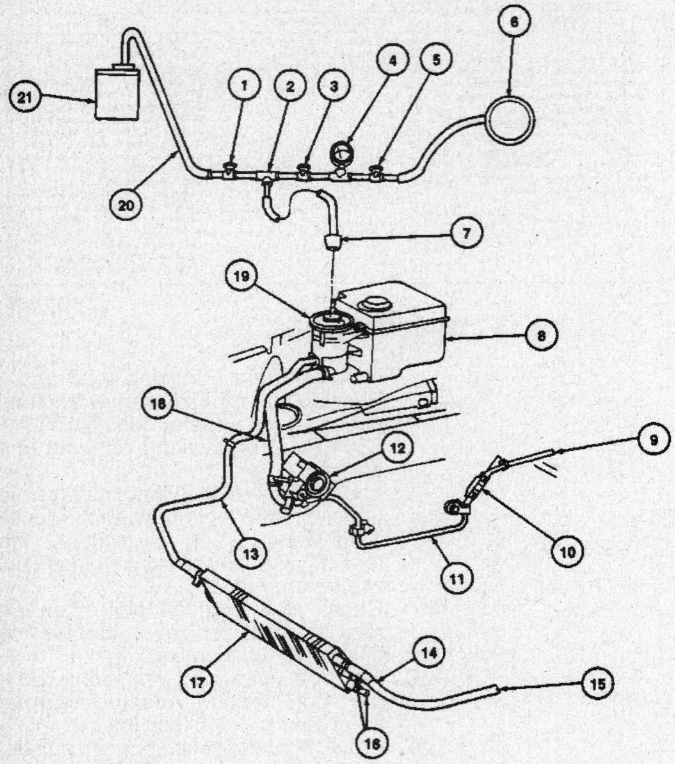

Item	Description
1	Valve No. 1
2	Tee
3	Valve No. 2
4	0 to 30 Inch Vacuum Gauge
5	Valve No. 3
6	Vacuum Source
7	No. 7 Stopper
8	Radiator Coolant Recovery Reservoir
9	Power Steering Left Turn Pressure Hose (To Auxiliary Actuator)
10	Intermediate Connection

Item	Description
11	Power Steering Pressure Hose
12	Power Steering Pump
13	Oil Cooler-To-Reservoir Hose
14	Power Steering Return Hose
15	From Power Steering Gear
16	Transmission Fluid Cooler Ports
17	Combination Power Steering and Automatic Transmission Fluid Cooler
18	Power Steering Reservoir Pump Hose

FM6029500266000X

Fig. 6 Pressure test connections. Continental

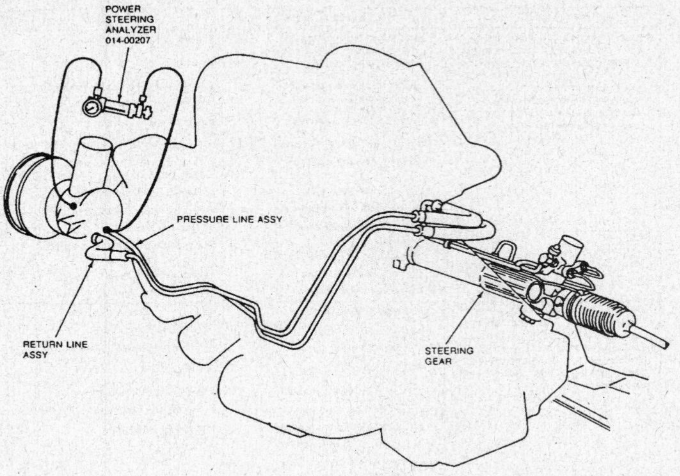

FM6029100090000X

Fig. 7 Pressure test connections. Sable & Taurus, except SHO

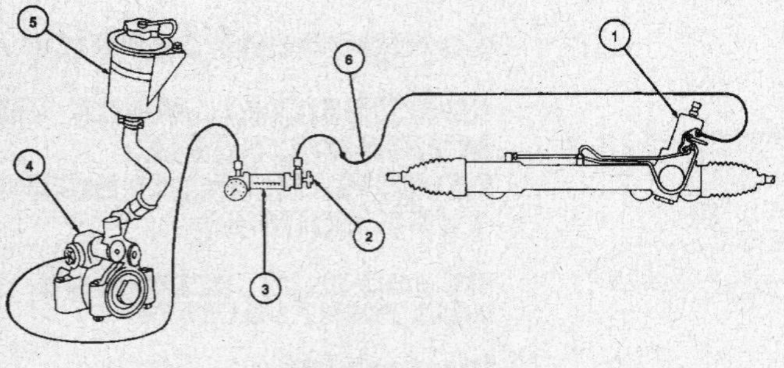

Item	Description
1	Steering Gear
2	Gate Valve
3	Rotunda Power Steering System Analyzer

Item	Description
4	Power Steering Pump
5	Power Steering Pump Auxiliary Reservoir
6	Existing High Pressure Hose

FM6029400202000X

Fig. 8 Pressure test connections. Contour, Mystique & 1999 Cougar

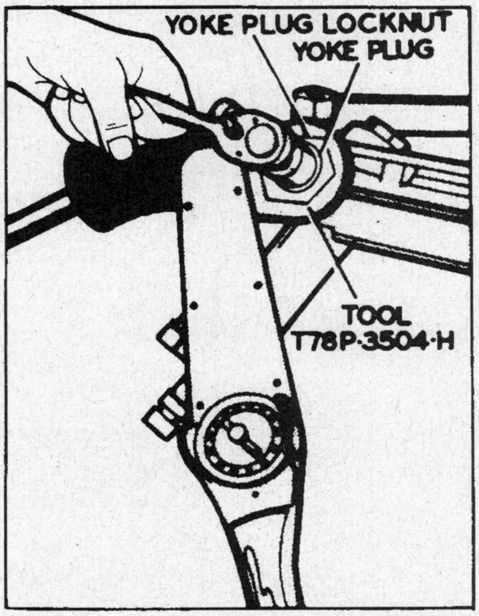

FM6029100092000X

Fig. 9 Yoke plug locknut removal. Continental, Mark VIII, Mustang, Sable, Taurus, Thunderbird & 1997 Cougar

5. If pinion is to be removed, remove pinion before proceeding as described under "Input Shaft & Valve Assembly."
6. Thread point of roll pin remover tool No. T78P-3504–N, or equivalent, into roll pin on ball socket and tighten too finger tight, then remove roll pins, **Fig. 10.**
7. if pinion was not removed, remove gear housing from holding fixture and place on bench to prevent damage to gear teeth.
8. Position rack so that several teeth are exposed. Hold rack using an adjustable wrench on end teeth while loosening ball sockets with nut wrench tool No. T74P-3504–U, or equivalent, **Fig. 11.**

Assemble

This procedure has been modified by a technical service bulletin.

1. **On models equipped with tie rods retained by a rivet or pin,** proceed as follows:

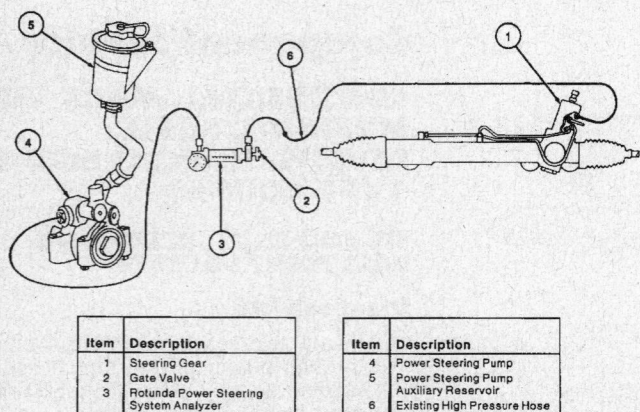

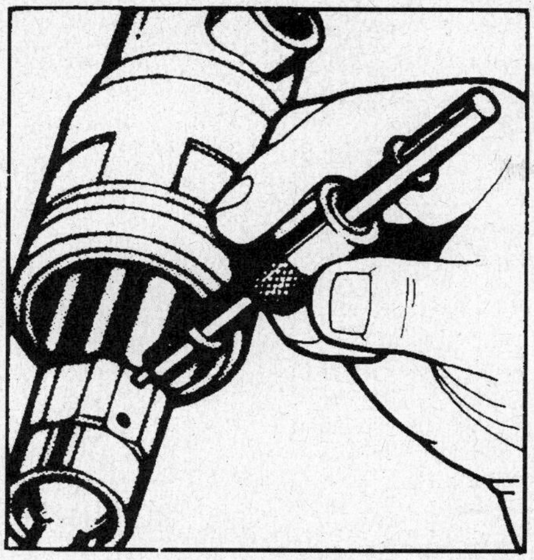

FM6029100093000X

Fig. 10 Roll pin from ball socket removal. Continental, Mark VIII, Mustang, Sable, Taurus, Thunderbird & 1997 Cougar

a. Install tie rod and ball socket assemblies onto rack. Hold one ball socket with 1 5⁄16 inch wrench while tightening other ball socket to specifications, using nut wrench tool No. T74P3504–U, or equivalent. Both ball socket assemblies will be torqued simultaneously using this method. **If pinion was not removed from housing, this step must be performed with the steering gear removed from the holding fixture and positioned on bench to prevent damage to gear teeth.**
b. Support ball housing using a wooden block, then install roll pins by tapping lightly with a plastic mallet.
c. If pinion was removed, install pinion as described under " Input Shaft and Valve Assembly."
d. Thoroughly clean rack and housing bore.
e. Apply lubricant to bellows clamp under cut on tie rod, then install bellows and breather tube.
f. Install clamps retaining bellows to steering gear. Use tool No. T63P-9171–A, or equivalent, to secure clamp to gear.
g. Install clamps retaining bellows to tie rods, then jam nuts and tie rod ends.

2. **On models equipped with tie rods, not retained by a rivet or pin,** proceed as follows:
   a. Turn rack to left stop, then place suitable adjustable wrench on rack to prevent turning during tightening procedures.
   b. Using a suitable wrench, tighten tie rod to rack to specifications.
   c. Install rack boots, then secure to rack body and tie rod using suitable clamps, tighten to specification.
   d. Install tie rod end jam nuts and tie rod ends to tie rods, tighten to specification after final adjustment.

STEERING GEAR

The steering gear on these models is not serviceable. Steering gear must be replaced as an assembly.

CONTOUR, MYSTIQUE & 1999 COUGAR

TIE ROD ENDS, BELLOWS & BALL JOINT SOCKETS

1. Secure steering gear in holding fixture tool No. T57L-500-B, or equivalent.
2. Loosen tie rod end jam nuts, then remove tie rod ends and jam nuts from tie rods. Record turns required to remove tie rod ends.
3. Remove rack boot clamps, then the rack boots.
4. Place a suitable adjustable wrench on end teeth of rack only, then using a suitable pipe wrench, loosen and remove tie rods. Do not allow rack to turn in gear.
5. Reverse procedure to install, tighten to specification.

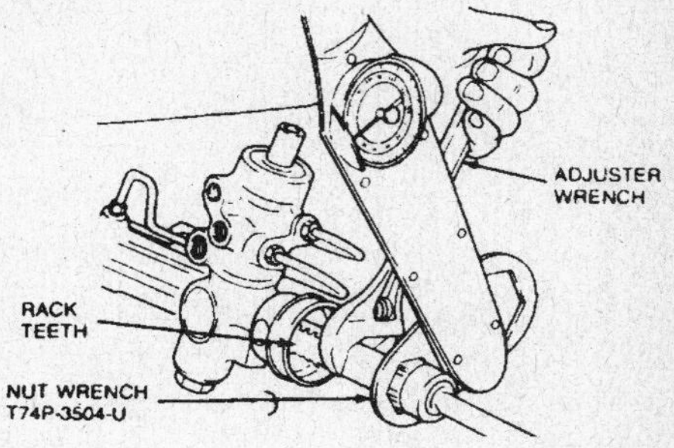

FM6029100094000X

Fig. 11 Tie rod & ball socket removal. Continental, Mark VIII, Mustang, Sable, Taurus, Thunderbird & 1997 Cougar

STEERING GEAR

The steering gear on these models is not serviceable. Steering gear must be replaced as an assembly.

ESCORT, TRACER & ZX2

TIE ROD ENDS, BELLOWS & BALL JOINT SOCKETS

1. Raise and support vehicle, then disconnect tie rod ends from knuckle using separator tool No. T85M-3395-A, or equivalent.
2. Loosen tie rod end jam nuts, then remove tie rod ends and jam nuts from tie rods. Record turns required to remove tie rod ends.
3. Remove rack boot clamps, then the rack boots.
4. Place a 20 mm crowfoot wrench, or equivalent, on end of rack, then using tie rod socket tool No. C3AZ-19578-A, or equivalent, loosen and remove tie rods. Do not allow rack to turn in gear.
5. Reverse procedure to install, tighten nuts and bolts to specification.

STEERING GEAR

The steering gear on these models is not serviceable. Steering gear must be replaced as an assembly.

TIGHTENING SPECIFICATIONS

Component	Torque/Ft. Lbs.
CONTINENTAL	
Bellows Clamp Screw	20–30①
Gear Hose Fittings	24–30
Gear Housing Return Line	20–25
Gear To Crossmember	100–144
Intermediate Shaft To Steering Column	15–24
Intermediate Shaft To Steering Gear	30–38
Pressure Line Fitting To Actuator Banjo Bolt	22–28
Pump Pressure Line Fitting	42–54
Tie Rod Ball Socket To Rack	②
Tie Rod End Jam Nut	35–48
Tie Rod End To Spindle Arm	35–47
VAPS Actuator	24–30

Continued

TIGHTENING SPECIFICATIONS—Continued

Component	Torque/Ft. Lbs.
CONTOUR, MYSTIQUE & 1999 COUGAR	
Bellows Clamp Screw	20–30①
Flexible Coupling Pinch Bolt	21
Gear Hose Fittings	23
Gear Housing Return Line	23
Gear Cover Plate Bolts	37
Gear To Crossmember	101
Pump Pressure Line Fitting	48
Tie Rod End Jam Nut	35–50
Tie Rod End To Spindle Arm	21
Escort, Tracer & ZX2	
A/C Compressor	15–22
High Pressure Line To Housing Flare Nut	21–25
Return Line To Housing Flare Nut	21–25
Tie Rod End Jam Nuts	25–37
Tie Rod To Rack	40–50
MARK VIII	
Bellows Clamp Screw	20–30①
Gear Hose Fittings	20–25
Gear To Crossmember	100–144
Steering Flex Coupling Bolt	20–30
Tie Rod End Jam Nut	35–46
Tie Rod End To Spindle Arm	35–49
Tie Rod Socket Assembly To Rack	②
1997-98 MUSTANG	
Bellows Clamp Screw	20–30①
Gear Hose Fittings	20–25
Gear To Crossmember	30–40
Pump Pressure Hose Fitting	26–33
Steering Flex Coupling Bolt	20–30
Tie Rod End Jam Nut	35–50
Tie Rod End To Spindle Arm	35–47
Tie Rod Socket Assembly To Rack	②
1999-2000 MUSTANG	
Front Wheel Spindle Tie Rod	74
Pressure Line Fitting	48
Steering Gear Mounting Nut	35
Steering Intermediate Shaft Coupling Pinch Bolt	25
Tie Rod End Castellated Nut	11
Tie Rod End Jam Nut	41
1997-99 SABLE & TAURUS	
Bellows Clamp Screw	20–30①
Gear Hose Fittings	15–25
Gear Housing Return Line	24–30
Gear To Crossmember	85–100
Intermediate Shaft To Steering Column	15–25
Intermediate Shaft To Steering Gear	30–38
Pressure Line Fitting To Actuator Banjo Bolt	22–28
Pump Pressure Line Fitting	42–54
Tie Rod Ball Socket To Rack	66–81
Tie Rod End Jam Nut	35–50
Tie Rod End To Spindle Arm	35–47
VAPS Actuator	24–30

Continued

TIGHTENING SPECIFICATIONS—Continued

Component	Torque/Ft. Lbs.
THUNDERBIRD & 1997 COUGAR	
Bellows Clamp Screw	20–30①
Gear Hose Fittings	20–25
Gear To Crossmember	100–144
Pump Pressure Hose Fitting	10–15
Steering Flex Coupling Bolt	20–30
Tie Rod End Jam Nut	35–50
Tie Rod End To Spindle Arm	39–54
Tie Rod Socket Assembly To Rack	②

① — Inch lbs.
② — Tie rod retained w/pin or rivet, 55-65 ft. lbs., tie rod not retained by a pin or rivet, 68–81 ft. lbs.

Type 3-Ford Torsion Bar Power Steering Gear

NOTE: On Air Bag Equipped Models, Refer To " Air Bag System Precautions" Located In The Front Of This Manual For System Disarming & Arming Procedures.

NOTE: Refer To "Computer Relearn Procedures " Located In The Front Of This Manual For Computer Relearn Procedures.

NOTE: Also Refer To "Type 1–Ford Variable Assist Electronic Variable Orifice (EVO) System."

INDEX

PRECAUTIONS

AIR BAG SYSTEMS

Refer to "Air Bag System Precautions" in the front of this manual for system disarming and arming procedures.

BATTERY GROUND CABLE

Prior to service, disconnect battery ground cable and isolate as required.

DESCRIPTION

The power steering unit, **Fig. 1,** is a torsion bar type of hydraulic-assisted system. This system furnishes power to reduce the amount of turning effort required at the steering wheel. It also reduces road shock and vibrations.

The unit includes a worm and one piece rack-piston which is meshed to the gear teeth on the steering sector shaft. The unit also includes a hydraulic valve, valve actuator, input shaft and torsion bar assembly which are mounted on the end of the worm shaft and operated by a twisting action of the torsion bar.

The gear unit is designed with the one piece rack-piston, worm and sector shaft in the one housing and the valve spool in an attaching housing. This makes possible internal fluid passages between valve and cylinder, thus eliminating all external lines and hoses except the pressure and return hoses between pump and gear.

The power cylinder is an integral part of the gear housing. The piston is double acting in that fluid pressure may be applied to either side of the piston.

OPERATION

The operation of the hydraulic control valve spool is governed by the twisting of a torsion bar. All effort applied to the steering wheel is transmitted directly through the input shaft and torsion bar to the worm and piston. Any resistance to the turning of the front wheels results in twisting of the bar.

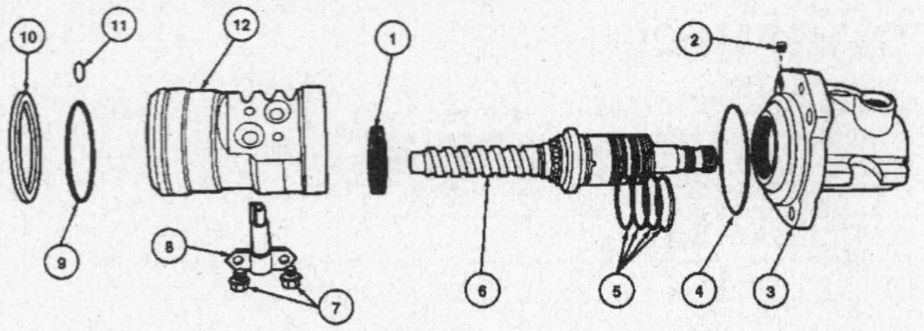

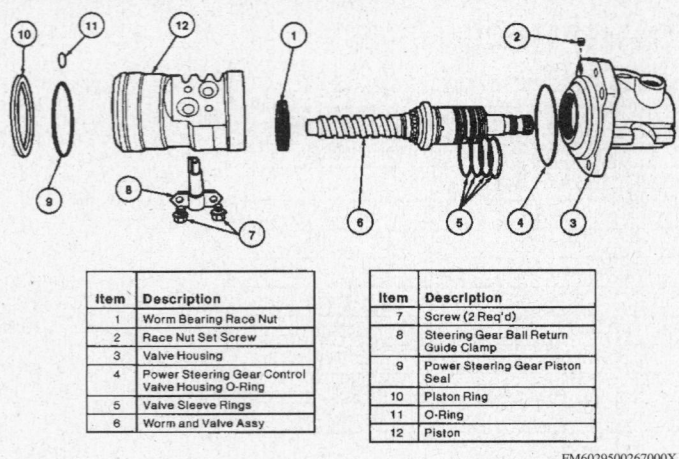

Item	Description
1	Worm Bearing Race Nut
2	Race Nut Set Screw
3	Valve Housing
4	Power Steering Gear Control Valve Housing O-Ring
5	Valve Sleeve Rings
6	Worm and Valve Assy

Item	Description
7	Screw (2 Req'd)
8	Steering Gear Ball Return Guide Clamp
9	Power Steering Gear Piston Seal
10	Piston Ring
11	O-Ring
12	Piston

FM6029500267000X

Fig. 1 Exploded view of Ford power steering gear

The twisting of the bar increases as the front wheel turning effort increases. The control valve spool, actuated by the twisting of the torsion bar, directs fluid to the side of the piston where hydraulic assistance is required.

As the torsion bar twists, its radial motion is transferred into axial motion by three helical threads. Thus, the valve is moved off center, and fluid is directed to one side of the piston or the other.

TROUBLESHOOTING

STEERING DRIFT/WANDER

1. Tire size and pressure.
2. Loose or worn tie rod ends or ball joints.
3. Steering gear mounting insulators or retaining bolts loose or damaged.
4. Loose front suspension lower arm struts.
5. Steering column gear input shaft coupling connecting bolts loose.
6. Steering gear input shaft coupling joints lose or worn.
7. Improper wheel alignment.
8. Excessive toe-in.
9. Excessive friction between components.

PULLS TO ONE SIDE

1. Improper tire pressure.
2. Improper tire size or type.
3. Vehicle is unevenly loaded.
4. Improper wheel alignment.
5. Damaged front or rear suspension components.
6. Steering gear valve effort out of adjustment.
7. Front or rear brakes operating improperly.
8. Bent rear axle housing, damaged or sagging front coil springs or damaged or worn rear suspension component.
9. loose or damaged rear suspension retaining fasteners.

FEEDBACK (RATTLE, CHUCKLE OR KNOCKING NOISES FROM STEERING GEAR)

1. Steering column gear input shaft coupling joints loose or worn.
2. Loose tie rod ends.
3. Steering gear retaining bolts loose or damaged.
4. Loose suspension bushings, fasteners or ball joints.
5. Improper steering gear adjustment.

POOR RETURNABILITY, STICKY FEEL

1. Improper tire pressure, tire size or tire type.
2. Misaligned steering column or column flange.
3. Steering column gear input shaft universal joints binding.
4. Steering column tube boot tears.
5. Binding or damaged tie rod ends.
6. Damaged or worn front suspension components.
7. Improper wheel alignment.
8. Column bearing binding.
9. Contamination in system.
10. Improper steering gear adjustment.

HEAVY STEERING EFFORT, POOR ASSIST OR LOSS OF ASSIST

1. Contamination of system by foreign objects in power steering oil reservoir or metallic particles in fluid being generated by cam pack discrepancies.
2. Low power steering fluid.
3. Steering gear assembly internal or external leak.
4. Improper drive belt tension.
5. Hose or cooler external leak or internal restriction.
6. Improper engine idle speed.
7. Power steering pump pulley loose or warped.
8. Power steering pump flow or pressure not to specifications.
9. Improper steering gear adjustments.
10. System contamination.
11. EVO power steering control valve actuator sticking.

POWER STEERING PUMP LEAKS AT EVO CONTROL VALVE ACTUATOR

1. Damaged power steering control valve actuator ring.
2. EVO power steering control valve actuator electrical connector damaged.
3. EVO power steering control valve actuator damaged.

NOISY PUMP

Swish Type Noise

A swish type noise may be created by the flow of excessive fluid into the bypass port of the pump valve housing with temperatures below 130.° This is a normal condition and will diminish when fluid temperature increases.

1. Low fluid level and possible leak.

Clicking Type Noise

1. Excessive power steering pump wear.

Moan or Whine Type Noise

1. Fluid aeration.
2. Power steering pump loose or misaligned with engine.
3. Low fluid.
4. Hose or steering column grounded.
5. Damaged internal components.

POWER STEERING SYSTEM SERVICE

Adjustments

MESHLOAD

1997–98

During vehicle break in period, some factory adjustments may change. These changes will not necessarily affect operation of the steering gear, but should excessive steering lash be encountered, a meshload adjustment may be required.

1. Disconnect steering gear sector shaft arm form steering gear sector shaft.
2. Disconnect fluid return line at reservoir and cap reservoir return line pipe.
3. Place end of return line in a clean container and cycle steering wheel in both directions as required to discharge fluid from gear.
4. Remove ornamental cover from wheel hub and turn steering wheel 45° from left stop.
5. Using an inch lb. torque wrench on steering wheel nut, determine torque required to rotate shaft slowly through an approximately ¼ turn from the 45° position.
6. Turn steering gear back to center, then determine torque required to rotate shaft back and forth across center position.
7. Loosen adjuster nut and turn adjusting screw, **Fig. 2,** until reading is as follows:

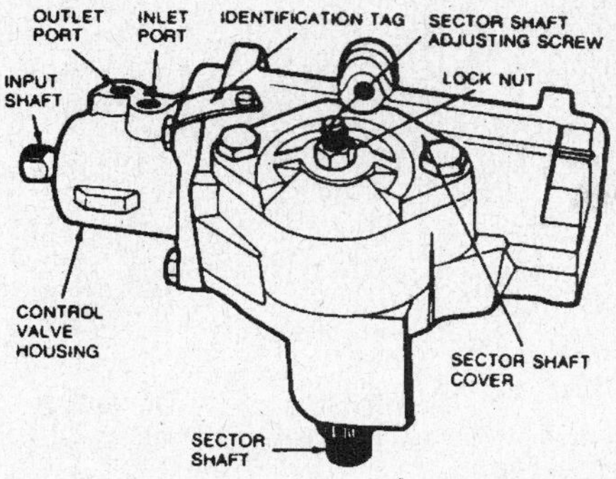

Fig. 2 Meshload adjustment

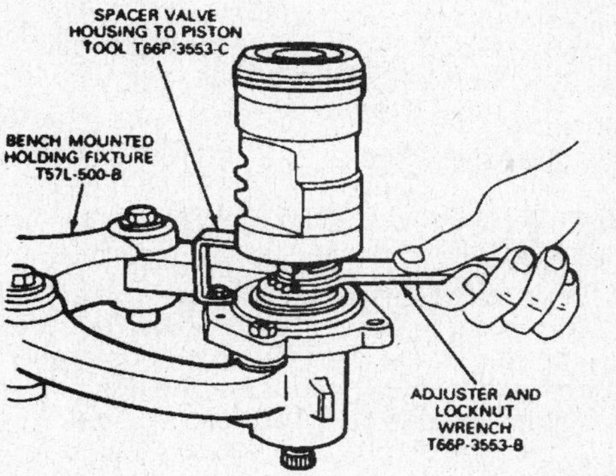

Fig. 4 Input shaft removal

a. **On models with 0–5000 miles,** reset if total meshload over mechanical center if not 15-24 inch lbs.
b. Set torque rocking across center to a values 11-15 inch lbs. greater than that measured 45° from right stop.
c. **On models with more than 5000 miles,** reset if meshload measured while rocking input shaft over center is less then 10 inch lbs. greater than the torque 45° from right stop.
d. Set torque measured rocking across center to a value of 10–14 inch lbs. greater than measured 45° from right stop.

8. **On all models,** recheck readings and replace pitman arm and steering wheel.
9. Connect fluid return line and replenish reservoir.

1999–2000

Perform the following adjustment with the steering gear and fluid lines disconnected from the vehicles steering system components.

1. Rotate input shaft either right or left to the stop.
2. Rotate the shaft in the opposite direction and count the number of turns.
3. Rotate the shaft back one half the number of turns counted.
4. Using a suitable inch lb. torque wrench, measure the torque required to rotate the input shaft 45° either side of center. If torque reading is not 12–16 inch lbs., turn sector shaft adjusting screw to adjust meshload.

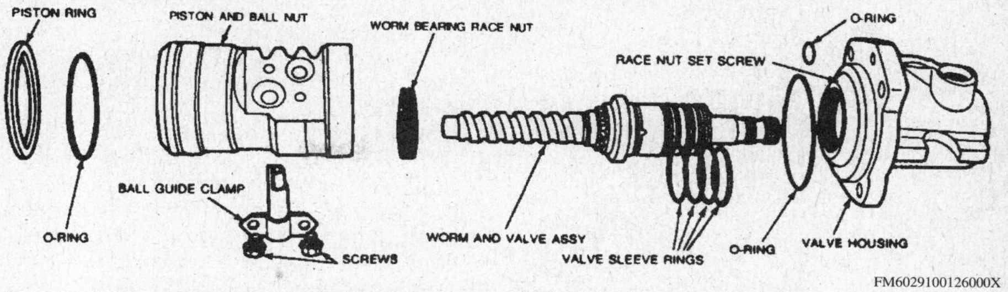

Fig. 3 Exploded view of ball nut & valve housing

Component Service

OVERHAUL

GEAR

Disassemble

1. Hold steering gear over drain pan in an inverted position and cycle input shaft six times to drain remaining fluid from gear.
2. Using suitable mounting pads for support, install gear in bench mounting fixture tool No. T57L-500-B, or equivalent.
3. Remove locknut from adjusting screw.
4. Turn input shaft to either stop, then turn it back approximately 1⅝ turns to center the gear. **Input shaft spline indexing flat should be facing downward.**
5. Remove sector shaft cover bolts.
6. Tap lower end of sector shaft with a soft-faced hammer to loosen it, then lift cover and shaft from housing as a unit. Discard O-ring.
7. Turn sector shaft cover counterclockwise off adjuster screw.
8. Remove valve housing attaching bolts. Lift valve housing from gear housing while holding piston to prevent it from rotating off worm shaft. Remove valve housing and lube passage O-rings and discard.
9. Remove valve housing attaching bolts and ID tag, while holding piston separate valve housing from housing, remove and discard O-rings.
10. With piston held, remove ball clamp screws and guide clamp, **Fig. 3.**
11. With finger over ball guide opening, turn piston so ball guide faces downward over clean container, then allow guide tubes to drop to container.
12. Rotate input shaft from stop to stop, until all balls fall from piston, then remove valve assembly from piston. **Ensure all balls have been removed. Worm may no longer be removed from piston.**
13. Install valve body to bench mounting fixture tool No. T57L-500-B, or equivalent, then loosen valve housing race nut lockscrew. Using adjuster locknut wrench tool No. T66P-3553-B and spacer valve housing tool No. T66P-3553-C, or equivalents, remove worm bearing race.
14. Slide input shaft, worm and valve assembly from valve housing, **Fig. 4.**

Assemble

1. Install worm and valve in housing.

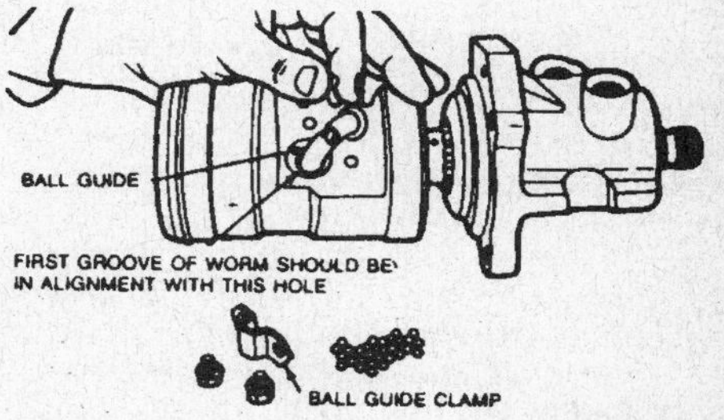

Fig. 5 Piston assembly on worm shaft

2. Install retaining nut in housing, then tighten nut using Adjuster and locknut wrench tool No. T66P-3553, or equivalent. Because length of tool required to tighten nut will affect torque wrench reading, the following formula must be used to determine torque. Torque (using tool T66P-3553-B, or equivalent) equals (length of torque wrench x 72 ft. lbs. length of torque wrench + 5.5 inches).
3. Install race nut screw and tighten to specifications.
4. Place piston on bench with ball guide holes facing up. Insert worm shaft into piston so that first groove is in alignment with hole nearest to center of piston, **Fig. 5.**
5. Place ball guide into piston. Place balls in guide (27 minimum), turning worm clockwise (viewed from input end of shaft). If all balls have not been fed into guide upon reaching right stop, rotate input shaft in one direction and then in the other while installing balls. After balls have been installed, do not rotate input shaft or piston more than 3½ turns off the right stop to prevent balls from falling out of circuit.
6. Secure guides to ball nut with clamp and tighten to specifications.
7. Apply petroleum jelly to piston seal.
8. Place a new O-ring on valve housing.
9. Slide piston and valve into gear housing, being careful not to damage seal.
10. Align lube passage in valve housing with one in gear housing, place O-ring in gear housing oil passage hole, then identification tag and install but do not tighten attaching bolts at this time.
11. Rotate ball nut so that teeth are in same plane as sector teeth. Tighten valve housing attaching bolts.
12. Position sector shaft cover O-ring in gear housing. Turn input shaft as required to center piston.

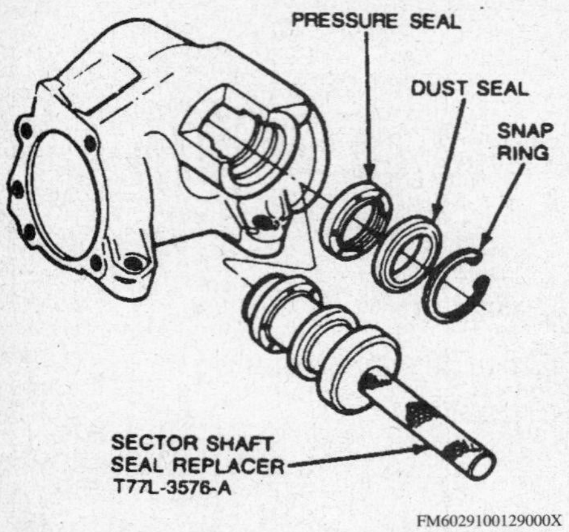

Fig. 6 Exploded view of steering gear housing

13. Apply petroleum jelly to sector shaft journal, then position sector shaft and cover into gear housing. Install air conditioner line mounting bracket, if equipped, and two sector shaft cover bolts, then tighten to specifications.
14. Attach an inch lb. torque wrench to input shaft and adjust mesh load as outlined previously.

GEAR HOUSING

1. Remove lower end housing snap ring, **Fig. 6.**
2. Using puller attachment tool No. T58L-101-B, or equivalent, remove and discard dust and pressure seals. **Bearing is not a serviceable and must be replaced as an assembly.**
3. Using suitable multi purpose grease, lubricate new pressure, dust seal and sector shaft seal bore.
4. Install dust seal on sector shaft, using seal replacer tool No. T77L-3576-A, or equivalent, with seal raised lip toward tool, then install pressure seal with lip away from tool, pressure seal flat side should be against flat side of dust deal.
5. Install tool to sector shaft bore, then drive tool until seals clear snap ring grooves. **Do not bottom seal against bearing or seals will not function properly.**
6. Install snap ring in housing groove.

REPLACEMENT

VALVE HOUSING

1. Using puller attachment tool No. T58L-101-B, or equivalent, remove and discard dust seal, **Fig. 7.**
2. Remove snap ring from valve housing, then turn fixture so valve housing is upside down.
3. Install bearing remover tool No. T65P-3524-A2 and installer tool No. T65P-3524-A3, or equivalents to valve body opposite the oil seal, then gently tap bearing and seal from housing, discard seal. **Exercise care when inserting and removing tool to prevent damage to valve bore in housing.**
4. Remove oil inlet and outlet tube seats with rack bushing holding Tool No. T74P-3504-L, or equivalent, if damaged.
5. Coat tube seats with petroleum jelly and position them in housing. Install and tighten tube nuts to press seats to proper location, using brass tube seat replacer tool No. T74P-3504-M, or equivalent.
6. Coat bearing and seal surface in housing with a film of petroleum jelly.
7. Install bearing with metal side that covers rollers facing downward, then using bearing installer tool No. T65P-3524-A, or equivalent, seat bearing, ensure smooth bearing operation.
8. Dip new oil seal in premium power steering fluid, or equivalent, then place it in housing with metal side of seal facing outward. Drive seal into housing until outer edge of seal does not quite clear snap ring.
9. Place snap ring in housing, then drive on ring until snap ring seats in its groove to locate seal properly.
10. Apply coating of suitable multipurpose grease between seals.
11. Place dust seal in housing with dished side (rubber side) facing outward. Drive dust seal in place so that it is located behind undercut in input shaft when it is installed.

WORM & VALVE SLEEVES

1. Cut valve sleeve rings from valve sleeve, then position worm end of assembly in soft jawed vice.
2. Using Tool Kit No. T75L-3517-A1, or equivalent, install four valve sleeve rings. After installing rings ensure they turn freely in grooves.

PISTON & BALL NUT

1. Remove plastic ring and O-ring from piston and ball nut, **Fig. 3.**
2. Dip a new O-ring in premium power steering fluid, or equivalent, lube and install on piston and ball nut.
3. Install new Teflon ring on piston and ball nut, being careful not to stretch it any more than necessary.

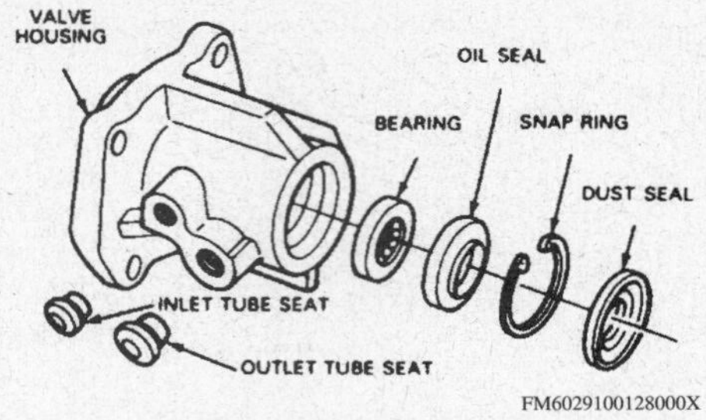

Fig. 7 Exploded view of valve housing

INSPECTION

VALVE SPOOL CENTERING CHECK

The "out of car" procedure for valve centering check is the same as for the "in car" except the torque and simultaneous pressure reading must be made at the right and left stops instead of either side of center.

1. Install a 2000 psi pressure gauge in pressure line between pump outlet port and steering gear inlet port. Ensure that valve on gauge in is fully open position.
2. Check fluid level in reservoir and replenish as required.
3. Start engine and cycle steering wheel from stop to stop to bring steering lubricant up to normal operating temperature. Stop engine and recheck reservoir. Add fluid as necessary.
4. With engine running at a fast idle speed (1000 RPM) and steering wheel centered, attach an inch pound torque wrench to steering wheel retaining nut. Apply sufficient torque to wrench in each direction (either side of center) to get a gauge reading of 250 psi.
5. The torque reading should be the same in both directions. If the difference between readings exceed 4 inch lbs., the shaft and control assemblies must be replaced.

TIGHTENING SPECIFICATIONS

Year	Component	Torque/Ft. Lbs.
1997–2000	Ball Return Guide Clamp Screw	42–70①
	Flex Coupling To Gear Input Shaft Bolt	20–30
	Gear To Side Rail Bolts	50–65
	Hose Clamps	12–24①
	Meshload Adjusting Screw Locknut	35–45
	Piston End Cap	70–110
	Pitman Arm To Sector Shaft Nut	200–250
	Pressure Hose To Gear	16–25
	Race Nut Setscrew	15–25①
	Race Retaining Nut	②
	Return Hose To Gear	16–25
	Sector Shaft Cover Bolts	55–70
	Valve Housing To Gear Housing	30–45

①— Inch lbs.
②— Refer to "Component Service."

Type 4-TSCL Rack & Pinion Steering Gear

NOTE: On Air Bag Equipped Models, Refer To " Air Bag System Precautions" Located In The Front Of This Manual For System Disarming & Arming Procedures.

NOTE: Refer To "Computer Relearn Procedures " Located In The Front Of This Manual For Computer Relearn Procedures.

INDEX

PRECAUTIONS

AIR BAG SYSTEMS

Refer to "Air Bag System Precautions" in the front of this manual for system disarming and arming procedures.

BATTERY GROUND CABLE

Prior to service, disconnect battery ground cable and isolate as required.

DESCRIPTION

The steering gear is operated and controlled by the hydraulic fluid supplied by the power steering pump.

The rack and pinion is held in position by two mounting brackets and rubber bushings. The gear uses an integral piston and rack design to provide power assisted steering control.

TROUBLESHOOTING

Refer to "Type 4-Aspire Vane-Type Pump" for troubleshooting procedures.

DIAGNOSIS & TESTING

POWER STEERING PRESSURE TEST

Refer to "Type 4-Aspire Vane-Type Pump" for power steering pressure test procedure.

POWER STEERING SYSTEM SERVICE

Adjustments

VALVE HOUSING

Perform this adjustment if the valve housing, steering gear housing or pinion control valve assembly have been replaced.

1. Measure valve housing, lower bearing and spacer and steering gear housing as shown in **Fig. 1.**
2. To determine proper thickness of shim needed, use this formula, T = A + C – B. Where T is shim thickness needed.
3. Shims are available in .0020 inch only.

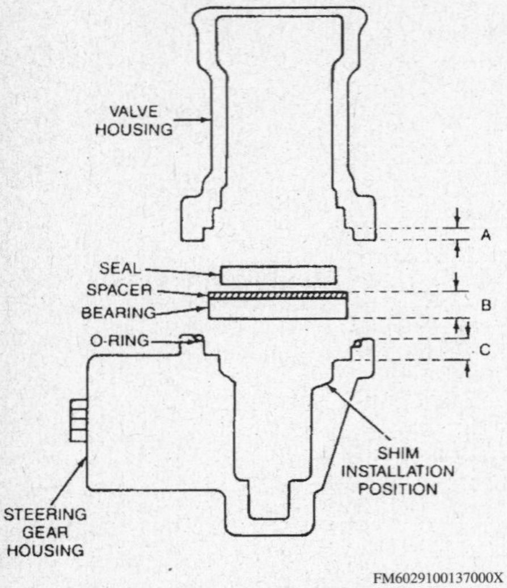

Fig. 1 Valve housing shim selection

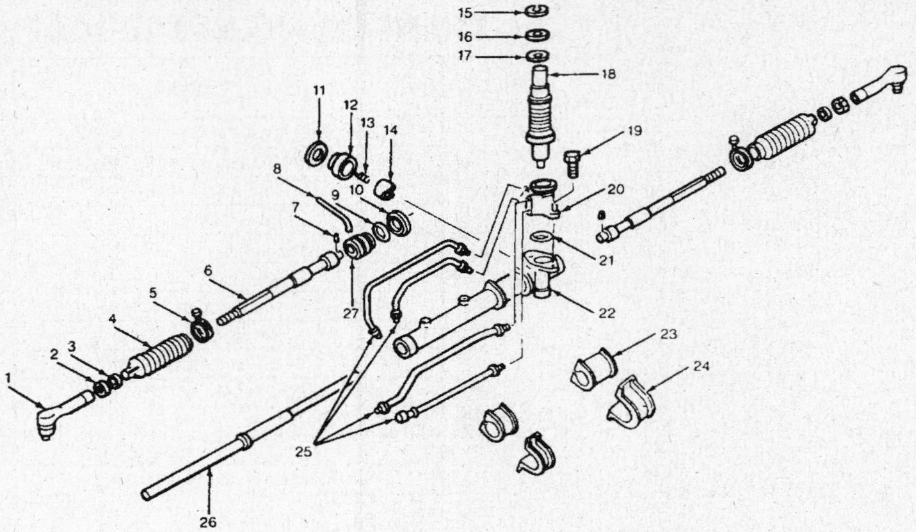

1. TIE ROD END
2. JAM NUT
3. BOOT CLIP
4. BOOT
5. BOOT WIRE
6. TIE ROD
7. LOCK PIN
8. RETAINING WIRE
9. O-RING
10. SEAL
11. LOCKNUT
12. YOKE PLUG
13. SPRING
14. SUPPORT YOKE
15. SNAP RING
16. SEAL
17. BEARING
18. PINION AND CONTROL VALVE ASSEMBLY
19. BOLT
20. VALVE HOUSING
21. O-RING
22. STEERING GEAR HOUSING
23. GROMMET
24. MOUNTING BRACKET
25. FLUID LINES
26. RACK
27. RACK BUSHING

FM6029100138000X

Fig. 2 Exploded view of steering rack

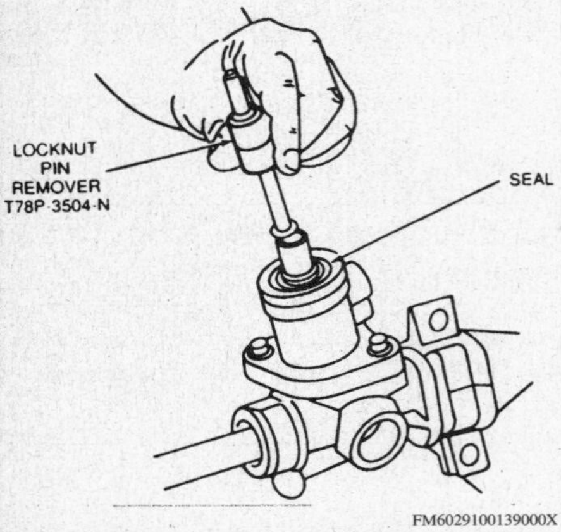

Fig. 3 . Control valve assembly O-ring removal

Determine number of shims using this formula, N = T / .0020 inch. Where N is number of shims needed. Round up or down to the closest full number.

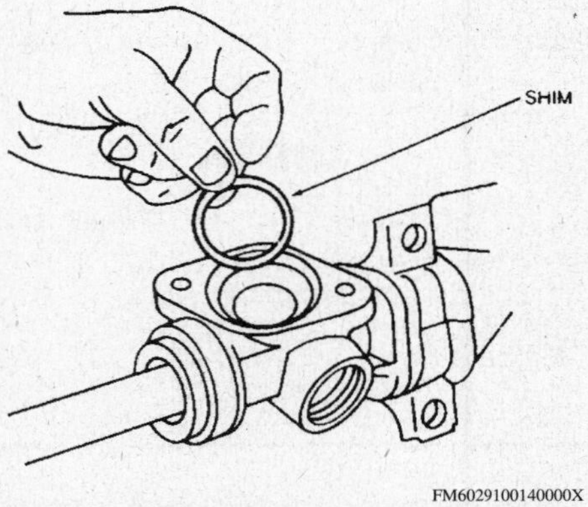

Fig. 4 Control valve assembly shims removal

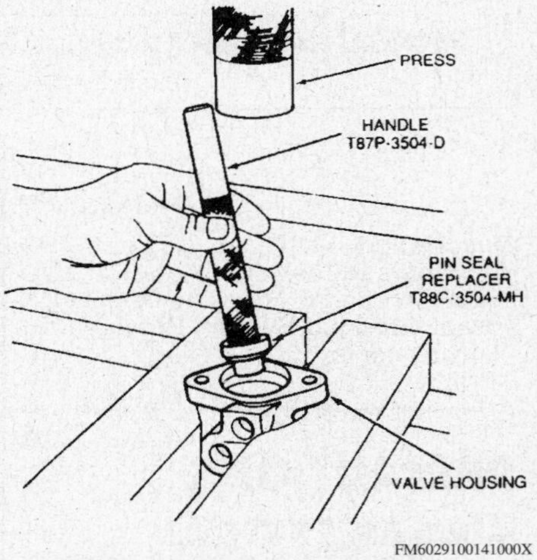

Fig. 5 Valve housing bearing removal

Component Service

STEERING GEAR

Disassemble

Refer to **Fig. 2** when performing the following procedure:

1. Secure steering gear on a soft jawed vise.
2. Remove fluid lines.
3. Place alignment marks on lefthand tie rod to ease installation.
4. Loosen jam nut and remove left tie rod end.
5. Remove boot clamps then the boot.
6. Using Lockpin Tool Removal No. T78P-3504-N, or equivalent, remove tie rod lockpins.
7. Remove tie rods from rack assembly.
8. Using yoke plug locknut removal tool No. T90C-3504-BH, or equivalent, remove yoke plug locknut.
9. Remove yoke plug, spring and support yoke.
10. Remove pinion and control valve assembly retaining snap ring.
11. Remove seal using locknut pin removal tool No. T78P-3504-N, or equivalent, **Fig. 3.**
12. Remove valve housing attaching bolts, then valve housing, pinion and control valve assembly.
13. If present, remove shim(s) from steering gear housing, **Fig. 4.**
14. Remove steering gear O-ring.
15. Remove pinion and control valve assembly from valve housing by lightly tapping with a rubber mallet.
16. Press bearing out of valve housing using pinion seal replacement tool No. T88P-3504-MH and Handle No. Y87P-3504-D, or equivalent, **Fig. 5.**
17. Using outer box torque adapter tool No. T88C-3504-CH, or equivalent, rotate rack bushing until hooked end of retaining wire is aligned with slot in steering gear housing, **Fig. 6.**
18. Pry retaining wire from bushing hole.
19. Rotate bushing and remove retaining wire, **Fig. 7.**
20. Remove rack from right side of steering gear.
21. Remove O-ring and seal using rack inner seal removal tool No. T87C-3504-A, or equivalent.

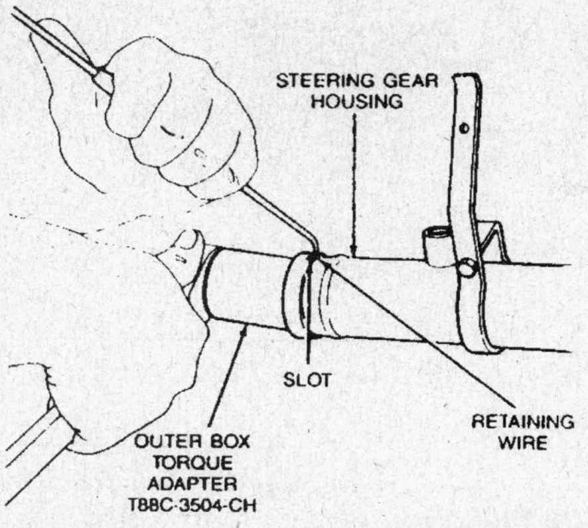

Fig. 6 Retaining wire alignment

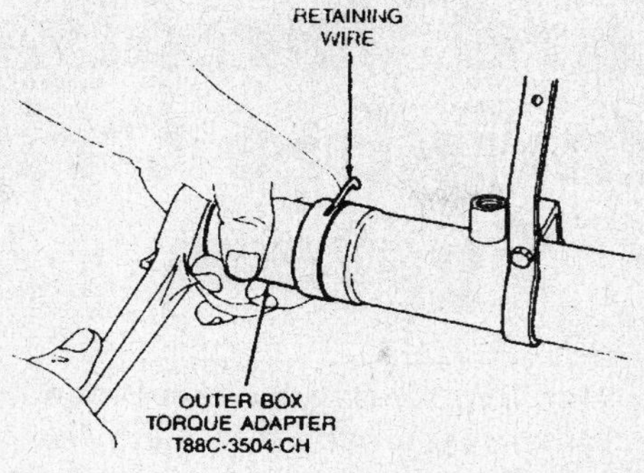

Fig. 7 Retaining wire removal

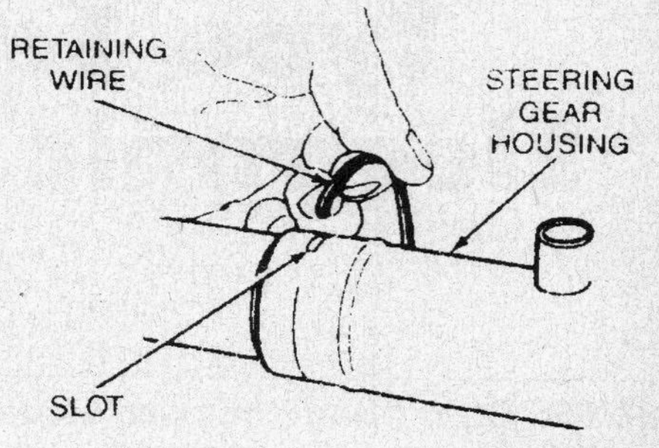

Fig. 8 Retainer wire installation

Assemble

1. Install a new seal and O-ring using a suitable seal and Teflon ring expander installer.
2. Install rack into steering gear.
3. Insert retaining wire through slot and into bushing hole, **Fig. 8.**
4. Install retaining wire using outer box torque adapter tool No. T88C-3504-CH, or equivalent.
5. If valve housing, steering gear housing or pinion and control valve assembly has been replaced, perform valve housing adjustment procedure as outlined under "Adjustments" in this section.

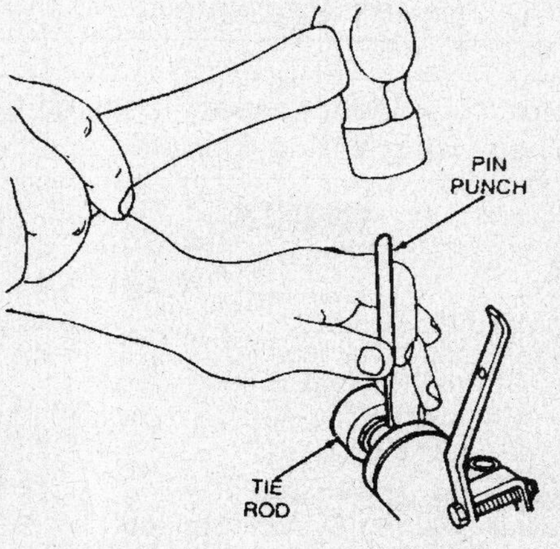

Fig. 9 Pinion seal installation

6. Insert pinion and control valve assembly into valve housing, ensure it seats properly.
7. Install a new O-ring.
8. Install valve housing, pinion and control valve assembly into steering gear and tighten to specifications.
9. Install bearing using pinion seal/torque adapter tool No. T88C-3504-BH, or equivalent.
10. Install seal using same tool, **Fig. 9.**
11. Install snap ring, support yoke, spring and yoke plug.
12. **Torque** yoke plug to 86 inch lbs. then loosen it.
13. **Torque** yoke to 38-48 inch lbs. then loosen it 45.°
14. Apply sealant to exposed threads of yoke plug.
15. Install yoke plug locknut and tighten to specifications.
16. Install tie rods using a suitable pin punch on lockpins.
17. Install boots, boot wires and clips.
18. Install left tie rod end and jam nut.
19. Install fluid lines.

TIGHTENING SPECIFICATIONS

Year	Component	Torque/Ft. Lbs.
1997	Actuator Housing	15–19
	Fluid Reservoir Bolts	60–84②
	Hose Nut	12–17
	Steering Gear Attaching Bolts	23–34
	Steering Gear Bracket Bolts	27–38
	Tie Rod End Nut	31–42
	Tie Rod End Jam Nut	25–36
	Yoke Plug	①
	Yoke Plug Locknut	36–43

① — Refer to "Component Service."

② — Inch lbs.

Type 1–Ford Variable Assist Electronic Variable Orifice (EVO) System

NOTE: On Air Bag Equipped Models, Refer To " Air Bag System Precautions" Located In The Front Of This Manual For System Disarming & Arming Procedures.

NOTE: Refer To "Computer Relearn Procedures " Located In The Front Of This Manual For Computer Relearn Procedures.

NOTE: "Electrical Symbol & Wire Color Code Identification" Located In The Front Of This Manual May Be Used As An Aid When Using Wiring Circuits Found In This Section.

INDEX

PRECAUTIONS

AIR BAG SYSTEMS

Refer to "Air Bag System Precautions" in the front of this manual for system disarming and arming procedures.

BATTERY GROUND CABLE

Prior to service, disconnect battery ground cable and isolate as required.

DESCRIPTION

The electronic variable orifice system, **Fig. 1 and 2,** is designed to vary the flow from the power steering pump based on vehicle speed and the rate of steering wheel rotation. The system provides full assist at low speed for light parking effort and minimum assist at high speed for good road feel and directional stability. In the event of system failure, full assist is provided.

TROUBLESHOOTING

COUGAR & THUNDERBIRD

Refer to symptom charts **Figs. 3 and 4** for troubleshooting procedures.

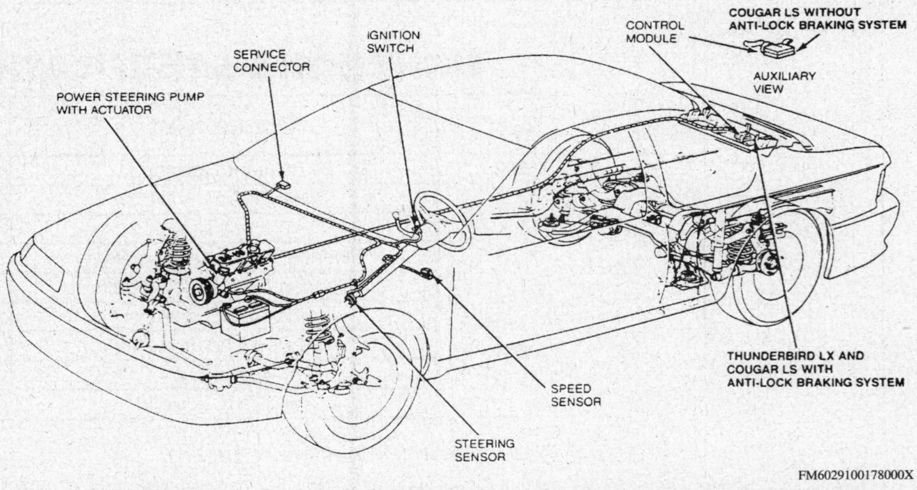

Fig. 1 Component locations electronic variable orifice system. Cougar & Thunderbird

1997 CROWN VICTORIA, GRAND MARQUIS & TOWN CAR

Refer to symptom charts, **Figs. 5 and 6** for troubleshooting procedures.

MARK VIII

Refer to symptom charts, **Figs. 7 and 8** for troubleshooting procedures.

DIAGNOSIS & TESTING

Wiring Diagrams

COUGAR & THUNDERBIRD

Refer to **Fig. 9** for wiring diagram.

CROWN VICTORIA & GRAND MARQUIS

Refer to **Figs. 10 and 11** for wiring diagrams.

MARK VIII

Refer to **Fig. 12** for wiring diagram.

TOWN CAR

Refer to **Figs. 13 and 14** for wiring diagram.

Pinpoint Tests

COUGAR & THUNDERBIRD

Refer to **Fig. 15** for symptom chart, **Figs. 16 through 18** for diagnosis and testing of the system.

CROWN VICTORIA & GRAND MARQUIS

1997-98

Diagnosis and testing requires the use of a Super Star II hand held diagnostic tester, Rotunda model No. 007-0041A, or equivalent, and a suitable digital volt ohm meter.

Refer to **Fig. 19** for symptom chart and **Figs. 20 through 30** for diagnosis and testing of the system.

1999-2000

If vehicle is equipped with air suspension perform the procedure as outlined in "Auto Test."

Refer to **Fig. 31** for symptom chart and **Figs. 31 through 44** for diagnosis and testing of the system.

MARK VIII

Refer to **Fig. 45** for symptom chart and **Figs. 46 through 49,** for diagnosis and testing of the system.

TOWN CAR

1997

Refer to "Crown Victoria & Grand Marquis" for pinpoint tests.

1998-99

Refer to **Fig. 50** for symptom chart and **Figs. 51 through 56** for pinpoint tests.

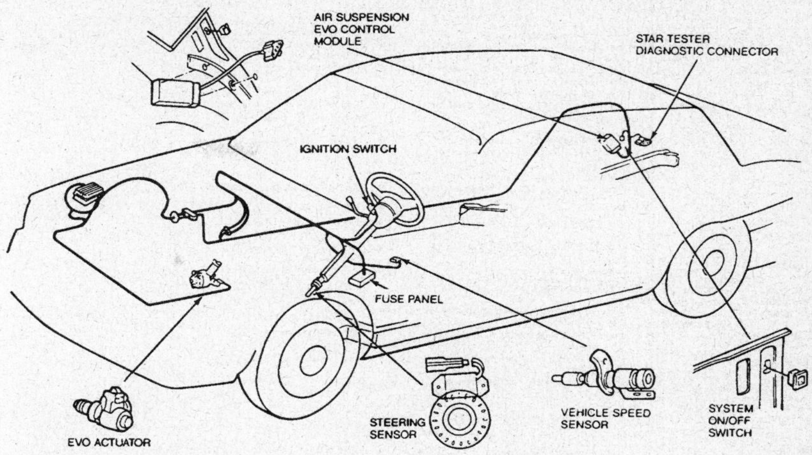

FM6029100179000X

Fig. 2 Component locations electronic variable orifice system. Except Cougar & Thunderbird

Condition	Possible Source	Action
• Pulls to One Side—Vehicle Tends to Pull to One Side When Driven on a Level Surface	• Improper tire pressure. • Improper tire size or different type.	• ADJUST tire pressure. • REPLACE as required.
	• Vehicle is unevenly or excessively loaded.	• ADJUST load.
	• Improper wheel alignment. • Damaged front suspension components or retainers. • Damaged rear suspension components or retainers.	• ADJUST as required.
	• Steering gear valve effort out of balance.	• PLACE transmission in NEUTRAL while driving and TURN engine off (coasting). If vehicle does not pull with the engine off, REPLACE the steering gear valve assembly. — If vehicle does drift with engine off, CROSS-SWITCH front tire / wheel assemblies. — If vehicle pulls to opposite side, CROSS-SWITCH tire / wheel assemblies that were on the rear to same side on the front. — If vehicle pull direction is not changed, CHECK front suspension components and wheel alignment.
	• Check front and rear brakes for proper operation.	• ADJUST if necessary.
	• Check for bent rear axle housing.	• REPLACE if necessary.
• Feedback (Rattle, Chuckle, Knocking Noises in Power Steering Short Rack) — Where Roughness is Felt in the Steering Wheel by the Driver When the Vehicle is Driven Over Rough Pavement	• Steering column intermediate shaft coupling loose / worn.	• REPLACE steering column intermediate shaft coupling assembly.
	• Loose front wheel spindle tie rods and / or tie rod inner ball joints.	• REPLACE front wheel spindle tie rods.
	• Steering gear mounting insulators and / or retaining bolts loose or damaged.	• REPLACE retaining bolts.
	• Steering column gear input shaft coupling connecting bolts loose.	• TIGHTEN bolts at power steering short rack to flex coupling and flex coupling to intermediate shaft.
	• Loose suspension bushings / fasteners or ball joints.	• TIGHTEN suspension fasteners, REPLACE worn bushings, or REPLACE ball joints.
	• Check steering column conditions.	

FM6029500246010X

Fig. 3 Steering systems symptom chart (Part 1 of 3). Cougar & Thunderbird

Auto Test

CROWN VICTORIA & GRAND MARQUIS

1999-2000

Open trunk, then connect New Generation Star (NGS) Tester to air suspension/steering test connector. Select "Air Suspension Auto Test." At the beginning of the automatic portion of the test, the air suspension module checks for a damaged air suspension control module, for unstable battery voltage, then for shorted or open circuits that would create DTC's 39–46 and DTC's 68–71. If shorts or opens are detected, the automatic portion of the test is ended and a DTC 13 is displayed on the Star Tester. If no shorts or opens are detected, the automatic portion of the test continues. The air suspension control module attempts to raise and lower the vehicle to verify that all three air suspension height sensor states (trim, high and low) can be reached. A properly functioning vehicle will be at trim height at the end of the Auto Test procedure. If all three states are not reached, the Auto Test will end and the Star Tester will display a DTC 13. If all systems are functional, a DTC 12 will be displayed. If all systems are functional, perform the manual input portion of the test by following the prompts on the display of the Star Tester.

After the Auto Test and the manual test have been performed, the DTC's will be displayed automatically. Each DTC detected will be displayed for approximately 15 seconds. The code display will continue until all DTC's have been displayed and will repeat until the Star tester button is released.

Condition	Possible Source	Action
• Poor Returnability, Sticky Feel — Steering Fails to Return to Center Following a Turn Without Manual Effort From the Driver. In Addition, When the Driver Returns the Steering Wheel to Center, it May Have a Sticky or Catchy Feel.	• Improper tire pressure. • Improper tire size or different type. • Misaligned steering column or column flange rubbing steering wheel and/or flange. • Steering column gear input shaft universal joints binding. • Check for steering column tube boot tears and/or evidence of binding or damage to front wheel spindle tie rods or ball joints. • Damaged/worn front suspension components. • Improper wheel alignment. • Column bearing binding. • Contamination in system.	• ADJUST tire pressures. • REPLACE as required. • ALIGN steering column. • REPLACE steering column gear input shaft coupling assembly. • REPLACE as necessary. • INSPECT control arm ball joints • ADJUST toe as required. • REPLACE steering column bearing. • FLUSH power steering system.
• Heavy Steering Efforts, Poor Assist or Loss of Assist — Condition Recognized by the Driver While Turning Corners and During Parking Maneuvers.	• Low power steering pump fluid. • Steering gear assembly external or internal leak. • Power steering pump external leak. • Improper drive belt tension • Hose or cooler external leak. • Improper engine idle speed. • Power steering pump pulley loose or warped. • Power Steering pump flow/pressure not to specifications. • Hose or cooler line restricted. • Check steering gear adjustments. • System contaminated. • EVO power steering control valve actuator sticking.	• FILL as required and CHECK for system leaks. • REPLACE power steering pump. • ADJUST drive belt tension. • SERVICE/REPLACE as necessary. • REPLACE power steering pump pulley. • CLEAN or REPLACE as necessary. • INSPECT system for foreign objects, kinked hose. —FLUSH system. • GO to Pinpoint Test A.
• Fluid Leakage	• Overfilled system. • Component leak.	• CORRECT fluid level as required. • LOCATE suspect component, and REFER to service procedures.
• Clicking Type Noise	• Excessive power steering pump wear.	• REPLACE power steering pump.

FM6029500246020X

Fig. 3 Steering systems symptom chart (Part 2 of 3). Cougar & Thunderbird

Condition	Possible Source	Action
• Drive Belt Squeal (Particularly at Full Wheel Travel and Stand Still Parking)	• Loose drive belt.	
• Chirp Noise in Power Steering Pump	• Loose or worn drive belt.	• REPLACE drive belt.
• Swish Type Noise	• A noise created by the flow of excessive fluid into the bypass port of the pump valve housing (with temperature below 54°C (130°F). The shearing effect of the cooler (heavier) oil is not detrimental to power steering pump operation.	• A normal condition. Noise will diminish with fluid temperature increase.
• Power Steering Pump — No or Poor Assist	• Contamination can be caused by foreign objects in the power steering oil reservoir or power steering pump, or metallic particles being generated by cam pack discrepancies.	• System must be flushed thoroughly when installing a serviced or new power steering pump.
• Moan or Whine Type Noise	• Fluid aeration. • Power steering pump loose. • Low fluid. • Hose grounded. • Steering column grounded. • Damaged internal components.	• PURGE the power steering system to reduce aeration noise. • TIGHTEN as required. • CHECK fluid level. • CHECK for hose being grounded. • CHECK steering column alignment. • REPLACE power steering pump.
• Power Steering Short Rack Hiss	• Check steering column intermediate shaft coupling and power steering short rack for alignment and binding. • Check for grounded or loose boot at cowl. • Input shaft and valve assembly.	• ADJUST steering column and/or steering column intermediate shaft coupling. • ALIGN boot or TIGHTEN fasteners as required. • REPLACE—Only if noise is extremely objectionable.
• Other Causes of Noise	• Improper assembly or failure of pump rotating group.	• REPLACE power steering pump.

FM6029500247000X

Fig. 4 Power steering pump noise symptom chart. Cougar & Thunderbird

Condition	Possible Source	Action
• Power Steering Pump and/or Remote Reservoir Leaks	• Excessive fluid fill. • Loose or damaged hose fittings. • Leak at shaft seal: — 1. Seal damage. — 2. Rotor shaft damage, such as helical grooving or the OD has an axial scratch. — Shaft bushing worn. • Damaged or missing outlet fitting O-rings. • Loose outlet fitting. • Outlet fitting, damaged. • Remote reservoir cracked/damaged.	• ADJUST fluid to proper level. • SERVICE or replace. • REPLACE power steering pump. • REPLACE O-rings. • TIGHTEN as required. • REPLACE outlet fitting. • REPLACE remote reservoir.
• Power Steering Pump Leaks, EVO Power Steering Control Valve Actuator	• Damaged EVO actuator O-rings. • EVO actuator electrical connector damaged. • EVO power steering control valve actuator damaged.	• REPLACE power steering control valve actuator. • REPLACE power steering control valve actuator. • REPLACE power steering control valve actuator.
• Noise/Rattle (Steering Column)	• Loose bolts/attaching brackets. • Looseness of ball bearings or insufficient lube. • Steering shaft insulators cracked or dry. • Flex coupling compressed or extended.	• TIGHTEN. • LUBE or REPLACE bearings. • REPLACE or LUBE insulators as required. • REPOSITION shaft assembly to flatten flex coupling.
• Noise/Squeak or Cracks (Steering Column)	• Dry bushings. • Loose or mispositioned shrouds. • Steering wheel rubbing against shrouds. • Dry shift lever grommets. • Insufficient lube on speed control slip ring. • Upper or lower bearing sleeve out of position.	• LUBE shaft seal and shift tube seal. • TIGHTEN or reposition shrouds as required. • REPLACE shroud(s) or steering wheel or REPOSITION shrouds as required. • LUBE grommets. • LUBE slip ring. • REPOSITION bearing sleeve.
• Excessive Travel of Shift Lever Out of Park Detent with Steering Column Locked	• Shift cane spacer clip too small or missing.	• REPLACE or ADD spacer clip.
• Ignition Lock Cylinder Binds in Lock and/or Accessory Position	• Shift cane spacer clip too large.	• REPLACE spacer clip.
• Power Steering Pump Leaks, EVO Power Steering Control Valve Actuator	• Damaged EVO actuator O-rings. • Damaged EVO actuator electrical connector. • Damaged EVO power steering control valve actuator.	• REPLACE power steering control valve actuator. • REPLACE power steering control valve actuator. • REPLACE power steering control valve actuator.

FM6029500246030X

Fig. 3 Steering systems symptom chart (Part 3 of 3). Cougar & Thunderbird

Condition	Possible Source	Action
• NOTE: Evaluation should be conducted on a level road (little road crown) Steering Drift/Wander — Condition Where the Vehicle Wanders Side-To-Side on the Roadway When it is Driven Straight Ahead While the Steering Wheel is Held in a Firm Position	• Check tire size and pressure. • Check if vehicle is unevenly loaded or overloaded. • Loose/worn tie rod ends or ball socket. • Steering gear mounting insulators and/or retaining bolts loose or damaged. • Loose front suspension lower arm struts or ball joint(s). • Steering column gear input shaft coupling connecting bolts loose. • Steering column gear input shaft coupling joints loose/worn. • Improper wheel alignment. • Excessive friction between components. • Excessive toe-in.	• Be sure tire sizes are correct and ADJUST tire pressures. • ADJUST load. • REPLACE tie rod end assembly as necessary. • REPLACE bolts. • REPLACE arm and ball joint assembly. • TIGHTEN at gear and at column. • REPLACE steering column intermediate shaft coupling assembly. • ADJUST as required. • REFER to Sensitive Steering Diagnostic and Service Procedure. • CHECK alignment.
• Pulls to One Side — A Condition Where the Vehicle Tends to Pull to One Side When Driven on a Level Surface	• Improper tire pressure. • Improper tire size or different type. • Vehicle is unevenly or excessively loaded. • Improper wheel alignment. • Damaged front suspension components. • Damaged rear suspension components. • Steering gear valve effort out of balance. • Check front and rear brakes for proper operation. • Check for bent rear axle housing and for damaged or sagging front coil springs in the front and/or rear suspension. • Check for damaged air spring in the front and/or rear suspension. • Check rear suspension for loose/worn rear shock absorber struts, suspension arm retaining fasteners.	• ADJUST tire pressure. • REPLACE as required. • ADJUST load. • ADJUST as required. • REFER to front suspension replacement. • REFER to rear suspension replacement. • PLACE transmission in NEUTRAL while driving and TURN engine off (coasting). If vehicle does not pull with the engine off, REPLACE the steering gear valve assembly. If vehicle does drift with engine off CROSS switch front tire/wheel assemblies. —If vehicle pulls to opposite side, CROSS switch tire/wheel assemblies that were on the rear to same side on the front. —If vehicle pull direction is not changed, CHECK front suspension components and wheel alignment. • ADJUST if necessary. • REPLACE if necessary. • REPLACE if necessary. • TIGHTEN all retaining fasteners.

FM6029600224020X

Fig. 5 Steering systems symptom chart (Part 1 of 3). 1997 Crown Victoria, Grand Marquis & Town Car

Condition	Possible Source	Action
• Feedback (Rattle, Chuckle, Knocking Noises in Steering Gear) — Condition Where Roughness is Felt in the Steering Wheel by the Driver When the Vehicle is Driven Over Rough Pavement	• Steering column gear input shaft coupling joints loose / worn. • Loose tie rod ends. • Steering gear retaining bolts loose or damaged. • Steering column gear input shaft coupling connecting bolts loose. • Loose suspension bushings / fasteners or ball joints. • Check steering gear adjustments. • Check steering column conditions.	• REPLACE steering column intermediate shaft coupling assembly. • REPLACE tie rod ends. • REPLACE retaining bolts and tighten. • TIGHTEN bolts to specification at steering gear and at steering column intermediate shaft coupling. • TIGHTEN suspension fasteners, REPLACE worn bushings, or REPLACE ball joints.
• Poor Returnability, Sticky Feel — Condition Noticed When the Steering Fails to Return to Center Following a Turn Without Manual Effort From the Driver. In Addition, When the Driver Returns the Steering Wheel to Center, it May Have a Sticky or Catchy Feel	• Improper tire pressure. • Improper tire size or incorrect type. • Misaligned steering column or column flange rubbing steering wheel and / or flange. • Steering column gear input shaft coupling universal joints binding. • Check for steering column tube boot tears and / or evidence of binding or damage to tie rod ends. • Damaged / worn front suspension components. • Improper wheel alignment. • Column bearing binding. • Contamination in system. • Check steering gear adjustments.	• ADJUST tire pressures. • REPLACE as required. • ALIGN steering column. • REPLACE steering column intermediate shaft coupling assembly. • REPLACE as necessary. • INSPECT control arm ball joints. • ADJUST toe as required. • REPLACE bearing. • FLUSH power steering system as outlined under Cleaning and Inspection.
• Light Steering Efforts at All Vehicle Speeds	• Electronic variable orifice (EVO actuator).	• Vehicles with air suspension, GO to Pinpoint Test B1. Vehicles without air suspension, GO to Pinpoint Test DTC 28.
• Excessive Steering Effort While Making Quick Maneuvers at High Speed	• Steering sensor.	• Vehicles with air suspension, GO to Pinpoint Test B. Vehicles without air suspension, GO to Pinpoint Test DTC 33.

FM6029600224030X

Fig. 5 Steering systems symptom chart (Part 2 of 3). 1997 Crown Victoria, Grand Marquis & Town Car

Condition	Possible Source	Action
• Drive Belt Squeal (Particularly at Full Steering Wheel Travel and Stand Still Parking)	• Loose drive belt.	• ADJUST drive belt tension to specification.
• Chirp Noise in Steering Pump	• Loose or worn drive belt.	• ADJUST drive belt tension to specification or REPLACE drive belt.
• Power Steering Pump Noisy	• Low fluid level and possible leak.	• REFILL to specified level. PURGE air from system. CHECK for leaks. SERVICE as required.
• Swish Type Noise	• A noise created by the flow of excessive fluid into the bypass port of the pump valve housing (with temperature below 55°C (130°F). The shearing effect of the cooler (heavier) fluid is not detrimental to power steering pump operation.	• A normal condition. Noise will diminish with fluid temperature increase.
• Clicking Type Noise	• Excessive power steering pump wear.	• REPLACE power steering pump.

FM6029600225010X

Fig. 6 Power steering pump noise symptom chart (Part 1 of 2). 1997 Crown Victoria, Grand Marquis & Town Car

CONDITION	POSSIBLE SOURCE	ACTION
• NOTE: Evaluation should be conducted on a level road (little road crown). Wander — Condition Where Vehicle Wanders Side-To-Side on Roadway When it is Driven Straight Ahead While Steering Wheel is Held in a Firm Position	• Check tire size and pressure. • Check if vehicle is unevenly loaded or overloaded. • Loose / worn front wheel spindle tie rods or ball socket. • Steering gear mounting insulators and / or retaining bolts loose or damaged. • Loose front suspension lower arm struts or ball joint(s). • Steering column gear input shaft coupling connecting bolts loose. • Steering column gear input shaft coupling joints loose / worn. • Improper wheel alignment.	• Be sure tire sizes are correct and ADJUST tire pressures. • ADJUST load. • REPLACE front wheel spindle tie rod or tie rod assembly as necessary. • REPLACE bolts. • REPLACE arm and ball joint assembly. • TIGHTEN at power steering short rack and at steering column. • REPLACE steering column gear input shaft coupling assembly. • ADJUST as required.

FM6029500238010X

Fig. 7 Steering systems symptom chart (Part 1 of 4). 1997 Mark VIII

Condition	Possible Source	Action
• Heavy Steering Efforts, Poor Assist or Loss of Assist — Condition Recognized by the Driver While Turning Corners and During Parking Maneuvers	• Low power steering pump fluid. • Steering gear assembly external or internal leak. • Power steering pump external leak. • Improper drive belt tension. • Hose or cooler external leak. • Improper engine idle speed. • Power steering pump pulley loose or warped. • Power steering pump flow / pressure not to specifications. • Hose or cooler line restriction. • Check steering gear adjustments. • System contamination. • EVO power steering control valve actuator sticking.	• FILL as required and CHECK for system leaks. • REPLACE power steering pump. • ADJUST drive belt tension. • SERVICE / REPLACE as necessary. • ADJUST idle. • REPLACE power steering pump pulley. • CLEAN or REPLACE as necessary. • INSPECT system for foreign objects, kinked hose, etc. —FLUSH system. • Vehicles with air suspension, GO to Pinpoint Test B. • Vehicles without air suspension, GO to Pinpoint Test A.
• Fluid Leakage	• Overfilled system. • Component leak.	• CORRECT fluid level as required. • LOCATE suspect component, and
• Power Steering Pump Leaks, EVO Power Steering Control Valve Actuator	• Damaged EVO power steering control valve actuator ring. • EVO power steering control valve actuator electrical connector damaged. • EVO power steering control valve actuator damaged.	• Vehicles without air suspension, GO to Pinpoint Test A. Vehicles with air suspension, GO to Pinpoint Test B.

FM6029600224040X

Fig. 5 Steering systems symptom chart (Part 3 of 3). 1997 Crown Victoria, Grand Marquis & Town Car

Condition	Possible Source	Action
• Power Steering Pump / Remote Power Steering Oil Reservoir Leaks	• Excessive fluid fill. • Fluid cap missing, loose, damaged or missing O-ring. • Loose or damaged hose fittings. • Leakage at shaft seal or any visible point on pump.	• ADJUST fluid to proper level. • SERVICE or REPLACE, if required. • SERVICE or REPLACE. • REPLACE power steering pump.
• Power Steering Pump — No or Poor Assist	• Contamination can be caused by foreign objects in the power steering oil reservoir or power steering pump or metallic particles being generated by cam pack discrepancies.	• Thoroughly flush system when installing a serviced or new power steering pump.
• Moan or Whine Type Noise	• Fluid aeration. • Power steering pump loose or misaligned on engine. • Low fluid. • Hose grounded. • Steering column grounded. • Damaged internal components.	• PURGE the power steering system to reduce aeration noise. • TIGHTEN or ALIGN as required. • CHECK fluid level. • CHECK for hose being grounded. • CHECK steering column tube alignment. • REPLACE power steering pump.

FM6029600225020X

Fig. 6 Power steering pump noise symptom chart (Part 2 of 2). 1997 Crown Victoria, Grand Marquis & Town Car

MARK VIII

1. Open hood and locate air suspension/steering test connector on righthand front shock tower. Install battery charger to power vehicle during testing.
2. Open trunk, then connect New Generation Star (NGS) Tester to air suspension/steering test connector. Select air suspension auto test.
3. Ensure both doors are closed, then turn air suspension switch OFF then to ON.
4. Turn ignition switch from OFF to Run, then press trigger button to begin auto test.
5. **Do not lean of vehicle or open doors while DTC 10 is displayed. This will introduce false errors into the test results.**
6. DTC 10 is displayed while the auto test is running. Any faults discovered by the auto test will halt test and the DTC's will be displayed.
7. When DTC 12 is displayed, open driver door, turn steering wheel a minimum of ¼ turn in both directions, exit vehicle and close the driver door, then open and close the passenger door and press trigger to continue test.
8. Read displayed DTC's. DTC 11 means vehicle has passed auto test, other DTC's retrieved indicate faults that must be repaired.
9. If vehicle passes auto test, exit diagnostics by turning ignition switch OFF

CONDITION	POSSIBLE SOURCE	ACTION
• Pulls to One Side — A Condition Where Vehicle Tends to Pull to One Side When Driven on a Level Surface	• Improper tire pressure. • Improper tire size or different type. • Vehicle is unevenly or excessively loaded. • Improper wheel alignment. • Damaged front suspension components. • Damaged rear suspension components. • Steering gear valve effort out of balance. • Check front and rear brakes for proper operation. • Check for damaged air spring in the front and/or rear suspension. • Check rear suspension for loose/worn rear shock absorber struts, rear suspension arm and bushing retaining fasteners.	• ADJUST tire pressure. • REPLACE as required. • ADJUST load. • ADJUST as required. • PLACE transmission in NEUTRAL while driving and TURN engine off (coasting). If vehicle does not pull with the engine off, REPLACE the power steering short rack assembly. • If vehicle does drift with engine off: — CROSS-SWITCH front tire/wheel assemblies. — If vehicle pulls to opposite side, CROSS-SWITCH tire/wheel assemblies that were on the rear to same side on the front. — If vehicle pull direction is not changed, CHECK front suspension components and wheel alignment. • ADJUST if necessary. • REPLACE if necessary. • TIGHTEN all retaining fasteners.
• Feedback (Rattle, Chuckle, Knocking Noises in Power Steering Short Rack — Condition Where Roughness is Felt in the Steering Wheel By the Driver When the Vehicle is Driven Over Rough Pavement	• Steering column gear input shaft coupling loose/worn. • Loose front wheel spindle tie rods and/or tie rod inner ball joints. • Steering gear mounting insulators and/or retaining bolts loose or damaged. • Steering column gear input shaft coupling connecting bolts loose. • Loose suspension bushings/fasteners or ball joints. • Check steering column conditions.	• REPLACE steering column gear input shaft coupling assembly. • REPLACE front wheel spindle tie rods. • REPLACE retaining bolts. • TIGHTEN bolts at power steering short rack to flex coupling and flex coupling to intermediate shaft. • TIGHTEN suspension fasteners, REPLACE worn bushings, or REPLACE ball joints.

FM6029500238020X

Fig. 7 Steering systems symptom chart (Part 2 of 4). 1997 Mark VIII

CONDITION	POSSIBLE SOURCE	ACTION
• Poor Returnability, Sticky Feel — Condition Noticed When the Steering Fails to Return to Center Following a Turn Without Manual Effort From the Driver. In Addition, When the Driver Returns the Steering Wheel to Center, it May Have a Sticky or Catchy Feel	• Improper tire pressure. • Improper tire size or different type. • Misaligned steering column or column flange rubbing steering wheel and/or flange. • Steering column gear input shaft universal joints binding. • Check for steering column tube boot tears and/or evidence of binding or damage to front wheel spindle tie rods or ball joints. • Damaged/worn front suspension components. • Improper wheel alignment. • Column bearing binding. • Contamination in system.	• ADJUST tire pressures. • REPLACE as required. • ALIGN steering column. • REPLACE steering column gear input shaft coupling assembly. • REPLACE as necessary. • INSPECT control arm ball joints. • ADJUST toe as required. • REPLACE steering column tube bearing. • FLUSH power steering system.
• Light Steering Efforts at All Vehicle Speeds	• Variable assist (EVO).	• REFER to Pinpoint Test B.
• Excessive Steering Effort While Making Quick Maneuvers at High Speed	• Variable assist (EVO).	• REFER to Pinpoint Test C.
• Heavy Steering Efforts, Poor Assist or Loss of Assist — Condition Recognized by the Driver While Turning Corners and During Parking Maneuvers	• Low power steering pump fluid. • Power steering short rack assembly external or internal leak. • Power steering pump external leak. • Improper drive belt tension • Hose or cooler external leak. • Improper engine idle speed. • Power steering pump pulley loose or warped. • Power steering pump flow/pressure not to specifications. • Hose or cooler line restricted. • Check steering gear adjustments. • System contaminated. • EVO power steering control valve actuator sticking.	• FILL as required and CHECK for system leaks. • REPLACE power steering pump. • CHECK drive belt tensioner. • SERVICE/REPLACE as necessary. • REPLACE power steering pump pulley. • CLEAN or REPLACE as necessary. • INSPECT system for foreign objects, kinked hose, etc. —FLUSH system. • GO to Pinpoint Test A.
• Fluid Leakage	• Overfilled system. • Component leak.	• CORRECT fluid level as required. • LOCATE suspect component, and
• Drive Belt Squeal	• Check drive belt for proper tension or glazing.	• CHECK automatic tensioner or REPLACE drive belt as required.
• Power Steering Pump Noisy	• Low fluid level and possible leak.	• REFILL to specified level. PURGE air from system. CHECK for leaks. SERVICE as required.
• Swish Type Noise	• Fluid flow into the bypass valve of the pump valve housing with fluid temperature below 54°C (130°F).	• Normal noise.

FM6029500238030X

Fig. 7 Steering systems symptom chart (Part 3 of 4). 1997 Mark VIII

CONDITION	POSSIBLE SOURCE	ACTION
• Whine Type Noise	• Aerated fluid, vacuum leak in system.	• PURGE system of air.
• Clicking Type Noise	• Excessive power steering pump wear.	• REPLACE power steering pump.
• Power Steering Pump/Remote Reservoir Leaks	• Excessive fluid fill. • Loose or damaged hose fittings. • Leak at shaft seal: — Seal damage. — Rotor shaft damage, such as helical grooving or the OD has an axial scratch. — Shaft bushing worn. • Damaged or missing outlet fitting O-rings. • Loose outlet fitting. • Outlet fitting, damaged. • Remote reservoir cracked/damaged.	• ADJUST fluid to proper level. • SERVICE or REPLACE. • REPLACE power steering pump. • REPLACE O-rings. • TIGHTEN as required. • REPLACE outlet fitting. • REPLACE remote reservoir.
• Power Steering Pump Leaks, EVO Power Steering Control Valve Actuator	• Damaged EVO actuator O-rings. • EVO actuator electrical connector damaged. • EVO power steering control valve actuator damaged.	• REPLACE power steering control valve actuator. • REPLACE power steering control valve actuator. • REPLACE power steering control valve actuator.

FM6029500238040X

Fig. 7 Steering systems symptom chart (Part 4 of 4). 1997 Mark VIII

CONDITION	POSSIBLE SOURCE	ACTION
• Drive Belt Squeal (Particularly at Full Wheel Travel and Stand Still Parking)	• Loose drive belt.	• CHECK automatic tensioner.
• Chirp Noise in Power Steering Pump	• Loose or worn drive belt.	• CHECK automatic tensioner or REPLACE drive belt.
• Swish Type Noise	• A noise created by the flow of excessive fluid into the bypass port of the pump valve housing (with temperature below 130°). The shearing effect of the cooler (heavier) oil is not detrimental to power steering pump operation.	• A normal condition. Noise will diminish with fluid temperature increase.
• Power Steering Pump — No or Poor Assist	• Contamination can be caused by foreign objects in the power steering oil reservoir or power steering pump, or metallic particles being generated by cam pack discrepancies.	• System must be flushed thoroughly when installing a serviced or new power steering pump.
• Moan or Whine Type Noise	• Fluid aeration. • Power steering pump loose. • Low fluid. • Hose grounded. • Steering column grounded. • Damaged internal components.	• PURGE the power steering system to reduce aeration noise. • TIGHTEN as required. • CHECK fluid level. • CHECK for hose being grounded. • CHECK steering column alignment. • REPLACE power steering pump.

FM6029500239010X

Fig. 8 Power steering pump noise symptom chart (Part 1 of 2). 1997 Mark VIII

and disconnecting New Generation Star (NGS) Tester.

POWER STEERING SYSTEM SERVICE

Component Service

CONTROL MODULE, REPLACE

Cougar & Thunderbird

1. Turn ignition switch to OFF position, then locate module on A/C evaporator housing behind glove compartment.
2. Remove two screws and power steering variable assist control and bracket from A/C evaporator housing.
3. Disconnect wiring and remove from vehicle.
4. Reverse procedure to install.

Crown Victoria, Grand Marquis & Town Car

The EVO control module and air suspension modules are one unit. Turn air suspension switch off, then proceed as follows:

1. **On 1997–98 models,** remove glove compartment, then detach control module from snap in fingers on bracket behind glove compartment.
2. **On 1999–2000 models,** remove lower dash panel, disconnect lamp from panel, disconnect wiring, then remove screws from module.
3. **On all models,** pull module out to gain access to connectors.
4. Disconnect each connector by pushing connector release button and pulling connector from module.
5. Reverse procedure to install. **Torque** attaching nuts to 60–84 inch lbs.

CONDITION	POSSIBLE SOURCE	ACTION
• Steering Gear Hiss	• Check steering column gear input shaft coupling and steering gear for alignment and binding. • Check for grounded or loose boot at dash panel. • Input shaft and valve assembly.	• ADJUST steering column and/or steering column gear input shaft coupling. • ALIGN boot or TIGHTEN fasteners as required. • REPLACE—Only if noise is extremely objectionable.
• Noise/Rattle (Steering Column)	• Loose bolts/attaching brackets. • Looseness of ball bearings or insufficient lube. • Steering shaft insulators cracked or dry. • Flex coupling compressed or extended.	• TIGHTEN. • LUBE or REPLACE bearings. • REPLACE or LUBE insulators as required. • REPOSITION shaft assembly to flatten flex coupling.
• Noise/Squeak or Cracks (Steering Column)	• Dry bushings. • Loose or mispositioned shrouds. • Steering wheel rubbing against shrouds. • Dry shift lever grommets. • Insufficient lube on speed control slip ring. • Upper or lower bearing sleeve out of position.	• LUBE shaft seal and shift tube seal. • TIGHTEN or REPOSITION shrouds as required. • REPLACE shroud(s) or steering wheel or REPOSITION shrouds as required. • LUBE grommets. • LUBE slip ring. • REPOSITION bearing sleeve.
• Excessive Travel of Shift Lever Out of Park Detent with Steering Column Locked	• Shift cane spacer clip too small or missing.	• REPLACE or ADD spacer clip.
• Ignition Lock Cylinder Binds in Lock and/or Accessory Position	• Shift cane spacer clip too large.	• REPLACE spacer clip.
• Other Causes of Noise	• Improper assembly of pump rotating group. • Imperfections on inside diameter or power steering pump CAM surface. • Damaged power steering pump rotor splines. • Hairline crack on cam inner surface. • Interference between power steering pump rotor and cam. • Excessively worn or scored pumping elements and power steering pump pressure plates. • Internal damage or component imperfection.	• REPLACE power steering pump as required. • REPLACE power steering pump. • REPLACE power steering pump. • REPLACE power steering pump. • REPLACE power steering pump. • REPLACE power steering pump. • REPLACE power steering pump.

FM6029500239020X

Fig. 8 Power steering pump noise symptom chart (Part 2 of 2). 1997 Mark VIII

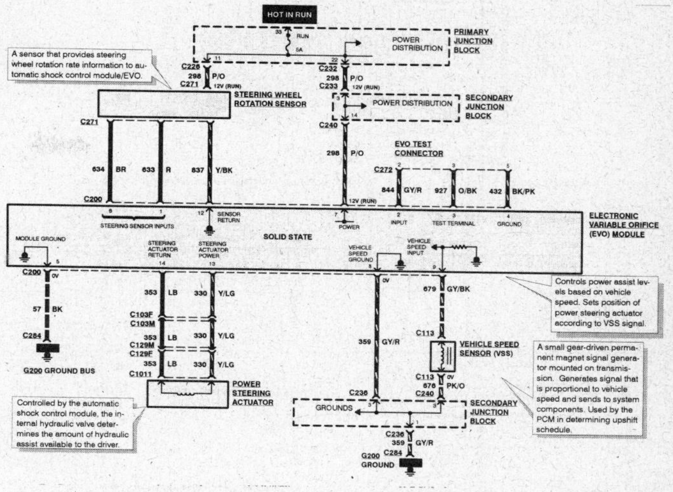

FM6029500243000X

Fig. 9 Wiring diagram. Cougar & Thunderbird

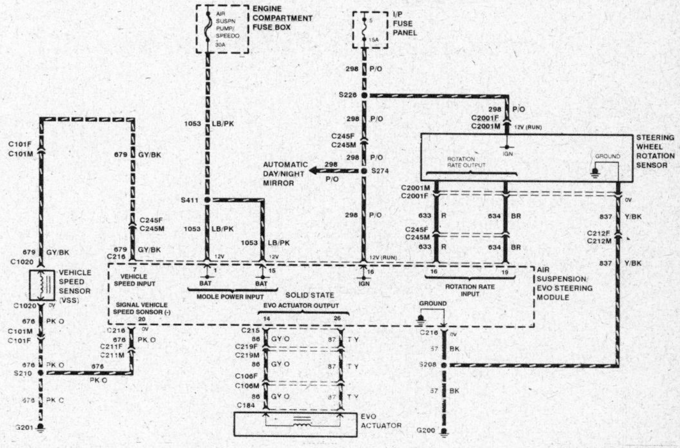

FM6029700284000X

Fig. 11 Wiring diagram. Crown Victoria & Grand Marquis w/air suspension

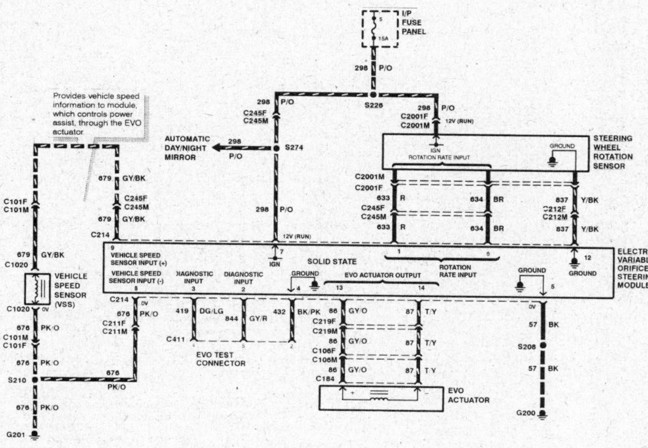

FM6029700283000X

Fig. 10 Wiring diagram. Crown Victoria & Grand Marquis less air suspension

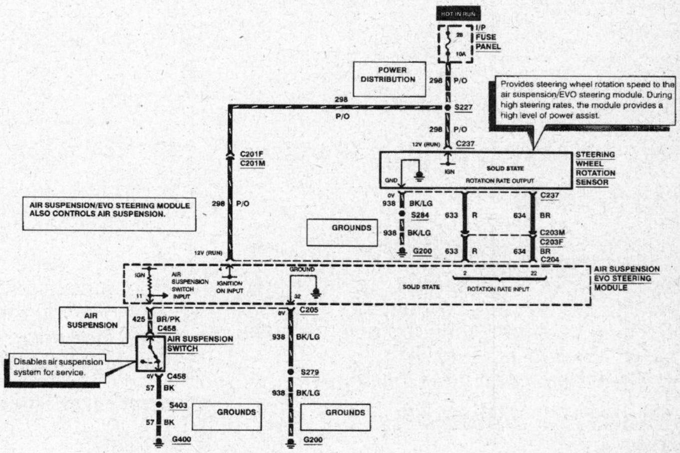

FM6029700273010X

Fig. 12 Wiring diagram (Part 1 of 2). Mark VIII

CONTROL VALVE ACTUATOR, REPLACE

1997–98

1. Disconnect EVO wiring harness connector from EVO actuator.
2. Disconnect return hose, then pressure hose from the power steering pump. Plug all openings.
3. Disconnect belt from pulley, then remove pump and pulley assembly.
4. Place power steering pump in a vise and remove EVO actuator assembly from power steering pump using a 6mm Allen hex from the back side of the actuator.
5. Install actuator assembly to pump housing, then **torque** to 10–15 ft. lbs.
6. Install pump and pulley assembly to engine. **Torque** four pump retaining bolts to 15–22 ft. lbs.
7. Remove plugs and connect return and pressure hoses to power steering pump.
8. Connect EVO wiring harness to EVO actuator assembly.
9. Purge power steering system of air.

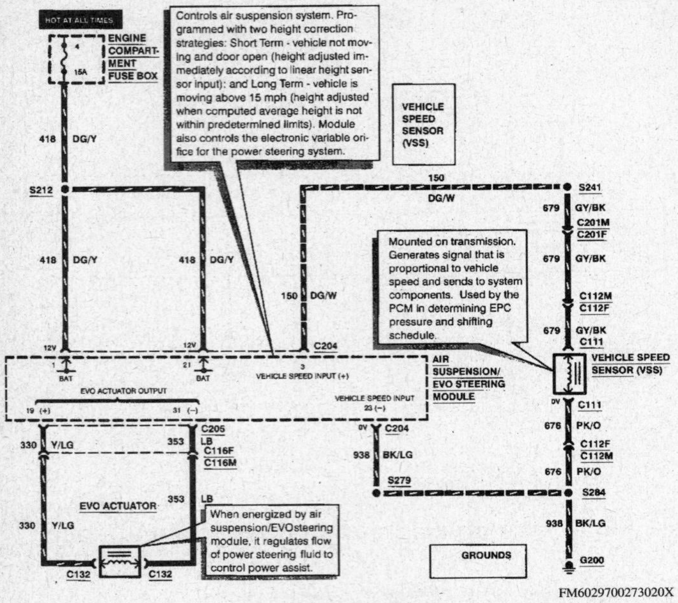

Fig. 12 Wiring diagram (Part 2 of 2). Mark VIII

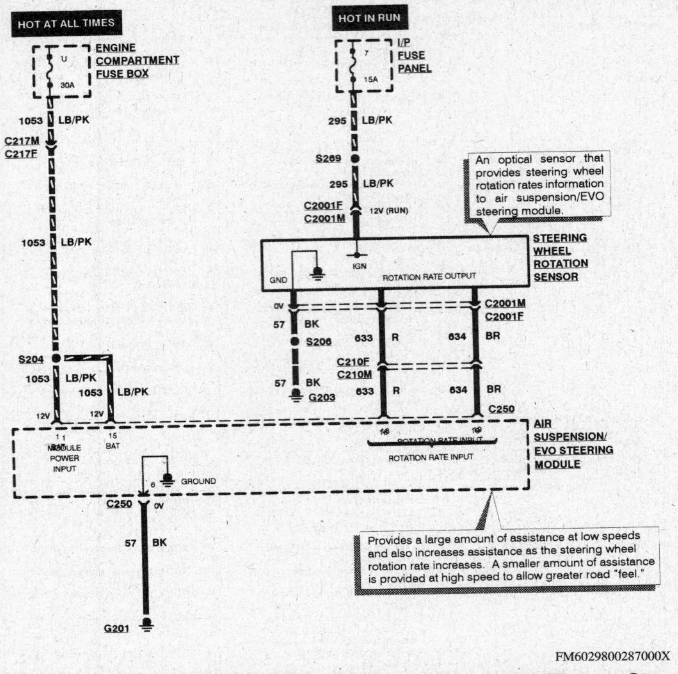

Fig. 13 Wiring diagram (Part 1 of 2). 1997 Town Car

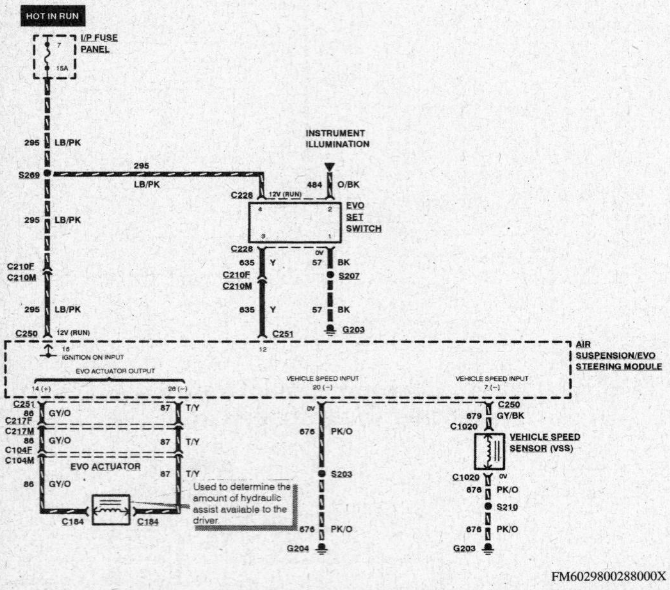

Fig. 13 Wiring diagram (Part 2 of 2). 1997 Town Car

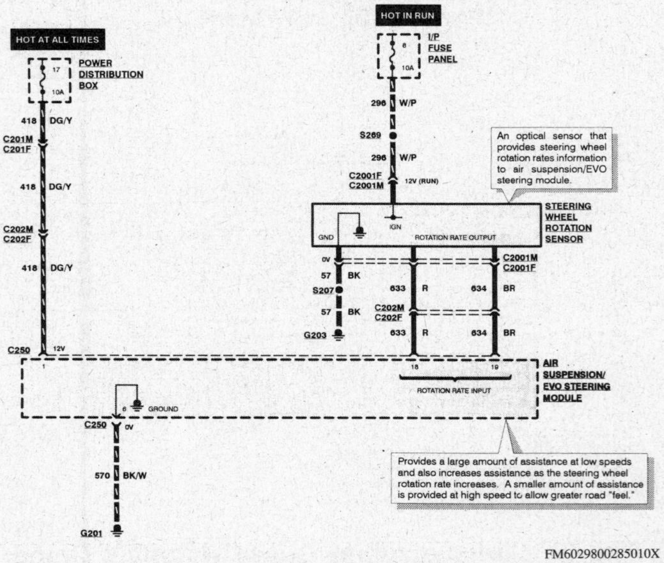

Fig. 14 Wiring diagram (Part 1 of 2). 1998–99 Town Car

1999–2000

1. Raise and support vehicle.
2. Remove engine oil filter.
3. Disconnect power steering auxiliary actuator electrical connector.
4. Remove screw, then the power steering auxiliary actuator.
5. Reverse procedure to install.

STEERING SENSOR, REPLACE

1. **On 1999–2000 models,** remove sound panel, finish panel and knee bolster and bracket from under steering column.
2. **On all models,** disconnect sensor electrical connector.
3. Remove sensor electrical connector from bracket under instrument panel.
4. Remove two sensor retaining screws, then the sensor, **Fig. 57.**
5. Reverse procedure to install.

STEERING SENSOR RING, REPLACE

1. Remove steering column as outlined under "Steering Column, Replace."
2. Remove steering shaft from steering column, then the sensor ring.
3. Reverse procedure to install.

SPEED SENSOR, REPLACE

1. Raise and support vehicle.
2. Remove speed sensor mounting clip retaining bolt.
3. Remove speed sensor and driven gear from transmission.
4. Disconnect electrical connector from speed sensor.
5. Remove driven gear retainer, then the driven gear.
6. Reverse procedure to install. Ensure internal O-ring is seated in sensor housing.

DIAGNOSTIC CHART INDEX

Code/Test	Description	Page No.	Fig. No.
COUGAR & THUNDERBIRD			
—	Symptom chart	16-36	15
Test A	Steering Very Difficult/Very Easy	16-36	16
Test B	Steering Does Not Vary w/Vehicle Speed	16-37	17
Test C	Steering Diagnostics Cannot Be Entered	16-37	18
MARK VIII			
—	Symptom Chart	16-49	45
35	EVO Power Steering Control Valve Actuator Concern	16-49	46
45	Steering Rotation Not Detected	16-50	47
Test A	EVO Power Steering Control Valve Actuator Concern	16-49	46
Test B	Steering Rotation Not Detected	16-50	47
Test C	Steering Diagnostics Cannot Be Entered	16-51	48
Test D	Steering Does Not Vary With Vehicle Speed	16-53	49
1997–98 CROWN VICTORIA & GRAND MARQUIS & 1997 TOWN CAR			
—	Symptom Chart	16-37	19
16	Steering Very Difficult Or Very Easy	16-39	30
17	Steering Very Difficult Or Very Easy	16-39	30
18	Steering Very Difficult Or Very Easy	16-39	30
27	Actuator Circuit Open	16-38	20
28	Actuator Circuit Shorted	16-38	21
29	Actuator High Side Short To Ground	16-38	22
30	Actuator Circuit Shorted To Battery	16-38	23
31	Actuator Circuit Low Side Shorted To Ground	16-38	24
33	Steering Wheel Rotation Not Detected	16-38	25
35	Vehicle Speed Above 15 MPH Not Detected	16-38	26
55	Steering Does Not Vary w/Vehicle Speed	16-38	27
74	Steering Wheel Rotation Not Detected	16-39	28
Test A	Steering Diagnostics Can Not Be Entered	16-39	29
Test B	Steering Very Difficult Or Very Easy	16-39	30
1999–2000 CROWN VICTORIA & GRAND MARQUIS			
—	Symptom Chart	16-41	31
16	EVO Actuator Shorted	16-43	36
17	EVO Actuator Shorted Or Open	16-43	36
18	EVO Actuator Resistance Out Of Range	16-43	36
27	EVO Actuator Circuit Open	16-44	37
28	EVO Actuator Circuit Shorted	16-44	38
29	EVO Actuator Circuit High Side Shorted To Ground	16-45	39
30	EVO Actuator Circuit Shorted To Battery	16-45	40
31	EVO Actuator Circuit Low Side Shorted To Ground	16-46	41
33	Steering Rotation Not Detected	16-46	42
35	Vehicle Speed Above 15 mph Not Detected	16-47	43
74	Steering Rotation Not Detected	16-48	44
Test A	No Communication With EVO Control Module	16-41	32
Test B	No Communication With Air Suspension Control Module	16-41	33
Test C	Unable To Enter Auto Test-EVO Control Module	16-42	34
Test D	Unable To Enter Auto Test-Air Suspension Control Module	16-42	35
1998–99 TOWN CAR			
—	Symptom Chart	16-54	50
1441	Steering Sensor Circuit Failure	16-54	51
1442	Steering Sensor Circuit Failure	16-54	51
1897	Steering VAPS II Circuit Loop Failure	16-56	52
Test A	Steering Sensor Circuit Failure	16-54	51
Test B	Steering VAPS II Circuit Loop Failure	16-56	52
Test C	Steering Is Very Difficult/Very Easy	16-56	53
Test D	Steering Does Not Vary w/Increased Wheel Rotation	16-57	54

Continued

DIAGNOSTIC CHART INDEX—Continued

Code/Test	Description	Page No.	Fig. No.
1998–99 TOWN CAR			
Test E	Steering Does Not Vary w/Vehicle Speed	16-57	55
Test F	No Communication w/Rear Air Suspension Control Module	16-57	56

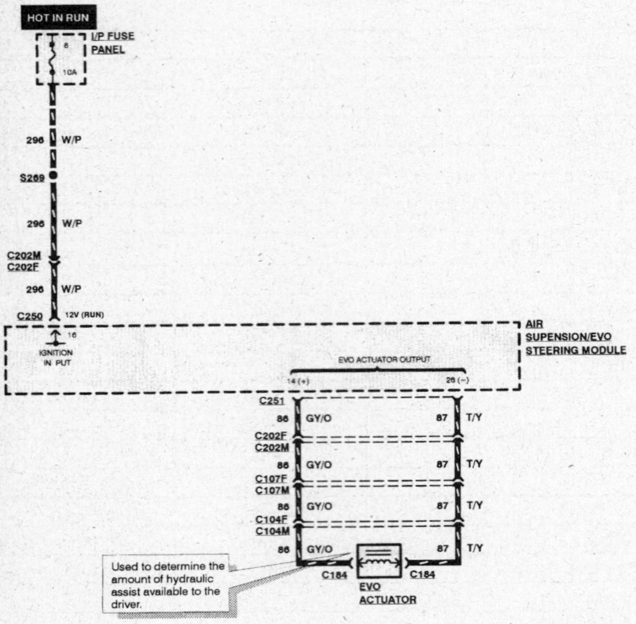

FM6029800286010X

Fig. 14 Wiring diagram (Part 2 of 2). 1998–99 Town Car

	Test Step	Result ▶	Action to Take
A1	CHECK CONNECTIONS		
	• Verify harness connector at EVO power steering control valve actuator on power steering pump is seated. • Verify harness connector on EVO control module is seated (located in luggage compartment). • **Is connector seated properly?** 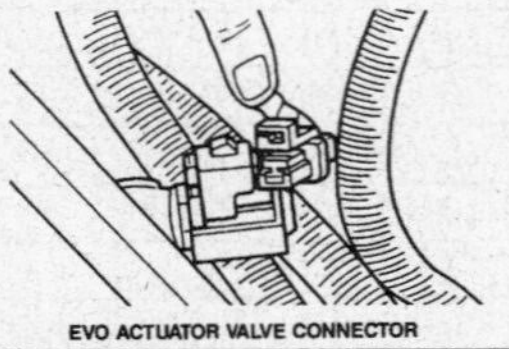 	Yes ▶ No ▶	GO to **A2.** MAKE proper connection. GO to **A2.**
A2	CONTROL MODULE CHECK		
	• Turn ignition switch to OFF position. • Locate data link connector located behind glove compartment. • Connect the EVO system tester to jumper and to the data link connector located behind glove compartment. • Start engine. When engine starts, the control module will turn on the diagnostic lamp for one second to indicate: — Control module is functional — Tester is functional • **Does lamp turn on steadily?**	Yes ▶ No ▶	GO to **A3.** GO to Pinpoint Test Step **C1.**
A3	ACTUATOR OUTPUT CIRCUIT CHECK		
	• After the one second control module check, the control module will perform the Actuator Output Test. If there is a short to ground or an open circuit, after two seconds delay, the diagnostic lamp will flash a Diagnostic Trouble Code 6 (on for 0.5 second and off for 0.5 second, 6 times) then delay two seconds and repeat continuously until the power is turned off. During this "failure mode" the control module output will be off and both speed and steering wheel rotation inputs will be disabled. Once this "failure mode" has occurred, the control module will be inoperable until power is removed and reapplied. • **Does lamp flash a Diagnostic Trouble Code 6?**	Yes ▶ No ▶	GO to **A8.** GO to **A4.**
A4	STEERING WHEEL SENSOR CHECK		
	• Start engine (transmission in PARK). • Vehicle speed: zero km/h (mph) • Turn steering wheel from lock to lock. The steering wheel must be rotated in one direction at least 220 degrees. • **Does diagnostic lamp turn on after sufficient steering wheel rotation?**	Yes ▶ No ▶	GO to **A5.** GO to **A17.**

FM6029500248010X

Fig. 16 Test A: Steering Very Difficult/Very Easy (Part 1 of 4). Cougar & Thunderbird

Condition	Possible Source	Action
• Steering Very Difficult / Very Easy	• Power steering control valve actuator. • Steering wheel rotation sensor. • Circuitry open / shorted. • EVO control module.	• GO to Pinpoint Test A.
• Steering Does Not Vary With Vehicle Speed	• Vehicle speed sensor. • Circuitry open / shorted. • EVO control module .	• GO to Pinpoint Test B.
• Steering Diagnostics Can Not Be Entered	• Circuitry open / shorted. • EVO control module.	• GO to Pinpoint Test C.
• Light Steering Efforts at All Vehicle Speeds	• Variable assist (EVO).	• GO to Pinpoint Test C.
• Excessive Steering Effort While Making Quick Maneuvers at High Speed	• Variable assist (EVO).	• GO to Pinpoint Test C.
• Wander — Vehicle Wanders Side-To-Side on Roadway When it is Driven Straight Ahead While Steering Wheel is Held in a Firm Position NOTE: Evaluation should be conducted on a level road (little road crown).	• Check tire size and pressure. • Check if vehicle is unevenly loaded or overloaded. • Loose / worn front wheel spindle tie rods or ball socket. • Steering gear mounting insulators and / or retaining bolts loose or damaged. • Loose front suspension lower arm struts or ball joint(s). • Steering column gear input shaft coupling connecting bolts loose. • Steering column gear input shaft coupling joints loose / worn. • Improper wheel alignment.	• Be sure tire sizes are correct and ADJUST tire pressures. • ADJUST load. • REPLACE tie rod end assembly as necessary. • REPLACE bolts. • REPLACE arm and ball joint assembly. • TIGHTEN at power steering short rack and at steering column. • REPLACE steering column intermediate shaft coupling assembly. • ADJUST as required.

FM6029500245000X

Fig. 15 Symptom chart. Cougar & Thunderbird

	Test Step	Result ▶	Action to Take
A5	VEHICLE SPEED SENSOR CHECK ABOVE 24 KM/H (10 MPH)		
	• Start engine. • Steering wheel rate: 0 rpm • Operate vehicle on road and apply vehicle speed of greater than 24 km/h (15 mph). • **Does diagnostic lamp turn on for all speeds greater than 24 km/h (15 mph)?**	Yes ▶ No ▶	GO to **A6.** GO to Pinpoint Test Step **B1.**
A6	VEHICLE SPEED SENSOR CHECK BELOW 16 KM/H (15 MPH)		
	• Reduce vehicle speed to below 16 km/h (10 mph) • **Does diagnostic lamp turn off when speed is below 16 km/h (10 mph)?**	Yes ▶ No ▶	Electrical portion of system is functioning. GO to Pinpoint Test Step **B1.**
A7	SERVICE POWER STEERING		
	• Refer to Service Procedures. • Perform Pump Flow and Pressure Tests. • **Are concerns found?**	Yes ▶ No ▶	SERVICE as required. System OK. RESTORE vehicle. TEST DRIVE vehicle.
A8	DTC 6 ACTIVATED: EVO ACTUATOR VALVE CHECK (SHORT TO GROUND OR AN OPEN CIRCUIT)		
	• Turn ignition switch to OFF position. • Verify harness connection on the EVO power steering control valve actuator on power steering pump is properly seated. • Check connector condition on power steering control valve actuator. • **Is connector properly seated?**	Yes ▶ No ▶	GO to **A9.** Make proper connection, GO to **A2.**
A9	CHECK RESISTANCE ACROSS ACTUATOR VALVE		
	• Ignition switch in OFF position. • Locate the control module behind glove compartment. • Using an ohmmeter, measure resistance across Pin 13 and Pin 14 of harness connector. Resistance should be 7-18 ohms. If the resistance is greater than 1000 ohms, the circuit is open. • **Is resistance 7-18 ohms?**	Yes ▶ No ▶	GO to **A10.** GO to **A11.**
A10	CHECK CONTINUITY OF WIRING		
	• Ignition switch in OFF position. • Disconnect EVO harness connector from EVO power steering control valve actuator located on power steering pump. • Test continuity of Circuits 330 (Y/LG) and 353 (LB) from the actuator connector to the control module connector. • **Is there continuity?**	Yes ▶ No ▶	GO to **A11.** SERVICE suspect circuit for open. GO to **A1.**

FM6029500248020X

Fig. 16 Test A: Steering Very Difficult/Very Easy (Part 2 of 4). Cougar & Thunderbird

Test Step		Result	Action to Take
A11	CHECK EVO ACTUATOR VALVE RESISTANCE		
	• Disconnect EVO harness connector from EVO power steering control valve actuator located on power steering pump. • Using an ohmmeter, measure resistance across the two actuator valve connector pins. • **Is resistance 5 to 20 ohms?** 	Yes ▶ No ▶	GO to **A12**. REPLACE EVO power steering control valve actuator. RESTORE vehicle. RETEST system.
A12	CHECK WIRE HARNESS FOR PROPER CONNECTION		
	• Ignition switch in OFF position. • EVO harness disconnected from EVO power steering control valve actuator. • Disconnect EVO control module from the connector in luggage compartment. • **Is module connected?**	Yes ▶ No ▶	GO to **A16**. GO to **A13**.
A13	CHECK WIRE HARNESS FOR SHORT TO GROUND CIRCUIT 330 (Y/LG)		
	• Using an ohmmeter, measure resistance between Pin 5 (ground) and Pin 13 harness connector. • **Is resistance 5 ohms or less?**	Yes ▶ No ▶	SERVICE Circuit 330 (Y/LG) for short. GO to **A14**. GO to **A14**.
A14	CHECK WIRE HARNESS FOR SHORT TO GROUND CIRCUIT 353 (LB)		
	• Using an ohmmeter, measure resistance between Pin 5 (ground) and Pin 14 of harness connector. • **Is resistance 5 ohms or less?**	Yes ▶ No ▶	SERVICE suspect circuit for short to B+. RESTORE vehicle. RETEST system. GO to **A15**.
A15	CHECK CIRCUITS 330 (Y/LG) AND 353 (LB) FOR SHORT TO B +		
	• Ignition switch in RUN position. • EVO harness disconnected from EVO power steering control valve actuator on power steering pump. • Using a voltmeter, measure the voltage across Pin 13 and Pin 5, Pin 14 and Pin 5. • **Is voltage greater than 5 volts?**	Yes ▶ No ▶	SERVICE suspect circuit for short to B+. GO to **A1**. GO to **A16**.
A16	CHECK FOR SHORT ACROSS CIRCUITS 330 (Y/LG) AND 353 (LB)		
	• Ignition switch in OFF position. • EVO harness disconnected from EVO actuator valve on power steering pump. • EVO control disconnected from harness connector. • Using an ohmmeter, measure resistance across Pin 13 and Pin 14 on harness connector. • **Is resistance 5 ohms or less?**	Yes ▶ No ▶	SERVICE wires for short. GO to **A1**. REPLACE EVO control module. RESTORE vehicle. RETEST system.
A17	CHECK STEERING WHEEL SENSOR CONNECTION		
	• Verify harness connection on steering wheel rotation sensor (located on lower portion of steering column) is properly seated. • **Is connector properly seated?**	Yes ▶ No ▶	GO to **A18**. MAKE proper connection. GO to **A1**.

FM6029500248030X

Fig. 16 Test A: Steering Very Difficult/Very Easy (Part 3 of 4). Cougar & Thunderbird

Test Step		Result	Action to Take
B1	CHECK SPEED SENSOR CONNECTION		
	• Make sure harness connection on vehicle speed sensor (located on the transmission) is properly seated. • **Is connector properly seated?**	Yes ▶ No ▶	GO to **B2**. MAKE proper connection. GO to Pinpoint Test Step **A1**.
B2	SPEED SENSOR CHECK		
	• Turn ignition switch to OFF position. • Disconnect the electrical connector from the EVO module (located in luggage compartment). • Make sure there is no damage to harness and that: — Circuit 679 is in Pin 9 — Circuits 359 and 676 are in Pin 8 • **Are wires crossed or damaged?**	Yes ▶ No ▶	SERVICE wires. GO to Pinpoint Test Step **A1**. GO to **B3**.
B3	TEST VEHICLE SPEED SENSOR GROUND CIRCUIT		
	• Test continuity of vehicle speed sensor ground Circuit 359 (GY/R) from Pin 8 of module connector to a known good ground. • **Is Circuit 359 (GY/R) continuous to ground?**	Yes ▶ No ▶	GO to **B4**. SERVICE wire to ground eyelet as necessary. GO to Pinpoint Test Step A1.
B4	TEST VEHICLE SPEED SENSOR		
	• Start engine. • Perform Speedometer Reads 0 MPH at All Speeds Pinpoint Test • **Are concerns found?**	Yes ▶ No ▶	SERVICE GO to Pinpoint Test Step **A1**. REPLACE EVO control module. RESTORE vehicle. RETEST system.

FM6029500249000X

Fig. 17 Test B: Steering Does Not Vary w/Vehicle Speed. Cougar & Thunderbird

Test Step		Result	Action to Take
A18	STEERING WHEEL ROTATION SENSOR CHECK		
	• Ignition switch in OFF position. • Disconnect EVO control module from connector—located in luggage compartment. • Examine wiring harness, verify that there is no damage and — Circuit 633 (R) is in Pin 1 — Circuit 634 (BR) is in Pin 6 — Circuit 837 (Y/BK) is in Pin 12 • **Are wires crossed or damaged?**	Yes ▶ No ▶	SERVICE wires as necessary. GO to **A1**. GO to **A19**.
A19	TEST STEERING WHEEL ROTATION SENSOR SIGNALS		
	• Using a jumper, connect Pin 12 to Pin 5 (connector disconnected). • Start engine. • While rotating the steering wheel slowly, and using an ohmmeter set to the 1K scale, measure the resistance from — Pin 1 to Pin 5 — Pin 6 to Pin 5 • **Does meter vary for both circuits?**	Yes ▶ No ▶	SHUT off engine. REPLACE EVO control module. RESTORE vehicle. RETEST system. GO to **A20**.
A20	STEERING WHEEL ROTATION SENSOR WIRE CHECK		
	• Ignition switch in the OFF position. • Disconnect steering sensor (located on lower steering column). • Check wires at steering sensor connector for damage and/or incorrect location. • Test continuity of Pin 1, Circuit 633 (R), Pin 6, Circuit 634 (BR), and Pin 12, Circuit 837 (Y/BK) from steering sensor to EVO control module connector. • **Is there continuity?**	Yes ▶ No ▶	SERVICE wires for open. GO to **A1**. GO to **A21**.
A21	CHECK FOR SHORT ACROSS CIRCUITS 633 (R) AND 634 (BR)		
	• Turn ignition switch to OFF position. • Steering sensor disconnected. • Disconnect control module connector. Measure resistance between — Pin 1 and Pin 6 — Pin 1 and Pin 12 — Pin 6 and Pin 12 • **Is resistance 5 ohms or less?**	Yes ▶ No ▶	SERVICE wires for short. GO to **A1**. GO to **A22**.
A22	TEST STEERING SENSOR POWER		
	• Using a jumper, connect Pin 12 to Pin 5 of the control module connector. (Connector disconnected.) • Turn ignition switch to RUN position. • Using a voltmeter, measure the voltage between Circuits 298 (P/O) and 837 (Y/BK) at the steering sensor connector. • **Are there 12 volts?**	Yes ▶ No ▶	GO to **A23**. SERVICE Circuit 298 (P/O) for open. GO to **A1**.
A23	TEST STEERING SENSOR POWER CIRCUIT		
	• Remove jumper and connect module connector. • Using a voltmeter, measure the voltage between Circuits 298 (P/O) and 837 (Y/BK) at the steering sensor connector. • **Are there 12 volts?**	Yes ▶ No ▶	REPLACE steering sensor. RESTORE vehicle. RETEST system. REPLACE control module. RESTORE vehicle. RETEST system.

FM6029500248040X

Fig. 16 Test A: Steering Very Difficult/Very Easy (Part 4 of 4). Cougar & Thunderbird

Test Step		Result	Action to Take
C1	DIAGNOSTIC LAMP CHECK		
	• Test the EVO Service Diagnostic Lamp or EVO system tester in another vehicle to see if the device is functional. • Check connection of bulb in tool. • **Are concerns found?**	Yes ▶ No ▶	REPLACE bulb or tester. GO to **C3**. GO to **C2**.
C2	RETEST CONTROL MODULE		
	• Turn ignition switch to OFF position. • Connect EVO system tester lamp to data link connector in luggage compartment. • Start engine. • **Does lamp turn on or flicker?**	Yes ▶ No ▶	GO to Pinpoint Test Step **A3**. GO to **C3**.
C3	EVO CONTROL MODULE CHECK		
	• Turn ignition switch to OFF position. • Make sure connector is properly connected to control module. • **Is connection properly secured?**	Yes ▶ No ▶	GO to **C4**. SECURE connection. GO to Pinpoint Test Step **A2**.
C4	CHECK POWER FEED		
	• Turn ignition switch to the OFF position. • Disconnect EVO control module connector. • Turn ignition switch to RUN position. • Using a voltmeter, measure voltage from Pin 7 (ignition in RUN only) to Pin 5 (ground) at control module connector. • **Are there 12 volts?**	Yes ▶ No ▶	REPLACE EVO control module. RESTORE vehicle. RETEST system. SERVICE short to ground or open in Circuit 298 (P/O) as necessary. GO to Pinpoint Test Step **A1**.

FM6029500250000X

Fig. 18 Test C: Steering Diagnostics Cannot Be Entered. Cougar & Thunderbird

Condition	Possible Source	Action
• Steering Very Difficult/Very Easy DTC 16, 17 or 18	• Power steering pump actuator valve. • Circuitry open/shorted. • EVO control module. • Computer controlled suspension.	• GO to EVO Steering Diagnosis. PERFORM Actuator Output Circuit Test, Steering Wheel Sensor Test and Vehicle Speed Sensor Test as outlined. PERFORM Pinpoint Test B
• Engine Stalls with High Wheel Rotation	• Inoperative idle speed control circuit.	
• Steering Does Not Vary with Increased Wheel Rotation Speed	• Steering wheel rotation sensor inoperative. • Open/shorted circuitry.	• GO to EVO Steering Diagnosis. PERFORM Steering Wheel Sensor Test as outlined. PERFORM Pinpoint Test B (vehicles with Computer Controlled Suspension System).
• Steering Does Not Vary With Vehicle Speed DTC 55 or DTC 35	• Vehicle speed sensor. • Circuitry open/shorted. • EVO control module.	• GO to EVO Steering Diagnosis. PERFORM Vehicle Speed Sensor Test as outlined (DTC 35) for vehicles without computer controlled suspension. PERFORM Pinpoint Test DTC 55 (vehicles with Computer Controlled Suspension System).
• Steering Diagnostics Can Not Be Entered	• Circuitry open/shorted. • EVO control module. • Computer controlled suspension.	• GO to Pinpoint Test A (vehicle without Computer Controlled Suspension).

FM6029600224010X

Fig. 19 Symptom chart. 1997–98 Crown Victoria, Grand Marquis & 1997 Town Car

Test Step		Result	Action to Take
27-1	CHECK EVO ACTUATOR CONNECTION		
	• Ignition switch OFF. • Access EVO actuator. • Check actuator harness connector. • **Is actuator harness connector firmly plugged into actuator?**	Yes	GO to **27-2**.
		No	INSTALL actuator harness connector correctly. REPEAT Actuator Output Circuit Test.
27-2	CHECK HIGH SIDE CIRCUIT CONTINUITY		
	• Access EVO control module. • Disconnect control module connector. • Access EVO actuator. • Disconnect actuator connector. • Measure resistance between Pin 13, Circuit 86 (GY/O) of control module and Circuit 86 (GY/O) at actuator. • **Is resistance less than 5 ohms?**	Yes	GO to **27-3**.
		No	SERVICE open high side circuit. GO to Pinpoint Test A.
27-3	CHECK LOW SIDE CIRCUIT CONTINUITY		
	• Measure resistance between Pin 14, Circuit 87 (T/Y) of control module and Circuit 87 (T/Y) at actuator. • **Is resistance less than 5 ohms?**	Yes	REPLACE EVO actuator. RESTORE vehicle. REPEAT Actuator Output Test.
		No	SERVICE open low side circuit. RESTORE vehicle. REPEAT Actuator Output Test.

FM6029600226000X

Fig. 20 Code 27: Actuator Circuit Open. 1997–98 Crown Victoria, Grand Marquis & 1997 Town Car

Test Step		Result	Action to Take
29-1	CHECK CIRCUIT 86 (GY/O)		
	• Ignition switch OFF. • Access EVO actuator and disconnect harness connector. • Access EVO control module and disconnect harness connector. • Measure resistance between Pin 13, Circuit 86 (GY/O) and Pin 5, Circuit 57 (BK). • **Is resistance less than 100K ohms?**	Yes	SERVICE Circuit 86 (GY/O) and/or Circuit 86 (GY/O) for short to ground. RESTORE vehicle. REPEAT Actuator Output Test.
		No	GO to **29-2**.

FM6029600228010X

Fig. 22 Code 29: Actuator High Side Short To Ground (Part 1 of 2). 1997–98 Crown Victoria, Grand Marquis & 1997 Town Car

Test Step		Result	Action to Take
30-1	CHECK ACTUATOR CIRCUIT 86 (GY/O)		
	• Ignition switch OFF. • Access EVO control module. • Disconnect harness connector. • Disconnect EVO actuator. • Measure voltage between Pin 13, Circuit 86 (GY/O) and Pin 5, Circuit 57 (BK). • **Is B+ present?**	Yes	SERVICE Circuit 86 (GY/O) for short to B+. RESTORE vehicle. REPEAT Actuator Output Test.
		No	GO to **30-2**.
30-2	CHECK ACTUATOR CIRCUIT 87 (T/Y)		
	• Measure voltage between Pin 14, Circuit 87 (T/Y) and Pin 5, Circuit 57 (BK). • **Is B+ present?**	Yes	SERVICE Circuit 87 (T/Y) for short to B+. RESTORE vehicle. REPEAT Actuator Output Test.
		No	REPLACE EVO control module. RESTORE vehicle. REPEAT Actuator Output Test.

FM6029600229000X

Fig. 23 Code 30: Actuator Circuit Shorted To Battery. 1997–98 Crown Victoria, Grand Marquis & 1997 Town Car

Test Step		Result	Action to Take
33-1	CHECK CIRCUIT CONTINUITY		
	• Ignition switch OFF. • Access EVO control module and disconnect harness connector. • Access steering wheel rotation sensor and disconnect harness connector. • Measure resistance of Circuit 633 (R/Y), 634 (BR) and 837 (Y/BK) between steering wheel rotation sensor connector and EVO control module connector. • **Is resistance less than 5 ohms?**	Yes	GO to **33-2**.
		No	SERVICE open or high resistance circuits. RESTORE vehicle. REPEAT Steering Wheel Sensor Test.

FM6029600231010X

Fig. 25 Code 33: Steering Wheel Rotation Not Detected (Part 1 of 2). 1997–98 Crown Victoria, Grand Marquis & 1997 Town Car

Test Step		Result	Action to Take
35-1	CHECK SPEEDOMETER OPERATION		
	• Check for proper speedometer operation. • **Does speedometer indicate vehicle speeds above 24 km/h (15 mph)?**	Yes	GO to **35-2**.
		No	SERVICE Circuits 679 (GY/BK) and/or 676 (PK/O) or vehicle speed sensor.
35-2	CHECK CIRCUIT 679 (GY/BK)		
	• Ignition switch OFF. • Access instrument cluster connector C2 and disconnect harness connector. • Access EVO control module and disconnect harness connector • Measure resistance between instrument cluster Pin C2-14 and EVO control module Pin 9. • **Is resistance 5 ohms or less?**	Yes	GO to **35-3**.
		No	SERVICE open in Circuit 679 (GY/BK) between instrument cluster and EVO control module. RESTORE vehicle. REPEAT Vehicle Speed Sensor Test.
35-3	CHECK CIRCUIT 676 (PK/O)		
	• Measure resistance between EVO control module Pin 8 and Pin 5. • **Is resistance 5 ohms or less?**	Yes	REPLACE EVO control module. RESTORE vehicle. REPEAT Vehicle Speed Sensor Test.
		No	SERVICE open Circuit 676 (PK/O). RESTORE vehicle. REPEAT Vehicle Speed Sensor Test.

FM6029600232000X

Fig. 26 Code 35: Vehicle Speed Above 15 mph Not Detected. 1997–98 Crown Victoria, Grand Marquis & 1997 Town Car

Test Step		Result	Action to Take
28-1	CHECK CIRCUIT RESISTANCE		
	• Ignition switch OFF. • Access EVO control module. • Disconnect harness connector. • Access EVO actuator. • Disconnect actuator connector. • Measure resistance between Pin 13, Circuit 86 (GY/O) and Pin 14, Circuit 87 (T/Y) of control module connector. • **Is resistance less than 100K ohms?**	Yes	SERVICE short between Circuit 86 (GY/O) and Circuit 87 (T/Y). RESTORE vehicle. REPEAT Actuator Output Test.
		No	GO to **28-2**.
28-2	CHECK ACTUATOR RESISTANCE		
	• Measure resistance of EVO actuator. • **Is resistance less than 5 ohms?**	Yes	REPLACE EVO actuator. RESTORE vehicle. REPEAT Actuator Output Test.
		No	REPLACE control module. RESTORE vehicle. REPEAT Actuator Output Test.

FM6029600227000X

Fig. 21 Code 28: Actuator Circuit Shorted. 1997–98 Crown Victoria, Grand Marquis & 1997 Town Car

Test Step		Result	Action to Take
29-2	CHECK ACTUATOR		
	• Reconnect EVO actuator. • Measure resistance between Pin 13, Circuit 86 (GY/O) and Pin 5, Circuit 57 (BK). • **Is resistance less than 100K ohms?**	Yes	REPLACE EVO actuator. RESTORE vehicle. REPEAT Actuator Output Test.
		No	REPLACE EVO control module. RESTORE vehicle. REPEAT Actuator Output Test.

FM6029600228020X

Fig. 22 Code 29: Actuator High Side Short To Ground (Part 2 of 2). 1997–98 Crown Victoria, Grand Marquis & 1997 Town Car

Test Step		Result	Action to Take
31-1	CHECK CIRCUIT 87 (T/Y)		
	• Ignition switch OFF. • Access EVO actuator and disconnect harness connector. • Access EVO control module and disconnect harness connector. • Measure resistance between Pin 14, Circuit 87 (T/Y) and Pin 5, Circuit 57 (BK). • **Is resistance less than 10K ohms?**	Yes	SERVICE Circuit 87 (T/Y) for short to ground. RESTORE vehicle. REPEAT Actuator Output Test.
		No	GO to **31-2**.
31-2	CHECK ACTUATOR		
	• Reconnect EVO actuator. • Measure resistance between Pin 14, Circuit 87 (T/Y) and Pin 5, Circuit 57 (BK). • **Is resistance less than 10K ohms?**	Yes	REPLACE EVO actuator. RESTORE vehicle. REPEAT Actuator Output Test.
		No	REPLACE control module. RESTORE vehicle. REPEAT Actuator Output Test.

FM6029600230000X

Fig. 24 Code 31: Actuator Circuit Low Side Shorted To Ground. 1997–98 Crown Victoria, Grand Marquis & 1997 Town Car

Test Step		Result	Action to Take
33-2	CHECK STEERING WHEEL ROTATION SENSOR SUPPLY		
	• Turn ignition switch to RUN. • Measure voltage at steering wheel rotation sensor Circuit 298 (P/O). • **Is B+ present?**	Yes	REPLACE sensor. RESTORE vehicle. REPEAT steering wheel sensor test.
		No	SERVICE Circuit 298 (P/O) between Fuse 17 (15A) of fuse junction panel and sensor. RESTORE vehicle. REPEAT Steering Wheel Sensor Test.

FM6029600231020X

Fig. 25 Code 33: Steering Wheel Rotation Not Detected (Part 2 of 2). 1997–98 Crown Victoria, Grand Marquis & 1997 Town Car

Test Step		Result	Action to Take
55-1	CHECK SPEED SENSOR CONNECTION (DTC 55 CONCERN)		
	• Make sure harness connection on vehicle speed sensor (located on the transmission) is properly seated. • **Is connector properly seated?**	Yes	GO to **55-2**.
		No	MAKE proper connection. GO to Pinpoint Test Step **B1**.
55-2	SPEED SENSOR CHECK		
	• Turn ignition switch to the OFF position. • Disconnect electrical connectors from the EVO module (located in luggage compartment). • Make sure there is no damage to harness and that: — Circuit 679 (GY/BK) is in Pin 7. — Circuit 676 (PK/O) is in Pin 20. • **Are wires damaged or crossed?**	Yes	SERVICE wires. GO to Pinpoint Test Step **B1**.
		No	GO to **55-3**.
55-3	TEST SPEED SENSOR GROUND CIRCUIT		
	• Test continuity of speed sensor ground Circuit 676 (PK/O) from Pin 20 to Pin 6. • **Is there continuity?**	Yes	GO to **55-4**.
		No	SERVICE wire or ground eyelet as necessary. GO to Pinpoint Test Step **B1**.

FM6029600233010X

Fig. 27 Code 55: Steering Does Not Vary w/Vehicle Speed (Part 1 of 2). 1997–98 Crown Victoria, Grand Marquis & 1997 Town Car

Test Step		Result		Action to Take
55-4	TEST VEHICLE SPEED SENSOR			
	• Turn ignition switch to RUN position. • Perform Speedometer / Odometer Reads Inaccurately Test. • **Are concerns found?**	Yes	▶	GO to Pinpoint Test Step
		No	▶	GO to **55-5**.
55-5	EVO CONTROL MODULE CHECK			
	• Turn ignition switch to OFF position. • Make sure harness connectors are properly connected to module. • Check air suspension switch connection. • Check if the air suspension switch is turned on. • **Is connector properly seated?**	Yes	▶	GO to **55-6**.
		No	▶	SECURE connection. GO to **55-6**.
55-6	CHECK POWER FEED			
	• Turn ignition switch to the OFF position. • Disconnect EVO control module connectors C1 and C2. • Turn ignition switch to RUN position. • Using Rotunda Digital Volt-Ohmmeter 014-00407 or equivalent, measure voltage from Pin 16, Circuit 295 (LB / PK) Town Car, Circuit 298 (P / O) Crown Victoria, Grand Marquis (ignition-run only) to Pin 6, Circuit 57 (BK) (ground) at pin connectors. • Measure voltage from Pin 1 to Pin 6. • If 12 volts from Pin 1 to Pin 6 connect, test light between Pins 1 and 6. • **Are there 12 volts with bright light?**	Yes	▶	REPLACE EVO control module. RESTORE vehicle. RETEST system.
		No	▶	SERVICE short to ground, high resistance or open in Circuit 298 (P / O), 295 (LB / PK) or 1053 (LB / PK) as necessary. GO to Pinpoint Test Step **B1**.

FM6029600233020X

Fig. 27 Code 55: Steering Does Not Vary w/Vehicle Speed (Part 2 of 2). 1997–98 Crown Victoria, Grand Marquis & 1997 Town Car

Test Step		Result		Action to Take
A1	DIAGNOSTIC LAMP CHECK			
	• Test the Rotunda Super Star II Tester 007-0041B or equivalent in another vehicle to see if the equipment is functional. • Check connection of tool to data link connector. • **Are concerns found?**	Yes	▶	REPLACE tester.
		No	▶	GO to **A2**.
A2	RETEST CONTROL MODULE			
	• Turn ignition switch to OFF position. • Connect Rotunda Super Star II Tester 007-0041B or equivalent to data link connector. • Start engine. • Latch HOLD / TEST button down. • **Does DTC 20 appear?**	Yes	▶	GO to Entering EVO Diagnostics.
		No	▶	GO to **A3**.
A3	EVO CONTROL MODULE CHECK			
	• Turn ignition switch to OFF position. • Make sure connector is properly connected to module. • **Is connection properly secured?**	Yes	▶	GO to **A4**.
		No	▶	SECURE connection. GO to Entering EVO Diagnostics.
A4	CHECK POWER FEED			
	• Turn ignition switch to the OFF position. • Disconnect EVO control module connector. • Turn ignition switch to RUN position. • Using Rotunda Digital Volt-Ohmmeter 014-00407 or equivalent, measure voltage from Pin 7, Circuit 298 (P / O) to Pin 5, Circuit 57 (BK) at harness connector. • **Are there 12 volts?**	Yes	▶	REPLACE EVO control module. RESTORE vehicle. RETEST system.
		No	▶	GO to **A5**.

FM6029600234010X

Fig. 29 Test A: Steering Diagnostics Can Not Be Entered (Part 1 of 2). 1997–98 Crown Victoria, Grand Marquis & 1997 Town Car

Test Step		Result		Action to Take
74-1	CHECK CIRCUIT RESISTANCE			
	• Ignition switch OFF. • Access EVO control module and disconnect harness Connector C216. • Access steering wheel rotation sensor and disconnect harness Connector C2001. • Measure resistance of Circuit 633 (R / Y) and 634 (BR) between steering wheel rotation sensor Connector C2001 and EVO control module Connector C216. • **Is resistance less than 5 ohms?**	Yes	▶	GO to **74-2**.
		No	▶	SERVICE open or high resistance circuits. RESTORE vehicle. REPEAT Steering Wheel Sensor Test.
74-2	CHECK STEERING WHEEL ROTATION SENSOR SUPPLY			
	• Turn ignition switch to RUN. • Measure voltage at steering wheel rotation sensor Circuit 298 (P / O). • **Is B+ present?**	Yes	▶	REPLACE sensor. RESTORE vehicle. REPEAT steering wheel sensor test.
		No	▶	SERVICE Circuit 298 (P / O) between Fuse 5 (15A) of fuse junction panel and sensor. RESTORE vehicle. REPEAT Steering Wheel Sensor Test.

FM6029700279000X

Fig. 28 Code 74: Steering Wheel Rotation Not Detected. 1997–98 Crown Victoria & Grand Marquis

Test Step		Result		Action to Take
A5	CHECK GROUND			
	• Measure resistance from Pin 5, Circuit 57 (BK) to a known good ground. • **Is resistance 5 ohms or less?**	Yes	▶	SERVICE Circuit 298 (P / O) for open. RESTORE vehicle. REPEAT Entering EVO Diagnostics.
		No	▶	SERVICE Circuit 57 (BK) for open. RESTORE vehicle. REPEAT Entering EVO Diagnostics.

FM6029600234020X

Fig. 29 Test A: Steering Diagnostics Can Not Be Entered (Part 2 of 2). 1997–98 Crown Victoria, Grand Marquis & 1997 Town Car

Test Step		Result		Action to Take
B1	DETERMINE REQUIRED TEST STEP (DTC 16, 17 AND 18)			
	• Enter EVO Steering Diagnosis as outlined. • Read and record displayed DTC(s). • Each DTC must be addressed individually. If more than one DTC is detected, perform the test step required for each DTC. • **Is DTC 16, 17 or 18 displayed?**	Yes	▶	GO to **B6**.
		No	▶	GO to **B2**.
B2	DETERMINE REQUIRED TEST STEP (DTC 74)			
	• Read and record displayed DTC(s). • Each DTC must be addressed individually. If more than one DTC is detected, perform the test step required for each DTC. • **Is DTC 74 displayed?**	Yes	▶	GO to **B22**.
		No	▶	GO to **B3**.
B3	DETERMINE REQUIRED TEST STEP (DTC 55)			
	NOTE: Code 55 is only generated in drive cycle test. • Cycle ignition on, then off. • Turn Star tester on with button raised. • Depress button. • Read and record displayed DTC(s). • Each DTC must be addressed individually. If more than one DTC is detected, perform the test step required for each DTC. • **Is DTC 55 displayed?**	Yes	▶	GO to Pinpoint Test DTC 55.
		No	▶	GO to **B4**.
B4	DETERMINE REQUIRED TEST STEP (DTC 11 / 15)			
	• Read and record displayed DTC(s). • Each DTC must be addressed individually. If more than one DTC is detected, perform the test step required for each DTC. • **Is DTC 11 or 15 displayed?**	Yes	▶	REFER to Pump Flow and Pressure Tests as outlined in Service Procedures.
		No	▶	GO to **B5**.
B5	DETERMINE REQUIRED TEST STEP (OTHER DTCs)			
	• Read and record displayed DTC(s). • Each DTC must be addressed individually. If more than one DTC is detected, perform the test step required for each DTC. • **Are DTCs other than 11, 15, 16, 17, 18, 55 or 74 detected?**	Yes	▶	suspension diagnostics.
		No	▶	GO to **B6**.
B6	EVO ACTUATOR VALVE CHECK (SHORT TO GROUND OR AN OPEN CIRCUIT) (DTC 16, 17 AND 18 CONCERN)			
	• Turn ignition switch to OFF position. • Verify harness connection on the EVO power steering control valve actuator on power steering pump is properly seated. • **Is connector properly seated?**	Yes	▶	GO to **B7**.
		No	▶	MAKE proper connection. GO to **B1**.
B7	DTC 16: EVO ACTUATOR VALVE CHECK (SHORT TO GROUND)			
	• Turn ignition switch to OFF position. • Read all DTCs. • **Is DTC 16 displayed?**	Yes	▶	GO to **B13**.
		No	▶	GO to **B8**.

FM6029600235010X

Fig. 30 Test B: Codes 16, 17 or 18: Steering Very Difficult or Very Easy (Part 1 of 5). 1997–98 Crown Victoria, Grand Marquis & 1997 Town Car

Step	Test Step	Result	Action to Take
B8	DTC 17: EVO ACTUATOR VALVE CHECK (SHORT TO GROUND OR AN OPEN CIRCUIT)		
	• Turn ignition switch to the OFF position. • Read all DTCs. • **Is DTC 17 displayed?**	Yes ▶ No ▶	GO to **B10.** GO to **B9.**
B9	DTC 18: EVO ACTUATOR VALVE CHECK (BAD VALVE INDUCTANCE)		
	• Turn ignition switch to OFF position. • Read all DTCs. • **Is DTC 18 displayed?**	Yes ▶ No ▶	**REPLACE EVO valve. RESTORE vehicle. RETEST system.** GO to **B10.**
B10	CHECK RESISTANCE ACROSS ACTUATOR VALVE		
	• Ignition switch in OFF position. • Locate the control module behind glove compartment. Harness connector can be disconnected from module without removing module. • Using an ohmmeter, measure resistance across Pin 14 and Pin 26 of harness connector. Resistance should be 7-18 ohms. If the resistance is greater than 1000 ohms, the circuit is open. • **Is resistance between 7-18 ohms?**	Yes ▶ No ▶	GO to **B11.** GO to **B12.**
B11	CHECK CONTINUITY OF WIRING		
	• Ignition switch in OFF position. • Disconnect EVO harness connector from EVO actuator valve located on power steering pump. • Test continuity of Circuits 86 (GY / O) and 87 (T / Y) from the actuator connector to the EVO control module connector. • **Is there continuity?**	Yes ▶ No ▶	GO to **B12.** **SERVICE wires as necessary. GO to B1.**
B12	CHECK EVO ACTUATOR VALVE		
	• Disconnect EVO harness connector from EVO power steering control valve actuator located on power steering pump. • Using an ohmmeter, measure resistance across the two actuator valve connector pins. • **Is resistance greater than 20 ohms or less than 5 ohms?**	Yes ▶ No ▶	**REPLACE EVO valve. RESTORE vehicle. RETEST system.** GO to **B14.**
B13	CHECK EVO ACTUATOR VALVE RESISTANCE		
	• Disconnect EVO harness connector from EVO power steering control valve actuator located on power steering pump. • Using an ohmmeter, measure resistance across the two actuator valve connector pins. • **Is resistance between 5-20 ohms?**	Yes ▶ No ▶	GO to **B14.** GO to **B17.**
B14	CHECK WIRE HARNESS		
	• Ignition switch in OFF position. • EVO harness disconnected from EVO power steering control valve actuator. • Disconnect EVO control module from the connector behind glove compartment. • **Was module not connected properly?**	Yes ▶ No ▶	**MAKE proper connection. RESTORE vehicle. RETEST system.** GO to **B15.**
B15	CHECK WIRE HARNESS FOR SHORT TO GROUND (PIN 14 RESISTANCE OVER 1000 OHMS)		
	• Using an ohmmeter, measure resistance between Pin 6 (ground) and Pin 14 of harness connector. • **Is resistance over 1000 ohms?**	Yes ▶ No ▶	GO to **B17.** GO to **B16.**

FM6029600235020X

Fig. 30 Test B: Codes 16, 17 or 18: Steering Very Difficult or Very Easy (Part 2 of 5). 1997–98 Crown Victoria, Grand Marquis & 1997 Town Car

Step	Test Step	Result	Action to Take
B16	CHECK WIRE HARNESS FOR SHORT TO GROUND (PIN 14 RESISTANCE LESS THAN 10 OHMS)		
	• Using an ohmmeter, measure resistance between Pin 6 (ground) and Pin 14 of harness connector. • **Is resistance less than 10 ohms?**	Yes ▶ No ▶	**SERVICE harness. RESTORE vehicle. RETEST system.** GO to **B19.**
B17	CHECK WIRE HARNESS FOR SHORT TO GROUND (PIN 26 RESISTANCE LESS THAN 10 OHMS)		
	• Using an ohmmeter, measure resistance between Pin 6 (ground) and Pin 26 of harness connector. • **Is resistance less than 10 ohms?**	Yes ▶ No ▶	**SERVICE harness. RESTORE vehicle. RETEST system.** GO to **B18.**
B18	CHECK WIRE HARNESS FOR SHORT TO GROUND (PIN 26 RESISTANCE OVER 1000 OHMS)		
	• Using an ohmmeter, measure resistance between Pin 6 (ground) and Pin 26 of harness connector. • **Is resistance over 1000 ohms?**	Yes ▶ No ▶	GO to **B19.** GO to **B20.**
B19	CHECK HARNESS FOR SHORT TO B+		
	• Ignition switch in RUN position. • EVO harness disconnected from EVO power steering control valve actuator on power steering pump. • Using a voltmeter, measure the voltage across — Pin 14 and Pin 6 — Pin 26 and Pin 6 • **Is either voltage greater than 5 volts?**	Yes ▶ No ▶	**SERVICE wires. GO to B1.** GO to **B20.**
B20	CHECK FOR SHORT ACROSS CIRCUITS 86 (GY / O) AND 87 (T / Y) (RESISTANCE LESS THAN 10 OHMS)		
	• Ignition switch in OFF position. • EVO harness disconnected from EVO power steering control valve actuator on power steering pump. • Using an ohmmeter, measure resistance across Pin 14 and Pin 26 on harness connector. • **Is resistance less than 10 ohms?**	Yes ▶ No ▶	**SERVICE wires. GO to B1.** GO to **B21.**
B21	CHECK FOR SHORT ACROSS CIRCUITS 86 (GY / O) AND 87 (T / Y) (RESISTANCE OVER 1000 OHMS)		
	• Ignition switch in OFF position. • EVO harness disconnected from EVO power steering control valve actuator on power steering pump. • Using an ohmmeter, measure resistance across Pin 14 and Pin 26 on harness connector. • **Is resistance over 1000 ohms?**	Yes ▶ No ▶	**REPLACE EVO control module. RESTORE vehicle. RETEST system.** GO to DTC 55-5.
B22	CHECK STEERING WHEEL SENSOR CONNECTION (DTC 74 CONCERN)		
	• Verify harness connection on steering wheel rotation sensor (located on lower portion of steering column) is properly seated. • **Is connector properly seated?**	Yes ▶ No ▶	GO to **B23.** **MAKE proper connection. GO to B1.**

FM6029600235030X

Fig. 30 Test B: Codes 16, 17 or 18: Steering Very Difficult or Very Easy (Part 3 of 5). 1997–98 Crown Victoria, Grand Marquis & 1997 Town Car

Step	Test Step	Result	Action to Take
B23	STEERING WHEEL ROTATION SENSOR CHECK		
	• Ignition switch in OFF position. • Disconnect EVO control module and leave connectors mated. • Examine wiring harness, verify that there is no damage and: • **Crown Victoria, Grand Marquis** — Circuit 633 (R) is in Pin 18. — Circuit 634 (BR) is in Pin 19. — Circuit 837 (Y / BK) is connected to Circuit 57 (BK). — Circuit 57 (BK) is in Pin 6 (ground). — Circuit 298 (P / O) is connected to steering sensor, supplying B+ with ignition switch in RUN. • **Town Car** — Circuit 633 (R) is in Pin 18. — Circuit 634 (BR) is in Pin 19. — Circuit 57 (BK) is in Pin 6 (ground). — Circuit 295 (LB / PK) is connected to steering sensor, B+ 12 volts with ignition switch in RUN. • **Are wires damaged or crossed?**	Yes ▶ No ▶	**SERVICE wires as necessary. GO to B1.** GO to **B24.**
B24	TEST STEERING WHEEL ROTATION SENSOR SIGNALS		
	• Start engine. • NOTE: The resistance values will vary between meters, but the needle on all meters should swing from a low to a higher resistance and back approximately every nine degrees of steering wheel rotation. While rotating the steering wheel slowly, and using an analog ohmmeter such as, Rotunda Inductive Dwell-Tach-Volt Ohmmeter 164-R0254 or equivalent, set to the 1K scale, measure the resistance from: — Pin 18 to Pin 6. — Pin 19 to Pin 6. • **Does meter needle swing for both circuits?**	Yes ▶ No ▶	**SHUT OFF engine. REPLACE EVO control module. RESTORE vehicle. RETEST system.** GO to **B25.**
B25	STEERING WHEEL ROTATION SENSOR WIRE CHECK		
	• Disconnect EVO control module from connectors C1 and C2 located under dash. • Turn ignition switch to OFF position. • Disconnect steering sensor (located on lower steering column). • Check wires at steering sensor connector for damage and / or incorrect location. • Test continuity of Circuits 633 (R), 634 (BR) and 57 (BK) from steering sensor to EVO control module connector. (Refer to Electrical Schematic). • Test continuity from Circuit 837 (Y / BK) to 57 (BK) (Crown Victoria, Grand Marquis). • **Is there continuity?**	Yes ▶ No ▶	GO to **B26.** **SERVICE wires as necessary. GO to B1.**
B26	CHECK FOR SHORT ACROSS CIRCUITS 834 (R / Y) AND 835 (R / W) (RESISTANCE OVER 1000 OHMS)		
	• Turn ignition switch to OFF position. • Steering sensor disconnected. • Disconnect pin connectors. Measure resistance between: — Pin 18 and Pin 19. — Pin 18 and Pin 6. — Pin 19 and Pin 6 of the pin connectors (in luggage compartment). • **Is resistance over 1000 ohms?**	Yes ▶ No ▶	GO to **B28.** GO to **B27.**

FM6029600235040X

Fig. 30 Test B: Codes 16, 17 or 18: Steering Very Difficult or Very Easy (Part 4 of 5). 1997–98 Crown Victoria, Grand Marquis & 1997 Town Car

Step	Test Step	Result	Action to Take
B27	CHECK FOR SHORT ACROSS CIRCUITS 834 (R / Y) AND 835 (R / W) (RESISTANCE LESS THAN 10 OHMS)		
	• Turn ignition switch to the OFF position. • Steering sensor disconnected. • Disconnect pin connectors. • Measure resistance between: — Pin 18 and Pin 19. — Pin 18 and Pin 6. — Pin 19 and Pin 6 of the harness connectors (in luggage compartment). • **Is resistance less than 10 ohms?**	Yes ▶ No ▶	**SERVICE wires as necessary. GO to B1.** GO to **B28.**
B28	TEST STEERING SENSOR POWER CIRCUIT		
	• Turn ignition switch to RUN position. • Using a voltmeter, measure the voltage between Circuits 295 (LB / PK) and 57 (BK) (Town Car) and 298 (P / O) and 837 (Y / BK) (Crown Victoria, Grand Marquis) at the steering sensor connector. • **Are there 12 volts?**	Yes ▶ No ▶	**REPLACE steering sensor. RESTORE vehicle. RETEST system.** **SERVICE Circuit 295 (LB / PK) (Town Car), Circuit 298 (P / O) (Crown Victoria, Grand Marquis). CHECK / REPLACE Fuse 17 (15A), Crown Victoria, Grand Marquis, 7 (15A), Town Car. GO to B1.**

FM6029600235050X

Fig. 30 Test B: Codes 16, 17 or 18: Steering Very Difficult or Very Easy (Part 5 of 5). 1997–98 Crown Victoria, Grand Marquis & 1997 Town Car

Condition	Possible Source	Action
• No communication with the EVO control module	• CJB Fuse: — 5 (15A). • Battery junction box (BJB) Fuse: — 8 (30A). • Circuitry. • EVO control module.	• GO to Pinpoint Test A.
• No communication with the air suspension control module	• CJB Fuse: — 5 (15A). • BJB Fuse: — 8 (30A). • Circuitry. • Air suspension control module.	• GO to Pinpoint Test B.
• Unable to enter auto test — EVO control module	• CJB Fuse: — 5 (15A). • BJB Fuse: — 8 (30A). • Circuitry. • EVO control module.	• GO to Pinpoint Test C.
• Unable to enter auto test — air suspension control module	• CJB Fuse: — 5 (15A). • BJB Fuse: — 8 (30A). • Circuitry. • Air suspension control module.	• GO to Pinpoint Test D.
• Steering very difficult/very easy	• Power steering pump actuator valve. • Circuitry open/shorted. • EVO control module. • Air suspension module.	• PERFORM actuator output test and steering wheel sensor test. PERFORM Pinpoint Test E (with air suspension).
• Steering does not vary with increased wheel rotation	• Steering wheel rotation sensor inoperative. • Open/shorted circuitry.	• PERFORM Steering Wheel Sensor Test. PERFORM Pinpoint Test E (with air suspension).

FM6029900334000X

Fig. 31 Symptom Chart. 1999–2000 Crown Victoria & Grand Marquis

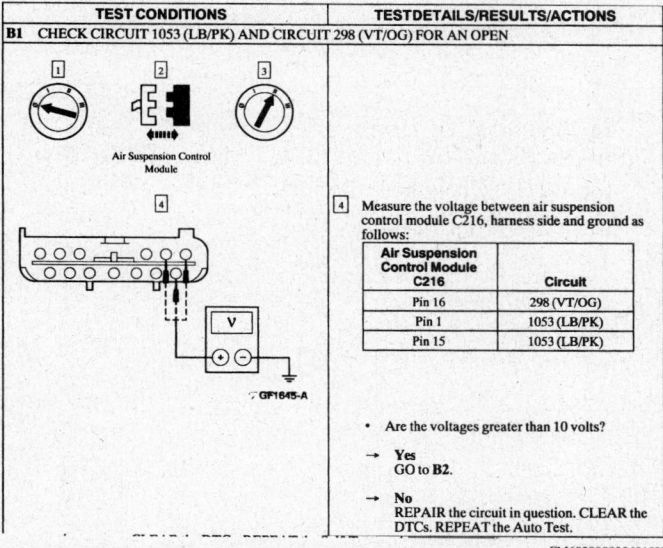

TEST CONDITIONS	TESTDETAILS/RESULTS/ACTIONS
A1 CHECK POWER FEED	
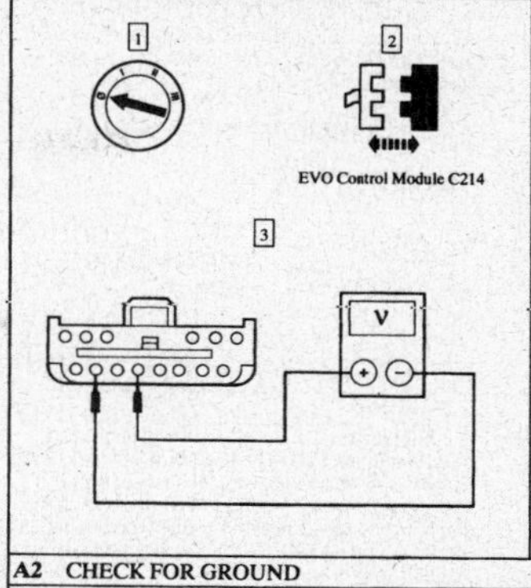	3 Measure the voltage between EVO control module C214 Pin 7, Circuit 298 (VT/OG), harness side and EVO control module C214 Pin 5, Circuit 57 (BK), harness side. • Is the voltage greater than 10 volts? → **Yes** INSTALL a new EVO control module. CLEAR the DTCs. REPEAT the Auto Test. → **No** GO to **A2**.
A2 CHECK FOR GROUND	
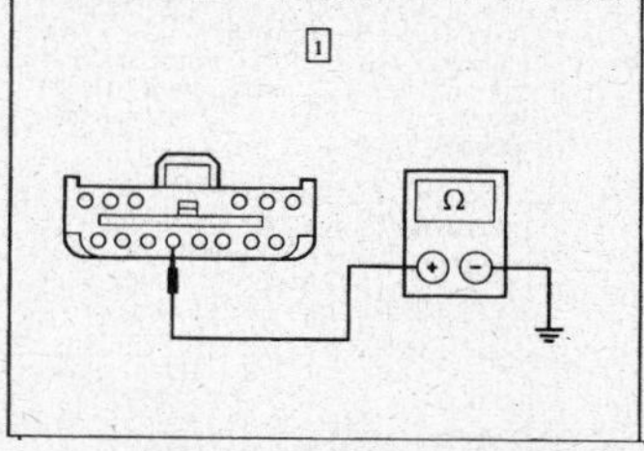	1 Measure the resistance between EVO control module C214 Pin 5, Circuit 57 (BK), harness side and ground. • Is the resistance less than 5 ohms? → **Yes** REPAIR Circuit 298 (VT/OG). CLEAR the DTCs. REPEAT the Auto Test. → **No** REPAIR Circuit 57 (BK). CLEAR the DTCs. REPEAT the Auto Test.

FM6029900335000X

Fig. 32 Test A: No Communication w/EVO Control Module. 1999–2000 Crown Victoria & Grand Marquis

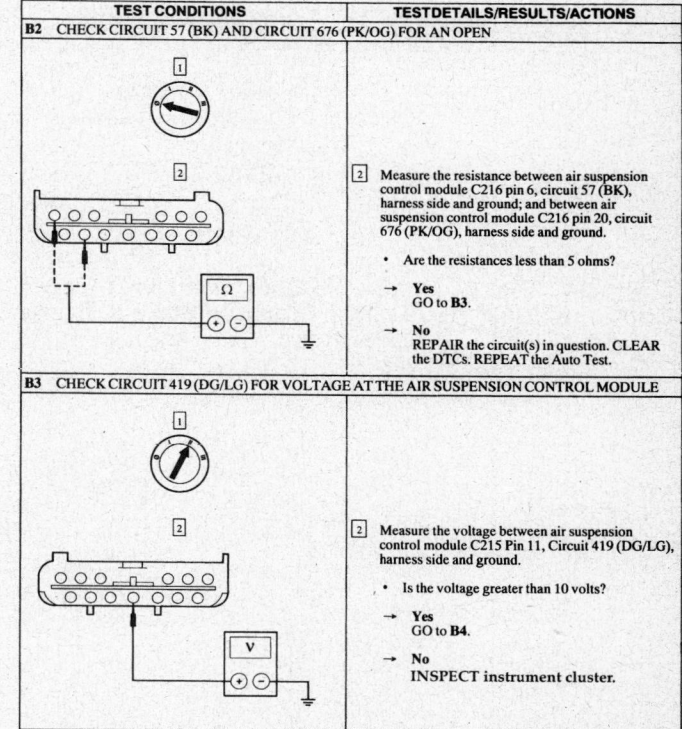

TEST CONDITIONS	TESTDETAILS/RESULTS/ACTIONS
B1 CHECK CIRCUIT 1053 (LB/PK) AND CIRCUIT 298 (VT/OG) FOR AN OPEN	
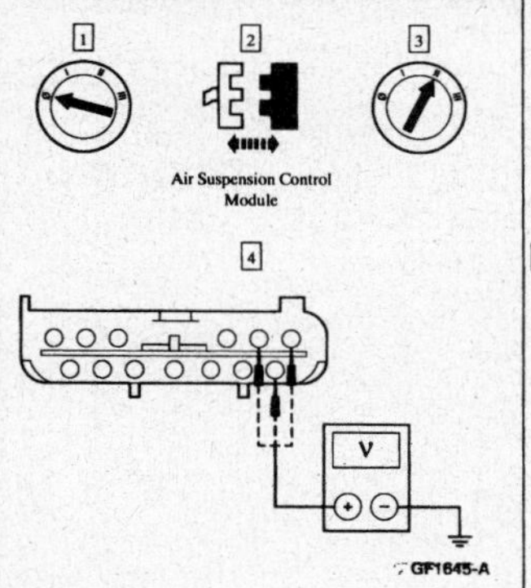	4 Measure the voltage between air suspension control module C216, harness side and ground as follows: Air Suspension Control Module C216 — Circuit Pin 16 — 298 (VT/OG) Pin 1 — 1053 (LB/PK) Pin 15 — 1053 (LB/PK) • Are the voltages greater than 10 volts? → **Yes** GO to **B2**. → **No** REPAIR the circuit in question. CLEAR the DTCs. REPEAT the Auto Test.

FM6029900336010X

Fig. 33 Test B: No Communication w/Air Suspension Control Module. (Part 1 of 4). 1999–2000 Crown Victoria & Grand Marquis

TEST CONDITIONS	TESTDETAILS/RESULTS/ACTIONS
B2 CHECK CIRCUIT 57 (BK) AND CIRCUIT 676 (PK/OG) FOR AN OPEN	
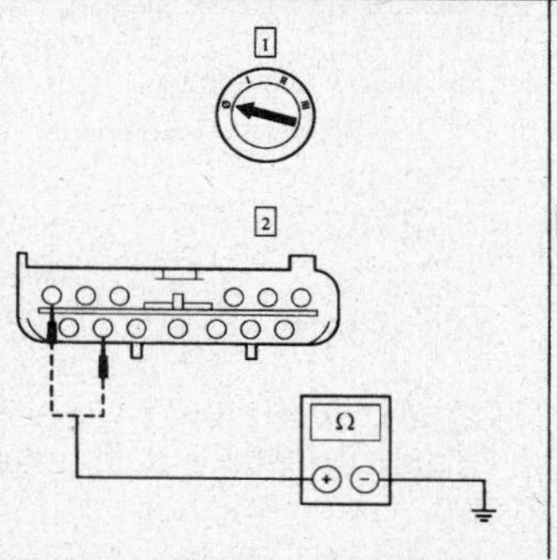	2 Measure the resistance between air suspension control module C216 pin 6, circuit 57 (BK), harness side and ground; and between air suspension control module C216 pin 20, circuit 676 (PK/OG), harness side and ground. • Are the resistances less than 5 ohms? → **Yes** GO to **B3**. → **No** REPAIR the circuit(s) in question. CLEAR the DTCs. REPEAT the Auto Test.
B3 CHECK CIRCUIT 419 (DG/LG) FOR VOLTAGE AT THE AIR SUSPENSION CONTROL MODULE	
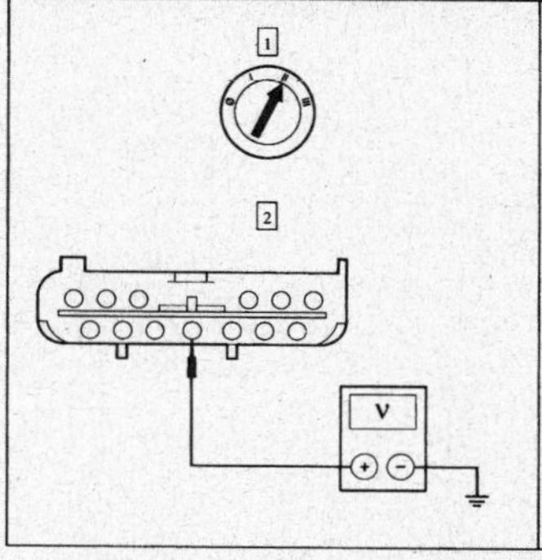	2 Measure the voltage between air suspension control module C215 Pin 11, Circuit 419 (DG/LG), harness side and ground. • Is the voltage greater than 10 volts? → **Yes** GO to **B4**. → **No** INSPECT instrument cluster.

FM6029900336020X

Fig. 33 Test B: No Communication w/Air Suspension Control Module. (Part 2 of 4). 1999–2000 Crown Victoria & Grand Marquis

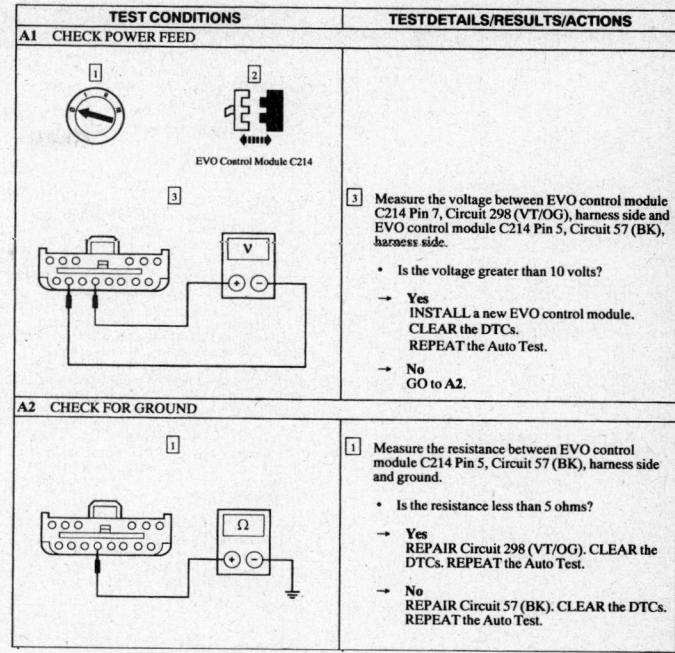

TEST CONDITIONS	TEST DETAILS/RESULTS/ACTIONS
B4 CHECK CIRCUIT 419 (DG/LG) FOR VOLTAGE AT THE AIR SUSPENSION TEST CONNECTOR	
1 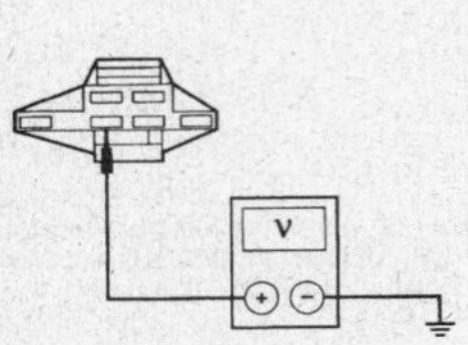	1 Measure the voltage between air suspension test connector C459 Pin 4, Circuit 419 (DG/LG), harness side and ground. • Is the voltage greater than 10 volts? → **Yes** GO to **B5**. → **No** REPAIR the circuit. CLEAR the DTCs. REPEAT the Auto Test.
B5 CHECK CIRCUIT 844 (GY/RD)	
1 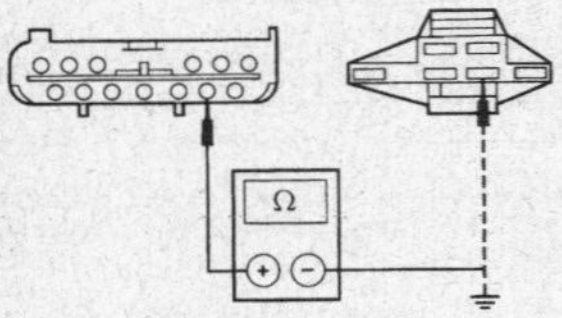	1 Measure the resistance between air suspension control module C215 Pin 9, Circuit 844 (GY/RD), harness side and air suspension test connector C459 Pin 5, Circuit 844 (GY/RD), harness side; and between air suspension control module C215 Pin 9, Circuit 844 (GY/RD), harness side and ground. • Is the resistance less than 5 ohms between air suspension control module and air suspension test connector; and greater than 10,000 ohms between air suspension control module and ground? → **Yes** GO to **B6**. → **No** REPAIR the circuit. CLEAR the DTCs. REPEAT the Auto Test.

FM6029900336030X

Fig. 33 Test B: No Communication w/Air Suspension Control Module. (Part 3 of 4). 1999–2000 Crown Victoria & Grand Marquis

TEST CONDITIONS	TEST DETAILS/RESULTS/ACTIONS
C1 CHECK COMMUNICATION TO THE EVO CONTROL MODULE	
	1 Check communication between the Super Star II Tester and the EVO control module. • Does the Super Star II Tester communicate? → **Yes** INSTALL a new EVO control module. REPEAT the Auto Test. → **No** GO to Pinpoint Test A.

FM6029900337000X

Fig. 34 Test C: Unable To Enter Auto Test-EVO Control Module. 1999–2000 Crown Victoria & Grand Marquis

TEST CONDITIONS	TEST DETAILS/RESULTS/ACTIONS
B6 CHECK CIRCUIT 432 (BK/PK)	
1 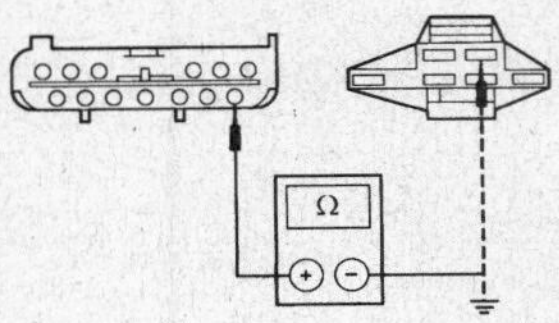	1 Measure the resistance between air suspension control module C215 Pin 8, Circuit 432 (BK/PK), harness side and air suspension test connector C459 Pin 2, Circuit 432 (BK/PK), harness side; and between air suspension control module C215 Pin 9, Circuit 432 (BK/PK), harness side and ground. • Is the resistance less than 5 ohms between air suspension control module and air suspension test connector; and greater than 10,000 ohms between air suspension control module and ground? → **Yes** INSTALL a new air suspension control module. REPEAT the Auto Test. → **No** REPAIR the circuit. CLEAR the DTCs. REPEAT the Auto Test.

FM6029900336040X

Fig. 33 Test B: No Communication w/Air Suspension Control Module. (Part 4 of 4). 1999–2000 Crown Victoria & Grand Marquis

TEST CONDITIONS	TEST DETAILS/RESULTS/ACTIONS
D1 CHECK COMMUNICATION TO THE AIR SUSPENSION CONTROL MODULE	
	1 Check communication between the Super Star II Tester and the air suspension control module. • Does the Super Star II Tester communicate? → **Yes** INSTALL a new air suspension control module. REPEAT the Auto Test. → **No** GO to Pinpoint Test B.

FM6029900338000X

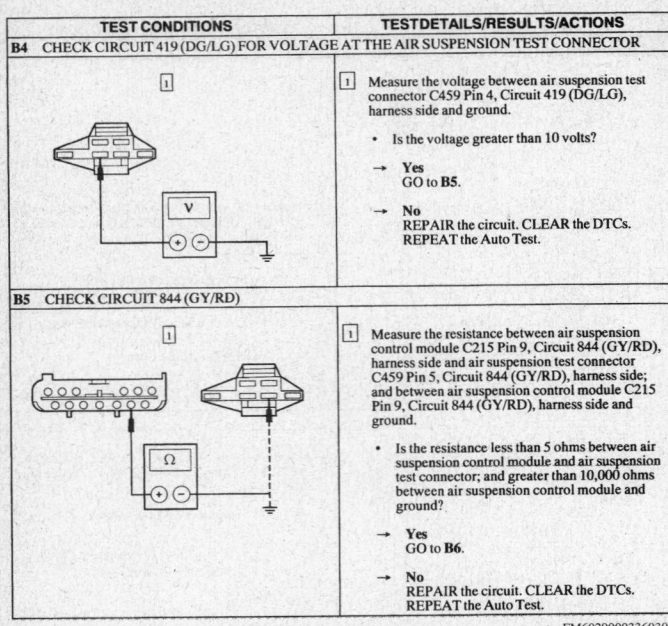

Fig. 35 Test D: Unable To Enter Auto Test-Air Suspension Control Module. 1999–2000 Crown Victoria & Grand Marquis

TEST CONDITIONS	TEST DETAILS/RESULTS/ACTIONS

E1 EVO ACTUATOR VALVE CHECK (DTC 16)

1

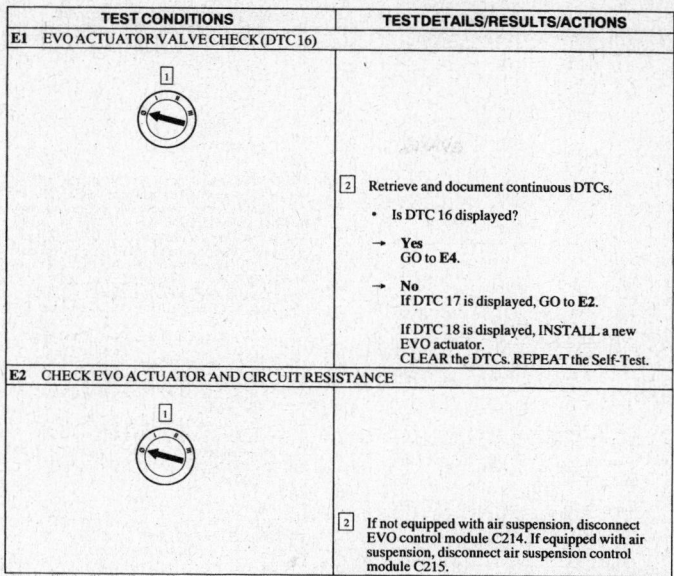

2 Retrieve and document continuous DTCs.

- Is DTC 16 displayed?

→ **Yes**
GO to **E4**.

→ **No**
If DTC 17 is displayed, GO to **E2**.

If DTC 18 is displayed, INSTALL a new EVO actuator.
CLEAR the DTCs. REPEAT the Self-Test.

E2 CHECK EVO ACTUATOR AND CIRCUIT RESISTANCE

1

2 If not equipped with air suspension, disconnect EVO control module C214. If equipped with air suspension, disconnect air suspension control module C215.

FM6029900339010X

Fig. 36 DTC 16: EVO Actuator Shorted; DTC 17: EVO Actuator Shorted or Open; DTC 18: EVO Actuator Resistance Out Of Range (Part 1 of 6). 1999–2000 Crown Victoria & Grand Marquis

TEST CONDITIONS	TEST DETAILS/RESULTS/ACTIONS

E2 CHECK EVO ACTUATOR AND CIRCUIT RESISTANCE

3

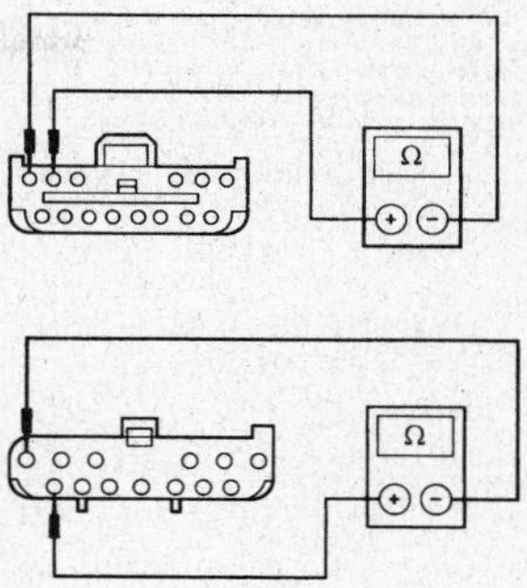

3 If not equipped with air suspension, measure the resistance between EVO control module C214 Pin 14, Circuit 87 (TN/YE), harness side and EVO control module C214 Pin 13, Circuit 86 (GY/OG), harness side. If equipped with air suspension, measure the resistance between air suspension control module C215 Pin 14, Circuit 86 (GY/OG), harness side and air suspension control module C215 Pin 26, Circuit 87 (TN/YE), harness side.

- Is the resistance between 5 and 20 ohms?

→ **Yes**
GO to **E3**.

→ **No**
GO to **E4**.

FM6029900339020X

Fig. 36 Test E-DTC 16: EVO Actuator Shorted; DTC 17: EVO Actuator Shorted or Open; DTC 18: EVO Actuator Resistance Out Of Range (Part 2 of 6). 1999–2000 Crown Victoria & Grand Marquis

TEST CONDITIONS	TEST DETAILS/RESULTS/ACTIONS

E3 CHECK CIRCUITS 86 (GY/OG) AND 87 (TN/YE)

1

EVO Actuator C184

2

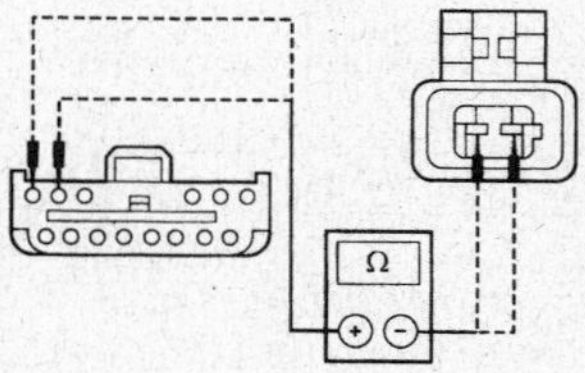

2 If not equipped with an air suspension, measure the resistance between the EVO control module C214, harness side and EVO actuator C184, harness side.

EVO Control Module C214	EVO Actuator C184	Circuit
Pin 14	Pin 1	87 (TN/YE)
Pin 13	Pin 2	86 (GY/OG)

3

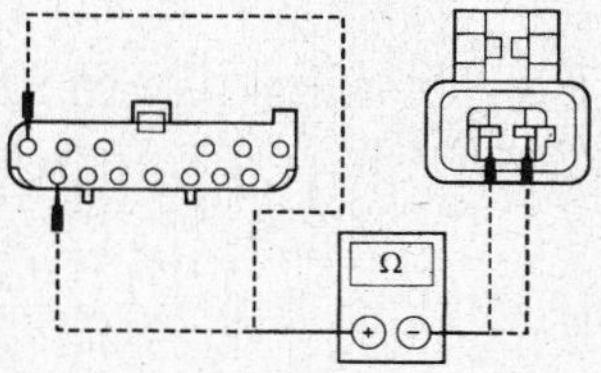

3 If equipped with an air suspension, measure the resistance between the air suspension control module C215, harness side and EVO actuator C184, harness side.

Air Suspension Control Module C215	EVO Actuator C184	Circuit
Pin 26	Pin 1	87 (TN/YE)
Pin 14	Pin 2	86 (GY/OG)

- Is the resistance less than 5 ohms?

→ **Yes**
GO to **E4**.

→ **No**
REPAIR the circuit(s) in question. CLEAR the DTCs. REPEAT the Auto Test.

FM6029900339030X

Fig. 36 Test E-DTC 16: EVO Actuator Shorted; DTC 17: EVO Actuator Shorted or Open; DTC 18: EVO Actuator Resistance Out Of Range (Part 3 of 6). 1999–2000 Crown Victoria & Grand Marquis

TEST CONDITIONS	TEST DETAILS/RESULTS/ACTIONS

E4 CHECK EVO ACTUATOR RESISTANCE

1

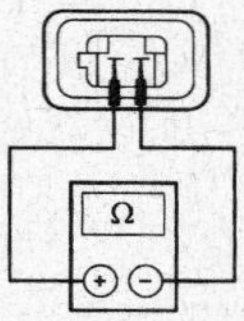

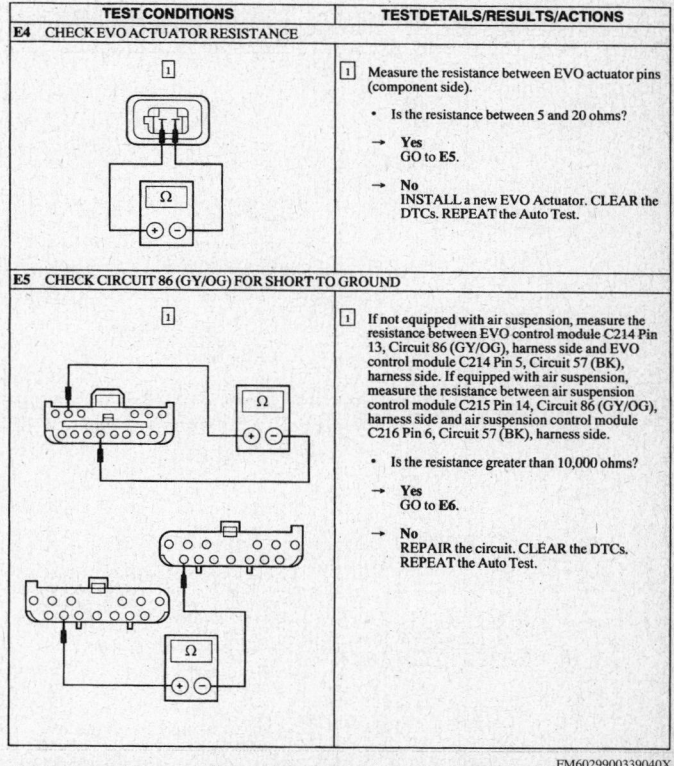

1 Measure the resistance between EVO actuator pins (component side).

- Is the resistance between 5 and 20 ohms?

→ **Yes**
GO to **E5**.

→ **No**
INSTALL a new EVO Actuator. CLEAR the DTCs. REPEAT the Auto Test.

E5 CHECK CIRCUIT 86 (GY/OG) FOR SHORT TO GROUND

1

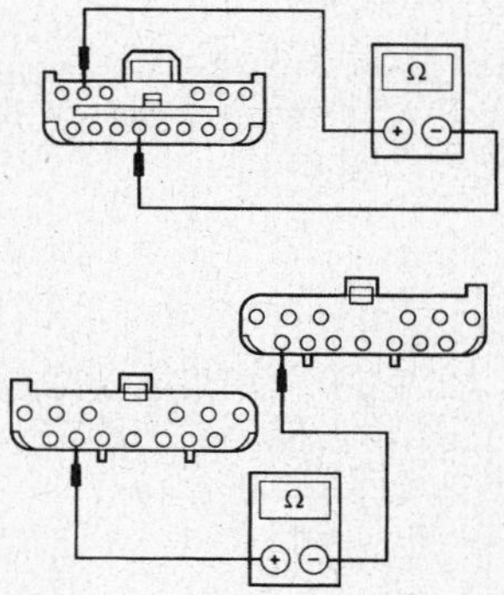

1 If not equipped with air suspension, measure the resistance between EVO control module C214 Pin 13, Circuit 86 (GY/OG), harness side and EVO control module C214 Pin 5, Circuit 57 (BK), harness side. If equipped with air suspension, measure the resistance between air suspension control module C215 Pin 14, Circuit 86 (GY/OG), harness side and air suspension control module C216 Pin 6, Circuit 57 (BK), harness side.

- Is the resistance greater than 10,000 ohms?

→ **Yes**
GO to **E6**.

→ **No**
REPAIR the circuit. CLEAR the DTCs. REPEAT the Auto Test.

FM6029900339040X

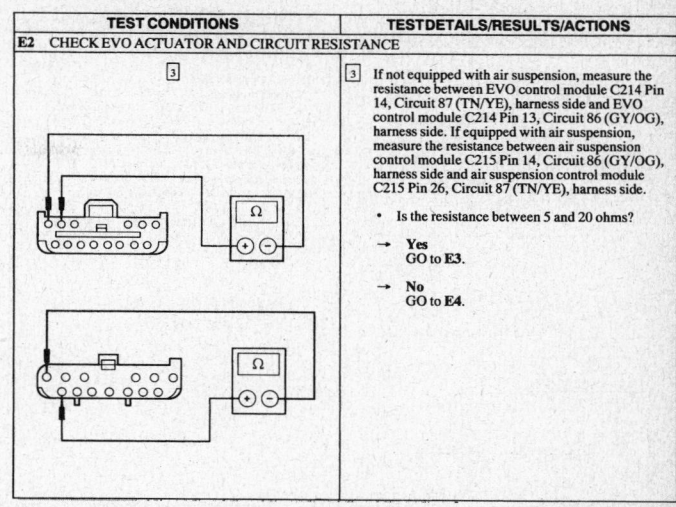

Fig. 36 Test E-DTC 16: EVO Actuator Shorted; DTC 17: EVO Actuator Shorted or Open; DTC 18: EVO Actuator Resistance Out Of Range (Part 4 of 6). 1999–2000 Crown Victoria & Grand Marquis

TEST CONDITIONS	TEST DETAILS/RESULTS/ACTIONS
E6 CHECK CIRCUIT 87 (TN/YE) FOR SHORT TO GROUND	
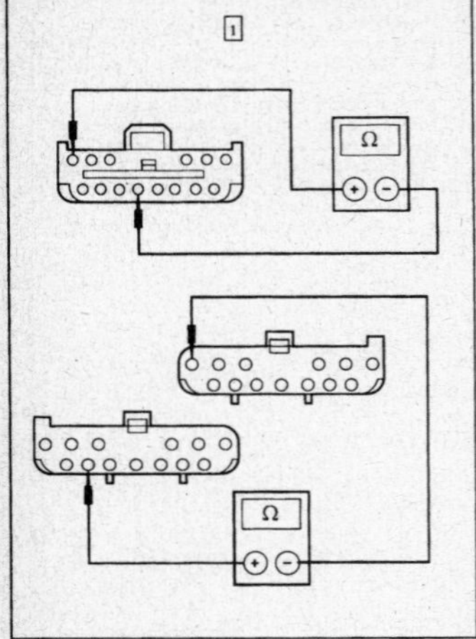	1 If not equipped with air suspension, measure the resistance between EVO control module C214 Pin 14, Circuit 87 (TN/YE), harness side and EVO control module C214 Pin 5, Circuit 57 (BK), harness side. If equipped with air suspension, measure the resistance between air suspension control module C215 Pin 26, Circuit 87 (TN/YE), harness side and air suspension control module C216 Pin 6, Circuit 57 (BK), harness side. • Is the resistance greater than 10,000 ohms? → **Yes** GO to **E7**. → **No** REPAIR the circuit. CLEAR the DTCs. REPEAT the Auto Test.

FM6029900339050X

Fig. 36 Test E-DTC 16: EVO Actuator Shorted; DTC 17: EVO Actuator Shorted or Open; DTC 18: EVO Actuator Resistance Out Of Range (Part 5 of 6). 1999–2000 Crown Victoria & Grand Marquis

TEST CONDITIONS	TEST DETAILS/RESULTS/ACTIONS
F1 CHECK EVO ACTUATOR FOR AN OPEN	
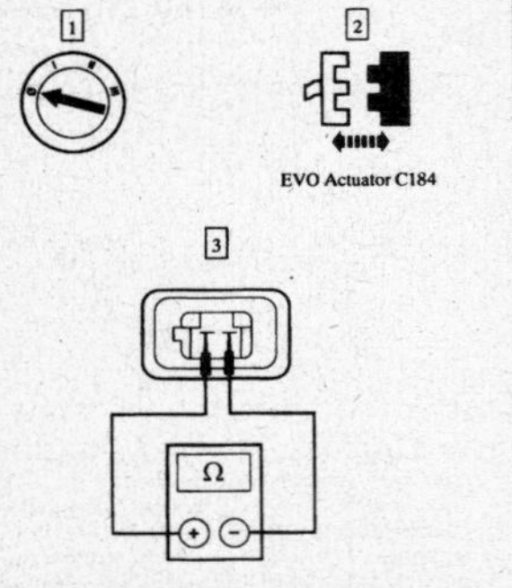	3 Measure the resistance between EVO actuator pins (component side). • Is the resistance between 5 and 20 ohms? → **Yes** GO to **F2**. → **No** INSTALL a new EVO actuator. CLEAR the DTCs. REPEAT the Auto Test.
F2 CHECK CIRCUIT 86 (GY/OG) FOR AN OPEN	
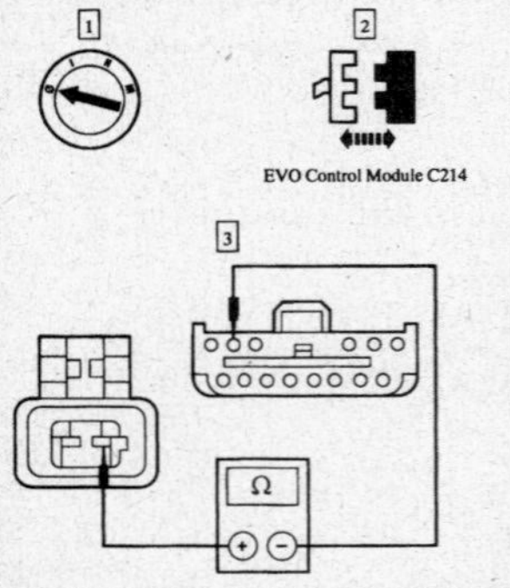	3 Measure the resistance between EVO control module C214 Pin 13, Circuit 86 (GY/OG), harness side and EVO actuator C184 Pin 2, Circuit 86 (GY/OG), harness side. • Is the resistance less than 5 ohms? → **Yes** GO to **F3**. → **No** REPAIR the circuit. CLEAR the DTCs. REPEAT the Auto Test.

FM6029900340010X

Fig. 37 DTC 27: EVO Actuator Circuit Open (Part 1 of 2). 1999–2000 Crown Victoria & Grand Marquis

TEST CONDITIONS	TEST DETAILS/RESULTS/ACTIONS
E7 CHECK FOR SHORT TO BATTERY	
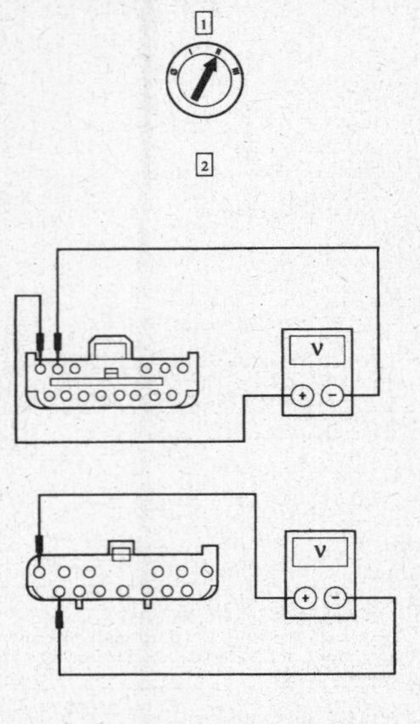	2 If not equipped with air suspension, measure the voltage between EVO control module C214 Pin 13, Circuit 86 (GY/OG), harness side and ground; and between EVO control module C214 Pin 14, Circuit 87 (TN/YE), harness side and ground. If equipped with air suspension, measure the voltage between air suspension control module C215 Pin 14, Circuit 86 (GY/OG), harness side and ground; and between air suspension control module C215 Pin 26, Circuit 87 (TN/YE), harness side and ground. • Are the resistances greater than 10,000 ohms? → **Yes** If not equipped with air suspension, INSTALL a new EVO control module. CLEAR the DTCs. REPEAT the Auto Test. If equipped with air suspension, INSTALL a new air suspension module. CLEAR the DTCs. REPEAT the Auto Test. → **No** REPAIR the circuit(s) in question. CLEAR the DTCs. REPEAT the Auto Test.

FM6029900339060X

Fig. 36 Test E-DTC 16: EVO Actuator Shorted; DTC 17: EVO Actuator Shorted or Open; DTC 18: EVO Actuator Resistance Out Of Range (Part 6 of 6). 1999–2000 Crown Victoria & Grand Marquis

TEST CONDITIONS	TEST DETAILS/RESULTS/ACTIONS
F3 CHECK CIRCUIT 87 (TN/YE) FOR AN OPEN	
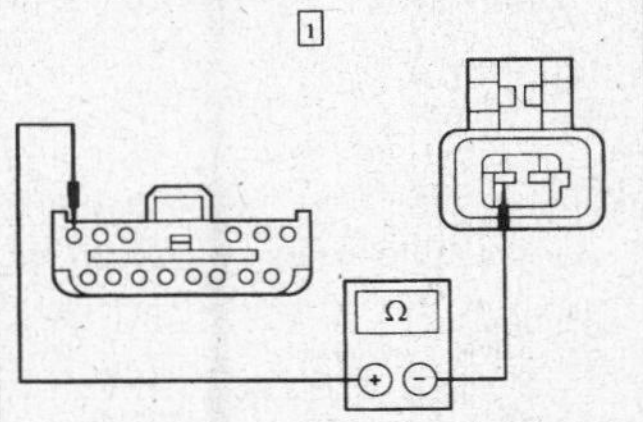	1 Measure the resistance between EVO control module C214 Pin 14, Circuit 87 (TN/YE), harness side and EVO actuator C184 Pin 1, Circuit 87 (TN/YE), harness side. • Is the resistance less than 5 ohms? → **Yes** INSTALL a new EVO control module. CLEAR the DTCs. REPEAT the Auto Test. → **No** REPAIR the circuit. CLEAR the DTCs. REPEAT the Auto Test.

FM6029900340020X

Fig. 37 DTC 27: EVO Actuator Circuit Open (Part 2 of 2). 1999–2000 Crown Victoria & Grand Marquis

TEST CONDITIONS	TEST DETAILS/RESULTS/ACTIONS
G1 CHECK EVO ACTUATOR FOR A SHORT	
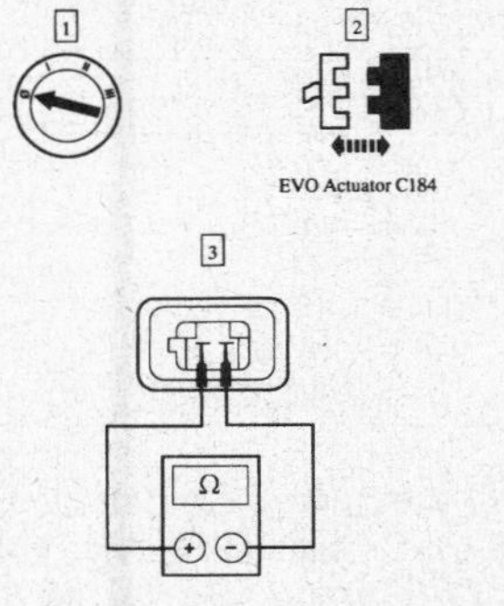	3 Measure the resistance between EVO actuator pins (component side). • Is the resistance between 5 and 20 ohms? → **Yes** GO to **G2**. → **No** INSTALL a new EVO actuator. CLEAR the DTCs. REPEAT the Auto Test.

FM6029900341010X

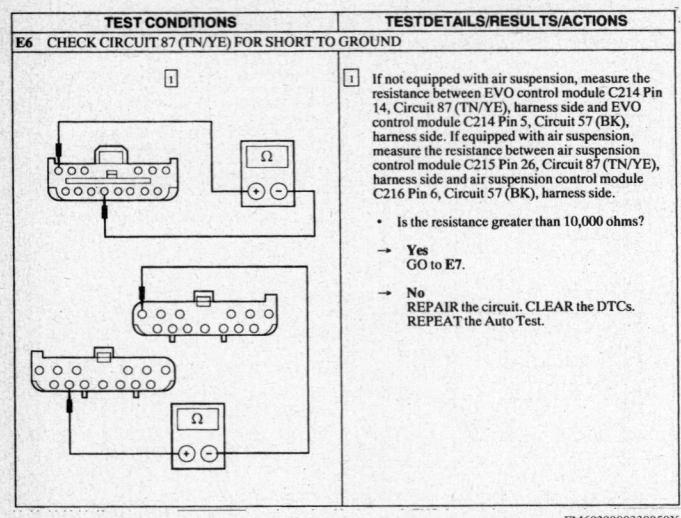

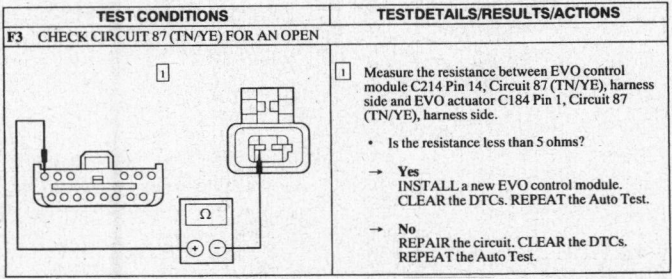

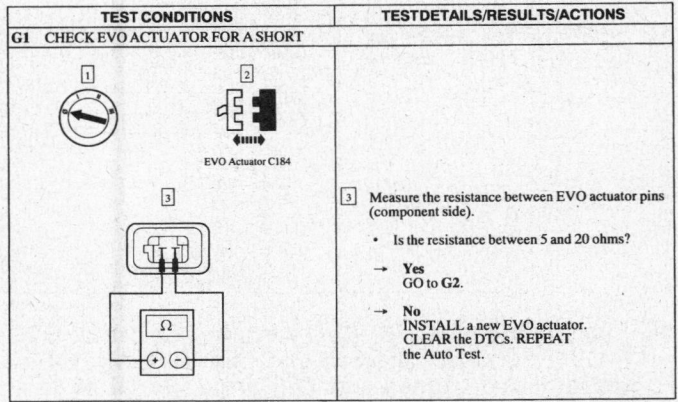

Fig. 38 DTC 28: EVO Actuator Circuit Shorted (Part 1 of 3). 1999–2000 Crown Victoria & Grand Marquis

TEST CONDITIONS	TESTDETAILS/RESULTS/ACTIONS
G2 CHECK CIRCUIT 86 (GY/OG) FOR A SHORT TO GROUND	
1 	
2 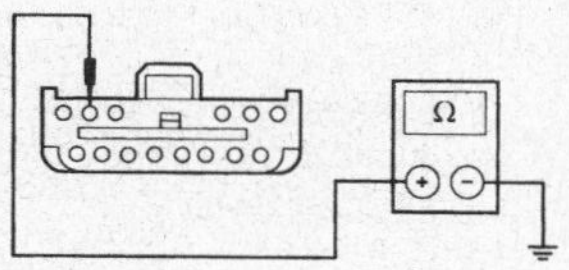	2 Measure the resistance between EVO control module C214 Pin 13, Circuit 86 (GY/OG), harness side and ground. • Is the resistance greater than 10,000 ohms? → **Yes** GO to **G3**. → **No** REPAIR the circuit. CLEAR the DTCs. REPEAT the Auto Test.
G3 CHECK CIRCUIT 87 (TN/YE) FOR A SHORT TO GROUND	
1 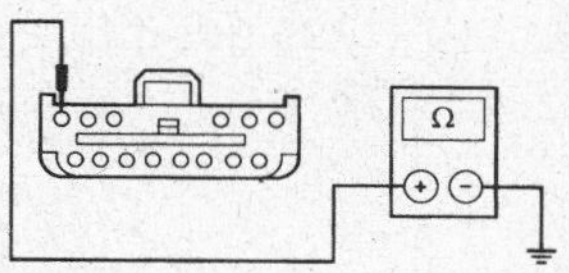	1 Measure the resistance between EVO control module C214 Pin 14, Circuit 87 (TN/YE), harness side and ground. • Is the resistance greater than 10,000 ohms? → **Yes** GO to **G4**. → **No** REPAIR the circuit. CLEAR the DTCs. REPEAT the Auto Test.

FM6029900341020X

Fig. 38 DTC 28: EVO Actuator Circuit Shorted (Part 2 of 3). 1999–2000 Crown Victoria & Grand Marquis

TEST CONDITIONS	TESTDETAILS/RESULTS/ACTIONS
H1 CHECK CIRCUIT 86 (GY/OG) FOR SHORT TO GROUND	
1 2 3 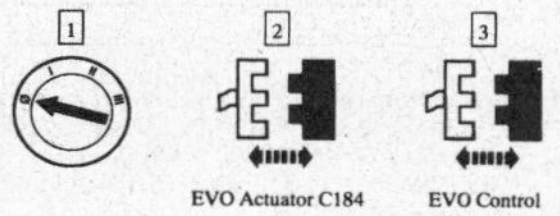	
4 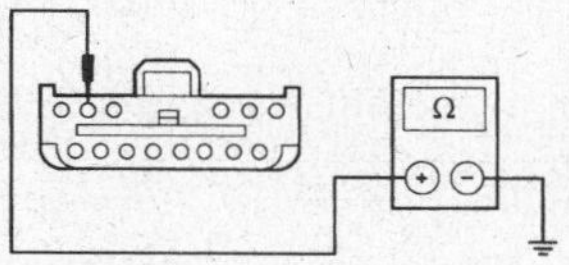	4 Measure the resistance between EVO control module C214 Pin 13, Circuit 86 (GY/OG), harness side and ground. • Is the resistance less than 10,000 ohms? → **Yes** REPAIR the circuit. CLEAR the DTCs. REPEAT the Auto Test. → **No** GO to **H2**.

FM6029900342010X

Fig. 39 DTC 29: EVO Actuator Circuit High Side Shorted To Ground (Part 1 of 2). 1999–2000 Crown Victoria & Grand Marquis

TEST CONDITIONS	TESTDETAILS/RESULTS/ACTIONS
G4 CHECK CIRCUIT RESISTANCE	
1 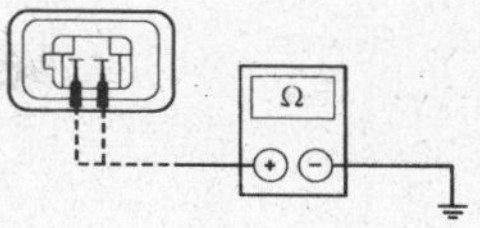	1 Measure the resistance between EVO actuator Pin 1, (component side) and ground; and between EVO actuator Pin 2, (component side) and ground. • Are the resistances greater than 10,000 ohms? → **Yes** INSTALL a new EVO control module. CLEAR the DTCs. REPEAT the Auto Test. → **No** INSTALL a new EVO actuator. CLEAR the DTCs. REPEAT the Auto Test.

FM6029900341030X

Fig. 38 DTC 28: EVO Actuator Circuit Shorted (Part 3 of 3). 1999–2000 Crown Victoria & Grand Marquis

TEST CONDITIONS	TESTDETAILS/RESULTS/ACTIONS
H2 CHECK EVO ACTUATOR FOR SHORT TO GROUND	
1 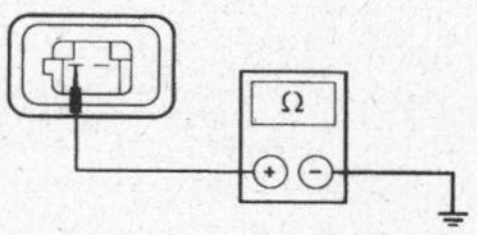	1 Measure the resistance between EVO actuator Pin 2, circuit 86 (component side) and ground. • Is the resistance greater than 10,000 ohms? → **Yes** INSTALL a new EVO control module. CLEAR the DTCs. REPEAT the Auto Test. → **No** REPAIR the circuit. CLEAR the DTCs. REPEAT the Auto Test.

FM6029900342020X

Fig. 39 DTC 29: EVO Actuator Circuit High Side Shorted To Ground (Part 2 of 2). 1999–2000 Crown Victoria & Grand Marquis

TEST CONDITIONS	TESTDETAILS/RESULTS/ACTIONS
I1 CHECK CIRCUIT 86 (GY/OG) FOR SHORT TO BATTERY	
1 2 3 	
4 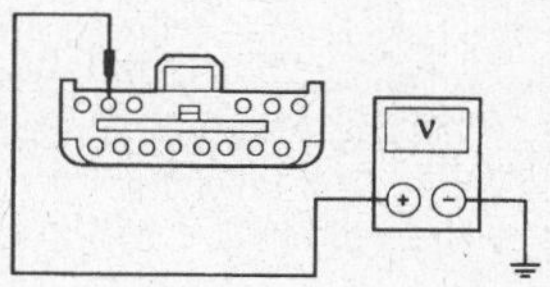	4 Measure the voltage between EVO control module C214 Pin 13, Circuit 86 (GY/OG), harness side and ground. • Is voltage present? → **Yes** REPAIR the circuit. CLEAR the DTCs. REPEAT the Auto Test. → **No** GO to **I2**.

FM6029900343010X

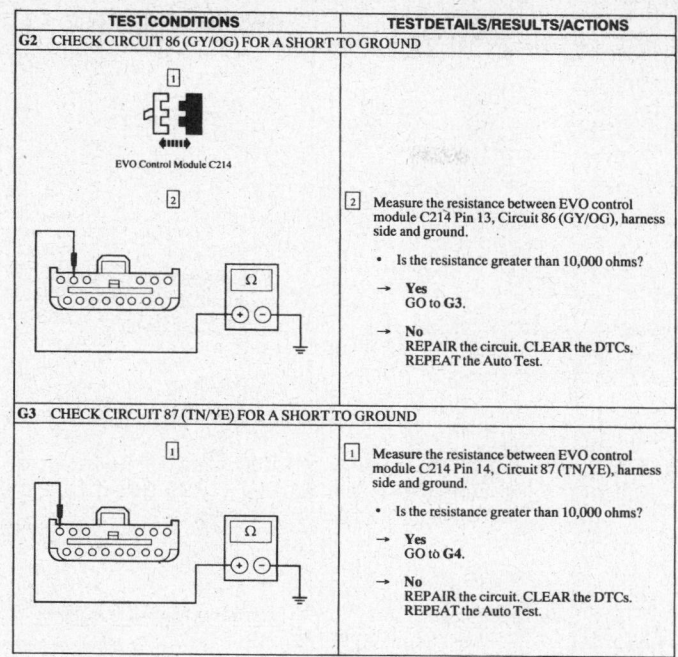

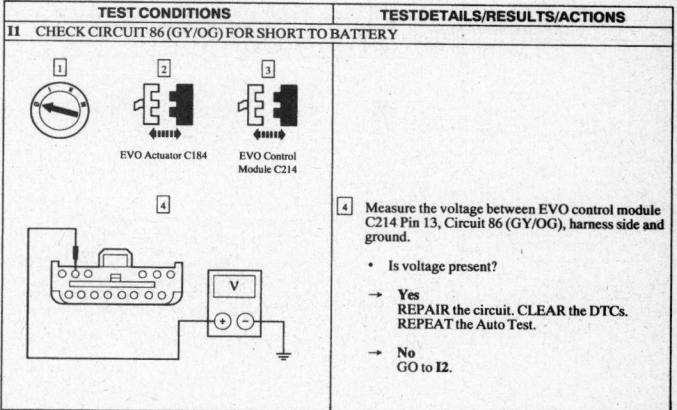

Fig. 40 DTC 30: EVO Actuator Circuit Shorted To Battery (Part 1 of 2). 1999–2000 Crown Victoria & Grand Marquis

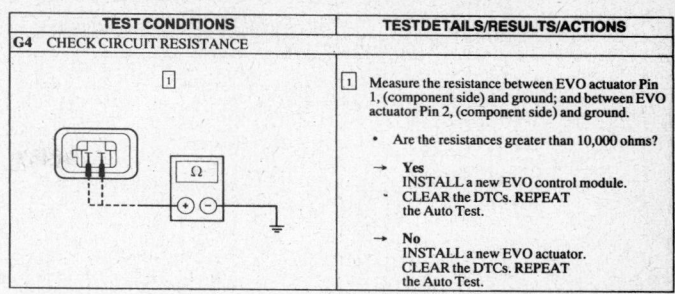

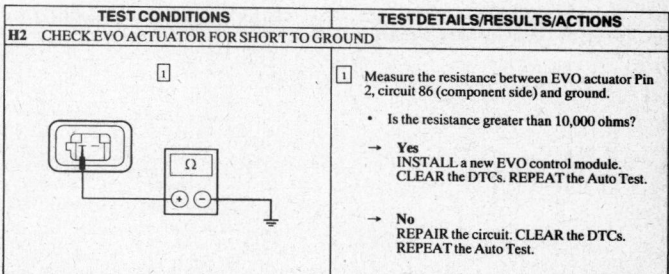

TEST CONDITIONS	TESTDETAILS/RESULTS/ACTIONS
I2 CHECK CIRCUIT 87 (TN/YE) FOR SHORT TO BATTERY	
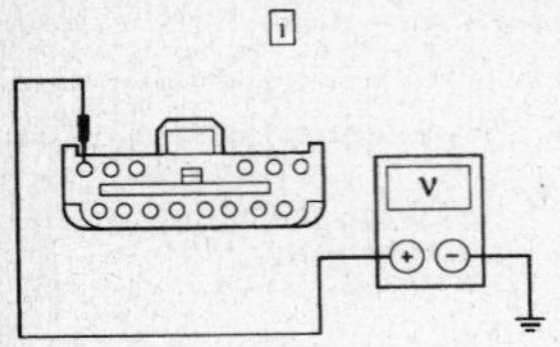	1 Measure the voltage between EVO control module C214 Pin 14, Circuit 87 (TN/YE), harness side and ground. • Is voltage present? → **Yes** REPAIR the circuit. CLEAR the DTCs. REPEAT the Auto Test. → **No** INSTALL a new EVO control module. CLEAR the DTCs. REPEAT the Auto Test.

FM6029900343020X

Fig. 40 DTC 30: EVO Actuator Circuit Shorted To Battery (Part 2 of 2). 1999–2000 Crown Victoria & Grand Marquis

TEST CONDITIONS	TESTDETAILS/RESULTS/ACTIONS
J2 CHECK EVO ACTUATOR FOR SHORT TO GROUND	
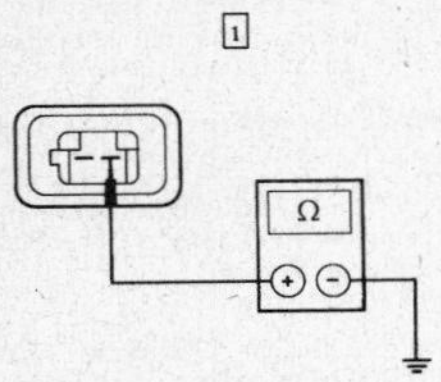	1 Measure the resistance between EVO actuator Pin 1, (component side) and ground. • Is the resistance greater than 10,000 ohms? → **Yes** INSTALL a new EVO control module. CLEAR the DTCs. REPEAT the Auto Test. → **No** REPAIR the circuit. CLEAR the DTCs. REPEAT the Auto Test.

FM6029900344020X

Fig. 41 DTC 31: EVO Actuator Circuit Low Side Shorted To Ground (Part 2 of 2). 1999-2000 Crown Victoria & Grand Marquis

TEST CONDITIONS	TESTDETAILS/RESULTS/ACTIONS
K1 CHECK CIRCUITS 633 (RD) AND 634 (BN) FOR CONTINUITY	
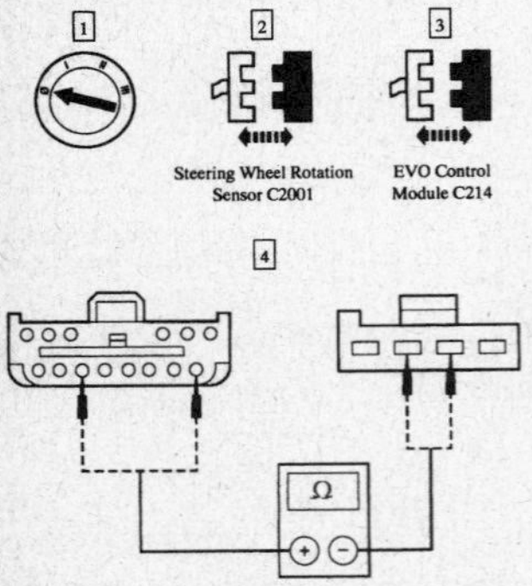	4 Measure the resistance between EVO control module C214 Pin 1, Circuit 633 (RD), harness side and steering wheel rotation sensor C2001 Pin 3, Circuit 633 (RD), harness side; and between EVO control module C214 Pin 6, Circuit 634 (BN), harness side and steering wheel rotation sensor C2001 Pin 2, Circuit 634 (BN), harness side. • Are the resistances less than 5 ohms? → **Yes** GO to **K2**. → **No** REPAIR the circuit(s) in question. CLEAR the DTCs. REPEAT the Auto Test.

FM6029900345010X

Fig. 42 DTC 33: Steering Rotation Not Detected (Part 1 of 4). 1999-2000 Crown Victoria & Grand Marquis

TEST CONDITIONS	TESTDETAILS/RESULTS/ACTIONS
J1 CHECK CIRCUIT 87 (TN/YE) FOR SHORT TO GROUND	
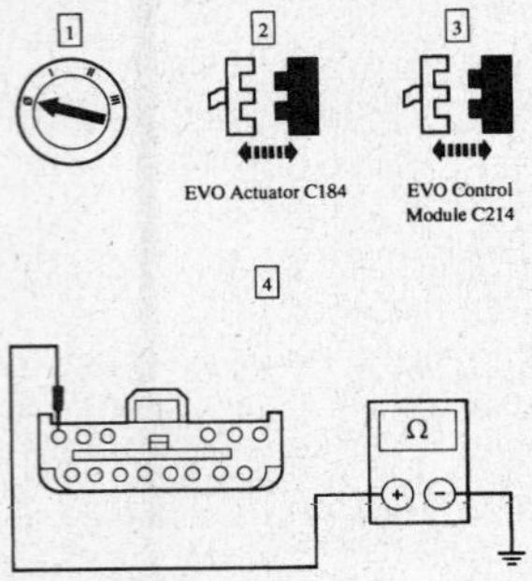	4 Measure the resistance between EVO control module C214 Pin 14, Circuit 87 (TN/YE), harness side and ground. • Is the resistance less than 10,000 ohms? → **Yes** REPAIR the circuit. CLEAR the DTCs. REPEAT the Auto Test. → **No** GO to **J2**.

FM6029900344010X

Fig. 41 DTC 31: EVO Actuator Circuit Low Side Shorted To Ground (Part 1 of 2). 1999-2000 Crown Victoria & Grand Marquis

TEST CONDITIONS	TESTDETAILS/RESULTS/ACTIONS
K2 CHECK CIRCUIT 837 (YE/BK) FOR CONTINUITY	
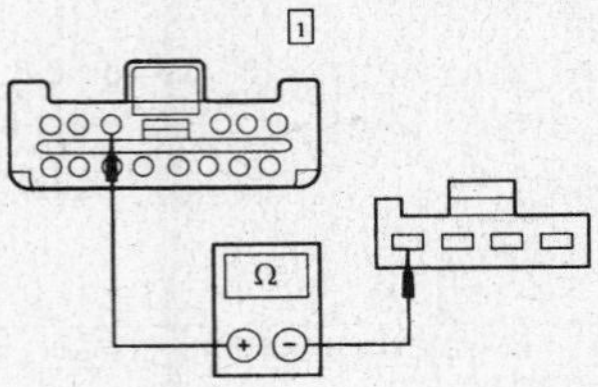	1 Measure the resistance between EVO control module C214 Pin 12, Circuit 837 (YE/BK), harness side and steering wheel rotation sensor C2001 Pin 1, Circuit 837 (YE/BK), harness side. • Is the resistance less than 5 ohms? → **Yes** GO to **K3**. → **No** REPAIR the circuit. CLEAR the DTCs. REPEAT the Auto Test.
K3 CHECK CIRCUITS 633 (RD) AND 634 (BN) FOR SHORT TO BATTERY	
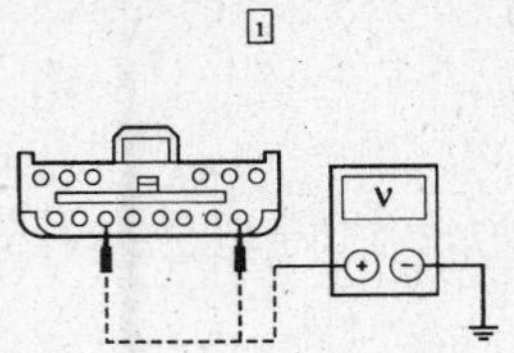	1 Measure the voltage between EVO control module C214 Pin 1, Circuit 633 (RD), harness side and ground; and between EVO control module C214 Pin 6, Circuit 634 (BN), harness side and ground. • Is voltage present? → **Yes** REPAIR the circuit(s) in question. CLEAR the DTCs. REPEAT the Auto Test. → **No** GO to **K4**.
K4 CHECK CIRCUITS 633 (RD) AND 634 (BN) FOR SHORT TO GROUND	
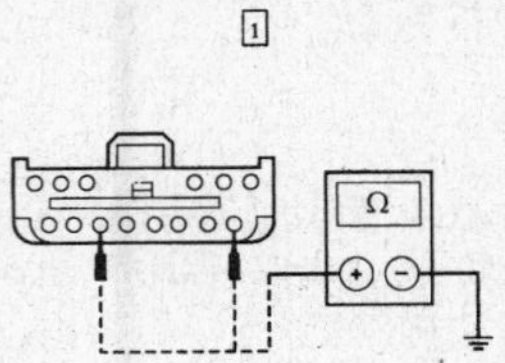	1 Measure the resistance between EVO control module C214 Pin 1, Circuit 633 (RD), harness side and ground; and between EVO control module C214 Pin 6, Circuit 634 (BN), harness side and ground. • Are the resistances greater than 10,000 ohms? → **Yes** GO to **K5**. → **No** REPAIR the circuit(s) in question. CLEAR the DTCs. REPEAT the Auto Test.

FM6029900345020X

Fig. 42 DTC 33: Steering Rotation Not Detected (Part 2 of 4). 1999-2000 Crown Victoria & Grand Marquis

TEST CONDITIONS	TEST DETAILS/RESULTS/ACTIONS
K5 CHECK CIRCUIT 298 (VT/OG) FOR VOLTAGE	
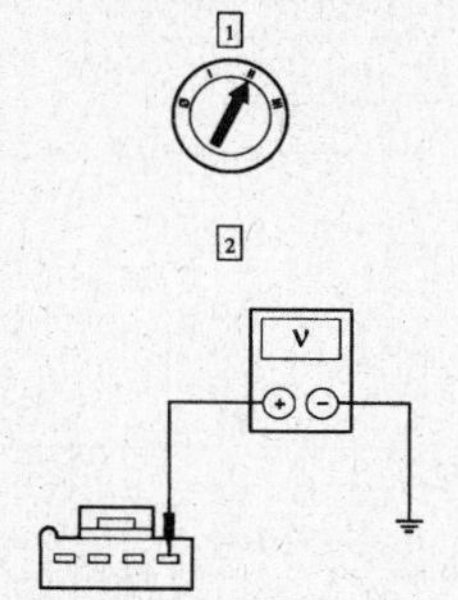	2 Measure the voltage between steering wheel rotation sensor C2001 Pin 4, Circuit 298 (VT/OG), harness side and ground. • Is the voltage greater than 10 volts? → **Yes** GO to **K6**. → **No** REPAIR the circuit(s) in question. CLEAR the DTCs. REPEAT the Auto Test.
K6 CHECK STEERING WHEEL ROTATION SENSOR	
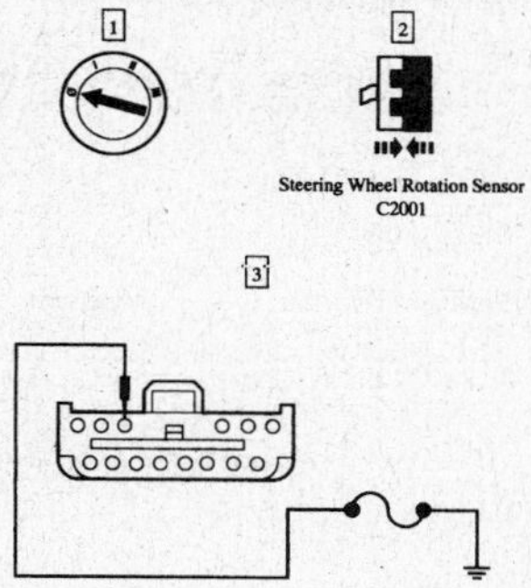	3 Connect a (5A) amp fused jumper wire between EVO control module C214 Pin 12, Circuit 837 (YE/BK), harness side and ground. 4 Place the 73 Digital Multimeter in the diode check position.

FM6029900345030X

Fig. 42 DTC 33: Steering Rotation Not Detected (Part 3 of 4). 1999-2000 Crown Victoria & Grand Marquis

TEST CONDITIONS	TEST DETAILS/RESULTS/ACTIONS
L1 CHECK SPEEDOMETER OPERATION	
	1 Drive the vehicle and check for correct speedometer operation. • Does the speedometer indicate vehicle speeds above 24 km/h (15 mph)? → **Yes** GO to **L2**. → **No** INSPECT instrument cluster. CLEAR the DTCs. REPEAT the Auto Test.

FM6029900346010X

Fig. 43 DTC 35: Vehicle Speed Above 15 mph Not Detected (Part 1 of 2). 1999-2000 Crown Victoria & Grand Marquis

TEST CONDITIONS	TEST DETAILS/RESULTS/ACTIONS
K6 CHECK STEERING WHEEL ROTATION SENSOR	
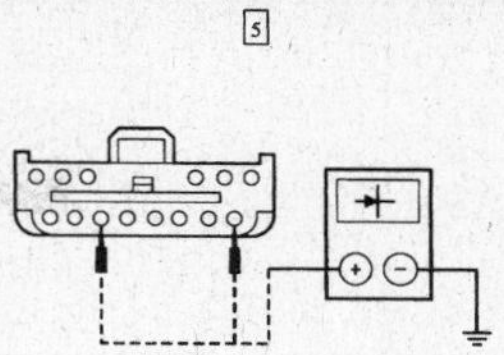	5 **Note:** Touch 73 Digital Multimeter leads together to be sure the audio (beep) function is operational. **Note:** The 73 Digital Multimeter should beep several times while rotating the steering wheel. Connect 73 Digital Multimeter leads between EVO control module C214 Pin 1, Circuit 633 (RD), harness side and ground; and between EVO control module C214 Pin 6, Circuit 634 (BN), harness side and ground. Listen for an audible beep while turning the steering wheel one quarter turn in each direction. • Does 73 Digital Multimeter beep multiple times in each direction? → **Yes** INSTALL a new EVO control module. CLEAR the DTCs. REPEAT the Auto Test. → **No** INSTALL a new steering wheel rotation sensor. CLEAR the DTCs. REPEAT the Auto Test.

FM6029900345040X

Fig. 42 DTC 33: Steering Rotation Not Detected (Part 4 of 4). 1999-2000 Crown Victoria & Grand Marquis

TEST CONDITIONS	TEST DETAILS/RESULTS/ACTIONS
L2 CHECK CIRCUIT 676 (PK/OG) FOR AN OPEN	
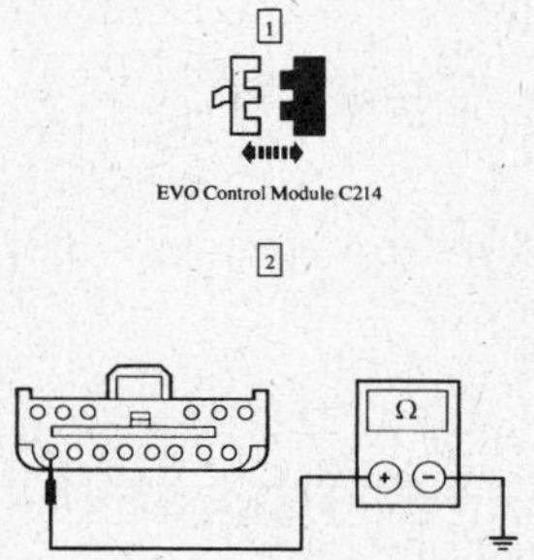	2 Measure the resistance between EVO control module C214 Pin 8, Circuit 676 (PK/OG), harness side and ground. • Is the resistance greater than 10,000 ohms? → **Yes** GO to **L3**. → **No** REPAIR the circuit. CLEAR the DTCs. REPEAT the Auto Test.
L3 CHECK CIRCUIT 679 (GY/BK) FOR AN OPEN	
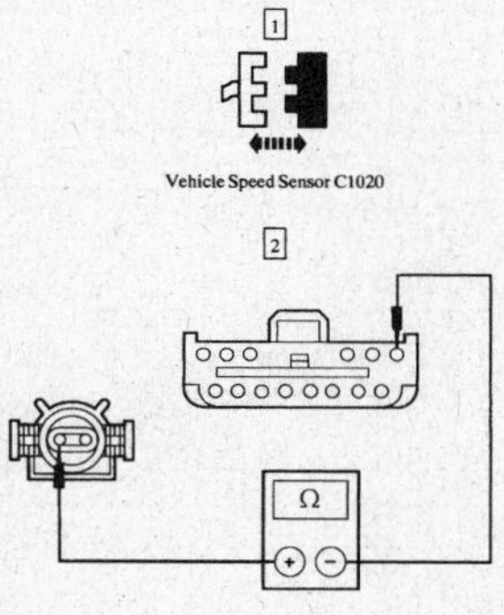	2 Measure the resistance between EVO control module C214 Pin 9, Circuit 679 (GY/BK), harness side and vehicle speed sensor C1020 Pin 1, Circuit 679 (GY/BK), harness side. • Is the resistance less than 5 ohms? → **Yes** INSTALL a new EVO control module. REFER to Section 211-02. CLEAR the DTCs. REPEAT the Auto Test. → **No** REPAIR the circuit. CLEAR the DTCs. REPEAT the Auto Test.

FM6029900346020X

Fig. 43 DTC 35: Vehicle Speed Above 15 mph Not Detected (Part 2 of 2). 1999-2000 Crown Victoria & Grand Marquis

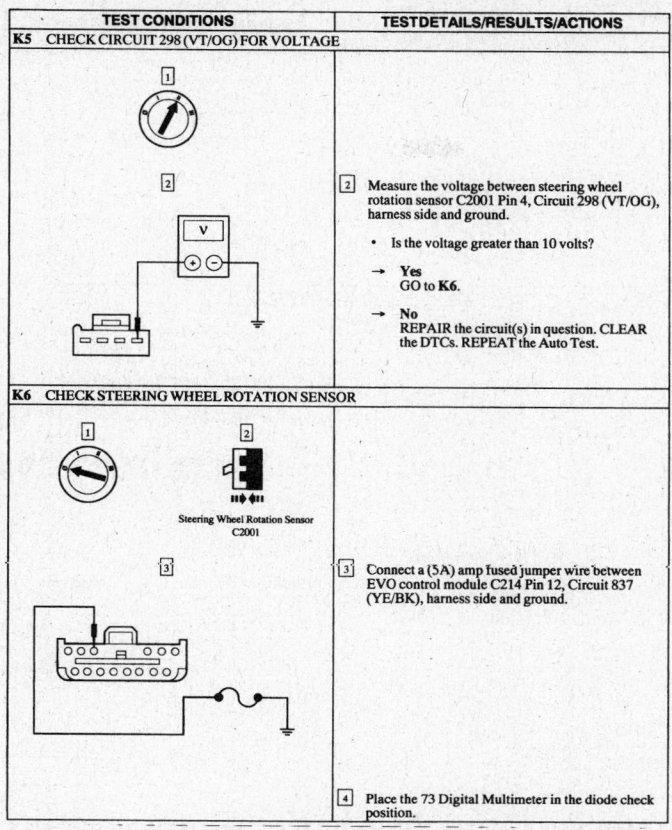

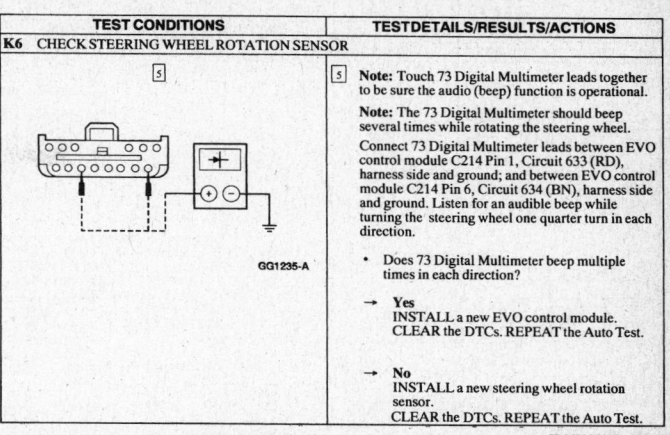

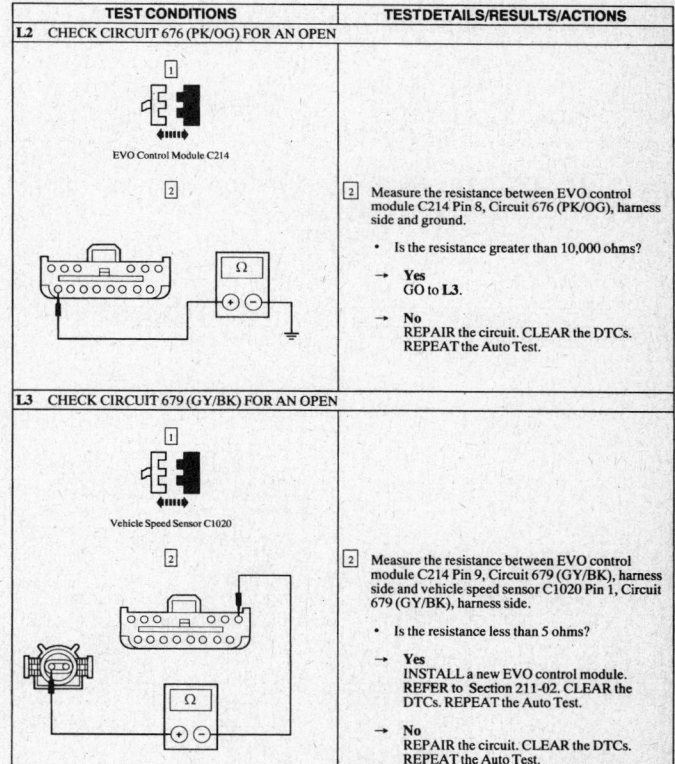

TEST CONDITIONS	TESTDETAILS/RESULTS/ACTIONS
M1 CHECK CIRCUITS 633 (RD) AND 634 (BN) FOR CONTINUITY	
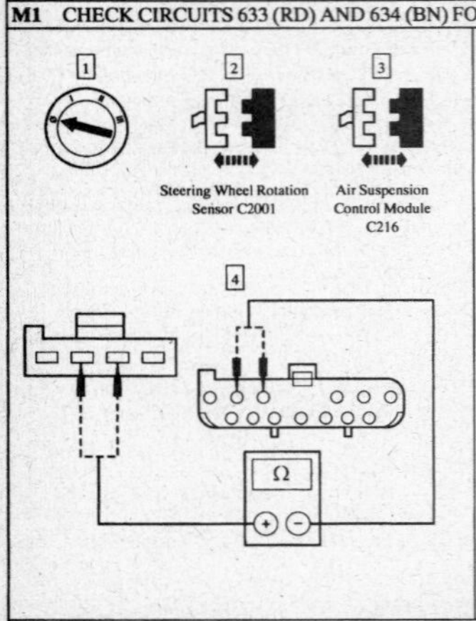	4 Measure the resistance between air suspension control module C216 Pin 18, Circuit 633 (RD), harness side and steering wheel rotation sensor C2001 Pin 3, Circuit 633 (RD), harness side; and between air suspension control module C216 Pin 19, Circuit 634 (BN), harness side and steering wheel rotation sensor C2001 Pin 2, Circuit 634 (BN), harness side. • Are the resistances less than 5 ohms? → **Yes** GO to **M2**. → **No** REPAIR the circuit(s) in question. CLEAR the DTCs. REPEAT the Auto Test.
M2 CHECK CIRCUIT 837 (YE/BK) FOR CONTINUITY	
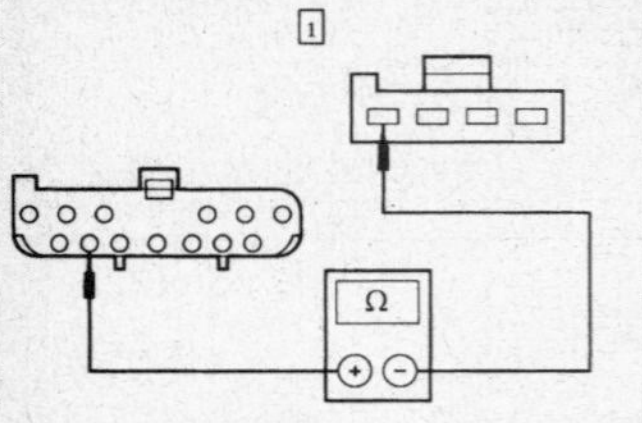	1 Measure the resistance between air suspension control module C216 Pin 6, Circuit 57 (BK), harness side and steering wheel rotation sensor C2001 Pin 1, Circuit 837 (YE/BK), harness side. • Is the resistance less than 5 ohms? → **Yes** GO to **M3**. → **No** REPAIR the circuit. CLEAR the DTCs. REPEAT the Auto Test.

FM6029900347010X

Fig. 44 DTC 74: Steering Rotation Not Detected (Part 1 of 4). 1999-2000 Crown Victoria & Grand Marquis

TEST CONDITIONS	TESTDETAILS/RESULTS/ACTIONS
M6 CHECK CIRCUIT 298 (VT/OG) FOR VOLTAGE	
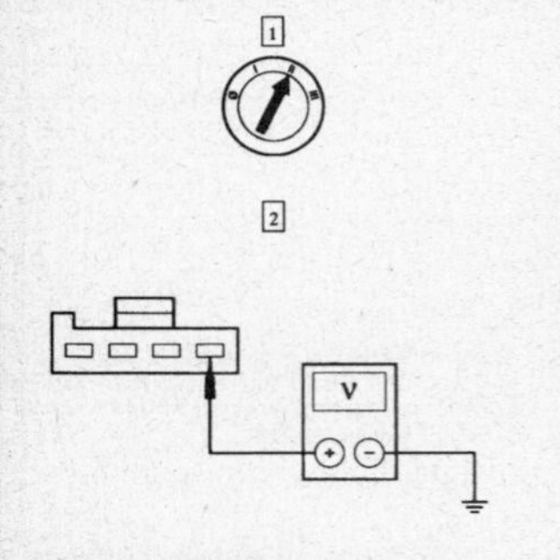	2 Measure the voltage between steering wheel rotation sensor C2001 Pin 4, Circuit 298 (VT/OG), harness side and ground. • Is the voltage greater than 10 volts? → **Yes** GO to **M7**. → **No** REPAIR the circuit(s) in question. CLEAR the DTCs. REPEAT the Auto Test.
M7 CHECK STEERING WHEEL ROTATION SENSOR	
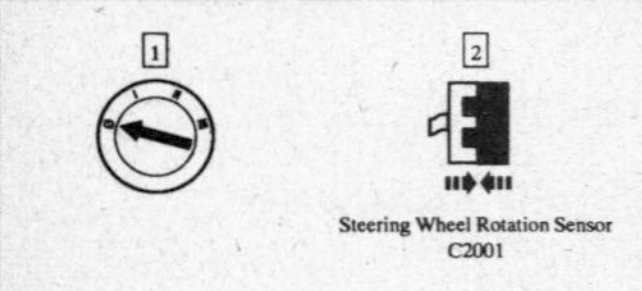	3 Place the 73 Digital Multimeter in the diode check position.

FM6029900347030X

Fig. 44 DTC 74: Steering Rotation Not Detected (Part 3 of 4). 1999-2000 Crown Victoria & Grand Marquis

TEST CONDITIONS	TESTDETAILS/RESULTS/ACTIONS
M3 CHECK CIRCUIT 837 (YE/BK) FOR GROUND	
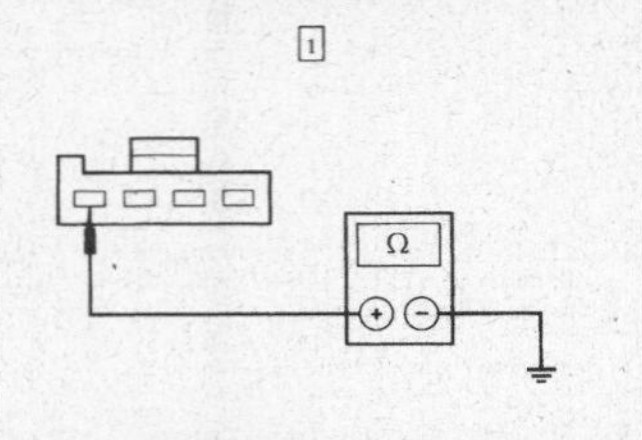	1 Measure the resistance between steering wheel rotation sensor C2001 Pin 1, Circuit 837 (YE/BK), harness side and ground. • Is the resistance greater than 10,000 ohms? → **Yes** GO to **M4**. → **No** REPAIR the circuit. CLEAR the DTCs. REPEAT the Auto Test.
M4 CHECK CIRCUITS 633 (RD) AND 634 (BN) FOR SHORT TO BATTERY	
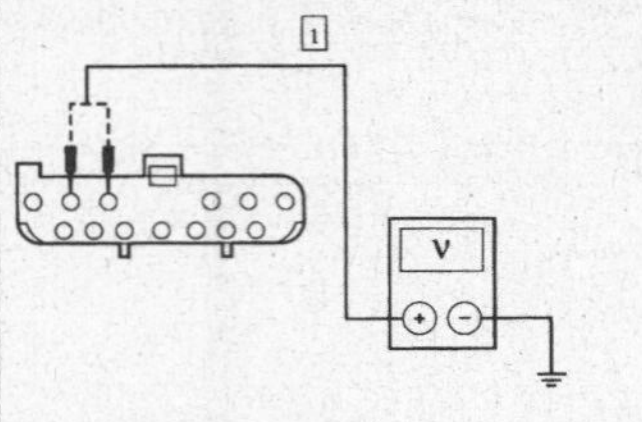	1 Measure the voltage between air suspension control module C216 Pin 18, Circuit 633 (RD), harness side and ground; and between air suspension control module C216 pin 19, circuit 634 (BN), harness side and ground. • Is voltage present? → **Yes** REPAIR the circuit(s) in question. CLEAR the DTCs. REPEAT the Auto Test. → **No** GO to **M5**.
M5 CHECK CIRCUITS 633 (RD) AND 634 (BN) FOR SHORT TO GROUND	
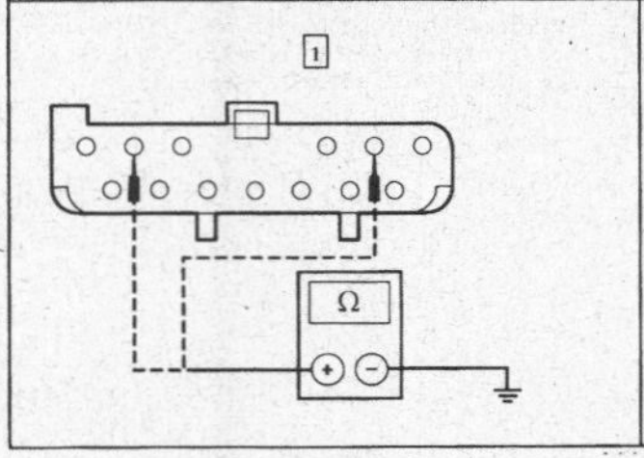	1 Measure the resistance between air suspension control module C216 Pin 18, Circuit 633 (RD), harness side and ground; and between air suspension control module C216 Pin 19, Circuit 634 (BN), harness side and ground. • Are the resistances greater than 10,000 ohms? → **Yes** GO to **M6**. → **No** REPAIR the circuit(s) in question. CLEAR the DTCs. REPEAT the Auto Test.

FM6029900347020X

Fig. 44 DTC 74: Steering Rotation Not Detected (Part 2 of 4). 1999-2000 Crown Victoria & Grand Marquis

TEST CONDITIONS	TESTDETAILS/RESULTS/ACTIONS
M7 CHECK STEERING WHEEL ROTATION SENSOR	
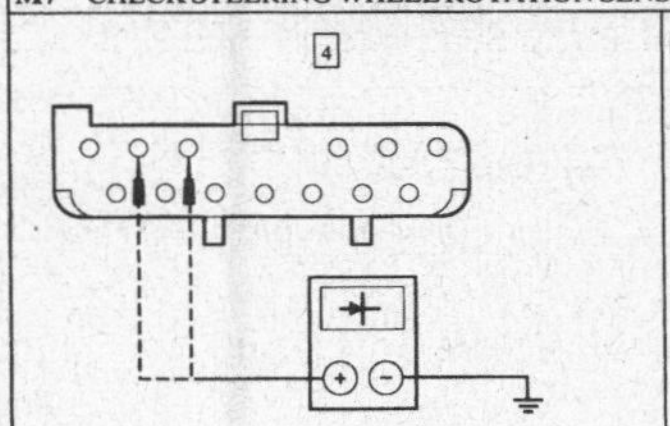	4 **Note:** Touch 73 Digital Multimeter leads together to be sure the audio (beep) function is operational. **Note:** The 73 Digital Multimeter should beep several times while rotating the steering wheel. Connect 73 Digital Multimeter leads between air suspension control module C216 Pin 18, Circuit 633 (RD), harness side and ground; and between air suspension control module C216 Pin 19, Circuit 634 (BN), harness side ground. Listen for an audible beep while turning the steering wheel one quarter turn in each direction. • Does 73 Digital Multimeter beep multiple times in each direction? → **Yes** INSTALL a new EVO control module. CLEAR the DTCs. REPEAT the Auto Test. → **No** INSTALL a new steering wheel rotation sensor. CLEAR the DTCs. REPEAT the Auto Test.

FM6029900347040X

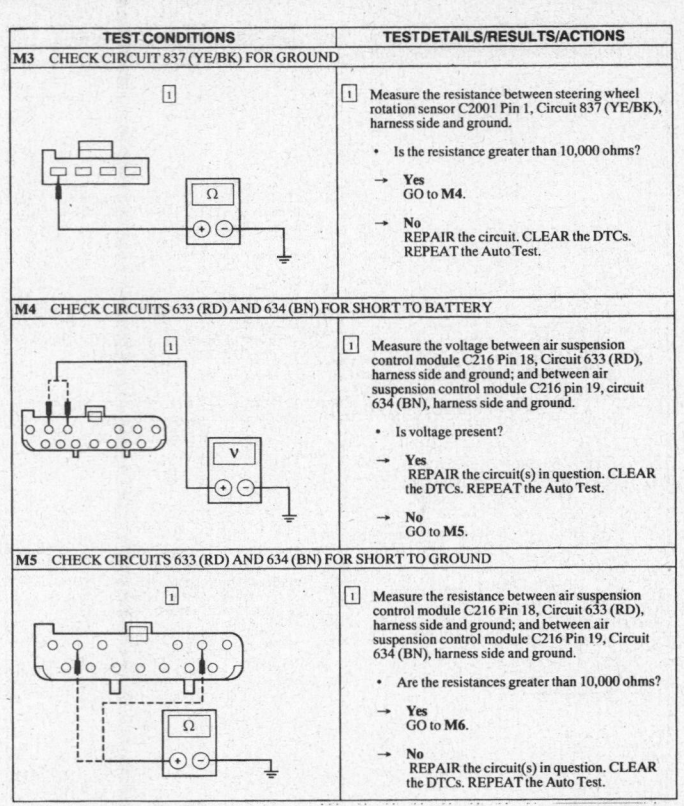

Fig. 44 DTC 74: Steering Rotation Not Detected (Part 4 of 4). 1999-2000 Crown Victoria & Grand Marquis

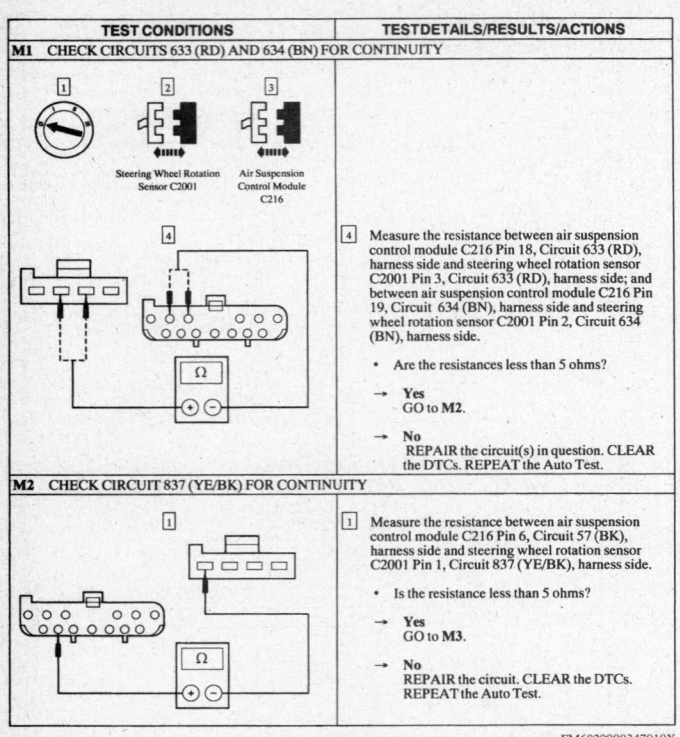

Code	Description	Error Handling	Generated	Validation
10	Auto test in progress		Auto Test	
11	Auto test passed		Auto Test	
12	Perform manual tests		Auto Test	
15	No faults stored in memory		Auto Test	
18	Control Module Detects Low Battery Voltage	Disable air suspension and EVO until senses more than 13 volts for 1 second	Auto Test	Less than 11 volts for 1 second continuous
19	Control Module Detects High Battery Voltage	Disable Air Suspension and EVO until senses less than 17.5 volts for 1 second	Auto Test	More than 19 volts for 1 second continuous
20	Control Module Memory Error 2	Disable Air Suspension	Drive Cycle Auto Test	More than 19 volts for 1 second continuous
25	Air Suspension Height Sensor Supply Not 5 Volts	Disable Air Suspension	Drive Cycle Auto Test	
29	Two Door Cycles Not Detected During Test		Auto Test	
35	EVO Power Steering Control Valve Actuator Concern	Air suspention normal, EVO full assist	Drive Cycle Auto Test	Fault after 1 second contin-uous / GO to Pinpoint Test A
45	Steering Rotation Not Detected		Auto Test	GO to Pinpoint Test B
50	LH Front Air Suspension Height Sensor Signal Out Of Range	Disable Air Suspension	Drive Cycle Auto Test	Fault after 1 second continuous
55	RH Front Air Suspension Height Sensor Signal Out Of Range	Disable Air Suspension	Drive Cycle Auto Test	Fault after 1 second continuous
60	LH Rear Air Suspension Height Sensor Signal Out Of Range	Disable Air Suspension	Drive Cycle Auto Test	Fault after 1 second continuous
70	Vent Solenoid Valve	Disable Air Suspension	Drive Cycle Auto Test	Fault after 1 second continuous
75	Compressor Relay Control Circuit	Disable Air Suspension	Drive Cycle Auto Test	Fault after 1 second continuous

FM6029700274010X

Fig. 45 Symptom chart (Part 1 of 2). Mark VIII

TEST CONDITIONS	TEST DETAILS/RESULTS/ACTIONS
A1 CHECK EVO POWER STEERING CONTROL VALVE ACTUATOR	
1 2 	
3 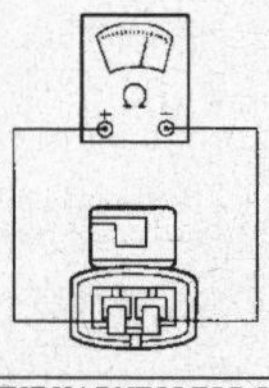	3 Connect an ohmmeter between the EVO actuator connector C132, Circuit 353 (LB) and Circuit 330 (Y/LG). • Is the resistance less than 8 ohms or more than 16 ohms? → **Yes** REPLACE the EVO power steering control valve actuator. REPEAT the Auto Test. → **No** GO to **A2**.
A2 CHECK THE HARNESS FOR SHORT TO B+	
1 2 	
3 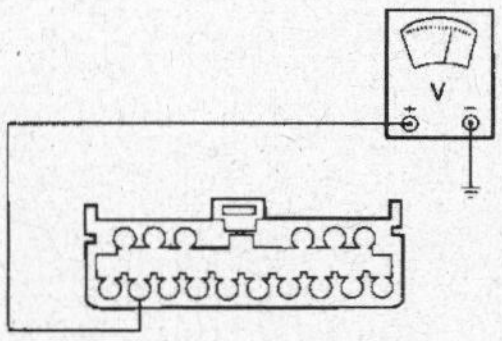	3 Connect a voltmeter to the air suspension/electronic variable orifice (EVO) control module connector Pin C205-19, Circuit 330 (Y/LG). Note the reading.

FM6029700275010X

Fig. 46 Test A: DTC 35, EVO Power Steering Control Valve Actuator Concern (Part 1 of 3). Mark VIII

• Steering Diagnostics Cannot Be Entered	• Circuitry open/shorted. • Control module.	• GO to Pinpoint Test C.
• Steering Does Not Vary With Vehicle Speed	• Vehicle speed sensor. • Circuitry open/shorted. • Control module.	• GO to Pinpoint Test D.

FM6029700274020X

Fig. 45 Symptom chart (Part 2 of 2). Mark VIII

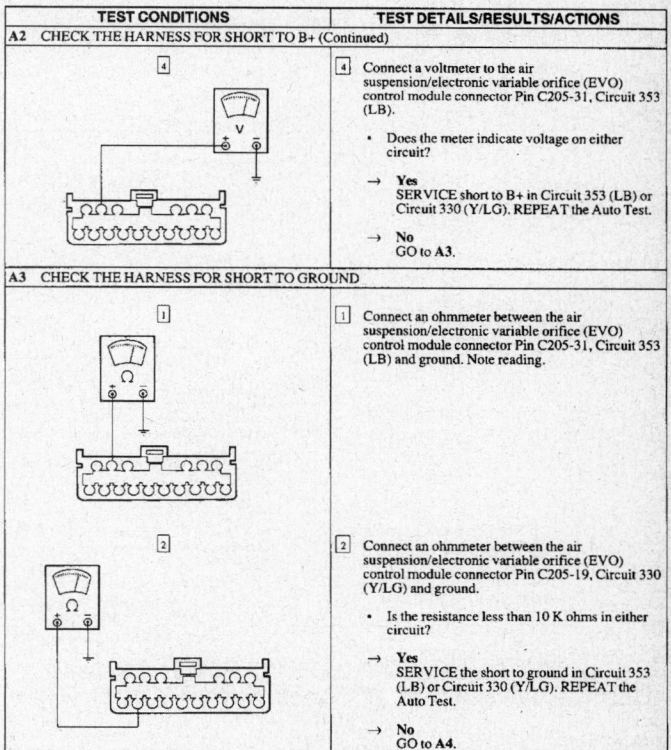

TEST CONDITIONS	TEST DETAILS/RESULTS/ACTIONS
A2 CHECK THE HARNESS FOR SHORT TO B+ (Continued)	
4 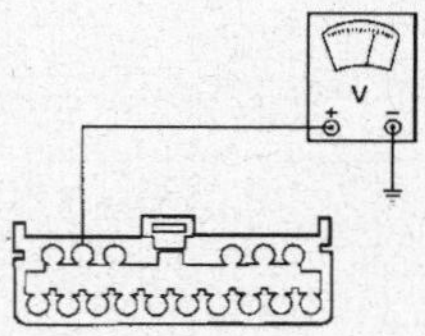	4 Connect a voltmeter to the air suspension/electronic variable orifice (EVO) control module connector Pin C205-31, Circuit 353 (LB). • Does the meter indicate voltage on either circuit? → **Yes** SERVICE short to B+ in Circuit 353 (LB) or Circuit 330 (Y/LG). REPEAT the Auto Test. → **No** GO to **A3**.
A3 CHECK THE HARNESS FOR SHORT TO GROUND	
1 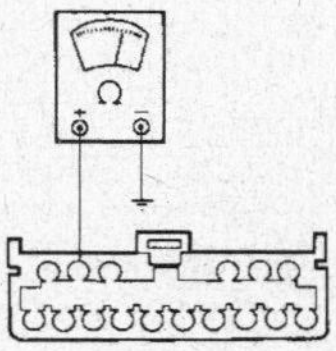	1 Connect an ohmmeter between the air suspension/electronic variable orifice (EVO) control module connector Pin C205-31, Circuit 353 (LB) and ground. Note reading.
2 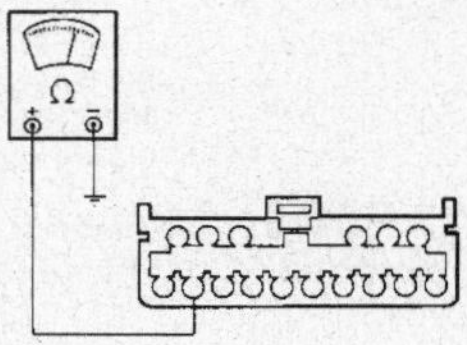	2 Connect an ohmmeter between the air suspension/electronic variable orifice (EVO) control module connector Pin C205-19, Circuit 330 (Y/LG) and ground. • Is the resistance less than 10 K ohms in either circuit? → **Yes** SERVICE the short to ground in Circuit 353 (LB) or Circuit 330 (Y/LG). REPEAT the Auto Test. → **No** GO to **A4**.

FM6029700275020X

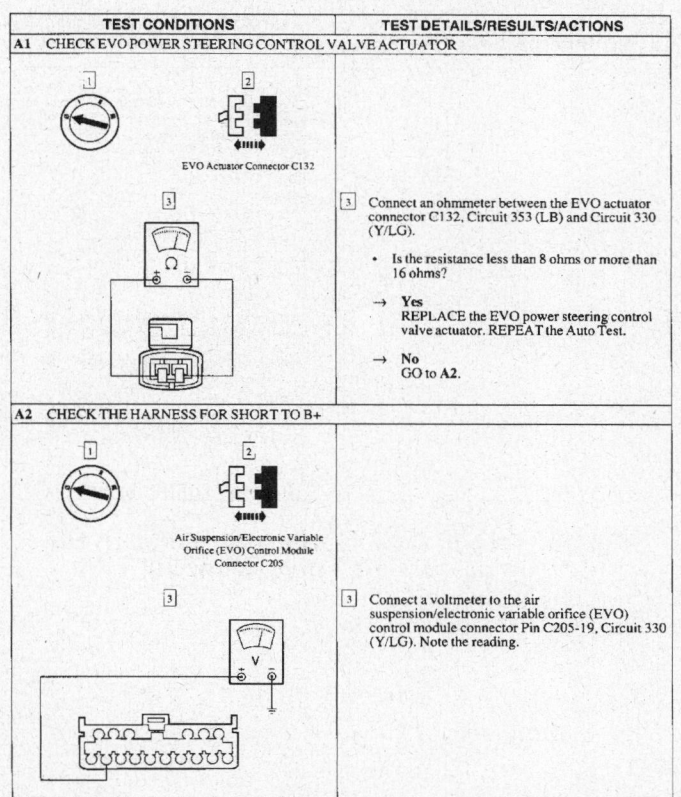

Fig. 46 Test A: DTC 35, EVO Power Steering Control Valve Actuator Concern (Part 2 of 3). Mark VIII

TEST CONDITIONS	TEST DETAILS/RESULTS/ACTIONS
A4 CHECK FOR SHORT BETWEEN CIRCUITS 353 (LB) AND 330 (Y/LG)	
1 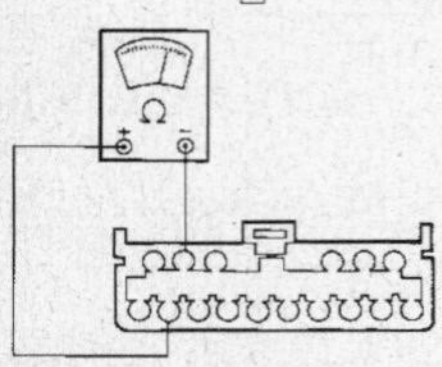	1 Connect an ohmmeter between the air suspension/electronic variable orifice (EVO) control module connector Pin C205-19, Circuit 330 (Y/LG) and Circuit C205-31, Circuit 353 (LB). • Is the resistance 10 K ohms or less? → **Yes** SERVICE short between Circuit 353 (LB) and Circuit 330 (Y/LG). REPEAT the Auto Test. → **No** GO to **A5**.
A5 CHECK FOR OPEN IN CIRCUIT 353 (LB) AND CIRCUIT 330 (Y/LG)	
1 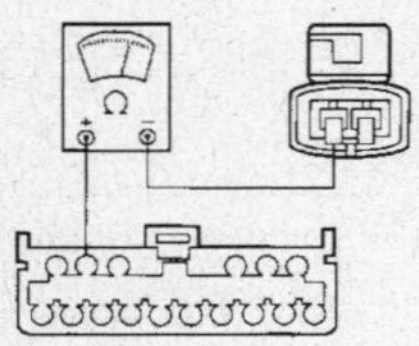	1 Connect an ohmmeter between the air suspension/electronic variable orifice (EVO) control module connector Pin C205-31 and the EVO actuator connector C132, Circuit 353 (LB). Note reading.
2 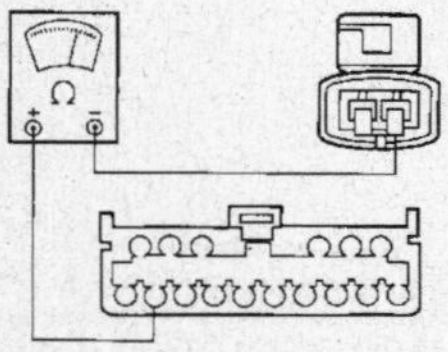	2 Connect an ohmmeter between the air suspension/electronic variable orifice (EVO) control module connector Pin C205-19 and the EVO actuator connector C132, Circuit 330 (Y/LG). • Is the resistance 5 ohms or less in each circuit? → **Yes** INSPECT the connector pins. CLEAN/SERVICE as required. REPEAT the Auto Test. If DTC 35 repeats, REPLACE the air suspension/electronic variable orifice (EVO) control module. → **No** SERVICE the open in Circuit 353 (LB) or 330 (Y/LG). REPEAT the Auto Test.

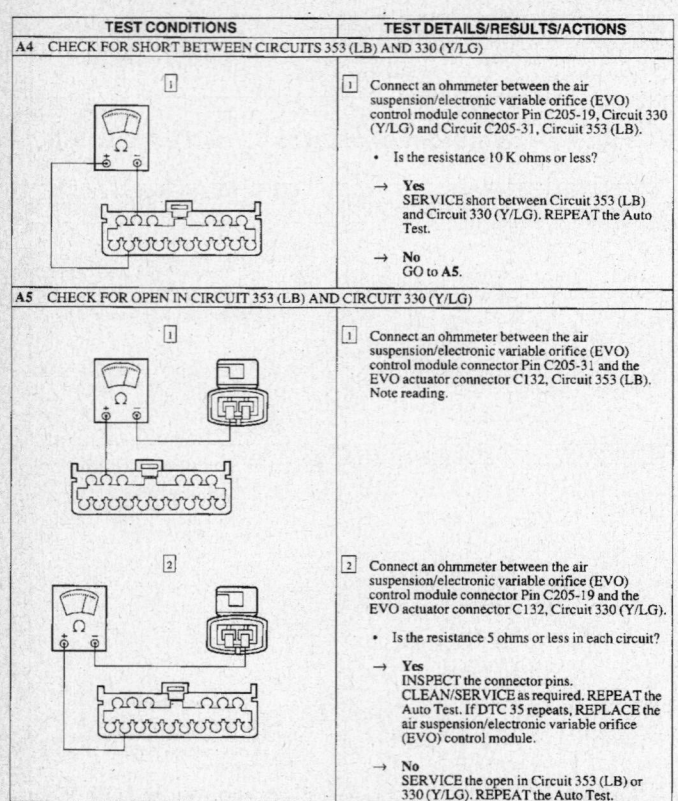

FM6029700275030X

Fig. 46 Test A: DTC 35, EVO Power Steering Control Valve Actuator Concern (Part 3 of 3). Mark VIII

TEST CONDITIONS	TEST DETAILS/RESULTS/ACTIONS
B3 CHECK CIRCUITS 633 (R) AND 634 (BR) FOR CHANGING VOLTAGE AT CONTROL MODULE	
1 2 	
3 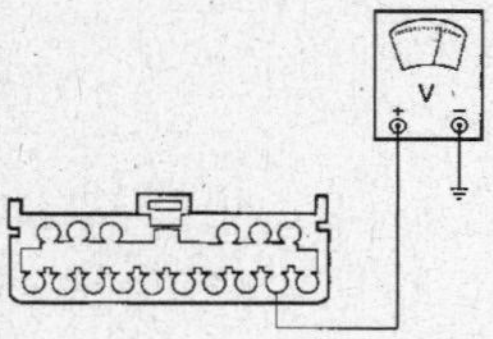	3 **NOTE:** The meter reading should change between 5 volts and zero volts several times while rotating the steering wheel. Connect a voltmeter to the air suspension/electronic variable orifice (EVO) control module connector Pin C204-2, Circuit 633 (R).
	4 Slowly rotate the steering wheel one quarter of a turn while observing the meter reading.

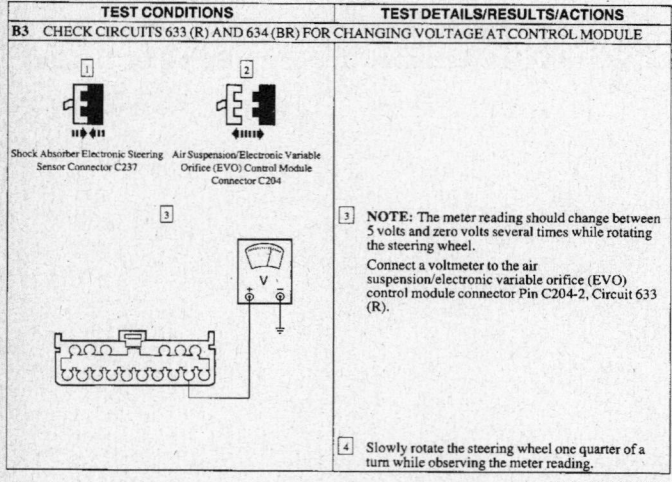

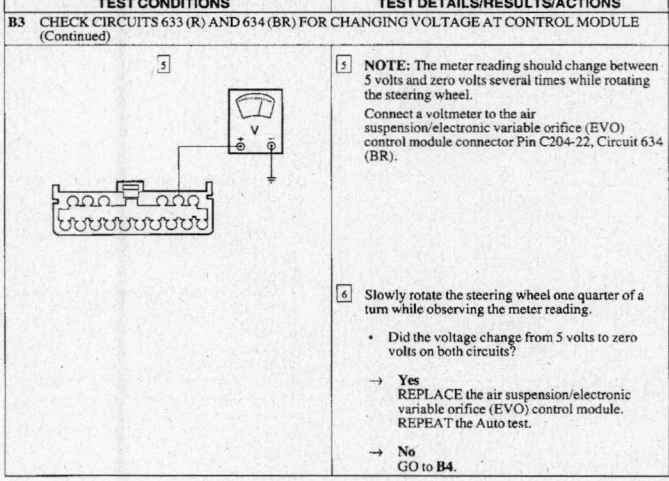

FM6029700276020X

Fig. 47 Test B: DTC 45, Steering Rotation Not Detected (Part 2 of 6). Mark VIII

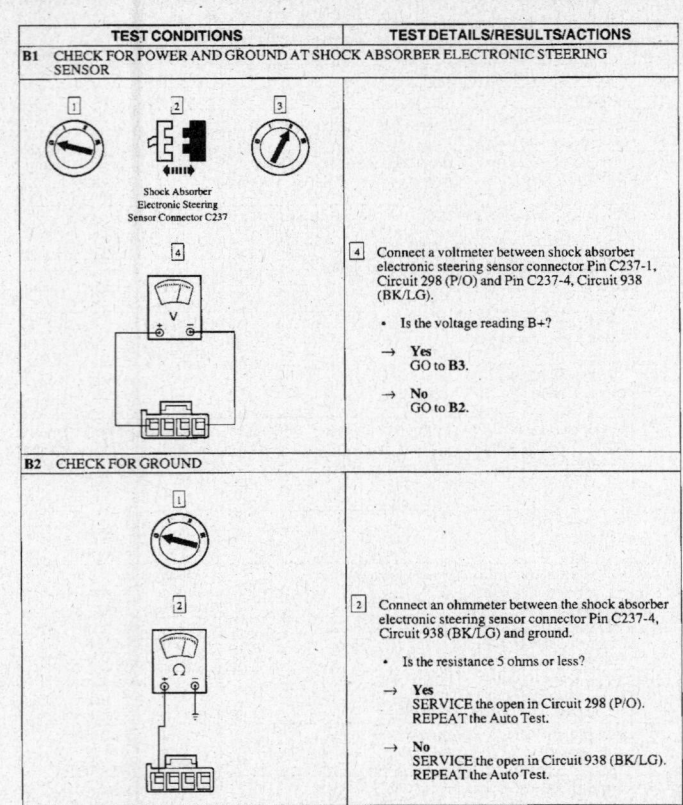

TEST CONDITIONS	TEST DETAILS/RESULTS/ACTIONS
B1 CHECK FOR POWER AND GROUND AT SHOCK ABSORBER ELECTRONIC STEERING SENSOR	
1 2 3 	
4 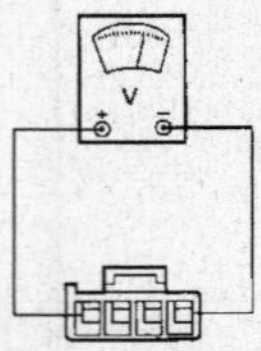	4 Connect a voltmeter between shock absorber electronic steering sensor connector Pin C237-1, Circuit 298 (P/O) and Pin C237-4, Circuit 938 (BK/LG). • Is the voltage reading B+? → **Yes** GO to **B3**. → **No** GO to **B2**.
B2 CHECK FOR GROUND	
1 	
2 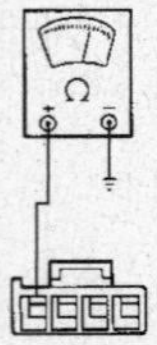	2 Connect an ohmmeter between the shock absorber electronic steering sensor connector Pin C237-4, Circuit 938 (BK/LG) and ground. • Is the resistance 5 ohms or less? → **Yes** SERVICE the open in Circuit 298 (P/O). REPEAT the Auto Test. → **No** SERVICE the open in Circuit 938 (BK/LG). REPEAT the Auto Test.

FM6029700276010X

Fig. 47 Test B: DTC 45, Steering Rotation Not Detected (Part 1 of 6). Mark VIII

TEST CONDITIONS	TEST DETAILS/RESULTS/ACTIONS
B3 CHECK CIRCUITS 633 (R) AND 634 (BR) FOR CHANGING VOLTAGE AT CONTROL MODULE (Continued)	
5 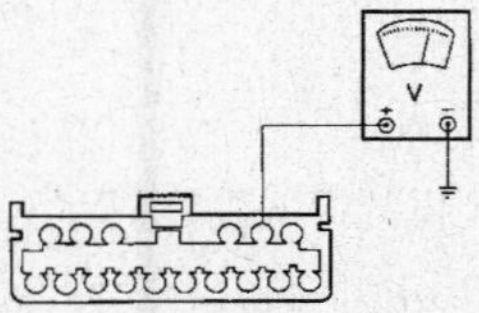	5 **NOTE:** The meter reading should change between 5 volts and zero volts several times while rotating the steering wheel. Connect a voltmeter to the air suspension/electronic variable orifice (EVO) control module connector Pin C204-22, Circuit 634 (BR).
	6 Slowly rotate the steering wheel one quarter of a turn while observing the meter reading. • Did the voltage change from 5 volts to zero volts on both circuits? → **Yes** REPLACE the air suspension/electronic variable orifice (EVO) control module. REPEAT the Auto test. → **No** GO to **B4**.

FM6029700276030X

Fig. 47 Test B: DTC 45, Steering Rotation Not Detected (Part 3 of 6). Mark VIII

TEST CONDITIONS	TEST DETAILS/RESULTS/ACTIONS
B4 CHECK VOLTAGE READING	
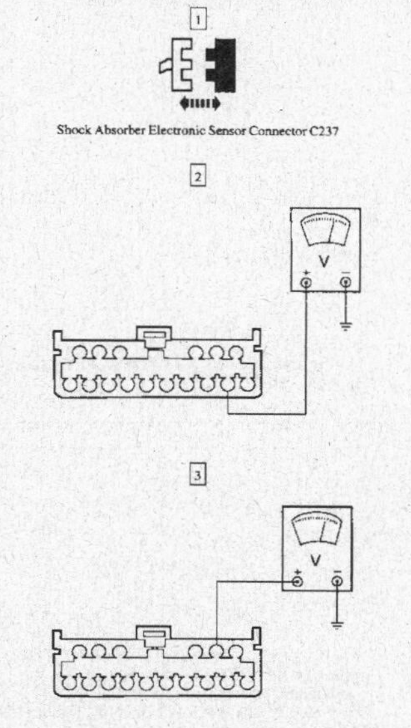	2 Connect a voltmeter to the air suspension/electronic variable orifice (EVO) control module connector Pin C204-2, Circuit 633 (R). 3 Connect a voltmeter to the air suspension/electronic variable orifice (EVO) control module connector Pin C204-22, Circuit 634 (BR). • Is the voltage reading on one or both circuits B+? → **Yes** SERVICE the short to B+ in Circuit 634 (BR) or 633 (R). REPEAT the Auto Test. → **No** GO to **B5**.

FM6029700276040X

Fig. 47 Test B: DTC 45, Steering Rotation Not Detected (Part 4 of 6). Mark VIII

TEST CONDITIONS	TEST DETAILS/RESULTS/ACTIONS
B6 CHECK FOR OPEN CIRCUIT ON 633 (R) OR 634 (BR) (Continued)	
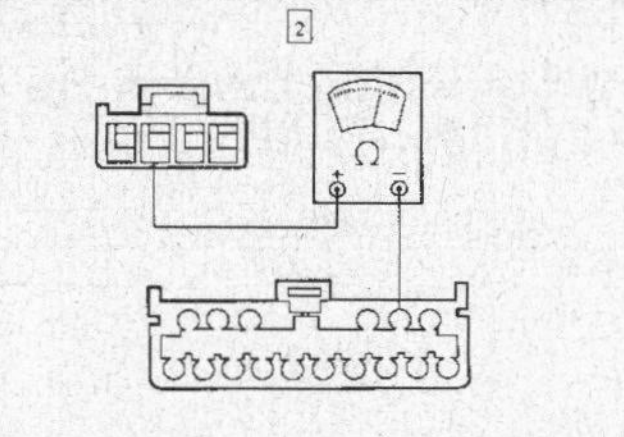	2 Connect an ohmmeter between the air suspension/electronic variable orifice (EVO) control module connector Pin C204-22 and shock absorber electronic steering sensor connector Pin C237-3, Circuit 634 (BR). • Is the resistance 5 ohms or less in each circuit? → **Yes** REPLACE the shock absorber electronic steering sensor. REPEAT the Auto Test. → **No** SERVICE Circuit 633 (R) or 634 (BR) for an open. REPEAT the Auto Test.

FM6029700276060X

Fig. 47 Test B: DTC 45, Steering Rotation Not Detected (Part 6 of 6). Mark VIII

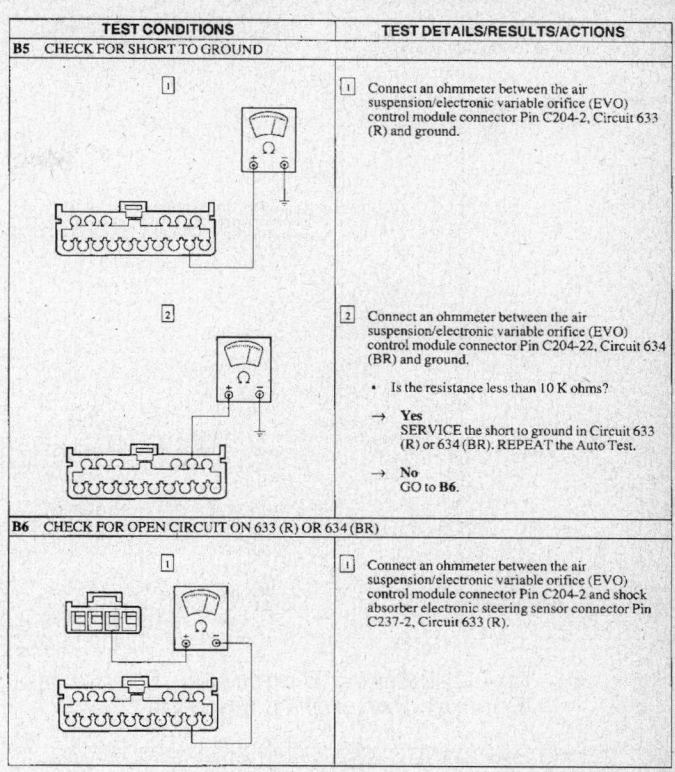

TEST CONDITIONS	TEST DETAILS/RESULTS/ACTIONS
B5 CHECK FOR SHORT TO GROUND	
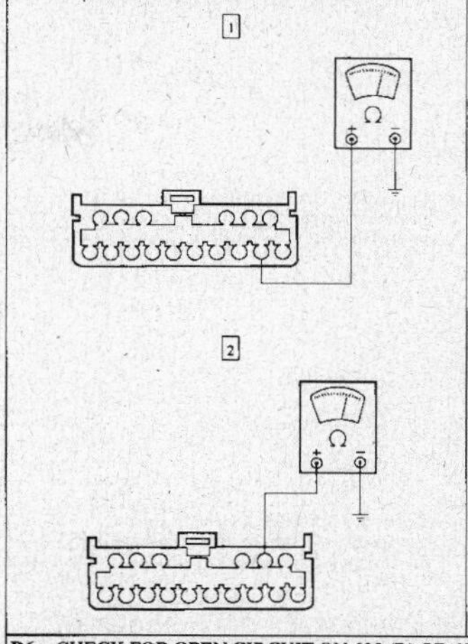	1 Connect an ohmmeter between the air suspension/electronic variable orifice (EVO) control module connector Pin C204-2, Circuit 633 (R) and ground. 2 Connect an ohmmeter between the air suspension/electronic variable orifice (EVO) control module connector Pin C204-22, Circuit 634 (BR) and ground. • Is the resistance less than 10 K ohms? → **Yes** SERVICE the short to ground in Circuit 633 (R) or 634 (BR). REPEAT the Auto Test. → **No** GO to **B6**.
B6 CHECK FOR OPEN CIRCUIT ON 633 (R) OR 634 (BR)	
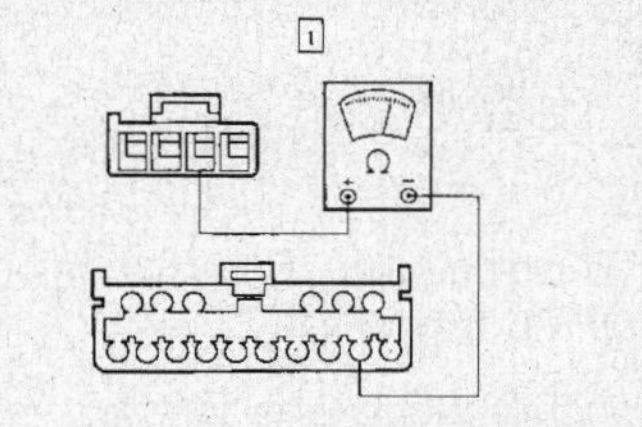	1 Connect an ohmmeter between the air suspension/electronic variable orifice (EVO) control module connector Pin C204-2 and shock absorber electronic steering sensor connector Pin C237-2, Circuit 633 (R).

FM6029700276050X

Fig. 47 Test B: DTC 45, Steering Rotation Not Detected (Part 5 of 6). Mark VIII

TEST CONDITIONS	TEST DETAILS/RESULTS/ACTIONS
C1 RECHECK AUTO TEST	
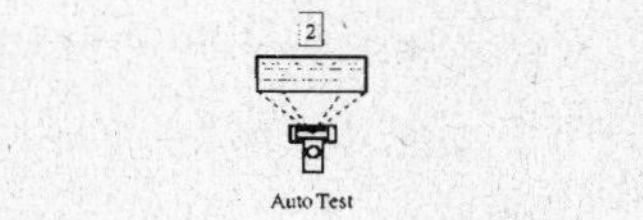	1 Make sure the air suspension service switch is ON. 2 If the function test codes 211 through 228 are continuously displayed Pin C2-11, Circuit 425 (BR/PK) is not at ground. Possibly caused by the air suspension switch or involved circuitry. • Are DTCs 211 through 228 displayed? → **Yes** GO to **C11**. → **No** GO to **C2**.
C2 CHECK FOR DTC	
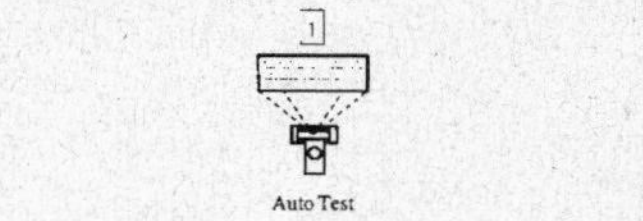	1 Perform the Auto Test and check for DTCs. • Are any DTCs retrieved? → **Yes** GO to the Air Suspension/Electronic Variable Orifice (EVO) Control Module Diagnostic Trouble Code Index. → **No** GO to C3.

FM6029700277010X

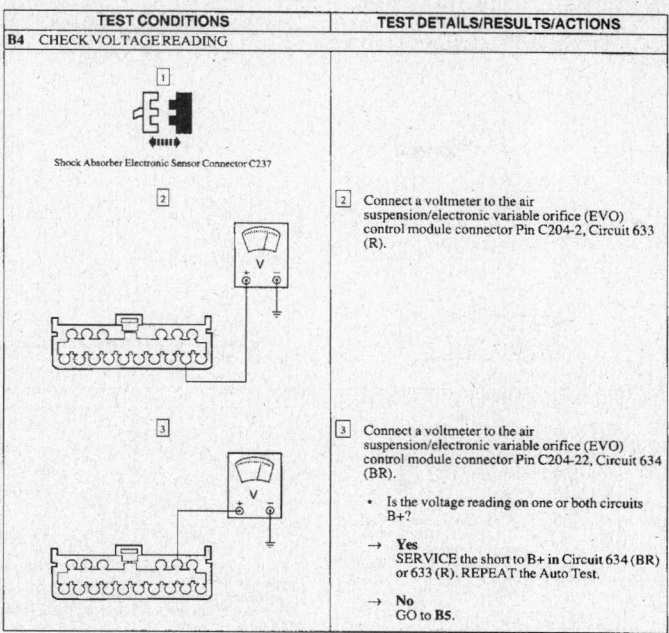

Fig. 48 Test C: Steering Diagnostics Cannot Be Entered (Part 1 of 7). Mark VIII

TEST CONDITIONS	TEST DETAILS/RESULTS/ACTIONS
C3 CHECK FOR B+ ON CIRCUIT 418 (DG/Y)	
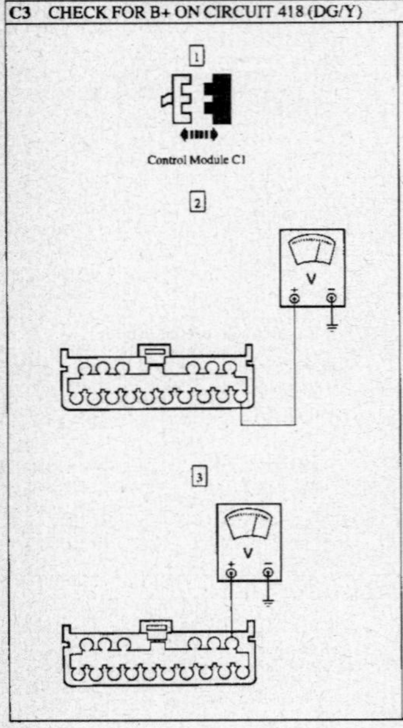	2 Connect a voltmeter to the air suspension/electronic variable orifice (EVO) control module connector Pin C204-1, Circuit 418 (DG/Y). 3 Connect a voltmeter to the air suspension/electronic variable orifice (EVO) control module connector Pin C204-21, Circuit 418 (DG/Y). • Is the voltage reading B+ on both circuits? → **Yes** GO to **C4**. → **No** SERVICE the open in Circuit 418 (DG/Y). REPEAT the Auto Test.

FM6029700277020X

Fig. 48 Test C: Steering Diagnostics Cannot Be Entered (Part 2 of 7). Mark VIII

TEST CONDITIONS	TEST DETAILS/RESULTS/ACTIONS
C6 CHECK LINE 419 (DG/LG) FOR SHORT TO GROUND	
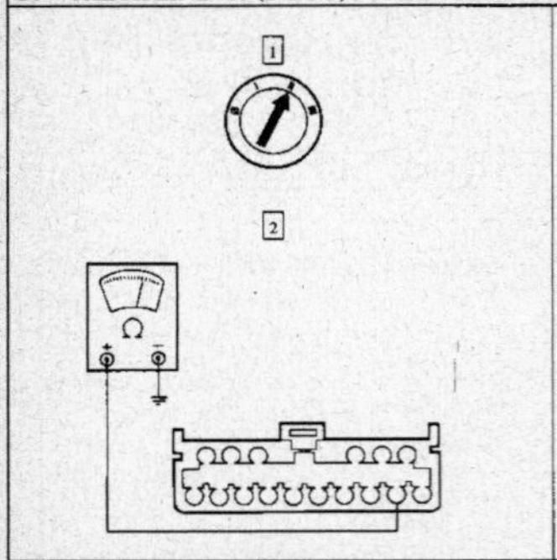	2 Connect a voltmeter to the air suspension/electronic variable orifice (EVO) control module connector Pin C205-12, Circuit 419 (DG/LG). • Is the voltage reading approximately 6 volts? → **Yes** GO to **C8**. → **No** GO to **C7**.
C7 ISOLATE SHORT TO GROUND **NOTE:** A short to ground in Circuit 419 (DG/LG) will cause CHECK AIR RIDE to be displayed in the message center, even if no air suspension system damage exists.	
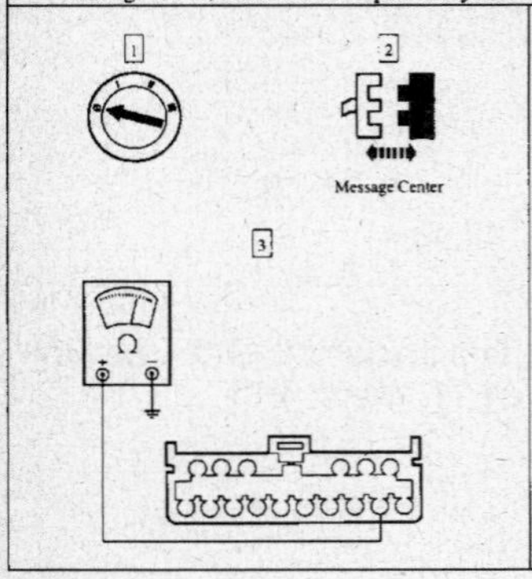	3 Connect an ohmmeter between the air suspension/electronic variable orifice (EVO) control module connector Pin C2-12, Circuit 419 (DG/LG) and ground. • Is the resistance 10 K ohms or more? → **Yes** DIAGNOSE a message service center. → **No** SERVICE the short to ground in Circuit 419 (DG/LG). REPEAT Auto Test.

FM6029700277040X

Fig. 48 Test C: Steering Diagnostics Cannot Be Entered (Part 4 of 7). Mark VIII

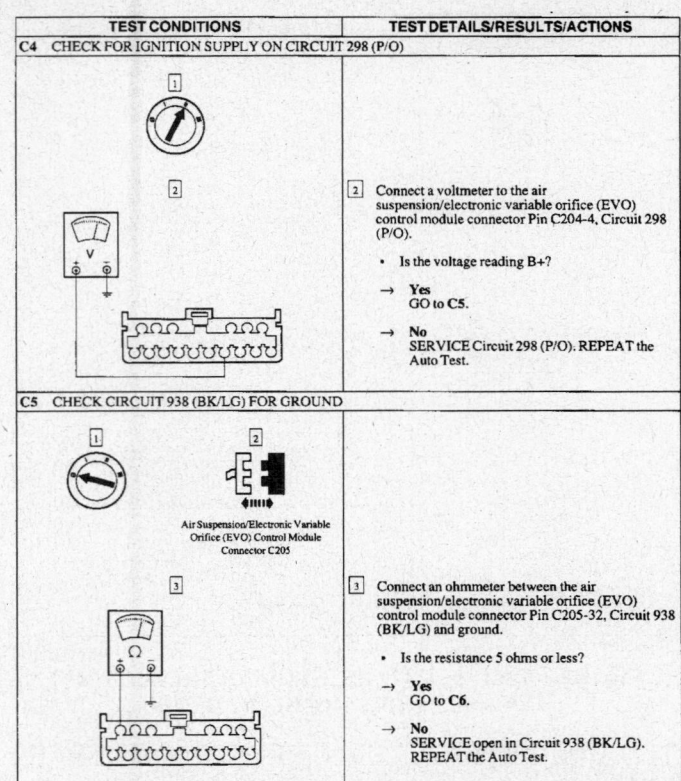

TEST CONDITIONS	TEST DETAILS/RESULTS/ACTIONS
C4 CHECK FOR IGNITION SUPPLY ON CIRCUIT 298 (P/O)	
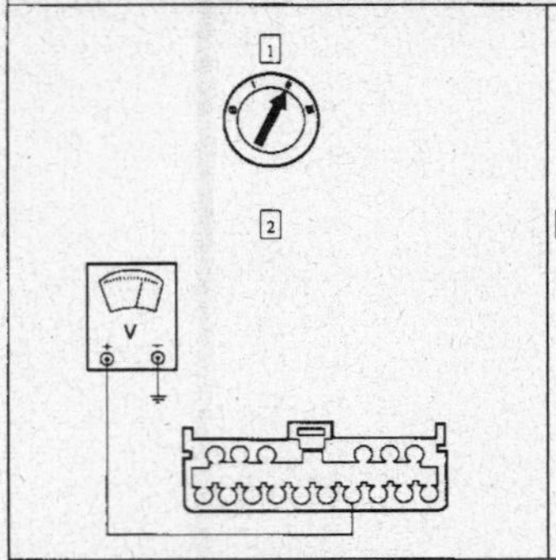	2 Connect a voltmeter to the air suspension/electronic variable orifice (EVO) control module connector Pin C204-4, Circuit 298 (P/O). • Is the voltage reading B+? → **Yes** GO to **C5**. → **No** SERVICE Circuit 298 (P/O). REPEAT the Auto Test.
C5 CHECK CIRCUIT 938 (BK/LG) FOR GROUND	
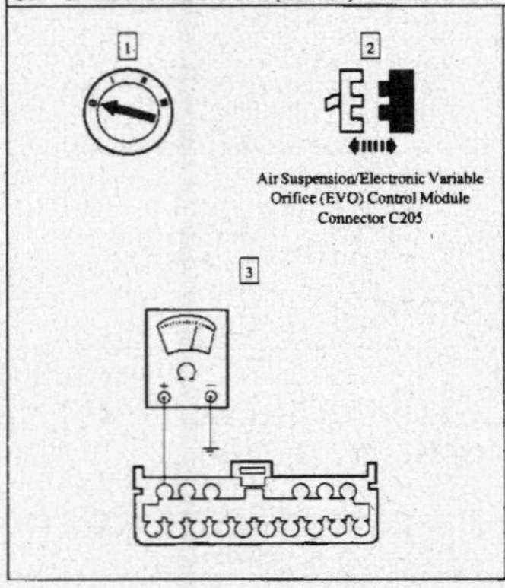	3 Connect an ohmmeter between the air suspension/electronic variable orifice (EVO) control module connector Pin C205-32, Circuit 938 (BK/LG) and ground. • Is the resistance 5 ohms or less? → **Yes** GO to **C6**. → **No** SERVICE open in Circuit 938 (BK/LG). REPEAT the Auto Test.

FM6029700277030X

Fig. 48 Test C: Steering Diagnostics Cannot Be Entered (Part 3 of 7). Mark VIII

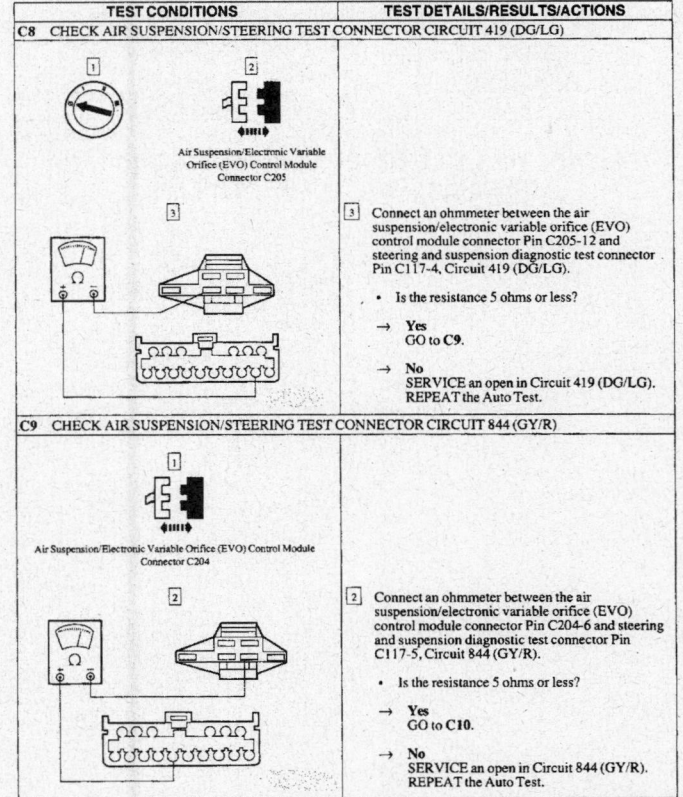

TEST CONDITIONS	TEST DETAILS/RESULTS/ACTIONS
C8 CHECK AIR SUSPENSION/STEERING TEST CONNECTOR CIRCUIT 419 (DG/LG)	
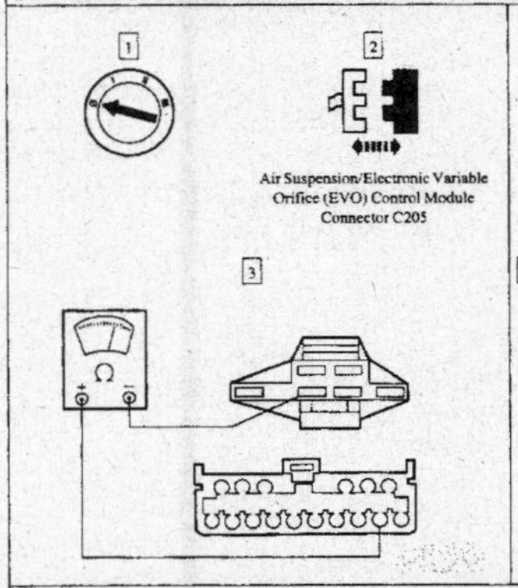	3 Connect an ohmmeter between the air suspension/electronic variable orifice (EVO) control module connector Pin C205-12 and steering and suspension diagnostic test connector Pin C117-4, Circuit 419 (DG/LG). • Is the resistance 5 ohms or less? → **Yes** GO to **C9**. → **No** SERVICE an open in Circuit 419 (DG/LG). REPEAT the Auto Test.
C9 CHECK AIR SUSPENSION/STEERING TEST CONNECTOR CIRCUIT 844 (GY/R)	
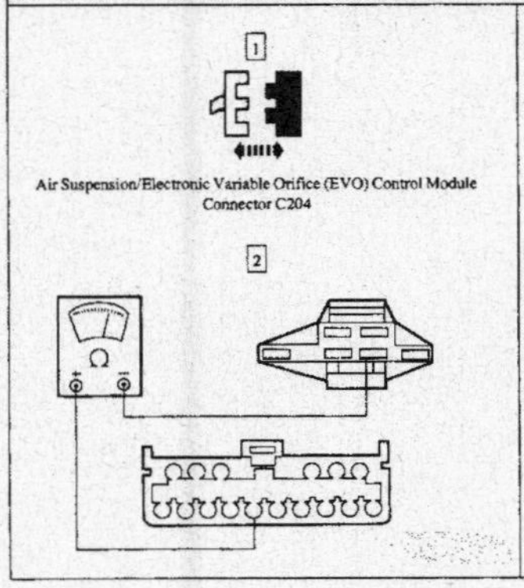	2 Connect an ohmmeter between the air suspension/electronic variable orifice (EVO) control module connector Pin C204-6 and steering and suspension diagnostic test connector Pin C117-5, Circuit 844 (GY/R). • Is the resistance 5 ohms or less? → **Yes** GO to **C10**. → **No** SERVICE an open in Circuit 844 (GY/R). REPEAT the Auto Test.

FM6029700277050X

Fig. 48 Test C: Steering Diagnostics Cannot Be Entered (Part 5 of 7). Mark VIII

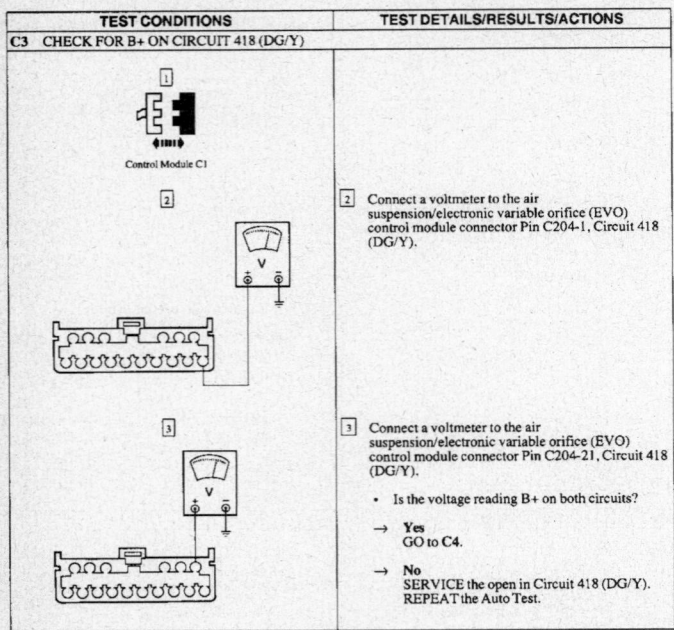

TEST CONDITIONS	TEST DETAILS/RESULTS/ACTIONS
C10 CHECK AIR SUSPENSION/STEERING TEST CONNECTOR CIRCUIT 938 (BK/LG)	
1 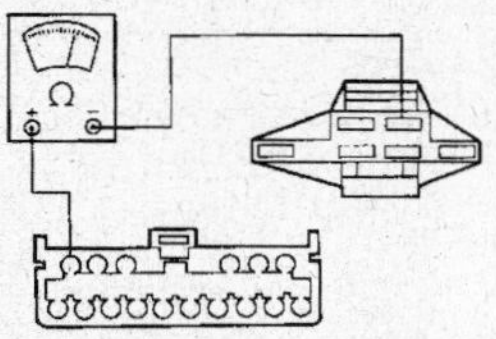	1 Connect an ohmmeter between the air suspension/electronic variable orifice (EVO) control module connector Pin C205-32 and steering and suspension diagnostic test connector Pin C117-2, Circuit 938 (BK/LG). • Is the resistance 5 ohms or less? → **Yes** GO to **C11**. → **No** SERVICE the open in Circuit 938 (BK/LG). REPEAT the Auto Test.
C11 CHECK AIR SUSPENSION SERVICE SWITCH	
1  2 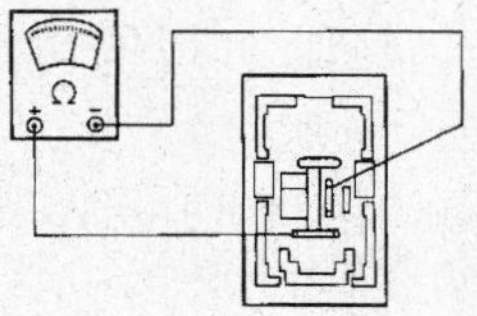	2 Connect an ohmmeter between the two terminals on the air suspension switch. Make sure the air suspension switch is in the ON position. • Is the resistance 5 ohms or less? → **Yes** GO to **C12**. → **No** REPLACE the air suspension switch. REPEAT the Auto Test.

FM6029700277060X

Fig. 48 Test C: Steering Diagnostics Cannot Be Entered (Part 6 of 7). Mark VIII

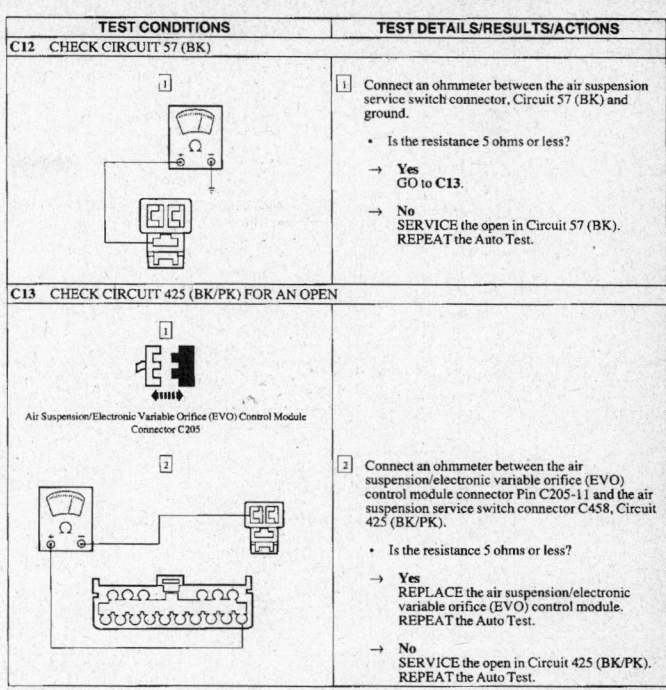

TEST CONDITIONS	TEST DETAILS/RESULTS/ACTIONS
C12 CHECK CIRCUIT 57 (BK)	
1 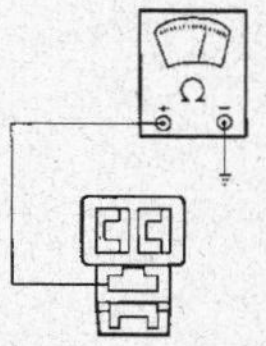	1 Connect an ohmmeter between the air suspension service switch connector, Circuit 57 (BK) and ground. • Is the resistance 5 ohms or less? → **Yes** GO to **C13**. → **No** SERVICE the open in Circuit 57 (BK). REPEAT the Auto Test.
C13 CHECK CIRCUIT 425 (BK/PK) FOR AN OPEN	
1  2 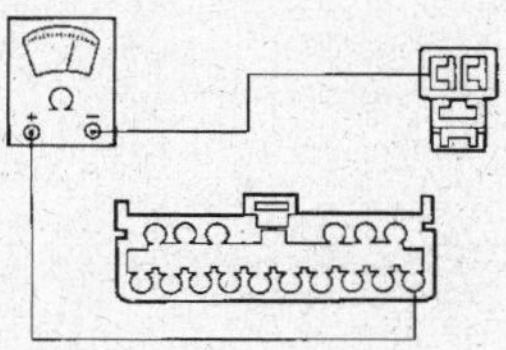	2 Connect an ohmmeter between the air suspension/electronic variable orifice (EVO) control module connector Pin C205-11 and the air suspension service switch connector C458, Circuit 425 (BK/PK). • Is the resistance 5 ohms or less? → **Yes** REPLACE the air suspension/electronic variable orifice (EVO) control module. REPEAT the Auto Test. → **No** SERVICE the open in Circuit 425 (BK/PK). REPEAT the Auto Test.

FM6029700277070X

Fig. 48 Test C: Steering Diagnostics Cannot Be Entered (Part 7 of 7). Mark VIII

TEST CONDITIONS	TEST DETAILS/RESULTS/ACTIONS
D1 CHECK SPEEDOMETER OPERATION	
1 2 	3 Test drive the vehicle and observe the speedometer. • Does the speedometer operate? → **Yes** GO to **D2**. → **No** DIAGNOSE speedometer.
D2 CHECK FOR SPEED SIGNAL AT CONTROL MODULE	
2 3 4 	1 Make sure air suspension switch is OFF. 4 Test drive the vehicle at speeds over 16 km/h (10 mph) and compare the speedometer and the New Generation Star (NGS) Tester readouts. • Do the displayed speeds agree? → **Yes** REFER to Symptom Chart to identify possible mechanical or hydraulic concerns. If no other concerns are identified REPLACE the air suspension/electronic variable orifice (EVO) control module. → **No** GO to **D3**.

FM6029700278010X

Fig. 49 Test D: Steering Does Not Vary w/Vehicle Speed (Part 1 of 5). Mark VIII

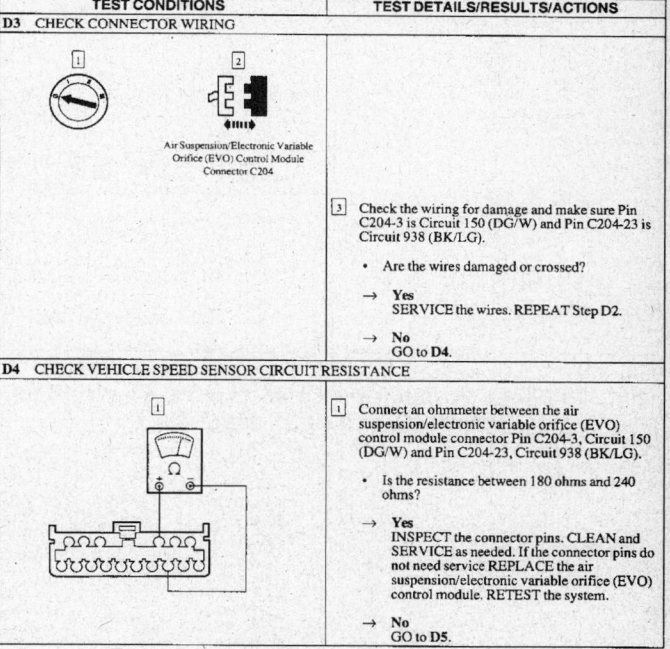

TEST CONDITIONS	TEST DETAILS/RESULTS/ACTIONS
D3 CHECK CONNECTOR WIRING	
1 2 	3 Check the wiring for damage and make sure Pin C204-3 is Circuit 150 (DG/W) and Pin C204-23 is Circuit 938 (BK/LG). • Are the wires damaged or crossed? → **Yes** SERVICE the wires. REPEAT Step D2. → **No** GO to **D4**.
D4 CHECK VEHICLE SPEED SENSOR CIRCUIT RESISTANCE	
1 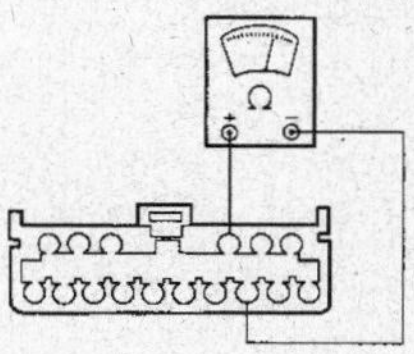	1 Connect an ohmmeter between the air suspension/electronic variable orifice (EVO) control module connector Pin C204-3, Circuit 150 (DG/W) and Pin C204-23, Circuit 938 (BK/LG). • Is the resistance between 180 ohms and 240 ohms? → **Yes** INSPECT the connector pins. CLEAN and SERVICE as needed. If the connector pins do not need service REPLACE the air suspension/electronic variable orifice (EVO) control module. RETEST the system. → **No** GO to **D5**.

FM6029700278020X

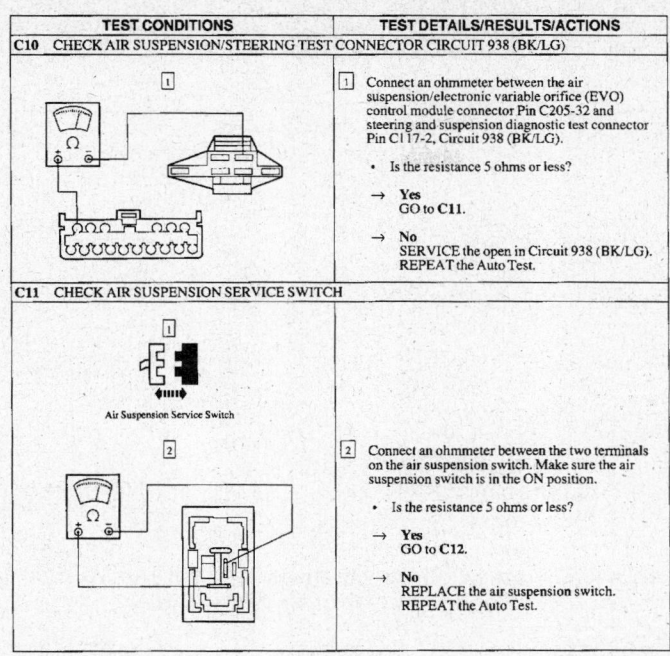

Fig. 49 Test D: Steering Does Not Vary w/Vehicle Speed (Part 2 of 5). Mark VIII

TEST CONDITIONS	TEST DETAILS/RESULTS/ACTIONS
D5 CHECK VEHICLE SPEED SENSOR RESISTANCE	
1  Vehicle Speed Sensor Connector C111	
2 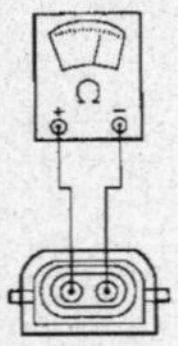	2 Connect an ohmmeter between the vehicle speed sensor terminals. • Is the resistance between 180 ohms and 240 ohms? → **Yes** GO to **D6**. → **No** REPLACE the vehicle speed sensor. RETEST the system.
D6 CHECK CIRCUIT 938 (BK/LG) FOR OPEN	
1 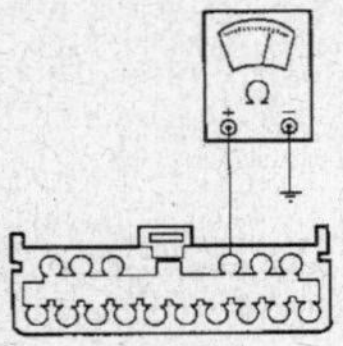	1 Connect an ohmmeter between the air suspension/electronic variable orifice (EVO) control module connector Pin C204-23, Circuit 938 (BK/LG) and ground. • Is the resistance 5 ohms or less? → **Yes** GO to D7. → **No** SERVICE Circuit 938 (BK/LG) for an open. RETEST the system.

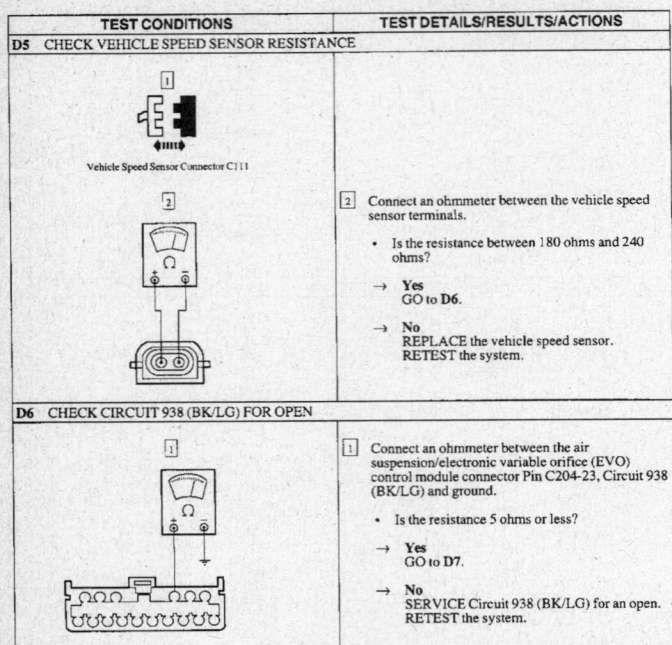

FM6029700278030X

Fig. 49 Test D: Steering Does Not Vary w/Vehicle Speed (Part 3 of 5). Mark VIII

TEST CONDITIONS	TEST DETAILS/RESULTS/ACTIONS
D9 CHECK FOR CIRCUIT TO CIRCUIT SHORT	
1  Vehicle Speed Sensor Connector C111	
2 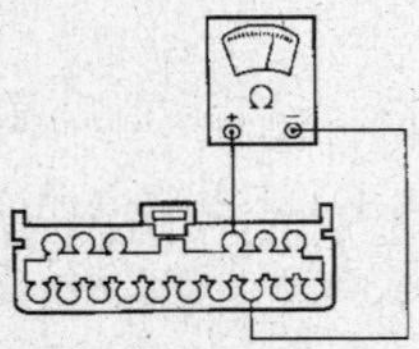	2 Connect an ohmmeter between the air suspension/electronic variable orifice (EVO) control module connector Pin C204-3, Circuit 150 (DG/W) and Pin C204-23, Circuit 938 (BK/LG). • Is the resistance less than 180 ohms? → **Yes** SERVICE Circuit 150 (DG/W) for a short to Circuit 938 (BK/LG). RETEST the system. → **No** RESTORE the vehicle. REPEAT step D2.

FM6029700278050X

Fig. 49 Test D: Steering Does Not Vary w/Vehicle Speed (Part 5 of 5). Mark VIII

TEST CONDITIONS	TEST DETAILS/RESULTS/ACTIONS
D7 CHECK CIRCUIT 150 (DG/W) FOR SHORT TO GROUND	
1 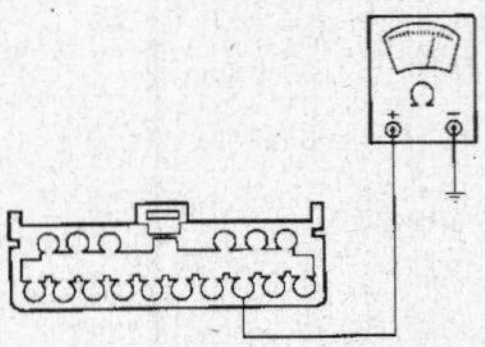	1 Connect an ohmmeter between the air suspension/electronic variable orifice (EVO) control module connector Pin C204-3, Circuit 150 (DG/W) and ground. • Is the resistance 10 K ohms or less? → **Yes** SERVICE circuit 150 (DG/W) for a short to ground. RETEST the system. → **No** GO to **D8**.
D8 CHECK CIRCUIT 150 (DG/W) FOR OPEN	
1 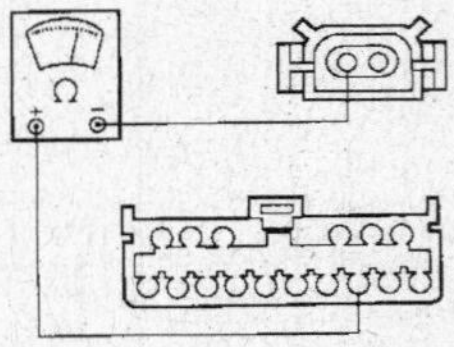	1 Connect an ohmmeter between the air suspension/electronic variable orifice (EVO) control module connector Pin 3 and the vehicle speed sensor connector C111, Circuit 150 (DG/W). • Is the resistance 5 ohms or less? → **Yes** GO to **D9**. → **No** SERVICE Circuit 150 (DG/W) for an open. RETEST the system.

FM6029700278040X

Fig. 49 Test D: Steering Does Not Vary w/Vehicle Speed (Part 4 of 5). Mark VIII

Condition	Possible Source	Action
• Steering Is Very Difficult/Very Easy	• Power steering pump. • Power steering linkage. • Steering gear.	• GO to Pinpoint Test C.
• Steering Does Not Vary With Increased Wheel Rotation	• Power steering pump. • Power steering hose(s).	• GO to Pinpoint Test D.
• Steering Does Not Vary With Vehicle Speed	• Circuitry. • Rear Air suspension control module.	• GO to Pinpoint Test E.
• No Communication With The Module — Rear Air Suspension Control Module	• Fuse. • Circuitry. • Rear Air suspension control module.	• GO to Pinpoint Test F.
• Power Steering Pump Noisy	• Low fluid level and possible leakage. • Plugged reservoir filter. • Power steering pump.	• REFILL to specified level. Refer to Final Fill. CHECK for leaks. REPAIR and/or REPLACE as necessary. • REPLACE the reservoir • REPLACE the power steering pump
• System Back Pressure	• Power steering pump. • Power steering gear. • Hoses or fittings. • Power steering pump.	• REFER to Pump Flow And Pressure Test.

FM6029800289000X

Fig. 50 Symptom Chart. 1998-99 Town car

TEST CONDITIONS	TEST DETAILS/RESULTS/ACTIONS
A1 CHECK FUSE JUNCTION PANEL FUSE 8 (10A)	
1  2  Fuse Junction Panel Fuse 8 (10A)	• Is the fuse OK? → **Yes** GO to **A2**. → **No** REPLACE the fuse. TEST the system for normal operation. If the fuse fails again, CHECK for short to ground. REPAIR as necessary. TEST the system for normal operation.
A2 CHECK STEERING WHEEL ROTATION SENSOR SIGNAL CIRCUIT 633 (R) AT THE REAR AIR SUSPENSION CONTROL MODULE	
1  Rear Air Suspension Control Module 2 	3 Place the 73 Digital Multimeter in the diode check position.

FM6029800290010X

Fig. 51 Pinpoint test A: DTC C1441, C1442, Steering Sensor Circuit Failure (Part 1 of 5). 1998–99 Town Car

TEST CONDITIONS	TEST DETAILS/RESULTS/ACTIONS
A2 CHECK STEERING WHEEL ROTATION SENSOR SIGNAL CIRCUIT 633 (R) AT THE REAR AIR SUSPENSION CONTROL MODULE (Continued)	
4 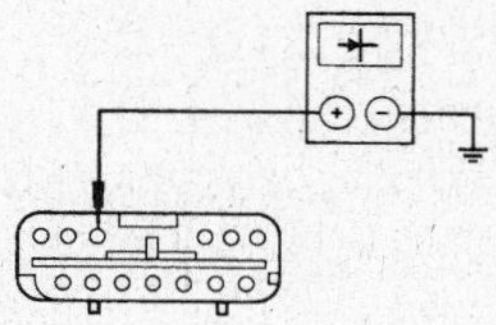	4 **NOTE:** Touch 73 Digital Multimeter leads together to be sure the audio (beep) function is operational. **NOTE:** The 73 Digital Multimeter should beep several times while rotating the steering wheel. Connect 73 Digital Multimeter leads between rear air suspension control module C250-18, circuit 633 (R), and ground, and listen for an audible beep while turning the steering wheel one quarter turn in each direction. • Does 73 Digital Multimeter beep multiple times in both directions? → **Yes** GO to **A3**. → **No** GO to **A4**.
A3 CHECK STEERING WHEEL ROTATION SENSOR SIGNAL CIRCUIT 644 (BR) AT THE REAR AIR SUSPENSION CONTROL MODULE	
1 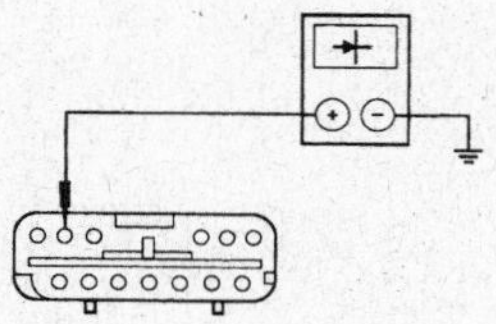	1 With 73 Digital Multimeter in the diode check position, connect 73 Digital Multimeter leads between rear air suspension control module C250-19, circuit 634 (BR), and ground, and listen for an audible beep while turning the steering wheel one quarter turn in each direction. • Does 73 Digital Multimeter beep multiple times in both directions? → **Yes** REPLACE the rear air suspension control module. TEST the system for normal operation. → **No** GO to **A9**.

FM6029800290020X

Fig. 51 Pinpoint test A: DTC C1441, C1442, Steering Sensor Circuit Failure (Part 2 of 5). 1998–99 Town Car

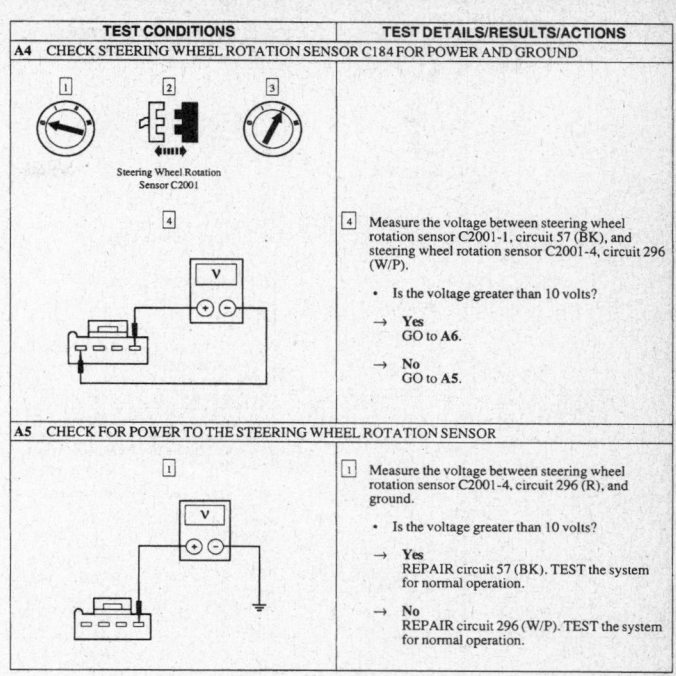

TEST CONDITIONS	TEST DETAILS/RESULTS/ACTIONS
A4 CHECK STEERING WHEEL ROTATION SENSOR C184 FOR POWER AND GROUND	
1 2 3 	
4 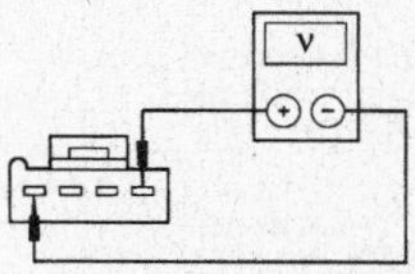	4 Measure the voltage between steering wheel rotation sensor C2001-1, circuit 57 (BK), and steering wheel rotation sensor C2001-4, circuit 296 (W/P). • Is the voltage greater than 10 volts? → **Yes** GO to **A6**. → **No** GO to **A5**.
A5 CHECK FOR POWER TO THE STEERING WHEEL ROTATION SENSOR	
1 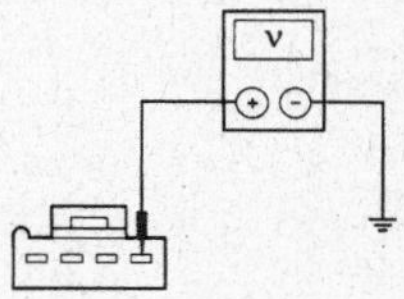	1 Measure the voltage between steering wheel rotation sensor C2001-4, circuit 296 (R), and ground. • Is the voltage greater than 10 volts? → **Yes** REPAIR circuit 57 (BK). TEST the system for normal operation. → **No** REPAIR circuit 296 (W/P). TEST the system for normal operation.

FM6029800290030X

Fig. 51 Pinpoint test A: DTC C1441, C1442, Steering Sensor Circuit Failure (Part 3 of 5). 1998–99 Town Car

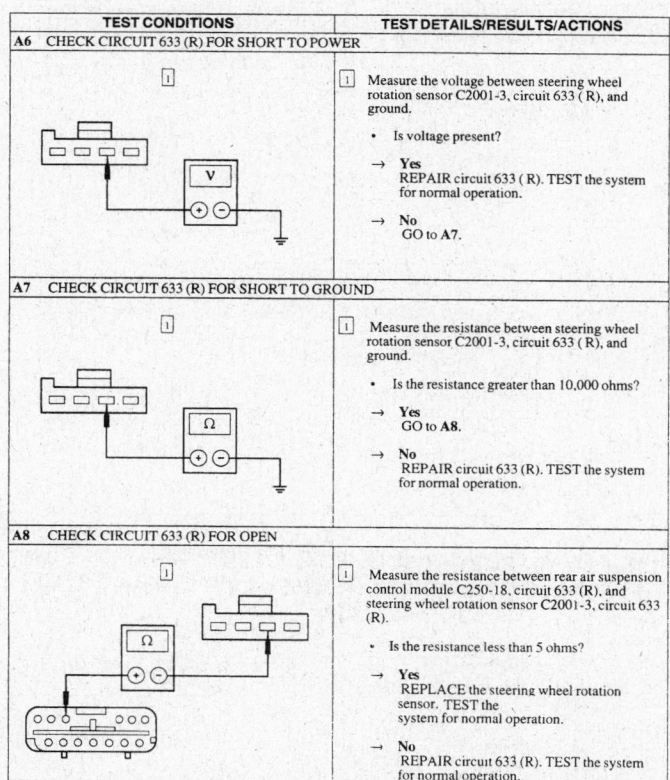

TEST CONDITIONS	TEST DETAILS/RESULTS/ACTIONS
A6 CHECK CIRCUIT 633 (R) FOR SHORT TO POWER	
1 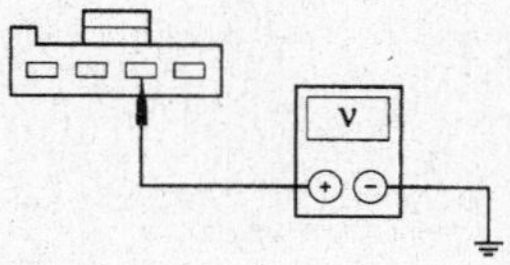	1 Measure the voltage between steering wheel rotation sensor C2001-3, circuit 633 (R), and ground. • Is voltage present? → **Yes** REPAIR circuit 633 (R). TEST the system for normal operation. → **No** GO to **A7**.
A7 CHECK CIRCUIT 633 (R) FOR SHORT TO GROUND	
1 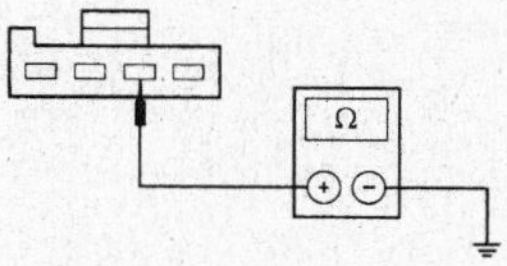	1 Measure the resistance between steering wheel rotation sensor C2001-3, circuit 633 (R), and ground. • Is the resistance greater than 10,000 ohms? → **Yes** GO to **A8**. → **No** REPAIR circuit 633 (R). TEST the system for normal operation.
A8 CHECK CIRCUIT 633 (R) FOR OPEN	
1 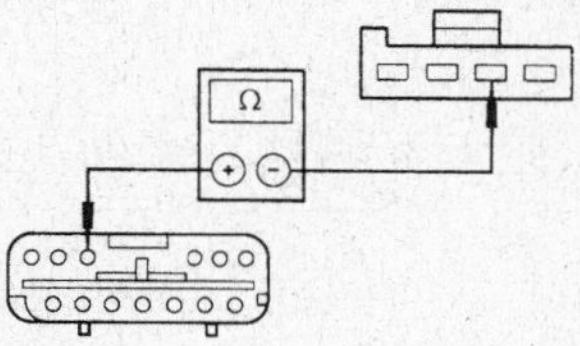	1 Measure the resistance between rear air suspension control module C250-18, circuit 633 (R), and steering wheel rotation sensor C2001-3, circuit 633 (R). • Is the resistance less than 5 ohms? → **Yes** REPLACE the steering wheel rotation sensor. TEST the system for normal operation. → **No** REPAIR circuit 633 (R). TEST the system for normal operation.

FM6029800290040X

Fig. 51 Pinpoint test A: DTC C1441, C1442, Steering Sensor Circuit failure (Part 4 of 5). 1998–99 Town Car

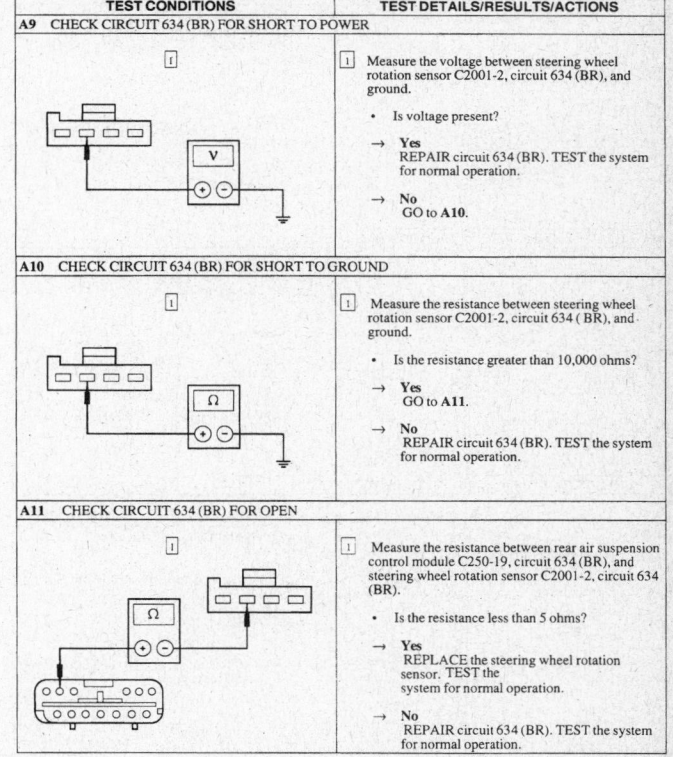

TEST CONDITIONS	TEST DETAILS/RESULTS/ACTIONS
A9 CHECK CIRCUIT 634 (BR) FOR SHORT TO POWER	
1 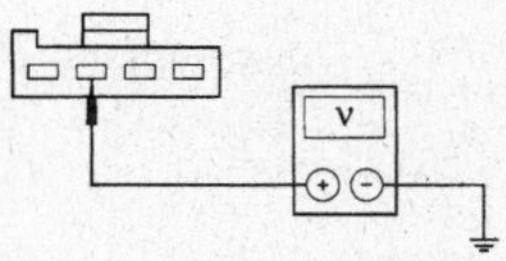	1 Measure the voltage between steering wheel rotation sensor C2001-2, circuit 634 (BR), and ground. • Is voltage present? → **Yes** REPAIR circuit 634 (BR). TEST the system for normal operation. → **No** GO to **A10**.
A10 CHECK CIRCUIT 634 (BR) FOR SHORT TO GROUND	
1 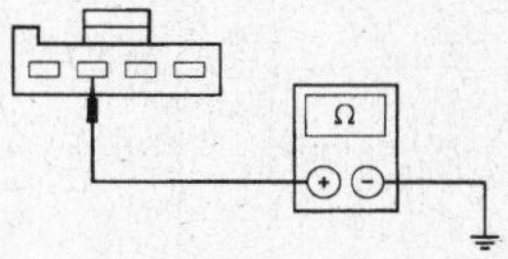	1 Measure the resistance between steering wheel rotation sensor C2001-2, circuit 634 (BR), and ground. • Is the resistance greater than 10,000 ohms? → **Yes** GO to **A11**. → **No** REPAIR circuit 634 (BR). TEST the system for normal operation.
A11 CHECK CIRCUIT 634 (BR) FOR OPEN	
1 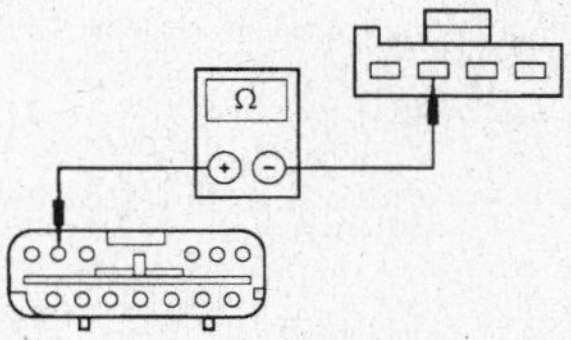	1 Measure the resistance between rear air suspension control module C250-19, circuit 634 (BR), and steering wheel rotation sensor C2001-2, circuit 634 (BR). • Is the resistance less than 5 ohms? → **Yes** REPLACE the steering wheel rotation sensor. TEST the system for normal operation. → **No** REPAIR circuit 634 (BR). TEST the system for normal operation.

FM6029800290050X

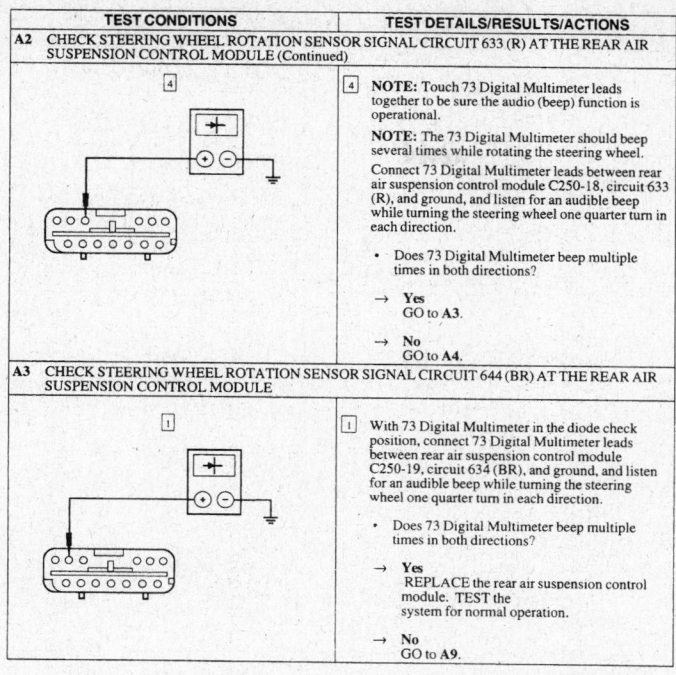

Fig. 51 Pinpoint test A: DTC C1441, C1442, Steering Sensor Circuit Failure (Part 5 of 5). 1998–99 Town Car

TEST CONDITIONS	TEST DETAILS/RESULTS/ACTIONS
B1 CHECK THE POWER STEERING CONTROL VALVE ACTUATOR	
1 2 	3 Check the power steering control valve actuator C184 for damaged pigtail, bent pins, dirt, or corrosion. • Are the connector and pigtail OK? → **Yes** GO to **B2**. → **No** REPAIR as necessary. TEST the system for normal operation.
B2 CHECK THE POWER STEERING CONTROL VALVE ACTUATOR FOR SHORT TO GROUND	
1 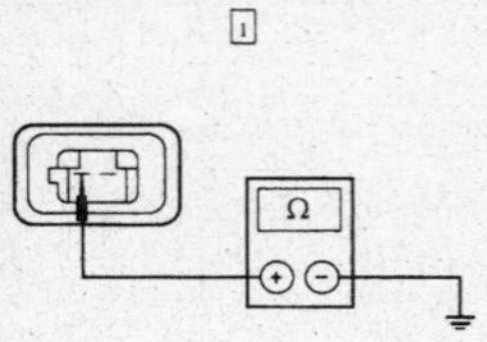	1 Measure the resistance between power steering control valve actuator terminal (component side), and ground. • Is the resistance greater than 10,000 ohms? → **Yes** GO to **B3**. → **No** REPLACE the power steering control valve actuator. TEST the system for normal operation.

FM6029800291010X

Fig. 52 Pinpoint test B: DTC C1897, Steering VAPS II Circuit Loop Failure (Part 1 of 4). 1998–99 Town Car

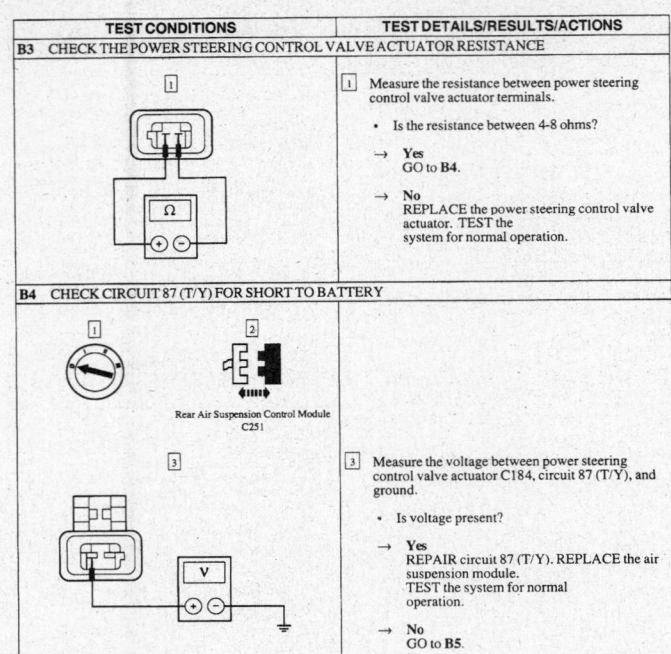

TEST CONDITIONS	TEST DETAILS/RESULTS/ACTIONS
B3 CHECK THE POWER STEERING CONTROL VALVE ACTUATOR RESISTANCE	
1 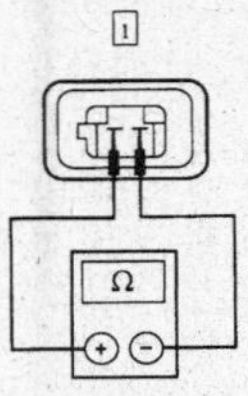	1 Measure the resistance between power steering control valve actuator terminals. • Is the resistance between 4-8 ohms? → **Yes** GO to **B4**. → **No** REPLACE the power steering control valve actuator. TEST the system for normal operation.
B4 CHECK CIRCUIT 87 (T/Y) FOR SHORT TO BATTERY	
1 2  3 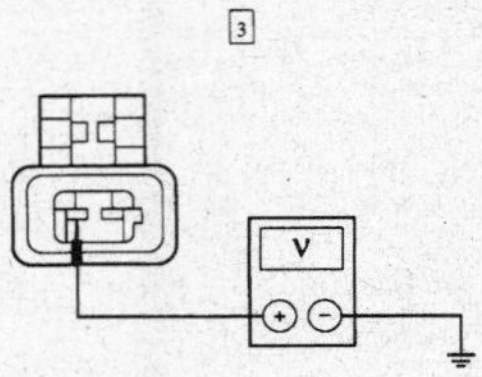	3 Measure the voltage between power steering control valve actuator C184, circuit 87 (T/Y), and ground. • Is voltage present? → **Yes** REPAIR circuit 87 (T/Y). REPLACE the air suspension module. TEST the system for normal operation. → **No** GO to **B5**.

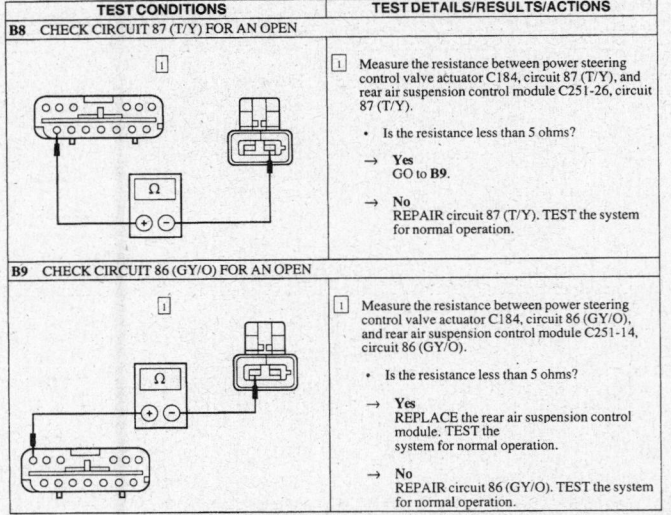

FM6029800291020X

Fig. 52 Pinpoint test B: DTC C1897, Steering VAPS II Circuit Loop Failure (Part 2 of 4). 1998–99 Town Car

TEST CONDITIONS	TEST DETAILS/RESULTS/ACTIONS
B5 CHECK CIRCUIT 86 (GY/O) FOR SHORT TO BATTERY	
1 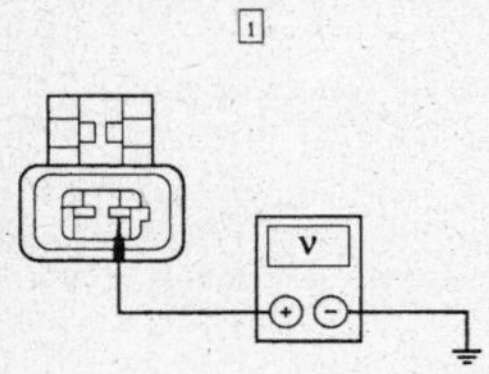	1 Measure the voltage between power steering control valve actuator C184, circuit 86 (GY/O), and ground. • Is voltage present? → **Yes** REPAIR circuit 86 (GY/O). TEST the system for normal operation. → **No** GO to **B6**.
B6 CHECK CIRCUIT 87 (T/Y) FOR SHORT TO GROUND	
1 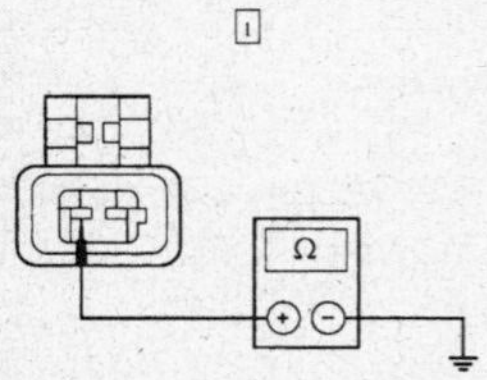	1 Measure the resistance between power steering control valve actuator C184, circuit 87 (T/Y), and ground. • Is the resistance greater than 10,000 ohms? → **Yes** GO to **B7**. → **No** REPAIR circuit 87 (T/Y). TEST the system for normal operation.
B7 CHECK CIRCUIT 86 (GY/O) FOR SHORT TO GROUND	
1 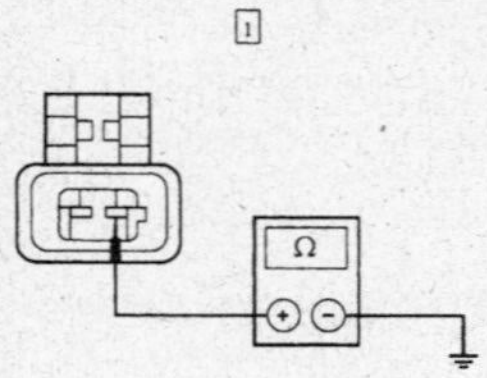	1 Measure the resistance between power steering control valve actuator C184, circuit 86 (GY/O), and ground. • Is the resistance greater than 10,000 ohms? → **Yes** GO to **B8**. → **No** REPAIR circuit 86 (GY/O). TEST the system for normal operation.

FM6029800291030X

Fig. 52 Pinpoint test B: DTC C1897, Steering VAPS II Circuit Loop Failure (Part 3 of 4). 1998–99 Town Car

TEST CONDITIONS	TEST DETAILS/RESULTS/ACTIONS
B8 CHECK CIRCUIT 87 (T/Y) FOR AN OPEN	
1 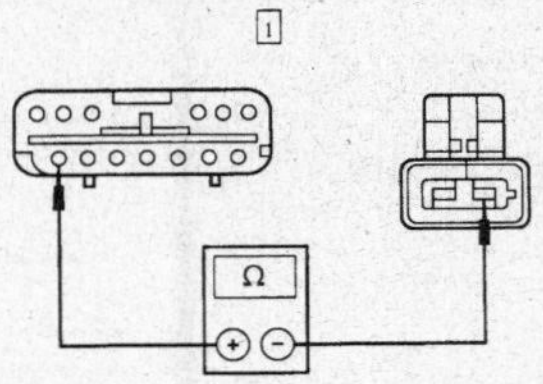	1 Measure the resistance between power steering control valve actuator C184, circuit 87 (T/Y), and rear air suspension control module C251-26, circuit 87 (T/Y). • Is the resistance less than 5 ohms? → **Yes** GO to **B9**. → **No** REPAIR circuit 87 (T/Y). TEST the system for normal operation.
B9 CHECK CIRCUIT 86 (GY/O) FOR AN OPEN	
1 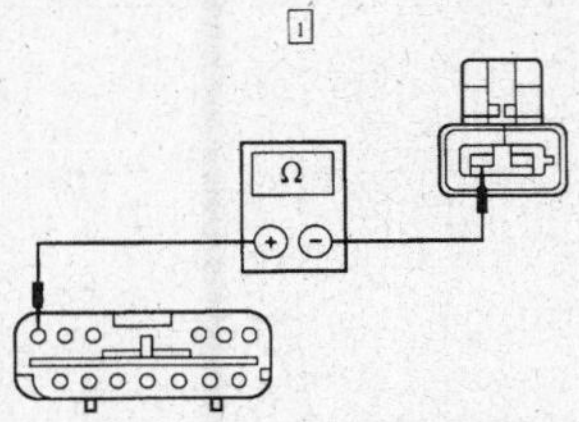	1 Measure the resistance between power steering control valve actuator C184, circuit 86 (GY/O), and rear air suspension control module C251-14, circuit 86 (GY/O). • Is the resistance less than 5 ohms? → **Yes** REPLACE the rear air suspension control module. TEST the system for normal operation. → **No** REPAIR circuit 86 (GY/O). TEST the system for normal operation.

FM6029800291040X

Fig. 52 Pinpoint test B: DTC C1897, Steering VAPS II Circuit Loop Failure (Part 4 of 4). 1998–99 Town Car

TEST CONDITIONS	TEST DETAILS/RESULTS/ACTIONS
C1 CHECK THE POWER STEERING PUMP	
1 	2 Check the power steering pump for leaks by rotating the steering wheel while observing the power steering pump.

FM6029800292010X

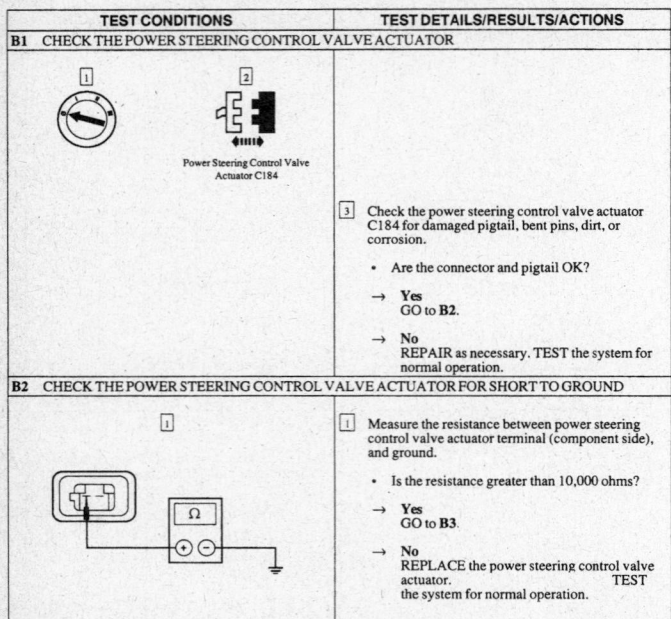

Fig. 53 Pinpoint test C: Steering Is Very Difficult/ Very Easy (Part 1 of 2). 1998-99 Town Car

TEST CONDITIONS	TEST DETAILS/RESULTS/ACTIONS
C4 CHECK THE STEERING GEAR (Continued)	
	2 Check the steering gear mounting fasteners for loose bolts. • Is the steering gear OK? → **Yes** If condition still exists, GO to the Symptom Chart. → **No** TIGHTEN and/or REPLACE the steering gear; TEST the system for normal operation.

FM6029800292020X

Fig. 53 Pinpoint test C: Steering Is Very Difficult/ Very Easy (Part 2 of 2). 1998-99 Town Car

TEST CONDITIONS	TEST DETAILS/RESULTS/ACTIONS
E1 CHECK THE SPEEDOMETER	
1 	2 Check the speedometer by driving the vehicle and observing the speedometer operation. • Does the speedometer operate properly? → **Yes** GO to **E2**. → **No**
E2 CHECK FOR DTC U1041	
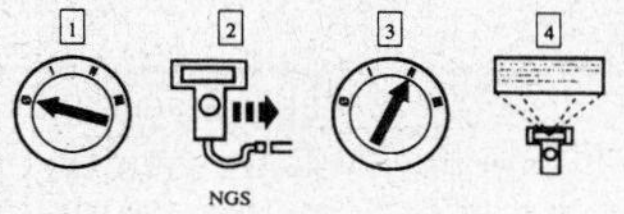	4 Retrieve and document DTCs. • Is DTC U1041 retrieved? → **Yes** → **No** If any DTCs are retrieved, **GO TO** (DTC) Index. If no DTCs are retrieved, REPLACE the rear air suspension control module. TEST the system for normal operation.

FM6029800294000X

Fig. 55 Pinpoint test E: Steering Does Not Vary w/Vehicle Speed. 1998-99 Town Car

TEST CONDITIONS	TEST DETAILS/RESULTS/ACTIONS
F3 CHECK CIRCUIT 418 (DG/Y) FOR AN OPEN	
1 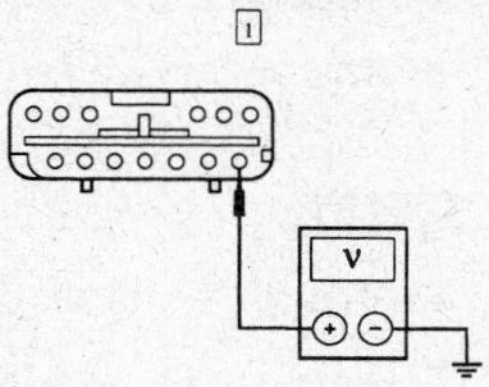	1 Measure the voltage between rear air suspension control module C250-1, circuit 418 (DG/Y), and ground. • Is the voltage greater than 10 volts? → **Yes** GO to **F4**. → **No** REPAIR circuit 418 (DG/Y). TEST the system for normal operation.
F4 CHECK CIRCUIT 57 (BK) FOR AN OPEN	
1 2 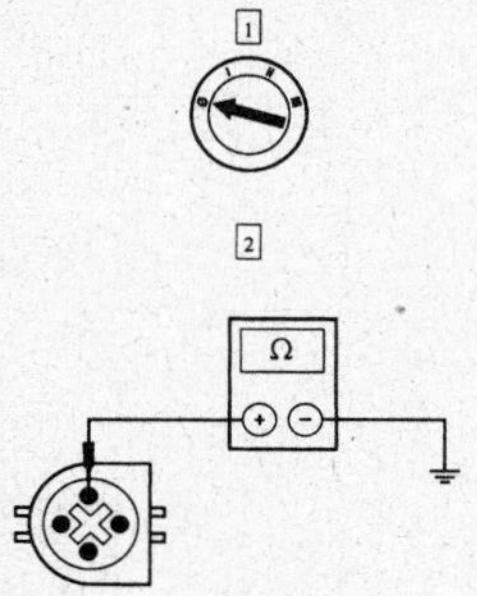	2 Measure the resistance between rear air suspension control module C250-6, circuit 57 (BK), and ground. • Is the resistance less than 5 ohms? → **Yes** → **No** REPAIR circuit 57 (BK). TEST the system for normal operation.

FM6029800295020X

Fig. 56 Pinpoint test F: No Communication w/Rear Air Suspension Control Module (Part 2 of 2). 1998–99 Town Car

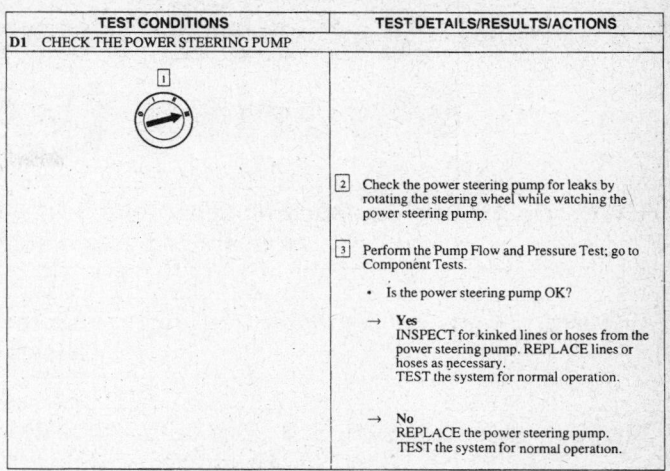

TEST CONDITIONS	TEST DETAILS/RESULTS/ACTIONS
D1 CHECK THE POWER STEERING PUMP	
1 	2 Check the power steering pump for leaks by rotating the steering wheel while watching the power steering pump. 3 Perform the Pump Flow and Pressure Test; go to Component Tests. • Is the power steering pump OK? → **Yes** INSPECT for kinked lines or hoses from the power steering pump. REPLACE lines or hoses as necessary. TEST the system for normal operation. → **No** REPLACE the power steering pump. TEST the system for normal operation.

FM6029800293010X

Fig. 54 Pinpoint test D: Steering Does Not Vary w/Increased Wheel Rotation. 1998-99 Town Car

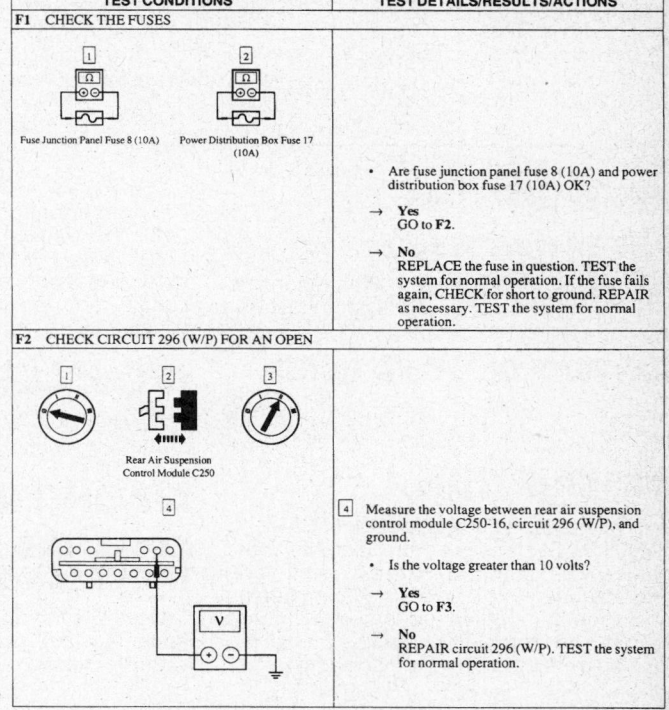

TEST CONDITIONS	TEST DETAILS/RESULTS/ACTIONS
F1 CHECK THE FUSES	
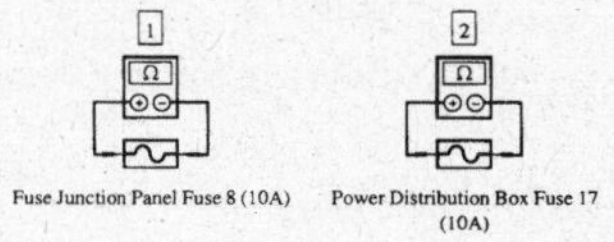	• Are fuse junction panel fuse 8 (10A) and power distribution box fuse 17 (10A) OK? → **Yes** GO to **F2**. → **No** REPLACE the fuse in question. TEST the system for normal operation. If the fuse fails again, CHECK for short to ground. REPAIR as necessary. TEST the system for normal operation.
F2 CHECK CIRCUIT 296 (W/P) FOR AN OPEN	
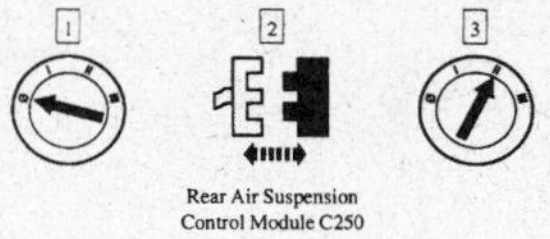 4 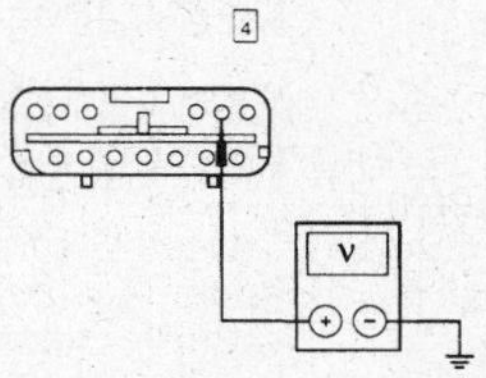	4 Measure the voltage between rear air suspension control module C250-16, circuit 296 (W/P), and ground. • Is the voltage greater than 10 volts? → **Yes** GO to **F3**. → **No** REPAIR circuit 296 (W/P). TEST the system for normal operation.

FM6029800295010X

Fig. 56 Pinpoint test F: No Communication w/Rear Air Suspension Control Module (Part 1 of 2). 1998–99 Town Car

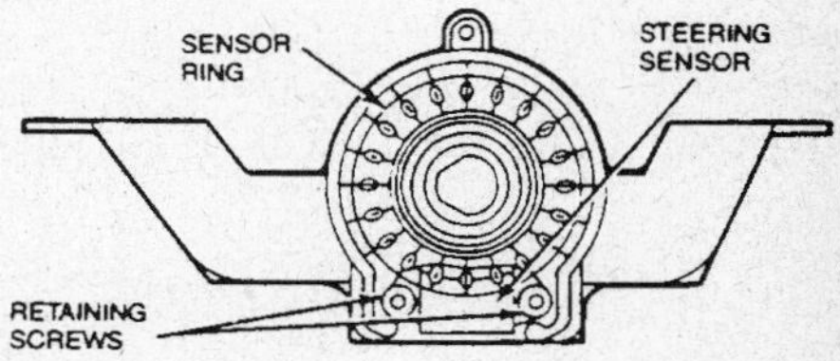

FM6029100190000X

Fig. 57 Steering sensor removal

Type 2–Ford Variable Assist Power Steering (VAPS II) System

NOTE: On Air Bag Equipped Models, Refer To " Air Bag System Precautions" Located In The Front Of This Manual For System Disarming & Arming Procedures.

NOTE: Refer To "Computer Relearn Procedures " Located In The Front Of This Manual For Computer Relearn Procedures.

NOTE: "Electrical Symbol & Wire Color Code Identification" Located In The Front Of This Manual May Be Used As An Aid When Using Wiring Circuits Found In This Section.

INDEX

PRECAUTIONS

AIR BAG SYSTEMS

Refer to "Air Bag System Precautions" in the front of this manual for system disarming and arming procedures.

BATTERY GROUND CABLE

Prior to service, disconnect battery ground cable and isolate as required.

DESCRIPTION

The Variable Assist Power Steering (VAPS II) System uses the Generic Electronics Module (GEM) to improve steering characteristics. The VAPS II system begins operation as soon as the ignition is turned to Run, and maintains control as long as the ignition switch is in the Run position.

The level of assist provided by the VAPS II system depends on vehicle speed. The faster the vehicle speed, the less assist provided by the VAPS II system. Vehicle speed is determined by the GEM based on signals received from the Vehicle Speed Sensor (VSS).

TROUBLESHOOTING

Refer to **Fig. 1** for troubleshooting procedures.

DIAGNOSIS & TESTING

ACCESSING DIAGNOSTIC TROUBLE CODES

Using Rotunda New Generation Star Tester No. 007–00500, or equivalent, perform diagnostic tests for GEM. The Diagnostic Link Connector (DLC) is located on the LH side of the steering wheel, under the instrument panel. The Generic Electronic Module (GEM) is located at the LH rear of the engine compartment.

DIAGNOSTIC TROUBLE CODE INTERPRETATION

Refer to **Fig. 2** for diagnostic trouble code interpretation.

WIRING DIAGRAM

Refer to **Figs. 3 and 4.** for wiring diagrams.

PINPOINT TESTS

Refer to **Figs. 5 through 14** for pinpoint tests.

Condition	Possible Source	Action
NOTE: Discolored Steering Fluid in a Rack-and-Pinion Steering System Should Not be Misdiagnosed as a Functional or Noise Concern When Steering Very Difficult / Very Easy. • High (Excessive) Power Steering Efforts at All Vehicle Speeds is Recognized While Turning Corners and During Low Speed Maneuvers and Especially While Parking. The Assist Concerns May Occur in Both Directions or Only in One Direction. They May be Intermittent, or Consistent	• Low power steering pump fluid.	• FILL as required and CHECK for system leaks.
	• Power rack and pinion steering gear assembly external or internal leak.	• REPLACE power rack and pinion steering gear.
	• Power steering pump external leak.	
	• Power steering pump pressure and flow improper.	• PERFORM Pump Flow and Pressure Tests SERVICE as required.
	• Improper drive belt tension.	• CHECK for proper drive belt tension.
	• Hose external leak.	• SERVICE or REPLACE as necessary.
	• Hose restriction.	• CLEAN and REPLACE as necessary.
	• Power steering pump pulley loose / warped.	• REPLACE power steering pump pulley.
	• Power steering pump drive belt loose / glazed / broken or water on drive belt.	• INSPECT, CHECK drive belt tension or REPLACE as required.
	• Engine idle too low.	• ADJUST idle. REFER to Powertrain Control / Emissions Diagnosis
	• Tires not properly inflated.	• INFLATE.
	• Suspension bent or interference.	• INSPECT, SERVICE or REPLACE as necessary.
	• System contaminated.	• INSPECT system for foreign object, kinked hose, etc. — FLUSH system.
	• Flex coupling rubbing against housing face.	• REPOSITION flex coupling.
	• Steering column misaligned or binding.	• ALIGN steering column assembly.
• Engine Stalls With High Wheel Rotation	• Inoperative idle speed control circuit. • Pressure switch or pressure hose blocked.	• REFER to Powertrain Control / Emissions Diagnosis
• No Communications With Generic Electronic Module	• Generic electronic module. • Circuits.	• GO to Pinpoint Test A.
• Steering Does Not Vary With Vehicle Speed	• Damaged vehicle speed sensor. • Power steering control valve actuator inoperative.	• GO to Pinpoint Test B.

FM6029400210010X

Fig. 1 Symptom troubleshooting chart (Part 1 of 7)

Condition	Possible Source	Action
NOTE: Clean Off the Steering Gear Before Performing ANY Steering Gear External Leakage Checks. • External Leakage	• Leaks between power steering control valve actuator and steering gear.	• NOTE: The only serviceable components on the VAPS power rack and pinion steering gear are the tie rod bellows, front wheel spindle tie rods, power steering control valve actuator, and actuator bolts and seals. All external leaks, which cannot be serviced by tightening tube fittings, are to be serviced by installing a power steering short rack assembly. • TIGHTEN actuator bolts.
	• Leaks between power steering control valve actuator and actuator bolts.	• TIGHTEN actuator bolts. • REPLACE two upper actuator seals.
	• Power rack and pinion steering gear fittings loose, cross threaded or stripped.	• INSPECT and TIGHTEN or REPLACE power steering short rack assembly
	• Leaks from power rack and pinion steering gear seals (input shaft, pinion or either rack seals).	• REPLACE power steering short rack assembly.
	• Steering gear housing cracked or leaking (due to a porous condition).	• REPLACE power steering short rack assembly.
NOTE: This Condition Should be Checked on Center Only. The Loose Condition Can be Detected With Greater Reliability With the Engine off and Steering Wheel Straight Ahead. A Very Light Touch on the Steering Wheel Should be Used in Checking for This Condition. • Loose On Center	• Power rack and pinion steering gear mounting bolts loose.	• TIGHTEN retaining nuts to specification.
	• Steering column intermediate shaft coupling connecting bolt loose.	• TIGHTEN.
	• Intermediate shaft spring loaded U-bolt distorted.	• REPLACE U-bolt.
	• Flex coupling clamp bolt loose.	• TIGHTEN.
	• Gear front wheel spindle tie rod inner ball socket loose.	• REPLACE gear front wheel spindle tie rod.
	• Steering column intermediate shaft coupling joints loose or worn.	• REPLACE steering column intermediate shaft coupling assembly.
	• Steering column clips missing or broken.	• REPLACE as required.
	• Flex coupling fractured.	• REPLACE as required.
	• Front wheel spindle tie rod loose or worn.	• TIGHTEN or REPLACE as required.
	• Wheel loose or worn.	• REPLACE as required.
	• Loose lug nuts.	• TIGHTEN.
• Steering Wheel Not Centered Properly NOTE: Groove on Steel Hub of Steering Wheel Must be in Line With Mark on Top End of Steering Shaft With Front Wh eels in Straight Ahead Position to Line Up Steering Wheel Spokes Properly. Steering Wheel Centerline Should be Within 10 Degrees of Vertical Plane After Toe-In is Adjusted.	• Incorrect toe setting.	• SET front end alignment.
	• Flex coupling clamp bolts loose / missing.	• REPLACE and TIGHTEN.
	• Pinion installed in rack off location.	• REPLACE power steering short rack assembly.
	• Improperly installed steering wheel.	• REPOSITION steering wheel.
	• Power rack and pinion steering gear loose on front sub-frame.	• TIGHTEN.
	• Steering column intermediate shaft coupling installed off location in column shaft V-block.	• INDEX shaft to correct position.

FM6029400210020X

Fig. 1 Symptom troubleshooting chart (Part 2 of 7)

Condition	Possible Source	Action
NOTE: Discolored Steering Fluid in Rack-and-Pinion Steering System Should Not Be Misdiagnosed as a Functional or Noise Concern. • Smoothness / Sticky Feeling — Condition of Momentary Build Up, Hitch, Lump or Hesitation in Steering Efforts, Usually Occurring Just as the Turn is Begun. It May Occur Right or Left, and in Rare Cases, Occur in Both Directions. It May be Noticed During Parking, Low Speed Turns or at Road Speeds. If This Condition is Detected During Parking Maneuvers, It May Also be Noticed During Higher Speed Driving	• Loose or worn drive belt.	• TIGHTEN or REPLACE.
	• Front suspension lower arm (LH) / front suspension lower arm (RH) ball joint worn.	• REPLACE front suspension lower arm (LH) / front suspension lower arm (RH) assembly.
	• Column trim rubbing steering wheel.	• REPOSITION trim on column.
	• Binding in steering gear control valve assembly.	• REPLACE power steering short rack assembly.
	• Water or oil on drive belt.	• CLEAN or REPLACE.
	• Steering column misaligned or binding.	• ALIGN steering column.
	• Flex coupling distorted or fractured.	• ALIGN or REPLACE as required.
	• Flex housing rubbing against housing face.	• ALIGN or REPOSITION flex coupling.
	• Steering column intermediate shaft coupling loose, worn or binding.	• REPLACE as required.
	• Steering column intermediate shaft coupling connecting bolt loose.	• TIGHTEN.
	• Steering linkage, front spring and shocks are loose, worn or binding.	• LUBRICATE, ADJUST or REPLACE as necessary.
	• Tight steering column bearings.	• LUBRICATE or REPLACE as required.
	• Steering column clips missing or damaged.	• SERVICE as required.
	• Steering gear retaining bolts loose or damaged.	• TIGHTEN.
	• Front wheel bearing loose or worn.	• REPLACE as required.
	• Loose lug nuts.	• TIGHTEN.
	• Bent or damaged power rack and pinion steering gear assembly.	• REPLACE power steering short rack assembly.
	• Low tire pressure.	• INFLATE.
	• Improper front end alignment.	• ALIGN front end.

FM6029400210030X

Fig. 1 Symptom troubleshooting chart (Part 3 of 7)

Condition	Possible Source	Action
NOTE: Perform the Following Test to Determine if Concern is Related to Power Rack and Pinion Steering Gear or Vehicle System: • Uneven Drive Efforts, Pulls or Leads to One Side — Condition Recognized by the Driver While Turning the Steering Wheel in a Left or Right Turn. This Condition Will Reveal Lighter Efforts in One Direction, Very Noticeable to the Driver. Vehicle Pulls or Leads to One Side. Keep in Mind Road Conditions and Wind. Pulls or Leads Refers to the Tendency of a Vehicle to Drift Consistently to One Side on a Reasonably Flat Road. It May or May Not be Accompanied by Unequal Effort Requirements at the Steering Wheel. At 24-88 km/h (15-55 mph) on a Flat Straight Surface, Set Vehicle in a Straight Line. Place Shift Selector in NEUTRAL Position and Turn Off Ignition. If the Vehicle Continues to Pull or Drift in the Same Direction as the Original Concern, Then the Power Rack and Pinion Steering Gear is Not the Cause. If the Vehicle Does Not Pull, but Remains on a Straight Line This Indicates a Power Rack and Pinion Steering Gear Concern and Steering Efforts Should Also be Noticeably Light in Direction of Pull. This Condition is Normally Due to an Unbalanced Power Rack and Pinion Steering Gear Valve Assembly.	• Radial tires (misaligned belts).	• REPLACE as necessary.
	• Front or rear end misaligned.	• ALIGN.
	• Steering gear valve efforts unbalanced. (Efforts will be lighter in one direction.)	• REPLACE power steering short rack assembly.
	• Front suspension components damaged.	• REPLACE as required.
	• Low tire pressure or incorrect front to rear.	• CHECK pressure and INFLATE / DEFLATE as necessary.
	• Incorrect tire size or incorrect type.	• CORRECT as required.
	• Check front and rear brakes for proper operation.	• ADJUST if necessary.
	• Check rear axle housing for damaged or sagging front coil springs in the front or rear suspension.	• REPLACE if necessary.
	• Check rear suspension for loose or worn rear shock absorber, suspension arm retaining fasteners.	• TIGHTEN all retaining fasteners.
	• Vehicle unevenly loaded.	• CORRECT as required.
	• Front wheel bearing or rear wheel bearing worn.	
	• Power rack and pinion steering gear retaining bolts loose or damaged.	• TIGHTEN.
	• Steering column misaligned or binding.	• ALIGN steering column assembly.
	• Halfshaft or CV joint bind.	• REPLACE CV joints.

FM6029400210040X

Fig. 1 Symptom troubleshooting chart (Part 4 of 7)

Condition	Possible Source	Action
NOTE: The Following Condition is Accompanied By a Momentary Build Up, Hitch, Lump, or Hesitation, in Steering Efforts Usually Occurring Just Off Center Either in One Direction or Both. Concern Occurs Only During Driving, and Not During Parking Maneuvers. • Poor Returnability is a Condition Noticed When the Vehicle Fails to Return to a Nearly Straight Ahead Position After a Corner Maneuver. The Steering Wheel Should Return Within a Reasonable Period of Time Without Undue Help From the Driver. Returnability Concerns May Occur From Both Directions or Only From One Direction.	• Column trim rubbing steering wheel.	• REPOSITION trim ring in steering column tube assembly slots.
	• Front suspension lower arm (LH) / front suspension lower arm (RH) worn.	• REPLACE front suspension lower arm (LH) / front suspension lower arm (RH).
	• Brinelled or binding upper strut bearing.	• REPLACE bearing.
	• Tight front wheel spindle tie rod and / or tie rod end ball joints.	• REPLACE front wheel spindle tie rod and / or tie rod ends.
	• Steering valve assembly off balance. Efforts will be light in one direction and return will be poor in light direction.	• REPLACE power steering short rack assembly.
	• Improper front end alignment.	• ALIGN front end.
	• Steering linkage, front spring and shocks, loose, worn or binding.	• LUBRICATE, ADJUST or REPLACE as necessary.
	• Tilt column bearing sideloaded by spring.	• REMOVE spring. If improved, REPLACE tilt yoke, shaft or steering wheel.
	• Steering column intermediate shaft coupling joints binding.	• REPLACE steering column intermediate shaft coupling assembly.
	• Bent or damaged front crossmember.	• REPLACE as necessary.
	• Steering column bearing binding.	• REPLACE as necessary.
	• Steering column misaligned or binding.	• ALIGN steering column assembly.
	• Low tire pressure or incorrect pressure front to rear.	• CHECK pressure and INFLATE / DEFLATE as necessary.
	• Steering wheel clear vision off location.	• ADJUST as required.
	• Incorrect tire size or incorrect type.	• REPLACE as required.

FM6029400210050X

Fig. 1 Symptom troubleshooting chart (Part 5 of 7)

CONDITION	POSSIBLE SOURCE	ACTION
• NOTE: A Common Noise in the Rack-and-Pinion Power Steering Short Rack is a Hissing Sound. The Sound is Most Evident at Static Position or During Parking Maneuvers. There is no Relationship Between This Noise and Performance of the Steering. "Hiss" May Occur at end of Steering Wheel Travel or When Slowly Turning at Stand Still, or at a Particular Position.	• Steering column gear input shaft coupling connecting bolt loose.	• TIGHTEN.
	• Column trim rubbing steering wheel.	• REPOSITION trim on steering column.
	• Loose or worn pump drive belt.	• ADJUST or REPLACE as required.
	• Front suspension lower arm (LH)/front suspension lower arm (RH) worn or binding.	• REPLACE as required.
	• Brinelled or binding upper strut bearing.	• REPLACE strut bearing.
	• Flex coupling distorted.	• ALIGN flex coupling.
Noise/Rattle/Clicks/Pops/Squeaks/Creaks/Clunk/Squawk/Hiss There are Many System Noises Which Can be Misdiagnosed as Originating From the Power Power Steering Short Rack. Most System Noises are RPM Sensitive. Therefore, Turning the Steering Wheel Will Vary the RPM and Consequently the Noise Pitch. Careful Diagnosis is Necessary to Prevent Unnecessary Services. Disconnecting of Belts and Re-evaluation is Essential in Many Cases, as is Partially Cycling the Steering Wheel With the Engine in OFF.	• Flex coupling clamp bolt loose.	• TIGHTEN.
	• Power steering pump support loose or misaligned.	• TIGHTEN and ALIGN.
	• Lack of lubricant where horn brush contacts rub steering wheel plate.	• LUBRICATE or ADJUST as required.
	• Column shaft clips missing.	• REPLACE as required.
	• Column U-joints loose.	• REPLACE if necessary.
	• Loose tie rod ends or ball joints.	• REPLACE tie rod assembly.
	• Power steering short rack assembly loose on frame.	• TIGHTEN.
	• Loose suspension struts.	• ADJUST or REPLACE as required.
	• Flex coupling fractured.	• REPLACE as required.
	• Loose lug nuts.	• TIGHTEN.
	• Pressure hose grounded against front fender or vacuum canister.	• REPOSITION pressure hoses.
	• Front wheel bearing loose or worn.	• REPLACE front wheel bearing.
	• Steering column misaligned or lower steering column tube bearing out of position.	• CORRECT as necessary.
	• Steering shaft insulators cracked or dry.	• REPLACE or LUBRICATE as required.
	• Kinked pressure hoses.	• REPOSITION pressure hoses.
	• Power steering short rack or power steering pump external leak.	• INSPECT and REPLACE or SERVICE as required.
	• Power steering pump pulley loose or warped.	• REPLACE power steering pump pulley assembly.
	• Aerated fluid.	• PURGE and EVACUATE system.
	• Water in steering fluid.	• PURGE and EVACUATE system.

FM6029400210060X

Fig. 1 Symptom troubleshooting chart (Part 6 of 7)

Condition	Possible Source	Action
NOTE: Pointing Characteristics are Normal with the Rack-and-Pinion Steering System Up to 10 Degrees Off-Center.	• Power rack and pinion steering gear retaining bolts loose or damaged.	• TIGHTEN.
• Wandering/Darting/Pointing—Condition Noticed When the Vehicle is Driven in a Straight Ahead Position With the Steering Wheel Held in a Firm Position, and the Vehicle Wanders to Either Side. Darting Refers to Down the Road Steering Feel, it is Not Smooth and Seems to be Sticky and the Driver Cannot Make Minor Correction With Ease. Pointing Refers to the Inability of the Vehicle to Return to a Straight Ahead Position After a Moderate to Higher Speed Lane Change.	• Improper front or rear end alignment.	• ALIGN.
	• Front lower control arm ball joint(s) worn.	• REPLACE as required.
	• Brinelled or binding strut upper bearing.	• REPLACE bearing.
	• Steering wheel clear vision off location.	• CORRECT as required.
	• Column trim rubbing steering wheel.	• REPOSITION trim on steering column assembly.
	• Loose suspension struts or ball joints binding.	• ADJUST or REPLACE as required.
	• Loose front wheel spindle tie rods.	• REPLACE front wheel spindle tie rods.
	• Steering column intermediate shaft coupling joint loose or worn.	• REPLACE steering column intermediate shaft coupling.
	• Steering column misaligned or binding.	• ALIGN steering column assembly.
	• Tie rod inner ball joint loose or worn.	• REPLACE front wheel spindle tie rod.
	• Steering column intermediate shaft coupling connecting bolt loose.	• TIGHTEN.
	• Low tire pressure or incorrect pressure front to rear.	• CHECK tire pressure and INFLATE/DEFLATE as necessary.
	• Incorrect tire size or incorrect type.	• CORRECT as required.
	• Radial tires (misaligned belts).	• REPLACE as required.
	• Front wheel bearing and/or rear wheel bearing loose or worn.	
	• Loose or worn rear suspension.	• TIGHTEN or REPLACE as necessary.
	• Loose flex coupling bolt.	• TIGHTEN.
	• Improper brake operation or adjustment.	• INSPECT and ADJUST. CORRECT as required.
	• Vehicle unevenly loaded.	• CORRECT as required.

FM6029400210070X

Fig. 1 Symptom troubleshooting chart (Part 7 of 7)

DTC	Description
B1301	Power Door Lock Circuit Failure
B1302	Delayed Accessory Relay Coil Circuit Failure
B1304	Delayed Accessory Relay Coil Circuit Short To Battery
B1309	All Door Lock Sense Circuit Short To Ground
B1310	Power Door Unlock Circuit Failure
B1314	Battery Saver Relay Coil Circuit Open
B1315	Battery Saver Relay Coil Circuit Short to Battery
B1316	Battery Saver Relay Coil Circuit Short to Ground
B1317	Battery Voltage High
B1318	Battery Voltage Low
B1322	Door Ajar LF Circuit Short to Ground
B1323	Door Ajar Lamp Circuit Failure
B1325	Door Ajar Lamp Circuit Short to Ground
B1330	Door Ajar RF Circuit Short to Ground
B1334	Liftgate/Decklid Ajar Circuit Short To Ground
B1338	Door Ajar RR Circuit Short to Ground
B1345	Heated Rear Window Switch Input Short to Ground
B1347	Heated Rear Window Switch Input Short to Ground
B1349	Heated Rear Window Relay Output Circuit Short to Battery
B1352	Ignition Key-In Circuit Failure
B1359	Ignition RUN/ACC Circuit Failure
B1365	Ignition Start Circuit Short to Battery
B1371	Illuminated Entry Relay Coil Circuit Failure
B1373	Illuminated Entry Relay Short to Battery
B1397	Power Door Unlock Circuit Short to Battery
B1398	LF Power Window One Touch Window Relay Circuit Failure

FM6029400211010X

Fig. 2 GEM DTC Index (Part 1 of 3)

DTC	Description
B1400	LF Power Window One Touch Window Relay Circuit Short to Battery
B1405	LF Power Window Down Input Short to Battery
B1408	LF Power Window Up Input Short to Battery
B1410	LF Power Window Motor Circuit Failure
B1426	Safety Belt Lamp Circuit Short to Battery
B1428	Safety Belt Lamp Circuit Failure
B1432	Wiper Brake/Run Relay Circuit Short to Battery
B1433	Wiper Brake/Run Relay Circuit Short to Ground
B1434	Wiper HI/LO Speed Relay Coil Circuit Failure
B1436	Wiper HI/LO Speed Relay Coil Circuit Short to Battery
B1438	Wiper Mode Select Switch Circuit Failure
B1441	Wiper Front Mode Select Switch Circuit Short To Ground
B1445	Door Handle Switch Circuit Short to Ground
B1446	Wiper Front Park Sense Circuit Failure
B1448	Wiper Front Park Sense Circuit Short to Battery
B1450	Wiper Wash/Delay Switch Circuit Failure
B1453	Wiper Wash/Delay Switch Circuit Short to Ground
B1458	Wiper Washer Pump Motor Relay Circuit Failure
B1460	Wiper Washer Pump Motor Relay Coil Circuit Short to Battery
B1462	Safety Belt Switch Circuit Failure
B1465	Wiper Run Relay Coil Circuit Open
B1466	Wiper HI/LO Speed Not Switching
B1473	Wiper Low Speed Motor Circuit Failure
B1474	Battery Saver Relay Power Output Circuit Short to Battery

FM6029400211020X

Fig. 2 GEM DTC Index (Part 2 of 3)

DTC	Description
B1475	Delayed Accessory Relay Contact Short to Battery
B1476	Wiper High Speed Motor Circuit Failure
B1555	Ignition RUN/START Circuit Failure
B1574	Door Ajar LR Circuit Short to Ground
B1577	Park Lamp Input Circuit Short to Battery
B1610	Illuminated Entry Input Circuit Short to Ground
B1833	Door Unlock/Disarm Switch Circuit Short to Ground
B1834	Door Unlock/Disarm Output Circuit Failure
B1836	Door Unlock/Disarm Output Circuit Short to Battery
B1838	Battery Saver Relay Power Circuit Failure
B1840	Wiper Front Power Circuit Failure
C1899	VAPS Circuit Short to Battery
C1928	VAPS Solenoid Actuator Return Circuit Short to Ground
P1882	Engine Coolant Level Switch Short to Ground
P1883	Engine Coolant Level Lamp Circuit Failure
P1884	Engine Coolant Level Lamp Short to Battery

FM6029400211030X

Fig. 2 GEM DTC Index (Part 3 of 3)

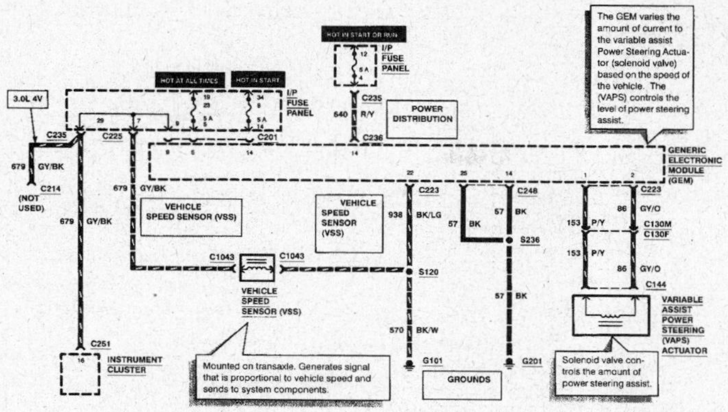

FM6029600280000X

Fig. 3 VAPS II wiring diagram. Sable & Taurus except SHO

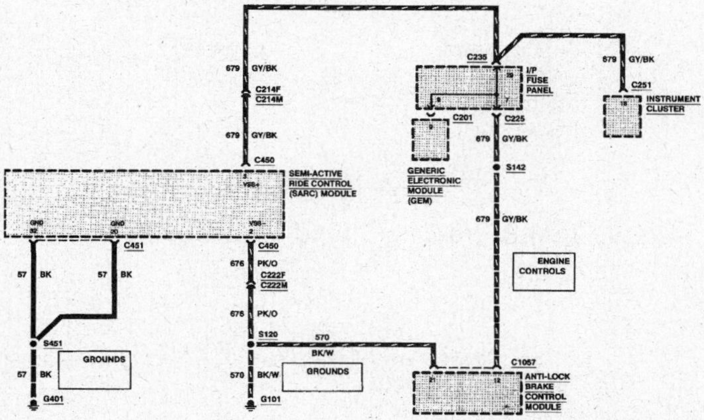

FM6029600281020X

Fig. 4 VAPS wiring diagram (Part 2 of 2). Taurus SHO

	Test Step	Result	Action to Take
A1	CHECK OUTPUT FUSE 23 (5A) FOR SHORT TO GROUND		
	• Remove Fuse 23 (5A) from fuse junction panel. • Using ohmmeter connected to good ground, measure resistance between output side (RH) pin of Fuse 23 and ground. • Observe ohmmeter reading. Reading should start above 1M ohm and drop to less than 3K ohm steadily. • **Does ohmmeter start above 1M ohm and drop to less than 3K ohm steadily?**	Yes No	GO to **A7**. GO to **A2**.
A2	CHECK RESISTANCE		
	• Set up as in A1. • Observe ohmmeter reading. • **Did ohmmeter read less than 10 ohms?**	Yes No	GO to **A4**. GO to **A3**.
A3	CHECK GENERIC ELECTRONIC MODULE		
	• Remove generic electronic module from fuse junction panel connector C1. • Disconnect and reconnect ohmmeter as in A1. • **Does ohmmeter read above 1M ohm? (May drop steadily to less than 3K ohms.)**	Yes No	REPLACE generic electronic module. RESTORE vehicle. REPEAT self test. GO to **A4**.
A4	CHECK FUSE JUNCTION PANEL		
	• Disconnect fuse junction panel connector C4. • Measure resistance between output side of Fuse 23 and ground. • **Is resistance less than 10K ohms?**	Yes No	REPLACE fuse junction panel. RESTORE vehicle. REPEAT self test. RECONNECT fuse junction panel connector C4. GO to **A5** if PATS/RAP equipped. GO to **A7** if not PATS/RAP equipped.
A5	CHECK PATS MODULE (IF EQUIPPED)		
	• Disconnect PATS module connector. • Disconnect and reconnect ohmmeter as in A1. • **Does ohmmeter read above 1M ohm and drop steadily to less than 3K ohms?**	Yes No	REPLACE PATS module. RESTORE vehicle. REPEAT self test. GO to **A6**.
A6	CHECK RAP MODULE (IF EQUIPPED)		
	• Disconnect RAP module connector C2. • Disconnect and reconnect ohmmeter as in A1. • **Does ohmmeter read above 1M ohm?**	Yes No	REPLACE RAP module. RESTORE vehicle. REPEAT self test. SERVICE Circuit 1001 (W/Y) for short to ground. RESTORE vehicle. REPEAT self test.

FM6029400212010X

Fig. 5 Test A: No Communication w/GEM (Part 1 of 2). 1997

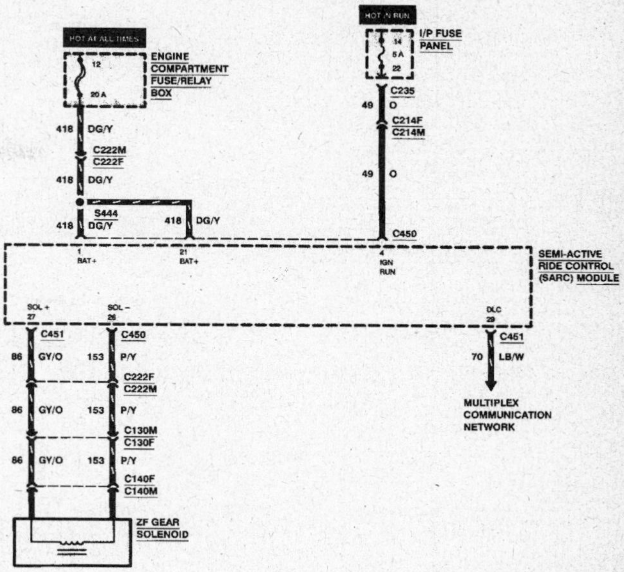

FM6029600281010X

Fig. 4 VAPS wiring diagram (Part 1 of 2). Taurus SHO

	Test Step	Result	Action to Take
A7	CHECK POWER GROUNDS		
	• Disconnect generic electronic module connector C2. • Using ohmmeter, measure resistance to ground of both C248-14 and C248-25, Circuit 57 (BK). • **Is resistance 5 ohms or less?**	Yes No	GO to **A8**. SERVICE either or both Circuits 57 (BK) for opens or high resistance. RESTORE vehicle. REPEAT self test.
A8	CHECK DEDICATED GROUND		
	• Disconnect generic electronic module connector C223. • Using ohmmeter, measure resistance to ground of Pin C223-12, Circuit 570 (BK/W). • **Is resistance 5 ohms or less?**	Yes No	GO to **A9**. SERVICE Circuit 570 (BK/W) for opens or high resistance. RESTORE vehicle. REPEAT self test.
A9	CHECK IGNITION START/RUN INPUT		
	• Disconnect generic electronic module connector C236. • Turn ignition switch to RUN. • Using voltmeter connected to a good ground, measure voltage at Pin C236-14. • **Is B+ present?**	Yes No	GO to **A11**. GO to **A10**.
A10	CHECK FUSE JUNCTION PANEL FUSE 12		
	• Remove fuse junction panel Fuse 12. • Measure resistance across fuse. • **Is fuse OK?**	Yes No	SERVICE Circuit 640 (R/Y) for open. RESTORE vehicle. REPEAT self test. SERVICE Circuit 640 (R/Y) for short to ground. REPLACE fuse 12. RESTORE vehicle. REPEAT self test.
A11	CHECK SIGNAL GROUND CIRCUIT 938 (BK/LG)		
	• Using ohmmeter connected to a good ground, measure resistance between Pin C223-22, Circuit 938 (BK/LG) and ground. • **Is resistance less than 5 ohms?**	Yes No	GO to Pinpoint Test C for diagnostic communication Circuit 70 (LB/W) diagnosis. SERVICE Circuit 938 (BK/LG) for open. RESTORE vehicle. REPEAT self test.

FM6029400212020X

Fig. 5 Test A: No Communication w/GEM (Part 2 of 2). 1997

	Test Step	Result	Action to Take
A1	CHECK THE FUSES		
	• Check the following I/P fuse panel fuses: fuse 23 (5A), fuse 20 (5A), and fuse 8 (5A). • **Are the resistances less than 5 ohms?**	Yes No	GO to **A2**. REPLACE the fuse(s). RETEST system. If the fuse(s) fail(s) again, CHECK for short to ground. REPAIR as necessary.
A2	CHECK CIRCUIT 640 (R/Y) FOR OPEN		
	• Key OFF. • Disconnect generic electronic module (GEM) C236. • Key ON. • Measure the voltage between GEM C236-14, circuit 640 (R/Y), and ground. • **Is the voltage greater than 10 volts?**	Yes No	GO to **A3**. REPAIR circuit 640 (R/Y). TEST the system for normal operation.
A3	CHECK THE I/P FUSE PANEL FOR VOLTAGE		
	• Key OFF. • Disconnect I/P fuse panel C201. • Key ON. • Measure the voltage between I/P panel terminal 5 and ground; and between terminal 15 and ground. • Measure the voltage between I/P fuse panel terminal 14 while holding the key in the start position. • **Are the voltages greater than 10 volts?**	Yes No	GO to **A4**. REPLACE the I/P fuse panel. TEST the system for normal operation.
A4	CHECK CIRCUIT 57 (BK) FOR OPEN		
	• Key OFF. • Disconnect GEM C248. • Measure the resistance between GEM C248-14, and C248-25, circuit 57 (BK), and ground. • **Is the resistance less than 5 ohms?**	Yes No	GO to **A5**. REPAIR circuit 57 (BK). TEST the system for normal operation.
A5	CHECK CIRCUIT 570 (BK/W) FOR OPEN		
	• Disconnect GEM C223. • Measure the resistance between GEM C223-12, circuit 570 (BK/W), and ground. • **Is the resistance less than 5 ohms?**	Yes No	GO to **A6**. REPAIR circuit 570 (BK/W). TEST the system for normal operation.
A6	CHECK CIRCUIT 938 (BK/LG) FOR OPEN		
	• Measure the resistance between GEM C223-22, circuit 938 (BK/LG), and ground. • **Is the resistance less than 5 ohm?**	Yes No	DIAGNOSE communication network. REPAIR circuit 938 (BK/LG). TEST the system for normal operation.

FM6029800282000X

Fig. 6 Test A: No Communication w/GEM. 1998

Step	Test Step	Result ▶	Action to Take
A1	CHECK FOR BATTERY VOLTAGE • Disconnect battery charger. • Measure voltage across battery terminals. • **Is the voltage greater than 11 volts?**	Yes No	▶ GO to **A2.** ▶ REPAIR the charging system.
A2	CHECK CIRCUIT 57 (BK) RESISTANCE • Turn ignition switch OFF. • Disconnect module from vehicle harness connectors C450 and C451. • Measure resistance between module Pin C451-32, C451-20, Circuit 57 (BK) and ground. • **Is resistance less than 5 ohms?**	Yes No	▶ GO to **A3.** ▶ REPAIR Circuit 57 (BK). REPEAT On-Demand Self-Test.
A3	CHECK CIRCUIT 418 (DG / Y) RESISTANCE • Remove power distribution box Fuse 12 (20A). • Check resistance from output side of Fuse 12 (20A) Circuit 418 (DG / Y) to Pin C450-1, Circuit 418 (DG / Y) module connector. • **Is resistance less than 5 ohms?**	Yes No	▶ GO to **A4.** ▶ REPAIR Circuit 418 (DG / Y). REPEAT On-Demand Self Test.
A4	CHECK CIRCUIT 49 (O) RESISTANCE • Remove fuse junction panel Fuse 14 (5A). • Check resistance from output side of Fuse 14 (5A) to Pin C450-4, Circuit 49 (O). • **Is resistance less than 5 ohms?**	Yes No	▶ **Diagnose Module Communications network.** ▶ REPAIR Circuit 49 (O). REPEAT On-Demand Self-Test.

FM6029900310000X

Fig. 7 Test A: No Communication w/Module. 1999 Taurus SHO

Step	Test Step	Result ▶	Action to Take
B3	CHECK CIRCUIT 679 (GY / BK) FOR SHORT TO GROUND • Using ohmmeter, measure resistance from Pin C3-7, Circuit 679 (GY / BK) to a known ground. • **Is resistance 10,000 ohms or more?**	Yes No	▶ GO to **B4.** ▶ SERVICE Circuit 679 (GY / BK) for short to ground. RESTORE vehicle. REPEAT **B1.**
B4	CHECK CIRCUIT 679 (GY / BK) FOR SHORT TO BATTERY • Using voltmeter connected to a known ground, measure voltage at Pin C3-7, Circuit 679 (GY / BK). • **Is B+ voltage present?**	Yes No	▶ SERVICE Circuit 679 (GY / BK) for short to battery. RESTORE vehicle REPEAT **B1.** ▶ GO to **B5.**
B5	CHECK FUSE JUNCTION PANEL FOR OPEN CIRCUIT • Disconnect GEM fuse junction panel connector C1. • Using ohmmeter, measure resistance between C1-9 and C3-7. • **Is resistance 5 ohms or less?**	Yes No	▶ GO to **B6.** ▶ REPLACE fuse junction panel. RESTORE vehicle. REPEAT **B1.**
B6	CHECK FUSE JUNCTION PANEL FOR INTERNAL SHORT TO BATTERY • Disconnect GEM from fuse junction panel. • Turn ignition switch to RUN. • Measure voltage between GEM fuse junction panel connector Pin C1-9 and a known ground. • **Is B+ voltage present?**	Yes No	▶ REPLACE internally shorted fuse junction panel. RESTORE vehicle. REPEAT **B1.** ▶ GO to **B7.**
B7	CHECK FUSE JUNCTION PANEL FOR INTERNAL OPEN CIRCUIT • Using ohmmeter connected to known ground, measure resistance at Pin C1-9. • **Is resistance less than 10,000 ohms?**	Yes No	▶ REPLACE grounded fuse junction panel. RESTORE vehicle. REPEAT B1. ▶ REPLACE vehicle speed sensor. RESTORE vehicle. REPEAT **B1.**

FM6029400213020X

Fig. 8 Test B: Steering Does Not Vary w/Vehicle Speed (Part 2 of 2). 1997–98

Step	Test Step	Result ▶	Action to Take
B1	CHECK GEM VEHICLE SPEED PID • NGS installed. • Access GEM PID VSS__GEM. • Drive vehicle while observing VSS__GEM PID. • **Does PID change and reflect vehicle speed when compared to speedometer?**	Yes No	▶ PERFORM on board diagnostic self test. SERVICE any DTC retrieved. REPEAT self test and test drive to confirm service. If symptom still present, condition is mechanical. GO to mechanical diagnostic procedures. ▶ TURN vehicle OFF. GO to **B2.**
B2	CHECK CIRCUIT 679 (GY / BK) FOR OPEN • Disconnect vehicle speed sensor connector. • Disconnect fuse junction panel connector C3. • Using ohmmeter, measure resistance between fuse junction panel Pin C3-7, Circuit 679 (GY / BK) and vehicle speed sensor connector Circuit 679 (GY / BK). • **Is resistance 5 ohms or less?**	Yes No	▶ GO to **B3**. ▶ SERVICE Circuit 679 (GY / BK) for open circuit. RESTORE vehicle. REPEAT B1.

FM6029400213010X

Fig. 8 Test B: Steering Does Not Vary w/Vehicle Speed (Part 1 of 2). 1997–98

Step	Test Step	Result ▶	Action to Take
B1	CONFIRM VEHICLE SPEED SIGNAL FUNCTION • Drive vehicle at normal city / highway speeds and observe speedometer. • **Is speedometer displaying correct speed?**	Yes No	▶ GO to **B2**. ▶ Diagnose Speedometer
B2	CHECK CONTINUITY IN CIRCUIT 676 (PK / O) AND CIRCUIT 570 (BK / W) • Disconnect module connector C450. • Using an ohmmeter, measure resistance between module connector Pin C450-2, Circuit 676 (PK / O), and ground. • **Is resistance less than 5 ohms?**	Yes No	▶ LEAVE module disconnected. GO to **B3**. ▶ REPAIR Circuit 676 (PK / O), and Circuit 570 (BK / W). REPEAT self-test.
B3	CHECK CIRCUIT 679 (GY / BK) FOR AN OPEN • Disconnect the anti-lock brake control module C1057. • Using an ohmmeter, measure resistance between module connector Pin C450-3, Circuit 679 (GY / BK), and anti-lock brake control module connector Pin C1057-12, Circuit 679 (GY / BK). • **Is resistance less than 5 ohms?**	Yes No	▶ REPLACE module. REPEAT self-test. ▶ REPAIR Circuit 679 (GY / BK). REPEAT self-test.

FM6029900308000X

Fig. 9 Test B: Vehicle Speed Signal Failure. 1999

DIAGNOSTIC CHART INDEX

Test Step		Result ▶	Action to Take
B1318-1	CHECK CHARGING SYSTEM OPERATION		
	• Have engine running. • Make sure lights, radio, and accessories are OFF. • Measure voltage between battery terminals. • **Is voltage less than 12.5 volts?**	Yes ▶ No ▶	REPAIR charging system. GO to **B1318-2**.
B1318-2	CHECK CONTROL MODULE SUPPLY		
	• Have engine running. • Make sure lights, radio, and accessories are OFF. • Disconnect module from harness. • Measure voltage between module connector Pins C450-1 and C450-21, Circuit 418 (DG/Y), and ground. • **Are the voltages greater than 10 volts?**	Yes ▶ No ▶	GO to **B1318-3**. REPAIR circuit 418 (DG/Y) and/or REPLACE the Power Distribution Box Fuse 12 (20A).
B1318-3	CHECK CIRCUIT RESISTANCE		
	• Measure resistance between module C451-20, and C451-32, Circuit 57 (BK), and ground. • **Are the resistances more than 5 ohms?**	Yes ▶ No ▶	REPAIR Circuit 57 (BK). RETEST system. If DTC B1318 is a continuous DTC and not encountered during self-test, CLEAR DTCs and REPEAT self-test. If DTC B1318 is a self-test DTC, REPLACE module. REPEAT self-test.

FM6029900306000X

Fig. 10 Code B1318: Battery Voltage Low. 1999

Test Step		Result ▶	Action to Take
C1897-1	CHECK STEERING SOLENOID CIRCUITS		
	• Disconnect module connectors C450 and C451. • Using an ohmmeter, measure the resistance between Pin C450-26, Circuit 153 (P/Y) and Pin C451-27, Circuit 86 (GY/O). • **Is resistance between 5 and 9 ohms?**	Yes ▶ No ▶	GO to **C1897-3**. GO to **C1897-2**.
C1897-2	CHECK RESISTANCE OF STEERING SOLENOID		
	• Disconnect steering solenoid 2-pin connector C140. • Using an ohmmeter, measure resistance of steering solenoid. • **Is resistance between 5 and 9 ohms?**	Yes ▶ No ▶	REPAIR Circuit 86 (GY/O), Circuit 153 (P/Y). REPEAT self-test. REPLACE steering solenoid. REPEAT self-test.
C1897-3	CHECK CIRCUIT 86 (GY/O) FOR SHORT		
	• Using an ohmmeter, measure resistance between module Pin C451-32, Circuit 57 (BK) and C451-27, Circuit 86 (GY/O). • **Is resistance greater than 10,000 ohms?**	Yes ▶ No ▶	GO to **C1897-4**. REPAIR Circuit 86 (GY/O). REPEAT self-test.
C1897-4	CHECK CIRCUIT 153 (P/Y) FOR SHORT		
	• Using an ohmmeter, measure resistance between module Pins C450-26, Circuit 153 (P/Y), C451-32, Circuit 57 (BK). • **Is resistance 10,000 ohms or more?**	Yes ▶ No ▶	GO to **C1897-5**. REPAIR Circuit 153 (P/Y). RETEST system.

FM6029900309010X

Fig. 12 Code C1897: Variable Assist Power Steering Circuit Loop Failure (Part 1 of 2). 1999

Test Step		Result ▶	Action to Take
B1342-1	CHECK FOR DTC B1342		
	• Clear stored DTCs from memory by cycling ignition switch to OFF, starting engine, and performing the "Clear Continuous DTCs" function under the DIAGNOSTIC TEST MODES menu on the NGS or equivalent. • Repeat ON-DEMAND SELF TEST under DIAGNOSTIC TEST MODES on the NGS or equivalent. • **Is DTC B1342 present?**	Yes ▶ No ▶	REPLACE module. RESTORE vehicle. RETEST system. Diagnosis complete. RESTORE vehicle. RETEST system.

FM6029900307000X

Fig. 11 Code B1342: ECU Internal Failure. 1999

Test Step		Result ▶	Action to Take
C1897-5	CHECK STEERING SOLENOID FOR SHORT TO BATTERY		
	• Using an ohmmeter, measure resistance between module Pins C450-26, Circuit 153 (P/Y), C451-27, Circuit 86 (GY/O) and Pin C450-1, Circuit 418 (DG/Y). • **Is resistance 10,000 ohms or more?**	Yes ▶ No ▶	GO to **C1897-6**. REPAIR Circuit 153 (P/Y) or Circuit 86 (GY/O). RETEST system.
C1897-6	CHECK FOR DAMAGED/CORRODED PINS		
	• Carefully inspect all connector pins for damage or corrosion. • **Are pins damaged or corroded?**	Yes ▶ No ▶	REPAIR/CLEAN pins as necessary. REPEAT self test. REPLACE module. REPEAT self test.

FM6029900309020X

Fig. 12 Code C1897: Variable Assist Power Steering Circuit Loop Failure (Part 2 of 2). 1999

Test Step		Result ▶	Action to Take
C1899-1	CHECK PID		
	• NGS installed. • Start engine. • Access GEM PID VAPSOUT. • Drive vehicle at various speeds. • Read VAPSOUT valve. • **Is PID VAPSOUT value constant at 100%?**	Yes ▶ No ▶	TURN engine OFF. GO to **C1899-2**. GO to **C1899-4**.
C1899-2	CHECK CIRCUIT 86 (GY / O)		
	• Disconnect GEM connector C4. • Using voltmeter attached to a known ground, measure voltage on Pin C4-2, Circuit 86 (GY / O). • **Is B+ present?**	Yes ▶ No ▶	SERVICE Circuit 86 (GY / O) for short to battery. GO to **C1899-3**.
C1899-3	READ PID WITH CIRCUIT OPEN		
	• Reconnect GEM connector C4. • Disconnect variable assist power steering actuator. • Start engine. • Access VAPSOUT PID. • **Is VAPSOUT value 100%?**	Yes ▶ No ▶	REPLACE GEM. RESTORE vehicle. REPEAT self-test. GO to **C1899-4**.
C1899-4	PERFORM WIGGLE TEST		
	• Reconnect variable assist power steering actuator. • Access GEM wiggle test. Follow directions displayed on NGS. • Tap actuators, connectors and flex harness from variable assist power steering actuator and GEM. • **Is DTC C1899 retrieved during wiggle test?**	Yes ▶ No ▶	NOTE: Both Circuit 153 (P / Y) and Circuit 86 (GY / O0 must be serviced. SERVICE connector, actuator or harness being agitated when DTC C1899 was recorded for short to battery. RESTORE vehicle. REPEAT self test. REPEAT on-board diagnostic self test. If DTC C1899 retrieved, REPLACE GEM. RESTORE vehicle. REPEAT self test.

FM6029400214000X

Fig. 13 Code C1899: VAPS Circuit Short To Battery

Test Step		Result ▶	Action to Take
C1928-1	ELIMINATE ACTUATOR		
	• Turn engine OFF. • Disconnect variable assist power steering actuator from harness. • Start engine. • Read VAPS__IN PID. • **Is PID VAPS__IN value 0?**	Yes ▶ No ▶	GO to **C1928-2**. REPLACE variable assist power steering actuator. (Actuator has internal short to ground.) RESTORE vehicle. REPEAT on demand self test.
C1928-2	CHECK CIRCUIT 153 (P / Y) FOR SHORT TO GROUND		
	• Ignition switch OFF. • Disconnect GEM connector C4. • Using ohmmeter attached to a known ground, measure resistance at Pin C4-1, Circuit 153 (P / Y). • **Is resistance less than 10,000 ohms?**	Yes ▶ No ▶	SERVICE Circuit 153 (P / Y) for short to ground. RESTORE vehicle. REPEAT on demand self test. REPLACE GEM. RESTORE vehicle. REPEAT on demand self test.

FM6029400215000X

Fig. 14 Code C1928: VAPS Solenoid Actuator Return Circuit Short To Ground

DISC BRAKES

NOTE: On Air Bag Equipped Models, Refer To "Air Bag System Precautions" Located In The Front Of This Manual For System Disarming & Arming Procedures.

TABLE OF CONTENTS

Front Disc Brakes

NOTE: Prior To Performing Any Service Operations Listed In This Section, Consult The "Technical Service Bulletins " Section For Related Information.

INDEX

PRECAUTIONS

AIR BAG SYSTEMS

Refer to "Air Bag System Precautions" in the front of this manual for system disarming and arming procedures.

BATTERY GROUND CABLE

Prior to service, disconnect battery ground cable and isolate as required.

SYSTEM DEPRESSURIZING

On models equipped with anti-lock brakes, hydraulic system must be depressurized prior to disconnecting any hydraulic lines or fittings, by pumping the brake pedal a minimum of 25 times with ignition in Off position.

DESCRIPTION

SINGLE PISTON CALIPERS

The caliper assembly consists of a pin sliding caliper housing, inner and outer shoe and lining assemblies and a single piston, **Figs. 1 through 3.** The caliper slides on two pins which also act as attaching bolts between caliper and the combination anchor plate and spindle. The outer brake shoe and lining assembly is longer than the inner brake shoe and lining assembly. Inner and outer shoe and lining assemblies are attached to the caliper by spring clips riveted to the shoe surfaces. The inner shoe is attached to the caliper by installing the spring clip to the inside of the caliper piston. The outer shoe clips directly to the caliper housing. A wear indicator is incorporated, which emits a noise when the lining is worn to a point for necessary replacement. Lefthand and righthand inner and outer shoes are not interchangeable.

DUAL PISTON CALIPERS

The caliper assembly consists of a sliding bridge type caliper housing with dual pistons, caliper mounting frame and inner and outer friction pad assemblies, **Figs. 4 and 5.** The caliper is located into and slides on the anchor frame by its thrust face and a locating pin and clip. The friction pads are retained into the anchor frame by the caliper sliding bridge assembly and use an anti-rattle spring clip to reduce brake noise. The friction pads are retained into the sliding bridge assembly by clips located on the back of the friction pad.

Righthand and lefthand caliper and inner and outer righthand and lefthand friction pads are unique and cannot be interchanged. When servicing this system, mark all parts with location marks for later reference and assembly.

TROUBLESHOOTING

BRAKE ROUGHNESS

Thickness Variation

If roughness or vibration is encountered during highway operation or if pedal pumping is experienced at low speeds, the disc may have excessive thickness variation. Measure the disc at 12 points with a micrometer at a radius approximately one inch from edge of disc. If thickness measurements vary by more than .0005 inch, replace the disk.

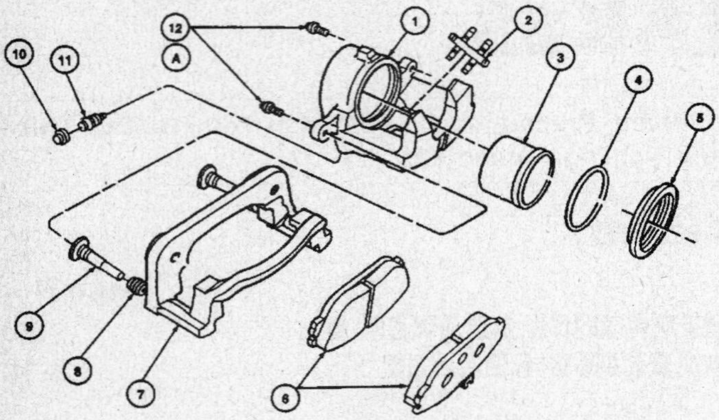

Item	Description
1	Disc Brake Caliper
2	Disc Brake Pad Anti-Rattle Clip
3	Caliper Piston
4	Brake Piston Seal
5	Front Disc Brake Caliper Boot
6	Brake Shoe and Lining
7	Front Disc Brake Caliper Anchor Plate

Item	Description
8	Locating Pin Boots
9	Disc Brake Caliper Locating Pin
10	Bleed Screw Cap
11	Wheel Cylinder Bleeder Screw
12	Caliper Guide Pin Bolt
A	Tighten to 28-36 N-m (21-26 Lb-Ft) (Tighten Bottom Caliper Guide Pin Bolt First)

FM4079500072000X

Fig. 1 Exploded view of single piston disc brake caliper. Continental, Contour, Cougar, Mark VIII, Mustang (except Cobra), Mystique, Sable, Taurus, Thunderbird & 1997 Crown Victoria, Grand Marquis & Town Car

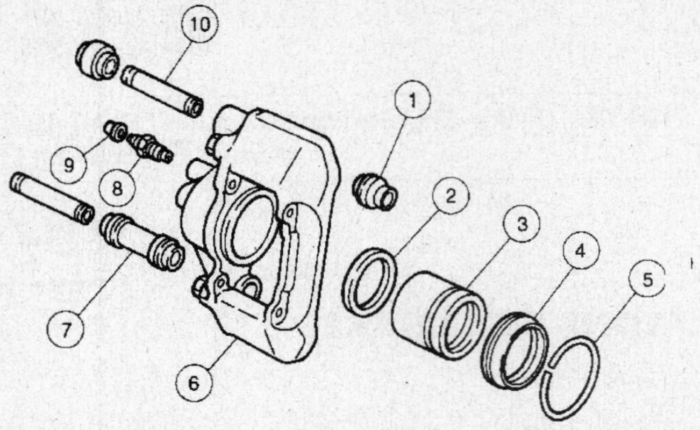

Item	Description
1	Boot
2	Piston Seal
3	Piston
4	Dust Seal
5	Snap Ring

Item	Description
6	Disc Brake Caliper
7	Boot
8	Brake Caliper Bleeder Screw
9	Brake Caliper Bleeder Screw Cap
10	Front Caliper Sleeve

FM4079500074000X

Fig. 2 Exploded view of front disc brake caliper. Aspire, Escort, Tracer & ZX2

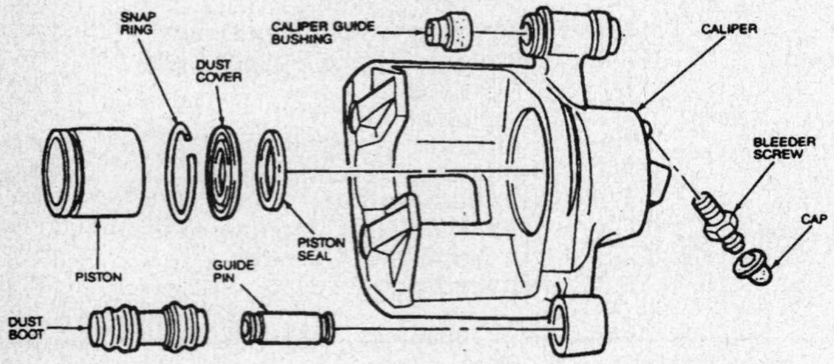

FM4079100022000X

Fig. 3 Exploded view of front brake caliper. Probe

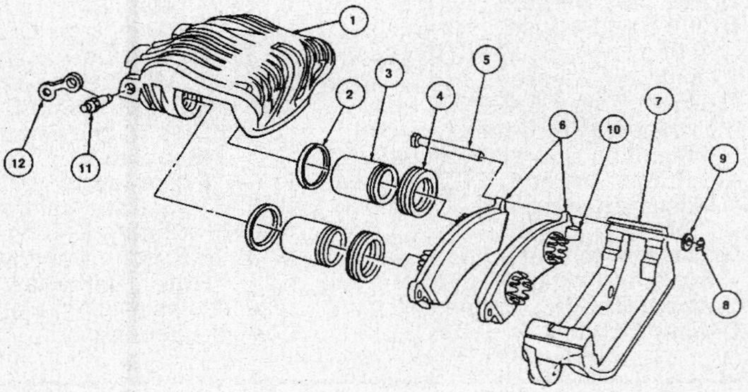

Item	Description
1	Caliper Housing (Part of 2B119)
2	Piston Seal (2 Req'd)
3	Caliper Piston (2 Req'd)
4	Dust Boot (2 Req'd)
5	Front Brake Locating Pin
6	Brake Shoe and Lining

Item	Description
7	Front Disc Brake Caliper Anchor Plate
8	Clip
9	Washer
10	Anti-Rattle Clip and Insulator
11	Wheel Cylinder Bleeder Screw
12	Cover

FM4079500073000X

Fig. 4 Exploded view of front disc brake caliper. Mustang Cobra

Lateral Runout

Excessive lateral runout of braking disc may cause a " knocking back" of the pistons, possibly creating increased pedal travel and vibration when brakes are applied.

Wheel Bearing Looseness

Adjust the wheel bearings, as outlined in appropriate "Front Steering & Suspension" section, before measuring lateral runout. The readjustment is important and will be required at the completion of the test to prevent bearing failure.

BRAKE BOOSTER OPERATION TEST

1. Inspect hydraulic system for leaks or insufficient fluid.
2. With transmission in park, stop engine.
3. Apply brakes several times to release all vacuum in system.
4. Depress brake pedal and hold in applied position.
5. Start engine and note whether brake pedal moves downward under constant foot pressure.
6. If no pedal movement is felt, brake booster system is inoperative.
7. Remove vacuum hose from power brake booster valve.
8. Inspect for vacuum at valve end of hose with engine at idle speed and transmission in neutral.
9. Ensure all unused vacuum ports are properly capped, and vacuum hoses are not cracked or deteriorated.
10. If manifold vacuum is present, and no pedal movement is noted during testing, replace power brake booster.
11. Operate engine a minimum of ten seconds at fast idle. Stop engine and let vehicle stand for ten minutes.
12. Apply brake pedal with approximately 20 lbs. of force.
13. The pedal feel should be the same as that noted with engine operating.
14. If the bake pedal feels hard (no power assist), replace check valve and repeat test.
15. If brake pedal still feels hard after check valve replacement, replace power brake booster.
16. If pedal movement feels spongy, bleed

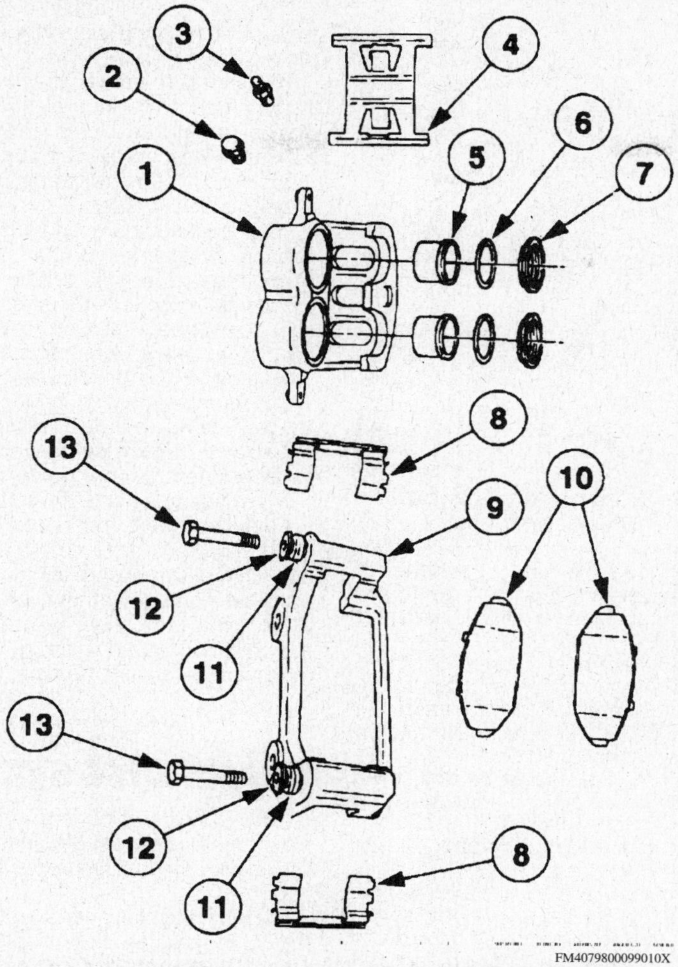

Fig. 5 Exploded view of front dual piston caliper (Part 1 of 2). LS & 1998–2000 Crown Victoria, Grand Marquis & Town Car

Item	Part Number	Description
1	2B120	Disc brake caliper
2	2L126	Bleeder screw cap
3	2208	Bleeder screw
4	2B164	Anti-rattle spring
5	2196	Caliper piston
6	2B115	Piston seal
7	2207	Piston dust boot
8	2L200	Shoe slipper
9	2B292	Front disc brake caliper anchor plate
10	2001	Brake pads
11	2A492	Guide pin boot
12	2B296	Guide pin
13	2N386	Caliper bolt

FM4079800099020X

Fig. 5 Exploded view of front dual piston caliper (Part 2 of 2). LS & 1998–2000 Crown Victoria, Grand Marquis & Town Car

hydraulic system to remove air from system.

BRAKE MASTER CYLINDER

Normal Conditions

The following conditions are considered normal and are not indications the brake master cylinder is malfunctioning:

1. A slight turbulence in brake master cylinder reservoir fluid occurring when the brake pedal is released. Turbulence occurs as brake fluid returns to master cylinder after releasing brakes.
2. A trace of brake fluid on booster shell below master cylinder mounting flange. This condition results from the lubricating action of the master cylinder wiping seal.

Abnormal Conditions

Prior to performing any diagnosis, ensure brake system warning indicator is functional.

Diagnostic procedures in this section use brake pedal feel, warning indicator illumination, and brake fluid level indicators in diagnosing brake system problems. The following conditions are considered abnormal:

1. **Brake pedal goes down fast.** Inspect for external or internal leak.
2. **Brake pedal eases down slowly.** Inspect for internal or external leak.
3. **Brake pedal is low or feels spongy.**
   a. Inspect fluid level in brake master cylinder reservoir.
   b. Inspect brake master cylinder reservoir cap vent holes for clogging.
   c. Inspect rear brake adjustment.
   d. Inspect for air in hydraulic system.
4. **Brake pedal effort is excessive.** Inspect for binding or obstructed brake pedal linkage or insufficient power brake booster vacuum.
5. **Rear brakes lock up during light brake pedal application.** Inspect for wrong tire pressure, worn tires, grease or fluid on brake linings, damaged linings, improperly adjusted parking brakes or damaged brake pressure control valve.
6. **Brake pedal effort is erratic.** Inspect for power brake booster malfunction, extreme caliper piston knock back or improperly installed disc brake shoe or lining.
7. **Brake warning indicator is on.** Inspect for low fluid level, ignition wire routing too close to fluid level indicator or float assembly damage.

Bypass Condition Inspection

1. Inspect fluid level in brake master cylinder reservoir. Fill if necessary.
2. Observe fluid level in brake master cylinder. If, after several brake applications the fluid level remains the same, measure wheel turning torque required to rotate wheels with brakes applied as follows:
   a. Place transmission in neutral.
   b. Raise vehicle on hoist.
   c. Apply brakes slowly to a minimum of 100 lbs. and hold for approximately 15 seconds.
   d. With brakes still applied, exert 75 ft. lbs. of torque on one front wheel and one rear wheel.
   e. If either wheel rotates, inspect internal components of brake master cylinder.
   f. Repair or replace as necessary.

Non-Pressure Leaks

An empty brake master cylinder reservoir condition may be caused by either of the following non-pressure external leaks:

1. Inspect for an external leak that may occur at the brake master cylinder reservoir cap due to improper positioning of gasket and cap.
2. Inspect for a leak at the brake master cylinder reservoir mounting grommets. Install new grommets if necessary.

BRAKE SYSTEM BLEED

Pressure bleeding is recommended for all hydraulic disc brake systems.

Do not reuse brake fluid drained from the hydraulic system when bleeding the brakes. Ensure disc brake pistons are returned to their normal positions and the shoe and lining assemblies are properly seated.

Do not shake the pressure bleeder tank while air is being added or after it has been pressurized. This will prevent air from the tank getting into the lines. Do not move the tank during the bleeding operation. The tank should be kept at least one third full.

On models equipped with power brakes, exhaust the vacuum in the power unit by pumping the brake pedal several times with the engine Off.

On vehicles equipped with disc brakes and master cylinders without proportioners or pressure control valves located in the master cylinder outlet port, the brake metering valve or combination valve must be held in position using a suitable tool.

On vehicles equipped with plastic reservoirs, do not exceed 25 psi bleeding pressure.

When bleeding without pressure, open the bleed valve three quarters of a turn, depress the pedal a full stroke, close the bleeder and allow the pedal to return slowly to its released position. Repeat until no more air is visible in fluid.

Discard drained or bled brake fluid. Do not spill fluid on vehicle surfaces, brake fluid will damage painted finishes.

Flushing is essential if there is water, mineral oil or other contaminants in the lines, and whenever new parts are installed in the hydraulic system. Fluid contamination is usually indicated by swollen and deteriorated cups and other rubber parts.

If air has entered system due to low fluid levels, or removal of master cylinder brake lines, all four wheels will require bleeding. If a line is disconnected at only one cylinder, then only that cylinder needs to be bled.

Master cylinders equipped with bleeder valves should be bled first before the wheel cylinders are bled. In all cases where a master cylinder has been overhauled, it must be bled. Where there is no bleeder valve, leave the lines loose, then actuate the brake pedal to expel the air. Tighten lines and repeat until no air is visible in expelled fluid.

SYSTEM PRIMING

When a new master cylinder is installed or if the brake system has been partially or completely emptied, fluid may not flow from the bleeder screws during normal bleeding. It may be necessary to prime the system using the following procedure:

1. Remove brake lines from master cylinder.
2. Install short brake lines in master cylinder and position them back into the reservoir. Ensure short brake line ends are submerged in reservoir brake fluid.
3. Fill reservoir with recommended brake fluid, then cover master cylinder fluid reservoir with shop towel.
4. Pump brakes until clear, bubble-free fluid comes out of both brake lines. If any brake fluid spills on paint, wash it off immediately with water.
5. Remove short brake lines, then install original brake lines.
6. Bleed each brake line at master cylinder using the following procedure:
   a. Have assistant pump brake pedal 10 times, then hold firm pressure on pedal.
   b. Open rearmost brake line fittings until stream of brake fluid comes out. Have assistant maintain pressure on brake pedal until brake line fitting is tightened.
   c. Repeat this operation until clear, bubble-free fluid comes out from around tube fitting.
   d. Repeat bleeding operation at front brake line fitting.
7. If any of brake lines or calipers have been removed, it may be necessary to prime system by gravity bleeding. Gravity bleed system after master cylinder is primed and bled. To prime system using gravity method, proceed as follows:
   a. Fill master cylinder with manufacturer recommended brake fluid or equivalent.
   b. Loosen both rear bleeder screws and leave open until clear brake fluid flows out. **Inspect reservoir fluid level frequently. Do not allow fluid level to drop below halfway.**
   c. Tighten rear bleeder screws.
   d. Loosen bleeder screw on front caliper and leave open until clear fluid flows out. **Bleed front calipers one side at a time.**
8. After master cylinder has been primed, lines bled at master cylinder and brake system primed, resume normal brake system bleeding at each wheel.

FM4079100009000X

Fig. 6 Rotor lateral runout inspection

WHEEL BLEEDING SEQUENCE

Rear Wheel Drive.....RR-LR-RF-LF
Front Wheel Drive....RR-LF-LR-RF

INSPECTION

Remove wheels and inspect brake disc, caliper and linings. Inspect wheel bearings and repack if necessary.

If the caliper is cracked or fluid leakage through the casting is evident, it must be replaced as a unit.

If caliper is removed when installing new parts, clean all parts in alcohol, then wipe dry using lint-free cloths. Blow out drilled passages and bores with compressed air. Inspect dust boots for punctures or tears, replace as necessary.

Inspect piston bores in both housings for scoring or pitting. Bores showing light scratches or corrosion can be cleaned with crocus cloth. Bores with deep scratches or scoring may be honed, provided the diameter of the bore is not increased more than .002 inch. If the bore does not clean up within this specification, replace the caliper. **Black stains on the bore walls are caused by piston seals and do not adversely affect caliper performance.**

When using a hone, install the hone baffle before honing the bore. The baffle is used to protect the hone stones from damage. Use extreme care in cleaning the caliper after honing. Remove all dust and grit by flushing the caliper with alcohol. Wipe the caliper dry with a clean lint-free cloth, then repeat cleaning procedure.

BRAKE DISC SERVICE

Disc brake service is critical due to the close tolerances required in machining the brake disc to ensure proper brake operation.

Maintaining close control of the shape of the rubbing surfaces is necessary to prevent brake roughness. In addition, the surface finish must be non-directional and maintained at a micro-inch finish. This is necessary to avoid pulls and erratic performance, and to promote long lining life and equal lining wear of both the lefthand and righthand brakes.

Do not attempt to refinish the rubbing surfaces unless precision equipment, capable of measuring in micro inches (millionths of an inch), is available.

To inspect the disc lateral runout, mount a dial indicator, so the indicator's plunger contacts the disc one inch from the outer edge, **Fig. 6.** If the total indicated runout exceeds specifications, install a new disc.

To inspect parallelism (thickness variation), mount dial indicators, **Fig. 7,** so the plunger contacts the rotor approximately one inch from the outer edge. If parallelism exceeds specifications, replace the rotor.

BRAKE PAD SERVICE

On models with anti-lock brakes, the brake hydraulic system must be depressurized before disconnecting any hydraulic lines or fittings. Depressurize the system by pumping the brake pedal a minimum of 25 times with the ignition in the Off position.

Fig. 7 Rotor parallelism (thickness variation) inspection

EXCEPT ASPIRE, CONTOUR, ESCORT, MUSTANG COBRA, MYSTIQUE, PROBE, TRACER & ZX2

Removal

1. Remove brake fluid until reservoir is half full.
2. **On Continental and Town Car,** turn air suspension service switch (if equipped) to Off.
3. **On all models,** raise and support front of vehicle, then remove wheel and tire assembly.
4. Remove two caliper anchor bracket mounting bolts and discard.
5. Lift front disc brake caliper anchor plate away from rotor using a rotating motion.
6. Remove outer brake shoe from disc brake caliper assembly by sliding brake shoe away from outer leg to disengage it from anchor plate.
7. Remove inner brake shoe and lining assembly by sliding brake shoe away from piston disengaging it from the caliper anchor plate.
8. Suspend caliper from inner fender housing with wire to avoid damaging brake hose.

Installation

1. Using a suitable C-clamp and block of wood 2¾ x 1 inch and approximately ¾ inch thick, seat caliper piston in bore, then remove C-clamp and wooden block. Some models have pistons made of phenolic material. Do not seat these pistons in bore by applying C-clamp directly to piston. Use extra care during this procedure to prevent damage to the piston. Metal or sharp objects should not come into direct contact with the piston or damage may result.
2. Install caliper anchor plate with caliper guide pin bolts. Tighten lower bolt first, then upper bolt to specifications.
3. Ensure anti-rattle spring and anti-rattle clip are seated in caliper lining inspection opening. Anti-rattle clips must be installed from lining side.
4. Engage brake shoe and lining in anchor plate by first engaging the side opposite anti-rattle clip. Press other end of brake shoe and lining to compress disc brake pad anti-rattle clip, then engage brake shoe lining in front anchor plate.
5. Inspect caliper and anchor plate assembly to ensure brake shoes and linings are properly installed.
6. Position caliper and anchor plate assembly over rotor. Install two new caliper anchor bracket bolts. Tighten mounting bolt to specifications.
7. Inspect caliper locating pin and pin boots. If caliper locating pin is binding, remove and clean.
8. Install wheel and tire assembly, then lower vehicle.
9. **On Continental, Sable and Taurus,** turn air suspension service switch (if equipped) On.
10. **On all models,** fill master cylinder, then pump brake pedal several times to position brake linings before moving vehicle.

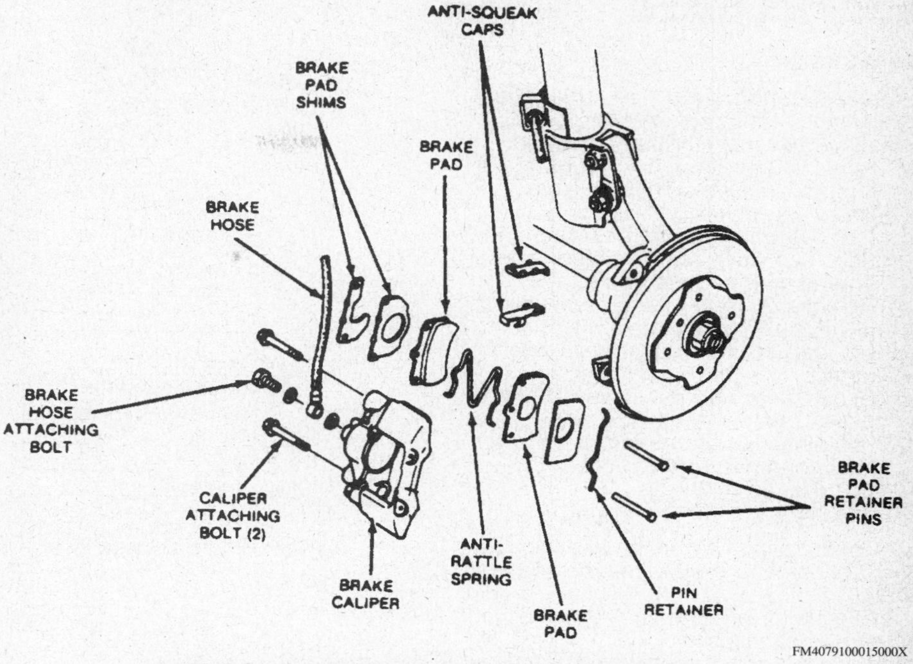

Fig. 8 Front disc brake assembly. Aspire

ASPIRE

Removal

1. Drain approximately ⅓ of brake fluid from master cylinder.
2. Raise and support front of vehicle, then remove tire and wheel.
3. Place C-clamp on caliper and tighten clamp to move caliper piston approximately .118 inch in cylinder bore, then remove clamp. **Do not use screwdriver or similar tool to pry caliper piston away from brake rotor.**
4. Disengage anti-rattle spring from brake pads, **Fig. 8.**
5. Remove brake pad pins and anti-rattle spring, then pull brake pads and shims out of caliper. **Do not discard shims found behind inner brake pad.**

Installation

1. Push piston fully back into caliper bore.
2. Apply suitable brake grease to both sides of inner shim and to back of inner brake pad.
3. Install brake pads and shims, ensure shims are positioned properly.
4. Install brake pad pins, anti-rattle spring and pin retainer.
5. Install wheel and lower vehicle.
6. Inspect and adjust master cylinder fluid level as required.

CONTOUR & MYSTIQUE

1. Raise and support vehicle.
2. Remove wheels.
3. Remove brake pad retaining clip.
4. Disconnect and detach brake pad wear sensor connector (if equipped).
5. Remove bolt covers and bolts, then the caliper.
6. Secure caliper out of way to prevent damage to flexible brake hose.
7. Remove outer and inner brake pads.
8. Reverse procedure to install.

ESCORT, TRACER & ZX2

Removal

1. Raise and support vehicle, then remove wheel and tire assembly.
2. Remove springs and brake pad retaining pins, **Fig. 9.**
3. Remove brake pads and shims from caliper assembly.

Installation

1. Push piston fully back into caliper bore.
2. Apply grease between shims and brake pad guide plates, then position brake pads and shims into caliper.
3. Install springs, two brake pad retaining pins, then wheel and tire assembly.

MUSTANG COBRA

Removal

Brake components are not interchangeable. Ensure each component is installed back in it's original location.

1. Remove approximately ½ of brake fluid from master cylinder reservoir.
2. Raise and support vehicle.
3. Remove wheel assemblies. **Use caution not to damage disc brake shields or bleeder screws.**
4. Remove clip and washer from caliper locating pin, then remove pin.
5. Lift caliper with pads from anchor frame.
6. Secure assembly out of way with wire or tie wrap.
7. Mark inner and outer friction pads for later reference, then remove pads.

Inspection

Inspect caliper piston and caliper pin boots for damage, replace boots as necessary.

Inspect rotor for wear and runout. Minor glazing of surfaces can be removed by hand sanding with a medium grit sandpaper.

Installation

1. Clean sliding and contact surfaces of brake components.
2. Remove protective paper from adhesive insulator material on friction pads. **Do not to contaminate adhesive surface.**
3. Install friction pads into caliper, ensure correct pad is fully seated into proper position of caliper.
4. Use a suitable C-clamp to compress pistons into caliper. Ensure sufficient clearance exists to allow pads to fit over rotor.
5. Place caliper into position on anchor frame, then install locating pin, washer and clip.
6. Install wheel assemblies, tighten lug nuts to specifications. **Use caution not to damage brake shields or bleeder screws.**
7. Lower vehicle, then pump brake pedal until a firm pedal is achieved. Inspect and adjust brake fluid level as needed.

PROBE

1. Remove approximately ⅔ of brake fluid from master cylinder.
2. Raise and support vehicle.
3. Remove wheel and tire assembly.
4. Using screwdriver, pry caliper outward. **Position front disc brake hose away from front disc brake caliper casting to avoid cracking front brake hose.**
5. Remove caliper mounting bolt, **Fig. 10,** then slide caliper upward.
6. Slide caliper off guide pin.
7. Mark anti-rattle shims to allow installation in original positions
8. Remove brake pads from caliper anchor.
9. Remove retaining clips from brake pads.

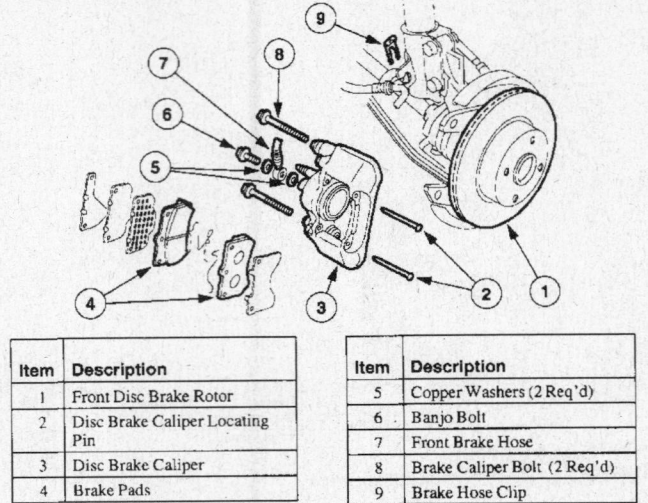

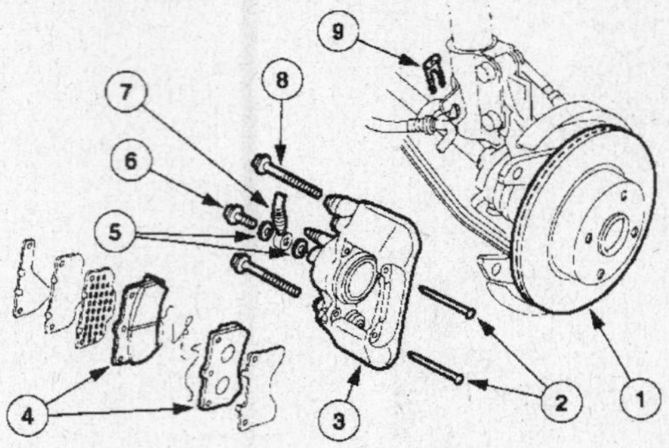

Item	Description
1	Front Disc Brake Rotor
2	Disc Brake Caliper Locating Pin
3	Disc Brake Caliper
4	Brake Pads

Item	Description
5	Copper Washers (2 Req'd)
6	Banjo Bolt
7	Front Brake Hose
8	Brake Caliper Bolt (2 Req'd)
9	Brake Hose Clip

FM4079500075000X

Fig. 9 Front disc brake assembly. Escort, Tracer & ZX2

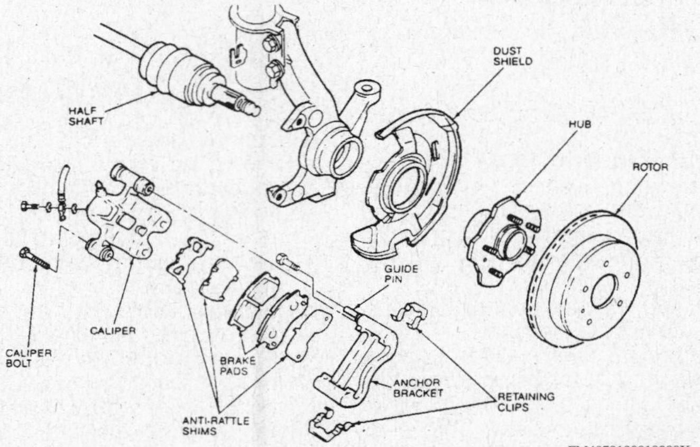

FM4079100018000X

Fig. 10 Front disc brake assembly. Probe

10. Reverse procedure to install, noting the following:
    a. Ensure wear indicators are located on inboard side of caliper anchor.
    b. Correct brake fluid level in master cylinder as necessary.
    c. Road test vehicle for proper operation.

CALIPER SERVICE

REPLACEMENT

On models with anti-lock brakes, the brake booster system must be depressurized before disconnecting any hydraulic lines or fittings. Depressurize the system by pumping the brake pedal a minimum of 25 times with the ignition in the Off position.

EXCEPT ASPIRE, CONTOUR, ESCORT, MUSTANG COBRA, MYSTIQUE, PROBE, TRACER & ZX2

Before removing calipers, mark lefthand and righthand calipers so they can be installed in the same position.

1. **On Continental and Town Car,** turn air suspension service switch off if equipped.
2. **On all models,** raise and support front of vehicle, then remove wheel and tire assembly.
3. Loosen brake tube fitting connecting brake tube to fitting on frame. Plug brake tube.
4. Remove retaining clip from brake hose and bracket, then disconnect brake hose from caliper.
5. Remove caliper locating pins.
6. Lift caliper from rotor and spindle anchor plate assembly.
7. **On models equipped with phenolic caliper piston,** do not pry directly against the piston or damage may result.
8. **On all models,** reverse procedure to install, noting the following:
    a. Install caliper assembly over rotor with outer shoe against rotor braking surface to prevent pinching piston boot between inner brake shoe and piston. **Ensure calipers are installed in proper position.**
    b. Bleed brake system as described under "Brake System Bleed."

c. Pump brake pedal several times to position brake shoes before moving vehicle.
9. Turn air suspension switch (if equipped) ON.

ASPIRE

1. Raise and support vehicle, then remove wheel and tire.
2. Remove brake pads as described under "Brake Pad Service."
3. Remove brake hose attaching bolt, then disconnect hose from caliper. Discard seal washers located between brake hose connection and caliper.
4. Remove caliper attaching bolts, then the caliper.
5. Remove anti-squeak caps.
6. Reverse procedure to install. Bleed brakes as described under "Brake System Bleed."

CONTOUR & MYSTIQUE

1. Raise and support vehicle.
2. Remove wheel and tire assembly.
3. Disconnect and detach brake pad wear sensor connector (if equipped).
4. Loosen brake hose union.
5. Remove brake pad retaining clip.
6. Remove bolt covers and bolts, then the caliper.
7. Remove outer and inner brake pad.
8. Disconnect and plug brake hose form caliper.
9. Reverse procedure to install.

ESCORT, TRACER & ZX2

1. Raise and support vehicle, then remove brake pads as described under "Brake Pad Service."
2. Using suitable needle nose vise grips, clamp center of brake flex hose to prevent brake fluid leakage.
3. Remove banjo bolt retaining brake flex hose to caliper.
4. Disconnect brake hose from caliper and discard two copper washers.
5. Remove two caliper bolts, then the caliper.
6. Reverse procedure to install, noting the following:
   a. Use new copper sealing washers.
   b. Bleed brakes as described under "Brake System Bleed."

MUSTANG COBRA

Brake components are unique, and are not interchangeable. Ensure each component is installed back in it's original location.

1. Remove brake pads as described under "Brake Pad Service."
2. Remove brake flex hose from caliper and discard copper sealing washers.
3. If necessary, remove two caliper anchor frame bolts, then lift caliper/anchor frame assembly off rotor.
4. Reverse procedure to install, noting the following:
   a. Use new copper sealing washers.
   b. Bleed brakes as described under "Brake System Bleed."

PROBE

1. Raise and support vehicle.
2. Remove wheel and tire assembly.
3. Remove brake hose to caliper bolt.
4. Remove two copper washers and discard.
5. Remove caliper bolts.
6. Pivot caliper off brake pads and slide caliper off guide pin.
7. Remove guide pin bushing dust boots and push out guide pin bushing.
8. Using high temperature grease D7AZ-19590-A or equivalent, lubricate guide pin bushings.
9. Reverse procedure to install. Bleed front brakes as described under "Brake System Bleed."

OVERHAUL

EXCEPT ASPIRE, ESCORT, MUSTANG COBRA, PROBE, TRACER & ZX2

Disassemble

1. Remove caliper assembly from vehicle as described under "Caliper, Replace."
2. Position fiber block and shop towels between caliper piston and caliper housing, then apply compressed air to caliper brake line fitting bore to force piston from caliper.
3. Remove dust boot from caliper assembly, **Fig. 1.**
4. Remove piston seal from cylinder and discard.

Inspection

1. Inspect piston for scratches, scoring or damage. Replace if necessary.
2. Inspect caliper bore for scratches, scoring or corrosion. Light scratches or slight corrosion can be polished out using crocus cloth.
3. Ensure bleeder screw and bleeder screw bore hole in caliper are fully open.
4. Inspect caliper bushings for corrosion and dust boot retaining ring for damage or tension loss. Replace parts as necessary.

Assemble

1. Lubricate piston seal with clean brake fluid, then install seal in caliper bore. **Ensure seal is firmly seated in groove.**
2. Install new dust boot in outer groove of caliper bore, **Fig. 1.**
3. Coat piston with clean brake fluid and install piston in caliper bore.
4. Spread dust boot over piston as it is installed, then seat dust boot in piston groove.
5. Install caliper assembly as described previously.
6. **On Continental and Town Car,** turn air suspension service switch (if equipped) ON.

ASPIRE

Disassemble

1. Remove caliper as described previously.
2. Remove bleeder screw and drain remaining fluid from caliper. Install screw.
3. Remove dust boot retaining ring, **Fig. 2.**
4. Position block of wood between piston and caliper, then apply compressed air to fluid inlet port to blow piston from caliper bore. **Apply only enough pressure to ease piston out of bore.**
5. Remove dust boot from piston, then use suitable wooden pick to carefully pry piston seal from caliper bore.
6. Remove bleeder screw, then the caliper bushings and bushing seals.
7. Wash all parts in denatured alcohol, then dry with compressed air.

Inspection

1. Inspect piston for scratches, scoring or damage. Replace if necessary.
2. Inspect caliper bore for scratches, scoring or corrosion. Light scratches or slight corrosion can be polished out using crocus cloth.
3. Ensure bleeder screw and bleeder screw bore hole in caliper are fully open.
4. Inspect caliper bushings for corrosion and dust boot retaining ring for damage or tension loss. Replace parts as necessary.

Assemble

1. Lubricate piston seal with suitable brake grease or clean brake fluid, then install into caliper bore.
2. Lubricate piston, then partially install into caliper bore. Ensure dust boot groove on piston remains above caliper bore.
3. Lubricate dust boot with suitable brake grease, then install onto piston.
4. Press piston fully inward until it bottoms in bore, then install dust boot retaining ring.
5. Install bleeder screw.
6. Install caliper bushings and new bushing seals. Lubricate inner surface of bushing seal and outer surface of bushings with suitable brake grease before installation. **Do not allow grease to enter piston bore.**

ESCORT, TRACER & ZX2

Disassemble

1. Remove front caliper as described previously.
2. Remove front caliper sleeves and dust boots.
3. Remove caliper bleed screw cap and screw.
4. Remove snap ring from caliper piston dust seal, then the seal.
5. Position wood block or shop towels between caliper and piston, then apply air pressure to brake hose fitting to remove piston from caliper. Use only enough air pressure to ease piston from caliper bore. **Keep hands and fingers away from piston, as personal injury may result.**

Inspection

1. Inspect piston for scratches, scoring or damage. Replace if necessary.
2. Inspect caliper bore for scratches,

scoring or corrosion. Light scratches or slight corrosion can be polished out using crocus cloth.
3. Ensure bleeder screw and bleeder screw bore hole in caliper are fully open.
4. Inspect caliper bushings for corrosion and dust boot retaining ring for damage or tension loss. Replace parts as necessary.

Assemble

1. Lubricate piston seal with brake fluid, then position seal in caliper bore groove.
2. Lubricate piston and caliper bore with brake fluid.
3. Install caliper assembly as described previously.

MUSTANG COBRA

Disassemble

1. Remove caliper assembly from vehicle as described previously.
2. Drain any remaining brake fluid from caliper.
3. Position fiber block and shop towels between caliper pistons and caliper housing, then apply compressed air to caliper brake line fitting bore to force pistons from caliper.
4. Remove dust boots from caliper assembly.
5. Remove piston seals from cylinder and discard.

Inspection

1. Inspect pistons for scratches, scoring or damage. Replace if necessary.
2. Inspect caliper bores for scratches, scoring or corrosion. Light scratches or slight corrosion can be polished out using crocus cloth.
3. Ensure bleeder screw and bleeder screw bore hole in caliper are fully open.

Assemble

1. Lubricate piston seals with clean brake fluid, then install seals in caliper bore. **Ensure seals are firmly seated in groove.**
2. Install new dust boots in outer groove of caliper bore.
3. Coat pistons with clean brake fluid and install pistons in caliper bore.
4. Install dust boots over piston as they are installed, then seat dust boots in piston groove.
5. Install caliper assembly as described previously.

PROBE

Disassemble

1. Open caliper bleed screw and drain caliper. Close bleed screw.
2. Remove caliper as described previously.
3. Remove caliper guide bushing and dust boots, **Fig. 3.**
4. Remove snap ring from caliper piston dust boot.
5. Position block of wood between piston and caliper.
6. Apply air pressure to brake hose fitting. **Do not use excessive air pressure to remove piston.**
7. Remove dust boot and discard.
8. Remove piston seal from caliper and discard.

Inspection

1. Inspect piston for scratches, scoring or damage. Replace if necessary.
2. Inspect caliper bore for scratches, scoring or corrosion. Light scratches or slight corrosion can be polished out using crocus cloth.
3. Ensure bleeder screw and bleeder screw bore hole in caliper are fully open.
4. Inspect caliper bushings for corrosion and dust boot retaining ring for damage or tension loss. Replace parts as necessary.

Assemble

1. Lubricate new piston seal with brake fluid and install seal in caliper groove. **Ensure seal does not become twisted in caliper bore.**
2. Lubricate caliper bore and piston with brake fluid.
3. Install dust boot on piston and slide dust boot into groove.
4. Install piston in caliper bore and push down into bottom of bore.
5. Slide dust boot over boss on caliper bore and install snap ring.
6. Install caliper guide bushing, dust boot and guide pin.
7. Install caliper bolt and tighten to specifications.
8. Bleed front brakes as described under "Brake System Bleed."
9. Pump brake pedal several times to seat brake pads.
10. Inspect fluid level and add if necessary.
11. With vehicle in Neutral, spin each rotor to ensure brakes are not dragging.
12. Install wheel and tire assemblies.

ROTOR

REPLACE

If caliper does not require servicing, do not disconnect brake hose or remove caliper from vehicle. Position caliper aside with wire or tie straps to avoid damaging caliper or hose.

If excessive force must be used to remove the rotor, then it should be inspected for lateral runout before installation.

REMOVAL

1. **On models with air suspension,** turn service switch Off.
2. **On all models,** raise and support vehicle, then remove wheel and tire assembly. **Use care to avoid damage or interference with caliper bleeder screw fitting and brake rotor shield.**
3. Remove caliper anchor bracket bolts. Position caliper aside and support with wire or tie straps to avoid damaging caliper and hose. **Use care to prevent deformation of rotor and nicking, scratching or contaminating brake lining and rotor surfaces.**
4. Remove front rotor from hub assembly by pulling it off hub studs, noting the following:
   a. If excessive force is necessary to remove rotor, inspect rotor for lateral runout prior to installation.
   b. If additional force is required to remove front disc brake rotor, apply suitable rust penetrant and inhibitor on front and rear rotor/hub mating surfaces.
   c. Strike rotor between studs with plastic hammer. If rotor still will not come off, install three-jaw puller tool No. D80L-1013-A, or equivalent, and remove rotor.

INSTALLATION

Failure to clean rust and foreign material from rotor and hub mounting surfaces when installing new or old rotors will result in high rotor lateral runout, which will speed up the development of brake roughness, shudder or vibration.

1. If front disc brake rotor is being replaced, remove protective coating from new rotor with suitable carburetor cleaner.
2. If original rotor is being installed, ensure rotor braking and mounting surfaces are clean.
3. Apply suitable lubricant to pilot diameter of front disc brake rotor, then install rotor on wheel hub assembly.
4. Install caliper and caliper anchor bracket bolts on rotor. Tighten caliper anchor bracket bolts to specifications.
5. Install wheel and tire assembly, then tighten wheel hub bolt nuts to specifications. **Failure to tighten wheel hub bolt nuts with torque wrench in star pattern may result in high rotor runout, which will speed development of brake roughness, shudder and vibration.**
6. Lower vehicle, then pump brake pedal to position brake linings prior to moving vehicle.
7. Turn air suspension service switch (if equipped) ON.
8. Road test vehicle.

TECHNICAL SERVICE BULLETINS

CLICKING DURING BRAKING AFTER DIRECTION CHANGE

1997–99 Escort & Tracer & 1998–99 ZX2

On some of these models, the front brakes may click during application after changing direction.

This condition may be caused by excessive clearance between caliper bracket and inned brake pad. To correct this condition, proceed as follows:

1. Raise and support vehicle, then remove front wheel and tire assemblies.
2. Measure clearance between steel

inner brake pad and steering knuckle while pushing brake pad to extreme side of knuckle. Clearance should be .016–.037 inch.

3. If clearance is more than .037 inch, proceed as follows:
   a. Remove caliper and inspect for missing guide plates between steering knuckle ears.
   b. If missing, install new guide plates.
   c. Measure gap as previously described. If clearance is more than .028, proceed to next step.
4. If clearance is more than .028 inch, proceed as follows:
   a. Remove caliper.
   b. Break all four tabs off new guide plate (part No. F5CZ-2B164-AA). Ensure to break tabs off to bottom of bend relief holes.
   c. Install revised guide plate inside another new guide plate.
   d. Install guide plates over steering knuckle ear. Outer guide plate can be slightly bent inward to improve retention.
   e. Install another new guide plate on outer ear. This plate may also be bent as long as assembled dimension does not become less than .016 inch.
   f. Remove inner brake pads and shims.
   g. Clean shims and inner pad mating surfaces with suitable brake cleaner.
   h. Apply silicone brake caliper grease and dielectric compound (part No. D7AZ-19A331-A, or equivalent) to inner brake pad back. Grease should entirely cover shim/inner pad interface, but not bleed out excessively when shims are pressed to inner pad back.
   i. Assemble caliper and inner pads/shims.
   j. Ensure gap is not less than .016 inch.

GROANING DURING CITY DRIVING

1997–99 Contour & Mystique & 1999 Cougar

On some of these models the front brakes may groan during city driving.

This condition may be caused by front brake pads' damping rate. To correct this condition, install revised pads (less pad wear warning, part No. XS8Z-2001-CA; with pad wear warning part, No. XS6Z-2001-DA).

SQUEALING OR MOANING/GROANING

1997–98 Continental

On some of these models, the front brakes may have a high frequency squealing or a moaning/groaning under moderate braking. This noise is not to be confused with intermittent squeals or groans during first few brake applications in morning or while braking in reverse.

This condition may be caused by high frequency response between the lining, caliper and rotor. To correct this condition, install revised front brake pads (part No. F3Z-2001-CB).

COMPOSITE ROTORS

Continental, Sable & Taurus

The disc rotor is a hat section-type of composite steel and cast iron. A Rotunda Rotor Mounting Adapter tool No. 054-00032, or equivalent, is required for use on the brake lathe for refinishing. **Failure to use the adapter will result in gouging the brake disc, making it unfit for use.**

A new design full-cast front disc brake rotor is now available for service use. If service is required, install the new full cast front disc rotors, part No. F10Y-1125-B **in pairs only. Never install a full cast rotor on one side of the vehicle with a composite rotor on the other side.**

IMPROVED BRAKE CALIPER SLIDE GREASE

When performing any disc brake service, lubricate all necessary components with silicone brake caliper grease and dielectric compound, part No. D7AZ-19A331-A, also known as Motorcraft WA-10. If this is not available, an equivalent meeting Ford specification ESE-M1C171-A should be used.

DISC BRAKE SPECIFICATIONS

Refer to "Rear Disc Brakes & Parking Brakes" for specification charts.

TIGHTENING SPECIFICATIONS

Component	Torque/Ft. Lbs.
Brake Hose Bolts	16–44
Caliper Bolts	②
Locating Pins③	18–25
Locating Pins④	45–65
Locating Pins⑤	40–60
Wheel Lug Nuts⑥	65–88
Wheel Lug Nuts⑦	85–104
Wheel Lug Nuts①	85–105
Wheel Lug Nuts⑧	66–88
Wheel Lug Nuts⑨	74–100
Wheel Lug Nuts⑩	100

① — Mustang Cobra, Thunderbird & Cougar.
② — Aspire, 29–36 ft. lbs.; Probe, 33–36 ft. lbs.; 1997 Escort & Tracer, 29–36 ft. lbs.; 1998–99 Escort, Tracer & ZX2 36–43 ft. lbs.
③ — Escort, Sable, Taurus, Tracer & 1997–98 Continental.
④ — Cougar, Mustang & Thunderbird.
⑤ — Crown Victoria, Grand Marquis & Town Car.
⑥ — Except Sable, Taurus & 1997–98 Mustang Cobra,
⑦ — Sable & Taurus.
⑧ — 1997 Escort & Tracer.
⑨ — 1998–99 Escort, Tracer & ZX2.
⑩ — LS.

Rear Disc Brakes & Parking Brakes

INDEX

PRECAUTIONS

AIR BAG SYSTEMS

Refer to "Air Bag System Precautions" in the front of this manual for system disarming and arming procedures.

BATTERY GROUND CABLE

Prior to service, disconnect battery ground cable and isolate as required.

SYSTEM DEPRESSURIZING

On models equipped with anti-lock brakes, hydraulic system must be depressurized prior to disconnecting any hydraulic lines or fittings, by pumping the brake pedal a minimum of 25 times with ignition in Off position.

DESCRIPTION

CONTINENTAL, COUGAR, LS, MARK VIII, MUSTANG, SABLE, TAURUS & THUNDERBIRD

Sliding caliper rear disc brakes are used on these models, **Fig. 1.** The caliper is basically the same as the larger front wheel caliper. However, a parking brake mechanism and a larger inner brake shoe anti-rattle spring have been added.

The parking brake lever, located at the rear of the caliper, is actuated by a cable system similar to rear drum brake applications. When the parking brake is applied, the cable rotates the lever and operating shaft, driving the caliper piston and brake shoe assembly against the rotor. An automatic adjuster in the assembly compensates for lining wear and maintains proper clearance in the parking brake mechanism.

The cast iron rotors are ventilated by curved fins located between the braking surfaces and are designed to cause the rotor to act as an air pump when the vehicle is traveling forward. The rotors are not interchangeable and are identified by a "Right or Left" marking cast inside the hat section of the rotor. The rotor is secured to the axle flange in the same manner as a rear brake drum. A splash shield is bolted to a forged axle adapter to protect the inboard rotor surface.

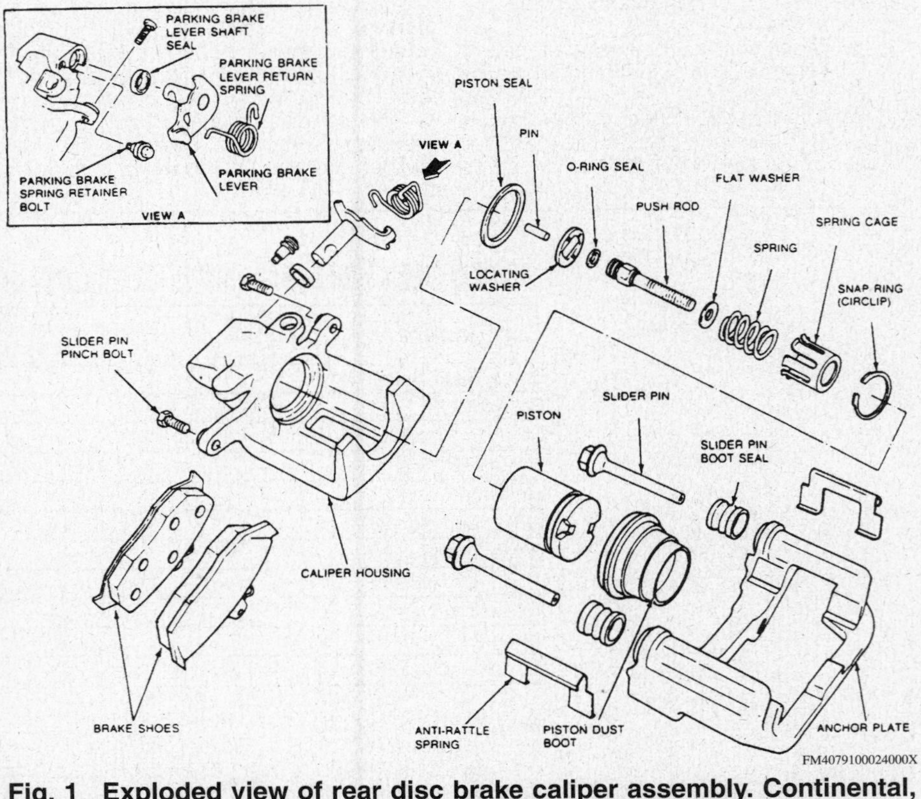

Fig. 1 Exploded view of rear disc brake caliper assembly. Continental, Cougar, LS, Mark VIII, Mustang, Sable, Taurus & Thunderbird

CONTOUR & MYSTIQUE

During normal operation, hydraulic pressure from the master cylinder pushes the

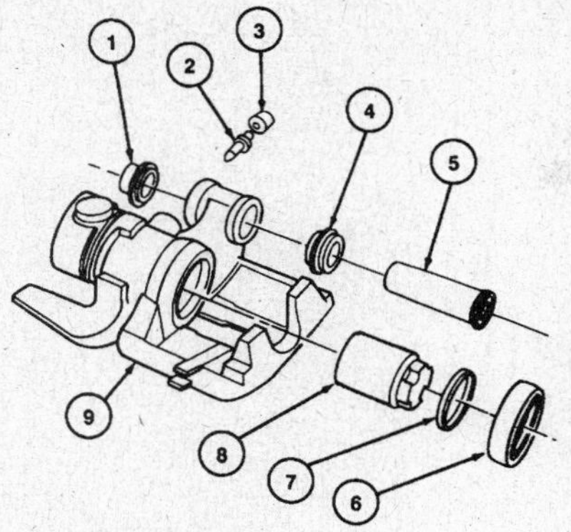

Item		Description
1		Disc Brake Caliper Locating Pin Seal
2		Brake Bleeder Screw
3		Brake Bleeder Screw Cap
4		Disc Brake Caliper Locating
5		Disc Brake Caliper Locating Pin
6		Caliper Piston Dust Cover
7		Caliper Piston Seal
8		Rear Disc Brake Caliper Piston and Adjuster
9		Disc Brake Caliper

FM4079300070010X

Fig. 2 Exploded view of rear brake caliper (Part 1 of 2). Contour & Mystique

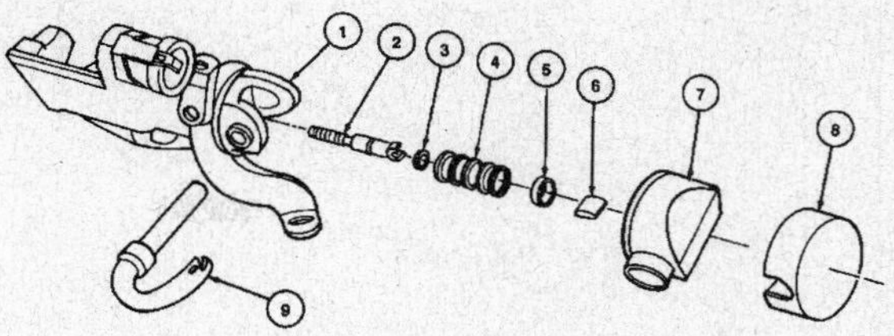

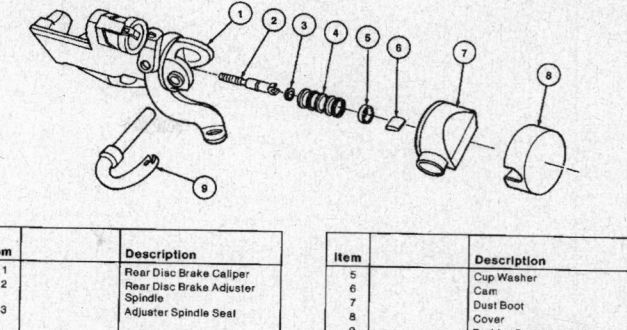

Item		Description
1		Rear Disc Brake Caliper
2		Rear Disc Brake Adjuster Spindle
3		Adjuster Spindle Seal
4		Brake Adjuster Springs

Item		Description
5		Cup Washer
6		Cam
7		Dust Boot
8		Cover
9		Parking Brake Actuator Lever

FM4079300070020X

Fig. 2 Exploded view of rear brake caliper (Part 2 of 2). Contour & Mystique

piston, **Fig. 2,** forward and applies pressure on the inboard brake pad. This pressure also causes the caliper to slide inward on the guide pins. As the brakes are applied, the square cut piston seal distorts. When the brake pedal is released, the square cut seal returns the piston to its normal position. If the piston moves no further than the square cut deformation limit, no self-adjustment takes place. If piston movement is greater than the deformation limit of the square cut seal, the piston and sleeve nut will travel on the threads of the spindle. When the brake pedal is released, the piston returns the amount the square cut seal was deformed but it does not return to its original position. The tightened adjuster spring does not allow the sleeve nut to rotate and travel on the thread. The piston can adjust outward from the caliper housing but it cannot move inward.

The parking brake cable is attached to the caliper at the operating lever. When the parking brake is applied, the operating lever pushes the connecting link against the piston which forces application of the brake pads. When the parking brake is released, pressure against the piston is released and the brake pads return to their normal position.

CROWN VICTORIA, GRAND MARQUIS & TOWN CAR

The rear disc brake system uses a pin slider-type caliper assembly, **Fig. 3,** and a cast iron rotor bolted to the rear axle shaft

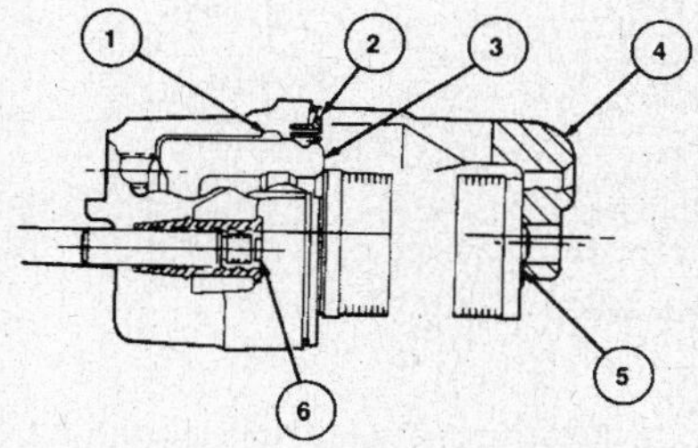

Item		Description
1		Piston Seal
2		Dust Boot
3		Inner Brake Shoe and Lining Assy (Must be Firmly Seated Against Piston)
4		Rear Disc Brake Caliper
5		Outer Brake Shoe and Lining Assy (Must be Seated Against Housing)
6		Disc Brake Caliper Locating Pin

FM4079300066000X

Fig. 3 Cutaway view of rear disc brake caliper assembly. Crown Victoria, Grand Marquis & Town Car

flange. The caliper has a phenolic piston with a seal and a press-in type dust boot.

The inner pads are interchangeable left to right and use a three-finger clip fit inside the caliper piston. The outer pads are interchangeable left to right and use a dual-purpose clip which holds the brake pads on the caliper housing and also prevents caliper rattle.

The flanges on both inner and outer pads slide on a machined surfaces of the brake adapter.

ESCORT, PROBE, TRACER & ZX2

The self-adjusting rear disc brake system consists of a disc rotor and a single piston caliper, **Figs. 4 and 5.** The brake pads are held in position between the caliper and the rotor by two guides, two shims and an anti rattle spring. It is not necessary to remove the caliper completely to replace the brake pads; they can be removed simply by pivoting the caliper on its mounting bracket.

On some models it may be necessary to disconnect the parking brake cable to allow full caliper rotation.

During normal operation, hydraulic pressure from the master cylinder pushes the piston forward and applies pressure on the inboard brake pad. This pressure also causes the caliper to slide inward on the guide pins. As the brakes are applied, the square cut piston seal distorts. When the brake pedal is released, The square cut seal returns the piston to its normal position. If the piston moves no further than the square cut deformation limit, no self-adjustment takes place. If piston movement is greater than the deformation limit of the square cut seal, the piston and sleeve nut will travel on the threads of the spindle. This is because the loosened adjuster spring allows the sleeve nut to rotate. When the brake pedal is released, the piston returns the amount the square cut seal was deformed but it does not return to its original position. This is because the tightened adjuster spring does not allow the sleeve nut to rotate and travel on the thread. The piston can adjust outward from the caliper housing but it cannot move inward.

The parking brake cable is attached to the caliper at the operating lever. When the parking brake is applied, the operating lever pushes the connecting link against the piston which forces application of the brake pads. When the parking brake is released, pressure against the piston is released and the brake pads return to their normal position.

TROUBLESHOOTING

BRAKE ROUGHNESS

If roughness or vibration is encountered during highway operation or if pedal pumping is experienced at low speeds, the disc may have excessive thickness variation. Measure the disc at 12 points with a micrometer at a radius approximately one inch from the edge of the disc. If thickness measurements vary by more than .0005 inch, replace the rotor.

Excessive lateral runout of braking disc may cause a " knocking back" of the pistons, possibly creating increased pedal travel and vibration when brakes are applied.

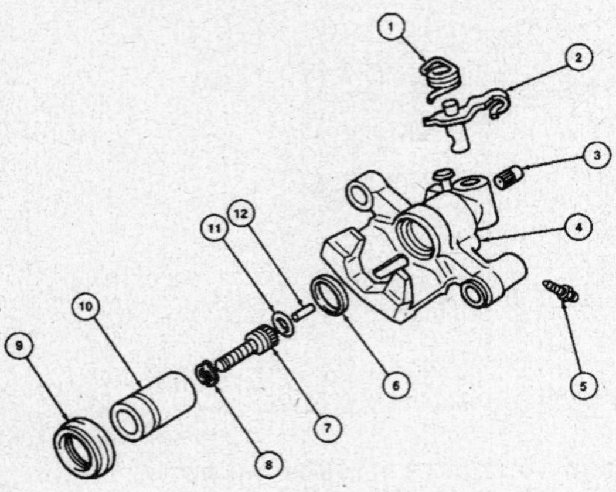

Item	Description
1	Rear Wheel Brake Caliper Spring
2	Rear Brake Operating Lever
3	Brake Adjuster Screw
4	Rear Disc Brake Caliper
5	Rear Disc Brake Caliper Bleeder Screw

Item	Description
6	Piston Seal
7	Rear Disc Brake Adjuster Spindle
8	Snap Ring
9	Dust Seal
10	Piston
11	O-Ring
12	Brake Connecting Link

FM4079300065000X

Fig. 4 Exploded view of rear disc brake assembly. Escort, Tracer & ZX2

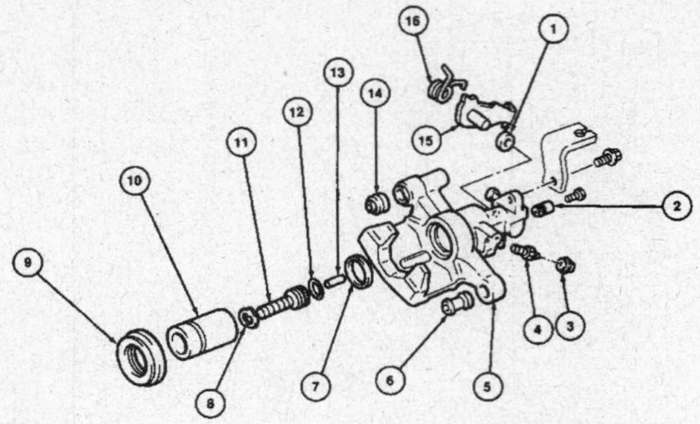

Item	Description
1	Rear Brake Operating Lever Boot
2	Brake Adjuster Screw
3	Bleeder Screw Cap
4	Bleeder Screw
5	Rear Disc Brake Caliper
6	Caliper Sleeve
7	Piston Seal
8	Snap Ring
9	Dust Cover

Item	Description
10	Rear Disc Brake Caliper Piston
11	Rear Disc Brake Adjuster Spindle
12	O-Ring
13	Brake Connecting Link
14	Brake Caliper Bolt Dust Boot
15	Rear Brake Operating Lever
16	Rear Wheel Brake Caliper Spring

FM4079300068000X

Fig. 5 Exploded view of rear disc brake assembly. Probe

Adjust the wheel bearings before inspecting the runout. The readjustment is very important and will be required at the completion of the test to prevent bearing failure. Adjust the wheel bearings as outlined in the " Front Suspension" section.

BRAKE SYSTEM BLEED

Pressure bleeding is recommended for all hydraulic disc brake systems.

Do not use brake fluid drained from the hydraulic system when bleeding the brakes. Ensure disc brake pistons are returned to their normal positions and the shoe and lining assemblies are properly seated. Before driving the vehicle, inspect the brake operation.

Do not shake the pressure bleeder tank while air is being added or after it has been pressurized. This will prevent air from the tank getting into the lines. Set the tank in the required location, then bring the air hose to the tank. Do not move the tank during the bleeding operation. The tank should be kept at least one third full.

On models equipped with power brakes, exhaust the vacuum in the power unit by pumping the brake pedal several times with the engine Off before starting to bleed the system.

On vehicles equipped with disc brakes and master cylinders without proportioners or pressure control valves located in the master cylinder outlet port, the brake metering valve or combination valve must be held in position using a suitable tool.

On vehicles equipped with plastic reservoirs, do not exceed 25 psi bleeding pressure.

When bleeding without pressure, open the bleed valve three quarters of a turn, depress the brake pedal a full stroke, then close the bleeder valve and allow the pedal to return slowly to its released position. Repeat as necessary until fluid is free of air bubbles.

Discard drained or bled brake fluid. Brake fluid will damage painted finishes. Do not spill fluid on vehicle surfaces.

Flushing is essential if there is water, mineral oil or other contaminants in the lines, and whenever new parts are installed in the hydraulic system. Fluid contamination is usually indicated by swollen and deteriorated cups and other rubber parts.

Bleeding is necessary on all four wheels if air has entered the system because of low fluid level or the line or lines have been disconnected. If a line is disconnected at any one wheel cylinder, only that cylinder needs to be bled.

Master cylinders equipped with bleeder valves should be bled first before the wheel cylinders are bled. In all cases where a master cylinder has been overhauled, it must be bled. Where there is no bleeder valve, this can be done by leaving the lines loose, actuating the brake pedal to expel the air then tightening the lines.

After overhauling a dual master cylinder used in conjunction with disc brakes, air may be trapped between the master cylinder pistons. Bleed the cylinder before installing it on the vehicle.

SYSTEM PRIMING

When a new master cylinder is installed or the brake system is partially or completely emptied, fluid may not flow from the bleeder screws during normal bleeding. If necessary, prime the system using the following procedure:

1. Remove brake lines from master cylinder.
2. Install short brake lines in master cylinder and position them back into the reservoir. Ensure short brake line ends are submerged in reservoir brake fluid.
3. Fill reservoir with recommended brake fluid, then cover master cylinder fluid reservoir with shop towel.
4. Pump brakes until clear, bubble-free fluid comes out of both brake lines. **If any brake fluid spills on paint, wash it off immediately with water.**
5. Remove short brake lines, then reinstall original brake lines.
6. Bleed each brake line at master cylinder as follows:
   a. Have assistant pump brake pedal 10 times, then hold firm pressure on pedal.
   b. Open rearmost brake line fittings with tubing wrench until stream of brake fluid comes out. Have assistant maintain pressure on brake pedal until brake line fitting is tightened.
   c. Repeat until clear, bubble-free fluid comes out from around tube fitting.
   d. Repeat bleeding operation at front brake line fitting.
7. If any of brake lines or calipers have been removed, it may be helpful to prime system by gravity bleeding. This should be done after master cylinder is primed and bled. To prime system using gravity method, use following procedure:
   a. Fill master cylinder with manufacturer's recommended brake fluid, or equivalent.
   b. Loosen both rear bleeder screws and leave open until clear brake fluid flows out. **Inspect reservoir fluid level frequently. Do not allow fluid level to drop below halfway.**
   c. Tighten rear bleeder screws.
   d. Loosen bleeder screw on front caliper and leave open until clear fluid flows out. **Bleed front calipers one side at a time.**

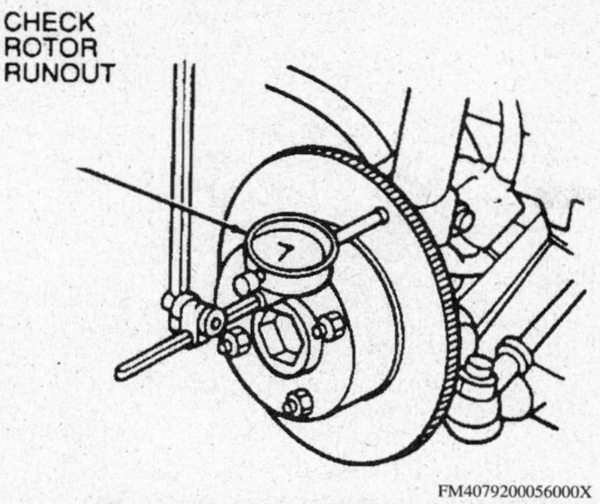

Fig. 6 Rotor lateral runout inspection

8. After master cylinder has been primed, lines bled at master cylinder and brake system primed, resume normal brake system bleeding at each wheel.

WHEEL BLEEDING SEQUENCE

Rear Wheel Drive.....RR-LR-RF-LF
Front Wheel Drive....RR-LF-LR-RF

INSPECTION

Remove wheels and inspect brake disc, calipers and linings. Inspect and repack wheel bearings if necessary.

If the caliper is cracked or fluid leakage through the casting is evident, it must be replaced as a unit.

If caliper was removed when installing new parts, clean all parts in alcohol, then wipe dry using lint-free cloths. Using an air hose, blow out drilled passages and bores. Inspect dust boots for punctures or tears. If punctures or tears are evident, install new boots during assembly.

Inspect piston bores in both housings for scoring or pitting. Bores showing light scratches or corrosion can usually be cleaned with crocus cloth. Bores with deep scratches or scoring may be honed, provided the diameter of the bore is not increased more than .002 inch. If the bore does not clean up within this specification, a new caliper housing should be installed. Black stains on the bore walls are caused by piston seals and will not adversely affect caliper performance.

When using a hone, install the hone baffle before honing the bore. The baffle is used to protect the hone stones from damage. Use extreme care in cleaning the caliper after honing. Remove all dust and grit by flushing the caliper with alcohol. Wipe the caliper dry with a clean lint-free cloth, then repeat cleaning procedure.

BRAKE DISC SERVICE

Disc brake service is critical due to the close tolerances required in machining the brake disc to ensure proper brake operation.

Maintaining close control of the shape of the rubbing surfaces is necessary to prevent brake roughness. In addition, the surface finish must be non-directional and maintained at a micro-inch finish. This is necessary to avoid pulls and erratic performance and promote long lining life and equal lining wear of both the lefthand and righthand brakes.

Do not attempt to refinish the rubbing surfaces unless precision equipment, capable of measuring in micro inches (millionths of an inch) is available.

To inspect the disc lateral runout, mount a dial indicator on a convenient part, such as a steering knuckle, tie rod, or caliper housing, so the indicator's plunger contacts the disc one inch from the outer edge, **Fig. 6.** If the total indicated runout exceeds specifications, install a new disc.

To inspect parallelism (thickness variation), mount dial indicators so the plunger contacts the rotor approximately one inch from the outer edge. If parallelism exceeds specifications, replace the rotor.

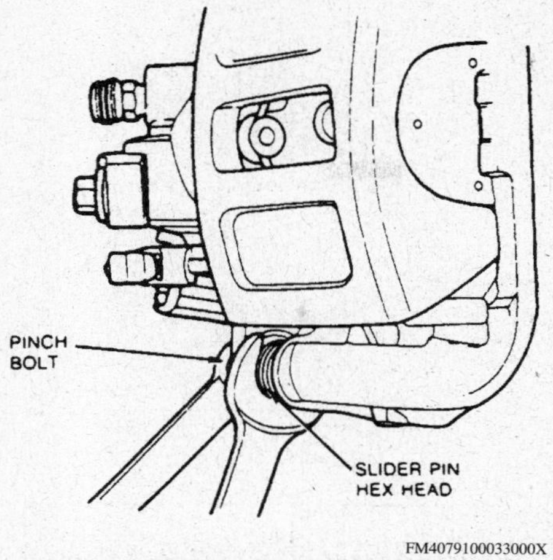

Fig. 7 Slider pin removal. Continental, Cougar, Mark VIII, Mustang, Sable, Taurus & Thunderbird

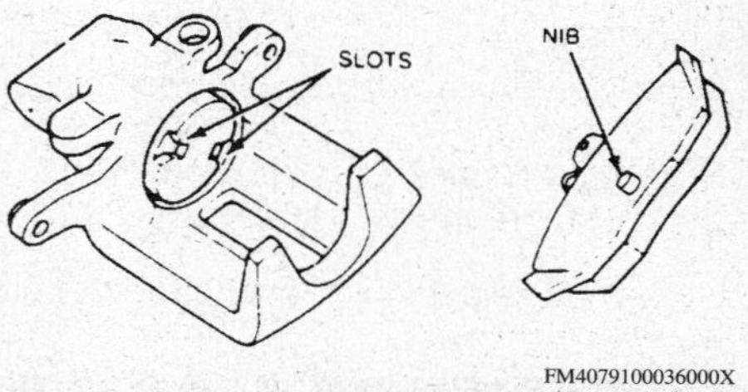

Fig. 9 Caliper piston to brake pad nib positioning. Continental, Cougar, Mark VIII, Mustang, Sable, Taurus & Thunderbird

BRAKE PAD SERVICE

On models with anti-lock brakes, the brake system power booster must be depressurized before disconnecting any hydraulic lines or fittings. Depressurize the system by pumping the brake pedal a minimum of 25 times with the ignition in the Off position.

After performing any service work, obtain a firm brake pedal before moving the vehicle.

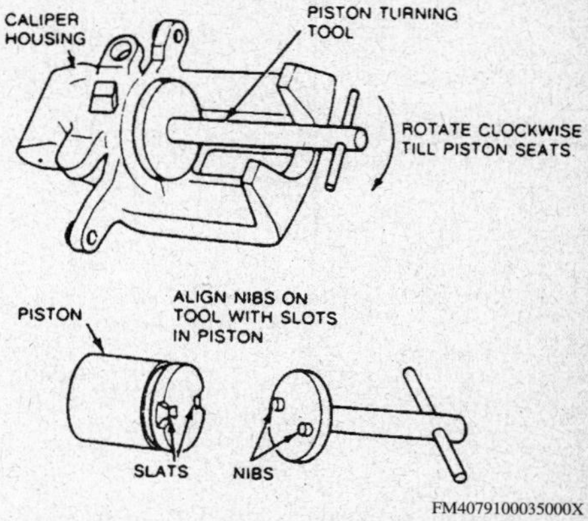

Fig. 8 Caliper piston seating. Continental, Cougar, Mark VIII, Mustang, Sable, Taurus & Thunderbird

CONTINENTAL, COUGAR, MARK VIII, MUSTANG, SABLE, TAURUS & THUNDERBIRD

Removal

On models with air suspension, turn service switch Off before beginning repairs.

1. Raise and support rear of vehicle, then remove wheel and tire assembly.
2. Remove brake hose bracket to shock unit bracket screw.
3. Remove retaining clip, then disconnect parking brake cable from lever.
4. Using open end wrench to hold slider pin in position, remove upper pinch bolt, **Fig. 7.** Loosen, but do not lower, slider pin pinch bolt.
5. Carefully rotate caliper away from rotor, then remover inner and outer brake pads and anti-rattle springs from anchor plate.

Installation

1. Using rear caliper piston adjuster tool No. T87P-2588-A, or equivalent, rotate caliper piston clockwise until fully seated, **Fig. 8.** Position one of two piston slots so it will engage nib on rear of brake pad, **Fig. 9.**
2. Position inner and outer brake pads on anchor plate, then install anti-rattle springs.
3. Carefully rotate caliper assembly over brake rotor. Ensure brake pads and anti-rattle springs are properly positioned, **Fig. 10.**
4. Apply suitable thread sealer and locking compound to pinch bolt threads. Install and tighten pinch bolts to specification, while holding slider pin in position with suitable open end wrench.
5. Position parking brake cable to lever, then install retaining clip.
6. Position brake hose and bracket to shock unit bracket and install attaching bolt.

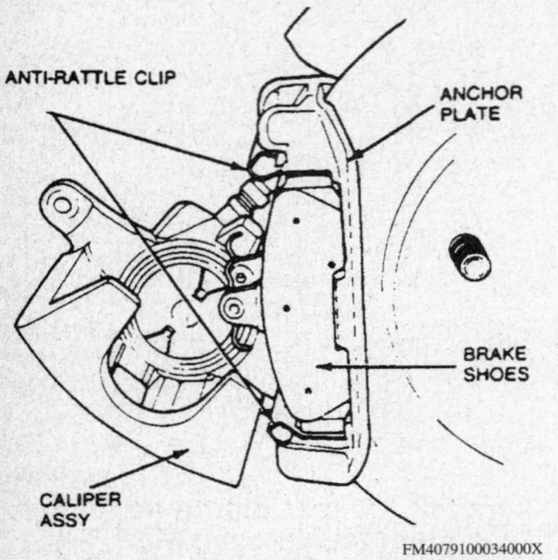

Fig. 10 Anti-rattle clip positioning. Continental, Cougar, Mark VIII, Mustang, Sable, Taurus & Thunderbird

7. Install wheel and tire assembly, then lower vehicle.
8. **On models with air suspension,** turn service switch On.
9. **On all models,** cycle brake pedal several times to position brake pads and caliper piston.

CONTOUR & MYSTIQUE

Removal

1. Remove a sufficient amount of fluid from brake fluid reservoir to prevent an overflow when retracting caliper pistons.
2. Raise and support vehicle.
3. Remove wheel and tire assemblies.
4. Remove guide pin, **Fig. 11.**
5. Remove caliper locating pin cover, then caliper locating pin.
6. Lift caliper from friction pads and anchor frame assembly.

Installation

1. Using rear caliper piston adjuster tool No. T87P-2588-A, or equivalent, rotate caliper piston clockwise until fully seated, **Fig. 8.** Position one piston slot so it will engage nib on rear of brake pad, **Fig. 9.**
2. Ensure all locating pin, guide pin, caliper and anchor frame mounting and sliding surfaces are clean.
3. Place inner and outer pads into position on anchor frame.
4. Place caliper into position on anchor frame.
5. Apply a suitable thread lock compound to mounting threads of locating pin, then apply a suitable brake lubricant to sliding surface of locating pin.
6. Install and tighten locating pin to specifications.
7. Install guide pin, then lock into place with suitable cotter pin.
8. Install wheel and tire assemblies, lower vehicle, then tighten lug nuts to specifications.
9. Apply brake pedal and parking brake several times to adjust rear brakes, adjust parking brake cable if necessary

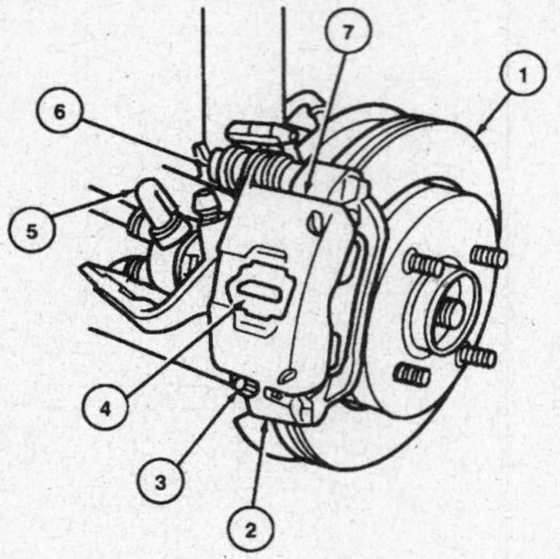

Item		Description
1		Rear Disc Brake Rotor
2		Rear Disc Brake Caliper Anchor Plate
3		Guide Pin
4		Anti-Rattle Clip
5		Parking Brake Lever
6		Disc Brake Caliper Locating Pin
7		Rear Disc Brake Caliper

FM4079300071000X

Fig. 11 Brake pad replacement. Contour & Mystique

as outlined under " Parking Brake Service."

CROWN VICTORIA, GRAND MARQUIS & TOWN CAR

Replacement

1. **On models with air suspension,** turn service switch Off before beginning repairs.
2. **On all models,** remove master cylinder cap and inspect fluid level in reservoir. Remove brake fluid until reservoir is half full.
3. Raise and support vehicle, then remove wheel and tire assembly.
4. Remove caliper as previously described.
5. Remove inner and outer brake linings.
6. Inspect both rotor braking surfaces. Minor scoring or buildup of lining material does not require machining or replacement of the rotor assembly. Hand sand glaze from both rotor braking surfaces using garnet paper 100-A (medium grit) or aluminum oxide 150-J (medium).
7. Suspend caliper inside fender housing with wire or tie straps. Use care not to damage caliper or stretch brake hose.
8. **Use care to prevent damaging plastic piston. Metal or sharp objects should not come in direct contact with piston surface or damage will result.** Using a suitable C-clamp and wood block approximately 2¾ inch x 1 inch and at least ¾ inch thick, seat caliper piston in piston bore. **This procedure must be done to provide clearance for caliper assembly to fit over rotor.**
9. Remove all rust buildup from inside of caliper legs (outer shoe contact area).
10. Install inner shoe and lining assembly

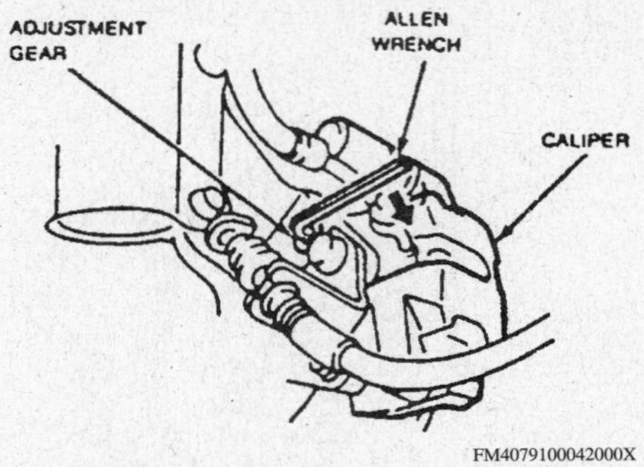

Fig. 12 Rear disc brake adjustment gear location. Escort, Probe, Tracer & ZX2

in caliper piston(s). Do not bend shoe clips during installation in piston or distortion and rattles may occur.
11. Install outer pad in caliper assembly. Ensure clips are properly seated.
12. Install caliper assembly as previously outlined.
13. Install wheels, and lower vehicle.
14. **On models with air suspension,** turn service switch On.

ESCORT, PROBE, TRACER & ZX2

Removal

1. Remove approximately two thirds of brake fluid from master cylinder.
2. Raise and support vehicle, then remove wheel and tire assembly.
3. Loosen parking brake cable housing adjusting nut, then remove cable housing from bracket and parking lever.
4. Turn brake adjuster screw counterclockwise with suitable Allen wrench to pull caliper piston inward, **Fig. 12.** Turn brake adjuster screw until it stops, this will fully retract caliper piston.
5. Remove lower caliper retaining bolt, then pivot caliper to clear brake pads. If necessary, pry caliper outward, **Fig. 13.**
6. If necessary remove caliper, then support caliper with wire from strut assembly.
7. Remove anti-rattle springs from disc pads, then the disc pads, anti-rattle shims and retaining clips. If disc pads and anti-rattle shims are to be used again, they must be installed in their original positions, **Figs. 14 and 15.**
8. If necessary, remove and resurface rotor at this time. **Rotor must be machined while it is bolted to hub. Rotor and hub are mounted as an assembly on lathe to decrease possibility of rotor runout.**

Installation

1. Install disc pad retaining clips, then position anti-rattle shims on disc pads.
2. Position disc pads into caliper anchor bracket.
3. Install anti-rattle springs into disc pads.
4. Lubricate guide pin bushings with high temperature grease part No. D7AZ-19590-A, or equivalent.
5. Install caliper on guide pin if caliper

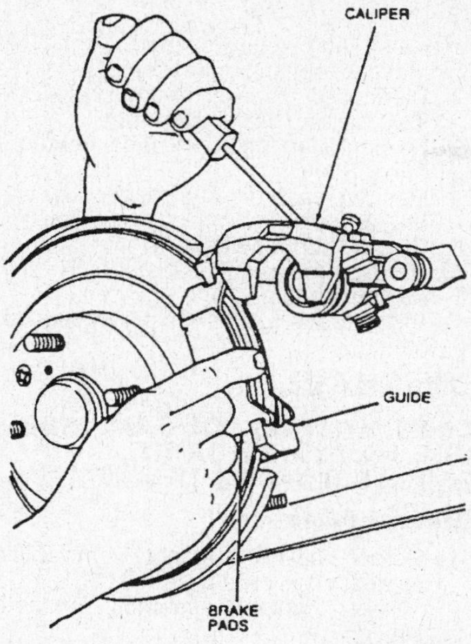

FM4079100043000X

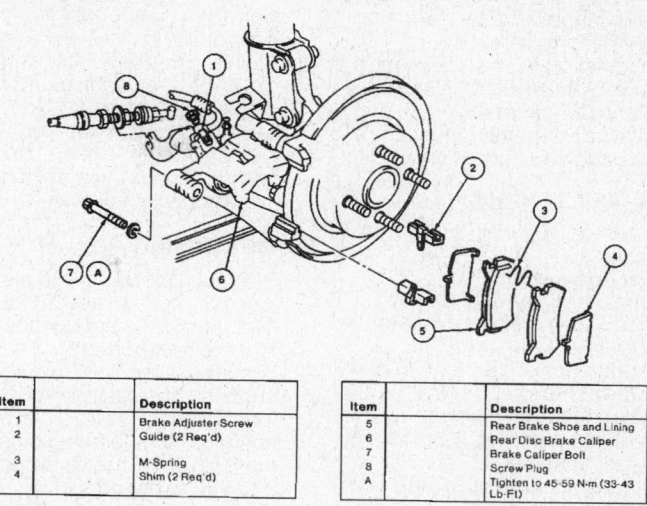

Fig. 13 Rear caliper rotating into position for brake pad replacement. Escort, Probe, Tracer & ZX2

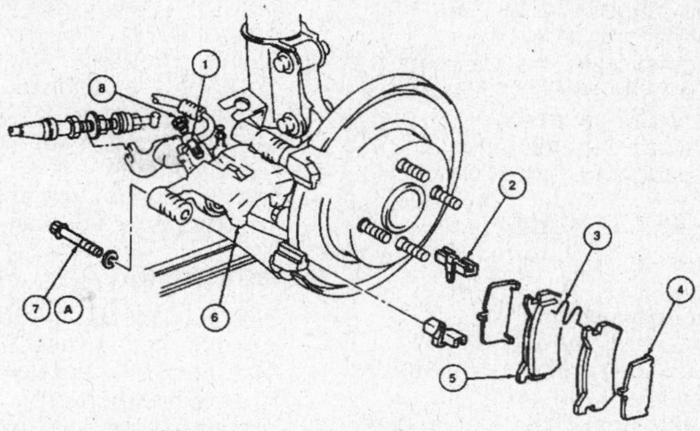

Item		Description
1		Brake Adjuster Screw
2		Guide (2 Req'd)
3		M-Spring
4		Shim (2 Req'd)

Item		Description
5		Rear Brake Shoe and Lining
6		Rear Disc Brake Caliper
7		Brake Caliper Bolt
8		Screw Plug
A		Tighten to 45-59 N·m (33-43 Lb-Ft)

FM4079300067000X

Fig. 14 Rear brake pad replacement. Escort, Tracer & ZX2

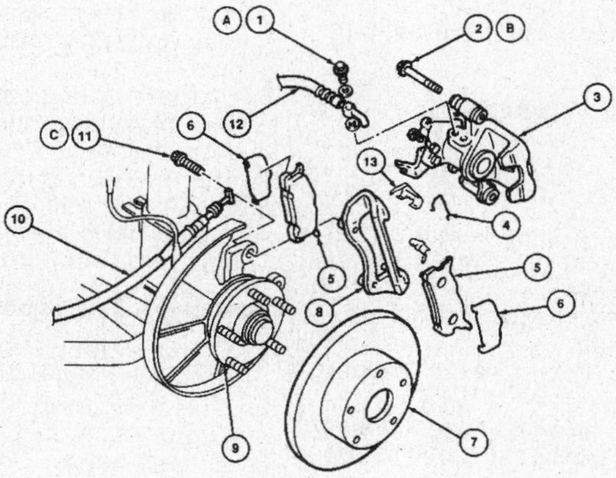

Item		Description
1		Banjo Bolt
2		Brake Caliper Bolt
3		Rear Disc Brake Caliper
4		Anti-Rattle Spring
5		Rear Brake Shoe and Lining
6		Shim
7		Rear Disc Brake Rotor
8		Rear Disc Brake Caliper Anchor Plate
9		Wheel Hub

Item		Description
10		Parking Brake Rear Cable and Conduit
11		Rear Disc Brake Caliper Anchor Plate Bolt (2 Req'd)
12		Rear Wheel Brake Hose
13		Clip
A		Tighten to 23-29 N·m (16-22 Lb-Ft)
B		Tighten to 34-39 N·m (25-29 Lb-Ft)
C		Tighten to 45-67 N·m (33-49 Lb-Ft)

FM4079300069000X

Fig. 15 Rear brake pad replacement. Probe

was removed, then pivot caliper over brake disc pads.

6. Install caliper retaining bolt, then tighten to specifications.
7. Bleed brake system.
8. Position parking brake cable into parking brake lever and bracket.
9. Adjust parking brake cable so there is no clearance between cable end and parking brake lever.
10. Tighten parking brake cable locknut to specification.
11. Install wheel and tire assembly.

LS

1. Raise and support vehicle, then remove wheel and tire assembly.
2. Remove mounting bolts and caliper. **Do not allow caliper to hang from brake hose.**
3. Remove brake pads.
4. Measure brake disc and resurface as required. **Use hub-mount brake lathe if required to machine brake disc.** Install new brake disc if beyond specification.
5. Compress disc brake piston and adjuster into the disc brake caliper using rear caliper piston adjuster tool No. T87P-2588-A, or equivalent.
6. Reverse procedure to install.

CALIPER SERVICE

REPLACEMENT

CONTINENTAL, COUGAR, MARK VIII, MUSTANG, SABLE, TAURUS & THUNDERBIRD

Removal

1. Raise and support rear of vehicle, then remove wheel and tire assembly.
2. Disconnect brake hose from caliper assembly.
3. Remove retaining clip, then disconnect parking brake cable from lever arm.
4. Using open end wrench to hold slider pin in position, remove pinch bolts, **Fig. 7.**
5. Lift caliper assembly from anchor plate, then remove slider pins and boots.

Installation

1. Apply suitable silicone dielectric compound to slider pins and inside of boots.
2. Place slider pins and boots on anchor plate, then position caliper assembly on anchor plate. Ensure brake pads and anti-rattle springs are properly positioned, **Fig. 10.**
3. Apply suitable sealer and thread locking compound to pinch bolt threads, then install pinch bolts.
4. Using open end wrench to hold slider pin in position, tighten pinch bolts to specifications.
5. Attach parking brake cable to lever arm, then install retaining clip.
6. Using replacement washers, connect

brake hose to caliper. Tighten retaining bolt to specifications.
7. Bleed brake system as described under "Brake System Bleed," then install wheel and tire assembly.
8. Cycle brake pedal several times to position brake pads and caliper piston.

CONTOUR & MYSTIQUE

Removal

1. Raise and support vehicle.
2. Remove wheel and tire assemblies.
3. Disconnect and remove parking brake cable from caliper.
4. Remove brake hose banjo bolt, discard sealing washers.
5. Remove guide pin, **Fig. 11.**
6. Remove caliper locating pin cover, then caliper locating pin.
7. Lift caliper from friction pads and anchor frame assembly.

Installation

1. Using rear caliper piston adjuster tool No. T87P-2588-A, or equivalent, position one piston slot so it will engage nib on rear of brake pad, **Fig. 9.**
2. Ensure all locating pin, guide pin, caliper and anchor frame mounting and sliding surfaces are clean and free of residues.
3. Place inner and outer pads into position on anchor frame.
4. Place caliper into position on anchor frame.
5. Apply a suitable thread lock compound to mounting threads of locating pin, then apply a suitable brake lubricant to sliding surface of locating pin.
6. Install and tighten locating pin to specifications.
7. Install guide pin, lock into place with suitable cotter pin.
8. Install parking brake cable.
9. Install brake hose using new sealing washers, then bleed brakes as outlined under "Brake System Bleed."
10. Install wheel and tire assemblies, lower vehicle, then tighten lug nuts to specifications.
11. Apply brake pedal and parking brake several times to adjust rear brakes, adjust parking brake cable if necessary as outlined under " Parking Brake Service."

CROWN VICTORIA, GRAND MARQUIS & TOWN CAR

Visually inspect caliper. If the caliper housing is leaking, it should be replaced. If a seal is leaking, the caliper must be disassembled and new seals and dust boot installed. If a piston is seized in the bore, replace caliper. Care must be taken when removing plastic piston.

Removal

1. **On models with air suspension,** turn service switch Off before beginning repairs.
2. **On all models,** raise and support vehicle, then remove wheel and tire assembly.
3. Remove flexible brake hose retaining bolt from caliper, then plug hose and caliper fitting.
4. Using Tore drive bit tool No. D79P-2100-T40, or equivalent, remove caliper locating pins.
5. Lift caliper off rotor and anchor plate using rotating motion. **Do not pry directly against plastic piston or piston damage will result.**

Installation

1. Retract piston fully into piston bore and position caliper assembly above rotor with anti-rattle spring located on lower adapter support arm.
2. Install caliper over rotor with rotating motion. Ensure inner shoe is properly positioned.
3. Install caliper locating pins. **Caliper locating pins must be inserted and started by hand.**
4. Tighten locating pins to specifications.
5. Remove plugs from caliper fittings, then install flexible brake hose on caliper with new gasket on each side of fitting outlet.
6. Insert retaining bolt through washers and fittings. Tighten bolt to specifications.
7. Bleed brake system as described under "Brake System Bleed."
8. Pump brake pedal to position brake linings before moving vehicle.
9. **On models with air suspension,** turn service switch On.

ESCORT, PROBE, TRACER & ZX2

Removal

1. Remove wheel and tire assembly, then the brake pads as described under "Brake Pad Service."
2. Remove brake flex hose clip from strut assembly bracket.
3. Remove brake flex hose to caliper banjo bolt.
4. Remove and discard two copper washers sealing flex hose banjo fitting.
5. Remove lower caliper bolt.
6. Using cold chisel, remove upper caliper guide pin dust cap to gain access to Allen head guide pin.
7. Using Allen wrench, loosen and remove upper caliper guide pin.
8. Lift caliper off rotor.

Installation

Before installation, remove upper and lower guide pin bushings and lubricate with high temperature grease D7AZ-19590-A, or equivalent.

1. Install brake pads and shims as described under " Brake Pad Service."
2. Position caliper over rotor, then install caliper retaining bolts and tighten to specifications.
3. Install two new copper washers, then the banjo bolt on flex hose banjo fitting.
4. Position flex hose on caliper and install banjo bolt. Tighten bolt to specifications.
5. Bleed brake system as described under "Brake System Bleed," then install wheel and tire assembly.

LS

1. Raise and support vehicle, then remove wheel and tire assembly.
2. Disengage parking brake cable end from parking brake lever arm.
3. Remove parking brake cable and conduit.
4. Remove caliper bolts, caliper flow bolt and caliper.
5. Discard copper washers.
6. Reverse procedure to install using new copper washers.
7. Bleed brake system as previously described.

OVERHAUL

CONTINENTAL, COUGAR, MARK VIII, MUSTANG, SABLE, TAURUS & THUNDERBIRD

Disassemble

1. Remove caliper assembly from vehicle as described previously.
2. Position caliper assembly in soft-jawed vise.
3. Using tool No. T75P-2588-B, or equivalent, rotate caliper piston counterclockwise to remove from caliper bore, **Fig. 8.**
4. Remove piston dust boot and seal from caliper piston bore, **Fig. 1.**
5. Remove snap ring retaining pushrod to caliper. Use care when removing, snap ring and spring cover are under spring load.
6. Remove spring cover, spring, washer, key plate and pushrod and strut pin from caliper.
7. Remove O-ring from pushrod.
8. Remove parking brake lever return spring, then the brake lever stop bolt and pull lever from caliper.

Cleaning & Inspection

1. Clean all metal components with isopropyl alcohol.
2. Use compressed air to clean out passages and grooves.
3. Inspect caliper bore for damage and excessive wear.
4. Inspect caliper piston for pitting, scoring or worn plating and replace as necessary.

Assemble

1. Apply light coating of silicone dielectric compound to parking brake lever bore and parking brake lever seal, then position seal into caliper bore, **Fig. 1.**
2. Apply silicone dielectric compound to parking brake lever shaft, then insert shaft into caliper housing bore.
3. Install O-ring into groove on pushrod, then apply silicone dielectric compound to recesses in pushed.
4. Place strut pin into caliper housing and into recess of parking brake lever shaft.
5. Position pushed into caliper housing bore, ensure strut pin is properly located between shaft recesses and recess at end of pushrod.
6. Position key plate over pushrod, so washer nib is located in hole in caliper housing.

7. Install flat washer, spring and spring cage into caliper bore.
8. Install snap ring using rear caliper spring compressor set No. T87P-2588-P, or equivalent. Ensure snap ring is properly seated in recess.
9. Lubricate replacement piston seal with clean brake fluid, then install seal into caliper bore groove.
10. Lubricate piston and dust boot with clean brake fluid, then install dust boot into caliper bore.
11. Position piston into dust boot, seating dust boot in piston groove.
12. Using rear caliper spring compressor set No. T75P-2588-B, or equivalent, turn piston in clockwise direction until piston is fully seated in caliper bore, **Fig. 8.**
13. Position one of two slots on piston so it will engage nib on rear of disc pad when caliper is installed, **Fig. 9.**
14. Install caliper assembly as described previously.

CONTOUR & MYSTIQUE

Disassemble

1. Remove caliper as outlined previously, then drain fluid from caliper.
2. Using rear caliper piston adjuster tool No. T87P-2588-A, or equivalent, rotate caliper piston counterclockwise to remove piston and adjuster from caliper and adjuster spindle, **Fig. 8.**
3. Remove and discard caliper piston dust seal and piston seal, **Fig. 2.**
4. Remove bleeder screw, then locating pin, pin dust seals and bushings.
5. Cut tie-wrap, then remove cover and dust seals from parking brake actuator.
6. Mount caliper in a suitable vice with soft jaws, positioned to access parking brake actuator.
7. Compress actuator spring, then remove parking brake actuator arm and cam.
8. Remove cup washer and adjuster springs from adjuster spindle, note position of components for later assembly.
9. Remove adjuster spindle and seal from caliper, then remove seal from spindle.

Cleaning & Inspection

1. Clean all metal components with isopropyl alcohol.
2. Use compressed air to clean out passages and grooves.
3. Inspect caliper bore for damage and excessive wear.
4. Inspect parking brake and adjuster components for damage and excessive wear.
5. Inspect caliper piston for pitting, scoring or worn plating and replace as necessary.

Assemble

1. Position caliper housing in a suitable vice with soft jaws.
2. Install a new seal to adjuster spindle, then install spindle into caliper.
3. Install adjuster springs and cup washer onto spindle in order of disassembly.
4. Compress cup washer and spring, then install parking brake actuator cam and arm.
5. Install parking brake actuator dust boot and cover, and secure with a suitable tie-wrap.
6. Replace any removed locating pin, bushings and seals, then lubricate with a suitable brake grease.
7. Install bleeder screw.
8. Install new caliper piston seal into groove, lubricate with clean brake fluid.
9. Install new piston dust seal onto piston, then pack seal with a suitable disc brake slide grease. Lubricate piston surfaces with clean brake fluid.
10. Using rear caliper piston adjuster tool No. T87P-2588-A, or equivalent, rotate caliper piston clockwise to install piston into caliper and onto adjuster spindle.
11. Seat piston dust seal into caliper.
12. Install caliper into vehicle as outlined under " Caliper, Replace."

CROWN VICTORIA, GRAND MARQUIS & TOWN CAR

Visually inspect caliper. If the caliper housing is leaking, it should be replaced. If a seal is leaking, the caliper must be disassembled and new seals and dust boot installed. If a piston is seized in the bore, replace the caliper. Care must be taken when removing the plastic piston.

Disassemble

On models with air suspension, turn service switch Off before beginning repairs.

1. Remove caliper from caliper mounting bracket as described previously.
2. Remove outer pad by slipping down caliper leg until clip is disengaged, then inner pad by pulling it straight out of piston.
3. Place shop towels between the caliper piston and caliper bridge. Do not place fingers between these areas. Two methods can be used to remove the piston from the caliper bore: one method is using low volume air pressure, the other is with hydraulic pressure. If air pressure is not available, slowly apply brake pedal until caliper piston is forced from bore. This method can only be done one caliper at a time. If air pressure is to be used, use following procedure:
   a. Disconnect flexible hose from caliper assembly, then remove caliper from vehicle.
   b. Using air nozzle, apply light air pressure to brake hose inlet until piston is free from caliper. **Do not use shop pressure if it cannot be adjusted down to a safe level (15–30 psi), or personal injury and/or damage to components could result.**
4. Remove seal and dust boot from caliper assembly.

Cleaning & Inspection

Clean all metal parts with Isopropyl alcohol. Dry grooves and passageways with compressed air. Ensure caliper bore and component parts are cleaned thoroughly. Inspect cylinder bore and piston for damage or excessive wear.

Examine piston for surface irregularities or small chips and cracks. Minor surface imperfections are allowable, provided they do not enter the dust boot groove area. Replace piston if damaged.

Assemble

1. Coat new seal and dust boot with clean brake fluid, then install in caliper assembly.
2. Coat piston with clean brake fluid, then place piston in caliper assembly and push firmly into caliper bore.
3. With piston seated, completely seat piston using a suitable C-clamp and a block of wood approximately 2¾ inch x 1 inch x ¾ inch thick.
4. Ensure dust boot is tight in boot groove on piston and in caliper.
5. Install brake pads as described under "Brake Pad Service," then the caliper as described previously.

ESCORT, PROBE, TRACER & ZX2

Disassemble

1. Remove caliper as previously described previously.
2. Open bleeder screw and drain brake fluid from caliper through brake flex hose fitting. After draining fluid, close bleeder screw.
3. Remove caliper guide bushing and dust boots, **Figs. 4 and 5.**
4. Pry retaining spring off dust boot with screwdriver, then remove piston.
5. Remove and discard dust boot.
6. Remove piston seal from caliper and discard. **Use plastic or wooden pick to remove seal. Metal tools can scratch or nick seal groove, resulting in a possible seal leak.**
7. Remove stopper snap ring.
8. Remove adjusting spindle, stopper and connecting link. Separate adjuster spindle and stopper.
9. Remove Oaring from adjuster spindle, then discard Oaring.
10. Remove parking brake return spring, then operating lever nut and lockjaws.
11. Mark relationship between operating lever and shaft, then remove lever from shaft.
12. Remove seal from caliper housing.
13. Remove shaft from caliper housing, then the needle bearings.

Inspection

1. Inspect caliper bore, piston seal groove and piston for cuts, deep scratches and pitting. Piston and piston bore may be lightly polished with crocus cloth. If deep scratches cannot be removed, replace caliper assembly.
2. Caliper seal groove must be free of deep scratches which would prevent seal from operating properly.
3. Inspect upper guide pin and lower guide pin bushing for wear.
4. Inspect bushing dust boots for damage or poor sealing.

Assemble

1. Lubricate needle bearings with orange grease included in caliper rebuilding kit part No. FOJY-2221-A.
2. Align opening in bearing with bore in caliper housing, then install needle bearings.
3. Install operating shaft into caliper housing.
4. Install operating lever. Align marks made during removal.
5. Install lockjaws nut.
6. Install connecting link into operating shaft.
7. Install Oaring onto adjuster spindle, then position stopper onto adjuster spindle so pin will align with caliper housing.
8. Install adjuster spindle in caliper by aligning adjuster spindle pins with caliper holes.
9. Install parking brake return spring.
10. Lubricate new piston seal with brake fluid and install in caliper groove, then lubricate caliper bore and caliper piston with brake fluid.
11. Install dust boot in caliper bore.
12. Install piston in caliper bore by rotating piston until seated.
13. Install upper guide pin dust boot, then the lower guide pin bushing dust boot.
14. Install caliper upper guide pin, then the lower guide pin bushing.
15. Install caliper as described previously.

LS

1. Remove brake caliper as previously described.
2. Drain brake fluid from caliper.
3. Secure brake caliper in suitable vise.
4. Turn brake piston counterclockwise with rear caliper piston adjuster tool No. T87P-2588-A, or equivalent.
5. Remove brake piston from caliper bore.
6. Remove and discard piston dust boot and piston seal from caliper bore.
7. Reverse procedure to assemble, noting the following:
   a. Install new seals and dust boots.
   b. Use new brake fluid when assembling and bleeding the brake system.

ROTOR

REPLACE

CONTINENTAL, COUGAR, MARK VIII, MUSTANG, SABLE, TAURUS & THUNDERBIRD

Removal

1. Remove rear disc brake caliper assembly as described under " Caliper Service." Do not disconnect flexible hose unless caliper requires service. Support caliper with wire or tie strap so flexible hose is not stretched or twisted.
2. Remove rear disc support bracket to wheel knuckle bolts, then the rear disc support bracket and brake shoes and linings.
3. Remove two nuts, then the rotor from rear hub.

Installation

1. If installing new rotor, remove protective coating from rotor with suitable carburetor cleaner.
2. Lubricate rear hub pilot diameter with suitable grease.
3. Install rotors on axle shaft flange, then the two nuts.
4. Install inner and outer brake shoes and linings in rear disc support bracket.
5. Install rear disc support bracket as follows:
   a. Clean rear disc support bracket and bolt threads, then add one drop of suitable sealer to each bolt.
   b. Install caliper/rear support bracket assembly to rear wheel knuckle.
   c. Install bolts, then tighten to specifications.
6. Install inner and outer brake shoes and linings as described under "Brake Pad Service."
7. Install rear disc brake caliper as described under " Caliper Service."

CONTOUR & MYSTIQUE

1. Remove caliper and friction pads as outlines under " Brake Pad Service."
2. Remove two bolts retaining caliper anchor frame, then the frame.
3. Remove rotor to hub retainers, then the rotor.
4. Reverse procedures to install, noting the following:
   a. Ensure rotor and mounting surfaces are clean and free of rust, fluids and Protestants.
   b. Lubricate hub pilot boss with a suitable brake grease.
   c. Tighten fasteners to specification.

ESCORT, TRACER & ZX2

1. Raise and support vehicle, then remove wheel and tire assembly.
2. Remove rear brake shoe and lining as described under " Brake Pad Service."
3. Remove two rear disc brake rotor screws.
4. Using screwdriver, pivot rear disc brake caliper on rear disc support bracket and remove rotor.
5. Reverse procedure to install.

CROWN VICTORIA, GRAND MARQUIS & TOWN CAR

Removal

1. Raise and support vehicle, then remove wheel and tire assembly.
2. Remove rear disc brake caliper assembly as described under "Caliper Service." Do not disconnect flexible hose unless caliper requires service. Position caliper aside and support wire or tie strap to avoid damaging caliper.
3. Remove rotor push nuts, then the disc brake rotor. If additional force is required, use following procedure:
   a. Apply rust penetrant and inhibitor part No. D7AZ-19A501-AA or equivalent to rotor/flange mating surface.
   b. Install three-jaw puller tool No. D80L-1013-A, or equivalent, then remove rear disc brake rotor. **If excessive force is necessary to remove rotor, it should be inspected for lateral runout prior to installation.**

Installation

1. If installing new rotor, remove protective coating with suitable carburetor cleaner. If installing original rotor, ensure rotor braking and mounting surfaces are clean.
2. Install rotor and push nuts.
3. Install caliper as described under "Caliper Service. "
4. Install wheel and tire assembly, then lower vehicle and tighten wheel hub bolt nuts to specifications.
5. Pump brake pedal to position brake shoes and linings before moving vehicle and road testing.

LS

1. Remove support bracket.
2. Remove and discard the pushrods, if equipped.
3. Remove brake disc.
4. Reverse procedure to install.

PROBE

Removal

1. Raise and support vehicle, then remove wheel and tire assembly.
2. Using a chisel, onstage, remove and discard rear axle wheel hub retainer.
3. Remove two anchor plate bolts, then the caliper and caliper anchor plate assembly. Support caliper with wire or tie strap from rear shock absorber. Do not disconnect brake hose from caliper.
4. Remove rotor.

Installation

1. Install rotor on wheel hub.
2. Install caliper and anchor plate assembly. Tighten anchor plate bolts to specifications.
3. Install new rear axle wheel hub retainer. Tighten to specifications.
4. Stake new retainer using cold chisel with rounded cutting edge. **If retainer splits or cracks after staking, it must be replaced with a new one.**
5. Install hub grease cap, then the wheel and tire assembly. Tighten wheel hub bolt nuts to specifications.

PARKING BRAKE SERVICE

PARKING BRAKE LININGS, REPLACE

CROWN VICTORIA, GRAND MARQUIS & TOWN CAR

1997

The parking brake system is a drum type design mounted in the hubs of the rear brake rotors.

1. Raise and support vehicle, then remove wheel and tire assembly.
2. Remove caliper as previously outlined, then the rotor assembly.
3. Drain differential fluid from axle by removing cover.
4. Remove lock bolt from differential pinion shaft, then shaft from differential.
5. Push axle shaft inward to access and remove axle shaft Clock.
6. Remove ABS speed sensor, then axle shaft from axle housing.
7. Disconnect brake cable from lever, then the brake shoe retaining pins and springs.
8. Set adjuster assembly to shortest length.
9. Pull shoe assemblies slightly away from backing plate, then spread to remove adjuster.
10. Lift shoe assemblies over support, then remove shoes and actuating lever as an assembly.
11. Install lower return springs and actuating lever to brake shoe assemblies.
12. Ensure actuator boot is properly positioned through backing plate.
13. Install shoe assemblies by first inserting lever through boot and lowering shoes into position.
14. Install upper return adjuster spring, then the adjuster assembly.
15. Install brake shoe retaining pins and springs.
16. Connect brake cable to lever.
17. Slide axle shaft into axle housing until spines enter side gear. **Ensure care is taken not to damage wheel bearing seal or ABS sensor ring.**
18. Push axle shaft at flange inward, then install Clock at end of shaft.
19. Pull shaft outboard until each Clock enters recess of side gears.
20. Apply stud and bearing mount part No. EOAZ-19554-BA, or equivalent to pinion shaft lock bolt, then install shaft and lock bolt.
21. Tighten pinion lock bolt to specifications.
22. Clean axle housing cover, then apply a 3/16 inch bead of silicone rubber sealant, part No. D6AZ-19562-B, or equivalent.
23. Install axle housing cover, then tighten bolts in diagonal pattern to specifications.
24. Fill axle with lubricant until fluid level is 1/4 inch below bottom of fill hole.
25. Center brake shoes on backing plate, then, using an eight inch micrometer, adjust shoes until a measurement of 7.065–7.072 inch is obtained.
26. Install rotor and caliper as previously described.

1998-2000

1. Remove tire and wheel assembly.
2. Remove brake rotor.
3. Remove brake shoe adjusting screw spring, then the brake shoe adjusting screw.
4. Remove brake shoe hold down springs.
5. Remove parking bake shoe and linings.
6. Reverse procedure to install noting the following:
   a. Lubricate brake shoe contact point before installation with silicone brake caliper grease and dielectric compound part No. D7AZ-19A331-A or equivalent.
   b. Use a brake adjusting gauge to set the rear brake shoe and lining diameter to .020 inch less than the inside diameter of drum portion of rear brake.
   c. Adjust parking brake cable tension.

ADJUSTMENTS

PARKING BRAKE

Cougar, Crown Victoria, Grand Marquis, Thunderbird & Town Car

1. Apply parking brake control fully with 100 lbs. foot pedal effort, then release brake control.
2. Place transmission in Neutral, then raise and support vehicle.
3. With parking brake control in Off position, grasp pensioner around housing. Using an hook tool place end into rounded end of clip between clip and housing. Unlock clip by pulling downward with tool and support pensioner.
4. The pensioner spring will take up cable slack and reload cables, while holding pensioner, lock clip by pushing up on bottom of clip. If clip does not slide up move assembly slightly to align closest groove on adjuster rod to clip.
5. Examine pensioner for remaining cable take up capability. If none is present, inspect all cables, parking brake control and brackets for possible damage or deflection.

Continental & Mark VIII

1. Fully release parking brake control, then raise and support vehicle.
2. Pull parking brake cable adjuster clip downward. The pensioner spring will take up cable slack and reload the cables.
3. Push up on bottom of clip to lock adjustment. If clip does not slide up, move assembly slightly to align closest groove on parking brake cable adjuster rod with clip.
4. Apply 157 lbs. of force to parking brake control, apply force for 20 minutes.
5. Repeat steps 2 and 3, then lower vehicle and verify operation of parking brake.

Contour & Mystique

The parking brake is self-adjusting. After brake system service, operate parking brake several times to adjust system.

Escort, Tracer & ZX2

1. Start engine and shift into Reverse position.
2. With vehicle moving in Reverse, depress brake pedal several times.
3. Shift into Park position, then stop engine.
4. Remove parking brake console.
5. Turn adjusting nut until parking brake lever stroke is five to seven notches when pulled with force of 22 lbs.
6. Install parking brake console.

Probe

Normal parking brake adjustment is made at hand lever between seats.

1. Remove six screws in center console, then the console.
2. Tighten parking brake adjusting nut on lefthand side of parking brake lever. This shortens equalizer cable. Tighten adjusting nut until it takes 7–10 notches to fully set parking brake.

Sable & Taurus

1. Ensure parking brake control is fully released, then raise and support vehicle.
2. Using Rotunda cable tension gauge tool No. 014–R1056, or equivalent, tighten adjusting nut against rear parking brake cable adjuster until cable tension is 34–46 lbs., **Fig. 16.**
3. Apply parking brake control fully, then release.
4. Verify cable tension is still within specification and their is no drag on rear brakes.
5. Lower vehicle and verify operation of parking brake.

Mustang

If any parking brake system component requires service or if the rear axle housing is removed, the cable tension must be released as follows:

1. Place parking brake control in released position.
2. Remove console top panel as follows:
   a. Carefully pry finish panel up from retaining clips, then disconnect electrical connectors.
3. Raise and support vehicle with assistant inside.
4. Have another assistant pull parking brake cable and equalizer rearward approximately 1–2 ½ inches, **Fig. 17,** to rotate self-adjuster reel backward.
5. Insert steel locking through holes in lever and parking brake control assembly to lock ratchet wheel in cable-released position. **Do not remove steel locking until rear cable and conduit are connected to parking brake cable and equalizer. Pin removal releases the tension in the ratchet wheel, causing spring to unwind and release tension. If pin is removed without rear cable and conduit attached, entire assembly must be removed to reset spring tension.**

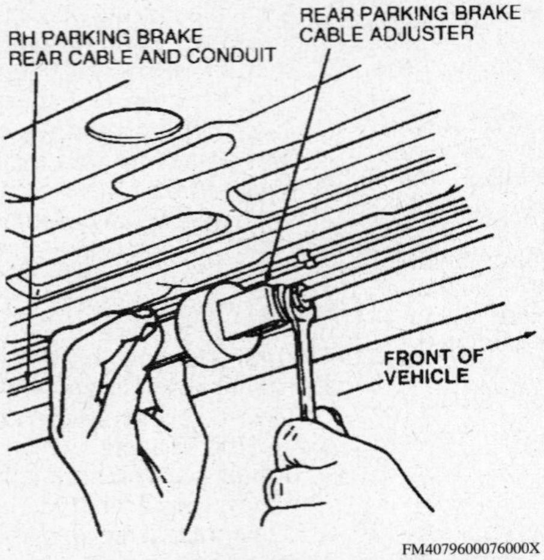

Fig. 16 Park brake adjustment. Sable & Taurus

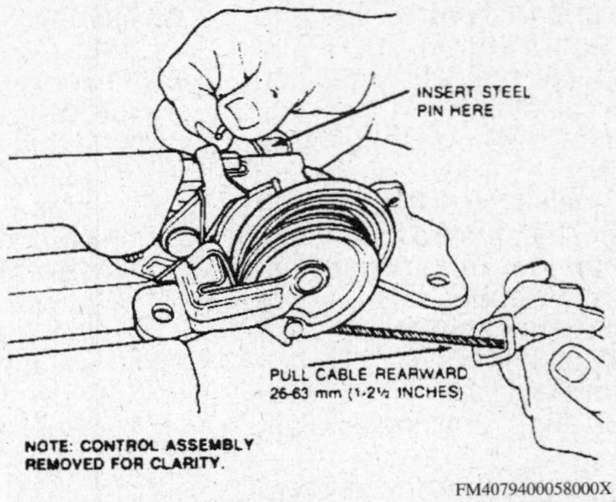

Fig. 17 Self-adjuster reel rotation. Mustang

DISC BRAKE SPECIFICATIONS

ROTOR SPECIFICATIONS

Model	Year	Nominal Thickness Inch	Minimum Refinish Thickness Inch①	Thickness Variation (Parallelism) Inch	Lateral Runout (T.I.R.) Inch	Finish (Micro-Inch)
FRONT						
Aspire	1997	—	④	.0010	.004	—
Continental	1997	1.020	.974	.0003	.002	15–125
	1998–2000	1.024	.974	.0003	.003	16–126
Contour & Mystique	1997–2000	.950	.870	.0006	.006	10–80
Cougar	1997	1.024	.974	.0004	.003	118
	1999–2000	.950	.870	.0006	.003	—
Crown Victoria & Grand Marquis	1997	1.024	.974	.0004	.002	16–126
	1998	1.1	1.01	.00035	.002	—
	1999–2000	1.063	1.01	—	—	—
Escort, Tracer & ZX2	1997–2000	.870	.790	—	.004	—
LS	2000	1.120	—	.0004	.001	—
Mark VIII	1997–98	1.024	.974	.0004	.003	16–126
Mustang	1997–1998③	1.030	.970	.0003	.001	10–80
	1997–1998②	1.100	1.040	.0003	.001	10–80
	1999–2000	1.1000	—	.00035	.002	—
Probe	1997	—	.860	.0010	.004	—
Sable & Taurus	1997–2000	1.020	.974	.0004	.003	15–125
Thunderbird	1997–98	1.024	.974	.0004	.003	⑤
Town Car	1997	1.024	.974	.0004	.002	16–126
	1998	1.10	1.01	.00035	—	—
	1999–2000	1.063	1.01	—	—	—
REAR						
Continental	1997	.550	.500	.0004	.001	16–25
	1998–2000	—	.502	.0004	.004	—
Contour & Mystique	1997–2000	.790	.710	.0006	.006	16–25
Cougar	1997	.709	.657	.00035	.003	16–126
	1999–2000	.790	.710	—	.003	—
Crown Victoria & Grand Marquis	1997	.550	.510	.0004	.005–.009	10–80
	1998	.550	.510	.0004	.002	—
	1999–2000	.550	.510	.0003	—	—
Escort, Tracer & ZX2	1997–2000	.350	.280	—	.002	—

Continued

DISC BRAKE SPECIFICATIONS

ROTOR SPECIFICATIONS—Continued

Model	Year	Nominal Thickness Inch	Minimum Refinish Thickness Inch①	Thickness Variation (Parallelism) Inch	Lateral Runout (T.I.R.) Inch	Finish (Micro-Inch)
REAR						
LS	2000	.740	—	.0004	.001	—
Mark VIII	1997–98	.709	.657	.0004	.002	16–25
Mustang	1997–1999③	.550	.500	.0003	.002	16–25
	1997–1998②	.710	.660	.0003	.002	16–25
	1999–2000	.550	—	.0004	.002	—
Probe	1997	—	.315	—	—	—
Sable & Taurus	1997–2000	.550	.500	.0004	.0004	16–125
Thunderbird	1997	.709	.657	.0004	.002	16–25
Town Car	1997	.550	.510	.0004	.005–.009	10–80
	1998	.550	.510	.0004	.002	10–80
	1999–2000	—	.510	—	.003	—

① — For reference only. Always use specification found on component.
② — Mustang Cobra.
③ — Except Mustang Cobra.
④ — Automatic transvalue, .817 inch; manual transvalue, .660 inch.
⑤ — 15 inch wheels, 10.87, 16 inch wheels, 11.57 inch.

CALIPER SPECIFICATIONS

Model	Year	Caliper Bore Diameter Inch
FRONT		
Aspire	1997	2.000
Continental	1997–2000	2.598
Contour & Mystique	1997–2000	2.360
Cougar	1997	2.598
	1999–2000	—
Crown Victoria & Grand Marquis	1997	2.599
	1998	1.89
	1999–2000	—
Escort, Tracer & ZX2	1997–2000	2.120
LS	2000	②
Mark VIII	1997–98	2.598
Mustang	1997–2000	①
Probe	1997	—
Sable & Taurus	1997–2000	2.598
Thunderbird	1997	2.598
Town Car	1997–98	2.599
	1999–2000	—
REAR		
Continental	1997–2000	1.690
Contour & Mystique	1997–98	1.420
	1999–2000	1.69
Cougar	1997	1.790
	1999–2000	—
Crown Victoria & Grand Marquis	1997–2000	1.890
Escort, Tracer & ZX2	1997–99	1.190
LS	2000	—
Mark VIII	1997–98	1.790
Mustang	1997–2000	1.500
Probe	1997	—
Sable & Taurus	1997–2000	1.690
Thunderbird	1997	1.790
Town Car	1997	1.890
	1998–2000	—

① — Except Mustang Cobra, 2.60 inches; Mustang Cobra w/dual pistons, 1.50 inches.
② — One piston is 1.492 inches; the other is 1.772 inches.

TIGHTENING SPECIFICATIONS

Component	Torque/Ft. Lbs.
CONTINENTAL	
Anchor Plate Bolt	64–88
Brake Adapter Retaining Bolt	44–60
Brake Hose Bracket To Shock	8–11
Brake Hose To Caliper (Banjo) Bolt	30–40
Brake Pin Retaining Bolt	23–26
Disc Brake Caliper Bolts	23–28
Disc Brake Shield	80–106①
Front Caliper Bleed Screw	9–13
Rear Caliper Bleeder Screw	12–18
CONTOUR & MYSTIQUE	
Anchor Plate Bolts	43
Brake Hose To Caliper (Banjo) Bolt	17–21
Caliper Retaining Bolts	20
Disc Brake Shield	60–84①
Wheel Lug	62
1999–2000 COUGAR	
Anchor Plate Bolts	89
Backing Plate Bolts	37
Caliper Brake Hose Union	120①
Caliper Locating Bolt	30
Shield Bolts	17
Rear Brake Cylinder Brake Tube Union	10
Rear Wheel Cylinder Bolts	108①
Rear Hub Nut	214
CROWN VICTORIA, GRAND MARQUIS & TOWN CAR	
Anchor Plate To Spindle	125–169
Brake Hose To Caliper (Banjo) Bolt	30–44
Caliper Bleed Screw	80–106①
Caliper Locating Pin	22–30
Hydraulic Tube Connections	9–11
Rear Caliper Anchor Plate Mounting Nuts	45–55
Wheel Lug	85–104
ESCORT, TRACER & ZX2	
Brake Hose To Caliper (Banjo) Bolt	16–22
Brake Caliper Bolts	33–43
Parking Brake Cable Lockout	14–21
Screw Plug	9–12
Wheel Lug	74–100
LS	
Anchor Plate	76
Axle Shaft	221
Caliper	26
Caliper Bleeder Screw	60–120①
Caliper Flow Bolt	35
Master Cylinder Tube Fitting	11–15
Support Bracket	36
Wheel Lug	100
MARK VIII	
Anchor Plate Bolt	64–88
Axle Nut	188–254
Brake Hose To Caliper (Banjo) Bolt	30–45
Brake Pin Retainer	23–26
Disc Shield Retaining Bolt	22–37
Parking Brake Lever Limiting Bolt	60–84①

Continued

TIGHTENING SPECIFICATIONS—Continued

Component	Torque/Ft. Lbs.
MARK VIII	
Wheel Lug	85–105
MUSTANG	
Anchor Plate Nut	64–88
Brake Hose To Axle Bolt	18–24
Brake Hose To Caliper (Banjo) Bolt	20–30
Brake Pin Retainer	30–35
Disc Brake Adapter Retaining Bolt	30–40
Limiting Bolt	60–84①
Parking Brake Cable To Axle Bracket	23–26
Rear Disc Shield	80–106①
Rear Disc Shield Support Bracket	64–88
Wheel Lug	85–105
PROBE	
Anchor Plate Bolt	33–49
Brake Hose To Caliper (Banjo) Bolt	16–22
Disc Shield Bolt	37–50
Rear Axle Hub Nut	130–174
Wheel Lug	65–87
SABLE & TAURUS	
Anchor Plate Bolt	64–88
Axle Nut	188–254
Brake Adapter Retaining Bolt	44–60
Brake Hose Bracket To Shock	8–11
Brake Hose To Caliper (Banjo) Bolt	30–40
Brake Pin Retaining Bolt	23–26
Disc Brake Shield	72–108①
Hub Nut	188–254
Park Brake Lever Limit Bolt	60–84①
Rear Anti-Lock Sensor	36–60①
THUNDERBIRD & 1997 COUGAR	
Anchor Frame Bolts	64–88
Axle Nut	188–254
Brake Hose To Caliper (Banjo) Bolt	30–45
Brake Pin Retainer	23–26
Disc Shield Retaining Bolts	22–37
Hub Nut	188–254
Parking Brake Lever Limiting Bolt	60–84①
Parking Brake Retainer	16–22

① — Inch lbs.

DRUM BRAKES

TABLE OF CONTENTS

Application Chart

Model	Year	Type
Aspire	1997	4
Contour	1997–2000	3
Cougar	1997	5
	1999–2000	3
Escort	1997–2000	2
Mystique	1997–2000	3
Probe	1997	1
Sable	1997–99	3
Taurus	1997–99	3
Thunderbird	1997	5
Tracer	1997–99	2
ZX2	1998–2000	2

Type 1

INDEX

PRECAUTIONS

AIR BAG SYSTEMS

Refer to "Air Bag System Precautions" in the front of this manual for system disarming and arming procedures.

BATTERY GROUND CABLE

Prior to service, disconnect battery ground cable and isolate as required.

SAFETY PRECAUTIONS

When working on or around brake assemblies, care must be taken to prevent breathing asbestos dust. Many manufacturers incorporate asbestos fibers in the production of brake linings. During routine service operations the amount of asbestos dust from brake lining wear is at a low level, due to a chemical breakdown during use. **Do not sand or grind brake linings unless suitable local exhaust ventilation equipment is used to prevent excessive asbestos exposure.**

1. Wear suitable respirator approved for asbestos dust use during all repair procedures.
2. When cleaning brake dust from brake parts, use vacuum cleaner with highly efficient filter system. If suitable vacuum cleaner is not available, use water-soaked rag. **Do not use compressed air or dry brush to clean brake parts.**
3. Keep work area clean, using same equipment as for cleaning brake parts.
4. Properly dispose of rags and vacuum cleaner bags by placing them in plastic bags.
5. **Never use gasoline, kerosene, alcohol, motor oil, transmission fluid, or any fluid containing mineral oil to clean brake system components. These fluids will damage rubber caps and seals. If system contamination is suspected, inspect brake fluid in reservoir for dirt, discoloration, or separation (breakdown) of brake fluid into distinct layers. Drain and flush hydraulic system with clean brake fluid if contamination is suspected.**

INSPECTION

1. Inspect components for damage and unusual wear. Replace as necessary.
2. Inspect wheel cylinders. Boots which are torn, cut, or heat damaged indicate need for wheel cylinder replacement. Fluid spilling from boot center hole or wetness around wheel cylinder ends indicates cup leakage and need for wheel cylinder replacement. **A small amount of fluid is always present and is considered normal, acting as lubricant for cylinder pistons.**
3. Inspect backing plate for evidence of seal leakage. If leakage exists, refer to "Probe" chassis chapters for axle seal replacement procedure.

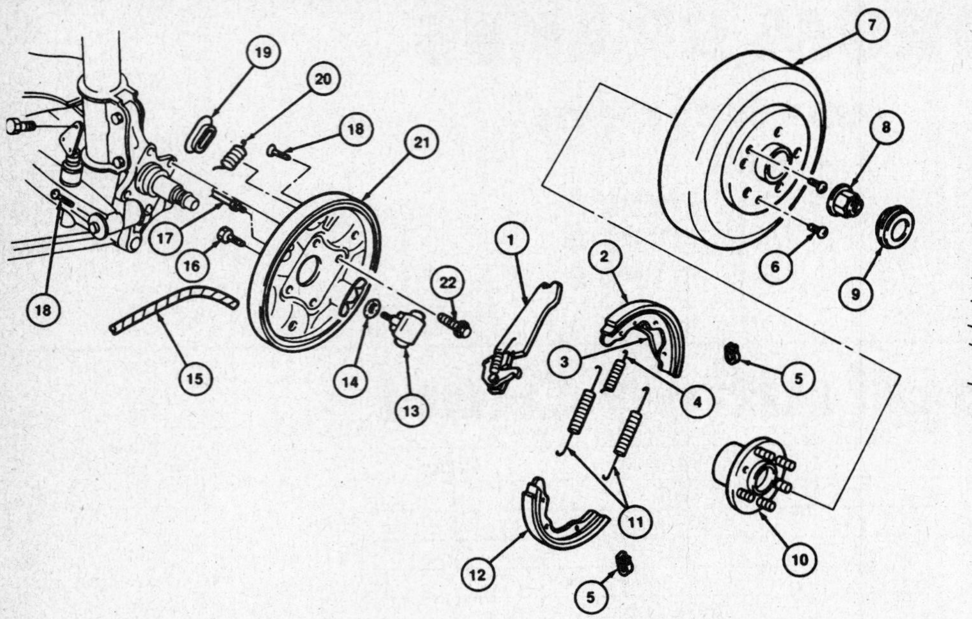

Item	Description
1	Rear Brake Strut and Quadrant
2	Trailing Brake Shoe and Lining
3	Parking Brake Lever
4	Parking Brake Return Spring
5	Brake Shoe Hold-Down Spring
6	Brake Drum Screw (2 Req'd)
7	Brake Drum
8	Rear Axle Wheel Hub Retainer
9	Hub Grease Cap
10	Wheel Hub
11	Brake Shoe Retracting Spring, Upper
	Brake Shoe Retracting Spring, Lower
12	Leading Brake Shoe and Lining

Item	Description
13	Rear Wheel Cylinder
14	Wheel Cylinder Gasket
15	Parking Brake Rear Cable and Conduit
16	Rear Wheel Cylinder Bolt (2 Req'd)
17	Brake Tube
18	Brake Shoe Hold-Down Spring Pin
19	Brake Adjusting Hole Cover
20	Right Hand Anti-Rattle Spring
21	Rear Brake Backing Plate
22	Brake Backing Plate Bolt (2 Req'd)

FM4089400018000X

Fig. 1 Exploded view of rear drum brake

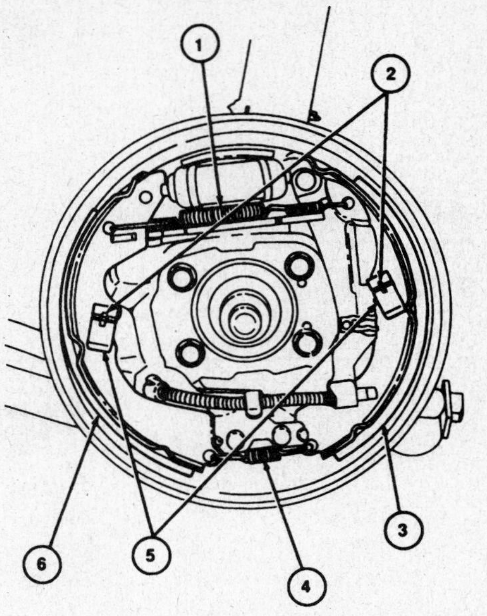

Item	Description
1	Brake Shoe Retracting Spring, Upper
2	Brake Shoe Hold-Down Spring Pin
3	Trailing Brake Shoe and Lining
4	Brake Shoe Retracting Spring, Lower
5	Brake Shoe Hold-Down Spring
6	Leading Brake Shoe and Lining

FM4089400019000X

Fig. 2 Brake shoe hold down pin removal

4. Inspect backing plate bolts and ensure they are tight.
5. Inspect adjuster screw operation. If satisfactory, lightly lubricate adjusting screw and washer with suitable brake lubricant. If operation is unsatisfactory, replace.
6. Using fine emery cloth or other suitable abrasive, clean rust and dirt from shoe contact surfaces on backing plate.

BRAKE SERVICE

REMOVAL

1. Raise and support vehicle, then remove wheel and tire assembly.
2. Remove grease hub cap.
3. Remove brake drum screws, then the drum, **Fig. 1.**
4. Remove wheel hub as described in "Probe" chassis section.
5. Remove brake shoe hold-down springs, **Fig. 2,** using screwdriver to push in and twist spring to disengage it from pin.
6. Remove parking brake rear cable and conduit from parking brake cable anchor plate. Remove brake shoe retracting spring.
7. Remove trailing brake shoe and lining from rear brake strut and quadrant, then the leading brake shoe and lining.

INSTALLATION

1. If brake shoes and linings are being reused, inspect shoes and linings and measure thickness. Ensure thickness meets specifications.
2. Clean rear brake backing plate with suitable vacuum, then lubricate brake shoe and lining contact points with high temperature lubricant, such as Motorcraft WA-10. Also lubricate rear brake backing plate where brake shoes and linings ride.
3. Ensure rear wheel cylinder bolts are tightened to specifications.
4. If new brake shoes and linings are being installed, brake drums should be resurfaced to remove glazing, ensuring an equal friction surface from side-to-side and correcting out-of-round and bell conditions.
5. Position trailing brake shoe and lining in rear brake strut and quadrant, then install brake shoe hold down spring pin.
6. Position leading brake shoe and lining against rear brake strut and quadrant and install brake shoe hold down spring pin.
7. Install upper and lower brake shoe retracting springs.
8. Measure brake drum with brake adjustment gauge tool No. D81L-1103-A, or equivalent, **Fig. 3.**
9. Adjust shoes and linings to same measurement of drum by inserting screwdriver into knurled quadrant of rear brake strut and quadrant.
10. Install wheel hub as described in "Probe" chassis section.
11. Install drum, then the drum screws. Tighten screws to specifications.
12. Install grease cap, then wheel and tire assembly.

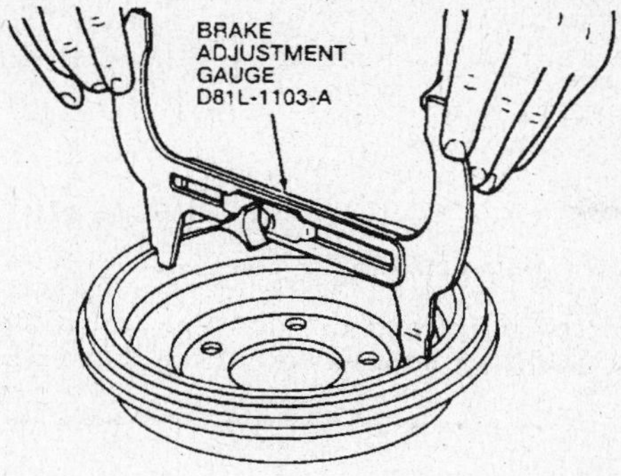

Fig. 3 Brake drum measurement

ADJUSTMENTS

PARKING BRAKE

1. Start engine and press brake pedal several times while vehicle is moving in Reverse, then stop engine.
2. Remove armrest base to armrest compartment screws.
3. Remove armrest base, then armrest compartment to ashtray bracket screws.
4. Remove armrest compartment, then unsnap coin tray from console finish panel.
5. Remove console panel nuts from console panel ashtray bracket.
6. **On models with manual transaxle,** unscrew shift control selector lever knob.
7. **On models with automatic transaxle,** remove console top panel.
8. **On all models,** engage parking brake, then gently pull up on console finish panel to separate it from console panel.
9. Remove instrument panel ashtray bulb and socket from console finish panel.
10. Disconnect cigar lighter knob and element electrical connectors, then remove console front finish panel screws.
11. Remove console panel screws, then the panel from vehicle.
12. Remove three parking brake lever boot screws, then the parking brake lever boot.
13. Turn parking brake control adjusting nut at front of parking brake control, **Fig. 4,** to shorten front parking brake control cable and conduit. Tighten adjusting nut until it takes 5–7 notches to fully set parking brake.
14. Turn ignition On, then pull parking brake control one notch to ensure parking brake warning lamp lights.
15. Ensure rear brakes do not drag.
16. To install console panel, reverse removal procedure.

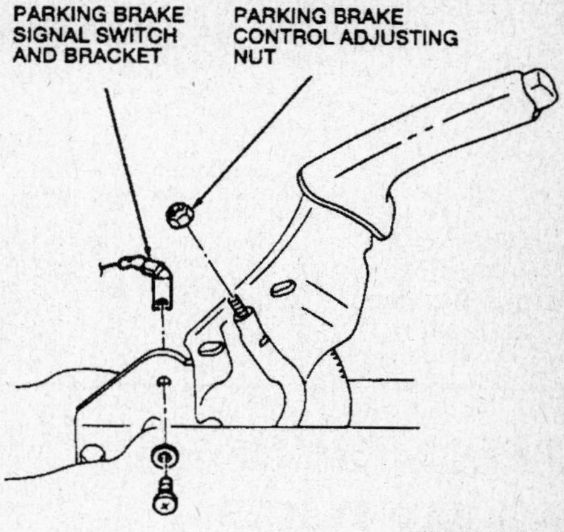

Fig. 4 Parking brake control adjustment

DRUM BRAKE SPECIFICATIONS

Year	Brake Drum		
	Inside Dia., Inch	Bore Limit (Max.), Inch①	Max. Runout, Inch
1997	9.000	9.060	.005

① — For reference only. Always use specifications found on component.

TIGHTENING SPECIFICATIONS

Year	Component	Torque/Ft. Lbs.
1997	Axle Nut	73–131
	Brake Backing Plate Bolts	31–47
	Brake Drum Screws	84–120①
	Hub Nut	73–131
	Wheel Cylinder Bolts	84–120①
	Wheel Lug Nuts	65–87

① — Inch lbs.

Type 2

INDEX

PRECAUTIONS

AIR BAG SYSTEMS

Refer to "Air Bag System Precautions" in the front of this manual for system disarming and arming procedures.

BATTERY GROUND CABLE

Prior to service, disconnect battery ground cable and isolate as required.

SAFETY PRECAUTIONS

When working on or around brake assemblies, care must be taken to prevent breathing asbestos dust. Many manufacturers incorporate asbestos fibers in the production of brake linings. During routine service operations, the amount of asbestos dust from brake lining wear is at a low level due to a chemical breakdown during use. **Do not sand or grind brake linings unless suitable local exhaust ventilation equipment is used to prevent excessive asbestos exposure.**

1. Wear suitable respirator approved for asbestos dust use during all repair procedures.
2. When cleaning brake dust from brake parts, use vacuum cleaner with highly efficient filter system. If suitable vacuum cleaner is not available, use water-soaked rag. **Do not use compressed air or dry brush to clean brake parts.**
3. Keep work area clean, using same equipment as for cleaning brake parts.
4. Properly dispose of rags and vacuum cleaner bags by placing them in plastic bags.
5. **Never use gasoline, kerosene, alcohol, motor oil, transmission fluid, or any fluid containing mineral oil to clean brake system components. These fluids will damage rubber caps and seals. If system contamination is suspected, inspect brake fluid in reservoir for dirt, discoloration, or separation (breakdown) of brake fluid into distinct layers. Drain and flush hydraulic system with clean brake fluid if contamination is suspected.**

INSPECTION

1. Inspect components for damage and unusual wear. Replace as necessary.
2. Inspect wheel cylinders. Boots which are torn, cut, or heat damaged indicate need for wheel cylinder replacement. Fluid spilling from boot center hole, or wetness around wheel cylinder ends indicates cup leakage and need for wheel cylinder replacement. **A small amount of fluid is always present and is considered normal, acting as lubricant for cylinder pistons.**
3. Inspect backing plate for evidence of seal leakage. If leakage exists, refer to "Escort, Tracer & ZX2" chassis chapters for axle seal replacement procedure.
4. Inspect backing plate bolts and ensure tightness.
5. Inspect adjuster screw operation. If satisfactory, lightly lubricate adjusting screw and washer with suitable brake lubricant. If operation is unsatisfactory, replace.
6. Using fine emery cloth or other suitable abrasive, clean rust and dirt from shoe contact surfaces on backing plate.

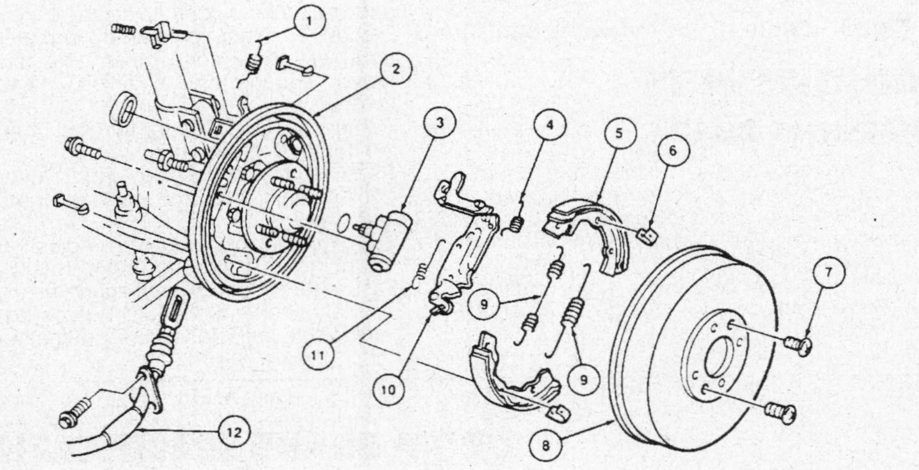

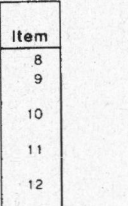

Item	Description
1	Parking Brake Link Spring
2	Brake Backing Plate
3	Rear Wheel Cylinder
4	Right Hand Anti-Rattle Spring
5	Rear Brake Shoe and Lining
6	Brake Shoe Hold Down Spring
7	Screw

Item	Description
8	Brake Drum
9	Brake Shoe Retracting Spring
10	Parking Brake Actuating Lever
11	Rear Brake Adjusting Quadrant Spring
12	Parking Brake Rear Cable and Conduit

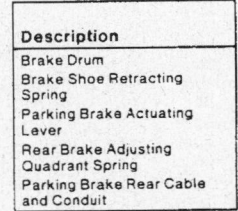

FM4089400016000X

Fig. 1 Exploded view of drum brake

BRAKE SERVICE

REMOVAL

1. Raise and support vehicle, then remove wheel and tire assembly.
2. Remove brake drum screws, then the brake drum.
3. Remove wheel hub as described in "Escort, Tracer & ZX2" chassis chapter.
4. Remove brake shoe retracting springs, **Fig. 1,** using screwdriver to push in and twist spring to disengage it from pin.
5. Remove righthand anti-rattle spring.
6. Push and turn brake shoe hold down springs, then remove them.
7. Remove primary rear shoe and lining

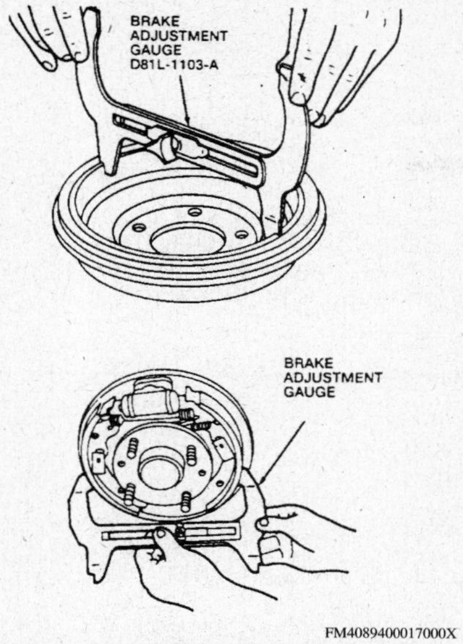

Fig. 2 Drum brake & shoe lining measurements

from backing plate, then the secondary shoe and lining.

INSTALLATION

1. If rear shoes and linings are to be used again, inspect them to ensure they meet specifications.
2. Clean backing plate with suitable brake vacuum, then lubricate shoe and lining contact points and areas where shoes and linings ride with suitable lubricant, such as Motorcraft WA-10.
3. Tighten wheel cylinder bolts to specifications.
4. If new shoes and linings are being installed, resurface drums to remove glazing and ensure an equal friction surface from side to side. Resurfacing will also correct out-of-round and bell conditions.
5. Position secondary rear shoe and lining on backing plate, then install one shoe hold-down spring.
6. Position primary rear shoe and lining on backing plate, then install other shoe hold-down spring.
7. Install righthand anti-rattle spring, then the upper and lower shoe retracting springs.
8. Measure drum, shoes and linings with brake adjustment gauge tool No. D81L-1103-A, or equivalent, **Fig. 2.**
9. Inset screwdriver into knurled quadrant of rear quad operating lever stopper, **Fig. 1,** then adjust shoes and linings to same measurement of drum.
10. Install wheel hub as described in "Escort, Tracer & ZX2" chassis section.
11. Install drum, then the drum screws. Tighten screws to specifications.
12. Install wheel and tire assembly.

ADJUSTMENTS

PARKING BRAKE

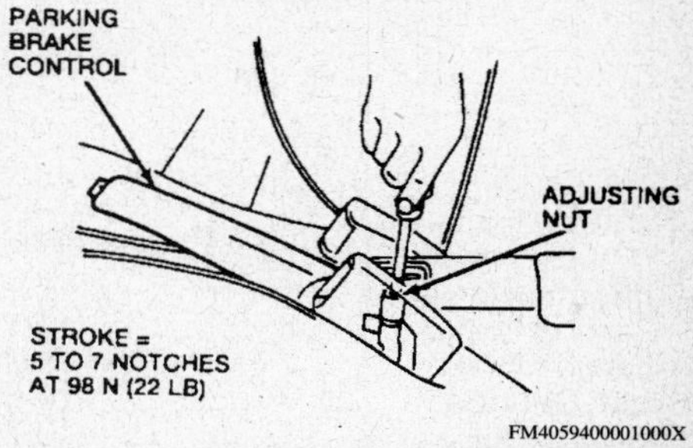

Fig. 3 Parking brake adjustment

1. Start engine and move shift control selector lever into Reverse position.
2. With vehicle moving in Reverse, press and release brake pedal several times.
3. Move shift control selector lever into Park position, then stop engine.
4. Position both front seats to rearmost position, then remove front console screws.
5. Recline both front seats, then remove rear console screws.
6. Unbuckle safety belts, then, with parking brake control engaged, remove console.
7. Turn adjusting nut, **Fig. 3,** until control stroke is five to seven notches when pulled with 22 lbs. of force.
8. Feed safety belt ends through proper holes in console, then install console over parking brake control.
9. Install console screws, then return both seats to original positions.

DRUM BRAKE SPECIFICATIONS

Year	Brake Drum		
	Inside Dia., Inch	Bore Limit (Max.), Inch①	Max. Runout, Inch
1997	7.87	7.91	.005①
1998–2000	9.00	9.04	—

① — For reference only. Always use specifications found on component.

TIGHTENING SPECIFICATIONS

Year	Component	Torque/ Ft. Lbs.
1997–2000	Axle Nut	130–174
	Backing Plate	33–43
	Bleeder Screws	53–77①
	Brake Drum Screws	84–120①
	Cable Bracket to Backing Plate	14–19
	Hose	12–16
	Hub Nut	130–174
	Rear Wheel Cylinder	84–108①
	Wheel Lug	②

① — Inch lbs.
② — 1997, 65–87 ft. lbs.; 1998–2000, 74–100 ft. lbs.

Type 3

INDEX

PRECAUTIONS

AIR BAG SYSTEMS

Refer to "Air Bag System Precautions" in the front of this manual for system disarming and arming procedures.

BATTERY GROUND CABLE

Prior to service, disconnect battery ground cable and isolate as required.

SAFETY PRECAUTIONS

When working on or around brake assemblies, care must be taken to prevent breathing asbestos dust, as many manufacturers incorporate asbestos fibers in the production of brake linings. During routine service operations the amount of asbestos dust from brake lining wear is at a low level, due to a chemical breakdown during use. A few precautions will minimize exposure. **Do not sand or grind brake linings unless suitable local exhaust ventilation equipment is used to prevent excessive asbestos exposure.**

1. Wear suitable respirator approved for asbestos dust use during all repair procedures.
2. When cleaning brake dust from brake parts, use vacuum cleaner with highly efficient filter system. If suitable vacuum cleaner is not available, use water-soaked rag. **Do not use compressed air or dry brush to clean brake parts.**
3. Keep work area clean, using same equipment as for cleaning brake parts.
4. Properly dispose of rags and vacuum cleaner bags by placing them in plastic bags.
5. **Never use gasoline, kerosene, alcohol, motor oil, transmission fluid, or any fluid containing mineral oil to clean brake system components. These fluids will damage rubber caps and seals. If system contamination is suspected, inspect brake fluid in reservoir for dirt, discoloration, or separation (breakdown) of brake fluid into distinct layers. Drain and flush hydraulic system with clean brake fluid if contamination is suspected.**

INSPECTION

1. Inspect components for damage and unusual wear. Replace as necessary.
2. Inspect wheel cylinders. Boots which are torn, cut, or heat damaged indicate need for wheel cylinder replacement. Fluid spilling from boot center hole, or wetness around wheel cylinder ends indicates cup leakage and need for wheel cylinder replacement. **A small amount of fluid is always present and is considered normal, acting as lubricant for cylinder pistons.**
3. Inspect backing plate for evidence of seal leakage. If leakage exists, refer to "Contour, Mystique & 1999–2000 Cougar" of "Sable & Taurus" chassis chapters for axle seal replacement procedure.
4. Inspect backing plate bolts and ensure they are tight.
5. Inspect adjuster screw operation. If satisfactory, lightly lubricate adjusting screw and washer with suitable brake lubricant. If operation is unsatisfactory, replace.
6. Using fine emery cloth or other suitable abrasive, clean rust and dirt from shoe contact surfaces on backing plate.

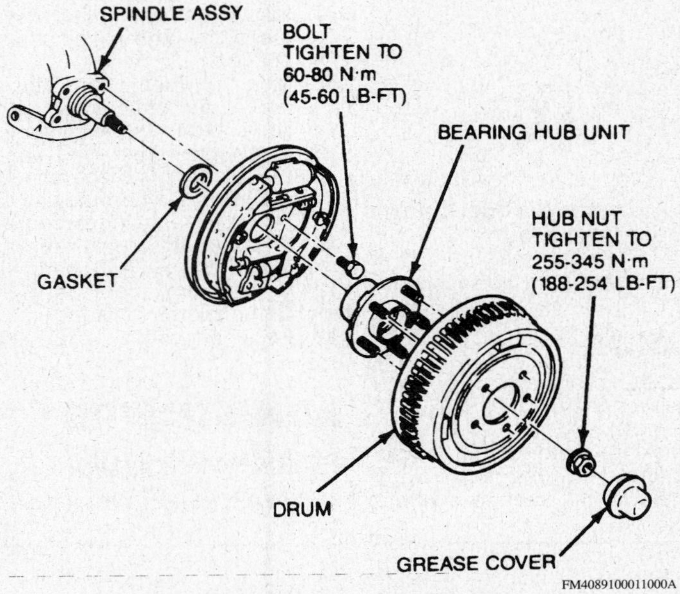

Fig. 1 Drum & hub assembly

BRAKE SERVICE

REMOVAL

1. Raise and support rear of vehicle, then remove tire and wheel assembly.
2. Remove drum retainer push nuts, then slide drum off hub, **Fig. 1.**
3. If drum is stuck to hub, use suitable hammer to lightly tap on face of drum in flange mounting area to release.
4. If brake lining is dragging on brake drum, back off brake adjustment by holding adjustment lever off star wheel, then loosen star wheel, **Fig. 2.**
5. Remove hub nut cover and discard.
6. Remove hub nut and discard, then slide hub and one-piece bearing assembly off spindle.
7. Install suitable wheel cylinder piston retainer tool.
8. Using suitable tool, remove shoe hold-down springs and pins.
9. Lift shoes, springs and adjuster assembly off backing plate and wheel cylinder assembly, being careful not to bend adjusting lever.
10. Remove parking brake cable from parking brake lever.
11. Remove retracting springs from lower shoe attachments and upper shoe to adjusting lever attachment points, then separate shoes and disengage adjuster mechanism.
12. Clean dirt from drum, backing plate and all other components. **Do not use compressed air or dry brush to clean brake parts. Many brake parts**

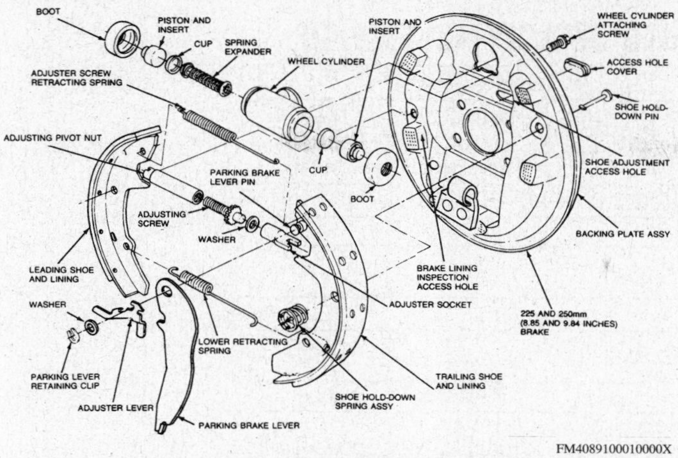

Fig. 2 Drum brake assembly

contain asbestos fibers which, if inhaled, can cause serious industry. Clean brake parts with water-soaked rag or suitable vacuum cleaner to minimize airborne dust.

INSTALLATION

1. Lightly lubricate backing plate shoe contact surfaces with suitable brake lubrication.
2. Apply thin uniform coat of suitable brake lubricant to adjuster screw threads and socket end of adjusting screw.
3. Install stainless steel washer over socket end of adjusting screw and install socket, then turn adjusting screw fully into adjusting pivot nut and back off ½ turn.
4. Assemble parking brake lever to trailing shoe and lining assembly by installing spring washer and a new horseshoe retaining clip. Crimp clip until it securely retains lever to shoe.
5. Attach parking brake cable to parking brake lever.
6. Attach lower shoe retracting spring to leading and trailing shoe assemblies and install on backing plate. It will be necessary to stretch retracting spring as shoes are installed downward over anchor plate to inside of shoe retaining plate.
7. Install adjuster screw assembly between leading shoe slot and the slot in trailing shoe and parking brake lever. Adjuster socket end slot must fit into the trailing shoe and parking brake lever. **Adjuster socket blade is marked "R" or "L" for righthand and lefthand brake assemblies. The R or L adjuster blade must be installed with letter R or L in upright position (facing wheel cylinder) on proper side to ensure deeper of two slots in adjuster sockets fits into parking brake lever.**
8. Assemble adjuster lever in groove located in parking brake lever pin and into slot of adjuster socket that fits into trailing shoe web.
9. Attach upper retracting spring to leading shoe slot and, using suitable tool, stretch other end of spring into notch on adjuster lever. **If adjuster lever does not contact star wheel after installing spring, adjuster socket may be improperly installed.**
10. Install hub to spindle, then tighten new hub nut to specifications.
11. Install new hub nut cover.
12. Install brake drum to hub, then install drum retainer push nuts.
13. Install tire and wheel assembly.
14. If any hydraulic connections have been opened, bleed system as described in "Hydraulic Brake System."
15. Adjust parking brake as described under "Adjustments."
16. Inspect all hydraulic lines and connections for leakage, repairing as necessary.
17. Inspect master cylinder fluid level and replenish as necessary.
18. Inspect brake pedal for proper feel and return.
19. Lower vehicle and road test. **Do not severely apply brakes immediately after installation of new linings or permanent damage may occur to linings, and/or drums may become scored. Brakes must be used moderately during first several hundred miles of operation to ensure proper burnishing of linings.**

ADJUSTMENTS

SERVICE BRAKES

Although the brakes are self-adjusting, an initial adjustment will be required after a brake repair. This adjustment is performed as follows:

1. Determine inside diameter of brake drum surface using brake shoe gauge tool No. D81L-1103-A, or equivalent. Adjust brake shoe diameter to fit gauge. Hold automatic adjusting lever out of engagement while rotating adjusting screw and ensure screw rotates freely.
2. Install brake drum, **Fig. 1,** then the tire and wheel assembly.

PARKING BRAKE

1. Ensure parking brake lever is released.
2. With transmission in Neutral, raise and support vehicle.
3. Tighten parking brake nut against brake equalizer until rear brakes drag, then loosen nut until rear brakes are fully released.
4. Lower vehicle, then inspect parking brake operation.

DRUM BRAKE SPECIFICATIONS

Year	Model	Brake Drum		
		Inside Dia., Inch	Bore Limit (Max.), Inch①	Max. Runout, Inch
CONTOUR & MYSTIQUE & 1999–2000 COUGAR				
1997	—	—	8.04	—
1998–2000	—	9.00	9.04	—
SABLE & TAURUS				
1997–99	Except Wagon	8.85	8.92	.005
	Wagon	9.84	9.90	.005

① — For reference only. Always use specifications found on component.

TIGHTENING SPECIFICATIONS

Year	Component	Torque/ Ft. Lbs.
CONTOUR & MYSTIQUE & 1999–2000 COUGAR		
1997–2000	ABS Sensor	120①
	Axle Nut	214
	Backing Plate Bolts	37
	Brake Hose	120①
	Hub Nut	214
	Wheel Cylinder Bolts	108①
	Wheel Lug Nuts	94
SABLE & TAURUS		
1997–99	ABS Sensor	72–96①
	Axle Nut	188–254
	Brake Backing Plate To Spindle Bolt	45–59
	Brake Hose	12–14
	Hub Nut	188–254
	Parking Brake Stop Bolt	96–108①
	Wheel Cylinder Attaching Bolts	9–13
	Wheel Lug Nuts	85–104

① — Inch lbs.

Type 4

INDEX

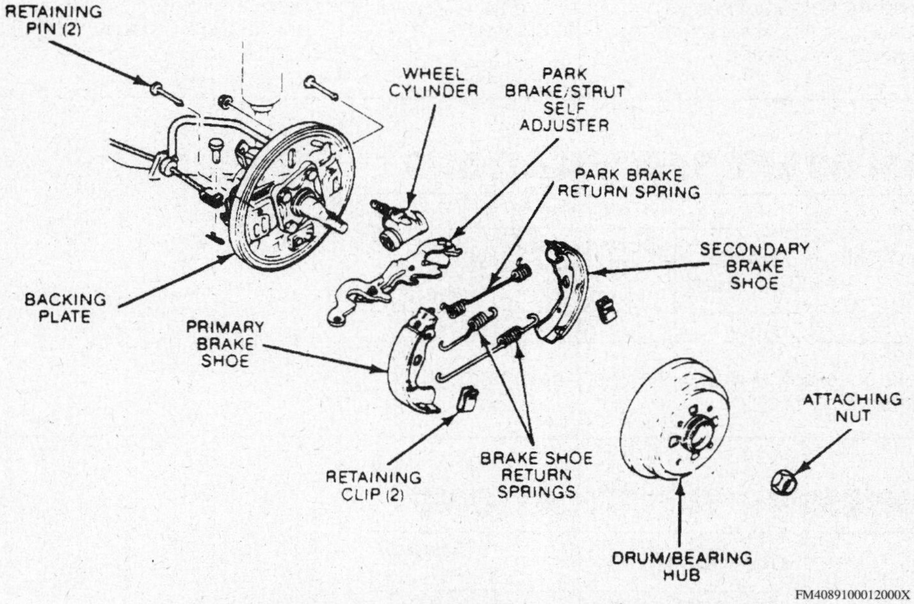

Fig. 1 Exploded view of drum brake assembly

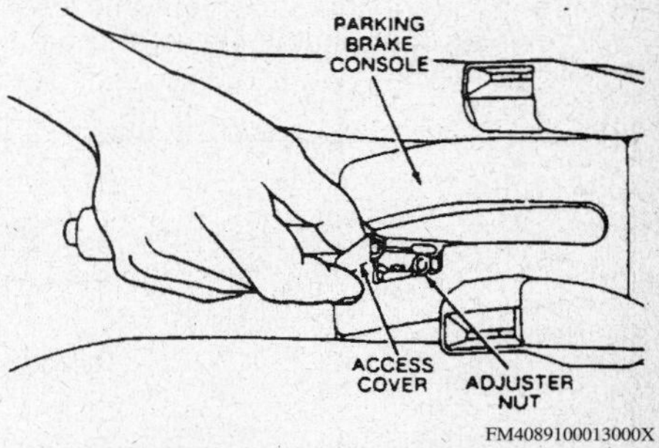

Fig. 2 Parking brake adjustment

PRECAUTIONS

AIR BAG SYSTEMS

Refer to "Air Bag System Precautions" in the front of this manual for system disarming and arming procedures.

BATTERY GROUND CABLE

Prior to service, disconnect battery ground cable and isolate as required.

SAFETY PRECAUTIONS

When working on or around brake assemblies, care must be taken to prevent breathing asbestos dust, as many manufacturers incorporate asbestos fibers in the production of brake linings. During routine service operations the amount of asbestos dust from brake lining wear is at a low level, due to a chemical breakdown during use and a few precautions will minimize exposure. **Do not sand or grind brake linings unless suitable local exhaust ventilation equipment is used to prevent excessive asbestos exposure.**

1. Wear suitable respirator approved for asbestos dust use during all repair procedures.
2. When cleaning brake dust from brake parts, use vacuum cleaner with highly efficient filter system. If suitable vacuum cleaner is not available, use water-soaked rag. **Do not use compressed air or dry brush to clean brake parts.**
3. Keep work area clean, using same equipment as for cleaning brake parts.
4. Properly dispose of rags and vacuum cleaner bags by placing them in plastic bags.
5. **Never use gasoline, kerosene, alcohol, motor oil, transmission fluid, or any fluid containing mineral oil to clean brake system components. These fluids will damage rubber caps and seals. If system contamination is suspected, inspect brake fluid in reservoir for dirt, discoloration, or separation (breakdown) of brake fluid into distinct layers. Drain and flush hydraulic system with clean brake fluid if contamination is suspected.**

INSPECTION

1. Inspect components for damage and unusual wear. Replace as necessary.
2. Inspect wheel cylinders. Boots which are torn, cut, or heat damaged indicate need for wheel cylinder replacement. Fluid spilling from boot center hole, or wetness around wheel cylinder ends indicates cup leakage and need for wheel cylinder replacement. **A small amount of fluid is always present and is considered normal, acting as lubricant for cylinder pistons.**
3. Inspect backing plate for evidence of seal leakage. If leakage exists, refer to "Aspire" chassis chapters for axle seal replacement procedure.
4. Inspect backing plate bolts and ensure they are tight.
5. Inspect adjuster screw operation. If satisfactory, lightly lubricate adjusting screw and washer with suitable brake lubricant. If operation is unsatisfactory, replace.
6. Using fine emery cloth or other suitable abrasive, clean rust and dirt from shoe contact surfaces on backing plate.

BRAKE SERVICE

REMOVAL

1. Raise and support vehicle, then remove rear wheel
2. Remove locknut and brake drum. **Locknut on righthand side of vehicle has lefthand threads. Turn locknut clockwise to remove.**
3. Remove hold-down clips and retaining pins, **Fig. 1.**
4. Remove all return springs, then the primary and secondary brake shoes.
5. Remove cotter pin, then the clevis pin from parking brake strut/self-adjuster. Disengage parking cable from self-adjuster.

INSTALLATION

1. Clean backing plate with factory approved vacuum cleaner.
2. Lubricate backing plate shoe pads with

suitable high temperature brake grease, such as Motorcraft WA-10.

3. Install and position parking brake strut/ self-adjuster onto backing plate.
4. Install upper return spring to primary brake shoe, then position shoe on backing plate and install retaining pin and hold-down clip, **Fig. 1.**
5. Connect upper return spring to secondary brake shoe, then position secondary shoe on backing plate and install retaining pin and hold-down clip.
6. Install parking brake return spring.
7. Install lower return spring onto primary and secondary shoes.
8. Connect parking cable onto self-adjuster, then install clevis and cotter pins.
9. Push on adjuster cam with screwdriver to position self-adjuster in fully released position.
10. Install brake drum and locknut.
11. Push brake pedal down several times to set self-adjuster, then install rear wheel.
12. Adjust parking brake as required.

ADJUSTMENTS

SERVICE BRAKES

These models are equipped with self-adjusting drum brake mechanisms which require no adjustment. The brakes are adjusted as necessary whenever the service brakes are applied.

PARKING BRAKE

1. Ensure parking lever is in fully released position.
2. Remove adjuster nut access cover from parking brake console, **Fig. 2.**
3. Remove adjuster nut locking clip, then raise and support rear of vehicle.
4. Tighten adjuster nut until slight drag is felt when rear wheels are rotated.
5. Loosen adjuster nut in small increments until brake drag is eliminated.
6. Inspect operation of parking brake. When properly adjusted, rear brakes should lock when parking brake lever is pulled upward eight to 11–16 clicks.
7. Lower vehicle, then install locking clip and access cover.

DRUM BRAKE SPECIFICATIONS

Model	Year	Brake Drum		
		Inside Dia., Inch	Bore Limit (Max.), Inch①	Max. Runout, Inch
Aspire	1997	7.87	7.93	—

① — For reference only. Always use specifications found on component.

TIGHTENING SPECIFICATIONS

Year	Component	Torque/ Ft. Lbs.
1997	Anti-Lock Sensor Bolt	12–16
	Wheel Cylinder Bolts	84–108①
	Wheel Lug Nuts	65–88
	Wheel Spindle Nuts	32–45

① — Inch lbs.

Type 5

INDEX

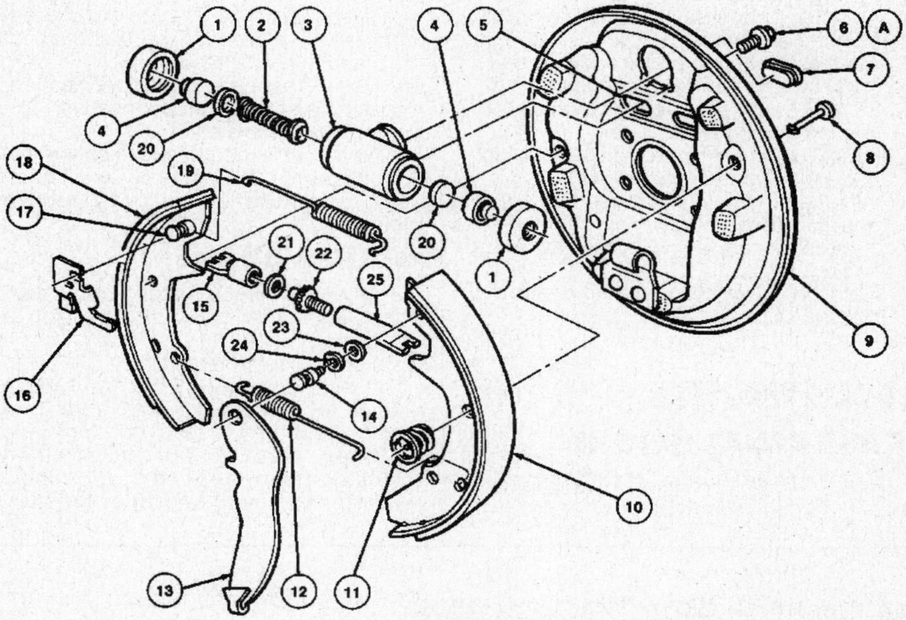

Item	Description
1	Boot
2	Spring Expander
3	Rear Wheel Cylinder
4	Piston and Insert
5	Shoe Adjustment Access Hole
6	Wheel Cylinder Retaining Screw (2 Req'd)
7	Brake Adjusting Hole Cover
8	Brake Shoe Hold-Down Spring Pin (2 Req'd)
9	Rear Brake Backing Plate
10	Trailing Shoe and Lining
11	Brake Shoe Hold-Down Spring (2 Req'd)
12	Brake Shoe Retracting Spring
13	Parking Brake Lever

Item	Description
14	Parking Brake Lever Pin (Inner)
15	Brake Shoe Adjusting Screw Socket
16	Brake Shoe Adjusting Lever
17	Parking Brake Lever Pin (Outer)
18	Leading Shoe and Lining
19	Brake Shoe Adjusting Screw Spring
20	Cup
21	Washer
22	Adjusting Screw
23	Washer
24	Parking Brake Lever Pin Retainer
25	Adjusting Pivot Nut
A	Tighten to 12-18 N·m (107-159 Lb-In)

FM4089500041000X

Fig. 1 Exploded view of brake drum assembly

PRECAUTIONS

AIR BAG SYSTEMS

Refer to "Air Bag System Precautions" in the front of this manual for system disarming and arming procedures.

BATTERY GROUND CABLE

Prior to service, disconnect battery ground cable and isolate as required.

SAFETY PRECAUTIONS

When working on or around brake assemblies, care must be taken to prevent breathing asbestos dust, as many manufacturers incorporate asbestos fibers in the production of brake linings. During routine service operations the amount of asbestos dust from brake lining wear is at a low level, due to a chemical breakdown during use and a few precautions will minimize exposure. **Do not sand or grind brake linings unless suitable local exhaust ventilation equipment is used to prevent excessive asbestos exposure.**

1. Wear suitable respirator approved for asbestos dust use during all repair procedures.
2. When cleaning brake dust from brake parts, use vacuum cleaner with highly efficient filter system. If suitable vacuum cleaner is not available, use water-soaked rag. **Do not use compressed air or dry brush to clean brake parts.**
3. Keep work area clean, using same equipment as for cleaning brake parts.
4. Properly dispose of rags and vacuum cleaner bags by placing them in plastic bags.
5. **Never use gasoline, kerosene, alcohol, motor oil, transmission fluid, or any fluid containing mineral oil to clean brake system components. These fluids will damage rubber caps and seals. If system contamination is suspected, inspect brake fluid in reservoir for dirt, discoloration, or separation (breakdown) of brake fluid into distinct layers. Drain and flush hydraulic system with clean brake fluid if contamination is suspected.**

INSPECTION

1. Inspect components for damage and unusual wear. Replace as necessary.
2. Inspect wheel cylinders. Boots which are torn, cut, or heat damaged indicate need for wheel cylinder replacement. Fluid spilling from boot center hole, or wetness around wheel cylinder ends indicates cup leakage and need for wheel cylinder replacement. **A small amount of fluid is always present and is considered normal, acting as lubricant for cylinder pistons.**
3. Inspect backing plate for evidence of seal leakage. If leakage exists, refer to "Crown Victoria, Grand Marquis, Thunderbird & 1997 Cougar" chassis chapter for axle seal replacement procedure.

4. Inspect backing plate bolts and ensure they are tight.
5. Inspect adjuster screw operation. If satisfactory, lightly lubricate adjusting screw and washer with suitable brake lubricant. If operation is unsatisfactory, replace.
6. Using fine emery cloth or other suitable abrasive, clean rust and dirt from shoe contact surfaces on backing plate.

BRAKE SERVICE

REMOVAL

1. Raise and support rear of vehicle, then remove tire and wheel assembly.
2. Remove brake drum.
3. Install suitable wheel cylinder clamp over ends of wheel cylinder to retain pistons in bore.
4. Disconnect parking brake cable from parking brake lever.
5. Remove two brake shoe hold-down retainers, springs and pins, **Fig. 1.**
6. Spread brake shoes over piston shoe guide slots, then lift shoes, springs and adjuster off backing plate as an assembly.
7. Remove adjuster spring.
8. Remove retracting springs to separate shoes.
9. Remove parking brake lever retaining clip, spring and washer.
10. Remove lever from pin.

INSTALLATION

1. Lightly lubricate backing plate shoe contact surfaces with suitable brake lubricant, such as Motorcraft WA-10.
2. Install parking brake lever to trailing shoe with spring washer and new retaining clip, **Fig. 1.**
3. Position trailing shoe or backing plate and attach hand brake cable.
4. Install adjuster assembly to slots in brake shoes. Socket end must fit into slot in leading shoe (wider slot). Slot in adjuster nut must fit into slots in trailing shoe and parking brake lever.
5. Install adjuster lever on pin on leading shoe and to slot in adjuster socket.
6. Install upper retracting spring in slot on trailing shoe and slot in adjuster lever. Adjuster lever should contact star and adjuster assembly.
7. Assemble parking brake cable to trailing shoe and parking brake lever.
8. Install lower retracting spring to leading-trailing shoe.
9. Install assembly to backing plate fitting shoes into wheel cylinder piston slots.
10. Install adjuster socket to leading shoe and lining assembly.
11. Install brake shoe anchor pins, springs and retainers.
12. Remove brake cylinder clamp and install brake drum.

ADJUSTMENTS

BRAKE PEDAL HEIGHT

1. Run engine at normal operating condition.
2. Measure distance to top center of brake pedal pad.
3. Free height should be approximately 7.35 inches.
4. If pedal height is not within specification, inspect pedal, booster or master cylinder to ensure proper parts are installed. Replace worn or damaged parts.

BRAKE PEDAL TRAVEL

1. With engine running in Neutral or Park position, block drive wheels, then release parking brake.
2. Install brake pedal effort gauge tool No. 014-R1051, or equivalent, and inspect pedal travel. With 25 lbs. of pressure applied to pedal, travel should not exceed three inches.
3. If pedal travel exceeds specification, make several Reverse stops with forward stop before each.
4. If travel still exceeds specification, remove drums and inspect brake adjusters. Hydraulic system may require bleeding.

PARKING BRAKE

1. Apply and release parking brake several times, then place transmission in Neutral position.
2. Raise and support vehicle.
3. Release tensioner by rotating locking lever away from threaded rod. Tensioner spring will take up slack and preload cables. **Do not pull down on locking lever, as it will pull cables down and cause improper tension.**

DRUM BRAKE SPECIFICATIONS

Model	Year	Brake Drum		
		Inside Dia., Inch	Bore Limit (Max.), Inch①	Max. Runout, Inch
Cougar & Thunderbird	1997	9.80	9.90	.005

① — For reference only. Always use specifications found on component.

TIGHTENING SPECIFICATIONS

Year	Component	Torque/Ft. Lbs.
1997	Axle Nut	188–254
	Backing Plate To Axle	44–59
	Bleeder Screw	8–15
	Brake Line Fitting	10–17
	Hub Nut	188–254
	Parking Brake Stop Bolt	96–108①
	Wheel Cylinder Attaching Bolts	96–120①
	Wheel Lug Nuts	85–105

① — Inch Lbs.

HYDRAULIC BRAKE SYSTEMS

NOTE: On Air Bag Equipped Models, Refer To " Air Bag System Precautions" Located In The Front Of This Manual For System Disarming & Arming Procedures.

NOTE: Refer To "Computer Relearn Procedures " Located In The Front Of This Manual For Computer Relearn Procedures.

INDEX

PRECAUTIONS

AIR BAG SYSTEMS

Refer to "Air Bag System Precautions" in the front of this manual for system disarming and arming procedures.

BATTERY GROUND CABLE

Prior to service, disconnect battery ground cable and isolate as required.

DESCRIPTION

This system operates on the same principles as conventional front and rear split systems using primary and secondary master cylinders moving simultaneously to exert hydraulic pressure on their respective systems, **Fig. 1**.

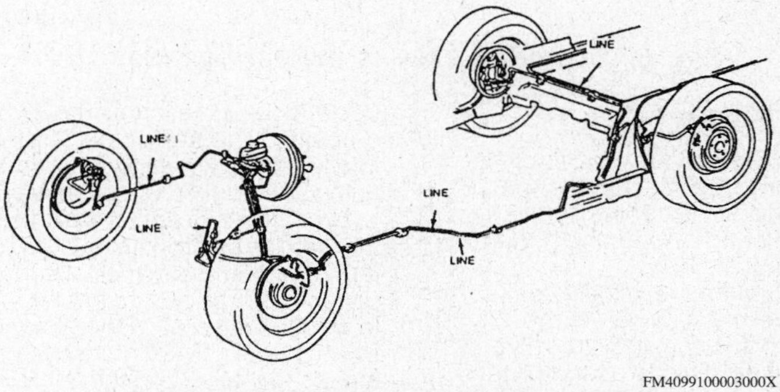

Fig. 1 Diagonally split brake system

The hydraulic brake lines on this system, however, have been diagonally split front to rear (left front to right rear and right front to left rear) in place of separate lines to the front and rear wheels.

In the event of a system failure this would cause the remaining good system to do all the braking on one front wheel and the opposite rear wheel, thus maintaining 50% of the total braking force. The hydraulic pressure loss would result in a pressure differential in the system and cause a warning light on the dashboard to glow as in front and rear split systems.

BRAKE WARNING LIGHT SYSTEMS

When a pressure differential occurs between the front and rear brake systems, the valves will shuttle toward the side with the low pressure. Movement of the differential valve forces the switch plunger upward over the tapered shoulder of the valve to close the switch contacts and light the dual brake warning lamp, signaling a brake system failure.

The valve assembly consists of two valves in a common bore that are spring loaded toward the centered position. The spring-loaded switch contact plunger rests on top of the valves in the centered position. When a pressure differential occurs between the front and rear brake systems, the valves will shuttle toward the side with the low pressure. The spring-loaded switch plunger is triggered and the ground circuit for the warning light is completed, lighting the lamp.

As pressure falls in one system, the other system's normal pressure forces the piston to the inoperative side, contacting the switch terminal, causing the warning light on the instrument panel to glow.

On front wheel drive models, a fluid level indicator replaces the pressure differential valve used in previous brake systems. It is contained inside the body of the master cylinder plastic reservoir and activates the brake warning light when fluid level is low.

Testing Warning Light Systems

If the parking brake light is connected into the service brake warning light system, the brake warning light will flash only when the parking brake is applied with the ignition turned ON. The same light will also glow should one of the two service brake systems fail when the brake pedal is applied.

To test the system, turn the ignition on and apply the parking brake. If the lamp fails to light, inspect for a burned out bulb, disconnected socket, a broken or disconnected wire at the switch.

To test the brake warning system, raise the car and open a wheel bleeder valve while a helper depresses the brake pedal and observes the warning light on the instrument panel. If the bulb fails to light, inspect for a burned out bulb, disconnected socket, or a broken or disconnected wire at the switch. If the bulb is not burned out, and wire continuity is proven, replace the brake warning switch.

COMBINATION VALVE

The combination valve is a metering valve, failure warning switch, and a proportioner in one assembly and is used on disc brake applications. The metering valve delays front disc braking until the rear drum brake shoes contact the drum. The failure warning switch is actuated in event of front or rear brake system failure, in turn activating a dash warning lamp. The proportioner balances front to rear braking action during rapid deceleration.

Combination valves used on diagonally split brake systems do not use metering valves instead two proportioning valves are used.

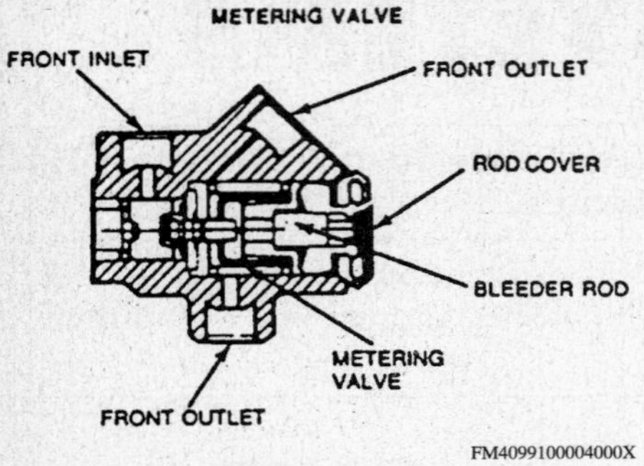

Fig. 2 Metering valve

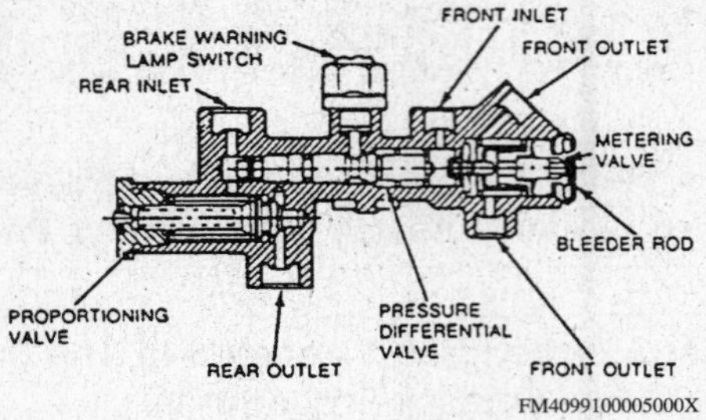

Fig. 3 Combination valve

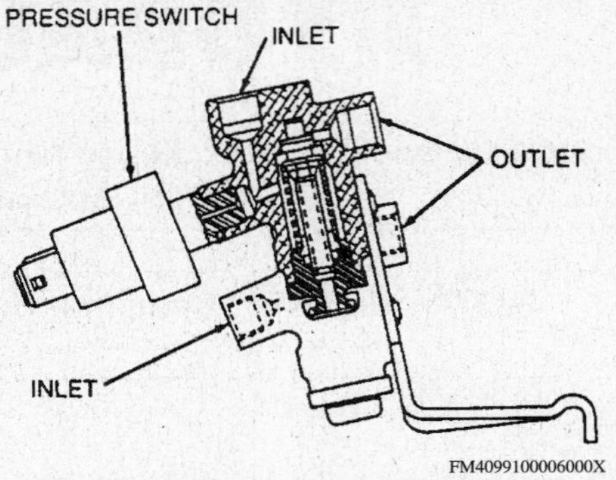

Fig. 4 Pressure control valve

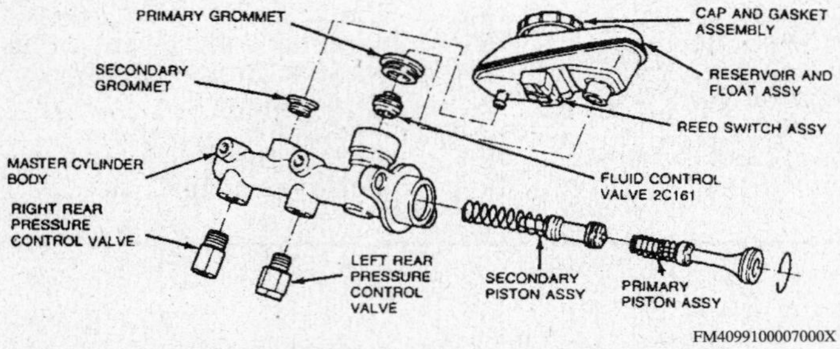

Fig. 5 Exploded view of master cylinder

Metering Valve

When the brakes are not applied, the metering valve, **Fig. 2,** permits the brake fluid to flow through the valve, thus allowing the fluid to expand and contract with temperature changes.

When the brakes are initially applied, the metering valve, stem moves to the left, preventing fluid to flow through the valve to the front disc brakes. This is accomplished by the smooth end of the metering valve stem contacting the metering valve seal lip at 4–30 psi. The metering valve spring holds the retainer against the seal until a predetermined pressure is produced at the valve inlet port which overcomes the spring pressure and permits hydraulic pressure to actuate the front disc brakes. The increased pressure into the valve is metered through the valve seal, to the front disc brakes, producing an increased force on the diaphragm. The diaphragm then pulls the pin, in turn pulling the retainer and reduces the spring pressure on the metering valve seal. Eventually, the pressure reaches a point at which the spring is pulled away by the diaphragm pin and retainer, leaving the metering valve unrestricted, permitting full pressure to pass through the metering valve.

On some applications, two-way or three-way combination valves are used. The three-way combination valve consists of a metering valve, failure warning switch and a proportioner mounted in an aluminum body, **Fig. 3.** The two-way combination valve consists of a failure warning switch and a proportioner. On models equipped with metering valves, the metering valve release rod must be pushed in during bleeding operations on the front wheels.

Failure Warning Switch

If the rear brake system fails, the front system pressure forces the switch piston to one side. The switch pin is then forced up into the switch, completing the electrical circuit and activates the dash warning lamp.

When repairs are made and pressure returns to the system, the piston moves to the left, resetting the switch. The detent on the piston requires approximately 100–450 psi to permit full reset of the piston. In event of front brake system failure, the piston moves to the left and the same sequence of events is followed as for rear system failure except the piston resets to the right.

Proportioner Or Pressure Control Valve

During rapid deceleration, a portion of vehicle weight is transferred to the front wheels. This resultant loss of weight at rear wheels must be compensated for to avoid early rear wheel skid. The proportioner or pressure control valve, **Fig. 4,** reduces rear brake system pressure, delaying rear wheel skid. When the proportioner or pressure control valve is incorporated in the combination valve assembly, pressure developed within the valve acts against the large end of the piston, overcoming the spring pressure, moving the piston. The piston then contacts the stem seat and restricts line pressure through the valve.

During normal braking operation, the proportioner or pressure control valve is not functional. Brake fluid flows into the proportioner or pressure control valve between the piston center hole and the valve stem, through the stop plate and to the rear brakes. Spring pressure loads the piston during normal braking, causing it to rest against the stop plate.

On diagonally split brake systems, two proportioners or pressure control valves are used. One controls the left rear brake, the other the right rear brake. On front wheel drive models less power brakes, the proportioners or pressure control valves are located in the combination valve. On front wheel drive models with power brakes, the proportioners or pressure control valves are installed in the master cylinder rear brake outlet ports, **Fig. 5.**

BRAKE DISTRIBUTION VALVE & SWITCH

This switch assembly which is used on some diagonally split brake systems, is connected to the outlet ports of the master cylinder and also to the brake warning light that warns the driver if either the primary or secondary brake system has failed.

When hydraulic pressure is equal in both primary and secondary brake systems, the switch remains centered. If pressure fails in one of the systems, hydraulic pressure moves the piston toward the inoperative side. The shoulder of the piston contacts the switch terminal, providing a ground and lighting the warning lamp.

PROPORTIONING VALVE & SWITCH

Description

The proportioning valve (when used), **Fig. 6,** provides balanced braking action between front and rear brakes under a wide range of braking conditions. The valve regulates the hydraulic pressure applied to the rear wheel cylinders, thus limiting rear braking action when high pressures are required at the front brakes. In this manner, premature rear wheel skid is prevented.

Testing

When a premature rear wheel slide is obtained on a brake application, it usually is an indication that the fluid pressure to the rear wheels is above the 50% reduction ratio for the rear line pressure and that malfunction has occurred within the proportioning valve.

To test the valve, install gauge set shown in **Fig. 6,** in brake line between master cylinder and proportioning valve, and at output end of proportioning valve and brake line as shown. Ensure all joints are fluid tight.

Have a helper exert pressure on brake pedal (holding pressure). Obtain a reading on master cylinder output of approximately 700 psi. While pressure is being held as above, reading on valve outlet should be

550–610 psi. If the pressure readings do not meet these specifications, the valve should be removed and a new valve installed.

COMPONENT REPLACEMENT

MASTER CYLINDER

Aspire

1. Disconnect master cylinder fluid level sensor electrical connectors.
2. Disconnect brake tubes, then cap tubes to prevent entry of contaminants.
3. Remove master cylinder attaching nuts, then the master cylinder.
4. Reverse procedure to install. After installation is complete, fill master cylinder with manufacturer recommended brake fluid and bleed brakes.

Continental, Crown Victoria, Grand Marquis, Mark VIII, Mustang, Thunderbird & Town Car & 1997 Cougar

1. **On models equipped with ABS,** depress brake pedal several times to exhaust all vacuum in the system.
2. **On all models,** disconnect brake lines from master cylinder, then all necessary electrical connectors.
3. **On models equipped with ABS,** disconnect hydraulic control unit supply hose at master cylinder. Secure hose in a position to prevent brake fluid loss.
4. **On models equipped with ABS and traction control,** remove two bolts which attach proportioning valve bracket to brake master cylinder. Secure proportioning valve and tubes in a position to prevent damage or loss of brake fluid.
5. **On all models,** remove nuts retaining master cylinder to brake booster.
6. Remove master cylinder.
7. Reverse procedure to install. After installation is complete, fill master cylinder with manufacturer recommended brake fluid and bleed brakes.

Contour, Mystique & 1999-2000 Cougar

1. Apply brake pedal several times to exhaust all vacuum in system.
2. Disconnect brake warning switch, then remove brake tubes from primary and secondary outlet ports of master cylinder.
3. **On models equipped with manual transaxle,** disconnect hose to hydraulic clutch master cylinder, then drain brake fluid into a suitable container.
4. **On all models,** remove brake lines.
5. Remove two nuts and master cylinder.
6. Reverse procedure to install. After installation is complete, fill master cylinder with manufacturer recommended brake fluid and bleed brakes.

Escort, Tracer & ZX2

1. **On 1998 models,** remove air cleaner assembly.

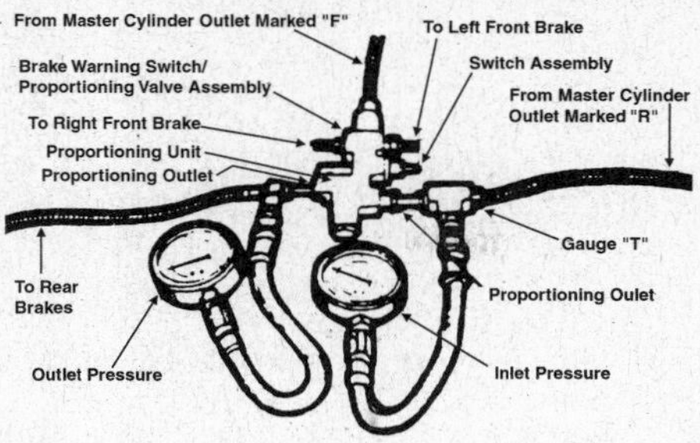

FM4079100011000X

Fig. 6 Proportioning valve test gauge connection

2. **On models equipped with manual transaxle,** disconnect clutch master cylinder hose from brake master cylinder reservoir.
3. **On all models,** disconnect master cylinder fluid level sensor and brake tubes from master cylinder.
4. Cap brake tubes and master cylinder ports.
5. Remove two master cylinder to power booster nuts and master cylinder.
6. Reverse procedure to install. After installation is complete, fill master cylinder with manufacturer recommended brake fluid and bleed brakes.

LS

1. Disconnect fluid level sensor connector.
2. Remove vapor management valve (VMV) nuts.
3. Remove VMV hose and position valve aside.
4. Disconnect brake tubes.
5. Disconnect brake master cylinder IVD solenoid electrical connector.
6. Remove brake master cylinder mounting nuts.
7. Unclip fuel line and vapor management hose from fastener, then position aside.
8. Remove brake master cylinder.
9. Reverse procedure to install. Bleed brake system.

Probe

1. Remove speed control cable from its bracket, if equipped.
2. **On models equipped with manual transaxle,** disconnect clutch reservoir supply hose.
3. **On all models,** disconnect fluid level sensor and brake tubes from master cylinder.
4. Cap brake tubes and ports, then remove two master cylinder nuts and master cylinder.
5. Reverse procedure to install. After installation is complete, fill master cylinder with manufacturer recommended brake fluid and bleed brakes.

Sable & Taurus

1. Apply brake several times to exhaust all vacuum in the system.
2. Remove brake tubes from primary and secondary outlet ports of brake master cylinder.
3. Disconnect brake fluid level warning switch connector.
4. Remove nut retaining cowl top inner panel tube to brake master cylinder.
5. Disconnect cowl top inner panel tube from cowl and remove.
6. Remove two nuts retaining brake master cylinder to power brake booster assembly.
7. Slide brake master cylinder forward and upward from vehicle.
8. Reverse procedure to install. After installation is complete, fill master cylinder with manufacturer recommended brake fluid and bleed brakes.

WHEEL CYLINDERS

Removal

1. Remove wheel, drum and brake shoes.
2. Disconnect hydraulic line at wheel cylinder. Do not pull metal line away from cylinder as the cylinder connection will bend metal line and make installation difficult. Line will separate from cylinder when cylinder is moved away from brake backing plate.
3. Remove screws holding cylinder to brake plate and remove cylinder.

Installation

1. Wipe end of hydraulic line to remove any foreign matter.
2. Place hydraulic cylinder in position. Enter tubing into cylinder and start connecting fitting.
3. Secure cylinder to backing plate and then complete tightening of tubing fitting.
4. Install brake shoes, drum and wheel.
5. Bleed system as outlined under "Brake System Bleed " and adjust brakes.

COMPONENT SERVICE

MASTER CYLINDER OVERHAUL

Disassemble

1. Clean outside of master cylinder thoroughly. Drain brake fluid from master cylinder.
2. Remove stop bolt and pressure control valves, if equipped.
3. Using a screwdriver, carefully pry up on reservoir and remove it from master cylinder body.
4. Remove fluid control valve, if equipped.
5. Depress primary piston and remove snap ring from retaining groove at open end of bore.
6. Remove primary and secondary piston assemblies from master cylinder. If secondary piston does not come out, apply air pressure to secondary outlet port to remove.

Inspection

When disassembled, wash all parts in clean brake fluid only. Use an air hose to blow out all passages, orifices and valve holes. Air dry and place parts on clean paper or lint-free cloth. Inspect master cylinder bore for scoring, rust, pitting or etching. Any of these conditions will require replacement of the housing. Inspect master cylinder pistons for scoring, pitting or distortion. Replace piston if any of these conditions exist.

If either master cylinder housing or piston is replaced, clean new parts with clean brake fluid and blow out all passages with air hose.

Examine reservoirs for foreign matter and check all passages for restrictions. If there is any suspicion of contamination or evidence of corrosion, completely flush hydraulic system as outlined below.

When overhauling a master cylinder, use all parts contained in repair kit. Before starting reassembly, dip all cups, seals, pistons, springs, check valves and retainers in clean brake fluid and place in a clean pan or on clean paper. Wash hands with soap and water only to prevent contamination of rubber parts from oil, kerosene or gasoline. During assembly, dip all parts in clean brake fluid.

Inspect through side outlet of dual master cylinder housing to make certain cup lips do not hang up on edge of hole or turn back, which would result in faulty operation. A piece of 3⁄16 inch rod with an end rounded off will be helpful in guiding cups past hole.

When overhauling aluminum master cylinders, carefully inspect master cylinder bore for corrosion. If corroded, replace master cylinder. Do not hone or use abrasives on the bore of these cylinders.

Assemble

1. Coat replacement piston assemblies in clean heavy duty DOT 3 brake fluid before assembly.
2. Install secondary piston assembly into bore, spring end first.
3. Install primary piston assembly, spring end first.
4. Depres primary piston and install snap ring.
5. **On all models except Escort, Tracer and ZX2,** install fluid control valve and **torque** to 96–120 inch lbs.
6. **On Escort, Tracer and ZX2 models,** install fluid control valve and **torque** to 33–39 ft. lbs.
7. **On all models,** install stop bolt and pressure control valves, if equipped.
8. Lubricate new reservoir grommets with brake fluid and install in master cylinder body.
9. Install reservoir into new grommets.
10. Fill and bench bleed master cylinder.

WHEEL CYLINDERS

Overhaul

1. Refer to **Fig. 7** as a guide, then remove boots, pistons, springs and cups from cylinder.
2. Place all parts, except cylinder casting in clean brake fluid. Wipe cylinder walls with clean brake fluid.
3. Examine cylinder bore. A scored bore may be honed providing the diameter is not increased more than .005 inch.

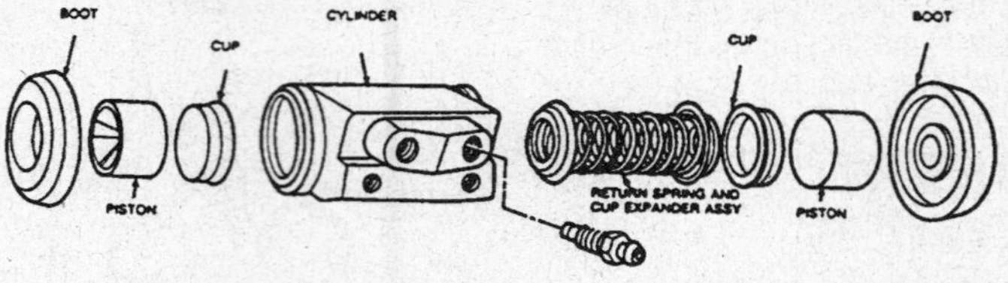

Fig. 7 Exploded view of typical wheel cylinder

Replace worn or damaged parts from the repair kit.

4. Before assembling, wash hands with soap and water only, as oil, kerosene or gasoline will contaminate rubber parts.
5. Lubricate cylinder wall and rubber cups with brake fluid.
6. Install springs, cups, pistons and boots in housing.

BRAKE SYSTEM BLEED

Pressure bleeding is recommended for all hydraulic brake systems. Ensure all dirt and contaminants are removed from master cylinder area prior to removing reservoir cap.

To prevent air from the pressure tank getting into the lines, do not shake the tank while air is being added to the tank or after it has been pressurized. Set the tank in the required location, bring the air hose to the tank, and do not move it during the bleeding operation. The tank should be kept at least one-third full.

On vehicles equipped with disc brakes and master cylinders without proportioners or pressure control valves located in the master cylinder outlet port, the brake metering valve or combination valve must be held in position using a suitable tool.

If air does get into the fluid, releasing the pressure will cause the bubbles to increase in size, rise to the top of the fluid, and escape. Pressure should not be greater than about 35 psi.

On vehicles equipped with plastic reservoirs, do not exceed 25 psi during bleeding pressure.

When bleeding without pressure, open the bleed valve three-quarters of a turn, depress the pedal a full stroke, then allow the pedal to return slowly to its released position. It is suggested that after the pedal has been depressed to the end of its stroke, the bleeder valve should be closed before the start of the return stroke. On models with power brakes, first reduce the vacuum in the power unit to zero by pumping the brake pedal several times with the engine off before starting to bleed the system.

Pressure bleeding eliminates the need for pedal pumping.

Discard drained or bled brake fluid. Care should be taken not to spill brake fluid, since this can damage the finish of the car.

Flushing is essential if there is water, mineral oil or other contaminants in the lines, and whenever new parts are installed in the hydraulic system. Fluid contamination is usually indicated by swollen and deteriorated cups and other rubber parts.

Wheel cylinders on disc brakes are equipped with bleeder valves, and are bled in the same manner as wheel cylinders for drum brakes.

Bleeding is necessary on all four wheels if air has entered the system because of low fluid level, or the line or lines have been disconnected. If a line is disconnected at any one wheel cylinder, that cylinder only need be bled. On brake reline jobs, bleeding is advisable to remove any air or contaminants.

Master cylinders equipped with bleeder valves should be bled first before the wheel cylinders are bled. In all cases where a master cylinder has been overhauled, it must be bled. Where there is no bleeder valve, this can be done by leaving the lines loose, actuating the brake pedal to expel the air and then tightening the lines.

After overhauling a dual master cylinder used in conjunction with disc brakes, it is advisable to bleed the cylinder before installing it on the car. The reason for this recommendation is that air may be trapped between the master cylinder pistons because there is only one residual pressure valve (check valve) used in these units.

SYSTEM PRIMING

When a new master cylinder has been installed or the brake system emptied or partially emptied, fluid may not flow from the bleeder screws during normal bleeding. It may be necessary to prime the system using the following procedure:

1. Using a tubing wrench, remove the brake lines from the master cylinder.
2. Install short brake lines in the master cylinder and position them back into the reservoir, ensure the short brake line ends are submerged in the reservoir brake fluid.
3. Fill the reservoir with recommended brake fluid, then cover master cylinder fluid reservoir with shop towel.
4. Pump the brakes until clear, bubble free fluid comes out of both brake lines. **If any brake fluid spills on paint, wash it off immediately with water.**
5. Remove the short brake lines, then reinstall original brake lines.
6. Bleed each brake line at the master cylinder using the following procedure:
   a. Have assistant pump brake pedal ten times, then hold firm pressure on the pedal.
   b. Open the rearmost brake line fittings with a tubing wrench until a stream of brake fluid comes out. Have assistant maintain pressure on the brake pedal until the brake line fitting is tightened again.
   c. Repeat this operation until clear,

bubble free fluid comes out from around tube fitting.

d. Repeat this bleeding operation at the front brake line fitting.

7. If any of the brake lines or calipers have been removed, it may be helpful to prime the system by gravity bleeding. this should be done after the master cylinder is primed and bled. To prime the system using the gravity method, proceed as follows:
   a. Fill the master cylinder with recommended brake fluid.
   b. Loosen both rear bleeder screws and leave them open until clear brake fluid flows out. **Check reservoir fluid level frequently; do not allow fluid level to drop below half full.**
   c. Tighten rear bleeder screws.
   d. Loosen bleeder screw on front caliper, leave open until clear fluid flows out. **Bleed front calipers one side at a time.**
8. After the master cylinder has been primed, the lines bled at the master cylinder and the brake system primed, normal brake system bleeding can be resumed at each wheel.

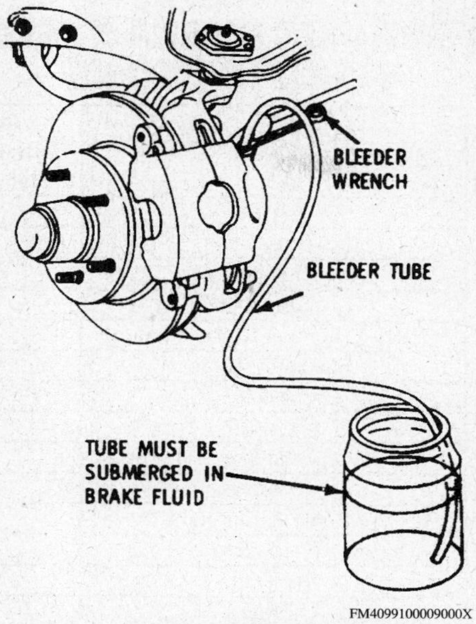

Fig. 8 Hydraulic brake system flushing

WHEEL BLEEDING SEQUENCE

Rear Wheel Drive .....RR-LR-RF-LF
Front Wheel Drive....RR-LF-LR-RF

HYDRAULIC BRAKE SYSTEM FLUSH

Whenever new brake components are installed in the hydraulic system, it is recommended that the entire hydraulic system be thoroughly flushed with clean brake fluid.

It may sometime become necessary to flush out the system due to the presence of mineral oil, kerosene, gasoline, etc., which will cause swelling of rubber piston cups and valves and render them inoperative.

Flushing is performed at each wheel in the same manner as the bleeding operation except that the bleeder valve is opened 1½ turns and the fluid is forced through the lines and bleeder valve until it emerges clear in color, **Fig. 8.** Approximately one quart of clean brake fluid is required to flush the hydraulic system. After completing the flushing operation at all bleeder valves, check to ensure the master cylinder is filled to the proper level.

HYDRAULIC BRAKE SYSTEM SPECIFICATIONS

Year	Model	Master Cylinder Bore Dia., Inch
1997–2000	Aspire	①
	Continental	—
	Contour & Mystique	—
	Cougar	—
	Crown Victoria & Grand Marquis	—
	Escort & Tracer	—
	LS	—
	Mark VIII	—
	Mustang	②
	Probe	—
	Sable & Taurus	—
	Thunderbird	—
	Town Car	—
	ZX2	—

① — Less ABS, 0.81 inch; w/ABS, 0.87 inch.
② — 3.8L engine 1.06 inch, 4.6L engines 1.00 inch.

POWER BRAKE UNITS

NOTE: On Models Equipped With Anti-Lock Brakes, Refer To "Anti-Lock Brake" Section.

NOTE: On Air Bag Equipped Models, Refer To " Air Bag System Precautions" Located In The Front Of This Manual For System Disarming & Arming Procedures.

INDEX

APPLICATION CHART

Model	Year	Power Brake Booster Type
Aspire	1997	Single Diaphragm
Continental	1997	Single Diaphragm
	1998–2000	Dual Diaphragm
Contour	1997–2000	Single Diaphragm
Cougar	1997	①
	1999–2000	Single Diaphragm
Crown Victoria	1997–2000	Bendix Tandem Diaphragm
Escort	1997–2000	Single Diaphragm
Grand Marquis	1997–2000	Bendix Tandem Diaphragm
LS	2000	Dual Diaphragm
Mark VIII	1997–98	Bendix Tandem Diaphragm
Mustang	1997–2000	②
Mystique	1997–2000	Single Diaphragm
Probe	1997	Single Diaphragm
Sable	1997–99	Bendix Single Diaphragm
Taurus	1997–99	Bendix Single Diaphragm
Thunderbird	1997	①
Town Car	1997–2000	Bendix Tandem Diaphragm
Tracer	1997–99	Single Diaphragm
ZX2	1998–2000	Single Diaphragm

① — Except models w/3.8L engine less ABS, Bendix Single Diaphragm; models w/3.8L engine & ABS, Bendix Tandem Diaphragm.

② — 3.8L engine, Bendix Tandem Diaphragm. 4.6L engine, Bendix Hydro-Boost system.

PRECAUTIONS

AIR BAG SYSTEMS

Refer to "Air Bag System Precautions" in the front of this manual for system disarming and arming procedures.

BATTERY GROUND CABLE

Prior to service, disconnect battery ground cable and isolate as required.

DESCRIPTION

VACUUM ASSIST DIAPHRAGM TYPE

The vacuum assist diaphragm assembly multiplies the force exerted on the master cylinder piston in order to increase the hydraulic pressure delivered to the wheel cylinders while decreasing the effort necessary to obtain acceptable stopping performance.

Vacuum assist units get their energy by opposing engine vacuum to atmospheric pressure. A piston, cylinder and flexible diaphragm utilize this energy to provide brake assistance. The diaphragm is balanced with engine vacuum until the brake pedal is depressed, allowing atmospheric pressure to unbalance the unit and apply force to the brake system.

Brakes will operate even if the power unit fails. This means the conventional brake system and the power assist system are completely separate. Troubleshooting conventional and power assist systems are exactly the same until the power unit is reached. As with conventional hydraulic brakes, a spongy pedal still means air is trapped in the hydraulic system. Power brakes give higher line pressure, making leaks more critical.

BENDIX DIAPHRAGM TYPES

These units are of the vacuum suspended type. Some units are of the single diaphragm type, while others are of the tandem diaphragm type. Both single piston and double piston or split system type master cylinders are used.

The vacuum suspended diaphragm type units utilize engine manifold vacuum and atmospheric pressure for its power. It consists of three basic elements combined into a single power unit. The three basic elements of the single diaphragm type are:

1. A vacuum power section which includes a front and rear shell, a power diaphragm, a return spring and a pushrod.
2. A control valve, built integral with the power diaphragm and connected through a valve rod to the brake pedal, controls the degree of brake application or release in accordance with the pressure applied to the brake pedal.
3. A hydraulic master cylinder, attached to the vacuum power section which contains all the elements of the conventional brake master cylinder except for the pushrod, supplies fluid under pressure to the wheel brakes in proportion to the pressure applied to the brake pedal.

Operation

Upon application of the brakes, the valve rod and plunger move to the lefthand in the power diaphragm to close the vacuum port and open the atmospheric port to admit air through the air cleaner and valve at the rear diaphragm chamber. With vacuum present in the rear chamber, a force is developed to move the power diaphragm, hydraulic pushrod and hydraulic piston or pistons to close the compensating port or ports and force fluid under pressure through the residual check valve or valves and lines into the front and rear wheel cylinders to actuate the brakes.

As pressure is developed within the master cylinder a counter force acting through the hydraulic pushrod and reaction disc against the vacuum power diaphragm and valve plunger sets up a reaction force opposing the force applied to the valve rod and plunger. This reaction force tends to close the atmospheric port and reopen the vacuum port. Since this force is in opposition to the force applied to the brake pedal by the driver it gives the driver a "feel" of the amount of brake applied. The proportion of reactive force applied to the valve plunger through the reaction disc is designed into the Master-Vac to ensure maximum power consistent with maintaining pedal feel. The

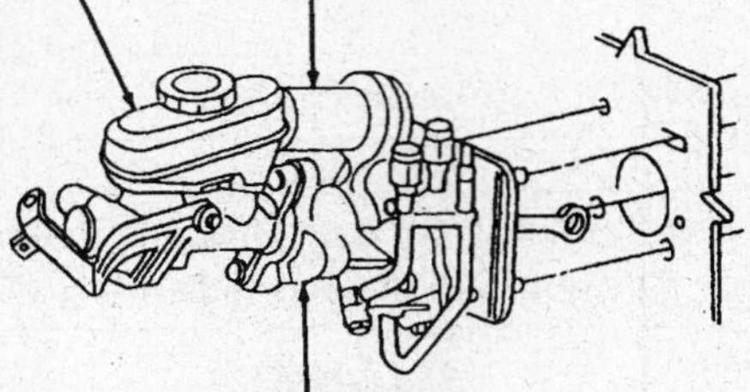

Fig. 1 Bendix Hydro-Boost

reaction force is in direct proportion to the hydraulic pressure developed within the brake system.

BENDIX HYDRO-BOOST SYSTEM

The Bendix Hydro-Boost System, **Fig. 1**, is a hydraulically operated booster with fluid provided by the power steering pump. If power steering fluid flow is interrupted, a reserve accumulator system stores enough fluid under pressure to provide at least two power-assisted stops. Manual brake application is permitted if the reserve system is depleted.

The Hydro-Boost booster, power steering pump and hydraulic hoses are all serviced separately. If the booster becomes inoperative or is damaged, it must be replaced as an assembly.

TROUBLESHOOTING

Complaints about power brake operation should be handled as if two separate systems exist. Inspect for faults in the hydraulic system first. If it is satisfactory, start inspecting the power brake circuit. For a quick inspection of proper power unit operation, press the brake pedal firmly and then start the engine. The pedal should fall away slightly and less pressure should be needed to maintain the pedal in any position.

Another inspection begins with installation of a suitable pressure gauge in the brake hydraulic system. Take a reading with the engine Off and the power unit not operating. Maintaining the same pedal height, start the engine and take another reading. There should be a substantial pressure increase in the second reading.

Pedal free travel and total travel are critical on models equipped with power brakes. Pedal travel should be kept strictly to specifications.

Take a manifold vacuum reading or inspect operation of the external vacuum pump if the power unit is not giving enough assistance. Remember, though, on currently produced emission controlled engines, manifold vacuum readings may be less than 15 inches Hg at idle. If manifold vacuum is abnormally low, tune the engine and then inspect the power brakes again. Naturally, loose vacuum lines and clogged air intake filters will cut down brake efficiency. Most units have a check valve that retains some vacuum in the system when the engine is Off. A vacuum gauge inspection of this valve will tell when it is restricted, stuck open or closed.

Failure of the brakes to release in most instances is caused by a tight or misaligned connection between the power unit and the brake linkage. If this connection is free, look for a broken piston, diaphragm or bellows and return spring.

A simple hydraulic system inspection should be made before proceeding. Loosen the connection between the master cylinder and the brake booster. If the brakes release, the trouble is in the power unit; if the brakes still will not release, look for a restricted brake line or similar difficulties in the regular hydraulic circuit.

A residual pressure check valve is usually included immediately under the brake line connection on hydraulic assist power brakes. This valve maintains a slight hydraulic pressure within the brake lines and wheel cylinders to give better pedal response. If it is sticking, the brakes may not release.

Power brakes that have a hard pedal are usually suffering from a milder form of the same ills that cause complete power unit failure. Collapsed or leaking vacuum lines or insufficient manifold vacuum, as well as punctured diaphragms or bellows and leaky piston seals, all lead to weak power unit operation. A steady hiss when the brake is held down means a vacuum leak that will cause poor power unit operation.

Do not immediately condemn the power unit if the brakes grab. First look for all the usual causes, such as greasy linings, scored rotors or drums. Then investigate the power unit. When the trouble has been traced to the power unit, inspect for a damaged reaction control. The reaction control is usually made up of a diaphragm, spring and valves that tends to resist pedal action. It is put in the system to give the pedal " feel."

On models equipped with the Bendix Hydro-Boost system, ensure engine is in Off position, then pressing and releasing the brake pedal several times to relieve all hydraulic pressure from the booster. Depress and hold the pedal with light pressure. Start engine and note pedal reaction. If it does not fall slightly and hold, press and release the pedal several times, then depress and hold with medium foot pressure. If the pedal now moves toward the floor, inspect for brake fluid leakage at master cylinder, brake hoses and all connections, **Fig. 2.**

To inspect the Hydro-Boost unit for leakage, idle the engine, then depress and hold the brake pedal for no more than five seconds with heavy foot pressure. If the booster shows any signs of fluid leakage, it must be replaced.

An accumulator reserve retention inspection requires operating the engine at idle, then depressing and holding the brake pedal for no more than five seconds with heavy foot pressure, or holding the steering wheel at full stop. Turn the ignition Off, then wait 8–12 hours. Depress the brake pedal

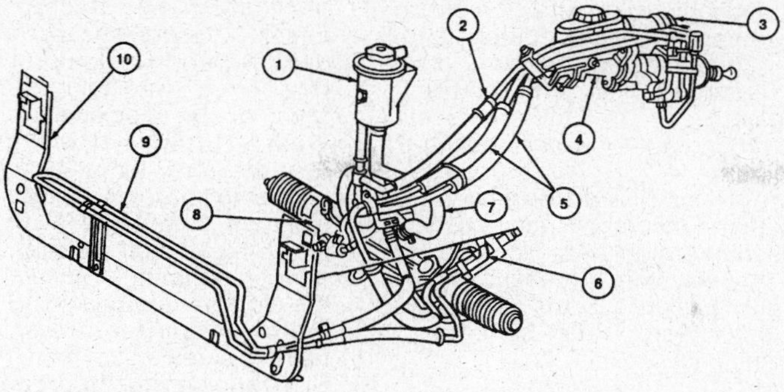

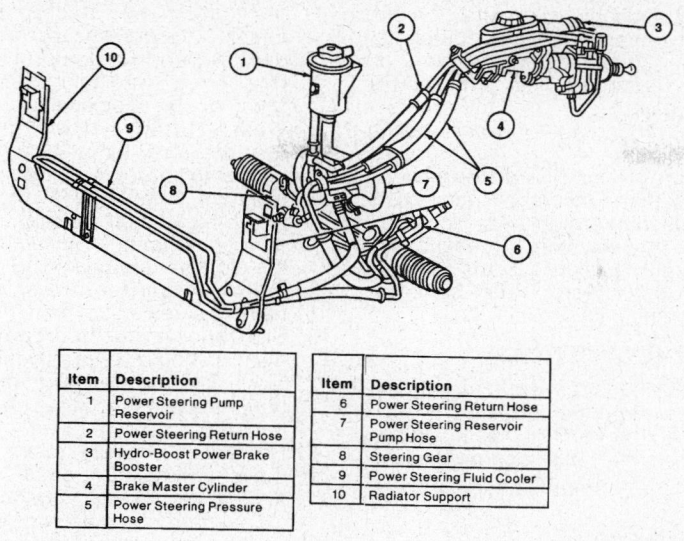

Item	Description
1	Power Steering Pump Reservoir
2	Power Steering Return Hose
3	Hydro-Boost Power Brake Booster
4	Brake Master Cylinder
5	Power Steering Pressure Hose
6	Power Steering Return Hose
7	Power Steering Reservoir Pump Hose
8	Steering Gear
9	Power Steering Fluid Cooler
10	Radiator Support

FM4099600013000X

Fig. 2 Hydro-Boost system fluid distribution. Mustang w/4.6L engine

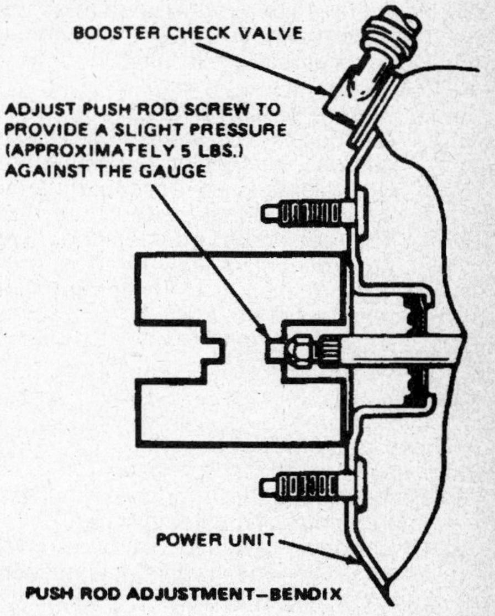
BOOSTER CHECK VALVE
ADJUST PUSH ROD SCREW TO PROVIDE A SLIGHT PRESSURE (APPROXIMATELY 5 LBS.) AGAINST THE GAUGE
POWER UNIT
PUSH ROD ADJUSTMENT—BENDIX

FM4099100010000X

Fig. 3 Master cylinder pushrod adjustment. Bendix type vacuum booster

and inspect for reserve. If no reserve is present, the booster is defective and must be replaced.

BENDIX DIAPHRAGM TYPES

Hard Pedal Or No Assist

1. Air cleaner element clogged.
2. Control valve faulty.
3. Defective diaphragm.
4. Worn or distorted reaction plate or levers.
5. Cracked or broken power piston or levers.
6. Internal or external leaks.

Brakes Grab

1. Control valve defective or sticking.
2. Bind in linkage.
3. Reaction diaphragm leaking.
4. Worn or distorted levers or plate.

No Or Slow Release

1. Pushrod adjustment improper.
2. Linkage binding.
3. Return spring defective.

BENDIX HYDRO-BOOST TYPE

No Power Assist

1. Power steering pump drive belt slipping or worn.
2. Power steering pump fluid level improper.
3. Linkage binding.
4. Hydro-Boost unit failure.

Erratic Booster Operation, Binding, Grabbing Or Sticking

1. Supply hose leakage or obstructions.
2. Hydro-Boost unit seal leakage.

ADJUSTMENTS

PUSHROD

Proper adjustment of the master cylinder pushrod is necessary to ensure proper operation of the power brake system. A pushrod that is too long will prevent the master cylinder piston from completely releasing hydraulic pressure, eventually causing the brakes to drag. A pushrod that is too short will cause excessive brake pedal travel and cause groaning noises to come from the booster when the brakes are applied. A properly adjusted pushrod that remains assembled to the booster with which is was matched during production should not require service adjustment. However, if the booster, master cylinder or pushrod are serviced, the pushrod may require adjustment.

If the power unit pushrod requires an adjustment the Power Unit Repair Kit for the unit being serviced includes a gauge. The gauge measures from the end of the pushrod to the power unit shell.

ESCORT, TRACER & ZX2

Refer to "Hydraulic Brake Systems" section for adjustment procedure.

EXCEPT ESCORT, TRACER & ZX2

Bendix Type

1. Disconnect master cylinder from booster leaving brake lines connected, and secure cylinder to prevent lines from being damaged.
2. Start engine and operate engine at idle speed.
3. With engine running, position gauge over pushrod. Gauge should bottom against booster housing with a force of approximately 5 lbs. applied to pushrod, **Fig. 3.**
4. If force required to seat gauge exceeds 5 lbs., shorten length of pushrod. If force required to seat gauge is less than 5 lbs., lengthen pushrod. **Ensure pushrod is properly seated in booster when performing gauge inspection.**
5. Install master cylinder, then remove reservoir cover.
6. With engine running, observe fluid surface in reservoir when brakes are applied and released rapidly. If no movement is observed on fluid surface, pushrod is adjusted too long.

Single Diaphragm Booster

1. Remove master cylinder as previously outlined.
2. Position master cylinder gauge T87C-2500-A, or equivalent, on end of master cylinder.
3. Loosen setscrew and push gauge plunger against bottom of primary piston.
4. While holding gauge in position, tighten setscrew.
5. Invert gauge and place over brake booster pushrod. Reading should be zero.
6. If clearance is not zero, loosen pushrod locknut and adjust pushrod.
7. Reverse procedure to install.

POWER BRAKE UNIT SERVICE

POWER BOOSTER, REPLACE

ASPIRE

Pump brake pedal several times to exhaust any vacuum in the booster.

1. Remove master cylinder as described in the "Hydraulic Brake Systems" section.
2. Disconnect vacuum hose from power brake unit.
3. From under instrument panel, remove brake pedal clevis pin, then detach pushrod from brake pedal.

4. Remove power brake unit attaching nuts, then remove power brake unit.
5. Reverse procedure to install noting the following:
   a. Ensure proper clearance between pushrod and master cylinder exists as described under "Adjustments."
   b. Bleed brakes as described in the "Hydraulic Brake Systems" section.
   c. **Torque** brake booster mounting nuts to 14–19 ft. lbs.
   d. **Torque** master cylinder mounting nuts to 7–12 ft. lbs.

CONTINENTAL

1997

Pump brake pedal several times to exhaust any vacuum in the booster.

1. Remove tubes from primary and secondary ports of master cylinder.
2. Disconnect manifold vacuum hose from booster check valve, then disconnect warning indicator.
3. Remove master cylinder retaining nuts and master cylinder.
4. Working under instrument panel, disconnect electrical connector from stop lamp switch.
5. Remove stop lamp switch retaining pin and white nylon washer. Slide switch off brake pedal pin enough so outer plate of switch clears the pin, then remove switch from pin.
6. Remove brake booster-to-dash panel attaching nuts, then slide booster pushrod and pushrod bushing off brake pedal pin.
7. Move booster assembly forwards until it clears dash panel, then remove booster.
8. Reverse procedure to install, noting the following:
   a. Ensure proper clearance between pushrod and master cylinder exists as described under "Adjustments."
   b. Bleed brake system as described in the "Hydraulic Brake Systems" section.
   c. **Torque** booster to dash panel retaining nuts to 18–26 ft. lbs.
   d. **Torque** master cylinder to booster locking nuts to 16–21 ft. lbs.

1998–2000

1. Remove battery, then disconnect speed control actuator electrical connector.
2. Remove two retaining nuts and speed control actuator cable and position aside.
3. Remove two strut tower brace nuts and brace.
4. Remove windshield wiper motor, then rubber grommet from lower cowl panel.
5. Remove lower cowl panel nut and bolts, then lower cowl panel.
6. Disconnect power brake booster check valve, then master cylinder.
7. Remove retaining nut and evaporative emission canister purge valve.
8. Disconnect EVAP electrical connector, then vacuum hoses.
9. Remove instrument close out panel pushpins and the panel.
10. Remove stoplight switch retaining pin, then slide stoplight switch and booster push rod from brake pedal pin.
11. Remove retaining nuts and power brake booster.
12. Reverse procedure to install, noting the following:
    a. Ensure proper clearance between pushrod and master cylinder exists as described under "Adjustments."
    b. Bleed brake system as described in "Hydraulic Brake Systems" section.
    c. **Torque** booster to dash panel retaining nuts to 19–25 ft. lbs.

CONTOUR & MYSTIQUE

Pump brake pedal several times to exhaust any vacuum in the booster.

1. Disconnect brake fluid level indicator.
2. **On models with 2.0L engine,** remove mass air flow sensor and air cleaner cover.
3. **On all models,** disconnect vacuum hose from booster unit.
4. Remove master cylinder.
5. Remove booster mounting bolts, then while an assistant holds and guides booster unit out of panel, remove brake booster pushrod retainer from rod.
6. Remove booster from vehicle.
7. Reverse procedure to install, noting the following:
   a. Ensure proper clearance between pushrod and master cylinder exists as described under "Adjustments."
   b. Bleed brake system as described in the "Hydraulic Brake Systems" section.
   c. **Torque** booster to dash panel retaining nuts to 29 ft. lbs.
   d. **Torque** master cylinder to booster locking nuts to 15–28 ft. lbs.

1999–2000 COUGAR

1. Remove air cleaner and mass air flow sensor.
2. Remove air cleaner outlet tube.
3. Disconnect engine wiring harness electrical connector.
4. **On models with automatic transaxle,** remove automatic transaxle fluid dipstick.
5. **On all models,** remove master cylinder.
6. Remove brake booster actuator rod retaining clip.
7. Disconnect vacuum hose from brake booster. **Do not pull on accelerator speed control cable.**
8. Remove brake booster.
9. Reverse procedure to install, noting the following:
   a. Bleed brake system.
   b. Ensure that brake booster connecting rod is correctly positioned through bulkhead rubber boot.

CROWN VICTORIA, GRAND MARQUIS & TOWN CAR

1997

Pump brake pedal several times to exhaust any vacuum in the booster.

1. Disconnect master cylinder from booster and position aside. **It is not necessary to disconnect brake lines, but care should be taken to avoid twisting or kinking them.**
2. Disconnect manifold vacuum hose from booster check valve.
3. Working under instrument panel, disconnect stop lamp switch electrical connector under instrument panel.
4. Remove stop lamp switch retaining pin. Slide switch off brake pedal pin enough so outer plate of switch clears the pin, then remove switch from pin.
5. Remove booster-to-dash panel attaching screws.
6. Slide booster pushrod, nylon washers and bushing off brake pedal pin.
7. Move booster forward until booster studs clear dash panel, then remove booster.
8. Reverse procedure to install, noting the following:
   a. Ensure proper clearance between pushrod and master cylinder exists as described under "Adjustments."
   b. **Torque** booster to dash panel retaining nuts and master cylinder nuts to 16–21 ft. lbs.

1998–2000

1. Disconnect fluid level sensor connector.
2. Position speed control cable out of way.
3. Disconnect power brake booster check valve.
4. Remove brake master cylinder nuts.
5. Remove wiring harness bracket and position aside.
6. Remove brake master cylinder and position aside.
7. Remove instrument close-out panel pushpins, then the panel.
8. Remove stoplight switch retaining pin.
9. Slide stoplight switch and booster push rod off brake pedal pin.
10. Remove brake booster retaining nuts, then the power brake booster.
11. Reverse procedure to install. **Torque** retaining nuts to 16–21 ft. lbs.

ESCORT, PROBE, TRACER & ZX2

Pump brake pedal several times to exhaust any vacuum in the booster.

1. Remove master cylinder as described in the "Hydraulic Brake Systems" section.
2. Disconnect rubber hose connecting intake manifold to power brake unit.
3. **On Escort, Tracer and ZX2 models,** remove instrument panel steering column cover.
4. **On all models,** remove spring clip in brake pedal clevis pin.
5. Remove brake pedal clevis pin, then brake pedal pushrod from brake pedal.
6. Remove power brake unit attaching nuts, then power brake unit from vehicle.
7. Reverse procedure to install, noting the following:
   a. **On Probe models,** ensure arrow on booster vacuum hose points toward intake manifold.
   b. **On all models,** ensure proper clearance between pushrod and

master cylinder exists as described under "Adjustments."
   c. **Torque** booster to dash panel retaining nuts to 14–19 ft. lbs.
   d. **Torque** master cylinder retaining nuts to 8–12 ft. lbs.

LS

Removal

1. Remove wiper arm nuts and remove wiper arms, then disconnect washer hose.
2. Remove pushpins, rubber trim and cowl cover.
3. Remove vacuum hose bracket nut and position bracket aside.
4. Remove cowl brace center and end bolts, then the bracket.
5. Disconnect coolant reservoir return hose.
6. Remove brake master cylinder.
7. Disconnect power brake booster check valve and electrical connector.
8. Remove coolant reservoir bolts and disconnect hose.
9. Remove coolant reservoir.
10. Remove clip and brake pedal pin.
11. Remove mounting nuts and power brake booster.

Installation

1. Install power brake booster and mounting nuts.
2. Install brake pedal pin and clip.
3. Install radiator coolant recovery reservoir mounting bolts and hose.
4. Connect power brake booster electrical connector and check valve.
5. Connect coolant reservoir return hose.
6. Install brake master cylinder.
7. Install cowl brace end and center bolts.
8. Install vacuum hose bracket nut.
9. Install cowl cover, rubber trim and pushpins.
10. Connect washer hose and install wiper arm nuts.
11. Bleed brake system.

MARK VIII

1. Remove windshield wiper motor.
2. Disconnect power brake booster check valve.
3. Disconnect fluid level sensor connector.
4. Remove nut retaining wire harness support bracket, then the bracket.
5. Remove nuts retaining brake master cylinder to power brake booster.
6. Position brake master cylinder out of the way.
7. Disconnect harness connectors.
8. Working inside vehicle below the instrument panel, remove retaining clip from the powertrain control module.
9. Remove power brake booster push rod from brake pedal.
10. Disconnect electrical connector from stoplight switch.
11. Remove hairpin retainer and push rod spacer.
12. Remove push rod, stoplight switch and push rod bushing.
13. Remove processor bracket to brake booster retaining nuts. Position bracket to the side.
14. Remove brake pedal support bracket to booster studs retaining nuts.
15. From inside the engine compartment, move power brake booster forward until booster studs clear the instrument panel.
16. Rotate front of power brake booster toward engine, then remove power brake booster.
17. Reverse procedures to install, noting the following:
    a. **Torque** power brake booster-to-instrument panel retaining nut to 16–21 ft. lbs.
    b. **Torque** break master cylinder-to-power brake booster locking nuts to 16–21 ft. lbs.
    c. **Torque** pedal support bracket-to-cowl bolt to 16–21 ft. lbs.
    d. **Torque** master cylinder brake tube fittings 13–17 ft. lbs.

MUSTANG

Vacuum Type System

Pump brake pedal several times to exhaust any vacuum in the booster.

1. Remove air cleaner assembly.
2. Disconnect manifold vacuum hose from power booster check valve.
3. Disconnect hydraulic lines from master cylinder and cap open lines and ports.
4. Remove master cylinder retaining nuts and master cylinder.
5. **On models with manual transmission,** remove clutch cable routing bracket and position cable aside.
6. **On all models,** disconnect accelerator cable at dash panel and accelerator pedal and shaft, then reposition to gain maneuvering room for brake booster.
7. Working under instrument panel, disconnect electrical connector from stop lamp switch.
8. Remove hairpin type retainer. Slide stop lamp switch off brake pedal pin just far enough for the switch outer hole to clear the pin, then lower switch away from pin.
9. Slide brake master cylinder pushrod bushing off of brake pedal pin.
10. Remove booster-to-dash panel attaching nuts.
11. **On models equipped with speed control,** unfasten control amplifier from lower outboard booster stud and position aside.
12. **On all models,** work from engine compartment and move booster forward until booster studs clear the dash panel, then raise front of unit and remove from vehicle.
13. Reverse procedure to install, noting the following:
    a. Ensure proper clearance between pushrod and master cylinder exists as described under "Adjustments."
    b. Bleed brake system as described in the "Hydraulic Brake Systems" section.
    c. **Torque** booster to dash panel retaining nuts and master cylinder to booster locking nuts to 15–23 ft. lbs.

Hydro-Boost System

The booster should not be carried by the accumulator, nor should it be dropped on this portion. The accumulator contains high pressure nitrogen gas and can be dangerous if mishandled.

If the accumulator is ready for disposal, it must be kept clear of excessive heat, fire or incineration. Before disposal, drill a 1/16 inch diameter hole in the accumulator can's end to relieve the gas pressure. Be sure to use wear safety glasses while performing this operation.

Do not activate the booster when the master cylinder has been removed.

1. Apply brake pedal several times to discharge accumulator.
2. Remove brake lines from proportioning valve's primary and secondary ports.
3. Disconnect fluid level sensor.
4. **On models with automatic transmission,** disconnect shift interlock cable.
5. **On models with manual transmission,** disconnect clutch cable from master cylinder routing bracket.
6. **On all models,** remove hose routing bracket from master cylinder.
7. Disconnect power steering pressure hoses and return line from Hydro-Boost unit. Move hoses out of the way.
8. Remove electrical connector from brake lamp switch.
9. Loosen four booster retaining nuts and brake pedal support bracket to cowl bolt.
10. Remove hairpin type retainer. Slide stop lamp switch off brake pedal pin just far enough for switch outer arm to clear pin, then remove switch.
11. Slide brake master cylinder pushrod bushing off brake pedal pin.
12. Remove booster to firewall attaching nuts.
13. Move booster and master cylinder forward and upward until booster's studs clear firewall. Remove unit from vehicle.
14. Reverse procedure to install, noting the following:
    a. **Torque** booster to firewall nuts to 16–21 ft. lbs.
    b. **Torque** brake pedal support bracket to cowl bolt to 14–19 ft. lbs.
    c. **Torque** brake line fittings in ports to 11–17 ft. lbs.
    d. **Torque** power steering pressure hoses and return line to booster tubes to 10–15 ft. lbs., **Fig. 2.**
    e. Bleed brake system. Check power brake operation and bleed booster of air if necessary.

SABLE & TAURUS

Pump brake pedal several times to exhaust any vacuum in the booster.

1. Disconnect vacuum hose from booster unit.
2. Disconnect air cleaner cover and position aside.
3. Remove speed control actuator nuts, then position actuator aside.
4. Disconnect brake fluid level sensor

from master cylinder.
5. Remove nut holding cowl top inner panel tube to master cylinder mounting stud, then remove master cylinder.
6. Working under instrument panel, disconnect electrical connector from stop lamp switch.
7. Remove stop lamp switch retaining pin and white nylon washer. Slide switch off brake pedal pin enough so outer plate of switch clears the pin, then remove switch from pin.
8. Remove brake booster-to-dash panel attaching nuts, then slide booster pushrod and pushrod bushing off brake pedal pin.
9. Slide booster out of panel.
10. Reverse procedure to install, noting the following:
    a. Ensure proper clearance between pushrod and master cylinder exists as described under "Adjustments."
    b. Bleed brake system as described in the "Hydraulic Brake Systems" section.
    c. **Torque** booster to dash panel retaining nuts and cowl top inner panel tube nut to 16–21 ft. lbs.
    d. **Torque** master cylinder to booster locking nuts to 19–28 ft. lbs.

THUNDERBIRD & 1997 COUGAR

Pump brake pedal several times to exhaust any vacuum in the booster.

1. Remove air cleaner.
2. Disconnect manifold vacuum hose from booster check valve.
3. Disconnect brake lines from primary and secondary outlet ports of master cylinder.
4. Remove master cylinder to booster attaching nuts and the master cylinder.
5. Remove windshield wiper motor.
6. **On models equipped with speed control,** unfasten control amplifier from lower outboard booster stud and position aside.
7. **On all models,** working under instrument panel, disconnect electrical connector from stop lamp switch.
8. Remove hairpin type retainer. Slide stop lamp switch off brake pedal pin just far enough for the switch outer hole to clear the pin, then lower switch away from pin.
9. Remove booster to dash panel attaching nuts.
10. Slide booster pushrod, bushing and inner nylon washer off brake pedal pin.
11. Move booster forward in engine compartment until booster studs clear dash panel, then rotate front of booster toward engine and remove booster.
12. Reverse procedure to install, noting the following:
    a. Ensure proper clearance between pushrod and master cylinder exists as described under "Adjustments."
    b. Bleed brake system as described in the "Hydraulic Brake Systems" section.
    c. **Torque** booster to dash panel retaining nuts to 20–25 ft. lbs.
    d. **Torque** master cylinder to booster locking nuts to 16–25 ft. lbs.

OVERHAUL

Overhaul is not required. If it has been determined that the brake booster is defective, replace power brake unit as an assembly. In some instances, the only service required is replacement of the check valve and grommet and pushrod adjustment.

AUTOMATIC TRANSMISSIONS/ TRANSAXLES

TABLE OF CONTENTS

Application Chart

Model	Year	Engine	Transmission/ Transaxle
Aspire	1997	All	ATX
Continental	1997–2000	All	AX4N
Contour	1997–2000	All	CD4E
Cougar	1997	All	4R70W
	1999–2000	All	CD4E
Crown Victoria	1997–2000	All	4R70W
Escort	1997	All	IF4E
	1998–2000	All	F4E-III
Grand Marquis	1997–2000	All	4R70W
LS	2000	All	5R55N
Mark VIII	1997–98	All	4R70W
Mustang	1997–2000	All	4R70W
Mystique	1997–2000	All	CD4E
Probe	1997	2.0L	CD4E
		2.5L	4EAT
Sable	1997–99	3.0L	①
Taurus	1997–99	3.0L	①
		3.4L	AX4N
Thunderbird	1997	All	4R70W
Tracer	1997	All	IF4E
	1998–99	All	F4E-III
Town Car	1997–2000	All	4R70W
ZX2	1998–2000	All	F4E-III

① — May use AX4S or AX4N. AX4S main control cover will be identified "AXOD METRIC," while AX4N will read "AX4N METRIC."

ATX Automatic Transaxle

NOTE: On Air Bag Equipped Models, Refer To " Air Bag System Precautions" Located In The Front Of This Manual For System Disarming & Arming Procedures.

NOTE: "Electrical Symbol & Wire Color Code Identification" Located In The Front Of This Manual May Be Used As An Aid When Using Wiring Circuits Found In This Section.

NOTE: Prior To Performing Any Service Operations Listed In This Section, Consult "Technical Service Bulletins " Section For Related Information.

INDEX

PRECAUTIONS

AIR BAG SYSTEMS

Refer to "Air Bag System Precautions" in front of this manual for system disarming and arming procedures.

BATTERY GROUND CABLE

Prior to service, disconnect battery ground cable and isolate as required.

DESCRIPTION

This automatic transaxle combines an automatic transmission and differential into a single powertrain unit. This unit is designed specifically for front-wheel drive applications. Transaxle housing is made of a lightweight aluminum alloy and is mounted transversely to engine.

TROUBLESHOOTING

SHIFT INTERLOCK SYSTEM DOES NOT RELEASE OR LOCK PROPERLY

Refer to wiring diagram **Fig. 1** and troubleshooting chart **Fig. 2.**

MAINTENANCE

FLUID CHECK

With vehicle on a level surface, start engine and operate at fast idle for several minutes. With engine at curb idle speed and brakes applied, move selector lever through all gear positions, then return lever to P. With engine still operating at curb idle speed, clean area around transaxle dipstick, then remove dipstick and check fluid level. Fluid level should be between L and F marks. Add Dexron Type II fluid, as necessary, to bring fluid level between L and F marks. After completing fluid level check, ensure transaxle dipstick is properly seated in dipstick tube.

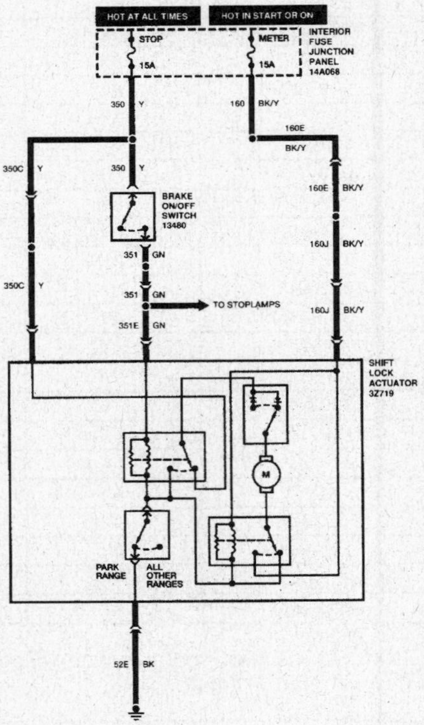

FM5029300957000X

Fig. 1 Shift interlock system wiring diagram

1. Bring engine to normal operating temperature.
2. Park vehicle on level surface, then place transaxle in Park.
3. Apply brakes, then shift gear selector lever through entire range twice.
4. Remove transaxle dipstick, wipe clean, then replace, ensure dipstick is fully seated in tube.
5. Remove transaxle dipstick, then read level indicator on dipstick.
6. If fluid level is low, add specified transaxle fluid.

FLUID CHANGE

Under normal operating circumstances, changing of transaxle fluid every 30,000 miles. Under severe conditions, transaxle fluid should be changed every 21,000 miles.

1. Raise and support front of vehicle.
2. Position suitable drain pan under transaxle, then remove drain plug and allow transaxle to drain.
3. Remove transaxle oil pan retaining bolts and carefully remove oil pan.
4. Clean oil pan and filter. If necessary, replace filter.
5. Position new gasket to transaxle oil pan, then install oil pan on transaxle. Tighten oil pan-to-transaxle retaining screws to specifications. **Do not use any sealer on transaxle oil pan gasket.**
6. Install new washer and oil pan drain plug, then tighten to specifications.
7. Lower vehicle.
8. Remove transaxle dipstick and add 3

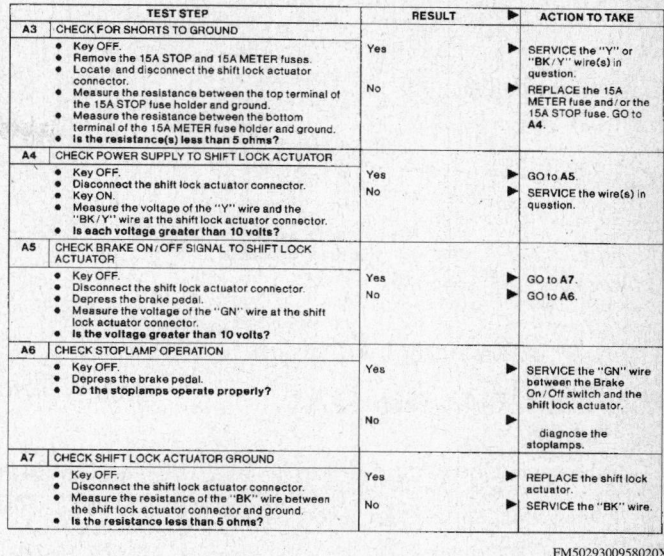

TEST STEP		RESULT	▶ ACTION TO TAKE
A1	CHECK FUSES		
	• Key OFF. • Check the 15A METER and the 15A STOP fuses located in the interior fuse junction panel. • **Are the fuses OK?**	Yes No	▶ GO to **A4**. ▶ GO to **A2**.
A2	CHECK SYSTEM		
	• Key OFF. • Replace the blown fuse(s). • Key ON. • **Do(es) the fuse(s) fail again?**	Yes No	▶ GO to **A3**. ▶ GO to **A4**.

FM5029300958010X

Fig. 2 Shift interlock system troubleshooting chart (Part 1 of 2)

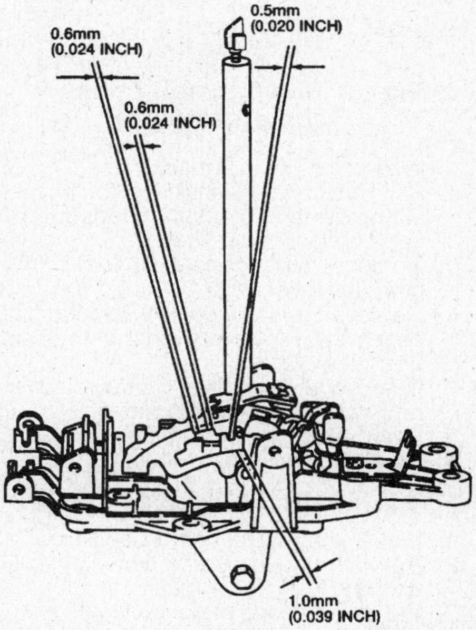

FM5019400510000X

Fig. 3 Transaxle shift control guide plate & pin clearance

TEST STEP		RESULT	▶ ACTION TO TAKE
A3	CHECK FOR SHORTS TO GROUND		
	• Key OFF. • Remove the 15A STOP and 15A METER fuses. • Locate and disconnect the shift lock actuator connector. • Measure the resistance between the top terminal of the 15A STOP fuse holder and ground. • Measure the resistance between the bottom terminal of the 15A METER fuse holder and ground. • **Is the resistance(s) less than 5 ohms?**	Yes No	▶ SERVICE the "Y" or "BK/Y" wire(s) in question. ▶ REPLACE the 15A METER fuse and/or the 15A STOP fuse. GO to **A4**.
A4	CHECK POWER SUPPLY TO SHIFT LOCK ACTUATOR		
	• Key OFF. • Disconnect the shift lock actuator connector. • Key ON. • Measure the voltage of the "Y" wire and the "BK/Y" wire at the shift lock actuator connector. • **Is each voltage greater than 10 volts?**	Yes No	▶ GO to **A5**. ▶ SERVICE the wire(s) in question.
A5	CHECK BRAKE ON/OFF SIGNAL TO SHIFT LOCK ACTUATOR		
	• Key OFF. • Disconnect the shift lock actuator connector. • Depress the brake pedal. • Measure the voltage of the "GN" wire at the shift lock actuator connector. • **Is the voltage greater than 10 volts?**	Yes No	▶ GO to **A7**. ▶ GO to **A6**.
A6	CHECK STOPLAMP OPERATION		
	• Key OFF. • Depress the brake pedal. • **Do the stoplamps operate properly?**	Yes No	▶ SERVICE the "GN" wire between the Brake On/Off switch and the shift lock actuator. ▶ diagnose the stoplamps.
A7	CHECK SHIFT LOCK ACTUATOR GROUND		
	• Key OFF. • Disconnect the shift lock actuator connector. • Measure the resistance of the "BK" wire between the shift lock actuator connector and ground. • **Is the resistance less than 5 ohms?**	Yes No	▶ REPLACE the shift lock actuator. ▶ SERVICE the "BK" wire.

FM5029300958020X

Fig. 2 Shift interlock system troubleshooting chart (Part 2 of 2)

quarts of Mercon ATF to transaxle through dipstick tube.

9. Start engine and allow to reach operating temperature, then check fluid level as outlined under "Oil Level Check."

ADJUSTMENTS

SHIFT CABLE

1. Engage parking brake.
2. Move transaxle selector lever into Park position, then remove shift console panel.
3. Remove shift lever knob screws, then gearshift lever knob.
4. Remove transaxle control selector dial screws. Ensure detent spring roller is in Park detent, then remove transaxle control selector dial bezel.
5. Loosen transaxle shift cable and bracket bolts, then adjust shift cable and bracket at shift lever and move to desired position.
6. Inspect shift cable and bracket for proper adjustment at shift lever, then inspect shift lever trunnion.
7. Press selector push rod and ensure guide plate and guide pin clearances are with specifications, **Fig. 3.**
8. Repeat previous step when transaxle selector lever is shifted to Neutral and Drive. If clearance is not as specified, adjust shift cable.

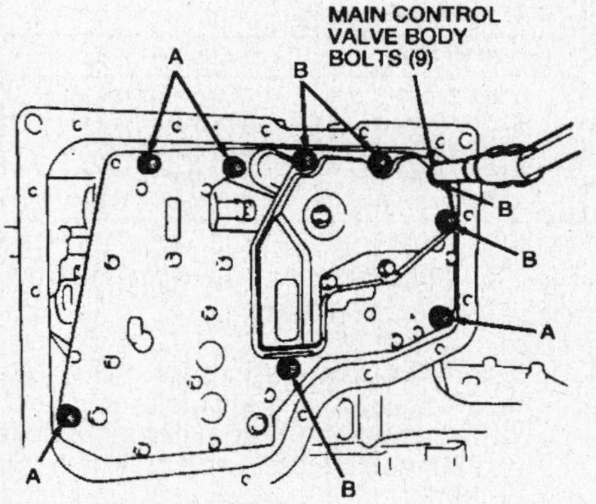

A = 30mm (1.18 INCH) BOLT
B = 40mm (1.57 INCH) BOLT

FM5029501141000X

Fig. 4 Valve body retaining bolt locations

9. Install shift quadrant, then shift quadrant bezel.

IN-VEHICLE REPAIRS

VALVE BODY, REPLACE

Removal

1. Raise and support vehicle.
2. Remove front fender and front splash shields to gain access to transaxle.
3. Drain transaxle fluid, then remove oil pan attaching bolts and oil pan.
4. Remove valve body retaining bolts, **Fig. 4,** then carefully remove valve. **Be careful not to lose throttle control valve rod or check ball and detent spring used for torque converter relief valve.**

Installation

1. Install throttle control rod into hole in case, then install ball and spring into slotted hole in transaxle case, **Fig. 5.**

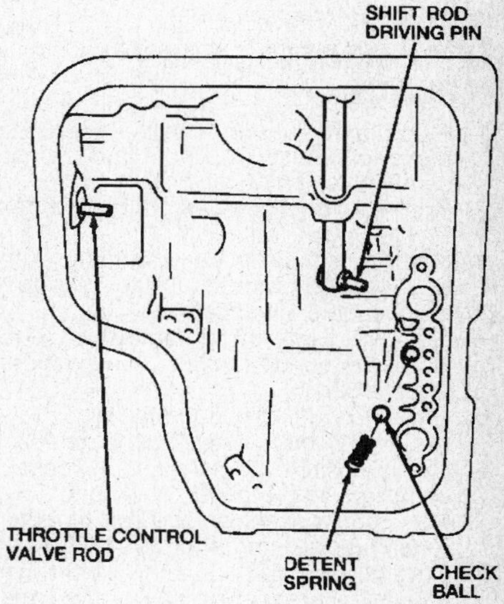

FM5029501142000X

Fig. 5 Throttle control rod, check ball & spring installation

Insert ball first, then spring. Use petroleum jelly to hold ball and spring in position.

2. Install valve body, mating manual valve groove with shift rod driving pin, then index dowel in transaxle case with mating holes in valve body holes, **Fig. 6.**
3. Install valve body retaining bolts and tighten to specifications.
4. Install oil pan and new gasket. Tighten oil pan retaining bolts to specifications. **Do not use any sealer on oil pan gasket.**
5. Install splash shields, then lower vehicle.
6. Add three quarts of Mercon ATF to transaxle, then start engine and check fluid level as outlined under "Oil Level Check."

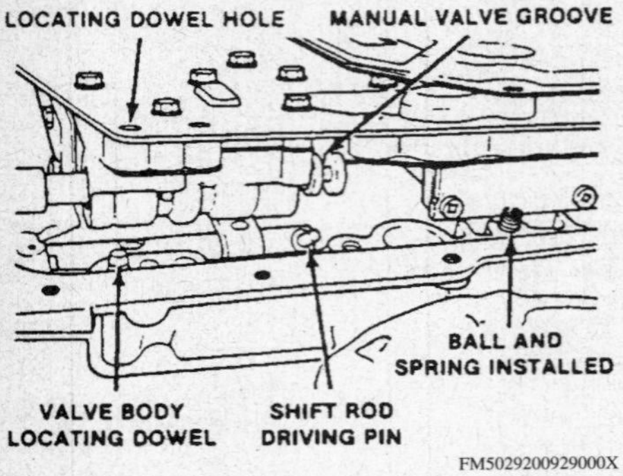

Fig. 6 Valve body installation

DIFFERENTIAL OIL SEAL, REPLACE

1. Raise and support front of vehicle.
2. Remove front wheel driveshaft and joint as described under " Front Wheel Drive Axles."
3. Use suitable flat blade screwdriver to remove differential oil seal.
4. Reverse procedure to install using differential seal replacer tool No. T87C-77000-H, or equivalent.

INTERMEDIATE SERVO, REPLACE

1. Raise and support vehicle, then remove lefthand front wheel and tire assembly.
2. Remove valve body as outlined under "Valve Body, Replace."
3. Remove stabilizer bar mounting nuts and bracket, then stabilizer support bracket bolts and bracket.
4. Remove front wheel driveshaft and joint as described under " Front Wheel Drive Axles."
5. Loosen band adjusting stop and locknut, **Fig. 7,** then remove band strut.
6. Using suitable C-clamp and socket, compress servo piston, then use suitable screwdriver, remove servo piston retaining snap ring, **Fig. 8.**
7. Carefully loosen C-clamp, then remove servo retainer, piston, spring and seal.
8. Reverse procedure to install, noting following:
   a. . Prior to installation, lubricate servo piston with Mercon ATF.
   b. Tighten band adjusting stop to specifications, then loosen bolt three turns.
   c. While holding anchor end bolt in position, tighten locknut to specifications.

VACUUM THROTTLE VALVE DIAPHRAGM, REPLACE

1. Drain transaxle fluid, then disconnect vacuum hose from vacuum diaphragm.
2. Unscrew vacuum unit by hand , while holding flange with suitable pliers, remove O-ring and vacuum diaphragm rod from case. **Diaphragm control rod is a selective component. If diaphragm is to be replaced refer to Fig. 9** for correct rod.

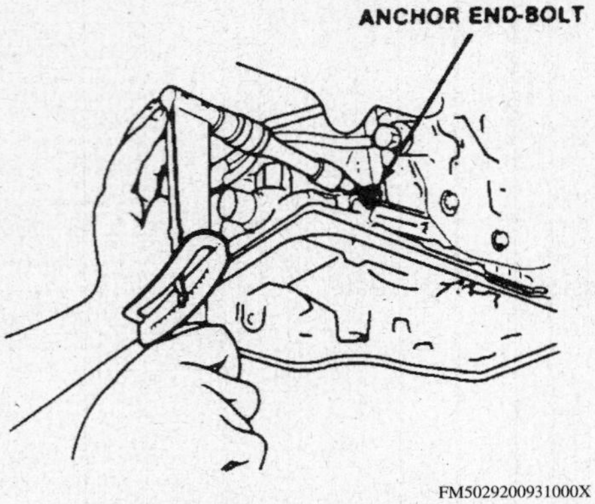

Fig. 7 Band adjusting stop loosening

MEASUREMENT	DIAPHRAGM ROD USED
Under 25.4 mm (1.000 in)	29.5 mm (1.160 in)
25.4 – 25.9 mm (1.000 – 1.020 in)	30.0 mm (1.180 in)
25.9 – 26.4 mm (1.020 – 1.039 in)	30.5 mm (1.200 in)
26.4 – 26.9 mm (1.039 – 1.059 in)	31.0 mm (1.220 in)
Over 26.9 mm (1.059 in)	31.5 mm (1.240 in)

PART NO.	DIAPHRAGM ROD
E7GZ-7A380-E	29.5 mm (1.160 in)
E7GZ-7A380-C	30.0 mm (1.180 in)
E7GZ-7A380-D	30.5 mm (1.200 in)
E7GZ-7A380-B	31.0 mm (1.220 in)
E7GZ-7A380-A	31.5 mm (1.240 in)

FM5028900830000X

Fig. 9 Diaphragm rod application chart

3. Insert vacuum diaphragm rod gauge tool No. T87C-77000-A, or equivalent, into vacuum diaphragm mounting hole (with beveled side facing out) until tool bottoms.
4. Place rod of special tool through opening of vacuum diaphragm rod gauge until it bottoms against valve.
5. Tighten lock knob on vacuum diaphragm tool, then remove tool and rod from transaxle case.
6. Use suitable depth gauge to measure distance from flat surface of vacuum diaphragm tool to end of rod.
7. Install vacuum diaphragm rod into transaxle case.
8. Lubricate new diaphragm O-ring with Mercon ATF, then install O-ring on vacuum unit.
9. Coat threads of vacuum unit with sealer part No. E1FZ-19562-A, or equivalent, then install vacuum unit into transaxle case and tighten with suitable pliers on crimped portion of diaphragm.
10. Connect vacuum hose to vacuum diaphragm.
11. Add three quarts of Mercon ATF into transaxle, then check fluid level.

SHIFT CABLE, REPLACE

1. Place transaxle shift lever in 1 position.
2. Remove instrument panel, then heater core.
3. Remove cotter pin, then gearshift cable mounting bracket from gearshift

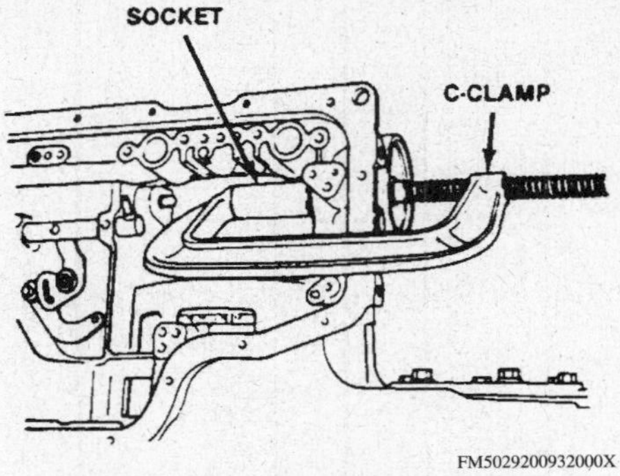

Fig. 8 Servo piston spring compression

lever trunnion on transaxle.

4. Remove transaxle locking clip, then lift shift cable and bracket from gear shift cable mounting bracket.
5. Remove shift console panel, then gearshift lever knob.
6. Remove transaxle control selector dial bezel, then transaxle shift cable and bracket locknut.
7. Remove shift cable and bracket, then rubber grommet from bulkhead.
8. Pull shift cable from vehicle.
9. Reverse procedure to install.

GEAR SELECTOR, REPLACE

1. Place gearshift lever in 1 position.
2. Remove parking brake console panel ashtray.
3. Remove parking brake console.
4. Lift shift console, then disconnect electrical connections.
5. Remove shift console, then gearshift knob.
6. Lift transaxle control dial bezel, then disconnect electrical connections.
7. Remove transaxle control dial bezel, then shift cable and bracket.
8. Disconnect shift lock actuator electrical connections, then remove shift lock actuator.
9. Loosen locknut "A," then remove ignition/shifter interlock cable, **Fig. 10. Do not loosen locknut "B." It is factory preset for proper shift interlock operation.**
10. Remove gearshift selector.
11. Reverse procedure to install.

SHIFT INTERLOCK CABLE, REPLACE

1. Remove shift console panel.
2. Loosen locknut "A" in **Fig. 10,** then disconnect interlock cable from bracket on shift lever. **Do not loosen locknut " B." It is factory preset for proper shift interlock operation.**
3. Attach suitable mechanic's wire to cable to aid installation, then remove two hold-down bracket screws attaching interlock cable to bulkhead.
4. Remove lower steering column shroud attaching screws, then separate upper and lower steering column shrouds.
5. Remove interlock cable to lock cylinder bolt at lock cylinder housing, then remove cable.
6. Reverse procedure to install.

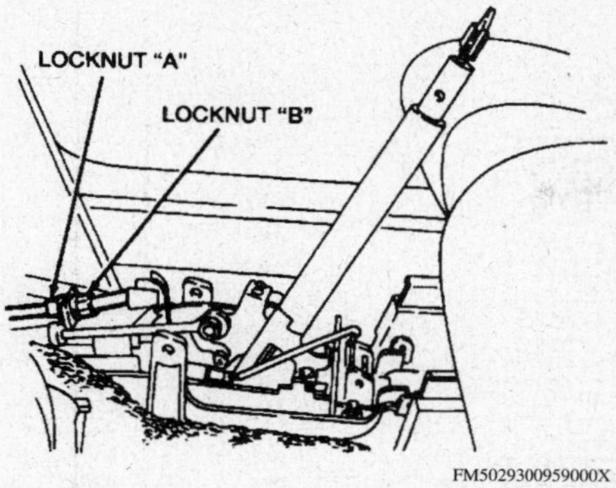

Fig. 10 Interlock cable removal

TRANSAXLE

REPLACE

1. Drain transmission fluid, then disconnect speedometer cable from transaxle.
2. Disconnect electrical connectors near governor, then ground wire from transaxle.
3. Disconnect transaxle vacuum hose, then shift lever nut from manual shaft assembly.
4. Remove shift cable from transaxle, then support engine using engine support bar tool No. D87L-6000-A, or equivalent.
5. Raise and support vehicle, then remove front wheels.
6. Remove lefthand splash shield, then stabilizer bar mounting nuts and brackets.
7. Remove lower arm clamp bolts and nuts. Pull lower arms down, separating lower arms from knuckles.
8. Remove cotter pin and nut, then disconnect tie rod end from knuckle.
9. Remove halfshafts, then install differential plug tools No. T87C-7025-C , or equivalent, between differential side gears.
10. Disconnect oil cooler hoses, then remove crossmember.
11. Remove gusset plate-to-transaxle bolts, then remove flywheel cover.
12. Remove torque converter bolts, then starter.
13. Remove engine-to-transaxle bolts, then transaxle from vehicle.
14. Reverse procedure to install.

TECHNICAL SERVICE BULLETINS

DELAYED ENGAGEMENT AFTER EXTENDED SHUT DOWN

On these models, there may be delayed transaxle engagement after sitting for extended period.

This condition may be caused by low torque converter fluid flow. To correct this condition, proceed as follows:

1. Inspect and adjust fluid level.
2. If fluid is burnt or discolored, diagnosis and repair transaxle as outlined in **MOTOR's Domestic Transmission Manual.**
3. Inspect line pressure at idle and stall. If pressures are not within specifications, **Fig. 11,** diagnosis and repair transaxle as outlined in **MOTOR's Domestic Transmission Manual.** If pressures are within specifications, proceed to next step.
4. Drain transmission fluid into suitable container.
5. Remove mounting bolts and pan, then discard gasket.

LINE PRESSURE SPECIFICATIONS			
	Control Pressure		
Engine State	"D" and "1"	"2"	"R"
At Idle	46-54 psi	76-95 psi	76-95 psi
At Stall (Wide Open Throttle)	141-157 psi	150-166 psi	251-263 psi

FMA059800088000X

Fig. 11 ATX line pressure specifications

6. Note main control valve body bolt locations for assembly.
7. Remove mounting bolts and main control valve body. Do not loss check ball and detent spring in slotted hole or throttle control valve rod.
8. Thoroughly clean oil pan gasket residue from case and pan.
9. Install revised check ball and seat assembly kit (part No. F4BZ-7K037-AA) in drain back hole. Use suitable petroleum jelly to hold assembly in place.
10. Install following kit parts in order: seat, sleeve, check ball and spring.
11. Install throttle control valve rod.
12. Install main control valve body in reverse order of disassembly with main control valve body bolts in original positions. Ensure spring is not crushed between main control valve body and case.
13. Tighten mounting bolts to specifications.
14. Install pan with kit supplied gasket. Do not use any sealer on gasket. If necessary, soak gasket in transmission fluid.
15. Tighten pan mounting bolts to specifications.
16. Fill transaxle with Mercon III automatic transmission fluid, or equivalent, to proper level.
17. Warm transaxle to operating temperature and adjust fluid level.

TIGHTENING SPECIFICATIONS

Year	Component	Torque/ Ft. Lbs.
1997	Adjuster Locknut	41–59
	Anchor End Bolt	9–11
	Anchor End Bolt Locknut	41–59
	Bearing Housing	14–19
	Bearing/Stator Support Bolts	96–120①
	Crossmember Attaching Bolts	47–66
	Differential Ring Gear Bolts	51–62
	Engine To Transaxle Bolts	41–59
	Flywheel Cover Attaching Bolts	72–86①
	Front Engine Mount To Crossmember Bolts	32–38
	Gasket Plate To Transaxle Bolts	27–38
	Governor Cover Attaching Bolts	69–15
	Idler Gear Locknut	94–130
	Intermediate Band Adjuster Bolt	9–11
	Lower Arm Ball Joint	40–50
	Manual Shaft Nut	22–29
	Manual Shaft Support Bolts	43–69①

Continued

TIGHTENING SPECIFICATIONS—Continued

Year	Component	Torque/ Ft. Lbs.
1997	Neutral Safety Switch	14–19
	Oil Filler Tube Retaining Bolt	60–84①
	Oil Pan Attaching Bolts	43–69①
	Oil Pump Cover Bolts	96–120①
	Oil Pump To Transaxle Bolts	11–16
	Parking Paw Actuator Support Bolts	9–12
	Rear Engine Mount To Crossmember Nut	21–34
	Shift Linkage To Manual Shift Bolt	34–57
	Speedometer Drive Gear Bolt	72–96①
	Stabilizer Body Bracket Nuts	43–52
	Stabilizer Mounting Nuts	40–50
	Tie Rod End Attaching Nut	26–30
	Torque Converter Attaching Nuts	26–36
	Transaxle Case To Clutch Housing Bolts	22–34
	Transaxle Drain Plug	29–40
	Valve Body Side Plate Bolts	22–30①
	Valve Body Retaining Bolts	72–96①

① — Inch lbs.

AX4N Automatic Transaxle

NOTE: On Air Bag Equipped Models, Refer To " Air Bag System Precautions" Located In The Front Of This Manual For System Disarming & Arming Procedures.

NOTE: Prior To Performing Any Service Operations Listed In This Section, Consult "Technical Service Bulletins " Section For Related Information.

INDEX

PRECAUTIONS

AIR BAG SYSTEMS

Refer to "Air Bag System Precautions" in front of this manual for system disarming and arming procedures.

BATTERY GROUND CABLE

Prior to service, disconnect battery ground cable and isolate as required.

IDENTIFICATION

Transaxle identification tag, **Fig. 1,** is located on top of converter housing.

FM5029601057000X

Fig. 1 Transaxle identification tag

DESCRIPTION

The AX4N automatic transaxle, **Fig. 2,** is a four-speed unit with automatic shift control. All upshifting, downshifting, line pressure and torque converter clutch operations are controlled by EEC-V electronic engine control system. transaxle control is separate from engine control strategy in PCM, although some input signals are shared.

TROUBLESHOOTING

BRAKE-SHIFT INTERLOCK SYSTEM

Refer to "AX4S (AXOD-E)) Automatic Overdrive Transaxle."

TRANSAXLE

Refer to **Figs. 3 through 47** for troubleshooting.

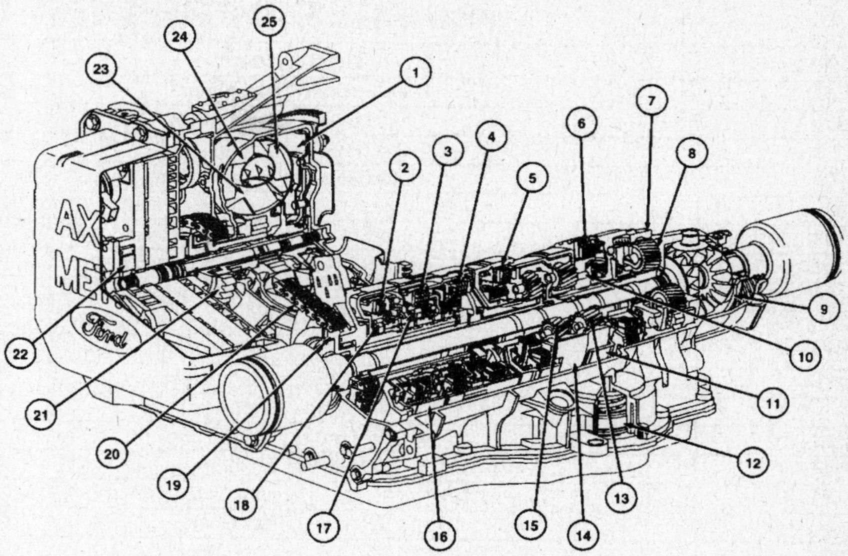

Item	Description
1	Torque Converter
2	Forward Clutch Assy
3	Direct Clutch Assy
4	Intermediate Clutch Assy
5	Reverse Clutch Assy
6	Low/Intermediate Clutch Assy
7	Final Drive Ring Gear
8	Final Drive Gearset
9	Differential Assy
10	Low/Intermediate One-Way Roller Clutch Assy
11	Coast Band
12	Coast Servo Piston
13	Rear Planetary Gearset
14	Rear Planetary Ring Gear
15	Front Planetary Gearset
16	Overdrive Band
17	Direct One-Way Roller Clutch Assy
18	Low One-Way Sprag Clutch
19	Driven Sprocket
20	Drive Chain
21	Drive Sprocket
22	Pump Assy
23	Reactor
24	Impeller
25	Turbine

FM5029601058000X

Fig. 2 Cross-sectional view of AX4N automatic transaxle

TROUBLESHOOTING TEST INDEX

Routine	Description	Page No.	Fig. No.
201/301	No Forward Engagement	21-9	3
202/302	No Reverse Engagement	21-9	4
203/303	Harsh Reverse Engagement	21-10	5
204/304	Harsh Forward Engagement	21-10	6
205/305	Delayed/Soft Reverse Engagement	21-10	7
206/306	Delayed/Soft Forward Engagement	21-11	8
207/307	No Forward & No Reverse Engagement	21-11	9
208/308	Harsh Forward & Reverse Engagement	21-12	10
209/309	Delayed/Soft Forward & Reverse Engagement	21-13	11
210/310	Some Or All Shifts Missing	21-13	12
211/311	Shift Timing Is Early/Late	21-14	13
212/312	Shift Timing Is Erratic/Hunting	21-15	14
213/313	Shift Feel Is Soft/Slipping	21-16	15
214/314	Shift Feel Is Harsh	21-16	16
215/315	No 1st Gear, Engages In Higher Gear	21-17	17
216/316	No Manual 1st Gear	21-17	18
220/320	No 1-2 Automatic Shift	21-17	19
221/321	No 2-3 Automatic Shift	21-18	20
222/322	No 3-4 Automatic Shift	21-18	21
223/323	No 4-3 Automatic Shift	21-19	22
224/324	No 3-2 Automatic Shift	21-19	23
225/325	No 2-1 Automatic Shift	21-19	24
226/326	Soft/Slipping 1-2 Shift	21-20	25
227/327	Soft/Slipping 2-3 Shift	21-20	26
228/328	Soft/Slipping 3-4 Shift	21-20	27
229/329	Soft/Slipping 4-3 Shift	21-21	28
230/330	Soft/Slipping 3-2 Shift	21-21	29
231/331	Soft/Slipping 2-1 Shift	21-21	30
232/332	Harsh 1-2 Shift	21-21	31
233/333	Harsh 2-3 Shift	21-22	32
234/334	Harsh 3-4 Shift	21-22	33
235/335	Harsh 4-3 Shift	21-23	34
236/336	Harsh 3-2 Shift	21-23	35
237/337	Harsh 2-1 Shift	21-23	36
240/340	No Torque Converter Apply	21-24	37
241/341	Torque Converter Always Applied/Stalls Vehicle	21-24	38
242/342	Torque Converter Cycling/Shudder/Chatter	21-24	39
250/350	No Engine Braking In 1st Gear Manual	21-25	40
251/351	Shift Lever Efforts High	21-25	41
252/352	External Leaks	21-26	42
253/353	Poor Vehicle Performance	21-26	43
254/354	Noise/Vibration In Forward/Reverse	21-26	44
255/355	Engine Will Not Crank	21-26	45
256/356	No Park Range	21-27	46
257/357	Transaxle Overheating	21-27	47

Possible Component	Reference/Action
201 — ELECTRICAL ROUTINE	
Powertrain Control System ● Electrical Inputs/Outputs, Vehicle Wiring Harnesses, Powertrain Control Module	● Run On-Board Diagnostics. **Refer to MOTOR'S Domestic Transmission Manual** for diagnosis. Using Rotunda Transmission Tester 007-00130 and Rotunda AX4N Cable and Overlay 007-00117 or equivalent, perform transmission voltage tests If DTC P1700 is present, check for low transaxle fluid level. Then, continue to Hydraulic/Mechanical Routines.
301 — HYDRAULIC/MECHANICAL ROUTINE	
Shift Linkage ● Damaged, out of adjustment	● Inspect and service as required. Verify linkage adjustment After servicing linkage, verify TR sensor is properly adjusted.

FM5029801602010X

Fig. 3 Routines 201 & 301: No Forward Engagement (Part 1 of 2)

Possible Component	Reference/Action
Improper Pressures ● Low Forward Clutch pressure, low line pressure, low EPC pressure	● Check pressure at line and EPC taps. Perform line pressures and stall speed tests. If pressures are low, check the following possible components: — main control valve body, — pump assembly, — low intermediate clutch assembly, — low intermediate apply tube and seal, N-D accumulator assembly.
Main Control Valve Body	
● Bolts out of torque specification	● Tighten bolts to specification.
● Gaskets and separator plate damaged, off location	● Inspect gasket for damage. Replace as required.
● Manual Control Valve damaged	● Inspect. Service as required.
Fluid Pump Assembly	
● Bolts out of torque specification	● Tighten bolts to specification.
● Gaskets and Separator Plate damaged, off location	● Inspect for damage. Replace as required.
● Porosity/cross leaks/ball missing or leaking	● Inspect for porosity and leaks. Replace as required.
● Components damaged	● Inspect for damage. Replace as required.
Low Intermediate One-Way Clutch Assembly	
● DTC P1700 present	
● Worn, damaged, misassembled	● Inspect for damage. Service as required.
● Roller—damaged	● Inspect for damage. Service as required.
● Case—damaged	● Inspect for damage. Service as required.
● Springs—damaged	● Inspect for damage. Service as required.
● Inner/Outer races—damaged	● Inspect for damage. Service as required.
Low Intermediate Clutch Assembly	
● Seals, Piston—damaged	● Perform Air Pressure Tests
● Fluid Tubes and Seals, Band, Anchor Pin—worn, damaged, loose, leaking	● Inspect. Replace as required.
● Friction elements—damaged, clearance check incorrect	● Inspect. Service as required.
● Wave Spring—damaged, missing	● Inspect. Service as required.
Low/Intermediate Accumulator Assembly	
● Piston Seals—damaged, leaking	● Inspect for damage. Service as required.
● Shaft or Bore—damaged, leaking	● Inspect for damage. Service as required.

FM5029801602020X

Fig. 3 Routines 201 & 301: No Forward Engagement (Part 2 of 2)

Possible Component	Reference/Action
202 — ELECTRICAL ROUTINE	
Powertrain Control System ● Electrical Inputs/Outputs, Vehicle Wiring Harnesses, Powertrain Control Module	● Run On-Board Diagnostics. **Refer to MOTOR'S Domestic Transmission Manual** for diagnosis. Using Rotunda Transmission Tester 007-00130 and Rotunda AX4N Cable and Overlay 007-00117 or equivalent, perform transmission voltage tests. If DTC P1700 is present, check for low transaxle fluid level. Then, continue to Hydraulic/Mechanical Routines.
302 — HYDRAULIC/MECHANICAL ROUTINE	
Shift Linkage (Internal/External) ● Damaged or out of adjustment	● Inspect and service as required. Verify linkage adjustment. After servicing linkage, verify that the TR sensor is properly adjusted.

FM5029801603010X

Fig. 4 Routines 202 & 302: No Reverse Engagement (Part 1 of 2)

Possible Component	Reference/Action
Improper Pressures ● Low line pressure, low EPC pressure	● Perform Line Pressure and Stall Speed Tests **Check pressure at line and EPC taps.** 401 for specifications. If pressures are low, check the following possible components: — main control valve body, — pump assembly, — reverse clutch assembly, — reverse apply tube and seal, N-R accumulator assembly.
Main Control Valve Body	
● Bolts out of torque specification	● Tighten bolts to specification.
● Gasket and Separator Plate—damaged, off location	● Inspect for damage. Replace as required.
● Manual Control Valve, Springs—stuck, damaged	● Inspect for damage. Service as required.
Pump Assembly	
● Bolts out of torque specification	● Tighten bolts to specification.
● Gasket damaged	● Inspect for damage and replace as required.
● Porosity/cross leaks, pump assembly leaking, plugged hole	● Replace pump assembly.
● Components damaged	● Inspect for damage and replace as required.
Reverse Clutch Assembly	● Perform Air Pressure Tests
● Seals, Piston, Springs damaged	● Inspect for damage. Service as required.
● Clearance Check out of specification	● Inspect. Perform clearance checks.
● Friction Elements damaged or worn	● Inspect for damage. Service as required.
● Reverse Apply Tube and Seal leaking or incorrectly installed	● Inspect. Service as required.
N-R Accumulator Assembly	
● Seals, Piston—damaged, leaking	● Inspect for damage. Service as required.
● Shaft or Bore—damaged, leaking	● Inspect for damage. Service as required.

FM5029801603020X

Fig. 4 Routines 202 & 302: No Reverse Engagement (Part 2 of 2)

Possible Component	Reference/Action
203 — ELECTRICAL ROUTINE	
Powertrain Control System	
• Electrical Inputs/Outputs, Vehicle Wiring Harnesses, Powertrain Control Module (PCM), EPC Solenoid, TFT, TSS, TP Sensor, MAF Sensor, VSS, IAT Sensor, ISC and PSP sensor, Engine rpm.	• Run On-Board Diagnostic. **Refer to MOTOR'S Domestic Transmission Manual** for diagnosis. Perform Pinpoint Tests B, E, and F using the Rotunda Transmission Tester 007-00130 and Rotunda AX4N Cable and Overlay 007-00117 or equivalent. Service as required. Clear codes. Road Test and rerun On-Board Diagnostic.
303 — HYDRAULIC/MECHANICAL ROUTINE	
Improper Pressures	
• High line pressure, high EPC pressure	• Perform Line Pressure and Stall Speed Tests Check pressure at line and EPC pressure taps. If high, check the following possible components: Main Control Valve Body, Fluid Filter and Fluid Pan Screen Ring.
Main Control	
• Bolts out of torque specification	• Tighten bolts to specification.
• Gasket and Separator Plate—damaged, off location	• Inspect for damage. Replace as required.
• B1 Check Ball, Pressure Failsafe Valve, Main Regulator Valve—stuck, damaged	• Inspect for damage. Service as required.
Pump Assembly	
• Bolts out of torque specification	• Tighten bolts to specification.
• Gasket damaged, off location	• Inspect for damage and replace as required.
• Components damaged	• Inspect for damage and replace as required.

FM5029801604010X

Fig. 5 Routines 203 & 303: Harsh Reverse Engagement (Part 1 of 2)

Possible Component	Reference/Action
204 — ELECTRICAL ROUTINE	
Powertrain Control System	
• Electrical Inputs/Outputs, Vehicle Wiring Harnesses, Powertrain Control Module (PCM), TP, MAF, IAT, ISC, VSS, PSP, EPC, TFT, TSS, Internal Harness	• Run On-Board Diagnostic. Refer to MOTOR Domestic Transmission Manual[18] for diagnosis. Perform Pinpoint Tests B, E and F using the Rotunda Transmission Tester 007-00130 and Rotunda AX4N Cable and Overlay 007-00117 or equivalent. Service as required. Clear codes, road test and rerun On-Board Diagnostic.
304 — HYDRAULIC/MECHANICAL ROUTINE	
Improper Pressures	
• High line pressure, high EPC pressure	• Perform Line Pressure Tests
• Check pressure at line and EPC pressure taps. If pressures are high, check the following possible components: Main Controls, Pump Assembly.	
Main Controls	
• Bolts out of torque specification	• Tighten bolts to specification.
• Gaskets and Separator Plate—damaged, off location	• Inspect for damage. Replace as required.
• Main Regulator Valve, Pressure Failsafe Valve	• Inspect. Service as required.
• B3 Check Ball—damaged, missing	• Inspect for damage and contamination. Service as required.
Pump Assembly	
• Bolts out of torque specification	• Tighten bolts to specification.
• Gaskets and Separator—damaged, off location	• Inspect for damage. Replace as required.
• EPC Solenoid—stuck, damaged	• Inspect for damage and contamination. Service as required. Activate solenoid using transmission tester. If solenoid operation cannot be felt when placing hard on solenoid, replace solenoid. Inspect O-rings for damage. Service as required.
Low Intermediate Clutch Assembly	
• Seals, Piston—worn, damaged	• Perform Air Pressure Tests
• Friction element—damaged	• Inspect for damage. Replace as required.
• Wave Spring—damaged	• Inspect for damage. Replace as required.
Neutral-to-Drive Accumulator	
• Piston stuck, seals or springs, missing, damaged	• Check for damage. Replace as required.

FM5029801605000X

Fig. 6 Routines 204 & 304: Harsh Forward Engagement

Possible Component	Reference/Action
• EPC Solenoid—stuck, damaged	• Inspect for damage. Perform Pinpoint Test E. **Refer to MOTOR'S Domestic Transmission Manual.** Service as required. Activate solenoid using Rotunda Transmission Tester 007-00130 and Rotunda AX4N Cable and Overlay 007-00117 or equivalent. If solenoid operation cannot be felt when placing hand on solenoid, replace solenoid. Inspect O-rings for damage. Service as required.
Reverse Clutch Assembly	• Perform Air Pressure Tests
• Piston damaged, stuck	• Inspect for damage. Service as required.
• Friction Elements damaged, worn	• Inspect for damage. Service as required.
• Return Spring Piston damaged, worn, stuck	• Inspect for damage. Service as required.
• Reverse Apply Tube leaking or incorrectly installed	• Inspect for damage. Service as required.
• Wave Spring—damaged, worn	• Inspect for damage. Service as required.
N-R Accumulator Assembly	
• Stuck, damaged, components missing	• Inspect for damage. Service as required.
• Shaft or Bore—damaged	• Inspect for damage. Service as required.

FM5029801604020X

Fig. 5 Routines 203 & 303: Harsh Reverse Engagement (Part 2 of 2)

Possible Component	Reference/Action
205 — ELECTRICAL ROUTINE	
Powertrain Control System	
• Electrical Inputs/Outputs, Vehicle Wiring Harnesses, Powertrain Control Module (PCM), EPC Solenoid, TFT, TR Sensor, Internal Harness	• Run On-Board Diagnostic. Refer to MOTOR's "Domestic Transmission Manual" for diagnosis. Perform Pinpoint Tests B, D and E using the Rotunda Transmission Tester 007-00130 and Rotunda AX4N Cable and Overlay 007-00117 and Rotunda Transmission Range (TR) Sensor Cable (MLP-B Cable) 007-00127 or (TRS-E Cable) 007-00111 or equivalent. Service as required. Clear codes. Road Test and rerun On-Board Diagnostic.
305 — HYDRAULIC/MECHANICAL ROUTINE	
Shift Linkage (Internal/External)	
• Damaged, out of adjustment	• Inspect and service as required. Verify linkage adjustment. After servicing linkage, verify that the TR sensor is properly adjusted.
Improper Pressures	
• Low line pressure, low EPC pressure	• Check pressure at line and EPC taps. Perform line pressure and stall speed tests. If pressures are low, check the following possible components: Main Control Valve Body, Pump Assembly, Reverse Clutch Assembly, Reverse Clutch Tube
Main Controls	
• Bolts out of torque specification	• Tighten bolts to specification.
• Gaskets and Separator Plate—damaged, off location	• Inspect for damage. Replace as required.
• Manual Control Valve, Main Regulator Valve, Converter Drain Back Valve, Springs—missing, damaged, misassembled	• Inspect for damage. Service as required.
Pump Assembly	
• Bolts out of torque specification	• Tighten bolts to specification.
• Porosity/cross leaks, oil pump leaking	• Replace pump assembly.
• Gaskets damaged, off location	• Inspect for damage and replace as required.
• EPC Solenoid—stuck, damaged	• Inspect for damage. Perform Pinpoint Test E. Service as required. Activate solenoid using Rotunda Transmission Tester 007-00130 and Rotunda AX4N Cable and Overlay 007-00117 or equivalent. If solenoid operation cannot be felt when placing hand on solenoid, replace solenoid. Inspect O-rings for damage. Service as required.
• Components damaged	• Inspect for damage and replace as required.
Reverse Clutch Assembly	• Perform Air Pressure Tests
• Seals, Piston, worn, damaged	• Inspect for damage. Service as required.
• Wave Spring damaged	• Inspect for damage. Service as required.
• Friction elements damaged or worn	• Inspect for damage. Service as required.
• Return Spring and Piston damaged or worn	• Inspect for damage. Service as required.
• Reverse Apply Tube or Seal leaking	• Inspect. Service as required.
Neutral-Drive Accumulator	
• Piston, Seals damaged, leaking	• Inspect for damage. Service as required.

FM5029801606000X

Fig. 7 Routines 205 & 305: Delayed/Soft Reverse Engagement

Possible Component	Reference/Action
206 — ELECTRICAL ROUTINE	
Powertrain Control System	
• Electrical Inputs/Outputs, Vehicle Wiring Harnesses, Powertrain Control Module (PCM), EPC Solenoid, TFT, TR Sensor, Internal Harness	• Run On-Board Diagnostic. Refer to MOTOR's "Domestic Transmission Manual" for diagnosis. Perform Service Manual Pinpoint Tests B, D and E using the Rotunda Transmission Tester 007-00130 and Rotunda AX4N Cable and Overlay 007-00117 and Rotunda Transmission Range (TR) Sensor Cable (MLP-B Cable) 007-00127 or (TRS-E Cable) 007-00111 or equivalent. Service as required. Clear codes. Road Test and rerun On-Board Diagnostic.
306 — HYDRAULIC/MECHANICAL ROUTINE	
Shift Linkage	
• Damaged, out of adjustment	• Inspect and service as required. Verify linkage adjustment. After servicing linkage, verify that the TR sensor is properly adjusted.
Improper Pressures	
• Low line pressure, low EPC pressure	• Check pressure at line and EPC taps. Perform line pressure and stall speed tests. If pressures are low, check the following possible components: Main Control Valve Body and Pump Assembly, Low/Intermediate Clutch.
Main Control Valve Body	
• Bolts out of torque specification	• Tighten bolts to specification.
• Gaskets and Separator Plate—damaged, off location	• Inspect for damage. Replace.
• Main Regulator Valve—stuck, damaged, missing	• Inspect. Service as required.
Pump Assembly	• Tighten bolts to specification.
• Bolts out of torque specification	• Inspect for porosity and leaks. Replace as required.
• Porosity/cross leaks	• Inspect for damage and replace as required.
• Gaskets damaged, off location	• Inspect for damage and replace as required.
• Components damaged	• Inspect for damage. Perform Pinpoint Test E. Refer to MOTOR'S Domestic Transmission Manual. Service as required. Activate solenoid using Rotunda Transmission Tester 007-00130 and Rotunda AX4N Cable and Overlay 007-00117 or equivalent. If solenoid operation cannot be felt when placing hand on solenoid, replace solenoid. Inspect O-rings for damage. Service as required.
• EPC Solenoid—stuck, damaged	
Low/Intermediate Clutch Assembly	
Perform Air Pressure Tests as described.	
• Seals, Piston—worn, damaged	• Inspect seals and piston for damage. Replace as required.
• Low/Intermediate Fluid Tubes and Seals—damaged, loose, leaking	• Inspect for damage. Service as required.
• Band, Anchor Pins—damaged	• Inspect for damage. Service as required.
• Wave Spring—damaged	• Inspect for damage. Service as required.
Neutral-Drive Accumulator	
• Seals, Bore—damaged, stuck, leaking	• Inspect for damage. Service as required.

FM5029801607000X

Fig. 8 Routines 206 & 307: Delayed/Soft Forward Engagement

Possible Component	Reference/Action
207—ELECTRICAL ROUTINE	
No Electrical Concerns	
307—HYDRAULIC/MECHANICAL ROUTINE	
Fluid	
• Improper level—low	• Adjust fluid to proper level.
Halfshaft	
• Splines—worn, damaged	• Inspect for damage. Service as required.
• Shaft—misassembled, incorrect	
Shift Linkage (Internal/External)	
• Damaged, out of adjustment, misassembled	• Inspect. Service as required. Verify linkage adjustment. After servicing linkage, verify that the TR sensor is properly adjusted.
Improper Pressures	
• Low line pressure, low EPC pressure	• Perform Line Pressure and Stall Tests
•	• Check pressure at line pressure and EPC tap. If pressures are low, check the following possible components: Fluid Filter and Seal Assembly, Main Control, Pump Assembly, Reverse Clutch Assembly, Forward Clutch Assembly.
Fluid Filter and Seal Assembly	
• Plugged, damaged	• Replace filter and seal assembly.
Main Controls	
• Bolts out of torque specification	• Tighten bolts to specification.
• Gaskets and Separator Plate—damaged, off location	• Inspect for damage. Replace as required.
• Pump Shaft—broken	• Inspect. Service/replace as required.
• Forward Clutch Control Valve, Manual Valve, Springs—stuck, damaged	• Inspect for damage. Service as required.
• Main Regulator Valve (only if line pressure is out of specification)—damaged	• Inspect for damage. Service as required.
• Components—damaged	• Inspect for damage. Service as required.
Pump Assembly	
• Bolts out of torque specification	• Tighten bolts to specification.
• Gaskets—damaged, off location	• Inspect for damage. Replace as required.
• Porosity/cross leaks—leaking, plugged hole	• Replace pump assembly.
• Components damaged	• Inspect for damage. Replace as required.
Support Assembly—Driven Sprocket	
• Bolts out of torque specification	• Tighten bolts to specification.
• Seals missing or damaged	• Inspect seals. Replace as required.
• Seal grooves damaged	• Inspect for damage. Service as required.
Forward Clutch Assembly	
• Seals, Piston and Seal Assembly	• Perform Air Pressure Tests
•	• Inspect for damage. Service as required.
• Wave Spring—missing	• Inspect for spring. Service as required.
• Check Balls	• Inspect for mislocation, poor seating and damage. Replace cylinder as required.
• Piston—cracked	• Inspect piston. Replace as required.
• Friction elements—worn, damaged	• Check for abnormal wear, damage. Replace as required.
• Retaining Ring missing	• Inspect for ring/damage. Service as required.

FM5029801608010X

Fig. 9 Routines 207 & 307: No Forward & No Reverse Engagement (Part 1 of 2)

Possible Component	Reference/Action
Low One-Way Clutch Assembly	
• Worn, damaged, misassembled	• Inspect for damage. Service as required.
Output Shaft	
• Splines damaged	• Inspect for damage. Service as required.
Other Possible Components	
• Turbine Shafts	• Inspect for damage. Service as required.
• Chain	• Inspect for damage. Service as required.
• Flywheel	• Inspect for damage. Service as required.
• Sprockets	• Inspect for damage. Service as required.
• Front Sun Gear and Shell Assembly	• Inspect for damage. Service as required.
• Front or Rear Planetaries	• Inspect for damage. Service as required.
• Rear Sun Drum and Race Assembly	• Inspect for damage. Service as required.
• Final Drive Assembly	• Inspect for damage. Service as required.
• Oil Pump Shaft Assembly	• Inspect for damage. Service as required.

FM5029801608020X

Fig. 9 Routines 207 & 307: No Forward & No Reverse Engagement (Part 2 of 2)

Possible Component	Reference/Action
208—ELECTRICAL ROUTINE	
Powertrain Control System	
• Electrical inputs/outputs, vehicle wiring harnesses, Powertrain Control Module (PCM), TP, MAF, VSS, IAT, PSP, TFT, TR sensor, internal harness, EPC solenoid, engine rpm, ISC.	• Run On-Board Diagnostics. Refer to MOTOR's "Domestic Transmission Manual" for diagnosis. Perform Pinpoint Tests B, D and E using Rotunda Transmission Tester 007-00130 and Rotunda AX4N Cable and Overlay 007-00117 and Rotunda Transmission Range (TR) Sensor Cable (MLP-B Cable) 007-00127 or (TRS-E Cable) 007-00111 or equivalent. Service as required. Clear codes, road test and rerun On-Board Diagnostics.
308—HYDRAULIC/MECHANICAL ROUTINE	
Fluid	
• Improper level	• Adjust fluid to proper level.
Improper Pressures	
• High line pressure, high EPC pressure	• Perform Line Pressure Tests.
•	• Check pressure at line and EPC pressure taps. If high, check the following possible components: Main Controls, Fluid Filter and Seal.
Main Controls	
• Bolts out of torque specification	• Tighten bolts to specification.
• Gaskets and Separator—damaged, off location	• Inspect for damage. Replace as required.
• B1, B4 Check Ball, Pressure Failsafe Valve, Main Regulator Valve—stuck, damaged, missing	• Inspect for damage. Service as required.
• Line Modulator Valve—stuck open	• Inspect for damage. Service as required.
Pump Assembly	
• Bolts out of torque specification	• Tighten bolts to specification.
• Gaskets—damaged, off location	• Inspect for damage. Replace as required.
• Components—damaged	• Inspect for damage. Replace as required.
• EPC Solenoid—stuck, damaged	• Inspect for damage and contamination. Service as required. Activate solenoid using transmission tester. If solenoid operation cannot be felt when placing hand on solenoid, replace solenoid. Inspect O-rings for damage. Service as required.
Forward Clutch Assembly	
• Seals, Piston—worn, damaged	• Inspect for damage. Service as required.
• Friction elements—damaged, worn	• Inspect for damage. Service as required.
• Return Spring Piston—damaged, worn	• Inspect for damage. Service as required.
• Check Ball—missing	• Inspect for damage. Service as required.
• Wave Spring—damaged	• Inspect for damage. Service as required.

FM5029801609000X

Fig. 10 Routines 208 & 308: Harsh Forward & Reverse Engagement

Possible Component	Reference/Action
209—ELECTRICAL ROUTINE	
Powertrain Control System	
• Electrical inputs/outputs, vehicle wiring harnesses, Powertrain Control Module (PCM), TFT, TR Sensor, internal harness, EPC solenoid.	• Run ON-Board Diagnostics. Refer to MOTOR's "Domestic Transmission Manual" for diagnosis. Perform Pinpoint Tests B, D and E using Rotunda Transmission Tester 007-00130 and Rotunda AX4N Cable and Overlay 007-00117 and Rotunda Transmission Range (TR) Sensor Cable (MLP-B Cable) 007-00127 or (TRS-E Cable) 007-00111 or equivalent. Service as required. Clear codes, road test and rerun On-Board Diagnostics.
309—HYDRAULIC/MECHANICAL ROUTINE	
Fluid	
• Improper level	• Adjust fluid to proper level.
• Condition	• Inspect. Service as required.
Shift Linkage (Internal/External)	
• Damaged, out of adjustment	• Inspect. Service as required. Verify linkage adjustment. After servicing linkage, verify that the TR sensor is properly adjusted.
Improper Pressures	
• Low line pressure, low EPC pressure	• Perform Line Pressure and Stall Tests.
•	• Check pressure at line and EPC tap. If pressures are low, check the following possible components: Main Control, Pump Assembly.
Fluid Filter and Seal Assembly	
• Plugged—damaged, not properly seated	• Replace filter and seal assembly.
• Filter Seal—damaged	
Main Controls	
• Bolts out of torque specification	• Tighten bolts to specification.
• Gaskets and Separator Plate—damaged, off location	• Inspect for damage. Replace as required.
• Seals, Manual Valve, Main Regulator Valve, Line Modulator Valve, Springs—missing, damaged or misassembled	• Inspect for damage. Service as required.
Pump Assembly	
• Bolts out of torque specification	• Tighten bolts to specification.
• Gaskets—damaged, off location	• Inspect for damage. Replace as required.
• Porosity/Cross Leaks—leaking	• Replace pump assembly.
• Components damaged	• Inspect for damage. Replace as required.
• EPC Solenoid—stuck, damaged	• Inspect for damage. Replace as required. Activate solenoid using Rotunda Transmission Tester 007-00130 and Rotunda AX4N Cable and Overlay 007-00117. If solenoid operation cannot be felt when placing hand on solenoid, replace solenoid. Inspect O-rings for damage. Service as required.
Forward Clutch Assembly	
• Assembly	• Perform Air Pressure Tests.
• Seals, Piston—damaged, worn	• Inspect seals for damage. Service as required.
• Check Ball—missing, damaged	• Inspect for mislocation, poor seating and damage. Replace cylinder as required.
• Piston—cracked	• Inspect piston. Replace as required.
• Friction elements—damaged, worn	• Check for abnormal wear, damage. Replace as required.

FM5029801610000X

Fig. 11 Routines 209 & 309: Delayed/Soft Forward & Reverse Engagement

Possible Component	Reference/Action
210 — ELECTRICAL ROUTINE	
Powertrain Control System	
• Electrical Inputs/Outputs, Vehicle Wiring Harnesses, Powertrain Control Module (PCM), Shift Solenoids, (SS1, SS2, SS3), TP, MAF, VSS, TR Sensor, Internal Wiring Harness.	• Run On-Board Diagnostic. Refer to MOTOR's "Domestic Transmission Manual" for diagnosis. Perform Service Manual Pinpoint Tests A and D using the Rotunda Transmission Tester 007-00130 and Rotunda AX4N Cable and Overlay 007-00117 and the Rotunda Transmission Range (TR) Sensor Cable (MLP-B Cable) 007-00127 or (TRS-E Cable) 007-00111 or equivalent. Service as required. Clear codes. Road Test and rerun On-Board Diagnostic. If DTC P1700 is present, check for low transmission fluid level.
310 — HYDRAULIC/MECHANICAL ROUTINE	
Fluid	
• Improper level	• Adjust fluid to proper level.
• Condition	• Inspect Fluid Condition.
Shift Linkage (Internal/External)	
• Damaged, out of adjustment	• Inspect and service as required. Verify linkage adjustment. After servicing linkage, verify that the TR sensor is properly adjusted.
Vehicle Speed Input	
• Speedometer Gear—DRIVE—damaged	• Refer to Disassembly and Assembly for teardown information on these gears. Also refer to the appropriate shift routines as described at the end of this routine.
• Speedometer Gear—DRIVEN—Gear and Shaft Assembly—damaged	
• Differential Assembly—damaged or missing	
• Speedometer DRIVE GEAR—damaged	
Filter and Seal Assembly	
• Plugged, missing	• Inspect. Service as required.
Apply and Release Fluid Tubes	
• Damaged, missing	• Inspect for damage. Service as required.
• Seal or O-ring—damaged	• Inspect for damage. Service as required.
Forward Support—Driven Sprocket	
• Seals—damaged	• Inspect for damage. Service as required.
• Holes—blocked	• Inspect for damage. Service as required.
Planetary Gear Sets	
• Damaged	• Inspect for damage. Service as required.
One-Way Clutch Assembly	
• Damaged	• Inspect for damage. Service as required.
Other Components	
• Clutches	• Inspect for damage. Service as required.
• Output Shafts (Differential)	• Inspect for damage. Service as required.
• Overdrive Band	• Inspect for damage. Service as required.
• Powerflow Components	• Inspect for damage. Service as required.
Go to Reference/Action	
	• For further diagnosis, refer to the appropriate shift routine(s):
• Shift Concern: No 1-2	• Routine 220/320
• Shift Concern: No 2-3	• Routine 221/321
• Shift Concern: No 3-4	• Routine 222/322
• Shift Concern: No 4-3	• Routine 223/323
• Shift Concern: No 3-2	• Routine 224/324
• Shift Concern: No 2-1	• Routine 225/325

FM5029801611000X

Fig. 12 Routines 210 & 310: Some Or All Shifts Missing

Possible Component	Reference/Action
211 — ELECTRICAL ROUTINE	
Powertrain Control System	
	● Perform Shift Point Road Test and Torque Converter Clutch Operation Test.
● Electrical Inputs/Outputs, Vehicle Wiring Harnesses, Powertrain Control Module (PCM), Shift Solenoids (SS1, SS2, SS3), TP, MAF, VSS, IAT, ECT, TFT, Internal Wire Harness, EPC Solenoid	● Run On-Board Diagnostic. Refer to MOTOR's "Domestic Transmission Manual" for diagnosis. Perform Pinpoint Tests A, B and E using the Rotunda Transmission Tester 007-00130 and Rotunda AX4N Cable and Overlay 007-00117 or equivalent. Service as required. Clear codes. Road Test and rerun On-Board Diagnostic.
311 — HYDRAULIC/MECHANICAL ROUTINE	
Other	
● Tire size or chain ratio—change, Speedometer Gear	● Refer to the specification decal and verify vehicle has original equipment. Changes in tire size and chain ratio will affect shift timing.
Fluid	
● Improper level	● Adjust fluid to proper level.
Shift Linkage	
● Damaged, out of adjustment	● Inspect. Service as required. Verify linkage adjustment. After servicing linkage, verify that the TR sensor is properly adjusted.
Main Controls	
● Bolts out of torque specification	● Tighten bolts to specification.
● Gaskets and Separator Plate—damaged, off location	● Inspect for damage. Replace.
● Valves, Accumulators, Seals, Springs, Clips—damaged, missing, misassembled	● Inspect for damage and contamination. Service as required.
	● Refer to the appropriate shift for further diagnosis:
	● Shift Concern: Soft/Slipping 1-2 Routine 226/326
	● Shift Concern: Soft/Slipping 2-3 Routine 227/327
	● Shift Concern: Soft/Slipping 3-4 Routine 228/328
	● Shift Concern: Soft/Slipping 4-3 Routine 229/329
	● Shift Concern: Soft/Slipping 3-2 Routine 230/330
	● Shift Concern: Soft/Slipping 2-1 Routine 231/331
Front Support—Driven Sprocket	
● Seals—damaged	● Inspect for damage. Service as required.
● Holes—blocked	● Inspect for damage. Service as required.
Planetary Gear Sets	
● Damaged	● Inspect for damage. Service as required.
One-Way Clutch Assembly	
● Damaged	● Inspect for damage. Service as required.
Other Components	
● Clutches	● Inspect for damage. Service as required.
● Output Shaft (differential)	● Inspect for damage. Service as required.
● Overdrive Band	● Inspect for damage. Service as required.
● Powerflow Components	● Inspect for damage. Service as required.
Vehicle Speed Input	
● Speedometer Gear—DRIVE—damaged	● Refer to Disassembly for teardown information on these gears. Also refer to the appropriate shift routines as noted under Main Controls.
● Speedometer Gear—DRIVEN—Gear and Shaft Assembly, damaged	
● Differential Assembly—damaged	
● Speedometer DRIVE GEAR—damaged	

FM5029801612010X

Fig. 13 Routines 211 & 311: Shift Timing Is Early/Late (Part 1 of 2)

Possible Component	Reference/Action
Filter and Seal Assembly	
● Plugged, missing	● Inspect. Service as required.
Apply and Release Fluid Tubes	
● Damaged, missing	● Inspect for damage. Service as required.
● Seal or O-ring—damaged	● Inspect for damage. Service as required.

FM5029801612020X

Fig. 13 Routines: 211 & 311: Shift Timing Is Early/Late (Part 2 of 2)

Possible Component	Reference / Action
212 — ELECTRICAL ROUTINE	
Powertrain Control System	
	• Perform Shift Point Road Test and Torque Converter Clutch Operation Test.
• Electrical Inputs / Outputs, Vehicle Wiring Harnesses, Powertrain Control Module (PCM), TCC and Shift Solenoids (SS1, SS2, SS3), TP, VSS, ECT, IAT, MAF, TR, TFT Sensors, Internal Wire Harness.	• Run On-Board Diagnostic. Refer to MOTOR's "Domestic Transmission Manual" for diagnosis. Perform Service Manual Pinpoint Tests A, B, C, D and F using the Rotunda Transmission Tester 007-00130 and Rotunda AX4N Cable and Overlay 007-00117 and the Rotunda Transmission Range (TR) Sensor Cable (MLP-B Cable) 007-00127 or (TRS-E Cable) 007-00111 or equivalent. Service as required. Clear codes. Road Test and rerun On-Board Diagnostic.
312 — HYDRAULIC / MECHANICAL ROUTINE	
Fluid	
• Improper level	• Adjust fluid to proper level.
• Condition	• Inspect. Service as required.
Shift Linkage (Internal / External)	
• Damaged, out of adjustment	• Inspect. Service as required. Verify linkage adjustment. After servicing linkage, verify that the TR sensor is properly adjusted.
Main Control Valve Body	
• Bolts out of torque specification	• Tighten bolts to specification.
• Gaskets and Separator Plate—damaged, off location	• Inspect for damage. Replace as required.
• Valves, Accumulators, Seals, Clips, Check Ball—stuck, damaged, contaminated	• Inspect for damage. Service as required.
Vehicle Speed Input	
• Speedometer Gear—DRIVE—damaged	• Refer to Disassembly and Assembly for teardown information on these gears. Also refer to the appropriate shift routines as noted below.
• Speedometer Gear—DRIVEN—Gear and Shaft Assembly, damage	
• Differential Assembly—damaged or missing	
• Speedometer DRIVE GEAR—damaged	
Torque Converter Clutch	
•	• Refer to Torque Converter Cycling (Routine 242 / 342).
Front Support—Driven Sprocket	
• Seals—damaged	• Inspect for damage. Service as required.
• Holes—blocked	• Inspect for damage. Service as required.
Planetary Gear Sets	
• Damaged	• Inspect for damage. Service as required.
One-Way Clutch Assembly	
• Damaged	• Inspect for damage. Service as required.
Other Components	
• Clutches	• Inspect for damage. Service as required.
• Output Shaft (differential)	• Inspect for damage. Service as required.
• Overdrive Band	• Inspect for damage. Service as required.
• Powerflow Components	• Inspect for damage. Service as required.

FM5029801613010X

Fig. 14 Routines 212 & 312: Shift Timing Is Erratic/Hunting (Part 1 of 2)

Possible Component	Reference / Action
Filter and Seal Assembly	
• Plugged, missing	• Inspect. Service as required.
Apply and Release Oil Tubes	
• Damaged, missing	• Inspect for damage. Service as required.
• Seal or O-ring—damaged	• Inspect for damage. Service as required.
For Diagnosis Related to a Specific Shift	• Refer to the appropriate routine for further diagnosis:
• Shift Concern: No 1-2	• Routine 220 / 320
• Shift Concern: No 2-3	• Routine 221 / 321
• Shift Concern: No 3-4	• Routine 222 / 322
• Shift Concern: No 4-3	• Routine 223 / 323
• Shift Concern: No 3-2	• Routine 224 / 324
• Shift Concern: No 2-1	• Routine 225 / 325
• Shift Concern: Soft / Slip 1-2	• Routine 226 / 326
• Shift Concern: Soft / Slip 2-3	• Routine 227 / 327
• Shift Concern: Soft / Slip 3-4	• Routine 228 / 328
• Shift Concern: Soft / Slip 4-3	• Routine 229 / 329
• Shift Concern: Soft / Slip 3-2	• Routine 230 / 330
• Shift Concern: Soft / Slip 2-1	• Routine 231 / 331
• Shift Concern: Harsh 1-2	• Routine 232 / 332
• Shift Concern: Harsh 2-3	• Routine 233 / 333
• Shift Concern: Harsh 3-4	• Routine 234 / 334
• Shift Concern: Harsh 4-3	• Routine 235 / 335
• Shift Concern: Harsh 3-2	• Routine 236 / 336
• Shift Concern: Harsh 2-1	• Routine 237 / 337

FM5029801613020X

Fig. 14 Routines 212 & 312: Shift Timing Is Erratic/Hunting (Part 2 of 2)

Possible Component	Reference/Action
213 — ELECTRICAL ROUTINE	
Powertrain Control System ● Electrical Inputs/Outputs, Vehicle Wiring Harnesses, Powertrain Control Module (PCM), EPC Solenoid, MAF, TP, ECT, IAT, TFT, Internal Harness, TSS.	● Perform Shift Point Road Test as described under Road Test Vehicle. ● Run On-Board Diagnostic. Refer to MOTOR's "Domestic Transmission Manual" for diagnosis. Perform Service Manual Pinpoint Tests B, E and F using the Transmission Tester 007-00130 and Rotunda AX4N Cable and Overlay 007-00117 or equivalent. Service as required. Clear codes. Road Test and rerun On-Board Diagnostic.
313 — HYDRAULIC/MECHANICAL ROUTINE	
Fluid ● Improper level ● Condition	● Adjust fluid to proper level. ● Inspect Fluid Condition.
Filter and Seal Assembly ● Damaged, partially plugged	● Inspect for damage. Service as required.
Shift Linkage (Internal/External) ● Damaged, out of adjustment	● Inspect. Service as required. Verify linkage adjustment. After servicing linkage, verify that the TR sensor is properly adjusted.
Improper Pressures ● Low line pressure, low EPC pressure	● Check pressures at line and EPC taps. If pressures are low or all shifts are soft/slipping, go to Main Control.

FM5029801614010X

Fig. 15 Routines 213 & 313: Shift Feel Is Soft/Slipping (Part 1 of 2)

Possible Component	Reference/Action
	● If pressures are OK and a specific shift is soft/slipping, refer to the following chart. **Soft/Slipping Shift** 1-2, **Routine** 226/326 **Soft/Slipping Shift** 2-3, **Routine** 227/327 **Soft/Slipping Shift** 3-4, **Routine** 228/328 **Soft/Slipping Shift** 4-3, **Routine** 229/329 **Soft/Slipping Shift** 3-2, **Routine** 230/330 **Soft/Slipping Shift** 2-1, **Routine** 231/331
Main Controls ● Bolts out of torque specification ● Gaskets and Separator Plate—damaged, off location ● Line Modulator Valve, 2-3 Capacity Modulator Valve, Accumulator/Regulator Valve, Main Regulator Valve, Check Balls, 3-2 Shift Timing Valve, Clips, Springs—damaged, missing	● Tighten bolts to specification. ● Inspect for damage. Replace as required. ● Inspect. Service as required.
Pump Assembly ● Bolts out of torque specification ● Gaskets and Separator—damaged, off location ● EPC Solenoid—stuck, damaged	● Tighten bolts to specification. ● Inspect for damage. Replace as required. ● Inspect for damage and contamination. Service as required. Activate solenoid using Rotunda Transmission Tester 007-00130 and Rotunda AX4N Cable and Overlay 007-00117 or equivalent. If solenoid operation cannot be felt when placing hand on solenoid, replace solenoid. Inspect O-rings for damage. Service as required.
Front Support Assembly—Drive ● Damaged	● Inspect for damage. Service as required.
Apply and Release Oil Supply Tubes ● Damaged, blocked ● Seal—leaking	● Inspect for damage. Service as required. ● Inspect for damage. Service as required.

FM5029801614020X

Fig. 15 Routines 213 & 313: Shift Feel Is Soft/Slipping (Part 2 of 2)

Possible Component	Reference/Action
214 — ELECTRICAL ROUTINE	
Powertrain Control System ● Electrical Inputs/Outputs, Vehicle Wiring Harnesses, Powertrain Control Module (PCM), EPC Solenoid, MAF, TP, VSS, ECT, IAT, PSP, TFT, TR Sensor, Internal Wire Harness and Shift Solenoid No. 3 (SS3), A/C	● Run On-Board Diagnostic. Refer to MOTOR's "Domestic Transmission Manual" for diagnosis. Perform Pinpoint Tests A, B, D and E using the Rotunda Transmission Tester 007-00130 and Rotunda AX4N Cable and Overlay 007-00117 and Rotunda Transmission Range (TR) Sensor Cable (MLP-B Cable) 007-00127 or (TRS-E Cable) 007-00111 or equivalent. Service as required. Clear codes. Road Test and rerun On-Board Diagnostic.
314 — HYDRAULIC/MECHANICAL ROUTINE	
Fluid ● Improper level	● Adjust fluid to proper level.
Improper Pressures ● High line pressure High EPC pressure	● Check pressures at line and EPC taps. Perform Line Pressure Test. If pressures are high or all shifts are harsh, go to Main Control Valve Body. ● If pressures are OK and a specific shift is harsh, refer to the appropriate shift routine in the following chart: **Harsh Shift** 1-2, **Routine** 232/332 **Harsh Shift** 2-3, **Routine** 233/333 **Harsh Shift** 3-4, **Routine** 234/334 **Harsh Shift** 4-3, **Routine** 235/335 **Harsh Shift** 3-2, **Routine** 236/336 **Harsh Shift** 2-1, **Routine** 237/337

FM5029801615010X

Fig. 16 Routines 214 & 314: Shift Feel Is Harsh (Part 1 of 2)

Possible Component	Reference/Action
Main Control Valve Body ● Bolts out of torque specification ● Gaskets and Separator Plate—damaged, off location ● 2-3 Capacity Modulator Valve, Main Regulator Valve, Line Modulator Valve, 3-2 Timing Valve, Springs, Clips, Check Balls—stuck, damaged	● Tighten bolts to specification. ● Inspect for damage. Replace as required. ● Inspect. Service as required.
Pump Assembly ● Bolts out of torque specification ● Gaskets and Separator—damaged, off location ● EPC Solenoid—stuck or damaged	● Tighten bolts to specification. ● Inspect for damage. Replace as required. ● Inspect for damage, contamination. Service as required. Activate solenoid using Rotunda Transmission Tester 007-00130 and Rotunda AX4N Cable and Overlay 007-00117. If solenoid operation cannot be felt when placing hand on solenoid, replace solenoid. Inspect O-rings for damage. Service as required.

FM5029801615020X

Fig. 16 Routines: 214 & 314: Shift Feel Is Harsh (Part 2 of 2)

Possible Component	Reference/Action
215 — ELECTRICAL ROUTINE	
Powertrain Control System • Electrical Inputs/Outputs, Vehicle Wiring Harnesses, Powertrain Control Module (PCM), Shift Solenoids, (SS1, SS2, SS3), VSS Sensor, Internal Wire Harness	• Run On-Board Diagnostic. Refer to MOTOR's "Domestic Transmission Manual" for diagnosis. Perform Service Manual Pinpoint Tests A using the Rotunda Transmission Tester 007-00130 and Rotunda AX4N Cable and Overlay 007-00117 or equivalent. Service as required. If DTC P1700 is present, check for low transmission fluid level, Then, continue to Hydraulic/Mechanical Routines. Clear codes. Road test and rerun on-board diagnostic.
315 — HYDRAULIC/MECHANICAL ROUTINE	
Main Control Valve Body • Bolts out of torque specification • Gaskets and Separator Plate—damaged, off location • Shift Valves, Forward Clutch Control Valve, Springs, Clips—stuck, damaged, missing, misassembled • Shift Solenoid—stuck, damaged • For diagnosis related to a specific gear, use the Transmission Tester to determine gear.	• Tighten bolts to specification. • Inspect for damage. Replace as required. • Inspect. Service as required. • Inspect for damage. Perform Pinpoint Test A. Service as required. Activate solenoid using transmission tester. If solenoid operation cannot be felt when placing hand on solenoid, replace solenoid. Inspect O-rings for damage. Service as required. • Refer to the following routines: **No Shift** 1-2, **Routine** 220/320 **No Shift** 2-3, **Routine** 221/321 **No Shift** 3-4, **Routine** 222/322
Mechanical • Fluid tubes—damaged • Bands, clutches or seals damaged or worn	• Inspect. Service as required. • Inspect. Service as required.

FM5029801616000X

Fig. 17 Routines 215 & 315: No 1st Gear, Engages In Higher Gear

Possible Component	Reference/Action
216 — ELECTRICAL ROUTINE	
Powertrain Control System • Electrical Inputs/Outputs, Vehicle Wiring Harnesses, Powertrain Control Module	• Run On-Board Diagnostics. Refer to MOTOR's "Domestic Transmission Manual" for diagnosis. Using Rotunda Transmission Tester 007-00130 and Rotunda AX4N Cable and Overlay 007-00117 or equivalent, perform transmission functional tests. If DTC P1700 is present, check for low transaxle fluid level. Then, continue to Hydraulic/Mechanical Routines.

FM5029801617010X

Fig. 18 Routines 216 & 316: No Manual 1st Gear (Part 1 of 2)

Possible Component	Reference/Action
316 — HYDRAULIC/MECHANICAL ROUTINE	
Shift Linkage (Internal/External) • Damaged or out of adjustment	• Inspect and service as required. Verify linkage adjustment. After servicing linkage, verify that the TR sensor is properly adjusted.
Improper Pressures • Low line pressure, low EPC pressure	• Check pressure at line and EPC pressure taps. Perform Line Pressure Test If pressures are low, check the following possible components: Main Control Valve Body.
Main Control Valve Body • Bolts out of torque specification • Gaskets and Separator Plate—damaged, off location • Manual Control Valve, Manual Downshift Valve, Springs, Shift Valves, Clips—stuck, damaged, missing • B8 Check Ball damaged, missing	• Tighten bolts to specification. • Inspect for damage. Replace as required. • Inspect for damage. Service as required. • Inspect for damage. Service as required.
Low/Intermediate One-Way Clutch Assembly • DTCs P1784, P1785 present • Worn, damaged, misassembled • Roller—damaged • Case—damaged • Springs—damaged • Inner/Outer races—damaged	• Inspect for damage. Service as required. • Inspect for damage. Service as required. • Inspect for damage. Service as required. • Inspect for damage. Service as required. • Inspect for damage. Service as required.

FM5029801617020X

Fig. 18 Routines 216 & 316: No Manual 1st Gear (Part 2 of 2)

Possible Component	Reference/Action
220 — ELECTRICAL ROUTINE	
Powertrain Control System • Electrical Inputs/Outputs, Vehicle Wiring Harnesses, Powertrain Control Module (PCM), Shift Solenoids, (SS1, SS2), TR Sensor, Internal Wire Harness NOTE: If SS1 is ON, it equals a third gear start.	• Run On-Board Diagnostic. Refer to MOTOR's "Domestic Transmission Manual" for diagnosis. Perform Pinpoint Tests A and D using the Rotunda Transmission Tester 007-00130 and Rotunda AX4N Cable and Overlay 007-00117 and Rotunda Transmission Range (TR) Sensor Cable (MLP-B Cable) 007-00127 or (TRS-E Cable) 007-00111 or equivalent as described. If DTC P1700 is present, check for low transaxle fluid level. Then, continue to Hydraulic/Mechanical Routines and service. Clear codes. Road Test and rerun On-Board Diagnostic.
320 — HYDRAULIC/MECHANICAL ROUTINE	
Improper Pressures • Line pressure, EPC pressure	• Check pressure at line, EPC and intermediate clutch taps. Perform Line Pressure Test. If not OK, check Main Control Valve Body.
Main Control Valve Body • Bolts out of torque specification • Gaskets and Separator Plate—damaged, off location • 1-2 Shift Valve, Springs, Clips—loose, stuck, missing, misassembled • SS1 and SS2 not functioning properly	• Tighten bolts to specification. • Inspect for damage. Replace as required. • Inspect. Service as required. • Activate solenoid using Rotunda Transmission Tester 007-00130 and Rotunda AX4N Cable and Overlay 007-00117. If solenoid operation cannot be felt when placing hand on solenoid, replace solenoid. Inspect O-rings for damage. Service as required.

FM5029801618010X

Fig. 19 Routines 220 & 320: No 1-2 Automatic Shift (Part 1 of 2)

Possible Component	Reference/Action
Pump Assy	
• Porosity/Cross Leaks	• Inspect. Replace as required.
• Gasket damaged—off location	• Inspect for damaged. Replace as required.
• Component damaged	• Inspect for damage, missing ball. Replace pump assembly if required.
1-2 Accumulator Assembly	• Perform Air Pressure Tests
• Piston Seals, Springs—damaged, missing	• Inspect for damage. Service as required.
Support Assembly—Driven Sprocket	
• Seals—damaged, missing • Holes blocked	• Inspect for damage, missing or blockage. Service as required.
Low One-Way Clutch Assembly	
• Not overrunning, damaged	• Inspect for damage. Replace as required.
Intermediate Clutch Assembly	• Perform Air Pressure Tests
• Seals—damaged	• Inspect for damage. Replace as required.
• Piston—damaged	• Inspect for damage. Replace as required.
• Check ball missing, damaged	• Inspect for damage. Replace as required.
• Friction—damaged, worn	• Inspect for damage. Replace as required.
• Cylinder Hub Lube Grooves—blocked, damaged	• Inspect for damage. Replace as required.
• Return Spring Assembly—damaged	• Inspect for damage. Replace as required.
Front Planet Carrier	
• Damaged	• Inspect for damage. Service as required.

FM5029801618020X

Fig. 19 Routines 220 & 320: No 1-2 Automatic Shift (Part 2 of 2)

Possible Component	Reference/Action
221 — ELECTRICAL ROUTINE	
Powertrain Control System	
• Electrical Inputs/Outputs, Vehicle Wiring Harnesses, Powertrain Control Module (PCM), Shift Solenoid (SS1), Internal Wire Harness	• Run On-Board Diagnostic. Refer to MOTOR's "Domestic Transmission Manual" for diagnosis. Perform Pinpoint Test A, using the Rotunda Transmission Tester 007-00130 and Rotunda AX4N Cable and Overlay 007-00117 or equivalent. Service as required. Clear codes. Road Test and rerun On-Board Diagnostic.
321 — HYDRAULIC/MECHANICAL ROUTINE	
Improper Pressures	
• Line pressure, EPC pressure	• Check pressure at EPC and line taps. Perform Line Pressure Test. If not OK, check the Main Control Valve Body.
Main Control Valve Body	
• Bolts out of torque specification	• Tighten bolts to specification.
• Gaskets and Separator Plate—damaged, off location	• Inspect for damage. Replace as required.
• 1-2 Shift Valve, 2-3 Shift Valve, 2-3 Capacity Modulator Valve—stuck, damaged	• Inspect. Service as required.
• B8 Check Ball—damaged, missing	• Inspect for damage. Service as required.
• SS1 damaged	• Activate solenoid using Rotunda Transmission Tester 007-00130 and Rotunda AX4N Cable and Overlay 007-00117 or equivalent. If solenoid operation cannot be felt when placing hand on solenoid, replace solenoid. Inspect O-rings for damage. Service as required.
Low Intermediate Servo Assembly	
• Wrong Apply Rod, Servo Bore or Piston damaged, Piston Seals damaged, Return Spring or Retaining Clip damaged, missing	• Inspect for damage. Service as required.

FM5029801619010X

Fig. 20 Routines 221 & 321: No 2-3 Automatic Shift (Part 1 of 2)

Possible Component	Reference/Action
Support Assembly—Driven Sprocket	
• Seals—damaged, missing, holes blocked	• Inspect for damage. Service as required.
Direct One-Way Clutch	
• Not holding, damaged	• Inspect for damage. Replace as required.
Direct Clutch Assembly	• Perform Air Pressure Tests.
• Seals—damaged	• Inspect for damage. Replace as required.
• Piston—damaged	• Inspect for damage. Replace as required.
• Friction plates damaged or worn	• Inspect for damage. Replace as required.
• Check Ball not seating	• Inspect for damage. Replace as required.
• Return Spring Assembly—damaged	• Inspect for damage. Replace as required.
2-3 Accumulator	
• Pistons, Seals—leaking, damaged	• Inspect for damage. Service as required.
• Rod or Bore, Spring—damaged	• Inspect for damage. Service as required.

FM5029801619020X

Fig. 20 Routines 221 & 321: No 2-3 Automatic Shift (Part 2 of 2)

Possible Component	Reference/Action
222 — ELECTRICAL ROUTINE	
Powertrain Control System	
• Electrical Inputs/Outputs, Vehicle Wiring Harnesses, Powertrain Control Module (PCM), Shift Solenoid SS3, TR Sensor, Internal Wire Harness, VSS	• Run On-Board Diagnostic. Refer to MOTOR's "Domestic TRansmission Manual" for diagnosis. Perform Pinpoint Tests A and D using the Rotunda Transmission Tester 007-00130 and Rotunda AX4N Cable and Overlay 007-00117 and Rotunda Transmission Range (TR) Sensor Cable (MLP-B Cable) 007-00127 or (TRS-E Cable) 007-00111 or equivalent. Service as required. Clear codes. Road Test and rerun On-Board Diagnostic.
322 — HYDRAULIC/MECHANICAL ROUTINE	
Overdrive Servo Assembly	• Perform Air Pressure Tests.
• Apply Rod incorrect	• Inspect. Replace if incorrect.
• Servo Bore or Piston damaged, incorrect	• Inspect for damage. Service as required.
• Piston Seals—damaged, missing	• Inspect for damage. Service as required.
• Return Spring Retaining Clip—broken, missing	• Inspect for damage. Service as required.
• Wave Spring—damaged	• Inspect for damage. Service as required.
Main Control Valve Body	
• Bolts out of torque specification	• Tighten bolts to specification.
• Gaskets and Separator Plate—damaged, off location	• Inspect for damage. Replace as required.
• 3-4 Shift Valve, Line Modulator Valve, Forward Clutch Control Valve—stuck, damaged	• Inspect. Service as required.
• SS3 not functioning properly	• Activate solenoid using Rotunda Transmission Tester 007-00130 and Rotunda AX4N Cable and Overlay 007-00117 or equivalent. If solenoid operation cannot be felt when placing hand on solenoid, replace solenoid. Inspect O-rings for damage. Service as required.
3-4 Accumulator Assembly	• Perform Air Pressure Tests.
• Accumulator Piston—damaged	• Inspect for damage. Service as required.
• Piston Seals—missing, damaged	• Inspect for damage. Service as required.
• Springs—damaged	• Inspect for damage. Service as required.
• Rod or Bore—damaged	• Inspect for damage. Service as required.
OD Band	
• OD Band—damaged, worn, misassembled	• Inspect for damage. Replace as required.
• Direct One-Way Clutch Assembly damaged	• Inspect for damage. Replace as required.

FM5029801620000X

Fig. 21 Routines 222 & 322: No 3-4 Automatic Shift

Possible Component	Reference/Action
223 — ELECTRICAL ROUTINE	
Powertrain Control System Perform Torque Converter Clutch Operation Test as described under ● Electrical Inputs/Outputs, Vehicle Wiring Harnesses, Powertrain Control Module (PCM), Shift Solenoid (SS3), TR sensor, Internal Wiring Harness, VSS	● Run On-Board Diagnostic. Refer to MOTOR's "Domestic Transmission Manual" for diagnosis. Perform Pinpoint Tests A and D using the Rotunda Transmission Tester 007-00130 and Rotunda AX4N Cable and Overlay 007-00117 and Rotunda Transmission Range (TR) Sensor Cable (MLP-B Cable) 007-00127 or (TRS-E Cable) 007-00111 or equivalent. Service as required. Clear codes. Road Test and rerun On-Board Diagnostic.
323 — HYDRAULIC/MECHANICAL ROUTINE	
Component Special Note ●	● Perform manual 4-3 pull in. If OK, Go to overdrive servo assembly in this routine. If not OK, Go to Main Control in this routine.
Main Control ● Bolts out of torque specification ● Gaskets and Separator Plate—damaged, off location ● 3-4 Shift Valve—stuck, damaged ● SS3—damaged	● Tighten bolts to specification. ● Inspect for damage. Replace. ● Inspect. Service as required. ● Inspect for damage and contamination. Service as required. Activate solenoid using Rotunda Transmission Tester 007-00130 and Rotunda AX4N Cable and Overlay 007-00117 or equivalent. If solenoid operation cannot be felt when placing hand on solenoid, replace solenoid. Inspect O-rings for damage. Service as required.
OD Band ● OD Band—damaged, worn, misassembled	● Inspect for damage. Replace as required.
Overdrive Servo Assembly ● Apply Rod—incorrect ● Servo Bore or Piston—damaged ● Piston Seals—damaged, missing ● Return Spring Retaining Clip—broken, missing	● Inspect Rod. ● Inspect for damage. Service as required. ● Inspect for damage. Service as required. ● Inspect for damage. Service as required.

FM5029801621000X

Fig. 22 Routines 223 & 323: No 4-3 Automatic Shift

Possible Component	Reference/Action
Low One-Way Clutch Assembly ● Not Overrunning—damaged	● Inspect for damage. Replace as required.
Forward Clutch Assembly ● Check Ball leaking	● Inspect for damage. Service as required.
Intermediate Clutch Assembly ● Damaged, burnt ● Check Ball damaged ● Seals, damaged	● Inspect for damage. Service as required. ● Inspect for damage. Service as required. ● Inspect for damage. Service as required.

FM5029801622020X

Fig. 23 Routines 224 & 324: No 3-2 Automatic Shift (Part 2 of 2)

Possible Component	Reference/Action
224 — ELECTRICAL ROUTINE	
● No Electrical Concerns.	● No action required.
324 — HYDRAULIC/MECHANICAL ROUTINE	
Improper Pressures ● EPC pressure ● Line pressure	● Perform Line Pressure Tests. ● Check pressure at line and EPC taps. If not within specification, check main control valve body.
Speedometer Gear—Drive ● Damaged	● Inspect for damage. Service as required.
Speedometer Gear—Driven ● Damaged	● Inspect for damage. Service as required.
Main Control Valve Body ● Bolts out of torque specification ● Gaskets and Separator Plate—damaged, off location ● 2-3 Shift Valves, 2-3 Capacity Modulator Valve—stuck, damaged	● Tighten bolts to specification. ● Inspect for damage. Replace as required. ● Inspect. Service as required.

FM5029801622010X

Fig. 23 Routines 224 & 324: No 3-2 Automatic Shift (Part 1 of 2)

Possible Component	Reference/Action
225 — ELECTRICAL ROUTINE	
Powertrain Control System ● Electrical Inputs/Outputs, Vehicle Wiring Harnesses, Powertrain Control Module (PCM), Shift Solenoids (SS1, SS2), VSS, TR Sensor	● Run On-Board Diagnostic. Refer to MOTOR's "Domestic Transmission Manual" for diagnosis. Perform Service Manual Pinpoint Tests A and D using the Rotunda Transmission Tester 007-00130 and Rotunda AX4N Cable and Overlay 007-00117 and Rotunda Transmission Range (TR) Sensor Cable (MLP-B Cable) 007-00127 or (TRS-E Cable) 007-00111 or equivalent. Service as required. Clear codes. Road Test and rerun On-Board Diagnostic.
325 — HYDRAULIC/MECHANICAL ROUTINE	
Main Control Valve Body ● Bolts out of torque specification ● Gaskets and Separator Plate—damaged, off location ● 1-2 Shift Valve ● SS1, SS2 damaged	● Tighten bolts to specification. ● Inspect for damage. Replace as required. ● Inspect. Service as required. ● Activate solenoid using transmission tester. If solenoid operation cannot be felt when placing hand on solenoid, replace solenoid. Inspect O-rings for damage. Service as required.
Intermediate Clutch Assembly ● Return Spring—damaged, misassembled ● Piston and Seal—damaged ● Balance Dam—damaged ● Friction element—damaged, worn	● Perform Air Pressure Tests. ● Inspect for damage. Replace as required. ● Inspect for damage. Replace as required. ● Inspect for damage. Replace as required. ● Inspect for damage. Replace as required.
Low One-Way Clutch Assembly ● Not holding, damaged	● Inspect for damage. Replace as required.

FM5029801623000X

Fig. 24 Routines 225 & 325: No 2-1 Automatic Shift

Possible Component	Reference/Action
226 — ELECTRICAL ROUTINE	
No Electrical Concerns	
326 — HYDRAULIC/MECHANICAL ROUTINE	
Improper Pressures	
• Line pressure, EPC pressure	• Perform Line Pressure and Stall Speed Test.
•	• Check pressure at line and EPC taps. If not OK, check the following possible component: Main Control
Main Control	
• Bolts out of torque specification	• Tighten bolts to specification.
• Gaskets and Separator Plate—damaged, off location	• Inspect gaskets for damage. Replace.
• 1-2 Shift Valve, Springs, Clips—loose, stuck, missing, misassembled	• Inspect. Service as required.

FM5029801624010X

Fig. 25 Routines 226 & 326: Soft/Slipping 1-2 Shift (Part 1 of 2)

Possible Component	Reference/Action
Pump Assembly	
• Porosity/Cross Leak	• Inspect. Replace as required.
• Gaskets—damaged, off location	• Inspect for damage. Replace as required.
• Components—damaged	• Inspect for damage, missing ball. Replace pump assembly if required.
1-2 Accumulator Assembly	
• Piston Seals, Springs—damaged, missing	• Inspect for damage. Service as required.
Support Assembly—Driven Sprocket	
• Seals—damaged, missing	• Inspect for damage, missing or blockage. Service as required.
• Holes—partially blocked	
Intermediate Clutch Assembly	
• Seals—damaged, leaking	• Inspect for damage. Replace as required.
• Piston—damaged	• Inspect for damage. Replace as required.
• Friction—damaged, worn	• Inspect for damage. Replace as required.
• Cylinder Hub Lube Groove—restricted	• Inspect for restriction. Service as required.

FM5029801624020X

Fig. 25 Routines 226 & 326: Soft/Slipping 1-2 Shift (Part 2 of 2)

Possible Component	Reference/Action
227 — ELECTRICAL ROUTINE	
No Electrical Concerns	
327 — HYDRAULIC/MECHANICAL ROUTINE	
Improper Pressures	
• Line pressure, EPC pressure	• Perform Line Pressure and Stall Speed Tests.
•	• Check pressure at EPC and line taps. If not OK, check the following possible component: Main Control
Main Control	
• Bolts out of torque specification	• Tighten bolts to specification.
• Gaskets and Separator Plate—damaged, off location	• Inspect gaskets and replace.
• 1-2 Shift Valve, 2-3 Shift Valve, Line Modulator Valve, 2-3 Capacity Modulator Valve, Spring—stuck, damaged	• Inspect. Service as required.
• B8 Check Ball—damaged, missing or hole damaged	• Inspect for damage. Service as required.
Support Assembly—Drive Sprocket	
• Seals—damaged, missing, holes partially blocked	• Inspect for damage. Service as required.
Direct Clutch Assembly	
• Seals—damaged, worn	• Inspect for damage. Replace as required.
• Piston—damaged, worn	• Inspect for damage. Replace as required.
• Friction—damaged, worn	• Inspect for damage. Replace as required.
• Check Ball—not seating	• Inspect for damage. Replace as required.
• Return Spring Assembly—damaged, worn	• Inspect for damage. Replace as required.
Direct/Intermediate Clutch Hub	
• Damaged or holes partially blocked	• Inspect for damage. Service as required.
2-3 Accumulator Assembly	
• Piston, Seals, Spring, Rod or Bore—damaged	• Inspect for damage. Service as required.

FM5029801625000X

Fig. 26 Routines 227 & 327: Soft/Slipping 2-3 Shift

Possible Component	Reference/Action
228 — ELECTRICAL ROUTINE	
No Electrical Concerns	
328 — HYDRAULIC/MECHANICAL ROUTINE	
Overdrive Servo Assembly	
• Apply Rod—damaged	• Inspect rod. Replace if incorrect.
• Servo Bore or Piston—damaged	• Inspect for damage. Service as required.
• Piston Seals—damaged, missing	• Inspect for damage. Service as required.
Main Control	
• Bolts out of torque specification	• Tighten bolts to specification.
• Gaskets and Separator Plate—damaged, off location	• Inspect gaskets for damage. Replace.
• 3-4 Shift Valve, Line Modulator Valve, Forward Clutch Control Valve—stuck, damaged	• Inspect. Service as required.
3-4 Accumulator Assembly	
• Accumulator Piston—stuck, damaged	• Inspect for damage. Service as required.
• Piston Seals—damaged, missing	• Inspect for damage. Service as required.
• Springs—damaged	• Inspect for damage. Service as required.
• Rod or Bore—damaged	• Inspect for damage. Service as required.
OD Band	
• OD Band—damaged, worn, misassembled	• Inspect for damage. Replace as required.

FM5029801626000X

Fig. 27 Routines 228 & 328: Soft/Slipping 3-4 Shift

Possible Component	Reference/Action
229 — ELECTRICAL ROUTINE	
No Electrical Concerns	
329 — HYDRAULIC/MECHANICAL ROUTINE	
Main Control	
• Bolts out of torque specification	• Tighten bolts to specification.
• Gaskets and Separator Plate—damaged, off location	• Inspect for damage. Replace.
• 3-4 Shift Valve, Line Modulator Valve—stuck, damaged	• Inspect. Service as required.
OD Band	
• OD Band—damaged, worn, misassembled	• Inspect for damage. Replace as required.
Overdrive Servo Assembly	
• Apply Rod—incorrect	• Inspect. Replace if incorrect.
• Servo Bore or Piston—damaged	• Inspect for damage. Service as required.
• Piston Seals—damaged, missing	• Inspect for damage. Service as required.
• Return Spring Retaining Clip—damaged, missing	• Inspect for damage. Service as required.
Direct Clutch Assembly	
• Direct Clutch assembly	• Perform Air Pressure Tests
• Damaged	• Inspect for damage. Service as required.
• Check Ball—damaged	• Inspect for damage. Service as required.
Support Assembly—Drive Sprocket	
• Seals—damaged, holes partially blocked	• Inspect for damage. Service as required.

FM5029801627000X

Fig. 28 Routines 229 & 329: Soft/Slipping 4-3 Shift

Possible Component	Reference/Action
230 — ELECTRICAL ROUTINE	
No Electrical Concerns	
330 — HYDRAULIC/MECHANICAL ROUTINE	
Main Control	
• Bolts out of torque specification	• Tighten bolts to specification.
• Gaskets and Separator Plate—damaged, off location	• Inspect for damage. Replace.
• 1-2 Shift Valve, 3-4 Shift Valve, Line Modulator Valve, 3-2 Timing Valve—stuck, damaged	• Inspect. Service as required.
Intermediate Clutch Assembly	
• Clutch Assembly—damaged	• Perform Air Pressure Tests
• Seals—leaking	• Inspect for damage. Service as required.
Support Assembly—Driven	
• Seals—damaged, leaking, hole partially blocked	• Inspect for damage. Service as required.
Forward Clutch Assembly	
•	• Perform Air Pressure Tests
• Check Ball—damaged, missing	• Inspect for damage. Service as required.
• Clutch Assembly—damaged	• Inspect for damage. Service as required.
• Friction Plates—damaged	• Inspect for damage. Service as required.

FM5029801628000X

Fig. 29 Routines 230 & 330: Soft/Slipping 3-2 Shift

Possible Component	Reference/Action
231 — ELECTRICAL ROUTINE	
No Electrical Concerns	
331 — HYDRAULIC/MECHANICAL ROUTINE	
Main Control	
• Bolts out of torque specification	• Tighten bolts to specification.
• Gaskets and Separator Plate—damaged, off location	• Inspect for damage. Replace.
• 1-2 Shift Valve, Line Modulator Valve, 3-2 Timing Valve—stuck, damaged	• Inspect. Service as required.
Low One-Way Clutch Assembly	
• Clutch Assembly—damaged	• Inspect for damage. Service as required.
Support Assembly—Drive Sprocket	
• Seals—damaged, leaking, hole partially blocked	• Inspect for damage. Service as required.
Forward Clutch Assembly	
• Forward Clutch assembly	• Perform Air Pressure Tests
• Check Ball—damaged, missing	• Inspect for damage. Service as required.
• Clutch Assembly—damaged	• Inspect for damage. Service as required.
• Friction—damaged	• Inspect for damage. Service as required.

FM5029801629000X

Fig. 30 Routines 231 & 331: Soft/Slipping 2-1 Shift

Possible Component	Reference/Action
232 — ELECTRICAL ROUTINE	
No Electrical Concerns	
332 — HYDRAULIC/MECHANICAL ROUTINE	
Improper Pressures	
• Line pressure, EPC pressure	• Perform Line Pressure test
•	• Check pressure at EPC and line taps. If not OK, check the following possible component: Main Control

FM5029801630010X

Fig. 31 Routines 232 & 323: Harsh 1-2 Shift (Part 1 of 2)

Possible Component	Reference/Action
Main Control	
• Bolts out of torque specification	• Tighten bolts to specification.
• Gaskets and Separator Plate—damaged, off location	• Inspect gaskets for damage. Replace.
• 1-2 Shift Valve, Springs, B10 Check Ball, Clips—stuck, missing, misassembled	• Inspect. Service as required.
Pump Assembly	
• Porosity/cross leak	• Inspect. Replace as required.
• Gaskets—damaged, off location	• Inspect for damage. Replace as required.
• Components—damaged	• Inspect for damage, missing ball. Replace pump assembly if required.
1-2 Accumulator Assembly	
• Piston Seals, Springs—damaged, missing	• Inspect for damage. Service as required.
• Piston or Rod—stuck, damaged	• Inspect for damage. Service as required.
Intermediate Clutch Assembly	
• Seals—damaged	• Inspect for damage. Replace as required.
• Piston—damaged	• Inspect for damage. Replace as required.
• Friction Plates—damaged, worn	• Inspect for damage. Replace as required.
• Return Spring—damaged, broken	• Inspect for damage. Service as required.

FM5029801630020X

Fig. 31 Routines 232 & 323: Harsh 1-2 Shift (Part 2 of 2)

Possible Component	Reference/Action
233 — ELECTRICAL ROUTINE	
No Electrical Concerns	
333 — HYDRAULIC/MECHANICAL ROUTINE	
Improper Pressures	
• Line Pressure, EPC pressure	• Perform Line Pressure.
•	• Check pressure at EPC and line taps. If not OK, check the following possible component: Main Control
Main Control	
• Bolts out of torque specification	• Tighten bolts to specification.
• Gaskets and Separator Plate—damaged, off location	• Inspect gaskets and replace.
• 2-3 Shift Valve, 2-3 Capacity Modulator Valve/Spring—stuck, damaged	• Inspect. Service as required.
• Line Modulator or Capacity Modulator Check Valves/Springs—damaged, missing	• Inspect for damage. Service as required.
Direct Clutch Assembly	
•	• Perform Air Pressure Tests.
• Seals—damaged, worn	• Inspect for damage. Replace as required.
• Piston—damaged, worn	• Inspect for damage. Replace as required.
• Friction—damaged, worn	• Inspect for damage. Replace as required.
• Return Spring Assembly—damaged, worn	• Inspect for damage. Replace as required.
2-3 Accumulator Assembly	
• Piston, Seals, Rod or Bore—damaged, stuck	• Inspect for damage. Replace as required.

FM5029801631000X

Fig. 32 Routines 233 & 333: Harsh 2-3 Shift

Possible Component	Reference/Action
234 — ELECTRICAL ROUTINE	
No Electrical Concerns	
334 — HYDRAULIC/MECHANICAL ROUTINE	
Overdrive Servo Assembly	
• Apply Rod—incorrect	• Inspect rod. Replace if incorrect.
• Return Spring Retaining Clip—broken, missing	• Inspect for damage. Service as required.

FM5029801632010X

Fig. 33 Routines 234 & 334: Harsh 3-4 Shift (Part 1 of 2)

Possible Component	Reference/Action
Main Control	
• Bolts out of torque specification	• Tighten bolts to specification.
• Gaskets and Separator Plate—damaged, off location	• Inspect for damage. Replace.
• 3-4 Shift Valve, Line Modulator Valve, Forward Clutch Control Valve—stuck, damaged	• Inspect. Service as required.
3-4 Accumulator Assembly	
• Accumulator Piston—stuck, damaged	• Inspect for damage. Service as required.
• Piston Seals—damaged	• Inspect for damage. Service as required.
• Springs—damaged, missing	• Inspect for damage. Service as required.
• Rod or Bore—damaged	• Inspect for damage. Service as required.
OD Band	
• OD Band—damaged, worn, misassembled	• Inspect for damage. Replace as required.

FM5029801632020X

Fig. 33 Routines 234 & 334: Harsh 3-4 Shift (Part 2 of 2)

Possible Component	Reference/Action
235 — ELECTRICAL ROUTINE	
No Electrical Concerns	
335 — HYDRAULIC/MECHANICAL ROUTINE	
Main Control	
• Bolts out of torque specification	• Tighten bolts to specification.
• Gaskets and Separator Plate—damaged, off location	• Inspect for damage. Replace.
• 3-4 Shift Valve, Line Modulator Valve,—stuck, damaged	• Inspect. Service as required.
OD Band	
• OD Band—damaged, worn, misassembled	• Inspect for damage. Replace as required.
Overdrive Servo Assembly	
• Apply Rod—incorrect	• Inspect rod. Service as required.
• Servo Bore or Piston—damaged	• Inspect for damage. Service as required.
• Piston Seals—damaged, missing	• Inspect for damage. Service as required.
• Return Spring Retaining Clip—damaged, missing	• Inspect for damage. Service as required.
Direct Clutch Assembly	
• Direct Clutch assembly	• Perform Air Pressure Tests as described.
• Damaged	• Inspect for damage. Service as required.
• Check Ball—damaged	• Inspect for damage. Service as required.
Support Assembly—Drive Sprocket	
• Seals—damaged, holes partially blocked	• Inspect for damage. Service as required.

FM5029801633000X

Fig. 34 Routines 235 & 335: Harsh 4-3 Shift

Possible Component	Reference/Action
236 — ELECTRICAL ROUTINE	
No Electrical Concerns	
336 — HYDRAULIC/MECHANICAL ROUTINE	
Main Control	
• Bolts out of torque specification	• Tighten bolts to specification.
• Gaskets and Separator Plate—damaged, off location	• Inspect for damage. Service as required.
• 3-2 Shift Timing Valve, Line Modulator Valve, 1-2, 3-4 Shift Valves,—stuck, damaged	• Inspect. Service as required.
Intermediate Clutch Assembly	
• Clutch Assembly—damaged	• Inspect for damage. Replace as required.
• Seals—leaking	• Inspect for damage. Service as required.

FM5029801634010X

Fig. 35 Routines 236 & 336: Harsh 3-2 Shift (Part 1 of 2)

Possible Component	Reference/Action
Support Assembly—Drive Sprocket	
• Seals—damaged, leaking, holes blocked, missing	• Inspect for damage, missing or blockage. Service as required.
Low One-Way Clutch Assembly	
• Not overrunning—damaged	• Inspect for damage. Replace as required.
Forward Clutch Assembly	
• Forward Clutch assembly	• Perform Air Pressure Tests.
• Clutch Assembly—damaged	• Inspect for damage. Replace as required.
• Check Ball—not functioning, missing	• Inspect for damage. Replace as required.

FM5029801634020X

Fig. 35 Routines 236 & 336: Harsh 3-2 Shift (Part 2 of 2)

Possible Component	Reference/Action
237 — ELECTRICAL ROUTINE	
No Electrical Concerns	
337 — HYDRAULIC/MECHANICAL ROUTINE	
Main Control	
• Bolts out of torque specification	• Tighten bolts to specification.
• Gaskets and Separator Plate—damaged, off location	• Inspect for damage. Replace.
• 1-2 Shift Valve, Line Modulator Valve, 3-2 Timing Valve—stuck, damaged	• Inspect. Service as required.
Support Assembly—Driven	
• Seals—damaged, holes blocked	• Inspect for damage. Service as required.
Forward Clutch Assembly	
• Forward Clutch assembly	• Perform Air Pressure Tests.
• Check Ball—damaged, missing	• Inspect for damage. Service as required.
• Friction element—damaged	• Inspect for damage. Service as required.
• Support Assembly—damaged	• Inspect for damage. Service as required.
Low One-Way Clutch Assembly	
• Not holding—damaged	• Inspect for damage. Replace as required.

FM5029801635000X

Fig. 36 Routines 237 & 337: Harsh 2-1 Shift

Possible Component	Reference/Action
240 — ELECTRICAL ROUTINE	
Powertrain Control System	• Perform Torque Converter Clutch Operation Test.
• Electrical Inputs/Outputs, Vehicle Wiring Harnesses, Powertrain Control Module (PCM), TP, TFT, TSS Sensor, BOO Switch, TCC Solenoid, Internal Wiring Harness	• Run On-Board Diagnostic. Refer to MOTOR's "Domestic Transmission Manual" for diagnosis. Perform Service Manual Pinpoint Tests B, C and F using the Rotunda Transmission Tester 007-00130 and Rotunda AX4N Cable and Overlay 007-00117 or equivalent. Service as required. Clear codes. Road Test and rerun On-Board Diagnostic.
340 — HYDRAULIC/MECHANICAL ROUTINE	
Improper Pressures	
• Low line pressure, low EPC pressure	• Perform Line Pressure.
•	• Check pressure at EPC and line taps. If low, check main control valve body.
Main Control Valve Body	
• Bolts out of torque specification	• Tighten bolts to specification.
• Gaskets and Separator Plate—damaged, off location	• Inspect gaskets. Service as required.
• Valve Body Pilot Sleeve—damaged, misaligned. Manual Valve, Converter Regulator Valve, Main Regulator Valve, Springs, Solenoid Regulator Valve, Bypass Clutch Control Valve—ctuck, damaged	• Inspect. Service as required.

FM5029801636010X

Fig. 37 Routines 240 & 340: No Torque Converter Apply (Part 1 of 2)

Possible Component	Reference/Action
• TCC Solenoid not functioning properly	• Activate solenoid using Rotunda Transmission Tester 007-00130 and Rotunda AX4N Cable and Overlay 007-00117 or equivalent. If solenoid operation cannot be felt when placing hand on solenoid, replace solenoid. Inspect O-rings for damage. Service as required.
Turbine Shaft	
• Seals—damaged, missing	• Inspect for damage. Replace as required.
• Holes—missing, plugged	• Inspect for damage. Service as required.
Pump Assembly	
• Seals, Bearing—damaged, missing	• Inspect seals for damage. Service as required
Converter	
• Refer to Reference/Action	• Inspect as described. Service as required.

FM5029801636020X

Fig. 37 Routines 240 & 340: No Torque Converter Apply (Part 2 of 2)

Possible Component	Reference/Action
241 — ELECTRICAL ROUTINE	
Powertrain Control System	
• Electrical Inputs/Outputs, Vehicle Wiring Harnesses, Powertrain Control Module (PCM), TCC Solenoid, Internal Wiring Harness	• Perform Torque Converter Clutch Operation Test. Run On-Board Diagnostic. Refer to MOTOR's "Domestic Transmission Manual" for diagnosis. Perform Pinpoint Test C using the Rotunda Transmission Tester 007-00130 and Rotunda AX4N Cable and Overlay 007-00117 or equivalent. Service as required. Clear codes. Road Test and rerun On-Board Diagnostic.
Main Controls	
• Bolts out of torque specification	• Tighten bolts to specification.
• Gaskets and Separator Plate—damaged, off location	• Inspect gaskets. Service as required.
• Bypass Clutch Control Valve and Plunger, Solenoid Regulator Valve, Converter Regulator Valve—stuck, damaged	• Inspect. Service as required.
• TCC Solenoid—not functioning properly	• Activate solenoid using Rotunda Transmission Tester 007-00130 and Rotunda AX4N Cable and Overlay 007-00117 or equivalent. If solenoid operation cannot be felt when placing hand on solenoid, replace solenoid.
Converter	
• No End Clearance to Turbine	• Check torque converter end play

FM5029801637000X

Fig. 38 Routine 241: Torque Converter Always Applied/Stalls Vehicle

Possible Component	Reference/Action
242 — ELECTRICAL ROUTINE	
Powertrain Control System	
• Electrical Inputs/Outputs, Vehicle Wiring Harnesses, Powertrain Control Module (PCM), TCC, TFT Sensor, BOO Switch, Internal Wiring Harness, TSS	• Perform Torque Converter Clutch Operation Test. Run On-Board Diagnostic. Refer to MOTOR's "Domestic Transmission Manual" for diagnosis. Perform Service Manual Pinpoint Tests B, C and F using the Rotunda Transmission Tester 007-00130 and Rotunda AX4N Cable and Overlay 007-00117 or equivalent. Service as required. Clear codes. Road Test and rerun On-Board Diagnostic.
342 — HYDRAULIC/MECHANICAL ROUTINE	
• Fluid condition	• Prior to performing this action, make sure all electrical diagnostics have been performed. Inspect fluid condition. If burnt, drain fluid and converter. Replace fluid and fluid filter assembly. Bring vehicle to normal operating temperature. Perform Transaxle Drive Cycle Test. Perform On-Board Diagnostic. If condition still exists, continue diagnostics.

FM5029801638010X

Fig. 39 Routines 242 & 342: Torque Converter Cycling/Shudder/Chatter (Part 1 of 2)

Possible Component	Reference/Action
Improper Pressures	
• Low line pressure, low EPC	• Check pressure at line and EPC taps. Perform Line Pressure and Stall Speed Tests.
	• If not OK, check the Main Control Valve Body.
Main Control Valve Body	
• Bolts out of torque specification	• Tighten bolts to specification.
• Gaskets and Separator Plate—damaged, off location	• Inspect for damage. Replace as required.
• Valve Body Pilot Sleeve—damaged, misaligned Manual Valve, Bypass Clutch Control Valve and Plunger, Converter Regulator Valve, Solenoid Regulator Valve—stuck, damaged	• Inspect. Service as required.
• TCC Solenoid not functioning properly	• Activate solenoid using Rotunda Transmission Tester 007-00130 and Rotunda AX4N Cable and Overlay 007-00117 or equivalent. If solenoid operation cannot be felt when placing hand on solenoid, replace solenoid. Inspect O-rings for damage. Service as required.
Turbine Shaft	
• Seals—damaged, missing	• Inspect for damage. Replace as required.
Pump Shaft	
• Seals—damaged, missing	• Inspect seals for damage. Service as required.
Torque Converter	
• Refer to Reference/Action	• Inspect. Service as required.

FM5029801638020X

Fig. 39 Routines 242 & 342: Torque Converter Cycling/Shudder/Chatter (Part 2 of 2)

Possible Component	Reference/Action
250 — ELECTRICAL ROUTINE	
• No Electrical Concerns	• No action required.
350 — HYDRAULIC/MECHANICAL ROUTINE	
Improper Pressures	
• Line pressure, EPC pressure	• Perform Line Pressure Test. Check pressure at line and EPC taps. If not OK, check Main Control Valve Body and Direct Clutch Assembly.
Main Control Valve Body	
• Bolts out of torque specification	• Tighten bolts to specification.
• Gaskets and Separator Plate—damaged, off location	• Inspect for damage. Replace as required.
• Shift Valve, Manual Downshift Modulator Valve, B8 Check Ball—stuck or damaged	• Inspect. Clean or service as required.
Direct Clutch Assembly	
• Refer to Routine 321	• Inspect. Service or replace as required.
Direct One-Way Clutch	
• Damaged, refer to Routine 321	• Inspect for damage. Service as required.
Coast Band	
• Band—damaged	• Inspect for damage. Service as required.
• Friction Plates—damaged	• Inspect for damage. Service as required.
• Coast Band Apply Tube/Seal—damaged, loose	• Inspect for damage. Service as required.
• Low/Intermediate Coast Band—damaged	• Inspect for damage. Service as required.
• Apply Servo, Cover, Seals—damaged	• Inspect for damage. Service as required.

FM5029801639000X

Fig. 40 Routines 250 & 350: No Engine Braking In 1st Gear Manual

Possible Component	Reference/Action
251 — ELECTRICAL ROUTINE	
• No Electrical Concerns	• No action required.

FM5029801640010X

Fig. 41 Routines 251 & 351: Shift Lever Efforts High (Part 1 of 2)

Possible Component	Reference/Action
351 — HYDRAULIC/MECHANICAL ROUTINE	
Shift Linkage (Internal, External)	
• Damaged or out of adjustment	• Inspect and service as required. Verify linkage adjustment. After servicing linkage, verify that the TR sensor is properly adjusted.
Manual Lever	
• External Retaining Pin damaged, Nut loose, Detent Spring—bent, damaged; or Park Mechanism damaged, improper lever used	• Inspect and service/replace as required.
Main Control Valve Body	
• Manual Valve stuck	• Inspect and service or replace as necessary.
• Bolts out of torque specification	• Tighten bolts to specification.
Brake Shift Interlock	
•	• Refer to "AX4S (AXOD-E) Automatic Overdrive Transmission."

FM5029801640020X

Fig. 41 Routines 251 & 351: Shift Lever Efforts High (Part 2 of 2)

Possible Component	Reference/Action
252 — ELECTRICAL ROUTINE	
• No Electrical Concerns	• No action required.
352 — HYDRAULIC/MECHANICAL ROUTINE	
Improper Fluid Level •	• Adjust fluid to proper level.
Seals/Gaskets • Converter, TSS, Halfshaft Axles, Gasket/Seal Manual Lever, Fluid Level Indicator, Servo Cover, Transaxle Pan, Improper Hub Seal, Chain Cover-to-Case	• Locate source. Service as required.
Other • Cooler Fitting, Pressure Taps, Transmission Connectors, Cooler Lines, Transaxle Pan, Case Porosity, Chain Cover Porosity, Case Cracked • Vent—blocked, damaged.	• Locate Source. Service as required. • Check vent for damage or blockage. Service as required.

FM5029801641000X

Fig. 42 Routines 252 & 352: External Leaks

Possible Component	Reference/Action
253 — ELECTRICAL ROUTINE	
Powertrain Control System • Electrical Inputs/Outputs, Vehicle Wiring Harnesses, Powertrain Control Module (PCM), TCC Solenoid, TP, VSS, MAF, IAT Sensors, Internal Wiring Harness	• Perform Shift Point Road Test and Torque Converter Clutch Operation Test. • Run On-Board Diagnostic. Refer to MOTOR's "Domestic Transmission Manual" for diagnosis. Perform Service Manual Pinpoint Test C using the Rotunda Transmission Tester 007-00130 and Rotunda AX4N Cable and Overlay 007-00117 or equivalent. Service as required. Clear codes. Road test and rerun On-Board Diagnostic.
353 — HYDRAULIC/MECHANICAL ROUTINE	
Fluid • Low Level	• Adjust to proper level
Verify Proper Shift Scheduling, Engagements, Line Pressures and Stall Speed •	• Go to the appropriate Diagnostic Routines per Index.
Converter Clutch Always Applied •	• Go to Routine 341.

FM5029801642000X

Fig. 43 Routines 253 & 353: Poor Vehicle Performance

Possible Component	Reference/Action
254 — ELECTRICAL ROUTINE	
• No electrical concerns	• No action required
354 — HYDRAULIC/MECHANICAL ROUTINE	
For Noises/Vibrations That Change With Engine Speed: • Converter components • Fluid level (low) — Pump cavitation • Pump Assembly • Engine drive accessories • Fluid Cooler Tubes grounding out • Flywheel	• Locate source of disturbance and service as required.
For Noises/Vibrations That Change With Vehicle Speed: • Engine Mounts — loose or damaged • Driveline concerns: — Halfshaft shudder — CV joints — Suspension — Modifications • Output/Halfshaft Splines worn or damaged • TSS incorrectly installed	• Locate source of disturbance and service as required. • Inspect. Service as required.
Other Noises/Vibrations: • Main Controls — Valve resonance • Shift Cable — Vibration, Grounding • Fluid Cooler Tubes grounding • Anti-Lock (ABS) Brake System • Power Steering Pump	• Locate source of disturbance and service as required. • Locate source of disturbance and service as required. • Locate source of disturbance and service as required. • Refer to "Anti-Lock Brakes." • Refer to Power Steering Pump.

FM5029801643000X

Fig. 44 Routines 254 & 354: Noise/Vibration In Forward/Reverse

Possible Component	Reference/Action
255 — ELECTRICAL ROUTINE	
Powertrain Control System • Electrical Inputs/Outputs, Vehicle Wiring Harnesses, Powertrain Control Module (PCM), TR Sensor	• Run On-Board Diagnostic. Refer to MOTOR's "Domestic Transmission Manual" for diagnosis. Perform Pinpoint Test D using the Rotunda Transmission Tester 007-00130 and Rotunda AX4N Cable and Overlay 007-00117 and the Rotunda Transmission Range (TR) Sensor Cable (MLP-B Cable) 007-00127 or (TRS-E Cable) 007-00111 or equivalent. Service as required. Clear codes. Road Test and rerun On-Board Diagnostic.
355 — HYDRAULIC/MECHANICAL ROUTINE	
Shift Linkage/Cable (Internal/External) • Damaged or out of adjustment	• Inspect and service as required. Verify linkage adjustment. After servicing linkage, verify that the TR sensor is properly adjusted.

FM5029801644000X

Fig. 45 Routines 255 & 355: Engine Will Not Crank

Possible Component	Reference/Action
256 — ELECTRICAL ROUTINE	
• No Electrical Concerns	• No action required

FM5029801645010X

Fig. 46 Routines 256 & 356: No Park Range (Part 1 of 2)

Possible Component	Reference/Action
356 — HYDRAULIC/MECHANICAL ROUTINE	
Shift Linkage (Internal/External) • Damaged or out of adjustment	• Inspect and service as required. Verify linkage adjustment. After servicing linkage, verify that the TR sensor is properly adjusted.
Park Mechanism • Park Brake Pawl, Parking Pawl Return Spring, Park Rod Abutment, Parking Pawl Shaft, Parking Pawl Actuating Rod, Manual Lever, Manual Lever Detent Spring—damaged	• Inspect. Service as required.

FM5029801645020X

Fig. 46 Routines 256 & 356: No Park Range (Part 2 of 2)

Possible Component	Reference/Action
257 — ELECTRICAL ROUTINE	
Refer to Electrical Routine 240, 340 Torque Converter No Applying •	• Refer to Electrical Routine 240, 340 Torque Converter - No Applying
357 — HYDRAULIC/MECHANICAL ROUTINE	
Fluid • Improper level • Condition	• Adjust fluid to proper level. • Inspect as described under Fluid Condition Check.
Cooler Lines • Damaged, blocked, reversed, leaking	• Inspect and service as required.
Auxiliary Cooler • Damaged, blocked, restricted or improperly installed	• Inspect and service as required.
Vehicle Concerns Causing Engine Overheating	
Main Control Valve Body • By-Pass Clutch Control Valve and Plunger, Converter Regulator Valve, Cooler Bypass Valve/spring-stuck, damaged	• Inspect and service as required.
Torque Converter Not Applying • Seized Converter One-Way Clutch	• See Routine 240/340. Inspect. Service as required.
Excessive Towing Loads	• Check gross vehicle weight (GVW).
Idle or Performance Concern	• Refer to MOTOR's "Domestic Transmission Manual."
Improper Clutch or Band Application or Oil Pressure Control System	• Perform Line Pressure Tests and Shift Point Road Tests

FM5029801646000X

Fig. 47 Routines 257 & 357: Transaxle Overheating

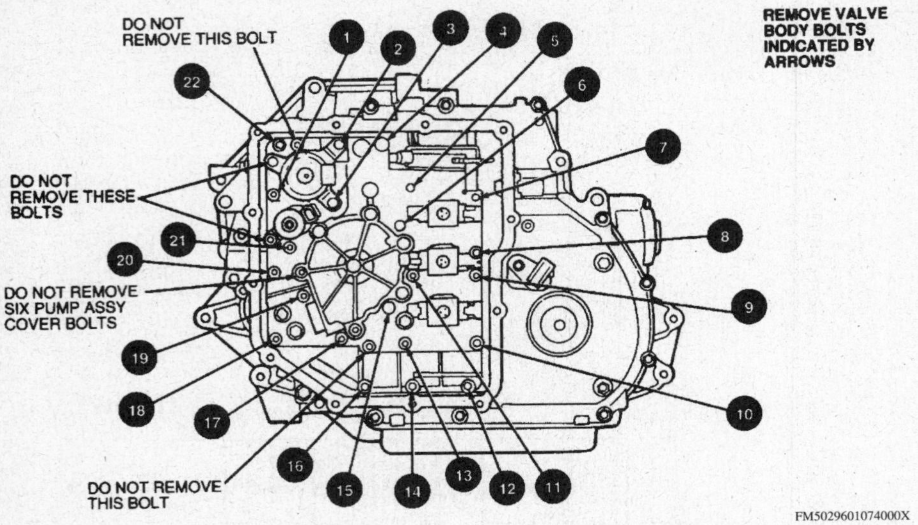

Fig. 48 Main control valve body bolt removal

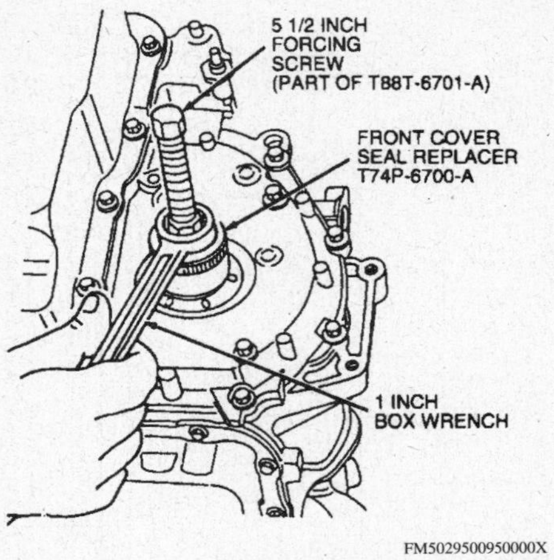

Fig. 49 Lefthand differential seal removal

MAINTENANCE

Ford Motor Company recommends use of Mercon type automatic transmission fluid in this transaxle. If Mercon type fluid is not available, Type H automatic transmission fluid may be used. Use of a fluid other than specified may result in transaxle malfunction or failure.

FLUID CHECK

Fluid level should be checked at normal operating temperature, with vehicle on a level surface.

1. Start engine and move gearshift selector through all ranges, allowing sufficient time for each position to engage.
2. Place gear selector in Park position and set parking brake.
3. With engine running, check fluid mark on transaxle dipstick. Fluid should be within crosshatched area of level indicator.
4. If fluid level is low, add Mercon ATF, or equivalent, automatic transmission fluid.
5. If fluid level is too high, disconnect transaxle fluid cooler "IN" line at cooler and drain.

FLUID CHANGE

1. Place transaxle range selector in Park and set parking brake.
2. **On models equipped with automatic air suspension,** place switch in Off position before raising vehicle.
3. **On all models,** raise and support vehicle.
4. Remove retainer clip from lower transaxle fluid cooler line and fitting.
5. On models equipped with 5⁄16 inch cooler lines, use disconnect tool No. T82L-9500-AH, or equivalent, to disconnect transaxle cooler line.
6. On models equipped with 3⁄8 inch cooler lines, pinch plastic retainer tabs of push connect fitting and pull cooler line to separate it from fitting.
7. Disconnect lower transaxle cooler line from cooler line fitting at transaxle.

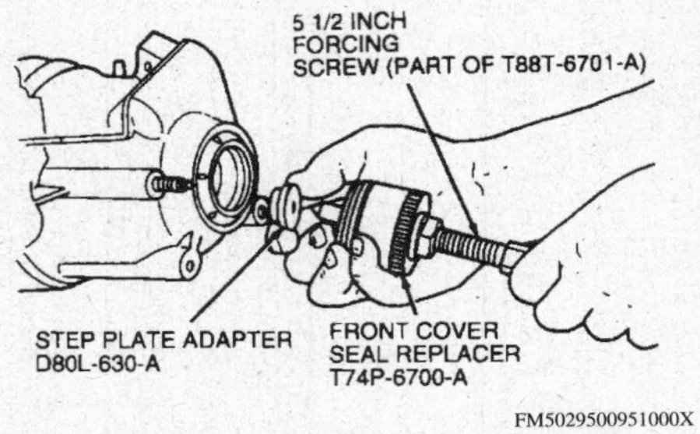

Fig. 50 Righthand differential seal removal

8. Attach flexible hose, about 3 ft. in length, to end of transaxle cooler line and gently fasten hose with clamp. Place opposite end of flexible hose into suitable container.
9. Plug transaxle cooler line fitting at transaxle.
10. Lower vehicle.
11. Place gear selector in Park and start engine. Run engine at idle for approximately 40–60 seconds until steady stream of fluid stops flowing from flexible drain hose, then turn engine off.
12. Fill transaxle with 10 quarts of suitable transaxle fluid, then repeat previous step. This should drain 10 quarts of fluid.
13. Raise and support vehicle, then remove plug from transaxle cooler line fitting.
14. Remove flexible hose from cooler line.
15. Install cooler line into transaxle cooler fitting.
16. Install retainer clip over cooler line and fitting.
17. Lower vehicle.
18. Add 2 quarts of suitable transaxle fluid.
19. Start engine and move gear selector through all ranges, allowing transaxle to engage in each position.
20. Check fluid level as described under "Fluid Check."
21. Place air suspension switch in On position, if equipped.

ADJUSTMENTS

MANUAL SHIFT LINKAGE

CONTINENTAL

Column Shifter

1. Place shift lever in OD position, then hang three-pound weight on shift lever to ensure lever is firmly in OD detent.
2. Loosen adjusting nut located on top of transaxle on gearshift lever.
3. Move gearshift lever to OD position, then tighten nut to specification.
4. Check operation of transaxle in each transaxle range and ensure Transaxle Range (TR) sensor is functioning properly.

Console Shifter

1. Place shift lever in OD position.
2. Loosen manual control lever to transaxle shift cable retaining nut.
3. Move gearshift lever to OD position, second detent from most rearward position.
4. Tighten retaining nut to specification.
5. Check operation of transaxle in each transaxle range and ensure Transaxle Range Sensor (TR) is functioning properly.

SABLE & TAURUS

Refer to "AX4S (AXOD-E) Automatic Overdrive Transaxle."

SHIFT INDICATOR CABLE

CONTINENTAL

Column Shift

1. Remove steering column tilt release lever.
2. Remove ignition switch lock cylinder, refer to "Ignition Lock, Replace" in "Electrical" section.
3. Remove upper and lower steering column shrouds.
4. Place shift lever in OD position, then hang three-pound weight on shift lever to ensure lever is firmly in OD detent.
5. Using adjustment wheel located on shift cable, adjust shift cable until shift

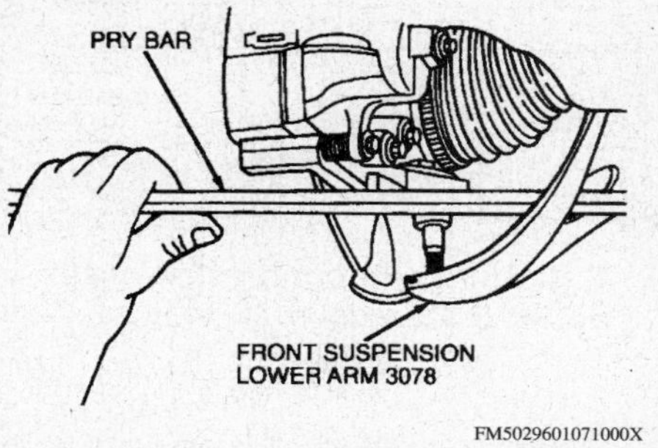

Fig. 51 Ball joint stud removal

indicator completely covers OD indicator and calibration dots show no red.

6. Cycle shift lever through all positions and check that shift indicator completely covers proper letter or number in each position.
7. Install steering column shrouds, ignition lock and tilt release lever.

IN-VEHICLE REPAIRS

PUMP ASSEMBLY & MAIN CONTROL VALVE BODY

1. Remove air cleaner assembly.
2. Remove battery and battery tray.
3. Disconnect transaxle range sensor and transaxle harness electrical connector. Position engine wire harness out of way.
4. Place TR sensor manual lever in Park position.
5. Install Rotunda three-bar engine support, tool No. D88L-6000-A, or equivalent, with Rotunda engine lift bracket set, tool No. 014-00796, or equivalent, and support engine assembly.
6. Remove transaxle side pan upper attaching bolts.
7. Raise and support vehicle.
8. Remove lefthand front tire and wheel.
9. Remove lefthand front splash shield.
10. Remove lefthand side engine support and insulator.
11. Position drain pan under transaxle side pan, then remove remaining lower transaxle side pan attaching bolts.
12. Remove transaxle side pan and gasket, then discard gasket.
13. Disconnect transaxle fluid temperature sensor from main control valve body and solenoid electrical connectors.
14. Remove transaxle wiring harness from chain cover.
15. Remove main control valve body retaining bolts, **Fig. 48. Do not remove pump assembly cover bolts.**
16. Disconnect manual valve linkage and carefully slide pump assembly and main control valve body off pump shaft and remove from transaxle.
17. Reverse procedure to install. Tighten valve body retaining bolts and transaxle side pan bolts to specifications.

TURBINE SHAFT SPEED SENSOR (TSS)

1. Remove battery and battery tray.

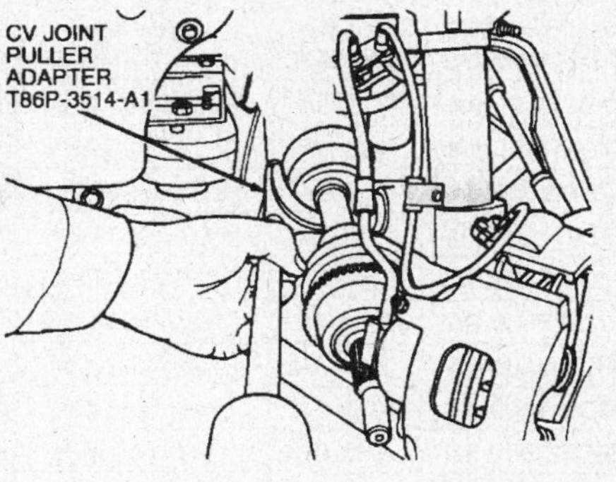

Fig. 52 CV joint puller adapter

PCM APPLICATION CHART				
Application	Old Calibration	Old Part Number (-12A650-)	New Calibration	New Part Number (-12A650-)
	R10			F6PZ
	R10			F6
1997 49-State	7-14A-R06	F7DF-GC	7-14A-R10	F7DZ-GD
1997 California	7-14S-R06	F7DF-HC	7-14S-R10	F7DZ-HD
Leaded Fuel California	7-LDA-QAB	F7DF-VB	7-LDA-QAC	F7DZ-VC

FMA009700053000A

Fig. 54 PCM reprogramming. 1997 Sable & Taurus w/24-valve 3.0L engine

2. Disconnect Turbine Shaft Speed Sensor (TSS) electrical connector.
3. Remove TSS retaining bolt, then TSS from transaxle.
4. Reverse procedure to install.

DIFFERENTIAL OIL SEALS

Do not begin this procedure unless following parts are available: new front axle hub nut, lower ball joint to lower suspension arm nut and driveshaft bearing retainer circlip. Once removed these parts must not be reused. Their torque-holding ability or retention capability is diminished during removal.

1. Raise and support vehicle.
2. Remove front tire and wheel assemblies.
3. Remove halfshaft assemblies as described in "Transaxle, Replace."
4. Install front cover seal replacer tool No. T74P-6700-A, or equivalent, with 5½ inches forcing screw tool No. T88T-6701-A, or equivalents into lefthand differential seal, **Fig. 49.**
5. Turn forcing screw until outer metal seal protector part of differential seal is removed. Remove outer metal seal protector from tool and discard.
6. Install seal replacer tool and forcing screw into seal portion of differential seal, then tighten forcing screw until seal portion is removed and discard seal.
7. Install step plate adapter tool No. D80L-630-A, or equivalent, into righthand differential fluid seal opening, **Fig. 50.**
8. Turn front cover seal replacer tool No. T74P-6700-A and forcing screw T88T-6701-A, or equivalents, into metal protector portion of seal.
9. Tighten forcing screw on end of tool

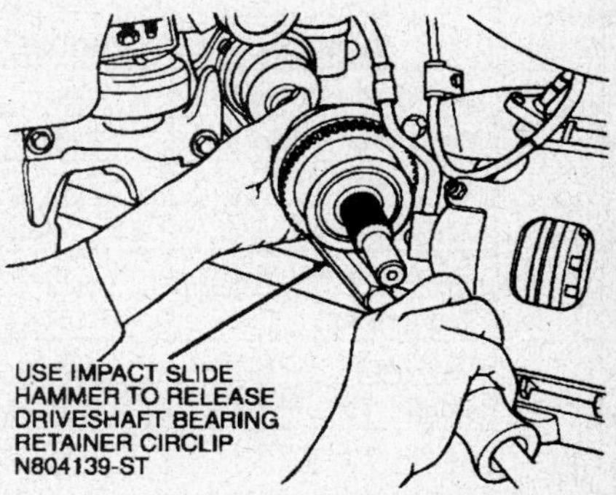

Fig. 53 Driveshaft bearing retainer clip removal

until metal portion of seal is removed.

10. Remove metal portion of seal from tool and discard.
11. Install seal removal tool into rubber portion of seal, then tighten tool until seal is removed from transaxle.
12. Reverse procedure to install, using output seal replacer tool No. T86P-1177-B , or equivalent, to install differential seals.

BRAKE-SHIFT INTERLOCK ACTUATOR/SOLENOID, REPLACE

1. Remove lower steering column shroud.
2. Remove steering column retaining nuts and lower steering column to floor.
3. Disconnect actuator/solenoid electrical connector.
4. Remove ignition/shifter interlock cable to steering column attaching screws.
5. Remove solenoid from solenoid retainer bracket.
6. Reverse procedure to install.

BRAKE-SHIFT INTERLOCK CABLE, REPLACE

Console Shift

1. Remove console finish panel retaining screw.
2. Move transaxle selector lever arm and support rearward.
3. Remove transaxle gear shift opening seal.
4. Remove console panel to console panel bracket attaching screws.
5. Disconnect console electrical connectors, then remove console panel.
6. Remove ignition/shifter interlock cable to shifter retaining screw, then interlock/shifter cable from shifter interlock cam.
7. Remove lower steering column shroud.
8. Remove steering column retaining nuts and lower steering column to floor.
9. Disconnect actuator/solenoid electrical connector.
10. Remove ignition/shifter interlock cable to steering column attaching screws.

MODEL YEAR	VEHICLE	ENGINE	ENGINEERING PART NUMBER	MODEL NUMBER	SERVICE PART NUMBER
1997	Continental – Column	4.6L	F7OP-7000-BA	PNB-GA	F7OZ-7000-BRM
	Continental – Floor	4.6L	F7OP-7000-AA	PNB-CA	F7OZ-7000-ARM
	Taurus SHO	3.4L	F7DP-7000-BA	PNB-EA	F7DZ-7000-BRM
	Taurus/Sable	3.0L Vulcan	F7DP-7000-CA	PNB-FA	F7DZ-7000-CRM
	Taurus/Sable – Column	3.0L Mod	F7DP-7000-DA	PNB-DA	F7DZ-7000-DRM
	Taurus/Sable – Floor	3.0L Mod	F7DP-7000-EA	PNB-HA	F7DZ-7000-ERM
1998	Continental – Column	4.6L	F8OP-7000-BA	PNB-GA	Not Available
	Continental – Floor	4.6L	F8OP-7000-AA	PNB-CA	Not Available
	Taurus SHO	3.4L	F8DP-7000-BA	PNB-EA	Not Available
	Taurus/Sable – Column	3.0L Mod	F8DP-7000-DA	PNB-DA	Not Available
	Taurus/Sable – Floor	3.0L Mod	F8DP-7000-EA	PNB-HA	Not Available
	Taurus/Sable – Column	3.0L Vulcan	F8DP-7000-CA	PNB-FA	Not Available
	Taurus/Sable – Floor	3.0L Vulcan	F8DP-7000-FA	PNB-KA	Not Available

FMA059800091000X

Fig. 55 AX4N application data. 1997–98 Continental, Sable & Taurus

RECALIBRATION CROSS REFERENCE			
Old Calibration	Old Part Number (-12A650-)	New Calibration	New Part Number (-12A650-)
7-14A-R10	F7DF-GD	7-14A-R10	F7PF-RA
7-14S-R10	F7DF-HD	7-14S-R10	F7PF-SA

FMA059800092000X

Fig. 56 PCM calibration. 1997 Sable & Taurus w/12-valve 3.0L engine

11. Remove solenoid from solenoid retainer bracket.
12. Pull ignition/shifter interlock cable out from under instrument panel and unhook it from retaining bracket.
13. Roll back carpet and slide cable out.
14. Reverse procedure to install, noting following:
    a. Tighten cable to steering column retaining screws to specifications.
    b. Tighten steering column retaining nuts to specifications.
    c. Check for proper interlock operation. Ignition key should be removable only with gearshift lever in Park. Gearshift lever should be locked in Park position with key removed.

TRANSAXLE

REPLACE

CONTINENTAL

1. Remove battery and battery tray.
2. **On 1997 models,** remove two accelerator control splash shield attaching screws.
3. **On all models,** open luggage compartment and ensure air suspension switch is turned off.
4. Disconnect intake air temperature sensor and mass air flow sensor electrical connectors from air cleaner assembly.
5. Disconnect air cleaner assembly hoses and tubes, then remove air cleaner assembly.
6. Disconnect transaxle harness and range sensor electrical connectors.
7. Remove shift actuator cable fitting, shift actuator cable nut and disconnect cable from shift cable bracket.
8. Install two engine lifting eyes tool No. D81L-6001-D, or equivalent, to front and rear of engine.
9. Install three-bar engine support bracket set tool No. D88L-6000-A, or equivalent, and support engine assembly.
10. Raise and support vehicle.
11. Place a drain pan under transaxle, then loosen lower pan retaining bolts and drain transaxle fluid.
12. Remove transaxle pan bolts.
13. After fluid has completely drained from transaxle, reinstall transaxle pan.
14. Remove front tire and wheel assemblies.
15. Depressurize air suspension system and disconnect height sensors.
16. Remove two cotter pins, two nuts and disconnect tie rod ends from steering knuckles.
17. Remove two nuts and disconnect stabilizer bar links from stabilizer bar.
18. Remove two nuts and separate lower control arm from steering knuckles.
19. Install puller tool No. T86P-3514-A1, or equivalent, between constant velocity joint and transaxle case. Turn steering hub and/or wire strut assembly out of way.
20. Screw extension tool No. T86P-3514-A2, or equivalent, into constant velocity joint puller and hand tighten. Screw impact slide hammer tool No. D79P-100-A, or equivalent, onto extension.
21. Remove constant velocity joint from transaxle.
22. Support end of halfshaft by suspending it from a conventional underbody component with a length or wire. **Do not allow shaft to hang unsupported, damage to outboard constant velocity joint may result.**
23. Separate outboard constant velocity joint from hub using front hub remover tools No. T81P-1104-C, T83P-1104-BH, T86P-1104-A1 and T81P-1104-A, or equivalents. **Never use a hammer to separate outboard constant velocity joint stub shaft from hub. Damage to constant velocity joint threads and internal components may result.**
24. Remove halfshaft assemblies from vehicle.
25. Disconnect three oxygen sensor electrical connectors.
26. Remove three bolts, nine nuts and Y-pipe assembly from vehicle.
27. Remove splash shield from front subframe and radiator support.
28. Support power steering gear with wire, to secure power steering housing in position.
29. Remove ball joint nut from under steering knuckle, then separate lower arm from steering knuckle.
30. Remove two nuts that attach power steering gear to front subframe.
31. Remove power steering return hose to front subframe retaining screws, then position hose of way.
32. Disconnect ride height sensor links at front suspension lower arms.
33. Remove lefthand and righthand front engine support insulator retaining nuts.
34. Remove engine and transaxle support insulator to front subframe attaching bolts.
35. Support front subframe with adjustable jacks.
36. Remove left and righthand front subframe body insulator braces.
37. Remove front subframe to body attaching bolts.
38. With help from an assistant lower subframe from vehicle.
39. Remove starter motor retaining nuts, then disconnect starter motor electrical connector.
40. Remove starter motor bolt and stud, then starter motor.
41. Position suitable transmission jack under transaxle.
42. Remove lower engine to transaxle bolts.
43. Remove two bolts and one nut on righthand side engine mount to transaxle case.
44. Slowly lower transaxle from vehicle, ensure no obstructions exist.
45. Reverse procedure to install. Tighten all fasteners to specifications.

SABLE & TAURUS

Removal

1. Remove battery and tray.
2. Remove air cleaner assembly.
3. Disconnect transaxle harness electrical connector and range sensor connector.
4. Remove shift actuator cable fitting and disconnect transaxle shift cable from shift cable bracket and transaxle.
5. Disconnect fluid cooler lines from transaxle.
6. **On models with 3.0L 12-valve engine,** remove one upper transaxle to engine stud.

7. **On models with 3.0L 24-valve and 3.4L engines,** remove five upper transaxle to engine bolts.
8. **On all models,** remove righthand cowl assembly, then install two Rotunda engine lift bracket set tool No. 014-00796, or equivalents, to front and rear locations on engine.
9. Install three-bar engine support tool No. D88L-6000-A, or equivalent, and suitably support engine assembly.
10. Raise and support vehicle on hoist.
11. Place drain pan under transaxle, then loosen transaxle pan retaining bolt and drain transaxle.
12. When fluid level is has drained to level of transaxle pan flange, remove remaining transaxle pan bolts.
13. When transaxle fluid has completely drained, reinstall transaxle pan.
14. Remove front tire and wheel assemblies.
15. Loosen lug nuts, then remove front axle wheel hub retainer.
16. Remove stabilizer bar link top retaining nut with box end wrench while holding stud with socket.
17. Remove stabilizer bar link from front strut and position out of way.
18. Install front hub remover/replacer and two stud adapter tool Nos. T81P-1104-C and T86P-1104-A1, or equivalents.
19. Install metric hub remover adapters and front hub replacer tool Nos. T83P-1104-BH and T81P-1104-A, or equivalents.
20. Push front wheel driveshaft joint only to point that splines are free in hub. Remove puller tool.
21. Remove and discard lower ball joint nut. Using pitman arm puller tool No. T64P-3590-F, or equivalent, separate lower ball joint from front suspension lower arm.
22. Insert pry bar through opening in front suspension lower arm. With end of pry bar on frame rail, push down on front suspension lower arm until ball joint stud is free from front suspension lower arm. Pull hub and strut outward, remove CV joint stub shaft from hub and rest halfshaft on frame rail, **Fig. 51.**
23. Assemble CV joint puller, extension and impact slide hammer tool Nos. T86P-3514-A1, T86P-3514-A2 and D79P-100-A, or equivalents. Insert CV joint puller adapter behind inboard CV joint housing, **Fig. 52.**
24. Use impact slide hammer to release driveshaft bearing retainer clip, **Fig. 53.**
25. Remove halfshaft assembly and tools from vehicle.
26. Disconnect four oxygen sensor electrical connectors.
27. Remove Y-pipe assembly from vehicle.
28. Disconnect two starter motor electrical connectors.
29. Remove starter motor from transaxle.
30. **On models with 3.0L 12-valve engine,** remove housing cover from transaxle.
31. **On all models,** remove front subframe.
32. Position Rotunda high lift transmission jack tool No. 014-00210, or equivalent, under transaxle and support transaxle.
33. Remove lower engine to transaxle bolts.
34. Remove four flywheel to torque converter nuts.
35. Remove rear engine support from transaxle.
36. Remove bolt from righthand engine mount brace, then slowly lower transaxle from vehicle.

Installation

1. Place transaxle on Rotunda high lift transmission jack tool No. 014-00210, or equivalent, and position under vehicle.
2. Slowly raise transaxle and align with engine block.
3. Install one bolt into righthand engine mount brace. Tighten to specifications.
4. Install rear engine support to transaxle and secure with three bolts and two nuts. Tighten to specifications.
5. Install torque converter to flywheel nuts and tighten to specifications.
6. **On models with 3.0L 12-valve engine,** install one lower transaxle to engine bolt. Tighten to specifications.
7. **On models with 3.0L 24-valve and 3.4L engines,** install four lower transaxle to engine bolts. Tighten to specifications.
8. **On all models,** install front subframe.
9. Remove jack from under transaxle.
10. **On models with 3.0L 12-valve engine,** install transaxle housing cover and secure with one bolt. Tighten to specifications.
11. **On all models,** install starter motor to transaxle. Tighten bolts to specifications.
12. Connect starter motor electrical connectors.
13. Install Y-pipe assembly into vehicle. Tighten to specifications.
14. Connect four oxygen sensor electrical connectors.
15. Install both halfshafts into vehicle.
16. Install front tire and wheel assemblies.
17. Lower vehicle.
18. Remove three-bar engine support from vehicle.
19. Remove engine lift bracket set from engine.
20. Install upper transaxle to engine bolts.
21. Connect fluid cooler lines from transaxle.
22. Install transaxle shift cable into shift cable bracket. Connect shift cable end to TR sensor manual lever. Secure with shift actuator cable fitting and one nut. Tighten to specifications.
23. Connect transaxle harness electrical connector and TR sensor connector.
24. Install air cleaner, battery and battery tray.

TECHNICAL SERVICE BULLETINS

HESITATION/STUMBLE OR DELAYED 4-2 DOWNSHIFT

1997 Sable & Taurus

On these models equipped with 24-valve 3.0L engine there may be acceleration hesitation or hesitation/stumble and delayed 4-2 downshifts.

This condition may be caused by Powertrain Control Module (PCM) calibration. To correct this condition, reprogram PCM according to **Fig. 54.**

HARSH SHIFTS & ENGAGEMENTS AFTER TRANSAXLE EXCHANGE

1997-98 Continental, Sable & Taurus

On these models, there may be harsh shifts and engagements after transaxle has been replaced. Diagnostic Trouble Codes (DTCs) 628, P07401 and/or P01744 may be stored.

This condition may be caused by incorrect transaxle being installed. To correct this condition, replace transaxle with correct unit, **Fig. 55.**

INTERMITTENT HARSH 1-2 SHIFT

1997 Sable & Taurus

On these models equipped with 12-valve 3.0L engine, there may be intermittent harsh 1-2 shift.

This condition may be caused by Powertrain Control Model (PCM) calibration. To correct this condition, reprogram calibration according to **Fig. 56.**

TRANSAXLE OIL COOLER LEAK

1997 Continental

On these models, transaxle oil cooler hoses may leak at cooler.

This condition may be caused by leaking hose attachment. To correct this condition, proceed as follows:

1. Clean fluid from tanks and lines.
2. Ensure clamp tightness.
3. Verify leak.
4. Replace radiator only if leak is at cooler-to-radiator end tank seal.

NO 4TH GEAR

1997-98 Continental, Sable & Taurus

On these models, there may be no 4th gear (3-4 upshift).

This condition may be caused by broken forward clutch control valve and spring retaining clip. To correct this condition, remove valve body and install revised retaining clip (part No. F8DZ-7F194-AA).

TIGHTENING SPECIFICATIONS

Year	Component	Torque/ Ft. Lbs.
1997–2000	Battery To Starter Terminal Nut④	8–10
	Case To Stator Support Bolts	84–108①
	Chain Cover To Case	②
	Control Arm To Steering Knuckle Nuts④	50–68
	Dust Cover To Case	84–108①
	Engine Mount Bolts	60–85
	Engine Mount To Support	55–75
	Filler Tube To Case	84–108①
	Ground Strap Nut④	13–17
	Hose Screws	20–30①
	Ignition Switch To Starter Terminal Nut④	40–56①
	Manual Cable Bracket Bolt	10–20
	Manual Lever To Manual Shaft	9–11
	Power Steering Line Bracket	40–50①
	Pressure Switch To Pump Body	84–108①
	Pressure Tap Plug For Chain Cover & Pump Body	60–72①
	Pump Body To Chain Cover	84–108①
	Righthand Engine Mount To Transaxle Case④	84–108①
	Rear Engine Support To Transaxle Bolts④	44–60
	Shaft Cable Stud	20–26
	Shift Cable To Manual Lever Nut	14–19
	Stabilizer U-Clamp To Bracket Bolt	23–29
	Steering Gear Bolts④	85–100
	Sub-Frame Bolt	55–75
	Tie Rod To Knuckle Bolt③	23–35
	Tie Rod To Knuckle Nut④	35–46
	Torque Converter To Flywheel Bolt	20–34
	Transaxle Cooler Line Fitting At Radiator	8–12
	Transaxle Cooler Line Fitting At Transaxle	13–17
	Transaxle Cooler Line Nut	13–18
	Transaxle Housing Cover Bolts	84–108①
	Transaxle Pan Bolts	84–108①
	Transaxle To Engine Bolt③	41–50
	TSS Sensor Bolt	84–120①
	Upper Transaxle To Engine Bolts④	25–34
	Valve Body To Chain Cover Bolts	84–108①
	Valve Body To Pump Bolts	84–108①
	Vehicle Speed Sensor Bolt	31–39①
	Wheel Hub Bolt Nuts	85–105
	Y-Pipe Assembly Nuts & Bolts	26–34

① — Inch lbs.

② — On Sable & Taurus, torque 10mm bolts to 17–21 ft. lbs. and 13mm bolts to 20–26 ft. lbs.; on Continental, torque Torx bolts to 96–108 inch. lbs., 10mm bolts to 18–23 ft. lbs. and 13mm bolts to 20–26 ft. lbs.

③ — Sable & Taurus.

④ — Continental.

AX4S (AXOD-E) Automatic Overdrive Transaxle

NOTE: On Air Bag Equipped Models, Refer To " Air Bag System Precautions" Located In The Front Of This Manual For System Disarming & Arming Procedures.

NOTE: "Electrical Symbol & Wire Color Code Identification" Located In The Front Of This Manual May Be Used As An Aid When Using Wiring Circuits Found In This Section.

NOTE: Prior To Performing Any Service Operations Listed In This Section, Consult "Technical Service Bulletins " Section For Related Information.

INDEX

PRECAUTIONS

AIR BAG SYSTEMS

Refer to "Air Bag System Precautions" in front of this manual for system disarming and arming procedures.

BATTERY GROUND CABLE

Prior to service, disconnect battery ground cable and isolate as required.

IDENTIFICATION

Identification tags, **Fig. 1,** located on top of converter housing, includes transaxle assembly number, serial number and build date.

DESCRIPTION

This automatic overdrive transaxle, **Fig. 2,** is a fully automatic transaxle with four forward speeds and one reverse, in addition to neutral and park.

AX4S (AXOD-E) transaxle has two planetary gear sets and a combination planetary/differential gear set. Four multiple plate clutches, two band assemblies and two one-way clutches.

A lockup torque converter is coupled to engine crankshaft and transmits engine power to gear train by means of a drive link assembly (chain) that connects drive and driven sprockets. Converter clutch application is controlled through an electronic control integrated in on-board EEC-IV system, **Fig. 3.** These controls, along with hydraulic controls in valve body, operate a piston plate clutch in torque converter to provide improved fuel economy by eliminating converter slip when applied.

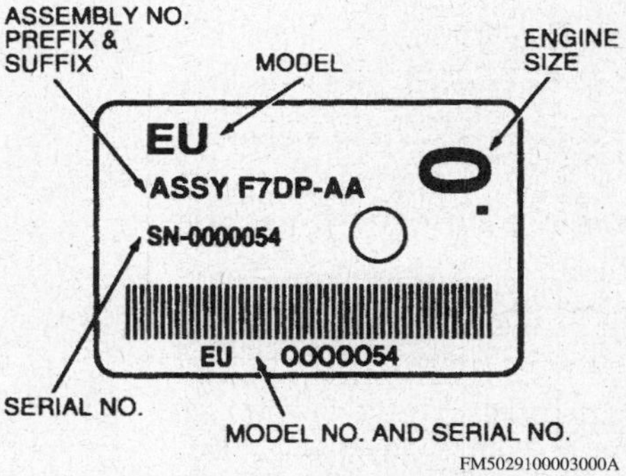

Fig. 1 Identification tag

TORQUE CONVERTER

Converter

Torque converter couples engine to turbine shaft. It also provides torque multiplication and absorbs engine shock of gear shifting.

Piston Plate Clutch & Damper Assembly

Piston plate clutch and damper assembly transmit engine power to turbine from converter cover during lockup.

Converter Cover

Converter cover transmits power from engine into converter. Also, oil pump driveshaft is splined to converter cover.

Turbine

Turbine is splined to drive sprocket turbine shaft and driven by fluid by impeller.

Impeller

Impeller is driven by converter cover, together with reactor it supplies torque multiplication.

Reactor

Reactor, also called stator, contains a one-way clutch to hold it stationary only when "reaction" is required. It also causes hydraulic reaction during torque multiplication.

GEAR TRAIN

Forward Clutch

Forward clutch locks driven sprocket to low one-way clutch.

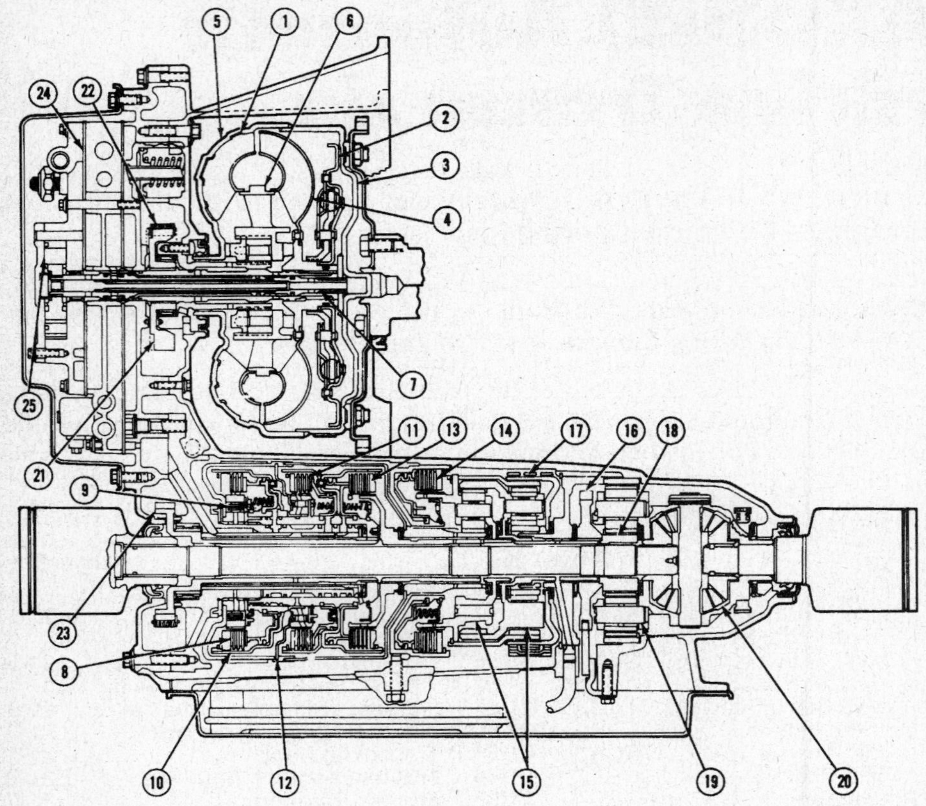

1. TORQUE CONVERTER
2. CONVERTER CLUTCH (PISTON PLATE CLUTCH AND DAMPER ASSEMBLY)
3. CONVERTER COVER
4. TURBINE
5. IMPELLER
6. REACTOR
7. OIL PUMP DRIVESHAFT
8. FORWARD CLUTCH
9. LOW ONE-WAY CLUTCH
10. OVERDRIVE BAND
11. DIRECT CLUTCH
12. DIRECT ONE-WAY CLUTCH
13. INTERMEDIATE CLUTCH
14. REVERSE CLUTCH
15. PLANETARY GEARS
16. PARKING GEAR
17. LOW-INTERMEDIATE BAND
18. FINAL DRIVE SUN GEAR
19. FINAL DRIVE PLANET
20. DIFFERENTIAL ASSEMBLY
21. DRIVE SPROCKET
22. DRIVE LINK ASSEMBLY (CHAIN)
23. DRIVEN SPROCKET
24. VALVE BODY (MAIN CONTROL ASSEMBLY)
25. OIL PUMP

FM5028800007000X

Fig. 2 Cross-sectional view of automatic transaxle

Gear	Low-Int Band	Overdrive Band	Forward Clutch	Intermediate Clutch	Direct Clutch	Reverse Clutch	Low One-Way Clutch	Direct One-Way Clutch
1st Gear Manual Low	Applied		Applied		Applied		Holding	
1st Gear (Drive)	Applied		Applied				Holding	
2nd Gear (Drive)	Applied		Applied	Applied			Overrunning	
3rd Gear (Drive)			Applied	Applied	Applied			Holding
4th Gear (Overdrive)		Applied		Applied	Applied			Overrunning
Reverse (R)			Applied			Applied	Holding	
Neutral (N)			Applied					
Park (P)			Applied					

FM5029501137000X

Fig. 3 Clutch & band application chart

Low One-Way Clutch

Low one-way clutch transmits torque from driven sprocket to sun gear of forward planetary gear set in first gear. It also provides engine braking in third gear in connection with forward clutch.

Overdrive Band

Overdrive band holds sun gear of forward planetary gear set stationary in fourth gear (overdrive).

Direct Clutch

Direct clutch locks sun gear of planetary assembly of forward planetary gear set to direct one-way clutch in third gear.

Direct One-Way Clutch

Direct one-way clutch transmits torque from driven sprocket to sun gear of forward planetary gear set in third gear, and provides engine braking in manual low.

Intermediate Clutch

Intermediate clutch locks driven sprocket to planetary assembly of forward planetary gear set in second and third gear.

Reverse Clutch

Reverse clutch holds planetary assembly of forward planetary gear set, and ring gear of rear planetary gear set stationary in reverse gear.

Planetary Gears

Two planetary gear sets are used to provide four forward speeds, including reverse, depending upon clutch and/or band applications.

Parking Gear

Parking gear allows output (axle) shaft to be mechanically locked by parking pawl anchored in case.

Low Intermediate Band

Low intermediate band holds sun gear of rear planetary gear set stationary in low, first and second gears.

Final Drive Sun Gear

Final drive sun gear transfers torque from transaxle output to final drive planetary assembly.

Final Drive Planet

Final drive planet drives differential assembly.

Differential Assembly

Differential assembly drives front axle shafts and provides differential action if driving wheels are turning at different speeds.

TORQUE CONVERTER & GEAR TRAIN

Drive Sprocket

Drive sprocket transmits power from converter to drive link assembly (chain).

Drive Link Assembly (Chain)

Drive link assembly transmits converter power to gear train.

Driven Sprocket

Driven sprocket transmits converter power to geartrain.

HYDRAULIC SYSTEM

Valve Body

Valve body or main control assembly directs fluid (oil) under pressure to torque converter, band servos, clutches and governor to control transaxle operation.

Oil Pump

Oil pump provides a supply of fluid (oil) under pressure to operate, lubricate and cool transaxle. Pump is a variable capacity vane and rotor pump with output flow proportional to demand. It is located within transaxle control valve and pump assembly.

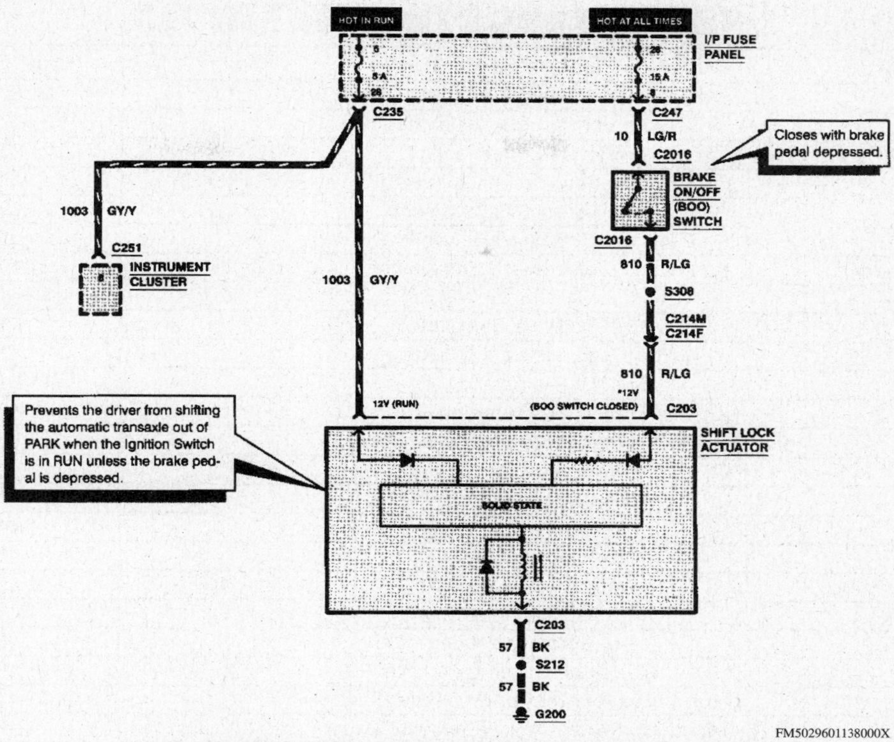

Fig. 4 Brake-shift interlock system wiring circuit

Overdrive Servo

Overdrive servo applies overdrive band in fourth gear.

Low-Intermediate Servo

Low-intermediate servo applies low-intermediate band in manual, low, first and second gears.

Governor

Governor provides a "road speed" signal to hydraulic control system for shift control, and is driven by a gear on differential assembly.

Reservoir

Two reservoir areas are used to control oil level, dependent on fluid temperature. Along with lower sump, a fluid reservoir is located in lower section of valve body cover. As fluid temperature in reservoir increases, a thermostatic element closes, retaining fluid in upper reservoir.

ELECTRICAL COMPONENT FUNCTION

Turbine Speed Sensor

Turbine speed sensor is a variable reluctance sensor used with vehicle electronic control system. Sensor, along with a rotating exciter wheel on driven sprocket, sends a signal to EEC microprocessor. EEC reads this signal and reacts to speed information it transmits by controlling clutch application.

Shift Control Solenoid

Shift control solenoids provide proper operating gear selection and are controlled by EEC. There are three shift control solenoids in this transaxle. They are three port, normally open feed to control flow of oil to a hydraulic spool valve.

Transaxle Oil Temperature Sensor

Transaxle oil temperature sensor informs EEC of transaxle oil temperature. It is a thermostat whose resistance varies according to temperature.

Variable Force Solenoid

Variable force solenoid is an analog pressure regulator that varies transaxle line pressure as directed by microprocessor.

Modulated Lock-Up Solenoid Or Modulated Converter Clutch Control

Solenoid receives an electronic signal from EEC microprocessor and uses this information to vary pressure which sets slip in converter clutch.

DOWNSHIFTS

Under certain conditions transaxle will downshift automatically to a lower gear range without moving shift selector lever. There are three different types of downshift categories:

Coastdown

Coastdown downshift occurs when vehicle is coasting down to a stop.

Torque Demand

Torque demand downshift occurs during part throttle acceleration when demand for torque is greater than engine can provide at that gear ratio. Transaxle will disengage converter clutch to provide added acceleration, if applied.

Kickdown

Kickdown downshift occurs when accelerator pedal is depressed fully to floor. A forced downshift into second gear is possible below 55 mph. Below approximately 25 mph a forced kickdown to first gear will occur. All shift speed specifications will vary due to tire size and engine calibration requirements.

TROUBLESHOOTING

BRAKE-SHIFT INTERLOCK SYSTEM

Refer to wiring diagrams **Fig. 4** and troubleshooting charts **Fig. 5.**

TRANSAXLE

Refer to **Figs. 6 through 36** for troubleshooting.

TROUBLESHOOTING TEST INDEX

	Test Step	Result	Action to Take
A1	CHECK ELECTRON IGN FUSE		
	• Check Fuse 5 (5A) located in fuse junction panel. • **Is fuse OK?**	Yes No	▶ GO to **A3**. ▶ GO to **A2**.
A2	CHECK FOR SHORT TO GROUND		
	• Turn ignition switch OFF. • Remove Fuse 5 (5A). • Disconnect shift-lock actuator connector C203 located to the right of steering column. • Measure resistance of the Circuit 1003 (GY/Y) between the correct terminal of Fuse 5 (5A) and ground. • **Is resistance greater than 10,000 ohms?**	Yes No	▶ REPLACE Fuse 5 (5A). GO to **A3**. ▶ SERVICE Circuit 1003 (GY/Y) wire between fuse junction panel and shift-lock actuator.
A3	CHECK POWER SUPPLY FROM FUSE 5 (5A)		
	• Reinstall Fuse 5 (5A). • Turn ignition switch to RUN. • Measure voltage on Circuit 1003 (GY/Y) wire and ground. • **Is voltage greater than 10 volts?**	Yes No	▶ GO to **A4**. ▶ SERVICE Circuit 1003 (GY/Y) wire between interior fuse panel and shift-lock actuator.
A4	CHECK POWER SUPPLY FROM FUSE 28 (15A)		
	• Turn ignition switch OFF. • Disconnect connector C2016. • Turn ignition switch ON. • Measure voltage on Circuit 10 (LG/R) and ground. • **Is voltage B+?**	Yes No	▶ GO to **A5**. ▶ SERVICE Circuit 10 (LG/R) for open. RESTORE vehicle and TEST system for normal operation.
A5	CHECK WIRE BETWEEN STOPLIGHT SWITCH AND SHIFT-LOCK ACTUATOR		
	• Turn ignition switch OFF. • Disconnect shift-lock actuator connector C203. • Apply brake pedal. • Measure voltage on Circuit 810 (R/LG) wire and ground. • **Is voltage greater than 10 volts with brake pedal applied and less than 1 volt with brake pedal released?**	Yes No	▶ GO to **A6**. ▶ SERVICE Circuit 810 (R/LG) wire between stoplight switch and shift-lock actuator.
A6	CHECK SHIFT-LOCK ACTUATOR GROUND		
	• Measure resistance of Circuit 57 (BK) and ground. • **Is resistance less than 5 ohms?**	Yes No	▶ REPLACE shift-lock actuator. ▶ SERVICE BK wire.

FM5029601139000X

Fig. 5 Brake-shift interlock system troubleshooting chart

Possible Component	Reference/Action
201 — ELECTRICAL ROUTINE	
Powertrain Control System	
• Electrical Inputs/Outputs, Vehicle Wiring Harnesses, powertrain control module.	• Run On-Board Diagnostics. Refer to MOTOR's Domestic Transmission Manual for diagnosis. Using the Rotunda Transmission Tester 007-00130 with AX4S Cable and Overlay 007-00087 or equivalent, perform transmission voltage tests. If DTC P1700 is present, check for a low transaxle fluid level. Then, continue to Hydraulic/Mechanical Routines.
301 — HYDRAULIC/MECHANICAL ROUTINE	
Fluid	
• Improper level, low	• Adjust fluid to proper level.
Driveshafts	
• Worn, damaged, misassembled	• Inspect for damage. Service as required.
Shift Linkage	
• Damaged, out of adjustment	• Inspect and service as required. Verify linkage adjustment After servicing linkage, verify Transmission Range sensor is properly adjusted.

FM5029801571010X

Fig. 6 Routines 201 & 301: No Forward Engagement (Part 1 of 2)

Possible Component	Reference/Action
Improper Pressures	
• Low Forward Clutch pressure, Low Line pressure, Low Intermediate Clutch pressure, Low EPC pressure	• Check pressure at line and EPC taps. Perform line pressures and stall speed tests. If pressures are low, check the following possible components: — fluid filter and fluid screen ring, — main control valve body, — pump assembly, — reverse clutch assembly, — low intermediate band servo, and — intermediate clutch assembly.
Fluid Filter and Fluid Filter Seal	
• Plugged, damaged	• Replace fluid filter and fluid filter seal.
• Fluid Filter Seal damaged	
Main Control Valve Body	
• Forward Clutch Pressure Tap Plug—damaged, loose or missing	• Inspect. Service as required.
• Bolts out of torque specifications	• Tighten bolts to specifications.
• Gaskets—damaged, off location	• Inspect gasket for damage. Replace as required.
• Pump assembly shaft—broken	• Service/replace as required.
• 3-4 Shift Valve, Main Regulator Valve, Forward Clutch Control Valve, Manual Control Valve, 2-3 Servo Regulator Valve—stuck, damaged	• Inspect. Service as required.
Pump Assembly	
• Bolts out of torque specification	• Tighten bolts to specification.
• Gaskets damaged, off location	• Inspect for damage. Replace as required.
• Porosity/cross leaks and ball missing or leaking	• Inspect for porosity and leaks. Replace as required.
• Components damaged	• Inspect for damage. Replace as required.
Support Assembly—Driven Sprocket	
• Bolts out of torque specifications	• Tighten bolts to specifications. Use sealant on two external chain cover bolts.
• Seals—missing, damaged	• Inspect seals. Replace as required.
• Seal grooves damaged	• Inspect for damage. Service as required.
Forward Clutch Assembly	
	• Perform Air Pressure Tests
• Seals, Piston	• Inspect seals for damage and replace as required.
• Check balls	• Inspect for mislocation, poor seating damage. Replace cylinder as required.
• Piston cracked	• Inspect piston. Replace as required.
• Friction Elements—damaged or worn	• Check for abnormal wear, damage. Replace as required.
Low One-Way Clutch Assembly	
• Worn, damaged or misassembled	• Inspect for damage. Service as required.
Low Intermediate Servo Assembly	
•	• Perform Air Pressure Tests
• Seals, Piston	• Inspect. Replace as required.
• Fluid Transfer Tubes, Band, Anchor Pins—worn, damaged, loose, leaking	• Inspect. Service as required.
• Apply Rod—incorrect length	• Replace as required.
Output Shaft	
• Splines damaged	• Inspect for damage. Service as required.

FM5029801571020X

Fig. 6 Routines 201 & 301: No Forward Engagement (Part 2 of 2)

Possible Component	Reference/Action
202 — ELECTRICAL ROUTINE	
Powertrain Control System	
• Electrical Inputs/Outputs, Vehicle Wiring Harnesses, powertrain control module.	• Run On-Board Diagnostics. Refer to MOTOR's Domestic Transmission Manual for diagnosis. Using the Rotunda Transmission Tester 007-00130 with AX4S cable and overlay 007-00087 or equivalent, perform transmission voltage tests. If DTC P1700 is present, check for a low transaxle fluid level. Then, continue to Hydraulic/Mechanical Routines.
302 — HYDRAULIC/MECHANICAL ROUTINE	
Fluid	
• Improper level	• Adjust fluid to proper level.
Halfshafts	
• Worn, damaged, misassembled	• Inspect for damage. Service as required.
Shift Linkage	
• Damaged or out of adjustment	• Inspect and service as required. Verify linkage adjustment. After servicing linkage, verify that the Transmission Range sensor is properly adjusted.
Improper Pressures	
• Low Reverse Clutch pressure, Low Line pressure, Low Forward Clutch pressure, Low EPC pressure	• Check pressure at line and EPC taps. Perform Line Pressure and Stall Speed Tests. If pressures are low, check the following possible components: — fluid filter and fluid screen ring, — main control valve body, — pump assembly, — reverse clutch assembly.
Fluid Filter and Fluid Filter Seal	
• Plugged or damaged	• Replace fluid filter and fluid filter seal.
Main Control Valve Body	
• Forward Clutch Pressure Tap Plug—damaged, loose, missing	• Inspect. Service as required.
• Bolts out of torque specification.	• Tighten bolts to specification.
• Gasket—damaged, off location	• Inspect for damage. Replace as required.
• Pump Assembly Shaft—broken	• Inspect. Service/replace as required.
• Forward Clutch Control Valve, Manual Control Valve, Main Regulator Valve, Springs—stuck, damaged	• Inspect for damage. Service as required.
Pump Assembly	
• Bolts out of torque specification.	• Tighten bolts to specification.
• Gasket damaged, off location	• Inspect for damage and replace as required.
• Porosity/cross leaks/ball missing or leaking, plugged hole	• Replace pump assembly.
• Components damaged	• Inspect for damage and replace as required.
Support Assembly—Driven Sprocket	
• Bolts out of torque specification	• Tighten bolts to specification. Use sealant on two external chain cover bolts.
• Seals missing or damaged	• Inspect seals. Replace as required.
• Seal grooves damaged	• Inspect for damage. Service as required.
Forward Clutch Assembly	• Perform Air Pressure Tests
• Seals, Piston	• Inspect seals for damage. Replace as required.
• Check Balls	• Inspect for mislocation, poor seating, and damage. Replace cylinder as required.
• Piston—cracked	• Inspect piston. Replace as required.
• Friction Elements—worn, damaged	• Check for abnormal wear, damage. Replace as required.

FM5029801572010X

Fig. 7 Routines 202 & 302: No Reverse Engagement (Part 1 of 2)

Possible Component	Reference/Action
Low-One-Way Clutch Assembly	
• Worn, damaged, misassembled or Code P1784 present	• Inspect for damage. Service as required.
Reverse Clutch Assembly	• Perform Air Pressure Tests
• Seals, Piston	• Inspect for damage. Service as required.
• Check Ball	
• Friction Elements damaged or worn	
• Reverse Clutch Apply Fluid Transfer Tube leaking or improperly installed	• Inspect. Service as required.
Output Shaft	
• Splines damaged	• Inspect for damage. Service as required.

FM5029801572020X

Fig. 7 Routines 202 & 302: No Reverse Engagement (Part 2 of 2)

Possible Component	Reference/Action
203 — ELECTRICAL ROUTINE	
Powertrain Control System	
• Electrical Inputs/Outputs, Vehicle Wiring Harnesses, Powertrain Control Module, EPC Solenoid, TFT, TSS, TR, PSP, TPS, MAF, VSS, IAT, ISC	• Run On-Board Diagnostic. Refer to MOTOR's Domestic Transmission Manual for diagnosis. Perform Pinpoint Tests A, B, D and F using the Rotunda Transmission Tester 007-00130 with AX4S cable and overlay 007-00087 and Transmission Range (TR) Sensor Cable (MLP-B Cable) (007-00127) or equivalents as described. Service as required. Clear codes. Road Test and rerun On-Board Diagnostic.
303 — HYDRAULIC/MECHANICAL ROUTINE	
Fluid	
• Improper level	• Adjust fluid to proper level.
• Condition	• Inspect Fluid Level and Condition.
Shift Linkage	
• Damaged or out of adjustment	• Inspect and service as required. Verify linkage adjustment. After servicing linkage, verify that the Transmission Range sensor is properly adjusted.
Improper Pressures	
• High Line pressure, High EPC pressure	• Check pressure at line and EPC pressure taps. Perform Line Pressure and Stall Speed Tests. If high, check the following possible components: Main Control Valve Body, Fluid Filter and Fluid Screen Ring.
Fluid Filter and Fluid Filter Seal	
• Plugged or damaged	• Replace fluid filter and fluid filter seal.
• Fluid Filter Seal damaged	
Main Control Valve Body	
• Bolts out of torque specification	• Tighten bolts to specification.
• Gasket—damaged, off location	• Inspect for damage. Replace as required.
• B1 Check Ball, Pressure Failsafe Valve, Manual Control Valve, Main Regulator Valve—stuck, damaged	• Inspect for damage. Service as required.
Pump Assembly	
• Bolts out of torque specification	• Tighten bolts to specification.
• Gasket damaged, off location	• Inspect for damage and replace as required.
• Porosity/cross leaks	• Replace pump assembly.
• Components damaged	• Inspect for damage and replace as required.

FM5029801573010X

Fig. 8 Routines 203 & 303: Harsh Reverse Engagement (Part 1 of 2)

Possible Component	Reference/Action
Reverse Clutch Assembly	• Perform Air Pressure Tests
• Seals, Piston	• Inspect for damage. Service as required.
• Friction Elements damaged, worn	
• Return Spring Piston damaged, worn	
• Reverse Clutch Apply Fluid Transfer Tube leaking or improperly installed	

FM5029801573020X

Fig. 8 Routines 203 & 303: Harsh Reverse Engagement (Part 2 of 2)

Possible Component	Reference/Action
204 — ELECTRICAL ROUTINE	
Powertrain Control System	
• Electrical Inputs/Outputs, Vehicle Wiring Harnesses, Powertrain Control Module, EPC Solenoid, TFT, TSS, TR, PSP, TPS, MAF, IAT, ISC	• Run On-Board Diagnostic. Refer to MOTOR's Domestic Transmission Manual for diagnosis. Perform Pinpoint Tests A, B, D and F using the Rotunda Transmission Tester 007-00130 with AX4S cable and overlay 007-00087 and Transmission Range (TR) Sensor Cable (MLP-B Cable) 007-00127 or equivalents. Service as required. Clear codes. Road Test and rerun On-Board Diagnostic.
304 — HYDRAULIC/MECHANICAL ROUTINE	
Fluid	
• Improper level	• Adjust fluid to proper level.
• Condition	• Inspect Fluid Level and Condition.
Shift Linkage	
• Damaged, out of adjustment	• Inspect. Service as required. Verify linkage adjustment. After servicing linkage, verify that the Transmission Range sensor is properly adjusted.
Improper Pressures	
• High Forward Clutch pressure, High Line pressure, High EPC pressure	• Check pressure at line, EPC and forward clutch pressure taps. Perform Line Pressure and Stall Speed Tests. If pressures are high, check the following possible components: Main Control Valve Body, Pump Assembly.
Main Controls	
• Bolts out of torque specification	• Tighten bolts to specification.
• Gaskets—damaged, off location	• Inspect for damage. Replace as required.
• Main Regulator Valve, Backout Valve, Pressure Failsafe Valve	• Inspect. Service as required.
• EPC Solenoid—stuck, damaged	• Inspect for damage and contamination. Service as required.
• 2-3 Servo Regulator Valve, Engagement Valve, B3 or B2 Check Ball—missing, damaged	• Inspect for damage and contamination. Service as required.
Pump Assembly	
• Bolts out of specification	• Tighten bolts to specification.
• Porosity/cross leaks	• Inspect for porosity/leaks. Replace pump assembly.
• Gaskets damaged, off location	• Inspect for damage and replace as required.
Low and Intermediate Servo	
	• Perform Air Pressure Tests as described.
• Seals, Piston	• Inspect for damage. Replace as required.
• Fluid Tubes—damaged, loose, leaking, misassembled	• Inspect for damage. Replace as required.
• Band, Anchor Pins	• Inspect for damage. Replace as required.
• Apply Rod—incorrect length	• Replace as required.

FM5029801574010X

Fig. 9 Routines 204 & 304: Harsh Forward Engagement (Part 1 of 2)

Possible Component	Reference/Action
Neutral to Drive Accumulator	
• Piston stuck, seals or springs—damaged, missing	• Check for damage. Replace as required.
Forward Clutch Assembly	
	• Perform Air Pressure Tests
• Check Ball	• Inspect for mislocation, poor seating, damage. Replace front clutch cylinder.
• Friction Element damaged or worn	• Check for wear or damage, replace as required.
• Spring, Rear Clutch Pressure damaged	• Check for damage, replace as required.
• Forward Clutch Return Spring damaged	• Check for damage, replace as required.
Low and Intermediate Band/Rear Sun Gear and Drum	
• Friction Elements—damaged, worn	• Check for damage. Replace as required.
• Drum damaged	

FM5029801574020X

Fig. 9 Routines 204 & 304: Harsh Forward Engagement (Part 2 of 2)

Possible Component	Reference/Action
205 — ELECTRICAL ROUTINE	
Powertrain Control System	
• Electrical Inputs/Outputs, Vehicle Wiring Harnesses, Powertrain Control Module, EPC Solenoid, TFT Sensor	• Run On-Board Diagnostic. Refer to MOTOR's Domestic Transmission Manual for diagnosis. Perform Pinpoint Tests B and E using the Rotunda Transmission Tester 007-00130 with AX4S cable and overlay 007-00087 or equivalent. Service as required. Clear codes. Road Test and rerun On-Board Diagnostic.
305 — HYDRAULIC/MECHANICAL ROUTINE	
Fluid	
• Improper level	• Adjust fluid to proper level.
• Condition	• Inspect as described under Fluid Check
Shift Linkage	
• Damaged, out of adjustment	• Inspect and service as required. Verify linkage adjustment. After servicing linkage, verify that the Transmission Range sensor is properly adjusted.
Improper Pressures	
• Low Reverse Clutch pressure, Low Line pressure, Low EPC pressure	• Check pressure at line and EPC taps. Perform Line Pressure and Stall Speed Tests. If pressures are low, check the following possible components: Main Control Valve Body, Pump Assembly, Reverse Clutch Assembly.
Fluid Filter and Fluid Filter Seal	
• Plugged or damaged	• Replace fluid filter and fluid filter seal.
• Fluid Filter Seal damaged	
Main Controls	
• Bolts out of torque specification	• Tighten bolts to specification.
• Gaskets—damaged, off location	• Inspect for damage. Replace as required.
• Seals, Manual Control Valve, Main Regulator Valve, B5 Check Ball, Converter Drain Back Valve, Springs—missing, damaged or misassembled	• Inspect for damage. Service as required.
• EPC Solenoid stuck, damaged	• Inspect for damage. Service as required.
• Failsafe Valve (Zero EPC Pressure Only) stuck, damaged	• Inspect for damage. Service as required.
Pump Assembly	
• Bolts out of torque specification	• Tighten bolts to specification.
• Porosity/cross leaks/ball missing or leaking	• Replace pump assembly.
• Gaskets damaged, off location	• Inspect for damage and replace as required.
• Components damaged	• Inspect for damage and replace as required.

FM5029801575010X

Fig. 10 Routines 205 & 305: Delayed/Soft Reverse Engagement (Part 1 of 2)

Possible Component	Reference/Action
Support Assembly—Driven Sprocket	
• Bolts out of torque specification	• Tighten bolts to specification. Use sealant on two external chain cover bolts.
• Seals missing or damaged	• Inspect seals. Replace as required.
• Seal grooves damaged	• Inspect for damage. Service as required.
Neutral to Drive Accumulator	
• Piston or seals damaged	• Inspect for damage. Service as required.
Forward Clutch Assembly	
	• Perform Air Pressure Tests
• Seals, Piston	• Inspect seals for damage. Service as required.
• Check Ball	• Inspect for mislocation, poor seating and damage. Replace cylinder as required.
• Piston cracked	• Inspect piston. Replace as required.
• Friction Elements—damaged, worn	• Check for abnormal wear, damage. Replace as required.
Reverse Clutch Assembly	
	• Perform Air Pressure Tests
• Seals, Piston	• Inspect for damage. Service as required.
• Check Ball	• Inspect for damage. Service as required.
• Friction Elements damaged or worn	• Inspect for damage. Service as required.
• Support and Spring and Piston damaged or worn	• Inspect for damage. Service as required.
• Reverse Clutch Apply Fluid Transfer Tube leaking or improperly installed	• Inspect. Service as required.

FM5029801575020X

Fig. 10 Routines 205 & 305: Delayed/Soft Reverse Engagement (Part 2 of 2)

Possible Component	Reference/Action
206 — ELECTRICAL ROUTINE	
Powertrain Control System	
• Electrical Inputs/Outputs, Vehicle Wiring Harnesses, Powertrain Control Module, EPC Solenoid, TFT Sensor	• Run On-Board Diagnostic. Refer to MOTOR's Domestic Transmission Manual for diagnosis. Perform Pinpoint Tests B and E using the Rotunda Transmission Tester 007-00130 with AX4S cable and overlay 007-00087 or equivalent as described. Service as required. Clear codes. Road Test and rerun On-Board Diagnostic.
306 — HYDRAULIC/MECHANICAL ROUTINE	
Fluid	
• Improper level	• Adjust fluid to proper level.
• Condition	• Inspect as described under Fluid Check.
Shift Linkage	
• Damaged, out of adjustment	• Inspect and service as required. Verify linkage adjustment. After servicing linkage, verify that the Transmission Range sensor is properly adjusted.
Improper Pressures	
• Low Forward Clutch pressure, Low Line pressure, Low EPC pressure	• Check pressure at line and EPC taps. Perform Line Pressure and Stall Speed Tests. If pressures are low, check the following possible components: Fluid Filter and Fluid Screen Ring, Main Control Valve Body and Pump Assembly.
Fluid Filter and Fluid Filter Seal	
• Plugged or damaged	• Replace fluid filter and fluid filter seal.
• Fluid Filter Seal damaged	

FM5029801576010X

Fig. 11 Routines 206 & 306: Delayed/Soft Forward Engagement (Part 1 of 2)

Possible Component	Reference/Action
Main Control Valve Body	
• Bolts out of torque specification	• Tighten bolts to specification.
• Gaskets—damaged, off location	• Inspect for damage. Replace.
• 3-4 Shift Valve, Backout Valve, Main Regulator Valve, Manual Control Valve, 2-3 Servo Regulator Valve, Engagement Valve, B5 Check Ball —stuck, damaged, missing	• Inspect. Service as required.
• EPC Solenoid—stuck, damaged	• Inspect for damage and contamination. Service as required.
• Pressure Failsafe Valve stuck or damaged	• Inspect for damage. Service as required.
Pump Assembly	
• Bolts out of torque specification	• Tighten bolts to specification.
• Porosity/cross leaks	• Inspect for porosity and leaks. Replace as required.
• Gaskets damaged, off location	• Inspect for damage and replace as required.
• Components damaged	• Inspect for damage and replace as required.
Low Intermediate Servo Assembly	
	• Perform Air Pressure Tests
• Seals, Piston	• Inspect seals and piston for damage. Replace as required.
• Fluid Transfer Tubes—damaged, loose, leaking	• Inspect for damage. Service as required.
• Band, Anchor Pins—damaged	• Inspect for damage. Service as required.
• Apply Rod—incorrect length	• Replace as required.
Neutral to Drive Accumulator	
• Seals, Bore—damaged, stuck	• Inspect for damage. Replace.
Support Assembly—Driven Sprocket	
• Bolts out of torque specification	• Tighten bolts to specification. Use sealant on two external chain cover bolts.
• Seals missing or damaged	• Inspect seals. Replace as required.
• Seal grooves damaged	• Inspect for damage. Service as required.
Forward Clutch Assembly	
	• Perform Air Pressure Tests
• Seals, Piston, front support	• Inspect seals for damage and replace as required.
• Check Balls	• Inspect for incorrect location, poor seating damage. Replace cylinder as required.
• Friction Elements—damaged or worn	• Check for abnormal wear or damage. Replace as required.
Low and Intermediate Band/Rear Sun Gear and Drum	
• Friction Elements—damaged, worn	• Inspect for damage. Service as required.
• Drum damaged	

FM5029801576020X

Fig. 11 Routines 206 & 306: Delayed/Soft Forward Engagement (Part 2 of 2)

Possible Component	Reference/Action
210 — ELECTRICAL ROUTINE	
Powertrain Control System	
• Electrical Inputs/Outputs, Vehicle Wiring Harnesses, Powertrain Control Module, Shift Solenoids, TR Sensor, TP, MAF, VSS	• Run On-Board Diagnostic. Refer to MOTOR's Domestic Transmission Manual for diagnosis. Perform Pinpoint Tests A and D using the Rotunda Transmission Tester 007-00130 with AX4S cable and overlay 007-00087 and Transmission Range (TR) Sensor Cable (MLP-B Cable) 007-00127 or equivalents. Service as required. Clear codes. Road Test and rerun On-Board Diagnostic. If DTC P1700 is present, check for a low transaxle fluid level. Then, continue.
310 — HYDRAULIC/MECHANICAL ROUTINE	
Fluid	
• Improper level	• Adjust fluid to proper level.
• Condition	• Inspect Fluid Condition and Condition.

FM5029801577010X

Fig. 12 Routines 210 & 310: Some Or All Shifts Missing (Part 1 of 2)

Possible Component	Reference/Action
Shift Linkage	
• Damaged, out of adjustment	• Inspect and service as required. Verify linkage adjustment. After servicing linkage, verify that the TR sensor is properly adjusted.
Vehicle Speed Input	
• Speedometer Gear—DRIVE—damaged	• Inspect gears.
• Speedometer Gear—DRIVEN—Gear and Shaft Assembly	
• Differential Assembly—damaged or missing	
• Speedometer DRIVE GEAR—damaged	
Go to Reference/Action to diagnose specific missing shifts	
• Shift Concern: 1-2 Shift (Automatic)	• Routine 220/320
• Shift Concern: 2-3 Shift (Automatic)	• Routine 221/321
• Shift Concern: 3-4 Shift (Automatic)	• Routine 222/322
• Shift Concern: 4-3 Shift (Automatic)	• Routine 223/323
• Shift Concern: 3-2 Shift (Automatic)	• Routine 224/324
• Shift Concern: 2-1 Shift (Automatic)	• Routine 225/325

FM5029801577020X

Fig. 12 Routines 210 & 310: Some Or All Shifts Missing (Part 2 of 2)

Possible Component	Reference/Action
211 — ELECTRICAL ROUTINE	
Powertrain Control System	
	• Perform Shift Point Road Test and Torque Converter Clutch Operation Test.
• Electrical Inputs/Outputs, Vehicle Wiring Harnesses, Powertrain Control Module, Shift Solenoids, TFT, TP, MAF, VSS, IAT, ECT	• Run On-Board Diagnostic. Refer to MOTOR's Domestic Transmission Manual for diagnosis. Perform Pinpoint Tests A and B using the Rotunda Transmission Tester 007-00130 with AX4S cable and overlay 007-00087 or equivalents. Service as required. Clear codes. Road Test and rerun On-Board Diagnostic.
311 — HYDRAULIC/MECHANICAL ROUTINE	
Other	
• Tire size change, Chain ratio change, Speedometer Gear	• Refer to the specification decal and verify vehicle has original equipment. Changes in tire size and chain ratio will affect shift timing.
Fluid	
• Improper level	• Adjust fluid to proper level.
Main Control Valve Body	
• Bolts out of torque specification	• Tighten bolts to specification.
• Gaskets—damaged, off location	• Inspect for damage. Replace.
• Valves, Accumulators, Seals, Springs, Clips—damaged, missing, misassembled	• Inspect for damage and contamination. Service as required.
	• Refer to the appropriate shift routine(s) for further diagnosis: **Shift** 1-2, **Routine** 220/320 **Shift** 2-3, **Routine** 221/321 **Shift** 3-4, **Routine** 222/322 **Shift** 4-3, **Routine** 223/323 **Shift** 3-2, **Routine** 224/324 **Shift** 2-1, **Routine** 225/325

FM5029801578000X

Fig. 13 Routines 211 & 311: Shift Timing Is Early/Late

Possible Component	Reference/Action
212 — ELECTRICAL ROUTINE	
Powertrain Control System	
	• Perform Shift Point Road Test and Torque Converter Clutch Operation Test.
• Electrical Inputs/Outputs, Vehicle Wiring Harnesses, Powertrain Control Module, Shift Solenoids, TR, TCC, TSS and TFT Sensor, TP, VSS, ECT, IAT, MAF	• Run On-Board Diagnostic. Refer to MOTOR's Domestic Transmission Manual for diagnosis. Perform Pinpoint Tests A, B, C, D and F using the Rotunda Transmission Tester 007-00130 with AX4S cable and overlay 007-00087 and Transmission Range (TR) Sensor Cable (MLP-B Cable) 007-00127 or equivalents. Service as required. Clear codes. Road Test and rerun On-Board Diagnostic.
312 — HYDRAULIC/MECHANICAL ROUTINE	
Fluid	
• Improper level	• Adjust fluid to proper level.
Main Control Valve Body	
• Bolts out of torque specifications	• Tighten bolts to specifications.
• Gaskets—damaged, off location	• Inspect for damage. Replace as required
• Valves, Accumulators, Seals, Clips, Intermediate Clutch Shuttle Valve —stuck, damaged	• Inspect for damage. Service as required.
Vehicle Speed Input	
• Speedometer Gear—DRIVE—damaged	• Inspect gears.
• Speedometer Gear—DRIVEN—Gear and Shaft Assembly	
• Differential Assembly—damaged or missing	
• Speedometer DRIVE GEAR—damaged	
Torque Converter Clutch (TCC)	• Refer to Routine 342, converter cycling.
Go to Reference/Action to diagnose specific missing shifts	
• Shift Concern: 1-2 Shift (Automatic)	• Routine 220/320
• Shift Concern: 2-3 Shift (Automatic)	• Routine 221/321
• Shift Concern: 3-4 Shift (Automatic)	• Routine 222/322
• Shift Concern: 4-3 Shift (Automatic)	• Routine 223/323
• Shift Concern: 3-2 Shift (Automatic)	• Routine 224/324
• Shift Concern: 2-1 Shift (Automatic)	• Routine 225/325

FM5029801579000X

Fig. 14 Routines 212 & 312: Shift Timing Is Erratic/Hunting

Possible Component	Reference/Action
213 — ELECTRICAL ROUTINE	
Powertrain Control System	
	• Perform Shift Point Road Test
• Electrical Inputs/Outputs, Vehicle Wiring Harnesses, Powertrain Control Module, EPC Solenoid, TFT, ECT, TP, MAF	• Run On-Board Diagnostic. Refer to MOTOR'S Diagnostic Transmission Manual for diagnosis. Perform Pinpoint Tests B and E using the Rotunda Transmission Tester 007-00130 with AX4S cable and overlay 007-00087 or equivalents. Service as required. Clear codes. Road Test and rerun On-Board Diagnostic.
313 — HYDRAULIC/MECHANICAL ROUTINE	
Fluid	
• Improper level	• Adjust fluid to proper level.
• Condition	• Inspect Fluid Level and Condition.

FM5029801580010X

Fig. 15 Routines 213 & 313: Shift Feel Is Soft/Slipping (Part 1 of 2)

Possible Component	Reference/Action
Shift Linkage	
• Damaged, out of adjustment	• Inspect. Service as required. Verify linkage adjustment After servicing linkage, verify that the transmission range sensor is properly adjusted.
Improper Pressures	
• Low Line pressure, Low EPC pressure	• Check pressures at line and EPC taps. Perform Line Pressure and Stall Speed Tests If pressures are low or all shifts are soft/slipping, go to Main Control Valve Body. • If pressures are OK and a specific shift is soft/slipping, refer to the appropriate routine(s) for additional diagnosis. **Shift** 1-2, **Routine** 220/320 **Shift** 2-3, **Routine** 221/321 **Shift** 3-4, **Routine** 222/322 **Shift** 4-3, **Routine** 223/323 **Shift** 3-2, **Routine** 224/324 **Shift** 2-1, **Routine** 225/325
Main Control Valve Body	
• Bolts out of torque specifications	• Tighten bolts to specifications.
• Gaskets—damaged, off location	• Inspect for damage. Service as required.
• 1-2 Capacity Modulator Valve, Accumulator/Regulator Valve, Main Regulator Valve, 2-3 Servo Regulator Valve, Check Balls, 3-2 Shift Timing Valve, Clips, Springs—damaged, misassembled, missing	• Inspect. Service as required.
• EPC Solenoid—stuck, damaged	• Inspect for damage and contamination. Service as required.
• Pressure Failsafe Valve (Zero EPC Pressure Only) stuck, damaged	• Inspect for damage. Service as required.

FM5029801580020X

Fig. 15 Routines 213 & 313: Shift Feel Is Soft/Slipping (Part 2 of 2)

Possible Component	Reference/Action
214 — ELECTRICAL ROUTINE	
Powertrain Control System ● Electrical Inputs/Outputs, Vehicle Wiring Harnesses, Powertrain Control Module, EPC Solenoid, TFT, TR Sensor and Shift Solenoid No. 3, MAF, TP, VSS, A/C, ECT, IAT, PSP	● Run On-Board Diagnostic. Refer to MOTOR'S Domestic Transmission Manual. for diagnosis. Perform Pinpoint Tests A, B, D and E using the Rotunda Transmission Tester 007-00130 with AX4S cable and overlay 007-00087 and Transmission Range (TR) Sensor Cable (MLP-B Cable) 007-00127 or equivalents Service as required. Clear codes. Road Test and rerun On-Board Diagnostic.
314 — HYDRAULIC/MECHANICAL ROUTINE	
Fluid ● Improper level	● Adjust fluid to proper level.
Improper Pressures ● High Line pressure High EPC pressure	● Check pressures at line and EPC taps. Perform Line Pressure Test If pressures are high or all shifts are harsh, go to Main Control Valve Body. ● If pressures are OK and a specific shift is harsh, refer to the appropriate shift routine in the following chart: **Shift** 1-2, **Routine** 220/320 **Shift** 2-3, **Routine** 221/321 **Shift** 3-4, **Routine** 222/322 **Shift** 4-3, **Routine** 223/323 **Shift** 3-2, **Routine** 224/324 **Shift** 2-1, **Routine** 225/325

FM5029801581010X

Fig. 16 Routines 214 & 314: Shift Feel Is Harsh (Part 1 of 2)

Possible Component	Reference/Action
Main Control Valve Body ● Bolts out of torque specifications ● Gaskets—damaged, off location ● 1-2 Capacity Modulator Valve, Accumulator Regulator Valve, Main Regulator Valve, 2-3 Servo Regulator Valve, 3-2 Timing Valve, Springs, Clips, Check Balls—stuck, damaged, misassembled ● EPC Solenoid, Shift Solenoid 3—stuck or damaged	● Tighten bolts to specifications. ● Inspect for damage. Replace as required. ● Inspect. Service as required. ● Inspect for damage, contamination. Service as required.

FM5029801581020X

Fig. 16 Routines 214 & 314: Shift Feel Is Harsh (Part 2 of 2)

Possible Component	Reference/Action
215 — ELECTRICAL ROUTINE	
Powertrain Control System ● Electrical Inputs/Outputs, Vehicle Wiring Harnesses, Powertrain Control Module, Shift Solenoids, TR Sensor, VSS	● Run On-Board Diagnostic. Refer to MOTOR'S Domestic Transmission Manual. for diagnosis. Perform Pinpoint Tests A and D using the Rotunda Transmission Tester 007-00130 with AX4S cable and overlay 007-00087 and Transmission Range (TR) Sensor Cable (MLP-B Cable) 007-00127 or equivalents. Service as required. Clear codes. Road Test and rerun On-Board Diagnostic. If DTC P1700 is present, check for a low transaxle fluid level. Then, continue to Hydraulic/Mechanical Routines.
315 — HYDRAULIC/MECHANICAL ROUTINE	
Shift Linkage ● Damaged or out of adjustment	● Inspect and service as required. Verify linkage adjustment After servicing linkage, verify that the Transmission Range sensor is properly adjusted.
Main Control Valve Body ● Bolts out of torque specifications ● Gaskets—damaged, off location ● Shift Valves, Intermediate Clutch Shuttle Valve, Forward Clutch Control Valve, Springs, Clips—stuck, damaged, misassembled ● For diagnosis related to a specific gear, use the Transmission Tester to determine gear	● Tighten to specifications. ● Inspect for damage. Replace as required. ● Inspect. Service as required. ● Refer to the following routines: **Shift** 1-2, **Routine** 220/320 **Shift** 2-3, **Routine** 221/321 **Shift** 3-4, **Routine** 222/322
Mechanical ● Bands, clutches or seals damaged or worn	● Refer to Transaxle Disassembly and Assembly.

FM5029801582000X

Fig. 17 Routines 215 & 315: No 1st Gear, Engages Higher Gear

Possible Component	Reference/Action
216 — ELECTRICAL ROUTINE	
Powertrain Control System ● Electrical Inputs/Outputs, Vehicle Wiring Harnesses, Powertrain Control Module and Shift Solenoids, Transaxle Internal Wiring Harness	● Run On-Board Diagnostic. MOTOR'S Domestic Transmission Manual for diagnosis. Perform Pinpoint Test A using the Rotunda Transmission Tester 007-00130 with AX4S cable and overlay 007-00087 or equivalent as described. Service as required. Clear codes. Road Test and rerun On-Board Diagnostic. If DTC P1700 is present, check for a low transaxle fluid level. Then, continue to Hydraulic/Mechanical Routines.

FM5029801583010X

Fig. 18 Routines 216 & 316: No Manual 1st Gear (Part 1 of 2)

Possible Component	Reference/Action
316 — HYDRAULIC/MECHANICAL ROUTINE	
Shift Linkage	
• Damaged or out of adjustment	• Inspect and service as required. Verify linkage adjustment After servicing linkage, verify that the Transmission Range sensor is properly adjusted.
Improper Pressures	
• Low Direct Clutch pressure, Low Line pressure, Low EPC pressure	• Check pressure at line and EPC pressure taps. Perform Line Pressure Test If pressures are low, check the following possible components: Main Control Valve Body, Support Assembly, Driven Sprocket, Direct Clutch Assembly.
Main Control Valve Body	
• Bolts out of torque specifications	• Tighten bolts to specifications.
• Gaskets—damaged, off location	• Inspect for damage. Replace as required.
• Manual Control Valve, Manual Low Relief Valve and Spring, Springs, Clips—stuck, damaged, missing	• Inspect for damage. Service as required.
Support Assembly—Driven Sprocket	
• Bolts out of torque specifications	• Tighten bolts to specifications. Use sealant on two external chain cover bolts.
• Seals missing or damaged	• Inspect seals. Replace as required.
• Seal grooves damaged	• Inspect for damage. Service as required.
Direct Clutch	
	• Perform Air Pressure Tests
• Check Ball, Piston, Piston Seals, Plates	• Inspect for damage. Service as required.
• Friction Elements—damaged, worn	• Inspect for damage. Service as required.
Low One-Way Clutch Assembly	
• Not Overrunning, damaged	• Inspect for damage. Service as required.
Low Intermediate Band	
• Damaged, worn, burned out or missassembled	• Inspect for damage. Service as required.
Forward Clutch Assembly	
	• Perform Air Pressure Tests
• Seals, Piston	• Inspect seals for damage. Service as required.
• Check Ball	• Inspect for mislocation, poor seating and damage. Replace cylinder as required.
• Piston cracked	• Inspect piston. Replace as required.
• Friction Elements—damaged, worn	• Check for abnormal wear, damage. Replace as required.

FM5029801583020X

Fig. 18 Routines 216 & 316: No Manual 1st Gear (Part 2 of 2)

Possible Component	Reference/Action
220 — ELECTRICAL ROUTINE	
Powertrain Control System	
• Electrical Inputs/Outputs, Vehicle Wiring Harnesses, Powertrain Control Module, Shift Solenoids, TR, TFT and EPC, TP, MAF	• Run On-Board Diagnostic. **Refer to MOTOR'S Domestic Transmission Manual.** for diagnosis. Perform Pinpoint Tests A, B, D and E using the Rotunda Transmission Tester 007-00130 with AX4S cable and overlay 007-00087 and Transmission Range (TR) Sensor Cable (MLP-B Cable) 007-00127 or equivalents If DTC P1700 is present, check for a low transaxle fluid level, then continue to Hydraulic/Mechanical Routine. Service as required. Clear codes. Road Test and rerun On-Board Diagnostic.

FM5029801584010X

Fig. 19 Routines 220 & 320: No Automatic 1-2 Shift (Part 1 of 2)

Possible Component	Reference/Action
320 — HYDRAULIC/MECHANICAL ROUTINE	
Shift Linkage • Damaged or out of adjustment	• Inspect and service as required. Verify linkage adjustment After servicing linkage, verify that the Transmission Range sensor is properly adjusted.
Speedometer Gear—Drive • Damaged	• Inspect for damage. Service as required.
Speedometer Gear—Driven • Damaged	• Inspect for damage. Service as required.
Improper Pressures • Intermediate Clutch pressure, Line pressure, EPC pressure	• Check pressure at line, EPC and intermediate clutch taps. Perform Line Pressure Test If not OK, check Main Control Valve Body.
Main Control Valve Body • Bolts out of torque specification • Gaskets—damaged, off location • Intermediate Clutch Tap—loose, missing • 1-2 Shift Valve, Accumulator Regulator Valve, 1-2 Capacity Modulator Valve, Main Regulator Valve, Intermediate Shuttle Valve, Springs, B10 Check Ball, Clips—loose, missing, stuck, misassembled • SS1 not functioning properly	• Tighten bolts to specification. • Inspect for damage. Replace as required. • Inspect. Service as required. • Inspect. Service as required. • Activate solenoid using NGS. If solenoid operation cannot be felt when placing hand on solenoid, replace solenoid. Inspect O-rings for damage. Service as required.
1-2 Accumulator Assembly • Piston Seals, Springs—damaged, missing	• Perform Air Pressure Tests • Inspect for damage. Service as required.
Support Assembly—Driven Sprocket • Seals—damaged, missing • Holes blocked	• Inspect for damage, missing or blockage. Service as required.
Pump Assembly • Porosity/cross leak • Gasket damaged, off location • Components damaged	• Inspect and replace as required. • Inspect for damage. Replace as required. • Inspect for damage or missing ball. Replace pump assembly if required.
Low One-Way Clutch Assembly • Not overrunning, damaged	• Inspect for damage. Replace as required.
Intermediate Clutch Assembly • Seals—damaged • Piston—damaged • Friction—damaged, worn • Check Ball—missing, damaged	• Perform Air Pressure Tests • Inspect for damage. Replace as required. • Inspect for damage. Replace as required. • Inspect for damage. Replace as required. • Inspect for damage. Service or replace as required.
Front Planet Carrier • Damaged	• Inspect for weld damage. Service as required.
Differential Assembly • Damaged or missing	• Inspect for damage. Service as required.
Speedometer Drive Gear • Damaged or missing	• Inspect for damage. Service as required.

FM5029801584020X

Fig. 19 Routines 220 & 320: No Automatic 1-2 Shift (Part 2 of 2)

Possible Component	Reference/Action
221 — ELECTRICAL ROUTINE	
Powertrain Control System • Electrical Inputs/Outputs, Vehicle Wiring Harnesses, Powertrain Control Module, Shift Solenoids, TFT, EPC, TP, MAF	• Run On-Board Diagnostic. Refer to MOTOR'S Domestic Transmission Manual, for diagnosis. Perform Pinpoint Tests A, B and E using the Rotunda Transmission Tester 007-00130 with AX4S cable and overlay 007-00087 and Transmission Range (TR) Sensor Cable (MLP-B Cable) 007-00127 or equivalents as described. Service as required. Clear codes. Road Test and rerun On-Board Diagnostic.
321 — HYDRAULIC/MECHANICAL ROUTINE	
Shift Linkage • Damaged or out of adjustment	• Inspect and service as required. Verify linkage adjustment After servicing linkage, verify that the Transmission Range sensor is properly adjusted.
Speedometer Gear—Drive • Damaged	• Inspect for damage. Service as required.
Speedometer Gear—Driven • Damaged	• Inspect for damage. Service as required.
Improper Pressures • Direct Clutch pressure, EPC pressure	• Check pressure at EPC and line taps. Perform Line Pressure Test If not OK, check the Main Control Valve Body.
Main Control Valve Body • Bolts out of torque specification • Gaskets—damaged, off location • 1-2 Shift Valve, 2-3 Shift Valve, 2-3 Servo Regulator Valve/Spring —stuck, damaged • B3, B8, B9, B10, B11 Check Balls—damaged, missing • SS1, SS2, SS3 not functioning properly	• Tighten bolts to specification. • Inspect for damage. Replace as required. • Inspect. Service as required. • Inspect for damage. Service as required. • Activate solenoid using NGS. If solenoid operation cannot be felt when placing hand on solenoid, replace solenoid. Inspect O-rings for damage. Service as required.
Low Intermediate Servo Assembly • Wrong Apply Rod, Servo Bore or Piston damaged, Piston Seals damaged or missing, Return Spring or Retaining Clip missing, broken	• Perform Air Pressure Tests • Inspect for damage. Service as required.
Support Assembly—Driven Sprocket • Seals—damaged, missing, holes blocked	• Inspect for damage. Service as required.
Direct One-Way Clutch • Not holding, damaged	• Perform Air Pressure Tests • Inspect for damage. Replace as required.
Direct Clutch Assembly • Seals • Piston • Friction damaged or worn • Check Ball not seating • Return Spring Assembly	• Perform Air Pressure Tests • Inspect for damage. Replace as required. • Inspect for damage. Replace as required. • Inspect for damage. Replace as required. • Inspect for damage. Replace as required. • Inspect for damage. Replace as required.
Case • Servo Release Passage blocked • Servo Release Tube—leaking, loose	• Inspect for damage. Replace case if damaged.

FM5029801585010X

Fig. 20 Routines 221 & 321: No Automatic 2-3 Shift (Part 1 of 2)

Possible Component	Reference/Action
Direct/Intermediate Clutch Hub • Seals damaged, missing or holes blocked	• Inspect for damage. Service as required.
Speedometer Drive Gear • Damaged	• Inspect for damage. Service as required.

FM5029801585020X

Fig. 20 Routines 221 & 321: No Automatic 2-3 Shift (Part 2 of 2)

Possible Component	Reference/Action
222 — ELECTRICAL ROUTINE	
Powertrain Control System	
• Electrical Inputs/Outputs, Vehicle Wiring Harnesses, Powertrain Control Module, Shift Solenoids, TR Sensor, EPC Solenoid, VSS	• Run On-Board Diagnostic. Refer to MOTOR'S Domestic Transmission Manual for diagnosis. Perform Pinpoint Tests A, D and E using the Rotunda Transmission Tester 007-00130 with AX4S cable and overlay 007-00087 and Transmission Range (TR) Sensor Cable (MLP-B Cable) 007-00127 or equivalents. Service as required. Clear codes. Road Test and rerun On-Board Diagnostic.
322 — HYDRAULIC/MECHANICAL ROUTINE	
Shift Linkage	
• Damaged or out of adjustment	• Inspect and service as required. Verify linkage adjustment After servicing linkage, verify that the TR sensor is properly adjusted.
Speedometer Gear—Drive	
• Damaged	• Inspect for damage. Service as required.
Speedometer Gear—Driven	
• Damaged	• Inspect for damage. Service as required.
Overdrive Servo Assembly	• Perform Air Pressure Tests
• Wrong Apply Rod	• Inspect. Replace if incorrect.
• Servo Bore or Piston damaged	• Inspect for damage. Service as required.
• Piston Seals—damaged, missing	• Inspect for damage. Service as required.
• Return Spring Retaining Clip—missing, broken	• Inspect for damage. Service as required.
Main Control Valve Body	
• Bolts out of torque specification	• Tighten bolts to specification.
• Gaskets—damaged, off location	• Inspect for damage. Replace as required.
• 3-4 Shift Valve, 1-2 Shift Valve, Accumulator Regulator Valve, Forward Clutch Control Valve—stuck, damaged	• Inspect. Service as required.
• SS3 not functioning properly	• Activate solenoid using NGS. If solenoid operation cannot be felt when placing hand on solenoid, replace solenoid. Inspect O-rings for damage. Service as required.
• EPC Solenoid stuck, damaged	• Inspect for damage. Service as required.
• B4, B11 Check Balls	• Inspect for damage. Replace as required.
3-4 Accumulator Assembly	• Perform Air Pressure Tests
• Accumulator Piston—stuck, damaged	• Inspect for damage. Service as required.
• Piston Seals—missing, damaged	• Inspect for damage. Service as required.
• Springs—missing, damaged, holes blocked	• Inspect for damage. Service as required.
Support Assembly—Driven Sprocket	
• Seals—damaged, missing, holes blocked	• Inspect for damage, missing or blockage. Service as required.
OD Band	
• OD Band—damaged, worn, misassembled	• Inspect for damage. Replace as required.
• Direct Overrunning Clutch Assembly damaged	• Inspect for damage. Replace as required.

FM5029801586010X

Fig. 21 Routines 222 & 322: No Automatic 3-4 Shift (Part 1 of 2)

Possible Component	Reference/Action
Differential Assembly	
• Damaged or missing	• Inspect for damage. Service as required.
Speedometer Drive Gear	
• Damaged	• Inspect for damage. Service as required.

FM5029801586020X

Fig. 21 Routines 222 & 322: No Automatic 3-4 Shift (Part 2 of 2)

Possible Component	Reference/Action
223 — ELECTRICAL ROUTINE	
Powertrain Control System	• Perform Torque Converter Clutch Operation Test
• Electrical Inputs/Outputs, Vehicle Wiring Harnesses, Powertrain Control Module, Shift Solenoids, TR sensor, TSS, EPC Solenoid, VSS	• Run On-Board Diagnostic. Refer to MOTOR'S Domestic Transmission Manual for diagnosis. Perform Pinpoint Tests A, D, E and F using the Rotunda Transmission Tester 007-00130 with AX4S cable and overlay 007-00087 and Transmission Range (TR) Sensor Cable (MLP-B Cable) 007-00127 or equivalents. Service as required. Clear codes. Road Test and rerun On-Board Diagnostic.
323 — HYDRAULIC/MECHANICAL ROUTINE	
Speedometer Gear—Drive	
• Damaged	• Inspect for damage. Service as required.
Speedometer Gear—Driven	
• Damaged	• Inspect for damage. Service as required.
Main Control Valve Body	
• Bolts out of torque specification	• Tighten bolts to specification.
• Gaskets—damaged, off location	• Inspect for damage. Replace as required.
• 1-2 Shift Valve, 3-4 Shift Valve, Accumulator Regulator Valve—stuck, damaged	• Inspect. Service as required.
• SS1 not functioning properly	• Activate solenoid using NGS. If solenoid operation cannot be felt when placing hand on solenoid, replace solenoid. Inspect O-rings for damage. Service as required.
• EPC Solenoid—stuck, damaged	• Inspect for damage. Perform Pinpoint Test E.
• B4, B11 Check Balls—damaged, missing	• Inspect for damage. Service as required.
Overdrive Band	
• Overdrive Band—damaged, worn, misassembled	• Inspect for damage. Replace as required.
• Direct One-Way Clutch Assembly damaged	• Inspect for damage. Service as required.
Overdrive Servo Assembly	
• Servo Cover, Seal, Rod and Piston Cushion Spring—damaged	• Perform Air Pressure Tests
	• Inspect for damage. Service as required.
• Apply Rod wrong	• Inspect Rod as described under Transaxle, Assembly.
• Servo Bore or Piston damaged	• Inspect for damage. Service as required.
• Piston Seals—damaged, missing	• Inspect for damage. Service as required.
• Return Spring Retaining Clip—missing, broken	• Inspect for damage. Service as required.
Torque Converter Clutch	
• Not releasing	• See: Converter Always Applied Diagnostic Routine 241/341.
Differential Assembly	
• Damaged	• Inspect for damage. Service as required.
Speedometer Drive Gear	
• Wrong or missing	• Inspect for damage. Service as required.

FM5029801587000X

Fig. 22 Routines 223 & 323: No Automatic 4-3 Shift

Possible Component	Reference/Action
224 — ELECTRICAL ROUTINE	
Powertrain Control System	
• Electrical Inputs/Outputs, Vehicle Wiring Harnesses, Powertrain Control Module, Shift Solenoids, TR Sensor, PSP, VSS	• Run On-Board Diagnostic. Refer to MOTOR'S Domestic Transmission Manual for diagnosis. Perform Pinpoint Tests A and D using the Rotunda Transmission Tester 007-00130 with AX4S cable and overlay 007-00087 and Transmission Range (TR) Sensor Cable (MLP-B Cable) 007-00127. Service as required. Clear codes. Road Test and rerun On-Board Diagnostic.
324 — HYDRAULIC/MECHANICAL ROUTINE	
• **Improper Pressures** — Direct Clutch — EPC pressure — Forward Clutch — Line pressure	• Check pressure at line, direct clutch and EPC taps. Perform Line Pressure and Stall Speed Tests if not within specification, check main control valve body.
Speedometer Gear—Drive	
• Damaged	• Inspect for damage. Service as required.
Speedometer Gear—Driven	
• Damaged	• Inspect for damage. Service as required.
Main Control Valve Body	
• Bolts out of torque specification	• Tighten bolts to specification.
• Gaskets—damaged, off location	• Inspect for damage. Replace as required.
• 3-2 Shift Timing Valve, Backout Valve, Forward Clutch Control, 1-2, 2-3 Shift Valves—stuck, damaged	• Inspect. Service as required.
• 3-2 Shift Timing Spring Clip—damaged, missing	• Inspect for damage. Service as required.
• B5 Check Ball	• Inspect. Service as required.
• SS1, SS2 or SS3 not functioning properly	• Activate solenoid using NGS. If solenoid operation cannot be felt when placing hand on solenoid, replace solenoid. Inspect O-rings for damage. Service as required.
Low/Intermediate Servo Assembly	• Perform Air Pressure Tests
• Spring, Bore, Piston—damaged, missing	• Inspect for damage. Replace as required.
• Incorrect Servo Apply Rod length	• Replace as required.
Support Assembly—Driven Sprocket	
• Seals—damaged, missing, holes blocked	• Inspect for damage, missing or blockage. Service as required.
Low One-Way Clutch Assembly	
• Not Overrunning—damaged	• Inspect for damage. Replace as required.
Forward Clutch Assembly	• Perform Air Pressure Tests
• Return Spring damaged	• Inspect for damage. Service as required.
• Friction Elements damaged	• Inspect for damage. Service as required.
• Seals/Piston damaged	• Inspect for damage. Service as required.
• Check Ball damaged, stuck or missing	• Inspect for damage. Service as required.
Direct Clutch Assembly	• Perform Air Pressure Tests
• Support and Spring damaged	• Inspect for damage. Replace as required.
• Support and Spring Retaining Ring out of position	• Inspect for damage. Replace as required.
• Check Ball not functioning	• Inspect for damage. Replace as required.
Low/Intermediate Band	
• Damaged, worn, burnt, misassembled	• Inspect for damage. Replace as required.
Differential Assembly	
• Damaged	• Inspect for damage. Service as required.
Speedometer Drive Gear	
• Damaged	• Inspect for damage. Service as required.

FM5029801588000X

Fig. 23 Routines 224 & 324: No Automatic 3-2 Shift

Possible Component	Reference/Action
225 — ELECTRICAL ROUTINE	
Powertrain Control System	
• Electrical Inputs/Outputs, Vehicle Wiring Harnesses, Powertrain Control Module, Shift Solenoids, TR Sensor, VSS, IAC, PSP	• Run On-Board Diagnostic. Refer to MOTOR'S Domestic Transmission manual for diagnosis. Perform Pinpoint Tests A and D using the Rotunda Transmission Tester 007-00130 with AX4S cable and overlay 007-00087 and Transmission Range (TR) Sensor Cable (MLP-B Cable) 007-00127. Service as required. Clear codes. Road Test and rerun On-Board Diagnostic.
325 — HYDRAULIC/MECHANICAL ROUTINE	
Speedometer Gear—Drive	
• Damaged	• Inspect for damage. Service as required.
Speedometer Gear—Driven	
• Damaged	• Inspect for damage. Service as required.
Main Control Valve Body	
• Bolts out of torque specification	• Tighten bolts to specification.
• Gaskets—damaged, off location	• Inspect for damage. Replace as required.
• 1-2 Shift Valve, Backout Valve, Intermediate Clutch Shuttle Valve, Main Regulator Valve	• Inspect. Service as required.
• SS1 not functioning properly	• Activate solenoid using transmission tester. If solenoid operation cannot be felt when placing hand on solenoid, replace solenoid. Inspect O-rings for damage. Service as required.
• B10 Check Ball—missing, damaged	• Inspect for damage. Service as required.
Intermediate Clutch Assembly	• Perform Air Pressure Tests
• Support and Spring—damaged, misassembled	• Inspect for damage. Replace as required.
• Friction Element—damaged, worn	• Inspect for damage. Replace as required.
• Check Ball damaged	• Inspect. Service as required.
Low One-Way Clutch Assembly	
• Not Holding, damaged	• Inspect for damage. Replace as required.
Differential Assembly	
• Damaged	• Inspect for damage. Service as required.
Speedometer Drive Gear	
• Damaged	• Inspect for damage. Service as required.

FM5029801589000X

Fig. 24 Routines 225 & 325: No Automatic 2-1 Shift

Possible Component	Reference/Action
240 — ELECTRICAL ROUTINE	
Powertrain Control System	• Perform Torque Converter Clutch Operation Test
• Electrical Inputs/Outputs, Vehicle Wiring Harnesses, Powertrain Control Module, TFT, TSS, TR, TCC, VSS, TP, ECT	• Run On-Board Diagnostic. Refer to MOTOR'S Domestic Transmission Manual for diagnosis. Perform Pinpoint Tests B, C, D and F using the Rotunda Transmission Tester 007-00130 with AX4S cable and overlay 007-00087 and Transmission Range (TR) Sensor Cable (MLP-B Cable) 007-00127 or equivalents. Service as required. Clear codes. Road Test and rerun On-Board Diagnostic.
340 — HYDRAULIC/MECHANICAL ROUTINE	
Improper Pressures	
• Low Line pressure, Low EPC	• Check pressure at line and EPC taps. Perform Line Pressure and Stall Speed Tests If low, check main control valve body.

FM5029801590010X

Fig. 25 Routines 240 & 340: No Torque Converter Apply (Part 1 of 2)

Possible Component	Reference/Action
Main Control Valve Body	
• Bolts out of torque specification	• Tighten bolts to specification.
• Gaskets—damaged, off location	• Inspect gaskets. Service as required.
• Valve Body Pilot Sleeve—damaged, misaligned. Manual Shift Valve, Torque Converter Clutch Control Valve and/or Plunger, Converter Regulator Valve, Springs, Solenoid Regulator Valve—stuck, damaged	• Inspect. Service as required.
• TCC Solenoid not functioning properly	• Activate solenoid using NGS. If solenoid operation cannot be felt when placing hand on solenoid, replace solenoid. Inspect O-rings for damage. Service as required.
Turbine Shaft	
• Seals—damaged, missing	• Inspect for damage. Replace as required.
Pump Assembly Shaft	
• Seals—damaged, missing	• Inspect seals for damage. Service as required
Torque Converter	
• Leakage, Friction Material, Internal Seals	• Inspect and replace as required.

FM5029801590020X

Fig. 25 Routines 240 & 340: No Torque Converter Apply (Part 2 of 2)

Possible Component	Reference/Action
242 — ELECTRICAL ROUTINE	
Powertrain Control System	• Perform Torque Converter Clutch Operation Test
• Electrical Inputs/Outputs, Vehicle Wiring Harnesses, Powertrain Control Module, TCC, TR Sensor, TFT, TSS, TP, ECT, VSS	• Run On-Board Diagnostic. **Refer to MOTOR'S Domestic Transmission Manual** for diagnosis. Perform Pinpoint Tests C and D using the Rotunda Transmission Tester 007-00130 with AX4S cable and overlay 007-00087 and Transmission Range (TR) Sensor Cable (MLP-B Cable) 007-00127. Service as required. Clear codes. Road Test and rerun On-Board Diagnostic.

FM5029801592010X

Fig. 27 Routines 242 & 342: Torque Converter Cycling/Shudder/Chatter (Part 1 of 2)

Possible Component	Reference/Action
241 — ELECTRICAL ROUTINE	
Powertrain Control System	• Perform Torque Converter Clutch Operation Test
• Electrical Inputs/Outputs, Vehicle Wiring Harnesses, Powertrain Control Module, TFT, TSS, TCC, TR, ECT, MAF	• Run On-Board Diagnostic. **Refer to MOTOR'S Domestic Transmission Manual** for diagnosis. Perform Pinpoint Tests B, C and F using the Rotunda Transmission Tester 007-00130 with AX4S cable and overlay 007-00087 or equivalents. Service as required. Clear codes. Road Test and rerun On-Board Diagnostic.
341 — HYDRAULIC/MECHANICAL ROUTINE	
Main Control Valve Body	
• Bolts out of torque specification	• Tighten bolts to specification.
• Gaskets—damaged, off location	• Inspect gaskets. Service as required.
• Torque Converter Clutch Control Valve or Plunger—stuck, damaged	• Inspect. Service as required.
• TCC Solenoid not functioning properly	• Activate solenoid using NGS. If solenoid operation cannot be felt when placing hand on solenoid, replace solenoid.
Torque Converter	
• No end clearance	• Inspect and replace as required.
• Piston Plate damaged/stuck to cover	• If cover is heat stained, replace converter.

FM5029801591000X

Fig. 26 Routines 241 & 341: Torque Converter Always Applied/Stalls Vehicle

Possible Component	Reference/Action
342 — HYDRAULIC/MECHANICAL ROUTINE	
Fluid Condition	• Inspect fluid condition. If burnt, drain fluid and converter. Replace fluid and fluid filter assembly. Bring vehicle to normal operating temperature. Perform Drive Cycle NGS. Perform On-Board Diagnostic. If condition still exists, continue diagnostics.
Improper Pressures	
• Low Line pressure, Low EPC	• Check pressure at line and EPC taps. Perform Line Pressure and Stall Speed Tests • If not OK, check the Main Control Valve Body.
Main Control Valve Body	
• Bolts out of torque specification	• Tighten bolts to specification.
• Gaskets—damaged, off location	• Inspect for damage. Replace as required.
• Valve Body Pilot Sleeve—damaged, misaligned Manual Shift Valve, Torque Clutch Control Valve and Plunger, Converter Regulator Valve—stuck, damaged	• Inspect. Service as required.
• TCC Solenoid not functioning properly	• Activate solenoid using NGS. If solenoid operation cannot be felt when placing hand on solenoid, replace solenoid. Inspect O-rings for damage. Service as required.
Turbine Shaft	
• Seals—damaged, missing	• Inspect for damage. Replace as required.
Pump Assembly Shaft	
• Seals—damaged, missing	• Inspect seals for damage. Service as required.
Torque Converter	
• End Clearance—excessive	• Inspect as described. Replace as required.
• Leakage, Friction Materials, Internal Seals	• Inspect as described. Replace as required.

FM5029801592020X

Fig. 27 Routine 242 & 342: Torque Converter Cycling/Shudder/Chatter (Part 2 of 2)

Possible Component	Reference/Action
249 — ELECTRICAL ROUTINE	
Powertrain Control System	
• Electrical Inputs/Outputs, Vehicle Wiring Harnesses, Powertrain Control Module, Shift Solenoid No. 3 (SS-3)	• Run On-Board Diagnostic. • **Refer to MOTOR'S Domestic Transmission Manual** for diagnosis. Perform Pinpoint Test A using the Rotunda Transmission Tester 007-00130 with AX4S cable and overlay 007-00087 . Service as required. Clear codes. Road Test and rerun On-Board Diagnostic.
349 — HYDRAULIC/MECHANICAL ROUTINE	
Shift Linkage Cable	
• TR Sensor—damaged, out of adjustment	• Inspect for damage. Service as required. Verify linkage adjustment. After servicing the linkage, verify that the transmission range sensor is properly adjusted.
Improper Pressures	
• Forward Clutch Pressure, Line Pressure	• Check pressure at line tap. Perform Line Pressure and Stall Speed Tests If not OK, check the following components: Main Controls and Forward Clutch Assembly.
Main Control Valve Body	
• Bolts out of torque specification	• Tighten bolts to specification.
• Gaskets—damaged, off location	• Inspect for damage. Replace gaskets.
• Shift Valves, Forward Clutch Control Valve damaged, stuck or misassembled.	• Inspect for damage. Service as required.

FM5029801593010X

Fig. 28 Routines 249 & 349: No Engine Braking In 3rd Gear D Position (Part 1 of 2)

Possible Component	Reference/Action
• SS-3 damaged, stuck	• Perform Pinpoint Test A.
Forward Clutch Assembly	
• Return Spring, Piston, Seals, Friction Elements, Check Ball—stuck, damaged, misassembled	• Perform Air Pressure Tests • Inspect for damage. Service as required.
Low One-Way Clutch Assembly	
• Not Overrunning, damaged	• Inspect for damage. Service as required.

FM5029801593020X

Fig. 28 Routines 249 & 349: No Engine Braking In 3rd Gear D Position (Part 2 of 2)

Possible Component	Reference/Action
250 — ELECTRICAL ROUTINE	
• No Electrical Concerns	• No action required
350 — HYDRAULIC/MECHANICAL ROUTINE	
Shift Linkage	
• Damaged or out of adjustment	• Inspect and service as required. Verify linkage adjustment After servicing linkage, verify that the TR sensor is properly adjusted.
Improper Pressures	
• Direct Clutch pressure	• Check pressure at direct clutch tap. Perform Line Pressure Test If not OK, check Main Control Valve Body and Direct Clutch Assembly.
Main Control Valve Body	
• Bolts out of torque specification	• Tighten bolts to specification.
• Gaskets—damaged, off location	• Inspect for damage. Replace as required.
• Manual Low Relief Valve, 1-2 Shift Valve, Pull-In Valve—stuck, damaged or misassembled	• Inspect. Clean or service as required.
Direct Clutch Assembly	
• Seals	• Inspect. Service or replace as required.
• Piston	• Inspect. Service or replace as required.
• Friction Damaged or worn	• Inspect. Service or replace as required.
• Check Ball Not Seating	• Inspect. Service or replace as required.
• Return Spring Assembly	• Inspect. Service or replace as required.
Direct One-Way Clutch	
• Damaged	• Inspect for damage. Service as required.

FM5029801594000X

Fig. 29 Routines 250 & 350: No Engine Braking In 1st Gear Manual

Possible Component	Reference/Action
251 — ELECTRICAL ROUTINE	
• No Electrical Concerns	• No action required
351 — HYDRAULIC/MECHANICAL ROUTINE	
Shift Linkage	
• Damaged or out of adjustment	• Inspect and service as required. Verify linkage adjustment After servicing linkage, verify that the transmission range sensor is properly adjusted.
Manual Control Lever	
• Retaining Pin damaged, Nut loose, Detent Spring—bent, damaged or Park Mechanism damaged	• Inspect and service as required.

FM5029801595010X

Fig. 30 Routines 251 & 351: Shift Lever Efforts High (Part 1 of 2)

Possible Component	Reference/Action
Main Control Valve Body	
• Manual Shift Valve stuck	• Inspect and service or replace as necessary.
• Bolts out of torque specification	• Tighten bolts to specification.
Brake Shift Interlock	

FM5029801595020X

Fig. 30 Routines 251 & 351: Shift Lever Efforts High (Part 2 of 2)

Possible Component	Reference/Action
252 — ELECTRICAL ROUTINE	
Engine Components • Vehicle Speed Sensor, Seals	• Inspect and service as required.
Transaxle Components • Transaxle Connector, TSS Seals	• Inspect and service as required.
352 — HYDRAULIC/MECHANICAL ROUTINE	
Seals/Gaskets • Converter, TSS, Pan, Extension Housing — Gasket/Seal, Manual Control Lever, Fluid Level Indicator, Servo Covers, Driveshaft Axles	• Locate source and service as required.
Other • Cooler Fitting, Pressure Taps, Transaxle Connectors, Speedometer Cover, Cooler Inlet and Outlet Tubes, Case Porosity, Case cracked	• Locate source and service as required.
• Vent blocked or damaged	• Check vent for damage or blockage; service as required.

FM5029801601000X

Fig. 31 Routines 252 & 352: External Leaks

Possible Component	Reference/Action
253 — ELECTRICAL ROUTINE	
Powertrain Control System • Electrical Inputs/Outputs, Vehicle Wiring Harnesses, Powertrain Control Module, TCC Solenoid	• Perform Shift Point Road Test and Torque Converter Clutch Operation Test • Run On-Board Diagnostic. **Refer to MOTOR'S Domestic Transmission Manual** for diagnosis. Perform Pinpoint Test C using the Rotunda Transmission Tester 007-00130 with AX4S cable and overlay 007-00087 or equivalents . Service as required. Clear codes. Road test and rerun On-Board Diagnostic.
353 — HYDRAULIC/MECHANICAL ROUTINE	
Verify proper shift scheduling and engagements	• Go to the appropriate Diagnostic Routines.
Torque Converter Clutch always applied	• Go to Routine 341.
Torque Converter Clutch • Damaged	• Replace converter if damaged.

FM5029801596000X

Fig. 32 Routines 253 & 353: Poor Vehicle Performance

Possible Component	Reference/Action
254 — ELECTRICAL ROUTINE	
• No electrical concerns	• No action required

FM5029801597010X

Fig. 33 Routines 254 & 354: Noise/Vibration In Forward/Reverse (Part 1 of 2)

Possible Component	Reference/Action
354 — HYDRAULIC/MECHANICAL ROUTINE	
For Noises/Vibrations That Change With Engine Speed: • Converter components • Fluid level (low) — Pump cavitation • Pump Assembly • Engine drive accessories • Cooler Inlet and Outlet Tubes grounding out • Flywheel	• Locate source of disturbance and service as required.
For Noises/Vibrations That Change With Vehicle Speed: • Engine Mounts — loose or damaged • Driveline concerns — Driveshaft shudder — Driveshaft Joint — Suspension — Modifications • Output/Driveshaft Splines worn or damaged	• Locate source of disturbance and service as required.
Other Noises/Vibrations: • Main Controls — Valve resonance • Cooler Inlet and Outlet Tubes grounding • Anti-Lock (ABS) Brake System • Power Steering Pump	• Locate source of disturbance and service as required. • Locate source of disturbance and service as required. • **Refer to ABS.** • **Refer to Power Steering**

FM5029801597020X

Fig. 33 Routines 254 & 354: Noise/Vibration In Forward/Reverse (Part 2 of 2)

Possible Component	Reference/Action
255 — ELECTRICAL ROUTINE	
Powertrain Control System • Electrical Inputs/Outputs, Vehicle Wiring Harnesses, Powertrain Control Module, TR Sensor	• Perform Torque Converter Clutch Operation Test Run On-Board Diagnostic. Refer to MOTOR'S **Domestic Transmission Manual** for diagnosis. Perform Pinpoint Test D using the Rotunda Transmission Tester 007-00130 with AX4S cable and overlay 007-00087 and Transmission Range (TR) Sensor Cable (MLP-B Cable) 007-00127 . Service as required. Clear codes. Road Test and rerun On-Board Diagnostic.
355 — HYDRAULIC/MECHANICAL ROUTINE	
Shift Linkage/Cable, TR Sensor • Damaged or out of adjustment	• Inspect and service as required. Verify linkage adjustment After servicing linkage, verify that the transmission range sensor is properly adjusted.

FM5029801598000X

Fig. 34 Routines 255 & 355: Engine Will Not Crank

Possible Component	Reference/Action
256 — ELECTRICAL ROUTINE	
• No Electrical Concerns	• No action required

FM5029801599010X

Fig. 35 Routines 256 & 356: No Park Range (Part 1 of 2)

Possible Component	Reference/Action
356 — HYDRAULIC/MECHANICAL ROUTINE	
Shift Linkage • Damaged or out of adjustment	• Inspect and service as required. Verify linkage adjustment After servicing linkage, verify that the transmission range sensor is properly adjusted.
Park Mechanism • Parking Pawl, Parking Pawl Return Spring, Park Rod Guide Cup, Parking Pawl Shaft, Parking Lever Actuating Rod, Manual Control Lever, Manual Lever Detent Spring—damaged	• Inspect and service as required.

FM5029801599020X

Fig. 35 Routines 256 & 356: No Park Range (Part 2 of 2)

Possible Component	Reference/Action
257 — ELECTRICAL ROUTINE	
Refer to Electrical Routine 240, Torque Converter Not Applying	• Refer to Electrical Routine 240, Torque Converter - No Applying
357 — HYDRAULIC/MECHANICAL ROUTINE	
Fluid • Improper level • Condition	 • Adjust fluid to proper level. • Inspect. Fluid Level and Condition.
Cooler Lines • Damaged, blocked or reversed	• Inspect and service as required.
Auxiliary Cooler • Damaged, blocked or restricted, improperly installed	• Inspect and service as required.
Vehicle Concerns Causing Engine Overheating	• Refer to appropriate chassis manual.
Main Control Valve Body • Torque Converter Clutch Control Valve and Plunger, Converter Regulator Valve stuck or damaged	• Inspect and service as required.
Torque Converter Clutch Not Applying • Seized Torque Converter Clutch	• See Routine 240/340. Inspect. Service as required.
Excessive Towing Loads	• Check gross vehicle weight.
Incorrect Idle or Performance	• Refer to MOTOR'S Auto Engine Performance & Driveability Manual.
Improper Clutch or Band Application or Fluid Pressure Control System	• Inspect. Service as required.

FM5029801600000X

Fig. 36 Routines 257 & 357: Transaxle Overheating

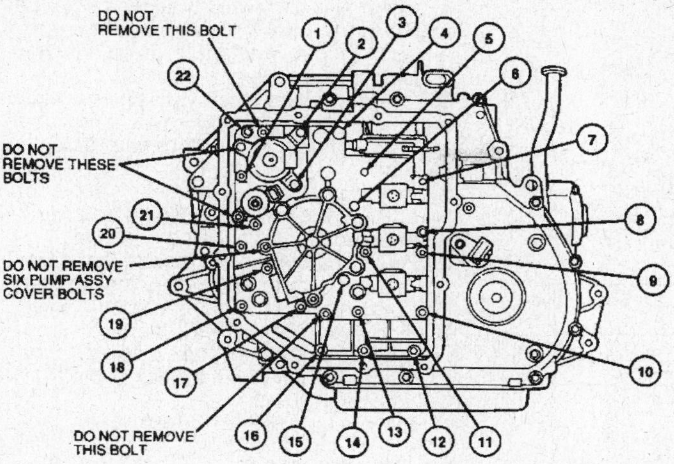

Fig. 37 Oil pump & valve body bolt removal

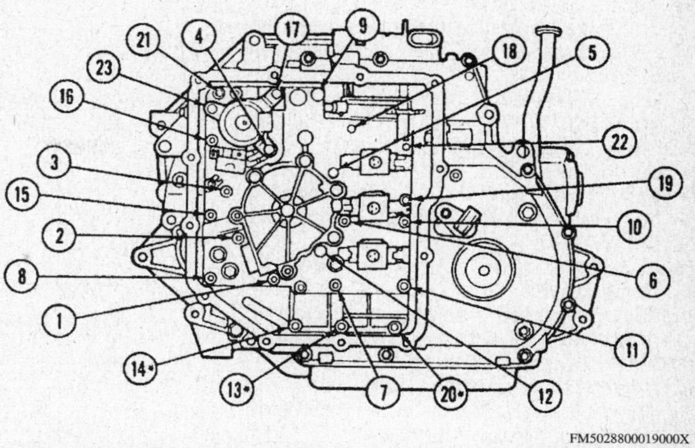

Fig. 38 Oil pump & valve body bolt tightening sequence

MAINTENANCE

Ford Motor Company recommends use of Mercon type automatic transmission fluid in this transaxle. If Mercon type fluid is not available, Type H automatic transmission fluid may be used. Use of a fluid other than specified may result in transaxle malfunction or failure.

FLUID CHECK

1. Start engine and allow to reach normal operating temperature.
2. Move transaxle selector lever through each range, allowing enough time in each range for transaxle to engage. Return selector lever to Park position and apply parking brake. **Do not turn off engine during fluid level check.**
3. Clean all dirt from transaxle fluid dipstick cap before removing dipstick from filler tube.
4. Remove dipstick from tube, wipe it clean, then push it all way back into tube. Ensure dipstick is fully seated.
5. Pull dipstick out of tube and check fluid level. Fluid should be between arrows.
6. If vehicle has been operating for an extended period at high speed or in city traffic in hot weather or vehicle is being used to tow a trailer, transaxle fluid must be allowed to cool for about 30 minutes after engine has been turned off for an accurate reading to be obtained.

FLUID CHANGE

Normal maintenance and lubrication requirements do not necessitate periodic fluid change. If vehicle is operated under abnormal conditions, fluid should be changed every 30,000 miles. If major failure has occurred in transaxle, it will have to be removed for service. At this time converter should be thoroughly flushed to remove any foreign matter.

1. Raise and support vehicle, then disconnect inlet line from radiator fitting or top auxiliary cooler fitting. Install 5/16 or 3/8 inch I.D. hose over end of cooler line and put opposite end into drain pan.
2. Lower vehicle, then start engine with transaxle in Park. Run engine between idle and 1500 RPM from approximately 4 minutes or until transaxle fluid is no longer being pumped out of hose.
3. Shut engine off as soon as fluid has stopped being pumped out to prevent damage to transaxle
4. Connect hoses and fill transaxle to specifications.

ADJUSTMENTS

SHIFT CONTROL LINKAGE

1. Place gearshift lever in Overdrive position. A weight of three-pound should be hung on gearshift lever to ensure lever is located firmly on Overdrive detent.
2. Loosen manual control lever-to-control cable retaining nut.
3. Move transaxle manual control lever to Overdrive position, second detent from most rearward position.
4. Tighten retaining nut to specifications. Check operation of transaxle in each range position. Ensure park mechanism and transaxle range sensor are functioning properly.

IN-VEHICLE REPAIRS

VALVE BODY, REPLACE

Oil pump and valve body are removed as an assembly.

Removal

1. Remove air cleaner assembly, then battery and battery tray.
2. Disconnect digital transaxle range sensor and transaxle harness electrical connectors and reposition engine wire harness.
3. Place digital TR sensor manual lever in Park position.
4. Install three-bar engine support D88L-6000-A or equivalent, with engine lifting brackets T70P-6000 or equivalent, and support engine assembly.
5. Remove main control cover upper retaining bolts, then raise and support vehicle.
6. Remove lefthand front wheel assembly, then lefthand front fender splash shield.
7. Remove lefthand engine support and insulator.
8. Position drain pan under transaxle main control cover and remove remaining lower transaxle main control cover bolts and transaxle main control cover and gasket.
9. Disconnect transaxle fluid temperature sensor from main control valve body and solenoid electrical connectors.
10. Remove transaxle wiring harness from chain cover.
11. Remove main control valve body retaining bolts in sequence, **Fig. 37,** then disconnect manual linkage and carefully slide pump assembly and main control valve body off of pump shaft.

Installation

1. Carefully slide pump assembly and main control valve body over pump shaft and onto chain cover.
2. **On models equipped with ABS,** hydraulic modulator may not afford enough clearance to be able to rotate pump assembly and main control valve body to complete engagement between pump shaft and pump assembly. It may be necessary to rotate crankshaft using a 7/8 inch deep well socket on crankshaft pulley to complete. Engagement pump shaft with pump assembly.
3. **On models less ABS models,** remove manual shift valve from main control valve body.
4. **On all models,** rotate main control valve body as necessary to allow engagement between pump shaft and pump assembly, if complete engagement has been obtained main control valve body should slide flush onto chain cover with little effort.
5. After full engagement between pump shaft and pump assembly has been obtained, align main control valve body to installation position and install manual shift valve.

6. Rotate pump assembly and main control valve body clockwise and connect manual valve link with manual shift valve.
7. Use valve body guide pin T86P-70100-C or equivalent, to position main control valve body and install pump assembly and main control valve body retaining bolts and tighten bolts in sequence, **Fig. 38,** to specifications.
8. Install transaxle wiring harness into chain cover, then connect transaxle fluid temperature sensor and solenoid electrical connectors to solenoids and main control valve body.
9. Install main control cover with new gasket to chain cover, then tighten side pan bolts to specifications.
10. Install lefthand engine support and insulator, then the lefthand front fender splash shield and tire assembly.
11. Lower vehicle, then remove three-bar engine support and engine lifting brackets.
12. Connect Transaxle Range (TR) sensor and transaxle harness electrical connectors and position engine wire harness.
13. Install battery tray, battery and air cleaner assembly.
14. Fill transaxle with specified transaxle fluid.
15. Start engine, move transaxle selector lever through all ranges, checking pump and valve body cover for leakage.

BRAKE-SHIFT INTERLOCK ACTUATOR/SOLENOID, REPLACE

1. Remove lower steering column shroud.
2. Remove steering column retaining nuts and lower steering column to floor.
3. Disconnect actuator/solenoid electrical connector.
4. Remove ignition/shifter interlock cable to steering column attaching screws.
5. Remove solenoid from solenoid retainer bracket.
6. Reverse procedure to install.

BRAKE-SHIFT INTERLOCK ACTUATOR, REPLACE

Column Shift

1. Remove mounting screws and upper steering column shroud.
2. Insert scratch awl into access hole located in bottom of lower steering column shroud.
3. Push in on ignition lock cylinder release pin and rotate ignition lock cylinder clockwise to Run position.
4. Remove ignition lock cylinder from steering column.
5. Remove lower shroud, then mounting screws and knee bolster from instrument panel.
6. Loosen shift indicator adjustment mechanism.
7. Disconnect shift indicator cable and

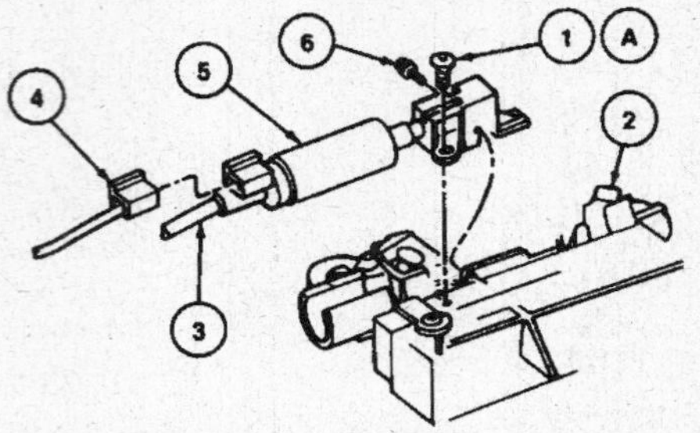

Item	Description
1	Screw
2	Steering Column Tube
3	Ignition / Shifter Interlock Cable
4	Ignition / Shifter Interlock Actuator Electrical Connector
5	Ignition / Shifter Interlock Actuator
6	Screw
A	Tighten to 2.0 N·m (17 Lb-In)

FM5029601140000X

Fig. 39 Brake-shift interlock cable replacement

adjustment mechanism from steering column lever.
8. Rotate shift indicator adjustment wheel clockwise until enough slack exists to disconnect shift indicator cable from steering column lever. Disconnect cable.
9. Rotate shift indicator adjustment wheel clockwise until shift indicator cable can be pulled through adjustment wheel and adjustment mechanism can fall away from steering column tube.
10. Remove mounting nuts and steering column absorber.
11. Remove mounting nuts and lower steering column assembly, then disconnect ignition/shifter interlock actuator electrical connector.
12. Remove Torx head screws and ignition/shifter interlock actuator from steering column tube.
13. Reverse procedure to install. Tighten Torx head bolts and steering column nuts to specifications.

Floor Shift

The ignition/shifter interlock actuator on floor shift vehicles is only serviced with ignition/shifter interlock cable. If ignition/shifter interlock actuator replacement on vehicles equipped with floor shift becomes necessary, ignition/shifter interlock cable must be replaced as an assembly.

BRAKE-SHIFT INTERLOCK CABLE, REPLACE

1. Unsnap and remove upper console bezels.
2. Disconnect ignition/shifter interlock cable conduit from bracket and pull cable from pink cam on transaxle range selector lever and housing.
3. Remove mounting screws and upper steering column shroud.
4. Insert scratch awl into access hole located in bottom of lower steering column shroud and push in on ignition lock cylinder release pin.
5. Rotate ignition lock cylinder clockwise to Run position and remove ignition lock cylinder from steering column tube.
6. Remove lower steering column shroud, then the mounting screws and knee bolster from instrument panel.
7. Remove steering column absorber mounting nuts, then steering column nuts and lower steering column.
8. Remove Torx head screws from ignition/shifter interlock actuator, then the ignition/shifter interlock cable from vehicle, **Fig. 39.**
9. Reverse procedure to install.

TRANSAXLE

REPLACE

1. Remove battery and tray.
2. Remove air cleaner.
3. Disconnect transaxle harness and transaxle range sensor electrical connectors.
4. Remove shift actuator cable fitting, then disconnect transaxle shift cable from shift cable bracket and transaxle.
5. Disconnect fluid cooler lines from transaxle.
6. Remove upper transaxle to engine bolts and transaxle to engine stud.
7. Install two engine lifting eyes from engine lift bracket set No. 014-00796 , or equivalent, to front and rear locations on engine.
8. Install three-bar engine support tool No. D88L-6000-A, or equivalent, and support engine assembly.
9. Raise and support vehicle.
10. Place suitable drain pan under transaxle.
11. Loosen lower transaxle pan retaining bolts and drain fluid from transaxle.
12. When fluid is drained to level of transaxle pan flange, remove remaining transaxle pan bolts gradually, allowing fluid to drain.
13. Remove transaxle oil pan.
14. When transaxle fluid has completely drained, reinstall transaxle pan.
15. Remove front tire and wheel assemblies.
16. Raise and support vehicle, then remove front wheels.
17. Remove and discard front axle retainer nut and washer.
18. Remove nut from stabilizer bar link at shock absorber end, then the link from shock and position aside.
19. Remove nut from lower ball joint, then loosen ball joint in lower control arm using suitable pitman arm type puller.
20. Place suitable pry bar through opening in lower control arm and under frame, then pry down on control arm to release lower ball joint
21. Remove outer CV joint from hub.
22. Do not use a hammer to drive joint from hub.
23. Do not allow driveshaft to hang from inner joint.
24. Remove inner joint from transaxle.

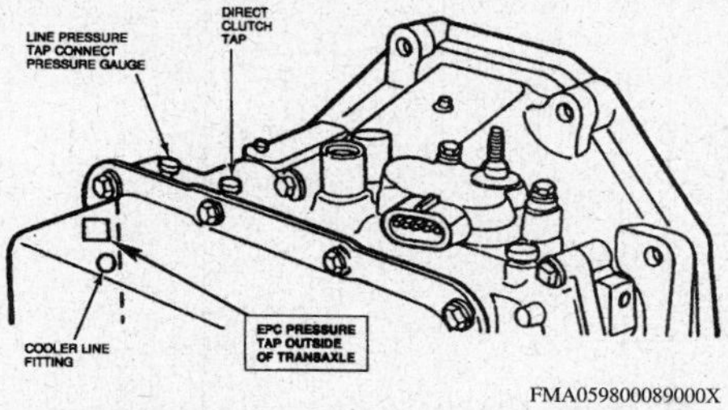

Fig. 40 EPC pressure port. 1997 Sable & Taurus

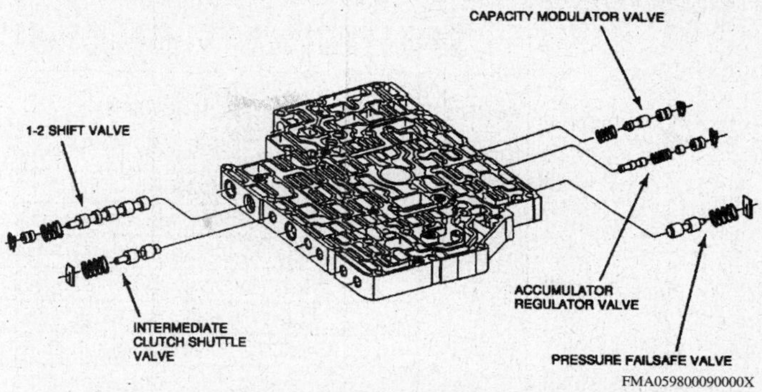

Fig. 41 Valve body inspection. 1997 Sable & Taurus

Model	Year	Engine	Engineering Part No.	Model No.	Service Part No.
Sable/ Taurus	1997	3.0L	F7DP-7000-AA	PNA-EU	F7DZ-7000-ARM
	1998	3.0L	F8DP-7000-AA	PNA-EV & EV1	N/A

Fig. 42 Transaxle application data. 1997–98 Sable & Taurus

25. Repeat procedure to remove other driveshaft
26. Disconnect heated oxygen sensor electrical connectors.
27. Remove bolts, nuts and Y-pipe assembly.
28. Disconnect starter motor electrical connectors.
29. Remove bolt, stud and starter motor.
30. Remove transaxle housing cover.
31. Position high lift transmission jack tool No. 014-00210, or equivalent, under transaxle and support transaxle.
32. Remove lower transaxle to engine mounting bolt.
33. Remove flywheel to torque converter mounting nuts.
34. Remove mounting bolts and nuts, then the rear engine support from transaxle.
35. Remove transaxle.
36. Reverse procedure to install, noting following:
    a. Tighten fasteners to specifications.
    b. Use new front axle retainer nut.
    c. Use new driveshaft bearing retainer circlip.
    d. Use new halfshaft ball joint nut.
    e. When installing driveshaft joints into transaxle use care not to damage seal.
    f. Check for proper engagement of lefthand driveshaft inner joint spline into transaxle side gears.
    g. Ensure proper engagement of transaxle shaft spline into righthand inner CV joint.
    h. Ensure bearing retainer circlips is properly seated.

TECHNICAL SERVICE BULLETINS

HARSH 3-2 DOWNSHIFT OR SHUDDER

Sable & Taurus

On some of these models there may be a harsh 3-2 downshift when coasting around a corner then accelerating away. There may also be a shudder on turns if the throttle is held to accelerate through the turn.

This condition may be caused by air entering the fluid filler pickup because of low fluid level. To correct this condition, ensure the fluid level is at the top of dipstick hatch marks.

HARSH 1-2 SHIFT

1997 Sable & Taurus

On these models, there may be harsh 1-2 upshift.

This condition may be caused by high Electronic Pressure Control (EPC) pressure in transaxle and/or main control valves sticking in valve body. To correct this condition, proceed as follows:

1. Install pressure gauge in transaxle EPC port, **Fig. 40.**
2. If EPC pressure is more than 10–20 psi, EPC solenoid is mechanically stuck or pressure failsafe valve is stuck.
3. If pressure is within specifications, remove valve body an inspect for sticking valves, metal chips and/or contamination.
4. Harsh 1-2 upshifts may be caused by 1-2 shift, valve, intermediate clutch shuttle valve, capacity modulator valve, accumulator regulator valve or pressure failsafe valve, **Fig. 41.**

HARSH SHIFTS & ENGAGEMENTS AFTER TRANSAXLE EXCHANGE

1997–98 Sable & Taurus

On these models, there may be harsh shifts and engagements after transaxle has been replaced. Diagnostic Trouble Codes (DTCs) 628, P07401 and/or P01744 may be stored.

This condition may be caused by incorrect transaxle being installed. To correct this condition, replace transaxle with correct unit, **Fig. 42.**

TIGHTENING SPECIFICATIONS

Year	Component	Torque/ Ft. Lbs.
1997–1999	Bracket Tubes To Case	84–108①
	Brake Hose Routing Clip	96①
	Brake-Shift Interlock Actuator,	17①
	Case To Chain Cover (10 mm)	84–108①
	Case To Chain Cover (13 mm)	24–26
	Case To Reverse Clutch Nut	25–35
	Case To Reverse Clutch Screw	84–108①
	Case To Stator Support	84–108①
	Chain Cover To Case (10 mm)	19–20
	Chain Cover To Case (13 mm)	25–35
	Chain Cover To Front Support (7 mm)	25–35
	Chain Cover To Front Support (13 mm)	20–22
	Control Arm To Knuckle	36–44
	Detent Spring To Chain Cover	84–108①
	Differential Brace To Case	26–37
	Dust Cover To Case	84–108①
	Dust Cover	15–21
	Engine To Case	41–50
	Filler Tube To Case	84–108①
	Governor Cover To Case	84–108①
	Insulator Bracket To Frame	40–50
	Insulator Mount To Transmission	25–33
	Insulator To Bracket	55–70
	Low/Intermediate Servo Cover To Case	84–108①
	Main Control Cover To Chain Cover	10–12
	Manual Cable Bracket	10–20
	Manual Lever To Manual Shaft	12–16
	Neutral Start Switch To Case	84–108①
	Oil Pan To Case	10–12
	Oil Pump Assembly To Main Control	84–108①
	Overdrive Servo Cover To Case	84–108①
	Park Abutment To case	20–22
	Pressure Switch To Pump Body	9–13
	Pressure Tap Plug For Chain Cover & Pump Body	9–13
	Pump Body To Chain Cover	84–108①
	Pump Cover To Pump Body	84–108①②
	Separator Plate To Main Control	84–108①
	Separator Plate To Pump Body	84–108①
	Shift Control Lever	13–17
	Solenoid To Main Control	84–108①
	Stabilizer To Control Arm	98–125
	Stabilizer U-Clamp To Bracket	60–70
	Starter	16–21
	Steering Column	10–21
	Tie Rod To Knuckle	23–35①
	Torque Converter To Flywheel	20–34
	Transaxle To Engine	39–53
	Valve Body/Solenoid To Chain Cover	84–108①

①— Tighten to minimum specified torque, then continue tightening to nearest cotter pin slot.

②— Refer to “Valve Body, Replace” for tightening sequence.

CD4E Automatic Transaxle

NOTE: On Air Bag Equipped Models, Refer To " Air Bag System Precautions" Located In The Front Of This Manual For System Disarming & Arming Procedures.

NOTE: "Electrical Symbol & Wire Color Code Identification" Located In The Front Of This Manual May Be Used As An Aid When Using Wiring Circuits Found In This Section.

NOTE: Prior To Performing Any Service Operations Listed In This Section, Consult "Technical Service Bulletins " Section For Related Information.

INDEX

PRECAUTIONS

AIR BAG SYSTEMS

Refer to "Air Bag System Precautions" in front of this manual for system disarming and arming procedures.

BATTERY GROUND CABLE

Prior to service, disconnect battery ground cable and isolate as required.

IDENTIFICATION

The CD4E automatic transaxle, **Fig. 1,** may be identified by a tag located at rear of transaxle case, on bottom of main control cover assembly.

DESCRIPTION

The CD4E transaxle is a four-speed, front wheel drive automatic overdrive unit with a three element torque converter and torque converter clutch. Its geartrain consists of a compound planetary gearset, pinion and side gear differential, chain drive and planetary gearset final drive.

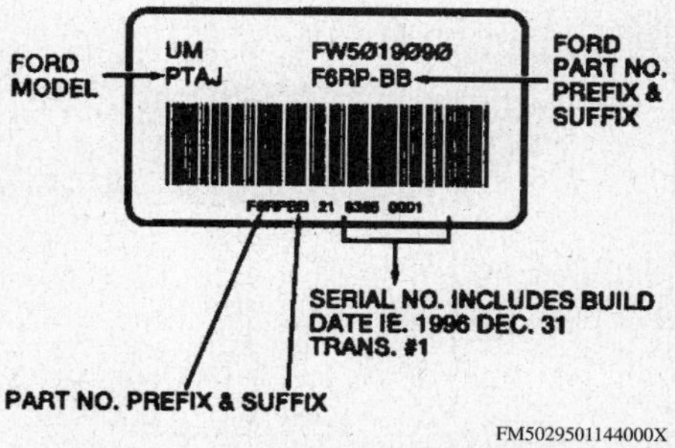

Fig. 1 CD4E identification tag

Both electronic and hydraulic control systems are employed by CD4E. Electronic functions include shift scheduling, 3-2 shift timing, coast braking, Electronic Pressure Control (EPC, for shift quality) and Torque Converter Clutch (TCC) control. Hydraulic functions include modification of line pressure and shift valve position for optimal shift feel and scheduling, modulated application of TCC, 3-2 shift timing and engine braking.

In addition, a control switch is provided which allows driver to prevent a shift into 4th (Overdrive) gear and uses engine braking to help slow vehicle.

TROUBLESHOOTING

SHIFT INTERLOCK SYSTEM

Contour & Mystique & 1999–2000 Cougar

Refer to wiring diagram, **Figs. 2 and 3,** and troubleshooting charts, **Figs. 4 and 5,** when troubleshooting shift interlock system.

Probe

Refer to wiring diagram, **Fig. 6,** and troubleshooting chart, **Fig. 7,** when troubleshooting shift interlock system.

TRANSAXLE

Refer to **Figs. 8 through 45** for transaxle troubleshooting.

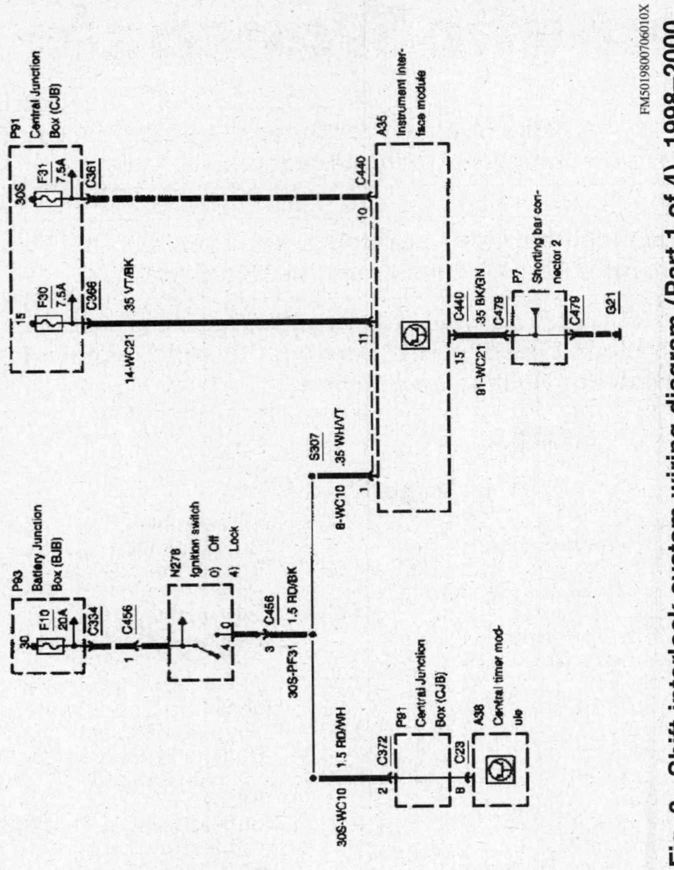

Fig. 3 Shift interlock system wiring diagram (Part 1 of 4). 1998–2000 Contour & Mystique & 1999–2000 Cougar

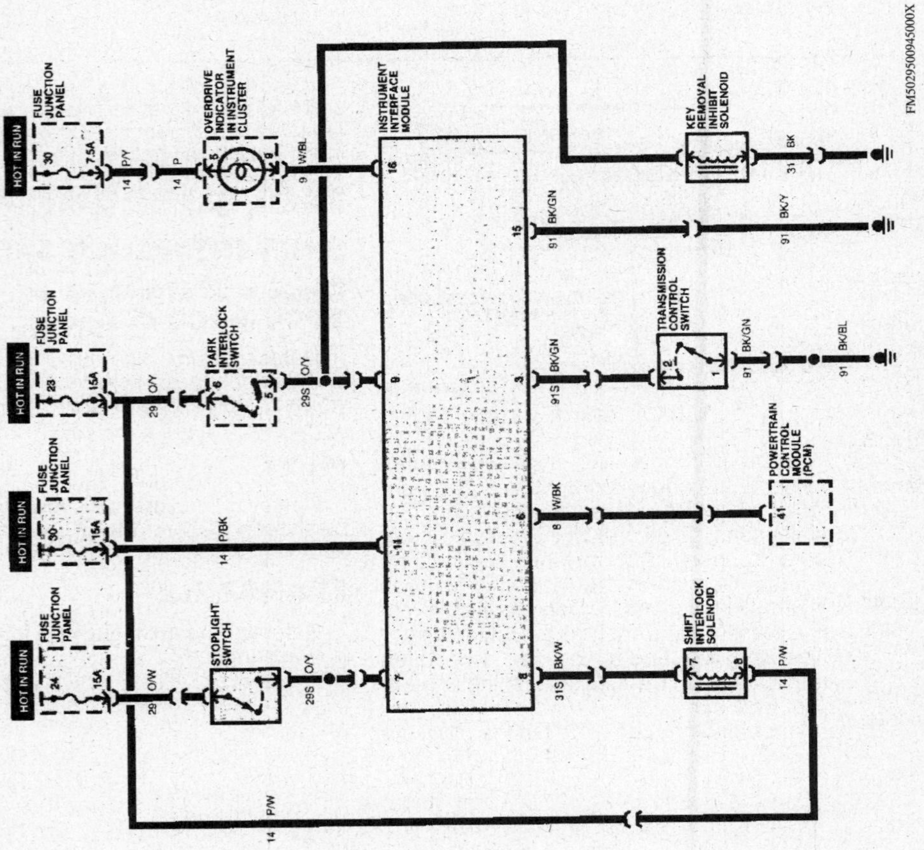

Fig. 2 Shift interlock system wiring diagram. 1997 Contour & Mystique

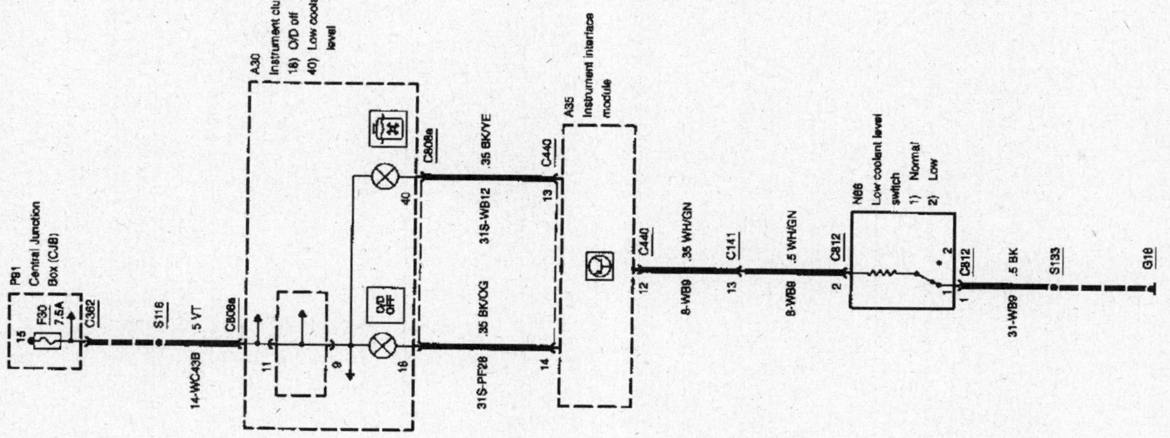

FM5019800706020X

Fig. 3 Shift interlock system wiring diagram (Part 2 of 4). 1998–2000 Contour & Mystique & 1999–2000 Cougar

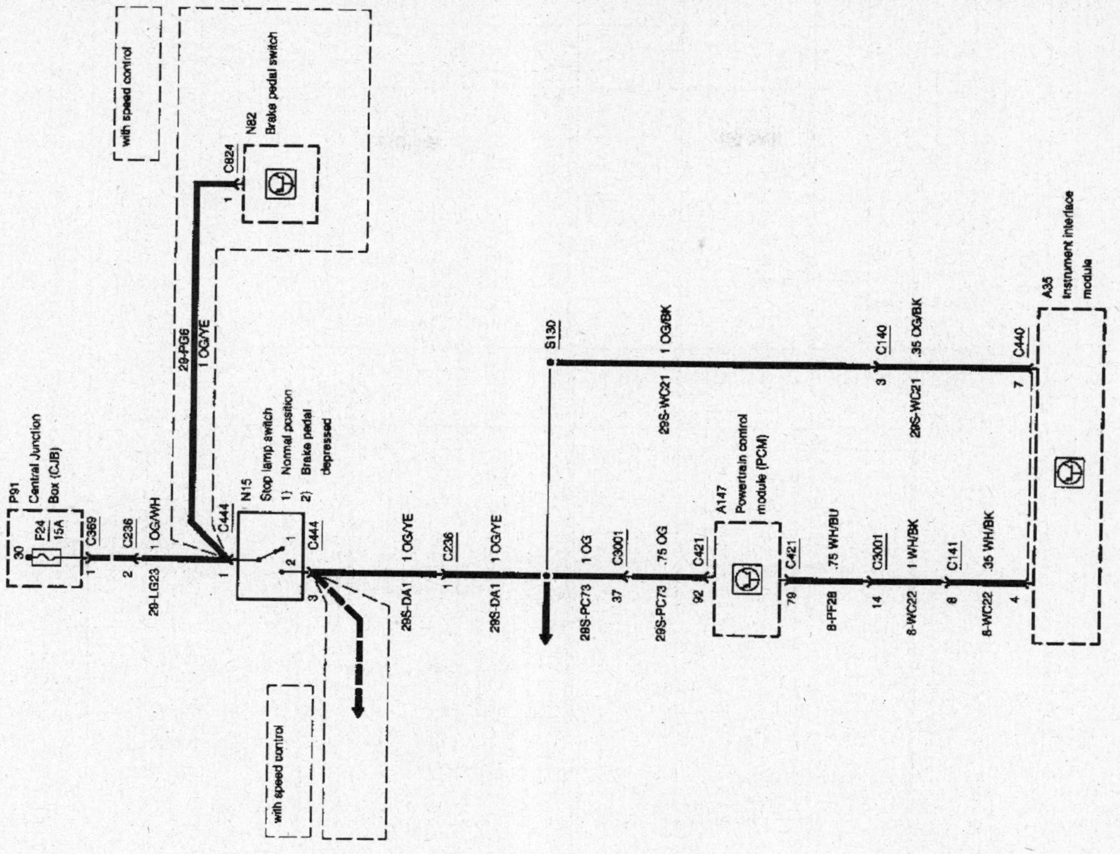

FM5019800706030X

Fig. 3 Shift interlock system wiring diagram (Part 3 of 4). 1998–2000 Contour & Mystique & 1999–2000 Cougar

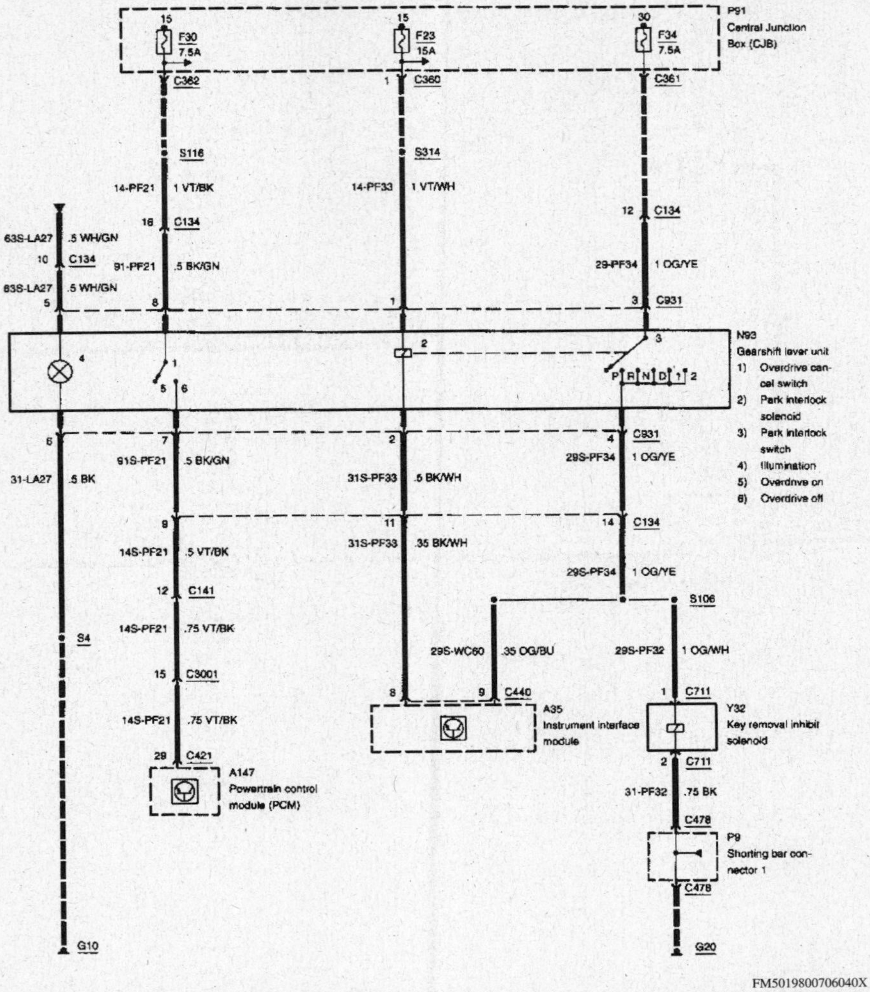

Fig. 3 Shift interlock system wiring diagram (Part 4 of 4). 1998–2000 Contour & Mystique & 1999–2000 Cougar

TROUBLESHOOTING TEST INDEX

Routine	Description	Page No.	Fig. No.
—	Shift Interlock System Troubleshooting Chart (1997 Contour & Mystique)	21-60	4
—	Shift Interlock System Troubleshooting Chart (1998–99 Contour & Mystique & 1999–2000 Cougar)	21-61	5
—	Shift Interlock System Troubleshooting Chart (Probe)	21-66	7
201/301	No Forward Engagement	21-67	8
202/302	No Reverse Engagement	21-67	9
203/303	Harsh Reverse Or Forward Engagement	21-68	10
205/304	Delayed/Soft Reverse Or Forward Engagement	21-68	11
207/307	No Forward & No Reverse Engagement	21-69	12
210/310	Some Or All Shifts Missing	21-69	13
211/311	Shift Timing Is Early/Late	21-70	14
212/312	Shift Timing Is Erratic/Hunting	21-70	15
213/313	Shift Feel Is Soft/Slipping	21-71	16
214/314	Shift Feel Is Harsh	21-71	17
215/315	No 1st Gear, Engages In Higher Gear	21-72	18
216/316	No Manual 1st Gear	21-72	19
220/320	No Automatic 1-2 Shift	21-72	20
221/321	No Automatic 2-3 Shift	21-73	21
222/322	No Automatic 3-4 Shift	21-73	22
226/326	Soft/Slipping 1-2 Only Shift	21-74	23
227/327	Soft/Slipping 2-3 Only Shift	21-74	24
228/328	Soft/Slipping 3-4 Only Shift	21-74	25
229/329	Soft/Slipping 4-3 Only Shift	21-75	26
230/330	Soft/Slipping 3-2 Only Shift	21-75	27
231/331	Soft/Slipping 2-1 Only Shift	21-76	28
232/332	Harsh 1-2 Shift Only	21-76	29
233/333	Harsh 2-3 Shift Only	21-77	30
234/334	Harsh 3-4 Shift Only	21-77	31
235/335	Harsh 4-3 Shift Only	21-78	32
236/336	Harsh 3-2 Shift Only	21-78	33
240/340	No Torque Converter Apply	21-79	34
241/341	Torque Converter Always Applied/Stalls Vehicle	21-79	35
251/351	Shift Lever Efforts High	21-79	36
252/352	External Leaks	21-80	37
253/353	Poor Vehicle Performance	21-80	38
254/354	Noise/Vibration In Forward/Reverse	21-80	39
255/355	Engine Will Not Crank	21-81	40
256/356	No Park Range	21-81	41
257/357	Transaxle Overheating	21-81	42
258/358	No Engine Braking In 1st Gear Manual Only	21-82	43
259/359	No Engine Braking In Drive w/TCS On Or Manual 2nd Position	21-82	44
262/362	Vehicle Movement w/Transaxle Range Selector In N Position	21-82	45

Test Step	Result	Action to Take
A1 CHECK SUPPLY FUSE		
• Check Fuse 30 (7.5A) located in fuse junction panel. • **Is fuse OK?**	Yes No	GO to **A3**. GO to **A2**.
A2 CHECK FOR SHORT TO GROUND		
• Turn ignition switch OFF. • Remove Fuse 30 (7.5A). • Disconnect instrument interface module connector. • Measure resistance of the Circuit 14 (P/BK) between the output terminal of Fuse 30 (7.5A) and ground. • **Is resistance greater than 10,000 ohms?**	Yes No	**REPLACE Fuse 30 (7.5A). GO to A3.** SERVICE Circuit 14 (P/BK) wire between fuse junction panel and instrument interface module.
A3 CHECK POWER SUPPLY FROM FUSE 30 (7.5A)		
• Turn ignition switch OFF. • Disconnect instrument interface module connector. • Turn ignition switch to RUN. • Measure voltage on Circuit 14 (P/BK) wire at instrument interface module connector. • **Is voltage greater than 10 volts?**	Yes No	GO to **A4**. SERVICE open Circuit 14 (P/BK) wire between fuse junction panel and instrument interface module.
A4 CHECK INSTRUMENT INTERFACE MODULE GROUND		
• Ignition switch in OFF position. • Measure the resistance between Circuit 91 (BK/GN) at the instrument interface module connector Pin 5 and ground. • **Is the resistance less than 5 ohms?**	Yes No	GO to **A5**. SERVICE Circuit 91 (BK/GN) for open. RESTORE vehicle. RETEST system.
A5 CHECK POWER SUPPLY FROM STOPLIGHT SWITCH		
• Turn ignition switch OFF. • Disconnect instrument interface module connector. • Press brake pedal. • Measure voltage on instrument interface module connector Pin 7, Circuit 29S (O/Y). • **Is voltage greater than 10 volts?**	Yes No	GO to **A7**. GO to **A6**.
A6 CHECK STOPLAMP OPERATION		
• Apply brake pedal. • Observe stoplamp operation. • **Do stoplamps operate correctly?**	Yes No	SERVICE Circuit 29S (O/Y) between stoplight switch and instrument interface module connector. RESTORE vehicle. RETEST interlock system. SERVICE stoplamp system.
A7 CHECK GEARSHIFT LEVER SWITCH INPUT		
• Ignition switch in OFF position. • Disconnect instrument interface module. • Shift to PARK position. • Turn ignition switch to RUN. • Measure voltage on instrument interface module connector Pin 9, Circuit 29S (O/BL). • Shift into any range other than PARK. • Measure voltage on instrument interface module connector Pin 9, Circuit 29S (O/BL). • **Is voltage zero volts PARK and B+ with gearshift lever in any other transmission range?**	Yes No	GO to **A8**. GO to A13.

FM5029601145010X

Fig. 4 Shift Interlock System Troubleshooting Chart (Part 1 of 3). 1997 Contour & Mystique

Test Step	Result	Action to Take
A8 CHECK INSTRUMENT INTERFACE MODULE FUNCTION		
• Turn ignition switch OFF. • Reconnect instrument interface module. • Disconnect gearshift lever unit connector located in console. • Turn ignition switch to RUN. • Apply brake pedal. • Use ohmmeter to check continuity to ground of gearshift lever connector Pin 2, Circuit 31S (BK/W). • **Is circuit continuous to ground with ignition switch in RUN, and brake pedal, and open with either brake pedal released or ignition switch OFF?**	Yes No	GO to **A11**. GO to **A9**.
A9 CHECK WIRE BETWEEN INSTRUMENT INTERFACE MODULE AND GEARSHIFT LEVER		
• Turn ignition switch OFF. • Disconnect instrument interface module connector. • Measure resistance of Circuit 31S (BK/W) wire between instrument interface module connector Pin 8 and gearshift lever connector Pin 2. • Measure resistance of Pin 8, Circuit 31S (BK/W) between instrument interface module connector and ground. • **Is resistance less than 5 ohms between instrument interface module connector and gearshift lever connector, and greater than 10,000 ohms between the instrument interface module connector and ground?**	Yes No	GO to **A10**. SERVICE Circuit 31S (BK/W). RESTORE vehicle. RETEST system.
A10 CHECK GEARSHIFT LEVER SUPPLY		
• Turn ignition switch OFF. • Disconnect gearshift lever connector. • Turn ignition switch to RUN position. • Measure voltage at Pin 1, Circuit 14 (P/W) between gearshift lever unit connector and ground. • **Is battery voltage present?**	Yes No	REPLACE gearshift lever. RESTORE vehicle. RETEST system. GO to **A11**.
A11 CHECK FUSE 23 (15A)		
• Check Fuse 23 (15A) in fuse junction panel. • **Is fuse blown (open)?**	Yes No	GO to **A12**. SERVICE open in Circuit 14 (P/W) wire to interlock solenoid.
A12 CHECK CIRCUIT 14 (P/W)		
• Remove Fuse 23 (15A). • Disconnect gearshift lever harness connector. • Measure resistance of Circuit 14 (P/W) from gearshift lever unit connector Pin 1 to ground. • **Does resistance measure 10,000 ohms or more?**	Yes No	GO to **A13**. SERVICE Circuit 14 (P/W) short to ground. RESTORE vehicle. RETEST system.
A13 CHECK POWER SUPPLY TO GEARSHIFT LEVER		
• Locate and disconnect the gearshift lever connector. • Turn ignition switch to RUN. • Measure the voltage on the gearshift lever connector Pin 3, Circuit 29 (O/Y). • **Is the voltage greater than 10 volts?**	Yes No	GO to **A16**. GO to **A14**.
A14 CHECK FUSE 34 (7.5A)		
• Turn headlamp switch to PARK position. • **Do parking lamps operate?**	Yes No	SERVICE Circuit 29 (O/Y) for open. RESTORE vehicle. RETEST system. GO to **A15**.

FM5029601145020X

Fig. 4 Shift Interlock System Troubleshooting Chart (Part 2 of 3). 1997 Contour & Mystique

Test Step		Result ▶	Action to Take
A15	CHECK CIRCUIT 29 (O / Y)		
	• Disconnect gear shift lever connector. • Remove Fuse 34 (7.5A). • Measure resistance to ground at Pin 3, Circuit 29 (O / Y) of gear shift lever connector. • **Is resistance less than 10K ohms?**	Yes ▶	SERVICE Circuit 29 (O / Y) for short to ground. RESTORE vehicle. RETEST system.
		No ▶	DIAGNOSE interior lighting.
A16	CHECK GEARSHIFT LEVER		
	• Disconnect gearshift lever connector. • Measure the resistance between Pins 3 and 4 of the gearshift lever connector with the gearshift lever in PARK. • Measure the resistance again with the gearshift lever in any range other than PARK. • **Is the resistance greater than 10K ohms in PARK and less than 5 ohms in the other ranges?**	Yes ▶	GO to **A17**.
		No ▶	REPLACE gearshift lever. RESTORE vehicle. RETEST system.
A17	CHECK CIRCUIT 29S (O / W) AND 29S (O / Y)		
	• Locate and disconnect the key removal inhibit solenoid connector. • Measure the resistance between the gearshift lever connector Pin 4, Circuit 29S (O / Y) and the key removal inhibit solenoid connector Circuit 29S (O / W). • Measure the resistance between the key removal inhibit solenoid connector Circuit 29S (O / W) and ground. • **Is the resistance less than 5 ohms between the connectors and greater than 10K ohms between the Circuit 29S (O / W) and ground?**	Yes ▶	Go to **A18**.
		No ▶	SERVICE Circuit 29S (O / W) or 29S (O / Y). RESTORE vehicle. RETEST system.
A18	CHECK GROUND 31 (BK)		
	• Measure the resistance between ground and the key removal inhibit solenoid connector Circuit 31 (BK). • **Is the resistance less than 5 ohms?**	Yes ▶	REPLACE the key removal inhibit solenoid. RESTORE vehicle. RETEST system.
		No ▶	SERVICE Circuit 31 (BK) for open. RESTORE vehicle. RETEST system.

FM5029601145030X

Fig. 4 Shift Interlock System Troubleshooting Chart (Part 3 of 3). 1997 Contour & Mystique

CONDITIONS	DETAILS/RESULTS/ACTIONS
A1 CHECK INTERIOR PANEL FUSE 23 (15A)	
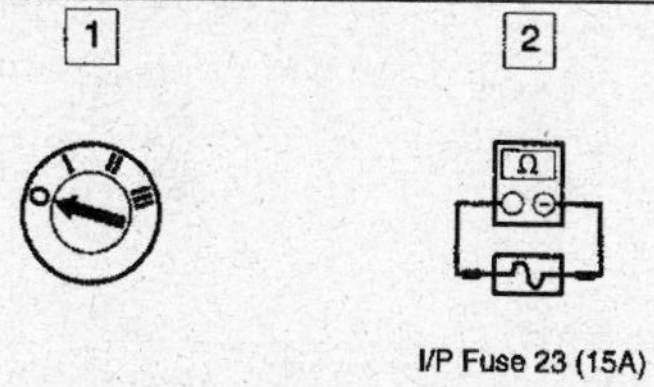	

FM5019800707010X

Fig. 5 Shift Interlock System Troubleshooting Chart (Part 1 of 10). 1998–2000 Contour & Mystique & 1999–2000 Cougar

CONDITIONS	DETAILS/RESULTS/ACTIONS
	• Is fuse OK? → **Yes** RECONNECT fuse. GO to **A2.** → **No** REPLACE fuse. If fuse fails again, CHECK circuit for short to ground. TEST the system for normal operation.
A2 CHECK INTERIOR PANEL FUSE 34 (7.5A)	
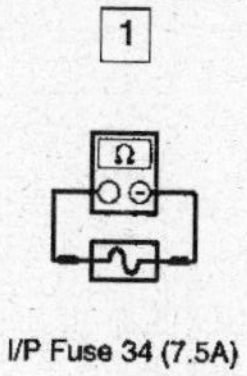	• Is fuse OK? → **Yes** RECONNECT fuse. GO to **A3.** → **No** REPLACE fuse. ATTEMPT to shift gearshift lever. If fuse fails again, CHECK circuit for short to ground. TEST the system for normal operation.
A3 CHECK INTERIOR PANEL FUSE 30 (7.5A)	
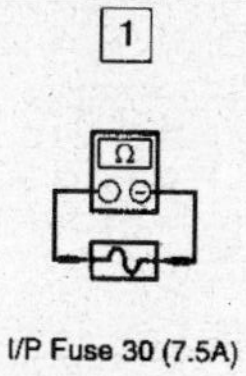	

FM5019800707020X

Fig. 5 Shift Interlock System Troubleshooting Chart (Part 2 of 10). 1998–2000 Contour & Mystique & 1999–2000 Cougar

CONDITIONS	DETAILS/RESULTS/ACTIONS
	• Is fuse OK? → **Yes** RECONNECT fuse. GO to **A4.** → **No** REPLACE fuse. If fuse fails again, CHECK circuit for short to ground. TEST the system for normal operation.
A4 CHECK POWER TO GEARSHIFT LEVER UNIT	
1 2 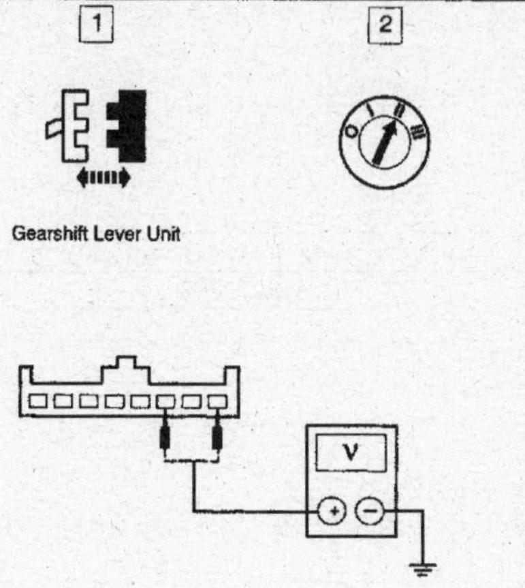	3 Measure the voltage between gearshift lever unit connector Pin 1, Pin 3, and ground. • Is voltage greater than 10 volts? → **Yes** GO to **A5.** → **No** REPAIR circuit 14 (VT/BL), circuit 14 (VT/WH), or circuit 29 (OG/YE) for open. TEST the system for normal operation.

FM5019800707030X

Fig. 5 Shift Interlock System Troubleshooting Chart (Part 3 of 10). 1998–2000 Contour & Mystique & 1999–2000 Cougar

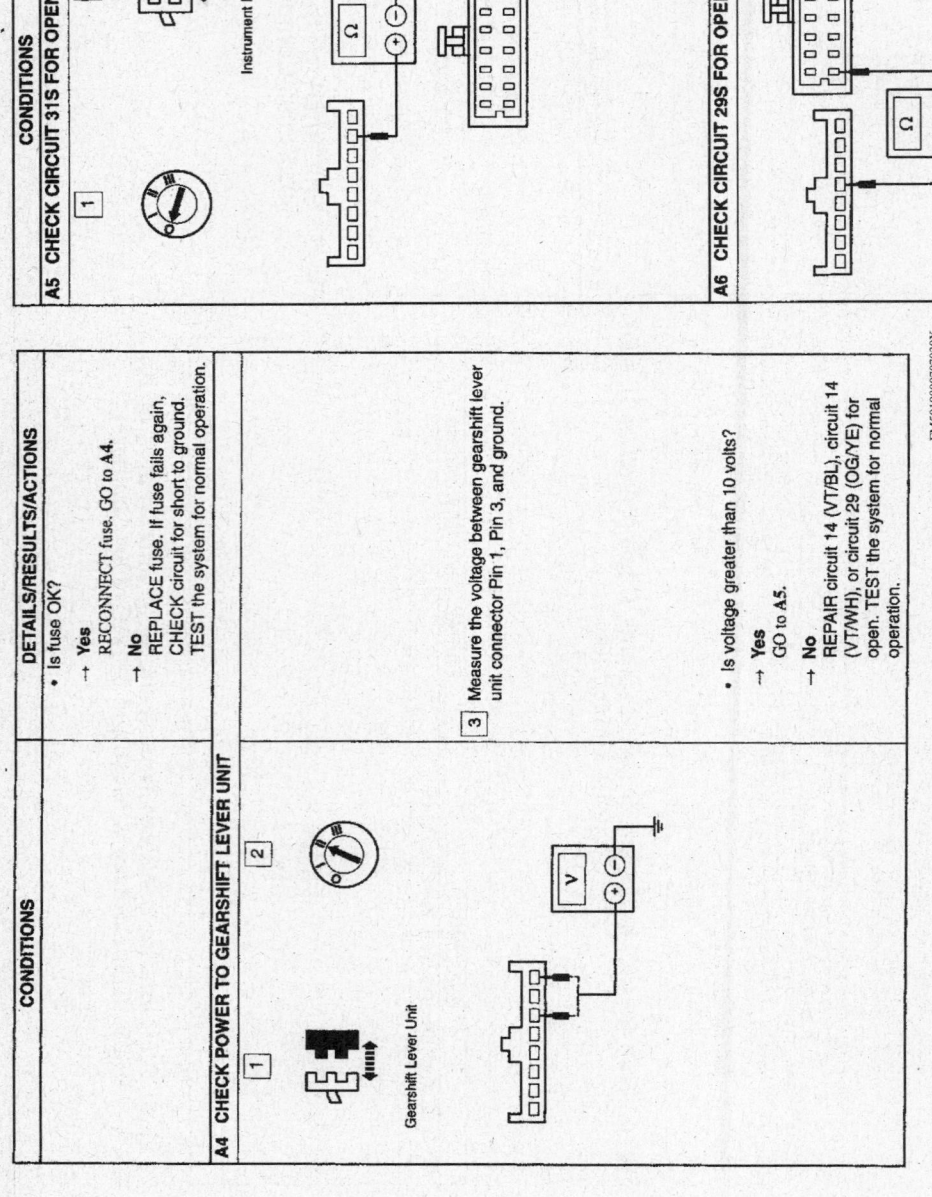

CONDITIONS	DETAILS/RESULTS/ACTIONS
A5 CHECK CIRCUIT 31S FOR OPEN	
1 2 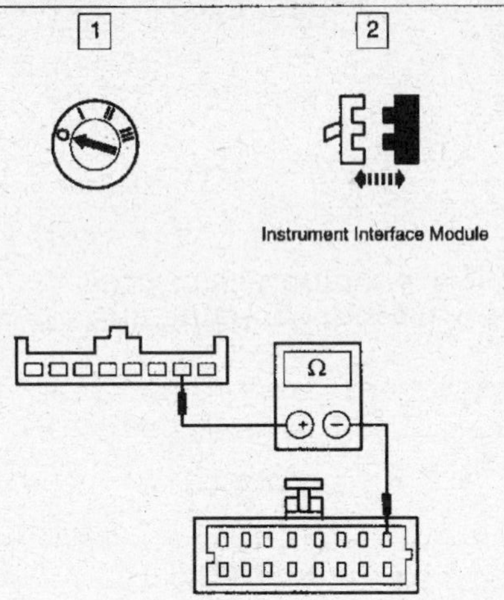	3 Measure the resistance between gearshift lever unit connector Pin 2, and instrument interface module connector Pin 8. • Is the resistance less than 5 ohms? → **Yes** GO to **A6.** → **No** REPAIR circuit 31S (BK/WH) for open. TEST the system for normal operation.
A6 CHECK CIRCUIT 29S FOR OPEN	
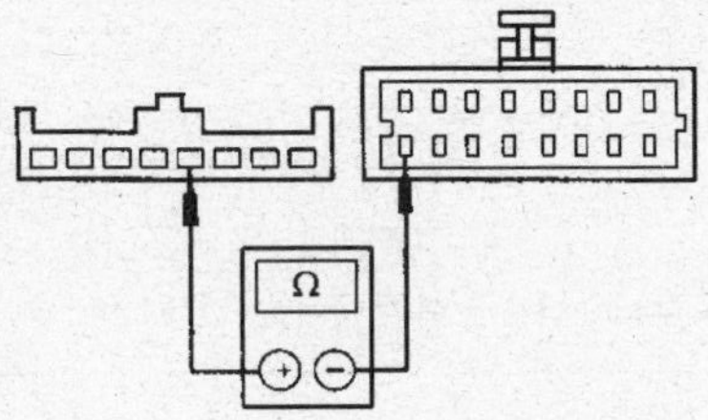	1 Measure the resistance between gearshift lever unit connector Pin 4, and instrument interface module connector Pin 9.

FM5019800707040X

Fig. 5 Shift Interlock System Troubleshooting Chart (Part 4 of 10). 1998–2000 Contour & Mystique & 1999–2000 Cougar

CONDITIONS	DETAILS/RESULTS/ACTIONS
	• Is the resistance less than 5 ohms? → **Yes** GO to **A7**. → **No** REPAIR circuit 29S (OG/YE), or circuit 29 (OG/BU) for open. TEST the system for normal operation.
A7 CHECK CIRCUIT 31S FOR SHORT TO POWER	
1 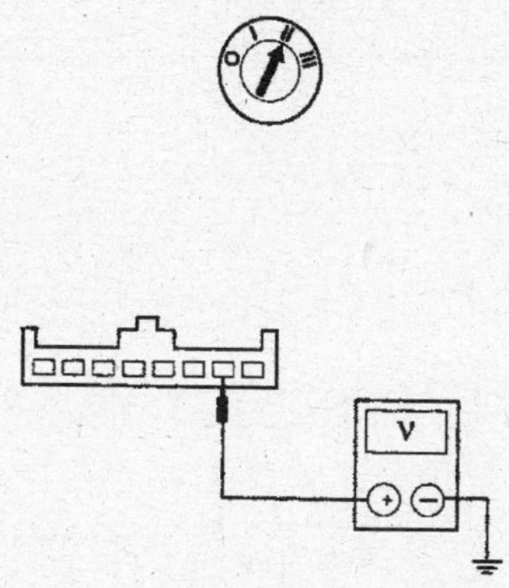	2 Measure the voltage between gearshift lever unit connector Pin 2, and ground. • Is voltage less than 1 volt? → **Yes** GO to **A8**. → **No** REPAIR circuit 31S (BK/WH) for short to power. TEST the system for normal operation.

FM5019800707050X

Fig. 5 Shift Interlock System Troubleshooting Chart (Part 5 of 10). 1998–2000 Contour & Mystique & 1999–2000 Cougar

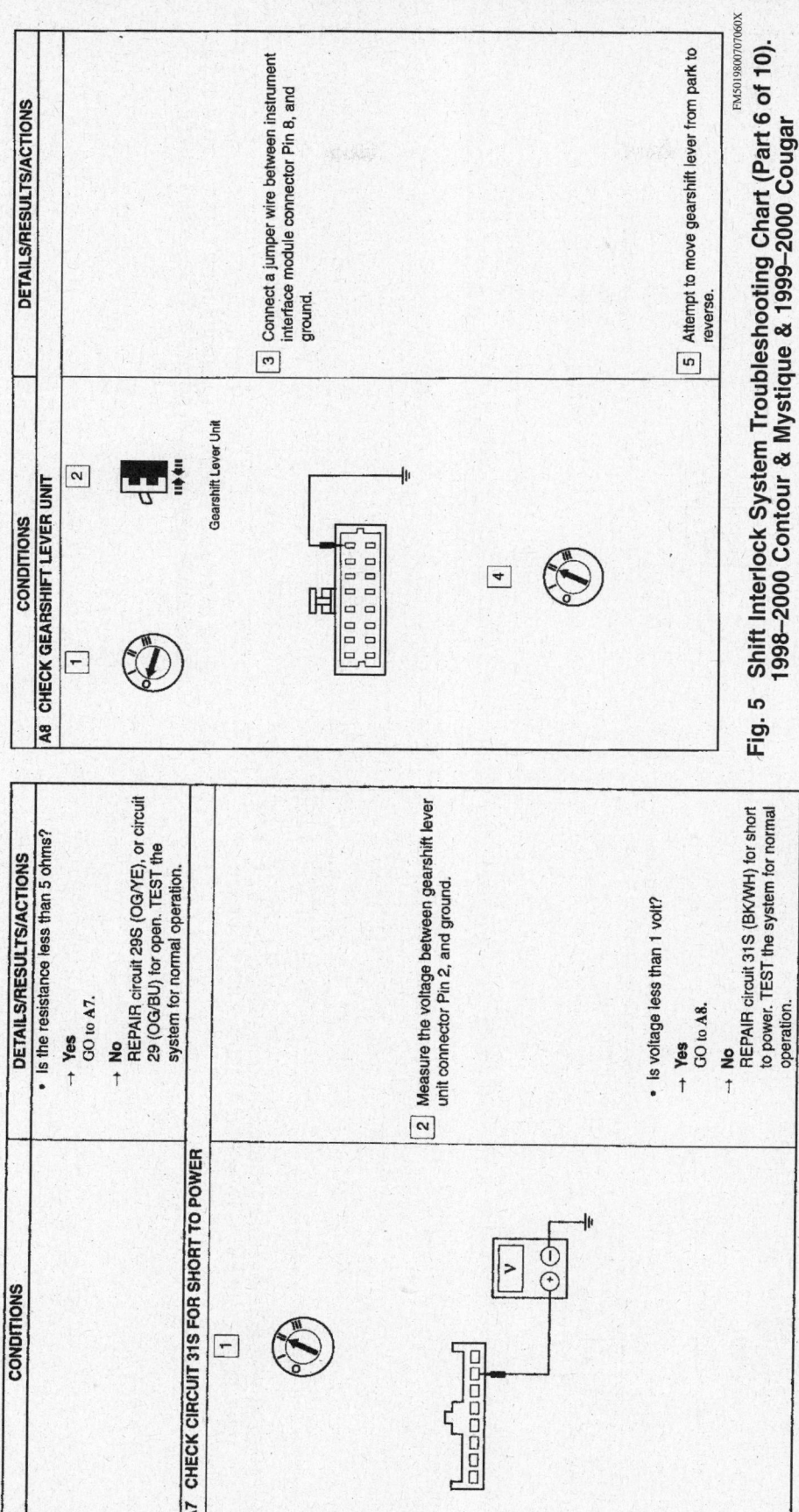

CONDITIONS	DETAILS/RESULTS/ACTIONS
A8 CHECK GEARSHIFT LEVER UNIT	
1 2 4 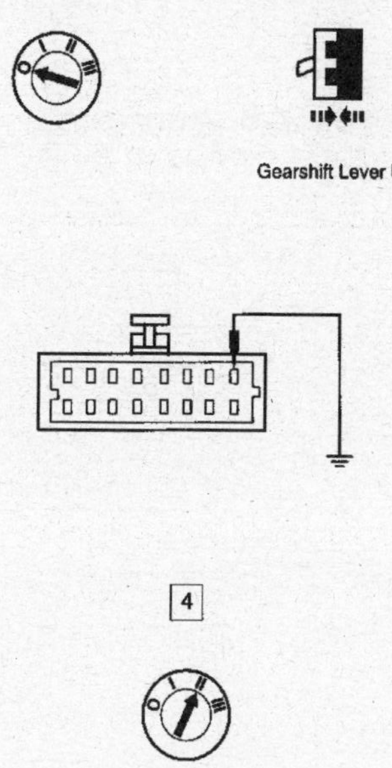 Gearshift Lever Unit	3 Connect a jumper wire between instrument interface module connector Pin 8, and ground. 5 Attempt to move gearshift lever from park to reverse.

FM5019800707060X

Fig. 5 Shift Interlock System Troubleshooting Chart (Part 6 of 10). 1998–2000 Contour & Mystique & 1999–2000 Cougar

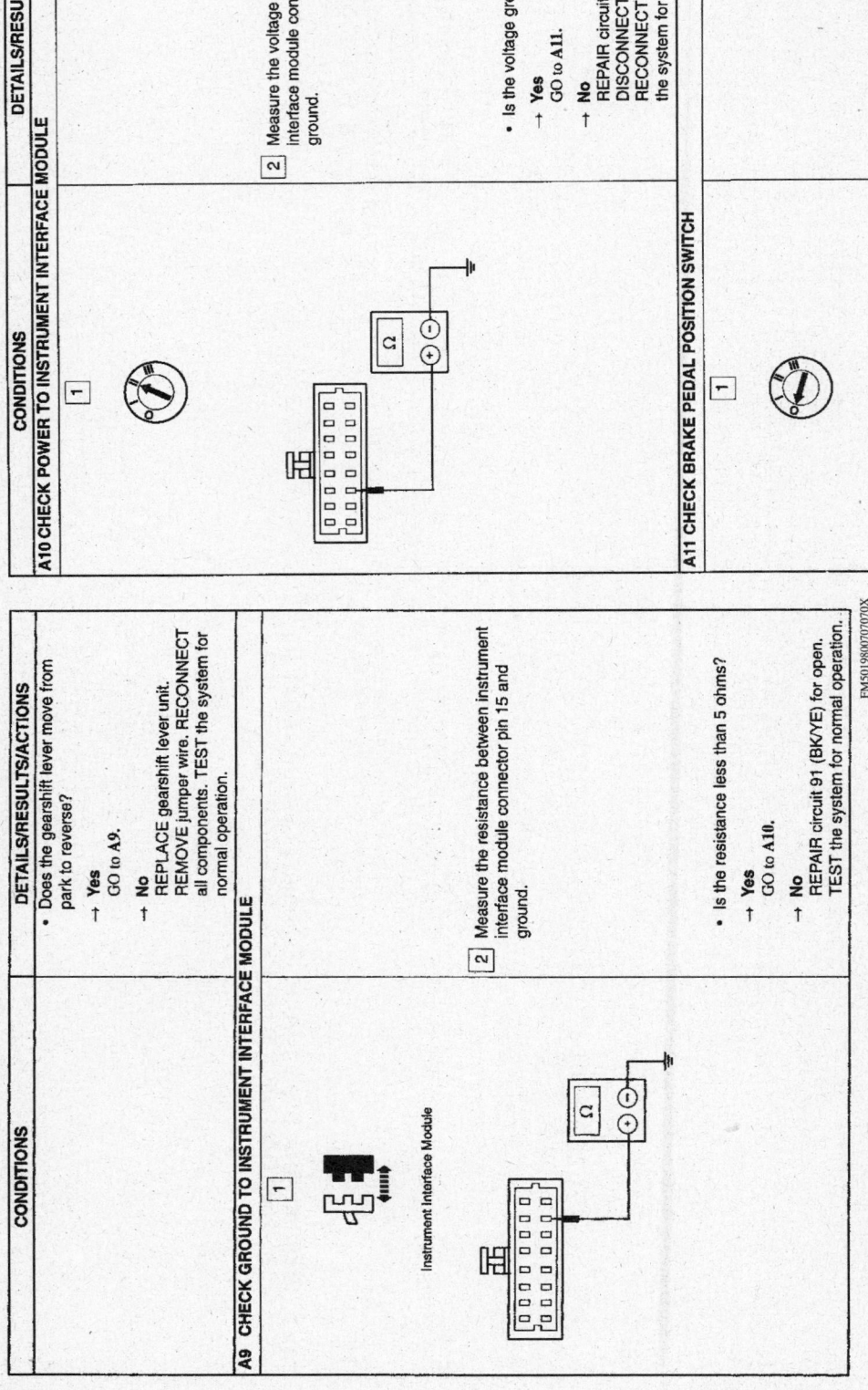

CONDITIONS	DETAILS/RESULTS/ACTIONS
	• Does the gearshift lever move from park to reverse? → **Yes** GO to **A9.** → **No** REPLACE gearshift lever unit. REMOVE jumper wire. RECONNECT all components. TEST the system for normal operation.
A9 CHECK GROUND TO INSTRUMENT INTERFACE MODULE	
1  Instrument Interface Module 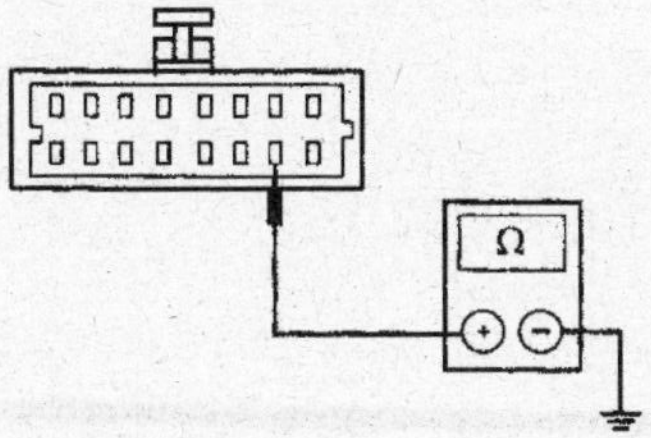	2 Measure the resistance between instrument interface module connector pin 15 and ground. • Is the resistance less than 5 ohms? → **Yes** GO to **A10.** → **No** REPAIR circuit 91 (BK/YE) for open. TEST the system for normal operation.

FM5019800707070X

Fig. 5 Shift Interlock System Troubleshooting Chart (Part 7 of 10). 1998–2000 Contour & Mystique & 1999–2000 Cougar

CONDITIONS	DETAILS/RESULTS/ACTIONS
A10 CHECK POWER TO INSTRUMENT INTERFACE MODULE	
1  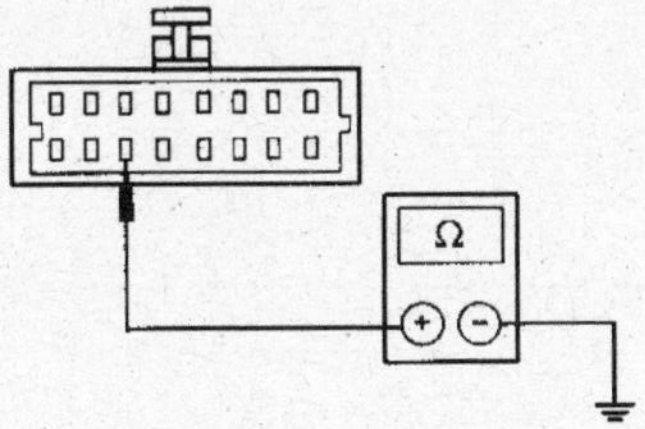	2 Measure the voltage between instrument interface module connector Pin 11, and ground. • Is the voltage greater than 10 volts? → **Yes** GO to **A11.** → **No** REPAIR circuit 14 for open. DISCONNECT breakout box. RECONNECT all components. TEST the system for normal operation.
A11 CHECK BRAKE PEDAL POSITION SWITCH	
1 	

FM5019800707080X

Fig. 5 Shift Interlock System Troubleshooting Chart (Part 8 of 10). 1998–2000 Contour & Mystique & 1999–2000 Cougar

CONDITIONS	DETAILS/RESULTS/ACTIONS
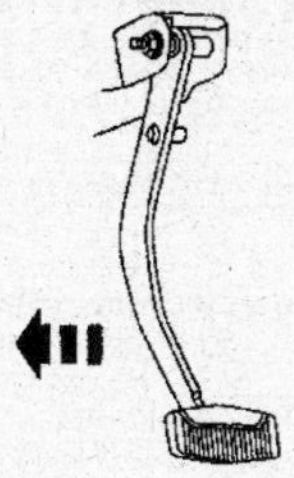	2 Depress brake pedal. 3 Observe stoplamps. • Are stoplamps on? → **Yes** GO to **A12.** → **No** Diagnose the brake pedal position switch.
A12 CHECK CIRCUIT 29S FOR OPEN	
1  PCM	2 Install breakout box to PCM wiring harness connector. Leave PCM disconnected.

FM5019800707090X

Fig. 5 Shift Interlock System Troubleshooting Chart (Part 9 of 10). 1998–2000 Contour & Mystique & 1999–2000 Cougar

CONDITIONS	DETAILS/RESULTS/ACTIONS
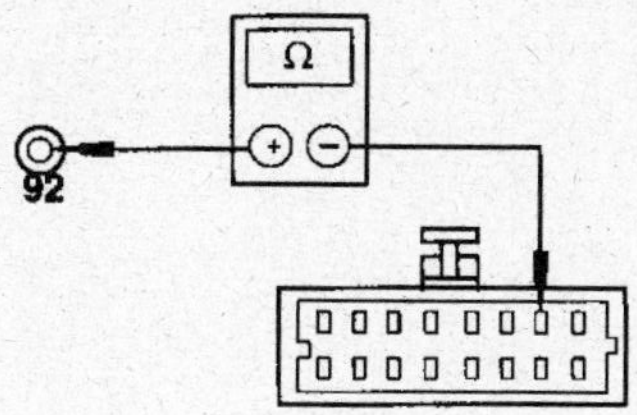	3 Measure the resistance between the breakout box Test Pin 92 and instrument interface module connector Pin 7. • Is the resistance less than 5 ohms? → **Yes** REPLACE instrument interface module. TEST the system for normal operation. → **No** REPAIR circuit 29S for open. DISCONNECT breakout box. RECONNECT all components. TEST the system for normal operation.

FM5019800707100X

Fig. 5 Shift Interlock System Troubleshooting Chart (Part 10 of 10). 1998–2000 Contour & Mystique & 1999–2000 Cougar

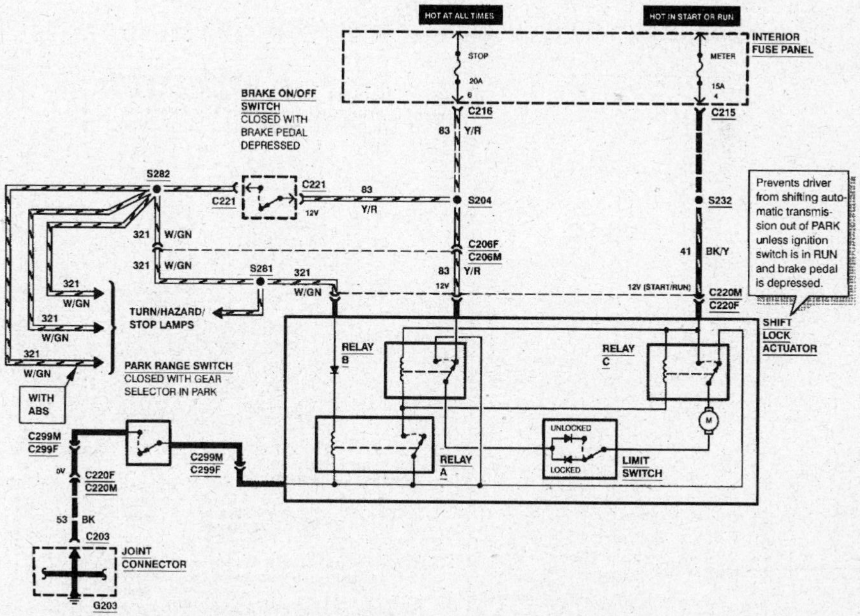

FM5029501146000X

Fig. 6 Shift interlock system wiring diagram. Probe

	Test Step	Result	Action to Take
A1	CHECK FUSES		
	• Key OFF. • Check the 15A METER and the 20A STOP fuses located in the interior fuse junction panel. • **Are the fuses OK?**	Yes No	▶ GO to **A4**. ▶ GO to **A2**.
A2	CHECK SYSTEM		
	• Key OFF. • Replace the blown fuse(s). • Key ON. • **Do(es) the fuse(s) fail again?**	Yes No	▶ GO to **A3**. ▶ GO to **A4**.

FM5029501147010X

Fig. 7 Shift Interlock System Troubleshooting Chart (Part 1 of 3). Probe

	Test Step	Result	Action to Take
A3	CHECK FOR SHORTS TO GROUND		
	• Key OFF. • Disconnect the interior fuse panelC215 and C216. • Locate and disconnect the shift lock actuator C220. 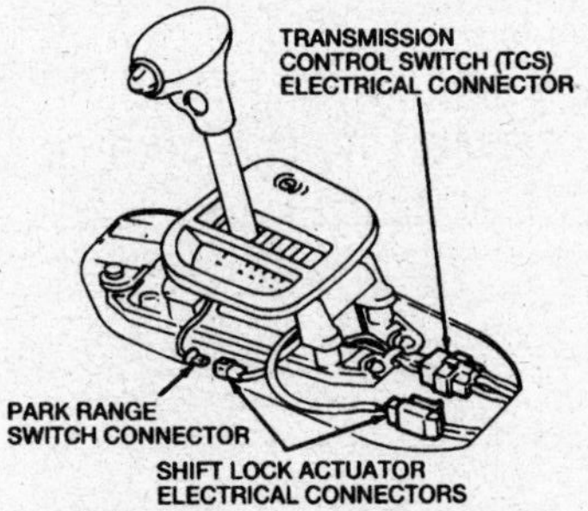 • Measure the resistance between the interior fuse junction panel C215-4, "BK/Y," C216-6, "Y/R," and ground. • **Is the resistance(s) less than 5 ohms?**	Yes No	▶ SERVICE the wire(s) in question. ▶ REPLACE the 15A METER fuse and/or the 20A STOP fuse. GO to **A4**.
A4	CHECK POWER SUPPLY TO SHIFT LOCK ACTUATOR		
	• Key OFF. • Reconnect the interior fuse panel C215 and C216, if disconnected in step A3. • Disconnect the shift lock actuator connector. • Key ON. • Measure the voltage at the shift lock actuator C220, "Y/R," and C220, "BK/Y." • **Is each voltage greater than 10 volts?**	Yes No	▶ GO to **A5**. ▶ SERVICE the wire(s) in question.
A5	CHECK BRAKE ON/OFF SIGNAL TO SHIFT LOCK ACTUATOR		
	• Key OFF. • Disconnect the shift lock actuator connector. • Depress the brake pedal. • Measure the voltage at the shift lock actuator C220, "W/GN." • **Is the voltage greater than 10 volts?**	Yes No	▶ GO to **A7**. ▶ GO to **A6**.
A6	CHECK STOPLAMP OPERATION		
	• Key OFF. • Depress the brake pedal. • **Do the stoplamps operate properly?**	Yes No	▶ SERVICE the "W/GN" wire between the Brake On/Off (BOO) switch and the shift lock actuator. ▶ diagnose the stoplamps.
A7	CHECK SHIFT LOCK ACTUATOR GROUND		
	• Key OFF. • Disconnect the shift lock actuator connector. • Measure the resistance between the shift lock actuator C299, "BK," and ground. • **Is the resistance less than 5 ohms?**	Yes No	▶ REPLACE the shift lock actuator. ▶ Go to **A8**.

FM5029501147020X

Fig. 7 Shift Interlock System Troubleshooting Chart (Part 2 of 3). Probe

	Test Step	Result	Action to Take
A8	CHECK PARK RANGE SWITCH		
	• Remove transmission control selector dial bezel. Refer to procedure in this section. Key on, engine off (KOEO). • Depress the brake pedal. • Move the transmission range selector to the 1 position. • Disconnect the park range switch C299. • Measure the resistance of the park range switch. 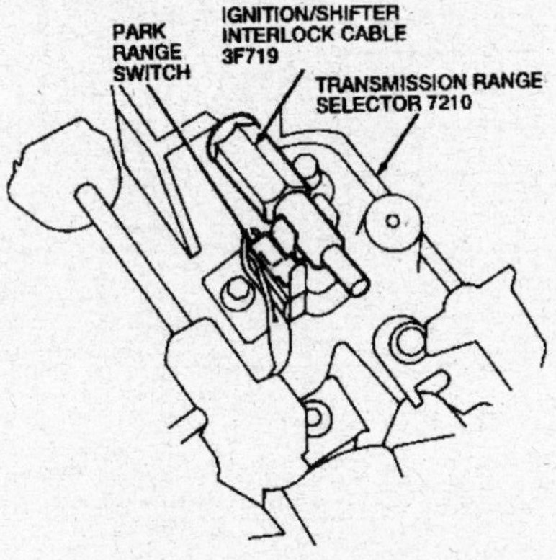 • Toggle the park range switch with your hand. • **Is the resistance less than 5 ohms when the park range switch is depressed and more than 10,000 ohms when released?**	Yes No	▶ SERVICE the "BK" wire(s). ▶ REPLACE park range switch.

FM5029501147030X

Fig. 7 Shift Interlock System Troubleshooting Chart (Part 3 of 3). Probe

Possible Component	Reference/Action
201 — ELECTRICAL ROUTINE	
No Electrical Concerns	
301 — HYDRAULIC/MECHANICAL ROUTINE	
Internal or External Shift Linkages	
• Damaged, misadjusted, misassembled	• INSPECT and SERVICE as required. ADJUST linkage. After servicing linkage, VERIFY that the transmission range (TR) sensor is properly adjusted.
Pump Assembly	
• Bolts out of torque specifications	• RETORQUE bolts to specifications.
• Gaskets damaged	• INSPECT for damage and replace.
• Porosity/cross leaks and/or ball plug missing or leaking, or a plugged hole	• INSPECT for porosity and leaks. REPLACE as required.
• Pump Support Seal Rings, No. 3 or No. 4, damaged	• INSPECT for damage. SERVICE as required.
Main Controls	
• Bolts out of torque specifications	• RETORQUE bolts to specifications.
• Gaskets damaged or leaking	• INSPECT for damage. SERVICE as required.
• Pressure Tap Plate/Gasket leaking or damaged	• INSPECT for damage. SERVICE as required.
• Separator Plates damaged	• INSPECT for damage. SERVICE as required.
• Hydraulic Passages damaged	• INSPECT for damage. SERVICE as required.
• Main Regulator Valve stuck, damaged or misassembled	• INSPECT for damage. SERVICE as required.
• Forward Accumulator leaking	• INSPECT for damage. SERVICE as required.
Forward Clutch and Coast Clutch Assembly	• PERFORM air pressure check.
• Seals or Pistons damaged	• INSPECT for damage. SERVICE as required.
• Forward Clutch Return Spring damaged	• INSPECT for damage. SERVICE as required.
• Ball Check Valve damaged	• INSPECT for mislocation, poor seating damage. REPLACE piston as required.
• Friction Elements severely damaged or worn	• CHECK for abnormal wear, damage. SERVICE as required.
• Forward/Coast/Direct clutch cylinder damaged, leaking, misassembled or binding	• INSPECT for damage. SERVICE as required.
• Cylinder to Hub Weld broken or Splines damaged	• INSPECT for damage. SERVICE as required.
Low OWC Assembly	
• Worn, damaged, misassembled	• INSPECT for damage. SERVICE as required.
Forward OWC Assembly	
• Worn, damaged, misassembled	• INSPECT for damage. SERVICE as required.
Low Intermediate Carrier	
• Damaged, misassembled	• INSPECT for damage. SERVICE as required.

FM5029801535000X

Fig. 8 Routines 201 & 302: No Forward Engagement

Possible Component	Reference/Action
202 — ELECTRICAL ROUTINE	
Powertrain Control System	
• Electrical Inputs/Outputs, Vehicle Wiring Harnesses, Powertrain Control Module, Shift Solenoid No. 1 (ON), transmission range (TR) sensor	• RUN OBD Tests. REFER to MOTOR's Domestic Transmission Manual for diagnosis. PERFORM Service Manual pinpoint tests "A and D" and the Engagement Test routine using the Transmission Tester (007-00130), CD4E Update Kit (007-00088) and TR Sensor Cable (007-0086A). SERVICE as required. CLEAR codes, ROAD TEST and RERUN OBD Tests.
302 — HYDRAULIC/MECHANICAL ROUTINE	
External Shift Linkage	
• Damaged, misadjusted	• INSPECT and SERVICE as required. After servicing linkage, VERIFY that the TR sensor is properly adjusted.
Improper Pressures	
• Low Line Pressure	• CHECK pressure at Line pressure tap. PERFORM Control Pressure and Stall Speed Tests. If pressure is low, CHECK the following possible components: Main Control, Oil Pump Assembly, Rev. Cl. Assembly, Low/Reverse Cl. Assembly.
Internal Shift Linkage	
• Damaged, misadjusted	• INSPECT and SERVICE as required. ADJUST linkage After servicing linkage, VERIFY that the TR sensor is properly adjusted.
Main Controls	
• Bolts out of torque specifications	• RETORQUE bolts to specifications.
• Gasket damaged	• INSPECT for damage and REPLACE as required.
• 1-2 Shift Valve, SS1, Main Regulator Valve, Low/Reverse Modulator Valve, Low/Reverse Accumulator Piston, Pressure Tap Plate damaged, missing, stuck, misassembled	• INSPECT for damage. SERVICE as required.
• Separator Plates damaged	• INSPECT for damage. SERVICE as required.
• Hydraulic Passages damaged	• INSPECT for damage. SERVICE as required.
Oil Pump Assembly	
• Bolts out of torque specifications	• RETORQUE bolts to specifications.
• Gasket damaged	• INSPECT for damage and REPLACE as required.
• Porosity/cross leaks/ball plug missing or leaking, plugged hole	• REPLACE oil pump assembly.
• Pump Support Seal Rings, No. 6 or No. 7, damaged	• INSPECT for damage. SERVICE as required.
Reverse Clutch Assembly	• PERFORM Air Pressure Test
• Seals - Piston damaged	• INSPECT for damage. SERVICE as required.
• Ball Check Valve damaged	• INSPECT for damage. SERVICE as required.
• Friction Elements worn, severely damaged or misassembled	• INSPECT for damage. SERVICE as required.
• Piston Return Spring damaged	• INSPECT for damage. SERVICE as required.
• Reverse Clutch Hub to Forward/Coast/Direct Hub Splines damaged	• INSPECT for damage. SERVICE as required.
Low/Reverse Clutch Assembly	• PERFORM Air Pressure Test.
• Seals or piston damaged	• INSPECT for damage. SERVICE as required.
• Friction elements worn or severely damaged	• INSPECT for damage. SERVICE as required.
• Piston Return Spring damaged	• INSPECT for damage. SERVICE as required.
• Wave Spring missing	• INSPECT for spring. SERVICE as required.
• Piston Bore damaged	• INSPECT for damage. SERVICE as required.
Forward/Coast/Direct Clutch Cylinder	
• Reverse Seal Rings damaged, missing, misassembled	• INSPECT for damage. SERVICE as required.
Case	• PERFORM Air Pressure Test.
• Reverse to Low/Reverse Clutch feeds have severe cross leakage or porosity	• INSPECT for damage. SERVICE as required.
Reverse/Overdrive Gear Set	
• Damaged	• INSPECT for damage. SERVICE as required.

FM5029801536000X

Fig. 9 Routines 202 & 302: No Reverse Engagement

Possible Component	Reference/Action
203 — ELECTRICAL ROUTINE	
Powertrain Control System • Electrical Inputs/Outputs, Vehicle Wiring Harnesses, Powertrain Control Module, EPC Solenoid, Transmission Fluid Temperature Sensor	• RUN OBD Tests. REFER to MOTOR's Domestic Transmission Manual for diagnosis. PERFORM Service Manual Pinpoint Tests "E and B" and the Engagement Test routine using the Transmission Tester (007-00130 and CD4E Update Kit 007-00088). SERVICE as required. CLEAR codes, ROAD TEST and RERUN OBD Tests.
303 — HYDRAULIC/MECHANICAL ROUTINE	
Fluid • Level • Condition	• ADJUST fluid to proper level. • INSPECT per Service Manual instructions under Fluid Condition Check.
CV Joints/ Front Wheel Driveshaft and Joint • Splines damaged	• INSPECT for damage. SERVICE as required.
Powertrain Mounts • Loose, broken, missing or misaligned • Powertrain contacting with other vehicle components	• INSPECT mounts per Service Manual procedures. SERVICE as required. • INSPECT for contact. SERVICE as required.
External Shift Linkage • Damaged, misadjusted	• INSPECT and SERVICE as required. ADJUST to linkage After servicing linkage, VERIFY that the transmission range (TR) sensor is properly adjusted.
Improper Pressures • Improper Line Pressure	• CHECK pressure at Line tap. PERFORM Control Pressure and Stall Speed Tests. If high, VERIFY Engagements at Minimum EPC using the Transmission Tester. If Line remains HIGH, CHECK the following component: Main Controls.
Internal Shift Linkages • Damaged, misadjusted	• INSPECT and SERVICE as required. ADJUST linkage. After servicing linkage, VERIFY that the TR sensor is properly adjusted.
Oil Filter and Seal Assembly • Filter/Seal damaged, plugged • Recirc Seal damaged, plugged or out of position	• REPLACE filter and seal assembly. • REPLACE Recirculation Seal.
Main Controls • Bolts out of torque specifications • Gaskets damaged • Low/Reverse Accumulator Piston and Spring (Reverse), Main Regulator Valve, Forward Accumulator Piston and Spring misassembled, stuck or damaged • EPC Solenoid stuck or damaged	• RETORQUE bolts to specifications. • INSPECT for damage and REPLACE as required. • INSPECT for damage. SERVICE as required. • INSPECT for damage, contamination. ACTIVATE solenoid using transmission tester. SERVICE as required.
Forward Cl. Assembly (Forward Only) • Forward Clutch Cylinder damaged • Piston Bore damaged • Friction Elements damaged, worn • Forward Clutch Return Spring damaged or missing • Ball Check damaged • Piston or Seals damaged	• PERFORM Air Pressure Test. • INSPECT for damage. SERVICE as required. • INSPECT for damage. SERVICE as required. • INSPECT for damage. SERVICE as required. • INSPECT for damage. SERVICE as required. • INSPECT for damage. SERVICE as required. • INSPECT for damage. SERVICE as required.
Reverse Cl. Assembly (Reverse Only) • Seals or Piston damaged • Reverse Piston damaged • Friction Elements damaged, worn, misassembled	• PERFORM Air Pressure Test. • INSPECT for damage. SERVICE as required. • INSPECT for damage. SERVICE as required. • INSPECT for damage. SERVICE as required.

FM5029801537010X

Fig. 10 Routines 203 & 303: Harsh Reverse Or Forward Engagement (Part 1 of 2)

Possible Component	Reference/Action
• Return Spring Assembly damaged, worn • Ball Check damaged, missing	• INSPECT for damage. SERVICE as required. • INSPECT for damage. SERVICE as required.
Low/Reverse Cl. Assembly (Reverse Only) • Seals or Reverse Clutch Piston damaged • Wave Spring damaged • Friction Elements damaged, worn, misassembled • Return Spring Assembly damaged, worn or misassembled • Piston Bore damaged	• PERFORM Air Pressure Test. • INSPECT for damage. SERVICE as required. • INSPECT for damage. SERVICE as required. • INSPECT for damage. SERVICE as required. • INSPECT for damage. SERVICE as required. • INSPECT for damage. SERVICE as required.
Direct Clutch Assembly (Reverse Only) • Friction Elements Severely damaged	• PERFORM Air Pressure Test. • INSPECT for damage. SERVICE as required.

FM5029801537020X

Fig. 10 Routines 203 & 303: Harsh Reverse Or Forward Engagement (Part 2 of 2)

Possible Component	Reference/Action
205 — ELECTRICAL ROUTINE	
No Electrical Concerns	
305 — HYDRAULIC/MECHANICAL ROUTINE	
Fluid • Improper level • Condition	• ADJUST fluid to proper level. • INSPECT per Service Manual instructions under Fluid Condition Check.
External Shift Linkages • Damaged, misadjusted or misassembled	• INSPECT and SERVICE as required. ADJUST linkage. After servicing linkage, VERIFY that the transmission range (TR) sensor is properly adjusted.
Improper Pressures • Low Line Pressure	• CHECK pressure at line tap. PERFORM Control Pressure and Stall Speed Tests. If pressure is low, CHECK the following possible components: Main Control, Oil Pump Assembly, Clutch Assemblies, Oil Filter and Seal Assembly, Recirculating Seal.
Internal Shift Linkages • Damaged, misadjusted or misassembled	• INSPECT and SERVICE as required. ADJUST linkage. After servicing linkage, VERIFY that the TR sensor is properly adjusted.
Oil Pump Assembly • Bolts out of torque specifications • Gaskets damaged • Porosity/cross leaks/ball plug missing or leaking, or passage blockage • Pump Support Seal Rings, No. 3 or No. 4 (Forward), or No. 6 or No. 7 (Reverse), damaged • Pump Gear/Pocket damaged • Separator Plate damaged	• RETORQUE bolts to specifications. • INSPECT for damage and REPLACE as required. • REPLACE oil pump assembly. • INSPECT for damage. SERVICE as required. • INSPECT for damage. SERVICE as required. • INSPECT for damage. SERVICE as required.
Oil Filter and Seal Assembly • Filter/Seal damaged, plugged • Recirculating Seal damage or out of position	• REPLACE filter and seal assembly. • REPLACE/RESEAT Recirculating Seal.
Main Controls • Bolts out of torque specifications • Gaskets damaged • Manual Valve, Main Regulator Valve, Low/Reverse Modulator Valve stuck, damaged or misassembled • Separator Plates damaged • Pressure Tap Plate/Gasket leaks, damaged, misassembled	• RETORQUE bolts to specifications. • INSPECT for damage and REPLACE as required. • INSPECT for damage. SERVICE as required. • INSPECT for damage. SERVICE as required. • INSPECT for damage. SERVICE as required.
Low/Reverse Cl. Assembly (Reverse Only)	• PERFORM Air Pressure Check.

FM5029801538010X

Fig. 11 Routines 205 & 305: Delayed/Soft Reverse Or Forward Engagement (Part 1 of 2)

Possible Component	Reference/Action
• Piston or Seals damaged	• INSPECT for damage. SERVICE as required.
• Friction Elements damaged, worn	• INSPECT for damage. SERVICE as required.
• Return Spring damaged	• INSPECT for damage. SERVICE as required.
• Piston Bore damaged	• INSPECT for damage. SERVICE as required.
• Excessive Cl. Pack End Clearance	• SERVICE as required.
Reverse Cl. Assembly (Reverse Only)	• PERFORM Air Pressure Check.
• Seals or Piston damaged	• INSPECT for damage. SERVICE as required.
• Check Ball damaged	• INSPECT for damage. SERVICE as required.
• Friction Elements damaged, worn	• INSPECT for damage. SERVICE as required.
• Return Spring worn, damaged	• INSPECT for damage. SERVICE as required.
• Piston Bore damaged	• INSPECT for damage. SERVICE as required.
• Excessive Cl. Pack End Clearance	• INSPECT. SERVICE as required.
Forward Clutch Assembly (Forward Only)	• PERFORM Air Pressure Check.
• Seals or Piston damaged	• INSPECT for damage. SERVICE as required.
• Ball check damaged, missing or not seating properly	• INSPECT for damage, proper seating or missing. REPLACE cylinder as required.
• Friction Elements damaged, worn or excessive end clearance	• INSPECT for damage and end clearance. SERVICE as required.
Forward/Coast/Direct Clutch Cylinder Assembly	
• Reverse Seal Ring damaged or missing	• INSPECT for damage. SERVICE as required.
• Cylinder damaged or leaking	• INSPECT for damage. SERVICE as required.

FM5029801538020X

Fig. 11 Routines 205 & 305: Delayed/Soft Reverse Or Forward Engagement (Part 2 of 2)

Possible Component	Reference/Action
• Recirculating Seal damaged or out of position	• REPLACE/RESEAT Recirculating Seal.
Main Controls	
• Bolts out of torque specifications	• RETORQUE bolts to specifications.
• Gaskets damaged	• INSPECT for damage and REPLACE as required.
• Pressure Plate/Gasket damaged or missing	• INSPECT for damage. SERVICE as required.
• Main Regulator Valve, Manual Valve stuck, damaged, plugged, missing; "Z" Link not connected	• INSPECT for damage. SERVICE as required.
Flywheel (Starter Gear)	
• Damaged, broken	• INSPECT for damage. SERVICE as required.
Torque Converter Assembly	
• Pump Drive Shaft Insert damaged	• INSPECT for damage. SERVICE as required.
• Studs broken or damaged • Splines damaged • Internal Blades damaged, broken	• INSPECT torque converter. If damaged, REPLACE.
Turbine Shaft to Forward/Coast/Direct Clutch Cylinder Hsg.	
• Splines damaged	• INSPECT for damage. SERVICE as required.
Chain and Sprocket Assembly	
• Broken, damaged	• INSPECT for damage. SERVICE as required.
Park Mechanism	
• Parking Pawl Return Spring damaged, missing or misassembled	• INSPECT for damage. SERVICE as required.
Front Wheel Drive Shafts and Joints	
• Broken or splines damaged	• INSPECT for damage. SERVICE as required.
Final Drive and Differential Assembly	
• Splines damaged	• INSPECT for damage. SERVICE as required.
• Gearset damaged	• INSPECT for damage. SERVICE as required.
Planetary Gearsets	
• Gear Teeth, Carriers, Splines damaged, or broken	• INSPECT for damage. SERVICE as required.

FM5029801539020X

Fig. 12 Routines 207 & 307: No Forward & No Reverse Engagement (Part 2 of 2)

Possible Component	Reference/Action
207 — ELECTRICAL ROUTINE	
No Electrical Concerns	
307 — HYDRAULIC/MECHANICAL ROUTINE	
Fluid	
• Improper level	• ADJUST fluid to proper level.
External Shift Linkages	
• Damaged, misadjusted or misassembled	• INSPECT and SERVICE as required. ADJUST linkage. After servicing linkage, VERIFY that the transmission range (TR) sensor is properly adjusted.
Improper Pressures	
• Low/No Line Pressure	• CHECK pressure at Line tap. PERFORM Control Pressure and Stall Speed Tests. If pressure is low, CHECK the following possible components: Oil Filter and Seal Assembly, Main Controls, Oil Pump Assembly. If OK, PROCEED to Turbine Shaft. • CHECK Flex Plate. • CHECK Torque Converter Pump Shaft and Assembly.
Internal Shift Linkages	
• Damaged, misadjusted or misassembled	• INSPECT and SERVICE as required. ADJUST linkage After servicing linkage, VERIFY that the TR sensor is properly adjusted.
Pump Assembly	
• Bolts out of torque specifications	• RETORQUE bolts to specifications.
• Gasket damaged, missing	• INSPECT for damage and REPLACE as required.
• Porosity/cross leaks or passage(s) blocked	• INSPECT for porosity, leaks, blockage. REPLACE pump as required.
• Pump Support Seal Rings missing	• INSPECT for damage. SERVICE as required.
• Pump Shaft broken, damaged	• INSPECT for damage. SERVICE as required.
Filter and Seal Assembly	
• Filter/Seal damaged, plugged, or missing	• REPLACE filter and seal assembly per Service Manual procedures.

FM5029801539010X

Fig. 12 Routines 207 & 307: No Forward & No Reverse Engagement (Part 1 of 2)

Possible Component	Reference/Action
210 — ELECTRICAL ROUTINE	
Powertrain Control System	• PERFORM Shift Point Test.
• Electrical Inputs/Outputs, Vehicle Wiring Harnesses, Powertrain Control Module, Shift Solenoids, Transmission Range (TR) sensor, throttle position sensor, VSS, TCS	• RUN OBD Tests. REFER to MOTOR's Domestic Transmission Manual for diagnosis. PERFORM Service Manual Pinpoint Tests "A and D" using Transmission Tester (007-00130 CD4E cable 007-00125) and the TR Sensor Cable (007-0086A). SERVICE as required. CLEAR codes, ROAD TEST and RERUN OBD Tests.
310 — HYDRAULIC/MECHANICAL ROUTINE	
Fluid	
• Improper level	• ADJUST fluid to proper level.
Internal and External Shift Linkages	
• Damaged, misadjusted or misassembled	• INSPECT and SERVICE as required. ADJUST linkage After servicing linkage, VERIFY that the TR sensor is properly adjusted.
Speedo Input	
• Speedometer Drive Gear damaged	• INSPECT for damage. SERVICE as required.
• Speedometer Gear damaged	• INSPECT for damage. SERVICE as required.
• Speedometer Driven Gear Retainer damaged or missing	• INSPECT for damage. SERVICE as required
Go to Reference/Action to diagnose specific missing shifts	
• Shift Concern: No 1-2 Shift	• Routine 220/320
• Shift Concern: No 2-3 Shift	• Routine 221/321
• Shift Concern: No 3-4 Shift	• Routine 222/322

FM5029801540000X

Fig. 13 Routines 210 & 310: Some Or All Shifts Missing

Possible Component	Reference/Action
211 — ELECTRICAL ROUTINE	
Powertrain Control System • Electrical Inputs/Outputs, Vehicle Wiring Harnesses, Powertrain Control Module, Throttle Position Sensor, Vehicle Speed Sensor, Transmission Fluid Temperature Sensor	• PERFORM Shift Point Test. • RUN OBD Tests. REFER to MOTOR's Domestic Transmission Manual for diagnosis. PERFORM Service Manual Pinpoint Tests "B" using the Transmission Tester (007-00130 and CD4E cable 007-00125) SERVICE as required. CLEAR codes, ROAD TEST and RERUN OBD Tests.
311 — HYDRAULIC/MECHANICAL ROUTINE	
Other • Tire Size change	• REFER to the spec. decal on door panel and VERIFY that vehicle has original equipment. Changes in tire size or speedometer gear will affect shift timing.
• Speedometer Gear broken or incorrect	• INSPECT for damage. SERVICE as required.
• Speedometer Drive Gear damaged	• INSPECT for damage. SERVICE as required.

FM5029801541000X

Fig. 14 Routines 211 & 311: Shift Timing Is Early/Late

Possible Component	Reference/Action
212 — ELECTRICAL ROUTINE	
Powertrain Control System • Engine Concerns	• REFER to MOTOR'S AEP & DM to diagnose erratic engine operations. • PERFORM Shift Point Test.
• Electrical Inputs/Outputs, Vehicle Wiring Harnesses, Powertrain Control Module, Shift Solenoids, Transmission Range (TR) Sensor, Brake On/Off Switch, TCC Solenoid, Vehicle Speed Sensor, Throttle Position Sensor, TSS, EPC, 3-2T/CCS	• RUN OBD Tests. REFER to MOTOR's Domestic Transmission Manual for diagnosis. PERFORM Service Manual Pinpoint Tests "A,C,D,F and G" using Transmission Tester (007-00130 and CD4E cable 007-00125) and the TR Sensor Cable (007-0086A). SERVICE as required. CLEAR codes, ROAD TEST and RERUN OBD Tests.
312 — HYDRAULIC/MECHANICAL ROUTINE	
Fluid • Improper level	• ADJUST fluid to proper level.
• Condition	• INSPECT Fluid Condition.
Vehicle Speed Input • Speedometer Drive Gear damaged	• INSPECT for damage. SERVICE as required.
• Speedometer Gear damaged	• INSPECT for damage. SERVICE as required.
Main Control • Bolts out of torque specifications	• RETORQUE bolts to specifications.
• Gaskets damaged	• INSPECT for damage and REPLACE as required.
• 3-2 Timing Valve, Pull-in Valve, 2-4 Accumulator, Servo Release Shuttle Valve, 3-2 Control Valve stuck, damaged, misassembled	• INSPECT for damage. SERVICE as required.
• Solenoid Screen blocked	• CLEAN or REPLACE screen.
• Separator Plates damaged, blocked	• INSPECT for damage. SERVICE as required.
• Pressure Tap Plate/Gasket damaged	• INSPECT for damage. SERVICE as required.
• SS1, SS2, 3-2T/CCS Solenoid malfunction, stuck, damaged	• ACTIVATE solenoids with tester. INSPECT for damage. SERVICE as required.
Go to Reference/Action to diagnose specific shift concern	
• Shift Concern: No 1-2 Shift	• Routine 220/320
• Shift Concern: No 2-3 Shift	• Routine 221/321
• Shift Concern: No 3-4 Shift	• Routine 222/322
• Shift Concern: Soft/Slip 1-2 Shift	• Routine 226/326
• Shift Concern: Soft/Slip 2-3 Shift	• Routine 227/327
• Shift Concern: Soft/Slip 3-4 Shift	• Routine 228/328
• Shift Concern: Soft/Slip 4-3 Shift	• Routine 229/329
• Shift Concern: Soft/Slip 3-2 Shift	• Routine 230/330
• Shift Concern: Soft/Slip 2-1 Shift	• Routine 231/331

FM5029801542010X

Fig. 15 Routines 212 & 312: Shift Timing Is Erratic/Hunting (Part 1 of 2)

Possible Component	Reference/Action
• Shift Concern: Harsh 1-2 Shift	• Routine 232/332
• Shift Concern: Harsh 2-3 Shift	• Routine 233/333
• Shift Concern: Harsh 3-4 Shift	• Routine 234/334
• Shift Concern: Harsh 4-3 Shift	• Routine 235/335
• Shift Concern: Harsh 3-2 Shift	• Routine 236/336

FM5029801542020X

Fig. 15 Routines 212 7 312: Shift Timing Is Erratic/Hunting (Part 2 of 2)

Possible Component	Reference/Action
213 — ELECTRICAL ROUTINE	
Powertrain Control System • Electrical Inputs/Outputs, Vehicle Wiring Harnesses, Powertrain Control Module, EPC Solenoid, Transmission Fluid Temperature Sensor, Throttle Position Sensor, Mass Air Flow Sensor	• PERFORM Shift Point Test. • RUN OBD Tests. REFER to MOTOR's Domestic Transmission Manual for diagnosis. PERFORM Service Manual Pinpoint Tests "B and E" using the Transmission Tester (007-00130 and CD4E cable 007-00125). SERVICE as required. CLEAR codes. ROAD TEST and RERUN OBD Tests.
313 — HYDRAULIC/MECHANICAL ROUTINE	
Fluid • Improper level • Condition	 • ADJUST fluid to proper level. • INSPECT Fluid Condition.
External Shift Linkage • Damaged, misadjusted or misassembled	• INSPECT and SERVICE as required. ADJUST linkage. After servicing linkage, VERIFY that the transmission range (TR) Sensor is properly adjusted.
Improper Pressures • Low Line Pressure	• CHECK pressures at Line tap. PERFORM Control Pressure Tests. If pressures are low or all shifts are soft/slipping, GO to Main Control, Oil Pump Assembly, Oil Filter/Seal Assembly. If pressures are OK and a specific shift is soft/slipping, REFER to the appropriate routine(s) for additional diagnosis. **Shift** 1-2, **Routine** 226/326 **Shift** 2-3, **Routine** 227/327 **Shift** 3-4, **Routine** 228/328 **Shift** 4-3, **Routine** 229/329 **Shift** 3-2, **Routine** 230/330 **Shift** 2-1, **Routine** 231/331
Internal Shift Linkage • Damaged, misadjusted or misassembled	• INSPECT and SERVICE as required. ADJUST linkage. After servicing linkage, VERIFY that the TR Sensor is properly adjusted.
Main Controls • Bolts out of torque specifications • Gaskets damaged • Main Regulator Valve, Line Modulator Valve stuck, damage or misassembled or springs missing, tangled or damaged • EPC Solenoid stuck or damaged • Separator Plates damaged, blocked • Pressure Tap Plate/Gasket damaged or missing	 • RETORQUE bolts to specifications. • INSPECT gaskets and REPLACE as required. • INSPECT for damage. SERVICE as required. • INSPECT for damage, contamination. ACTIVATE solenoid using the trans tester. SERVICE as required. • INSPECT for damage. SERVICE as required. • INSPECT for damage. SERVICE as required.
Oil Pump Assembly • Bolts out of torque specifications • Gaskets damaged	 • RETORQUE bolts to specifications. • INSPECT for damage and REPLACE as required.

FM5029801543010X

Fig. 16 Routines 213 & 313: Shift Feel Is Soft/Slipping (Part 1 of 2)

Possible Component	Reference/Action
• Porosity/cross leaks	• INSPECT for porosity. SERVICE as required.
Oil Filter/Seal Assembly • Filter/Seal damaged, plugged or missing • Recirculating Seal damaged or out of position	 • REPLACE filter and seal assembly. • REPLACE Recirculating Seal.

FM5029801543020X

Fig. 16 Routines 213 & 313: Shift Feel Is Soft/Slipping (Part 2 of 2)

Possible Component	Reference/Action
214 — ELECTRICAL ROUTINE	
Powertrain Control System • Electrical Inputs/Outputs, Vehicle Wiring Harnesses, Powertrain Control Module, EPC Solenoid, Transmission Fluid Temperature Sensor, TSS, Throttle Position Sensor, Vehicle Speed Sensor, Mass Air Flow Sensor, TCC Solenoid, Transmission Range (TR) Sensor, 3-2T/CCS	• PERFORM Torque Converter Clutch Operation Test. • RUN OBD Tests. REFER to MOTOR's Domestic Transmission Manual for diagnosis. PERFORM Service Manual Pinpoint Tests "B, C, D, E, F and G" using Transmission Tester (007-00130 and CD4E cable 007-00125) and TR Sensor Cable (007-0086A). SERVICE as required. CLEAR codes, ROAD TEST and RERUN OBD Tests.
314 — HYDRAULIC/MECHANICAL ROUTINE	
Fluid • Improper level • Condition	 • ADJUST fluid to proper level. • Inspect Fluid Condition.
CV Joint/Front Wheel Driveshafts and Joints • Damaged, loose, splines damaged	• INSPECT for damage. SERVICE as required.
Powertrain Mounts • Damaged, loose, missing	• INSPECT for damage. SERVICE as required.
Improper Pressures • High Line Pressure	• CHECK pressure at Line tap. PERFORM Control Pressure Test and Stall Speed Tests. If pressures are high or all shifts are harsh, GO to Main Control. • If pressures are OK and a specific shift is harsh. **Shift** 1-2, **Routine** 232/332 **Shift** 2-3, **Routine** 233/333 **Shift** 3-4, **Routine** 234/334 **Shift** 4-3, **Routine** 235/335 **Shift** 3-2, **Routine** 236/336 **Shift** 2-1, **Routine** 237/337
Main Controls • Bolts out of torque specifications • Gaskets damaged • Main Regulator Valve, By-Pass Valve, Line Modulator Valve stuck damaged or misassembled. Springs tangled, missing, damaged • EPC Solenoid stuck or damaged • Hydraulic Passages damaged • Separator Plate damaged, blocked	 • RETORQUE bolts to specifications. • INSPECT for damage. SERVICE as required. • INSPECT for damage. SERVICE as required. • INSPECT for damage, contamination. ACTIVATE solenoid using transmission tester. SERVICE as required. • INSPECT for damage. SERVICE as required. • INSPECT for damage. SERVICE as required.
Torque Converter Assembly NOTE: If TCC Applied during shifts • Piston damaged • Pump Support Seal No. 1 (CBY circuit) leaking, missing or damaged • Case leakage • Converter Assembly damaged	 • INSPECT for damage. SERVICE as required. • INSPECT for damage. SERVICE as required. • INSPECT for damage. SERVICE as required. • If heat stained, REPLACE converter.

FM5029801544000X

Fig. 17 Routines 214 & 314: Shift Feel Is Harsh

Possible Component	Reference/Action
215 — ELECTRICAL ROUTINE	
Powertrain Control System • Electrical Inputs/Outputs, Vehicle Wiring Harnesses, Powertrain Control Module, Shift Solenoids, Transmission Range (TR) Sensor	• RUN OBD Tests. REFER to MOTOR's Domestic Transmission Manual for diagnosis. PERFORM Service Manual Pinpoint Tests "A and D" using the Transmission Tester (007-00130 and CD4E cable 007-00125) and the TR Sensor Cable (007-0086A). SERVICE as required. CLEAR codes, ROAD TEST and RERUN OBD Tests.
315 — HYDRAULIC/MECHANICAL ROUTINE	
External Shift Linkages • Damaged, misadjusted or misassembled	• INSPECT for proper adjustment. SERVICE as required. ADJUST After servicing linkage, VERIFY that the TR Sensor is properly adjusted.
Main Controls • Bolts out of torque specifications • Gaskets damaged • Pull In Valve, Solenoid Regulator Valve, Shift Valves stuck, damaged, misassembled • Solenoid Filter Gasket damaged or misassembled • Hydraulic Passages damaged • SS1, SS2 Solenoid malfunction	• RETORQUE bolts to specifications. • INSPECT for damage and REPLACE as required. • INSPECT for damage. SERVICE as required. • INSPECT for damage. SERVICE as required. • INSPECT for damage. SERVICE as required. • ACTIVATE solenoid with transmission tester. SERVICE as required.
For diagnosis related to a specific gear, use Transmission Tester (007-00130) to determine gear	• REFER to the following routines: **Shift** 1-2, **Routine** 220/320 **Shift** 2-3, **Routine** 221/321 **Shift** 3-4, **Routine** 222/322
Mechanical • Seals, Clutches damaged, worn • Direct Clutch, 2/4 Band, 2/4 Servo damaged, stuck on	• SERVICE as required.

FM5029801545000X

Fig. 18 Routines 215 & 315: No 1st Gear, Engages In Higher Gear

Possible Component	Reference/Action
216 — ELECTRICAL ROUTINE	
Powertrain Control System • Electrical Inputs/Outputs, Vehicle Wiring Harnesses, Powertrain Control Module, Shift Solenoids, Transmission Range (TR) Sensor	• RUN OBD Tests. REFER to MOTOR's Domestic Transmission Manual for diagnosis. PERFORM Service Manual Pinpoint Tests "A and D" using the Transmission Tester (007-00130 and CD4E cable 007-00125) and the TR Sensor Cable (007-0086A). SERVICE as required. CLEAR codes, ROAD TEST and RERUN OBD Tests.
316 — HYDRAULIC/MECHANICAL ROUTINE	
Internal and External Shift Linkages • Damaged, misadjusted or misassembled	• INSPECT and SERVICE as required. ADJUST linkage After servicing linkage, VERIFY that the TR sensor is properly adjusted. REFER to Disassembly/Assembly procedures
Main Controls • Bolts out of torque specifications • Gaskets damaged • Pull-in Valve stuck, damaged • SS2 stuck "ON" • Hydraulic Passages damaged • Separator Plates damaged, blocked	• RETORQUE bolts to specifications. • INSPECT for damage and REPLACE as required. • INSPECT for damage. SERVICE as required. • ACTIVATE solenoid using transmission tester. SERVICE as required. • INSPECT for damage. SERVICE as required. • INSPECT for damage. SERVICE as required.

FM5029801546000X

Fig. 19 Routines 216 & 316: No Manual 1st Gear

Possible Component	Reference/Action
220 — ELECTRICAL ROUTINE	
Powertrain Control System • Electrical Inputs/Outputs, Vehicle Wiring Harnesses, Powertrain Control Module, Shift Solenoids, Transmission Range (TR) Sensor	• RUN OBD Tests. REFER to MOTOR's Domestic Transmission Manual for diagnosis. PERFORM Service Manual Pinpoint Tests "A and D" using the Transmission Tester (007-00130 and CD4E cable and overlay 007-00125) and the TR Sensor Cable (007-0086A). SERVICE as required. CLEAR codes, ROAD TEST and RERUN OBD Tests.
320 — HYDRAULIC/MECHANICAL ROUTINE	
Improper Pressures • Line Pressure	• CHECK pressure at Line tap. PERFORM Control Pressure and Stall Speed Tests. If not OK, CHECK the following possible components: Main Control.
Main Control • Bolts out of torque specifications • Gaskets damaged • 1-2 Shift Valve, 2-4 Accumulator, Main Regulator Valve stuck, damaged, or misassembled • SS1 malfunction • Pressure Tap Plate/Gasket damaged • Separator Plates damaged • Hydraulic Passages damaged	• RETORQUE bolts to specifications. • INSPECT for damage and REPLACE as required. • INSPECT for damage. SERVICE as required. • INSPECT for damage. ACTIVATE solenoid by using transmission tester. • INSPECT for damage. SERVICE as required. • INSPECT for damage. SERVICE as required. • INSPECT for damage. SERVICE as required.
Int/OD Band and Servo Assembly NOTE: Also No 4th gear • Seals damaged, missing • Piston damaged • Band damaged, worn • Springs damaged • Servo Rod or Rod Bore damaged	• INSPECT for damage. SERVICE as required. • INSPECT for damage. SERVICE as required. • INSPECT for damage. SERVICE as required. • INSPECT for damage. SERVICE as required. • INSPECT for damage. SERVICE as required.
Low OWC Assembly • Damaged	• INSPECT for damage. SERVICE as required.
OD/Reverse Sun Gear and Shell • Damaged, weld broken • Lugs damaged	• INSPECT for damage. SERVICE as required.
Case • Low and Intermediate Band Anchor Area damaged • Porosity/leakage in Servo Apply, Servo Release circuits	• INSPECT for damage. If damaged REPLACE the case. • INSPECT case for leakage/porosity. PERFORM Air Pressure Tests. REPLACE case as required.

FM5029801547000X

Fig. 20 Routines 220 & 320: No Automatic 1-2 Shift

Possible Component	Reference/Action
221 — ELECTRICAL ROUTINE	
Powertrain Control System	
• Electrical Inputs/Outputs, Vehicle Wiring Harnesses, Powertrain Control Module, Shift Solenoids, Transmission Range (TR) Sensor	• RUN OBD Tests. REFER to MOTOR's Domestic Transmission Manual for diagnosis. PERFORM Service Manual Pinpoint Tests "A and D" using the Transmission Tester (007-00130 and CD4E cable and overlay 007-00125) and the TR Sensor Cable (007-0086A) as outlined in this manual. SERVICE as required. CLEAR codes, ROAD TEST and RERUN OBD Tests.
321 — HYDRAULIC/MECHANICAL ROUTINE	
Improper Pressures	

FM5029801548010X

Fig. 21 Routines 221 & 321: No Automatic 2-3 Shift (Part 1 of 2)

Possible Component	Reference/Action
• Line Pressure	• CHECK pressure at Line pressure tap. PERFORM Control Pressure Tests. If NOT OK, CHECK the following possible component: Main Control.
Main Control	
• Bolts out of torque specifications	• RETORQUE bolts to specifications.
• Gasket leaks	• INSPECT for damage and REPLACE as required.
• 2-3 Shift Valve (also No 4th), Main Regulator Valve stuck, damaged, misassembled	• INSPECT for damage. SERVICE as required.
• SS2 malfunction (also no 4th)	• INSPECT for damage. ACTIVATE solenoid by using transmission tester.
• Separator Plates damaged	• INSPECT for damage. SERVICE as required.
• Pressure Tap Plate/Gasket leaks	• INSPECT for damage. SERVICE as required.
• Hydraulic Passages damaged	• INSPECT for damage. SERVICE as required.
Oil Pump Assembly	
• Bolts out of torque specifications	• RETORQUE bolts to specifications.
• Gaskets damaged	• INSPECT for damage and REPLACE as required.
• Porosity/cross leaks	• INSPECT for damage. SERVICE as required.
• Pump Support Seal Rings, No. 4 or No. 5, damaged	• INSPECT for damage. SERVICE as required.
Direct Clutch Assembly	• PERFORM Air Pressure Check.
• Seals or Piston damaged	• INSPECT for damage. SERVICE as required.
• Piston Bore damaged	• INSPECT for damage. SERVICE as required.
• Friction severely damaged, worn	• INSPECT for damage. SERVICE as required.
• Ball Check not seating properly	• INSPECT for damage. SERVICE as required.
• Return Spring Assembly damaged	• INSPECT for damage. SERVICE as required.
• Cylinder Bore/Splines damaged	• INSPECT for damage. SERVICE as required.
• Shell/Hub damaged	• INSPECT for damage. SERVICE as required.
INT/OD Servo	
• Piston or Piston Bore damaged	• INSPECT for damage. SERVICE as required.
• Rod Bore or Rod damaged, leaking	• INSPECT for damage. SERVICE as required.
Case	
• Leakage in the Servo Apply, Servo Release or Direct Clutch Circuits	• INSPECT case for damage. PERFORM Air Pressure Tests. SERVICE or REPLACE case as required.

FM5029801548020X

Fig. 21 Routines 221 & 321: No Automatic 2-3 Shift (Part 2 of 2)

Possible Component	Reference/Action
222 — ELECTRICAL ROUTINE	
Powertrain Control System	
• Electrical Inputs/Outputs, Vehicle Wiring Harnesses, Powertrain Control Module, Shift Solenoids, Transmission Range (TR) Sensor, Transmission Control Switch (TCS).	• RUN OBD Tests. REFER to MOTOR's Domestic Transmission Manual for diagnosis. PERFORM Service Manual Pinpoint Tests "A and D" using the Transmission Tester (007-00130 and CD4E cable and overlay 007-00125) and the TR Sensor Cable (007-0086A) SERVICE as required. CLEAR codes, ROAD TEST and RERUN OBD Tests.
322 — HYDRAULIC/MECHANICAL ROUTINE	
Improper Pressures	
• Line pressure	• CHECK pressure at Line tap. PERFORM Control Pressure Tests. If out of specification CHECK Main Control.
Main Control	
• Bolts out of torque specifications	• RETORQUE bolts to specifications.
• Gasket leaks	• INSPECT for damage and REPLACE as required.
• 3-4 Shift Valve, Main Regulator Valve stuck, damaged or misassembled	• INSPECT for damage. SERVICE as required.
• SS1 malfunction (also No 1st)	• ACTIVATE solenoid using transmission tester. SERVICE as required.

FM5029801549010X

Fig. 22 Routines 222 & 322: No Automatic 3-4 Shift (Part 1 of 2)

Possible Component	Reference/Action
• Separator Plates damaged or Orifice blocked	• INSPECT for damage. SERVICE as required.
INT/OD Band and Servo Assembly	
NOTE: Also No 2nd gear	
• INT/OD Band damaged, worn	• INSPECT for damage. SERVICE as required.
• Servo Rod or Rod Bore damaged	• INSPECT for damage. SERVICE as required.
• Servo Piston or Cover damaged or leaking	• INSPECT for damage. SERVICE as required.
• Springs damaged	• INSPECT for damage. SERVICE as required.
Coast Clutch Assembly	
• Seals damaged, missing	• INSPECT for damage. SERVICE as required.
• Piston damaged	• INSPECT for damage. SERVICE as required.
• Friction severely damaged, worn	• INSPECT for damage. SERVICE as required.
• Check ball severely damaged	• INSPECT for damage. SERVICE as required.
Forward OWC Assembly	
• Damaged	• INSPECT for damage. SERVICE as required.
Case (Also No 2nd gear)	
• Band anchor damaged	• INSPECT for damage. PERFORM Air Pressure Checks. SERVICE as required.
• Servo Apply and Servo Release circuits leaking	• INSPECT for damage. SERVICE as required.

FM5029801549020X

Fig. 22 Routines 222 & 322: No Automatic 3-4 Shift (Part 2 of 2)

Possible Component	Reference/Action
226 — ELECTRICAL ROUTINE	
Powertrain Control System	
• Electrical Inputs/Outputs, Vehicle Wiring Harnesses, Powertrain Control Module, EPC Solenoid, Transmission Fluid Temperature Sensor	• RUN OBD Tests. PERFORM Stall Speed Tests. PERFORM Pinpoint Tests "B and E" using the Transmission Tester (007-00130 and CD4E cable and overlay 007-00125) and the TR Sensor (MLP Sensor) Cable (007-0086A). SERVICE as required. CLEAR codes, ROAD TEST and RERUN OBD Tests.
326 — HYDRAULIC/MECHANICAL ROUTINE	
Main Control	
• Bolts out of torque specifications	• RETORQUE bolts to specifications.
• Gaskets damaged	• INSPECT for damage and REPLACE as required.
• 2-4 Accumulator Piston Plug and Seal (also soft 3-4 shift), Main Regulator Valve, Line Modulator Valve (also soft 3-4 shift) stuck, damaged or misassembled	• INSPECT for damage. SERVICE as required.
• Hydraulic Passages damaged	• INSPECT for damage. SERVICE as required.
• Pressure Tap Plate/Gasket damaged	• INSPECT for damage. SERVICE as required.
• Separator Plates damaged	• INSPECT for damage. SERVICE as required.
INT/OD Band and Servo Assembly	
• Piston, Seals or Piston Bore damaged, missing	• INSPECT for damage. SERVICE as required.
• Servo Rod or Rod Bore damaged	• INSPECT for damage. SERVICE as required.
• Intermediate/Overdrive Band and/or Reverse Clutch Drum Assembly worn, damaged or misassembled	• INSPECT for damage. SERVICE as required.
• Springs damaged	• INSPECT for damage. SERVICE as required.
• Servo Cover and Seal damaged	• INSPECT for damage. SERVICE as required.
Forward OWC Assembly (slips in 1st)	
• Not holding or damaged	• INSPECT for damage. SERVICE as required.
Forward Clutch Assembly (slips in 1st)	• PERFORM Air Pressure Check.
• Seals damaged	• INSPECT for damage. SERVICE as required.
• Return Spring damaged	• INSPECT for damage. SERVICE as required.
• Friction elements damaged	• INSPECT for damage. SERVICE as required.
• Pump Supports Seals No. 3, No. 4 damaged	• INSPECT for damage. SERVICE as required.
Low OWC Assembly	

FM5029801550010X

Fig. 23 Routines 226 & 326: Soft/Slipping 1-2 Only Shift (Part 1 of 2)

Possible Component	Reference/Action
• Not overrunning, damaged	• INSPECT for damage. SERVICE as required.
Low Reverse Clutch Assembly	
• Friction elements severely damaged	• INSPECT for damage. SERVICE as required.
Case	
• Band Anchor damaged	• INSPECT for damage. If damaged REPLACE the case.
• Porosity/Leakage in Servo Apply, Servo Release circuits	• INSPECT case for leakage/porosity. PERFORM Air Pressure checks. REPLACE case as required.

FM5029801550020X

Fig. 23 Routines 226 & 326: Soft/Slipping 1-2 Only Shift (Part 2 of 2)

Possible Component	Reference/Action
227 — ELECTRICAL ROUTINE	
Powertrain Control System	
• Electrical Inputs/Outputs, Vehicle Wiring Harnesses, Powertrain Control Module, EPC Solenoid, Transmission Fluid Temperature Sensor	• RUN OBD Tests. REFER to MOTOR's Domestic Transmission Manual for diagnosis. PERFORM Service Manual Pinpoint Tests "B and E" using the Transmission Tester (007-00130 and CD4E cable and overlay 007-00125). SERVICE as required. CLEAR codes, ROAD TEST and RERUN OBD Tests. PERFORM Stall Speed Test.
327 — HYDRAULIC/MECHANICAL ROUTINE	
Oil Pump Assembly	
• Bolts out of torque specifications	• RETORQUE bolts to specifications.
• Gaskets damaged	• INSPECT for damage and REPLACE as required.
• Pump support seals No. 4 or No. 5 damaged, missing	• INSPECT for damage. SERVICE as required.
Main Control	
• Bolts out of torque specifications	• RETORQUE bolts to specifications.
• Gasket Leaks	• INSPECT for damage and REPLACE as required.
• Line Modulator Valve (also soft 1-2 and 3-4 shifts), Servo Release Shuttle Valve stuck damaged or misassembled	• INSPECT for damage. SERVICE as required.
• Hydraulic passages damaged	• INSPECT for damage. SERVICE as required.
• Separator Plates damaged	• INSPECT for damage. SERVICE as required.
• Pressure Tap Plate/Gasket leaks	• INSPECT for damage. SERVICE as required.
Direct Clutch Assembly	• PERFORM Air Pressure Check.
• Seals or Piston damaged	• INSPECT for damage. SERVICE as required.
• Piston bore damaged	• INSPECT for damage. SERVICE as required.
• Friction element damaged, worn or excessive end clearance	• INSPECT for damage. CHECK end clearance. SERVICE as required.
• Check ball not seating properly	• INSPECT for damage. SERVICE as required.
• Return Spring Assembly damaged	• INSPECT for damage. SERVICE as required.
INT/OD Servo	
• Piston or piston bore damaged	• INSPECT for damage. SERVICE as required.
• Servo rod or rod bore damaged	• INSPECT for damage. SERVICE as required.
Case	
• Leakage in the Servo Apply, Servo Release or Direct Clutch circuits	• INSPECT case for damage. PERFORM Air Pressure Checks. SERVICE or REPLACE case as required.
Forward OWC Assembly	
• Not holding, damaged	• INSPECT for damage. SERVICE as required.

FM5029801551000X

Fig. 24 Routines 227 & 327: Soft/Slipping 2-3 Only Shift

Possible Component	Reference/Action
228 — ELECTRICAL ROUTINE	
Powertrain Control System	

FM5029801552010X

Fig. 25 Routines 228 & 328: Soft/Slipping 3-4 Only Shift (Part 1 of 2)

Possible Component	Reference/Action
• Electrical Inputs/Outputs, Vehicle Wiring Harnesses, Powertrain Control Module, EPC Solenoids, Transmission Fluid Temperature Sensor	• RUN OBD Tests. REFER to MOTOR's Domestic Transmission Manual for diagnosis. PERFORM Service Manual Pinpoint Tests "B and E" using the Transmission Tester (007-00130 and CD4E cable and overlay 007-00125). SERVICE as required. CLEAR codes, ROAD TEST and RERUN OBD Tests.
328 — HYDRAULIC/MECHANICAL ROUTINE	
Main Control	
• Bolts out of torque specifications	• RETORQUE bolts to specifications.
• Gasket Leaks	• INSPECT for damage and REPLACE as required.
• Line Modulator Valve, 2-4 Accumulator Valve Plug and Seal (also soft 1-2 shift), stuck, damaged or misassembled	• INSPECT for damage. SERVICE as required.
• Pressure Tap Plate/Gasket leaks	• INSPECT for damage. SERVICE as required.
• Hydraulic passages damaged	• INSPECT for damage. SERVICE as required.
• Separator Plates damaged or Orifice blocked	• INSPECT for damage. SERVICE as required.
INT/OD Band and Servo Assembly	
• INT/OD Band and/or Reverse Clutch Drum Assembly worn, damaged or misassembled	• INSPECT for damage. SERVICE as required.
• Piston, Seals or Piston Bore damaged, missing	• INSPECT for damage. SERVICE as required.
• Servo Cover or Seal damaged	• PERFORM Air Pressure Check. INSPECT for damage. SERVICE as required.
• Servo Rod or Rod Bore damaged	• INSPECT for damage. SERVICE as required.
• Springs damaged	• INSPECT for damage. SERVICE as required.
Direct Clutch Assembly NOTE: May also have 3rd gear slip	• PERFORM Air Pressure Check.
• Seals damaged, missing	• INSPECT for damage. SERVICE as required.
• Piston damaged	• INSPECT for damage. SERVICE as required.
• Check Ball damaged, missing or leaking	• INSPECT for damage. SERVICE as required.
• Return Spring damaged	• INSPECT for damage. SERVICE as required.
• Friction elements damaged	• INSPECT for damage. SERVICE as required.
Case	
• Band anchor damaged	• INSPECT for damage. SERVICE as required.
• Servo apply and servo release circuits leaking	• INSPECT for damage. PERFORM Air Pressure Check. SERVICE as required.

FM5029801552020X

Fig. 25 Routines 228 & 328: Soft/Slipping 3-4 Only Shift (Part 2 of 2)

Possible Component	Reference/Action
• Servo Return Spring broken	• INSPECT for damage. SERVICE as required.
• Servo Rod damaged	• INSPECT for damage. SERVICE as required.
• Piston seal damaged	• INSPECT for damage. SERVICE as required.
Direct Clutch Assembly	• PERFORM Air Pressure Check.
• Seals damaged, missing	• INSPECT for damage. SERVICE as required.
• Piston damaged	• INSPECT for damage. SERVICE as required.
• Check Ball damaged, missing or leaking	• INSPECT for damage. SERVICE as required.
• Return Spring damaged	• INSPECT for damage. SERVICE as required.
• Friction elements damaged	• INSPECT for damage. SERVICE as required.
Forward/Coast Clutch Assembly	• PERFORM Air Pressure Check.
• Seals damaged, missing	• INSPECT for damage. SERVICE as required.
• Piston damaged	• INSPECT for damage. SERVICE as required.
• Friction Elements worn, damaged	• INSPECT for damage. SERVICE as required.
• Check Ball not functioning	• INSPECT for damage. SERVICE as required.
• Forward Clutch Piston and Return Spring damaged	• INSPECT for damage. SERVICE as required.
Case	
• Porosity/cross leaks in Servo Apply, Servo Release, Direct Clutch circuits	• INSPECT for damage. PERFORM Air Pressure Check. SERVICE as required.

FM5029801553020X

Fig. 26 Routines 229 & 329: Soft/Slipping 4-3 Only Shift (Part 2 of 2)

Possible Component	Reference/Action
229 — ELECTRICAL ROUTINE	
Powertrain Control System	
• Electrical Inputs/Outputs, Vehicle Wiring Harnesses, Powertrain Control Module, EPC Solenoid, Vehicle Speed Sensor, Mass Air Flow Sensor, Throttle Position Sensor	• RUN OBD Tests. REFER to MOTOR's Domestic Transmission Manual for diagnosis. PERFORM Service Manual Pinpoint Test "E" using the Transmission Tester (007-00130 and CD4E cable and overlay 007-00125). SERVICE as required. CLEAR codes, ROAD TEST and RERUN OBD Tests.
329 — HYDRAULIC/MECHANICAL ROUTINE	
Main Control	
• Bolts out of torque specifications	• RETORQUE bolts to specifications.
• Gasket Leaks	• INSPECT for damage and REPLACE as required.
• Servo Release Shuttle Valve, Main Regulator Valve stuck, damaged, or misassembled	• INSPECT for damage. SERVICE as required.
• Hydraulic passages damaged	• INSPECT for damage. SERVICE as required.
• Pressure Tap Plate/Gasket leaks, or damaged	• INSPECT for damage. SERVICE as required.
• Separator Plates damaged, blocked	• INSPECT for damage. SERVICE as required.
INT/OD Band and Servo Assembly	
• INT/OD Band and Reverse Clutch Drum Assembly worn, damaged or misassembled	• INSPECT for damage. SERVICE as required.

FM5029801553010X

Fig. 26 Routines 229 & 329: Soft/Slipping 4-3 Only Shift (Part 1 of 2)

Possible Component	Reference/Action
230 — ELECTRICAL ROUTINE	
Powertrain Control System	
• Electrical Inputs/Outputs, Vehicle Wiring Harnesses, Powertrain Control Module, EPC Solenoid, Throttle Position Sensor, Vehicle Speed Sensor, Mass Air Flow Sensor, 3-2 Timing/Coast Clutch Solenoid (3-2T/CCS)	• RUN OBD Tests. REFER to MOTOR's Domestic Transmission Manual for diagnosis. PERFORM Service Manual Pinpoint Tests "E and G" using the Transmission Tester (007-00130 and CD4E cable and overlay 007-00125. SERVICE as required. CLEAR codes, ROAD TEST and RERUN OBD Tests.
330 — HYDRAULIC/MECHANICAL ROUTINE	
Main Control	
• Bolts out of torque specifications	• RETORQUE bolts to specifications.
• Gasket damaged	• INSPECT for damage and REPLACE as required.
• 3-2 Timing Valve, Solenoid Regulator Valve, 3-2 Control Valve stuck, damaged or misassembled	• INSPECT for damage. SERVICE as required.
• 3-2T/CCS Solenoid malfunction	• ACTIVATE solenoid using Transmission Tester (007-00130 and CD4E cable and overlay 007-00125). SERVICE as required.
• Pressure Tap Plate/Gasket leaks or damaged	• INSPECT for damage. SERVICE as required.
• Separator Plates damaged, blocked	• INSPECT for damage. SERVICE as required.
Direct Clutch Assembly	• PERFORM Air Pressure Check.
• Return Spring damaged, broken	• INSPECT for damage. SERVICE as required.
• Friction elements damaged, worn	• INSPECT for damage. SERVICE as required.
• Ball check not releasing	• INSPECT for damage. SERVICE as required.
• Piston or seal damaged	• INSPECT for damage. SERVICE as required.
INT/OD Band and Servo Assembly	
• INT/OD Band and/or Reverse Clutch Drum Assembly worn, damaged or misassembled	• INSPECT for damage. SERVICE as required.
• Servo piston damaged	• INSPECT for damage. SERVICE as required.
• Servo Return and Cushion Springs damaged, misassembled	• INSPECT for damage. SERVICE as required.
• Springs damaged, misassembled	• INSPECT for damage. SERVICE as required.
• Servo rod bent, damaged	• INSPECT for damage. SERVICE as required.
Oil Pump Assembly	
• Bolts out of torque specifications	• RETORQUE bolts to specifications.
• Gaskets damaged	• INSPECT for damage and REPLACE as required.
• Porosity/cross leaks	• INSPECT for porosity, leaks. REPLACE pump as required.

FM5029801554010X

Fig. 27 Routines 230 & 330: Soft/Slipping 3-2 Only Shift (Part 1 of 2)

Possible Component	Reference/Action
• Pump Support seal rings No. 4, 5, 6 damaged or misassembled • Forward to direct passage leaks	• INSPECT for damage. SERVICE as required. • INSPECT for damage. SERVICE as required.
Case • Band Anchor damaged • Leakage in servo apply/release circuits • Case bore damaged (Servo Rod)	• INSPECT for damage. SERVICE as required. • INSPECT for leaks. PERFORM Air Pressure Check. SERVICE as required. • INSPECT for damage. SERVICE as required.

FM5029801554020X

Fig. 27 Routine 230 & 330: Soft/Slipping 3-2 Only Shift (Part 2 of 2)

Possible Component	Reference/Action
232 — ELECTRICAL ROUTINE	
Powertrain Control System • Electrical Inputs/Outputs, Vehicle Wiring Harnesses, Powertrain Control Module, EPC Solenoids, Transmission Fluid Temperature Sensor, Vehicle Speed Sensor, TSS, Throttle Position Sensor, Mass Air Flow Sensor, TCC solenoid, Transmission Range (TR) Sensor	• RUN OBD Tests. REFER to MOTOR's Domestic Transmission Manual for diagnosis. PERFORM Service Manual Pinpoint Tests "B, C, D, E and F" with Transmission Tester (007-00130 and CD4E cable and overlay 007-00125) and the TR Sensor Cable. SERVICE as required. CLEAR codes, ROAD TEST and RERUN OBD Tests. PERFORM Stall Speed Tests.
332 — HYDRAULIC/MECHANICAL ROUTINE	
Main Control • Bolts out of torque specifications • Gasket leaks • 2-4 Accumulator Valve, 3-2 Control Valve (also harsh 3-4 shift) stuck, damaged or misassembled • Separator plates damaged • Hydraulic passages damaged	• RETORQUE bolts to specifications. • INSPECT for damage and REPLACE as required. • INSPECT for damage. SERVICE as required. • INSPECT for damage. SERVICE as required. • INSPECT for damage. SERVICE as required.
Pump • Bolts out of torque specifications • Gasket damaged • Pump support seal rings No. 3 or No. 4 damaged • Porosity/cross leaks	• RETORQUE bolts to specifications. • INSPECT for damage and REPLACE as required. • INSPECT for damage. SERVICE as required. • INSPECT for damage. SERVICE as required.

FM5029801556010X

Fig. 29 Routines 232 & 332: Harsh 1-2 Shift Only (Part 1 of 2)

Possible Component	Reference/Action
231 — ELECTRICAL ROUTINE	
Powertrain Control System • Electrical Inputs/Outputs, Vehicle Wiring Harnesses, Powertrain Control Module, EPC Solenoid, Transmission Fluid Temperature Sensor, Throttle Position Sensor, Mass Air Flow Sensor	• RUN OBD Tests. REFER to MOTOR's Domestic Transmission Manual for diagnosis. PERFORM Service Manual Pinpoint Tests "B and E" using the Transmission Tester (007-00130 and CD4E cable and overlay 007-001215). SERVICE as required. CLEAR codes, ROAD TEST and RERUN OBD Tests.
331 — HYDRAULIC/MECHANICAL ROUTINE	
Pump • Gaskets damaged • Porosity/cross leaks • Pump support seals No. 3 or 4 leaking, misassembled, damaged	• INSPECT for damage and REPLACE as required. • INSPECT for leak/porosity. REPLACE as required. • INSPECT for damage. SERVICE as required.
Intermediate OD Servo and Band Assembly • Servo Piston damaged • Servo Piston Return Spring damaged	• INSPECT for damage. SERVICE as required. • INSPECT for damage. SERVICE as required.
Forward Clutch Assembly • Piston or Seals damaged • Friction Elements damaged	• PERFORM Air Pressure Check. • INSPECT for damage. SERVICE as required. • INSPECT for damage. SERVICE as required.
Low OWC • Damaged, not holding	• INSPECT for damage. SERVICE as required.

FM5029801555000X

Fig. 28 Routines 231 & 331: Soft/Slipping 2-1 Only Shift

Possible Component	Reference/Action
INT/OD Band and Servo Assembly • Cushion return springs damaged • INT/OD Band damaged, worn • INT/OD Band and/or Reverse Clutch Drum Assembly worn, damaged or misassembled	• INSPECT for damage. SERVICE as required. • INSPECT for damage. SERVICE as required. • INSPECT for damage. SERVICE as required.
Forward Clutch Assembly • Seals damaged • Return Spring damaged • Friction elements damaged	• PERFORM Air Pressure Check. • INSPECT for damage. SERVICE as required. • INSPECT for damage. SERVICE as required. • INSPECT for damage. SERVICE as required.
Case • Band Anchor Area damaged	• INSPECT for damage. If damaged, REPLACE the case.

FM5029801556020X

Fig. 29 Routines 232 & 332: Harsh 1-2 Shift Only (Part 2 of 2)

Possible Component	Reference/Action
233 — ELECTRICAL ROUTINE	
Powertrain Control System	
• Electrical Inputs/Outputs, Vehicle Wiring Harnesses, Powertrain Control Module, EPC Solenoid, Transmission Range (TR) Sensor, Vehicle Speed Sensor, Transmission Fluid Temperature Sensor, Mass Air Flow Sensor, TCC solenoid, TSS	• RUN OBD Tests. REFER to MOTOR's Domestic Transmission Manual for diagnosis. PERFORM Service Manual Pinpoint Tests "B, C, D, E and F" with Transmission Tester (007-00130 and CD4E Update kit 007-00088) and the TR Sensor (MLP Sensor) Cable. SERVICE as required. CLEAR codes, ROAD TEST and RERUN OBD Tests.
333 — HYDRAULIC/MECHANICAL ROUTINE	
Main Control	
• Bolts out of torque specifications	• RETORQUE bolts to specifications.
• Gasket leaks	• INSPECT for damage and REPLACE as required.
• Line Modulator Valve (also 1-2 and 3-4 harsh shift), Servo Release Shuttle Valve stuck, damaged or misassembled	• INSPECT for damage. SERVICE as required.
• Separator plates damaged	• INSPECT for damage. SERVICE as required.
• Hydraulic passages damaged	• INSPECT for damage. SERVICE as required.
Pump	
• Bolts out of torque specifications	• RETORQUE bolts to specifications.
• Gasket damaged	• INSPECT for damage and REPLACE as required.
• Porosity/cross leaks	• INSPECT for damage. SERVICE as required.
• Pump support seal rings No. 4 or No. 5 damaged	• INSPECT for damage and REPLACE as required.
Direct Clutch Assembly	• PERFORM Air Pressure Check.
• Piston or piston bore damaged	• INSPECT for damage. SERVICE as required.
• Friction elements damaged, worn	• INSPECT for damage. SERVICE as required.
• Ball check not seating properly	• INSPECT for damage. SERVICE as required.
• Return Spring damaged	• INSPECT for damage. SERVICE as required.
• Clutch cylinder splines damaged	• INSPECT for damage. SERVICE as required.
INT/OD Servo	
• Servo Piston or Piston Bore damaged	• INSPECT for damage. SERVICE as required.
• Servo rod damaged	• INSPECT for damage. SERVICE as required.
Case	
• Leakage in the Servo Apply, Servo Release or Direct Clutch circuits	• INSPECT case for damage. PERFORM Air Pressure Check. SERVICE or REPLACE case as required.
• Servo Rod Bore damaged	• INSPECT for damage. SERVICE as required.

FM5029801557000X

Fig. 30 Routines 233 & 333: Harsh 2-3 Shift Only

Possible Component	Reference/Action
234 — ELECTRICAL ROUTINE	
Powertrain Control System	

FM5029801558010X

Fig. 31 Routines 234 & 334: Harsh 3-4 Shift Only (Part 1 of 2)

Possible Component	Reference/Action
• Electrical Inputs/Outputs, Vehicle Wiring Harnesses, Powertrain Control Module, EPC Solenoid, Vehicle Speed Sensor, 3-2T/CCS, Transmission Range (TR) Sensor, Transmission Fluid Temperature Sensor, TSS, Throttle Position Sensor, Mass Air Flow Sensor, TCC solenoid	• RUN OBD Tests. REFER to MOTOR's Domestic Transmission Manual for diagnosis. PERFORM Service Manual Pinpoint Tests "B, C, D, E, F and G" with Transmission Tester (007-00130 and CD4E cable and overlay 007-00125) and the TR Sensor Cable as outlined in this manual. SERVICE as required. CLEAR codes, ROAD TEST and RERUN OBD Tests.
334 — HYDRAULIC/MECHANICAL ROUTINE	
Main Control	
• Bolts out of torque specifications	• RETORQUE bolts to specifications.
• Gasket leaks	• INSPECT for damage and REPLACE as required.
• Line Modulator Valve (also 1-2 and 2-3 harsh shift), 3-2 Control Valve, 2-4 Accumulator Valve, Coast Clutch Valve, stuck, damaged or misassembled	• INSPECT for damage. SERVICE as required.
• Hydraulic passages damaged	• INSPECT for damage. SERVICE as required.
• Separator plates damaged, blocked	• INSPECT for damage. SERVICE as required.
Pump	
• Bolts out of torque specifications	• RETORQUE bolts to specifications.
• Gasket damaged	• INSPECT for damage and REPLACE as required.
• Porosity/cross leaks	• INSPECT for damage. SERVICE as required.
• Coast Clutch Teflon seals damaged	• INSPECT for damage and REPLACE as required.
INT/OD Band and Servo Assembly	
• INT/OD Band and Reverse Clutch Drum Assembly, damaged, worn, misassembled	• INSPECT for damage. SERVICE as required.
• Servo Piston or Cover damaged or leaking	• INSPECT for damage. SERVICE as required.
• Springs damaged	• INSPECT for damage. SERVICE as required.
Coast Clutch Assembly	
• Piston or Seals damaged, missing	• INSPECT for damage. SERVICE as required.
• Friction elements damaged, worn	• INSPECT for damage. SERVICE as required.
• Check Ball not functioning	• INSPECT for damage. SERVICE as required.
Direct Clutch Assembly	• PERFORM Air Pressure Check.
• Piston or seals damaged, missing	• INSPECT for damage. SERVICE as required.
• Check Ball damaged, missing or leaking	• INSPECT for damage. SERVICE as required.
• Return Spring damaged	• INSPECT for damage. SERVICE as required.
• Friction elements damaged	• INSPECT for damage. SERVICE as required.
• Clutch Cylinder splines damaged	• INSPECT for damage. SERVICE as required.
Case	
• Band Anchor damaged	• INSPECT for damage. SERVICE as required.

FM5029801558020X

Fig. 31 Routines 234 & 334: Harsh 3-4 Shift Only (Part 2 of 2)

Possible Component	Reference/Action
235 — ELECTRICAL ROUTINE	
Powertrain Control System	
• Electrical Inputs/Outputs, Vehicle Wiring Harnesses, Powertrain Control Module, EPC Solenoid, Transmission Range (TR) Sensor, Vehicle Speed Sensor, 3-2T/CCS, Transmission Fluid Temperature Sensor, TSS, Throttle Position Sensor, Mass Air Flow Sensor, TCC solenoid	• RUN OBD Tests. Refer to MOTOR'S Domestic Transmission Manual. PERFORM Service Manual Pinpoint Tests "B, C, D, E, F and G" with Transmission Tester (007-00130 and CD4E cable and overlav 007-00125) and the TR Sensor Cable SERVICE as required. CLEAR codes, ROAD TEST and RERUN OBD Tests.
335 — HYDRAULIC/MECHANICAL ROUTINE	
Main Control	
• Bolts out of torque specifications	• RETORQUE bolts to specifications.
• Gasket leaks	• INSPECT for damage and REPLACE as required.
• Servo Release Shuttle Valve, 3-2 Timing/Coast Clutch Valve stuck, damaged or misassembled	• INSPECT for damage. SERVICE as required.
• Hydraulic passages damaged	• INSPECT for damage. SERVICE as required.

FM5029801559010X

Fig. 32 Routines 235 & 335: Harsh 4-3 Shift Only (Part 1 of 2)

Possible Component	Reference/Action
• Separator plates damaged, blocked	• INSPECT for damage. SERVICE as required.
Pump	
• Bolts out of torque specifications	• RETORQUE bolts to specifications.
• Porosity/cross leaks, Seal Rings damaged, missing or leaking ball plug	• INSPECT pump for damage. SERVICE or REPLACE pump as required.
• Gasket damaged	• INSPECT for damage and REPLACE as required.
• Pump Support Seal Rings No. 2, 3, 4, or No. 5 (Coast and Direct Clutch circuits) damaged	• INSPECT for damage. SERVICE as required.
INT/OD Band and Servo Assembly	
• Servo Rod bent, damaged	• INSPECT for damage. SERVICE as required.
• Servo Return Spring Broken	• INSPECT for damage. SERVICE as required.
Coast Clutch Assembly	
• Seals damaged, missing	• INSPECT for damage. SERVICE as required.
• Piston damaged	• INSPECT for damage. SERVICE as required.
• Friction elements worn, damaged	• INSPECT for damage. SERVICE as required.
• Check Ball not functioning	• INSPECT for damage. SERVICE as required.
• Forward clutch piston and Return Spring damaged	• INSPECT for damage. SERVICE as required.
Case	
• Porosity/cross leaks in servo apply, servo release, direct clutch, coast clutch circuits	• INSPECT for damage. PERFORM Air Pressure Check. SERVICE as required.

FM5029801559020X

Fig. 32 Routines 235 & 335: Harsh 4-3 Shift Only (Part 2 of 2)

Possible Component	Reference/Action
236 — ELECTRICAL ROUTINE	
Powertrain Control System	
• Electrical Inputs/Outputs, Vehicle Wiring Harnesses, Powertrain Control Module, EPC Solenoid, Transmission Range (TR) Sensor, Vehicle Speed Sensor, 3-2T/CCS, Transmission Fluid Temperature Sensor, TSS, throttle position sensor, Mass Air Flow Sensor, TCC solenoid	• RUN OBD Tests. REFER to MOTOR's Domestic Transmission Manual for diagnosis. PERFORM Service Manual Pinpoint Tests "B, C, D, E, F and G" with Transmission Tester (007-00130 and CD4E cable and overlay 007-00125) and the TR Sensor Cable. SERVICE as required. CLEAR codes, ROAD TEST and RERUN OBD Tests.
336 — HYDRAULIC/MECHANICAL ROUTINE	
Main Control	
• Bolts out of torque specifications	• RETORQUE bolts to specifications.
• Gasket damaged	• INSPECT for damage and REPLACE as required.
• 3-2 Timing Valve, Solenoid Regulator Valve, 3-2 Control Valve stuck, damaged, misassembled	• INSPECT for damage. SERVICE as required.
• Hydraulic passages damaged	• INSPECT for damage and REPLACE as required.
• Separator plates damaged or blocked	• INSPECT for damage. SERVICE as required.
• 3-2T/CCS Solenoid malfunction	• ACTIVATE solenoid using Transmission Tester. If Coast Clutch operation is OK PROCEED to Direct Clutch Assembly.
Direct Clutch Assembly	• PERFORM Air Pressure Check.
• Return Spring damaged, broken	• INSPECT for damage. SERVICE as required.
• Friction Elements damaged, worn	• INSPECT for damage. SERVICE as required.
• Check Ball not exhausting	• INSPECT for damage. SERVICE as required.
INT/OD Band and Servo Assembly	
• INT/OD Band and/or Reverse Clutch Drum Assembly damaged, worn or misassembled	• INSPECT for damage. SERVICE as required.
• Servo Piston damaged	• INSPECT for damage. SERVICE as required.
• Servo Return and Cushion Springs damaged, misassembled	• INSPECT for damage. SERVICE as required.
• Springs damaged, misassembled	• INSPECT for damage. SERVICE as required.
• Servo Rod bent or damaged	• INSPECT for damage. SERVICE as required.
Oil Pump Assembly	
• Bolts out of torque specifications	• RETORQUE bolts to specifications.
• Gaskets damaged	• INSPECT for damage and REPLACE as required.

FM5029801560010X

Fig. 33 Routines 236 & 336: Harsh 3-2 Shift Only (Part 1 of 2)

Possible Component	Reference/Action
• Porosity/cross leaks	• INSPECT for porosity, leaks. REPLACE as required.
• Pump Support Seal Rings damaged or misassembled	• INSPECT for damage. SERVICE as required.
Case	
• Band Anchor damaged	• INSPECT for damage. SERVICE as required.
• Servo Rod Bore damaged	• INSPECT for damage. SERVICE as required.

FM5029801560020X

Fig. 33 Routines 236 & 336: Harsh 3-2 Shift Only (Part 2 of 2)

Possible Component	Reference/Action
240 — ELECTRICAL ROUTINE	
Powertrain Control System	
• Electrical Inputs/Outputs, Vehicle Wiring Harnesses, Powertrain Control Module, Transmission Fluid Temperature Sensor, TCC solenoid, Brake On/Off (BOO) Switch, TSS	• PERFORM Torque Converter Control Operation Tests. RUN OBD Tests. Refer to MOTOR'S Domestic Transmission Manual. PERFORM Service Manual Pinpoint Tests "B, C and F" with Transmission Tester (007-00130 and CD4E cable and overlay 007-00125) SERVICE as required. CLEAR codes, ROAD TEST and RERUN OBD Tests.
340 — HYDRAULIC/MECHANICAL ROUTINE	
Main Control	
• Bolts out of torque specifications	• RETORQUE bolts to specifications.
• Gasket damaged	• INSPECT for damage and REPLACE as required.
• Solenoid Pressure Regulator Valve, Bypass Clutch Control Valve and Plunger, Converter Regulator Valve stuck, damaged, misassembled	• INSPECT for damage. SERVICE as required.
• TCC Solenoid malfunction	• ACTIVATE solenoid using Transmission Tester. SERVICE as required.
• Hydraulic passages damaged	• INSPECT for damage and REPLACE as required.
• Separator plates damaged or blocked	• INSPECT for damage. SERVICE as required.
Torque Converter Assembly	
• Leakage, Internal damage	• INSPECT for damage and leakage. PERFORM Converter checks REPLACE as required

FM5029801561000X

Fig. 34 Routines 240 & 340: No Torque Converter Apply

Possible Component	Reference/Action
• Pump Support No. 1 Seal Ring damaged, missing, misassembled	• INSPECT for damage. SERVICE as required.
Torque Converter Assembly	
• Internal Seals damaged	• INSPECT. SERVICE as required.
• Piston Plate damage/stuck to Cover	• If cover is heat stained, REPLACE converter.
Case	
• Porosity/cross leaks from the CBY circuit	• INSPECT for porosity/leaks. SERVICE or REPLACE case as required.

FM5029801562020X

Fig. 35 Routines 241 & 341: Torque Converter Always Applied/Stalls Vehicle (Part 2 of 2)

Possible Component	Reference/Action
240 — ELECTRICAL ROUTINE	
Powertrain Control System	
• Electrical Inputs/Outputs, Vehicle Wiring Harnesses, Powertrain Control Module, Transmission Fluid Temperature Sensor, TCC solenoid, Brake On/Off (BOO) Switch, TSS	• PERFORM Torque Converter Control Operation Tests. RUN OBD Tests. REFER to MOTOR Domestic Transmission Manual for diagnosis. PERFORM Service Manual Pinpoint Tests "B, C and F" with Transmission Tester (007-00130 and CD4E cable and overlay 007-00125) SERVICE as required. CLEAR codes, ROAD TEST and RERUN OBD Tests.
340 — HYDRAULIC/MECHANICAL ROUTINE	
Main Control	
• Bolts out of torque specifications	• RETORQUE bolts to specifications.
• Gasket damaged	• INSPECT for damage and REPLACE as required.
• Solenoid Pressure Regulator Valve, Bypass Clutch Control Valve and Plunger, Converter Regulator Valve stuck, damaged, misassembled	• INSPECT for damage. SERVICE as required.
• TCC Solenoid malfunction	• ACTIVATE solenoid using Transmission Tester. SERVICE as required.
• Hydraulic passages damaged	• INSPECT for damage and REPLACE as required.
• Separator plates damaged or blocked	• INSPECT for damage. SERVICE as required.
Torque Converter Assembly	
• Leakage, Internal damage	• INSPECT for damage and leakage. PERFORM Converter checks as outlined in this manual. REPLACE as required.

FM5029801562010X

Fig. 35 Routines 241 & 341: Torque Converter Always Applied/Stalls Vehicle (Part 1 of 2)

Possible Component	Reference/Action
251 — ELECTRICAL ROUTINE	
No Electrical Concerns	
351 — HYDRAULIC/MECHANICAL ROUTINE	
Brake Shift Interlock	• REFER to "Troubleshooting" in this section.
Internal and External Shift Linkages	
• Damaged, misadjusted or misassembled	• INSPECT and SERVICE as required. ADJUST linkage as outlined in Service Manual. After servicing linkage, VERIFY that the transmission range (TR) sensor is properly adjusted.
• Manual Control Lever damaged, park mechanism damaged, Shaft bent, Detent Lever Shaft Bore (in case) damaged, Detent Spring bent/damaged, Nut Loose	• INSPECT for damage. SERVICE as required.
Main Control	
• Bolts out of torque specifications	• RETORQUE bolts to specifications.
• Manual Valve stuck, damaged	• INSPECT for damage. SERVICE as required.

FM5029801563000X

Fig. 36 Routines 251 & 351: Shift Lever Efforts High

Possible Component	Reference/Action
252 — ELECTRICAL ROUTINE	
No Electrical Concerns	
352 — HYDRAULIC/MECHANICAL ROUTINE	
Fluid • Improper level	• ADJUST fluid to proper level.
Seals/Gaskets • Differential Seals, Speedometer Gear, Retainer Seal, Pump, Main Control Cover, Servo Cover, Split Flange Gasket, Converter Impeller Hub, Manual Lever Shaft Seal, Oil Level Indicator Tube.	• LOCATE source of leak. SERVICE as required. If Differential Seal or Converter Impeller Hub is leaking, INSPECT drain back holes in Case/Converter Housing, INSPECT surface of linkshaft or front wheel driveshaft and joint for a rough surface. Rough surface may cause seal leakage. SERVICE as required.
Other • Oil Tube Fitting, Line Pressure Tap, Pressure Port Plugs, Drain Plug, Fluid Cooler Tubes, Case porosity, Case cracked • Vent blocked or damaged • Bolts at Split Flange or Main Control Cover leaking	• LOCATE source of leak. SERVICE as required. • CHECK vent for damage or blockage. SERVICE as required. • INSPECT for leaks. SERVICE as required.
Sensors/Connectors • Transmission Connector, Transmission Range (TR) Sensor, TSS or Seal	• LOCATE source of leak. SERVICE as required.

FM5029801564000X

Fig. 37 Routines 252 & 352: External Leaks

Possible Component	Reference/Action
253 — ELECTRICAL ROUTINE	
Powertrain Control System • Base Engine Concerns.	• REFER to MOTOR's Auto Engine Performance & Driveability Manual.

FM5029801565010X

Fig. 38 Routines 253 & 353: Poor Vehicle Performance (Part 1 of 2)

Possible Component	Reference/Action
• Electrical Inputs/Outputs, Vehicle Wiring Harnesses, Powertrain Control Module, Transmission Fluid Temperature Sensor, TCC Solenoid, Transmission Range (TR) Sensor, Throttle Position Sensor	• PERFORM Torque Converter Clutch Operation Test. RUN OBD Tests. REFER to MOTOR's Domestic Transmission Manual for diagnosis. PERFORM Service Manual Pinpoint Tests "B, C, D" using the Transmission Tester (007-00130 and CD4E cable and overlay 007-00125) and the TR Sensor Cable (007-0086A). CLEAR codes, ROAD TEST and RERUN OBD Tests.
353 — HYDRAULIC/MECHANICAL ROUTINE	
Internal and External Shift Linkages or TR Sensor • Damaged, misadjusted or misassembled	• INSPECT and SERVICE as required. ADJUST linkage as outlined in Service Manual. After servicing linkage, VERIFY that the TR Sensor is properly adjusted.
Verify Proper Shift Scheduling and Engagements	• GO to the appropriate Diagnostic Routines per Index.
Torque Converter Clutch Always Applied	• GO to Routine No. 341.
Torque Converter OWC Clutch • Damaged	• PERFORM Service Manual inspection procedures. SERVICE or REPLACE as required.

FM5029801565020X

Fig. 38 Routines 253 & 353: Poor Vehicle Performance (Part 2 of 2)

Possible Component	Reference/Action
254 — ELECTRICAL ROUTINE	
No Electrical Concerns	
354 — HYDRAULIC/MECHANICAL ROUTINE	
For Noises/Vibrations that Change with Engine Speed: • Torque Converter Components • Fluid Level (Low) Pump cavitation • Oil Pump Assembly • Engine Drive Accessories • Fluid Cooler Tubes grounding out • Flywheel • Inspection Cover	• LOCATE source of disturbance. SERVICE as required.
For Noises/Vibrations that Change with Vehicle Speed: • Powertrain Mounts Loose, Damaged • Tires • Driveline Concerns: Front Wheel Driveshaft and Joint or Linkshaft, Differential: Final Drive/Chain, Suspension, Modifications • Planetary Gear Sets • Chain grounding to Chain Pan • FWD OWC • Torque Converter Assembly • LH and RH Front Wheel Driveshaft and Joint Splines worn, damaged • Speedometer Cable or Gears	• LOCATE source of disturbance. SERVICE as required. For Specific Shifts or Torque Converter concerns, • INSPECT Chain Pan for signs of damage or misinstallation. SERVICE as required. • INSPECT for damage. SERVICE as required.
Other Noises/Vibrations: • Shift Cable and Bracket Vibration, Grounding. • Cooler Lines Grounding	• LOCATE source of disturbance. SERVICE as required.

FM5029801566000X

Fig. 39 Routines 254 & 354: Noise/Vibration In Forward/Reverse

Possible Component	Reference/Action
255 — ELECTRICAL ROUTINE	
Powertrain Control System • Base Engine Concerns	• REFER to MOTOR's Auto Engine Performance & Driveability Manual.

FM5029801567010X

Fig. 40 Routines 255 & 355: Engine Will Not Crank (Part 1 of 2)

Possible Component	Reference/Action
• Electrical Inputs/Outputs, Vehicle Wiring Harnesses, Powertrain Control Module, Transmission Range (TR) Sensor (damaged/misadjusted)	• RUN OBD Tests. REFER to MOTOR's Domestic Transmission Manual for diagnosis. PERFORM Pinpoint-Test "D" using the TR Sensor Cable. SERVICE as required. CLEAR codes, ROAD TEST and RERUN OBD Tests.
355 — HYDRAULIC/MECHANICAL ROUTINE	
Starter/Flywheel • Damaged or misassembled	• INSPECT for damage, misassembly. SERVICE as required.
Internal and External Shift Linkages or TR Sensor • Damaged, misadjusted or misassembled	• ADJUST linkage. After servicing linkage, VERIFY that the transmission range (TR) sensor is properly adjusted.

FM5029801567020X

Fig. 40 Routines 255 & 355: Engine Will Not Crank (Part 2 of 2)

Possible Component	Reference/Action
256 — ELECTRICAL ROUTINE	
No Electrical Concerns	
356 — HYDRAULIC/MECHANICAL ROUTINE	
Internal or External Shift Linkages • Damaged, misadjusted or misassembled	• INSPECT and SERVICE as required. ADJUST linkage as outlined in Service Manual. After servicing linkage, VERIFY that the transmission range (TR) sensor is properly adjusted.
Park Mechanism • Park Gear on Driven Sprocket Assembly, Parking Pawl Return Spring, Park Pawl Ratcheting Springs, Parking Pawl Shaft, Manual Control Lever, Cam Apply Lever, Manual Lever Detent Spring, TR Sensor, Parking Pawl Apply Cam, Manual Shaft nut damaged, missing or misassembled	• INSPECT for damage. SERVICE as required.

FM5029801568000X

Fig. 41 Routines 256 & 356: No Park Range

Possible Component	Reference/Action
257 — ELECTRICAL ROUTINE	
Powertrain Control System • Electrical Inputs/Outputs, Vehicle Wiring Harnesses, Powertrain Control Module, TCC Solenoid, Transmission Fluid Temperature Sensor, TSS	• RUN OBD Tests. REFER to PC/ED Manual[35] for diagnosis. PERFORM Service Manual Pinpoint Tests "B, C and F" using the Transmission Tester (007-00130 and CD4E cable and overlay 007-00125) as outlined in this manual. SERVICE as required. CLEAR codes, ROAD TEST and RERUN OBD Tests.
357 — HYDRAULIC/MECHANICAL ROUTINE	
Vehicle Concerns Causing Engine Overheating	• REFER to Engine section of Service Manual for diagnosis.
Fluid • Improper level • Condition	• ADJUST fluid to proper level. • INSPECT per Service Manual instructions under Fluid Condition Check. If fluid is aerated, CHECK Thermo Valve and Filter Seals. SERVICE as required.
Oil Cooler Tubes • Damaged, blocked, reversed	• INSPECT for damage. SERVICE as required.
Intake Cooler • Damaged, blocked, restricted or leaking	• INSPECT for damage. SERVICE as required.
Auxiliary Cooler (If equipped) • Damaged, blocked, restricted, improperly installed	• INSPECT for damage or improper installation. SERVICE as required.
Main Control • Bolts out of torque specifications	• RETORQUE bolts to specifications.

FM5029801569010X

Fig. 42 Routines 257 & 357: Transaxle Overheating (Part 1 of 2)

Possible Component	Reference/Action
• Main Regulator Valve, Bypass Clutch Control Valve, Converter Regulator Valve stuck, damaged, misassembled • Hydraulic Passages damaged • Separator Plates/Gaskets damaged • TCC Solenoid malfunction (OFF)	• INSPECT for damage. SERVICE as required. • INSPECT for damage. SERVICE as required. • INSPECT for damage. SERVICE as required. • ACTIVATE solenoid using Transmission Tester. SERVICE as required.
Torque Converter Clutch - No Apply	• SEE Routine No. 240/340.
Oil Pump Assembly • Gasket damaged • Rear Lube Passage blocked	• INSPECT for damage and REPLACE as required. • INSPECT for damage. SERVICE as required.
Chain Pan • Missing	• INSPECT for missing pan. INSTALL pan if missing.
Thermostatic Oil Level Control Valve • Stuck open or damaged • Gasket damaged or missing • Bolt or bracket damaged, missing, or improperly installed	• INSPECT for damage. SERVICE as required. • INSPECT for damage and REPLACE as required. • INSPECT for damage. SERVICE as required.
Case/Converter Housing/Stator Support • Front Lube Passage blocked or restricted	• INSPECT passages. SERVICE as required.

FM5029801569020X

Fig. 42 Routines 257 & 357: Transaxle Overheating (Part 2 of 2)

Possible Component	Reference/Action
258 — ELECTRICAL ROUTINE	
Powertrain Control System	
• Electrical Inputs/Outputs, Vehicle Wiring Harnesses, Powertrain Control Module, 3-2 Timing/Coast Clutch Solenoid	• RUN OBD Tests. REFER to MOTOR's Domestic Transmission Manual for diagnosis. PERFORM Service Manual Pinpoint Test "G" using the Transmission Tester (007-00130 and CD4E cable and overlay 007-00125). SERVICE. CLEAR codes, ROAD TEST and RERUN OBD Tests. PERFORM Stall Speed Tests.
358 — HYDRAULIC/MECHANICAL ROUTINE	
Main Controls	
• Bolts out of torque specifications	• RETORQUE bolts to specifications.
• Gaskets damaged	• INSPECT for damage and REPLACE as required.
• Low/Reverse Modulator Valve, Coast Clutch Valve stuck damaged or misassembled	• INSPECT for damage. SERVICE as required.
• 3-2 Timing/Coast Clutch Solenoid stuck or damaged	• INSPECT for damage, contamination. ACTIVATE solenoid with Transmission Tester. SERVICE as required.
• Hydraulic Passages damaged	• INSPECT for damage. SERVICE as required.
• Pressure Tap Plate/Gasket damaged	• INSPECT for damage. SERVICE as required.
• Separator Plate/Gasket damaged	• INSPECT for damage. SERVICE as required.
Coast Clutch Assembly	
• Assembly misassembled, damaged	• INSPECT for damage. SERVICE as required.
• Forward Clutch Hub Seal damaged	• INSPECT for damage. SERVICE as required.
• Piston or Seals damaged	• INSPECT for damage. SERVICE as required.
• Ball check damaged, missing	• INSPECT for damage. SERVICE as required.
Low/Reverse Clutch Assembly	• PERFORM Air Pressure Check.
• Assembly misassembled, damaged	• INSPECT for damage. SERVICE as required.
• Piston or Seals damaged	• INSPECT for damage. SERVICE as required.
Oil Pump Assembly	
• Pump Support No. 2 or No. 3 Seal Rings for the Coast Clutch circuit damaged, missing	• INSPECT for damage. SERVICE as required.

FM5029801570000X

Fig. 43 Routines 258 & 358: No Engine Braking In 1st Gear Manual Only

Possible Component	Reference/Action
259 — ELECTRICAL ROUTINE	
Powertrain Control System	
• Electrical Inputs/Outputs, Vehicle Wiring Harnesses, Powertrain Control Module, 3-2 Timing/Coast Clutch Solenoid	• RUN OBD Tests. REFER to MOTOR's Domestic Transmission Manual for diagnosis. PERFORM Service Manual Pinpoint Test "G" using the Transmission Tester (007-00130 and CD4E cable and overlay 007-00125). SERVICE as required. CLEAR codes, ROAD TEST and RERUN OBD Tests. PERFORM Stall Speed Tests.
359 — HYDRAULIC/MECHANICAL ROUTINE	
Internal or External Shift Linkages	
• Damaged, misadjusted or misassembled	• INSPECT and SERVICE as required. ADJUST linkage. After servicing linkage, VERIFY that the transmission range (TR) sensor is properly adjusted.
Main Controls	
• 3-4 Shift Valve, 1-2 Shift Valve, Pull-in Valve, Coast Clutch Control Valve stuck, damaged	• INSPECT for damage. SERVICE as required.
• 3-2 Timing/Coast Clutch Solenoid stuck or damaged	• INSPECT for damage, contamination. ACTIVATE solenoid with Transmission Tester. SERVICE as required.
Forward OWC Assembly	
• Damaged, misassembled	• INSPECT for damage. SERVICE as required.
Coast Clutch Assembly	
• Assembly misassembled, damaged	• INSPECT for damage. SERVICE as required.
• Forward Clutch hub Seal damaged	• INSPECT for damage. SERVICE as required.
• Piston or Seals damaged	• INSPECT for damage. SERVICE as required.
• Ball check damaged, missing	• INSPECT for damage. SERVICE as required.
Pump Assembly	
• Pump Support No. 2 or No. 3 Seal Rings for the Coast Clutch circuit damaged, missing	• INSPECT for damage. SERVICE as required.

FM5029801647000X

Fig. 44 Routines 259 & 359: No Engine Braking In Drive w/TCS On Or Manual 2nd Position

Possible Component	Reference/Action
262 — ELECTRICAL ROUTINE	
No Electrical Concerns	
362 — HYDRAULIC/MECHANICAL ROUTINE	
Internal or External Shift Linkages	
• Damaged, misadjusted or misassembled	• INSPECT and SERVICE as required. ADJUST linkage. After servicing linkage, VERIFY that the transmission range (TR) sensor is properly adjusted.
Oil Pump Assembly	
• Gaskets severely damaged	• INSPECT for damage and REPLACE as required.
• Pump Support Seal Ring No. 2, leakage from Lube Circuit into FC Circuit	• INSPECT for damage. SERVICE as required.
Forward/Coast Clutch Assembly	
• Friction plates severely damaged	• INSPECT for damage. SERVICE as required.
• Return Spring damaged	• INSPECT for damage. SERVICE as required.
• Ball Check damaged, missing	• INSPECT for damage. SERVICE as required.

FM5029801648000X

Fig. 45 Routines 262 & 362: Vehicle Movement w/Transaxle Range Selector In N Position

MAINTENANCE

FLUID CHECK

Under ordinary circumstances, transaxle fluid level need not be checked. However, if transaxle is not functioning properly or if external fluid leakage is indicated, check fluid as follows:

1. With vehicle on a level surface, start engine and move selector lever through all gear ranges. Allow each gear to engage completely.
2. Place selector lever in Park position, then lock parking brake.
3. With engine still running, remove dipstick from tube and wipe end clean, then slide dipstick back in tube. ensure it seats properly.
4. Remove dipstick from tube and note fluid level. **If level is below bottom hole on dipstick and outside temperature is above 50°F, vehicle should not be driven.**
5. If vehicle has been driven until reaching normal operating temperature, fluid level should be within cross-hatched "hot" area on dipstick. If vehicle has not been driven and outside temperature is above 50°F, fluid level should be above bottom hole on dipstick.
6. Check fluid condition as follows:
   a. Observe fluid color and check for burned odor. If fluid is dark brown or black, or if odor is detected, overheating or component failure is indicated.
   b. Wipe dipstick and examine stain for solid particles, gum or varnish. If these are present, change and inspect fluid as described under " Fluid Change."

FLUID CHANGE

Automatic transaxle fluid should bechanged every 30,000 miles if vehicle operates for prolonged periods at idle or below 30°F, is driven regularly in dusty conditions or on salted, muddy or rough road surfaces or if contamination is suspected.

1. Raise and support vehicle, then place suitable container beneath transaxle drain plug.
2. Remove plug and allow fluid to drain. **If an internal transaxle problem is suspected, drain fluid through suitable paper filter. While a small accumulation of metal or friction particles may indicate normal wear, an excessive amount warrants further internal transaxle service.**
3. Clean drain plug threads and apply a thin coat of Teflon pipe sealant No. D8AZ-19554-A, or equivalent. Install drain plug and tighten to specifications.
4. Lower vehicle, then add 6 quarts of Mercon ATF, or equivalent, to transaxle.
5. Start engine, then move selector lever through all gear ranges. Check fluid as described under "Fluid Check" and add as required.

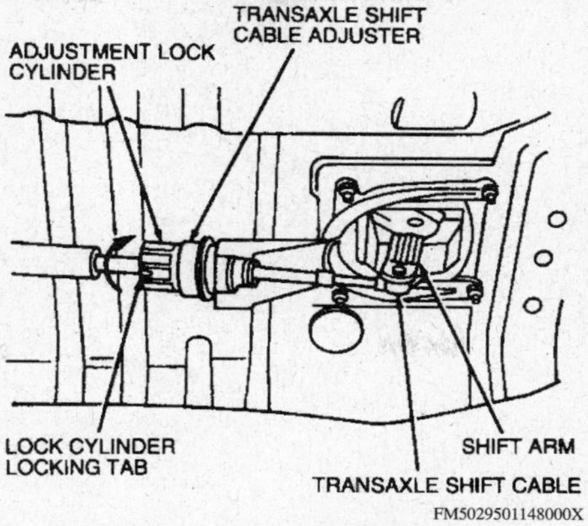

Fig. 46 Shift control linkage adjustment. Contour & Mystique & 1999–2000 Cougar

ADJUSTMENTS

SHIFT CONTROL LINKAGE

Contour & Mystique & 1999–2000 Cougar

1. Verify that transaxle is in D position by viewing TR sensor. alignment marks will be aligned with D arrow on TR sensor body when transaxle is in full Drive position.
2. Have someone hold gearshifter lever in D position, then raise and support vehicle.
3. Remove transaxle shift cable from shift arm using suitable screwdriver.
4. Depress two locking tabs on adjustment lock cylinder and rotate adjustment lock cylinder, **Fig. 46,** shift cable is now unlocked and free to slide in retainer.
5. Make sure assistant is holding gearshift lever so that indicator is centered on D.
6. Grasp cable forward of adjustment lock cylinder and move as necessary to align cable eye with pin on shift arm.
7. Install shift cable end to shift arm by pressing on by hand . Rotate adjustment lock cylinder clockwise until it snaps into place.
8. Lower vehicle, then shift transaxle through all transaxle ranges to make sure shift control linkage operation is correct and indicator is properly aligned.

SHIFT CABLE & BRACKET

Probe

1. Remove console finish panel.
2. Shift transaxle range selector to Drive position, then remove transaxle control selector dial bezel mounting screws and lift selector dial bezel out of way.
3. Slide lock cover back and disconnect set button, **Fig. 47.**
4. Slide transaxle range selector to adjust position, then connect set button.
5. Slide lock cover to lock set button in place, then install transaxle control selector dial bezel and selector dial bezel screws.
6. Tighten selector dial bezel screws to specifications.
7. Verify proper operation of shift cable and bracket.

TRANSAXLE RANGE SENSOR

Contour & Mystique & 1999–2000 Cougar

1. Turn manual control lever to Neutral.
2. Remove engine air intake resonator and mass air flow sensor.
3. Loosen transaxle range sensor retaining bolts.
4. Align sensor slots using transaxle range sensor adjustment tool No. T94P-70010-AH, or equivalent.
5. Tighten bolts to specification, then install air intake resonator and mass air flow sensor.
6. Check for proper operation with parking brake control engaged. Engine should start in Park or Neutral only, and backup lamps should activate only in Reverse.

Probe

1. Remove air cleaner assembly.
2. Place selector lever in Neutral position, then disconnect Transmission Range (TR) sensor electrical connector and loosen sensor bolts.
3. Install TR sensor alignment tool No. T92P-70010-AH, or equivalent, **Fig. 48,** to align sensor on shaft and transaxle case, then tighten sensor bolts to specifications.
4. Remove alignment tool, then connect TR sensor electrical connector.
5. Install air cleaner assembly.

IN-VEHICLE REPAIRS

SELECTOR LEVER & HOUSING, REPLACE

CONTOUR & MYSTIQUE & 1999–2000 COUGAR

1. Raise and support vehicle.
2. Remove center underbody heat shield retaining nuts.
3. Disconnect shift cable and bracket from transaxle range selector lever stud.
4. Remove four bracket retaining nuts.
5. Remove bracket with transaxle shift cable connected, then position aside.
6. Lower vehicle.
7. Using a screwdriver, pry bezel from console assembly.
8. Lift gearshift lever out of console assembly to access transaxle control switch wiring harness connector.
9. Disconnect transaxle control switch wiring harness connector, then remove gearshift lever.
10. Reverse procedure to install.

PROBE

Refer to **Fig. 49** throughout following procedure.

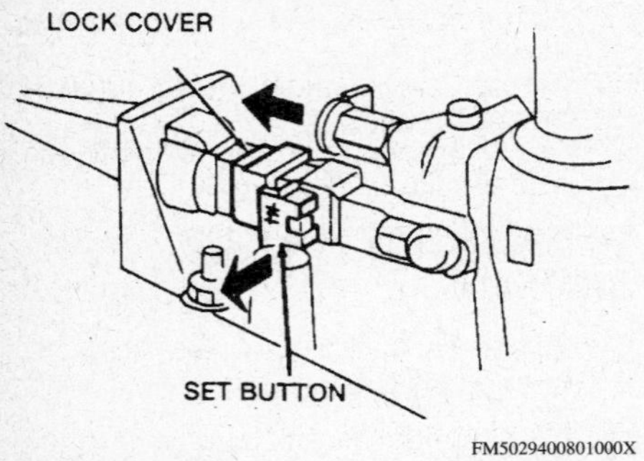

Fig. 47 Lock cover & set button location. Probe

1. Remove console finish panel.
2. Remove transaxle control selector dial bezel screws, then disconnect park range switch, overdrive switch and emergency override switch electrical connectors.
3. Using suitable screwdriver, pry shift cable and bracket from selector lever and housing.
4. Remove lock tab cover, then squeeze tabs on shift cable and bracket to remove from selector lever and housing.
5. Loosen interlock cable locknut, **Fig. 50,** then disconnect shift lock actuator electrical connector.
6. Remove selector lever and housing nuts and bolt, then lift lever, housing and seal off studs.
7. Reverse procedure to install, noting following:
   a. Tighten bolt, nuts and screws to specifications.
   b. Adjust shift cable and bracket.

SHIFT CABLE & BRACKET, REPLACE

CONTOUR & MYSTIQUE & 1999–2000 COUGAR

1. Raise and support vehicle.
2. Remove center underbody heat shield retaining nuts.
3. Remove front underbody heat shield retaining nuts.
4. Disconnect shift cable and bracket from transaxle range selector lever stud.
5. Pull transaxle shift cable and bracket plastic snap retainer from bracket.
6. Lower vehicle, then disconnect shift cable and bracket from manual control lever stud on transaxle.
7. Remove two bolts attaching shift cable and bracket to transaxle case.
8. Remove shift cable and bracket by guiding out through engine compartment.
9. Reverse procedure to install.

DIFFERENTIAL OIL SEALS, REPLACE

1. Raise and support vehicle, then remove front wheels and drain transaxle fluid into suitable container.
2. Remove front wheel driveshaft and joint, then use converter seal remover tool No. T94P-77000-B and impact slide hammer tool No. T50T-100-A, or equivalents, to remove differential oil seal. Discard seal.
3. Reverse procedure to install, noting following:
   a. Apply a thin film of petroleum jelly to outer diameter and lip of new oil seal.
   b. Tap seal into place using output seal replacer tool No. T86P-1177-B, or equivalent.
   c. Fill transaxle with suitable ATF.

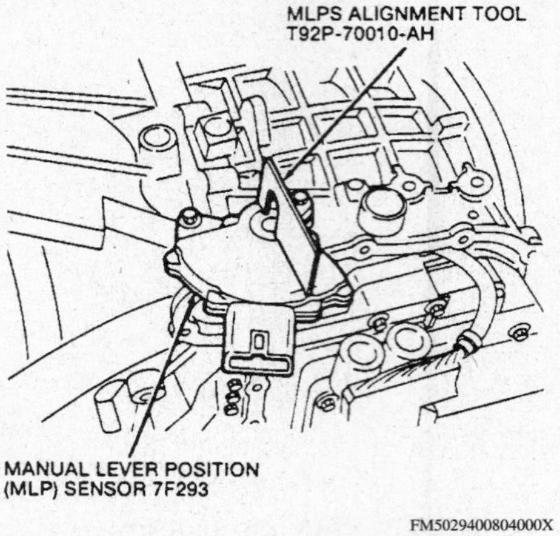

Fig. 48 TR sensor alignment tool installation

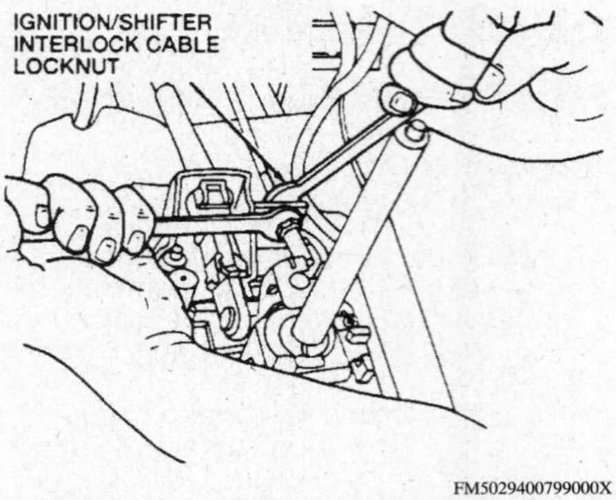

Fig. 50 Interlock cable locknut. Probe

TRANSAXLE RANGE SENSOR, REPLACE

CONTOUR & MYSTIQUE & 1999–2000 COUGAR

1. Place manual control lever in Neutral.
2. Remove engine air intake resonator and mass air flow sensor.
3. Disconnect electrical harness from transaxle range sensor.
4. Remove range sensor retaining bolts, then sensor.
5. Reverse procedure to install.

PROBE

1. Remove air cleaner assembly.
2. Disconnect Transaxle Range (TR) sensor electrical connector, then remove two sensor bolts.
3. Remove TR sensor.
4. Reverse procedure to install.

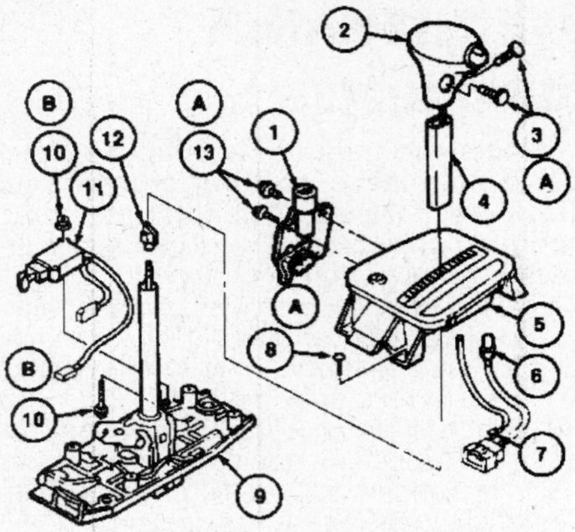

Item	Description
1	Lockout Switch
2	Transmission Range Selector Knob
3	Transmission Range Selector Knob Screws (2 Req'd)
4	Transmission Range Selector Cover
5	Transmission Control Selector Dial Bezel
6	Transmission Range Indicator Lamp Bulb
7	Transmission Control Switch (TCS) Electrical Connector
8	Transmission Control Selector Dial Bezel Screws (4 Req'd)
9	Transmission Range Selector
10	Shift Lock Actuator Nut and Bolt (2 Req'd)
11	Shift Lock Actuator
12	Shift Lever Cam
13	Lockout Switch Screw (2 Req'd)
A	Tighten to 2-2.9 N·m (17-26 Lb-In)
B	Tighten to 1.3-1.8 N·m (11-16 Lb-In)

FM5029400698010A

Fig. 49 Selector lever assembly. Probe

TURBINE SHAFT SPEED SENSOR, REPLACE

1. Raise and support vehicle.
2. **On Probe models,** remove lefthand front fender splash shield.
3. **On all models,** place suitable drain pan beneath Turbine Shaft Speed Sensor (TSS), then disconnect TSS electrical connector.
4. Remove TSS bolt and TSS from transaxle.
5. Reverse procedure to install, noting following:
   a. Replace TSS O-ring if damaged or worn. Apply a thin film of petroleum jelly to O-ring before installation.
   b. Tighten TSS bolt to specifications.
   c. Check and adjust transmission fluid

TIGHTENING SPECIFICATIONS

Year	Component	Torque, Ft. Lbs.
CONTOUR & MYSTIQUE		
1997–2000	ABS Wire Loom	35
	A/C Suction Accumulator/Drier Bracket	48–72①
	Battery Tray	72–84①
	Bumper Bracket	84①
	Cooler Lines	17
	Drain Plug	19–21
	Engine Mount Bracket, Righthand	35
	Lower Radiator Support Brackets	20
	Main Control Valve Body	84–96①
	Mount Through Bolt	87
	Power Steering Hydraulic Line	56–76
	Shift Cable Mounting Bracket	15–19
	Steering Gear	96
	Steering Gear Heat Shield	18
	Starter Motor (2.0L Engine)	15–20
	Starter Motor (2.5L Engine)	43–58
	Strut Upper Mounting	34
	Sub-Frame	96
	Suspension Arm To Knuckle Pinch Bolts	61
	Tie Rod End To Front Knuckle	23–35
	Transaxle Cooler Inlet Line Fitting	17
	Transaxle Range Sensor	108①
	Transaxle (2.0L Engine)	30
	Transaxle (2.5L Engine)	35
	Turbine Shaft Speed (TSS) Sensor	108–120①
	Torque Converter To Flywheel	23–29
	Vehicle Speed Sensor (VSS)	43–53①
	Wheel Lug Nut	62
COUGAR		
1999–2000	ABS Wire Loom	35
	A/C Suction Accumulator/Drier Bracket	48–72①
	Battery Tray	72–84①
	Bumper Bracket	84①
	Cooler Lines	17
	Drain Plug	19–21
	Engine Mount Bracket, Righthand	35
	Lower Radiator Support Brackets	20
	Main Control Valve Body	84–96①
	Mount Through Bolt	87
	Power Steering Hydraulic Line	56–76
	Shift Cable Mounting Bracket	15–19
	Steering Gear	96
	Steering Gear Heat Shield	18
	Starter Motor (2.0L Engine)	15–20
	Starter Motor (2.5L Engine)	43–58
	Strut Upper Mounting	34
	Sub-Frame	96
	Suspension Arm To Knuckle Pinch Bolts	61
	Tie Rod End To Front Knuckle	23–35
	Transaxle Cooler Inlet Line Fitting	17
	Transaxle Range Sensor	108①
	Transaxle (2.0L Engine)	30
	Transaxle (2.5L Engine)	35

Continued

TIGHTENING SPECIFICATIONS—Continued

Year	Component	Torque, Ft. Lbs.
COUGAR		
1999-2000	Turbine Shaft Speed (TSS) Sensor	108–120①
	Torque Converter To Flywheel	23–29
	Vehicle Speed Sensor (VSS)	43–53①
	Wheel Lug Nut	62
PROBE		
1997	Battery Tray	72–84①
	Crossmember	68–96
	Drain Plug	11–26
	Front Transaxle Support Bracket	28–38
	Front Transaxle Mount Through Bolt	63–86
	Intake Manifold Support	27–38
	Lefthand Engine Mount Bolts	28–38
	Lefthand Engine Mount Nuts	12–17
	Lefthand Engine Mount Through Bolt	63–86
	Lower Starter Motor	23–34
	Main Control Valve Body	72–86①
	Manual Control Lever	18–22
	Manual Control Lever Shaft	49–60
	Oil Filler Tube	60–84①
	Rear Engine Mount	50–68
	Rear Transaxle Mount Through Bolt	63–86
	Selector Dial Bezel	17–26①
	Starter Battery Terminal	12–17
	Torque Converter To Flywheel	24–30
	Transaxle To Engine	③
	Transaxle Range (TR) Sensor	96–120①
	Turbine Shaft Speed (TSS) Sensor	9–11
	Upper Starter Motor	23–34
	Vehicle Speed Sensor	44–53①
	Wheel Lug Nuts	66–86

① — Inch lbs.

② — Bolts A, 68–86 ft. lbs.; B, 28–38 ft. lbs. & C, 14–18 ft. lbs. Refer to "Transaxle, Replace" for tightening application.

F4E-III & IF4E Automatic Transaxles

NOTE: Prior To Performing Any Service Operations Listed In This Section, Consult The "Technical Service Bulletins " Section For Related Information.

NOTE: On Air Bag Equipped Models, Refer To " Air Bag System Precautions" Located In The Front Of This Manual For System Disarming & Arming Procedures.

NOTE: "Electrical Symbol & Wire Color Code Identification" Located In The Front Of This Manual May Be Used As An Aid When Using Wiring Circuits Found In This Section.

INDEX

PRECAUTIONS

AIR BAG SYSTEMS

Refer to "Air Bag System Precautions" in front of this manual for system disarming and arming procedures.

BATTERY GROUND CABLE

Prior to service, disconnect battery ground cable and isolate as required.

IDENTIFICATION

The IF4E and F4E-III automatic transaxles can be identified by a tag located on top of transaxle case, **Fig. 1**.

FM5029701111000X

Fig. 1 Identification tag

DESCRIPTION

The IF4E and F4E-III automatic transaxles are four-speed transaxles, using a combination of electronic, hydraulic and mechanical systems to control forward and reverse gear shifting, torque converter lockup and self-diagnosis, **Fig. 2**.

TROUBLESHOOTING

BRAKE-SHIFT INTERLOCK SYSTEM

Refer to **Figs. 3 and 4,** when troubleshooting brake-shift interlock system.

TRANSAXLE

Refer to **Figs. 5 through 8,** when troubleshooting.

MAINTENANCE

Ford Motor Company recommends use of Mercon multi-purpose automatic transmission fluid XT-2-QDX, or Mercon equivalent, in this transaxle.

FLUID CHECK

If vehicle has been operated for an extended period at high speeds, in city traffic, in hot weather or pulling a trailer, allow ATF to cool for approximately 30 minutes after engine has been turned off to obtain accurate reading.

1. Park vehicle on a level surface, apply parking brake and block wheels.
2. Start engine, depress brake pedal and move gearshift lever through each range, allowing each range to engage, then return to P.
3. Allow ATF to reach normal operating temperature. Do not turn engine off while checking level.
4. Clean dirt from transaxle fluid level indicator cap, then pull dip stick from filler tube, wipe clean and push back into tube until seated.
5. Pull dip stick from filler tube and check fluid level.
6. If fluid is low, add ATF in ½ pint increments to avoid over filling.

FLUID CHANGE

According to manufacturer, "Normal maintenance and lubrication requirements do not require periodic automatic transaxle fluid change. If a major repair is required, such as clutch band, bearing, etc., transaxle will have to be removed for service. At this time, torque converter, oil pan, fluid cooler, and fluid cooler tubes must be thoroughly flushed to remove any contamination."

1. Remove fluid level indicator, then raise and support vehicle.
2. Place suitable drain pan under transaxle, remove drain plug and washer. Discard washer. **It may be useful to measure amount of ATF drained from transaxle.**
3. Install new washer and drain plug, then lower vehicle.
4. Fill transaxle with approximately same amount of ATF drained.
5. Check fluid level.

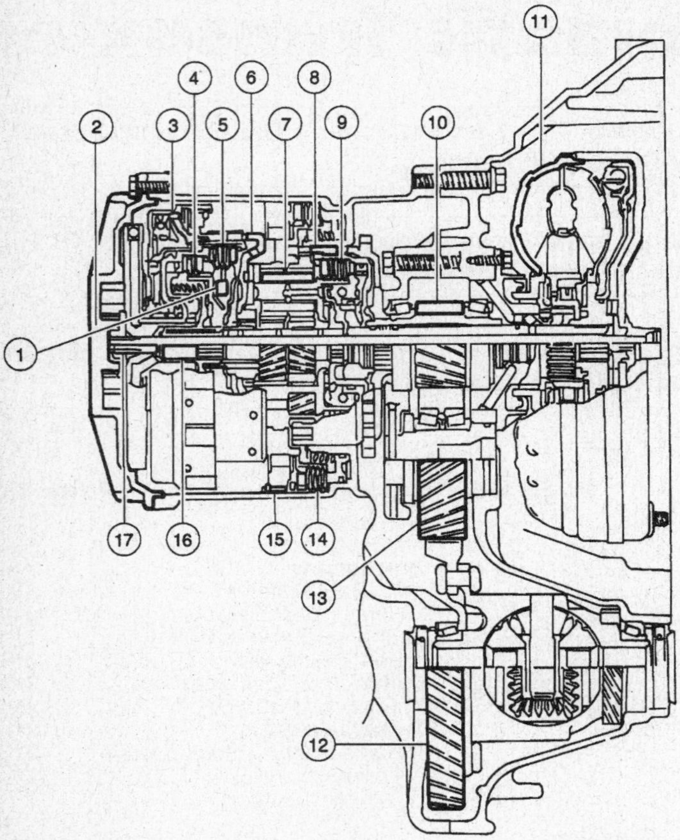

FM5029701112010X

Fig. 2 Cross-sectional view (Part 1 of 2)

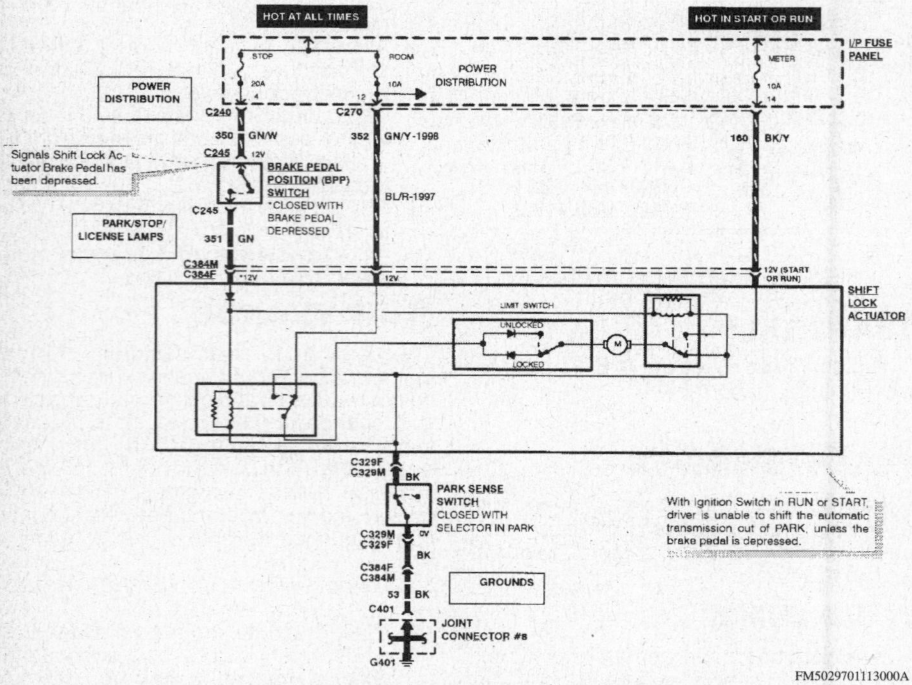

FM5029701113000A

Fig. 3 Brake-shift interlock wiring diagram

Item	Description
1	One-Way Clutch
2	Oil Pump
3	Reverse Clutch
4	Coasting Clutch
5	Forward Clutch
6	2-4 Band
7	Front Planet
8	Front Sun Shell
9	3-4 Clutch

Item	Description
10	Output Gear
11	Torque Converter
12	Differential
13	Idler Gear
14	Low/Reverse Clutch
15	One-Way Clutch
16	Turbine Shaft
17	Oil Pump Shaft

FM5029701112020X

Fig. 2 Cross-sectional view (Part 2 of 2)

ADJUSTMENTS

SHIFT CABLE & BRACKET

1. With gearshift lever in P position, loosen transaxle range switch cable nut.
2. Move shift cable toward rear as far as possible.
3. Check cable for tension or movement restriction, then tighten to specifications.

TRANSAXLE CONTROL SELECTOR DIAL BEZEL

1. Place gearshift lever in P.
2. Loosen transaxle control selector dial bezel screws.
3. Place stiff wire in slider panel and position slider panel pointer to align with P position on transaxle control selector dial bezel.
4. Tighten screws to specifications.

THROTTLE VALVE CONTROL ACTUATOR CABLE

1. Remove square head plug "L" and install transmission test adapter No. D87C-77000-A, or equivalent, and suitable pressure gauge.
2. With all accessories off, shift gearshift lever to P and warm engine to normal operating temperature. Use NGS tester, or equivalent, to verify transaxle fluid is 140–160°F.
3. Apply parking brake and ensure idle is 670–730 RPM.
4. Loosen bolt "1," then "2," **Fig. 9.**
5. Ensure throttle plate is fully closed, then tighten bolt "1" to specification.
6. Pull cable conduit until line pressure slightly exceeds 81 psi, then push cable until line pressure decreases to 71 psi with engine at idle.
7. Tighten bolt "2" to specification.
8. Ensure all slack is removed from cable by apply slight downward pressure on cable.
9. Turn engine off and ensure throttle valve control actuating cable moves smoothly.
10. Start engine, press accelerator slightly and return engine to idle.
11. Ensure line pressure is 62–81 psi.
12. Turn engine off, remove pressure gauge and adapter, then install new square head plug and tighten to specifications.

TEST CONDITIONS	TEST DETAILS/RESULTS/ACTIONS
A1 CHECK FUSE STOP (15A), ROOM (10A) AND METER (10A)	
1 	2 Check 10A METER, 10A ROOM and 15A STOP fuses. • Are the fuses OK? → **Yes** GO to **A2**. → **No** REPLACE the fuse in question. TEST the system for normal operation. If the fuse fails again, CHECK for a short to ground. REPAIR as necessary. TEST the system for normal operation.
A2 CHECK VOLTAGE TO SHIFT LOCK ACTUATOR FROM THE INTERIOR FUSE JUNCTION PANEL	
1 2 3  4 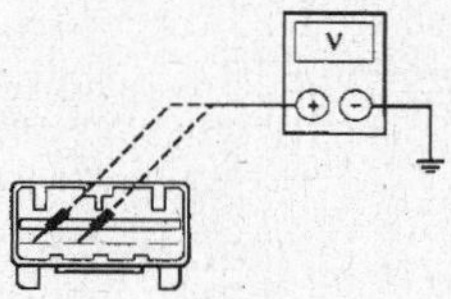	4 Measure the voltage between shift lock actuator C384-4, circuit 352 (GN/Y or BL/R), and ground; between C384-3, circuit 160 (BK/Y), and ground. • Are the voltages greater than 10 volts? → **Yes** GO to **A3**. → **No** REPAIR the circuit in question. TEST the system for normal operation.

FM5029701115010A

Fig. 4 Shift Interlock System Does Not Release Or Lock Properly (Part 1 of 3)

TEST CONDITIONS	TEST DETAILS/RESULTS/ACTIONS
A3 CHECK THE VOLTAGE TO SHIFT LOCK ACTUATOR FROM THE BPP SWITCH — CIRCUIT 351 (GN)	
1  2 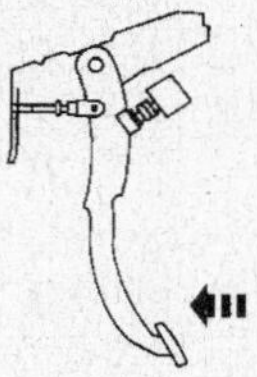	2 Depress and hold the brake pedal.
3 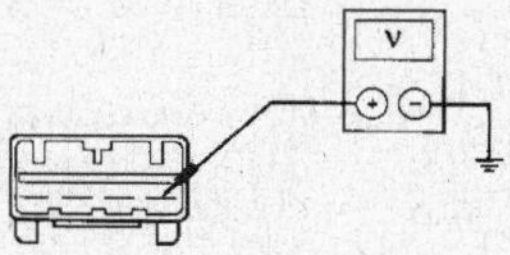	3 Measure the voltage between shift lock actuator C384-1, circuit 351 (GN), and ground. • Is the voltage greater than 10 volts? → **Yes** RELEASE the brake pedal; GO to **A4**. → **No** DIAGNOSE brake switch.

FM5029701115020A

Fig. 4 Shift Interlock System Does Not Release Or Lock Properly (Part 2 of 3)

TEST CONDITIONS	TEST DETAILS/RESULTS/ACTIONS
A4 CHECK THE PARK RANGE SWITCH GROUND FOR OPEN — CIRCUIT 53 (BK)	
1  2 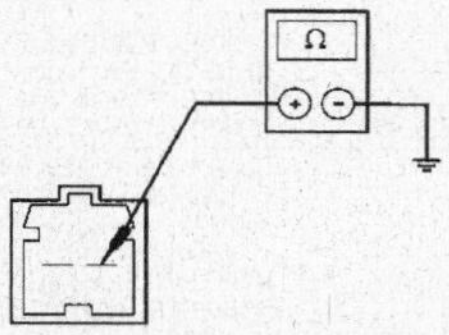	2 Measure the resistance between park range switch C329, circuit 53 (BK), and ground. • Is the resistance less than 5 ohms? → **Yes** GO to **A5**. → **No** REPAIR circuit 53 (BK). TEST the system for normal operation.
A5 CHECK THE PARK RANGE SWITCH	
1 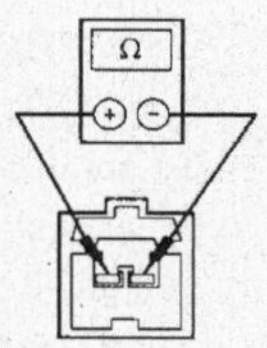	1 Measure the resistance between the park range switch terminals, with the park release button out, and with the park release button in or the shifter in the R, Ⓓ, D, and L positions. • Is the resistance less than 5 ohms with the park release button out, and greater than 10,000 ohms with the park release button in or the shifter in the R, Ⓓ, D, and L positions? → **Yes** REPLACE the shift lock actuator. TEST the system for normal operation. → **No** REPLACE the gearshift lever. TEST the system for normal operation.

FM5029701115030A

Fig. 4 Shift Interlock System Does Not Release Or Lock Properly (Part 3 of 3)

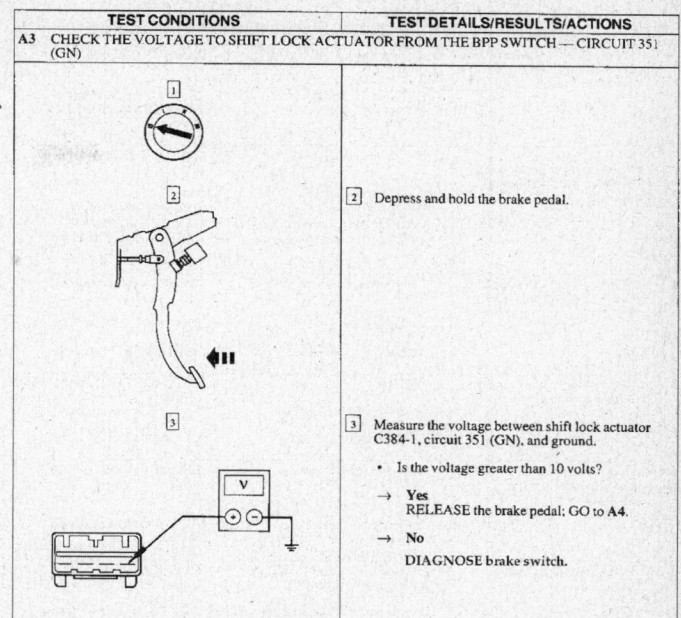

Condition	Possible Source	Action
• Engine Does Not Crank in Park (P) and/or Neutral (N)	• Gearshift lever and linkage out of adjustment. • Transmission range (TR) switch does not operate or is disconnected. • TR switch not correctly aligned to the transaxle.	• CONFIRM the selector or linkage adjustment and operation. • ADJUST the TR switch.
• Engine Starts in Gearshift Lever Positions Other Than Park (P) or Neutral (N)	• Gearshift lever or linkage damaged or out of adjustment. • TR switch damaged or out of adjustment.	• CONFIRM the gearshift lever or linkage adjustment and operation. • CONFIRM the TR switch adjustment and operation.
• Vehicle Moves in Park (P) Range or Transaxle Stays in Park (P) When not in Park (P) Range	• Gearshift lever and linkage out of adjustment. • Parking pawl is damaged.	• CONFIRM the gearshift lever or linkage adjustment and operation. • INSPECT the parking pawl;
• Vehicle Moves in Neutral (N)	• Gearshift lever and linkage out of adjustment. • Control valve damaged. • Torque converter damaged. • Forward clutch damaged.	• CONFIRM the gearshift lever or linkage adjustment and operation. • INSPECT the control valve. REPAIR or REPLACE as required. • INSPECT the forward clutch. REPAIR or REPLACE as required.
• Vehicle Does Not Move in Overdrive Ⓓ, Drive (D), Low (L) and Reverse (R)	• Transmission shift cable damaged. • Control valves. • Automatic transmission fluid (ATF) level. • Oil pump dirty, broken, or damaged seals. • Torque converter damaged.	• INSPECT the transaxle shift cable. REPAIR or REPLACE as required. • INSPECT the control valves. • CHECK ATF level and FILL as necessary. • INSPECT the oil pump. REPAIR or REPLACE as required. • INSPECT the torque converter. REPAIR or REPLACE as required.
• Vehicle Does Not Move in Any Forward Gearshift Lever Position, but Reverse (R) Is OK	• Control valves. • Forward clutch worn or damaged. • One-way clutch No. 1 worn or damaged. • Oil flow to forward clutch blocked.	• INSPECT the control valves. • INSPECT the clutch. • INSPECT the one-way clutch.

FM5029701118010X

Fig. 5 Automatic Concerns (Part 1 of 5)

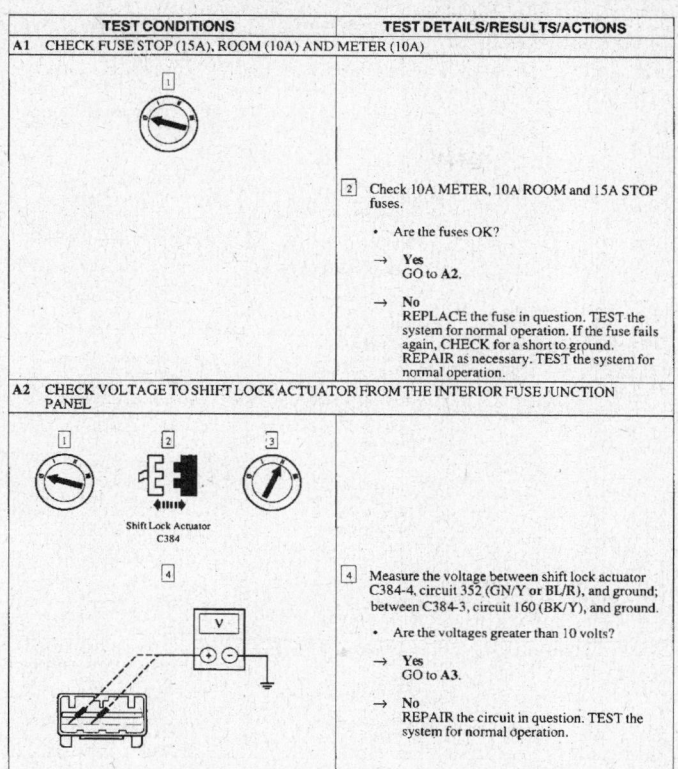

Condition	Possible Source	Action
• Vehicle Does Not Move in Reverse (R), but Forward Positions Are OK	• Reverse clutch worn or damaged.	• INSPECT reverse clutch.
	• LOW and REVERSE clutch slipping or damaged.	• INSPECT the LOW and REVERSE clutch pack clearance.
• Noise Severe Under Acceleration or Deceleration, but OK in Park (P), Neutral (N), or at a Steady Speed	• Engine mounts grounding out.	• REPLACE the engine mounts;
	• Torque converter failure.	• EXAMINE/REPLACE.
	• Gear or reverse clutch failure.	• EXAMINE/REPLACE.
	• Selector cable grounding out.	• INSTALL and ROUTE the cable as specified.
• Noise in Park (P) or Neutral (N) — Does Not Stop in Drive (D)	• Loose flex plate-to-converter nuts.	• TIGHTEN to specification.
	• Oil pump worn.	• EXAMINE/REPLACE the oil pump.
	• Torque converter failure.	• EXAMINE/REPLACE the torque converter.
• Noise in All Gears — Changes Acceleration to Deceleration	• ATF level.	• CHECK ATF level and FILL as necessary.
	• Front wheel driveshaft and joint.	• REPLACE as required.
	• Final drive gear set worn.	• EXAMINE/SERVICE the final drive gear set.
• Noise in All Gears — Does Not Change Acceleration to Deceleration	• Defective vehicle speed sensor (VSS).	• EXAMINE/REPLACE the VSS.
	• Bearings worn or damaged.	• EXAMINE/REPLACE the bearings.
	• Front planet worn.	• REPLACE the front planet.
• Harsh Shifts (Any Gears)	• Throttle valve control actuating cable out of adjustment.	• CHECK the throttle valve control actuating cable adjustment.
	• Idle air control valve sticking.	• INSPECT the idle air control valve.
	• Engine mounts loose.	• REPLACE as required;
	• Front wheel driveshaft and joint.	• REPLACE as required;
	• Line pressure incorrect.	
	• Band adjustment.	• CHECK the band adjustment.
	• Main control valve body.	• INSPECT the main control valve body.
	• 2-4 band.	• INSPECT the 2-4 band.
	• Sticking accumulator piston.	• INSPECT the accumulator piston.

FM5029701118020X

Fig. 5 Automatic Concerns (Part 2 of 5)

Condition	Possible Source	Action
• **NOTE:** Excessive overheating may cause damage to the internal components. Always retest the automatic transaxle for other symptoms after the overheating problem is resolved and the burnt fluid is replaced. Transaxle Overheating	• ATF level.	• CHECK ATF level and FILL as necessary.
	• Poor engine performance.	• ADJUST according to specifications.
	• Restriction in oil cooler lines.	REPAIR or REPLACE the oil cooler lines.
	• Worn clutch, incorrect band application, or poor oil pressure control.	
• Drags in Reverse (R) as if Parking Brake Is Applied	• Brakes partially applied.	
	• 2-4 band adjustment incorrect.	• INSPECT the 2-4 band adjustment.
• Drags in Forward Gears as if Parking Brake Is Applied	• Brakes partially applied.	
	• 2-4 band adjustment incorrect.	• INSPECT the 2-4 band adjustment.
• Engine Runaway or Flare-up on Upshift	• Transmission fluid temperature sensor.	• INSPECT the transmission fluid temperature sensor.
	• ATF level low.	• CHECK ATF level.
	• Main control valve body damaged or sticking valves.	• INSPECT the main control valve body and solenoid valves.
	• Oil pump pressure inadequate.	
	• Clutches slipping.	• INSPECT the clutches.
• Engine Runaway or Flare-up on Downshift	• ATF level low.	• CHECK ATF level and FILL as necessary.
	• Oil pump pressure inadequate.	
	• Clutches slipping.	• INSPECT the clutches.
• Excessive Creep	• Ignition timing and idle speed.	• CHECK and ADJUST as necessary.
	• Throttle valve control actuating cable out of adjustment.	• INSPECT the throttle valve control actuating cable adjustment.
	• Manual valve misadjusted.	• ADJUST the manual valve.

FM5029701118040X

Fig. 5 Automatic Concerns (Part 4 of 5)

Condition	Possible Source	Action
• Soft Shifts (Any Gears)	• ATF level.	• CHECK ATF level and FILL as necessary.
	• Throttle valve control actuating cable out of adjustment.	• CHECK the throttle valve control actuating cable adjustment.
	• Idle air control valve sticking.	• INSPECT the idle air control valve.
	• Line pressure.	
	• Band adjustment.	• CHECK the band adjustment.
	• Band servo.	• INSPECT the band servo.
	• Pressure regulator damaged.	• INSPECT the pressure regulator.
	• Main control valve body.	• INSPECT the main control valve body.
	• Sticking accumulator piston.	• INSPECT the accumulator piston.
	• Internal ATF leakage.	• INSPECT the automatic transaxle.
	• Oil pump worn.	• INSPECT the oil pump.
• Erratic Shifting, Incorrect Shift Points, Incorrect Shift Sequence	• ATF level and quality.	• CHECK ATF level and condition and FILL as necessary.
	• Throttle valve control actuating cable out of adjustment.	• CHECK the throttle valve control actuating cable adjustment.
	• Throttle position sensor (TP sensor) out of range.	• INSPECT throttle position sensor signal.
	• Line pressure.	
	• 2-4 band adjustment.	• CHECK the band adjustment.
	• Control valves.	• INSPECT the control valves.
	• Clutches slipping.	• INSPECT the clutches.
• Improper Lockup	• Throttle position sensor out of range.	• INSPECT throttle position sensor signal.
	• Control valves.	• INSPECT the control valves.
	• Torque converter.	• INSPECT, REPLACE the torque converter.
• Skipping Gears (For Example, Shift 1st to 3rd, or 2nd to Overdrive (O))	• Transmission fluid temperature sensor.	• EXAMINE/REPLACE the transmission fluid temperature sensor.
	• Main control valve body.	• INSPECT the main control valve body.
	• Control valves.	• INSPECT the control valves.
	• 2-4 band.	• CHECK the 2-4 band adjustment.

FM5029701118030X

Fig. 5 Automatic Concerns (Part 3 of 5)

Condition	Possible Source	Action
• No Creep	• Parking brakes partially applied.	• INSPECT the brake adjustment.
	• ATF level and condition.	• CHECK ATF level and condition and FILL as necessary.
	• Throttle valve control actuating cable out of adjustment.	• INSPECT the throttle valve control actuating cable adjustment.
	• Gearshift lever and linkage out of adjustment.	• CONFIRM the gearshift lever and linkage adjustment and operation.
	• Ignition timing idle speed.	
	• Main control valve body.	• INSPECT the main control valve body.
	• Control valves.	• INSPECT the control valves.
	• Forward clutch.	• INSPECT the clutch.
	• Reverse clutch.	• INSPECT the reverse clutch.
	• Oil pump.	• INSPECT the oil pump.
• Engine Stalls When Put Into Gear	• Main control valve body.	• INSPECT the main control valve body.
	• Timing idle speed.	
	• Control valves.	• INSPECT the control valves.
	• Torque converter.	• INSPECT, REPLACE torque converter.
	• Oil pump.	• INSPECT the oil pump.
• No Kickdown	• Main control valve body.	• INSPECT main control valve body.
• Poor Fuel Economy	• Brake on/off (BOO) switch.	• INSPECT BOO switch.
	• Torque converter clutch (TCC) solenoid.	• INSPECT TCC solenoid.
	• Engine performance.	
• Lack of Power	• Engine performance.	
	• Torque converter.	
	• Forward clutch.	• INSPECT forward clutch.
• Surges While Cruising	• TCC solenoid.	• INSPECT TCC solenoid.
	• Main control valve body.	• INSPECT main control valve body.
• Poor Acceleration	• Engine performance.	
	• TCC solenoid.	• INSPECT TCC solenoid.
	• Main control valve body.	• INSPECT main control valve body.
	• Torque converter.	• INSPECT/REPLACE torque converter.

FM5029701118050X

Fig. 5 Automatic Concerns (Part 5 of 5)

Condition	Possible Source	Action
• Shift Shock in All Ranges	• Low fluid. • Throttle valve control actuating cable out of adjustment. • Idle air control valve sticking or damaged. • Front wheel driveshaft and joint or engine mounts. • 2-4 band and servo. • Pressure regulator sticking or damaged. • Control valves. • Coasting clutch. • Accumulator piston. • Low/Reverse clutch. • 3-4 clutch.	• CHECK fluid level. • INSPECT the cable adjustment. • CLEAN, REPAIR or REPLACE the throttle valve. • REPAIR or REPLACE front wheel driveshaft and joint or engine mounts. • CHECK the adjustment. • CLEAN, REPAIR, or REPLACE. • CHECK for clogging, blockage; REPAIR as required. • CHECK for wear; REPLACE coasting clutch. • CLEAN, REPAIR, or REPLACE. • CHECK for adjustment, wear, and damage; REPAIR as required. • INSPECT, REPAIR, or REPLACE.
• Harsh 1-2 Shift	• Throttle valve control actuating cable broken or out of adjustment. • 1-2 accumulator piston sticking or damaged. • Idle speed.	• CHECK the throttle valve control actuating cable adjustment. • INSPECT and REPAIR or REPLACE.
• Harsh Engagement NEUTRAL-REVERSE	• NEUTRAL-REVERSE accumulator sticking or damaged. • Idle speed.	• INSPECT, REPAIR or REPLACE.
• Harsh Engagement NEUTRAL-OVERDRIVE (D)	• N-D accumulator sticking or damaged.	• INSPECT, REPAIR or REPLACE.
• 2-3 Shift Shock	• 2-3 accumulator piston sticking or damaged.	• INSPECT and REPAIR or REPLACE.
• Erratic Shifts	• Throttle valve control actuating cable broken or out of adjustment. • Main control valve body.	• INSPECT the throttle valve control actuating cable adjustment. • INSPECT the main control valve body and solenoid valves.
• Soft Shift in All Ranges	• Low fluid. • Throttle valve control actuating cable broken or out of adjustment. • Idle air control valve sticking or damaged. • Pressure regulator valve sticking or damaged. • Main control valve body.	• CHECK fluid level. • INSPECT the cable adjustment. • CLEAN, REPAIR, or REPLACE. • CLEAN, REPAIR, or REPLACE. • INSPECT the main control valve body and solenoid valves.

FM5029701119010X

Fig. 6 Shift Feel Concerns (Part 1 of 2)

Condition	Possible Source	Action
• Engine Has Momentary Runaway During 3-2 Downshift	• 2-4 band damaged or misadjusted.	• INSPECT for adjustment or damage; REPAIR or REPLACE.
• Hesitation in 3-2 Shift	• Main control valve body.	• INSPECT the main control valve body and solenoid valves. REPLACE as required.
• No Engine Braking (D) to DRIVE	• Fluid blockage to coasting clutch or failed coasting clutch. • Main control valve body.	• CHECK for blockage and coasting clutch condition. • INSPECT the main control valve body and solenoid valves. REPLACE as required.
• No Engine Braking DRIVE to LOW	• Fluid blockage to coasting clutch or failed coasting clutch. • 2-4 band. • Main control valve body. • Control valve.	• INSPECT coasting clutch for blockage or damage. • CHECK adjustment and INSPECT condition. • INSPECT the main control valve body and solenoid valves. REPLACE as required. • INSPECT, CLEAN or REPAIR.

FM5029701120000X

Fig. 7 Downshift Concerns

TRANSAXLE RANGE (TR) SWITCH

1. Remove air cleaner.
2. Remove shift cable and bracket nut, then control cable front clamp.
3. Rotate manual control lever to neutral position and loosen TR switch bolts.
4. Disconnect TR switch electrical connector.
5. Connect suitable ohmmeter between TR switch terminals A and H, then adjust TR switch until there is no continuity by rotating housing on manual control lever.
6. While holding switch in place, tighten TR switch bolts to specifications.
7. Install shift cable and bracket, then tighten nut to specification.
8. Install air cleaner.

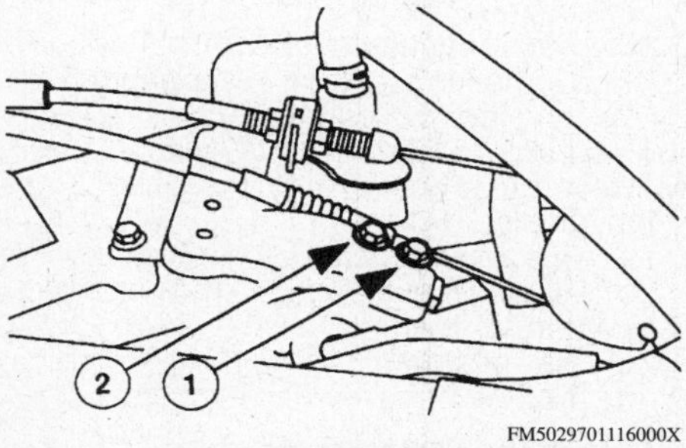

Fig. 9 Throttle valve control actuator cable adjustment

Condition	Possible Source	Action
• 1-2 Soft Shift	• 2-4 band is too loose. • Main control valve body.	• INSPECT the adjustment. • INSPECT the main control valve body and solenoid valves.
• 2-3 Soft Shift	• 2-3 accumulator sticking or damaged. • Main control valve body.	• INSPECT, CLEAN, REPAIR, or REPLACE. • INSPECT the main control valve body and solenoid valves.
• Neutral (N)-Reverse (R) Soft Shift	• N-D accumulator piston sticking or damaged.	• INSPECT, CLEAN, REPAIR, or REPLACE.
• No Lockup	• Lockup valve sticking or damaged. • Torque converter.	• INSPECT, CLEAN, REPAIR, or REPLACE. • INSPECT the torque converter.
• Drags in REVERSE as if Parking Brake Is Applied	• 2-4 band is too tight.	• CHECK adjustment.
• Slow to Engage in REVERSE	• Reverse clutch. • LOW and REVERSE clutch.	• INSPECT for damage or wear; REPAIR or REPLACE. • INSPECT for damage or wear; REPAIR or REPLACE.

FM5029701119020X

Fig. 6 Shift Feel Concerns (Part 2 of 2)

Condition	Possible Source	Action
• No 2-3 Upshift	• 3-4 clutch damaged. • Main control valve body.	• CHECK clutch adjustment for damage. • INSPECT the main control valve body and solenoid valves. REPLACE as required.
• No 2nd Gear (Transaxle Shifts 1-3)	• Loose 2-4 band. • Main control valve body.	• ADJUST 2-4 band. • INSPECT the main control valve body and solenoid valves. REPLACE as required.
• No Lockup	• Torque converter clutch (TCC) solenoid not functioning. • Torque converter.	• INSPECT the TCC solenoid and related hydraulic circuit. • INSPECT the torque converter.
• Shift Points Incorrect	• 2-4 band out of adjustment. • Main control valve body.	• CHECK 2-4 band adjustments. • INSPECT the main control valve body and solenoid valves. REPLACE as required.
• Engine Runaway When Upshifting	• Park/neutral position switch. • Main control valve body. • One-way clutch. • 2-4 band and servo. • 3-4 clutch.	• CHECK the adjustment and condition. • CLEAN, INSPECT, REPAIR or REPLACE. • INSPECT, REPAIR or REPLACE. • CHECK the adjustment and condition. • CHECK the condition and REPAIR.
• No Upshift Into Overdrive	• One-way clutch. • Main control valve body.	• CHECK one-way clutch. • CHECK orifices, solenoid valves and main control valve body.
• Delayed 1-2 Shift	• 2-4 band damaged or misadjusted. • Main control valve body.	• INSPECT for damage or misadjustment. REPAIR or REPLACE. • INSPECT valve body and solenoid valves. REPLACE as required.

FM5029701121000X

Fig. 8 Upshift Concerns

IN-VEHICLE REPAIRS

SHIFT LOCK ACTUATOR, REPLACE

1. Remove shift console.
2. Remove righthand and front gearshift lever knob screws, then knob.
3. Remove transaxle control selector dial bezel attaching screws, then disconnect miniature bulb from bezel.
4. Disconnect shift lock actuator and park range switch electrical connectors, then screws and shift lock actuator.
5. Revere procedure to install, noting following:
   a. Using threadlock and sealer part No. EOAZ-19554-AA, or equivalent, on gearshift lever knob screws.
   b. Adjust transaxle control selector dial bezel.
   c. Tighten nuts, bolts and screws to specifications.

SHIFT CABLE & BRACKET

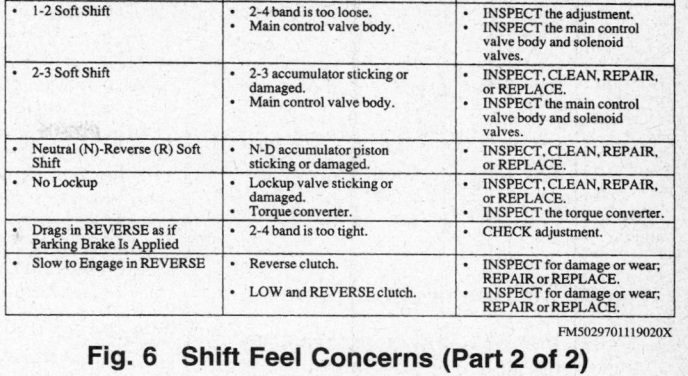

1. Remove Powertrain Control Module

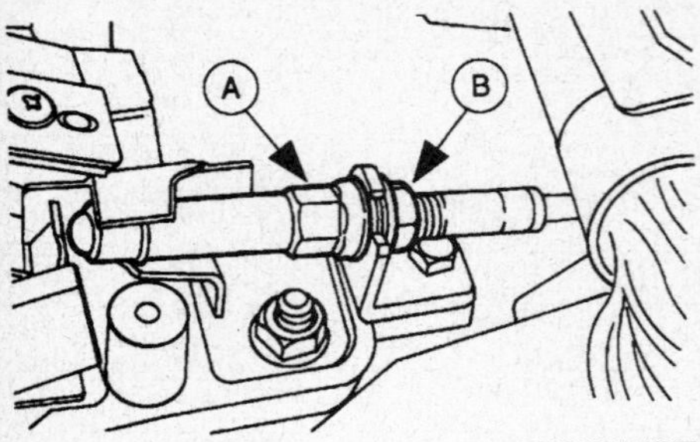

Fig. 10 Interlock cable removal

(PCM), then air bag diagnostic monitor and bracket.
2. Remove rear air bag safing sensor and bracket.
3. Remove shift console.
4. Remove righthand and front gearshift lever knob screws, then knob.
5. Remove transaxle control selector dial bezel attaching screws, then bezel.
6. Remove gearshift lever cable nut, cable floorpan bracket bolts and cable bulkhead bracket nuts.
7. Remove transaxle range switch cable nut and control cable front clamp, then shift cable and bracket.
8. Revere procedure to install, noting following:
   a. Apply threadlock and sealer part No. EOAZ-19554-AA, or equivalent, on gearshift lever knob screws.
   b. Adjust shift cable and bracket.
   c. Adjust transaxle control selector dial bezel.
   d. Tighten fasteners to specifications.

GEARSHIFT LEVER

1. Remove shift console.
2. Remove righthand and front gearshift lever knob screws, then knob.
3. Remove transaxle control selector dial bezel attaching screws, then bezel.
4. Disconnect shift lock actuator and park range switch electrical connectors.
5. Remove screws and shift lock actuator.
6. Remove gearshift lever cable nut and cable floorpan bracket bolts. **Do not kink shift cable and bracket.**
7. Loosen ignition/shift interlock cable locknut "B ", **Fig. 10. Do not loosen locknut "A" from factory setting. Do not kink cable.**
8. Remove gearshift lever nuts, then gearshift lever.
9. Reverse procedure to install, noting following:
   a. Use threadlock and sealer part No. EOAZ-19554-AA, or equivalent, on gearshift lever knob screws.
   b. Adjust shift cable and bracket.
   c. Adjust transaxle control selector dial bezel.
   d. Tighten fasteners to specifications.

IGNITION/SHIFTER INTERLOCK CABLE

1. Remove shift console.
2. Remove righthand and front gearshift lever knob screws, then knob.
3. Remove transaxle control selector dial bezel attaching screws, then bezel.
4. Loosen ignition/shift interlock cable locknut "B, " **Fig. 10. Do not loosen locknut "A" from factory setting. Do not kink cable.**
5. Remove steering column shroud screws and shroud.
6. Remove hood latch control handle nut, then position cable aside.
7. Remove instrument panel steering column cover screw and cover.
8. Remove ignition/shifter interlock cable bracket nut and cable.
9. Reverse procedure to install, noting following:
   a. Apply threadlock and sealer part No. EOAZ-19554-AA, or equivalent, to gearshift lever knob screws.
   b. Adjust shift cable and bracket.
   c. Adjust transaxle control selector dial bezel.
   d. Tighten fasteners to specifications.

MAIN CONTROL VALVE BODY, REPLACE

1. Raise and support vehicle.
2. Position suitable drain pan under transaxle, then remove plug and washer.
3. With suitable pan under transaxle oil pan, remove all bolts except corner bolts, then remove two rear corner bolts and allow pan to drain.
4. Remove remaining bolts and oil pan, then remove and discard case gasket.
5. Remove bolts holding wire retainers to main control valve body, then disconnect solenoid electrical connectors.
6. Remove remaining valve body bolts and carefully remove valve body.
7. Reverse procedure to install, noting following:
   a. Position main control valve body into transaxle case, ensure manual valve aligns with detent lever pin.
   b. Install valve body bolts, ensure those in locations "A" are 1.18 inches long below head, while those in " C" are 1.97 inches, **Fig. 11.**

TRANSAXLE RANGE (TR) SWITCH, REPLACE

1. Remove air cleaner outlet tube.
2. Remove shift cable and bracket nut, then control cable front clamp.
3. Remove manual lever control nut and shift outer lever, then disconnect TR switch electrical connector.
4. Remove switch bolts and switch.
5. Reverse procedure to install, noting following:
   a. Ensure transaxle is in Neutral.
   b. Align TR switch mark with manual control lever.
   c. Adjust switch.
   d. Tighten bolts to specifications.

TURBINE SHAFT SPEED (TSS) SENSOR, REPLACE

1. Remove air cleaner outlet rube and air cleaner, then battery tray.
2. Remove TSS sensor bolt and sensor.
3. Reverse procedure to install. Use new O-ring.

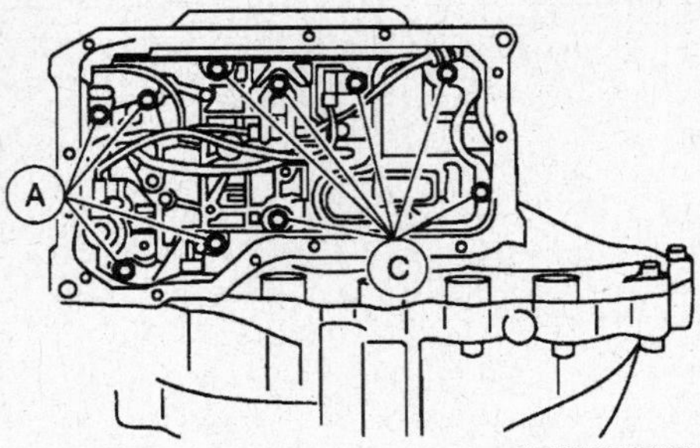

Fig. 11 Valve body installation

VEHICLE SPEED SENSOR

1. Raise and support vehicle.
2. Disconnect vehicle speed sensor electrical connector.
3. Unclip heated oxygen sensor wire clip from VSS bracket.
4. Remove VSS bolt, then gently pry VSS out of transaxle case.
5. Reverse procedure to install.

DIFFERENTIAL OIL SEALS, REPLACE

1. Install three-bar engine support No. D88L-6000-A, or equivalent, then raise and support vehicle.
2. Remove front tires and wheels.
3. Remove lefthand splash shield.
4. Remove transaxle case plug and washer, then drain ATF.
5. Remove front wheel driveshaft and joints. Refer to " Front Wheel Drive Axles."
6. Carefully pry differential seal from case.
7. Reverse procedure to install. Use differential seal replacer No. T87C-7700-H, or equivalent, to tap in new seals.

THROTTLE VALVE CONTROL ACTUATING CABLE, REPLACE

1. Loosen throttle valve control actuating nuts, then remove cable from throttle control lever.
2. Remove cable bolt from transaxle.
3. Remove main control valve body as outlined under " Main Control Valve Body, Replace."
4. Remove cable from throttle control lever and remove cable.
5. Reverse procedure to install.

TRANSAXLE

REPLACE

1. Remove battery tray, air cleaner outlet tub and air cleaner.
2. Disconnect computer control relay module (CCRM) electrical connector.
3. Remove bracket bolt and nut, then CCRM and bracket.
4. Remove shift cable and bracket nut from manual control shift outer lever, then shift cable and bracket clip.
5. Disconnect Transaxle Range (TR) switch, transaxle solenoid, turbine shaft speed (TSS) sensor, heated oxygen sensor and vehicle speed sensor (VSS) electrical connectors.

6. Remove starter motor.
7. **On 1997 models,** remove throttle valve control actuating cable bolts, then disconnect throttle valve control actuating cable from throttle cam.
8. **On all models,** install three-bar engine support No. D88L-6000-A, or equivalent.
9. Place suitable drain pan under transaxle, then disconnect fluid cooler lines from transaxle.
10. Remove lefthand engine support insulator nuts and washers, then two upper transaxle to engine bolts.
11. Raise and support vehicle, then remove front tire and wheel assemblies.
12. Remove lefthand splash shields.
13. Remove case plug, then drain transaxle fluid.
14. Remove front wheel driveshaft and joints as outlined under " Front Wheel Drive Axles."
15. Install two transaxle plugs No. T88C-7025-AH, or equivalent, into transaxle to hold different side gears. **Failure to install transaxle plugs may cause differential side gears to become improperly positioned.**
16. Disconnect heated oxygen sensor wire clip.
17. Remove front engine crossmember bolts and crossmember.
18. Disconnect A/C line from retainer on front engine crossmember.
19. Remove engine support crossmember bolts and nuts, then lefthand engine mount and transaxle mount nuts.
20. Remove transaxle housing cover bolts and cover.
21. Remove four flywheel to converter retaining nuts.
22. Remove lower transaxle to engine bolts.
23. Remove upper front transaxle to engine bolt. Bolt remains in block.
24. Position hi-lift transaxle jack No. 014-00210, or equivalent, and secure transaxle to jack.
25. Remove middle transaxle to engine bolts, then carefully lower transaxle from vehicle.
26. Reverse procedure to install, noting following:
    a. Lubricate torque converter pilot hub with multi-purpose grease No. DOAZ-19584-AA, or equivalent.
    b. Align torque converter studs to flywheel.
    c. To ease installation, loosen front transaxle support insulator through bolt and transaxle insulator bolt.
    d. Tighten nuts and bolts to specifications.

TECHNICAL SERVICE BULLETINS

ERRATIC SHIFT WITH DTC P0712

1998 Escort & Tracer

On some of these models, the transaxle may have erratic shifts with Diagnostic Trouble Code (DTC) P0712.

This condition may be caused by the Transmission Fluid Temperature (TFT) wire being pinched on the valve body spring clip. To correct this condition, proceed as follows:

1. Remove transaxle pan.
2. Remove TFT sensor retaining clip and inspect wire for chaffing or breaks.
3. Repair wire and install ¼ or ⅜ inch plastic conduit around affected area.
4. Install clip being careful to not pinch wire.
5. Install transaxle pan.

TIGHTENING SPECIFICATIONS

Year	Component	Torque/ Ft. Lbs.
1997–2000	Drain Plug	29–39
	Engine Mount	50–68
	Engine Support Crossmember	48–65
	Fluid Cooler Line	24–34
	Front Engine Crossmember	69–97
	Gearshift Lever	12–16
	Gearshift Lever Knob	18–26 ①
	Lefthand Engine Mount	28–38
	Oil Pan	72–86①
	Pressure Port Plug	44–86①
	Shift Cable	72–96①
	Shifter Interlock Cable	7–11①
	Shifter Interlock Cable Bracket	38–54①
	Shift Lock Actuator	12–16①
	Throttle Cable	60–84①
	Transaxle Case-To-Converter	28–38
	Transaxle Mount	28–38
	Transaxle-To-Engine	41–59
	Transmission Control Selector Dial Bezel	18–26①
	Transmission Range Switch	72–84①
	Transmission Range Switch Cable	12–16
	Transmission Range Switch Manual Control Lever	33–47
	Turbine Shaft Speed Sensor	72–84①
	Valve Body	72–96①
	Vehicle Speed Sensor	72–108①
	Wheel Lug Nuts	66–87

① — Inch lbs.

4EAT Automatic Transaxle

NOTE: On Air Bag Equipped Models, Refer To " Air Bag System Precautions" Located In The Front Of This Manual For System Disarming & Arming Procedures.

NOTE: "Electrical Symbol & Wire Color Code Identification" Located In The Front Of This Manual May Be Used As An Aid When Using Wiring Circuits Found In This Section.

INDEX

PRECAUTIONS

AIR BAG SYSTEMS

Refer to "Air Bag System Precautions" in front of this manual for system disarming and arming procedures.

BATTERY GROUND CABLE

Prior to service, disconnect battery ground cable and isolate as required.

IDENTIFICATION

All vehicles are equipped with a vehicle certification label affixed to lefthand door jamb below latch striker, **Fig. 1.** Refer to code below space marked "TR." For additional information, such as model, service ID level, or build date, refer to transaxle service ID tag, **Fig. 2.** Transaxle service ID tag is located on transaxle case.

DESCRIPTION

The 4EAT electronically controlled automatic transaxle system features a combination of electronic and mechanical systems to control forward gear shifting and torque converter lockup for quietness and economy, and self-diagnosis capability for simplifying diagnostic procedures, **Fig. 3.** These transaxles are equipped with a manual switch for slow driving on steep or slippery surfaces.

A unique mechanical feature of 4EAT automatic transaxle is single compact combination type four-speed planetary gear instead of typical two planetary gears used in three-speed transaxles. This allows for an overall size reduction. Another unique feature is variable capacity oil pump. This pump provides a constant oil quantity at and above medium speed to reduce power losses caused by pumping more oil than necessary at higher speeds.

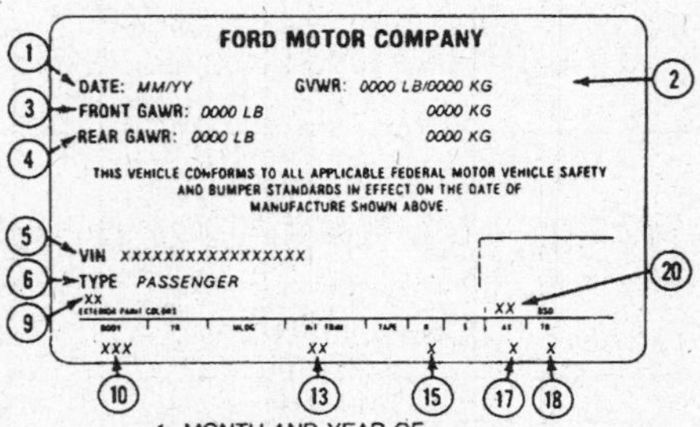

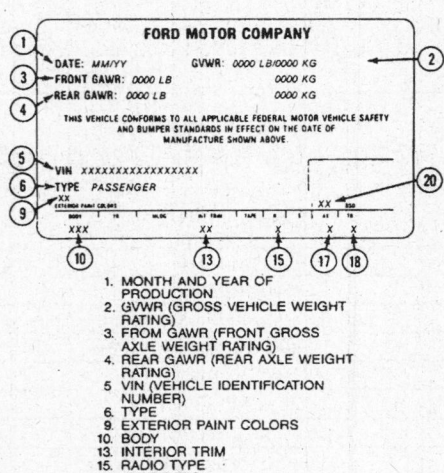

1. MONTH AND YEAR OF PRODUCTION
2. GVWR (GROSS VEHICLE WEIGHT RATING)
3. FROM GAWR (FRONT GROSS AXLE WEIGHT RATING)
4. REAR GAWR (REAR AXLE WEIGHT RATING)
5. VIN (VEHICLE IDENTIFICATION NUMBER)
6. TYPE
9. EXTERIOR PAINT COLORS
10. BODY
13. INTERIOR TRIM
15. RADIO TYPE
17. AXLE RATIO
18. TRANSMISSION
20. DSO (SPECIAL ORDER CODE)

FM5028800297000X

Fig. 1 Vehicle certification label

Electronic system controls transaxle shifting in forward speeds and controls torque converter lockup through solenoid operated valves. When energized (on), solenoid valves actuate clutches and bands to control planetary gear shifting. Shift timing and torque converter lockup are regulated by control unit with programmed logic and in response to input sensors and switches to produce optimum driveability.

TROUBLESHOOTING

SHIFT INTERLOCK

Shift Interlock System Does Not Release Or Lock Properly

Refer to "CD4E Automatic Transaxle" section for system troubleshooting.

TRANSAXLE

Vehicle Does Not Move In OD, D, L Or R Range

1. Fluid level too low or fluid contaminated.
2. Incorrectly adjusted selector lever.
3. Malfunctioning control valve(s).
4. Defective oil pump.
5. Problem in hydraulic circuit.
6. Defective torque converter.
7. Defective forward clutch.
8. Defective reverse clutch.
9. Defective one-way clutch No. 1
10. Defective one-way clutch No. 2
11. Defective parking gear.

Vehicle Moves In N Range

1. Incorrectly adjusted selector lever.
2. Malfunctioning control valve(s).

Excessive Creep

1. Incorrectly adjusted throttle cable.
2. Check idle speed and ignition timing.
3. Defective torque converter.

No Creep At All

1. Fluid level too low or fluid contaminated.
2. Incorrectly adjusted selector lever.
3. Incorrectly adjusted throttle cable.
4. Malfunctioning control valve(s).
5. Defective oil pump.
6. Problem in hydraulic circuit.
7. Defective forward clutch.
8. Defective reverse clutch.

No Shift

1. Defective inhibitor switch.
2. Defective hold switch.
3. Defective 1-2 solenoid.
4. Defective 2-3 solenoid.
5. Defective 3-4 solenoid.
6. Fluid level too low or fluid contaminated.
7. Incorrectly adjusted selector cable.

FM5029000591000X

Fig. 2 Transaxle Identification tag

8. Malfunctioning control valve(s).
9. Defective oil pump.

Abnormal Shift Sequence

1. Defective inhibitor switch.
2. Defective hold switch.
3. Defective throttle sensor.
4. Defective cruise control switch.
5. Defective water temperature switch.
6. Defective pulse generator.
7. Defective 1-2 solenoid.
8. Defective 2-3 solenoid.
9. Defective 3-4 solenoid.
10. Fluid level too low or fluid contaminated.
11. Incorrectly adjusted selector lever.
12. Malfunctioning control valve(s).
13. Defective 2-4 brake band and/or servo.

Frequent Shifting

1. Defective inhibitor switch.
2. Defective mode switch.
3. Defective throttle sensor.
4. Defective cruise control switch.
5. Defective pulse generator.
6. Defective 1-2 solenoid.
7. Defective 2-3 solenoid.
8. Defective 3-4 solenoid.
9. Defective lockup solenoid.
10. Malfunctioning control valve(s).

Excessively High Or Low Shift Point

1. Defective inhibitor switch.
2. Defective mode switch.
3. Defective hold switch.
4. Defective idle switch.
5. Defective throttle sensor.
6. Defective throttle generator.
7. Defective 1-2 solenoid.
8. Defective 2-3 solenoid.
9. Defective 3-4 solenoid.
10. Incorrectly adjusted selector cable.

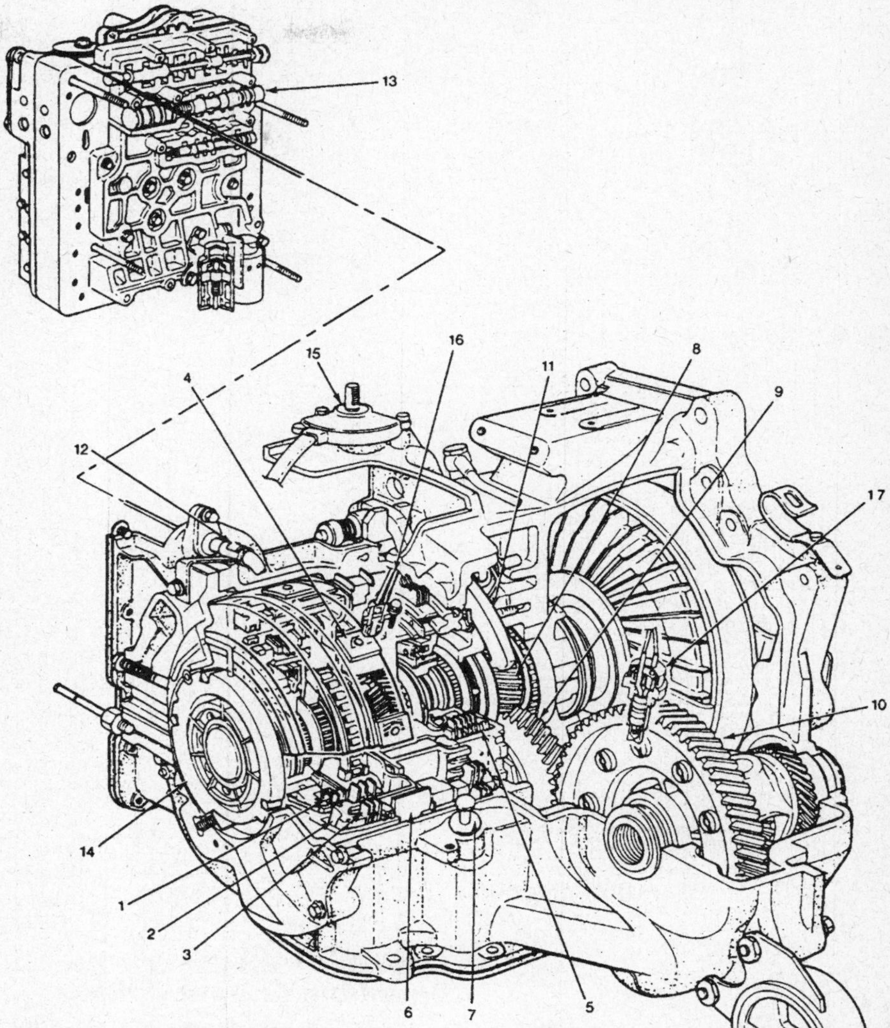

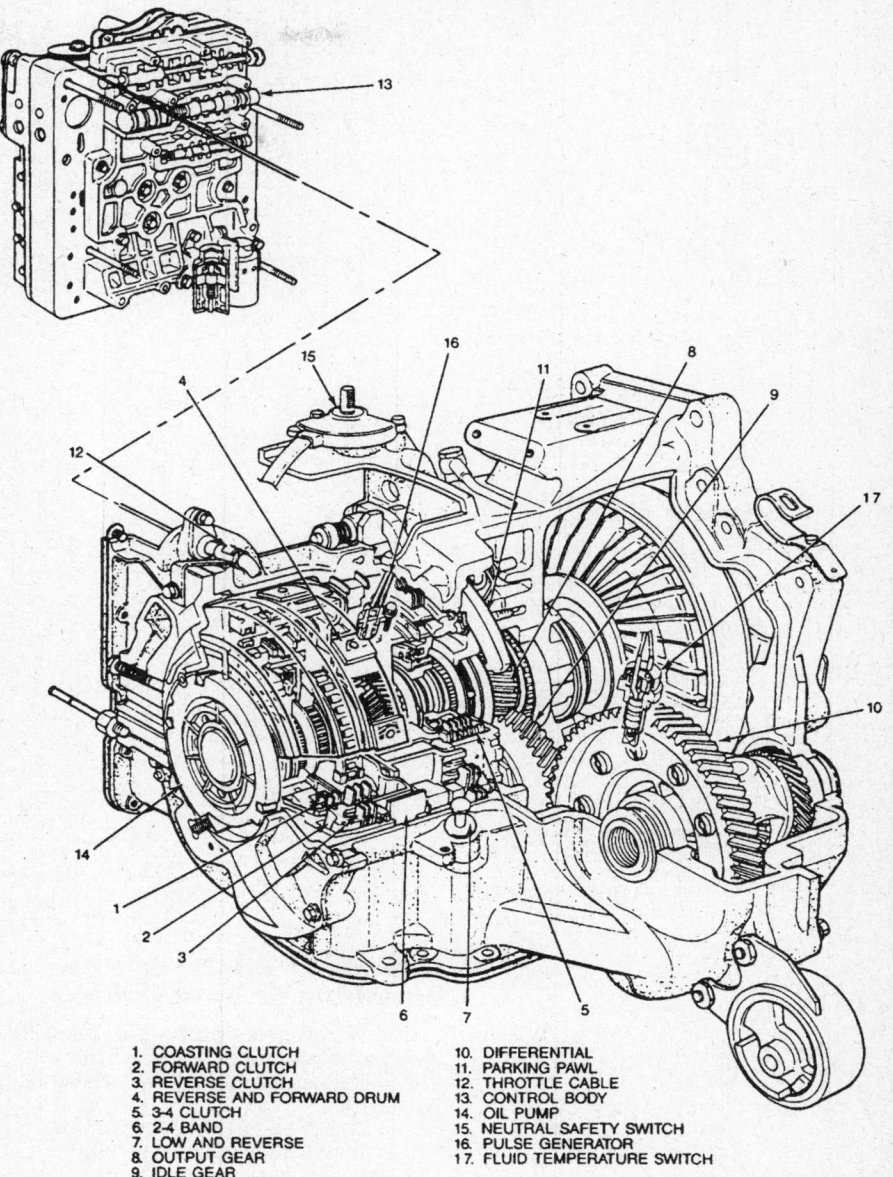

1. COASTING CLUTCH
2. FORWARD CLUTCH
3. REVERSE CLUTCH
4. REVERSE AND FORWARD DRUM
5. 3-4 CLUTCH
6. 2-4 BAND
7. LOW AND REVERSE
8. OUTPUT GEAR
9. IDLE GEAR
10. DIFFERENTIAL
11. PARKING PAWL
12. THROTTLE CABLE
13. CONTROL BODY
14. OIL PUMP
15. NEUTRAL SAFETY SWITCH
16. PULSE GENERATOR
17. FLUID TEMPERATURE SWITCH

FM5028800298000X

Fig. 3 Cross-sectional view of 4EAT automatic transaxle

11. Malfunctioning control valve(s).

No Lock-Up

1. Defective brake light switch.
2. Defective throttle sensor.
3. Defective cruise control switch.
4. Defective water temperature switch.
5. Defective pulse generator.
6. Defective 1-2 solenoid.
7. Defective 2-3 solenoid.
8. Defective 3-4 solenoid.
9. Defective lockup solenoid.
10. Incorrectly adjusted selector lever.
11. Defective torque converter.

No Kickdown

1. Defective inhibitor switch.
2. Defective hold switch.
3. Defective throttle sensor.
4. Incorrectly adjusted selector lever.

Engine Runaway Or Slip When Starting Vehicle

1. Defective inhibitor switch.
2. Fluid level too low or fluid contaminated.
3. Malfunctioning control valve(s).
4. Defective oil pump.
5. Defective forward clutch.
6. Defective one-way clutch No. 1.

Engine Runaway Or Slip When Upshifting Or Downshifting

1. Defective inhibitor switch.
2. Fluid level too low or fluid contaminated.
3. Malfunctioning control valve(s).
4. Defective oil pump.
5. Defective forward clutch.
6. Defective reverse clutch.
7. Defective 3-4 clutch.

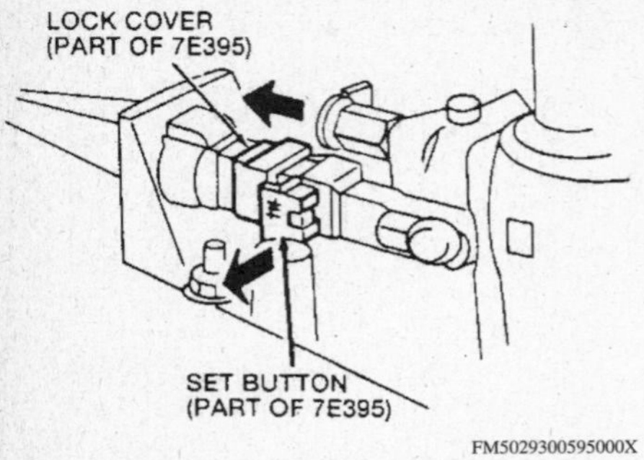

Fig. 4 Sliding back lock cover

Test Step		Result	Action to Take
A1	CHECK BATTERY		
	• Check the battery. • **Is the battery OK?**	Yes ▶ No ▶	GO to **A2**. CHARGE or REPLACE the battery.
A2	CHECK START SIGNAL TO TRANSMISSION RANGE SWITCH		
	• Key OFF. • Disconnect the transmission range (TR) switch connector. • Key in START position. • Measure the voltage of the "GN" wire at the TR switch connector. • **Is the voltage greater than 10 volts with the key in the START position?**	Yes ▶ No ▶ ▶	GO to **A3**. For vehicles with anti-theft system diagnose the starter interrupt relay. All others diagnose the ignition switch START position.

FM5029501104010X

Fig. 5 TR switch diagnosis (Engine will not crank, Part 1 of 2)

Test Step		Result	Action to Take
A3	CHECK TRANSMISSION RANGE SWITCH		
	• Key OFF. • Disconnect the TR switch connector. • Measure the resistance between terminal 9 and terminal 6 at the TR switch. 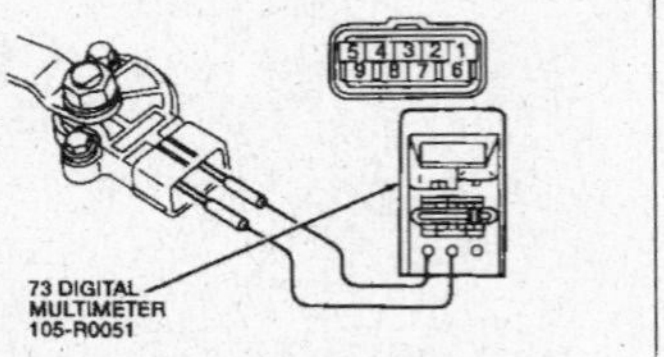 • Shift the gearshift lever through all positions. • **Is the resistance less than 5 ohms when the gearshift lever is in PARK (P) and NEUTRAL (N), and greater than 10,000 ohms when the gearshift lever is in all other ranges?**	Yes ▶ No ▶	GO to **A4**. REPLACE the TR switch.
A4	CHECK START SIGNAL TO STARTER MOTOR		
	• Key OFF. • Reconnect the TR switch connector. • Disconnect the starter motor connector. • Place the gearshift lever into PARK (P). • Key in START position. • Measure the voltage of the "BK/R" wire at the starter motor connector. • **Is the voltage greater than 10 volts with the key in the START position?**	Yes ▶ No ▶	diagnose the starter motor. SERVICE the "BK/R" wire between the TR switch and the starter motor.

FM5029501104020X

Fig. 5 TR switch diagnosis (Engine will not crank, Part 2 of 2)

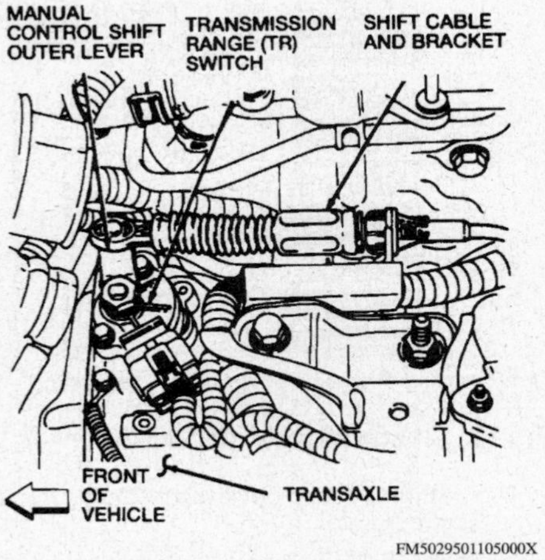

Fig. 6 Shift cable, manual control lever & TR switch

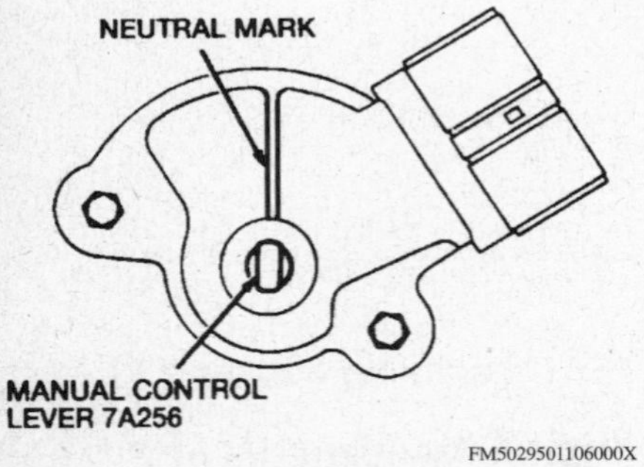

Fig. 7 TR switch alignment

8. Defective 2-4 brake band and/or servo.
9. Defective one-way clutch No. 1.

Excessive N To D Or N To R Shift Shock

1. Fluid level too low or fluid contaminated.
2. Check idle speed and ignition timing.
3. Malfunctioning control valve(s).
4. Defective accumulator(s).
5. Defective forward clutch.
6. Defective reverse clutch.

Excessive Shift Shock When Upshifting Or Downshifting

Following procedure has been revised by a Technical Service Bulletin.

1. Fluid level too low or fluid contaminated.
2. Incorrectly adjusted throttle cable.
3. Malfunctioning control valve(s).
4. Defective accumulator(s).
5. Defective coasting clutch.
6. Defective 3-4 clutch.
7. Defective 2-4 brake band and/or servo.
8. Weak servo return spring.

Excessive Shift Shock When Changing Ranges

1. Defective inhibitor switch.
2. Incorrectly adjusted selector lever.
3. Malfunctioning control valve(s).
4. Defective coasting clutch.
5. Defective low and reverse brake.

Transaxle Noisy In N Or P Range

1. Fluid level too low or fluid contaminated.
2. Defective oil pump.
3. Defective torque converter.

Key Position	Terminals 1	2	3	4	5	6	7	8	9
P						O	—	—	O
R		O	—	—	O				
N						O	—	—	O
D				O	O				
2					O	—	—	O	
1			O	—	O				

O—O: Indicates Continuity

FM5029501107000X

Fig. 8 TR switch continuity chart

4. Defective differential assembly.

Transaxle Noisy In OD, D, L Or R Range

1. Fluid level too low or fluid contaminated.
2. Defective forward clutch.
3. Defective one-way clutch No. 1
4. Defective planetary gear.

No Engine Braking

1. Defective 2-3 solenoid.
2. Defective 3-4 solenoid.
3. Malfunctioning control valve(s).
4. Problem in hydraulic circuit.
5. Defective coasting clutch.

6. Defective low and reverse brake.

No Mode Change

1. Defective inhibitor switch.
2. Defective mode switch.
3. Defective hold switch.
4. Defective throttle sensor.
5. Defective water temperature switch.
6. Defective vehicle speed sensor.
7. Defective pulse generator.
8. Defective 1-2 solenoid.
9. Defective 2-3 solenoid.
10. Defective 3-4 solenoid.
11. Defective lockup solenoid.

Transaxle Overheats

1. Defective lockup solenoid.
2. Fluid level too low or fluid contaminated.
3. Malfunctioning control valve(s).
4. Defective oil pump.
5. Defective torque converter.

Vehicle Moves In P, Or Parking Gear Not Disengaged When P Is Disengaged

1. Incorrectly adjusted selector lever.
2. Defective parking gear.

Hold Indicator Flashes

1. Defective throttle sensor.
2. Defective vehicle speed sensor.
3. Defective pulse generator.
4. Defective 1-2 solenoid.
5. Defective 2-3 solenoid.
6. Defective 3-4 solenoid.
7. Defective lockup solenoid.

Engine Will Not Start

1. Defective inhibitor switch.
2. Incorrectly adjusted selector lever.

Vehicle Drags In Forward & Reverse Gears

1. Bands improperly adjusted.
2. Improper brake function.

MAINTENANCE

FLUID CHECK

1. Start engine and allow transaxle to reach normal operating temperature.
2. With engine idling and parking brake applied, move selector lever through all ranges, then return to P position.
3. With engine idling, remove dipstick and check fluid level. Fluid level should be between full and low marks.
4. Add specified automatic transaxle fluid as necessary to bring level within specifications.

FLUID CHANGE

Normal maintenance and lubrication do not require periodic automatic transaxle fluid changes. If major service, such as a clutch band, bearing, etc. is required, transaxle will have to be removed for service. **At this time torque converter, cooler and oil cooler tubes must be thoroughly flushed to remove any contamination.**

When used after 30,000 miles under continuous or severe conditions, transaxle

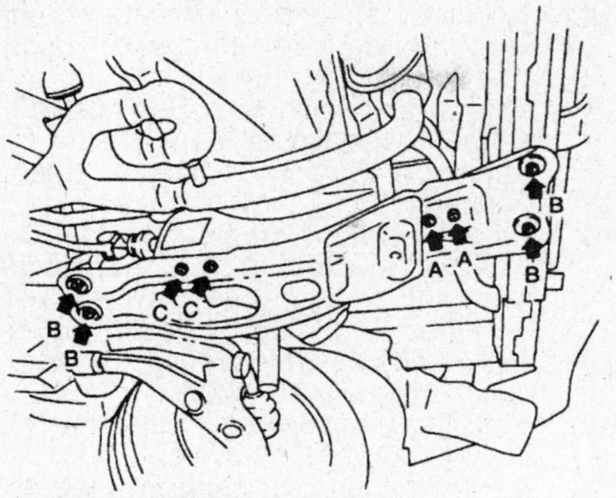

Fig. 9 Tightening transaxle cradle nuts & bolts. 2.5L engines

and torque converter should be drained and refilled with automatic transaxle fluid. Refer to "Lubricant Data Chart" in this manual.

Following procedure is for partial drain and refill due to in-vehicle service operation.

1. Raise and support vehicle, then remove drain plug and washer. Discard washer. **Avoid spilling hot transaxle fluid.**
2. Loosen oil pan bolts and drain fluid.
3. Slowly loosen oil pan bolts, allowing pan to drop and oil to drain.
4. Remove pan, then thoroughly clean.
5. Remove and discard oil pan to case gasket, oil pan screen and oil pan screen ring. **Do not reuse or clean oil pan screen. Filter element material will contaminate transaxle.**
6. Reverse procedure to install, noting following:
   a. Install new oil pan screen, oil pan screen ring, oil pan to case gasket and drain plug washer.
   b. Tighten oil pan bolts and drain plug to specifications.
   c. Add transaxle fluid to specifications. Refer to " Lubricant Data Chart" in this manual.

ADJUSTMENTS

2-4 BRAKE BAND

1. Raise and support vehicle.
2. Remove oil pan and loosen locknut.
3. **Torque** piston stem to 9-11 ft. lbs.
4. Loosen piston stem 1½ turns.
5. Tighten locknut to specifications.

SELECTOR LINKAGE

1. Remove floor console.
2. Shift selector lever to P position, then remove position indicator mounting screws and lift position indicator out of way.
3. Slide lock cover back, then disconnect set button, **Fig. 4.**
4. Slide selector lever to adjust P position, then connect set button.
5. Slide lock cover to lock set button in place.
6. Reverse procedure to install. Tighten position indicator mounting screws to specifications.

TRANSAXLE RANGE (TR) SWITCH

If vehicle will not start in Park/Neutral, refer to **Fig. 5** for TR switch diagnosis. Use following procedure to adjust TR switch.

1. Remove engine air cleaner.
2. Using a screwdriver, pry shift cable and bracket from manual control shift outer lever, **Fig. 6.**
3. Disconnect TR switch electrical connector, then rotate TR switch shaft to Neutral mark, **Fig. 7.**
4. Loosen TR switch bolts.
5. Using an ohmmeter, check continuity between TR switch terminals. Continuity between terminals should be as shown in **Fig. 8.** If continuity is not as specified, replace TR switch as described in "Transaxle Range (TR) Switch, Replace."
6. Tighten TR switch bolts to specifications, then connect TR switch electrical connector. **Ensure TR switch shaft is still aligned with Neutral mark.**
7. Install shift cable, then air cleaner.

IN-VEHICLE REPAIRS

DIFFERENTIAL OIL SEALS, REPLACE

Removal

1. Raise and support vehicle, then remove front wheels.
2. Drain transmission fluid, then remove either lefthand or righthand halfshaft and joint.
3. Remove differential oil seals with flat-tip screwdriver.

Installation

1. Use differential seal replacer tool No. T87C-77000-H, or equivalent, to install new differential oil seals.
2. Replace halfshaft bearing retainer circlip on end of lefthand halfshaft and joint, then install halfshaft.
3. Install front wheels, then tighten wheel hub bolt nuts to specifications.
4. Lower vehicle, then add specified transaxle fluid.
5. Add specified transaxle fluid, check for leaks and check fluid level.

VALVE BODY, REPLACE

Removal

1. Raise and support vehicle.
2. Remove lefthand splash shield, then drain transaxle fluid.
3. Disconnect and plug transaxle cooler inlet and outlet hoses, then remove transaxle cooler hose mounting bracket from top righthand side of valve body cover.
4. Disconnect vent hose from top lefthand side of valve body cover.
5. Loosen valve body cover mounting

bolts and allow any transaxle fluid to drain from cover.
6. Remove valve body cover mounting bolts and cover, then discard gasket.
7. Disconnect transaxle oil temperature sensor connector, then solenoid connectors. **Note color and position of connectors to ease installation.**
8. Remove valve body mounting bolts, then valve body.

Installation

1. Position valve body in transaxle case. **Ensure manual valve is aligned with manual plate.**
2. Install valve body mounting bolts and tighten to specifications.
3. Connect vent hose to top lefthand side of valve body cover, then install oil cooler hose mounting bracket on top righthand side of valve body cover.
4. Remove plugs from oil cooler inlet and outlet hoses, then connect hoses.
5. Connect solenoid and TOT sensor connectors.
6. Install new gasket on valve body cover. **Do not use any type of sealer on valve body cover or gasket.**
7. Install valve body cover and tighten mounting bolts to specifications.
8. Install lefthand splash shield. Tighten screws to specifications.
9. Lower vehicle.
10. Fill transaxle with specified transaxle fluid, then check for leaks.

SHIFT LOCK ACTUATOR, REPLACE

Refer to "CD4E Automatic Transaxle" section for replacement procedure.

TRANSAXLE

REPLACE

REMOVAL

1. Remove battery hold-down, battery and battery tray from vehicle.
2. Remove air cleaner assembly.
3. Remove shift cable from TR switch arm. Use screwdriver to pry cable from switch arm.
4. Remove shift cable from cable bracket as follows:
   a. Remove lock tab retainer.
   b. Press in on lock tabs to release cable, then pull cable through bracket.
5. Disconnect TR switch electrical connector.
6. Disconnect two heated oxygen sensor electrical connectors.
7. Disconnect electrical connector, then remove wiring harness bracket from cable bracket.
8. Remove starter motor, then disconnect vehicle speed sensor.
9. Remove ground wire bracket, then ground wire.
10. Remove harness support bracket to generator located at rear transaxle mount.
11. Disconnect and plug oil cooler outlet and inlet hoses, then remove four transaxle to engine mount bolts.
12. Install three-bar Engine Support tool No. 014-00750, or equivalent.
13. Remove lefthand transaxle mount nuts and bolts, then through bolt.
14. Remove fuel filter bracket nuts from lefthand transaxle mount, then position fuel filter and bracket aside.
15. Remove lefthand transaxle mount, then disconnect pulse signal generator electrical connector.
16. Raise and support vehicle, then remove front wheel and tire assemblies and both splash shields.
17. Remove transverse member, then transaxle cradle.
18. Remove transaxle lower mount bolts, then lower mount.
19. Remove halfshafts, then Install transaxle plug set tool No. T88C-7025-AH, or equivalent, into differential side gears. **Failure to install transaxle plugs may allow differential side gears to become improperly positioned.**
20. Disconnect transaxle vent hose and dipstick tube.
21. Remove inspection cover and four torque converter to flex plate nuts.
22. Position transmission jack under transaxle, then secure transaxle to jack.
23. Remove engine-to-transaxle and transaxle to engine mounting bolts.
24. Remove three rear transaxle mount bolts.
25. Separate transaxle from engine block, then slightly tilt transaxle and engine to ease removal.
26. Remove transaxle from engine, then lower transaxle from vehicle.

INSTALLATION

1. Place transaxle on transmission jack. **Ensure transaxle is secure.**
2. Raise transaxle to proper height, then align torque converter studs and flexplate holes.
3. Install engine to transaxle mounting bolts. Tighten bolts to specifications.
4. Install rear transaxle mount bolts. Tighten bolts to specifications, then install inspection cover.
5. Connect transaxle vent hose, then install dipstick tube. Tighten dipstick mounting bolts to specifications.
6. Remove transaxle plugs, then install halfshafts.
7. Install transaxle lower mount. Tighten lower mount to specifications.
8. Remove jack from under transaxle.
9. Install transaxle cradle. **Torque** cradle bolts (A) to 55–77 ft. lbs., (B) to 50–68 ft. lbs. and (C) to 32–44 ft. lbs., **Fig. 9.**
10. Install transverse member. Tighten bolts to specifications.
11. Install splash shields. Tighten mounting screws to specifications.
12. Install front wheel and tire assemblies. Tighten wheel lug nuts to specifications.
13. Lower vehicle.
14. Install transaxle to engine mounting bolts. Tighten bolts to specifications.
15. Connect vehicle speed sensor, then install ground wire bracket and ground wire.
16. Connect pulse signal generator electrical connector.
17. Install harness support bracket to generator located at rear transaxle mount.
18. Install lefthand transaxle mount, nuts and bolt. Tighten nuts and bolts to specifications.
19. Install lefthand transaxle mount through bolt. Tighten through bolt to specifications.
20. Remove engine support bar.
21. Install fuel filter bracket to lefthand transaxle mount. Tighten bracket bolts to specifications.
22. Connect oil cooler outlet and inlet hoses.
23. Install starter motor then connect electrical connector.
24. Connect two heated oxygen sensor electrical connectors.
25. Install shift cable to cable bracket as follows:
    a. Insert shift cable through cable bracket.
    b. Pull cable until lock tabs engage, then install lock tab retainer.
26. Install shift cable on TR switch arm, then connect TR switch electrical connector.
27. Snap wiring harness bracket on cable bracket, then install air cleaner assembly.
28. Install battery tray, battery and battery hold-down.
29. Add specified transaxle fluid, then check for leaks and check fluid level.

TIGHTENING SPECIFICATIONS

Year	Component	Torque/ Ft. Lbs.
1997	Battery Tray Bolts	72–84①
	Bearing Housing	21–25
	Case Plug	30–36
	Center Transaxle Mount Bolts	27–40
	Center Transaxle Mount Nuts	47–66
	Converter Cover	72–120①
	Crossmember Bolts	27–40
	Crossmember Nuts	55–69
	Dipstick Tube	60–84①
	Drain Plug	29–43
	Fluid Temperature Switch	22–29
	Gusset Plate To Transaxle	27–38
	Left Mount To Bracket	49–69
	Line Pressure Plug	43–87①
	Manual Shaft Plate	30–41
	Oil Cooler Line Plug	23–35
	Oil Pan	72–120①
	Oil Pump	14–19
	Pulse Generator	72–120①
	Range Selector To Transaxle	22–29
	Right Transaxle Mount	63–86
	Switch Box	12–17
	Throttle Cable Bracket	14–19
	Throttle Cam	61–87①
	Torque Converter	32–45
	Transaxle Case To Converter Housing	27–38
	Transaxle To Engine	50–73
	Transaxle To Left Mount	63–86
	Transaxle Range Switch Bolts	72–96①
	Valve Body	60–72①

① — Inch lbs.

4R70W (AODE-W) Automatic Overdrive Transmission

NOTE: On Air Bag Equipped Models, Refer To " Air Bag System Precautions" Located In The Front Of This Manual For System Disarming & Arming Procedures.

NOTE: "Electrical Symbol & Wire Color Code Identification" Located In The Front Of This Manual May Be Used As An Aid When Using Wiring Circuits Found In This Section.

NOTE: Prior To Performing Any Service Operations Listed In This Section, Consult "Technical Service Bulletins " Section For Related Information.

INDEX

PRECAUTIONS

AIR BAG SYSTEMS

Refer to "Air Bag System Precautions" in front of this manual for system disarming and arming procedures.

BATTERY GROUND CABLE

Prior to service, disconnect battery ground cable and isolate as required.

IDENTIFICATION

These transmissions may be identified by tag attached to upper righthand extension housing to transmission case bolt. Tags include model prefix and suffix, a service identification number and a build date code, **Fig. 1.** Service identification number indicates changes to service details which affect interchangeability when transmission model is not changed. For interpretation of this number Ford Master Parts Catalog should be consulted.

DESCRIPTION

This unit is a four-speed automatic transmission incorporating an integral overdrive feature. With selector lever in 1 position, transmission will start and remain in first gear until selector lever is moved to another position. In 3 position, transmission will automatically shift through 1-2-3 range, but will not engage overdrive. In D position, transmission will automatically select appropriate time to shift into overdrive (4th gear). Design of transmission features a split torque path in third gear, where 40% of engine torque is transmitted hydraulically through torque converter and 60% is transmitted mechanically through solid connections (direct drive input shaft) to driveshaft. When transmission is in overdrive (4th gear), 100% of engine torque is transmitted through direct drive input shaft.

Transmission consists of a torque converter assembly, compound planetary gear train and a hydraulic control system, **Fig. 2.** For gear control transmission has four friction clutches, two one-way roller clutches and two bands. Overdrive is accomplished by addition of a band to lock reverse sun gear while driving planet carrier. Torque converter operation is similar to other types of automatic transmission, but has an added damper assembly and input shaft for 3rd gear and overdrive. Direct drive input shaft couples engine directly to direct clutch. This shaft is driven by torque converter cover through damper assembly which cushions engine shock to transmission.

The 4R70W (AODE-W) transmission is an AOD-E transmission with wide ratio gears and is a four-speed rear wheel drive automatic with an electronic shift, torque converter clutch control and line pressure controls. This transmission uses a double pinion compound gearset to produce four forward speeds and reverse. Two bands, two one-way roller clutches and four friction clutches are used to hold or drive various planetary gearset members.

For safety purposes, 4R70W also incorporates a brake shift interlock system. This prevents gear shift lever from being shifted from Park (with key in On position) unless brake pedal is applied. Brake shift interlock system includes an actuator mounted at base of steering column that runs continuously while ignition is in On position.

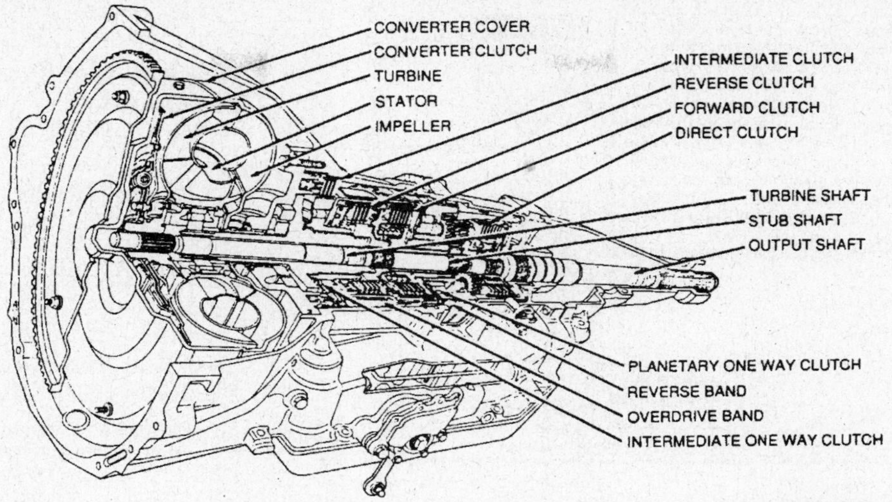

FM5029200634000X

Fig. 2 Cross-sectional view of automatic overdrive transmission

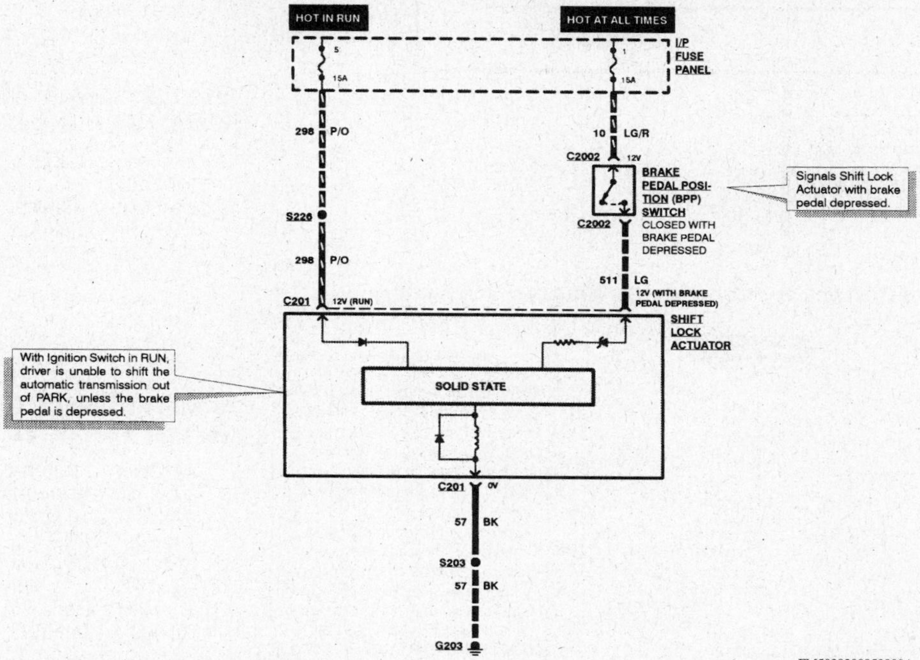

FM5029300953000A

Fig. 3 Shift interlock system wiring diagram. Thunderbird & Mark VIII & 1997–98 Crown Victoria, Grand Marquis & Town Car & 1997 Cougar

TROUBLESHOOTING

SHIFT INTERLOCK SYSTEM

THUNDERBIRD & MARK VIII & 1997–98 CROWN VICTORIA, GRAND MARQUIS & TOWN CAR & 1997 COUGAR

Refer to wiring diagrams **Figs. 3 through 5,** and troubleshooting chart **Figs. 6 through 8** when troubleshooting brake shift interlock system.

1999–2000 CROWN VICTORIA, GRAND MARQUIS & TOWN CAR

Refer to wiring diagram **Fig. 3.**

Test A1: Test Brake Lights

1. Turn ignition switch to On position.
2. Apply brake pedal and view brake lights.
3. If brake lights illuminate go to Test A7.
4. If brake lights do not illuminate go to Test A2.

Test A2: Test Fuse 10 (20A)

1. Turn ignition switch to On position.
2. Measure resistance of fuse 10 (20A).
3. If resistance of fuse is 5 ohms or less go to Test A4.
4. If resistance of fuse is 5 ohms or more go to Test A3.

Test A3: Test Circuit 10 (LG/R) For Short To Ground

1. Turn ignition switch to On position.
2. Disconnect Brake Pedal Position (BPP) switch connector C2002.
3. Measure resistance of circuit 10 (LG/R) at connector C2002.
4. If resistance is 10 K ohms or less, check circuit 10 (LG/R) for short to ground, then test system for normal operation.

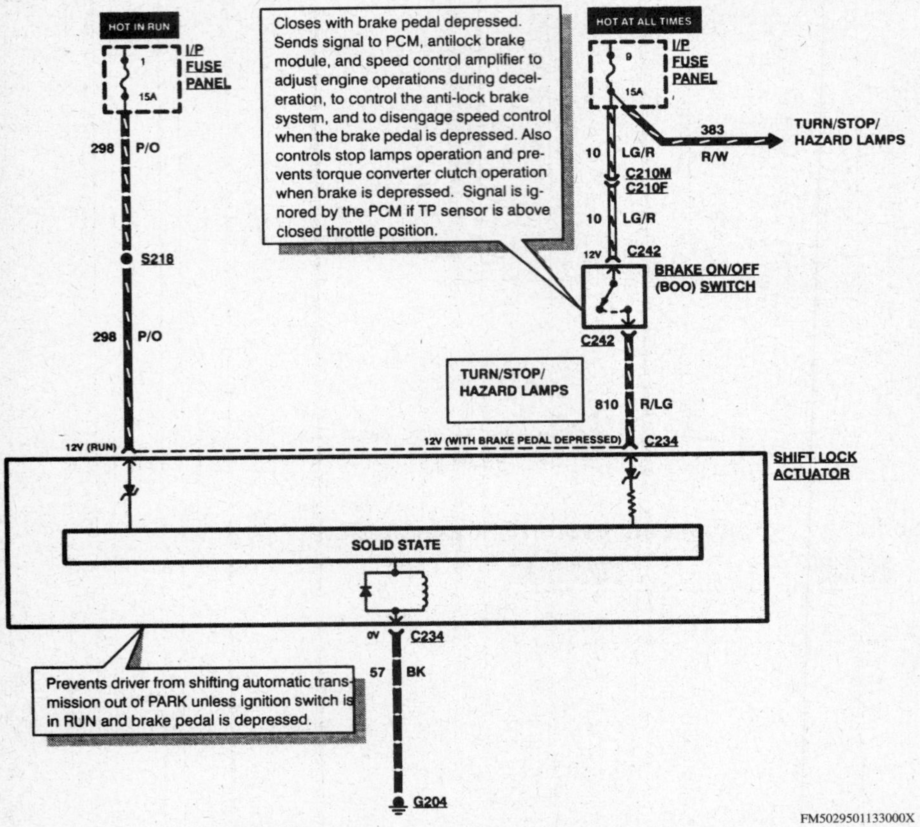

Fig. 4 Shift interlock system wiring diagram. Mustang

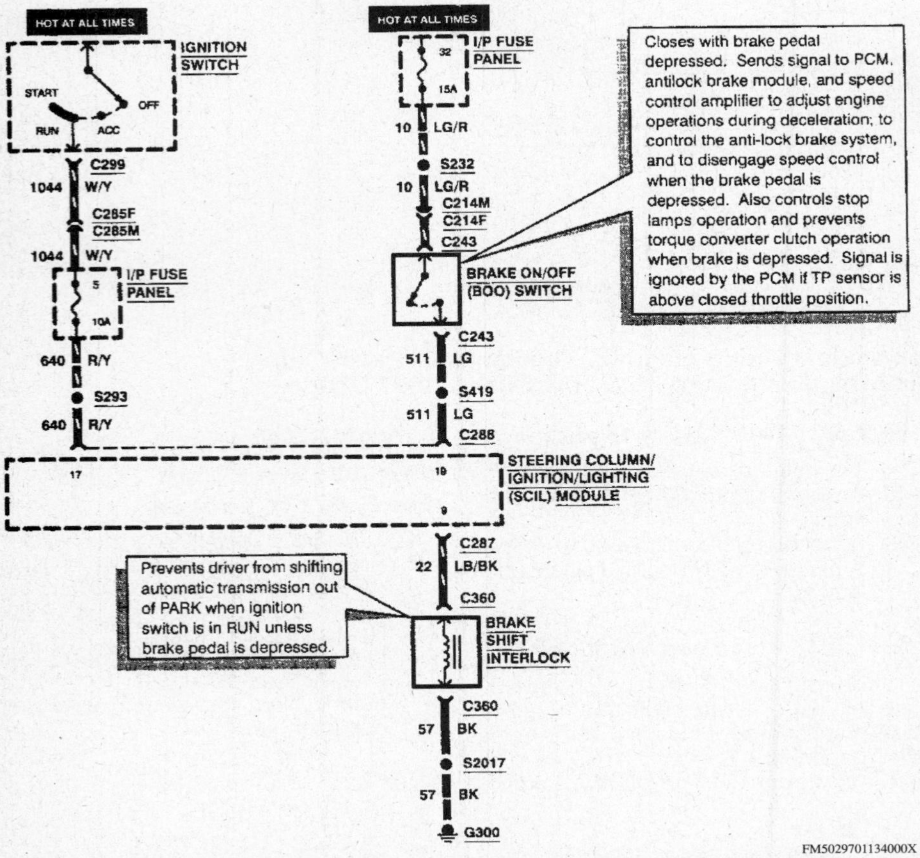

Fig. 5 Shift interlock system wiring diagram. Mark VIII

5. If resistance is 10 K ohms or more, go to Test A4.

Test A4: Test Circuit 10 (LG/R) For Open

1. Measure resistance between output side of fuse 10 (20A) and Brake Pedal Position (BPP) switch connector C2002, circuit 10 (LG/R).
2. If resistance is 5 ohms or less, go to Test A5.
3. If resistance is 5 ohms or more, check circuit 10 (LG/R) for open, then test system for normal operation.

Test A5: Test Brake Pedal Position (BPP) Switch

1. Measure resistance of BPP switch while open (Off) and closed (On).
2. If resistance of switch is greater than 10 K ohms while Off and 5 ohms or less while On, go to Test A8.
3. If resistance of switch is less than 10 K ohms while Off and 5 ohms or more while On, replace BPP switch, then test system for normal operation.

Test A6: Check Circuit 810 (R/LG) For Short To Ground

1. Disconnect shift lock actuator connector C232.
2. Measure resistance of circuit 810 (R/LG), pin C232-1.
3. If resistance is 10 K ohms or less, check circuit 810 (R/LG) for short to ground, then test system for normal operation.
4. If resistance is 10 K ohms or more, go to Test A7.

Test A7: Check Circuit 810 (R/LG) For Open

1. Measure resistance of circuit 810 (R/LG) between shift lock actuator pin C232-1 and brake On/Off switch connector C2002.
2. If resistance is 5 ohms of less, go to Test A8.
3. If resistance is 5 ohms of more, check circuit 810 (R/LG) for open, then test system for normal operation.

Test A8: Test For B+ On Circuit 296 (W/P)

1. Measure voltage at shift lock actuator pin C298-3, circuit 296 (W/P).
2. If B+ is present, go to Test A12.
3. If B+ is not present, go to Test A9.

Test A9: Test Fuse 6 (5A)

1. Turn ignition switch to On position.
2. Measure fuse 20 (7.5A) resistance.
3. If resistance of fuse is 5 ohms or less, go to Test A11.
4. If resistance of fuse is 5 ohms or more, go to Test A10.

Test A10: Test Circuit 296 (W/P) For Short To Ground

1. Measure resistance at Pin C232-3, circuit 296 (W/P).
2. If resistance is 10 K ohms or less, check circuit 296 (W/P) for short to

ground, then test system for normal operation.
3. If resistance is 10 K ohms or more, go to Test A11.

Test A11: Test Circuit 296 (W/P) For Open

1. Measure resistance of circuit 296 (W/P) between output side of fuse 20 (7.5A) and shift lock actuator pin C232-3.
2. If resistance is 5 ohms or less, go to Test A12.
3. If resistance is 5 ohms or more, check circuit 296 (W/P) for open, then test system for normal operation.

Test A12: Test Circuit 57 (BK) For Open

1. Measure resistance of shift lock actuator connector C232-2, circuit 57 (BK).
2. If resistance is 5 ohm or less, replace shift lock actuator, then test system for normal operation.
3. If resistance is 5 ohm or more, check circuit 57 (BK) for open, then test system for normal operation.

1999-2000 MUSTANG

Refer to wiring diagram **Fig. 7.**

Test A1: Test Brake Lights

1. Turn ignition switch to On position.
2. Apply brake pedal and view brake lights.
3. If brake lights illuminate go to Test A2.
4. If brake lights do not illuminate inspect brake light operation.

Test A2: Check Circuit 511 (LG) For Open

1. Measure voltage of circuit 511 (LG) between shift lock actuator pin C234-1 harness side and ground while pressing and releasing brake pedal.
2. If measurement is more than 10 volts with brake pedal pressed and zero volts with pedal released, go to Test A3.
3. If measurement is not more than 10 volts with brake pedal pressed and zero volts with pedal released, repair circuit.

Test A3: Test Circuit 294 (WH/LB) For Open

1. Measure voltage at shift lock actuator pin C234-3, circuit 294 (WH/LB).
2. If measurement is more than 10 volts, go to Test A4.
3. If measurement is less than 10 volts, repair circuit.

Test A4: Test Circuit 57 (BK) For Open

1. Measure resistance of shift lock actuator connector C232-2, circuit 57 (BK).
2. If resistance is 5 ohm or less, replace shift lock actuator, then test system for normal operation.
3. If resistance is 5 ohm or more, check circuit 57 (BK) for open, then test system for normal operation.

TRANSMISSION

1997

Rough Initial Engagement

1. Improper fluid level.
2. High engine idle.
3. Loose driveshaft, engine mounts or U-joints.
4. Sticking or dirty valve body.
5. Improper clutch or band application, or low oil control pressure.
6. Incorrectly adjusted automatic choke.

Slow Initial Engagement

1. Improper fluid level.
2. Damaged or improperly adjusted linkage.
3. Contaminated fluid.
4. Low main control pressure or improper clutch and band application.

Harsh Engagements w/Warm Engine

1. Improper fluid level.
2. Damaged or improperly adjusted linkage.
3. High engine idle.
4. Sticking or dirty valve body.
5. Throttle linkage return spring disconnected.
6. Valve body bolts improperly tightened, loose or too tight.

No Or Delayed Forward Engagement

1. Improper fluid level.
2. Damaged or improperly adjusted linkage.
3. Low main control pressure.
4. Forward clutch stator support seal rings Nos. 3 and/or 4 leaking.
5. Burned and/or damaged forward clutch assembly.
6. Forward clutch cylinder check ball and/or piston seal rings leaking.
7. Valve body bolts improperly tightened.
8. Valve body dirty or valves sticking.
9. Clogged transmission filter.
10. Damaged or leaking pump.

No Or Delayed Reverse Engagement

1. Improper fluid level.
2. Damaged or improperly adjusted linkage.
3. Low main control pressure.
4. Leaking high reverse clutch or reverse clutch stator support seal rings Nos. 1 and/or 2.
5. Burned or worn reverse clutch assembly.
6. Leaking reverse clutch piston check ball and/or piston seal rings.
7. Valve body bolts improperly tightened.
8. Valve body dirty or valves sticking.
9. Clogged transmission filter.
10. Damaged pump.

No Or Delayed Reverse Engagement And/Or No Engine Braking In Manual Low

1. Improper fluid level.
2. Damaged or improperly adjusted linkage.
3. Leaking low reverse servo piston seal.
4. Burned or worn low reverse servo piston.
5. Damaged planetary low one-way clutch.
6. End play clearance too tight.

No Engine Braking In Manual 2nd

1. Improper fluid level.
2. Damaged or improperly adjusted linkage.
3. Improper clutch or band application.
4. Improper control system pressure.
5. Leaking intermediate servo.
6. Damaged intermediate one-way clutch.

Forward Engagement Slips, Shudders And/Or Chatters

1. Improper fluid level.
2. Incorrectly adjusted or damaged linkage.
3. Low main control pressure.
4. Valve body bolts improperly tightened.
5. Valve body dirty or valves sticking.
6. Forward clutch piston check ball leaking and/or not seating.
7. Cut and/or worn forward clutch piston seal.
8. Leaking forward clutch stator support seal rings Nos. 3 and 4.
9. Damaged low one-way clutch (planetary).

Reverse Shudders, Chatters And/Or Slips

1. Improper fluid level.
2. Low main control pressure in reverse.
3. Leaking low reverse servo.
4. Damaged planetary low one-way clutch.
5. Damaged reverse clutch drum bushing.
6. Worn or damaged reverse clutch stator support seal rings or grooves.
7. Cut and/or worn reverse clutch piston.
8. Damaged reverse band.
9. Loosen driveshaft, engine mounts or U-joints.

No Drive, Slips Or Chatters In 1st Gear In D Or Overdrive

1. Damaged planetary low one-way clutch.

No Drive, Slips Or Chatters In 2nd Gear

1. Worn or damaged friction clutch or one-way clutch.
2. Intermediate clutch piston belled hole clogged or not positioned at 12 o'clock.
3. Control pressure or improper band or clutch application.
4. Internal leakage.
5. Dirty valve body or sticking valves.

Initial Drive In 2nd Or 3rd

1. Improper fluid level.
2. Damaged or improperly adjusted linkage.

3. Oil pressure control system or improper clutch and/or band application.
4. Intermediate clutch pack clearance too tight.
5. Damaged, worn or sticking governor.
6. Sticking or dirty valve body.
7. Valve body bolts too loose.
8. Cross leaks between valve body and case mating surface.

Improper Shift Points

1. Improper fluid level.
2. Damaged or improperly adjusted linkage.
3. Improper speedometer gear installed.
4. Improper clutch or band application.
5. Improper control system pressure.
6. Damaged or worn governor.
7. Sticking or dirty valve body.

Harsh, Delayed Or No Upshifts

1. Improper fluid level.
2. Damaged or improperly adjusted linkage.
3. Throttle return spring disconnected.
4. Damaged or incorrectly adjusted manual linkage.
5. Governor sticking.
6. High main control pressure.
7. Valve body bolts improperly tightened.
8. Sticking or dirty valve body.

Mushy And/Or Early Upshifts Or Upshift Pileup

1. Improper fluid level.
2. Damaged or improperly adjusted linkage.
3. Low main control pressure.
4. Sticking throttle control valve or valve body.
5. Sticking governor valve.
6. Valve body bolts improperly tightened.

No 1-2 Upshifts

1. Improper fluid level.
2. Damaged or improperly adjusted linkage.
3. Low main control pressure to intermediate friction clutch.
4. Sticking, leaking or bent diaphragm unit.
5. Sticking or dirty valve body.
6. Burned intermediate clutch, band or servo.
7. Valve body bolts improperly tightened.

Rough, Harsh And/Or Delayed 1-2 Upshift

1. Improper fluid level.
2. Poor engine performance.
3. Incorrectly adjusted or damaged throttle linkage.
4. Main control pressure too high.
5. Sticking governor valve.
6. Valve body bolts improperly tightened.
7. Valve body dirty or valves sticking.

Mushy, Early, Soft And/Or Slipping 1-2 Upshift

1. Improper fluid level.
2. Improperly tuned engine.
3. Damaged or improperly adjusted linkage.
4. Incorrect main control pressure.
5. Sticking governor valve.
6. Valve body bolts improperly tightened.
7. Valve body dirty or valves sticking.
8. Worn or burned intermediate friction clutch.
9. Damaged intermediate servo.

No 2-3 Upshifts

1. Improper fluid level.
2. Low main control pressure to direct clutch.
3. Valve body bolts improperly tightened.
4. Sticking or dirty valve body.
5. Burned or worn direct or reverse-high clutch assembly.
6. Broken weld on converter damper hub.

Harsh And/Or Delayed 2-3 Upshift

1. Incorrect engine performance.
2. Incorrectly adjusted, sticking or damaged throttle linkage.
3. Plugged or missing 2-3 accumulator apply passage.
4. Cut or worn 2-3 accumulator piston seals.
5. Damaged 2-3 accumulator.
6. Valve body bolts improperly tightened.
7. Valve body dirty.
8. Sticking 2-3 capacity modulator valve.
9. Bent, sticking or leaking vacuum diaphragm or TV control rod.

Soft, Early And/Or Mushy 2-3 Upshift

1. Improper fluid level.
2. Improperly tuned engine.
3. Damaged or improperly adjusted linkage.
4. Valve body bolts improperly tightened.
5. Burned or worn direct clutch assembly or reverse/high clutch.
6. Damaged accumulator.
7. Dirty or sticking valve body.
8. Bent, sticking or leaking vacuum diaphragm or TV control rod.

No 3-4 Upshifts

1. Low fluid level.
2. Damaged or improperly adjusted linkage.
3. Direct clutch circuit leakage.
4. Sticking or dirty valve body.
5. Distorted main control gasket.
6. Distorted case.
7. Leaking governor.

Harsh And/Or Delayed 3-4 Upshift

1. Improper fluid level.
2. Damaged or improperly adjusted linkage.
3. Throttle return spring disconnected.
4. Valve body bolts improperly tightened.
5. Valve body dirty or valves sticking.
6. Incorrect engine performance.
7. Cut or worn 3-4 accumulator piston seals.
8. Clogged 3-4 accumulator piston drain passage.

Slipping 4th Gear

1. Overdrive circuit leakage or blocked passage.
2. Overdrive servo piston and/or band not applying.
3. Overdrive band incorrectly located.
4. Converter damper plate and hub damaged.
5. Distorted direct driveshaft splines.

Erratic Shifts

1. Improper fluid level.
2. Improperly tuned engine.
3. Damaged or improperly adjusted linkage.
4. Dirty or sticking valve body.
5. Sticking governor valve.
6. Damaged output shaft collector body seal rings.
7. Valve body bolts improperly tightened.

Shifts 1-3 In Overdrive

1. Improper fluid level.
2. Damaged or burned intermediate friction clutch.
3. Damaged intermediate one-way clutch.
4. Improper control system pressure or clutch application.
5. Sticking or dirty valve body.
6. Sticking governor valve.

Engine Overspeeds On 2-3 Shift

1. Improper fluid level.
2. Damaged or improperly adjusted linkage.
3. Improper control system pressure or clutch application.
4. Damaged or worn high clutch or intermediate servo.
5. Sticking or dirty valve body.
6. Broken converter damper hub.
7. Cut or leaking intermediate servo piston seals.

Shift Hunting 3-4 Or 4-3

1. Improperly tuned engine.
2. Damaged or improperly adjusted linkage.
3. Worn or damaged EGR solenoid.

No Forced Downshifts

1. Improper fluid level.
2. Damaged or improperly adjusted linkage.
3. Improper control system pressure or clutch application.
4. Sticking or dirty valve body.
5. Sticking or dirty governor.

Rough Shudder 3-1 Shift At Closed Throttle In Overdrive

1. Improper fluid level.
2. Improperly tuned engine.
3. Damaged or improperly adjusted linkage.
4. Improper control system pressure or clutch application.
5. Improper governor operation.
6. Sticking or dirty valve body.

Rough Or Mushy 4-2 Or 3-1 Shift

1. Improper fluid level.
2. Improperly tuned engine.

3. Damaged or improperly adjusted linkage.
4. Improper application of intermediate friction and one-way clutch.
5. Sticking or dirty valve body.

High Shift Effort

1. Damaged or improperly adjusted linkage.
2. Loose manual lever nut.
3. Damaged manual lever retainer pin.

Transmission Overheats

1. Improper fluid level.
2. Improperly tuned engine.
3. Improper control system pressure or clutch application.
4. Restricted cooler or lines.
5. Seized converter one-way clutch.
6. Sticking or dirty valve body.

Clunk Or Squawk In 1-2 Or 2-3

1. Blocked intermediate bleed hole or bleed hole not at 12 o'clock position.
2. Incorrectly aligned anti-clunk spring.

Harsh Downshift Coasting Clunk

1. Improperly seated anti-clunk spring.
2. Damaged or improperly adjusted linkage.

Poor Vehicle Acceleration

1. Improperly tuned engine.
2. Seized torque converter one-way clutch.

Slipping Shift Followed By Sudden Engagement

Throttle valve linkage set too short.

Transmission Noisy, Valve Resonance

Gauges may aggravate any hydraulic resonance.

1. Improper fluid level.
2. Damaged or improperly adjusted linkage.
3. Improper control system pressure or clutch application.
4. Cooler lines contacting frame, floor pan or other components.
5. Sticking or dirty valve body.
6. Internal leakage or pump cavitation.

Transmission Noisy, Except Valve Resonance

1. Improper fluid level.
2. Damaged or improperly adjusted linkage.
3. Contaminated fluid.
4. Loose converter to flywheel housing bolts or nuts.
5. Loose or worn speedometer driven gear.
6. Damaged or worn extension housing bushing seal or driveshaft.
7. Damaged or worn front or rear planetary and/or one-way clutch.

Harsh Coasting Downshift Clunk

1. Improperly seated anti-clunk spring.
2. Incorrectly adjusted throttle linkage.
3. Sticking throttle linkage return spring.

Initial Engagement Clunk w/Engine Warm

1. Engine idle speed incorrect.
2. Incorrectly adjusted throttle linkage.
3. Worn, damaged or loose universal joints, slip yoke, rear axle or suspension.
4. Excessive transmission endplay.

Vehicle Will Not Start

1. Incorrectly adjusted ignition switch.
2. Defective ignition switch.
3. Defective neutral start switch.

1998–2000

Refer **Figs. 9 through 38** for troubleshooting.

TROUBLESHOOTING TEST INDEX

SHIFT INTERLOCK SYSTEM

Test	Description	Page No.	Fig. No.
THUNDERBIRD & 1997–98 CROWN VICTORIA, GRAND MARQUIS & TOWN CAR & 1997 COUGAR SHIFT INTERLOCK			
—	Shift Interlock System Troubleshooting Chart	21-113	6
MUSTANG SHIFT INTERLOCK			
—	Shift Interlock System Troubleshooting Chart	21-114	7
MARK VIII SHIFT INTERLOCK			
—	Shift Interlock System Troubleshooting Chart	21-114	8
1999–2000 CROWN VICTORIA & GRAND MARQUIS & 1997–99 TOWN CAR SHIFT INTERLOCK			
Test A1	Test Brake Lights	21-107	—
Test A2	Test Fuse 10 (20A)	21-107	—
Test A3	Test Circuit 10 (LG/R) For Short To Ground	21-107	—
Test A4	Test Circuit 10 (LG/R) For Open	21-108	—
Test A5	Test Brake Pedal Position (BPP) Switch	21-108	—
Test A6	Check Circuit 810 (R/LG) For Short To Ground	21-108	—
Test A7	Check Circuit 810 (R/LG) For Open	21-108	—
Test A8	Test For B+ On Circuit 296 (W/P)	21-108	—
Test A9	Test Fuse 6 (5A)	21-108	—
Test A10	Test Circuit 296 (W/P) For Short To Ground	21-108	—
Test A11	Test Circuit 296 (W/P) For Open	21-109	—
Test A12	Test Circuit 57 (BK) For Open	21-109	—
1999–2000 MUSTANG			
Test A1	Test Brake Lights	21-109	—
Test A2	Check Circuit 511 (LG) For Open	21-109	—
Test A3	Test Circuit 294 (WH/LB) For Open	21-109	—
Test A4	Test Circuit 57 (BK) For Open	21-109	—

TRANSMISSION

Routine	Description	Page No.	Fig. No.
1997 TRANSMISSION			
—	Clunk Or Squawk In 1-2 Or 2-3	21-111	—
—	Engine Overspeeds On 2-3 Shift	21-110	—
—	Erratic Shifts	21-110	—
—	Forward Engagement Slips, Shudders And/Or Chatters	21-109	—
—	Harsh And/Or Delayed 2-3 Upshift	21-110	—
—	Harsh And/Or Delayed 3-4 Upshift	21-110	—
—	Harsh Coasting Downshift Clunk	21-111	—
—	Harsh, Delayed Or No Upshifts	21-110	—
—	Harsh Downshift Coasting Clunk	21-111	—
—	Harsh Engagements w/Warm Engine	21-109	—
—	High Shift Effort	21-111	—
—	Improper Shift Points	21-110	—
—	Initial Drive In 2nd Or 3rd	21-109	—
—	Initial Engagement Clunk w/Engine Warm	21-111	—
—	Mushy And/Or Early Upshifts Or Upshift Pileup	21-110	—
—	Mushy, Early, Soft And/Or Slipping 1-2 Upshift	21-110	—
—	No Drive, Slips Or Chatters In 1st Gear, D or Overdrive	21-109	—
—	No Drive, Slips Or Chatters In 2nd Gear	21-109	—
—	No Engine Braking In Manual 2nd	21-109	—
—	No Forced Downshifts	21-110	—
—	No Or Delayed Forward Engagement	21-109	—
—	No Or Delayed Reverse Engagement And/Or No Engine Braking In Manual Low	21-109	—
—	No 1-2 Upshift	21-110	—
—	No 2-3 Upshift	21-110	—
—	No 3-4 Upshifts	21-110	—
—	Poor Vehicle Acceleration	21-111	—
—	Reverse Shudders, Chatters And/Or Slips	21-109	—
—	Rough, Harsh And/Or Delayed 1-2 Upshift	21-110	—
—	Rough Initial Engagement	21-109	—
—	Rough Or Mushy 4-2 Or 3-1 Shift	21-110	—
—	Rough Shudder 3-1 Shift At Closed Throttle In Overdrive	21-110	—
—	Shift Hunting 3-4 Or 4-3	21-110	—
—	Shifts 1-3 In Overdrive	21-110	—
—	Slipping 4th Gear	21-110	—
—	Slipping Shift Followed By Sudden Engagement	21-111	—
—	Slow Initial Engagement	21-109	—
—	Soft, Early And/Or Mushy 2-3 Upshift	21-110	—
—	Transmission Noisy, Except Valve Resonance	21-111	—
—	Transmission Noisy, Valve Resonance	21-111	—
—	Transmission Overheats	21-111	—
—	Vehicle Will Not Start	21-111	—
1998–2000 TRANSMISSION			
201/301	No Forward Engagement	21-118	9
202/302	No Reverse Engagement	21-119	10
203/303	Harsh Reverse Engagement	21-120	11
204/304	Harsh Forward Engagement	21-121	12
205/305	Delayed/Soft Reverse Engagement	21-121	13
206/306	Delayed/Soft Forward Engagement	21-122	14
210/310	Some Or All Shifts Missing	21-123	15
212/312	Shift Timing Is Erratic/Hunting	21-124	16
213/313	Shift Feel Is Soft/Slipping	21-125	17
214/314	Shift Feel Is Harsh	21-125	18
215/315	No 1st Gear, Engages In Higher Gear	21-126	19
216/316	No Manual 1st Gear	21-127	20

Continued

TRANSMISSION—Continued

	Test Step	Result	Action to Take
A1	CHECK RUN FUSE		
	• CHECK RUN Fuse (5A) located in fuse junction panel. • **Is fuse OK?**	Yes ▶ No ▶	GO to **A3**. GO to **A2**.
A2	CHECK RESISTANCE OF CIRCUIT 298 (P/O)		
	• Turn ignition switch OFF. • Remove RUN Fuse (5A). • Disconnect shiftlock actuator connector C209. • Measure resistance of Circuit 298 (P/O) and ground. • **Is resistance greater than 10,000 ohms?**	Yes ▶ No ▶	GO to **A3**. SERVICE Circuit 298 (P/O) for short to ground. RESTORE vehicle. RETEST system.
A3	CHECK POWER SUPPLY FROM RUN FUSE (5A)		
	• Reinstall RUN Fuse (5A). • Disconnect shiftlock actuator connector C209. • Measure voltage on Circuit 298 (P/O) and ground. • Turn ignition ON. • **Is voltage B+?**	Yes ▶ No ▶	GO to **A4**. SERVICE Circuit 298 (P/O) for open. RESTORE vehicle. RETEST system.
A4	CHECK STOP LAMP OPERATION		
	• Press brake pedal. • **Does stoplamp operate?**	Yes ▶ No ▶	GO to **A5**. SERVICE stoplamp circuit.
A5	CHECK POWER SUPPLY BETWEEN BRAKE PEDAL AND SHIFTLOCK ACTUATOR		
	• Apply brake pedal. • Measure voltage on Circuit 511 (LG) and ground. • **Is voltage B+ with brake pedal applied?**	Yes ▶ No ▶	GO to **A6**. SERVICE Circuit 511 (LG) for open. RESTORE vehicle. RETEST sytsem.
A6	MEASURE RESISTANCE IN GROUND CIRCUIT		
	• With C209 disconnected, measure resistance of Circuit 57 (BK) and ground. • **Is resistance less than 5 ohms?**	Yes ▶ No ▶	REPLACE shiftlock actuator. SERVICE Circuit 57 (BK) for open. RESTORE vehicle. RETEST system.

FM5029300954000A

Fig. 6 Shift Interlock System Troubleshooting Chart. Thunderbird & 1997–98 Crown Victoria, Grand Marquis & Town Car & 1997 Cougar

Test Step		Result	Action to Take
A1	CHECK FUSE 1 (15A)		
	• Check Fuse 1 (15A) located in fuse junction panel. • **Is fuse OK?**	Yes No	▶ GO to **A3**. ▶ GO to **A2**.
A2	CHECK RESISTANCE IN CIRCUIT 298 (P / O)		
	• Turn ignition switch OFF. • Remove Fuse 1 (15A). • Disconnect shift lock actuator connector C234. • Measure resistance of the Circuit 298 (P / O) and ground. • **Is resistance greater than 10,000 ohms?**	Yes No	▶ GO to **A3**. ▶ SERVICE Circuit 298 (P / O) for short to ground. RESTORE vehicle. RETEST system.
A3	CHECK POWER SUPPLY FROM FUSE 1 (15A)		
	• Reinstall RUN Fuse 1 (15A). • Disconnect shift lock actuator connector C234. • Measure voltage on Circuit 298 (P / O) and ground. • Turn ignition ON. • **Is voltage B+?**	Yes No	▶ GO to **A4**. ▶ SERVICE Circuit 298 (P / O) for open. RESTORE vehicle. RETEST system.
A4	CHECK STOPLAMP OPERATION		
	• Press brake pedal. • **Does stoplamp operate?**	Yes No	▶ GO to **A5**. ▶ SERVICE stoplamp circuit.
A5	CHECK POWER SUPPLY BETWEEN BRAKE PEDAL AND SHIFT LOCK ACTUATOR		
	• Apply brake pedal. • Measure voltage on Circuit 810 (R / LG) and ground. • **Is voltage B+ with brake pedal applied?**	Yes No	▶ GO to **A6**. ▶ SERVICE Circuit 810 (R / LG) for open. RESTORE vehicle. RETEST system.
A6	MEASURE RESISTANCE IN GROUND CIRCUIT		
	• With C234 disconnected, measure resistance of Circuit 57 (BK) and ground. • **Is resistance less than 5 ohms?**	Yes No	▶ REPLACE shift lock actuator. ▶ SERVICE Circuit 57 (BK) for open. RESTORE vehicle. RETEST system.

FM5029501135000X

Fig. 7 Shift Interlock System Troubleshooting Chart. Mustang

TEST CONDITIONS	TEST DETAILS/RESULTS/ACTIONS
C1 CHECK THE BRAKE SHIFT INTERLOCK IN THE ACC POSITION	
1  2 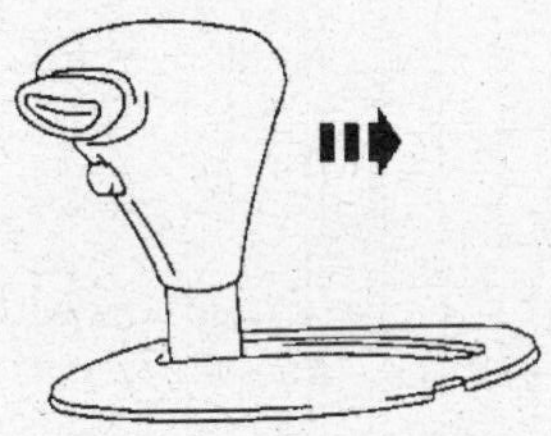	2 With the brake pedal released, attempt to move the transmission range selector lever to REVERSE. • Did the transmission range selector lever move to REVERSE? → **Yes** GO to C3. → **No** GO to C2.
C2 CHECK FOR THE PROPER OPERATION	
1  2 	2 Press the brake pedal.

FM5029701136010X

Fig. 8 Shift Interlock System Troubleshooting Chart (Part 1 of 6). Mark VIII

TEST CONDITIONS	TEST DETAILS/RESULTS/ACTIONS
C2 CHECK FOR THE PROPER OPERATION (Continued)	
3 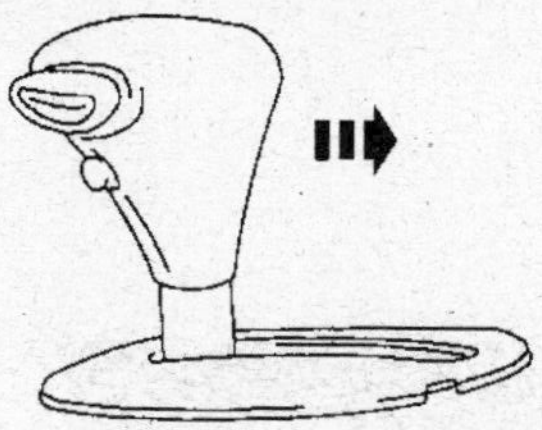	3 Move the transmission range selector lever to REVERSE. • Did the transmission range selector lever move to REVERSE? → **Yes** The brake shift interlock system is operating properly. CHECK for intermittent or loose connections. CHECK the transmission range selector alignment and the adjustment. → **No** GO to **C9.**
C3 CHECK THE STEERING COLUMN ADJUSTMENT	
	1 Actuate the steering column adjustment switch to the tilt or the telescope position. • Does the steering column adjust? → **Yes** GO to **C4.** → **No** **Diagnose steering column.**

FM5029701136020X

Fig. 8 Shift Interlock System Troubleshooting Chart (Part 2 of 6). Mark VIII

TEST CONDITIONS	TEST DETAILS/RESULTS/ACTIONS
C4 CHECK THE STOPLIGHT SWITCH OPERATION	
1  Steering Column/Ignition/Lighting Control Module PID BOO__SCI 2 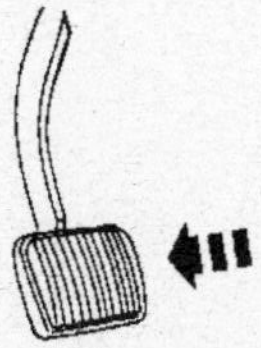	2 Press down on the brake pedal while monitoring PID BOO __SCI. • Does the PID BOO__SCI change from OFF to ON when the brake pedal is pressed? → **Yes** GO to **C5.** → **No** **Diagnose brake light switch.**
C5 CHECK THE STEERING COLUMN/IGNITION/LIGHTING CONTROL MODULE OUTPUT	
1  Brake Shift Interlock Solenoid Connector C360 2 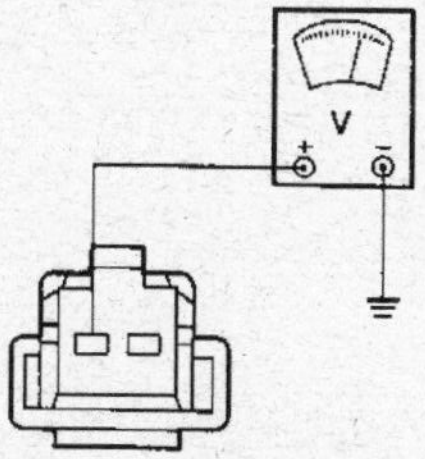	2 Connect a voltmeter to the brake shift interlock connector C360, Circuit 22 (LB/BK).

FM5029701136030X

Fig. 8 Shift Interlock System Troubleshooting Chart (Part 3 of 6). Mark VIII

TEST CONDITIONS	TEST DETAILS/RESULTS/ACTIONS
C5 CHECK THE STEERING COLUMN/IGNITION/LIGHTING CONTROL MODULE OUTPUT (Continued)	
3  Steering Column/Ignition/Lighting Control Module Active Command BRAKE SYSTEM 4  Trigger BRK/SHIFT On	• Is the voltage reading B+? → **Yes** GO to **C8.** → **No** GO to **C6.**
C6 CHECK CIRCUIT 22 (LB/BK) FOR A SHORT TO THE GROUND	
1  Steering Column/Ignition/Lighting Control Module Connector C287 2 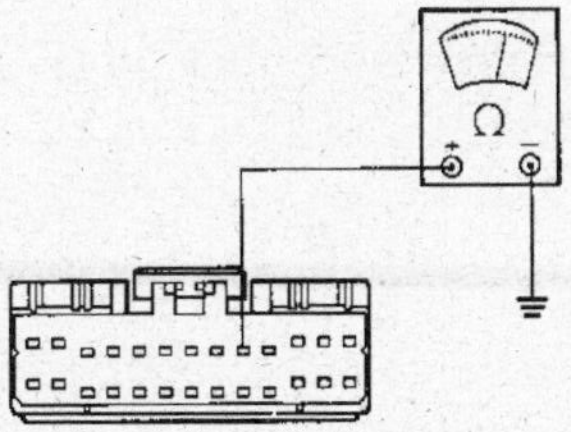	2 Connect an ohmmeter between the steering column/ignition/lighting control module connector Pin C287-9 and ground. • Is resistance reading 10 K ohms or less? → **Yes** SERVICE Circuit 22 (LB/BK) for a short to the ground. RETEST the system. → **No** GO to C7.

FM5029701136040X

Fig. 8 Shift Interlock System Troubleshooting Chart (Part 4 of 6). Mark VIII

TEST CONDITIONS	TEST DETAILS/RESULTS/ACTIONS
C7 CHECK CIRCUIT 22 (LB/BK) FOR AN OPEN	
1 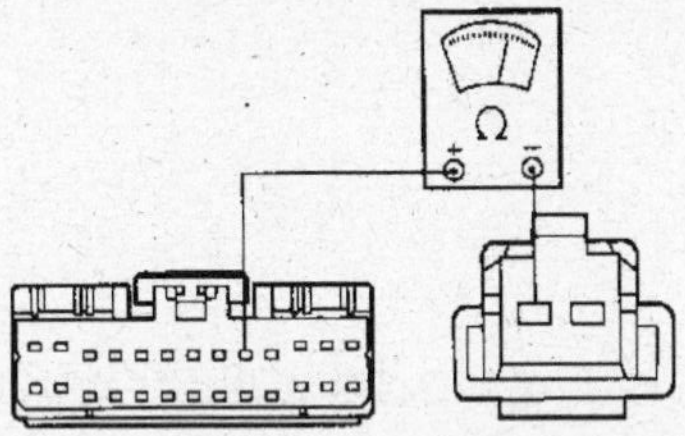	1 Connect an ohmmeter between the steering column/ignition/lighting control module connector Pin C287-9 and the brake shift interlock solenoid connector C360, Circuit 22 (LB/BK). • Is the resistance 5 ohms or less? → **Yes** REPLACE the steering column/ignition/lighting control module. RETEST the system. → **No** SERVICE Circuit 22 (LB/BK) for an open. RETEST the system.
C8 CHECK CIRCUIT 57 (BK) FOR AN OPEN	
1 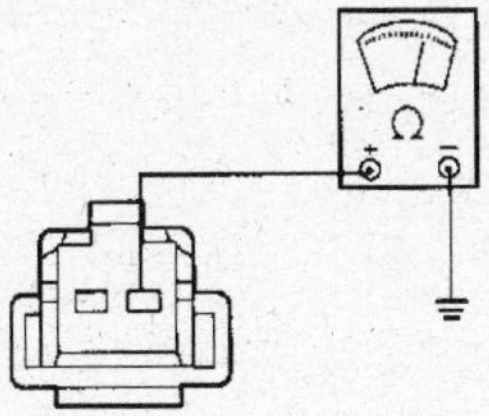	1 Connect an ohmmeter between the brake shift interlock solenoid connector C360, Circuit 57 (BK) and the ground. • Is the resistance 5 ohms or less? → **Yes** REPLACE the brake shift interlock solenoid. RETEST the system. → **No** SERVICE Circuit 57 (BK) for an open. RETEST the system.

FM5029701136050X

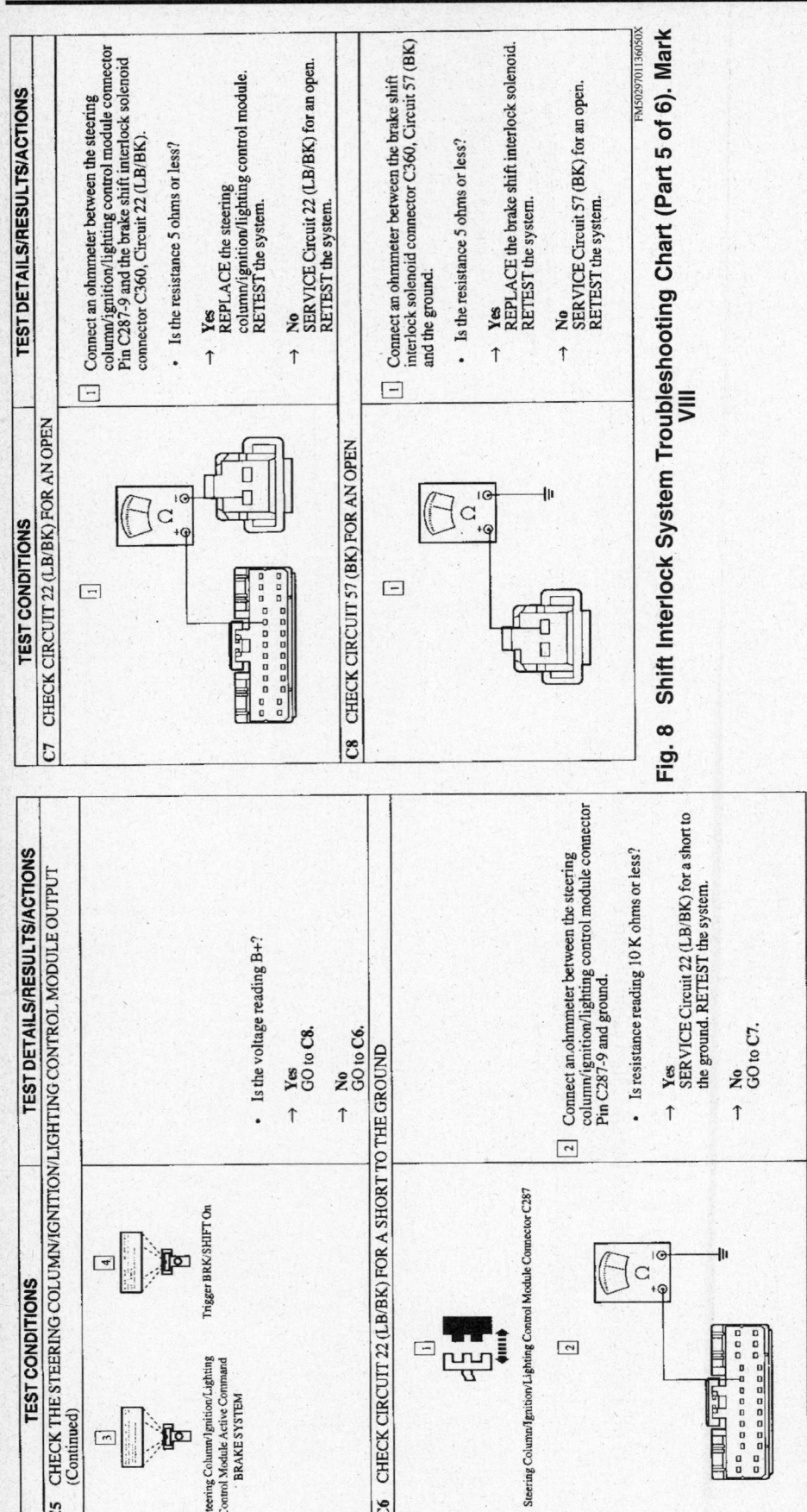

Fig. 8 Shift Interlock System Troubleshooting Chart (Part 5 of 6). Mark VIII

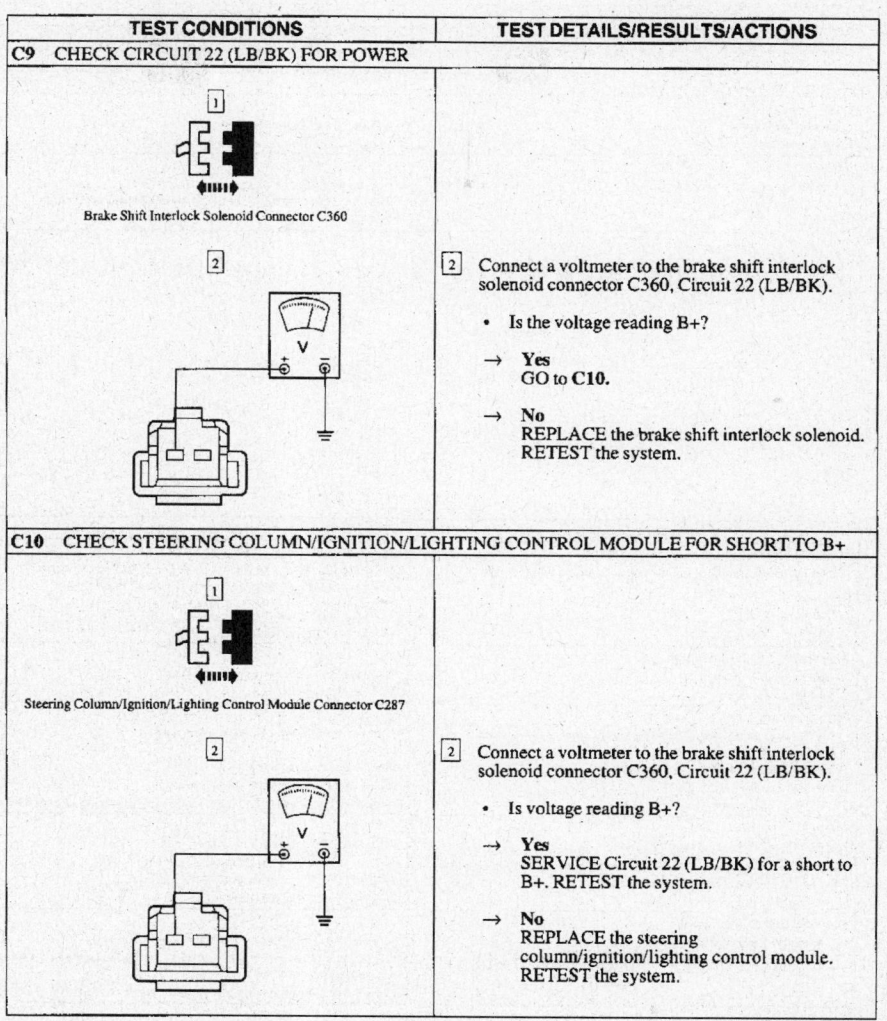

TEST CONDITIONS	TEST DETAILS/RESULTS/ACTIONS
C9 CHECK CIRCUIT 22 (LB/BK) FOR POWER	
1  Brake Shift Interlock Solenoid Connector C360	
2 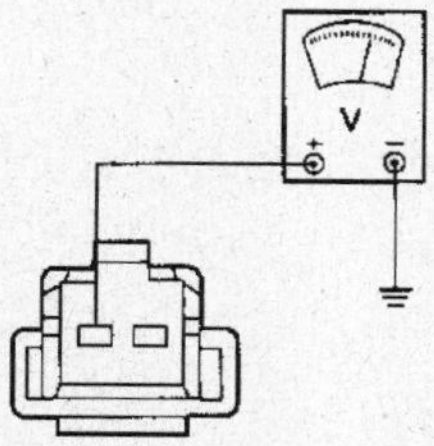	2 Connect a voltmeter to the brake shift interlock solenoid connector C360, Circuit 22 (LB/BK). • Is the voltage reading B+? → **Yes** GO to **C10.** → **No** REPLACE the brake shift interlock solenoid. RETEST the system.
C10 CHECK STEERING COLUMN/IGNITION/LIGHTING CONTROL MODULE FOR SHORT TO B+	
1  Steering Column/Ignition/Lighting Control Module Connector C287	
2 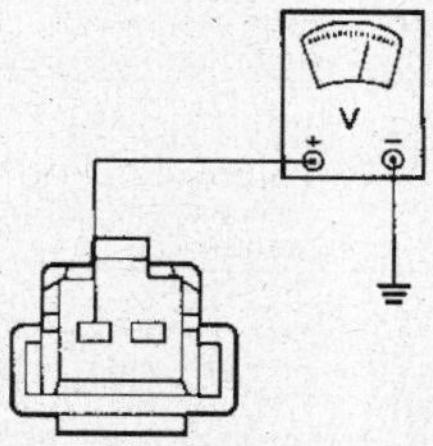	2 Connect a voltmeter to the brake shift interlock solenoid connector C360, Circuit 22 (LB/BK). • Is voltage reading B+? → **Yes** SERVICE Circuit 22 (LB/BK) for a short to B+. RETEST the system. → **No** REPLACE the steering column/ignition/lighting control module. RETEST the system.

FM5029701136060X

Fig. 8 Shift Interlock System Troubleshooting Chart (Part 6 of 6). Mark VIII

Possible Component	Reference/Action
201 — ELECTRICAL ROUTINE	
• No Electrical Concerns	
301 — HYDRAULIC/MECHANICAL ROUTINE	
Fluid • Improper level • Condition	 • Adjust fluid to proper level. • Inspect Fluid Condition.
Shift Linkage • Damaged, out of adjustment	• Inspect and service as required. Verify linkage adjustment After servicing linkage, verify Digital TR sensor is properly adjusted.

FM50298015040I0X

Fig. 9 Routines 201 & 301: No Forward Engagement (Part 1 of 2). 1998–2000

Possible Component	Reference/Action
Improper Pressures • Low forward clutch pressure, low line pressure	• Check pressure at line and forward clutch tap. If pressures are low, check the following possible components: — fluid filter and seal assembly, — main controls, pump assembly, — forward clutch assembly.
Fluid Filter and Seal Assembly • Plugged, damaged • Filter seal damaged	• Replace fluid filter and seal assembly.
Main Controls • 3-4 shift valve, main regulator valve, manual valve stuck, damaged • Bolts out of torque specification • Gaskets damaged • 2-3 accumulator and seals damaged	• Inspect for damage. Service as required. • Tighten bolts to specification. • Inspect gasket for damage and replace. • Inspect piston, seals and bore for damage. Service as required.
Pump Assembly • Bolts out of torque specification • Porosity/cross leaks and ball missing or leaking, plugged hole • No. 3 and No. 4 seal rings damaged • Gaskets damaged	• Tighten bolts to specification. • Inspect for porosity and leaks. Service as required. • Inspect seals for damage. Service as required. • Inspect for damage and replace.
Forward Clutch Assembly • Seals, piston damaged • Check balls damaged, missing, mislocated, not seating properly • Friction elements damaged or worn	• Inspect seals for damage. Service as required. • Inspect for mislocation, poor seating, damage. Replace cylinder as required. • Check for abnormal wear, damage. Service as required.
Low One-Way Clutch Assembly (Planetary) • Worn, damaged or misassembled	• Inspect for damage. Service as required.
Output Shaft • Damaged	• Inspect for damage. Service as required.

FM50298015040 20X

Fig. 9 Routines 201 & 301: No Forward Engagement (Part 2 of 2). 1998–2000

Possible Component	Reference/Action
202 — ELECTRICAL ROUTINE	
• No Electrical Concerns	
302 — HYDRAULIC/MECHANICAL ROUTINE	
Fluid	
• Improper level	• Adjust fluid to proper level.
• Condition	• Inspect Fluid Condition.
Shift Linkage	
• Damaged or out of adjustment	• Inspect and service as required. Verify linkage adjustment. After servicing linkage, verify that the Digital TR sensor is properly adjusted.
Improper Pressures	
• Low reverse clutch pressure, low reverse band pressure, low line pressure	• Check pressure at line pressure tap. If pressures are low, check the following possible components: — fluid filter and seal assembly, — main controls, — reverse servo, — pump assembly, — reverse clutch assembly.

FM5029801505010X

Fig. 10 Routines 202 & 302: No Reverse Engagement (Part 1 of 2). 1998–2000

Possible Component	Reference/Action
Fluid Filter and Seal Assembly	
• Plugged, damaged	• Replace filter and seal assembly.
Main Controls	
• No. 6 shuttle ball, manual valve, main regulator valve, 1-2 accumulator seals stuck or damaged	• Inspect for damage. Service as required.
• Bolts out of torque specification	• Tighten bolts to specification.
• Gasket damaged	• Inspect for damage and replace.
Low Reverse Servo	
• Seals (piston and cover) damaged	• Inspect for damage. Service as required.
• Servo cover retaining ring damaged	
• Anchor pins (case) damaged	
Pump Assembly	
• Bolts out of torque specification	• Tighten bolts to specification.
• Porosity/cross leaks/ball missing or leaking, plugged hole	• Inspect pump assembly. Replace as required.
• Gasket damaged	• Inspect for damage and replace.
• No. 1 and 2 seal rings damaged	• Inspect for damage. Service as required.
Reverse Clutch Assembly	
• Seals, piston damaged	• Inspect for damage. Service as required.
• Check ball missing or damaged	
• Friction elements damaged or worn	
Low Reverse Band	
• Band, servo, anchor pins damaged or worn	• Inspect for damage. Service as required.

FM5029801505020X

Fig. 10 Routines 202 & 302: No Reverse Engagement (Part 2 of 2). 1998–2000

Possible Component	Reference/Action
203 — ELECTRICAL ROUTINE	
Powertrain Control System • Electrical inputs/outputs, vehicle wiring harnesses, PCM, TP, MAF, EI system, EPC solenoid, TFT sensor	• Run Self-Test. Refer to MOTOR's Domestic Transmissions for diagnosis. Perform engagement test, EPC test and Pinpoint Tests B and E using Rotunda Transmission Tester 007-00130, or equivalent. Service as required. Clear codes, road test and rerun self-test.
303 — HYDRAULIC/MECHANICAL ROUTINE	
Fluid • Improper level • Condition	• Adjust fluid to proper level. • Inspect Fluid Condition.
Shift Linkage • Damaged or out of adjustment	• Inspect and service as required. Verify linkage adjustment. After servicing linkage, verify that the Digital TR sensor is properly adjusted.
Improper Pressures • High line pressure, high EPC pressure	• Check pressure at line and EPC pressure taps. Refer to Reference: If high, check the following possible components: main controls, oil filter and seal assembly.
Oil Filter and Seal Assembly • Plugged or damaged • Filter seal damaged	• Replace filter and seal assembly.
Main Controls • No. 6 Shuttle ball, No. 5 check ball, manual valve, main regulator valve stuck, damaged or missing • Loose bolts • Gasket damaged	• Inspect for damage. Service as required. • Tighten bolts to specification. • Inspect for damage and replace.

FM5029801506010X

Fig. 11 Routines 203 & 303: Harsh Reverse Engagement (Part 1 of 2). 1998–2000

Possible Component	Reference/Action
• EPC solenoid stuck or damaged	• Inspect for damage, contamination. Perform EPC test in Routine No. 203. Service as required.
Low Reverse Servo • Seals (piston and cover) damaged • Servo cover retaining ring damaged • Anchor pins (case) damaged	• Inspect for damage. Service as required.
Pump Assembly • Loose bolts • Porosity/cross leaks • Gasket damaged • No. 1 and No. 2 seal rings damaged	• Tighten bolts to specification. • Inspect pump assembly. Replace as required. • Inspect for damage and replace. • Inspect for damage. Service as required.
Reverse Clutch Assembly • Seals, piston damaged • Check ball missing or damaged • Friction elements damaged, worn • Return spring piston damaged, worn	• Inspect for damage. Service as required.
Low Reverse Band • Band, servo, anchor pin damaged or worn	• Inspect for damage. Service as required.

FM5029801506020X

Fig. 11 Routines 203 & 303: Harsh Reverse Engagement (Part 2 of 2). 1998–2000

Possible Component	Reference/Action
204 — ELECTRICAL ROUTINE	
Powertrain Control System • Electrical inputs/outputs, vehicle wiring harnesses, PCM, TFT sensor, EPC solenoid	• Run Self-Test. Refer to MOTOR's Domestic Transmission Manual for diagnosis. Perform engagement test, EPC test and Pinpoint Tests B and E using Rotunda Transmission Tester 007-00130, or equivalent. Service as required. Clear codes, road test and rerun self-test.
304 — HYDRAULIC/MECHANICAL ROUTINE	
Fluid • Improper level • Condition	• Adjust fluid to proper level. • Inspect as described under Fluid Condition Check.
Improper Pressures • High forward clutch pressure, high line pressure, high EPC pressure	• Check pressure at line, EPC and forward pressure taps. If pressures are high, check the following possible components: main controls, pump assembly.
Main Controls • Main regulator valve, 2-3 backout valve, 2-3 accumulator seal/retainer stuck, damaged • Bolts out of torque specification • Gaskets damaged • EPC solenoid stuck or damaged	• Inspect and service as required. • Tighten bolts to specification. • Inspect for damage and replace. • Inspect for damage or contamination. Perform EPC test in Routine No. 204. Service as required.
Pump Assembly • Bolts out of torque specification • Porosity/cross leaks • Gaskets damaged • No. 3 and No. 4 seal ring damage	• Tighten bolts to specification. • Inspect for porosity/leaks. Replace pump assembly as required. • Inspect for damage and replace.
Forward Clutch Assembly • Check balls missing or damaged • Friction element damaged or worn • Forward clutch wave spring damaged • Forward clutch return spring damaged	• Inspect for mislocation, poor seating, damage. Replace forward clutch cylinder. • Inspect for damage. Service as required. • Inspect for damage. Service as required. • Inspect for damage. Service as required.

FM5029801507000X

Fig. 12 Routines 204 & 304: Harsh Forward Engagement. 1998–2000

Possible Component	Reference/Action
205 — ELECTRICAL ROUTINE	
• No Electrical Concerns	
305 — HYDRAULIC/MECHANICAL ROUTINE	
Fluid • Improper level • Condition	• Adjust fluid to proper level. • Inspect Fluid Condition.
Shift Linkage • Damaged, out of adjustment	• Inspect and service as required. Verify linkage adjustment. After servicing linkage, verify that the Digital TR sensor is properly adjusted.
Improper Pressures • Low reverse clutch pressure, low reverse band pressure, low line pressure	• Check pressure at line tap. If pressures are low, check the following possible components: main controls, pump assembly, reverse clutch assembly, reverse servo.
Fluid Filter and Seal Assembly • Plugged, damaged • Fluid filter seal damaged	• Replace fluid filter and seal assembly.
Main Controls • No. 6 shuttle ball, 1-2 accumulator seals, manual valve, main regulator valve stuck or damaged • Bolts out of torque specification • Gaskets damaged	• Inspect for damage. Service as required. • Tighten bolts to specification. • Inspect for damage and replace.
Low Reverse Servo • Seals (piston and cover) damaged • Servo cover retaining ring assembled wrong.	• Inspect for damage. Service as required.
Pump Assembly • Bolts out of torque specification • Porosity/cross leaks/ball missing or leaking • Gaskets damaged • No. 1 and No. 2 seal rings damaged	• Tighten bolts to specification. • Inspect pump assembly. Replace as required. • Inspect for damage and replace. • Inspect for damage. Service as required.
Reverse Clutch Assembly • Seals, piston damaged • Check ball missing or damaged • Friction elements damaged, worn • Return spring and piston damaged, worn	• Inspect for damage. Service as required.
Low Reverse Band • Damaged, worn	• Inspect for damage. Service as required.

FM5029801508000X

Fig. 13 Routines 205 & 305: Delayed/Soft Reverse Engagement. 1998–2000

Possible Component	Reference/Action
206 — ELECTRICAL ROUTINE	
• No Electrical Concerns	
306 — HYDRAULIC/MECHANICAL ROUTINE	
Fluid • Improper level • Condition	• Adjust fluid to proper level. • Inspect Fluid Condition.
Shift Linkage • Damaged, out of adjustment	• Inspect and service as required. Verify linkage adjustment. After servicing linkage, verify that the Digital TR sensor is properly adjusted.

FM5029801509010X

Fig. 14 Routines 206 & 306: Delayed/Soft Forward Engagement (Part 1 of 2). 1998–2000

Possible Component	Reference/Action
Improper Pressures • Low forward clutch pressure, low line pressure, low EPC pressure	• Check pressure at line, forward clutch and EPC taps. If pressures are low, check the following possible components: fluid filter and seal assembly, main controls and pump assembly.
Fluid Filter and Seal Assembly • Plugged, damaged • Fluid filter seal damaged	• Replace fluid filter and seal assembly.
Main Controls • 3-4 shift valve, main regulator valve • Bolts out of torque specification • Gaskets damaged • 2-3 or 1-2 accumulator, bore damaged or stuck	• Inspect and service as required. • Tighten bolts to specification. • Inspect for damage and replace. • Inspect for damage. Service as required.
Pump Assembly • Bolts out of torque specification • Porosity/cross leaks • Gaskets damaged • No. 3, No. 4 seal rings damaged	• Tighten bolts to specification. • Inspect pump assembly. Replace as required. • Inspect for damage and replace. • Inspect for damage. Service as required.
Forward Clutch Assembly • Seals, piston damaged • Check balls missing, damaged • Friction elements damaged, worn	• Inspect for damage. Service as required. • Inspect for mislocation, poor seating, damage. Replace cylinder as required. • Check for damage. Service as required.

FM5029801509020X

Fig. 14 Routines 206 & 306: Delayed/Soft Forward Engagement (Part 2 of 2). 1998–2000

Possible Component	Reference/Action
210 — ELECTRICAL ROUTINE	
Powertrain Control System	
• Electrical inputs/outputs, vehicle wiring harnesses, powertrain control module, shift solenoids, output shaft speed (OSS) sensor, Digital TR sensor	• Run self-test. Refer to MOTOR's Domestic Transmission Manual for diagnosis. Perform Pinpoint Tests A, D and F using Rotunda Transmission Tester 007-00130 with Rotunda Transmission Range (TR) Sensor Cable "E" 007-00111 and Digital (TR) Sensor Overlay 007-00131, or equivalent. Service as required. Clear codes, road test and rerun self-test.
310 — HYDRAULIC/MECHANICAL ROUTINE	
Fluid	
• Improper level	• Adjust fluid to proper level.
• Condition	• Inspect as described under Fluid Condition Check.
Shift Linkage, Digital TR Sensor	
• Damaged, out of adjustment	• Inspect and service as required. Verify linkage adjustment. After servicing linkage, verify that the Digital TR sensor is properly adjusted. • Refer to the following shift routine(s) for further diagnosis: **Shift** 1-2, **Routine** 220/320 **Shift** 2-3, **Routine** 221/321 **Shift** 3-4, **Routine** 222/322 **Shift** 4-3, **Routine** 223/323 **Shift** 3-2, **Routine** 224/324 **Shift** 2-1, **Routine** 225/325

FM5029801510010X

Fig. 15 Routines 210 & 310: Some Or All Shifts Missing (Part 1 of 2). 1998–2000

Possible Component	Reference/Action
211 — ELECTRICAL ROUTINE	
Powertrain Control System	
• Electrical inputs/outputs, vehicle wiring harnesses, powertrain control module, shift solenoids, EPC solenoid, TFT sensor, OSS	• Run self-test. Refer to MOTOR's Domestic Transmission Manual for diagnosis. Perform Pinpoint Tests A, B, E and F using Rotunda Transmission Tester 007-00130 or equivalent. Service as required. Clear codes, road test and rerun Self-Test.
311 — HYDRAULIC/MECHANICAL ROUTINE	
Other	
• Tire size change, axle ratio change	• Verify vehicle has original equipment. Refer to Certification Label and Safety Standard Certification Label. Changes in tire size, axle ratio will affect shift timing.
Fluid	
• Improper level	• Adjust fluid to proper level.
• Condition	• Inspect Fluid Condition.
Improper Pressures	
• Line pressure, EPC pressure	• Check pressure at line and EPC taps. If not OK, check the main controls. If OK, refer to the following shift routine(s) for further diagnosis: **Shift** 1-2, **Routine** 320 **Shift** 2-3, **Routine** 321 **Shift** 3-4, **Routine** 322 **Shift** 4-3, **Routine** 323 **Shift** 3-2, **Routine** 324 **Shift** 2-1, **Routine** 325
Main Controls	
• EPC solenoid, stuck or damaged hydraulically or mechanically	• Inspect for damage, contamination. Perform EPC tests in Routine No. 211. Service as required.
• Valves, accumulators, seals stuck or damaged or misassembled	• Inspect for damage. Service as required.
• Gaskets damaged	• Inspect for damage and replace.
• Solenoid screen (in valve body) blocked or damaged	• Clean or replace screen.

FM5029801510020X

Fig. 15 Routines 210 & 310: Some Or All Shifts Missing (Part 2 of 2). 1998–2000

Possible Component	Reference/Action
212 —ELECTRICAL ROUTINE	
Powertrain Control System • Electrical inputs/outputs, vehicle wiring harnesses, powertrain control module, shift solenoids, TCC solenoid, digital TR sensor, OSS	• Run self-test. Refer to MOTOR's Domestic Transmission Manual for diagnosis. Perform Pinpoint Tests A, D and F using Rotunda Transmission Tester 007-00130, with Rotunda Transmission Range (TR) Sensor Cable "E" 418-F107 (007-00111) and Digital (TR) Sensor Overlay 007-00131 or equivalent. Service as required. Clear codes, road test and rerun self-test.
312 —HYDRAULIC/MECHANICAL ROUTINE	
Fluid • improper level • Condition	 • Adjust fluid to proper level. • Inspect Fluid Condition.
Main Controls • Valves, accumulators, seals, misassembled, stuck or damaged • Gaskets damaged • Solenoid screen (in valve body) blocked or damaged	 • Inspect for damage. Service as required. • Inspect for damage and replace. • Clean or replace screen.
Torque Converter Clutch • Torque converter	 • Refer to Hydraulic/Mechanical Routine 342, Converter Cycling/Shudder/Chatter.

FM5029801511010X

Fig. 16 Routines 212 & 312: Shift Timing Is Erratic/Hunting (Part 1 of 2). 1998–2000

Possible Component	Reference/Action
Specific Shifts	• Refer to the following shift routine(s) for further diagnosis: **Shift** 1-2, **Routine**, 320 **Shift** 2-3, **Routine**, 321 **Shift** 3-4, **Routine**, 322 **Shift** 4-3, **Routine**, 323 **Shift** 3-2, **Routine**, 324 **Shift** 2-1, **Routine**, 325

FM5029801511020X

Fig. 16 Routines 212 & 312: Shift Timing Is Erratic/Hunting (Part 2 of 2). 1998–2000

Possible Component	Reference/Action
213 — ELECTRICAL ROUTINE	
Powertrain Control System	
• Electrical inputs/outputs, vehicle wiring harnesses, powertrain control module, EPC solenoid, OSS	• Run Self-Test. Refer to MOTOR's Domestic Transmission Manual for diagnosis. Perform Pinpoint Tests E and F using Rotunda Transmission Tester 007-00130 or equivalent. Service as required. Clear codes, road test and rerun Self-Test.
313 — HYDRAULIC/MECHANICAL ROUTINE	
Fluid	
• Improper level	• Adjust fluid to proper level.
• Condition	• Inspect as described under Fluid Check.
Improper Pressures	
• Low line pressure, low EPC pressure	• Check pressures at line and EPC taps. If pressures are low or all shifts are soft/slipping, go to Main Controls. If pressures are OK and a specific shift is soft/slipping, refer to the following routine(s) for further diagnosis: **Shift** 1-2, **Routine**, 320 **Shift** 2-3, **Routine**, 321 **Shift** 3-4, **Routine**, 322 **Shift** 4-3, **Routine**, 323 **Shift** 3-2, **Routine**, 324 **Shift** 2-1, **Routine**, 325
Main Controls	
• 1-2 accumulator, 2-3 backout valve, main regulator valve, overdrive servo regulator valve stuck, damaged or misassembled	• Inspect for damage. Service as required.
• EPC solenoid stuck or damaged	• Inspect for damage and contamination. Perform EPC tests in Routine No. 213. Service as required.

FM5029801512000X

Fig. 17 Routines 213 & 313: Shift Feel Is Soft/Slipping. 1998–2000

Possible Component	Reference/Action
214 — ELECTRICAL ROUTINE	
Powertrain Control System	
• Electrical inputs/outputs, vehicle wiring harnesses, EPC solenoid, OSS	• Run self-test. Refer to MOTOR's Domestic Transmission Manual for diagnosis. Perform Pinpoint Tests E and F using Rotunda Transmission Tester 007-00130 or equivalent. Service as required. Clear codes, road test and rerun Self-Test.
314 — HYDRAULIC/MECHANICAL ROUTINE	
Fluid	
• Improper level	• Adjust fluid to proper level.
• Condition	• Inspect Fluid Condition.

FM5029801513010X

Fig. 18 Routines 214 & 314: Shift Feel Is Harsh (Part 1 of 2). 1998–2000

Possible Component	Reference/Action
Improper Pressures • High line pressure, high EPC pressure	• Check pressures at line and EPC taps. If pressures are high or all shifts are harsh, go to Main Controls. If pressures are OK and a specific shift is harsh, refer to the following shift routine(s) for further diagnosis: **Shift** 1-2, **Routine**, 320 **Shift** 2-3, **Routine**, 321 **Shift** 3-4, **Routine**, 322 **Shift** 4-3, **Routine**, 323 **Shift** 3-2, **Routine**, 324 **Shift** 2-1, **Routine**, 325
Main Controls • 1-2 accumulator, 2-3 backout valve, main regulator valve, overdrive servo regulator valve stuck, damaged or misassembled • EPC solenoid stuck or damaged	• Inspect for damage. Service as required. • Inspect for damage, contamination. Perform EPC tests in Routine 214. Service as required.

FM5029801513020X

Fig. 18 Routines 214 & 314: Shift Feel Is Harsh (Part 2 of 2). 1998–2000

Possible Component	Reference/Action
215 — ELECTRICAL ROUTINE	
Powertrain Control System • Electrical inputs/outputs, vehicle wiring harnesses, powertrain control module, shift solenoids, digital TR sensor	• Run Self-Test. Refer to MOTOR's Domestic Transmission Manual for diagnosis. Perform Pinpoint Tests A and D using Rotunda Transmission Tester 007-00130, with Rotunda Transmission Range (TR) Sensor Cable "E" 418-F107 (007-00111) and Digital (TR) Sensor Overlay 007-00131 or equivalent. Service as required. Clear codes, road test and rerun Self-Test.
315 — HYDRAULIC/MECHANICAL ROUTINE	
Shift Linkage, Digital TR Sensor • Damaged or out of adjustment	• Inspect and service as required. Verify linkage adjustment as After servicing linkage, verify that the digital TR sensor is properly adjusted.
Improper Pressures • Low reverse clutch pressure, low reverse band pressure,low line pressure	• Check for which pressures are on as follows and corresponding routines •
• **Forward** Off, **Intermediate**Off,**Direct** X	• 324, 301
• **Forward** Off, **Intermediate**X,**Direct** Off	• 325, 301
• **Forward** Off, **Intermediate**X,**Direct** X	• 323, 324, 325, 301
• **Forward** X, **Intermediate**Off, **Direct** X	• 324
• **Forward** X, **Intermediate**X,**Direct** Off	• 325
• **Forward** X, **Intermediate**X,**Direct** X	• 323, 324, 325
• **Forward** X, **Intermediate**Off, **Direct** Off	• Refer to appropriate Mechanical Diagnosis
Mechanical • Bands, clutches or seals damaged or worn	• Refer to MOTOR's Domestic Transmission Manual.

FM5029801514000X

Fig. 19 Routines 215 & 315: No 1st Gear, Engages In Higher Gear. 1998–2000

Possible Component	Reference/Action
216 — ELECTRICAL ROUTINE	
Powertrain Control System • Electrical inputs/outputs, vehicle wiring harnesses, PCM, shift solenoids, Digital TR sensor	• Run self-test. Refer to MOTOR's Domestic Transmission Manual for diagnosis. Perform Pinpoint Tests A and D using Rotunda Transmission Tester 007-00130 with Rotunda Transmission Range (TR) Sensor Cable "E" 007-00111 and Digital (TR) Sensor Overlay 007-00131 or equivalent. Service as required. Clear codes, road test and rerun self-test.
316 — HYDRAULIC/MECHANICAL ROUTINE	
Shift Linkage, Cable, Digital TR Sensor • Damaged or out of adjustment	• Inspect and service as required. Verify linkage adjustment. After servicing linkage, verify that the Digital TR sensor is properly adjusted.
Improper Pressures • Low reverse clutch pressure, low reverse band pressure, low line pressure, low EPC pressure	• Check pressure at line and EPC pressure taps. If pressures are low, check the following possible components: oil filter and seal assembly, main controls, reverse clutch assembly and reverse servo assembly.
Oil Filter and Seal Assembly • Plugged or damaged	• Replace filter and seal assembly.
Main Controls • No. 6 shuttle ball, manual valve, main regulator valve, low servo modulator valve stuck, damaged • Loose bolts • Gaskets damaged	• Inspect for damage. Service as required. • Tighten bolts to specification. • Inspect for damage and replace.
Low Reverse Servo • Seals (piston and cover) damaged • Servo cover retaining ring damaged • Anchor pins (case) damaged	• Inspect for damage. Service as required.

FM5029801515000X

Fig. 20 Routines 216 & 316: No Manual 1st Gear. 1998–2000

Possible Component	Reference/Action
217 — ELECTRICAL ROUTINE	
Powertrain Control System • Electrical inputs/outputs, vehicle wiring harnesses, powertrain control module (PCM), shift solenoids, Digital TR sensor	• Run Self-Test. Refer to MOTOR's Domestic Transmission Manual for diagnosis. Perform Pinpoint Tests A and D using Rotunda Transmission Tester 007-00130 with Rotunda Transmission Range (TR) Sensor Cable "E" 007-00111 and Digital (TR) Sensor Overlay 007-00131 or equivalent Service as required. Clear codes, road test and rerun self-test.
317 — HYDRAULIC/MECHANICAL ROUTINE	
Shift Linkage, Cable, Digital TR Sensor • Damaged, out of adjustment	• Inspect and service as required. Verify linkage adjustment After servicing linkage, verify that the Digital TR sensor is properly adjusted.
Main Controls • 3-4 shift valve, 1-2 and 2-3 shift valve, 3-4 capacity modulator valve stuck, damaged or misassembled • Bolts out of torque specification • Gaskets damaged	• Inspect for damage. Service as required. • Tighten bolts to specification. • Inspect for damage and replace.

FM5029801516000X

Fig. 21 Routines 217 & 317: No Manual 2nd Gear. 1998–2000

Possible Component	Reference/Action
220 — ELECTRICAL ROUTINE	
Powertrain Control System • Electrical inputs/outputs, vehicle wiring harnesses, PCM, MAF, TP, VSS, OSS, Digital TR sensor, shift solenoids, EI system	• Run self-test. Refer to MOTOR's Domestic Transmission Manual for diagnosis. Perform Pinpoint Tests A, D and F using Rotunda Transmission Tester 007-00130 Rotunda Transmission Range (TR) Sensor Cable "E" 007-00111 and Digital (TR) Sensor Overlay 007-00131 or equivalent. Service as required. Clear codes, road test and rerun self-test.
320 — HYDRAULIC/MECHANICAL ROUTINE	
Shift Linkage, Digital TR Sensor • Damaged or out of adjustment	• Inspect and service as required. Verify linkage adjustment After servicing linkage, verify that the Digital TR sensor is properly adjusted.
Improper Pressures • Intermediate clutch pressure, line pressure	• Check pressure at line and intermediate clutch taps. If not OK, check the Main Controls.
Main Controls • 1-2 shift valve, 1-2 accumulator valve stuck or damaged • Loose bolts • SS1 malfunction • Gasket damaged • No. 8 ball not seating	• Inspect for damage. Service as required. • Tighten bolts to specification. • Activate solenoid using transmission tester. If solenoid operation cannot be felt when placing hand on solenoid, replace solenoid. Inspect O-rings for damage. Service as required. • Inspect for damage and replace. • Inspect for damage and service as required.
Pump • Porosity/cross leaks, balls missing, damaged or leaking • Gasket damaged	• Inspect for porosity/leaks, balls missing. Replace pump as required. • Inspect for damage and replace.
Intermediate Clutch Assembly • Seals damaged • Piston damaged • Friction elements damaged or worn	• Inspect for damage. Service as required. • Inspect for damage. Service as required. • Inspect for damage. Service as required.
Intermediate One-Way Clutch Assembly • Not holding or damaged	• Inspect for damage. Service as required.
Low One-Way Clutch Assembly • Not overrunning or damaged	• Inspect for damage. Service as required.

FM5029801517000X

Fig. 22 Routines 220 & 320: No Automatic 1-2 Shift. 1998–2000

Possible Component	Reference/Action
221 — ELECTRICAL ROUTINE	
Powertrain Control System • Electrical inputs/outputs, vehicle wiring harnesses, PCM, TP, MAF, VSS, OSS, Digital TR sensor, shift solenoids, EI system	• Run self-test. Refer to MOTOR's Domestic Transmission Manual for diagnosis. Perform Pinpoint Tests A, D and F using Rotunda Transmission Tester 007-00130 with Rotunda Transmission Range (TR) Sensor Cable "E" 007-00111 and Digital (TR) Sensor Overlay 007-00131 or equivalent. Service as required. Clear codes, road test and rerun self-test.
321 — HYDRAULIC/MECHANICAL ROUTINE	
Shift Linkage • Damaged or out of adjustment	• Inspect and service as required. Verify linkage adjustment After servicing linkage, verify that the Digital TR sensor is properly adjusted.

FM5029801533010X

Fig. 23 Routines 221 & 321: No Automatic 2-3 Shift (Part 1 of 2). 1998–2000

Possible Component	Reference/Action
Improper Pressures	
• Direct clutch pressure	• Check pressure at direct clutch tap. If not OK, check the main controls.
Main Controls	
• 2-3 shift valve, check ball No. 3 or No. 9, solenoid pressure regulator valve, 2-3 backout valve, 2-3 modulator valve, damaged or misassembled	• Inspect for damage. Service as required.
• Loose bolts	• Tighten bolts to specification.
• SS2 malfunction	• Activate solenoid using transmission tester. If solenoid operation cannot be felt when placing hand on solenoid, replace solenoid. Inspect O-rings for damage. Service as required.
• Gaskets damaged	• Inspect for damage and replace.
• Output shaft seals damaged or cup plug leaking or missing	• Inspect for damage and service as required.
• 2-3 accumulator damaged or stuck	• Inspect piston seal and bore for damage. Service as required.
• Solenoid screen (in main control) blocked or damaged	• Clean or replace screen.
Intermediate One-Way Clutch Assembly	
• Not overrunning or damaged	• Inspect for damage. Service as required
Output Shaft	
• Seal rings damaged • Cup plug damaged or missing	• Inspect for damage. Service as required.
Direct Clutch Assembly	
• Seals or piston damaged	• Inspect for damage. Service as required.
• Friction elements worn or damaged	• Inspect for damage. Service as required.
• Check ball not seating	• Inspect for damage. Service as required.
• Return spring assembly damaged	• Inspect for damage. Service as required.
Case	
• Output shaft rear seals leaking or damaged	• Inspect for damage. Service as required. Inspect case for damaged seal area. If damaged, replace case.

FM5029801533020X

Fig. 23 Routines 221 & 321: No Automatic 2-3 Shift (Part 2 of 2). 1998–2000

Possible Component	Reference/Action
222 — ELECTRICAL ROUTINE	
Powertrain Control System	
• Electrical inputs/outputs, vehicle wiring harnesses, PCM, TP, MAF, VSS, OSS, Digital TR sensor, TCS, shift solenoids, EI system	• Run self-test. Refer to MOTOR's Domestic Transmission Manual for diagnosis. Perform Pinpoint Tests A, D and F using Rotunda Transmission Tester 007-00130 with Rotunda Transmission Range (TR) Sensor Cable "E" 007-00111 and Digital (TR) Sensor Overlay 007-00131 or equivalent. Service as required. Clear codes, road test and rerun self-test.
322 — HYDRAULIC/MECHANICAL ROUTINE	
Shift Linkage, Digital TR Sensor	
• Damaged or out of adjustment	• Inspect and service as required. Verify linkage adjustment. After servicing linkage, verify that the Digital TR sensor is properly adjusted.
Improper Pressures	
• Forward clutch pressure, direct clutch pressure, line pressure	• Check line, direct and forward clutch pressures at appropriate taps. If pressures are out of specification, check main controls.
Main Controls	
• 3-4 shift valve, solenoid pressure regulator valve, OD servo regulator, 3-4 capacity modulator valve, 2-3 backout valve, 1-2 and 2-3 shift valves stuck, damaged	• Inspect for damaged and service as required.
• Loose bolts	• Tighten bolts to specification.

FM5029801518010X

Fig. 24 Routines 222 & 322: No Automatic 3-4 Shift (Part 1 of 2). 1998–2000

Possible Component	Reference/Action
• SS1 or SS2 malfunction	• Activate solenoid using transmission tester. If solenoid operation cannot be felt when placing hand on solenoid, replace solenoid. Inspect O-rings for damage. Service as required.
• Gaskets damaged	• Inspect for damage and replace.
• OD servo cover, rod and piston cushion spring or seals damaged	• Inspect for damage. Service as required.
• No's 2, 4, 7, and 9 check balls damaged or missing	• Inspect for damage. Service as required.
• Solenoid screen (in main control) blocked or damaged	• Clean or replace screen.
Pump	
• Porosity/cross leaks, balls missing, damaged or leaking	• Inspect for porosity/leaks, balls missing. Replace pump as required.
• Gaskets damaged	• Inspect for damage. Replace as required.
OD Band	
• OD band and reverse clutch drum assembly damaged, worn	• Inspect for damage and service as required.
• Intermediate one-way clutch assembly damaged	• Inspect for damage. Service as required.
Forward Clutch Assembly	
• Seals or piston damaged	• Inspect for damage. Service as required.
• Friction elements worn or damaged	• Inspect for damage. Service as required.
• Check ball stuck, damaged or not seating properly	• Inspect for damage. Service as required.
Input Shaft	
• Seals damaged	• Inspect for damage. Service as required.

FM5029801518020X

Fig. 24 Routines 222 & 322: No Automatic 3-4 Shift (Part 2 of 2). 1998–2000

Possible Component	Reference/Action
223 — ELECTRICAL ROUTINE	
Powertrain Control System	
• Electrical inputs/outputs, vehicle wiring harnesses, PCM, TP, MAF, VSS, OSS, Digital TR sensor, TCS, shift solenoids, EI system.	• Run Self-Test. Refer to MOTOR's Domestic Transmission Manual for diagnosis. Perform Pinpoint Tests A, D and F using Rotunda Transmission Tester 007-00130 with Rotunda Transmission Range (TR) Sensor Cable "E" 007-00111 and Digital (TR) Sensor Overlay 007-00131 or equivalent, as described. Service as required. Clear codes, road test and rerun self test.
323 — HYDRAULIC/MECHANICAL ROUTINE	
Improper Pressures	
• Forward clutch pressure, line pressure	• Check line and forward clutch at pressure taps. If out of specification, check main controls.
Main Controls	
• 3-4 shift valve, solenoid pressure regulator valve, OD servo regulator, 3-4 capacity modulator, 2-3 backout valve, 1-2, 2-3 shift valves stuck, damaged	• Inspect for damage. Service as required.
• Check balls No. 2, No. 7, No. 9 damaged, missing or not seating properly	• Inspect for damage. Service as required.
• Loose bolts	• Tighten bolts to specification.
• SSA/SS1, malfunction	• Activate solenoid using transmission tester. If solenoid operation cannot be felt when placing hand on solenoid, replace solenoid. Inspect O-rings for damage. Service as required.
• Gaskets damaged	• Inspect for damage and replace.
• OD servo, seal, rod damaged	• Inspect for damage. Service as required.
• Solenoid screen (in main control) blocked or damaged	• Clean or replace screen.
Pump	
• Porosity/cross leaks, balls missing, damaged or leaking	• Inspect for porosity/leaks, balls missing. Replace pump as required.
• Seal rings damaged.	• Inspect for damage. Service as required.
• Gaskets damaged	• Inspect for damage and replace.

FM5029801519010X

Fig. 25 Routines 223 & 323: No Automatic 4-3 Shift (Part 1 of 2). 1998–2000

Possible Component	Reference/Action
Overdrive Band	
• OD band and reverse clutch assembly damaged, worn	• Inspect for damage. Service as required.
• Intermediate one-way clutch assembly damaged	• Inspect for damage. Service as required.
Forward Clutch Assembly	
• Seals or piston damaged	• Inspect for damage. Service as required.
• Friction elements damaged, worn	• Inspect for damage. Service as required.
• Check ball stuck, damaged or not seating properly	• Inspect for damage. Service as required.
• Forward clutch piston and return spring damaged	• Inspect for damage. Service as required.
Input Shaft	
• Seals damaged	• Inspect for damage. Service as required.

FM5029801519020X

Fig. 25 Routines 223 & 323: No Automatic 4-3 Shift (Part 2 of 2). 1998–2000

Possible Component	Reference/Action
224 — ELECTRICAL ROUTINE	
Powertrain Control System	
• Electrical inputs/outputs, vehicle wiring harnesses, PCM, TP, MAF, VSS, OSS, Digital TR sensor, shift solenoids, EI system.	• Run self-test. Refer to MOTOR's Domestic Transmission Manual for diagnosis. Perform Pinpoint Tests A, D and F using Rotunda Transmission Tester 007-00130 with Rotunda Transmission Range (TR) Sensor Cable "E" 007-00111 and Digital (TR) Sensor Overlay 007-00131 or equivalent. Service as required. Clear codes, road test and rerun self test.
324 — HYDRAULIC/MECHANICAL ROUTINE	
Improper Pressures	
• Direct clutch	• Check pressure at direct clutch tap. If not within specification, check Main Controls.
Main Controls	
• 2-3 shift valve stuck or damaged	• Inspect for damage. Service as required
• Check balls damaged or missing	• Inspect for damage. Service as required.
• Loose bolts	• Tighten bolts to specification.
• SSB/SS2 malfunction	• Activate solenoid using transmission tester. If solenoid operation cannot be felt when placing hand on solenoid, replace solenoid. Inspect O-rings for damage. Service as required.
• Gaskets damaged	• Inspect for damage and replace.
Intermediate One-Way Clutch	
• Not holding or damaged	• Inspect for damage. Service as required.
Direct Clutch Assembly	
• Seals or piston damaged	• Inspect for damage. Service as required.
• Friction element damaged, worn	• Inspect for damage. Service as required.
• Check ball stuck, damaged or not seating properly	• Inspect for damage. Service as required.

FM5029801520000X

Fig. 26 Routines 224 & 324: No Automatic 3-2 Shift. 1998–2000

Possible Component	Reference/Action
225 — ELECTRICAL ROUTINE	
Powertrain Control System	
• Electrical inputs/outputs, vehicle wiring harnesses, PCM, TP, MAF, VSS, OSS, Digital TR sensor, shift solenoids, EI system.	• Run self-test. Refer to MOTOR's Domestic Transmission Manual for diagnosis. Perform Pinpoint Tests A, D and F using Rotunda Transmission Tester 007-00130 with Rotunda Transmission Range (TR) Sensor Cable "E" 007-00111 and Digital (TR) Sensor Overlay 007-00131 or equivalent. Service as required. Clear codes, road test and rerun self test.

FM5029801521010X

Fig. 27 Routines 225 & 325: No Automatic 1-2 Shift (Part 1 of 2). 1998–2000

Possible Component	Reference/Action
325 — HYDRAULIC/MECHANICAL ROUTINE	
Improper Pressures	
• Intermediate clutch	• Check pressure at intermediate clutch tap. If not within specifications, check Main Controls and Pump.
Main Controls	
• 1-2 shift valve, 1-2 accumulator solenoid pressure regulator valve stuck, damaged	• Inspect for damage. Service as required.
• Loose bolts	• Tighten bolts to specification.
• SS1 malfunction	• Activate solenoid using transmission tester. If solenoid operation cannot be felt when placing hand on solenoid, replace solenoid. Inspect O-rings for damage; service as required.
• Gaskets damaged	• Inspect for damage and replace.
Pump	
• Gaskets damaged	• Inspect for damage and replace.
• Porosity/cross leaks	• Inspect for leak/porosity. Replace pump as required.
Intermediate Clutch Assembly	
• Piston damaged	• Inspect for damage. Service as required.
• Friction elements damaged, worn	• Inspect for damage. Service as required.
• End clearance improper	• Inspect and correct.
Intermediate One-Way Clutch	
• Damaged	• Inspect for damage. Service as required.
Low One-Way Clutch	
• Not holding or damaged	• Inspect for damage. Service as required.

FM5029801521020X

Fig. 27 Routines 225 & 325: No Automatic 1-2 Shift (Part 2 of 2). 1998–2000

Possible Component	Reference/Action
240 — ELECTRICAL ROUTINE	
Powertrain Control System	
• Electrical inputs/outputs, vehicle wiring harnesses, PCM, TP, MAF, VSS, OSS, Digital TR sensor, TFT sensor, TCC solenoids, EI system.	• Run self-test. Refer to MOTOR's Domestic Transmission Manual for diagnosis. Perform Pinpoint Tests B, D and F using Rotunda Transmission Tester 007-00130 with Rotunda Transmission Range (TR) Sensor Cable "E" 007-00111 and Digital (TR) Sensor Overlay 007-00131 or equivalent. Service as required. Clear codes, road test and rerun self test.
340 — HYDRAULIC/MECHANICAL ROUTINE	
Shift Linkage	
• Damaged, out of adjustment	• Inspect and service as required. Verify linkage adjustment. After servicing linkage, verify that the Digital TR sensor is properly adjusted.
Improper Pressures	
• Low line pressure, low EPC pressure	• Check pressure at line and EPC taps. If pressure is low, check EPC and main regulator valve. If within specification, check Main Controls.
Main Controls	
• Solenoid pressure regulator valve, manual valve, torque converter clutch control valve and plunger, converter pressure limit valve, drain back valve stuck, damaged	• Inspect for damage and service as required.
• Loose bolts	• Tighten bolts to specification.
• Solenoid screen (in valve body) blocked or damaged	• Clean or replace screen.
• TCC solenoid malfunction	• Activate solenoid using transmission tester. If solenoid operation cannot be felt when placing hand on solenoid, replace solenoid. Inspect O-rings for damage. Service as required.

FM5029801522010X

Fig. 28 Routines 240 & 340: No Torque Converter Apply (Part 1 of 2). 1998–2000

Possible Component	Reference/Action
• Gaskets damaged	• Inspect for damage and replace.
Pump Assembly	
• Loose bolts	• Tighten bolts to specification.
• Porosity/cross leaks, balls leaking	• Inspect for porosity/leaks, ball missing. Replace pump as required.
• Gaskets damaged	• Inspect for damage and replace.
Input Shaft	
• Seals damaged	• Inspect for damage. Service as necessary.
Torque Converter Assembly	
• Leakage, friction material damaged, internal seals damaged	• Inspect torque converter. Service or replace as required.

FM5029801522020X

Fig. 28 Routines 240 & 340: No Torque Converter Apply (Part 2 of 2). 1998–2000

Possible Component	Reference/Action
241 — ELECTRICAL ROUTINE	
Powertrain Control System	
• Electrical inputs/outputs, vehicle wiring harnesses, PCM, TP, MAF, VSS, OSS, Digital TR sensor, TCS, shift solenoids, EI system.	• Run self-test. Refer to MOTOR's Domestic Transmission Manual for diagnosis. Perform Pinpoint Tests A, D and F using Rotunda Transmission Tester 007-00130 with Rotunda Transmission Range (TR) Sensor Cable "E" 007-00111 and Digital (TR) Sensor Overlay 007-00131 or equivalent. Service as required. Clear codes, road test and rerun self test.
341 — HYDRAULIC/MECHANICAL ROUTINE	
Main Controls	
• Drain back valve, torque converter clutch and plunger stuck, damaged	• Inspect for damage and service as required.
• Loose bolts	• Tighten bolts to specification.
• TCC solenoid malfunction	• Activate solenoid using transmission tester. If solenoid operation cannot be felt when placing hand on solenoid, replace solenoid. Inspect O-rings for damage. Service as required.
• No. 7 ball improper seating	• Inspect for damage. Service as required.
• Gaskets damaged	• Inspect for damage and replace.
Pump Assembly	
• Loose bolts	• Tighten bolts to specification.
• Ball missing, leaking, porosity/cross leaks	• Inspect for porosity/leaks, balls missing. Replace pump as required.
• Gaskets damaged	• Inspect for damage and replace.
Input Shaft	
• Seals damaged	• Inspect for damage. Service as required.
Torque Converter Assembly	
• No end clearance	• Inspect converter as described and replace as required.
• Piston plate damaged or stuck to cover	• If cover is heat-stained, replace converter.

FM5029801523000X

Fig. 29 Routines 241 & 341: Torque Converter Always Applied/Stalls Vehicle. 1998–2000

Possible Component	Reference/Action
242 —ELECTRICAL ROUTINE	
Powertrain Control System	
• Electrical inputs/outputs, vehicle wiring harnesses, powertrain control module, torque converter clutch (TCC) solenoid, OSS	• Run Self-Test. Refer to MOTOR's Domestic Transmission Manual for diagnosis. Perform Pinpoint Test F using Rotunda Transmission Tester 007-00130 or equivalent. Service as required. Clear codes, road test and rerun Self-Test.

FM5029801524010X

Fig. 30 Routines 242 & 342: Torque Converter Cycling/Shudder/Chatter (Part 1 of 2). 1998–2000

Possible Component	Reference/Action
342 —HYDRAULIC/MECHANICAL ROUTINE	
Fluid	
• Condition	• Inspect fluid condition. If burnt, drain fluid and converter. Replace fluid and filter assembly. Bring vehicle to normal operating temperature. Perform Transmission Drive Cycle Test
Main Controls	
• Solenoid pressure regulator valve, No. 7 check ball, bypass clutch control valve and plunger, converter pressure limit valve stuck, damaged or misassembled	• Inspect for damage. Service as required.
• Bolts out of torque specification	• Tighten bolts to specification.
• Solenoid screen (in valve body) blocked or damaged	• Clean or replace screen.
• TCC solenoid not functioning properly	• Activate solenoid using transmission tester. If solenoid operation cannot be felt when placing hand on solenoid, replace solenoid. Inspect O-rings for damage. Service as required.
• Gaskets damaged	• Inspect for damage and replace.
Pump Assembly	
• Bolts out of torque specification	• Tighten bolts to specification.
• Porosity/cross leaks, balls missing or leaking	• Inspect for porosity/leaks or balls missing. Replace pump assembly as required.
• Gaskets damaged	• Inspect for damage and replace.
Input Shaft	
• Seals damaged	• Inspect for damage. Service as required.
Torque Converter	
• Excessive end clearance	• Inspect converter as described. Replace as required.

FM5029801524020X

Fig. 30 Routines 242 & 342: Torque Converter Cycling/Shudder/Chatter (Part 2 of 2). 1998–2000

Possible Component	Reference/Action
250 — ELECTRICAL ROUTINE	
• No Electrical Concerns	
350 — HYDRAULIC/MECHANICAL ROUTINE	
Shift Linkage	
• Damaged or out of adjustment	• Inspect and service as required. Verify linkage adjustment After servicing linkage, verify that the Digital TR sensor is properly adjusted.
Main Controls	
• 3-4 shift valve, 1-2 and 2-3 shift valve, gaskets, 3-4 capacity modulator valve, stuck or damaged or misassembled	• Inspect for damage. Service as required.
• OD servo assembly damaged or stuck	• Inspect cover, piston and seal for damage. Service as required.
Overdrive	
• OD band, reverse clutch drum assembly worn or damaged	• Inspect for damage. Service as required.
• Intermediate overrunning clutch assembly damaged	• Inspect for damage. Service as required.
Reverse Band (Manual 1st Only)	
• Damaged, misadjusted	• Inspect for damage. Service as required.

FM5029801525000X

Fig. 31 Routines 250 & 350: No Engine Braking In 2nd Gear, Manual 2nd Or Manual 1st. 1998–2000

Possible Component	Reference/Action
251 — ELECTRICAL ROUTINE	
• No Electrical Concerns	

FM5029801526010X

Fig. 32 Routines 251 & 351: Shift Lever Efforts High (Part 1 of 2). 1998–2000

Possible Component	Reference/Action
351 — HYDRAULIC/MECHANICAL ROUTINE	
Shift Linkage, Digital TR Sensor • Damaged or out of adjustment	• Inspect and service as required. Verify linkage adjustment After servicing linkage, verify that the Digital TR sensor is properly adjusted.
Manual Lever • Retaining pin damaged, nut loose, detent spring bent or damaged or PARK mechanism damaged	• Inspect for damage. Service as required.
Main Controls • Manual valve stuck or damaged • Bolts out of torque specification	• Inspect for damage. Service as required. • Tighten bolts to specification.

FM5029801526020X

Fig. 32 Routines 251 & 351: Shift Lever Efforts High (Part 2 of 2). 1998–2000

Possible Component	Reference/Action
252 — ELECTRICAL ROUTINE	
Powertrain Control System • Electrical inputs/outputs, sensor seals leaking (Digital TR, OSS, VSS or transmission connector)	• Inspect for leakage and service as required.
352 — HYDRAULIC/MECHANICAL ROUTINE	
Seals, Gaskets • Torque converter, pump assembly, pan, extension housing - gasket/seal, manual lever, fluid level indicator tube	• Locate source of leak. Service as required.
Other • Cooler fitting, pressure taps, converter drain plug, band anchor pins, cooler lines, case porosity, case cracked • Vent blocked or damaged	• Locate source of leak. Service as required. • Check vent for damage or blockage. Service as required.

FM5029801527000X

Fig. 33 Routines 252 & 352: External Leaks. 1998–2000

Possible Component	Reference/Action
253 — ELECTRICAL ROUTINE	
Powertrain Control System • Electrical inputs/outputs, vehicle wiring harnesses, shift solenoids, Digital TR sensor, torque converter clutch (TCC) solenoid, transmission fluid temperature (TFT) sensor	• Run Self-Test. Refer to MOTOR's Domestic Transmission Manual for diagnosis. Perform Pinpoint Tests A, B and D using Rotunda Transmission Tester 007-00130 with Rotunda Transmission Range (TR) Sensor Cable "E" 007-00111 and Digital (TR) Sensor Overlay 007-00131,or equivalent. Service as required. Clear codes, road test and rerun Self-Test. Also refer to Routines 241/341 Torque Converter Operation Concern: Always Applied/Stalls Vehicle.
353 — HYDRAULIC/MECHANICAL ROUTINE	
Shift Linkage, Digital TR Sensor • Damaged or out of adjustment	• Inspect and service as required. Verify linkage adjustment After servicing linkage, verify that the Digital TR sensor is properly adjusted.
Verify Proper Shift Scheduling and Engagements	• Go to the appropriate Diagnostic Routines.
Torque Converter Clutch Always Applied	• Go to Hydraulic/Mechanical Routine 241/341.
Torque Converter Clutch • Damaged	• Inspect torque converter

FM5029801528000X

Fig. 34 Routines 253 & 353: Poor Vehicle Performance. 1998–2000

Possible Component	Reference/Action
254 — ELECTRICAL ROUTINE	
• No Electrical Concerns	
354 — HYDRAULIC/MECHANICAL ROUTINE	
For Noises/Vibrations That Change With Engine Speed: • Converter components • Fluid level (low) pump cavitation • Pump assembly • Engine drive accessories • Cooler lines grounding out • Flywheel	• Locate source of disturbance. Service as required.
For Noises/Vibrations That Change With Vehicle Speed: • Engine mounts loose or damaged • Driveline concerns: — u-joints — rear axle — suspension — modifications • First Gear: — low one-way clutch — gearset — friction elements • Second Gear: — intermediate one-way clutch — intermediate clutch piston bleed hole out of 12 O'clock position — friction elements • Third Gear: — torque converter — anti-clunk spring — friction elements • Fourth Gear: — gear set — friction elements — torque converter • Reverse: — gear set — friction elements • Output shaft splines worn or damaged	• Locate source of disturbance and service as required. • For specific shift or torque converter concerns, refer to the following routine(s) for further diagnosis: **Shift** 1-2,**Routine**, 320 **Shift** 2-3, **Routine**, 321 **Shift** 3-4, **Routine**, 322 **Shift** 4-3, **Routine**, 323 **Shift** 3-2, **Routine**, 324 **Shift** 2-1, **Routine**, 325 **Torque Converter Cycling** 242/342
Other Noises/Vibrations: • Main Controls, valve resonance • Shift Cable: — vibration — grounding — cooler lines — grounding	• Locate source of disturbance and service as required.

FM5029801529000X

Fig. 35 Routines 254 & 354: Noise/Vibration In Forward Or Reverse. 1998–2000

Possible Component	Reference/Action
255 — ELECTRICAL ROUTINE	
Powertrain Control System • Electrical inputs/outputs, vehicle wiring harnesses, engine starting system hardware, Digital TR sensor	• Run Self-Test. Refer to MOTOR's Domestic Transmission Manual for diagnosis. Perform Pinpoint Test D using Rotunda Transmission Range (TR) Sensor Cable "E" 007-00111 and Digital (TR) Sensor Overlay 007-00131 or equivalent Service and adjust as required.
355 — HYDRAULIC/MECHANICAL ROUTINE	
Shift Linkage, Digital TR Sensor • Damaged or out of adjustment	• Inspect and service as required. Verify linkage adjustment After servicing linkage, verify that the Digital TR sensor is properly adjusted.

FM5029801530000X

Fig. 36 Routines 255 & 355: Engine Will Not Crank. 1998–2000

Possible Component	Reference/Action
256 — ELECTRICAL ROUTINE	
• No Electrical Concerns	
356 — HYDRAULIC/MECHANICAL ROUTINE	
Shift Linkage, Digital TR Sensor • Damaged or out of adjustment	• Inspect and service as required. Verify linkage adjustment After servicing linkage, verify that the Digital TR sensor is properly adjusted.
Park Mechanism • Output shaft ring, park brake pawl, parking pawl return spring, park rod guide cup, parking pawl shaft, parking pawl actuating rod, manual lever, manual lever detent spring damaged or misassembled	• Inspect for damage or misassembly and service as required.

FM5029801531000X

Fig. 37 Routines 256 & 356: No Park Range. 1998–2000

Possible Component	Reference/Action
257 — ELECTRICAL ROUTINE	
Refer to Routine 240/340, Torque Converter Operation Concern: No Apply	
357 — HYDRAULIC/MECHANICAL ROUTINE	
Fluid • Improper level • Condition	• Adjust fluid to proper level. • Inspect Fluid Condition.
Cooler Lines • Damaged, blocked or reversed	• Inspect for damage and proper installation. Service as required.
Auxiliary Cooler • Damaged, blocked or restricted or improperly installed	• Inspect for damage and proper installation. Service as required.
Vehicle Concerns Causing Engine Overheating	• Inspect Cooling System.
Main Controls • Drain back valve, torque clutch control valve, converter limit valve stuck, damaged or misassembled	• Inspect for damage and service as required.
Torque Converter • No Apply	• Refer to Routine 240/340.

FM5029801532000X

Fig. 38 Routines 257 & 357: Transmission Overheating. 1998–2000

MAINTENANCE

Ford Motor Company recommends use of Mercon V type automatic transmission fluid in this transmission. Use of a fluid other than that meeting Ford Mercon V specifications may result in transmission malfunction or failure.

BRAKE SHIFT INTERLOCK SYSTEM

Inspection

1. With engine Off, turn ignition switch to Run position.
2. Place gear shift lever in Park, brake not applied, and verify lever cannot be shifted from Park.
3. With brake pedal applied, ensure gear shift lever can be shifted from Park.
4. Shift to Reverse, verify ignition switch cannot be turned to Lock position.
5. Shift to Park, verify ignition switch can be turned to Lock position.

TRANSMISSION FLUID COOLER FLOW INSPECTION

Linkage, fluid and control pressure must be within specification before performing this flow check.

1. Remove transmission dipstick from filler tube, then place funnel in filler tube.
2. Raise and support vehicle, then remove cooler return line from its fitting in case.
3. Attach hose to cooler return line and fasten free end of hose to funnel installed in filler tube.
4. Start engine and set idle speed at 1000 RPM with transmission in Neutral.
5. Observe fluid flow at funnel. When flow is solid, air bleeding has been completed, flow should be liberal. If there is not a liberal flow at 1000 RPM in Neutral, low pump capacity, main circuit system leakage, or cooler system restriction is indicated.
6. To separate transmission trouble from cooler system trouble, observe flow at transmission case converter out fitting.

FLUID CHECK

1. With transmission at operating temperature, park vehicle on level surface.
2. Operate engine at idle speed with parking brake applied and move selector lever through each detent position. Return selector lever to Park.
3. With engine idling, remove dipstick and check fluid level. Fluid level should be between arrows on dipstick.
4. Add fluid as necessary to bring fluid to proper level.

FLUID CHANGE

Normal maintenance and lubrication requirements do not necessitate periodic fluid changes. If vehicle accumulates 5,000 or more miles per month or it is used in continuous stop and go service, change fluid every 30,000 miles.

When filling a dry transmission and converter, install approximately 12 quarts of specified fluid. Start engine, shift selector lever through all ranges and place it at P position. Check fluid level and add enough to raise level in transmission to F (full) mark on dipstick. When a partial drain and refill is required, proceed as follows:

1. Loosen oil pan bolts and allow pan to drain.
2. Working from rear and both sides of transmission oil pan, remove bolts, allowing pan to drop and drain slowly.
3. Remove and clean pan and replace screen.
4. Place a new gasket on pan and install pan and screen.
5. Add three quarts of specified fluid to transmission.
6. Run engine at a fast idle until it reaches normal operating temperature.
7. Shift selector lever through all ranges and then place it in P position.
8. Add fluid as required to bring level to full mark.

ADJUSTMENTS

MANUAL LINKAGE

Column Shift

1. Place steering column selector lever in Overdrive and hold selector lever in position by placing three-pound weight on lever.
2. Raise and support vehicle.
3. Loosen shift cable retaining nut at manual control lever.
4. Move manual control lever to Overdrive position, second detent from most forward position.
5. Tighten shift cable retaining nut to specifications.
6. Check shift lever for proper operation.

Floor Shift

1. Place transmission selector lever in Drive position. Hold in position with three-pound rearward load.
2. Raise and support vehicle.
3. Loosen transmission shift cable and bracket to cable bracket retaining nut.
4. Move transmission manual control lever to Drive position third detent from full clockwise position.
5. Tighten retaining nut to specifications.
6. Check transmission operation in all selector lever positions.

IN-VEHICLE REPAIRS

BRAKE SHIFT LOCK ACTUATOR, REPLACE

CROWN VICTORIA, GRAND MARQUIS, MARK VIII & TOWN CAR

1. Remove steering column as outlined in "Steering Columns."
2. Remove mounting bolts, then insert plate and shift lock actuator.
3. Remove insert plate and discard shift lock actuator clip.
4. Reverse procedure to install. Tighten mounting bolts to specifications.

MUSTANG

1. Remove shifter top control panel and disconnect electrical connectors.
2. Remove shifter bezel and bulb, then disconnect electrical connector.
3. Remove mounting screw and handle. **Do not pull handle too far or overdrive cancel button may be damaged.**
4. Remove brake shift interlock cable mounting clip and bolt, then disconnect cable.
5. Remove mounting screws and instrument panel steering column cover.
6. Remove mounting screws and instrument panel reinforcement.
7. Remove mounting nuts and lower steering column.
8. Remove mounting screws and brake shift cable interlock actuator.
9. Reverse proceed to install.

IGNITION/SHIFT INTERLOCK CABLE, REPLACE

THUNDERBIRD & 1997 COUGAR

1. Open console glove compartment door and remove console finish panel attaching screws.
2. Lift rear of console finish panel off of retainers.
3. Reach under console finish panel and disconnect electrical connectors.
4. Lift rear of console finish panel and slide rearward to release two front locating tabs, then remove console finish panel from vehicle.
5. Remove lefthand lower instrument panel trim and lower steering column shroud.
6. Remove interlock cable retaining

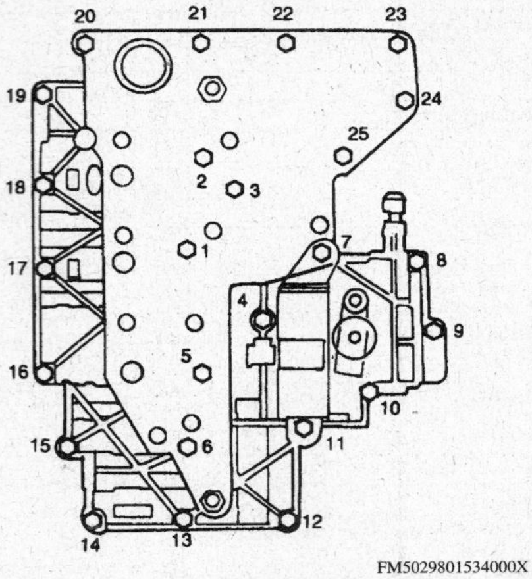

Fig. 39 Valve body tightening sequence

screws and clip, then disconnect ignition/shifter interlock cable from lever cam.
7. Remove steering column retaining nuts and lower steering column to floor.
8. Disconnect interlock solenoid electrical connector.
9. Remove ignition/shifter interlock cable retaining screws from steering column.
10. Guide ignition/shifter interlock cable from under floor carpet and remove cable from vehicle.
11. Reverse procedure to install.

MUSTANG

1. Remove two access covers at rear of console, then armrest retaining bolts.
2. Remove four armrest to floor bracket retaining bolts, then armrest assembly.
3. Remove gearshift lever opening finish panel and shift knob, then slide finish panel up to remove.
4. Place emergency brake lever in up position, remove four retaining screws and lift top finish panel up, then disconnect electrical connectors and remove top finish panel.
5. Remove two console to rear floor bracket retaining screws, then insert a small screwdriver into two notches at bottom of front upper finish panel and snap out.
6. **On models equipped with radio opening cover plate with stowage bin,** use a small screwdriver to pry cover plate out of console.
7. **On models equipped with radio with stowage bin or radio with graphic equalizer,** install radio remover tool No. T87P-19061-A, or equivalent, into radio face plate. Push radio remover in approximately one inch to release clips, apply a light spreading force and pull radio out of dash, then disconnect electrical connectors.
8. **On all models,** open glove compartment door and drop glove compartment assembly down, then remove two console to instrument panel retaining screws.
9. Remove four console to bracket retaining screws, then console from vehicle.
10. Remove lefthand lower instrument panel trim and steering column lower shroud.
11. Remove interlock cable retaining screw, then disconnect cable from shift lever cam.
12. Remove steering column retaining nuts, then lower column to floor.
13. Remove cable retaining clip, then disconnect electrical connector at solenoid.
14. Remove cable retaining screw from steering column, then guide interlock cable out from under console brackets.
15. Reverse procedure to install. Tighten mounting nuts to specifications.

SHIFT LINKAGE, REPLACE

1997-98 CROWN VICTORIA, GRAND MARQUIS & TOWN CAR

Removal

1. Remove cable plastic terminal from gearshift lever pivot ball by prying with suitable screwdriver between cable plastic terminal and range selector lever under instrument panel.
2. Remove cable and bracket from steering column tube.
3. Raise and support vehicle.
4. Remove shift cable and bracket from transmission shift cable bracket by unlocking lock tabs and sliding cable out.
5. Remove cable to transmission manual control lever stud retaining nut, then cable from stud.
6. Remove shift cable and bracket from torque converter housing and frame rail.
7. Lower vehicle.
8. Unseat cable grommet from cowl, then shift cable and bracket on engine compartment side.
9. Pull cable out of cowl.

Installation

1. Feed plastic terminal end of cable through cowl from engine compartment.
2. Pull rubber grommet on transmission range selector cable into dash panel opening and seat it securely from passenger compartment.
3. Install transmission range selector cable into steering column transmission shift cable bracket. Ensure locking tab seats fully.
4. Install shift cable and bracket to steering column casting.
5. Apply small amount of suitable grease to column selector lever pivot ball or cable terminal.
6. Attach cable plastic terminal to shift lever pivot ball.
7. Place transmission range selector lever in Overdrive position and hang three-pound weight on end.
8. Route shift cable to bracket on crossmember and through fuel rail bracket clip.
9. Insert cable clip into bracket and position cable so white band is 21 inches from ground.
10. Raise and support vehicle.

11. Install cable in shift cable bracket, then clip bracket into transmission bracket. Ensure locking tabs fully seat.
12. Place transmission in Overdrive by rotating lever counterclockwise to stop, then clockwise two stops.
13. Align transmission shift cable paddle slot on manual control lever stud shoulders while tightening nut to specifications.
14. Lower vehicle and remove three-pound weight.

1999–2000 CROWN VICTORIA, GRAND MARQUIS & TOWN CAR

1. Disconnect transmission shift cable from selector lever and support.
2. Disconnect cable from steering column instrument panel bracket.
3. Disconnect cable shift actuator cable fitting.
4. Push rubber grommet and cable through bulkhead.
5. Raise and support vehicle.
6. Disconnect shift cable from manual control lever.
7. Disconnect shift actuator cable fitting and release cable.
8. Disconnect shift cable from transmission shift cable bracket.
9. Remove mounting bolts and bracket.
10. Reverse procedure to install. Tighten mounting bolts to specifications.

MARK VIII

1. Remove transmission control selector dial bezel.
2. Slide retaining clip and pull shift cable from lever cam.
3. Remove shift cable and shifter nut, then shift cable bracket clip.
4. Remove shift cable and bracket, then nut from transmission shift cable bracket.
5. Reverse procedure to install. Tighten mounting nuts to specifications.

MUSTANG

Removal

1. Place transmission range selector lever in Drive position.
2. Raise and support vehicle.
3. Remove shift cable and bracket mounting bolts from shifter mounted bracket.
4. Disconnect cable from shift lever ball stud.
5. Remove shift cable and bracket mounting bolts from transmission bracket.
6. Remove cable retaining nut from manual control lever, then cable.

Installation

1. Install shift cable shifter mounted bracket and tighten mounting screws to specifications.
2. Connect shift cable and bracket to transmission range selector lever ball stud.
3. Install shift cable mounted bracket to transmission and tighten mounting nuts to specifications.
4. Place transmission manual control lever in Drive position and apply three-pound rearward force to lever.
5. Connect shift cable and bracket to transmission manual control lever and tighten mounting nut to specifications.

THUNDERBIRD & 1997 COUGAR

1. Remove console finish panel.
2. Remove transmission control selector dial bezel mounting screws.
3. Remove transmission range selector lever and housing to floorpan mounting screws.
4. Remove shift cable and bracket-to-transmission range selector lever and housing mounting screws.
5. Disconnect cable from range selector lever.
6. Raise and support vehicle.
7. Disconnect shift cable and bracket from control selector connecting rod adjustment rod.
8. Remove mounting nut from cable and bracket at transmission.
9. Reverse procedure to install. Tighten mounting nuts and bolts to specifications.

VALVE BODY, REPLACE

1997

Removal

1. Raise and support vehicle.
2. Drain transmission fluid into suitable container.
3. Remove pan, filter and magnet.
4. Disconnect solenoid and sensor connectors by grasping and pulling straight out.
5. Remove mounting bolts, then manual control valve detent lever spring.
6. Remove mounting bolt and Electronic Pressure Control (EPC) solenoid bracket.
7. Remove mounting bolts and main control valve body. Discard pump outlet screen.

Installation

1. Position gasket and main control valve body using two alignment bolts.
2. Loosely install mounting bolts. Do not tighten now.
3. Install EPC solenoid bracket, then loosely install mounting bolt.
4. Install manual control valve detent lever spring and mounting bolt.
5. Tighten valve body mounting bolts to specifications in sequence, **Fig. 39.**
6. Connect Transmission Fluid Temperature (TFT) sensor, then the shift, Torque Converter clutch (TCC) and EPC solenoid wiring connectors.
7. Install filter and grommet
8. Position magnet, then install gasket and pan.
9. Tighten pan mounting bolts to specifications.
10. Lower vehicle and fill transmission with suitable fluid.

1998–2000

Removal

1. Raise and support vehicle.
2. Drain transmission fluid into suitable container.
3. Remove pan, filter and magnet.
4. Carefully pry up locking tabs, then disconnect following leads. **Do not pull on molded lead frame.**
   a. Shift solenoid SSA/SS1 and SSB/SS2.
   b. TCC solenoid.
   c. EPC solenoid.
   d. Bulkhead inter-connector.
5. Remove mounting bolts, then the shift and TCC solenoids.
6. Remove mounting bolts, then the manual control valve detent lever spring.
7. Remove mounting bolts and main control valve body. Discard pump outlet screen.

Installation

1. Position gasket and main control valve body using two alignment bolts.
2. Ensure manual valve detent lever assembly drive pin engages manual valve properly before installing mounting bolts.
3. Loosely install mounting bolts. Do not tighten now.
4. Install manual control valve detent lever spring and mounting bolt.
5. Tighten valve body mounting bolts to specifications in sequence, **Fig. 39.**
6. Install shift and TCC solenoid, then the mounting bolts.
7. Connect molded lead frame inter-connector, then to EPC, TCC and shift solenoids.
8. Install filter seal.
9. If transmission is being service for contamination-related failure, use new filter and seal. **Carefully remove main control bore grommet with suitable small screwdriver.**
10. Position magnet, then install gasket and pan.
11. Tighten pan mounting bolts to specifications.
12. Lower vehicle and fill transmission with suitable fluid.

EXTENSION HOUSING SEAL & GASKET, REPLACE

1. Turn air suspension switch to Off position, if equipped.
2. Raise and support vehicle.
3. Drain transmission fluid into suitable container.
4. Mark rear driveshaft yoke and axle flange alignment for assembly.
5. Remove mounting bolts and separate driveshaft from transmission.
6. Remove exhaust system as necessary.
7. Support transmission with suitable jack.
8. Remove transmission mounting nuts, then mounting bolts and transmission crossmember.
9. Lower transmission to access extension housing bolts.
10. Remove extension housing seal using

PCM CALIBRATION CHART				
Application	Old Calibration	Old Part Number (-12A650-)	New Calibration	New Part Number (-12A650-)
1997 Crown Victoria/Grand Marquis				
49S/Canada/High Altitude	7-18F-R10	F7AF-BD	7-18F-R11	F7AZ-BE
49S/Canada/High Altitude	7-18H-R10	F7AF-CD	7-18H-R11	F7AZ-CE
Mexico	7-18H-R10	F7AF-DD	7-18H-R11	F7AZ-DE
Police	7-18I-R10/R11	F7AF-EF	7-18I-R11	F7AZ-EF
California	7-18M-R10	F7AF-FD	7-18M-R11	F7AZ-FE
California	7-18N-R10	F7AF-GD	7-18N-R11	F7AZ-GE
1997 Town Car				
49S/Canada/High Altitude	7-18J-R10	F7VF-AD	7-18J-R11	F7VZ-AE
49S/Canada/Mexico/High Altitude	7-18E-R10	F7VF-BD	7-18E-R11	F7VZ-BE
California	7-18Q-R10	F7VF-CD	7-18Q-R11	F7VZ-CE
California	7-18S-R10	F7VF-DD	7-18S-R11	F7VZ-DE

FMA059800087010X

Fig. 40 PCM calibration (Part 1 of 2). 1997 Cougar, Crown Victoria, Grand Marquis, Thunderbird & Town Car

PCM CALIBRATION CHART (Cont'd.)				
Application	Old Calibration	Old Part Number (-12A650-)	New Calibration	New Part Number (-12A650-)
1997 3.8L Thunderbird/Cougar				
49S/Canada/Mexico/High Altitude	6-16F-R05/R10	F6SF-AE	7-16F-R10	F6SZ-AF
California	6-16T-R05/R10	F6SF-BE	7-16T-R10	F6SZ-BF
1997 4.6L Thunderbird/Cougar				
49S/Canada/Mexico/High Altitude	7-18B-R05 through R10	F7SF-AA	7-18B-R11	F7SZ-AB
California	7-18P-R05 through R10	F7SF-BA	7-18P-R11	F7SZ-BB

FMA059800087020X

Fig. 40 PCM calibration (Part 2 of 2). 1997 Cougar, Crown Victoria, Grand Marquis, Thunderbird & Town Car

oil seal remover tool No. T74O-77248-A, or equivalent, and suitable slide hammer.

11. Remove mounting bolts and nuts, then extension housing and gasket.
12. Reverse procedure to install, noting following:
    a. Install seal using extension housing seal replacer tool No. T61L-7657-B, or equivalent.
    b. Tighten mounting bolts and nuts to specifications.
    c. Ensure output shaft and driver shaft removal marks are aligned properly.

ELECTRONIC PRESSURE CONTROL (EPC) SOLENOID, REPLACE

1. Remove manual control lever as outlined under "Manual Control Lever Shaft & Seal, Replace."
2. **On 1997 models,** grasp, pull and remove EPC solenoid connector.
3. **On 1998–2000 models,** carefully pry up locking tabs, then disconnect following leads. **Do not pull on molded lead frame.**
    a. Shift solenoid SSA/SS1 and SSB/SS2.
    b. TCC solenoid.
    c. EPC solenoid.
    d. Bulkhead inter-connector.
4. **On all models,** remove EPC solenoid.
5. Reverse procedure to install.

MANUAL CONTROL LEVER SHAFT & SEAL, REPLACE

1. Turn air suspension switch to Off position, if equipped.
2. Raise and support vehicle.
3. Drain transmission fluid into suitable container.
4. Remove pan and filter.
5. Disconnect digital Transmission Range (TR) sensor electrical connector.
6. Disconnect transmission shift linkage.
7. Remove mounting nuts and digital TR sensor.
8. Remove mounting nut and manual control valve detent lever spring.
9. Remove manual lever shaft retaining pin. Use suitable shop cloth to protect transmission case surface.
10. Remove nut and slide manual control lever shaft out.
11. **On 1998–2000 models,** remove manual valve detent lever, then parking lever actuating rod.
12. **On all models,** carefully pry seal out using suitable screwdriver in seal lower edge. **Do not damage bore with prying tool.**
13. Reverse procedure to install, noting following:
    a. Install seal using oil seal replacer tool No. T74P-77498-A, or equivalent.
    b. Tighten nuts to specifications.
    c. Align digital TR sensor using digital TR sensor alignment tool No. T97L-70010-A, or equivalent, as outlined under "Digital Transmission Range (TR) Sensor, Replace."

DIGITAL TRANSMISSION RANGE (TR) SENSOR, REPLACE

1. Position manual control lever in Neutral position.
2. Raise and support vehicle.
3. Remove mounting nut and position manual shift cable aside.
4. Remove mounting bolts, lower digital TR sensor and disconnect electrical harness.
5. Remove TR sensor.
6. Reverse procedure to install, noting following:
    a. Align digital TR sensor using digital TR sensor alignment tool No. T97L-70010-A, or equivalent.
    b. Tighten mounting nuts and bolts to specifications.

REVERSE SERVO, REPLACE

REMOVAL

1. Remove main control valve body as previously described.
2. Compress servo spring with servo piston remover/replacer tool No. T92P-70023-A, or equivalent.
3. Remove reverse band servo retaining ring.
4. Remove cover, piston and rod, and reverse band spring.

INSTALLATION

This procedure does not compensate for band wear.

Piston rods are three different length grades. Do not install in any transmission other than one from which they were removed.

1. Lubricate piston seal.
2. Install reverse servo piston and return spring. **Do not install cover.**
3. Install servo piston selection tool No. T80L-77030-A, or equivalent, and tighten apply bolt to specifications.
4. Attach suitable dial indicator with bracket.
5. Position indicator stem on reverse servo piston flat portion and zero dial.
6. Loosen bolt until piston stops against tool.
7. Measure and record piston travel.
8. If piston travel is not .211–.237 inch, select proper servo assembly to bring piston travel within specifications. Piston rod lengths are as follows:
    a. One groove pistons have rods 2.936 inches long.
    b. Two groove pistons have rods 2.989 inches long.
    c. Three groove pistons have rods 3.043 inches long.
9. Remove dial indicator and tool.
10. Install proper servo piston assembly spring, cover and seal.
11. Compress servo spring using servo piston remover/replacer tool No. T92P-70023-A, or equivalent.
12. Install retaining ring, then main control valve body.

OVERDRIVE SERVO, REPLACE

1. Remove main control valve body as previously described.
2. Compress servo spring with servo piston remover/replacer tool No. T92P-70023-A, or equivalent.
3. Remove reverse band servo retaining ring.
4. Remove piston and return spring.
5. Reverse procedure to install.

1-2 ACCUMULATOR, REPLACE

1. Remove main control valve body as previously described.
2. Compress 1-2 accumulator cover with servo piston remover/replacer tool No. T92P-70023-A, or equivalent.
3. Remove retaining ring and cover.
4. Remove lower spring, piston and upper spring.
5. Reverse procedure to install.

2-3 ACCUMULATOR, REPLACE

1. Remove main control valve body as previously described.
2. Remove piston retainer.
3. Remove piston and upper spring.
4. Reverse procedure to install.

CROSSMEMBER, REPLACE

Refer to "Extension Housing Seal & Gasket, Replace " for crossmember replacement.

TRANSMISSION

REPLACE

CROWN VICTORIA, GRAND MARQUIS, MUSTANG, THUNDERBIRD & TOWN CAR & 1997 COUGAR

Removal

1. Raise and support vehicle.
2. Drain transmission fluid into suitable container.
3. Remove exhaust system as necessary.
4. Remove converter access cover and engine oil pan adapter plate bolts.
5. Remove flywheel-to-converter mounting nuts, noting following:
   a. Use suitable socket and breaker bar on crankshaft pulley mounting bolt.
   b. Rotate crankshaft clockwise as viewed from front to access each nut.
   c. **Never rotate crankshaft counterclockwise.**
6. Mark rear driveshaft yoke and axle companion flange for original position assembly.
7. Remove mounting bolts and driveshaft.
8. Disconnect transmission shift linkage, then remove shift cable bracket.
9. Disconnect Output Shaft Speed (OSS) and Vehicle Speed Sensor (VSS) connectors.
10. Remove torque converter access plug and drain fluid into suitable container.
11. Disconnect transmission wiring harness.
12. Remove mounting bolts and position starter motor out of way.
13. Raise transmission slightly with suitable jack.
14. Remove engine rear support-to-crossmember mounting bolts.
15. Remove crossmember mounting bolts.
16. Remove transmission support insulator, engine and transmission support, and engine damper mounting body bracket.
17. Lower jack and allow transmission to hang.
18. Position suitable jack to front and raise engine to gain access to upper converter housing mounting bolts.
19. Disconnect cooler lines at transmission and plug all openings.
20. Remove lower converter housing mounting bolts.
21. Remove transmission fluid filler tube.
22. Secure transmission to suitable jack.
23. Support engine with suitable safety stand and wood block.
24. Disconnect Heated Oxygen Sensor (HO2S) connectors.
25. Remove upper converter housing bolts.
26. Move transmission to rear to disengage dowel pins and torque converter from flywheel.
27. Install torque converter holding tool No. T97T-7902-A, or equivalent.
28. Lower transmission.
29. Remove holding tool and torque converter.

Installation

1. Apply multi-purpose grease No. DOAZ-19584-AA, or equivalent, to pilot hub.
2. Tighten converter housing drain plug to specifications.
3. Install torque converter, pushing and at same time rotating through what feels like two notches or bumps.
4. Ensure torque converter centering spigot is approximately .4375–.5625 inch inside housing.
5. Secure transmission to suitable jack and install torque converter holding tool No. T97T-7902-A, or equivalent.
6. Ensure torque converter drive studs and housing access plug align with flywheel holes.
7. Align converter stud and flywheel bolt holes with balancing marks.
8. Move transmission and torque converter forward, squarely against flywheel.
9. Remove converter holding tool.
10. Ensure torque converter is properly seated by grasping stud, then moving back and forth. If there is no metallic clank noise and converter will not move, proceed as follows:
    a. Remove transmission.
    b. Reposition torque converter so impeller hub is properly engaged in pump gear.
    c. Install transmission.
11. Install converter housing mounting bolts and tighten to specifications.
12. Remove jack safety chain.
13. Connect HO2S connectors.
14. Install fluid filler tube and tighten mounting bolt to specifications.
15. Install cooler lines and tighten to specifications.
16. Remove jack support from engine front.
17. Raise transmission and install transmission support insulator, engine and transmission support, and engine damper mounting body bracket.
18. Lower transmission and install rear engine crossmember nut.
19. Remove transmission jack.
20. Connect transmission wiring harness.
21. Install starter motor.
22. Install flywheel-to-converter mounting nuts and tighten to specifications.
23. Install access cover and tighten mounting bolts to specifications.
24. Install exhaust system.
25. Install vehicle speed sensor and connect wiring.
26. Install driveshaft.
27. Lower vehicle and fill transmission.

MARK VIII

Removal

1. Place transmission range selector in Neutral position.
2. Raise and support vehicle.
3. Disconnect transmission harness electrical connector.
4. If transmission is to be disassembled, drain fluid into suitable container.
5. Mark rear driveshaft yoke and axle companion flange for original position assembly.
6. Remove mounting bolts and position rear driveshaft yoke aside
7. Remove rear differential retaining nuts and bolts and separate driveshaft from transmission.
8. Remove mounting bolts and inspection cover.
9. Remove torque converter mounting nuts. Rotate crankshaft to access nuts.
10. Disconnect electrical connectors, then remove mounting bolts and starter motor.
11. Disconnect transmission shift linkage.
12. Disconnect transmission cooler lines.
13. Disconnect Heated Oxygen Sensor (HO2S) connectors.
14. Position suitable jack under transmission assembly.
15. Remove transmission-to-crossmember mounting bolts, then mounting bolts and crossmember.
16. Remove mounting bolts and transmission mount.
17. Remove dual converter Y pipe.
18. Remove transmission housing mounting bolts.
19. Install torque converter holding tool No. T97T-7902-A, or equivalent.
20. Remove mounting bolt and fluid filler tube.
21. Lower and remove transmission.

Installation

1. Ensure torque converter is held securely in position with converter holding tool No. T97T-7902-A, or equivalent.
2. Raise transmission, then align converter stud and flywheel bolt holes.
3. Move transmission into position and ensure torque converter is squarely fitted to flywheel.
4. Install fluid filler tube.
5. Install transmission holding bolts and tighten to specifications.
6. Remove torque converter holding tool.
7. Install dual converter Y pipe.
8. Position transmission mount and exhaust pipe bracket, then tighten mounting bolts to specifications.
9. Install crossmember and tighten mounting bolts to specifications.
10. Tighten transmission-to-crossmember mounting nuts to specifications.
11. Remove transmission jack.
12. Connect HO2S electrical connectors.
13. Connect transmission cooler lines.

14. Slide transmission shift linkage into cable bracket until tabs are fully seated, then connect shift cable to manual lever. Manual lever must be in Overdrive position.
15. Install starter, tighten mounting bolts to specifications and connect wires.
16. Install torque converter mounting nuts and tighten to specifications.
17. Install transmission inspection cover and tighten bolts to specifications.
18. Position driveshaft on transmission, then tighten rear differential nuts and bolts to specifications.
19. Position driveshaft to rear differential and tighten driveshaft bolts to specifications.
20. Lower vehicle and connect transmission harness electrical connector.

TECHNICAL SERVICE BULLETINS

VIBRATION OR EXTENSION HOUSING FLUID LEAK

1999 Crown Victoria Police Vehicles

On some of these models there may be a vibration and/or extension housing seal leak.

This condition may be caused by extension housing bushing or seal walking or spinning out because extended high speed operation and excessive driveshaft flexing. To correct this condition, replace extension housing assembly (part No. F5UZ-7A039-A) and gasket (part No. F7AZ-7086-A). Also ensure vehicle has "GNX" (part No. F8AZ-5560-GA) level rear springs and that an revised Metal Matric Composite (MMC) driveshaft (part No. XW7Z-4602-AA) is installed.

DELAYED OR NO 2-3 UPSHIFT

Crown Victoria, Grand Marquis, Mark VIII, Mustang & Town Car

On some of these models, there may a delayed or no 2-3 upshift, specially when the transmission is cold. Diagnostic Trouble Code (DTC) P0782 may be stored.

This condition may be caused by fluid pressure leakage past the 2-3 accumulator larger diameter seal. To correct this condition, replace the 2-3 accumulator using the revised piston (part No. F7AZ-7H292-AB).

Thunderbird & 1997-98 Crown Victoria, Grand Marquis, Mark VIII, Mustang & Town Car & 1997 Cougar w/Remanufactured Transmissions

On some of these models with remanufactured transmissions (serial Nos. Between R0475797–R0771887), there may a delayed or no 2-3 upshift, specially when the transmission is cold. Diagnostic Trouble Code (DTC) P0782 may be stored.

This condition may be caused by fluid pressure leakage past the 2-3 accumulator larger diameter seal. To correct this condition, replace the 2-3 accumulator using the revised piston (part No. F7AZ-7H292-AB).

TRANSMISSION FLUID LEAK AT RADIATOR

1997-99 Mustang

On some of these models, there may be a transmission fluid leak at the radiator transmission oil cooler connection joint between the radiator and cooler fitting (not the cooler line into fitting).

This condition may be caused by insufficient thread sealer on the fitting. To correct this condition, install an O-ring (part No. W705181-S300) onto the oil cooler line fitting.

SHUDDER OR VIBRATION

1997 Cougar, Crown Victoria, Grand Marquis, Thunderbird & Town Car

On these models there may be torque converter clutch shudder or vibration under light to moderate acceleration above 35 mph in 3rd or 4th gears.

This condition may be caused by transmission fluid breakdown and/or Powertrain Control Module (PCM) calibration. To correct this condition, proceed as follows:

1. Completely drain transmission, converter, cooler and lines. Residual fluid in coolers and lines will cause shudder to return.
2. Remove transmission pan, then clean pan and magnet.
3. Inspect transmission gasket and filter, then replace as necessary.
4. Install filter, gasket and pan.
5. **On Crown Victoria, Grand Marquis and Town Car models,** install new transmission fluid cooler (part No. F8VZ-7A095-AA) and transmission fluid cooler installation kit (Crown Victoria and Grand Marquis part No. F8AZ-7K177-AA; Town Car part No. F8VZ-7K177-AA) according to kit instructions if vehicle operates under following conditions:
   a. Mostly stop-and-go traffic.
   b. High ambient temperatures.
   c. High humidity.
   d. Or in Alabama, Arkansas, Florida, Georgia, Hawaii, Louisiana, Mississippi, North Carolina, Oklahoma, South Carolina, Tennessee or Texas,
6. **On all models,** fill transmission with Mercon V automatic transmission fluid, or equivalent. Ensure bulk fluid does not have moisture contamination.
7. Ensure PCM calibration is current. If not, reprogram PCM according to **Fig. 40.**

ERRATIC OR PROLONGED 1-2 SHIFT

1997

On these models there may be erratic or prolonged 1-2 shift.

This condition may be caused by premature accumulator seal wear. To correct this condition, proceed as follows:

1. Remove transmission pan and gasket.
2. Remove 1-2 accumulator piston retainer using suitable snap ring removal tool. Spring load will pop cover and bottom accumulator spring out of bore.
3. Remove piston and top accumulator spring.
4. Replace piston and top accumulator spring with new bonded piston (part No. A7AZ-7F251-AA).
5. If not damaged, install bottom accumulator spring and cover, then the retaining spring.
6. Install gasket and pan.

TRANSMISSION OIL COOLER FLUID LEAK

Thunderbird & 1997 Cougar

On these models transmission oil cooler may leak fluid at radiator.

This condition may be caused by transmission oil cooler gasket. To correct this condition, proceed as follows:

1. Drain cooling system and remove radiator as outlined under "Crown Victoria, Grand Marquis, Thunderbird & 1997 Cougar."
2. Lay radiator flat on bench. Do not damage cooling fins or tubes.
3. Remove oil cooler line fitting, jam nut and washer.
4. Push transmission oil cooler down and slide to side under end tank lip.
5. Remove gasket.
6. Install new gasket (part No. E77Z-8C242-AA), placing gasket over fitting, pushing down on oil cooler and carefully working gasket around fitting into position.
7. Install jam nut and washer, then tighten to specifications.
8. Install oil cooler line fitting and tighten to specifications.
9. Repeat procedure to other oil cooler line fitting, if necessary.
10. Install radiator, then fill transmission and cooling system

TIGHTENING SPECIFICATIONS

Year	Component	Torque/ Ft. Lbs.
1997–2000	Brake Shift Lock Actuator	60–96①
	Cooler Lines	15–19
	Crossmember	35–46
	Detent Spring	84–120①
	Digital Transmission Range Sensor	60–84①
	Driveshaft	76
	Extension Housing	19–22
	Filler Tube	28–37
	Filter	84–120①
	Front Pump	15–19
	Governor Body Cover	20–30①
	Governor Body To Counterweight	50–60①
	Inspection Cover	23–29
	Manual Control Lever	14–19
	Manual Lever Shaft	20–27
	Neutral Start Switch	8–11
	Oil Cooler Line	17–24
	Oil Cooler Line Fitting Jam Nut	11–14
	Oil Pan	9–11
	Outer Throttle Lever To Shaft	12–16
	Pressure Plug	6–12
	Push Connect Fitting	18–23
	Rear Differential Bolts	57–75
	Rear Differential Nuts	45–59
	Reinforcing Plate To Valve Body	84–120①
	Reverse Servo Selection Tool Apply Band	50①
	Shift Cable	13–17
	Shift Cable Bracket	17–23
	Shifter Mounted Bracket	108①
	Shifter Transmission Bracket	19–25
	Solenoid	84–96①
	Stator Support	15–19
	Transmission To Crossmember	25–34
	Transmission To Engine	40–50
	Torque Converter Drain Plug	21–22
	Torque Converter Housing	41–50
	Torque Converter Housing Access Cover	16–22
	Torque Converter To Flywheel	20–33
	Valve Body	84–96①

① — Inch lbs.

5R55N Automatic Transmission

NOTE: On Air Bag Equipped Models, Refer To " Air Bag System Precautions" Located In The Front Of This Manual For System Disarming & Arming Procedures.

NOTE: "Electrical Symbol & Wire Color Code Identification" Located In The Front Of This Manual May Be Used As An Aid When Using Wiring Circuits Found In This Section.

NOTE: Prior To Performing Any Service Operations Listed In This Section, Consult "Technical Service Bulletins " Section For Related Information.

INDEX

PRECAUTIONS

AIR BAG SYSTEMS

Refer to "Air Bag System Precautions" in the front of this manual for system disarming and arming procedures.

BATTERY GROUND CABLE

Prior to service, disconnect battery ground cable and isolate as required.

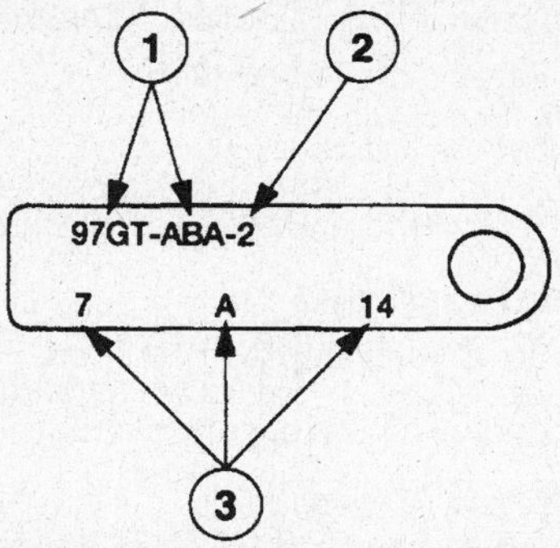

Item	Description
1	Assy. Part No. Prefix and Suffix
2	Line Shift Code
3	Build Date Code (Year, Month, Day)

FM5029701129000X

Fig. 1 Transmission tag location

Item	Description
1	Color Code
2	Part Number Prefix and Suffix
3	Test Procedure Number
4	Transmission Number Bar Code
5	Transmission Number
6	Date
7	Transmission Code
8	Daily Serial Number

FM5029701130000X

Fig. 2 Transmission fluid pan label location

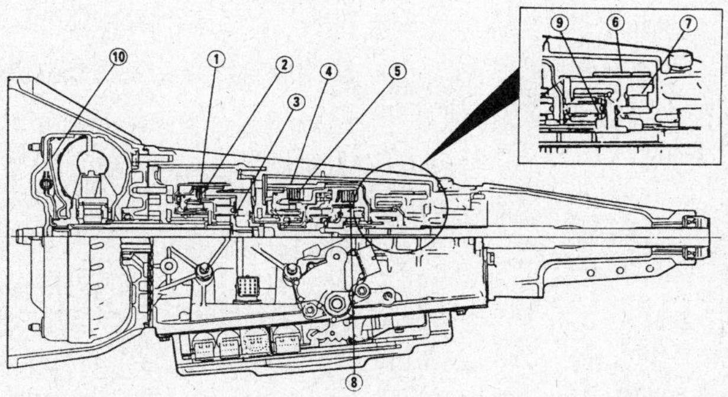

1. Front band (5R55E)
2. Coasting clutch
3. Overdrive one-way clutch
4. Intermediate band
5. Direct clutch (5R55E)
6. Low and reverse band
7. Rear one-way clutch
8. Forward clutch
9. Sleeve
10. Torque converter clutch

TK5029701145000X

Fig. 3 Cross-sectional view of 5R55N transmission

IDENTIFICATION

Refer to **Figs. 1 and 2** for transmission identification location.

DESCRIPTION

The 5R55N automatic transmission is a new five-speed, non-synchronous transmission. The internal structure of this transmission is very similar to its parent transmission, the 5R55E, **Fig. 3.** However, the 5R55N shares very few common components with the 5R55E.

The 5R55N has the following features: five forward speeds: electronic shift, pressure and torque converter clutch controls: three compound planetary gearsets: three bands: four multi-plate clutches, and three one-way clutches.

All hydraulic functions are directed by electronic solenoids to control: static engagement feel; shift feel; shift scheduling; modulated torque converter clutch (TCC) applications; engine braking utilizing the coast clutch and band, and manual first and second timing.

TROUBLESHOOTING

Brake Shift Interlock

Refer to **Fig. 4** for brake shift interlock wiring diagram.

TEST D1: CHECK DTCS

1. Retrieve Diagnostic Trouble Codes (DTCs).
2. If DTCs are present, repair as required.
3. If DTCs are not present, go to Test D2.

TEST D2: CHECK FOR VOLTAGE ON CIRCUIT 7S-TA33 (YE/VT)

1. Turn ignition switch to Off position.
2. Disconnect brake shift interlock connector C322.
3. Turn ignition switch to II position.
4. Measure voltage between brake shift interlock connector C322 pin No. 2 circuit 7S-TA33 (YE/VT), harness side and ground.
5. If measurement is more than 10 volts, go to Test D5.
6. If measurement is not more than 10 volts, go to Test D3.

TEST D3: CHECK CIRCUIT 7S-TA33 (YE/VT) FOR SHORT TO GROUND

1. Measure resistance between brake shift interlock connector C322 pin No. 2 circuit 7S-TA33 (YE/VT), harness side and ground.
2. If resistance is more than 10,000 ohms, go to Test D4.
3. If resistance is less than 10,000 ohms, repair circuit as required.

TEST D4: CHECK CIRCUIT 7S-TA33 (YE/VT) FOR OPEN

1. Measure resistance between brake shift interlock connector C322 pin No. 2 circuit 7S-TA33 (YE/VT), harness side and Front Electrical Module (FEM) C201f pin No. 15, circuit 7S-TA33 (YE/VT), harness side.
2. If resistance is less than 5 ohms, install new FEM.
3. If resistance is more than 5 ohms, repair circuit as required.

TEST D5: CHECK CIRCUIT 31-TA33 (BK) FOR OPEN

1. Measure resistance between brake shift interlock connector C322 pin No. 1 circuit 31-TA33 (BK), harness side and ground.
2. If resistance is less than 5 ohms, install new brake shift interlock actuator.
3. If resistance is more than 5 ohms, repair circuit as required.

Transmission

NO FORWARD IN D5 OR D4 ONLY

ELECTRICAL

PCM, vehicle wiring harnesses, pressure control solenoid B.

HYDRAULIC/MECHANICAL

Fluid

Incorrect level condition.

Forward Clutch Assembly

1. Seals, piston damaged.
2. Check ball damaged, missing, not

seating, off location.
3. Friction elements damaged or worn.
4. Return springs damaged.

OD Servo

1. Servo retaining ring damaged.
2. Seals (piston and cover) damaged.
3. Anchor pins in case damaged.

OD Band

1. Band damaged.
2. Servo worn or damaged.
3. Not adjusted correctly.
4. Anchor pins damaged or worn.

Case

Damaged.

NO FORWARD

ELECTRICAL

PCM, vehicle wiring harnesses, pressure control solenoid B.

HYDRAULIC/MECHANICAL

Main Control

1. Bolt not tightened to specifications.
2. Separator plate damaged.
3. Contamination.
4. Valves, springs damaged, misassembled, missing, stuck or bore damaged.

Center Support

1. Screw not tightened to specification.
2. Seal rings or bearing damaged.
3. Outside diameter of case bore damage.
4. Support damaged or leaking.

Forward Clutch Assembly

1. Seals, piston damaged.
2. Check ball damaged, missing, not seating, off location.
3. Friction elements damaged or worn.
4. Return springs damaged.

Forward Planetary Assembly

Planetary damage.

Intermediate Clutch Assembly

1. Seals, piston damaged.
2. Check ball damaged, missing, not seating, off location.
3. Friction elements damaged or worn.
4. Return springs damaged.

Low One-Way Clutch

Worn, damaged or assembled incorrectly.

NO REVERSE

ELECTRICAL

PCM, vehicle wiring harnesses, pressure control solenoid C (PC C), shift solenoid B (SSB).

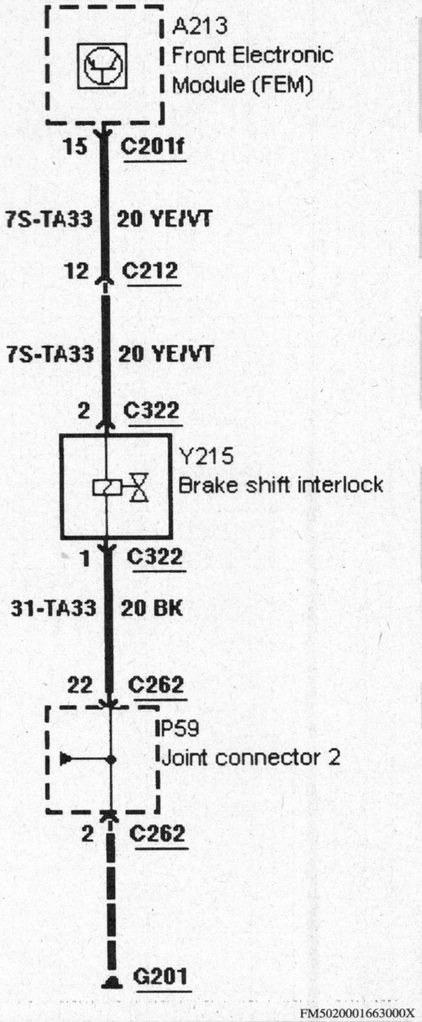

Fig. 4 Brake shift interlock wiring diagram

HYDRAULIC/MECHANICAL

Main Control

1. Bolts not tightened to specifications.
2. Separator plate damaged.
3. Contamination.
4. Valves, springs damaged, misassembled, missing, stuck, or bore damage.

Direct Clutch Assembly

1. Seals, piston damaged.
2. Check ball damaged, missing, not seating, off location.
3. Friction elements damaged or worn.
4. Return springs damaged.

Forward Clutch Assembly

1. Seals, piston damaged.
2. Check ball damaged, missing, not seating, off location.
3. Friction elements damaged or worn.
4. Return springs damaged.

Intermediate Clutch Assembly

1. Seals, piston damaged.
2. Check ball damaged, missing, not seating, off location.
3. Friction elements damaged or worn.
4. Return springs damaged.

Reverse Servo

1. Servo retaining ring damaged.
2. Seals (piston and cover) damaged.
3. Anchor pins in case damaged.

Reverse Band

1. Band damaged.
2. Servo worn or damaged.
3. Not adjusted correctly.
4. Anchor pins damaged or worn.

Reverse Clutch Assembly

1. Seals, piston damaged.
2. Check ball damaged, missing, not seating, off location.
3. Friction elements damaged or worn.
4. Return springs damaged.

HARSH REVERSE ONLY

ELECTRICAL

PCM, vehicle wiring harnesses, pressure control solenoid C (PC C)

HYDRAULIC/MECHANICAL

Incorrect Pressures

High pressures.

Main Control

1. Bolts not tightened to specification.
2. Separator plate damaged.
3. Contamination.
4. Valves, spring damaged, misassembled, missing, stuck or bore damaged.

Direct Clutch Assembly

1. Seals, piston damaged.
2. Check ball damaged, missing not seating, off location.
3. Friction elements damaged or worn.
4. Return springs damaged.

Forward Clutch Assembly

1. Seals, piston damaged.
2. Check ball damaged, missing, not seating, off location.
3. Friction elements damaged or worn.
4. Return springs damaged.

Intermediate Clutch Assembly

1. Seals, piston damaged.
2. Check ball damaged, missing, not seating, off location.
3. Friction elements damaged or worn.
4. Return springs damaged.

Reverse Servo

1. Servo retaining ring damaged.
2. Seals (piston and cover) damaged.
3. Anchor pins in case damaged.

Reverse Band

1. Band damaged.
2. Servo worn or damaged.
3. Not adjusted correctly.
4. Anchor pins damaged or worn

Reverse Clutch Assembly

1. Seals, piston damaged.
2. Check ball damaged, missing, not seating, off location.
3. Friction elements damaged or worn.
4. Return springs damaged.

HARSH FORWARD ONLY

ELECTRICAL

PCM, vehicle wiring harnesses, Pressure Control Solenoid A (PC A), Pressure Control Solenoid C (PC C).

HYDRAULIC/MECHANICAL

Incorrect Pressures

High Pressures.

Main Control

1. Bolts not tightened to specification.
2. Separator plate damaged.
3. Contamination.
4. Valves, springs damaged, misassembled, missing, stuck or bore damaged.

OD Servo

1. Servo retaining ring damaged.
2. Seals (piston and cover) damaged.
3. Anchor pins in case damaged.

OD Band

1. Band damaged.
2. Servo worn or damaged.
3. Not adjusted correctly.
4. Anchor pins damaged or worn.

Center Support

1. Screw not tightened to specification.
2. Seal rings or bearing damage.
3. Outside diameter of case bore damage.
4. Support damaged or leaking.

Forward Clutch Assembly

1. Seals, piston damaged.
2. Check ball damaged, missing, not seating, off location.
3. Friction elements damaged or worn.
4. Return springs damaged.

Intermediate Clutch Assembly

1. Seals, piston damaged.
2. Check ball damaged, missing, not seating, off location.
3. Friction elements damaged or worn.
4. Return springs damaged.

HARSH MANUAL 1ST GEAR ONLY

ELECTRICAL

PCM, vehicle wiring harnesses, Pressure Control Solenoid B (PC B), Turbine Shaft Speed (TSS) sensor

HYDRAULIC/MECHANICAL

No hydraulic or mechanical concerns

DELAYED OR SOFT REVERSE ONLY

ELECTRICAL

PCM, vehicle wiring harnesses, Pressure Control Solenoid C (PC C)

HYDRAULIC/MECHANICAL

Incorrect pressures

Low pressure

Main Control

1. Bolts not tightened to specification.
2. Separator plate damaged.
3. Contamination.
4. Valves, springs damaged, misassembled, missing, stuck or bore damaged.

Direct Clutch Assembly

1. Seals, piston damaged.
2. Check ball damaged, missing not seating, off location.
3. Friction elements damaged or worn.
4. Return springs damaged.

Reverse Servo

1. Servo retaining ring damaged.
2. Seals (piston and cover) damaged.
3. Anchor pins in case damaged.

Reverse Band

1. Band damaged.
2. Servo worn or damaged.
3. Not adjusted correctly.
4. Anchor pins damaged or worn.

DELAYED/SOFT FORWARD ONLY

ELECTRICAL

PCM, vehicle wiring harnesses, Pressure Control Solenoid B (PC B).

HYDRAULIC/MECHANICAL

Incorrect Pressures

Low pressures.

Main Control

1. Bolts not tightened to specification.
2. Separator plate damaged.
3. Contamination.
4. Valves, spring damaged, misassembled, missing, stuck or bore damaged.

OD Servo

1. Servo retaining ring damaged.
2. Seals (piston and cover) damaged.
3. Anchor pins in case damaged.

OD Band

1. Band damaged.
2. Servo worn or damaged.
3. Not adjusted correctly.
4. Anchor pins damaged or worn.

Center Support

1. Screw not tightened to specification.
2. Seal rings or bearing damaged.
3. Outside diameter of case bore damage.
4. Support damaged or leaking.

Forward Clutch Assembly

1. Seals, piston damaged.
2. Check ball damaged, missing, not seating, off location.
3. Friction element damaged or worn.
4. Return springs damaged.

NO FORWARD & NO REVERSE

ELECTRICAL

PCM, vehicle wiring harnesses, Pressure Control Solenoid B (PC B).

HYDRAULIC/MECHANICAL

Fluid

1. Incorrect level.
2. Condition.

Shift Cable/Digital TR Sensor

Cable system or digital TR sensor damaged, misaligned.

Main Control

1. Bolts not tightened to specification.
2. Separator plate damaged.
3. Contamination.
4. Valve, springs damaged, misassembled, missing, stuck, or bore damaged.

Input Shaft

Damaged.

Fluid Pump Assembly

1. Bolts not tightened to specifications.
2. Gasket damaged.
3. Porosity, cross leaks, ball missing, plugged hole.

OD Planetary Assembly

Planetary damaged.

Center Shaft Assembly

Damaged. One-way clutch damaged

Forward Clutch Assembly

1. Seals, piston damaged.
2. Check ball damaged, missing, not seating, off location.

3. Friction elements damaged or worn.
4. Return springs damaged.

Forward Planetary Assembly

Planetary damaged.

Intermediate Clutch Assembly

1. Seals, piston damaged.
2. Check ball damaged, missing, not seating, off location.
3. Friction elements damaged or worn.
4. Return springs damaged.

Reverse Planetary Assembly

Planetary damaged.

Output Shaft

Damaged.

Torque Converter

1. Damaged flexplate or adapter plate.
2. Damaged impeller hub.
3. Damaged turbine hub.

Direct One-way Clutch

Worn, damaged or assembled incorrectly.

ENGAGEMENT CONCERN: HARSH FORWARD & HARSH REVERSE

ELECTRICAL

PCM, vehicle wring harnesses, digital TR sensor, Transmission Fluid (TFT) sensor.

HYDRAULIC/MECHANICAL

FluidIncorrect level.

1. Condition.

Incorrect Pressures

High pressures.

Main Control

1. Bolts not tightened to specifications.
2. Separator plate damaged.
3. Contamination.
4. Valves, springs damaged, misassembled, missing, stuck, or bore damaged.

Forward Clutch Assembly

1. Seals, piston damaged.
2. Check ball damaged, missing, not seating, off location.
3. Friction elements damaged or worn.
4. Return springs damaged.

Intermediate Clutch Assembly

1. Seals, piston damaged.
2. Check ball damaged, missing, not seating, off location.
3. Friction elements damaged or worn.
4. Return springs damaged.

DELAYED FORWARD & DELAYED REVERSE

ELECTRICAL

PCM, vehicle wiring harnesses, Transmission Fluid Temperature (TFT) sensor.

HYDRAULIC/MECHANICAL

Fluid

1. Incorrect level.
2. Condition.

Incorrect Pressures

High pressures

Main Control

1. Bolts not tightened to specifications.
2. Separator plate damaged.
3. Contamination.
4. Valves and springs damaged, misassembled, missing, stuck, or bore damaged.

Fluid Pump Assembly

1. Bolts not tightened to specifications.
2. Gasket damaged.
3. Porosity, cross leaks, ball missing, plugged hole.

SOME/ALL SHIFTS MISSING (AUTOMATIC MODE ONLY)

ELECTRICAL

PCM, vehicle wiring harnesses, Shift Solenoids A, B, C, Torque Converter Clutch (TCC) solenoid, Pressure Control Solenoids A, B, C, Output Shaft Speed (OSS) sensor, digital TR sensor, IAT sensor, VSS input.

HYDRAULIC/MECHANICAL

Some Shifts Missing ONLY

If only some shifts are missing, determine which shift(s) is missing: Refer to appropriate routine(s).

Fluid

1. Incorrect level.
2. Condition.

Shift Cable/Digital TR Sensor

Cable system or digital TR sensor damaged, misaligned.

Incorrect Pressures

High/Low pressures.

Main Control

1. Bolts not tightened to specification.
2. Separator plate damaged.
3. Contamination.
4. Valve, springs damaged, misassembled, missing, stuck, or bore damaged.

Fluid Pump Assembly

1. Bolts not tightened to specifications.
2. Gasket damaged.
3. Porosity, cross leaks, ball missing, plugged hole.

OD Planetary Assembly

Planetary damaged.

Center Support

1. Screw not tightened to specification.
2. Seal rings or bearing damaged.
3. Outside diameter of case bore damaged.
4. Support damaged or leaking.

Direct Clutch Assembly

1. Seals, piston damaged.
2. Check ball damaged, missing, not seating, off location.
3. Friction elements damaged or worn.
4. Return springs damaged.

Intermediate Clutch Assembly

1. Seals, piston damaged.
2. Check ball damaged, missing, not seating, off location.
3. Friction elements damaged or worn.
4. Return springs damaged.

Intermediate One-Way Clutch

Worn, damaged or assembled incorrectly.

EARLY/LATE TIMING

ELECTRICAL

PCM, vehicle wiring harnesses, Output Shaft Speed (OSS) sensor, IAT sensor.

HYDRAULIC/MECHANICAL

Some Shifts Early/Late Only

If only some shifts are early/late, determine which shift(s) is missing: Refer to appropriate condition(s).

Fluid

1. Incorrect level.
2. Condition.

Main Control

1. Bolts not tightened to specification.
2. Separator plate damaged.
3. Contamination.
4. Valve, springs damaged, misassembled, missing, stuck, or bore damaged.

OD Servo

1. Servo retaining ring damaged.
2. Seals (piston and cover) damaged.
3. Anchor pins in case damaged.

OD Band

1. Band damaged.
2. Servo worn or damaged.
3. Not adjusted correctly.
4. Anchor pins damaged or worn.

ERRATIC/HUNTING (SOME/ALL) SHIFT TIMING

ELECTRICAL

PCM, vehicle wiring harnesses, Output Shaft Speed (OSS) sensor, IAT sensor.

HYDRAULIC/MECHANICAL

Fluid

1. Incorrect level.
2. Condition.

Main Control

1. Bolts not tightened to specification.
2. Separator plate damaged.
3. Contamination.
4. Valve, springs damaged, misassembled, missing, stuck, or bore damaged.

Further Diagnosis

For further diagnosis for timing issues, refer to appropriate condition.

SOFT/SLIPPING (SOME/ALL) ENGAGEMENT

ELECTRICAL

PCM, vehicle wiring harnesses, Shift Solenoids A, B, C, Pressure Control Solenoids A, B, C, D, Intermediate Shaft Speed (ISS) sensor, Transmission Fluid Temperature (TFT) sensor, IAT Sensor, VSS input.

HYDRAULIC/MECHANICAL

Some Shifts Soft/Slipping Only

If only some of the shifts are soft/slipping, determine which shift(s) is missing: Refer to appropriate conditions(s).

Fluid

1. Incorrect level.
2. Condition.

Incorrect Pressures

High/Low pressures.

Main Control

1. Bolts not tightened to specifications.
2. Separator plate damaged.
3. Contamination.
4. Valves, springs damaged, misassembled, missing, stuck, or bore damaged.

Fluid Pump Assembly

1. Bolts not tightened to specification.
2. Gasket damaged.
3. Porosity, cross leaks, misassembled ball missing, plugged hole.

Coast Clutch Assembly

1. Seals, piston damaged.
2. Check ball damaged, missing, not seating, off location.
3. Friction elements damaged or worn.
4. Return springs damaged.

Center Support

1. Screw not tightened to specification.
2. Seal rings or bearings damaged.
3. Outside diameter of case bore damage.
4. Support damaged or leaking.

Intermediate Servo

1. Servo retaining ring damaged.
2. Seals (piston and cover) damaged.
3. Anchor pins in case damaged.

Intermediate Band

1. Band damaged.
2. Servo worn or damaged.
3. Not adjusted correctly.
4. Anchor pins damaged or worn.

Direct Clutch Assembly

1. Seals, piston damaged.
2. Check ball damaged, missing, not seating, off location.
3. Friction elements damaged or worn.
4. Return springs damaged.

Forward Clutch Assembly

1. Seals, piston damaged.
2. Check ball damaged, missing, not seating, off location.
3. Friction elements damaged or worn.
4. Return springs damaged.

Intermediate Clutch Assembly

1. Seals, piston damaged.
2. Check ball damaged, missing, not seating, off location.
3. Friction elements damaged or worn.
4. Return springs damaged.

Reverse Servo

1. Servo retaining ring damaged.
2. Seals (piston and cover) damaged.
3. Anchor pins in case damaged.

Reverse Band

1. Band damaged.
2. Servo worn or damaged.
3. Not adjusted correctly.
4. Anchor pins worn or damaged.

Case

Damaged.

HARSH SHIFT (SOME/ALL)

ELECTRICAL

PCM, vehicle wiring harnesses, Shift Solenoids A, B, C, Pressure Control Solenoids A, B, C, D, Intermediate Shaft Speed (ISS) sensor, digital TR sensor, Transmission Fluid Temperature (TFT) sensor, IAT sensor, VSS input.

HYDRAULIC/MECHANICAL

Some Shifts Harsh Only

If only some of the shifts are harsh, determine which shift(s) is missing: Refer to appropriate routine(s).

Incorrect Pressures

High/Low pressures.

Main Control

1. Bolts not tightened to specification.
2. Separator plate damaged.
3. Contamination.
4. Valves, springs damaged, misassembled, missing, stuck, or bore damaged.

Input Shaft

Damaged

OD Servo

1. Servo retaining ring damaged.
2. Seals (piston and cover) damaged.
3. Anchor pins in case damaged.

OD Band

1. Band damaged.
2. Servo worn or damaged.
3. Not adjusted correctly.
4. Anchor pins worn or damaged.

Center Shaft Assembly

1. Center shaft assembly damaged.
2. One-way clutch damaged.

Intermediate Servo

1. Servo retaining ring damaged.
2. Seals (piston and cover) damaged.
3. Anchor pins in case damaged.

Intermediate Band

1. Band damaged.
2. Servo worn or damaged.
3. Not adjusted correctly.
4. Anchor pins damaged or worn.

Forward Clutch Assembly

1. Seals, piston damaged.
2. Check ball damaged, missing, not seating, off location.
3. Friction elements damaged or worn.
4. Return springs damaged.

Intermediate Clutch Assembly

1. Seals, piston damaged.
2. Check ball damaged, missing, not seating, off location.
3. Friction elements damaged or worn.
4. Return springs damaged.

Reverse Servo

1. Servo retaining ring damaged.
2. Seals (piston and cover) damaged.
3. Anchor pins in case damaged.

Reverse Band

1. Band damaged.
2. Servo worn or damaged.
3. Not adjusted correctly.
4. Anchor pins damaged or worn.

Output Shaft

Damaged.

Case

Damaged.

NO 1ST & 2ND GEAR IN DRIVE, ENGAGES IN HIGHER GEAR

ELECTRICAL

PCM, vehicle wiring harnesses, Shift Solenoids A, B, C, digital TR sensor.

HYDRAULIC/MECHANICAL

Incorrect Pressures

High/Low pressures

Main Control

1. Bolts not tightened to specification.
2. Separator plate damaged.
3. Contamination.
4. Valves/springs damaged, misassembled, missing, stuck, or bore damaged.

Intermediate Clutch Assembly

1. Seals, piston damaged.
2. Check ball damaged, missing, not seating, off location.
3. Friction elements damaged or worn.
4. Return springs damaged.

Direct One-way Clutch

Worn, damaged or assembled incorrectly.

Low One-Way Clutch

Worn, damaged or assembled incorrectly

NO 1ST GEAR IN MANUAL 1 POSITION

ELECTRICAL

PCM, vehicle wiring harnesses, Shift Solenoids A, B, Pressure Control Solenoids B, C.

HYDRAULIC/MECHANICAL

Incorrect Pressures

High/Low pressures

Main Control

1. Bolts not tightened to specification.
2. Separator plate damaged.
3. Contamination.
4. Valves, springs damaged, misassembled, missing, stuck or bore damaged.

OD Planetary Assembly

Planetary damaged

Direct One-Way Clutch

Worn, damaged or assembled incorrectly.

Low One-Way Clutch

Worn, damaged or assembled incorrectly.

NO 2ND GEAR IN MANUAL 2 POSITION

ELECTRICAL

PCM, vehicle wiring harnesses, Shift Solenoids A, B, C, Pressure Control Solenoid B.

HYDRAULIC/MECHANICAL

Incorrect Pressure

High/Low pressures.

Main Control

1. Bolts not tightened to specification.
2. Separator plate damaged.
3. Contamination.
4. Valves, springs damaged, misassembled, missing, stuck or bore damaged.

OD Servo

1. Servo retaining ring damaged.
2. Seals (piston and cover) damaged.
3. Not adjusted correctly.
4. Anchor pins in case damage.

OD Band

1. Band damaged.
2. Servo worn or damaged.
3. Not adjusted correctly.
4. Anchor pins damaged or worn.

Direct One-Way Clutch

Worn, damaged or assembled incorrectly.

Low One-Way Clutch

Worn, damaged or assembled incorrectly

TORQUE CONVERTER DOES NOT APPLY

ELECTRICAL

PCM, vehicle wiring harnesses, Torque Converter Clutch (TCC) solenoid, Transmission Fluid Temperature (TFT) sensor.

HYDRAULIC/MECHANICAL

Incorrect Pressures

High/Low pressures

Main Control

1. Bolts not tightened to specification.
2. Separator plate damaged.
3. Contamination.
4. Valve, springs damaged, misassembled, missing, stuck, or bore damaged.

Fluid Pump Assembly

1. Bolts not tightened to specification.
2. Gasket damaged.
3. Porosity, cross leaks, ball missing, plugged hole.

Torque Converter Assembly

Torque Converter internal failure preventing engagement, piston application.

TORQUE CONVERTER ALWAYS APPLIED/STALLS VEHICLE

ELECTRICAL

PCM, vehicle wiring harnesses, Torque Converter Clutch (TCC) solenoid.

HYDRAULIC/MECHANICAL

Main Control

1. Bolts not tightened to specifications.
2. Separator plate damaged.
3. Contamination.
4. Valve, springs damaged, misassembled, missing, stuck, or bore damaged.
5. Low one-way clutch.

Torque Converter Assembly

Torque Converter internal failure preventing engagement, piston release.

Low One-Way Clutch

Worn, damaged or assembled incorrectly

TORQUE CONVERTER CYCLING/SHUDDER/CHATTER

ELECTRICAL

PCM, vehicle wiring harnesses, Torque Converter Clutch (TCC) solenoid.

HYDRAULIC/MECHANICAL

Fluid

Condition—contaminated, degraded.

Main Control

1. Bolts not tightened to specifications.
2. Separator plate damaged.
3. Contamination.

4. Valve, springs damaged, misassembled, missing, stuck, or bore damaged.

Torque Converter Assembly

Torque converter internal leakage, clutch material damaged.

SHIFT LEVER EFFORTS HIGH

ELECTRICAL

PCM, vehicle wiring harnesses, digital TR sensor.

HYDRAULIC/MECHANICAL

Shift Cable, Digital TR sensor

Cable system or digital TR sensor damaged, misaligned.

Main Control

1. Bolts not tightened to specification.
2. Separator plate damaged.
3. Contamination.
4. Valve/springs damaged, misassembled, missing, stuck, or bore damaged.

Case

1. Manual control lever assembly damage, manual valve inner lever pin bent, manual valve inner lever damaged, spring rod damaged.
2. Manual valve lever shaft retaining pin damaged.

EXTERNAL LEAKS

ELECTRICAL

Output Shaft Speed (OSS) sensor, Intermediate Shaft Speed (ISS), Turbine Shaft Speed (TSS) sensor, digital TR sensor.

HYDRAULIC/MECHANICAL

Fluid

Incorrect level

Case

Case vent damaged

Seals/Gaskets

Leakage at gaskets, seals, etc.

POOR VEHICLE PERFORMANCE

ELECTRICAL

PCM, vehicle wiring harnesses, Shift Solenoids A, B, C, Pressure Control Solenoids A, B, C, Output Shaft Speed (OSS) sensor, Turbine Shaft Speed (TSS) sensor, Transmission Fluid Temperature (TFT) sensor, digital TR sensor.

HYDRAULIC/MECHANICAL

Fluid

Incorrect level

Input Shaft

Damaged.

Center Shaft Assembly

Damaged. One-way clutch damaged.

Forward Clutch Assembly

1. Seals, piston damaged.
2. Piston check ball damaged, missing, not seating, off location.
3. Friction elements damaged or worn.
4. Return springs damaged.

Intermediate Clutch Assembly

1. Seals, piston damaged.
2. Check ball damaged, missing, not seating, off location.
3. Friction elements damaged or worn.
4. Return springs damaged.

Torque Converter Assembly

1. Torque Converter one-way clutch slipping.
2. Incorrect torque converter used in rebuild.

NOISE/VIBRATION— FORWARD OR REVERSE

ELECTRICAL

PCM, vehicle wiring harnesses, Torque Converter Clutch (TCC) solenoid, Pressure Control Solenoids A, B, C.

HYDRAULIC/MECHANICAL

Fluid Pump Assembly

1. Bolts not tightened to specification.
2. Gasket damaged.
3. Porosity, cross leaks, ball missing, plugged hole.

Intermediate Clutch Assembly

1. Seals, piston damaged.
2. Check ball damaged, missing, not seating, off location.
3. Friction elements damaged or worn.
4. Return springs damaged.

Low One-Way Clutch

Worn, damaged or assembled incorrectly.

Flexplate or Adapter Plate

1. Damaged.
2. Adapter Plate not aligned correctly.

ENGINE WILL NOT CRANK

ELECTRICAL

PCM, vehicle wiring harnesses, digital TR sensor.

HYDRAULIC/MECHANICAL

Shift Cable/Digital TR Sensor

Cable system or digital TR Sensor damaged, misaligned.

Fluid Pump Assembly

Seized.

Flexplate or Adapter Plate

Damaged.

NO PARK RANGE

ELECTRICAL

No electrical concerns.

HYDRAULIC/MECHANICAL

Shift Cable/Digital TR sensor

able system or digital TR sensor damaged, misaligned.

Case

1. Manual control lever assembly damage, manual valve inner lever pin bent, manual valve inner lever damaged, spring rod damaged.
2. Manual valve lever shaft retaining pin damaged.

Park System

1. Park gear, parking pawl, parking pawl return spring, park or guide plate, parking actuating rod, parking pawl shaft, manual lever, manual lever detent spring damaged or misassembled.
2. External linkages/brackets damaged.

TRANSMISSION OVERHEATING

ELECTRICAL

PCM, vehicle wiring harnesses, Torque Converter Clutch (TCC) solenoid, Pressure Control Solenoids A, B, C, Transmission Fluid Temperature (TFT) sensor.

HYDRAULIC/MECHANICAL

Fluid

Incorrect level

Incorrect Pressures

High/low pressures

Main Control

1. Bolts not tightened to specification.
2. Separator plate damaged.
3. Contamination.
4. Valves/springs damaged, misassembled, missing, stuck, or bore damaged.

Fluid Pump Assembly

1. Bolts not tightened to specification.
2. Gasket damaged.

3. Porosity, cross leaks, ball missing, plugged hole.

Case

Case vent damaged.

Torque Converter Assembly

1. Sized torque converter one-way clutch.
2. Excessive slip detected.

Transmission Cooling System

1. Restriction in the transmission cooling system.
2. Excessive trailer tow load.
3. Poor engine performance.

NO ENGINE BRAKING IN MANUAL 3RD POSITION

ELECTRICAL

PCM, vehicle wiring harnesses, shift solenoids A, B, C, Reverse Pressure (RP) switch, pressure control solenoids A, B.

HYDRAULIC/MECHANICAL

Fluid

Incorrect level

Incorrect Pressures

High/Low pressures

Main Control

1. Bolts not tightened to specification.
2. Separator plate damaged.
3. Contamination.
4. Valve/springs damaged, misassembled, missing, stuck, or bore damaged.

Fluid Pump Assembly

1. Bolts not tightened to specification.
2. Gasket damaged.
3. Porosity, cross leaks, ball missing, plugged hole.

Coast Clutch Assembly

1. Seals, piston damaged.
2. Check ball damaged, missing, not seating, off location.
3. Friction elements damaged or worn.
4. Return springs damaged.

Center Support

1. Screw not tightened to specification.
2. Seals rings or bearing damaged.
3. Outside diameter of case bore damage.
4. Support damaged or leaking.

Intermediate Servo

1. Servo retaining ring damaged.
2. Seals (piston and cover) damaged.
3. Anchor pins in case damaged.

Intermediate Band

1. Band damaged.
2. Servo worn or damaged.
3. Not adjusted correctly.
4. Anchor pins damaged or worn.

Intermediate Clutch Assembly

1. Seals, piston damaged.
2. Check ball damaged, missing, not seating, off location.
3. Friction elements damaged or worn.
4. Return springs damaged.

Low One-Way Clutch

Worn, damaged, or assembled incorrectly.

NO ENGINE BRAKING IN MANUAL 4TH (D4) POSITION

ELECTRICAL

PCM, vehicle wiring harnesses, Shift Solenoid D, Reverse Pressure (RP) switch, Pressure Control Solenoid B.

HYDRAULIC/MECHANICAL

Fluid

Improper level

Main Control

1. Bolts not tightened to specification.
2. Separator plate damaged.
3. Contamination.
4. Valve/springs damaged, misassembled, missing, stuck, or bore damaged.

Fluid Pump Assembly

1. Bolts not tightened to specification.
2. Gasket damaged.
3. Porosity, cross leaks, ball missing, plugged hole.

Coast Clutch Assembly

1. Seals, piston damaged.
2. Check ball damaged, missing, not seating, off location.
3. Friction elements damaged or worn.
4. Return springs damaged.

Forward Clutch Assembly

1. Seals, piston damaged.
2. Check ball damaged, missing, not seating, off location.
3. Friction elements damaged or worn.
4. Return springs damaged.

NO ENGINE BRAKING IN MANUAL 2ND POSITION

ELECTRICAL

PCM, vehicle wiring harnesses, Shift Solenoids A, C, D, Pressure Control Solenoid A.

HYDRAULIC/MECHANICAL

Fluid

Incorrect level.

Incorrect Pressures

High/low pressures.

Reverse Servo

1. Servo retaining ring damaged.
2. Seals (piston and cover) damaged.
3. Anchor pins in case damaged.

Reverse Band

1. Band damaged.
2. Servo worn or damaged.
3. Not adjusted correctly.
4. Anchor pins damaged or worn.

NO ENGINE BRAKING IN MANUAL 1ST POSITION

ELECTRICAL

PCM, vehicle wiring harnesses, Shift Solenoids A, C, D, Pressure Control Solenoids A, B.

HYDRAULIC/MECHANICAL

Fluid

Incorrect level.

Incorrect pressures

High/low pressures.

Fluid Pump Assembly

1. Bolts not tightened to specification.
2. Gasket damaged.
3. Porosity, cross leaks, ball missing, plugged hole.

Coast Clutch Assembly

1. Seals, piston damaged.
2. Check ball damaged, missing, not seating, off location.
3. Friction elements damaged or worn.
4. Return springs damaged.

Reverse Servo

1. Servo retaining ring damaged.
2. Seals (piston and cover) damaged.
3. Anchor pins in case damaged.

Reverse Band

1. Band damaged.
2. Servo worn or damaged.
3. Not adjusted correctly.
4. Anchor pins damaged or worn.

FLUID VENTING/FOAMING

ELECTRICAL

No Electrical concerns.

HYDRAULIC/MECHANICAL

Fluid

1. Incorrect level.
2. Condition.

Fluid Pump Assembly

1. Bolts not tightened to specification.
2. Gasket damaged.
3. Porosity, cross leaks, ball missing, plugged hole.

Intermediate Servo

1. Servo retaining ring damaged.
2. Seals (piston and cover) damaged.
3. Anchor pins in case damaged.

Intermediate Band

1. Band damaged.
2. Servo worn or damaged.
3. Not adjusted correctly.
4. Anchor pins damaged or worn.

Case

Case vent damaged.

Other

Transmission overheating.

VEHICLE MOVEMENT WITH GEAR SELECTOR IN "N" POSITION

ELECTRICAL

No Electrical concerns

HYDRAULIC/MECHANICAL

Fluid

Incorrect level

Incorrect pressures

High/low pressures

SLIPS/CHATTERS IN MANUAL 1ST POSITION

ELECTRICAL

PCM, vehicle wiring harnesses, Pressure Control Solenoids A, B

HYDRAULIC/MECHANICAL

Fluid

1. Incorrect level.
2. Condition.

Incorrect Pressures

High/Low pressures

Main Control

1. Bolts not tightened to specification.
2. Separator plate damaged.
3. Contamination.
4. Valve/springs damaged, misassembled, missing, stuck, or bore damaged.

Fluid Pump Assembly

1. Bolts not tightened to specification.
2. Gasket damaged.
3. Porosity, cross leaks, ball missing, plugged hole.

Forward Clutch Assembly

1. Seals, piston damaged.
2. Check ball damaged, missing, not seating, off location.
3. Friction elements damaged or worn.
4. Return springs damaged.

Reverse Servo

1. Servo retaining ring damaged.
2. Seals (piston and cover) damaged.
3. Anchor pins in case damaged.

Reverse Band

1. Band damaged.
2. Servo worn or damaged.
3. Not adjusted correctly.
4. Anchor pins damaged or worn.

Direct One-Way Clutch

Worn, damaged or assembled incorrectly

Low One-Way Clutch

Worn, damaged or assembled incorrectly.

SLIPS/CHATTERS IN MANUAL 2ND POSITION

ELECTRICAL

PCM, vehicle wiring harnesses, Pressure Control Solenoids A, B.

HYDRAULIC/MECHANICAL

Fluid

1. Incorrect level.
2. Condition.

Incorrect Pressures

High/low pressures

Fluid Pump Assembly

1. Bolts not tightened to specification.
2. Gasket damaged.
3. Porosity, cross leaks, ball missing, plugged hole.

OD Servo

1. Servo retaining ring damaged.
2. Seals (piston and cover) damaged.
3. Anchor pins in case damaged.

OD Band

1. Band damaged.
2. Servo worn or damaged.
3. Not adjusted correctly.
4. Anchor pins damaged or worn.

OD Planetary Assembly

Planetary damaged

Forward Clutch Assembly

1. Seals, piston damaged.
2. Check ball damaged, missing, not seating, off location.
3. Friction elements damaged or worn.
4. Return springs damaged.

Reverse Servo

1. Servo retaining ring damaged.
2. Seals (piston and cover) damaged.
3. Anchor pins in case damaged.

Reverse Band

1. Band damaged.
2. Servo worn or damaged.
3. Not adjusted correctly.
4. Anchor pins damaged or worn.

Low One-Way Clutch

Worn, damaged or assembled incorrectly.

SLIP/CHATTERS IN MANUAL 3RD POSITION

ELECTRICAL

PCM, vehicle wiring harnesses, Pressure Control Solenoids A, B.

HYDRAULIC/MECHANICAL

Fluid

1. Incorrect level.
2. Condition.

Incorrect Pressures

High/Low pressures

Fluid Pump Assembly

1. Bolts not tightened to specification.
2. Gasket damaged.
3. Porosity, cross leaks, ball missing, plugged hole.

OD Servo

1. Servo retaining ring damaged.
2. Seals (piston and cover) damaged.
3. Anchor pins in case damaged.

OD Band

1. Band damaged.
2. Servo worn or damaged.
3. Not adjusted correctly.
4. Anchor pins damaged or worn.

Intermediate Servo

1. Servo retaining ring damaged.
2. Seals (piston and cover) damaged.
3. Anchor pins in case damaged.

Intermediate Band

1. Band damaged.
2. Servo worn or damaged.
3. Not adjusted correctly.
4. Anchor pins damaged or worn.

Forward Clutch Assembly

1. Seals, piston damaged.
2. Check ball damaged, missing, not seating, off location.
3. Friction elements damaged or worn.
4. Return springs damaged.

Intermediate Clutch Assembly

1. Seals, piston damaged.
2. Check ball damaged, missing, not seating, off location.
3. Friction elements damaged or worn.
4. Return springs damaged.

Direct One-way Clutch

Worn, damaged or assembled incorrectly.

Low One-way Clutch

Worn, damaged or assembled incorrectly.

ENGINE BRAKING IN ALL GEARS

ELECTRICAL

PCM, vehicle wiring harnesses, Shift Solenoid D

HYDRAULIC/MECHANICAL

No hydraulic/mechanical concerns.

NO 2ND & 5TH GEARS

ELECTRICAL

PCM, vehicle wiring harnesses, Pressure Control Solenoids A, B.

HYDRAULIC/MECHANICAL

Intermediate Clutch Assembly

1. Seals, piston damaged.
2. Check ball damaged, missing, not seating, off location.
3. Friction elements damaged or worn.
4. Return springs damaged.

NO 3RD, 4TH & 5TH GEARS

ELECTRICAL

PCM, vehicle wiring harnesses, Pressure Control Solenoids A, B.

HYDRAULIC/MECHANICAL

Fluid Pump Assembly

1. Bolts not tightened to specification.
2. Gasket damaged.
3. Porosity, cross leaks, ball missing, plugged hole.

OD Band

1. Band damaged.
2. Servo worn or damaged.
3. Not adjusted correctly.
4. Anchor pins damaged or worn.

OD Planetary Assembly

Planetary damaged

HARSH 1-2 SHIFT

ELECTRICAL

PCM, vehicle wiring harnesses, Shift Control Solenoid C, Pressure Control Solenoids B, Turbine Shaft Speed (TSS) sensor, Digital TR sensor, Transmission Fluid Temperature (TFT) sensor.

HYDRAULIC/MECHANICAL

Incorrect Pressures

High/Low pressures

Main Control

1. Bolts not tightened to specification.
2. Separator plate damaged.
3. Contamination.
4. Valve/springs damaged, misassembled, missing, stuck, or bore damaged.

OD Servo

1. Servo retaining ring damaged.
2. Seals (piston and cover) damaged.
3. Anchor pins in case damaged.

OD Band

1. Band damaged.
2. Servo worn or damaged.
3. Not adjusted correctly.
4. Anchor pins damaged or worn.

Direct Clutch Assembly

1. Seals, piston damaged.
2. Check ball damaged, missing, not seating, off location.
3. Friction elements damaged or worn.
4. Return springs damaged.

Intermediate Clutch Assembly

1. Seals, piston damaged.
2. Check ball damaged, missing, not seating, off location.
3. Friction elements damaged or worn.
4. Return springs damaged.

HARSH 2-3 SHIFT

ELECTRICAL

PCM, vehicle wiring harnesses, Shift Control Solenoid B, Pressure Control Solenoids A, Turbine Shaft Speed (TSS) sensor, Intermediate Shaft Speed (ISS) sensor, Digital TR sensor, Transmission Fluid Temperature (TFT) sensor.

HYDRAULIC/MECHANICAL

Incorrect Pressures

High/Low pressures

Main Control

1. Bolts not tightened to specification.
2. Separator plate damaged.
3. Contamination.
4. Valve/springs damaged, misassembled, missing, stuck, or bore damaged.

Direct Clutch Assembly

1. Seals, piston damaged.
2. Check ball damaged, missing, not seating, off location.
3. Friction elements damaged or worn.
4. Return springs damaged.

Intermediate Clutch Assembly

1. Seals, piston damaged.
2. Check ball damaged, missing, not seating, off location.
3. Friction elements damaged or worn.
4. Return springs damaged.

Direct One-Way Clutch

Worn, damaged or assembled incorrectly.

HARSH 3-4 SHIFT

ELECTRICAL

PCM, vehicle wiring harnesses, Shift Control Solenoid A, Pressure Control Solenoids C, Digital TR sensor, Transmission Fluid Temperature (TFT) sensor

HYDRAULIC/MECHANICAL

Incorrect Pressures

High/low pressures

Main Control

1. Bolts not tightened to specification.
2. Separator plate damaged.
3. Contamination.
4. Valve/springs damaged, misassembled, missing, stuck, or bore damaged.

Center Support

1. Screws not tightened to specification.
2. Seal rings or bearing damaged.
3. Outside diameter of case bore damage.
4. Support damaged or leaking.

Direct Clutch Assembly

1. Seals, piston damaged.
2. Check ball damaged, missing, not seating, off location.
3. Friction elements damaged or worn.
4. Return springs damaged.

Intermediate Clutch Assembly

1. Seals, piston damaged.
2. Check ball damaged, missing, not seating, off location.
3. Friction elements damaged or worn.
4. Return springs damaged.

HARSH 4-5 SHIFT

ELECTRICAL

PCM, vehicle wiring harnesses, Shift Solenoid C, Pressure Control Solenoid B, Turbine Shaft Speed (TSS) sensor, Digital TR sensor, Transmission Fluid Temperature (TFT) sensor

HYDRAULIC/MECHANICAL

Incorrect Pressures

High/Low pressures

Main Control

1. Bolts not tightened to specification.
2. Separator plate damaged.
3. Contamination.
4. Valve/springs damaged, misassembled, missing, stuck, or bore damaged.

OD Servo

1. Servo retaining ring damaged.
2. Seal (piston and cover) damaged.
3. Anchor pins in case damaged.

OD Band

1. Band damaged.
2. Servo worn or damaged.
3. Not adjusted correctly.
4. Anchor pins damaged or worn.

HARSH 5-4 SHIFT

ELECTRICAL

PCM, vehicle wiring harnesses, Shift Control Solenoid C, Pressure Control Solenoid C, Turbine Shaft Speed (TSS) sensor, Digital TR sensor, Transmission Fluid Temperature (TFT) sensor.

HYDRAULIC/MECHANICAL

Incorrect Pressures

High/low pressures

Main Control

1. Bolts not tightened to specification.
2. Separator plate damaged.
3. Contamination.
4. Valve/springs damaged, misassembled, missing, stuck, or bore damaged.

Direct Clutch Assembly

1. Seals, piston damaged.
2. Check ball damaged, missing, not seating, off location.
3. Friction elements damaged or worn.
4. Return springs damaged.

Direct One-Way Clutch

Worn , damaged or assembled incorrectly

HARSH 4-3 SHIFT

ELECTRICAL

PCM, vehicle wiring harnesses, Shift Solenoid A, Pressure Control Solenoid A, Digital TR sensor, Transmission Fluid Temperature (TFT) sensor.

HYDRAULIC/MECHANICAL

Incorrect Pressures

High/Low pressures.

Main Control

1. Bolts not tightened to specification.
2. Separator plate damaged.
3. Contamination.
4. Valves, springs damaged, misassembled, missing, stuck, or bore damaged.

Direct Clutch Assembly

1. Seals, piston damaged.
2. Check ball damaged, missing, not seating, off location.
3. Friction elements damaged or worn.
4. Return springs damaged.

Intermediate Clutch Assembly

1. Seals, piston damaged.
2. Check ball damaged, missing, not seating, off location.
3. Friction elements damaged or worn.
4. Return springs damaged.

HARSH 3-2 SHIFT

ELECTRICAL

PCM, vehicle wiring harnesses, Shift Control Solenoid C, Pressure Control Solenoid B, Turbine Shaft Speed (TSS) sensor, Intermediate Shaft Speed (ISS) sensor, Digital TR sensor, Transmission Fluid Temperature (TFT) sensor.

HYDRAULIC/MECHANICAL

Incorrect Pressures

High/Low pressures

Main Control

1. Bolts not tightened to specification.
2. Separator plate damaged.
3. Contamination.
4. Valve/springs damaged, misassembled, missing, stuck, or bore damaged.

OD Servo

1. Servo retaining ring damaged.
2. Seals (piston and cover) damaged.
3. Anchor pins in case damaged.

OD Band

1. Band damaged.
2. Servo worn or damaged.
3. Not adjusted correctly.
4. Anchor pins damaged or worn.

Direct Clutch Assembly

1. Seals, piston damaged.
2. Check ball damaged, missing, not seating, off location.
3. Friction elements damaged or worn.
4. Return springs damaged.

Intermediate Clutch Assembly

1. Seals, piston damaged.
2. Check ball damaged, missing, not seating, off location.
3. Friction elements damaged.
4. Return springs damaged.

HARSH 2-1 SHIFT

ELECTRICAL

PCM, vehicle wiring harnesses, Shift Control Solenoid C, Pressure Control Solenoid B, Turbine Shaft Speed (TSS) sensor, Digital TR sensor, Transmission Fluid Temperature (TFT) sensor.

HYDRAULIC/MECHANICAL

Incorrect Pressures

High/Low pressures

Main Control

1. Bolts not tightened to specification.
2. Separator plate damaged.
3. Contamination.
4. Valve/springs damaged, misassembled, missing, stuck, or bore damaged.

Direct Clutch Assembly

1. Seals, piston damaged.
2. Check ball damaged, missing, not seating, off location.
3. Friction elements damaged or worn.
4. Return springs damaged.

Intermediate Clutch Assembly

1. Seals, piston damaged.
2. Check ball damaged, missing, not seating, off location.
3. Friction elements damaged or worn.
4. Return springs damaged.

Direct Clutch One-Way Clutch

Worn, damaged or assembled incorrectly

NO 1-2 SHIFT

ELECTRICAL

PCM, vehicle wiring harnesses, Shift Solenoid C, Pressure Control Solenoid B, Output Shaft Speed (OSS) sensor, Digital TR sensor, IAT sensor, VSS input.

HYDRAULIC/MECHANICAL

Fluid

Incorrect level

Incorrect Pressures

High/Low pressures

Main Control

1. Bolts not tightened to specification.
2. Separator plate damaged.
3. Contamination.
4. Valve/springs damaged, misassembled, missing, stuck, or bore damaged.

OD Servo

1. Servo retaining ring damaged.
2. Seals (piston and cover) damaged.
3. Anchor pins in case damaged.

OD Band

1. Band damaged.
2. Servo worn or damaged.
3. Not adjusted correctly.
4. Anchor pins damaged or worn.

OD Planetary Assembly

Planetary damaged.

Forward Clutch Assembly

1. Seals, piston damaged.
2. Check ball damaged, missing, not seating, off location.
3. Friction elements damaged or worn.
4. Return springs damaged.

Intermediate Clutch Assembly

1. Seals, piston damaged.
2. Check ball damaged, missing, not seating, off location.
3. Friction elements damaged or worn.
4. Return springs damaged.

NO 2-3 SHIFT

ELECTRICAL

PCM, vehicle wiring harnesses, Shift Solenoid B, Torque Converter Clutch (TCC) solenoid, Pressure Control Solenoid A, Output Shaft Speed (OSS) sensor, Digital TR sensor

HYDRAULIC/MECHANICAL

Incorrect Pressures

High/low pressures

Main Control

1. Bolts not tightened to specification.
2. Separator plate damaged.
3. Contamination.
4. Valve/springs damaged, misassembled, missing, stuck, or bore damaged.

Forward Clutch Assembly

1. Seals, piston damaged.
2. Check ball, damaged, missing, not seating, off location.
3. Friction elements damaged or worn.
4. Return springs damaged.

Intermediate Clutch Assembly

1. Seals, piston damaged.
2. Check ball, damaged, missing, not seating, off location.
3. Friction elements damaged or worn.
4. Return springs damaged.

Intermediate One-Way Clutch

Worn, damaged or assembled incorrectly

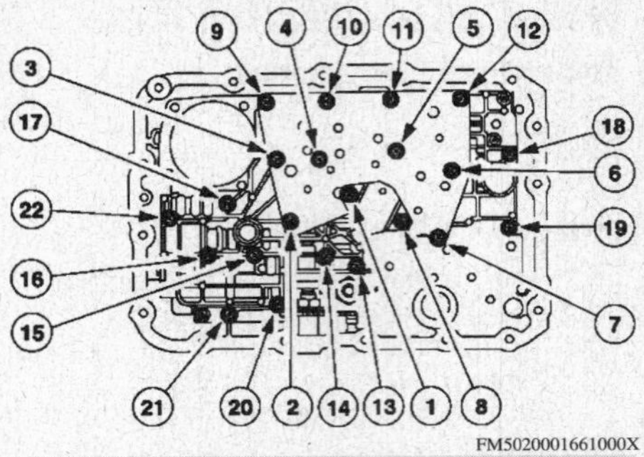

Fig. 5 Valve body mounting screws tightening sequence

NO 3-4 SHIFT

ELECTRICAL

1. PCM, vehicle wiring harnesses, Shift Solenoid A, Pressure Control Solenoid C, Output Shaft Speed (OSS) sensor, Digital TR sensor.
2. Transmission Control Switch (TCS).

HYDRAULIC/MECHANICAL

Incorrect Pressures

High/Low pressures

Main Control

1. Bolts not tightened to specification.
2. Separator plate damaged.
3. Contamination.
4. Valve/springs damaged, misassembled, missing, stuck, or bore damaged.

Center Support

1. Screws not tightened to specification.
2. Seal rings or bearing damaged.
3. Outside diameter of case bore damaged.
4. Support damaged or leaking.

Direct Clutch Assembly

1. Seals, piston damaged.
2. Check ball damaged, missing, not seating, off location.
3. Friction elements damaged or worn.
4. Return springs damaged.

Forward Clutch Assembly

1. Seals, piston damaged.
2. Check ball damaged, missing, not seating, off location.
3. Friction elements damaged or worn.
4. Return springs damaged.

Intermediate Clutch Assembly

1. Seals, piston damaged.
2. Check ball damaged, missing, not seating, off location.
3. Friction elements damaged or worn.
4. Return springs damaged.

NO 4-5 SHIFT

ELECTRICAL

1. PCM, vehicle wiring harnesses, Shift Solenoid C, Pressure Control Solenoid B, Output Shaft Speed (OSS) sensor, Digital TR sensor.
2. Transmission Control Switch (TCS).

HYDRAULIC/MECHANICAL

Incorrect Pressures

High/Low pressures.

Main Control

1. Bolts not tightened to specification.
2. Separator plate damaged.
3. Contamination.
4. Valve/springs damaged, misassembled, missing, stuck, or bore damaged.

OD Servo

1. Servo retaining ring damaged.
2. Seals (piston and cover) damaged.
3. Anchor pins in case damaged.

OD Band

1. Band damaged.
2. Servo worn or damaged.
3. Not adjusted correctly.
4. Anchor pins damaged or worn.

NO 5-4 SHIFT

ELECTRICAL

1. PCM, vehicle wiring harnesses, Shift Solenoid C, Pressure Control Solenoid C, Output Shaft Speed (OSS) sensor, Digital TR sensor.
2. Transmission Control Switch (TCS).

HYDRAULIC/MECHANICAL

Incorrect Pressures

High/Low pressures.

Main Control

1. Bolts not tightened to specification.
2. Separator plate damaged.
3. Contamination.
4. Valves/springs damaged, misassembled, missing, stuck, or bore damaged.

Direct Clutch Assembly

1. Seals, piston damaged.
2. Check ball damaged, missing, not seating, off location.
3. Friction elements damaged or worn.
4. Return springs damaged.

NO 4-3 SHIFT

ELECTRICAL

1. PCM, vehicle wiring harnesses, Shift Solenoid A, Pressure Control Solenoid A, Output Shaft Speed (OSS) sensor, Digital TR sensor.

2. Transmission Control Switch (TCS).

HYDRAULIC/MECHANICAL

Incorrect Pressures

High/Low pressures.

Main Control

1. Bolts not tightened to specification.
2. Separator plate damaged.
3. Contamination.
4. Valves/springs damaged, misassembled, missing, stuck, or bore damaged.

Forward Clutch Assembly

1. Seals, piston damaged.
2. Check ball damaged, missing, not seating, off location.
3. Friction elements damaged or worn.
4. Return springs damaged.

Intermediate Clutch Assembly

1. Seals, piston damaged.
2. Check ball damaged, missing, not seating, off location.
3. Friction elements damaged or worn.
4. Return springs damaged.

NO 3-2 SHIFT

ELECTRICAL

PCM, vehicle wiring harnesses, Shift Solenoid C, Pressure Control Solenoid B, Output Shaft Speed (OSS) sensor, Digital TR sensor.

HYDRAULIC/MECHANICAL

Incorrect Pressures

High/low pressures.

Main Control

1. Bolts not tightened to specification.
2. Separator plate damaged.
3. Contamination.
4. Valves/springs damaged, misassembled, missing, stuck, or bore damaged.

OD Servo

1. Servo retaining ring damaged.
2. Seals (piston and cover) damaged.
3. Anchor pins in case damaged.

OD Band

1. Band damaged.
2. Servo worn or damaged.
3. Not adjusted correctly.
4. Anchor pins damaged or worn.

Forward Clutch Assembly

1. Seals, piston damaged.
2. Check ball damaged, missing, not seating, off location.
3. Friction elements damaged or worn.
4. Return springs damaged.

Intermediate Clutch Assembly

1. Seals, piston damaged.
2. Check ball damaged, missing, not seating, off location.

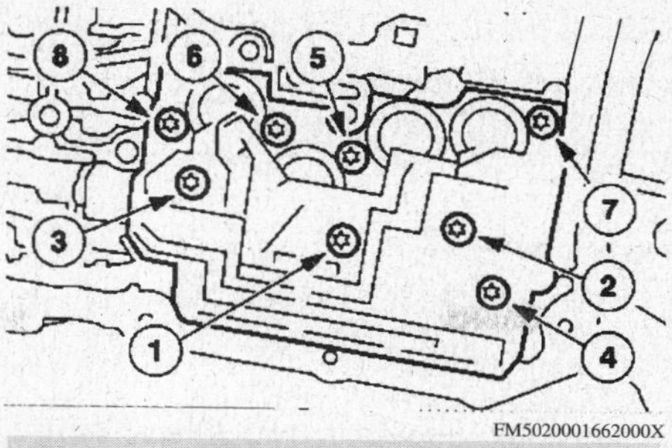

Fig. 6 Solenoid body mounting bolts tightening sequence

3. Friction elements damaged or worn.
4. Return springs damaged.

NO 2-1 SHIFT

ELECTRICAL

PCM, vehicle wiring harnesses, Shift Solenoid C, Pressure Control Solenoid B, Output Shaft Speed (OSS) sensor, Digital TR sensor.

HYDRAULIC/MECHANICAL

Incorrect Pressures

High/Low pressures.

Main Control

1. Bolts not tightened to specification.
2. Separator plate damaged.
3. Contamination.
4. Valves/springs damaged, misassembled, missing, stuck, or bore damaged.

Forward Clutch Assembly

1. Seals, piston damaged.
2. Check ball damaged, missing, not seating, off location.
3. Friction elements damaged or worn.
4. Return springs damaged.

Intermediate Clutch Assembly

1. Seals, piston damaged.
2. Check ball damaged, missing, not seating, off location.
3. Friction elements damaged or worn.
4. Return springs damaged.

SOFT/SLIPPING 1-2 SHIFT

ELECTRICAL

PCM, vehicle wiring harnesses, Shift Solenoid C, Pressure Control Solenoid B, Transmission Fluid Temperature (TFT) sensor, IAT sensor, VSS input.

HYDRAULIC/MECHANICAL

Fluid

1. Incorrect level.
2. Condition.

Incorrect Pressures

High/Low pressures

Main Control

1. Bolts not tightened to specification.
2. Separator plate damaged.
3. Contamination.
4. Valve/springs damaged, misassembled, missing, stuck, or bore damaged.

OD Servo

1. Servo retaining ring damaged.
2. Seals (piston and cover) damaged.
3. Anchor pins in case damaged.

OD Band

1. Band damaged.
2. Servo worn or damaged.
3. Not adjusted correctly.
4. Anchor pins damaged or worn.

SOFT/SLIPPING 2-3 SHIFT

ELECTRICAL

PCM, vehicle wiring harnesses, Shift Solenoid A, Pressure Control Solenoid A, Intermediate Shaft Speed (ISS) sensor, Transmission Fluid Temperature (TFT) sensor.

HYDRAULIC/MECHANICAL

Incorrect Pressures

High/Low pressures

Main Control

1. Bolts not tightened to specification.
2. Separator plate damaged.
3. Contamination.
4. Valve/springs damaged, misassembled, missing, stuck, or bore damaged.

Intermediate Servo

1. Servo retaining ring damaged.
2. Seals (piston and cover) damaged.
3. Anchor pins in case damaged.

Intermediate Band

1. Band damaged.
2. Servo worn or damaged.
3. Not adjusted correctly.
4. Anchor pins damaged or worn.

Intermediate Clutch Assembly

1. Seals, piston damaged.
2. Check ball damaged, missing, not seating, off location.
3. Friction elements damaged or worn.
4. Return springs damaged.

Direct One-Way Clutch

Worn, damaged or assembled incorrectly.

SOFT/SLIPPING 3-4 SHIFT

ELECTRICAL

PCM, vehicle wiring harnesses, Shift Solenoid A, Pressure Control Solenoid C,

Transmission Fluid Temperature (TFT) sensor.

HYDRAULIC/MECHANICAL

Incorrect Pressures

High/Low pressures.

Main Control

1. Bolts not tightened to specification.
2. Separator plate damaged.
3. Contamination.
4. Valves/springs damaged, misassembled, missing, stuck, or bore damaged.

Center Support

1. Screw not tightened to specification.
2. Seal rings or bearing damaged.
3. Outside diameter of case bore damage.
4. Support damaged or leaking.

Direct Clutch Assembly

1. Seals, piston damaged.
2. Check ball damaged, missing, not seating, off location.
3. Friction elements damaged or worn.
4. Return springs damaged.

SOFT/SLIPPING 4-5 SHIFT

ELECTRICAL

PCM, vehicle wiring harnesses, Shift Solenoid C, Pressure Control Solenoid B, Transmission Fluid Temperature (TFT) sensor.

HYDRAULIC/MECHANICAL

Incorrect Pressures

High/Low pressures.

Main Control

1. Bolts not tightened to specification.
2. Separator plate damaged.
3. Contamination.
4. Valves/springs damaged, misassembled, missing, stuck, or bore damaged.

OD Servo

1. Servo retaining ring damaged.
2. Seals (piston and cover) damaged.
3. Anchor pins in case damaged.

OD Band

1. Band damaged.
2. Servo worn or damaged.
3. Not adjusted correctly.
4. Anchor pins damaged or worn.

SOFT/SLIPPING 5-4 SHIFT

ELECTRICAL

PCM, vehicle wiring harnesses, Shift Solenoid C, Pressure Control Solenoid C, Transmission Fluid Temperature (TFT) sensor.

HYDRAULIC/MECHANICAL

Incorrect Pressures

High/Low pressures.

Main Control

1. Bolts not tightened to specification.
2. Separator plate damaged.
3. Contamination.
4. Valves/springs damaged, misassembled, missing, stuck, or bore damaged.

Direct Clutch Assembly

1. Seals, piston damaged.
2. Check ball damaged, missing, not seating, off location.
3. Friction elements damaged or worn.
4. Return springs damaged.

Direct One-Way Clutch

Worn, damaged or assembled incorrectly.

SOFT/SLIPPING 4-3 SHIFT

ELECTRICAL

PCM, vehicle wiring harnesses, Shift Solenoid A, Pressure Control Solenoid A, Transmission Fluid Temperature (TFT) sensor.

HYDRAULIC/MECHANICAL

Incorrect Pressures

High/Low pressures.

Main Control

1. Bolts not tightened to specification.
2. Separator plate damaged.
3. Contamination.
4. Valves/springs damaged, misassembled, missing, stuck, or bore damaged.

Intermediate Clutch Assembly

1. Seals, piston damaged.
2. Check ball damaged, missing, not seating, off location.
3. Friction elements damaged or worn.
4. Return springs damaged.

SOFT/SLIPPING 3-2 SHIFT

ELECTRICAL

PCM, vehicle wiring harnesses, Shift Solenoid C, Pressure Control Solenoid B, Intermediate Shaft Speed (ISS) sensor, Transmission Fluid Temperature (TFT) sensor.

HYDRAULIC/MECHANICAL

Incorrect Pressures

High/Low pressures

Main Control

1. Bolts not tightened to specification.
2. Separator plate damaged.
3. Contamination.
4. Valves/springs damaged, misassembled, missing, stuck, or bore damaged.

OD Servo

1. Servo retaining ring damaged.
2. Seals (piston and cover) damaged.
3. Anchor pins in case damaged.

OD Band

1. Band damaged.
2. Servo worn or damaged.
3. Not adjusted correctly.
4. Anchor pins damaged or worn.

Direct One-Way Clutch

Worn, damaged or assembled incorrectly

SOFT/SLIPPING 2-1 SHIFT

ELECTRICAL

PCM, vehicle wiring harnesses, Shift Solenoid C, Pressure Control Solenoid B, Transmission Fluid Temperature (TFT) sensor.

HYDRAULIC/MECHANICAL

Incorrect Pressures

High/Low pressures.

Main Control

1. Bolts not tightened to specification.
2. Separator plate damaged.
3. Contamination.
4. Valves/springs damaged, misassembled, missing, stuck, or bore damaged.

MAINTENANCE

Ford Motor Company recommends use of Mercon V type automatic transmission fluid in this transmission. Use of a fluid other than that meeting Ford Mercon V specifications may result in transmission malfunction or failure.

FLUID LEVEL CHECK

1. Run engine until operating temperature is 80–120F.
2. Move selector through gears and place selector lever in Park
3. Raise and support vehicle. ensure vehicle is level.
4. Place suitable drain pan under transmission.
5. Remove fluid level indicator plug with transmission in Park and engine running.
6. Allow fluid to drain.
7. When fluid comes out as thin stream or drip it is at correct level.
8. If no fluid comes out hole, fluid will need to be added as follows:
   a. Remove fill plug.
   b. Fill transmission to correct fluid level.
   c. When fluid starts to drain from fluid level hole, transmission is full.
9. Install fill and fluid level indicator plug.
10. Lower vehicle, check transmission operation and inspect for leaks.

FLUID CHANGE

1. Run engine until operating temperature is 80–120F.
2. Move selector through gears and place selector lever in Park
3. Raise and support vehicle. Ensure vehicle is level.
4. Place suitable drain pan under transmission.
5. Remove drain plug and allow fluid to drain.
6. Remove converter housing plug.
7. Remove drain plug and discard.
8. Once fluid has drained, install new converter drain plug. **New converter drain plug must be used to prevent leakage.**
9. Install drain and converter housing access plugs.
10. Remove fluid level indicator and fill plugs.
11. Fill transmission to correct fluid level. When fluid starts to drain from fluid level hole, transmission is full.
12. Perform fluid level check as previously described.

ADJUSTMENTS

SELECTOR CABLE

1. Place selector lever in D5 position.
2. Raise and support vehicle, then disconnect selector cable from manual control lever.
3. Place control lever in D5 position, three positions from most rearward position.
4. Disconnect cable from selector lever.
5. Connect cable to manual control lever.
6. Unlock cable end adjuster.
7. Connect cable to shifter and lock end adjuster.
8. Lower vehicle.
9. Carefully move control lever from detent to detent and compare with transmission settings.
10. Ensure vehicle will start in Park or Neutral.
11. Ensure backup lamps light in Reverse.
12. If adjustments are not correct, repeat procedure and adjust digital Transmission Range (TR) sensor in Neutral as described under " In-Vehicle Repairs."

IN-VEHICLE REPAIRS

CONTROL SWITCH, REPLACE

1. Remove center console.
2. Remove PRNDL indicator bulb and disconnect electrical connector.
3. Disconnect switches and remove harness.
4. Reverse procedure to install.

SELECTOR LEVER, REPLACE

1. Remove center console.
2. Slide cover down, then remove mounting screws, handle and cover.
3. Remove shift bezel and PRNDL indicator bulb, then the rear A/C air duct.
4. Remove shift interlock cable from bracket and disconnect cable.
5. Raise and support vehicle, then disconnect transmission shift cable.
6. Lower vehicle, then remove mounting bolts and shifter assembly.
7. Reverse procedure and adjust cable as described under " Adjustments."

SHIFT CABLE, REPLACE

1. Raise and support vehicle.
2. Disconnect transmission shift cable from selector lever and bracket.
3. Remove mounting bolts and allow heat shield to rest on exhaust.
4. Remove shift cable bracket and cable mounting bolts, then the cable and bracket.
5. Reverse procedure to install. Tighten mounting bolts to specifications.
6. Adjust cable as described under "Adjustments."

BRAKE SHIFT INTERLOCK ACTUATOR, REPLACE

1. Disconnect traction control switch, if equipped.
2. Remove center console.
3. Remove PRNDL indicator bulb, rear A/C air duct and shifter bezel.
4. Remove shift interlock cable from bracket and disconnect cable.
5. Remove lower steering column mounting screws.
6. Remove instrument panel steering column cover.
7. Disconnect electrical connector.
8. Remove mounting screws, then position hood release cable and bracket aside.
9. Remove floor heat duct mounting screw and lower reinforcement panel.
10. Remove inner and outer instrument panel finish panels.
11. Disconnect power mirror switch and remove inner trim support panel.
12. Remove mounting screws and ignition switch.
13. Remove shift lock actuator cable mounting screws and disconnect electrical connector.
14. Remove cable from bracket.
15. Reverse procedure to install.

TRANSMISSION PAN, REPLACE

Removal

1. Raise and support vehicle.
2. Place suitable drain pan under transmission fluid pan.
3. Remove drain plug and drain fluid.
4. Remove bracket, fluid pan and gasket.
5. Remove and discard transmission fluid filter.
6. Clean and inspect transmission fluid pan and magnet.
7. Remove converter housing and drain plugs.

Installation

1. Install new converter drain plug. **New converter drain plug must be used to prevent leakage.**
2. Install converter housing access plug.
3. Lubricate fluid filter O-rings and seals with Mercon V automatic transmission fluid, then install transmission fluid filter. Ensure fluid filter O-rings are correctly seated on filter.
4. Install oil pan magnet in transmission fluid pan.
5. Install transmission fluid pan and gasket, then loosely fit mounting screws. Gasket is reusable, clean and inspect for damage.
6. Tighten pan mounting screws to specifications in crisscross sequence.
7. Install shifter cable bracket.
8. Remove fill, drain and fluid level indicator plugs.
9. Fill transmission to correct fluid level. When fluid starts to drain from fluid level hole transmission is full.
10. Perform fluid level check as described under "Maintenance."

VALVE BODY, REPLACE

Removal

1. Raise and support the vehicle, then drain transmission fluid as previously described.
2. Remove converter housing and drain plugs.
3. Remove shifter cable bracket.
4. Clean area around solenoid body connector, then Disconnect transmission connector.
5. Disconnect digital TR sensor connector.
6. Remove transmission fluid pan and gasket, then the transmission fluid filter.
7. Disconnect connector and Remove reverse pressure switch and discard.
8. Remove solenoid body, valve body cover plate and gasket. Note bolt sizes and locations for installation.
9. Remove reverse servo.
10. Remove detent spring, main control valve body, separator plate and gasket.
11. Remove intermediate clutch spring and seal. Intermediate clutch spring and seal will fall out of case.

Installation

Failure to correctly seat the intermediate clutch fluid inlet tube seal and spring will cause an internal fluid leak and transmission damage. Correctly install and seat the intermediate clutch fluid inlet tube seal and spring into the case using a suitable drift punch.

1. Install two .248 inch valve body guide pin tools No. T95L-70010-C, or equivalent, into transmission case.
2. Install main control valve body and loosely fit mounting screws.
3. Remove guide pin tools and loosely fit remaining mounting screws.
4. Install valve body cover plate and gasket and loosely fit mounting screws.
5. Install reverse pressure switch and loosely fit mounting screws.
6. Tighten mounting screws to specifications in sequence, **Fig. 5.**
7. Install reverse servo and tighten mounting bolts in crisscross pattern.
8. Install manual control valve detent spring.
9. Install new solenoid body connector

O-rings. Lubricate O-rings with clean Mercon V automatic transmission fluid.

10. Inspect transmission case bore to ensure it is free of debris and not damaged.
11. Install solenoid body and tighten mounting bolts to specifications in sequence, **Fig. 6.**
12. Connect reverse pressure switch connector.
13. Lubricate fluid filter O-rings and seals with Mercon V automatic transmission fluid, then install transmission fluid filter. Ensure fluid filter O-rings are correctly seated on filter.
14. Install oil pan magnet in transmission fluid pan.
15. Install transmission fluid pan and gasket, then loosely fit mounting screws. Gasket is reusable, clean and inspect for damage.
16. Tighten pan mounting screws to specifications in crisscross sequence.
17. Install new converter drain plug. **New converter drain plug must be used to prevent leakage.**
18. Install converter housing access plug.
19. Connect digital TR sensor connector.
20. Clean area around connector to prevent contamination of solenoid body connector.
21. Lubricate new O-rings with suitable petroleum jelly and install on transmission connector.
22. Connect connector. **Do not tighten mounting screw above specifications.**
23. Install shift cable bracket.
24. Lower vehicle.
25. Fill transmission to correct fluid level and check for correct operation.

EXTENSION HOUSING SEAL, REPLACE

Removal

1. Raise and support vehicle, then remove exhaust and driveshaft.
2. Remove flange nut and discard.
3. Remove output flange using output flange remover tool No. 307-408, or equivalent.
4. Remove seal using convertor seal remover tool No. T94P-77001-BH, and impact slide hammer tool No. T50T-100-A, or equivalents.

Installation

1. Install new extension housing seal using extension housing bushing replacer tool No. T74P-77052-A, or equivalent.
2. Install output flange using output shaft flange installer tool No. T307-404, or equivalent.
3. Install new flange nut and tighten to specifications.
4. Install drive shaft and exhaust.
5. Lower vehicle and adjust transmission fluid level as required.

EXTENSION HOUSING GASKET, REPLACE

Removal

1. Raise and support vehicle, then remove exhaust and driveshaft.
2. Support transmission with suitable transmission jack.
3. Remove center rear mount mounting bolt, then the outer mounting bolts.
4. Disconnect shift cable.
5. Remove flange nut and discard.
6. Remove output flange using output flange remover tool No. 307-408, or equivalent.
7. Remove extension housing. **Parking pawl, parking pawl return spring and parking pawl shaft may fall out during removal.**
8. Remove and discard extension housing gasket.

Installation

1. Clean extension housing and install new extension housing gasket. **Ensure park pawl is installed correctly.**
2. Install the extension housing. **Ensure parking lever actuating rod is correctly seated into case parking rod guide cup.**
3. Install shift cable.
4. Install rear mount and tighten mounting bolts to specifications.
5. Install output flange using output shaft flange installer tool No. T307-404, or equivalent.
6. Install new flange nut and tighten to specifications.
7. Install driveshaft and exhaust.
8. Fill transmission to correct fluid level and check for correct operation.

SOLENOID BODY, REPLACE

Replace solenoid body as previously described under " Valve Body, Replace."

DIGITAL TRANSMISSION RANGE (TR) SENSOR, REPLACE

Removal

1. Raise and support vehicle, then remove exhaust and drive shaft.
2. Support transmission with suitable transmission jack. **Secure transmission to transmission jack with suitable safety chain.**
3. Remove mount and lower transmission enough to gain access to digital TR sensor.
4. Disconnect shift cable.
5. Disconnect connector and remove digital TR sensor.

Installation

The digital transmission range sensor must fit flush against the boss on the case to prevent damage to the sensor.

1. Install digital TR sensor and loosely fit mounting screws.
2. Ensure manual lever is in Neutral position.
3. Align digital TR sensor using TRS alignment tool No. T97L-70010-A, or equivalent, and tighten mounting screws in alternating sequence. **Tightening one screw before tightening other may cause sensor to bind or become damaged.**
4. Connect digital TR sensor connector and shift cable.
5. Install rear mount.
6. Ensure shift cable is adjusted as described under " Adjustments."
7. Install drive shaft and exhaust.
8. Lower vehicle.

REVERSE SERVO, REPLACE

Replace reverse servo as previously described under " Valve Body, Replace."

PARK SYSTEM, REPLACE

Removal

1. Raise and support the vehicle, then drain transmission fluid as previously described.
2. Remove converter housing and drain plugs.
3. Remove shifter cable bracket.
4. Remove exhaust and drive shaft.
5. Support transmission with suitable transmission jack. **Secure transmission to transmission jack with suitable safety chain.**
6. Remove shift cable bracket.
7. Remove transmission mount.
8. Disconnect shift cable and digital TR sensor connector.
9. Remove transmission fluid pan and gasket, then the transmission fluid filter.
10. Remove digital TR sensor.
11. Remove manual control valve detent spring.
12. Remove nut and manual lever shaft retaining pin. **Ensure wrench does not strike manual valve inner lever pin.**
13. Partially remove manual control lever shaft.
14. Disconnect manual valve inner lever from parking lever actuating rod.
15. Remove manual valve inner lever.
16. Remove flange nut and discard.
17. Remove output flange using output flange remover tool No. 307-408, or equivalent.
18. Remove extension housing and discard gasket. **The parking pawl, parking pawl return spring and parking pawl shaft may fall out during extension housing removal.**
19. **If damage is found to parking gear, transmission must be removed and disassembled.**
20. Inspect parking pawl, parking pawl return spring and parking pawl shaft. Discard components if damaged or worn.
21. Remove parking lever actuating rod.

Installation

1. Install parking lever actuating rod and manual control lever.
2. Assemble manual valve inner lever and parking lever actuating rod.
3. Align manual inner lever flats with manual control lever shaft flats, then install manual valve inner lever and parking lever actuating rod onto manual control lever shaft.
4. Install manual valve inner lever onto manual shaft and loosely fit mounting nut.
5. Align manual control lever shaft alignment groove with manual control lever shaft spring pin bore in transmission case.
6. Install manual control lever shaft spring pin.
7. Tap manual control lever shaft spring pin into transmission case.
8. **Do not to damaged fluid pan rail surface when installing retaining pin.**
9. Tighten mounting nut. **Do not allow wrench to strike manual valve inner lever pin.**
10. Install manual valve detent spring.
11. Clean extension housing and install new extension housing gasket. **Ensure parking pawl is correctly installed.**
12. Install extension housing.**Ensure parking lever actuating rod is correctly seated into case parking rod guide cup.**
13. Lubricate fluid filter O-rings and seals with Mercon V automatic transmission fluid, then install transmission fluid filter. Ensure fluid filter O-rings are correctly seated on filter.
14. Install oil pan magnet in transmission fluid pan.
15. Install transmission fluid pan and gasket, then loosely fit mounting screws. Gasket is reusable, clean and inspect for damage.
16. Tighten pan mounting screws to specifications in crisscross sequence.
17. Install converter housing access plug.
18. Install digital TR sensor and loosely fit mounting screws.
19. Ensure manual lever is in Neutral position.
20. Align digital TR sensor using TRS alignment tool No. T97L-70010-A, or equivalent, and tighten mounting screws in alternating sequence. **Tightening one screw before tightening other may cause sensor to bind or become damaged.**
21. Connect digital TR sensor connector.
22. Install new converter drain plug. **New converter drain plug must be used to prevent leakage.**
23. Install converter housing access plug.
24. Install shift cable.
25. Install rear mount and tighten bolts to specifications.
26. Install shift cable bracket.
27. Install output flange using output shaft flange installer tool No. T307-404, or equivalent.
28. Install new flange nut and tighten to specifications.
29. Install driveshaft and exhaust.
30. Fill transmission to correct fluid level and check for correct operation.

TRANSMISSION

REPLACE

REMOVAL

If the transmission is to be removed for a period of time, support the engine with a suitable safety stand and wood block.

1. Raise and support vehicle, then remove exhaust.
2. If transmission disassembly is necessary, drain transmission fluid as preciously described.
3. Remove drive shaft.
4. Support transmission with suitable transmission jack. **Secure transmission to transmission jack with suitable safety chain.**
5. Remove mounting bolts and transmission mount.
6. Disconnect shift cable.
7. Lower transmission enough to gain access to sensors, then disconnect TSS, OSS and ISS harness connectors.
8. Remove harness screw.
9. Disconnect transmission connector. **Clean area around connector to prevent contamination of solenoid body connector.**
10. Disconnect harness retainers. and remove HO2S connector.
11. Remove shifter cable bracket and disconnect shifter cable from manual lever.
12. Disconnect digital TR sensor connector.
13. Disconnect transmission cooler line bracket and transmission cooler tubes. **Do not damage the cooler tubes.**
14. Remove access cover and apply identifying mark on nut, stud, and adapter plate for installation alignment.
15. Remove mounting nuts and bolts.
16. Lower and remove transmission.
17. Backflush and clean transmission fluid cooler.

INSTALLATION

Secure the transmission to the transmission jack with a safety chain.

1. Raise and position transmission.
2. Align flexplate to converter marks made during removal.
3. Install mounting bolts and nuts, then tighten to specifications.
4. Install access cover.
5. Install transmission cooler tubes. **Do not to bend or force cooler tubes otherwise damage to cooler tubes and transmission may result.**
6. Tighten cooler tube to specifications.
7. Install transmission cooler line bracket.
8. Connect digital TR sensor connector.
9. Clean area around connector to prevent contamination of solenoid body connector.
10. Lubricate new O-rings with suitable petroleum jelly and install on transmission connector.
11. Connect connector. **Do not tighten mounting screw above specifications.**
12. Install shift cable bracket and connect shifter cable.
13. Install HO2S connector and connect harness retainers, then install harness mounting screw.
14. Connect TSS, OSS, and ISS connectors.
15. Install rear transmission mount.
16. Install shift cable.
17. Tighten rear transmission mount mounting bolts to specifications.
18. Remove transmission jack and Install drive shaft.
19. Install exhaust system.
20. Lower vehicle.
21. Conduct fluid level check as described under "Maintenance. "
22. Ensure shift cable is correctly adjusted as described under " Adjustments."
23. Check transmission operation and inspect for leaks.

TIGHTENING SPECIFICATIONS

Year	Description	Torque, Ft. Lbs.
2000	Band Adjustment Locknut	40
	Case To Center Support	96①
	Converter Drain Plug	89①
	Digital Transmission Range (TR) Sensor	89①
	Extension Housing	29
	Extension Housing Fill Plug	15
	Fluid Level Indicator Plug	89①
	Fluid Pan Drain Plug	12
	Heat Shield	89①
	Main Control	89①②
	Main Control Separator	89①
	Main Control Valve Detent Spring	89①
	Manual Control Lever	35
	Output Flange	97
	Overdrive Band Adjustment	120①
	Pressure Tap Plug	120①
	Reverse Servo	89①
	Shift Cable Bracket	18
	Shift Lock Actuator	80①
	Shifter	62①
	Solenoid Body	71①②
	Speed Sensor	89①
	Transmission Cooler Fitting	35
	Transmission Cooler Line Bracket (V6 Engine)	89①
	Transmission Cooler Line Bracket (V8 Engine)	13
	Transmission Cooler Tube	26
	Transmission Fluid Filter	89①
	Transmission Fluid Pan	108①
	Transmission Mount-To-Extension Housing Center Screw	30
	Transmission Mount-To-Extension Housing Screw	37
	Transmission Mount	41
	Transmission To Engine	35
	Vehicle Harness	44①

① — Inch lbs.
② — Refer to "Valve Body, Replace" for tightening sequence.

FRONT WHEEL DRIVE AXLES

TABLE OF CONTENTS

Aspire

NOTE: On Air Bag Equipped Models, Refer To " Air Bag System Precautions" Located In The Front Of This Manual For System Disarming & Arming Procedures.

INDEX

PRECAUTIONS

AIR BAG SYSTEMS

Refer to "Air Bag System Precautions" in the front of this manual for system disarming and arming procedures.

BATTERY GROUND CABLE

Prior to service, disconnect battery ground cable and isolate as required.

DESCRIPTION

The front wheel driveshaft and joints mechanically link engine torque from the transaxle to the front wheels, **Fig. 1.** At the transaxle end, the front wheel driveshaft joint is splined to the differential side gears. Disengagement of the tripod type front wheel driveshaft joint from the differential side gear is prevented by an expanding spring steel driveshaft bearing retainer circlip.

The wheel ends of the righthand and lefthand front driveshaft and joints are splined to the wheel hubs which are supported on opposed tapered front wheel bearing inner and outer cone and rollers. Disengagement of the driveshaft and joint from the wheel hub is prevented by the front axle wheel hub washer and retainer.

Backlash between the wheel hubs and driveshaft joint is eliminated by the splines. The front wheel hub splines are machined straight while the driveshaft joint splines are machined with a slight helical cut. The difference in splines provides a tight, backlash-free coupling without the replacement problems associated with an interference fit.

TROUBLESHOOTING

IMPROPER FRONT WHEEL DRIVESHAFT & JOINT OPERATION

1. Broken ball joint.
2. Worn or seized front wheel driveshaft joint.

ABNORMAL NOISE FROM FRONT WHEEL DRIVESHAFT & JOINT

1. Insufficient grease or front wheel driveshaft joint or spline.
2. Excessive backlash on spline.
3. Worn front wheel driveshaft joint.
4. Loose dynamic damper.

STEERING WHEEL PULLS LEFT OR RIGHT WHILE DRIVING STRAIGHT OR LEVEL

1. Improper front wheel bearing inner and outer cone and roller preload adjustment.
2. Bent steering linkage.
3. Fatigued front coil spring.
4. Front suspension lower arm mounting bolt bushing worn or damaged.
5. Bent front wheel knuckle.
6. Bent front suspension lower arm or loose mounting.
7. Improper toe adjustment.
8. Improper tire pressure.
9. Unevenly worn tires (difference between lefthand and righthand tire wear).
10. Brake dragging.

UNSTABLE HANDLING

1. Improper front wheel bearing inner and outer cone and roller preload adjustment.
2. Bent steering linkage.
3. Lower steering column shaft worn or damaged.
4. Improper steering gear preload adjustment.
5. Fatigued front coil spring.
6. Worn rear spring and shock absorber assemblies.
7. Front suspension lower arm mounting bolt bushing worn or damaged.
8. Improper toe adjustment.
9. Improper tire pressure.
10. Wheels bent or out of balance.

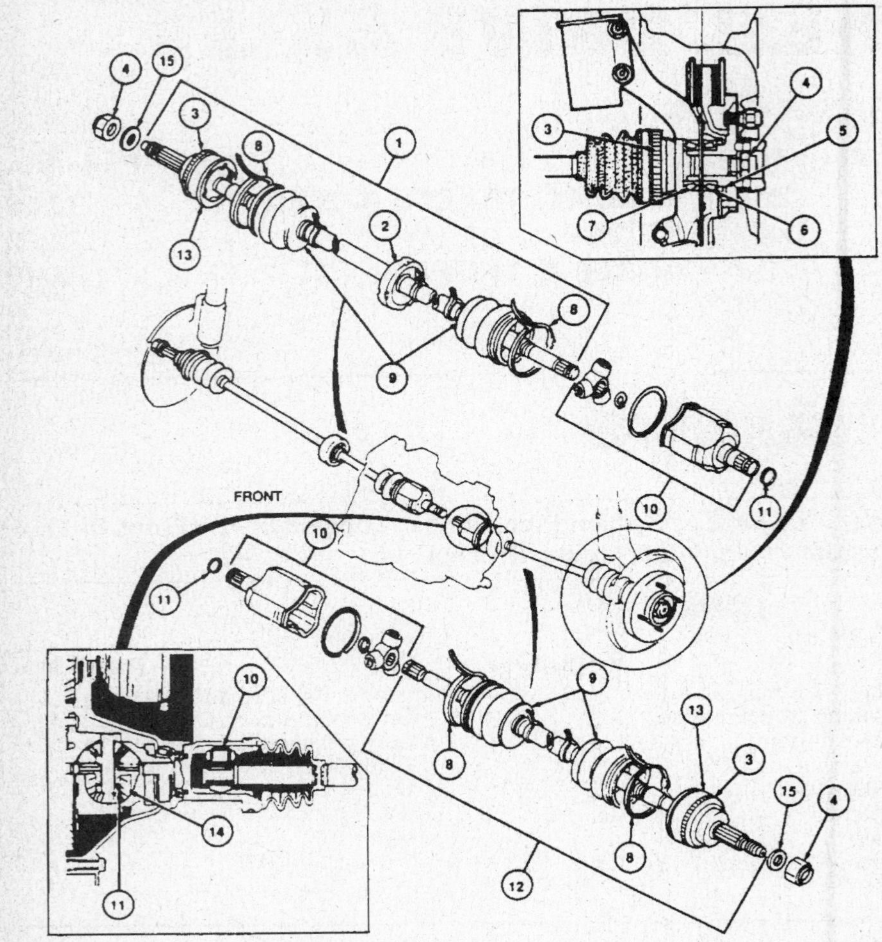

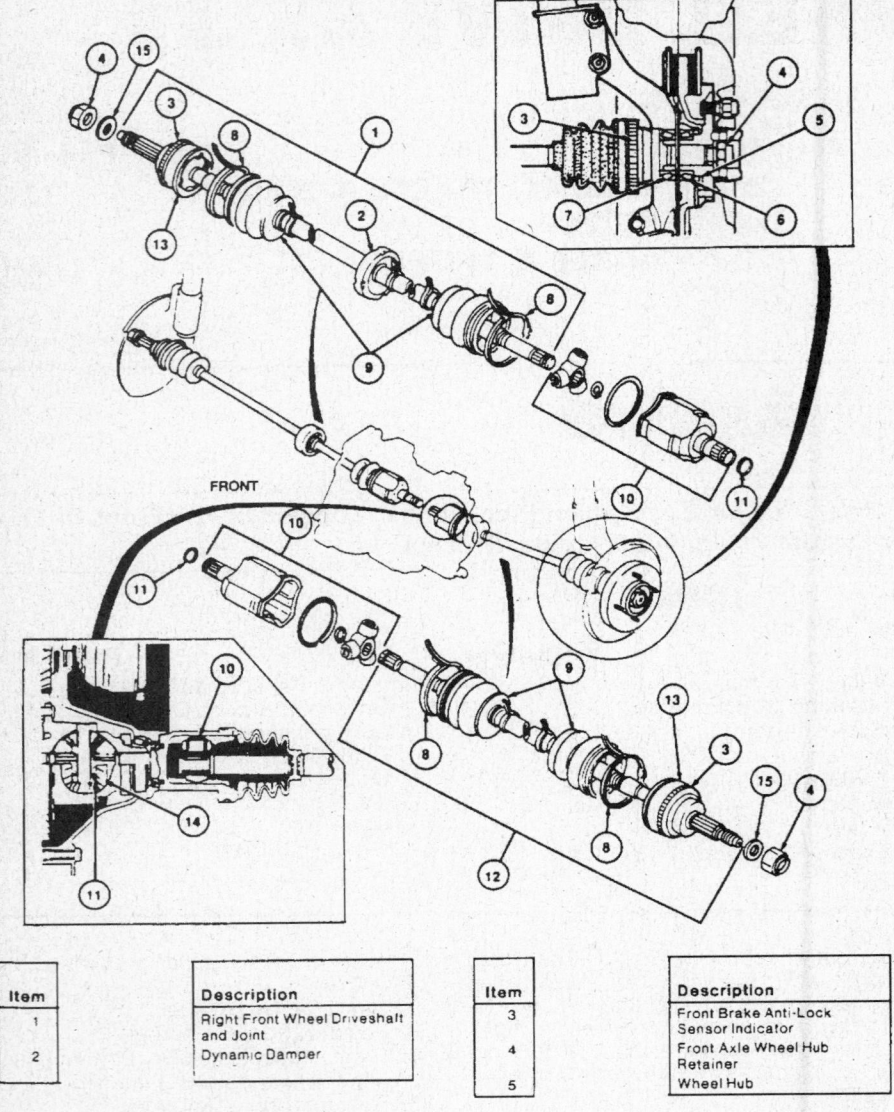

Item	Description
1	Right Front Wheel Driveshaft and Joint
2	Dynamic Damper
3	Front Brake Anti-Lock Sensor Indicator
4	Front Axle Wheel Hub Retainer
5	Wheel Hub

FM3039400237000X

Fig. 1 Exploded view of front wheel driveshaft & joint

EXCESSIVE STEERING WHEEL PLAY

1. Loose front wheel bearing inner and outer cone and roller.
2. Improper steering gear preload adjustment.
3. Steering gear worn.
4. Lower steering column shaft worn or damaged.
5. Front suspension lower arm mounting bolt bushing worn or damaged.

TIRES WORN EXCESSIVELY OR UNEVENLY

1. Improper front wheel bearing inner and outer cone and roller preload adjustment.
2. Improper toe adjustment.
3. Improper tire pressure.
4. Wheels out of balance.

ABNORMAL NOISE FROM WHEEL HUB

1. Faulty front wheel bearing inner and outer cone and roller.

DRIVESHAFT

REPLACE

REMOVAL

1. Raise and support vehicle.
2. Drain transmission fluid from transaxle.
3. Remove front wheel and tire assemblies.
4. Use small cape chisel to carefully raise staked portion of front axle wheel hub retainer.
5. While applying brakes, loosen but do not remove front axle wheel hub retainer.

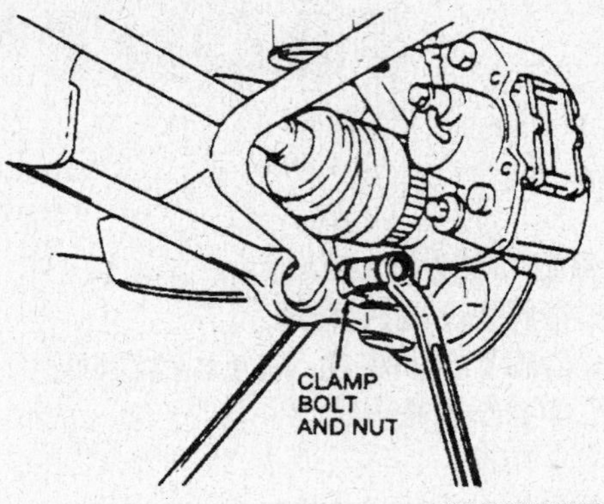

FM3039400238000X

Fig. 2 Clamp bolt & nut removal

6. Remove clamp bolt and nut, **Fig. 2.**
7. Carefully pry down on front suspension lower arm to separate ball joint from front wheel knuckle, **Fig. 3.**
8. **Separate driveshaft and joint from transaxle gradually. If driveshaft is yanked from transaxle, differential oil seal may be damaged.**
9. Use pry bar to separate driveshaft and joint from transaxle.
10. Remove front axle wheel hub retainer and washer.
11. If necessary, use suitable drift and hammer to tap driveshaft and joint from front wheel hub.
12. Pry driveshaft bearing retainer circlip off of driveshaft joint.
13. Install differential plugs.

INSTALLATION

1. Before installing driveshaft, inspect and/or replace differential and inner wheel bearing oil seals.
2. Install new driveshaft bearing retainer circlip on driveshaft joint.
3. Lubricate end of driveshaft joint with grease.
4. Remove differential plugs.
5. Install end of driveshaft joint into differential side gear.
6. Lubricate end of driveshaft and joint.
7. Insert end of driveshaft and joint into wheel hub.
8. Install front axle wheel hub retainer and washer onto front wheel driveshaft and joint. Tighten by hand.
9. Install front suspension lower arm by placing ball joint into front wheel knuckle.
10. Install clamp nut and bolt on front suspension lower arm.
11. While applying brakes, tighten front axle wheel hub retainer nut.
12. Use suitable cape chisel with cutting edge rounded to stake front axle wheel hub retainer.
13. Install front wheel and tire assemblies. Tighten wheel hub bolts.
14. Fill transaxle to proper level with specified grade of transmission fluid.

DRIVESHAFT SERVICE

DISASSEMBLE

Do not remove front brake anti-lock

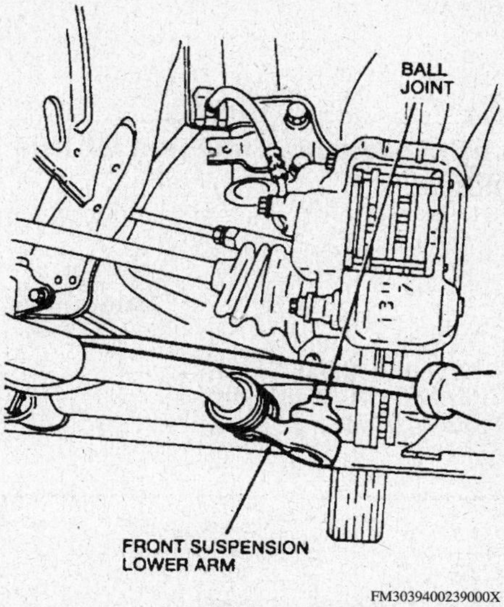

Fig. 3 Ball joint separation from wheel knuckle

sensor indicator if it does not need to be replaced. Any time it is removed, it must be replaced.

1. Clamp driveshaft and joint in a soft-jaw vise to prevent damage to any parts.
2. Peel driveshaft joint boot clamp away from front wheel driveshaft joint boot.
3. Remove large joint boot clamp and discard.
4. Roll driveshaft joint boot back over driveshaft and joint.
5. Remove wire ring bearing retainer.
6. Paint alignment marks on outer race and tripod bearing, **Fig. 4.**
7. Remove outer race and snap ring.
8. Use suitable drift and hammer to gently tap tripod bearing from driveshaft.
9. If necessary, remove small driveshaft joint boot and clamp.

ASSEMBLE

1. Align marks on tripod bearing and driveshaft.
2. Use suitable soft faced hammer to gently tap tripod bearing onto driveshaft.
3. Use snap ring pliers to remove snap ring.
4. Fill outer race with 3.5 ounces of CV joint grease No. E43Z-19590-A, or equivalent, meeting Ford specification ESP-M1C207-A.
5. Install outer race over tripod bearing and install wire ring bearing retainer.

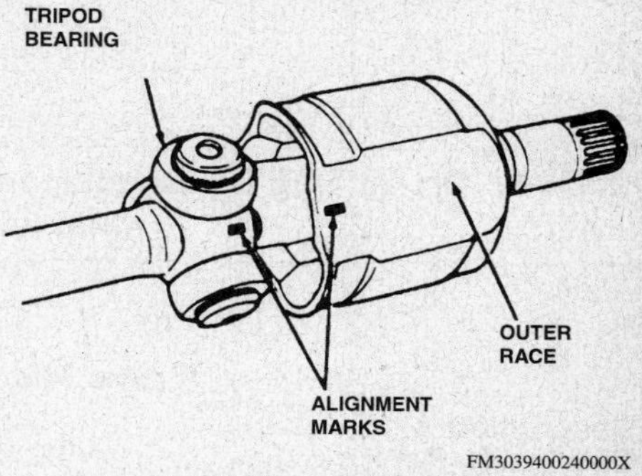

Fig. 4 Outer race & tripod bearing alignment marks

6. Position driveshaft joint boot so that it is fully seated in driveshaft grooves and outer race.
7. Extend or compress driveshaft as necessary until distance between joint boot clamp grooves is 4.11 inches.
8. Insert dull screwdriver between driveshaft joint boot and outer race to allow trapped air to escape.
9. Install new driveshaft joint boot clamps.

TIGHTENING SPECIFICATIONS

Component	Torque/Ft. Lbs.
Axle Nut	116–174
Ball Joint Pinch Bolt	40–50
Driveshaft Nut	116–174
Hub Nut	116–174
Tie Rod End Nut	31–42
Wheel Lug Nut	65–87

Continental

NOTE: On Air Bag Equipped Models, Refer To " Air Bag System Precautions" Located In The Front Of This Manual For System Disarming & Arming Procedures.

INDEX

PRECAUTIONS

AIR BAG SYSTEMS

Refer to "Air Bag System Precautions" in the front of this manual for system disarming and arming procedures.

BATTERY GROUND CABLE

Prior to service, disconnect battery ground cable and isolate as required.

DESCRIPTION

Each front wheel driveshaft employs Constant Velocity (CV) joints at both inboard (differential side) and outboard (wheel side) for vehicle operating smoothness. The CV joints are connected by an interconnecting shaft which is splined at both ends and retained in the inboard and outboard CV joints by snap rings, **Fig. 1.**

Inboard CV joint is permanently retained by the interconnecting shaft. The service components of the CV joint include the shaft and the driveshaft joint boot. The joint and outboard boot will need to be removed to replace the boot, joint or shaft.

TROUBLESHOOTING

Refer to **Fig. 2** for troubleshooting chart.

DRIVESHAFT

REPLACE

REMOVAL

If removing both righthand and lefthand driveshafts, install plugs tool No. T81P-1177B, or equivalent. Failure to do so may result in dislocation of differential side gears, necessitating transaxle disassembly to align the gears again. Should the gears become misaligned, the differential will have to be removed from the transaxle for alignment.

Do not begin this procedure unless a new hub retainer nut, lower control arm to steering knuckle attaching bolt and nut and a new inboard CV joint stub shaft snap ring are available. Once removed, these components must not be reused during assembly/installation. Their torque holding ability or retention capability is diminished during removal.

1. Turn air suspension system switch Off.
2. Raise and support vehicle. Remove tire and wheel assemblies.
3. Remove hub retainer nut and washer. Discard nut after removal.
4. Remove attaching nut from ball joint to steering knuckle attaching bolt.
5. Using a punch and a hammer, drive bolt out of steering knuckle. **Discard bolt and nut.**
6. Remove anti-lock brake sensor from steering knuckle. Remove height sensor link at lower arm ball stud attachment.
7. Remove stabilizer bar link at stabilizer bar.
8. Separate ball joint from steering knuckle using a pry bar. **Position end of pry bar outside of bushing pocket**

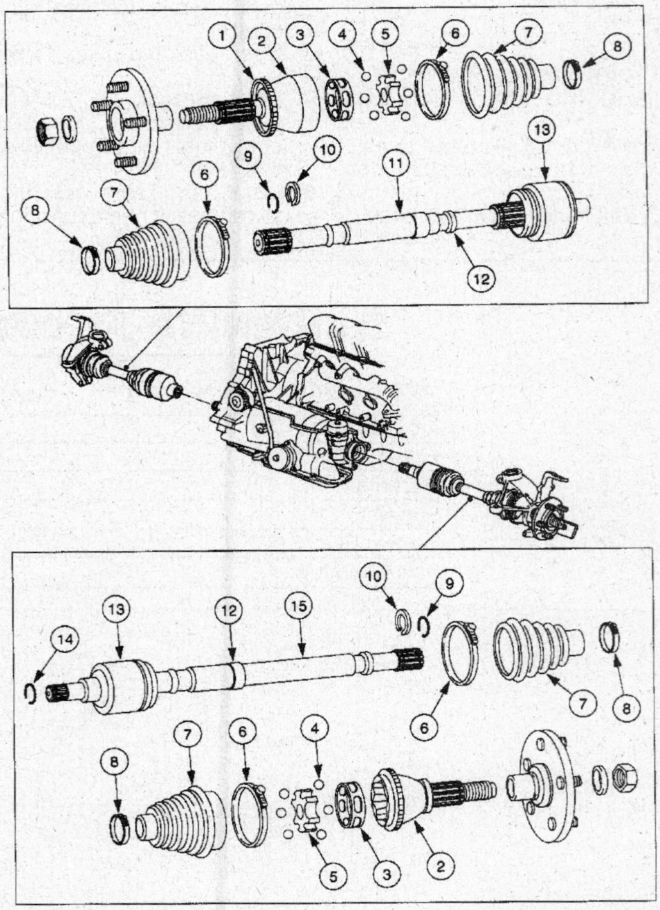

Fig. 1 Exploded view of driveshaft assemblies (Part 1 of 2)

Item	Description
1	Front Brake Anti-Lock Sensor Indicator
2	Front Wheel Driveshaft Joint
3	Ball Cage
4	Balls (6 Req'd)
5	Race
6	Front Wheel Driveshaft Joint Boot Clamp (Large)
7	Front Wheel Driveshaft Joint Boot
8	Front Wheel Driveshaft Joint Boot Clamp (Small)

Item	Description
9	Circlip
10	Stop Ring
11	Interconnecting Shaft
12	Halfshaft Identification Label
13	Inboard CV Joint Housing
14	Circlip
15	Interconnecting Shaft

FM3039500309020X

Fig. 1 Exploded view of driveshaft assemblies (Part 2 of 2)

Condition	Possible Source
• Clicking, Popping or Grinding Noises While Turning	• Inadequate or contaminated lube in outboard front wheel driveshaft joint or inboard front wheel driveshaft joint. • Another component contacting halfshaft assembly. • Worn, damaged or improperly installed wheel bearings, brakes, suspension or steering components.
• Vibration at Highway Speeds	• Out of balance front wheels or tires. • Out of round front tires. • Improperly seated outboard front wheel driveshaft joint in front wheel hub.
• Shudder Vibration During Acceleration	• Excessively high front wheel driveshaft joint operating angles caused by improper ride height. • Excessively worn or damaged inboard front wheel driveshaft and joint or outboard front wheel driveshaft joint.
• Front Wheel Drive Shaft Joint Pullout	• Inboard driveshaft bearing retainer circlip missing or not properly seated in differential side gear. • Engine / transaxle assembly mispositioned. • Frame rail or shock tower out of position or damaged. • Front suspension components worn or damaged.

FM3039500310000X

Fig. 2 Troubleshooting chart

to avoid bushing damage.

9. Install puller tool No. T86P-3514-A1, or equivalent, between CV joint and transaxle case. Turn steering hub and/or wire strut assembly out of way.
10. Screw extension tool No. T86P-3514-A2, or equivalent, into CV joint puller and hand tighten. Screw impact slide hammer tool No. D79P-100-A, or equivalent, onto extension.
11. Remove CV joint from transaxle.
12. Support end of shaft by suspending it from a conventional underbody component with a length or wire. **Do not allow shaft to hang unsupported. Damage to outboard CV joint may result.**
13. Separate outboard CV joint from hub using front hub remover tool Nos. T81P-1104-A, T83P-1104-BH1, T86P-1104-A1 and T81P-1104-C, or equivalents. **Never use a hammer to separate outboard CV joint stub shaft from hub. Damage to joint threads and internal components may result.**
14. Remove driveshaft assembly from vehicle.

INSTALLATION

1. Install a new snap ring onto inboard CV joint stub shaft and/or link shaft. **Outboard CV joint stub shaft does not have a snap ring. To properly install snap ring, start one end in groove and work ring over stub shaft end and into groove. This will avoid overexpanding snap ring. The old snap ring must not be reused. A new snap ring must be installed each time inboard CV joint is installed into transaxle differential.**
2. Carefully align splines of inboard CV joint stub shaft or link shaft with splines in differential. Exerting force, push CV joint into differential until snap ring seats in differential side gear. **Use care to prevent damage to differential oil seal. A plastic hammer or equivalent may be used to aid in seating snap ring into side gear groove.**
3. Carefully align splines of outboard CV joint stub shaft with splines in hub and push shaft into hub as far as possible.
4. Temporarily attach rotor to hub with washers and two wheel lug nuts. Insert a steel rod into rotor and rotate clockwise to contact steering knuckle to prevent rotor from turning during CV joint installation.
5. Install hub nut washer and a new hub retainer nut. Manually thread retainer onto CV joint shaft as far as possible. **A new hub retainer nut must be installed.**
6. Connect control arm to steering knuckle. Install a new nut and bolt. **A new nut and bolt must be installed.**
7. Connect stabilizer bar link to stabilizer bar.
8. Connect ride height sensor link.
9. Install anti-lock sensor link into control arm and tighten retaining bolt.
10. Install tire and wheel assembly, then lower vehicle.
11. Fill transaxle to operating level with proper fluid as required.

DRIVESHAFT SERVICE

OUTBOARD JOINT

Disassemble

CV joint components are matched during manufacturing and cannot be interchanged with components from another joint. Do not intermix or substitute components between joints.

1. Clamp driveshaft into a vise. Do not allow vise jaws to contact boot or clamp.
2. Cut large boot clamp and peel away from boot.
3. Support interconnecting shaft in a soft jaw vise and angle CV joint to expose inner bearing race.
4. Using a brass drift and hammer, give a sharp tap to inner bearing race to dislodge internal snap ring and separate CV joint from interconnecting shaft. The boot can now be removed from shaft.
5. Inspect CV joint grease for contamination. If CV joints are operating satisfactorily, and grease does not appear to be contaminated, add grease and replace boot. If grease appears contaminated or has a gritty feeling, inspect for worn components and replace as necessary.
6. Remove snap ring located near end of shaft. Discard snap ring. A new snap ring is supplied with both boot replacement kit and CV joint. **The stop ring, located just below snap ring, should only be removed if it is damaged.**
7. Clamp CV joint stub shaft in a vise with outer facing pointing upward. Care should be taken not to damage dust seal.
8. Press down on inner race until it tilts enough to allow removal of ball.
9. With cage tilted, remove ball from cage. Repeat until all six balls are removed.
10. Pivot cage and inner race assembly until it is facing straight up and down in outer race. Align cage windows with outer race lands while pivoting bearing race. With cage pivoted and aligned, lift assembly from outer race.
11. Rotate inner race up and out of cage.

Assemble

Because CV joint components are matched as a set during assembly, individual components are not available for service. If inspection determines a part to be worn or damaged, CV joint should

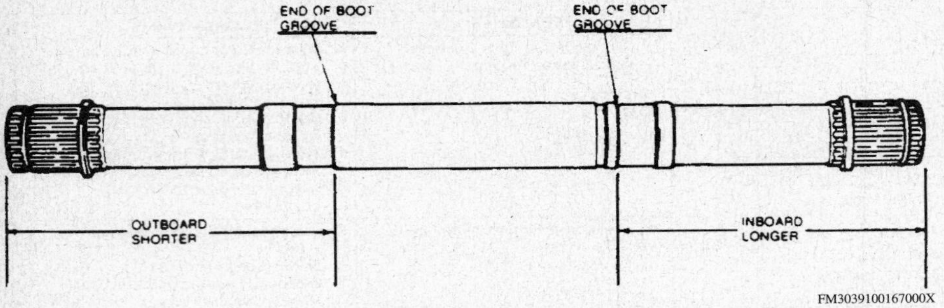

Fig. 3 Interconnecting shaft identification

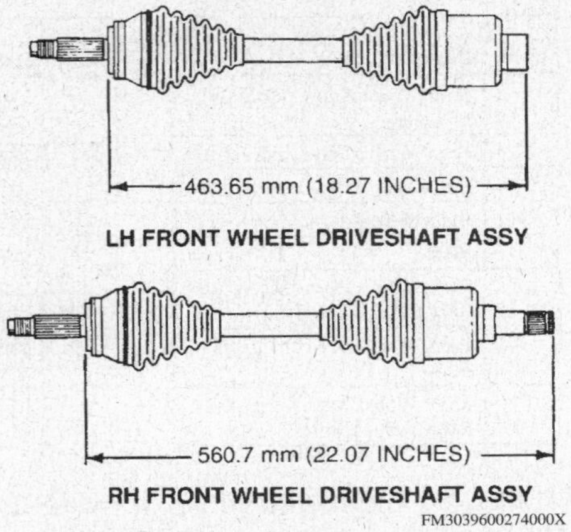

Fig. 4 Driveshaft assembled lengths

be replaced as an assembly. Do not replace a joint if components appear polished. Shiny areas in ball races and cage spheres are normal. A CV joint should be replaced only if inspection determines a component to be cracked, broken, severely pitted, worn or otherwise unserviceable.

1. Apply a light coat of grease onto inner and outer ball races. **Use only Ford CV grease No. E43Z-19590-A, or equivalent.**
2. Install inner race into bearing cage.
3. Install inner race and cage assembly into outer race.
4. Install assembly vertically and pivot 90° into position.
5. Align bearing cage and inner race with outer race.
6. Tilt inner race and cage, then install a ball. Repeat this step until all six balls are installed.
7. Lefthand and righthand interconnecting shafts are not same end-for-end. The outboard end is shorter from end of shaft to end of boot groove than inboard end. Take a measurement to ensure proper inboard and outboard CV joint to shaft installation, **Fig. 3.**
8. If removed, install CV joint boot after removing stop ring.
9. Ensure boot is properly seated in its groove and clamp into position.
10. If removed, install stop ring. If not removed, ensure stop ring is properly seated in groove.
11. Install a new snap ring, supplied with service kit, in groove nearest end of shaft.
12. Do not overexpand or twist snap ring during installation.
13. Before positioning boot over CV joint, pack CV joint and boot with grease supplied in service kit. Add 3.52 ounces.
14. With boot peeled back, position CV joint on shaft and tap into position. **CV joint is completely seated when snap ring locks in groove cut into CV joint inner race. Inspect for snap ring seating by trying to pull joint from shaft.**
15. Remove all excess grease from CV joint external surfaces.
16. Position boot over CV joint.
17. Ensure boot is seated in its groove and clamp in position.

DUST SEAL

Removal

Using a hammer, gently and evenly tap around dust seal until unseated.

Installation

Using seal installation tool Nos. T83T-3132-A1 and T86P-1104-A4, or equivalents, install dust seal. **Dust seal flange must face outboard.**

SPEED INDICATOR RING

Removal

1. Remove outboard CV joint as described under "Outboard Joint."
2. Position press tool No. T88P-2020-A, or equivalent, onto a press.
3. Position CV joint onto tool.
4. With joint in position, use press ram to apply pressure to joint and remove speed indicator ring.

Installation

1. With press tool No. T88P-2020-A, or equivalent, positioned on press, place sensor ring on tool.
2. Position joint into speed indicator ring tool. Allow joint to rest on ring.
3. With joint installed on tool, place a steel plate across joint's back face. Press joint until it bottoms out in tool. Ring will be properly installed when bottomed out in tool.

INBOARD JOINT

Disassemble

Inboard CV joint is permanently retained to interconnecting shaft. The service CV joint includes shaft and driveshaft joint boot. Joint and outboard boot will require removal to replace the boot, joint or shaft.

1. Cut and remove both boot clamps, then slide boot back on shaft.
2. Remove stop ring and driveshaft bearing retainer circlip.
3. Slide boot off interconnecting shaft.

Assemble

1. Install driveshaft boot on interconnecting shaft, then position boot to allow for inboard joint housing installation.
2. Position boot in small boot groove.
3. Position small boot clamp and install with boot clamp replacer tool No. T95P-3514-A, or equivalent. Tighten tool through bolt until tool is in closed position.
4. Fill inboard joint housing with Ford High Temperature CV Joint Grease part No. E43Z-19590-A, or equivalent, meeting Ford specification ESP-M1C207-A. Spread remainder evenly inside driveshaft joint boot for a total combined fill of 16 ¾ ounces.
5. Remove all excess grease from CV joint external surfaces. Position boot over joint and move joint inward and outward as necessary to specified length **Fig. 4.** Before installing driveshaft joint boot clamp, ensure any air pressure which may have built up in boot is relieved as follows:
   a. Insert a dull tip screwdriver blade between boot and outer bearing race, allow trapped air to escape from boot.
   b. Air should be released from boot only after adjusting to specified dimension.
6. Locate clamp tabs in slots. Hand tighten clamps.
7. Ensure boot is properly seated in its groove and clamp is in position.
8. Use boot clamp replacer tool No. T95P-3514-A, or equivalent, and tighten tool through bolt until tool is in closed position.
9. Work CV joint through several angles through its full travel range. Joint should compress, extend and flex smoothly.

TIGHTENING SPECIFICATIONS

Component	Torque/Ft. Lbs.
ABS Sensor Mounting Bolt	40–60①
Ball Joint Pinch Bolt	39–53
Hub Nut	180–200
Stabilizer Bar Link	57–75
Wheel Lug Nut	80–105

① — Inch lbs.

Contour & Mystique

NOTE: On Air Bag Equipped Models, Refer To " Air Bag System Precautions" Located In The Front Of This Manual For System Disarming & Arming Procedures.

INDEX

PRECAUTIONS

AIR BAG SYSTEMS

Refer to "Air Bag System Precautions" in the front of this manual for system disarming and arming procedures.

BATTERY GROUND CABLE

Prior to service, disconnect battery ground cable and isolate as required.

DESCRIPTION

These models use equal length driveshafts to minimize torque steer and to provide a smooth transfer of power to the front driving wheels. An intermediate driveshaft and support bearing are used on the righthand side to compensate for transaxle offset, **Fig. 1**

Inner CV joints are of the tripod type, while outer joints are of the ball and race type. **Outer joints contain matched components and must not be intermixed.**

TROUBLESHOOTING

Refer to **Fig. 2** for troubleshooting chart.

DRIVESHAFT

REPLACE

In all service operations the driveshaft bearing retainer circlips **Fig. 1, must be replaced with a new part. Do not begin this procedure unless a new hub retainer nut, lower control arm to steering knuckle attaching bolt and nut, and the circlips are available. Once removed, these components must not be reused during assembly/installation. Their torque holding ability or retention capability is diminished during removal.**

LEFTHAND DRIVESHAFT

1. Raise and support vehicle, then remove front wheel assemblies.
2. Remove front axle retainer nut and washer, discard nut.
3. Remove nut from stabilizer bar link at shock absorber end, then using a suitable tie rod end puller, remove link from shock and position aside.
4. Remove nut from tie rod end, then using a suitable tie rod end puller, remove tie rod from knuckle and position aside.
5. Remove and discard lower ball joint pinch bolt, then pry lower ball joint from knuckle.
6. Remove outer joint from hub using tools shown in **Fig. 3** or their equivalents, noting the following:
   a. Do not use a hammer to drive joint from hub.
   b. Do not allow driveshaft to hang from inner joint.
7. Remove inner joint from transaxle using tools shown in **Figs. 4 and 5,** or their equivalents. **Use caution when positioning tool to avoid transaxle speed sensor damage.**
8. Remove drive axle from vehicle.
9. Reverse procedure to install, noting the following:
   a. New front axle retainer nut must be used.
   b. New driveshaft bearing retainer circlips must be used.
   c. New ball joint pinch nut and bolt must be used.
   d. Use care when installing lefthand driveshaft joint into transaxle not to damage seal.
   e. Ensure proper engagement of lefthand driveshaft inner joint spline into transaxle side gears and that bearing retainer circlip is properly seated.
   f. Check transaxle fluid, add if needed.

RIGHTHAND DRIVESHAFT

1. Raise and support vehicle, then remove front wheel assemblies.
2. Remove and discard front axle retainer nut.
3. Remove nut from stabilizer bar link at shock absorber end, then using a suitable tie rod end puller, remove link from shock and position aside.
4. Remove nut from tie rod end, then using a suitable tie rod end puller, remove tie rod from knuckle and position aside.
5. Remove and discard lower ball joint pinch bolt, then pry lower ball joint from knuckle.
6. Remove outer joint from hub using tools shown in **Fig. 3** or their equivalents, noting the following:
   a. Do not use a hammer to drive joint from hub.
   b. Do not allow driveshaft to hang from inner joint.
7. Remove inner joint from intermediate shaft using tools shown in **Fig. 4** or their equivalents.
8. Remove driveshaft from vehicle.
9. Reverse procedure to install, noting the following:

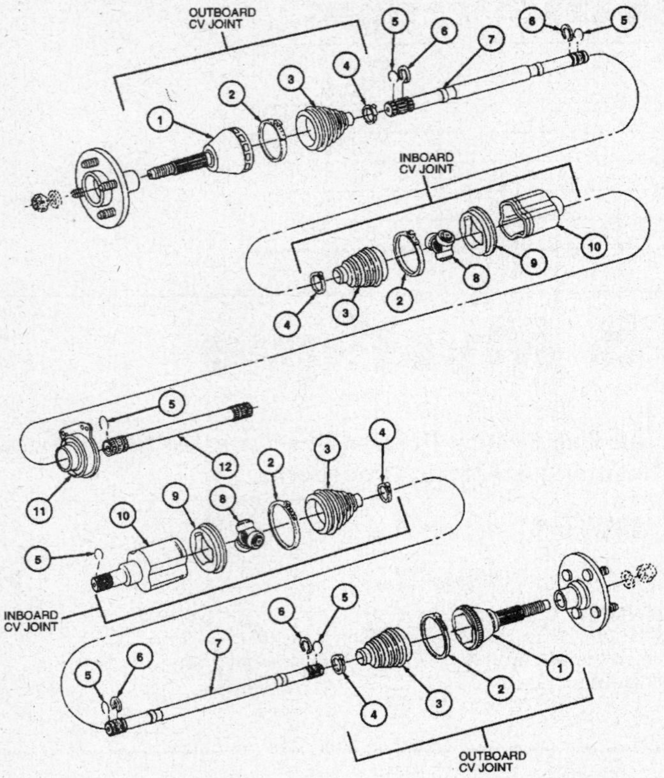

FM3039600257010X

Fig. 1 Exploded view of driveshaft assemblies (Part 1 of 2)

Item	Description
1	Front Wheel Driveshaft Joint
2	Front Wheel Driveshaft Joint Boot Clamp (Large)
3	Front Wheel Driveshaft Joint Boot
4	Front Wheel Driveshaft Joint Boot Clamp (Small)
5	Driveshaft Bearing Retainer Circlip
6	Stop Ring
7	Halfshaft
8	Tri-Pot Assembly
9	Tri-Lobe Insert
10	Inboard CV Joint Stub Shaft Pilot Bearing Housing
11	Intermediate Halfshaft Bearing
12	Intermediate Halfshaft

FM3039600257020X

Fig. 1 Exploded view of driveshaft assemblies (Part 2 of 2)

Condition	Possible Source
• Clicking, Popping or Grinding Noises While Turning	• Inadequate or contaminated lube in outboard front wheel driveshaft joint or inboard front wheel driveshaft joint. • Another component contacting driveshaft assembly. • Worn, damaged or improperly installed wheel bearings, brakes, suspension or steering components.
• Vibration at Highway Speeds	• Out-of-balance front wheels or tires. • Out-of-round front tires. • Improperly seated outboard front wheel driveshaft joint in front wheel hub.
• Shudder Vibration During Acceleration	• Excessively high CV joint operating angles caused by improper ride height. • Excessively worn or damaged inboard front wheel driveshaft joint or outboard front wheel driveshaft joint.
• Halfshaft Joint Pullout	• Inboard driveshaft bearing retainer circlip missing or not properly seated in differential side gear. • Engine / transaxle assembly mispositioned. • Frame rail or shock tower out of position or damaged. • Front suspension components worn or damaged.

FM3039500311000X

Fig. 2 Troubleshooting chart

a. New front axle retainer nut must be used.
b. New driveshaft bearing retainer circlips must be used.
c. New ball joint pinch nut and bolt must be used.
d. Check transaxle fluid, add if needed.

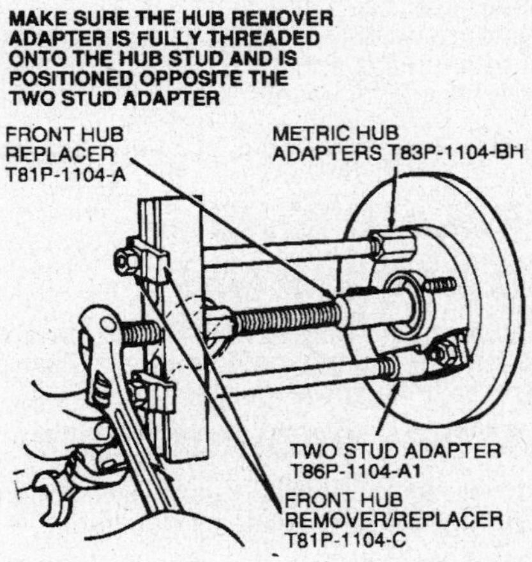

FM3039600258000X

Fig. 3 Outer joint removal from hub

INTERMEDIATE DRIVESHAFT

1. Remove righthand driveshaft as outlined under "Driveshaft Replace."
2. Remove intermediate driveshaft support bearing nuts and bearing shield.
3. **On models with 2.0L engine,** remove exhaust clamp and two bolts.
4. **On all models,** if necessary to achieve clearance, remove intermediate driveshaft support bearing bracket and three bolts.
5. Remove intermediate driveshaft from transaxle.
6. Remove and discard driveshaft bearing retainer circlip.
7. Reverse procedure to install, noting the following:
   a. New front axle retainer nut must be used.
   b. New driveshaft bearing retainer circlip must be used.
   c. New ball joint pinch nut and bolt

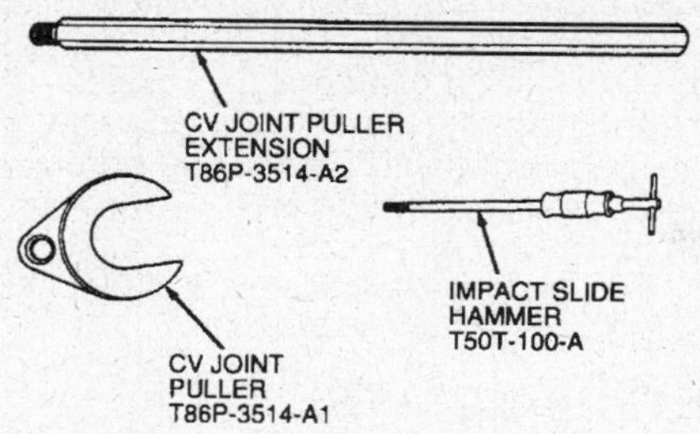

Fig. 4 Inner CV joint pulling tools

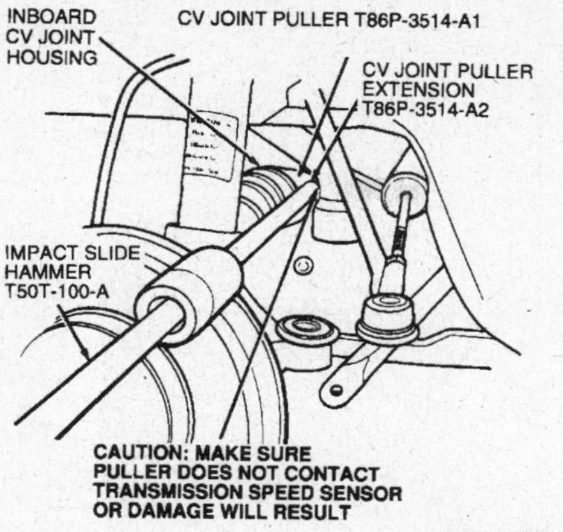

Fig. 5 Inner CV joint removal

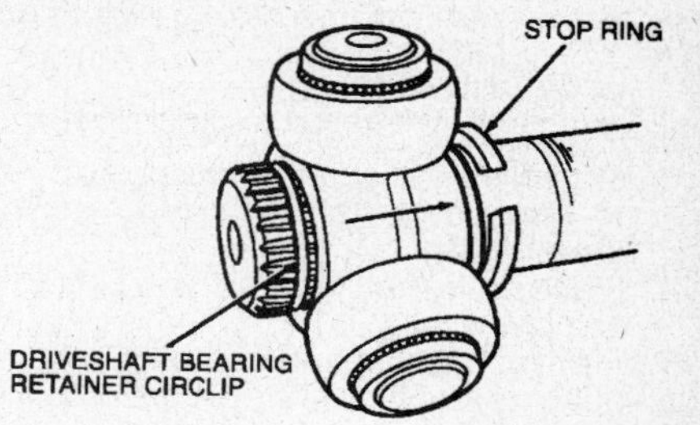

Fig. 6 Tripod removal

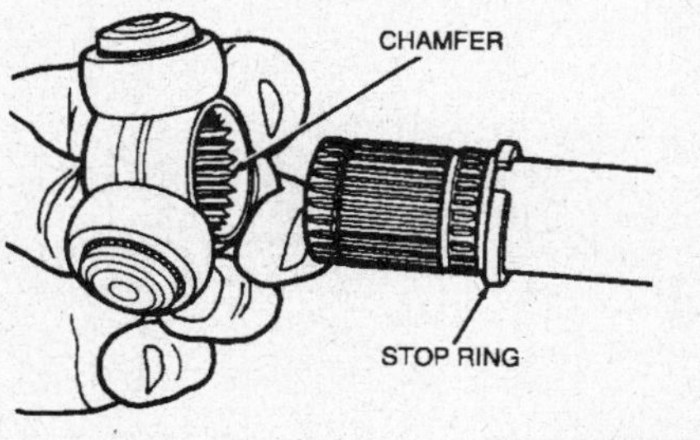

Fig. 7 Tripod installation

must be used.

d. Use care when installing intermediate driveshaft into transaxle not to damage seal.
e. Ensure proper engagement of intermediate driveshaft spline into transaxle side gears and that bearing retainer circlip is properly seated.

DRIVESHAFT SERVICE

INNER JOINT & BOOT

Removal

1. Remove both clamps from inner joint boot.
2. Pull inner joint outer housing out of boot and off tripod assembly.
3. Use suitable snap ring pliers to remove stop ring from groove, **Fig. 6,** then slide ring inward on shaft.
4. Slide tripod assembly inward on shaft splines to expose driveshaft bearing retainer circlip.
5. Remove and discard driveshaft bearing retainer circlip, then remove tripod assembly from shaft.
6. Remove stop ring, then inner joint boot from shaft.

Inspection

1. Clean and dry all components.
2. Inspect boot for cracks, splits and abrasion.
3. Inspect joint components for wear, cracks and broken parts.
4. Inspect shaft for worn splines and bending.

Installation

1. Place small boot clamp on shaft, then slide boot onto shaft and into position groove on shaft.
2. Place small clamp into position on boot, then using suitable boot clamp ring pliers, tighten clamp ring securely. **Use caution not to overtighten clamp ring and cut or deform boot.**
3. Place stop ring onto shaft, slide stop ring past stop ring groove to allow room for installation of tripod assembly and driveshaft bearing retainer circlip.
4. Slide tripod assembly onto shaft splines, ensure chamfered side of tripod assembly is toward stop ring, **Fig. 7.**
5. Place a new driveshaft bearing retainer circlip onto shaft. **Use caution not to stretch or deform circlip during installation.**
6. Pull tripod assembly into position over driveshaft bearing retainer circlip. It may be necessary to compress driveshaft bearing retainer circlip to allow tripod assembly to move into position.
7. Place stop ring into place using suitable snap ring pliers.
8. Place trilobe boot insert into place on joint outer housing, **Fig. 8,** then fill housing and boot with suitable quantity and type CV joint grease.
9. Place joint outer housing onto tripod assembly, then position boot onto trilobe insert.
10. Ensure boot is in a relaxed position (not stretched, compressed or dimpled). If necessary, pry up edge of boot using a blunt flat tool and allow air pressure to equalize. This ensures proper joint outer housing positioning over tripod assembly.
11. Clean any excess grease from outside of joint and boot.
12. Place large clamp into position on boot, then using suitable boot clamp ring pliers, tighten clamp ring securely. **Do not overtighten clamp ring or cut or deform boot.**
13. **On lefthand axle,** place a new driveshaft bearing retainer circlip onto joint housing. **Use caution not to stretch or deform circlip during installation.**
14. **On all axles,** ensure joint moves freely with no binding or excessive looseness.

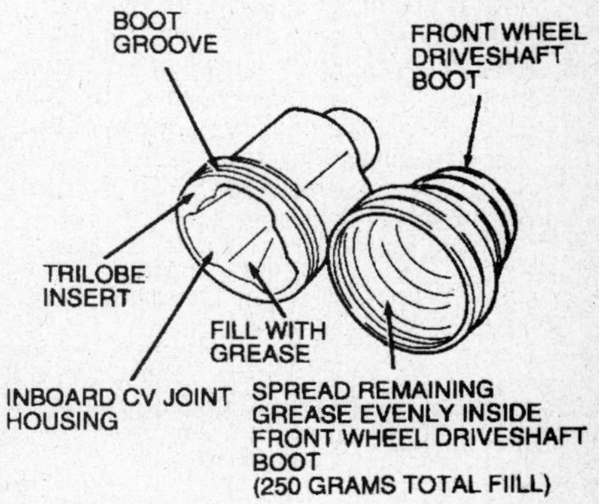

Fig. 8 Trilobe insert installation

OUTER JOINT & BOOT

Outer CV joint is composed of matched components. Interchanging components is not recommended.

Removal

1. Place driveshaft assembly into a suitable soft jaw vice.
2. Remove both clamps from inner joint boot.
3. Pull large end of boot back and off joint assembly.
4. Support driveshaft assembly in soft jaw vice as shown in **Fig. 9,** then tap on inner race of joint using a suitable drift punch to release driveshaft bearing retainer circlip.
5. Slide joint assembly off shaft splines to expose driveshaft bearing retainer circlip.
6. Remove and discard driveshaft bearing retainer circlip.
7. Remove joint boot from shaft.

Inspection

1. Clean and dry all components.
2. Inspect boot for cracks, splits and abrasion.
3. Inspect joint components for wear, cracks and broken parts.
4. Inspect shaft for worn splines and deformities.

Installation

1. Place small boot clamp on shaft, then slide boot onto shaft and into position groove on shaft.
2. Place small clamp into position on boot, then using suitable boot clamp ring pliers, tighten clamp ring securely.

Do not overtighten clamp ring or cut or deform boot.

3. Place a new driveshaft bearing retainer circlip onto shaft. **Use caution not to stretch or deform circlip during installation.**
4. Place driveshaft in a vertical position in soft jaw vice.
5. Fill joint housing and boot with suitable quantity and type CV joint grease.
6. Place joint on driveshaft, aligning splines, then tap joint onto shaft using a soft face hammer, until driveshaft bearing retainer circlip engages joint.
7. Position boot onto outer joint.
8. Ensure boot is in a relaxed position (not stretched, compressed or dimpled). If necessary, pry up edge of boot using a blunt flat tool and allow air pressure to equalize. This ensures proper joint positioning.

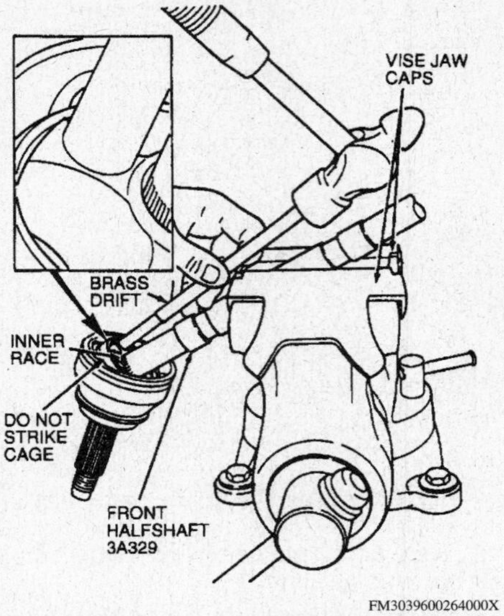

Fig. 9 Outer CV joint removal from driveshaft

9. Clean any excess grease from outside of joint and boot.
10. Place large clamp into position on boot, then using suitable boot clamp ring pliers, tighten clamp ring securely. **Do not overtighten clamp ring or cut or deform boot.**
11. Ensure joint moves freely with no binding or excessive looseness.

INTERMEDIATE DRIVESHAFT BEARING

Use suitable press and press tools to press intermediate driveshaft out of, then back into, bearing and dust shield.

TIGHTENING SPECIFICATIONS

Component	Torque/Ft. Lbs.
Ball Joint Pinch Bolt	54–67
Hub Nut	220
Intermediate Shaft Bracket Bolts	15–23
Intermediate Shaft Support Bracket Nuts	17–22
Stabilizer Bar Link Nut	14–23
Tie Rod End Nut	20
Wheel Lug Nut	62

Cougar

NOTE: On Air Bag Equipped Models, Refer To " Air Bag System Precautions" Located In The Front Of This Manual For System Disarming & Arming Procedures.

INDEX

PRECAUTIONS

AIR BAG SYSTEMS

Refer to "Air Bag System Precautions" in the front of this manual for system disarming and arming procedures.

BATTERY GROUND CABLE

Prior to service, disconnect battery ground cable and isolate as required.

DESCRIPTION

The front drive halfshafts transmit torque from the engine to the wheels. In order to allow vertical movement of the wheels and engine, the front drive halfshafts operate at varying lengths and angles. The tripod joints allow for changes in driveshaft length during axial movements.

To reduce running friction, the front drive halfshafts are fitted with constant velocity (CV) joints at both ends. Tripod joints (with tripod, running rollers and tripod housing) are fitted on the transaxle side. Fix joints (with ball star, ball cage and ball shell) are fitted on the wheel side. The lefthand tripod joint is secured in the differential with a snap ring. The intermediate shaft (right - hand side) is not secured in the differential, but is secured by the intermediate shaft bearing bracket. The tripod joint of the right-hand front drive halfshaft is secured in the intermediate shaft with a snap ring. The wheel - side constant velocity joints are attached to the wheel hubs.

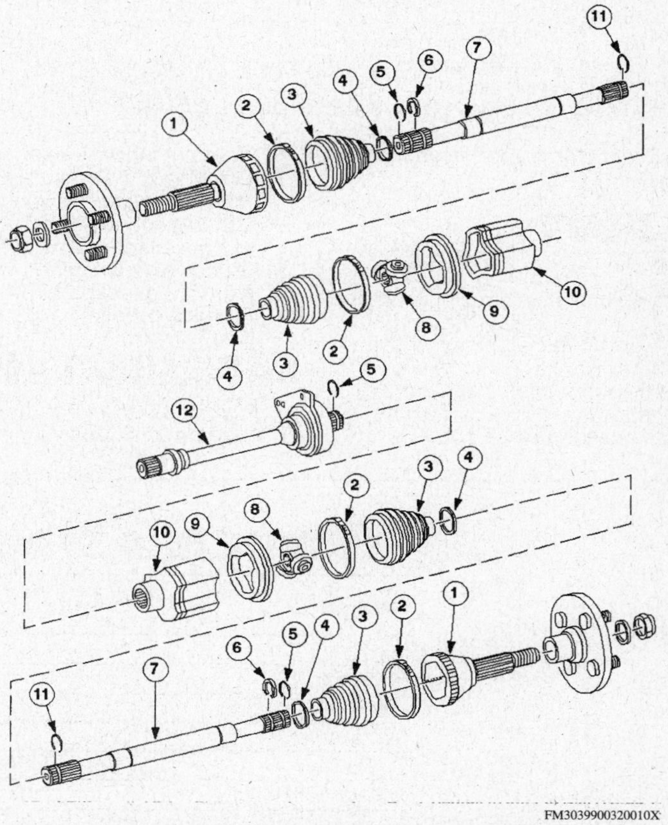

Fig. 1 Exploded view of driveshafts (Part 1 of 2)

TROUBLESHOOTING

CLICKING, POPPING OR GRINDING NOISES WHILE TURNING

1. Another component contacting half-shaft assembly.
2. Inadequate or contaminated lube in outboard/inboard front wheel halfshaft joint.
3. Inspect wheel bearings, brakes, suspension or steering components.

VIBRATION AT HIGHWAY SPEEDS

1. Out of balance front wheels or tires.
2. Out of round tires.
3. Incorrectly seated outboard front wheel halfshaft joint in front wheel hub.

SHUDDER VIBRATION DURING ACCELERATION

1. Excessively high CV joint operating angles caused by incorrect ride height.
2. Excessively worn or damaged inboard front wheel halfshaft joint or outboard front wheel halfshaft joint.

HALFSHAFT JOINT PULLOUT

1. Inboard halfshaft bearing retainer circlip missing or not correctly seated in differential side gear.
2. Engine/transaxle assembly misaligned.
3. Frame rail or strut tower out of position or damaged.

Item	Part Number	Description
1	-	Fix joint
2	-	Boot clamp (large)
3	-	Boot
4	-	Boot clamp (small)
5	-	Halfshaft joint snap ring
6	-	Snap ring
7	-	Front drive halfshaft
8	-	Tripod
9	-	Tripod housing insert
10	-	Tripod housing
11	-	Halfshaft joint snap ring
12	-	Intermediate shaft

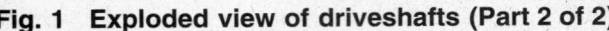

FM3039900320020X

Fig. 1 Exploded view of driveshafts (Part 2 of 2)

4. Front suspension components worn or damaged.

DRIVESHAFT

REPLACE

1. Loosen suspension strut locknut five turns.
2. Loosen driveshaft stub nut and front wheel nuts.
3. Raise and support vehicle.
4. Remove front wheel.
5. Remove driveshaft stub nut.
6. Remove fender splash shields.
7. Disconnect lower suspension arm ball joint from wheel knuckle.
8. Disconnect ABS wiring harness bracket from suspension strut.
9. Disconnect driveshaft from transaxle.
10. Remove driveshaft from vehicle.
11. Reverse procedure to install.

DRIVESHAFT SERVICE

1. Cut small and large boot clamps and discard them, **Fig. 1.**

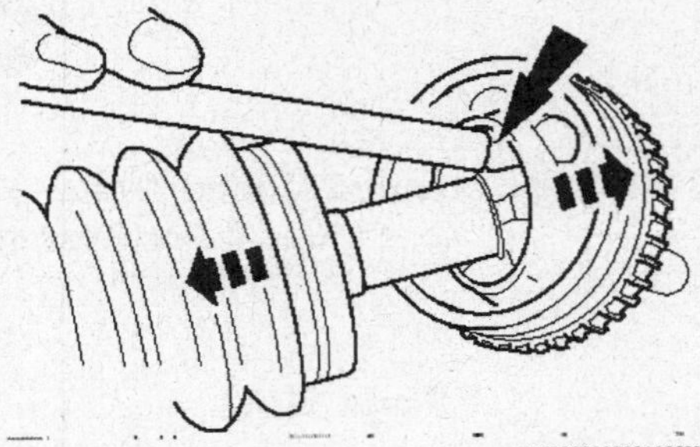

FM3039900321000X

Fig. 2 Driveshaft joint removal

2. Slide boot back, then pull out tripod joint.
3. Remove snap ring, then using suitable puller, pull off tripod assembly.
4. Loosen driveshaft joint at wheel end.
5. Cut boot clamps and remove.
6. Slide boot back.
7. Unseat driveshaft joint from snap ring seat using suitable brass drift, **Fig. 2.**
8. Remove driveshaft joint.
9. Remove snap ring.
10. Remove stop ring.
11. Pull off boot.
12. Reverse procedure to install noting the following:
    a. Install new snap rings and boot clamps when servicing joints.
    b. Pack tripod joint with 6 ounces of high temperature Constant velocity joint grease.

TIGHTENING SPECIFICATIONS

Component	Torque/Ft. Lbs.
Ball Joint	61
Driveshaft Nut	214
Hub Nut	214
Stabilizer Link	35
Tie Rod	19
Upper Strut Mount	34

Escort, Tracer & ZX2

NOTE: On Air Bag Equipped Models, Refer To " Air Bag System Precautions" Located In The Front Of This Manual For System Disarming & Arming Procedures.

INDEX

PRECAUTIONS

AIR BAG SYSTEMS

Refer to "Air Bag System Precautions" in the front of this manual for system disarming and arming procedures.

BATTERY GROUND CABLE

Prior to service, disconnect battery ground cable and isolate as required.

TROUBLESHOOTING

NOISE & VIBRATION ON TURNS

Clicking, popping or grinding noises while turning may be caused by the following:

1. Cut or damaged CV joint boots, resulting in contaminated lube in outboard or inboard joints.
2. Loose joint clamps.
3. Worn, damaged or improperly installed wheel bearings.
4. Halfshaft assembly connecting component.

VIBRATION AT HIGHWAY SPEEDS

1. Front wheels or tires out of balance.
2. Front tires out of round.

SHUDDER OR VIBRATION ON ACCELERATION

1. Excessively worn or damaged inboard or outboard CV joint.
2. Excessively high CV joint operating angles caused by improper ride height.

HALFSHAFT OR CV JOINT PULL-OUT

Engine Or Transaxle Misaligned

1. Inspect engine mounts for damage.

Front Suspension Components Worn Or Damaged

1. Inspect for worn bushings or bent front suspension components.

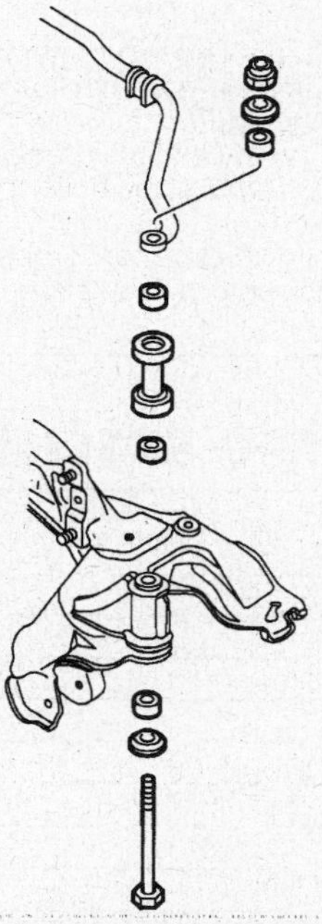

FM3039800319000X

Fig. 1 Stabilizer bar removal

Improperly Installed Or Missing Retainers

1. Inspect for CV joint circlip missing or not properly seated in transaxle side gear.

DRIVESHAFT

REPLACE

1. Raise and support vehicle.
2. Remove front tire and wheel.
3. Raise staked portion of front axle wheel hub retainer.
4. Remove and discard front axle wheel hub retainer.
5. Remove cotter pin and tie rod end nut.
6. Using suitable tie rod end remover, separate tie rod end from front wheel knuckle.
7. Remove stabilizer bar as follows:
   a. Remove front stabilizer bar end nut, **Fig. 1.**
   b. Remove front stabilizer bar end bolt.
   c. Remove upper front stabilizer bar end retainer.
   d. Remove front stabilizer bar end bushing above front stabilizer bar.
   e. Remove front stabilizer bar end bushing below front stabilizer bar.
   f. Remove front stabilizer bar end bushing.
   g. Remove front stabilizer bar end bushing above front sub-frame.
   h. Remove front stabilizer bar end bushing below front sub-frame.
   i. Remove lower front stabilizer bar end retainer.
8. Remove ball joint nut and pinch bolt.
9. Separate front suspension lower arm ball joint from steering knuckle.
10. Pull driveshaft and joint from steering knuckle.
11. Insert pry bar between front wheel driveshaft and joint and transaxle case and pry outward, releasing front wheel driveshaft and joint from differential side gears.
12. **On ZX2 models with manual transaxles,** proceed as follows:
    a. Remove bolts from center support bearing.
    b. Lower driveshaft assembly and remove halfshaft from differential side gears.
    c. Separate driveshaft and joint from center support bearing and halfshaft.
13. **On all models,** reverse procedure to install.

DRIVESHAFT SERVICE

CV JOINT

Disassemble

1. Secure driveshaft in soft-jawed vise.
2. Use a punch to remove ABS sensor ring from joint housing, then discard sensor.
3. Remove boot clamps, then slide boot back to expose joint.
4. Mark joint to shaft for reference to ensure proper installation, then use soft-face hammer to separate outboard joint by gently tapping it from shaft.

Transaxle	Model	Location	Length, Inches
Automatic	Except ZX2	Lefthand	24.96
		Righthand	35.93
Manual	Except ZX2	Lefthand	24.87
		Righthand	36.59
Automatic	ZX2	Lefthand	24.47
		Righthand	36.59
Manual	ZX2	Lefthand	24.49
		Righthand	24.49

Fig. 2 Halfshaft specifications

5. Remove and discard bearing retainer circlip.
6. Remove snap ring from outboard side of shaft.
7. Wrap outboard shaft splines with suitable tape before sliding boot from shaft.

Assemble

1. Clean and inspect outboard bearings and cage for grit in grease or any signs of cracking or pitting. Replace if needed.
2. Lubricate outboard joint bearings with Ford CV Joint Grease part No. E43Z-19590-A, or equivalent, meeting Ford specification ESP-M1C207-A.
3. Wrap outboard shaft splines with suitable tape to protect joint boot from damage, then install boot on shaft.
4. Install snap ring on outboard side of shaft.
5. Install a new bearing retainer circlip.
6. Use soft-face hammer to gently install joint onto shaft.
7. Remove any excess grease on mating surfaces and slide boot forward onto joint.
8. Refer to **Fig. 2** for proper halfshaft lengths before adjusting boots and clamps.
9. After adjusting boot spacing, remove any excess air trapped in boot with a dull screwdriver.
10. Install new boot clamps with pliers tool No. D87P-1098-A, or equivalent.
11. Use replacer tool No. T94P-20202-B, or equivalent, to install a new ABS sensor indicator.

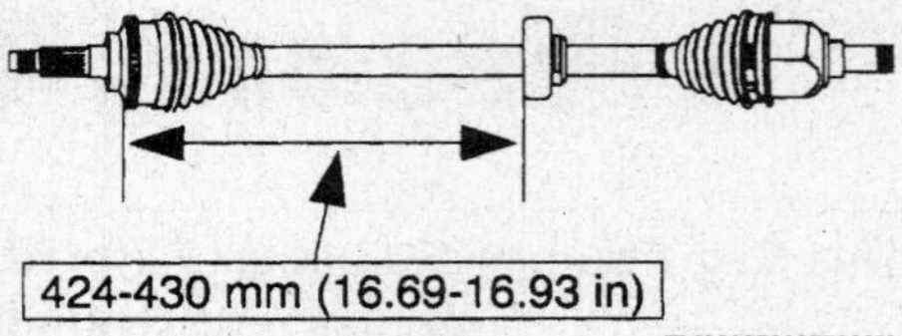

Fig. 3 Righthand damper installation

DYNAMIC DAMPER BEARING

1. Remove outboard driveshaft joint.
2. Remove and discard damper retaining clamp, then remove damper.
3. Install damper as shown, **Fig. 3. Use new retainer to hold band in place.**
4. Install driveshaft.

TIGHTENING SPECIFICATIONS

Component	Torque/Ft. Lbs.
Ball Joint Pinch Bolt	32–43
Crossmember	69–93
Dynamic Damper Bearing	31–46
Hub Nut	174–235
Tie Rod End Nut (1997)	25-33
Tie Rod End Nut (1998-2000)	32-41
Wheel Lug Nut (1997)	65-87
Wheel Lug Nut (1998-2000)	74-100

Probe

NOTE: On Air Bag Equipped Models, Refer To " Air Bag System Precautions" Located In The Front Of This Manual For System Disarming & Arming Procedures.

INDEX

PRECAUTIONS

AIR BAG SYSTEMS

Refer to "Air Bag System Precautions" in the front of this manual for system disarming and arming procedures.

BATTERY GROUND CABLE

Prior to service, disconnect battery ground cable and isolate as required.

DESCRIPTION

The front wheel driveshaft and joints mechanically link engine torque from the transaxle to the front wheels. At the transaxle end, the front wheel driveshaft joint is splined to the differential side gears. Disengagement of the tripod type front wheel driveshaft joint from the differential side gear is prevented by an expanding spring steel driveshaft bearing retainer circlip.

The wheel ends of the righthand and lefthand front driveshaft and joints are splined to the wheel hubs which are supported on opposed tapered front wheel bearing inner and outer cone and rollers. Disengagement of the driveshaft and joint from the wheel hub is prevented by the front axle wheel hub washer and retainer.

Backlash between the wheel hubs and driveshaft joint is eliminated by the splines. The front wheel hub splines are machined straight while the driveshaft joint splines are machined with a slight helical cut. The difference in splines provides a tight, backlash-free coupling without the replacement problems associated with an interference fit.

All outboard joints are the Birfield type. On models equipped with automatic transaxles are equipped with tripod inboard joints, while double offset type joints are found on those with manual transaxles. A front axle bearing is installed between the righthand driveshaft and the halfshaft to help prevent engine vibration to the body and reduce torque steer.

The tripod and double offset joints can be disassembled and serviced. Other than the driveshaft boot, the outboard Birfield type shaft and joint is serviced only as an assembly with the shaft and joint.

Condition	Possible Source
• Front Wheel Driveshaft and Joint Vibrates or Does Not Move	• Damaged ball joint. • Worn or seized joint.
• Abnormal Noise	• Insufficient grease in joint or spline. • Bent front wheel driveshaft and joint. • Worn or damaged front wheel bearing. • Worn or damaged front wheel driveshaft and joint.
• Steering Wheel Pulls or One-sided Braking	• Worn or damaged front wheel bearing. • Excessive front wheel bearing play. • Improper tire air pressure. • Unevenly worn tires. • Brakes dragging. • Incorrect front wheel bearing preload adjustment. • Incorrect toe-in adjustment. • Bent steering linkage. • Fatigued front coil spring. • Front suspension lower arm mounting bolt bushing worn or damaged. • Bent front suspension lower arm.
• Unstable Handling	• Improper tire air pressure. • Wheels bent or unbalanced. • Incorrect front wheel bearing preload. • Incorrect toe-in adjustment. • Bent steering linkage. • Worn or damaged joint in steering system. • Incorrect rack yoke preload adjustment. • Fatigued front coil spring. • Worn front shock absorber. • Front suspension lower arm mounting bolt bushings worn or damaged.
• Excessive Steering Wheel Play	• Worn front wheel bearing. • Worn or damaged joint in steering system. • Incorrect rack yoke preload adjustment. • Steering gear worn. • Front suspension lower arm mounting bolt bushings worn or damaged.
• Tires are Excessively Worn or Worn Unevenly	• Improper tire air pressure. • Unbalanced wheels. • Incorrect toe-in adjustment. • Incorrect front wheel bearing preload adjustment (excessively loose).

FM3039500304010X

Fig. 1 Troubleshooting chart (Part 1 of 2)

Condition	Possible Source
• Grease Leakage From Front Wheel Driveshaft Joint Boot	• Damaged front wheel driveshaft joint boot. • Damaged front wheel driveshaft joint boot clamp. • Excessive grease.
• Noise and Vibration in Turns	• Inadequate or contaminated lube in front wheel driveshaft joint. • Loose front wheel driveshaft joint boot clamps. • Another component contacting front wheel driveshaft and joint. • Worn, damaged or improper preloaded front wheel bearing.
• Vibration at Highway Speeds	• Front wheels or tires unbalanced. • Tires out of round.
• Shudder or Vibration During Acceleration	• Worn or damaged inboard or outboard front wheel driveshaft joint. • Excessively high front wheel driveshaft joint operating angles caused by improper ride height.
• Front Wheel Driveshaft and Joint Pullout	• Engine / transaxle assembly misaligned. • Frame rail or strut tower out of position or damaged. • Front suspension components (bushings, front suspension lower arm, etc.) worn or damaged. • Inboard driveshaft bearing retainer circlip improperly seated in transaxle.

FM3039500304020X

Fig. 1 Troubleshooting chart (Part 2 of 2)

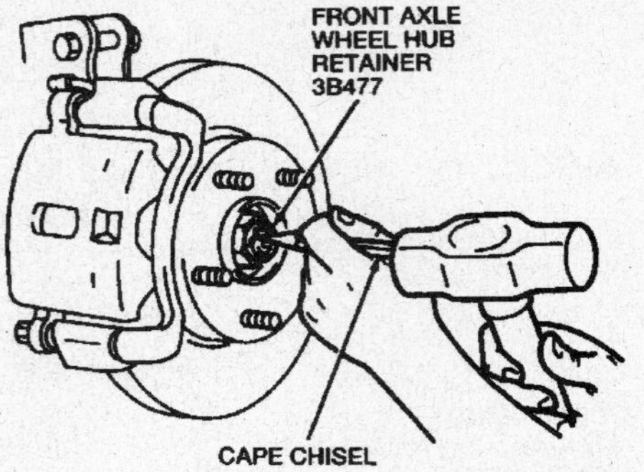

FM3039500305000X

Fig. 2 Axle nut unstaking

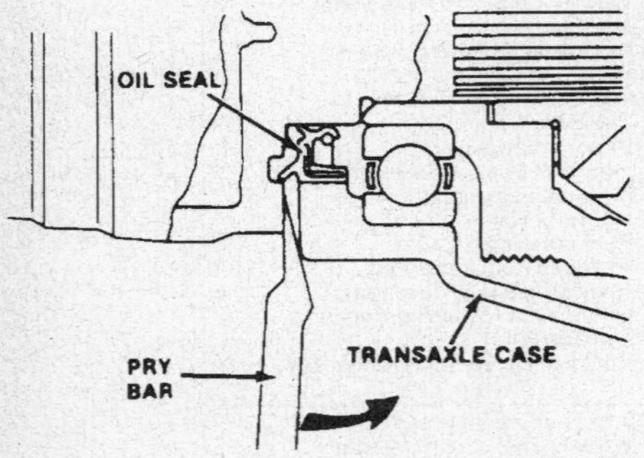

FM3039100183000X

Fig. 3 Pry bar insertion for driveshaft separation

TROUBLESHOOTING

Refer to **Fig. 1** for troubleshooting chart.

DRIVESHAFT

REPLACE

When removing driveshafts, install differential plugs tool No. T87C-7025-AH, or equivalent. Failure to do so may result in fluid leakage and dislocation of differential side gears, necessitating transaxle disassembly to align the gears again. Should the gears become misaligned, the differential will have to be removed from the transaxle for alignment.

Do not begin this procedure unless a new hub retainer and a new inboard driveshaft bearing retainer circlip are available. Once removed, these components must not be reused during assembly/installation. Their torque holding ability or retention capability is diminished during removal.

REMOVAL

1. Raise and support front of vehicle, then remove wheel and tire assembly.
2. Using a chisel, raise staked portion of axle nut, then with brakes applied, loosen but do not remove nut, **Fig. 2.**
3. Remove and discard front axle wheel hub retainer.
4. Remove stabilizer bar link from front suspension lower arm to ease separation of ball joint from ball joint clamp.
5. Pry ball joint from front wheel knuckle. **Never strike front wheel driveshaft and joint with any object.**
6. Separate front wheel driveshaft and joint from wheel hub, if front wheel driveshaft and joint splines bind use 2 jaw puller tool No. D80L-1002–L or equivalent.
7. Hold front wheel knuckle and brake assembly outward to separate the assemblies.
8. Pivot front wheel driveshaft and joint rearward to ease front wheel driveshaft and joint removal.
9. Remove lefthand driveshaft and joint by using an angled prybar or a suitable tool between front wheel driveshaft joint outer race and transaxle case. Carefully tap prybar end only enough to unseat driveshaft bearing retainer circlip on differential end of lefthand driveshaft and joint, **Fig. 3.**
10. No driveshaft bearing retainer circlip is used on transaxle end of the righthand halfshaft. Remove three front axle bearing bracket bolts.
11. Separate righthand driveshaft and joint from differential by carefully prying halfshaft from transaxle.
12. Support and slide righthand driveshaft and joint out of transaxle.
13. Remove both front wheel driveshaft and joints from vehicle and position them on a flat and protected work area.
14. Install transaxle plugs T88C-7025–AH into differential side gears.

2.0L Models

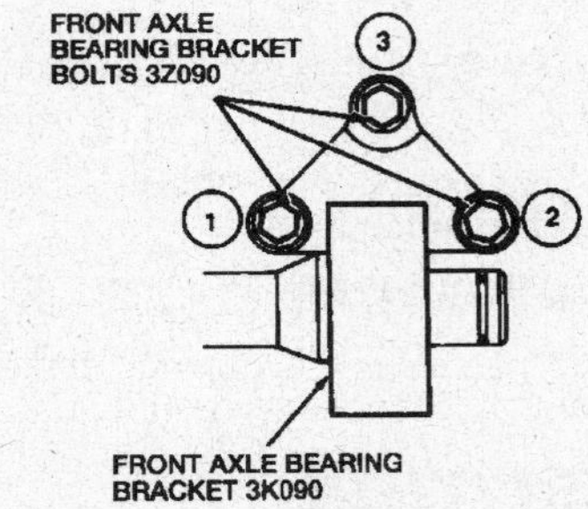

2.5L Models

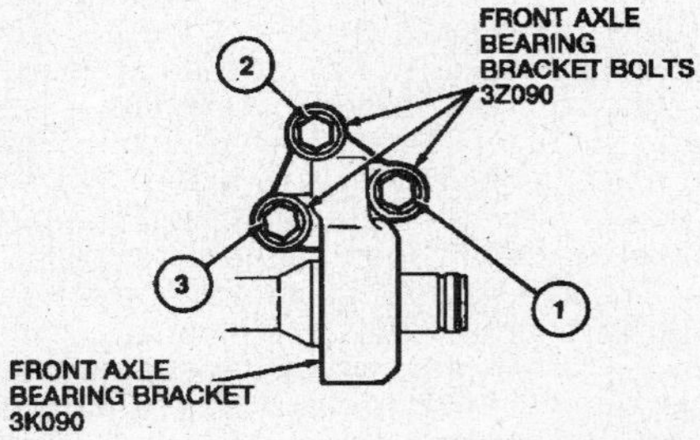

FM3039500306000X

Fig. 4 Axle bearing bracket bolt tighten sequence

INSTALLATION

1. Install new driveshaft bearing retainer circlip on lefthand driveshaft and joint only.
2. Inspect driveshaft joint boots and ensure correct type and amount of driveshaft joint lubricant is used on driveshaft joints.
3. Remove transaxle plugs, then inspect differential oil seals if they show any sign of wear or damage replace them.
4. Ensure driveshaft bearing retainer circlip gap is positioned at top of lefthand driveshaft and joint splines and lubricate splines with proper lubricant.
5. Carefully align driveshaft and joint splines with differential side gear splines and push driveshaft and joint into differential. Locking of driveshaft

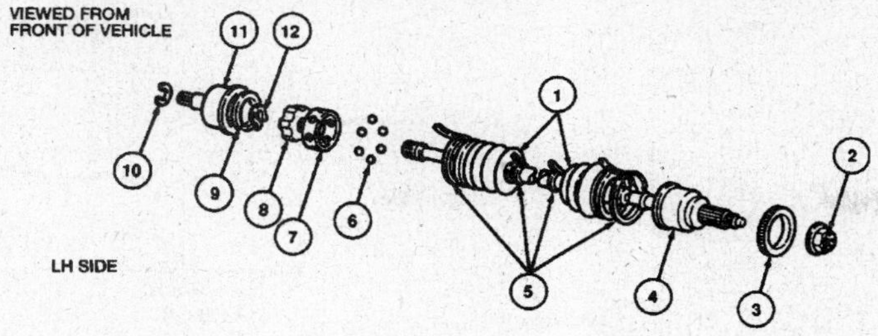

Item	Description
1	Front Wheel Driveshaft Joint Boots
2	Front Axle Wheel Hub Retainer
3	Front Brake Anti-Lock Sensor Indicator
4	Birfield-Type Front Wheel Driveshaft Joint
5	Front Wheel Driveshaft Joint Boot Clamps
6	Ball Bearing

Item	Description
7	Bearing Cage
8	Inner Race
9	Wire Ring Bearing Retainer
10	Driveshaft Bearing Retainer Circlip
11	Outer Race
12	Snap Ring
A	Tighten to 235-319 N-m (174-235 Lb-Ft)

FM3039500307000X

Fig. 5 Exploded view of halfshaft. Manual transaxle

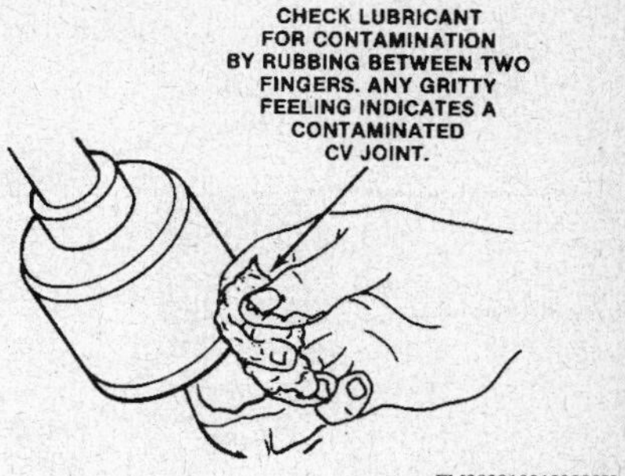

FM3039100189000X

Fig. 6 CV joint lubricant contamination inspection

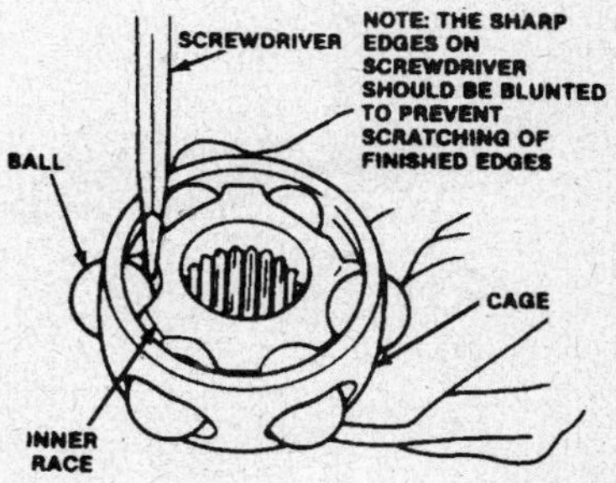

FM3039100192000X

Fig. 9 Ball bearing removal from cage

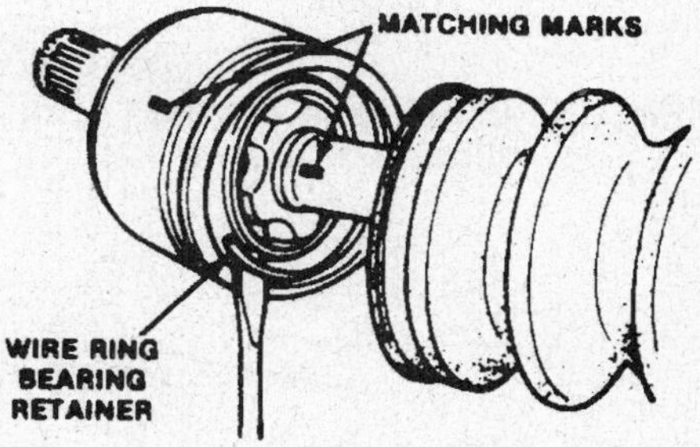

FM3039100190000X

Fig. 7 Bearing retaining ring removal

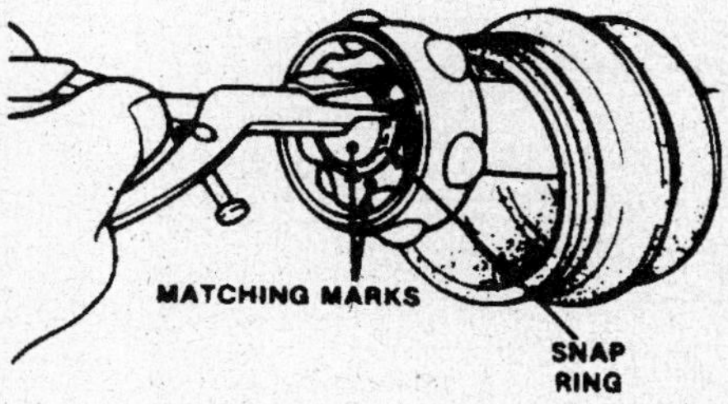

FM3039100191000X

Fig. 8 Inner bearing race snap ring removal

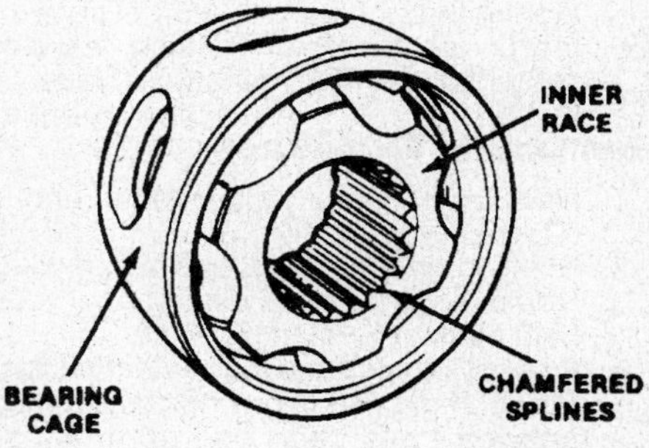

FM3039100193000X

Fig. 10 Inner bearing race to cage positioning

bearing retainer circlip into lefthand differential side gear groove can be felt which indicates that lefthand driveshaft is fully installed.

6. Position driveshaft and joint through wheel hub and install new front axle hub retainer. Do not tighten axle hub retainer at this time.
7. On righthand side position front axle bearing bracket and install three front axle bearing bracket bolts. **Torque** three axle bearing bracket bolt to 31–46 ft. lbs. in sequence, **Fig. 4.**
8. Position ball joint to knuckle and install ball joint clamp bolt.
9. Install stabilizer bar link to lower arm, then install front axle hub retainer.
10. Stake hub retainer nut with chisel.
11. Check transaxle fluid level and check for leaks.
12. Install wheel and tire assembly.
13. Lower vehicle.

DRIVESHAFT SERVICE

CONSTANT VELOCITY (CV) JOINTS

Manual Transaxle

1. Remove driveshaft as described under "Driveshaft, Replace."
2. Position driveshaft in a soft jawed vise.
3. Remove large boot clamp, then roll boot back over shaft, **Fig. 5.**
4. Inspect joint grease for contamination, **Fig. 6.** If grease is not contaminated and joint has been operating satisfactorily, add required amount of lubricant and install a replacement bolt. If grease is contaminated, CV boot must be disassembled and inspected.
5. Place alignment marks on bearing outer race and driveshaft, then remove bearing retaining ring, **Fig. 7.**
6. Remove outer race.
7. Place alignment marks on bearing inner race and driveshaft, then remove snap ring, **Fig. 8.**
8. Remove inner race, bearing cage and ball bearing assembly.
9. Using a screwdriver with sharp edges filed down, pry ball bearings from cage, **Fig. 9.**
10. Place alignment marks on bearing inner race and bearing cage.
11. Rotate bearing cage inner race to align bearing lands, then remove inner race through large end of cage.
12. If necessary, remove small clamp and boot from driveshaft. If boot is to be reused, wrap driveshaft splines with tape before removing.
13. Inspect all bearing components for wear and damage. Bearing components are matched during manufacturing process, therefore components from another CV should not be interchanged. If bearing is found to unsatisfactory, replace CV joint assembly.
14. Cover driveshaft spline with tape and install boot, if removed.
15. Lubricate inner race, bearing cage and ball bearings with lubricant E43Z-19590-A, or equivalent.
16. Aligning mark made during disassembly, position inner race into bearing cage. Inner race chamfered splines should face large end of cage, **Fig. 10.**
17. Using hand pressure, press ball bearings into cage windows.
18. Aligning marks on inner race and driveshaft made during disassembly, position inner race, cage and ball bearing assembly onto driveshaft, then insert snap ring into driveshaft groove. When install bearing assembly on driveshaft, chamfered end of cage should face snap ring, **Fig. 11.**
19. Apply 1.4 to 2.1 ounces of lubricant E43Z-19590-A, or equivalent to outer

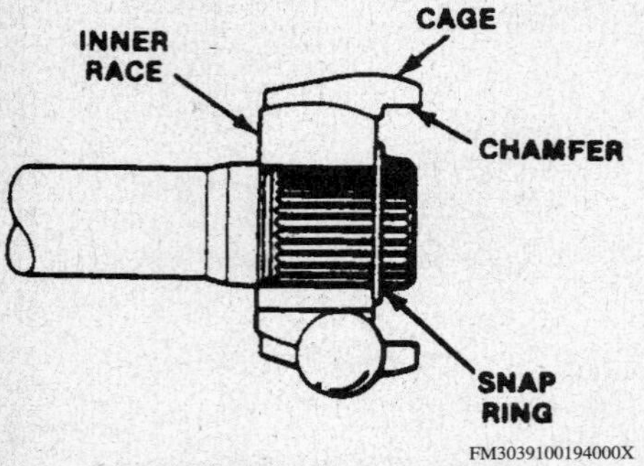

Fig. 11 Bearing cage to driveshaft positioning

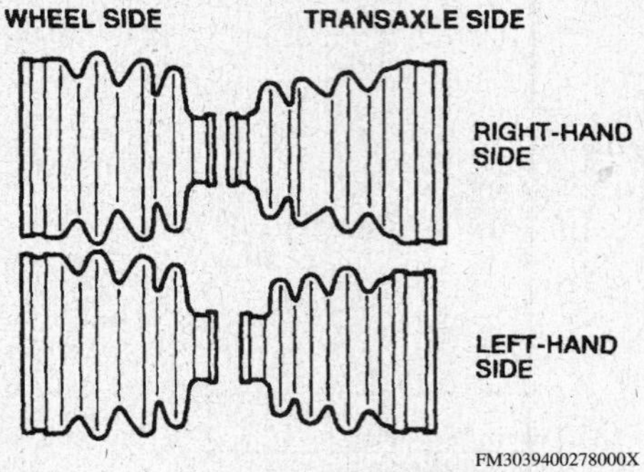

Fig. 12 Joint boot installation

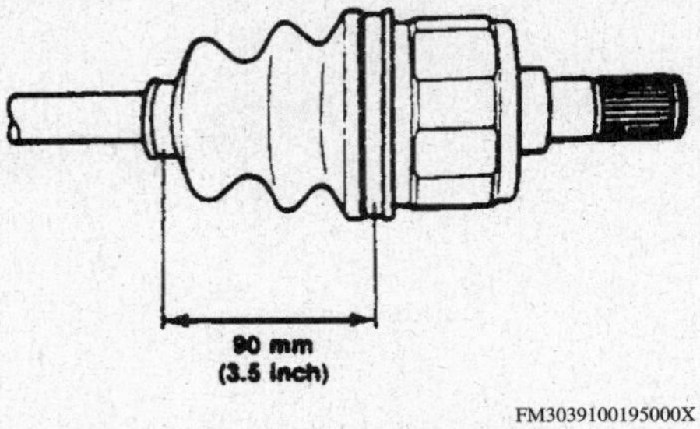

Fig. 13 CV joint positioning on driveshaft

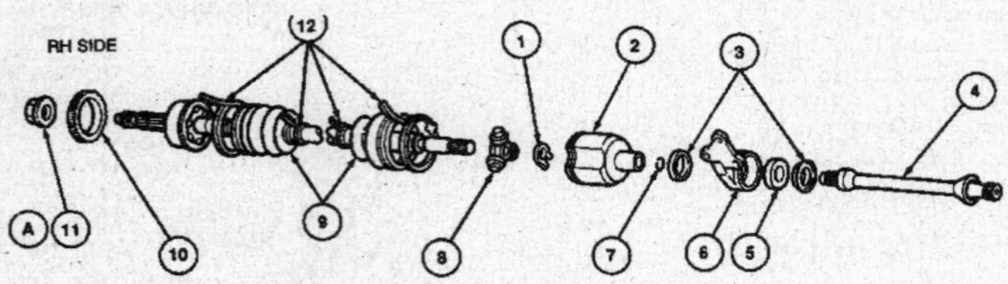

Item	Description
1	Snap Ring
2	Outer Race
3	Driveshaft Inner Dust Seals
4	Halfshaft
5	Front Axle Bearing
6	Front Axle Bearing Bracket
7	Driveshaft Bearing Retainer Circlip
8	Tripot Bearing

Item	Description
9	Front Wheel Driveshaft Joint Boots
10	Front Brake Anti-Lock Sensor Indicator (If Equipped)
11	Front Axle Wheel Hub Retainer
12	Front Wheel Driveshaft Joint Boot Clamps
A	Tighten to 235-319 N-m (174-236 Lb-Ft)

FM3039500308000X

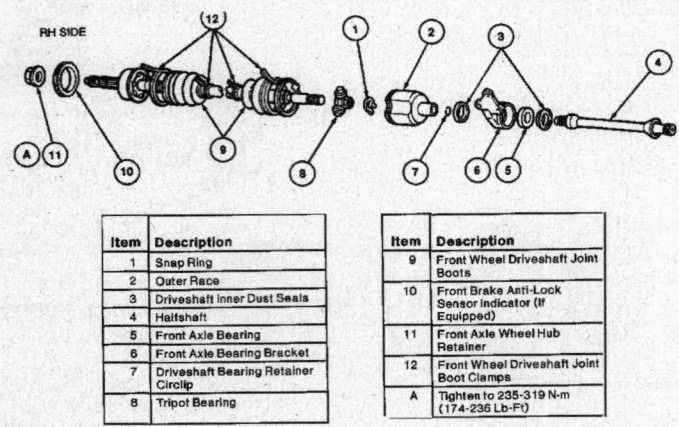

Fig. 14 Exploded view of halfshaft. Automatic transaxle

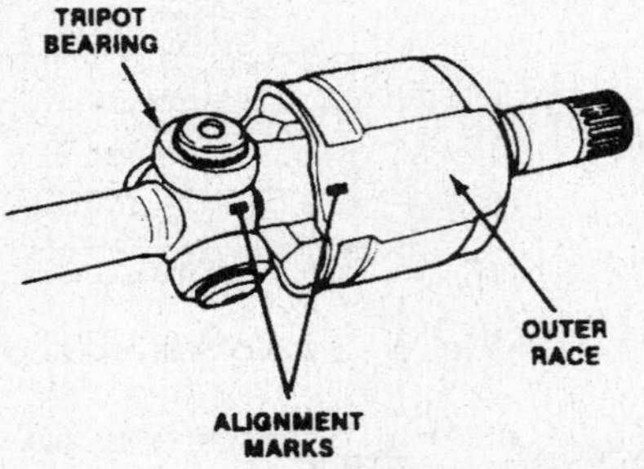

Fig. 15 Outer race & tripod joint alignment marks

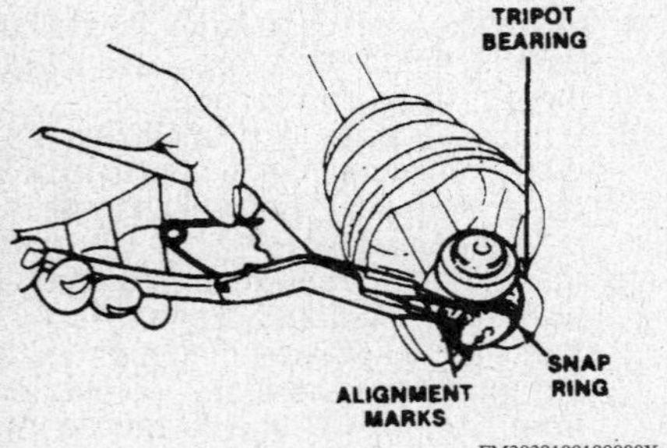

Fig. 16 Tripod joint snap ring removal

race, then install outer race over inner race, cage and ball bearing assembly.

20. Add approximately .7 to 1 ounce of lubricant specified in step 19 to outer race, then install outer race bearing retaining ring.
21. Ensure all boots are properly installed in their locations, **Fig. 12.**
22. Seat boot in grooves on driveshaft and outer race, then extend CV joint until distance between boot grooves is 3½ inches, **Fig. 13.** Keep joint at this distance until after boot clamps have been installed.
23. Using a screwdriver with sharp edges filed off, pry up on boot at outer race to allow trapped air to escape.
24. Install and lock boot clamps.
25. Inspect CV joint for smoothness of operation through its full range of travel.
26. Install driveshaft on vehicle as described under " Driveshaft, Replace."

Automatic Transaxle

1. Remove halfshaft as described under "Driveshaft, Replace."
2. Position halfshaft in a soft jawed vise.
3. Remove large boot clamp, then roll boot back over shaft, **Fig. 14.**
4. Inspect joint grease for contamination, **Fig. 6. If grease is not contaminated and joint has been operating satisfactorily, add required amount of lubricant and install a replacement boot. If grease is contaminated, CV joint must be disassembled and inspected.**
5. Remove bearing retaining ring.
6. Place alignment marks on outer race and tripod joint, then remove outer race, **Fig. 15.**
7. Place alignment mark on tripod bearing and halfshaft, then remove snap ring, **Fig. 16.**
8. Using a brass drift, carefully drive tripod joint from halfshaft, **Fig. 17.**
9. If necessary, remove boot small clamp, then wrap tape around halfshaft splines and remove boot.
10. Inspect tripod joint for wear and damage and replace as necessary.
11. If removed, wrap halfshaft splines with

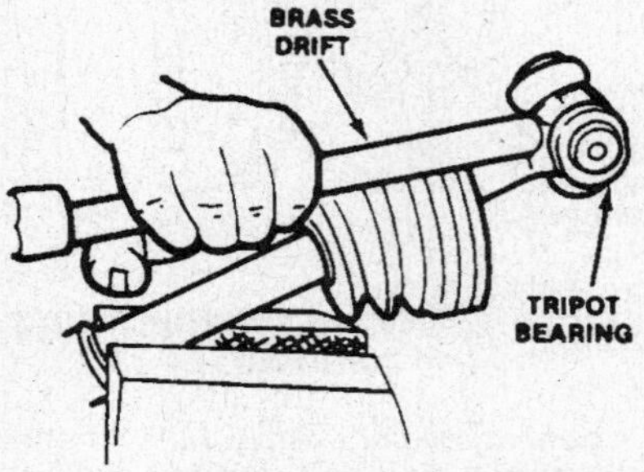

Fig. 17 Tripod joint removal from halfshaft

tape and install boot to halfshaft groove.

12. Align marks on halfshaft and tripod joint made during removal.
13. Using a brass drift, drive tripod joint into position on halfshaft, then install snap ring.
14. Fill outer race with 3.5 ounces of lubricant E43Z-19590-A, or equivalent, then position outer race over tripod joint, aligning marks made during removal.
15. Install bearing retaining ring, then position boot in groove on outer race.
16. Position joint so that distance between halfshaft boot groove and outer race groove is 3½ inches, **Fig. 13.**
17. Using a screwdriver with sharp edges filed off, pry up on boot at outer race end to allow trapped air to escape.
18. Install and lock boot clamps, then inspect joint for smoothness of operation through its full range of travel.
19. Install halfshaft on vehicle as described under " Driveshaft, Replace."

TIGHTENING SPECIFICATIONS

Component	Torque/Ft. Lbs.
Ball Joint Pinch Bolt	25–42
Bearing Support Bracket	31–46
Hub Nut	174–235
Stabilizer Bar Link Bolt	27–40
Wheel Lug Nut	65–87

Sable & Taurus

NOTE: On Air Bag Equipped Models, Refer To " Air Bag System Precautions" Located In The Front Of This Manual For System Disarming & Arming Procedures.

INDEX

PRECAUTIONS

AIR BAG SYSTEMS

Refer to "Air Bag System Precautions" in the front of this manual for system disarming and arming procedures.

BATTERY GROUND CABLE

Prior to service, disconnect battery ground cable and isolate as required.

TROUBLESHOOTING

NOISE & VIBRATION ON TURNS

Clicking, popping or grinding noises while turning may be caused by the following:

1. Cut or damaged CV joint boots, resulting in contaminated lube in outboard or inboard CV joints.
2. Loose CV joint clamps.
3. Worn, damaged or improperly installed wheel bearings.
4. Foreign object contacting driveshaft assembly.

VIBRATION AT HIGHWAY SPEEDS

1. Front wheels or tires out of balance.
2. Improperly seated outboard CV joint in front wheel hub.
3. Bent interconnecting shaft.
4. Front tires out of round.

SHUDDER OR VIBRATION ON ACCELERATION

1. Excessively worn or damaged inboard or outboard CV joint.

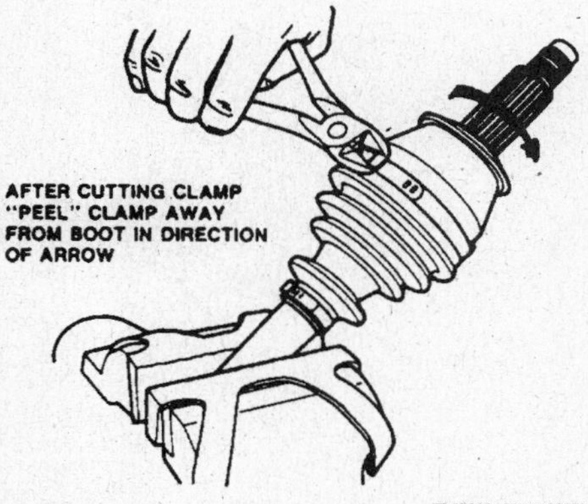

AFTER CUTTING CLAMP "PEEL" CLAMP AWAY FROM BOOT IN DIRECTION OF ARROW
FM3039100151000X

Fig. 1 Boot clamp removal

2. Excessively high CV joint operating angles caused by improper ride height.

DRIVESHAFT OR CV JOINT PULL-OUT

1. Inboard CV joint circlip missing or improperly seated in transaxle side gear.
2. Engine or transaxle improperly positioned. Inspect engine mounts.
3. Frame rail or strut tower improperly positioned or damaged.
4. Front suspension components worn or damaged.

DRIVESHAFT

REPLACE

1. Raise and support vehicle, then remove front wheels.
2. Remove and discard front axle retainer nut and washer.
3. **On SHO models,** remove wiring harness from routing clip on front shock absorber, then air suspension height sensor from height sensor ball studs.
4. **On all models,** remove nut from stabilizer bar link at shock absorber end, then remove link from shock and position aside.
5. Remove nut from lower ball joint, then using a suitable pitman arm type puller, loosen ball joint in lower control arm.
6. Place a suitable pry bar through opening in lower control arm and under frame, then pry down on control arm to release lower ball joint
7. Remove outer CV joint from hub noting the following:
   a. Do not use a hammer to drive joint from hub.
   b. Do not allow driveshaft to hang from inner joint.
8. Remove inner joint from transaxle.
9. Reverse procedure to install, noting the following:
   a. New front axle retainer nut must be used.
   b. New driveshaft bearing retainer circlip must be used.
   c. New ball joint nut must be used.
   d. Use care not to damage seal when installing driveshaft joints into transaxle.
   e. Ensure proper engagement of lefthand driveshaft inner joint spline into transaxle side gears and that bearing retainer circlip is properly seated.
   f. Ensure proper engagement of transaxle shaft spline into righthand inner CV joint and that bearing retainer circlip is properly seated.
   g. Check transaxle fluid, add if necessary.

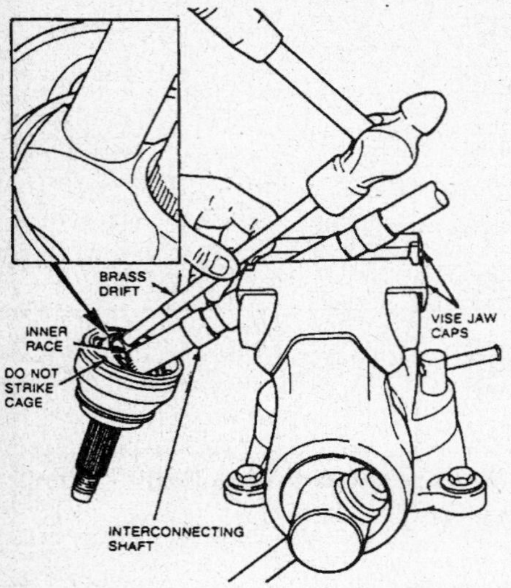

Fig. 2 Internal snap ring removal

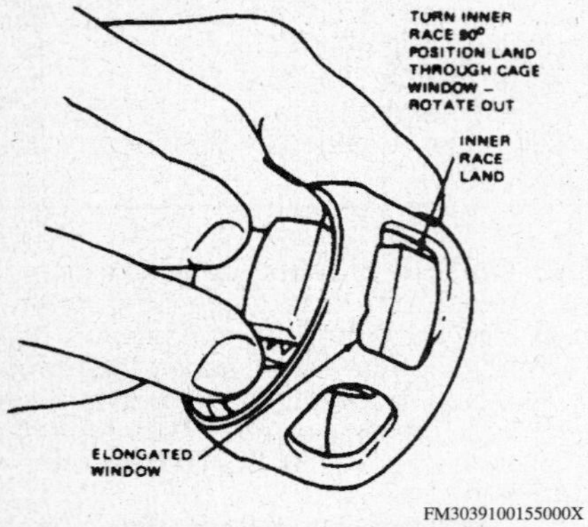

Fig. 5 Inner race replacement

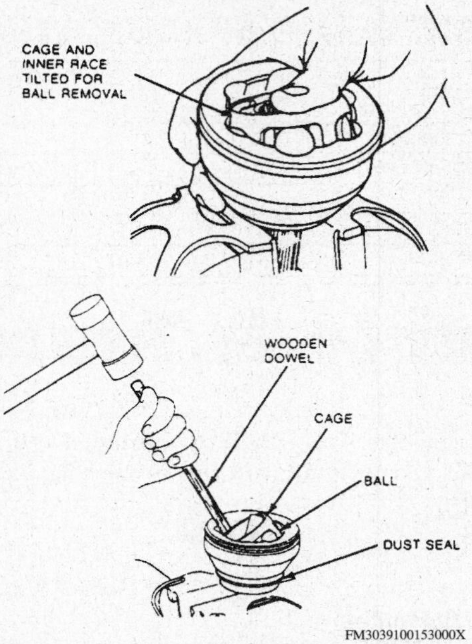

Fig. 3 CV joint ball removal

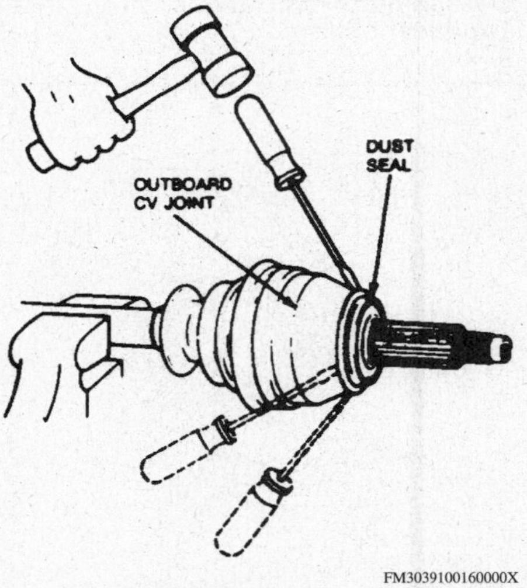

Fig. 7 Dust seal removal

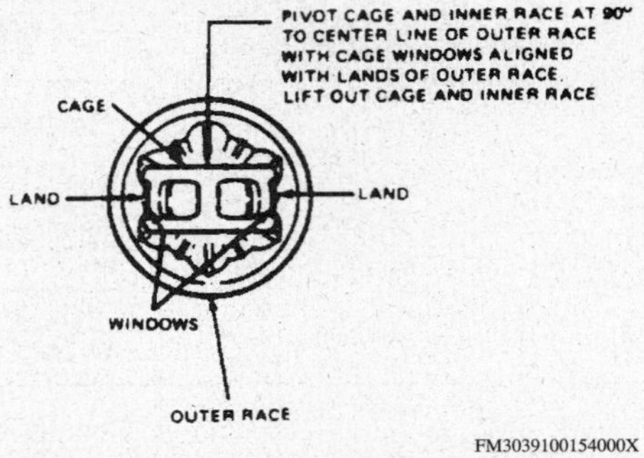

Fig. 4 Cage & inner race removal

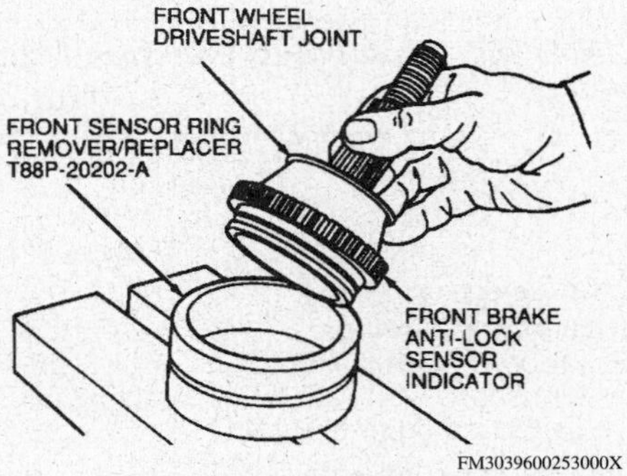

Fig. 6 Anti-Lock brake sensor wheel removal

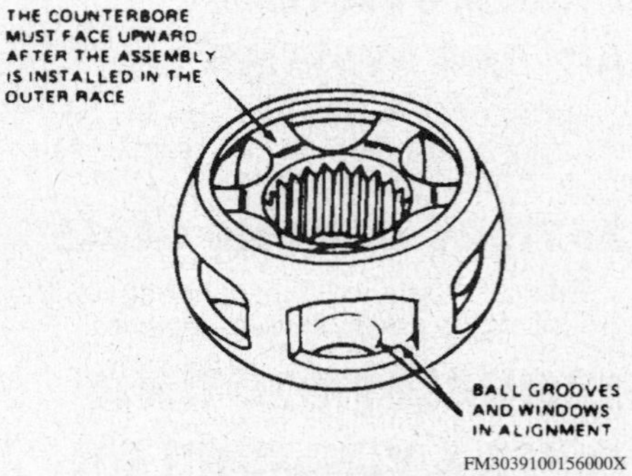

Fig. 8 Inner race & cage assembly

DRIVESHAFT SERVICE

OUTBOARD JOINT & BOOT

REMOVAL

CV Joint

During manufacturing, CV joint components are matched. Components cannot be interchanged with another joint's components. If a joint component is faulty, entire joint should be replaced.

1. Install soft vise jaw caps in vise to prevent damage to driveshaft, then position driveshaft in vise. Do not allow vise to contact CV joint boot or clamps.
2. Using side cutting pliers, cut large boot clamp and peel away from boot. Roll boot back over driveshaft, **Fig. 1.**
3. Turn driveshaft over in vise, then angle CV joint so that inner bearing race is exposed, **Fig. 2.** Using a brass drift and a hammer, give a sharp rap to inner bearing race to dislodge internal snap ring.
4. Separate CV joint from driveshaft.
5. Remove CV boot from shaft.
6. Inspect CV joint grease for contamination. If grease appears contaminated or has a gritty feeling, inspect for worn components and replace as necessary. If grease is not contaminated and joint was operating satisfactorily, add grease and replace boot.
7. Remove and discard circlip from end of shaft. Inspect stop ring located below circlip, if it is worn or damaged, replace it.
8. Clamp CV joint stub axle in vise with soft vise jaw caps. Be careful not to damage dust seal.
9. Push down on CV joint inner race until it tilts enough to allow ball removal, **Fig. 3. If inner race is tight, it can be tilted by tapping inner race with wooden dowel and hammer. Do not hit cage.**
10. Remove balls from cage. If balls are tight, use blunt screwdriver to pry balls from cage.
11. Pivot cage and inner race assembly until it is straight up, **Fig. 4.** Align cage windows with outer race lands while pivoting bearing cage, then lift out cage and inner race.
12. Rotate inner race up and out of cage, **Fig. 5.**

Anti-Lock Brake Sensor Wheel

1. Remove outer CV joint as outlined.
2. Place CV joint into removal tool No.T88P-20202-A, **Fig. 6,** or equivalent.
3. Using a suitable press, push CV joint out of sensor wheel.
4. Use caution not to damage sensor wheel teeth.

Dust Seal

With driveshaft removed, use a light duty hammer and screwdriver to tap evenly around seal until unseated and remove seal, **Fig. 7.**

INSPECTION

During manufacturing, CV joints components are matched. Components cannot be

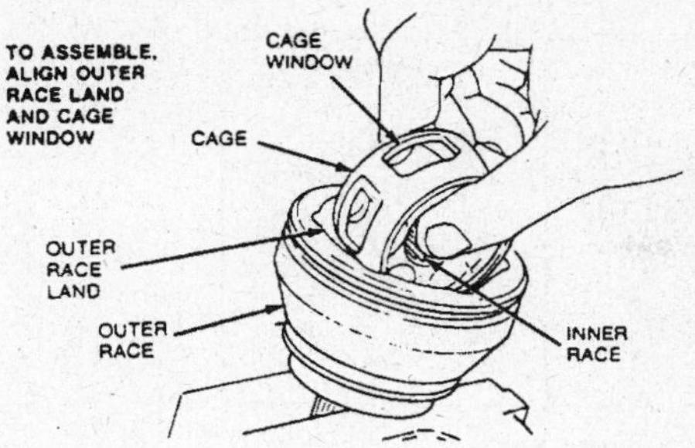

FM3039100157000X

Fig. 9 CV joint assembly installation into outer race

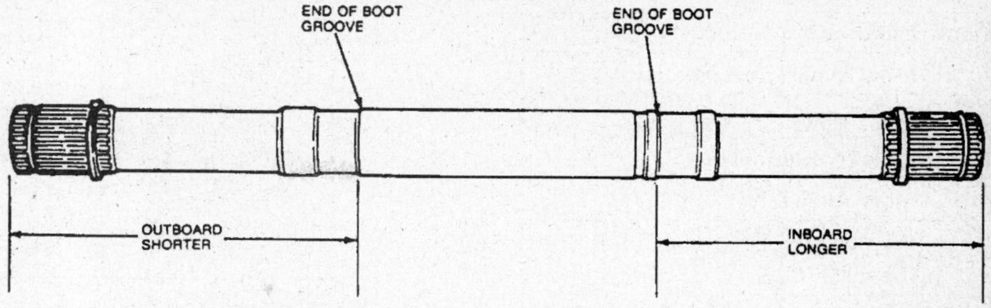

FM3039100158000X

Fig. 10 Driveshaft end identification

interchanged with another joint's components. If a component is faulty, entire joint should be replaced.

Inspect all parts. If any parts are cracked, broken, severely pitted, worn or otherwise unserviceable, replace CV joint. If any parts appear polished, do not replace joint as this is a normal condition.

If anti-lock brake sensor wheel's teeth are chipped or cracked, install a replacement sensor wheel.

INSTALLATION

CV Joint

1. Apply light coating of Ford CV joint grease No. E2FZ-19590-A or equivalent on inner and outer races, then install inner race in bearing cage, **Fig. 5.**
2. Install inner race and cage assembly in outer race, **Fig. 8.**
3. Install CV joint assembly into outer race and pivot 90° into position, **Fig. 9.**
4. Align bearing cage and inner race with outer race, then tilt inner race and install a ball, followed by remaining five balls.
5. Determine which end of driveshaft is for outboard CV joint. The outboard joint side has a shorter end of boot groove to end of shaft dimension, **Fig. 10.**
6. Install CV joint boot and small boot clamp. If stop ring was removed, install at this time. If stop ring was not removed, ensure it is seated properly in groove.
7. Install new circlip.
8. Pack CV joint with Ford CV joint grease No. E2FZ-19590-A, or equivalent. Spread any remaining grease evenly inside CV boot.
9. With boot peeled back, position CV joint on driveshaft and tap into position with a plastic hammer. Joint is properly seated when circlip locks into position. Inspect for proper retention by attempting to pull off joint.
10. Remove all excess grease from external surfaces, then position boot over joint. Ensure boot is seated in its groove, then install clamp.

Anti-Lock Brake Sensor Wheel

1. Position sensor wheel onto remover replacer tool No. T88P-20202-A, or equivalent.
2. Position CV joint into sensor wheel and tool.
3. Using a suitable press, push joint into sensor wheel until joint bottoms in tool.
4. Use caution not to damage sensor wheel teeth.

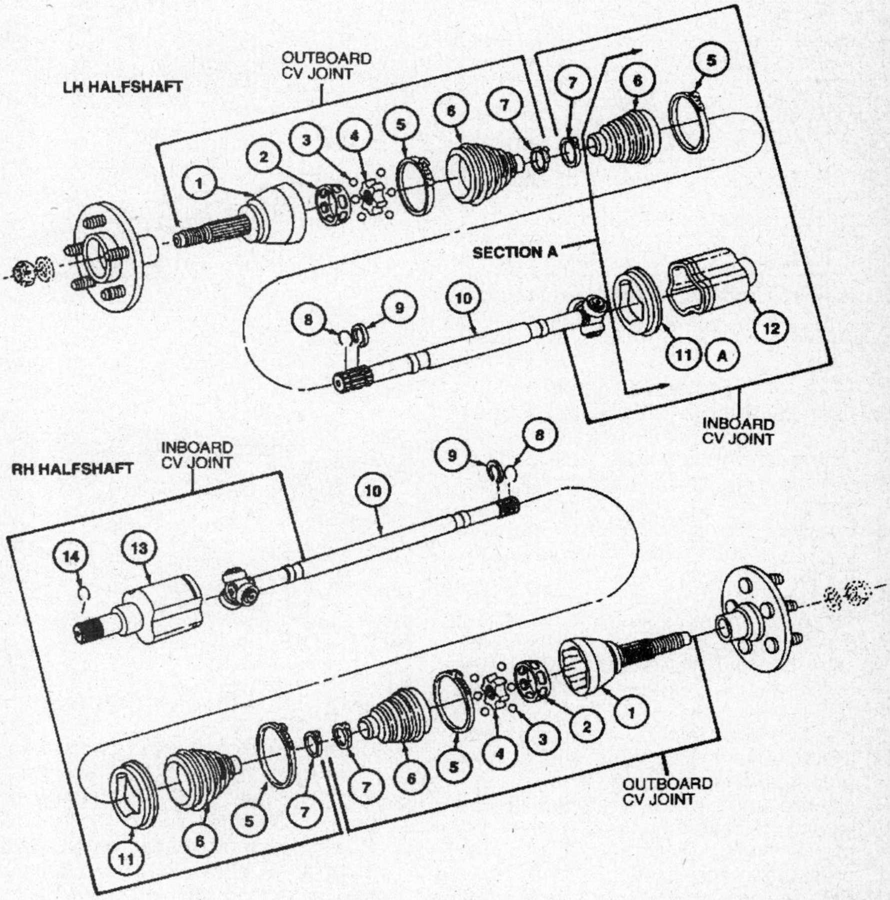

FM3039600254010X

Fig. 11 Exploded view of driveshaft assemblies (Part 1 of 2)

Dust Seal

Install dust seal using spindle/axle seal tool No. T83T-3132-A1, and dust seal installer tool No. T83P-3425-AH, or equivalents.

INBOARD JOINT & BOOT

REMOVAL

The tripod is a unit with driveshaft. If either tripod or driveshaft are damaged, entire assembly must be replaced, **Fig. 11.**

Three types of boots and CV joints, **Fig. 12,** are used on these models. These components are not interchangeable. Always use matching type when replacing components.

1. Remove large and small boot clamp as necessary, then remove inner joint outer housing.
2. If boot replacement is necessary, remove outer CV joint as outlined under "Outboard Joint & Boot," then remove outer joint stop ring.
3. Remove old boot by sliding off outboard end of driveshaft.

INSTALLATION

1. If boot replacement is required, slide

Item	Description
1	Front Wheel Driveshaft Joint
2	Ball Cage
3	Balls (6 required)
4	Inner Race
5	Front Wheel Driveshaft Joint Boot Clamp (Large)
6	Front Wheel Driveshaft Joint Boot
7	Front Wheel Driveshaft Joint Boot Clamp (Small)
8	Circlip
9	Stop Ring
10	Interconnecting Shaft
11	Tri-Lobe Insert
12	LH Inboard CV Joint Housing
13	RH Inboard CV Joint Housing
14	Circlip
A	Part Used Only With Ford Design Conventional Boot

FM3039600254020X

Fig. 11 Exploded view of driveshaft assemblies (Part 2 of 2)

new boot onto shaft and into position groove of shaft from outer end of driveshaft.

2. Position new small boot clamp onto boot from outer end of driveshaft, then tighten clamp.
3. Fill inner CV joint and boot with a total of 8.8 oz. of a suitable CV joint grease.
4. If inner boot was replaced, install outer joint stop ring, then outer CV joint as outlined under "Outboard Joint & Boot."
5. Position inner joint outer housing onto tripod, then install large end of boot onto joint outer housing.
6. Ensure boot is not stretched or collapsed, if necessary use a blunt flat tool to pry up lip of boot to allow air pressure to equalize.
7. Ensure driveshaft length is proper, **Fig. 13.**

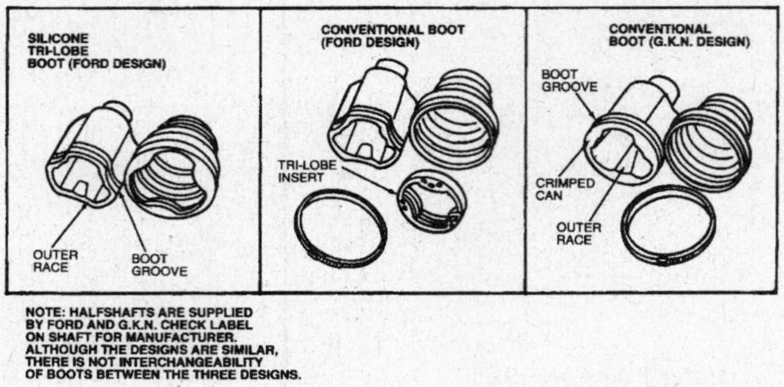

FM3039600255000X

Fig. 12 CV joint & boot types

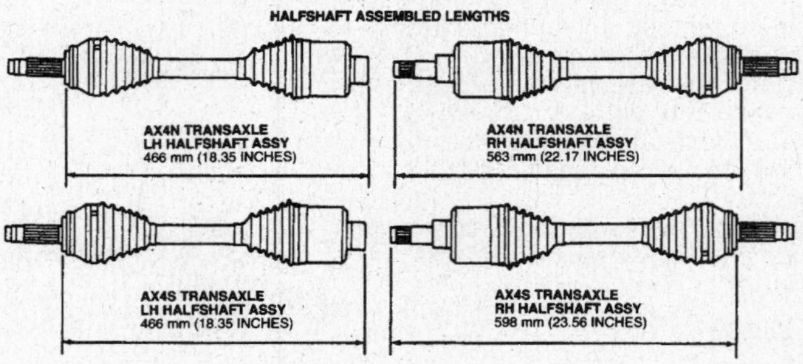

FM3039600256000X

Fig. 13 Driveshaft assembled length

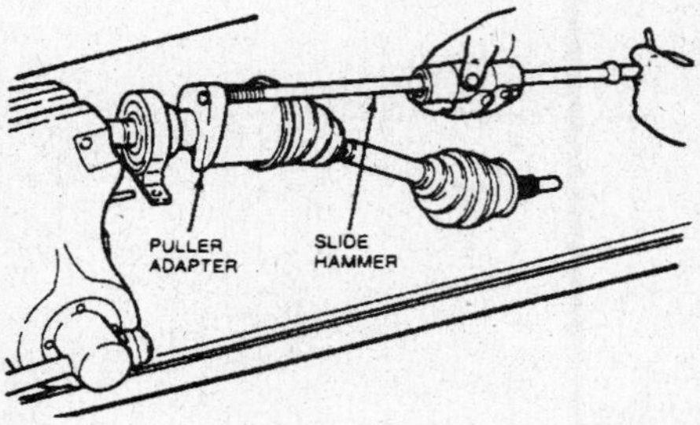

FM3039100165000X

Fig. 14 Linkshaft removal

8. Clean any excess grease from outside of boot.
9. Position new large boot clamp onto boot, then tighten clamp.
10. Position clamp replacer tool No. T95P-3514-A, or equivalent, on clamp ear and tighten tool through bolt until tool is in closed position.

LINKSHAFT

DISASSEMBLE

1. Clamp linkshaft in vise with driveshaft supported on workbench. Using puller adapter tool No. T86P-3514-A and slide hammer tool No. D79P-100-A, or equivalents, separate linkshaft from driveshaft, **Fig. 14.**
2. Pry seal from linkshaft with screwdriver.
3. Position linkshaft in an arbor press, then press off bearing.

ASSEMBLE

1. Press on new bearing and bearing seal with arbor press.
2. Coat shaft splines with Ford CV joint grease No. E2FZ-19590-A, or equivalent, then assemble linkshaft to driveshaft.

TIGHTENING SPECIFICATIONS

Component	Torque/Ft. Lbs.
Ball Joint Nut	50–68
Hub Nut	180–200
Stabilizer Bar Joint Nut	57–75
Wheel Lug Nut	85–105

DRIVE AXLES

NOTE: On Air Bag Equipped Models, Refer To " Air Bag System Precautions" Located In The Front Of This Manual For System Disarming & Arming Procedures.

NOTE: Refer To "Computer Relearn Procedures " Located In The Front Of This Manual For Computer Relearn Procedures.

INDEX

IDENTIFICATION

REAR AXLE TAG

The plant code shown on the axle identification tag in **Fig. 1** is used to identify the axle assembly. The plant code will not change as long as that particular axle assembly never undergoes an external design change. If an internal design change is made to an axle during its production life and that internal change affects service parts interchangeability, a dash and numerical suffix will be added to the plant code, **Fig. 2.**

Information on axle ratio, differential type and ring gear diameter may also be found on this tag.

VEHICLE CERTIFICATION LABEL

Information on axle ratio and differential type may be found on the vehicle certification label, which is affixed to the lefthand front door lock panel or door pillar. A code found in the "AX" box on the label will identify the originally installed axle. Refer to **Fig. 3** for axle identification.

TROUBLESHOOTING

Refer to troubleshooting chart, **Fig. 4,** for rear axle symptoms.

AXLE NOISE

Noise Acceptability

Drive axles produce a certain amount of noise, as all gear-driven parts do. Some noise is acceptable and may be audible at certain speeds or under various driving conditions, such as a newly paved blacktop road. The slight noise is in no way detrimental to rear axle operation and may be considered normal.

With Traction-Lok limited slip differential axle, slight chatter noise on slow, tight turns after extended highway driving is considered acceptable and has no detrimental effect on the axle's locking function.

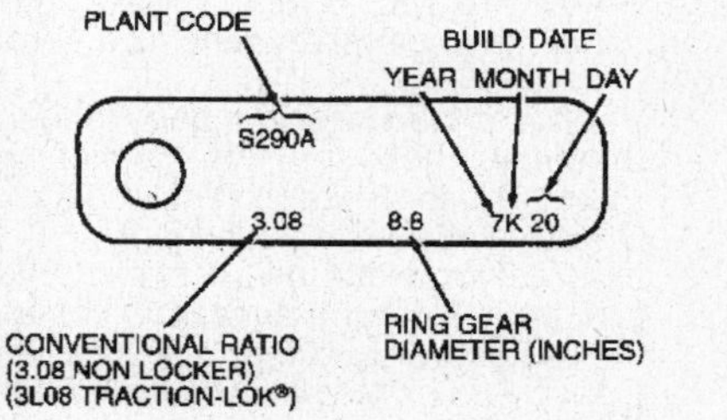

FM3039100118000A

Fig. 1 Rear axle identification tag

Axle Code	Differential Type	Gear Ratio
8	Conventional	2.73
M	Traction-Lok	2.73
Y	Conventional	3.08
Z	Traction-Lok	3.08
5	Conventional	3.27
E	Traction-Lok	3.27
F	Conventional	3.45
R	Traction-Lok	3.45
2	Conventional	3.55
K	Traction-Lok	3.55
6	Conventional	3.73
W	Traction-Lok	3.73

Fig. 3 Drive axle identification

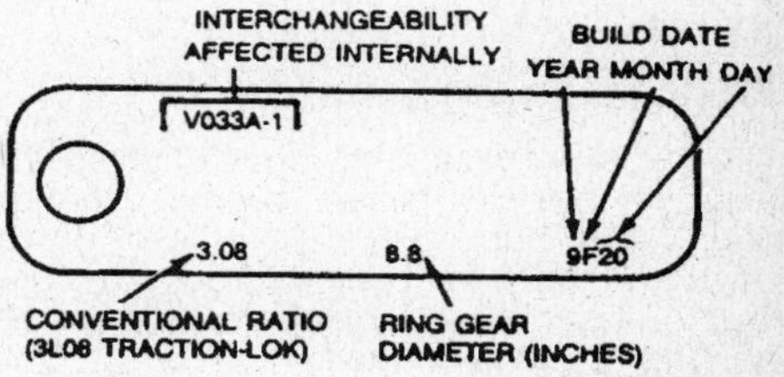

FM3039100119000X

Fig. 2 Internally modified rear axle identification tag

Gear Noise

Gear noise is the typical "howling" or " whining" of the ring gear and pinion due to an improper gear pattern, gear damage or improper bearing preload. It can occur at various speeds and driving conditions or it can be continuous.

Chuckle

Chuckle is a particular "rattling" noise that sounds like a stick against the spokes of a bicycle wheel. It occurs while decelerating from 40 mph and can be heard all the way to a stop. The frequency varies with the vehicle's speed.

Knock

Knock is very similar to chuckle, though it may be louder and occurs on acceleration or deceleration.

Clunk

Clunk may be a metallic noise heard when the automatic transmission is engaged in Reverse or Drive or it may occur when the throttle is applied or released. It is caused by backlash somewhere in the driveline or loose suspension components.

Condition	Possible Source	Action
• Excessive Rear Axle Noise	• Differential carrier.	• ROAD TEST vehicle to make sure concern is rear axle noise rather than other system noise. Refer to Road Test procedure.
• Loud Clunk in Driveshaft When Shifting from REVERSE to DRIVE	• Driveshaft. • Rear axle shafts.	• RAISE vehicle, ROTATE driveshaft by hand to isolate concern as a driveshaft or rear axle concern. SERVICE or REPLACE as required. • REMOVE and INSPECT. SERVICE as required.
• Limited-Slip or Traction-Lok® Axle Does Not Work in Snow, Mud or on Ice	• Differential.	• PERFORM Traction-Lok® Differential Operation Inspection. SERVICE as required.
• On Turns, the Rear Axle Has a High-Pitched Chattering Noise (Limited-Slip or Traction-Lok Axles Only). Slight Chatter Noise on Slow Turns after Extended Highway Driving is Considered Acceptable and Has No Detrimental Effect on the Locking Axle Function	• Lubricant. • Differential.	• ROAD TEST vehicle—DRIVE vehicle in tight circles—five clockwise and five counterclockwise. If chatter is still evident, FLUSH axle and REPLACE with SAE80W-90, Premium Rear Axle Lubricant XY-80W90-QL or -KL or equivalent meeting Ford specification WSP-M2C197-A—plus 118.2 ml (4 oz) C8AZ-19B546-A Additive Friction Modifier or equivalent meeting Ford specification EST-M2C118-A. • REMOVE differential, SERVICE as required.

FM3039500311000A

Fig. 4 Troubleshooting chart

Bearing Whine

Bearing whine is a high pitched sound similar to a whistle. It is usually caused by malfunctioning pinion bearings, which are operating at driveshaft speed. Bearing noise occurs at all driving speeds. This distinguishes it from gear whine, which usually comes and goes as speed changes.

Bearing Rumble

Bearing rumble sounds like marbles being tumbled. This condition is usually caused by a malfunctioning wheel bearing. The lower pitch is because the wheel bearing turns at only about one third of driveshaft speed. In addition, wheel bearing noise may be high pitched, similar to gear noise but will be evident in all four driving modes.

Chatter On Cornering

Chattering noise when cornering is a condition where the whole rear end vibrates only when the vehicle is moving. The vibration is plainly felt as well as heard. In conventional axles, extra differential thrust washers cause a partial lockup condition which creates this chatter. Chatter noise on Traction-Lok axles can usually be traced to erratic movement between adjacent clutch plates and can be corrected with a lubricant change.

Click At Engagement

Click at engagement is a condition on axles of a slight noise, distinct from a "clunk" that happens in Reverse or Drive engagement. It can be corrected by installing a slinger between the companion flange and front pinion bearing.

LEAKAGE CONDITIONS

Most rear axle leakage conditions can be corrected without a teardown. However, it is important to clean the leaking area enough to identify the exact source of the leak.

A plugged or seized jiggle cap vent will cause excessive seal lip wear due to internal pressure buildup. When a leak occurs, inspect cap by pressing down on it with index finger. If the cap moves up and down freely, it is working properly. If it does not move freely, it must be replaced.

Inspect axle lubricant level, which should be 9⁄16 inch below bottom of filler hole.

Drive Pinion Seal

If the drive pinion seal leaks, it is usually because of improper installation or because of poor quality of the seal journal surface. Any damage to the seal bore, such as dings, dents and gouges, will distort the seal casing and allow leakage past the outer edge of the seal.

Pinion Nut

Some models may experience oil leakage past the threads of the pinion nut. The condition can be corrected by removing the nut and applying pipe sealant with Teflon part No. D8AZ-19554-A, or equivalent, on the pinion threads and nut face. **Ensure the proper procedure for setting the bearing preload is followed when the nut is installed.**

Porous Casting

The differential carrier may leak through small pockets in the metal. These pockets (casting leakage) are caused by gas bubbles in the casting process.

Because the axle's sound characteristics may be changed if torn down to replace the carrier, servicing the porosity is preferable. Below are two recommended procedures that may be employed to fix a porous axle:

1. Peen a small amount of body lead into the hole, then seal the pocket with Epoxy Sealer Metallic Plastic part No. C6A7-A9554-A, or equivalent.
2. In larger pockets, drill a shallow hole and tap it for a small setscrew. Install the setscrew and seal it over with Epoxy Sealer Metallic Plastic part No. C6A7-A9554-A, or equivalent.

Axle Vent

There have been some occurrences of lubricant leaking through the axle vent. This may be caused by a clogged or sticking axle vent cap. If this is the case, the vent assembly should be replaced. Use Stud and Bearing Mount part No. EOAZ-19554-BA, or equivalent, on vent's threads to ensure retention.

VIBRATION CONDITIONS

Few vibration conditions are caused by the axle. Most rear end vibration is caused by the tires or driveline angle.

Vehicles equipped with a Traction-Lok differential will always have both wheels driving. If, while the vehicle is being serviced, only one wheel is raised off the floor and the rear axle is driven by the engine, the wheel on the floor could drive the vehicle off the safety stand. Ensure both rear wheels are raised off the floor.

Tires

Some vehicles are equipped with directional tires. See tire rotation arrows on tire sidewall. If a directional tire is removed for service, it must be mounted in its original location.

Do not balance the rear wheels and tires while they are mounted on the vehicle. Possible tire disintegration and/or differential failure could result, causing personal injury and/or extensive component damage. Use only an off-vehicle wheel and tire balancer.

A vibration can sometimes be corrected by properly rotating or inflating the tires. The best tires should be placed on the rear to minimize vibration, especially on vehicles with rear coil springs.

Driveline Angle

An improper driveline (pinion) angle can often be detected by the driving condition when vibration occurs.

1. A vibration during coasting from 35–45 mph is often caused by a high pinion angle.
2. A vibration during acceleration from 35–45 mph may indicate a lower than specified pinion angle.

TRACTION-LOK DIFFERENTIAL OPERATION INSPECTION

A Traction-Lok differential can be inspected for proper operation without removing it from the axle housing using procedure outlined below:

1. Raise and support one rear wheel, then remove the wheel cover.
2. Install adapter for Traction-Lok differential tool No. T59L-4204-A, or equivalent, then connect a torque wrench of at least a 200 ft. lbs. capacity.
3. Rotate the axle shaft. **Ensure transmission is in Neutral, one wheel is on floor and other rear wheel is raised off floor.**
4. Breakaway torque required to start rotation should be at least 20 ft. lbs. The initial breakaway torque may be higher than continuous turning torque. This is considered normal.
5. Axle shaft should turn with even pressure throughout inspection without slipping or binding. If torque reading is less than specified, inspect differential for improper assembly.

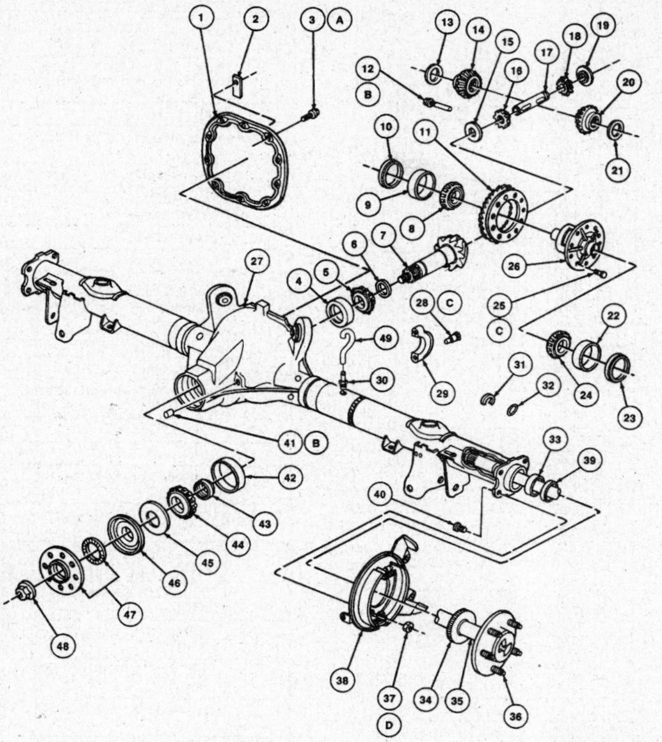

FM3039500279010X

Fig. 5 Exploded view of 8.8 inch rear axles (Part 1 of 2). Crown Victoria, Grand Marquis & Town Car

Item	Description
1	Axle Housing Cover
2	I.D.Tag
3	Axle Housing Cover Bolt
4	Rear Axle Pinion Bearing Cup
5	Differential Pinion Bearing
6	Drive Pinion Bearing Adjustment Shim
7	Drive Pinion (Part of 4209)
8	Differential Bearing (RH)
9	Differential Bearing Cup
10	Differential Bearing Shim
11	Ring Gear (Part of 4209)
12	Differential Pinion Shaft Lock Pin
13	Differential Side Gear Thrust Washer
14	Differential Side Gear
15	Differential Pinion Thrust Washer
16	Differential Pinion Gear
17	Differential Pinion Shaft
18	Differential Pinion Gear
19	Differential Pinion Thrust Washer
20	Differential Side Gear
21	Differential Side Gear Thrust Washer
22	Differential Bearing
23	Differential Bearing Shim
24	Differential Bearing (LH)
25	Rear Axle Differential Gear Case Bolt
26	Differential Case
27	Rear Axle Housing
28	Bolt
29	Differential Bearing Cap (Part of 4010)
30	Rear Axle Housing Vent
31	U-Washer
32	Rear Axle Shaft O-Ring
33	Rear Wheel Bearing
34	Rear Brake Anti-Lock Sensor Indicator
35	Axle Shaft
36	Lug Bolt
37	Nut
38	Rear Wheel Disc Brake Adapter
39	Inner Wheel Bearing Oil Seal
40	Bolt
41	Fill Plug
42	Differential Drive Pinion Bearing Cup
43	Differential Drive Pinion Collapsible Spacer
44	Differential Pinion Bearing
45	Rear Axle Drive Pinion Shaft Oil Slinger
46	Rear Axle Drive Pinion Seal
47	Rear Axle Universal Joint Flange
48	Drive Pinion Nut
49	Formed Vent Hose
A	Tighten to 38-52 N·m (28-38 Lb-Ft)
B	Tighten to 20-41 N·m (15-30 Lb-Ft)
C	Tighten to 95-115 N·m (70-85 Lb-Ft)
D	Tighten to 27-40 N·m (20-30 Lb-Ft)

FM3039500279020X

Fig. 5 Exploded view of 8.8 inch rear axles (Part 2 of 2). Crown Victoria, Grand Marquis & Town Car

DISASSEMBLE

CROWN VICTORIA, GRAND MARQUIS, MUSTANG & TOWN CAR

Differential Case

1. Raise and support rear of vehicle, then loosen axle housing cover bolts and allow lubricant to drain into suitable container, **Figs. 5 and 6.**
2. Remove axle housing cover, then proceed as follows:
   a. Wipe excess lubricant from inside axle housing, then visually inspect parts for wear and/or damage.
   b. Rotate gears and inspect for roughness, indicating damaged bearings or gears.
   c. Install suitable dial indicator on axle housing cover flange, then inspect and record ring gear back face runout. Maximum back face runout is .004 inch.
3. Remove rear axles and propeller shaft. Refer to “ Rear Axle & Suspension” section for procedures.
4. Scribe reference marks on differential bearing caps for assembly reference, then loosen bearing cap bolts. **Observe and record direction the arrows are facing on the bearing caps. During installation, arrows must face in same direction.**
5. Using suitable tool, pry differential case, bearing cups and shims out of housing until loose in bearing caps. Remove bearing caps, then differential assembly. Mark which side cups and shims came from for reference during assembly.

Drive Pinion

1. Scribe reference mark between drive pinion and companion flange. Hold flange with holding tool No. T78P-4851-A, or equivalent, then remove pinion nut and pinion flange.
2. Using suitable soft faced hammer, drive pinion out of front bearing cone and remove from rear of axle housing.
3. Remove oil seal and front bearing cone and roller from pinion housing.
4. Using suitable arbor press and adapters, remove rear pinion bearing.
5. Using suitable micrometer, measure and record thickness of shim which is found under rear bearing cone.
6. Remove pinion bearing cups from pinion housing with suitable brass drift. Install cups using suitable bearing cup installer. Cups are not properly installed if a .015 feeler gauge can be inserted between cup and bottom of bore at any point around the cup. **If any bearing cups are replaced, the respective cone and roller must also be replaced.**

LS

Extreme care must be taken not to damage aluminum rear axle housing while carrying out these procedures.

1. Remove differential housing cover.
2. Install dial indicator with bracketry tool No. 4201-C, or equivalent.
3. Measure and record ring gear runout, **Fig. 13.**
4. Attach housing spreader adapters tool No. T93P-4000-A, or equivalent, to rear axle housing with four cover bolts.
5. Attach housing spreader adapters to holding fixture tool No. T57L-500-B, or equivalent, with two 3/8 inch x 1-1/2 inch bolts.
6. Install differential carrier spreader tool No. T4000-E, or equivalent, onto housing spreader adapters with spreader pins aligned with housing spreader adapters holes.
7. **On models equipped with aluminum axle,** proceed as follows:
   a. Install dial indicator tool and attach clutch housing alignment adapter tool No. T75L-4201-A, or equivalent to dial indicator with tip positioned in spreader adapter hole.
   b. Tighten and loosen housing spreader adapter screw to normalize housing spreader adapters prior

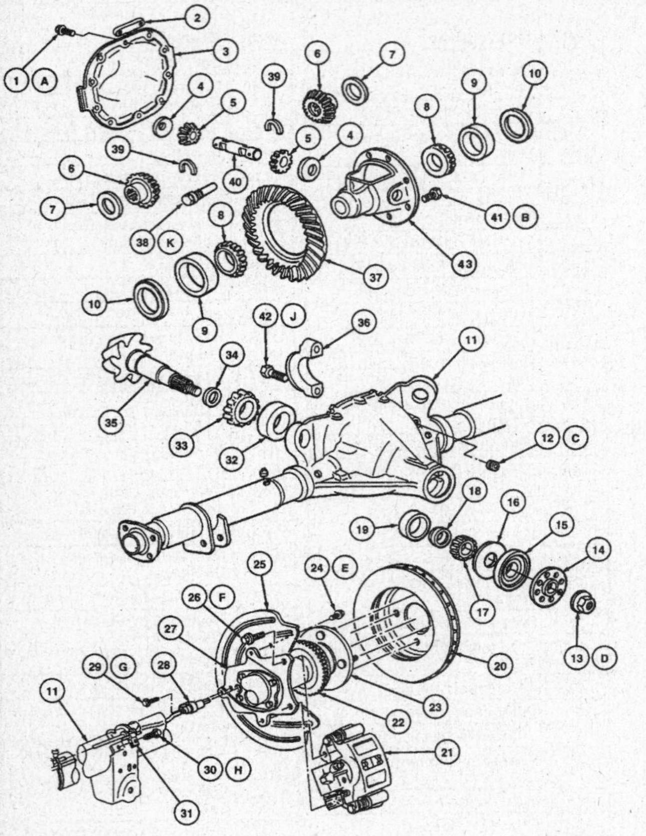

FM3039800326010X

Fig. 6 Exploded view of 7½ & 8.8 inch rear axles (Part 1 of 2). Mustang

Item	Description
1	Axle Housing Cover Bolt
2	Rear Axle Brake Line Clip
3	Axle Housing Cover
4	Differential Pinion Thrust Washer
5	Differential Pinion Gear
6	Differential Side Gear
7	Differential Side Gear Thrust Washer
8	Differential Bearing
9	Differential Bearing Cup
10	Differential Bearing Shim
11	Rear Axle Housing
12	Filler Plug
13	Pinion Nut
14	Rear Axle Universal Joint Flange
15	Rear Axle Drive Pinion Seal
16	Rear Axle Drive Pinion Shaft Oil Slinger
17	Differential Pinion Bearing
18	Differential Drive Pinion Collapsible Spacer
19	Differential Drive Pinion Bearing Cup
20	Rear Disc Brake Rotor
21	Rear Disc Brake Caliper
22	Rear Brake Anti-Lock Sensor Indicator
23	Axle Shaft Flange
24	Bolt (3 Req'd)
25	Rear Wheel Disc Brake Shield
26	Caliper Anchor Bolt
27	Left Hand Rear Disc Brake Adapter
28	Rear Brake Anti-Lock Sensor

Item	Description
29	Bolt
30	Bolt
31	Clip
32	Rear Axle Pinion Bearing Cup
33	Differential Pinion Bearing
34	Drive Pinion Bearing Adjustment Shim
35	Drive Pinion
36	Bearing Cap
37	Ring Gear
38	Differential Pinion Shaft Lock Pin
39	U-Washer
40	Differential Pinion Shaft
41	Rear Axle Differential Gear Case Bolt
42	Bearing Cap Bolt
43	Differential Case
A	Tighten to 38-52 N·m (28-38 Lb-Ft)
B	Tighten to 95-115 N·m (70-84 Lb-Ft)
C	Tighten to 20-41 N·m (15-30 Lb-Ft)
D	Tighten to 190 N·m (140 Lb-Ft)
E	Tighten to 8-12 N·m (70-106 Lb-In)
F	Tighten to 87-119 N·m (65-87 Lb-Ft)
G	Tighten to 4.5-6.8 N·m (40-60 Lb-In)
H	Tighten to 10-14 N·m (89-123 Lb-In)
J	Tighten to 102-122 N·m (76-89 Lb-Ft)
K	Tighten to 20-41 N·m (15-30 Lb-Ft)

FM3039800326020X

Fig. 6 Exploded view of 7½ & 8.8 inch rear axles (Part 2 of 2). Mustang

to final dial indicator reading. **Over-spreading can damage rear axle housing.**

c. Adjust dial indicator to zero and tighten housing spreader screw until rear axle housing is spread to .030 inch. Remove dial indicator.

8. **On models equipped with nodular iron axle,** housing spreader adapters are used to give the rear axle housing stability. **Do not spread rear axle housing.**
9. **On all models,** mark position of bearing caps as arrows may not be visible. Bearing caps must be installed in their identical locations and positions.
10. Remove retaining bolts and bearing caps.
11. **On models equipped with aluminum axle,** proceed as follows:
    a. Position wood blocks on top and bottom of differential. **Wood blocks must be used to avoid rear axle housing damage.**
    b. Pry differential case and differential bearing shims out of rear axle housing, **Fig. 9.**
    c. Remove special tool.
12. **On models equipped with nodular iron axle,** remove differential case.
13. **On all models,** remove 10 ring gear bolts.
14. Insert suitable punch in bolt holes and drive ring gear off. **Do not damage bolt hole threads.**
15. Remove differential bearing using two-jaw puller tool No. D97L-4221-A and step plate tool No. D83T-4205-C2, or equivalents.
16. Repeat proceeding procedure on other side.
17. Remove differential lock bolt, pinion shaft, gears and side gears.
18. Install suitable torque wrench on pinion nut and record torque necessary to maintain rotation of drive pinion gear through several revolutions.
19. Install flange holding tool No. 205-478, or equivalent. **Ensure to insert cotter key in special tool.**
20. Remove pinion nut using suitable breaker bar. **After removing pinion nut, discard it. Use new nut for installation.**
21. Mark pinion flange in relation to drive pinion stem to ensure correct alignment during assembly.
22. Remove pinion flange using flange remover tool No. 307-408l, or equivalent.
23. Install pinion thread protector tool No. 205-460, or equivalent.
24. Drive pinion out of front bearing cone using suitable soft-faced hammer and remove it through rear of housing.
25. Remove rear axle drive pinion shaft oil slinger, rear axle drive pinion seal and collapsible spacer.
26. Position pinion bearing cone remover tool No. T71P-4621-B, or equivalent, under pinion bearing.
27. Remove pinion bearing using suitable press.
28. Remove front pinion bearing.
29. Measure and record thickness of drive pinion bearing adjustment shim found under differential pinion bearing.
30. Remove drive pinion bearing adjustment shim.
31. If required, remove damaged rear axle pinion bearing cups from rear axle housing using pinion outer bearing cup remover tool No. 205-482 and pinion inner bearing cup remover tool No. 205-481, or equivalents.

MARK VIII, THUNDERBIRD, 1997 COUGAR

Differential Case

1. Remove rear axle assembly as outlined under "Rear Axle & Suspension" section, then remove axle cover, **Fig. 7.**
2. Place axle carrier in holding fixture tool No. T57L-500-B, or equivalent, with housing spreader adapters tool No.

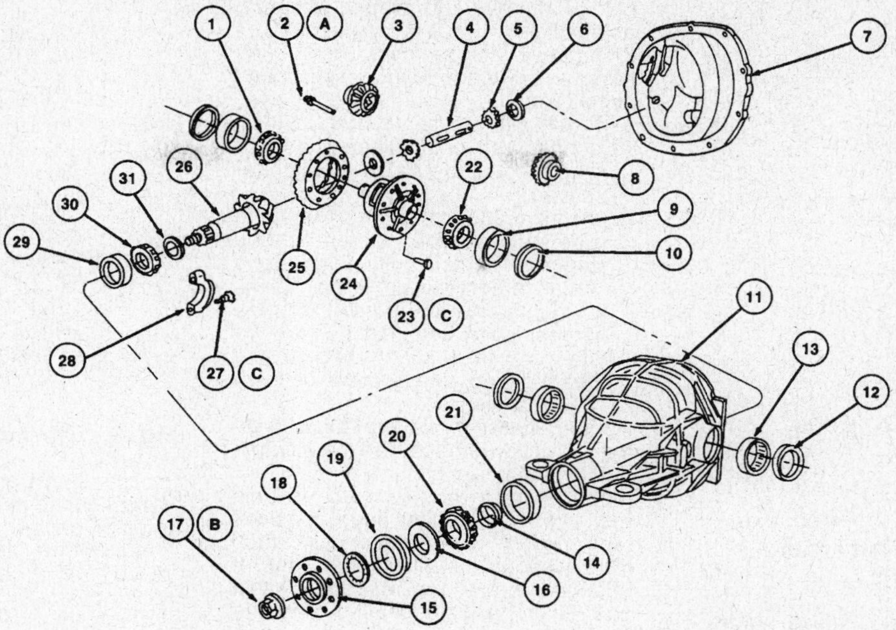

Item	Description
1	Differential Bearing (RH)
2	Differential Pinion Shaft Lock Pin
3	Differential Side Gear (RH)
4	Differential Pinion Shaft
5	Differential Pinion Gear
6	Differential Pinion Thrust Washer
7	Axle Housing Cover
8	Differential Side Gear (LH)
9	Differential Bearing Cup
10	Differential Bearing Shim
11	Rear Axle Housing
12	Inboard Cv Joint Stub Shaft Pilot Bearing Housing Seal
13	Pilot Bearing
14	Differential Drive Pinion Collapsible Spacer
15	Rear Axle Universal Joint Flange
16	Rear Axle Drive Pinion Shaft Oil Slinger
17	Pinion Nut

Item	Description
18	Drive Pinion Oil Seal Deflector
19	Rear Axle Drive Pinion Seal
20	Differential Pinion Bearing
21	Differential Drive Pinion Bearing Cup
22	Differential Bearing (LH)
23	Rear Axle Differential Gear Case Bolt
24	Differential Case
25	Ring Gear (Part of 4209)
26	Pinion (Part of 4209)
27	Bolt
28	Rear Axle Housing)
29	Rear Axle Pinion Bearing Cup
30	Differential Pinion Bearing
31	Drive Pinion Bearing Adjustment Shim
A	Tighten to 20-41 N·m(15-30 Lb-Ft)
B	Tighten to 190 N·m (140 Lb-Ft)
C	Tighten to 95-115 N·m (70-85 Lb-Ft)

FM3039500280000X

Fig. 7 Exploded view of 7 1/2 & 8.8 inch rear axles. Mark VIII, Thunderbird, 1997 Cougar

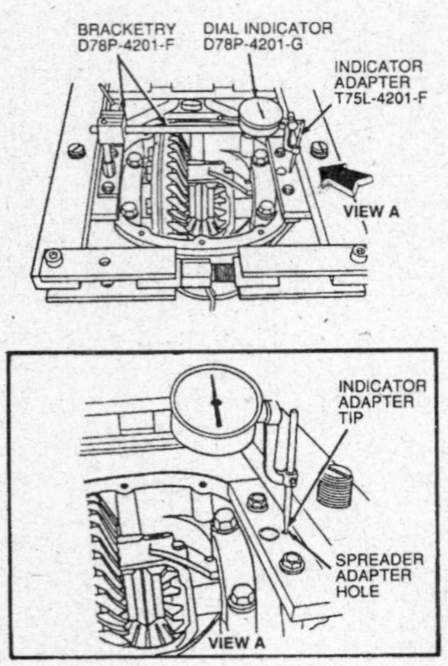

FM3039300265000X

Fig. 8 Differential carrier spreading

T93P-4000-A and dial indicator base tool No. D78P-4201-F, or equivalents, attached.

3. Install carrier spreader tool No. T4000-E, or equivalent, to spreader adapters, then install a suitable dial gauge and brackets as shown in **Fig. 8.**
4. Zero dial gauge, then spread differential carrier .030 inch.
5. Mark differential bearing caps righthand and lefthand, noting direction of arrows cast into bearing caps.
6. Place wood blocks into differential carrier, **Fig. 9,** then pry differential case out of housing. **Wood blocks must be used to prevent damage to carrier.**
7. Place differential case into a suitable soft jaw vice, then remove ring gear bolts.
8. Use a suitable drift punch to tap ring gear from case.

Drive Pinion

1. Remove differential case as outlined under "Differential Case Assembly."
2. If pinion shaft is to be used again, place match marks on shaft and companion flange. Use companion flange holding tool No. T78P-4851-A, or equivalent, to loosen, but not remove, pinion nut.
3. Using a suitable puller, pull companion flange loose from splines, then remove flange and nut from pinion shaft.
4. Use a soft face hammer to tap pinion shaft from differential carrier.

SUBASSEMBLY SERVICE

CONVENTIONAL DIFFERENTIAL

CROWN VICTORIA, GRAND MARQUIS, MUSTANG & TOWN CAR

Differential Case Bearings

1. If differential bearings are to be replaced, remove and replace with suitable puller.
2. If ring gear backlash measured during removal exceeded .015 inch, proceed as follows:
   a. Install differential bearing cups on cones, then install differential case in rear housing with drive pinion removed.
   b. Install a .265 inch shim on lefthand side of case, then install bearing cap and tighten bolts finger-tight. Install progressively larger shims on righthand side of case until the largest shim selected can be installed with a slight drag. Install bearing cap and **torque** bolts to 70–85 ft. lbs.
3. Rotate differential several turns in either direction to ensure free rotation and to seat bearings.
4. Mount suitable dial indicator to axle housing, then inspect ring gear back face runout. Ring gear back face runout should be within .004 inch. If ring gear back face runout is within specifications, the original reading was caused by insufficient differential bearing preload. If ring gear back face runout is still not within specifications, proceed as follows:
   a. Inspect differential case runout, which should be within .004 inch.
   b. If runout is within specifications, ring gear is out of specifications and should be replaced.
   c. If runout is not within specifications, the differential case is damaged and should be replaced.
5. Remove differential case from axle housing, then remove ring gear. Install differential case less ring gear in housing following procedures given above.
6. Inspect differential case runout. Runout should be within .004 inch. If runout is within specifications, ring gear is out of specifications and should be replaced. If runout is not within specifications, the differential case is damaged and should be replaced.

Drive Pinion Depth Determination

Prior to determining drive pinion depth, clean pinion bearing cups and differential bearing pedestals thoroughly to ensure an accurate reading. Apply only a light oil film to bearing assemblies to avoid false readings.

1. Assemble aligning adapter, gauge disc and gauge block to tool No. T79P-4020-A, or equivalent, **Fig. 10.**
2. Place rear pinion bearing over aligning adapter, then insert tool and bearing in rear pinion bearing cup in pinion housing bore. Place front pinion bearing over screw in front pinion bearing cup and assemble tool handle onto screw. **Torque** handle to 20 inch lbs. Ensure tool is mounted securely between front and rear bearings.
3. Rotate gauge block several half turns to ensure bearings are seated properly. Rotational torque should be 20 inch lbs. with new bearings. Set gauge block at an angle approximately 45° from horizontal, **Fig. 11.**

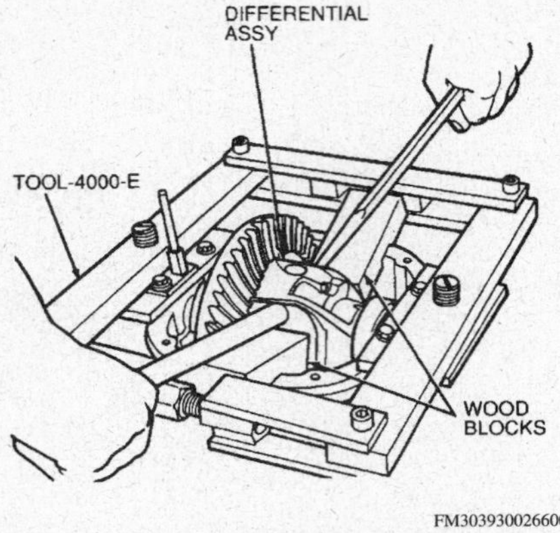

FM3039300266000X

Fig. 9 Differential case removal

4. Install gauge tube in differential bearing mounts, then install bearing caps and bearing cap bolts.
5. Use pinion shims to determine pinion depth by inserting shims between gauge block and gauge tube. The proper shim will fit with a slight drag. Do not attempt to force a shim between block and tube. **Do not use shims that are bent, dirty, nicked or mutilated as a gauge.**
6. Make note of proper shim size and remove tool from axle housing.
7. Using suitable arbor press and adapters, remove rear pinion bearing.
8. Install shim determined in previous step on pinion shaft, then install bearing using arbor press. **The rear pinion bearing used to determine drive pinion depth must be used in the final assembly of the axle.**

Drive Pinion Installation

1. Lubricate pinion bearings with suitable axle lubricant, then install pinion shaft and rear bearing, collapsible spacer and front bearing.
2. Install slinger (if equipped) and pinion oil seal, then insert pinion flange in seal and hold firmly in place against front bearing. From rear of housing, insert pinion shaft into flange.
3. Install pinion (yoke) nut. While holding pinion flange, tighten nut only enough to remove bearing endplay. When an increase in pinion nut turning effort is noted, stop tightening pinion nut. Rotate pinion several times in both directions to seat bearings.
4. Continue to tighten pinion nut in very small increments, then, occasionally, using suitable torque wrench, measure pinion rotational torque. The rotating torque must not exceed 20 inch lbs. **Do not exceed specified preload torque. Do not loosen pinion nut if preload torque is exceeded. If preload torque is exceeded, remove pinion nut, yoke, oil seal, slinger (if equipped) and collapsible spacer. Replace collapsible spacer and oil seal with new ones and repeat procedure.**

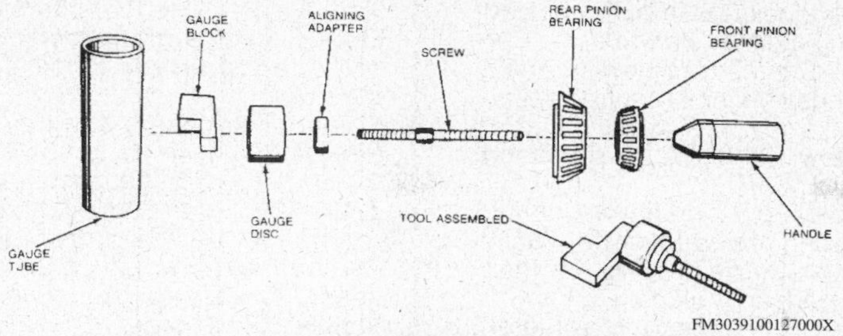

Fig. 10 Rear axle pinion depth gauge

LS

Take extreme care not to damage aluminum rear axle housing while carrying out these procedures.

1. Lubricate differential side gear thrust washers with Premium Long-Life Grease XG-1-C, or equivalent, prior to installation.
2. Install differential side gears in differential case.
3. Lubricate differential pinion thrust washers with Premium Long-Life Grease XG-1-C, or equivalent, prior to installation.
4. Install differential pinion gears with differential pinion thrust washers in differential case.
5. If new pinion shaft lock bolt is unavailable, coat threads with Threadlock and Sealer EOAZ-19554-AA, or equivalent, prior to installation.
6. Install differential pinion shaft and new differential pinion shaft lock bolt.
7. Install differential bearing on differential case using differential side bearing replacer tool No. T57L-4221-A2, or equivalent. Repeat for other side.
8. Start two of ring gear bolts through differential case and into ring gear to ensure ring gear bolt holes align with differential case bolt holes correctly then press ring gear on differential case.
9. Install the ring gear bolts. Apply Stud and Bearing Mount EOAZ-19554-BA, or equivalent, to bolts.
10. With pinion removed, place differential case/gear subassembly with differential bearing and rear axle pinion bearing cups in rear axle housing.
11. Install differential bearing shim of thickness shown on lefthand side of differential case.
12. Install lefthand bearing cap finger-tight.
13. Apply pressure toward lefthand side to fully seat differential bearing cup.
14. Install progressively larger differential bearing shims on righthand side until largest differential bearing shim selected can be assembled with slight drag feel.
15. Install righthand bearing cap and **torque** bearing caps to 77 ft. lbs.
16. Rotate differential assembly to ensure it rotates freely.
17. Install dial indicator with bracketry tool No. T4201-C, or equivalent.
18. Measure and record ring gear runout, **Fig. 13.**
19. If runout is .003 inch, original out-of-specification runout was caused by insufficient bearing preload.
20. If runout is more than .003 inch, proceed as follows:
    a. Remove differential case.
    b. Remove ring gear.
    c. Install differential case without ring gear.
    d. Rotate differential case to correctly seat differential bearings.
    e. Measure differential case flange runout using dial indicator.
    f. If runout is .003 inch, install new ring gear and pinion.
    g. If runout is more than .003 inch, ring gear is true and concern is due to either damaged differential case or differential bearings.
    h. Inspect differential bearings.
    i. If differential bearings are not damaged, install new differential case and differential bearings.
    j. Measure runout with new differential case and differential bearings.
21. Install new inner rear axle pinion bearing cup in rear axle housing using pinion inner bearing cup tool No. 205-480 and cup replacer tool No. T71P-4616-A, or equivalents.
22. Install new outer rear axle pinion bearing cup in rear axle housing using cup replacer tools.
23. Coat new rear axle pinion bearing cup with SAE 5W-30 Super Premium Motor Oil XO-5W30-QSP, or equivalent.
24. Position rear axle pinion bearing cup on handle tool No. T76P-4020-A11, screw tool No. T76P-4020-A9, pinion depth gauge aligner tool No. 205-477, pinion depth gauge disc tool No. 205-476, and gauge block tool No. T76P-4020-A10, or equivalent, **Fig. 10.**
25. Position bearing cup replacer in rear axle housing and tighten special tool to fully seat rear axle pinion bearing cup in bore.
26. Apply light film of SAE 75W140 Synthetic Rear Axle Lubricant F1TZ-19580-B, or equivalent, on front differential pinion bearing and rear differential pinion bearing assemblies.
27. Thread handle onto screw and torque to 20 inch lbs.
28. Rotate gauge block tool several half turns to correctly seat the pinion bearings, **Fig. 11. Gauge block tool must be offset to obtain an accurate reading.**

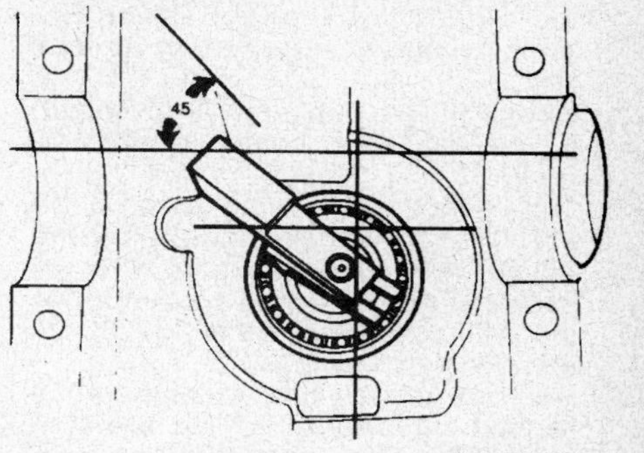

Fig. 11 Pinion depth gauge block installation

29. Position gauge tube tool No. T93P-4020-A, or equivalent, on differential bearing seat of rear axle housing.
30. Install differential bearing caps and cap bolts. Torque cap bolts to 77 ft. lbs.
31. Slight drag should be felt for correct shim selection. Remove special tool.
32. Same pinion bearings and drive pinion bearing adjustment shim used in drive pinion shim selection procedure must be used in final axle assembly.
33. Position drive pinion bearing adjustment shim, pinion bearing, and bearing/seal service plate tool No. T75L-1165-B and universal bearing puller tool No. T53T-4621-C, or equivalents, on pinion stem.
34. Firmly seat drive pinion bearing adjustment shim and pinion bearing on pinion stem using suitable press.
35. Install front pinion bearing, rear axle drive pinion shaft oil slinger and rear axle drive pinion seal.
36. Ensure pinion stem splines are free of burrs. If burrs are evident, remove using fine crocus cloth, work in rotational motion.
37. Install new drive pinion collapsible spacer on pinion stem against pinion stem shoulder.
38. Install drive pinion and drive pinion collapsible spacer into rear axle housing.
39. Master bearings are marked LH and RH.
40. Remove differential bearings and install right master bearing tool No. T93P-4222-B and left master bearing tool No. T93P-4222-A, or equivalents, on differential case.
41. Lubricate rear axle pinion flange splines using SAE 75W140 Synthetic Rear Axle Lubricant F1TZ-19580-B, or equivalent.
42. Align rear axle pinion flange with drive pinion shaft and install rear axle pinion flange. Disregard scribe marks if new rear axle pinion flange is being installed.
43. With drive pinion in place in rear axle housing, install rear axle pinion flange using pinion flange installer tool No. 205-479 and flange holding tool No. 205-478, or equivalents.
44. Tighten pinion nut using flange holding

tool No. 205-478, or equivalent. **Ensure to insert cotter key in special tool.**
45. Rotate pinion occasionally to ensure differential pinion bearings seat correctly.
46. Take frequent differential pinion bearing torque preload readings by rotating pinion with suitable torque wrench. Preload **torque** should be 8–10 inch lbs. with used bearings or 16–28 inch lbs. with new bearings.
47. **Do not under any circumstance loosen pinion nut to reduce preload. If it is necessary to reduce preload, install new collapsible spacer and pinion nut.**
48. **On models equipped with aluminum axle,** proceed as follows:
    a. Place differential case and dial indicator into rear axle housing. Position dial indicator on outside mounting hole.
    b. Attach dial indicator with indicator tip positioned on machined surface of differential case flange.
    c. Move differential case to left and right as far as possible.
    d. Repeat this procedure until consistent reading is obtained.
    e. Record reading.
    f. Remove special tool and differential case from rear axle housing.

MARK VIII, THUNDERBIRD & 1997 COUGAR

Differential Case Bearings

Pinion depth and bearing preload must be determined as outlined under "Pinion Shaft Bearings," before performing this operation. The pinion must be properly installed into the carrier.

1. If differential bearings are to be replaced, remove from differential case with suitable puller.
2. Place righthand and lefthand master bearings onto differential case, **Fig. 12.**
3. Install differential case with master bearings into carrier.
4. Install a suitable dial gauge, then measure total end play **Fig. 13. Record this measurement as dimension A.**
5. Remove differential case from carrier and place in a suitable fixture or soft jaw vice for ring gear installation.
6. Use a suitable fine flat file to remove burrs on mounting surface of ring gear and differential case.
7. Place ring gear into position on differential case, then loosely install three bolts to position ring gear to differential case.
8. Place differential case with ring gear in a suitable press fixture, then press ring gear onto differential case.
9. Install remaining ring gear bolts, then **torque** bolts to 70–85 ft. lbs.
10. Place differential case, with ring gear and master bearings installed, into carrier.
11. Install a suitable dial gauge, then measure total end play between ring gear and pinion gear. **Record this measurement as dimension B.**
12. Subtract dimension B from dimension A to determine dimension C.
13. Determine thickness of new differential case bearings and their required shims as follows:
    a. Mark new bearings as righthand and lefthand.
    b. Assemble new righthand bearing into bearing preload tool No. T93P-4220-A, or equivalent, **Fig. 14,** then **torque** preload tool to 25 ft. lbs.
    c. Using a suitable depth micrometer, measure thickness of bearing. **Record this dimension as D, righthand side.**
    d. Repeat above procedure on lefthand bearing. **Record this dimension as D, lefthand side.**
14. Determine thickness of righthand bearing shim as follows:
    a. Subtract dimension D righthand side from master bearing standard thickness of .8695. **Record this measurement as dimension E, righthand side.**
    b. Add dimension E, righthand side, dimension C and preload standard of .0200. Result is righthand shim initial thickness.
    c. Round off initial shim thickness to nearest available shim thickness for final righthand side shim size.
15. Determine thickness of lefthand bearing shim as follows:
    a. Subtract dimension D, lefthand side from master bearing standard thickness of .8695. . **Record this measurement as dimension E, lefthand side.**
    b. Add dimension E, lefthand side to dimension B, then subtract backlash standard of .006 to determine lefthand shim initial thickness.
    c. Round off initial shim thickness to nearest available shim thickness for final righthand side shim size.
16. Mark lefthand and righthand shims for later assembly.
17. Place righthand and lefthand differential case bearings onto their proper positions, then using a suitable press seat bearings onto differential case.

Drive Pinion Depth Determination

Refer to "Crown Victoria, Grand Marquis, Mustang & Town Car."

Drive Pinion Installation

Refer to "Crown Victoria, Grand Marquis, Mustang & Town Car."

TRACTION-LOK LIMITED SLIP DIFFERENTIAL

For differential case and ring gear runout inspections and differential bearing replacement, refer to "Except Traction-Lok Limited Slip Differential."

1. Remove and discard ring gear to differential case attaching bolts.
2. Tap on ring gear using a suitable mallet and remove ring gear from case.
3. Remove pinion shaft lock screw and pinion shaft.
4. Remove preloaded "S" shaped spring, **Fig. 15. Use caution when removing "S" shaped spring, since it is under tension.**
5. Rotate pinion gears and thrust washers using 12 inch socket extension inserted into pinion gear rotator tool No. T80P-4205-A, or equivalent, until they can be removed through access hole.
6. Remove lefthand and righthand side gears, clutch packs and shims, **Fig. 16.** Note order of removal and side removed from and tag for reference during assembly.
7. Apply suitable lubricant to clutch plates, then install lefthand side gear, clutch pack and new shim into differential case. Repeat procedure for righthand hand side.
8. Install pinion gears and thrust washers 180° apart and in contact with side gears.
9. Align gears with pinion shaft bore, **Fig. 17,** using 12-inch socket extension inserted in pinion shaft rotator.
10. Install "S" shaped preload spring into differential using soft faced hammer.

CLEANING & INSPECTION

CONVENTIONAL DIFFERENTIAL

Clean all parts in suitable solvent. Dry all parts except bearings with compressed air or shop towels. Allow bearings to air dry or use shop towels. Do not use compressed air to dry bearings as damage may result.

Inspect differential bearings and cups for wear, pitting, galling, flat spots or cracks. Any bearing or cup showing any signs of wear or damage must be replaced. Bearings and respective cups must be replaced as an assembly only. Do not attempt to interchange bearings and cups as bearing life will be affected.

Inspect non-machined differential case surfaces for nicks and burrs which can be removed with an oil stone or fine tooth file. Inspect pinion shaft bore to ensure it is not elongated or worn. If damage is evident, differential case must be replaced. Inspect machined differential surfaces and counterbores. They must be smooth and free of nicks, gouges, cracks and other visible damage. If damage is evident, differential case must be replaced.

Inspect pinion shaft for excessive wear, scoring or galling. Ensure shaft is smooth and concentric. If any wear or damage is evident, replace the shaft. Inspect pinion shaft lockpin for damage and to ensure it has a snug fit in the differential case. Replace lockpin or case as necessary.

Inspect pinion and ring gears for worn or chipped teeth, cracks, damaged bearing journals or attaching bolt threads. If any of the above are evident, replace ring gear and pinion as a matched set.

Inspect pinion and side gears. Gears must exhibit a uniform contact pattern without any signs of cracks, wear, scoring or galling. If any of the above are evident, replace all the gears. Inspect thrust washers for wear and replace as necessary.

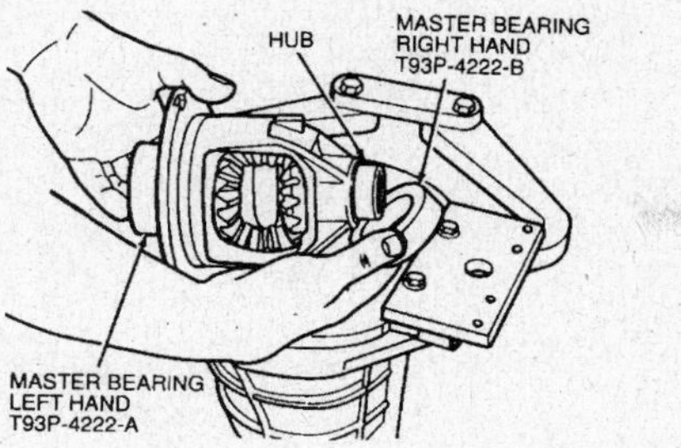

Fig. 12 Master bearing onto differential case installation

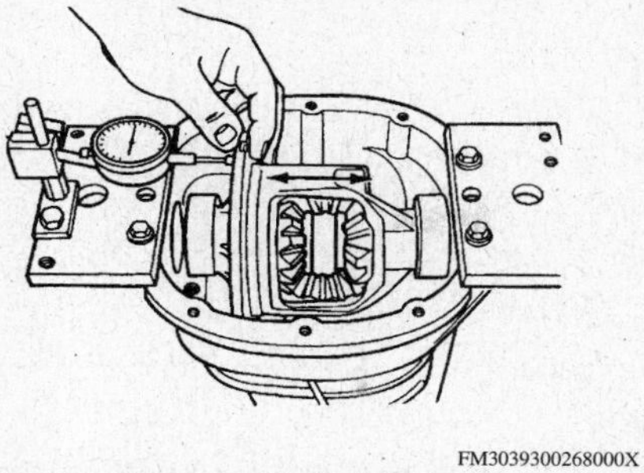

Fig. 13 Differential case end play measurement

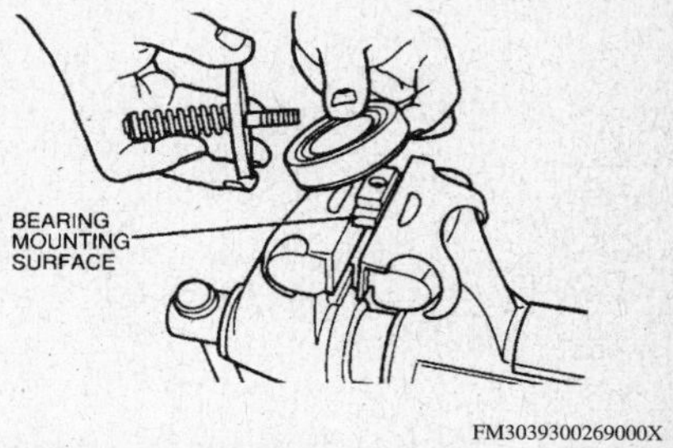

Fig. 14 Differential case bearing thickness measurement

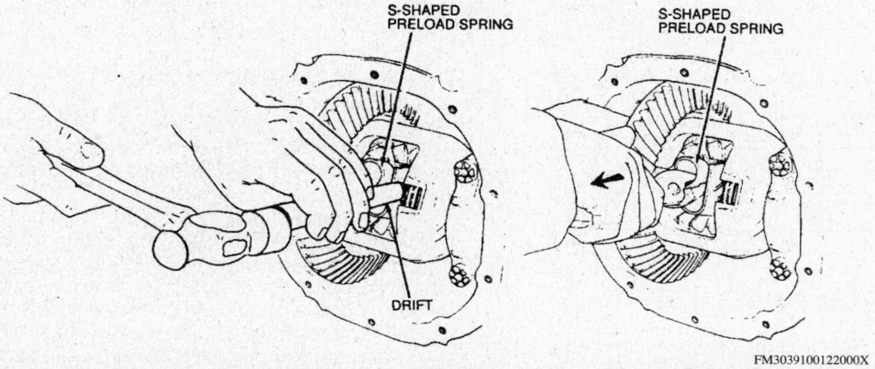

Fig. 15 C-clips "S" shaped preload spring removal. Traction-Lok

Inspect pinion and ring gears for worn or chipped teeth, cracks, damaged bearing journals or attaching bolt threads. If any of the above are evident, replace ring gear and pinion as a matched set.

Inspect axle shaft C-locks (if equipped) for signs of cracks or wear and replace as necessary.

TRACTION-LOK LIMITED SLIP DIFFERENTIAL

The cleaning and inspection of these units is the same as for conventional differentials except that cleaning solvent should not be allowed to contact the clutch plates. The clutch plates should be wiped clean only. In addition, the following steps should be performed which only apply to the Traction-Lok differential.

Visually inspect clutch packs, side gears, pinion gears and pinion shaft for damage or wear and replace as necessary.

Place each clutch pack without shims into tool No. T80P-4946-A, or equivalent, **Fig. 18. Torque** nut to 5 ft. lbs. Using feeler gauge, determine thickness of new shims by inserting thickest blade possible between clutch pack and tool, **Fig. 19,** then note size for use during assembly.

ASSEMBLE

CROWN VICTORIA, GRAND MARQUIS, MUSTANG & TOWN CAR

1. Install replacement ring gear (if removed). Apply suitable locking compound to new bolts and **torque** to 70–85 ft. lbs.
2. Apply suitable axle lubricant to differential bearing bores.
3. Place differential bearing cups on bearings, then set differential assembly in axle housing. **If ring gear and pinion gear have punch marks, assemble ring gear in carrier so marked tooth on pinion is indexed between the marked teeth of ring gear.**
4. Inspect and adjust backlash as follows:
   a. Mount suitable dial indicator on axle housing cover flange, then measure ring gear backlash. If backlash is within specifications, **Fig. 20,** proceed to step f. If backlash is not within specifications, proceed to step c. If backlash is zero, proceed to step b.
   b. If backlash measured above is zero, add .020 inch (.5 mm) to righthand side of case and subtract .020 inch (.5 mm) from lefthand side of case, then inspect backlash again. If backlash now ranges within specifications, proceed to step d.
   c. If backlash is not within specifications, correct by increasing thickness of one shim and decreasing thickness on the other shim by the same amount. Refer to **Fig. 21,** for approximate shim change.
   d. Install shims and bearing caps. **Torque** bearing cap bolts to 70–85 ft. lbs., then rotate differential case assembly several turns in both directions.
   e. Inspect backlash. If backlash is within specifications, proceed to step f. If not within specifications, repeat step c.
   f. Increase both lefthand and righthand side shims by .006 inch to provide proper differential bearing preload. Ensure shims are fully seated and the case assembly turns freely.
   g. Using suitable white marking compound applied to ring gear, inspect tooth mesh contacting pattern. **Tooth mesh contacting pattern can be improved by installing the propeller shaft and axle assemblies and rotating both tires in the drive and coast direction.**
   h. Contacting pattern should be within the primary area of the ring gear tooth surface avoiding narrow contact with the outer perimeter of tooth. Inspect pattern on the drive (pull) side of the ring gear. If serious error is determined, inspect pinion shim selection.
5. Install axle housing cover, driveshaft and axle assemblies.
6. Fill rear axle assembly with axle lubricant recommended by manufacturer. **On models equipped with 7½ inch Traction-Lok differential,** subtract 3 ounces of axle lubricant and replace with 3 ounces of Friction Modifier part No. C8AZ-19546-A, or equivalent.

LS

Aluminum

1. Draw-file differential ring gear mounting surface to remove any nicks or burrs.
2. Place ring gear onto differential case, then hand start three bolts to align ring gear holes and differential case.
3. Place differential case and ring gear onto press bed blocks with ring gear teeth facing down.
4. Press ring gear into place
5. Install remaining ring gear bolts and **torque** to 77 ft. lbs.
6. **On models equipped with aluminum axle,** proceed as follows:
   a. Place the differential case, left master bearing tool No. T93P-4222-A, right master bearing tool No. T93P-4222-B, or equivalents, and ring gear into rear axle housing.

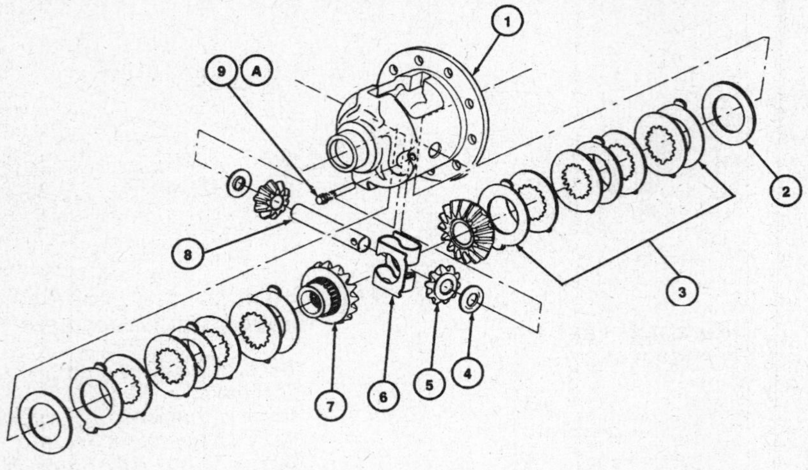

Item	Description
1	Differential Case
2	Rear Axle Differential Clutch Shim
3	Differential Clutch Pack
4	Differential Pinion Thrust Washer
5	Differential Pinion Gear

Item	Description
6	Differential Clutch Spring
7	Differential Side Gear
8	Differential Pinion Shaft
9	Differential Pinion Shaft Lock Pin
A	Tighten to 20-41 N·m (15-30 Lb-Ft)

FM3039100123000A

Fig. 16 Exploded view of Traction-Lok

b. Ring gear bolt heads inside rear axle housing may interfere. If so, remove 3–5 bolts to provide clearance.
c. Attach dial indicator with the indicator tip positioned on machined surface of the case flange.
d. Rock ring gear to allow full mesh with pinion gear.
e. With gears in full mesh, set dial indicator to zero.
f. Move differential case as far as possible to the and record reading.
g. Record reading for differential bearing shim selection procedure.
h. Remove dial indicator and differential case from rear axle housing.
i. Stand height of both differential bearings must be measured prior to installation.
j. Place bearing preload tool No. T93P-4220-AR, or equivalent, base in suitable soft-jawed vise with bearing mounting surface above vise jaws.
k. Position differential bearing on bearing preload tool base.
l. Attach bolt, spring, washers and spacer, then tighten bolt.
m. Mark differential bearings left and right before measuring.
n. Invert bearing preload tool No. T93P-4220-AR, or equivalent, and clamp bolt head in suitable vise.
o. Position suitable depth micrometer flat on differential bearing.
p. Measure stand height of both differential bearings and record for differential bearing shim selection.
q. Press left and righthand differential bearing on differential case.
r. Install differential carrier spreader tool No. T4000-E, or equivalent, and dial indicator.
s. **Overspreading may damage rear axle housing.**
t. Tighten and loosen housing spreader adapter screw to normalize housing spreader adapters prior to final dial indicator reading.
u. Adjust dial indicator to zero and tighten the differential carrier spreader screw to spread rear axle housing to .030 inch.
v. Remove dial indicator.

7. **On all models,** apply light coating of Premium Long-Life Grease XG-1-C, or equivalent, to differential bearing shim to help hold in place.
8. Select correct size lefthand side differential bearing shim as follows:
   a. Add end play and bearing height.
   b. Subtract backlash.
   c. Round off initial thickness to nearest shim thickness.
9. Select correct size righthand side differential bearing shim as follows:
   a. Add end play and bearing height.
   b. Add backlash.
   c. Round off initial thickness to nearest shim thickness.
10. Install differential bearing shims in rear axle housing.
11. Position differential bearing cups on differential bearings.
12. Lower differential case in place between differential bearing shims.
13. Install bearing caps in original positions and **torque** bolts to 77 ft. lbs.
14. Tighten bearing cap bolts prior to releasing housing spreader.
15. Remove differential carrier spreader

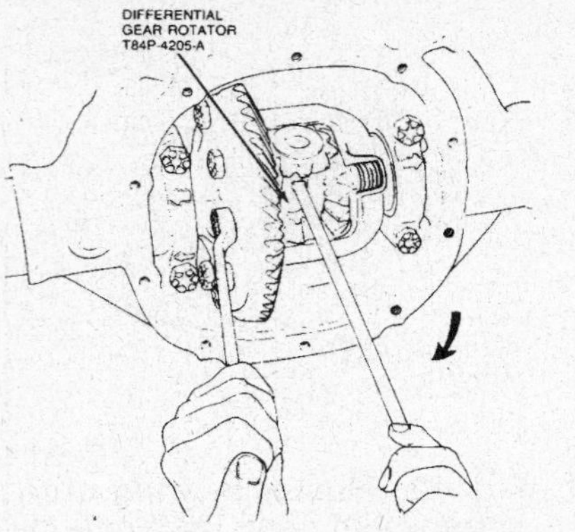

FM3039100126000X

Fig. 17 Pinion gear removal & installation. Traction-Lok

and move dial indicator to 12 o'clock position.
16. Position indicator needle centrally on drive tooth and zero indicator.
17. Turn ring gear without turning pinion gear.
18. Record indicator reading.
19. Measure ring gear backlash at four places to obtain consistent reading.
20. If backlash is not .004 inch, correct by increasing thickness of one differential bearing shim and decreasing thickness of other differential bearing shim by the same amount.
21. Ensure machined surfaces on both rear axle housing and differential housing cover are clean and free of oil before installing new silicone sealant.
22. Inside of rear axle must be covered when cleaning machined surface to prevent contamination.
23. Apply new continuous bead of Silicone Rubber D6AZ-19562-AA, or equivalent, sealant to differential housing cover.
24. Install differential housing cover.
25. Install rear axle and refill.

MARK VIII, THUNDERBIRD & 1997 COUGAR

Do not interchange righthand and lefthand side components during assembly.

1. Place differential case bearing shims into proper locations using a light film of suitable grease to hold them into place.
2. Install carrier spreader, **Fig. 8,** and spread case .030 inch.
3. Place differential case into place. **Use no force or aluminum carrier may be damaged.**
4. With carrier still spread, place differential bearing caps into place and **torque** bolts to 70–85 ft. lbs.
5. Remove carrier spreader, then install a suitable dial gauge and inspect ring gear backlash.
6. If backlash is not within specifications, **Fig. 20,** refer to **Fig. 21** for shim correction table.

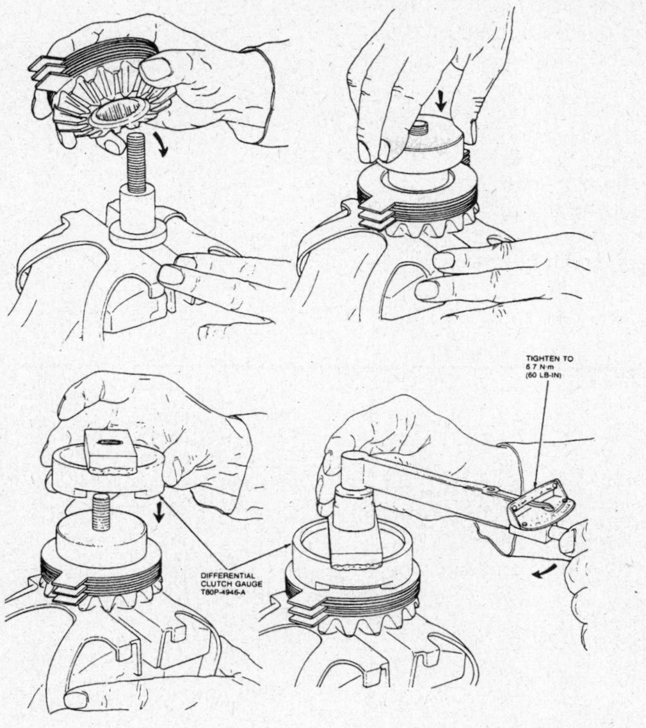

FM3039100124000X

Fig. 18 Shim thickness measuring. Traction-Lok

Description	inches
Maximum Runout of Backface of Ring Gear	0.004
Differential Side Gear Thrust Washer Thickness	0.030-0.032
Differential Pinion Gear Thrust Washer Thickness	0.030-0.032
Maximum Differential Case Runout	0.003
Nominal Pinion Locating Shim	0.030
Backlash Between Ring Gear and Pinion Teeth	0.008-0.015
Maximum Backlash Variation Between Teeth	0.004
Maximum Radial Runout of Companion Flange in Assembly	0.010 TIR

FM3039400281000X

Fig. 20 Rear axle specifications & tolerances

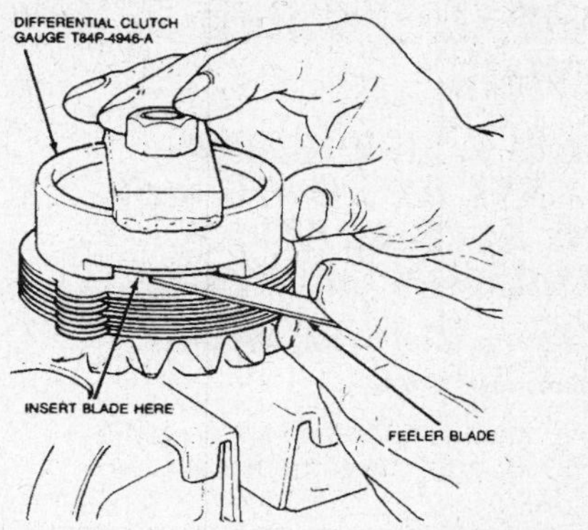

FM3039100125000X

Fig. 19 Shim thickness measurement using tool No. T80P-4946-A, or equivalent. Traction-Lok

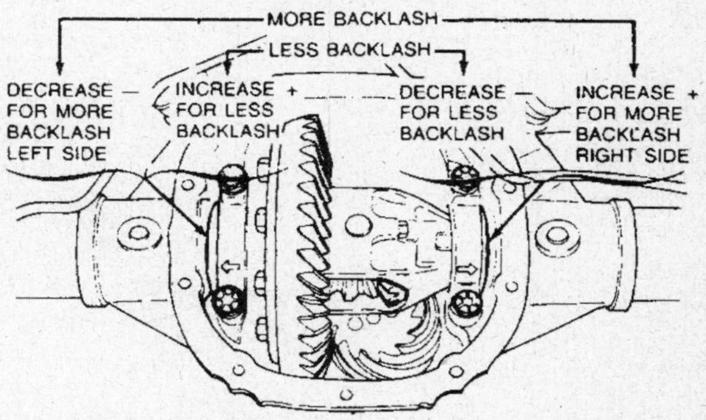

BACKLASH CHANGE REQUIRED	THICKNESS CHANGE REQUIRED	BACKLASH CHANGE REQUIRED	THICKNESS CHANGE REQUIRED
.001	.002	.009	.012
.002	.002	.010	.014
.003	.004	.011	.014
.004	.006	.012	.016
.005	.006	.013	.018
.006	.008	.014	.018
.007	.010	.015	.020
.008	.010		

FM3039100129000X

Fig. 21 Rear axle backlash adjustment

TECHNICAL SERVICE BULLETINS

WHINING NOISE HEARD FROM AXLE AT 50–65 mph DURING ACCELERATION, DECELERATION OR CRUISE

1997 Crown Victoria, Grand Marquis & Town Car

A whining noise is heard from axle while driving at 50–65 mph during acceleration, deceleration or cruise. This may be caused by the axle transmitting the noise through the driveshaft and frame to the interior of the vehicle.

Correct axle noise as follows:

1. Install frame brace kit No. F7AZ-4B410–AA, or equivalent to No. 4 frame crossmember. Refer to instructions included with kit for installation.
2. Verify effectiveness of repair. If axle noise still exists, proceed with normal diagnosis.

ENGINE REBUILDING SPECIFICATIONS

NOTE: For Engine Tightening Specifications, Refer To The Engine Section In The Appropriate Chassis Chapter Of This Manual.

INDEX

CYLINDER HEAD, VALVE GUIDE & VALVE SEATS

All Measurements Given In Inches, Unless Otherwise Specified.

Engine Liter	Year	Cylinder Head Warpage Limit	Valve Guides			Valve Seats					
			Inside Diameter	Stem to Guide Clearance		Seat Angle °	Seat Width		Run-Out	Seat Insert Bore Diameter	
				Intake	Exhaust		Intake	Exhaust		Intake	Exhaust
1.3L	1997	.006	.2760–.2768	.0080	.0080	45	.043–.067	.043–.067	.002	—	—
2.0L⑤	1997	.002	.2366–.2374	.0010–.0024	.0300–.0650	45	.035–.051	.035–.051	—	—	—
2.0L②	1997–2000	①	—	.0007–.0025	.0014–.0032	45	—	—	—	—	—
2.0L⑦	1997–2000	.005	.3170–.3190	.0008–.0027	.0018–.0037	45	.069–.091	.069–.091	.002	1.572–1.573	1.375–1.573
2.5L⑤	1997	.006	—	.0010–.0023	.0012–.0025	45	.032–.055	.032–.055	—	—	—
2.5L ⑥	1997–2000	①	—	.0007–.0027	.0017–.0037	44.75	.043–.055	.055–.066	.001	—	—
3.0L (2V)	1997–99	.007	.3140–.3150	.0010–.0028	.0015–.0033	45	.060–.080	.080–.100	.001	—	—
3.0L (4V)	1997–99	①	—	.0007–.0027	.0017–.0037	44.75	.043–.055	.055–.066	.001	—	—
3.0L (4V)⑧	2000	—	—	—	—	—	—	—	—	—	—
3.4 SHO	1997–99	—	—	.0010–.0023	.0012–.0025	45	.039–.055	.039–.055	—	—	—
3.8L	1997–98	.007	.3433–.3443	.0010–.0028	.0015–.0033	44.5	.060–.080	.060–.080	.003	1.8532–1.8542	1.5645
3.9L	2000	—	—	—	—	—	—	—	—	—	—
4.6L	1997–2000	—	—	.0008–.0027	.0018–.0037	45	③	③	④	—	—

① — .002 inch for each six inches of length.
② — Contour, Cougar, Mystique & ZX2.
③ — 16-valve engine, .075–.083 inch; 32-valve engine, .071–.087 inch.
④ — 16-valve engine, .001 inch; 32-valve engine, .002 inch.
⑤ — Probe.
⑥ — Contour, Cougar & Mystique.
⑦ — Escort & Tracer.
⑧ — LS.

VALVE SPRINGS

All Measurements Given In Inches, Unless Otherwise Specified.

Engine Liter	Year	Free Length	Installed Height	Seated Pressure Pounds @ Inches	Comp. Pressure Pounds @ Inches	Out Of Square Limit
1.3L	1997	1.172	—	—	—	.059
2.0L⑥	1997	1.732	—	—	—	.061
2.0L②	1997–2000	1.700	1.35	①	③	2°
2.0L④	1997–2000	1.860	1.42–1.54	95 @ 1.46	200 @ 1.09	5°
2.5L⑩	1997–2000	⑤	—	—	—	.064
2.5L⑥	1997	1.840	1.57	51 @ 1.57	153 @ 1.18	.010
3.0L (2V)	1997–99	1.840	1.58	65 @ 1.58	180 @ 1.16	—
3.0L (4V)	1997–99	1.840	1.57	51 @ 1.57	153 @ 1.18	.010
3.0L (4V)⑪	2000	—	—	—	—	—
3.4L SHO	1997–99	1.730	1.36	39 @ 1.36	89 @ 1.00	—
3.8L	1997–98	2.020	1.65	85 @ 1.65	220 @ 1.18	—
3.9.L	2000	—	—	—	—	—
4.6L	1997–2000	⑦	—	⑧	⑨	.056

① — Intake, 33 lbs. @ 1.35 inch; exhaust, 41 lbs. @ 1.35 inch.
② — Contour, Cougar, Mystique & ZX2.
③ — Intake, 82 lbs. @ 1.00 inch; exhaust, 95 lbs. @ 1.03 inch.
④ — Escort, Tracer.
⑤ — Intake, 1.729 inch; exhaust, 1.847 inch.
⑥ — Probe.
⑦ — 16-valve engine, 1.95 inch; 32-valve engine, 1.66 inch.
⑧ — 16-valve engine, 54 lbs. @ 1.57 inch; 32-valve engine, 55 lbs. @ 1.42 inch.
⑨ — 16-valve engine, 132 lbs. @ 1.10 inch; 32-valve engine, 160 lbs. @ 1.03 inch.
⑩ — Contour, Cougar & Mystique.
⑪ — LS.

VALVES

All Measurements Given In Inches, Unless Otherwise Specified.

Engine Liter	Year	Valves: Stem Diameter Intake	Stem Diameter Exhaust	Maxi-Tip Refinish	Face Angle	Margin① Int.	Margin① Exh.	Clearance Int.	Clearance Exh.
1.3L	1997	.2744–.2750	.2742–.2748	—	45.0°	—	—	⑥	⑥
2.0L④	1997	.2350–.2356	.2348–.2354	—	45.0°	—	—	⑥	⑥
2.0L⑤	1997–2000	.2375–.2381	.2368–.2374	—	91°	—	—	.039②	.039②
2.0L③	1997–2000	.3159–.3167	.3149–3156	—	45.6°	—	—	⑥	⑥
2.5L④	1997	.2351–.2356	.2349–.2354	—	45.0°	—	—	⑥	⑥
2.5L⑦	1997–2000	.2350–.2358	.2343–.2350	—	45.5°	—	—	.019–.043②	.019–.043②
3.0L (2V)	1997–99	.3126–.3134	.3121–.3129	—	44.0°	—	—	.085–.185②	.085–.185②
3.0L (4V)	1997–99	.2350–.2358	.2343–.2350	—	45.5°	—	—	.019–.043②	.019–.043②
3.0L (4V)⑧	2000	—	—	—	—	—	—	—	—
3.4L SHO	1997–99	.2346–.2352	.2344–.2350	—	45.5°	.020	.020	.006–.010	.010–.014
3.8L	1997–98	.3415–.3423	.3410–.3418	—	45.8°	—	—	.089–.189②	.089–.189②
3.9L	2000	—	—	—	—	—	—	—	—
4.6L	1997–2000	.2746–.2750	.2736–.2744	—	45.5°	—	—	.080–.120②	.080–.120②

① — Minimum.
② — With cylinder @ top dead center, hold steady pressure on lifter until fully collapsed to check clearance.
③ — Escort & Tracer.
④ — Probe.
⑤ — Contour, Cougar, Mystique & ZX2.
⑥ — Not adjustable, zero lash hydraulic lifters used.
⑦ — Contour, Cougar & Mystique.
⑧ — LS.

CAMSHAFT

All Measurements Given In Inches unless Otherwise Specified.

Engine Liter	Year	Camshaft Journal Diameter	Camshaft Bearing Inside Diameter	Camshaft Bearing Clearance	Camshaft Endplay	Lifter Bore Diameter	Lifter Diameter	Lifter To Bore Clearance
1.3L	1997	①	—	—	.0020–.0070	—	—	—
2.0L⑨	1997	1.0213–1.0222	—	.0014–.0032	.0031–.0079	—	—	—
2.0L④	1997–2000	1.0228–1.0236	—	.0007–.0028	.0031–.0086	—	1.1171–1.1178	.0010–.0028
2.0L⑧	1997–2000	1.8007–1.8017	—	.0013–.0033	.0008–.0078	—	.8740–.8745	.0009–.0026
2.5L⑨	1997	⑥	—	⑦	.0020–.0039	—	—	.0010–.0025
2.5L⑩	1997–2000	1.0600–1.0610	1.0620–1.0630	.0010–.0029	.0010–.0064	—	.6290–.6294	.0007–.0027
3.0L (2V)	1997–99	2.0074–2.0084	2.0094–2.0104	.0010–.0030	.0010–.0050	.8752–.8767	.8740	.0007–.0027
3.0L (4V)	1997–99	1.0600–1.0610	1.062–1.063	.0010–.0029	.0010–.0064	—	.6290–6294	.0007–.0027
3.0L (4V)⑪	2000	—	—	—	—	—	—	—
3.4L SHO	1997–99	②	—	⑤	.0039–.0094	—	—	—
3.8L	1997–98	2.0505–2.0515	2.0525–2.0535	.0010–.0030	③	.8767–.8752	.8740–.8745	.0007–.0027
3.9L	2000	—	—	—	—	—	—	—
4.6L	1997–2000	1.0604–1.0614	1.0624–1.0635	.0010–.0030	.0010–.0064	—	.6294–.6299	.0007–.0027

① — Nos. 1 & 3, 1.7103–1.7112 inch; No. 2, 1.7091–1.7100 inch.
② — Front 1.1992–1.1998 inch, Others .9826–.9833 inch.
③ — No endplay. Camshaft is retained by spring.
④ — Contour, Cougar, Mystique & ZX2.
⑤ — Front .0010–.0024 inch, Others .0008–.0024 inch.
⑥ — Righthand cylinder head: No. 1 intake, 1.180–1.1811 inch; No. 1 exhaust, 1.0213–1.0220 inch; Nos. 2, 3, & 4 intake & exhaust, 1.0201–1.0209 inch; No. 5 intake & exhaust, 1.0213–1.0220 inch. Lefthand cylinder head: No. 1 intake, 1.0213–1.0220 inch; No. 1 exhaust, 1.1802–1.1809 inch; Nos. 2, 3, & 4 intake & exhaust, 1.0201–1.0209 inch; No. 5 intake & exhaust, 1.0213–1.0220 inch.
⑦ — Nos. 1 & 5, .0016–.0032 inch; Nos. 2, 3, & 4, .0028–.0044 inch.
⑧ — Escort & Tracer.
⑨ — Probe.
⑩ — Contour, Cougar & Mystique.
⑪ — LS.

CRANKSHAFT, BEARINGS & RODS

All Measurements Given In Inches, Unless Otherwise Specified.

Engine Liter	Year	Crankshaft				Bearing Clearance			Connecting Rods	
		Main Bearing Journal Diameter	Connecting Rod Journal Diameter	Max. Out of Round All	Max. Taper All	Main Bearings	Connecting Rod Bearings	Crankshaft Endplay	Pin Bore Diameter	Side Clearance
1.3L	1997	1.9661–1.9668	1.5724–1.5731	.0020	.0020	.0009–.0017	.0009–.0017	.0031–.0111	.7854–.7859	.0120
2.0L⑧	1997	2.2022–2.2029	1.8874–1.8880	.0001	.0002	①	.0005–.0015	.0031–.0110	.7476–.7480	.0043–.0103
2.0L ③	1997–2000	2.2844–2.2852	1.8439–1.8518	—	—	.0007–.0017	.0006–.0027	.0035–.0102	.7521–7883	.0035–.0126
2.0L⑨	1997–2000	2.2827–2.2835	1.7279–1.7287	.0003	.0003	.0003	.0008–.0026	.0040–.0120	.8098–.8114	.004–.011
2.5L⑧	1997	2.4385–2.4392	—	.0020	.0020	.0015–.0022	.0009–.0017	.0032–.0111	.7864–.7866	.0070–.0130
2.5L⑤	1997–2000	2.4670–2.2790	1.9670–1.9680	—	—	.0009–.0017	.0010–.0025	.0040–.0090	.8270–.8280	.0039–.0118
3.0L (2V)	1997–99	2.5190–2.5198	2.1253–2.1261	.0003	.0003	.0010–.0014	.0010–.0014	.0040–.0080	.9096–.9112	.0060–.0140

Continued

CRANKSHAFT, BEARINGS & RODS—Continued

All Measurements Given In Inches, Unless Otherwise Specified.—Continued

Engine Liter	Year	Crankshaft				Bearing Clearance			Connecting Rods	
		Main Bearing Journal Diameter	Connecting Rod Journal Diameter	Max. Out of Round All	Max. Taper All	Main Bearings	Connecting Rod Bearings	Crankshaft Endplay	Pin Bore Diameter	Side Clearance
3.0L (4V)	1997–99	2.4670–2.4790	1.9670–1.9680	—	—	.0009–.0017	.0010–.0025	.0040–.0090	.8270–.8280	.0039–.0118
3.0L (4V)⑪	2000	—	—	—	—	—	—	—	—	—
3.4L SHO	1997–99	2.4794–2.4803	1.9675–1.9685	.0008	.0008	⑩	⑥	.0024–.0103	.8274–.8280	④
3.8L	1997–98	2.519–2.5198	2.3103–2.3111	.0006	.0003	.0010–0014	.0010–.0014	.0040–.0080	.9096–.9112	.0047–.0114
3.9L	2000	—	—	—	—	—	—	—	—	—
4.6L	1997–2000	2.6570	2.0866	.0019	—	⑦	.0011–.0027	.0051–.0119	②	.0006–.0177

① — Nos. 1, 2, 4 & 5, .0009–.0020 inch; No. 3, .0012–.0022 inch.
② — Except 32-valve engine, .8645–.8653 inch; 32-valve engine, .8664–.8668 inch.
③ — Contour, Cougar, Mystique & ZX2.
④ — Standard .006–.012 inch, Service Limit .0137 inch.
⑤ — Contour, Cougar & Mystique.
⑥ — Desired .0009–.0023 inch, Allowable .0031 inch.
⑦ — Except 32-valve engine, .0011–.0026 inch; 32-valve engine, .0010–.0018 inch.
⑧ — Probe.
⑨ — Escort & Tracer.
⑩ — Desired .0004–.0012 inch, Allowable .0024 inch.
⑪ — LS.

PISTONS, PINS & RINGS

All Measurements Given In Inches, Unless Otherwise Specified.

Engine Liter	Year	Piston Diameter (Std.)	Piston Clearance	Piston Pin Diameter	Pin To Piston Clearance	Piston End Ring Gap①		Piston Ring Side Clearance	
						Comp.	Oil	Comp.	Oil
1.3L	1997	2.7930–2.7940	.0060	.7864–.7866	.0000–.0010	.006	.008	.0010–.0030	—
2.0L⑬	1997	3.2659–3.2667	.0015—.0020	.7470–.7472	—	.006	.008	.0014–.0026	—
2.0L⑫	1997–2000	㉘	㉙	㉚	.0004–.0006	⑯	.016–.055	㉕	⑭
2.0L④	1997–2000	3.3374–3.3386	.0008–.0027	.8119–.8122	.0003–.0005	.010–.030	.010–.030	.0015–.0035	.0015–.0032
2.5L ⑬	1997	3.3250–3.3261	.0012–.0022	.7470–.7472	.0004–.0010	㉗	.008	⑤	—
2.5L⑰	1997–2000	⑥	.0005–.0009	.8278–.8279	.0001–.0005	⑦	.006–.025	⑧	⑭
3.0L (2V)	1997–99	⑪	.0014–.0022	.9119–.9124	.0002–.0005	.010	.010	⑧	⑭
3.0L (4V)	1997–99	㉖	.0005–.0009	.8278–.8279	.0000–.0001	⑦	.006–.025	.0012–.0031	—
3.0L (4V)㉛	2000	—	—	—	—	—	—	—	—
3.4L SHO	1997–99	③	⑨	.8272–.8273	⑩	.008–.014	.008–.028	②	.0024–.0059
3.8L	1997–98	⑮	.0014–.0032	.9119–.9124	.01	⑱	.015	.0016–.0034	—
3.9L	2000	—	—	—	—	—	—	—	—
4.6L	1997–2000	⑲	.0008–.0018	⑳	㉑	㉒	㉓	㉔	.0006

① — Minimum.

② — Top ring, .0018–.0031 inch; 2nd ring, .0012–.0028 inch.

③ — Coded Grade 3 (Brown) 3.2437–3.2441 inch, Coded Grade 2 (None) 3.2433–3.2437 inch, Coded Grade 1 (Green) 3.2429–3.2433 inch.

④ — Escort & Tracer.

⑤ — Top ring, .0008–.0026 inch; 2nd ring, .0012–.0026 inch.

⑥ — Measured 90° from pin bore, 1.7 inches down from top of piston;

grade 1, 3.2436–3.2444 inch;
grade 2, 3.2440–3.2449 inch;
grade 3, 3.2444–3.2452 inch.

⑦ — Top ring, .0039–.0098 inch; 2nd ring, .0106–.0165 inch.

⑧ — Top ring, .0015–.0029 inch; 2nd ring, .0015–.0033 inch.

⑨ — Standard .0008–.0016 inch, Max Service Limit .0028 inch.

⑩ — Press Fit — .00024 to +.00008

⑪ — Coded red, 3.5024–3.5031 inch; coded blue, 3.5035–3.5041 inch; coded yellow, 3.5045–3.5051 inch.

⑫ — Contour, Cougar, Mystique & ZX2.

⑬ — Probe.

⑭ — Snug fit.

⑮ — Coded red, 3.8095–3.8101 inch; coded blue, 3.8107–3.8113 inch; coded yellow, 3.8119–3.8125 inch.

⑯ — Top ring, .008–.010 inch; 2nd ring .012–.020 inch.

⑰ — Contour, Cougar & Mystique.

⑱ — Top ring, .011 inch; 2nd ring, .009 inch.

⑲ — Coded red, 3.5498–3.5503 inch; coded blue, 3.5503–3.5509 inch; coded yellow, 3.5509–3.5514 inch.

⑳ — Except 32-valve engine, .8659–.8661 inch; 32-valve engine, .8662–.8663 inch.

㉑ — Except 32-valve engine, .0002–.0039 inch; 32-valve engine, .0001–.0007 inch.

㉒ — Except 32-valve engine: top & 2nd ring, .009 inch; 32-valve engine: top ring, .010 inch; 2nd ring, .009 inch.

㉓ — Except 32-valve engine, .010 inch; 32-valve engine, .006 inch.

㉔ — Top ring, .002–.004 inch; 2nd ring, .001–.003 inch.

㉕ — Top ring, .0016–.0028 inch; 2nd ring, .0008–.0020 inch.

㉖ — Coated pistons, measure 90° from pin bore, 1.7 inches down from top of piston; grade 1, 3.5035–3.5043 inch; grade 2, 3.5038–3.5048 inch; grade 3, 3.5043–3.5051 inch.

㉗ — Top ring, .006 inch; 2nd ring, .010 inch.

㉘ — Measured 90° from pin bore, 1.7 inches down from top of piston; grade 1, 3.3399–3.3403 inch; grade 2, 3.3403–3.3407 inch; grade 3, 3.3407–3.3411 inch.

㉙ — Coated piston, .0004–.0011 inch; non coated piston, .0008–.0016 inch.

㉚ — White, .8125–.8126 inch; red, .8126–.8127 inch; blue, .8127–.8131 inch.

㉛ — LS.

CYLINDER BLOCK

All Measurements Given In Inches, Unless Otherwise Specified.

Engine Liter	Year	Cylinder Bore Diameter (Std.)	Cylinder Bore Taper Max.	Cylinder Bore Out of Round Max.
1.3L	1997	2.7953–2.7960	.0007	.0007
2.0L⑤	1997	3.2677–3.2685	.0004	.0004
2.0L①	1997–2000	④	.0010	.0010
2.0L⑥	1997–2000	3.3400	.0005	.0010
2.5L⑤	1997	3.3268–3.3276	.0008	.0008
2.5L⑦	1997–2000	③	.0002	.0007
3.0L (2V)	1997–99	3.5040	.0020	.0020
3.0L (4V)	1997–99	—	.0007	.0008
3.0L (4V)⑧	2000	—	—	—
3.4L SHO	1997–99	②	.0002	.0005
3.8L	1997–98	3.8100	.0020	.0020
3.9L	2000	—	—	—
4.6L	1997–2000	3.5510	.0006	.0020

① — Contour, Cougar, Mystique & ZX2.
② — Grade 1: 3.2441–3.2445 inch,
Grade 2: 3.2445–3.2449 inch,
Grade 3: 3.2449–3.2453 inch.
③ — Grade 1 bore, 3.2465–3.2469;
grade 2 bore, 3.2469–3.2473;
grade 3 bore, 3.2473–3.2477.
④ — Grade 1 bore, 3.3411–3.3415;
grade 2 bore, 3.3415–3.3419;
grade 3 bore, 3.3419–3.3423
⑤ — Probe.
⑥ — Escort & Tracer.
⑦ — Contour, Cougar & Mystique.
⑧ — LS.

OIL PUMP

All Measurements Given In Inches, Unless Otherwise Specified.

Engine Liter	Year	Rotor Back-lash	Rotor To Body Clear-ance	Rotor End-play①	Driveshaft To Pump Body Clearance	Relief Valve To Body Clearance	Relief Spring Pressure Lbs. @ Inch-es
1.3L	1997	—	.0087	.0050	—	—	—
2.0L②	1997	—	—	—	—	—	—
2.0L③④	1997–2000	—	—	—	—	—	—
2.0L⑤	1997–2000	—	.0029–.0063	.0005–.0035	—	.0008–.0031	9.3–10.3 @ 1.11
2.5L②	1997	.0078	.0087	.0051	—	—	—
2.5L⑧④	1997–2000	—	—	—	—	—	—
3.0L (2V)	1997–99	.0080–.0012	.0020–.0055	.0005–.0055	⑥	.0017–.0029	9.1–10.1 @ 1.11

Continued

OIL PUMP—Continued

All Measurements Given In Inches, Unless Otherwise Specified.

Engine Liter	Year	Rotor Back-lash	Rotor To Body Clear-ance	Rotor End-play①	Driveshaft To Pump Body Clearance	Relief Valve To Body Clearance	Relief Spring Pressure Lbs. @ Inch-es
3.0L (4V)④	1997–99	—	—	—	—	—	—
3.0L (4V)⑨	2000	—	—	—	—	—	—
3.4L SHO	1997–99	.0024–.0071	.0012–.0035	.0039–.0069	.0012–.0035	.0020–.0035	52.5 Per Inch
3.9L	2000	—	—	—	—	—	—
3.8L	1997–98	.0080–.0012	.0020–.0055	.0005–.0055	⑦	.0017–.0029	15.2–17.1 @ 1.20
4.6L④	1997–2000	—	—	—	—	—	—

① — Measured between pump cover mounting surface & end of gear, using straightedge & feeler gauge.
② — Probe.
③ — Contour, Cougar, Mystique & ZX2.
④ — Not a service item, replaced as an assembly.
⑤ — Escort & Tracer.
⑥ — Driver shaft to body clearance, .0005–.0019 inch; idler shaft to idler clearance, .0004–.0017 inch.
⑦ — Driver shaft to body clearance, .0015–.0030 inch; idler shaft to idler clearance, .0005–.0017 inch.
⑧ — Contour, Cougar & Mystique.
⑨ — LS.

GENERAL MOTORS CORP.

GENERAL MOTORS CORP.

ACHIEVA, ALERO, CUTLASS, GRAND AM, MALIBU & SKYLARK

NOTE: Refer To Rear Of This Manual For Vehicle Manufacturer's Special Service Tool Suppliers.

INDEX OF SERVICE OPERATIONS

ACHIEVA, ALERO, CUTLASS, GRAND AM, MALIBU & SKYLARK

Specifications

GENERAL ENGINE SPECIFICATIONS

Engine Liter/VIN Code①	Fuel Injection System	Bore & Stroke	Compression Ratio	Net H.P. @ RPM②	Maximum Torque Ft. Lbs. @ RPM	Normal Oil Pressure psi
1997–98						
2.4L/T	SFI	3.54 × 3.70	9.5	150 @ 5600	155 @ 4400	④
3.1L/M	SFI	3.50 × 3.31	9.5	155 @ 5200	185 @ 4000	60③
1999						
2.4L/T	SFI	3.54 × 3.70	9.5	150 @ 5600	155 @ 4400	④
3.1L/M	SFI	3.50 × 3.31	9.5	150 @ 4800	185 @ 4000	60③
3.4L/E	SFI	3.62 × 3.31	9.5	170 @ 5200	195 @ 4000	⑤
2000						
2.4L/T	SFI	3.54 × 3.70	9.5	150 @ 5600	155 @ 4400	④
3.1L/J	SFI	3.50 × 3.31	9.6	170 @ 5200	190 @ 4000	⑤
3.4L/E	SFI	3.62 × 3.31	9.5	170 @ 4800	200 @ 4000	⑤

SFI — Sequential Fuel Injection
① — The eighth digit denotes engine code.
② — Ratings are as installed in vehicle.
③ — 1850 RPM with engine at operating temperature.
④ — 10 psi minimum @ 900 RPM; 30 psi minimum @ 3000 RPM.
⑤ — 15 psi at 1100 RPM.

TUNE UP SPECIFICATIONS

Year & Engine/VIN Code①	Spark Plug Gap, Inch	Ignition Timing, ° BTDC				Curb Idle Speed RPM③		Fast Idle Speed RPM		Fuel Pump Pressure, psi	Valve Lash
		Firing Order, Fig.	Man. Trans.	Auto. Trans.	Mark Fig.	Man. Trans.	Auto. Trans.	Man. Trans.	Auto Trans.		
1997–98											
2.4L/T	.060	A	⑦	⑦	⑧	④	④	④	④	41–47⑤	⑥
3.1L/M	.060	②	⑦	⑦	⑧	④	④	④	④	41–47⑨	⑥
1999											
2.4L/T	.050	A	⑦	⑦	⑧	④	④	④	④	41–47⑤	⑥
3.1L/M	.060	②	⑦	⑦	⑧	④	④	④	④	41–47⑨	⑥
3.4L/E	.060	②	—	⑦	⑧	—	④	—	④	41–47⑩	⑥
2000											
2.4L/T	.050	A	⑦	⑦	⑧	④	④	④	④	48–55⑩	⑥
3.1L/J	.060	②	⑦	⑦	⑧	④	④	④	④	48–55⑩	⑥
3.4L/E	.060	②	—	⑦	⑧	—	④	—	④	48–55⑩	⑥

BTDC — Before Top Dead Center
① — The eighth digit of the Vehicle Identification Number (VIN) denotes engine code.
② — Cylinder numbering from front of engine to rear: righthand bank, 1-3-5; lefthand bank, 2-4-6. Firing order: 1-2-3-4-5-6. Refer to **Fig. B** for spark plug wire connections at ignition coil.
③ — P: Park. When adjusting idle speed, set parking brake & block drive wheels.
④ — Idle speed is controlled by an idle air control (IAC) valve or an idle speed control (ISC) motor.
⑤ — Loosen fuel tank filler cap. Raise & support vehicle, then disconnect fuel pump electrical connector. Start engine & operate until fuel

supply is depleted. Crank engine for approximately three seconds, then turn ignition Off. Connect fuel pump electrical connector and disconnect battery ground cable. Disconnect fuel line quick connect fittings and install fuel pressure test gauge tool No. J-29658-D, or a suitable equivalent. Tighten fuel tank filler cap & connect battery ground cable. Turn ignition On & inspect for leaks at gauge connections. Note fuel pressure reading with ignition turned On.

⑥ — Vehicle is equipped w/hydraulic valve lifters. No adjustment is required.

⑦ — Ignition timing is controlled by Powertrain Control Module (PCM).

⑧ — Equipped with crankshaft position sensor.

⑨ — With shop towel wrapped around fuel pressure valve to prevent fuel spillage, connect a suitable fuel pressure gauge to fuel pressure valve. Inspect fuel pressure with ignition On, but engine not running.

⑩ — Disconnect and isolate battery ground cable. Loosen fuel filler cap. Remove fuel pressure connection cap. Wrap shop towel around fuel pressure connection while connecting pressure gauge tool No. J-34730-1A, or equivalent. Connect battery ground cable and inspect fuel pressure with ignition On, but engine not running.

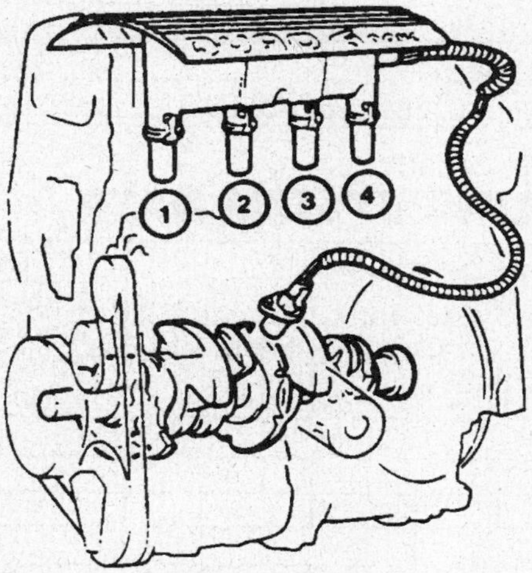

Firing order 1-3-4-2

GC1139300353000X

Fig. A

FIRING ORDER 1-2-3-4-5-6

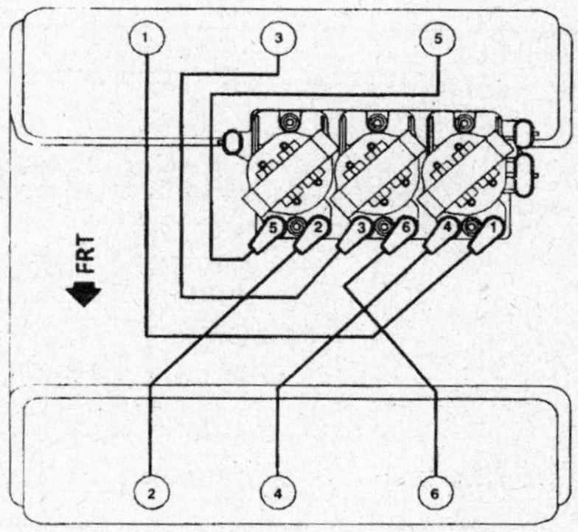

GC1139300604000X

Fig. B

FRONT WHEEL ALIGNMENT SPECIFICATIONS

Model	Caster Angle, Degrees		Camber Angle, Degrees		Total Toe, Degrees	Ball Joint Wear
	Limits	Desired	Limits	Desired		
1997						
Achieva, Grand Am & Skylark	+.45 to +2.45	+1.45	–1.00 to +1.00	0	–.25 to +.25	①
Cutlass & Malibu	+3.30 to +5.30	+4.30	–1.20 to +.80	–.20	–.25 to +.25	①
1998						
Achieva, Grand Am & Skylark	+.45 to +2.45	+1.45	–1.00 to +1.00	0	–.25 to +.25	①
Cutlass & Malibu	+3.10 to +5.10	+4.10	–1.20 to +.80	–.20	–.15 to +.35	①
1999–2000						
All	+3.10 to +5.10	+4.10	–1.20 to +.80	–.20	–.15 to +.35	①

① — Refer to "Front Suspension & Steering" section for ball joint inspection procedure.

REAR WHEEL ALIGNMENT SPECIFICATIONS

Model	Camber Angle, Degrees		Total Toe, Degrees	Thrust Angle, Degrees
	Limits	Desired		
1997				
Achieva, Grand Am & Skylark	–1.15 to +.35	–.40	–.1 to +.5	–.25 to +.25
Cutlass & Malibu	–.90 to +.10	–.40	–.20 to +.20	–.20 to +.20
1998				
Achieva, Grand Am & Skylark	–1.15 to +.35	–.40	–.1 to +.5	–.25 to +.25
Cutlass & Malibu	–.90 to +.10	–.20	–.26 to +.14	–.20 to +.20
1999				
Alero & Grand Am	–.70 to +.30	–.20	–.26 to +.14	–.20 to +.20
Cutlass & Malibu	–.90 to +.10	–.20	–.26 to +.14	–.20 to +.20
2000				
All	–.70 to +.30	–.20	–.26 to +.14	–.20 to +.20

FLUID CAPACITIES & COOLING SYSTEM DATA

Year	Engine/VIN Code⑤	Coolant Capacity, Qts.	Surge Tank Cap Relief Pressure, psi	Thermo. Opening Temp. Deg. F	Fuel Tank Gals.	Engine Oil Refill Qts.	Transaxle Oil	
							5 Speed Manual Transaxle Pts.	Auto. Transaxle Qts.①
ACHIEVA & SKYLARK								
1997–98	2.4L/T	10.4	15	180	15.2	4②	4	③
	3.1L/M	13.1	15	195	15.2	4②	4	④
ALERO & GRAND AM								
1997–98	2.4L/T	10.4	15	180	15.2	4②	4	③
	3.1L/M	13.1	15	195	15.2	4②	4	④
1999	2.4L/T	11.3	15	185	15	4	—	⑦
	3.4L/E	13.6	15	195	15	4.5	—	⑦
2000	2.4L/T	11.3	15	185	14.3	4		⑦
	3.4L/E	13.6	15	195	14.3	4.5	—	⑦
CUTLASS & MALIBU								
1997–99	2.4L/T	11.3	15	180	15.2	4②	—	⑥
	3.1L/M	13.6	15	195	15.2	4②	—	⑥
2000	3.1L/J	13.6	15	195	15	4.5	—	⑦

① — Approximate. Make final inspection with dipstick.
② — When changing filter, additional oil may be required.
③ — On models with 3T40 transaxle oil pan capacity, 4 qts.; total capacity, 7 qts.; dry, 9 qts. On models with 4T60E oil pan capacity, 6 qts.; total capacity, 8 qts.; dry, 10 qts.
④ — Oil pan capacity 6 qts.; total capacity 8 qts.; dry, 10 qts.
⑤ — The eighth digit denotes engine code.
⑥ — Oil pan capacity, 7.4 qts.; total capacity, 10.6 qts.
⑦ — Pan capacity 6.9 qts.; total capacity 9.5 qts.; dry 12.9 qts.

LUBRICANT DATA

Year	Model	Lubricant Type				
		Transaxle		Clutch Hydraulic System	Power Steering System	Brake System
		Automatic	Manual			
1997–98	All	Dexron III	①	③	Power Steering Fluid ②	DOT 3
1999	All	Dexron III	①	③	Power Steering Fluid④	DOT 3
2000	All	Dexron III	—	—	Power Steering Fluid④	DOT 3

①— Synchromesh transaxle fluid GM part No. 12345349, or equivalent.
②— Meeting GM specification 9985010 or equivalent. In cold climates use GM part No. 12345867 or 12345866, or equivalents. System must be flushed, refilled & bled prior to installation of cold climate fluid.
③— Hydraulic clutch fluid GM part No. 12345347, or equivalent.
④— GM part No. 1052884 (pint), 1050017 (quart), or equivalent.

Electrical

NOTE: On Air Bag Equipped Models, Refer To "Air Bag System Precautions" Located In The Front Of This Manual For System Disarming & Arming Procedures.

NOTE: Refer To "Computer Relearn Procedures " Located In The Front Of This Manual For Computer Relearn Procedures.

INDEX

PRECAUTIONS

AIR BAG SYSTEMS

Refer to "Air Bag System Precautions" in the front of this manual for system disarming and arming procedures.

BATTERY GROUND CABLE

Prior to service, disconnect battery ground cable and isolate as required.

FUSE PANEL & FLASHER LOCATION

ACHIEVA, SKYLARK & 1997-98 GRAND AM

The fuse panel is located behind the left-hand side of instrument panel. The turn signal flasher is located in the convenience center next to the hazard flasher. The hazard warning flasher is located on the convenience center, behind the lefthand side of the instrument panel to the left of the steering column.

ALERO, CUTLASS, MALIBU & 1999-2000 GRAND AM

The fuse panel is located behind the left-hand side of instrument panel. The turn and hazard flasher is an internal part of the hazard switch located in the center of the instrument panel.

FUEL PUMP RELAY LOCATION

ACHIEVA, ALERO, GRAND AM & SKYLARK

The fuel pump relay is located in the engine compartment relay center on the left-hand side of the engine compartment, **Fig. 1.**

CUTLASS & MALIBU

The fuel pump relay is located in the underhood bussed electrical center on the lefthand side of the engine compartment, **Fig. 2.**

RELAY CENTER LOCATION

The relay center is located on the left-hand side of the engine compartment.

STARTER

REPLACE

2.4L ENGINE

1. Remove air inlet duct from throttle body.
2. Remove starter upper mounting bolt.
3. Raise and support vehicle.
4. Remove all required shrouding and closeout panels.
5. Remove starter lower mounting bolt.
6. Position engine wiring harness aside.
7. Move starter to access solenoid wiring and remove starter electrical wiring.
8. Remove starter.
9. Reverse procedure to install, noting the following:
    a. **Torque** cable to solenoid nut to 8.8 ft. lbs.
    b. **Torque** lower mounting bolt to 66 ft. lbs.
    c. **Torque** upper mounting bolt to 66 ft. lbs.

3.1L ENGINE

1. Raise and support vehicle.
2. Remove starter motor mounting bolts, then lower the starter.
3. Disconnect starter electrical connectors and remove starter.
4. Reverse procedure to install. **Torque** mounting bolts to 37 ft. lbs.

3.4L ENGINE

Removal

1. Raise and safely support vehicle.
2. Remove flywheel inspection cover.
3. Remove all electrical connectors from starter.
4. Remove starter mounting bolts, then the starter.

Installation

1. Tighten nut next to cap on solenoid BAT terminal while starter is still on bench.
2. Secure electrical terminal on solenoid.
3. **Torque** solenoid battery terminal inside nut to seven ft. lbs.
4. Install electrical connectors to starter.
5. **Torque** solenoid battery terminal outside nut to seven ft. lbs.
6. **Torque** solenoid "S" terminal outside nut to 22 inch lbs.
7. Install starter onto engine and **torque** mounting bolts to 32 ft. lbs.
8. Install inspection cover and **torque** bolts to 7.4 ft. lbs.

ALTERNATOR

REPLACE

2.4L ENGINE

1. Remove serpentine drive belt using tool No. J-37059, or equivalent to rotate tensioner.
2. Remove mounting bolts and studs, **Fig. 3.**
3. Disconnect electrical leads and remove alternator.
4. Reverse procedure to install. **Torque** mounting bolts to 37 ft. lbs.

3.1L ENGINE

1. Remove serpentine drive belt.
2. Disconnect alternator electrical connectors and power steering line clip.
3. Remove alternator rear brace.
4. Disconnect alternator air inlet connector.
5. Remove mounting bolts and nuts, then the alternator.
6. Reverse procedure to install. **Torque** mounting bolts to 18 ft. lbs. and nut to 37 ft. lbs.

3.4L ENGINE

1. Remove cruise control module as required.
2. Remove engine mount as required.
3. Using a suitable ⅜ inch breaker bar, rotate serpentine drive belt tensioner in a clockwise direction and remove belt.
4. Disconnect alternator electrical connectors and power steering line clip.
5. Remove mounting bolts and nuts, then the alternator.
6. Reverse procedure to install, noting the following:
    a. **Torque** alternator mounting bolts to 37 ft. lbs.
    b. **Torque** alternator mounting nuts to 22 ft. lbs.
    c. **Torque** engine mount to body bolt to 96 ft. lbs.
    d. **Torque** engine mount to body nut to 49 ft. lbs.
    e. **Torque** engine mount bracket support bolts to 96 ft. lbs.

COIL PACK

REPLACE

2.4L ENGINE

Removal

1. Remove accelerator and cruise control cables from their hold-down clip.
2. Remove fuel line retainer clip bolt.
3. Disconnect electronic Ignition Control Module (ICM) 11-pin electrical connector.
4. Remove ICM and coil assembly to camshaft housing bolts, **Fig. 4.**
5. If spark plug boots adhere to plugs, use remover tool No. J-36011, or equivalent to twist, then pull upward on retainers.
6. Remove coil and ICM assembly.
7. Remove housing to cover screws. Ensure ground strap remains in place.
8. Disconnect coil harness electrical connector, **Fig. 5,** then remove housing from cover.
9. Remove ignition coil(s) from housing, **Fig. 6.**
10. Disconnect coil electrical connectors.
11. Remove contact springs from housing.
12. Remove coil seals from coils.

Installation

1. Install new seals into ignition coils.
2. Install contact springs into housing using petroleum jelly to keep them in place.
3. Connect coil electrical connector.
4. Install coils into housing.
5. Connect ground strap if it was not done during removal.
6. Connect coil(s) electrical connector to ICM, ensuring ground strap stays in place.
7. Install housing to cover.
8. Install housing to cover screws. **Torque** to 35 inch lbs.
9. Install spark plug boots and retainers to housing.
10. Install coil and ICM assembly to engine while carefully aligning boots to plug terminals.
11. Coat coil and ICM assembly to camshaft housing bolts with GM Loctite sealant part No. 12346004, or equivalent.
12. Install bolts with isolator washer rubber sides facing down, then **torque** to 16 ft. lbs.
13. Connect ICM 11-pin electrical connector.
14. Install fuel line retainer clip bolt.

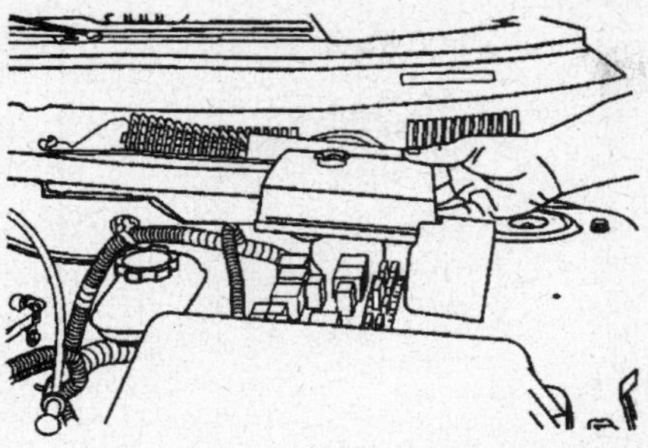

Fig. 1 Fuel pump relay location. Achieva, Alero, Grand Am & Skylark

15. Install accelerator and cruise control cables into their hold-down clip.

3.1L ENGINE

1. Remove electrical connectors from ignition control module.
2. Remove spark plug wires from ignition coils.
3. Remove screws securing ignition coils to ignition module, then the coils.
4. Reverse procedure to install. **Torque** coil to module screws to 40 inch lbs.

3.4L ENGINE

1. Tag spark plug wires to ensure proper routing, then disconnect them from ignition coils.
2. Remove screws retaining ignition coils to ignition module, then the coils.
3. Reverse procedure to install. **Torque** retaining screws to 40 inch lbs.

IGNITION LOCK

REPLACE

ACHIEVA, SKYLARK & 1997–98 GRAND AM

Less Ignition Key

1. Remove ignition switch assembly wiring harness and steering column.
2. Drill a 9⁄32 inch hole in steering column housing assembly back, **Fig. 7.**
3. Insert retainer spring tool No. J-41253, or equivalent into hole, then engage and remove lock retainer spring.
4. Hold steering column vertical and tap on housing assembly to dislodge lock retainer. It may be necessary to remove retainer with suitable needle nose pliers.
5. Pull lock cylinder from housing assembly, then clean metal shavings from drilled hole.
6. Reverse procedure to install.

With Ignition Key

1. Remove lower lefthand insulator panel screws and disconnect two-way yellow SIR connectors.
2. Remove tilt lever, upper and lower steering column trim covers.
3. Turn lock cylinder to Run position, push locking button on steering column back and remove lock cylinder.

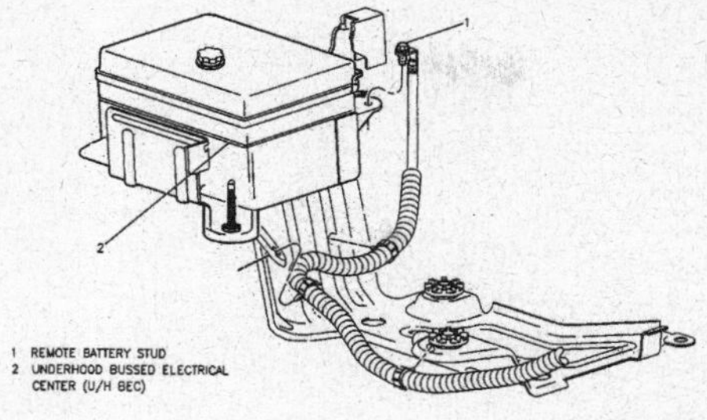

Fig. 2 Fuel pump relay location. Cutlass & Malibu

4. Reverse procedure to install.

ALERO, CUTLASS, MALIBU & 1999–2000 GRAND AM

Refer to "Ignition Switch, Replace."

IGNITION SWITCH

REPLACE

ACHIEVA, SKYLARK & 1997–98 GRAND AM

1. Remove steering wheel and covers as outlined under "Steering Wheel, Replace."
2. Turn ignition to Off/Lock.
3. Remove ignition switch wire harness.
4. Remove tapping screws and ignition switch, **Fig. 8.**
5. Reverse procedure to install. **Torque** screws to 12 inch lbs.

ALERO & 1999–2000 GRAND AM

1. Remove lefthand sound insulator.
2. Remove ignition switch trim ring.
3. Remove accessory trim plate.
4. Remove upper steering column cover.
5. Remove instrument cluster trim plate.
6. Remove instrument cluster.
7. Remove ignition switch retaining bolts, then the switch.
8. Disconnect electrical connectors.
9. Disconnect ignition lock cable from switch.
10. Insert key into ignition lock cylinder and turn to Run position.
11. Depress cylinder release plunger. This is located at four o'clock position on switch.
12. Pull on key to remove cylinder from switch.
13. Reverse procedure to install.

CUTLASS & MALIBU

1. Remove lefthand sound insulator, ignition switch trim ring and accessory trim plates, then the instrument cluster.
2. Remove mounting bolts and electrical connectors, then the console trim plate.
3. Remove ignition lock cable from shift lever and bracket at console front.
4. Remove ignition switch.
5. Reverse procedure to install. **Torque** ignition switch mounting bolts to 18 inch lbs.

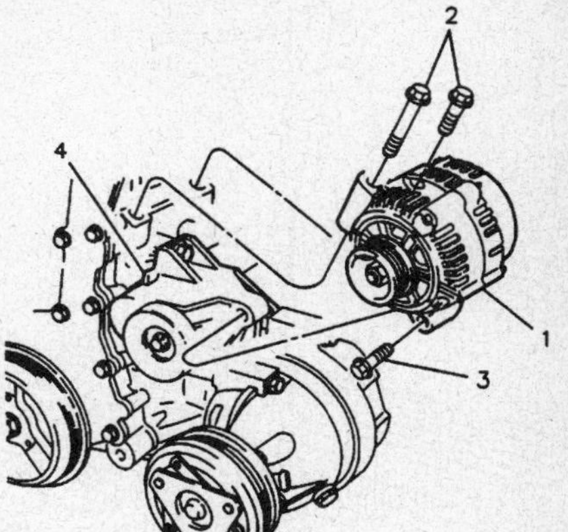

1 GENERATOR
2 UPPER GENERATOR BOLTS
3 LOWER GENERATOR BOLTS
4 BELT TENSIONER

GC1129600064000X

Fig. 3 Alternator replacement. 2.4L engine

CLUTCH START SWITCH

REPLACE

1. Disconnect switch electrical connector.
2. Remove nuts attaching switch to mounting, then remove switch.
3. Reverse procedure to install. After installation, inspect switch for proper operation.

NEUTRAL SAFETY SWITCH

REPLACE

REMOVAL

1. Disconnect switch electrical connector.
2. Remove shift linkage retaining nut, then the linkage.
3. Remove shift linkage lever.
4. Note switch orientation and make alignment marks as required to ease installation.
5. Remove mounting screws and switch.

INSTALLATION

1. Place shift shaft in Neutral position, then align flats on shaft with those on the switch.
2. Loosely install switch with marks properly aligned.
3. If original switch is being installed, insert a 3⁄32 inch drill bit into switch adjustment hole. Move switch until drill bit drops to depth of 9⁄64 inch. **Torque** switch mounting screws to 18 ft. lbs., then remove drill bit.
4. New switches are pinned in Neutral position. If installation is difficult, ensure shift shaft is in Neutral. Do not rotate switch. **Torque** switch mounting screws to 18 ft. lbs.

Fig. 4 Ignition coil & control module assembly removal. 2.4L engine

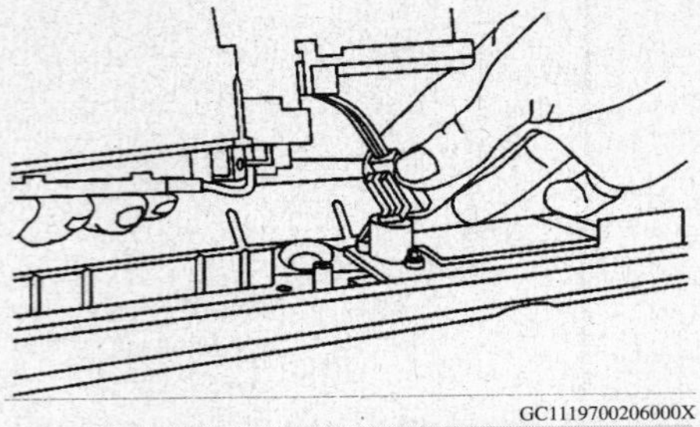

Fig. 5 Coil harness electrical connector disconnection. 2.4L engine

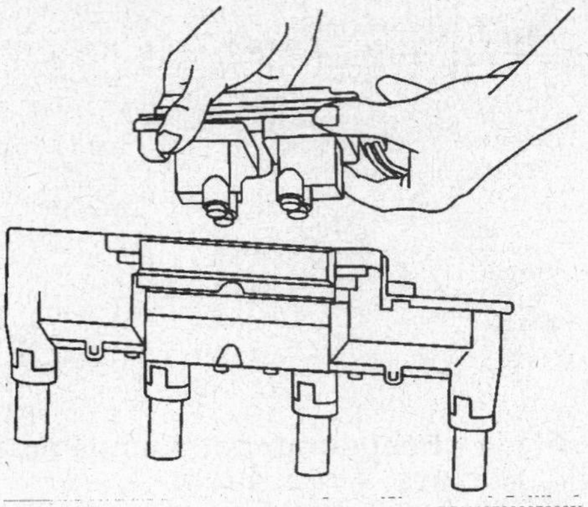

Fig. 6 Ignition coil removal. 2.4L engine

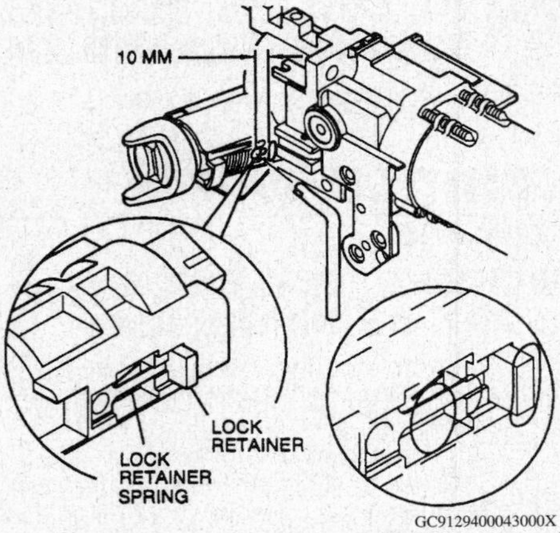

Fig. 7 Lock cylinder removal. Achieva, Skylark & 1997–98 Grand Am

HEADLAMP SWITCH

REPLACE

ACHIEVA, CUTLASS, MALIBU, SKYLARK & 1997–98 GRAND AM

1. Remove instrument cluster trim plate retaining screws, then the trim plate.
2. Disconnect headlamp switch electrical connector.
3. Remove headlamp switch from instrument panel.
4. Reverse procedure to install.

ALERO & 1999–2000 GRAND AM

Removal

1. Place turn signal and multi-function switch in center of Off position.
2. Remove steering column air bag module.
3. Remove steering wheel using puller tool No. J-1859-A and legs tool No. J-42120, or equivalent.
4. Remove steering column lower cover retaining bolts.
5. Tilt lower cover down and slide it rearwards to disengage locking tabs, then remove cover.
6. Remove upper column cover retaining bolts.
7. Remove wiring harness strap.
8. Remove two wiring harness straps from column harness.
9. Disconnect switch electrical connectors from column bulkhead connector as required.
10. Remove bolts from turn signal and multi-function switches, then the switches.

Installation

1. Use a suitable small flat-bladed screwdriver to compress turn signal and multi-function switch electrical contact, then move switches into position.
2. Ensure electrical contact rests on cancelling cam.
3. Install turn signal and multi-function switch bolts, then **torque** to 53 inch lbs.
4. Connect switch electrical connectors at column bulkhead connector.
5. Connect column bulkhead connector to vehicle main harness.
6. Install two wiring harness straps at column harness.
7. Install wiring harness strap.
8. Install upper and lower column covers.
9. Place turn signal and multi-function switch in center of Off position.
10. Install steering wheel.
11. **On 1997–98 models, torque** nut to 30 ft. lbs.
12. **On 1999 models, torque** nut to 29 ft. lbs.
13. **On 2000 models, torque** nut to 27 ft. lbs.
14. **On all models,** install air bag module. **Torque** screws to 89 inch lbs.

STOP LIGHT SWITCH

REPLACE

ACHIEVA, SKYLARK & 1997–98 GRAND AM

1. Disconnect electrical connectors from switch, then pull switch out of retaining clip on brake pedal support.
2. Depress brake pedal and push replacement switch into retainer until switch shoulder is bottomed against bracket.
3. Adjust switch by pulling brake pedal back against stop.
4. Ensure switch has continuity when pedal is depressed from normal rest position and stop lamps turn off when pedal returns to full rest.

ALERO, CUTLASS, MALIBU & 1999–2000 GRAND AM

Removal

1. Remove lefthand side instrument panel insulator.
2. Disconnect stop lamp switch electrical connector.
3. Remove switch retainer by grasping and turning 90° counterclockwise and pulling toward rear of vehicle.
4. Remove stop lamp switch.

Installation

1. Insert stop lamp switch into retainer until switch body has seated onto retainer.
2. Pull brake pedal upward against its internal stop.
3. Adjust switch so its plunger extends no more than .78 inch beyond threaded portion when brake pedal is fully released.
4. Rotate switch 90° clockwise until it locks into position.
5. Connect switch electrical connector.

MULTI-FUNCTION SWITCH

REPLACE

ACHIEVA, CUTLASS, MALIBU, SKYLARK & 1997–98 GRAND AM

1. Remove horn pad and steering wheel as outlined under "Steering Wheel, Replace."

2. Remove tilt lever from steering column, if equipped. If required, position spark plug boot or other suitable device over tilt lever (to prevent damage) and remove tilt lever using locking pliers.
3. Remove steering column upper and lower covers, then the dampener assembly.
4. Remove attaching screw and switch assembly, **Fig. 9.**
5. Reverse procedure to install.

ALERO & 1999–2000 GRAND AM

Refer to "Headlamp Switch, Replace" for replacement procedure.

TURN SIGNAL SWITCH

REPLACE

ACHIEVA, CUTLASS, MALIBU, SKYLARK & 1997–98 GRAND AM

Refer to "Multi-Function Switch, Replace" for replacement procedure.

ALERO & 1999–2000 GRAND AM

Refer to "Headlamp Switch, Replace" for replacement procedure.

DIMMER SWITCH

REPLACE

ACHIEVA, CUTLASS, MALIBU, SKYLARK & 1997–98 GRAND AM

Refer to "Multi-Function Switch, Replace" for replacement procedure.

ALERO & 1999–2000 GRAND AM

Refer to "Headlamp Switch, Replace" for replacement procedure.

STEERING WHEEL

REPLACE

1. Remove attaching screws for horn pad or inflator module.
2. **On models equipped with radio controls,** remove wire protector plate connector.
3. **On all models,** remove horn pad or inflator module and horn lead, then the steering wheel retainer and nut.
4. Remove steering wheel using puller tool No. J-1859-A and legs tool No. J-42120, or equivalent.
5. Reverse procedure to install, noting the following:
   a. **On 1997–98 models, torque** steering wheel nut to 30 ft. lbs.
   b. **On 1999 models, torque** steering wheel nut to 29 ft. lbs.
   c. **On 2000 models, torque** steering wheel nut to 27 ft. lbs.
   d. **On all models,** install air bag module. **Torque** screws to 89 inch lbs.

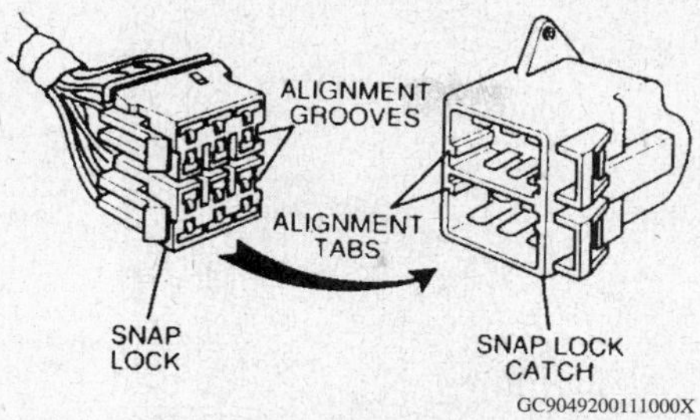

Fig. 8 Ignition switch & electrical connections. Achieva, Skylark & 1997–98 Grand Am

BACK-UP LAMP SWITCH

REPLACE

AUTOMATIC TRANSAXLE

Refer to "Neutral Safety Switch, Replace" for replacement procedure.

MANUAL TRANSAXLE

1. Disconnect back-up lamp switch electrical connector.
2. Using a suitable socket, remove back-up lamp switch from top of transaxle case. **Do not use an open-end wrench.**
3. Reverse procedure to install. Prior to installation, apply pipe sealant part No. 1052080, or equivalent to switch threads.

INSTRUMENT CLUSTER

REPLACE

1. Remove mounting screws, electrical connectors and instrument panel cluster trim plates.
2. Remove instrument cluster to instrument panel mounting screws.
3. Disconnect cluster electrical connectors and remove instrument cluster.
4. Reverse procedure to install.

RADIO

REPLACE

ACHIEVA & SKYLARK

1. Remove mount screws, disconnect electrical connectors and remove instrument panel cluster trim plate.
2. Twist fastener ¼ turn, remove accelerator pedal nut, courtesy lamp and lefthand sound insulator.
3. Twist fastener ¼ turn, remove courtesy lamp and righthand sound insulator.
4. Remove screws and bolts, then the lower instrument panel cluster trim pad, **Fig. 10.**
5. Remove HVAC control and radio housing attaching screws, **Fig. 11.**
6. Remove attaching nuts, then pull radio rearward.
7. Disconnect all electrical connectors and antenna lead-in, then remove radio assembly.
8. Reverse procedure to install. **Torque** radio to radio bracket attaching nuts to 17 inch lbs.

ALERO & 1999–2000 GRAND AM

1. Remove accessory trim plate.
2. Remove radio mounting screws.
3. Pull radio rearward.
4. Disconnect all electrical connectors and antenna lead-in.
5. Reverse procedure to install.

CUTLASS & MALIBU

1. Remove ignition key trim cover using a suitable flat-bladed pry tool.
2. Pull accessory trim plate to rear and remove.
3. Remove mounting screws and pull radio to rear.
4. Disconnect all electrical connectors and antenna lead-in.
5. Remove radio.
6. Reverse procedure to install.

1997–98 GRAND AM

1. Remove mounting screws, disconnect electrical connectors and remove instrument panel cluster trim plate, **Fig. 12.**
2. Remove HVAC control and radio housing attaching screws, **Fig. 13.**
3. Remove attaching nuts, pull radio to rear, disconnect antenna and electrical connectors and remove radio assembly.
4. Reverse procedure to install. **Torque** radio to radio bracket attaching nuts to 17 inch lbs.

WIPER MOTOR

REPLACE

ACHIEVA, CUTLASS, MALIBU, SKYLARK & 1997–98 GRAND AM

1. Remove wiper arm and blade assemblies.
2. Remove cowl cover assembly.
3. Use wiper transmission separator tool No. J-39232, or equivalent to disconnect drive link from crank arm.
4. Disconnect wiper motor electrical connectors.
5. Remove mounting screws and wiper motor.
6. Reverse procedure to install, noting the following:
   a. **Torque** motor mounting screws to seven ft. lbs.
   b. Use wiper transmission installer tool No. J-39529, or equivalent to connect drive link to crank arm.

ALERO & 1999–2000 GRAND AM

1. Remove wiper arms from shafts.
2. Remove cowl air inlet grille.
3. Disconnect wiper motor electrical connector.
4. Remove three wiper drive system assembly to vehicle mounting screws, then the wiper assembly from vehicle.

5. Remove wiper transmission assembly from crank arm using separator tool No. J-39232, or equivalent.
6. Remove two motor to tube frame mounting screws, then the motor from frame.
7. Reverse procedure to install, noting the following:
   a. Install motor onto tube frame. **Torque** screws to 88 inch lbs.
   b. Install transmission assembly onto crank arm using installer tool No. J-39529, or equivalent.
   c. Install drive system module onto vehicle. **Torque** screws to 88 inch lbs.

WIPER SWITCH

REPLACE

1. Remove multi-function switch as outlined under "Multi-Function Switch, Replace."
2. Remove attaching screws and windshield wiper and washer switch, **Fig. 9.**
3. Reverse procedure to install.

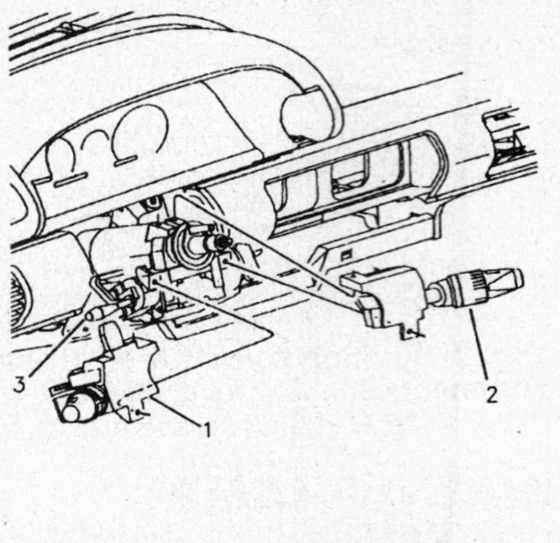

1 HEADLAMP/TURN SIGNAL/CRUISE CONTROL HAZARD SWITCH
2 WINDSHIELD WIPER/WASHER SWITCH
3 TILT LEVER (IF EQUIPPED)

GC9049200112000A

Fig. 9 Multi-function switch replacement. Achieva, Cutlass, Malibu, Skylark & 1997–98 Grand Am

WIPER TRANSMISSION

REPLACE

ACHIEVA, SKYLARK & 1997-98 GRAND AM

1. Remove wiper arm and blades assemblies.
2. Remove cowl cover assembly and disconnect drive link from crank arm using wiper transmission separator tool No. J-39232, or equivalent.
3. Remove attaching screws and guide linkage out through access hole.
4. Reverse procedure to install. **Torque** mounting screws to six ft. lbs.

ALERO & 1999-2000 GRAND AM

1. Remove wiper arms from transmission shafts.
2. Remove air inlet screen from cowl panel.
3. Disconnect wiper motor electrical connector.
4. Remove wiper transmission retaining screws, then the transmission from the vehicle.
5. Using separator tool No. J-39232, or equivalent, disconnect motor crank arm from transmission assembly.
6. Remove transmission assembly cap.
7. Remove four screws and transmission assembly from tube frame.
8. Remove three grommets from tube frame and transmission assembly.
9. Remove motor assembly from tube frame.
10. Reverse procedure to install, noting the following:
    a. **Torque** wiper transmission to tube frame screws to 79 inch lbs.
    b. Install transmission onto crank arm using installer tool No. J-39529, or equivalent.
    c. **Torque** wiper transmission mounting screws to 79 inch lbs.

CUTLASS & MALIBU

1. Remove wiper arm and blades assemblies.
2. Remove cowl cover assembly and disconnect wiper motor connector.
3. Remove mounting screws and wiper drive system module.
4. Remove wiper motor as outlined under "Wiper Motor, Replace."
5. Remove transmission assembly caps, wiper motor grommets and transmission assembly.
6. Reverse procedure to install. **Torque** mounting screws to six ft. lbs.

BLOWER MOTOR

REPLACE

ACHIEVA, SKYLARK & 1997-98 GRAND AM

1. **On models equipped with 3.1L engine,** remove serpentine belt, attaching bolts and alternator and set aside.
2. **On all models,** disconnect blower motor electrical connectors and position engine wiring harness aside.
3. Partially cut blower motor case cover as indicated in **Fig. 14.** The cutting pattern is also indicated on the blower case cover. Cover thickness is approximately ⅛ inch. Cut just through thickness of cover. Any cut deeper than thickness of cover may cause damage to cooling tube.
4. Move cut portion of cover downward and disconnect blower motor cooling tube.
5. Remove retaining screws and blower motor.
6. Reverse procedure to install. Use three retaining clips to attach cut portion of blower motor cover.

ALERO, CUTLASS, MALIBU & 1999-2000 GRAND AM

The blower motor and fan are located in the lower righthand corner of the HVAC module. The fan and motor are serviced only as a complete assembly.

1. Remove righthand closeout panel and insulator as required.
2. Position Body Control Module (BCM) aside.
3. Disconnect blower motor electrical connectors.
4. Remove blower motor attaching screws, then the motor and fan assembly.
5. Reverse procedure to install. **Torque** blower motor attaching screws to 45 inch lbs.

HEATER CORE

REPLACE

ACHIEVA, SKYLARK & 1997-98 GRAND AM

1. Drain coolant into an approved container.
2. Raise and support vehicle.
3. Disconnect heater hoses from heater core assembly and remove drain tube.
4. Lower vehicle, apply parking brake and block drive wheels.
5. Position transaxle shift lever in Neutral.
6. **On models equipped with automatic transaxle,** remove retaining clip and shift lever handle.
7. **On models equipped with manual transaxle,** turn shift lever handle counterclockwise to remove from lever.
8. **On all models,** carefully pry upward on outer edges of console trim plate.
9. Disconnect electrical connectors and ashtray lamp from console trim plate, then remove trim plate from console.
10. Remove attaching screws and console.
11. Remove attaching screws, then disconnect cruise control module electrical connector and lamp and remove lefthand sound insulator panel.
12. Remove attaching screws and nuts, disconnect EVO controller electrical connector and lamp and remove righthand sound insulator panel.
13. Remove attaching screws and steering column filler panel.
14. Remove floor outlet duct.
15. Remove attaching screws and heater core cover.
16. Remove mounting clamps and heater core.
17. Reverse procedure to install.

ALERO & 1999-2000 GRAND AM

1. Drain coolant into an approved container.
2. Raise and safely support vehicle.
3. Drain tube from heater case.
4. Disconnect heater hoses at heater core.
5. Lower the vehicle.

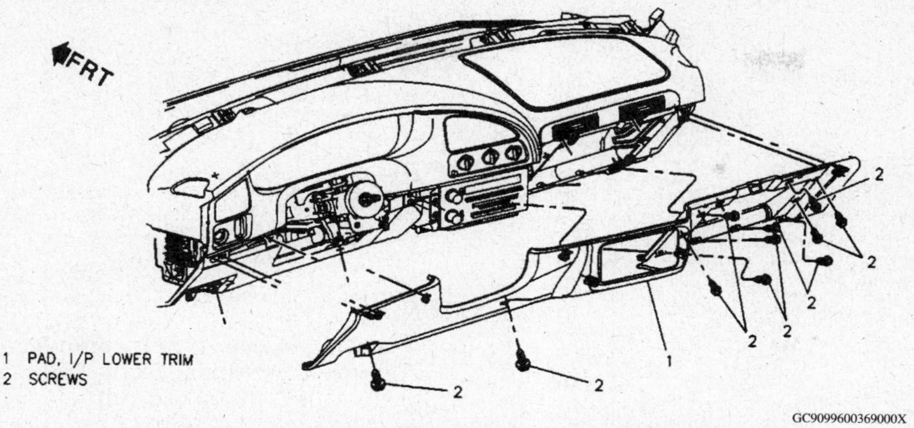

Fig. 10 Lower trim pad removal. Achieva & Skylark

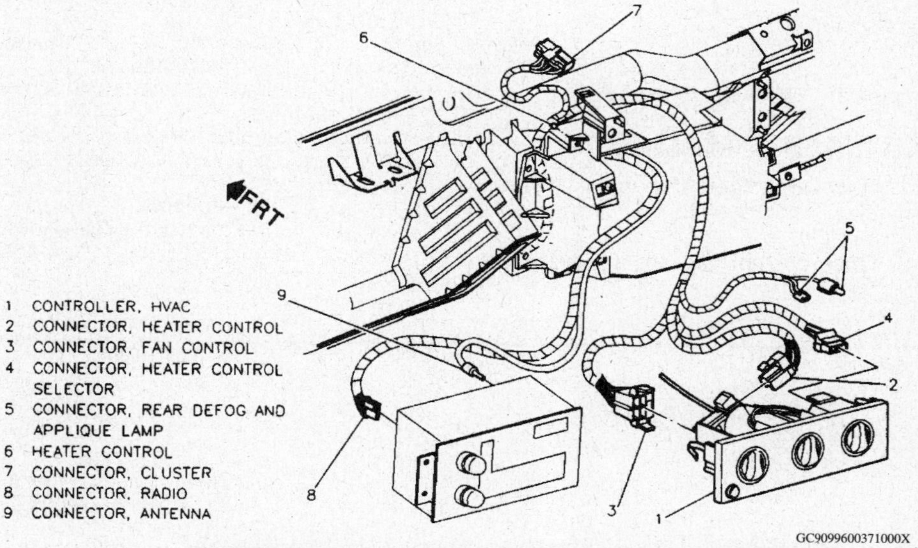

Fig. 11 HVAC control & radio removal. Achieva & Skylark

6. **On models equipped with console,** partially remove console as required.
7. **On all models,** remove righthand and lefthand closeout and insulator panels.
8. Remove steering column opening filler.
9. Remove floor air outlet duct.
10. Remove heater core cover. One mounting screw is located in a recess in center of cover.
11. Remove core mounting clamps, then the core.
12. Reverse procedure to install, noting the following:
    a. **Torque** core mounting clamps to 12 inch lbs.
    b. **Torque** cover screws to 12 inch lbs.
    c. **Torque** floor air outlet screws to 12 inch lbs.
    d. Close radiator petcock, fill cooling system and inspect for leaks.

CUTLASS & MALIBU

1. Drain coolant into an approved container.
2. Remove heater hoses and drain tube.
3. Remove instrument panel and console as outlined in "Dash Panel Service."

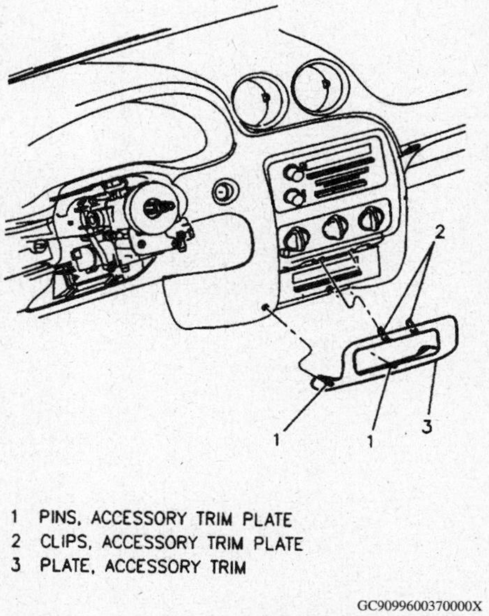

Fig. 12 Lower trim plate removal. 1997–98 Grand Am

4. Remove heater outlet, mounting screw and heater core cover.
5. Remove mounting clamps and heater core.
6. Reverse procedure to install.

EVAPORATOR CORE

REPLACE

ACHIEVA, SKYLARK & 1997–98 GRAND AM

1. Recover refrigerant charge using recycling station tool No. J-39500, or equivalent.
2. Raise and support vehicle. Remove front exhaust system heat shield.
3. Remove attaching bolts and swing cradle cross brace aside.
4. Disconnect refrigerant lines from evaporator and lower vehicle.
5. Remove righthand under dash insulator panel.
6. Disconnect heater core cover electrical connector.
7. Remove lefthand side insulator panel, steering column filler panel and center console.
8. Remove floor duct and heater core cover, then the heater shroud and straps.
9. Remove evaporator core. Use care when removing evaporator core, as heater core is only suspended by heater core pipes.
10. Reverse procedure to install. When connecting refrigerant lines, use new O-rings.

ALERO & 1999–2000 GRAND AM

1. Recover refrigerant charge using recycling station tool No. J-39500, or equivalent.
2. Raise and safely support vehicle.
3. Remove evaporator drain tube.
4. Remove lines from evaporator and discard O-rings.
5. Lower the vehicle.
6. Remove righthand and lefthand closeout and insulator panels.
7. Remove electrical junction box at heater core cover.
8. Remove steering column filler.
9. **On models equipped with console,** partially remove console to access floor duct and heater core cover.
10. **On all models,** remove floor air duct.
11. Remove heater core cover. One mounting screw is located in a recess in center of cover.
12. Remove heater core shroud and straps.
13. Remove evaporator assembly.
14. Reverse procedure to install, noting the following:
    a. **Torque** evaporator assembly screws to 12 inch lbs.
    b. **Torque** heater core shroud and straps screws to 12 inch lbs.
    c. **Torque** heater cover screws to 12 inch lbs.
    d. **Torque** floor duct screws to 12 inch lbs.

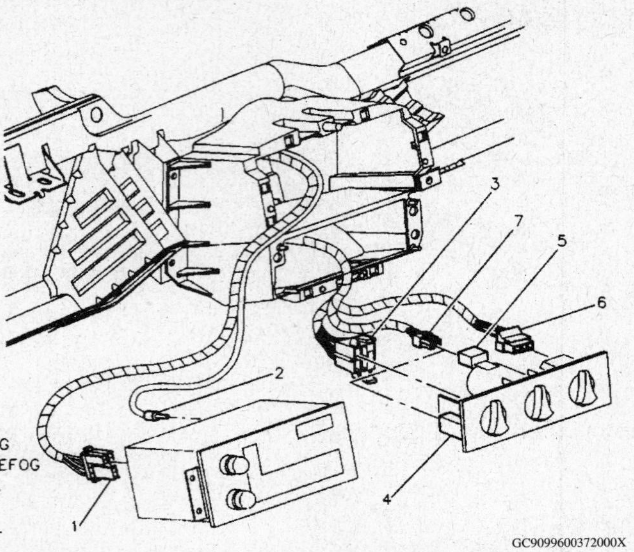

1 CONNECTOR, RADIO
2 CONNECTOR, ANTENNA
3 CONNECTOR, FAN SPEED CONTROL
4 CONNECTOR, WITH REAR DEFOG
5 CONNECTOR, WITHOUT REAR DEFOG
6 CONNECTOR, HEATER CONTROL SELECTOR
7 CONNECTOR, HEATER CONTROL

Fig. 13 HVAC control & radio removal. 1997–98 Grand Am

e. **On 1999 models, torque** evaporator inlet line fitting to 14 ft. lbs. and outlet line fitting to 35 ft. lbs.
f. **On 2000 models, torque** evaporator hose fitting bolt to 18 ft. lbs.
g. **On all models,** evacuate and charge refrigerant system.

CUTLASS & MALIBU

1. Recover refrigerant charge using recycling station tool No. J-39500, or equivalent.
2. Drain coolant into an approved container.

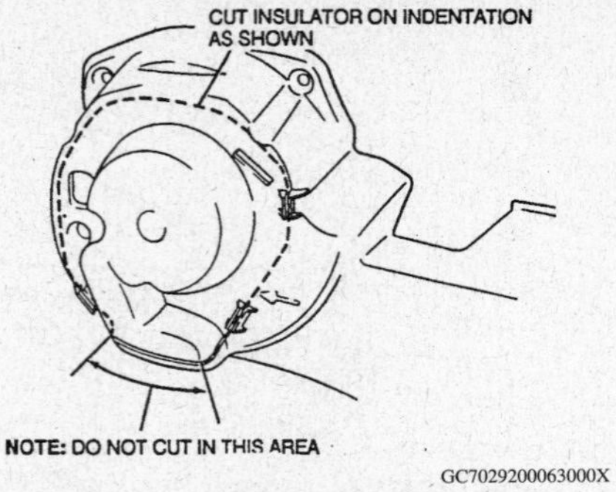

Fig. 14 Blower motor removal pattern. Achieva, Skylark & 1997–98 Grand Am

3. Remove heater core hoses, evaporator block fitting, seal plate and moisture drain tube.
4. Remove instrument panel and console as outlined in "Dash Panel Service."
5. Remove heater outlet, mounting screw and heater core cover.
6. Remove clamps and heater core, then the mounting screw and heater core shroud.
7. Remove evaporator core.
8. Reverse procedure to install using new sealing washers. **Torque** evaporator hose to evaporator fitting nut to 18 ft. lbs.

2.4L Engine

NOTE: On Air Bag Equipped Models, Refer To "Air Bag System Precautions" Located In The Front Of This Manual For System Disarming & Arming Procedures.

NOTE: Refer To "Computer Relearn Procedures " Located In The Front Of This Manual For Computer Relearn Procedures.

INDEX

PRECAUTIONS

AIR BAG SYSTEMS

Refer to "Air Bag System Precautions" in the front of this manual for system disarming and arming procedures.

FUEL SYSTEM PRESSURE RELIEF

Failure to relieve system pressure prior to disconnecting fuel system components may cause fire or personal injury.

1. Loosen fuel tank filler cap to relieve tank pressure.
2. Raise and safely support vehicle.
3. Disconnect fuel pump electrical connector.
4. Lower the vehicle.
5. Start and operate engine until fuel supply is consumed.
6. Crank engine for approximately three seconds to relieve remaining pressure.
7. Disconnect battery ground cable, then connect fuel pump connector.

BATTERY GROUND CABLE

Prior to service, disconnect battery ground cable and isolate as required.

COMPRESSION PRESSURE

When inspecting cylinder compression, the engine should be at room temperature, the throttle should be open, all spark plugs removed and the battery at or near full charge. The lowest reading cylinder should not be less than 70% of the highest and no cylinder reading should be less than 100 psi. Turn ignition key until engine cranks through four compression cycles. Normal compression builds up quickly and evenly to specified compression on each cylinder.

ENGINE MOUNT

REPLACE

FRONT MOUNT

1. Remove coolant recovery tank attaching bolt and position tank aside with hoses connected.
2. Install engine support tool No. J-28467-360, or equivalent then raise engine off the mount.
3. Remove mount to body attaching nuts.
4. Remove engine bracket to mount attaching bolts.
5. Remove engine mount assembly.
6. Reverse procedure to install. Tighten nuts and bolts to specifications.

ENGINE MOUNT STRUT

1. Raise and support vehicle.
2. Remove righthand front splash shield.
3. Remove engine mount strut bolts, **Fig. 1.**
4. Remove engine mount strut.
5. Reverse procedure to install. Tighten bolts to specifications.

ENGINE

REPLACE

ACHIEVA, MALIBU, SKYLARK & 1997–98 GRAND AM

1. Recover refrigerant charge using recycling station tool No. J-39500, or equivalent.
2. Drain coolant into an approved container.
3. **On models equipped with manual transaxle,** remove lefthand sound insulator and disconnect clutch push rod from pedal assembly.
4. **On all models,** disconnect heater hose at thermostat housing.
5. Disconnect radiator upper inlet hose.
6. Remove air cleaner assembly.
7. Remove coolant fan.
8. Disconnect compressor/condenser hose assembly at compressor and discard O-rings.
9. Disconnect vacuum hoses from front of engine.
10. Disconnect alternator, A/C compressor, injector harness, Idle Air Control (IAC) and Throttle Position (TP) sensors at throttle body, Manifold Air Pressure (MAP) and Intake Air Temperature (IAT) sensors, EVAP

Canister Purge solenoid, starter solenoid and ground cables.
11. Disconnect battery ground cable from transaxle, Electronic Ignition Coil and Module ASM, two Engine Coolant Temperature sensors, oil pressure sensor/switch, oxygen sensor (O2S), Crankshaft Position (CP) sensor, back-up lamp switch and camshaft position sensor.
12. Disconnect power brake vacuum hose from throttle body.
13. Disconnect throttle cable and bracket.
14. Remove power steering bolts and pump. Position pump aside with lines attached.
15. Disconnect fuel lines. Refer to "Precautions" for fuel system pressure relief.
16. Disconnect shift cables.
17. **On models equipped with manual transaxle,** disconnect clutch actuator line.
18. **On all models,** remove exhaust manifold and heat shield.
19. Disconnect radiator lower outlet hose.
20. Install engine support fixture No. J-28467-360, or equivalent.
21. Remove coolant recovery tank attaching bolt and position tank aside with hoses intact.
22. Remove engine mount assembly as outlined under "Engine Mount, Replace."
23. Raise and support vehicle.
24. Remove front wheel and tire assemblies.
25. Remove righthand splash shield.
26. Disconnect vehicle speed and sensors, starter solenoid and front ABS wheel speed sensor electrical connectors.
27. Remove engine mount strut and transaxle mount as outlined under "Engine Mount Replace."
28. Separate ball joints from steering knuckles.
29. Remove suspension supports, crossmember and stabilizer shaft as an assembly.
30. Remove heater outlet hose from radiator outlet pipe.
31. **On models equipped with manual transaxle,** disconnect axle shaft from transaxle and intermediate shaft and position aside.
32. **On all models,** remove flywheel housing cover.
33. Position suitable support below engine, then lower vehicle onto support.
34. Mark threads on support fixture hooks so setting can be duplicated when installing engine. Remove engine support fixture J-hooks.
35. Raise vehicle slowly off engine and transaxle assembly. Note that it may be necessary to move engine/transaxle assembly rearward to clear intake manifold.
36. Separate engine from transaxle.
37. Reverse procedure to install. Tighten all fasteners to specifications. Fill all drained fluids and inspect for leaks.

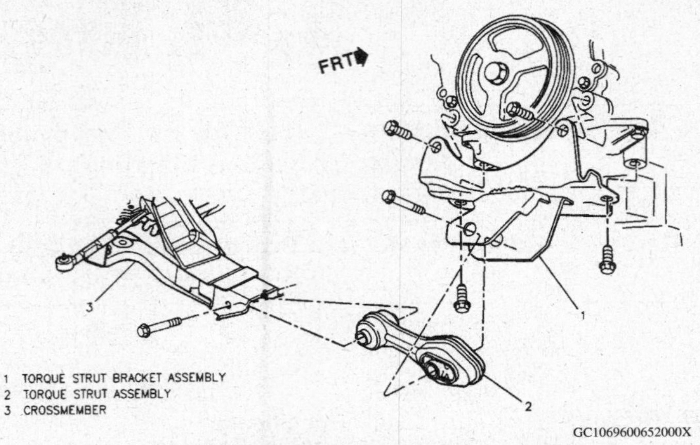

Fig. 1 Engine mount strut & bracket

ALERO & 1999–2000 GRAND AM

1. Relieve fuel system pressure as outlined under "Precautions."
2. Drain coolant into an approved container.
3. Drain engine oil using approved containers and methods.
4. Remove fuel rail assembly, then the air intake duct from air cleaner.
5. Disconnect and remove ignition coil and module assembly, then the Camshaft Position Sensor (CMP) electrical connector.
6. Remove power steering pump mounting fasteners, then position pump aside with lines and hoses intact.
7. Disconnect oil pressure sender electrical connector.
8. Remove air intake duct bracket, then the cruise control assembly and position aside.
9. Install engine support fixture tool No. J-28467-360, or equivalent.
10. Remove engine mount assembly.
11. Disconnect vacuum hose at fuel pressure regulator.
12. Raise engine using support fixture "J" hook.
13. Remove engine mount bracket, then lower the engine.
14. Raise and safely support vehicle.
15. Remove serpentine drive belt using tensioner tool No. J-36018, or equivalent.
16. Remove front tires and wheels, then the righthand front splash shield.
17. Remove harmonic balancer using puller tool No. J-24420-C, or equivalent.
18. Lower the vehicle.
19. Disconnect electrical connectors at MAP, IAT and EGR sensors, then at EVAP canister.
20. Remove alternator.
21. Remove and discard accelerator cable. **Manufacturer recommends cable replacement when engine is removed and installed.**
22. Position cruise control cable aside to avoid damage.
23. Remove accelerator cable bracket, then the starter motor.
24. Remove exhaust brace bolt from exhaust manifold, then the exhaust manifold heat shield.
25. Disconnect exhaust pipe at manifold.
26. Remove intake coolant pipe.
27. Remove torque converter bolts.
28. Raise and safely support vehicle.
29. Remove O2 sensor.
30. Remove A/C compressor bolts, then position compressor aside with lines intact.
31. Remove oil pan to bellhousing bolts.
32. Remove transaxle mount.
33. Remove transaxle to engine attaching bolts.
34. Install a suitable lifting device to engine.
35. Raise engine and separate it from transaxle.
36. If engine will be mounted onto a stand, remove flexplate mounting bolts and flexplate, then mount engine on suitable stand.
37. Reverse procedure to install, noting the following:
    a. If flexplate was removed, install it and its bolts. Tighten bolts evenly to specifications while holding flexplate in place with holder tool No. J-38122, or equivalent.
    b. Tighten all fasteners to specifications.
    c. Start engine and inspect for fluid leaks.

INTAKE MANIFOLD

REPLACE

1. Remove air cleaner duct.
2. Disconnect electrical connectors at MAP, IAT and EVAP sensors and fuel injector harness.
3. Disconnect vacuum hoses from fuel regulator and EVAP canister purge solenoid to canister.
4. Remove throttle cable bracket.
5. Disconnect coolant lines from throttle body as required.
6. Remove stud-ended alternator mount bolt.
7. Remove pipe from EGR adapter.
8. Raise and support vehicle.
9. Remove intake manifold support brace, then lower the vehicle.
10. Remove manifold retaining nuts, bolts, manifold and gasket, **Fig. 2.**

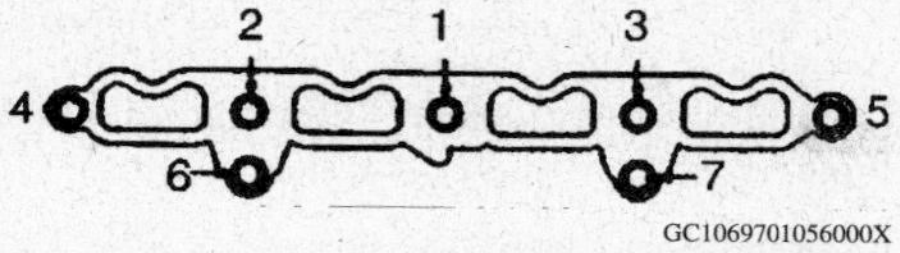

Fig. 2 Intake manifold installation & bolt tightening sequence

11. Reverse procedure to install. Tighten intake manifold bolts in sequence outlined in **Fig. 2.**

EXHAUST MANIFOLD

REPLACE

1. Disconnect electrical connector from O2 sensor.
2. Raise and safely support vehicle.
3. Remove exhaust manifold brace to manifold bolts.
4. Remove upper heat shield.
5. Remove exhaust pipe to manifold retaining nuts, then pull down and back on pipe to disengage from manifold. **Do not bend exhaust flex coupler more than 3° in any direction.**
6. Lower the vehicle and remove exhaust manifold to cylinder head retaining nuts, manifold, seals and gaskets.
7. Reverse procedure to install. Tighten exhaust manifold attaching nuts in sequence outlined in **Fig. 3.**

CYLINDER HEAD

REPLACE

1. Drain coolant into an approved container.
2. Remove air cleaner duct.
3. Disconnect heater inlet and throttle body hoses from coolant outlet.
4. Disconnect power brake vacuum hose.
5. Disconnect MAP, IAT, CMP sensor and EVAP canister purge solenoid electrical connectors.
6. Remove alternator stud-ended bolt.
7. Remove brace and intake manifold as outlined under "Intake Manifold, Replace."
8. Install alternator stud-ended bolt.
9. Install engine support tool No. J-28467-360, or equivalent.
10. Remove exhaust manifold as outlined under "Exhaust Manifold, Replace."
11. Remove electrical connectors, mounting bolts and ignition coil and module.
12. Remove power steering pump as outlined under "Front Suspension & Steering."
13. Remove fuel pressure regulator vacuum line and fuel injector harness connectors.
14. Remove fuel line retaining clamp and fuel rail mounting bolts on top of intake camshaft housing.
15. Cover injector openings and injector nozzles.
16. Remove fuel rail with lines attached and position aside.
17. **On Alero and 1999–2000 Grand Am models,** proceed as follows:
    a. Remove timing chains as outlined under "Timing Chain, Replace."
    b. Remove timing sprockets.
    c. Remove water pump as outlined under "Water Pump, Replace."
18. **On all models except Alero and 1999–2000 Grand Am,** disconnect timing chain housing at intake camshaft housing. **Do not remove it from vehicle.**
19. **On all models,** remove intake and exhaust camshaft housings.
20. Remove valve lifters.
21. Disconnect oil pressure switch and ECT sensor electrical connectors.
22. **On models equipped with automatic transaxle,** remove transaxle fluid level indicator tube if required.
23. **On all models,** disconnect upper radiator hose and ECT sensor connectors.
24. Remove mounting bolts in reverse of tightening sequence, **Fig. 4.**
25. Reverse procedure to install. Tighten cylinder head attaching bolts using torque angle meter tool No. J-36660, or equivalent as outlined in **Fig. 4.**

CAMSHAFT LOBE LIFT SPECIFICATIONS

Engine/VIN	Int., Inch	Exh., Inch
2.4L/T	.354	.346

VALVE ADJUSTMENT

These engines are equipped with hydraulic valve lash adjusters. No adjustment is required.

VALVE GUIDES

Valve guides are an integral part of the cylinder head and are not removable. If valve stem clearance becomes excessive, the valve guide should be reamed to the next oversize and the appropriate oversize valves installed.

VALVE LASH ADJUSTERS

These engines use hydraulic valve lash adjusters. The valve lash adjusters can be replaced after the appropriate camshaft and housing are removed. Refer to "Camshaft, Replace."

FRONT COVER

REPLACE

1. Drain coolant into an approved container.
2. Remove coolant reservoir or surge tank.
3. Remove serpentine drive belt.
4. Attach engine support tool Nos. J-28467-360 and J-28467-400, or equivalents onto alternator stud-ended bolt.
5. Remove front cover upper attaching screws.
6. Remove engine mount assembly and bracket adapter. Discard adapter bolts.

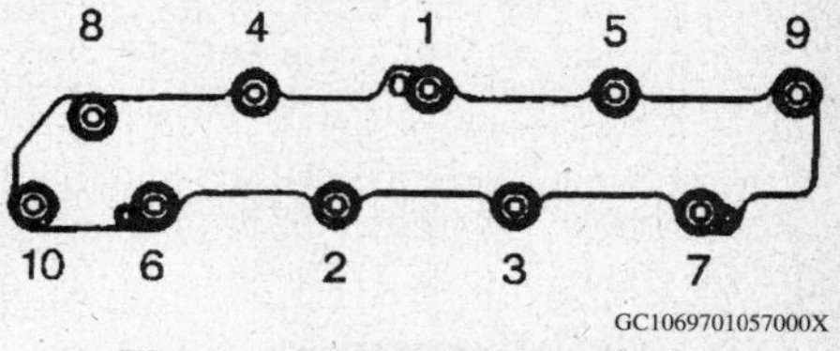

Fig. 3 Exhaust manifold installation & bolt tightening sequence

7. Raise and safely support vehicle.
8. Remove righthand front wheel and tire assembly, then the righthand splash shield.
9. Using harmonic balancer tool No. J-38122, or equivalent to hold balancer in position, remove retaining bolt and balancer using puller tool No. J-24420-C, or equivalent.
10. Remove fasteners attaching lower portion of front cover.
11. Lower the vehicle.
12. Remove front cover and gaskets.
13. Reverse procedure to install, noting the following:
    a. Engine mount bracket adapter bolts are designed to permanently stretch when tightened. Always use proper fasteners in this particular location. Do not use stronger bolts. Components will not tighten properly if improper bolts are used.
    b. Using torque angle meter tool No. J-36660 or equivalent, **torque** engine mount bracket adapter bolts to 81 ft. lbs., then rotate an additional 90°.
    c. Tighten all remaining fasteners to specifications.

TIMING CHAIN

REPLACE

REMOVAL

1. Remove front cover as outlined under "Front Cover, Replace."
2. Rotate crankshaft in clockwise direction until camshaft sprocket timing dowel pin holes line up with timing chain housing holes, **Fig. 5.**
3. Remove timing chain guides.
4. Raise and support vehicle.
5. Ensure all timing chain slack is above tensioner, then remove tensioner, **Fig. 6.**
6. Timing chain must be disengaged from grooves in tensioner shoe to permit removal of shoe. Position a suitable screwdriver under timing chain while pulling shoe outward to disengage.
7. If removing tensioner shoe is difficult, proceed as follows:
    a. Lower the vehicle.
    b. Hold intake camshaft sprocket in position with camshaft sprocket wrench tool No. J-39579, or equivalent.
    c. Remove sprocket bolt and washer.
    d. Remove washer and install bolt into camshaft by hand.
    e. Position a suitable three-jaw puller into intake camshaft sprocket relief

holes and remove sprocket. Do not pry on camshaft sprocket as damage to sprocket or timing chain housing may result.

8. Remove mounting bolts and tensioner assembly. Use care when removing, as tensioner is spring loaded.
9. Mark timing chain and crankshaft sprocket for installation.
10. Remove timing chain.

INSTALLATION

Do not interchange timing chains between model years on this engine. There are differences in the sprockets. The links' shape matches the sprockets. Be sure the crankshaft sprocket and timing chain are assembled in the same orientation as they were removed.

1. Hold camshaft sprocket in position with camshaft sprocket tool No. J-39579, or equivalent, then install attaching bolt and washer. Use adhesive sealant compound part No. 12345493, or equivalent on bolt. Tighten to specifications.
2. Install camshaft sprocket timing alignment pin tools No. J-36800, or equivalent through holes in camshaft sprockets into timing chain housing holes to position camshafts for proper timing, **Fig. 5.**
3. If camshafts are out of position and must be rotated more than 1/8 turn, proceed as follows:
   a. Rotate crankshaft clockwise to 90° off TDC.
   b. Position camshafts and install dowels.
   c. Rotate crankshaft **counterclockwise** back to TDC. **Rotating crankshaft clockwise to TDC will damage valves and pistons.**
4. Place timing chain over exhaust camshaft sprocket, coolant pump or idler sprocket and crankshaft sprocket.
5. Remove intake camshaft timing pin and attach camshaft sprocket tool No. J-39579, or equivalent.
6. Rotate intake camshaft sprocket counterclockwise with tool until timing chain can be installed over sprocket.
7. Release tool. The timing chain tension between camshaft sprockets should tighten.
8. Timing pin should easily fit through intake camshaft sprocket timing hole into timing chain housing timing hole. If timing pin does not fit easily, repeat procedure.
9. With timing pins installed, raise and support vehicle.
10. With slack removed from timing chain between intake camshaft sprocket and crankshaft sprocket, timing marks on crankshaft and engine block should be aligned. If crankshaft timing marks are not aligned, move timing chain one tooth forward or rearward to remove slack, then align marks.
11. **On Achieva, Malibu, Skylark and 1997–98 Grand Am models,** proceed as follows:
   a. Load tensioner assembly to zero position by forming a keeper out of heavy gauge wire.

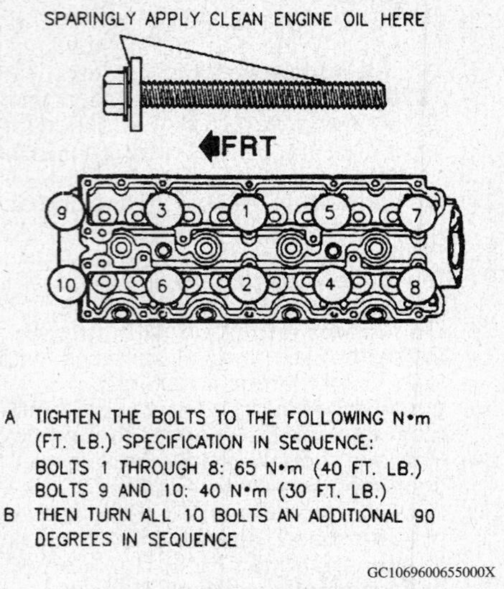

SPARINGLY APPLY CLEAN ENGINE OIL HERE
FRT
9
3
1
5
7
10
6
2
4
8
A TIGHTEN THE BOLTS TO THE FOLLOWING N•m (FT. LB.) SPECIFICATION IN SEQUENCE:
BOLTS 1 THROUGH 8: 65 N•m (40 FT. LB.)
BOLTS 9 AND 10: 40 N•m (30 FT. LB.)
B THEN TURN ALL 10 BOLTS AN ADDITIONAL 90 DEGREES IN SEQUENCE
GC1069600655000X

Fig. 4 Cylinder head bolt tightening sequence

   b. Apply slight force on tensioner blade to compress plunger.
   c. Insert small screwdriver into reset access hole and pry ratchet pawl away from ratchet teeth while forcing the plunger completely in the hole.
   d. Install keeper between access hole and blade.
   e. Install tensioner assembly to chain housing and inspect plunger assembly installation once again, ensuring long end is toward crankshaft.
   f. Tighten timing chain tensioner bolts to specifications.
12. **On Alero and 1999–2000 Grand Am models,** proceed as follows:
   a. Assemble tensioner plunger and tensioner body.
   b. With tensioner plunger fully extended, rotate tensioner with plunger down on a flat surface.
   c. Press down on tensioner body until plunger full seats in body.
   d. Install assembled tensioner onto timing chain housing.
   e. Apply hand pressure to tensioner shoe until locking tab seats into stud groove.
   f. Install tensioner bolts and **torque** to 89 inch lbs.
   g. Release plunger.
   h. Use a flat-bladed screwdriver or similar tool to press firmly against plunger's face. Press down until plunger releases against rear of tensioner shoe. **Do not damage face.**
13. **On all models,** lower vehicle enough to remove alignment dowel pins.
14. Rotate crankshaft two revolutions clockwise.
15. Align crankshaft keyway with cylinder block alignment mark and insert timing pins through camshaft sprockets into timing chain housing timing holes.
16. Timing pins should slide easily through timing holes. If timing pins cannot be easily inserted, repeat procedure to properly time engine.
17. Install timing chain guides and front cover.

CAMSHAFT

REPLACE

Whenever camshaft housing to cylinder head attaching bolts are loosened, the camshaft housing to cylinder head gasket must be replaced.

INTAKE

1. Drain coolant into an approved container.
2. Disconnect ignition coil and module electrical connectors.
3. Remove mounting bolts and pull upward on ignition coil and module assembly, **Fig. 4.** If connectors are stuck to spark plugs, remove them using spark plug connector remover tool No. J-36011, or equivalent. Always pull straight upward.
4. Disconnect camshaft position electrical sensor.
5. Remove power steering pump and position aside with hoses attached.
6. Disconnect vacuum line from fuel pressure regulator and fuel injector wiring harness electrical connector.
7. Remove fuel line bracket from top of intake camshaft housing.
8. Remove fuel rail retaining bolts and fuel rail. Leave fuel lines attached and position fuel rail over master cylinder. Cover openings in cylinder head and injector nozzles.
9. Disconnect timing chain housing at intake camshaft housing. **Do not remove from vehicle.**
10. Remove front cover as outlined under "Front Cover, Replace."
11. Raise and safely support vehicle.
12. Disconnect heater hose at thermostat housing and drain cylinder block completely.
13. Remove timing chain tensioner and timing chain as outlined under "Timing Chain, Replace."
14. Remove water pump mounting nuts as outlined under "Water Pump, Replace."
15. Remove timing chain housing to block bolts and oil pan to front cover bolts.
16. Remove lowest front cover retaining stud.
17. Lower the vehicle.
18. Remove camshaft sprocket retaining bolts and washers while holding sprockets with camshaft sprocket tool No. J-39579, or equivalent.
19. Remove camshaft sprockets. They are identical and interchangeable.
20. Remove chain housing to camshaft housing bolts. Do not remove timing chain housing.
21. Remove camshaft housing cover attaching bolts, **Fig. 7,** and note positioning of all gaskets.
22. Loosen camshaft housing to cylinder head attaching bolts in reverse order of tightening sequence, **Fig. 8.**

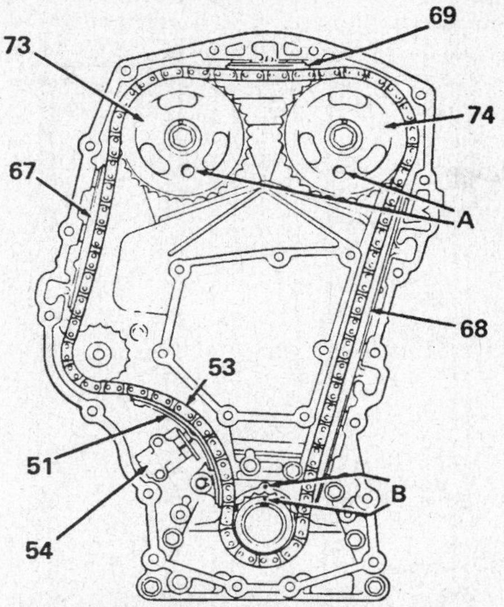

A. CAMSHAFT TIMING ALIGNMENT PIN LOCATIONS
B. CRANKSHAFT GEAR TIMING MARKS
51. SHOE ASM. TIMING CHAIN TENSIONER
53. TIMING CHAIN
54. TENSIONER, TIMING CHAIN
67. GUIDE – R.H. TIMING CHAIN
68. GUIDE – L.H. TIMING CHAIN
69. GUIDE – UPPER TIMING CHAIN
73. SPROCKET, EXHAUST CAMSHAFT
74. SPROCKET, INTAKE CAMSHAFT

GC1069100417000X

Fig. 5 Valve timing marks

23. Leave two camshaft housing to cylinder head attaching bolts loosely installed. Thread four camshaft housing to cylinder head bolts into tapped camshaft housing cover holes and push cover off housing. Remove loosely installed bolts. Note positioning of all gaskets, then remove and discard gasket.
24. Loosely install one camshaft housing to cylinder head bolt to retain housing during camshaft and lifter removal.
25. Note timing chain sprocket dowel pin position for assembly and remove camshaft, using care not to damage journals.
26. Remove valve lash adjuster. Keep adjusters in order for future assembly. Store them in the upside down position on a level surface in clean engine oil to minimize lifter bleed-down.
27. Remove camshaft housing and gasket.
28. Reverse procedure to install, noting the following:
    a. Lubricate entire camshaft and valve lash adjusters with lubricant part No. 12345501, or equivalent.
    b. Apply suitable sealant to threads of camshaft housing, cover retaining, ignition coil and module assembly attaching bolts.
    c. install camshaft housing cover to camshaft housing, noting seal positioning is as noted during removal.
    d. **Torque** camshaft housing to cylinder head bolts in sequence outlined in **Fig. 8,** to 16 ft. lbs., then rotate an additional 90° using torque angle meter tool No. J-36660, or equivalent. **Torque** camshaft housing cover to camshaft housing bolts to 16 ft. lbs., then rotate an additional 30°.
    e. Apply a ¼ inch bead of sealer part No. 12346286, or equivalent onto joint at end of camshaft housing halves before installing power steering pump and face seal.
    f. Tighten timing chain housing to engine and camshaft housing fasteners to specifications.
    g. Apply pipe sealant part No. 1052080, or equivalent onto ignition coil and bolts securing module cover assembly to camshaft housing.
    h. If a new camshaft was installed, add engine oil supplement part No. 1052367, or equivalent to engine oil.

EXHAUST

1. Drain coolant into an approved container.
2. Disconnect ignition coil and module electrical connectors.
3. Remove mounting bolts, then pull upward on ignition coil and module assembly, **Fig. 4.** If connectors are stuck to spark plugs, use spark plug connector remover tool No. J-36011, or equivalent by pulling straight upward to remove them.
4. Disconnect oil pressure switch electrical connector.
5. Remove front cover as outlined under "Front Cover, Replace."
6. Raise and safely support vehicle.
7. Disconnect heater hose at thermostat housing and drain cylinder block completely.
8. Disconnect timing chain housing at exhaust camshaft housing, but do not remove components from vehicle.
9. **On models equipped with automatic transaxle,** remove transaxle fluid level indicator tube assembly from exhaust camshaft cover and position aside.
10. **On all models,** lower the vehicle.
11. Remove exhaust camshaft housing cover and gasket.
12. Loosen camshaft housing to cylinder head attaching bolts in reverse order of tightening sequence, **Fig. 8.**
13. Leave two camshaft housing to cylinder head attaching bolts loosely installed. Thread four camshaft housing to cylinder head bolts into tapped camshaft housing cover holes and push cover off housing. Remove loosely installed bolts, note gasket positioning, then discard gasket.
14. Loosely install one camshaft housing to cylinder head bolt to retain housing during camshaft and lifter removal.
15. Note timing chain sprocket dowel pin position for assembly and remove camshaft, using care not to damage journals.
16. Remove valve lash adjuster. Keep them in order for reassembly. Store them in the upside down position, on a level surface in clean engine oil to prevent lifter bleed-down.

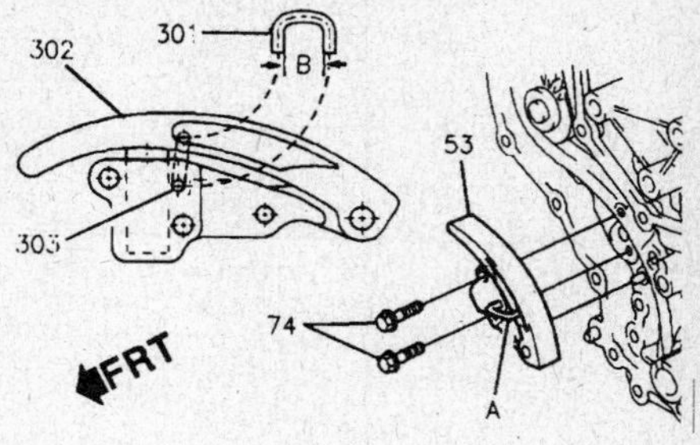

A AFTER INSTALLATION, REMOVE ANTI-RELEASE FROM TENSIONER ASM. TO RELEASE TENSIONER
B 13 mm (1/2 INCH)

53 TIMING CHAIN TENSIONER AND SHOE ASSEMBLY
74 BOLTS – 10 N m (89 LBS. IN.)
301 ANTI-RELEASE KEEPER – FABRICATED FROM HEAVY GAGE WIRE OR STEEL ROD
302 SHOE
303 RESET ACCESS HOLE

GC1069600656000X

Fig. 6 Timing chain tensioner spring & retainer

17. Remove camshaft housing and gasket.
18. Reverse procedure to install, noting the following:
    a. Lubricate entire camshaft and valve lash adjusters with lubricant part No. 12345501, or equivalent.
    b. Apply suitable sealant to threads of camshaft housing, cover retaining, ignition coil and module assembly attaching bolts.
    c. When installing camshaft housing cover to camshaft housing, ensure seals are positioned as was noted during removal.
    d. **Torque** camshaft housing to cylinder head bolts in sequence outlined in **Fig. 8** to 11 ft. lbs., then rotate an additional 90° using torque angle meter tool No. J-36660, or equivalent. **Torque** camshaft housing cover to camshaft housing bolts to 11 ft. lbs., then rotate an additional 30°.
    e. Tighten timing chain housing to engine and camshaft housing fasteners to specifications.
    f. Apply pipe sealant part No. 1052080, or equivalent on camshaft housing and threads of cover retainer bolt.
    g. Tighten timing chain housing to engine and camshaft housing fasteners to specifications.
    h. If a new camshaft was installed, add engine oil supplement part No. 1052367, or equivalent to engine oil.

VALVE LIFTER BREAK-IN

If new lifters have been installed or if they bled down while the engine was disassembled some excessive noise might be heard when first starting up again. This is normal and no engine damage should occur. To purge trapped air from the lifters, proceed as follows:

1. Start engine and allow it to idle and

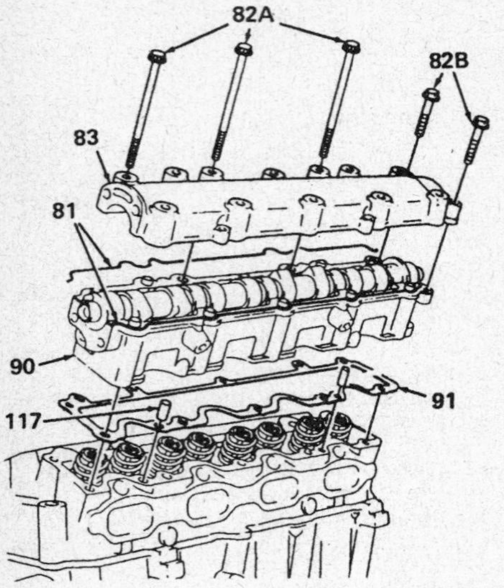

81. SEALS, CAMSHAFT HOUSING TO CAMSHAFT HOUSING COVER (EACH SEAL IS DIFFERENT)
82A. BOLT, CAMSHAFT HOUSING TO CYLINDER HEAD
82B. BOLT, CAMSHAFT HOUSING COVER TO CAMSHAFT HOUSING
83. COVER, CAMSHAFT
90. CAMSHAFT HOUSING (INTAKE SHOWN)
91. GASKET, CAMSHAFT HOUSING TO CYLINDER HEAD
117. DOWEL PIN (2)

GC1069100422000X

Fig. 7 Camshaft housing & cover

warm up for five minutes.
2. Increase engine speed to 2000 RPM until lifter noise disappears.
3. Return engine to idle for another five minutes or perform a road test.

BALANCE SHAFT

REPLACE

REMOVAL

1. Remove oil pan as outlined in "Oil Pan, Replace."
2. Remove mounting nut, bolt and balance shaft chain cover.
3. Loosen but do not remove balance shaft chain tensioner.
4. Remove oil pump and cover.
5. Rotate engine crankshaft until No. 1 piston is at TDC.
6. Use balance shaft holding tool No. J-41088, or equivalent to prevent balance shafts from turning while loosening bolt.
7. Mark driven sprocket's surface if it will be used again, then remove lefthand threaded driven sprocket bolt from shaft.
8. Loosen balance shaft housing bolts.
9. Remove fasteners and balance shaft housing.
10. Remove bolts and separate housing.
11. Remove balance shaft and gear subassemblies from lower housing, then the bearings, bolts and thrust plate.

INSTALLATION

1. Install thrust plate and tighten bolts to specifications.
2. Mount a suitable dial indicator and measure shaft endplay at rear side of shafts.
3. If endplay is not within .0073–.0179 inch, inspect and replace thrust plate.
4. Install balance shaft and gear subassemblies, ensuring gear timing marks are properly aligned.
5. Apply thread locker part No. 12345493, or equivalent to mounting bolts and install housing on block, then proceed as follows:
   a. **Torque** housing bolt Nos. 1, 2, 4, 5, 6 and 7, **Fig. 9,** 11 ft. lbs., then rotate an additional 40° using torque angle meter tool No. J-36660, or equivalent.
   b. **Torque** housing bolt Nos. 3 and 8 to 7.4 ft. lbs., then rotate an additional 40°.
   c. **Torque** housing bolt Nos. 1, 2 and 4, **Fig. 10,** to 18 ft. lbs., then rotate an additional 70°.
   d. **Torque** bolt 3, **Fig. 10,** to 30 inch lbs., then rotate an additional 60°.
   e. **Torque** bolt 5, **Fig. 10,** to 39 ft. lbs.
6. Rotate balance shafts and ensure they spin freely.
7. Ensure No. 1 piston is at TDC.
8. Install balance shaft holder tool No. J-41088, or equivalent to prevent shaft rotation.
9. **Torque** balance shaft driven sprocket bolt to 22 ft. lbs., then rotate an additional 45°. **Bolt is lefthand threaded and must be tightened by rotating counterclockwise.**
10. Adjust balance shaft chain tension with three lbs. of force to .040 inch using a brass feeler gauge between guide and chain.
11. **Torque** balance shaft chain tensioner bolt to 9.6 ft. lbs.
12. Install balance shaft chain cover and **torque** bolt to 9.6 ft. lbs.
13. Install oil pan with a new gasket. Tighten fasteners to specifications as outlined in **Fig. 13.**

PISTON & ROD ASSEMBLY

Assemble piston to rod with arrow on piston toward front of engine and oil squirt hole on rod toward exhaust side of engine, **Fig. 11.**

Upon installation, use a suitable feeler gauge to measure connecting rod side clearance, which should be .0059–.0177 inch.

PISTONS, PINS & RINGS

Pistons and rings are available in standard size and oversize. Pistons and their pins are serviced as an assembly.

MAIN & ROD BEARINGS

Main and rod bearings are available in standard size only.

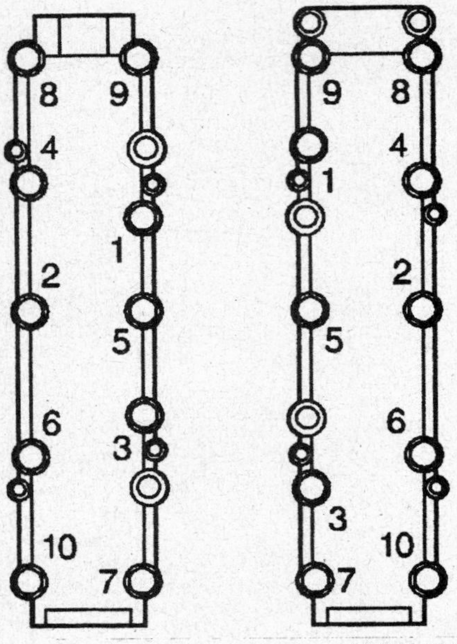

GC1069701058000X

Fig. 8 Camshaft housing bolt tightening sequence

CRANKSHAFT REAR OIL SEAL

REPLACE

1. Remove transaxle assembly as outlined under "Transaxle, Replace."
2. **On models equipped with manual transaxle,** remove clutch as outlined under "Clutch, Replace."
3. **On all models,** remove mounting bolts and flywheel using holder tool No. J-38122, or equivalent.
4. Remove oil pan to crankshaft rear seal housing mounting bolts.
5. Remove mounting screws, crankshaft rear seal housing and gasket, **Fig. 12.**
6. Support crankshaft rear seal housing on two wooden blocks of equal thickness with crankshaft side facing upward and drive seal out through transaxle side of housing.
7. Reverse procedure to install, noting the following:
   a. If silicone strips across top of aluminum carrier oil pan, at cylinder block and at seal housing 3-way joint are damaged they can be restored to their original dimensions using silicone sealant part No. 12345739, or equivalent.
   b. Lubricate seal lips with engine oil prior to installing housing.
   c. Press replacement seal into housing using rear crankshaft seal installer No. J-36005, or equivalent.
   d. If using old flywheel to crankshaft bolts, coat their threads with adhesive sealant compound part No. 12345493, or equivalent.
   e. Tighten all fasteners to specifications.

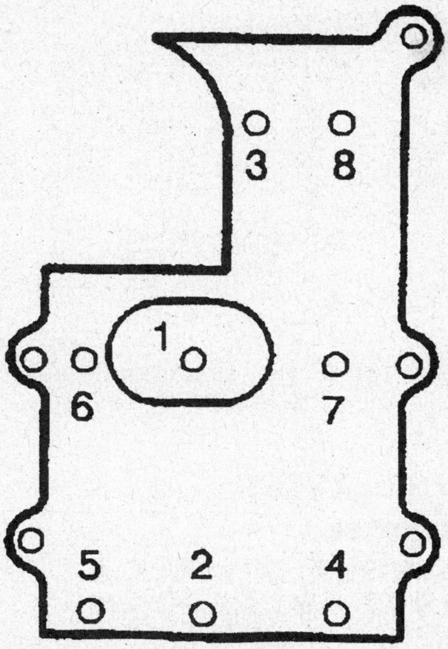

Fig. 9 Balance shaft housing bolt tightening sequence

OIL PAN

REPLACE

1. Drain crankcase and cooling system into approved containers.
2. Support engine using engine support fixture tool No. J-28467-360, or equivalent.
3. Remove flywheel housing inspection cover.
4. Remove righthand front wheel and tire assembly, then the splash shield.
5. Remove serpentine drive belt.
6. Remove A/C compressor lower mounting bolts from bracket and support with refrigerant hoses attached.
7. **On Alero and 1999–2000 Grand Am models,** remove engine to transaxle brace.
8. **On all models,** remove engine mount strut bracket bolts and position bracket aside.
9. Raise engine approximately 1½ inches.
10. Remove bolts and radiator outlet pipe.
11. Remove exhaust manifold brace.
12. Remove oil pan to flywheel cover nut and bolt.
13. **On Alero and 1999–2000 Grand Am models,** remove flywheel cover stud for clearance.
14. **On all models,** remove radiator outlet pipe from lower radiator hose and oil pan.
15. Disconnect oil level sensor electrical connector.
16. Remove mounting bolts and oil pan.
17. Reverse procedure to install, noting the following:
    a. **Torque** M8 × 1.25 × 80 bolts (1), **Fig. 13,** to 18 ft. lbs.
    b. **Torque** M8 × 1.25 × 22 bolts (2) to 18 ft. lbs.
    c. **Torque** M6 × 1.00 × 25 bolts (3) to 8.8 ft. lbs.
    d. **Torque** bolt (4) to 19 ft. lbs.

OIL PUMP

REPLACE

1. Remove oil pan as outlined under "Oil Pan, Replace."
2. Remove balance shaft chain cover.
3. Remove balance shaft chain tensioner assembly.
4. Remove oil pump cover, mounting bolts and pump, **Fig. 14.**
5. Reverse procedure to install, noting the following:
    a. **Torque** cover to balance shaft housing bolts to 40 ft. lbs.
    b. Adjust balance shaft tension as outlined under "Balance Shaft, Replace."
    c. Tighten remaining bolts to specifications.

OIL PUMP SERVICE

1. Remove oil pump as outlined under "Oil Pump, Replace."
2. Disassemble pump gerotor cover from housing.
3. Remove pump from balance shaft housing.
4. Disassemble pressure relief valve.
5. Remove roll pin with punch.
6. Pry out remaining bottom half of valve using suitable tool.
7. Clean all components in suitable cleaning solvent. Remove varnish, sludge and dirt.
8. Inspect pump cover and housing for cracks, scoring, porous or damaged casting, damaged threads, excessive wear or galling and replace if needed.
9. Inspect relief valve for physical damage and replace if needed.
10. Inspect gerotor for chipping, galling or excessive wear and replace if needed.
11. Measure gerotor cavity depth, **Fig. 15.**
12. **On 1997 models,** depth should be .6736–.6756 inch.
13. **On 1998–2000 models,** depth should be .6023–.6043 inch.
14. **On all models,** measure inner gerotor tip clearance, **Fig. 16,** which should be .0059 inch maximum.
15. Measure outer gerotor diameter clearance, **Fig. 17.**
16. **On 1997 models,** diameter clearance should be .0013–.0052 inch.
17. **On 1998–2000 models,** diameter clearance should be .0019–.0059 inch.
18. **On all models,** replace any worn part if any measurement is not within specifications.

BELT TENSION DATA

1. Turn off all accessories.
2. Bring engine to operating temperature.
3. Turn engine off.
4. Using tension gauge tool No. J-23600-B or equivalent, measure belt tension halfway between alternator and power steering pump.
5. Start engine and allow temperature to stabilize for 15 seconds.
6. Turn engine off.
7. Using a 15 mm socket, apply clockwise force to tensioner pulley bolt.
8. Release force and measure belt tension without disturbing tensioner position.
9. Using 15 mm socket, apply counterclockwise force to tensioner pulley bolt and raise pulley to eliminate all tension.
10. Slowly lower pulley to belt and measure belt tension without disturbing tensioner position.
11. Average out all three readings.
12. If average reading is less than 30–50 lbs., replace belt tensioner.

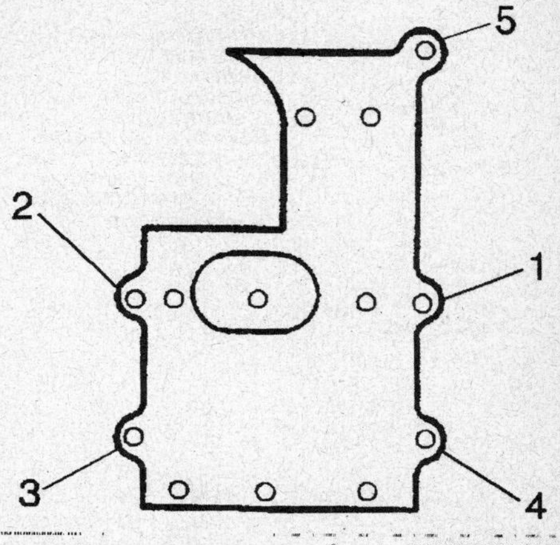

Fig. 10 Balance shaft housing to block bolt tightening sequence

SERPENTINE DRIVE BELT

Refer to **Fig. 18** for drive belt replacement. **Use a tight fitting 13 mm wrench at least 18 inches long.**

COOLING SYSTEM BLEED

After filling cooling system, start engine and allow it to reach operating temperature with surge tank pressure cap removed. Air will bleed through surge cap opening. Add coolant as required to bring to proper level, then install surge tank pressure cap.

THERMOSTAT

REPLACE

1. Drain coolant into an approved container until level falls below thermostat.
2. Remove exhaust manifold heat shield.
3. Remove inlet housing bolt through exhaust manifold.
4. Raise and support vehicle.
5. **On Alero and 1999–2000 Grand Am models,** proceed as follows:

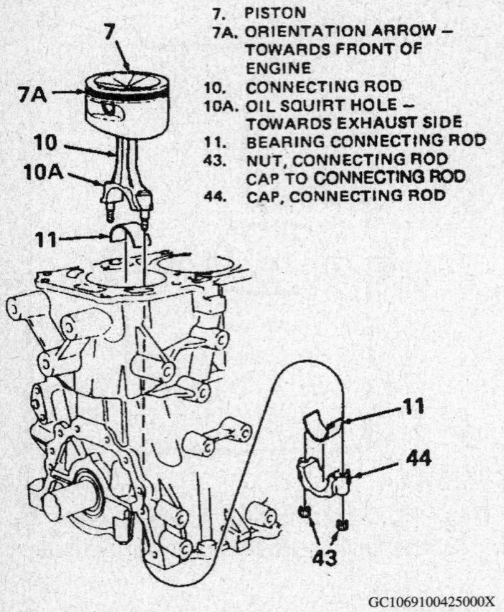

Fig. 11 Piston & rod assembly

a. Remove coolant inlet housing stud from oil pan.
b. Remove tire and wheel.
c. Remove splash shield.
d. Remove transaxle to engine block brace.

6. **On all models,** remove radiator outlet pipe stud.
7. Remove second coolant inlet housing bolt and inlet housing.
8. Remove thermostat, **Fig. 19.**
9. Reverse procedure to install, noting the following:
   a. **Torque** coolant inlet housing stud to oil pan to 19 ft. lbs.
   b. **Torque** coolant inlet housing bolts through exhaust manifold to 10 ft. lbs.
   c. Bring engine to operating temperature and inspect for leaks.

WATER PUMP

REPLACE

REMOVAL

1. Drain coolant into an approved container.
2. Remove drive belt as outlined under "Serpentine Drive Belt, Replace."
3. Compress tensioner and hold while removing tensioner mounting bolts and tensioner.
4. Disconnect all required electrical connectors.
5. Remove required exhaust manifold heat shields.
6. Remove heat wrap from heater hose.
7. Disconnect all required heater hoses.
8. Remove coolant inlet housing bolt through exhaust manifold.
9. Raise and safely support vehicle.
10. Remove exhaust manifold brace mounting bolt.
11. Remove exhaust pipe to manifold studs.
12. **On Alero and 1999–2000 Grand Am models,** remove heater outlet pipe bracket to transmission bolt.

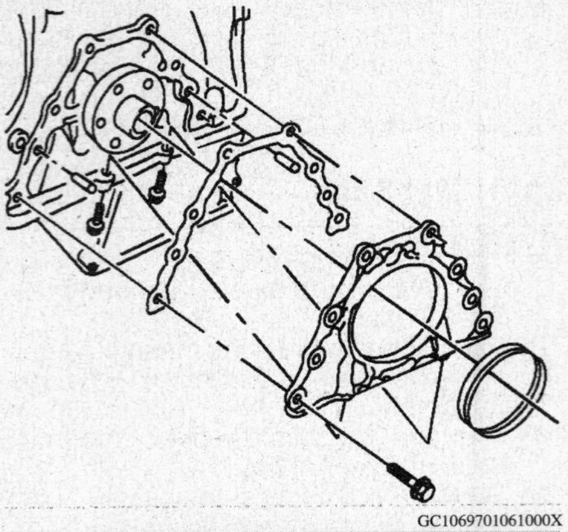

Fig. 12 Crankshaft rear oil seal replacement

13. **On all models,** pull down and back on exhaust pipe to disengage from manifold bolts. **To avoid damage do not rotate flex coupling more than 3°.**
14. **On models equipped with manual transaxle,** remove exhaust manifold brace.
15. **On all models,** remove radiator outlet pipe from oil pan and transaxle. Leave lower radiator hose attached and pull down gently on radiator outlet pipe to disengage it from water pump. Leave outlet pipe hanging.
16. Lower the vehicle and remove brake vacuum pipe from cam housing.
17. Remove mounting nuts, exhaust manifold, seals and gaskets.
18. Remove engine front cover as outlined under "Front Cover, Replace," then compress timing chain tensioner.
19. Remove cover bolts, timing chain housing nuts, water pump and cover, **Fig. 20.**

INSTALLATION

Read through this entire procedure before installing the water pump. Pay particular attention to the unusual tightening sequence.

1. Install water pump cover to pump assembly. Hand tighten bolts.
2. Install cover to block bolts hand tight.
3. Install pump to timing chain housing. Hand tighten nuts.
4. Lubricate coolant inlet pipe O-ring with clean antifreeze, then slide pipe into pump cover. Hand tighten bolts.
5. **Torque** pump assembly to timing chain housing nuts to 19 ft. lbs.
6. **Torque** pump cover to pump bolts to 10 ft. lbs.
7. **Torque** pump cover to engine block bottom bolt to 19 ft. lbs., then **torque** remaining bolts to 19 ft. lbs.
8. **Torque** coolant inlet pipe assembly to pump cover bolts to 10 ft. lbs.
9. Reverse remaining removal steps to complete installation. Tighten all fasteners to specifications.

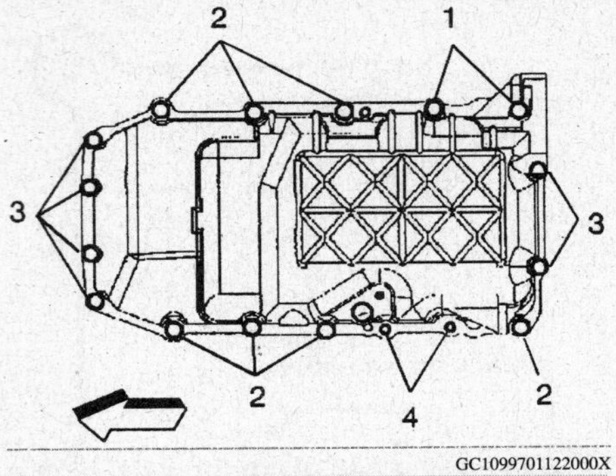

Fig. 13 Oil pan bolt identification & locations

RADIATOR

REPLACE

ACHIEVA, SKYLARK & 1997–98 GRAND AM

1. Drain coolant into an approved container.
2. Remove air intake duct assembly.
3. Disconnect upper transaxle cooler line.
4. Disconnect upper radiator hose.
5. Lower transaxle cooler line.
6. Disconnect cooling fan electrical connector and remove cooling fan mounting bolts.
7. Remove cooling fan.
8. Remove splash guard below lower radiator hose.
9. Disconnect lower radiator hose from radiator.
10. Remove condenser line retaining clip.
11. Remove condenser to radiator attaching bolts.
12. Disconnect coolant surge tank hose.
13. Remove mounting bolts and radiator.
14. Reverse procedure to install. Tighten all fasteners to specifications.

ALERO & 1999–2000 GRAND AM

1. Recover refrigerant charge using recycling station tool No. J-39500, or equivalent.
2. Drain coolant into an approved container.
3. Remove battery and battery tray.
4. Remove upper radiator hose.
5. Remove upper transaxle cooler line.
6. Remove coolant surge tank hose.
7. Remove condenser inlet fitting from discharge hose.
8. Disconnect cooling fan electrical connector.
9. Raise and safely support vehicle.
10. Remove lower closeout panel.
11. Remove lower radiator hose from radiator.
12. Remove lower transaxle cooler line.
13. Remove evaporator line from condenser outlet.
14. Remove radiator lower mounting panel.
15. Remove Condenser Radiator Fan

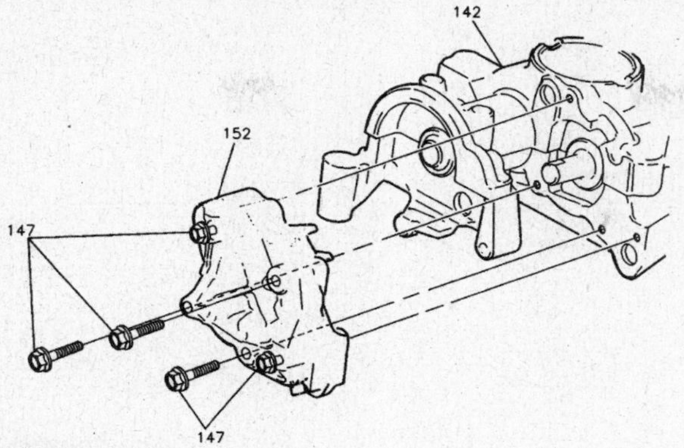

Fig. 14 Oil pump replacement

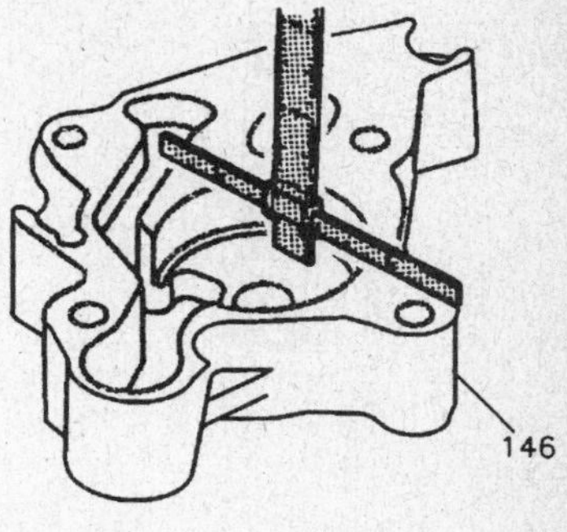

Fig. 15 Gerotor cavity depth measurement

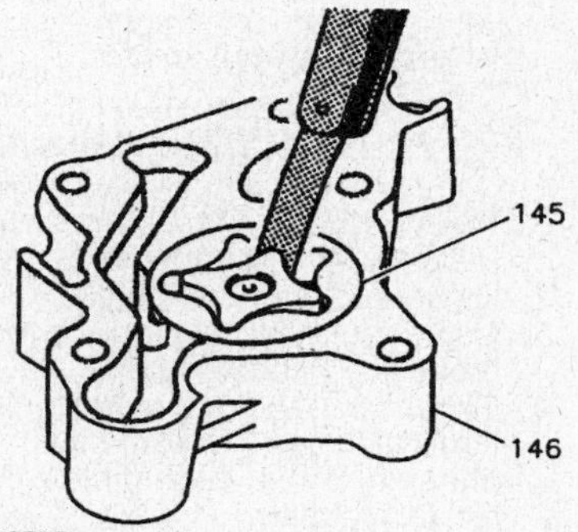

Fig. 16 Inner gear tip clearance measurement

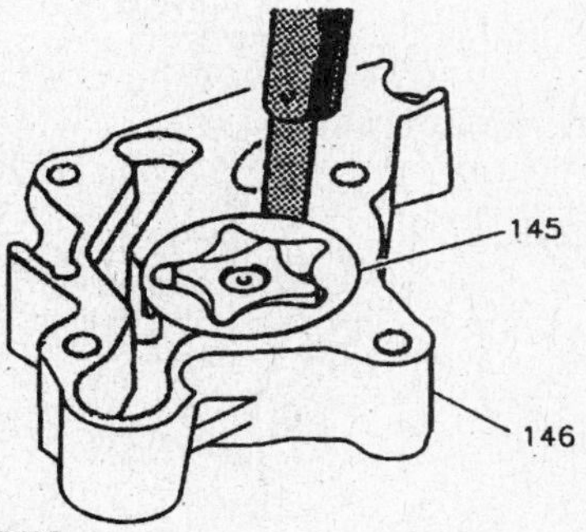

Fig. 17 Outer gerotor diameter clearance measurement

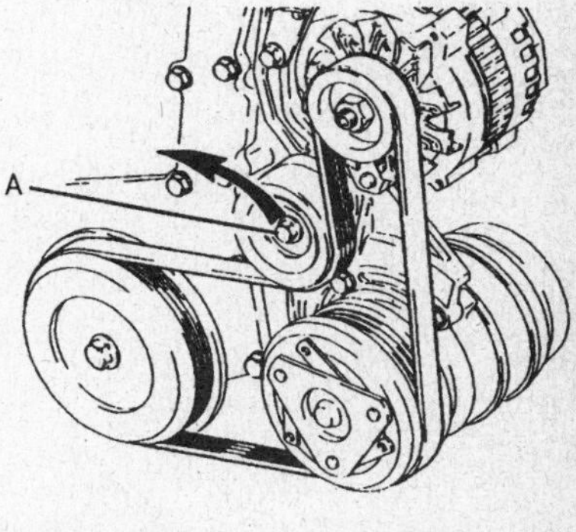

Fig. 18 Serpentine belt replacement

Module (CRFM) from vehicle.

16. Remove condenser and fan shroud from radiator.
17. Reverse procedure to install, noting the following:
    a. **Torque** condenser to radiator bolt to 44 inch lbs.
    b. **Torque** radiator lower mounting panel bolts to 89 inch lbs.
    c. **Torque** condenser outlet to evaporator line bolt to 18 ft. lbs.
    d. **Torque** transaxle cooler line bolts to 22 ft. lbs.
    e. **Torque** condenser inlet fitting to discharge hose bolt to 18 ft. lbs.
    f. Close radiator petcock, fill cooling system and inspect for leaks.

CUTLASS & MALIBU

1. Recover refrigerant charge using recycling station tool No. J-39500, or equivalent.
2. Drain coolant into an approved container.
3. Remove upper radiator hose and transaxle cooler line, then the surge tank hose.
4. Remove condenser inlet fitting from discharge hose and lower transaxle cooler line.
5. Disconnect cooling fan electrical connector.
6. Raise and support vehicle.
7. Remove lower closeout panel, then the lower radiator hose and evaporator line.
8. Remove lower radiator mounting plate and condenser fan radiator module.
9. Remove condenser, fan shroud and radiator.
10. Reverse procedure to install. Tighten bolts to specifications.

FUEL PUMP

REPLACE

The fuel pump is part of the fuel sender assembly and must be replaced as a complete unit.

1. Relieve fuel system pressure as outlined under "Fuel System Pressure Relief."
2. Drain fuel from tank into an approved container.
3. Disconnect all required electrical connectors.
4. Remove ground wire retaining screw from underbody.
5. Disconnect hoses from tank meter assembly, tank filler and vent pipes.
6. Support fuel tank and disconnect fuel tank retaining straps.
7. Remove fuel tank from vehicle.
8. The modular fuel sender assembly might spring up from its original position. Have a shop towel ready to absorb spills because reservoir bucket is full of fuel. Tip assembly slightly to avoid float damage.
9. Using lock ring tool No. J-39765, or equivalent, remove fuel tank sending unit and pump assembly by holding it down and removing lock ring from designated retainer slots.
10. Reverse procedure to install, noting the following:
    a. Install a new O-ring on sender tank flange.
    b. Align tab on front of fuel sender with slot on front of retainer lock ring.
    c. Slowly apply pressure to top of spring loaded sender until sender aligns flush with tank retainer.
    d. Insert lock ring into proper slots.
    e. Inspect for fuel leaks as outlined under "Fuel Leak Inspection."

FUEL LEAK INSPECTION

After fuel tank has been removed and replaced, proceed as follows:

1. Turn ignition On for two seconds.
2. Turn ignition Off for 10 seconds.
3. Turn ignition On.
4. Look for and correct any fuel leaks.

FUEL FILTER

REPLACE

The fuel filter is located below the rear of the vehicle, rearward of the fuel tank.

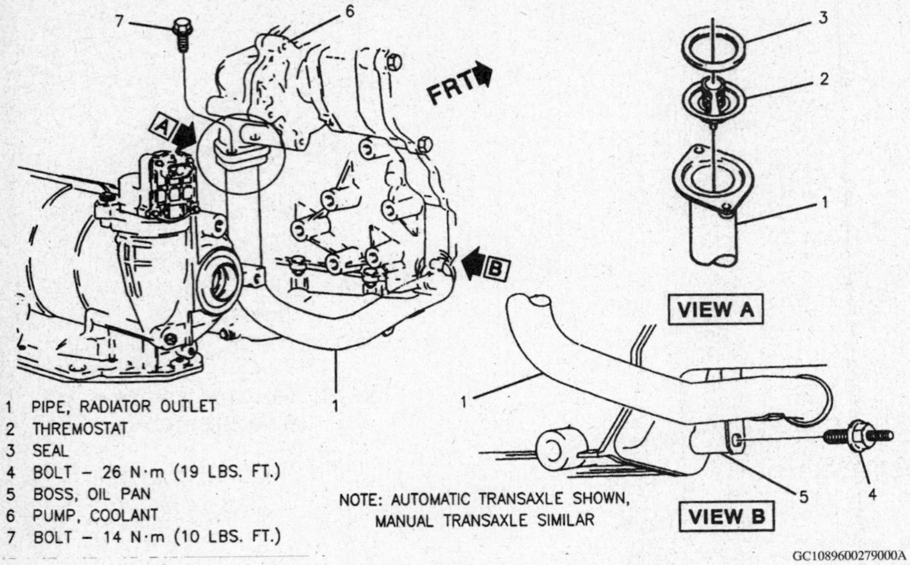

Fig. 19 Thermostat replacement

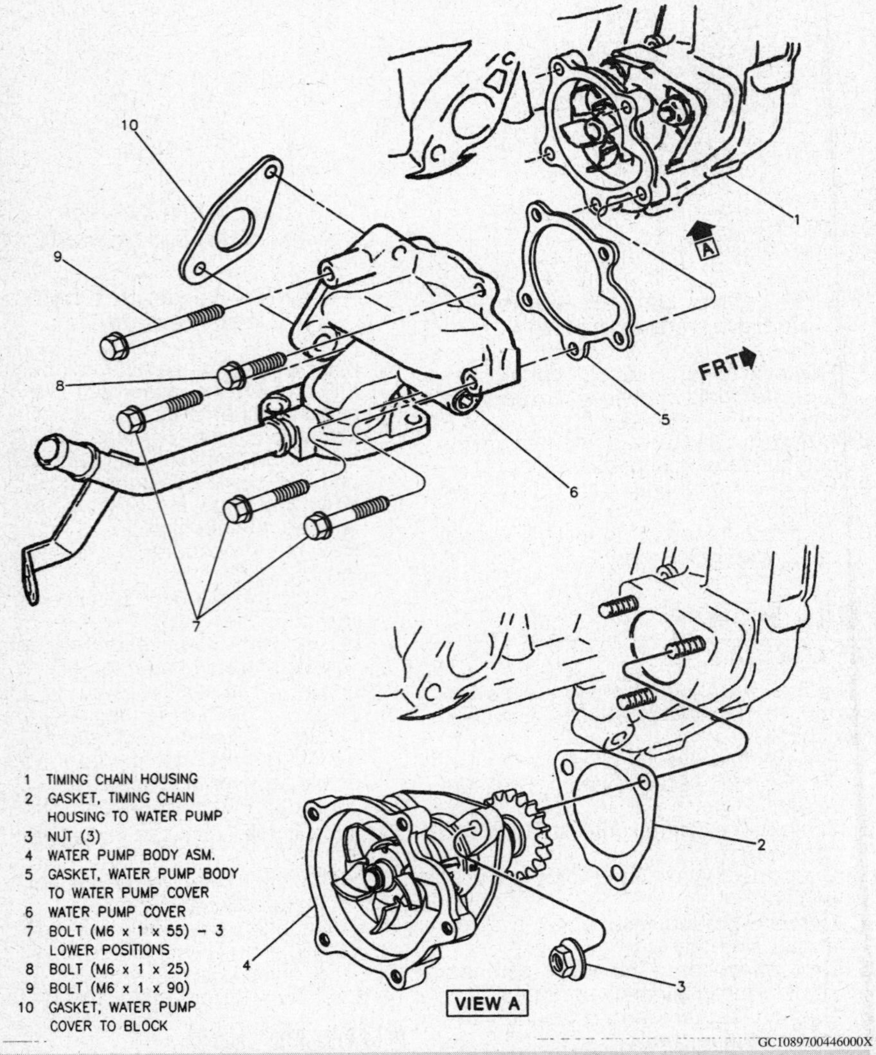

Fig. 20 Water pump replacement

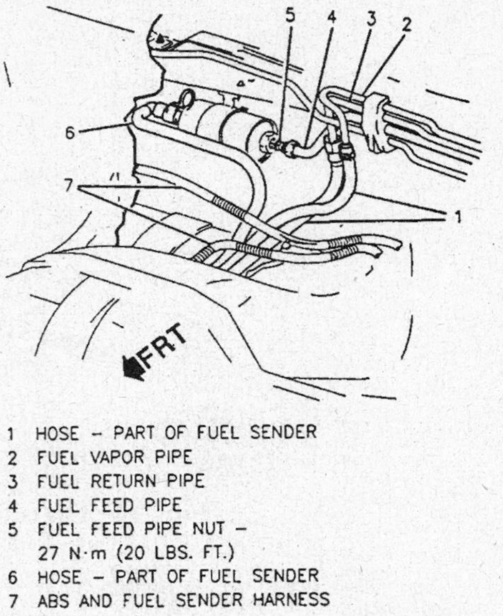

Fig. 21 Fuel filter replacement

1. Relieve fuel system pressure as outlined under "Precautions."
2. Raise and support vehicle.
3. Using suitable back-up wrench, remove fuel filter fitting, **Fig. 21.**
4. Grasp filter and one nylon fuel connection line fitting, then twist quick connect fitting 1/4 turn in each direction to loosen dirt in fitting.
5. Using compressed air, clean dirt from quick connect fitting.
6. Depress quick connect fitting plastic tabs of male end connector and pull apart.
7. Remove fuel filter.
8. Reverse procedure to install, noting the following:
   a. Apply a few drops of clean engine oil to male pipe ends before connection to reduce risk of leakage and fire.
   b. Tighten filter fitting to specifications.
   c. Inspect for fuel leaks as outlined under "Fuel Leak Inspection."

TIGHTENING SPECIFICATIONS

Year	Component	Torque/Ft. Lbs.
1997-2000	Balance Shaft Cover	10
	Balance Shaft Housing	⑤
	Balance Shaft Mounting	⑤
	Balance Shaft Sprocket	⑤
	Camshaft Housing & Cover	⑦
	Camshaft Position Sensor	89⑨
	Camshaft Sprocket To Cam Bolt	52
	Connecting Rod Nuts	②
	Coolant Inlet To Oil Pan	19
	Coolant Inlet To Water Pump	10
	Coolant Outlet To Cylinder Head	19
	Crankshaft Balancer To Crankshaft	129③
	Crankshaft Bearing Cap Bolts	15③
	Crankshaft Position Sensor	80⑨
	Cylinder Head Bolts	④
	Engine Mount Bracket	99
	Engine Mount To Bracket	46
	Engine Mount To Body	49
	Exhaust Camshaft Housing Rear Cover	⑦
	Exhaust Manifold Brace To Manifold Bolt	41
	Exhaust Manifold Brace To Oil Pan Nuts	19
	Exhaust Manifold Heat Shield Bolts	10
	Exhaust Manifold To Cylinder Head Nuts	41
	Exhaust Manifold To Cylinder Head Studs	11
	Exhaust Manifold To Oil Pan	19
	Exhaust Manifold Studs To Manifold	19
	Exhaust Pipe To Manifold	26
	Flexplate To Clutch Cover	22
	Flexplate To Converter	46
	Flexplate To Crankshaft	22⑥
	Front Cover To Timing Chain Housing	9
	Fuel Filter Fitting	20
	Fuel Pipe Bracket To Camshaft Housing	11①
	Fuel Pipe To Fuel Rail Nut	22
	Fuel Rail To Camshaft Housing	19
	Ignition Coil & Module Assembly To Camshaft Housing	16
	Intake Manifold Brace Bolts	19
	Intake Manifold To Cylinder Head Nuts	19
	Intake Manifold To Cylinder Head Studs	96⑨
	Knock Sensor	15
	Oil/Air Separator To Intake Manifold	19
	Oil/Air Separator To Block	19
	Oil Filter Connector To Block	21
	Oil Pan Bolts	17
	Oil Pan Bolts (Second Set)	106⑨
	Oil Pan Drain Plug	19
	Oil Pan Studs	19
	Oil Passage Plug Bolt	22
	Oil Passage Plugs, ⅛ × 27	89⑨
	Oil Passage Plugs, ¼ × 18	15
	Oil Passage Plugs, ⅜ × 18	22

Continued

TIGHTENING SPECIFICATIONS—Continued

Year	Component	Torque/Ft. Lbs.
1997–2000	Oil Pump To Balance Shaft Housing, Long Bolts (Alero & 1999–2000 Grand Am)	106⑨
	Oil Pump To Balance Shaft Housing, Short Bolts (Alero & 1999–2000 Grand Am)	89⑨
	Oil Pump To Block (1997–98)	40
	Oil Pump Cover To Oil Pump Body (1997–98)	108⑨
	Oxygen Sensor To Exhaust Manifold	31
	Radiator Mounting Bolts	89⑨
	Rear Crankshaft Seal Housing To Block	108⑨
	Spark Plugs	13
	Starter	66
	Thermostat Housing	19
	Throttle Body To Intake Manifold	89⑨
	Timing Chain Housing To Block Or Camshaft Housing	19
	Timing Chain Housing To Block Stud	21
	Timing Chain Tensioner To Housing & Block	89⑨
	Transaxle To Block Bolt	44
	Transaxle To Block Nut	49
	Transaxle To Block Stud	115⑨
	Water Pump Cover	⑧
	Water Pump Cover To Block	⑧
	Water Pump To Timing Chain Housing	⑧

① — Tighten an additional 30°.

② — Tighten an additional 80°.

③ — Tighten an additional 90°.

④ — Refer to "Cylinder Head, Replace."

⑤ — Refer to "Balance Shaft, Replace."

⑥ — Tighten an additional 45°.

⑦ — Refer to "Camshaft, Replace."

⑧ — Refer to "Water Pump, Replace."

⑨ — Inch lbs.

3.1L Engine

NOTE: On Air Bag Equipped Models, Refer To "Air Bag System Precautions" Located In The Front Of This Manual For System Disarming & Arming Procedures.

NOTE: For Procedures Not Found In This Section, Refer To "3.1L Engine" Section In The "Century, Cutlass Supreme, Grand Prix, Impala, Intrigue, Lumina, Monte Carlo & Regal" Chapter.

NOTE: Refer To "Computer Relearn Procedures " Located In The Front Of This Manual For Computer Relearn Procedures.

INDEX

PRECAUTIONS

AIR BAG SYSTEMS

Refer to "Air Bag System Precautions" in the front of this manual for system disarming and arming procedures.

FUEL SYSTEM PRESSURE RELIEF

Failure to relieve system pressure prior to disconnecting fuel system components may cause fire or personal injury.

1. Loosen fuel tank filler cap to relieve tank pressure.
2. Raise and safely support vehicle.
3. Disconnect fuel pump electrical connector.
4. Lower vehicle.
5. Start and operate engine until fuel supply is consumed.
6. Crank engine for approximately three seconds to relieve remaining pressure.
7. Disconnect battery ground cable and connect fuel pump connector.

BATTERY GROUND CABLE

Prior to service, disconnect battery ground cable and isolate as required.

COMPRESSION PRESSURE

When inspecting cylinder compression, the throttle should be open, all spark plugs removed and the battery at or near full charge. The lowest reading cylinder should not be less than 70% of the highest and no cylinder reading should be less than 100 psi. Turn ignition key until engine cranks through four compression cycles. Normal compression builds up quickly and evenly to specified compression on each cylinder.

ENGINE MOUNT

REPLACE

1. Support engine by oil pan and remove engine mount assembly to engine mount bracket support bolts, **Fig. 1.**
2. Remove engine mount to body bolts and nut.
3. Remove engine mount assembly.
4. Reverse procedure to install. Tighten nuts and bolts to specifications.

ENGINE MOUNT STRUT

REPLACE

1. Raise and support vehicle.
2. Remove righthand splash shield.
3. Remove engine mount strut bolts, **Fig. 2.**
4. Remove engine mount strut.
5. Reverse procedure to install. Tighten bolts to specifications.

ENGINE

REPLACE

1. Relieve fuel system pressure as outlined under "Precautions."
2. Remove upper half of air cleaner assembly and throttle body duct.
3. Drain coolant into an approved container.
4. Disconnect upper radiator hose from engine and position aside.
5. Disconnect lower radiator hose from engine and position aside.
6. Disconnect coolant inlet line from surge tank.
7. Disconnect vacuum modulator, EVAP canister purge and power brake booster vacuum hoses.
8. Disconnect heater outlet hose from water pump.
9. Remove serpentine drive belt.
10. Disconnect accelerator and cruise control cable from throttle linkage.
11. Disconnect electrical connectors at electronic ignition, heated oxygen sensor, injector harness, IAC, throttle position sensor, engine coolant temperature sensor, PNP switch, transaxle shift solenoid, TCC solenoid and EGR and battery ground cable at transaxle.
12. Remove alternator as outlined under "Alternator, Replace" in "Electrical" section.
13. Disconnect power steering lines at power steering pump.
14. Disconnect fuel lines.
15. Remove cooling fan assembly.
16. Disconnect shift cable linkage and cable from mounting bracket. Transaxle should be in low gear for better accessibility.
17. Disconnect transaxle vent tube from transaxle.
18. Disconnect vacuum hose at vacuum reservoir.
19. Remove engine support fixture.
20. Loosen but do not remove upper two A/C compressor bolts.
21. Raise and support vehicle.
22. Remove front tire and wheel assemblies.
23. Remove righthand and lefthand splash shields.
24. Remove engine mount strut as outlined under "Engine Mount Strut, Replace."
25. Remove both front ABS speed sensor connectors and harness from suspension supports.
26. Remove both ball joints.

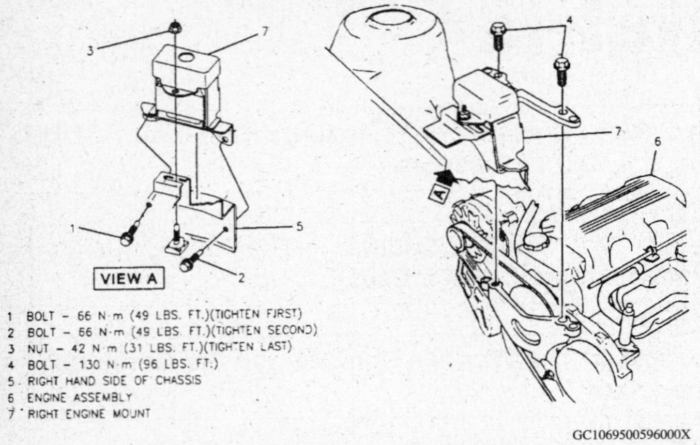

Fig. 1 Engine mount assembly

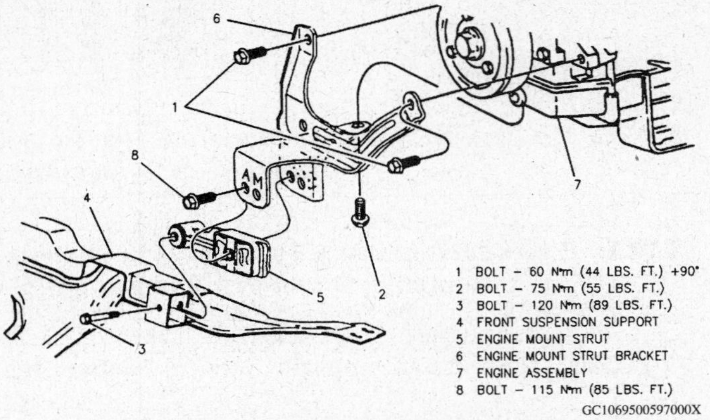

Fig. 2 Engine mount strut bolt removal

27. Remove suspension support assembly.
28. Remove drive axles from transaxle and support.
29. Remove oil filter and adapter.
30. Remove transaxle converter cover.
31. Remove starter as outlined under "Starter, Replace " in "Electrical" section.
32. Disconnect knock sensor, front crankshaft position sensor, side crankshaft position sensor, oil level sensor, VSS and transaxle ground cable.
33. Disconnect heater hoses.
34. Remove A/C compressor lower bolts and position compressor aside.
35. Remove vacuum reserve tank.
36. Remove exhaust pipe from manifold and position aside.
37. Remove engine mount strut bracket.
38. Disconnect transaxle cooling lines at radiator.
39. Remove fluid level indicator and tube.
40. Lower vehicle and engine/transaxle onto suitable table.
41. Remove transaxle mount to body bolts, **Fig. 1.**
42. Remove intermediate bracket from righthand engine mount support bracket.
43. Raise and support vehicle, leaving powertrain on table.
44. Separate engine and transaxle assembly.
45. Reverse procedure to install, noting the following:
    a. After connecting engine to transaxle, loosely install serpentine drive belt to hold components together.
    b. Tighten engine fasteners and components to specifications.
    c. Bleed power steering system after engine installation.

INTAKE MANIFOLD

REPLACE

1997

1. Relieve fuel system pressure as outlined under "Precautions."
2. Remove upper half of air cleaner assembly and throttle body duct.
3. Drain coolant into an approved container.
4. Disconnect EGR pipe from exhaust manifold.
5. Remove serpentine drive belt.
6. Disconnect brake vacuum pipe at plenum.
7. Disconnect power steering lines at alternator bracket.
8. Remove alternator as outlined under "Alternator, Replace" in "Electrical" section.
9. Disconnect secondary ignition wires from spark plugs and harness at plenum.
10. Remove electronic ignition coil/module assembly and the EVAP canister purge solenoid.
11. Disconnect upper engine wire harness connectors.
12. Disconnect vacuum modulator, fuel pressure regulator and PCV vacuum lines.
13. Remove MAP sensor from upper intake manifold.
14. Remove upper intake manifold, **Fig. 3.**
15. Disconnect fuel lines at fuel rail and remove from bracket.
16. Install engine support fixture.
17. Remove engine mount assembly as outlined under "Engine Mounts, Replace."
18. Remove power steering pump mounting bolts and position pump aside.
19. Disconnect coolant inlet pipe from coolant outlet housing.
20. Remove coolant bypass at coolant pump and cylinder head.
21. Disconnect radiator hose at coolant outlet housing.
22. Remove coolant outlet housing.
23. Remove both valve rocker covers.
24. Remove lower intake manifold bolts.
25. Loosen rocker arms and remove pushrods.
26. Remove intake manifold and gasket.
27. Reverse procedure to install. Tighten intake manifold upper and lower bolts to specifications.

1998–2000

Upper

1. Disconnect vacuum lines.
2. Remove electrical connector, mounting screws and MAP sensor.
3. Remove pipe, bolts, EGR valve and gaskets.
4. Remove spark plug wires.
5. Remove mounting nuts, bolts and electronic ignition control module.
6. Remove mounting nuts, studs, upper intake manifold and gasket.
7. Reverse procedure to install. Tighten nuts and bolts to specifications.

Lower

1. Remove fuel feed and return pipe mounting bolt and clip, then the mounting bolts and fuel injector rail assembly.
2. Remove mounting nut and heater inlet pipe.
3. Remove mounting bolts and lower intake manifold.
4. Reverse procedure to install. Tighten nuts and bolts to specifications.

EXHAUST MANIFOLD

REPLACE

LEFTHAND

1. Remove upper half of air cleaner assembly and throttle cable duct.
2. Partially drain coolant into an approved container and disconnect radiator hose from thermostat housing.
3. Disconnect coolant bypass pipe at coolant pump and from exhaust manifold.
4. Remove exhaust crossover heat shield.
5. Remove exhaust crossover pipe from manifold.
6. Disconnect secondary ignition wires from spark plugs.
7. Remove exhaust manifold heat shield, **Fig. 4.**
8. Remove retaining nuts and exhaust manifold.
9. Reverse procedure to install. Tighten exhaust manifold and heat shield to specifications.

RIGHTHAND

1. Remove upper half of air cleaner assembly and throttle cable duct.
2. Remove exhaust crossover heat shield.

3. Remove crossover at exhaust manifold.
4. Remove heated oxygen sensor.
5. Disconnect EGR pipe at exhaust manifold.
6. Raise and support vehicle.
7. Remove transaxle oil fill tube and level indicator assembly.
8. Remove exhaust pipe from exhaust manifold.
9. Disconnect exhaust pipe from converter flange and support converter.
10. Remove converter heat shield from body.
11. Remove exhaust manifold heat shield.
12. Remove exhaust manifold mounting nuts, **Fig. 4,** then pull manifold from bottom of vehicle.
13. Reverse procedure to install.

RADIATOR

REPLACE

Refer to "2.4L Engine" section for this procedure.

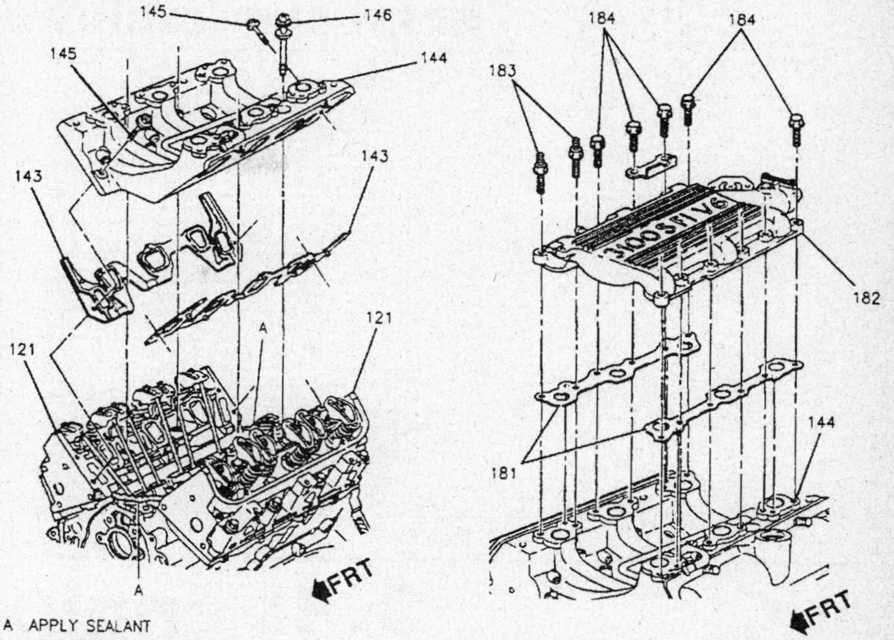

A APPLY SEALANT
121 HEAD ASSEMBLY, CYLINDER
143 GASKET, LOWER INTAKE MANIFOLD
144 BOLT, LOWER INTAKE
145 BOLT, LOWER INTAKE MANIFOLD
146 BOLT, LOWER INTAKE MANIFOLD

144 MANIFOLD, LOWER INTAKE
181 GASKET, UPPER INTAKE MANIFOLD
182 MANIFOLD, UPPER INTAKE
183 STUD, UPPER INTAKE MANIFOLD
184 BOLT, UPPER INTAKE MANIFOLD

GC1069500599000X

Fig. 3 Intake manifold assembly. 1997

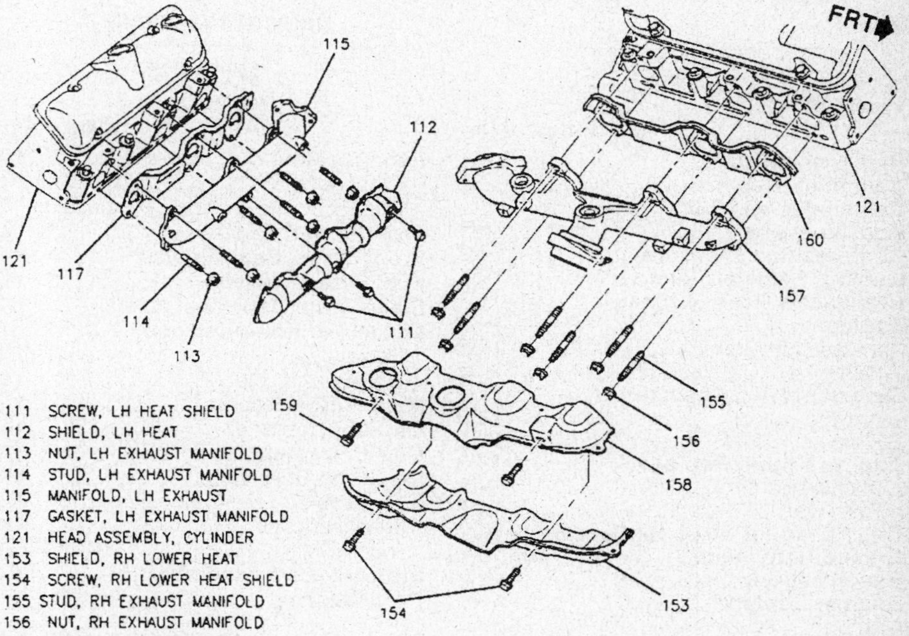

111 SCREW, LH HEAT SHIELD
112 SHIELD, LH HEAT
113 NUT, LH EXHAUST MANIFOLD
114 STUD, LH EXHAUST MANIFOLD
115 MANIFOLD, LH EXHAUST
117 GASKET, LH EXHAUST MANIFOLD
121 HEAD ASSEMBLY, CYLINDER
153 SHIELD, RH LOWER HEAT
154 SCREW, RH LOWER HEAT SHIELD
155 STUD, RH EXHAUST MANIFOLD
156 NUT, RH EXHAUST MANIFOLD
157 MANIFOLD, RH EXHAUST
158 SHIELD, RH UPPER HEAT
159 SCREW, RH UPPER HEAT SHIELD
160 GASKET, RH EXHAUST MANIFOLD

GC1069500600000X

Fig. 4 Exhaust manifold assembly

TIGHTENING SPECIFICATIONS

Year	Component	Torque/Ft. Lbs.
1997-2000	Accelerator Cable Bracket Nuts & Bolts	89①
	Coolant Drain Plug	14
	Coolant Outlet Bolt	18
	Drive Belt Tensioner Bolt	37
	Engine Mount Strut Bolts	52
	Engine Mount To Body Bolts	49
	Engine Mount To Body Nut	31
	Exhaust Manifold Bolts	12
	Exhaust Manifold Heat Shield	84①
	Lower Intake Manifold Bolts	10
	Oil Filter	9–10
	Upper Intake Manifold Bolts	18
	Water Pump Bolts	89①
	Water Pump Pulley Bolts	18

① — Inch lbs.

3.4L Engine

NOTE: On Air Bag Equipped Models, Refer To "Air Bag System Precautions" Located In The Front Of This Manual For System Disarming & Arming Procedures.

NOTE: Refer To "Computer Relearn Procedures " Located In The Front Of This Manual For Computer Relearn Procedures.

INDEX

PRECAUTIONS

AIR BAG SYSTEMS

Refer to "Air Bag System Precautions" in the front of this manual for system disarming and arming procedures.

FUEL SYSTEM PRESSURE RELIEF

Failure to relieve system pressure prior to disconnecting fuel system components may cause fire or personal injury.

1. Loosen fuel tank filler cap to relieve tank pressure.
2. Raise and safely support vehicle.
3. Disconnect fuel pump electrical connector.
4. Lower the vehicle.
5. Start and operate engine until fuel supply is consumed.
6. Crank engine for approximately three seconds to relieve remaining pressure.
7. Disconnect and isolate battery ground cable, then connect fuel pump electrical connector.

BATTERY GROUND CABLE

Prior to service, disconnect battery ground cable and isolate as required.

COMPRESSION PRESSURE

When inspecting cylinder compression, the throttle should be open, all spark plugs removed and the battery at or near full charge. The lowest reading cylinder should not be less than 70% of the highest and no cylinder reading should be less than 100 psi. Crank engine until it runs through four compression cycles. Normal compression builds up quickly and evenly to specified compression on each cylinder.

ENGINE MOUNT

REPLACE

REMOVAL

1. Support engine with a wooden block and a suitable floor jack positioned below oil pan.
2. Remove cruise control module.
3. Remove engine mount assembly to bracket support bolts.
4. Remove engine mount to body fasteners.
5. Remove engine mount assembly.

INSTALLATION

1. Install body fasteners to mount assembly. **Torque** bolts to 96 ft. lbs. **Torque** nuts to 49 ft. lbs.
2. Install mount bracket support bolts to mount. **Torque** bolt to 96 ft. lbs.
3. Install cruise control module.
4. Remove jack and wooden block.

ENGINE MOUNT STRUT

REPLACE

1. Raise and safely support vehicle.
2. Remove righthand splash shield.
3. Remove engine mount strut bolts.
4. Remove engine mount strut.
5. Reverse procedure to install. **Torque** strut bolts to 74 ft. lbs., then rotate an additional 90° using torque angle meter tool No. J-36660, or equivalent.

ENGINE

REPLACE

1. Relieve fuel system pressure as outlined under "Precautions."
2. Drain coolant into an approved container.
3. Remove engine air cleaner assembly.
4. Remove hood.
5. Remove serpentine belt.
6. Remove hoses from surge tank.
7. Remove cruise control module.
8. Remove engine wiring harness from upper side of engine and position it aside.
9. Disconnect throttle and cruise control cables. **Manufacturer recommends throttle cable replacement when engine is removed and installed.**
10. Raise and safely support vehicle.
11. Remove starter motor.
12. Remove A/C compressor with lines intact and position aside.
13. Disconnect engine lower wiring harness and position it aside.
14. Disconnect catalytic converter flange from rear exhaust manifold.
15. Remove inspection cover.
16. Remove torque converter to flexplate bolts.
17. Remove engine splash shields.
18. Remove transaxle to engine brace.
19. Remove two outer transaxle mounting bolts.
20. Disconnect upper and lower radiator hoses.
21. Lower the vehicle.
22. Disconnect fuel lines from engine.
23. Disconnect vacuum hoses at brake booster.
24. Disconnect heater hoses.
25. Install engine support fixture tool No. J-28467-360, or equivalent.
26. Raise engine.
27. Remove engine mount and adapter.
28. Remove power steering pump.
29. Install suitable engine lifting device.
30. Remove engine support fixture.
31. Remove transaxle to engine bolts.
32. Carefully remove engine from vehicle.
33. If engine will be mounted onto a stand, remove flexplate mounting bolts and flexplate, then mount engine on suitable stand.
34. Reverse procedure to install, noting the following:
    a. If flexplate was removed, install it and its bolts. Tighten bolts evenly to specifications.
    b. Tighten all fasteners to specifications.
    c. Start engine and inspect for fluid leaks.

INTAKE MANIFOLD

REPLACE

UPPER

1. Drain coolant into an approved container.
2. Remove upper half of air cleaner assembly.
3. Remove EGR valve.
4. Remove brake vacuum pipe at plenum.
5. Disconnect fuel pressure regulator vacuum hose from regulator and at PCV valve.
6. Mark and disconnect spark plug wires at plugs.
7. Remove spark plug wires from plenum harness.
8. Remove electronic ignition coil and module assembly.
9. Remove EVAP canister purge solenoid.
10. Disconnect TP and IAC sensor electrical connectors.
11. Disconnect injector harness.
12. Disconnect ECT and CMP sensor electrical connectors.
13. Disconnect vacuum modulator.
14. Disconnect MAP sensor vacuum line and electrical connector.
15. Remove MAP sensor mounting bolts, then the sensor.
16. Remove upper intake manifold mounting bolts, then the manifold with its gaskets.
17. Reverse procedure to install, noting the following:
    a. Apply thread locker part No. 12345382, or equivalent to intake manifold mounting bolt threads.
    b. **Torque** intake manifold mounting bolts evenly to 18 ft. lbs.
    c. Start engine and inspect for leaks.

LOWER

Removal

1. Relieve fuel system pressure as outlined under "Precautions."
2. Remove upper intake manifold as outlined under "Intake Manifold, Replace."
3. Remove fuel lines at fuel rail and bracket, then the rail with injectors.
4. Remove engine mount as outlined under "Engine Mount, Replace."
5. Remove power steering pump mounting bolts, then position pump aside.
6. Remove heater inlet pipe from coolant outlet housing.
7. Remove heater bypass at coolant pump and at cylinder head.
8. Remove radiator hose at heater outlet housing.
9. Remove water outlet housing.
10. Remove valve covers as outlined under "Valve Cover, Replace."
11. Remove lower intake manifold bolts, **keeping washers in same orientation on center bolts.**
12. Remove lower intake manifold.
13. Loosen rocker arm bolts.
14. Remove pushrods, keeping them in order. Intakes have yellow stripes and are 5.75 inches long. Exhausts have

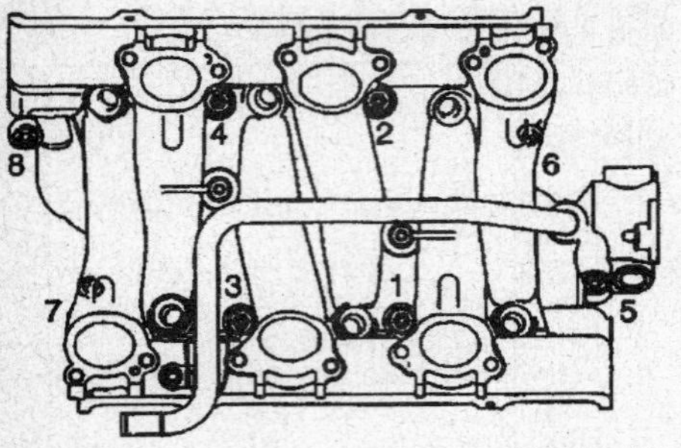

Fig. 1 Lower intake manifold bolt tightening sequence

green stripes and are six inches long.
15. Remove intake manifold gaskets.

Installation

1. Clean all gasket material from mating surfaces.
2. Remove excess RTV sealer from front and rear block ridges.
3. Clean sealing surfaces using a suitable degreasing compound.
4. Place a .079–.118 inch bead of RTV sealer part No. 12345739, or equivalent on each manifold-to-block contact ridge.
5. Install new manifold gaskets.
6. Coat pushrod ends with prelube part No. 1052356, or equivalent.
7. Install pushrods in proper sequence. Intakes have yellow stripes and are 5.75 inches long. Exhausts have green stripes and are six inches long.
8. Install rocker arm bolts. **Torque** to 14 ft. lbs., then rotate an additional 30° using torque angle meter tool No. J-36660, or equivalent.
9. Place lower intake manifold in position, then proceed as follows:
   a. Apply sealant part No. 12345382, or equivalent to lower intake manifold bolt threads.
   b. **Torque** vertical bolts to 9.6 ft. lbs. in sequence outlined in **Fig. 1. Always tighten vertical bolts before the horizontals to avoid an oil leak.**
   c. **Torque** horizontal bolts to 9.6 ft. lbs. in sequence outlined in **Fig. 1. Always tighten horizontal bolts after the verticals to avoid an oil leak.**
10. Install valve covers.
11. Install heater outlet housing.
12. Install heater inlet pipe to thermostat housing.
13. Install fuel lines to fuel rail and bracket.
14. Install upper intake manifold as outlined under "Intake Manifold, Replace."
15. Start engine and inspect for leaks.

EXHAUST MANIFOLD

REPLACE

FRONT

1. Partially drain coolant into an approved container.
2. Remove complete air cleaner assembly and TBI duct.
3. Remove exhaust crossover heat shield.
4. Remove crossover pipe at exhaust manifold.
5. Remove upper radiator hose from thermostat housing.
6. Tag and disconnect spark plug wires from front spark plugs, then position aside.
7. Remove exhaust manifold heat shield.
8. Remove exhaust manifold attaching nuts, then the manifold from bottom of vehicle. Discard manifold to head gasket.
9. Reverse procedure to install, noting the following:
   a. Clean head and manifold mating surfaces.
   b. Install a new manifold mounting gasket.
   c. Install manifold and tighten nuts to specifications.
   d. Tighten heat shield nuts to specifications.
   e. Start engine and inspect for leaks.

REAR

1. Remove complete air cleaner assembly and throttle body duct.
2. Remove O2 sensors using socket tool No. J-39194-B, or equivalent.
3. Remove exhaust crossover heat shield.
4. Disconnect EGR pipe from manifold.
5. Remove exhaust crossover pipe from manifold.
6. Remove exhaust manifold heat shield.
7. Remove exhaust manifold attaching nuts, then the manifold.
8. Reverse procedure to install, noting the following:
   a. Clean head and manifold mating surfaces.
   b. Install a new manifold mounting gasket.
   c. Install manifold, then tighten nuts to specifications.
   d. Tighten heat shield nuts to specifications.
   e. Start engine and inspect for leaks.

CYLINDER HEAD

REPLACE

FRONT

Removal

1. Relieve fuel system pressure as outlined under "Precautions."
2. Drain coolant into an approved container.
3. Remove upper half of engine air cleaner assembly.
4. Remove TBI unit duct.
5. Remove exhaust crossover.
6. Remove upper and lower intake manifolds as outlined under "Intake Manifold, Replace."
7. Remove valve cover as outlined under "Valve Cover, Replace." Use a soft rubber mallet or palm of the hand to bump cover if it will not easily budge.

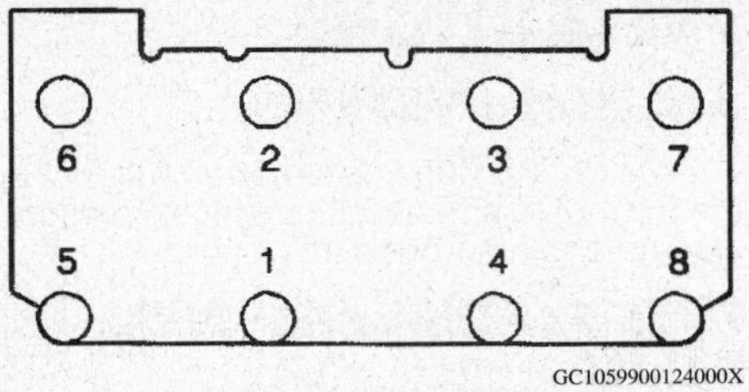

Fig. 2 Cylinder head bolt tightening sequence

8. Remove rocker arm bolts, pivot balls and arms.
9. Remove pushrods, keeping them in order. Intakes have yellow stripes and are 5.75 inches long. Exhausts have green stripes and are six inches long.
10. Remove front exhaust manifold as outlined under "Exhaust Manifold, Replace."
11. Remove cylinder head attaching bolts, then the head.

Installation

1. Clean mating surfaces of head, block and intake manifold.
2. Clean cylinder head bolts and their threads.
3. Place head gasket into position over dowel pins with "THIS SIDE UP" notice properly oriented.
4. Carefully place head into position.
5. Coat head bolt threads with sealer part No. 1052080, or equivalent.
6. Install head bolts. **Torque** to 33 ft. lbs. in sequence outlined in **Fig. 2,** then rotate them an additional 90° using torque angle meter tool No. J-36660, or equivalent.
7. Install intake manifold gaskets.
8. Install pushrods in proper sequence. Intakes have yellow stripes and are 5.75 inches long. Exhausts have green stripes and are six inches long.
9. Install rocker arms, pivot balls and bolts. **Torque** to 14 ft. lbs., then rotate an additional 30° using torque angle meter tool No. J-36660, or equivalent.
10. Install intake manifolds as outlined under "Intake Manifold, Replace."
11. Install exhaust manifold as outlined under "Exhaust Manifold, Replace."
12. Install crossover pipe and heat shield.
13. Fill cooling system.
14. Install TBI unit duct.
15. Install upper half of air cleaner assembly.
16. Start engine and inspect for leaks.

REAR

Removal

1. Relieve fuel system pressure as outlined under "Precautions."
2. Drain coolant into an approved container.
3. Remove exhaust crossover pipe.
4. Raise and safely support vehicle.
5. Remove rear exhaust manifold as outlined under "Exhaust Manifold, Replace."
6. Lower the vehicle.

7. Remove serpentine drive belt as outlined under "Serpentine Drive Belt."
8. Remove valve cover as outlined under "Valve Cover, Replace." Use a soft rubber mallet or palm of the hand to bump cover if it will not easily budge.
9. Remove rocker arm bolts, pivot balls and arms.
10. Remove pushrods, keeping them in order. Intakes have yellow stripes and are 5.75 inches long. Exhausts have green stripes and are six inches long.
11. Remove upper and lower intake manifolds as outlined under "Intake Manifold, Replace."
12. Remove cylinder head attaching bolts, then the head.

Installation

1. Clean mating surfaces of head, block and intake manifold.
2. Clean cylinder head bolts and their threads.
3. Place head gasket into position over dowel pins with "THIS SIDE UP" notice properly oriented.
4. Carefully place head into position.
5. Coat head bolt threads with sealer part No. 1052080, or equivalent.
6. Install head bolts. **Torque** to 33 ft. lbs. in sequence outlined in **Fig. 2,** then rotate them an additional 90° using torque angle meter tool No. J-36660, or equivalent.
7. Install intake manifold gaskets.
8. Install pushrods in proper sequence. Intakes have yellow stripes and are 5.75 inches long. Exhausts have green stripes and are six inches long.
9. Install rocker arms, pivot balls and bolts. **Torque** to 14 ft. lbs., then rotate an additional 30° using torque angle meter tool No. J-36660, or equivalent.
10. Install intake manifolds as outlined under "Intake Manifold, Replace."
11. Install valve cover with a new gasket.
12. Connect spark plug wires.
13. Install serpentine belt.
14. Raise and safely support vehicle.
15. Install exhaust manifold as outlined under "Exhaust Manifold, Replace."
16. Install crossover pipe and heat shield.
17. Fill cooling system.
18. Install TBI unit duct.
19. Install upper half of air cleaner assembly.
20. Start engine and inspect for leaks.

VALVE COVER

REPLACE

FRONT

1. Partially drain coolant into an approved container.
2. Remove rear ignition wire harness and spark plug wires at spark plugs.
3. Remove heater bypass intake.
4. Disconnect PCV vacuum hose.
5. Remove valve cover retaining bolts, then the cover. If cover is stubborn, tap it lightly with palm of hand or a soft rubber mallet to break it loose.
6. Reverse procedure to install, noting the following:

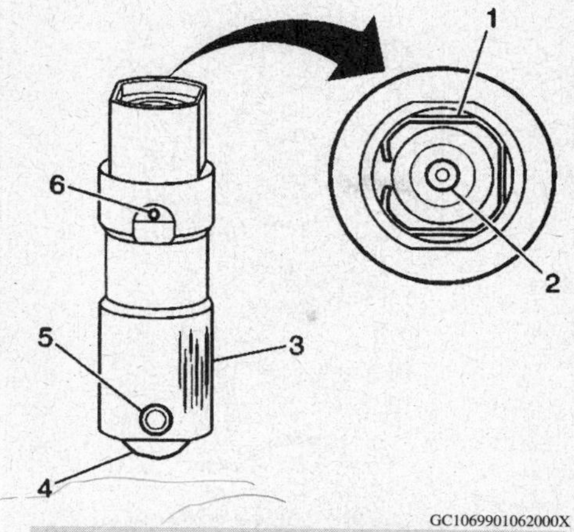

Fig. 3 Valve lifter inspection locations

a. Install a new gasket and grommets onto cover.
b. Apply sealer part No. 12346192, or equivalent in cover notch.
c. Tighten cover bolts to specifications.

REAR

1. Remove serpentine belt.
2. Remove alternator as outlined under "Alternator, Replace" in electrical section.
3. Remove alternator bracket.
4. Remove rear bank spark plug wires.
5. Remove ignition coils and bracket.
6. Remove purge and vacuum canister solenoids.
7. Remove vacuum hose from rear bank valve cover grommet.
8. Remove serpentine belt tensioner.
9. Remove valve cover retaining bolts, then the cover. If cover is stubborn, tap it lightly with palm of hand or a soft rubber mallet to break it loose.
10. Reverse procedure to install, noting the following:
    a. Install a new gasket and grommets onto cover.
    b. Apply sealer part No. 12345739, or equivalent at cylinder head to lower intake manifold joints.
    c. Tighten cover bolts to specifications.

VALVE ARRANGEMENT

FRONT TO REAR

Cowl side ....E-I-E-I-I-E
Radiator side ....E-I-I-E-I-E

VALVE LIFTERS

Roller type valve lifters, **Fig. 3,** are used in this engine and must be replaced whenever the camshaft is replaced. They must be kept in order so they will be installed in their original positions.

Inspect the lifters and look for a bent or broken clip (1), worn pushrod socket (2), scuffed or worn sides (3), flat spots on the roller (4), a loose or damaged pin, (5) a plugged oil hole (6) or worn or damaged roller bearing. Ensure the roller can rotate freely with no binding or rough operation. If the lifter show side wear the block lifter bores should also be inspected for damage or wear. Replace any lifter which does not pass these inspections.

Valve lifters must be kept in order so they will be installed in their original positions.

CAMSHAFT LOBE LIFT SPECIFICATIONS

Intake .... .2727
Exhaust .... .2727

VALVE ADJUSTMENT

These engines are equipped with hydraulic valve lash adjusters. No adjustment is required.

PUSH RODS

1. Remove rocker arm covers and rocker arms, identifying components so they will be installed in same location.
2. Remove rocker arm pivot balls and rocker arms, then the pushrods. Intakes have yellow stripes and are 5.75 inches long. Exhausts have green stripes and are six inches long.
3. Reverse procedure to install, noting the following:
    a. Ensure pushrods seat in lifters.
    b. Coat bearing surfaces of rocker arms and pivot balls with Molykote part No. 1052356, or an equivalent lubricant.
    c. Tighten rocker arm bolts to specifications.

FRONT COVER

REPLACE

1. Recover refrigerant charge using recycling station tool No. J-39500, or equivalent.
2. Drain coolant into an approved container.
3. Install engine support tool No. J-28467-360, or equivalent.
4. Remove engine mount assembly as outlined under "Engine Mount, Replace."
5. Remove engine mount bracket support.
6. Remove serpentine drive belt as outlined under "Serpentine Drive Belt."
7. Remove complete engine air cleaner assembly.
8. Remove TBI unit tube.
9. Disconnect power steering lines at power steering pump, allowing fluid to drain into a suitable container.
10. Loosen upper two A/C compressor mounting bolts.
11. Remove alternator as outlined under "Alternator, Replace."
12. Remove alternator bracket.
13. Raise and safely support vehicle.
14. Drain engine oil using approved methods and equipment.
15. Remove righthand front tire and wheel.

16. Remove righthand front splash shield.
17. Remove flexplate inspection cover.
18. Remove harmonic balancer using puller tool No. J-24420-C, or equivalent.
19. Remove serpentine belt tensioner.
20. Disconnect righthand front wheel speed sensor electrical connector and wiring harness from suspension support.
21. Remove righthand front ball joint as outlined under "Ball Joint, Replace."
22. Remove righthand stabilizer shaft from righthand suspension support and control arm.
23. Remove righthand suspension support.
24. Separate righthand outer tie rod from knuckle if required.
25. Remove A/C compressor to oil pan bolts.
26. Remove oil filter and adapter.
27. Remove starter motor as outlined under "Starter, Replace."
28. Remove lower A/C compressor mounting bolts, then position compressor aside.
29. Remove evaporator to accumulator A/C line.
30. Remove righthand front and righthand rear engine cradle bolts.
31. Remove oil pan.
32. Remove CKP sensor.
33. Remove front cover lower bolts.
34. Lower the vehicle.
35. Remove coolant bypass to coolant pump and manifold.
36. Remove radiator hose to coolant outlet housing.
37. Remove front cover retaining bolts.
38. Carefully remove front cover.
39. Using a suitable large screwdriver or a prying tool, remove and discard front cover crankshaft oil seal.
40. Reverse procedure to install, noting the following:
    a. Clean all gasket mating surfaces using a suitable degreaser.
    b. Lubricate a new front cover crankshaft oil seal with clean engine oil.
    c. Using crankshaft seal installer and centering tool No. J-36468, or equivalent, install crankshaft oil seal with lip facing engine.
    d. Apply RTV sealer part No. 1052080, or equivalent to both sides of front cover gasket's lower tabs.
    e. Tighten all fasteners to specifications.
    f. Fill cooling system, power steering reservoir and crankcase.
    g. Start engine and inspect for leaks.

FRONT COVER SEAL

REPLACE

1. Raise and safely support vehicle.
2. Remove righthand front tire and wheel.
3. Remove righthand front splash shield.
4. Using torsional dampener remover tool No. J-24420-C, or equivalent, remove crankshaft balancer.
5. Remove crankshaft key from keyway.
6. Pry out seal using suitable tool, being careful not to damage crankshaft or front cover.

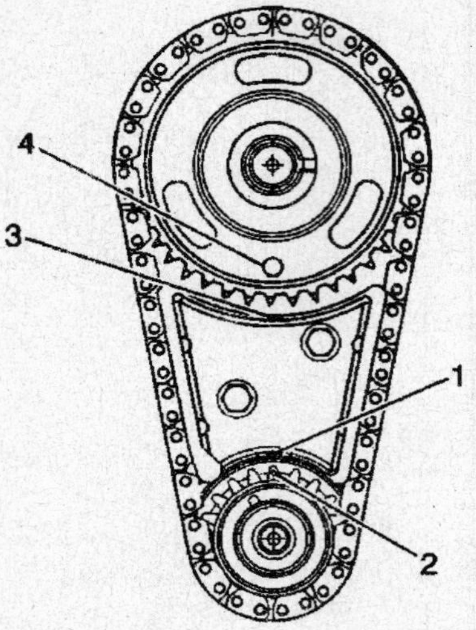

1. DAMPER LOWER TIMING MARK
2. CRANKSHAFT TIMING MARK
3. DAMPER UPPER TIMING
4. CAMSHAFT GEAR

GC1059900125000X

Fig. 4 Timing mark alignment

7. Reverse procedure to install, noting the following:
    a. Install a new key if old one is damaged or worn.
    b. Lubricate new seal with clean engine oil and insert in front cover with lip facing engine.
    c. Use front cover alignment and oil seal installer tool No. J-35468, or equivalent to drive seal into place.

TIMING CHAIN

REPLACE

REMOVAL

1. Remove engine front cover as outlined under "Front Cover, Replace."
2. Turn engine in normal direction of rotation until No. 1 piston reaches TDC. This is the No. 4 cylinder firing position.
3. Align camshaft gear timing mark, **Fig. 4,** with mark on top of chain damper and crankshaft gear timing mark with damper's lower mark.
4. Remove camshaft gear retaining bolt.
5. Remove camshaft gear and timing chain.
6. Remove crankshaft gear using puller tool No. J-5825-A, or equivalent. If gear is stubborn, gently tap lower edge with a plastic mallet to dislodge it.

INSTALLATION

1. Apply prelube part No. 12345501, or equivalent to crankshaft gear thrust surface.
2. Install crankshaft gear using installer tool No. J-38612, or equivalent.
3. Install timing chain damper. Tighten bolts to specifications.
4. Ensure all timing gear and damper marks are properly aligned.
5. Hold camshaft gear with chain hanging down.
6. Install chain to crankshaft gear.
7. Align camshaft dowel with camshaft gear dowel hole.
8. Draw camshaft gear onto camshaft by tightening retaining bolt. Tighten to specifications.
9. Install front cover. Tighten all fasteners to specifications.
10. Fill cooling system, power steering reservoir and crankcase.
11. Start engine and inspect for leaks.

CAMSHAFT

REPLACE

1. Remove engine as outlined under "Engine, Replace."
2. Remove valve lifters.
3. Remove front cover.
4. Remove timing chain and gears.
5. Remove camshaft.
6. Reverse procedure to install, noting the following:
    a. If installing a new camshaft, also install new valve lifters. **Never use old lifters with a new camshaft.**
    b. Coat camshaft lobes with engine oil supplement part No. 12345501, or equivalent.
    c. Lubricate camshaft journals with engine oil.

PISTON & ROD ASSEMBLY

When installing piston and rod assemblies into cylinder block, ensure arrow on top of piston faces toward front of engine, **Fig. 5.** Ensure flat area on bottom of piston aligns with the small dimple above the connecting rod crankshaft bearing bore.

MAIN & ROD BEARINGS

Engine bearings are of the precision insert type. They are available for service usage in standard and various undersizes.

To determine proper replacement insert size, bearing clearance must be measured as follows:

1. Measure crankshaft journal diameter in several places, approximately 90° apart and average the measurements.
2. Measure taper and runout, which should be .0002 inch maximum.
3. Install bearing inserts and tighten rod and main bearing cap bolts to specifications, then measure I.D. with an inside micrometer. Measure connecting rod I.D. in same direction as length of rod.
4. Select a suitable set of inserts to provide specified clearance limits. **Do not mix inserts of different nominal size in same bearing bore.** If clearance limits cannot be met, crankshaft journal must be reconditioned and undersize bearing inserts installed.

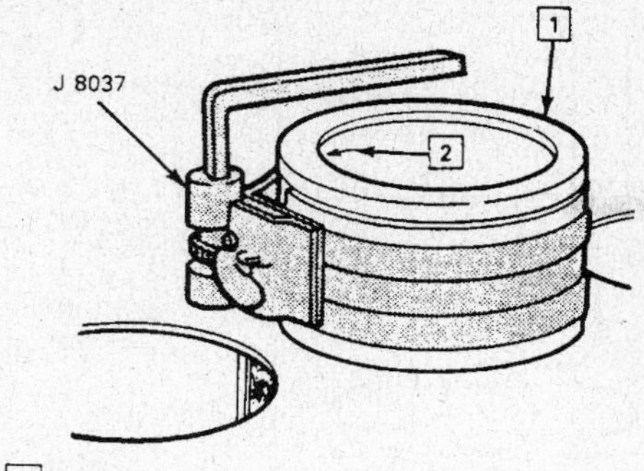

1 PISTON
2 ARROW TOWARDS FRONT OF ENGINE

GC1069100455000X

Fig. 5 Piston marking

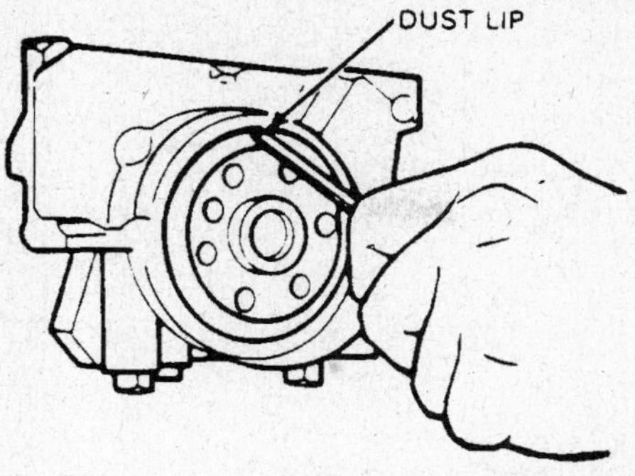

GC1069100456000X

Fig. 6 Rear main seal removal

CRANKSHAFT REAR OIL SEAL

REPLACE

REMOVAL

1. Using engine support fixture tool No. J-28467-360 and fixture adapters tool No. J-28467-90, or equivalents, safely support engine, then remove transaxle as outlined in "Automatic Transmissions/Transaxles" chapter.
2. Remove flexplate.
3. Using a screwdriver or suitable tool, remove seal by inserting tool in through dust lip at an angle, **Fig. 6,** then prying seal out by moving handle of tool toward end of crankshaft pilot, repeating around circumference of seal as required. **Be careful not to damage crankshaft O.D. surface or the chamfer.**

INSTALLATION

1. Inspect I.D. of bore for nicks or burrs and repair as required.
2. Inspect crankshaft for burrs or nicks on surface which contacts seal, repairing or replacing crankshaft as required.
3. Install seal as follows:
   a. Apply clean engine oil to I.D. and O.D. of new seal, then slide seal over mandrel until rear of seal bottoms squarely against collar of rear main bearing seal installer tool No. J-34686, or equivalent, **Fig. 7.**
   b. Align dowel pin of tool with dowel pin in crankshaft by hand, then **torque** attaching screws to 45 inch lbs., **Fig. 7.**
   c. Turn "T" handle of tool so collar pushes seal into bore, turning handle until collar is tight against case.
   d. Loosen "T" handle of tool until it comes to a stop, then remove attaching screws.
   e. Ensure seal is seated squarely in bore.
4. Install flexplate and transaxle.

OIL PAN

REPLACE

1. Recover refrigerant charge using recycling station tool No. J-39500, or equivalent.
2. Drain coolant into an approved container.
3. Remove serpentine belt as outlined under "Serpentine Drive Belt, Replace."
4. Install engine support tool No. J-28467-360, or equivalent.
5. Raise and safely support vehicle.
6. Drain engine oil using approved methods and equipment.
7. Remove righthand front tire and wheel.
8. Remove righthand front splash shield.
9. Remove righthand front wheel speed sensor harness from righthand front suspension support.
10. Separate righthand front ball joint from control arm.
11. Separate righthand outer tie rod end from knuckle.
12. Remove A/C compressor and position aside with hoses intact.
13. Remove evaporator to accumulator line.
14. Remove flexplate inspection cover.
15. Remove righthand front and rear engine cradle bolts.
16. Remove harmonic balancer using puller tool No. J-24420-C, or equivalent.
17. Remove starter motor.
18. Remove all oil pan retaining and side bolts, then the oil pan.
19. Reverse procedure to install, noting the following:
   a. Clean oil pan flanges and rail, front cover, rear main cap and all bolt holes.
   b. Install a new oil pan gasket. If installing rear main cap, install sealer part No. 1052080, or equivalent on tabs that insert into cap's outer gasket grooves.
   c. Install oil pan. **Torque** retaining bolts to 18 ft. lbs. **Torque** side bolts to 37 ft. lbs.

OIL PUMP

REPLACE

1. Remove oil pan as outlined under "Oil Pan, Replace."
2. Remove oil pump mounting bolt, then the oil pump and drive shaft extension.
3. Reverse procedure to install. Tighten pump mounting bolt to specifications.

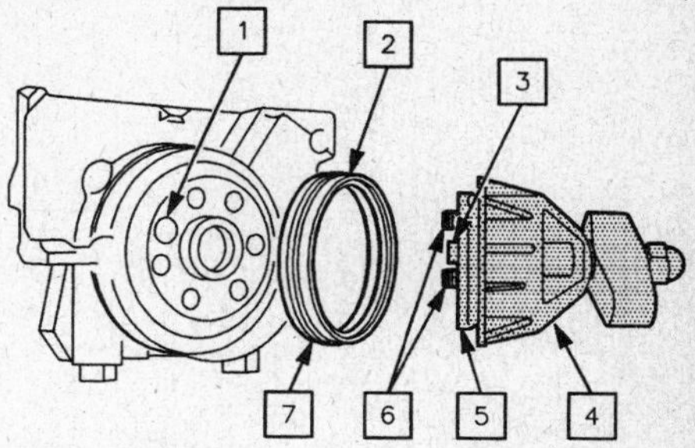

1 ALIGNMENT HOLE
2 DUST LIP
3 DOWEL PIN
4 COLLAR
5 MANDRIL
6 ATTACHING SCREWS
7 SEAL

GC1069701063000X

Fig. 7 Rear main seal installation

OIL PUMP SERVICE

DISASSEMBLE

1. Drain oil from pump into an approved container.
2. Remove pump driveshaft.
3. **Do not remove pickup tube from cover unless it is broken or loose.**
4. Remove pump cover and pump gears.
5. Remove pressure regulator valve and spring. If valve is stuck, soak pump housing in carburetor cleaning solvent. **Pressure regulator valve spring may be under pressure. Remove retaining pin carefully.**
6. Clean sludge, oil and varnish from all components. Varnish may be removed by soaking in carburetor cleaning solvent.

INSPECTION

1. Inspect pump housing and cover for casting imperfections, cracks or damaged threads, replacing as required. **Do not attempt to repair pump housing.** Replace spring as required.
2. Inspect idler gear shaft. If loose in housing, replace pump.
3. Inspect pressure regulator valve for scoring or sticking. Burrs may be removed with a fine oil stone.
4. Inspect pressure regulator valve spring for loss of tension or bending.
5. Inspect suction pipe and screen assembly for looseness if permanently pressed into pump body. If pipe is loose or has been removed, pump body cover must be replaced. Inspect for broken wire mesh or screen.
6. Inspect gears for chipping, galling or wear.
7. Measure gear lash in several positions, **Fig. 8,** which should be .0037–.0077 inch.
8. Measure pump housing gear pocket depth, **Fig. 9,** which should be 1.202–1.204 inches.
9. Measure pump housing gear pocket

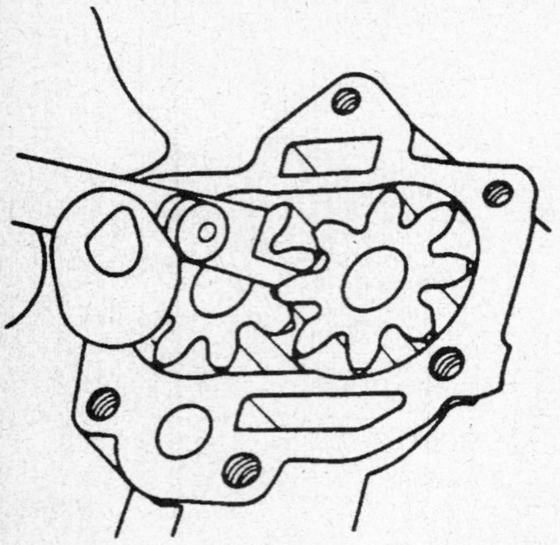

GC1099100076000X

Fig. 8 Oil pump gear lash measurement

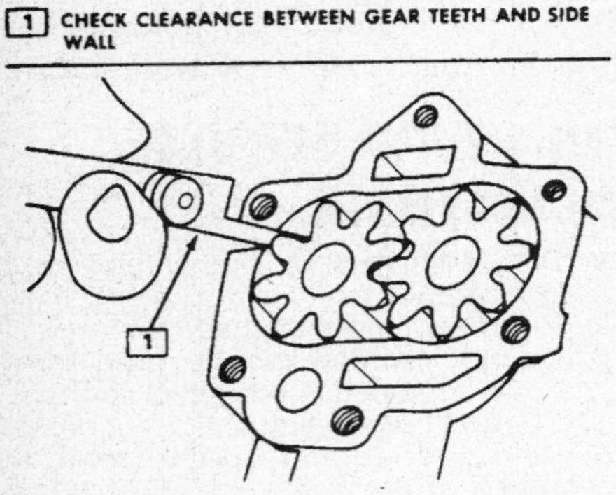

GC1099100079000X

Fig. 11 Gear side clearance measurement

diameter, **Fig. 9.** Pump housing diameter should be 1.503–1.505 inches.

10. Measure pump gear diameters, **Fig. 10,** which should be 1.498–1.500 inches.
11. Measure pump gear side clearance, **Fig. 11,** which should be .001–.003 inch.
12. Measure oil pump end clearance, **Fig. 12,** which should be .002–.005 inch.

ASSEMBLE

1. Lubricate all internal components with clean engine oil.
2. Install pump gears.
3. Install cover and gasket. **Use only original equipment gaskets since gasket thickness is critical to proper pump operation.** Tighten pump cover attaching bolts to specifications.
4. Install pressure spring retaining pin, ensuring it is properly secured.
5. If installing a new pickup screen and tube, apply sealer part No. 1050026, or equivalent to tube. Drive new tube into position using plastic hammer and tube installer tool No. J-21882, or equivalent.

BELT TENSION DATA

Belt tension is maintained automatically

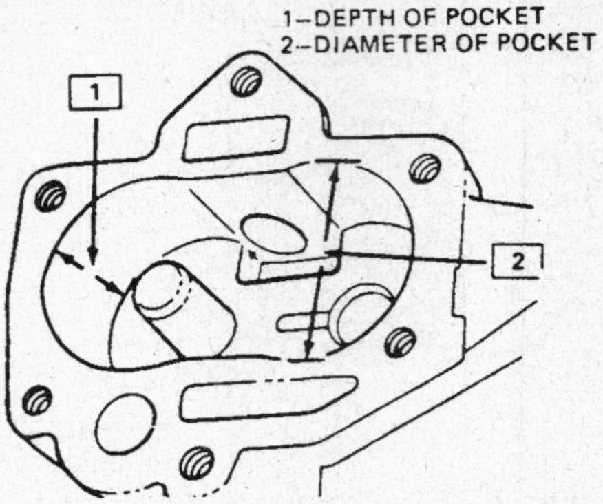

GC1099100077000X

Fig. 9 Oil pump gear pocket measurement

by a spring tensioned idler pulley. Serpentine belt adjustment is not required.

If belt slippage is indicated and belt tensioner indicator is within normal operating range, measure belt tension as follows:

1. Bring engine to operating temperature, then turn ignition Off.
2. Measure belt tension halfway between alternator and power steering pump using belt tension gauge tool No. J-23600-B, or equivalent.
3. Run engine for 15 seconds with all accessories turned Off.
4. Using a ⅜ inch breaker bar, apply clockwise force to tensioner pulley arm.
5. Release force and immediately measure belt tension without disturbing tensioner position.
6. Use breaker bar to apply a counterclockwise force to tensioner pulley arm and raise pulley arm to release all tension.
7. Slowly lower pulley to belt and measure tension without disturbing tensioner position.
8. Average out all three belt tension measurements, which should be 30–50 lbs.
9. If belt tension is not as specified, replace belt tensioner.

SERPENTINE DRIVE BELT

1. Remove cruise control module as required.
2. Remove engine mount as outlined under "Engine Mount, Replace."
3. Rotate belt tensioner in a clockwise direction using a suitable ⅜ inch breaker bar.
4. Remove serpentine belt.
5. Reverse procedure to install. Route belt around power steering pump pulley last of all.

COOLING SYSTEM BLEED

1. Close radiator petcock.
2. If engine block drain plugs were previously removed, coat their threads with pipe sealer part No. 12346004, or equivalent.
3. Open coolant air bleed valve located on top of thermostat bypass heater pipe assembly. **Close this valve as soon as a continuous coolant stream flows from it.**
4. Fill surge tank to base of filler neck.
5. Start engine while pressure cap is still off.
6. Operate engine until upper radiator hose starts to feel hot.
7. If surge tank coolant level is low it will need to be brought up to "full cold" line by adding proper coolant mix.
8. **On models equipped with intermittent low coolant lamp,** this lamp may occasionally light during some extreme driving conditions. This might be eliminated by removing surge tank cap and adding coolant to a level just at or above "full cold" line when system is cold.
9. **On all models,** install surge tank cap hand tight.

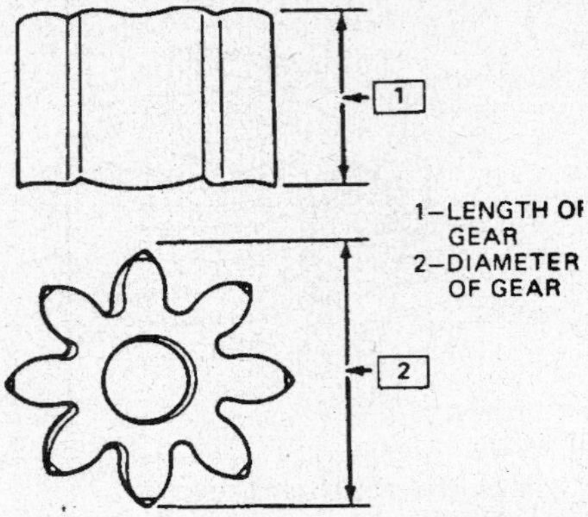

GC1099100078000X

Fig. 10 Oil pump gear measurement

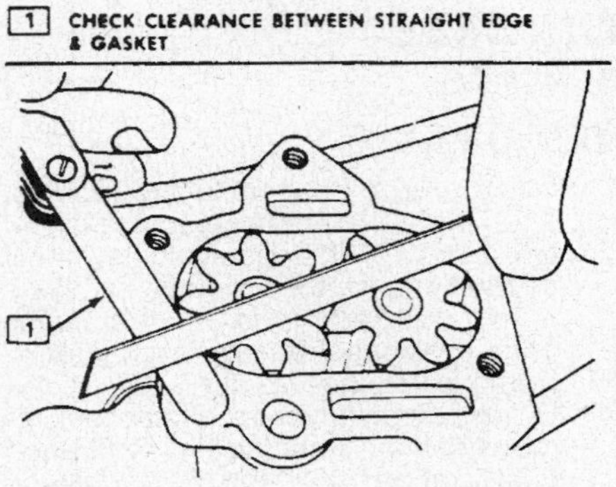

GC1099100080000X

Fig. 12 Oil pump end clearance measurement

THERMOSTAT

REPLACE

1. Drain coolant into an approved container.
2. Remove complete engine air cleaner assembly.

3. Remove surge tank line from coolant outlet.
4. Remove coolant outlet to manifold bolts, then the outlet.
5. Remove thermostat.
6. Clean all gasket mating surfaces.
7. Reverse procedure to install. Tighten coolant outlet bolts to specifications.

WATER PUMP

REPLACE

1. Drain coolant into an approved container.
2. Remove serpentine belt as outlined under "Serpentine Drive Belt."
3. Remove water pump pulley bolts, then the pulley.
4. Remove water pump to front cover bolts, then the pump.
5. Clean all gasket mating surfaces.
6. Reverse procedure to install, noting the following:
   a. Tighten water pump to front cover bolts to specifications.
   b. Tighten water pump pulley bolts to specifications.
   c. Fill and bleed cooling system, then inspect for leaks.

RADIATOR

REPLACE

Refer to "2.4L Engine" section for this procedure.

FUEL PUMP

REPLACE

Refer to "2.4L Engine" section for this procedure.

FUEL FILTER

REPLACE

Refer to "2.4L Engine" section for this procedure.

TIGHTENING SPECIFICATIONS

Year	Component	Torque/Ft. Lbs.
1997- 2000	Accelerator Cable Bracket Nuts & Bolts	89⑤
	Alternator Bracket & Front Engine Lift Hook Bolt	37
	CKP Sensor To Front Cover Bolt	89⑤
	CKP Sensor To Block Side Bolt	96⑤
	CKP Sensor Wiring Bracket Bolt	37
	CMP Sensor Bolt	89⑤
	Camshaft Sprocket	103
	Camshaft Thrust Plate	89⑤
	Connecting Rod Bearing Cap Nuts	①
	Coolant Drain Plug	14
	Coolant Outlet Bolt	19
	Crankshaft Balancer	76
	Crankshaft Oil Deflector Nut	18
	Cylinder Head Bolts	37②
	ECT Sensor	17
	EGR Valve To Valve Pipe Bolt	18
	EGR Valve Adapter Pipe To Exhaust Manifold Nut	18
	Engine Mount Bracket Bolts	43
	Engine Mount Lower Nuts	32
	Engine Mount Strut & Lift Bracket Bolt, LH Rear Of Engine	52
	Engine Mount Upper Nut	35
	Engine Mount Strut Bolts & Nuts	35
	Engine Mount Strut Bracket Bolt @ RH Vehicle Side	37
	Engine Mount Strut Bracket Bolt @ Upper Radiator Support	21
	Exhaust Manifold Heat Shield	89⑤
	Exhaust Manifold Nut	12
	Exhaust Manifold Stud	13
	Exhaust Crossover Nut & Stud	18
	Flexplate Bolts	52
	Front Cover Bolts (Large)	41
	Front Cover Bolts (Medium)	35
	Front Cover Bolts (Small)	15
	Fuel Feed Pipe To Injector Rail Nut	13

Continued

TIGHTENING SPECIFICATIONS—Continued

Year	Component	Torque/Ft. Lbs.
1997-2000	Fuel Injector Rail Bolt	89⑤
	Fuel Pipe Bracket Bolt & Stud	37
	Fuel Pipe Clip Bolt	72⑤
	Fuel Return Pipe To Fuel Injector Rail Nut	13
	HO2S	31
	Heater Inlet Pipe Nut	18
	Ignition Coil Bracket Fasteners	18
	Lower Intake Manifold Bolts	115⑤
	Upper Intake Manifold Bolts & Studs	18
	Main Bearing Cap Bolts	③
	Oil Cooler Connector	37
	Oil Cooler Hose Fitting	14
	Oil Cooler Pipe Bracket Bolt	89⑤
	Oil Filter Fitting	29
	Oil Filter	10
	Oil Gallery Plugs, ¼ Inch	14
	Oil Gallery Plugs, ⅜ Inch	24
	Oil Level Indicator Stud	18
	Oil Level Sensor Bolt	89⑤
	Oil Pan	18
	Oil Pan Drain Plug	18
	Oil Pressure Indicator Switch	10
	Oil Pump To Block	30
	Oil Pump Cover	89⑤
	Oil Pump Drive Clamp Bolt	27
	Rocker Arm Bolt	④
	Rocker Arm Covers	89⑤
	Serpentine Drive Belt Shield Bolt	89⑤
	Serpentine Drive Belt Tensioner Bolt	37
	Spark Plugs	20
	Thermostat Bypass Pipe To Cylinder Head Nut	18
	Thermostat Bypass Pipe To Front Cover Bolt	108⑤
	Thermostat Bypass Pipe To TBI Unit Nut	18
	Thermostat Housing Bolt	19
	Timing Chain Damper	15
	Valve Lifter Guide Bolt	89⑤
	Water Pump To Front Cover Bolts	89⑤
	Water Pump Pulley Bolts	18

① — Tighten each bolt an additional 75°.

② — Tighten an additional 90°.

③ — Tighten an additional 77°.

④ — Tighten an additional 30°.

⑤ — Inch lbs.

Clutch & Manual Transaxle

NOTE: For Service Procedures Refer To "Clutch & Manual Transaxle" Section In The "Cavalier & Sunfire" Chapter.

Rear Axle & Suspension

INDEX

DESCRIPTION

ACHIEVA, SKYLARK & 1997-98 GRAND AM

The rear suspension, **Fig. 1,** is the semi-independent type consisting of an axle assembly with trailing arms and cross beam, coil springs and shock absorbers. A single unit hub and bearing assembly is bolted to each end of the axle assembly. The hub and bearing assembly is a sealed, non-serviceable unit and must be replaced as an assembly.

ALERO, CUTLASS, MALIBU & 1999-2000 GRAND AM

The rear suspension, **Fig. 2,** uses coil springs over struts and lightweight aluminum knuckles. Each wheel is mounted to a tri-link independent suspension system. The three links include the inverted U-channel trailing arms and front and rear stamped lateral links.

The knuckles are machined aluminum castings. **Do not use hammers or pry bars to loosen any components from them.**

REAR AXLE

REPLACE

ACHIEVA, SKYLARK & 1997-98 GRAND AM

1. Raise and support vehicle. Support rear suspension with suitable jack.
2. Remove rear wheel and tire assembly.
3. Disconnect brake lines from axle brackets.
4. Remove shock absorber to lower mounting bracket attaching bolts and disconnect shock absorbers from axle assembly
5. Disconnect parking brake cable.
6. Carefully lower rear axle assembly and remove coil springs and insulators.
7. Disconnect parking brake and equalizer.
8. Remove righthand tire and wheel assembly.
9. Disconnect ABS electrical connector.
10. Disconnect brake lines at wheels.
11. With assistants helping out, remove mounting bolts, then the axle assembly.
12. Reverse procedure to install, noting the following:
    a. Tighten all fasteners to specifications.
    b. Bleed brake system as outlined in "Hydraulic Brake Systems" chapter.
    c. Road test vehicle to ensure proper operation.

HUB & BEARING

REPLACE

1. Raise and safely support vehicle.
2. Remove wheel and tire assembly.
3. **On models equipped with rear drum brakes,** proceed as follows:
    a. Remove brake drum. **Do not hammer on drum since damage to bearing may result.**
    b. Disconnect ABS wheel sensor electrical connector.
    c. Remove attaching bolts, then the hub and bearing assembly from axle. **Partially remove hub and bearing assembly prior to removing the upper rear hub attaching bolt.**
4. **On models equipped with rear disc brakes,** proceed as follows:
    a. Remove brake rotor as outlined in the "Disc Brakes " chapter.
    b. Disconnect parking brake cable from parking brake lever.
    c. Disconnect ABS wheel sensor electrical connector.
    d. Remove hub assembly to knuckle bolts, then the hub from knuckle.
    e. Remove Torx head bolts from rear of hub assembly, then the hub assembly from backing plate.
5. **On all models,** reverse procedure to install. Tighten all fasteners to specifications. **Avoid dropping and damaging hub and bearing assembly.**

STRUT

REPLACE

ALERO, CUTLASS, MALIBU & 1999-2000 GRAND AM

Do not hammer or pry on the machined aluminum knuckle casting or any of the components attached to it.

1. Raise and support vehicle.
2. Remove tire and wheel assembly.
3. Scribe knuckle to strut position for assembly.
4. Open luggage compartment and remove strut mount nut.
5. Remove mounting bolts from wheelwell.
6. Remove strut knuckle mounting bolts, then the strut.

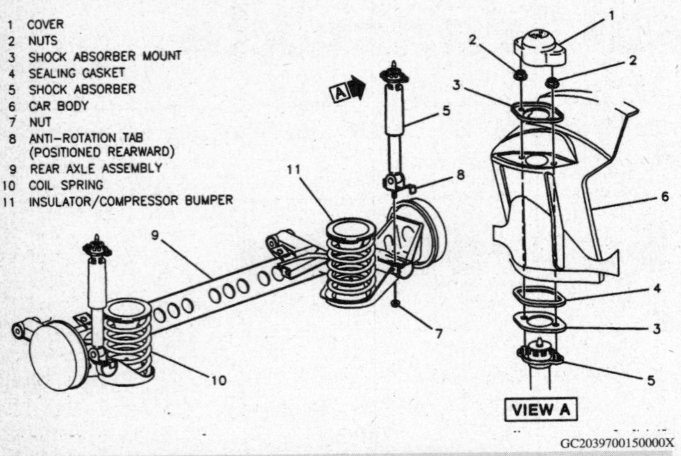

Fig. 1 Exploded view of rear suspension. Achieva, Skylark & 1997–98 Grand Am

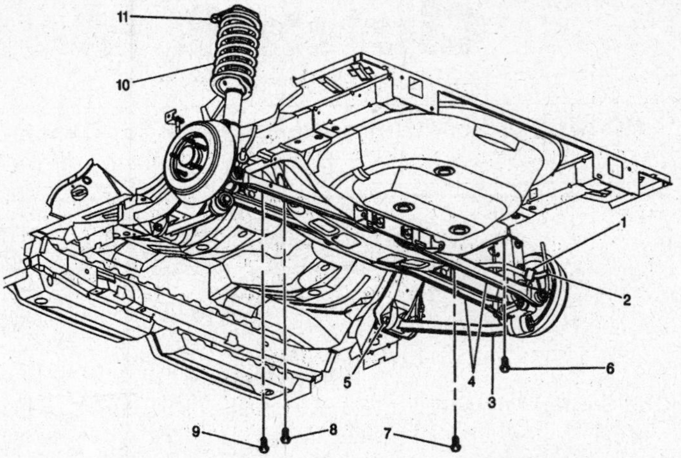

(1) Link Assembly, Rear Stabilizer Shaft
(2) Stabilizer Shaft, Rear
(3) Arm, Rear Suspension Trailing
(4) Link, Lateral
(5) Bolt, Rear Suspension Support
(6) Bolt, Rear Suspension Support
(7) Bolt, Rear Suspension Support
(8) Bolt, Rear Suspension Support
(9) Bolt, Rear Suspension Support
(10) Spring, Coil
(11) Mount, Upper Strut

GC2039700141000X

Fig. 2 Exploded view of rear suspension. Alero, Cutlass, Malibu & 1999–2000 Grand Am

7. Reverse procedure to install. Ensure scribe marks are properly aligned.

STRUT SERVICE

Refer to "Strut Service" in "Front Suspension & Steering."

SHOCK ABSORBER

REPLACE

ACHIEVA, SKYLARK & 1997–98 GRAND AM

If replacing both shock absorbers, remove one at a time.

1. Remove trim cover and shock absorber upper retaining nut from inside luggage compartment.
2. Raise rear of vehicle and support rear axle using a suitable jack.
3. Remove shock absorber lower attaching bolt and disconnect shock absorber from mounting bracket, **Fig. 1.**
4. Remove shock absorber from vehicle.
5. Reverse procedure to install. Tighten attaching bolt to specifications.

COIL SPRING

REPLACE

ACHIEVA, SKYLARK & 1997–98 GRAND AM

1. Raise and support rear of vehicle.
2. Support rear axle using a suitable jack.
3. Remove wheel and tire assemblies.
4. Remove brake line bracket attaching bolts from body and allow brake lines to hang freely.
5. Disconnect shock absorbers from axle assembly at lower mounting bracket. **Do not suspend rear axle by brake hoses since damage to hoses will result.**
6. Carefully lower rear axle assembly, then remove springs and insulators.
7. Reverse procedure to install. Upper ends of spring must be properly positioned in spring seat and within 9/16 inch of spring stop.

ALERO, CUTLASS, MALIBU & 1999–2000 GRAND AM

The coil spring is part of the strut assembly. Remove the spring as outlined under "Strut Service" in the "Front Suspension & Steering" section.

CONTROL ARM BUSHING

REPLACE

ACHIEVA, SKYLARK & 1997–98 GRAND AM

1. Raise rear of vehicle and support rear axle under front side of spring seat using a suitable jack.
2. Remove wheel and tire assembly.
3. If righthand side bushing is to be replaced, disconnect brake line bracket from body.
4. If lefthand side bushing is to be replaced, disconnect brake line bracket from body and parking brake cable at hook guide.
5. Remove control arm to mounting bracket attaching nut, bolt and washer, then allow control arm to rotate downward.
6. Remove bushing using rear control arm bushing service set tool No. J-29376-A, long nut tool No. J-21474-18 and long bolt and bearing tool No. J-21474-19, or equivalents, **Fig. 3.**
7. Reverse procedure to install, noting the following:
   a. When installing bushing, installer arrow must align with arrow on receiver, **Fig. 3.**
   b. Tighten bolts to specifications.
   c. **Control arm attaching bolt must be tightened after vehicle is lowered to floor and is in its standing height position.**

KNUCKLE

REPLACE

ALERO, CUTLASS, MALIBU & 1999–2000 GRAND AM

Removal

1. Raise and support vehicle, then remove tire and wheel assembly.
2. Scribe strut to knuckle position for installation reference.
3. Remove rear lateral link nut, bolt and washer, then the drum or rotor.
4. Remove ABS electrical connector and rear wheel hub.
5. Remove trailing arm from knuckle.
6. Remove strut nuts and bolts.
7. Remove knuckle.

Installation

1. Install knuckle onto vehicle.
2. Install strut to knuckle nuts and bolts. Hand tighten the bolts.
3. Install stabilizer shaft link.
4. Install trailing arm to knuckle bolt, washer and bushing. Tighten bolt to specifications.
5. Install hub assembly.
6. **On models equipped with rear disc brakes,** connect parking brake cable to parking brake lever.
7. **On all models,** install rotor or drum.
8. Install lateral links to knuckle nut, bolt and washer. Tighten nut to specifications.
9. Connect wheel speed sensor harness.
10. Tighten strut to knuckle bolts to specifications.
11. Install tire and wheel.
12. Lower the vehicle.
13. Inspect rear wheel alignment.

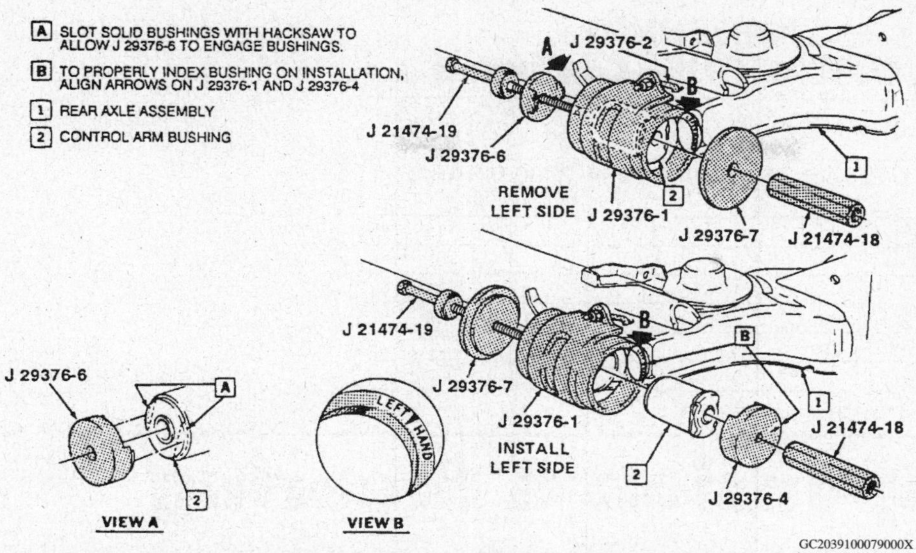

Fig. 3 Control arm bushing replacement. Achieva, Skylark & 1997–98 Grand Am

REAR CROSSMEMBER

REPLACE

ALERO, CUTLASS, MALIBU & 1999–2000 GRAND AM

1. Raise and support vehicle, then remove tire and wheel assemblies.
2. Remove tailpipe if required.
3. Remove brake lines and parking brake cables from crossmember.
4. Remove stabilizer shaft as outlined under "Stabilizer Shaft, Replace."
5. Disconnect rear wheel speed sensor electrical connectors, then position harness aside.
6. Remove front and rear lateral links as outlined under "Lateral Link, Replace."
7. Remove bolt from EVAP canister.
8. Support crossmember with suitable jack stands.
9. Remove mounting bolts and rear crossmember.
10. Reverse procedure to install. Tighten bolts to specifications.

TRAILING ARM

REPLACE

ALERO, CUTLASS, MALIBU & 1999–2000 GRAND AM

1. Raise and support vehicle.
2. Remove trailing arm knuckle bolt, washer and bushing.
3. Remove body bolt, then the trailing arm.
4. Reverse procedure to install. Tighten bolts to specifications.

STABILIZER SHAFT

REPLACE

ALERO, CUTLASS, MALIBU & 1999–2000 GRAND AM

1. Raise and support vehicle, then remove tire and wheel assemblies if required.
2. Remove link bolts.
3. Remove mounting nuts and insulator brackets.
4. Remove stabilizer shaft.
5. Reverse procedure to install. Tighten bolts to specifications.

LATERAL LINK

REPLACE

ALERO, CUTLASS, MALIBU & 1999–2000 GRAND AM

1. Raise and support vehicle, then remove tire and wheel assembly.
2. If removing front lateral line and trailing arm, remove ABS wire harness.
3. Remove knuckle bolt, nut and washer. Push bolt forward enough for removal clearance.
4. Remove crossmember nut and rear lateral link and trailing arm.
5. Reverse procedure to install.

TIGHTENING SPECIFICATIONS

Component	Torque/Ft. Lbs.
ACHIEVA, SKYLARK & 1997–98 GRAND AM	
Axle To Body Bracket	68
Control Arm To Underbody Nuts	59①
Hub & Bearing To Axle Bolts	37
Shock Absorber Lower Mounting Bolt To Axle	35
Shock Absorber Upper Mounting Bolt To Body	13
Shock Absorber Upper Mounting Nut	21
Wheel Lug Nuts	100
ALERO, CUTLASS, MALIBU & 1999–2000 GRAND AM	
Crossmember	89
Disc Brake Caliper To Bracket Bolt	81
Disc Brake Caliper To Knuckle Bolt	85
Lateral Link To Crossmember	89
Lateral Link To Knuckle	89
Stabilizer Shaft Bracket	39
Stabilizer Shaft Link	51
Strut Nut	89

Continued

TIGHTENING SPECIFICATIONS—Continued

Component	Torque/Ft. Lbs.
ALERO, CUTLASS, MALIBU & 1999–2000 GRAND AM	
Strut To Body	18
Strut To Knuckle	89
Trailing Arm To Body	48①
Trailing Arm To Knuckle	51
Wheel Hub To Knuckle	70
Wheel Lug Nuts	100

① — Tighten an additional 120°.

Front Suspension & Steering

NOTE: Refer To "Computer Relearn Procedure " Located In The Front Of This Manual For Computer Relearn Procedures.

INDEX

PRECAUTIONS

AIR BAG SYSTEMS

Refer to "Air Bag System Precautions" in the front of this manual for system disarming and arming procedures.

BATTERY GROUND CABLE

Prior to service, disconnect battery ground cable and isolate as required.

DESCRIPTION

The front suspension on these vehicles, **Fig. 1,** is of the strut and spring design. The lower control arms pivot from the lower side rails through rubber bushings. The upper end of the strut is isolated by a rubber mount incorporating a bearing for wheel turning. The tie rods connect to the steering arm on the strut, below the spring seat. The lower end of the steering knuckle pivots on a ball stud which is retained to the lower control arm by rivets and is secured to the steering knuckle with a nut and cotter pin. The sealed wheel bearings are integral with the hub and are serviced as an assembly.

WHEEL BEARING

REPLACE

1. Raise and safely support vehicle.
2. Remove wheel and tire assembly.
3. Install modified outer seal protector tool No. J-34754, or equivalent.
4. Place shop towels under outer joint to protect it from sharp edges.
5. Insert suitable drift punch into caliper and rotor to prevent turning and remove axle shaft nut and washer, **Fig. 2.**
6. Remove lower ball joint cotter pin and nut, then loosen joint from steering knuckle using joint separator tool No. J-38892, or equivalent.
7. If lefthand drive axle shaft is being remove, turn wheel to right. If righthand drive axle shaft is being removed, turn wheel left.
8. Remove ABS sensor wire and disconnect stabilizer link.
9. Position a suitable pry bar between suspension support and lower control arm and separate lower ball joint from steering knuckle.
10. Use front hub knuckle remover tool No. J-28733-B, or equivalent to separate drive axle shaft from hub and bearing assembly, **Fig. 3.**
11. When removing righthand axle shaft, use slide hammer tool No. J-2619-01 and axle shaft removal tool No. J-33008, or equivalents.
12. Separate drive axle shaft from hub and wheel bearing assembly and move strut and knuckle assembly rearward. Use wire or rope to suspend drive axle shaft from underbody. Use care not to overextend driveshaft joints.
13. Remove caliper attaching bolts and brake caliper with brake hose attached. Use wire to suspend caliper from underbody. Do not allow caliper to hang from brake hose.
14. Remove brake rotor, hub and bearing assembly attaching bolts, **Fig. 4.**
15. Remove hub and bearing assembly.
16. Reverse procedure to install, noting following:
    a. Tighten attaching fasteners to specifications.
    b. Inspect front wheel alignment and adjust as required.

BALL JOINT INSPECTION

Ball joints must be replaced if any looseness is detected in the joint or the seal is cut.

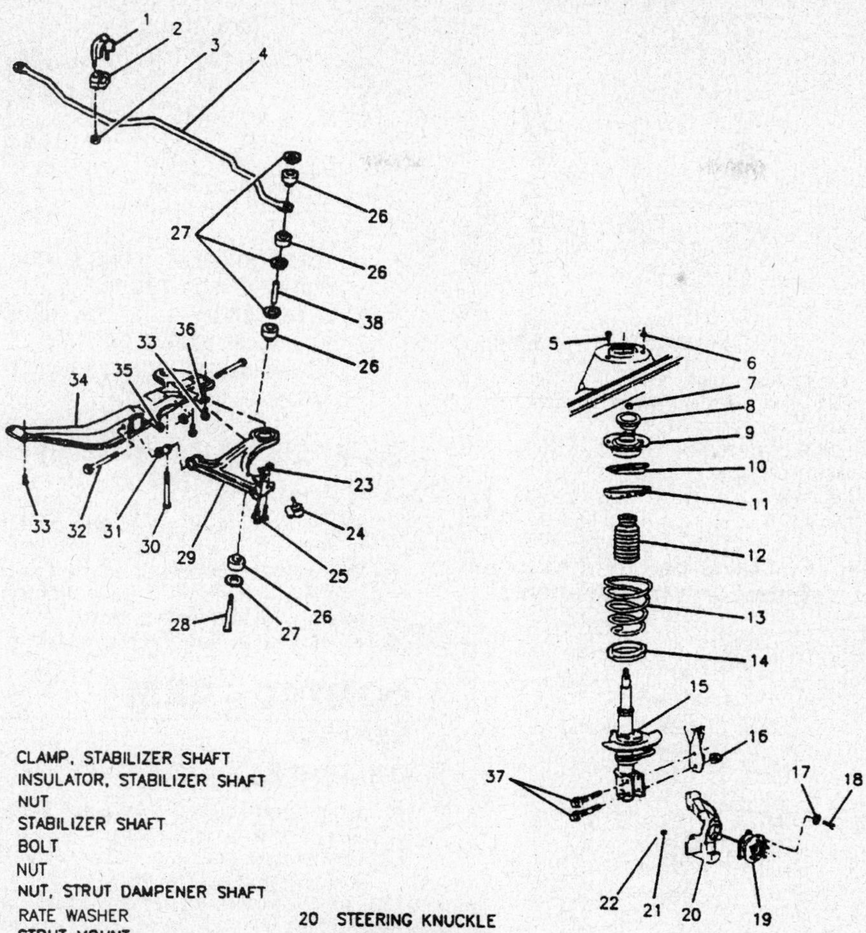

1 CLAMP, STABILIZER SHAFT
2 INSULATOR, STABILIZER SHAFT
3 NUT
4 STABILIZER SHAFT
5 BOLT
6 NUT
7 NUT, STRUT DAMPENER SHAFT
8 RATE WASHER
9 STRUT MOUNT
10 UPPER SPRING SEAT
11 UPPER SPRING INSULATOR
12 DUST TUBE ASSEMBLY
13 SPRING
14 LOWER SPRING INSULATOR
15 STRUT
16 NUT
17 WASHER
18 BOLT
19 HUB AND BEARING ASSEMBLY
20 STEERING KNUCKLE
21 NUT, BALL JOINT
22 COTTER PIN
23 NUT
24 BALL JOINT
25 BOLT
26 INSULATOR, STABILIZER LINK
27 WASHER, STABILIZER LINK
28 BOLT, STABILIZER LINK
29 CONTROL ARM
30 BOLT
31 BUSHING, CONTROL ARM
32 BOLT
33 BOLT
34 SUSPENSION SUPPORT
35 NUT
36 WASHER
37 BOLT
38 SPACER, STABILIZER LINK

GC2029700271000X

Fig. 1 Exploded view of front suspension

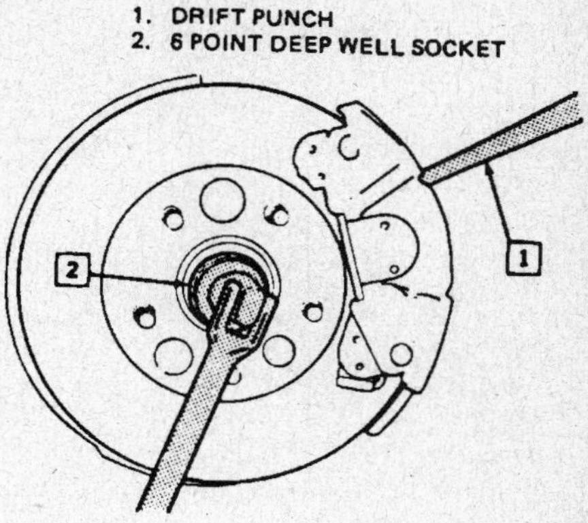

GC3039100240000X

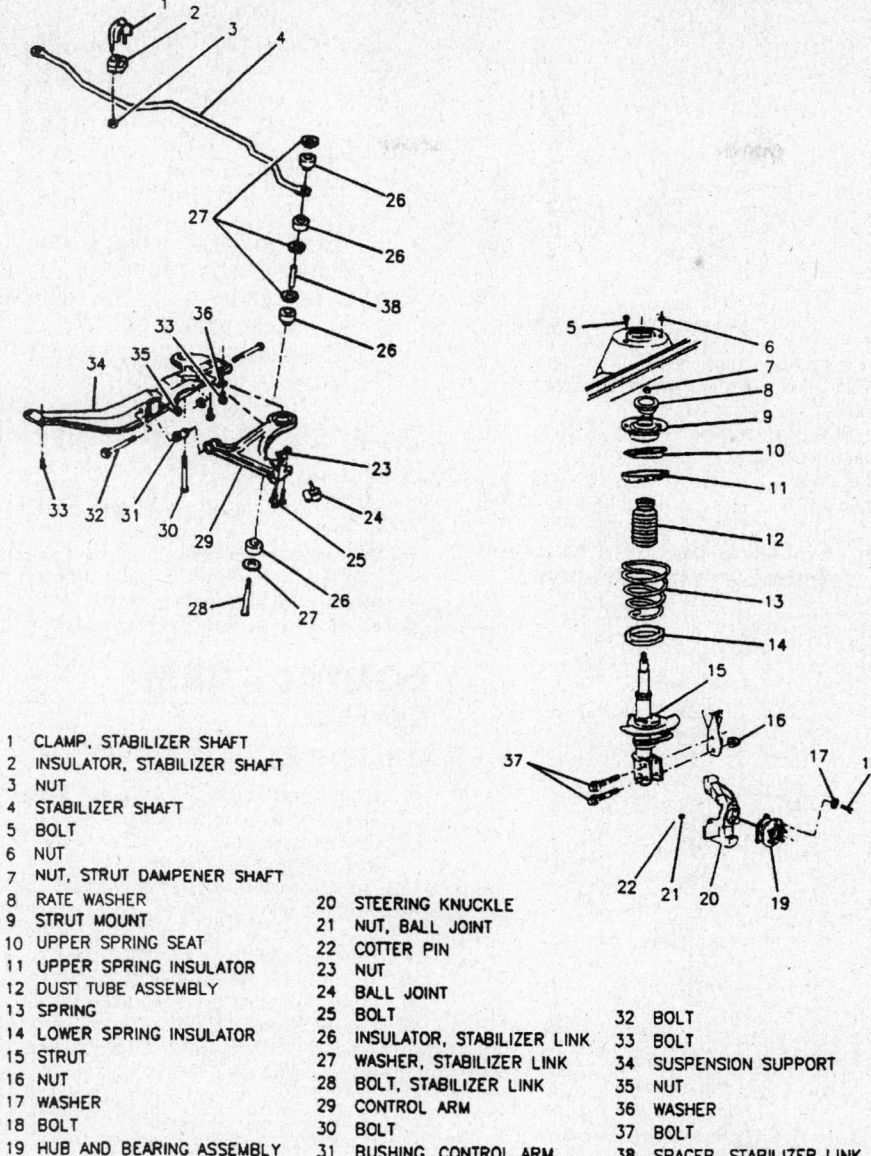

Fig. 2 Drive axle shaft nut replacement

To inspect the ball joints, raise the front of the vehicle allowing the suspension to hang free. Grasp the tire at the top and bottom and move the top of tire with an in-and-out motion. Look for any horizontal movement of the steering knuckle relative to the front lower control arm.

If the ball stud is disconnected from the steering knuckle and any looseness is detected or if the ball stud can be twisted in its socket using finger pressure, replace the ball joint.

Ball stud tightness in the steering knuckle boss should also be inspected when inspecting the ball joint. This may be done by shaking the wheel and feeling for movement of the stud end or castellated nut at the knuckle boss. Inspecting the fastener torque at the castellated nut is an alternative method of inspecting for wear. A loose nut can indicate a bent stud or an opened-up hole in the knuckle boss. Worn or damaged ball joints and knuckles must be replaced.

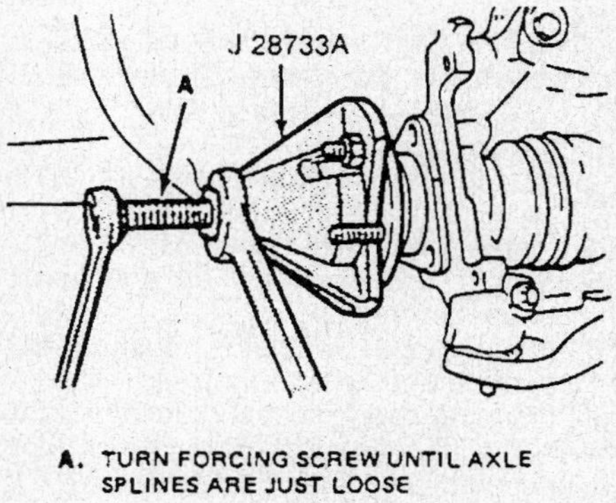

GC3039100241000X

Fig. 3 Drive axle shaft removal from hub

BALL JOINT

REPLACE

1. Raise and support vehicle. Remove tire and wheel assembly.
2. Remove lower ball joint cotter pin and nut.
3. **On models equipped with ABS,** position wheel speed sensor wiring aside as required.
4. **On all models,** using ball joint separator tool No. J-43828, or equivalent, separate lower ball joint from steering knuckle, **Fig. 5.**
5. Locate center of rivet body and mark with a center punch.
6. Using a ⅛ inch drill bit, drill pilot holes completely through rivets. **Avoid damaging CV joint boots.**
7. Using a ½ inch drill bit, drill final holes through rivets to ensure proper fitting of new ball joint.
8. Remove nut attaching stabilizer shaft link.
9. Remove ball joint from knuckle and lower control arm.
10. Reverse procedure to install using bolts provided in service package. Tighten all fasteners to specifications.

STRUT

REPLACE

1. Remove strut assembly body attaching nuts and bolt.
2. Raise and support vehicle.
3. Place jack stands under front crossmember, then lower vehicle slightly so it rests on stands, not on control arms.
4. Remove wheel and tire. Install modified outer seal protector tool No. J-34754, or equivalent if required.
5. Remove tie rod end cotter pin and nut, then, using tie rod puller tool No. J-24319-01, or equivalent, disconnect tie rod from strut assembly.
6. Remove brake line bracket.
7. Scribe alignment marks on strut flange, **Fig. 6.**

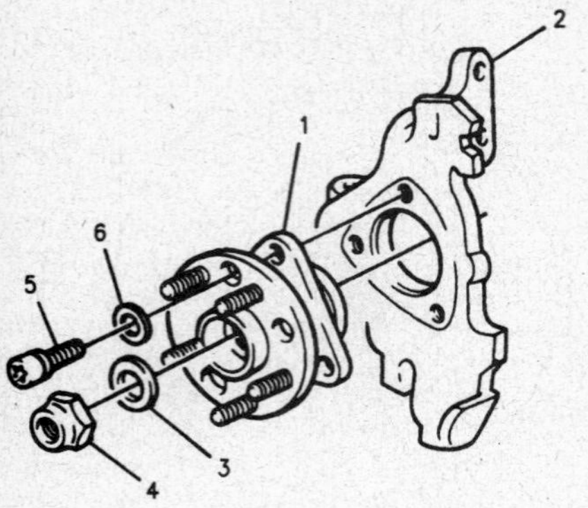

Fig. 4 Front hub & wheel bearing replacement

8. Remove attaching bolts and strut, **Fig. 1.** Use care not to damage spring coating.
9. Reverse procedure to install, noting the following:
   a. Align marks on strut flange and steering knuckle made during removal.
   b. Tighten all fasteners to specifications.
   c. Inspect wheel alignment and adjust as required.

STRUT SERVICE

DISASSEMBLE

1. **On Achieva, Skylark and 1997–98 Grand Am models,** position strut compressor tool No. J-34013-B in holding fixture J-3289-20, or equivalent, then position strut in strut compressor. Use care not to damage spring coating.
2. **On Alero, Cutlass, Malibu and 1999–2000 Grand Am models,** position strut compressor tool No. J-34013-B in holding fixture J-3289-20 with adapter tool No. J-34013-88, or equivalents.
3. **On all models,** compress strut to approximately half of its height. Use care not to bottom spring or damper rod.
4. Remove nut from strut dampener shaft and position alignment rod tool No. J-34013-27, or equivalent on dampener shaft. Use guide rod tool to position dampener shaft down through bearing cap while compressing coil spring.
5. Remove strut components, **Figs. 7 and 8.**

ASSEMBLE

1. Install bearing cap.
2. Mount strut to strut compressor tool using bottom locking pin only.
3. Extend dampener shaft and install dampener rod clamp tool No. J-34013-20, or equivalent.
4. Install spring over dampener.
5. Swing strut assembly up and install upper locking pin.
6. Install upper insulator, dust shield, bumper and upper spring seat. The flat on upper spring seat should face in the same direction as centerline of strut assembly knuckle, **Fig. 9.**
7. Install guide rod tool onto dampener shaft, then compress strut unit until dampener shaft threads are visible. Remove guide rod tool and install retaining nut.
8. While holding dampener shaft in position with a suitable wrench, tighten retaining nut to specifications.
9. Remove dampener rod clamp tool.

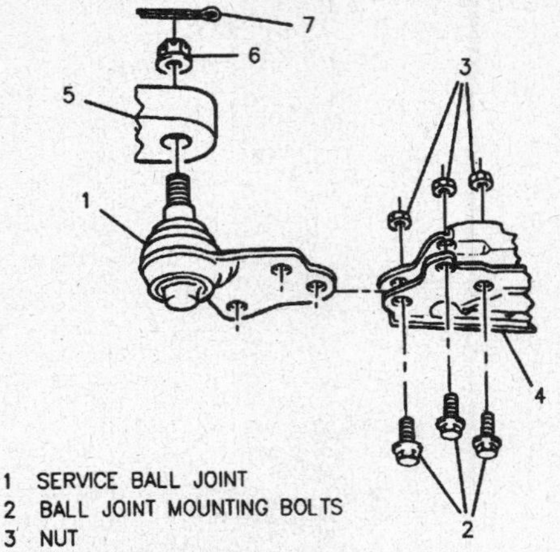

Fig. 5 Lower ball joint to lower control arm replacement

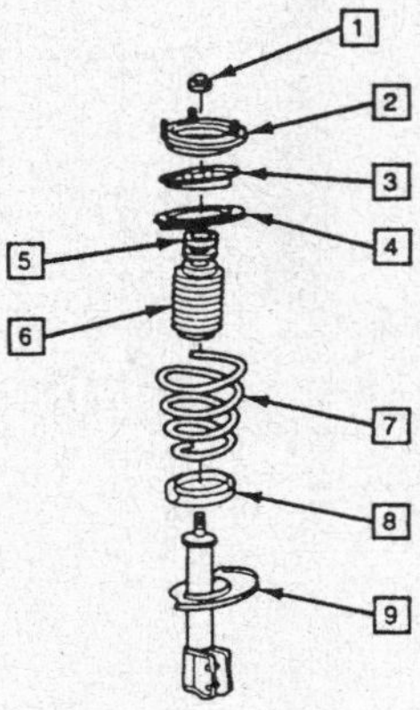

Fig. 7 Exploded view of strut assembly. Achieva, Skylark & 1997–98 Grand Am

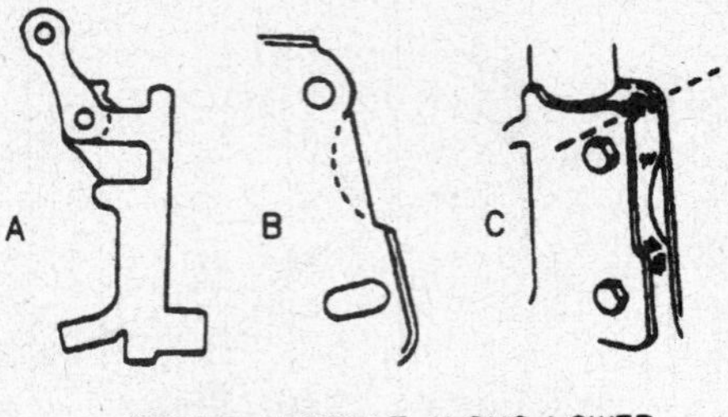

Fig. 6 Strut & knuckle alignment marks

CONTROL ARM

REPLACE

REMOVAL

1. Raise and support vehicle. Remove wheel and tire assembly.
2. Disconnect stabilizer bar at lower control arm and control arm support.
3. Remove ball joint cotter pin and nut.
4. Separate ball joint from steering knuckle with ball joint separator tool No. J-43828, or equivalent.
5. Remove mounting bolts, support and control arm as an assembly, **Fig. 10.**
6. **On Achieva, Skylark and 1997–98 Grand Am models,** separate control arm from support and use lower control arm front bushing set tool No. J-29792, or equivalent to remove bushings from control arm.

INSTALLATION

1. **On Achieva, Skylark and 1997–98 Grand Am models,** proceed as follows:
   a. Install control arm into position and loosely install mounting bolts.
   b. Install ball joint to knuckle nut. Tighten to specifications and install cotter pin.
   c. Install stabilizer link nut and tighten to specifications.
   d. If vehicle is sitting on a suspension contact hoist, raise vehicle slightly, then remove jack stands from under suspension supports.
   e. Install tire and wheel.
   f. Lower the vehicle to the ground, then tighten, in order, the center, front and rear suspension support mounting bolts to specifications.
   g. Tighten, in order, the control arm front and rear mounting bolts to specifications.

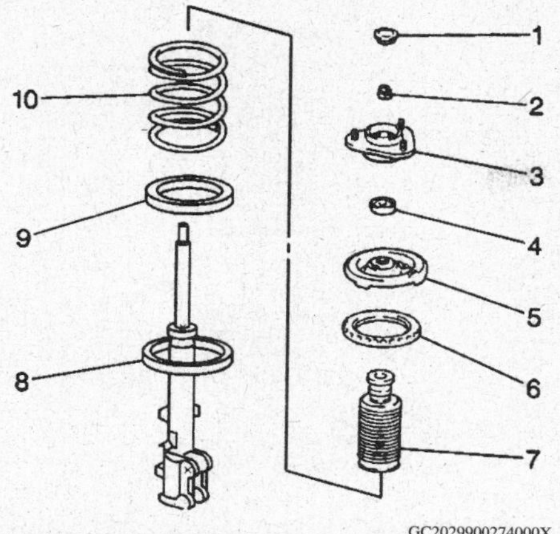

Fig. 8 Exploded view of strut assembly (1-cap, 2-nut, 3-support, 4-seal, 5-seat, 6-insulator, 7-bumper, 8-strut, 9-insulator, 10-spring). Alero, Cutlass, Malibu & 1999–2000 Grand Am

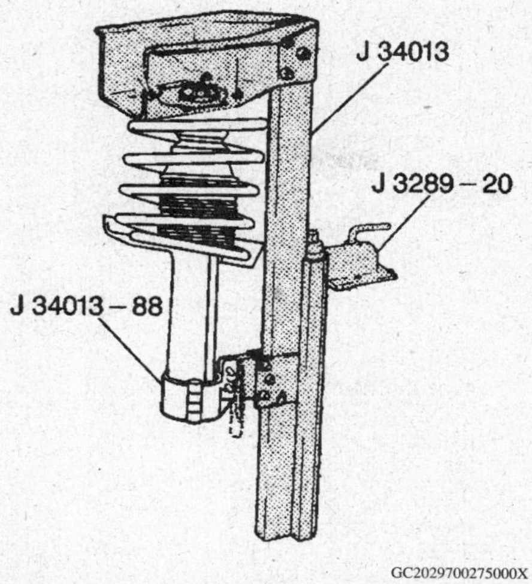

Fig. 9 Strut unit assembly

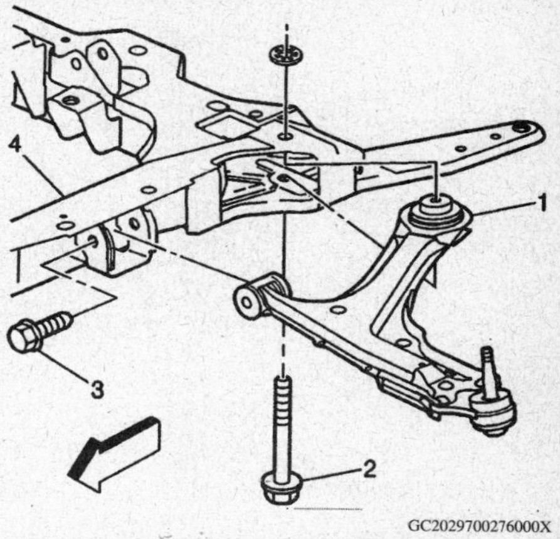

Fig. 10 Lower control arm replacement (1-arm, 2- rear mounting bolt, 3-front mounting bolt, 4-crossmember)

2. **On Alero, Cutlass, Malibu and 1999–2000 Grand Am models,** proceed as follows:
   a. Install control arm into position and hand tighten rear mounting bolt.
   b. Install and hand tighten front mounting bolt.
   c. Install stabilizer shaft link.
   d. Install lower ball joint to knuckle.
   e. Raise vehicle slightly, then remove jack stands from under crossmember.
   f. Install tire and wheel.
   g. Lower the vehicle to the ground, then tighten, in order, the control arm front and rear mounting bolts to specifications.
3. **On all models,** inspect front wheel alignment and adjust as required.

STEERING KNUCKLE

REPLACE

1. Raise and support vehicle. Remove wheel and tire.
2. Remove front hub and bearing as outlined under "Wheel Bearing, Replace."
3. Remove steering knuckle to strut mounting bolts, then the knuckle.
4. Reverse procedure to install. Tighten all fasteners to specifications.

STABILIZER BAR

REPLACE

1. Raise and support vehicle, allowing control arms to hang free.
2. Remove front wheels and tires.
3. **On Alero, Cutlass, Malibu and 1999–2000 Grand Am models,** proceed as follows:
   a. Remove stabilizer shaft links.
   b. Using separator tool No. J-24319-01, or equivalent, separate tie rod ends from knuckles.
   c. Remove transaxle rear mount bolt.
   d. Remove power steering line bracket from crossmember.
4. **On all models,** disconnect stabilizer bar at control arms and suspension support assemblies, **Fig. 11.**
5. Loosen front and remove rear and center bolts from suspension support assembly. Lower support enough to allow stabilizer bar removal.
6. Remove stabilizer bar with insulators.
7. Reverse procedure to install, noting the following:
   a. **On Achieva, Skylark and 1997–98 Grand Am models,** tighten, in order, the center, front and rear suspension support mounting bolts to specifications. Tighten, in order, the stabilizer shaft clamp nuts and control arm nuts to specifications.
   b. **On Alero, Cutlass, Malibu and 1999–2000 Grand Am models,** tighten, in order, the lefthand rear, righthand rear, lefthand front and righthand front crossmember mounting bolts to specifications.

POWER STEERING GEAR

REPLACE

ACHIEVA, SKYLARK & 1997–98 GRAND AM

1. Remove lefthand sound insulator and steering shaft coupling pinch bolt.
2. Remove line retainer, then the master cylinder from brake booster and position aside with lines attached.
3. Move power brake booster away from cowl and remove brake pedal pushrod from pedal.
4. Remove inner tie rod bolts, lock plates and washers.
5. Remove steering gear mounting clamps, **Fig. 12.**
6. Disconnect steering gear hydraulic lines.
7. Move steering gear slightly forward, remove lower pinch bolt from flexible coupling, detach coupling from steering gear stub shaft and remove dash seal.
8. Remove steering gear through lefthand wheel opening.
9. Reverse procedure to install, noting the following:
   a. If steering gear mounting clamp studs have backed out during removal, install studs to cowl and tighten until stud is fully seated.
   b. Torque should not exceed 15 ft. lbs.
   c. After second use of studs, thread locking kit No. 1052624 or equivalent must be used.

ALERO, CUTLASS, MALIBU & 1999–2000 GRAND AM

1. Carefully siphon fluid from power steering reservoir.
2. Raise and support vehicle, then remove front tires and wheels.
3. Remove stabilizer shaft links from control arms.
4. Using separator tool No. J-24319-01, or equivalent, remove tie rods from knuckles.
5. Remove intermediate shaft lower pinch bolt.
6. Support rear of crossmember with suitable jack stands.
7. Remove stabilizer shaft.
8. Remove steering gear mounting bolts.
9. **On Cutlass and Malibu models, if required,** proceed as follows:
   a. Remove transaxle mount-to-crossmember bolt.
   b. Remove rear crossmember to body bolts to provide pipe and hose removal clearance.
   c. Loosen front crossmember bolts.
10. **On all models,** remove steering gear mounting bolts.
11. Place a suitable drain pan below steering gear, then disconnect power steering fluid hoses from gear.
12. Remove steering gear through lefthand wheel opening.
13. Reverse procedure to install. Tighten all fasteners to specifications.

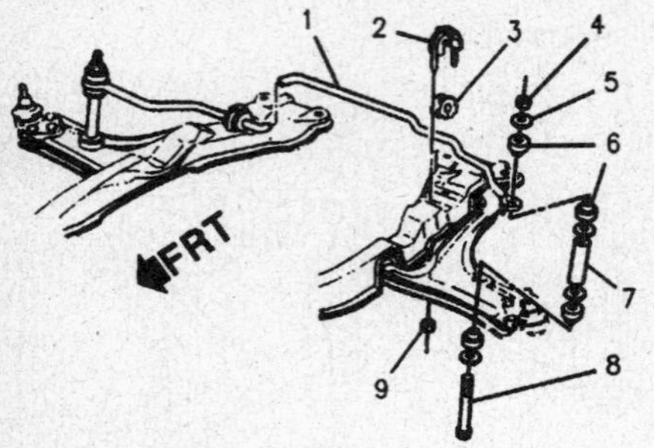

1 SHAFT, STABILIZER
2 CLAMP
3 INSULATOR, STABILIZER SHAFT
4 NUT
5 WASHER
6 INSULATOR, STABILIZER LINK
7 SPACER
8 BOLT
9 NUT

GC2029700277000X

Fig. 11 Typical stabilizer bar replacement

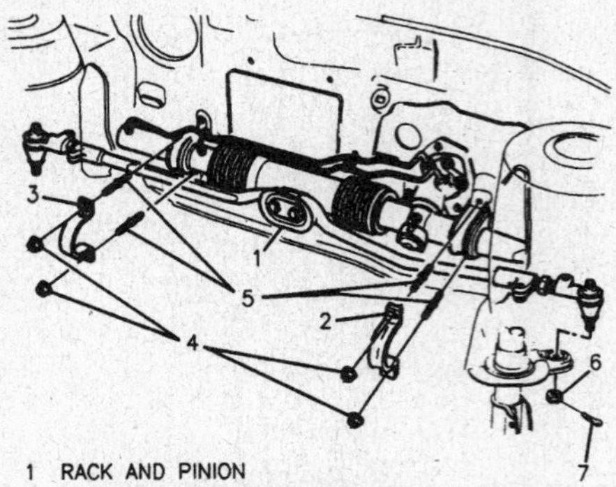

1 RACK AND PINION
2 L.H. CLAMP – HORIZONTAL SLOT AT TOP
3 R.H. CLAMP – HORIZONTAL SLOT AT TOP
4 NUT – HAND START ALL NUTS. TIGHTEN LEFT HAND SIDE CLAMP NUTS FIRST, THEN TIGHTEN RIGHT SIDE NUTS.
5 STUD – AFTER SECOND REUSE OF STUD, THREAD LOCKING KIT NO. 1052624 MUST BE USED.
6 NUT
7 COTTER PIN

GC2029700278000X

Fig. 12 Power rack & pinion steering gear mounting. Achieva, Skylark & 1997–98 Grand Am

1 CLAMP, HOSE
2 HOSE, OUTLET
3 HOSE, INLET (NON EVO)
4 HOSE, INLET (EVO)

GC6039700056000A

Fig. 13 Power steering pump removal. 2.4L engine

POWER STEERING PUMP

REPLACE

2.4L ENGINE

1. Siphon as much power steering fluid as possible from reservoir.
2. **On models equipped with variable effort steering,** disconnect variable effort steering electrical connector.
3. **On all models,** place a suitable drain pan in position, then disconnect power steering pump lines at pump, **Fig. 13.**
4. Remove power steering pump mounting bolts, then the pump.
5. Reverse procedure to install, noting the following:
   a. Tighten pump mounting bolts and hose connections to specifications.
   b. Fill pump with proper fluid and bleed air as required.
   c. Inspect for fluid leaks.

3.1L & 3.4L ENGINES

1. Siphon as much power steering fluidas possible from reservoir.
2. Remove engine mount as outlined under "Engine Mount, Replace."
3. Remove serpentine belt as outlined under "Serpentine Drive Belt."
4. Remove alternator bracket retaining hose nut.
5. Remove power steering pump bolts to ease power steering line removal.
6. Place a suitable drain pan in position, then disconnect power steering pump lines at pump and remove pump.
7. Remove transfer pulley if required.
8. Reverse procedure to install. Tighten all fasteners to specifications.

TIGHTENING SPECIFICATIONS

Component	Torque/Ft. Lbs.
ACHIEVA, SKYLARK & 1997–98 GRAND AM	
Axle Nut	185
Ball Joint Stud Nut (1997)	①
Ball Joint Stud Nut (1998)	41–48
Control Arm To Suspension Support Bolts At Front Bushing (1997)	89
Control Arm To Suspension Support Bolts At Front Bushing (1998)	55②
Control Arm To Suspension Support Bolts At Rear Vertical Bushing	125
Control Arm Pivot Bolt	61
Disc Brake Caliper Bolts	38
Driveshaft Nut (1997)	185
Driveshaft Nut (1998)	74③
Hub & Bearing Assembly To Knuckle Bolts	70
Hub Nut	185
Power Steering Line Fittings	20
Power Steering Pump (2.4L)	19
Power Steering Pump (3.1L)	25

Continued

TIGHTENING SPECIFICATIONS—Continued

Component	Torque/Ft. Lbs.
ACHIEVA, SKYLARK & 1997–98 GRAND AM	
Stabilizer Shaft To Control Arm	15
Stabilizer Shaft Link to Support Nuts	22
Steering Coupling To Steering Column	30
Steering Coupling To Stub Shaft	30
Stabilizer To Support Assembly	16
Steering Knuckle To Strut Assembly	133
Strut Assembly To Body	18
Strut Cartridge Retaining Nut	65
Suspension Support Assembly	89
Tie Rod End To Steering Knuckle	37
Tie Rod End To Strut Nut (1997)	44
Tie Rod End To Strut Nut (1998)	42
Tie Rod Inner Bolts	65
Tie Rod Pinch Bolts	41
Wheel Lug Nuts	100
ALERO, CUTLASS, MALIBU & 1999–2000 GRAND AM	
Axle Nut	284
Ball Joint To Knuckle (Alero & 1999–2000 Grand Am)	41
Ball Joint To Knuckle For Cotter Pin Installation (1997–98 Cutlass & Malibu)	7④
Control Arm Pivot Bolt At Front Bushing (1997–98 Cutlass & Malibu)	44⑤
Control Arm Pivot Bolt At Rear Vertical Bushing (1997–98 Cutlass & Malibu)	74④
Control Arm To Frame Bolts At Front Bushing (Alero & 1999–2000 Grand Am)	79
Control Arm To Frame Bolts At Rear Bushing (Alero & 1999–2000 Grand Am)	81
Disc Brake Caliper Bolts	85
Disc Brake Caliper To Bracket Bolt	23
Driveshaft Nut	284
Hub & Bearing Assembly To Knuckle Bolts	70
Hub Nut	284
Power Steering Line Fittings	20
Power Steering Pump (2.4L Engine)	19
Power Steering Pump (3.1L & 3.4L Engines)	25
Stabilizer Shaft To Control Arm	13
Stabilizer Shaft Bushing Clamp To Crossmember Support Nuts	49
Stabilizer Shaft Link to Control Arm Nuts	13
Steering Gear Bolts	89
Steering Gear Mounting Clamp	22
Steering Column Upper & Lower Pinch Bolts	16
Steering Knuckle To Strut Assembly	133
Strut Assembly To Body	18
Suspension Crossmember (Alero & 1999–2000 Grand Am)	81
Suspension Support Assembly Bushing (1997–98 Cutlass & Malibu)	74④
Strut Nut To Strut Rod	52
Tie Rod End To Steering Knuckle Nut (1997–98 Cutlass & Malibu)	15④
Tie Rod End To Steering Knuckle Nut (1999 Alero & Grand Am)	33
Tie Rod End To Steering Knuckle Nut (2000)	15

Continued

TIGHTENING SPECIFICATIONS—Continued

Component	Torque/Ft. Lbs.
ALERO, CUTLASS, MALIBU & 1999–2000 GRAND AM	
Tie Rod End To Strut Nut (1997–98 Cutlass & Malibu)	15④
Tie Rod Jam Nuts	50
Transaxle Front Mount Bolt (1997–98 Cutlass & Malibu)	89
Transaxle Mount Bolt (Alero & Grand Am)	89
Wheel Lug Nuts	100

① — Tighten an additional 60°.
② — Tighten an additional 90°.
③ — Tighten an additional 40°.
④ — Tighten an additional 180°.
⑤ — Tighten an additional 120°.

Wheel Alignment

INDEX

PRELIMINARY INSPECTION

Ensure all tires are properly inflated.

Before measuring and setting front wheel alignment, rest front wheels on turn plates.

Before setting rear toe, rest rear wheels on slider plates or turn plates.

Before setting any alignment angle, jounce the vehicle three times at each end to establish trim height.

Special adapters are available for using a magnetic hub gauge at rear wheels. Depending on type of equipment used, these may not be required. After removing hub cap and bearing cap, hub gauge will snap into place on brake drum. Magnetic mounting toe gauges may also be installed in the same manner.

Always perform wheel alignment on a level alignment rack. Before doing alignment, proceed as follows:

1. Inspect for worn suspension components.
2. Inspect standing curb height.
3. Remove heavy weights from trunk.
4. Inspect wheel bearings for excessive freeplay.
5. Ensure gas tank is full.
6. Place front seats in full rear position.
7. Inspect rear toe adjustment.
8. Always road test vehicle after adjusting alignment. If vehicle still pulls, switch front tires. If vehicle still pulls in same direction, inspect alignment and rear tracking. If vehicle pulls in opposite direction, rotate tires and road test.

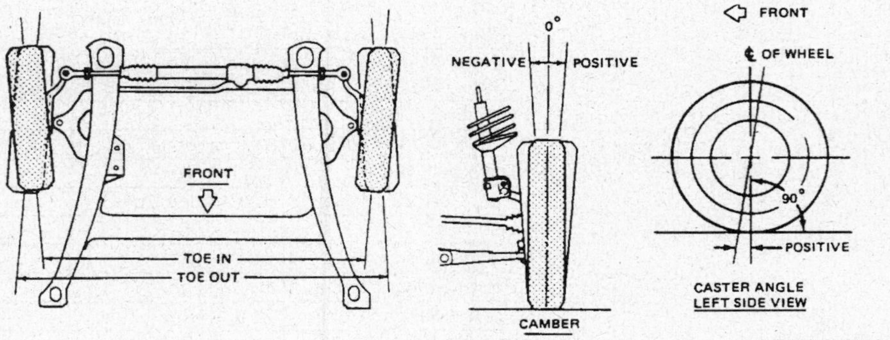

GC2049100100000X

Fig. 1 Caster, camber & toe angles

FRONT WHEEL ALIGNMENT

CASTER

Caster angle is not adjustable. If caster angle, **Fig. 1**, is not within specifications, inspect suspension support for improper alignment and suspension components for damage. Replace damaged components as required.

CAMBER

Toe setting is the only adjustment normally required. However, in special circumstances, such as damage due to road hazard or collision, camber angle, **Fig. 1**, may be adjusted by modifying strut assembly.

1. If strut is on vehicle, disconnect strut from steering knuckle. If strut is off vehicle, secure bottom of strut assembly in a suitable vise.
2. Enlarge bottom holes in outer flanges with a round file, until holes in outer flanges match slots in inner flanges, **Fig. 2.**
3. Install or connect strut to steering knuckle and install bolts finger tight.
4. Grasp top of tire firmly and move tire inboard or outboard until proper camber reading is obtained. Tighten retaining bolts enough to secure camber setting.

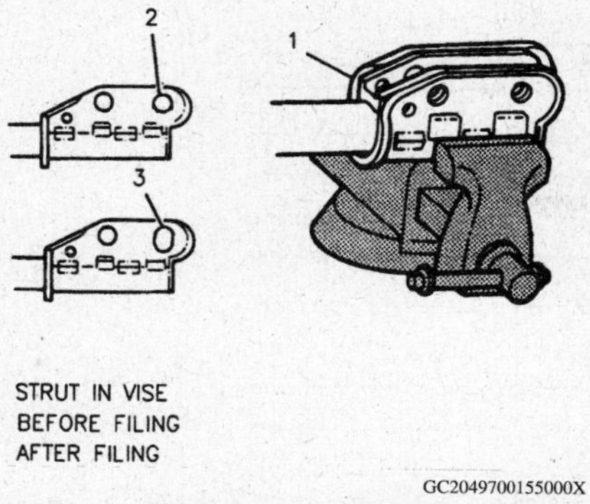

Fig. 2 Strut bracket modification for camber adjustment

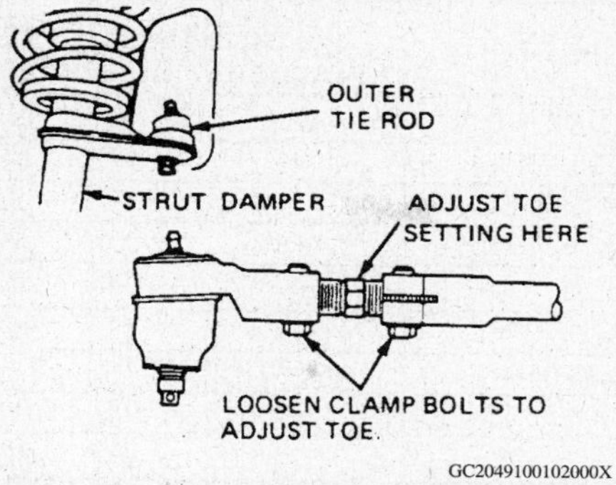

Fig. 3 Toe adjustment. Achieva, Skylark & 1997–98 Grand Am

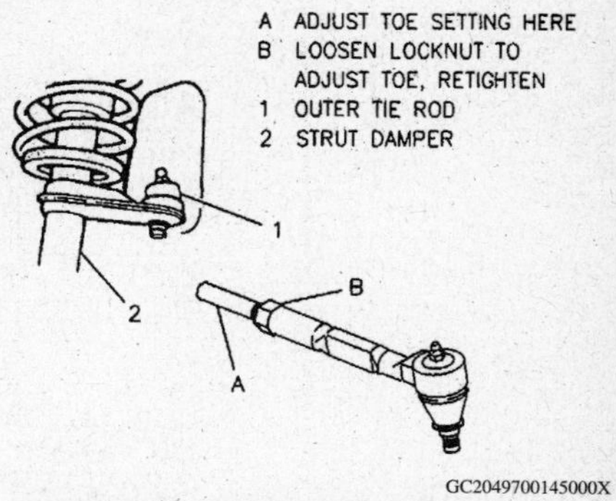

Fig. 4 Toe adjustment. Alero, Cutlass, Malibu & 1999–2000 Grand Am

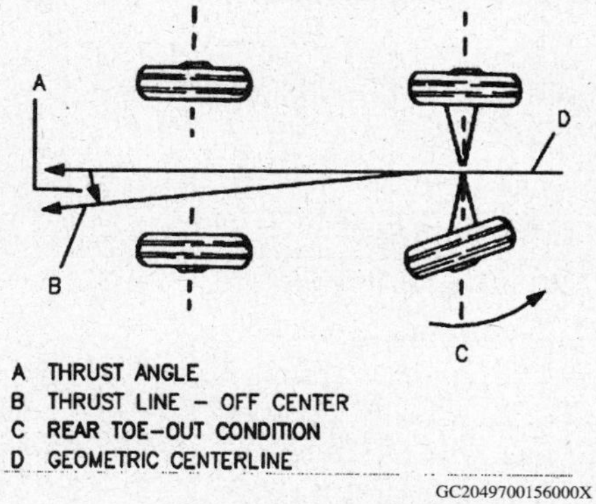

Fig. 5 Thrust angle

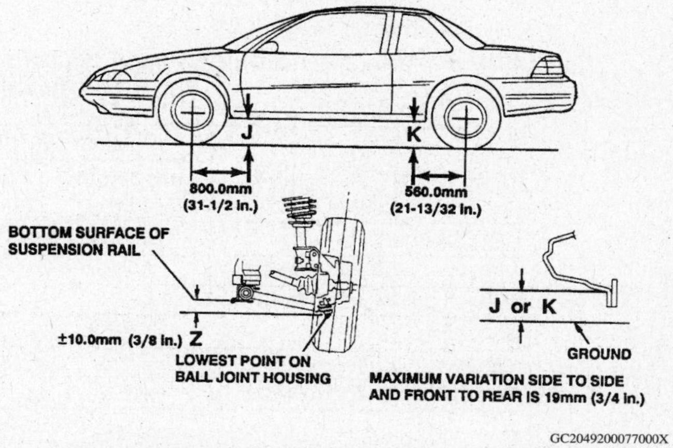

Fig. 6 Vehicle ride height measurement locations. Achieva, Skylark & 1997–98 Grand Am

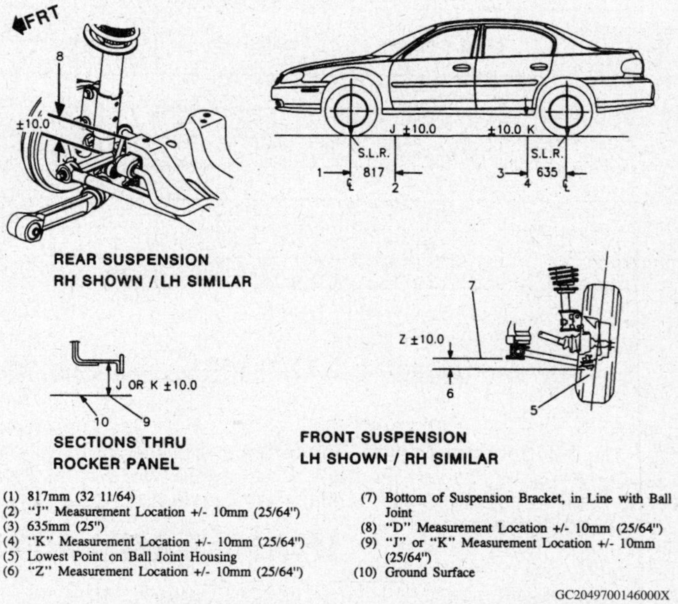

Fig. 7 Vehicle ride height measurement locations. Alero, Cutlass, Malibu & 1999–2000 Grand Am

5. Remove wheel and tire assembly if required and tighten strut to steering knuckle retaining bolts to specifications.

TOE

Toe, **Fig. 1,** is controlled by tie rod position.

Achieva, Skylark & 1997-98 Grand Am

1. Loosen clamp bolts at steering knuckle end of tie rods.
2. Rotating rods to obtain proper toe setting, **Fig. 3.**
3. **Torque** clamp bolts to 31 ft. lbs.

Alero, Cutlass, Malibu & 1999-2000 Grand Am

1. Ensure front wheels are in straight-ahead position.
2. Loosen jam nut, **Fig. 4.**
3. Turn adjuster to obtain proper toe setting.
4. **On 1997–98 Cutlass and Malibu models, torque** jam nut to 89 inch lbs., then rotate an additional 210° using torque angle meter tool No. J-36660, or equivalent.
5. **On Alero and 1999–2000 Grand Am models, torque** jam nut to 50 ft. lbs.

REAR WHEEL ALIGNMENT

After front wheel alignment has been inspected or adjusted, rear wheel alignment

Year	Tire Size	Ride Height Measurements, Inches①		
		Dimension Z	Dimension J	Dimension K
ACHIEVA				
1997–98	P195/70R14	9/16	9.37	9.57
	P195/65R15	5/16	9.37	9.57
	P205/55R16	15/64	9.37	9.57
GRAND AM				
1997–98	P195/70R14	9/16	9.37	9.57
	P195/65R15	5/16	9.37	9.57
	P205/55R16	15/64	9.37	9.57
SKYLARK				
1997–98	P195/70R14	9/16	9.37	9.57
	P195/65R15	11/32	9.37	9.57
	P205/55R16	9/32	9.37	9.57

① — ± 3/8 inch.

Fig. 8 Vehicle ride height specifications. Achieva, Skylark & 1997–98 Grand Am

Year	Tire Size	Ride Height Measurements, Inches①			
		Dimension D	Dimension Z	Dimension J	Dimension K
CUTLASS					
1997	P215/60R15	4 59/64	1/8	9 29/64	9 27/32
1998–2000	P215/60R15	4 27/32	0	9 21/64	9 39/64
MALIBU					
1997	P215/60R15	4 41/64	1/8	9 21/64	9 29/64
1998–2000	P215/60R15	4 27/32	0	9 21/64	9 39/64

① — ± 3/8 inch.

Fig. 9 Vehicle ride height specifications. Cutlass & Malibu

Year	Suspension Code	Tire Size	Engine	Ride Height Measurements, Inches①			
				Dimension Z	Dimension D	Dimension J	Dimension K
ALERO							
1999–2000	FE2	P215/60R15	2.4L	0	4 27/32	9 21/64	9 39/64
	FE3	P225/50R16	3.4L	–13/64	4 49/64	9 21/64	9 39/64
GRAND AM							
1999–2000	2-Door w/FE2	P215/60R15	2.4L & 3.4L	0	4 27/32	9 21/64	9 39/64
	4-Door w/FE2	P225/50R16	2.4L & 3.4L	–15/64	4 3/4	9 21/64	9 39/64
	FE3	P225/50R16	3.4L	–13/64	4 49/64	9 21/64	9 39/64

① — ± 3/8 inch.

Fig. 10 Vehicle ride height specifications. Alero & 1999–2000 Grand Am

angles should be inspected if vehicle still does not track properly or if excessive rear tire wear is present. Rear wheels should be parallel to and the same distance from the vehicle centerline.

Rear wheel alignment is not adjustable. If alignment angles are not within specification, inspect for bent or damaged suspension arms, components or underbody.

THRUST ANGLE

The vehicle is steered by the front wheels. The path the rear wheels follow is the thrust angle, **Fig. 5**. In an ideal setting, the thrust angle would be aligned with that of the vehicle centerline.

VEHICLE RIDE HEIGHT

Refer to **Figs. 6 and 7** for vehicle ride height measurements and **Figs. 8 through 10** for specifications. When inspecting ride height measurements, fuel tank should be full, tires at should be proper pressure, front seat should be in the rearward position, trunk should be empty except for spare tire and jack and vehicle should be on level ground. If fuel tank is not full, add weight to trunk to compensate for amount of fuel below the full level.

Prior to inspecting ride height, lift front bumper upward approximately 1 ½ inches and gently release. Repeat twice. Inspect front ride height. Push front bumper downward approximately 1 ½ inches and gently release. Repeat twice. Inspect front ride height. Average both readings to determine vehicle ride height. Inspect rear ride height in same manner, lifting and pushing rear bumper.

AURORA & RIVIERA

NOTE: Refer To The Rear Of This Manual For Manufacturer's Special Service Tool Supplies.

INDEX OF SERVICE OPERATIONS

Specifications

GENERAL ENGINE SPECIFICATIONS

Engine Liter/VIN Code①	Fuel System	Bore & Stroke	Compression Ratio	Net H.P. @ RPM②	Maximum Torque Ft. Lbs. @ RPM	Normal Oil Pressure, psi
1997–99						
3800/K	SFI	3.80 X 3.40	9.4	205 @ 5200	230 @ 4000	⑤
3800/1③	SFI	3.80 X 3.40	8.5	240 @ 5200	280 @ 3600	⑤
4.0L/C	SFI	3.43 X 3.31	10.3	250 @ 5600	260 @ 4000	④

① — Eighth digit of VIN denotes engine code.

② — Ratings are net-as installed in vehicle.

③ — Supercharged.

④ — 5 psi @ idle speed, 35 psi @ 2000 RPM.

⑤ — 60 psi @ 1850 RPM, using 10W-30 engine oil, w/engine @ operating temperature.

TUNE UP SPECIFICATIONS

Engine Liter/VIN Code①	Spark Plug Gap	Ignition Timing: Firing Order	Ignition Timing: Wire Connections Fig.	Idle Speed	Fuel Pump Pressure, psi⑤	Valve Clearance, Inch
1997-99						
3800/K	.060	②	A	③	48–55	⑦
3800/1	.060	②	A	③	48-55	⑦
4.0L/C	.050	④	B	⑥	⑧	⑦

① — Eighth digit of VIN denotes engine code.

② — Cylinder numbering from left to right as viewed front of vehicle, front bank 1, 3, 5; rear bank 2, 4, 6. Firing order, 1-6-5-4-3-2

③ — Idle speed is controlled by the Idle Air Control Valve.

④ — Cylinder numbering from left to right as viewed from front of vehicle, front bank 2, 4, 6, 8; rear bank 1, 3, 5, 7. Firing order, 1-2-7-3-4-5-6-8.

⑤ — With shop towel wrapped around fuel pressure gauge & fuel pressure test port to prevent spillage, connect fuel pressure gauge to fuel pressure test port. Check fuel pressure w/ignition key in the On position and engine not running.

⑥ — Idle speed is controlled by the Idle Speed Control Actuator.

⑦ — Equipped w/hydraulic valve lifters; no adjustment necessary.

⑧ — 1997 & 1999 models, 48–55 psi., 1998 models 41–47 psi

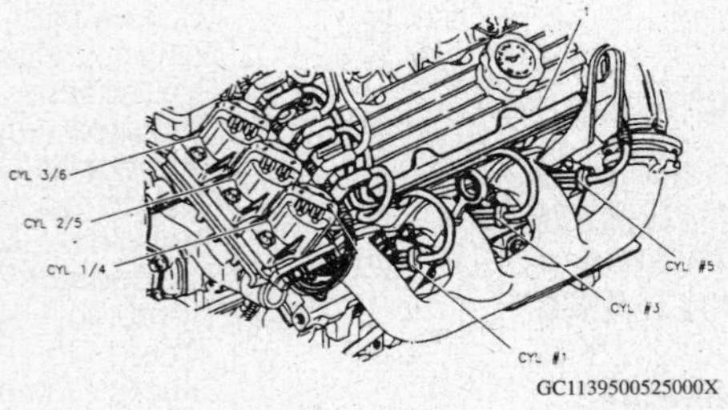

Fig. A

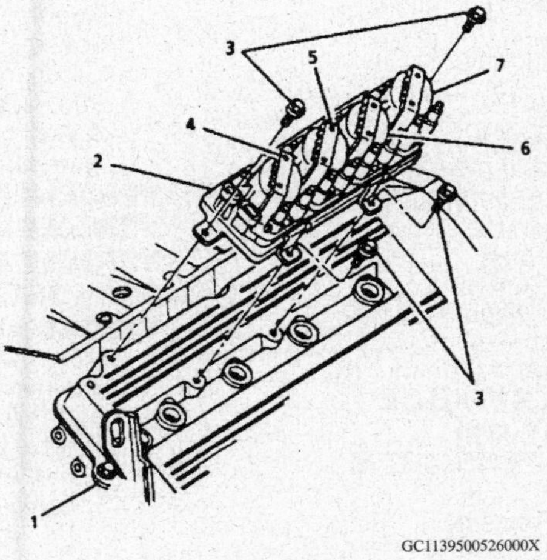

Fig. B

FRONT WHEEL ALIGNMENT SPECIFICATIONS

Year	Model	Caster Angle, Degrees		Camber Angle, Degrees		Total Toe, Degree	Steering Angle, Degrees	Ball Joint Wear
		Limits	Desired	Limits	Desired			
1997–99	All	+5.5 to +6.5	+6	-.3 to +.7	+.2	-.2 to +.2	-3 to +3	①

① — Refer to "Ball Joint Inspection" in "Front Suspension & Steering" section.

REAR WHEEL ALIGNMENT SPECIFICATIONS

Year	Model	Camber Angle, Degrees		Total Toe, Degrees	Thrust Angle, Degrees
		Limits	Desired		
1997–99	All	–.8 to +.2	-.3	0 to +.4	-.1 to +.1

FLUID CAPACITIES & COOLING SYSTEM DATA

Model	Engine Liter/VIN Code①	Coolant Capacity, Qts.	Radiator Cap Relief Pressure, Lbs.	Thermo Opening Temp.	Fuel Tank, Gallons	Engine Oil Refill, Qts. ⑧	Auto Transaxle, Qts.
1997							
Aurora	4.0L/C	13⑤⑦	15	185	19.4	7.0	③
Riviera	3800/K & 1	13⑦	16	195	20.0	4.5	②
1998-99							
Aurora	4.0L/C	13⑤⑦	15	185	19.4	7.5	④
Riviera	3800/K & 1	13⑦	16	195	19.4	4.5	⑥

① — Eighth digit of VIN denotes engine code.
② — Drain & refill, 6 qts.; overhaul, 8 qts.; total dry, 11 qts.
③ — Drain & refill, 8 qts.; overhaul, 12.6 qts.; total dry, 15 qts.
④ — Drain & refill, 11 qts.; overhaul, 10 qts.; total dry, 15 qts.
⑤ — Add three pellets of GM coolant supplement sealant part No. 3634621, or equivalent.
⑥ — Drain & refill, 7.4 qts.; overhaul, 10 qts.; total dry 13.4 qts.
⑦ — DEX-COOL, or equivalent, silicant-free antifreeze conforming to GM specification No. 6277M.
⑧ — With filter change.

LUBRICANT DATA

Year	Model	Lubricant Type			
		Automatic Transmission	Power Steering System	Supercharger	Brake System
1997–99	All	Dexron III	GM Part No. 1052884	Synthetic Oil GM Part No. 12345982	DOT 3

Electrical

NOTE: On Air Bag Equipped Models, Refer To " Air Bag System Precautions" Located In The Front Of This Manual For System Disarming & Arming Procedures.

NOTE: Refer To "Computer Relearn Procedures " Located In The Front Of This Manual For Computer Relearn Procedures.

INDEX

PRECAUTIONS

AIR BAG SYSTEMS

Refer to "Air Bag System Precautions" in the front of this manual for system disarming and arming procedures.

BATTERY GROUND CABLE

Prior to service, disconnect battery ground cable and isolate as required.

FUSE PANEL & FLASHER LOCATION

The instrument panel fuse block is located behind the lefthand side of the instrument panel, behind the trim panel. The rear fuse block is located under the rear seat.

The hazard flasher is located behind the lefthand side of the instrument panel, right of the steering column support. The turn signal flasher is located behind the lefthand side of the instrument panel, attached to the lefthand sound insulator.

FUEL PUMP RELAY LOCATION

The fuel pump relay is in the passenger compartment relay center, located below the rear seat.

RELAY CENTER LOCATION

The passenger compartment relay center is located under the rear seat. The engine compartment relay center is located on the front righthand side of the engine compartment.

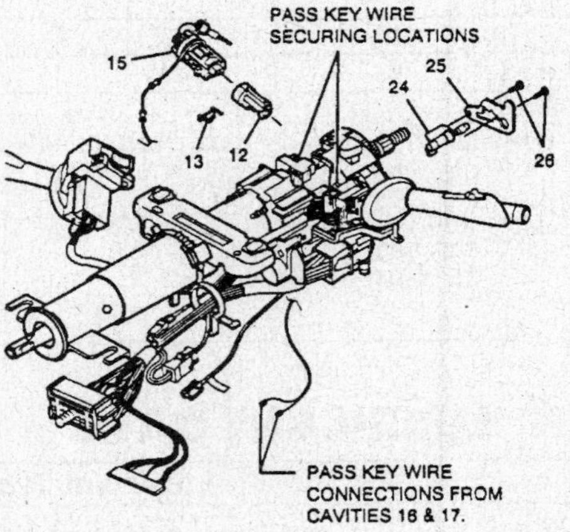

12 ACTUATOR ASM, IGNITION LOCK
13 SPRING, LOCK PRE-LOAD
15 LOCK CYL SET, STRG COLUMN
24 BOLT ASM, LOCK
25 BRACKET, LOCK BOLT SUPPORT
26 SCREW, TAPPING

GC6049500152000X

Fig. 1 Lock cylinder & lock bolt removal

STARTER

REPLACE

3800 ENGINE

1. Raise and support vehicle.
2. Remove splash shield
3. Remove mounting bolts and flywheel inspection cover.
4. Disconnect starter wiring.
5. Remove mounting bolts and starter.
6. Reverse procedure to install, noting the following:
   a. **Torque** starter to engine bolts to 32 ft. lbs.
   b. **Torque** nut on solenoid battery terminal to 12 ft. lbs.
   c. **Torque** nut on solenoid S terminal to 22 inch lbs.
   d. **Torque** flywheel inspection cover bolts to 22 inch lbs.

4.0L ENGINE

1. Remove intake manifold as outlined under "Intake Manifold, Replace" in "4.0L Engine" section.
2. Disconnect electrical connectors from starter solenoid S and battery terminals.
3. Remove mounting bolts and starter.
4. Reverse procedure to install, noting the following:
   a. **Torque** inner nuts on solenoid terminals to 6 ft. lbs.
   b. **Torque** S terminal nut to 26 inch lbs.
   c. **Torque** battery terminal nut to 6 ft. lbs.
   d. **Torque** starter mounting bolts to 22 ft. lbs.

COIL PACK

REPLACE

3800 ENGINE

1. Disconnect coil pack (ignition control module) 14-way electrical connector.

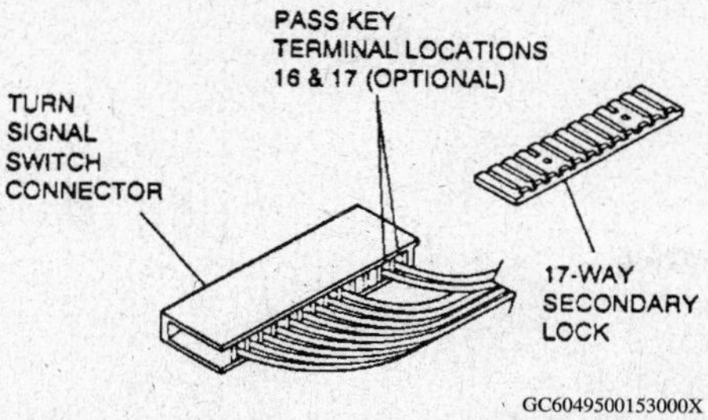

Fig. 2 Pass Key wire connector removal

2. Mark and disconnect spark plug wires at coils.
3. Remove screws mounting ignition coil assemblies to ignition control module.
4. Remove coil assemblies from control module.
5. Remove ignition control module mounting screws.
6. Reverse procedure to install.

4.0L ENGINE

1. Disconnect four electrical connectors from (ignition control module).
2. Mark and disconnect spark plug wires at coils.
3. Remove mounting bolts and ignition coils from ignition control module.
4. Reverse procedure to install. **Torque** retaining bolts to 9 ft. lbs.

IGNITION LOCK

REPLACE

REMOVAL

1. Tilt column to center position.
2. Remove mounting screws and upper steering column cover.
3. Remove pivot and pulse switch as outlined under " Pivot & Pulse Switch, Replace," allow switch to hang freely from column.
4. Turn lock cylinder to Run position.
5. Push against locking button located on back side of bearing and housing assembly and remove lock cylinder.
6. Remove lock preload spring, **Fig. 1.**
7. To remove Pass Key wiring harness from steering column, proceed as follows:
   a. Disconnect bulkhead connector from vehicle wire harness.
   b. Disconnect gray turn signal switch connector from bulkhead connector, **Fig. 2.**
   c. Remove 17-way secondary lock from turn signal switch connector.
   d. Disconnect two Pass Key terminals from cavities 16 and 17 of gray turn signal switch connector.
   e. Disconnect Pass Key wire harness from wire harness strap, multi-function switch and upper head housing assembly.
8. Using needle nose pliers, remove ignition lock actuator assembly from upper head housing assembly.
9. Remove lock bolt assembly as follows:

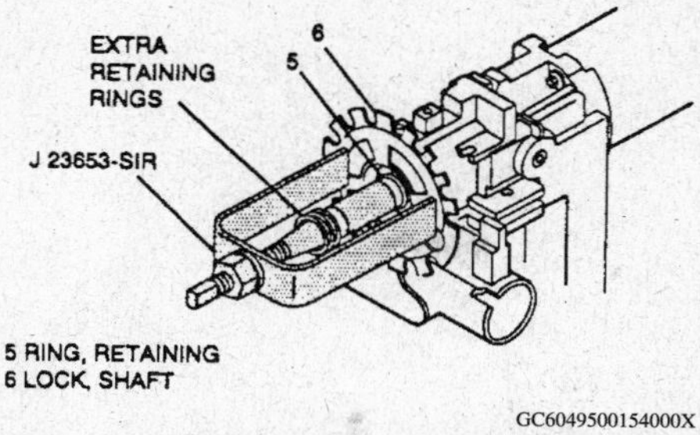

Fig. 3 Shaft lock retaining ring removal & installation

   a. Remove mounting screw and tilt lever knob.
   b. Pry close out knob locking tabs from bearing and housing assembly and remove close out knob.
   c. Remove mounting screws and steering column lower cover.
   d. Remove steering wheel as outlined under "Steering Wheel, Replace."
   e. Remove retaining ring and SIR coil assembly from column. Allow coil assembly to hang freely from steering column.
   f. Using lock plate compressor tool No. J-23653-SIR, or equivalent, to push down shaft lock, remove shaft lock retaining ring, **Fig. 3.**
   g. Remove shaft lock from steering column.
   h. Remove turn signal cancel cam, upper bearing spring, upper bearing inner race seat, inner race and tilt lever bracket, **Fig. 4.**
   i. Remove mounting bolts and lock bolt support bracket.
   j. Remove lock bolt from housing assembly.

INSTALLATION

1. Install lock bolt and support bracket into housing assembly, **torque** support bracket mounting screws to 46 inch lbs.
2. Ensure end of lock bolt is flush with support bracket, **Fig. 1,** install ignition lock actuator assembly into housing,
3. Rotate actuator counterclockwise until it pushes out lock bolt and actuator seats into housing assembly.
4. Rotate actuator clockwise to Run position.
5. Align inner block tooth of lock plate to block tooth of upper shaft assembly.
6. Install tilt lever bracket, inner race, upper bearing inner race seat, upper bearing spring and turn signal cam assembly.
7. Lubricate shaft lock with suitable synthetic grease and install shaft lock into housing.
8. Using lock plate compressor tool No. J-23653-SIR, or equivalent, push down shaft lock and install shaft lock retaining ring, **Fig. 3. Ensure ring is seated firmly in groove on shaft.**
9. Insert key into lock cylinder and with lock cylinder in RUN position, align locking tab with slot in housing assembly and push into position.
10. Insert Pass Key wire harness into col-

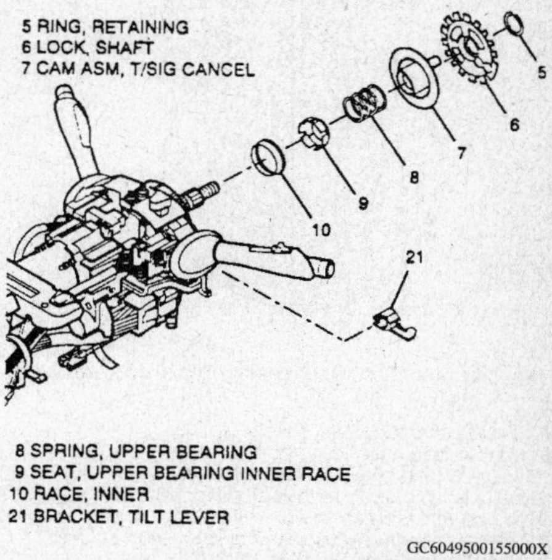

Fig. 4 Upper steering shaft components

umn and route wire harness through wiring protector.
11. Secure wiring harness to housing assembly and multi-function switch and route through wiring harness strap.
12. Connect terminals of wiring harness to cavities 16 and 17 in gray turn signal switch connector.
13. Install 17-way secondary lock onto turn signal switch connector.
14. Connect gray turn signal switch connector to bulkhead connector.
15. Connect bulkhead connector to vehicle wiring harness.
16. Install pivot and pulse switch assembly as outlined under " Pivot & Pulse Switch, Replace."
17. Install upper steering column cover, **torque** cover mounting screws to 46 inch lbs.
18. Install multi-function switch as outlined under " Multi-Function Switch, Replace."
19. Install and center SIR coil assembly as shown in **Fig. 5.**
20. Install steering wheel as outlined under "Steering Wheel, Replace."

IGNITION SWITCH

REPLACE

1. Tilt column to center position.
2. Remove mounting screws and upper steering column cover.
3. Remove mounting screw and tilt lever knob.
4. Pry close out knob locking tabs from bearing and housing assembly and remove close out knob.
5. Remove mounting screws and lower steering column cover.
6. Remove two wire straps from steering column wiring harness, **Fig. 6.**
7. Disconnect steering column bulkhead connector from vehicle wiring harness.
8. Disconnect ignition key and alarm switch assembly from wire harness strap.
9. Disconnect gray and black connectors of turn signal and multi-function switch from column bulkhead connector.
10. Remove mounting screws and ignition and key alarm switch from column.

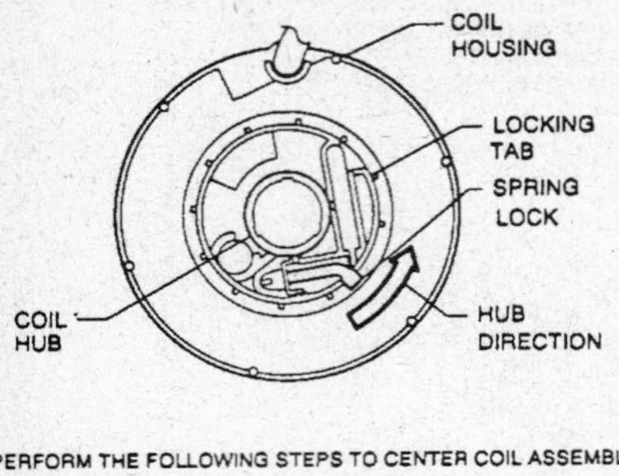

Fig. 5 SIR coil assembly installation

11. Reverse procedure to install.

NEUTRAL SAFETY SWITCH

REPLACE

1. Set parking brake and set gear selector to N position.
2. Remove linkage cable bracket to transaxle shaft retaining nut.
3. Remove linkage cable bracket from transaxle shaft.
4. Remove park/neutral position switch mounting bolts.
5. Disconnect park/neutral position switch electrical connector.
6. Remove terminal nut on starter solenoid and disconnect cable from starter.
7. Remove park/neutral position switch from vehicle.
8. Reverse procedure to install.

STOP LIGHT SWITCH

REPLACE

1. Remove lefthand instrument panel sound insulator.
2. Disconnect switch electrical connectors, **Fig. 7.**
3. Disconnect vacuum hose from switch.
4. Remove switch from brake pedal support.
5. Reverse procedure to install, adjust switch as follows:
   a. After installing switch, press brake pedal rearward until no audible clicks remain and release pedal.
   b. Press brake pedal again to ensure no clicks are heard.
   c. Compare switch adjustment to **Fig. 7.**
   d. Only notch should be visible. If plunger is visible or notch is not, repeat adjustment.

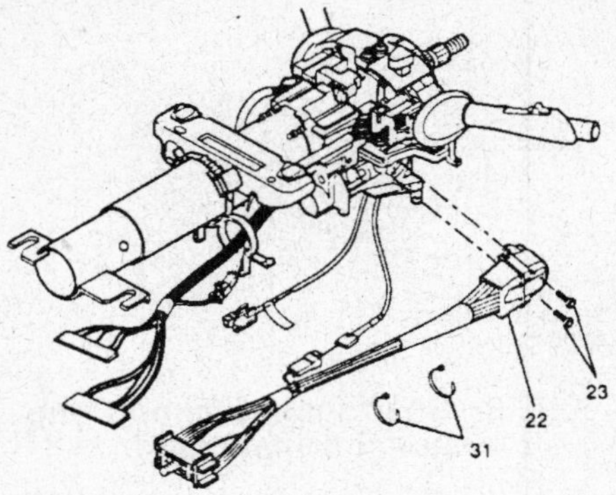

Fig. 6 Ignition & key alarm switch removal

PIVOT & PULSE SWITCH

REPLACE

1. Tilt column to center position.
2. Remove mounting screws and upper steering column cover.
3. Remove two wire straps from steering column wire harness.
4. Disconnect pivot and pulse switch connector from turn signal and multi-function switch wire harness connector.
5. Disconnect pivot and pulse switch harness from wire harness strap.
6. Remove mounting screws and pivot and pulse switch assembly from column, **Fig. 8.**
7. Reverse procedure to install.

MULTI-FUNCTION SWITCH

REPLACE

1997–98

1. Tilt column to center position.
2. Remove mounting screws and upper steering column cover.
3. Remove two wire straps from steering column wire harness.
4. Disconnect steering column bulkhead connector from vehicle wiring harness.
5. Disconnect turn signal and multi-function switch wiring harness from wiring harness strap.
6. Disconnect pivot and pulse switch assembly connector from multi-function switch wire harness connector.
7. Disconnect gray and black multi-function switch connectors from column bulkhead connector.
8. Remove 17-way secondary lock from turn signal switch connector.
9. Disconnect two Pass Key terminals from cavities 16 and 17 of gray turn signal switch connector.

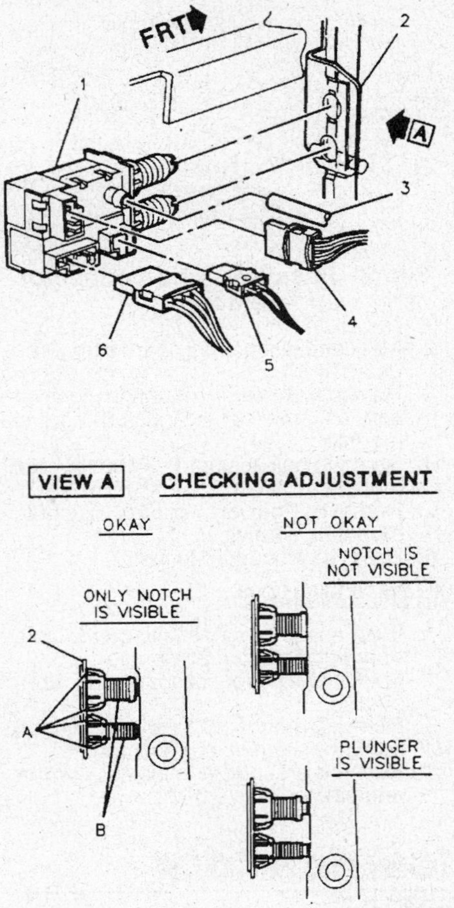

Fig. 7 Stop lamp switch removal & adjustment

10. Remove mounting screws and multi-function switch from column, **Fig. 9.**
11. Reverse procedure to install.

1999

1. Remove steering wheel as outlined under "Steering Wheel Replace."
2. Remove tilt lever by pulling straight out.
3. Remove torx screws, then the lower column shroud.
4. Remove torx screws, then the upper column shroud.
5. Remove IP trim panel, then torx bolts from multi-function switch.
6. Disconnect electrical connector from switch.

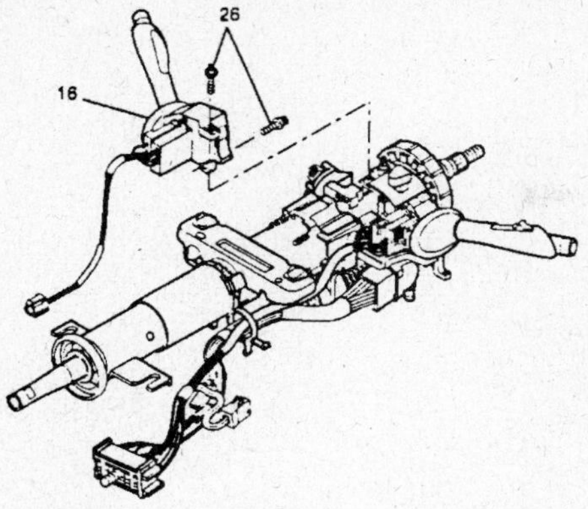

Fig. 8 Pivot & pulse switch assembly removal

7. Remove multi-function switch.
8. Reverse procedure to install.

STEERING WHEEL

REPLACE

1. Remove air bag as outlined in "Passive Restraints Systems" chapter.
2. Remove steering wheel retaining nut, place match marks on shaft and steering wheel.
3. Using pulling tools Nos. J-1859-03 and J-38720, or equivalents, remove steering wheel from steering shaft.
4. Reverse procedure to install, noting the following:
   a. Align mark on steering shaft with steering wheel.
   b. **Torque** steering wheel retaining nut to 30 ft. lbs.

INSTRUMENT CLUSTER

REPLACE

AURORA

1. Remove knee bolster from under steering column.
2. Remove upper steering column bracket nuts and lower steering column.
3. Remove trunk/fuel door release and interior lamp trim plates by pulling rearward and disconnecting electrical connectors, **Fig. 10.**
4. Remove center A/C outlet trim panel.
5. Pull instrument panel cluster trim plate rearward, **Fig. 11.**
6. Remove instrument cluster mounting screws.
7. Pull cluster rearward and disconnect two electrical connectors.
8. Remove cluster from vehicle, **Fig. 12.**
9. Reverse procedure to install

RIVIERA

1. Remove switches and air deflectors from cluster trim plate, **Fig. 13.**
2. Remove mounting screws and cluster trim plate from instrument panel.
3. Remove instrument cluster retaining screws.

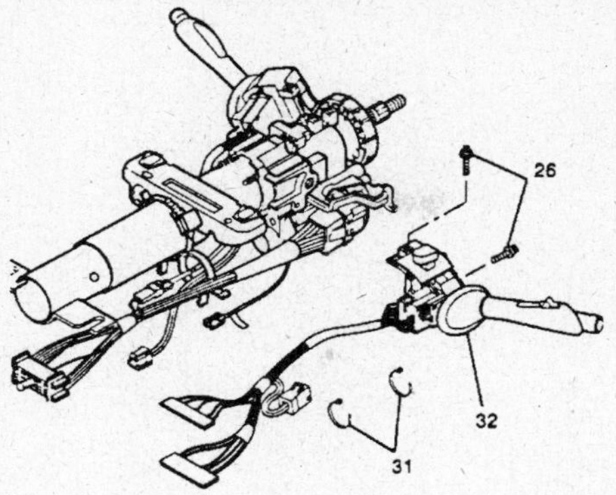

Fig. 9 Turn signal & multi-function switch removal

4. Disconnect cluster electrical connectors, **Fig. 14.**
5. Remove instrument cluster from vehicle.
6. Reverse procedure to install.

RADIO

REPLACE

AURORA

1. Remove instrument panel center trim plate by pulling rearward to disengage retainers.
2. Remove two radio assembly retaining screws.
3. Pull radio outward and disconnect antenna lead and electrical connectors.
4. Remove radio from vehicle.
5. Reverse procedure to install.

RIVIERA

1. Remove instrument cluster trim plate as outlined under " Instrument Cluster, Replace."
2. Remove two radio assembly retaining screws.
3. Pull radio outward and disconnect antenna lead and electrical connectors.
4. Remove radio from vehicle.
5. Reverse procedure to install.

WIPER MOTOR

REPLACE

1. Turn ignition switch to Accessory position and set wiper switch to Pulse position.
2. Turn ignition switch off when wiper arms are at bottom and not moving.
3. Lift wiper blade assembly up from windshield.
4. Pull out retaining latch with a screwdriver.
5. Pull wiper arm assembly off transmission driveshaft.
6. Disconnect hose from washer hose.
7. Remove five air inlet panel retainers.
8. Push washer hose into firewall.
9. Remove air inlet panel from vehicle.
10. Using wiper transmission separator tool No. J-39232, or equivalent, remove transmission drive link socket from wiper motor crank arm.
11. Pull two harness connector retainers out of wiper motor connector.
12. Disconnect two harness connectors from wiper motor.
13. Remove bolts and stud, then wiper motor.
14. Reverse procedure to install.

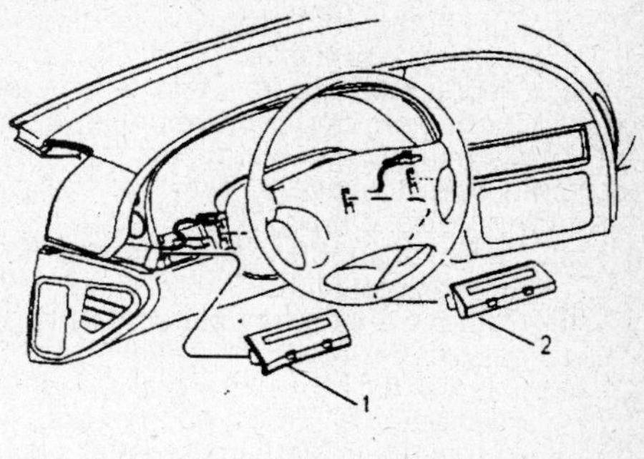

Fig. 10 Instrument panel trim plate removal. Aurora

BLOWER MOTOR

REPLACE

1. Remove righthand sound insulator.
2. Disconnect blower motor electrical connector.
3. Disconnect cooling tube from blower motor.
4. Remove blower motor to heater and A/C control module mounting screws.
5. Remove blower motor and fan assembly from vehicle.
6. Reverse procedure to install.

HEATER CORE

REPLACE

1. Drain cooling system.
2. Disconnect heater hoses from heater core.
3. Remove left and righthand sound insulators.
4. Remove heater core cover from heater and A/C module.
5. Remove heater core retaining straps.
6. Remove heater core from vehicle.
7. Reverse procedure to install. To aid installation sound insulator seal may be cut in half. Each half should be placed into respective sides of heater and A/C module.

EVAPORATOR CORE

REPLACE

1. Remove storage compartment bin from center console.
2. Remove retainer and shifter handle.
3. Disconnect shift handle electrical connector and remove handle.
4. **On Aurora models,** remove shifter trim plate as follows:

   a. Pull shifter trim plate up to disengage retaining tabs.
   b. Disconnect all trim plate electrical connectors and remove shifter trim plate from center console.
5. **On Riviera models,** remove shifter trim plate as follows:
   a. Remove upper console trim plate by pulling outward.
   b. Remove shifter trim plate mounting screws.
   c. Pull shifter trim plate upward and disconnect electrical connectors.
   d. Remove trim plate from center console.
6. **On all models,** remove center console mounting nuts and bolts.
7. Disconnect console electrical connectors and remove console assembly from vehicle.
8. Remove cluster trim plate as outlined under "Instrument Cluster, Replace."
9. **On Aurora models,** remove mounting screws and upper trim pad mounting screws.
10. **On Riviera models,** remove instrument panel upper trim pad as follows:
    a. Pry windshield defroster grill upward.
    b. Disconnect sunload temperature and twilight sentinel sensors from defroster grill.
    c. Remove defroster grill from vehicle.
    d. Remove upper trim pad to instrument panel mounting screws.
    e. Remove upper trim pad from instrument panel.
11. **On all models,** remove A pillar trim pads.
12. Remove left and righthand sound insulators.
13. **On Aurora models,** remove mounting screws and knee bolster.
14. **On Riviera models,** remove knee bolster mounting screws. Disconnect electrical connectors, traction control switch and air temperature sensor and remove knee bolster.
15. **On all models,** remove glove box from instrument panel.
16. Remove radio as outlined under "Radio, Replace."
17. Remove HVAC control head retaining screws.
18. Disconnect connector and remove HVAC control head from instrument panel.
19. Remove instrument panel to dash panel mounting screws.
20. Pull instrument panel carrier away from dash and disconnect electrical connectors and antenna cable.
21. Remove instrument panel from vehicle.
22. Recover refrigerant as outlined under "Air Conditioning."
23. Remove engine compartment vacuum tank.
24. Remove multi-use bracket to gain access to A/C lines.
25. Remove A/C lines from evaporator and drain cooling system.
26. Disconnect heater hoses from heater core.

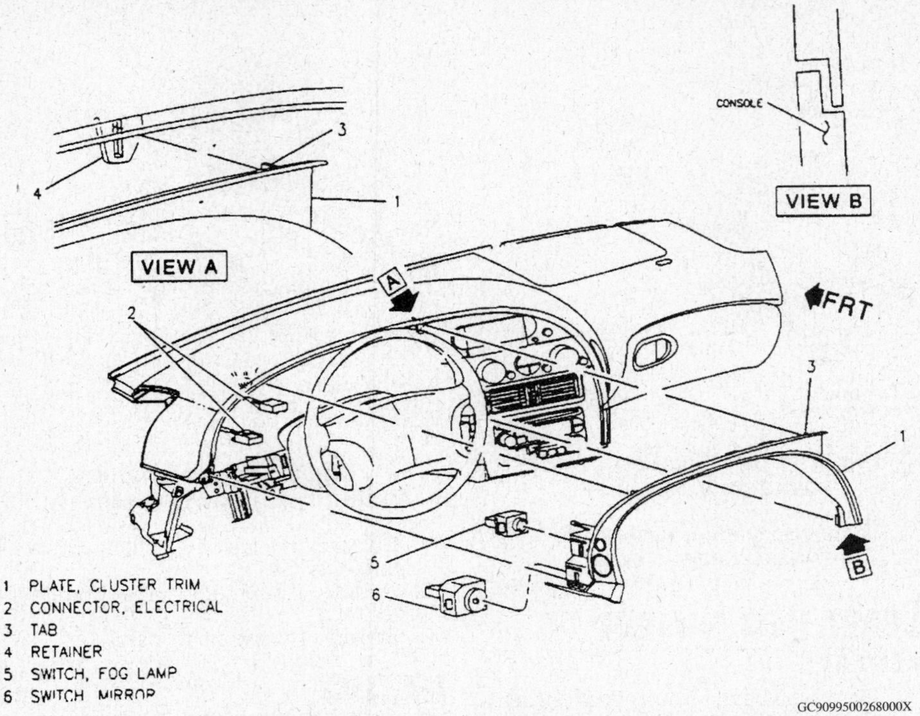

Fig. 11 Instrument cluster trim plate removal. Aurora

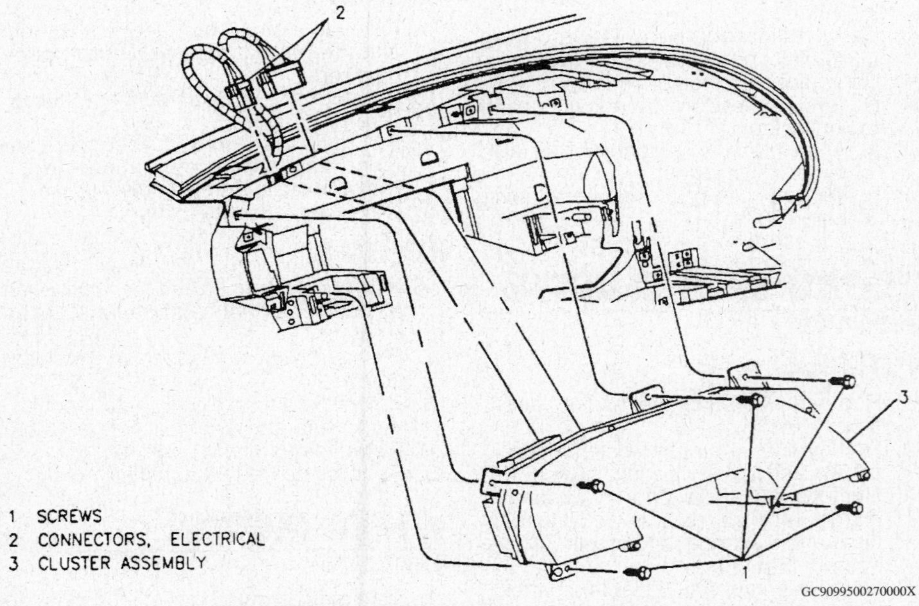

Fig. 12 Instrument cluster removal. Aurora

27. Remove PCM/Programmer bracket.
28. Remove mounting screws and passenger air bag module.
29. Remove defroster duct and disconnect electrical connector near blower housing.
30. Remove connector duct from case and floor.
31. Remove side window ducts.
32. Remove righthand center instrument panel mounting bracket.
33. Remove heater and A/C module retaining nuts.
34. Remove heater and A/C module.
35. Remove evaporator access panel from heater and A/C module.
36. Remove mounting straps and evaporator from heater and A/C module.
37. Reverse procedure to install.

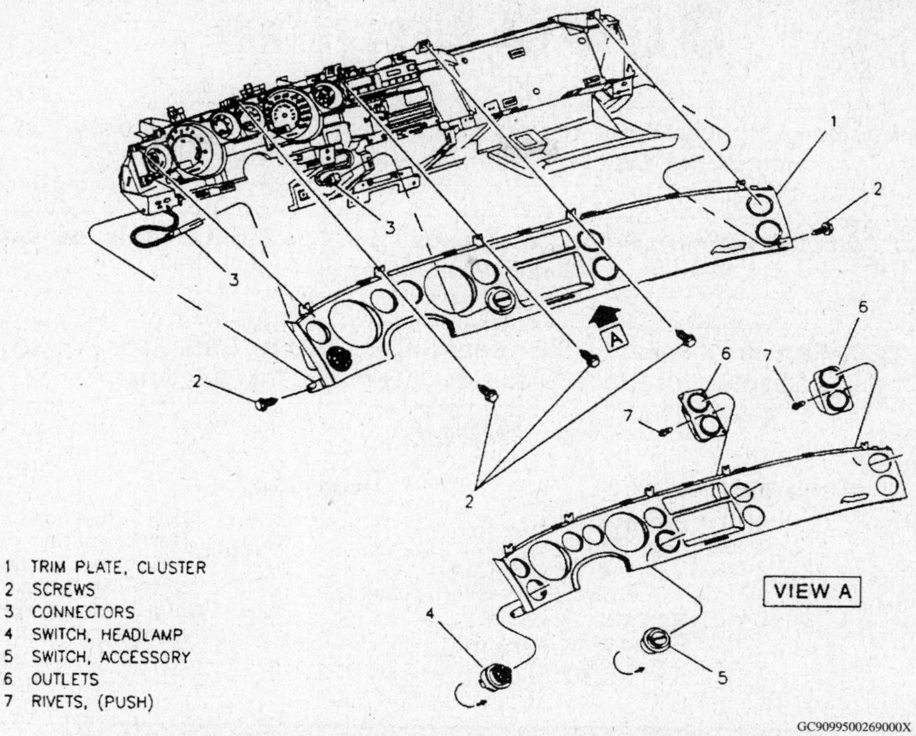

Fig. 13 Instrument panel cluster trim plate removal. Riviera

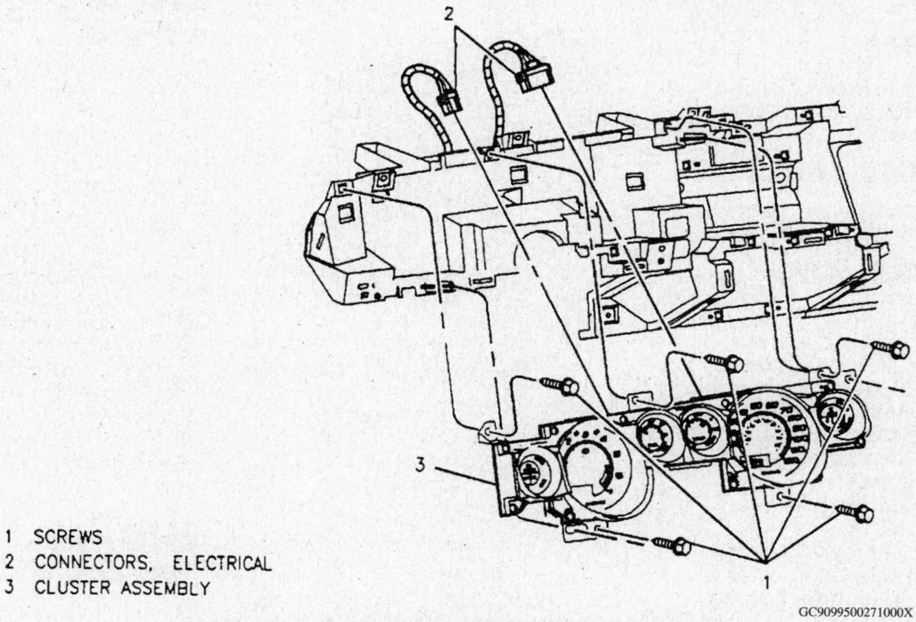

Fig. 14 Instrument cluster removal. Riviera

3800 Engine

NOTE: On Air Bag Equipped Models, Refer To "Air Bag System Precautions" Located In The Front Of This Manual For System Disarming & Arming Procedures.

NOTE: Refer To "Computer Relearn Procedures" Located In The Front Of This Manual For Computer Relearn Procedures.

NOTE: Refer To "3800 Engine" Section In The "Bonneville, LeSabre, LSS, Park Avenue, 88 & Regency" Chapter For Procedures Not Covered In This Section.

INDEX

PRECAUTIONS

AIR BAG SYSTEMS

Refer to "Air Bag System Precautions" in the front of this manual for system disarming and arming procedures.

BATTERY GROUND CABLE

Prior to service, disconnect battery ground cable and isolate as required.

FUEL SYSTEM PRESSURE RELIEF

After relieving fuel system pressure, a small amount of fuel may be released when servicing fuel pipes or connections. In order to reduce the risk of personal injury, cover fuel pipe fittings with shop towel before disconnecting to catch any fuel that may leak.

1. Loosen fuel filler cap to relieve tank pressure.
2. Connect suitable fuel pressure gauge to fuel pressure test connector. **Wrap a shop towel around connection to avoid fuel spillage.**
3. Insert bleed hose into a suitable container and open valve to bleed system.
4. Drain any fuel remaining in fuel gauge into suitable container.

COMPRESSION PRESSURE

When checking compression, the lowest cylinder must be within 70 percent of the highest cylinder with a minimum pressure of 100 psi. Perform compression test with engine at normal operating temperature, spark plugs removed and throttle wide open.

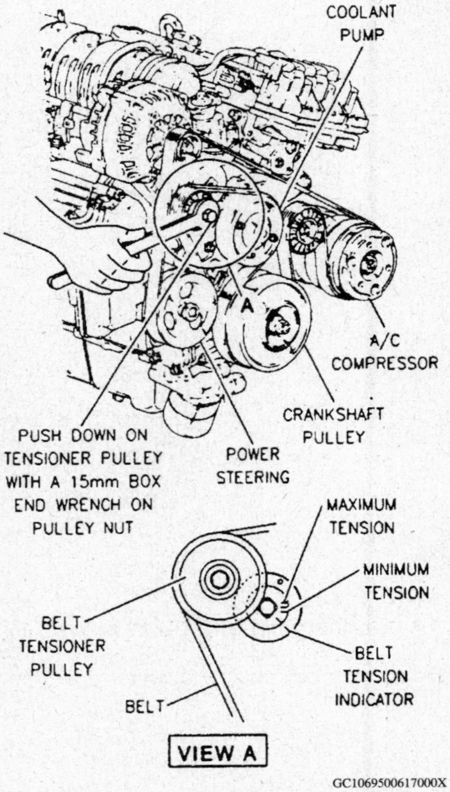

Fig. 1 Serpentine drive belt inspection. Less supercharged engine

ENGINE MOUNT

REPLACE

1. Raise engine slightly using the following engine support tools, or equivalents:
   a. Engine support fixture tool No. J-28467- 360, or equivalent.
   b. Engine support fixture adapter tool No. J-28467–94, or equivalent.
   c. Engine support fixture adapter tool No. J-28467-330, or equivalent.
   d. Engine support fixture adapter tool No. J-28467-350, or equivalent.
2. Remove bottom bolts on mount.
3. Remove front engine mount through bolt from mount.
4. Remove rear engine mount through bolt from mount.
5. Remove engine mount from bracket.
6. Reverse procedure to install.

ENGINE

REPLACE

1. Remove engine hood. Mark hood for installation reference.
2. Relieve fuel system pressure as outlined under "Precautions."
3. Drain coolant and engine oil into suitable containers.
4. Remove radiator and heater hoses.
5. Disconnect battery ground cable from engine.
6. Disconnect engine harness at bulkhead connector.
7. Remove serpentine drive belt.
8. Remove power steering pump from engine and position aside.
9. Remove air flow duct.
10. Disconnect throttle cable from throttle

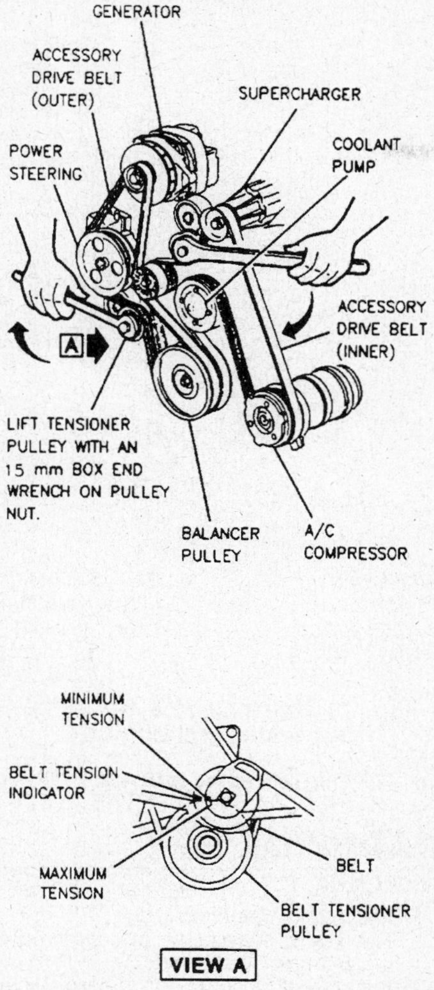

Fig. 2 Serpentine drive belt inspection. Supercharged engine

linkage mounting bracket and other applicable cables.

11. Disconnect the following wiring harness connectors:
    a. MAT sensor.
    b. Throttle position sensor.
    c. Idle air control valve.
    d. Oxygen sensor.
    e. A/C compressor.
    f. Oil pressure switch.
    g. Power steering cutout switch.
    h. Vehicle speed sensor.
    i. Low oil level sensor.
12. Disconnect ignition coil ground strap from fender inner panel mounting screws.
13. Disconnect fuel feed and return lines from fuel rail and fuel pressure regulator.
14. Disconnect emission control canister hoses from throttle body connections.
15. Disconnect brake booster and heater control hoses from engine vacuum connections.
16. Disconnect vacuum hoses from cruise control and servo assembly.
17. Raise and support vehicle.
18. Remove exhaust pipe from righthand

Fig. 3 Drive belt routing. Less supercharged engine

exhaust manifold.

19. Remove A/C compressor and position aside.
20. Remove righthand front engine to transaxle bracket.
21. Remove flywheel cover, then starter motor as outlined under " Starter, Replace" in "Electrical" section.
22. Remove flywheel to torque converter bolts. Scribe marks on flywheel and torque converter for reassembly reference.
23. Lower vehicle.
24. Attach suitable lifting device to engine lifting brackets
25. Raise engine slightly and remove torque axis engine mount.
26. Support transaxle and remove engine to transaxle bolts.
27. Separate engine from transaxle and remove engine.
28. Reverse procedure to install.

SERPENTINE DRIVE BELT

BELT TENSION INSPECTION

1. Run engine, with no accessories on, until engine is warmed up.
2. Shut engine off and read belt tension using belt tension gauge tool No. J-23600-B, or equivalent.
3. **On models less supercharged engine,** place gauge between alternator and power steering pump.
4. **On models with supercharged engine,** check inner belt tension between supercharger and idler pulley.
5. **On all models,** note readings and remove belt tension gauge.
6. Start engine with accessories off and allow system to stabilize for 15 seconds.
7. Turn engine off and use 15mm socket to apply clockwise force to tensioner pulley bolt, **Figs. 1 and 2.**
8. Release force and immediately take tension reading without disturbing belt tensioner position.
9. Use same socket to apply counter-

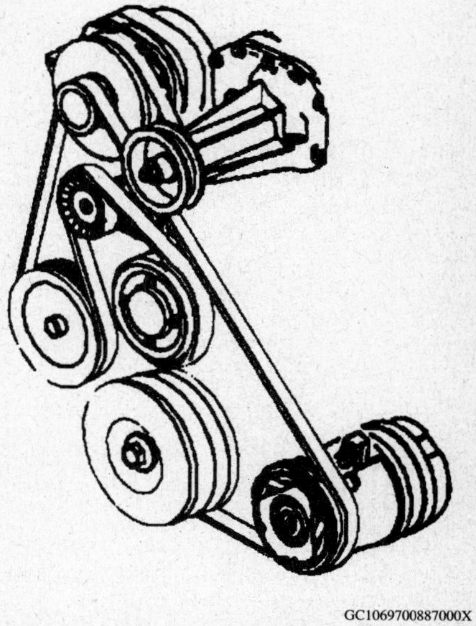

Fig. 4 Inner drive belt routing. Supercharged engine

clockwise force to tensioner pulley bolt and raise pulley to eliminate all tension.

10. Slowly lower pulley to belt and take tension reading without disturbing belt tensioner position.
11. Average three readings. If average reading is not 50–70 lbs. and belt is within tensioners operating range, replace tensioner.

BELT, REPLACE

1. Place a jack with suitable wood block under engine oil pan.
2. Remove engine mounting bracket torque axis bolt.
3. Disconnect crank sensor electrical connector.
4. Remove engine mounting bracket lower stud and lower engine to allow stud to clear frame rail.
5. Raise engine and install torque axis bolt.
6. Lower engine and remove spacer.
7. **On models with supercharged engine,** remove outer and inner belts. **Outer belt drives supercharger, while inner belt drives alternator, power steering pump, water pump and air conditioning compressor.**
8. **On models less supercharged engine,** remove belt.
9. **On all models,** reverse procedure to install. Use belt routings shown in **Figs. 3 through 5.**

BELT TENSIONER, REPLACE

Less Supercharged Engine

1. Drain engine coolant and remove drive belt as outlined under " Belt, Replace."
2. Remove alternator.
3. Remove heater hoses.
4. Remove mounting bolts and tensioner.
5. Reverse procedure to install.

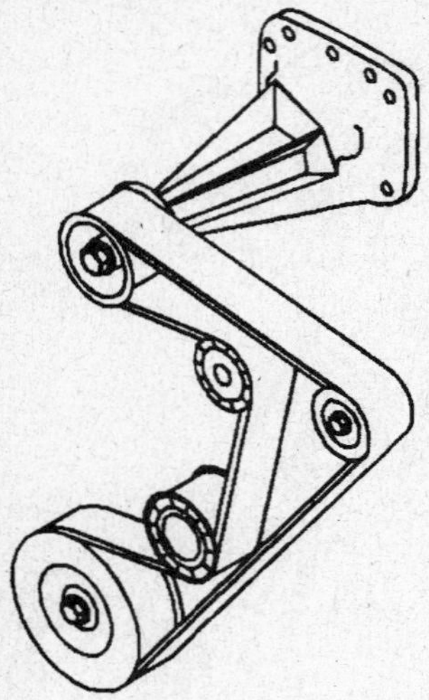

GC1069700888000X

Fig. 5 Outer driver belt routing. Supercharged engine

Supercharged Engine

1. Drain engine coolant and remove drive belts as outlined under "Belt, Replace."
2. Remove ignition module.
3. Remove mounting bolts and tensioner.
4. Reverse procedure to install.

COOLING SYSTEM BLEED

1. After filling cooling system, place heater and A/C control to any A/C mode except MAX. Set temperature to its highest setting.
2. Allow engine to continue idling until lower radiator hose to coolant pump is hot.
3. Cycle engine speed up to about 3000 RPM and back to idle five times.
4. Slowly open bleed valve on rear of thermostat housing for approximately 15 seconds to expel any air in cooling system.
5. After air has been expelled, fill cooling system.

THERMOSTAT

REPLACE

1. Drain cooling system into suitable container.
2. Remove upper radiator hose from thermostat housing.
3. Remove mounting bolts, housing and thermostat, **Figs. 6 and 7.**
4. Reverse procedure to install.

WATER PUMP

REPLACE

LESS SUPERCHARGED ENGINE

1. Drain cooling system, then remove air cleaner assembly.
2. Disconnect coolant hoses from water pump.
3. Remove water pump belt cover, then the drive belt as outlined under "Serpentine Drive Belt."
4. Remove bypass hose, then the lower radiator hose from thermostat housing.
5. Remove mounting bolts and water pump, **Fig. 8.**
6. Reverse procedure to install, tighten mounting bolts as shown in **Fig. 8.**

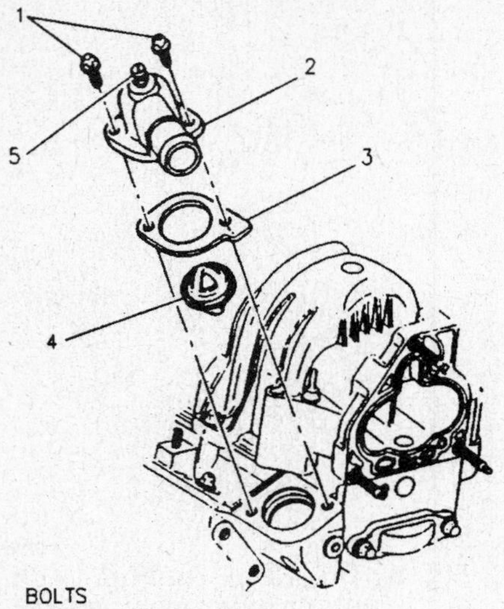

1 BOLTS
2 OUTLET NECK
3 GASKET
4 THERMOSTAT
5 BLEEDER VALVE

GC1089500245000X

Fig. 6 Thermostat & housing. Less supercharged engine

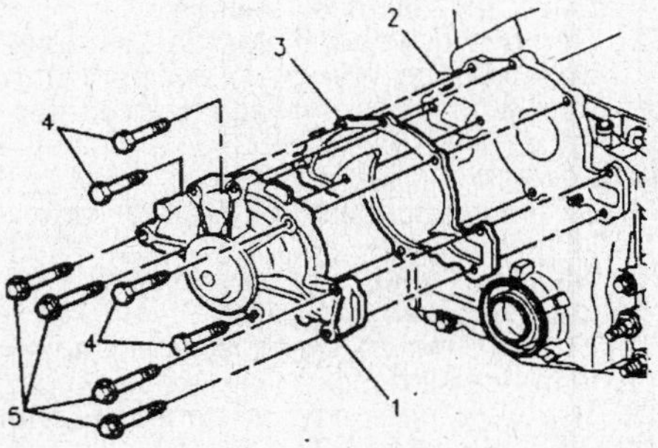

1 COOLANT PUMP
2 ENGINE FRONT COVER
3 GASKET
4 11 N·m (97 LB. IN.)
5 39 N·m (29 LB. FT.)

GC1089500247000X

Fig. 8 Water pump replacement

SUPERCHARGED ENGINE

1. Drain cooling system and remove drive belts as outlined under "Serpentine Drive Belt."
2. Position coil pack out of way and remove supercharger belt tensioner.
3. Remove engine mount and power steering pump.
4. Remove engine mount bracket and idler pulley.
5. Remove pulley and water pump, **Fig. 8.**

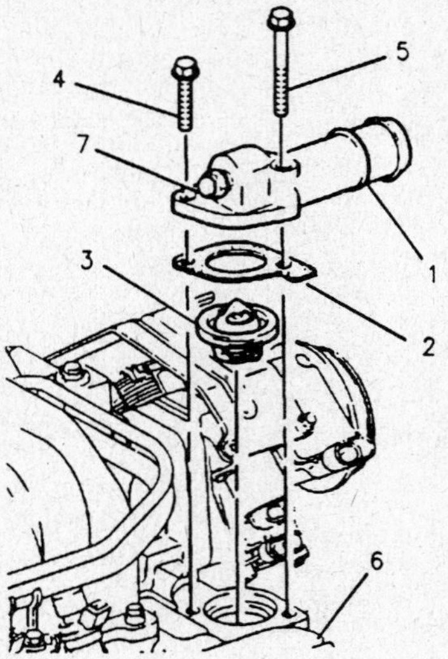

1 OUTLET
2 GASKET
3 THERMOSTAT
4 BOLT/SCREW
5 BOLT/SCREW
6 INTAKE MANIFOLD
7 BLEEDER VALVE

GC1089500246000X

Fig. 7 Thermostat & housing. Supercharged engine

6. Reverse procedure to install.

RADIATOR

REPLACE

1. Raise and support vehicle.
2. Remove lower air dam and drain cooling system.
3. Install lower air dam and lower vehicle.
4. Remove upper tie bar.
5. Disconnect cooling fan electrical connectors.
6. Remove left and righthand cooling fans.
7. Disconnect coolant level sensor electrical connector.
8. Disconnect coolant recovery hose from radiator filler neck.
9. Remove upper and lower radiator hoses from radiator.
10. Remove condenser to radiator mounting bolts.
11. Remove transaxle cooler lines from radiator.
12. **On models equipped with engine cooler lines,** disconnect from radiator.
13. **On all models,** remove radiator from vehicle.
14. Reverse procedure to install.

FUEL PUMP

REPLACE

1. Drain fuel tank to at least ¾ of a tank.
2. Relieve fuel system pressure as outlined under "Precautions."
3. Remove spare tire cover, jack and tire.
4. Pull back trunk liner and remove fuel sender access panel.
5. Disconnect quick-connect fittings from fuel pump as shown in **Fig. 9.**

6. Disconnect fuel pump electrical connectors.
7. Using retaining ring removal tool No. J-39765, or equivalent, remove fuel pump retaining ring.
8. Pull fuel pump straight up and hold while pumping fuel from reservoir. **When removing fuel pump from fuel tank, reservoir bucket on fuel pump is full of fuel. It must be tipped slightly during removal to avoid damage to float assembly. Place remaining fuel into an approved container once fuel pump is removed from fuel tank. Discard fuel pump assembly gasket.**
9. Reverse procedure to install.

FUEL FILTER

REPLACE

1. Relieve fuel system pressure as outlined under " Precautions."
2. Raise and support vehicle.
3. Disconnect quick-connect fittings from fuel filter shown in **Fig. 9.**
4. Disconnect fuel feed pipe from fuel filter and drain any remaining fuel into an approved container.
5. Remove fuel filter.
6. Reverse procedure to install.

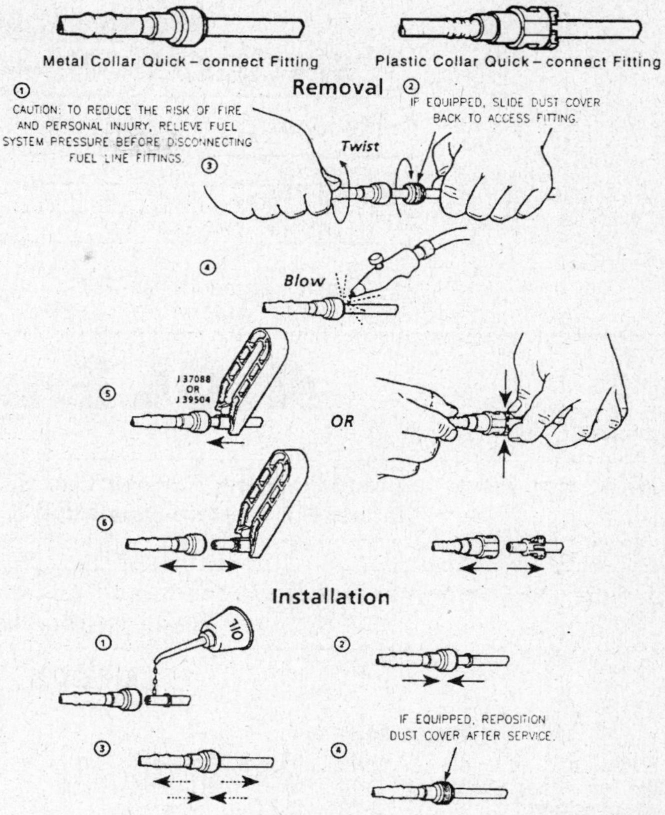

Fig. 9 Servicing fuel line quick-connect fittings

TIGHTENING SPECIFICATIONS

Component	Torque/Ft. Lbs.
Alternator Support Through Alternator	36
Alternator Support To Cylinder Head	11
Coolant Temperature Sensor	15
Drive Belt Tensioner To Cylinder Block Bracket	37
Engine Mount Front (Torque Axis) Through Bolt	64
Engine Mount Rear (Torque Axis) Through Bolt	52
Engine Mount Rear (Torque Axis) To Cylinder Block	65
Exhaust Pipe To Manifold	18
Flywheel Cover	22①
Flywheel To Crankshaft	11②
Fuel Feed & Return Pipes	22
Heater Hose Fitting To Intake	11
Ignition Module To Alternator	18
Oil Cooler Adapter Connector	37
Oil Pan Drain Plug	22
Power Steering Hoses	20
Power Steering Mounts	20
Starter Motor	32
Supercharger Bolt/Stud	17
Supercharger Bypass Valve Nut	72①
Thermostat Housing	15
Torque Converter To Flywheel	46
Transaxle Oil Cooler	20
Transaxle To Cylinder Block	55

Continued

TIGHTENING SPECIFICATIONS—Continued

Component	Torque/Ft. Lbs.
Upper Tie Bar	89
Water Pump Pulley	108①
Water Pump To Front Cover	③

① — Inch lbs.
② — Tighten an additional 50.°
③ — Refer to "Water Pump, Replace."

4.0L Engine

NOTE: On Air Bag Equipped Models, Refer To " Air Bag System Precautions" Located In The Front Of This Manual For System Disarming & Arming Procedures.

NOTE: Refer To "Computer Relearn Procedures " Located In The Front Of This Manual For Computer Relearn Procedures.

INDEX

PRECAUTIONS

AIR BAG SYSTEMS

Refer to "Air Bag System Precautions" in the front of this manual for system disarming and arming procedures.

BATTERY GROUND CABLE

Prior to service, disconnect battery ground cable and isolate as required.

CAMSHAFT TIMING & TIMING CHAIN

With the timing chain removed or loosened, avoid turning the camshaft or crankshaft. If movement is required, exercise extreme caution to avoid valve damage caused by piston contact.

FUEL SYSTEM PRESSURE RELIEF

After relieving fuel system pressure, a small amount of fuel may be released when servicing fuel pipes or connections. In order to reduce the risk of personal injury, cover fuel pipe fittings with shop towel before disconnecting to catch any fuel that may leak.

1. Loosen fuel filler cap to relieve tank pressure.
2. Connect suitable fuel pressure gauge to fuel pressure test connector. **Wrap a shop towel around connection to avoid fuel spillage.**
3. Insert bleed hose into a suitable container and open valve to bleed system.
4. Drain any fuel remaining in fuel gauge into suitable container.

COMPRESSION PRESSURE

When checking compression, the lowest cylinder must be within 70 percent of the highest cylinder with a minimum pressure of 100 psi. Perform compression test with engine at normal operating temperature, spark plugs removed and throttle wide open.

ENGINE MOUNT

REPLACE

1. Install engine support fixture tool No. J-28467-A, core support wedges tool No. J-28467-350 and core support bar tool No. J-28467-330, or equivalents, lifting devices to engine.
2. Remove windshield washer reservoir.

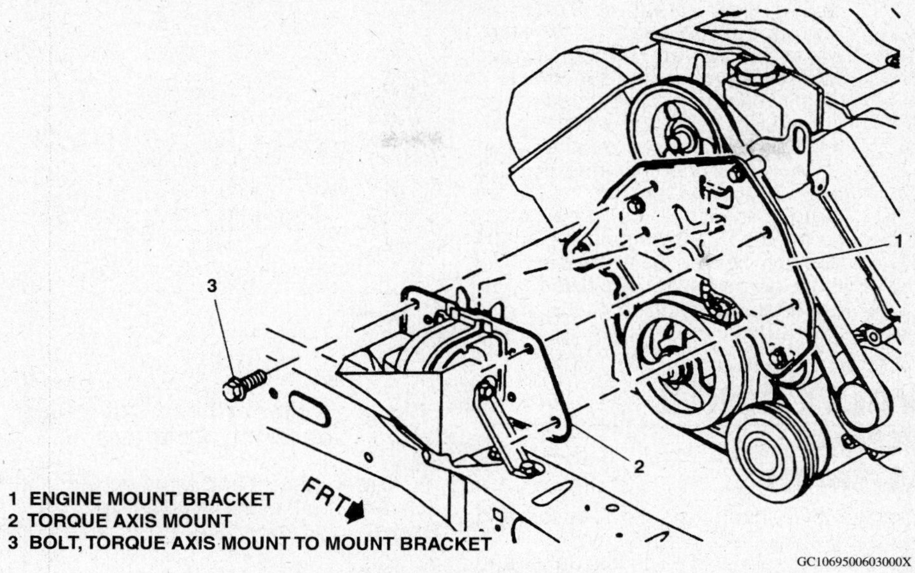

Fig. 1 Front engine mount

3. Remove engine mount to body through bolt.
4. Remove torque axis engine mount from engine mount bracket, **Fig. 1.**
5. Raise and support vehicle.
6. Remove righthand front tire and wheel assembly.
7. Remove splash shield from wheelwell.
8. Remove lower center air deflector.
9. Remove lefthand transaxle mount to cradle through bolt.
10. Remove lower retaining bolt/nut from engine mount bracket.
11. Remove power steering pump and set aside.
12. Raise engine with support fixture.
13. Remove engine mount bracket from engine.
14. Remove torque axis mount from body.
15. Reverse procedure to install.

ENGINE

REPLACE

1. Drain cooling system and oil from crankcase.
2. Relieve fuel system pressure as outlined under " Precautions."
3. Recover refrigerant as outlined under "Air Conditioning. "
4. Disconnect fuel feed and return lines.
5. Disconnect vacuum harness from rear of intake.
6. Disconnect engine wire harness at bulkhead.
7. Disconnect coolant hoses from overflow reservoir.
8. Remove upper radiator hose from coolant crossover.
9. Remove lower radiator hose at thermostat housing.
10. Disconnect upper transaxle cooler hose at radiator.
11. Disconnect lower transaxle cooler hose at transaxle.
12. Remove heater hoses from coolant pipes at rear of engine.
13. Disconnect brake booster vacuum hose.
14. Remove shift control cable retaining bracket from transaxle.
15. Remove shift control cable from lever on transaxle.
16. Remove vacuum reservoir.
17. Disconnect vacuum and electrical connectors at cruise control servo.
18. Install engine support fixture.
19. Disconnect positive battery cable at junction block.
20. Remove through bolt from front engine mount.
21. Remove front engine mount bolts from front plate.
22. Disconnect battery ground cable from engine block.
23. Raise and support vehicle.
24. Remove both front wheels.
25. Remove left and right splash shields.
26. Disconnect steering gear electrical connector.
27. Remove cotter pin from lefthand and righthand ball joints and separate ball joints from steering knuckle.
28. Remove hub assembly from righthand and lefthand axle shafts.
29. Remove exhaust pipe to exhaust manifold mounting bolts and nuts and separate exhaust system from exhaust manifold.
30. Remove engine oil cooler hoses at adapter.
31. Remove engine to transaxle braces at oil pan, then at front and rear of engine.
32. Remove flywheel cover.
33. Remove flywheel to converter bolts, then transaxle to engine bolts.
34. Remove oil filter, then oil filter adapter from engine block.
35. Disconnect A/C hose and muffler from rear of A/C compressor.
36. Position cradle support table under engine and lower vehicle.
37. Remove lefthand transaxle mount.
38. Support front of lower engine with a block of wood.
39. Release engine support.
40. Remove engine cradle bolts.
41. Raise vehicle and remove engine and transaxle assembly from under vehicle.
42. Reverse procedure to install. **When refilling cooling system refer to "Cooling System Bleed."**

INTAKE MANIFOLD

REPLACE

1. Remove intake manifold cover.
2. Relieve fuel system pressure as outlined under " Precautions."
3. Remove air intake duct from throttle body, then transaxle vent hose and shift cable.
4. Disconnect throttle position sensor and IAC valve connectors.
5. Disconnect accelerator and cruise control cables. Position cables out of way.
6. Remove lefthand spark plug wires and position out of way.
7. Drain cooling system into a suitable container.
8. Disconnect throttle body coolant hoses and surge tank pipe, then EGR pipe and crankcase ventilation pipe at throttle body spacer.
9. Disconnect intake manifold brake booster vacuum hose.
10. Disconnect righthand cylinder head fuel rail ground wire.
11. Disconnect fuel rail quick connect fittings and fuel rail EGR valve bracket.
12. Disconnect intake manifold PCV hose and injector harness main connector.
13. Remove mounting bolts, studs and intake manifold.
14. Reverse procedure to install. When tightening bolts and studs, start at center and work outward in circular pattern.

EXHAUST MANIFOLD

REPLACE

LEFTHAND

1. Remove drive belt as outlined under "Serpentine Drive Belt."
2. Remove alternator upper retaining bolt.
3. Raise and support vehicle.
4. Remove righthand wheelwell splash shield and lower center air deflector.
5. Remove alternator rear bracket and lower mounting bolt and position alternator aside.
6. Remove exhaust manifold to crossover exhaust pipe bolts.
7. Disconnect oxygen sensor electrical connector.
8. Remove exhaust manifold to cylinder head mounting bolts.
9. Remove exhaust manifold and gasket from cylinder head.
10. Remove oxygen sensor from manifold.
11. Reverse procedure to install, coat oxygen sensor threads with suitable high temperature anti-seize lubricant prior to installation.

RIGHTHAND

1. Raise and support vehicle. Support catalytic converter.

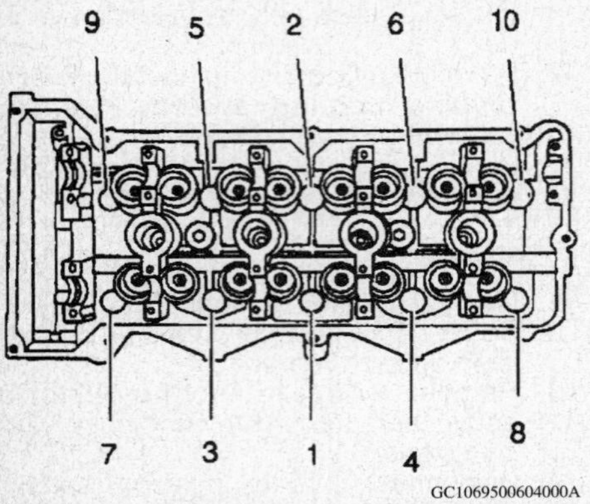

Fig. 2 Cylinder head tightening sequence. Righthand

2. Remove mounting bolts and exhaust manifold Y pipe from front of catalytic converter and crossover exhaust pipe, then crossover pipe.
3. Disconnect oxygen sensor electrical connector.
4. Remove mounting nuts, exhaust manifold and gasket, then oxygen sensor.
5. Reverse procedure to install. Coat oxygen sensor threads with suitable high temperature anti-seize lubricant prior to installation.

CYLINDER HEAD

REPLACE

Align all timing marks before removing cylinder heads and timing chains. Especially if only removing one cylinder head.

Do not turn engine with timing chains loose or removed. Valve damage may occur.

1. Remove engine as outlined under "Engine, Replace."
2. Remove intake manifold as outlined under "Intake Manifold, Replace."
3. Remove valve covers as outlined under "Valve Cover, Replace."
4. Remove crankshaft damper as outlined under "Crankshaft Damper, Replace."
5. Remove front cover as outlined under "Front Cover, Replace."
6. Remove oil pump as outlined under "Oil Pump, Replace."
7. Remove chain tensioner from timing chain, then cam sprocket. Timing chain should remain in crankcase.
8. Remove timing chain guides and lever. Access for retaining bolts is through plugs at front of cylinder head.
9. Remove water crossover.
10. Remove exhaust manifold.
11. Remove bolts, cylinder head and gasket.
12. Reverse procedure to install, noting the following:
    a. Clean any remaining gasket material from cylinder head and cylinder head mating surface. **Extreme care must be taken when cleaning aluminum gasket surfaces to prevent damage to sealing surfaces. Use only plastic, wood or dull gasket scrapers. Chemical agents can be used to dissolve gasket materials, follow manufacturers recommendations.**
    b. Coat washers and underside of cylinder head bolts with suitable anti-seize lubricant, prior to installation.
    c. Using sequence shown in **Figs. 2 and 3, torque** ten M11 cylinder head bolts to 22 ft. lbs., then tighten an additional 60°, then another 60° and final tighten an additional 60.°
    d. **On all models, torque** three cylinder head M6 bolts to 9 ft. lbs.

VALVE COVER

REPLACE

LEFTHAND

1. Remove intake manifold cover and partially drain cooling system.
2. Remove oil level dipstick, tube and upper radiator hose.
3. Disconnect lefthand spark plug wires.
4. Remove upper core support brace.
5. Remove PCV fresh air tube from valve cover, then air intake hose and EGR outlet pipe.
6. Remove water pump drive belt shield and drive belt, then belt tensioner and water pump pulley using tool No. J-38825 or equivalent.
7. Remove retainer screws and camshaft seal.
8. Remove valve cover mounting bolts.
9. Move cam drive end of valve cover up and pivot entire cover around water pump drive shaft. Continue moving cover upward and pivoting such that edge of cover closely follows lefthand edge of intake manifold cover. Remove cover, **Fig. 4.**
10. Reverse procedure to install, noting the following:
    a. Use fingers to guide valve cover up over cylinder head edge. **Use care to prevent valve cover seal exposed section from being damaged by cylinder head casting edge.**
    b. Work cover into position by allowing cover top edge to follow intake manifold lefthand edge.
    c. **When refilling cooling system refer to " Cooling System Bleed."**

RIGHTHAND

1. Remove intake manifold cover.
2. Remove vacuum reservoir.
3. Remove cruise control servo and position aside.
4. Disconnect DIS ignition module wiring connectors and remove DIS module mounting bolts.
5. Remove DIS ignition module and spark plug wires from valve cover.
6. Remove PCV valve and fuel vapor canister purge solenoid from valve cover.
7. Raise and support vehicle.
8. Disconnect knock sensor, vehicle speed sensor and power steering pressure switch electrical connectors.

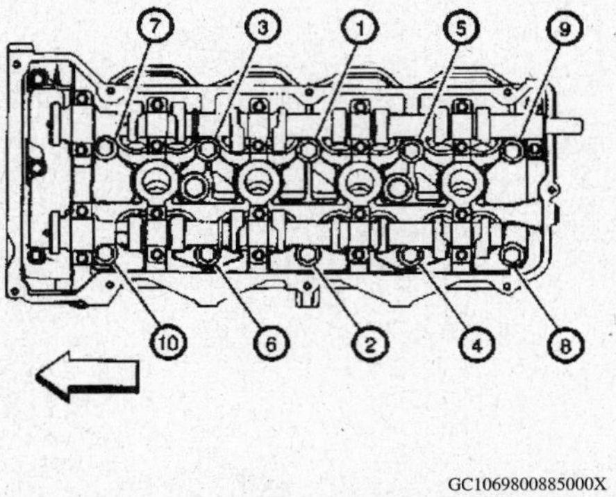

Fig. 3 Cylinder head tightening sequence. Lefthand

9. Lower vehicle and remove wiring harness retainers from cover.
10. Remove mounting bolts and valve cover.
11. Reverse procedure to install.

VALVE CLEARANCE SPECIFICATIONS

These engines are equipped with hydraulic valve lifters. Valve clearance should be zero.

VALVE ADJUSTMENT

These engines are equipped with hydraulic valve lifters. No adjustment is required.

VALVE GUIDES

Check valve stem to valve guide clearance. Clearance should be .005 inch or less. Service valves are available in standard size (.235 inch). If clearance is excessive and new standard size valve stem will not bring clearance within specifications, cylinder head must be replaced.

HYDRAULIC LIFTERS

REPLACE

If camshafts remain in cylinder head, some valves will always be held open and cylinder head cannot be set on workbench with cylinder head face down. Damage to valves and/or gasket surface will result.

Do not mix cam bearing caps between positions or between heads. Each cap must be reassembled in the position from which it was removed and in the original orientation (arrow points toward front of engine).

1. Remove cylinder head as outlined under "Cylinder Head, Replace."
2. Place matchmarks on all bearing caps.
3. Remove intake and exhaust camshafts by alternately loosening each cam bearing cap bolt two turns at a time until valve spring pressure is completely released.

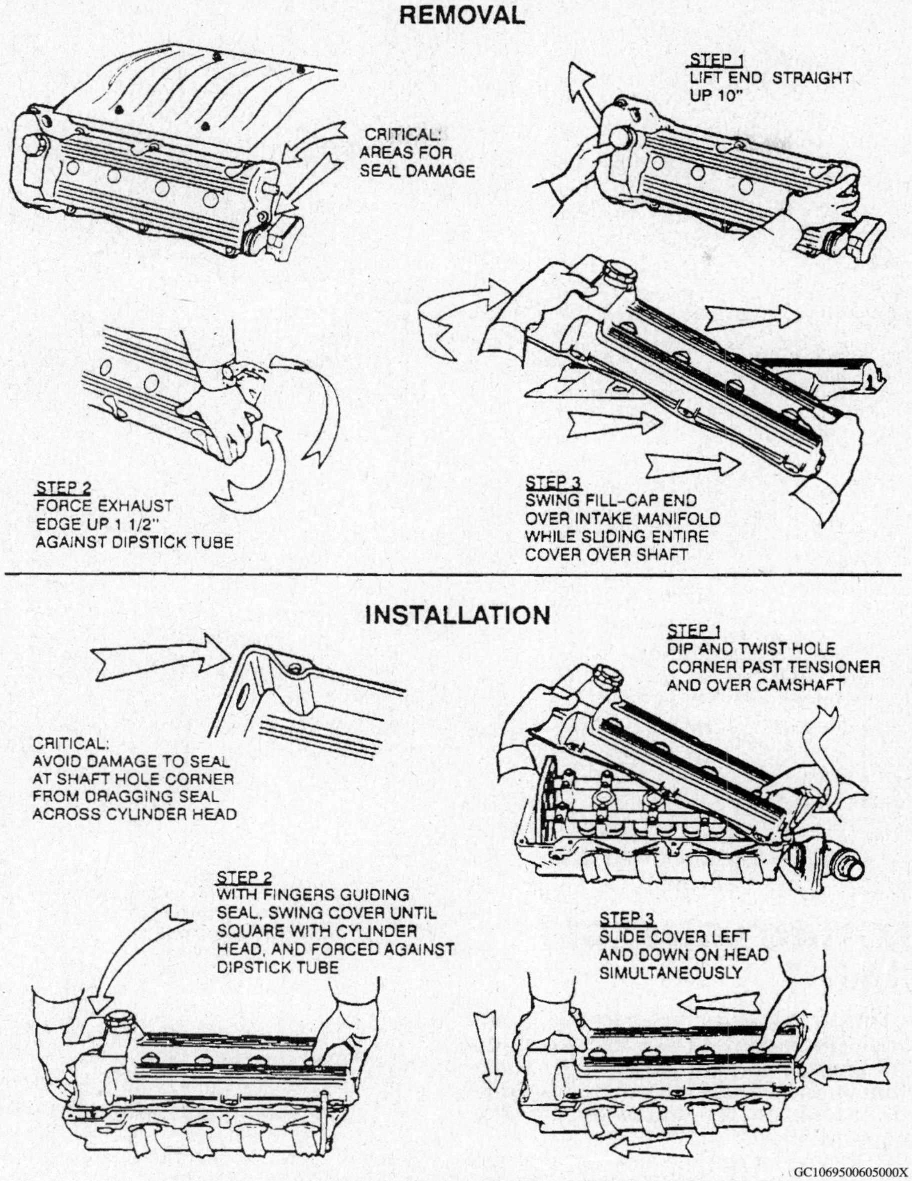
REMOVAL
STEP 1
LIFT END STRAIGHT UP 10"
CRITICAL: AREAS FOR SEAL DAMAGE
STEP 2
FORCE EXHAUST EDGE UP 1 1/2" AGAINST DIPSTICK TUBE
STEP 3
SWING FILL-CAP END OVER INTAKE MANIFOLD WHILE SLIDING ENTIRE COVER OVER SHAFT
INSTALLATION
STEP 1
DIP AND TWIST HOLE CORNER PAST TENSIONER AND OVER CAMSHAFT
CRITICAL: AVOID DAMAGE TO SEAL AT SHAFT HOLE CORNER FROM DRAGGING SEAL ACROSS CYLINDER HEAD
STEP 2
WITH FINGERS GUIDING SEAL, SWING COVER UNTIL SQUARE WITH CYLINDER HEAD, AND FORCED AGAINST DIPSTICK TUBE
STEP 3
SLIDE COVER LEFT AND DOWN ON HEAD SIMULTANEOUSLY
GC1069500605000X

Fig. 4 Lefthand valve cover replacement

4. Remove valve lifters and arrange them so they may be installed in their original position.
5. Reverse procedure to install, noting the following:
   a. Lubricate camshaft bearing journals with engine oil prior to installation.
   b. Alternately tighten camshaft bearing cap bolts one turn at a time to specifications.

CRANKSHAFT DAMPER

REPLACE

1. Release accessory drive belt tension.
2. Remove torque axis engine mount as outlined under " Engine Mount, Replace."
3. Remove brace between engine oil pan and transaxle case and install flywheel holder tool No. J-39411, or equivalent.
4. Remove crankshaft damper mounting bolt.
5. Lower engine at support fixture to obtain clearance for pulling tool J-38416-A, or equivalent, below body rail.
6. Install pilot tool No. J-39344-2, or equivalent, into end of crankshaft.
7. Install pulling tool No. J-38416-A, or equivalent, onto balancer and remove balancer from end of crankshaft.
8. Reverse procedure to install, noting the following:
   a. Thoroughly clean balancer bolt threads.
   b. Apply clean engine oil to balancer bolt threads prior to installation.
   c. Tighten bolt to specification.

FRONT COVER

REPLACE

1. Remove accessory drive belt as outlined under "Serpentine Drive Belt."
2. Remove crankshaft damper as outlined under "Crankshaft Damper, Replace."
3. Remove drive belt tensioner and idler pulley.
4. Remove mounting bolts, front cover and gasket.
5. Reverse procedure to install. Front cover seal is reusable, do not discard unless seal is damaged.

FRONT COVER SEAL

REPLACE

1. Remove crankshaft damper as outlined under "Crankshaft Damper, Replace."
2. Use a suitable flat-bladed screwdriver to pry seal out of front cover, **Fig. 5.**
3. Reverse procedure to install, noting the following:
   a. Lubricate seal lips with clean engine oil prior to installation.
   b. Use seal installer tool No. J-38818, or equivalent, to push seal into front cover until tool bottoms on cover.

TIMING CHAIN

REPLACE

CAMSHAFT PRIMARY DRIVE CHAIN

1. Remove front cover as outlined under "Front Cover, Replace."
2. Remove oil pump as outlined under "Oil Pump, Replace. "
3. Remove valve covers as outlined under "Valve Cover, Replace."
4. Remove timing chain tensioners and camshaft sprockets.
5. Remove secondary drive chains as outlined under " Camshaft Secondary Drive Chain."
6. Remove bolt from intermediate shaft sprocket and slide gears and primary drive chain off crankshaft and intermediate shaft, **Fig. 6.**
7. Reverse procedure to install. Set camshaft timing as outlined under "Setting Camshaft Timing."

CAMSHAFT SECONDARY DRIVE CHAIN

1. Remove front cover as outlined under "Front Cover, Replace."
2. Remove valve covers as outlined under "Valve Cover, Replace."
3. Remove bolts and tensioners.
4. Remove chain guide access plugs noting O-ring seal.
5. Remove camshaft position sensor.
6. Remove mounting bolts and chain guides
7. Remove mounting bolts and slide sprockets off camshafts.
8. Remove sprockets and secondary drive chain together. Leave intermediate sprocket in place.
9. Reverse procedure to install, set camshaft timing as outlined under "Setting Camshaft Timing."

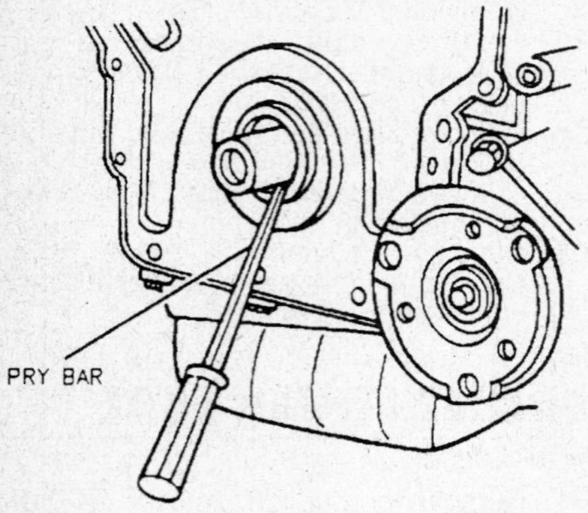

GC1069500606000X

Fig. 5 Front cover seal removal

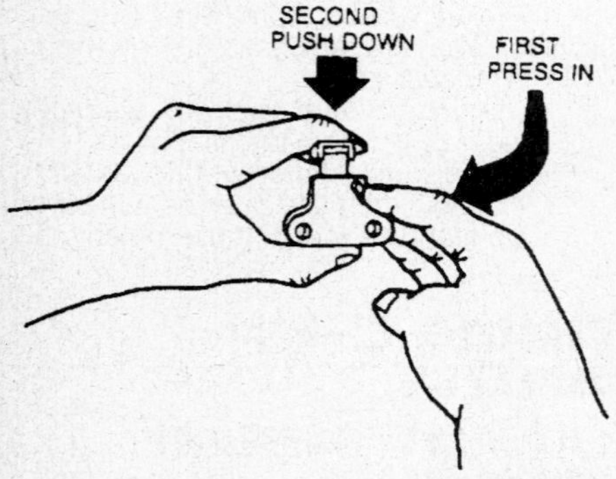

GC1069500609000X

Fig. 8 Rotating tensioner release lever

TIMING CHAIN TENSIONER

REPLACE

REMOVAL

1. Remove front cover as outlined under "Front Cover, Replace."
2. Remove transaxle to oil pan brace.
3. Lock flywheel with flywheel holder tool No. J-39411, or equivalent,
4. Remove mounting bolts and tensioner, **Fig. 7.**

INSTALLATION

1. Rotate ratchet release lever counterclockwise and hold, **Fig. 8.**
2. Collapse tensioner retainer shoe and hold.
3. Release ratchet lever and slowly release shoe pressure.
4. Hold tensioner shoe at first click hold, insert suitable pin through hole and release lever, **Fig. 9.**
5. Ensure release lever is facing you, install tensioner and bolts. Tighten to specifications.
6. Remove retaining pin allowing tensioner shoe to extend.
7. Remove flywheel holding tool and install pan brace.
8. Install front cover.

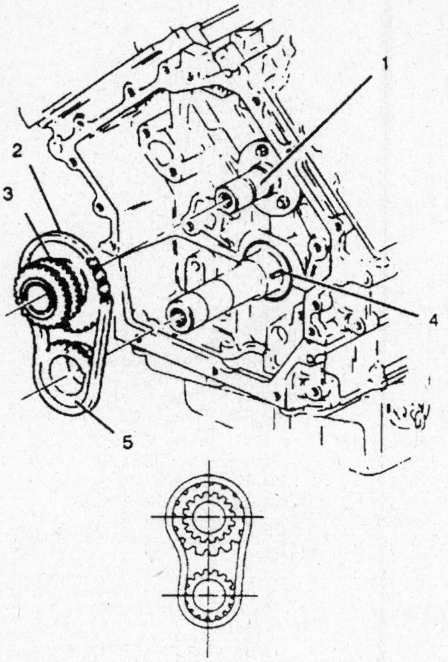

1 INTERMEDIATE SHAFT
2 PRIMARY CHAIN
3 INTERMEDIATE SHAFT SPROCKET
4 CRANKSHAFT SPROCKET KEY
5 SPROCKET

GC1069500607000X

Fig. 6 Primary drive chain removal

SETTING CAMSHAFT TIMING

This engine is an interference fit engine. The engine is not free spinning and pistons will strike valves if crankshaft is rotated with camshaft drive disconnected or if camshafts are not properly timed.

1. Remove valve covers as outlined under "Valve Cover, Replace."
2. Remove front engine mount as outlined under "Engine Mount, Replace."
3. Support front of engine and remove front cover as outlined under "Front Cover, Replace."
4. Remove three chain tensioners. Chain tensioners may remain in their installed position, but must be fully retracted.
5. Remove oil pump as outlined under "Oil Pump, Replace."
6. Install crankshaft sprocket drive key. If necessary, tap into place with suitable small hammer until key bottoms in shaft.
7. Using suitable socket, rotate crankshaft until piston No. 1 is at Top Dead Center (TDC) and sprocket drive key is at approximately one o'clock position.
8. Align crankshaft and intermediate shaft sprockets and install with primary drive chain, **Fig. 10.** Rotate crankshaft as necessary to engage crankshaft key in sprocket without changing timing marks relationship.
9. Install bolt and tighten intermediate sprocket retainer bolt to specification.
10. Install primary chain tensioner and release tensioner shoe as outlined under "Timing Chain Tensioner, Replace."
11. Lock crankshaft into position with flywheel holding tool No. J-39411 or equivalent.
12. If necessary, install secondary camshaft drive chain guides and access plugs.
13. Route lefthand cylinder head secondary drive chain over inner row of intermediate shaft teeth and chain guide.
14. Install lefthand exhaust cam sprocket to chain so camshaft drive pin engages sprocket notch marked LE. There should be no slack in lower chain section and cam drive pin must be perpendicular to cylinder head face. Camshaft drive pin must be perpendicular to cylinder head face.
15. Install intake cam sprocket into chain

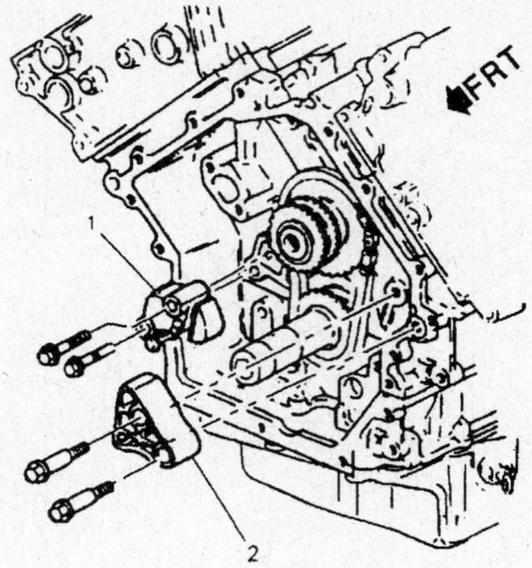

1 PRIMARY CHAIN TENSIONER
2 PRIMARY CHAIN GUIDE

GC1069500608000X

Fig. 7 Primary chain tensioner removal

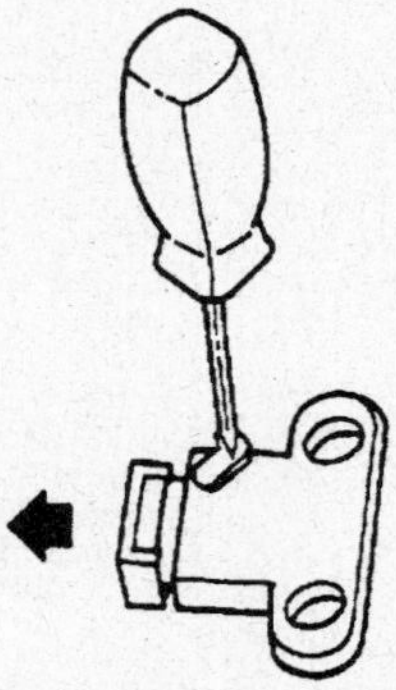

1 RELEASE TO FIRST CLICK
2 INSTALL LOCK PIN

GC1069500610000X

Fig. 9 Locking tensioner

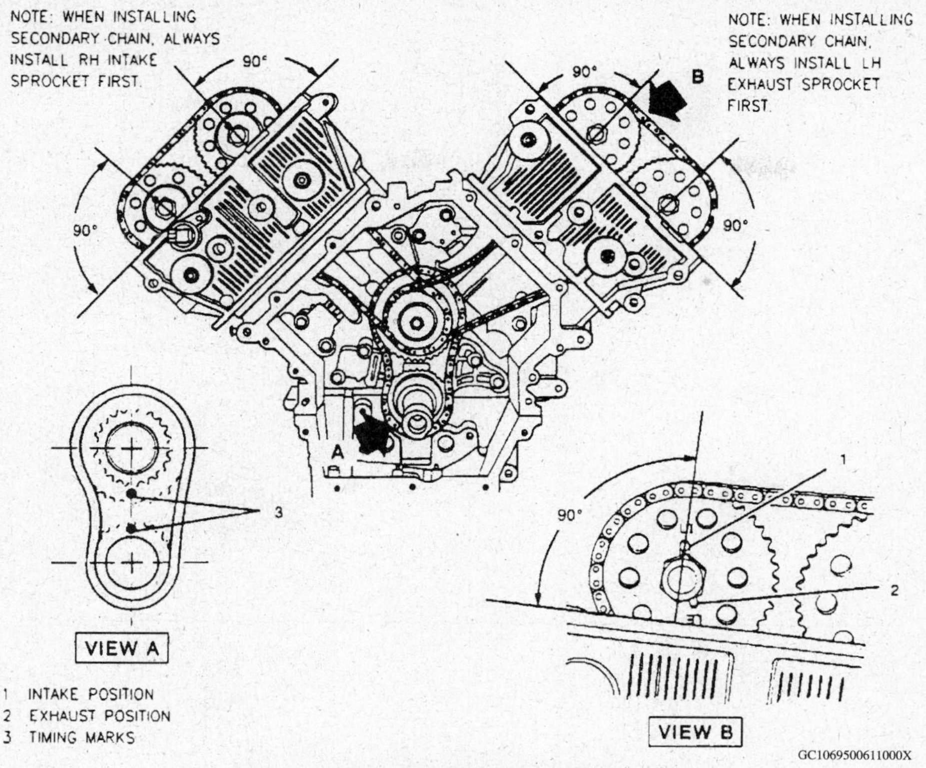

Fig. 10 Setting camshaft timing

so sprocket notch marked LI engages cam drive pin. Pin must be perpendicular to cylinder head face. A hex is cast into camshaft behind lobes for cylinder No. 2 so an open end wrench may be used to provide minor camshaft repositioning.

16. Loosely install intake and exhaust cam sprocket retainer bolts.
17. Install chain tensioner and release tension on shoe as outlined under "Timing Chain Tensioner, Replace."
18. Route secondary drive chain for right-hand cylinder head over outer row of intermediate shaft teeth.
19. Install righthand exhaust cam sprocket to chain so camshaft drive pin engages sprocket notch marked RI. There should be no slack in lower chain section and cam drive pin must be perpendicular to cylinder head face. Camshaft drive pin must be perpendicular to cylinder head face.
20. Install intake cam sprocket into chain so sprocket notch marked RE engages cam drive pin. Pin must be perpendicular to cylinder head face. A hex is cast into camshaft behind lobes for cylinder No. 1 so an open end wrench may be used to provide minor camshaft repositioning.
21. Ensure RE sprocket contains camshaft position sensor pickup and install camshaft position sensor.
22. Loosely install intake and exhaust cam sprocket retainer bolts.
23. Install chain tensioner and release tension on shoe as outlined under "Timing Chain Tensioner, Replace."
24. Install oil pump as outlined under "Oil Pump, Replace."
25. Install front cover as outlined under "Front Cover, Replace."
26. Install valve covers as outlined under "Valve Cover, Replace."
27. Install front engine mount as outlined under "Engine Mount, Replace."

CAMSHAFT

REPLACE

1. Remove valve cover as outlined under "Valve Cover, Replace."
2. Set engine at piston No. 1 TDC and align timing marks to correct position.
3. Secure cam sprocket to timing chain using tie-raps through cam sprocket holes. Use two tie-raps per sprocket. **Sprocket to chain relationship must be maintained throughout this procedure or camshaft timing will be lost and require further engine disassembly for timing.**
4. Working behind sprockets, install cam chain holder J-38822, or equivalent, so it is positioned between chain tensioner and chain guide, **Fig. 11.** Apply tension to tool by tightening tension adjusting screw. **When using cam chain holder tool on righthand cylinder bank it is necessary to remove wiper motor to gain clearance.**
5. Remove camshaft sprocket bolts. Note relative location of cam drive pins in ends of camshafts.
6. Work sprockets off camshaft using chain play.
7. Alternately loosening each cam bearing cap bolt two turns at a time until valve spring pressure is completely released. **Do not mix cam bearing caps between positions or between heads. Each cap must be reassembled in position from which it was removed and in original orientation (arrow points toward front of engine).**
8. Remove camshafts.
9. Reverse procedure to install.

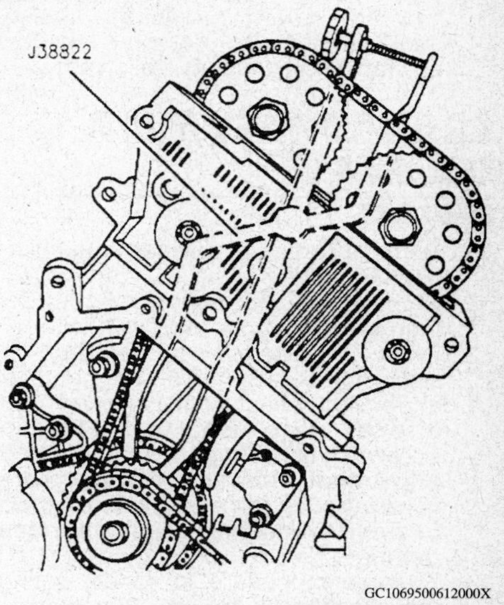

Fig. 11 Holding drive chain tension

PISTON & ROD ASSEMBLY

Refer to **Fig. 12,** for piston and rod assembly. Refer to **Fig. 13,** for piston installation.

MAIN & ROD BEARINGS

Shell type main bearings of steel backed aluminum are used at all positions. The upper and lower bearing halves are all interchangeable except for the upper bearing in the No. 3 position as this is the thrust bearing. Maximum crankshaft endplay is .019 inch.

With the crankcase disassembled the main bearing clearance can be measured using a suitable plastic gauging material as follows:

1. Wipe oil from crankshaft journals and bearing inserts.
2. Place plastic gauging material across journals to be measured.
3. Install lower crankcase and oil manifold.
4. Install main bearing bolts and using sequence shown in **Fig. 14.** tighten bolts to specifications.
5. Determine clearance by comparing width of flattened plastic gauging material with measurement increments on plastic gauging package.
6. If bearing clearance is greater than .0025 inch and new bearings do not reduce clearance to .0006–.0020 inch a

new crankshaft is required. Undersized bearings are not available and no crankshaft grinding is allowed.

CRANKSHAFT REAR OIL SEAL

REPLACE

1. Remove engine as outlined under "Engine, Replace."
2. Remove mounting bolts and transaxle, then mounting bolts and flywheel.
3. Drill a 1/8 inch hole in seal metal body of seal and use a suitable slide hammer to remove seal. **Seal removal can also be done using a flat-bladed screwdriver between seal lip and crankshaft. However, extreme care is required when using this method to avoid crankshaft sealing surface damage.**
4. Reverse procedure to install, noting the following:
   a. Place a small amount of RTV sealant at crankcase split line across end of upper and lower crankcase seal.
   b. Lubricate rear main seal with clean engine oil prior to installation.

OIL PAN

REPLACE

1. Remove transaxle as outlined in "Automatic Transmission/Transaxle" chapter.
2. Drain engine oil into a suitable container.
3. Remove exhaust crossover pipe.
4. Remove mounting bolts and oil pan.
5. Reverse procedure to install. Gasket is reusable unless damaged. **Do not remove gasket from oil pan groove unless replacement is required.** If replacing gasket do not expose new gasket to oil before inserting gasket into pan groove, gasket will expand when exposed to oil and will not stay in pan groove.

OIL PUMP

REPLACE

1. Remove front cover as outlined under "Front Cover, Replace."
2. Remove oil pump mounting bolts.
3. Remove oil pump and drive spacer, **Fig. 15.**
4. Reverse procedure to install.

OIL PUMP SERVICE

DISASSEMBLE

1. Remove drive spacer and screws holding pump housing halves together.
2. Remove inner (drive) and outer (driven) rotors out of housing and mark mating surfaces for assembly.
3. Remove pressure relief valve cap retaining pin and plug without damaging O-ring seal.
4. Slide pressure relief valve spring and piston out of bore.

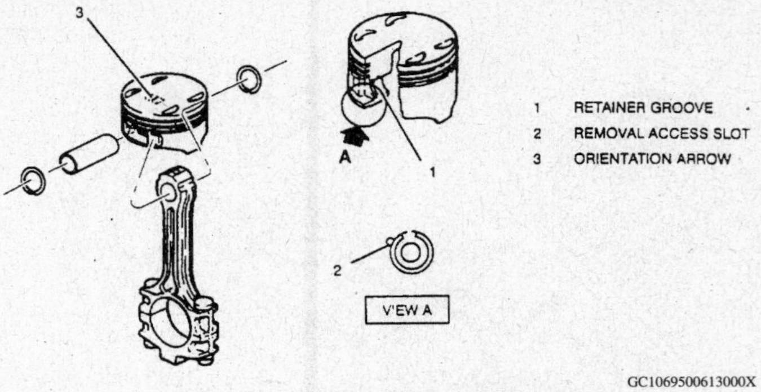

Fig. 12 Piston & rod assembly

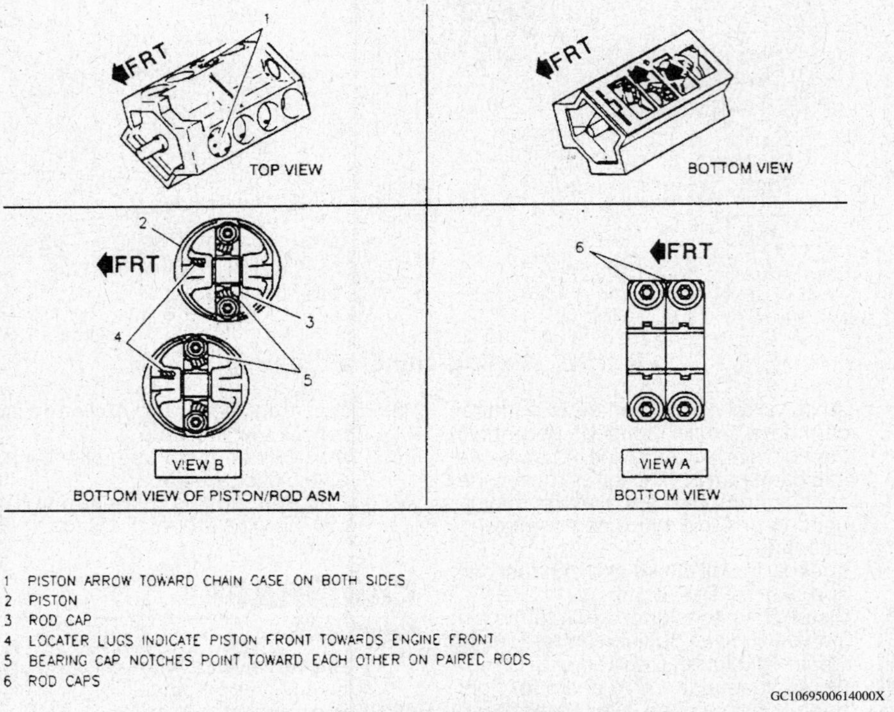

Fig. 13 Piston installation

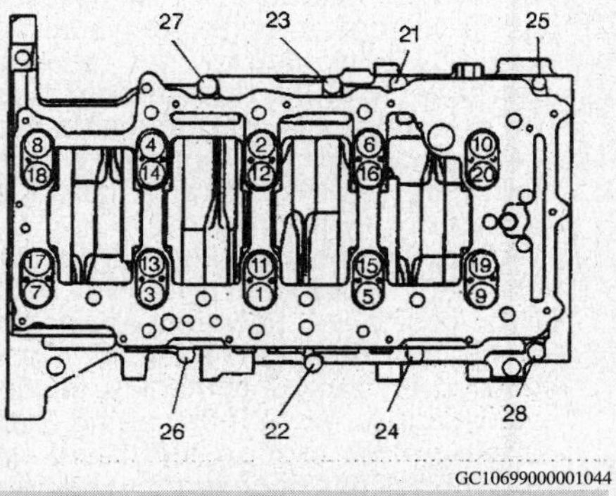

Fig. 14 Main bearing bolt tightening sequence

ASSEMBLE

1. Install inner and outer rotors to pump cover in same position as they were removed (dimples out). Chamfered edge of outer rotor must be face down (closest to engine rear).
2. Install pressure relief valve piston, spring and retaining cap in pump housing.
3. Pack housing with suitable white petroleum jelly.
4. Assemble housing and cover over locating dowel.
5. Insert a 3/8 inch drill in pump mounting hole on opposite side to aid in alignment of housing and cover.
6. Install screws and tighten to specifications.

SERPENTINE DRIVE BELT

BELT, REPLACE

1. Release belt tension and remove belt from power steering and alternator pulleys. Twist belt to get between tensioner and front cover and between

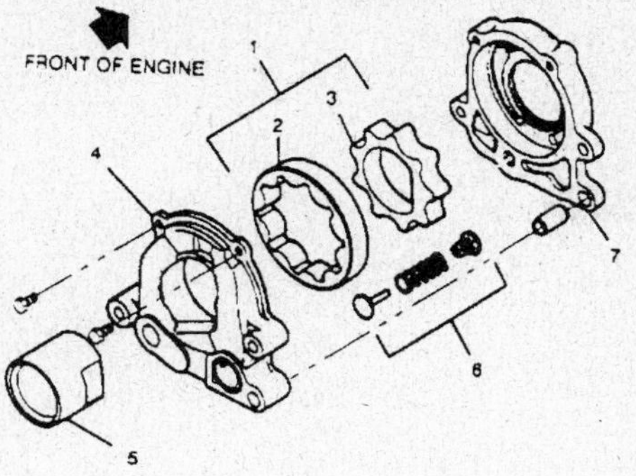

1 GEROTOR ASSEMBLY
2 OUTER GEAR
3 INNER GEAR
4 HOUSING
5 DRIVE SPACER
6 RELIEF VALVE
7 COVER

GC1069500616000X

Fig. 15 Exploded view of oil pump

power steering pulley and engine mount bracket.

2. Raise and support vehicle.
3. Turn wheel to extreme right and remove righthand splash shield.
4. Remove belt from crankshaft and A/C compressor pulleys. Twist belt to get between idler pulley and engine mount bracket.
5. Lower vehicle.
6. Twisting new belt to get past front cover, install belt around power steering pump pulley, **Fig. 16.** Allow belt to hang free.
7. Twist belt to get between tensioner and front cover, wrap belt around alternator.
8. Remove belt from power steering pulley and set aside.
9. Raise and support vehicle.
10. Twist belt to get between tensioner and front cover, wrap belt around crankshaft and A/C compressor pulleys.
11. Install right side splash shield and lower vehicle.
12. Position belt around power steering pulley and release tensioner.

COOLING SYSTEM BLEED

This engine does not require a cooling system bleed procedure. However, when refilling the cooling system on aluminum engines a special coolant solution along with GM coolant supplement (sealant) part No. 3634621, or equivalent, must be used. **Failure to add the sealant or the approved coolant solution could result in major engine damage.** When refilling cooling system add three pellets of engine coolant supplement (sealant) to lower radiator hose.

THERMOSTAT

REPLACE

1. Drain cooling system.
2. Remove air intake duct.

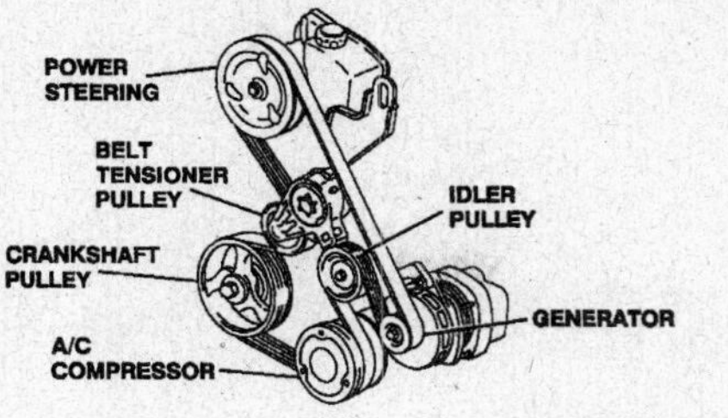

GC1069500815000X

Fig. 16 Serpentine drive belt routing

3. Disconnect radiator hose from thermostat housing.
4. Remove mounting bolts and thermostat housing, **Fig. 17.**
5. Remove thermostat from thermostat housing.
6. Reverse procedure install. **When refilling cooling system refer to "Cooling System Bleed."**

WATER PUMP

REPLACE

1. Drain engine coolant.
2. Remove air intake duct.
3. Remove coolant pump drive belt cover and belt.
4. Remove lower radiator and bypass hoses, then water pump cover.
5. Turn coolant remover/installer tool No. J-38816, or equivalent, clockwise and remove water pump, seal and gasket, **Fig. 18.**
6. Reverse procedure to install. **When refilling cooling system refer to "Cooling System Bleed."**

RADIATOR

REPLACE

1. Raise and support vehicle.
2. Remove lower air dam and drain cooling system.
3. Install lower air dam and lower vehicle.
4. Remove upper tie bar.
5. Disconnect cooling fan electrical connectors.
6. Remove left and righthand cooling fans.
7. Disconnect coolant level sensor electrical connector.
8. Disconnect coolant recovery hose from radiator filler neck.
9. Remove upper and lower radiator hoses from radiator.
10. Remove condenser to radiator mounting bolts.
11. Remove transaxle cooler lines from radiator.
12. Remove radiator from vehicle.
13. Reverse procedure to install. **When refilling cooling system refer to "Cooling System Bleed."**

FUEL PUMP

REPLACE

Refer to "Fuel Pump, Replace" in " 3800 Engine" section for fuel pump replacement procedure.

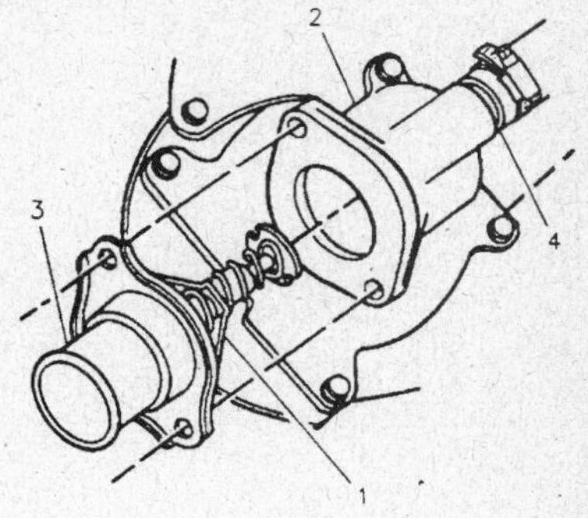

1 THERMOSTAT
2 THERMOSTAT HOUSING
3 COOLANT PUMP INLET
4 THERMOSTAT BY-PASS HOSE

GC1089500248000X

Fig. 17 Thermostat removal

FUEL FILTER

REPLACE

Refer to "Fuel Filter, Replace" in " 3800 Engine" section for fuel filter replacement procedure.

TECHNICAL SERVICE BULLETINS

LACK OF POWER & LOSS OF OIL PRESSURE

Some of these vehicles may exhibit low oil pressure which may display a "Low Oil Pressure" message and/or a Malfunction Indicator Lamp (MIL) illumination. These messages will illuminate at engine speeds over 1000 RPM.

This low oil pressure condition could be caused by particles from the engine manufacturing process sticking the oil pump relief valve or a loose harmonic balancer (crankshaft damper) bolt which will cause the oil pump not to spin.

To correct this condition, inspect crankshaft damper bolt tightening as outlined under "Tightening Specifications." If bolt is tightened correctly, use the following procedure to correct this condition.

1. Add an additional 10–12 quarts of engine oil to engine. This will completely immerse oil pump in oil.
2. Start engine and repeatedly open throttle from idle to 3500 RPM. This will allow pump to prime, cycling relief valve forces any debris from relief valve. **Do not rev engine above 3500 RPM, this will aerate engine oil and force excess engine oil into PCV system. Do not drive vehicle with additional oil in engine.**
3. After engine has sufficient oil pressure, drain crankcase.
4. Install drain plug and refill engine oil.

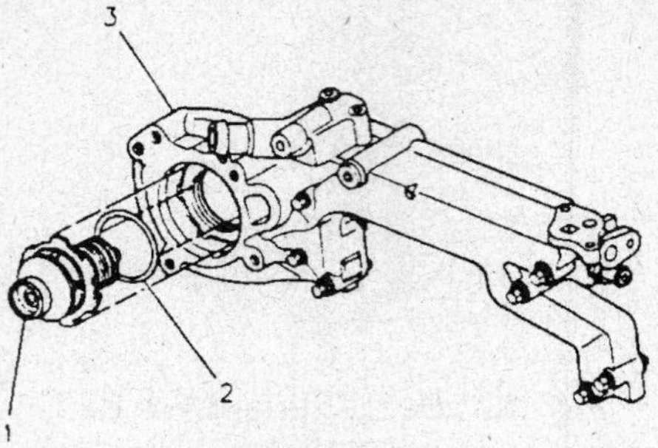

Fig. 18 Coolant pump removal

TIGHTENING SPECIFICATIONS

Component	Torque/Ft. lbs.
Belt Idler Pulley	37
Belt Tensioner	37
Camshaft Bearing Cap	108⑦
Camshaft Drive Chain Tensioner	18
Camshaft Sprocket Bolts	89
Connecting Rod Bearing Cap	⑥
Crankshaft Damper	37②
Cylinder Head	④
Exhaust Manifold To Cylinder Head	18
Flywheel To Converter	③
Front Cover	84⑦
Intake Manifold	84⑦
Intermediate Sprocket	44
Main Bearing Cap	15①
Oil Filter Adapter	12
Oil Manifold	84⑦
Oil Pan	84⑦
Oil Pump	7⑤
Oxygen Sensor	30
Primary Chain Tensioner	18
Upper Crankcase To Lower Crankcase	22
Valve Cover Bolts	84⑦

① — Tighten an additional 65.°

② — Tighten an additional 150.°

③ — Tighten an additional 50.°

④ — Refer to "Cylinder Head, Replace."

⑤ — Tighten an additional 35.°

⑥ — 1997, 18 ft. lbs. plus an additional 110°; 1998–99, 22 ft. lbs., then back to zero, then 18 ft. lbs. plus an additional 110.°

⑦ — Inch lbs.

Rear Suspension

INDEX

DESCRIPTION

These models utilize an independent rear suspension, **Fig. 1,** that is secured to the vehicle body at four points. Control arms, a stabilizer bar and adjustment links are connected to the rear suspension support assembly to provide side to side stability and to allow for rear toe adjustment.

The Electronic Level Control (ELC) system employs rear air adjustable shocks which are anchored at the control arms and allow the system to maintain proper vehicle ride height under various load conditions. The shocks are not manually adjustable and must be replaced if they lose their resistance or begin leaking fluid.

The rear wheel bearings have been integrated into the hubs to eliminate the necessity of adjustments and periodic maintenance. This integral hub and bearing also incorporates a wheel speed sensor ring for anti-lock brake operation.

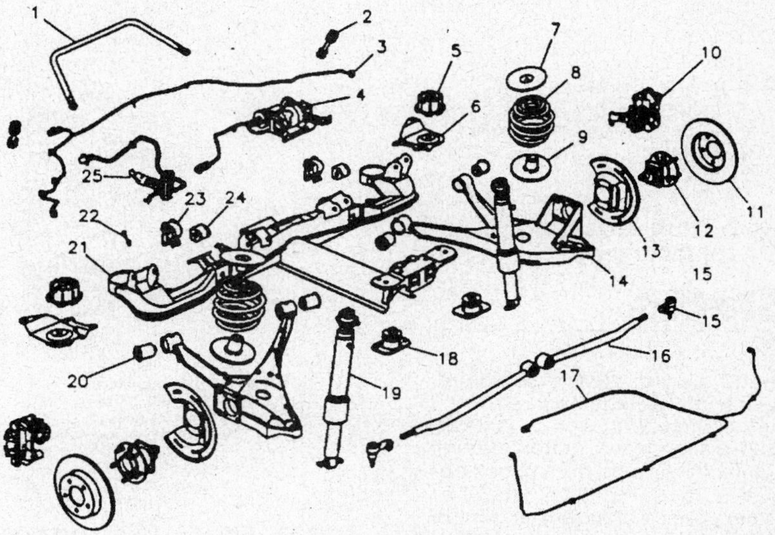

1 STABILIZER BAR
2 STABILIZER BAR LINK
3 ABS ELECTRICAL HARNESS
4 ELC COMPRESSOR
5 FORWARD BODY MOUNT
6 SUPPORT BRACKET
7 JOUNCE BUMPER
8 SPRING
9 LOWER SPRING INSULATOR
10 BRAKE CALIPER
11 BRAKE ROTOR
12 HUB AND BEARING
13 BRAKE SHIELD
14 CONTROL ARM
15 OUTER ADJUSTMENT LINK
16 INNER ADJUSTMENT LINK
17 ELC AIR LINE
18 REAR BODY MOUNT
19 SHOCK
20 CONTROL ARM BUSHING
21 REAR SUSPENSION SUPPORT ASSEMBLY
22 ELC HEIGHT SENSOR LINK
23 STABILIZER BAR CLAMP
24 STABILIZER BAR INSULATOR
25 ELC HEIGHT SENSOR

GC2039500107000X

Fig. 1 Exploded view of rear suspension

HUB & BEARING

REPLACE

1. Raise and support vehicle.
2. Remove wheel and disc brake caliper. **It is not necessary to disconnect hydraulic line from caliper; support caliper assembly from frame to prevent hydraulic line damage.**
3. Remove brake rotor and ABS sensor wire connector.
4. Remove bolts, lift hub and bearing assembly, then brake shield from control arm, **Fig. 2.**
5. Reverse procedure to install. Tighten bolts and wheel lug nuts to specifications.

WHEEL BEARING

ADJUST

Because the hub and bearing are integral parts, the bearing is non-adjustable and is not independently serviceable. If the bearing requires service, the entire hub assembly must be replaced.

REAR SUSPENSION

REPLACE

1. Raise and support vehicle. Remove rear wheels and disconnect exhaust system components as necessary to provide clearance.
2. Remove rear springs as outlined under "Coil Spring, Replace."
3. Remove brake calipers from control arms. **It is not necessary to disconnect hydraulic line at caliper; support caliper from frame to prevent hydraulic line damage.**
4. Disconnect parking brake cables at calipers and at rear suspension support assembly.
5. Disconnect rear suspension support assembly electrical connectors from electrical harness, then Electronic Level Control (ELC) electrical connector and vent hose.
6. Disconnect ELC air tube from ELC compressor and support rear suspension assembly with a suitable jack, **Fig. 3.**
7. Remove support bracket to body bolts from each side of vehicle.
8. Remove front and rear anchor bolts and lower rear suspension support assembly from vehicle.
9. Reverse procedure to install. Tighten mounting bolts and nuts to specifications.

SHOCK ABSORBER

REPLACE

1. Raise and support vehicle. Remove wheel and support control arm with a suitable jack stand.
2. Disconnect Electronic Level Control (ELC) air tube from shock absorber and remove shock to control arm bolts, **Fig. 4.**
3. Remove luggage compartment trim as necessary to gain access to shock absorber upper mounting nuts, then shock upper cover.
4. Remove upper mounting nuts and reinforcement, then shock absorber.
5. Reverse procedure to install. Tighten mounting bolts and nuts to specifications.

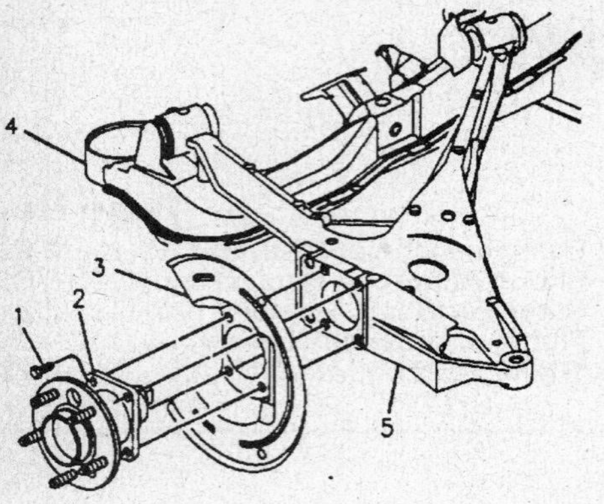

1 BOLT
2 HUB & BEARING
3 BRAKE SHIELD
4 REAR SUSPENSION SUPPORT ASSEMBLY
5 CONTROL ARM

GC2039500108000X

Fig. 2 Hub & bearing replacement

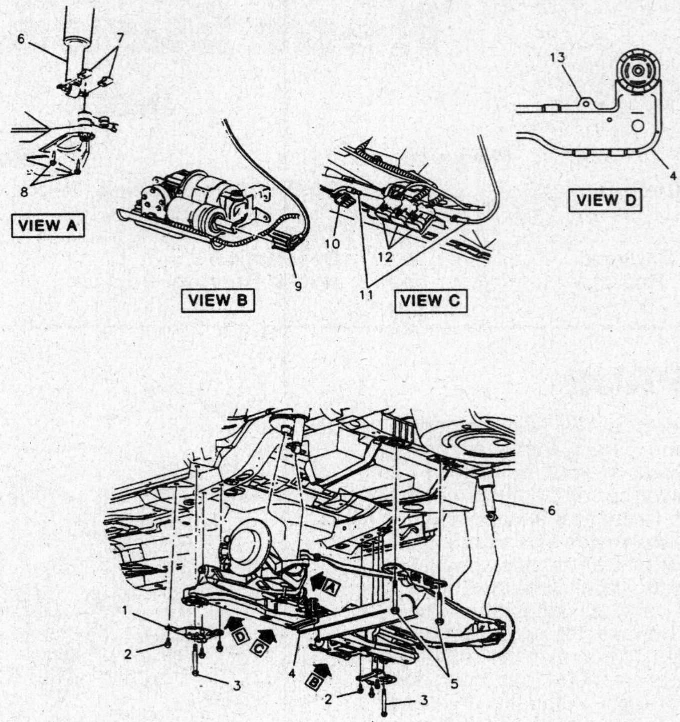

1 SUPPORT BRACKET
2 BOLT 86 N•m (63 LB. FT.)
3 BOLT 191 N•m (141 LB. FT.)
4 REAR SUSPENSION SUPPORT ASSEMBLY
5 BOLT 165 N•m (122 LB. FT.)
6 SHOCK
7 U-NUT
8 BOLT 24 N•m (18 LB. FT.)
9 ELC AIR LINE
10 ELC COMPRESSOR ELECTRICAL CONNECTOR
11 ELC COMPRESSOR VENT TUBE
12 ELECTRICAL CONNECTORS, (ELC HEIGHT SENSOR, FUEL PUMP, ABS HARNESS)
13 GAUGE HOLE

GC2039500109000X

Fig. 3 Rear suspension assembly replacement

COIL SPRING

REPLACE

1. Raise and support vehicle so control arm hangs freely. Remove wheel.
2. Support control arm with a suitable jack and disconnect Electronic Level Control (ELC) air tube from shock absorber.
3. Disconnect shock absorber at control arm and remove cotter pin and slotted nut securing adjustment link to knuckle.
4. Using universal steering linkage puller tool No. J-24319-B, or equivalent, separate adjustment link from knuckle and slowly lower control arm until it bottoms on rear suspension support assembly.
5. Pry under lower coil spring insulator and remove spring with insulator, **Fig. 5;** then, if necessary, remove jounce bumper by pulling downward.
6. Reverse procedure to install. Tighten all bolts and nuts to specifications.

CONTROL ARM

REPLACE

1. Remove rear suspension support assembly as outlined under " Rear Suspension, Replace."
2. If lefthand control arm is being replaced, remove Electronic Level Control (ELC) height sensor link.
3. Remove stabilizer link bolt and nut and disconnect ABS electrical connector.
4. Remove hub and bearing assembly as outlined under " Hub & Bearing, Replace," then bolt and nut securing control arm to rear suspension support assembly.
5. Reverse procedure to install, noting the following:
   a. Tighten control arm nuts with vehicle weight resting on rear wheels.
   b. Tighten all bolts and nuts to specifications.

CONTROL ARM BUSHING

REPLACE

REMOVAL

1. Remove control arm as outlined under "Control Arm, Replace," and assemble bushing replacement tools as shown in **Fig. 6.**
2. Tighten nut until bushing is driven from control arm and remove bushing replacement tools.

INSTALLATION

1. Start new bushing into control arm with flat on bushing positioned vertically and rearward.
2. Assemble bushing tools as shown in **Fig. 6,** and tighten bolt until bushing is seated fully in control arm.
3. Remove bushing tools and install control arm as outlined under "Control Arm, Replace."

STABILIZER SHAFT

REPLACE

1. Raise and support vehicle. Remove wheels and disconnect Electronic Level Control (ELC) height sensor link at control arm.
2. Remove bolts and position ELC height sensor aside.
3. Remove stabilizer shaft link assembly bolt, nut, retainer and insulators from control arm, **Fig. 7.**
4. Remove clamp bolt and bend open end of clamp upward and remove stabilizer shaft and insulators.
5. Reverse procedure to install, noting the following:
   a. Ensure stabilizer shaft is centered before tightening clamp bolt.
   b. Tighten all bolts and nuts to specifications.

ADJUSTMENT LINK

REPLACE

INNER

1. Raise and support vehicle. Remove wheel.
2. Loosen pinch bolt.
3. Support exhaust and rear suspension support assembly with a wood block at least seven inches long.
4. Remove exhaust hangers and rear suspension support assembly mounting bolts.

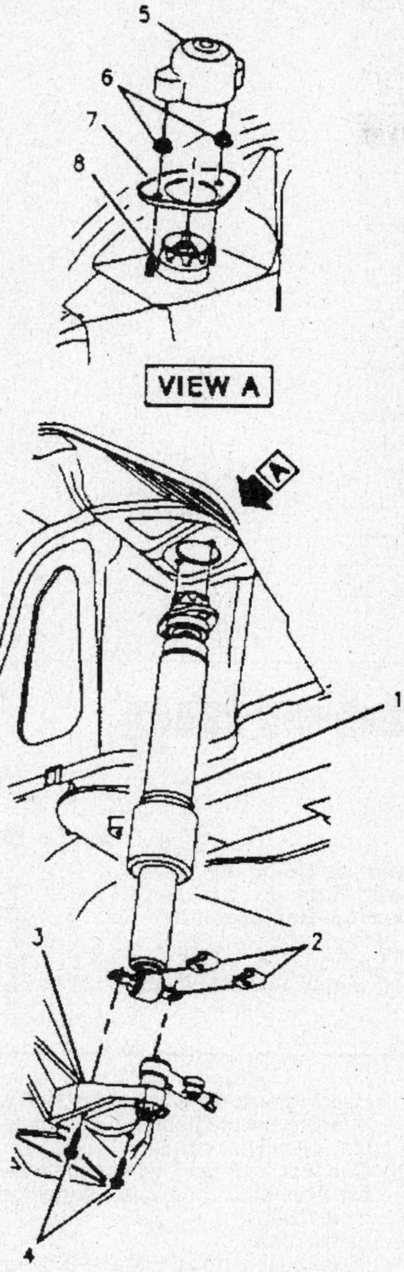

Fig. 4 Shock absorber replacement

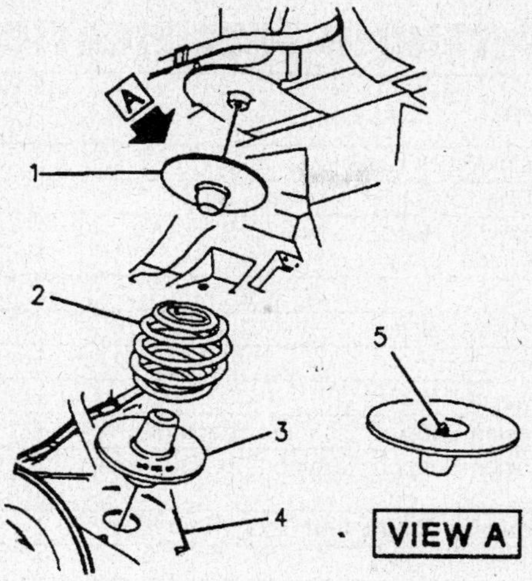

Fig. 5 Coil spring replacement

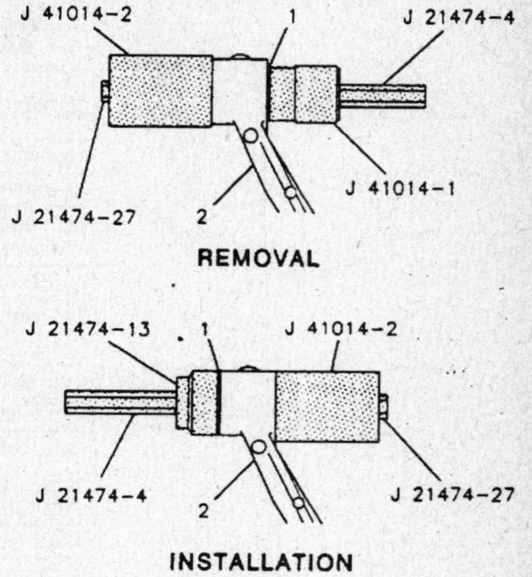

Fig. 6 Control arm bushing replacement tool installation

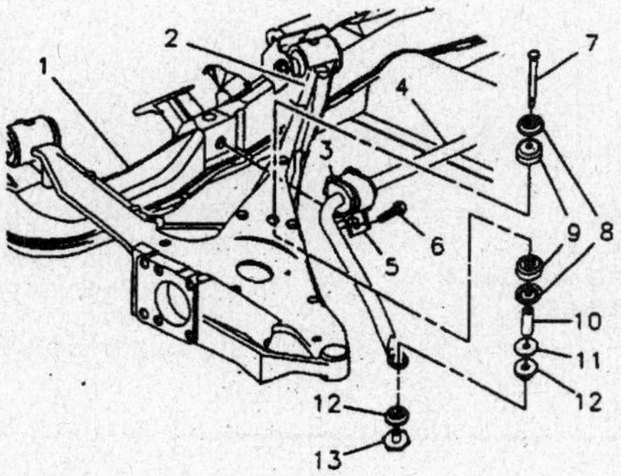

Fig. 7 Stabilizer shaft replacement

5. Lower support and exhaust together.
6. Remove cam bolt and nut, then adjustment link.
7. Remove inner from outer link. Note number of turns for assembly.
8. Reverse procedure to install. Inspect and adjust rear toe as outlined under "Wheel Alignment."

OUTER

1. Raise and support vehicle. Remove wheel.
2. Loosen pinch bolt.
3. Remove cotter pin and clotted hex nut.
4. Use universal steering linkage puller tool No. J-24319-B, or equivalent, to separate adjustment link from knuckle. **Do not drive wedge between joint and attached part.**
5. Remove outer from inner link. Note number of turns for assembly.
6. Reverse procedure to install. Inspect and adjust rear toe as outlined under "Wheel Alignment."

TIGHTENING SPECIFICATIONS

Component	Torque/Ft. Lbs.
Adjustment Link Pinch Bolt	36
Adjustment Link To Control Arm Nut	7–8①
Adjustment Link To Rear Suspension Support Assembly	55
Control Arm Nuts	78
ELC Height Sensor Bolts	60②
Hub & Bearing Bolts	52
Rear Body Mount Bolts	38
Rear Suspension Support Assembly Bracket Bolts	63
Rear Suspension Support Assembly To Body Rear Bolts	141
Shock Absorber To Control Arm Bolts	18
Shock Tower Mounting Nut	15
Stabilizer Link Bolt	10
Stabilizer Shaft Clamp Bolt	24
Stabilizer Shaft Link Bolt	9–10
Wheel Lug Nuts	100

①— Plus an additional 1/2 turn.
②— Inch lbs.

Front Suspension & Steering

INDEX

HUB & BEARING

REPLACE

REMOVAL

1. Raise and support vehicle. Remove tire and wheel assembly.
2. Insert suitable drift punch or screwdriver into caliper and rotor to prevent rotor from turning.
3. Remove drive axle nut, **Fig. 1.**
4. Remove bolts and support caliper with mechanics wire.
5. Remove rotor.
6. Disconnect ABS front wheel speed sensor connector and unclip from dust shield.
7. Remove hub and bearing retaining bolts and dust shield.
8. Place transmission in P position.
9. Using front hub spindle remover tool No. J-28733-B, or equivalent, separate hub and bearing from axle.

INSTALLATION

1. Install hub and bearing to drive axle and apply a thin layer of grease to knuckle bore.

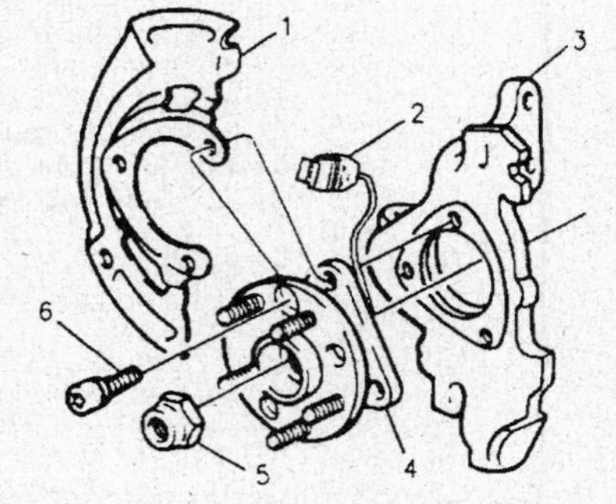

Fig. 1 Hub & bearing replacement

2. Install new drive axle nut, draw hub and bearing onto axle.
3. Place transmission in N position.
4. Install dust shield. **Do not damage bearing outboard lip seal or hub and bearing bolts.** Tighten hub and bearing bolts to specification.
5. Connect ABS front wheel speed sensor connector and clip connector to dust shield.
6. Install rotor.
7. Install caliper and tighten bolts to specification.
8. Insert a drift punch into caliper and rotor to prevent rotor from turning and tighten drive axle nut to specification.
9. Install wheel and tire. Tighten wheel nuts to specifications.

BALL JOINT INSPECTION

Replace ball joints if any looseness is detected in the joint or ball joint seal is cut. Complete the following steps in order to inspect ball joint.

1. Raise front of vehicle.
2. Allow suspension to hang free.
3. Grasp tire at top and bottom and move it in and out.

4. Inspect for any horizontal movement in knuckle relative to control arm.
5. Replace ball joint if ball stud is disconnected from knuckle and looseness is detected or ball stud twists in its socket while using finger pressure.
6. Inspect for ball stud tightness in knuckle boss. Shake wheel and feel for movement of stud end or nut at knuckle boss. Replace any worn or damaged ball joints and knuckles.

BALL JOINT

REPLACE

The ball joint is not serviced separate of the control arm. Refer to "Control Arm Replace."

1. Raise vehicle allowing control arm to hang free.
2. Remove cotter pin from ball joint and loosen nut.
3. Use ball joint separator remover tool No. J-43828, or equivalent, to remove ball joint from knuckle.
4. Reverse procedure to install.

STRUT

REPLACE

Care should be taken to avoid chipping or cracking spring coating. Failure to observe may result in spring breakage.

1. Remove strut mount bolts at strut to body.
2. Raise vehicle and support vehicle with control arms hanging free.
3. Remove tire and wheel assembly.
4. Disconnect ABS front wheel speed sensor connector.
5. Remove speed sensor bracket from strut.
6. Remove brake line bracket from lefthand strut.
7. Remove strut-to-knuckle bolts. **The knuckle must be retained after strut-to-knuckle bolts have been removed. Failure to observe this may cause ball joint and/or drive axle damage.**
8. Remove strut.
9. Reverse procedures to install, tightening nuts to specification.

CONTROL ARM

REPLACE

Use only recommended tools for separating ball joint from knuckle. Failure to do so may cause damage to joint and seal.

1. Raise and support vehicle with control arms hanging free. Remove wheel and tire.
2. Disconnect stabilizer link to control arm bolt.
3. Remove cotter pin and loosen nut from ball stud. **Care must be exercised to prevent Tri-Pot joints from being over extended, resulting in separation of internal parts and possible joint failure.**
4. Using ball joint separator tool No. J-43828, or equivalent, remove ball joint from knuckle.

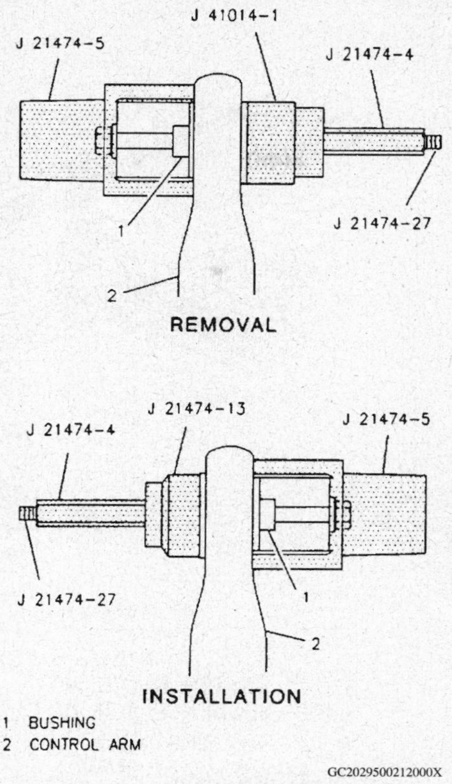

Fig. 2 Control arm bushing replacement

5. Remove mounting bolts and control arm.
6. Reverse procedure to install.

CONTROL ARM BUSHING

REPLACE

The rear control bushing is serviced with the control arm and cannot be serviced separately.

1. Remove control arm from vehicle as outlined under " Control Arm, Replace."
2. Assemble bolt assembly tool No. J-21474-27 with a washer through bushing receiver tool No. J-21474-5, or equivalents, with larger diameter end over bushing against control arm, **Fig. 2.**
3. Lubricate bolt threads with high pressure lubricant.
4. Install bushing remover tool No. J-41014-1 (large end facing bushing), thrust bearing and nut tool No. J-21474-4 onto bolt assembly tool No. J-21474-27, or equivalents.
5. Tighten nut until bushing is driven out of control arm.
6. Remove bushing tools.
7. Reverse procedure to install.

STABILIZER BAR

REPLACE

1. Raise and support vehicle with control arms hanging free. Remove front wheels and tires.
2. Remove left and righthand stabilizer link bolts.
3. Remove left and righthand stabilizer bar brackets.
4. Use universal steering linkage puller tool No. J-24319-B, or equivalent, to remove lefthand tie rod end from knuckle.
5. Remove exhaust pipe from manifold and immediate exhaust hangers and lower exhaust pipe.
6. Turn lefthand strut completely to right and slide stabilizer shaft outboard over lefthand steering knuckle until righthand end comes free.
7. Remove stabilizer shaft out of center of vehicle.
8. Reverse procedures to install.

TIE ROD

REPLACE

INNER

1. Remove steering gear as outlined under "Power Steering Gear, Replace."
2. Remove outer tie rod.
3. Remove inner tie rod assembly jam nut and end clamp.
4. Remove boot clamp with side cutters and discard.
5. Mark breather tube location on steering gear for assembly.
6. Remove rack and pinion boot and breather tube.
7. Loosen inner tie rod assembly shock dampener and slide back on rack.
8. Hold rack in suitable vice.
9. With one wrench on rack assembly flats and another on inner tire rod housing flats, turn inner tie rod housing counterclockwise and remove.
10. Reverse procedure to install. Gap between rack and housing stakes should be .01 inch.

OUTER

1. Remove cotter pin and hex slotted nut.
2. Loosen jam nut.
3. Use universal steering linkage puller tool No. N-24319-01, or equivalent, to remove outer tie rod from steering knuckle.
4. Remove outer from inner tie rod.
5. Reverse procedure to install.

POWER STEERING GEAR

REPLACE

1. Raise and support vehicle. Remove front tires and wheels.
2. Disconnect exhaust system from exhaust manifold.
3. Remove fasteners and fold back wheelhouse splash shield enough to allow removal of steering gear.
4. Using puller tool No. J-24319-B, or equivalent, disconnect tie rod ends from steering knuckles.
5. Disconnect intermediate shaft lower connection. **Vehicle wheels must be straight ahead and steering column**

in lock position before disconnecting steering column or intermediate shaft from steering gear. Failure to disconnect intermediate shaft from rack and pinion stub shaft can result in damage to steering gear and/or intermediate shaft which can cause loss of steering control.

6. Unsnap and remove power steering heat shield.
7. Disconnect Magnasteer electrical connector.
8. Disconnect steering gear outlet and inlet hoses.
9. Remove steering gear mounting bolts, **Fig. 3.**
10. **On 1997–98 models,** support rear of frame, remove rear bolts and lower rear of frame to allow steering gear removal. **Do not lower rear of frame too far or engine components may be damaged by cowl,**
11. Remove steering gear through right-hand wheel opening.
12. **On 1999 models,** remove steering gear through lefthand wheel opening.
13. **On all models,** reverse procedure to install. Tighten bolts to specification.

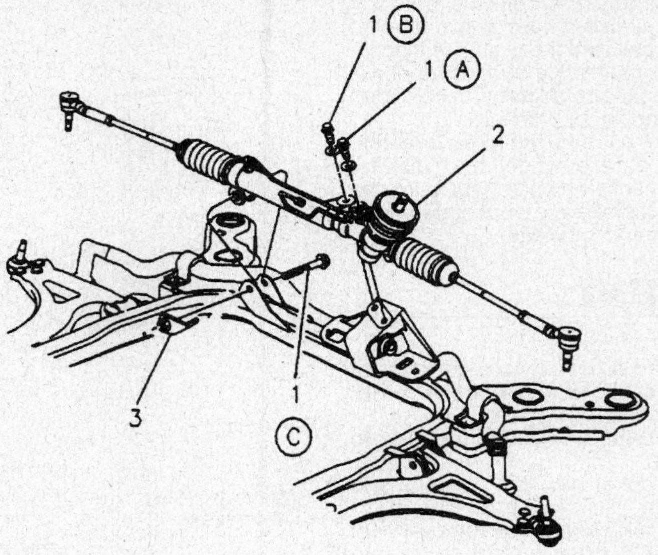

1 BOLT, 65 N•m (48 LB. FT.) TIGHTEN BOLTS IN SEQUENCE A THRU C
2 STEERING GEAR
3 TAB NUT

GC2029800224000X

Fig. 3 Steering gear removal

POWER STEERING PUMP

REPLACE

AURORA

1. Remove drive belt as outlined under "Serpentine Drive Belt" in "4.0 Engine" section.
2. Remove power steering gear outlet and inlet hoses from pump, **Fig. 4.**
3. Remove mounting bolts.
4. Remove pump and bracket from engine.
5. Reverse procedures to install.

RIVIERA

1. Remove drive belt as outlined under "Serpentine Drive Belt" in "3800 Engine" section.
2. Remove power steering gear outlet and inlet hoses from pump.
3. Remove mounting bolts.
4. Raise and support vehicle.
5. Remove pump from under engine and transfer pulley as needed.
6. Reverse procedure to install.

TIGHTENING SPECIFICATIONS

Component	Torque ft. Lbs.
Ball Joint Nut	84②
Ball Joint To Control Arm Nuts	50
Brake Line & Speed Sensor Bracket Bolts	13
Caliper Mounting Bolts	38
Control Arm Bolt	117
Control Arm Nut	93
Drive Axle Nut	107
Frame To Underbody Bolts	141
Hub & Bearing Bolts	70
Hub Nut	107
Intermediate Steering Shaft Pinch Bolt	35
Power Steering Gear Hose Connections	20
Power Steering Gear Mounting Bolts	48
Power Steering Pump Bolts	20
Stabilizer Bracket Bolts	28
Stabilizer Shaft Link Nut	13
Strut To Body Attaching Nuts	35
Strut To Knuckle Bolts	136

Continued

TIGHTENING SPECIFICATIONS—Continued

Component	Torque ft. Lbs.
Tie Rod End To Knuckle Nuts	35–52①
Wheel Lug Nuts	100

① — Do not counter-rotate nut for cotter pin insertion.
② — Inch lbs.

Wheel Alignment

INDEX

PRELIMINARY INSPECTION

Inspect all tires for proper inflation.

Inspect tie rods for lateral end motion relative to the steering knuckle and tie rod end seals for any visible signs of damage. Replace tie rod end if either of these conditions exist.

Inspect runout of wheels and tires.

Inspect trim height. If out of specifications, correct before alignment. Inspect shocks, rack and pinion and control arms for looseness and proper operation. Replace any damaged steering/suspension components.

If any excess weight is normally carried in the trunk of vehicle, alignment is recommended with load in place.

Ensure vehicle is level.

FRONT WHEEL ALIGNMENT

CASTER

1. Remove top strut nuts and washers.
2. Raise and support front of vehicle to separate strut from inner wheel housing.
3. Drill two 12/32 inch holes at front and rear of oval strut mounting hole on left and righthand strut towers, **Fig. 1,** and file excess metal to create slotted holes. **Paint exposed metal with rust resistant paint or primer.**
4. Lower front of vehicle.
5. Install strut mounting nuts, but do not tighten at this time.
6. Adjust caster by moving top of strut forward or rearward. A .040 inch position change at tower is approximately .1° change in caster.
7. When caster is within specifications, **torque** strut mounting nuts to 35 ft. lbs.

CAMBER

1. Loosen both strut to steering knuckle nuts and install camber adjusting tool No. J-39601, J-29862 or equivalent, **Fig. 2** and set camber to specifications.
2. **Torque** strut to steering knuckle bolts to 136 ft. lbs.

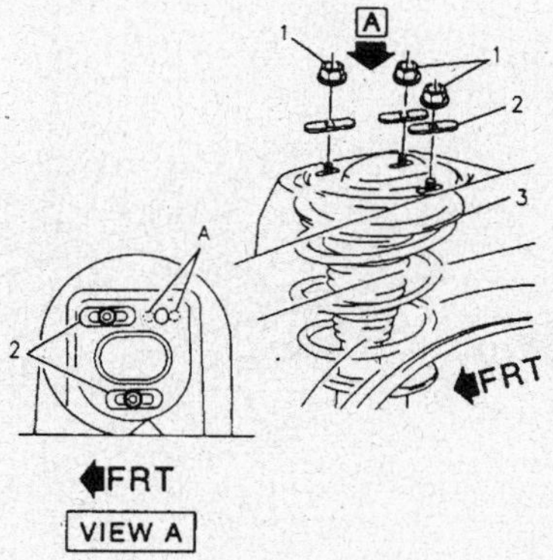

Fig. 1 Front caster adjustment

TOE

1. Loosen lock nuts on tie rod ends. **Ensure boots are not twisted or damaged during adjustment.**
2. Rotate inner tie rod, **Fig. 2,** to adjust toe to specifications.
3. **Torque** lock nuts to 47 ft. lbs.

REAR WHEEL ALIGNMENT

Make left and right toe adjustments separately, per wheel.

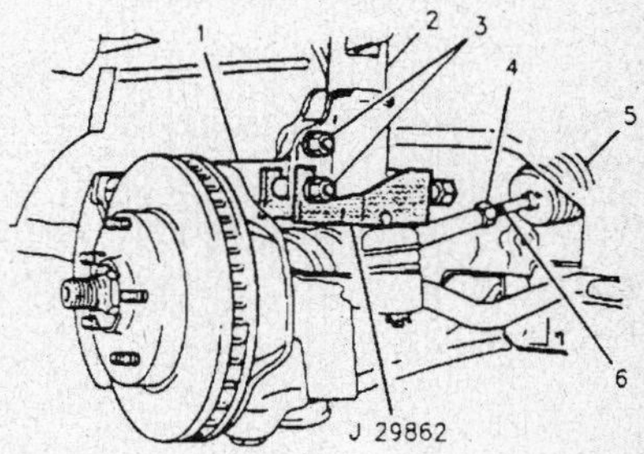

Fig. 2 Camber & toe adjustment

1. Loosen inner adjustment link cam nut, **Fig. 3.**
2. Rotate cam bolt using an 18 mm wrench or socket and adjust toe to specifications.
3. **Torque** cam nut to 55 ft. lbs.

VEHICLE RIDE HEIGHT

Refer to **Fig. 4,** while inspecting vehicle ride height. Ensure vehicle is on level ground and fuel tank is full. Ensure no extra weight is in passenger compartment or trunk.

On vehicle equipped with electronic level control (ELC), ensure ELC is functioning properly.

1. Place front seat to rear position.
2. Bounce vehicle three times at front and rear to normalize suspension.
3. Make measurement D, C, S and Z, **Fig. 4.**
4. Refer to **Fig. 5** for specifications.

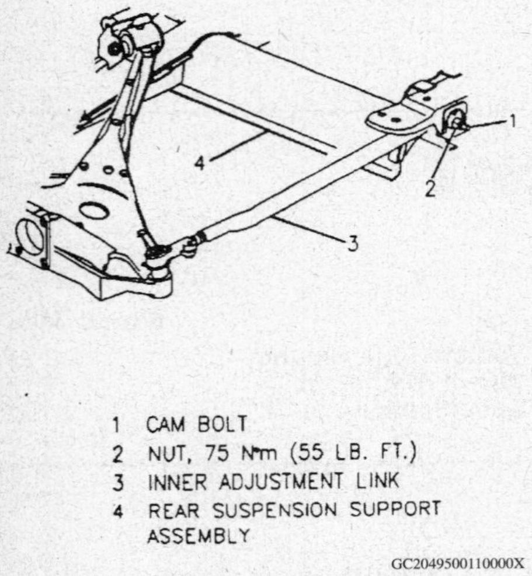

Fig. 3 Rear toe adjustment

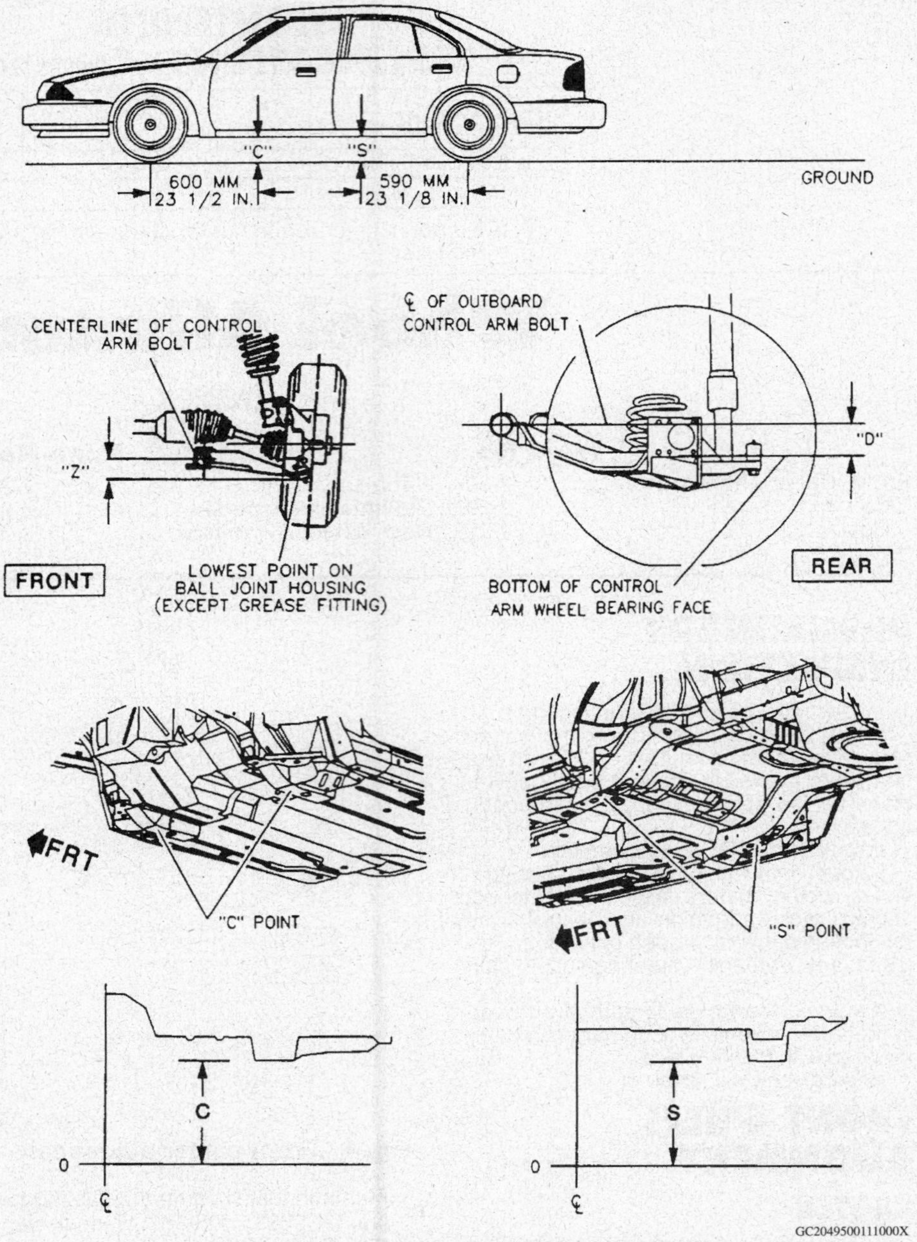

Fig. 4 Vehicle ride height measurement

Year	Model	Ride Height, Inches①			
		C	D	S	Z
1997–99	Aurora	6 11/16 to 7 1/2	3 to 3 3/4	8 5/8 to 9 13/32	1 3/16 to 2
	Riviera	6 7/16 to 7 1/4	3 to 3 3/4	8 3/8 to 9 3/16	1 3/16 to 2

① — Maximum side-to-side and front-to-rear variation, 3/4 inch.

Fig. 5 Vehicle ride height specifications

BONNEVILLE, EIGHTY EIGHT, LESABRE, LSS, PARK AVENUE & REGENCY

NOTE: Refer To The Rear Of This Manual For Vehicle Manufacturer's Special Service Tool Suppliers.

INDEX OF SERVICE OPERATIONS

Specifications

GENERAL ENGINE SPECIFICATIONS

Year	Engine		Fuel System	Bore & Stroke	Compression Ratio	Net H.P. @ RPM②	Maximum Torque Ft. Lbs. @ RPM	Normal Oil Pressure psi
	Liter	VIN Code①						
1997–2000	3800	K	SFI	3.80 x 3.40	9.4	205 @ 5200	230 @ 4000	60③
	3800	1	SFI	3.80 x 3.40	8.5	240 @ 5200	280 @ 3200	60③

MFI — Multi-Point Fuel Injection
SFI — Sequential Port Fuel Injection
① — The eighth digit denotes engine code.
② — Ratings are net-as installed in vehicle.
③ — At 1850 RPM using SAE 10W-30 motor oil.

TUNE UP SPECIFICATIONS

Engine/VIN Code①	Spark Plug Gap	Ignition Timing			Curb Idle Speed	Fast Idle Speed	Fuel Pump Pressure	Valve Clearance, Inch
		Firing Order Fig.②	°BTDC	Mark Fig.				
3800/K & 1	.060	⑥	⑦	⑧	③	③	48–55⑤	④

BTDC — Before Top Dead Center
① — The eighth digit of the Vehicle Identification Number (VIN) denotes engine code.
② — Before removing wires from distributor cap, determine location of No. 1 wire in cap, as distributor position may have been altered from that shown at the end of this chart.
③ — Idle speed is controlled by an idle speed control (ISC) motor or an idle air control (IAC) valve.
④ — Equipped w/hydraulic valve lifters, there is no provision for adjustment.
⑤ — With shop towel wrapped around fuel pressure valve to prevent fuel spillage, connect a suitable fuel pressure gauge to fuel pressure valve. Check fuel pressure w/ignition switch in the On position, engine not running.
⑥ — Cylinder numbering left to right as viewed in Figs. A & B from front of vehicle, front bank, 1, 3, 5; rear bank, 2, 4, 6. Firing order 1-6-5-4-3-2. Two different types computer controlled coil ignition systems are used. Refer to **Figs. A and B** for spark plug wire connections at coil unit.
⑦ — Computer controlled, no adjustment.
⑧ — Equipped w/crankshaft position sensor.

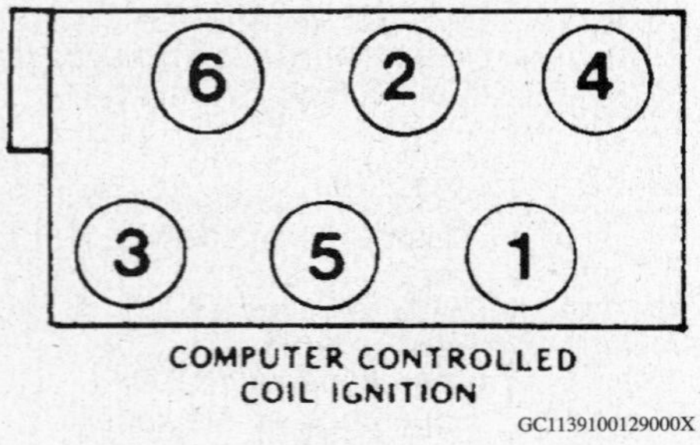

Fig. A

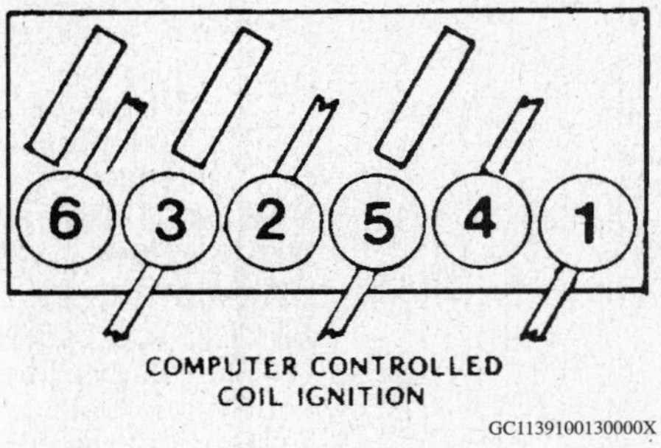

Fig. B

FRONT WHEEL ALIGNMENT SPECIFICATIONS

Year	Model	Caster Angle, Degrees		Camber Angle, Degrees				Total Toe, Degree	Ball Joint Wear
		Limits	Desired	Limits		Desired			
				Left	Right	Left	Right		
1997–99	Bonneville, Eighty Eight, LeSabre, LSS & Regency	+2.5 to +3.5	+3	-.3 to +.7②	-.3 to +.7②	+.2	+.2	0	①
	Park Avenue	+5.5 to +6.5	+6	-.5 to +.5	-.5 to +.5	0	0	+.2	①
2000	Bonneville, LeSabre & Park Avenue	+5.5 to +6.5	+6	-.7 to +.3	-.7 to +.3	-.2	-.2	+.2	①

① — Refer to "Ball Joint Inspection" in "Front Suspension & Steering" section.

② — Cross caster or camber (LH-RH), 0° (+/- .75°).

REAR WHEEL ALIGNMENT SPECIFICATIONS

Year	Model	Camber Angle, Degrees		Total Toe, Degrees	Thrust Angle, Degrees	Ball Joint Wear
		Limits	Desired			
1997–99	All	-.8 to +.2	–.3	+.2	-.1 to +.1	①
2000	Bonneville, LeSabre & Park Avenue	-.8 to +.2	–.3	+.2	-.1 to +.1	①

① — Refer to "Ball Joint Inspection" in "Rear Suspension" section.

FLUID CAPACITIES & COOLING SYSTEM DATA

Year	Model	Engine	Coolant Capacity, Qts.	Radiator Cap Relief Pressure, Lbs.	Thermo. Opening Temp.	Fuel Tank Gals.	Engine Oil Refill Qts.	Auto. Transaxle Qts.①
1997	All	3800	13	15	195	18	4.5⑤	③
1998–99	Bonneville, Eighty Eight, LeSabre, LSS & Regency	3800	13	15	195	19.4	4.5⑤	③
	Park Avenue	3800	13	15	195	④	4.5⑤	②
2000	Bonneville, LeSabre & Park Avenue	3800	13	⑦	188	18.5	4.0⑤	⑥

① — Approximate, make final check w/dipstick.

② — Oil pan capacity, 6.0 qts.; total capacity, 11.0 qts.

③ — Oil pan capacity, 7.4 qts.; total capacity, 10 qts.

④ — VIN 1 engine, 19 gallons; VIN K engine, 18 gallons.

⑤ — Add .5 qt. w/filter change.

⑥ — Drain and refill, 7.4 qts.; overhaul, 10 qts.; dry, 13.4 qts.

⑦ — Relief pressure specification is stamped on cap.

LUBRICANT DATA

Year	Model	Lubricant Type		
		Automatic Transaxle	Power Steering	Brake System
1997–99	All	Dexron III	Power Steering Fluid①	DOT 3
2000	All	Dexron III	Power Steering Fluid ①	②

① — Meeting GM specification 1052884, or equivalent.

② — Delco Supreme II GM No. 12377967, or equivalent.

Electrical

NOTE: On Air Bag Equipped Models, Refer To " Air Bag System Precautions" Located In The Front Of This Manual For System Disarming & Arming Procedures.

NOTE: Refer To "Computer Relearn Procedures " Located In The Front Of This Manual For Computer Relearn Procedures.

INDEX

PRECAUTIONS

AIR BAG SYSTEMS

Refer to "Air Bag System Precautions" in the front of this manual for system disarming and arming procedures.

BATTERY GROUND CABLE

Prior to service, disconnect battery ground cable and isolate as required.

FUSE PANEL & FLASHER LOCATION

The instrument panel fuse panel is located behind the lefthand side of the instrument panel, behind the trim panel. The engine compartment fuse panel is located at the rear center of the engine compartment.

The hazard flasher is located behind the lefthand side of the instrument panel, on the righthand side of the steering column. The turn signal flasher is located behind the lefthand side of the instrument panel, left of the steering column.

RELAY CENTER LOCATION

The passenger compartment relay center is located behind the righthand side of the instrument panel, on the multi-use bracket. The engine compartment relay center is located at the rear center of the engine compartment.

FUEL PUMP RELAY LOCATION

The fuel pump relay is located on the passenger compartment relay center, behind the righthand side of the instrument panel.

STARTER

REPLACE

When removing starter, note if any shims are used between the starter and mounting surface. If shims are found, reinstall in original locations.

If starter is noisy during cranking, remove one .015 inch double shim or add one .015 inch single shim to the outer bolt. If starter makes a high pitched whine after engine start, add .015 inch double shims until noise ceases.

1. Raise and support vehicle.
2. Remove starter braces, shields or other components that may hinder starter removal.
3. Support starter and remove mounting bolts.
4. Lower starter and disconnect solenoid wires and battery cable.
5. Remove starter from vehicle.
6. Reverse procedure to install.

COIL PACK

REPLACE

1. Remove electrical connectors from ignition control module.
2. Remove spark plug wires from ignition coils.
3. Remove screws securing ignition coils to ignition module, then the coils.
4. Reverse procedure to install.

IGNITION LOCK

REPLACE

EIGHTY EIGHT, LESABRE, LSS, PARK AVENUE & REGENCY

Removal

1. Remove steering wheel as described under "Steering Wheel, Replace."
2. Disconnect SIR wiring harness from wiring protector and wire harness strap.
3. Lower or remove steering column from vehicle.
4. Remove tilt lever if equipped.
5. Remove mounting screws from lower shroud, then the shroud.
6. Remove two mounting screws from upper shroud, then the shroud.
7. Remove lock cylinder as follows:
   a. Insert ignition key and hold in Start position.
   b. Using a 1/16 inch Allen wrench, push on lock cylinder retaining tab, refer to **Fig. 1.**
   c. Release key to Run position and pull lock cylinder from lock module assembly.

Installation

1. Install upper shroud, **torque** mounting screws to 12 inch lbs.
2. Install lower shroud, ensure slots on lower shroud engage with tabs on upper shroud.
3. Install lower shroud mounting screws, torque both screws to 53 inch lbs.
4. Install shift and multi-function lever seals to column shrouds.
5. Install tilt lever.
6. Raise or install steering column into vehicle.
7. Install lock cylinder as follows:
   a. Insert key into lock cylinder.
   b. Ensure sector in lock module assembly is in Run position.
   c. Align locking tabs, position tab with slots in lock module assembly and push cylinder into position.
   d. Install lock cylinder through upper shroud and into lock module assembly.

BONNEVILLE

1997-99

Refer to procedure listed under "Eighty Eight, LeSabre, LSS, Park Avenue & Regency."

2000

1. Apply parking brake.
2. Remove instrument panel cluster trim bezel.
3. Remove radio.
4. Remove fasteners from ignition switch.
5. Rotate switch in instrument panel.
6. Disconnect electrical connectors from switch.
7. Remove ignition switch bulb from side of switch, then remove switch through radio opening.

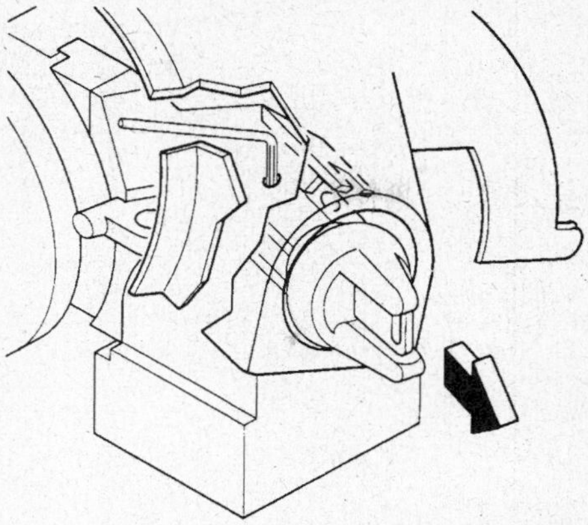

GC9049700157000X

Fig. 1 Lock cylinder removal. Eighty Eight, LeSabre, LSS, Park Avenue & Regency

8. Remove ignition switch from bracket.
9. Reverse procedure to install.

IGNITION SWITCH

REPLACE

1. Remove lock cylinder assembly, refer to "Lock Cylinder, Replace."
2. Remove control coded key wire harness from slot in steering column.
3. Remove control coded key connector from wire harness.
4. Pry retaining clip on key alarm switch with suitable screwdriver, then rotate alarm switch 1/4 turn and remove.
5. Remove ignition switch mounting screws, then the ignition and key alarm switch assembly.
6. Reverse procedure to install.

NEUTRAL SAFETY SWITCH

REPLACE

1. Disconnect shift cable from transaxle.
2. Disconnect electrical connector from switch.
3. Remove two switch mounting bolts, then the switch.
4. Align flats on switch with flats on transaxle shaft and push switch over shaft and fully seat on transaxle.
5. Install and **torque** switch mounting bolts to 20 ft. lbs. **If switch was rotated and pin is broken, switch will be automatically reset to neutral position as follows:**
   a. Place transaxle shaft in neutral position.
   b. Install switch on transaxle as outlined previously and loosely install mounting bolts.
   c. Insert a 3/32 inch gauge pin into service adjustment hole of switch.
   d. Rotate switch until pin drops in detent.
   e. **Torque** mounting bolts to 20 ft. lbs.

BACK-UP LAMP SWITCH

REPLACE

Refer to "Neutral Safety Switch, Replace" for procedure.

HEADLAMP SWITCH

REPLACE

BONNEVILLE, EIGHTY EIGHT, LSS & REGENCY

1997-98

1. Remove instrument panel molding fasteners in instrument panel compartment, **Fig. 2.**
2. Remove instrument panel molding by carefully puling rearward.
3. Remove cluster trim plate by removing screws and tilting top of trim plate rearward then pulling bottom of trim plate rearward.
4. Remove HVAC control head and headlamp/parklamp switch from connectors.
5. Remove HVAC control head vacuum harness connector, then remove control head by carefully pushing one side outward.
6. Remove headlamp/parklamp switch by carefully pushing one side outward.
7. Reverse procedure to install.

1999

1. Remove instrument panel cluster trim panel.
2. Remove fuel door/trunk release switch screws (3) and electrical connector (1), then the switch (2), **Fig. 3.**
3. Remove headlamp switch screws, then pull rearward to remove switch (4).
4. Reverse procedure to install.

LESABRE & PARK AVENUE

1997-98

Refer to "Eighty Eight, LSS & Regency" under "Headlamp Switch, Replace."

1999

1. Remove door trim panel.
2. Disconnect electrical connector, **Fig. 4**, then remove fasteners (2), **Fig. 5**, that retain cover to inner side of trim panel.
3. Remove switch attaching screws, then the switch.
4. Reverse procedure to install.

2000

1. Remove left instrument panel accessory trim plate.
2. Remove headlamp switch fasteners, then the switch.
3. Reverse procedure to install.

BONNEVILLE

1997-98

Refer to **Fig. 6** for switch replacement.

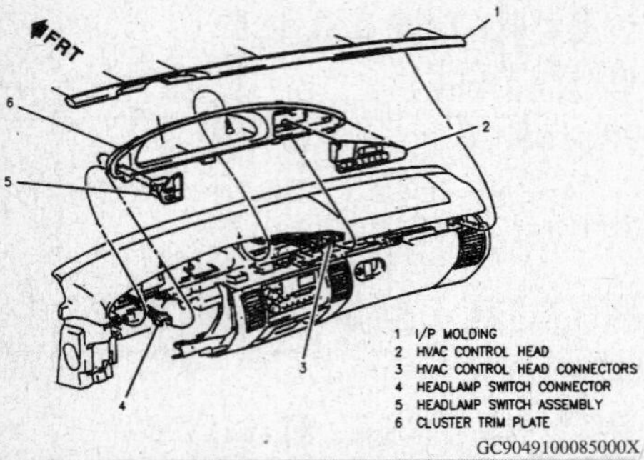

Fig. 2 Headlamp switch removal. 1997–98 Bonneville, Eighty Eight, LeSabre, LSS, Park Avenue & Regency

1999

Refer to "1999 Eighty Eight, LSS & Regency."

2000

1. Remove left instrument panel accessory trim plate.
2. Remove headlamp switch fasteners, then the switch.
3. Reverse procedure to install.

TURN SIGNAL SWITCH

REPLACE

EIGHTY EIGHT, LSS & REGENCY

1. Remove upper and lower steering column shrouds, refer to " Lock Cylinder, Replace."
2. Remove retaining ring (30), SIR coil, wave washer and retaining ring (4).
3. Remove shaft lock shield assembly.
4. Remove turn signal cancel cam.
5. Remove turn signal switch connector from shifter.
6. Remove turn signal switch mounting screws, then the switch.
7. Reverse procedure to install noting the following:
   a. Turn signal electrical contact must rest on canceling assembly.
   b. **Torque** turn signal switch mounting screws to 53 inch lbs.

BONNEVILLE, LESABRE & PARK AVENUE

1997–99

Refer to "Eighty Eight, LSS & Regency" for replacement procedure.

2000

1. Remove steering wheel and tilt lever.
2. Remove two Torx screws from lower shroud, then tilt shroud down and slide back to disengage locking tabs.
3. Remove shroud protector.
4. Remove two Torx screws from upper shroud, then remove shroud.
5. Remove instrument panel trim panel.
6. Remove two Torx screws from multi-function switch, disconnect electrical connectors, then remove switch.
7. Reverse procedure to install.

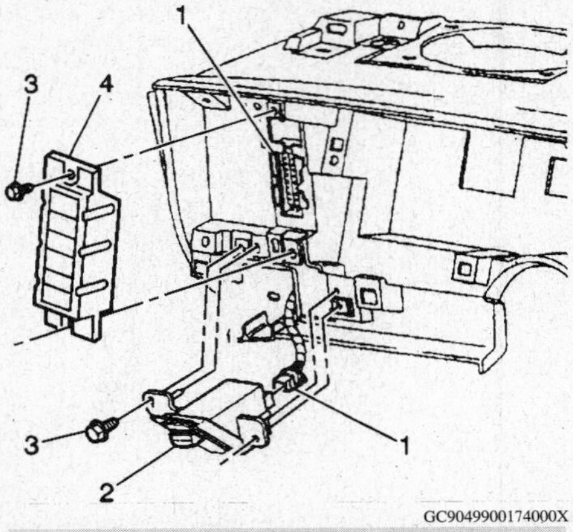

Fig. 3 Headlamp switch replacement. 1999 Bonneville, Eighty Eight, LSS & Regency

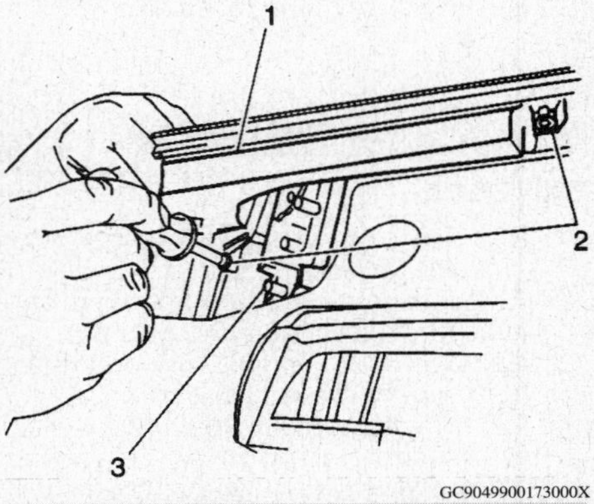

Fig. 5 Headlamp switch attaching hardware. 1999 LeSabre & Park Avenue

DIMMER SWITCH

REPLACE

Refer to "Turn Signal Switch, Replace" for procedure.

STEERING WHEEL

REPLACE

EIGHTY EIGHT, LSS & REGENCY

1. Remove module retaining screws from back of steering wheel.
2. Remove module from steering wheel, then disconnect horn contact, by pushing slightly and twisting counterclockwise.
3. Remove connector position assurance, then disconnect coil assembly connector, **Fig. 7.**
4. Remove steering wheel retaining nut.
5. Using suitable steering wheel puller, remove wheel.

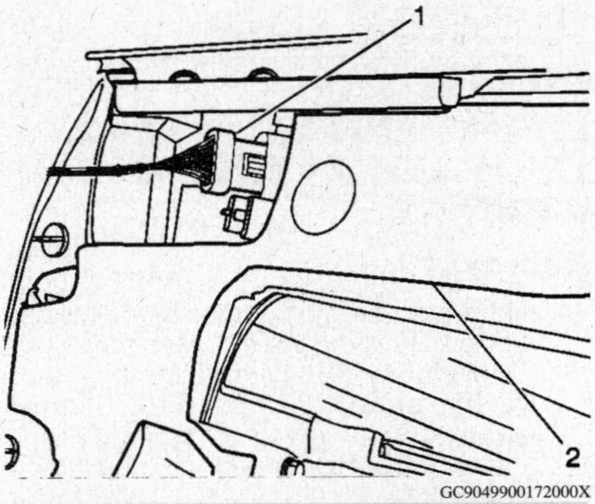

Fig. 4 Headlamp switch electrical connector. 1999 LeSabre & Park Avenue

6. Reverse procedure to install.

BONNEVILLE, LESABRE & PARK AVENUE

1997–99

Refer to "Eighty Eight, LSS & Regency" for replacement procedure.

2000

1. Disable the SIR system, then remove inflator module from steering wheel.
2. Remove weight block from steering wheel base, if equipped.
3. Remove nut from steering wheel.
4. Note mark on steering shaft and steering wheel for installation reference.
5. Use a suitable steering wheel puller to disengage steering wheel from shaft.
6. Reverse procedure to install, noting the following:
   a. Route wiring through steering wheel.
   b. Align mark on steering wheel with mark on steering shaft.
   c. Install nut and **torque** to 30 ft. lbs.

INSTRUMENT CLUSTER

REPLACE

LESABRE & PARK AVENUE

1997–98

1. Remove instrument panel trim plates.
2. Remove PRNDL cable.
3. Remove instrument panel dimmer switch.
4. Remove instrument cluster.
5. Reverse procedure to install.

1999

1. Remove instrument panel trim plates.
2. Remove PRNDL cable.
3. Remove panel lights twilight sentinel/traction control switch.
4. Remove instrument cluster.
5. Reverse procedure to install.

2000

1. Remove instrument panel upper trim pad.

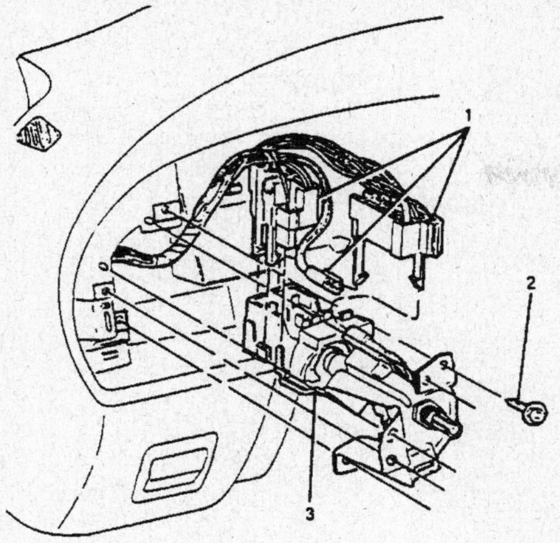

1 CONNECTORS
2 SCREW
3 HEADLAMP SWITCH

GC9049200089000X

Fig. 6 Headlamp switch removal. 1997–98 Bonneville

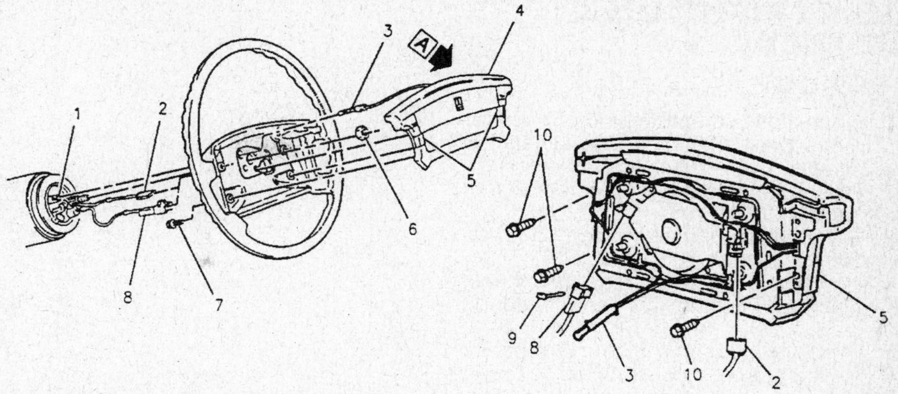

1 CAM TOWER
2 CONNECTOR, SWITCH
3 HORN CONTACT LEAD
4 INFLATOR MODULE
5 SWITCH ASM
6 NUT
7 BOLT/SCREW
8 CONNECTOR, SIR INFLATOR MODULE
9 RETAINER, CPA
10 BOLT/SCREW

GC6049100144000X

Fig. 7 Inflator module assembly. Eighty Eight, LSS & Regency

2. Remove instrument panel cluster trim panel.
3. Remove four instrument panel cluster pins and pull cluster rearward to remove.
4. Reverse procedure to install.

EIGHTY EIGHT, LSS & REGENCY

1997–98

1. Remove instrument panel molding attaching screws, then pull instrument panel molding rearward.
2. Pry defroster grill upward and remove sunload and twilight sentinel sensors.
3. Remove defroster grill from upper trim panel.
4. Tilt top of instrument cluster trim plate rearward, then pull bottom of trim plate rearward.
5. Disconnect HVAC control head and headlamp switch electrical connectors.
6. Disconnect HVAC control head vacuum harness connector.
7. Remove HVAC control head and headlamp switch from instrument cluster trim plate.
8. Remove instrument cluster trim plate.
9. Remove instrument panel upper trim pad attaching screws, then the trim pad from the instrument panel, **Fig. 8.**
10. Disconnect PRNDL cable.
11. Remove instrument cluster attaching screws, then the cluster from instrument panel.
12. Reverse procedure to install.

1999

1. Remove instrument panel cluster trim plate.
2. Remove PRNDL cable, if equipped.
3. Remove instrument cluster attaching screws, then the cluster by puling cluster rearward and disconnecting cluster connector.
4. Reverse procedure to instal.

BONNEVILLE

1997–98

1. Remove steering column lower filler attaching screws, then the filler panel.
2. Remove steering column support attaching bolts, then lower steering column and cover to prevent damage.
3. Remove instrument panel trim plate attaching screws.
4. Pull headlamp dimmer and twilight sentinel control knob rearward.
5. Pull panel cluster plate rearward to remove.
6. Remove headlamp switch attaching screws and pull rearward, then remove dimmer and twilight sentinel control knob from switch.
7. Remove instrument panel cluster trim plate.
8. Remove instrument cluster attaching screws, then pull righthand side of cluster rearward, **Fig. 9.**
9. Depress cluster electrical connector locking tab through top right side of assembly.
10. Pull bottom of cluster rearward, then rotate cluster to face upward, then pull rearward to remove.
11. Reverse procedure to install.

1999

1. Remove steering column filler panel.
2. Lower steering column. Remove steering column lower mounting bolts prior to removing upper steering column mounting bolts or damage to power steering column bearing may occur.
3. Remove instrument panel cluster trim plate.
4. Remove instrument cluster attaching screws, then pull right end of cluster rearward and rotate cluster assembly to face upward.
5. Reach around top or bottom right side of cluster assembly to disconnect cluster connector.
6. Remove instrument cluster by sliding toward center of vehicle.
7. Reverse procedure to install.

2000

Refer to model year 2000 under "LeSabre & Park Avenue" for replacement procedure.

RADIO

REPLACE

LESABRE & PARK AVENUE

1997–98

1. Remove instrument panel lower trim plates and four air vent deflectors by prying with suitable tool.
2. Remove bolts and screws that attach glove box to the instrument panel, **Fig. 10.**
3. Remove five instrument panel trim plate attaching screws.
4. Remove five radio to instrument panel attaching bolts and nuts, **Fig. 10.**
5. Pull radio straight back and disconnect electrical connectors and antenna.
6. Reverse procedure to install.

1999

1. Remove instrument panel cluster trim panel.
2. Remove radio attaching fasteners, then pull radio rearward.
3. Disconnect electrical connectors and antenna lead, then remove radio.
4. If replacing radio, transfer mounting bracket to new radio.
5. Reverse procedure to instal.

2000

1. Remove instrument panel cluster trim plate.
2. Depress spring clip retainers at side of radio.
3. Remove radio from instrument panel.
4. Reverse procedure to install.

EIGHTY EIGHT, LSS & REGENCY

1997–98

1. Open glove compartment door and remove two center trim plate attaching screws.
2. Pull center trim plate off of instrument panel.
3. Remove radio to instrument panel attaching screws.
4. Pull radio rearward and disconnect electrical connectors and antenna lead.
5. Remove radio from instrument panel.
6. Reverse procedure to install.

1999

Refer to "LeSabre & Park Avenue" , for radio replacement.

BONNEVILLE

1997–98

1. Pry instrument panel trim panel, pull panel upward, then rearward to remove.
2. Remove radio attaching screws, then pull rearward.
3. Disconnect electrical connector and antenna lead.
4. Remove radio assembly, **Fig. 11.**
5. Reverse procedure to install.

1999–2000

Refer to " LeSabre & Park Avenue" , for radio replacement.

WIPER MOTOR

REPLACE

EIGHTY EIGHT, LSS & REGENCY

1. Remove wiper arms.
2. Remove cowl cover.
3. Remove air inlet screen assembly.
4. Disconnect wiper arm drive link from crank arm.
5. Disconnect motor electrical connectors.
6. Remove wiper motor attaching screws, then the motor guiding cranking arm through hole.
7. Reverse procedure to install.

PARK AVENUE

1997–1999

Refer to "Eighty Eight, LSS & Regency" for replacement procedure.

2000

1. Remove wipers and air inlet grille.
2. Remove transmission drive link socket from wiper motor assembly crank arm using removal tool No. J-39232, or equivalent.
3. Remove electrical connector from motor.
4. Remove attaching bolts, then the motor.
5. Reverse procedure to install.

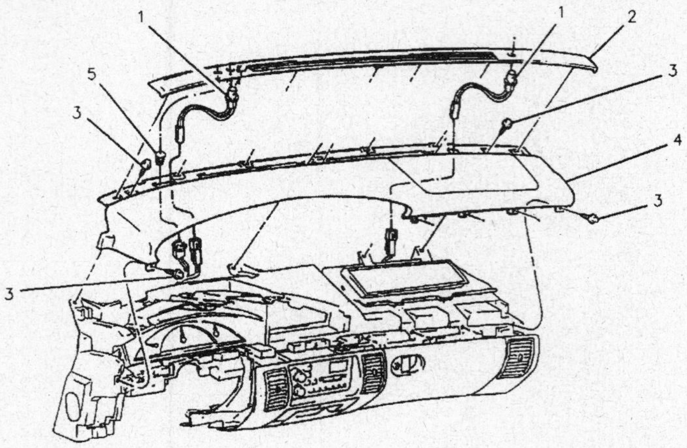

1 SUNLOAD SENSOR
2 WINDSHIELD DEFROSTER GRILLE
3 SCREW
4 UPPER PAD ASSEMBLY
5 TWILIGHT SENTINEL SENSOR

GC9099400375000X

Fig. 8 I/P upper trim pad removal. 1997–98 Eighty Eight, LSS & Regency

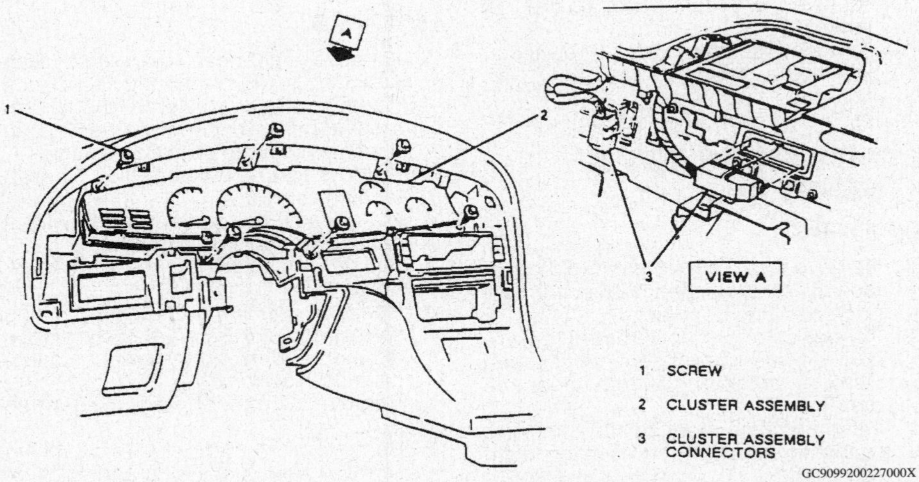

Fig. 9 Cluster removal. 1997–98 Bonneville

BONNEVILLE & LESABRE

1997–99

Refer to "Eighty Eight, LSS, & Regency," for replacement procedure.

2000

1. Remove wiper arms and air inlet grille panel.
2. Remove three bolts and two nuts retaining windshield frame reinforcement.
3. Remove windshield frame reinforcement.
4. Pull or push on wiper transmission linkage to rotate wiper motor crank arm opposite from park position.
5. Remove harness grommet from hole in plenum.
6. Disconnect wiper motor harness connector, then push harness and grommet through hole in plenum.
7. Remove three screws retaining wiper system drive module, then the module.
8. Remove drive link from wiper motor crank arm with wiper transmission separator tool No. J-39232, or equivalent.
9. Remove screws retaining wiper motor, then remove wiper motor from wiper drive system module.
10. Reverse procedure to install.

WIPER SWITCH

REPLACE

EIGHTY EIGHT, LESABRE, LSS, PARK AVENUE & REGENCY

1. Remove turn signal switch as outlined under "Turn Signal Switch, Replace" procedure.
2. Refer to **Figs. 12 through 15** for switch replacement.

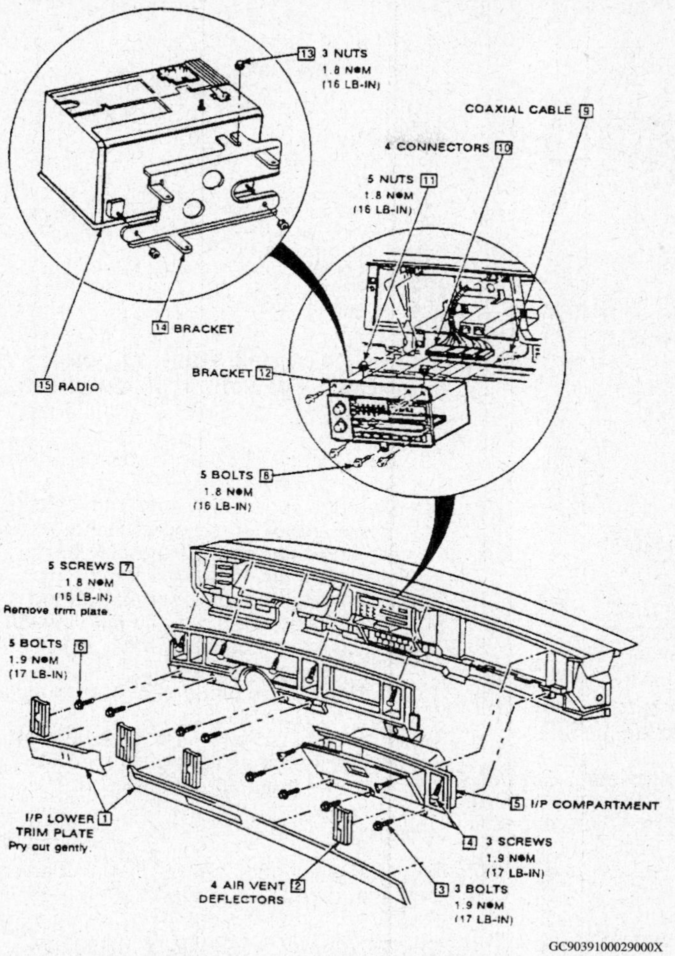

Fig. 10 Radio replacement. 1997–98 LeSabre & Park Avenue

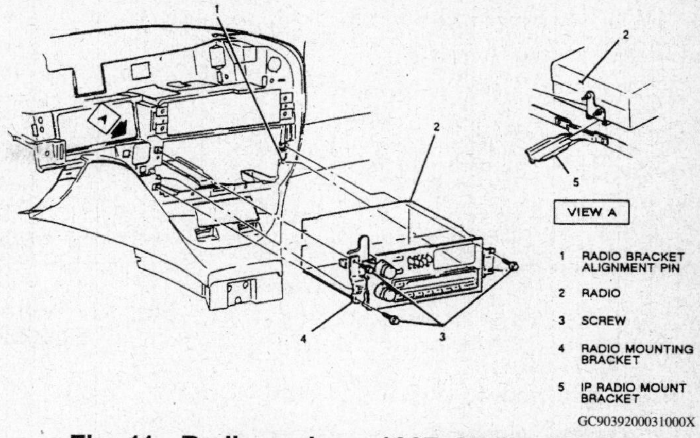

Fig. 11 Radio replace. 1997–98 Bonneville

BONNEVILLE

1997–99

Refer to "Eighty Eight, LeSabre, LSS, Park Avenue & Regency" for replacement procedure.

2000

1. Remove upper and lower steering column shrouds.
2. Remove wire harness assembly from wire restraint clip.
3. Remove wire harness straps.
4. Disconnect switch electrical connector.
5. Press on locking tabs of wiper switch assembly, then pull switch assembly out of mounting bracket.
6. Reverse procedure to install.

WIPER TRANSMISSION

REPLACE

EIGHTY EIGHT, LESABRE, LSS, PARK AVENUE & REGENCY

1. Disconnect washer hoses.
2. Remove wiper arms.
3. Remove air inlet screen assembly.
4. Disconnect drive link from motor crank arm.
5. Remove linkage attaching screws, then pull transmission through access hole in shroud upper panel.
6. Reverse procedure to install.

BONNEVILLE

1997–99

Refer to "Eighty Eight, LeSabre, LSS, Park Avenue & Regency" for replacement procedure.

2000

Refer to "2000 Bonneville & LeSabre" under "Wiper Motor, Replace" for replacement procedure.

BLOWER MOTOR

REPLACE

EIGHTY EIGHT, LSS & REGENCY

1. Remove cross car support brace.
2. **On 1999 models,** remove rear spark plug wires and bracket and set aside.
3. **On all models,** disconnect electrical connector and cooling tube from motor.
4. Remove blower motor attaching bolts, then the blower motor.
5. Reverse procedure to install.

PARK AVENUE

1997–99

Refer to "Eighty Eight, LSS & Regency" for replacement procedure.

2000

1. Remove right sound insulator from inside of vehicle.
2. Disconnect electrical connector and cooling hose from motor.
3. Remove screws that attach blower motor to heater and A/C module.
4. Remove blower and fan assembly.
5. Reverse procedure to install.

BONNEVILLE & LESABRE

1997–99

Refer to "Eighty Eight, LeSabre, LSS, Park Avenue & Regency" for replacement procedure.

2000

1. Remove right side closeout/insulator panel as follows:
   a. Remove fasteners at rear edge of insulator to disengage from lower instrument panel.
   b. Pry out retainers to release panel.
   c. Turn heater temperature sensor ¼ turn to release and allow to remain connected to it's wire.
   d. Disconnect electrical connectors, then slide insulator panel rearward to disengage.
2. Pull back carpet near blower motor.
3. Remove glove compartment.
4. Remove dash integration module (DIM) from bracket, then remove DIM bracket to allow for removal of blower motor.
5. Disconnect blower motor electrical connector.
6. Remove blower motor retaining screws, lower blower motor and rotate counter clockwise to remove from vehicle.

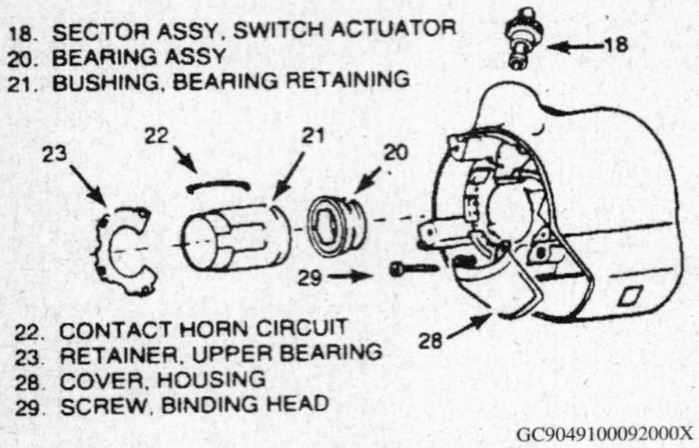

Fig. 12 Lock housing cover removal. Standard column

7. Reverse procedure to install.

HEATER CORE

REPLACE

EIGHTY EIGHT, LSS & REGENCY

1. Drain cooling system.
2. Remove right sound insulator.
3. Remove center and lower instrument panel trim plates.
4. **On models with automatic climate control,** proceed as follows:
   a. Remove speaker grille and speaker for access to programmer attaching bolt.
   b. Disconnect wiring and hoses from programmer.
   c. Remove programmer linkage cover and disconnect linkage.
   d. Remove programmer attaching bolt, then the programmer.
5. **On all models,** remove heater core cover, then the splash cover for access to heater hoses.
6. Disconnect heater hoses from heater core.
7. Remove heater core cover, then the heater core.
8. Reverse procedure to install.

BONNEVILLE, LESABRE & PARK AVENUE

1997–99

Refer to "Eighty Eight, LSS & Regency" for replacement procedure.

2000

1. Drain cooling system into suitable container.
2. Remove fuel injector sight shield.
3. Remove heater hose clamps with suitable hose clamp pliers.
4. Remove heater hoses.
5. From inside of vehicle, remove right and left side sound insulators.
6. **On models equipped with rear air,** remove front console assembly and auxiliary air distribution duct adapter.
7. **On all models,** remove instrument panel lower trim plate.
8. Remove air distributor duct screws (right side screw is difficult to remove and may be left out during reassembly), then the air duct.

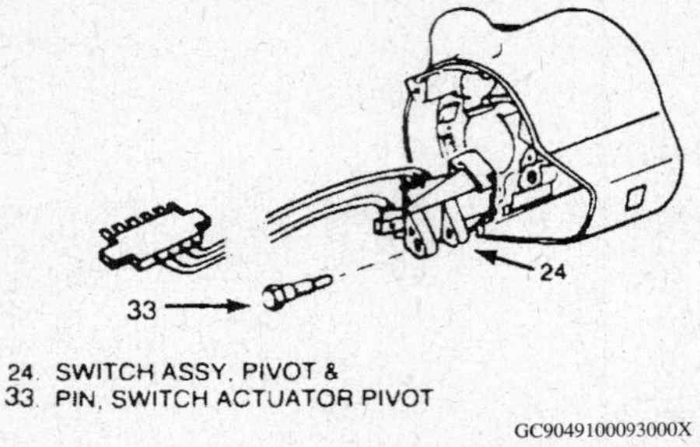

Fig. 13 Wiper switch removal. Standard column

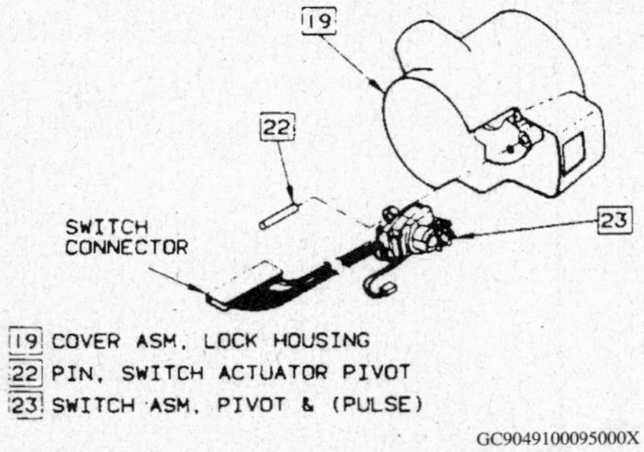

Fig. 15 Wiper switch removal. Tilt column & columns w/SIR

9. Remove heater core shield screws, then the shield.
10. Remove heater core cover screws, then the cover.
11. Remove retaining screw and strap from heater core.
12. Remove heater core.
13. Reverse procedure to install.

EVAPORATOR CORE

REPLACE

EIGHTY EIGHT, LSS & REGENCY

1997–98

Brazed fittings are used on the condenser and evaporator. These fittings cannot be turned. It is important that the service technician recognize which fitting is to be turned and use back-up wrenches. The brazed fitting that should not be turned is always the same color as the pipe it is brazed to.

1. Recover A/C refrigerant as outlined under "Air Conditioning."
2. Remove engine rear sight shield.
3. Disconnect electrical connector from pressure cycling switch.
4. Remove accumulator clamp screw.
5. Disconnect accumulator inlet and outlet connections.
6. Remove accumulator from vehicle.
7. Remove blower motor resistor, then the vacuum tank.
8. Remove engine coolant reservoir, then the evaporator tube from condenser outlet.

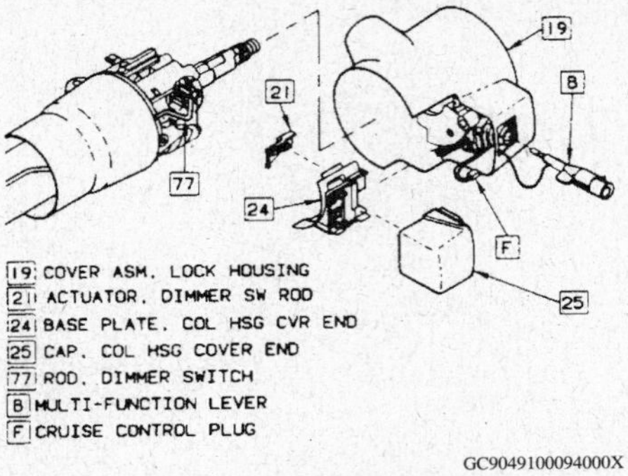

Fig. 14 Lock housing cover removal. Tilt column & columns w/SIR

9. Disconnect A/C lines from clamp near shock tower.
10. Remove evaporator tube from vehicle.
11. Remove blower motor, then the brackets and heat shield from blower module assembly, **Fig. 16**
12. Cut blower module assembly along indicated line, then remove bolts attaching blower module assembly to front of dash (driver's side only).
13. Remove large piece of blower module assembly insulation.
14. Remove screws from evaporator cover, then the evaporator.
15. Reverse procedure to install.

1999

1. Using suitable A/C recovery station, recover A/C refrigerant.
2. Remove cross car support brace.
3. Remove fuse box cover.
4. Remove accumulator as follows:
   a. Remove sight shield of rear engine.
   b. Loosen retaining clamp screw.
   c. Use dual O-ring joint separator tool No. J–38042, or equivalent, to disconnect accumulator inlet and outlet connections.
   d. Remove retaining clamp screw, then the accumulator.
5. Remove positive booster cable from multi-use relay center.
6. Position under hood fuse block out of way.
7. Remove evaporator tube from evaporator.
8. Remove wire harness clip from HVAC module.
9. Remove accumulator bracket.
10. Remove heat shield of HVAC module.
11. Following cut line, cut top side of HVAC module cover.
12. Raise and support vehicle.
13. Following cut line, cut bottom side of HVAC module cover.
14. Lower vehicle.
15. Remove fuel line clip from HVAC module, then remove insulator from the module.
16. Remove bolt that attaches heater and A/C module assembly to inside of vehicle.
17. Remove blower module from HVAC module assembly.

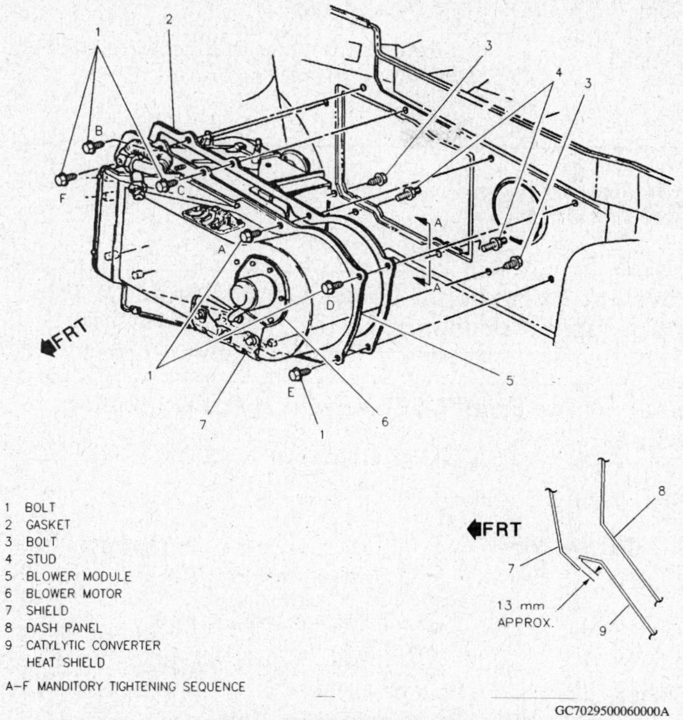

Fig. 16 Evaporator/heater module assembly. 1997–98 Eighty Eight, LSS, Park Avenue & Regency

18. Remove evaporator core.
19. Reverse procedure to install.

BONNEVILLE & LESABRE

1997–99

Refer to "Eighty Eight, LSS & Regency" for replacement procedure.

2000

1. Remove blower control module assembly as follows:
   a. Recover A/C refrigerant from A/C system using suitable A/C recovery station.
   b. Remove evaporator hose nut, then disconnect evaporator hose connection at evaporator.
   c. Remove heater hoses from heater core using suitable hose clamp pliers, pinch off hoses to minimize leakage of coolant.
   d. Raise and support vehicle.
   e. Remove drain tube from A/C module.
   f. Lower vehicle.
   g. Remove instrument panel assembly.
   h. Remove defroster duct and air distributor duct.
   i. Disconnect blower control module connection and instrument panel to A/C module connection.
   j. Remove HVAC module retaining nuts, then the module assembly
2. Remove seal from around heater core and evaporator tubes.
3. Remove upper A/C evaporator case, then the evaporator core.
4. Reverse procedure to install.

PARK AVENUE

1997–98

Brazed fittings are used on condenser and evaporator. These fittings cannot be turned. It is important that the service technician recognize which fitting is to be turned and use back-up wrenches. The brazed fitting that should not be turned is always the same color as the pipe it is brazed to.

1. Recover A/C refrigerant as outlined under "Air Conditioning."
2. Remove vacuum tank.
3. Remove rear sight shield, then disconnect positive battery booster cable from underhood fuse block.
4. Remove underhood fuse block from relay bracket and position aside.
5. Remove relay bracket from dash panel, then the blower resistor from top of evaporator/heater module casing.
6. Disconnect A/C module to accumulator tube from accumulator.
7. Disconnect A/C compressor and condenser hose from accumulator.
8. Remove clamp from accumulator, then disconnect electrical connector from pressure cycling switch.
9. Disconnect evaporator to condenser tube from evaporator case and condenser.
10. Disengage tube from clips holding evaporator tube to fender, then remove tube from vehicle.
11. Remove blower motor, then all brackets from evaporator/heater module, **Fig. 16.**
12. Remove heat shield from bottom of evaporator/heater module, then the three screws attaching bottom of module to dash panel.
13. Remove five screws attaching top and side of module to dash panel.
14. Cut insulator on module along line indicated, **Fig. 17.**
15. Remove four module to insulator attaching screws, located behind insulator.
16. Remove Electronic Brake Control Module (EBCM) as follows:
    a. Remove two screws attaching Assembly Line Diagnostic Link (ALDL) connector to righthand side sound insulator.
    b. Remove push-on nuts and attaching bolts from left and right sound insulators, **Fig. 17.**
    c. Remove righthand footwell courtesy light and oil life module from right side sound insulator, then the insulator from vehicle.
    d. Remove left footwell courtesy light from left side sound insulator, then the insulator.
    e. Remove two floor outlet assembly to instrument panel attaching screws.
    f. Remove four EBCM bracket to instrument panel attaching screws.
    g. Pull bracket away from instrument panel and remove EBCM to bracket

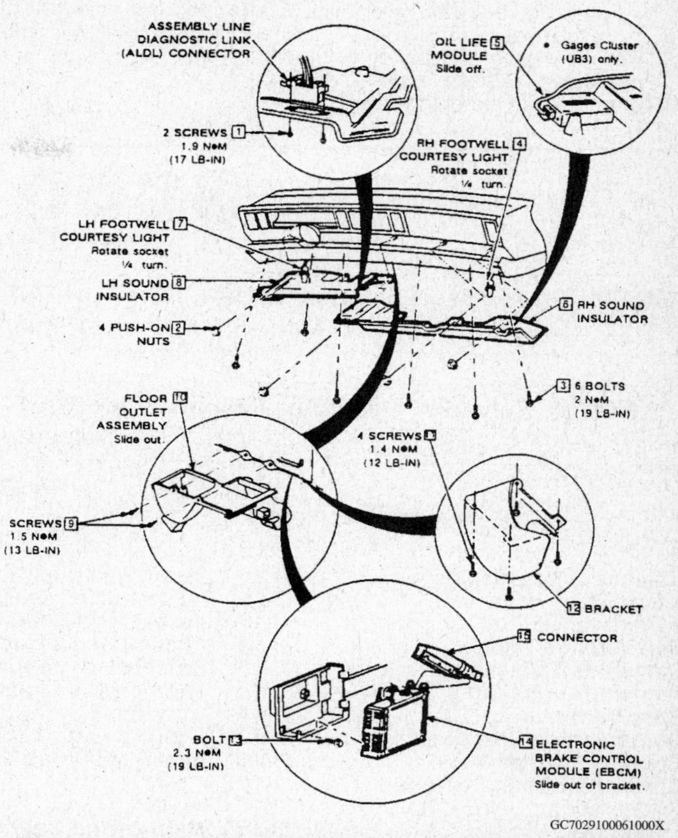

Fig. 17 Electronic Brake Control Module (EBCM) assembly removal. Park Avenue

attaching bolt, then slide EBCM out of bracket.

17. Pull down rug and padding, then remove dash panel to evaporator/heater module case attaching screw.
18. Pull module case away from dash panel and remove evaporator.
19. Reverse procedure to install.

1999–2000

Refer to "Bonneville & LeSabre" for replacement procedure.

3800 Engine

NOTE: On Air Bag Equipped Models, Refer To " Air Bag System Precautions" Located In The Front Of This Manual For System Disarming & Arming Procedures.

NOTE: Refer To "Computer Relearn Procedures " Located In The Front Of This Manual For Computer Relearn Procedures.

INDEX

PRECAUTIONS

AIR BAG SYSTEMS

Refer to "Air Bag System Precautions" in the front of this manual for system disarming and arming procedures.

FUEL SYSTEM PRESSURE RELIEF

After relieving fuel system pressure, a small amount of fuel may be released when servicing fuel pipes or connections. In order to reduce the risk of personal injury, cover fuel pipe fittings with a suitable shop towel before disconnecting to catch any fuel that may leak.

1. Loosen fuel filler cap to relieve tank pressure.
2. Connect fuel pressure gauge tool No. J-34370-1 or equivalent, to fuel pressure connection. Wrap fitting in suitable shop towel.
3. Install bleed hose to suitable container, then open valve and bleed off pressure.
4. Disconnect fuel pressure gauge, then drain gauge in suitable container.

BATTERY GROUND CABLE

Prior to service, disconnect battery ground cable and isolate as required.

COMPRESSION PRESSURE

When checking compression, lowest cylinder must be within 70 percent of the highest cylinder with a minimum pressure of 100 psi. Perform compression test with engine at normal operating temperature, spark plugs removed and throttle wide open.

ENGINE MOUNT

REPLACE

1997

1. Attach suitable lifting equipment to engine, then raise engine slightly to remove weight from engine mounts.
2. Remove accessory drive belt.
3. Remove through bolt from front engine mount, **Fig. 1.**
4. Lift engine until power steering reservoir touches strut tower cross brace, then loosen bottom two bolts on front engine mount.
5. Remove A/C line clip.
6. Remove top two attaching bolts from front engine mount, then mount.
7. Reverse procedure to install.

1998–99

Mount

1. Install engine support fixture No. J28467–360, or equivalent.
2. Remove mount to bracket bolt.
3. Remove mount to frame bolts, then the engine mount.
4. Reverse procedure to install

Bracket

1. Remove fuel injector sight shield.
2. Using suitable lifting equipment, raise engine slightly to relieve stress on mount.
3. Remove engine mount to bracket nuts,

then engine mount to bracket studs.
4. Remove engine mount brackets, then engine mount bracket studs and spacers.
5. Remove drive belt, then supercharger drive belt tensioner if necessary.
6. Without disconnecting lines, remove power steering pump and secure aside.
7. Disconnect coil pack assembly, then secure aside.
8. Remove coolant pump pulley, then engine mount bracket.
9. Remove engine mount nuts and bolts, then engine mount.
10. Reverse procedure to install, noting the following:
    a. **Torque** engine mount bolt nuts to 58 ft. lbs.
    b. **Torque** engine mount bracket stud nuts closest to A/C compressor to 33 ft. lbs.
    c. **Torque** engine mount bracket nuts to 58 ft. lbs.
    d. **Torque** engine mount to engine mount bracket nuts to 58 ft. lbs.

2000

Bonneville & LeSabre

1. Remove fuel injector sight shield.
2. Install suitable engine support fixture.
3. Raise and support vehicle.
4. Remove lower engine mount nut from stud.
5. Remove upper horizontal mount bolt in frame rail.
6. Remove nuts from vertical bolts.
7. Lower vehicle.
8. Remove two bolts from vertical bolt flanges on top of frame rail.
9. Raise and support vehicle.
10. Push two vertical bolts upward to clear mount.
11. Remove engine mount through wheel well.
12. Reverse procedure to install.

Park Avenue

1. Remove fuel injector sight shield.
2. Install suitable engine support fixture.
3. Remove engine mount to engine mount bracket nuts, studs and spacers.
4. **On models equipped with VIN 1 engine,** remove supercharger drive belt tensioner.
5. **On all models,** remove power steering pump and set aside.
6. Disconnect coil pack assembly and set aside.
7. Remove water pump pulley.
8. Remove engine mount bracket, engine mount nuts and bolts, then the engine mount.
9. Reverse procedure to install.

ENGINE

REPLACE

1. Relieve fuel pressure as outlined under "Precautions."
2. Scribe alignment marks on hood for installation reference, then remove hood.

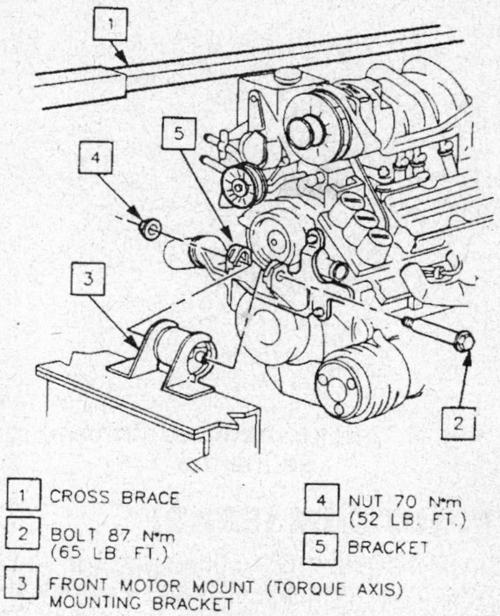

Fig. 1 Engine mount. 1997

3. Drain engine coolant.
4. Disconnect windshield washer, radiator and heater supply hoses.
5. Disconnect starter electrical connector and wiring.
6. Disconnect main engine harness and battery harness electrical connectors at relay center.
7. Remove accessory drive belt.
8. Remove power steering pump and position aside.
9. Remove air intake duct and air cleaner assembly.
10. Remove throttle cable from linkage bracket, then other applicable cables.
11. Disconnect electrical connectors from the following:
    a. MAT sensor.
    b. Throttle position switch.
    c. Idle air control valve.
    d. Oxygen sensor.
    e. A/C compressor.
    f. Oil pressure switch.
    g. Power steering cutout switch.
    h. Vehicle speed sensor.
    i. Low oil level sensor.
12. Remove ignition coil ground strap attaching screws.
13. Disconnect fuel feed and return lines from fuel rail and pressure regulator.
14. Disconnect throttle body canister hoses.
15. Disconnect brake booster and heater control hoses from engine vacuum connection.
16. Disconnect cruise control servo vacuum hoses.
17. Raise and support vehicle.
18. Remove exhaust pipe from right manifold.
19. Install suitable engine lifting equipment, then raise engine slightly.
20. Remove A/C compressor and position aside.
21. Disconnect engine oil cooler lines, if equipped.
22. Remove front engine mount.
23. Remove right front engine to transaxle bracket.
24. Using suitable jack stands, support transaxle.
25. Remove engine to transaxle attaching bolts.
26. Remove flywheel cover.
27. Scribe flywheel installation alignment mark, then remove torque converter to flywheel attaching bolts.
28. Lower vehicle and remove torque axis engine mount.
29. Separate engine from transaxle.
30. Remove engine assembly.
31. Reverse procedure to install.

INTAKE MANIFOLD

REPLACE

VIN K

The two bolts which fasten the lower intake manifold to the cylinder head are accessible only after removing the upper intake manifold. The bolts are located in the right front and the left rear corners of the lower intake manifold.

1. Remove upper intake manifold as described under "Upper Intake Manifold, Replace."
2. Drain cooling system and remove upper radiator hose from coolant outlet.
3. Remove alternator and set aside.
4. Remove drive belt tensioner.
5. Remove EGR valve outlet pipe.
6. Remove intake manifold bolts, then manifold.
7. Reverse procedure to install, noting the following:
    a. Clean cylinder block, heads and intake manifold sealing surface of all oil using a suitable solvent.
    b. Remove adhesive compound from intake manifold bolts and bolt holes.
    c. Apply thread lock compound part No. 12345493 or equivalent, to intake manifold bolt threads prior to installation.
    d. Tighten intake manifold bolts in two steps to specifications in sequence shown in **Fig. 2.**

VIN 1

The two bolts which fasten the lower intake manifold to the cylinder head are accessible only after removing the upper intake manifold. The bolts are located in the right front and the left rear corners of the lower intake manifold.

1. Relieve fuel pressure as outlined under "Precautions."
2. Remove fuel injector sight shield.
3. Remove plastic engine cover and air intake duct.
4. Disconnect manifold vacuum source, then drain cooling system.
5. Disconnect righthand side spark plug wires and position aside.
6. Remove fuel rail, then exhaust manifold heat shield.
7. Disconnect upper radiator and bypass hoses from coolant outlet.

8. Disconnect electrical connectors from the following:
   a. Throttle position sensor.
   b. Idle air control valve.
   c. Fuel injectors.
   d. MAP sensor.
9. Remove EGR outlet pipe.
10. Remove throttle and cruise control cables.
11. Remove throttle bracket with power steering reservoir and set aside.
12. Remove inner accessory drive belt, then disconnect heater hose from intake.
13. Using standard double nut procedure, remove tensioner bracket to supercharger retaining stud.
14. Remove intake manifold attaching bolts, then manifold.
15. Reverse procedure to install, noting the following:
    a. Clean cylinder block, heads and intake manifold sealing surface of all oil using a suitable solvent.
    b. Remove adhesive compound from intake manifold bolts and bolt holes.
    c. Apply thread lock compound part No. 12345493 or equivalent, to intake manifold bolt threads prior to installation.
    d. Tighten intake manifold bolts in two steps to specifications in sequence shown in **Fig. 2.**

UPPER INTAKE MANIFOLD

REPLACE

VIN K

1. Relieve fuel pressure as outlined under "Precautions."
2. Remove fuel injector sight shield and air intake duct.
3. Remove spark plug wires on right (rear) side of engine and position aside.
4. Remove fuel rail, then exhaust manifold heat shield.
5. Remove throttle cable bracket to cylinder head mounting bolt.
6. Remove throttle body support bracket.
7. Remove upper intake manifold attaching bolts, then manifold, **Fig. 3.**
8. Reverse procedure to install, tighten in sequence to specification.

EXHAUST MANIFOLD

REPLACE

LEFT SIDE (FRONT)

1. Relieve fuel pressure as outlined under "Precautions."
2. Remove two crossover pipe to manifold attaching bolts (Vin K) or two left exhaust manifold to right exhaust manifold attaching bolts (Vin 1).
3. Disconnect spark plug wires at spark plugs.
4. Remove oil dipstick tube and dipstick.
5. Remove manifold attaching bolts, then manifold.
6. Reverse procedure to install.

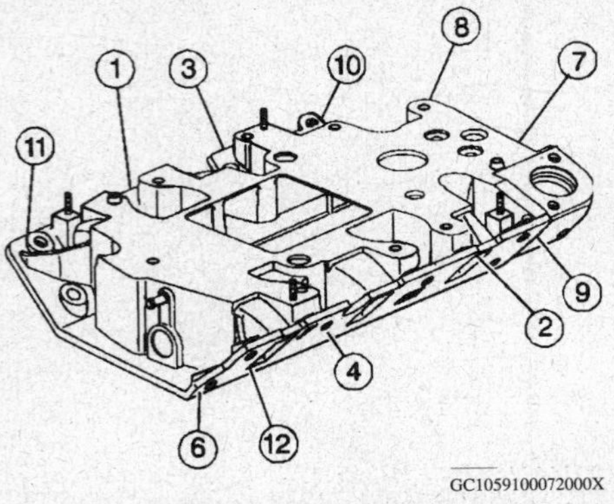

Fig. 2 Intake manifold tightening sequence

RIGHT SIDE (REAR)

Inspect the EGR outlet pipe for leaks whenever the pipe is removed from the right hand exhaust manifold. If a leak exists, replace the EGR adapter.

1. Disconnect spark plug wires from the spark plugs.
2. Remove transaxle oil level dipstick and tube.
3. Disconnect oxygen sensor electrical connector.
4. Remove bolts attaching right exhaust manifold to crossover pipe.
5. Raise and support vehicle.
6. Remove front exhaust pipe to exhaust manifold attaching nuts, then remove exhaust pipe from manifold.
7. Lower vehicle.
8. Remove engine lift bracket.
9. Remove exhaust manifold studs, then the exhaust manifold.
10. Reverse procedure to install.

CYLINDER HEAD

REPLACE

1. Relieve fuel pressure as outlined under "Precautions."
2. Remove intake and exhaust manifolds as described previously.
3. Remove left and right valve covers.
4. Remove any additional wiring or bracketry as necessary.
5. Remove rocker arm assemblies, guide plate and pushrods.
6. Remove and discard cylinder head attaching bolts.
7. Remove cylinder head.
8. Reverse procedure to install, noting the following:
   a. Clean all gasket mating surfaces and cylinder head bolt holes in block.
   b. Clean threads in block with appropriate tap.
   c. Apply suitable sealant to new bolt threads.
   d. Install new head gasket with arrow pointing towards front of engine.
   e. **Torque** cylinder head bolts to 37 ft. lbs. in sequence shown in **Fig. 4.**
   f. Using torque angle meter No. J36660, or equivalent, tighten each bolt an additional 130° in sequence.
   g. Using torque angle meter, tighten center four bolts an additional 30° in sequence.

CAMSHAFT LOBE LIFT SPECIFICATIONS

Engine	Year	Int.	Exh.
3800	1997	.250	.255
	1998–2000	.258	.255

VALVE CLEARANCE SPECIFICATIONS

These engines are equipped with hydraulic valve lifters, valve clearance should be zero.

VALVE ADJUSTMENT

These engines are equipped with hydraulic valve lifters, there is no provision for adjustment.

ROCKER ARMS

Rocker arms are pedestal mounted, over support plates, **Fig. 5.** To replace rocker arms, remove valve cover, pedestal retaining bolt(s), pedestal and the rocker arm. Replace rocker arms and pedestals as an assembly if they are damaged or excessively worn. If rocker arms are to be reused, they must be installed in original position.

VALVE GUIDES

The valve guides are an integral part of the cylinder head and cannot be replaced. If excessive valve stem clearance is noted, the valve guide must be reamed and an oversize valve guide installed. Valves are available in an oversize of .010 inch.

FRONT COVER

REPLACE

1. Remove torque axis mount and bracket.
2. Remove drive belt.
3. Remove drive belt idler pulley/tensioner assembly.
4. Remove crankshaft balancer.
5. Remove crankshaft sensor shield, then the crankshaft sensor.
6. Remove oil pan to front cover bolts.
7. Remove engine front cover attaching bolts, then the front cover.
8. Inspect timing chain for overall in and out movement. Movement should not exceed one inch.
9. Inspect sprockets for visible signs of wear or damage.
10. Clean gasket mating surfaces at timing chain cover and cylinder block.
11. If oil pan gasket is excessively swollen, oil pan must be removed and the gasket replaced.
12. Reverse procedure to install, noting the following:
    a. Apply sealer No. 12346004, or equivalent, to bolt threads.
    b. Install engine front cover bolts and

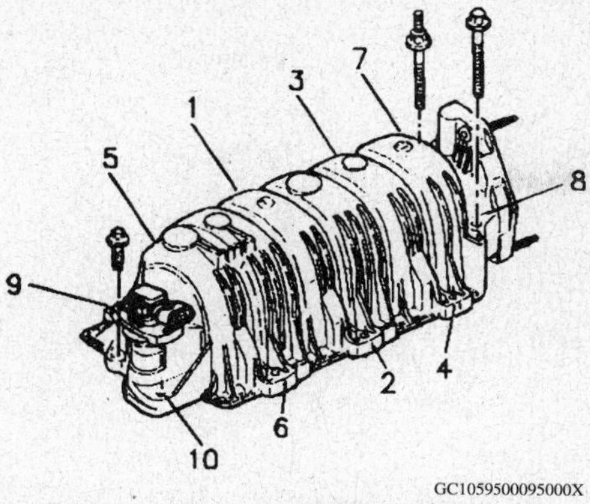

Fig. 3 Upper intake manifold. VIN K

torque to 11 ft. lbs. Then using torque angle meter No. J36660, or equivalent, tighten an additional 40.°

c. Install oil pan to front engine cover bolts and **torque** to 125 inch lbs.
d. Install crankshaft sensor and shield. **Do not adjust crankshaft sensor.**
e. Crankshaft sensor bolt is designed to permanently stretch when installed, do not install a standard bolt. If improper bolt is used, parts will not be tightened correctly.

TIMING CHAIN

REPLACE

1. Remove front cover as outlined under "Front Cover, Replace."
2. Align timing marks on sprockets, **Fig. 6,** so they are as close together as possible.
3. Remove timing chain dampener.
4. Remove camshaft sprocket bolts, **Fig. 7.**
5. Remove camshaft sprocket and chain, then crankshaft sprocket.
6. Reverse procedure to install, noting the following:
   a. Ensure No. 1 piston is at TDC.
   b. Assemble timing chain on sprockets with their timing marks aligned, **Fig. 6.**
   c. Tighten camshaft sprocket bolts specifications.

CAMSHAFT

REPLACE

1. Relieve fuel pressure as outlined under "Precautions."
2. Remove intake manifold as outlined under "Intake Manifold, Replace."
3. Remove valve cover, rocker arms, pushrods and valve lifters.
4. Remove crankshaft pulley and crankshaft sensor cover.
5. Remove front cover, timing chain and sprockets.
6. Remove camshaft thrust plate and camshaft. **When removing or installing camshaft, avoid marring bearing surface.**
7. Reverse procedure to install, coating camshaft and valve lifters with prelube part No. 1052365 or equivalent, prior to installation.

BALANCE SHAFT

REPLACE

REMOVAL

1. Remove engine as outlined under "Engine, Replace."
2. Remove flywheel, then intake manifold.
3. Remove lifter guide retainer, then front cover.
4. Remove balance shaft drive gear bolt, **Fig. 8,** then camshaft sprocket and timing chain.
5. Remove balance shaft retainer bolts, retainer and gear.
6. Using slide hammer tool J-6125-B, or equivalent, remove balance shaft. **The balance shaft and both bearings are serviced as a complete package. Use only correct tools for bearing and shaft removal and installation. Inspect balance shaft drive gear and camshaft drive gear for nicks and burrs.**
7. Remove balance shaft rear plug.
8. Using tool J-36995-5, remove balance shaft rear bearing.

INSTALLATION

1. Dip balance shaft rear bearing in clean engine oil, then, using balance shaft bearing remover/installer tool No. J-36995-1, or equivalent, install bearing with rolled edge facing into engine and Manufacturer's markings facing flywheel side.
2. Dip front balance shaft bearing into clean engine oil, then, using tool J-36996, install balance shaft into block.
3. Temporarily install balance shaft bearing retainer and bolts.
4. Install balance shaft drive gear, then apply suitable sealant to and install bolt, tightening to specifications.
5. Install balance shaft rear plug.
6. Measure balance shaft endplay, **Fig. 9.** Endplay should be 0–.008 inch.
7. Measure balance shaft radial play at both front and rear, **Figs. 10 and 11.** Front radial play should be 0–.0011 inch and rear radial play should be .0005–.0047 inch.
8. Turn camshaft so, with camshaft sprocket temporarily installed, timing mark is straight down.
9. With camshaft sprocket and camshaft gear removed, turn balance shaft so timing mark on gear points straight down.
10. Install camshaft gear, aligning marks on balance shaft gear and camshaft gear by turning balance shaft, **Fig. 6.**
11. Turn crankshaft so No. 1 piston is at TDC.
12. Install timing chain and camshaft sprocket.
13. Measure gear lash, **Fig. 12,** at four places, every ¼ turn. Lash should be .002–.005 inch.

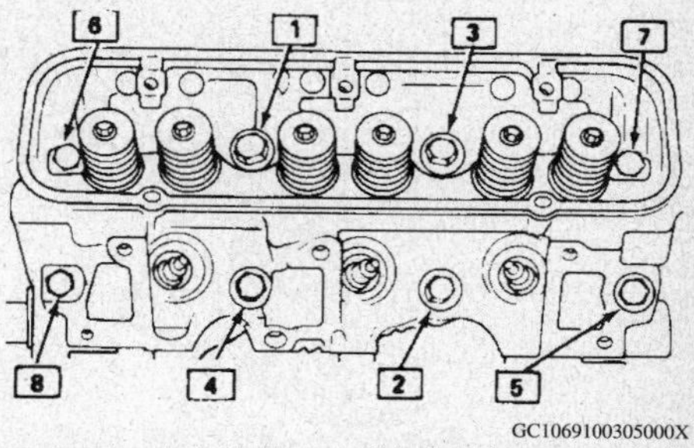

Fig. 4 Cylinder head tightening sequence

14. Install balance shaft front bearing retainer and bolts, then tighten to specifications.
15. Install front cover, then lifter guide retainer.
16. Install intake manifold, then flywheel. Tighten flywheel bolts to specifications.
17. Install engine in vehicle.

PISTON & ROD ASSEMBLY

1. Coat piston pin with oil.
2. Install one piston pin retainer into retainer groove.
3. Install connecting rod and piston pin, rod can be installed in either direction.
4. Push piston pin in until it bottoms against installed piston pin retainer.
5. Ensure piston moves freely.

PISTONS, PINS & RINGS

Pistons and ring are available in standard sizes and oversizes of .010. Piston pins are supplied with piston and are available in standard size only.

To check piston fit in bore, measure bore diameter using suitable telescoping gauges and record reading. Measure piston across skirt at a point ¾ inch below piston pin center line and record reading. Subtract piston diameter from bore diameter and compare to specified clearance.

MAIN & ROD BEARINGS

Main & rod bearings are available in standard sizes and a variety of undersizes.

CRANKSHAFT SEAL

REPLACE

REMOVAL

1. Remove transaxle assembly and flywheel/flexplate.
2. Pry out seal using a suitable screwdriver or other flat bladed tool.
3. Clean surfaces and inspect for visual damage or excessive wear, repair or replace components as necessary.

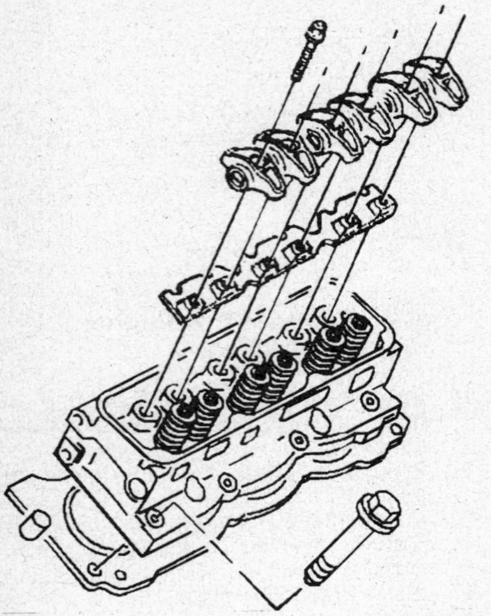

Fig. 5 Rocker arm assembly

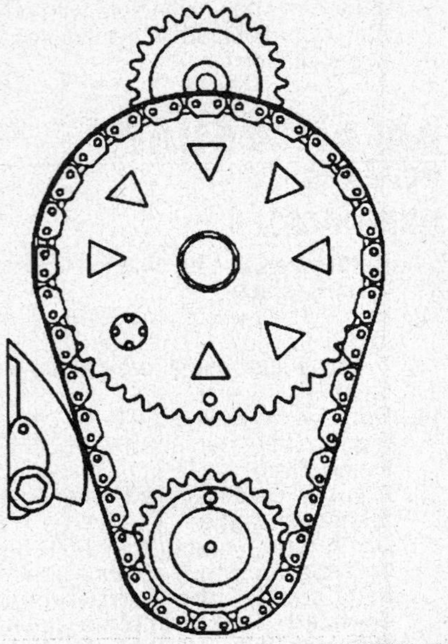

Fig. 6 Timing gear alignment marks

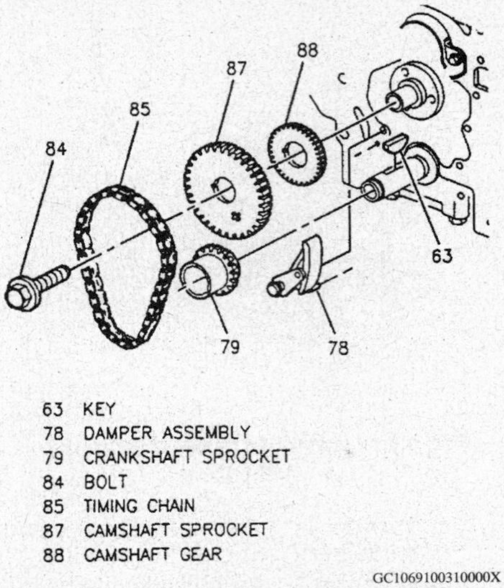

Fig. 7 Timing chain & sprockets

INSTALLATION

1. Apply engine oil to both sides of new seal.
2. Slide seal over mandrel of rear main oil seal installer tool No. J38196, or equivalent, until back of seal bottoms squarely against collar of tool.
3. Attach main seal oil installer tool to crankshaft by hand or torque attaching screws to 54 inch lbs.
4. Turn T-handle of tool so that collar pushes seal into bore.
5. Turn handle until collar is tight against case.
6. Loosen T-handle until it comes to a stop, then remove attaching screws.

OIL PAN

REPLACE

1. Raise vehicle and drain engine oil into suitable container.
2. Remove flywheel cover.
3. Remove oil level sensor located in oil pan before oil pan is removed. Damage to sensor will occur if pan is removed with sensor installed.
4. Remove oil filter.
5. Remove oil pan bolts, then the oil pan.
6. Remove oil pump pipe and screen.
7. Remove old oil pan gasket.
8. Clean oil pan and cylinder block mating surfaces.
9. Reverse procedure to install.

OIL PUMP SERVICE

REMOVAL & INSPECTION

1. Remove front cover, refer to "Front Cover, Replace" procedure.
2. Remove oil filter adapter, pressure regulator valve and spring.
3. Remove oil pump cover attaching screws, then cover and gears, **Fig. 13.**
4. Check pump cover and housing for cracks, scoring, porous or damaged casting, damaged threads or excessive wear or galling. Replace as required.
5. Check pressure regulator valve for scoring, burrs or sticking in valve bore. Replace as required.
6. Check pressure regulator valve spring for tension loss or bending. Replace spring as required.
7. Check gears for chipping galling or excessive wear. Replace as required.

ASSEMBLY & INSTALLATION

1. Measure oil pump inner gear tip clearance, **Fig. 14.** Maximum clearance should be .006 inch.
2. Measure oil pump outer gear diameter clearance, **Fig. 15.** Clearance should be .008–.015 inch.
3. Measure oil pump gear end clearance with gear dropped in housing, **Fig. 16.** Clearance should be .0010–.0035 inch.
4. Measure pressure regulator valve for valve to bore clearance of .0015–.003 inch.
5. Lubricate all gears with clean motor oil, then install gears in housing.
6. Pack pump cavity with suitable petroleum jelly.
7. Install pump cover and cover attaching screws. Tighten cover attaching screws to specifications.
8. Install pressure regulator valve and spring.
9. Install oil filter adapter using a new gasket. Tighten oil filter adapter attaching bolts to specifications.
10. Install front cover on engine. **During front cover installation, ensure inner pump gear is properly engaged on crankshaft sprocket.**

BELT TENSION DATA

This engine is equipped with an automatic belt tensioner.

SERPENTINE DRIVE BELT

BELT ROUTING

Refer to **Figs. 17 and 18** for serpentine drive belt routing.

BELT TENSIONER, REPLACE

VIN 1

1. Remove supercharger belt.
2. Remove ignition module.
3. Remove tensioner bolts, then the tensioner.
4. Reverse procedure to install.

VIN K

1. Raise and support vehicle.
2. Remove lower splash shield, then drain coolant into suitable container.
3. Install front splash shield, lower vehicle.
4. Remove drive belt, alternator and heater hoses.
5. Remove drive belt tensioner bolts, then the tensioner.
6. Reverse procedure to install, tighten tensioner bolts to specification.

COOLING SYSTEM BLEED

1. Fill cooling system and leave radiator cap off.
2. Turn A/C-heater control to any A/C mode and set temperature to highest setting.
3. Start engine and allow engine to idle until bottom radiator hose is hot.
4. Cycle engine speed up to 3000 RPM and back to idle five times.
5. Slowly open bleed valve on back of

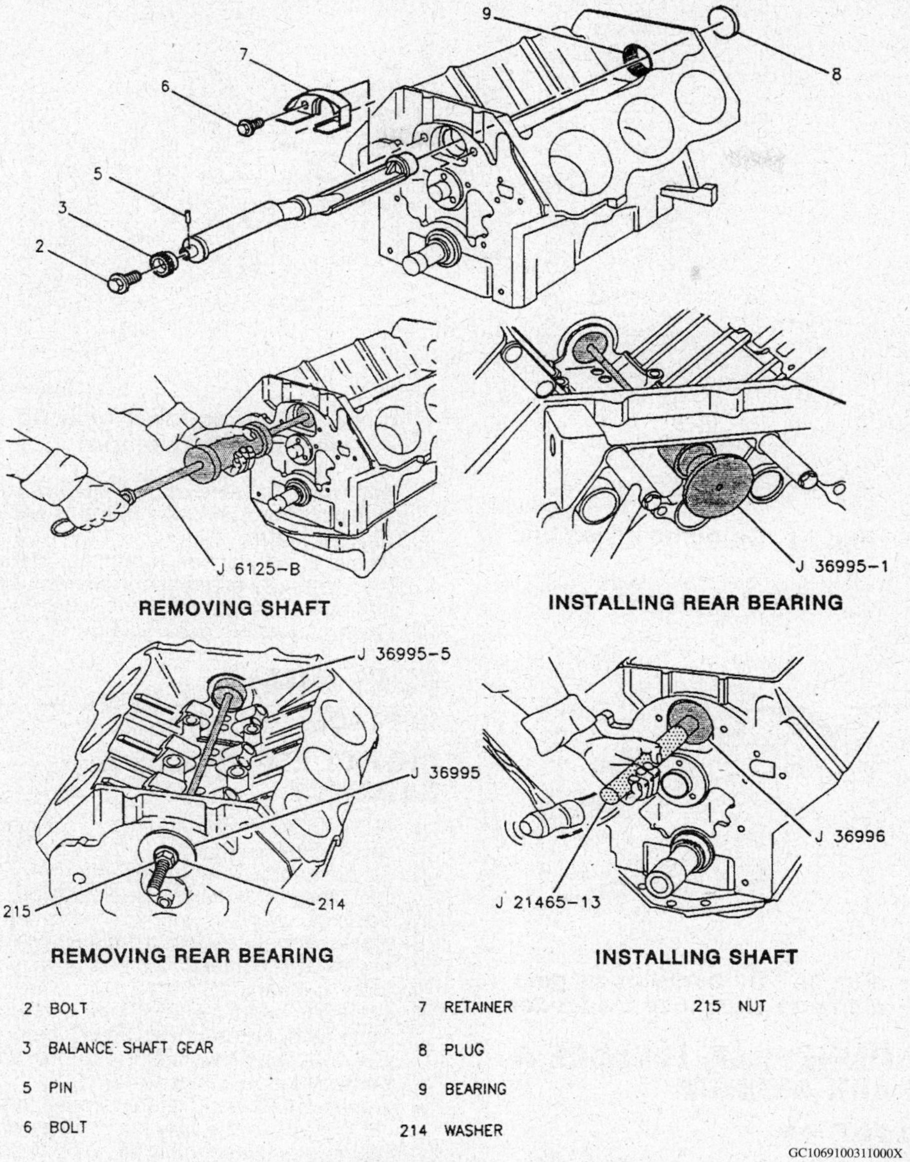

Fig. 8 Balance shaft service

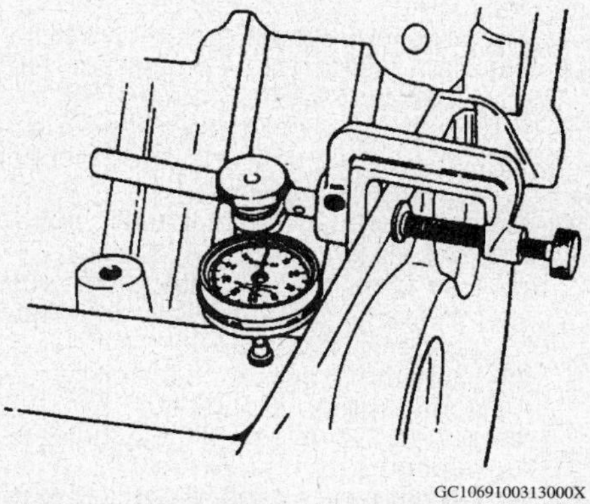

Fig. 10 Balance shaft front radial play measurement

thermostat housing for approximately 15 seconds to expel any trapped air in cooling system.

6. Refill radiator and install pressure cap.
7. Allow engine to return to outside temperature, then fill coolant reservoir to FULL COLD mark.

THERMOSTAT

REPLACE

1. **On 1998–2000 models,** remove engine cover.
2. **On all models,** with engine cool, drain engine coolant below thermostat level. **Never open cooling system with engine hot. Failure to follow this warning may cause personal injury.**
3. Disconnect radiator hose from thermostat housing.
4. Remove thermostat housing retaining bolt(s), then the housing, gasket and thermostat.
5. Reverse procedure to install noting the following:

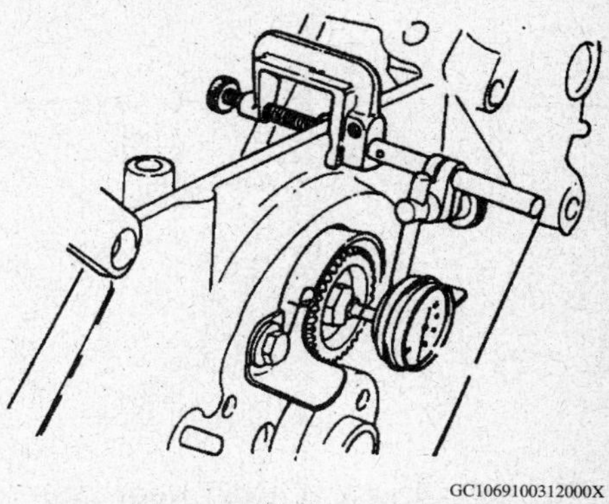

Fig. 9 Balance shaft endplay measurement

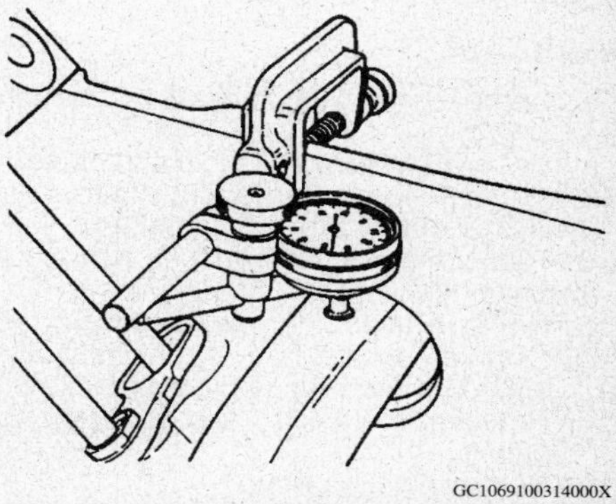

Fig. 11 Balance shaft rear radial play measurement

a. Prior to installation, ensure thermostat gasket area is thoroughly clean.
b. Install thermostat with new gasket.
c. Tighten thermostat housing retaining bolt(s) to specifications.
d. Refill and bleed cooling system as needed.

WATER PUMP

REPLACE

VIN K

Removal

1. Drain cooling system into suitable container.
2. Remove drive belt.
3. Remove water pump pulley bolts, then the water pump pulley.
4. Remove water pump bolts, then the water pump.
5. Clean gasket mating surfaces.

Installation

1. Install new gasket then place water pump in place on engine.
2. Install bolts and **torque** bolts (1) to 11 ft. lbs., and bolt (2) to 22 ft. lbs., **Fig. 19.**
3. Install drive belt.
4. Fill cooling system, run engine and inspect for leaks.

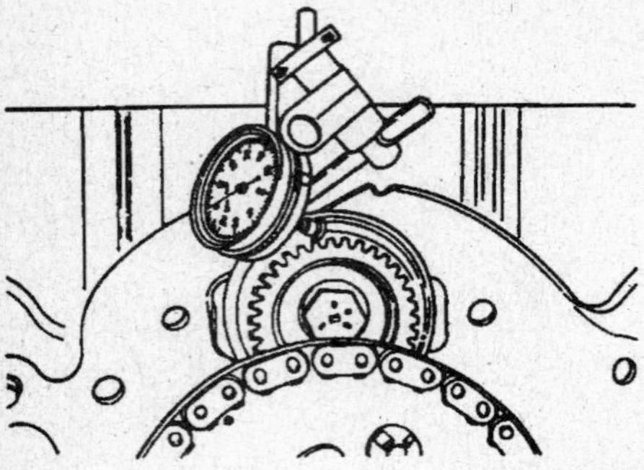

Fig. 12 Balance shaft gear lash inspection

VIN 1

Removal

1. Remove A/C compressor splash shield.
2. Drain coolant into suitable container.
3. Remove supercharger drive belt.
4. Remove accessory drive belt.
5. Remove coil pack mounting hardware and position coil pack out of way.
6. Remove supercharger belt tensioner.
7. Remove engine mount, power steering pump and engine mount bracket.
8. Remove idler pulley and water pump pulley.
9. Remove water pump.
10. Clean gasket mating surfaces.

Installation

1. Install new gasket, then position water pump on engine.
2. Install bolts and **torque** bolts (1) to 11 ft. lbs., and bolt (2) to 22 ft. lbs., **Fig. 19.**
3. Install water pump pulley, tighten bolts to specification.
4. Install idler pulley, tighten bolt to specification.
5. Install engine mount bracket, power steering pump and engine mount.
6. Install supercharger belt tensioner.
7. Install accessory drive belt, then the supercharger belt.
8. Fill cooling system.
9. Install A/C compressor splash shield.
10. Start engine and inspect for leaks.

RADIATOR

REPLACE

EIGHTY EIGHT, LSS & REGENCY

1. Drain engine coolant.
2. Remove upper fan mounting bolts.
3. Remove upper radiator panel.
4. Remove coolant hoses from radiator and coolant recovery tank hose from radiator neck.
5. Disconnect coolant fan electrical connector.
6. Disconnect transaxle oil cooler lines from radiator side tank.
7. Remove radiator from vehicle.
8. Reverse procedure to install.

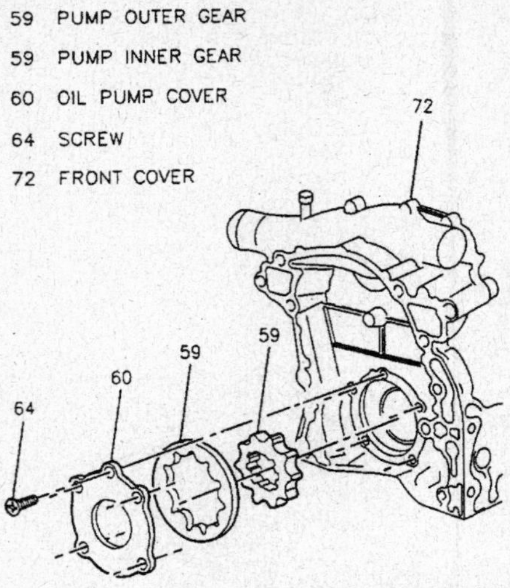

Fig. 13 Oil pump assembly

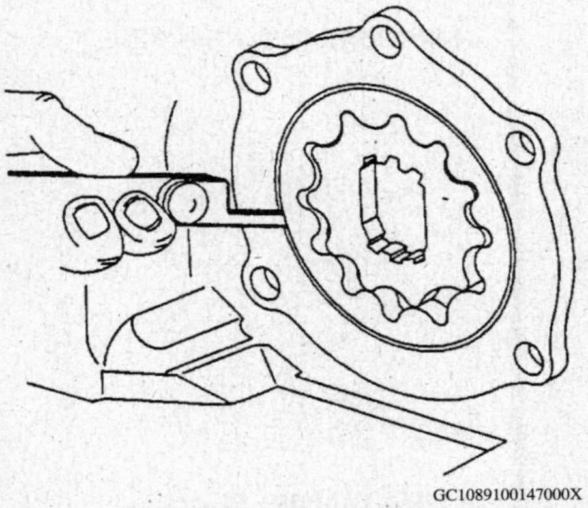

Fig. 15 Oil pump outer gear diameter clearance inspection

BONNEVILLE, LESABRE & PARK AVENUE

1997–99

Refer to "Eighty Eight, LSS & Regency" for replacement procedure.

2000

1. Drain engine coolant into suitable container.
2. Remove upper radiator seal.
3. **On Park Avenue models,** remove upper two bolts from hood latch support.
4. **On all models,** remove upper radiator support bar.
5. Disconnect and plug coolant overflow hose from radiator.
6. Disconnect upper and lower radiator hoses from radiator and position out of way.
7. Remove bolt from transmission oil cooler pipe clip at lower radiator tie bar.
8. Remove cooling fans.
9. Remove transmission cooler lines from radiator and position out of way.
10. **The bolt retaining the condenser to radiator end tank is a special length and must be used upon installation. Use of other bolts may damage radiator end tank.**
11. Remove condenser mounting bolts, then separate condenser from radiator and remove radiator from vehicle.
12. Reverse procedure to install.

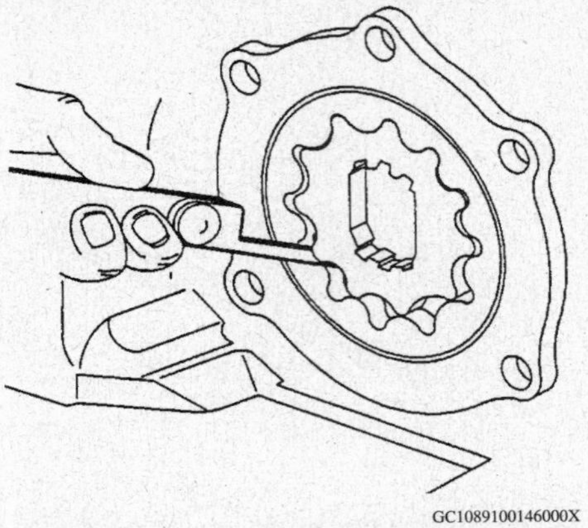

Fig. 14 Oil pump inner gear tip clearance inspection

FUEL PUMP

REPLACE

EIGHTY EIGHT, LSS & REGENCY

1. Relieve fuel pressure as outlined under "Precautions."
2. Do not handle fuel sender assembly by fuel pipes or damage to fuel pipe joints could occur.
3. Replace fuel sender O-rings when installing fuel sender.
4. Drain fuel tank.
5. Clean all fuel pipe and hose connections and surrounding areas before disconnecting connections to prevent contamination to fuel system.
6. Support fuel tank, then remove fuel tank straps and slowly lower tank until fuel line quick-connect fittings are accessible.
7. Disconnect fuel line fittings, then remove fuel tank from vehicle.
8. Remove fuel sender assembly retaining cam using fuel sender spanner wrench No. J35731, or equivalent.
9. Remove and discard fuel sender assembly O-ring, clean and inspect O-ring sealing surfaces.
10. Reverse procedure to install, noting the following:
    a. Use care not to fold over or twist fuel pump strainer when installing sender assembly.
    b. Use new O-ring when installing fuel sender/pump assembly.
    c. Attach fuel lines with original type fasteners and hardware.
    d. Do not repair sections of fuel pipe.
    e. Upon completion of repairs, turn ignition switch to On position for two seconds, then Off for 10 seconds. Turn ignition switch back to On position and inspect for leaks.

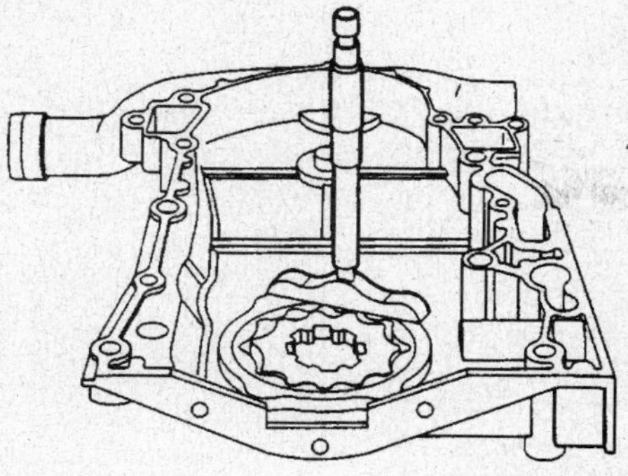

Fig. 16 Oil pump gear end clearance inspection

BONNEVILLE, LESABRE & PARK AVENUE

1997–99

Refer to “Eighty Eight, LSS & Regency” for replacement procedure.

2000

1. Clean fuel pipe connections, hose connections and surrounding areas to prevent fuel system contamination.
2. Do not handle fuel sender/pump assembly by fuel pipes or damage to pipe joints could occur.
3. Replace fuel sender O-rings when installing fuel sender to avoid damage to fuel sender assembly.
4. Relieve fuel system pressure as outlined in “Precautions.”
5. Drain fuel tank to approximately ¾ full.
6. Remove spare tire cover, jack and spare tire.
7. Remove rear compartment floor trim.
8. Remove fuel sender/pump access panel.
9. Remove quick connect fittings and electrical connector at fuel sender/pump assembly.
10. Remove electrical connector at fuel tank pressure sensor.
11. Remove fuel sender/pump retaining ring and assembly retaining cam with fuel sender locknut wrench No. J-39765, or equivalent.
12. Remove fuel sender/pump from vehicle.
13. Reverse procedure to install.

FUEL FILTER

REPLACE

1. Relieve fuel pressure as outlined under “Precautions.”
2. Raise and support vehicle.
3. Remove quick-connect fitting at fuel feed line (2), **Fig. 20.**
4. Remove threaded connection (5) at in-line fuel filter.
5. Inspect fuel lines and O-rings for cuts, swelling, cracks and distortion.

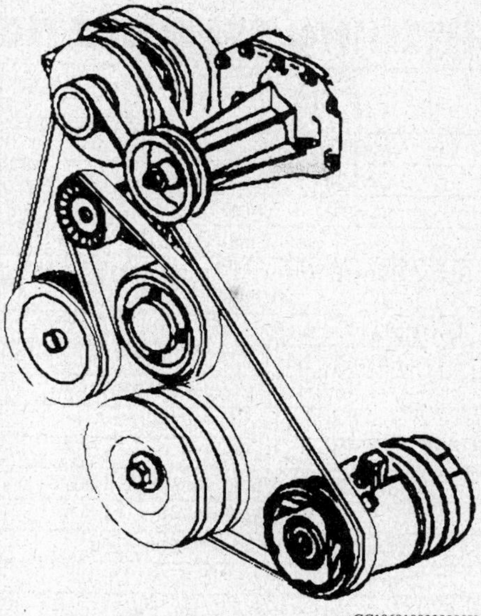

Fig. 17 Serpentine belt routing & replacement. VIN 1

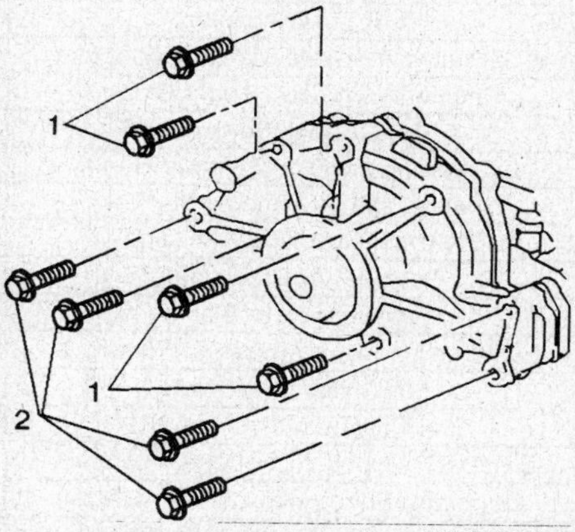

Fig. 19 Water pump bolt tightening orientation

6. Inspect fuel return line and fuel vent pipe.
7. Drain any remaining fuel into suitable container.
8. Reverse procedure to install, tighten fuel filter outlet nut to specification.

SUPERCHARGER

REPLACE

1. Relieve fuel pressure as outlined under “Precautions.”
2. Remove engine cover.
3. Remove supercharger belt.
4. Disconnect right side spark plug wires from ignition module and set aside
5. Remove alternator brace.

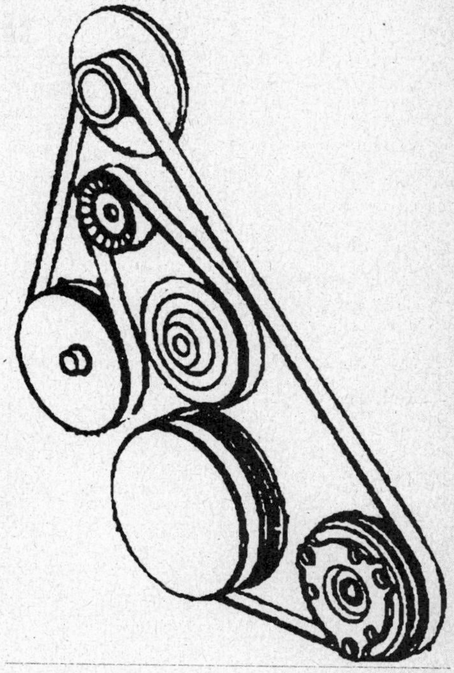

Fig. 18 Serpentine belt routing & replacement. VIN K

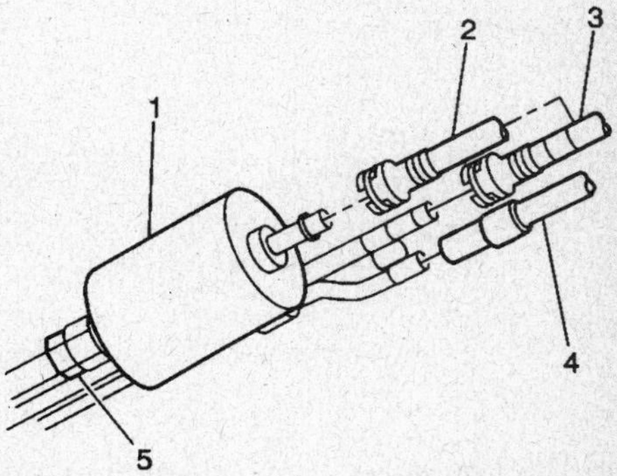

Fig. 20 Fuel filter replacement

6. Disconnect electrical connectors from fuel injectors.
7. Remove MAP sensor bracket.
8. Remove fuel rail mounting bolts and the fuel rail with the injectors.
9. Remove boost control solenoid.
10. Remove throttle body nuts.
11. Remove supercharger.
12. Clean intake manifold and supercharger mating surfaces.
13. Reverse procedure to install, noting the following:
    a. Do not use any sealer on supercharger gasket.
    b. Install supercharger bolts, then tighten to specification.

TIGHTENING SPECIFICATIONS

Year	Component	Torque/ Ft. Lbs.
1997–2000	Accessory Drive Belt Tensioner	37
	Balance Shaft Gear Bolt	16①
	Balance Shaft Retainer	22
	Belt Tensioner	37
	Boost Control Solenoid To Bypass Actuator (VIN 1)	22
	Bypass Actuator To Supercharger (VIN 1)	22
	Camshaft Sensor To Front Cover	72②
	Camshaft Sprocket Bolts	74⑤
	Connecting Rod Bolts	20⑥
	Coolant Plug	32
	Coolant Temperature Sensor To Intake	15
	Crankshaft Balancer	110⑦
	Crankshaft Sensor Clamp Bolt	40②
	Crankshaft Sensor To Front Cover	22
	Cylinder Block Drain Plug	25
	Cylinder Head To Block	③
	EGR Pipe To EGR Valve	22
	EGR Pipe To Exhaust Manifold	15
	EGR Valve Adapter	37
	EGR Valve To Intake Manifold Adapter	22
	Engine Mount To Cylinder Block	70
	ESC Knock Sensor	13
	Exhaust Manifold To Cylinder Head	38
	Exhaust Pipe To Exhaust Manifold	18
	Flywheel Cover To Transaxle	48②
	Flywheel To Crankshaft	11⑥
	Front Cover To Block	22
	Fuel Feed & Return Pipes To Fuel Rail	22
	Fuel Filter Outlet Nut	22
	Fuel Rail To Intake Manifold	11
	Generator Support Through Generator	36
	Generator Support To Cylinder Head	36
	Heater Hose Fitting To Intake	11
	Ignition Module To Generator Support	18
	Intake Manifold To Cylinder Head	84②
	Intake Manifold (Upper) To Lower Manifold	22
	Main Bearing Cap Bolts (1997–98)	26④
	Oil Filter Adapter To Front Cover	22
	Oil Galley Plugs	25
	Oil Level Indicator Tube	11
	Oil Level Sensor To Oil Pan	16
	Oil Pan Drain Plug	30
	Oil Pan To Block	10
	Oil Pan To Front Cover	10
	Oil Pressure Switch	24
	Oil Pump Cover To Front Cover	96②
	Oil Screen Housing To Cylinder Block	11
	Oxygen Sensor	31
	Pulley Assembly To Crankshaft	110⑦
	Right Exhaust Manifold To Left Exhaust Manifold	15
	Rocker Arm Cover	88②
	Rocker Arm Pedestal	19⑤
	Spark Plug	12
	Starter Motor	35
	Supercharger To Lower Intake Manifold	17

Continued

TIGHTENING SPECIFICATIONS—Continued

Year	Component	Torque/ Ft. Lbs.
1997–2000	Thermostat Housing	20
	Throttle Body Adapter To Intake	20
	Throttle Body To Throttle Body Adapter	20
	Throttle Cable Bracket	35②
	Timing Chain Damper	16
	Torque Converter To Flywheel	46
	Transaxle To Cylinder Block	55
	Valve Lifter Guide Bolts	22
	Water Pump Cover To Timing Chain Cover	11
	Water Pump Pulley	114②

① — Tighten an additional 70.°
② — Inch lbs.
③ — Refer to "Cylinder Head, Replace."
④ — Tighten an additional 50.°
⑤ — Tighten an additional 90.°
⑥ — Tighten an additional 50.°
⑦ — Tighten an additional 76.°

Rear Suspension

INDEX

DESCRIPTION

These vehicles use an independent rear suspension consisting of lower control arms, coil springs, toe links, suspension knuckles, superlift struts and stabilizer bar, **Fig. 1.** The hub and wheel bearing is an assembly and does not require periodic lubrication.

HUB & BEARING

REPLACE

WITH DRUM BRAKES

1. Raise and support rear of vehicle.
2. Remove wheel assembly and brake drum. **Do not hammer on drum as damage to bearing may occur.**
3. Disconnect ABS sensor wire.
4. Remove four hub and bearing assembly to axle attaching bolts. **These four bolts also support brake assembly. When removing these bolts, support brake assembly with a wire. Do not let brake line or ABS electrical wire support brake assembly.**
5. Remove hub and bearing assembly from axle, **Fig. 2.**
6. Reverse procedure to install. Tighten attaching bolts to specifications.

WITH DISC BRAKES

1. Raise and support rear of vehicle.
2. Remove wheel and tire assembly.
3. Remove caliper and secure aside.
4. Remove rotor, then disconnect wheel speed sensor connector.
5. Remove four bolts holding hub and bearing assembly.
6. Remove hub and bearing assembly, then brake shield.
7. Clean control arm face and bore to remove any debris.
8. Reverse procedure to install.

STRUT

REPLACE

1. Raise and support vehicle and remove wheel.
2. Remove rear seat cushion and seat back to gain access to strut tower mounting nuts.
3. Disconnect air tube from strut, **Fig. 3.**
4. Support lower control arm with suitable jack stand.
5. Remove two strut tower mount nuts.

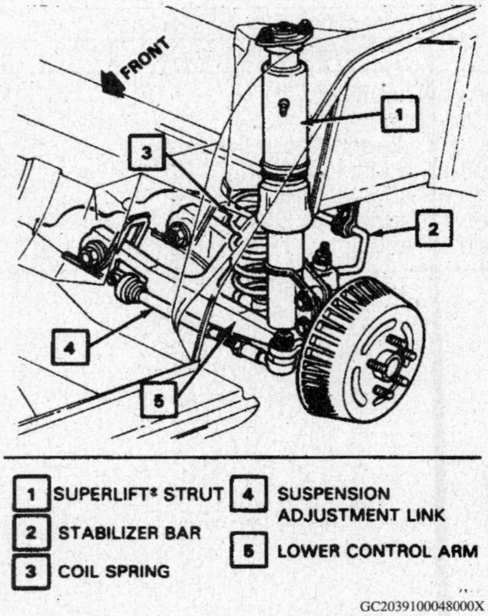

Fig. 1 Rear suspension

6. Remove two strut anchor bolts, washers and nuts from knuckle, then knuckle bracket.
7. Remove strut from vehicle.
8. Reverse procedure to install.

SHOCK ABSORBER

REPLACE

1. Raise and support vehicle.
2. Remove rear wheels and tires, then support control arm.
3. Remove Electronic Level Control air tube from shock.
4. Remove two bolts securing shock to control arm.
5. Remove trunk interior trim in order to gain access to shock upper mounting nuts.
6. Remove upper shock cover, two mounting nuts and reinforcement from top of shock.
7. Reverse procedure to install, tighten mounting hardware to specification.

COIL SPRING

REPLACE

1. Raise and support vehicle.
2. Remove rear wheels and tires.
3. Support control arm with suitable jack.
4. Remove Electronic Level Control (ELC) air tube from shock.
5. Remove two bolts securing shock to control arm.
6. Remove cotter pin and slotted hex nut from tie rod.
7. Using linkage puller tool No. J-24319-01 or equivalent, separate tie rod from lower control arm.
8. Slowly lower control arm until it bottoms on support assembly.
9. Pry under lower spring insulator and remove spring with insulator.
10. Reverse procedure to install, tighten all hardware to specifications.

BALL JOINT INSPECTION

The ball joint has a visual wear indicator. Checking the condition of the ball joint is a simple procedure but must be followed accurately to prevent unnecessary ball joint replacement.

The vehicle must be supported by the wheels during inspection to ensure vehicle weight is properly loading the ball joints.

The ball joint is inspected for wear by visual observation alone. Wear is indicated by retraction of the ½ inch diameter nipple into the ball joint cover (the ball joint grease fitting is threaded into this nipple).

The nipple protrudes .050 inch beyond the surface of the ball joint cover on a new unworn joint. Normal wear will result in the surface of this nipple retracting very slowly inward. The ball joint should be replaced if the nipple is flush or below the cover surface, **Fig. 4.**

Ball stud tightness in the knuckle boss should also be checked when inspecting the ball joint. This may be done by shaking the wheel and feeling for movement of the stud end or castellated nut at the knuckle boss.

Checking the fastener tightness at the castellated nut is an alternative method of inspecting (a loose nut can indicate a bent stud or an "opened up" hole in the knuckle boss). If worn, the ball joint and knuckle must be replaced.

If the ball joint is separated from the knuckle for suspension service, the ball joint seal should be inspected for damage. A damaged seal will cause joint failure. If seal damage is found the ball joint should be replaced.

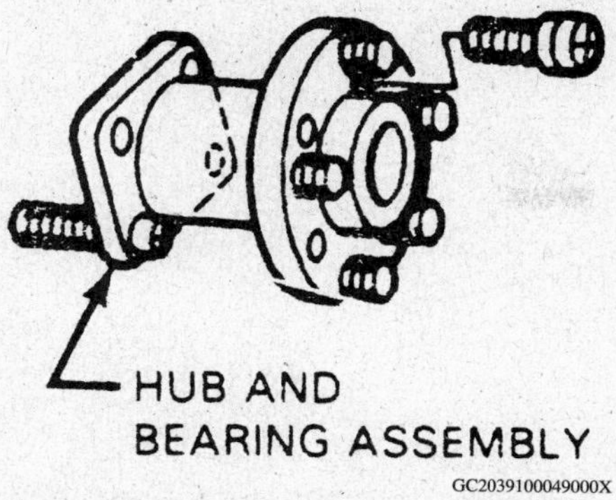

Fig. 2 Hub & bearing assembly

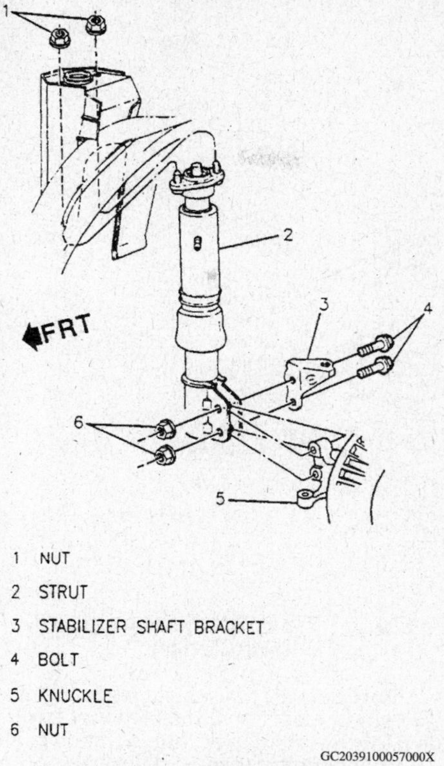

Fig. 3 Strut assembly

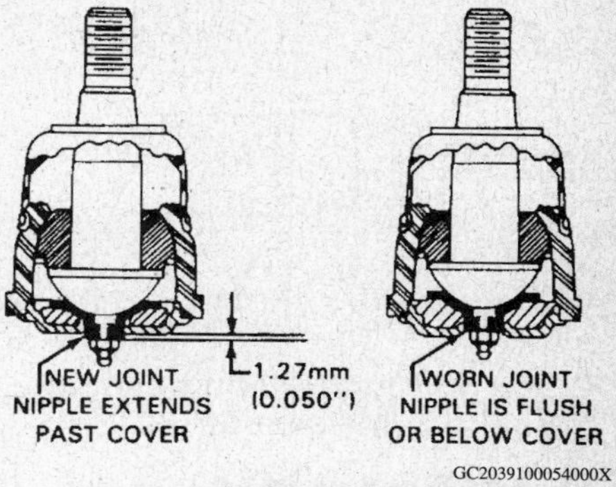

Fig. 4 Ball joint inspection

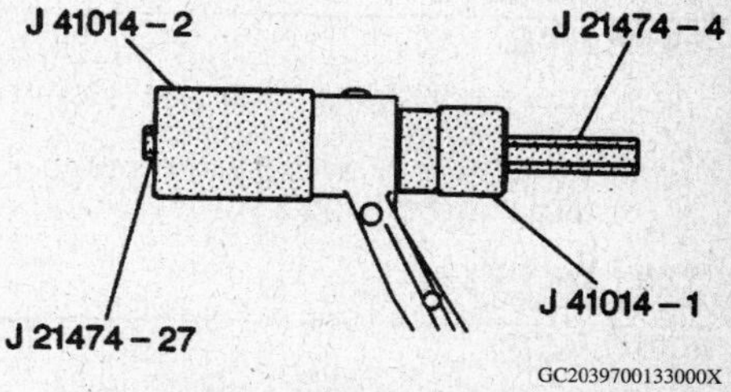

Fig. 7 Control arm bushing removal

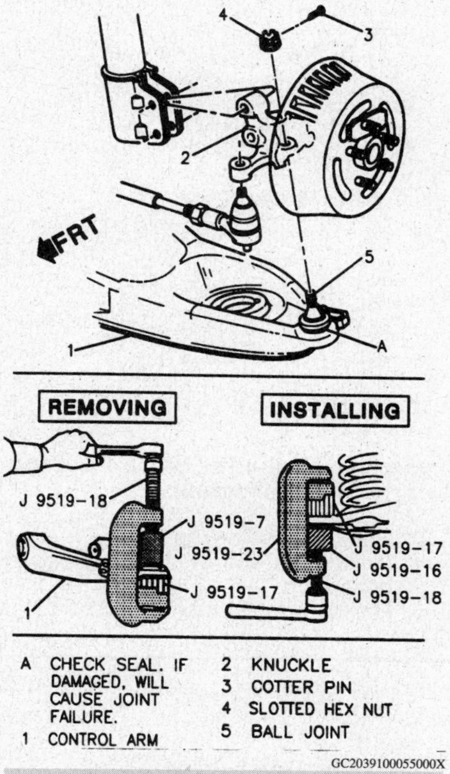

Fig. 5 Rear ball joint replacement.

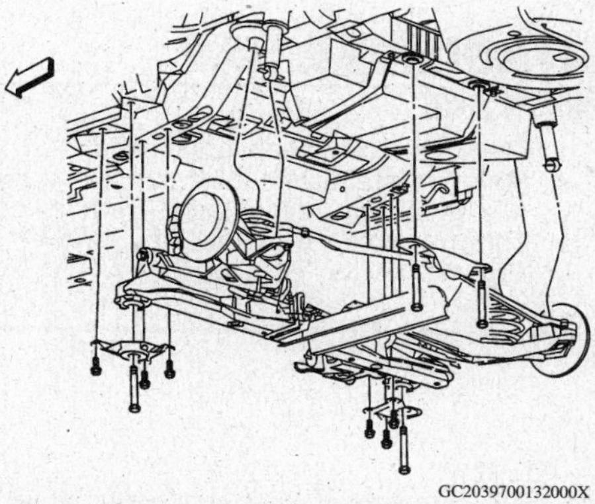

Fig. 6 Rear suspension support assembly removal. Park Avenue, LeSabre & 2000 Bonneville

BALL JOINT

REPLACE

1. Raise and support vehicle.
2. Remove wheel and tire.
3. **On models equipped with electronic level control,** remove height sensor link from right control arm.
4. **On all models,** remove parking brake cable retaining clip at left control arm.
5. Using universal steering linkage puller No. J24319–01, or equivalent, separate adjustment link from knuckle, **Fig. 5.**
6. Support control arm with a suitable jack to prevent spring from forcing it downward.
7. Remove cotter pin and slotted hex nut from ball joint.
8. Using ball joint separator tool No. J34505, or equivalent, separate knuckle from ball joint stud.
9. Install suitable ball joint removal tools and press ball joint out of control arm, **Fig. 5.**
10. Reverse procedure to install.

CONTROL ARM

REPLACE

EIGHTY EIGHT, LSS, REGENCY & 1997–1999 BONNEVILLE

1. Remove adjustment link from lower control arm.
2. Remove spring.
3. Using ball joint separator tool No. J34505, or equivalent, separate ball joint stud from knuckle.
4. Remove control arm.
5. Reverse procedure to install.

PARK AVENUE, LESABRE & 2000 BONNEVILLE

1. Raise and support vehicle, then remove rear tires and wheels.
2. Remove exhaust system.
3. Remove coil springs, refer to "Coil Spring, Replace."
4. Remove rear brake calipers from control arms, then parking brake cables from calipers.
5. Disconnect electrical connectors from wiring harness.
6. Remove Electronic Level Control electrical connector and vent hose.
7. Remove Electronic Level Control air tube from compressor.
8. Support rear suspension support assembly with suitable jack.
9. Remove three bolts per side, securing support assembly brackets to body of vehicle, **Fig. 6**
10. Remove front and rear suspension support assembly bolts, then support assembly.
11. On left control arm, remove Electronic Level Control height sensor.
12. Remove stabilizer link bolts and nuts.
13. Remove ABS electrical connectors.
14. Remove hub and bearing, refer to "Hub & Bearing, Replace."
15. Remove bolt and nut securing control arm to rear suspension support assembly, then control arm.
16. Reverse procedure to install.

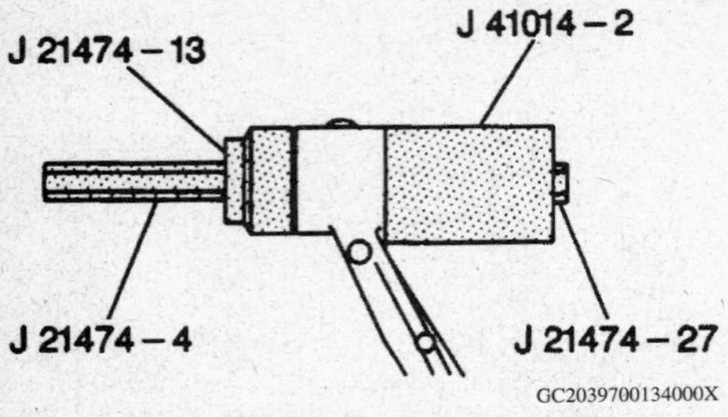

Fig. 8 Control arm bushing installation

CONTROL ARM BUSHING

REPLACE

1. Remove control arm, refer to "Control Arm, Replace "
2. Refer to **Figs. 7 and 8** when servicing control arm bushings.

TIE ROD

REPLACE

1. Raise and support vehicle.
2. Remove wheel assembly, cotter key and castle nut, **Fig. 9.**
3. Using steering linkage puller tool No. J-24319-01, or equivalent, disconnect outer tie rod/adjustment from lower control arm or knuckle. **When disconnecting tie rod/adjustment from lower control arm or knuckle, do not use a wedge since seal damage will occur.**
4. Remove rod/link assembly retaining nut and retainer.
5. Remove rod/link assembly from lower control arm.
6. Reverse procedure to install. Tighten link retaining nut to specifications and **torque** castellated nut securing ball stud to 37 ft. lbs. Install cotter pin retaining castellated nut, tightening nut as needed to insert pin through hole in stud. Do not loosen nut to align slots with hole.

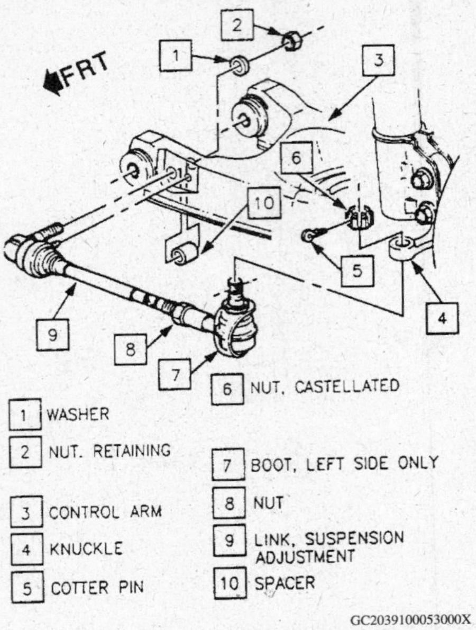

Fig. 9 Tie rod/adjustment link installation

STABILIZER BAR

REPLACE

1. Remove rear wheels and tires.
2. Remove stabilizer shaft support bolt, nut, retainer and insulators from lower control arm or knuckle bracket, **Fig. 10.**

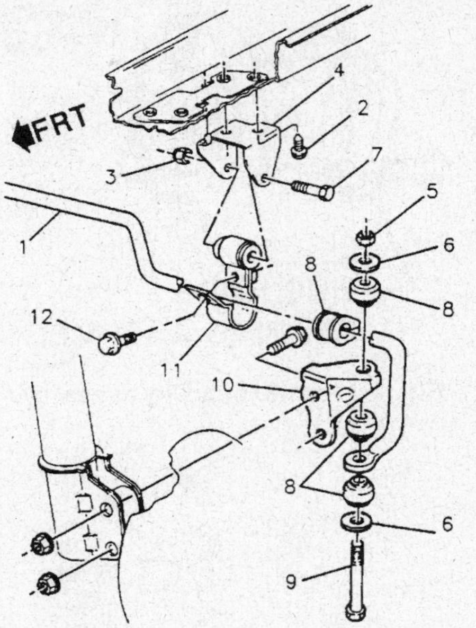

1	STABILIZER SHAFT	7	BOLT
2	BOLT	8	INSULATOR
3	NUT	9	BOLT
4	BRACKET	10	STABILIZER SHAFT BRACKET
5	NUT	11	LINK
6	RETAINER	12	BOLT

GC2039100056000X

Fig. 10 Stabilizer bar & bushing assembly

3. Remove bushing clip bolt.
4. Bend open end of support assembly downward.
5. Remove stabilizer shaft and bushings.

TIGHTENING SPECIFICATIONS

Year	Component	Torque/ Ft. Lbs.
PARK AVENUE		
1997–2000	Adjustment Link Lock Nut	48
	Adjustment Link To Control Arm	63
	Adjustment Link To Knuckle	33
	Adjustment Link To Pinch Bolt	35
	Adjustment Link To Suspension Support Assembly	55
	Body Mount Bolts	38
	Control Arm Nut	78
	Hub Mounting Bolts	52
	Shock To Control Arm Bolts	18
	Shock Tower Mounting Nut	15
	Stabilizer Shaft Clamp Bolt	24
	Stabilizer Shaft Link Bolt	10
	Suspension Support Assembly To Body Front Bolts	141
	Suspension Support Assembly To Body Rear Bolts (1997–98)	122
	Suspension Support Assembly To Body Rear Bolts (1999)	141
	Suspension Support Assembly To Bracket Bolts	63
	Tie Rod Pinch Bolt	35
	Tie Rod To Rear Suspension Support Assembly	55
	Wheel Lug Nuts	100
BONNEVILLE, EIGHTY EIGHT, LESABRE, LSS & REGENCY		
1997–2000	Adjustment Link Locknut	48
	Adjustment Link To Control Arm	63
	Adjustment Link To Knuckle	33
	Ball Joint	40
	Control Arm Bolts (Optional Torque)	134
	Control Arm Nuts	85
	Hub & Bearing Bolts	52
	Stabilizer Shaft Insulator Link Bolt	17
	Stabilizer Shaft Link Assembly	35
	Stabilizer Shaft Link Nut At Bracket	13
	Stabilizer Shaft Mounting Bracket To Body	14
	Strut To Knuckle	140
	Strut Tower Mounting Nut	35
	Tie Rod Retaining Nut	63
	Tie Rod Slotted Hex Nut	33
	Wheel Lug Nuts	100

Front Suspension & Steering

NOTE: On Air Bag Equipped Models, Refer To " Air Bag System Precautions" Located In The Front Of This Manual For System Disarming & Arming Procedures.

NOTE: Refer To "Computer Relearn Procedures " Located In The Front Of This Manual For Computer Relearn Procedures.

INDEX

PRECAUTIONS

AIR BAG SYSTEMS

Refer to "Air Bag System Precautions" in the front of this manual for system disarming and arming procedures.

BATTERY GROUND CABLE

Prior to service, disconnect battery ground cable and isolate as required.

DESCRIPTION

The front suspension is of the McPherson design, **Fig. 1.** The control arm pivots from the cradle and is mounted in rubber bushings. The upper end of the strut is isolated by a rubber mount and contains a non-serviceable bearing to allow for rotation. The lower end of the steering knuckle pivots on a ball joint riveted to the control arm. The ball joint is fastened to the steering knuckle with a castle nut and cotter pin.

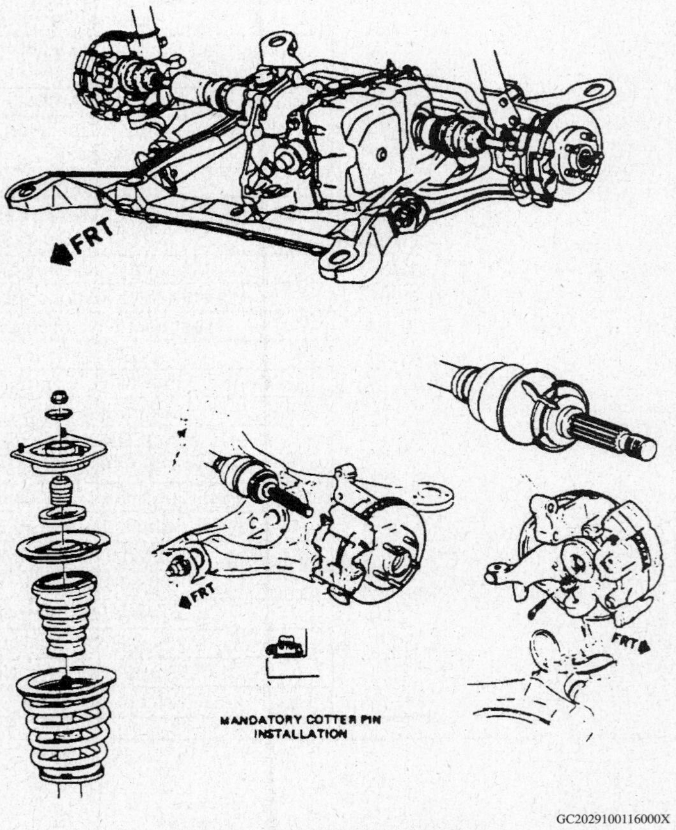

Fig. 1 Front suspension

HUB & BEARING

REPLACE

1. Raise and support vehicle and remove wheel assembly.
2. Clean and lubricate drive axle threads.
3. Insert a suitable drift into caliper and rotor to prevent assembly from rotating, then remove hub nut and washer.
4. Remove caliper bracket mounting bolts, caliper and bracket assembly and rotor. Then secure assembly aside taking care not to stretch or damage brake hose.
5. Disconnect ABS front wheel speed sensor connector and unclip connector from dust shield.
6. Remove hub and bearing retaining bolts and dust shield, **Fig. 2.**
7. Place transmission in park.
8. Using front hub spindle removal tool No. J28733–B, or equivalent, separate hub and bearing from drive axle, **Fig. 3.**
9. Clean face and bore of knuckle to remove any debris before assembly.
10. Reverse procedure to install. Fill area between seal and bearing assembly with GM lubricant part NO. 1052497 or equivalent. Tighten hub attaching bolts, caliper bolts and hub nut to specifications.

BALL JOINT INSPECTION

Ball joints must be replaced if any looseness is detected or ball joint seal is cut or damaged.

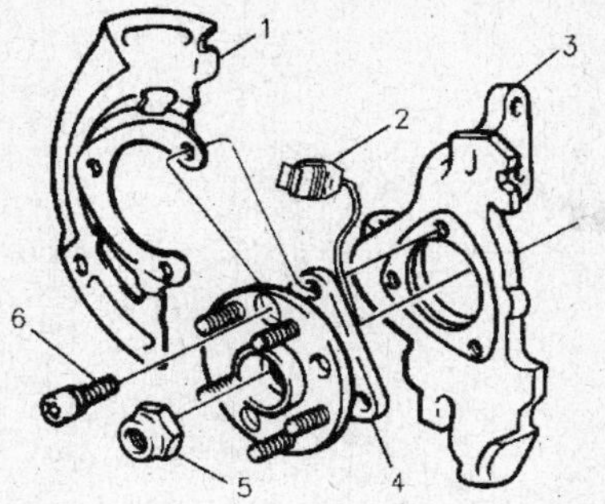

1 DUST SHIELD
2 WHEEL SPEED SENSOR CONNECTOR
3 STEERING KNUCKLE
4 HUB AND BEARING
5 NUT, DRIVE AXLE
6 RETAINING BOLT

GC2029300228000X

Fig. 2 Hub & bearing assembly

1. J-28733
2. TURN FORCING SCREW UNTIL AXLE SPLINES ARE JUST LOOSE

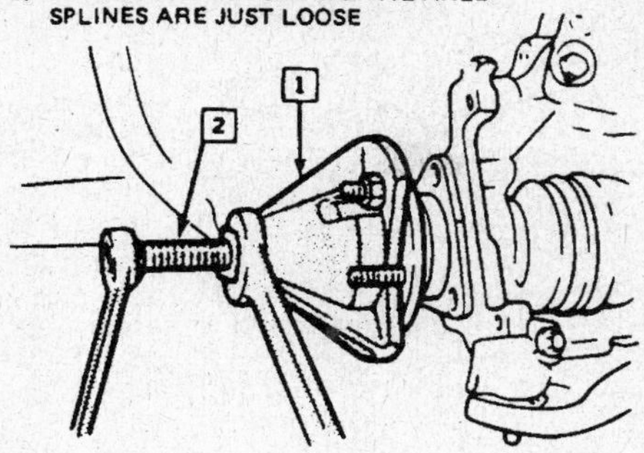

GC2029100117000X

Fig. 3 Separating drive axle from hub

1. J 36226 BALL JOINT SEPARATOR

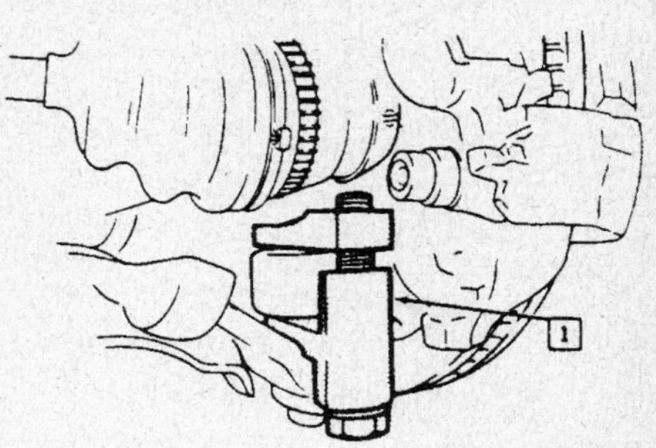

GC2029100119000X

Fig. 4 Separating ball joint from steering knuckle. Eighty Eight, LSS & Regency

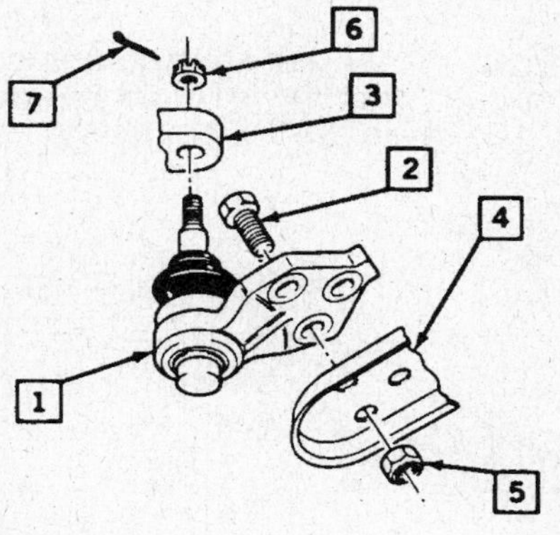

1. SERVICE BALL JOINT
2. BALL JOINT MOUNTING BOLTS MUST FACE DOWN
3. STEERING KNUCKLE
4. CONTROL ARM
5. BALL JOINT MOUNTING NUTS 68 N·m (50 LBS. FT.)
6. BALL JOINT TO STEERING KNUCKLE NUT 110 N·m (81 LBS. FT.) BEFORE COTTER PIN INSTALLATION
7. COTTER PIN

GC2029100120000X

Fig. 5 Service ball joint attachment. Eighty Eight, LeSabre, LSS & Regency

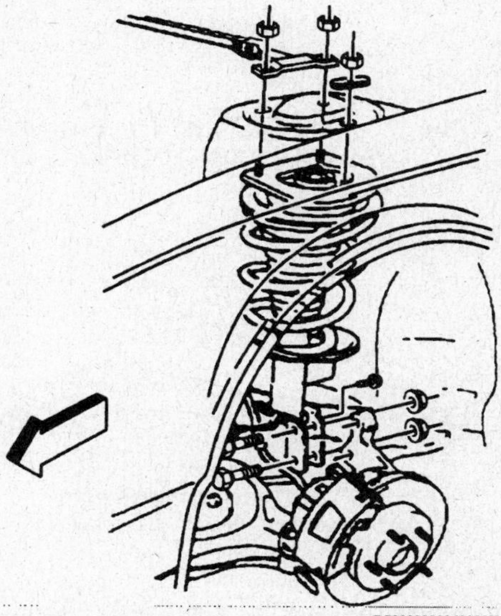

GC2029900260000X

Fig. 6 Strut housing tie bar through bolts. 1997–99 Bonneville, Eighty Eight, LeSabre, LSS & Regency

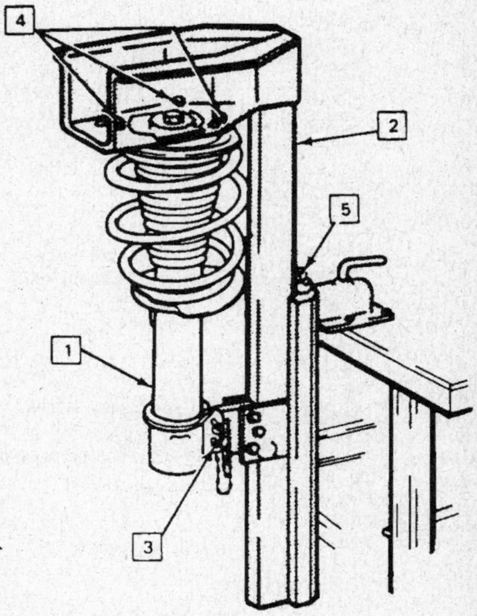

1. STRUT ASSEMBLY
2. STRUT COMPRESSOR J-34013
3. Install LOCKING PINS through STRUT ASSEMBLY
4. Tighten NUTS till flush with STRUT COMPRESSOR
5. COMPRESSOR FORCING SCREW

GC2029100126000X

Fig. 7 Disassembling strut

To inspect ball joints, raise the front of the vehicle, allowing suspension to hang freely. Grasp the tire at the top and bottom, an move the top of the tire in an in and out motion. Check for any horizontal movement of the knuckle relative to the control arm. If the ball stud is disconnected from the knuckle and looseness is detected or if the ball stud can be twisted using finger pressure, replace the ball joint.

Ball stud tightness in the knuckle boss should also be inspected. This may be done by shaking the wheel and feeling for movement of the stud end or nut at the knuckle boss. Worn or damaged ball joints and knuckles must be replaced.

BALL JOINT

REPLACE

EIGHTY EIGHT, LSS & REGENCY

1. Raise and support vehicle and place jackstands under cradle. **Vehicle weight should not be placed on control arms.**
2. Remove wheel assembly.
3. Install drive axle boot protectors.
4. Remove cotter key from ball joint nut and, using ball joint separator tool J-34505, or equivalent, separate ball joint from steering knuckle, **Fig. 4.**
5. Drill out ball joint retaining rivets.
6. Remove stabilizer bar bushing to control arm bolt.
7. Pull control arm downward and remove ball joint from steering knuckle and control arm.
8. Reverse procedure to install. Tighten new ball joint attaching nuts to specifications, **Fig. 5.**

LESABRE

1997–99

Refer to "Eighty Eight, LSS & Regency" for replacement procedure.

2000

The ball joint is serviced only with the control arm and cannot be serviced separately. Refer to "Control Arm, Replace " for replacement information.

PARK AVENUE

The ball joint is serviced with the control arm and cannot be serviced separately. Refer to "Control Arm, Replace" for replacement information.

BONNEVILLE

1997–99

Refer to "Eighty Eight, LSS & Regency," for replacement procedure.

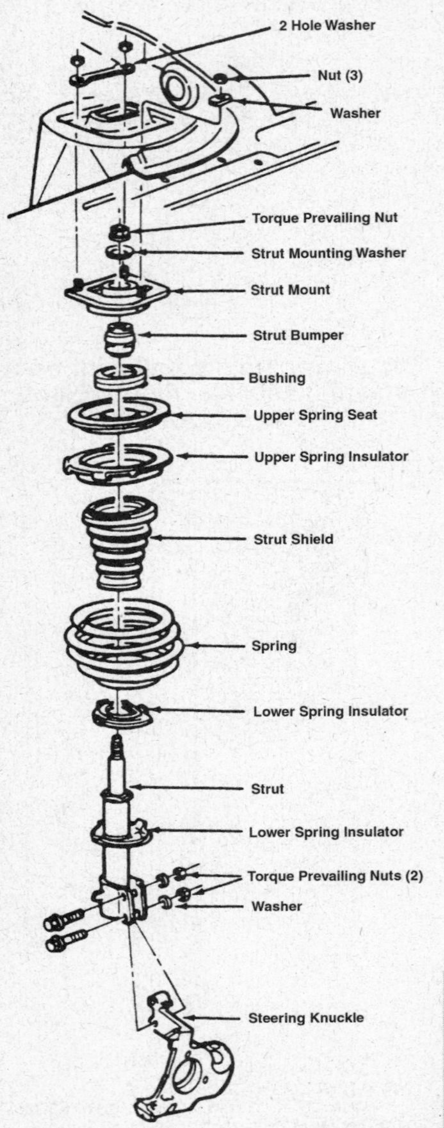

Fig. 8 Exploded view of strut assembly

2000

The ball joint is serviced only with the lower control arm and cannot be serviced separately. Refer to "Control Arm, Replace" for service procedure.

STRUT

REPLACE

1. **On 1997–99 Bonneville, Eighty Eight, LeSabre, LSS and Regency models,** loosen strut housing tie bar through bolts on both ends of tie bar, **Fig. 6.**
2. **On models equipped with CCR,** disconnect CCR connector.
3. **On all models,** remove three strut mount to body nuts.
4. Raise and support vehicle.
5. Remove wheel and tire.
6. Remove ABS front wheel speed sensor connector.

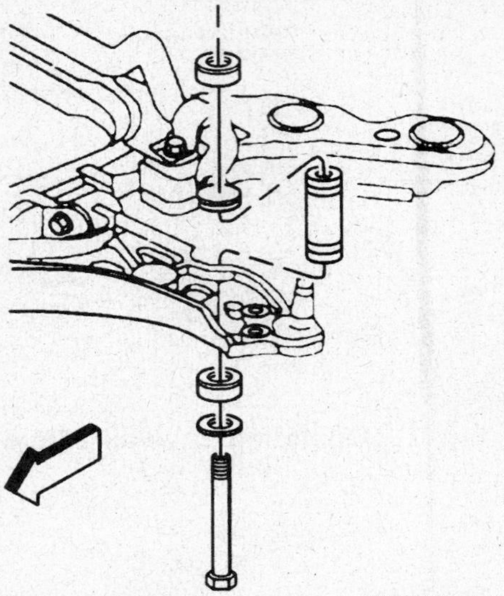

Fig. 9 Stabilizer link to control arm bolt. Park Avenue

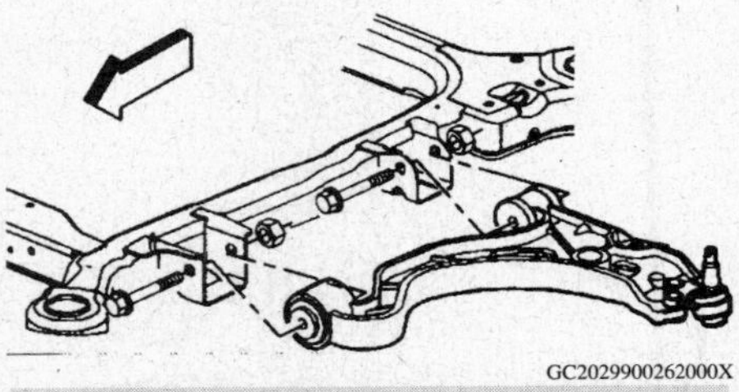

Fig. 11 Lower control arm replacement. Park Avenue

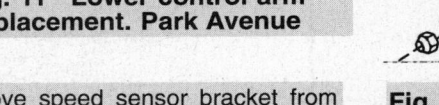

7. Remove speed sensor bracket from strut.
8. Remove brake line bracket from strut.
9. Retain knuckle in position to prevent damage to ball joint and/or drive axle.
10. Remove strut to knuckle bolts.
11. Remove strut from vehicle.
12. Reverse procedure to instal, noting the following:
    a. Avoid cracking or chipping spring coating when handling front suspension coil spring.

STRUT SERVICE

Refer to **Figs. 7 and 8** when performing the following procedure.

1. Remove strut as outlined under "Strut, Replace" procedure.
2. Mount strut in compressor tool J-34013 and holding fixture J-3289-20, or equivalents.
3. Rotate compressor forcing screw until spring compresses slightly.
4. Hold damper shaft from rotating and remove nut from top of strut assembly.
5. Use alignment rod tool J-34013-38, or equivalent, to guide damper shaft from assembly.
6. Loosen compressor forcing screw while guiding damper shaft from assembly. Continue to loosen nut until strut damper and spring can be removed.

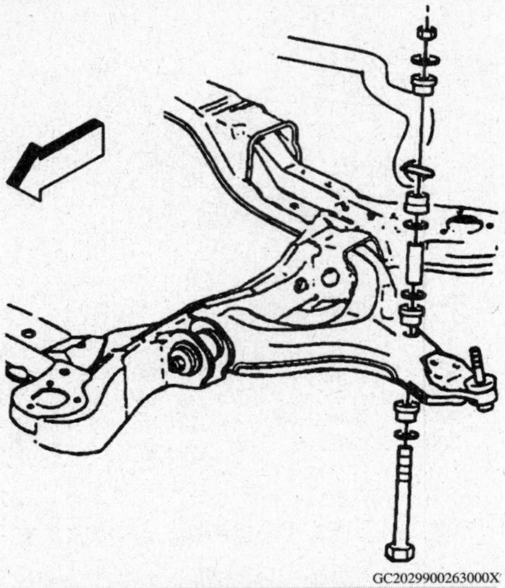

Fig. 10 Stabilizer shaft to control arm bolt. Bonneville, Eighty Eight, LeSabre, LSS & Regency

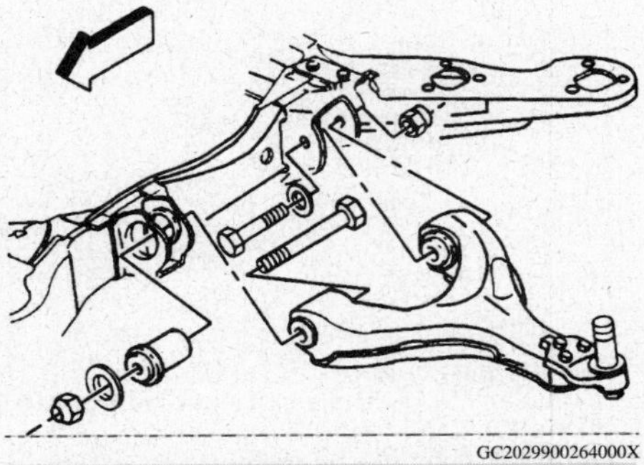

Fig. 12 Control arm replacement. Bonneville, Eighty Eight, LeSabre, LSS & Regency

7. Reverse procedure to assemble. When assembling spring, flat on upper spring seat must face outward 90 degrees from centerline of vehicle or when mounted in strut compressor, seat faces in same direction as steering knuckle mounting flange.

CONTROL ARM

REPLACE

1. Raise and support vehicle.
2. Remove wheel and tire.
3. Disconnect stabilizer link to control arm bolt, **Figs. 9 and 10.**
4. Remove cotter pin and loosen nut from ball joint stud.
5. Using a suitable ball joint separator tool, remove ball joint from steering knuckle.
6. Remove control arm mounting bolts, then remove control arm from frame, **Figs. 11 and 12.**
7. Reverse procedure to install, noting the following:
    a. Install control arm to frame and loosely install mounting bolts, washers and nuts.

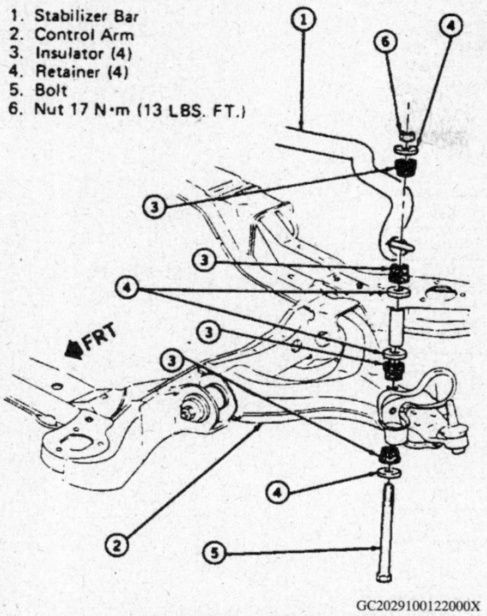

Fig. 13 Stabilizer bar bushing assembly

b. Do not tighten control arm nuts at this time. Weight of vehicle must be supported by the control arms so that vehicle design trim heights are obtained before tightening control arm mounting bolts.
c. Install all remaining control arm hardware, then lower vehicle to ground.
d. Check trim height.
e. Tighten control arm nuts to specification.

STABILIZER BAR

REPLACE

1. Raise and support vehicle and place jackstands under cradle. Vehicle weight should not be placed on control arms.
2. Remove wheel assembly.
3. Install drive axle boot protectors.
4. Remove nuts, washers, bushings and bolt securing stabilizer shaft to each control arm, **Fig. 13.**
5. Remove stabilizer bar mounting bolts, two bolts from each side, **Fig. 14.**
6. Disconnect tie rods from steering knuckles.
7. Remove exhaust pipe between exhaust manifold and catalytic converter.
8. Rotate right side strut assembly completely to right.
9. Slide stabilizer bar to right over steering knuckle and pull downward on left side until stabilizer bar clears cradle, **Fig. 15.**
10. Reverse procedure to install.

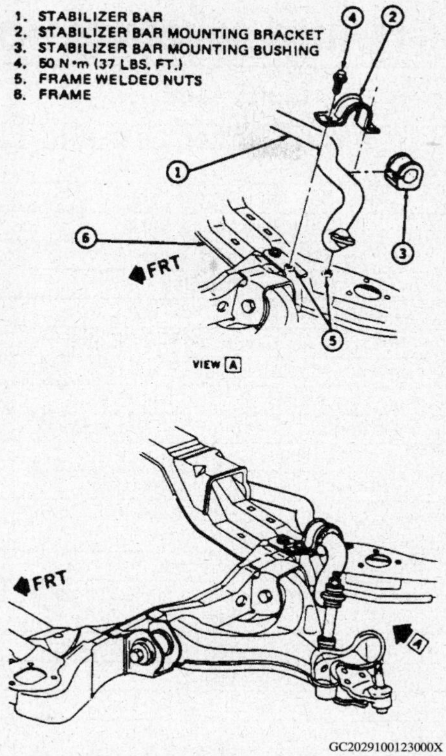

Fig. 14 Stabilizer bar mounting

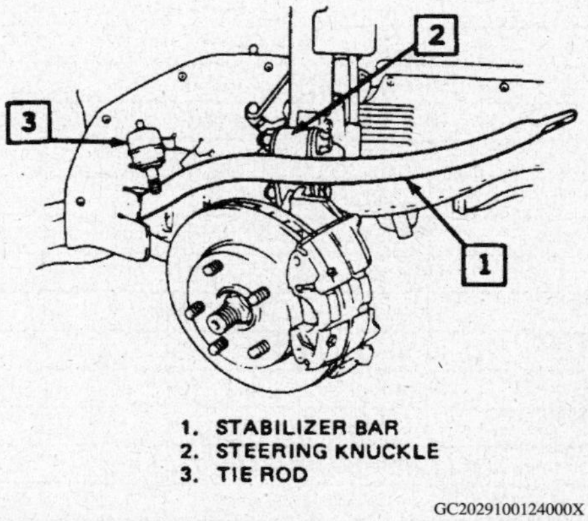

Fig. 15 Stabilizer bar replacement

POWER STEERING GEAR

REPLACE

1. Raise and support vehicle with weight resting on suspension.
2. Remove front wheel assemblies.
3. Disconnect intermediate shaft from steering gear stub shaft.
4. Disconnect both tie rod ends from steering knuckles.
5. Remove line retainers and disconnect hydraulic lines from steering gear.
6. Remove five steering gear attaching bolts, **Fig. 16.**
7. Remove steering gear from vehicle by sliding out of side.
8. Reverse procedure to install. Refer to **Fig. 16** for tightening sequence.

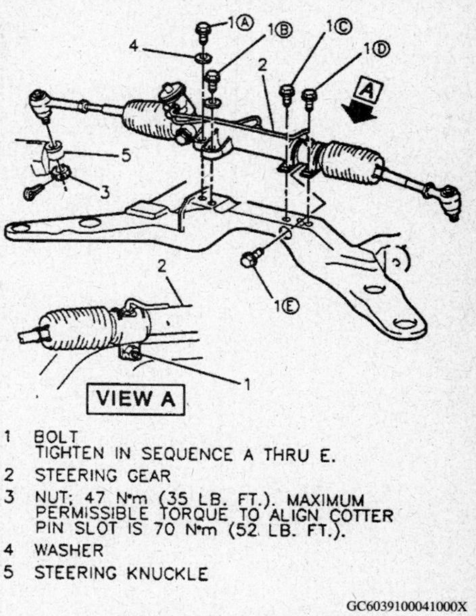

Fig. 16 Steering gear replacement

POWER STEERING PUMP

REPLACE

1. Remove air cleaner, if necessary.
2. Remove alternator drive belt and alternator.
3. Raise and support vehicle.
4. Disconnect hydraulic lines from pump.
5. Remove rear pump adjustment bracket to pump nut.
6. Remove pump drive belt.
7. Lower vehicle.
8. Remove pump rear adjustment bracket.
9. Remove power steering pump from vehicle.
10. Reverse procedure to install.

TIGHTENING SPECIFICATIONS

Year	Component	Torque/ Ft. Lbs.
BONNEVILLE, EIGHTY EIGHT, LESABRE, LSS & REGENCY		
1997	Ball Joint To Knuckle	50
	Brake Bracket To Strut	13
	Brake Caliper To Knuckle	38
	Drive Axle Nut	107
	Front Lower Control Arm Front Nut	140
	Front Lower Control Arm Rear Nut	91
	Front Wheel Speed Sensor Bracket To Strut	13
	Hub And Bearing To Knuckle	70
	Intermediate Steering Shaft Pinch Bolt	35
	Outer Tie Rod Lock Nut	52
	Power Steering Cooler Mounting	71①
	Power Steering Gear Hose Fittings To Pump And Steering Gear	20
	Power Steering Gear Inlet/Outlet Hose	70①
	Power Steering Gear Outlet Hose Clamp To Pump	15
	Power Steering Pump Mounting Bolts	22
	Shield Bolts	71①
	Stabilizer Shaft Bracket Bolt	35
	Stabilizer Shaft Link Nut	13
	Steering Gear Mounting Bolts	50
	Strut Housing Tie Bar Through Bolts	27
	Strut Housing Upper Tie bar	18
	Strut Mount Nut	55
	Strut Mount To Body Nuts	18
	Strut To Knuckle Nuts	140
	Tie Rod End To Knuckle Nut	35②
	Wheel Lug Nut	100
1998–2000	Ball Joint To Knuckle	50
	Brake Bracket To Strut	13
	Brake Caliper To Knuckle	38
	Control Arm Front Nut	140
	Control Arm Rear Nut	91
	Drive Axle Nut	107
	Hub And Bearing To Knuckle	70
	Inner Tie Rod	74
	Power Steering Gear Hose Fittings To Pump And Steering Gear	20
	Power Steering Gear Mounting Bolts	48
	Power Steering Inlet/Outlet Hose Retainer Bolts	53①
	Power Steering Outer Hose Retaining Clamp Nuts	15
	Power Steering Pump Mounting Bolts	20
	Rack And Pinion Adjuster Plug Nut	50
	Rack And Pinion Cylinder End Fittings	20
	Rack And Pinion Preload	16
	Stabilizer Shaft Bracket Bolt	35
	Stabilizer Shaft Link Nut	13
	Strut Housing Tie Bar Through Bolts	27
	Strut Mount Nut	55
	Strut Mount To Body Nuts	18
	Strut To Knuckle Nuts	140
	Tie Rod Lock Nut	50

Continued

TIGHTENING SPECIFICATIONS—Continued

Year	Component	Torque/ Ft. Lbs.
BONNEVILLE, EIGHTY EIGHT, LESABRE, LSS & REGENCY		
1998–2000	Tie Rod End Slotted Hexagon Nut	35
	Tie Rod To Knuckle	35②
	Wheel Speed Sensor Bracket To Strut	13
	Wheel Lug Nut	100
PARK AVENUE		
1997–2000	Ball Joint Mounting Nuts	50
	Ball Joint To Knuckle	50
	Brake Bracket To Strut	13
	Brake Caliper To Knuckle	38
	Control Arm Front Nut	93
	Control Arm Rear Bolt	117
	Drive Axle Nut	107
	Hub And Bearing To Knuckle	70
	Intermediate Steering Shaft Pinch Bolt	35
	Power Steering Gear Hose Fittings To Pump And Steering Gear	20
	Power Steering Inlet/Outlet Hose Retainer Bolts	53①
	Power Steering Outer Hose Retaining Clamp Nuts	15
	Power Steering Pump Mounting Bolts	20
	Stabilizer Shaft Bracket Bolt	30
	Stabilizer Shaft Link Nut	13
	Steering Gear Mounting Bolts	48
	Strut Mount Nut	55
	Strut Mount To Body Nuts	35
	Strut To Knuckle Nuts	136
	Tie Rod End To Knuckle Nut	35
	Wheel Lug Nut	100
	Wheel Speed Sensor Bracket To Strut	13

① — Inch lbs.

② — Tighten nut for cotter pin alignment; 52 ft. lbs. maximum.

Wheel Alignment

INDEX

PRECAUTIONS

AIR BAG SYSTEMS

Refer to "Air Bag System Precautions" in the front of this manual for system disarming and arming procedures.

PRELIMINARY INSPECTION

1. Inspect tires for proper inflation and similar tread wear.
2. Inspect hub and bearing for excessive wear, repair as required.
3. Inspect ball joints.
4. Inspect tie rod ends for excessive looseness.
5. Check wheel and tire runout.
6. Inspect vehicle ride height.
7. Inspect rack and pinion for looseness at frame.
8. Ensure proper strut operation.
9. Inspect control arm bushings.
10. Inspect stabilizer shaft for loose or missing parts.
11. Check suspension and steering components for damage, replace as required.

FRONT WHEEL ALIGNMENT

CASTER

1. Loosen cross brace assembly through bolts, **Fig. 1.**
2. Remove inboard strut nuts, then brace assembly.
3. Remove remaining nut over oval strut mounting hole, **Fig. 2.**
4. Lift front of vehicle by body to separate strut from inner wheelhouse.
5. **On Eighty Eight, LSS, Regency & 1997–99 Bonneville & LeSabre models,** drill two 11/32 inch holes at front and rear of oval strut mounting hole.
6. **On 1997–98 Park Avenue models,** drill two 13/32 inch holes at front and rear of oval strut mounting hole.
7. **On 1999–2000 Park Avenue & Bonneville & 2000 LeSabre models,** remove two guide pins and file to make slotted holes.

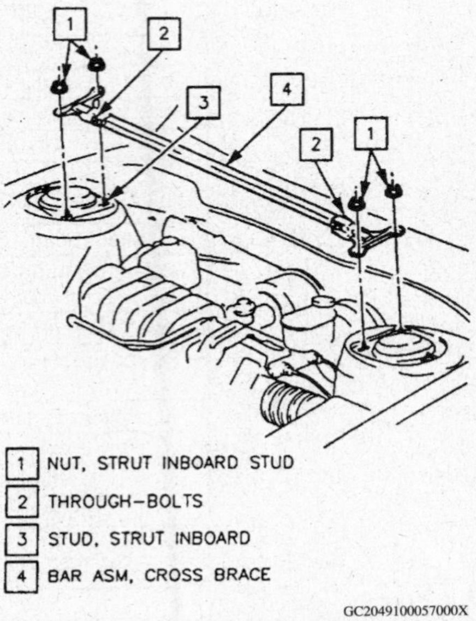

Fig. 1 Cross brace removal

8. **On all models,** file excess metal to elongate original holes, then paint exposed metal with primer.
9. Lower front of vehicle.
10. Place cross brace assembly on inboard strut studs and install strut attaching nuts.
11. Set caster to specifications by moving strut forward or rearward as necessary.
12. **Torque** strut attaching nuts to 18 ft. lbs.
13. **Torque** cross brace bar through bolts to 21 ft. lbs.

CAMBER

Except 1999–2000 Bonneville, LeSabre & Park Avenue

1. Loosen both strut to knuckle attaching nuts, **Fig. 3.**
2. Install camber adjusting tool J-39601, or equivalent.
3. Set camber to specifications.
4. Remove adjusting tool and **torque** strut to knuckle attaching nuts to 144 ft. lbs.
5. Recheck camber.

1999–2000 Bonneville, LeSabre & Park Avenue

1. Raise and support vehicle.
2. Remove wheel and tire.
3. Separate strut from knuckle, do not allow bolts to turn or damage to serrated shoulder will occur.
4. Using a round file or die grinder, file or grind the inner metal plate to outside plates diameters.
5. File excess metal to make slotted holes.
6. Paint the exposed metal with rust preventive paint or primer.
7. Replace strut to knuckle.
8. Install both upper and lower bolts, do not tighten at this time.
9. Install camber adjustment tool No. J 39601, or equivalent to bottom strut bolt, **Fig. 3**
10. Set camber to specification, **torque** upper strut to knuckle bolt to 166 ft. lbs.

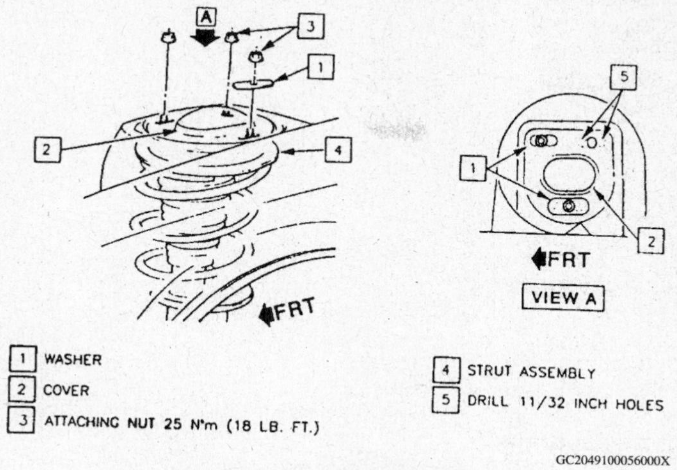

Fig. 2 Caster adjustment

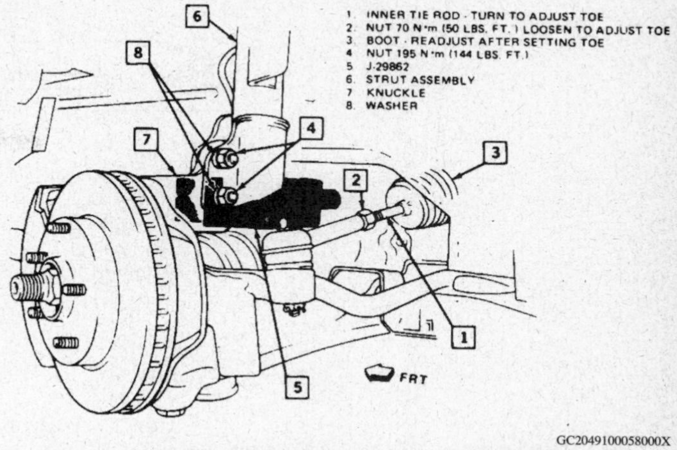

Fig. 3 Camber adjustment. Except 1999–2000 Bonneville, LeSabre & Park Avenue

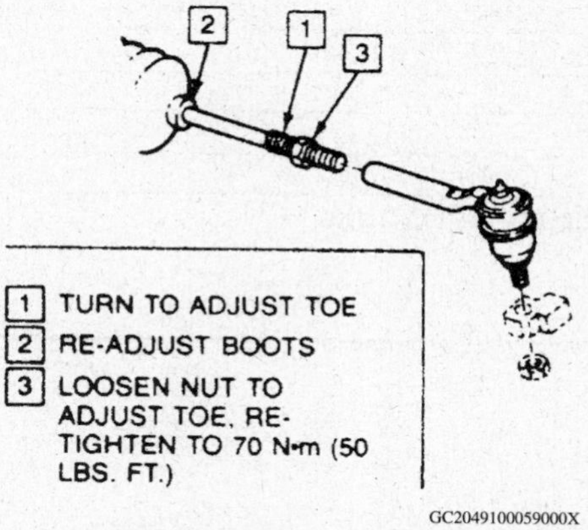

Fig. 4 Toe adjustment

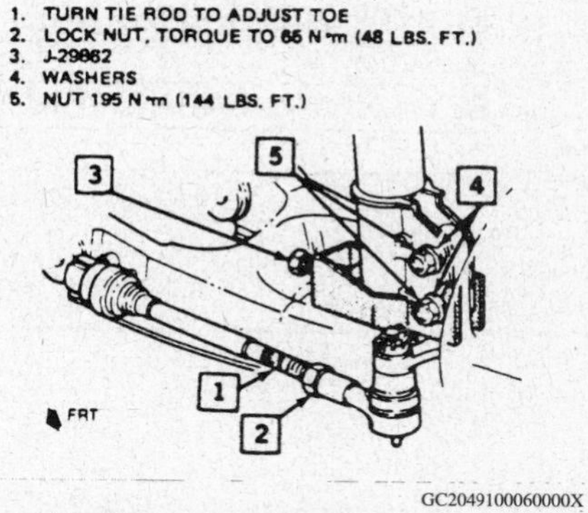

Fig. 5 Rear camber & toe adjustments

11. Remove camber adjusting tool, **torque** lower strut to knuckle bolt to 166 ft. lbs.
12. Recheck camber.

TOE

1. Loosen locknuts on both inner tie rods, **Fig. 4.**
2. Adjust toe to specifications by rotating inner tie rod.
3. **Torque** locknuts to 50 ft. lbs.
4. Recheck toe setting.

REAR WHEEL ALIGNMENT

When checking rear wheel alignment, the electronic leveling system must have the superlift struts inflated with residual pressure only.

Place a weight in trunk and turn ignition on and move transmission selector from Park to Reverse position and back. This will activate the compressor. Turn ignition to Off position and remove weight from trunk. Wait 30 seconds for the system to exhaust. Roll vehicle forward one complete wheel rotation. Jounce vehicle before checking alignment.

CAMBER

1. Loosen strut to knuckle attaching nuts.
2. Install camber adjusting tool J-29862, or equivalent, **Fig. 5.**
3. Move strut to set camber to specifications.
4. Remove camber adjusting tool and **torque** strut to knuckle nuts to 144 ft. lbs.
5. Recheck camber setting.

TOE

Toe adjustment is made by loosening the locknut at tie rod end and turning inner tie rod to set toe to specifications, **Fig. 5.**

VEHICLE RIDE HEIGHT

Refer to **Figs. 6 and 7** for ride height specifications and measurement locations. Check ride height as follows:

1. Ensure vehicle is on level ground.
2. Ensure tires are inflated to proper pressures.
3. Fuel tank should be full to obtain accurate readings.
4. Trunk should be empty except for spare tire and jack.
5. Place front seat in far rearward position, then turn ignition to On position to activate electronic level control, if equipped.
6. Bounce car three times at front and rear to normalize suspension.
7. Measure from lowest point on ball joint housing to control arm bolt centerline, "D" and "Z" positions.
8. Measure from level floor to rocker panel at "J" and "K" positions.

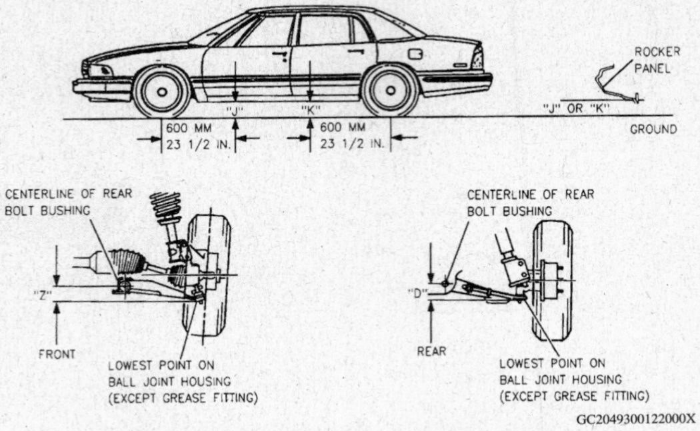

Fig. 6 Ride height measurements

Dimension D, Inches	Dimension J, Inches	Dimension K, Inches	Dimension Z, Inches
EIGHTY EIGHT, LESABRE, LSS & BONNEVILLE			
$2\frac{11}{16}$-$3\frac{7}{16}$	9-$9\frac{13}{16}$	$9\frac{9}{32}$-$10\frac{1}{16}$	$1\frac{15}{16}$-$2\frac{3}{4}$
REGENCY & PARK AVENUE			
3-$3\frac{3}{4}$	$6\frac{7}{16}$-$7\frac{1}{4}$	$8\frac{3}{8}$-$9\frac{3}{16}$	$1\frac{3}{16}$-2

Fig. 7 Vehicle ride height specifications

CAMARO & FIREBIRD

NOTE: Refer to Rear Of This Manual For Vehicle Manufacturer's Special Service Tool Suppliers

INDEX

Specifications

GENERAL ENGINE SPECIFICATIONS

Year	Engine		Fuel System	Bore & Stroke	Comp-ression Ratio	Net Brake H.P. @ RPM②	Maximum Torque	Normal Oil Pressure, psi
	Liter	VIN Code①						
1997	3800	K	SFI	3.80 x 3.40	9.4	200 @ 5200	225 @ 4000	⑤
	5.7L⑥	P	SFI	4.00 x 3.48	10.4	285 @ 5000	325 @ 2400	③
	5.7L④	P	SFI	4.00 x 3.48	10.4	305 @ 5400	335 @ 3200	③
1998–2000	3800	K	SFI	3.80 x 3.40	9.4	200 @ 5200	225 @ 4000	⑤
	5.7L⑥	G	SFI	3.89 x 3.62	10.1	305 @ 5200	335 @ 4000	③
	5.7L④	G	SFI	3.89 x 3.62	10.1	320 @ 5200	345 @ 4400	③

SFI — Sequential Fuel Injection

① — The eighth digit of the VIN denotes engine code.

② — Ratings are net-as installed in vehicle.

③ — Minimum, 6 psi @ 1000 RPM; 18 psi @ 2000 RPM; 24 psi @ 4000 RPM.

④ — Models w/ram air.

⑤ — Minimum of 60 psi @ 1850 RPM w/10W-30 motor oil.

⑥ — Models less ram air.

TUNE UP SPECIFICATIONS

Year & Engine Liter (VIN Code)①	Spark Plug Gap	Ignition Timing BTDC				Curb Idle Speed②		Fast Idle Speed		Fuel Pump Pressure, psi	Valve Clear-ance, Inch
		Firing Order Fig.③	Man. Trans.	Auto. Trans.	Mark	Man. Trans.	Auto. Trans.	Man. Trans.	Auto. Trans.		
1997											
3800 (K)	.060	⑪	④	④	⑧	⑤	⑤	⑤	⑤	48-55⑥⑩	⑦
5.7L (P)	.050	⑫	④	④	⑧	⑤	⑤	⑤	⑤	41-47 ⑥	⑦
1998–2000											
3800 (K)	.060	⑪	④	④	⑧	⑤	⑤	⑤	⑤	48-55	⑦
5.7L (G)	.060	⑨	④	④	⑧	⑤	⑤	⑤	⑤	55-60	⑦

BTDC — Before Top Dead Center
D — Drive
N — Neutral
① — The eighth digit of Vehicle Identification Number (VIN) denotes engine code.
② — When adjusting idle speed, set parking brake & block drive wheels.
③ — Before disconnecting wires from distributor cap, determine location of No. 1 wire in cap, as distributor position may have been altered from that shown at the end of this chart.
④ — Computer controlled, no adjustment.
⑤ — Idle speed is controlled by an Idle Speed Control (ISC) motor, Idle Air Control (IAC) valve or Idle Load Compensator (ILC).
⑥ — With shop towel wrapped around fuel pressure valve to prevent fuel spillage, connect a suitable fuel pressure gauge to fuel pressure valve. Check fuel pressure w/ignition switch On, engine not running.
⑦ — Equipped w/hydraulic lifters.
⑧ — Equipped w/crankshaft sensor.
⑨ — Refer to **Fig. C** for cylinder numbering. Firing order: 1–8–7–2–6–5–4–3.
⑩ — Reading taken at fuel rail quick connect.
⑪ — Cylinder numbering left to right as viewed from front of vehicle: Front bank, 1, 3, 5; rear bank, 2, 4, 6. Firing order: 1–6–5–4–3–2. Refer to **Fig. B** for spark plug wire connections at coil unit.
⑫ — Refer to **Fig. A** for cylinder numbering. Firing order: 1–8–7–2–6–5–4–3.

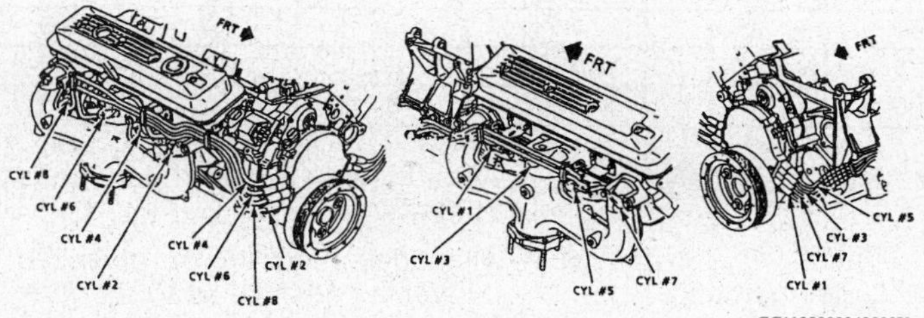

GC1138800343000X

Fig. A

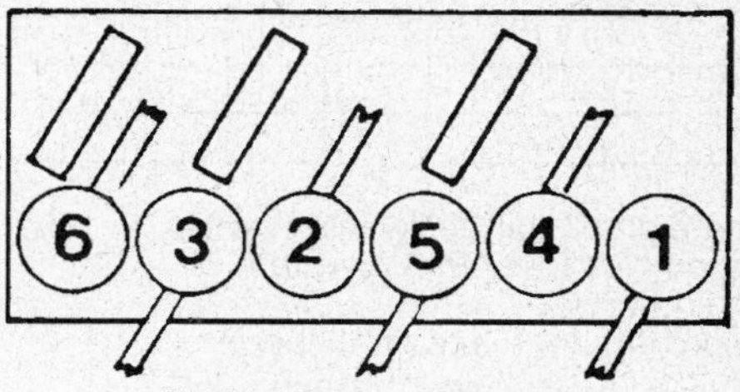

GC1139100130000X

Fig. B

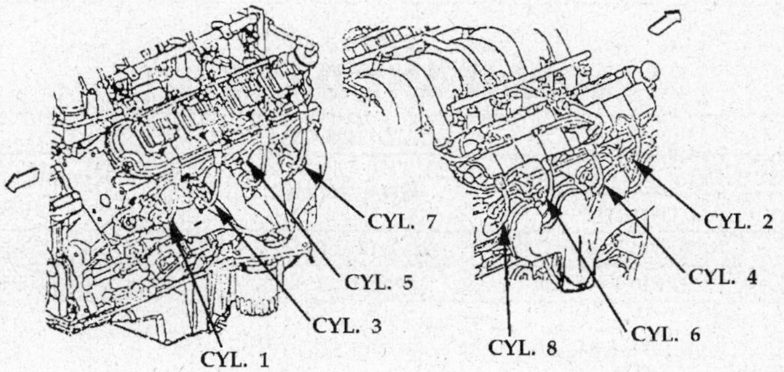

GC1139800673000X

Fig. C

FRONT WHEEL ALIGNMENT SPECIFICATIONS

Year	Caster Angle, Degrees		Camber Angle, Degrees		Total Toe, Degrees	Ball Joint Wear	
	Limits	Desired	Limits	Desired		Lower	Upper
All	+4.5 to +5.5	+5	-.1 to +.9	+.4	-.2 to +.2	②	①

① — Deflection on dial indicator, when positioned against wheel rim, should not exceed .125 inch while moving top of wheel in & out.

② — While reading dial indicator, pry between lower control arm & steering knuckle. Vertical movement should not exceed .046875 inches.

REAR WHEEL ALIGNMENT SPECIFICATIONS

Year	Camber Angle, Degrees		Total Toe, Degrees		Thrust Angle
	Limits	Desired	Limits	Desired	
All	-.6 to +.6	0	-.3 to +.3	0	-.15 to +.15

FLUID CAPACITIES & COOLING SYSTEM DATA

Year	Engine Liter (VIN)①	Coolant Capacity, Qts.		Radiator Cap Relief Pressure, psi	Thermo. Opening Temp. °F	Fuel Tank, Gals.	Engine Oil Refill Qts.	Transmission Oil		Rear Axle, Pts.⑨
		Less A/C	With A/C					Man Trans., Pts.	Auto. Trans., Qts.②	
1997	3800 (K)	⑦	⑦	18	195	15.5	4③	6.8	④	3.5
	5.7 (P)	⑧	⑧	18	180	15.5	4⑤	8	⑥	3.5
1998–2000	3800 (K)	⑦	⑦	18	195	15.5	4.5⑩	8.2	⑥	3.5
	5.7 (G)	⑧	⑧	18	180	15.5	5.5⑩	8.2	⑥	3.5

① — The eighth digit of Vehicle Identification Number (VIN) denotes engine code.

② — Approximate, make final check w/dipstick.

③ — Additional oil may be required to bring oil level to full mark when changing filter.

④ — Total capacity, 8.35 qts.; pan only, 5 qts.

⑤ — Add 1 qt. w/filter change.

⑥ — Total capacity, 11.2 qts.; pan only, 5 qts.

⑦ — Auto. trans., 12.3 qts.; Man. trans., 12.5 qts.

⑧ — Auto. trans., 15.1 qts.: Man. trans., 15.3 qts.

⑨ — All models require 4 oz. of limited differential additive lubricant part No. 1052358, or equivalent.

⑩ — With filter change.

LUBRICANT DATA

Year	Lubricant Type				
	Transmission		Rear Axle	Power Steering System	Brake System
	Manual	Automatic			
1997–98	Dexron III	Dexron III	80W-90 GL-5①	Power Steering Fluid②	DOT 3
1999–2000	Dexron III	Dexron III	75w-90 GL-5①	Power Steering Fluid②	DOT 3

① — Limited slip differentials also require 4 oz. of lubricant additive (GM part No. 1052358, or equivalent).

② — Meeting GM specification 9985010.

Electrical

NOTE: On Air Bag Equipped Models, Refer To " Air Bag System Precautions" Located In The Front Of This Manual For System Disarming & Arming Procedures.

NOTE: Refer To "Computer Relearn Procedures " Located In The Front Of This Manual For Computer Relearn Procedures.

INDEX

PRECAUTIONS

AIR BAG SYSTEMS

Refer to "Air Bag System Precautions" in the front of this manual for system disarming and arming procedures.

BATTERY GROUND CABLE

Prior to service, disconnect battery ground cable and isolate as required.

FUSE PANEL & FLASHER LOCATION

The instrument panel fuse block is attached to a bracket on the left front hinge pillar and is accessed through a removable panel on the instrument panel carrier. The vehicle speed sensor (VSS) and hazard lamp flasher are attached to the relay center (convenience center), located on the lefthand side of the steering column. The turn signal flasher is mounted behind the instrument panel to the right of the steering column on the driver knee bolster bracket.

FUEL PUMP RELAY LOCATION

1997

The fuel pump relay is located in front of lefthand side kick panel, mounted on foot rest bracket, under carpet.

1998–2000

The fuel pump relay is located in the underhood number 2 relay center, **Fig. 1.**

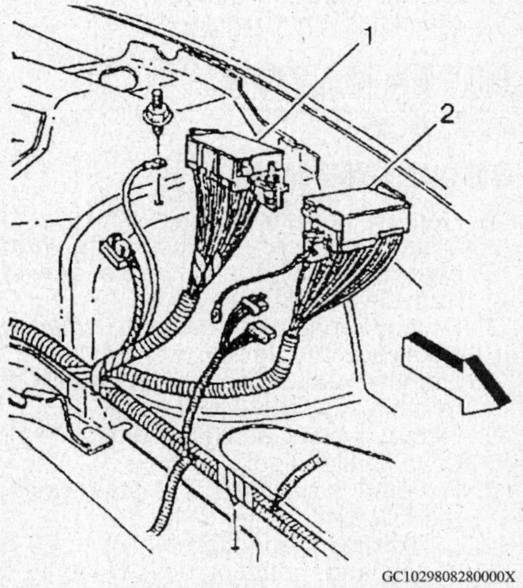

Fig. 1 Fuel pump relay location. 1998–2000

RELAY CENTER LOCATION

1997

The relay center (convenience center) is located on the cowl below the instrument panel carrier to the left of the steering column.

1998–2000

The number 1 and 2 relay centers are located under the hood on the left fenderwell, **Fig. 1.**

STARTER

REPLACE

This vehicle was designed for starter mounting without shims. If single or double shims have been added to correct a noise or engagement problem, they should be reinstalled in their original positions to ensure proper pinion to flywheel assembly engagement.

REMOVAL

1. Raise and support vehicle.
2. **On 1997 models,** disconnect exhaust crossover pipe at manifolds.

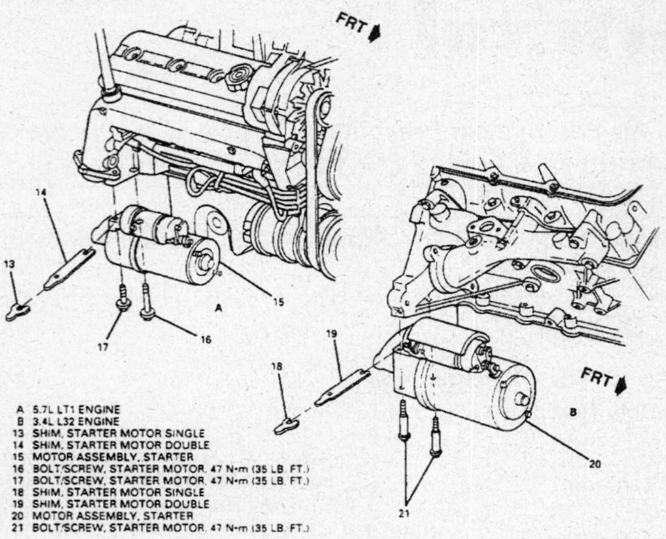

GC1129300041000X

Fig. 2 Starter motor replacement. 1997

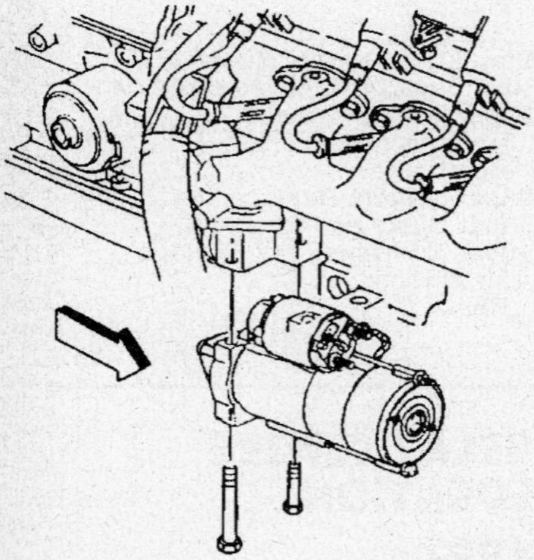

GC1129800077000X

Fig. 4 Starter motor replacement. 1998–2000 w/5.7L engine

3. **On 1998–2000 models equipped with 5.7L engine,** remove left catalytic converter.
4. **On models equipped with 3800 engine,** remove starter shield.
5. **On all models,** remove starter motor attaching bolts and lower starter motor assembly, **Figs. 2 through 4.**
6. Disconnect electrical connectors from starter motor assembly, then remove starter motor assembly.

INSTALLATION

Before connecting electrical connectors, tighten inner nuts on the solenoid terminals. If the nuts are not tight, the solenoid cap may be damaged during installation of connectors.

1. Connect electrical connectors to starter motor assembly, then **torque** BAT terminal nut to 7 ft. lbs. and S terminal nut to 18 inch lbs.
2. Install starter motor assembly.
3. **On 1997 models, torque** mounting bolts to 40 ft. lbs.
4. **On 1998–2000 models equipped with 3800 engine, torque** starter bolt to 35 ft. lbs., and stud to 33 ft. lbs.
5. **On 1998–2000 models equipped with 5.7L engine, torque** starter bolts to 37 ft. lbs.
6. **On all models,** measure pinion to flywheel clearance, **Fig. 5,** adding shims if necessary. On 1997 models, clearance should be .200 inch. On 1998–2000 models, clearance should be .010–.160 inch.
7. **On models equipped with 3800 engine,** install starter shield.
8. **On all models,** connect exhaust to manifolds, then lower vehicle.

ALTERNATOR

REPLACE

3800 ENGINE

1. Remove serpentine drive belt.
2. Disconnect electrical connector from alternator and battery positive terminal from "BAT" terminal.
3. Remove charcoal canister solenoid from alternator brace.
4. Remove bolt attaching alternator to rear brace, **Fig. 6.**
5. Remove bolts attaching alternator to drive belt tensioner.
6. Reverse procedure to install, noting the following:
   a. **Torque** mounting bolt (8) to 20 ft. lbs. and mounting bolt (11) to 38 ft. lbs.
   b. **Torque** rear brace bolt to 22 ft. lbs.

5.7L ENGINE

1997

Refer to **Fig. 7** for alternator replacement.

1998-2000

1. Remove accessory drive belt.
2. Raise and support vehicle.

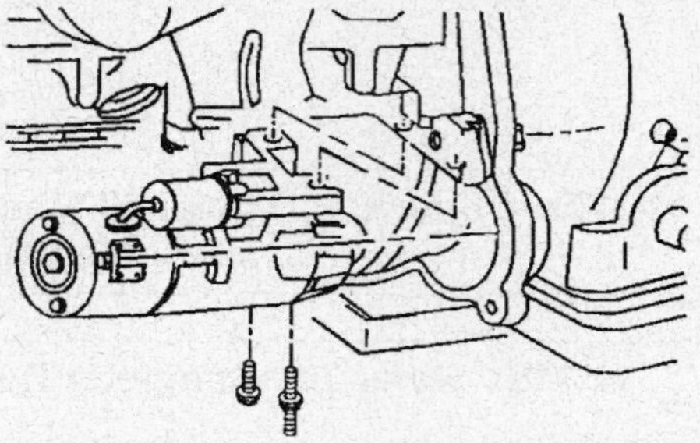

GC1129800076000X

Fig. 3 Starter motor replacement. 1998–2000 w/3800 engine

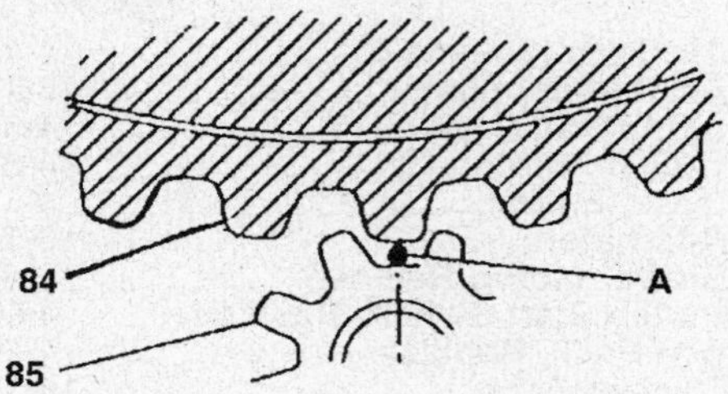

A INSERT WIRE GAGE HERE TO CHECK
84 FLYWHEEL ASSEMBLY
85 PINION, STARTER DRIVE

GC1129800075000X

Fig. 5 Flywheel assembly to pinion clearance inspection

3. Remove alternator rear bracket bolt, **Fig. 8.**
4. Remove alternator mounting bolts.
5. Disconnect alternator electrical connectors, then remove from vehicle.
6. Reverse procedure to install. **Torque** mounting bolts to 37 ft. lbs. and bracket to 18 ft. lbs.

DISTRIBUTOR

REPLACE

Prior to distributor removal, the ventilation vacuum system must be checked for proper operation. Check for proper routing and/or kinks. If OK, check the ventilation system for possible restriction by disconnecting vacuum harness at the air intake duct and check for vacuum. The gauge needle should move slowly toward manifold vacuum. If no vacuum is present, replace vacuum harness.

REMOVAL

1. Check the distributor ventilation vacuum system for proper operation.
2. Ensure ignition switch is in Off or Lock position, then remove water pump assembly as outlined under "Water Pump, Replace" in the "5.7L Engine" section.
3. Remove crankshaft balancer assembly as outlined in " 5.7L Engine" section.
4. Disconnect spark plug wire assemblies and the four-terminal ECM/PCM connector from distributor assembly.
5. Disconnect vacuum harness.

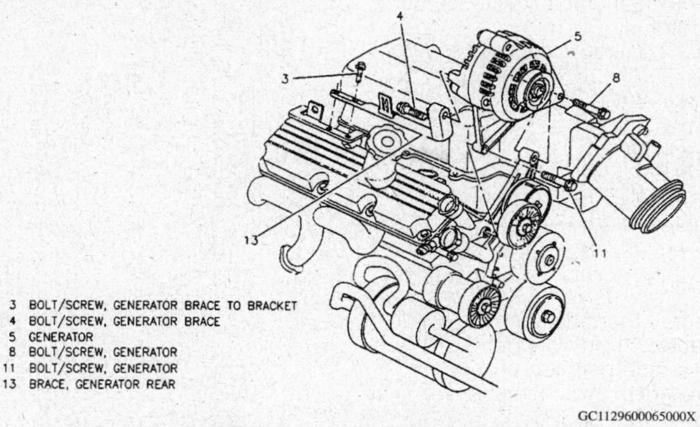

Fig. 6 Alternator replacement. 3800 engine

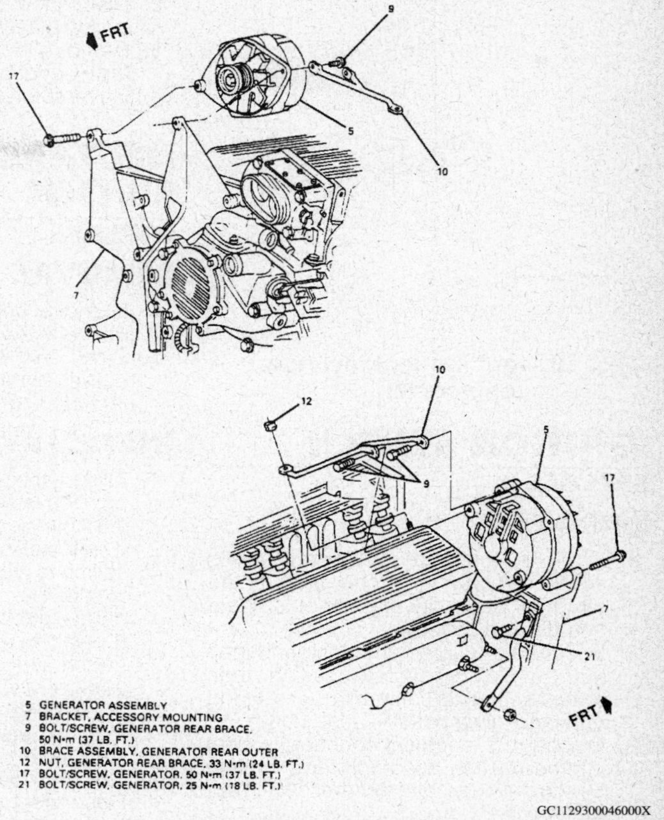

Fig. 7 Alternator replacement. 1997 5.7L engine

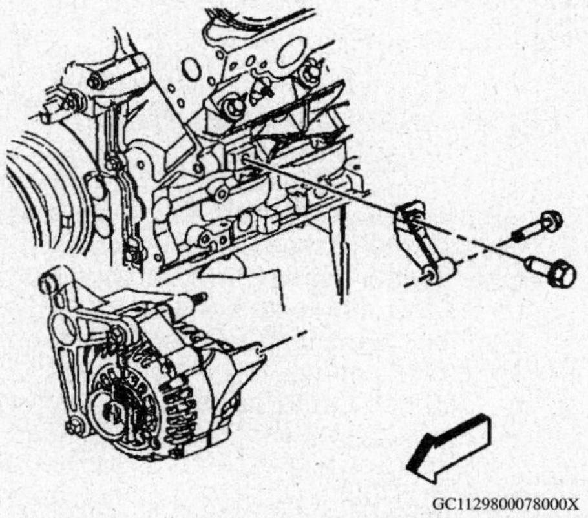

Fig. 8 Alternator replacement. 1998–2000 5.7L engine

6. Remove distributor assembly bolts, then pull distributor assembly forward until driveshaft disengages from end of camshaft assembly, **Fig. 9.**

INSTALLATION

1. Install distributor with driveshaft in end of camshaft. Rotate distributor coupling until camshaft sprocket pin slot aligns with camshaft sprocket pin, then slide distributor onto end of camshaft until fully seated on engine front cover. **If distributor will not seat by hand, it is not properly aligned with camshaft. Proceed as follows:**
   a. Rotate crankshaft until engine is at No. 1 cylinder TDC (camshaft sprocket pin at 9 o'clock position).
   b. Rotate the distributor coupling until the camshaft sprocket pin slot aligns with the distributor base timing mark.
   c. **Install distributor using hand pressure to fully seat.**
2. Install and **torque** distributor bolts to 8 ft. lbs.
3. Connect four-terminal ECM connector and spark plug wire assemblies to distributor assembly.
4. Install crankshaft balancer assembly as outlined in " 5.7L Engine" section.
5. Install water pump assembly as outlined under "5.7L Engine" section.

COIL PACK

REPLACE

1. Remove spark plug wire harness from coil pack/ignition control module.
2. Disconnect electrical harness from coil pack/ignition control module.
3. Remove coil pack/ignition control module attaching bolts, then the coil pack/control module.
4. Reverse procedure to install, noting the following:
   a. **On 3800 and 1997 5.7L engines, torque** coil pack/ignition control module attaching bolts to 22 ft. lbs.
   b. **On 1998–2000 5.7L engines, torque** coil attaching bolts to 8.8 ft. lbs.

IGNITION LOCK

REPLACE

1. Remove steering wheel as outlined under "Steering Wheel, Replace."
2. Remove turn signal switch as outlined under "Turn Signal Switch, Replace."
3. Remove buzzer switch retaining clip, then the buzzer switch.
4. Place ignition switch in Lock position.
5. Remove lock cylinder retaining screw, **Fig. 10.**
6. Disconnect terminal electrical connector at bulkhead connection to provide slack.

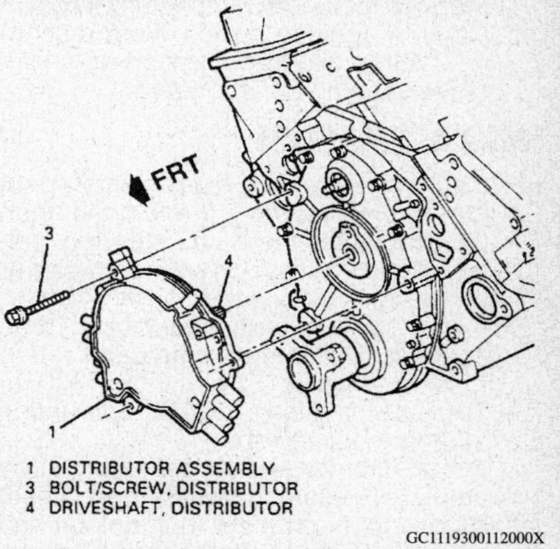

Fig. 9 Distributor replacement. 5.7L engine

7. Remove wiring connector from steering column.
8. Attach a suitable length of mechanic wire to ignition lock electrical connector for use during installation. Detach wire retaining clip, then carefully pull ignition lock wiring through housing shroud, steering column and lock housing cover.
9. Remove lock cylinder.
10. Reverse procedure to install. Ensure lock cylinder wiring is properly routed through steering column. **Torque** lock cylinder retaining screw to 22 inch lbs.

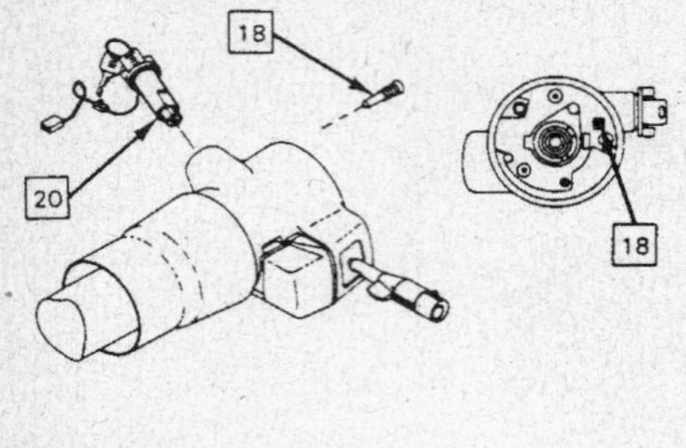

18 LOCK RETAINING SCREW
20 VATS LOCK CYLINDER SET

GC9129100016000X

Fig. 10 Ignition lock cylinder replacement

IGNITION SWITCH

REPLACE

REMOVAL

1. Remove lefthand instrument panel sound insulator assembly, then the instrument panel driver knee bolster assembly and deflector.
2. Ensure steering column lock and ignition switch are in Lock position, then remove steering column upper support nuts and lower column assembly.
3. Disconnect electrical connectors from dimmer switch assembly and ignition switch, then remove dimmer switch actuator rod.
4. Remove dimmer switch assembly, then the ignition switch actuator rod.
5. Remove ignition switch, then disconnect automatic transmission park lock cable assembly, if equipped.

INSTALLATION

1. Connect automatic transmission park lock cable assembly, if equipped, then ensure ignition switch, steering column lock and ignition cylinder assembly are in Lock position.
2. Install ignition switch to jacket, then connect ignition switch actuator rod to ignition switch.
3. **Torque** ignition switch mounting screws to 22 inch lbs.
4. Install dimmer switch assembly, then adjust by pressing switch mechanism slightly to insert a 3/32 inch drill bit and moving dimmer switch assembly to remove tool.
5. **Torque** dimmer switch mounting screws to 35 inch lbs.
6. Install dimmer switch actuator rod, then connect electrical connectors to dimmer switch assembly and ignition switch.
7. Raise column assembly and install upper support nuts.
8. Install instrument panel driver knee bolster assembly and deflector, then the lefthand instrument panel sound insulator assembly.

CLUTCH START SWITCH

REPLACE

1. Remove instrument panel driver knee bolster.
2. Disconnect clutch pedal position switch electrical connector.
3. Remove clutch pedal position switch from pedal bracket.
4. Reverse procedure to install.

NEUTRAL SAFETY SWITCH

REPLACE

REMOVAL

1. Remove floor console, then disconnect electrical connectors from switch.
2. Place shift lever in Neutral position of detent plate, then remove switch attaching screws and switch, **Fig. 11.**

INSTALLATION

1. Ensure the shift lever is in Neutral, then position switch on shift lever making sure pin on shaft is in slot of switch.
2. If reinstalling existing switch, rotate switch to align service adjustment hole with carrier tang hole. Insert a 3/32 inch gauge pin and rotate switch until pin drops in to a depth of 19/32 inch. **Torque** switch attaching nut to 18 inch lbs., then remove gauge pin.
3. If installing a new switch, **torque** attaching nuts to 18 inch lbs., then move shift lever out of Neutral to shear pin which is part of new switch.
4. Reconnect electrical connectors to switch, then apply parking brake and start engine. Check back-up lights and seat belt warning system for proper operation and ensure engine will start only in Park or Neutral.
5. Turn ignition off and install floor console.

HEADLAMP SWITCH

REPLACE

CAMARO

1. Remove switch assembly from bezel assembly, **Figs. 12 and 13.**
2. Disconnect electrical connector from switch assembly.
3. Reverse procedure to install.

FIREBIRD

1. Remove switch assembly from carrier, **Fig. 14.**
2. Disconnect electrical connector from switch assembly.
3. Reverse procedure to install.

STOP LIGHT SWITCH

REPLACE

1. Remove lefthand instrument panel sound insulator assembly, then disconnect electrical connectors, **Fig. 15.**
2. Remove release switch assembly, stop lamp and TCC switch assembly and clutch switch assembly, or clutch anticipate switch assembly, if equipped, from pedal assembly with bracket.
3. Install release switch assembly, stop lamp and TCC switch assembly and clutch switch assembly, or clutch anticipate switch assembly, if equipped, to pedal assembly with bracket.
4. Connect electrical connectors, then adjust switches as follows:
   a. Depress brake pedal assembly or clutch pedal assembly and insert release switch assembly, stop lamp and TCC switch assembly and clutch switch assembly, or clutch anticipate switch assembly into pedal assembly with bracket until retainer is fully seated.
   b. Slowly pull brake or clutch pedal assembly rearward with a force of 50 lbs. until click sounds can no longer be heard.
   c. Measure release switch assembly and stop lamp and TCC switch assembly contacts, should be open 1 inch or less of pedal assembly travel, and should occur at the same time or before onset of braking.
5. Install lefthand instrument panel sound insulator assembly.

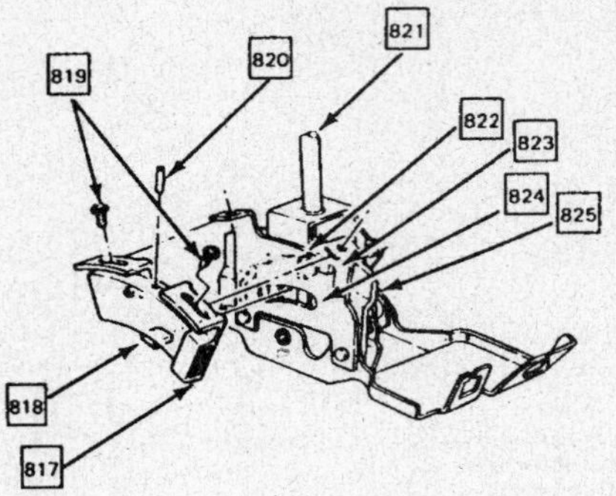

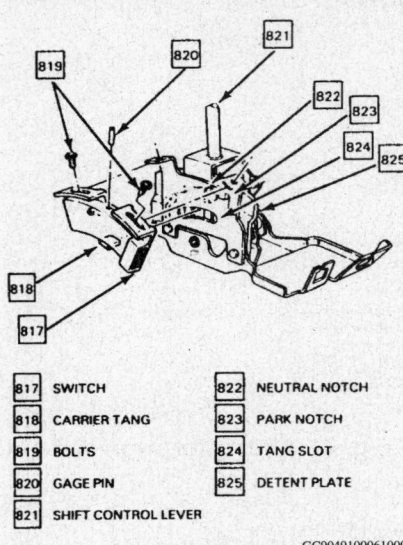

817 SWITCH
818 CARRIER TANG
819 BOLTS
820 GAGE PIN
821 SHIFT CONTROL LEVER
822 NEUTRAL NOTCH
823 PARK NOTCH
824 TANG SLOT
825 DETENT PLATE

GC9049100061000X

Fig. 11 Neutral safety switch replacement

TURN SIGNAL SWITCH

REPLACE

1. Remove steering wheel as outlined under "Steering Wheel, Replace."
2. Place ignition switch in Lock position to retain coil assembly in the centered position.
3. Remove coil assembly retaining ring, **Fig. 16.**
4. Lift coil assembly from steering shaft and allow to hang from wire, then remove wave washer.
5. Using a suitable tool, compress lock plate and remove snap ring (C-ring on tilt models), **Fig. 17.**

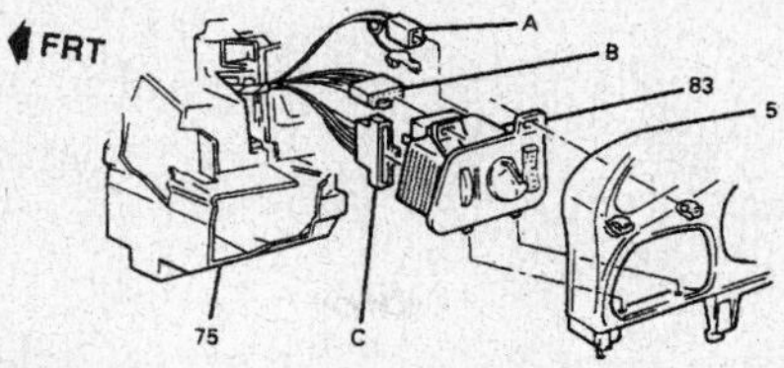

A CONNECTOR, INSTRUMENT PANEL WIRING HARNESS FOG LAMP ELECTRICAL
B CONNECTOR, INSTRUMENT PANEL WIRING HARNESS ELECTRICAL
C CONNECTOR, INSTRUMENT PANEL WIRING HARNESS DIMMER SWITCH ELECTRICAL
5 BEZEL ASSEMBLY, INSTRUMENT PANEL CLUSTER TRIM PLATE
75 CARRIER, INSTRUMENT PANEL
83 SWITCH ASSEMBLY, HEADLAMP AND INSTRUMENT PANEL LAMP DIMMER

GC9049300056000X

Fig. 12 Headlamp switch replacement. 1997 Camaro

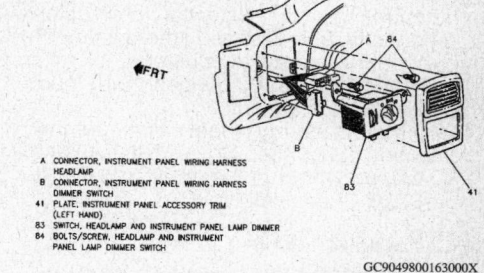

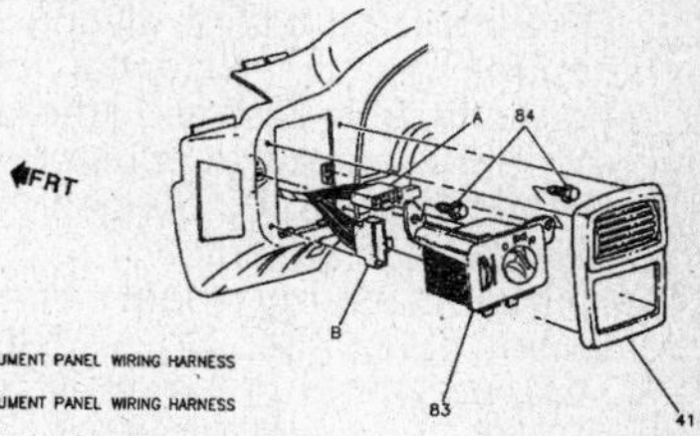

A CONNECTOR, INSTRUMENT PANEL WIRING HARNESS HEADLAMP
B CONNECTOR, INSTRUMENT PANEL WIRING HARNESS DIMMER SWITCH
41 PLATE, INSTRUMENT PANEL ACCESSORY TRIM (LEFT HAND)
83 SWITCH, HEADLAMP AND INSTRUMENT PANEL LAMP DIMMER
84 BOLTS/SCREW, HEADLAMP AND INSTRUMENT PANEL LAMP DIMMER SWITCH

GC9049800163000X

Fig. 13 Headlamp switch replacement. 1998–2000 Camaro

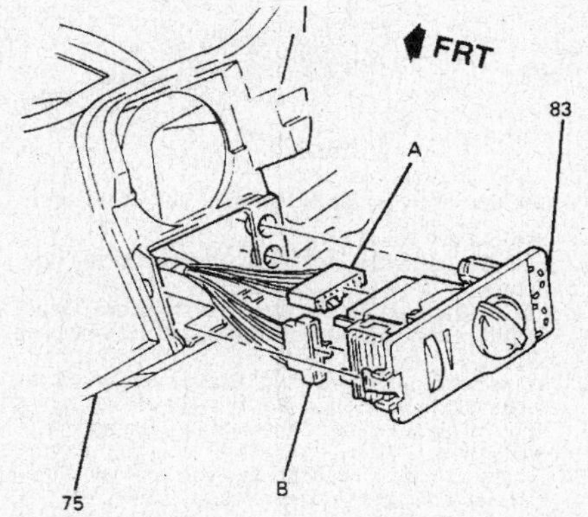

A CONNECTOR, INSTRUMENT PANEL WIRING HARNESS ELECTRICAL
B CONNECTOR, INSTRUMENT PANEL WIRING HARNESS ELECTRICAL
75 CARRIER, INSTRUMENT PANEL
83 SWITCH ASSEMBLY, HEADLAMP AND INSTRUMENT PANEL LAMP DIMMER

GC9049300058000X

Fig. 14 Headlamp switch replacement. Firebird

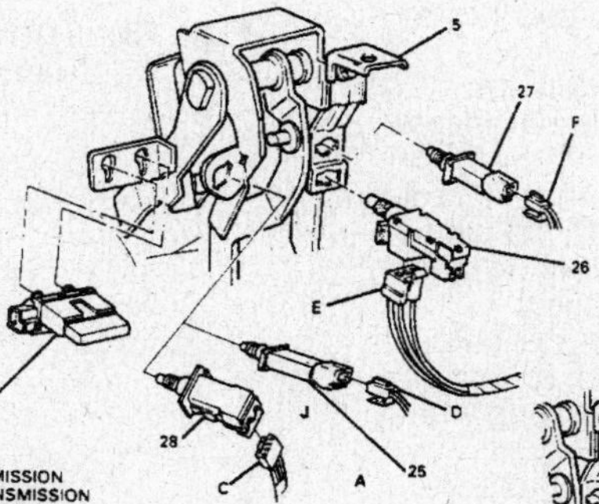

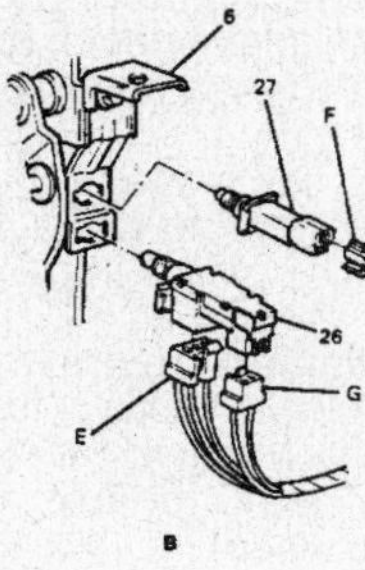

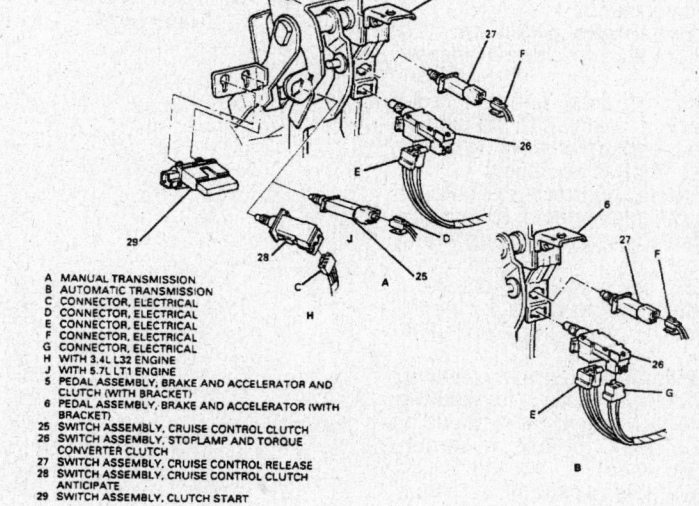

A MANUAL TRANSMISSION
B AUTOMATIC TRANSMISSION
C CONNECTOR, ELECTRICAL
D CONNECTOR, ELECTRICAL
E CONNECTOR, ELECTRICAL
F CONNECTOR, ELECTRICAL
G CONNECTOR, ELECTRICAL
H WITH 3.4L L32 ENGINE
J WITH 5.7L LT1 ENGINE
5 PEDAL ASSEMBLY, BRAKE AND ACCELERATOR AND CLUTCH (WITH BRACKET)
6 PEDAL ASSEMBLY, BRAKE AND ACCELERATOR (WITH BRACKET)
25 SWITCH ASSEMBLY, CRUISE CONTROL CLUTCH
26 SWITCH ASSEMBLY, STOPLAMP AND TORQUE CONVERTER CLUTCH
27 SWITCH ASSEMBLY, CRUISE CONTROL RELEASE
28 SWITCH ASSEMBLY, CRUISE CONTROL CLUTCH ANTICIPATE
29 SWITCH ASSEMBLY, CLUTCH START

GC9049300060000X

Fig. 15 Stop lamp switch replacement

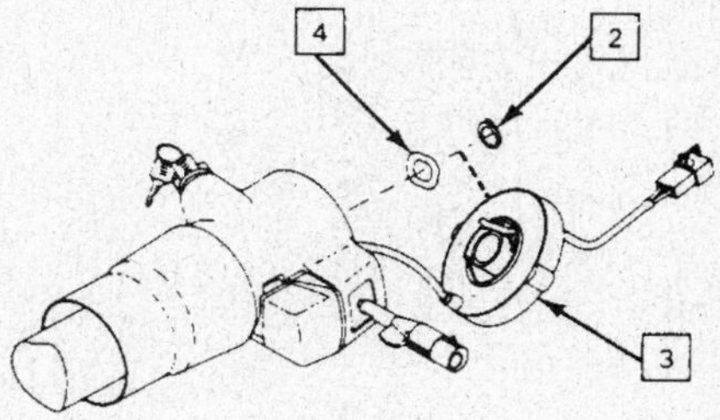

2 RETAINING RING
3 COIL ASSEMBLY
4 WAVE WASHER

GC9049100062000X

Fig. 16 Coil assembly removal

6. Remove lock plate, turn signal canceling cam and upper bearing spring, inner race seat and inner race.
7. Place turn signal lever in right hand turn position, then remove multifunction lever and hazard warning flasher knob.
8. Remove turn signal switch lever attaching screw, then remove lever.
9. Remove turn signal switch attaching screws.
10. Disconnect turn signal switch electrical connector at lower portion of steering column.
11. Remove turn signal switch wiring protector cover from steering column, **Fig. 18.**
12. Carefully pull turn signal switch wiring up and out of steering column.
13. Reverse procedure to install. If coil assembly has become uncentered, refer to **Fig. 19** for centering procedure.

DIMMER SWITCH

REPLACE

Refer to "Ignition Switch, Replace."

STEERING WHEEL

REPLACE

REMOVAL

When removing steering wheel, use only specified puller. Do not hammer on end of steering column shaft. Hammering on shaft may damage plastic injections, affecting column assembly rigidity.

When attaching specified puller to steering wheel, use caution to prevent threading bolts through steering wheel hub into Supplemental Inflatable Restraint (SIR) coil assembly, damaging coil assembly.

1. Remove screws from back of steering wheel assembly using a No. 30 Torx driver, then the inflatable restraint steering wheel module assembly from steering wheel assembly.
2. Disconnect SIR coil assembly electrical connector and retainer from inflatable restraint steering wheel module assembly.

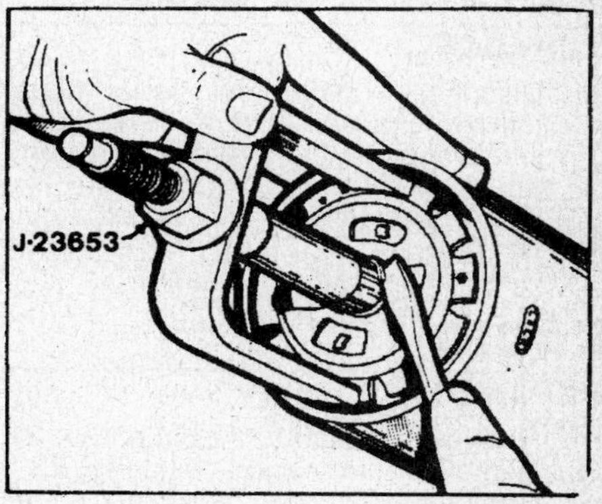

GC9049100063000X

Fig. 17 Lock plate retaining ring removal

3. **On Firebird models,** disconnect radio control switch electrical connector from inflatable restraint steering wheel module assembly, if equipped.
4. **On all models,** disconnect horn lead from column assembly.
5. Remove steering wheel using steering wheel puller tool No. J 1859-A and steering wheel puller bolts tool No. J 38720, or equivalents.

INSTALLATION

1. Route SIR coil assembly electrical connector to steering wheel, then install steering wheel, aligning block tooth on steering wheel with block tooth on steering column shaft within one female serration.
2. Install nut and **torque** to 32 ft. lbs.
3. Connect horn lead to column assembly.
4. **On Firebird models,** connect radio control switch electrical connector from inflatable restraint steering wheel module assembly, if equipped.
5. **On all models,** connect SIR coil assembly electrical connector and retainer to inflatable restraint steering wheel module assembly.
6. Secure SIR coil assembly electrical connector to steering wheel by inserting thick section of wire into existing retainers.
7. Position inflatable restraint steering wheel module assembly to steering wheel, ensure wiring is not exposed or trapped between module assembly and steering wheel.
8. Install inflatable restraint steering wheel module assembly screws and **torque** to 25 inch lbs.

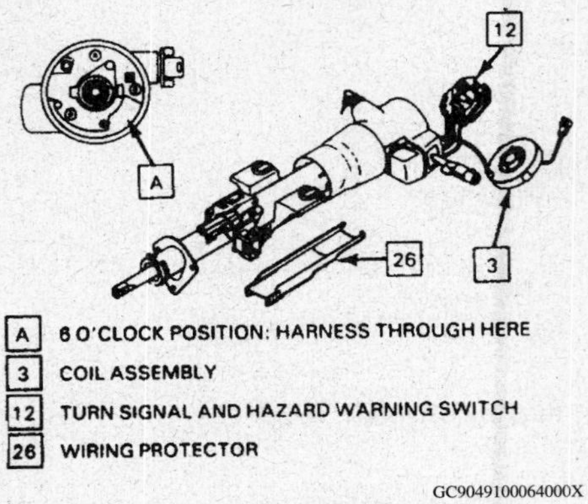
12
A
26
3
A 6 O'CLOCK POSITION: HARNESS THROUGH HERE
3 COIL ASSEMBLY
12 TURN SIGNAL AND HAZARD WARNING SWITCH
26 WIRING PROTECTOR
GC9049100064000X

Fig. 18 Turn signal switch removal

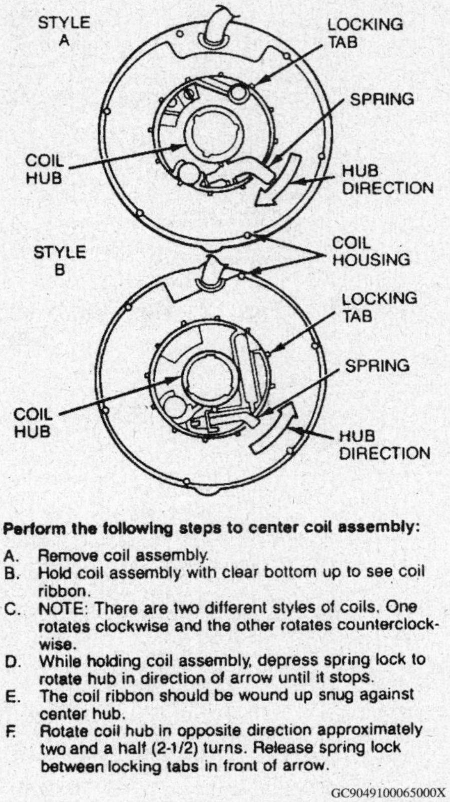
STYLE A
LOCKING TAB
SPRING
COIL HUB
HUB DIRECTION
COIL HOUSING
STYLE B
LOCKING TAB
SPRING
COIL HUB
HUB DIRECTION
Perform the following steps to center coil assembly:
A. Remove coil assembly.
B. Hold coil assembly with clear bottom up to see coil ribbon.
C. NOTE: There are two different styles of coils. One rotates clockwise and the other rotates counterclockwise.
D. While holding coil assembly, depress spring lock to rotate hub in direction of arrow until it stops.
E. The coil ribbon should be wound up snug against center hub.
F. Rotate coil hub in opposite direction approximately two and a half (2-1/2) turns. Release spring lock between locking tabs in front of arrow.
GC9049100065000X

Fig. 19 Coil assembly centered position

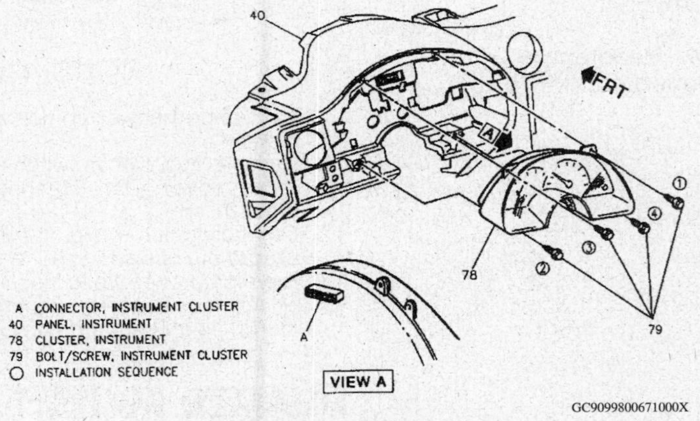

Fig. 20 Instrument cluster

INSTRUMENT CLUSTER

REPLACE

1. Disconnect instrument panel upper trim panel assembly from lower windshield support, then remove from carrier.
2. Remove instrument cluster assembly from carrier, **Fig. 20.**
3. Reverse procedure to install.

RADIO

REPLACE

1. Remove accessory trim plate, **Fig. 21.**
2. Remove radio bracket bolts, **Fig. 22.**
3. Remove radio from instrument panel, then disconnect antenna cable and electrical connectors.
4. Reverse procedure to install noting the following:
   a. **On Firebird models,** install radio bracket bolts in following order; lower left, upper right, upper left.
   b. **Torque** radio bracket bolts to 16 inch lbs.

WIPER MOTOR

REPLACE

REMOVAL

1. Remove wiper arm and blade assemblies as follows:
   a. Operate wipers at lowest delay setting, then shut Off wipers at inner wipe (end of sweep) position.
   b. Mark windshield at tip of blade assembly to aid installation, then lift wiper arm nut cover and remove nut.
   c. Remove wiper arm from linkage drive shaft using wiper arm puller J 39637.
2. Remove lefthand cowl panel and hood seal.
3. Disconnect washer hose assembly from lefthand cowl panel, then the electrical connector from wiper motor assembly.
4. Remove screw and nut from lefthand linkage assembly, **Fig. 23,** then disconnect socket of righthand linkage assembly from ball of lefthand linkage assembly using wiper linkage separator tool No. J–39232, or equivalent.
5. Remove lefthand linkage assembly, then the screw from wiper motor assembly.
6. Pull wiper motor assembly free from slots of bracket, then disconnect socket of righthand linkage assembly from crank arm ball of wiper motor assembly using wiper linkage separator.

INSTALLATION

When installing wiper motor assembly, ensure crank arm is in inner wipe

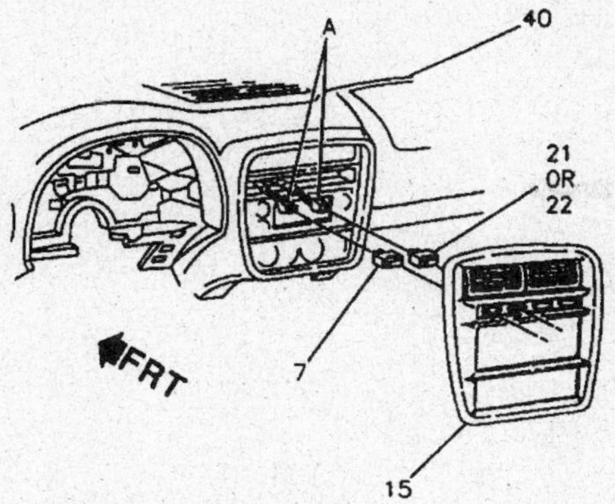

A CONNECTORS, INSTRUMENT PANEL WIRING HARNESS
7 SWITCH, FOG LAMP
15 PLATE, INSTRUMENT PANEL ACCESSORY TRIM
21 SWITCH, TRACTION CONTROL
22 SWITCH, SECOND GEAR START
40 PANEL, INSTRUMENT

GC9099800672000X

Fig. 21 Accessory trim plate removal

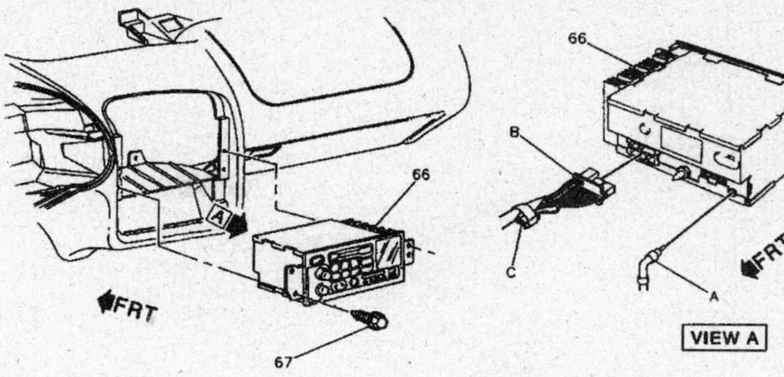

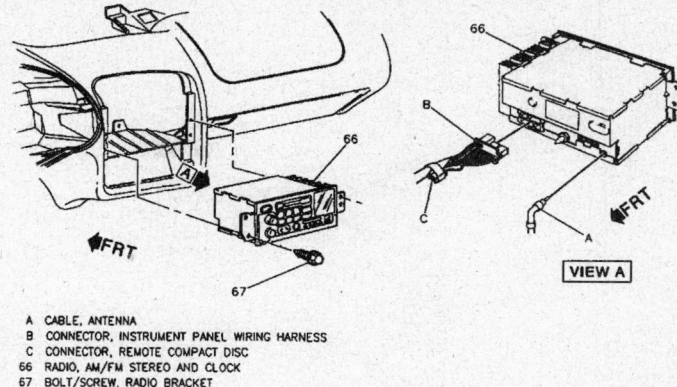

A CABLE, ANTENNA
B CONNECTOR, INSTRUMENT PANEL WIRING HARNESS
C CONNECTOR, REMOTE COMPACT DISC
66 RADIO, AM/FM STEREO AND CLOCK
67 BOLT/SCREW, RADIO BRACKET

GC9099800673000X

Fig. 22 Radio replacement

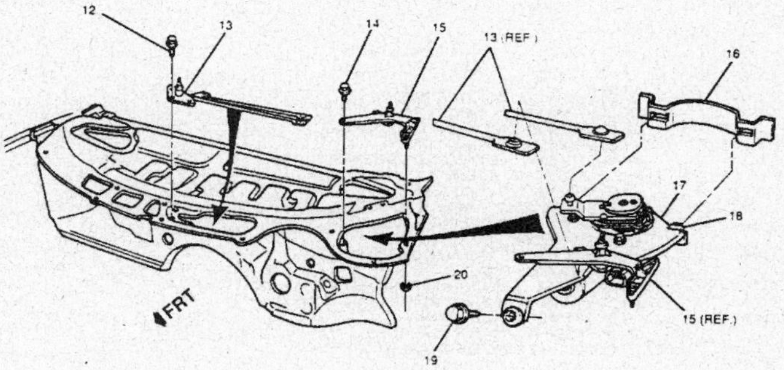

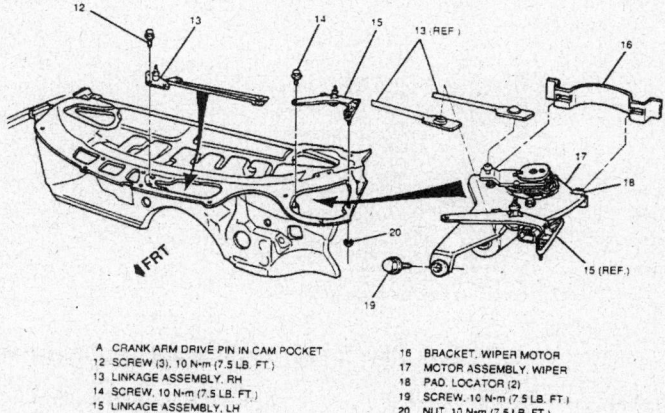

A CRANK ARM DRIVE PIN IN CAM POCKET
12 SCREW (3), 10 N•m (7.5 LB. FT.)
13 LINKAGE ASSEMBLY, RH
14 SCREW, 10 N•m (7.5 LB. FT.)
15 LINKAGE ASSEMBLY, LH
16 BRACKET, WIPER MOTOR
17 MOTOR ASSEMBLY, WIPER
18 PAD, LOCATOR (2)
19 SCREW, 10 N•m (7.5 LB. FT.)
20 NUT, 10 N•m (7.5 LB. FT.)

GC9099300207000X

Fig. 23 Windshield wiper motor/transmission assembly

position. Crank arm drive pin must be engaged in cam pocket.

1. Press socket of righthand linkage assembly into engagement with crank arm ball of wiper motor assembly using wiper linkage installer tool No. J 39529, or equivalent.
2. Install wiper motor assembly with two locator pads pressed fully into slots of bracket, then the mounting screw and **torque** to 7.5 ft. lbs.
3. Install lefthand linkage assembly without attaching parts, then press socket of righthand linkage assembly into engagement with ball of lefthand linkage assembly using wiper linkage installer.
4. Attach lefthand linkage assembly with screw and nut and **torque** to 7.5 ft. lbs.
5. Connect electrical connector to wiper motor assembly, then the washer hose assembly to lefthand cowl panel and washer nozzle.
6. Install lefthand cowl panel and hood seal.
7. Install wiper arm and blade assemblies as follows:
   a. Install wiper arm and blade assembly onto linkage drive shaft, with tip of blade assembly aligned with mark made at removal.
   b. Install nut on linkage drive shaft and **torque** to 24 ft. lbs. while holding wiper arm.
   c. Close nut cover, then run wipers and check for proper wipe pattern. Turn wipers Off and check for correct park position.

WIPER SWITCH

REPLACE

1. **On models equipped with cruise control,** remove tilt wheel release lever and access cover, then disconnect electrical connectors.
2. **On all models,** remove wiper switch by grasping firmly and pulling straight out.
3. Reverse procedure to install, noting the following:
   a. Ensure wiper switch is in Off position before installing.
   b. Position tilt lever ± 5° from centerline of column assembly.

WIPER TRANSMISSION

REPLACE

REMOVAL

1. Remove wiper arm and blade assemblies as follows:
   a. Operate wipers at lowest delay setting, then turn wipers Off at inner wipe (end of sweep) position.
   b. Mark windshield at tip of blade assembly to aid installation, then lift wiper arm nut cover and remove nut.
   c. Remove wiper arm from linkage drive shaft using wiper arm puller J 39637.
2. Remove lefthand cowl panel and hood seal, then disconnect washer hose assembly from lefthand cowl panel.
3. Remove screw and nut from lefthand linkage assembly, **Fig. 23,** then disconnect socket of righthand linkage assembly from ball of lefthand linkage assembly using wiper linkage separator tool No. J–39232, or equivalent.
4. Remove lefthand linkage assembly, then the screws securing righthand linkage assembly.
5. Disconnect socket of righthand linkage assembly from crank arm ball of wiper motor assembly using wiper linkage separator, then remove righthand linkage assembly from slotted plenum access hole.

INSTALLATION

1. Install righthand linkage assembly from slotted plenum access hole, then the screws securing righthand linkage assembly finger tight.
2. Align righthand linkage assembly, then press socket of righthand linkage assembly into engagement with crank arm ball of wiper motor assembly using wiper linkage installer J 39529.
3. Install lefthand linkage assembly without attaching parts, then press socket

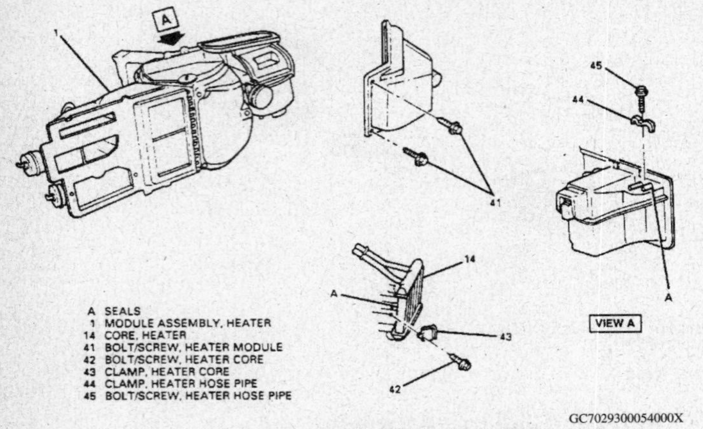

Fig. 24 Heater core replacement

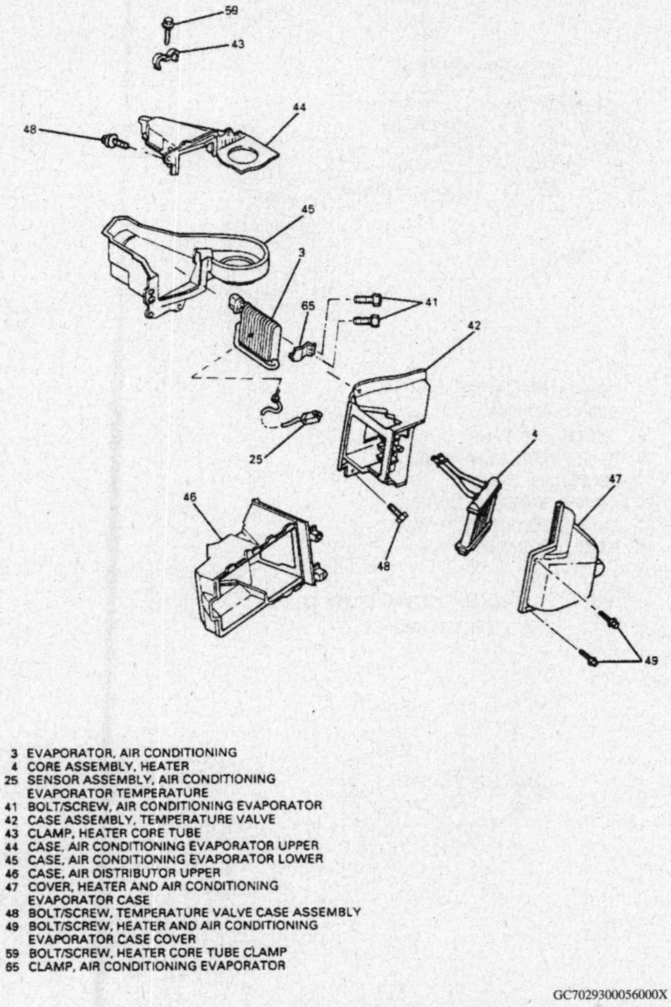

Fig. 25 Evaporator core replacement

of righthand linkage assembly into engagement with ball of lefthand linkage assembly using wiper linkage installer.
4. Attach lefthand linkage assembly with screw and nut and **torque** to 7.5 ft. lbs.
5. Connect washer hose assembly to lefthand cowl panel and washer nozzle.
6. Install lefthand cowl panel and hood seal.
7. Install wiper arm and blade assemblies as follows:
   a. Install wiper arm and blade assembly onto linkage drive shaft, with tip of blade assembly aligned with mark made at removal.
   b. Install nut on linkage drive shaft and **torque** to 24 ft. lbs. while holding wiper arm.
   c. Close nut cover, then run wipers and check for proper wipe pattern. Shut off wipers and check for correct park position.

BLOWER MOTOR

REPLACE

1. Ensure ignition switch is in Off position, then remove righthand instrument panel sound insulator assembly and side trim panel.
2. Remove blower motor mounting bolts, then the blower motor.
3. Reverse procedure to install. **Torque** mounting bolts to 20 inch lbs.

HEATER CORE

REPLACE

1997

1. Open instrument panel compartment by pushing in on sides of compartment to release it.
2. Drain coolant.
3. Remove heater module bolts, then the heater module assembly cover, **Fig. 24.**
4. **On models equipped with A/C,** remove evaporator temperature sensor from heater and air conditioning cover and remove air inlet valve actuator.
5. **On all models,** remove heater core bolt and heater core clamp, then the hose pipe clamp bolt and hose pipe clamp.
6. Disconnect hose heater hose assembly from heater hose pipes, then carefully pull heater core toward you to remove.
7. Reverse procedure to install, noting the following:
   a. Ensure seals around heater pipes stay in place when installing core.
   b. **Torque** hose pipe clamp bolt and heater core bolt to 16 inch lbs. and heater module bolts to 18 inch lbs.
   c. Operate engine and check for coolant leaks, then check coolant level, adding coolant as necessary.

1998–2000

1. Drain cooling system.
2. Remove heater hoses from heater core.
3. Push in on sides of instrument panel compartment, then remove.
4. Remove heater module bolts and screws, then the module cover.
5. Remove heater core bolt and clamp, then the heater core.
6. Reverse procedure to install. Ensure seal is correctly installed.

EVAPORATOR CORE

REPLACE

1. Discharge refrigerant into a recovery station, then drain coolant.
2. Remove righthand instrument panel sound insulator panel assembly, then disconnect heater hoses at heater core assembly.
3. Remove instrument panel compartment, then the heater core as previously described.
4. Remove evaporator temperature sensor assembly, **Fig. 25,** then disconnect temperature control cable assembly at temperature valve case assembly.
5. Remove bolts (located in engine compartment) from temperature valve case assembly, then the temperature valve case assembly by sliding case assembly downward to disengage upper case clip.
6. Remove thermostatic expansion valve assembly.
7. Using a small hand saw, remove perforated section of evaporator module assembly as one piece and retain for reuse.

8. Remove bolts retaining evaporator, then the evaporator from module assembly by sliding evaporator to left and pulling out through opening cut in module.
9. Reverse procedure to install, noting the following:
   a. If replacing evaporator, transfer condensate screen to new evaporator.
   b. If replacing evaporator, add 3 fluid ounces of polyalkalene glycol (PAG) synthetic refrigerant oil to new evaporator.
   c. Apply sealer No. 3012078, or equivalent, between evaporator upper and lower case just behind thermostatic expansion valve assembly to prevent air entry from engine compartment.
   d. Use epoxy glue to adhere perforated section of module assembly to module assembly.
   e. Fill radiator and bleed cooling system.
   f. Partially charge system and perform a leak test, then recover refrigerant and evacuate and charge system.

3800 Engine

NOTE: On Air Bag Equipped Models, Refer To " Air Bag System Precautions" Located In The Front Of This Manual For System Disarming & Arming Procedures.

NOTE: For Procedures Not Found In This Section, Refer To The 3800 Engine Section In The "Bonneville, Eighty Eight, LeSabre, LSS, Park Ave. & Regencey (C & H Cars)" Chapter.

NOTE: Refer To "Computer Relearn Procedures " Located In The Front Of This Manual For Computer Relearn Procedures.

INDEX

PRECAUTIONS

AIR BAG SYSTEMS

Refer to "Air Bag System Precautions" in the front of this manual for system disarming and arming procedures.

BATTERY GROUND CABLE

Prior to service, disconnect battery ground cable and isolate as required.

FUEL SYSTEM PRESSURE RELIEF

Refer to the 3800 Engine Section in the "Bonneville, Eighty Eight, LeSabre, LSS, Park Ave. & Regencey (C & H Cars)" chapter for fuel system pressure relief procedure.

ENGINE SUPPORT

When raising the engine for any reason, do not use a jack under the oil pan, crankshaft balancer or any sheet metal, this may result in damage to engine. Always use universal support fixture tool No. J 28467–A and engine support adapter tool No. J 41044, or equivalents.

COMPRESSION PRESSURE

When checking compression, lowest cylinder must be within 70 percent of the highest cylinder with a minimum pressure of 100 psi. Perform compression test with engine at normal operating temperature, spark plugs removed and throttle wide open.

ENGINE MOUNT

REPLACE

1. Remove alternator, then the ignition control module.
2. Raise and suitably support vehicle.
3. Disconnect exhaust catalytic converter system.
4. Remove engine mount nuts.
5. Disconnect transmission oil cooler lines, if necessary.
6. Loosen air conditioning compressor and slide forward, if necessary.
7. Install universal support fixture tool No. J 28467-A along with engine support adapter tool No. J 41044, or equivalents, and support engine to allow for engine mount bolts/bracket removal and raise engine.
8. Remove engine mount bolts and screws, then remove mounts from engine cradle.
9. Remove engine bracket bolts and screws, then the studs and brackets.
10. Reverse procedure to install, noting the following:
    a. **Torque** bolts and screws (13) and studs (11), **Fig. 1,** to 74 ft. lbs.
    b. **Torque** bolts and screws (14) to 37 ft. lbs. and engine mount bolts (18) to 43 ft. lbs.

ENGINE

REPLACE

1. Recover refrigerant, if necessary, then relieve fuel pressure as outlined under "Precautions."
2. Disconnect A/C compressor and condenser hose from accumulator, if necessary.

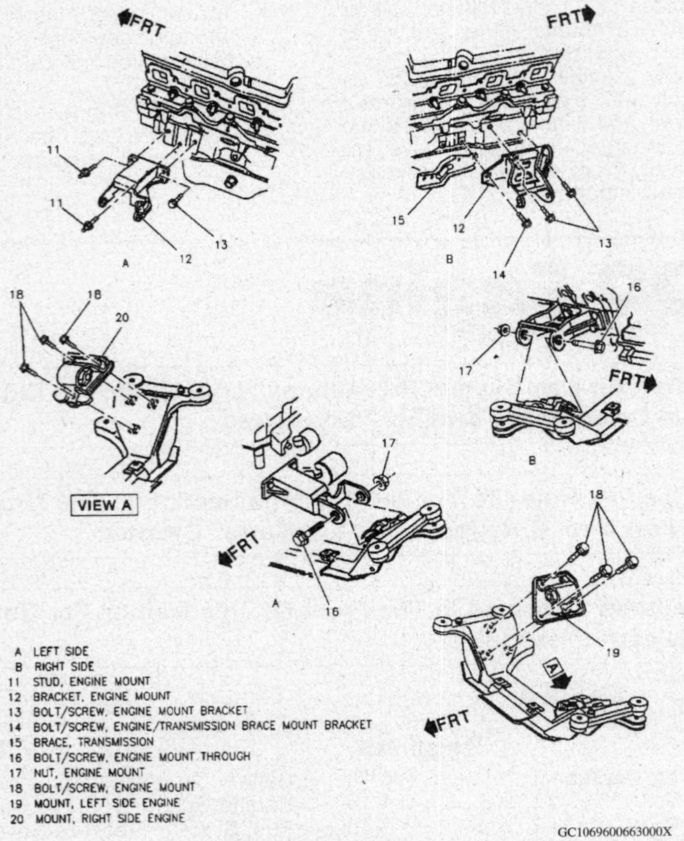

Fig. 1 Engine mount fasteners

3. Raise and support vehicle and remove front wheels.
4. Drain coolant, engine oil and disconnect 3-way catalytic converter.
5. Disconnect transmission converter and front fascia lower deflectors.
6. Disconnect stabilizer bar bushing bolts and transmission fluid cooler lines from radiator.
7. Remove radiator inlet hose, shift linkage from transmission and propeller shaft.
8. Disconnect rear axle torque arm from transmission and steering gear coupling shaft from rack and pinion assembly.
9. Disconnect power steering gear inlet and outlet hoses from power steering gear.
10. Disconnect starter motor and electrical ground strap from engine block.
11. Disconnect A/C compressor and condenser hoses, if necessary.
12. Remove battery negative cable from rear of A/C compressor and engine coolant heater cord from block.
13. Lower vehicle, remove serpentine belt and any heater hoses/brackets from tensioner.
14. Remove air cleaner outlet rear duct and resonator duct.
15. Remove fuel lines at fuel rail and cruise/accelerator cables from throttle body.
16. Disconnect radiator outlet hose from thermostat housing and brake booster vacuum hose.
17. Disconnect ABS combination valve from brake lines, clips and hydraulic modulator.
18. Remove righthand body hinge pillar trim panel and the three (blue, black and white) wiring harness connectors.
19. Disconnect the forward lamp wiring harness connectors and PCM and place on top of engine.
20. Disconnect engine wiring harness in passenger compartment and place on top of engine.
21. Disconnect positive lead at alternator.
22. Remove lower shock bolt from lower control arm.
23. Remove upper control arm ball stud from steering knuckle and secure struts.
24. Disconnect electrical connectors to wheel speed sensor at engine frame.
25. Using tool No. J 39580, or equivalent, position lift table under engine and frame.
26. Remove engine frame to transmission support bolts.
27. Raise vehicle from engine, transmission and engine frame.
28. Remove transmission.
29. **On models equipped with manual transmission,** remove clutch.
30. **On all models,** remove engine mount through-bolt and separate engine from engine frame.
31. Reverse procedure to install, noting the following:
    a. When installing wiring harness back through front of dash, the rubber grommet must be installed correctly. If grommet is torn or damaged, it must be replaced.
    b. Tighten fasteners to specifications.
    c. Align wheels.

INTAKE MANIFOLD

REPLACE

UPPER

1. Remove right side spark plug wires, then the manifold vacuum source.
2. Remove rear alternator mounting bracket bolts.
3. Remove EGR outlet pipe bolt and nut, then separate from intake manifold.
4. Remove throttle body and gasket.
5. Remove fuel rail with injectors attached.
6. Remove upper intake manifold bolts.
7. Remove upper intake manifold and gasket.
8. Reverse procedure to install, noting the following:
    a. **Torque** vertical bolts in sequence, **Fig. 2** to 11 ft. lbs.
    b. **Torque** water outlet bolts in sequence, **Fig. 2** to 20 ft. lbs.
    c. **Torque** side bolts in sequence, **Fig. 2** to 22 ft. lbs.

LOWER

To remove the lower intake manifold, the upper manifold must be removed first.

1. Remove upper intake manifold as outlined in the " Upper" section of this manual to access two hidden bolts.
2. Remove lower intake manifold bolts, then manifold.
3. Reverse procedure to install, noting the following:
    a. Use a suitable thread locking compound on intake manifold bolts prior to assembly.
    b. **Torque** bolts in sequence shown, **Fig. 3** to 11 ft. lbs.

EXHAUST MANIFOLD

REPLACE

RIGHT SIDE

1. Remove exhaust manifold heat shield nuts and then the shield.
2. Raise and support vehicle.
3. Remove exhaust catalytic converter pipe.
4. Remove heated oxygen sensor electrical connector from bracket.
5. Lower vehicle and remove exhaust manifold studs/bolts and then manifold.
6. Remove exhaust manifold gasket and clean cylinder head mating surface.
7. Reverse procedure to install.

LEFT SIDE

1. Remove EGR valve adapter from exhaust manifold.

2. Remove oil level indicator and tube.
3. Remove exhaust manifold heat shield nuts and then the shield.
4. Raise and support vehicle.
5. Remove exhaust catalytic converter pipe and oxygen sensor connector.
6. Disconnect spark plug wires and lower vehicle.
7. Remove exhaust manifold studs/bolts and then the manifold.
8. Remove exhaust manifold gasket and clean mating surfaces.
9. Reverse procedure to install, noting the following:
   a. Install new exhaust manifold gasket.
   b. Inspect EGR outlet tube for leaks.

CYLINDER HEAD

REPLACE

1. Remove upper and lower intake manifolds.
2. Remove exhaust manifold.
3. Remove rocker arm covers, rocker arms and push rods.
4. Remove and discard cylinder head bolts.
5. Remove cylinder head.
6. Reverse procedure to install, noting the following:
   a. Clean threads in block with proper size tap.
   b. Install new head gasket with the lefthand gasket, marked " L" and an arrow, pointing forward. The right-hand gasket has just the arrow marking. These head gaskets are not interchangeable.
   c. Install new cylinder head bolts, then using sequence shown in **Fig. 4, torque** cylinder head bolts to 37 ft. lbs.
   d. **On 1997 models,** using torque angle meter tool No. J 36660, or equivalent, tighten each bolt in sequence an additional 130°, finally, tighten four center bolts an additional 30.°
   e. **On 1998–2000 models,** using torque angle meter tool No. J 36660, or equivalent, tighten each bolt in sequence an additional 120°.

CRANKSHAFT DAMPER

REPLACE

1. Remove drive belt, then raise and support vehicle.
2. Remove starter motor and transmission braces.
3. Remove transmission access cover.
4. Hold flywheel using tool No. J 37096, or equivalent.
5. Remove crankshaft balancer/damper bolt and washer. **Note the relationship of the balancer/damper and crankshaft key as the balancer is removed.**
6. Remove crankshaft balancer using puller tool No. J38197, or equivalent. **The crankshaft damper is serviced as an assembly, do not separate pulley from balancer hub.**

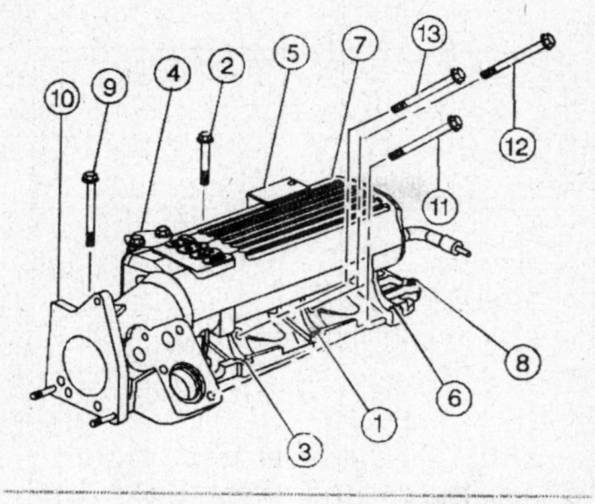

Fig. 2 Upper intake manifold tightening sequence

7. Reverse procedure to install, noting the following:
   a. Lubricate balancer and crankshaft mating surface with clean motor oil.
   b. Tighten balancer bolt to specifications.

FRONT COVER

REPLACE

1997

1. Drain cooling system.
2. Remove air cleaner, then the outlet and resonator ducts.
3. Remove radiator hose from front cover.
4. Remove drive belt tensioner if necessary.
5. Raise and support vehicle.
6. Remove crankshaft damper, **Fig. 5,** using tool No. J 38197, or equivalent.
7. Remove oil pan to front cover attaching bolts.
8. Lower vehicle, then disconnect electrical connectors from front cover.
9. Remove crankshaft position sensor shield.
10. Remove water pump.
11. Remove front cover bolts and cover, **Fig. 6.**
12. Reverse procedure to install, noting the following:
    a. Install front cover applying sealant GM P/N 12346004, or equivalent, to cover bolts.
    b. Tighten bolts to specifications, then using torque angle meter tool No. J 36660, or equivalent tighten an additional 40.°

1998–2000

1. Drain engine oil and coolant into suitable containers.
2. Disconnect IAT sensor electrical connector.
3. Remove air intake duct.
4. Loosen water pump pulley bolts.
5. Remove drivebelt tensioner.
6. Using puller No. J 25034–B, or equivalent, remove power steering pulley.
7. Place suitable container under power steering pump, then disconnect inlet and return hoses from pump.
8. Remove power steering pump, then raise and support vehicle.
9. Remove crankshaft damper as outlined under "Crankshaft Damper, Replace."
10. Disconnect CKP sensor electrical connector, then remove CKP sensor shield.
11. Remove CKP sensor, then the oil pan to front cover bolts.
12. Loosen oil pans bolts slightly to lower oil pan as an installation aid for front cover.
13. Lower vehicle, then remove water pump pulley.
14. Remove radiator outlet hose from front cover.
15. Remove front cover mounting studs and bolts.
16. Remove front cover and gasket.
17. Remove components from front cover as required if replacing cover.
18. Reverse procedure to install, noting the following:
    a. Apply sealant No. 12346004, or equivalent, to threads of front cover bolts and studs.
    b. Torque front cover bolts to 15 ft. lbs., then using torque angle meter No. J36660, or equivalent, tighten bolts and studs an additional 40°.

BALANCE SHAFT

REPLACE

1. Recover refrigerant as outlined under "Air Conditioning " section of this manual.
2. Remove A/C compressor.
3. Remove A/C hoses from condenser.
4. Remove radiator, condenser and condenser support.
5. **On models equipped with automatic transmissions,** remove transmission as outlined under "Automatic Transaxles/Transmissions, " then the flywheel.
6. **On models equipped with manual transmissions,** remove transmission as outlined under "Clutch & Manual Transmission," then the clutch and flywheel.
7. **On all models,** remove oil pan as outlined under "Oil Pan, Replace."
8. Remove crankshaft rear oil seal housing, **Fig. 7.**
9. Remove upper and lower intake manifold as outlined under " Intake Manifold, Replace."
10. Remove valve covers, rocker arms and pushrods. Ensure parts are kept in order so they may be installed to their original positions.
11. Remove valve lifter guides, then the valve lifters. Ensure lifters are reinstalled to their original position.
12. Remove front cover as outlined under "Front Cover, Replace."
13. Remove balance shaft gear attaching bolt.

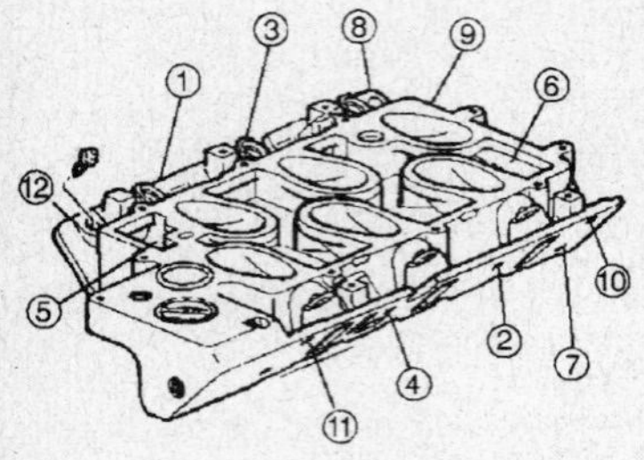

GC1069901046000X

Fig. 3 Lower intake manifold tightening sequence

14. Remove camshaft sprocket and timing chain, then the balance shaft driven gear.
15. Remove balance shaft retainer bolts, then the retainer and gear.
16. Using a suitable slide hammer, remove balance shaft.
17. Remove balance shaft rear plug, then the rear bushing using removal tool No. J36995, or equivalent. **Balance shaft, front bearing and rear bushing are serviced as a set.**
18. Reverse procedure to install noting the following:
    a. Coat rear bushing with engine oil, then install using bushing installer tool Nos. J36995 and J36995–8, or equivalents, **Fig. 8.** Ensure lubrication hole is facing flywheel side. Bushing is fully installed when installation tool fully contacts balance shaft bore.
    b. Using balance shaft installation tool No. J36996, or equivalent, install shaft to engine block, **Fig. 8.** Apply engine oil to front bearing and inner race before installation.
    c. Temporarily install balance shaft retainer and bolts.
    d. Install balance shaft drive gear and bolt, using suitable thread locking compound and **torque** to 16 ft. lbs. plus an additional 70° using a suitable torque angle meter.
    e. Inspect balance shaft end play and radial play at both front and rear. End play should be .0–.008 inch, front radial play should be .0–.0011 inch and rear play should be .0005–.0047 inch. Refer to **Fig. 9** for balance shaft measurements.
    f. With camshaft sprocket temporarily installed, rotate camshaft so timing mark is straight down.
    g. With the camshaft sprocket and gear removed, rotate balance shaft so timing mark, **Fig. 10,** is straight down.
    h. Install camshaft gear and turn crankshaft so No. 1 piston is at TDC.
    i. Install timing chain and camshaft sprocket. Timing gear lash is .002–.005 inch, measured at four places, every ¼ turn.

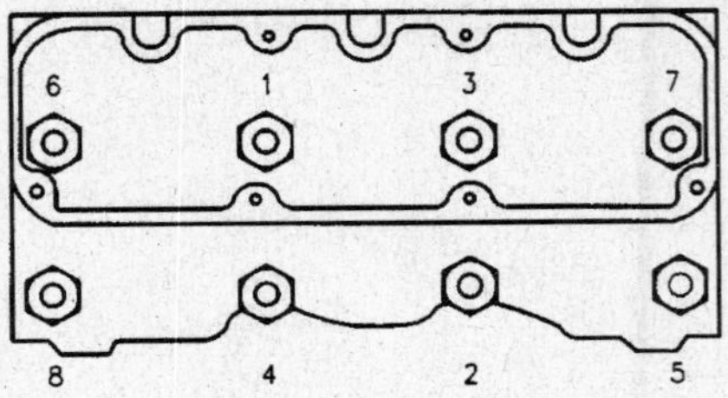

GC1069600665000X

Fig. 4 Cylinder head bolt tightening sequence

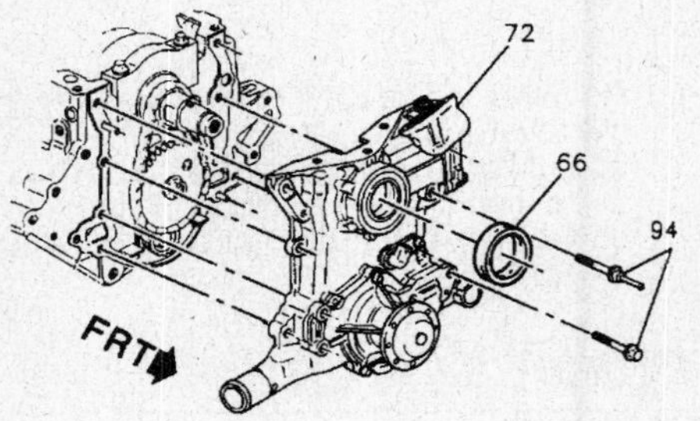

GC1069600667000X

Fig. 6 Front cover replacement

OIL PAN

REPLACE

1. Remove ignition coils.
2. Install engine support fixture tool No. J28467–A, or equivalent.
3. Raise and support vehicle.
4. Drain engine oil, then remove torque converter cover.
5. Remove exhaust crossover pipe.
6. Remove engine mount through bolts.
7. Raise engine using support fixture.
8. Remove oil level sensor, then the oil pan bolts.
9. Lower rear of oil pan, then rotate outward and remove pan.
10. Reverse procedure to install. Tighten all bolts and nuts to specifications.

SERPENTINE DRIVE BELT

BELT, REPLACE

Cracks appearing perpendicular to the belt ribs indicate normal wear. If sections of rib are missing or if the belt is slipping, the belt must be replaced. The belt tensioner has a wear indicator, and if it is out of limits, either the belt or tensioner must be replaced.

1. Using a ratchet and socket, push tensioner clockwise and remove serpentine belt, **Fig. 11.**
2. Reverse procedure to install.

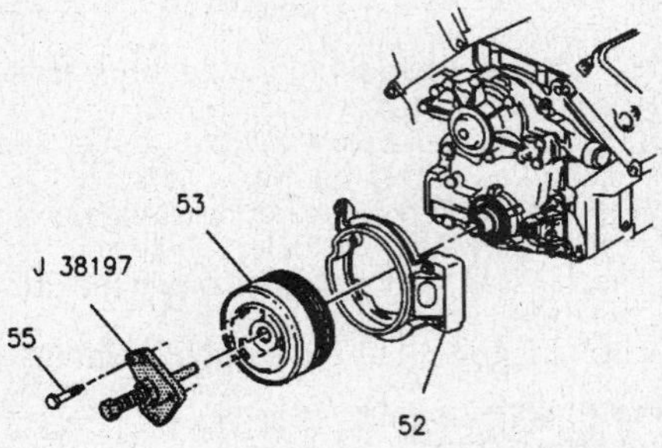

GC1069600666000X

Fig. 5 Crankshaft balancer assembly

TENSIONER, REPLACE

1. Drain engine coolant and remove drive belt.
2. Remove transmission oil dipstick and oil filler neck from rocker arm cover.
3. Remove manifold absolute pressure (MAP) sensor from alternator bracket and remove alternator.
4. Remove heater hoses from belt drive tensioner.
5. Remove belt drive tensioner bolts and tensioner, **Fig. 12.**
6. Reverse procedure to install.

RADIATOR

REPLACE

1997

1. Remove air intake duct and air cleaner.
2. Raise and support vehicle.
3. Drain coolant and remove electrical connectors at engine coolant fans.
4. Remove radiator upper mounting panel, **Figs. 13 and 14.**
5. Remove electric engine coolant fan, transmission oil cooler lines and coolant level indicator module, if equipped.
6. Lower vehicle and loosen receiver dehydrator bracket.
7. Remove upper radiator hose and lower radiator hose at water pump.
8. Remove overflow tube, then the condenser from radiator.
9. Remove radiator from vehicle.
10. Reverse procedure to install, noting the following:
    a. Ensure radiator is seated on radiator insulators.
    b. Add engine coolant and inspect for leaks.
    c. **Torque** upper mounting panel to 9 ft. lbs.

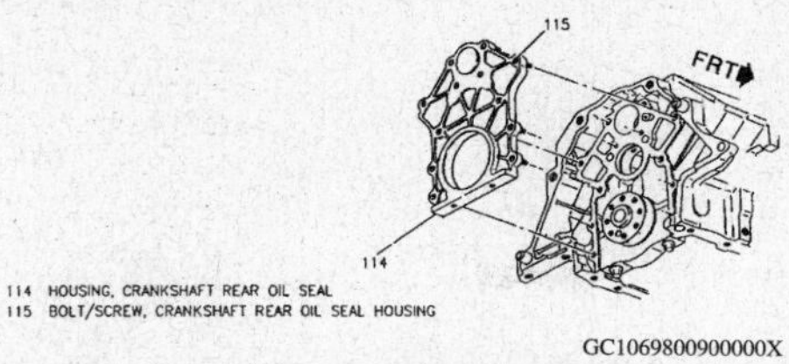

Fig. 7 Crankshaft rear oil seal housing removal

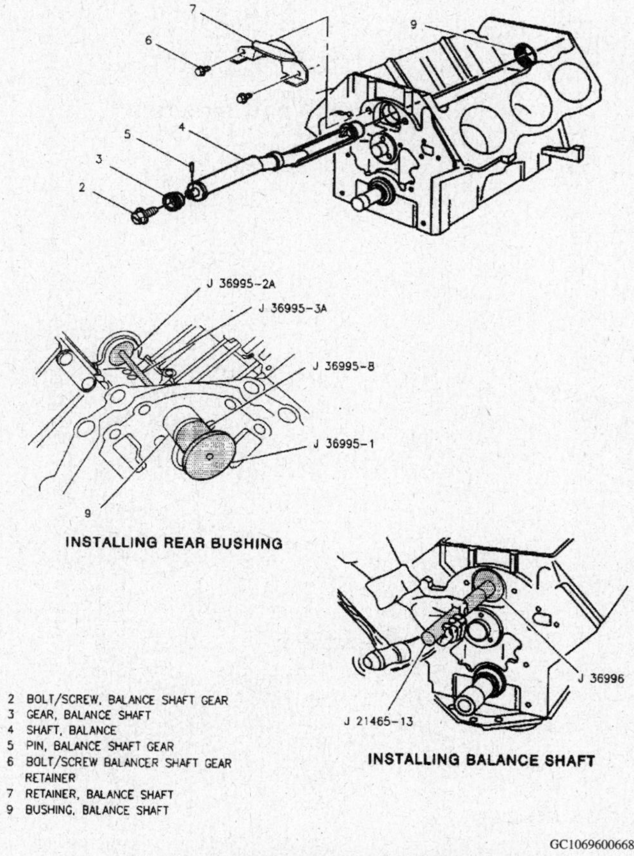

Fig. 8 Balance shaft installation

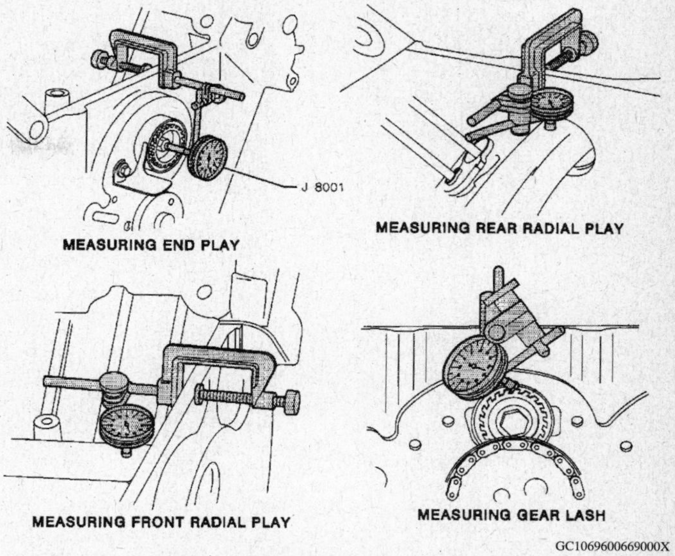

Fig. 9 Balance shaft clearance measurements

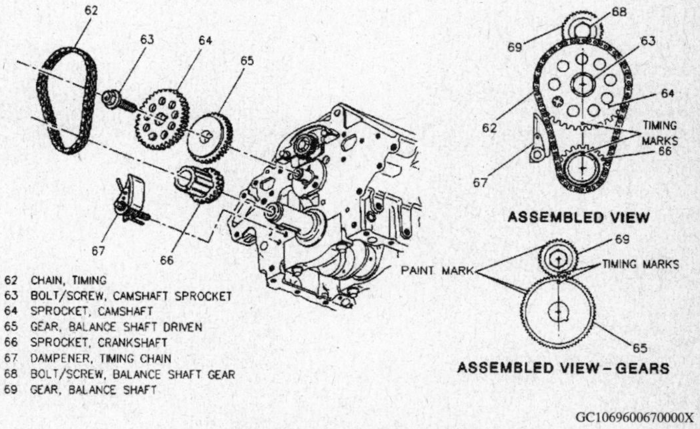

Fig. 10 Timing assembly

1998–2000

1. Recover refrigerant as outlined under "Air Conditioning."
2. Drain cooling system, then remove radiator hoses.
3. Remove upper evaporator tube bracket bolt, **Fig. 15.**
4. Remove evaporator tube from condenser.
5. Remove upper and lower oil cooler lines from radiator, if equipped.
6. Remove condenser tube from condenser, **Fig. 16.**
7. Remove overflow hose from radiator.
8. Remove air intake duct and air cleaner assembly, then disconnect cooling fan electrical connectors.
9. Remove electric cooling fans, then the coolant level indicator module if equipped.
10. Remove radiator and condenser.
11. Reverse procedure to install.

FUEL PUMP

REPLACE

1. Relieve fuel system pressure as outlined under "Precautions."
2. Raise and support vehicle.
3. Drain fuel tank and remove.
4. Remove fuel sender retaining nuts, retaining ring, sender seal (discard seal) and sender assembly.
5. Reverse procedure to install, noting the following:
   a. **Always replace fuel sender seal when servicing sending unit. Do not handle fuel sender assembly by the sender pipes, as this may damage the solder joints.**
   b. Clean fuel sender assembly sealing surfaces.
   c. Fuel pump strainer must be in horizontal position. Ensure fuel pump strainer does not block full travel of float arm.
   d. Gently fold strainer over itself and insert into fuel tank making sure strainer is not damaged or trapped by sump walls.
   e. Inspect for leaks.

FUEL FILTER

REPLACE

1. Relieve fuel system pressure as outlined under "Precautions," then raise and support vehicle.
2. Clean all inline fuel filter connections to avoid contaminating fuel system.
3. Remove quick-connect fitting at filter inlet using quick disconnect tool No. J37088–A, or equivalent, then the threaded fitting from filter outlet. Slide fuel filter from bracket.
4. Reverse procedure to install, noting the following:
   a. Inspect fuel pipe O-ring for cuts, nicks, swelling or distortion and replace, if necessary.
   b. Inspect for leaks.

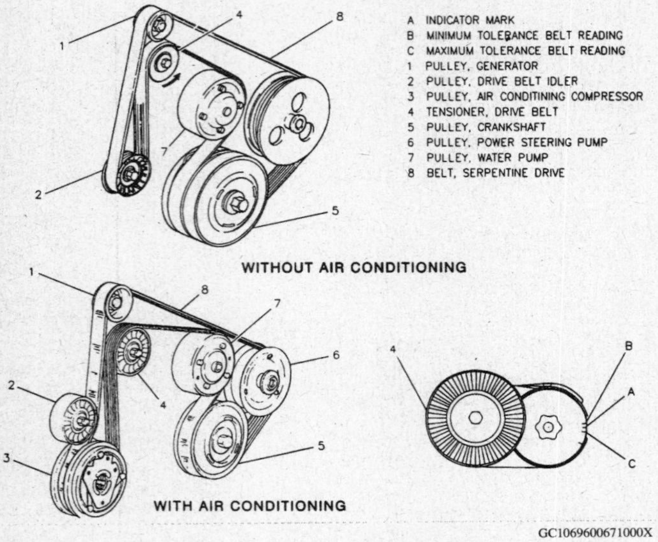

Fig. 11 Serpentine belt routing

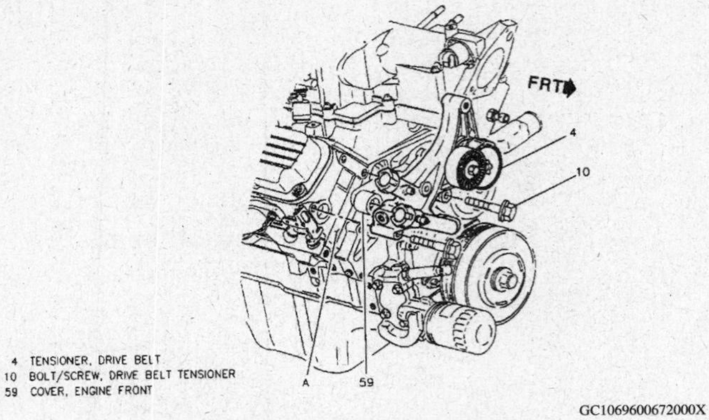

Fig. 12 Serpentine belt tensioner

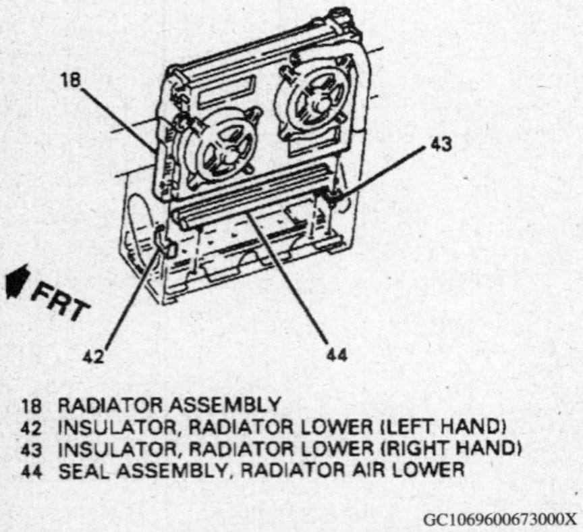

Fig. 13 Radiator insulators & seal

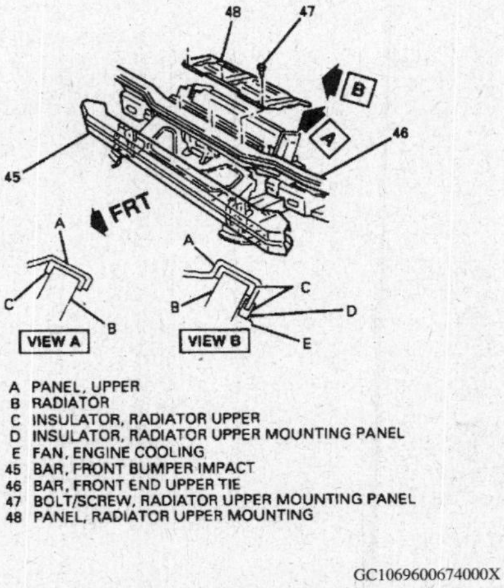

Fig. 14 Radiator upper mounting panel

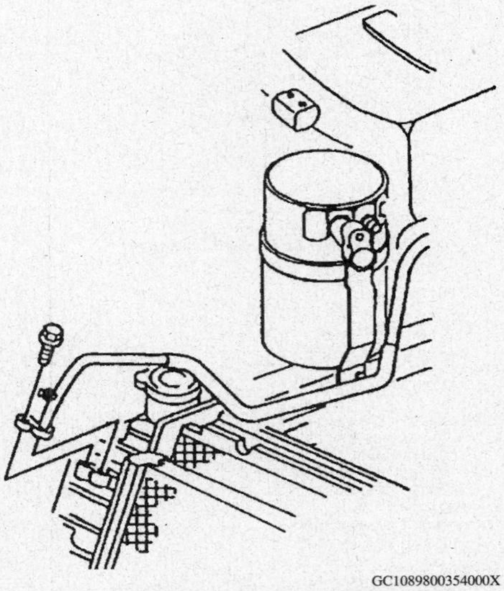

Fig. 15 Evaporator line removal

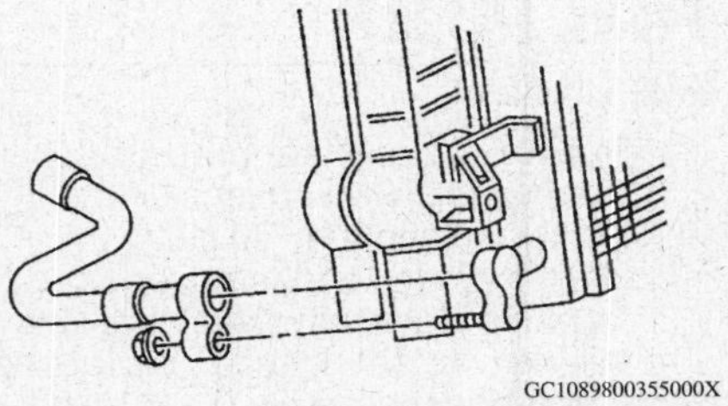

Fig. 16 Condenser tube removal

TIGHTENING SPECIFICATIONS

Year	Component	Torque/ Ft. Lbs.
1997– 2000	Balance Shaft Gear	16③
	Balance Shaft Retainer	22
	Camshaft Position Sensor	84⑫
	Camshaft Sprocket	⑩
	Connecting Rod Bearing Cap	20⑦
	Coolant Outlet	20
	Crankshaft Balancer	⑨
	Crankshaft Main Bearing Bolt	⑪
	Crankshaft Main Bearing Side Bolt	11④
	Crankshaft Position Sensor Stud	22
	Cylinder Head	①
	Drive Belt Tensioner	37
	EGR Valve Nut	21
	Engine Coolant Temperature Sensor	10
	Engine Front Cover	11⑥
	Engine Mount Bolts	43
	Engine Mount Through Bolt	70
	Engine Mount Through Bolt Nut	59
	Engine Oil Pressure Sensor	10
	ESC Knock Sensor	13
	Exhaust Manifold	⑧
	Flywheel Bolts (New)	11⑦
	Lower Intake Manifold	11
	Oil Pan	10
	Oil Pump Cover	96⑫
	Oxygen Sensor	31
	Throttle Body	84⑫
	Timing Chain Dampener	16
	Upper Intake Manifold (Two Side Bolts)	22
	Upper Intake Manifold (Two Water Outlet Bolts)	20
	Upper Intake Manifold (10 Vertical Bolts)	11
	Valve Lifter Guide Retainer	22
	Valve Rocker Arm	11⑤
	Water Pump	11 ②

① — Refer to "Cylinder Head, Replace."
② — Tighten an additional 80.°
③ — Tighten an additional 70.°
④ — Tighten an additional 45.°
⑤ — Tighten an additional 90.°
⑥ — Tighten an additional 40°
⑦ — Tighten an additional 50.°
⑧ — 1997, 8 ft. lbs.; 1998–2000, 22 ft. lbs.
⑨ — 111 ft. lbs. plus an additional 76°; 1998–2000 w/manual transmission, 111 ft. lbs. plus an additional 114.°
⑩ — 1997, 74 ft. lbs.; 1998–2000 74 ft. lbs. plus an additional 90.°
⑪ — Torque cap bolts to 51 ft. lbs. to seat bearings, then loosen each bolt 1 turn. **To ensure cap seats properly, do not tighten each bolt completely at one time. Make several passes until specified torque is achieved.** Torque to 30 ft. lbs. Using a suitable torque angle meter, tighten in following steps; 35°, an additional 35°, then an additional 40.°
⑫ — Inch lbs.

5.7L (VIN P) Engine

NOTE: On Air Bag Equipped Models, Refer To " Air Bag System Precautions" Located In The Front Of This Manual For System Disarming & Arming Procedures.

NOTE: Refer To "Computer Relearn Procedures " Located In The Front Of This Manual For Computer Relearn Procedures.

INDEX

PRECAUTIONS

AIR BAG SYSTEMS

Refer to "Air Bag System Precautions" in the front of this manual for system disarming and arming procedures.

BATTERY GROUND CABLE

Prior to service, disconnect battery ground cable and isolate as required.

FUEL SYSTEM PRESSURE RELIEF

Failure to relieve system pressure prior to disconnecting fuel system components may cause fire or personal injury. Remove fuel tank filler cap to release fuel tank pressure. Connect pressure gauge tool No. J-34730-1, or equivalent, to pressure tap on fuel rail, position bleed hose into suitable container and slowly relieve fuel system pressure. Prior to disconnecting fuel line, position shop towel over fitting.

COMPRESSION PRESSURE

When checking compression, lowest cylinder must be within 70 percent of the highest cylinder with a minimum pressure of 100 psi. Perform compression test with engine at normal operating temperature, spark plugs removed and throttle wide open.

ENGINE MOUNT

REPLACE

Do not raise or support engine by positioning jack under oil pan, crankshaft damper or other sheet metal components. Raise engine only enough to provide sufficient clearance for mount removal. Check for interference between rear of engine and cowl panel which could result in distributor damage.

1. Raise and support vehicle.
2. Remove engine mount through bolt, then raise front of engine to release weight from mount.
3. Remove mount to engine bolts, then the mount, **Fig. 1.**
4. Reverse procedure to install.

ENGINE

REPLACE

1. Remove air intake duct, then raise and support vehicle and remove wheels.
2. Drain coolant and engine oil, then remove exhaust crossover pipe assembly.
3. **On models with automatic transmission,** remove converter cover and converter bolts.
4. **On all models,** remove front fascia lower deflectors, stabilizer bar bolts and the serpentine drive belt.
5. Remove secondary air injection pump assembly, then disconnect A/C hose assembly from condenser and compressor.
6. **On models with automatic transmission,** disconnect transmission cooler lines from radiator.
7. **On all models,** disconnect lower radiator hose from radiator and lower heater hose from water pump, then the electrical ground straps from right side of engine block and electrical connections from starter motor.
8. Disconnect electrical connectors from knock sensor, oxygen sensor, coolant temperature sensor, wheel speed sensor, engine oil level switch and fuel pump switch/engine oil pressure gauge sensor assemblies.
9. Disconnect left front brake line from caliper brake hose, then the wiring harness from transmission.
10. Disconnect shift linkage from transmission, then the propeller shaft from transmission. **Scribe alignment marks on propeller shaft before disconnecting.**
11. Disconnect torque arm from transmission, then the intermediate steering shaft from rack and pinion assembly.
12. Disconnect electrical ground straps from left side of engine block and frame rail, then lower vehicle.
13. Disconnect fuel lines from fuel rail assembly.
14. Disconnect cruise and accelerator control cables from throttle body, then the upper and lower radiator hoses and upper heater hose from water pump.
15. Disconnect coolant air bleed pipe hose from radiator assembly.
16. Disconnect brake booster vacuum hose, then the alternator.

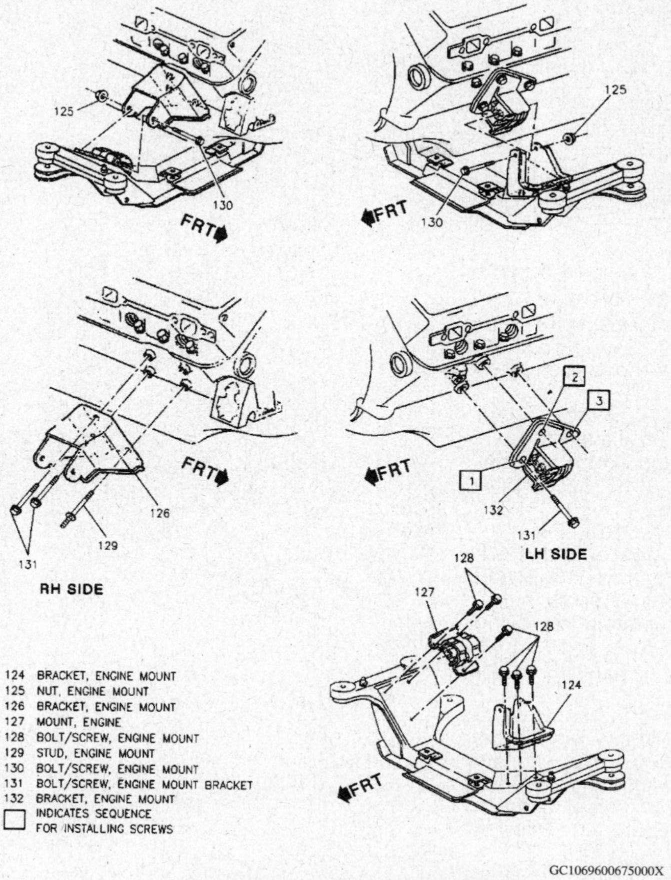

Fig. 1 Engine mounts & brackets

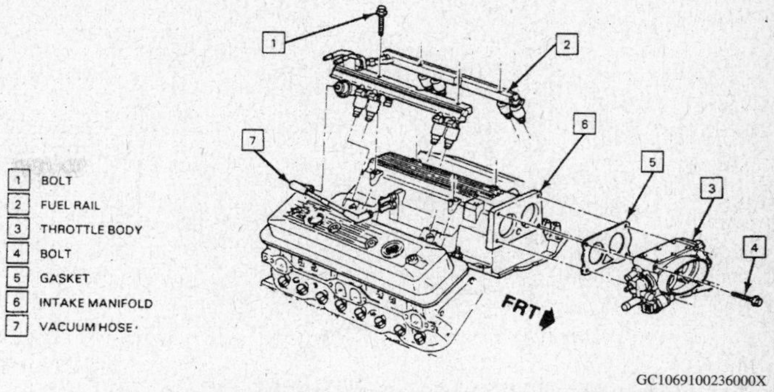

Fig. 2 Fuel rail & throttle body replacement

17. Disconnect engine wiring harness connectors and reposition harness.
18. Disconnect A/C receiver and dehydrator hose from condenser, A/C hose from expansion tube, then the power steering reservoir and reposition.
19. Remove brake master cylinder and reposition, then the upper bolts and nuts from strut assemblies.
20. Disconnect right front brake line from modulator valve assembly and clips, then raise and support vehicle.
21. Place a lift table under engine and engine frame assembly, then remove engine frame and transmission support bolts.
22. Raise vehicle from engine, transmission and engine frame assemblies, then secure strut assemblies to engine frame.
23. Disconnect transmission TV cable from throttle body, then remove transmission assembly.
24. **On models with manual transmission,** remove clutch housing and clutch assembly.
25. **On all models,** disconnect hose assemblies from A/C compressor, then remove compressor.
26. Disconnect power steering lines from power steering pump.
27. Remove engine mount through bolts, then the engine assembly from engine frame.
28. Reverse procedure to install, noting the following:
    a. Tighten fasteners to specifications.
    b. Bleed brake and power steering systems.
    c. Align wheels.

INTAKE MANIFOLD

REPLACE

1. Drain cooling system.
2. Remove throttle body air duct, then disconnect electrical connectors from fuel injectors.
3. Disconnect left and righthand wiring harness and position aside.
4. Remove accelerator cable bracket and disconnect cable from throttle body.
5. Disconnect hoses from AIR diverter valve.
6. Disconnect ground strap from intake manifold.
7. Remove attaching bolts from fuel rail.
8. Disconnect vacuum hose from fuel pressure regulator.
9. Relieve fuel system pressure as outlined under " Precautions," then disconnect and cap fuel lines at fuel rail.
10. Remove fuel injectors and fuel rail from intake manifold and position aside, **Fig. 2.**
11. Disconnect vacuum and PCV hoses from intake manifold.
12. Remove EGR solenoid bracket and fuel vapor canister purge solenoid bracket.
13. Remove EGR valve.
14. Disconnect air pipe from intake manifold and righthand exhaust manifold.
15. Remove alternator brace.
16. Disconnect coolant hoses from throttle body.
17. Remove throttle body to intake manifold attaching bolts, then remove throttle body and gasket, **Fig. 2.**
18. Remove intake manifold to engine block attaching bolts and studs, then remove intake manifold and gasket, **Fig. 3.**
19. Reverse procedure to install. Prior to installation, apply a 3/16 inch bead of sealer 1052366, or equivalent to front and rear of engine block. Extend bead of sealer 1/2 inch up each cylinder head to seal and retain gaskets. Install manifold and tighten bolts to specifications in sequence shown in **Fig. 4.**

EXHAUST MANIFOLD

REPLACE

The following service procedure has been revised by a "Technical Service Bulletin."

LEFT SIDE

1. Raise and support vehicle, then disconnect catalytic converter from exhaust manifold.
2. Lower vehicle, then remove air intake duct.
3. Remove serpentine drive belt.
4. Remove center panel front lefthand wheelwell.
5. Remove alternator and A/C compressor upper brace.
6. Remove A/C compressor and position aside with refrigerant hoses attached.
7. Disconnect air pipe, check valve and hose as an assembly from exhaust manifold.
8. Disconnect spark plug wires from spark plugs and wire clips from supports.
9. Remove accessory and A/C compressor bracket braces.
10. Remove spark plug wire supports, then remove spark plugs from cylinder head.
11. Remove exhaust manifold attaching bolts and studs, **Fig. 5.**

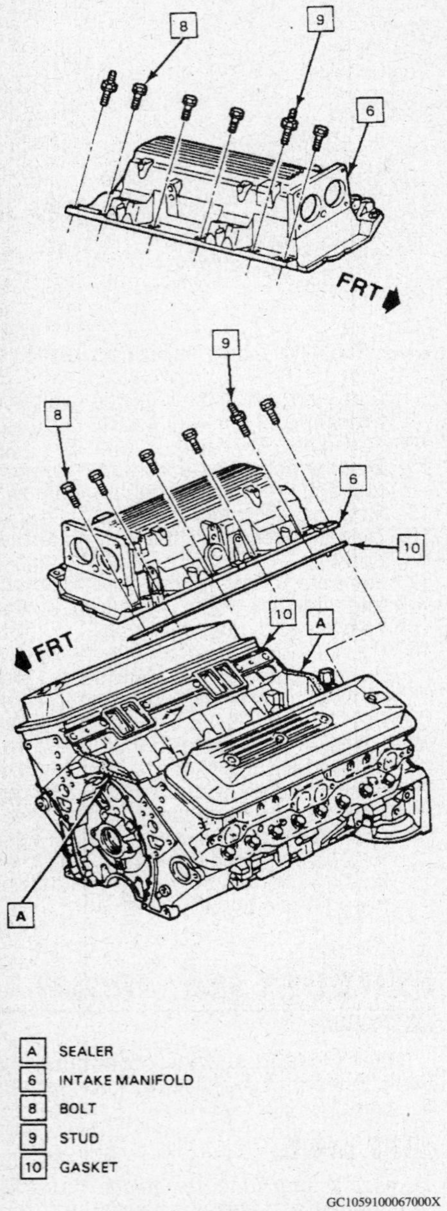

Fig. 3 Intake manifold replacement

12. Remove heat shields, exhaust manifold and gasket.
13. Reverse procedure to install. Check **torque** on the three exhaust manifold heat shield bolts, 6–9 ft. lbs.

RIGHT SIDE

1. Raise and support vehicle, then disconnect catalytic converter from exhaust manifold.
2. Lower vehicle, then disconnect electrical connectors from fuel injectors.
3. Disconnect vacuum hose from fuel pressure regulator.
4. Relieve fuel system pressure as outlined under " Precautions," then disconnect and cap fuel lines at fuel rail.
5. Remove fuel rail to intake manifold at-

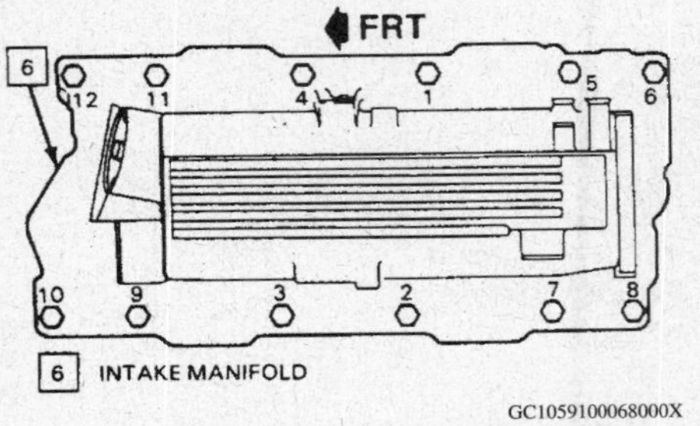

Fig. 4 Intake manifold bolt tightening sequence

taching bolts, then remove fuel injectors and rail.

6. Remove spark plug wires from spark plugs and wire clips from supports.
7. Remove spark plugs from cylinder head, then remove front spark plug wire bracket and bolt.
8. Remove oil level dipstick and tube.
9. Disconnect air pipe, gasket and check valve as an assembly from intake and exhaust manifolds and cylinder head.
10. Remove exhaust manifold attaching bolts and studs, **Fig. 5.**
11. Remove heat shields, exhaust manifold and gasket.
12. Reverse procedure to install. Prior to installing oil level dipstick and tube, apply sealer 1052080, or equivalent around tube approximately ½ inch below bead. **Torque** three exhaust manifold heat shield bolts to 6–9 ft. lbs.

CYLINDER HEAD

REPLACE

LEFT SIDE

1. Raise and support vehicle, then disconnect catalytic converter from exhaust manifold.
2. Drain cooling system, then lower vehicle.
3. Disconnect upper radiator hose, then remove serpentine drive belt.
4. Remove intake manifold as outlined under "Intake Manifold, Replace."
5. Remove center panel from lefthand wheelwell.
6. Remove A/C compressor and position aside with refrigerant hoses attached.
7. Remove alternator and A/C compressor brace.
8. Remove spark plug wire bracket, then disconnect spark plug wires from spark plugs.
9. Remove spark plugs from cylinder head.
10. Remove lefthand exhaust manifold as describe under " Exhaust Manifold, Replace."
11. Remove alternator and brace.
12. Disconnect AIR diverter valve hose.
13. Remove valve cover, then remove drive belt tensioner and idler pulley.
14. Remove power steering pump attaching bolts, then disconnect hoses and remove power steering pump.
15. Disconnect spark plug wires and coil wire at distributor.

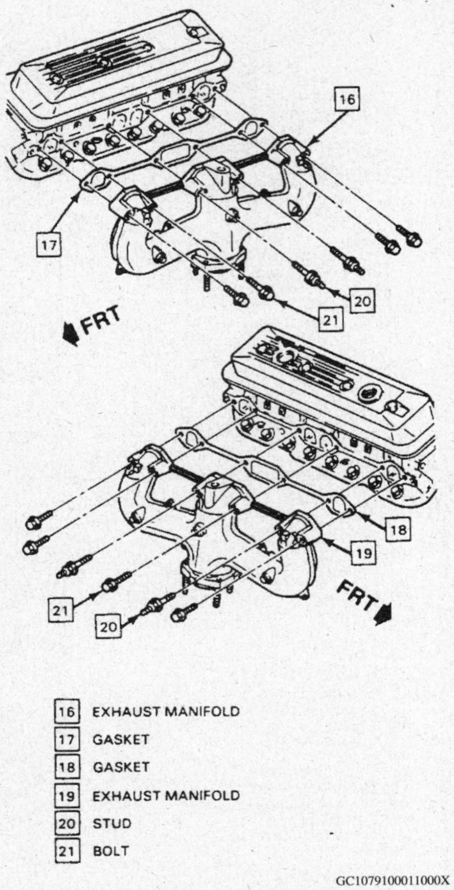

Fig. 5 Exhaust manifold replacement

16. Remove accessory attaching bracket.
17. Remove rocker arms and pushrods. Tag rocker arms and pushrods so they can be installed in the same positions.
18. Remove cylinder head attaching bolts, then remove cylinder head and gasket.
19. Reverse procedure to install, noting the following:
    a. When installing cylinder head gasket, position over dowel pins with bead facing upward.
    b. Prior to installing cylinder head bolts, coat threads with sealer 1052080, or equivalent.
    c. Using sequence shown in **Fig. 6,** tighten cylinder bolts in two steps; first step **torque** all bolts to 22 ft. lbs., second step tighten all short bolts (Nos. 3, 4, 7, 8, 11, 12, 15, 16) an additional 67°, then tighten all medium and long bolts (Nos. 1, 2, 5, 6, 9, 10, 13, 14 & 17) an additional 80.°

RIGHT SIDE

1. Raise and support vehicle, then disconnect catalytic converter from exhaust manifold.
2. Drain cooling system, then lower vehicle.
3. Disconnect lower radiator and heater hoses.

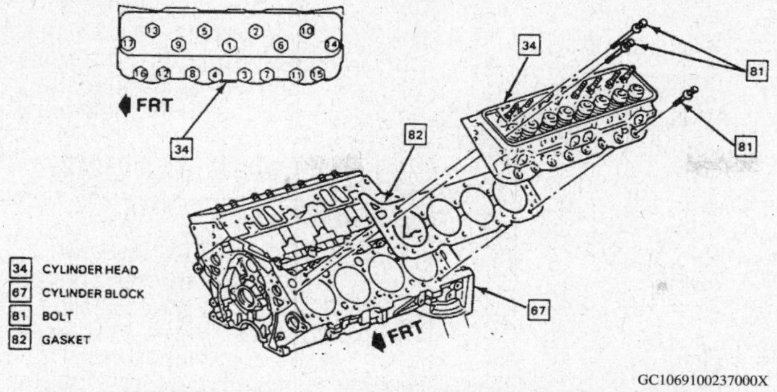

Fig. 6 Cylinder head bolt tightening sequence

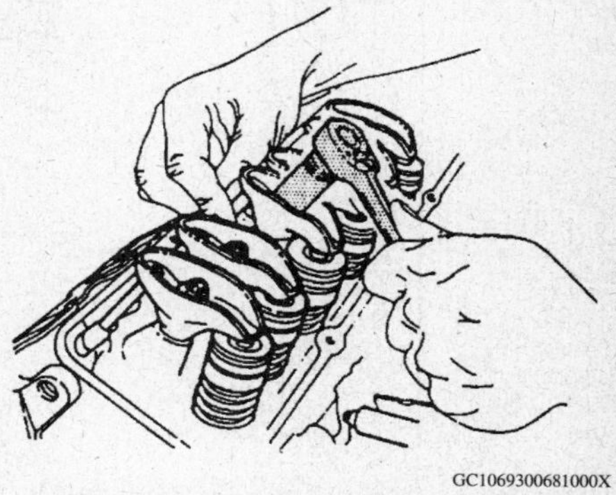

Fig. 7 Rocker arm adjustment

4. Remove power steering pump reservoir from cylinder head and position out of way.
5. Remove coil and bracket.
6. Remove intake manifold as outlined under "Intake Manifold, Replace."
7. Remove spark plug wires from clips, then remove front spark plug wire bracket.
8. Remove oil level dipstick and tube.
9. Disconnect spark plug wire, then remove spark plugs from cylinder head.
10. Remove righthand exhaust manifold as outlined under " Exhaust Manifold, Replace."
11. Remove cylinder head rear vent pipe and valve cover.
12. Remove power steering pump attaching bolts, then disconnect hoses and remove power steering pump.
13. Remove rocker arms and pushrods. Tag rocker arms and pushrods so they can be installed in the same positions.
14. Remove cylinder head attaching bolts, then remove cylinder head and gasket.
15. Reverse procedure to install, noting the following:
    a. When installing cylinder head gasket, position over dowel pins with bead facing upward.
    b. Prior to installing cylinder head bolts, coat threads with sealer 1052080, or equivalent.
    c. Using sequence shown in **Fig. 6,** tighten cylinder bolts in two steps; first step **torque** all bolts to 22 ft. lbs., second step tighten all short bolts (Nos. 3, 4, 7, 8, 11, 12, 15, 16) an additional 67°, then tighten all medium and long bolts (Nos. 1, 2, 5, 6, 9, 10, 13, 14 & 17) an additional 80.°

VALVE ARRANGEMENT

FRONT TO REAR

All..............................E-I-I-E-E-I-I-E

CAMSHAFT LOBE LIFT SPECIFICATIONS

Engine (VIN Code)	Engine	Int.	Exh.
5.7L (P)	5.7L	.298	.306

VALVE CLEARANCE SPECIFICATIONS

Engine/VIN	Valve Clearance
5.7L (P)	1 Turn①

① — Turn rocker arm stud nut until all lash is eliminated, then tighten nut additional turn listed, plus or minus 1/4 turn.

VALVE ADJUSTMENT

After the engine has been thoroughly warmed up, the valves may be adjusted with the engine turned off, as follows: with engine in position to fire No. 1 cylinder the following valves may be adjusted: Exhaust 1-3-4-8, intake 1-2-5-7. Then crank the engine one more complete revolution which will bring No. 6 cylinder to the firing position at which time the following valves may be adjusted: Exhaust 2-5-6-7, intake 3-4-6-8.

The following procedure, performed with the engine running, should be done only if readjustment is required.

1. After engine has been warmed up to operating temperature, remove valve cover and install a new valve cover gasket.
2. With engine running at idle speed, back off valve rocker arm nut, **Fig. 7,** until rocker arm starts to clatter.
3. Turn rocker arm nut down slowly until the clatter just stops. This is the zero lash position.
4. Turn nut down ¼ additional turn and pause 10 seconds until engine runs smoothly. Repeat additional ¼ turns, pausing 10 seconds each time, until nut has been turned down the number of turns listed in the Valve Adjustment Specifications Chart from the zero lash position. **This preload adjustment must be done slowly to allow the lifter to adjust itself to prevent the possibility of interference between the intake valve head and top of piston, which might result in internal damage and/or bent pushrods. Noisy lifters should be replaced.**

ROCKER ARMS

Tag rocker arms and components **Fig. 7** during removal so they can be installed in the same positions. When replacing rocker arms or rocker arm balls, bearing surfaces of rocker arms and balls should be coated with prelube 1052365, or equivalent.

ROCKER ARM STUDS

Rocker arm studs with damaged threads should be replaced. Threads of replacement rocker arms studs should be coated with sealing compound 1052080, or equivalent prior to installation. Looseness can be corrected by installing the proper size Heli-Coil insert or by replacing cylinder head.

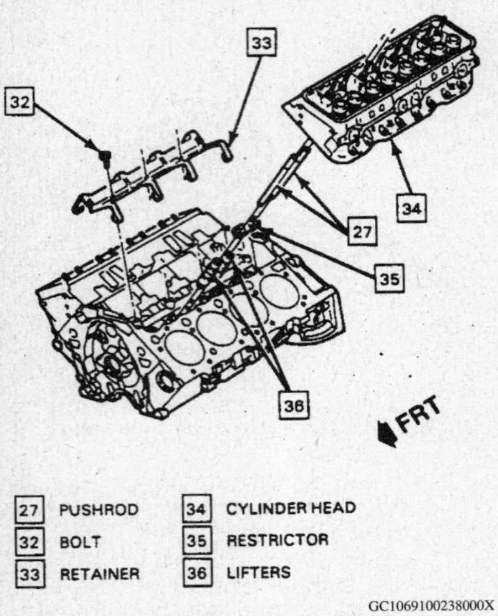

Fig. 8 Valve lifter replacement

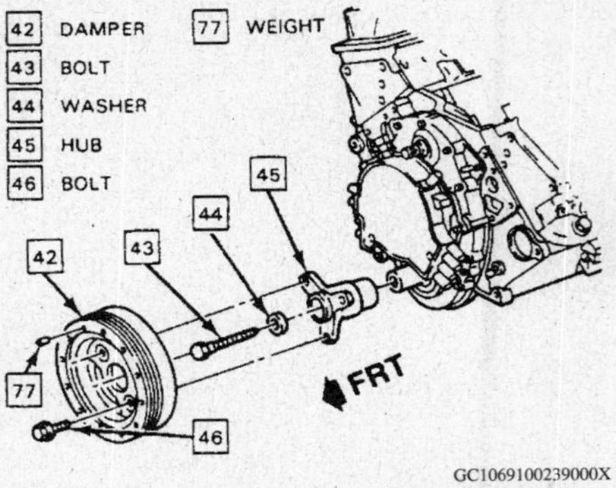

Fig. 9 Crankshaft damper & hub replacement

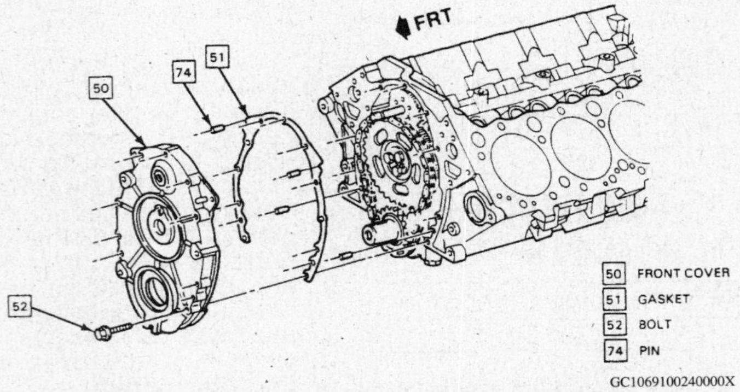

Fig. 10 Engine front cover replacement

PUSH RODS

Tag pushrods during remove so they can be installed in the same positions. When installing, ensure pushrod is seated in lifter sockets.

VALVE GUIDES

Valves operate in guide holes bored in the head. If clearance becomes excessive, use the next oversize valve and ream the bore to fit. Valves with oversize stems are available in .003, .015 and .030 inch.

HYDRAULIC LIFTERS

REPLACE

Valve lifters, **Fig. 8,** can be lifted from their bores after removing rocker arms, pushrods, intake manifold and valve lifter retainer. When removing, position valve lifters in rack so they may be installed at the same location. Adjustable pliers with protected jaws may be used to remove lifters which are stuck due to carbon or varnish deposits. When installing replacement valve lifters, coat roller with prelube 1052365, or equivalent.

CRANKSHAFT DAMPER & HUB

REPLACE

1. Remove air intake duct, then remove serpentine drive belt.
2. Raise and support vehicle, then remove engine mount nuts.
3. Remove power steering fluid cooler.
4. Attach suitable engine lifting device, then raise engine slightly to provide tool access to damper attaching bolts.
5. Remove damper to hub attaching bolts, then remove damper, **Fig. 9.**
6. Disconnect power steering line from steering gear.
7. Place alignment marks on damper hub and front cover for use during installation. **After placing alignment marks on hub and front cover do not rotate crankshaft, as an engine imbalance may result.**
8. Remove crankshaft hub bolt and washer, then remove crankshaft hub using tool No. J39046, or equivalent.
9. Reverse procedure to install. If crankshaft was accidentally rotated after placing alignment marks, position No. 1 cylinder at top dead center, then install hub with arrow casting at 12 o'clock position. If a replacement damper is to be installed, balance weights of the same size as the original damper must be install in the same locations on the new damper.

FRONT COVER

REPLACE

1. Drain cooling system.
2. Remove throttle body air duct.
3. Remove water pump as outlined under "Water Pump, Replace."
4. Remove crankshaft damper and hub as outlined under "Crankshaft Damper and Hub, Replace."
5. Remove ignition distributor as outlined under "Distributor, Replace" in the "Electrical" section.
6. Remove oil pan as outlined under "Oil Pan, Replace."
7. Remove front cover attaching screws and the front cover, **Fig. 10.**
8. Reverse procedure to install.

FRONT COVER SEAL

REPLACE

1. Remove front cover as outlined under "Front Cover, Replace."
2. Remove oil seal for crankshaft, water pump shaft and distributor shaft as necessary.
3. Properly support front cover in seal area.
4. Using tool seal installer tool No. J-35468, or equivalent, install crankshaft oil seal.
5. Using seal tool No. J-39090, or equivalent, install distributor shaft oil seal.
6. Using seal tool No. J-39088, or equivalent, install water pump oil seal.
7. Install engine front cover.

TIMING CHAIN

REPLACE

1. Remove front cover as outlined previously.
2. Remove crankshaft oil slinger.
3. Rotate engine until timing marks on sprockets are in alignment, **Fig. 11.**
4. Remove camshaft to sprocket bolts, **Fig. 11.**
5. Remove camshaft sprocket and timing chain together. Do not rotate crankshaft after timing chain has been removed.
6. If crankshaft sprocket is to be replaced, remove it with a suitable gear puller. Install new sprocket, aligning key and keyway.
7. If water pump driven gear is to be replaced, remove attaching bolts, then remove gear using a suitable gear puller. Install new gear using gear installer tool No. J3092, or equivalent, then install attaching bolts.
8. Install chain on camshaft sprocket. Hold sprocket vertical with chain hanging below and shift around to align the timing marks on sprockets. Align dowel in camshaft with dowel hole in sprocket and install sprocket on camshaft. **When installing camshaft sprocket**

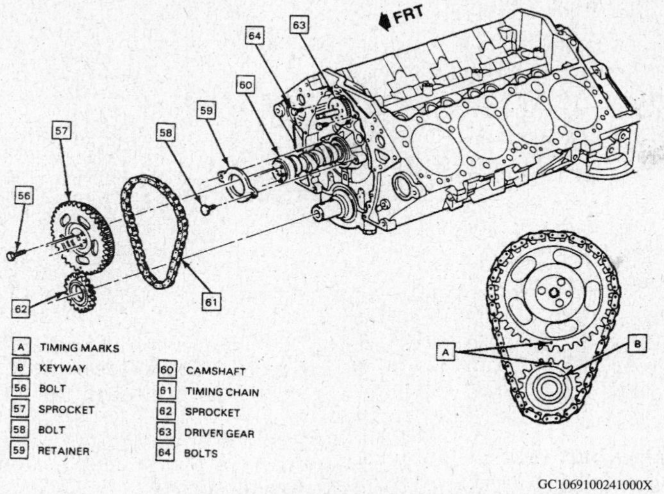

Fig. 11 Camshaft, sprockets & timing chain

onto camshaft, ensure teeth camshaft sprocket and water pump driven gear mesh. Do not attempt to drive sprocket on camshaft as welch plug at rear of engine can be dislodged.

9. Using tool No. J39089, or equivalent, install water pump driven gear O-ring.
10. Lubricate timing chain with engine oil, then install front cover.

CAMSHAFT

REPLACE

1. Remove surge tank cap and drain cooling system.
2. Remove engine front cover as outlined under "Front Cover, Replace."
3. Remove intake manifold as outlined under "Intake Manifold, Replace."
4. Remove oil pump stub shaft attaching bolt, then remove stub shaft, **Fig. 12.**
5. Remove valve covers, rocker arms and pushrods. Tag rocker arms and pushrods so they can be installed in the same locations.
6. Remove camshaft sprocket and timing chain as outlined under "Timing Chain, Replace."
7. Remove air cleaner assembly, then disconnect reservoir hose from radiator.
8. From lefthand side of radiator support, remove relay bracket.
9. Remove AIR pump inlet duct, then remove AIR pump attaching bolts and position AIR pump out of way.
10. Disconnect electrical connectors from engine cooling fans.
11. Remove bolt attaching accumulator bracket to upper radiator support.
12. Remove fan shroud to radiator upper support attaching screws.
13. Remove access plug from upper part of radiator.
14. Disconnect radiator bleed hose, then remove bolts and nuts attaching upper radiator support to front side member.
15. Remove screws attaching upper radiator support to lower support, then remove upper radiator support.
16. Disconnect hoses from radiator.

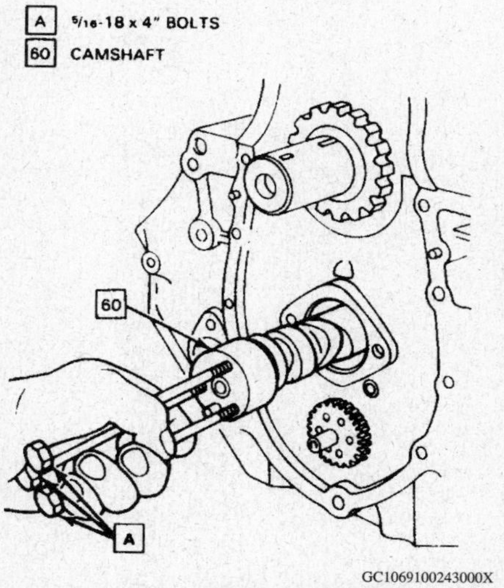

Fig. 13 Camshaft removal & installation

17. **On models with automatic transmission,** disconnect transmission fluid cooler lines from radiator.
18. **On all models,** remove radiator from vehicle.
19. Raise and support vehicle, then remove lower fan shroud attaching bolts.
20. Lower vehicle, then remove fan shroud and fans.
21. Detach A/C condenser line bracket from front crossmember.
22. Remove engine mount stud nuts, then using a suitable engine lifting fixture, raise front of engine slightly to provide clearance for camshaft removal.
23. Remove camshaft retainer bolts and retainer, **Fig. 11.**
24. Install three 5/16 18 x 4 inch bolts into camshaft bolt holes, **Fig. 13.**
25. Carefully rotate and pull camshaft from engine. Use care when removing camshaft to prevent damage to camshaft bearings.
26. Reverse procedure to install. Prior to installation, coat camshaft and bearings with engine oil. If installing a new camshaft, coat lobes with Molykote, or equivalent and replace roller lifters.

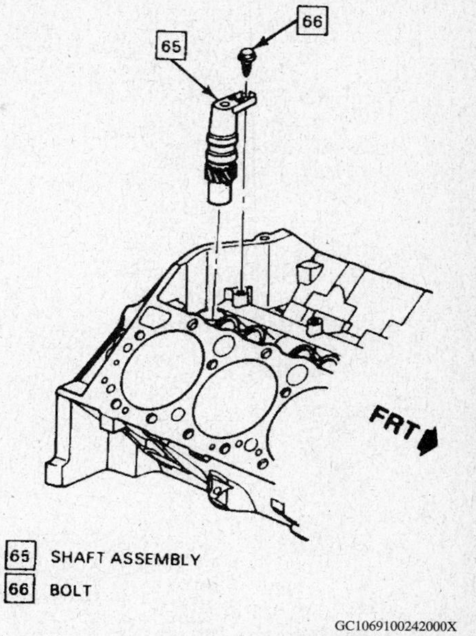

Fig. 12 Oil pump stub shaft location

PISTON & ROD ASSEMBLY

Assemble pistons to connecting rods as shown in **Fig. 14.**

Upon installation, measure the connecting rod side clearance using a suitable feeler gauge. Refer to "Engine Rebuilding Specifications " section for connecting rod side clearance.

PISTONS, PINS & RINGS

Pistons are available in standard and oversizes of .010 and .030 inch.

Piston rings are available in standard and oversizes of .030 inch.

MAIN & ROD BEARINGS

Connecting rod bearings are available in standard and undersizes of .001, .002, .010 and .020 inch.

Main bearings are available in standard and undersizes of .001, .002, .009, .010 and .020 inch.

CRANKSHAFT REAR OIL SEAL

REPLACE

This engine is equipped with a one-piece, lip type seal mounted in a separate seal retainer. Seal replacement requires removal of the transmission.

1. Raise and support vehicle, then remove transmission, clutch assembly and flywheel, as equipped.

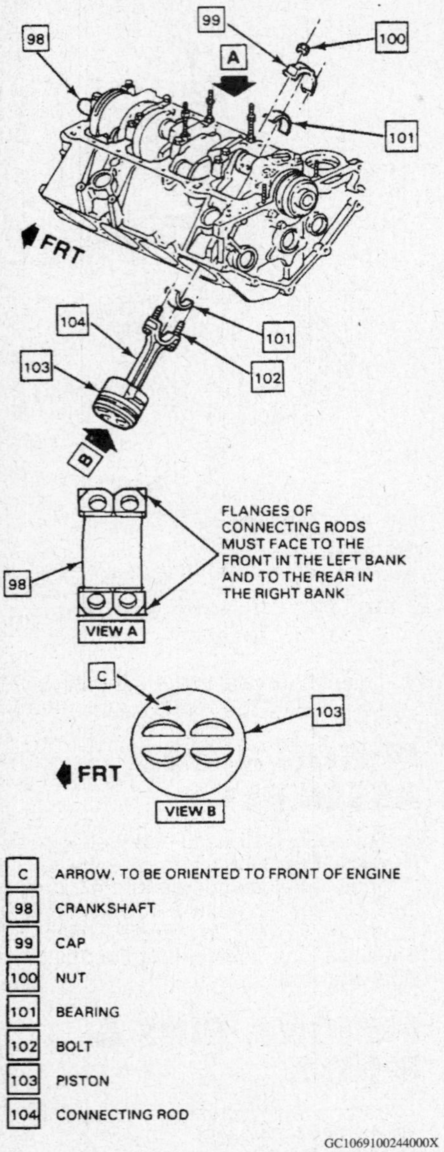

Fig. 14 Piston & rod assembly

2. Pry seal from retainer, inserting screwdriver in notches provided in seal retainer, **Fig. 15.**
3. Lubricate replacement seal with engine oil, then mount seal on tool No. J-35621, or equivalent, **Fig. 16.**
4. Mount tool on rear of crankshaft, tightening screws snugly to ensure seal will be installed squarely on crankshaft.
5. Tighten wing nut on tool until it bottoms, then remove tool from crankshaft.
6. Reverse remaining procedure to complete installation.

OIL PAN

REPLACE

1. Raise and support vehicle, then drain crankcase.
2. Disconnect oil level sensor electrical connector, then remove oil level sensor, **Fig. 17.**

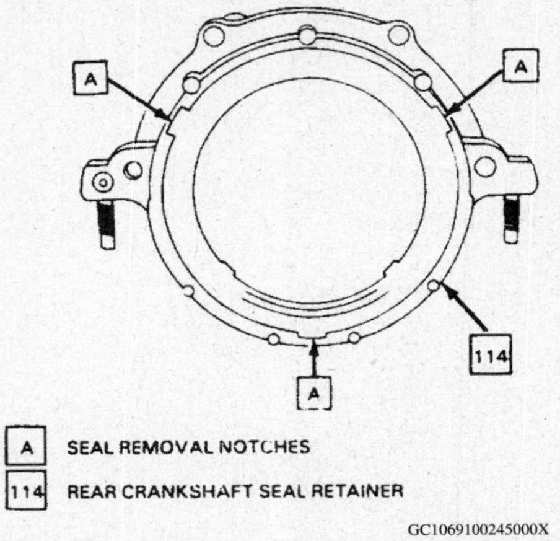

Fig. 15 Crankshaft rear oil seal removal

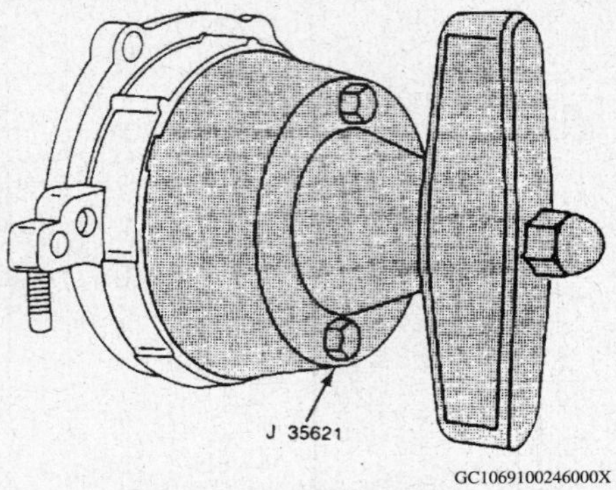

Fig. 16 Crankshaft rear oil seal installation

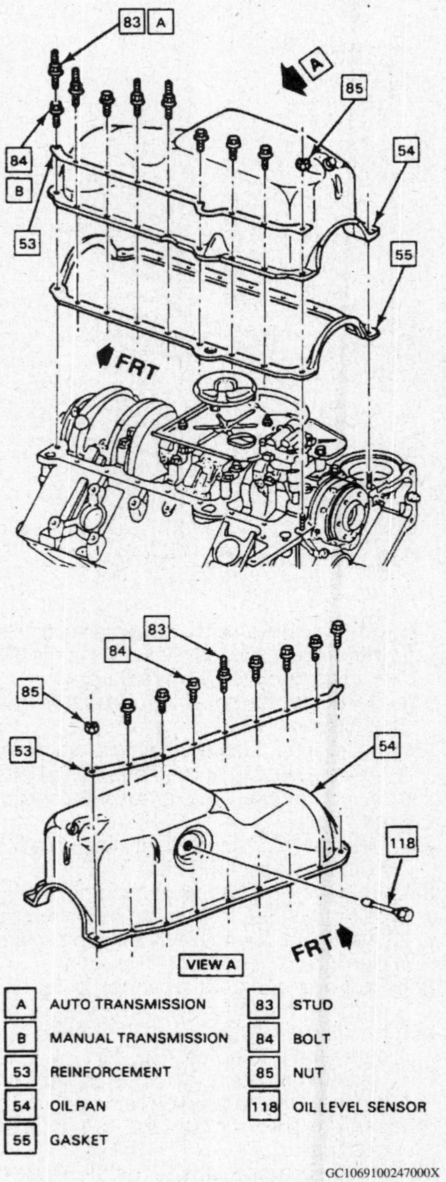

Fig. 17 Oil pan installation

3. Remove oil filter.
4. Remove starter motor, then remove flywheel cover.
5. Disconnect catalytic converters at exhaust manifolds.
6. Remove nuts from engine mount studs.
7. Remove oil pan attaching bolts, nuts and studs, then the oil pan.
8. Reverse procedure to install. Prior to installation apply a small amount of sealer 1052914, or equivalent to front cover to engine mating surface and rear seal retainer to engine mating surface. Apply sealer 1 inch in each direction of the radius cavity of these mating surfaces. Tighten oil pan attaching bolts to specifications.

OIL PUMP

REPLACE

1. Remove oil pan as outlined previously.
2. Remove oil pan baffle nuts.
3. Remove pump to rear main bearing cap bolt and remove oil pan baffle, pump intermediate shaft and retainer, **Fig. 18.**
4. Reverse procedure to install. Prime oil pump with clean engine oil prior to installation.

OIL PUMP SERVICE

1. Remove oil pump as outlined previously.
2. Remove pump cover screws and pump cover, **Fig. 19.**
3. Mark gear teeth so they can be reassembled with same teeth indexing, then remove drive gear, idler gear and shaft.
4. Remove pressure regulator valve attaching pin, pressure regulator valve and related parts.
5. If pickup screen and pipe require replacement, mount pump in a soft-jawed vise and extract pipe from pump.
6. Wash all parts in cleaning solvent and dry with compressed air.
7. Inspect pump body and cover for cracks and excessive wear.
8. Inspect pump gears for damage or excessive wear.
9. Check drive gear shaft for looseness in pump body.

10. Inspect inside of pump cover for wear that would allow oil to leak past the ends of the gears.
11. Inspect pickup screen and pipe assembly for damage to screen, pipe or relief grommet.
12. Check pressure regulator valve for fit in pump housing.
13. Reverse procedure to assemble. Turn driveshaft by hand to check for smooth operation. **The pump gears and body are not serviced separately. If the pump gears or body are damaged or worn, the pump assembly should be replaced. Also, if the pick-up screen and pump assembly was removed, it should be replaced with a new one as loss of the press fit condition could result in an air leak and loss of oil pressure.**

SERPENTINE DRIVE BELT

ROUTING

Refer to **Fig. 20** for serpentine drive belt routing.

REPLACEMENT

1. Using a suitable socket and handle on tensioner pulley bolt, lift tensioner upward in the clockwise direction, then remove serpentine drive belt, **Fig. 20.**
2. Reverse procedure to install. Ensure belt tension indicator marks are within limit lines on belt tensioner indicator.

COOLING SYSTEM BLEED

Open bleed valves, **Fig. 21,** on thermostat housing and throttle body prior to adding coolant. Add coolant through radiator surge tank opening until level is at base of tank neck. Close each bleed valve as solid flow of coolant is emitted from valve. Start engine and operate with surge tank cap removed until engine coolant level is maintained at base of surge tank neck. Add coolant as necessary, then install surge tank cap with arrows facing overflow tube. Fill coolant recovery reservoir to proper level. Start engine and allow reach operating temperature. Turn engine off and allow to cool, then recheck coolant level.

THERMOSTAT

REPLACE

1. Disconnect intake air temperature sensor electrical connector.
2. Remove air cleaner and intake duct assembly.
3. Remove pressure cap from surge tank, then drain cooling system.

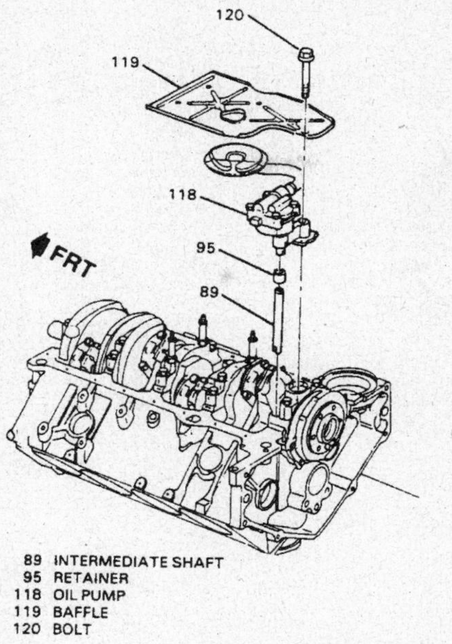

Fig. 18 Oil pump replacement

4. Disconnect lower radiator hose from thermostat housing on water pump.
5. Remove thermostat housing attaching bolts, then remove housing, **Fig. 22.**
6. Remove thermostat and seal.
7. Reverse procedure to install. When installing thermostat seal, position seal with taper facing upward. Bleed cooling system as outlined under "Cooling System Bleed."

WATER PUMP

REPLACE

1. Disconnect intake air temperature sensor electrical connector.
2. Remove air cleaner and duct assembly.
3. Remove radiator surge tank cap, then drain cooling system and remove knock sensor.
4. Disconnect upper and lower radiator hose, heater hose and coolant sensor electrical connector from water pump.
5. Remove coolant sensor wire retainer from front of water pump.
6. Using a ⅝ inch box wrench on serpentine drive belt tensioner, left tensioner upward and remove belt from alternator pulley.
7. Remove six water pump to engine attaching bolts, then remove water pump, **Fig. 22.**
8. Reverse procedure to install. Prior to assembling coupling to pump, apply a light coat of grease seals and splines. When installing coupling, white band should face toward engine, **Fig. 22.** Install water pump gaskets with tabs facing upward. After installation bleed cooling system.

RADIATOR

REPLACE

1. **On models equipped with ram air,** remove hold down bolts, air box cover and air filter.
2. **On all models,** remove air intake duct and air cleaner.
3. **On models equipped with ram air,** proceed as follows:
   a. Disconnect electrical connector from air temperature sensor.
   b. Remove vent hose clamp and hose from lower air box.
   c. Remove clamp attaching rubber shoulder from lower air box to mass air flow sensor.
   d. Remove bolt attaching lower air box to radiator support and lower box from vehicle.
4. **On all models,** raise and support vehicle.
5. Drain coolant and remove electrical connectors at engine coolant fans.
6. Remove radiator upper mounting panel.
7. Remove electric engine coolant fan, transmission oil cooler lines and coolant level indicator module, if equipped.
8. Lower vehicle and loosen receiver dehydrator bracket.
9. Remove upper radiator hose and lower radiator hose at water pump.
10. Remove overflow tube, then the condenser from radiator.
11. Remove radiator from vehicle.
12. Reverse procedure to install, noting the following:
    a. Ensure radiator is seated on radiator insulators.
    b. Add engine coolant and inspect for leaks.
    c. **Torque** upper mounting panel to 9 ft. lbs.

FUEL FILTER

REPLACE

1. Relieve fuel pressure as outlined under "Precautions, " then raise and support vehicle.
2. Clean both fuel feed pipe connections and surrounding areas, then remove fuel filter bracket.
3. Disconnect quick-disconnect fitting at fuel filter inlet, **Fig. 23,** then the threaded outlet from chassis fuel pipe.
4. Remove fuel filter.
5. Reverse procedure to install. Tighten fittings to specifications.

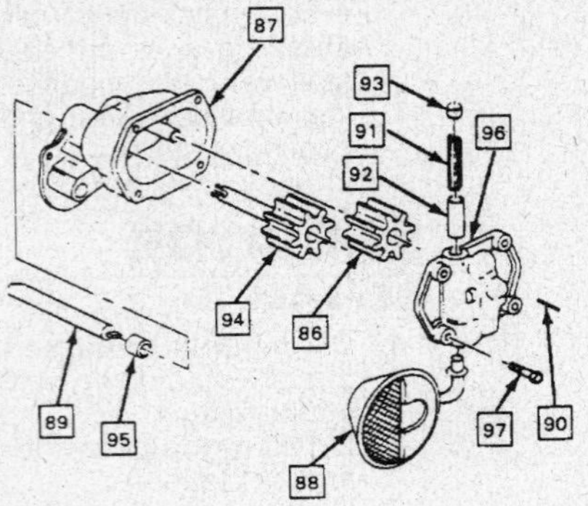

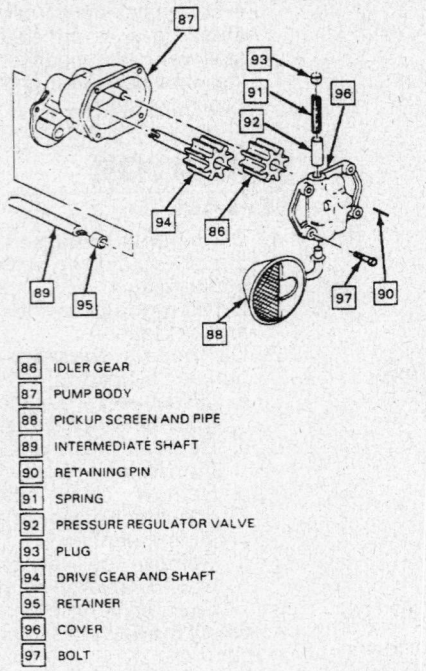

86 IDLER GEAR
87 PUMP BODY
88 PICKUP SCREEN AND PIPE
89 INTERMEDIATE SHAFT
90 RETAINING PIN
91 SPRING
92 PRESSURE REGULATOR VALVE
93 PLUG
94 DRIVE GEAR AND SHAFT
95 RETAINER
96 COVER
97 BOLT

GC1099100029000X

Fig. 19 Exploded view of oil pump

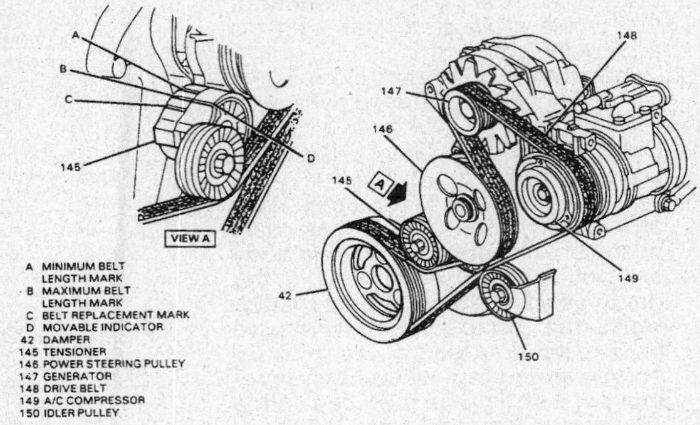

GC1069100248000X

Fig. 20 Serpentine drive belt replacement

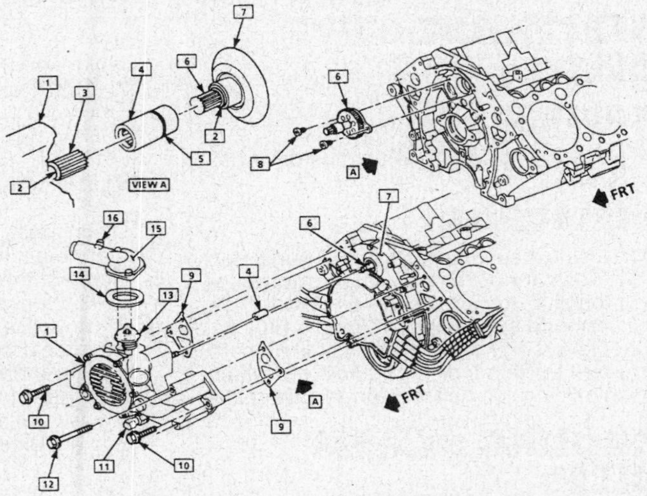

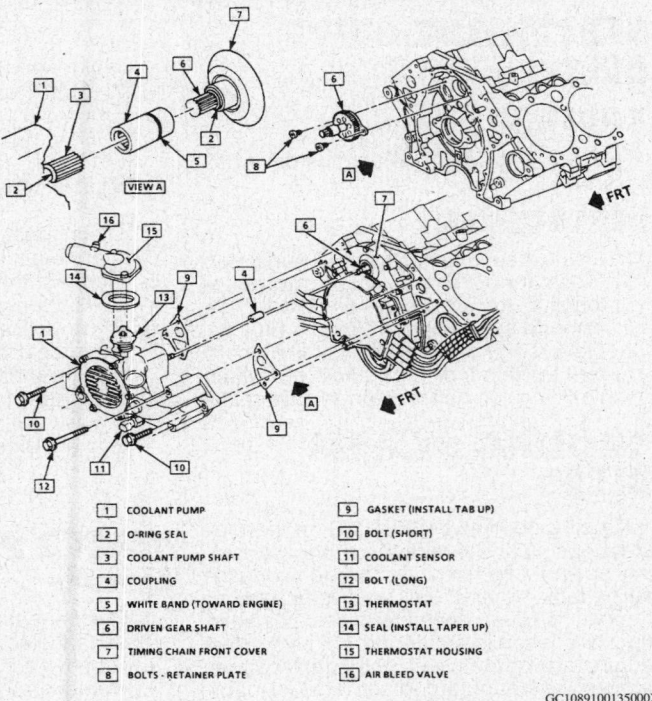

1 COOLANT PUMP
2 O-RING SEAL
3 COOLANT PUMP SHAFT
4 COUPLING
5 WHITE BAND (TOWARD ENGINE)
6 DRIVEN GEAR SHAFT
7 TIMING CHAIN FRONT COVER
8 BOLTS - RETAINER PLATE
9 GASKET (INSTALL TAB UP)
10 BOLT (SHORT)
11 COOLANT SENSOR
12 BOLT (LONG)
13 THERMOSTAT
14 SEAL (INSTALL TAPER UP)
15 THERMOSTAT HOUSING
16 AIR BLEED VALVE

GC1089100135000X

Fig. 22 Water pump & thermostat replacement

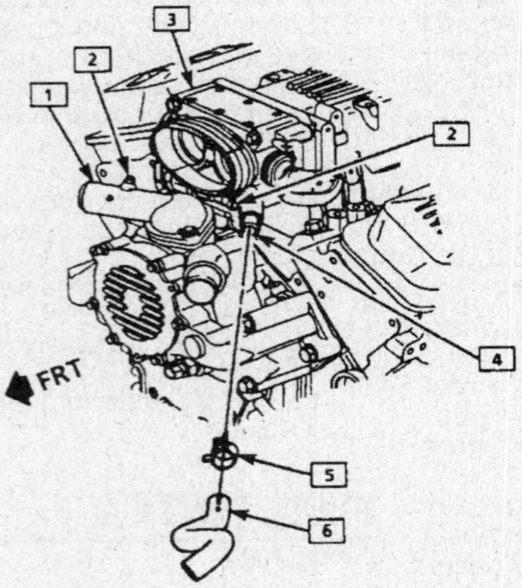

1 THERMOSTAT HOUSING
2 AIR BLEED VALVE
3 THROTTLE BODY ASSEMBLY
4 THROTTLE BODY NIPPLE
5 CLAMP - THROTTLE BODY
6 THROTTLE BODY HOSE

GC1089100134000X

Fig. 21 Cooling system bleed valve locations

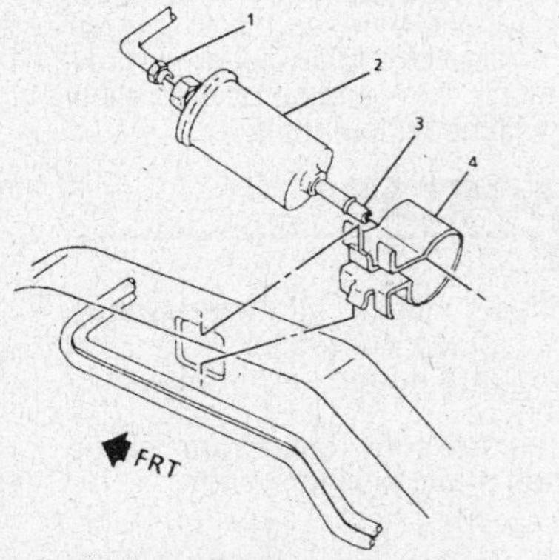

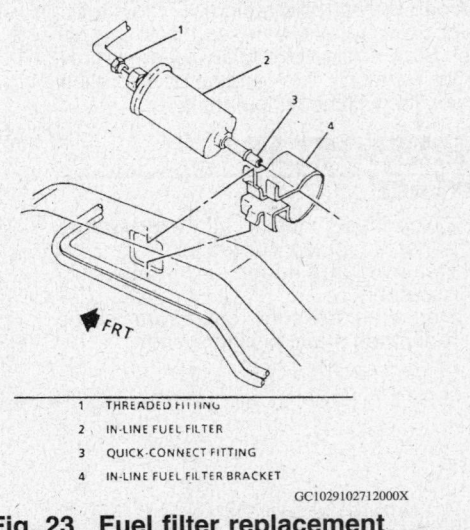

1 THREADED FITTING
2 IN-LINE FUEL FILTER
3 QUICK-CONNECT FITTING
4 IN-LINE FUEL FILTER BRACKET

GC1029102712000X

Fig. 23 Fuel filter replacement

TIGHTENING SPECIFICATIONS

Year	Component	Torque/Ft. Lbs.
1997– 2000	Camshaft Sprocket Bolt	18
	Catalytic Converter to Exhaust Manifold Nut	15
	Crankshaft Balancer Hub Bolt	74
	Drive Belt Idler Pulley Bolt	37
	Drive Belt Tensioner Bolt	18
	Engine Front Cover Bolt	9
	Engine Mount Through Bolts	70
	Engine Mount to Frame Bolts	43
	Engine Oil Level Sensor	26
	Exhaust Manifold Bolts	30
	Fuel Filter Fittings	20
	Intake Manifold Bolt	①
	Knock Sensor	15
	Oil Pan Bolts (Side Rail)	9
	Oil Pan Bolts (Corner Bolts)	15
	Oil Temperature Sensor	9
	Starter Motor Bolt	35
	Valve Rocker Arm Cover	9
	Valve Rocker Arm Stud	50
	Water Pump Bolt	33

① — Torque first to 71 inch lbs., then to 35 ft. Lbs.

5.7L (VIN G) Engine

NOTE: On Air Bag Equipped Models, Refer To " Air Bag System Precautions" Located In The Front Of This Manual For System Disarming & Arming Procedures.

NOTE: For Procedures Not Found In This Section, Refer To The 5.7L VIN G Engine Section In The Corvette (Y) Chapter.

NOTE: Refer To "Computer Relearn Procedures " Located In The Front Of This Manual For Computer Relearn Procedures.

INDEX

PRECAUTIONS

AIR BAG SYSTEMS

Refer to "Air Bag System Precautions" in the front of this manual for system disarming and arming procedures.

BATTERY GROUND CABLE

Prior to service, disconnect battery ground cable and isolate as required.

FUEL SYSTEM PRESSURE RELIEF

Failure to relieve system pressure prior to disconnecting fuel system components may cause fire or personal injury. Remove fuel tank filler cap to release fuel tank pressure. Connect pressure gauge tool No. J-34730-1A, or equivalent, to pressure tap on fuel rail, position bleed hose into suitable container and slowly relieve fuel system pressure. Prior to disconnecting fuel line, position shop towel over fitting.

COMPRESSION PRESSURE

When checking compression, lowest cylinder must be within 70 percent of the highest cylinder with a minimum pressure of 100 psi. Perform compression test with engine at normal operating temperature, spark plugs removed and throttle wide open.

ENGINE MOUNT

REPLACE

LEFT

1. Disconnect MAF and IAT sensor electrical connectors.
2. Remove air duct from throttle body and air cleaner box.
3. Support engine using engine fixture tool Nos. 42451, 28467, 36462 and 41044, or equivalents.
4. Raise and support vehicle, then remove left catalytic converter.
5. Remove engine mount bracket to crossmember bolts.
6. Lower vehicle.
7. Raise left side of engine using fixture tools.
8. Raise and support vehicle, then remove engine mount heat shield.
9. Remove engine mount bracket to block studs.
10. Remove engine mount from vehicle, then separate upper and lower mounts.
11. Reverse procedure to install.

RIGHT

1. Using engine support tool Nos. J42451, J41044 and J36462, or equivalent, support engine.
2. Raise and support vehicle.
3. Remove starter as outlined in "Electrical" section.

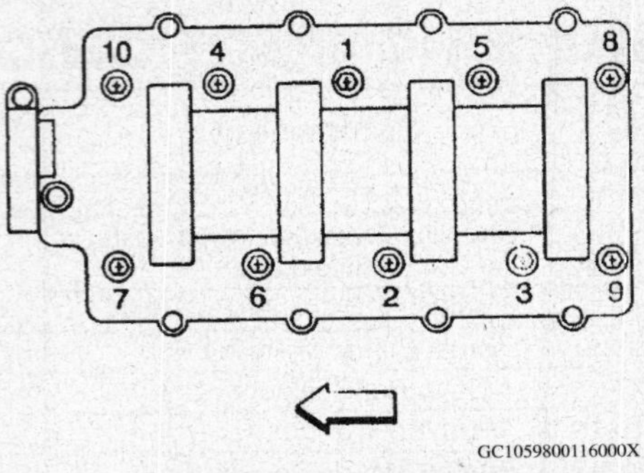

Fig. 1 Intake manifold tightening sequence

4. Remove negative battery cable from engine block.
5. Remove engine mount bracket to crossmember attaching bolts, then lower vehicle.
6. Using support tool, raise right side of engine.
7. Raise and support vehicle.
8. Remove engine mount to bracket bolts, then the mount from vehicle.
9. Reverse procedure to install. Tighten all bolts and nuts to specifications.

ENGINE

REPLACE

The engine and transmission are removed as an assembly.

The accelerator control cable must be replaced whenever the engine is removed.

1. Disconnect IAT and MAF sensor electrical connectors.
2. Remove air intake duct resonator.
3. Recover refrigerent as outlined under "Air Conditioning. "
4. Relieve fuel pressure, then raise and support vehicle.
5. Drain engine oil into suitable container, then remove front wheel and tire assemblies.
6. Drain engine coolant into suitable container, then remove right catalytic converter.
7. **On models equipped with manual transmission,** drain transmission fluid.
8. **On all models,** remove driveshaft and torque arm.
9. Remove starter motor.
10. **On models equipped with automatic transmission,** remove transmission range select cable.
11. **On models equipped with manual transmission,** remove clutch actuator line using special tool No. 36221, or equivalent.
12. **On all models,** remove left side front air deflector.
13. Remove stabilizer bar brackets.
14. Remove intermediate steering shaft bolt and shaft from rack.
15. Remove ground bolt and straps from front rail.
16. Disconnect front wheel speed sensors.
17. Remove condenser hose bolt from A/C compressor.
18. Remove fuel line heat shield, then remove brake lines from retainer clip.
19. Lower vehicle, then remove A/C compressor hose from accumulator.
20. Remove inlet and outlet heater hoses from water pump.
21. Disconnect fuel line from fuel rail and vapor line from purge valve.
22. Remove accelerator and cruise control cables from throttle lever.
23. Remove accelerator and cruise control cables from servo adjuster as required.
24. Remove inlet hose from water pump.
25. Remove outlet hose from engine.
26. Remove brake booster vacuum hose, then disconnect two front brake lines from brake pressure modulator valve.
27. Disconnect forward lamp wiring harness from engine wiring harness.
28. Disconnect engine harness vacuum tube from bottom of vacuum check valve.
29. Disconnect PCM electrical connectors, then remove PCM.
30. Remove right side insulator panel, then hinge pillar trim panel.
31. Disconnect engine wiring harness from instrument panel harness.
32. Remove engine harness through front of dash.
33. **On models equipped with automatic transmission,** remove floor shift control.
34. **On models equipped with manual transmission,** remove shift control.
35. **On all models,** raise and support vehicle.
36. Remove right and left lower shock bolts.
37. Remove cotter pins and nuts from right and left upper ball joints.
38. Using separator No. 39549, or equivalent, separate upper control arms from knuckles.
39. Remove both steering knuckles, then place engine support No. 39580, or equivalent, under vehicle.
40. Lower vehicle until crossmember is resting on support fixture.
41. Place engine wiring harness on top of engine.
42. Remove front crossmember bolts.
43. Remove transmission support bolts.
44. Raise vehicle to remove engine and transmission from vehicle.
45. Secure crossmember to support fixture.
46. Separate engine and transmission.
47. Reverse procedure to install.

INTAKE MANIFOLD

REPLACE

1. Drain cooling system, then disconnect fuel lines from rail.
2. Disconnect IAT and MAF sensor electrical connectors.
3. Remove air intake duct.
4. Disconnect throttle body electrical connectors.
5. Remove accessory drive belt, then disconnect EGR valve connector.
6. Remove EGR valve tube.
7. Remove accelerator and cruise control cables from throttle lever.

8. Remove accelerator and cruise control cable bracket.
9. Disconnect fuel injector electrical connectors.
10. Disconnect MAP sensor electrical connector and vacuum hose.
11. Disconnect knock sensor and all remaining intake manifold electrical connectors.
12. Remove PCV tube, then the fresh air hose from throttle body.
13. Remove throttle body coolant hoses, then the EVAP purge tube.
14. Remove canister purge valve and bracket.
15. Remove intake manifold bolts, then the fuel rail stop bracket.
16. Remove intake manifold and gaskets.
17. Reverse procedure to install noting the following:
    a. Install new intake manifold gaskets.
    b. Apply GM threadlock P/N 12345383, or equivalent to intake manifold bolts.
    c. **Torque** intake manifold bolts to 44 inch lbs. in sequence as shown in **Fig. 1.**
    d. **Torque** intake manifold bolts to 7.5 ft. lbs. in sequence as shown in **Fig. 1.**

EXHAUST MANIFOLD

REPLACE

LEFT

1. Remove fuel lines from vehicle.
2. Disconnect PCV hose from valve cover.
3. Remove spark plug wires, then the spark plugs.
4. Remove AIR hose and pipe.
5. Remove coolant sensor from cylinder head.
6. Remove exhaust manifold bolts, then raise and support vehicle.
7. Remove oxygen sensor from manifold, then the exhaust manifold to exhaust pipe attaching nuts.
8. Remove catalytic converter to exhaust pipe attaching nuts.
9. Remove exhaust manifold from vehicle.
10. Reverse procedure to install noting the following:
    a. Install new gasket, then the manifold.
    b. Apply GM threadlock P/N1234493, or equivalent to exhaust manifold bolt threads. Ensure threadlock does not contact first three threads of bolts.
    c. Tighten all fasteners to specifications.

RIGHT

1. Remove dipstick and tube.
2. Raise and support vehicle.
3. Remove exhaust manifold to exhaust pipe attaching nuts, then lower vehicle.
4. Remove AIR pipe and hose, then disconnect coil harness main connector.
5. Remove spark plug wires and spark plugs.

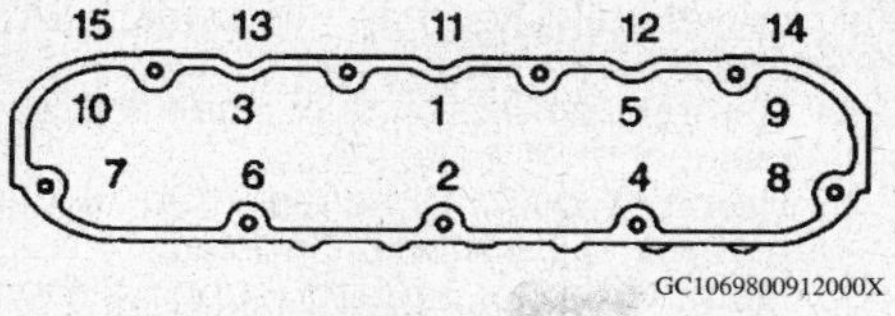

Fig. 2 Cylinder head bolt tightening sequence

6. Remove valve cover as outlined under "Valve Cover, Replace."
7. Disconnect EGR valve connector, then remove EGR valve and pipe.
8. Remove exhaust manifold bolts, then the manifold and gasket.
9. Reverse procedure to install noting the following:
    a. Install new gasket, then the manifold.
    b. Apply GM threadlock P/N1234493, or equivalent to exhaust manifold bolt threads. Ensure threadlock does not contact first three threads of bolts.
    c. Tighten all fasteners to specifications.

CYLINDER HEAD

REPLACE

LEFT

1. Remove intake manifold as outlined under "Intake Manifold, Replace."
2. Remove vapor vent tube from engine.
3. Remove power steering pump pulley using a suitable puller.
4. Remove power steering pump and bracket.
5. Remove rocker arms, pedestals and pushrods as outlined under " Rocker Arm & Push Rod, Replace."
6. Remove exhaust manifold as outlined under "Exhaust Manifold, Replace."
7. Remove ground straps from rear of cylinder head.
8. Remove spark plugs.
9. Remove cylinder head bolts, then the cylinder head. Discard M11 head bolts.
10. Reverse procedure to install noting the following:
    a. Clean cylinder head bolt holes, then ensure locating pins are in proper position.
    b. Ensure new gasket is installed facing proper direction.
    c. Install new M11 cylinder head bolts, then apply GM threadlock P/N 12345382, or equivalent to M8 cylinder head bolts and install. M11 cylinder head bolts are identified as 1–10 and M8 bolts are 11–15, **Fig. 2.**
    d. **Torque** M11 head bolts in sequence shown in **Fig. 2** to 22 ft. lbs.
    e. Tighten M11 cylinder head bolts in sequence an additional 90° using torque angle meter tool No. J36660, or equivalent.
    f. Tighten M11 head bolts 1–8 an additional 90° and bolts 9 and 10 50° using torque angle meter tool No. J36660, or equivalent.
    g. **Torque** M8 head bolts in sequence to 22 ft. lbs.

RIGHT

1. Remove intake manifold as outlined under "Intake Manifold, Replace."
2. Remove vapor vent tube from engine.
3. Remove exhaust manifold as outlined under "Exhaust Manifold, Replace."
4. Remove rocker arms, pedestals and pushrods as outlined under " Rocker Arm & Push Rod, Replace."
5. Remove spark plugs.
6. Remove cylinder head bolts, then the cylinder head. Discard M11 head bolts.
7. Reverse procedure to install noting the following:
    a. Clean cylinder head bolt holes, then ensure locating pins are in proper position.
    b. Ensure new gasket is installed facing proper direction.
    c. Install new M11 cylinder head bolts, then apply GM threadlock P/N 12345382, or equivalent to M8 cylinder head bolts and install. M11 cylinder head bolts are identified as 1–10 and M8 bolts are 11–15, **Fig. 2.**
    d. **Torque** M11 head bolts in sequence shown in **Fig. 2** to 22 ft. lbs.
    e. Tighten M11 cylinder head bolts in sequence an additional 90° using torque angle meter tool No. J36660, or equivalent.
    f. Tighten M11 head bolts 1–8 an additional 90° and bolts 9 and 10 50° using torque angle meter tool No. J36660, or equivalent.
    g. **Torque** M8 head bolts in sequence to 22 ft. lbs.

VALVE COVER

REPLACE

LEFT

1. Remove fuel lines from vehicle.
2. Remove PCV hose, then disconnect ignition coil main harness connector.
3. Remove spark plug wires, then the AIR hose and pipe.
4. Remove valve cover bolts, then the valve cover.
5. Reverse procedure to install. Tighten to specification.

RIGHT

1. Remove AIR hose and pipe.
2. Disconnect ignition coil main harness.
3. Remove spark plug wires, then the valve cover bolts and valve cover.
4. Reverse procedure to install. Tighten to specifications.

CAMSHAFT LOBE LIFT SPECIFICATIONS

Year & Engine (VIN Code)	Engine	Int.	Exh.
1998–2000 5.7L (G)	5.7L	.292	.292

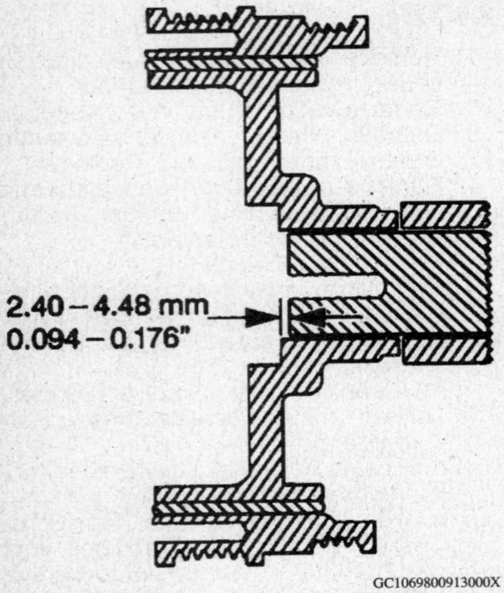

Fig. 3 Crankshaft damper installation

VALVE ADJUSTMENT

This engine is equipped with hydraulic lifters, no adjustment is required.

CRANKSHAFT DAMPER

REPLACE

1. Remove accessory drive belts.
2. Raise and support vehicle, then remove starter.
3. Remove right torque converter cover, then the transmission oil cooler lines from radiator.
4. Remove power steering cooler if equipped.
5. Install flywheel holder tool No. J42386.
6. Remove crankshaft balancer bolt.
7. Install puller tool Nos. J41816 and J41816–2, or equivalent, then remove damper.
8. Reverse procedure to install noting the following:
   a. Install crankshaft damper using pulley installation tool No. J41665, or equivalent.
   b. Transfer pulley weights if applicable.
   c. **Torque** crankshaft damper to 240 ft. lbs. using old damper bolt.
   d. Remove and discard damper bolt, then ensure nose of crankshaft extends .094–.176 inch into balancer bore, **Fig. 3.**
   e. If measurement is not as specified, repeat installation procedure.
   f. **Torque** new crankshaft damper bolt to 37 ft. lbs., then an addition 240 ft. lbs., then a final 140° using torque angle meter tool No. J36660, or equivalent.

FRONT COVER

REPLACE

1. Raise and support vehicle.
2. Remove cooling fan electrical connectors.
3. Drain cooling system, then engine oil.
4. Lower vehicle, then disconnect IAT and MAF sensors.
5. Remove air intake duct, then the accessory drive belts.
6. Remove coolant hoses from water pump and thermostat housing.
7. Remove upper radiator support, then the cooling fans and belt tensioner.
8. Disconnect overflow hose from radiator.
9. Remove throttle body coolant hoses and idler pulley.
10. Remove water pump as outlined under "Water Pump, Replace."
11. Remove crankshaft damper as outlined under "Crankshaft Damper, Replace."
12. Raise and support vehicle, then remove starter.
13. Remove right torque converter cover, then loosen oil pan attaching bolts.
14. Remove front cover bolts, then the front cover and gasket.
15. Remove front oil seal.
16. Reverse procedure to install noting the following:
    a. Install front cover and gasket to engine, then finger tighten bolts.
    b. Install front cover alignment tool No. J41480, or equivalent and **torque** to 18 ft. lbs.
    c. Install seal alignment tool No. J41476, or equivalent and finger tighten.
    d. **Torque** front cover bolts to 18 ft. lbs.
    e. Place a suitable straightedge across engine block and front cover oil pan sealing surfaces. Avoid contact with portion of gasket that extends into oil pan surface. Insert a suitable feeler gauge between front cover and straightedge. Ensure cover is flush with oil pan surface or .020 inch maximum below flush. If measurements are not as specified, repeat alignment procedure.
    f. Install new crankshaft oil seal using installer tool No. J41478, or equivalent.

MAIN BEARINGS

When replacing crankshaft bearings, it is essential that correct tolerances are achieved. If bearing clearance is not within specification, crankshaft position sensor signals may be affected. When replacing main bearings, the M8 bearing cap side bolts must be replaced. Refer to " Engine Rebuilding Specifications" for correct bearing clearance and to **Fig. 4** for main bearing cap tightening sequence.

When replacing main bearings, proceed as follows:

1. Finger tighten M10 main bearing cap bolts, then tap caps into place using a suitable plastic hammer.
2. Install new M8 bearing cap side bolts.
3. **Torque** inner main bearing cap M10 bolts to 15 ft. lbs. using sequence shown in **Fig. 4.**
4. Using a suitable plastic hammer, tap crankshaft backward and then forward to align thrust bearings.
5. Tighten M10 inner main bearing cap bolts an additional 80° in sequence using a suitable torque angle meter.
6. **Torque** outer main bearing cap M10 bolts to 15 ft. lbs. using sequence shown in **Fig. 4.**
7. Tighten M10 outer main bearing cap bolts an additional 53° in sequence using a suitable torque angle meter.
8. **Torque** M8 bearing cap side bolts to 18 ft. lbs. Tighten cap side bolt, then proceed to opposite side.

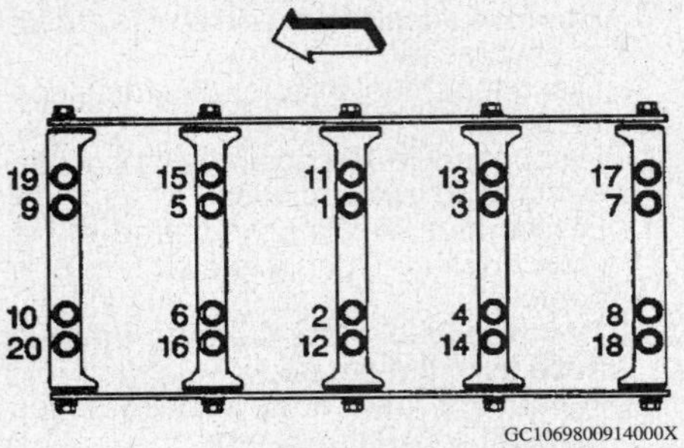

Fig. 4 Main bearing tightening sequence

REAR COVER

REPLACE

1. Place alignment marks on flywheel and crankshaft for installation reference.
2. Remove flywheel.
3. Remove rear cover attaching bolts, then the cover and gasket.
4. Remove oil seal from cover.
5. Reverse procedure to install noting the following:
   a. Install cover and gasket to engine, then finger tighten bolts.
   b. Install cover alignment tool No. J41480, or equivalent and **torque** to 18 ft. lbs.
   c. Rotate crankshaft until two opposing flywheel bolt holes are parallel to oil pan surface.
   d. Install seal alignment tool No. J41476, or equivalent and finger tighten.
   e. **Torque** rear cover bolts to 18 ft. lbs.
   f. Place a suitable straightedge across engine block and rear cover oil pan sealing surfaces. Avoid contact with portion of gasket that extends into oil pan surface. Insert a suitable feeler gauge between cover and straightedge. Ensure cover is flush with oil pan surface or .010 inch maximum below flush. If measurements are not as specified, repeat alignment procedure.
   g. Install new crankshaft oil seal using installer tool No. J41479, or equivalent.

CRANKSHAFT SEAL

REPLACE

Refer to "Front Cover, Replace" for front crankshaft seal replacement.

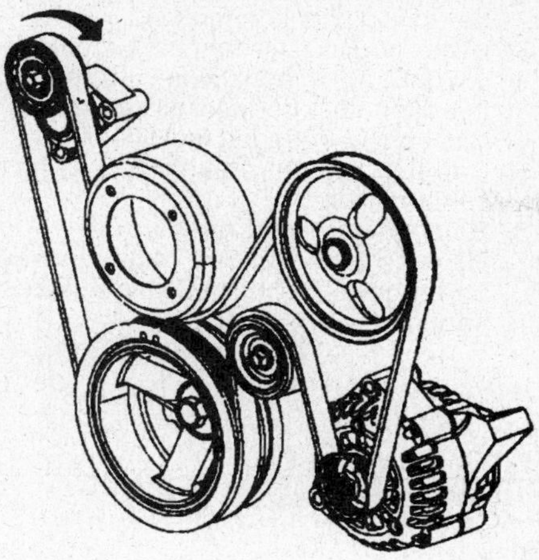

Fig. 5 Accessory drive belt routing (Part 1 of 2)

CRANKSHAFT REAR OIL SEAL

REPLACE

Refer to "Rear Cover, Replace" for rear crankshaft seal replacement.

OIL PAN

REPLACE

1. Support engine using engine support tool Nos. J41044, J36462–A, J42451 and J28467–B, or equivalent.
2. Raise and support vehicle.
3. Remove oil filter, then drain engine oil.
4. Remove right and left engine mount to cradle bolts, then the lower shock bolts.
5. Remove intermediate steering shaft bolt, then support engine cradle.
6. Disconnect and remove oil level sensor.
7. Remove starter, then the right and left torque converter covers.
8. Loosen six cradle bolts. Lower cradle and raise engine as necessary.
9. Remove oil pan attaching bolts, then the oil pan.
10. Reverse procedure to install noting the following:
    a. Apply a .200 inch bead of GM sealant P/N 12378190, or equivalent where front and rear covers meet engine block.
    b. Install gasket to oil pan. Ensure gasket is properly aligned.
    c. Install oil pan bolts through gasket, then oil pan to engine block. Tighten bolts finger tight.
    d. Using a suitable straight edge, ensure oil pan is flush with rear of engine block. Using a suitable feeler gauge, ensure gap between straight edge and oil pan does not exceed .020 inch. If measurement is not within specification, remove oil pan and repeat alignment procedure.
    e. **Torque** oil pan bolts as follows; oil pan to front cover and block, 18 ft. lbs.; oil pan to rear cover, 8.8 ft. lbs.

Fig. 5 Accessory drive belt routing (Part 2 of 2)

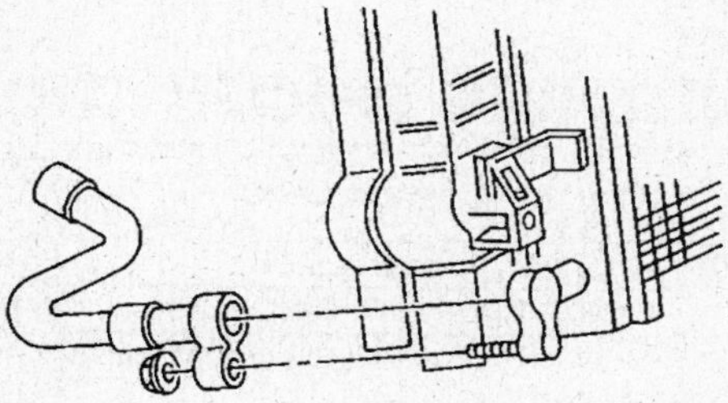

Fig. 7 Condenser tube removal

SERPENTINE DRIVE BELT

ROUTING

Refer to **Fig. 5** for drive belt routing.

REPLACEMENT

1. Rotate drive belt tensioner in clockwise direction.
2. Remove belt, then clean drive belt surfaces.
3. Reverse procedure to install. Refer to **Fig. 5** for drive belt routing.

COOLING SYSTEM BLEED

1. Fill radiator to below fill neck.
2. Fill coolant recovery bottle to FULL HOT mark.
3. Install coolant recovery reservoir cap.
4. Operate engine with radiator cap off until operating temperature is reached.
5. While engine is at idle, add coolant to radiator until coolant level reaches bottom of fill neck.
6. Install radiator cap and inspect system for leaks.

WATER PUMP

REPLACE

1. Raise and support vehicle.
2. Disconnect cooling fan electrical connectors, then drain cooling system.
3. Lower vehicle.
4. Disconnect IAT and MAF sensor electrical connectors.
5. Remove air intake duct, then the radiator hose from thermostat housing.
6. Remove water pump inlet hose, then the air cleaner assembly.

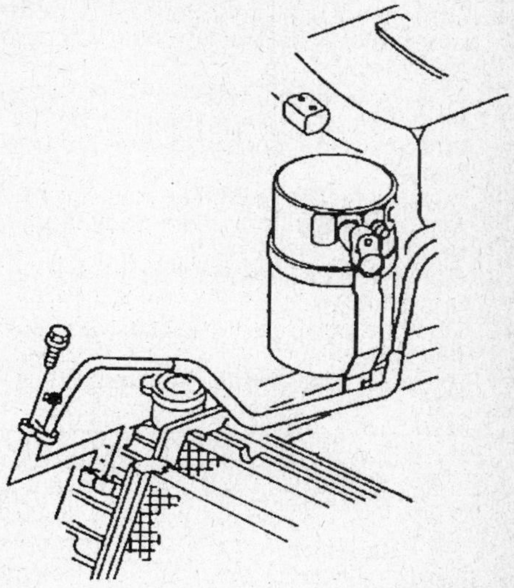

Fig. 6 Evaporator line removal

7. Remove radiator inlet hose, then the electric cooling fans.
8. Remove accessory drive belts.
9. Remove tensioner from water pump, then the overflow hose from radiator.
10. Remove water pump pulley.
11. Remove water pump attaching bolts, then the water pump.
12. Reverse procedure to install.

RADIATOR

REPLACE

1. Recover refrigerant as outlined under "Air Conditioning."
2. Drain cooling system, then remove radiator hoses.
3. Remove upper evaporator tube bracket bolt, **Fig. 6.**
4. Remove evaporator tube from condenser.
5. Remove upper and lower oil cooler lines from radiator, if equipped.
6. Remove condenser tube from condenser, **Fig. 7.**
7. Remove overflow hose from radiator.
8. Remove air intake duct and air cleaner assembly, then disconnect cooling fan electrical connectors.
9. Remove electric cooling fans, then the coolant level indicator module if equipped.
10. Remove radiator and condenser.
11. Reverse procedure to install.

FUEL PUMP

REPLACE

1. Drain fuel tank, then remove fuel tank filler pocket.
2. Raise and support vehicle, then remove filler pipe shield.
3. Remove exhaust system and shields from converter to muffler.
4. Remove rear axle as outlined under "Rear Axle, Replace."
5. Clean all fuel and EVAP lines, then disconnect and cap.

6. Disconnect fuel tank vent hose from rear brake hose bracket, then remove rear line clip.
7. Disconnect fuel electrical harness from fuel tank flange, then the sender and pressure sensor electrical connectors.
8. Support fuel tank, then remove left fuel tank strap bolt from under body bracket.
9. Remove EVAP canister vent solenoid and bracket.
10. Remove right fuel tank strap, then the fuel tank.
11. Remove fuel sender retaining nuts, then the retaining ring, sender assembly and seal.
12. Reverse procedure to install noting the following:
    a. Clean all sealing surfaces and install new seal.
    b. Tighten bolts and nuts to specifications.
    c. Inspect fuel system for leaks.

FUEL FILTER

REPLACE

1. Raise and support vehicle.
2. Clean fuel filter connections.
3. Using quick disconnect tool No. J37088–A, or equivalent, disconnect fuel filter quick connect fitting.
4. Disconnect threaded fuel filter line.
5. Cap fuel lines to prevent fuel system contamination.
6. Remove fuel filter from bracket.
7. Reverse procedure to install. Inspect and replace fuel filter O-ring if necessary.

TIGHTENING SPECIFICATIONS

Year	Component	Torque/Ft. Lbs.
1997– 2000	A/C Compressor Bolts	37
	A/C Compressor Bracket Bolts	37
	Air Injection Tube To Exhaust Manifold Bolts	15①
	Alternator Bracket	37
	Belt Tensioner Bolts	37
	Camshaft Retainer Bolts	18
	Camshaft Sensor Bolt	18
	Camshaft Sprocket Bolt	18
	Catalytic Converter Nut	18
	Connecting Rod Bolts	15①
	Coolant Temperature Gauge Sensor	15
	Crankshaft Balancer Bolt	②
	Crankshaft Bearing Cap Bolt	③
	Crankshaft Position Sensor	18
	Cylinder Head Bolts	④
	EGR Pipe To Cylinder Head	37
	EGR Valve	18
	Engine Mount Stud To Engine Block	37
	Engine Mount Through Bolts	70
	Engine Mount Through Bolt Nuts	59
	Engine Mount To Engine Block Bolts	37
	Exhaust Manifold	18
	Flywheel Bolts	⑤
	Front Cover	18
	Fuel Sender	58⑥
	Fuel Tank Straps	24
	Ignition Coil	106⑥
	Intake Manifold	⑦
	Lifter Guide Bolts	106⑥
	Oil Filter	22
	Oil Level Sensor	26
	Oil Pan	⑧
	Oil Pan Drain Plug	18
	Oil Pressure Sensor	13
	Oil Pump To Engine Block	18
	Oil Pump Screen To Pump	106⑥
	Oxygen Sensor	31
	Power Steering Pump	18
	Rear Cover Bolts	18
	Rocker Arms	22
	Spark Plugs	12

Continued

TIGHTENING SPECIFICATIONS—Continued

Year	Component	Torque/Ft. Lbs.
1997-2000	Starter Motor	37
	Thermostat Housing	11
	Throttle Body	106⑥
	Valve Cover	106⑥
	Water Pump	18
	Water Pump Pulley	89⑥

① — Tighten additional 60.°
② — Refer to "Crankshaft Damper, Replace."
③ — Refer to "Main Bearings."
④ — Refer to "Cylinder Head, Replace."
⑤ — Tighten in three steps; 1st step, 15 ft. lbs., 2nd step, 37 ft. lbs., 3rd step 74 ft. lbs.
⑥ — Inch lbs.
⑦ — Refer to "Intake Manifold, Replace."
⑧ — Refer to "Oil Pan, Replace."

Clutch & Manual Transmission

NOTE: On Air Bag Equipped Models, Refer To " Air Bag System Precautions" Located In The Front Of This Manual For System Disarming & Arming Procedures.

INDEX

PRECAUTIONS

AIR BAG SYSTEMS

Refer to "Air Bag System Precautions" in the front of this manual for system disarming and arming procedures.

BATTERY GROUND CABLE

Prior to service, disconnect battery ground cable and isolate as required.

ADJUSTMENTS

The hydraulic clutch system sets the clutch pedal height and provides automatic clutch adjustment. No adjustment of clutch or clutch pedal assembly is necessary.

HYDRAULIC SYSTEM SERVICE

CLUTCH SYSTEM BLEED

1. Fill clutch master cylinder with GM clutch fluid P/N 12345347, or equivalent.
2. Raise and support vehicle.
3. Attach a suitable hose to clutch bleeder screw, then submerge opposite end in approved container of GM clutch fluid.
4. Slowly depress clutch pedal and hold, then loosen bleeder screw, **Figs. 1 and 2.**
5. Allow air to escape, then tighten bleeder screw.
6. Repeat steps 1–4 until no air is present from bleeder hose. Ensure clutch master cylinder is kept full during bleed procedure.

CLUTCH MASTER & ACTUATOR CYLINDER, REPLACE

1. Remove instrument panel driver knee bolster assembly.
2. Disconnect clutch master cylinder pushrod from clutch pedal assembly, then remove clutch master cylinder nuts from dash panel assembly.
3. Remove clutch master cylinder U-bolt from dash panel assembly, then the clutch master cylinder from dash panel assembly.
4. Remove clutch master cylinder reservoir retainer, then the clutch master cylinder reservoir from lefthand hood strut bracket.
5. Raise and support vehicle, then remove clutch actuator cylinder from clutch housing.
6. Remove clutch master and actuator cylinder assembly from vehicle.
7. Reverse procedure to install, noting the following:
   a. Tighten fasteners to specifications.
   b. Bleed hydraulic clutch system.

CLUTCH

REPLACE

1. Raise and support vehicle.
2. Remove transmission assembly, then the clutch actuator cylinder and retain with mechanics wire.
3. Remove transmission brace, then the flywheel housing cover and flywheel housing assembly, **Figs. 3 and 4.**
4. Remove clutch pressure plate, then the clutch disc.
5. Reverse procedure to install, noting the following:
   a. Tighten fasteners to specifications.
   b. **On models equipped with 5-speed transmission,** align clutch disc and pressure plate

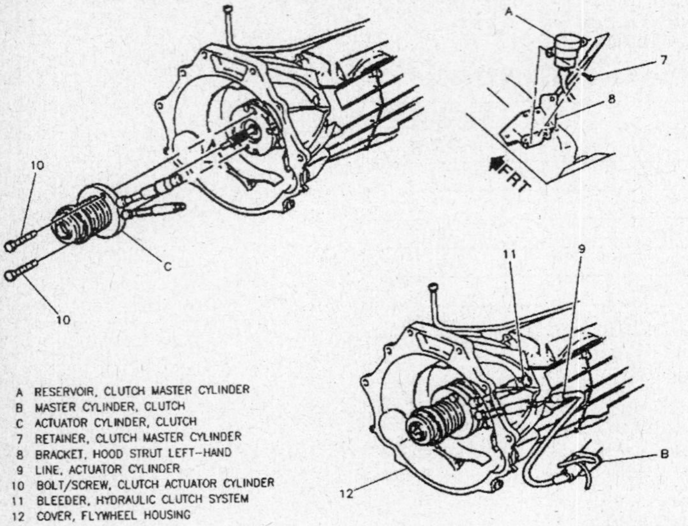

A RESERVOIR, CLUTCH MASTER CYLINDER
B MASTER CYLINDER, CLUTCH
C ACTUATOR CYLINDER, CLUTCH
7 RETAINER, CLUTCH MASTER CYLINDER
8 BRACKET, HOOD STRUT LEFT–HAND
9 LINE, ACTUATOR CYLINDER
10 BOLT/SCREW, CLUTCH ACTUATOR CYLINDER
11 BLEEDER, HYDRAULIC CLUTCH SYSTEM
12 COVER, FLYWHEEL HOUSING

GC5049800094000X

Fig. 1 Clutch hydraulic system. 5-speed transmission

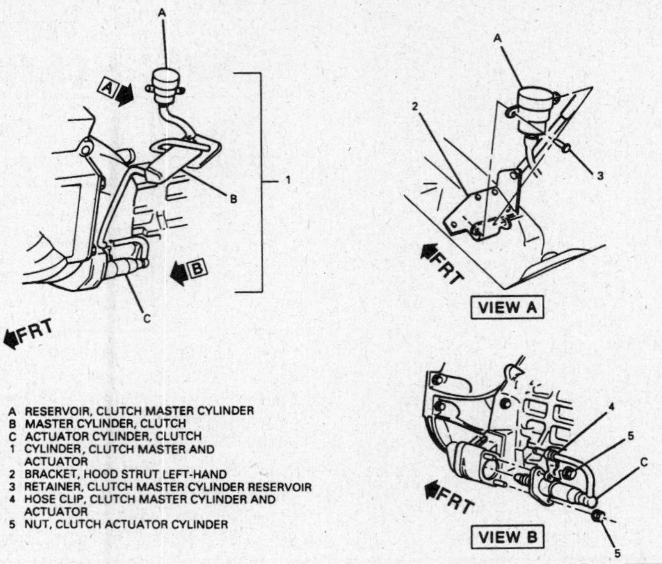

A RESERVOIR, CLUTCH MASTER CYLINDER
B MASTER CYLINDER, CLUTCH
C ACTUATOR CYLINDER, CLUTCH
1 CYLINDER, CLUTCH MASTER AND ACTUATOR
2 BRACKET, HOOD STRUT LEFT-HAND
3 RETAINER, CLUTCH MASTER CYLINDER RESERVOIR
4 HOSE CLIP, CLUTCH MASTER CYLINDER AND ACTUATOR
5 NUT, CLUTCH ACTUATOR CYLINDER

GC5049800095000X

Fig. 2 Clutch hydraulic system. 6-speed transmission

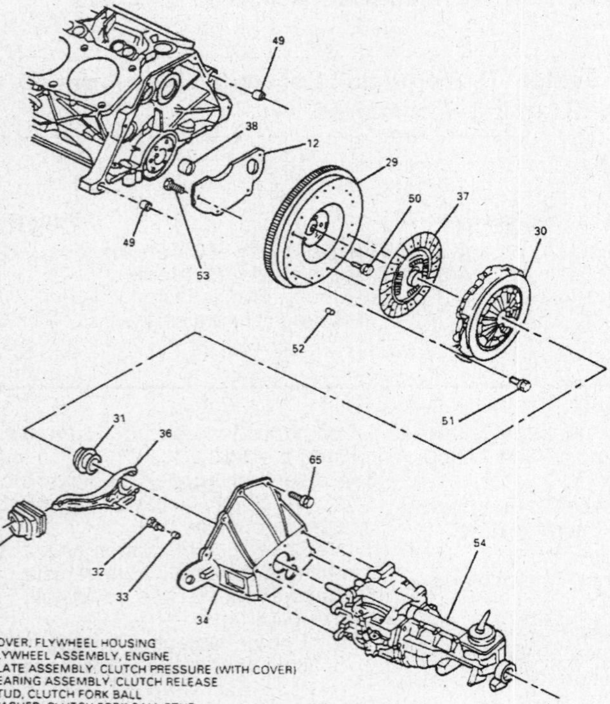

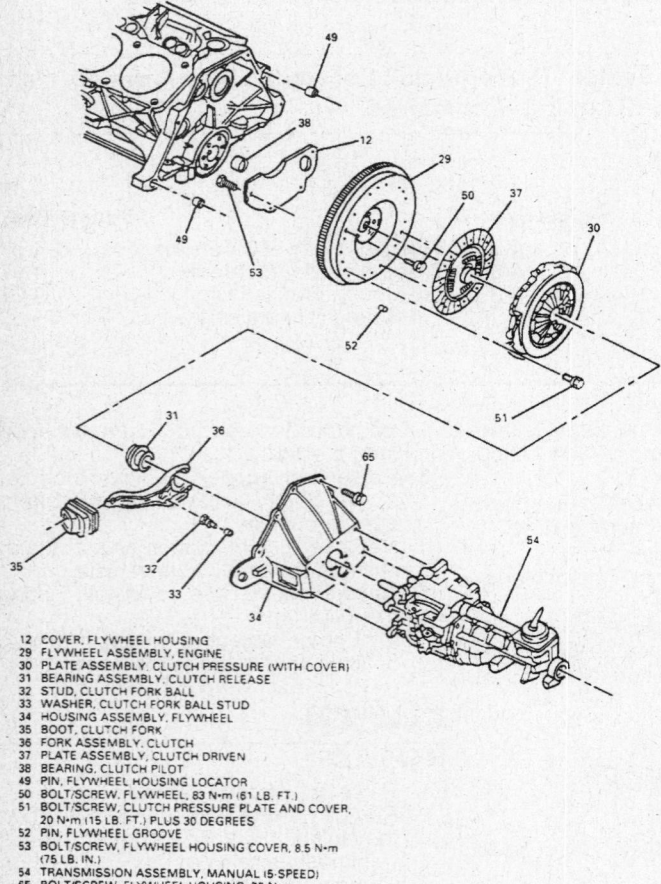

12 COVER, FLYWHEEL HOUSING
29 FLYWHEEL ASSEMBLY, ENGINE
30 PLATE ASSEMBLY, CLUTCH PRESSURE (WITH COVER)
31 BEARING ASSEMBLY, CLUTCH RELEASE
32 STUD, CLUTCH FORK BALL
33 WASHER, CLUTCH FORK BALL STUD
34 HOUSING ASSEMBLY, FLYWHEEL
35 BOOT, CLUTCH FORK
36 FORK ASSEMBLY, CLUTCH
37 PLATE ASSEMBLY, CLUTCH DRIVEN
38 BEARING, CLUTCH PILOT
49 PIN, FLYWHEEL HOUSING LOCATOR
50 BOLT/SCREW, FLYWHEEL, 83 N•m (61 LB. FT.)
51 BOLT/SCREW, CLUTCH PRESSURE PLATE AND COVER, 20 N•m (15 LB. FT.) PLUS 30 DEGREES
52 PIN, FLYWHEEL GROOVE
53 BOLT/SCREW, FLYWHEEL HOUSING COVER, 8.5 N•m (75 LB. IN.)
54 TRANSMISSION ASSEMBLY, MANUAL (5-SPEED)
65 BOLT/SCREW, FLYWHEEL HOUSING, 75 N•m (55 LB. FT.)

GC5049300035000X

Fig. 3 Clutch disc, pressure plate & housing assembly. 5-speed transmission

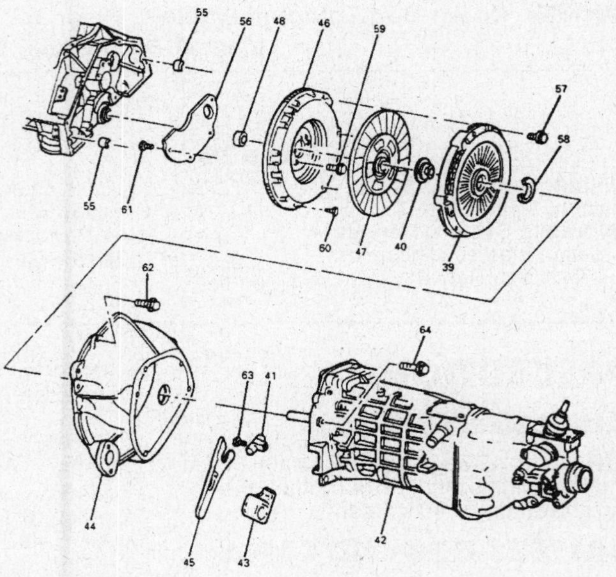

39 PLATE ASSEMBLY, CLUTCH PRESSURE (WITH COVER)
40 BEARING ASSEMBLY, CLUTCH RELEASE
41 T-STUD, CLUTCH FORK
42 TRANSMISSION ASSEMBLY, MANUAL (6-SPEED)
43 SPACER, CLUTCH ACTUATOR CYLINDER
44 HOUSING ASSEMBLY, FLYWHEEL
45 FORK ASSEMBLY, CLUTCH
46 FLYWHEEL ASSEMBLY, ENGINE
47 PLATE ASSEMBLY, CLUTCH DRIVEN
48 BEARING, CLUTCH PILOT
55 PIN, FLYWHEEL HOUSING LOCATOR
56 COVER, FLYWHEEL HOUSING
57 BOLT/SCREW, CLUTCH PRESSURE PLATE AND COVER 30 N•m (22 LB. FT.)
58 RETAINER, CLUTCH RELEASE BEARING
59 BOLT/SCREW, FLYWHEEL, 100 N•m (74 LB. FT.)
60 PIN, FLYWHEEL GROOVE
61 BOLT/SCREW, FLYWHEEL HOUSING COVER, 8.5 N•m (75 LB. IN.)
62 BOLT/SCREW, FLYWHEEL HOUSING, 47 N•m (35 LB. FT.)
63 BOLT/SCREW, CLUTCH FORK T-STUD, 24 N•m (18 LB. FT.)
64 BOLT/SCREW, TRANSMISSION, 35 N•m (26 LB. FT.)

GC5049300036000X

Fig. 4 Clutch disc, pressure plate & housing assembly. 6-speed transmission

using clutch alignment arbor tool No. J-33169, or equivalent.

c. **On models equipped with 6-speed transmission,** align clutch disc and pressure plate using clutch alignment arbor tool No. J-38836, or equivalent.

d. **On all models,** check for proper clutch fork to clutch release bearing engagement.

TRANSMISSION

REPLACE

5-SPEED TRANSMISSION

1. **On 1997 models,** disconnect intake air temperature (IAT) sensor and intake air duct.
2. **On all models,** remove front floor console trim plate assembly.
3. Raise and support vehicle, then drain fluid from transmission.
4. Disconnect propeller shaft assembly, then support rear axle assembly with a jack stand.
5. Remove rear axle torque arm assembly, then the catalytic converter hanger assembly.
6. Disconnect electrical connectors from back-up lamp switch and speed sensor, then support engine assembly with a jack stand.
7. Remove transmission support and mount assembly, then lower transmission enough to reach control bolts.
8. Remove transmission control bolts, then lower transmission and remove control assembly. **Control must be held while lowering transmission as control is not retained in vehicle and could drop damaging component.**
9. Remove transmission assembly.
10. Reverse procedure to install, noting the following:
    a. Tighten fasteners to specifications.
    b. Apply a continuous 1⁄8 inch bead of RTV sealant part No. 12345739 to extension housing to control assembly sealing surface.

6-SPEED TRANSMISSION

1. **On 1997 models,** disconnect intake air temperature (IAT) sensor and intake air duct.
2. **On all models,** remove front floor console trim plate assembly.
3. Remove control lever handle, then raise and support vehicle.
4. Drain fluid from transmission, then support rear axle assembly with a jack stand.
5. Disconnect propeller shaft assembly, then remove rear axle torque arm.
6. Remove catalytic converter hanger assembly, then disconnect electrical connectors from back-up lamp switch and reverse lockout solenoid.
7. Disconnect clutch master cylinder pushrod from clutch pedal assembly, then remove clutch actuator cylinder and retain with mechanics wire.
8. Remove actuator spacer, then pull clutch fork assembly down to disengage release bearing.
9. Disconnect electrical connector from electronic speed sensor, then support engine assembly with a jack stand.
10. Support transmission assembly with a jack stand, then remove transmission support and mount assembly.
11. Remove transmission assembly.
12. Reverse procedure to install. Tighten fasteners to specifications.

TIGHTENING SPECIFICATIONS

Year	Component	Torque/Ft. Lbs.
5-SPEED TRANSMISSIONS		
1997–2000	Actuator Cylinder Nuts	①
	Clutch Master Cylinder Nuts	20
	Flywheel Housing Bolts	55
	Flywheel Housing Cover Bolts	72④
	Pressure Plate To Flywheel	②
	Shift Control Lever Bolt	15
	Transmission Brace Nut & Bolt	37
	Transmission To Flywheel Housing Bolt	55
6-SPEED TRANSMISSIONS		
1997–2000	Actuator Cylinder Nuts	15
	Clutch Master Cylinder Nuts	20
	Flywheel Housing Bolts	35
	Flywheel Housing Cover Bolts	72④
	Pressure Plate To Flywheel	③
	Shift Control Lever Bolt	15
	Transmission To Flywheel Housing Bolt	26

① — 1997, 15 ft. lbs.; 1998–2000, 5.9 ft. lbs.

② — 1997, 15 ft. lbs.; 1998–2000, 15 ft. lbs. plus additional 45.°

③ — 1997, 22 ft. lbs.; 1998–2000, 15 ft. lbs. plus additional 45.°

④ — Inch lbs.

Rear Axle & Suspension

INDEX

REAR AXLE

REPLACE

1997

Construction of the axle assembly is such that service operations may be performed with the housing installed in the vehicle or with the housing removed and installed in a holding fixture. The following procedure is necessary only when the housing requires replacement.

1. Raise and support vehicle, then support rear axle with a suitable jack.
2. Disconnect shock absorbers from lower mountings.
3. Remove track bar.
4. Disconnect brake line from axle housing junction block and the parking brake cable.
5. Disconnect lower control arms from axle housing attachments.
6. Remove propeller shaft.
7. Lower axle slowly until springs can be moved. Roll axle assembly out from under vehicle.
8. Reverse procedure to install.

1998–2000

1. Raise and support vehicle, then remove rear wheels.
2. Remove driveshaft, then the stabilizer shaft.
3. Support axle using a suitable jack.
4. Remove rear shock absorbers, then the track bar.
5. Disconnect brake hose from rear brake hose junction block.
6. Remove coil springs as outlined under "Coil Spring, Replace."
7. Remove parking brake cables from axle housing.
8. Disconnect wheel speed sensors if equipped.
9. Remove torque arm, then the lower control arms.
10. Lower axle from vehicle.
11. Reverse procedure to install noting the following:
    a. Tighten to specifications.
    b. Bleed brake system as outlined under "Hydraulic Brake Systems."

REAR AXLE SHAFT

REPLACE

If the vehicle is equipped with acceleration slip regulation (ASR) traction control, care must be taken not to damage rear wheel speed sensor reluctor wheel. The sensing wheel is located on the axle shaft and must be replaced if damage occurs.

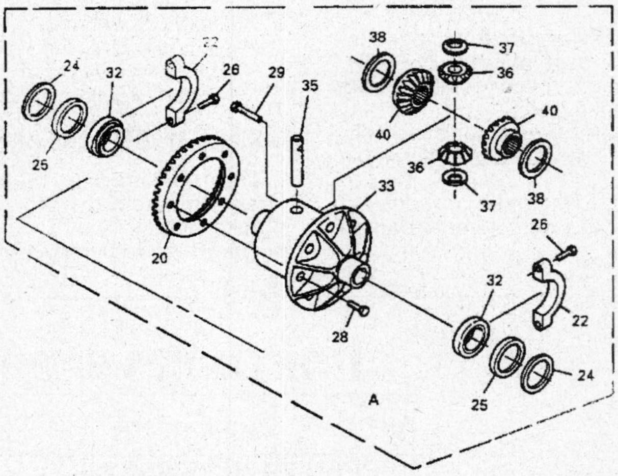

GC2039600116000X

Fig. 1 Pinion gear shaft & lock bolt removal

1. Raise and support vehicle.
2. Clean axle housing cover and disconnect parking brake guide.
3. Remove cover bolts and pry cover loose.
4. Drain lubricant, clean old gasket from both sealing surfaces.
5. Remove rear wheels and brake assembly.
6. **On models less traction control,** install exciter ring protector kit tool No. J 39446, or equivalent, to speed sensor reluctor wheel and remove.
7. **On all models,** remove differential pinion gear shaft lock bolt (29) from case (33) and then the pinion gear shaft (35), **Fig. 1.**
8. Remove axle shaft lock by pushing flanged end of axle shaft into housing.
9. Slide axle shaft from housing. Take care in removal as splines on end of shaft may damage seal.
10. Reverse procedure to install, noting the following:
    a. Ensure axle shaft splines mesh with splines on side gears.
    b. When installing axle shaft lock, ensure it seats inside counterbore of side gear.
    c. Use Loctite 242, or equivalent, when installing pinion gear shaft bolt and **torque** to 27 ft. lbs.

PROPELLER SHAFT

REPLACE

1. Raise and support vehicle, then mark relationship of propeller shaft assembly to pinion gear yoke.
2. Remove center support bearing and washers from torque arm assembly.
3. **On two-piece propeller shafts,** remove bolts from center support bearing.
4. **On all propeller shafts,** remove bolts and retainers, then the propeller shaft.
5. Reverse procedure to install, noting the following:
    a. Tighten fasteners to specifications.
    b. Lubricate slip yoke with .6 ounces of propeller shaft slip yoke lubricant 1050169, or equivalent.
    c. Align marks on pinion gear yoke and propeller shaft.

SHOCK ABSORBER

REPLACE

1. Fold down seat back frame, then remove quarter trim panel.
2. Pull folding carpet back, then raise and support vehicle.
3. Support rear axle, then remove shock absorber.
4. Reverse procedure to install. Tighten fasteners to specifications.

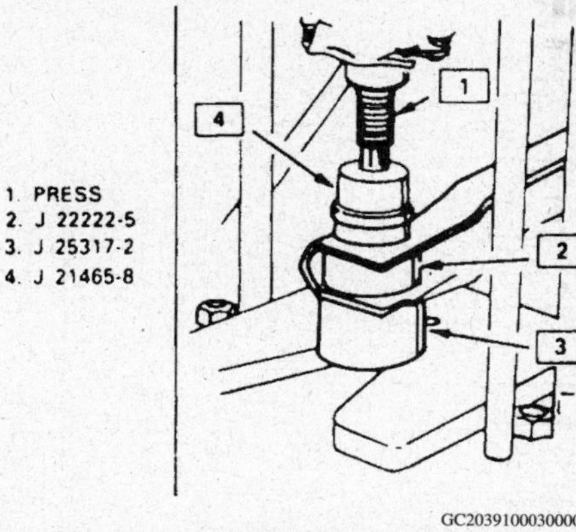

Fig. 2 Control arm bushing removal

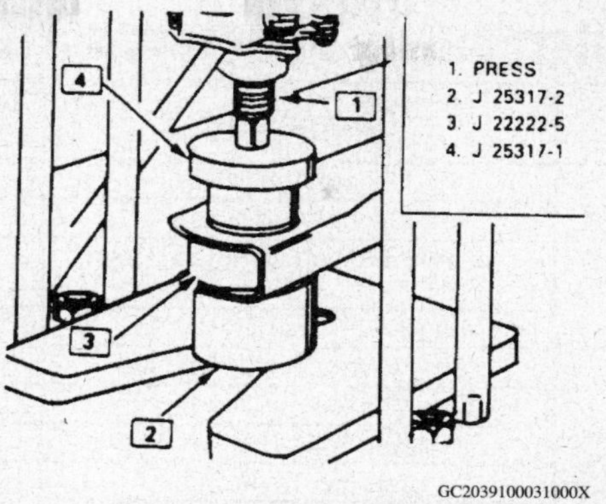

Fig. 3 Control arm bushing installation

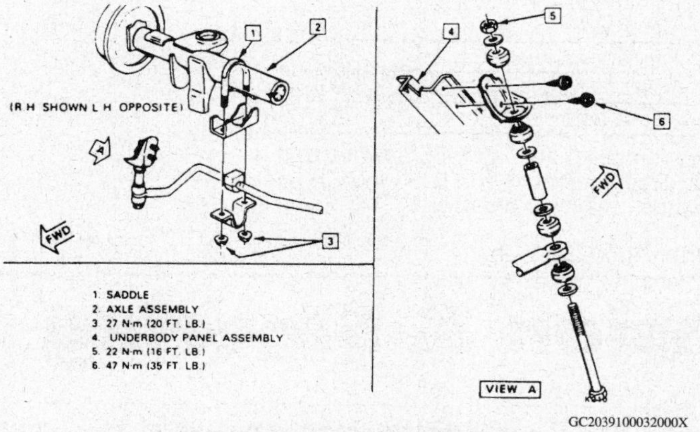

Fig. 4 Stabilizer bar installation

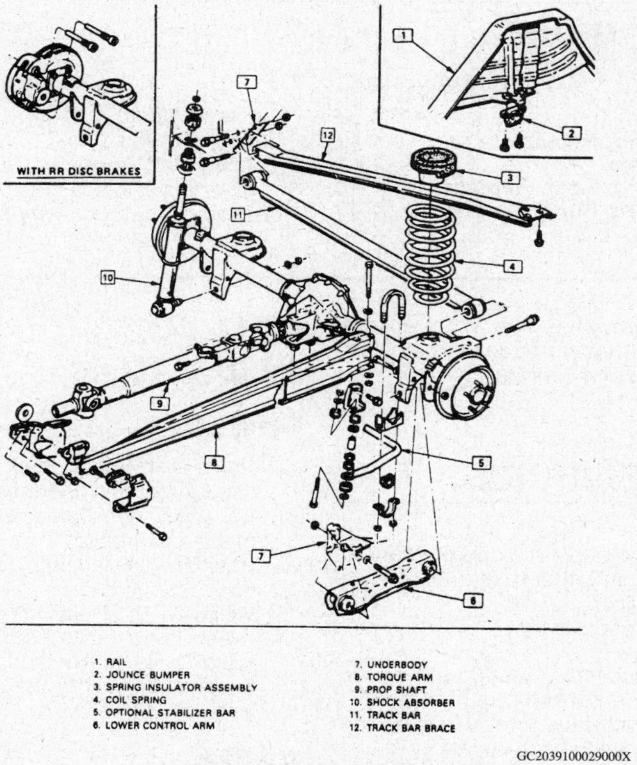

Fig. 5 Track rod replacement

COIL SPRING

REPLACE

1. Raise and support vehicle, then support rear axle with an adjustable lifting device. **Do not use twin post type hoist.**
2. Remove shock absorber nuts from rear axle, then lower rear axle.
3. Remove upper insulator assembly, then the rear spring.
4. Reverse procedure to install. Tighten fasteners to specifications.

CONTROL ARM

REPLACE

LOWER

If both control arms are to be removed, remove one control arm at a time to prevent axle from slipping or rolling.

1. Raise vehicle and support at frame pads. Support nose of axle housing to prevent assembly from twisting when control arm is removed.
2. Remove bolts securing control arm to chassis and rear axle, and the control arm.
3. Reverse procedure to install.

BUSHINGS

1. Raise and support vehicle and remove control arm as outlined previously.
2. Press bushings out of control arm using suitable tools as shown in **Fig. 2.**
3. Reverse procedure to install, ensure bushing is properly seated in control arm, **Fig. 3. If replacement bushing fits loosely in control arm, or if mounting areas are damaged or deformed, control arm must be replaced.**

STABILIZER BAR

REPLACE

1. Raise and support vehicle.
2. Remove link bolt nuts, washers, bushings, spacers and link bolts securing stabilizer to chassis, **Fig. 4.**
3. Remove clamps securing stabilizer shaft to rear axle and stabilizer shaft.
4. Reverse procedure to install. Tighten link bolts and U-bolt nuts to specifications.

TRACK ROD

REPLACE

1. Raise vehicle and support rear axle at curb height.
2. Remove track bar mounting bolt and nut from rear axle and from body bracket, then remove track rod, **Fig. 5.**
3. Remove heat shield attaching screws from track bar brace.
4. Remove three track bar to body brace screws.
5. Remove nut and bolt from body bracket, then remove track bar brace.
6. Reverse procedure to install.

TIGHTENING SPECIFICATIONS

Year	Component	Torque/Ft. lbs.
1997– 2000	Control Arm Bolts	②
	Control Arm Nuts	60
	Differential Pinion Gear Shaft Lock Bolt	27
	Shock Absorber Lower Nut	66
	Shock Absorber Upper Nut	13
	Stabilizer Link	16
	Stabilizer Shaft Bracket Bolts	17
	Stabilizer Shaft Nuts	18
	Torque Arm To Rear Axle Bolts	96
	Torque Arm To Transmission Center Bolt	20
	Torque Arm To Transmission Lower & Upper Bolts	37
	Torque Arm To Transmission Nuts	30
	Wheel Lug Nuts	100
	Yoke Nut	①

① — Tighten until endplay is near 0, then measure preload. If using new bearings, preload should be 15–30 inch lbs. If reinstalling old bearings, ensure preload is 10–15 inch lbs.

② — 1997, 74 ft. lbs., 1998–2000, 80 ft. lbs.

Front Suspension & Steering

NOTE: **On Air Bag Equipped Models, Refer To " Air Bag System Precautions" Located In The Front Of This Manual For System Disarming & Arming Procedures.**

INDEX

PRECAUTIONS

AIR BAG SYSTEMS

Refer to "Air Bag System Precautions" in the front of this manual for system disarming and arming procedures.

BATTERY GROUND CABLE

Prior to service, disconnect battery ground cable and isolate as required.

DESCRIPTION

The short/long arm (SLA) front suspension assembly, **Fig. 1,** is designed to allow each wheel to compensate for changes in road surface level without significantly affecting the opposite wheel. Each wheel is independently connected to the frame by a steering knuckle, wheel hub, shock absorber and spring, upper and lower ball studs and upper and lower control arms.

HUB & BEARING

REPLACE

1. Raise and support vehicle, then remove tire and wheel assembly on side to be serviced.
2. Remove brake caliper assembly and brake disc.
3. Disconnect wheel speed sensor electrical connector and secure aside.
4. Remove bolts and screws from hub assembly, then the hub assembly.
5. Reverse procedure to install, **torque** retaining bolts to 63 ft. lbs.

BALL JOINT INSPECTION

LOWER

1. Raise and support vehicle by positioning floor stands under both lower control arms, then wipe grease fitting free of dirt and grease.
2. Position dial indicator against wheel rim.
3. While reading dial indicator, pry between lower control arm and steering knuckle. Vertical movement should not exceed .047 inch, if so, replace ball joint.

UPPER

1. Raise front end of vehicle and position

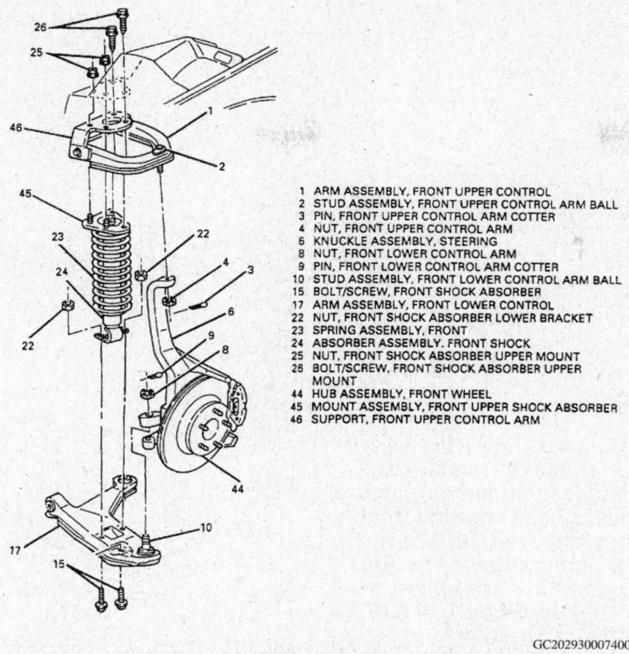

Fig. 1 Exploded view of front suspension

floor stands under both lower control arms as near to ball joints as possible.

2. Position a dial indicator against wheel rim as shown in **Fig. 2.** Push in on bottom of tire while pulling out at top, then reverse procedure.
3. Deflection on dial indicator should not exceed .125 inch. If deflection exceeds specification, replace ball joint.
4. If ball joint is disconnected from steering knuckle, check for looseness or see if ball joint can be twisted in its socket using your fingers.
5. If either of the above conditions exist, replace ball joint.

BALL JOINT

REPLACE

LOWER

1. Raise vehicle and support at frame, and remove wheel and tire.
2. Position a suitable jack under lower control arm spring seat, and raise jack to compress coil spring. **Jack must remain in place during ball joint replacement to hold spring and lower control arm in position.**
3. Remove cotter pin and nut securing ball joint stud to steering knuckle, then disconnect joint from knuckle using a suitable tool.
4. Lift knuckle assembly from ball stud, guiding control arm out of splash shield, then support knuckle aside to allow clearance for joint removal.
5. Remove grease fitting, then press ball joint assembly out of lower control arm using a suitable tool, **Fig. 3.**
6. Press replacement joint into arm by reversing removal tools, fit spindle over ball stud, install washer, if equipped, and retaining nut.
7. Tighten retaining nut to specifications.
8. Tighten nut up to an additional 1⁄16 turn, if necessary, to align hole in ball stud with nut, then install cotter pin.

UPPER

1. Raise and support vehicle, then remove wheel.
2. Place a floor jack under shock absorber mounting location on lower control. **Jack must remain in place during ball joint replacement to hold spring and lower control arm in position.**
3. Loosen ball joint from steering knuckle, then remove cotter pin and nut.
4. Support steering knuckle with floor stands, then disconnect ball joint from upper control arm using ball joint/tie rod separator tool No. J 39549, or equivalent.
5. With upper control arm in raised position, drill out four rivets approximately 1⁄4 inch deep using a 1⁄8 inch drill bit.
6. Drill off rivet heads using a 1⁄2 inch drill bit, then punch out rivets using a small punch and remove ball joint.
7. Position new ball joint and install bolts and nuts supplied with new ball joint.
8. Remove support from steering knuckle, then connect ball joint to steering knuckle.
9. Tighten nut enough to align slot with stud hole, then tighten nut to specifications and install cotter pin.

STRUT SERVICE

1. If servicing driver's side strut, remove brake master cylinder nuts, then move master cylinder aside.
2. Remove upper shock absorber mounting nuts and bolts, then raise and support vehicle.
3. Remove tire and wheel assembly, then disconnect stabilizer shaft link.

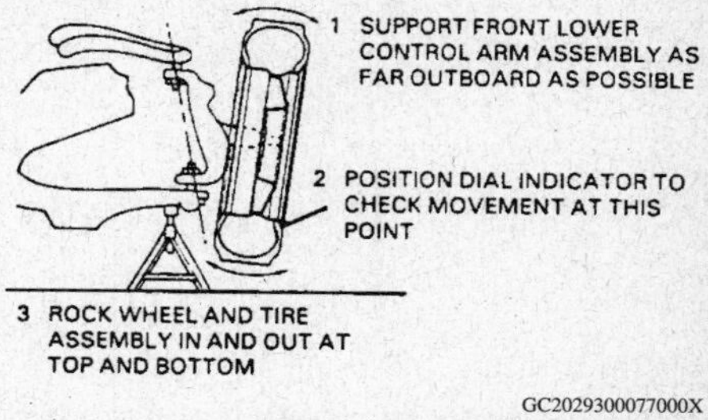

Fig. 2 Upper ball joint inspection

4. Remove lower shock absorber mounting nuts and bolts, then separate lower ball joint from steering knuckle.
5. Mark lower mount location relative to upper mount location, then remove shock absorber and spring assembly.
6. Proceed as follows to disassemble shock absorber assembly:
   a. Install modular shock assembly compressor adapter tool No. J 34013-114, or equivalent, onto strut spring compressor tool No. J 34013-B, or equivalent, using wing nuts to secure tool to mounting holes C-H in lower left corner and P in upper right corner for driver side shock absorber assembly, **Figs. 4 and 5,** or to holes A-X-P in upper left corner and C-H in lower right corner for passenger side shock absorber assembly, **Fig. 6.**
   b. Install strut compressor adapter tool No. J 34013-88, or equivalent, and modular shock support tool No. J 34013-218, or equivalent, onto strut spring compressor, **Fig. 7. Ensure strut compressor adapter and modular shock support are aligned so that they can open and close together. If tools are not properly aligned, they will not open.**
   c. Install shock absorber assembly to top of modular shock assembly compressor adapter, **Figs. 8 and 9. Ensure top of shock absorber assembly is flat against modular shock assembly compressor adapter. Shock absorber assembly will not be aligned properly if it does not lay flat against tool.**
   d. Install shock absorber assembly into strut compressor adapter and modular shock support, **Fig. 10,** then close strut compressor adapter and modular shock support and install locking pin. **Ensure mounting ears of shock absorber assembly are facing downward toward rear of strut spring compressor or shock absorber assembly will not align properly.**
   e. Turn screw on strut spring compressor counterclockwise to raise shock absorber assembly up to modular shock assembly compressor adapter. Ensure studs go through guide holes in modular shock assembly compressor adapter and top of shock absorber assembly is flat against tool.
   f. Compress front spring assembly

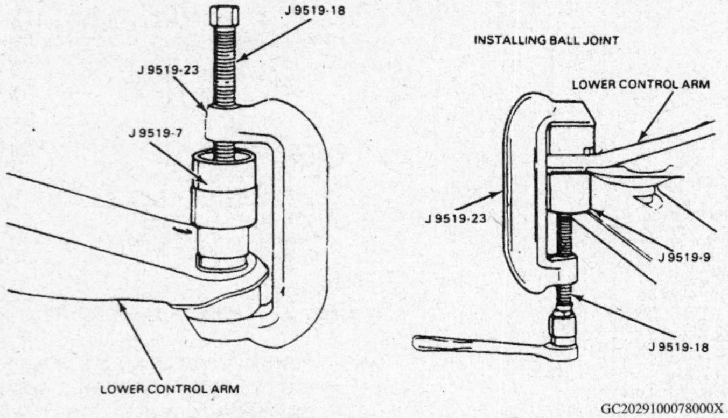

Fig. 3 Lower ball joint replacement

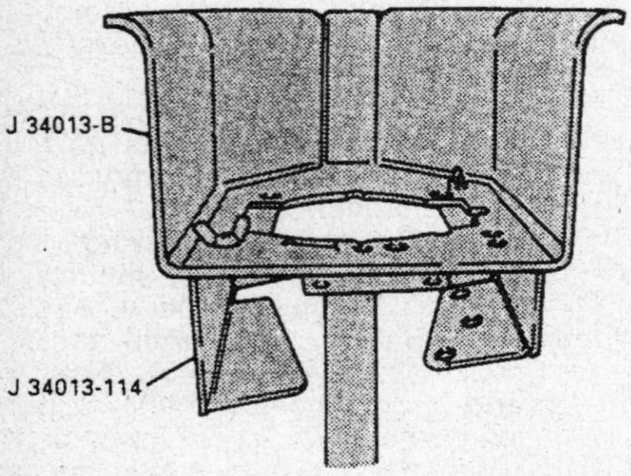

Fig. 5 Modular shock absorber assembly compressor adapter, driver side

approximately ½ inch or three or four complete turns of screw on modular shock assembly compressor adapter. **Do not over compress front spring assembly. Severe overloading may cause tool failure, possibly resulting in personal injury.**

g. Insert J 39642-1 from modular shock nut removal set tool No. J 39642, or equivalent, on shock absorber nut, then insert tool No. J 39642-2, or equivalent, from modular shock nut removal set tool Nos. J 39642 through J 39642-1, or equivalents, to hold shock absorber rod in place.

h. Remove shock absorber nut and discard, then turn strut spring compressor clockwise to relieve spring pressure.

7. Proceed as follows to assemble shock absorber assembly:

a. Install shock absorber to strut compressor adapter and modular shock support. **Ensure mounting ears of shock absorber assembly are facing downward toward rear of strut spring compressor or shock absorber assembly will not align properly.**

b. Close strut compressor adapter and modular shock support and install locking pin, then ensure upper and lower spring seats are positioned correctly.

c. Assemble shock absorber assembly to top of modular shock assembly compressor adapter. **Ensure top of shock absorber assembly is flat against modular shock assembly compressor adapter. Shock absorber assembly will not be aligned properly if it does not lay flat against tool.**

d. Turn screw on strut spring compressor counterclockwise to raise shock absorber assembly up to modular shock assembly compressor adapter without compressing spring assembly. Ensure studs on shock absorber assembly go through guide holes in modular shock assembly compressor adapter. **Only turn screw until shock absorber assembly is held in strut spring compressor by itself. Do not load spring assembly.**

e. Place modular shock assembly alignment rod J 34013-115 down through top of strut spring compressor, through top of shock absorber assembly and onto shock absorber rod, **Fig. 11. Ensure shock assembly alignment rod is straight with shock absorber assembly. If shock assembly alignment rod is angled, repeat preceding steps until tool is straight.**

f. Turn operating screw clockwise to compress spring assembly until threaded portion of shock absorber rod is through top of shock absorber assembly. **Do not over compress front spring assembly. Severe overloading may cause tool failure, possibly resulting in personal injury.**

g. Remove modular shock assembly alignment rod, then insert a new shock absorber nut on shock absorber rod. **Always replace shock absorber nut. Do not turn shock absorber rod when tightening nut or shock absorber assembly could be damaged. Retain shock absorber rod in a stationary position when tightening nut.**

h. Place tool No. J 39642-1, or equivalent, from modular shock nut removal set tool No. J 39642, or

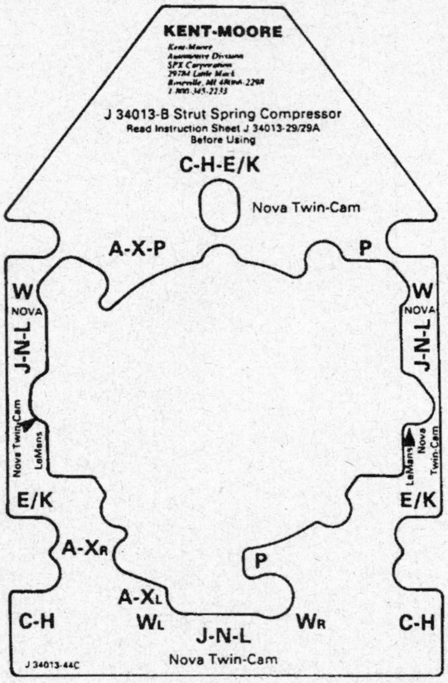

Fig. 4 Modular shock absorber assembly compressor mounting hole locations

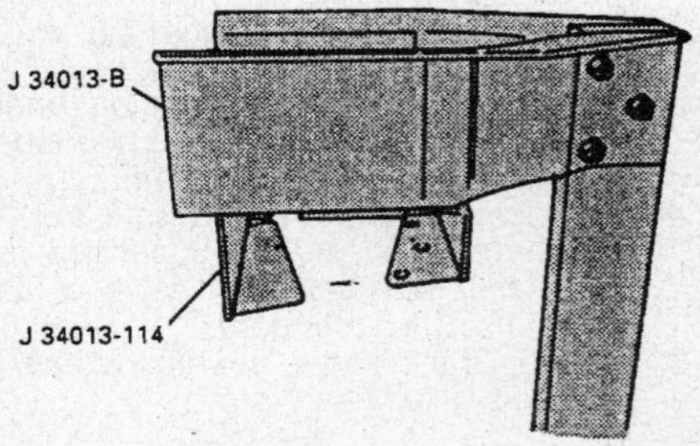

Fig. 6 Modular shock absorber assembly compressor adapter, passenger side

equivalent, on shock absorber nut, then insert J 39642-2 from modular shock nut removal set J–39642 through J 39642-1 to hold shock absorber rod in place and tighten nut to specifications.

i. Remove shock absorber assembly from strut spring compressor.

8. Reverse steps 1 through 5 to install. Tighten fasteners to specifications

STABILIZER BAR

REPLACE

1. Raise and support vehicle.
2. Remove nut from link bolt located at each side, then remove bolt, grommets and bushings, **Fig. 12.**
3. Remove stabilizer shaft to body bolts, then remove stabilizer bar.
4. Reverse procedure to install.

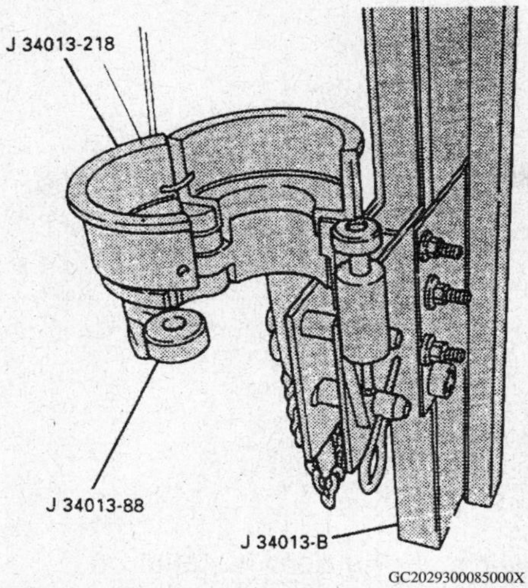

Fig. 7 Strut compressor adapter & modular shock support to strut spring compressor mounting

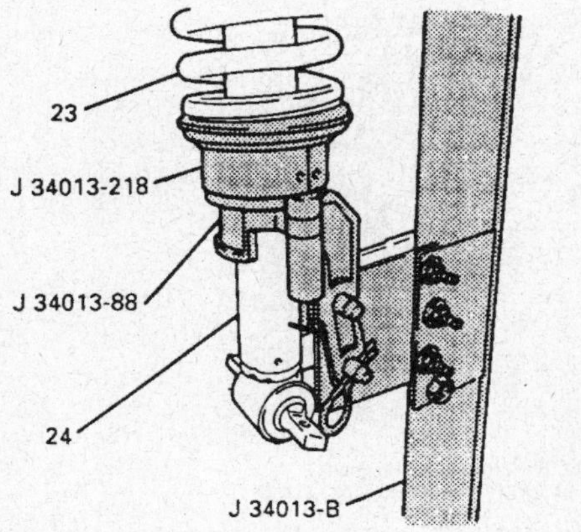

Fig. 10 Shock absorber assembly to strut spring compressor installation

POWER STEERING GEAR

REPLACE

1. Raise and support vehicle, then remove wheels.
2. Disconnect inlet and outlet hoses from

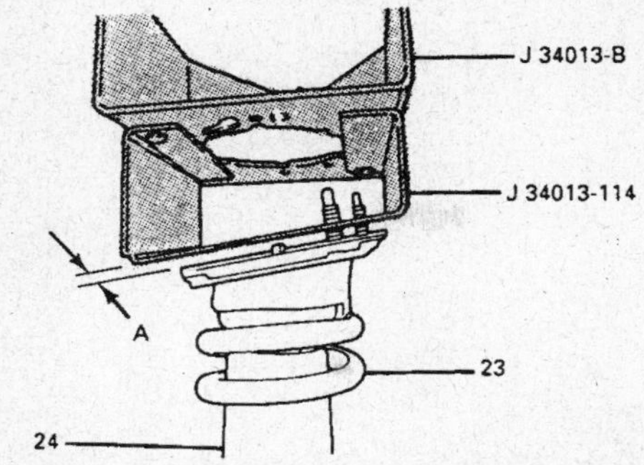

Fig. 8 Upper driver side shock absorber assembly to strut spring compressor installation

steering gear, then the steering linkage outer tie rods from steering knuckles, **Fig. 13.**
3. Disconnect steering gear coupling shaft from steering gear, then remove steering gear.
4. Reverse procedure to install, noting the following:
   a. Tighten fasteners to specifications.
   b. Adjust steering gear so that it aligns as straight as possible with steering gear coupling shaft.
   c. Refill and bleed power steering system.

POWER STEERING PUMP

REPLACE

1. **On models equipped with 5.7L engine,** raise and support vehicle, then drain engine coolant.
2. **On all models,** remove serpentine belt, then lower vehicle and remove front air intake duct.
3. **On models equipped with 5.7L engine,** remove alternator, radiator outlet hose and heater inlet/outlet hoses from water pump. Also, remove throttle body heater return from heater outlet hose and pump bolts.
4. **On models equipped with 3800 engine,** remove pulley from pump and mounting nuts.
5. **On all models,** remove pump mounting bolts, **Figs. 14 and 15,** then discon-

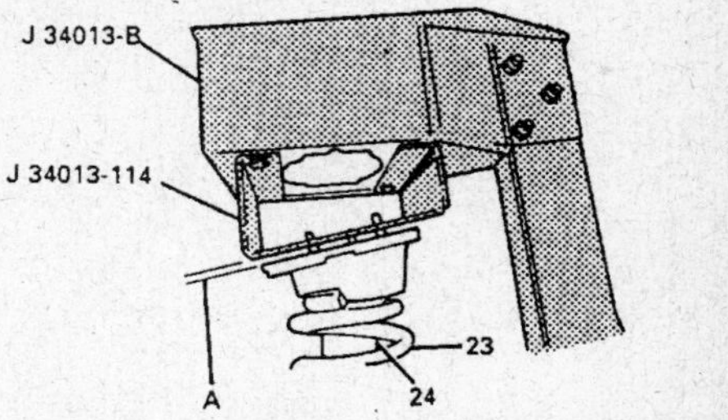

Fig. 9 Upper passenger side shock absorber assembly to strut spring compressor installation

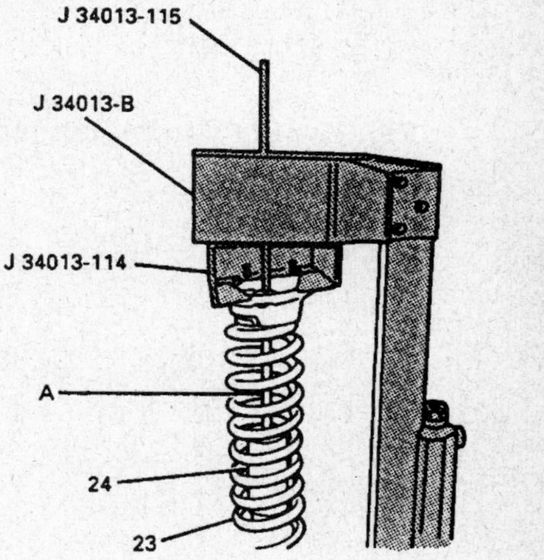

Fig. 11 Modular shock assembly alignment rod installation

nect inlet and reservoir hoses from pump and remove pump.
6. Reverse procedure to install, noting the following:
   a. Tighten fasteners to specifications.
   b. Refill and bleed power steering system.

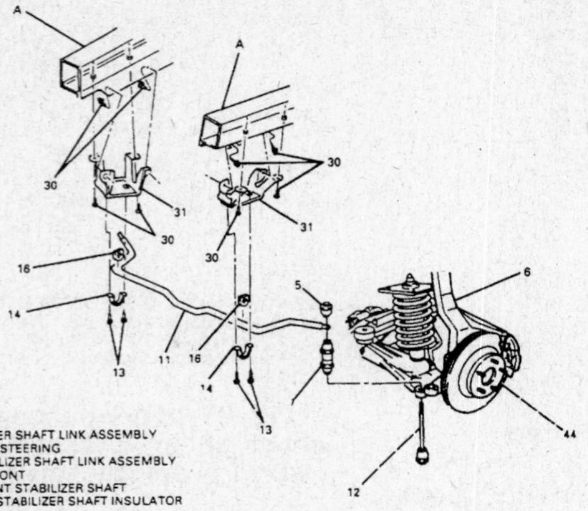

A SIDE RAIL
5 NUT, FRONT STABILIZER SHAFT LINK ASSEMBLY
6 KNUCKLE ASSEMBLY, STEERING
7 SLEEVE, FRONT STABILIZER SHAFT LINK ASSEMBLY
11 STABILIZER SHAFT, FRONT
12 LINK ASSEMBLY, FRONT STABILIZER SHAFT
13 BOLT/SCREW, FRONT STABILIZER SHAFT INSULATOR CLAMP
14 CLAMP, FRONT STABILIZER SHAFT INSULATOR
16 INSULATOR, FRONT STABILIZER SHAFT
30 BOLT/SCREW, FRONT STABILIZER SHAFT BRACKET
31 BRACKET ASSEMBLY, FRONT STABILIZER SHAFT
44 HUB ASSEMBLY, FRONT WHEEL

GC2029500206000X

Fig. 12 Stabilizer shaft replacement

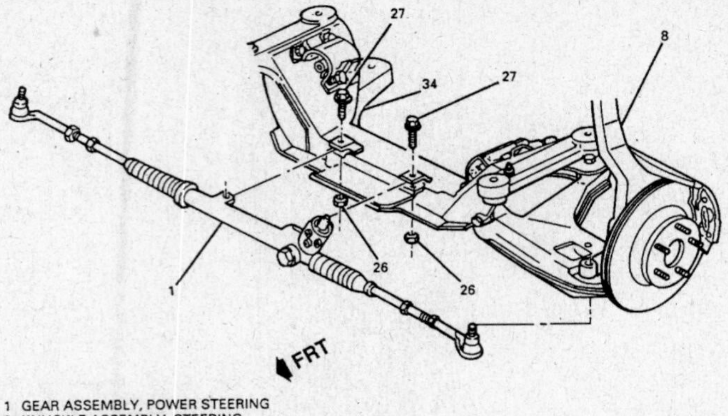

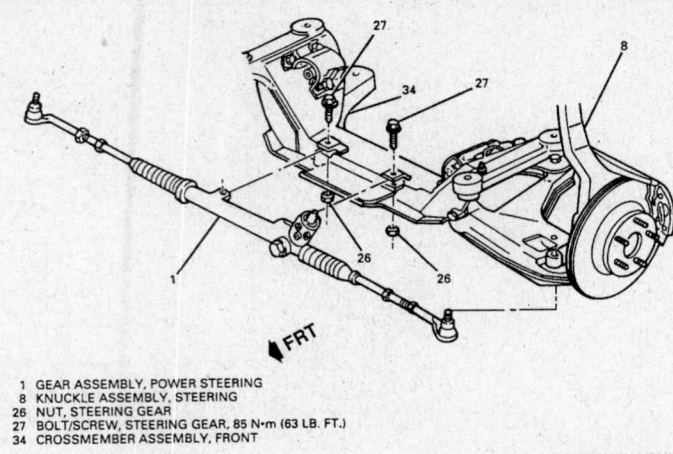

1 GEAR ASSEMBLY, POWER STEERING
8 KNUCKLE ASSEMBLY, STEERING
26 NUT, STEERING GEAR
27 BOLT/SCREW, STEERING GEAR, 85 N·m (63 LB. FT.)
34 CROSSMEMBER ASSEMBLY, FRONT

GC6049300136000X

Fig. 13 Power steering gear installation

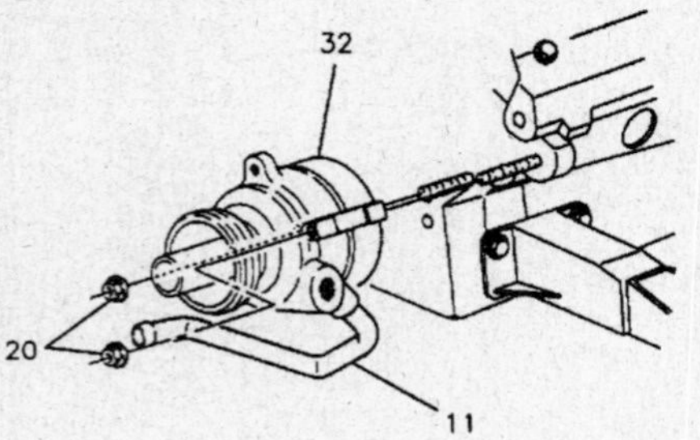

11 HOSE, POWER STEERING FLUID RESERVOIR
20 NUT, POWER STEERING PUMP
32 PUMP, POWER STEERING

GC6049600174000X

Fig. 14 Power steering pump replacement. 3800 engine

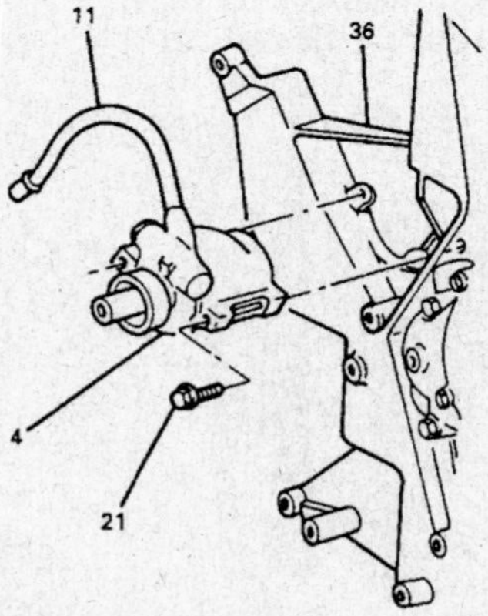

4 PUMP ASSEMBLY, POWER STEERING
11 HOSE ASSEMBLY, POWER STEERING FLUID RESERVOIR
21 BOLT/SCREW, POWER STEERING PUMP, 25 N·m (18 LB. FT.)
36 BRACKET ASSEMBLY, GENERATOR AND AIR CONDITIONER COMPRESSOR AND POWER STEERING PUMP AND DRIVE BELT TENSIONER

GC6049300140000X

Fig. 15 Power steering pump replacement. 5.7L engine

TIGHTENING SPECIFICATIONS

Year	Component	Torque/Ft. Lbs.
1997– 2000	Lower Ball Joint Nut	81
	Lower Shock Absorber Nuts	48
	Power Steering Gear Mounting Bolts	63
	Power Steering Pump Bolts (V6 Engine)	①
	Power Steering Pump Bolts (V8 Engine)	18
	Power Steering Pump Support To Pump Nuts & Bolts	37
	Stabilizer Bracket To Frame Bolts	41
	Stabilizer Clamp To Stabilizer Bracket Bolts	41
	Stabilizer Link Nut	17
	Upper Ball Joint Nut	39
	Upper Shock Absorber Mount To Strut Tower Bolts	37
	Upper Shock Absorber Mount To Strut Tower Nuts	32
	Wheel Lug Nuts	100

① — 1997, 37 ft. lbs., 1998–2000, 23 ft. lbs.

Wheel Alignment

INDEX

PRELIMINARY INSPECTION

Prior to checking or adjusting front suspension alignment, inspect suspension components for damage or excessive wear, and replace as needed. Ensure tire pressures and wheel bearings are properly adjusted, then raise and release front bumper several times to allow vehicle to assume normal ride height.

FRONT WHEEL ALIGNMENT

CASTER

1. Jounce front bumper three times to allow vehicle to return to normal ride height, then raise and support vehicle.
2. Loosen front lower control arm nuts, then install camber/caster adjuster tool No. J 38658, or equivalent, to slot holes in lower control arm and front crossmember, **Fig. 1.**
3. Adjust caster to specifications by rotating turnbuckle on camber/caster adjuster. Clockwise increases caster, counterclockwise decreases caster.
4. Remove camber/caster adjuster, then **torque** front lower control arm nuts to 96 ft. lbs.

CAMBER

1. Jounce front bumper three times to allow vehicle to return to normal ride height, then raise and support vehicle.
2. Loosen front lower control arm nuts, then install camber/caster adjuster tool No. J 38658, or equivalent, to slot holes in lower control arm and front crossmember, **Fig. 2.**
3. Adjust camber to specifications by rotating turnbuckle on camber/caster adjuster. Clockwise increases caster, counterclockwise decreases caster.
4. Remove camber/caster adjuster, then **torque** front lower control arm nuts to 96 ft. lbs.

TOE-IN

Toe adjustments are made separately at each individual wheel.

1. Ensure steering wheel is set in a straight ahead position within ± 3.5.°
2. Loosen nut on inner tie rod, then adjust toe to specifications. Left and right toe adjustment should be equal within ± .2.°
3. Ensure steering gear boot is not twisted, then **torque** inner tie rod nut to 35 ft. lbs.

REAR WHEEL ALIGNMENT

After front wheel alignment has been checked or adjusted, rear wheel alignment angles should be checked if vehicle still does not track properly or if excessive rear tire wear is present. Rear wheels should be parallel to and the same distance from the vehicle centerline, **Fig. 3.**

Rear wheel alignment is not adjustable. If alignment angles are not within specification, check for bent or damaged suspension arms, axle housing or frame.

THRUST ANGLE

If the thrust angle is not within specifications, inspect upper and lower control arms for damage. If control arms are not damaged, check frame dimensions.

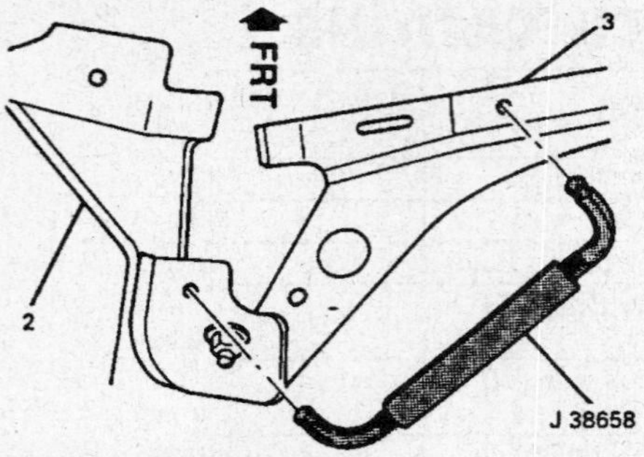

Fig. 1 Front caster adjustment tool installation

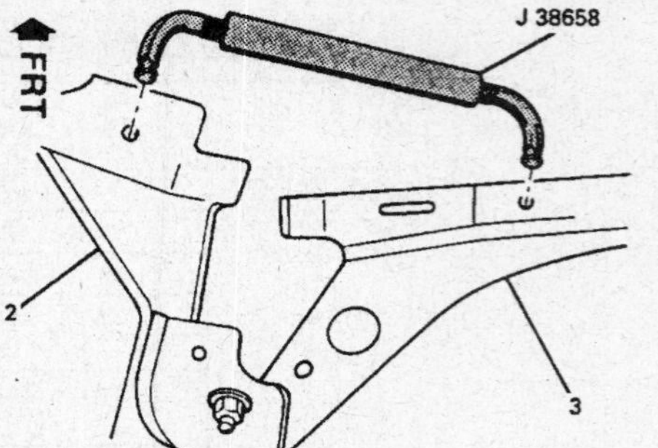

Fig. 2 Front camber adjustment tool installation

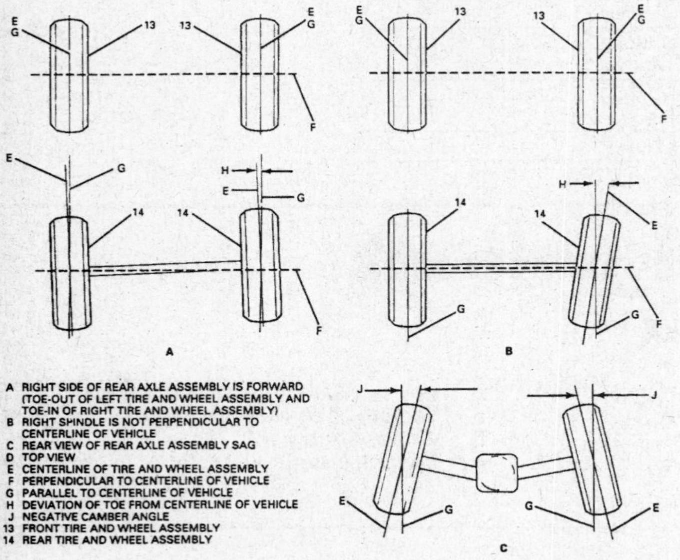

Fig. 3 Rear wheel alignment inspection

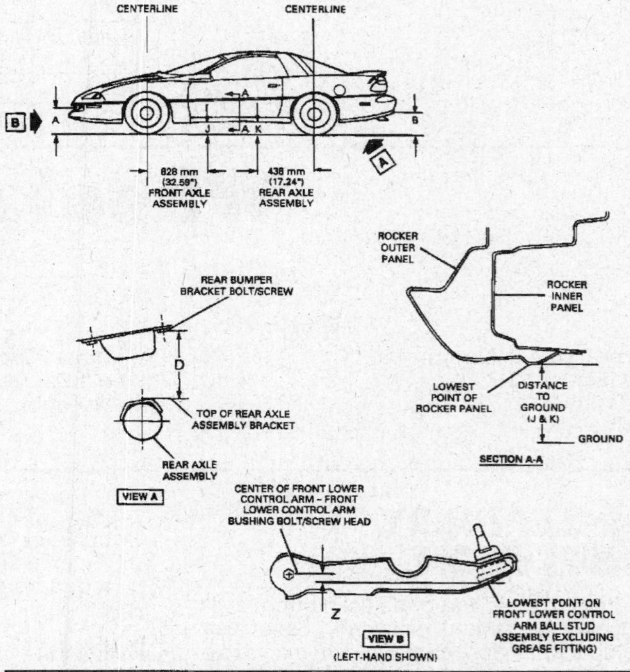

SUSPENSION	TIRE	A		B		Z		D		J		K	
		mm	inch	mm	inch	mm	inch	mm	inch	mm	inch	mm	inch
F41	215-60	420	16.5	367	14.4	32	1.3	121	4.8	204	8.0	208	8.2
	235-55	420	16.5	367	14.4	30	1.2	118	4.6	204	8.0	208	8.4
FE2	235-55	420	16.5	367	14.4	31	1.2	118	4.6	204	8.0	208	8.4
	245-50	420	16.5	367	14.4	37	1.5	125	4.9	204	8.0	208	8.4

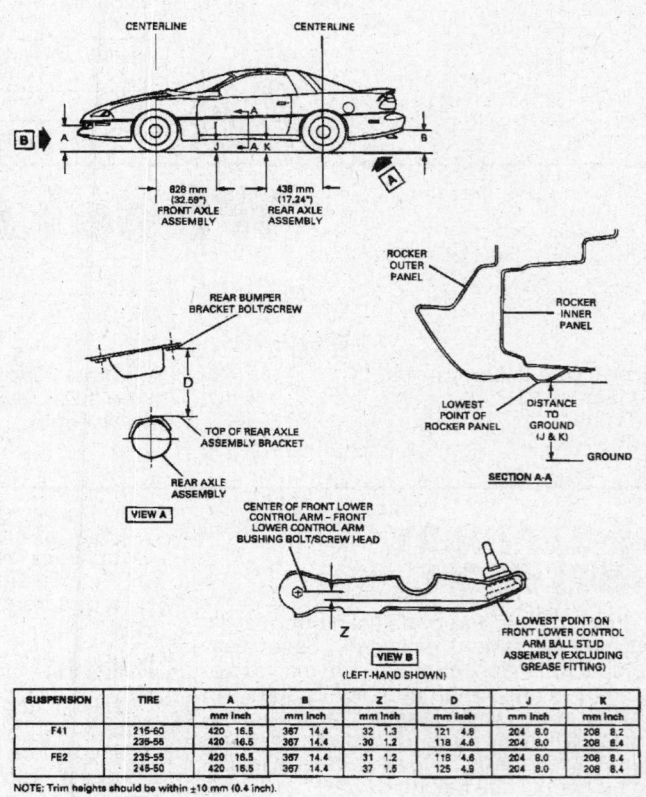

NOTE: Trim heights should be within ±10 mm (0.4 inch).

GC2049600117000X

Fig. 4 Vehicle ride height inspection

VEHICLE RIDE HEIGHT

Trim height should be checked when steering and vibration complaints are not solved through wheel balancing and front/ rear alignments. To measure correct trim height, proceed as follows:

1. Fuel tank is full and tires are inflated properly.
2. Ensure vehicle is on level ground and passenger compartment and trunk is empty except for spare tire.
3. Seats should be in full back position and all doors, hood and rear deck are closed.
   a. All dimensions shown in **Fig. 4** are measured vertical to the ground and should be within ± .4 inches to be considered correct.
   b. Lift front bumper approximately 1½ inches and slowly remove hands, repeat a second time.
   c. Measure dimensions Z, J and A.
   d. Push front bumper down approximately 1½ inches and slowly remove hands, repeat a second time.
   e. Again, measure dimensions Z, J and A.
   f. Calculate trim height by taking the average of high and low measurements
   g. Verify and correct trim heights as necessary.
   h. Repeat procedure for measurements D, K and B.

CATERA

NOTE: Refer To The Rear Of This Manual For Manufacturer's Special Service Tool Suppliers.

INDEX OF SERVICE OPERATIONS

Specifications

GENERAL ENGINE SPECIFICATIONS

Engine	Fuel System	Bore × Stroke, Inches	Comp. Ratio	Net HP @ RPM	Maximum Torque, Ft. Lbs. @ RPM	Minimum Oil Pressure, psi①
3.0L	SMPI	3.3858 × 3.3464	10.0	200 @ 6000	192 @ 3600	21.7

SMPI — Sequential Multi-Port Fuel Injection

① — At idle.

TUNE UP SPECIFICATIONS

Engine	Spark Plug Gap, Inch	Ignition Timing		Idle Speed, RPM	Fuel Pressure, psi	Valve Clearance, Inch
		Firing Order	°BTDC			
3.0L	.035–.043	1-2-3-4-5-6	①	③	④	②

BTDC — Before Top Dead Center

① — Not adjustable. Refer to **Fig. A** for spark plug wire harness routing.

② — Zero lash valve train. Not adjustable.

③ — Refer to Vehicle Emission Control Information (VECI) label in engine compartment.

④ — 1997–98 models, 46–59 psi., 1999–2000 models 40–48 psi.

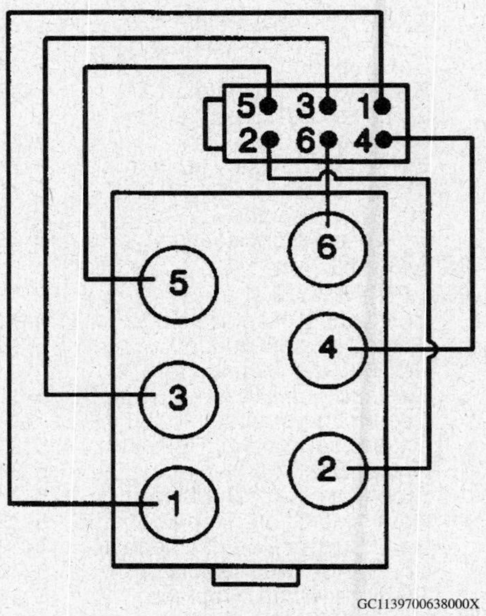

Fig. A

FRONT WHEEL ALIGNMENT SPECIFICATIONS

Year	Caster, Degrees①	Camber, Degrees		Toe, Degrees		Ball Joint Inspection
		Left & Right	Max. Cross Camber	Individual	Total	
1997–98	+3.90 to +4.90	+1.00 to +2.00	+1.00	−.03 to +.13	−.04 to +.26	②
1999–2000	+4.00 to +6.00	−1.15 to 1.35	+1.00	+.04 to +.20	+.09 to +.41	②

① — Not adjustable.

② — Refer to "Front Suspension & Steering" section for inspection procedure.

REAR WHEEL ALIGNMENT SPECIFICATIONS

Year	Camber, Degrees	Toe, Degrees	
		Individual	Total
1997–98	−1.50 to −2.30	−.03 to +.13	−.04 to +.26
1999–2000	−1.08 to −2.42	−.05 to .11	−.10 to .22

FLUID CAPACITIES & COOLING SYSTEM DATA

Engine	Coolant Capacity, Qts.	Coolant Recovery Reservoir Cap Pressure, Lbs.	Thermo. Opening Temp., °F	Fuel Tank Capacity, Gals.	Engine Oil Refill, Qts.①	Trans. Oil Refill, Qts.	Rear Axle Oil, Qts.
3.0L	10	14	194	18	5.3	7	1.74

① — With oil filter change.

LUBRICANT DATA

Year	Engine	Transmission	Rear Axle	Power Steering	Brake System
All	API 10W-30	Dexron III ATF	SAE 80W-90 GL-5	Dexron III ATF	DOT 3

Electrical

NOTE: Refer To "Air Bag System Precautions " Located In The Front Of This Manual For System Disarming & Arming Procedures.

NOTE: Refer To "Computer Relearn Procedure " Located In The Front Of This Manual For Computer Relearn Procedures.

INDEX

PRECAUTIONS

AIR BAG SYSTEMS

Refer to "Air Bag System Precautions" in the front of this manual for system disarming and arming procedures.

BATTERY GROUND CABLE

Prior to service, disconnect battery ground cable and isolate as required.

FUSE PANEL & FLASHER LOCATION

The fuse panel is located below the lefthand side of the instrument panel, near the lower lefthand portion of the steering column. The turn signal flasher is mounted on the relay box, which is below the instrument panel and to the right of the steering column.

FUEL PUMP RELAY LOCATION

The fuel pump relay is located at the lefthand front of the engine compartment, in the Engine Control Module (ECM) housing.

RELAY CENTER LOCATION

The relay centers, **Fig. 1,** are located behind the lefthand side of the instrument panel.

STARTER

REPLACE

1. Raise and support vehicle.
2. Remove terminal nuts and disconnect electrical leads at starter.
3. Remove righthand catalytic converter and righthand engine mount nuts, then lower vehicle.
4. Remove resonance chamber to throttle body ducts, then install engine support fixture tool No. J-28467-A and adapter tool No. J-28467-450, or equivalents.
5. Raise righthand side of engine approximately 1½ inches, then raise and support vehicle.
6. Remove engine mount from bracket and cradle, then remove bracket bolts and position bracket aside to gain working clearance.
7. Remove starter.
8. Reverse procedure to install, noting the following:
   a. **Torque** starter mounting bolts to 44 ft. lbs.
   b. Refer to "3.0L Engine" section for engine mount tightening specifications.
   c. When lowering engine, guide mount into position and ensure locator tab engages in cradle slot.

ALTERNATOR

REPLACE

1. Remove pre-volume chamber.
2. Remove serpentine drive belt from alternator pulley as outlined in "3.0L Engine" section.
3. Raise and support vehicle.
4. Remove terminal nuts and disconnect leads at alternator. **Identify leads for installation reference.**
5. Remove alternator air cooling duct, then the upper nut, **Fig. 2.**
6. Remove lower bolt and nut, then separate alternator from engine and slide upper bolt out through bracket.
7. Lower vehicle, then remove alternator.
8. Reverse procedure to install, noting the following:
   a. **Torque** alternator mounting bolts and nuts to 30 ft. lbs.
   b. Refer to "3.0L Engine" section for serpentine drive belt routing and installation procedure.

COIL PACK

REPLACE

1. Remove wiper arms, then the lefthand and righthand air inlet grilles.
2. Remove wiper motor as outlined under "Wiper Motor, Replace" in this section.
3. Disconnect power brake booster vacuum line at intake plenum and spark plug wiring harness at ignition coil.
4. Disconnect coil electrical connector and remove mounting bolts.
5. Remove coil.
6. Reverse procedure to install. **Torque** coil mounting bolts to 72 inch lbs.

IGNITION LOCK

REPLACE

1. **On 1997 models,** remove steering wheel as outlined under "Steering Wheel, Replace," then the steering column covers and tilt lever as outlined under "Turn Signal Switch, Replace."
2. **On all models,** remove Supplemental Inflatable Restraint (SIR) coil.
3. Insert suitable pointed tool into lock

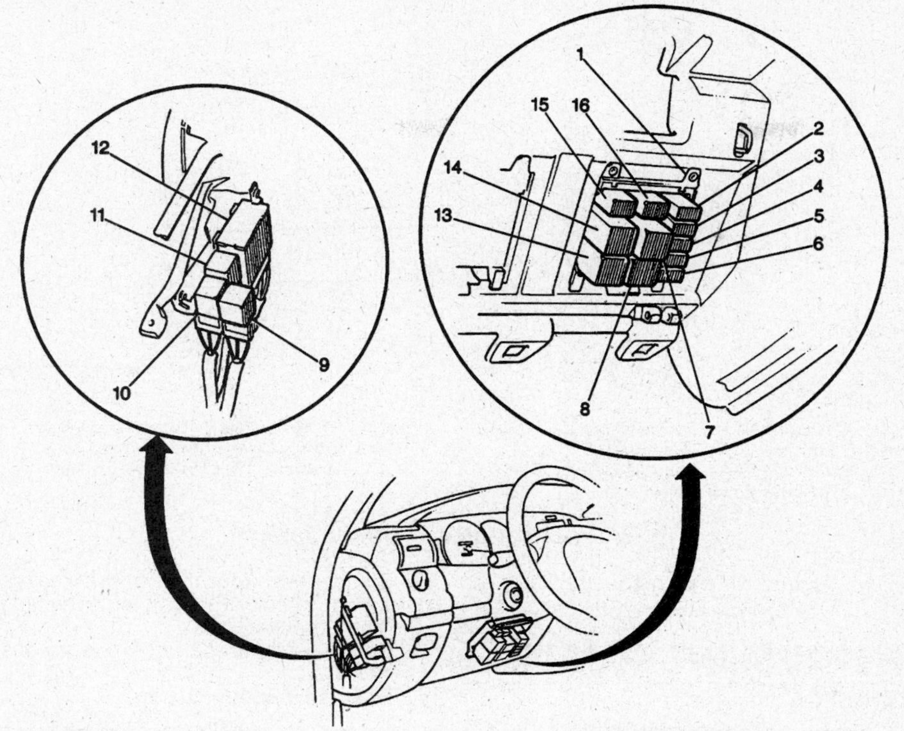

(1) Relay Center
(2) Park Lamp Relay
(3) Low Beam Relay
(4) Not Used
(5) Not Used
(6) LH Headlamp (High Beam) Relay
(7) Turn Signal Lamp Flasher
(8) Horn Relay
(9) Passenger Seat Heater Relay
(10) Driver Seat Heater Relay
(11) Power Steering Control Relay
(12) Multifunction Relay Module
(13) RH Headlamp (High Beam) Relay
(14) Heated Outside Rear View Mirror and Rear Window Defogger Relay
(15) Daytime Running Lamp Relay
(16) Rear Suspension Leveling Air Compressor Relay

GC9049700156000X

Fig. 1 Relay center location

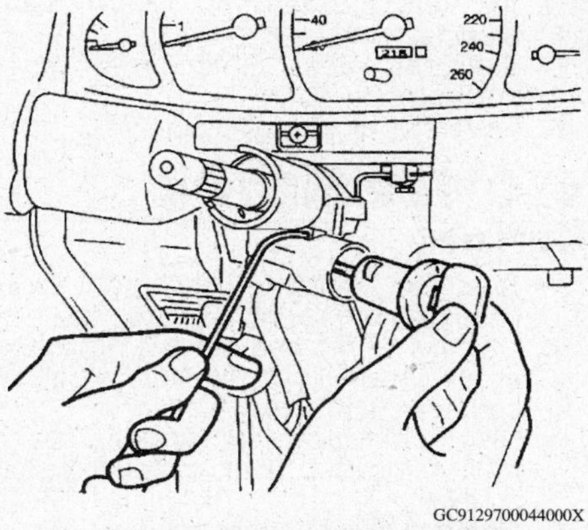

GC9129700044000X

Fig. 3 Ignition lock cylinder removal

cylinder release pin hole, then remove cylinder, **Fig. 3.**

4. Reverse procedure to install. Prior to installation, reset wheel locking device as follows:
   a. Locate locking lever in lock cylinder bore.
   b. Carefully push lever down, **Fig. 4,** until click is heard.

IGNITION SWITCH

REPLACE

1. **On 1997 models,** remove steering wheel as outlined under "Steering Wheel, Replace," then the steering column covers and tilt lever as outlined under "Turn Signal Switch, Replace."
2. **On all models,** remove Supplemental Inflatable Restraint (SIR) coil and ignition switch setscrew.
3. Turn ignition On, then depress connector locking tab with suitable flat-bladed screwdriver.
4. Disconnect electrical connector, then remove switch assembly.
5. Reverse procedure to install.

NEUTRAL SAFETY SWITCH

REPLACE

The transmission control selector switch incorporates the functions of a neutral safety and back-up lamp switch.

1. Apply parking brake and place selector lever in Neutral position.

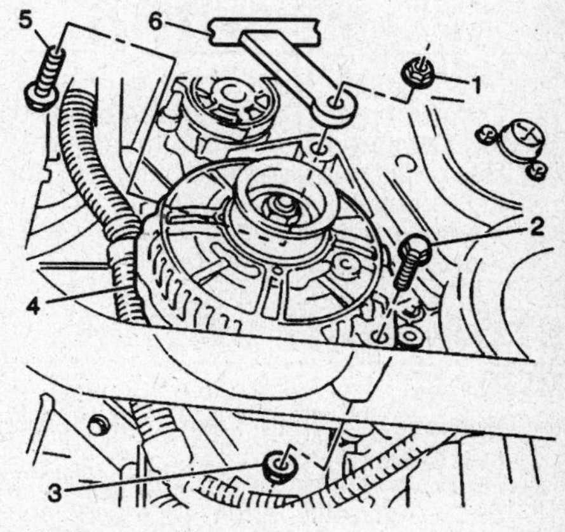

(1) Generator Upper Nut
(2) Generator Lower Bolt
(3) Generator Lower Nut
(4) Generator
(5) Generator Upper Bolt
(6) AIR Injection Crossover Pipe

GC1129700068000X

Fig. 2 Alternator & mounting hardware

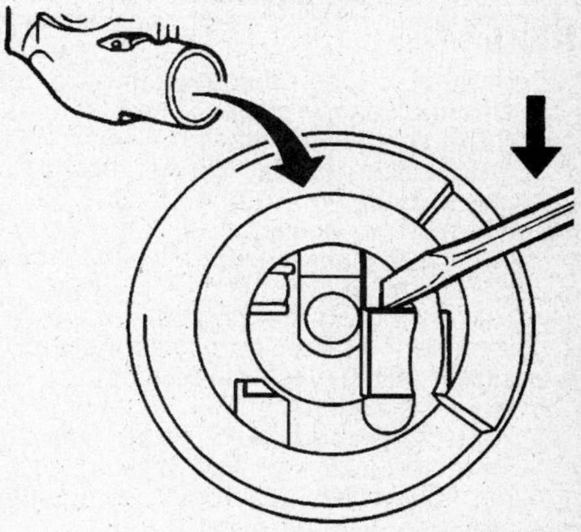

GC9129700045000X

Fig. 4 Steering wheel lock reset

2. Raise and support vehicle, then separate muffler from catalytic converter.
3. Support transmission assembly with suitable jack, then remove transmission crossmember to body bolts.
4. Lower transmission enough to access switch, then remove switch cover.
5. Disconnect switch wire harness at bracket with suitable pry tool.
6. Remove control selector shaft nut and remove lever from shaft.
7. Remove switch bolts, then the switch.
8. Reverse procedure to install, noting the following:
   a. Install bolts loosely, place transmission in Neutral position and align switch shaft and housing slots, then insert 3/32 inch drill bit to ensure alignment is proper during installation.
   b. **Torque** switch bolts to 96–108 inch lbs., crossmember to body bolts to 33 ft. lbs. and muffler to catalytic converter bolts to 30 ft. lbs.

HEADLAMP SWITCH

REPLACE

1. Carefully pry on lefthand side of switch to disengage from instrument panel. Use a suitable cloth to protect trim during removal.
2. Remove switch from instrument panel.
3. Reverse procedure to install.

STOP LIGHT SWITCH

REPLACE

1. Remove lefthand instrument panel sound insulator.
2. Remove lefthand front floor air outlet duct, then disconnect electrical connector at switch.
3. Using suitable angled pliers, compress both locking tabs and remove switch.
4. Reverse procedure to install. **Do not push actuating pin into switch. Pin will adjust itself when brake pedal is released.**

TURN SIGNAL SWITCH

REPLACE

1. Remove caps and screws from upper steering column cover.
2. Carefully thread tilt lever out of tilt mechanism. It may be necessary to use suitable non-marring tool.
3. Remove protective cover from lock cylinder and screws from lower steering column cover.
4. Remove lower steering column cover, then depress tabs and disconnect turn signal switch electrical connector.
5. Remove switch.
6. Reverse procedure to install. Coat tilt lever threads with GM locking compound part No. 12345382, or equivalent, prior to installation.

STEERING WHEEL

REPLACE

1. Remove air bag module Torx screws from rear of steering wheel.
2. Disconnect air bag module electrical connector and carefully remove module from steering wheel, noting the following:
   a. **Do not carry module by wires or connector.**
   b. **When handling module, ensure opening panel points away from all personnel in case of accidental deployment.**
3. Mark relationship between steering wheel and column for alignment during installation.
4. Disengage steering wheel nut locking tab, then remove nut and tab.
5. Using puller tool No. J-1859-A and puller legs tool No. J-36541-A, or equivalents, remove steering wheel from shaft. **Never hammer on steering shaft for any reason.**
6. Reverse procedure to install, noting the following:
   a. **Torque** steering wheel nut to 21 ft. lbs.
   b. **Torque** air bag module screws to 72 inch lbs.

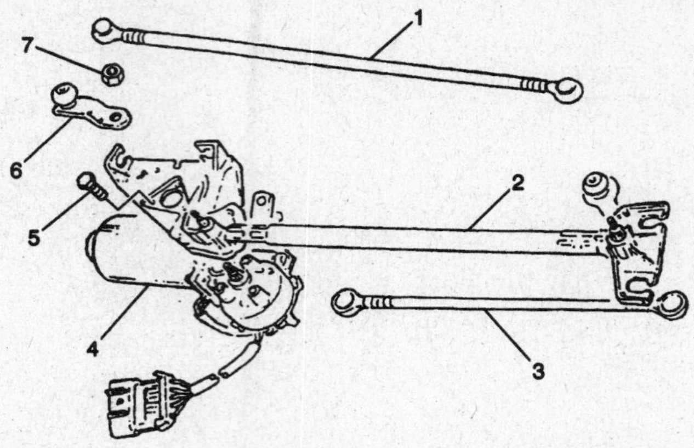

(1) Windshield Wiper Transmission Link (Upper)
(2) Windshield Wiper Transmission
(3) Windshield Wiper Transmission Link (Lower)
(4) Windshield Wiper Motor
(5) Windshield Wiper Motor Bracket Bolt
(6) Windshield Wiper Motor Crank Arm
(7) Windshield Wiper Transmission Nut

GC9029700443000X

Fig. 5 Wiper motor & transmission

INSTRUMENT CLUSTER

REPLACE

1. Remove center air deflector.
2. Remove righthand instrument cluster screw, then turn steering wheel as required to access upper steering column cover screws.
3. Remove screw plugs and screws from upper column cover, then lift cover away from column.
4. Remove screw from upper column cover collar, then the collar.
5. Disengage righthand side of cluster from dash panel, then disconnect cluster electrical connector.
6. Slide cluster assembly toward righthand side until lefthand side clears vent housing, then gently move cluster out of instrument panel.
7. Reverse procedure to install.

RADIO

REPLACE

1. Apply parking brake.
2. Move gear selector lever to full rearward position, then remove instrument panel center bezel.
3. Remove radio mounting screws, then separate radio from HVAC control head bracket.
4. Disconnect antenna lead and electrical harness at radio, then remove radio.
5. Reverse procedure to install.

WIPER MOTOR

REPLACE

1. Remove wiper transmission as outlined under "Wiper Transmission, Replace."
2. Disconnect wiper transmission upper link at wiper motor crank arm and remove wiper transmission nut from motor.
3. Disconnect wiper motor crank arm at wiper motor, **Fig. 5,** then remove motor bracket bolts.
4. Remove wiper motor from wiper transmission.
5. Reverse procedure to install.

WIPER TRANSMISSION

REPLACE

1. Remove air inlet grilles and disconnect brake booster hose.
2. Disconnect wiper motor harness connector.
3. Remove wiper transmission screws, then the wiper motor and transmission as an assembly.
4. Remove wiper transmission upper link, **Fig. 5,** then the wiper motor bracket bolts.
5. Separate wiper motor from wiper transmission.
6. Reverse procedure to install.

BLOWER MOTOR

REPLACE

1. Remove righthand side passenger compartment sound insulator.
2. Disengage clip and remove righthand front floor air outlet, then remove glove compartment.
3. Disconnect supply duct at side air vent, then remove blower motor housing screws.
4. Remove blower motor housing.
5. Remove blower motor to housing attaching screws, then separate motor from housing.
6. Reverse procedure to install.

HEATER CORE

REPLACE

1. Drain engine coolant into suitable container.
2. Disconnect heater hoses at heater core pipes. **Exercise caution when pulling on quick connect fittings.**
3. Remove steering column as outlined under "Steering Columns."

4. Remove front assist handles, windshield pillar moldings and righthand access panel.
5. Remove righthand air deflector and glove compartment.
6. Remove righthand air ducts, then the inflatable restraint module trim cover and fasteners.
7. Disconnect inflatable restraint module orange harness connector, then remove module.
8. Remove center console and center air duct.
9. Remove radio as outlined under "Radio, Replace," then disconnect and remove climate control head.
10. Remove center air deflector, lefthand access panel and lefthand air deflector.
11. Remove headlamp switch as outlined under "Headlamp Switch, Replace."
12. Remove lefthand vent bracket, then remove instrument cluster as outlined under "Instrument Cluster, Replace."
13. Remove fuse and relay panel mounting screws, then the panel.
14. Remove steering column support bracket nuts and instrument panel carrier bolts.
15. Remove headlamp automatic control ambient light sensor, then disconnect carrier wiring harness and disengage clips.
16. Pull carrier assembly rearward to access heater core. **It is not necessary to completely remove carrier assembly or to remove instrument panel wiring harness when servicing heater core.**

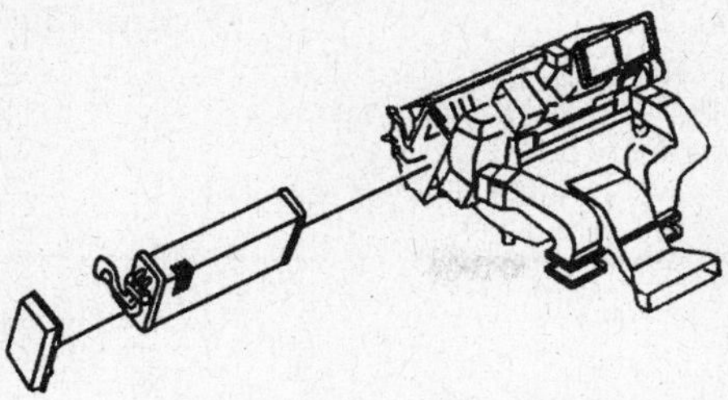

Fig. 6 Evaporator core replacement

17. Remove blower motor and housing as an assembly, then remove heater core pipe bracket.
18. Remove inlet and outlet pipes and instrument panel support brace bolts.
19. Remove instrument panel support brace, support bracket and heater core retaining screw.
20. Remove heater core and plug ports to prevent coolant spillage, then the rubber seal from cavity.
21. Reverse procedure to install, noting the following:
    a. **Torque** passenger air bag module fasteners to 84–96 inch lbs.
    b. When installing steering column, use new shear bolt and **torque** rear support bracket bolt, forward support strap nut and coupler to shaft clamp bolt to 16 ft. lbs. Shear bolt head should snap off at torque of approximately 15 ft. lbs.
    c. When connecting heater hoses, ensure quick disconnects are fully seated and retaining sleeves are in locked position.
    d. Fill and bleed cooling system as outlined in "3.0L Engine" section.

EVAPORATOR CORE

REPLACE

1. Discharge and recover A/C system as outlined under " Air Conditioning."
2. **On 1997 models,** proceed as follows:
    a. Remove evaporator line extension bolt and sound insulator.
    b. Disengage clip and remove lefthand front floor air outlet.
    c. Remove vacuum solenoid and cutoff valve actuator screws, then position actuators aside.
    d. Remove evaporator access panel and evaporator line screw, then disconnect line.
3. **On all models,** remove Thermal Expansion Valve (TXV) screws, then the TXV.
4. Remove steering column as outlined under "Steering Columns."
5. Remove brake pedal and bracket as an assembly.
6. Plug evaporator fittings to prevent oil spillage, then carefully remove evaporator core, **Fig. 6.**
7. Reverse procedure to install, noting the following:
    a. When installing TXV and evaporator line, use new O-rings lubricated with 525 viscosity mineral oil.
    b. Evacuate and recharge A/C system.

3.0L Engine

NOTE: Refer To "Air Bag System Precautions " Located In The Front Of This Manual For System Disarming & Arming Procedures.

NOTE: Refer To "Computer Relearn Procedure " Located In The Front Of This Manual For Computer Relearn Procedures.

INDEX

PRECAUTIONS

AIR BAG SYSTEMS

Refer to "Air Bag System Precautions" in the front of this manual for system disarming and arming procedures.

BATTERY GROUND CABLE

Prior to service, disconnect battery ground cable and isolate as required.

FUEL SYSTEM PRESSURE RELIEF

In order to avoid personal injury and possible vehicle damage, fuel system pressure must be relieved prior to servicing any part of the fuel system.

1. Loosen fuel filler cap to release tank pressure.
2. Connect fuel pressure gauge tool No. J-34730-1A with adapter hose tool No. J-42242, or equivalents, to fuel pressure service port on fuel crossover pipe, **Fig. 1.** Wrap shop towel around fitting to prevent spillage during connection.
3. Place end of bleed hose into an approved gasoline container and open valve to bleed system pressure.
4. Drain residual fuel from gauge tool into container, then connect battery ground cable.

COMPRESSION PRESSURE

INSPECTION

1. Run engine until normal operating temperature is reached.
2. Shut engine off, then disable fuel and ignition systems and remove spark plugs.
3. Disconnect air ducts at throttle body and block throttle plates open.
4. Install compression tester tool No. J-38722, or equivalent, in spark plug hole.
5. Crank engine through at least four compression strokes for test cylinder, noting gauge readings at each stroke.
6. Remove gauge and repeat test for each remaining cylinder. **Minimum pressure for any one cylinder is 100 psi. Compression is acceptable if lowest cylinder reading for all cylinders is within 70% of highest.**
7. Remove block from throttle plates and connect air ducts to throttle body.
8. Install spark plugs and tighten to specifications, then enable fuel and ignition systems.

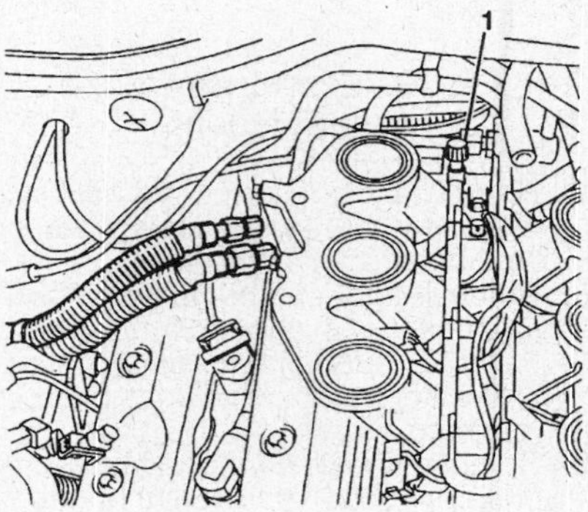

(1) Fuel Pressure Service Connection

GC1069700824000X

Fig. 1 Fuel pressure service port

ENGINE MOUNT

REPLACE

REMOVAL

1. Raise and support vehicle, then remove engine mount lower nut.
2. Lower vehicle and install engine support fixture tool No. J-28467-A, or equivalent, to support engine assembly.
3. Raise and support vehicle once again, then remove engine mount upper nut.
4. Remove engine mount.

INSTALLATION

1. With vehicle raised and supported, install engine mount with upper nut, tighten nut to specifications.
2. Lower vehicle, then lower engine and remove support fixture tool. **Ensure engine mount guide pin engages in crossmember guide hole, Fig. 2.**
3. Raise and support vehicle, then install engine mount lower nut. Tighten to specifications.

ENGINE

REPLACE

1. Drain engine coolant and oil into suitable containers, then remove wiper arms.
2. Remove lefthand and righthand air inlet grilles, then the hood. Mark hood position for installation reference.
3. Remove battery, then recover A/C system as outlined under " Air Conditioning."
4. Disconnect black wiring harness connector and body ground wire at battery ground cable end. Identify harnesses and wires for installation reference.
5. Disconnect four power supply wires at battery positive cable end and identify for installation reference.
6. Siphon power steering fluid from reservoir, then disconnect power steering suction hose and remove clamp.
7. Disconnect power steering discharge hose at pump, then remove threaded brake booster fitting from intake manifold plenum.
8. Disconnect vacuum lines at power brake booster hose. Identify lines for installation reference.
9. Disconnect intake plenum switchover valve vacuum and electrical connections, then remove switchover valve bolts.
10. Remove switchover valve and Engine Control Module (ECM), then remove relays and disconnect wiring harness at electrical center. Identify relays and connections for installation reference.
11. Disconnect blue and white wiring harness connectors, then disengage accelerator and cruise control cable retaining clips.
12. Disconnect accelerator and cruise control cables at throttle body, then relieve fuel system pressure as outlined under "Precautions. "
13. Using suitable back-up tool to prevent fuel rail damage, disconnect and remove fuel supply and return hoses.
14. Disconnect coolant return hose at throttle body and vacuum hose at ventilation chamber purge valve.
15. Disconnect vacuum hose at hot water control valve and coolant reservoir hose at coolant intake pipe.
16. Disconnect heater hoses at heater core pipes.
17. Disconnect Mass Air Flow (MAF) and Intake Air Temperature (IAT) sensor electrical connectors.
18. Disconnect resonance chamber air intake hose at air cleaner housing and MAF sensor, then disconnect Idle Air Control (IAC) inlet hose.
19. Disconnect intake plenum air inlet hoses.
20. Disconnect switchover valve electrical connector and all remaining vacuum connections. Identify connections for installation reference.
21. Remove mounting nuts, then the resonance chamber.
22. Remove radiator as outlined under "Radiator, Replace, " then disconnect A/C compressor/condenser hose bracket at body and position aside.
23. Disconnect A/C compressor hose quick connect fittings at compressor/condenser hose and at evaporator line extension.
24. Install engine support fixture tool No. J-28467-A, or equivalent, then raise and support vehicle.
25. Remove splash shield and disconnect

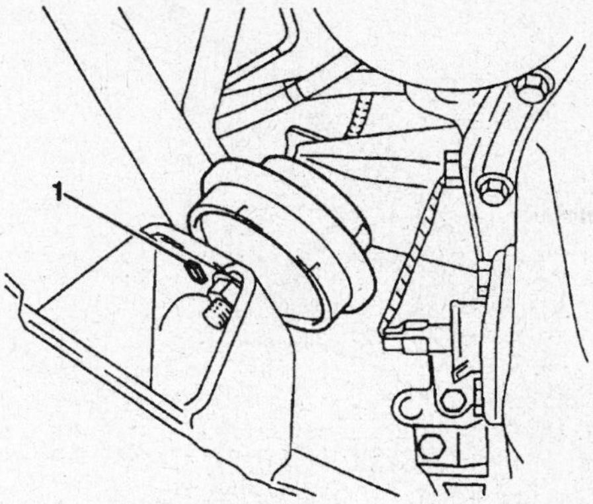

Fig. 2 Engine mount guide pin

A/C compressor electrical connector.
26. Drain transmission fluid into suitable container.
27. Disconnect transmission shift lever rod, then remove propeller shaft coupling bolts.
28. Separate propeller shaft coupling from drive flange using suitable pry tool, then remove transmission oil pan and bellhousing access plugs.
29. Remove flexplate to torque converter bolts. Mark relationship between flexplate and converter for installation reference.
30. Disconnect oil cooler inlet and outlet pipes at center pipes.
31. Disconnect oxygen sensor electrical connectors, then remove catalytic converters.
32. Remove transmission housing to engine oil pan bolts, then install transmission support.
33. Remove transmission crossmember to mount nuts and crossmember to body bolts, then the crossmember.
34. Lower transmission to access transmission housing to engine block bolts, then disconnect ventilation hose at transmission.
35. Disconnect transmission control selector switch, adapter case, main case and speed sensor electrical connectors.
36. With front of engine supported, remove transmission housing to engine block bolts.
37. Remove transmission.
38. Lower vehicle, then connect engine lift chains to three support lift shackles.
39. When weight of engine is supported by engine lift, remove support fixture tool.
40. Remove engine mount nuts, then the engine.
41. Reverse procedure to install, noting the following:
    a. Tighten all engine and transmission mounting bolts and nuts to specifications.
    b. Tighten fuel line connections to specifications, using suitable backup tool to prevent fuel rail damage.
    c. Fill engine, power steering fluid reservoir and transmission with proper amount and type of lubricant.
    d. With vehicle raised and supported, adjust shift lever rod by placing selector lever in Park position and loosening adjustment bolt, **Fig. 3,** to allow adjuster to slide freely. Hold transmission selector lever at rear stop and **torque** adjustment bolt to 72 inch lbs.
    e. Fill and bleed cooling system as outlined under " Cooling System Bleed."
    f. Evacuate and charge A/C system.

INTAKE MANIFOLD

REPLACE

1997–99

1. Relieve fuel system pressure as outlined under " Precautions."
2. Disconnect Idle Air Control (IAC) inlet hose and electrical connector, then the intake plenum air inlet hoses from throttle body.
3. Disengage accelerator and cruise control cable clips from throttle body linkage, then remove accelerator cable from bracket.
4. Remove accelerator and cruise control cable bracket, then disconnect Throttle Position Sensor (TPS) electrical connector.
5. Disconnect brake booster threaded vacuum hose at plenum, then remove wiper arms.
6. Remove lefthand and righthand air inlet grilles, then disconnect vacuum and crankcase ventilation hoses at intake plenum. Identify hoses for installation reference.
7. Remove wiring channel bolts from intake plenum, then disconnect switchover valve solenoid vacuum and electrical connections.
8. Disconnect fuel pressure regulator vacuum hose, then remove intake plenum caps and bolts.
9. Remove throttle body, intake plenum and plenum O-rings.
10. Disconnect fuel supply and return hoses at fuel rail, using suitable backup tool to prevent fuel rail damage.
11. Disconnect fuel injector harness electrical connector, then remove intake manifold mounting bolts.
12. Remove intake manifold, noting the following:
    a. Mask off intake manifold spacer ports to prevent entry of foreign matter.
    b. Clean intake manifold sealing surfaces using suitable nonabrasive tool or solvent.
    c. Ensure machined aluminum surfaces are not damaged.
13. Reverse procedure to install. Tighten intake manifold and plenum bolts to specifications.

2000

1. Remove clamps and intake plenum air inlet hose from throttle body.
2. Remove brake booster vacuum fitting from intake plenum.
3. Remove mounting bolts and position wiring harness channel out of way.

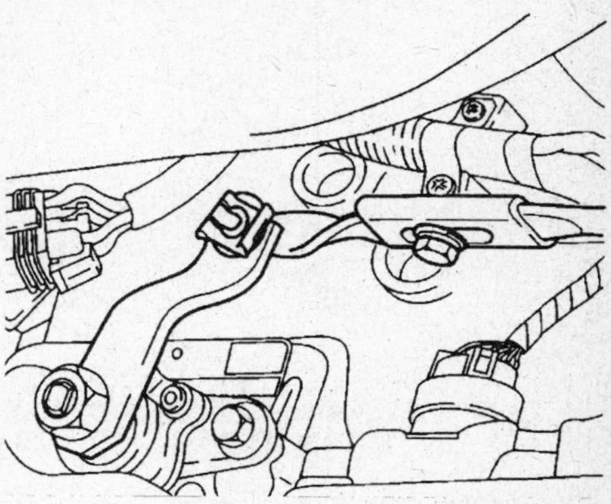

Fig. 3 Shift lever rod adjustment bolt

4. Disconnect switchover valve electrical connections and vacuum hose.
5. Disconnect throttle body control electrical connection.
6. Remove mounting bolts and throttle body from plenum.
7. Remove crankcase vent tube adaptor cover by gently prying up on side.
8. Unclip clamp from righthand side plenum bracket and position heater hoses out of way.
9. Remove caps, mounting bolts and intake plenum. Remove O-rings.
10. Relieve fuel system pressure as outlined under " Precautions."
11. Remove fuel supply and return hoses from fuel rail.
12. Disconnect fuel injector electrical harness and fuel pressure regulator vacuum connections.
13. Remove mounting bolts and intake manifold, noting the following:
    a. Mask intake manifold spacer ports to prevent entry of foreign matter.
    b. Clean intake manifold sealing surfaces using suitable nonabrasive tool or solvent.
    c. Ensure machined aluminum surfaces are not damaged.
14. Reverse procedure to install. Tighten intake manifold and plenum bolts to specifications.

EXHAUST MANIFOLD

REPLACE

LEFTHAND

1. Remove engine as outlined under "Engine, Replace."
2. Remove manifold lower and upper heat shields.
3. Remove Secondary Air Injection (AIR) pipe bolts, then separate pipe from exhaust manifold to access manifold mounting nuts.
4. Remove coolant pipe/engine lift bracket bolt from cylinder head, then remove dipstick tube by pulling firmly upward.
5. Remove exhaust manifold mounting nuts, then the manifold.
6. Reverse procedure to install, noting the following:
    a. Tighten manifold mounting nuts to specifications.
    b. Coat AIR pipe and heat shield bolts

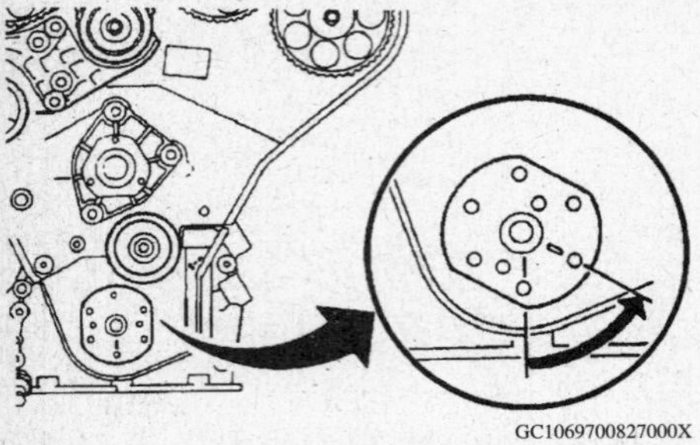

Fig. 4 Crankshaft alignment to 60° BTDC

with GM high temperature anti-seize compound part No. 5613695, or equivalent, then tighten to specifications.

RIGHTHAND

1. Remove transmission as outlined under "Engine, Replace," then remove coolant intake pipe.
2. Raise and support vehicle, then remove exhaust manifold lower heat shield.
3. Remove catalytic converter hanger bolt, then the two lower rear manifold mounting nuts.
4. Lower vehicle, then remove two lower front manifold mounting nuts.
5. Remove exhaust manifold upper heat shield bolts to access Secondary Air Injection (AIR) pipe. Allow shield to remain in place.
6. Remove AIR pipe bolts, then separate pipe from exhaust manifold.
7. Remove three upper manifold mounting nuts, then the manifold.
8. Reverse procedure to install, noting the following:
   a. Tighten manifold mounting nuts to specifications.
   b. Coat AIR pipe and heat shield bolts with GM high temperature anti-seize compound part No. 5613695, or equivalent, then tighten to specifications.

CYLINDER HEAD

REPLACE

LEFT

1. Remove intake plenum as outlined under "Intake Manifold, Replace."
2. Remove resonance chamber as outlined under "Engine, Replace" and intake manifold as outlined under " Intake Manifold, Replace."
3. Remove intake manifold spacer, coolant bridge and lefthand valve cover.
4. Remove front timing belt cover and timing belt as outlined under "Timing Belt, Replace."
5. **Position crankshaft at 60° Before Top Dead Center (BTDC), Fig. 4,** to prevent valve and piston interference when cylinder head is installed.
6. Remove timing belt tensioner bracket.
7. Remove gears from intake and exhaust camshaft Nos. 3 and 4, then from Nos. 1 and 2 as outlined under "Camshaft, Replace."
8. Remove water pump as outlined under "Water Pump, Replace."
9. Remove timing belt rear cover.
10. Disconnect camshaft sensor electrical connector, then remove exhaust camshaft No. 4 as outlined under "Camshaft, Replace."
11. Remove coolant pipe/engine lift bracket from cylinder head, then grasp dipstick tube firmly and pull upward to remove.
12. Disconnect upper radiator hose from coolant intake pipe, then twist pipe to remove.
13. Separate lefthand exhaust manifold from engine block as outlined under "Exhaust Manifold, Replace." **Because this procedure is performed with engine in vehicle, exhaust manifold cannot be completely removed. It is not necessary to remove engine to service manifold during this procedure.**
14. Disconnect ignition coil electrical connector, then remove cylinder head bolts in reverse order of tightening sequence outlined, **Fig. 5. Discard old cylinder head bolts. They are not reusable.**
15. Lift cylinder head off engine and remove gasket, then remove ignition coil and bracket from head.
16. Reverse procedure to install, noting the following:
    a. **Ensure crankshaft is still at 60° BTDC, Fig. 4, to prevent valve and piston interference when cylinder head is installed.**
    b. A new cylinder head gasket must be installed. Ensure " OBEN/TOP" imprint on gasket faces front of engine.
    c. **Torque** new cylinder head bolts to 18 ft. lbs. in sequence, **Fig. 5.**
    d. Tighten bolts an additional 90° in sequence.
    e. Tighten bolts an additional 90° in sequence.
    f. Tighten bolts another 90° in sequence.
    g. Tighten bolts an additional 15° in sequence.
    h. Install new sealing rings on coolant pipe and lubricate with coolant.
    i. Install new valve cover seals and O-rings as outlined under " Valve Cover, Replace."

RIGHTHAND

1. Remove resonance chamber as outlined under "Engine, Replace."
2. Remove intake plenum and manifold as outlined under " Intake Manifold, Replace," then remove manifold spacer.
3. Remove coolant bridge and righthand valve cover, then remove front timing belt cover and timing belt as outlined under "Timing Belt, Replace."
4. Remove timing belt tensioner bracket.
5. **Position crankshaft at 60° Before Top Dead Center (BTDC), Fig. 4, to prevent valve and piston interference when cylinder head is installed.**
6. Remove camshaft gears for shaft Nos. 3 and 4, then for shaft Nos. 1 and 2 as outlined under "Camshaft, Replace."
7. Remove water pump as outlined under "Water Pump, Replace," then remove rear timing belt cover.
8. Remove exhaust camshaft No. 1 as outlined under " Camshaft, Replace."
9. Remove coolant intake pipe.
10. Separate exhaust manifold from cylinder head as outlined under "Exhaust Manifold, Replace," then remove cylinder head bolts in reverse order of tightening sequence outlined, **Fig. 5. Discard old cylinder head bolts. They are not reusable.**
11. Remove cylinder head and gasket from engine block.
12. Reverse procedure to install, noting the following:
    a. **Ensure crankshaft is still at 60° BTDC, Fig. 4, to prevent valve and piston interference when cylinder head is installed.**
    b. A new cylinder head gasket must be installed. Ensure " OBEN/TOP" imprint on gasket faces rear of engine.
    c. **Torque** new cylinder head bolts to 18 ft. lbs. in sequence, **Fig. 5.**
    d. Tighten bolts an additional 90° in sequence.
    e. Tighten bolts an additional 90° in sequence.
    f. Tighten bolts an additional 90° in sequence.
    g. Tighten bolts an additional 15° in sequence.
    h. Install new valve cover seals and O-rings as outlined under " Valve Cover, Replace."

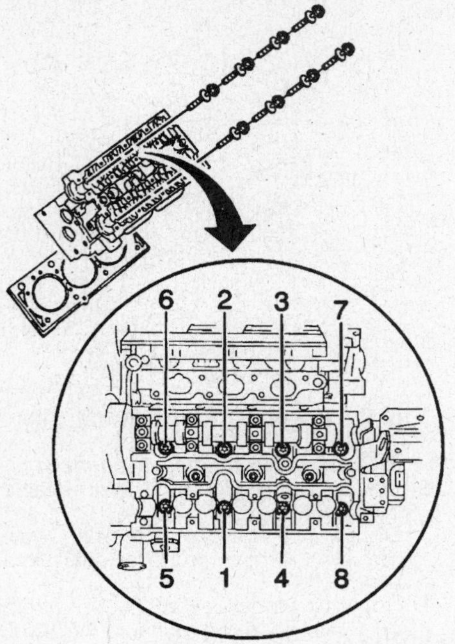

Fig. 5 Cylinder head bolt tightening sequence

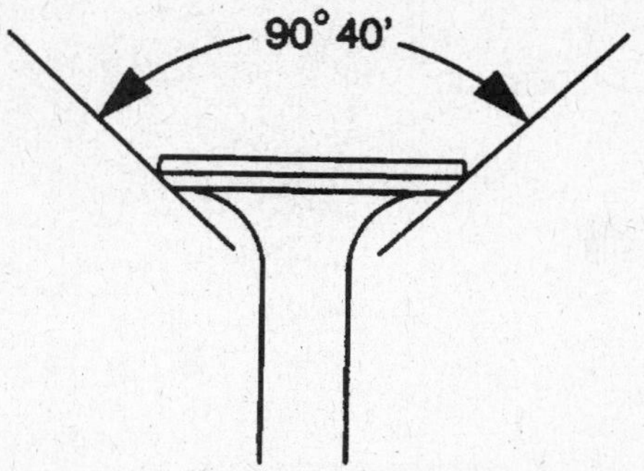

Fig. 6 Valve grinding angle

COMPONENT SERVICE

CYLINDER HEAD

Disassemble

1. Remove lifters and store in suitable rack. Identify for installation reference.
2. Using valve spring compressor tool No. J-8062 and adapter tool No. J-41774, or equivalents, compress valve springs and carefully remove stem keys.
3. Remove valve stem caps, springs and seals.
4. Remove valve spring seats and valves from cylinder head. Store valves in suitable rack and identify for installation reference.
5. Using suitable brush, clean carbon from combustion chambers and valve train components. Do not scratch combustion chamber surface.
6. Clean valve guides, then use buffing wheel to clean valve stems and heads.
7. Clean cylinder head bolt holes.

Inspection

1. Inspect cylinder head exhaust ports, combustion chambers and water chamber for cracks. Most cracks occur between exhaust valves or between exhaust valve and spark plug orifice.
2. Inspect valves for burned heads, cracked facing and damaged stems.
3. Ensure valve seats are tight and are not cracked.
4. Inspect valve springs for squareness as follows:
   a. Place spring on level surface next to square.
   b. Rotate spring and measure deviation from square.
   c. If deviation is .062 inch or less, spring squareness is satisfactory. If not, spring should be replaced.
5. Using valve spring tester tool No. J-9666, or equivalent, measure valve spring tension. Replace spring if length is less than 1.338 inches when 56.6 lbs. of force is applied.
6. Measure valve stem to guide clearance as follows:
   a. Clamp dial indicator tool No. J-8001, or equivalent, on exhaust port side of cylinder head.
   b. Position indicator plunger where side to side valve stem movement will be indicated.
   c. With valve protruding .39 inch above seat, move valve stem from side to side with light pressure and note clearance reading.
   d. Intake valve clearance should be .0011–.0022 inch and exhaust valve clearance should be .0015–.0026 inch. If not, valve and/or valve guide must be serviced. Proceed to next step.
7. If valve stem to guide clearance is not as indicated, measure valve stem diameter in three locations, noting the following:
   a. If intake valve stem diameter is below .2344 inch at narrowest point, replace valve.
   b. If exhaust valve stem diameter is below .2340 inch at narrowest point, replace valve.
   c. If valve stem diameters are above minimum specification, valve guides should be serviced. Proceed to next step.
8. If valve stem to guide clearance is not as indicated and valve stem diameter is satisfactory, use oversize valves and ream valve guides as follows:
   a. Clean guide thoroughly and insert reamer tool No. J-42096, or equivalent, from top of cylinder head.
   b. Rotate reamer with light hand pressure until it is completely through valve guide.
   c. Remove reamer, then clean valve guide and combustion chamber to ensure all metal shavings are removed.
9. If clearances are satisfactory and original valves are to be used, valves and seats can be ground to ensure valve seating is optimal. Note the following:
   a. Valves should be ground at 90 ⅔° angle, **Fig. 6,** and seats should be ground at 90° angle.
   b. Intake valve seat width should be .039–.055 inch and exhaust valve seat width should be .055–.070 inch.
   c. Control valve seat widths with 30° and 60° stones, **Fig. 7.**

Assemble

1. Lubricate valve stems with clean engine oil, then install valves.
2. Install valve spring seat, then use seal installer tool No. J-41775, or equivalent, to install new valve seal into cylinder head. **New seal sets provide protective sleeve to prevent valve stem grooves from damaging seals during installation.**
3. Install valve springs and caps, then compress springs using spring compressor tool No. J-8062 and adapter tool No. J-41774, or equivalents.
4. Install valve stem keys and use suitable grease to hold them in place while removing spring compressor and adapter. Ensure keys seat properly in upper groove.
5. Install lifters.

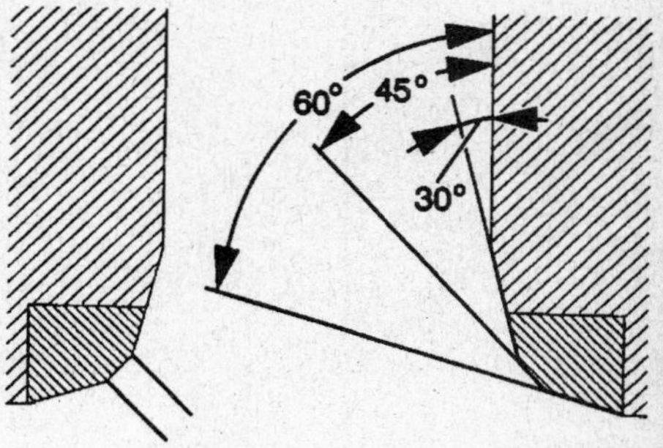

Fig. 7 Valve seat angle

VALVE COVER

REPLACE

1997

1. Remove intake plenum and manifold as outlined under " Intake Manifold, Replace."
2. Disconnect spark plug wires at plugs and disengage from routing clips.
3. If lefthand valve cover is to be removed, remove oil filler spout by unlocking tab and twisting counterclockwise.
4. Remove valve cover mounting bolts, then the cover and seals. Discard seals and O-rings.
5. Reverse procedure to install, noting the following:
   a. Use new seals and O-rings lightly coated with clean engine oil.
   b. Apply thin film of GM silicone sealer part No. 12345997, or equivalent, to front and rear of seals, **Fig.8.**
   c. Tighten valve cover bolts to specifications.

1998–2000

1. Remove throttle body retaining bolts, then the throttle body and gasket.
2. Remove crankcase vent tube adapter.
3. Remove intake plenum retaining bolts, then the plenum.
4. Remove intake manifold as outlined under "Intake Manifold, Replace."
5. **On lefthand side valve cover,** remove oil filler spout by unlocking tab and twisting counter clockwise.
6. Disconnect camshaft position sensor electrical connection and plastic ties.
7. **On both valve covers,** remove spark plug boots from spark plugs, then the wires from routing retainers.
8. Remove knock sensor wire harness bracket nut, then the valve cover retaining bolts.
9. Remove valve cover. **Ensure all eight sealing O-rings are accounted for.**

VALVE GUIDES

Refer to "Component Service" for valve guide service information.

VALVE SEATS

Refer to "Component Service" for valve seat service information.

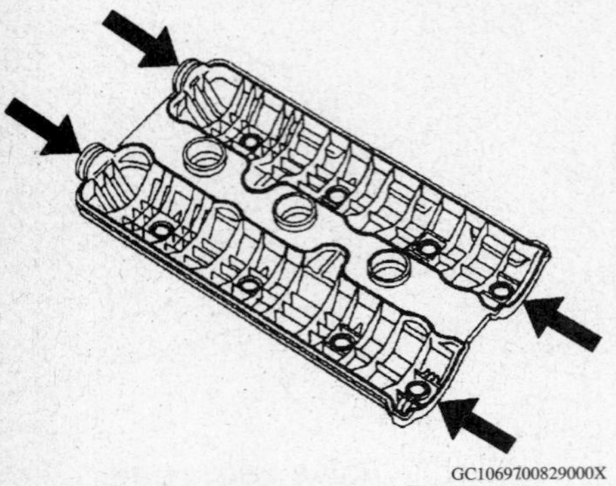

Fig. 8 Valve cover sealant application points

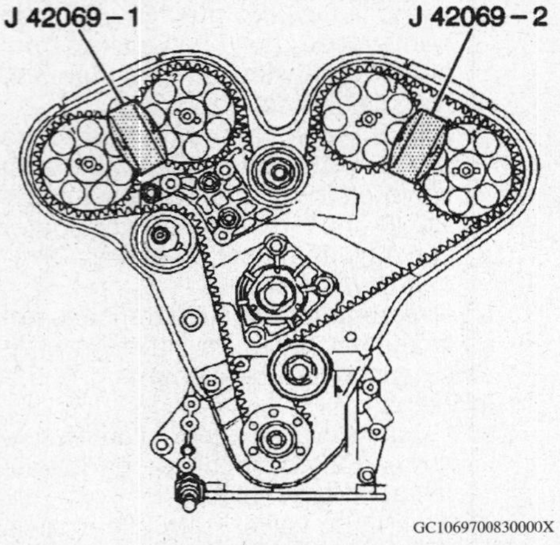

Fig. 9 Camshaft gear locking tool installation

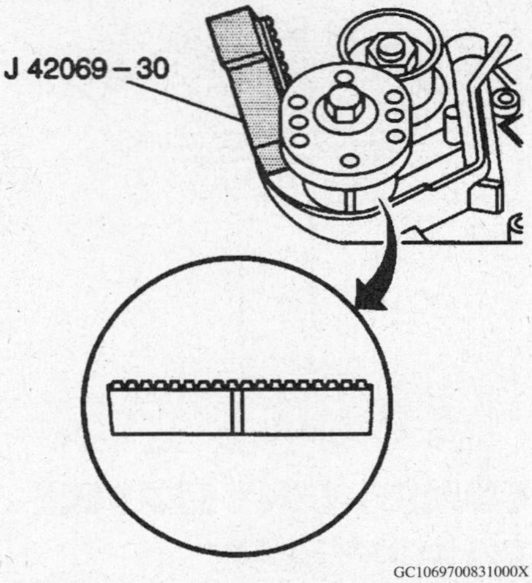

Fig. 10 Timing belt & pinch tool installation

FRONT COVER

REPLACE

Refer to "Timing Belt, Replace" for timing belt front cover replacement procedures.

TIMING BELT

REPLACE

With the timing belt removed, avoid turning the camshaft or crankshaft. If movement is required, exercise extreme caution to avoid valve damage caused by piston contact.

REMOVAL

1. Remove resonance chamber as outlined under "Engine, Replace."
2. Raise and support vehicle, then remove splash shield.
3. Remove Secondary Air Injection (AIR) crossover pipe bracket nut from alternator bolt. Use suitable back-up wrench on bolt.
4. Remove AIR crossover pipe bushing nut from bracket and pipe clamps from rubber hose connections, then separate pipe from rubber hose.
5. Lower vehicle, then remove AIR diverter hose clamp and crossover pipe.
6. Loosen, but do not remove, water pump and power steering pump pulley bolts, then remove A/C compressor hose support strap bolt from AIR crossover bracket.
7. Remove serpentine drive belt as outlined under " Serpentine Drive Belt."
8. Remove righthand lower wiring harness extension by releasing clips and pulling forward, then separate harness from channel. Note routing for installation reference.
9. Remove water pump and power steering pump pulley bolts, then the pulleys.
10. Remove serpentine drive belt tensioner, front timing belt cover and transfer wiring harness channel.
11. Remove harmonic balancer from crankshaft drive gear, then turn crankshaft to 60° Before Top Dead Center (BTDC), **Fig. 4.**
12. Install timing belt alignment kit tool No. J-42069-10, or equivalent, on crankshaft drive gear with knurled bolt.
13. Using crank hub socket tool No. J-42098, or equivalent, carefully turn crankshaft in direction of normal operation until alignment tool lever contacts water pump pulley flange, then secure lever to flange.
14. **Ensure crankshaft is not positioned 180° from desired alignment. Camshaft gear alignment marks must align with notches on timing belt rear cover.**
15. Install camshaft gear locking tools, **Fig. 9,** to lock camshaft gears. If gear teeth interfere with tool installation, proceed as follows:
    a. Loosen corresponding timing belt idler pulley and turn eccentric until tool can be inserted.
    b. Tighten idler pulley to specifications.
16. Loosen timing belt tensioner and remove timing belt.

INSTALLATION

1. Remove timing belt alignment kit tool No. J-42069-10, or equivalent, then raise and support vehicle.
2. Begin installing timing belt at crankshaft drive gear. Ensure Top Dead Center (TDC) mark is aligned with oil pump and belt drive gear marks, **Fig. 10.**
3. Use timing belt alignment kit pinch tool No. J-42069-30, or equivalent, to prevent belt from jumping splines, **Fig.10.**
4. Lower vehicle and route belt through idler pulleys for camshaft Nos. 3 and 4, then through gears for camshaft Nos. 3 and 4.
5. If timing belt marks do not align with marks on camshaft gears and timing belt rear cover, loosen timing belt idler pulley or move camshaft gears slightly with cam locking tools still in place. If idler pulley is loosened, tighten only until snug.
6. If belt deflection between camshaft No. 4 gear and idler pulley for camshaft Nos. 3 and 4, **Fig. 11,** exceeds .4 inch, adjust by rotating idler pulley eccentric counterclockwise with timing belt alignment kit tool No. J-42069-40, or equivalent.
7. **After adjustment, ensure belt deflection does not exceed .4 inch.**
8. Route timing belt through idler pulley for camshaft Nos. 1 and 2, then through camshaft gears.
9. If timing belt marks, **Fig. 12,** do not align with marks on camshaft gears and timing belt rear cover, loosen timing belt idler pulley or move camshaft gears slightly with cam locking tools still in place. Note the following:
    a. Using alignment kit tool No. J-42069-40, or equivalent, turn idler pulley eccentric for camshaft Nos. 1 and 2 counterclockwise and apply enough tension to prevent belt from slipping off gears.
    b. If idler pulley is loosened, tighten only until snug.
10. Route timing belt through timing belt tensioner, then apply initial belt tension by rotating tensioner eccentric counterclockwise until marks are set, **Fig. 13.**
11. Tighten timing belt tensioner nut to specifications, then ensure timing belt alignment marks are properly aligned with marks on camshaft gears, rear timing belt cover and oil pump housing.
12. Remove timing belt kit pinch tool and camshaft locking tools, then turn engine through two full revolutions in direction of normal operation and stop at 60° Before Top Dead Center (BTDC), **Fig. 4.**
13. Install timing belt alignment kit tool No. J-42069-10, or equivalent, on crankshaft drive gear with knurled bolt.
14. Using crank hub socket tool No. J-42098, or equivalent, carefully turn crankshaft in direction of normal operation until alignment tool lever contacts water pump pulley flange, then secure lever to flange.
15. Inspect alignment marks once again, noting the following:
    a. Timing belt alignment marks will no longer be aligned with camshaft gear marks after one or more engine revolutions.
    b. **It is extremely important that camshaft gear marks and rear timing belt cover notches are**

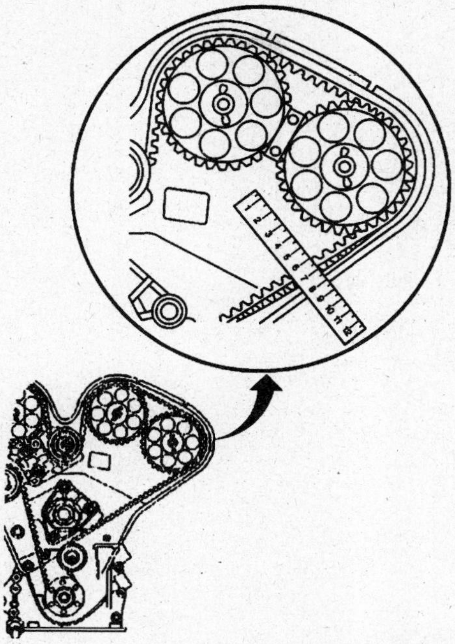

Fig. 11 Timing belt deflection measurement

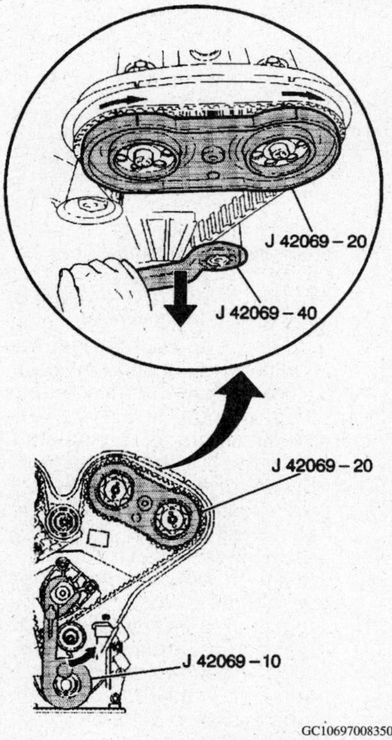

Fig. 14 Camshaft gear Nos. 3 & 4 aligned BTDC

aligned and that crankshaft drive gear and oil pump housing marks are also aligned.

16. To determine if timing belt needs adjustment, proceed as follows:
    a. Install gauge tool No. J-42069-20, or equivalent, on camshaft gear Nos. 3 and 4.
    b. If gear marks do not align perfectly with marks on gauge tool, belt adjustment will be required.
    c. If gear marks are perfectly aligned with marks on gauge tool, install tool on camshaft gear Nos. 1 and 2.
    d. If gear marks do not align perfectly with marks on gauge tool, belt adjustment will be required.
    e. If gear marks are perfectly aligned with marks on gauge tool, belt adjustment will not be required and camshaft gear alignment steps can be bypassed.
    f. If it is determined that belt adjustment will be required, camshaft Nos. 3 and 4 must be adjusted first.
17. If marks on camshaft gear Nos. 3 and 4 aligned to left (BTDC) of marks on gauge tool, correct alignment as follows:
    a. Loosen timing belt idler pulley for camshaft gear Nos. 3 and 4.
    b. Use alignment kit tool No. J-42069-40, or equivalent, to turn pulley eccentric counterclockwise until marks on camshaft gears and gauge tool align perfectly.
    c. Tighten timing belt idler pulley bolt to specifications.
    d. Remove alignment kit tools and gauge tool, then turn crankshaft two full revolutions in direction of normal engine operation and stop at 60° BTDC, **Fig. 4.**

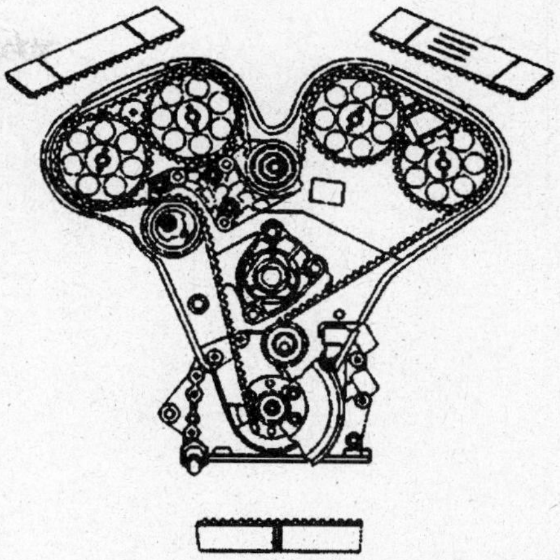

Fig. 12 Timing belt alignment marks

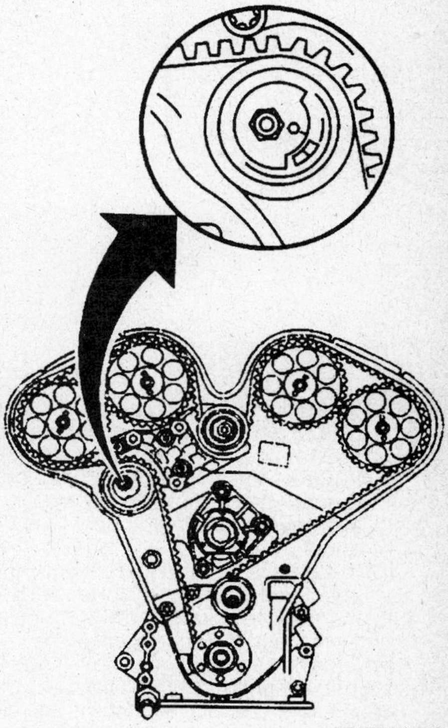

Fig. 13 Timing belt tensioner initial adjustment

e. Install timing belt alignment kit tool No. J-42069-10, or equivalent, on crankshaft drive gear with knurled bolt.
f. Using crank hub socket tool No. J-42098, or equivalent, carefully turn crankshaft in direction of normal operation until alignment tool lever contacts water pump pulley flange, then secure lever to flange.
g. Install gauge tool No. J-42069-20,

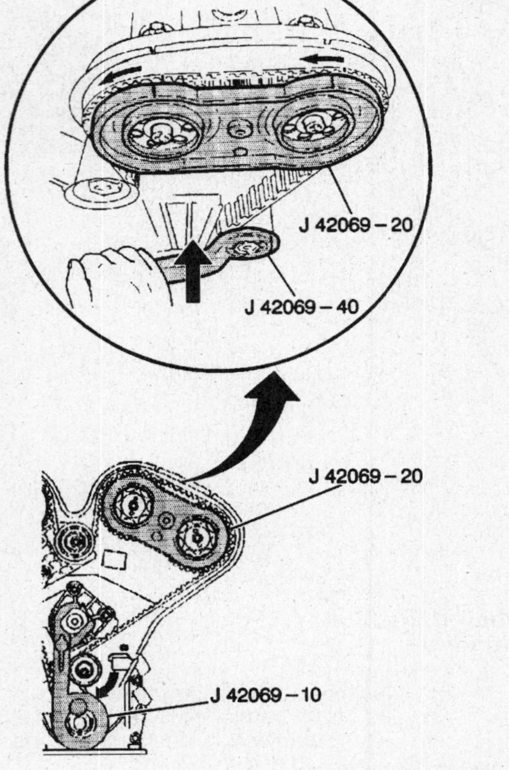

Fig. 15 Camshaft gear Nos. 3 & 4 aligned after TDC

or equivalent, on camshaft gear Nos. 3 and 4 to inspect alignment, **Fig.14.**

h. If marks are not perfectly aligned, repeat procedure for correcting alignment of camshaft gear Nos. 3 and 4.
i. If marks are perfectly aligned, inspect and, if required, correct alignment of camshaft gear Nos. 1 and 2 as outlined in subsequent steps.

18. If marks on camshaft gear Nos. 3 and 4 aligned to right (after TDC) of marks on gauge tool, correct alignment as follows:
   a. Loosen timing belt idler pulley for camshaft gear Nos. 3 and 4.
   b. Use alignment kit tool No. J-42069-40, or equivalent, to turn pulley eccentric clockwise until marks on camshaft gears travel to farthest point toward marks on gauge tool.
   c. Once farthest adjustment point is reached, tighten idler pulley bolt to specifications.
   d. Remove alignment kit tools and gauge tool, then turn crankshaft two full revolutions in direction of normal engine operation and stop at 60° BTDC, **Fig. 4.**
   e. Install timing belt alignment kit tool No. J-42069-10, or equivalent, on crankshaft drive gear with knurled bolt.
   f. Using crank hub socket tool No. J-42098, or equivalent, carefully turn crankshaft in direction of normal operation until alignment tool lever contacts water pump pulley flange, then secure lever to flange.
   g. Install gauge tool No. J-42069-20, or equivalent, on camshaft gear Nos. 3 and 4 to inspect alignment, **Fig.15.**
   h. If marks are not perfectly aligned, repeat procedure for correcting alignment of camshaft gear Nos. 3 and 4.
   i. If marks are perfectly aligned, inspect and, if required, correct alignment of camshaft gear Nos. 1 and 2 as outlined in subsequent steps.
19. When proper alignment of camshaft gear Nos. 3 and 4 has been verified, inspect alignment of camshaft gear Nos. 1 and 2 with gauge tool No. J-42069-20, or equivalent.
20. If marks on camshaft gear Nos. 1 and 2 aligned to left (BTDC) of marks on gauge tool, proceed as follows:
   a. Loosen timing belt idler pulley for camshaft gear Nos. 1 and 2.
   b. Use alignment kit tool No. J-42069-40, or equivalent, to turn pulley eccentric counterclockwise until marks on camshaft gears and gauge tool align perfectly.

c. Tighten timing belt idler pulley bolt to specifications.
d. Remove alignment kit tools and gauge tool, then turn crankshaft two full revolutions in direction of normal engine operation and stop at 60° BTDC, **Fig. 4.**
e. Install timing belt alignment kit tool No. J-42069-10, or equivalent, on crankshaft drive gear with knurled bolt.
f. Using crank hub socket tool No. J-42098, or equivalent, carefully turn crankshaft in direction of normal operation until alignment tool lever contacts water pump pulley flange, then secure lever to flange.
g. Install gauge tool No. J-42069-20, or equivalent, on camshaft gear Nos. 1 and 2 to inspect alignment, **Fig.16.**
h. If marks are not perfectly aligned, repeat procedure for correcting alignment of camshaft gear Nos. 1 and 2.
i. If marks are perfectly aligned, adjust timing belt tensioner and complete installation as outlined in subsequent steps.

21. If marks on camshaft gear Nos. 1 and 2 aligned to right (after TDC) of marks on gauge tool, correct alignment as follows:
    a. Loosen timing belt idler pulley for camshaft gear Nos. 1 and 2.
    b. Use alignment kit tool No. J-42069-40, or equivalent, to turn pulley eccentric clockwise until marks on camshaft gears travel to farthest point toward marks on gauge tool.
    c. Once farthest adjustment point is reached, tighten idler pulley bolt to specifications.
    d. Remove alignment kit tools and gauge tool, then turn crankshaft two full revolutions in direction of normal engine operation and stop at 60° BTDC, **Fig. 4.**
    e. Install timing belt alignment kit tool No. J-42069-10, or equivalent, on crankshaft drive gear with knurled bolt.
    f. Using crank hub socket tool No. J-42098, or equivalent, carefully turn crankshaft in direction of normal operation until alignment tool lever contacts water pump pulley flange, then secure lever to flange.
    g. Install gauge tool No. J-42069-20, or equivalent, on camshaft gear Nos. 1 and 2 to inspect alignment, **Fig.17.**
    h. If marks are not perfectly aligned, repeat procedure for correcting alignment of camshaft gear Nos. 1 and 2.
    i. If marks are perfectly aligned, adjust timing belt tensioner and complete installation as outlined in subsequent steps.
22. Loosen timing belt tensioner eccentric locking nut, then turn eccentric until marks are set turn, **Fig. 18.**
23. Tighten timing belt tensioner locking nut to specifications, then remove all inspection tools.
24. Perform final inspection as follows:
    a. Turn crankshaft two full revolutions in direction of normal engine operation and stop at 60° BTDC, **Fig.4.**
    b. Install timing belt alignment kit tool No. J-42069-10, or equivalent, on crankshaft drive gear with knurled bolt.
    c. Using crank hub socket tool No. J-42098, or equivalent, carefully turn crankshaft in direction of normal operation until alignment tool lever contacts water pump pulley flange, then secure lever to flange.
    d. **Reference marks on both sets of camshaft gears must be perfectly aligned with marks on gauge tool No. J-42069-20, or equivalent.**
    e. If marks are not aligned, repeat preceding adjustment operations as required.
    f. If marks are aligned, no further belt or tensioner adjustment is required. Continue installation procedure.
25. Ensure timing belt idler pulley bolts are tightened to specifications and all inspection tools are removed.
26. Install harmonic balancer on crankshaft drive gear and tighten bolts to specifications.
27. Install timing belt front cover and serpentine drive belt tensioner. Tighten bolts to specifications.
28. Install power steering and water pump pulleys and tighten to specifications, then route wiring harness into channel.
29. Install wiring harness channel cover and extension, then install serpentine drive belt as outlined under "Serpentine Drive Belt."
30. Install A/C compressor hose support strap bolt in Secondary Air Injection (AIR) crossover bracket and tighten to specifications.

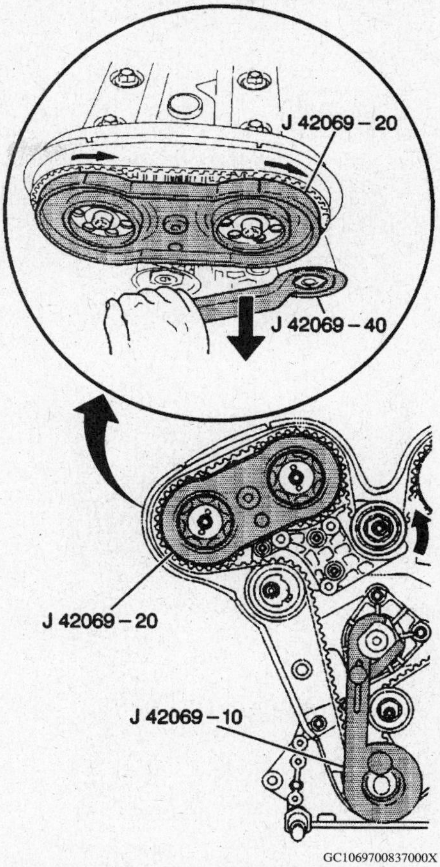

Fig. 16 Camshaft gear Nos. 1 & 2 aligned BTDC

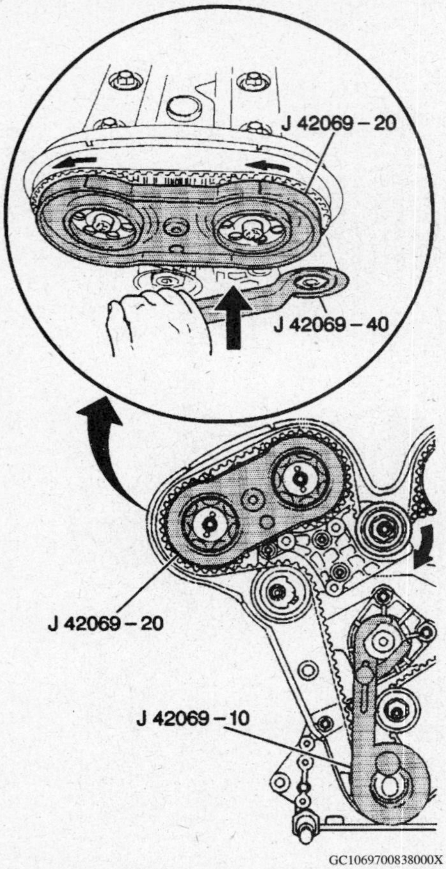

Fig. 17 Camshaft gear Nos. 1 & 2 aligned after TDC

30. Connect AIR diverter hose and install clamps, then raise and support vehicle.
31. Connect AIR crossover pipe to rubber hose and install clamps.
32. Install AIR crossover pipe bushing nut on alternator bolt and tighten to specifications.
33. Install AIR crossover pipe support bracket nut and tighten to specifications. Use suitable back-up wrench on alternator bolt.
34. Install splash shield, then lower vehicle.
35. Install resonance chamber as outlined under "Engine, Replace," then connect battery ground cable.

CAMSHAFT

REPLACE

REMOVAL

1. Remove intake plenum as outlined under "Intake Manifold, Replace."
2. Remove resonance chamber as outlined under "Engine, Replace" and appropriate valve cover as outlined under "Valve Cover, Replace."
3. Remove timing belt and front cover as outlined under "Timing Belt, Replace," then turn crankshaft counterclockwise to 60° BTDC, **Fig. 4.**
4. Install camshaft gear locking tool Nos. J-42069-1 and J-42069-2, or equivalents, to lock gears in place, then remove gear bolt.
5. Remove camshaft gear, noting the following:
   a. If righthand intake (No. 2) camshaft is being serviced, ensure camshaft pin points toward 11 o'clock position.
   b. If lefthand intake (No. 3) camshaft is being serviced, ensure camshaft pin points toward seven o'clock position.
   c. If lefthand exhaust (No. 4) camshaft is being serviced, ensure camshaft pin points toward 12 o'clock position and disconnect camshaft sensor electrical connector.
   d. Ensure camshaft is under no pressure from lifters.

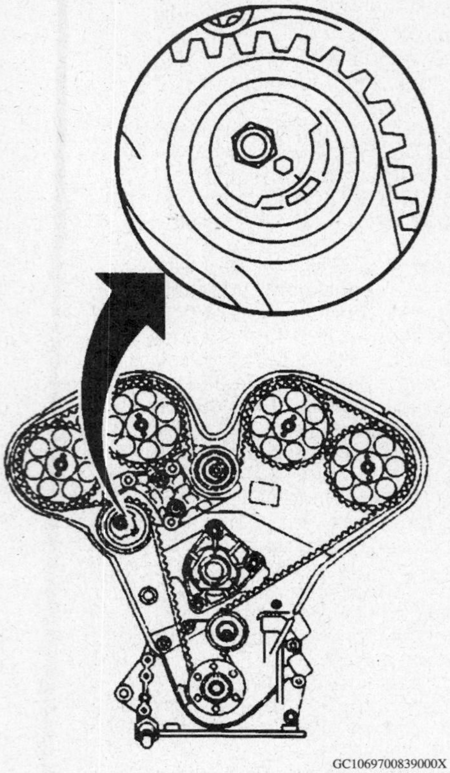

Fig. 18 Timing belt tensioner final adjustment

6. Starting from center and moving outward in spiral pattern, remove camshaft bearing cap bolts and caps.
7. Remove camshaft with seal, then separate seal from shaft.

INSTALLATION

1. Lubricate camshaft lobes and lifter contact points with GM lubricant part No. 12345501, or equivalent, and bearing surfaces with GM assembly fluid part No. 1052367, or equivalent.
2. If installing righthand exhaust (No. 1) camshaft, ensure camshaft pin points toward one o'clock position before installing bearing caps.
3. If installing righthand intake (No. 2) camshaft, ensure camshaft pin points toward 11 o'clock position before installing bearing caps.
4. If installing lefthand intake (No. 3) camshaft, ensure camshaft pin points toward seven o'clock position before installing bearing caps.
5. If installing lefthand exhaust (No. 4) camshaft, ensure camshaft pin points toward 12 o'clock position before installing bearing caps.
6. Apply Loctite sealant part No. 573, or equivalent, to bearing cap forward edges prior to installation. **Prevent sealant from entering oil journal.**

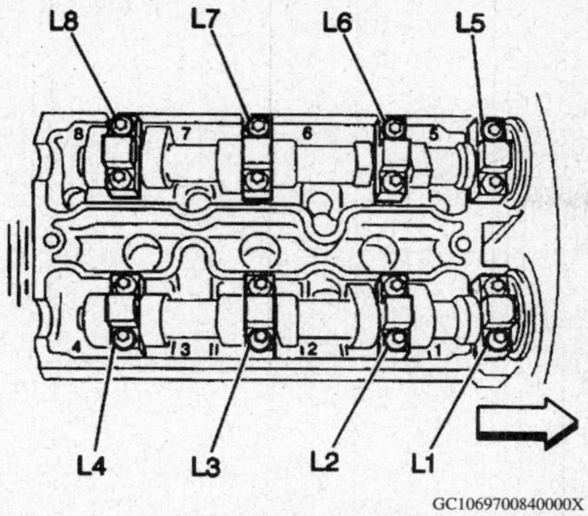

Fig. 19 Righthand bank camshaft bearing cap reference marks

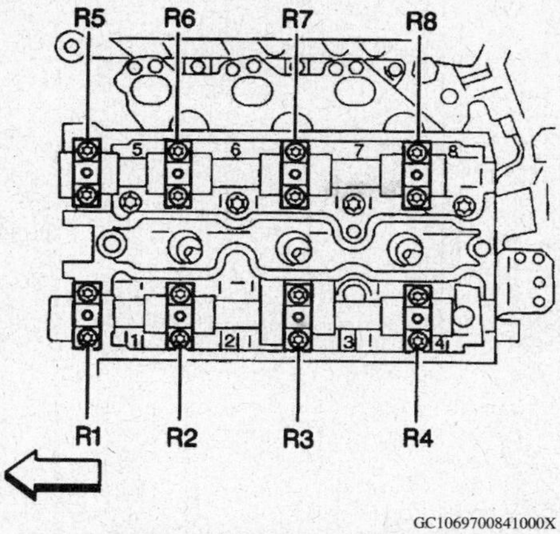

Fig. 20 Lefthand bank camshaft bearing cap reference marks

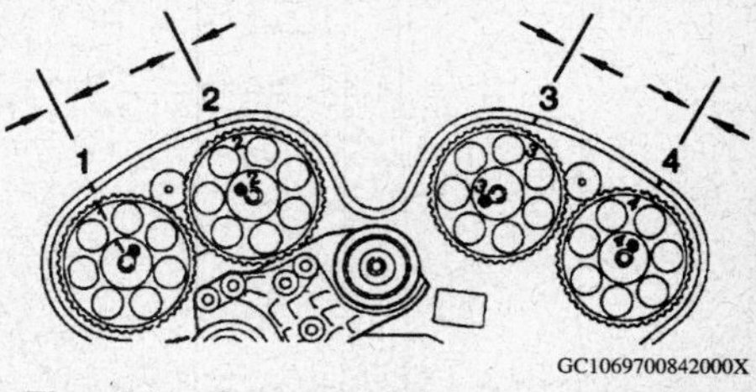

Fig. 21 Camshaft pin orientation

CYLINDER BORE	PISTON SIZE
(8) 85.976 - 85.985 mm (3.3848 - 3.3852 inch)	(8) 85.940 - 85.950 mm (3.3834 - 3.3838 inch)
(99) 85.985 - 85.995 mm (3.3852 - 3.3856 inch)	(99) 85.950 - 85.960 mm (3.3838 - 3.3842 inch)
(00) 85.995 - 86.005 mm (3.3856 - 3.3860 inch)	(00) 85.960 - 85.970 mm (3.3842 - 3.3846 inch)
(01) 86.005 - 86.015 mm (3.3860 - 3.3864 inch)	(01) 85.970 - 85.980 mm (3.3846 - 3.3850 inch)
(02) 86.015 - 86.025 mm (3.3864 - 3.3868 inch)	(02) 85.980 - 85.990 mm (3.3850 - 3.3854 inch)
† (7 + 0.5) 86.465 - 86.475 mm (3.4041 - 3.4045 inch)	† (7 + 0.5) 86.430 - 86.440 mm (3.4027 - 3.4031 inch)

GC1069700845000X

Fig. 22 Piston selection chart

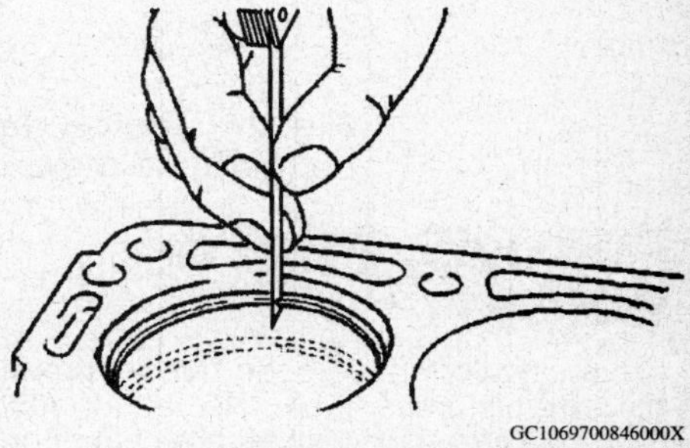

Fig. 23 Piston ring end gap measurement

7. Position bearing caps over camshafts with reference marks in proper locations, **Figs. 19 and 20. Ensure "L" coded caps are installed on passenger's side and "R" coded caps are installed on driver's side.**
8. Tighten camshaft bearing cap bolts to specifications in spiral pattern, starting from center bolts and moving outward.
9. If installing lefthand exhaust (No. 4) camshaft, connect camshaft sensor electrical connector.
10. Coat lip of camshaft seal with suitable chassis grease and tap into place with camshaft seal installer tool No. J-35268-A, or equivalent. Ensure seal is seated completely and evenly.
11. Ensure camshaft pins are positioned turn, **Fig. 21,** then install camshaft gear with new bolt.
12. Install camshaft gear locking tool Nos. J-42069-1 and J-42069-2, or equivalents, to prevent gear rotation while tightening bolt.
13. Tighten camshaft gear bolt as follows:
    a. **Torque** camshaft gear bolt to 37 ft. lbs.
    b. Tighten bolt an additional 60°.
    c. Finally, tighten bolt an additional 15°.
14. Turn crankshaft clockwise to Top Dead Center (TDC) position using crank hub socket tool No. J-42098, or equivalent, then install and adjust timing belt as outlined under "Timing Belt, Replace."
15. Install timing belt front cover as outlined under "Timing Belt, Replace" and valve cover as outlined under " Valve Cover, Replace."
16. Install resonance chamber as outlined under "Engine, Replace" and intake plenum as outlined under "Intake Manifold, Replace."
17. Connect battery ground cable.

PISTON & ROD ASSEMBLY

REMOVAL

1. With engine removed and only crankshaft, pistons and rods remaining in block, turn crankshaft until rod bearing cap bolts are accessible.
2. Remove rod bearing cap bolts, cap and insert, then use suitable block of wood to drive piston and rod assembly from block.
3. If piston and connecting rod are to be separated, refer to " Pistons, Pins & Rings" for related information.

INSTALLATION

1. With piston rings installed and oriented as outlined under " Pistons, Pins & Rings," install guide pin tool No. J-41742, or equivalent, in connecting rod end.
2. Install upper rod bearing on rod, then coat piston, rings, cylinder bore and bearing surfaces with GM Engine Oil Supplement (EOS) part No. 1052368, or equivalent.
3. Compress piston rings with ring compressor tool No. J-8037, or equivalent, then gently tap piston into cylinder bore while guiding connecting rod onto crankshaft. **Ensure arrow mark on top of piston faces front of engine.**
4. Remove rod guide pin tool and install connecting rod cap with bearing. **Ensure bumps on connecting rod and cap face rear of engine.**
5. Install new connecting rod cap bolts, then tighten bolts alternately as follows:
    a. **Torque** bolts to 26 ft. lbs.
    b. Tighten bolts an additional 45°.
    c. Finally, tighten bolts an additional 15°.

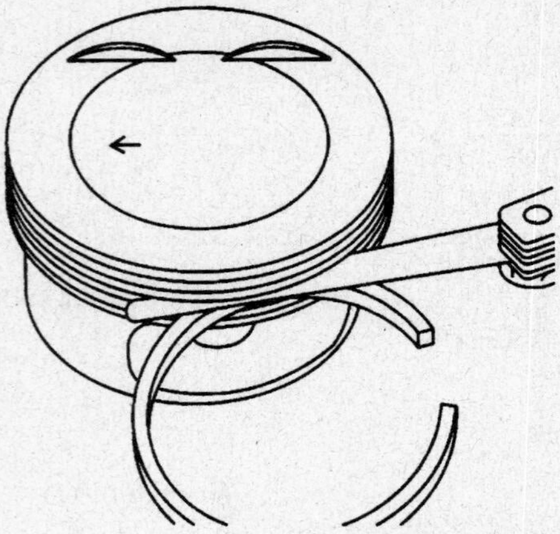

Fig. 24 Piston ring groove clearance measurement

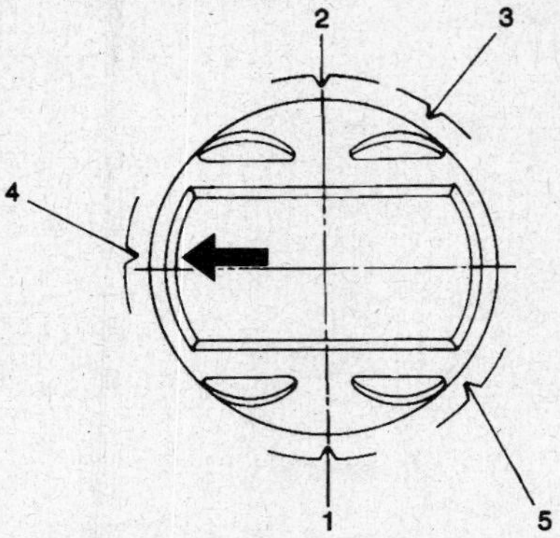

Fig. 25 Piston ring orientation

PISTONS, PINS & RINGS

1. If cylinders have been honed, proper size piston must be selected for each bore. Measure cylinder bore after honing and select corresponding piston size from chart, **Fig. 22.**
2. If piston must be separated from connecting rod, note the following:
   a. Heat end of connecting rod to facilitate piston pin replacement.
   b. Use press tool No. J-24086-C, or equivalent, to press piston pin out of and into piston and connecting rod.
   c. When assembling piston and rod, ensure arrow mark on top of piston and bumps on connecting rod face in opposite directions. Piston arrow mark will face front of engine, while connecting rod bumps will face rear.
3. Inspect piston pin bore to piston pin clearance with suitable micrometers. Maximum clearance is .0003 inch. If clearance is excessive, replace piston and pin.
4. After cylinders have been honed, inspect piston ring end gap clearances as follows:
   a. Install compression rings in cylinder bore and measure gap, **Fig. 23,** which should be .0118–.0196 inch.
   b. Install oil control ring in cylinder bore and measure gap, **Fig. 23,** which should be .0157–.0551 inch.
   c. Rings should be replaced if end gap is not as indicated.
5. Inspect piston ring groove clearance, **Fig. 24,** noting the following:
   a. Compression ring groove clearances should be .0008–.0015 inch.
   b. Oil control ring groove clearance should be .0004–.0012 inch.
   c. Replace piston if groove clearance is not as indicated.
6. When rings are installed on piston, they must be positioned turn, **Fig. 25.**

MAIN & ROD BEARINGS

MAIN BEARING CLEARANCE INSPECTION

1. Select piece of gauging plastic that is full width of crankshaft bearing, then place on journal, **Fig. 26.**
2. Measure all five bearing clearances simultaneously. **Do not turn crankshaft with gauging plastic installed between journal and crankshaft bearing.**
3. Install bearing caps and torsional bearing bridge in original positions.
4. Tighten main bearing cap bolts as follows:
   a. **Torque** main bearing cap bolts to 37 ft. lbs.
   b. Tighten bolts an additional 60°.
   c. Finally, tighten bolts an additional 15°.
5. Tighten torsional bearing bridge bolts to specifications, then remove bearing bridge and bearing caps for gauging plastic inspection.
6. Measure gauging plastic at widest point with scale provided in plastic gauge kit, noting the following:
   a. Bearing clearance should be .0006–.0017 inch.
   b. Crankshaft main journal diameter should be 2.6763–2.6766 inches (green) or 2.6766–2.6770 inches (brown).
7. If gauging plastic indicates excessive clearance or clearance irregularity exceeding .0010 inch and crankshaft main journal diameter is as indicated, use standard size bearings. **Always replace upper and lower crankshaft bearings as set.**
8. If specified clearance cannot be achieved with standard bearing, grind crankshaft again and use an undersize bearing, available in .010 and .020 inch undersizes.

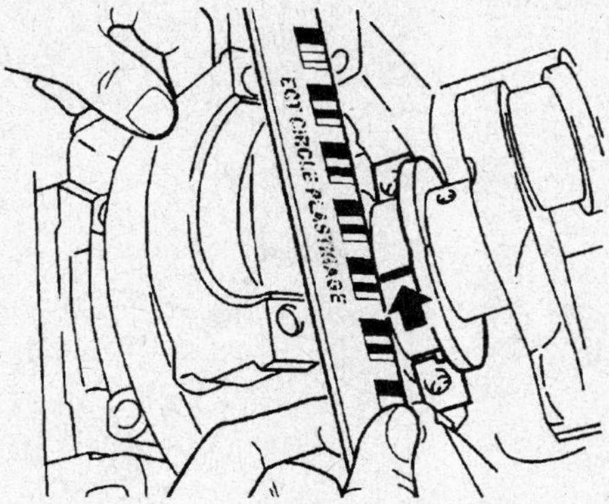

Fig. 26 Main journal gauging plastic installation

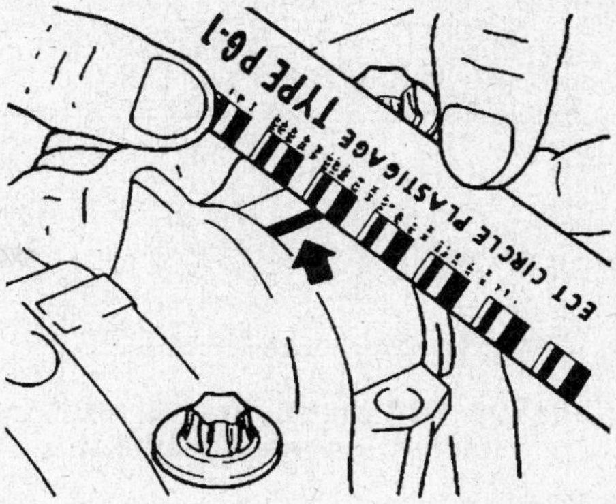

Fig. 27 Rod bearing gauging plastic installation

ROD BEARING CLEARANCE INSPECTION

If the lower half of the connecting rod bearing is worn or damaged, both halves should be replaced. Clearance must be measured at each connecting rod bearing to determine proper sizes, as factory installed bearing sizes may vary between journals.

Using Gauging Plastic

Perform this procedure with pistons and connecting rods installed in engine block. Refer to "Piston & Rod Assembly" for installation procedure.

1. Select piece of gauging plastic that is full width of crankshaft rod bearing and place on journal, **Fig. 27.**
2. Install rod bearing cap in original position. **Do not turn crankshaft while gauging plastic is between journal and bearing.**
3. Tighten bearing cap bolts as outlined under "Piston & Rod Assembly," then remove bearing caps.
4. Measure gauging plastic at widest point using scale provided in plastic gauge kit, noting the following:
   a. Connecting rod bearing clearance should be .0005–.0024 inch.
   b. Connecting rod journal diameter should be 1.9270–1.9280 inches.
5. If gauging plastic indicates excessive clearance or clearance irregularity exceeding .0010 inch and connecting rod journal diameter is satisfactory, use standard size bearing. **Always replace upper and lower bearings as set.**
6. If proper clearance cannot be achieved using standard size bearings, grind crankshaft again and use undersize bearings, available in .010 and .020 inch undersizes.

Using Micrometer

1. Install connecting rod bearings into rod and cap, then install cap and tighten bolts as outlined under "Piston & Rod Assembly."
2. Using suitable inside micrometer, measure inside diameter of connecting rod bearings in at least two places 90° apart, noting the following:
   a. If diameter varies more than .0012 inch, remove bearings and measure connecting rod inside diameter. If variance is still greater than .0012 inch, replace rod.
   b. If diameter does not vary more than .0012 inch, connecting rod is satisfactory.
3. Subtract rod bearing journal diameter from rod bearing inside diameter to obtain bearing clearance.
4. If bearing clearance is not as indicated, replace bearings with new, standard size bearings and measure clearance once again.
5. If clearance is still not as indicated, grind crankshaft again and use undersize bearings.

CRANKSHAFT REAR OIL SEAL

REPLACE

1. Remove transmission as outlined under "Engine, Replace."
2. Using crank hub socket tool No. J-42098, or equivalent, hold crankshaft in position and remove flexplate bolts.
3. Remove flexplate, then center punch rear oil seal steel ring.
4. Carefully drill small, shallow pilot hole into steel ring, then thread in self-tapping screw.
5. Use suitable pliers to pull on screw and extract oil seal from block.
6. Reverse procedure to install, noting the following:
   a. Coat lip of seal with suitable chassis grease prior to installation.
   b. Install seal with rear main oil seal installer tool No. J-42067, or equivalent.

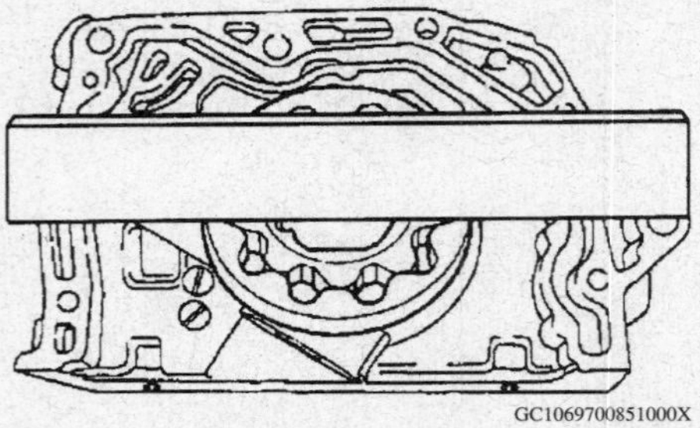

Fig. 28 Oil pump gear to housing clearance measurement

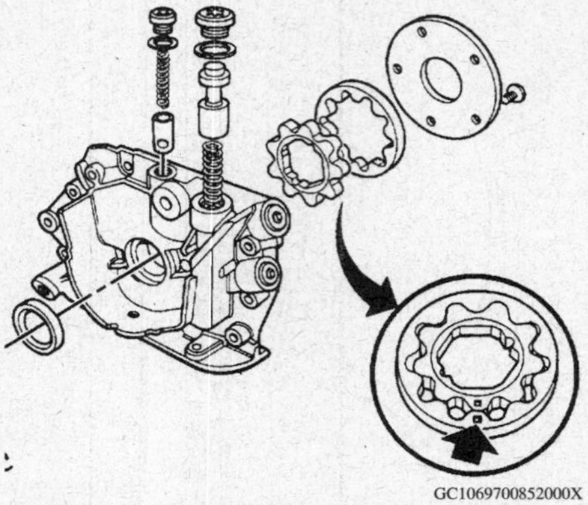

Fig. 29 Oil pump gear orientation

OIL PAN

REPLACE

LOWER

1. Raise and support vehicle, then remove mounting bolts and splash shield.
2. Drain engine oil into suitable container.
3. Disconnect oil level sensor and remove electrical connector C-clip from upper oil pan.
4. Remove mounting bolts and lower oil pan from upper.
5. Pull oil level sensor electrical connector from upper oil pan.
6. Remove mounting bolts and oil level sensor from oil pan.
7. Remove oil level sensor from oil pan.
8. Reverse procedure to install, noting the following:
    a. Install new oil pan gasket and oil level sensor O-ring.
    b. Tighten oil pan bolts to specifications and ensure crankcase is filled with oil.

UPPER

1. Remove lower oil pan as previously described.
2. Remove engine mount lower nuts from frame bracket. **Not alignment tab orientation for installation.**
3. Remove air condition compressor hose strap bolt from upper oil pan front.
4. Remove four transmission mounting bolts from upper oil pan.
5. Remove all but four corner upper oil pan mounting bolts.
6. Mark propeller shaft for alignment for installation, then remove mounting bolts and slide shaft rearward. Secure propeller shaft in place.
7. Remove catalytic converter mounting bolts from hanger bracket and nuts from exhaust manifold.
8. Lower catalytic converter and secure with suitable mechanic wire.
9. Remove two idler arm mounting bolts from frame and lower relay rod out of way.
10. Lower vehicle.
11. Support and raise engine using support fixture tool No. J-28467-A, engine support fixture adapter tool No. J-28467-450 and lift bracket tools No. J-36857, or equivalents. **Do not damage surrounding components.**
12. Raise and support vehicle.
13. Remove remaining upper oil pan mounting bolts.
14. Remove mounting bolts and oil intake pipe.
15. Remove upper oil pan toward vehicle front. **Do not damage aluminum mating surfaces.**
16. Remove rubber seal and RTV sealant.
17. Thoroughly clean oil pan housing and engine block.
18. Reverse procedure to install, noting the following:
    a. Apply bead of silicone sealing compound No. 12346286, or equivalent, in upper oil pan groove bottom.
    b. **Keep bead at least .4 inch from bolt holes.**
    c. **Oil pan must be installed within 10 minutes of applying sealant.**
    d. Install new seal.
    e. Tighten mounting bolts to specifications.

OIL PUMP

REPLACE

1. Drain engine coolant into suitable container.
2. Remove resonance chamber as outlined under "Engine, Replace" and timing belt as outlined under "Timing Belt, Replace."
3. Remove rear timing belt cover, then install crank hub holding tool No. J-42065, or equivalent, and remove crankshaft drive gear bolt with crank hub socket tool No. J-42098, or equivalent.
4. Remove crankshaft drive gear and lower alternator bolt.
5. Raise and support vehicle, then remove splash shield and drain engine oil into suitable container.
6. Remove oil pan as outlined under "Oil Pan, Replace. "
7. Remove engine mount lower nuts from frame bracket.
8. Remove oil intake pipe and A/C compressor hose support strap bolt.
9. Remove oil pan housing bolts, leaving four corner bolts in place, then make corresponding marks on propeller shaft and transmission output flange.
10. Remove propeller shaft to transmission flange bolts, then slide shaft rearward and secure away from transmission.
11. Remove catalytic converter hanger bolts, then lower vehicle.
12. Raise engine slightly and support with support fixture tool No. J-28467-A, or equivalent, then raise and support vehicle.
13. Remove remaining oil pan housing bolts, then the housing and gasket.
14. Remove oil pump housing bolts, then the pump.
15. Remove front main oil seal from oil pump.
16. Reverse procedure to install, noting the following:
    a. Tighten oil pump housing bolts to specifications.
    b. Install front main oil seal with oil seal installer tool No. J-35268-A, or equivalent.
    c. Apply GM sealant part No. 12345997, or equivalent, to engine block and oil pump joints.
    d. Tighten oil pan housing, catalytic converter, propeller shaft, A/C compressor hose support strap, oil intake pipe and lower alternator bolts to specifications.
    e. Install crank hub holding tool No. J-42065, or equivalent.
    f. Install new crankshaft drive gear bolt, **torque** to 184 ft. lbs.
    g. Finally, tighten gear bolt an additional 15°.
    h. Adjust timing belt as outlined under "Timing Belt, Replace."
    i. Fill and bleed cooling system as required.

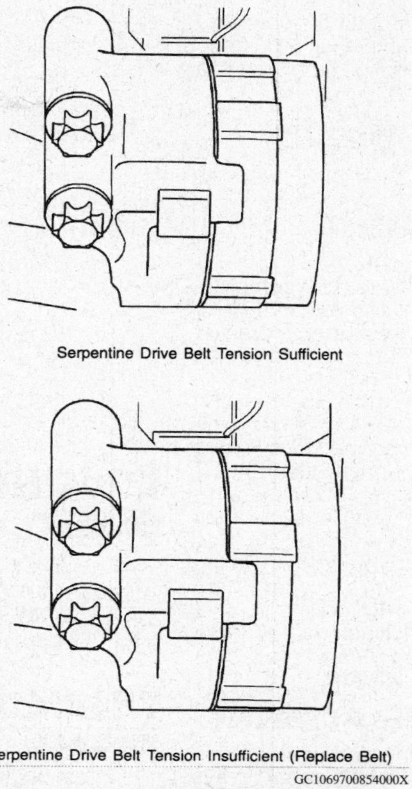

Fig. 30 Serpentine drive belt tensioner wear indicator

OIL PUMP SERVICE

1. Remove oil pump pressure regulating valve plug, seal, valve and spring.
2. Remove oil pump pressure relief valve plug, seal, spring and valve.
3. Remove oil pump cover bolts, then the cover and inner and outer gears.
4. Measure oil pump inner and outer gear to housing clearance using suitable feeler gauge and straightedge, **Fig. 28.** Maximum clearance is .003 inch for inner gear and .004 inch for outer gear.
5. Inspect oil pressure regulating and relief valves and springs for excessive wear and damage. Replace if required.
6. Install inner and outer gears with marks facing cover, **Fig. 29,** then install cover and tighten bolts to specifications.
7. Install pressure relief and regulating valves, springs, seals and plugs.

OIL COOLER

REPLACE

1. Remove intake plenum and manifold as outlined under " Intake Manifold, Replace."
2. Drain engine coolant and oil into suitable containers.
3. Disconnect coolant temperature sensor and sender electrical connectors, then disconnect throttle body and heater inlet hoses at coolant bridge.
4. Remove engine coolant bridge bolts and upper seals, then the bridge and lower seals.
5. Loosen lefthand exhaust manifold upper heat shield bolts, then disconnect oil feed and return lines at oil cooler.
6. Raise and support vehicle, then remove lefthand catalytic converter and exhaust pipe.
7. Remove oil filter, crank sensor and engine oil cooler line clamp.
8. Disconnect oil feed and return lines at engine block, then remove lines and lower the vehicle.
9. Remove oil cooler inlet and outlet nuts, cover and cooler assembly.
10. Reverse procedure to install, noting the following:
    a. Apply .08 inch bead of GM silicone sealer part No. 12345997, or equivalent, to oil cooler cover groove in place of original seal.
    b. Use four new seals on oil cooler oil feed and return line fittings.
    c. Tighten oil cooler cover bolts and inlet and outlet nuts to specifications.
    d. Tighten oil feed and return line fittings, crank sensor bolt, coolant bridge bolts and oil filter to specifications.
    e. Fill coolant reservoir and engine crankcase.

BELT TENSION DATA

The serpentine drive belt tensioner features wear indicator marks, **Fig. 30.** These should be used to determine if belt tension is sufficient.

SERPENTINE DRIVE BELT

BELT REPLACEMENT

1. Raise and support vehicle.
2. Remove splash shield, A/C compressor hose strap bolt and Secondary Air Injection (AIR) crossover pipe bracket nut. Use suitable back-up wrench on alternator bolt.
3. Remove AIR crossover pipe bushing nut from bracket and crossover pipe from rubber hose connections. Move pipe aside to gain working clearance.
4. Turn tensioner pulley clockwise, to release serpentine belt tension, then slide belt off pulleys.
5. Reverse procedure to install, noting the following:
   a. Route belt turn, **Fig. 31.**
   b. Turn tensioner clockwise to facilitate installation. Install belt over water pump pulley last.

TENSIONER REPLACEMENT

1. Remove serpentine drive belt as outlined under " Belt Replacement" in this section, then remove tensioner bolts.
2. Remove tensioner from engine.
3. Reverse procedure to install. Tighten tensioner bolts to specifications.

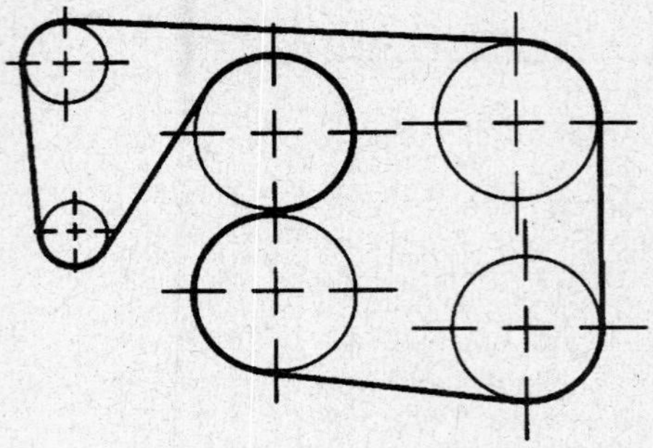

Fig. 31 Serpentine drive belt routing

COOLING SYSTEM BLEED

The cooling system will bleed automatically during engine warm-up. If reservoir is not full, it may be necessary to add coolant after the engine has cooled.

THERMOSTAT

REPLACE

1. Drain engine coolant into suitable container, then remove intake plenum as outlined under "Intake Manifold, Replace."
2. Remove intake manifold bolts as outlined under " Intake Manifold, Replace," then lift and support manifold while removing seals.
3. Disconnect radiator inlet hose at thermostat outlet pipe, then remove pipe.
4. Remove thermostat housing bolts, then the housing and thermostat assembly.
5. Remove seal ring.
6. Reverse procedure to install, noting the following:
   a. Install new thermostat seal ring.
   b. Tighten thermostat housing and outlet pipe bolts to specifications.
   c. Install new intake manifold seal.
   d. Fill cooling system as required.

WATER PUMP

REPLACE

1. Drain engine coolant into suitable container.
2. Remove resonance chamber as outlined under "Engine, Replace."
3. Remove timing belt front cover as outlined under " Timing Belt, Replace," then remove water pump bolts.
4. Remove water pump.
5. Reverse procedure to install, noting the following:
   a. Tighten water pump bolts to specifications.
   b. Fill cooling system as required.

RADIATOR

REPLACE

1. Remove battery.
2. Remove upper radiator covers, then drain engine coolant into suitable container.
3. Remove resonance chamber as outlined under "Engine, Replace," then disconnect primary cooling fan and cooling fan control switch electrical connectors.
4. Disconnect air bleed hose and transmission oil cooler pipes at radiator, then remove pipe seals.
5. Disconnect coolant hose at secondary auxiliary coolant pump, then remove Secondary Air Injection (AIR) cutoff valve bracket bolts from fan housing.
6. Remove condenser to radiator bracket bolts, then disconnect radiator inlet and outlet hoses.
7. Disconnect secondary auxiliary coolant pump electrical connector.
8. Using rocking motion, lift radiator and primary fan assembly away from radiator support.
9. Remove upper retainers, primary fan assembly and cooling fan control switches from radiator.
10. Reverse procedure to install, noting the following:
    a. Tighten cooling fan control switches, primary fan bolts and oil cooler pipe fittings to specifications.
    b. Fill cooling system as required.

FUEL PUMP

REPLACE

The fuel pump is located inside the modular fuel sender. Refer to "Electrical" section for fuel pump relay location.

1. Relieve fuel system pressure as outlined under " Precautions."
2. Drain fuel from tank with suitable hand operated pump, then raise and support vehicle.
3. Remove rear bumper fascia and rear frame support, then disconnect fuel feed line at fuel filter and fuel return line near filter.
4. Disconnect fuel tank breather and vent hoses and fuel sender electrical connector.
5. With fuel tank supported, remove tank retaining strap front bolts, then both straps.
6. Lower fuel tank and disconnect Evaporative Emission (EVAP) tank pressure sensor connector.
7. Remove spring loaded clamp at fuel tank boot, then remove sending unit and wiring harness from tank using fuel tank sender wrench tool No. J-42219, or equivalent.
8. Remove seal from sending unit cover and drain fuel from sender reservoir into suitable container.
9. Remove fuel level sensor from sender assembly, then disconnect fuel feed hose at fuel pump.
10. Disconnect fuel pump electrical connectors, then remove damper ring and fuel pump assembly from sender.
11. Remove fuel pump bracket and strainer.
12. Reverse procedure to install, noting the following:
    a. Install new fuel pump strainer and sending unit lip seal. Apply thin film of oil to inner diameter of lip seal prior to installation.
    b. Tighten fuel tank sender nut and fuel tank straps to specifications.

FUEL FILTER

REPLACE

1. Relieve fuel system pressure as outlined under " Precautions," then grasp filter firmly and remove fuel line fitting bolts.
2. Loosen fuel filter retaining strap, then remove filter.
3. Reverse procedure to install.

TIGHTENING SPECIFICATIONS

Year	Component	Torque/ Ft. Lbs.
1997–2000	Accelerator & Cruise Control Cable Bracket	72②
	Accessory Bracket Bolt	30
	A/C Compressor Bracket	30
	A/C Compressor Hose Support Strap	72②
	AIR Injection Crossover Pipe Bushing	108②
	AIR Injection Crossover Pipe Support Bracket	30
	AIR Injection Pipe	15
	Alternator	30
	Camshaft Bearing Cap	72②
	Camshaft Gear	③
	Catalytic Converter	15
	Connecting Rod Caps	⑤
	Coolant Bridge	22
	Cooling Fan Control Switches	16
	Crank Sensor	72②
	Crankshaft Drive Gear	⑥
	Cylinder Head	①
	Cylinder Head Cover	72②
	Engine Mount Lower Nut	41
	Engine Mount Upper Nut	30
	Exhaust Manifold	15
	Exhaust Manifold Heat Shield	72②
	Flexplate To Torque Converter	22
	Fuel Tank Sender	37
	Fuel Tank Straps	26
	Harmonic Balancer	15
	Intake Manifold	15
	Intake Manifold Spacer	15
	Intake Plenum	72②
	Intake Plenum Switchover Valve	72②
	Main Bearing Caps	④
	Oil Cooler Cover	22
	Oil Cooler Inlet & Outlet Nuts	15
	Oil Feed & Return Lines	22
	Oil Filter	11
	Oil Intake Pipe	72②
	Oil Pan	72②
	Oil Pan Baffle	72②
	Oil Pan Drain Plug	41
	Oil Pan Housing	11
	Oil Pump Cover	72②
	Oil Pump Housing	53②
	Power Steering Pump Pulley	15
	Primary Cooling Fan To Radiator	35②
	Propeller Shaft Coupling	70

Continued

TIGHTENING SPECIFICATIONS—Continued

Year	Component	Torque/ Ft. Lbs.
1997-2000	Resonance Chamber	27②
	Serpentine Drive Belt Tensioner	30
	Spark Plug	19
	Thermostat Housing	15
	Thermostat Outlet Pipe	15
	Timing Belt Cover	72②
	Timing Belt Idler Pulley	30
	Timing Belt Tensioner	15
	Timing Belt Tensioner Bracket	30
	Torsional Bearing Bridge	15
	Transmission Crossmember To Body	33
	Transmission Crossmember To Mount	15
	Transmission Housing To Engine Block	44
	Transmission Housing To Engine Oil Pan	15
	Transmission Oil Cooler Pipes To Radiator	18
	Valve Cover	72②
	Water Pump	18
	Water Pump Pulley	72②

AIR: Secondary Air Injection

① — Refer to "Cylinder Head, Replace" for tightening procedure & specifications.

② — Inch lbs.

③ — Refer to "Camshaft, Replace" for tightening procedure & specifications.

④ — Refer to "Main & Rod Bearings" for tightening procedure & specifications.

⑤ — Refer to "Piston & Rod Assembly" for tightening procedure & specifications.

⑥ — Refer to "Oil Pump, Replace" for tightening procedure & specifications.

Rear Axle & Suspension

INDEX

DESCRIPTION

The rear axle and suspension assembly, **Fig. 1,** is fully independent and is isolated from the vehicle body by rubber bushings at all mounting points. The differential is supported by cradle, which is also the mounting point for stabilizer shaft. Sealed tie rod ends and wheel bearings eliminate the need for periodic lubrication.

The two drive axle assemblies are essentially inner and outer Constant Velocity (CV) joints joined by shaft. The CV joints do not require periodic lubrication and, although the outer joint can be serviced independently of the axle, the inner joint and axle shaft are non-serviceable items.

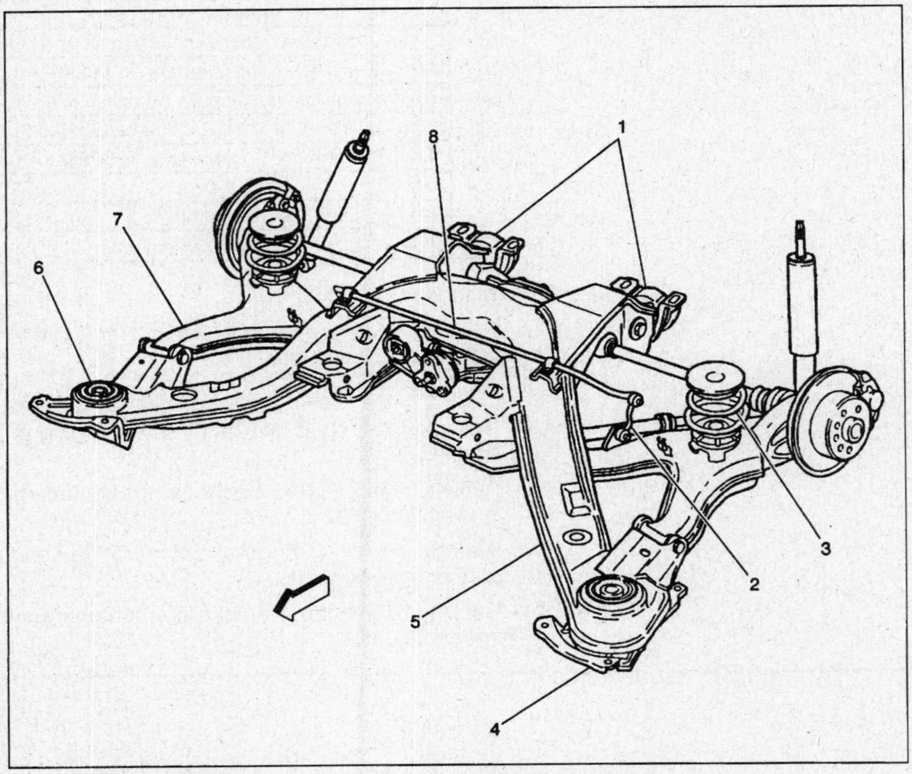

(1) Rear Axle Cradle Mount
(2) Stabilizer Shaft Link
(3) Spring
(4) Rear Axle Support Bushing Flange
(5) Rear Axle Cradle
(6) Rear Axle Support Bushing
(7) Rear Lower Control Arm
(8) Stabilizer Shaft

GC2039700121000X

Fig. 1 Rear axle & suspension assembly

REAR AXLE SHAFT

REPLACE

1. Place gear selector lever in Neutral position, then raise and support vehicle.
2. Remove wheel, then install hub flange holding adapter tool No. J-42066, or equivalent, on flange with wheel bolts.
3. Hold flange holding adapter tool with suitable ratchet and remove flange bolts.
4. Separate drive axle outer end from wheel bearing hub inner flange.
5. Using drive axle separator tool No. J-42071, or equivalent, and suitable hammer, separate drive axle from differential. **Ensure beveled side of tool is against differential and not against drive axle.**
6. Reverse procedure to install, noting the following:
   a. Lubricate drive axle spline and seal surfaces with suitable differential lubricant.
   b. Use rubber mallet to drive axle into differential bore. **Do not use more force than required to seat axle fully in bore.**
   c. Tighten bolts to specifications.

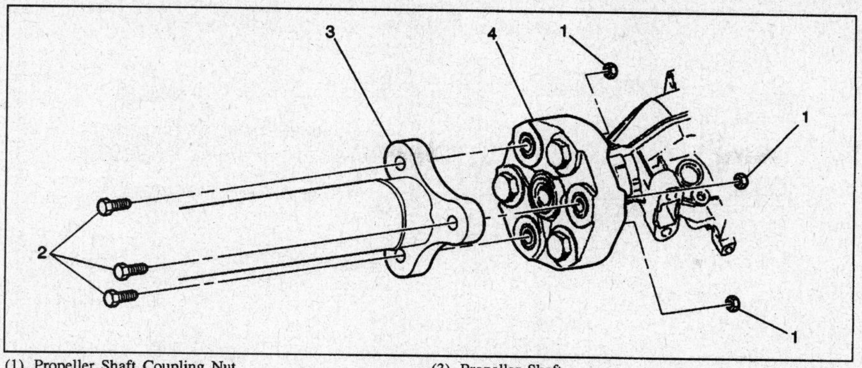

(1) Propeller Shaft Coupling Nut
(2) Propeller Shaft Coupling Bolt
(3) Propeller Shaft
(4) Propeller Shaft Coupling

GC2039700122000X

Fig. 2 Propeller shaft coupling

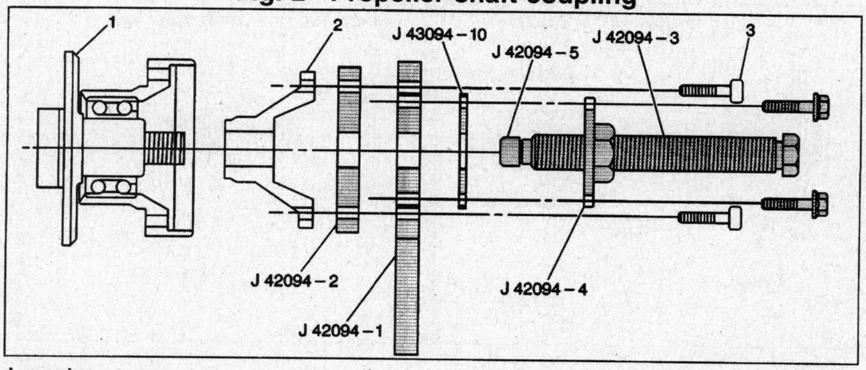

Legend

(1) Rear Wheel Hub
(2) Rear Wheel Hub Flange
(3) Driveshaft Bolt

GC2039700123000X

Fig. 3 Hub flange removal tools

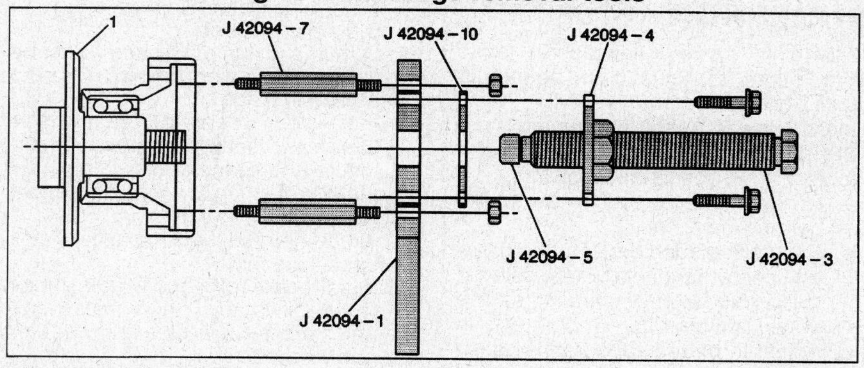

(1) Rear Wheel Hub

GC2039700124000X

Fig. 4 Hub removal tools

DIFFERENTIAL CARRIER

REPLACE

1. Raise and support vehicle, then support differential assembly with suitable transmission jack.
2. Disconnect anti-lock brake system electrical connectors, then remove drive axles as outlined under "Rear Axle Shaft, Replace."
3. Remove propeller shaft as outlined under "Propeller Shaft, Replace," then the coupling.
4. Remove differential support bracket bolts from bracket and bushing bolts from differential.
5. Remove differential carrier.
6. Reverse procedure to install, noting the following:
   a. Tighten differential bushing bolts to specifications.
   b. Tighten support bracket bolts to specifications.

PROPELLER SHAFT

REPLACE

1. Place gear selector lever in Neutral position, then raise and support vehicle.
2. Remove heat shields and bolts securing propeller shaft bearing bracket to underbody.
3. Remove front propeller shaft coupling nuts and bolts from shaft, **Fig. 2,** then pry front half of shaft rearward until it clears coupling.
4. Remove rear propeller shaft coupling nuts and bolts, then move rear half of shaft forward slightly.
5. Remove shaft by sliding it between exhaust system components and underbody surface.
6. Reverse procedure to install. Tighten front and rear coupling bolts to specifications.

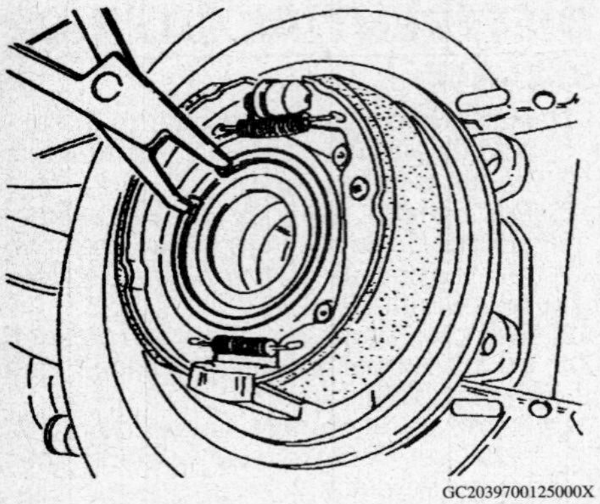

Fig. 5 Wheel bearing retaining ring replacement

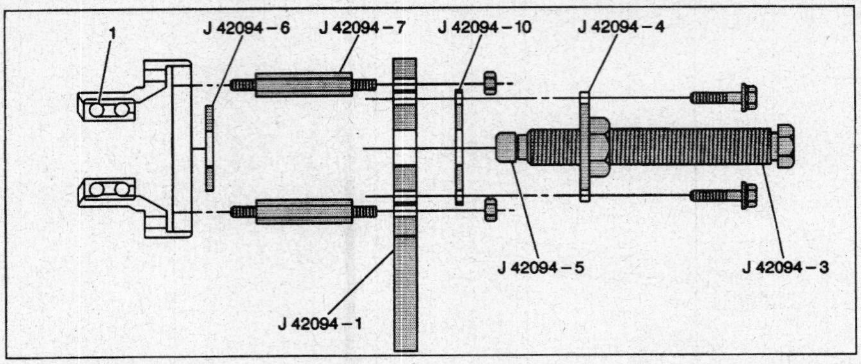

(1) Wheel Bearing

GC2039700126000X

Fig. 6 Wheel bearing removal tools

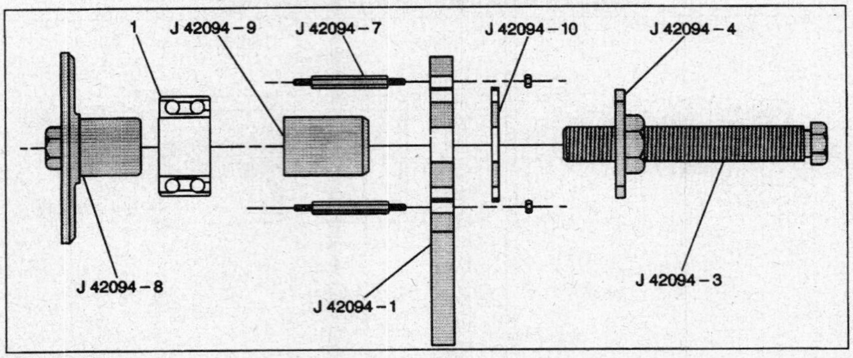

Legend

(1) Wheel Bearing

GC2039700127000X

Fig. 7 Wheel bearing installation tools

HUB & BEARING

REPLACE

REMOVAL

1. Raise and support vehicle, then remove wheel.
2. Using holding tool No. J-42066, or equivalent, and suitable breaker bar, remove driveshaft bolts.
3. Separate driveshaft from rear wheel hub flange and suspend in an upward direction. **Do not allow shaft to hang freely.**
4. Disengage clip and separate brake pipe from lower control arm, then remove disc brake pads and caliper. **Suspend caliper aside. It is not necessary to open hydraulic system.**
5. Loosen setscrew and slide rotor off hub, then use socket tool No. J-42072, or equivalent, to back out three of four brake backing plate bolts approximately .47 inch.
6. Install spacer tool No. J-42094-2 and holding fixture tool No. J-42094-1, or equivalents, on rear wheel hub flange, then remove hub nut.
7. Install flange removal tools, **Fig. 3,** then remove flange from hub by turning threaded driver tool.
8. Install hub removal tools, **Fig. 4,** then press out hub with threaded driver tool. **Damage may occur to wheel bearing seal during hub removal. If original bearing is to be used again, inspect seal carefully.**
9. Remove wheel bearing retaining ring, **Fig. 5,** then install wheel bearing removal tools, **Fig. 6.**
10. Turn threaded driver tool clockwise to remove wheel bearing.

INSTALLATION

1. Assemble bearing installation tools, **Fig.7,** then use tools to pull bearing in until it is fully seated.
2. Install wheel bearing retaining ring, **Fig. 5,** then assemble hub installation tools, **Fig. 8,** noting the following:
   a. Ensure installer tool is on wheel bearing inner ring.
   b. Ensure threaded driver tool is properly centered inside wheel bearing to prevent hub from binding as it is drawn into bearing.
   c. Adjust threaded spacer pins as required.
3. Draw hub into bearing by holding threaded driver and turning arbor clockwise, then remove tool assembly.
4. Assemble flange installation tools, **Fig. 9,** then install flange on hub by holding threaded driver while turning arbor clockwise. **Ensure splines are properly aligned.**
5. Remove arbor, driver and thrust bearing tools, leaving holding fixture and spacer in place.
6. Install rear wheel hub nut and tighten to specifications, then remove holding fixture and spacer tools.
7. Install retaining washer and stake to hub.
8. Tighten brake backing plate bolts to specifications.
9. Install brake rotor and tighten setscrew to specifications, then install caliper and secure brake pipe to lower control arm with clip.
10. Connect driveshaft to rear wheel hub flange, then install bolts.
11. Tighten driveshaft bolts to specifications.
12. Install wheel, then lower vehicle.

REAR SUSPENSION

REPLACE

The following procedure is for removal of the differential and axle cradle as a unit. If required, the differential can be replaced independently as outlined under "Differential Carrier, Replace."

1. Raise and support vehicle, allowing working clearance around rear axle support flange bolts.
2. Remove rear wheels, then disconnect wheel speed sensor electrical connectors.
3. Remove propeller shaft disc joint bolts from rear differential flange, then disconnect exhaust system at rubber body mounts.
4. Disengage clips and separate brake pipes from lower control arms, then release parking brake cables from actuator brackets.
5. Remove disc brake pads and caliper mounting bolts, then separate caliper from rotor and suspend aside to prevent damage to brake pipe. **Do not open hydraulic system.**
6. Scribe mark around perimeter of axle cradle mount for installation reference, then support cradle and each lower control arm.
7. Remove shock absorber lower mounting bolts and cradle mounting bolts, then pivot cradle to allow for removal of springs.
8. Remove springs, then lower vehicle and continue supporting axle cradle.
9. Remove axle support flange and bushing bolts, then the axle cradle.
10. Reverse procedure to install, noting the following:
    a. Tighten axle support bushing and flange bolts, shock absorber lower mount and propeller shaft disc joint bolts to specifications.
    b. Inspect and adjust wheel alignment as outlined in " Wheel Alignment" section.

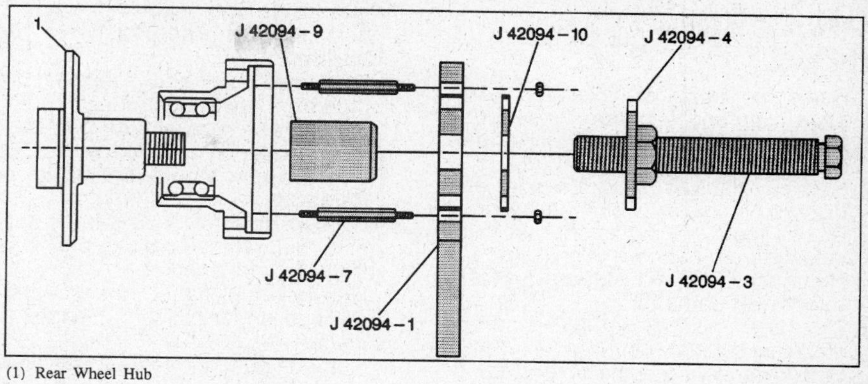

(1) Rear Wheel Hub

GC2039700128000X

Fig. 8 Hub installation tools

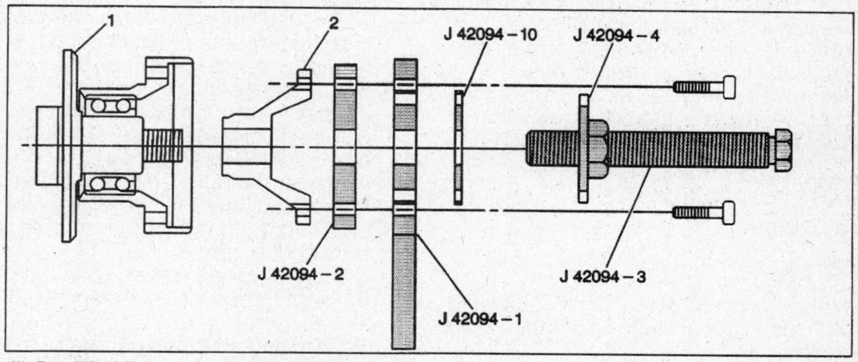

(1) Rear Wheel Hub (2) Rear Wheel Hub Flange

GC2039700129000X

Fig. 9 Hub flange installation tools

SHOCK ABSORBER

REPLACE

1. Move rear seat backrest forward to access upper shock absorber mount, then remove protective cap from tower.
2. Remove upper shock absorber mounting nut, washer and grommet, then raise and support vehicle.
3. Disconnect Automatic Level Control (ALC) air line.
4. Remove lower shock absorber mounting bolt, then the shock absorber.
5. Reverse procedure to install. Tighten mounting nut and bolt to specifications.

COIL SPRING

REPLACE

1. Raise and support vehicle, then disengage clips and separate brake pipes from lower control arms. **Do not open hydraulic system.**
2. Remove stabilizer shaft link bolts and disconnect link at lower control arms.
3. Disengage exhaust system rubber insulators from hangers to gain working clearance. **Support exhaust system to prevent damage.**
4. Disconnect rear wheel speed sensor electrical connectors.
5. With lower control arms supported, remove shock absorber lower mount bolt, then remove control arm supports and support differential instead.
6. Remove bolts securing rear axle cradle to vehicle body, then lower differential until springs can be removed.
7. Remove spring and seat assembly, then separate seat from spring.
8. Reverse procedure to install.

CONTROL ARM

REPLACE

LOWER

1. Raise and support vehicle, allowing rear axle support flange bolts to remain accessible.
2. Remove wheel, then hold rear wheel hub using holding tool No. J-42066, or equivalent, and remove driveshaft bolts.
3. Separate driveshaft from rear wheel hub flange and support in an upward position. **Do not suspend from spring.**
4. Disengage clip and separate brake pipe from lower control arm, then remove brake pads and caliper. **Do not open brake hydraulic system. Suspend caliper to prevent brake pipe damage.**
5. Loosen setscrew and slide rotor off hub, then release parking brake cable from actuator bracket.
6. Remove hub, flange and bearing as outlined under " Hub & Bearing, Replace."
7. Remove parking brake shoes and related hardware.
8. Using socket tool No. J-42072, or equivalent, remove rear backing plate bolts, then separate parking brake anchor from rear brake backing plate.
9. Remove backing plate from control arm, then disengage exhaust system hangers from rubber body mounts. **Support exhaust system components to prevent damage.**
10. Remove rear outer tie rod nut, then use tie rod puller tool No. J-6627-A, or equivalent, to remove outer tie rod from control arm.
11. Disconnect stabilizer shaft link at control arm, then support cradle assembly at differential.
12. Scribe marks around perimeter of cradle mounts for installation reference, then remove cradle to vehicle body mounting bolts.
13. With lower control arm supported, remove lower shock absorber mounting bolt, then lower rear cradle to allow for spring removal.
14. Remove rear spring with differential and control arms supported.
15. **On 1997 models,** proceed as follows:
    a. Remove underbody heat shields.
    b. Remove propeller shaft center bearing bolts.
    c. Remove rear support flange bolts and rear support bushing bolt.
16. **On all models,** lower control arm to access outboard control arm bolt, then remove inboard and outboard control arm bolts.
17. Remove control arm.
18. Reverse procedure to install, noting the following:
    a. Tighten control arm, support bushing, support flange, propeller shaft center bearing bracket, axle cradle mount and shock absorber lower mount bolt to specifications.
    b. **Torque** steering linkage installer tool No. J-42089, or equivalent, to 22 ft. lbs. to seat outer tie rod ball stud taper. **Use new self-locking tie rod nut.**
    c. Tighten outer tie rod nut to specifications.
    d. Tighten brake backing plate and driveshaft bolts as outlined under "Hub & Bearing, Replace."
    e. Tighten brake rotor setscrew and caliper mounting bolts to specifications.
    f. Adjust parking brake as required.
    g. Adjust wheel alignment as outlined in "Wheel Alignment " section.

CONTROL ARM BUSHING

REPLACE

REMOVAL

1. Remove lower control arm as outlined under "Control Arm, Replace," then cut off inboard bushing collar, **Fig. 10.**
2. Cut off outboard control arm rubber collar, then use bushing receiver tool No. J-21474-5 and lower control arm bushing replacement tool No. J-42200, or equivalents, to press out bushing.

INSTALLATION

1. Coat new bushings with suitable lubricant, then position inboard bushing with collar toward rear differential.
2. Assemble special tools, **Fig. 11,** and press in new bushing.
3. Lubricate outboard bushing with silicone spray, then press into place, **Fig. 11.**
4. Install lower control arm as outlined under "Control Arm, Replace."

TIE ROD

REPLACE

INNER

1. Raise and support vehicle, then remove inner tie rod bolt from axle cradle.
2. Separate inner tie rod from cradle, then loosen adjuster nut and remove tie rod from adjuster. **Record number of turns required to remove tie rod.**
3. Reverse procedure to install, noting the following:
   a. Thread inner tie rod into adjuster with same number of turns recorded during removal.
   b. Tighten adjuster nut and inner tie rod bolt to specifications.
   c. Adjust wheel alignment as outlined in "Wheel Alignment " section.

OUTER

1. Raise and support vehicle, then remove outer tie rod nut from rear lower control arm.
2. Using tie rod puller tool No. J-6627-A, or equivalent, separate outer tie rod from lower control arm.
3. Loosen adjuster nut, then remove tie rod from adjuster. **Record number of turns required to remove tie rod.**
4. Reverse procedure to install, noting the following:
   a. Thread inner tie rod into adjuster with same number of turns recorded during removal.
   b. Tighten adjuster nut and outer tie rod nut to specifications.
   c. **Torque** steering linkage installer tool No. J-42089, or equivalent, to 22 ft. lbs. to seat ball stud taper. **Use new self-locking tie rod nut.**
   d. Adjust wheel alignment as outlined in "Wheel Alignment " section.

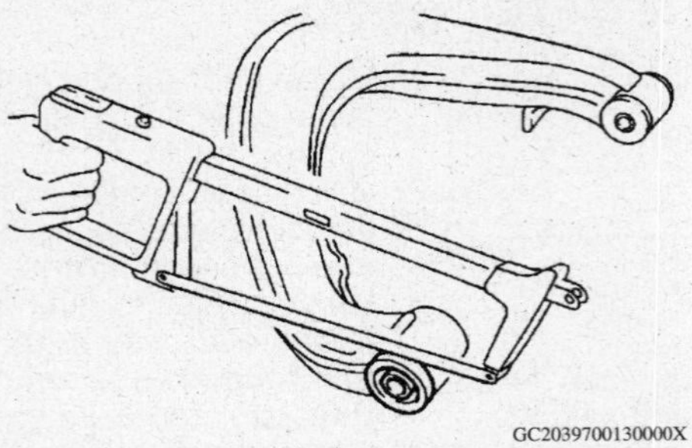

Fig. 10 Control arm bushing collar removal

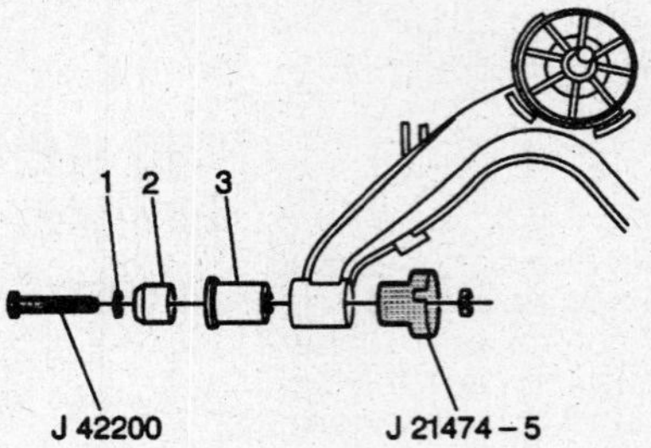

(1) Washer
(2) 30 mm Socket
(3) Bushing

GC2039700131000X

Fig. 11 Control arm bushing installation

STABILIZER SHAFT

REPLACE

1. Raise and support vehicle, then support rear axle cradle at differential.
2. Scribe mark around perimeter of cradle for installation reference, then remove bolts securing cradle to vehicle body.
3. Lower cradle slightly, then remove cradle mount protective shields.
4. Remove stabilizer shaft link bolts from lower control arm, then separate link from control arm.
5. Lower cradle, then remove bolts from stabilizer shaft mounting brackets.
6. Remove stabilizer shaft.
7. Reverse procedure to install, noting the following:
   a. Tighten stabilizer shaft, link and cradle bolts to specifications.
   b. Adjust wheel alignment as outlined in "Wheel Alignment" section.

TIGHTENING SPECIFICATIONS

Year	Component	Torque/Ft. Lbs.
1997–2000	Axle Nut	221
	Brake Backing Plate	37③
	Brake Caliper	59
	Brake Rotor Setscrew	35④
	Differential Bushing To Differential	74
	Differential Support Bracket (Lower Bolt)	66①
	Differential Support Bracket (Upper Bolt)	74
	Drive Axle	37②
	Driveshaft Bolts	37⑤
	Driveshaft Nut	221
	Hub Nut	221
	Inner Tie Rod	66
	Lower Control Arm	74
	Outer Tie Rod	44
	Propeller Shaft Bearing Insulator	16
	Propeller Shaft Center Bearing Bracket	15
	Propeller Shaft Couplings	70
	Propeller Shaft Disc Joint To Differential	70
	Rear Axle Cradle Mount To Body	48
	Rear Axle Cradle Mount To Cradle	74
	Rear Axle Filler Plug	15
	Rear Axle Support Bushing	92
	Rear Axle Support Flange	48
	Shock Absorber Lower Mount	81
	Shock Absorber Upper Mount	15
	Stabilizer Shaft Link	15
	Stabilizer Shaft Mounting Bracket	16
	Tie Rod Adjuster	11
	Wheel To Hub	81

① — Tighten an additional 38.°
② — Tighten an additional 67.
③ — Torque to 37 ft. lbs., then tighten an additional 40.°
④ — Inch lbs.
⑤ — Torque to 37 ft. lbs., then tighten an additional 70.°

Front Suspension & Steering

NOTE: Refer To "Air Bag System Precautions" Located In The Front Of This Manual For System Disarming & Arming Procedures.

NOTE: Refer To "Computer Relearn Procedure" Located In The Front Of This Manual For Computer Relearn Procedures.

INDEX

PRECAUTIONS

AIR BAG SYSTEMS

Refer to "Air Bag System Precautions" in the front of this manual for system disarming and arming procedures.

BATTERY GROUND CABLE

Prior to service, disconnect battery ground cable and isolate as required.

DESCRIPTION

The front suspension features McPherson struts with hydraulic bushings in the lower control arms and gas preloaded dampers. The speed sensitive steering system utilizes recirculating ball type steering gear.

HUB, BEARING & SEAL

REPLACE

1. Raise and support vehicle, then remove front wheel.
2. Remove brake pad wear indicator wire and brake hose from strut bracket, then remove caliper bracket assembly from steering knuckle. **Do not open brake hydraulic system. Suspend caliper aside to prevent brake pipe damage.**
3. Loosen set screw and remove brake rotor, dust cap and wheel hub nut.
4. Remove wheel hub, bearing and seal assembly.
5. Reverse procedure to install, noting the following:
   a. It may be necessary to use suitable socket to press outer bearing ring into wheel hub.
   b. Tighten wheel hub nut and brake rotor setscrew to specifications.
   c. Thread an M12 × 1.5 tap through caliper bolt holes to remove old locking compound, then install new caliper bolts coated in GM Threadlocker 272, or equivalent.
   d. Tighten caliper bracket bolts to specifications.

BALL JOINT INSPECTION

The following procedure applies only to the lower control arm ball stud. Before inspecting the ball stud, ensure the corresponding wheel bearing is in satisfactory condition.

1. Raise and support vehicle, then grasp wheel at top and bottom.
2. Move wheel in and out while observing steering knuckle and lower control arm.
3. If steering knuckle moves up and down independently of control arm, proceed as follows:
   a. Inspect steering knuckle pinch bolt area for ball stud slot movement or distortion. Repair as required.
   b. If pinch bolt area is satisfactory but ball stud movement is noted, replace ball stud.
4. If no vertical movement is observed between steering knuckle and control arm while moving wheel, ball stud and slot are satisfactory.

BALL STUD

REPLACE

1. Raise and support vehicle, then remove front wheel.
2. Remove control arm as outlined under "Control Arm, Replace."
3. Drill out three rivet heads securing ball stud to lower control arm, then remove stud.
4. Reverse procedure to install, noting the following:
   a. Secure ball stud to control arm with bolts inserted from upper side of lower control arm.
   b. Tighten bolts to specifications.

COIL SPRING

REPLACE

The coil spring is part of the strut assembly. Refer to " Strut, Replace" if the entire assembly is to be replaced, or to "Coil Spring & Strut Service" if the spring must be replaced independently.

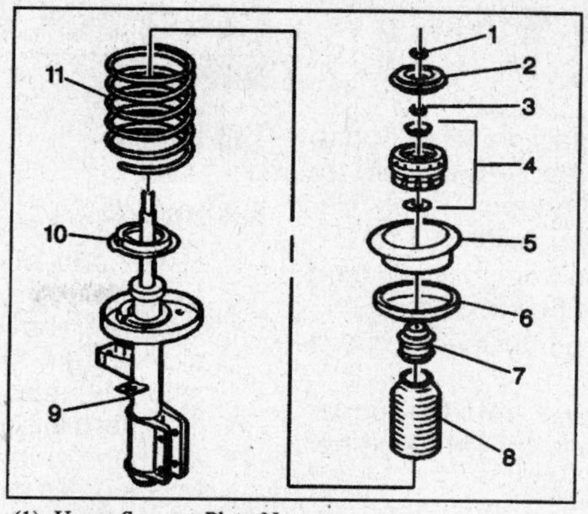

(1) Upper Support Plate Nut
(2) Upper Support Plate
(3) Upper Bearing Support Nut
(4) Bearing and Bearing Plate Assembly
(5) Upper Spring Support Plate
(6) Upper Insulator
(7) Strut Bumper
(8) Strut Cover
(9) Strut
(10) Lower Insulator
(11) Spring

GC2029700219000X

Fig. 1 Coil spring & strut components

STRUT

REPLACE

1. Raise and support vehicle, then remove front wheel.
2. Disconnect wheel speed sensor and brake wear indicator electrical connectors, then disengage brake flex hose from clip at strut.
3. Remove caliper bolts, then separate caliper from knuckle. **Do not open brake hydraulic system. Support caliper aside to prevent brake hose damage.**
4. Remove stabilizer shaft link nut, then separate link from strut.
5. Remove strut lower mounting bolts, then lower vehicle and remove upper support plate cap and nut.
6. Remove upper support plate, then the strut assembly.
7. Reverse procedure to install, noting the following:
   a. Tighten upper support and stabilizer shaft link nuts to specifications.
   b. Use new bolts to secure strut to steering knuckle and install from front of vehicle toward rear, then tighten only until snug. Final tightening will occur after wheel alignment procedures have been performed.
   c. Install and tighten caliper assembly as outlined under " Hub, Bearing & Seal, Replace."
   d. Adjust wheel alignment as outlined in "Wheel Alignment " section, then tighten strut to steering knuckle bolts to specifications.

COIL SPRING & STRUT SERVICE

1. Place strut assembly in strut spring compressor tool No. J-34013-A, or equivalent, with adapter tool No. J-34013-88, or equivalent.
2. Prevent strut piston from rotating, then remove upper bearing support nut.
3. Compress strut spring, then remove bearing and plate.
4. Release spring and remove upper support plate, insulator, strut bumper and cover, **Fig. 1.**
5. Separate spring from strut, then remove lower insulator.
6. Reverse procedure to assemble, noting the following:
   a. **Do not allow coil spring protective coating to be chipped or scratched. Premature spring failure may result.**
   b. Tighten bearing nut to specifications.

CONTROL ARM

REPLACE

LOWER

Removal

1. Raise and support vehicle, then remove front tire and wheel assembly.
2. Separate brake pad wear indicator sleeve from strut, then remove wheel speed sensor.
3. Separate brake hose from strut bracket, then remove caliper from steering knuckle. **Do not open brake hydraulic system. Suspend caliper to prevent brake hose damage.**
4. Remove outer tie rod ball stud nut, then use tie rod separator tool No. J-6627-A, or equivalent, to separate tie rod from knuckle.
5. Remove stabilizer shaft link nut from shaft and steering knuckle bolts from strut.
6. Remove lower control arm ball stud pinch bolt, then separate steering knuckle from ball stud. Allow hub and brake rotor to remain in place.
7. Loosen control arm horizontal and vertical bolts, then remove horizontal bolt and turn arm away from support bracket.
8. Remove vertical bolt, then the control arm.

Installation

1. Install lower control arm and new vertical bolt, then tighten bolt only until snug. Final tightening will occur after horizontal bolt installation.
2. Position front of control arm in support bracket, then install new horizontal bolt from rearward side of vehicle.
3. Ensure control arm is in horizontal position, then tighten bolts to specifications.
4. Connect steering knuckle to lower control arm ball stud, using new pinch bolt inserted from rearward side of vehicle. Tighten pinch bolt to specifications.
5. Connect steering knuckle to strut with new bolts installed from front of vehicle toward rear. Tighten bolts only until snug.

6. Connect stabilizer shaft link to shaft, then install nut and tighten to specifications.
7. Connect outer tie rod to steering knuckle, then position linkage installer tool No. J-42089, or equivalent, over tie rod ball stud.
8. **Torque** installer tool to 22 ft. lbs. to seat ball stud taper, then remove tool from ball stud.
9. Install new self-locking tie rod nut and tighten to specifications, then install caliper assembly on steering knuckle as outlined under "Hub, Bearing & Seal, Replace."
10. Attach brake hose to strut bracket, then install wheel speed sensor and tighten to specifications.
11. Attach brake pad wear indicator sleeve to strut, then install front wheel and lower vehicle.
12. Adjust wheel alignment as outlined in "Wheel Alignment" section.

CONTROL ARM BUSHING

REPLACE

1. Remove control arm as outlined under "Control Arm, Replace," then install bushing replacement tools turn, **Figs. 2 and 3.**
2. Press bushing out of control arm.
3. Reverse procedure to install. Ensure bushing is installed flush with control arm.

STEERING KNUCKLE

REPLACE

1. Raise and support vehicle, then remove front wheel.
2. Remove hub as outlined under "Hub, Bearing & Seal, Replace," then the brake rotor splash shield.
3. Remove ball stud nut from outer tie rod, then use tie rod separator tool No. J-6627-A, or equivalent, to separate tie rod from knuckle.
4. Remove steering knuckle to strut bolts, then separate knuckle from strut.
5. Remove lower control arm ball stud pinch bolt, then separate knuckle from control arm ball stud.
6. Reverse procedure to install, noting the following:
   a. Install new control arm ball stud pinch bolt and strut to steering knuckle bolts.
   b. Tighten control arm ball stud pinch bolt to specifications, but do not tighten strut to steering knuckle bolts until wheel alignment is complete.
   c. To attach tie rod to knuckle, position linkage installer tool No. J-42089, or equivalent, over tie rod ball stud and **torque** to 22 ft. lbs. to seat taper, then install new self-locking tie rod nut and tighten to specifications.
   d. Adjust wheel alignment as outlined in "Wheel Alignment" section, then tighten strut to steering knuckle bolts as outlined under "Strut, Replace."

STABILIZER BAR

REPLACE

1997

1. Install suitable engine support fixture, then raise and support vehicle.
2. Remove front wheels, then disengage wheel speed sensor and brake pad wear indicator wires from strut clips.
3. Disconnect and remove wheel speed sensors, then disengage brake flex hose clips and hoses from struts.
4. Remove brake calipers from steering knuckles. **Do not open brake hydraulic system. Suspend calipers aside to prevent damage to brake hoses.**
5. Remove outer tie rod nuts, then separate tie rod ball studs from knuckles with tie rod separator tool No. J-6627-A, or equivalent.
6. Remove lower control arm ball stud pinch bolts, then separate steering knuckles from control arm ball studs.
7. Remove stabilizer bar link nuts and separate links from bar, then remove engine mount nuts.
8. With engine crossmember frame supported, remove frame mounting bolts, then carefully lower frame.
9. Remove stabilizer bar insulator bolts, then the bar and insulators.
10. Reverse procedure to install, noting the following:
    a. Use new stabilizer bar insulator bolts and engine crossmember frame bolts.
    b. **Torque** stabilizer bar insulator bolts to 15 ft. lbs., then tighten an additional 37° using torque/angle meter tool No. J-36660, or equivalent.
    c. **Torque** engine crossmember frame to body bolts to 111 ft. lbs., then tighten an additional 37° using torque/angle meter tool.
    d. **Torque** engine crossmember frame to radiator support bolts to 48 ft. lbs., then tighten an additional 37° using suitable torque/angle meter tool.
    e. Tighten stabilizer bar link nuts and new lower control arm ball stud pinch bolts to specifications. Refer to "3.0L Engine" section for engine mount tightening specifications.
    f. To attach tie rod to knuckle, position linkage installer tool No. J-42089, or equivalent, over tie rod ball stud and **torque** to 22 ft. lbs. to seat taper, then install new self-locking tie rod nut and tighten to specifications.
    g. Tighten outer tie rod nuts and wheel speed sensor bolts to specifications. Refer to "Hub, Bearing & Seal, Replace" for caliper installation and tightening specifications.

1998–2000

1. Raise and support vehicle.
2. Attach engine support fixture tool No. J28467-A, or equivalent, at engine lift points.
3. Raise and support vehicle, then remove front wheel and tire assemblies.
4. Remove wheel speed sensor from strut assembly, then the brake wear indicator wires.
5. Remove brake flex hose clips and hose from strut assembly, then the wheel speed sensors.
6. Remove brake caliper, then the outer tie rods using tie rod/wheel stud puller tool No. J6627-A, or equivalent.
7. Remove lower control arm ball stud pinch bolts, then the steering knuckles from lower control arm ball studs.
8. Remove stabilizer shaft links from stabilizer shaft, then the engine mount nuts.
9. Support crossmember frame.
10. Remove front crossmember frame bolts, then the crossmember.
11. Remove stabilizer shaft insulator bolts, then the stabilizer shaft.
12. Reverse procedures to install. Tighten bolts to specifications.

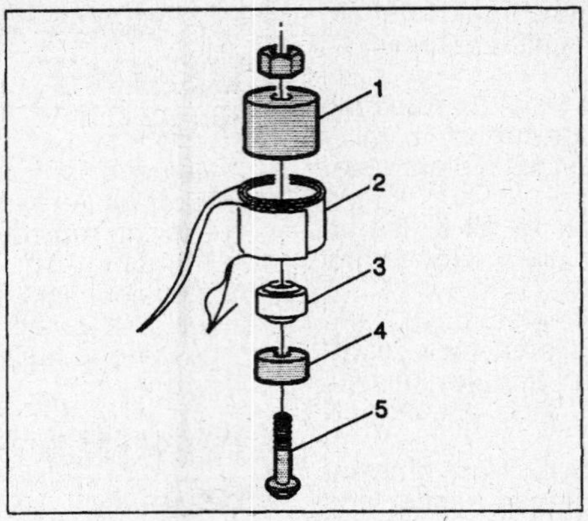

(1) J 42092-1, Receiver
(2) Lower Control Arm
(3) Bushing
(4) J 42092-2, Bushing Remover/Installer Tool
(5) J 42200, Rear Lower Control Arm Bushing Remover/Installer Bolt

GC2029700220000X

Fig. 2 Control arm horizontal bushing replacement

STABILIZER BAR BUSHING

REPLACE

Refer to "Stabilizer Bar, Replace" for bar and bushing replacement procedures.

TIE ROD

REPLACE

Never attempt to separate a steering linkage joint by driving a wedge between components. Seal damage may result.

INNER

1. Raise and support vehicle, then loosen tie rod clamp bolt at end of tie rod adjuster.
2. Remove tie rod ball stud nut, then separate ball stud from relay rod with tie rod separator tool No. J-6627-A, or equivalent.
3. Remove tie rod from adjuster, counting number of turns for installation reference.
4. Reverse procedure to install, noting the following:
   a. Lubricate tie rod adjuster threads with suitable Extra Pressure (EP) chassis lubricant.
   b. To connect tie rod ball stud to relay rod, position linkage tool No. J-42089, or equivalent, over ball stud and **torque** tool to 22 ft. lbs. This will seat taper.
   c. Install new self-locking tie rod ball stud nut and tighten to specifications.
   d. With adjuster and clamps positioned turn, **Fig. 4,** tighten adjuster clamp bolt to specifications, then adjust toe as outlined in "Wheel Alignment" section.

OUTER

1. Raise and support vehicle, then loosen tie rod clamp bolt near tie rod end.
2. Remove tie rod ball stud nut, then separate tie rod from knuckle with tie rod puller tool No. J-6627-A, or equivalent.
3. Remove tie rod from adjuster, noting the following:
   a. Outer tie rod has lefthand threads.
   b. Count number of turns required to remove tie rod for installation reference.
4. Reverse procedure to install, noting the following:
   a. Lubricate tie rod adjuster threads with Extra Pressure (EP) chassis lubricant.
   b. To connect tie rod ball stud to steering knuckle, position linkage tool No. J-42089, or equivalent, over ball stud and **torque** tool to 22 ft. lbs. to seat taper in knuckle, then install new self-locking ball stud nut and tighten to specifications.
   c. With adjuster and clamps positioned turn, **Fig. 4,** tighten clamp bolts to specifications, then adjust toe as outlined under "Wheel Alignment."

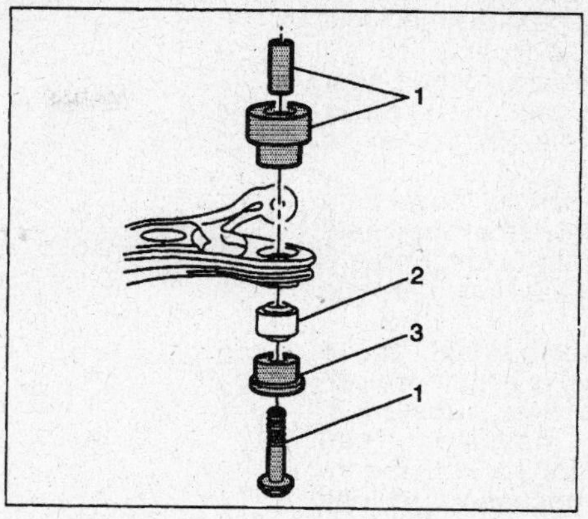

(1) J 21474, Universal Bushing Remover/Installer Kit
(2) Bushing
(3) J 42112-4, Rear Differential Bushing Remover/Installer Tool

GC2029700221000X

Fig. 3 Control arm vertical bushing replacement

POWER STEERING GEAR

REPLACE

1. Remove windshield wiper assembly.
2. Disconnect three body harness electrical connectors, **Fig. 5,** and remove Engine Control Module (ECM) from electrical box.
3. Drain engine coolant into suitable container, then remove upper radiator hose.
4. Discharge and recover A/C system as outlined under "Air Conditioning." Remove A/C evaporator line extension bolt, **Fig. 6.**
5. Siphon power steering fluid from reservoir, then remove reservoir bracket bolt and position reservoir aside.
6. Siphon brake fluid from reservoir, then disconnect brake booster vacuum line at intake plenum.

7. Disconnect brake pipes and electrical connector at master cylinder.
8. Make mating marks on steering gear splines and lower steering coupler, then disengage tabs and remove sound insulator.
9. Remove steering coupler bolts from coupler. **Do not allow steering wheel to turn when coupler is disconnected. Air bag clockspring damage may result.**
10. Place steering wheel in straight ahead position and lock in place, then remove ignition key. **Because substantial steering wheel movement can occur before ignition locking mechanism sets, it is necessary to lock steering wheel with suitable external locking device.**
11. Carefully spread coupler clamp ears apart until steering shaft can be moved upward and away from steering gear.
12. Remove retaining clip and pin, then disconnect brake pedal from booster link rod.
13. Remove lefthand instrument panel knee bolster, then remove fuse and relay panel screws and position panels away from upper vacuum booster nuts.
14. Remove vacuum booster and master cylinder as an assembly, then disconnect A/C evaporator line extension quick connect fitting.

Fig. 4 Tie rod adjuster & clamp orientation

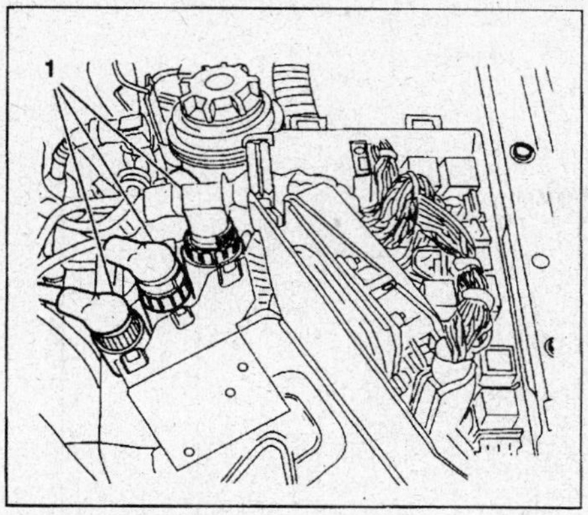

(1) Body Harness Electrical Connector

GC6029700118000X

Fig. 5 Body harness electrical connectors

15. Disconnect power steering hoses at steering gear and position away from Electronic Brake/Traction Control Module (EBTCM)/Brake Pressure Modulator Valve (BPMV) assembly, then remove EBTCM/BPMV.
16. Remove upper heat shield bolt, then raise and support vehicle.
17. Make mating marks on pitman arm and steering gear splines, then remove pitman arm nut and washer.
18. Using suitable pitman arm puller, remove arm from steering gear.
19. Remove lower heat shield nuts and lower steering gear bolts, nuts and washers.
20. Lower vehicle and remove heat shield, then disconnect power steering fluid flow control valve actuator electrical connector.
21. Remove upper steering gear bolt and shims. Note shim positions for installation reference.
22. Remove steering gear.
23. Reverse procedure to install, noting the following:
    a. Prior to installation, turn stub shaft from stop to stop and count number of turns, then turn shaft back ½ that number of turns. Align stub shaft mark with steering gear case "V" mark to center gear.
    b. Upper steering gear bolt should be installed and tightened until snug, but final tightening should not occur until remaining bolts are installed.
    c. Tighten steering gear bolts, heat shield, pitman arm nut, steering gear inlet and outlet hoses and coupler bolts to specifications.
    d. When connecting A/C evaporator line extension fittings, use new O-rings lubricated in 525 viscosity mineral oil.
    e. Ensure cooling, power steering and brake systems are filled with appropriate fluid and are bleed as required. Refer to "Power Steering System Bleed" in this section for steering system bleed procedures.

POWER STEERING PUMP

REPLACE

1. Siphon power steering fluid from reservoir.
2. Loosen power steering pump pulley bolts, then remove serpentine drive belt as outlined in "3.0L Engine" section.
3. Remove bolts and pulley from pump, then disconnect gear inlet hose at pump.
4. **On 1998–2000 models,** remove fluid reservoir inlet hose clamp, then the fluid reservoir inlet hose from power steering pump.

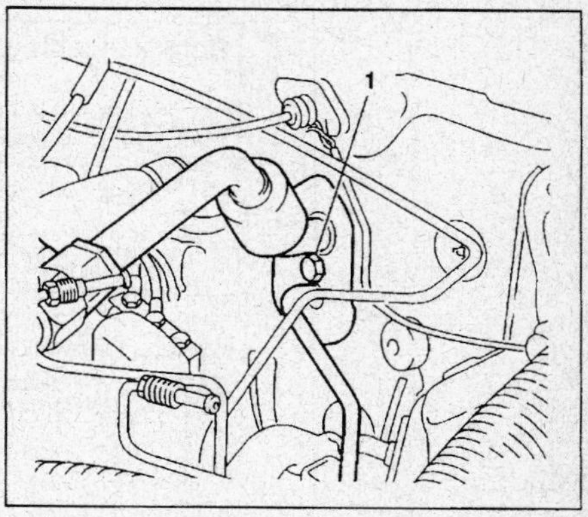

(1) Evaporator Line Extension to Cowl Bolt

GC6029700119000X

Fig. 6 Evaporator line extension bolt

5. **On all models,** raise and support vehicle, then remove Secondary Air Injection (AIR) crossover pipe support bracket.
6. Remove power steering pump mounting bolts, then the pump.
7. Reverse procedure to install, noting the following:
    a. Tighten pump mounting bolts and hose connections to specifications.
    b. Bleed system as outlined under "Power Steering System Bleed."

POWER STEERING SYSTEM BLEED

Refer to **Fig. 7** for power steering system bleed procedures. If the power steering system has been serviced, the system must be bled to obtain an accurate fluid level reading and to ensure proper system operation.

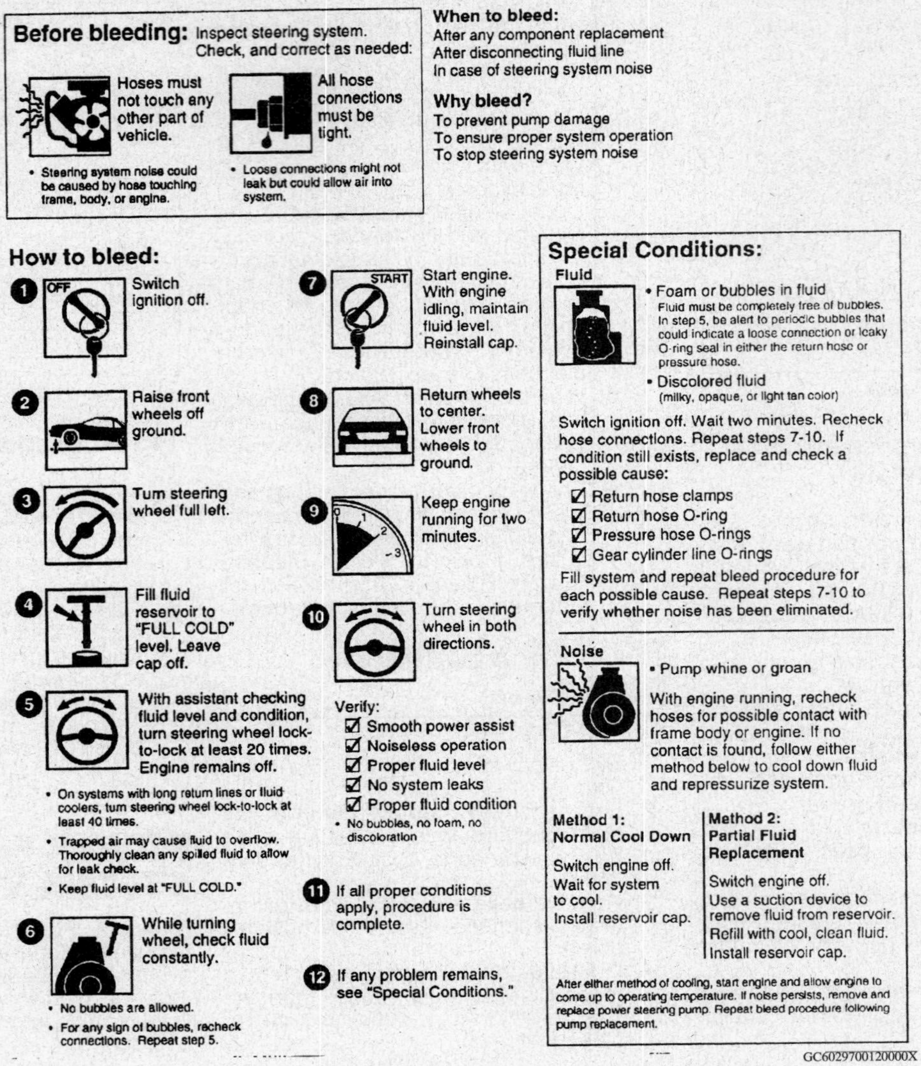

Before bleeding: Inspect steering system.
Check, and correct as needed:
Hoses must not touch any other part of vehicle.
• Steering system noise could be caused by hose touching frame, body, or engine.
All hose connections must be tight.
• Loose connections might not leak but could allow air into system.
When to bleed:
After any component replacement
After disconnecting fluid line
In case of steering system noise
Why bleed?
To prevent pump damage
To ensure proper system operation
To stop steering system noise
How to bleed:
1
OFF
Switch ignition off.
2
Raise front wheels off ground.
3
Turn steering wheel full left.
4
Fill fluid reservoir to "FULL COLD" level. Leave cap off.
5
With assistant checking fluid level and condition, turn steering wheel lock-to-lock at least 20 times. Engine remains off.
• On systems with long return lines or fluid coolers, turn steering wheel lock-to-lock at least 40 times.
• Trapped air may cause fluid to overflow. Thoroughly clean any spilled fluid to allow for leak check.
• Keep fluid level at "FULL COLD."
6
While turning wheel, check fluid constantly.
• No bubbles are allowed.
• For any sign of bubbles, recheck connections. Repeat step 5.
7
START
Start engine. With engine idling, maintain fluid level. Reinstall cap.
8
Return wheels to center. Lower front wheels to ground.
9
0
1
2
3
Keep engine running for two minutes.
10
Turn steering wheel in both directions.
Verify:
☑ Smooth power assist
☑ Noiseless operation
☑ Proper fluid level
☑ No system leaks
☑ Proper fluid condition
• No bubbles, no foam, no discoloration
11
If all proper conditions apply, procedure is complete.
12
If any problem remains, see "Special Conditions."
Special Conditions:
Fluid
• Foam or bubbles in fluid
Fluid must be completely free of bubbles. In step 5, be alert to periodic bubbles that could indicate a loose connection or leaky O-ring seal in either the return hose or pressure hose.
• Discolored fluid
(milky, opaque, or light tan color)
Switch ignition off. Wait two minutes. Recheck hose connections. Repeat steps 7-10. If condition still exists, replace and check a possible cause:
☑ Return hose clamps
☑ Return hose O-ring
☑ Pressure hose O-rings
☑ Gear cylinder line O-rings
Fill system and repeat bleed procedure for each possible cause. Repeat steps 7-10 to verify whether noise has been eliminated.
Noise
• Pump whine or groan
With engine running, recheck hoses for possible contact with frame body or engine. If no contact is found, follow either method below to cool down fluid and repressurize system.
Method 1: Normal Cool Down
Switch engine off.
Wait for system to cool.
Install reservoir cap.
Method 2: Partial Fluid Replacement
Switch engine off.
Use a suction device to remove fluid from reservoir.
Refill with cool, clean fluid.
Install reservoir cap.
After either method of cooling, start engine and allow engine to come up to operating temperature. If noise persists, remove and replace power steering pump. Repeat bleed procedure following pump replacement.
GC6029700120000X

Fig. 7 Power steering system bleed

TIGHTENING SPECIFICATIONS

Year	Component	Torque/Ft. Lbs.
1997–2000	A/C Evaporator Line Extension Bolt	15
	Ball Stud To Lower Control Arm	26
	Brake Caliper	70②
	Brake Pipes To Master Cylinder	12
	Brake Rotor Setscrew	35①
	Brake Rotor Splash Shield	35①
	Brake Vacuum Booster	15
	Heat Shield Lower Nuts	11
	Heat Shield Upper Bolt	72①
	Hub (Wheel Bearing)	236
	Lower Control Arm	103
	Lower Control Arm Ball Stud Pinch Bolt	74
	Pitman Arm	118
	Power Steering Fluid Reservoir Clamp	60①
	Power Steering Gear Hoses	21
	Power Steering Pump	15
	Power Steering Pump Pulley	15
	Stabilizer Shaft Insulator Bolts	15②
	Stabilizer Shaft Link To Shaft	48
	Steering Gear	30
	Strut Assembly Bearing	52
	Strut To Steering Knuckle	66③
	Strut Upper Support	41
	Tie Rod Adjuster Clamp	11
	Tie Rod Ball Studs	44
	Wheel Speed Sensor	72①
	Wheel To Hub	80

① — Inch lbs.
② — Tighten an additional 37.°
③ — Tighten an additional 52.°

Wheel Alignment

INDEX

PRELIMINARY INSPECTION

1. Ensure all tires are of recommended size and are inflated to proper pressure.
2. Inspect all tires for damage and uneven tread wear.
3. Ensure wheel bearings, control arm ball studs and bushings, relay rods and tie rod ends are in satisfactory condition. Looseness must be corrected before wheels can be aligned.
4. Inspect wheel and tire radial and lateral runout. With wheel and tire assembly off vehicle, runout should be approximately .050 inch. When on vehicle, runout should be approximately .060 inch.
5. If wheel and tire assembly runout specifications cannot be met, separate tire from wheel and measure wheel runout. Wheel runout should be approximately .030 inch.
6. Inspect vehicle ride height as outlined under "Vehicle Ride Height." If corrections are required, complete them prior to setting wheel alignment.
7. Ensure steering gear is not loose at frame mounting.
8. Inspect stabilizer shafts for loose or missing components.
9. Ensure struts and shocks are not leaking or excessively worn and strut upper mounts are in satisfactory condition.
10. Inspect all remaining suspension and steering components for damage and repair or replace prior to setting wheel alignment.
11. Ensure fuel tank is full or compensating ballast is added for proper weight distribution.
12. Ensure vehicle is on level surface and all loads that are normally carried inside vehicle are present.
13. Jounce front and rear of vehicle three times before beginning wheel alignment procedures.

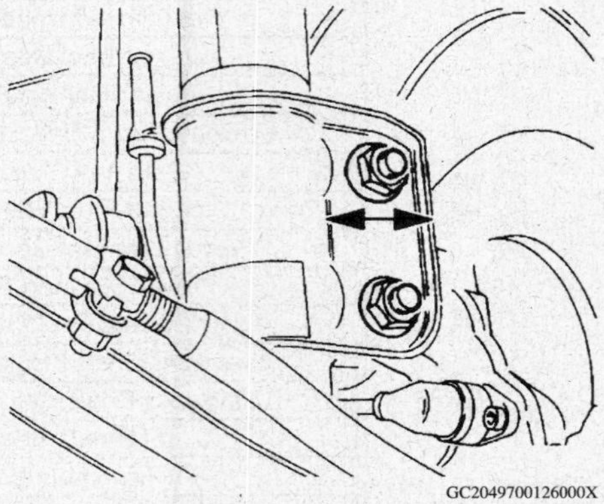

Fig. 1 Front camber adjustment

FRONT WHEEL ALIGNMENT

Caster must be satisfactory prior to adjusting camber. Likewise, camber settings must be satisfactory prior to adjusting toe. **Adjust rear toe before adjusting front camber or toe.**

Fig. 2 Front tie rod adjuster & clamp orientation

CASTER

Caster angles can be measured but cannot be adjusted. If angles are improper, service suspension components as required.

CAMBER

1. Raise and support vehicle, then remove front wheel and separate brake caliper from knuckle. **Do not open brake hydraulic system. Suspend caliper aside to prevent brake hose damage.**
2. Remove strut lower mounting bolts, then insert new bolts from front toward rear of vehicle and **torque** to 15 ft. lbs.
3. Inspect brake caliper mounting hole threads in steering knuckle and remove any residual locking compound.
4. Install caliper with new mounting bolts. Coat bolts with suitable thread locking compound and **torque** to 70 ft. lbs. then tighten an additional 37°.
5. Install wheel and **torque** bolts to 80 ft. lbs., then set camber turn, **Fig. 1.**
6. **Torque** strut lower mounting bolts to 66 ft. lbs., then tighten an additional 52°.

TOE

Toe adjustments are made separately for each wheel.

1. Set steering wheel in straight ahead position, then turn inner and outer tie rod sockets to limit of control arm ball stud travel.
2. Loosen clamp bolts at each end of tie rod adjuster, then turn adjuster until proper toe setting is achieved.
3. Position tie rod adjuster and clamps as shown, **Fig. 2,** then **torque** clamp bolts to 11 ft. lbs.
4. Ensure same number of threads are exposed on either side of adjuster and outer tie rod ends are at right angles to steering knuckles.

REAR WHEEL ALIGNMENT

Adjust rear toe before performing procedures outlined under "Front Wheel Alignment."

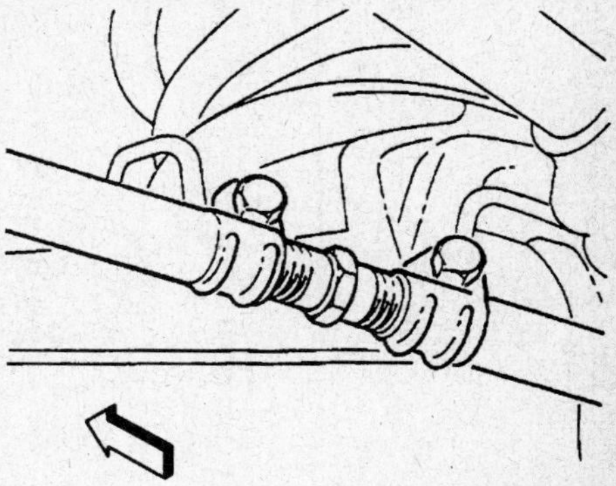

Fig. 3 Rear tie rod adjuster & clamps

TOE

1. Loosen both tie rod adjuster clamps, **Fig. 3,** then turn threaded sleeve until proper toe is achieved.
2. **Torque** tie rod adjuster clamp bolts to 11 ft. lbs.

VEHICLE RIDE HEIGHT

1. Ensure tire pressures are proper and fuel tank is full. Compensating weight may be added to simulate weight of full fuel tank.

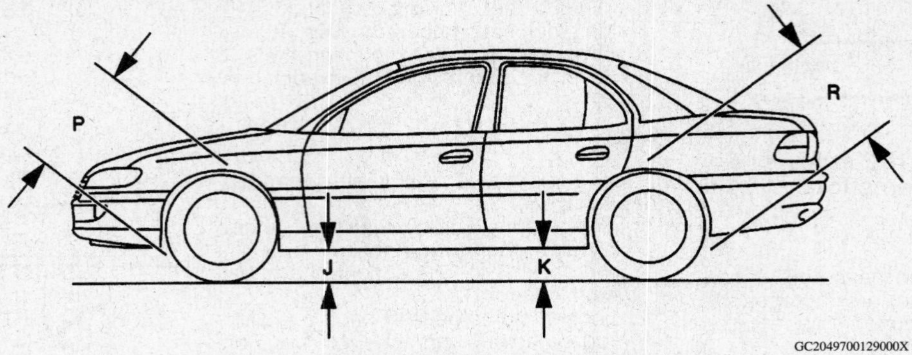

Fig. 4 Vehicle ride height dimensions

2. Slide front seats to full rearward position and ensure trunk contains only spare tire and factory jack.
3. Park vehicle on level surface with
4. Push front bumper down approximately 1.5 inches by hand, then allow vehicle to rise.
5. Measure dimensions J and P, **Fig. 4.** Dimension J should be 6.5 inches and P should be 27.3 inches.
6. If dimensions are as indicated, proceed to next step. If not, front springs must be replaced to correct ride height.
7. Lift rear bumper approximately 1.5 inches by hand, then allow vehicle to settle gently.
8. Push rear bumper down approximately 1.5 inches by hand, then allow vehicle to rise.
9. Measure dimensions K and R, **Fig. 4.** Dimension K should be 6.9 inches and R should be 27.3 inches.
10. If dimensions are as indicated, ride height is satisfactory. If not, rear springs must be replaced to correct ride height. doors, hood and trunk lid closed.
11. Lift front bumper approximately 1.5 inches by hand, then allow vehicle to settle gently.

CAVALIER & SUNFIRE

NOTE: Refer To The Rear Of This Manual For Manufacturer's Special Service Tool Suppliers.

INDEX OF SERVICE OPERATIONS

Specifications

GENERAL ENGINE SPECIFICATIONS

Year	Engine		Fuel System	Bore × Stroke	Comp-ression Ratio	Net H.P. @ RPM③	Maximum Torque Ft. Lbs. @ RPM	Normal Oil Pressure psi
	Liter	VIN Code②						
1997	2.2L	4	SFI	3.50 × 3.46	9.0	120 @ 5200	130 @ 4000	56④
	2.4L	T	SFI	3.54 × 3.70	9.5	150 @ 6000	155 @ 4400	①
1998	2.2L	4	SFI	3.50 × 3.46	9.0	115 @ 5000	135 @ 3600	56④
	2.4L	T	SFI	3.54 × 3.70	9.5	150 @ 5600	155 @ 4400	①
1999–2000	2.2L	4	SFI	3.50 × 3.46	8.85	115 @ 5000	135 @ 3600	56④
	2.4L	T	SFI	3.54 × 3.70	9.5	150 @ 5600	155 @ 4400	①

SFI — Sequential fuel injection
① — 10 @ 900 RPM; 30 @ 3000 RPM.
② — The eighth digit denotes engine code.
③ — Ratings are net as installed in vehicle.
④ — At 3000 RPM.

TUNE UP SPECIFICATIONS

Year & Engine	Spark Plug Gap	Firing Order Fig.	Ignition Timing BTDC	Timing Mark Fig.	Curb Idle Speed	Fast Idle Speed	Fuel Pump Pressure	Valve Lash
1997								
2.2L	.060	②	⑦	⑥	④	④	41–47③	①
2.4L	.060	⑤	⑦	⑥	④	④	41–47③	①
1998								
2.2L	.040	②	⑦	⑥	④	④	41–47③	①
2.4L	.050	⑤	⑦	⑥	④	④	41–47③	①
1999–2000								
2.2L	.040	②	⑦	⑥	④	④	41–47③	①
2.4L	.050	⑤	⑦	⑥	④	④	52–58③	①

BTDC — Before Top Dead Center

① — Equipped w/hydraulic valve lifters. No adjustment is required.

② — Cylinder numbering from front of engine to rear of engine, 1,2,3,4. Firing order 1–3–4–2. Coil connections are stamped on the coil assemblies.

③ — Relieve fuel system pressure as outlined under "Fuel System Pressure Relief" under "Precautions" in the appropriate engine section. Then, connect suitable fuel pressure gauge between fuel line and fuel rail. Connect battery ground cable. Turn ignition On and note fuel pressure reading.

④ — Idle speeds are controlled by the Idle Air Control (IAC) valve.

⑤ — Cylinder numbering from front of engine to rear of engine, 1, 2, 3, 4. Firing order 1–3–4–2. Refer to **Fig. A** for spark plug wire connection at coil unit.

⑥ — Equipped w/crankshaft sensor.

⑦ — No adjustment.

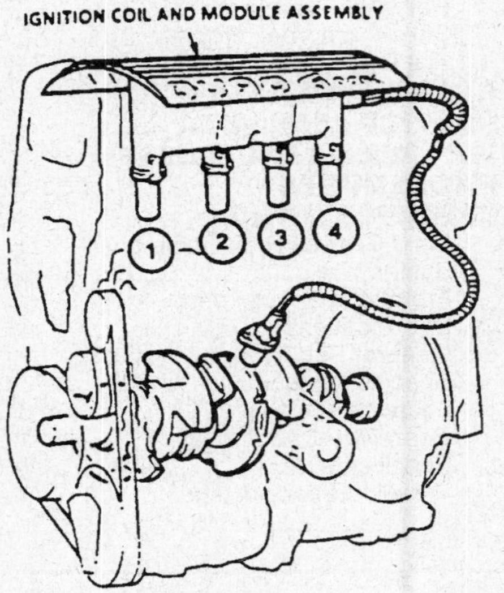

Firing order 1-3-4-2

GC1139500573000X

Fig. A

FRONT WHEEL ALIGNMENT SPECIFICATIONS

Year	Caster Angle, Degrees		Camber Angle, Degrees		Total Toe, Degrees	Ball Joint Wear
	Limits	Desired	Limits	Desired		
1997	+3.3 to +5.3①	4.3①	−1.20 to +.80	−.2	.05	②
1998–99	+.45 to +2.45①	+1.45①	−1 to +1	0	0	②
2000	+3.3 to +5.3①	4.3①	−1 to +1	0	0	②

① — Non-adjustable. For inspection purposes only.

② — Refer to the "Front Suspension & Steering" section for ball joint specifications and inspection procedure.

REAR WHEEL ALIGNMENT SPECIFICATIONS

Year	Camber Angle, Degrees①		Thrust Angle, Degrees①		Total Toe, Degrees①	
	Limits	Desired	Limits	Desired	Limits	Desired
1997	−1 to +.5	−.25	−.25 to +.25	0	−.1 to +.5	+.2
1998–2000	−1.15 to +.35	−.4	−.25 to +.25	0	−.1 to +.5	+.2

① — Non-adjustable. For inspection purposes only.

FLUID CAPACITIES & COOLING SYSTEM DATA

Year	Engine	Coolant Capacity, Qts.	Radiator Cap Relief Pressure, Lbs.	Thermo. Opening Temp.	Fuel Tank Gals.	Engine Oil Refill Qts.②	Transaxle Oil	
							Manual Pts.	Automatic Qts.①
1997–98	2.2L	10.5	15	180	15.2	4	4	③
	2.4L	10.5	15	180	15.2	4	4	③
1999–2000	2.2L	10.3	15	180	15	4	4	④
	2.4L	10.7	15	180	15	4	4	④

① — Approximate. Make final inspection w/dipstick.

② — When changing engine oil filter additional oil may be required.

③ — 3T40 auto. trans.: oil pan only, 4 qts. after overhaul, 7 qts. 4T40E auto. trans.: oil pan only, 7.4 qts. after overhaul, 10.6 qts.

④ — 3T40 auto. trans.: oil pan only, 4 qts., after overhaul 7 qts. 4T40E auto. trans.: oil pan only, 6.9 qts., after overhaul 9.5 qts.

LUBRICANT DATA

Year	Lubricant Type			
	Transaxle		Power Steering	Brake System
	Manual	Automatic		
1997–2000	①	DEXRON III	②	DOT-3

① — Manual transmission fluid GM part No. 12345349, or equivalent.

② — Power steering fluid GM part No. 1052884, or equivalent.

Electrical

NOTE: On Air Bag Equipped Models, Refer To "Air Bag System Precautions" Located In The Front Of This Manual For System Disarming and Arming Procedures.

NOTE: Refer To "Computer Relearn Procedure " Located In The Front Of This Manual For Computer Relearn Procedures.

INDEX

PRECAUTIONS

AIR BAG SYSTEMS

Refer to "Air Bag System Precautions" in the front of this manual for system disarming and arming procedures.

BATTERY GROUND CABLE

Prior to service, disconnect battery ground cable and isolate as required.

FUSE PANEL & FLASHER LOCATION

The fuse panel is located on the lefthand side of the instrument panel. To access the panel, pivot the access door downward.

The turn signal and hazard flasher is located under the instrument panel on the lefthand side of steering column.

FUEL PUMP RELAY LOCATION

The fuel pump relay is located in the front lefthand corner of the engine compartment, in the engine compartment relay center.

RELAY CENTER LOCATION

The relay center is located in the front lefthand corner of the engine compartment, by the strut tower.

STARTER

REPLACE

1997 2.2L ENGINE

1. Raise and support vehicle, then remove bolts attaching starter motor and bracket to engine.
2. Lower starter motor and disconnect leads at solenoid.
3. Remove starter motor from vehicle. Note position of shims for installation, if equipped.
4. Reverse procedure to install.

1997 2.4L ENGINE & 1998-2000 MODELS

1. Remove air inlet duct to throttle body.
2. Remove top starter bolt, then raise and support vehicle.
3. Remove lower starter bolt and position starter aside.
4. Disconnect electrical wiring and remove starter.
5. Reverse procedure to install.

ALTERNATOR

REPLACE

1. Disconnect electrical connections to alternator, then the drive belt.
2. Remove alternator attaching bolts, then the alternator.
3. Reverse procedure to install.

COIL PACK

REPLACE

2.2L ENGINE

1. Raise and support vehicle.
2. Remove spark plug cables. Mark cables for installation reference.
3. Remove ignition coil to ignition module attaching screws, then the coils from the module.
4. Disconnect ignition module electrical connectors, then remove ignition module to assembly plate attaching bolts.
5. Remove ignition module from assembly plate.
6. Reverse procedure to install.

2.4L ENGINE

1. Remove accelerator and speed control cables from hold-down clip.
2. Remove fuel line retainer clip bolt.
3. Disconnect Ignition Control Module (ICM) 11-pin electrical connector.
4. Remove ignition coil and ignition control module assembly to camshaft housing attaching bolts.
5. Remove ignition coil and ICM assembly from camshaft housing. If spark plug boots stick to spark plugs use removal tool No. J-36011, or equivalent, to separate boots from spark plugs.
6. Reverse procedure to install.

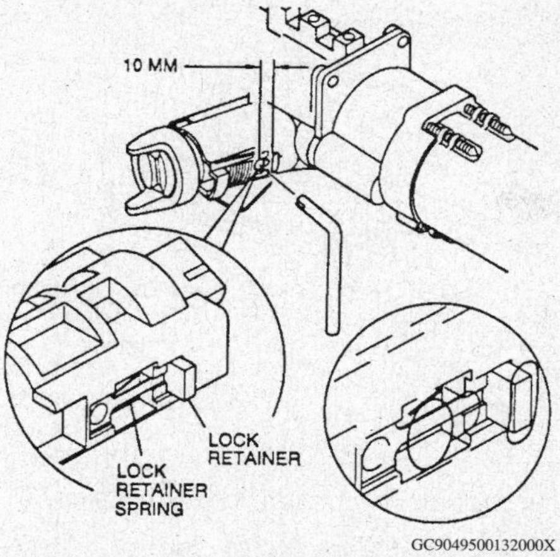

Fig. 1 Lock cylinder removal

IGNITION LOCK

REPLACE

KEY UNAVAILABLE

1. Disconnect wiring harness from ignition switch assembly.
2. Disconnect steering column from body as outlined under " Steering Columns."
3. Drill a 9⁄32 hole on back of steering column housing assembly.
4. Insert tool No. J-41253, or equivalent, **Fig. 1,** into hole to retain lock retainer spring, then turn tool to remove retainer spring.
5. Hold column vertical and tap on housing assembly to dislodge retainer.
6. Remove lock retainer and lock cylinder from housing.
7. Reverse procedure to install.

KEY AVAILABLE

1. **On models equipped with tilt column,** remove tilt lever.
2. **On all models,** remove steering column upper and lower trim covers.
3. Turn lock cylinder to Run.
4. Push against locking button on rear side of bearing and housing assembly, then remove lock cylinder by pulling it out of column.
5. Disconnect lock cylinder electrical connector.
6. Reverse procedure to install, noting the following:
   a. Turn lock cylinder to Run, then depress locking button.
   b. Gently push cylinder into place while rotating key approximately 5° counterclockwise.
   c. Inspect for proper operation.

IGNITION SWITCH

REPLACE

Refer to **Fig. 2** for ignition switch replacement.

CLUTCH START SWITCH

REPLACE

1997–98

1. Disconnect clutch start switch electrical connector.
2. Remove clutch bracket and switch attaching nuts, then the switch.
3. Reverse procedure to install. Ensure starter cranks only when clutch pedal is fully depressed.

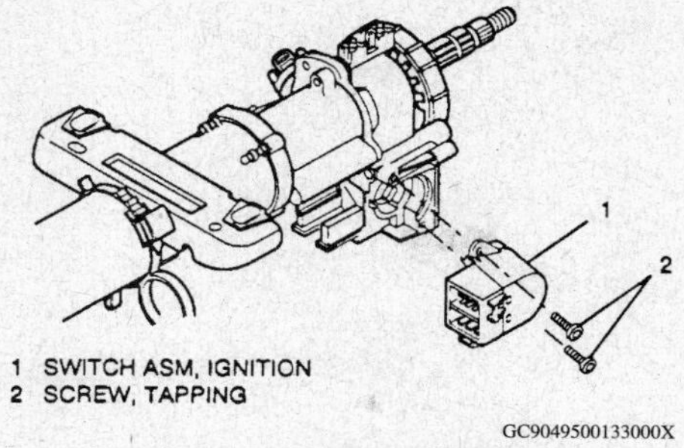

Fig. 2 Ignition switch replacement

1999–2000

1. Remove driver's instrument panel knee bolster.
2. Disconnect clutch start switch electrical connector.
3. Remove clutch start switch from pedal bracket.
4. Reverse procedure to install. Ensure starter cranks only when clutch pedal is fully depressed.

NEUTRAL SAFETY SWITCH

REPLACE

On models equipped with automatic transmission, the neutral start and back-up lamp switches are combined into one unit and must be replaced as an assembly.

1. Disconnect shift linkage.
2. Disconnect electrical connector from switch.
3. Remove switch attaching bolts, then the switch assembly, **Fig. 3.**
4. If same switch is to be installed again, proceed as follows:
   a. Place shift shaft in Neutral position.
   b. Align flats of shift shaft with switch, then install switch.
   c. Loosely install attaching bolts.
   d. Insert gauge pin, **Fig. 3,** or a 3⁄32 inch drill bit in service adjustment hole and rotate switch until pin drops in to a depth of 9⁄64 inch (9 mm).
   e. **Torque** attaching bolts to 18 ft. lbs.
5. If a new switch is to be installed, proceed as follows:
   a. Place shift shaft in Neutral position.
   b. Align flats of shift shaft with switch, then install switch.
   c. If bolt holes do not align with mounting boss on transaxle, ensure shift shaft is in Neutral position and do not rotate switch. Switch is pinned in Neutral position. If switch has been rotated and the pin has broken, use procedure outlined in step 4.
   d. **Torque** attaching bolts to 18 ft. lbs.

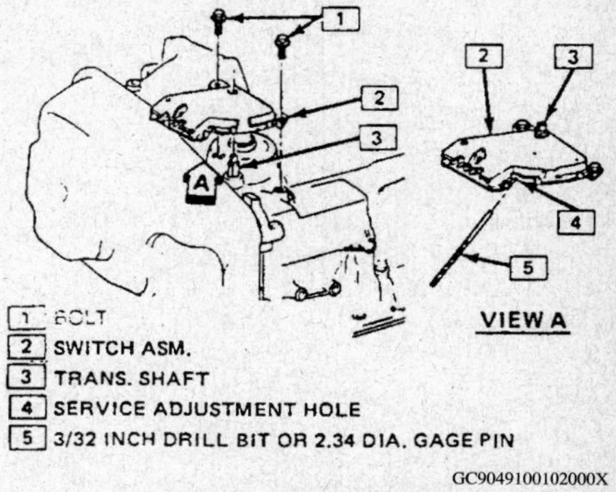

Fig. 3 Back-up lamp/neutral start switch replacement

6. Ensure engine will start only in Park or Neutral positions.

HEADLAMP SWITCH

REPLACE

The headlamp switch is part of the turn signal lever assembly and is not serviceable. The headlamp switch, turn signal lever and cruise control switch must be replaced as an assembly.

STOP LIGHT SWITCH

REPLACE

1. Remove drivers' side hush panel.
2. Disconnect switch electrical connector.
3. Remove switch from brake pedal support bracket. It may be necessary to rotate switch 90° counterclockwise, then pull it rearward.
4. Reverse procedure to install. Adjust switch as follows:
   a. Insert stop lamp switch in retainer until switch body seats on retainer.
   b. **On 1997 models,** pull brake pedal upward against internal pedal stop. Switch will be moved in retainer providing proper adjustment. Proper switch adjustment is achieved when no audible clicks are heard when the pedal is pulled upward and the brake lamps do not remain on without brake application.
   c. **On 1998–2000 models,** ensure the brake pedal is fully released and the stop lamp switch is fully depressed against brake pedal shanks. Insert switch and speed control switch into brake pedal bracket, then push pedal forward to set brake pushrod into booster. Pull brake pedal upward against internal pedal stop.
   d. **On all models,** inspect stop lamps for proper operation.

TURN SIGNAL SWITCH

REPLACE

1. Remove steering wheel as outlined under "Steering Wheel, Replace."
2. **On models with tilt steering,** remove tilt lever.

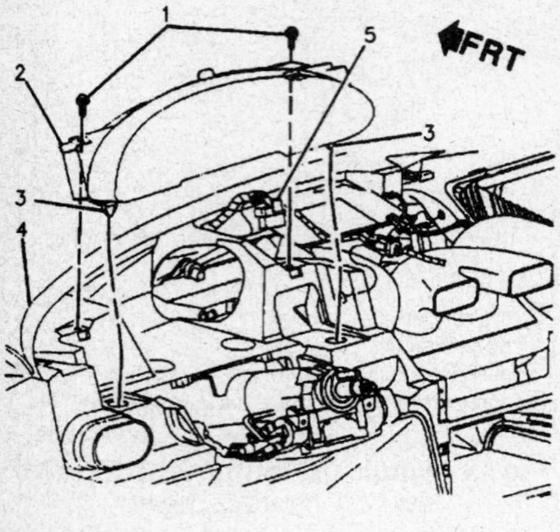

Fig. 4 Instrument cluster. Cavalier

3. **On all models,** remove upper and lower steering column covers.
4. **On 1997 models,** remove dampener assembly, then the switch assembly.
5. **On 1998–2000 models,** remove Torx head screws from multi-function switch, then the switch.
6. **On all models,** disconnect electrical connectors from switch.
7. Reverse procedure to install. Tighten fasteners to specifications.

DIMMER SWITCH

REPLACE

Refer to "Ignition Switch, Replace" for procedure.

STEERING WHEEL

REPLACE

1. Remove steering wheel center pad attaching screws.
2. Remove inflator module as outlined in "Air Bag Systems."
3. Disconnect horn electrical connector, then remove steering wheel center pad.
4. Remove steering wheel attaching nut and retainer.
5. Remove steering dampener, if equipped.
6. Scribe alignment marks on steering wheel and shaft to ease installation.
7. Using tool No. J-1859-A, or equivalent, remove steering wheel from shaft.
8. Reverse procedure to install. **On 1997 models, torque** steering wheel attaching nut to 30 ft. lbs. **On 1998–2000 models, torque** steering wheel attaching nut to 29 ft. lbs.

INSTRUMENT CLUSTER

REPLACE

1. **On Cavalier models,** remove instrument panel cluster trim plate, **Fig. 4.**

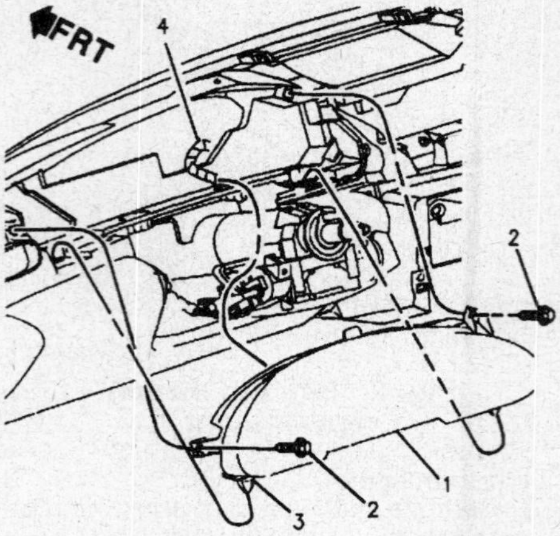

Fig. 5 Instrument cluster. Sunfire

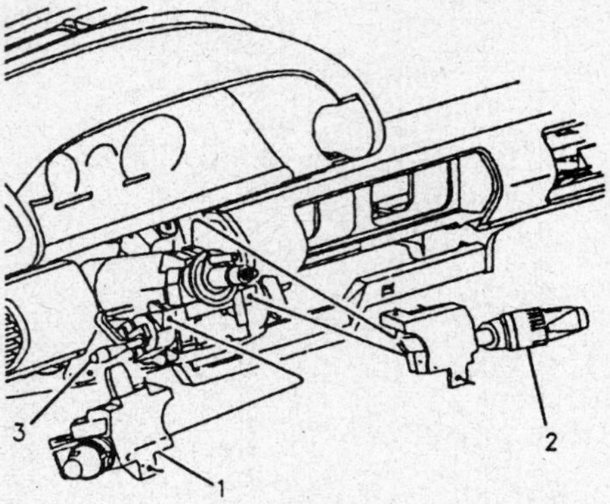

Fig. 6 Wiper switch removal

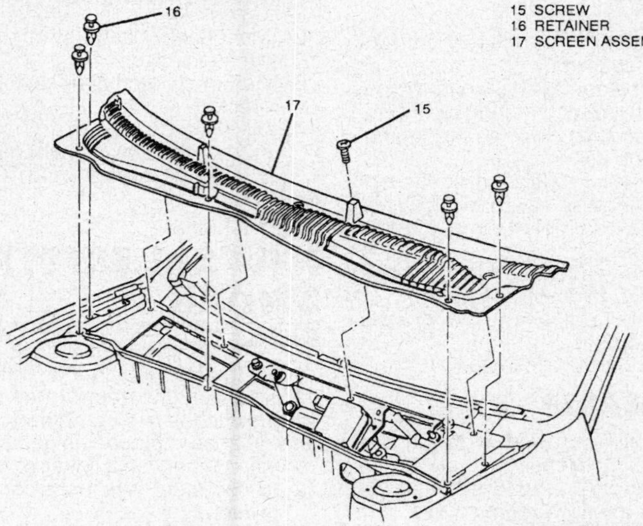

Fig. 7 Air inlet screen removal

2. **On Sunfire models,** remove instrument panel trim pad, **Fig. 5.**
3. **On all models,** remove screws from top of cluster.
4. Pull cluster rearward and disconnect electrical connectors, then remove cluster from instrument panel.
5. Reverse procedure to install.

WIPER MOTOR

REPLACE

1. Remove wiper arms from transmission spindle shafts.
2. Remove shroud top vent grille panel and screen.
3. **On 1997 models,** loosen, but do not remove, transmission drive link to motor crank arm attaching nuts, then pull drive link out of motor crank arm.
4. **On 1998–2000 models,** remove wiper transmission from crank arm using tool No. J-39232, or equivalent.
5. **On all models,** disconnect wiper motor electrical connections and remove wiper motor attaching bolts.
6. Rotate wiper motor upward and outward, then remove from vehicle.
7. Reverse procedure to install. **Torque** wiper motor attaching bolts to 84 inch lbs.

WIPER SWITCH

REPLACE

1. Remove horn pad and steering wheel as described under " Steering Wheel, Replace."
2. **On models equipped with tilt column,** remove tilt lever from column.
3. **On all models,** remove upper and lower steering column covers, **Fig. 6.**
4. Remove dampener assembly, then the headlamp switch assembly.
5. Remove windshield wiper switch assembly.
6. Reverse procedure to install.

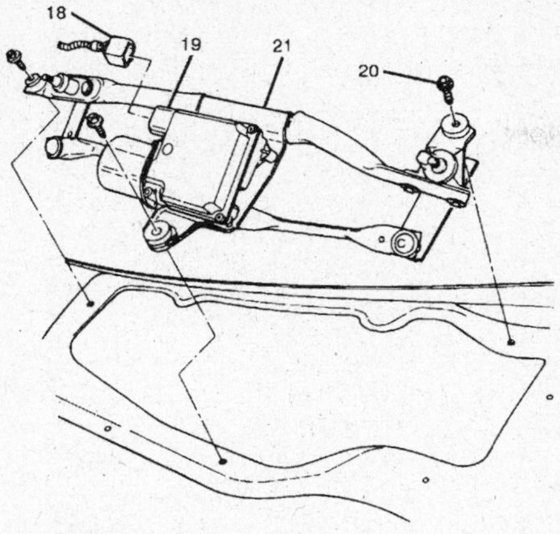

Fig. 8 Wiper motor connector

WIPER TRANSMISSION

REPLACE

1. Remove wiper arm assemblies from wiper transmission assembly drive shafts.
2. Remove air inlet screen attaching screws and retainers, then the air inlet screen, **Fig. 7.**
3. Disconnect wiper motor electrical connector, **Fig. 8.**
4. Remove three wiper module attaching screws, then the module, **Fig. 9.**
5. Using puller tool No. J-39232, or equivalent, remove wiper transmission assembly from wiper motor crank arm, **Fig. 10.**
6. Remove cap from wiper transmission assembly.
7. Remove four wiper transmission assembly to tube frame attaching screws, **Fig. 11.**
8. Remove three grommets from tube frame and transmission assembly.
9. Reverse procedure to install.

BLOWER MOTOR

REPLACE

1. Disconnect blower motor electrical connections.
2. Remove sound insulator and hush panels as required.
3. Remove blower motor attaching screws, then the blower motor and fan assembly.
4. Reverse procedure to install.

HEATER CORE

REPLACE

1. Drain cooling system into an approved container.

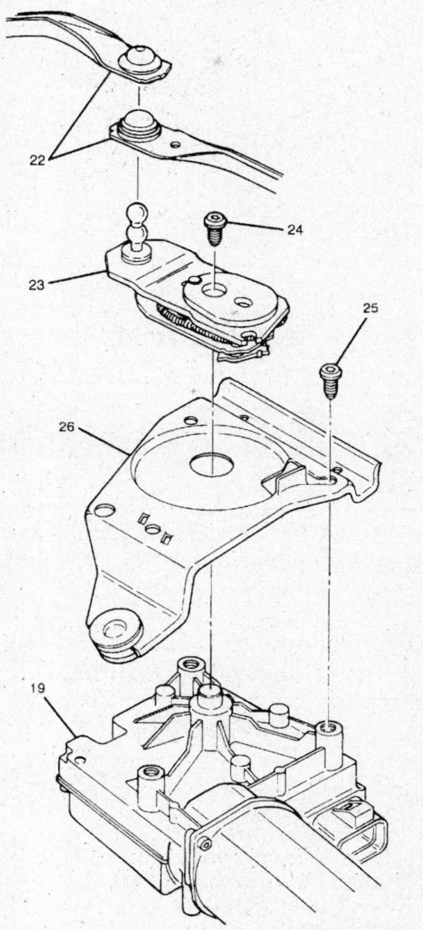

Fig. 9 Wiper module removal

2. Raise and support vehicle.
3. Disconnect heater hoses at heater core.
4. Lower the vehicle.
5. Remove defroster grille.
6. Remove instrument panel end caps.
7. **On Cavalier models,** remove instrument panel trim pad.
8. **On Sunfire models,** remove accessory trim plate.
9. **On all models,** remove cluster trim plate.
10. Remove HVAC control head and radio.
11. Remove air distribution ducts.
12. Remove steering wheel as outlined under "Steering Wheel, Replace" in this section.
13. Remove multi-function switches from steering column.

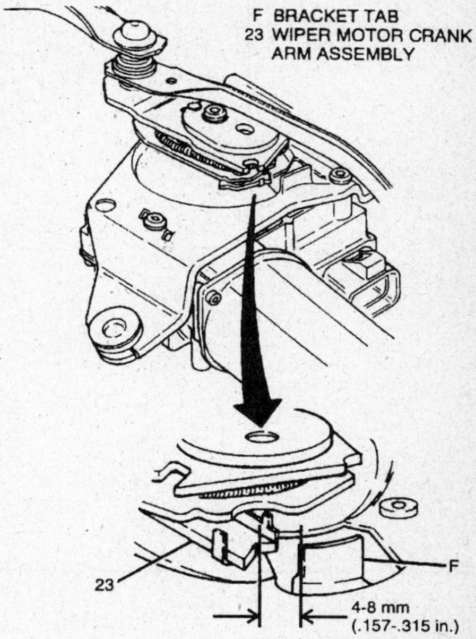

Fig. 10 Wiper transmission removal

14. Remove glove compartment lamp electrical connector.
15. Remove instrument panel to tie bar screws, then the instrument panel.
16. Remove heater core outlet.
17. Remove heater core cover. **There is a mounting screw hiding in a recess in center of cover.**
18. Remove heater core mounting clamps, then the core.
19. Reverse procedure to install.

EVAPORATOR CORE

REPLACE

1. Recover refrigerant.
2. Drain cooling system into an approved container.
3. Raise and support vehicle.
4. Disconnect heater hoses at heater core.
5. Disconnect evaporator lines at evaporator core. Discard O-rings.
6. Disconnect heater and evaporator assembly drain tube.
7. Lower the vehicle.
8. Remove defroster grille.
9. Remove heater core as outlined under "Heater Core, Replace" in this section.
10. Remove heater core shroud.
11. Remove evaporator cover and core. **There is a mounting screw located at center of front of dash.**
12. Reverse procedure to install. Install new evaporator O-rings lubricated in clean 525 viscosity refrigerant oil.

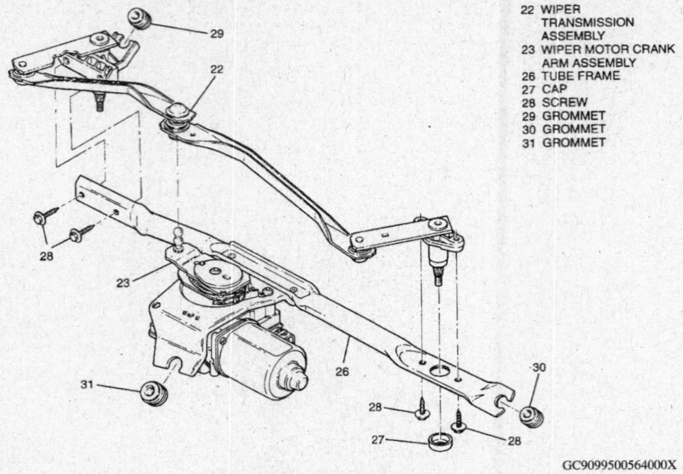

Fig. 11 Wiper assembly removal

2.2L Engine

NOTE: On Air Bag Equipped Models, Refer To " Air Bag System Precautions" Located In The Front Of This Manual For System Disarming and Arming Procedures.

NOTE: Refer To "Computer Relearn Procedures " Located In The Front Of This Manual For Computer Relearn Procedures.

INDEX

PRECAUTIONS

AIR BAG SYSTEMS

Refer to "Air Bag System Precautions" in the front of this manual for system disarming and arming procedures.

BATTERY GROUND CABLE

Prior to service, disconnect battery ground cable and isolate as required.

FUEL SYSTEM PRESSURE RELIEF

1. **On 1997 models,** loosen fuel filler cap.
2. **On all models,** raise and support vehicle.
3. Disconnect fuel pump electrical connector.
4. Start engine and run until remaining fuel is consumed.
5. Engage starter for approximately three seconds to ensure relief of any remaining pressure.
6. Disconnect and isolate battery ground cable to avoid possible fuel discharge if any attempt is made to start the engine.

COMPRESSION PRESSURE

When inspecting cylinder compression,

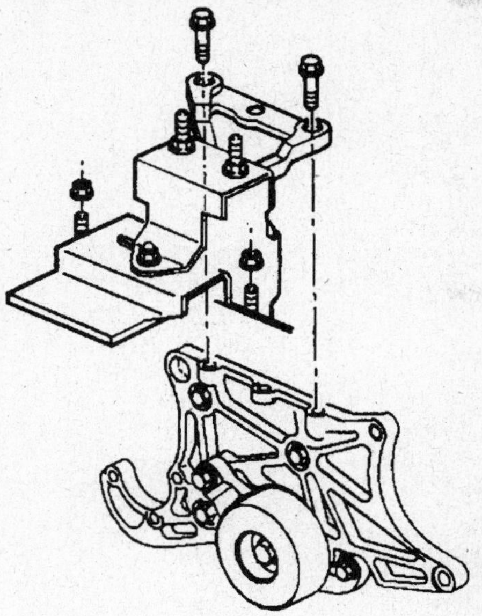

GC1069800901000X

Fig. 1 Engine mount removal

the throttle should be open, all spark plugs removed and the battery at or near full charge. The lowest reading cylinder should not be less than 70% of the highest and no cylinder reading should be less than 100 psi. Turn ignition key until engine cranks through four compression cycles. Normal compression builds up quickly and evenly to specifications on each cylinder.

ENGINE MOUNT

REPLACE

1. Install engine support fixture tool No. J-28467-360, or equivalent.
2. Raise engine at front lift hook in order to remove weight from engine mount assembly.
3. Remove coolant recovery tank attaching bolt.
4. Position coolant recovery tank aside with hoses attached.
5. Remove engine mount to drive belt tensioner bracket.
6. Remove two nuts on top of engine mount assembly, **Fig. 1.**
7. Remove engine mount to body nuts.
8. Remove engine mount bracket and engine mount.
9. Reverse procedure to install.

ENGINE MOUNT STRUT & STRUT BRACKET

REPLACE

1. Raise and support vehicle.
2. Remove righthand splash shield.
3. Remove engine mount strut bolts and engine mount strut, **Fig. 2.**
4. Remove A/C compressor with lines attached and position aside.
5. Remove transmission brace from engine.
6. Remove engine mount strut bracket bolts and strut bracket.
7. Reverse procedure to install.

ENGINE

REPLACE

AUTOMATIC TRANSAXLE

1. Relieve fuel system pressure as outlined under "Precautions."
2. Recover A/C refrigerant.
3. Drain and recover coolant in suitable container.
4. Mark positions of hinge to hood locations to ease installation, then remove hood.
5. Remove air cleaner assembly.
6. Disconnect brake booster vacuum line at intake manifold.
7. Disconnect accelerator control cable.
8. Disconnect speed control cable, then position it aside.
9. Remove fuel injector rail cover.
10. Remove accelerator and speed control cables from cable bracket. **Discard accelerator cable. It cannot be used again.**
11. Disconnect all required electrical connectors from engine components.
12. Remove cruise control module.
13. Disconnect refrigerant lines from accumulator. Discard O-rings.
14. Mark running direction, then remove engine accessory drive belt.
15. Remove coolant surge tank.
16. Remove upper and lower radiator hoses.
17. Remove fuel feed lines from engine.
18. Raise and support vehicle.
19. Remove coolant pipe assembly.
20. Remove righthand front wheel and tire.
21. Remove righthand front splash shield.
22. Remove engine mount strut as outlined under "Engine Mount Strut & Strut Bracket, Replace" in this section.
23. Remove flexplate inspection cover.
24. Remove exhaust pipe and hanger from exhaust manifold.
25. Remove starter.
26. Remove and support A/C compressor with hoses intact.
27. Remove A/C compressor bracket.
28. Drain engine oil into an approved container.
29. Remove torque convertor to flexplate bolts.
30. Remove transaxle to engine support brace.
31. Remove transaxle to engine lower bolts.
32. Lower the vehicle.
33. Support transaxle using a suitable jack.
34. Install a suitable engine lifting device to engine lifting eyes.
35. Remove engine front upper mount.
36. Remove remaining transaxle to engine bolts.
37. Separate engine from transaxle, then carefully lift engine up and out of vehicle.
38. Reverse procedure to install, noting the following:
    a. Install a new accelerator cable.
    b. Install new evaporator O-rings lubricated in clean 525 viscosity refrigerant oil.
    c. Ensure oil pan drain plug is intact with its gasket in place, then fill crankcase.
    d. Close radiator petcock, then fill cooling system.
    e. Start engine and inspect for any fluid leaks.

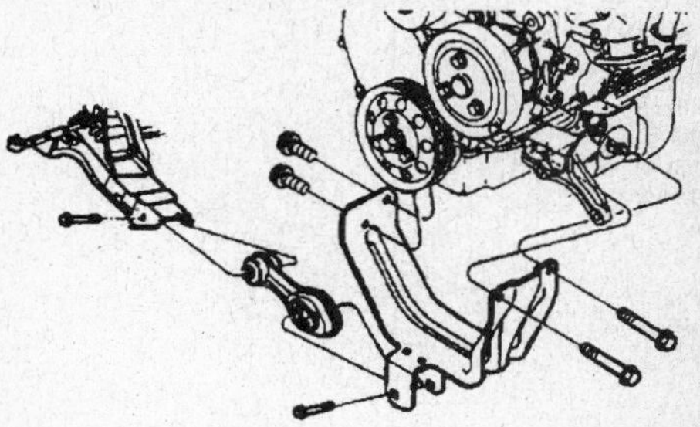

GC1069800902000X

Fig. 2 Engine mount strut & strut bracket removal

MANUAL TRANSAXLE

1. Relieve fuel system pressure as outlined under "Precautions."
2. Drain and recover coolant in a suitable container.
3. Remove air cleaner outlet duct.
4. Remove upper radiator hose at coolant outlet.
5. Disconnect brake booster vacuum hose.
6. Disconnect IAC electrical connection.
7. Disconnect alternator electrical connector.
8. Disconnect TPS, MAP, EVAP, EGR, ECT, TCC and O2 sensor electrical connectors.
9. Disconnect injector harness electrical connectors.
10. Disconnect engine ground electrical connections.
11. Remove drive belt as outlined under "Serpentine Drive Belt."
12. Remove transmission shift control cable from range select lever and bracket.
13. Remove coolant surge tank and hose.
14. Disconnect vacuum line near master cylinder.
15. Install engine support fixture tool No. J-28467-360, or equivalent.
16. Disconnect lower radiator hose from coolant pump.
17. Raise and support vehicle, then remove front wheels.
18. Remove splash shields.
19. Remove exhaust pipe at exhaust manifold and catalytic converter.
20. Remove engine mount strut as outlined under "Engine Mount Strut & Strut Bracket, Removal."
21. Remove wheel speed sensor wire harness from control arms.
22. Separate ball joints from steering knuckles as outlined under "Ball Joint, Replace" in the "Front Suspension & Steering" section.
23. Separate tie rod ends from struts.
24. Remove brake lines from suspension support below rack and pinion unit.
25. Remove A/C compressor and position aside with lines attached.
26. Disconnect electronic ignition module,

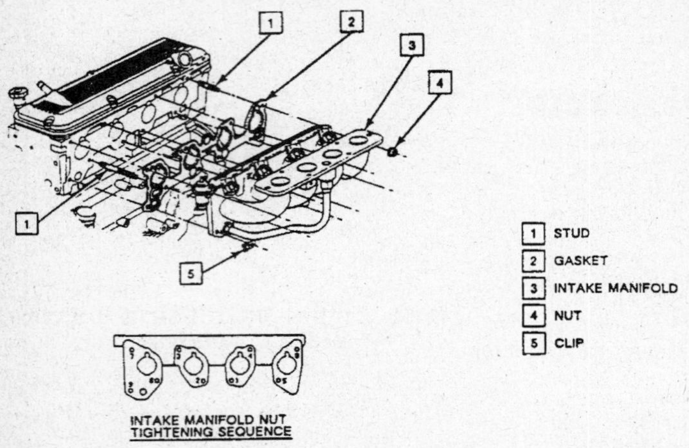

GC1059200078000X

Fig. 3 Intake manifold bolt tightening sequence. 1997

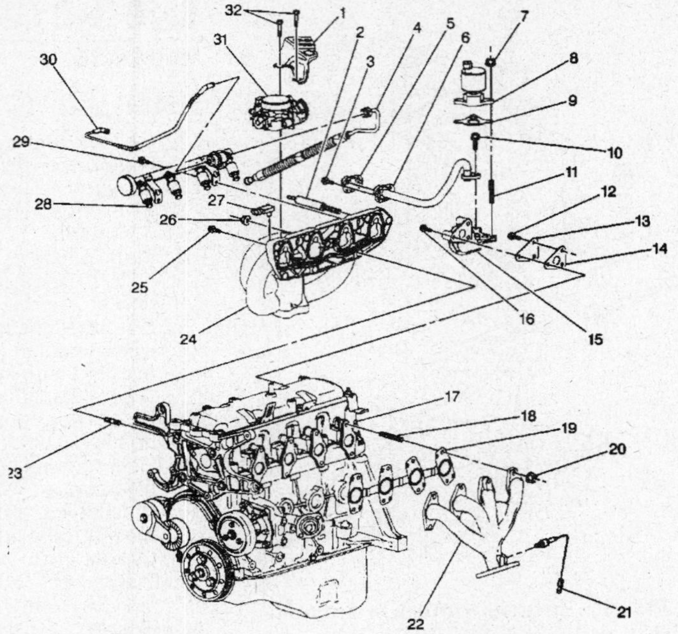

(1) Throttle Cable Bracket
(2) Bolt, Intake Manifold Fuel Rail Bracket
(3) Bolt, EGR Pipe
(4) Fuel Line
(5) Retainer, EGR Pipe
(6) EGR Pipe
(7) Nut, EGR Valve
(8) EGR Valve
(9) Gasket, EGR Valve
(10) Bolt, EGR Pipe
(11) Stud, EGR Valve
(12) Bolt, EGR Adapter
(13) EGR Port Cover (EXPORT ONLY)
(14) Gasket, EGR Adapter
(15) EGR Adapter
(16) Bolt, EGR Adapter
(17) Engine Block
(18) Stud, Exhaust Manifold
(19) Gasket, Exhaust Manifold
(20) Nut Exhaust Manifold
(21) Oxygen Sensor
(22) Exhaust Manifold
(23) Stud, Intake Manifold
(24) Intake Manifold
(25) Bolt, Intake Manifold
(26) Nut, Intake Manifold
(27) MAP Sensor
(28) Fuel Rail And Fuel Injectors
(29) Bolt, Fuel Rail
(30) Vacuum Harness
(31) Throttle Body
(32) Bolts, Throttle Body

GC1069800904000X

Fig. 4 Exploded view of intake and exhaust manifold components. 1998–2000

VSS, cooling fan, starter, A/C compressor, oil pressure sensor, oil level sensor and ground wire electrical connections.

27. Disconnect power steering lines from rack and pinion assembly.
28. Remove flexible coupling joint from rack and pinion assembly.
29. Remove accelerator and cruise control cables from accelerator control bracket.
30. Remove suspension support assembly.
31. Disconnect heater hoses from firewall.
32. Remove drive axles from transaxle and position aside.
33. Disconnect fuel lines and transaxle cooler lines, then cap them to prevent contamination.
34. Remove transmission mount.
35. Remove engine mount assembly as outlined under " Engine Mount, Replace."
36. Lower vehicle until engine rests lightly on a suitable support.
37. Remove engine support fixture from engine.
38. Raise vehicle, then remove engine and transmission assembly.
39. Place on bench and remove transmission.
40. Reverse procedure to install, noting the following:
    a. Close radiator petcock, then fill cooling system.
    b. Ensure all fluids are up to their proper levels.
    c. Start engine and inspect for any fluid leaks.

INTAKE MANIFOLD

REPLACE

1997

1. Remove air intake duct.
2. Drain coolant and disconnect all attaching vacuum lines and wires.
3. Disconnect throttle linkage, then remove MAP sensor and EGR solenoid valve.
4. Remove the power steering pump and position aside.
5. Remove upper intake manifold assembly, EGR valve injector, fuel injector retainer bracket, regulator injectors and fuel lines.
6. Disconnect accelerator and TV cables, then remove cable bracket.
7. Raise and support vehicle.
8. Remove intake manifold lower nuts, then lower vehicle.
9. Remove intake manifold upper nuts.
10. Remove lower intake manifold and gasket.
11. Reverse procedure to install. Tighten bolts to specifications in sequence outlined in **Fig. 3.**

1998–2000

1. Relieve fuel system pressure as outlined under " Precautions."
2. Remove air cleaner inlet duct.
3. Remove resonator and resonator bracket.
4. Remove accelerator and cruise control cables from accelerator control bracket.
5. Disconnect vacuum hoses at throttle body.
6. Disconnect MAP, TPS and IAC electrical connectors.
7. Remove throttle bracket attaching bolts and bracket, **Fig. 4.**
8. Remove throttle body attaching bolts and throttle body.
9. Remove fuel feed.
10. Remove fuel inlet pipe attaching bolts.
11. Remove intake manifold attaching nuts and bolts, then the manifold from engine.
12. Reverse procedure to install, noting the following:
    a. Clean mating surface of intake manifold and cylinder head.
    b. Inspect manifold for damage and replace as required.

EXHAUST MANIFOLD

REPLACE

1. Disconnect oxygen sensor lead, then remove the sensor.
2. Remove serpentine belt.
3. Remove alternator mounting bolts, then position aside.
4. Remove alternator rear brace.
5. **On 1998–2000 models,** partially drain

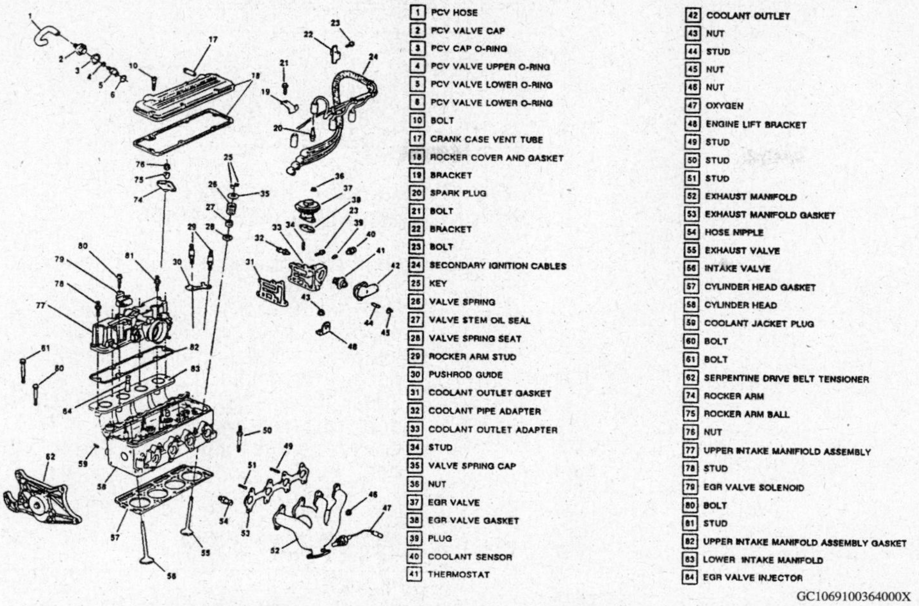

Fig. 5 Exploded view of cylinder head assembly. 1997

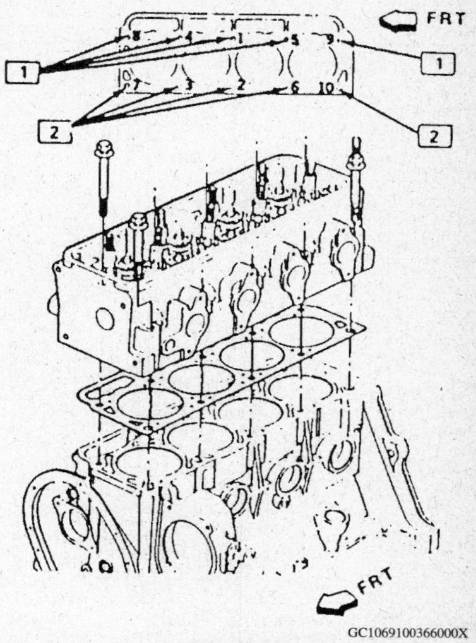

Fig. 6 Cylinder head bolt tightening sequence. 1997

coolant into an approved container, then remove radiator inlet pipe.
6. **On all models,** raise and support vehicle.
7. Disconnect exhaust pipe from the exhaust manifold, then lower the vehicle.
8. Remove oil fill tube, exhaust manifold attaching bolts and exhaust manifold.
9. Reverse procedure to install. Tighten manifold attaching bolts to specifications.

CYLINDER HEAD

REPLACE

1997

1. Loosen fuel filler cap to relieve tank vapor pressure.
2. Remove air cleaner assembly, then drain cooling system.
3. Disconnect attaching vacuum hoses, electrical connectors and accelerator cable.
4. Remove coolant reservoir tank.
5. Remove serpentine belt.
6. Remove alternator attaching bolts and alternator.
7. Loosen power steering pump attaching bolts, then position away.
8. Remove serpentine belt tensioner.
9. Remove ignition wires and canister purge line beneath manifold.
10. Remove upper radiator hose, then upper and lower heater hose at manifold.
11. Remove throttle body cables from bracket.
12. Remove cylinder head coolant inlet hose.
13. Remove intake manifold brace to power steering bracket attaching bolts.
14. Remove fuel lines. **Place shop towel over fuel line and fitting when disconnecting.**
15. Remove rocker arm cover attaching bolts and cover, **Fig. 5.**
16. Remove rocker arms and pushrods.
17. Remove ignition cable bracket.
18. Disconnect exhaust pipe at exhaust manifold.
19. Remove cylinder head attaching bolts.
20. **On models equipped with automatic transaxle,** remove transaxle fluid level indicator bracket.
21. **On all models,** remove cylinder head assembly.
22. Reverse procedure to install. Using sequence outlined in **Fig. 6,** torque cylinder head bolts in two steps: first, **torque** long bolts to 46 ft. lbs. and short bolts to 43 ft. lbs.; second, rotate all bolts an additional 90.°

1998–2000

1. Relieve fuel system pressure as outlined under " Precautions."
2. Drain and recover engine coolant into suitable container.
3. Remove accessory drive belt as outlined under "Serpentine Drive Belt."
4. Remove air cleaner outlet duct.
5. Remove engine mount as outlined under "Engine Mount, Replace" in this section.
6. Remove intake manifold as outlined under "Intake Manifold, Replace."
7. Remove exhaust manifold as outlined under "Exhaust Manifold, Replace."
8. Disconnect ECT sensor electrical connector.
9. Raise and support vehicle.
10. Lower the vehicle, then remove valve cover, **Fig. 7.**
11. Remove rocker arms and pushrods. Be sure to keep in order for proper installation.
12. Remove alternator rear brace and alternator.
13. Remove power steering pump and position aside with lines intact.
14. Remove radiator inlet pipe.
15. Remove ignition coil assembly.
16. Remove accessory bracket.
17. Reference mark each spark plug wire, then remove from spark plugs.
18. Install engine support fixture tool No. J-28467-360, or equivalent.
19. Using opposite sequence of one outlined in **Fig. 8,** remove cylinder head bolts and cylinder head.
20. Reverse procedure to install noting the following:
    a. Clean cylinder head to engine block and valve cover mating surfaces.
    b. Using sequence outlined in **Fig. 8, torque** cylinder head bolt Nos. 1, 4, 5, 8 and 9 to 46 ft. lbs., then bolt Nos. 2, 3, 6, 7 and 10 to 43 ft. lbs. Finally, rotate all bolts an additional 90° in sequence using tool No. J-3660, or equivalent.

VALVE CLEARANCE SPECIFICATIONS

This engine is equipped with hydraulic lifters. Clearance is zero.

VALVE ADJUSTMENT

Valve lash is obtained through the use of hydraulic valve lifters. No adjustment is required.

VALVE GUIDES

Valve guides are an integral part of the cylinder head and are not removable. If valve stem clearance becomes excessive, the valve guide should be reamed to the next oversize and the appropriate oversize valves installed. Valves are available in several different oversizes.

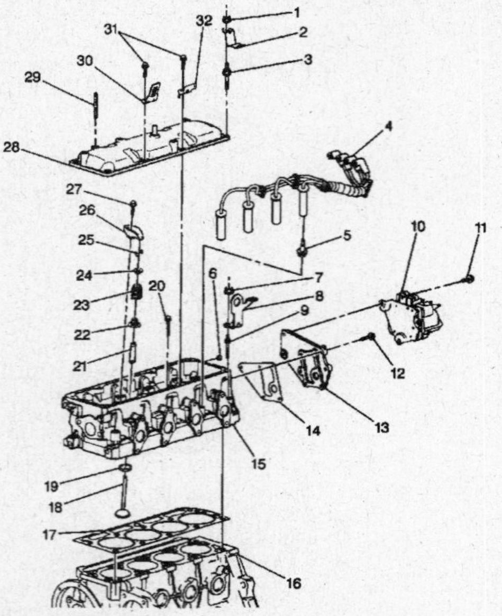

(1) Nut, Secondary Ignition Harness Bracket
(2) Secondary Ignition Harness Bracket
(3) Bolt, Valve Rocker Arm Cover
(4) Secondary Ignition Harness
(5) Spark Plug
(6) Oil Passage Plug
(7) Nut, Engine Lift Hook
(8) Engine Lift Hook
(9) Bolt, Cylinder Head
(10) Ignition Module And Coil Assembly
(11) Bolt, Ignition Coil Bracket
(12) Bolt, Rear Cylinder Head Cover
(13) Rear Cylinder Head Cover
(14) Gasket, Rear Cylinder Head Cover
(15) Cylinder Head
(16) Cylinder Block
(17) Gasket, Cylinder Head
(18) Valve
(19) Valve Seat
(20) Bolt, Cylinder Head
(21) Valve Guide
(22) Valve Guide Seal
(23) Valve Spring
(24) Valve Spring Retainer
(25) Valve Spring Keepers
(26) Valve Rocker Arm
(27) Bolt, Rocker Arm
(28) Valve Rocker Arm Cover
(29) Stud, Fuel Rail Bracket
(30) Bracket, Secondary Ignition Harness
(31) Bolts, Secondary Ignition and Fuel Injector Harness Brackets
(32) Bracket, Fuel Injector Harness

GC1069800905000X

Fig. 7 Exploded view of cylinder head components. 1998–2000

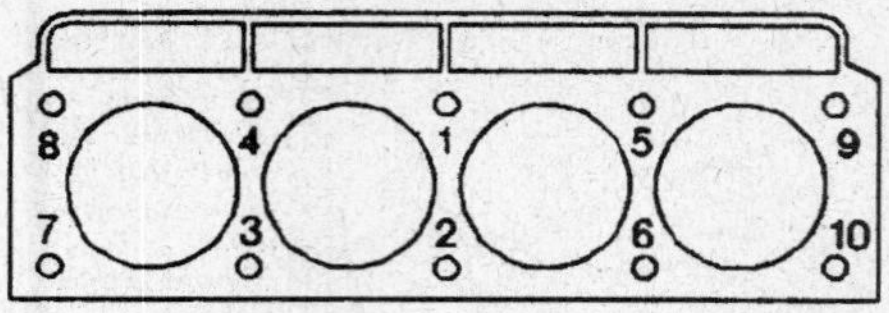

GC1069800903000X

Fig. 8 Cylinder head bolt tightening sequence. 1998–2000

HYDRAULIC LIFTERS

REPLACE

1997

1. Remove crankcase vent valve (PCV) and pipe assembly.
2. Remove rocker arm cover bolts, cover and gasket.
3. Loosen rocker arm nut and swing rocker arm aside.
4. Remove pushrods.
5. Remove cylinder head. Refer to "Cylinder Head, Replace."
6. Remove anti-rotation brackets and valve lifters.
7. Inspect lifter for any signs of damage or wear, replacing as required.
8. Reverse procedure to install.

1998–2000

1. Remove cylinder head. Refer to "Cylinder Head, Replace."
2. Remove anti-rotation brackets and valve lifters. Keep lifters in order.
3. Inspect lifters for any signs of damage or wear, replacing as required.
4. Reverse procedure to install.

CRANKSHAFT DAMPER

REPLACE

REMOVAL

Refer to **Fig. 9** when performing the following procedures:

1. Remove serpentine belt, then raise and support vehicle.
2. Remove righthand front wheel and tire assembly, then inner fender splash shield.
3. Remove three crankshaft pulley attaching bolts.
4. Remove crankshaft pulley hub bolt, then the crankshaft pulley.
5. Install crankshaft pulley puller tool No. J-24420-B, or equivalent on hub.
6. Turn puller screw and remove hub.

INSTALLATION

1. Coat front cover seal contact area with engine oil.
2. Apply RTV sealer No. 1052917, or equivalent, to keyway in pulley hub.
3. Place crankshaft pulley hub into position over key on crankshaft.
4. Install crankshaft pulley installer tool No. J-29113, or equivalent into crankshaft so a minimum of 1/4 inch of thread is engaged.
5. Pull pulley hub into position and remove tool from crankshaft.
6. Install crankshaft pulley, then three pulley attaching bolts.
7. Install inner slash shield, then wheel and tire assembly.
8. Lower vehicle and install serpentine belt.

FRONT COVER

REPLACE

1. Remove serpentine belt, then the belt tensioner.
2. Install engine support fixture tool No. J-28467-360, or equivalent.
3. Remove engine mount assembly as outlined under "Engine Mount, Replace" in this section.
4. Remove alternator rear brace.
5. Remove alternator, then position aside.
6. Remove power steering pump, then position aside with lines intact.
7. Raise and support vehicle, then remove oil pan as described in "Oil Pan, Replace."
8. Remove crankshaft pulley and hub.
9. Remove front cover attaching bolts, then the front cover.
10. Reverse procedure to install.

TIMING CHAIN

REPLACE

1. Remove crankcase front cover as described in "Front Cover, Replace."
2. Align marks on crankshaft sprocket and camshaft sprocket, **Fig. 10.**
3. **Before removing chain and sprockets,** measure distance between hole in bracket and unworn tensioner shoe surface. If this distance is more than 0.314 inch, replace both sprockets, tensioner and timing chain.
4. Remove timing chain tensioner bolts.
5. Remove camshaft sprocket and timing chain.
6. Remove tensioner Torx bolt, then the tensioner.
7. Using puller tool No. J-22888-20, or equivalent, remove crankshaft sprocket.
8. Reverse procedure to install, noting the following:
   a. Using sprocket installer tool No.

J-5590, or equivalent, install crankshaft sprocket fully seated against crankshaft.

b. Compress tensioner spring, then install a cotter pin or nail into hole "A" as shown in **Fig. 11.**
c. Align marks on camshaft and crankshaft sprockets with tabs on tensioner as shown in **Fig. 11.**
d. Align dowel in camshaft with dowel hole camshaft sprocket.
e. Draw camshaft sprocket onto camshaft using the attaching bolt. Tighten to specifications.

CAMSHAFT

REPLACE

REMOVAL

1. Remove engine assembly as described in "Engine, Replace."
2. Drain engine oil and remove oil filter.
3. Remove serpentine belt.
4. Remove alternator and related brackets.
5. Remove power steering pump.
6. Remove drive belt tensioner.
7. Remove water pump pulley.
8. Remove crankshaft pulley and hub.
9. Remove cylinder head.
10. Remove valve lifters.
11. Remove camshaft sprocket, timing chain and tensioner.
12. Remove oil pump drive.
13. Remove thrust plate.
14. Remove CMP sensor.
15. Carefully remove camshaft. **Avoid damaging camshaft bearings.**
16. Inspect camshaft for galling, gouges, overheating and wear. If any of these conditions exist, replace the camshaft.

INSTALLATION

Reverse procedure to install, noting the following:

1. **Coat camshaft lobes and bearings with camshaft lube No. 1051396, or equivalent. Insert camshaft with extreme care to avoid personal injury and gouging of the camshaft bearings.** Install camshaft and thrust plate.
2. Tighten thrust plate to specifications, then install camshaft sprocket and timing chain.
3. Replace valve lifters. Lifters must be installed in the same bores from which they were removed. **If a new camshaft is installed, replace all valve lifters. Some lifters may be oversized. Verify marking near the lifter bore.**
4. Install valve mechanism. Components must be installed in the same position and with the same mating surfaces from which they were removed.
5. Replace oil filter.
6. Ensure oil pan drain plug and gasket are intact.

PISTON & ROD ASSEMBLY

Assemble piston to rod with arrow on piston facing toward front of engine, **Fig. 12.** Upon installation, measure connecting rod side clearance using a feeler gauge, which should be .0039–.0149 inch.

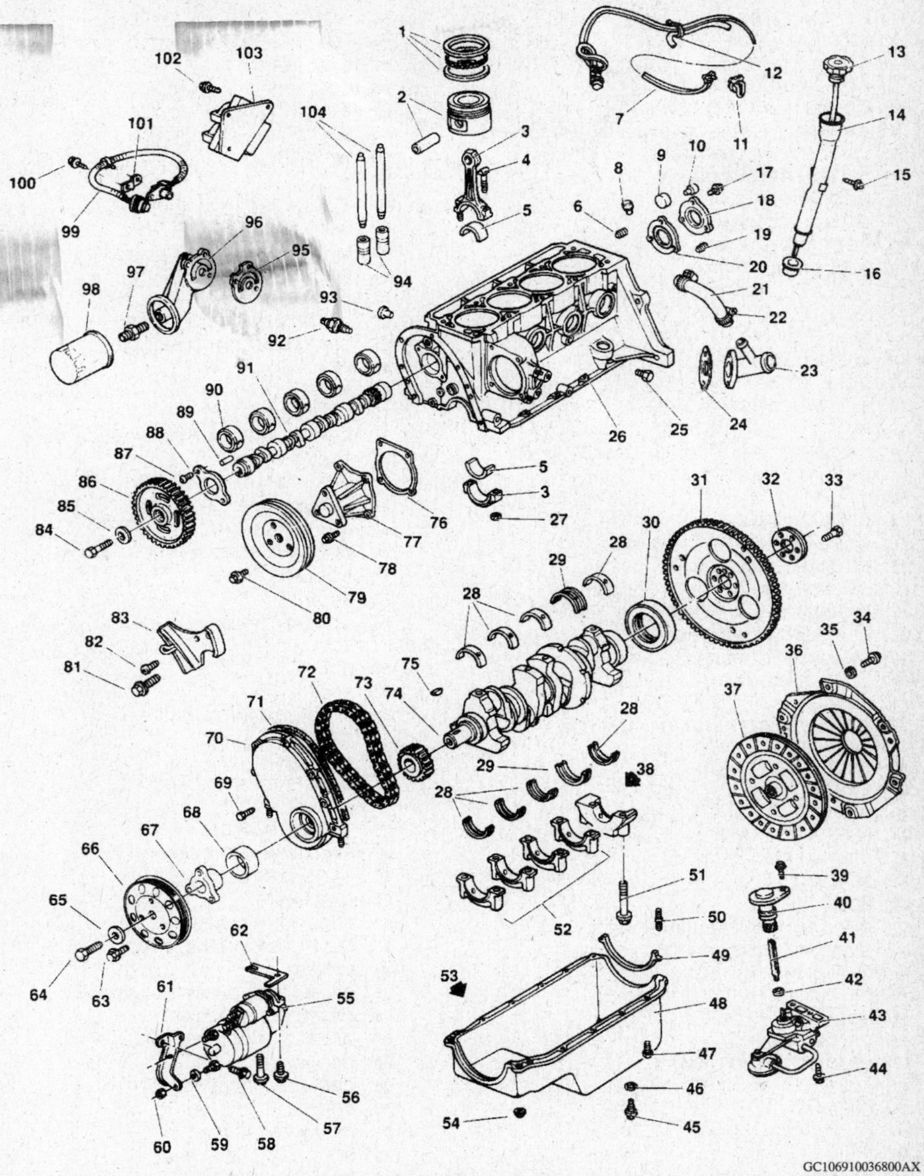

Fig. 9 Exploded view of cylinder block assembly (Part 1 of 2)

PISTONS, PINS & RINGS

Pistons are available in standard size and oversizes of .0015 inch (.04 mm), .002 inch (.5 mm) and .004 inch (1 mm). Piston pins are available in standard size only.

CRANKSHAFT REAR OIL SEAL

REPLACE

1. **On models equipped with automatic transaxle,** remove transaxle as outlined in the "Automatic Transaxle" section.
2. **On models equipped with manual transaxle,** remove transaxle, pressure plate and clutch disc as outlined in the "Clutch & Manual Transaxle" section.
3. **On all models,** remove flywheel attaching bolts and flywheel.
4. Insert a screwdriver or similar tool in through the dust lip as shown in **Fig. 13,** then pry seal out.
5. Reverse procedure to install, noting the following:
   a. Lubricate seal bore to seal surface with clean engine oil.
   b. Using seal installation tool No. J-34686, or equivalent, align dowel pin of tool with dowel pin hole in crankshaft and attach tool to crankshaft.
   c. **On 1997–98 models, torque** tool attaching screws to 27–62 inch lbs., then tighten tool T-handle to push seal into bore. Continue to tighten

1. PISTON RINGS
2. PISTON AND PIN
3. CONNECTING ROD
4. CONNECTING ROD BOLT
5. CONNECTING ROD BEARING
6. CYLINDER BLOCK OIL GALLERY HOLE PLUG
7. COOLANT HEATER CORD
8. CYLINDER HEAD DOWEL PIN
9. COOLANT JACKET PLUG
10. CLUTCH HOUSING PIN
11. COOLANT HEATER
12. ADJUSTABLE RETAINER
13. OIL LEVEL RETAINER
14. OIL FILL TUBE
15. BOLT
16. OIL FILL TUBE SEAL
17. BOLT
18. CAMSHAFT REAR COVER
19. PLUG
20. CAMSHAFT REAR COVER GASKET
21. COOLANT INLET HOSE
22. CLAMP
23. COOLANT INLET
24. COOLANT INLET GASKET
25. COOLANT DRAIN PLUG
26. CYLINDER BLOCK
27. CONNECTING ROD NUT
28. CRANKSHAFT BEARING
29. CRANKSHAFT BEARING
30. CRANKSHAFT REAR OIL SEAL
31. FLYWHEEL
32. FLYWHEEL RETAINER (AUTOMATIC TRANSAXLE)
33. BOLT
34. BOLT
35. WASHER
36. PRESSURE PLATE
37. CLUTCH DISC
38. SEALANT
39. BOLT
40. OIL PUMP DRIVE ASSEMBLY
41. OIL PUMP DRIVE SHAFT
42. RETAINER
43. OIL PUMP
44. BOLT
45. OIL DRAIN PLUG
46. OIL DRAIN PLUG GASKET
47. BOLT
48. OIL PAN
49. OIL PAN REAR SEAL
50. STUD
51. BOLT
52. MAIN BEARING CAP
53. SEALER
54. NUT
55. STARTER MOTOR
56. BOLT
57. BOLT
58. BOLT
59. WASHER
60. NUT
61. STARTER MOTOR BRACKET
62. SHIM
63. BOLT
64. BOLT
65. WASHER
66. CRANKSHAFT PULLEY
67. CRANKSHAFT PULLEY HUB
68. SEAL
69. BOLT
70. CRANKCASE
71. CRANKCASE FRONT COVER OIL SEAL
72. TIMING CHAIN
73. CRANKSHAFT SPROCKET
74. CRANKSHAFT
75. KEY
76. COOLANT PUMP GASKET
77. COOLANT PUMP
78. BOLT
79. COOLANT PUMP PULLEY
80. BOLT
81. BOLT
82. BOLT
83. TIMING CHAIN TENSIONER
84. BOLT
85. WASHER
86. CAMSHAFT SPROCKET
87. SCREW
88. THRUST PLATE
89. PIN CAMSHAFT BEARING
90. CAMSHAFT BEARING
91. CAMSHAFT
92. FUEL PUMP SWITCH
93. OIL FILTER BY-PASS VALVE
94. LIFTER
95. OIL FILTER ADAPTER GASKET
96. OIL FILTER ADAPTER
97. OIL FILTER CONNECTOR
98. OIL FILTER
99. CRANKSHAFT SENSOR
100. BOLT
101. RETAINER
102. BOLT
103. COIL
104. PUSHROD

GC106910036800BX

Fig. 9 Exploded view of cylinder block assembly (Part 2 of 2)

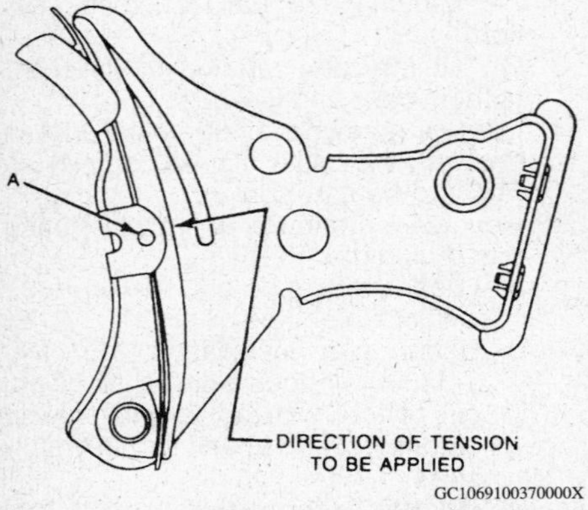

Fig. 11 Timing chain tensioner

until tool is flush against block.

d. **On 1999–2000 models,** tighten tool T-handle to push seal into bore. Continue to tighten until tool collar is flush against block.

OIL PAN

REPLACE

1. Raise and support vehicle.
2. Drain engine oil.
3. Remove righthand front tire and wheel.
4. Remove righthand front splash shield.
5. Remove starter bracket at block.
6. Remove starter and position aside.
7. Remove flywheel inspection cover.
8. Remove engine mount strut bracket.
9. Remove oil level sensor.
10. Remove oil pan attaching bolts and nuts, then the oil pan.

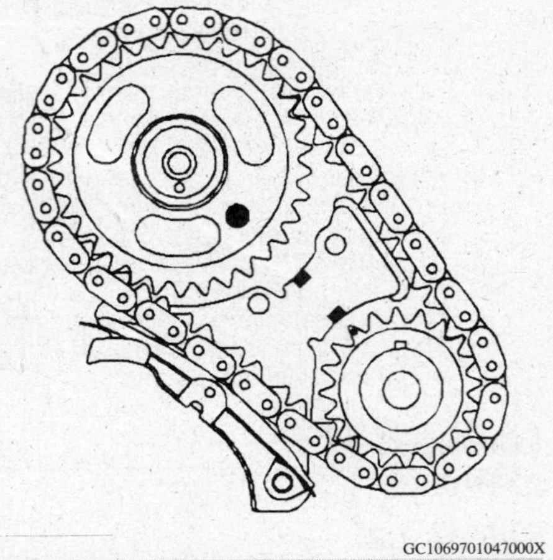

Fig. 10 Timing chain & sprockets

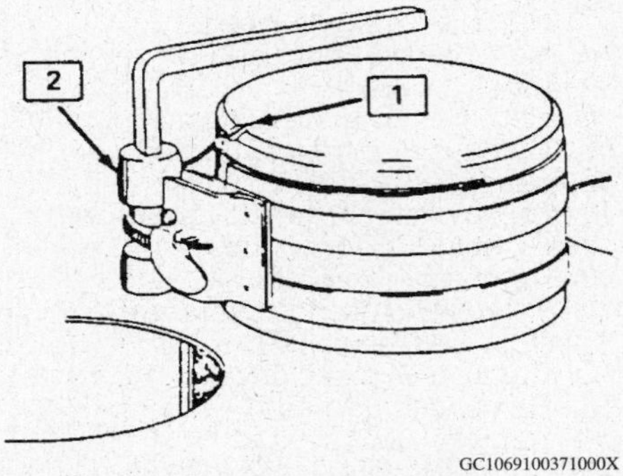

Fig. 12 Piston installation

11. Reverse procedure to install, noting the following:
    a. Clean all crankcase, front cover and pan sealing surfaces. Ensure all old RTV has been removed from blind attaching holes.
    b. Apply a 1⁄16 inch diameter bead of Loctite 5900 RTV sealer, or equivalent on oil pan to block sealing flanges, **but not at rear seal mounting surface.**
    c. Install a new oil pan rear seal and apply Loctite 5900 RTV sealer, or equivalent to ends down to ears.

OIL PUMP SERVICE

REMOVAL

1. Remove oil pan as described previously.
2. Remove pump to rear main bearing cap bolt, then the pump, extension shaft and retainer.

DISASSEMBLE

1. Drain oil from pump, then remove driveshaft, **Fig. 14.**
2. Remove pump cover, **Do not remove pickup tube from cover unless loose or broken.**
3. Remove pump gears, then the pressure regulator valve. **The pressure regulator valve spring is under**

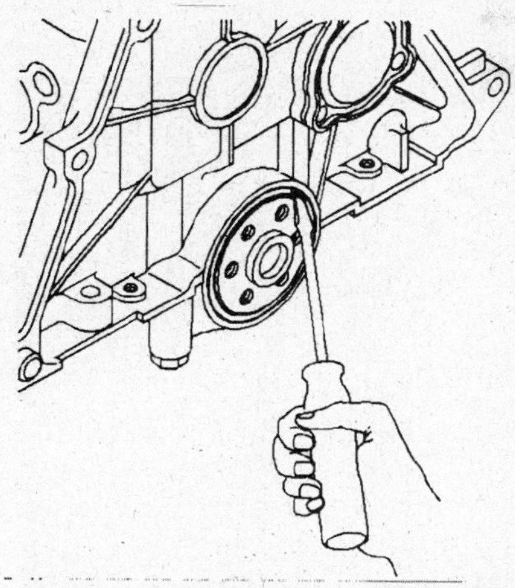

GC1069701048000X

Fig. 13 Crankshaft rear seal removal

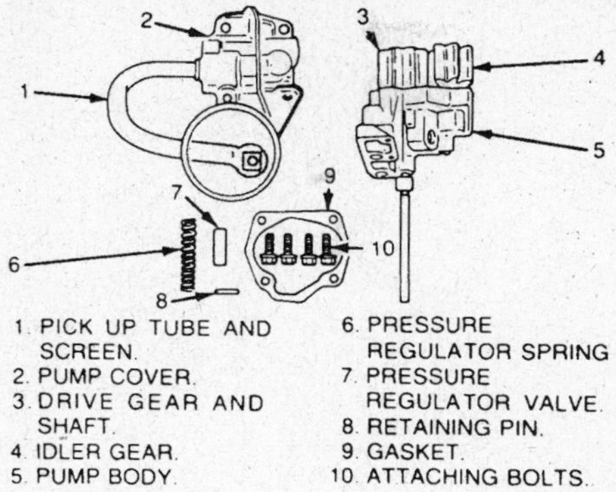

GC1099100051000X

Fig. 14 Exploded view of oil pump

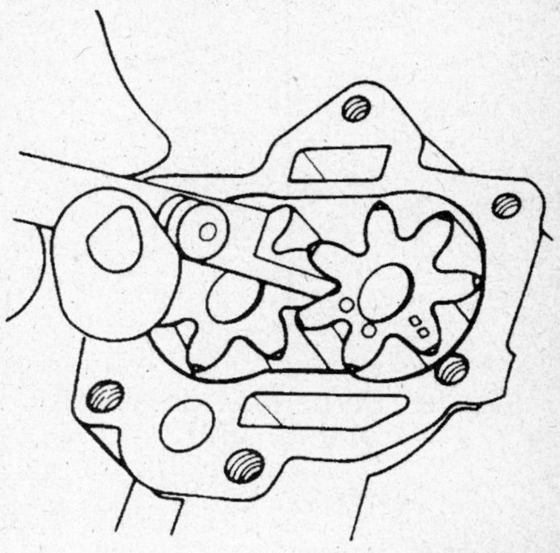

GC1099100052000X

Fig. 15 Oil pump gear lash measurement

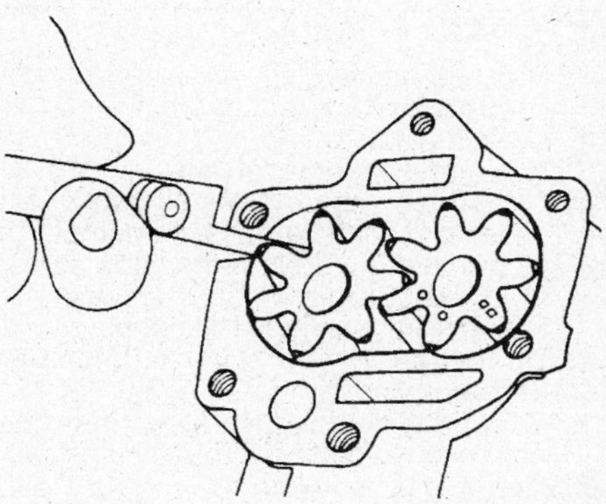

GC1099100053000X

Fig. 16 Gear side clearance measurement

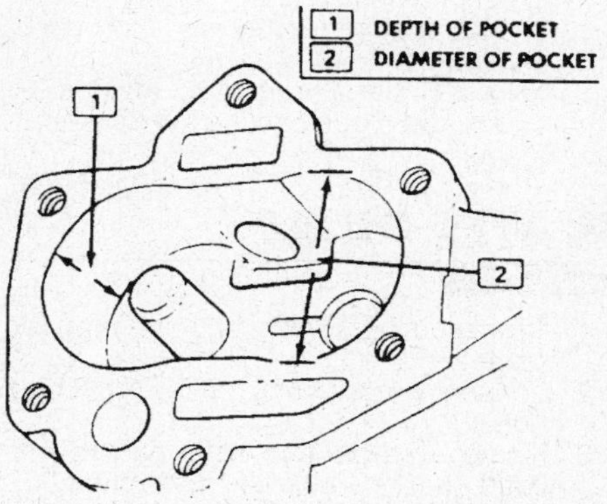

GC1099100054000X

Fig. 17 Oil pump gear pocket measurement

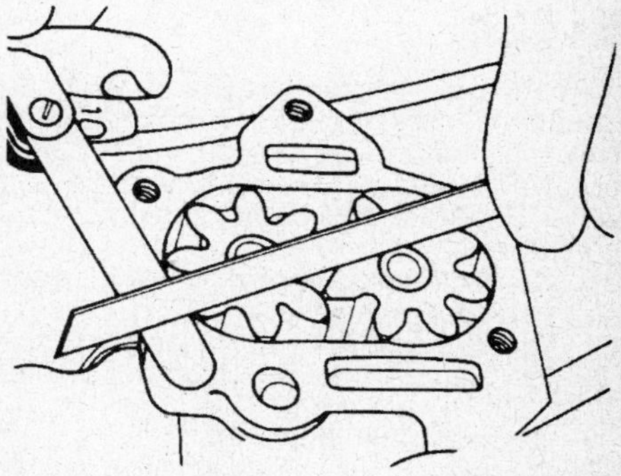

GC1099100055000X

Fig. 18 Oil pump end clearance measurement

pressure. Exercise caution when removing the retaining pin as bodily injury may result.

4. Remove plug, spring and valve. If valve is stuck, soak the pump housing in carburetor cleaning solvent.

INSPECTION

Thoroughly clean all oil pump components and inspect them for excessive wear or damage.

1. Using a straightedge and feeler gauge, inspect oil pump clearances as shown in **Figs. 15 through 18.**
2. Install gears and measure lash in several places, which should be within .004–.008 inch.
3. Measure depth and diameter of oil pump gear pocket. Depth should be 1.195–1.198 inches. Diameter should be 1.503–1.506 inches.
4. Measure gear side clearance, which should be .001–.004.
5. Measure gear end clearance, which should be .002–.006. When determining pump serviceability based on end clearance, consider depth of wear pattern in the pump cover and/or cover plate.

ASSEMBLE

1. Lubricate all internal components with engine oil during assembly.
2. Install pump gears. **To avoid engine damage, all pump cavities must be packed with petroleum jelly before installing gears to ensure priming.**
3. Install oil pump cover and gasket.
4. Install pressure regulator valve, spring and retaining pin.
5. Tighten pump cover bolts to specifications. Whenever the oil pump is overhauled, clear the oil pan of oil and sludge, replace oil filter and fill crankcase with clean oil.

INSTALLATION

1. Heat retainer in hot water, but not so hot it would crack during installation.
2. Install retainer to extension shaft.
3. Install extension to oil pump.
4. Tighten main bearing cap bolt to specifications.
5. Install oil pan.
6. Start engine and ensure oil pressure is as specified.

BELT TENSION DATA

The serpentine belt is automatically adjusted by a spring tensioner. No adjustment is required.

SERPENTINE DRIVE BELT

BELT, REPLACE

1. **On 1997 models,** remove coolant reservoir.
2. **On all models,** rotate tensioner clockwise with a suitable wrench and slide belt from alternator pulley. Release tensioner and remove belt.
3. Reverse procedure to install, routing belt as shown in **Figs. 19 through 21.**

TENSIONER, REPLACE

1997–98

1. Remove drive belt as outlined under "Serpentine Drive Belt."
2. Remove tensioner bolts.
3. Remove tensioner.
4. Reverse procedure to install.

1999–2000

1. Remove serpentine belt as described under "Serpentine Drive Belt."
2. Remove alternator, then position aside.
3. Raise and support vehicle.
4. Remove oil filter.
5. Remove idler pulley.
6. Remove A/C compressor mounting bolt, then position compressor aside

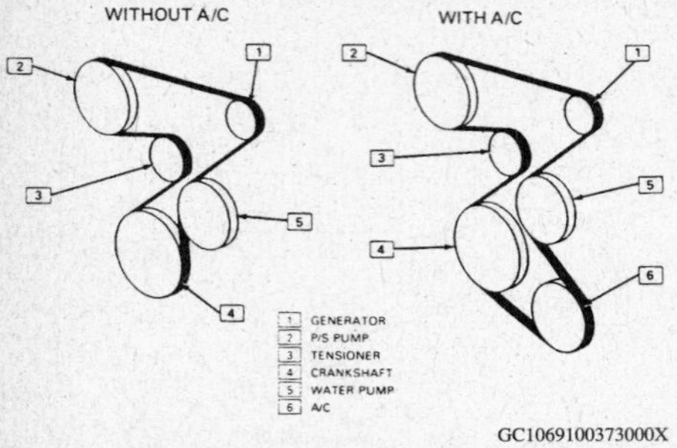

Fig. 19 Serpentine drive belt routing. 1997

with lines intact.

7. Remove tensioner mounting bolts, then the tensioner.
8. Reverse procedure to install.

COOLING SYSTEM BLEED

To ensure sufficient engine cooling and to enhance freezing and corrosion protection, maintain the protection level at –34°F or lower. Use a solution of antifreeze and water. Ensure solution is no more than 70% antifreeze.

1. **On models equipped with a bleeder valve,** open the valve.
2. **On all models,** fill surge tank or radiator to approximately 1 inch below filler neck.
3. Close bleeder valve.
4. Block the drive wheels and apply parking brake.
5. **On models equipped with automatic transaxle,** place shifter in Park position.
6. **On models equipped with manual transaxle,** place shifter in Neutral position.
7. **On all models,** start engine and turn HVAC controls to HEATER and FULL HOT.
8. Allow engine to run until upper radiator hose is hot.
9. Turn engine off, then inspect level of coolant in surge tank or radiator.
10. Allow engine to cool, then add coolant as required.

THERMOSTAT

REPLACE

1. Remove air intake duct.
2. With engine cool, drain engine coolant below thermostat level. **Never open cooling system with engine hot. Failure to follow this warning may cause personal injury.**
3. Disconnect radiator hose or outlet pipe from thermostat housing.
4. Remove thermostat housing attaching nuts, then the housing, gasket and thermostat.
5. Reverse procedure to install, noting the following:

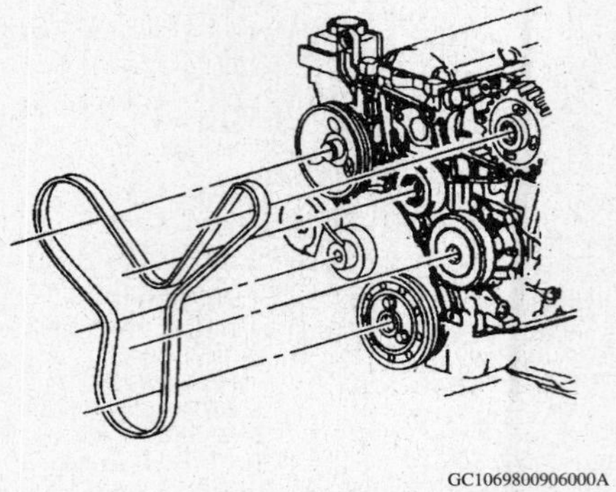

Fig. 20 Serpentine drive belt routing. 1998–2000 Less A/C

a. Prior to installation, ensure thermostat gasket area is thoroughly clean.
b. Install thermostat with new gasket.
c. Fill and bleed cooling system as required.

WATER PUMP

REPLACE

1. Drain cooling system into an approved container.
2. Loosen water pump pulley attaching bolts.
3. Remove serpentine drive belt as outlined under "Serpentine Drive Belt."
4. Remove alternator and mounting bracket.
5. Remove water pump pulley attaching bolts, then the pulley, **Fig. 22.**
6. Remove water pump attaching bolts, then the water pump.
7. Reverse procedure to install.

RADIATOR

REPLACE

1. Drain and recover engine coolant into suitable container.
2. Remove hood latch support from mounting plate.
3. Remove both headlamp assemblies.
4. Remove radiator upper mounts.
5. Raise and support vehicle.
6. Disconnect forward discriminating sensor electrical connector.
7. Remove cooling fan assembly.
8. Remove lower radiator hose from radiator.
9. Remove lower transaxle oil cooler line from radiator, then lower the vehicle.
10. Remove hood latch support bracket and forward discriminating sensor with electrical harness.
11. Disconnect upper transaxle oil cooler line from radiator.
12. Remove upper radiator hose and overflow hose from radiator.
13. Remove condenser from radiator, if equipped.
14. Remove radiator from vehicle.

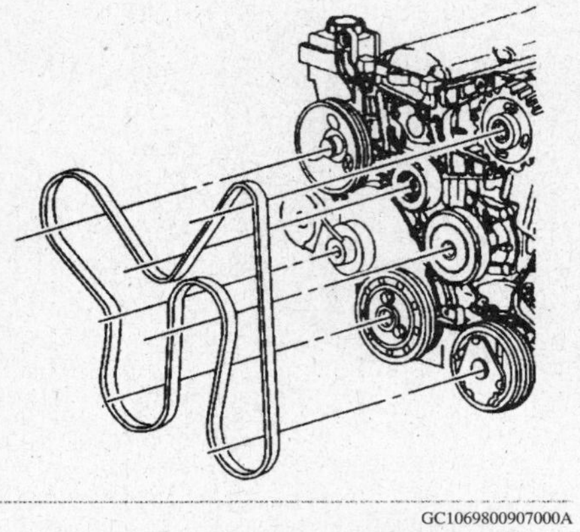

Fig. 21 Serpentine drive belt routing. 1998–2000 with A/C

15. Reverse procedure to install.

FUEL PUMP

REPLACE

1. Release fuel system pressure as outlined under " Precautions."
2. Drain fuel tank.
3. Raise and support vehicle.
4. Disconnect tank meter assembly harness from body harness connector.
5. Remove ground wire attaching screw from underbody, then disconnect hoses from fuel meter assembly.
6. Disconnect hoses at tank from filler and vent pipes.
7. Support fuel tank with jack, then disconnect two fuel tank retaining straps.
8. Remove tank assembly.
9. Remove fuel tank sending unit and pump assembly by turning cam lock ring counterclockwise. **Sending unit assembly might pop up from its position. Reservoir bucket may be full of fuel.** Tip the sending unit slightly to avoid float damage.
10. Lift assembly from fuel tank.
11. Reverse procedure to install.

FUEL FILTER

REPLACE

1. Release fuel system pressure as outlined under " Precautions."
2. Raise and support vehicle.
3. Using back-up wrench, remove filter fitting. If nylon fuel lines become kinked and cannot be straightened, they must be replaced.
4. Twist quick-connect fitting ¼ turn in each direction to loosen dirt within fitting.
5. Using compressed air, clean quick-connect fitting at ends of filter.
6. Disconnect quick-connect fittings by squeezing plastic tabs of male end connector and pulling apart.
7. Remove fuel filter, **Fig. 23.**
8. Reverse procedure to install.

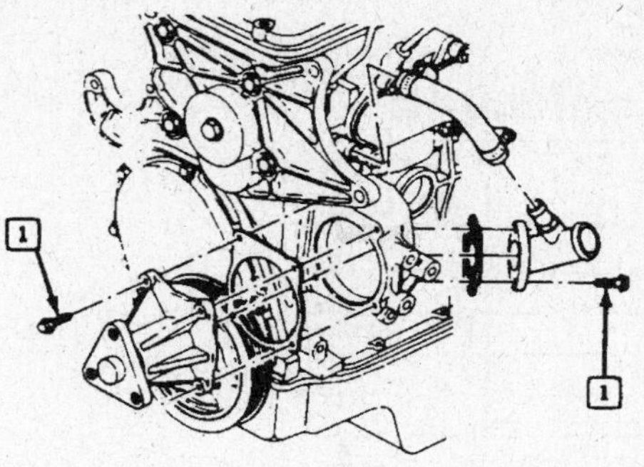

Fig. 22 Water pump installation

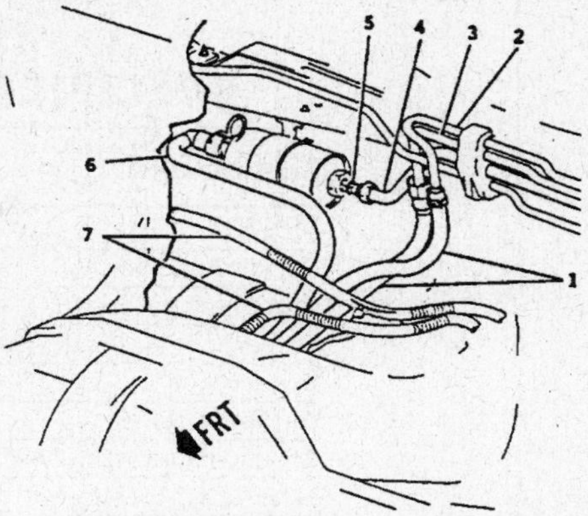

Fig. 23 Fuel filter replacement

TIGHTENING SPECIFICATIONS

Component	Torque/ Ft. Lbs.
1997	
Battery Ground Cable	13
Brake Booster Vacuum Fitting	10
Camshaft Pulley	77
Camshaft Thrust Plate	108⑤
Connecting Rod Cap Bolts	38
Coolant Drain Plug (Cylinder Block)	11
Coolant Outlet To Cylinder Head	96⑤
Crankcase Front Cover Bolts	96⑤
Crankshaft Pulley & Hub To Crankshaft	77
Crankshaft Pulley To Hub	37
Cylinder Head Bolts	①
DIS Coil Assembly	18
Engine Mount Bracket To Engine, Front	50
Engine Mount, Lower, To Bracket, Rear	18
Engine Mount To Bracket, Front	74
Engine Mount To Bracket, Rear	50
Exhaust Manifold Nuts	10
Exhaust Manifold Studs	9–10
Exhaust Pipe To Manifold	18
Flywheel To Crankshaft, A/T	52
Flywheel To Crankshaft, M/T	55
Fuel Filter Fitting	20
Intake Manifold	22
Main Bearing Cap Bolts	70
Oil Fill Tube To Cylinder Block	18
Oil Filter Adapter To Cylinder Block	18
Oil Pan Bolts	72⑤
Oil Pump Cover Bolts	84⑤
Oil Pump Drive Assembly Bolt	18
Oil Pump To Bearing Cap	32
Pressure Plate To Flywheel	15
Rear Engine Lift Bracket	32
Rocker Arm Cover	84⑤

Continued

TIGHTENING SPECIFICATIONS—Continued

Component	Torque/ Ft. Lbs.
1997	
Rocker Arm Nuts	22
Rod Bearing Cap Nut	38
Serpentine Tensioner Assembly	37
Spark Plugs	11
Tensioner bolts	37
Thermostat housing Nuts	90⑤
Timing Chain Cover	96⑤
Timing Chain Tensioner	18
Water Pump	18
Water Pump Inlet	18
Wheel Lug Nuts	100
1998–2000	
Accelerator Cable Mounting Bracket	90⑤
Accessory Bracket Bolts	37
Accessory Drive Belt Idler Pulley	37
Camshaft Position Sensor To Block Bolt	90⑤
Camshaft Rear Cover Bolts	108⑤
Camshaft Sprocket	96
Camshaft Thrust Plate Bolts	108⑤
Clutch Cover & Pressure Plate Assembly Bolts	④
Connecting Rod Cap Nuts	38
Crankcase Front Cover Bolts	96⑤
Crankshaft Main Bearing Cap Bolts	70
Crankshaft Pulley Hub To Crankshaft Bolts	77
Crankshaft Pulley To Hub Bolt	37
Crankshaft Sensor Bolt	72⑤
Cylinder Head Bolts	①
Direct Ignition System Coil Assembly	18
EGR Pipe To Adapter Bolt	18
EGR Pipe To Manifold Bolts	90⑤
EGR Valve Adapter	96⑤
EGR Valve Adapter To Cylinder Head Bolts	90⑤
EGR Valve To Adapter Nuts	19
Engine Lift Bracket Nut	37
Engine Mount Assembly Cage Nuts	33
Engine Mount Assembly To Accessory Bracket Bolts	③
Engine Mount Assembly To Body Nuts (1998)	49
Engine Mount Assembly To Body Nuts (1999)	55
Engine Mount Strut Bolts	②
Engine Mount Strut Bracket Bolts (Front)	49
Engine Mount Strut Bracket Bolts (Rear)	44
Exhaust Manifold Nuts	10
Flexplate Or Flywheel Bolts	55
Fuel Filter Fitting	20
Intake Manifold Bolts	17
Intake Manifold Nuts	17
Intake Manifold Studs	108⑤
Knock Sensor	26
Large Oil Gallery Plug (Rear Of Engine Block)	24
Lifter Guide	96⑤
Oil Fill Tube	37
Oil Filter	13
Oil Filter Adapter	26
Oil Gallery Plugs (Side Of Block Above Oil Filter)	15

Continued

TIGHTENING SPECIFICATIONS—Continued

Component	Torque/ Ft. Lbs.
1998–2000	
Oil Pan	90⑤
Oil Pump Cover Bolts	90⑤
Oil Pump Drive Assembly	18
Oil Pump Mounting Bolt	32
Oil Pressure Sensor Switch	108⑤
Oxygen Sensor	31
Rocker Arm Bolts	19
Rocker Arm Cover Bolts	90⑤
Serpentine Drive Belt Tensioner Bolt	37
Small Oil Gallery Plug (Rear Of Engine Block)	11
Spark Plugs	13
Thermostat Housing Nuts	10.3
Throttle Body To Intake Manifold Bolts	90⑤
Timing Chain Tensioner Bolts	18
Water Jacket Drain Plug	11
Water Outlet Pipe	19
Water Pump	18
Water Pump Inlet	18
Water Pump Pulley Bolts	22

①— Refer to "Cylinder Head, Replace" for tightening sequence and procedure.
②— Torque to 74 ft. lbs., then rotate an additional 90°.
③— Torque to 44 ft. lbs., then rotate an additional 90°.
④— Torque to 15 ft. lbs., then rotate an additional 45°.
⑤— Inch lbs.

2.4L Engine

NOTE: On Air Bag Equipped Models, Refer To "Air Bag System Precautions" Located In The Front Of This Manual For System Disarming and Arming Procedures.

NOTE: Refer To "Computer Relearn Procedures " Located In The Front Of This Manual For Computer Relearn Procedures.

NOTE: Refer To "Cutlass, Grand Am & Malibu" Section Of This Manual For Any Procedure Not Covered Here.

INDEX

PRECAUTIONS

AIR BAG SYSTEMS

Refer to "Air Bag System Precautions" in the front of this manual for system disarming and arming procedures.

BATTERY GROUND CABLE

Prior to service, disconnect battery ground cable and isolate as required.

FUEL SYSTEM PRESSURE RELIEF

1. **On 1997 models,** loosen fuel filler cap.
2. **On all models,** raise and support vehicle.
3. Disconnect fuel pump electrical connector.
4. Start engine and run until remaining fuel is consumed.
5. Engage starter for approximately three seconds to ensure relief of any remaining pressure.
6. Disconnect and isolate battery ground cable to avoid possible fuel discharge if any attempt is made to start the engine.

COMPRESSION PRESSURE

When inspecting cylinder compression, the throttle should be open, all spark plugs removed and the battery at or near full charge. The lowest reading cylinder should not be less than 70% of the highest and no cylinder reading should be less than 100 psi. Turn ignition key until engine cranks through four compression cycles. Normal compression builds up quickly and evenly to specifications on each cylinder.

ENGINE MOUNT

REPLACE

ENGINE MOUNT ASSEMBLY

1. Remove bolt attaching coolant recovery tank and position tank aside.
2. Install engine support tool No. J-28467-360, or equivalent, then raise engine off mount.
3. Remove body to mount attaching nuts, engine bracket to mount bolts, then the mount assembly.
4. Reverse procedure to install. Tighten fasteners to specifications.

ENGINE MOUNT STRUT

1. Raise and support vehicle.
2. Remove righthand front splash shield.
3. Remove engine mount strut bolts and engine mount strut.
4. Reverse procedure to install. Tighten fasteners to specifications.

ENGINE

REPLACE

1. Drain engine coolant into an approved container.
2. **On models equipped with air conditioning,** evacuate and recover refrigerant, then disconnect compressor/condenser hose assembly at compressor.
3. **On all models,** remove lefthand sound insulator and disconnect clutch pushrod from pedal assembly.
4. Disconnect heater hose at thermostat housing, then the upper radiator hose.
5. Remove air cleaner and coolant fan assembly.
6. Disconnect all vacuum hoses and electrical connectors.
7. Disconnect throttle cable and bracket.
8. Remove power steering rear bracket and power brake vacuum tube as an assembly.
9. Disconnect and position aside power steering pump.
10. Relive fuel pressure as outlined under "Precautions, " then disconnect fuel lines.
11. **On models equipped with automatic transaxle,** disconnect shift cables.
12. **On models equipped with manual transaxle,** disconnect clutch actuator line.
13. **On all models,** remove exhaust manifold and heat shields.
14. Disconnect lower radiator hose, then install engine support tool No. J-28467-360, or equivalent and remove engine mount assembly.
15. Raise and support vehicle, then remove both front tire and wheel assemblies.
16. Remove righthand side splash shield and radiator air deflector.
17. Remove engine and transaxle mount, then separate ball joints from steering knuckles.
18. Remove suspension supports, crossmember and stabilizer shaft as an assembly.
19. Disconnect air conditioning lines from oil pan.
20. Remove air flywheel housing cover.
21. Position suitable support beneath engine and carefully lower vehicle.
22. Mark threads on support fixture hooks so setting can be duplicated when installing engine.
23. Remove engine support "J" hooks, then slowly raise vehicle away from engine and transaxle assembly.
24. Reverse procedure to install.

RADIATOR

REPLACE

Refer to "Radiator, Replace" in the "2.2L Engine" section.

TIGHTENING SPECIFICATIONS

Component	Torque/Ft. Lbs.
Engine Mount Bracket To Block	44①
Engine Mount Front Bolts	49
Engine Mount Lower Bolts	96
Engine Mount To Body Nuts	55
Engine Mount Strut Bolts (1997–98)	74
Engine Mount Strut Bolts (1999–2000)	74①

① — Rotate an additional 90°.

Clutch & Manual Transaxle

NOTE: On Air Bag Equipped Models, Refer To "Air Bag System Precautions" Located In The Front Of This Manual For System Disarming and Arming Procedures.

NOTE: Refer To "Computer Relearn Procedures " Located In The Front Of This Manual For Computer Relearn Procedures.

INDEX

PRECAUTIONS

AIR BAG SYSTEMS

Refer to "Air Bag System Precautions" in the front of this manual for system disarming and arming procedures.

BATTERY GROUND CABLE

Prior to service, disconnect battery ground cable and isolate as required.

ADJUSTMENTS

CLUTCH PEDAL

These models use a hydraulic clutch system consisting of a dash mounted master cylinder with integral reservoir, a transmission mounted slave cylinder and high pressure tubing to connect the two components.

The hydraulic clutch system provides automatic clutch adjustment. There is no provision for adjustment.

HYDRAULIC SYSTEM SERVICE

HYDRAULIC SYSTEM BLEED

1. Clean dirt and foreign substances from reservoir cap.
2. Fill reservoir with hydraulic clutch fluid part No. 12345347, or a suitable DOT 3 type brake fluid.
3. Attach a hose to clutch actuator assembly bleeder screw, then submerge other end in a container of clutch fluid.
4. Have an assistant depress and hold clutch pedal.
5. Fully loosen bleeder screw located on slave cylinder near inlet connection.
6. While maintaining reservoir fluid level, allow fluid to flow from bleeder valve until a steady stream of fluid with no air bubbles is present, then tighten bleeder screw.
7. Fill reservoir to proper level, then start engine.
8. Depress clutch for approximately nine seconds, then select reverse gear. If no gear clash is present, system is satisfactory. If gear clash is present, repeat bleeding procedure.

CLUTCH MASTER CYLINDER, REPLACE

Removal

1. Remove sound insulator from inside of vehicle.
2. Disconnect clutch master cylinder pushrod from clutch pedal.
3. Remove clutch master cylinder attaching nuts at front of dash and disconnect remote reservoir.
4. Disconnect fluid master line from actuator line by pushing release slide in, then holding and disconnecting the halves.
5. Remove clutch master cylinder from vehicle.

Installation

1. Install clutch master cylinder to front of dash.
2. Connect fluid master line to actuator line by pushing release slide in, then holding and connecting the halves.
3. Connect remote reservoir.
4. Remove pedal restrictor from pushrod, then lubricate pushrod bushing on clutch pedal.
5. Connect pushrod with clutch pedal and install retaining clip.
6. Install sound insulator.
7. Bleed clutch fluid line as outlined under "Hydraulic System Bleed."

CLUTCH ACTUATOR CYLINDER, REPLACE

Removal

1. Disconnect fluid master line from actuator line by pushing release slide in, then holding and disconnecting the halves.
2. Remove transaxle assembly as outlined under "Transaxle, Replace."
3. Remove clutch actuator cylinder to bellhousing attaching bolts, then the actuator.

Installation

1. Lubricate inner diameter of release bearing with clutch bearing lubricant part No. 12345777, or equivalent.
2. Install clutch actuator cylinder to bellhousing.
3. Install transaxle assembly.
4. Connect fluid master line from actuator line by pushing release slide in, then holding and connecting the halves.
5. Bleed clutch fluid line as outlined under "Hydraulic System Bleed."

CLUTCH

REPLACE

1. Remove hush panel from driver's footwell as required, then disconnect clutch master cylinder pushrod from clutch pedal.
2. Remove transaxle as outlined under "Transaxle, Replace " procedure.
3. Mark position of pressure plate to flywheel to ease assembly.
4. Gradually loosen pressure plate to flywheel attaching bolts until spring tension is relieved.
5. Support pressure plate and remove attaching bolts, pressure plate and driven disc, **Fig. 1.**
6. Clean pressure plate and flywheel mounting surfaces. Inspect bearing retainer outer surface of the transaxle.
7. Align flywheel Heavy Side, stamped with an "X," with the clutch cover Light Side, marked with paint.
8. Place pressure plate and driven disc in position and support with tool No. J-29074, or equivalent, **Fig. 2. The driven disc is installed with the damper springs offset toward the transaxle. Stamped letters found on the driven disc identify the " Flywheel Side."**
9. Install and gradually tighten the pressure plate to flywheel attaching bolts. Remove support tool.

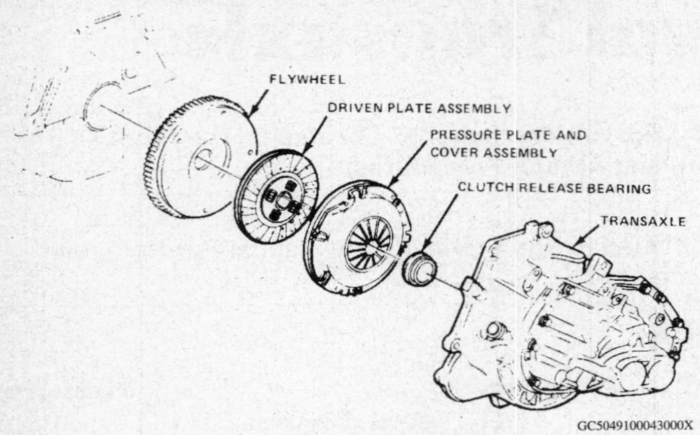

Fig. 1 Clutch assembly

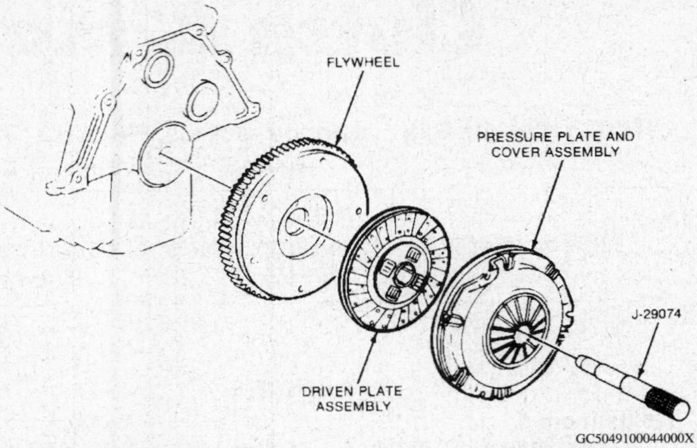

Fig. 2 Clutch disc & pressure plate alignment

10. Lubricate the release bearing outside diameter groove and inside diameter recess with lubricant part No. 12345777, or equivalent.
11. Install transaxle.
12. Bleed clutch fluid system as outlined under "Hydraulic System Bleed."

TRANSAXLE

REPLACE

1. Install engine support fixture tool No. J-28467-360, or equivalent, then raise engine enough to take pressure off motor mounts.
2. Remove air cleaner and duct assembly at TBI unit.
3. Remove wiring harness from mount bracket.
4. **On 1999–2000 models,** drain coolant into an approved container, then remove radiator upper hose.
5. **On all models,** remove transaxle upper mount and mount bracket attaching bolts.
6. Disconnect clutch fluid master line from actuator line by pushing release slide in, then holding and disconnecting the halves.
7. Remove shift cables and retaining clamp at transaxle.
8. Remove ground cable at transaxle attaching bolts, then disconnect back-up lamp switch electrical connector.
9. Remove transaxle vent tube.
10. **On 1999–2000 models,** remove starter.
11. **On all models,** remove transaxle to engine rear bolts.
12. Using support fixture tool, lower the engine at least 30 turns to ease removal and installation of transaxle.
13. Raise and support vehicle, then drain transaxle fluid into an approved container.
14. Remove front tires and wheels.
15. Remove lefthand front inner splash shield.
16. Disconnect front ABS and WSS harness electrical connectors, then position harnesses aside.
17. Remove clutch housing cover attaching bolts.
18. Disconnect Vehicle Speed Sensor (VSS) at transaxle.
19. **On 1997 models,** using ball joint separator tool No. J-38892, or equivalent, separate lefthand and righthand ball joints at knuckles.
20. **On 1998–2000 models,** using ball joint separator tool No. J-43828, or equivalent, separate lefthand and righthand ball joints at knuckles.
21. **On all models,** remove stabilizer link pins.
22. Disconnect power steering lines as required.
23. Disconnect steering gear at column coupler.
24. Remove suspension support attaching bolts.
25. Remove drive axles from transaxle.
26. Remove transaxle front lower mount.
27. Position suitable jack under transaxle, then remove transaxle to engine attaching bolts.
28. Slide transaxle away from engine, then carefully lower it away from vehicle.
29. Reverse procedure to install, noting the following:
    a. When installing transaxle, carefully guide righthand drive axle shaft into transaxle bore as transaxle is being raised.
    b. The righthand drive axle shaft cannot be installed once the transaxle has been connected to the engine.

TIGHTENING SPECIFICATIONS

Component	Torque/Ft. Lbs.
Back-Up Switch Assembly To Transaxle	24
Clutch Bleed Screw	18③
Clutch Cover To Flywheel (2.2L)	15①
Clutch Cover To Flywheel (2.4L)	15②
Clutch Cover To Transaxle	89③
Clutch Master Cylinder	15
Clutch Release Lever	37
Clutch Slave Cylinder Nut	16
Front Transaxle Strut To Transaxle	38
Front Transaxle To Body Bolt	38
Rear Mount Bracket To Transaxle	38
Rear Transaxle Mount To Body	55
Shift Cable Grommet To Shroud	12③

Continued

TIGHTENING SPECIFICATIONS—Continued

Component	Torque/Ft. Lbs.
Shift Control Box To Transaxle	13
Shift Control To Floor	18
Shift Linkage Retainer To Transaxle Case	17
Shift Retainer To Transaxle Case	18
Shift Shaft Lever Nut	61
Speedometer/VSS Housing To Transaxle	80③
Steering Column Lower Pinch Bolt (1997)	30
Steering Column Lower Pinch Bolt (1998–2000)	16
Steering Rack & Pinion Mounting Bolts	89
Transaxle Mount To Transaxle	55
Transaxle Shift Cable Bracket To Cables	89③
Transaxle Shift Lever To Cable Stud	89③
Transaxle To Engine Bolts And Studs	55
Transaxle To Engine Bolts And Studs	66
Wheel Lugnuts	100

① — Plus an additional 30°.
② — Plus an additional 45°.
③ — Inch lbs.

Rear Axle & Suspension

NOTE: On Air Bag Equipped Models, Refer To "Air Bag System Precautions" Located In The Front Of This Manual For System Disarming and Arming Procedures.

NOTE: Refer To "Computer Relearn Procedures " Located In The Front Of This Manual For Computer Relearn Procedures.

INDEX

PRECAUTIONS

AIR BAG SYSTEMS

Refer to "Air Bag System Precautions" in the front of this manual for system disarming and arming procedures.

BATTERY GROUND CABLE

Prior to service, disconnect battery ground cable and isolate as required.

DESCRIPTION

The rear suspension is a semi-independent type consisting of an axle assembly with trailing arms and twisting cross beam, coil springs and "coil-over" shock absorbers. A stabilizer bar is available and is attached to the inside of the axle beam and to the lower end of the control arms. A single unit hub and bearing assembly is bolted to each end of the axle assembly. The hub and bearing assembly is a sealed, non-serviceable unit and must be replaced as an assembly.

REAR AXLE

REPLACE

1. Raise and support vehicle on a hoist.
2. Remove rear wheels and tires.
3. Remove brake drums. **Do not hammer on drums since this might damage bearings.**
4. Remove brake fluid pipe retainer bolts from axle.
5. Disconnect brake pipe at brake hose.
6. Disconnect wheel speed sensor harnesses at sensors.
7. Remove wheel speed sensor harness from retainers on axle.
8. Disconnect parking brake cables from equalizers.
9. Remove parking brake cables from axle.
10. Support rear suspension with suitable jack.
11. Remove shock absorber lower mounting bolts.
12. Remove mounting bolts, washers and nuts from axle.
13. Carefully lower rear axle assembly from vehicle.
14. Remove control arm to underbody bracket bolts, then lower the rear axle assembly and remove from vehicle.
15. Remove hub to rear axle attaching bolts, then the hubs, bearings and backing plates from rear axle assembly.
16. Reverse procedure to install. Bleed brake system.

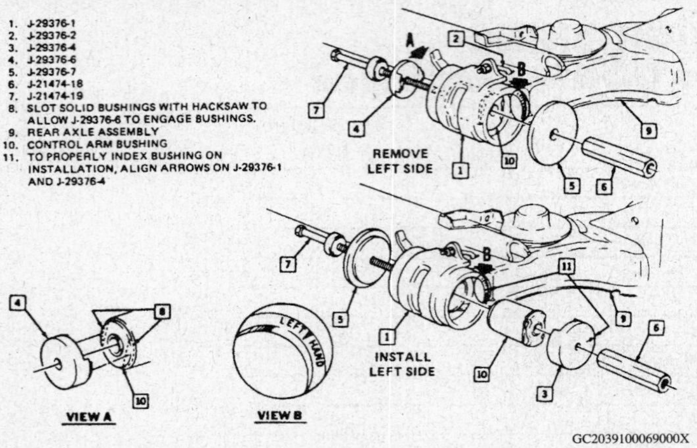

Fig. 1 Control arm bushing replacement

HUB & BEARING

REPLACE

1. Raise and support vehicle, then remove wheel and tire assembly and brake drum. **Do not hammer brake drum since damage to bearing may result.**
2. Disconnect wheel speed sensor electrical connector.
3. Remove hub/bearing assembly to rear axle attaching bolts, then the hub/bearing assembly from axle. **The upper rear hub attaching bolt may not clear brake shoe when removing hub and bearing assembly. Partially remove hub and bearing assembly prior to removing this bolt.**
4. Reverse procedure to install. Tighten hub attaching bolts to specifications. **Use care not to drop hub/bearing assembly since damage to bearing may result.**

SHOCK ABSORBER

REPLACE

1. Open luggage compartment lid, then remove trim cover and shock absorber upper attaching nuts.
2. Raise rear of vehicle and support rear axle using a suitable jack.
3. Remove shock absorber lower attaching bolt, then disconnect shock absorber from mounting bracket and remove shock absorber from vehicle.
4. Reverse procedure to install. Tighten attaching bolts to specifications.

CONTROL ARM BUSHING

REPLACE

Remove and install one control arm bushing at a time by proceeding as follows:

1. Raise and support vehicle.
2. Support rear axle with suitable jack.
3. Remove wheels and tires.
4. If replacing righthand bushings, disconnect brake fluid lines at body.
5. If replacing lefthand bushings, disconnect brake fluid line bracket from body and parking brake cable from guide hook on body.
6. Remove control arm to body nut, bolt and washer, then rotate control arm downward. **Do not allow axle to hang by brake hose.**
7. The bushing can now be replaced using tools shown in **Fig. 1.** When installing bushing, the arrow on the installer must align with arrow on the receiver, **Fig. 1.** Use high pressure lubricant part No. J-23444-A, or equivalent if required.
8. Reverse procedure to complete installation, noting the following:
   a. Press bushing into control arm by turning bolt. When bushing reaches its proper position the end flange will sit flush against control arm face.
   b. Ensure bushing washer and nut are installed on outboard side.
   c. **The control arm attaching bolt must be tightened after vehicle is lowered to floor and is in its standing height position.** Tighten attaching bolt to specifications.

TIGHTENING SPECIFICATIONS

Component	Torque/Ft. Lbs.
Brake Line Bracket To Axle	11
Brake Line Bracket To Body (1997)	97①
Brake Line Bracket To Body (1998–2000)	50①
Brake Fluid Pipe Fittings (1997)	17
Brake Fluid Pipe Fittings (1998–2000)	20
Control Arm To Body Nuts (1997)	44②
Control Arm To Body Nuts (1998–2000)	52
Hub & Bearing Assembly	44
Shock Absorber Bolt At Axle	125
Shock Absorber Mount To Body (1997)	21
Shock Absorber Mount To Body (1998–2000)	18
Stabilizer Shaft Clamp Bolts At Axle	13
Stabilizer Shaft Clamp Nuts	16
Wheel Lugnuts	100

① — Inch lbs.

② — Rotate an additional 120°.

Front Suspension & Steering

NOTE: On Air Bag Equipped Models, Refer To "Air Bag System Precautions" Located In The Front Of This Manual For System Disarming and Arming Procedures.

NOTE: Refer To "Computer Relearn Procedures " Located In The Front Of This Manual For Computer Relearn Procedures.

INDEX

PRECAUTIONS

AIR BAG SYSTEMS

Refer to "Air Bag System Precautions" in the front of this manual for system disarming and arming procedures.

BATTERY GROUND CABLE

Prior to service, disconnect battery ground cable and isolate as required.

DESCRIPTION

The front suspension on these models, **Fig. 1,** is a combination strut and spring design. The control arms pivot from the crossmember. The upper end of the strut is isolated by a rubber mount incorporating a non-serviceable bearing for wheel turning. On base models the lower control arm pivots have conventional rubber bushings. Upgraded models have a cross axis bearing rather than bushings. The tie rods connect to the steering arm on the strut, below the spring seat. The lower end of the steering knuckle pivots on a ball stud which is retained to the lower control arm by rivets and is secured to the steering knuckle with a nut and cotter pin. The sealed wheel bearings are integral with the hub and are serviced as an assembly.

WHEEL BEARING

REPLACE

REMOVAL

1. Raise and support vehicle.
2. Remove tire and wheel assembly, then install modified outer seal protector No. J-34754, or equivalent, **Fig. 2.**
3. Insert a drift punch through the rotor, **Fig. 3,** then remove axle shaft nut and washer.
4. **On 1997 models,** using ball joint separator tool No. J-38892, or equivalent, separate ball joint from knuckle.
5. **On 1998–2000 models,** using ball joint separator tool No. J-43828, or equivalent, separate ball joint from knuckle.
6. **On all models,** using tool No. J-28733-A, or equivalent, disengage axle from hub and bearing assembly.
7. Move axle shaft inward, then remove caliper attaching bolts and support caliper.
8. Remove brake rotor, then hub and bearing assembly attaching bolts.
9. Remove hub and bearing assembly.

INSTALLATION

1. Install hub and bearing assembly. Tighten attaching bolts to specifications.
2. Install hub and bearing seal, then the brake rotor.
3. Install caliper, tighten attaching bolts to specifications.
4. Move axle shaft outward, then insert drift punch through rotor, **Fig. 3.**
5. Install washer and new shaft nut, tighten shaft nut to specifications.
6. Install ball joint, then remove drift punch and seal protector.
7. Install tire and wheel assembly, then lower the vehicle.

BALL JOINT INSPECTION

1. Raise and support vehicle so suspension is allowed to hang free.
2. Grasp wheel and tire assembly at top and bottom, then rock top of wheel and tire assembly inward and outward.
3. While rocking wheel and tire assembly, observe movement between steering knuckle and control arm. If any horizontal movement is present, replace ball joint.
4. If ball joint is disconnected from steering knuckle, use finger to try to twist ball joint in its socket. If ball joint can be twisted in its socket, replace ball joint.

BALL JOINT

REPLACE

1. Raise and support vehicle, then remove wheel and tire.
2. Install modified tool No. J-34754, or equivalent, then remove ball joint attaching cotter pin.
3. Remove ball joint stud attaching nut.
4. **On 1997 models,** using ball joint separator tool No. J-38892, or equivalent, separate ball joint from knuckle.
5. **On 1998–2000 models,** using ball joint separator tool No. J-43828, or equivalent, separate ball joint from knuckle.
6. **On all models,** using a ⅛ inch drill bit, bore pilot holes completely through the rivets. Using a ½ inch drill bit, bore final holes through rivets to ensure fitting of new ball joint.
7. Remove ball joint from control arm.
8. Assemble new ball joint to lower control arm with bolts provided in service package, **Fig. 4.** Tighten bolts to specifications.
9. Insert ball joint stud into steering knuckle and tighten nut to specifications.
10. Install wheel and tire.

STRUT

REPLACE

1. Raise hood, then remove strut protective cap and strut to body attaching nuts.
2. Raise and support vehicle, then lower it slightly with its suspension support weight on suitable jack stands.
3. Remove wheel and tire assembly, then

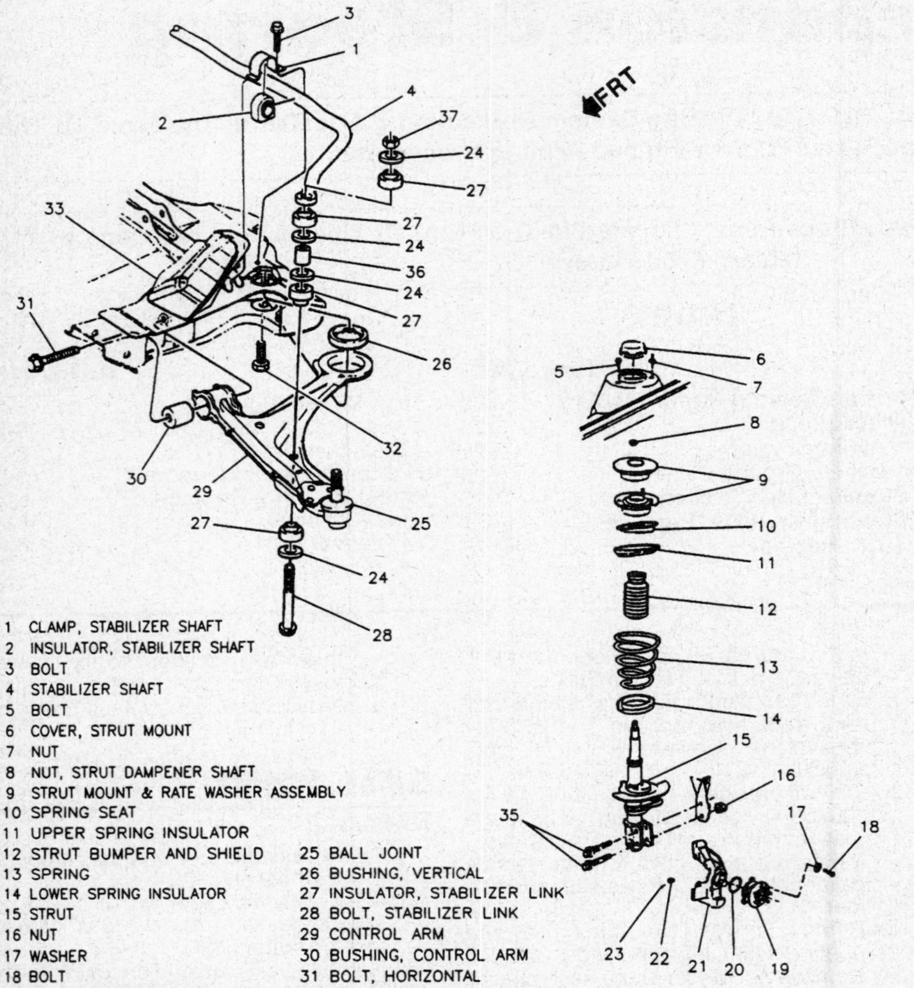

1 CLAMP, STABILIZER SHAFT
2 INSULATOR, STABILIZER SHAFT
3 BOLT
4 STABILIZER SHAFT
5 BOLT
6 COVER, STRUT MOUNT
7 NUT
8 NUT, STRUT DAMPENER SHAFT
9 STRUT MOUNT & RATE WASHER ASSEMBLY
10 SPRING SEAT
11 UPPER SPRING INSULATOR
12 STRUT BUMPER AND SHIELD
13 SPRING
14 LOWER SPRING INSULATOR
15 STRUT
16 NUT
17 WASHER
18 BOLT
19 HUB AND BEARING ASSEMBLY
20 SEAL (PART OF 24)
21 STEERING KNUCKLE
22 NUT, BALL JOINT
23 COTTER PIN
24 WASHER
25 BALL JOINT
26 BUSHING, VERTICAL
27 INSULATOR, STABILIZER LINK
28 BOLT, STABILIZER LINK
29 CONTROL ARM
30 BUSHING, CONTROL ARM
31 BOLT, HORIZONTAL
32 BOLT, VERTICAL BUSHING
33 SUSPENSION SUPPORT
34 WASHER
35 BOLT
36 SPACER, STABILIZER LINK
37 NUT, STABILIZER LINK

GC2029600214000A

Fig. 1 Exploded view of front suspension

install modified inner drive joint boot protector tool No. J-34754, or equivalent.

4. Remove brake fluid line bracket.
5. Using tool No. J-24319-01, or equivalent, disconnect tie rod from strut assembly.
6. Using a suitable sharp tool, scribe outlines of strut to knuckle relationship to ease installation.
7. Remove strut to steering knuckle attaching bolts, then the strut from vehicle. Avoid chipping or scratching spring coating.
8. Reverse procedure to install, noting the following:
   a. Ensure strut mounts to knuckle with all scribe marks properly aligned.
   b. Tighten all fasteners to specifications.
   c. Inspect wheel alignment.

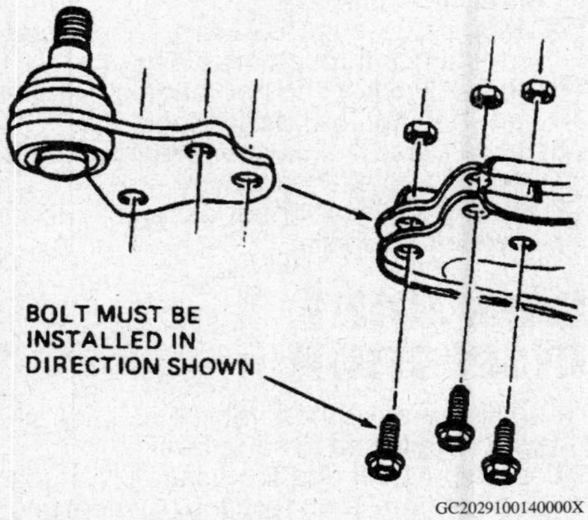

Fig. 4 Lower ball joint to control arm assembly

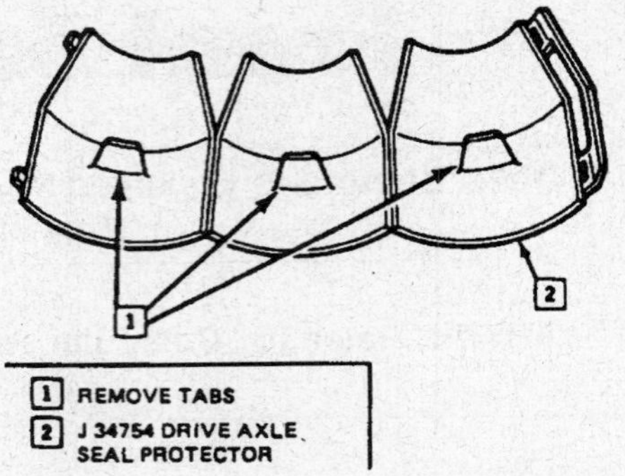

Fig. 2 Modified outer seal protector

1. DRIFT PUNCH
2. 6 POINT DEEP WELL SOCKET

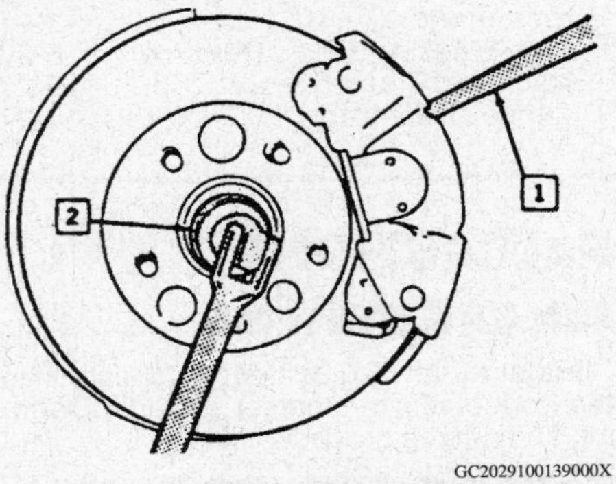

Fig. 3 Shaft nut replacement

STRUT SERVICE

DISASSEMBLE

1. Position strut compressor tool No. J-34013-B in holding fixture tool No. J-3289-20, or equivalents.
2. Position strut in strut compressor, then compress strut to approximately ½ of its height. Avoid bottoming out spring or damper rod.
3. Remove nut from strut dampener shaft, then position guide rod tool No. J-34013-88, or equivalent, on dampener shaft. Use guide rod tool to position dampener shaft down through bearing cap while compressing coil spring.
4. Remove components from coil strut unit.

ASSEMBLE

1. Position bearing cap on strut compressor.
2. Position strut to strut compressor and install compressor bottom locking pin.
3. Extend dampener shaft and install clamp tool No. J-34013-20, or equivalent, to hold shaft in position.
4. Position spring over dampener, then position strut to strut compressor upper locking pin hole and install pin.
5. Install upper insulator, shield, bumper and upper spring seat. The flat on the

upper spring seat should face in the same direction as the centerline of the strut assembly spindle.
6. Install guide rod tool No. J-34013-88, or equivalent, onto dampener shaft, then compress strut unit until dampener shaft threads are visible. Remove guide rod and install attaching nut.
7. Pack strut support with wheel bearing lubricant part No. 1051344, or equivalent.
8. While holding dampener shaft in position with a suitable wrench, tighten attaching nut to specifications. After tightening nut, remove clamp from dampener shaft clamp tool.

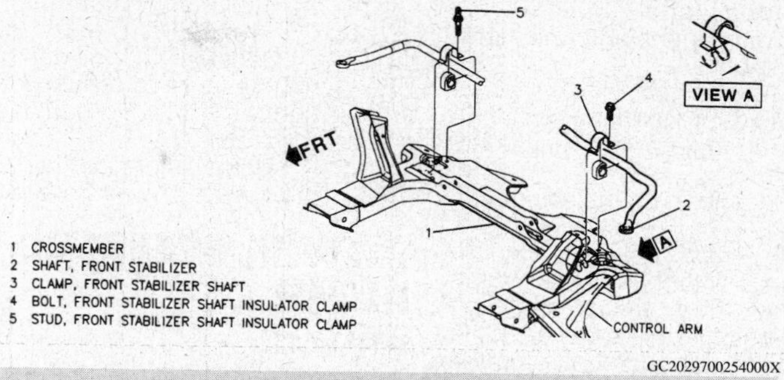

Fig. 5 Stabilizer bar installation

CONTROL ARM

REPLACE

1. Raise and support vehicle on a hoist, then remove wheel and tire.
2. Disconnect stabilizer bar at lower control arm and control arm support.
3. Install modified seal protector tool No. J-34754, or equivalent.
4. **On 1997 models,** using ball joint separator tool No. J-38892, or equivalent, separate ball joint from knuckle.
5. **On 1998–2000 models,** using ball joint separator tool No. J-43828, or equivalent, separate ball joint from knuckle.
6. **On all models,** remove control arm to chassis attaching bolts, then the control arm.
7. Attach new lower control arm to control arm support.
8. Install control arm support to chassis. Tighten all fasteners to specifications.
9. Reverse procedure to complete installation. Inspect toe setting and adjust as required.

STEERING KNUCKLE

REPLACE

1. Raise and support vehicle, then remove wheel and tire.
2. Remove front hub and bearing as outlined under "Wheel Bearing, Replace" in this section.
3. **On 1997 models,** using ball joint separator tool No. J-38892, or equivalent, separate ball joint from knuckle.
4. **On 1998–2000 models,** using ball joint separator tool No. J-43828, or equivalent, separate ball joint from knuckle.
5. **On all models,** using tool No. J-24319-01, or equivalent, disconnect tie rod from strut assembly.
6. Using a suitable sharp tool, scribe outlines of strut to knuckle relationship to ease installation.
7. Remove strut to steering knuckle attaching bolts, then disconnect strut from steering knuckle.
8. Assemble strut to new steering knuckle and install attaching bolts finger tight.
9. Insert ball joint stud into steering knuckle and tighten stud nut to specifications.
10. Tighten strut to steering knuckle bolts to specifications.
11. Reverse removal procedure to complete installation.

STABILIZER BAR

REPLACE

1. Raise and support vehicle, allowing control arms to hang freely.
2. Remove front wheels and tires.
3. Remove stabilizer shaft links.
4. Support front suspension support with a suitable jack.
5. Remove suspension support rear, center and front mounting bolts in this order.
6. Lower front suspension support to ease shaft removal.
7. Disconnect stabilizer bar at control arms and control arm supports, **Fig. 5.**
8. Remove stabilizer bar with insulators.
9. Reverse procedure to install, noting the following:
   a. Install stabilizer shaft to vehicle.
   b. Install and hand tighten shaft to suspension support clamp bolts.
   c. Install and hand tighten suspension support front, center and rear mounting bolts in this order.
   d. **On 1997 models, torque** suspension support lefthand rear, righthand rear, front upper and rear inboard bolts in this order to 71 ft. lbs., then rotate each bolt at same time an additional 90°.
   e. **On 1998–2000 models, torque** suspension support lefthand rear, righthand rear, lefthand front and righthand front bolts in this order to 71 ft. lbs.
   f. **On all models, torque** stabilizer shaft clamp bolts to 49 ft. lbs.
   g. **Torque** links to 13 ft. lbs.

POWER STEERING GEAR

REPLACE

AUTOMATIC TRANSAXLE

1. Raise and support vehicle on a hoist.
2. Remove front tires and wheels.
3. Remove righthand and lefthand splash shields.
4. Remove engine strut from lower engine mount and frame.
5. Remove front exhaust pipe.
6. Disconnect ABS wiring harness from wheel speed sensor and body.
7. Remove steering column lower pinch bolt at steering gear.
8. **On 1997 models,** using ball joint separator tool No. J-38892, or equivalent, separate ball joint from knuckle.
9. **On 1998–2000 models,** using ball joint separator tool No. J-43828, or equivalent, separate ball joint from knuckle.
10. **On all models,** using tool No. J-24319-01, or equivalent, disconnect tie rods from knuckles.
11. Remove brake fluid lines from frame retainers.
12. Disconnect power steering hoses from steering gear.
13. Remove front suspension support brace.
14. Lower the vehicle until front suspension support brace rests on jack stands.
15. Remove front suspension support mounting bolts.
16. Raise vehicle up from front suspension support.
17. Remove steering gear to suspension support mounting bolts, then the gear.
18. Reverse procedure to install, noting the following:
   a. **On 1997 models, torque** suspension support lefthand rear, righthand rear, front upper and rear inboard bolts in this order to 71 ft. lbs., then rotate each bolt at same time an additional 90°.
   b. **On 1998–2000 models, torque** suspension support lefthand rear, righthand rear, lefthand front and righthand front bolts in this order to 71 ft. lbs.
   c. Fill power steering fluid reservoir, then bleed any air from system.

MANUAL TRANSAXLE

1. Raise and support vehicle on a hoist.
2. Remove front tires and wheels.
3. Remove power steering hoses from steering gear.
4. Using tool No. J-24319-01, or equivalent, disconnect tie rods from knuckles.
5. Remove brake fluid lines from frame retainers.
6. Remove steering column lower pinch bolt at steering gear.
7. Support front suspension support with

a suitable jack stand.
8. Remove front suspension crossmember mounting bolts.
9. Lower the suspension enough to access steering gear mounting bolts.
10. Remove steering gear mounting bolts, then the gear.
11. Reverse procedure to install, noting the following:
    a. **On 1997 models, torque** suspension support lefthand rear, righthand rear, front upper and rear inboard bolts in this order to 71 ft. lbs., then rotate each bolt at same time an additional 90°.
    b. **On 1998–2000 models, torque** suspension support lefthand rear, righthand rear, lefthand front and righthand front bolts in this order to 71 ft. lbs.
    c. Fill power steering fluid reservoir, then bleed any air from system.

POWER STEERING PUMP

REPLACE

1. **On models equipped with 2.2L engine,** mark the running direction, then remove serpentine belt.
2. **On all models,** remove power steering fluid lines.
3. Remove power steering pump attaching bolts.
4. Remove pump assembly, then transfer pulley if required.
5. Reverse procedure to install. Tighten attaching bolts to specifications.

TIGHTENING SPECIFICATIONS

Component	Torque/ Ft. Lbs.
Ball Joint To Knuckle	41–50
Caliper Bolts	38
Control Arm To Crossmember Bolts (1997)	①
Control Arm To Crossmember Bolts (1998–2000)	②
Hub & Bearing Assembly	70
Hub Nut	185
Steering Column Pinch Bolt (1997)	30
Steering Column Pinch Bolt (1998–2000)	16
Stabilizer Shaft To Control Arm	13
Stabilizer To Support Assembly	49
Steering Knuckle To Strut Assembly	133
Strut Assembly To Body	18
Strut Piston Nut	34
Tie Rod Jam Nuts (1998–2000)	50
Tie Rod Pinch Bolts (1997)	31
Tie Rod Stud Nuts (1997)	37
Tie Rod Stud Nuts (1998–2000)	33
Wheel Lugnuts	100

① — Torque front bushing bolt to 89 ft. lbs., then rotate an additional 180°. Torque rear vertical bushing bolt to 125 ft. lbs.

② — Torque front bushing bolt to 79 ft. lbs. Torque rear vertical bushing bolt to 125 ft. lbs.

Wheel Alignment

INDEX

FRONT WHEEL ALIGNMENT

CASTER

Caster is not adjustable. If caster angle is not within specifications, inspect for suspension support misalignment or front suspension damage.

CAMBER

Toe setting is the only adjustment normally required. However, in special circumstances, such as damage due to road hazard or collision, camber may be adjusted by modifying the strut assembly. Proceed as follows:

1. Secure bottom of strut assembly in a suitable vise.
2. Enlarge bottom holes in outer flanges with a round file until holes in outer flanges match slots in inner flanges, **Fig. 1.**
3. Connect strut to steering knuckle and install bolts finger tight.
4. Grasp top of tire firmly, then move tire inboard or outboard until proper camber reading is obtained. Tighten attaching bolts enough to secure camber setting.
5. Remove wheel and tire and tighten strut to steering knuckle attaching bolts. **Torque** strut to steering knuckle attaching bolt to 133 ft. lbs.

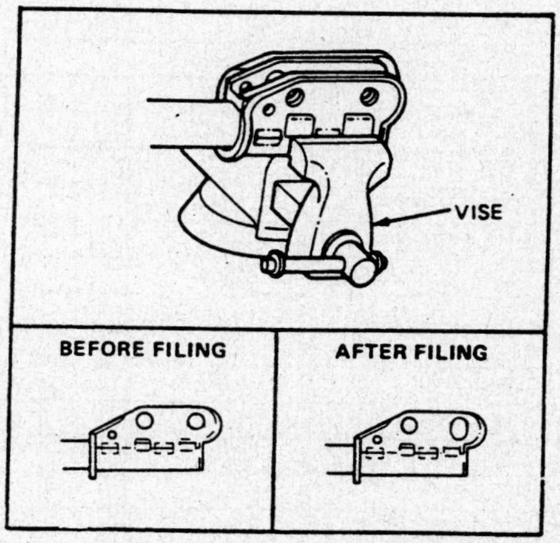

Fig. 1 Strut bracket modification for camber adjustment

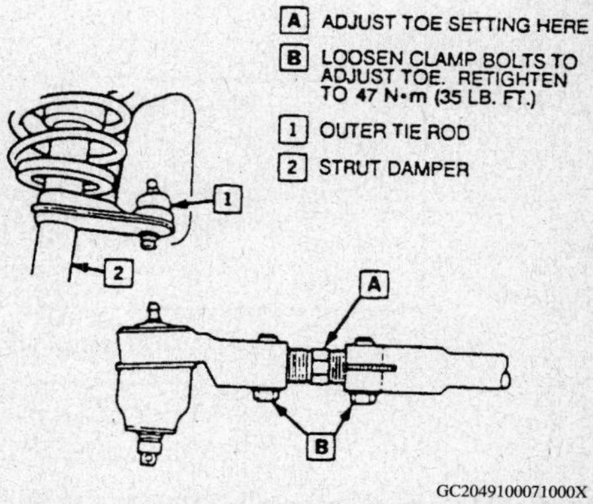

Fig. 2 Typical toe adjustment

TOE

Toe-out is controlled by tie rod position. Adjustment is made by loosening the clamp bolts or jam nuts at the steering knuckle end of the tie rods and rotating the rods to obtain proper toe setting, **Fig. 2.** After proper toe setting is obtained, tighten fasteners to specifications.

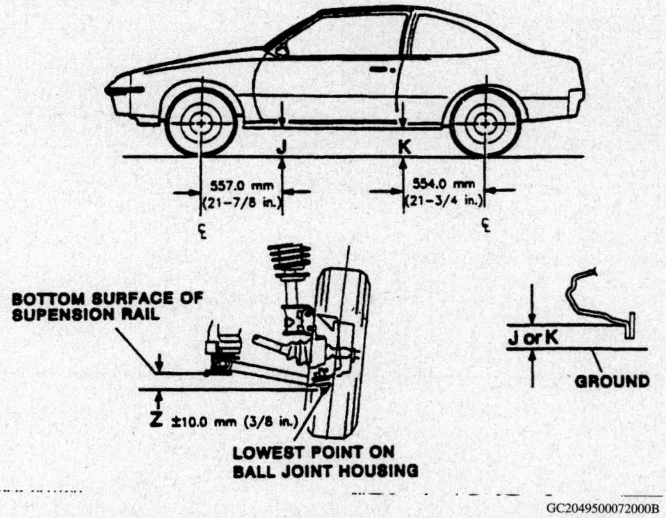

Fig. 3 Vehicle ride height measurement locations

VEHICLE RIDE HEIGHT

Refer to **Fig. 3** for ride height measurement points and to **Fig. 4** for the specifications. When inspecting ride height measurements, fuel tank should be full, tires should be at proper inflation, front seat should be in rearward position, luggage compartment should be empty except for spare tire and jack, and the vehicle should be on level ground. If fuel tank is not full, add weight to luggage compartment to compensate for missing fuel.

Prior to measuring ride height, lift front bumper upward approximately 1.5 inches and gently release (3 times), then measure front ride height. Push front bumper downward approximately 1.5 inches and gently release (3 times), then measure front ride height again. Average of both readings to determine vehicle ride height. Measure rear ride height in same manner, lifting and pushing rear bumper.

Year	Model	Body Type	Tire Size	Engine	Ride Height Measurements, Inches①		
					Dimension Z	Dimension J	Dimension K
1997	Cavalier	Base Coupe & Sedan	195/70R × 14	All	7/16	9.17	9.44
			195/65R × 15	All	3/16	9.17	9.44
		LS Sedan	195/65R × 15	2.4L	9/32	9.17	9.44
		Convertible	195/65R × 15	All	9/32	9.17	9.44
		LS Coupe & Z24	205/55R × 16	2.4L	1/8	9.17	9.44
	Sunfire	SE Coupe & Sedan	195/70R × 14	All	15/32	9.17	9.45
		SE Coupe, Convertible & Sedan	195/65R × 15	All	1/4	9.17	9.45
		GT Convertible	205/55R × 16	2.4L	5/32	9.17	9.45
1998–99	Cavalier	Convertible	195/65R × 15	2.2L	13/64	9.38	9.64
				2.4L	9/32	9.44	9.64
		Coupe②	195/70R × 14	2.2L	5/32	9.17	9.44
		Coupe④	205/55R × 16	2.4L	5/64	9.44	9.44
		Sedan②	195/65R × 15	2.2L	0	9.17	9.44
		Sedan③	195/65R × 15	2.4L	3/64	9.17	9.44
	Sunfire	Convertible	195/65R × 15	2.2L	13/64	9.44	9.64
				2.4L	9/32	9.44	9.64
		Coupe②	195/70R × 14	2.2L	5/32	9.17	9.44
		Coupe③	195/65R × 15	2.4L	3/64	9.17	9.44
		Coupe④	205/55R × 16	2.4L	5/64	9.17	9.44
		Sedan②	195/65R × 15	2.2L	5/64	9.17	9.44
		Sedan③	195/65R × 15	2.4L	3/64	9.17	9.44
2000	Cavalier & Sunfire	Convertible②	195/65R × 15	2.4L	9/32	9.37	9.64
		Coupe②	195/70R × 14	2.2L	5/32	9.17	9.44
			195/65R × 15	2.2L	0	9.17	9.44
		Coupe③	195/65R × 15	2.4L	3/64	9.17	9.44
		Coupe④	205/55R × 16	2.4L	5/64	9.17	9.44
		Sedan②	195/70R × 14	2.2L	5/32	9.17	9.44
			195/65R × 15	2.2L	5/64	9.17	9.44
		Sedan③	195/65R × 15	2.4L	3/64	9.17	9.44

① — Maximum variation side to side and front to rear is 3/4 inch.
② — Models w/FE0 suspension.
③ — Models w/FE1 suspension.
④ — Models w/FE2 suspension.

Fig. 4 Vehicle ride height specifications

CENTURY, CUTLASS SUPREME, GRAND PRIX, IMPALA, INTRIGUE, LUMINA, MONTE CARLO & REGAL

NOTE: Refer To Rear Of This Manual For Vehicle Manufacturer's Special Service Tool Suppliers.

INDEX OF SERVICE OPERATIONS

Specifications

GENERAL ENGINE SPECIFICATIONS

Year	Engine Displacement	Engine VIN Code②	Fuel System	Bore & Stroke	Compression Ratio	Net H.P. @ RPM③	Maximum Torque Ft. Lbs. @ RPM	Normal Oil Pressure, psi
1997	3.1L	M	SFI	3.50 x 3.31	9.6	160 @ 5200	185 @ 4000	15⑤
	3.4L	M	SFI	3.62 x 3.31	9.7	215 @ 5200	220 @ 4000	15⑤
	3800 ①	1	SFI	3.80 x 3.40	8.5	240 @ 5200	280 @ 3200	60④
	3800	K	SFI	3.80 x 3.40	9.4	195 @ 5200	220 @ 4000	60④
1998	3.1L	M	SFI	3.50 x 3.31	9.6	160 @ 5200	185 @ 4000	15⑤
	3800 ①	1	SFI	3.80 x 3.40	8.5	240 @ 5200	280 @ 3200	60④
	3800	K	SFI	3.80 x 3.40	9.4	195 @ 5200	220 @ 4000	60④
1999	3.1L	M	SFI	3.50 x 3.31	9.5	160 @ 5200	185 @ 4000	15⑤
	3.5L	H	SFI	3.52 x 3.62	9.3	215 @ 5600	234 @ 4400	⑥
	3800①	1	SFI	3.80 x 3.40	8.5	240 @ 5200	280 @ 3200	60④
	3800	K	SFI	3.80 x 3.40	9.4	200 @ 5200	220 @ 4000	60④
2000	3.1L	M	SFI	3.50 x 3.31	9.5	160 @ 5200	185 @ 4000	15⑤
	3.4L	E	SFI	3.62 x 3.31	9.5	180 @ 5200	205 @ 4000	15⑤
	3.5L	H	SFI	3.52 x 3.62	9.3	215 @ 5600	234 @ 4400	⑥
	3800①	1	SFI	3.80 x 3.40	8.5	240 @ 5200	280 @ 3200	60④
	3800	K	SFI	3.80 x 3.40	9.4	200 @ 5200	220 @ 4000	60④

MFI — Multi-Port Fuel Injection
SFI — Sequential-Port Fuel Injection
① — Supercharged engine.
② — The eighth digit of the VIN denotes engine code.
③ — Ratings are net as installed in vehicle.
④ — At 1850 RPM. Engine at operating temperature using 10W-30 engine oil.
⑤ — Minimum @ 1100 RPM. Engine at operating temperature.
⑥ — 35 @ 600 RPM, 80 @ 3600 RPM

TUNE UP SPECIFICATIONS

Year, Engine & VIN Code①	Spark Plug Gap, Inch	Ignition Timing			Curb Idle Speed②	Fast Idle Speed	Fuel Pump Pressure, Psi	Valve Clearance, Inch
		Firing Order Fig.③	°BTDC	Mark Fig.				
1997								
3.1L (M)	.060	⑩	④	⑤	⑥	⑥	41–47⑦	⑪
3.4L (X)	.045	⑨	④	⑤	⑥	⑥	48–55⑦	⑪
3800 (K)	.060	⑧	④	⑤	⑥	⑥	48–55⑦	⑪
3800 (1)	.060	⑧	④	⑤	⑥	⑥	48–55⑦	⑪
1998-99								
3.1L (M)	.060	⑩	④	⑤	⑥	⑥	41–47⑦	⑪
3.5 L (H)	.050	⑫	④	⑤	⑥	⑥	48–55⑦	⑪
3800 (K)	.060	⑧	④	⑤	⑥	⑥	48–55⑦	⑪
3800 (1)	.060	⑧	④	⑤	⑥	⑥	48–55⑦	⑪
2000								
3.1L (M)	.060	⑩	④	⑤	⑥	⑥	41–47⑦	⑪
3.4L (E)	.060	⑩	④	⑤	⑥	⑤	41–47⑦	⑪
3.5L (H)	.050	⑫	④	⑤	⑥	⑥	48–55⑦	⑪
3800 (K)	.060	⑧	④	⑤	⑥	⑥	48–55⑦	⑪
3800 (1)	.060	⑧	④	⑤	⑥	⑥	48–55⑦	⑪

BTDC — Before Top Dead Center

① — The eighth digit of Vehicle Identification Number (VIN) denotes engine code.

② — Idle speed is adjusted in Drive. When adjusting idle speed, set parking brake & block drive wheels. Where two idle speeds are listed, the higher speed is w/the idle or A/C solenoid energized.

③ — Before removing wires from distributor cap, determine location of No. 1 wire in cap, as distributor position may have been altered from that shown at the end of this chart.

④ — Computer controlled, no adjustment.

⑤ — Equipped w/crankshaft position sensor.

⑥ — Idle speed is controlled by an idle air control (IAC) valve or idle speed control (ISC) motor.

⑦ — Loosen fuel tank filler cap to relieve fuel vapor pressure. With shop towel wrapped around fuel pressure valve to prevent fuel spillage, connect a suitable fuel pressure gauge to fuel pressure valve. Check fuel pressure w/ignition switch On, engine not running.

⑧ — Cylinder numbering as viewed from front of vehicle, front bank, 1, 3, 5; rear bank, 2, 4, 6. Firing order 1-6-5-4-3-2. Two different types of computer controlled coil ignition systems are used. Refer to B & C for spark plug wire connections at coil unit.

⑨ — Cylinder numbering left to right as viewed from front of vehicle: front bank, 2, 4, 6; rear bank, 1, 3, 5. Firing order: 1-2-3-4-5-6. Refer to D for spark plug wire connections at coil unit.

⑩ — Cylinder numbering left to right as viewed from front of vehicle: front bank, 2, 4, 6; rear bank, 1, 3, 5. Firing order: 1-2-3-4-5-6. Refer to A for spark plug wire connections at coil unit.

⑪ — Equipped w/hydraulic valve lash adjusters. There is no provision for valve lash adjustment. If valve lash exists, inspect pushrod & rocker arm for excessive wear & check for an inoperative lifter.

⑫ — Cylinder numbering left to right as viewed from front of vehicle: front bank, 2, 4, 6; rear bank, 1, 3, 5. Firing order: 1-2-3-4-5-6.

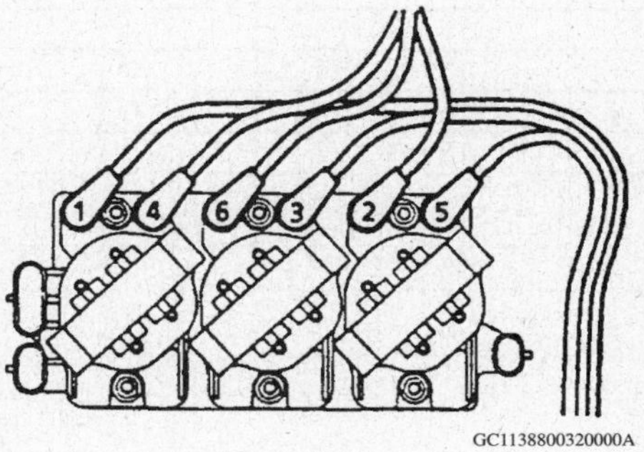

Fig. A

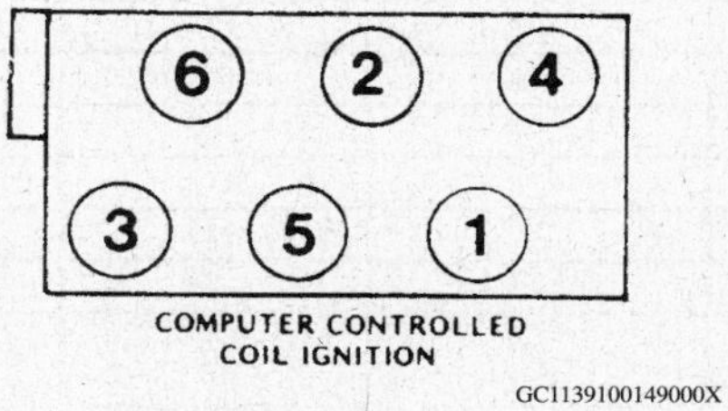

Fig. B

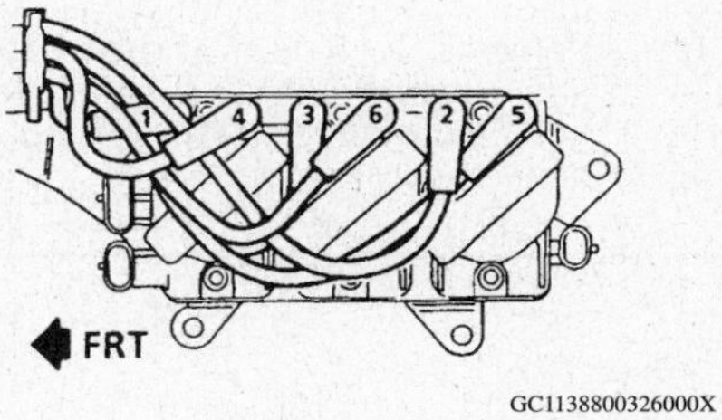

Fig. D

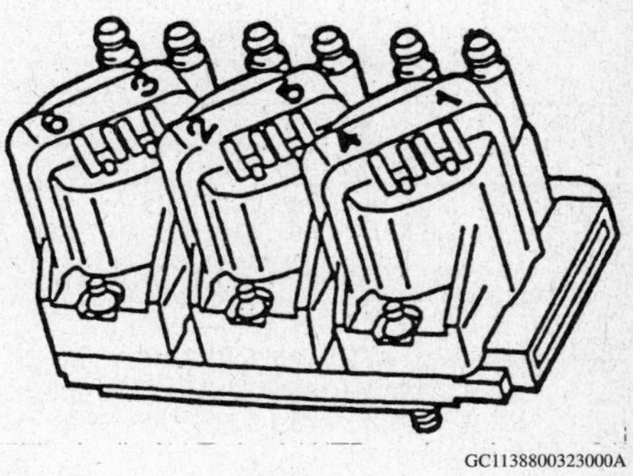

Fig. C

FRONT WHEEL ALIGNMENT SPECIFICATIONS

Year	Model	Caster Angle, Degrees		Camber Angle, Degrees		Toe-In, Degrees	Steering Angle, Degrees		Ball Joint Wear
		Limits	Desired	Limits	Desired		Limits	Desired	
1997	Century	+2.5 to +3.5	+3.0	-1.35 to -.35	-.85	-.2 to +.2	-3.5 to +3.5	0	①
	Cutlass Supreme	+1.5 to +2.5	+2	+.2 to +1.2	+.7	-.2 to +.2	-3.5 to +3.5	0	①
	Grand Prix & Regal	+2.5 to +3.5	+3.0	②	②	-.1 to +.3	-3.5 to +3.5	0	①
	Lumina & Monte Carlo	+1.3 to +2.3	+1.8	+.2 to +1.2	+.7	-.2 to +.2	-3.5 to +3.5	0	①
1998	Century, Grand Prix & Regal	+2.5 to +3.7	③	②	②	-.1 to +.3	-3.5 to +3.5	0	①
	Intrigue	+2.5 to + 3.5	③	-1.4 to -.4	-.9	-.15 to +.25	-3.5 to +3.5	0	①
	Lumina & Monte Carlo	+1.3 to +2.3	③	+.2 to +1.2	+.7	-.2 to +.2	-3.5 to +3.5	0	①
1999	Century, Lumina, Monte Carlo & Regal	+2.7 to +3.7	③	②	②	-.10 to +.30	-3.5 to +3.5	0	①
	Grand Prix & Intrigue	+2.5 to +3.5	+3.0	-1.40 to -.40	-.90	+.30 to -.10	-3.5 to +3.5	0	①
2000	Century, Impala, Lumina, Monte Carlo & Regal	+2.7 to +3.7	③	②	②	-.10 to +.30	-3.5 to +3.5	0	①
	Grand Prix & Intrigue	+2.5 to +3.5	+3.0	-1.40 to -.40	-.90	+.30 to -.10	-3.5 to +3.5	0	①

① — With vehicle raised & supported to allow front suspension to hang freely, grasp wheel at top & bottom, attempt to move bottom of wheel inward & outward. Ball joints must be replaced if looseness is observed between knuckle & control arm.

② — Vehicles w/15 inch wheels, -1.35° to -.35°; desired angle -.85.° Vehicles w/16 inch wheels, -1.44° to -.44°; desired angle -.94.°

③ — Not Adjustable.

REAR WHEEL ALIGNMENT SPECIFICATIONS

Year	Model	Camber Angle, Degrees		Total Toe, Degrees	Thrust Angle, Degrees	
		Limits	Desired		Limits	Desired
1997	Century	-1.4 to -.4	-.9	+.1	-.15 to +.15	0
	Cutlass Supreme, Lumina & Monte Carlo	-.4 to +.6	+.1	-.1	-.15 to +.15	0
	Grand Prix & Regal	②	②	+1.0	-.15 to +.15	0
1998	Century, Grand Prix & Regal	②	②	+1.0	-.15 to +.15	0
	Intrigue	-1.0 to 0	-.5	0	-.15 to +.15	0
	Lumina & Monte Carlo	①	①	0	-.15 to +.15	0
1999	Century, Lumina & Monte Carlo	②	②	+.10	-.15 to +.15	0
	Grand Prix & Intrigue	-1.4 to -.4	-.9	0	-.15 to +.15	0
2000	Century, Impala, Lumina & Monte Carlo	②	②	+.10	-.15 to +.15	0
	Grand Prix & Intrigue	-1.4 to -.4	-.9	0	-.15 to +.15	0

① — Vehicles w/15 inch wheels, -.85 to .15°; desired angle -.35.° Vehicles w/16 inch wheels, -.95° to .05°; desired angle -.45.°

② — Vehicles w/15 inch wheels, -1.4 to -.4°; desired angle -.9.° Vehicles w/16 inch wheels, -1.5 to -.50°; desired angle -1.0.°

FLUID CAPACITIES & COOLING SYSTEM DATA

Year	Engine/ VIN①	Coolant Capacity, Qts.	Radiator Cap Relief Pressure, psi	Thermostat Opening Temp. °F	Fuel Tank Gals.	Engine Oil Refill Qts.③	Transaxle Qts.②	
							Drain & Refill	Total Capacity
1997	3.1L (M)	11.6	15	195	④	4	⑤	⑥
	3.4L (X)	12.3	15	195	17.1	5	6	8
	3800 (K)	10.7	15	195	17.1	4	6	8
	3800 (1)	12.3	15	195	18	5	6	8
1998-99	3.1L (M)	11.6	15	195	17	4.5	⑦	⑧
	3.5L (H)	9.6	15	195	17	6	7.4	10
	3800 (K)	12.3	15	195	17	4.5	⑦	⑧
	3800 (1)	12.3	15	195	17	4.5	⑦	⑧
2000	3.1L (M)	11.6	15	195	17	4.5	⑦	⑧
	3.4L (E)	11.3	15	195	17	4.5	7.4	10
	3.5L (H)	9.6	15	195	17	6	7.4	10
	3800 (K)	12.3	15	195	17	4.5	⑦	⑧
	3800 (1)	12.3	15	195	17	4.5	⑦	⑧

① — The eight digit of vehicle identification number (VIN) denotes engine code.

② — Capacity approximate. Make final check w/dipstick & add fluid as necessary.

③ — Additional oil may be required to bring oil level to full mark when changing oil filter.

④ — Cutlass Supreme, Grand Prix & Regal, 17.1 gals.; Lumina & Monte Carlo, 16.1 gals.

⑤ — THM 3T40 transaxle, 4 qts.; THM 4T60–E, 6 qts.

⑥ — THM 3T40 transaxle, 7 qts.; THM 4T60–E, 8 qts.

⑦ — THM 4T60–E transaxle, 7 qts.; THM 4T65–E, 7.4 qts.

⑧ — THM 4T60–E transaxle, 9.6 qts.; THM 4T65–E, 10 qts.

LUBRICANT DATA

Year	Lubricant Type		
	Transaxle	Power Steering	Brake System
1997–2000	Dexron III	Power Steering Fluid①	DOT 3

① — Use power steering fluid meeting GM specification 9985010. For cold climates, use GM power steering fluid part No. 12345866 or 12345867, or equivalent. System should be drained, flushed, refilled & bled when changing to cold climate type fluid.

Electrical

NOTE: On Air Bag Equipped Models, Refer To " Air Bag System Precautions" Located In The Front Of This Manual For System Disarming & Arming Procedures.

NOTE: Refer To "Computer Relearn Procedures " Located In The Front Of This Manual For Computer Relearn Procedures.

INDEX

PRECAUTIONS

AIR BAG SYSTEMS

Refer to "Air Bag System Precautions" in the front of this manual for system disarming and arming procedures.

RADIO THEFT DETERRENT SYSTEM

Anti-theft radios have a coded theft deterrent circuit. **The security code number must be obtained before disconnecting battery, removing radio fuse or removing radio.**

After service procedure has been performed, reconnect radio power supply, and turn it to its ON position. When "LOC" is displayed, enter security code to reactivate radio.

BATTERY GROUND CABLE

Prior to service, disconnect battery ground cable and isolate as required.

FUSE PANEL & FLASHER LOCATION

CENTURY, GRAND PRIX, INTRIGUE & REGAL

The fuse panel is located behind the instrument panel, under the glove compartment. The hazard and turn signal flasher is located behind the lefthand side of the instrument panel, mounted on the multipurpose bracket, near the Body Control Module (BCM).

CUTLASS SUPREME, LUMINA & MONTE CARLO

The fuse panel is located behind the instrument panel, under the glove compartment. The hazard and turn signal flasher is located behind the lefthand side of the instrument panel, mounted on the bulkhead.

IMPALA

The lefthand side relay/fuse center is located behind the lefthand side instrument panel cluster trim plate, left of the steering column. The righthand side relay/fuse center is located behind the fuse block access opening cover, right of the glove compartment. The hazard and turn signal flasher is part of the hazard switch assembly, The hazard switch assembly is located behind the lefthand side of the instrument panel, mounted on the bulkhead.

FUEL PUMP RELAY LOCATION

The fuel pump relay is located in the underhood electrical center, on the righthand side of the engine compartment.

RELAY CENTER LOCATION

Relays are located in the underhood electrical center. The electrical center is mounted to the strut tower, on the righthand side of the engine compartment

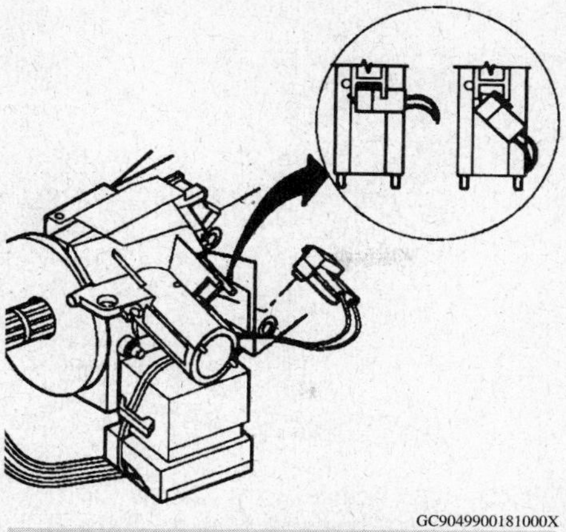

Fig. 1 Key alarm connector. Century, Grand Prix & Regal

6. Reverse procedure to install.

3.5L ENGINE

1. Raise and support vehicle.
2. Disconnect starter motor electrical connectors.
3. Remove torque converter cover.
4. Remove starter motor bolts and shims, then the starter motor.
5. Reverse procedure to install. **Torque** starter motor attaching bolts to 32 ft. lbs.

3800 ENGINE

1. Remove cooling fan assembly.
2. Remove serpentine drive belt.
3. Remove A/C compressor upper support brace.
4. Lay A/C compressor in fan opening.
5. Raise and support vehicle.
6. Disconnect engine oil cooler lines at flex connection.
7. Remove bolts from flywheel inspection cover.
8. Remove bolts from starter.
9. Disconnect starter motor wiring.
10. Remove starter motor.
11. Reverse procedure to install. **Torque** starter motor attaching bolts to 32 ft. lbs.

STARTER

REPLACE

3.1L ENGINE

1. Remove air cleaner assembly.
2. Raise and support vehicle.
3. **On models equipped with engine oil cooler,** proceed as follows:
   a. Position a suitable drain pan under vehicle, then remove oil filter.
   b. Position hose next to starter motor aside.
4. **On all models,** remove nut attaching starter brace to A/C compressor.
5. Remove nut attaching starter brace to engine, then the brace.
6. Remove bolts attaching flywheel inspection cover, then the cover.
7. Remove starter motor attaching bolts, lower starter and disconnect starter wiring.
8. Remove starter motor and shims (if used).
9. Reverse procedure to install, noting the following:
   a. When removing starter, note if any shims are used between starter and mounting surface. If shims are found, reinstall in original location.
   b. **Torque** starter motor attaching bolts to 32 ft. lbs.
   c. **Torque** starter brace nuts to 22 ft. lbs.
   d. **On models equipped with oil cooler,** check engine oil level, adding oil as necessary.

3.4L ENGINE

1997

1. Remove air cleaner assembly.
2. Raise and support vehicle.
3. Place a suitable drain pan under vehicle and remove oil filter.
4. Disconnect electrical connections from oil pressure sensor.
5. Disconnect crank sensor wire from ignition module.
6. Remove oil cooler adapter stud and set oil cooler aside.
7. Remove wiring harness from bellhousing clamp and lower radiator tie bar.
8. Disconnect power steering oil cooler lines from front crossmember.
9. Remove flywheel inspection cover.
10. Disconnect electrical connections from starter. **Disconnect and move electrical connections on cooling fan if necessary to gain access.**
11. Remove starter mounting bolts and starter assembly from vehicle.
12. Reverse procedure to install. **Torque** starter mounting bolts to 32 ft. lbs.

2000

1. Raise and support vehicle.
2. Remove front lower air deflector panel.
3. Remove torque converter covers from transaxle.
4. Remove retaining nuts, then disconnect starter motor electrical connectors from solenoid.
5. Remove starter motor attaching bolts, then the starter motor.

ALTERNATOR

REPLACE

3.1L ENGINE

1. Remove serpentine belt at alternator assembly.
2. Remove bolts from alternator assembly.
3. Remove power steering gear clip and nut.
4. Remove alternator stud, then disconnect alternator wiring.
5. Loosen alternator front and rear braces from upper intake manifold.
6. Remove alternator assembly.
7. Reverse procedure to install.

3.4L ENGINE

1997

1. Remove air cleaner assembly.
2. Remove coolant recovery tank, then the serpentine belt.
3. Disconnect power steering gear pipes from clip mounted to upper alternator stud.
4. Loosen alternator upper stud.
5. Raise and support vehicle, then remove right side tire and wheel assembly.
6. Remove right side engine splash shield, then front exhaust pipe and converter.
7. Remove alternator cooling duct, if equipped.
8. Loosen alternator rear brace.
9. Disconnect intermediate shaft lower pinch bolt at steering gear.
10. Install suitable jack to support engine, then remove rear cradle bolts.
11. Remove steering gear heat shield assembly.
12. Disconnect electrical connector from alternator regulator terminal.
13. Disconnect electrical connector from speed sensor.
14. Remove power steering gear pipe clip from steering gear.
15. Disconnect power steering gear inlet hose assembly from steering gear.
16. Remove alternator assembly.
17. Reverse procedure to install.

2000

1. Remove engine compartment cross vehicle brace.
2. Remove serpentine belt.
3. Remove coolant recovery reservoir attaching bolts, then position reservoir aside.
4. Remove alternator attaching bolts, then disconnect alternator electrical connector.
5. Remove retaining nut, then disconnect battery lead.
6. Remove alternator.
7. Reverse procedure to install.

3.5L ENGINE

The AD237 (KG7) alternator cannot be serviced and must be replaced as an assembly.

1. Drain coolant into suitable container, then remove right diagonal brace.
2. Position washer solvent reservoir aside, then remove accessory drive belt as outlined under "Serpentine Drive Belt."
3. Remove thermostat and radiator outlet hose.
4. Remove battery hold down retainer, battery and battery tray.
5. Remove outboard alternator bolt, then loosen inboard alternator bolt.
6. Remove idler pulley bolt and idler pulley.
7. Disconnect electrical terminals and connectors from alternator.
8. Remove inboard alternator, then the alternator.
9. Reverse procedure to install, **torquing**

idler pulley bolt and alternator bolts to 37 ft. lbs.

3800 ENGINE

The CS130 alternator cannot be serviced and must be replaced as an assembly.

1. Remove serpentine belt, then disconnect alternator electrical connections.
2. Remove bolts from alternator, then the alternator
3. Reverse procedure to install.

COIL PACK

REPLACE

1. Disconnect ignition control module electrical connectors.
2. Remove spark plug wires from ignition coils.
3. Remove screws securing ignition coils to ignition module, then the coils.
4. Reverse procedure to install.

IGNITION LOCK

REPLACE

1. Remove steering column from vehicle as outlined in " Steering Columns."
2. Remove and discard two lower spring retainers.
3. Remove lower bearing spring and lower bearing seat.
4. Remove nut retainer and jam nut, then the steering wheel.
5. Remove cancel cam assembly, then the hazard knob screw and hazard warning knob.
6. Position turn signal switch so turn signal switch screws and housing screw can be removed through opening in switch.
7. Remove housing screw and column housing cover, then the turn signal switch screws.
8. Remove wiring protector from opening in instrument panel bracket on jacket assembly and separate from wires.
9. Disconnect pivot/pulse switch connector then remove pivot screw and pivot/pulse switch assembly.
10. Disconnect turn signal switch connector from ignition and dimmer switch assembly connector.
11. Disconnect 17 way secondary lock from turn signal connector.
12. Using terminal remover tool No. J-35689-A or equivalent, disconnect wires on buzzer switch from turn signal connector and wrap wire ends with tape.
13. Remove turn signal switch assembly from column.
14. Remove and discard two lower spring retainers.
15. Remove lower bearing spring and seat.
16. Remove adapter screws then the adapter and bearing assembly.
17. **On models equipped with tilt column,** proceed as follows:
    a. Insert Phillips head screwdriver into square opening in spring retainer, push down and turn left to release retainer and wheel tilt spring.

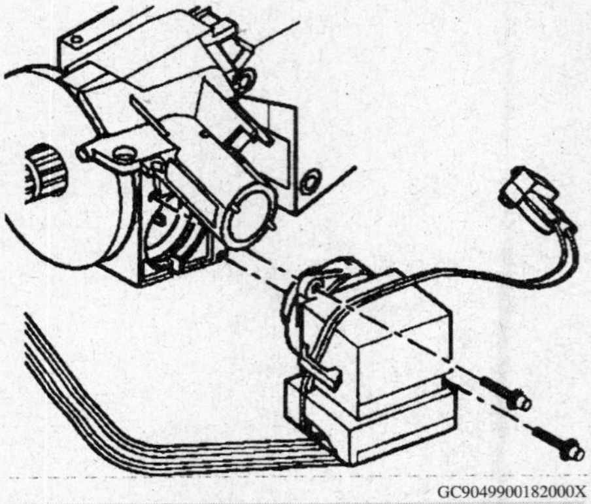

Fig. 2 Ignition & key alarm switch removal. Century, Grand Prix & Regal

    b. Remove spring retainer, tilt spring and tilt spring guide.
    c. Using pivot pin remover tool No. J-21854-01, or equivalent, remove two pivot pins.
18. **On all models,** place lock cylinder in Run position.
19. **On models equipped with tilt column,** pull tilt lever to release steering column housing. Remove steering shaft assembly and steering column housing as a complete unit.
20. **On models equipped without tilt column,** proceed as follows:
    a. Place opening in retaining ring over flat on steering shaft.
    b. Remove retaining ring using a suitable screwdriver.
    c. Remove thrust washer, upper bearing spring and washer.
    d. Remove steering shaft from lower end of jacket and bowl assembly.
    e. Remove housing screws and steering column housing.
    f. Remove housing spacer bearing using a suitable drift. Discard bearing.
21. **On all models,** place lock cylinder in Off-Lock position and remove key.
22. Remove buzzer switch by lifting switch tab with screwdriver and pulling gently on wires.
23. Remove lock retaining screw and lock cylinder.
24. Reverse procedure to install, noting the following:
    a. **Torque** lock retaining screw to 22 inch lbs.
    b. **Torque** steering column housing screws to 88 inch lbs.
    c. **Torque** turn signal switch and column housing cover screws to 35 inch lbs.
    d. **Torque** hazard knob screw to 7 inch lbs.
    e. **Torque** jam nut to 30 ft. lbs.
    f. Install new lower spring retainers, compressing spring until retainers are positioned 1.14 inches from lower end of steering shaft.

IGNITION SWITCH

REPLACE

CENTURY, GRAND PRIX & REGAL

1. Remove inflatable restraint steering wheel module as outlined in "Air Bag Systems."
2. Remove steering wheel as outlined in steering wheel replace.
3. Remove upper and lower steering column shrouds.
4. Remove turn signal and multi-function wire harness retaining straps from steering column and wire harness assembly.
5. Slide turn signal and multi-function switch assembly connectors out of bulkhead connector.
6. Rotate key alarm connector 90°, then pull key alarm connector out of lock module assembly, **Fig. 1.**
7. Remove two ignition and key alarm switch assembly retaining screws, then the ignition and key alarm switch assembly from steering column, **Fig. 2.**
8. Reverse procedure to install.

CUTLASS SUPREME, LUMINA & MONTE CARLO

Removal

1. Place shift lever in P position and lock cylinder in Off-Lock position.
2. Remove steering column from vehicle.
3. Disconnect turn signal switch connector from ignition and dimmer switch assembly connector.
4. Disconnect pivot and pulse switch connector from ignition and dimmer switch connector.
5. Remove bowl shield screw, bowl shield nut and bowl shield.
6. Remove dimmer switch nut, then the upper mounting stud.
7. Remove dimmer switch, then the dimmer switch actuator rod.
8. Remove lower mounting stud, then the ignition switch from ignition switch actuator rod.

Installation

Lock cylinder set must be in the Off-Lock position when installing ignition switch to ensure proper switch slider positioning.

1. Place ignition switch slider in far left position and move back one detent to right, then insert a 3/32 inch drill bit in adjustment hole on ignition switch to hold switch slider in proper position during installation.
2. Install ignition switch to switch rod.
3. Install ignition switch to steering column jacket assembly with lower mounting stud. **Torque** to 35 inch lbs.
4. Remove adjustment tool from ignition switch.
5. Install dimmer switch actuator rod through hole in instrument panel bracket and into hole in dimmer switch rod cap.
6. Install dimmer switch assembly on

lower mounting stud with dimmer switch nut and upper mounting stud but do not tighten.
7. To adjust dimmer switch, insert a 3/32 inch drill bit and push switch against actuator rod to remove all lash.
8. **Torque** dimmer switch nut and upper mounting stud to 35 inch lbs., then remove adjustment tool from dimmer switch.
9. Install bowl shield to column bowl and upper mounting stud, then install shield screw. **Torque** to 35 inch lbs.
10. Install bowl shield nut. **Torque** to 35 inch lbs.
11. Connect turn signal switch connector to ignition and dimmer switch assembly connector and snap in place.
12. Connect pivot and pulse switch connector to ignition and dimmer switch connector.
13. Install steering column and connect battery ground cable.

IMPALA

1. Remove steering column filler panel.
2. Remove knee bolster and bracket from under steering column.
3. Apply parking brake.
4. **On models equipped with column shift,** position shift lever in the "1" position.
5. **On all models,** remove ignition switch cylinder bezel.
6. Remove left and right fuse/relay panel access covers.
7. Remove instrument cluster trim plate bezel attaching screws, then pull cluster trim plate bezel away from instrument panel trim pad.
8. Remove ignition switch retaining bolts, then lower switch away from instrument panel.
9. Insert ignition key and turn switch to the RUN position.
10. Depress detent on bottom of ignition switch housing to release ignition lock cylinder from housing.
11. Disconnect electrical connector from switch housing and remove switch.
12. Reverse procedure to install.

INTRIGUE

1. Remove instrument panel center trim plate.
2. Remove radio as outlined under "Radio, Replace."
3. Remove heater and A/C control assembly retaining screws, then pull assembly away from instrument panel and disconnect electrical connectors.
4. Remove heater and A/C control assembly from instrument panel.
5. Remove push-in retainers from instrument panel insulators, then the insulators from under instrument panel, **Fig. 3.**
6. Remove steering column filler panel from under steering column.
7. Remove knee bolster bracket.
8. Turn ignition switch lock cylinder to the ACC position and pull park lock cable from ignition switch.
9. Turn ignition switch lock cylinder to the ON position.

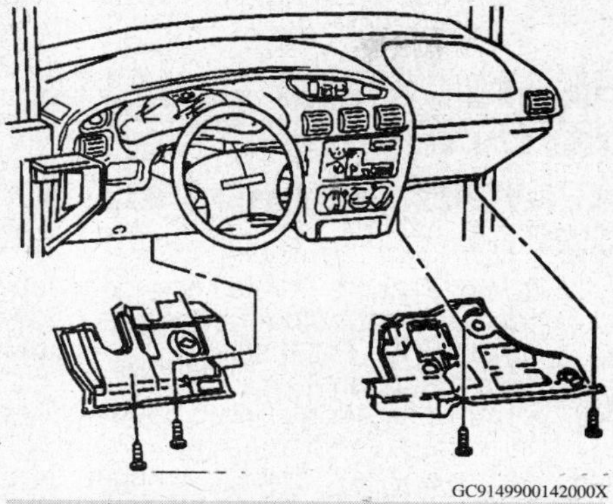

Fig. 3 I/P insulator panel removal. Intrigue

10. Insert a small flat-bladed tool through access hole on right side of ignition switch.
11. Depress locking tab and pull ignition lock cylinder from ignition switch.
12. Disconnect ignition switch electrical connector.
13. Pull ignition switch away from instrument panel.
14. Remove ignition switch to bracket attaching screws, then the bracket from ignition switch.
15. Reverse procedure to install.

PARK/NEUTRAL POSITION (PNP) SWITCH

REPLACE

1. Apply parking brake and block drive wheels.
2. Place selector lever in the NEUTRAL position.
3. Remove throttle body air inlet duct.
4. Remove automatic transaxle range selector cable from switch assembly.
5. Disconnect switch electrical connectors.
6. Remove range selector lever from switch assembly.
7. Remove switch assembly retaining screws, then the switch from transaxle.
8. Reverse procedure to install, noting the following:
   a. **Do not rotate a new switch assembly. The new switch is pinned to the NEUTRAL position. If bolts do not align with mounting boss on transaxle, ensure transaxle shaft is in the NEUTRAL position.**
   b. Align flats of shift shaft to flats of switch.
   c. **Torque** switch mounting bolts to 18 ft. lbs.

TRANSAXLE RANGE (TR) SWITCH

REPLACE

Refer to "Park/Neutral Position (PNP) Switch, Replace " for transaxle range switch replacement.

HEADLAMP SWITCH

REPLACE

CENTURY, GRAND PRIX & REGAL

1. Remove push-in retainers from lefthand side instrument panel sound insulator, then the insulator from under instrument panel.
2. Remove steering column opening filler panel from under steering column.
3. Remove knee bolster bracket from under lefthand side of instrument panel.
4. Remove steering column support to instrument panel retaining bolts, then lower steering column.
5. Pull bottom edge of instrument cluster trim plate away from instrument panel to release retainer clips.
6. Disconnect fog lamp switch electrical connector, then remove instrument cluster trim plate from instrument panel.
7. Pull headlamp switch away from instrument panel and disconnect electrical connector.
8. Reverse procedure to install.

IMPALA

1. Remove instrument cluster trim plate as outlined in " Ignition Switch, Replace."
2. Remove headlamp switch housing retaining screws, then the switch housing from instrument panel.
3. Disconnect electrical connector from headlamp switch housing and fog lamp switch.
4. Remove headlamp switch from instrument panel using a suitable flat-bladed tool.
5. Reverse procedure to install.

INTRIGUE

1. Remove push-in retainers from lefthand instrument panel sound insulator.
2. Remove sound insulator from instrument panel.
3. Remove steering column filler panel from under steering column.
4. Remove switch bank retaining screws, then the switch bank from instrument panel.
5. Reverse procedure to install.

LUMINA & MONTE CARLO

1. Move shift lever to the L1 position.
2. Tilt steering column to its lowest position.
3. Unsnap instrument panel cluster trim plate by pulling panel towards the rear.
4. Remove instrument cluster trim plate from instrument panel.
5. Depress headlamp switch locking tabs, then pull switch away from instrument panel and disconnect electrical connector.
6. Reverse procedure to install.

STOP LIGHT SWITCH

REPLACE

1. Remove push-in retainers from left-hand instrument panel sound insulator.
2. Remove sound insulator from under lefthand side of instrument panel.
3. Remove brake lamp switch to brake pedal bracket retaining screws.
4. Remove brake lamp switch.
5. Reverse procedure to install, adjust brake and cruise control switches as follows:
   a. Push brake pedal as far forward as possible to set brake push rod into booster.
   b. Pull brake pedal to the rear, against the internal stop. Stop light and cruise control switches are now adjusted.
   c. Ensure brake lamps operate properly.

MULTI-FUNCTION SWITCH

REPLACE

1. Remove steering wheel as outlined under "Steering Wheel, Replace."
2. Remove upper and lower steering column trim covers.
3. Remove wire harness straps from wiring harness and upper tilt head assembly.
4. Remove multi-function switch assembly retaining screws, then the switch assembly from steering column.
5. Reverse procedure to install. **Torque** retaining screws to 62 inch lbs.

TURN SIGNAL SWITCH

REPLACE

Refer to "Multi-Function Switch, Replace" for turn signal switch replacement procedure.

STEERING WHEEL

REPLACE

1. Turn ignition switch to the OFF position.
2. Remove inflatable restraint module as outlined in "Air Bag Systems" chapter.
3. Scribe an alignment mark on steering wheel hub inline with slash mark on steering shaft.
4. Loosen steering wheel nut, positioning it flush with end of shaft.
5. Using a suitable puller, loosen steering wheel. **When removing a steering wheel with accessory controls in the hub, use caution to avoid damaging electronic circuits. Steering wheel puller bolts should be turned in no more than four to six threads to avoid contact with electronic circuits.**
6. Remove steering shaft nut and steering wheel.
7. Reverse procedure to install, noting the following:
   a. Align scribe mark.
   b. **Torque** steering shaft nut to 30 ft. lbs.

INSTRUMENT CLUSTER

REPLACE

CENTURY, GRAND PRIX & REGAL

1. Remove push-in retainers from left-hand side instrument panel sound insulator, then the insulator from under instrument panel.
2. Remove steering column opening filler panel from under steering column.
3. Remove knee bolster bracket from under lefthand side of instrument panel.
4. Remove steering column support to instrument panel retaining bolts, then lower steering column.
5. Pull bottom edge of instrument cluster trim plate away from instrument panel to release retainer clips.
6. Disconnect fog lamp switch electrical connector, then remove instrument cluster trim plate from instrument panel.
7. Remove instrument cluster retaining screws.
8. Pull instrument cluster towards the rear and upwards to disengage retaining clips.
9. Disconnect cluster electrical connectors and remove cluster from instrument panel.
10. Reverse procedure to install.

IMPALA

1. Remove instrument cluster trim plate bezel as outlined in " Ignition Switch, Replace."
2. Remove instrument cluster attaching bolts.
3. Gently pull cluster away from instrument panel and disconnect electrical connector.
4. Remove cluster from instrument panel.
5. Reverse procedure to install.

INTRIGUE

1. Remove push-in retainers from left-hand instrument panel sound insulator.
2. Remove sound insulator from instrument panel.
3. Remove steering column filler panel from under steering column.
4. Remove trip odometer and reset switch from instrument cluster trim plate.
5. Remove instrument cluster trim plate attaching screws, then the instrument cluster trim plate.
6. Remove instrument cluster retaining screws.
7. Pull cluster towards the rear and disconnect electrical connectors.
8. Remove cluster from instrument panel.
9. Reverse procedure to install.

LUMINA & MONTE CARLO

1. Move shift lever to the L1 position.
2. Tilt steering column to lowest position.
3. Unsnap instrument panel cluster trim plate by pulling panel towards the rear.
4. Remove instrument cluster trim plate from instrument panel.
5. Remove instrument cluster retaining screws.
6. Pull cluster away from instrument panel and disconnect electrical connectors.
7. Reverse procedure to install.

RADIO

REPLACE

CENTURY & REGAL

1. Remove push-in retainers from left-hand side instrument panel sound insulator, then the insulator from under instrument panel.
2. Remove steering column opening filler panel from under steering column.
3. Remove instrument panel accessory trim panel attaching screws.
4. Pull accessory trim plate rearward and release two retaining tabs.
5. Remove accessory trim plate from instrument panel.
6. Remove radio retaining screws.
7. Pull radio away from instrument panel, then disconnect electrical connectors and antenna.
8. Reverse procedure to install.

CUTLASS SUPREME

1. Remove radio mounting screws.
2. Pull radio out far enough to disconnect antenna, speaker and electrical connectors, then remove radio.
3. Reverse procedure to install.

GRAND PRIX

1. Remove push-in retainers from left-hand side instrument panel sound insulator, then the insulator from under instrument panel.
2. Remove steering column opening filler panel from under steering column.
3. Remove knee bolster bracket from under lefthand side of instrument panel.
4. Remove steering column support to instrument panel retaining bolts, then lower steering column.
5. Pull bottom edge of instrument cluster trim plate away from instrument panel to release retainer clips.
6. Disconnect fog lamp switch electrical connector, then remove instrument cluster trim plate from instrument panel.
7. Remove radio retaining screws.
8. Pull radio away from instrument panel and disconnect electrical connectors and antenna.
9. Remove radio from instrument panel.
10. Reverse procedure to install.

IMPALA

1. Remove instrument cluster trim plate bezel as outlined in " Ignition Switch, Replace."
2. Remove radio retaining screws.

3. Pull radio away from instrument panel, then disconnect electrical connectors and antenna.
4. Reverse procedure to install.

INTRIGUE

1. Remove traction control switch from center console trim plate.
2. Open front floor console compartment and remove console trim plate attaching screws.
3. Pull up on trim plate to release retaining clips, then remove console trim plate from console.
4. Remove instrument panel accessory trim plate, then the radio attaching screws.
5. Disconnect electrical connectors, then remove radio.
6. Reverse procedure to install.

LUMINA & MONTE CARLO

1. Move shift lever to the L1 position.
2. Tilt steering column to lowest position.
3. Unsnap instrument panel cluster trim plate by pulling panel towards the rear.
4. Remove instrument cluster trim plate from instrument panel.
5. Remove radio retaining screws.
6. Pull radio away from instrument panel and disconnect electrical connectors and antenna.
7. Remove radio from instrument panel.
8. Reverse procedure to install.

WIPER MOTOR

REPLACE

1. Remove wiper module as outlined in "Wiper Module, Replace."
2. Remove wiper motor crank arm from wiper transmission using wiper transmission separator tool No. J 39232, or equivalent.
3. Remove wiper motor crank arm to wiper motor retaining nut.
4. Remove wiper motor bracket attaching screws, then the wiper motor assembly from tube frame.
5. Reverse procedure to install.

WIPER SWITCH

REPLACE

Refer to procedure outlined under "Multi-Function Switch, Replace."

WIPER TRANSMISSION

REPLACE

1. Remove wiper module as outlined under "Wiper Motor, Replace."
2. Remove two transmission socket screws, then remove socket from link ball.
3. Remove right, left and bellcrank mounting screws, then the transmission from module.
4. Connect new transmission to module.
5. Ensure wiper motor is in innerwipe position.
6. Using suitable tool, align holes in module and bellcrank and install transmission socket screws.
7. Ensure body seal is in proper place on righthand side of module and install wiper module.
8. Install passenger side wiper arm and blade. Measure from tip of blade to bottom edge of glass. Ensure distance is approximately 9⅛ inches (231 mm), then tighten nut install protective cap and reconnect washer hose.
9. Install driver side wiper arm and blade. Measure from tip of blade to bottom edge of glass. Ensure distance is approximately 2 inches (53 mm), then tighten nut, install protective cap and reconnect washer hose.
10. Run wiper at high and low speeds with wet and tacky windshield. Ensure wiper parks properly and there is no interference between blades.

WIPER MODULE

REPLACE

The windshield wiper module consists of both the wiper motor and the wiper transmission.

1. Turn ignition switch to the ACCY position, then set wiper switch to the PULSE/DELAY position.
2. With wiper arms are in innerwipe position and not moving, turn ignition switch off.
3. Remove hose from nozzle on wiper arm driveshaft.
4. Remove covers from wiper arm retaining nuts.
5. Remove wiper arm retaining nuts, then the wiper arms from wiper transmission driveshaft.
6. Remove inlet shroud attaching bolts, then the inlet shroud from vehicle.
7. Disconnect wiper motor electrical connectors.
8. Remove wiper module assembly attaching bolts, then the wiper module assembly from vehicle.
9. Reverse procedure to install.

BLOWER MOTOR

REPLACE

1. Remove right sound insulator panel from under instrument panel.
2. **On models equipped with convenience center,** remove rear retaining screws from electrical convenience center, then loosen front screw and slide convenience center out.
3. **On all models,** disconnect electrical connector at motor and remove harness from clip.
4. Disconnect blower motor cooling hose.
5. Remove blower motor mounting screws and blower motor.
6. Reverse procedure to install.

HEATER CORE

REPLACE

1. **On models equipped with 3.1L engine and 2000 models with 3.4L engine,** remove air cleaner and duct assembly.
2. **On 1997 models with 3.4L engine,** remove throttle body as follows:
   a. Drain engine coolant and remove air intake tube.
   b. Disconnect IAC valve and TP sensor electrical connectors.
   c. Remove accelerator control and cruise control cables.
   d. Remove accelerator control cable bracket.
   e. Remove throttle body to intake manifold attaching bolts and nuts, then the throttle body.
3. **On models equipped with 3.5L and 3800 engines,** remove fuel injector sight shield as follows:
   a. Remove oil fill cap.
   b. Remove fuel injector sight shield to fuel injector rail brace stud retaining nut.
   c. Lift fuel injector sight shield up at front and slide tab out of engine bracket.
   d. Install oil fill cap.
4. **On all models,** drain cooling system, then disconnect heater hoses from heater core.
5. **On models equipped with center console,** proceed as follows:
   a. Position transaxle shift lever in the LOW position.
   b. Remove floor console storage compartment rubber mat, then the floor console front attaching bolts.
   c. Remove floor console rear mounting bracket bolts located behind transaxle shift lever.
   d. Remove floor console left and right attaching bolts.
   e. Disconnect console electrical connectors.
   f. Pull console towards the rear and remove from vehicle.
6. **On all models,** remove push-in retainers from instrument panel insulators, then the insulators from under instrument panel.
7. Position heater core outlet cover downward and rearward.
8. Remove heater core outlet cover retaining screws, then disconnect outlet cover from floor duct assembly.
9. Remove heater core cover attaching screws, then the cover.
10. Remove and discard seals from heater core cover and heater core.
11. Remove heater core line clamp retaining screw, heater core retaining clamp and heater core pipe retainer clamp screw.
12. Remove heater core from HVAC lower case.
13. Remove and discard heater core lower, center, upper and side seals from HVAC case.
14. Reverse procedure to install, noting the following:
    a. Install all new seals.
    b. **Torque** heater core line clamp screw to 13 inch lbs.
    c. **Torque** heater core mounting clip screw to 13 inch lbs.
    d. **Torque** heater core cover screws to 13 inch lbs.

EVAPORATOR CORE

REPLACE

CENTURY, CUTLASS SUPREME, INTRIGUE, LUMINA, MONTE CARLO & REGAL

1. Recover A/C refrigerant as outlined in "Air Conditioning" section.
2. Remove air cleaner and duct assembly.
3. Drain engine coolant.
4. Remove instrument panel as outlined in "Dash Panel Service."
5. Remove passenger side air bag module as outlined in "Air Bag Systems."
6. Unclip fuse block and position aside.
7. Remove brake pedal bracket and reinforcement.
8. Remove BCM bracket attaching bolts, then position bracket aside.
9. Release instrument panel wiring harness retaining clips, then position harness aside.
10. Remove HVAC module center support bracket attaching bolts, then the support bracket.
11. Remove HVAC module upper support bracket attaching bolts, then the HVAC module from cross vehicle beam support.
12. Remove support braces from top of engine compartment.
13. Disconnect refrigerant lines from evaporator block fitting.
14. Disconnect heater hoses at heater core.
15. Remove HVAC module to dash panel retaining nuts.
16. Disconnect HVAC module electrical connectors and vacuum hoses. **Note location for installation reference.**
17. Remove HVAC module to cross vehicle support beam attaching bolts and nuts, then the module.
18. Remove all HVAC module outer seals, then the air inlet housing.
19. Unclip and remove heater/defrost valve vacuum actuator from HVAC module.
20. Remove HVAC module case upper screws, then separate module case.
21. Remove module seal and evaporator core from lower case.
22. Remove and discard all evaporator core seals and water core filter.
23. Reverse procedure to install, noting the following:
    a. Replace all seals.
    b. **Torque** HVAC case screws to 13 inch lbs.
    c. Recharge A/C system refrigerant.

IMPALA

1. Remove lefthand fender diagonal brace.
2. Remove cross vehicle brace.
3. Recover A/C refrigerant as outlined in "Air Conditioning" section.
4. Drain cooling system.
5. Disconnect A/C lines from evaporator block fitting, then the heater hoses from heater core.
6. Remove instrument panel as outlined in "Dash Panel Service."
7. Remove cross vehicle beam.
8. Disconnect vacuum hoses and electrical connectors from HVAC module.
9. Disconnect instrument panel wiring harness from HVAC module retainers.
10. Remove evaporator drain elbow.
11. Remove HVAC module to dash panel retaining nuts.
12. Pull HVAC module rearward and disengage from mounting studs.
13. Position dash insulator pad away from HVAC module air inlet opening.
14. Roll HVAC module downward and rearward, then remove heater outlet cover from rear floor air outlet duct.
15. Remove outer HVAC module seals.
16. Remove air inlet housing and heater/defroster valve vacuum actuator from HVAC module.
17. Remove HVAC module case upper screws.
18. Separate module upper case from and lower case.
19. Remove seal from module lower case.
20. Remove evaporator core from case.
21. Reverse procedure to install.

3.1L Engine

NOTE: Prior To Performing Any Service Operations Listed In This Section, Consult The "Technical Service Bulletins " Section For Related Information.

NOTE: On Air Bag Equipped Models, Refer To " Air Bag System Precautions" Located In The Front Of This Manual For System Disarming & Arming Procedures.

NOTE: Refer To "Computer Relearn Procedures " Located In The Front Of This Manual For Computer Relearn Procedures.

INDEX

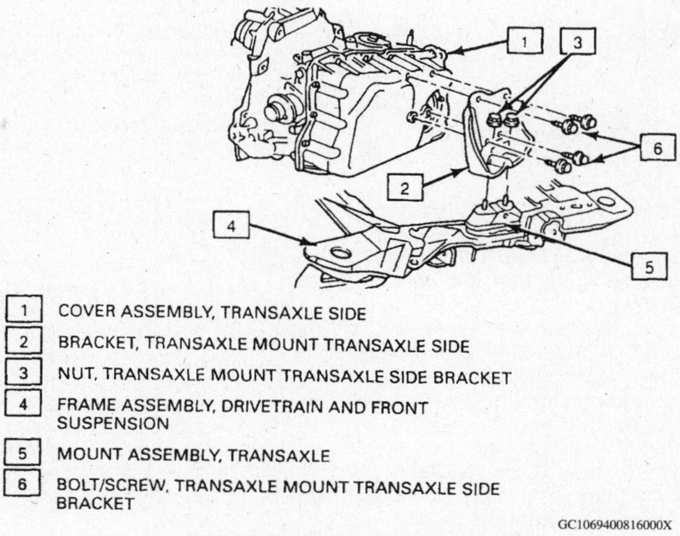

Fig. 1 Transaxle mount

PRECAUTIONS

AIR BAG SYSTEMS

Refer to "Air Bag System Precautions" in the front of this manual for system disarming and arming procedures.

BATTERY GROUND CABLE

Prior to service, disconnect battery ground cable and isolate as required.

FUEL SYSTEM PRESSURE RELIEF

To reduce the risk of fire and personal injury, it is necessary to relieve the fuel system pressure before servicing fuel system components.

1. Loosen fuel tank filler cap to relieve tank pressure.
2. Connect fuel pressure gauge tool No. J-34730-1, or equivalent, to fuel pressure valve. Wrap a shop towel around fitting while connection gauge to avoid spillage.
3. Install bleed hose into an approved

container and open valve to bleed system pressure.

IDLE LEARN PROCEDURE

If vehicle power is interrupted, the programmed position of the Idle Air Control (IAC) valve pintle is lost. The following procedures must be performed to update the ECM memory with the correct IAC valve pintle position for the vehicle and provide a stable idle speed.

1. Restore vehicle power.
2. Connect TECH I scan tool to ALDL connector located under lefthand side of dash panel.
3. Select "IAC System."
4. Select "Idle Learn" in the " Misc. Test" mode.
5. Proceed as directed.

COMPRESSION PRESSURE

When checking compression, lowest cylinder must be within 70 percent of the highest cylinder with a minimum pressure of 100 psi. Perform compression test with engine at normal operating temperature, spark plugs removed and throttle wide open.

ENGINE MOUNT

REPLACE

ENGINE MOUNT

1. Remove throttle body air inlet duct, then the engine mount struts.
2. Raise and support vehicle, then remove right front wheel and tire assembly.
3. Remove catalytic converter pipe from rear exhaust manifold.
4. Remove right engine splash shield, then the engine mount lower nuts.
5. Place a block of wood under the oil pan, then raise engine with suitable floor jack stand.
6. Remove engine mount bracket to oil pan bolts, then the engine mount and engine mount bracket.
7. Remove engine upper mount nuts, then the engine mount from engine mount bracket.
8. Reverse procedure to install.

ENGINE STRUT

1. Remove bolt from engine mount strut bracket, then bolt from bracket.
2. Remove strut assembly.
3. Reverse procedure to install. Tighten to specifications.

TRANSAXLE MOUNT

1. Support transaxle with suitable jack.
2. Remove crossmember to mount attaching nuts, **Fig. 1.**
3. Remove bracket to transaxle attaching bolts.
4. Remove mount and bracket assembly.
5. Separate mount from bracket.
6. Reverse procedure to install. Tighten nuts and bolts to specifications.

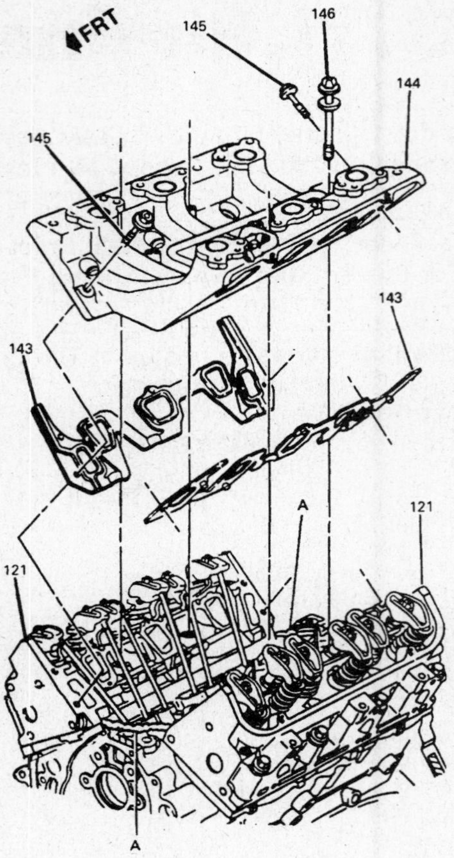

A APPLY SEALANT
121 HEAD ASSEMBLY, CYLINDER
143 GASKET, LOWER INTAKE MANIFOLD
144 BOLT, LOWER INTAKE
145 BOLT, LOWER INTAKE MANIFOLD
146 BOLT, LOWER INTAKE MANIFOLD
GC1059400113000X

Fig. 2 Intake manifold replacement

ENGINE

REPLACE

1. Drain engine coolant into a suitable container, then the engine oil.
2. Relieve fuel pressure as outlined under "Precautions."
3. Scribe alignment marks, then remove hood.
4. Remove air flow tube from air cleaner and throttle valve, then the air cleaner assembly.
5. Remove transaxle filler tube assembly.
6. Disconnect necessary electrical wiring, then the throttle and TV cables.
7. Remove engine mount strut bracket.
8. Disconnect fuel lines.
9. Remove AIR pump belt, then the serpentine drive belt cover and belt.
10. Disconnect radiator hoses at engine.
11. Remove A/C compressor bolts from front bracket.
12. Remove power steering pump and position aside.
13. Disconnect heater hoses from engine.
14. Disconnect brake booster vacuum supply line.
15. Disconnect EGR from exhaust.
16. Raise and support vehicle.
17. Remove starter motor assembly.
18. Remove A/C compressor bolts at rear bracket, then position compressor aside.
19. Remove flywheel cover, then disconnect starter and position aside.
20. Remove torque converter bolts, then the transaxle mount bracket.
21. Remove engine front mount retaining nuts.
22. Disconnect exhaust pipe at crossover, then lower vehicle.
23. Remove coolant recovery bottle.
24. Disconnect accelerator control cable bracket and move assemblies aside.
25. Disconnect crossover pipe at left manifold.
26. Remove serpentine belt, then the alternator.
27. Remove power steering pump assembly.
28. Remove plastic cover from front shock tower, then remove automatic transaxle modulator pipe assembly.
29. **On Century, Cutlass Supreme and Grand Prix models,** pull engine assembly forward and support in this position.
30. **On all models,** disconnect crossover pipe at right manifold.
31. Disconnect bulkhead connector.
32. **On Century, Cutlass Supreme and Grand Prix models,** remove engine support and allow engine to roll to normal position.
33. **On all models,** remove engine to transaxle attaching bolts, attach lifting device to engine and support transaxle.
34. Remove engine assembly.
35. Reverse procedure to install.

INTAKE MANIFOLD

REPLACE

UPPER

1. Disconnect vacuum hose from throttle body air inlet duct, then the wiring harness from intake air temperature sensor.
2. Remove throttle body air inlet duct, then drain engine coolant into a suitable container.
3. Remove accelerator control and cruise control cables with bracket from throttle body.
4. Disconnect wiring harness connectors from throttle body, then the front spark plug wires.
5. Disconnect wiring harness attachment clips from camshaft position sensor, front spark plug wire harness and engine wiring harness.
6. Disconnect thermostat bypass pipe coolant hoses from throttle body.
7. Remove ignition coil bracket with coils, purge solenoid and vacuum canister solenoid.
8. Disconnect vacuum hose at MAP sensor and upper intake manifold, then remove MAP sensor and bracket.

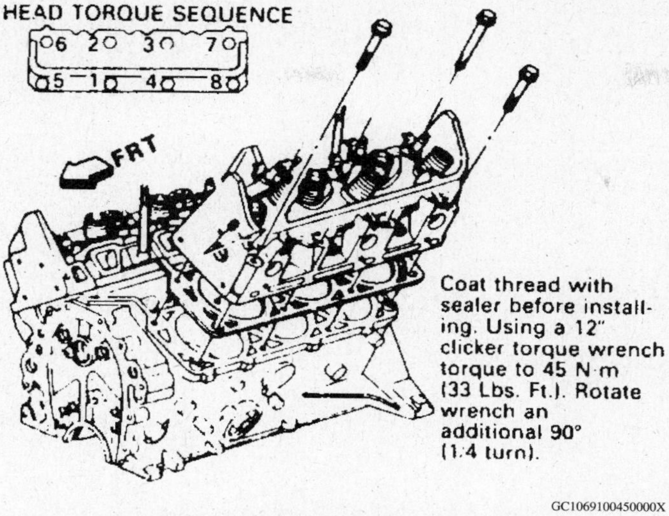
HEAD TORQUE SEQUENCE
6 2 3 7
5 1 4 8
FRT
Coat thread with sealer before installing. Using a 12" clicker torque wrench torque to 45 N·m (33 Lbs. Ft.). Rotate wrench an additional 90° (1/4 turn).
GC1069100450000X

Fig. 3 Cylinder head installation

9. Disconnect emission control vacuum harness, then the upper intake manifold to vacuum booster vacuum hose.
10. Disconnect automatic transaxle vacuum modulator hose.
11. Disconnect heater/air conditioning vacuum source hose and fuel pressure regulator vacuum hose.
12. Remove front and rear alternator braces, then the alternator bracket.
13. Remove EGR valve, then the upper intake manifold bolts and studs.
14. Remove upper intake manifold and gaskets.
15. Reverse procedure to install.

LOWER

1. Relieve fuel system pressure as outlined under " Precautions."
2. Remove upper intake manifold as outlined under " Upper Intake Manifold, Replace."
3. Remove both valve covers, then disconnect ECT wiring harness.
4. Remove fuel pipe clip bolt, then the fuel pipe clip.
5. Disconnect fuel feed and fuel return pipes from fuel injector rail.
6. Remove fuel injector rail, then the power steering pump from front engine cover and set aside.
7. Disconnect heater inlet pipe with heater hose from lower intake manifold and position aside.
8. Disconnect radiator inlet hose from engine, then the thermostat bypass hose from thermostat bypass pipe and lower intake manifold pipe.
9. Remove lower intake manifold bolts, then the lower intake manifold.
10. Remove pushrods, then the lower intake manifold gaskets and seals.
11. Reverse procedure to install, noting the following:
    a. Apply sealant as shown in **Fig. 2**
    b. Tighten lower intake manifold mounting bolts to specification.

EXHAUST MANIFOLD

REPLACE

LEFT

1. Remove throttle body air inlet duct, then drain engine coolant into a suitable container.
2. Remove right engine mount strut bracket, then disconnect radiator inlet hose from engine.
3. Remove automatic transaxle vacuum modulator pipe, then the thermostat bypass pipe.
4. Remove exhaust crossover pipe heat shield, then the exhaust crossover bolts to exhaust manifold.
5. Remove exhaust manifold heat shied bolts, then the heat shield.
6. Remove exhaust manifold nuts, then the exhaust manifold and gasket.
7. Reverse procedure to install.

RIGHT

1. Remove throttle body air inlet duct, then drain engine coolant into a suitable container.
2. Remove right engine mount strut bracket, then disconnect radiator inlet hose from engine.
3. Remove automatic transaxle vacuum modulator pipe, then the thermostat bypass pipe.
4. Remove exhaust crossover pipe heat shield, then the exhaust crossover bolts to exhaust manifold.
5. Remove exhaust manifold heat shied bolts, then the heat shield.
6. Disconnect heated oxygen sensor wiring harness connector, then raise and support vehicle.
7. Remove EGR tube from exhaust manifold, then the exhaust manifold upper heat shield bolts and upper heat shield.
8. Remove exhaust lower heat shield bolts and lower heat shield, then the exhaust manifold nuts and exhaust manifold.
9. Reverse procedure to install. Tighten to specifications.

CYLINDER HEAD

REPLACE

LEFT

1. Drain engine coolant into a suitable container, then the engine oil.
2. Remove upper and lower intake manifolds as outlined under " Intake Manifold, Replace."
3. Remove valve cover as outlined under "Valve Cover, Replace."
4. Remove exhaust crossover, then the oil lever indicator bracket.
5. Remove left exhaust manifold as outlined under " Exhaust Manifold, Replace."
6. Disconnect plug wires at left head, then remove pushrods. Intake and exhaust pushrods are different lengths (exhaust pushrods are longer). Intake pushrods are marked orange and are 5.68 inches long, exhaust pushrods are marked blue and are 6 inches long.
7. remove cylinder head attaching bolts, then the cylinder head.
8. Reverse procedure to install, noting the following:
    a. Clean gasket surfaces on head, cylinder block and intake manifold, cylinder block bolt threads and cylinder head bolts.
    b. Place gasket in position over dowel pins with "This Side Up" marking facing upward.
    c. Coat cylinder head bolt threads with suitable sealant.
    d. **On 1997 models,** using sequence shown in **Fig. 3, torque** cylinder head bolts in two steps; first step to 33 ft. lbs., second step an additional 90.°
    e. **On 1998–2000 models,** using sequence shown in **Fig. 3, torque** cylinder head bolts in two steps; first step to 37 ft. lbs., second step an additional 90.°
    f. **On all models,** tighten rocker arm nuts or bolts to specifications.

RIGHT

1. Raise and support vehicle, then drain engine coolant into a suitable container.
2. Drain engine oil, then lower vehicle.
3. Remove upper and lower intake manifolds as outlined under " Intake Manifold, Replace."
4. Disconnect plug wires at left head, then remove pushrods. Intake and exhaust pushrods are different lengths (exhaust pushrods are longer). Intake pushrods are marked orange and are 5.68 inches long, exhaust pushrods are marked blue and are 6 inches long.
5. Remove exhaust crossover pipe, then the right head spark plug wires and plugs.
6. Remove cylinder head attaching bolts, then the cylinder head.

7. Reverse procedure to install, noting the following:
   a. Clean gasket surfaces on head, cylinder block and intake manifold, cylinder block bolt threads and cylinder head bolts.
   b. Place gasket in position over dowel pins with "This Side Up" marking facing upward.
   c. Coat cylinder head bolt threads with suitable sealant.
   d. Using sequence shown in **Fig. 3, torque** cylinder head bolts in two steps; 1997, first step to 33 ft. lbs., second step an additional 90°; 1998–2000, first step to 37 ft. lbs., second step an additional 90.°
   e. Tighten rocker arm nuts or bolts to specifications.

VALVE COVER

REPLACE

LEFT

1. Remove lefthand side spark plug wires, then the automatic transaxle vacuum modulator pipe.
2. Remove PCV valve, then the left valve cover bolts.
3. Remove left valve cover and gasket.
4. Reverse procedure to install, noting the following:
   a. Clean sealing surfaces on cylinder head and cover.
   b. Use new gasket. Ensure gasket is seated properly in rocker cover groove.
   c. Apply suitable sealer in notch in cylinder head.

RIGHT

1. Remove serpentine drive belt, then the alternator braces.
2. Remove alternator, then the right head spark plug wires.
3. Remove ignition coil bracket with coils, then the purge solenoid and vacuum canister solenoid.
4. Remove vacuum hose from grommet in valve cover, then the valve cover bolts.
5. Remove valve cover and gasket.
6. Reverse procedure to install, noting the following:
   a. Clean sealing surfaces on cylinder head and cover.
   b. Use new gasket. Ensure gasket is seated properly in rocker cover groove.
   c. Apply suitable sealer in notch in cylinder head.

VALVE ARRANGEMENT

FRONT TO REAR

Cowl side ....E-I-E-I-I-E
Radiator side ....E-I-I-E-I-E

VALVE LIFTERS

Roller type valve lifters, **Fig. 4,** are used in this engine. Valve lifters must be replaced whenever camshaft is replaced.

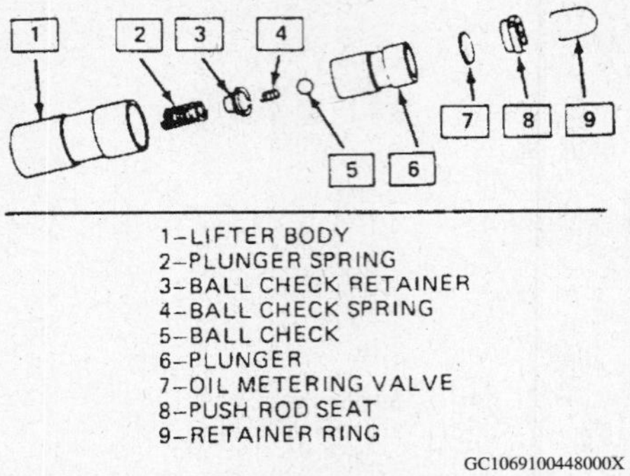

Fig. 4 Exploded view of valve lifter

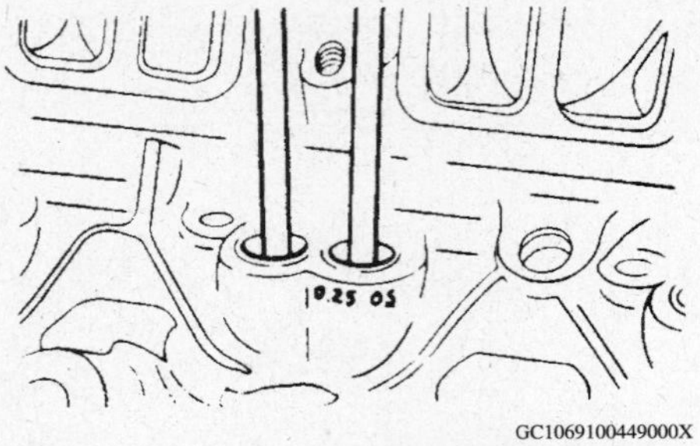

Fig. 5 Oversize lifter marking

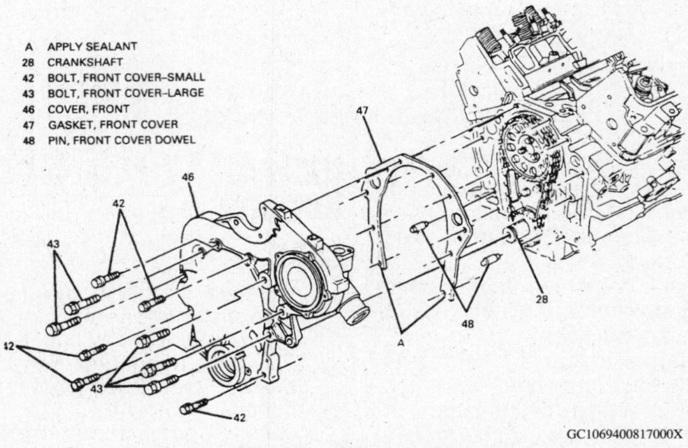

Fig. 6 Front cover installation

Valve lifters should be kept in order so they will be reinstalled in their original positions. Some engines will have both standard and .010 inch oversize valve lifters.

Where oversize lifters are used, the cylinder case will be marked ".25 OS" with white paint on the lifter boss, **Fig. 5.**

If lifters are removed, they must be installed in their original location. If replacement is necessary, use lifters with a narrow flat ground along the lower ¾ of the lifter. These flats provide additional oil to the cam lobe and lifter surfaces.

CAMSHAFT LOBE LIFT SPECIFICATIONS

1997

Intake.................................... .2727
Exhaust .... .2727

1998–2000

Intake.................................... .2500
Exhaust .... .2550

VALVE CLEARANCE SPECIFICATIONS

This engine is equipped with hydraulic lifters; valve lash should always be zero. If valve lash exists, inspect pushrod and rocker arm for excessive wear and check for inoperative lifters.

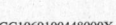

VALVE ADJUSTMENT

There is no valve adjustment for these engines.

PUSH RODS

1. Remove rocker arm covers and rocker arms, identifying components so they can be installed in same location.
2. Remove rocker arm pivot balls and rocker arms, then the pushrods. Intake and exhaust pushrods are different lengths (exhaust pushrods are longer). Intake pushrods are marked orange, exhaust pushrods are marked blue.
3. Reverse procedure to install, noting the following:
   a. Ensure pushrods seat in lifter.
   b. Coat bearing surfaces of rocker arms and pivot balls with Molykote or equivalent lubricant.
   c. Tighten rocker arm nuts or bolts to specifications.

FRONT COVER

REPLACE

1. Drain engine coolant into a suitable container.
2. Remove serpentine drive belt cover, then the drive belt.
3. Remove serpentine drive belt tensioner, then the alternator.
4. Detach power steering pump and position aside.

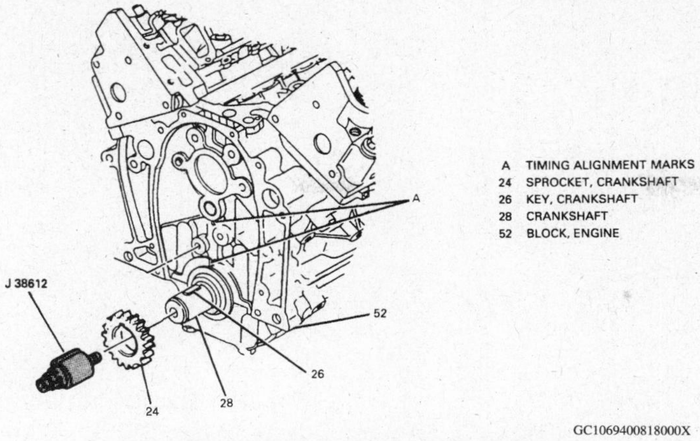

Fig. 7 Timing chain installation

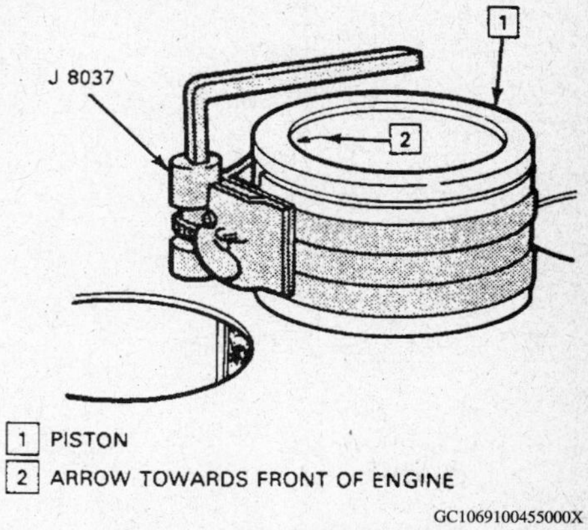

Fig. 8 Piston marking

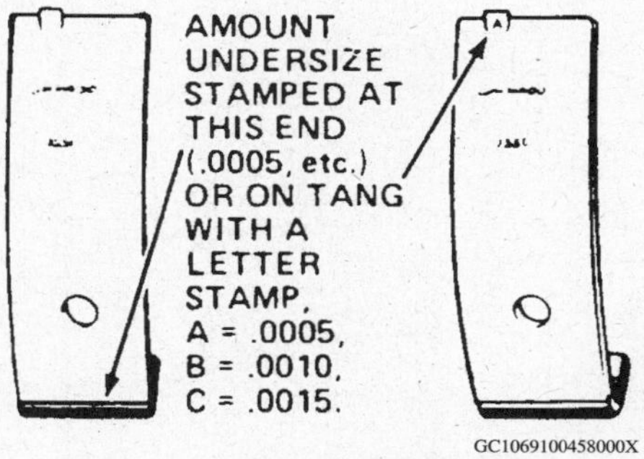

Fig. 9 Main bearing insert markings

5. Raise and support vehicle.
6. Remove inner splash shield, then the flywheel cover.
7. Remove starter; then, using torsional dampener remover tool No. J-24420, or equivalent, remove crankshaft balancer.
8. Remove serpentine drive belt idler pulley.
9. Remove lower timing cover attaching bolts, then lower vehicle.
10. Disconnect radiator hose at water pump and heater coolant hose from cooling system fill pipe.
11. Disconnect bypass, overflow and canister purge hoses.
12. Remove upper timing cover attaching bolts, then the cover.
13. Reverse procedure to install, noting the following:
    a. Clean sealing surfaces on front cover and cylinder block.
    b. Use new gasket and be careful not to damage sealing surfaces.
    c. Apply sealant and tighten timing cover attaching bolts to specifications, **Fig. 6**

FRONT COVER SEAL

REPLACE

1. Remove inner splash shield.
2. Using torsional dampener remover tool No. J-24420, or equivalent, remove crankshaft balancer.
3. Using suitable tool, pry out seal, being careful not to damage crankshaft.
4. Reverse procedure to install, noting the following:
    a. Lubricate new seal with clean engine oil and insert in front cover with lip facing engine.
    b. Use front cover alignment and oil seal installer tool No. J-35468, or equivalent, to drive seal into place.

TIMING CHAIN

REPLACE

REMOVAL

1. Remove timing cover as outlined under "Front Cover, Replace."
2. Remove camshaft sprocket retaining bolt, then the sprocket and timing chain.
3. Remove timing chain dampener bolts, then the dampener.
4. Using sprocket removal tool No. J-5825-A, or equivalent, remove crankshaft sprocket.

INSTALLATION

1. Install new crankshaft sprocket using sprocket installer tool No. J-38612 or equivalent, until sprocket is fully seated on flange of crankshaft.
2. Coat camshaft and crankshaft sprockets with engine oil.
3. Hold camshaft sprocket with chain hanging down and align marks on camshaft and crankshaft sprockets with cast timing marks on engine block, **Fig. 7**
4. Tighten bolts to specifications
5. Install front cover, refer to "Front Cover, Replace."

CAMSHAFT

REPLACE

1. Remove engine as outlined under "Engine, Replace."
2. Remove valve lifters, then the timing cover as previously outlined.
3. Remove timing chain and sprocket as previously outlined, then the camshaft.
4. Reverse procedure to install, noting the following:
    a. If installing new camshaft, coat camshaft lobes with GM E.O.S. part No. 1052367, or equivalent.
    b. Lubricate camshaft journals with engine oil.

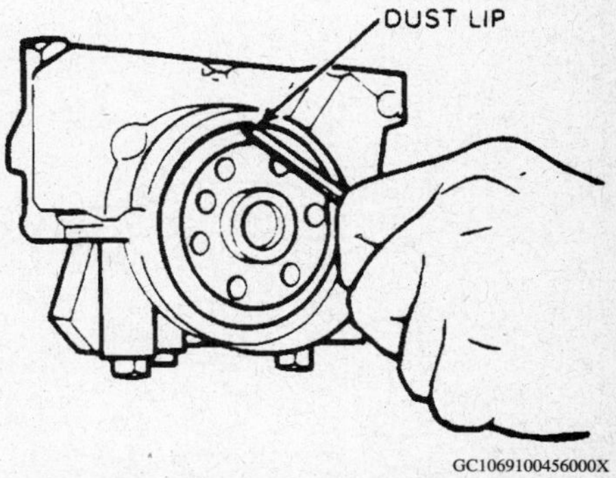

Fig. 10 Rear main seal removal

PISTON & ROD ASSEMBLY

When installing piston and rod assemblies into cylinder block, ensure arrow on top of piston faces toward front of engine, **Fig. 8.**

MAIN & ROD BEARINGS

Engine bearings are of the precision insert type. They are available for service use in standard and various undersizes, **Fig. 9.**

To determine correct replacement insert size, bearing clearance must be measured as follows:

1. Measure crankshaft journal diameter in several places, approximately 90° apart and average the measurements.
2. Measure taper and runout, which should be .0002 inch (maximum).
3. Install bearing inserts and tighten rod and main bearing cap bolts to specifications, then measure I.D. with an inside micrometer. Measure connecting rod I.D. in same direction as length of rod.
4. Select a suitable set of inserts to provide specified clearance limits. **Do not mix inserts of different nominal size in same bearing bore.** If clearance

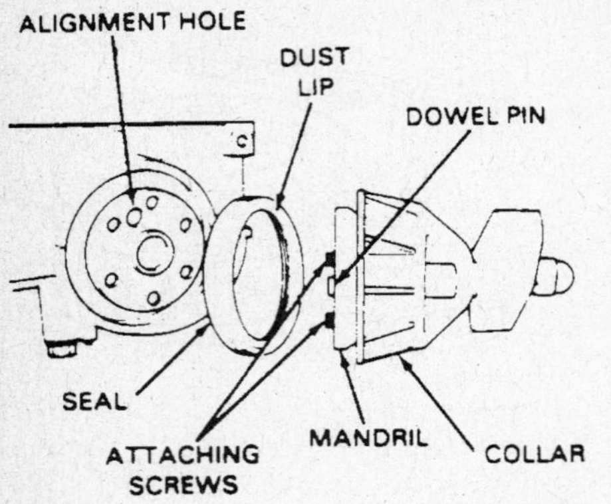

GC1069100457000X

Fig. 11 Rear main seal installation

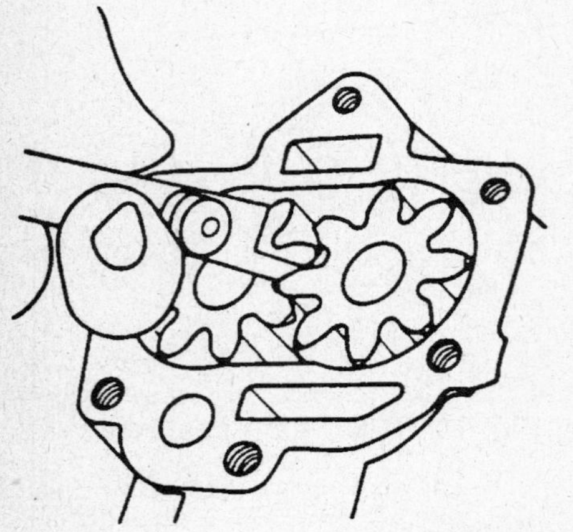
GC1099100076000X

Fig. 14 Oil pump gear lash measurement

limits cannot be met, crankshaft journal must be reconditioned and undersized bearing inserts installed.

CRANKSHAFT REAR OIL SEAL

REPLACE

REMOVAL

1. Using engine support fixture tool No. J-28467, or equivalent, and an extra support leg, support engine, then remove transaxle.
2. Remove flywheel.
3. Using suitable tool, remove seal by inserting tool in through dust lip at an angle, **Fig. 10,** and pry seal out by moving handle of tool toward end of crankshaft pilot, repeating around circumference of seal as necessary. **Be careful not to damage crankshaft O.D. surface.**

INSTALLATION

1. Check I.D. of bore for nicks or burrs and repair as required.
2. Inspect crankshaft for burrs or nicks on surface which contacts seal, repairing or replacing crankshaft as necessary.
3. Install seal as follows:

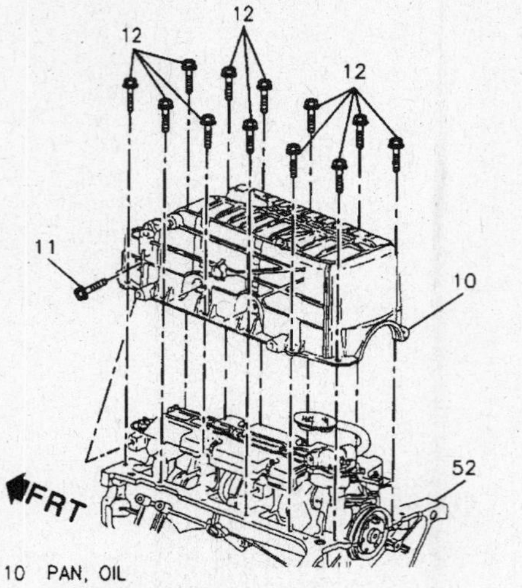

10 PAN, OIL
11 BOLT, OIL PAN SIDE
12 BOLT, OIL PAN RETAINING
52 BLOCK, ENGINE

GC1069600676000X

Fig. 12 Oil pan installation

   a. Apply engine oil to I.D. and O.D. of new seal, then slide seal over mandrel until back of seal bottoms squarely against collar of rear main bearing seal installer tool No. J-34686, or equivalent, **Fig. 11.**
   b. Align dowel pin of tool with dowel pin in crankshaft by hand, then **torque** attaching screws to 45 inch lbs., **Fig. 11.**
   c. Turn "T" handle of tool so collar pushes seal into bore, turning handle until collar is tight against case.
   d. Loosen "T" handle of tool until it comes to a stop, then remove attaching screws.
   e. Ensure seal is seated squarely in bore.
4. Install flywheel, then the transaxle.

OIL PAN

REPLACE

1. Remove engine mount struts from engine, then the A/C compressor mounting bolts and set compressor aside.
2. Install engine support fixture tool No. J 28467–A, engine support fixture adapter tool No. J28467–90 and engine support adapter leg tool No. J 36462, or equivalents.
3. Raise and support vehicle, then disconnect three way catalytic converter pipe from rear exhaust manifold.
4. Drain engine oil, then remove oil level sensor harness connector.
5. Remove starter as outlined under "Starter, Replace, " then the transaxle brace from oil pan.
6. Remove transaxle mount lower nuts, then the engine mount lower nuts.
7. Raise engine using engine support fixture in order to gain access for oil pan removal.
8. Remove engine mount bracket with engine mount from oil pan.

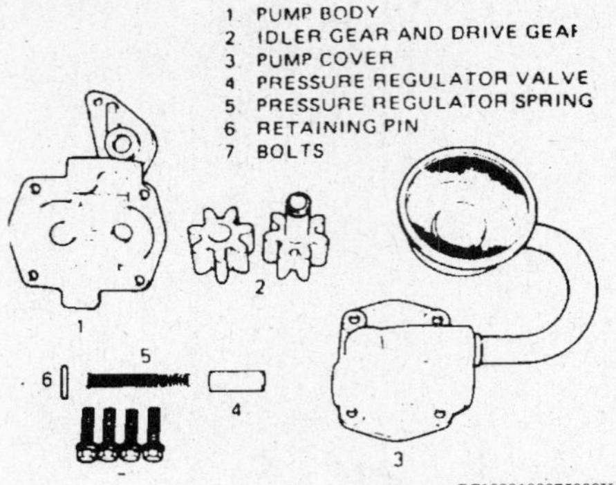

GC1099100075000X

Fig. 13 Exploded view of oil pump

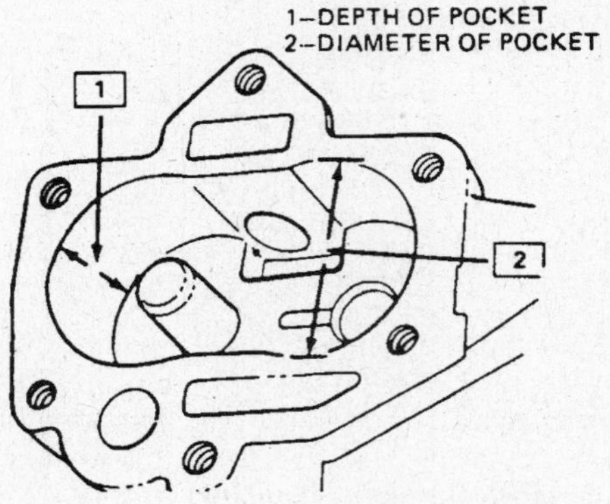

GC1099100077000X

Fig. 15 Oil pump gear pocket measurement

9. Remove rear oil pan side bolts, then the front oil pan side bolts.
10. Remove oil pan retaining bolts, then the oil pan and gasket.
11. Reverse procedure to install, noting the following:
    a. Clean oil pan flanges, oil pan rail, front cover, rear main bearing cap and the threaded holes.
    b. Use new gasket.
    c. Install oil pan as shown in **Fig. 12.**

OIL PUMP

REPLACE

1. Remove oil pan as described under "Oil Pan, Replace. "
2. Remove crankshaft oil deflector retaining nuts, then the deflector.
3. Remove oil pump mounting bolt, then the oil pump and drive rod.
4. Reverse procedure to install. Tighten bolts to specifications

OIL PUMP SERVICE

DISASSEMBLE

1. Drain oil from pump.
2. Remove pump cover and pump gears, **Fig. 13.**
3. Remove pressure regulator valve. If valve is stuck, soak pump housing in carburetor cleaning solvent. **Pressure**

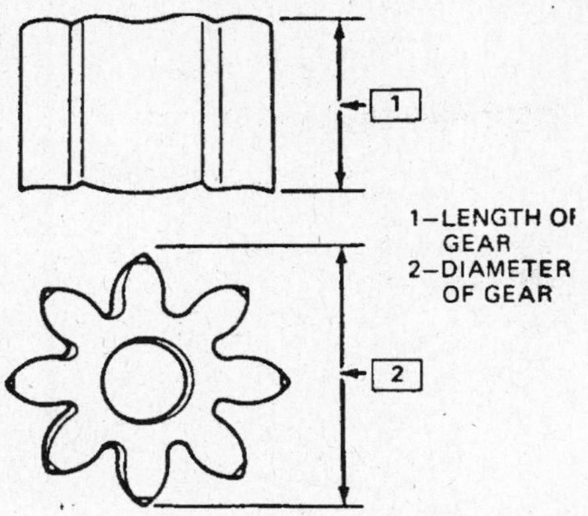

GC1099100078000X

Fig. 16 Oil pump gear measurement

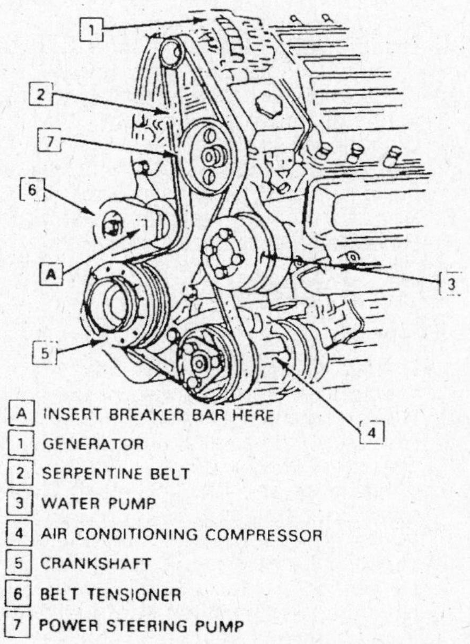

GC1069100459000X

Fig. 19 Serpentine drive belt routing

regulator valve spring may be under pressure. Remain retaining pin carefully.

4. Clean sludge, oil and/or varnish from all parts. Varnish may be removed by soaking in carburetor or cleaning solvent.

INSPECTION

1. Inspect pump housing and cover for cracks or damaged threads, replacing as necessary. **Do not attempt to repair pump housing.** Replace spring as necessary.
2. Inspect idler gear shaft. If loose in housing, replace pump.
3. Inspect pressure regulator valve for scoring or sticking. Burrs may be removed with a fine oil stone.
4. Inspect pressure regulator valve spring for loss of tension or bending.
5. Inspect suction pipe and screen assembly for looseness if permanently pressed into pump body. If pipe is

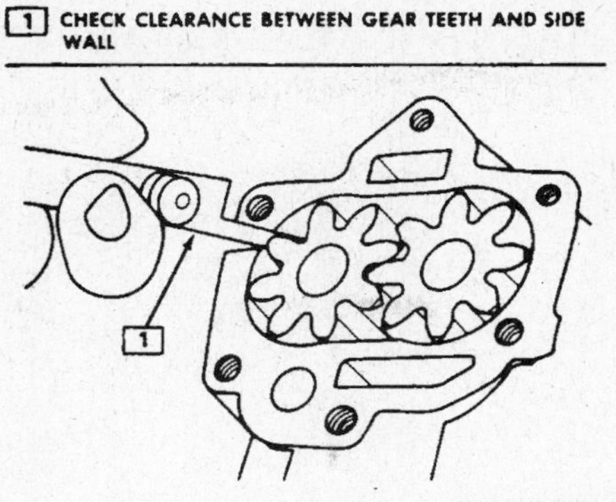

GC1099100079000X

Fig. 17 Gear side clearance measurement

loose or has been removed, pump body cover must be replaced. Check for broken wire mesh or screen.
6. Inspect gears for chipping, galling or wear.
7. Measure gear lash in several positions, **Fig. 14.** Gear lash should be .0037–.0077 inch.
8. Measure pump housing gear pocket depth, **Fig. 15.** Depth should be as follows:
   a. **On models equipped with an aluminum pump body,** pump depth should be 1.195–1.198 inches.
   b. **On models equipped with a cast pump body,** pump depth should be 1.202–1.204 inches.
9. **On all models,** measure pump housing gear pocket diameter, **Fig. 15.** Pump housing diameter should be 1.503–1.505 inches.
10. Measure pump gear diameters, **Fig. 16.** Gear diameter should be 1.498–1.500 inches.
11. Measure pump gear side clearance, **Fig. 17.** Gear side clearance should be .001–.003 inch.
12. Measure oil pump end clearance, **Fig. 18,** as follows:
    a. **On models equipped with an aluminum pump body,** end clearance should be .0016–.0067 inch.
    b. **On models equipped with a cast pump body,** end clearance should be .0020–.0050 inch.

ASSEMBLE

1. Lubricate all internal parts with engine oil.
2. Install pump gears.
3. Prime engine oil galleries by removing engine oil pump drive unit and rotating oil pump, using drill motor, appropriate socket and extension.
4. Install cover and gasket. **Use only original equipment gaskets as gasket thickness is critical to proper pump operation.**
5. Install pin. Ensure pin is properly secured.
6. **Torque** pump cover attaching bolts to 8 ft. lbs.

BELT TENSION DATA

Belt tension is maintained automatically

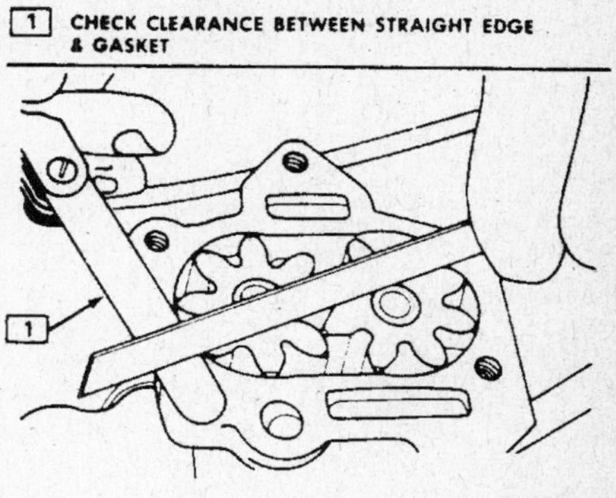

GC1099100080000X

Fig. 18 Oil pump end clearance measurement

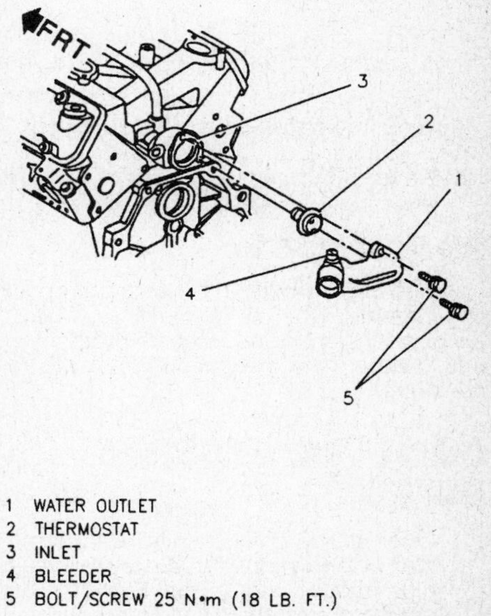

GC1089100172000X

Fig. 20 Cooling system bleed vent

by a spring tensioned idler pulley. Adjustment of serpentine belt is not necessary.

If belt slippage is indicated and belt tensioner indicator is within normal operating range, measure belt tension as follows:

1. Run engine for ten minutes, then shut off and measure belt tension between any two pulleys using V-belt tension gauge tool No. J 23600-B, or equivalent.
2. Run engine for 30 seconds and repeat measurement.
3. Repeat preceding step, then average all three belt tension measurements. Average tension should be 30–50 lbs.
4. If belt tension is not as specified, replace serpentine drive belt.

SERPENTINE DRIVE BELT

REPLACEMENT

1. Lift or rotate tensioner using a ½ inch breaker bar.
2. Remove serpentine belt.

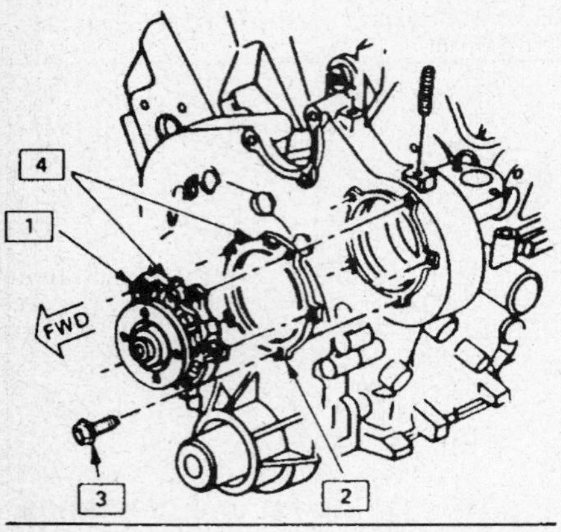

1. WATER PUMP
2. GASKET
3. 10 N·m (89 LB. IN.)
4. LOCATOR – MUST BE VERTICAL

GC1089100171000X

Fig. 21 Water pump mounting

3. Reverse procedure to install, routing drive belt as shown in **Fig. 19.**

ADJUSTMENT

There is no provision for serpentine belt adjustment. Refer to " Belt Tension Data" for belt tension measurement procedures and to determine whether belt requires replacement.

COOLING SYSTEM BLEED

1. Open vent valves located on thermostat housing and throttle body return pipe above water pump, **Fig. 20.** Turn both vents screws two to three turns.
2. Fill cooling system to base of radiator neck.
3. Close both vent valves. **Do not over tighten vent valves.**
4. Install radiator cap.
5. Add sufficient coolant to recovery tank.
6. Start engine and observe low coolant warning lamp.
7. If lamp remains illuminated, repeat bleed procedure.

THERMOSTAT

REPLACE

1. Drain engine coolant into a suitable container.
2. Disconnect radiator hose from thermostat housing.
3. Remove thermostat housing bolts, thermostat housing and thermostat.
4. Reverse procedure to install.

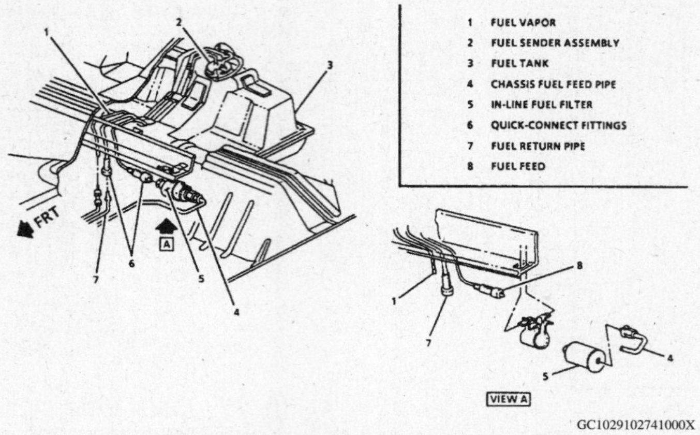

Fig. 22 Fuel filter replacement

WATER PUMP

REPLACE

1. Drain engine coolant into a suitable container.
2. Remove serpentine drive belt, then disconnect radiator and heater hose.
3. Remove water pump attaching bolts, then the water pump, **Fig. 21.**
4. Reverse procedure to install, noting the following:
   a. Clean water pump mating surfaces.
   b. Tighten water pump attaching bolts to specifications.

RADIATOR

REPLACE

1. Remove air cleaner assembly, then drain engine coolant into a suitable container.
2. Remove engine strut upper brace bolts from upper tie bar and rotate strut and brace rearward.
3. Disconnect upper radiator mounting panel bolts and clamps.
4. Disconnect cooling fan electrical connector.
5. Remove cooling fan mounting bolts and fan, then upper radiator bracket.
6. Remove upper and lower radiator hoses at radiator.
7. Disconnect low coolant sensor wiring.
8. Disconnect oil cooler lines, then remove radiator.
9. Reverse procedure to install.

FUEL PUMP

REPLACE

1. Relieve fuel system pressure as outlined under " Precautions."
2. Remove spare tire cover, jack and spare tire, then the trunk liner.
3. Remove seven fuel pump access panel retaining nuts, then the fuel pump access panel.
4. Disconnect fuel tank pressure sensor electrical connector, then clean fuel pipes and fuel pump assembly to prevent fuel contamination.
5. Disconnect quick connect fittings at fuel pump assembly, then remove fuel pump retaining snap ring.
6. Remove modular fuel pump assembly.
7. Reverse procedure to install.

FUEL FILTER

REPLACE

1. Relieve fuel system pressure as outlined under " Precautions."
2. Raise and support vehicle.
3. Remove bracket attaching screw and filter bracket, **Fig. 22.**
4. Grasp filter and fuel line fitting. Twist quick-connect fitting 1/4 turn in each direction to loosen any dirt within fitting.
5. Using compressed air, blow out dirt from quick-connect fitting.
6. Remove feed pipe nut from fuel filter, then drain any remaining fuel into a suitable container.
7. Remove fuel filter.
8. Reverse procedure to install.

TECHNICAL SERVICE BULLETINS

COMPOSITE ROCKER COVER ENGINE OIL LEAKS

On some of these models, there may be a rocker cover oil leak. This condition may be caused by the rocker cover material composition.

To correct this condition, install replacement aluminum rocker covers (lefthand, part No. 24504669; righthand, part No. 24504670).

TIGHTENING SPECIFICATIONS

Year	Component	Torque/Ft. Lbs.
1997– 2000	Camshaft Sprocket	⑤
	Camshaft Thrust Plate	96③
	Connecting Rod Bearing Cap Nuts	15⑥
	Crankshaft Balancer	76
	Cylinder Head Bolts	②
	Engine Mount Bracket Bolts	43
	Engine Mount Nuts	35
	Exhaust Manifold Heat Shield	96③
	Exhaust Manifold Nut	12
	Exhaust Manifold Stud	12
	Flywheel Bolts	⑦
	Front Cover (Large)	35
	Front Cover (Small)	15
	Lower Intake Manifold Bolts	10
	Upper Intake Manifold Bolt	18
	Upper Intake Manifold Stud	18
	Main Bearing Cap Bolts	37④
	Oil Cooler Connector	①
	Oil Filter	10
	Oil Filter Adapter	29
	Oil Level Indicator Retainer Nut	18
	Oil Level Sensor Screw	96③
	Oil Pan (Lower)	18
	Oil Pan (Side)	35
	Oil Pan Drain Plug	18
	Oil Pump	30
	Oil Pump Cover	96③
	Oil Pump Drive Assembly Bolt	27
	Rocker Arm Bolt	7.5⑧
	Rocker Arm Covers	96③
	Serpentine Drive Belt Tensioner Bolt	40
	Spark Plugs	15
	Timing Chain Dampener	18
	Valve Lifter Guide Bolt	96③
	Water Pump	96③

①— 1997, 29 ft. lbs.; 1998–2000, 50 ft. lbs.

②— Refer to "Cylinder Head, Replace" for tightening procedure.

③— Inch lbs.

④— Tighten an additional 77.°

⑤— 1997, 81 ft. lbs.; 1998–2000, 103 ft. lbs.

⑥— Tighten an additional 75.°

⑦— 1997, 61 ft. lbs.; 1998–2000, 52 ft. lbs.

⑧— Tighten an additional 30.°

3.4L Engine

NOTE: On Air Bag Equipped Models, Refer To " Air Bag System Precautions" Located In The Front Of This Manual For System Disarming & Arming Procedures.

NOTE: Refer To "Computer Relearn Procedures " Located In The Front Of This Manual For Computer Relearn Procedures.

INDEX

PRECAUTIONS

AIR BAG SYSTEMS

Refer to "Air Bag System Precautions" in the front of this manual for system disarming and arming procedures.

BATTERY GROUND CABLE

Prior to service, disconnect battery ground cable and isolate as required.

FUEL SYSTEM PRESSURE RELIEF

To reduce the risk of fire and personal injury, it is necessary to relieve the fuel system pressure before servicing fuel system components.

1. Loosen fuel tank filler cap to relieve tank pressure.
2. **On 2000 models,** remove fuel injection sight shield.
3. **On all models,** connect fuel pressure gauge tool No. J-34730-1, or equivalent, to the fuel pressure valve. Wrap a shop towel around fitting while connection gauge to avoid spillage.
4. Install bleed hose into an approved container and open valve to bleed system pressure.

IDLE LEARN PROCEDURE

If vehicle power is interrupted, the programmed position of the Idle Air Control (IAC) valve pintle is lost. The following procedures must be performed to update the ECM memory with the correct IAC valve pintle position for the vehicle and provide a stable idle speed.

1. Restore vehicle power.
2. Connect TECH I scan tool to ALDL connector located under lefthand side of dash panel.
3. Select "IAC System."
4. Select "Idle Learn" in the " Misc. Test" mode.
5. Proceed as directed by scan tool.

COMPRESSION PRESSURE

When checking compression, lowest cylinder must be within 70 percent of the highest cylinder with a minimum pressure of 100 psi. Perform compression test with engine at normal operating temperature, spark plugs removed and throttle wide open.

ENGINE MOUNT

REPLACE

1997

Front

1. Remove air cleaner assembly.
2. Disconnect engine torque strut.
3. Install engine support tool Nos. J-28467, J-28467-90 and J-36462, or equivalents.
4. Raise and support vehicle.
5. Remove right front tire and wheel assembly.
6. Remove righthand engine splash shield.
7. Drain engine oil into a suitable container and remove oil filter.
8. Remove front engine mount nuts at mount bracket and frame, **Fig. 1.**
9. Install drive axle boot protector and lower vehicle.
10. Raise engine.
11. Raise and support vehicle.
12. Remove front mount.
13. Reverse procedure to install.

Rear

1. Remove air cleaner assembly and disconnect engine torque strut.
2. Install engine support tool Nos. J-28467, J-28467-90 and J-36462, or equivalents, then raise and support vehicle.
3. Remove right front tire and wheel assembly, righthand engine and drive axle splash shields.
4. Install drive axle boot protector.
5. Remove engine mount nuts at frame, **Fig. 2.**
6. Lower vehicle and raise engine.
7. Raise and support vehicle.

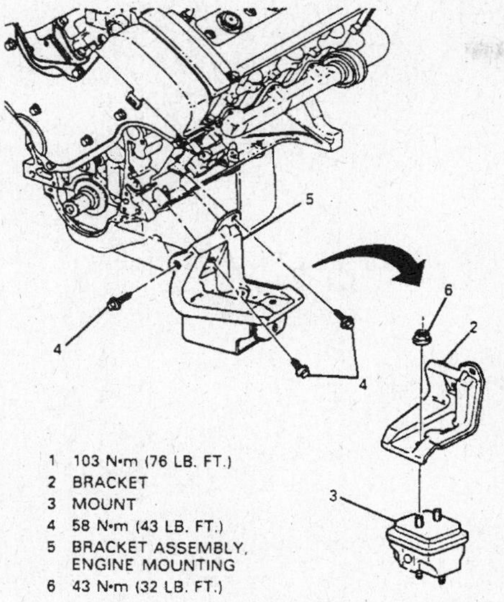

GC1069100460000X

Fig. 1 Front engine mounting bracket. 1997

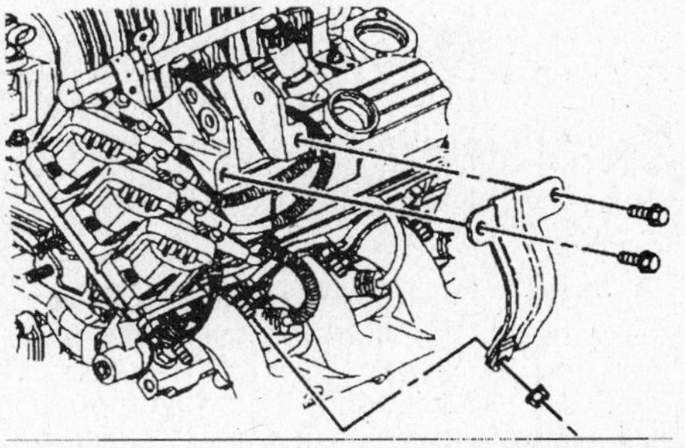

GC1060001065000X

Fig. 4 Right lower engine mount removal. 2000

8. Remove power rack and pinion mounting bolts and hang rack on frame.
9. Disconnect right ball joint from lower control arm.
10. Install a suitable jack under righthand side of frame.
11. Remove righthand frame mounting bolts.
12. Loosen lefthand frame mounting bolts.
13. Lower righthand side of frame approximately three inches.
14. Remove upper engine mount nuts at mount.
15. Remove mount.
16. Reverse procedure to install.

2000

Left

1. Remove engine mount strut from engine mount strut bracket.
2. Remove engine exhaust crossover pipe.
3. Remove thermostat housing as outlined in "Thermostat, Replace."
4. Remove engine mount strut bracket attaching bolts, **Fig. 3.**
5. Remove engine mount strut bracket.
6. Reverse procedure to install.

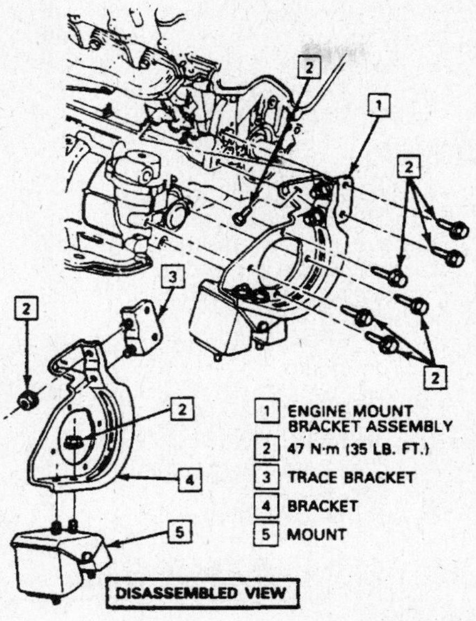

GC1069100462000X

Fig. 2 Rear engine mounting bracket. 1997

Right Lower

1. Remove right lower engine mount strut bracket attaching bolts, **Fig. 4.**
2. Remove engine mount retaining nut, then the engine mount.
3. Reverse procedure to install.

Right Upper

1. Remove right engine mount strut from upper engine strut mount bracket,
2. Remove fuel injector sight shield.
3. Remove EVAP emissions canister purge valve.
4. Remove right upper engine mount strut bracket bolts, then the bracket, **Fig. 5.**
5. **On models equipped with oil cooler,** remove oil cooler pipe bracket bolt from right engine mount strut bracket.
6. **On all models,** remove A/C compressor mounting bolts and position aside.
7. Remove vertical bolt from right engine mount strut bracket, **Fig. 6.**
8. Remove right engine mount bracket.
9. Reverse procedure to install.

Front Lower

1. Disconnect air inlet duct from throttle body.
2. Remove left and right engine mount struts.
3. Raise and support vehicle.
4. Disconnect catalytic converter pipe from right exhaust manifold.
5. Remove right front wheel and tire assembly.
6. Remove right side engine splash shield.
7. Remove engine mount to subframe nuts.
8. Lower vehicle, then install engine lifting tool No. J 28467-B, or equivalent.
9. Raise engine until mount is clear of subframe.
10. Raise and support vehicle.

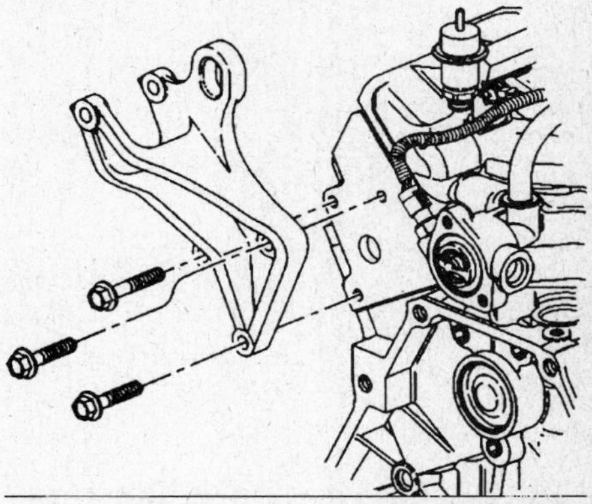

GC1060001064000X

Fig. 3 Left engine mount removal. 2000

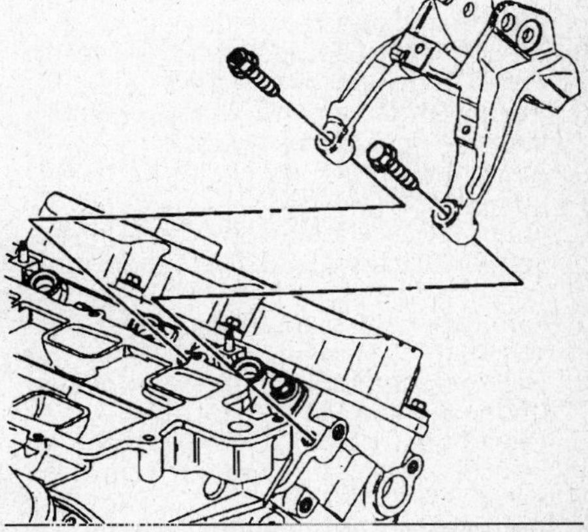

GC1060001066000X

Fig. 5 Right upper engine mount bracket. 2000

11. Remove engine mount attaching bolts, **Fig. 7.**
12. Reverse procedure to install.

ENGINE

REPLACE

1. Relieve fuel system pressure as outlined under " Precautions."
2. Remove air cleaner assembly.
3. Mark and remove hood assembly.
4. Drain engine coolant into a suitable container.
5. Recover A/C system as outlined in "Air Conditioning " section, then remove coolant recovery tank.
6. Remove heater hoses from engine.
7. Disconnect engine torque strut mount and stud.
8. Disconnect and remove engine cooling fans.
9. Remove radiator hoses from engine.
10. Disconnect control cables from bracket and throttle body.
11. Disconnect bulkhead connections from cowl.
12. Disconnect fuel lines from engine.
13. Remove exhaust crossover pipe.

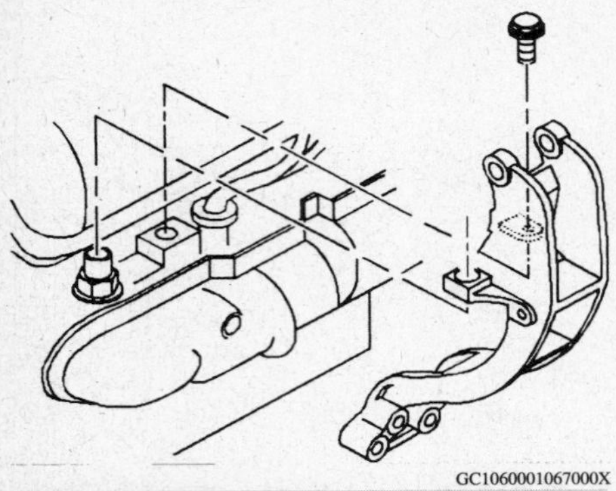

Fig. 6 Right engine mount strut bracket. 2000

14. Remove lower transaxle to engine bolts including ground wires.
15. Remove power steering pump from engine and position aside.
16. Disconnect EGR pipe from EGR valve.
17. Raise and support vehicle.
18. Remove right tire and wheel assembly, then the right splash shield.
19. Disconnect A/C manifold from A/C compressor.
20. Remove flywheel and steel torque converter inspection covers then starter.
21. Remove front exhaust pipe and converter.
22. Disconnect motor mounts as outlined under "Engine Mount, Replace."
23. Disconnect electrical connections at front and rear of engine then from alternator.
24. Remove torque converter bolts.
25. Remove right ball joint bolt and separate joint from control arm.
26. Remove drive axle assembly.
27. Lower vehicle.
28. Support transaxle using a suitable jack and install lifting device on engine.
29. Disconnect quick connects near ECM.
30. Remove remaining transaxle to engine bolts.
31. Disconnect necessary vacuum lines from rear of engine.
32. Remove engine assembly.
33. Reverse procedure to install.

INTAKE MANIFOLD

REPLACE

UPPER

1. Relieve fuel system pressure, refer to "Fuel System Pressure Relief."
2. Remove air cleaner assembly, then drain engine coolant.
3. Remove throttle body control cables at upper intake manifold.
4. Remove fuel rail cover bolts, then the fuel rail cover.
5. Remove fuel lines at fuel rail.
6. Remove heater hose at lower intake manifold.
7. Remove PCV valve and vacuum line.
8. Disconnect AIR solenoid, EGR valve, canister purge solenoid, MAP sensor and TPS electrical connectors.
9. Remove vacuum hoses and wiring loom bracket for rear spark plug wires.
10. Remove upper intake manifold bolts, then the manifold and gaskets, **Fig. 8**
11. Reverse procedure to install.

LOWER

1. Relieve fuel system pressure, refer to "Fuel System Pressure Relief."
2. Remove upper intake manifold.
3. Remove fuel rail.
4. Remove radiator hose from thermostat housing.
5. Disconnect temperature sensor electrical connector.
6. Remove heater pipe nut at throttle body.
7. Remove lower intake manifold mounting bolts, then the manifold and gaskets, **Fig. 9**
8. Reverse procedure to install.

EXHAUST MANIFOLD

REPLACE

FRONT

1. Remove air cleaner assembly.
2. Remove exhaust crossover pipe.
3. Remove engine torque strut bracket to frame bolts and lift strut out of the way.
4. Remove upper radiator shroud, right side cooling fan heat shield and right cooling fan assembly.
5. Remove exhaust manifold nuts, then the manifold and heat shield.
6. Reverse procedure to install.

REAR

1. Remove air cleaner and duct assembly, then the exhaust crossover pipe.
2. Raise and support vehicle.
3. Disconnect front exhaust pipe at manifold.
4. Lower vehicle.
5. Disconnect oxygen sensor connector.
6. Remove rear alternator brace.
7. Remove intermediate shaft from steering gear, then lower engine cradle assembly.
8. Remove steering gear heat shield.
9. Remove exhaust manifold nuts, then the manifold and heat shield.
10. Reverse procedure to install.

CYLINDER HEAD

REPLACE

FRONT

1. Relieve fuel system pressure as outlined under " Precautions."
2. Remove intake manifold, camshaft carrier and exhaust manifold as outlined under "Intake Manifold, Replace," " Camshaft, Replace" and "Exhaust Manifold, Replace. "
3. Remove right cooling fan assembly.
4. Remove oil level indicator tube.
5. Disconnect temperature sending unit connector.
6. Remove cylinder head bolts, then the cylinder head.
7. Reverse procedure to install, noting the following:

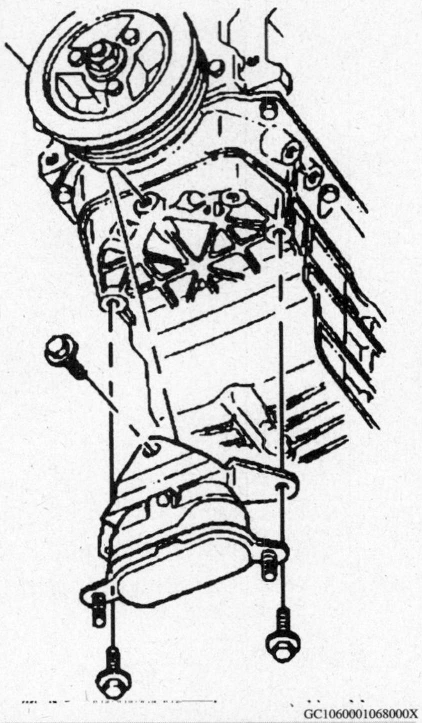

Fig. 7 Front lower engine mount. 2000

   a. Install cylinder head gasket with metal tabs between cylinders facing up.
   b. **On 1997 models,** using sequence shown in **Fig. 10,** tighten bolts in two steps; first step **torque** to 44 ft. lbs., second step an additional 90° turn using torque/angle meter tool No. J-36660, or equivalent.
   c. **On 2000 models,** using sequence shown in **Fig. 10,** tighten bolts in two steps; first step **torque** to 37 ft. lbs., second step an additional 120° turn using torque/angle meter tool No. J-36660, or equivalent.

REAR

1. Relieve fuel system pressure as outlined under " Precautions."
2. Remove intake manifold, camshaft carrier and exhaust manifold as outlined under "Intake Manifold, Replace," " Camshaft Carrier, Replace" and "Exhaust Manifold, Replace."
3. Disconnect oxygen sensor connector.
4. Remove rear timing belt tensioner bracket.
5. Remove cylinder head bolts then the cylinder head and gasket.
6. Reverse procedure to install, noting the following:
   a. Install cylinder head gasket with metal tabs between cylinders facing up.
   b. Using sequence shown in **Fig. 10, torque** bolts in two steps; first step to 44 ft. lbs., second step an additional 90° turn using torque/angle meter tool No. J-36660, or equivalent.

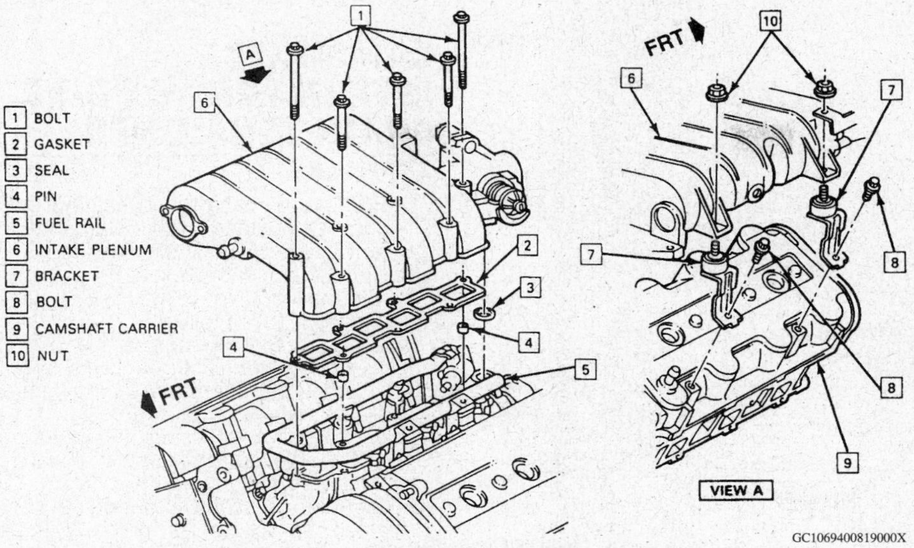

Fig. 8 Upper intake manifold assembly

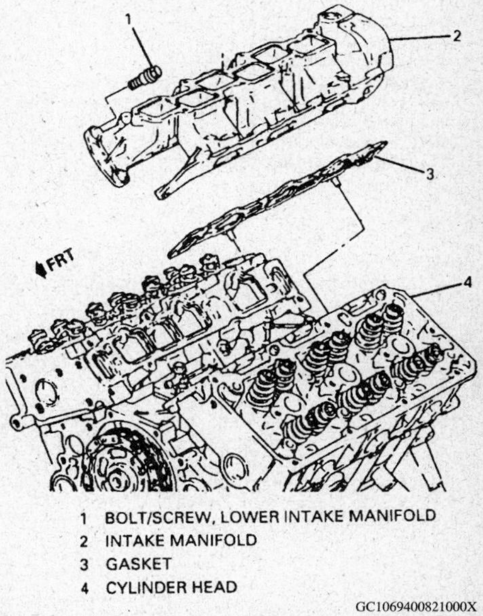

Fig. 9 Lower intake manifold assembly

VALVE LIFTERS

LIFTER REPLACEMENT

1. Remove camshaft carrier as outlined under "Camshaft, Replace."
2. Remove six lifter hold-down hoses.
3. Remove lifters.
4. Reverse procedure to install.

VALVE STEM OIL SEAL & SPRING REPLACEMENT

Head On Engine

1. Remove camshaft carrier as outlined under "Camshaft Carrier, Replace."
2. Remove spark plugs and install spark plug port adapter tool No. J-22794, or equivalent, and apply compressed air to hold valves in place.
3. Compress valve spring using valve spring compressor tool No. J-38606, or equivalent.
4. Remove valve stem locks and release spring tension.
5. Remove valve cap, valve spring and valve stem oil seal. **Wrap tape over valve lock grooves to prevent damage to valve seals.**
6. Reverse procedure to install.

Head Off Engine

1. Compress valve spring using valve spring compressor tool No. J-38606, or equivalent.
2. Remove valve stem locks and release spring tension.
3. Remove valve cap, valve spring and valve stem oil seal. **Wrap tape over valve lock grooves to prevent damage to valve seals.**
4. Reverse procedure to install.

CAMSHAFT LOBE LIFT SPECIFICATIONS

Intake................................ .370 inch

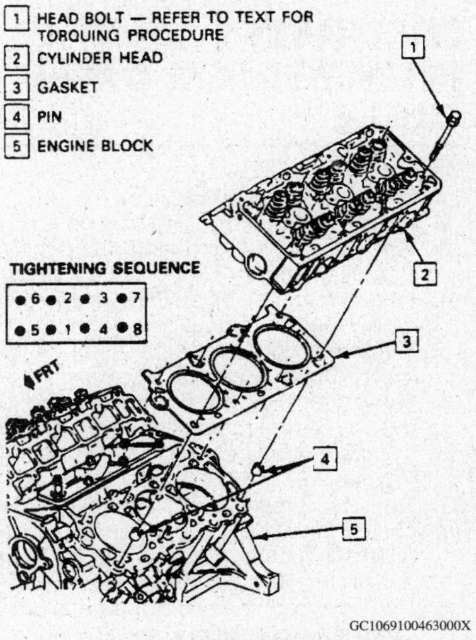

Fig. 10 Cylinder head bolt tightening sequence

Exhaust........................... .370 inch

CRANKSHAFT DAMPER

REPLACE

1. Remove serpentine drive belt as outlined under "Serpentine Drive Belt."
2. Raise and support vehicle.
3. Remove right tire and wheel assembly then the engine splash shield.
4. Remove starter as outlined under "Starter, Replace" in the "Electrical" section.
5. Remove crankshaft damper bolt using flywheel holding tool No. J-37096, or equivalent.
6. Remove crankshaft pulley bolt and pulley.
7. Remove crankshaft damper using crankshaft damper removal tool No. J-24430, or equivalent.
8. Reverse procedure to install, noting the following:
   a. Coat front cover oil seal with engine oil.
   b. Install suitable sealant to keyway of damper before installation.
   c. Install damper using crankshaft damper installer tool No. J-29113, or equivalent.

FRONT COVER

REPLACE

1. Remove secondary timing belt tensioner mounting bracket and idler pulleys as outlined under "Timing Belt, Replace."
2. Remove engine front lift hook.
3. Remove engine torque strut bracket from frame and pull strut and bracket out of the way.
4. Remove upper radiator support.
5. Remove righthand cooling fan heat shield then the cooling fan assembly.
6. Remove lower radiator hose from coolant pump.
7. Remove heater hose at front cover and heater pipe bracket at frame.
8. Raise and support vehicle.
9. Remove right tire and wheel assembly then the engine splash shield.
10. Remove crankshaft pulley and damper as outlined under "Crankshaft Damper, Replace."
11. Drain engine oil into a suitable container and remove oil filter.
12. Remove A/C compressor mounting bolts.

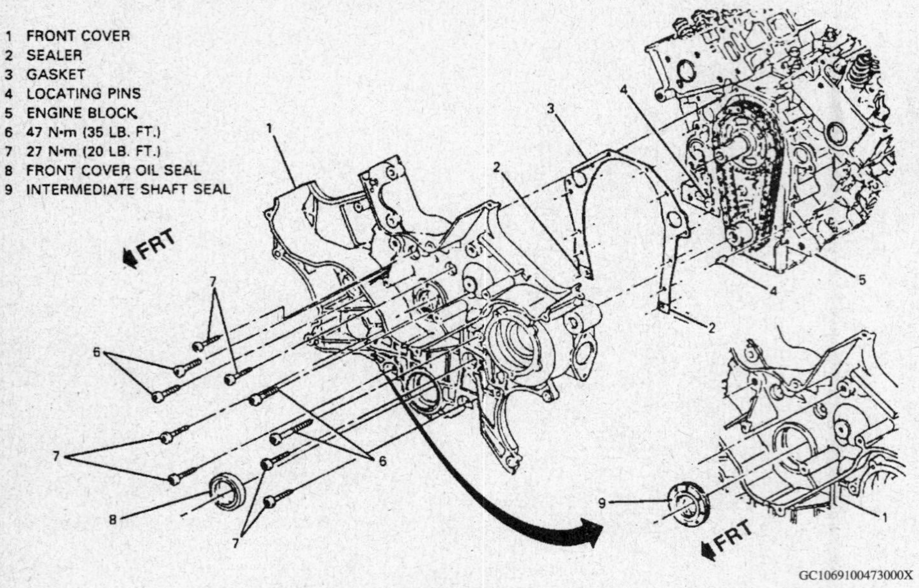

Fig. 11 Front cover & oil seal

13. Remove lower front cover bolts, **Fig. 11.**
14. **On models equipped with automatic transaxle,** remove drive axle assembly.
15. **On all models,** remove rear alternator bracket, then the starter motor.
16. Lower vehicle.
17. Remove intermediate timing belt sprocket as outlined under "Camshaft, Replace."
18. Remove upper alternator retaining bolts.
19. Remove forward lamp relay center screws and position relay center aside.
20. Remove oil cooler hose from front cover.
21. Remove water pump pulley.
22. Remove front cover upper bolts then the front cover and gasket.
23. Reverse procedure to install, noting the following:
    a. Apply GM sealer part No. 1052080, or equivalent, to lower edges of sealing surface of front cover.
    b. Apply suitable thread sealant to large bolts.
    c. Tighten attaching bolts to specifications.

FRONT COVER SEAL

REPLACE

1. Remove crankshaft pulley and damper as outlined under "Crankshaft Damper, Replace."
2. Pry out seal using a suitable pry tool.
3. Reverse procedure to install, noting the following:
    a. Lubricate seal with oil.
    b. Install seal using seal installer tool No. J-34995, or equivalent.

CAMSHAFT INTERMEDIATE DRIVE CHAIN

REPLACE

1. Raise and support vehicle.
2. Remove starter and flywheel cover.
3. Remove oil pan as outlined under "Oil Pan, Replace."
4. Remove engine as outlined under "Engine, Replace."
5. Remove front cover as outlined under "Front Cover, Replace."
6. Mark reference points on the intermediate sprocket, chain link, front face of cylinder and crankshaft sprocket, **Fig. 12.**
7. Retract camshaft intermediate drive chain tensioner as outlined under "Camshaft Intermediate Drive Chain Tensioner, Replace."
8. Remove camshaft intermediate drive chain and crankshaft sprocket using universal puller bridge tool No. J-8433, or equivalent, and special legs and protector tool No. J-38611, or equivalent. If intermediate gear does not slide off easily with timing chain, rotate crankshaft back and forth to help loosen gear.
9. Reverse procedure to install, noting the following:
    a. Aligning marks made during disassembling.
    b. Large chamfer and counterbore of crankshaft sprocket are installed toward crankshaft.
    c. Intermediate shaft sprocket spline sockets are installed away from case.
    d. Crankshaft sprocket must be pressed on for final .31 inch to seated position using crankshaft gear installer tool No. J-38612, or equivalent.

CAMSHAFT INTERMEDIATE DRIVE CHAIN TENSIONER

REPLACE

1. Remove camshaft intermediate drive chain as outlined under "Camshaft Intermediate Drive Chain, Replace."
2. Retract tensioner shoe using tensioner retractor tool No. J-33875, or equivalent, **Fig. 13,** as follows:
    a. Insert tool on both sides of tensioner. Pull on through pin in tensioner arm to retract spring located in tensioner arm.
    b. While compressing spring, use a suitable tool and insert in hole to retain spring.
3. Remove camshaft intermediate drive chain sprockets as outlined under "Camshaft Intermediate Drive Chain, Replace."
4. Remove tensioner mounting bolts, then the tensioner.
5. Inspect tensioner for wear, cracks or other damage.
6. With tensioner shoe retracted, install tensioner to engine block.
7. Lightly coat tensioner chain surfaces with oil.
8. Install camshaft intermediate drive chain as outlined under "Camshaft Intermediate Drive Chain, Replace."

TIMING BELT

REPLACE

With the timing belt removed, avoid turning the camshaft or crankshaft. If movement is required, exercise extreme caution to avoid valve damage caused by piston contact.

1. Remove air cleaner assembly, then drain coolant into suitable container.
2. Remove fuel injector sight shield, then disconnect throttle body cables.
3. Relieve fuel pressure as outlined under "Precautions."
4. Disconnect fuel lines from fuel rail, then remove fuel line bracket.
5. Remove EGR valve bolts and position aside.
6. Disconnect MAP sensor and EVAP purge solenoid electrical connectors.
7. Disconnect vacuum lines from upper intake manifold tee.
8. Remove wire loom for left side spark plugs.
9. Disconnect power brake vacuum hose.
10. Remove upper intake manifold support retaining bolts.
11. Remove EVAP purge solenoid and bracket.
12. Disconnect spark plug wires from coils. Reference mark for installation.
13. Remove control module, coils and bracket.
14. Remove upper intake manifold.

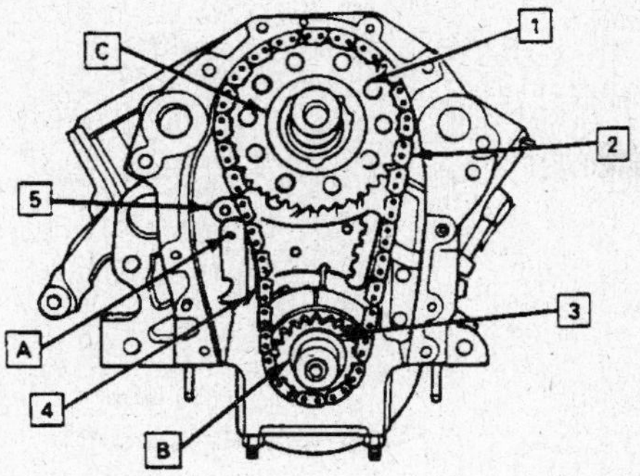

1 INTERMEDIATE SHAFT SPROCKET
2 TIMING CHAIN
3 CRANKSHAFT SPROCKET
4 TIMING CHAIN TENSIONER
5 25 N·m (18 LB. FT.)
A SPRING PIN HOLE
B CHAMFER AND COUNTER BORE INWARD
C SPROCKETS OUTWARD

GC1069100469000X

Fig. 12 Camshaft intermediate drive chain assembly

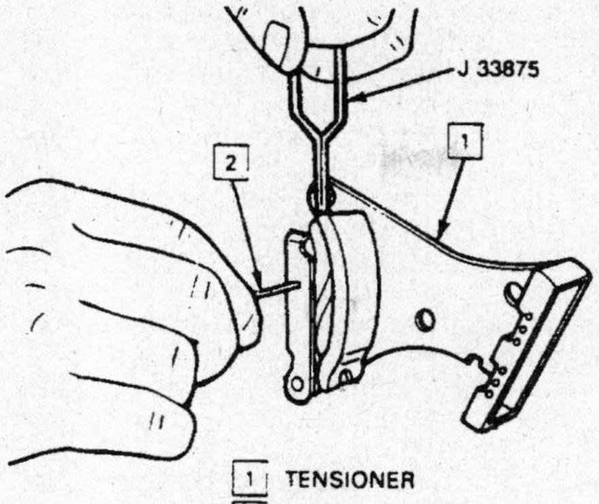

1 TENSIONER
2 PIN

GC1069100470000X

Fig. 13 Camshaft intermediate drive chain tensioner retraction

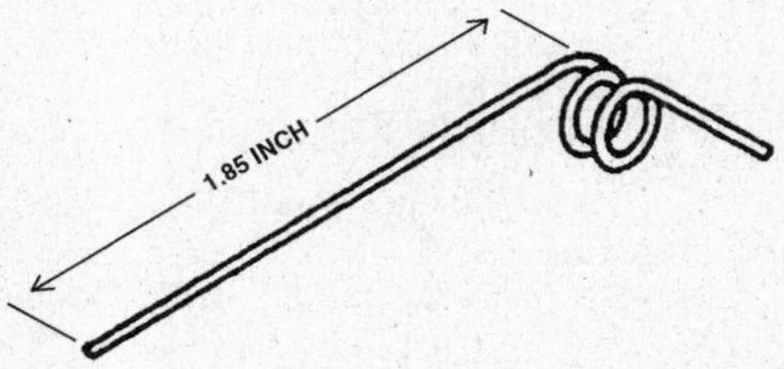

GC1069900988000X

Fig. 15 Tensioner tool fabrication

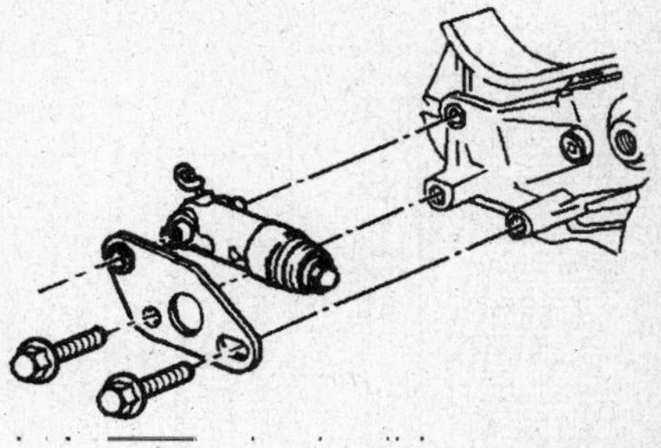

GC1069900987000X

Fig. 14 Timing belt actuator & plate

15. Remove coolant recovery reservoir.
16. Remove serpentine drive belt as outlined under " Serpentine Drive Belt."
17. Remove serpentine drive belt tensioner.
18. Position ignition control wiring harness near power steering pump aside.
19. Disconnect power steering lines, then position power steering pump aside.
20. Disconnect PCM electrical connectors and position aside.
21. Disconnect spark plug wires from spark plugs. Reference mark for installation.
22. Detach wiring harness cover at right strut tower, then remove fuel line bracket.
23. Remove upper timing belt covers and power steering line retaining clip from alternator mounting stud.
24. Remove front timing belt cover, then disconnect breather hose from rear camshaft carrier cover.
25. Disconnect crankcase vent hose from breather manifold.
26. Remove front and rear camshaft carrier covers.
27. Remove bolts and side plate from tension actuator, **Fig. 14.**
28. Rotate tension actuator from pulley socket and out of mounting base.
29. Remove tension actuator pulley bolt, then the pulley.
30. Lightly clamp tension actuator body in suitable vise with rod tip facing downward. Allow actuator oil to drain to the boot end for at least five minutes before refilling. **The tension actuator uses a tapered bushing between the actuator and mounting base. Use care not to damage or lose bushing when removing actuator.**
31. Fabricate locking tool from standard .032 inch paper clip without serrations to dimensions shown, **Fig. 15.**
32. Remove rubber end plug from rear of tension actuator, then push fabricated tool through center hole of vent plug into pilot hole. **Do not remove vent plug.**
33. Position suitable small screwdriver into screw slot inside actuator at rubber plug end.
34. Rotate screw clockwise until actuator plunger is fully retracted. Push on fabricated tool and slowly rotate screw counterclockwise until tool engages.
35. Remove timing belt and timing marks from camshaft and intermediate sprockets.
36. Position crankshaft so No. 1 cylinder is at top dead center on compression stroke. Mark timing indicator with white paint, or equivalent, on crankshaft balancer and front cover.
37. Position camshafts so flat spots are facing upward.
38. Install special tool No. J38613–A, or equivalent as shown, **Fig. 16.**
39. Remove camshaft sprocket bolts and taper lock rings, then the sprocket by lightly tapping with soft faced mallet.
40. Install camshaft sprockets with taper lock rings and bolts finger tight.
41. Install timing belt in counterclockwise direction around sprockets, **Fig. 17. Ensure timing belt teeth fully engage sprocket teeth.**
42. Install timing belt tension actuator pulley. **Torque** retaining bolt to 37 ft. lbs.
43. Add oil to tension actuator through end hole as required. Fill to bottom plug hole only when tension actuator is fully retracted and pin is installed. Use 5W-30 synthetic oil.
44. Push end plug onto rear of tension actuator until plug is flush and snapped into place.
45. Install tension actuator bushing into side plate. **Ensure bushing holes are clean. Do not lubricate.**
46. Install tension actuator and side plate onto front cover. **Ensure tapered fulcrum of tension actuator is properly seated in tension actuator bracket bushing. Torque** side plate bolts to 18 ft. lbs.
47. Rotate pulley into timing belt a maximum of 11 ft. lbs. to permit engagement of actuator shaft into pulley arm sprocket.
48. Pull lock pin from tension actuator. **Retorque** pulley to 11 ft. lbs. in counterclockwise direction to seat pulley against timing belt.
49. **Torque** both left camshaft sprockets to 96 ft. lbs.
50. Remove camshaft holding tool from left camshaft carrier.
51. Rotate crankshaft 360° in clockwise direction, aligning marks placed on crankshaft sprocket and front cover. **Ensure both left camshaft flats are facing down.**
52. **Torque** both right camshaft sprockets to 96 ft. lbs.
53. Remove camshaft holding tool from right camshaft carrier.
54. Rotate crankshaft 720° in clockwise direction, aligning marks placed on crankshaft sprocket and front cover. **Ensure both camshaft flats on one side are facing down, while the other side is facing up.**
55. Install camshaft carrier covers.
56. Connect breather hose to rear of camshaft carrier cover and crankcase vent to breather manifold.
57. Install timing belt covers.
58. Install fuel line bracket and wiring harness at right strut tower.
59. Connect spark plug wires to spark plugs and PCM electrical connectors.
60. Reposition power steering pump, then connect power steering lines.
61. Install serpentine drive belt as outlined under " Serpentine Drive Belt."
62. Install coolant recovery reservoir, then connect power brake vacuum hose.
63. Connect vacuum lines to upper intake manifold tee.
64. Connect MAP sensor and EVAP purge solenoid electrical connectors.
65. Install EGR and PCV valves, then connect vacuum line to throttle body.

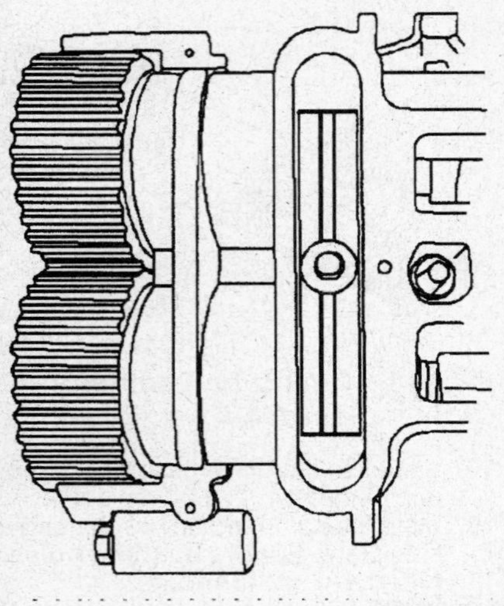

Fig. 16 Camshaft hold down tool installation

66. Install fuel line bracket, then connect fuel lines to fuel rail.
67. Install fuel injector sight shield, then connect accelerator cable to throttle body.
68. Install air cleaner assembly, then fill coolant system as required.
69. Fill power steering pump reservoir as required and bleed system.
70. Start engine and check for proper operation.

CAMSHAFT

REPLACE

1. Remove lefthand camshaft carrier as follows:
   a. Disconnect oil/air breather hose from cover.
   b. Remove spark plug wires from plugs.
   c. Remove rear spark plug wire cover.
   d. Remove camshaft carrier cover bolts, then the cover and O-ring.
   e. Remove secondary timing belt.
   f. Install fuel line hoses under camshaft and between lifters to hold lifters in carrier as shown in **Fig. 18.**
   g. Remove exhaust crossover pipe.
   h. Remove engine torque strut and strut bracket on engine.
   i. Remove camshaft carrier bolts and nut, then the camshaft carrier and gasket.
2. Remove righthand camshaft carrier as follows:
   a. Remove intake plenum as outlined under "Intake Manifold, Replace."
   b. Remove timing belt right cover as outlined under " Timing Belt, Replace."
   c. Remove spark plug wires and oil/air separator hose at camshaft cover.
   d. Remove camshaft cover bolts then the camshaft cover and gaskets.
   e. Remove secondary timing belt.
   f. Install fuel line hoses under camshaft and between lifters to hold lifters in carrier as shown in **Fig. 18.**
   g. Remove front engine lift hook.
   h. Remove camshaft carrier bolts and nut, then the camshaft carrier and gasket.
3. Remove lifters as outlined under "Hydraulic Lifter, Replace."
4. Install cam shaft hold-down tool No. J-38613, or equivalent.
5. Remove camshaft sprockets as follows:
   a. Remove clamping device from sprocket.
   b. Rotate camshafts so flats on camshaft to be serviced are facing up, **Fig. 19.**
   c. Install camshaft hold-down tool No. J-38613, or equivalent, and **torque** bolt to 22 ft. lbs., **Fig. 18.**
   d. Remove camshaft sprocket bolt and washer using camshaft holding tool Nos. J38613 and J-38614, or equivalents.
   e. Remove camshaft sprocket using sprocket remover tool No. J-38616, or equivalent.
   f. Remove flat ring from sprocket bore.
6. Remove camshaft carrier thrust plate cover, **Fig. 19.**
7. Remove thrust plate and bolts, **Fig. 19.**
8. Remove camshaft hold-down tool.
9. Remove camshaft by carefully removing it out the back of carrier. **All camshaft journals are same diameter and care must be taken when removing camshaft to avoid damage to bearing surfaces.**
10. If camshaft oil seal requires replacement, proceed as follows:
    a. Pull seal out with a suitable screwdriver.
    b. Install seal using seal installation tool No. J-38619, or equivalent.
11. Reverse procedure to install, noting the following:
    a. When installing carriers, remove oil from camshaft carrier to cylinder head bolt holes, **Fig. 19.**
    b. Use petroleum jelly in lifter bores, along with hoses to keep lifters in place.
    c. Install new camshaft sprocket flat ring to large bore of sprocket.
    d. Wipe camshaft noses with a light coat of oil prior to installing sprockets.
    e. Coat camshaft lobes and journals with GM engine oil supplement (EOS), or equivalent.

INTERMEDIATE SHAFT BELT SPROCKET & OIL SEAL

Removal

1. Verify relationship of intermediate sprocket to front cover.
2. Raise and support vehicle.
3. Remove starter motor and install flywheel holding tool No. J-37096, or equivalent.
4. Lower vehicle.
5. Rotate engine and position to factory alignment marks. Remove sprocket bolt and washer.
6. Mark position of sprocket on nose end of intermediate shaft.
7. Remove secondary timing belt.
8. Reverse center bolt and engage self-tapping screws of sprocket remover tool No. J-38616, or equivalent, into three equally spaced holes on belt sprocket and remove intermediate shaft timing belt sprocket.
9. Remove intermediate shaft belt sprocket oil seal.

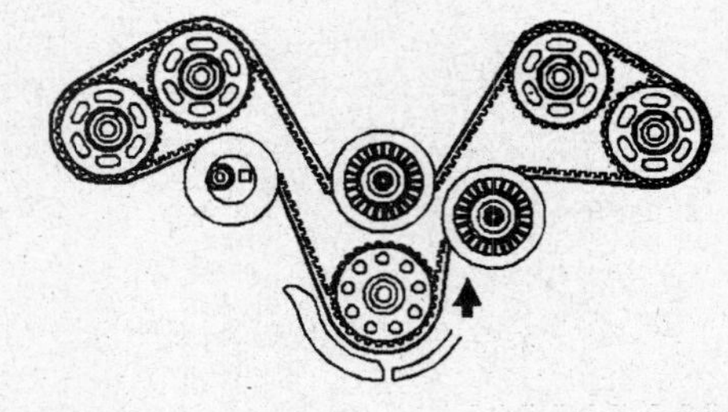

Fig. 17 Timing belt routing

Installation

1. Install oil seal using seal installer tool No. J-38619, or equivalent.
2. Lubricate seal surfaces of intermediate shaft sprocket.
3. Align timing marks and install sprocket into position engaging locating tangs of sprocket into mating sockets of chain sprocket.
4. Verify engagement by measuring from face of belt sprocket to front cover. If measurement is more than 1.65 inches, tangs are not engaged.
5. Install O-ring in position on end of intermediate shaft.
6. Lightly lubricate threads of sprocket bolt and tighten bolt to specifications.
7. Raise and support vehicle. Remove flywheel holding tool and install starter assembly.
8. Lower vehicle and install secondary timing belt and covers.

INTERMEDIATE SHAFT & BEARINGS

1. Remove engine assembly as outlined under "Engine, Replace."
2. Remove oil pump drive assembly as outlined under " Oil Pump Service."
3. Remove camshaft intermediate drive chain as outlined under " Camshaft Intermediate Drive Chain, Replace."
4. Remove intermediate shaft thrust plate and screws.
5. Remove intermediate shaft. **All intermediate shaft journals are the same diameter and care should be taken not to damage bearings or journals during removal.**
6. Remove intermediate shaft bearing using bearing remover/installer tool No. J-33049, or equivalent.
7. Reverse procedure to install, noting the following:
   a. Align oil holes in bearing with oil holes in cylinder block. install oil feed holes at 4 and 7 o'clock for front bearing and 4 o'clock for bearings 2, 3 and 4.

b. Apply oil to intermediate shaft journals prior to installation.
c. Replace O-ring seal after sprocket installation.

INTERMEDIATE SHAFT REAR COVER

1. Remove transaxle assembly as outlined under "Automatic Transmissions/ Transaxles" section.
2. Remove intermediate shaft rear cover bolts, then the cover and gasket.
3. Reverse procedure to install.

PISTON & ROD ASSEMBLY

When installing piston and rod assemblies into cylinder block, ensure arrow on top of piston faces toward the front of the engine, **Fig. 20.**

MAIN & ROD BEARINGS

Connecting rod and main bearing are of the precision insert type. They are available for service use in standard and two undersizes of .016 and .032 inch. Bearing undersize amount is stamped at either end of the bearing, **Fig. 21.**

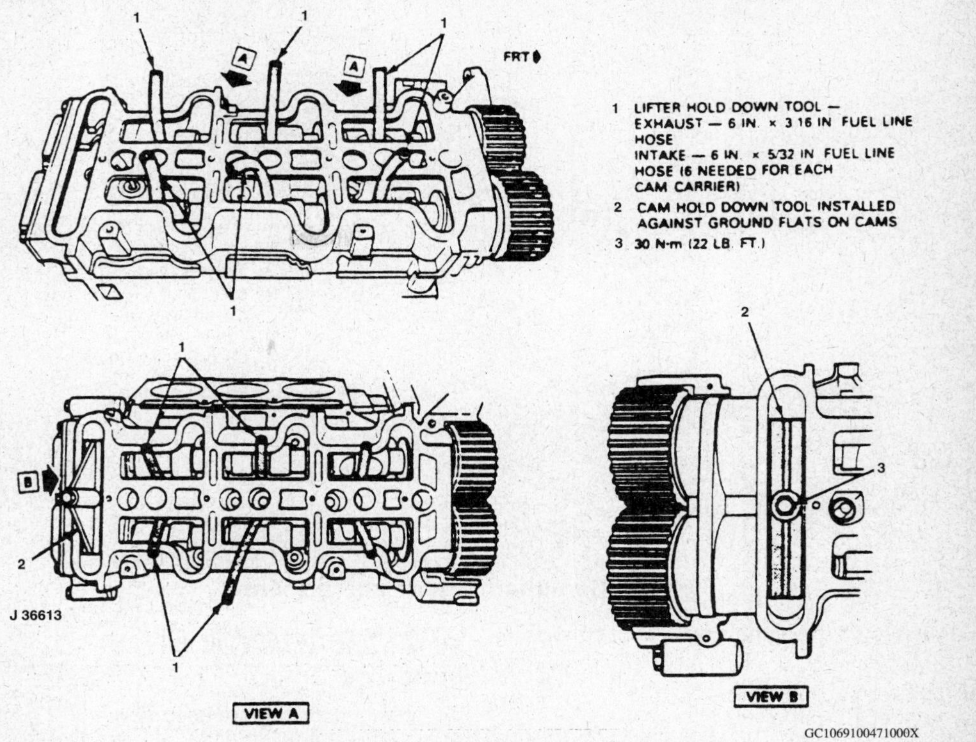

Fig. 18 Lifter & camshaft hold-down tool

CRANKSHAFT REAR OIL SEAL

REPLACE

1. Remove transaxle assembly as outlined under "Automatic Transmissions/ Transaxles" section.
2. Remove flywheel assembly.
3. Remove oil seal using a suitable pry tool as shown in **Fig. 22.**
4. Reverse procedure to install using seal installer tool No. J-34686, or equivalent.

OIL PAN

REPLACE

1. Remove air cleaner assembly.
2. Install engine support fixture tool Nos. J-28467-A, J-28467-90 and J-36462, or equivalents.
3. Raise and support vehicle.
4. Remove right tire and wheel assembly and steering gear heat shield.
5. Remove steering gear bolts then hang steering gear from frame.
6. Separate ball joints from control arms.
7. Remove power steering cooler line clips from frame.
8. Disconnect engine mounts at frame as outlined under " Engine Mount, Replace."
9. Support frame assembly and remove frame bolts then remove frame assembly.
10. Disconnect and remove starter assembly.
11. Remove flywheel cover.
12. Remove oil pan nuts and bolts then the oil pan and gasket.
13. Remove oil baffle nuts. Rotate pick up tube and remove oil baffle.
14. Reverse procedure to install. Tighten oil pan bolts to specifications shown in **Fig. 23.**

OIL PUMP

REPLACE

1. Remove oil pan and baffle as outlined under "Oil Pan & Baffle, Replace."
2. Remove oil pump bolt then the oil pump and driveshaft extension.
3. Install shaft extension on oil pump, engage shaft extension into drive gear.
4. Tighten oil pump bolt to specifications.
5. Install oil pan and baffle.

BELT TENSION DATA

Belt tension is maintained automatically by a spring tensioned idler pulley. No adjustment of serpentine belt is necessary.

If belt slippage is indicated and belt tensioner indicator is within normal operating range, measure belt tension as follows:

1. Run engine for ten minutes, then shut off and measure belt tension between any two pulleys using V-belt tension gauge tool No. J 23600-B, or equivalent.
2. Run engine for 30 seconds and repeat measurement.
3. Repeat preceding step, then average all three belt tension measurements. Average tension should be 35–55 lbs.
4. If belt tension is not as specified, replace serpentine drive belt.

SERPENTINE DRIVE BELT

BELT REPLACEMENT

1. Remove coolant recovery reservoir.
2. Rotate tensioner clockwise using a box end wrench.
3. Remove serpentine belt.
4. Reverse procedure to install, routing belt as shown in **Fig. 24.**

TENSIONER REPLACEMENT

1. Remove serpentine drive belt as outlined in this section.
2. Remove tensioner bolt, then the tensioner, **Fig. 25.**
3. Reverse procedure to install.

COOLING SYSTEM BLEED

1. Open air bleed vents on thermostat housing and heater water inlet pipe.
2. Fill system with water and coolant until level of coolant has reached base of radiator neck.
3. Close bleed vents and add clean water if necessary to bring coolant level to base of radiator neck.

THERMOSTAT

REPLACE

1. Remove air cleaner and duct assembly.
2. Drain engine coolant as a suitable container.

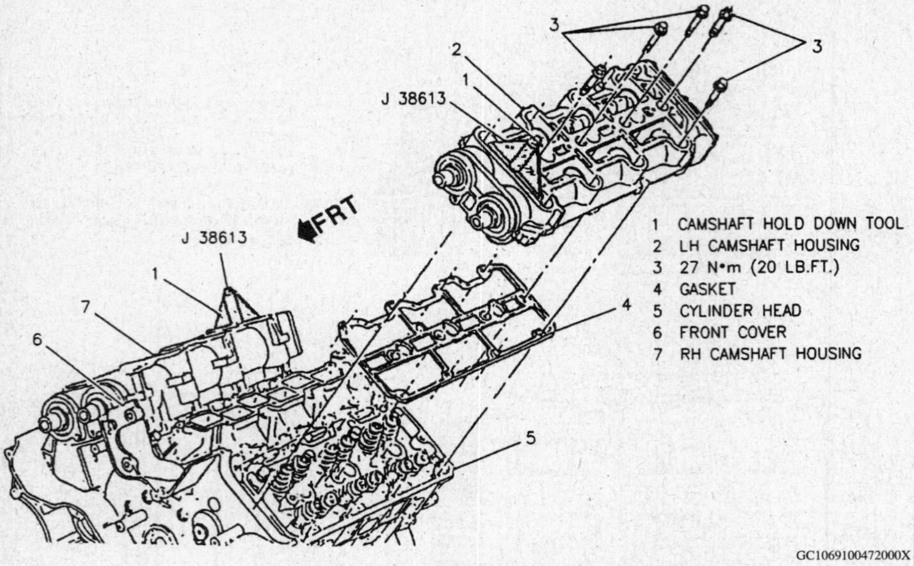

Fig. 19 Camshaft carrier components

3. Remove engine torque strut bolt at engine.

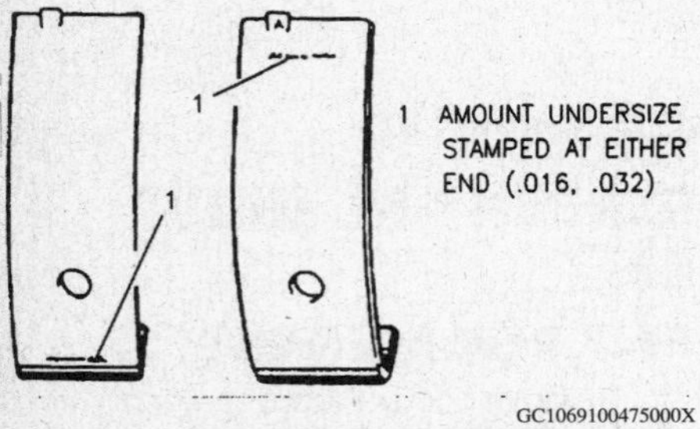

Fig. 21 Bearing marking

4. Disconnect upper radiator hose at thermostat housing.
5. Release fuel pressure as described under "Precautions."
6. Disconnect fuel lines at fuel rail.
7. Remove heater hose bracket at thermostat housing stud.
8. Disconnect heater hose at throttle body.
9. Remove thermostat housing bolts, thermostat housing and thermostat.
10. Reverse procedure to install.

WATER PUMP

REPLACE

1. Remove air cleaner assembly.
2. Drain engine coolant into a suitable container.
3. Remove serpentine drive belt as outlined under "Serpentine Drive Belt."
4. Remove water pump pulley.
5. Remove water pump bolts then the water pump and gasket, **Fig. 26.**
6. Reverse procedure to install.

RADIATOR

REPLACE

1. Remove air cleaner assembly, then drain engine coolant into a suitable container.
2. Remove engine strut upper brace bolts from upper tie bar and rotate strut and brace rearward.
3. Disconnect upper radiator mounting panel bolts and clamps.
4. Disconnect cooling fan electrical connector.
5. Remove cooling fan mounting bolts and fan, then upper radiator bracket.

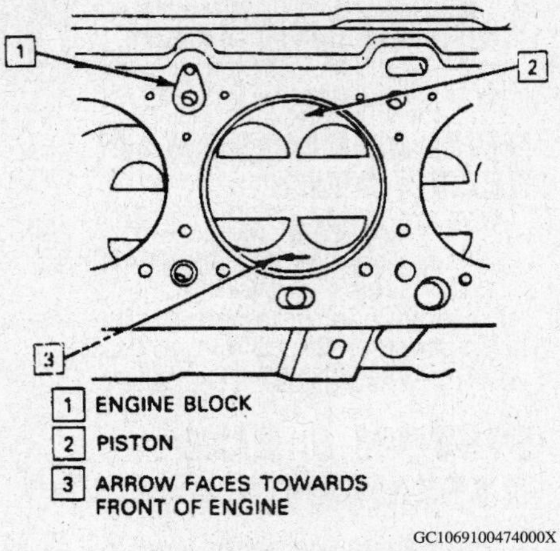

Fig. 20 Piston marking

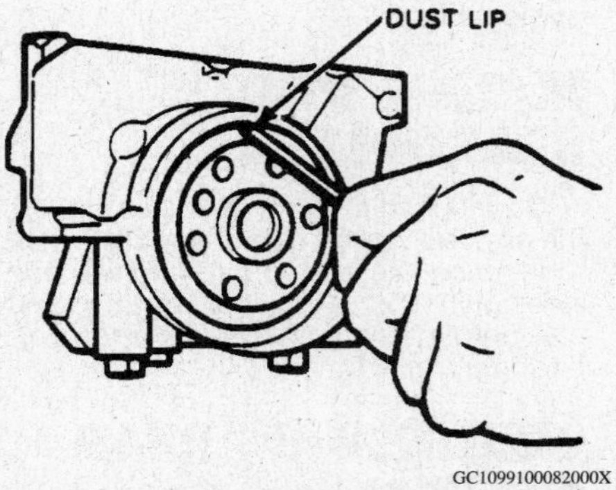

Fig. 22 Rear main seal removal

6. Remove upper and lower radiator hoses at radiator.
7. Disconnect low coolant sensor wiring.
8. Disconnect oil cooler lines, then remove radiator.
9. Reverse procedure to install.

FUEL PUMP

REPLACE

1997

1. Relieve fuel system pressure as outlined under "Precautions."
2. Drain fuel tank, then remove fuel tank assembly.
3. Remove fuel sender assembly.

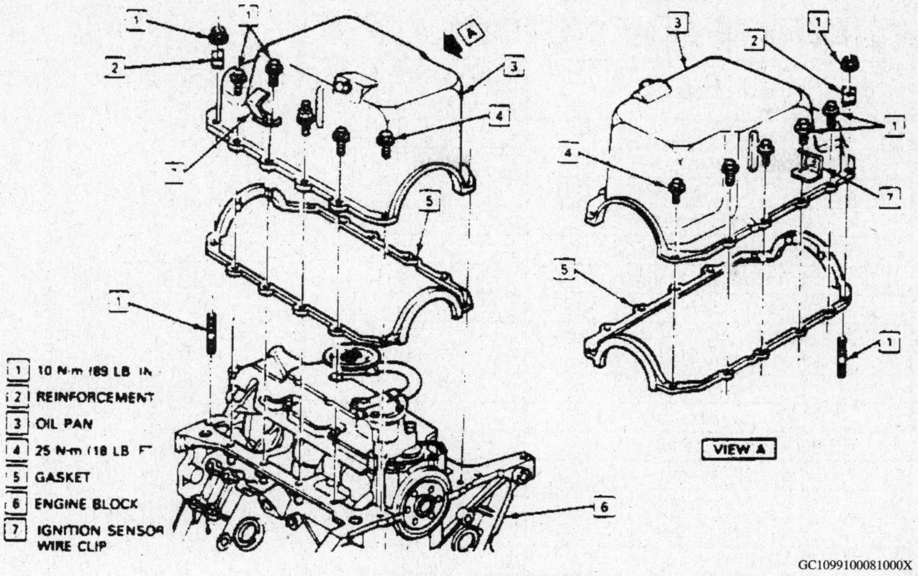

Fig. 23 Oil pan assembly

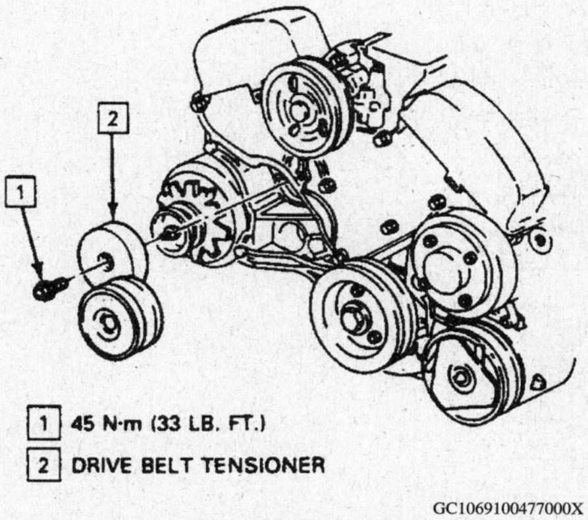

Fig. 25 Serpentine drive belt tensioner

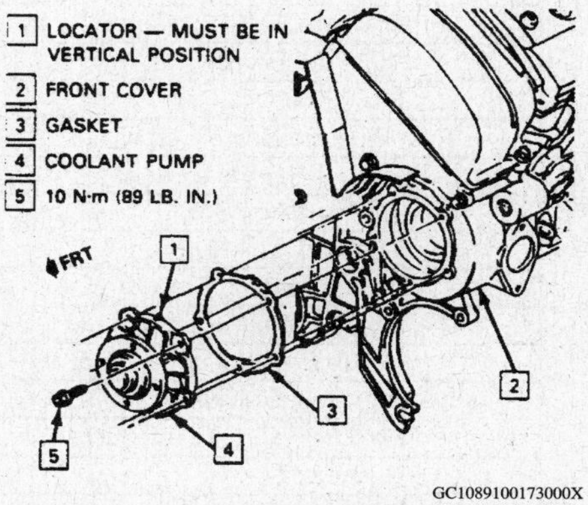

Fig. 26 Water pump assembly

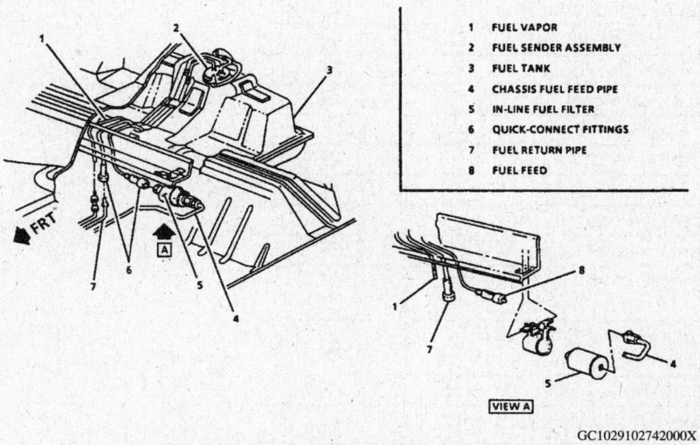

Fig. 27 Fuel filter replacement

4. Reverse procedure to install.

2000

1. Remove fuel pump/sender assembly access cover from luggage compartment.
2. Remove fuel pump/sender assembly attaching bolts.
3. Pull assembly upward and disconnect electrical connector.
4. Remove pump/sender assembly from fuel tank.

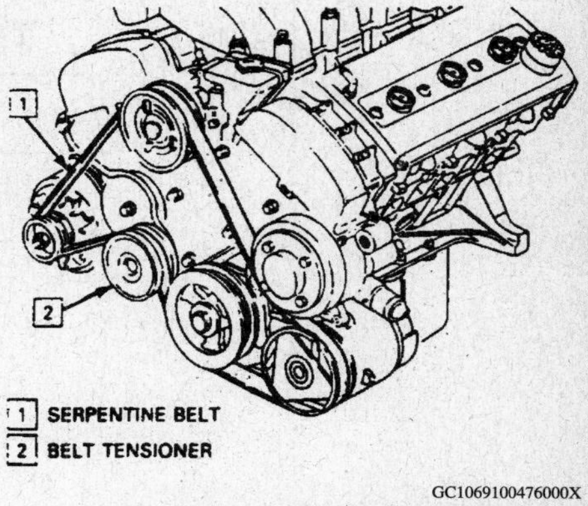

Fig. 24 Serpentine drive belt routing

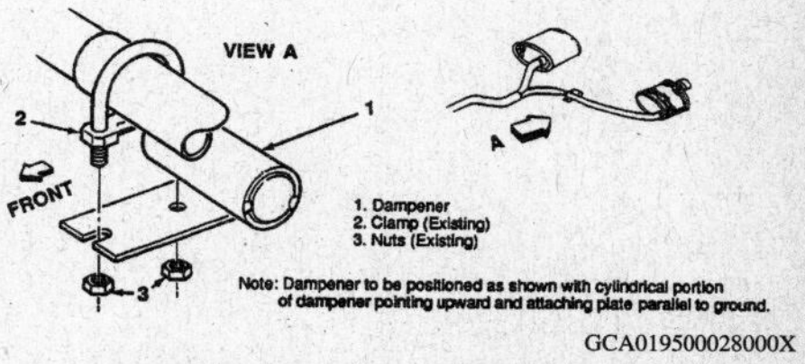

Fig. 28 Exhaust dampener installation

5. Reverse procedure to install.

FUEL FILTER

REPLACE

1. Relieve fuel system pressure as outlined under "Precautions."
2. Raise and support vehicle.
3. Remove bracket attaching screw and filter bracket, **Fig. 27.**
4. Grasp filter and fuel line fitting. Twist quick-connect fitting 1/4 turn in each direction to loosen any dirt within fitting.
5. Using compressed air, blow out dirt from quick-connect fitting.
6. Remove feed pipe nut from fuel filter, then drain any remaining fuel into a suitable container.
7. Remove fuel filter.
8. Reverse procedure to install.

TECHNICAL SERVICE BULLETINS

EXHAUST BOOM & MOAN

On some models an exhaust boom and moan noise may be heard in the passenger compartment. This condition may be caused by exhaust system vibration. To correct this condition, install dampener (part No. 10199232), **Fig. 28. Torque** nuts to 37 ft. lbs.

TIGHTENING SPECIFICATIONS

Year	Component	Torque/Ft. Lbs.
1997	Camshaft Carrier Bolt	20
	Camshaft Carrier Cover Bolt	96①
	Camshaft Carrier Thrust Plate Bolt	96①
	Camshaft Sprocket Bolt	96
	Connecting Rod Cap Nut	39
	Crankshaft Damper Mounting Bolt	79
	Crankshaft Main Cap Bolt	②
	Crankshaft Pulley To Crankshaft Damper Bolt	44
	Cylinder Head Bolt	③
	EGR Tube Assembly Bolt	18
	EGR Valve Assembly Bolt	18
	Exhaust Crossover Nut	84①
	Exhaust Heat Shield Nut	10
	Exhaust Mounting Nut	10
	Exhaust Stud	13
	Flywheel To Engine Bolt	60
	Front Cover Bolts (Large)	35
	Front Cover Bolts (Small)	20
	Fuel Filter	22
	Fuel Pipe Clip Bolt	60①
	Fuel Pipe Retaining Screw	21①
	Fuel Rail Bolt	96①
	Ignition Coil Bolt	18
	Ignition Coil Nut	18
	Intake Manifold Bolt	18
	Intake Plenum Bolt	18
	Intake Plenum Nut	96①
	Intermediate Shaft Belt Sprocket Bolt	96①
	Intermediate Shaft Thrust Plate Screw	96①
	Knock Sensor	15
	Oil Cooler Connector	30
	Oil Cooler Fitting	18
	Oil Distribution Cover Bolt	20
	Oil Level Indicator Bolt	96①
	Oil Pan Baffle Nut	18
	Oil Pan Bolt	④
	Oil Pan Drain Plug	18
	Oil Pan Nut	96①
	Oil Pump Drive Bolt	27
	Oil Pump To Rear Main Bolt	40
	Power Steering Pump To Bracket Bolt	25
	Rear Camshaft Cover Bolt	96①
	Rear Engine Mounting Brace To Bracket Bolt	60
	Rear Engine Mounting Brace To Bracket Nut	35
	Secondary Timing Belt Idler Bolt	37
	Secondary Timing Belt Tensioner Bracket Bolt	37
	Secondary Timing Belt Tensioner Pulley Bolt	37
	Secondary Timing Belt Tensioner Side Plate Bolt	96
	Serpentine Drive Belt Tensioner Bolt	37
	Spark Plug	15

Continued

TIGHTENING SPECIFICATIONS—Continued

Year	Component	Torque/Ft. Lbs.
1997	Starter Mounting Bolt	32
	Tensioner Mounting Bolt	18
	Timing Belt Cover Bolt	96①
	Timing Chain Tensioner Bolt	20
	Torque Strut and Engine Lift Bracket Bolt	52
	Trace Bracket To Rear Engine Mounting Bracket Bolt	35
	Upper Radiator Mounting Panel Bolt	96①
	Water Bypass Nut	18
	Water Outlet Bolt	20
	Water Pump Bolt	96①
2000	Alternator Brace Bracket	37
	Balance Shaft Gear Bolt	16⑤
	Balance Shaft Retainer Bolt	22
	Camshaft Position Sensor Bolt	89①
	Camshaft Sprocket Bolt	74⑥
	Camshaft Thrust Plate Bolt	11
	Connecting Rod Cap Bolt	20⑦
	Crankshaft Balancer Bolt	111⑧
	Crankshaft Main Bearing Cap Bolt	30⑨
	Crankshaft Main Bearing Cap Bolt (Side)	11⑩
	Crankshaft Position Sensor Stud	22
	Crankshaft Rear Oil Seal Housing	11⑩
	Cylinder Head Bolts	③
	Drive Belt Tensioner Bracket Bolt	37
	EGR Valve Adapter Bolt	37
	EGR Valve Nut	21
	Engine Block Coolant Drain Plug	13
	Engine Flywheel Bolt	11⑩
	Engine Front Cover	15⑪
	Engine Lift Bracket	22
	Engine Mount Bracket	75
	Engine Mount Nut	37
	Engine Mount Strut Bolt/Nut	35
	Engine Oil Gallery Plug	22
	Engine Oil Pressure Sensor	12
	Exhaust Crossover Heat Shield	15
	Exhaust Crossover	13
	Exhaust Manifold	22
	Exhaust Manifold Heat Shield	15
	Exhaust Manifold Pipe Stud	53①
	Fuel Injector Rail Assembly Nut	89①
	Fuel Injector Rail Stud	18
	Heated Oxygen Sensor	31
	Ignition Control Module Bracket Stud	22
	Ignition Control Module Assembly Bolt	37
	Lower Intake Manifold	11
	MAP Sensor Bolt	27①
	MAP Sensor Bracket Bolt	22
	Oil Cooler Adapter Connector	37
	Oil Filter Adapter Bolt	11⑩
	Oil Level Indicator Tube Nut	14
	Oil Level Sensor	15

Continued

TIGHTENING SPECIFICATIONS—Continued

Year	Component	Torque/Ft. Lbs.
2000	Oil Pan	10
	Oil Pan Drain Plug	22
	Oil Pump Cover	98①
	Power Brake Booster Heat Shield Nut	15
	Side Main Cap Bolt	11⑩
	Starter Motor Heat Shield Bolt	22
	Throttle Body Bolt/Nut	89①
	Timing Chain Dampener Bolt	18
	Valve Lifter Guide Retainer	22
	Valve Rocker Arm Bolt	11⑥
	Valve Rocker Arm Cover	89①
	Water Outlet Bolt	20
	Water Pump	11⑫
	Water Pump Pulley	10

① — Inch lbs.
② — Tighten an additional 75.°
③ — Refer to "Cylinder Head, Replace."
④ — Except two rear bolts, 8 ft. lbs.; two rear bolts, 18 ft. lbs.
⑤ — Tighten an additional 70.°
⑥ — Tightens an additional 90.°
⑦ — Tighten an additional 50.°
⑧ — Tighten an additional 76.°
⑨ — Tighten an additional 110.°
⑩ — Tighten an additional 45.°
⑪ — Tighten an additional 40.°
⑫ — Tighten an additional 80.°

3.5L Engine

NOTE: On Air Bag Equipped Models, Refer To " Air Bag System Precautions" Located In The Front Of This Manual For System Disarming & Arming Procedures.

NOTE: Refer To "Computer Relearn Procedures " Located In The Front Of This Manual For Computer Relearn Procedures.

INDEX

PRECAUTIONS

AIR BAG SYSTEMS

Refer to "Air Bag System Precautions" in the front of this manual for system disarming and arming procedures.

BATTERY GROUND CABLE

Prior to service, disconnect battery ground cable and isolate as required.

FUEL SYSTEM PRESSURE RELIEF

To reduce the risk of fire and personal injury, it is necessary to relieve the fuel system pressure before servicing fuel system components.

1. Loosen fuel tank filler cap to relieve tank pressure.
2. Connect fuel pressure gauge tool No. J-34730-1, or equivalent, to fuel pressure valve. Wrap a shop towel around fitting while connection gauge to avoid spillage.
3. Install bleed hose into an approved container and open valve to bleed system pressure.

IDLE LEARN PROCEDURE

If vehicle power is interrupted, the programmed position of the Idle Air Control (IAC) valve pintle is lost. The following procedures must be performed to update the ECM memory with the correct IAC valve pintle position for the vehicle and provide a stable idle speed.

1. Restore vehicle power.
2. Connect TECH I scan tool to ALDL connector located under lefthand side of dash panel.
3. Select "IAC System."
4. Select "Idle Learn" in " Misc. Test" mode.
5. Proceed as directed.

COMPRESSION PRESSURE

When checking compression, lowest cylinder must be within 70 percent of the highest cylinder with a minimum pressure of 140 psi. Perform compression test with engine at normal operating temperature, spark plugs removed and throttle wide open.

ENGINE MOUNT

REPLACE

ENGINE MOUNT

1. Remove engine mount strut as outlined under "Engine Mount, Replace."
2. Install engine support fixture No. J28467–B using adapter set Nos. J36462–A and J28467–90A, or equivalents.
3. Raise and support vehicle, then remove lower engine mount nuts.
4. Lower vehicle, then raise engine to gain access to engine mount.
5. Raise and support vehicle, then remove upper engine mount nuts.
6. Remove engine mount from bracket.
7. Reverse procedure to install, tightening to specifications.

ENGINE MOUNT STRUT & BRACKETS

1. Remove bolt and nut from engine mount strut at engine bracket.
2. Remove bolt and nut from engine mount strut at radiator support bracket.
3. Remove engine mount strut, then the bracket from radiator support.
4. Reverse procedure to install.

ENGINE

REPLACE

The throttle cable must be replaced when removing or replacing the engine.

1. Remove fuel injector sight shield and throttle body air inlet duct.
2. Remove engine mount strut as outlined under "Engine Mount, Replace."
3. Relieve fuel pressure as outlined under "Precautions, " then disconnect fuel lines from fuel rail and position aside.
4. Disconnect fuel vapor line, then remove throttle and cruise control cables with mounting brackets from throttle body.
5. Disconnect automatic range selector from park/neutral position switch and vacuum booster hose from engine.
6. Disconnect A/C vacuum hose from engine, then the wiring harness connectors from engine and transmissions.
7. Drain coolant into suitable container, then disconnect radiator inlet hose from engine.
8. Disconnect transaxle cooler lines from radiator, surge tank inlet hose and heater hoses from engine.
9. Raise and support vehicle, then drain engine oil.
10. Remove lower radiator air deflector, then disconnect AIR pipe from AIR inlet valve.
11. Remove battery cables from retainers, then disconnect radiator outlet hose from engine.
12. Remove A/C compressor from engine and secure to frame of vehicle.
13. Remove torque converter cover, then disconnect starter motor electrical connectors and remove starter motor.
14. Reference mark flywheel to torque converter location, then remove flywheel to torque converter attaching bolts.
15. Remove catalytic converter pipe from rear exhaust manifold, then the lower engine to transaxle bolts.
16. Remove front wheel and tire assemblies and the inner fender splash shield.
17. Disconnect fog lamp electrical connectors, then remove wheel speed sensor harness conduits from retainers in lower control arms.
18. Remove tie rod ends and lower ball joints from steering knuckles.
19. Disconnect drive axles from transaxle and secure to vehicle.
20. Remove pinch bolt at intermediate shaft, then disconnect intermediate shaft from steering gear. **This step must be performed to avoid possible damage to the steering gear and intermediate shaft.**
21. Place universal engine support table No. J39580, or equivalent, under engine/transaxle/frame, then lower vehicle to universal engine support table to support engine/transaxle/frame.
22. Suitably secure vehicle to hoist, then remove frame to body bolts.
23. Raise and support vehicle, then remove universal engine support table with engine/transaxle/frame from under vehicle.
24. Remove engine mount bracket to engine bolts, then the transaxle brace.
25. Remove serpentine drive belt and power steering pump from engine and position aside.
26. Remove alternator and upper engine to transaxle bolts.
27. Remove engine from transaxle/frame.
28. Reverse procedure to install. **Ensure intermediate shaft is fully seated prior to installing pinch bolt.**

INTAKE MANIFOLD

REPLACE

1. Disconnect throttle body air inlet duct, then partially drain coolant into suitable container.
2. Remove fuel injector sight shield, then disconnect throttle and cruise control cables from throttle body.
3. Relieve fuel pressure as outlined under Precautions, then disconnect fuel lines and coolant hoses from throttle body.
4. Disconnect fuel vapor line from EVAP canister purge solenoid.
5. Disconnect vacuum hose from brake booster and A/C vacuum hose from intake manifold.
6. Disconnect surge tank inlet pipe retainer from fuel rail.
7. Disconnect electrical connectors from the following:
   a. Fuel injectors.
   b. Throttle position sensor.
   c. IAC valve.
   d. EVAP canister purge solenoid.
   e. MAP sensor.
8. Remove engine wiring harness and channel from valve cover and position aside.
9. Disconnect fuel pressure regulator vacuum line from regulator and throttle body.
10. Remove PCV valve and feed tubes from valve cover and intake manifold.
11. Remove EGR valve outlet pipe and water crossover from intake manifold.
12. Disconnect fuel rail snap lock retainers by pushing toward valve cover and lifting.
13. Remove fuel rail and injectors as an assembly.
14. Remove intake manifold bolts, then the intake manifold.
15. Reverse procedure to install. Remove

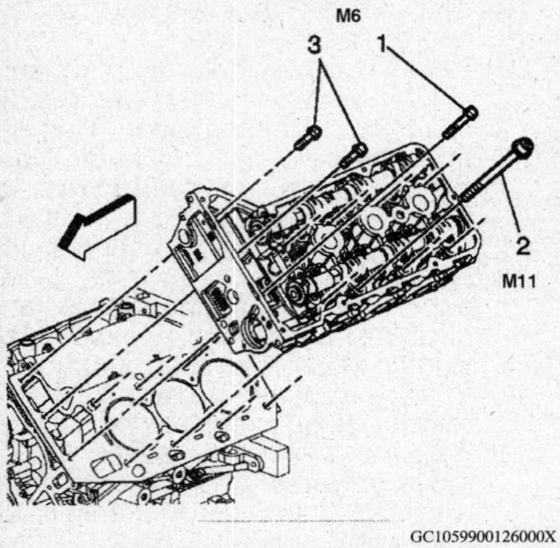

Fig. 1 Cylinder head bolt removal

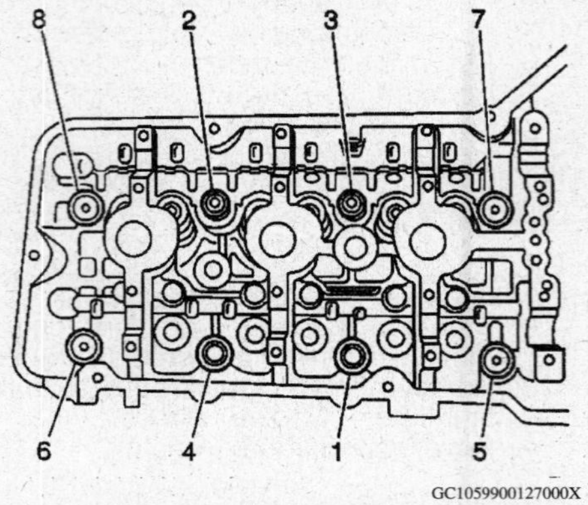

Fig. 2 Cylinder head tightening sequence

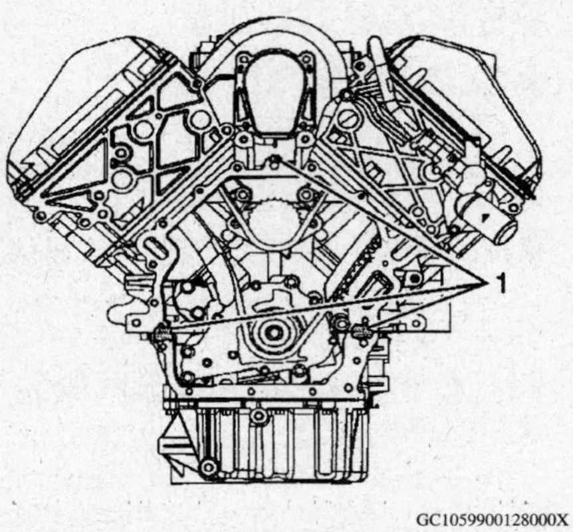

Fig. 3 RTV application points

all sensors, brackets and throttle body from intake manifold and transfer to new one.

EXHAUST MANIFOLD

REPLACE

LEFT

1. Remove engine as outlined under "Engine, Replace."
2. Remove left exhaust manifold crossover pipe from right exhaust manifold.
3. Disconnect EGR valve pipe from exhaust crossover pipe.
4. Remove left exhaust manifold retaining bolts, then the manifold.
5. Remove O2 sensor and replace as required.
6. Replace exhaust manifold studs as required.
7. reverse procedure to install.

RIGHT

1. Remove fuel injector sight shield, then the engine mount strut and bracket.
2. Drain coolant into suitable container, then remove engine cooling fans.
3. Remove radiator inlet and outlet hoses.
4. Remove transaxle cooler lines from radiator.
5. Remove radiator from vehicle.
6. Remove alternator as outlined under "Alternator, Replace."
7. Remove exhaust manifold heat shield and oil level indicator tube.
8. Disconnect vacuum tube from AIR control valve.
9. Disconnect feed pipe nut from exhaust manifold.
10. Remove AIR control from engine mount strut bracket.
11. Loosen exhaust manifold retaining bolts.
12. Remove exhaust manifold crossover pipe flange retaining studs.
13. Remove exhaust manifold bolts, then the manifold.
14. Reverse procedure to install.

CYLINDER HEAD

REPLACE

1. Remove intake manifold as outlined under "Intake Manifold, Replace."
2. Remove water outlet housing and engine mount strut bracket from right cylinder head.
3. Remove water crossover pipe.
4. Remove exhaust manifold as outlined under " Exhaust Manifold, Replace."
5. Remove camshaft covers, then install camshaft holding fixture No. J42038, or equivalent.
6. Remove primary camshaft drive chain, then the camshafts.
7. Remove rocker arms and lifters.
8. Remove coolant temperature sensor from left cylinder head.
9. Remove and discard M6 and M11 bolts, **Fig. 1. Do not reuse the cylinder head bolts.**
10. Remove cylinder head and ensure no dowel pins are stuck in the cylinder head.
11. Reverse procedure to install, noting the following:
    a. Ensure cylinder head locating pins are secured in cylinder block, then install cylinder head and gasket.
    b. Install new M6 and M11 bolts as shown, **Fig. 1.**
    c. Using sequence shown in **Fig. 2,** tighten M11 bolts in four steps, first step **torque** to 22 ft. lbs., second step an additional 60°, third step an additional 60°, fourth step an additional 60°.
    d. **Torque** long M6 bolt to 22 ft. lbs.
    e. **Torque** short M6 bolts to 108 inch lbs.

VALVE COVER

REPLACE

LEFT

1. Remove fuel injector sight shield and bracket.
2. Disconnect PCV feed tube from left valve cover.
3. Disconnect Inlet hose from coolant over flow tank.
4. Remove coolant over flow tank retaining nuts, then position tank aside.
5. Release clips from power steering lines, then position lines aside.
6. Remove engine wiring harness channel bolt from left valve cover, then position harness aside.
7. Remove engine wiring harness from retainers at left rear camshaft cover.
8. Disconnect O2 sensor, then remove left coil assembly from valve cover.
9. Remove left valve cover retaining bolts, then lift evenly off of cylinder head.
10. Reverse procedure to install.

RIGHT

1. Remove fuel injector sight shield.
2. Remove oil tube bolt, then adjust tube for access.
3. Disconnect PCV valve and feed tube from right valve cover.
4. Remove coil assembly from left valve cover.
5. Remove engine harness channel bolt from left valve cover, then position harness aside.
6. Remove engine harness from retainers on left valve cover and position aside.
7. Remove left valve cover retaining bolts, then lift cover off evenly.
8. Reverse procedure to install.

VALVE ARRANGEMENT

On lefthand side of engine, exhaust valves are on the left, intake valves on the right. On righthand side of engine, intake valves are on the left, exhaust valves on the right.

CAMSHAFT LOBE LIFT SPECIFICATIONS

Exhaust ....394 inch
Intake ....413 inch

VALVE ADJUSTMENT

There is no valve adjustment for these engines.

FRONT COVER

REPLACE

1. Drain coolant into suitable container, then remove right diagonal brace.
2. Remove battery and battery tray.

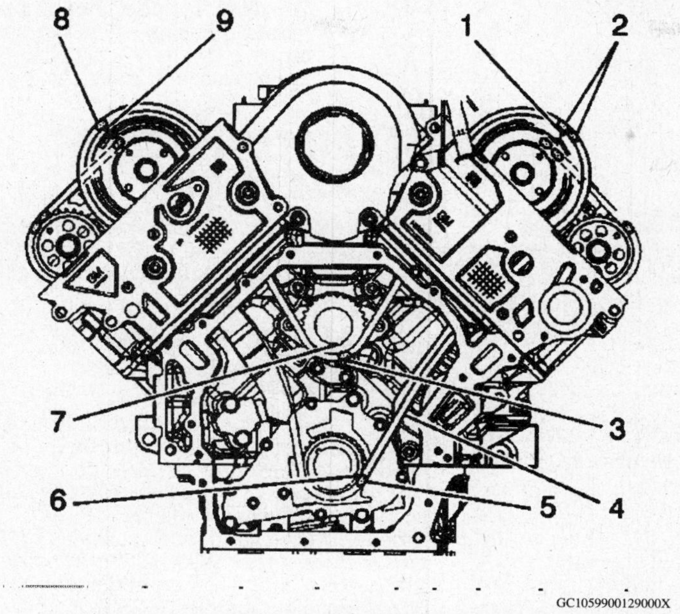

Fig. 4 Primary timing chain alignment

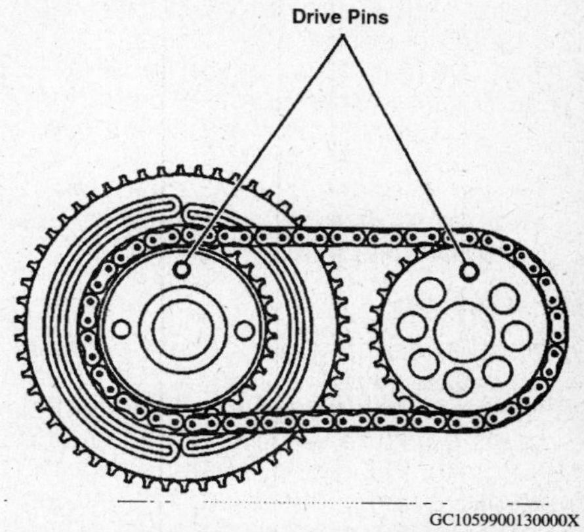

Fig. 5 Secondary sprocket drive pin alignment

3. Remove engine coolant and washer solvent reservoirs.
4. Reposition underhood accessory wiring junction block for access, then remove serpentine drive belt.
5. Remove power steering pump pulley and serpentine drive belt idler pulley.
6. Remove water pump pulley retaining bolts, then the pulley.
7. Remove water pump and housing as an assembly.
8. Support engine cradle, then remove right side cradle bolts.
9. Lower engine cradle, then remove crankshaft balancer.
10. Remove coolant drain plug from front cover and drain coolant from engine block into suitable container.
11. Remove ten perimeter bolts from front cover.
12. Remove front cover and gasket from engine. **Use plastic scraper when removing remaining gasket material to avoid damage to sealing surfaces.**
13. Reverse procedure to install. Apply short beads of RTV to engine block in locations shown, **Fig. 3.**

FRONT COVER SEAL

REPLACE

1. Remove crankshaft balancer.
2. Carefully pry out seal using small pry bar or flat screwdriver.
3. Install new seal using installer No. J42041, or equivalent.
4. The seal should not be flush with front cover, rather it should protrude .039–.078 inch.
5. Install crankshaft balancer.

TIMING CHAIN

REPLACE

PRIMARY

REMOVAL

1. Remove valve covers as outlined under "Valve Cover, Replace."
2. Install camshaft holding fixture No. J42038, or equivalent.
3. Remove front cover as outlined under "Front Cover, Replace."
4. Remove front engine lift bracket and camshaft position sensor.
5. Remove left cylinder exhaust camshaft sprocket bolt.
6. Remove four chain guide access plugs in cylinder heads.
7. Loosen both primary tensioner bolts, then remove lower tensioner bolt and allow tensioner to swing downward and expand.
8. Remove upper tensioner bolt, then the tensioner.
9. Remove primary timing chain tensioner shoe bolt, then the tensioner shoe by pushing the guide downward slightly and pulling up through cylinder head.
10. Remove primary timing chain from left camshaft sprocket and allow chain to fall into oil pump area of cylinder block.
11. Remove primary timing chain.

INSTALLATION

1. Install primary timing chain.
2. Set base engine timing by rotating crankshaft until cylinder No. 1 is at top dead center as indicated by crankshaft sprocket timing mark (6) in the position shown, **Fig. 4.**
3. Rotate balance shaft until timing mark (7) is in the position shown, **Fig. 4.**
4. Ensure painted marks on timing chain face toward front of engine.
5. Center timing mark on right camshaft sprocket between pair of painted marks on primary timing chain, then wrap chain around sprocket.
6. Fabricate hook tool out of wire, then pull primary timing chain up through left cylinder head to camshaft sprocket.
7. While pulling primary timing chain up, align painted marks with timing marks on balance shaft sprocket and crankshaft sprocket, **Fig. 4.**
8. Wrap primary timing chain around left camshaft sprocket and align painted link with timing mark on sprocket, **Fig. 4.**
9. Install primary timing chain tensioner shoe and retaining bolt through access hole in cylinder head. Ensure all timing marks on sprockets are aligned with painted marks on timing chain.
10. Collapse primary timing chain tensioner as follows:
    a. Rotate ratchet release lever counterclockwise and hold.
    b. Collapse tensioner shoe and hold.
    c. Release ratchet lever and slowly release pressure on shoe.
    d. As ratchet lever moves to first click, hold shoe inward and insert pin through hole in release lever.
    e. The locked ratchet mechanism should hold shoe in collapsed position.
11. Install primary timing chain tensioner.
12. Ensure all timing marks are aligned, then release pin holding tensioner to tighten any slack in primary timing chain.
13. Install four chain guide plugs and front engine lift bracket.
14. Install camshaft position sensor, then remove camshaft holding fixture tool No. J42038.
15. Install valve covers and front cover.

SECONDARY

LEFT

Removal

1. Remove left valve cover as outlined under "Valve Cover, Replace."

2. Install camshaft holding fixture No. J42038, or equivalent.
3. Remove camshaft position sensor.
4. Remove camshaft sprocket bolts, then install sprocket holding fixture No. J42042, or equivalent.
5. Evenly slide secondary drive chain and camshaft sprockets off camshafts on to sprocket holding fixture.

Installation

1. Install secondary timing chain, aligning drive pins as shown, **Fig. 5.**
2. Slide camshaft sprockets off sprocket holding fixture and onto camshafts, then align drive pins in camshafts.
3. Remove sprocket holding fixture, then install intake camshaft sprocket retaining bolts.
4. Remove camshaft holding fixture, then install camshaft position sensor.
5. Install valve cover.

RIGHT

Removal

1. Partially drain coolant into suitable container, then remove thermostat housing.
2. Remove right valve cover as outlined under "Valve Cover, Replace."
3. Install camshaft holding fixture tool No. J42038, or equivalent onto right camshafts.
4. Remove camshaft sprocket bolts, then install sprocket holding fixture No. J42042, or equivalent.
5. Evenly slide secondary drive chain and sprockets onto sprocket holding fixture.

Installation

1. Install secondary timing chain, aligning drive pins as shown, **Fig. 5.**
2. Slide camshaft sprockets off sprocket holding fixture and onto camshafts, then align drive pins in camshafts.
3. Remove sprocket holding fixture, then install intake camshaft sprocket retaining bolts.
4. Remove camshaft holding fixture, then install valve cover.
5. Install thermostat housing. Refill coolant system.

CAMSHAFT

REPLACE

REMOVAL

1. Remove valve cover as outlined under "Valve Cover, Replace."
2. **On right cylinder head,** partially drain coolant into suitable container, then remove thermostat housing.
3. **On left cylinder head,** remove camshaft position sensor.
4. **On all models,** remove camshaft sprockets as outlined under "Timing Chain, Replace."
5. Remove camshaft bearing caps. Identification markings and positions are as follows:
   a. I indicates intake camshaft. E indicates exhaust camshaft.

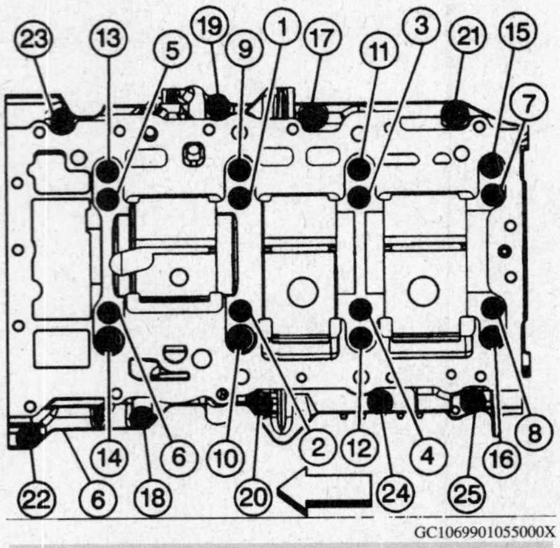

Fig. 6 Lower crankcase bolt tightening sequence

   b. Number indicates journal position from front of engine.
   c. Raised feature goes toward outboard side of engine.
   d. The cap closest to front of engine is the thrust cap and cannot be installed in any other position.
6. Remove camshafts.

INSTALLATION

1. Apply liberal amount of clean engine oil to rocker arms, then position on lifter and valve tip.
2. Camshafts for right and left cylinder heads are different lengths and identified as follows:
   a. Right cylinder head camshafts are longer than left cylinder head camshafts.
   b. Intake camshaft identification rings are between the first and second sets of lobes.
   c. Exhaust camshaft identification rings are between the second and third sets of lobes.
3. Apply liberal amount of clean engine oil to camshaft journals and camshaft carriers, then install camshafts.
4. Place camshafts in position with notch for camshaft sprocket drive pins at top of rotation.
5. Install camshaft bearing thrust caps in first journal of each camshaft. Thrust caps are wider and have machined undercuts not present on other caps.
6. Tighten bearing caps to specifications.
7. Using hex cast into camshaft, rotate camshaft so rear flat on camshaft is facing cylinder head.
8. Install camshaft holding fixture tool No. J42038, or equivalent.
9. Compress secondary timing chain tensioner and lock into position by inserting wire pin into access hole on side of tensioner.
10. Slowly release pressure on tensioner shoes.
11. Install camshaft sprockets as outlined under "Timing chain, Replace."
12. Remove wire pin from tensioner and allow tensioner shoes to expand.
13. **On left cylinder head,** install camshaft position sensor.
14. **On right cylinder head,** install thermostat housing, then fill coolant system.
15. **On all models,** install valve covers.

PISTON & ROD ASSEMBLY

When installing piston and rod assemblies into cylinder block, ensure arrow on top of piston faces toward front of engine.

MAIN & ROD BEARINGS

Engine bearings are of the precision insert type. Undersized bearings are not available. Crankshaft or connecting rod replacement is required if bearing clearances exceed specifications.

Using sequence shown in **Fig. 6, torque** lower crankcase bolts numbered 1–16 to 15 ft. lbs., then an additional 70°. **Torque** bolts numbered 17–25 to 22 ft. lbs.

CRANKSHAFT SEAL

REPLACE

FRONT

Refer to "Front Cover Seal, Replace" in this section.

REAR

Removal

1. Remove transaxle as outlined under "Automatic Transmission/Transaxle. "
2. Install crankshaft rear oil seal remover tool No. J42841, or equivalent.
3. Using variable speed drill with socket adapter, install eight 1 inch self tapping screws into seal using guide holes in remover tool.
4. Tighten center screw on removal tool to pull seal off end of crankshaft.

Installation

1. Place small amount of gasket maker PN 1052942, or equivalent, at crankcase split line across end of upper/lower crankcase seal.
2. Coat outer diameter of cylinder block rear crankshaft seal area with clean engine oil.
3. Coat outer rubber surface of rear crankshaft seal with clean engine oil. **Do not put any oil on green coating of seal. This coating is a sealant that cannot be contaminated.**
4. Loosen center bolt of seal installer No. J42842, or equivalent.
5. Thread three mounting bolts of seal installer into crankshaft flange and tighten until seal installer is firmly mounted on crankshaft.
6. Install seal by tightening center bolt of seal installer until installer bottoms against crankcase.
7. Loosen center bolt, then remove installer tool.

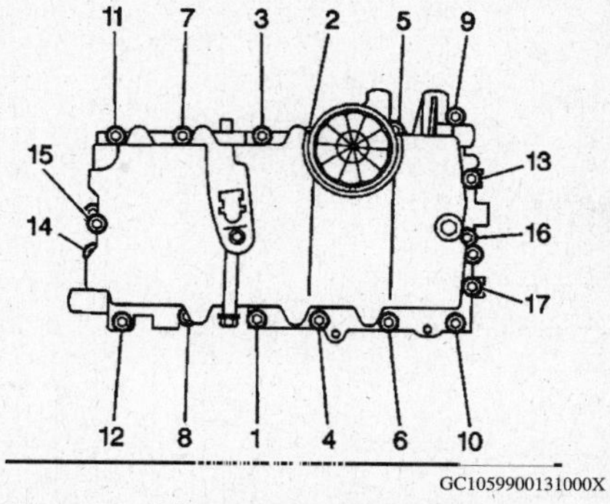

Fig. 7 Oil pan bolt tightening sequence

8. Inspect seal to ensure installation depth is equal around the seal circumference.
9. Install transaxle as outlined in "Automatic Transmission/Transaxle " section.

OIL PAN

REPLACE

1. Raise and support vehicle, then drain engine oil.
2. Remove oil filter cap, then discard oil filter element.
3. Disconnect oil level sensor electrical connector. then remove transaxle brace.
4. Remove oil pan retaining bolts, then the oil pan.
5. Transfer oil level switch to new oil pan as required.
6. Reverse procedure to install, noting the following:
   a. Ensure rear edge of oil pan is flush with rear of cylinder block face.
   b. Press forward part of oil pan against transaxle brace when tightening.
   c. Tighten oil pan retaining bolts to specifications using sequence shown, **Fig. 7.**

OIL PUMP

REPLACE

1. Remove front cover as outlined under "Front Cover, Replace."
2. Remove valve covers as outlined under "Valve Cover, Replace."
3. Install camshaft holding fixture tool No. J42038, or equivalent.
4. Remove camshaft drive chain tensioner.
5. Remove primary timing chain from drive sprocket.
6. Remove four large oil pump housing bolts, then slide pump housing with drive sprocket off of crankshaft.
7. Reverse procedure to install, noting the following:
   a. Align crankshaft sprocket splines with oil pump gerotor when installing drive sprocket into oil pump.
   b. Ensure crankshaft sprocket is aligned with drive pin in crankshaft.
   c. Crankshaft sprocket should protrude from oil pump and face of sprocket should be behind machined step in crankshaft.

OIL PUMP SERVICE

The internal components of the oil pump are not serviceable. The oil pump is replaced as an assembly only.

BELT TENSION DATA

Belt tension is maintained automatically by a spring tensioned idler pulley. Adjustment of serpentine belt is not necessary.

If belt slippage is indicated and belt tensioner indicator is within normal operating range, measure belt tension as follows:

1. Run engine for ten minutes, then shut off and measure belt tension between any two pulleys using V-belt tension gauge tool No. J 23600-B, or equivalent.
2. Run engine for 30 seconds and repeat measurement.
3. Repeat preceding step, then average all three belt tension measurements. Average tension should be 30–50 lbs.
4. If belt tension is not as specified, replace serpentine drive belt.

SERPENTINE DRIVE BELT

REPLACEMENT

1. Lift or rotate tensioner using a ½ inch breaker bar.
2. Remove serpentine belt.
3. Reverse procedure to install, routing drive belt as shown in **Fig. 8.**

ADJUSTMENT

There is no provision for serpentine belt adjustment. Refer to " Belt Tension Data" for belt tension measurement procedures and to determine whether belt requires replacement.

COOLING SYSTEM BLEED

1. Open radiator bleed valve.
2. Fill cooling system until coolant starts to come out of bleed valve.
3. Close bleed valve, then slowly add coolant until level reaches FULL COLD mark.
4. Run engine to operating temperature while adding coolant to FULL mark. Shut engine off and wait 2 minutes.
5. Recheck level and add coolant as required to restore level to FULL COLD mark.
6. Inspect coolant level after engine completes three thermal cycles and add coolant as required.

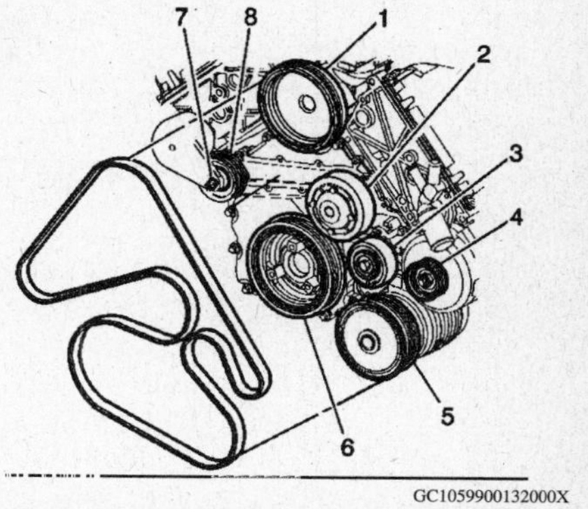

Fig. 8 Serpentine belt routing

THERMOSTAT

REPLACE

1. Partially drain coolant into suitable container, then remove hoses from water outlet housing.
2. Remove water housing outlet bolts, then the housing.
3. Replace thermostat and housing as an assembly.
4. Reverse procedure to install.

WATER PUMP

REPLACE

1. Partially drain coolant into suitable container, then loosen water pump pulley bolts.
2. Remove drive belt, idler pulley bolt and idler pulley.
3. Remove water pump pulley bolts and pulley.
4. Remove water pump bolts, then the pump.
5. Reverse procedure to install.

RADIATOR, REPLACE

1. Drain coolant into suitable container, then remove engine mount strut.
2. Remove engine mount strut bracket from upper radiator support, then disconnect cooling fan electrical connector.
3. Disconnect hoses from radiator, then remove cooling fan shroud, motors and fans from radiator.
4. Disconnect transaxle cooler lines from radiator, then remove radiator mounting brackets.
5. Remove radiator and mounts.
6. Reverse procedure to install.

FUEL PUMP

REPLACE

Refer to "Fuel Pump Replace" in the " 3.1L Engine" section.

FUEL FILTER

REPLACE

Refer to "Fuel Filter Replace" in the " 3.1L Engine" section.

TIGHTENING SPECIFICATIONS

Year	Component	Torque/Ft. Lbs.
1999- 2000	Accelerator Cable Bracket	84⑦
	Camshaft Bearing Caps	44①
	Camshaft Position Sensor	84⑦
	Camshaft Sprocket Bolt	18②
	Connecting Rod Bolt	⑥
	Coolant Temperature Sensor	15
	Cylinder Head	⑤
	EGR to Crossover Pipe	44
	Engine Mount Nuts	35
	Engine Mount Strut Bolt	35
	Engine Mount Strut Bracket Bolt	21
	Engine to Transaxle Bolts	55
	Exhaust Manifold Bolt	18
	Exhaust Manifold Crossover Stud	18
	Exhaust Manifold Stud	53③
	EVAP Canister Purge Solenoid	72⑦
	Front Cover Bolt	11
	Front Cover Coolant Drain Plug	96⑦
	Front Lift Bracket Hex Bolt	37
	Front Lift Bracket Internal Drive Bolt	18
	Idler Pulley Bolt	37
	Intake Manifold Bolt	60⑦
	Lower Crankcase	④
	Oil Gallery Plug	41
	Oil Level Sensor	84⑦
	Oil Pan	18
	Oxygen Sensor	30
	Radiator Bracket Bolt	18
	Throttle Body Bolt	108⑦
	Timing Chain Tensioner Bolt	18
	Timing Chain Tensioner Shoe Bolt	22
	Transaxle Brace	18
	Valve Cover	84⑦
	Water Pump Bolt	11
	Water Pump Pulley Bolt	108⑦
	Water Outlet Housing	84⑦

① — Tighten an additional 30.°

② — Tighten an additional 45.°

③ — Inch lbs.

④ — Refer to "Main & Rod Bearings" for tightening procedure.

⑤ — Refer to "Cylinder Head, Replace" for tightening procedure.

⑥ — First pass, 22 ft. lbs.; second pass, loosen completely; third pass, 18 ft. lbs.; final pass, an additional 110.°

⑦ — Inch lbs.

3800 Engine

NOTE: Prior To Performing Any Service Operations Listed In This Section, Consult The "Technical Service Bulletins " Section For Related Information.

NOTE: On Air Bag Equipped Models, Refer To " Air Bag System Precautions" Located In The Front Of This Manual For System Disarming & Arming Procedures.

NOTE: For Procedures Not Found In This Section, Refer To The "3800 Engine" Section In the " Bonneville, LeSabre, LSS, Park Avenue, 88 & Regency " Chapter.

NOTE: Refer To "Computer Relearn Procedures " Located In The Front Of This Manual For Computer Relearn Procedures.

INDEX

PRECAUTIONS

AIR BAG SYSTEMS

Refer to "Air Bag System Precautions" in the front of this manual for system disarming and arming procedures.

BATTERY GROUND CABLE

Prior to service, disconnect battery ground cable and isolate as required.

FUEL SYSTEM PRESSURE RELIEF

To reduce the risk of fire and personal injury, it is necessary to relieve the fuel system pressure before servicing fuel system components.

1. Loosen fuel tank filler cap to relieve tank pressure.
2. Connect fuel pressure gauge tool No. J-34730-1, or equivalent, to fuel pressure valve. Wrap a shop towel around fitting while connection gauge to avoid spillage.
3. Install bleed hose into an approved container and open valve to bleed system pressure.

COMPRESSION PRESSURE

When checking compression, lowest cylinder must be within 70 percent of the highest cylinder with a minimum pressure of 100 psi. Perform compression test with engine at normal operating temperature, spark plugs removed and throttle wide open.

ENGINE MOUNT

REPLACE

ENGINE BLOCK MOUNTS

1. Remove engine mount struts, then install engine support fixture tool No. J 28467–A, engine support fixture adapter tool No. J28467–90 and engine support adapter leg tool No. J 36462, or equivalents.
2. Raise and support vehicle, then remove right front wheel and tire assembly.
3. Remove right engine splash shield, then the engine mount lower retaining nuts from frame.
4. Raise and support engine, then remove A/C compressor and position aside.
5. Remove front engine mount bracket bolts, then the rear engine mount bracket from engine.
6. Remove engine mount with engine mount bracket from engine, then the engine mount upper retaining nuts.
7. Remove engine mount from engine mount bracket.
8. Reverse procedure to install.

TRANSAXLE MOUNT

1. Remove engine torque strut from engine.
2. Raise and support vehicle.
3. Remove left tire and wheel assembly and lower splash shield.
4. Support transaxle using a suitable jack.
5. Remove mount nuts then the mount.
6. Reverse procedure to install. Tighten to specifications.

ENGINE

REPLACE

1. Mark and remove hood assembly.
2. Remove air cleaner assembly.
3. Relieve fuel system pressure as described under " Precautions."
4. Remove fuel lines from rail and mounting bracket.
5. Remove coolant bottle and inner fender electrical cover.
6. Remove fuel injector sight cover.
7. Remove throttle cables, bracket and vacuum line from throttle body.
8. Remove heat shield from exhaust crossover pipe then crossover pipe.
9. Remove engine torque strut from engine.
10. Remove engine cooling fan.
11. Remove vacuum line from transaxle module.
12. Remove serpentine drive belt.
13. Remove power steering pump and alternator from engine.
14. Disconnect all necessary electrical connectors.
15. Remove upper and lower radiator and heater hoses from engine.
16. Remove transaxle to engine bolts and ground wire harness with bolt.
17. Raise and support vehicle.
18. Remove right tire and wheel assembly and inner splash shield.
19. Remove flywheel cover and scribe torque converter to flywheel for installation.
20. Remove flywheel to converter bolts.
21. Disconnect wire harness clamps from frame near radiator.
22. Remove A/C compressor and position aside.
23. Remove starter motor.

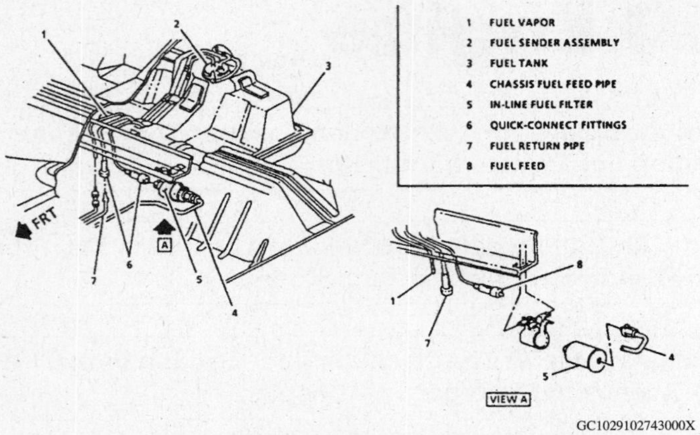

Fig. 1 Fuel filter replacement

24. Remove transaxle to engine bolt through wheelwell using suitable extension.
25. Disconnect engine mount to frame nuts.
26. Remove oil filter.
27. Disconnect front exhaust pipe from manifold.
28. Disconnect oil cooler piper from hose connections.
29. Lower vehicle.
30. Install lifting device and remove engine assembly.
31. Reverse procedure to install, noting the following:
    a. Align engine with transaxle dowel pins.
    b. **Torque** torque strut bolts to 41 ft. lbs.
    c. **Torque** flywheel to converter bolts to 46 ft. lbs.

FUEL PUMP

REPLACE

Refer to "Fuel Pump, Replace" in the " 3.1L Engine" section.

FUEL FILTER

REPLACE

1. Relieve fuel system pressure as outlined under " Precautions."
2. Raise and support vehicle.
3. Remove bracket attaching screw and filter bracket, **Fig. 1.**
4. Grasp filter and fuel line fitting. Twist quick-connect fitting 1/4 turn in each direction to loosen any dirt within fitting.
5. Using compressed air, blow out dirt from quick-connect fitting.
6. Remove feed pipe nut from fuel filter, then drain any remaining fuel into a suitable container.
7. Remove fuel filter.
8. Reverse procedure to install.

Rear Axle & Suspension

NOTE: Prior To Performing Any Service Operations Listed In This Section, Consult The "Technical Service Bulletins " Section For Related Information.

INDEX

DESCRIPTION

These vehicles use a tri-link independent rear suspension system with a transverse leaf spring and tubular struts with large lateral links attached to the body crossmember. The three mounting points are the crossmember, strut tower and trailing arm. The crossmember is stamped steel and the composite fiberglass mono leaf spring is transversely mounted to the under side of the crossmember, with its padded ends free riding on the cast knuckle assembly.

HUB & BEARING

REPLACE

The rear hub and bearing assembly is not serviceable. If the hub and/or bearing is damaged, the complete assembly must be replaced.

1. Raise and support vehicle, then remove tire and wheel assembly.
2. Remove brake caliper, leaving hose attached, and suspend out of way.
3. Remove brake rotor.
4. Disconnect anti-lock brake system electrical harness connector.

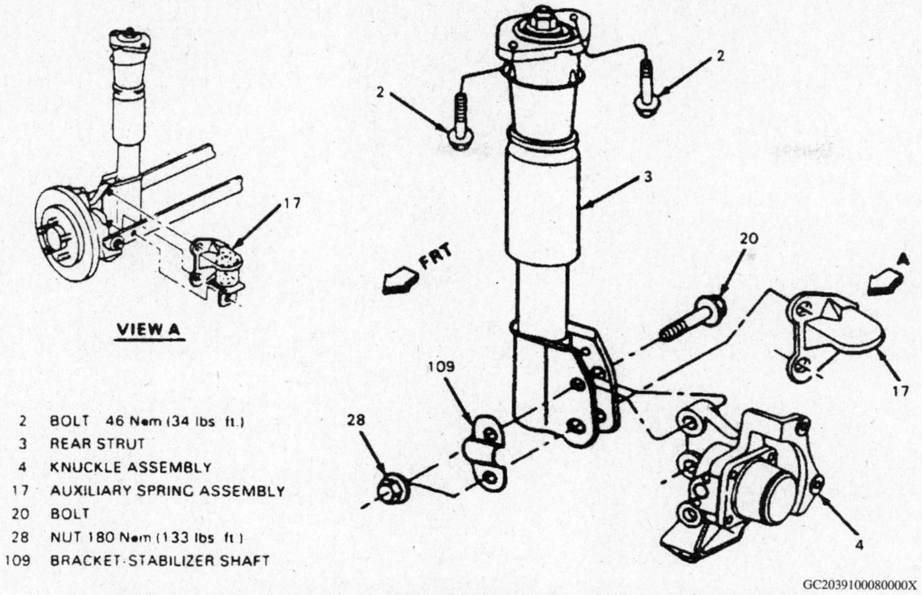

Fig. 1 Auxiliary spring replacement. Cutlass Supreme

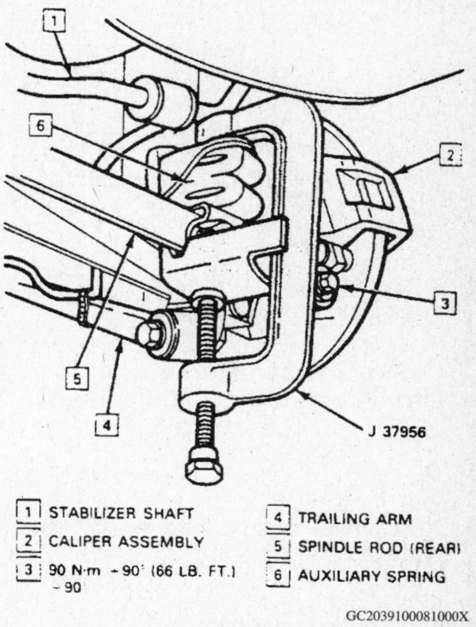

Fig. 2 Auxiliary spring compression. Cutlass Supreme

5. Remove hub and bearing to knuckle bolts.
6. Remove parking brake lever bracket, then the parking brake actuator.
7. Remove hub and bearing assembly.
8. Reverse procedure to install.

STRUT

REPLACE

CENTURY, GRAND PRIX, IMPALA, INTRIGUE & REGAL

1. Remove three strut to body mount retaining nuts.
2. Raise and support vehicle, then remove rear wheel and tire assembly.
3. Disconnect stabilizer shaft link from strut.
4. Scribe matching marks on strut and knuckle.
5. Remove strut to knuckle bolts, then the strut from vehicle.
6. Reverse procedure to install. Check rear wheel alignment as outlined in "Wheel Alignment" section.

CUTLASS SUPREME

1. Remove upper strut mount cover from inside rear compartment, then raise and support vehicle and remove tire and wheel assembly.
2. Place scribe marks on strut and knuckle to ensure installation in same position.
3. Remove jack pad.
4. Install rear leaf spring compressor tool No. J-35778, or equivalent, onto transverse spring assembly and tighten to hold spring pressure. **Do not remove spring or retention plates.**
5. Remove auxiliary spring as outlined under "Leaf Spring Service."
6. Remove brake hose bracket at strut.
7. Remove upper strut attaching bolts at body and allow assembly to drop down.
8. Remove stabilizer shaft bracket by removing strut to knuckle attaching nuts.
9. Remove strut to knuckle attaching bolts, then the strut assembly.
10. Reverse procedure to install. Tighten upper strut attaching bolts to specifications.

LUMINA & MONTE CARLO

1. Raise and support vehicle, then remove wheel and tire assemblies.
2. Place scribe marks on strut and knuckle for installation reference.
3. Remove brake hose bracket at strut, then the strut mount to body nuts.
4. Remove strut/stabilizer shaft bracket from knuckle, then the strut from body.
5. Reverse procedure to install.

STRUT SERVICE

1. Position strut assembly into strut spring compressor tool No. J 34013–B, or equivalent.
2. Compress spring assembly approximately ½ inch.
3. Holding shaft with T-45 Torx bit, remove and discard shaft nut.
4. Release spring tension and remove upper mount plate, spring, baffle and lower mount plate.
5. Reverse procedure to assemble.

COIL SPRING

REPLACE

Refer to "Strut Service" for coil spring replacement.

LEAF SPRING SERVICE

CUTLASS SUPREME

Auxiliary Spring Assembly, Replace

1. Raise and support vehicle, then remove wheel and tire assembly.
2. Remove leaf spring rear retention plate bolt.
3. Remove leaf spring retention bolt only enough to rotate plate clear of rod.
4. Install rear auxiliary spring compressor tool No. J-37956, or equivalent. Ensure pin in stationary end of clamp is inserted in hole of upper auxiliary spring bracket, **Figs. 1 and 2.**
5. Remove plug from upper bracket, then seat rod in tool channel and hand tighten.
6. Remove rod to knuckle bolt, then loosen tool forcing screw to allow spring to expand.
7. Remove auxiliary spring attaching bolts, then the spring and tool. **When removing auxiliary spring, ensure rod/bushing clears transverse spring and boss on knuckle.**
8. Reverse procedure to install, noting the following:
   a. Compress auxiliary spring with spring compressor tool enough to install rod to knuckle bolt.
   b. Install rod to knuckle bolt, using Loctite or equivalent. Tighten to specifications.
   c. Properly position leaf spring retention plate, install bolt and tighten to specifications.

Transverse Spring Assembly, Replace

Do not use corrosive cleaning agents, engine degreaser or solvents on or near the fiberglass leaf spring.

1. Raise and support vehicle.

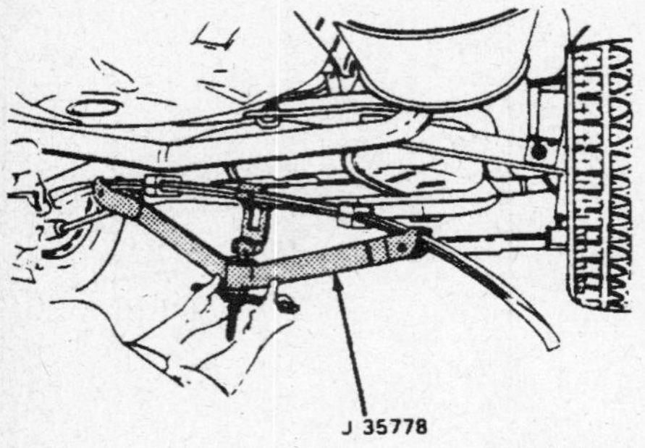

GC2039100082000X

Fig. 3 Transverse spring assembly removal. Cutlass Supreme

2. Remove three jack pad attaching bolts and the pad.
3. Remove left and right spring retention plate attaching bolts.
4. Remove right side trailing link to knuckle attaching nut and bolt.
5. Disconnect anti-lock brake system electrical harness connector.
6. Assemble rear spring leaf spring compressor tool No. J-35778, or equivalent, to transverse spring.
7. Loosen tool handle to base of tool shank.
8. Hang center shank of tool at spring center. It is not necessary to separate tool body and shank. **Attach from front side of vehicle only.**
9. Attach tool body to spring. **Always center spring on roller of tool.**
10. Fully compress spring, then slide spring to left side. It may be necessary to pry the spring, using a screwdriver/pry bar, to the opposite side, using wheel for leverage.
11. Relax the spring until removal clearance is achieved, then remove spring, **Fig. 3.**
12. Reverse procedure to install, noting the following:
    a. Tighten trailing link to knuckle attaching bolt to specifications.
    b. Tighten spring retention plate mounting bolts to specifications. **Rear spring retention plates are designed with tabs on one end. Tabs must be aligned with support assembly.**
    c. Tighten jack pad mounting bolts to specifications.

3 REAR STRUT
4 KNUCKLE ASSEMBLY
8 TRAILING ARM
12 FRONT LATERAL LINK
13 REAR LATERAL LINK
17 AUXILIARY SPRING
20 BOLT
21 BOLT 213 N•m (157 lbs ft)
22 WASHER
23 WASHER
24 BOLT 213 N•m (157 lbs ft)
25 BOLT
26 WASHER
27 NUT 260 N•m (192 lbs ft)
28 NUT 180 N•m (133 lbs ft)
108 STABILIZER SHAFT
109 BRACKET STABILIZER SHAFT
110 INSULATOR

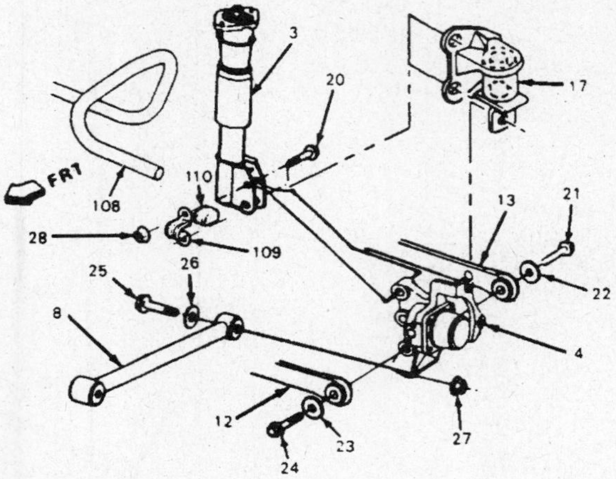

GC2039100084000X

Fig. 4 Exploded view of tri-link suspension assembly. Cutlass Supreme

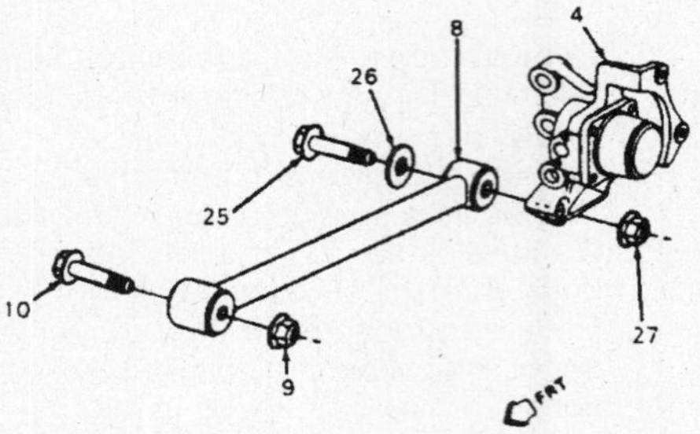

4 KNUCKLE ASSEMBLY
8 TRAILING LINK
9 65 N•m (48 lbs. ft.)
10 BOLT
25 BOLT
26 WASHER
27 NUT 260 N•m (192 lbs. ft.)

GC2039100085000X

Fig. 5 Trailing arm removal

KNUCKLE

REPLACE

CENTURY, GRAND PRIX, INTRIGUE & REGAL

1. Raise and support vehicle.
2. Remove wheel and tire assembly.
3. Scribe matching marks on strut and knuckle assembly, for installation reference.
4. Disconnect rear spindle rods from knuckle.
5. Remove brake caliper and bracket, then the brake rotor.
6. Disconnect ABS electrical connector.
7. Remove wheel hub and bearing.
8. Disconnect trailing arm from knuckle.
9. Remove rear suspension strut to knuckle bolts.
10. Remove knuckle assembly.
11. Reverse procedure to install.

CUTLASS SUPREME

1. Raise and support vehicle, then remove tire and wheel assembly.
2. Place scribe marks on strut and knuckle to ensure installation in same position.
3. Remove jack pad.
4. Install rear leaf spring compressor tool No. J-35778, or equivalent, onto transverse spring assembly and tighten to hold spring pressure. **Do not remove spring or retention plates.**
5. Remove auxiliary spring as outlined under "Leaf Spring Service."
6. Disconnect front link from knuckle.
7. Remove brake caliper, leaving hose attached, and suspend caliper out of way.
8. Disconnect anti-lock brake system electrical harness connector.
9. Remove brake rotor, then the hub and bearing assembly as described under "Hub & Bearing, Replace."
10. Disconnect trailing link from knuckle, **Fig. 4.**
11. Remove strut to knuckle attaching nuts, then the stabilizer shaft bracket.
12. Remove strut to knuckle attaching bolts, then the knuckle.
13. Reverse procedure to install. Tighten strut to knuckle attaching bolts and trailing link retaining nut to specifications.

IMPALA, LUMINA & MONTE CARLO

1. Raise and support vehicle, then remove wheel and tire assemblies.
2. Place scribe marks on strut and knuckle to ensure installation in same position.
3. Remove rear wheel spindle rods from knuckle, then the caliper and rotor (brake hose bracket and drum if so equipped).
4. Disconnect ABS connector, then remove rear wheel hub.
5. Disconnect trailing arm from knuckle.
6. Remove strut to knuckle nuts, then the knuckle.
7. Reverse procedure to install, noting the following:
    a. **Torque** trailing arm to knuckle to 66 ft. lbs., then using torque angle meter tool No. J 36660, or equivalent, tighten an additional 75.°
    b. Tighten rear wheel hub bolts to specifications.
    c. Tighten strut to knuckle nuts to specifications.

TRAILING ARM

REPLACE

1. Raise and support vehicle.
2. Disconnect ABS electrical harness connector.

3. Remove trailing arm to knuckle attaching nut and bolt, then the trailing rod (link) to body attaching nut and bolt, **Figs. 4 and 5.**
4. Remove trailing arm.
5. Reverse procedure to install. Tighten trailing arm to body nut and trailing link to knuckle nut to specifications.

STABILIZER BAR

REPLACE

1. Raise and support vehicle, then remove rear wheel and tire assemblies.
2. Remove right and lefthand stabilizer shaft link bolts, then open brackets to remove insulator.
3. Remove right and lefthand strut to knuckle to stabilizer shaft nuts, **Fig. 6. Do not remove strut to knuckle bolts.**
4. Remove insulator brackets from bolts and from stabilizer shaft, then the stabilizer shaft.
5. Reverse procedure to install, noting the following:
   a. It may be necessary to pry stabilizer shaft to one side for installation clearance at strut. Use caution when prying.
   b. Tighten stabilizer shaft link bolts and strut to knuckle bolts to specifications.

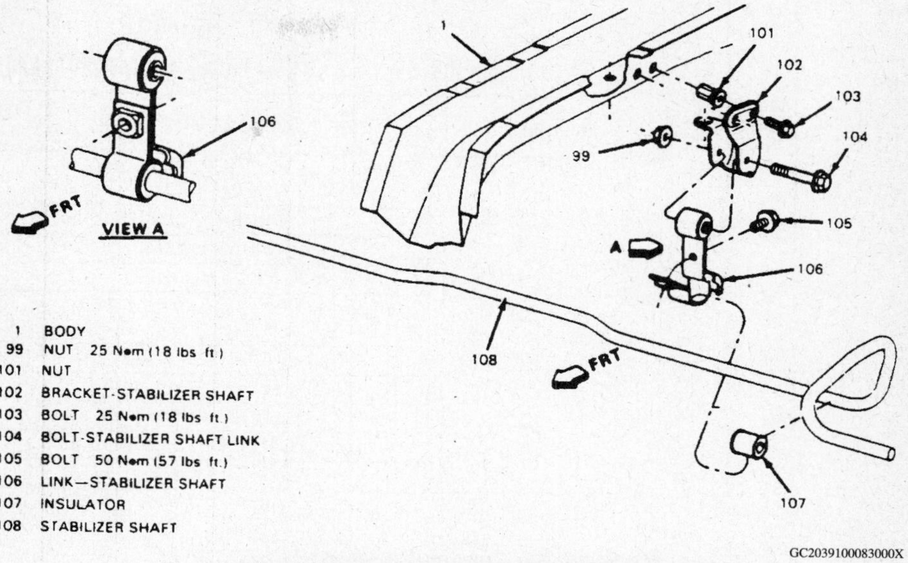

Fig. 6 Stabilizer shaft assembly replacement

LATERAL LINK

REPLACE

FRONT

1. Raise and support vehicle, then remove tire and wheel assembly.
2. Remove rod to knuckle bolt, then the exhaust pipe heat shield.
3. Lower fuel tank to gain access.
4. Remove lateral link to knuckle attaching bolt.
5. Remove lateral link to suspension crossmember attaching nut and bolt, then the lateral link.
6. Reverse procedure to install. Tighten lateral link to suspension crossmember nut and lateral link to knuckle bolt to specifications.

REAR

1. Raise and support vehicle, then remove tire and wheel assembly.
2. Remove transverse spring as outlined under "Leaf Spring Service."
3. Remove lower auxiliary spring bracket from rod.
4. Remove rear lateral link attaching nut from crossmember.
5. Push bolt forward enough to provide clearance for link removal, then remove rear lateral link.
6. Reverse procedure to install.

TECHNICAL SERVICE BULLETINS

REAR STRUT THUMPING OR SQUEAKING

On some of these models, the rear struts may have a muted thumping noise, oil canning or squeak, especially at low speed over irregular road surfaces.

This condition may be caused by the strut jounce bumper system. To correct this condition, replace both rear strut jounce bumper assemblies with revised units, service kit (part No. 22063945).

TIGHTENING SPECIFICATIONS

Year	Component	Torque/Ft. Lbs.
1997– 2000	Caliper Bleeder Valve	60⑤
	Front Caliper Mounting Bolt	79
	Front Caliper Mounting Bracket To Knuckle	148
	Jack Pad Bolt	18
	Lateral Link To Knuckle	157
	Lateral Link To Suspension Crossmember	140
	Proportioning Valve Caps	20
	Rear Caliper Mounting Bolt	92
	Rod To Knuckle	66②
	Rod To Support Crossmember	81①
	Spring Retention Plate Bolt	15
	Stabilizer Shaft Link Bolt	40③
	Stabilizer Shaft Link Bolt	26④
	Stabilizer Shaft Link To Body Bracket Nut	18③

Continued

TIGHTENING SPECIFICATIONS—Continued

Year	Component	Torque/Ft. Lbs.
1997-2000	Stabilizer Shaft Link To Body Bracket Nut	35④
	Strut Mount To Body	37
	Strut To Knuckle Nut	133③
	Strut To Knuckle Nut	82④
	Suspension Crossmember To Body Bolt	85
	Trailing Arm To Knuckle	192
	Trailing Link To Body Nut	48
	Upper Strut Bolt	34
	Wheel/Hub/Bearing To Knuckle Bolt	52
	Wheel Lug Nuts	100

① — Tighten an additional 60°.
② — Tighten an additional 90°.
③ — Cutlass Supreme.
④ — Except Cutlass Supreme.
⑤ — Inch lbs.

Front Suspension & Steering

NOTE: **Prior To Performing Any Service Operations Listed In This Section, Consult The "Technical Service Bulletins " Section For Related Information.**

NOTE: **On Air Bag Equipped Models, Refer To " Air Bag System Precautions" Located In The Front Of This Manual For System Disarming & Arming Procedures.**

NOTE: **Refer To "Computer Relearn Procedures " Located In The Front Of This Manual For Computer Relearn Procedures.**

INDEX

PRECAUTIONS

AIR BAG SYSTEMS

Refer to "Air Bag System Precautions" in the front of this manual for system disarming and arming procedures.

DESCRIPTION

The front suspension system on these vehicles is of the McPherson strut design. This design incorporates McPherson struts with coil springs and a one piece configuration with lower control arms. The use of tapered top coil springs on top of the struts provides a well controlled ride and allows a lower hood profile.

HUB & BEARING

REPLACE

IMPALA & INTRIGUE

1. Raise and support vehicle, then remove tire and wheel assembly.
2. Disconnect wheel speed sensor electrical connector.
3. Remove wheel speed sensor electrical connector from bracket.
4. Remove brake caliper and position aside.
5. Remove caliper bracket and brake rotor.
6. Remove driveshaft nut. Discard nut.
7. Attach front hub spindle remover tool No. J 28733-B, or equivalent, to wheel hub and bearing assembly.
8. Push driveshaft out of wheel hub and bearing assembly.
9. Remove hub and bearing assembly attaching bolts, then the hub and bearing assembly from steering knuckle. Discard attaching bolts.
10. Reverse procedure to install.

FRONT WHEEL DRIVESHAFT BEARING

REPLACE

CENTURY, GRAND PRIX & REGAL

1. Raise and support vehicle, then remove tire and wheel assembly.
2. Loosen driveshaft axle nut one turn. **Do not remove axle nut at this time, removing axle nut at this time may cause bearing damage.**
3. Remove brake caliper retaining pins, then the brake caliper assembly. Position aside.
4. Remove caliper bracket attaching bolts, bracket and brake rotor.
5. Remove drive axle shaft nut.
6. Push axle splines back out of front wheel drive shaft bearing, using front hub spindle remover tool No. J 28733, or equivalent.
7. Remove front wheel drive shaft bearing to knuckle attaching bolts.
8. Remove front wheel drive shaft bearing.
9. Reverse procedure to install.

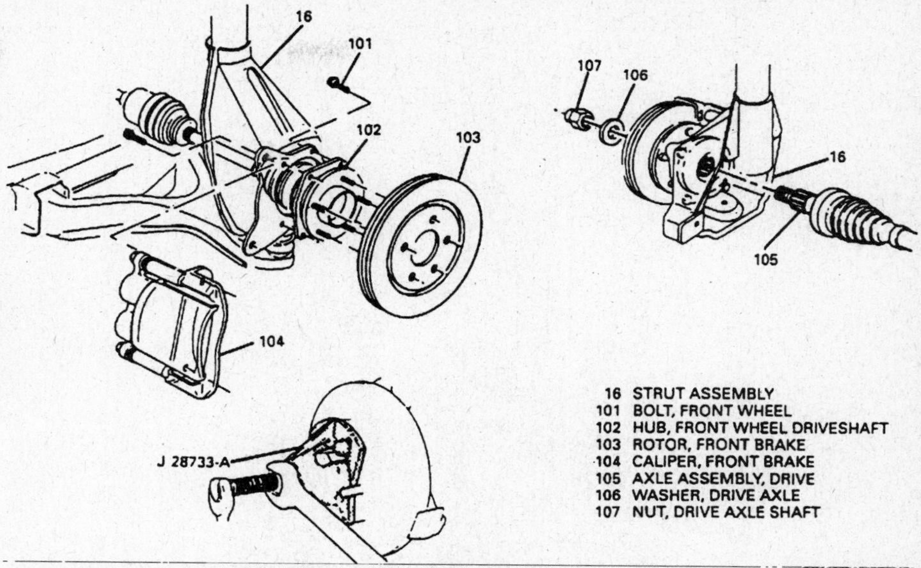

Fig. 1 Front wheel driveshaft bearing replacement. Cutlass Supreme, Lumina & Monte Carlo

CUTLASS SUPREME, LUMINA & MONTE CARLO

1. Raise and support vehicle, then remove wheel and tire assembly.
2. Loosen drive axle shaft nut one turn.
3. Remove brake caliper and position aside, **Fig. 1.**
4. Remove brake caliper mounting bracket bolts, then the caliper mounting bracket.
5. Remove brake rotor, then the drive axle shaft nut. Discard nut.
6. Loosen front wheel driveshaft bearing to knuckle attaching bolts.
7. Push axle splines back out of bearing assembly, using front hub spindle removal tool No. J 28733-A, or equivalent.
8. Remove driveshaft bearing to knuckle attaching bolts.
9. Remove ABS sensor mounting bolts, then the sensor. Position sensor aside.
10. Remove driveshaft bearing assembly from knuckle.
11. Reverse procedure to install.

BALL JOINT INSPECTION

With vehicle raised and supported to allow front suspension to hang freely, grasp wheel at top and bottom and attempt to move bottom of wheel inward and outward. **Ball joints must be replaced if looseness is observed between knuckle and control arm.**

BALL JOINT

REPLACE

CENTURY, GRAND PRIX, IMPALA, INTRIGUE & REGAL

1. Raise and support vehicle.
2. Remove control arm as outlined under "Control Arm, Replace."
3. Drill out three retaining rivets holding ball joint to control arm, then remove ball joint from control arm.
4. Reverse procedure to install.

CUTLASS SUPREME, LUMINA & MONTE CARLO

1. Raise and support vehicle, then remove wheel and tire assembly.
2. Remove ball joint heat shield attaching bolts, then the heat shield.
3. Remove lower ball joint cotter pin and retaining nut.
4. Loosen stabilizer shaft bushing bolts. **Do not remove bolts.**
5. Separate ball joint from lower control arm using tie rod puller/ball joint remover tool No. J 35917, or equivalent.
6. Drill out four rivets retaining ball joint to steering knuckle. Use a 1/8 inch drill bit to make a pilot hole, then use a 1/2 inch drill bit to finish drilling rivets.
7. Reverse procedure to install.

STRUT

REPLACE

CENTURY, GRAND PRIX, IMPALA, INTRIGUE & REGAL

1. Remove three strut to body nuts, **Fig. 2.**
2. Raise and support vehicle, then remove tire and wheel assembly.
3. Remove strut to knuckle attaching bolts. **After removing bolts, retain knuckle in its original position. Failure to retain knuckle could cause ball joint or drive axle damage.**
4. Remove strut assembly from vehicle.
5. Reverse procedure to install.

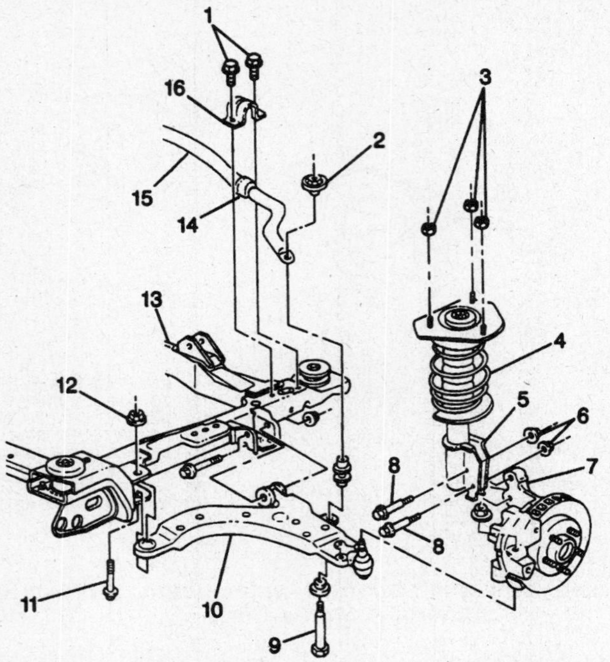

(1) Front Stabilizer Shaft Insulator Clamp Bolt/screw
(2) Front Stabilizer Shaft Link Nut
(3) Front Suspension Strut Mount Nut
(4) Front Suspension Spring
(5) Front Suspension Strut
(6) Strut To Knuckle Nut
(7) Front Steering Knuckle
(8) Strut To Knuckle Bolt/screw
(9) Front Stabilizer Shaft Link]
(10) Front Lower Control Arm
(11) Front Lower Control Arm Bolt/screw
(12) Front Lower Cotrol Arm Nut
(13) Frame
(14) Front Stabilizer Shaft Insulator
(15) Front Stabilizer Shaft
(16) Front Stabilizer Shaft Clamp

GC2029700266000X

Fig. 2 Front suspension. Century, Grand Prix, Impala, Intrigue & Regal

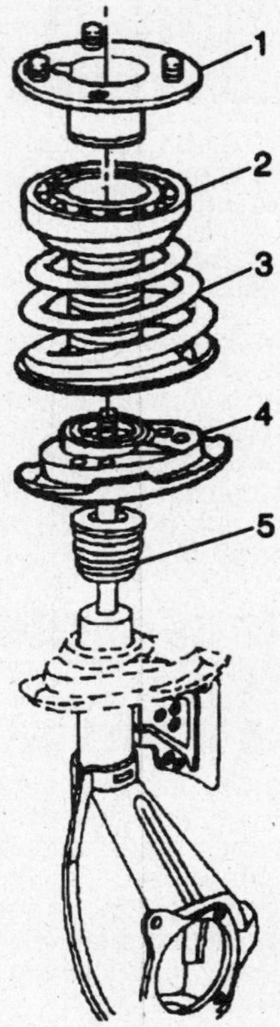

(1) Front Suspension Strut Mount Retainer
(2) Front Spring Upper Insulator
(3) Front Spring
(4) Front Spring Seat
(5) Front Suspension Strut Bumper

GC2029700267000X

Fig. 3 Exploded view of strut assembly. Cutlass Supreme, Lumina & Monte Carlo

CUTLASS SUPREME, LUMINA & MONTE CARLO

1. Scribe alignment marks on cover plate, then loosen cover plate retaining nuts, **Fig. 3.**
2. Raise and support vehicle.
3. Remove tire and wheel assembly.
4. Remove brake caliper and position aside. **Do not disconnect brake hose.**
5. Remove brake rotor, then the hub and bearing as outlined under"Hub & Bearing, Replace."
6. Separate axle from transaxle, then remove tie rod to knuckle attaching nut.
7. Separate tie rod from steering knuckle, using tie rod puller/ball joint removal tool No. J-35917, or equivalent.
8. Remove lower ball joint to knuckle attaching nut.
9. Separate lower ball joint from lower control arm, using tie rod puller/ball joint removal tool No. J-35917, or equivalent.
10. Remove cover plate retaining nuts, then the strut/knuckle assembly.
11. Reverse procedure to install.

STRUT CARTRIDGE

REPLACE

CUTLASS SUPREME, LUMINA & MONTE CARLO

Do not service strut unless weight of vehicle is on suspension.

Removal

1. Scribe alignment marks on cover plate, remove cover plate retaining nuts, then the cover plate.
2. Using No. 50 Torx bit and strut rod remover/installer tool No. J-35669, or equivalents, remove strut shaft.
3. Remove strut mount bushing by prying with suitable tool.
4. Using strut mount plate wrench tool No. J-35670, or equivalent, remove jounce bumper retainer.
5. Attach strut extension rod tool No. J-35668, or equivalent, to strut shaft and compress shaft down into cartridge, then remove tool and pull out jounce bumper.
6. Attach strut extension rod tool No. J-35668, or equivalent, to strut shaft and extend shaft, then remove tool and, using strut cap nut wrench tool No. J-35671, or equivalent, unscrew closure nut.
7. Remove strut cartridge.
8. Remove oil from strut tube using suction device.

Installation

1. Using strut cap nut wrench tool No. J-35671, or equivalent, install self contained replacement cartridge.
2. Install jounce bumper, then using strut mount plate wrench tool No. J-35670, or equivalent, the jounce bumper retainer.
3. Install strut mount bushing. If necessary, use strut extension rod tool No. J-35668, or equivalent after bushing is partially installed and position strut shaft as required. Lubricate bushing with a soap solution to ease installation.
4. Using No. 50 Torx bit and strut rod

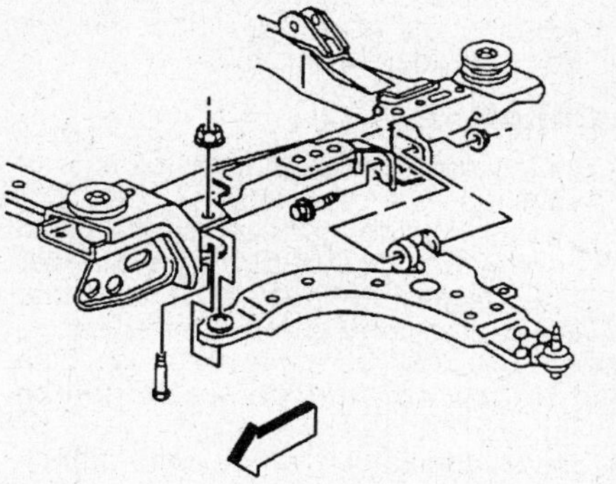

GC2029800225000X

Fig. 4 Lower control arm installation. Century, Grand Prix, Intrigue & Regal

remover/installer tool No. J-35669, or equivalents, install strut shaft nut and tighten to specifications.

5. Install strut mount cover, aligning scribe marks. Tighten cover plate nuts to specifications.

STRUT SERVICE

CENTURY, GRAND PRIX, IMPALA, INTRIGUE & REGAL

Disassemble

Springs are under high tension. Do not remove strut shaft nut without using a suitable spring compressing tool.

1. Mount strut and knuckle assembly into strut spring compressor tool No. J-34013-A and strut compressor adapter tool No. J-34013-88, or equivalents, then compress spring with compressor forcing screw just enough to release tension from upper spring insulator.
2. Using Torx bit and strut rod nut remover/installer tool No. J-35669, or equivalents, remove strut shaft nut.
3. Relieve all spring tension, then remove spring and strut components.

Assemble

1. Install spring seat and bearing.
2. Install lower spring insulator. Lower spring coil end must be visible between step and first retention tab of insulator.
3. Install front suspension spring.
4. Install dust shield to lower spring seat.
5. Install jounce bumper.
6. Install upper spring insulator. Upper spring coil end must be between step and location mark on insulator.
7. Using strut mount plate wrench tool No. J-35670, or equivalent, install jounce bumper retainer to strut mount.
8. Install strut mount and upper strut mount bushing.
9. Using strut spring compressor and strut compressor adapter tools Nos. J-34013-A and J-34013-38, or equivalents, compress strut assembly.
10. Align strut cartridge shaft with strut extension rod tool No. J-35668, or equivalent.
11. Using strut rod nut remover/installer tool No. J-35669, or equivalent, and Torx bit, install strut shaft nut and tighten to specifications.

CONTROL ARM

REPLACE

CENTURY, GRAND PRIX, IMPALA, INTRIGUE & REGAL

1. Raise and support vehicle, then remove wheel and tire assembly.
2. Remove steering gear outer tie rod from steering knuckle, then the stabilizer shaft to lower control arm insulator bracket bolts.
3. Disconnect ABS speed sensor, then remove control arm mounting bolts.
4. Remove cotter pin, then loosen nut from ball joint, **Fig. 2.**
5. Separate front lower control arm ball joint from steering knuckle, using ball joint separator tool No. J 41820, or equivalent.
6. Remove control arm from frame.
7. Reverse procedure to install, noting the following:
   a. Lower control arm to frame bolts must be installed as shown, **Fig. 4.**
   b. **Torque** lower ball joint nut 40 ft. lbs., then further tighten to align next slot in nut with cotter pin hole in stud. **Do not tighten more than 60° to align with hole and do not loosen nut at any time during installation.**

CUTLASS SUPREME, LUMINA & MONTE CARLO

1. Raise and support vehicle, then remove wheel and tire assembly.
2. Remove engine splash shields.
3. Remove stabilizer shaft to lower control arm insulator bracket bolts.
4. Remove lower ball joint cotter pin and nut, then, using tie rod puller/ball joint remover tool No. J-35917, or equivalent, separate ball joint from lower control arm.
5. Remove lower control arm to frame attaching nuts and bolts, then the lower control arms.
6. Reverse procedure to install, noting the following:
   a. Lower control arm to frame bolts must be installed as shown, **Fig. 5.**
   b. Tighten lower control arm to frame bolts to specifications.
   c. **Torque** lower ball joint nut 15 ft. lbs. and tighten an additional 90°, then further tighten to align next slot in nut with cotter pin hole in stud. **Do not tighten more than 60° to align with hole and do not loosen nut at any time during installation.**
   d. Tighten stabilizer shaft bolts and wheel lug nuts to specifications.

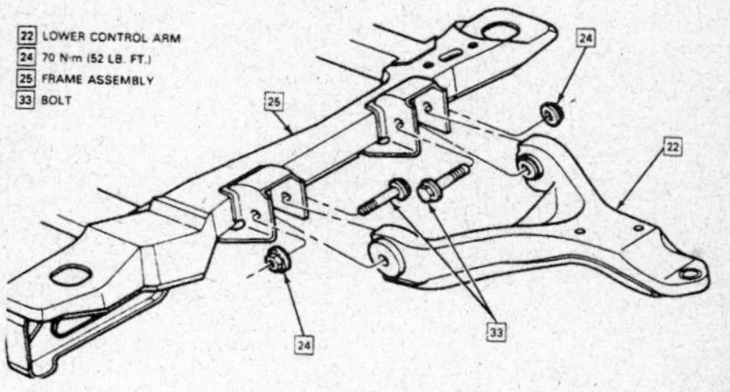

GC2029100174000X

Fig. 5 Lower control arm installation. Cutlass Supreme, Lumina & Monte Carlo

STEERING KNUCKLE

REPLACE

CENTURY, GRAND PRIX, IMPALA, INTRIGUE & REGAL

1. Raise and support vehicle, then remove wheel and tire assembly.
2. **On Century, Grand Prix and Regal models,** remove front wheel driveshaft bearing as outlined under "Front Wheel Driveshaft Bearing, Replace."
3. **On Impala and Intrigue models,** remove hub and bearing assembly as outlined under "Hub & Bearing, Replace."
4. **On all models,** remove lower control arm ball joint cotter pin and retaining nut.
5. Separate ball joint from control arm, using ball joint stud separator tool No. J 41820, or equivalent.
6. Separate outer tie rod end from steering knuckle, using universal steering linkage puller tool No. J 24319-B, or equivalent.
7. Scribe matching marks on strut and steering knuckle for installation reference.
8. Remove strut to knuckle attaching bolts, then the steering knuckle from vehicle.
9. Reverse procedure to install.

CUTLASS SUPREME, LUMINA & MONTE CARLO

Refer to "Strut, Replace" for strut/knuckle assembly replacement.

STABILIZER BAR

REPLACE

CENTURY, GRAND PRIX, IMPALA, INTRIGUE & REGAL

Removal

1. Raise and support vehicle, then remove tire and wheel assembly.
2. Move steering shaft dust seal to access lower intermediate shaft pinch bolt, then remove pinch bolt.
3. Loosen all insulator clamp attaching nuts and bolts, **Fig. 6.**

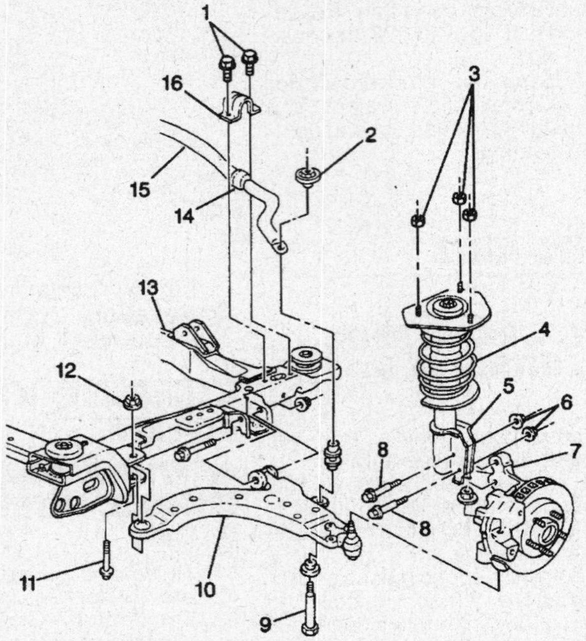

(1) Front Stabilizer Shaft Insulator Clamp Bolt/Screw
(2) Front Stabilizer Shaft Link Nut
(3) Front Suspension Strut Mount Nut
(4) Front Suspension Spring
(5) Front Suspension Strut
(6) Strut-to-Knuckle Nut
(7) Front Steering Knuckle
(8) Strut-to-Knuckle Bolt/Screw
(9) Front Stabilizer Shaft Link
(10) Front Lower Control Arm
(11) Front Lower Control Arm Bolt/Screw
(12) Front Lower Control Arm Nut
(13) Frame
(14) Front Stabilizer Shaft Insulator
(15) Front Stabilizer Shaft
(16) Front Stabilizer Shaft Clamp

GC2029800226000X

Fig. 6 Stabilizer shaft & insulators replacement. Century, Grand Prix, Impala, Intrigue & Regal

21 WELD NUTS
22 LOWER CONTROL ARM
25 FRAME
26 CLAMP BOLT
27 CLAMP
28 INSULATOR
29 STABILIZER SHAFT
30 BOLT 47 N•m (35 lbs. ft.)
31 CLAMP
32 INSULATOR
34 NUT 47 N•m (35 lbs. ft.)

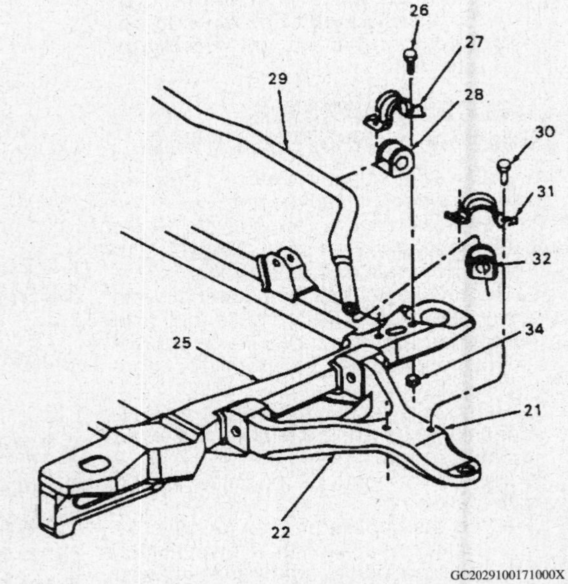

GC2029100171000X

Fig. 7 Stabilizer shaft & insulators replacement. Cutlass Supreme, Lumina & Monte Carlo

4. Place a jackstand under center of rear frame crossmember.
5. Loosen two front frame to body attaching bolts four turns.
6. Remove two rear frame to body attaching bolts, then lower rear of frame enough to remove stabilizer shaft. Discard frame to body bolts.
7. Remove insulators and clamps from frame.
8. Remove stabilizer bar links from control arms.
9. Pull stabilizer shaft rearward, the swing shaft downward and remove from left side of vehicle.

Installation

1. Install stabilizer shaft from left side of vehicle.
2. Loosely install stabilizer shaft link to control arm. **Do not tighten stabilizer link retaining nut at this time. Weight of vehicle must be supported by control arms so that trim height is obtained before tightening link nut.**
3. Install insulator clamps onto frame, then raise frame into position while guiding steering shaft onto steering gear.
4. Install new frame to body attaching bolts and remove jackstand.
5. Install intermediate shaft pinch bolt.
6. Install dust seal onto steering gear.
7. Support vehicle weight with control arms and tighten stabilizer link nut to specification.
8. Install tire and wheel assembly.

CUTLASS SUPREME, LUMINA & MONTE CARLO

1. Raise and support vehicle, then remove wheel and tire assembly.
2. Move steering shaft dust shield to gain access to pinch bolt.
3. Remove pinch bolt from lower intermediate steering shaft.
4. Loosen all insulator clamp attaching nuts and bolts, **Fig. 7.**
5. Place suitable jack under center of rear frame crossmember.
6. Loosen two front frame to body bolts four turns.
7. Remove two rear frame to body bolts.
8. Lower rear of frame just enough to gain access for stabilizer shaft removal.
9. Remove insulators and clamps from frame and control arms.
10. Pull stabilizer shaft rearward, swing down and remove from left side of vehicle.
11. Reverse procedure to install, noting the following:
    a. Coat new insulators with rubber lubricant.
    b. Tighten clamp to frame nuts and clamp to lower control arm bolts to specifications.
    c. Tighten frame to body bolts, pinch bolt and wheel lug nuts to specifications.
    d. **Torque** lug nuts to 100 ft. lbs.

TIE ROD END

REPLACE

INNER

Refer to the "Power Steering Gears" chapter for inner tie rod end replacement.

OUTER

1. Raise and support vehicle, then remove tire and wheel assembly.
2.
3. Remove hex torque prevailing nut,

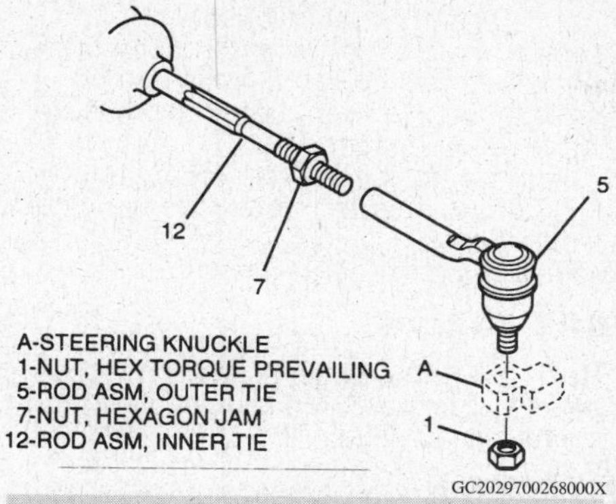

Fig. 8 Tie rod end replacement

then loosen jam nut, **Fig. 8.** Discard hex torque prevailing nut.

4. Separate tie rod end from steering knuckle, using universal steering linkage puller tool No. J 24319-01, or equivalent.
5. Remove outer tie rod from inner tie rod end.
6. Reverse procedure to install.

POWER STEERING GEAR

REPLACE

CENTURY, GRAND PRIX, IMPALA, INTRIGUE & REGAL

1. Set steering wheel to the 12 o'clock position with wheels straight ahead, then turn ignition switch to the LOCK position.
2. Raise and support vehicle, then remove left wheel and tire assembly.
3. Remove steering shaft lower bolt at steering gear.
4. Separate steering shaft from power steering gear. **Failure to disconnect intermediate shaft from rack and pinion shaft stub may result in damage to steering gear and/or intermediate shaft. This damage can cause loss of steering control.**
5. Remove hex torque prevailing nuts, then separate both outer tie rod ends from steering knuckle, using tie rod end puller/ball joint remover tool No. J 35917, or equivalent.
6. Support frame with suitable jackstands.
7. Remove frame bolts, then lower rear of frame. **Do not lower frame too far as damage to engine components nearest to the cowl may result.**
8. Remove pipe retaining clip from steering gear.
9. Remove inlet pipes and outlet line from steering gear.
10. Remove steering gear attaching bolts and nuts.
11. Remove power steering gear through wheel opening.
12. Reverse procedure to install. After completing installation, bleed power steering system as outlined under "Power Steering System Bleed."

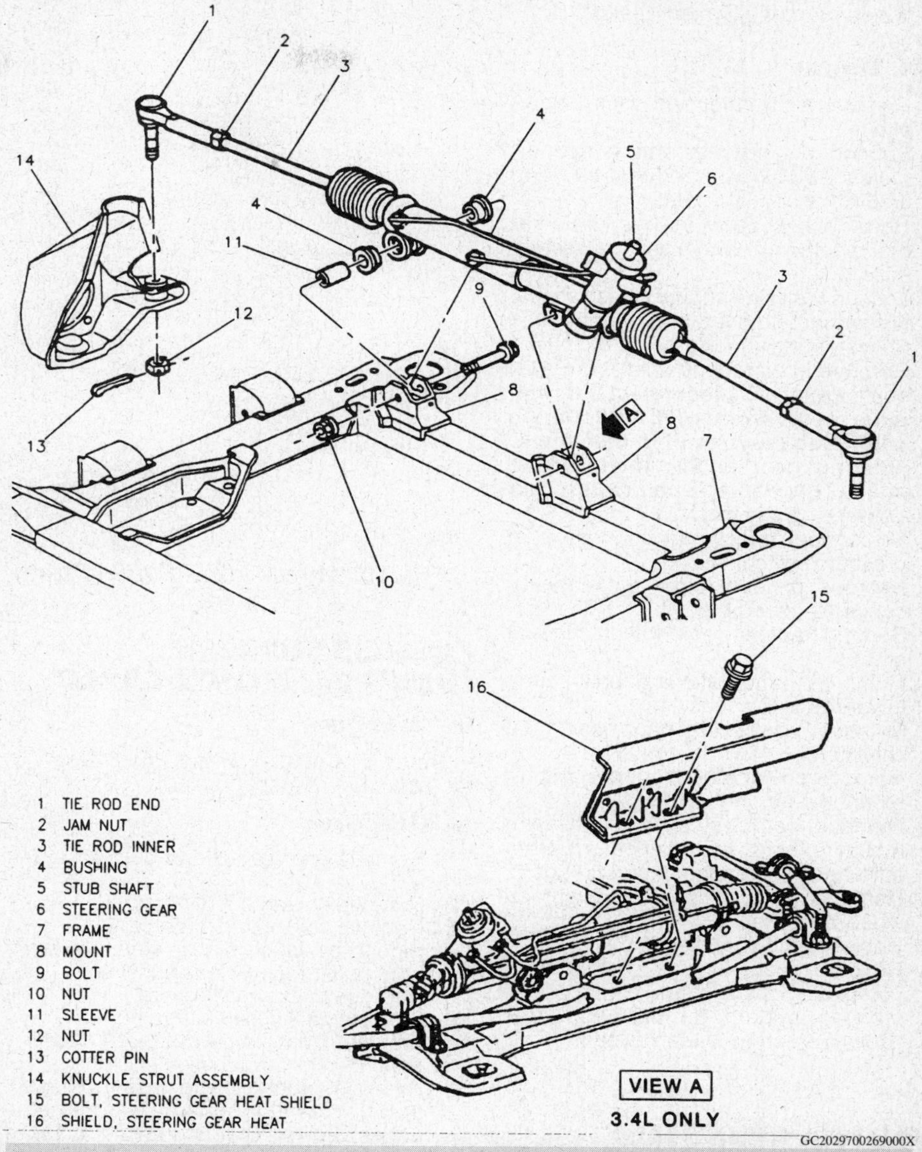

Fig. 9 Power steering gear replacement. Cutlass Supreme, Lumina & Monte Carlo

CUTLASS SUPREME, LUMINA & MONTE CARLO

3.1L & 3800 Engines

1. Raise and support vehicle. **Provide additional support at rear of vehicle.**
2. Remove front wheel and tire assemblies.
3. Remove intermediate shaft lower pinch bolt at steering gear, **Fig. 9.**
4. Remove intermediate shaft from stub shaft. **Failure to disconnect intermediate shaft from rack and pinion shaft stub may result in damage to steering gear and/or intermediate shaft. This damage can cause loss of steering control.**
5. Disconnect tie rod ends from knuckle and strut assembly, using tie rod puller/ball joint remover tool No. J-35917, or equivalent.
6. Support body with suitable stands, then remove rear frame mounting bolts and lower rear frame no more than 5 inches. **Do not lower rear of frame too far. Damage to engine components nearest to cowl may result.**
7. Remove heat shield, then the pipe retaining clip from steering gear.
8. Disconnect inlet pipes and outlet line from power steering gear.
9. Remove remaining brackets and clips.
10. Remove rack and pinion mounting nuts and bolts, then the rack and pinion assembly through the left wheel opening.
11. Reverse procedure to install. After completing installation, bleed power steering system as outlined under

"Power Steering System Bleed."

3.4L Engine

1. Remove air cleaner and duct assembly.
2. Support engine with engine support tools J-28467-A, J-28467-90 and J-36462, or equivalents.
3. Raise and support vehicle, then remove both front wheel and tire assemblies.
4. Loosen right side engine splash shield.
5. Disconnect both left and right tie rods from steering knuckles, **Fig. 9.**
6. Remove intermediate shaft from stub shaft. **Failure to disconnect intermediate shaft from rack and pinion shaft stub may result in damage to steering gear and/or intermediate shaft. This damage can cause loss of steering control.**
7. Disconnect electrical connector at pressure switch.
8. Remove exhaust pipe and catalytic converter assembly.
9. Support frame at center rear using jack stands.
10. Remove frame retaining bolts, then lower frame 3 inches.
11. Remove power steering gear heat shield.
12. Remove power steering line clamp at steering gear.
13. Remove both power steering gear mounting bolts, then disconnect pressure and return lines at steering gear.
14. Remove steering gear through left wheel opening.
15. Replace stub shaft seals.
16. Reverse procedure to install. After completing installation, bleed power steering system as outlined under "Power Steering System Bleed."

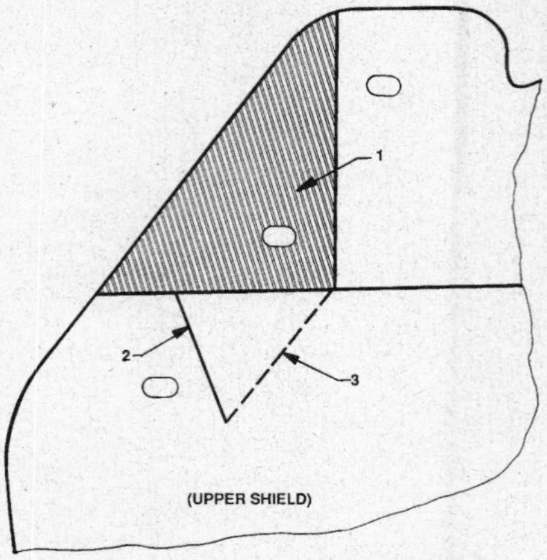
1
2
3
(UPPER SHIELD)
1. SHADED AREA TO REMOVED FROM UPPER SPLASH SHIELD.
2. CUT ALONG LENGTH OF LINE TO PROVIDE A SLIT IN SHIELD.
3. FOLD LINE.
GCA099400003000X

Fig. 10 Upper splash shield trim area

POWER STEERING PUMP

REPLACE

CENTURY, GRAND PRIX & REGAL

1. **On models equipped with 3.1L engine,** remove coolant recovery reservoir and position aside.
2. **On all models,** remove accessory drive belt from pump.
3. **On models equipped with 3.1L engine,** disconnect ignition control wiring harness near pump and position aside.
4. **On all models,** disconnect inlet and outlet hoses from pump.
5. Remove pump assembly attaching bolts, then the pump.
6. Transfer pulley to new pump, if necessary.
7. Reverse procedure to install. Bleed power steering system as outlined under "Power Steering System, Replace."

CUTLASS SUPREME, LUMINA & MONTE CARLO

3.1L Engine

Refer to "Century, Grand Prix & Regal" for replacement procedure.

3.4L Engine

1. Remove air cleaner and duct assembly.
2. Remove coolant recovery tank.
3. Remove serpentine drive belt.
4. Siphon as much power steering fluid from pump reservoir as possible.
5. Remove pump from bracket.
6. Disconnect fluid lines from pump.
7. Transfer pulley to new pump, if necessary.
8. Reverse procedure to install. Bleed power steering system as outlined under "Power Steering System, Replace."

3800 Engine

1. Remove accessory drive belt.
2. Raise and support vehicle, then remove tire and wheel assembly.
3. Place a drain pan under vehicle, then disconnect pressure and return lines from power steering pump.
4. Remove power steering pump mounting bolts, then the pump assembly.
5. Remove fluid reservoir from pump, then the pulley.
6. Transfer pulley and reservoir to new pump, if necessary.
7. Reverse procedure to install. Bleed power steering system as outlined under "Power Steering System, Replace."

IMPALA

3.4L Engine

1. Place a drain pan under vehicle, then remove coolant recovery reservoir.
2. Remove accessory drive belt from power steering pump pulley.
3. Remove ignition wiring harness from retainer near power steering pump.
4. Disconnect power steering pressure and return hoses.
5. Remove power steering pump mounting bolts, then the pump from engine mounting.
6. Reverse procedure to install.

3800 Engine

Refer to "3800 Engine" under "Cutlass Supreme, Lumina & Monte Carlo" for replacement procedure.

INTRIGUE

3.5L Engine

1. Place a drain under vehicle, then remove coolant surge tank.
2. Remove fuel injector sight shield.
3. Remove accessory drive belt, then the accessory wiring junction block, position junction block aside.
4. Remove power steering pump pulley, using power steering pump pulley remover tool No. J 25034–C, or equivalent.
5. Remove pressure and return lines from pump.
6. Remove pump mounting bolts, then the pump and reservoir.
7. Remove reservoir from pump.
8. Reverse procedure to install. Bleed power steering system as outlined under "Power Steering System, Replace."

3800 Engine

Refer to "3800 Engine" under " Cutlass Supreme, Lumina & Monte Carlo" for replacement procedure.

POWER STEERING SYSTEM BLEED

1. Turn wheels all the way to left.
2. Add power steering to Cold mark on fluid level indicator.
3. Start engine and run at fast idle, then add fluid, if necessary, to bring level to Cold mark.
4. Bleed system by turning wheels from side to side without hitting stops. Keep fluid level at Cold mark.
5. Return wheels to center position and continue running engine for 2–3 minutes.
6. Road test vehicle to ensure steering functions normally and is free of noise.
7. Check fluid level and ensure level is at Hot mark after system has stabilized at its normal operating temperature.

TECHNICAL SERVICE BULLETINS

RUBBING DURING FULL RIGHTHAND TURN OR METALLIC CLICKING DURING SHARP/HARSH ROAD INPUTS

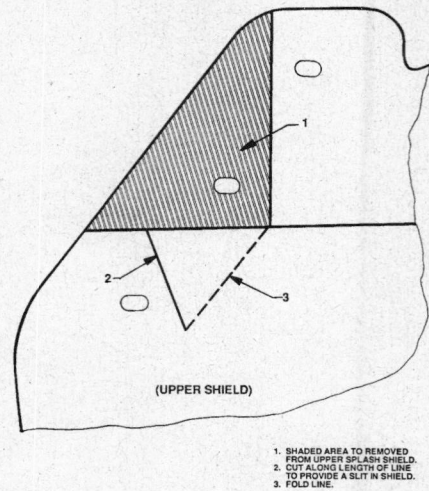

On some models equipped with 3.4L

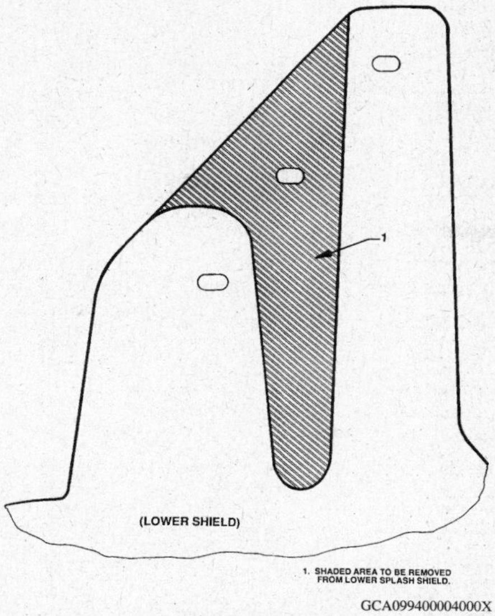

Fig. 11 Lower splash shield trim area

(VIN X) engine, there may be a rubbing during full righthand turns and/or a metallic clicking during sharp/harsh front suspension road inputs.

This condition may be caused by the tire contacting the engine compartment rubber splash shield or the shield fasteners contacting the suspension control arm. Use the following procedure to correct this condition.

1. Raise and support vehicle, then remove right front wheel and tire.
2. Remove four screws securing rear portion of upper and lower splash shields to wheelwell.
3. Remove shaded areas and cut slits as shown in **Figs. 10 through 12.**
4. Fold upper splash shield along indicated line and tuck tab under body rail, then position upper and lower splash shields in wheel well.
5. **Torque** three screws to 26 inch lbs., then remove two screws and two J-nuts holding lower splash shield to

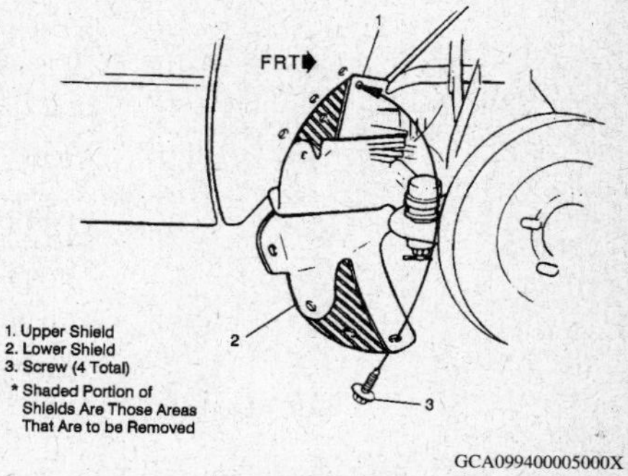

Fig. 12 Splash shield mounting

upper directly behind brake caliper above control arm forward surface.

6. Install two plastic rivets through lower and upper shield holes.
7. Install wheel and tire, then lower vehicle.

TIGHTENING SPECIFICATIONS

Year	Component	Torque/Ft. Lbs.
CENTURY, GRAND PRIX & REGAL		
1997– 2000	Ball Joint Heat Shield Retaining Nuts	54①
	Ball Joint To Lower Control Arm	50
	Ball Joint To Steering Knuckle	40
	Drive Axle Nut	151
	Frame To Body Bolt	100
	Front Wheel Driveshaft Bearing Bolts	96
	Heat Shield Screws	54①
	Inner Tie Rod To Rack	74
	Intermediate Shaft Pinch Bolt	35
	Lower Ball Joint Nut	40
	Lower Control Arm To Frame Bolts	②
	Outer Tie Rod End To Steering Knuckle Nut	18③
	Power Steering Pipe Fittings	20
	Pump Mounting Bolt	25
	Stabilizer Shaft Bracket Bolts	35
	Stabilizer Shaft Link Nut	17
	Steering Gear Mounting Bolt	59
	Strut To Body Mount Nuts	30
	Strut To Knuckle Bolts	90
	Tie Rod End Jam Nut	50
	Wheel Lug Nuts	100
CUTLASS SUPREME, LUMINA & MONTE CARLO		
1997– 2000	Ball Joint Heat Shield Bolts	62①
	Ball Joint Nut	63
	Drive Axle Nut	151
	Front Wheel Driveshaft Bearing To Knuckle	52
	Inner Tie Rod End Nut	74

Continued

TIGHTENING SPECIFICATIONS—Continued

Year	Component	Torque/Ft. Lbs.
CUTLASS SUPREME, LUMINA & MONTE CARLO		
1997-2000	Intermediate Shaft Pinch Bolt	35
	Lower Control Arm To Frame Bolts	52
	Outer Tie Rod End Nut	84①⑤
	Power Steering Line Fittings	20
	Stabilizer Shaft Bushing Clamp Bolt	35
	Stabilizer Shaft To Insulator Bracket To Frame	27
	Stabilizer Shaft To Insulator Clamp To Frame	35
	Stabilizer Shaft To Insulator Clamp To Lower Control Arm	35
	Steering Gear Heat Shield	54①
	Steering Gear Mounting Bolts	59
	Strut Closure Nut	82
	Strut Cover Plate Nuts	24
	Strut Piston Shaft Nut	59
	Strut To Knuckle Nuts	90
	Tie Rod End Jam Nut	46
	Wheel Lug Nuts	100
IMPALA		
2000	Front Wheel Driveshaft Bearing Nut	96
	Intermediate Shaft Lower Pinch Bolt	35
	Intermediate Shaft Upper Pinch Bolt	35
	Lower Control Arm Ball Stud To Control Arm	50
	Lower Control Arm Ball Stud To Knuckle	15④
	Lower Control Arm Mounting Nuts	77
	Power Steering Gear Mounting Bolts	59
	Power Steering Pressure Line To Pump	20
	Power Steering Pressure Line To Steering Gear	20
	Power Steering Pump Mounting Bolts	18
	Power Steering Return Line To Gear	20
	Power Steering Return Line To Pump	20
	Stabilizer Shaft Bracket Bolt	35
	Stabilizer Shaft Link Nut	17
	Strut Mount Nut	52
	Strut To Body Mount Nuts	24
	Strut To Steering Knuckle	90
	Tie Rod End Nut	22④
	Wheel Lug Nuts	100
INTRIGUE		
1998– 2000	Ball Joint Stud To Steering Knuckle	15④
	Ball Joint To Lower Control Arm Nut	50
	Front Wheel Driveshaft Bearing Nut	96
	Intermediate Shaft Lower Pinch Bolt	35
	Intermediate Shaft Upper Pinch Bolt	35
	Lower Control Arm Mounting Nuts	77
	Power Steering Cooler Pipe Retainer Bolt	53①
	Power Steering Gear Mounting Bolts	59
	Power Steering Pressure Line To Steering Gear	20

Continued

TIGHTENING SPECIFICATIONS—Continued

Year	Component	Torque/Ft. Lbs.
INTRIGUE		
1998-2000	Power Steering Pressure Line To Pump	20
	Power Steering Pump Mounting Bolts	18
	Power Steering Return Line To Gear	20
	Power Steering Return Line To Pump	20
	Stabilizer Shaft Bracket Bolt	35
	Stabilizer Shaft Link Nut	17
	Strut To Body Mount Nuts	24
	Strut Mount Nut	52
	Strut To Steering Knuckle Bolts	90
	Tie Rod End Nut	22④
	Wheel Lug Nuts	100

① — Inch lbs.
② — Refer to "Control Arm, Replace."
③ — Plus an additional 180° turn.
④ — Tighten an additional 120° turn.
⑤ — Tighten an additional 210° turn.

Wheel Alignment

INDEX

PRECAUTIONS

When adjusting wheel alignment, always adjust both front and rear alignment. Begin with rear wheel camber, then proceed to rear wheel toe and tracking and, finally, adjustment of front wheel camber and toe.

PRELIMINARY INSPECTION

1. Ensure tires are inflated to correct pressure, and check for uneven wear.
2. Check front wheel bearings and related suspension components for damage and replace as necessary, to eliminate improper alignment due to faulty components.
3. Check ball joints and tie rods.
4. Check vehicle trim heights.
5. Check steering gear for looseness at frame.
6. Check struts for improper operation.
7. Check for loose control arms.
8. Check for loose or missing stabilizer shaft attachments.

FRONT WHEEL ALIGNMENT

CAMBER

Century, Grand Prix, Impala, Intrigue & Regal

1. Remove strut assembly as outlined in "Front Suspension & Steering" section.
2. Place strut assembly in a suitable vise.
3. File lower strut to knuckle attaching hole oblong, **Fig. 1.**
4. Install strut assembly and adjust camber as necessary.
5. **Torque** strut to knuckle bolts to 88 ft. lbs.

Cutlass Supreme, Lumina & Monte Carlo

1. Open hood and remove three strut cover plate nuts and cover plate.
2. Lift front of vehicle just to the point that strut stud clears strut tower and cover top of strut. **Do not over extend drive axle. Do not lift by suspension.**
3. Use strut alignment template tool No. J-36892, or equivalent, to mark holes, then file three holes. File inboard or outboard of existing hole depending or camber requirement. Do not file more than .2 inch in either direction. **Paint exposed metal with red oxide primer and, after primer has dried, paint area with paint matching body color.**
4. Lower front of vehicle and guide strut studs into slotted holes.
5. Install three strut cover plate nuts.
6. Set camber to specifications by moving strut, then **torque** strut cover plate nuts to 24 ft. lbs.

TOE

1. Remove power steering gear seal clamps.
2. With steering wheel in straight ahead position, loosen jam nuts on tie rods.
3. Rotate inner tie rod to obtain proper toe angle, then ensure number of threads showing on each tie rod is approximately equal.
4. Ensure tie rod ends are square, then **torque** jam nuts to 46 ft. lbs.

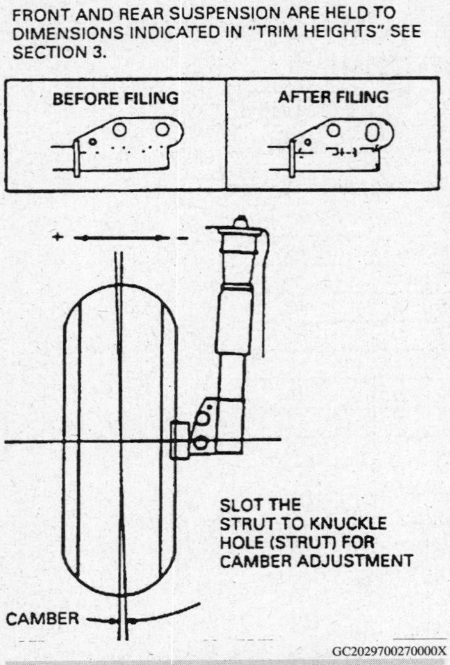

Fig. 1 Front camber adjustment. Century, Grand Prix, Impala, Intrigue & Regal

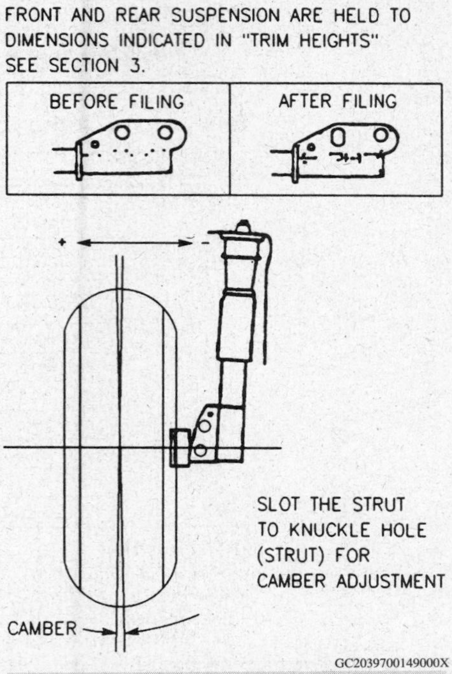

Fig. 2 Rear camber adjustment. Century, Grand Prix, Impala, Intrigue & Regal

5. Ensure seals are not twisted and install seal clamps.

REAR WHEEL ALIGNMENT

CAMBER

Century, Grand Prix, Impala, Intrigue & Regal

1. Remove strut assembly as outlined in "Rear Suspension " section.
2. Place strut assembly in a suitable vise.
3. File upper strut to knuckle attaching hole oblong, **Fig. 2.**
4. Install strut assembly and adjust camber as necessary.
5. **Torque** strut to knuckle bolts to 88 ft. lbs.

Cutlass Supreme, Lumina & Monte Carlo

1. Raise and support vehicle.
2. Remove tire and wheel assembly.
3. Remove strut assembly as outlined in "Rear Suspension " section.
4. Remove strut/upper auxiliary spring bracket/stabilizer shaft bracket.
5. Place strut in vise.
6. File lower strut to knuckle attaching hole oblong, **Fig. 3.**
7. Place auxiliary spring assembly in vise.
8. File lower strut attaching hole oblong.
9. Place stabilizer bracket in vise.
10. File lower stabilizer bracket to strut attaching hole oblong.
11. Attach strut assembly/stabilizer shaft bracket/upper auxiliary spring bracket to knuckle.
12. Install strut to body bolts and break hose bracket.
13. Install auxiliary spring and install tire and wheel assembly.
14. Adjust camber, then **torque** strut to knuckle nuts to 136 ft. lbs.
15. Check and adjust toe if necessary.

TOE

Century, Grand Prix, Impala, Intrigue & Regal

1. Loosen hex nuts at rear wheel spindle rod.
2. Adjust toe to specifications.
3. **Torque** hex nuts to 37 ft. lbs.

Cutlass Supreme, Lumina & Monte Carlo

1. Install rear toe adjusting tool No. J-38118, or equivalent, after lubricating threads.
2. Hand tighten turnbuckle portion of tool in direction of adjustment. Equal amounts of threads should be showing on both sides of turnbuckle.
3. Loosen rear rod nut at crossmember a minimum of four turns.
4. Rotate turnbuckle portion of tool to reach correct toe specification.
5. **Torque** rear rod to crossmember nut to 81 ft. lbs. plus an additional 60° turn.
6. Remove tool.

VEHICLE RIDE HEIGHT

1. Ensure vehicle is on level ground.
2. Ensure tires are inflated to proper pressures.
3. Fuel tank should be full to obtain accurate readings.
4. Trunk should be empty except for spare tire and jack.
5. Bounce car three times at front and rear to normalize suspension.
6. Measure from lowest point on the ball joint housing to control arm bolt centerline ("D" and "K" positions), **Fig. 4.**
7. Measure from level floor to rocker panel at "Z" and "J" positions.
8. Refer to for ride height measurement location and **Figs. 5 through 11** for specification charts.

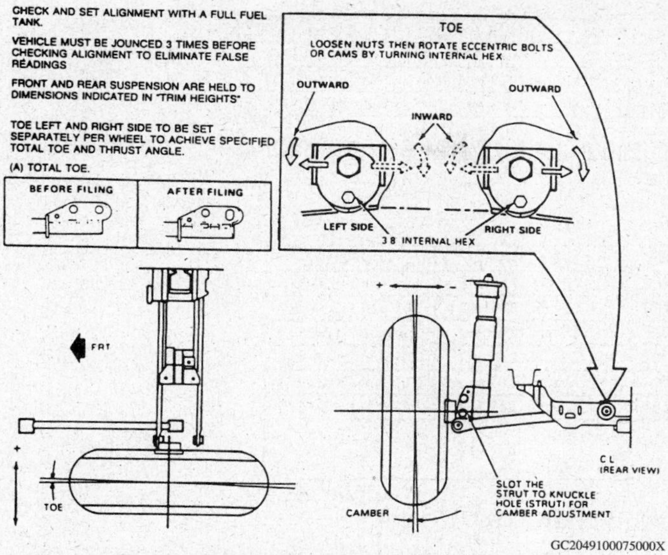

GC2049100075000X

Fig. 3 Rear alignment inspection & adjustment. Cutlass Supreme, Lumina & Monte Carlo

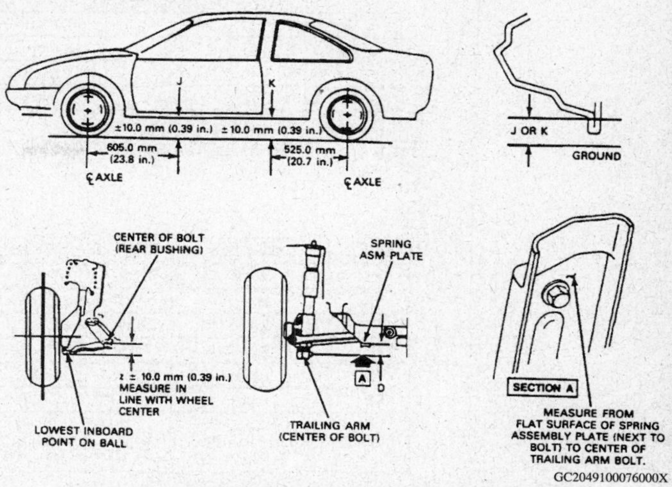

GC2049100076000X

Fig. 4 Ride height measurement location

SUSP	MODEL	ENGINE	STYLE	TIRE	Z (CURB)	D (CURB)
FE1	Cutlass Supreme w/o BYP	L82	2 DR.	P205/70R15	73 mm (2.87 in.)	261 mm (10.28 in.)
FE1	Cutlass Supreme with BYP	L82	2 DR.	P215/60R16	72 mm (2.83 in.)	261 mm (10.28 in.)
FE3	Cutlass Supreme w/o BYP	LQ1	2 DR.	P225/60R16	68 mm (2.67 in.)	256 mm (10.07 in.)
FE3	Cutlass Supreme with BYP	LQ1	2 DR.	P225/60R16	68 mm (2.67 in.)	256 mm (10.07 in.)
FE3	Cutlass Supreme w/o BYP	L82	2 DR.	P225/60R16	65 mm (2.60 in.)	257 mm (10.11 in.)
FE3	Cutlass Supreme with BYP	LQ1	2 DR.	P225/60R16	69 mm (2.72 in.)	257 mm (10.11 in.)
FE1	Cutlass Supreme w/o BYP	L82	4 DR.	P205/70R15	73 mm (2.87 in.)	262 mm (10.31 in.)
FE1	Cutlass Supreme with BYP	L82	4 DR.	P215/60R16	73 mm (2.87 in.)	261 mm (10.27 in.)
FE3	Cutlass Supreme w/o BYP	LQ1	4 DR.	P225/60R16	68 mm (2.68 in.)	256 mm (10.07 in.)
FE3	Cutlass Supreme with BYP	LQ1	4 DR.	P225/60R16	68 mm (2.68 in.)	256 mm (10.07 in.)

* NOTE: All measurements are ±10 mm (0.39 in.).
* NOTE: "J" and "K" curb heights are 249 mm (9.80 in.) for all model combinations.

GC2049600120000X

Fig. 5 Ride height specification chart. 1997 Cutlass Supreme

SUSP	MODEL	ENGINE	STYLE	TIRE	Z (CURB)	D (CURB)
FE1	MONTE CARLO LS	L82	2 DR.	P205/70R15	75 mm (2.96 in.)	272 mm (10.70 in.)
FE1	MONTE CARLO LS	L82	2 DR.	P225/60R16	68 mm (2.68 in.)	266 mm (10.49 in.)
F41	MONTE CARLO Z34	LQ1	2 DR.	P225/60R16	70 mm (2.76 in.)	267 mm (10.51 in.)
FE1	LUMINA LS	L82	4 DR.	P205/70R15	75 mm (2.95 in.)	272 mm (10.72 in.)
FE1	LUMINA LS	L82	4 DR.	P225/60R16	69 mm (2.72 in.)	267 mm (10.52 in.)
F41	LUMINA LS	LQ1	4 DR.	P225/60R16	70 mm (2.76 in.)	266 mm (10.49 in.)
FE1	LUMINA	L82	4 DR.	P205/70R15	75 mm (2.95 in.)	272 mm (10.72 in.)
FE1	LUMINA	L82	4 DR.	P225/60R16	69 mm (2.72 in.)	267 mm (10.52 in.)
F41	LUMINA WITH 9C3	L82	4 DR.	P215/65R15	75 mm (2.96 in.)	273 mm (10.75 in.)
F41	LUMINA WITH 9C6	L82	4 DR.	P205/70R15	76 mm (3.00 in.)	272 mm (10.72 in.)
F41	LUMINA WITH 9C6	L82	4 DR.	P215/65R15	75 mm (2.95 in.)	273 mm (10.75 in.)

* NOTE: All measurements are ±10 mm (0.39 in.).
* NOTE: "J" curb heights are 254 mm (10.00 in.) for all model combinations.
* NOTE: "K" curb heights are 259 mm (10.20 in.) for all model combinations.

GC2049600118000X

Fig. 6 Ride height specification chart. Lumina & Monte Carlo

SUSPENSION	STYLE	D (CURB)	J (CURB)	K (CURB)	Z (CURB)
FE1	2 DR	262.7 mm (10.34")	213.3 mm (8.40")	213.3 mm (8.40")	54.3 mm (2.14")
FE3	2 DR	257.4 mm (10.13")	213.3 mm (8.40")	213.3 mm (8.40")	46.4 mm (1.83")
FE1	4 DR	262.7 mm (10.34")	213.3 mm (8.40")	213.3 mm (8.40")	53.0 mm (2.08")
FE3	4 DR	257.4 mm (10.13")	213.3 mm (8.40")	213.3 mm (8.40")	46.3 mm (1.83")

GC2049700125000X

Fig. 7 Ride height specification chart. 1997 Grand Prix

Tire Size	Style	D (curb)	J (curb)	K (curb)	Z (curb)
P22560R16	2 door	255 mm (10.04")	213.3 mm (8.40")	213.3 mm (8.40")	48 mm (1.89")
P20570R15	4 door	261 mm (10.28")	213.3 mm (8.40")	213.3 mm (8.40")	55.0 mm (2.13")
P22560R16	4 door	255 mm (10.04")	213.3 mm (8.40")	213.3 mm (8.40")	48 mm (1.89")

GC2049800141000X

Fig. 8 Ride height specification chart. 1998–2000 Grand Prix, Impala & Intrigue

SUSP	MODEL	ENGINE	STYLE	TIRE	Z (CURB)	D (CURB)
FE1	Regal	L82	4 DR.	P205/70R15	73 mm (2.87 in.)	262 mm (10.31 in.)
FE1	Regal	L27	4 DR.	P205/70R15	73 mm (2.87 in.)	262 mm (10.31 in.)
FE3	Regal	L82/L27	4 DR.	P225/60R16	67 mm (2.64 in.)	256 mm (10.08 in.)
FE1	Regal	L82	2 DR.	P205/70R15	73 mm (2.87 in.)	261 mm (10.28 in.)
FE1	Regal	L27	2 DR.	P205/70R15	73 mm (2.87 in.)	261 mm (10.28 in.)
FE3	Regal	L82/L27	2 DR.	P225/60R16	67 mm (2.63 in.)	255 mm (10.04 in.)

* NOTE: All measurements are ±10 mm (0.39 in.).
* NOTE: "J" and "K" curb heights are 249 mm (9.80 in.) for all model combinations.

GC2049600121000X

Fig. 9 Ride height specification chart. 1997 Regal

SUSPENSION	STYLE	D (CURB)	J (CURB)	K (CURB)	Z (CURB)
FE1	4 DR	272 mm (10.70")	218 mm (8.58")	223 mm (8.77")	57 mm (2.24")
FE2	4 DR	266 mm (10.47")	223 mm (8.77")	224 mm (8.81")	57 mm (2.24")
FE3	4 DR	267 mm (10.51")	223 mm (8.77")	224 mm (8.81")	57 mm (2.24")

GC2049700142000X

Fig. 10 Ride height specification chart. 1997 Century

Tire Size	Style	D (curb)*	J (curb)	K (curb)	Z (curb)**
P22560R16	2 door	255 mm (10.04")	213.3 mm (8.40")	213.3 mm (8.40")	48 mm (1.89")
P20570R15	4 door	261 mm (10.28")	213.3 mm (8.40")	213.3 mm (8.40")	55.0 mm (2.13")
P22560R16	4 door	255 mm (10.04")	213.3 mm (8.40")	213.3 mm (8.40")	48 mm (1.89")

GC2049800143000X

Fig. 11 Ride height specification chart. 1998–2000 Century & Regal

CORVETTE

NOTE: Refer To The Rear Of This Manual For Vehicle Manufacturer's Special Tool Suppliers.

INDEX OF SERVICE OPERATIONS

Specifications

GENERAL ENGINE SPECIFICATIONS

Year	Engine		Fuel System	Bore & Stroke	Compression Ratio	Net Brake H.P. @ RPM②	Maximum Torque	Normal Oil Pressure psi
	Liter	VIN Code①						
1997–2000	5.7L	G	SFI	3.898 x 3.622	10.1	345 @ 5600	350 @ 4400	③

SFI — Sequential Fuel Injection
VIN — Vehicle Identification Number
① — The eighth digit of the VIN denotes engine code.
② — Ratings are net, as installed in vehicle.
③ — Engine hot, minimum oil pressure @ 1000 RPM, 6 psi.; @ 2000 RPM, 18 psi.; @ 4000 RPM, 24 psi.

TUNE UP SPECIFICATIONS

Year	Engine (VIN Code)①	Spark Plug Gap	Ignition Timing BTDC				Curb Idle Speed③		Fast Idle Speed		Fuel Pump Pressure psi	Valve Clearance Inch
			Firing Order	Man. Trans.	Auto. Trans.	Mark Fig.	Man. Trans.	Auto. Trans.	Man. Trans.	Auto. Trans.		
1997–2000	5.7L (G)	.060	1-8-7-2-6-5-4-3	⑥	⑥	—	④	④	④	④	55–61⑤	②

BTDC — Before Top Dead Center
VIN — Vehicle Identification Number
① — The eighth digit of the VIN denotes engine code.
② — Equipped w/hydraulic lifters. No adjustment is required.
③ — When inspecting idle speed, set parking brake & block drive wheels.
④ — Idle speed is controlled by an idle speed control motor.
⑤ — With shop towel wrapped around fuel pressure fitting to prevent fuel spillage, connect a suitable fuel pressure gauge. Inspect fuel pressure with ignition On, but engine not running.
⑥ — Computer controlled. No adjustment.

FRONT WHEEL ALIGNMENT SPECIFICATIONS

Year	Caster Angle, Degrees		Camber Angle, Degrees		Toe Per Wheel, Degrees		Steering Wheel Angle, Degrees	Ball Joint Wear	
	Limits	Desired	Limits	Desired	Limits	Desired		Upper	Lower
1997	+5.6 to +6.6	+6.1①	–.25 to –.15	–.20①	–.06 to +.14	+.04	–1 to +1	②	②
1998	+6.1 to +7.1	+6.6①	–.7 to .3	–.20	–.06 to +.14	+.04	–1 to +1	②	②
1999–2000	+6.4 to +7.4	+6.9①	–.7 to .3	–.20	–.06 to +.14	+.04	–1 to +1	②	②

① — Maximum variation between wheels is .5.°
② — Refer to "Front Suspension" for ball stud inspection procedure.

REAR WHEEL ALIGNMENT SPECIFICATIONS

Year	Camber Angle, Degrees		Toe Per Wheel, Degrees		Thrust Angle, Degrees	
	Limits	Desired	Limits	Desired	Limits	Desired
1997–2000	–.68 to .32	–.18	–.11 to +.09	–.01	–.1 to +.1	0

FLUID CAPACITIES & COOLING SYSTEM DATA

Year	Model Or Engine (VIN)①	Coolant Capacity, Qts.	Radiator Cap Relief Pressure, psi	Thermo. Opening Temp. °F	Fuel Tank, Gals.	Engine Oil, Qts.②		Transmission Oil			Rear Axle Pts.
						Less Filter Change	With Filter Change	Man Trans. Pts.	Auto. Trans. Qts.③		
									Drain & Refill	Total Cap-acity	
1997	5.7L (G)	⑤	15	187	19.1	6④	6.5④	8.2	5	10.8	3.4
1998–2000	5.7L (G)	⑥	15	187	19.1	6④	6.5④	8.2	5	10.8	3.4

VIN — Vehicle Identification Number
① — The eighth digit of the VIN denotes engine code.
② — After refilling, inspect oil level again.
③ — Approximate. Make final inspection w/dipstick.
④ — Recommended engine oil SG SAE 5W-30 synthetic engine oil meeting GM specification GM4718M.
⑤ — On models w/A/T, 12.6 qts.; w/M/T, 12.9 qts.
⑥ — On models w/A/T, 12.3 qts.; w/M/T, 12.6 qts.

LUBRICANT DATA

Year	Lubricant Type				
	Transmission		Rear Axle	Power Steering System	Brake System
	Automatic	Manual			
1997	Dexron III	Dexron III	①	Synthetic Power Steering Fluid②	DOT 3 Brake Fluid
1998	Dexron III	Dexron III	③	④	DOT 3 Brake Fluid
1999–2000	Dexron III	Dexron III	⑤	④	DOT 3 Brake Fluid

① — 80W-90 GL-5 gear lubricant & lubricant additive part No. 1052358, or equivalent.
② — Meeting GM specification 12345866 or 12345867.
③ — Axle lubricant part No. 12345977 & lubricant additive part No. 1052358, or equivalents.
④ — Power steering fluid part No. 1052884, 1050017 or equivalents.
⑤ — 75W-90 synthetic axle lubricant part No. 12378261, or an equivalent meeting GM specification 9986115. When completely draining & filling add 4 ounces of lubricant additive part No. 1052358, or equivalent.

Electrical

NOTE: On Air Bag Equipped Models, Refer To " Air Bag System Precautions" Located In The Front Of This Manual For System Disarming & Arming Procedures.

NOTE: Refer To "Computer Relearn Procedures " Located In The Front Of This Manual For Computer Relearn Procedures.

INDEX

PRECAUTIONS

AIR BAG SYSTEMS

Refer to "Air Bag System Precautions" in the front of this manual for system disarming and arming procedures.

BATTERY GROUND CABLE

Prior to service, disconnect battery ground cable and isolate as required.

FUSE PANEL & FLASHER LOCATION

The fuse panel is located behind the far righthand corner of the instrument panel. The turn signal and hazard flasher is incorporated into the hazard warning switch.

FUEL PUMP RELAY LOCATION

The fuel pump relay is located in the underhood electrical center.

RELAY CENTER LOCATION

The relay center, or underhood electrical center, is located on the righthand side of the engine compartment, in front of the battery.

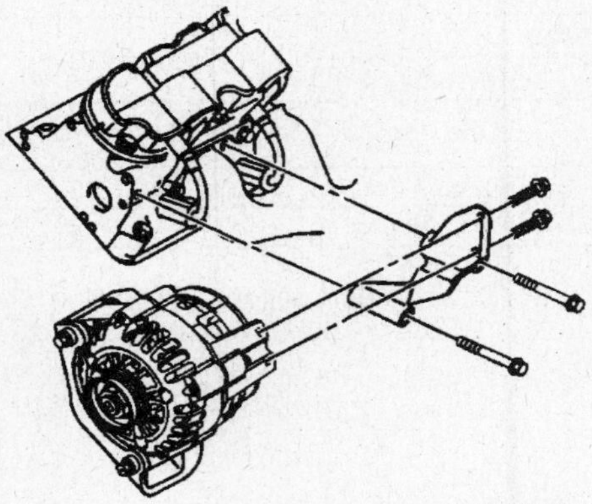

GC1129700074000X

Fig. 1 Alternator mounting bracket removal

STARTER

REPLACE

1. Raise and support vehicle.
2. Disconnect HO2S electrical connectors.
3. Remove takedown pipe flange nuts.
4. Remove intermediate pipe to rear pipe mounting bolts.
5. Remove front exhaust hanger bolts from takedown pipe bracket.
6. Remove rear exhaust hanger bolts from rear intermediate exhaust pipes.
7. Remove intermediate pipe assembly.
8. Remove rear HO2S from intermediate pipe.
9. Note orientation of wiring, then remove nuts and disconnect electrical connections from starter motor.
10. Remove starter motor mounting bolts while supporting starter motor.
11. Remove starter motor.
12. Reverse procedure to install, noting the following:
    a. **On 1997 models, torque** starter motor mounting bolts to 35 ft. lbs.
    b. **On 1998–2000 models, torque** starter motor mounting bolts to 37 ft. lbs.
    c. **On all models, torque** S-terminal mounting nut to 35 inch lbs.
    d. **Torque** battery cable mounting nuts to 11 ft. lbs.

ALTERNATOR

REPLACE

1. Disconnect regulator electrical connector and battery to alternator terminal from back of alternator.
2. Release accessory drive belt tensioner.
3. Remove accessory drive belt from alternator pulley.
4. Remove alternator rear mounting bracket and mounting bolts, **Fig. 1.**
5. Remove alternator mounting bolts, **Fig. 2.**
6. Remove alternator from bracket.
7. Reverse procedure to install, noting the following:
    a. **Torque** alternator mounting bolts to 37 ft. lbs.
    b. **Torque** battery terminal nut to 10 ft. lbs.
    c. **Torque** battery cable bolt to 11 ft. lbs.

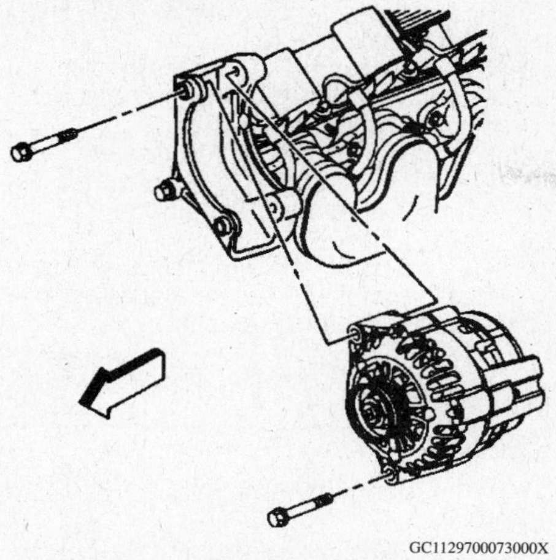

Fig. 2 Alternator removal

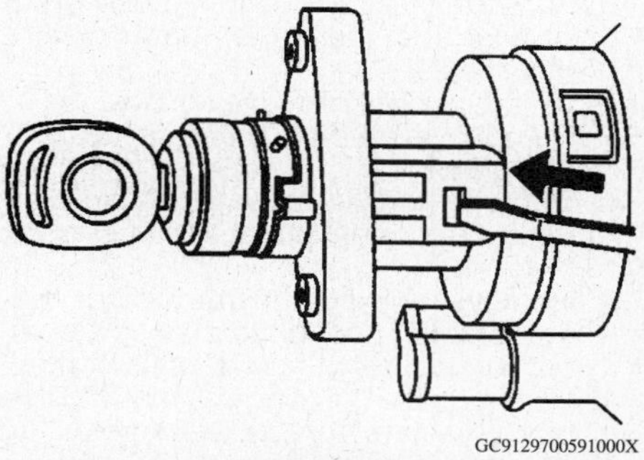

Fig. 5 Ignition lock cylinder removal

COIL PACK

REPLACE

1. Remove fuel rail cover.
2. Disconnect ignition coil harness electrical connector.
3. Disconnect spark plug wires at ignition coils.
4. Remove ignition coil mounting bolts, **Figs. 3 and 4.**
5. Remove ignition coils.
6. Reverse procedure to install. **Torque** coil mounting bolts to 106 inch lbs.

IGNITION LOCK

REPLACE

1. Apply parking brake and remove console.
2. Remove instrument panel accessory trim plate.
3. Remove driver's knee bolster trim panel.
4. Note routing of ignition switch lock cylinder wire wraps around switch bezel.
5. Remove ignition switch lock cylinder electrical connector from mounting tab on ignition switch.
6. Disconnect lock cylinder electrical connector.
7. Insert key and turn to run position.
8. Depress and hold ignition lock cylinder mounting tab located on righthand lower side of switch, using flat-bladed screwdriver or other suitable tool, **Fig. 5.**

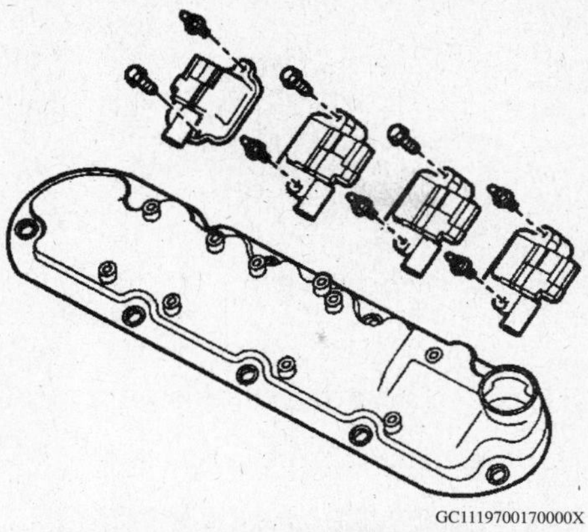

Fig. 3 Coil pack removal. 1997–98

9. Pull to remove ignition lock cylinder.
10. Remove ignition switch bezel. Carefully pull to unsnap it.
11. Reverse procedure to install, noting the following:
    a. Wrap ignition switch wire around base of switch bezel as in original fashion.
    b. Align bezel slots to cylinder pins, then push to secure in place.
    c. Press cylinder into place and listen for retaining tab to produce definite click.

IGNITION SWITCH

REPLACE

1. Remove ignition lock cylinder as previously described under "Ignition Lock, Replace."
2. Remove hazard warning switch wiring harness from ignition switch retainer.
3. Disconnect ignition switch electrical connectors.
4. **On models equipped with automatic transmission,** disconnect park lock cable from ignition switch using suitable screwdriver to depress retaining tab, **Fig. 6.**
5. **On all models,** remove ignition switch mounting bolts.
6. Remove ignition switch.
7. Reverse procedure to install. **Torque** ignition switch mounting bolts to 49 inch lbs.

CLUTCH START SWITCH

REPLACE

1. Disconnect clutch start switch electrical connector.
2. Insert feeler gauge between switch and clutch pedal bracket to release switch tab.
3. Remove clutch start switch by lifting slightly then pulling.
4. Reverse procedure to install.

NEUTRAL SAFETY SWITCH

REPLACE

1. Raise and support vehicle.
2. Disconnect HO2S connectors.

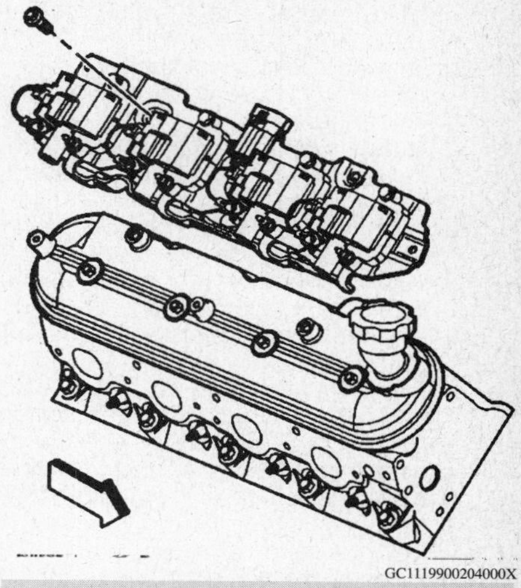

Fig. 4 Coil pack removal. 1999–2000

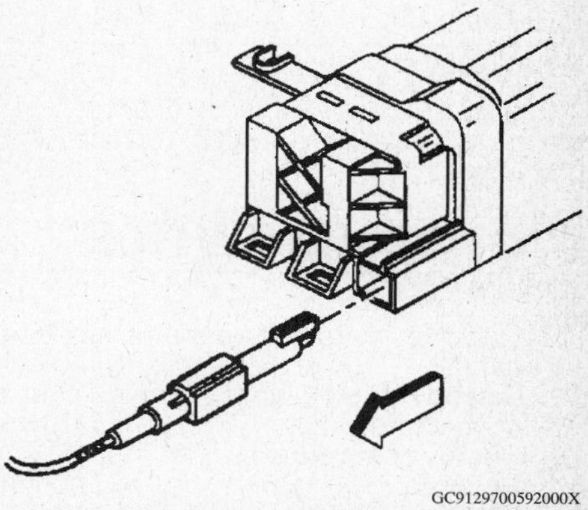

Fig. 6 Park lock cable removal

3. Remove exhaust takedown pipe flange nuts.
4. Remove intermediate pipe to rear pipe mounting bolts.
5. Remove front exhaust hanger bolts from takedown pipe bracket.
6. Remove rear exhaust hanger bolts from rear intermediate exhaust pipe.
7. Remove intermediate pipe assembly.
8. Remove rear HO2S from intermediate pipe.
9. Shift transmission to Neutral position.
10. Remove transmission shift control cable bracket to transmission nuts.
11. Disconnect transmission shift control cable from transmission range selector lever. Unsnap to release cable. **Use extra caution during these steps. Rod end guide tubes cannot endure much abuse.**
12. Position transmission shift cable and bracket aside.
13. Disconnect neutral safety switch electrical connectors.
14. Use wrench on manual shaft flats to prevent rotation, then remove range selector shift lever mounting nut and lever.
15. Ensure transmission is still in neutral.

16. Remove neutral safety switch mounting bolts.
17. Slide switch off manual shaft.
18. Reverse procedure to install, noting the following:
    a. Install switch alignment tool No. J-41364-A, or equivalent, to neutral safety switch.
    b. Align two lower slots on switch with two lower tabs on tool.
    c. Turn tool until its upper pin aligns with slot on top of switch.
    d. Ensure transmission is still in neutral.
    e. Ensure switch hub flats align with those on shaft, then install switch and tool onto manual shaft until switch mounting bracket meets transmission case mounting bosses.
    f. **Torque** switch mounting bolts to 20 ft. lbs.
    g. Remove alignment tool.
    h. Install range selector lever, then **torque** nut to 15 ft. lbs.

HEADLAMP SWITCH

REPLACE

Refer to "Multi-Function Switch, Replace" for headlamp switch replacement procedure.

STOP LIGHT SWITCH

REPLACE

1. Remove instrument panel lower trim panel.
2. Disconnect stop lamp switch electrical connectors.
3. Remove stop lamp switch.
4. Reverse procedure to install, noting the following:
    a. While keeping brake pedal depressed, insert switch into retainer until switch body has seated.
    b. Listen for clicks as threaded portion of switch travels through retainer.
    c. Slowly pull brake pedal fully rearward until clicks have stopped. Switch will move in retainer and self-adjust.

MULTI-FUNCTION SWITCH

REPLACE

1. Release tilt wheel lever locking tab using suitable small screwdriver, then slide lever straight out from steering column .
2. Remove steering wheel as outlined under "Steering Wheel, Replace."
3. Remove driver's side knee bolster trim panel.
4. Remove upper and lower steering column covers.
5. Disconnect multi-function turn signal switch electrical connectors.
6. Release upper and lower retaining clips.
7. Slide multi-function turn signal switch away from steering column lock module.

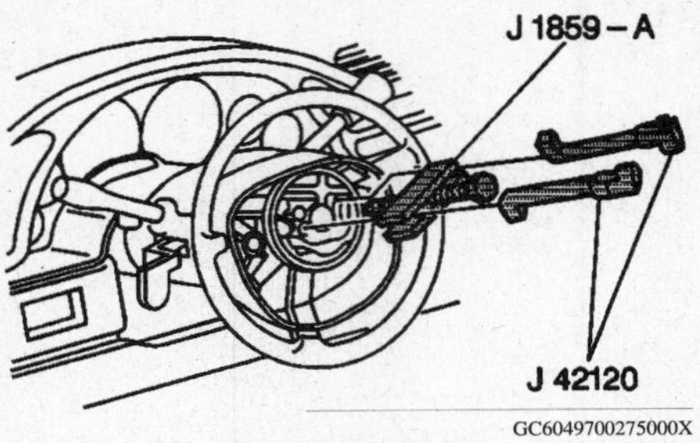

Fig. 7 Steering wheel removal

8. Reverse procedure to install.

TURN SIGNAL SWITCH

REPLACE

Refer to "Multi-Function Switch, Replace" for procedure.

DIMMER SWITCH

REPLACE

1. Remove instrument panel cluster.
2. Disconnect electrical connectors at instrument panel dimmer switch and driver information center switch.
3. Remove instrument panel cluster bezel mounting screws, then the bezel.
4. Remove instrument panel dimmer switch mounting screws, then the switch.
5. Reverse procedure to install.

STEERING WHEEL

REPLACE

REMOVAL

1. Remove driver's air bag module as described under "Air Bag, Replace."
2. Disconnect horn wiring harness from steering column.
3. Disconnect ground wire from steering column.
4. Remove and discard steering wheel set nut.
5. Install steering wheel puller and legs tool Nos. J-1859-A and J-42120, or equivalents, **Fig. 7.**
6. Tighten puller center screw against steering column shaft until wheel slides off shaft.

INSTALLATION

1. Install steering wheel onto column.
2. Install new steering wheel set nut.
3. **Torque** steering wheel set nut to 30 ft. lbs.
4. Connect horn electrical connector.
5. Install air bag as described under "Air Bag, Replace. "

INSTRUMENT CLUSTER

REPLACE

1. Remove instrument panel upper trim pad.
2. **On models equipped with Head Up Display (HUD),** carefully lift HUD electrical harness from between cluster and display, then disconnect HUD electrical connector.
3. **On all models,** remove Instrument Panel Cluster (IPC) to steering column bracket mounting screws.
4. Lift rear of IPC slightly to release locator tab, then lift IPC to access and disconnect electrical connectors.
5. Remove IPC.
6. Reverse procedure to install, ensuring cluster retaining tab is properly positioned to steering column bracket.

RADIO

REPLACE

1. **On 1998–2000 models,** proceed as follows:
    a. Remove front floor kick-up panel.
    b. Remove instrument panel electrical center cover.
    c. Remove RDO/CD Mini-Fuse No. 5 fuse from instrument panel electrical center.
2. **On all models,** remove console.
3. Remove instrument panel accessory trim plate.
4. Remove screws mounting radio control to instrument panel center support bracket.
5. Remove radio control from center support bracket enough to access electrical connectors at rear of radio control.
6. Disconnect electrical, audio and coaxial connectors from radio control.
7. Remove radio control.
8. Reverse procedure to install.

WIPER MOTOR

REPLACE

1. Remove wiper arm assemblies.
2. Remove air inlet screen.
3. Remove wiper motor module.
4. Disconnect wiper transmission linkage from crank arm, using linkage separator tool No. J-39232, or equivalent.
5. Remove three wiper motor to wiper motor module mounting screws.
6. Remove wiper motor from wiper motor module.
7. Reverse procedure to install, noting the following:
    a. Install motor into module.
    b. Connect linkage to crank arm using linkage installer tool No. J-39529, or equivalent.

WIPER SWITCH

REPLACE

1. Remove tilt wheel lever. Refer to "Steering Columns " for removal procedure.
2. Remove driver's side knee bolster trim panel.
3. Remove upper and lower steering column covers.
4. Disconnect electrical connector from wiring harness.
5. Release upper and lower mounting clips, then slide wiper washer switch from steering column lock module.
6. Reverse procedure to install.

WIPER TRANSMISSION

REPLACE

1. Remove wiper arm assemblies.
2. Remove air inlet screen.
3. Remove wiper motor module assembly.
4. Remove righthand wiper transmission mounting bolts.
5. Remove righthand wiper transmission from wiper transmission linkage.
6. Disconnect wiper transmission linkage from wiper motor module assembly using linkage separator tool No. J-39232, or equivalent.
7. Remove lefthand wiper transmission mounting bolts.
8. Disconnect lefthand wiper transmission from wiper transmission linkage.
9. Reverse procedure to install, using linkage installer tool No. J-39529, or equivalent, to connect linkage to crank arm.

BLOWER MOTOR

REPLACE

1. **On 1998–2000 models equipped with manual A/C,** remove front floor kick-up panel.
2. **On all models,** remove passenger floor hush panel.
3. Disconnect blower motor electrical connectors.
4. Remove cooling tube.
5. Remove blower motor to evaporator and heater core module mounting screws.
6. Remove blower motor and fan from module.
7. Reverse procedure to install.

HEATER CORE

REPLACE

1997

1. Evacuate refrigerant from air conditioning system.
2. Drain cooling system.
3. Remove battery and heat shield.
4. Remove intake manifold.
5. Disconnect heater hose pipe assembly from module.
6. Disconnect accumulator hose assembly from module. Discard O-rings.
7. Remove drain tube from module.
8. Remove instrument panel upper pad and air distribution duct assembly.
9. Disconnect electrical connector from instrument cluster.
10. Remove instrument cluster assembly.
11. Remove lefthand inboard side window glass defroster duct from windshield defroster duct.
12. Remove righthand inboard side window glass defroster duct from windshield defroster duct.
13. Disconnect DRL electrical connector from windshield defroster duct, if equipped.
14. Disconnect sun load temperature sensor from windshield defroster duct, if equipped.
15. Remove windshield defroster duct from module.
16. Remove inside air temperature sensor duct from module.
17. Disconnect electrical connector from passenger air bag module.
18. Remove passenger air bag bracket and module assembly.
19. Remove instrument panel center support bracket.
20. Disconnect electrical and vacuum connections from HVAC control head.
21. Remove driver side knee bolster.
22. Remove instrument panel center support bracket.
23. Remove driver side floor hush panel.
24. Remove lefthand floor air outlet duct from module.
25. Remove passenger floor hush panel.
26. Unsnap lower righthand floor air duct from upper righthand air duct.
27. Remove upper righthand floor air duct from module.
28. Disconnect electrical connector from blower motor.
29. Remove blower motor from module.
30. Disconnect electrical connector from temperature door control motor, if equipped.
31. Disconnect electrical connection to vacuum solenoid, if equipped.
32. Disconnect vacuum source line connection from instrument panel harness.
33. Disconnect electrical connector from temperature door control motor.
34. Remove lefthand and righthand rear floor air ducts from module.
35. Remove bolts and nuts mounting evaporator and heater core module to bulkhead and instrument panel brace.
36. Remove evaporator and heater core module.
37. Remove and discard air inlet, drain and plumbing seals.
38. Remove heater core cover.
39. Remove and discard cavity, whistle and permagum seals.
40. Remove and discard outer heater core seal, if equipped.
41. Remove heater core mounting clip screws.
42. Remove heater core pipe screw.
43. Remove heater core.
44. Remove and discard lower, center, upper and side heater core seals from heater evaporator module.
45. Reverse procedure to install.

1998–2000

1. Evacuate refrigerant from air conditioning system.
2. Drain coolant into an approved container.
3. Remove battery and heat shield.
4. Remove intake manifold.
5. Remove heater pipe to dash panel bracket nut.
6. Position heater pipe bracket aside.
7. Remove heater pipe to core retaining bolt.
8. Cap or plug heater pipe and core to prevent contamination and spillage.
9. Remove accumulator hose to evaporator retaining bolt.
10. Disconnect accumulator hose and evaporator tube-rear from evaporator. Cap or tape over all open A/C lines.
11. Remove evaporator and HVAC module drain tube from module.
12. Remove floor console.
13. Remove instrument panel accessory trim plate.
14. Remove glove compartment.
15. Remove righthand hush panel.
16. Remove driver's side knee bolster trim panel.
17. Remove lefthand hush panel.
18. Remove instrument panel upper trim pad.
19. Remove instrument cluster to steering column bracket retaining screws.
20. Position cluster to allow room for HVAC module removal.
21. Remove lefthand side window defroster lower outlet duct.
22. **On models equipped with Automatic Temperature Control (ATC),** remove inside air temperature sensor aspirator duct and muffler.
23. **On all models,** disconnect Daytime Running Lamp (DRL) sensor electrical connector from lefthand side of windshield defroster duct.
24. Disconnect temperature valve actuator electrical connector.
25. Remove instrument panel center support bracket.
26. Remove ignition switch housing bracket.
27. Remove lefthand floor air outlet duct retaining screws, then the duct.
28. Remove lefthand rear floor air outlet duct by rotating it 90° clockwise.
29. Remove righthand side window defroster lower outlet.
30. Remove passenger's air bag module bracket and knee bolster bracket.
31. **On models equipped with ATC,** disconnect sunload sensor electrical connector from righthand side of windshield defroster duct.
32. **On all models,** remove righthand floor air outlet duct retaining screws, then the duct.
33. Pull front floor carpet away from righthand side of floor tunnel.
34. Remove righthand rear floor air outlet duct by rotating 90° counterclockwise.
35. Remove blower motor.
36. Disconnect instrument panel vacuum harness from HVAC module harness.
37. Disconnect vacuum electric solenoid electrical connector.
38. Remove windshield defroster duct retaining screws, then the duct.
39. If required, position A/C refrigerant lines to ease removal of HVAC module retaining and sealing nuts from dash panel.
40. Remove HVAC module retaining screws from instrument panel upper support beam.
41. Carefully remove HVAC module.
42. Remove and discard seals at module air inlet, drain and plumbing seals.
43. Remove heater core outlet cover retaining screws, then the cover.
44. Remove heater core cover retaining screws, then the cover.

45. Remove and discard cavity, whistle and permagum seals from heater core cover.
46. Remove and discard heater core outer seal from core.
47. Remove heater core retaining clamp screw, clamp and pipe retainer clamp screw.
48. Remove heater core from HVAC module lower case.
49. Remove and discard heater core lower, center, upper and side seals at HVAC module lower case.
50. Release retaining tab using suitable flat-bladed screwdriver and open up heater core pipe retainer clamp, then remove clamp from pipes.
51. Reverse procedure to install, noting the following:
    a. Replace all gaskets, O-rings and seals.
    b. **Torque** heater core cover and outlet retaining screws to 14 inch lbs.
    c. Ensure cutouts on dash mat are properly aligned so air inlet, drain and plumbing seals are seated directly against dash panel, not dash mat.
    d. Ensure dash panel drain opening aligns with HVAC module drain.
    e. Coat new refrigerant line O-rings with suitable 525 viscosity refrigerant oil.

EVAPORATOR CORE

REPLACE

1. Remove HVAC module as previously described under "Heater Core, Replace."
2. Release vacuum harness retainers on HVAC case below air inlet housing.
3. Remove upper heater evaporator module screws.
4. Separate upper and lower heater evaporator module halves.
5. Remove and discard seal.
6. Remove evaporator core from module.
7. Remove and discard lower, side and upper evaporator core seals.
8. Remove and discard water core filter from evaporator core.
9. Reverse procedure to install.

5.7L Engine

NOTE: On Air Bag Equipped Models, Refer To "Air Bag System Precautions" Located In The Front Of This Manual For System Disarming & Arming Procedures.

NOTE: Refer To "Computer Relearn Procedures " Located In The Front Of This Manual For Computer Relearn Procedures.

INDEX

PRECAUTIONS

FUEL SYSTEM PRESSURE RELIEF

Failure to relieve system pressure prior to disconnecting fuel system components may cause fire or personal injury.

1. Disconnect and isolate battery ground cable.
2. Remove fuel tank filler cap to release fuel tank pressure.
3. Remove lefthand fuel rail cover.
4. Prior to disconnecting fuel line, position shop towel over fitting.
5. Connect pressure gauge tool No. J-34730-1A, or equivalent, to pressure tap on fuel rail.
6. Position bleed hose into suitable container.
7. Slowly relieve fuel system pressure.

BATTERY GROUND CABLE

Prior to service, disconnect battery ground cable and isolate as required.

COMPRESSION PRESSURE

When measuring compression, lowest cylinder must be within 70% of the highest cylinder with a minimum pressure of 100 psi. Compression test results will fall into one of the following categories:

1. Normally, compression builds up quickly and evenly to specifications on each cylinder.

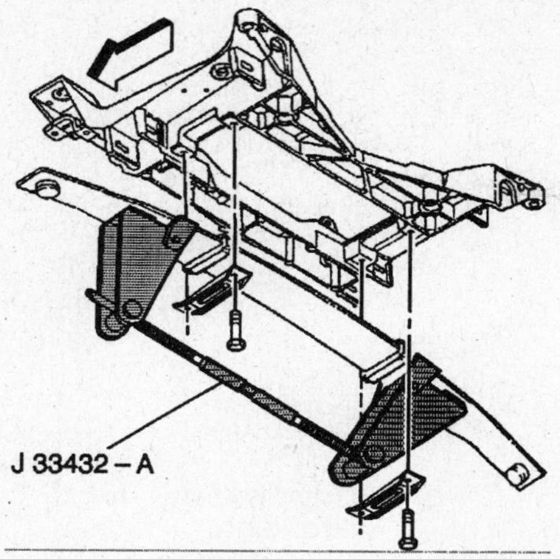

Fig. 1 Transverse spring compression

2. If piston rings are faulty, compression will be low on first stroke, then build up on following strokes but will not reach specifications. Improvement is considerable with addition of oil, approximately three squirts from plunger type oil can.
3. If valves are faulty, compression will be low on first stroke and will not tend to build up on following strokes. It will not improve much with addition of oil.
4. Perform compression test, noting the following:
   a. Ensure battery is fully charged.
   b. Bring engine to operating temperature.
   c. Disconnect electrical connector at crankshaft ignition timing sensor.
   d. Disable fuel injection system.
   e. Remove spark plugs.
   f. Ensure throttle is wide open.
   g. Install compression gauge tool No. J-38722, or equivalent, crank engine through four complete compression strokes, then record results for each cylinder.

ENGINE MOUNT

REPLACE

1. Remove alternator from accessory mount bracket.
2. **On 1998–2000 models,** proceed as follows:
   a. Remove windshield washer reservoir.
   b. Disconnect coolant switch electrical connector and position wiring aside.
   c. Disconnect headlamp electrical connector and position wiring aside.
3. **On all models,** support engine using engine support tool Nos. J-41803 and J-28467-B, or equivalent.
4. Raise and support vehicle.
5. Remove front wheels.
6. Remove tie rod end nuts.
7. Remove tie rod ends from steering knuckles using separator tool No. J-42188, or equivalent.

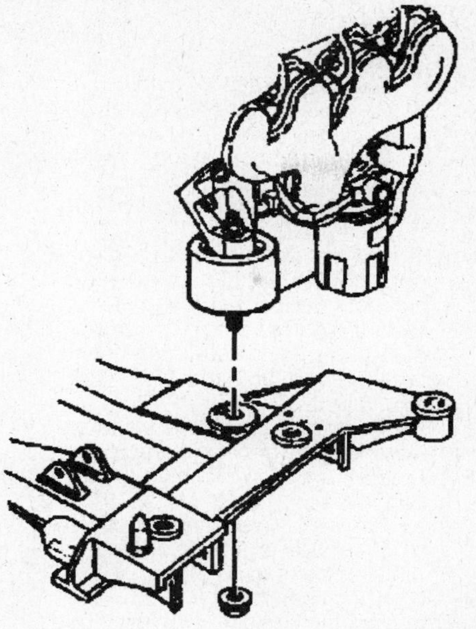

Fig. 2 Engine mount to cradle removal

8. Remove stabilizer bar bolts and straps.
9. Disconnect stabilizer from cradle.
10. Remove power steering cooler bolts.
11. Disconnect power steering cooler from cradle and position it upward.
12. Remove power steering gear from cradle and position it upward.
13. Install transverse leaf spring compressor tool No. J-33432-A, or equivalent, then carefully compress spring, **Fig. 1.**
14. Remove shock absorber lower mounting bolts.
15. **On 1997 models,** remove lower ball joint nuts.
16. **On 1998–2000 models,** loosen, but do not remove, lower ball joint nuts.
17. **On all models,** separate lower ball joints using separator tool No. J-42188, or equivalent, then remove tool and ball joint nuts.
18. Disconnect all electrical connectors from crossmember.
19. **On 1997 models,** remove transverse leaf spring compressor tool.
20. Disconnect all electrical harnesses from cradle.
21. **On 1998–2000 models,** remove brake pressure valve modulator valve bracket bolts, then position valve and bracket away from crossmember.
22. **On all models,** remove motor mount to cradle nuts, **Fig. 2.**
23. Support cradle with suitable transmission jack, or equivalent.
24. Remove cradle nuts, then the cradle.
25. Remove upper engine mount nut, **Fig. 3.**
26. Remove engine mount.
27. Remove motor mount bracket bolts from engine block, then the bracket.
28. Reverse procedure to install. Tighten fasteners to specifications.

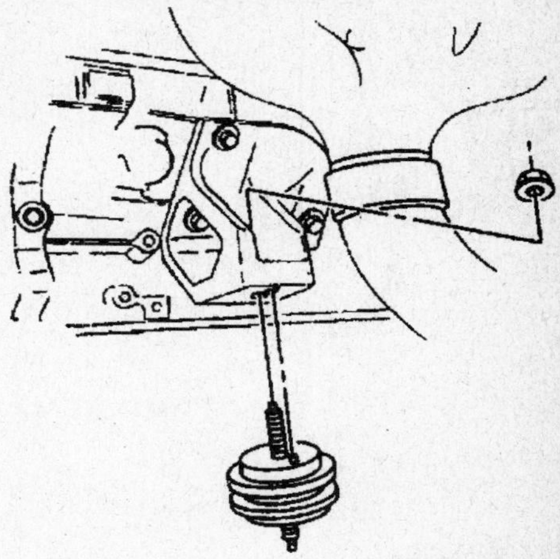

Fig. 3 Upper engine mount removal

ENGINE

REPLACE

1997

1. Evacuate A/C system.
2. Raise and support vehicle.
3. Drain engine coolant into an approved container, then lower vehicle.
4. Disconnect IAT and MAF sensor electrical connectors.
5. Disconnect fuel regulator purge line from air intake duct.
6. Remove air intake duct and air cleaner assembly.
7. Remove accessory drive belt.
8. Remove fuel rail covers.
9. Relieve fuel system pressure as described under “Precautions.”
10. Disconnect fuel lines at fuel rail.
11. Disconnect radiator and heater hoses from water pump.
12. Disconnect the following electrical connectors:
    a. Fuel injectors.
    b. Ignition coil main connectors.
    c. EVAP solenoid.
    d. Electric throttle motor.
    e. Throttle position sensor.
    f. ECT sensor.
    g. A/C compressor.
    h. Alternator.
13. Remove alternator rear bracket bolts and bracket.
14. Remove alternator mounting bolts and alternator.
15. Disconnect brake booster vacuum hose from brake booster.
16. Remove intermediate shaft to steering gear bolt.
17. Disconnect intermediate steering shaft from steering gear and position aside.
18. Disconnect AIR hose from lefthand exhaust manifold.
19. Raise and support vehicle and remove front wheels.
20. Remove intermediate exhaust pipe.
21. Remove closeout panel bolts, then the panel.
22. Remove starter electrical connectors.

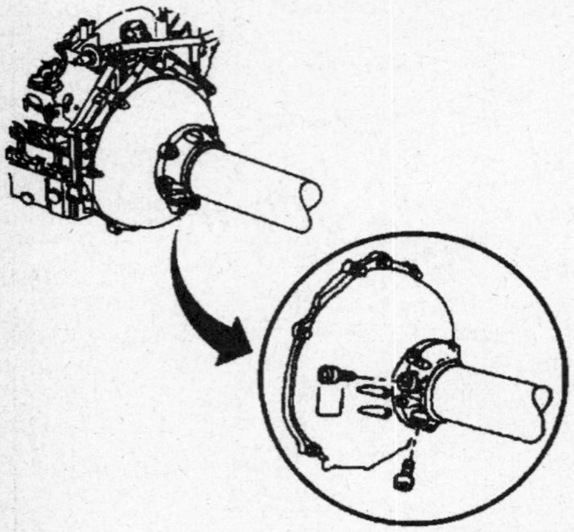

GC1069700892000X

Fig. 4 Propeller shaft support bolt installation

23. Remove all grounds from righthand side of engine block.
24. Remove starter bolts and starter.
25. Disconnect oil level sensor connector.
26. Disconnect crank position sensor connector.
27. Disconnect righthand front HO2S connector.
28. Remove A/C compressor hose retaining bolts.
29. Remove A/C compressor hose from A/C compressor.
30. Disconnect engine oil temperature sensor connector.
31. Disconnect all grounds from lefthand side of engine block.
32. Disconnect lefthand front HO2S connector.
33. Remove front stabilizer bar bolts and straps.
34. Disconnect front stabilizer bar from cradle.
35. Disconnect electrical connectors and harness from electric cooling fans.
36. Remove electric cooling fan bolts.
37. Remove both electric cooling fans.
38. Install transverse spring compressor tool No. J-33432-A, or equivalent, to front spring, **Fig. 1.**
39. Compress front transverse spring.
40. Remove tie rod end nuts.
41. Remove tie rod ends from steering knuckles using ball joint separator tool No. J-42188, or equivalent.
42. Disconnect ABS electrical connectors at cradle.
43. Disconnect EVO connector at cradle.
44. Disconnect RTD connectors at cradle, if equipped.
45. Remove lower shock absorber mounting bolts.
46. Separate lower ball joints using ball joint separator tool No. J-42188, or equivalent.
47. Remove J-33432-A from front spring.
48. Disconnect automatic transmission cooler lines at engine flywheel housing junction, if equipped.
49. Disconnect automatic transmission cooler lines from radiator.
50. **On models equipped with automatic transmissions,** proceed as follows:
    a. Remove two plugs in driveline support assembly.
    b. Install an M10 × 1.5 bolt, 55 mm or longer in each location, **Fig. 4. Torque** bolts to 26 ft. lbs.
    c. Remove engine flywheel housing access plug.
    d. Position transmission flywheel hub collar to access bolt.
    e. Loosen transmission flywheel hub collar bolt.
51. **On all models,** install driveline support tool No. 42203, or equivalent, to closeout panel flange, **Fig. 5.**
52. Partially lower vehicle and support engine and front cradle assembly on engine support table tool No. J-39580, or equivalent.
53. Remove front cradle nuts and partially lower engine and front cradle.
54. Disconnect the following electrical connectors:
    a. Engine oil pressure gauge.
    b. Camshaft position sensor.
    c. MAP sensor.
    d. Knock sensor.
    e. Ground on rear of lefthand head.
    f. All remaining electrical connections.
55. Remove front driveline support assembly bolts.
56. Slide engine and cradle assembly forward to clear propeller shaft spline.
57. Raise vehicle completely off of engine and cradle assembly.
58. Remove power steering pump and reservoir from engine and tie to cradle.
59. Remove engine mount to cradle nuts.
60. Remove engine from cradle.
61. Reverse procedure to install. Tighten fasteners to specifications.

1998–2000

1. Raise and support vehicle.
2. Drain coolant into an approved container.
3. Lower vehicle.
4. Recover A/C refrigerant charge.
5. Disconnect electrical connectors at IAT and MAF sensors.
6. Disconnect fuel pressure regulator purge tube from air intake duct.
7. Position air intake duct and air cleaner assembly forward.
8. Remove radiator as outlined under "Radiator, Replace."
9. **On 1998 models equipped with front-mounted Electronic Brake Control Module and Brake Pressure Modulator Valve (EBTCM/BPMV) and all 1999–2000 models,** remove EBTCM/BPMV and bracket. Position brake pipes aside as required. Cap and plug all open lines.
10. **On all models,** remove serpentine belt.
11. Remove lefthand fuel line from connector at front of firewall. Cap and plug fittings and openings.
12. Remove engine appearance covers.
13. Relieve fuel system pressure as outlined under "Precautions."
14. Disconnect fuel lines at fuel rail. Cap and plug fittings and openings.
15. Disconnect radiator hoses and heater hoses at water pump.

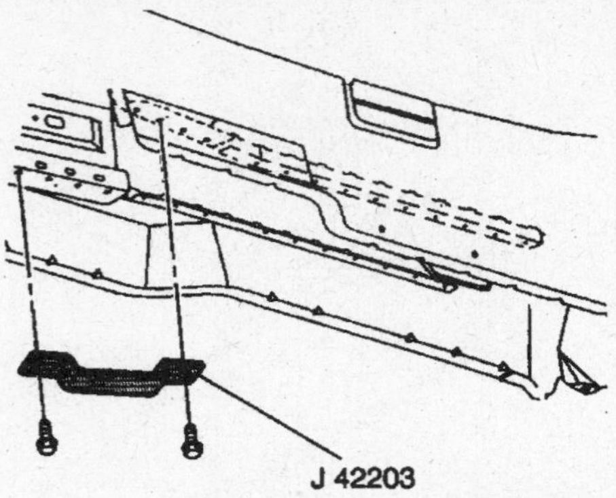

GC1069700893000X

Fig. 5 Driveline support installation

16. Disconnect the following electrical connectors:
    a. Fuel injectors.
    b. Ignition coil main connectors.
    c. EVAP solenoid.
    d. Electric throttle motor.
    e. Throttle position sensor.
    f. ECT sensor.
    g. A/C compressor.
    h. Alternator.
17. Remove alternator rear bracket bolts and bracket.
18. Remove alternator mounting bolts and alternator.
19. Disconnect brake booster vacuum hose from brake booster.
20. Remove steering intermediate shaft to steering gear bolt.
21. Disconnect steering intermediate shaft from steering gear and position it to left onto frame rail.
22. Disconnect AIR hose from lefthand exhaust manifold.
23. Raise and support vehicle, then remove front tires and wheels.
24. Disconnect and unclip HO2S electrical connectors from intermediate exhaust pipes.
25. Remove intermediate exhaust pipes.
26. Remove mounting bolts and closeout panel.
27. Disconnect starter electrical connectors and wiring.
28. Remove mounting bolts and starter.
29. Disconnect all righthand and read engine block wiring harness clips.
30. Disconnect oil level, CKP and righthand HO2S sensors electrical connectors.
31. Remove mounting bolt and A/C compressor hose assembly.
32. Disconnect engine oil temperature and lefthand HO2S sensors electrical connectors.
33. Remove mounting bolts and straps, then disconnect front stabilizer bar from cradle.
34. Disconnect electric cooling fans' electrical connectors and harness.
35. Slide up and remove electric cooling fans.
36. Loosen nuts and remove tie rod ends from steering knuckles using ball joint separator tool No. J-42188, or equivalent.

37. Disconnect ABS electrical, EVO and RTD connectors clips from at cradle.
38. Remove lower shock absorber mounting bolts.
39. Compress and remove front transverse spring using transverse spring compressor tool No. J-33432-A, or equivalent, **Fig. 1.**
40. **On models equipped with automatic transmission,** proceed as follows:
    a. Disconnect fluid cooler lines at bellhousing junction.
    b. Disconnect cooler pipe clamps from front and rear of engine oil pan.
    c. Disconnect cooler pipes from radiator.
    d. Remove two plugs in driveline support assembly.
    e. Install M10 1.5 × 55 mm, or longer bolt, in each plug location, **Fig. 4** and **torque** to 26 ft. lbs.
    f. Remove bellhousing lower inspection cover.
    g. Position transmission flexplate hub collar downward to access and loosen mounting bolt.
    h. Unclip wiring harness from engine and position it to driveline.
41. **On models equipped with manual transmission,** proceed as follows:
    a. Unclip hydraulic clutch actuator hose from bellhousing clip.
    b. Depress white circular release ring on actuator hose using hydraulic clutch line separator tool No. J-36221, or equivalent, while pulling lightly on master cylinder hose. This will separate two portions.
    c. Plug both open hydraulic hose ends.
    d. Remove bellhousing bolts from driveline support assembly.
42. **On all models,** install driveline support tool No. J-42203, or equivalent, to closeout panel flange, **Fig. 5. Do not support engine weight with driveline line support tool.**
43. Slowly lower vehicle to engine support table tool No. J-39580 and table top tool No. J-39580-500, or equivalents.
44. Support engine and cradle with table tools.
45. Remove front and rear cradle nuts **by hand.**
46. Partially raise vehicle.
47. Remove and reposition AIR tube bracket bolt to access and remove lefthand rear ground strap at cylinder head.
48. Disconnect following electrical connectors:
    a. Engine oil pressure sensor.
    b. Camshaft position sensor.
    c. MAP sensor.
    d. Knock sensor.
    e. Ground on rear of lefthand head.
    f. All remaining electrical connections.
49. Remove front driveline support assembly bolts from driveline.
50. Insert suitable flat-bladed screwdriver, or similar tool, between edge of driveline support assembly and bellhousing, then carefully pry engine loose from driveline.

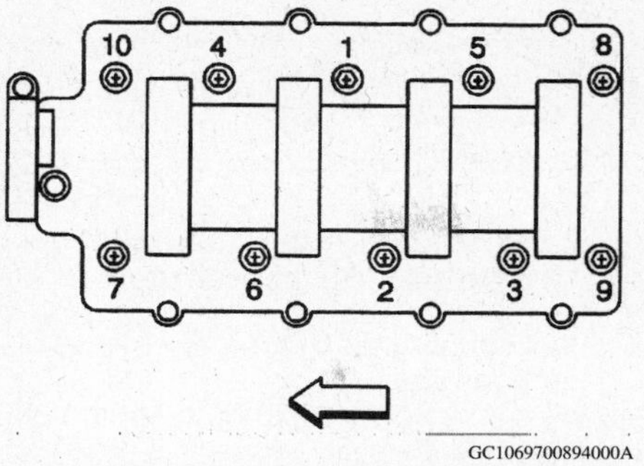

Fig. 6 Intake manifold bolt tightening sequence

51. Slowly and carefully pull engine away from driveshaft.
52. Slowly raise vehicle as soon as input shaft clears bellhousing.
53. Slide engine and cradle assembly forward to clear driveshaft spline.
54. **Ensure all wiring harnesses are free and clear,** then carefully raise vehicle completely off engine and cradle assembly.
55. Remove pulley from power steering pump using pulley removal tool No. J-25034-B, or equivalent.
56. Remove power steering pump bolts, then position pump and reservoir aside.
57. Remove A/C compressor belt.
58. Remove A/C compressor bolts and nut.
59. Remove A/C compressor stud and compressor from engine.
60. Remove AIR tube mounting bolts and tube from exhaust manifolds.
61. Install engine lifting brackets tool No. J-41798, or equivalent.
62. Install suitable lifting device to lifting brackets.
63. Mark locations and disconnect wires, then remove spark plugs.
64. Remove engine mount to cradle nuts, then the engine from cradle.
65. Reverse procedure to install, noting the following:
    a. **Only use hand tools to install new engine cradle nuts.**
    b. **On models equipped with automatic transmission,** tighten flexplate hub collar bolt by hand after bellhousing to driveline support assembly bolts have been tightened.
    c. After running engine to operating temperature, then allowing to cool to room temperature, tighten hub collar bolt to specifications.
    d. **On all models,** tighten all mounting bolts and nuts to specifications.

INTAKE MANIFOLD

REPLACE

1. Raise and support vehicle.
2. Drain cooling system, then lower vehicle.
3. Disconnect IAT and MAF sensors electrical connectors.
4. Disconnect fuel regulator purge line from air intake duct.
5. Remove air intake duct and air cleaner assembly.
6. Remove fuel rail covers.
7. Relieve fuel system pressure as described under "Precautions."
8. Disconnect fuel lines from fuel rail, then cap and plug all open fittings to prevent fuel contamination.
9. Remove vacuum and PCV hoses.
10. Remove throttle body coolant outlet hose from throttle body.
11. Disconnect fuel injector and knock sensor electrical connectors.
12. Disconnect all remaining electrical connectors from intake manifold.
13. Remove intake manifold bolts and fuel rail stop bracket.
14. Remove PCV valve pipe from lefthand and righthand valve covers.
15. Remove coolant air bleed hose from throttle body.
16. Remove throttle body heater outlet hose from throttle body.
17. Remove intake manifold and gaskets.
18. Remove manifold to cylinder head gaskets from intake manifold, then discard.
19. Reverse procedure to install, noting the following:
    a. Install new intake manifold to cylinder head gaskets.
    b. Apply threadlocker part No. 12345383, or equivalent, to intake manifold bolt threads.
    c. **Torque** intake manifold bolts to 44 inch lbs. in sequence, **Fig. 6.**
    d. Final **torque** bolts to 89 inch lbs. in sequence.
    e. Lubricate MAP sensor grommet with clean engine oil before installing.
    f. Install new fuel injector O-rings lubricated with clean engine oil.

EXHAUST MANIFOLD

REPLACE

LEFTHAND SIDE

1. Raise and support vehicle.
2. Remove lefthand intermediate exhaust pipe flange nuts from exhaust manifold studs.
3. Disconnect HO2S electrical connector and remove HO2S.
4. Lower vehicle and remove lefthand fuel rail cover.
5. Relieve fuel system pressure as described under "Precautions."
6. **On 1997 models,** disconnect fuel lines, then cap and plug lines to prevent fuel contamination.
7. **On all models,** remove accessory drive belt.
8. Remove alternator as previously described in "Electrical."
9. Remove Secondary Air Injection (SAI) hoses from SAI pipe.
10. Remove SAI pipe, bolts and gasket from exhaust manifold and position aside.
11. Remove spark plug wires from coils and spark plugs.
12. Remove spark plugs from cylinder head.

13. Remove No. 5 coil bolts and position coil aside.
14. Remove exhaust manifold and mounting bolts, then discard gasket.
15. Reverse procedure to install, noting the following:
    a. Install new exhaust manifold gasket.
    b. Apply threadlocker part No. 12345493, or equivalent, to exhaust manifold bolt threads.
    c. **Torque** exhaust manifold bolts to 11 ft. lbs. beginning with center two bolts, then alternate from side to side and work toward outside bolts.
    d. Final **Torque** to 18 ft. lbs. in same sequence.
    e. Bend over exposed edge of exhaust manifold gasket at rear of lefthand cylinder head using flat punch.
    f. Install AIR pipe and gasket and **torque** to 15 ft. lbs.

RIGHTHAND SIDE

1. Raise and support vehicle.
2. Remove intermediate exhaust pipe nuts from exhaust manifold studs.
3. Remove HO2S from manifold.
4. Lower vehicle.
5. Remove AIR pipe, bolts and gasket from righthand exhaust manifold.
6. Remove spark plug wires from spark plugs.
7. Remove engine oil dipstick from tube.
8. Remove dipstick tube mounting bolt, then the tube.
9. Remove exhaust manifold and mounting bolts, then discard gasket.
10. Reverse procedure to install, noting the following:
    a. Install new exhaust manifold gasket.
    b. Apply threadlocker part No. 12345493, or equivalent, to exhaust manifold bolt threads.
    c. **Torque** exhaust manifold bolts to 11 ft. lbs. beginning with center two bolts, then alternate from side to side and work toward outside bolts.
    d. Final **torque** to 18 ft. lbs. in same sequence.
    e. Bend over exposed edge of exhaust manifold gasket at front of righthand cylinder head using flat punch.
    f. Install AIR pipe and gasket and **torque** to 15 ft. lbs.

CYLINDER HEAD

REPLACE

LEFTHAND SIDE

Removal

1. Remove valve cover, rocker arms, pedestal and pushrods.
2. Remove lefthand exhaust manifold from cylinder head as previously described.
3. Remove intake manifold as previously described.
4. Remove vapor vent pipe.
5. Remove power steering pump pulley using pulley puller tool No. J-25034-B, or equivalent.
6. Remove power steering pump mounting bolts.
7. Remove power steering reservoir bracket bolts, then position pump and reservoir assembly aside.
8. Remove lower accessory mounting bracket bolts, then the accessory mounting bracket.
9. Remove ground wire bolt from rear of cylinder head.
10. Remove spark plugs from cylinder head.
11. Remove and discard cylinder head bolts.
12. Remove cylinder head, then discard gasket.

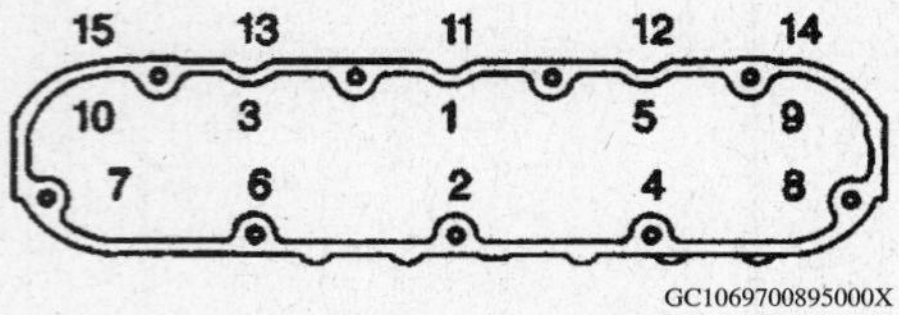

Fig. 7 Cylinder head bolt tightening sequence

Installation

1. Clean cylinder head bolt holes with compressed air.
2. Inspect cylinder head locating pins for proper installation.
3. Install new lefthand cylinder head gasket onto locating pins. When properly installed, tab on lefthand cylinder head gasket will be located left of center or closer to front of engine.
4. **On 1999–2000 models,** ensure "THIS SIDE UP" and engine displacement are visible.
5. **On all models,** install cylinder head onto locating pins and gasket.
6. Install M11 cylinder head bolts.
7. Apply threadlocker part No. 12345382, or equivalent, to threads of M8 cylinder head bolts.
8. Install M8 cylinder head bolts.
9. Tighten cylinder head bolts as follows:
    a. **Torque** M11 cylinder head bolts to 22 ft. lbs. in sequence, **Fig. 7.**
    b. Tighten M11 cylinder head bolts in sequence to 90° using torque angle meter tool No. J-36660, or equivalent.
    c. Tighten M11 cylinder head bolts 1, 2, 3, 4, 5, 6, 7 and 8 an additional 90°, and bolts 9 and 10 an additional 50° in sequence.
    d. **Torque** M8 cylinder head bolts 11, 12, 13, 14 and 15 to 22 ft. lbs. beginning with center bolt 11, then alternating side to side while working outward.
10. Install spark plugs into cylinder head.
11. Install ground wire bolt into rear of cylinder head.
12. Install accessory mounting bracket.
13. Install lower accessory mounting bracket bolts.
14. Install power steering reservoir bracket bolts.
15. Install power steering pump mounting bolts.
16. Install power steering pump pulley.
17. Install vapor vent pipe.
18. Install intake manifold as previously described.
19. Install lefthand exhaust manifold to cylinder head as previously described.
20. Install valve rocker arms, pedestal and pushrods.

RIGHTHAND SIDE

Removal

1. Remove valve rocker arms, pedestal and pushrods.
2. Remove righthand exhaust manifold from cylinder head as previously described.
3. Remove intake manifold as previously described.
4. Remove vapor vent pipe.
5. Remove spark plugs from cylinder head.
6. Remove and discard cylinder head bolts.
7. Remove cylinder head, then discard gasket.

Installation

1. Clean cylinder head bolt holes with compressed air.
2. Inspect cylinder head locating pins for proper installation.
3. Install new righthand cylinder head gasket onto locating pins. When properly installed, tab on righthand cylinder head gasket will be located left of center or closer to front of engine.
4. **On 1999–2000 models,** ensure "THIS SIDE UP" and engine displacement are visible.
5. **On all models,** install cylinder head onto locating pins and gasket.
6. Install M11 cylinder head bolts.
7. Apply threadlocker part No. 12345382, or equivalent, to threads of M8 cylinder head bolts.
8. Install M8 cylinder head bolts.
9. Tighten cylinder head bolts as follows:
    a. **Torque** M11 cylinder head bolts to 22 ft. lbs. in sequence, **Fig. 7.**
    b. Tighten M11 cylinder head bolts an additional 90° in sequence to using torque angle meter tool No. J-36660, or equivalent.
    c. Tighten M11 cylinder head bolts 1, 2, 3, 4, 5, 6, 7 and 8 an additional 90°, and bolts 9 and 10 an additional 50°.
    d. **Torque** M8 cylinder head bolts 11, 12, 13, 14 and 15 to 22 ft. lbs. beginning with center bolt 11, then alternating side to side while working outward.
10. Install spark plugs into cylinder head.
11. Install vapor vent pipe.
12. Install intake manifold as previously described.
13. Install righthand exhaust manifold to cylinder head as previously described.
14. Install valve rocker arms, pedestal and pushrods.

VALVE COVER

REPLACE

LEFTHAND SIDE

1. Remove lefthand fuel rail cover.
2. Relieve fuel system pressure as outlined under "Precautions."
3. Disconnect fuel lines from fuel rail.
4. **On 1997 models,** remove alternator rear bracket and bolts.
5. **On all models,** disconnect electrical connectors at alternator and coolant temperature sensors.
6. Disconnect secondary AIR hose from check valve.
7. Remove PCV valve pipe from lefthand valve cover.
8. Disconnect spark plug wires from ignition coils.
9. Disconnect ignition coil main harness electrical connector.
10. Disconnect EVAP purge solenoid valve hoses.
11. Remove EVAP purge solenoid from intake manifold.
12. Remove crankcase vent vacuum tube from grommet.
13. Remove valve rocker arm cover bolts and cover.
14. Remove and discard crankcase vent valve grommet from lefthand cover.
15. Remove ignition coil wire harness.
16. Remove ignition coils and bolts from cover.
17. Remove gasket and bolt grommets from cover.
18. Discard gasket. Bolt grommets may be used again if not damaged.
19. Reverse procedure to install, noting the following:
    a. Always install new cover gasket and PCV valve grommet.
    b. Install valve cover. **Torque** mounting bolts to 108 inch lbs.
    c. When installing ignition coils, **torque** mounting bolts to 108 inch lbs.

RIGHTHAND SIDE

1. Remove righthand fuel rail cover.
2. Remove secondary AIR hose from exhaust manifold.
3. Disconnect AIR hose from check valve.
4. Remove PCV hoses from breather pipes in valve cover.
5. Remove spark plug wires from ignition coils.
6. Disconnect ignition coil main harness electrical connector.
7. Remove ignition coil, bracket assembly and bolts.
8. Remove valve rocker arm cover bolts and cover.
9. Remove oil fill cap and tube, if required. Discard tube.
10. Remove gasket and bolt grommets from cover.
11. Discard gasket. Bolt grommets may be used again if not damaged.
12. Remove ignition coil bolts, wire harness and coils.
13. Reverse procedure to install, noting the following:
    a. Always install new cover gasket.
    b. Install new oil fill tube, if required.
    c. Install valve cover. **Torque** mounting bolts to 108 inch lbs.
    d. When installing ignition coils, **torque** mounting bolts to 108 inch lbs.

VALVE ARRANGEMENT

FRONT TO REAR

All..............................I-E-I-E-I-E-I-E

CAMSHAFT LOBE LIFT SPECIFICATIONS

Year & Engine (VIN Code)	Engine	Int.	Exh.
1997–99 (G)	5.7L	.277	.281

VALVE CLEARANCE SPECIFICATIONS

This engine is equipped with hydraulic valve lash adjusters. No adjustment is required.

VALVE ADJUSTMENT

This engine is equipped with hydraulic valve lash adjusters. No adjustment is required.

ROCKER ARMS

REMOVAL

Keep all components in original order if they will be installed again.

1. Remove valve rocker arm bolts and arms.
2. Remove valve rocker arm pedestals.

INSTALLATION

When using valve train components over again, always install them into original location and position. Valve lash is net build. No valve adjustment is required.

1. Lubricate valve rocker arms with clean engine oil.
2. Lubricate flange of valve rocker arm bolts with clean engine oil.
3. Lubricate flange or washer surface of bolt that will contact valve rocker arm.
4. Install valve rocker arm pedestals.
5. Install rocker arms and bolts. Ensure pushrods seat properly to valve lifter sockets and in ends of rocker arms.
6. Turn crankshaft until number one piston is at top dead center of compression stroke. Cylinders 1, 3, 5 and 7 are lefthand in bank. Cylinders 2, 4, 6 and 8 are in righthand bank. In this position sprocket marks on crankshaft and camshaft will be aligned.
7. With engine in number one firing position, proceed as follows:
    a. **Torque** exhaust valve rocker arm bolts 1, 2, 7 and 8 to 22 ft. lbs.
    b. **Torque** intake valve rocker arm bolts 1, 3, 4 and 5 to 22 ft. lbs.
8. Rotate crankshaft 360°, then proceed as follows:
    a. **Torque** exhaust valve rocker arm bolts 3, 4, 5 and 6 to 22 ft. lbs.
    b. **Torque** intake valve rocker arm bolts 2, 6, 7 and 8 to 22 ft. lbs.

PUSH RODS

REMOVAL

Keep all components in original order if they will be installed again.

1. Remove valve rocker arm bolts, arms and pedestals as previously described.
2. Remove pushrods.

INSTALLATION

When using valve train components over again, always install them into original location and position. Valve lash is net build. No valve adjustment is required.

1. Lubricate valve rocker arms and pushrods with clean engine oil.
2. Lubricate flange of valve rocker arm bolts with clean engine oil.
3. Lubricate flange or washer surface of bolt that will contact valve rocker arm.
4. Install valve rocker arm pedestal.
5. Install rocker arms and bolts.
6. Install pushrods. Ensure pushrods seat properly to valve lifter sockets and in ends of rocker arms.
7. Turn crankshaft until number one piston is at top dead center of compression stroke. Cylinders 1, 3, 5 and 7 are lefthand in bank. Cylinders 2, 4, 6 and 8 are in righthand bank. In this position sprocket marks on crankshaft and camshaft will be aligned.
8. With engine in number one firing position, proceed as follows:
    a. **Torque** exhaust valve rocker arm bolts 1, 2, 7 and 8 to 22 ft. lbs.
    b. **Torque** intake valve rocker arm bolts 1, 3, 4 and 5 to 22 ft. lbs.
9. Rotate crankshaft 360°, then proceed as follows:
    a. **Torque** exhaust valve rocker arm bolts 3, 4, 5 and 6 to 22 ft. lbs.
    b. **Torque** intake valve rocker arm bolts 2, 6, 7 and 8 to 22 ft. lbs.

HYDRAULIC LIFTERS

REPLACE

1. Remove cylinder head as previously described.
2. Remove valve lifter guide bolts.
3. Remove valve lifters and guide. If lifters stick in their bores use valve lifter removal tool No. J-3049-A, or equivalent, to remove them.
4. Remove valve lifters from guide.
5. Organize or mark components so that they can be installed in same location from which they were removed.
6. Reverse procedure to install, noting the following:
    a. Lubricate valve lifters and their bores with clean engine oil.

b. Align flat sides of lifters with corresponding flat areas in bores.

CRANKSHAFT DAMPER

REPLACE

1. Release accessory drive belt tensioner and remove drive belt.
2. **On 1998–2000 models,** remove electronic brake control module from its bracket, then position aside. Cap and plug all open lines.
3. **On all models,** remove power steering gear.
4. Remove starter motor.
5. Remove power steering cooler mounting bolts and cooler from front crossmember and position aside.
6. Release A/C drive belt tensioner and remove drive belt.
7. Install flywheel holding tool No. J-42386, or equivalent, then the flywheel retaining bolts. **Torque** bolts to 37 ft. lbs.
8. Remove crankshaft damper bolt.
9. Mark crankshaft damper and end of crankshaft. Note damper installed position on crankshaft for assembly. Also note location of any weights, which must return to original positions.
10. Remove crankshaft damper using crankshaft end protector and damper removal tool Nos. J-41816 and J-41816-2, or equivalents.
11. Reverse procedure to install, noting the following:
    a. Install damper using crankshaft balancer and sprocket installer tool No. J-41665, or equivalent.
    b. Install used crankshaft damper bolt and to ensure balancer is completely installed **torque** to 240 ft. lbs.
    c. Remove bolt and measure for properly installed damper, **Fig. 8.**
    d. Install new crankshaft damper bolt and **torque** to 37 ft. lbs.
    e. Tighten bolt an additional 140° using torque angle meter tool No. J-36660, or equivalent.
    f. **On 1997 models,** tighten bolt an additional 120° using torque angle meter tool No. J-36660, or equivalent.
    g. **On 1998–2000 models,** tighten bolt an additional 140° using torque angle meter tool No. J-36660, or equivalent.

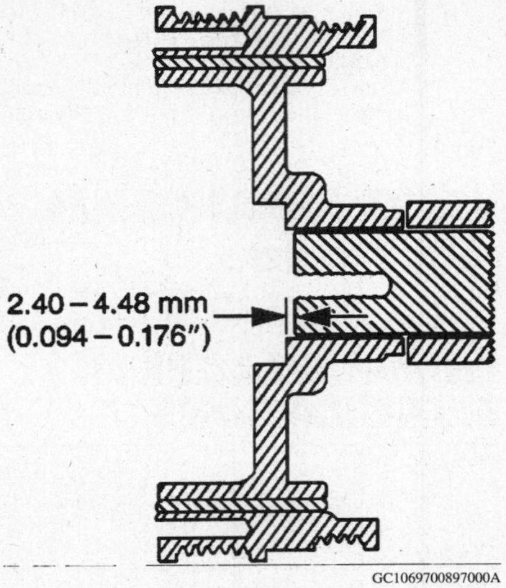

Fig. 8 Damper installed measurement

FRONT COVER

REPLACE

REMOVAL

1. Drain coolant into an approved container.
2. Disconnect fuel regulator purge line from air intake duct.
3. Remove air intake duct and air cleaner assembly.
4. Remove crankshaft damper as previously described.
5. Remove radiator and heater hoses from water pump.
6. Remove water pump mounting bolts, pump and gaskets.
7. Remove front cover bolts.
8. Remove front cover and gasket, then discard gasket. **Avoid sliding front cover or gasket across oil pan gasket.**
9. Remove and discard crankshaft oil seal.

INSTALLATION

1. Apply .20 inch bead of GM silicone gasket part No. 12378190, or equivalent, to corner where oil pan meets engine block.
2. Install new gasket, front cover and mounting bolts to engine block. Tighten bolts finger tight.
3. Align cover alignment tool No. J-41476, or equivalent, on front of crankshaft.
4. Install crankshaft damper bolt and tighten it finger tight.
5. Hand tighten oil pan to cover bolts so cover properly positions itself at pan rail.
6. **Torque** front cover bolts to 18 ft. lbs.
7. Remove alignment tool from cover.
8. Install crankshaft oil seal using oil seal installer tool No. J-41478, or equivalent. **Do not lubricate oil seal sealing surface.**
9. Install water pump, gaskets and mounting bolts.
10. Install radiator and heater hoses to water pump.
11. Fill cooling system.
12. Install crankshaft damper as previously described.
13. Install air intake duct and air cleaner assembly.
14. Connect fuel regulator purge line to air intake duct.

REAR COVER

REPLACE

REMOVAL

1. Mark crankshaft end and flywheel for assembly, then remove flywheel.
2. Remove engine rear cover mounting bolts and cover. Discard gasket.
3. Remove and discard crankshaft rear cover oil seal.

INSTALLATION

1. Apply .20 inch bead of GM silicone gasket part No. 12378190, or equivalent, to corner were oil pan meets engine block.
2. Install rear cover, gasket and bolts onto engine, tightening bolts finger tight.
3. Rotate crankshaft until two opposing flywheel bolt holes are parallel to oil pan surface.
4. Install cover alignment tool No. J-41476, or equivalent, and bolts onto rear of crankshaft. Tighten tool mounting bolts finger tight.
5. Hand tighten oil pan to cover bolts so cover properly positions itself at pan rail.
6. **Torque** oil pan to cover bolts to 108 inch lbs.
7. **Torque** rear cover mounting bolts to 18 ft. lbs.
8. Remove tool from crankshaft.
9. Install crankshaft rear oil seal using rear oil seal installer tool No. J-41479, or equivalent.
10. Install flywheel as follows:
    a. Align alignment mark made during removal and install mounting bolts finger tight.
    b. **Torque** flywheel mounting bolts to 15 ft. lbs. in sequence, **Fig. 9.**
    c. **Torque** flywheel mounting bolts to 37 ft. lbs. in sequence.
    d. **Torque** flywheel mounting bolts to 74 ft. lbs. in sequence.

TIMING CHAIN

REPLACE

REMOVAL

1. Remove oil pump as described under "Oil Pump, Replace."
2. Rotate crankshaft until crankshaft and camshaft sprocket timing marks are aligned.
3. Remove camshaft sprocket bolts.
4. Remove camshaft sprocket and timing chain.
5. Remove crankshaft sprocket using puller tool Nos. J-8433, J-21427-01, J-41816-2 and J-41558, or equivalents.
6. Remove crankshaft sprocket key if required.

INSTALLATION

1. Install key into crankshaft keyway.
2. Install crankshaft sprocket onto front of crankshaft, aligning key with keyway.
3. Install crankshaft sprocket using sprocket installation tool No. J-41665, or equivalent, ensuring sprocket fully seats against crankshaft flange.
4. Rotate crankshaft sprocket until alignment mark is in 12 o'clock position.
5. Install camshaft sprocket and timing chain, noting the following:
    a. Properly locate camshaft sprocket

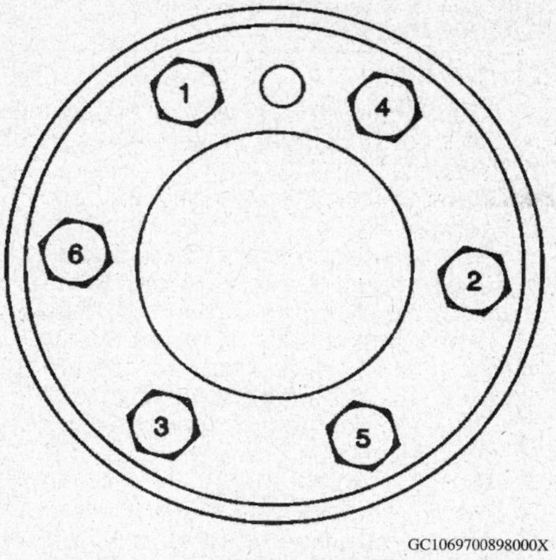

Fig. 9 Flywheel tightening sequence

locating pin with camshaft sprocket alignment hole.

b. Sprocket teeth and timing chain must mesh properly.

c. Camshaft and crankshaft sprocket alignment marks must be aligned properly, **Fig. 10.** Locate camshaft sprocket alignment mark in 6 o'clock position.

6. Install camshaft sprocket bolts.
7. Install oil pump as described under "Oil Pump, Replace. "

CAMSHAFT

REPLACE

1. Remove valve lifters as previously described under "Hydraulic Lifters, Replace."
2. Remove radiator.
3. Remove timing chain and sprockets as previously described.
4. Remove camshaft sensor bolt and sensor.
5. Remove camshaft retainer plate bolts and retainer.
6. Install three M8 1.25 × 100 mm bolts in camshaft front bolt holes.
7. Carefully rotate and pull camshaft out of engine block using bolts as handle.
8. Remove bolts from camshaft.
9. Reverse procedure to install, noting the following:
   a. Ensure camshaft journals are lubricated with clean engine oil before installation.
   b. Install camshaft retainer plate with sealing gasket facing engine block.
   c. Lubricate camshaft sensor O-ring with clean engine oil.

PISTON & ROD ASSEMBLY

1. Insert piston onto piston pin press tool No. J-24086-C, or equivalent. Note location of alignment mark on top of piston.
2. Apply mild heat to pin end of connecting rod using torch. This will ease piston and pin assembly.
3. Position connecting rod so that flat area on bolt flange faces front of engine block.
4. Press pin into connecting rod using piston pin press tool.
5. Measure piston, pin and connecting rod for proper assembly as follows:
   a. Place piston and connecting rod with flat top of piston on flat surface.
   b. Slide connecting rod and pin to one side and hold firmly against inside of piston.
   c. Measure pin for proper installation. Properly installed piston pin should protrude .05 inch from side of piston.
6. Install piston ring assembly onto piston as follows:
   a. Install oil control ring spacer in groove. Ends of oil control ring spacer should not overlap.
   b. Install upper and lower control rings. Oil control rings do not have dimple or orientation mark and may be installed in either direction.
   c. Stagger three oil control ring end gaps minimum of 90°.
   d. Install upper and lower compression rings. Upper compression ring does not have dimple or orientation mark and may be installed in either direction.
   e. Stagger compression ring end gaps minimum of 1 inch.

PISTONS, PINS & RINGS

Pistons are available in standard and .010 inch oversize.

Piston rings are available in standard and .010 inch oversize.

MAIN & ROD BEARINGS

Connecting rod bearings are available in standard size only.

Main bearings are available in standard size only.

CRANKSHAFT SEAL

REPLACE

Refer to "Front Cover, Replace" for crankshaft front seal replacement.

CRANKSHAFT REAR OIL SEAL

REPLACE

Refer to "Rear Cover, Replace" for crankshaft rear seal replacement.

OIL PAN

REPLACE

1. Drain oil from engine and remove oil filter.
2. Remove engine cradle as previously described under "Engine Mount, Replace.".
3. **On models equipped with automatic transmission,** remove fluid cooler line front and rear retaining clamp bolts.

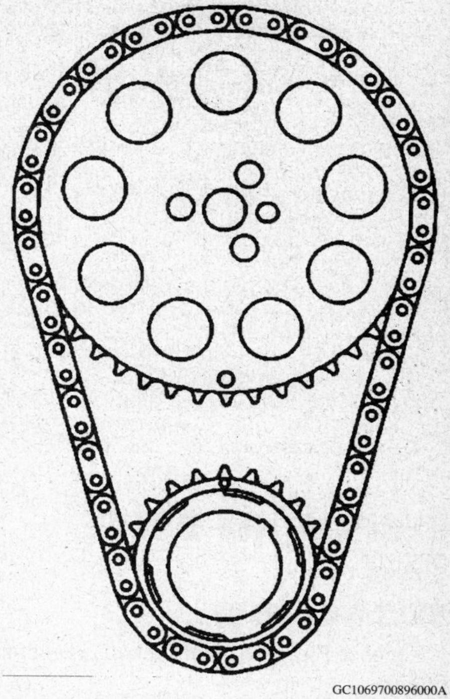

Fig. 10 Camshaft & crankshaft sprocket alignment

4. **On all models,** remove engine flywheel housing to oil pan bolts.
5. Remove engine flywheel housing cover bolts.
6. Remove lefthand and righthand closeout cover bolts and covers.
7. Disconnect engine oil level sensor electrical connector, then remove the sensor.
8. Disconnect engine oil temperature sensor electrical connector.
9. Remove oil pan mounting bolts and oil pan.
10. Remove and discard oil pan gasket and pan rivets.
11. Remove oil pan baffle bolt and baffle.
12. Reverse procedure to install, noting the following:
    a. Ensure rear of block and rear of oil pan are flush or even. **Rear of pan must never protrude beyond block and bellhousing plane.**
    b. Apply .20 inch wide by .80 inch long beads of GM silicone gasket sealer part No. 12378190, or equivalent, to front and rear cover gasket surfaces where covers attach to oil pan mating surface.
    c. Install gasket to oil pan and oil pan mounting bolts through oil pan and gasket before installation.

OIL PUMP

REPLACE

1. Remove engine front cover as previously described.
2. Remove oil pan as previously described.

3. Remove oil pump screen bolt and nuts.
4. Remove oil pump screen with O-ring seal.
5. Remove O-ring seal from pump screen.
6. Discard O-ring seal.
7. Remove remaining crankshaft oil deflector nuts.
8. Remove crankshaft oil deflector.
9. Remove oil pump bolts.
10. Reverse procedure to install, noting the following:
    a. Ensure all pump and oil gallery passages are clean and free from obstructions.
    b. Align crankshaft sprocket's splined surfaces with oil pump's.
    c. Install oil pump onto crankshaft sprocket until pump housing contacts face of engine block.

SERPENTINE DRIVE BELT

BELT ROUTING

Refer to **Fig. 11** for serpentine drive belt routing.

BELT REPLACEMENT

1. **On 1997 models,** loosen accessory drive belt tensioners Nos. 3 and 10, **Fig. 11,** to reduce tension on accessory drive belts.
2. **On 1998–2000 models,** using suitable hex-head socket, rotate tensioner away from belts to reduce their tension.
3. **On all models,** remove accessory drive belts.
4. Clean accessory drive belt surfaces.
5. Install accessory drive belts. Note running direction or arrow markings.
6. Tighten accessory drive belt tensioners to increase tension on accessory drive belts.
7. Ensure accessory drive belts are aligned in proper pulley grooves.

COOLING SYSTEM BLEED

1. Park vehicle on level surface.
2. After filling cooling system, start engine and let idle for one minute.
3. Install radiator surge tank cap.
4. Cycle RPM from idle to 3000 RPM in 30 second intervals until engine coolant reaches 210°F.
5. Shut off engine, then carefully remove radiator surge tank cap.
6. Start engine and idle for one minute, then fill surge tank to ½ inch above COLD FULL mark.
7. Install radiator surge tank cap and cycle RPM as previously described.
8. Shut off engine and remove radiator surge tank cap.
9. Fill surge tank to ½ inch above cold full line.
10. Rinse away any excess coolant from engine and compartment.

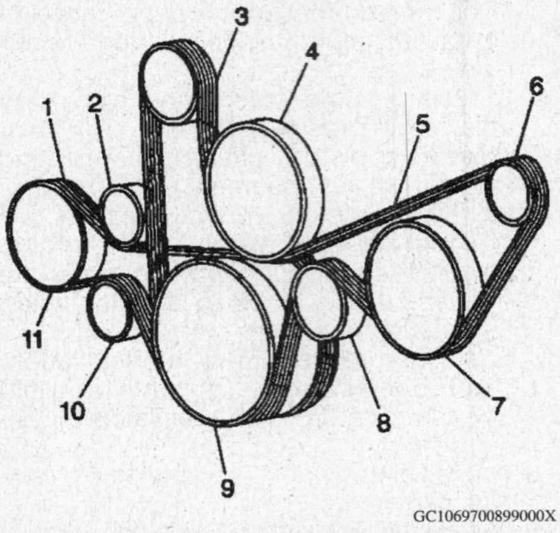

Fig. 11 Serpentine drive belt routing

THERMOSTAT

REPLACE

1. Drain cooling system into an approved container.
2. Remove radiator outlet hose clamp at thermostat housing using clamp pliers tool No. J-38185, or equivalent.
3. Disconnect radiator outlet hose from thermostat housing.
4. Remove thermostat housing mounting bolts and housing.
5. Note position of thermostat before removing it.
6. Remove and discard thermostat housing gasket.
7. Reverse procedure to install.

WATER PUMP

REPLACE

1. Drain cooling system into an approved container.
2. Disconnect IAT and MAF sensor electrical connectors.
3. Remove fuel regulator purge line from air intake duct.
4. Remove air intake duct cleaner assembly.
5. Remove drive belts as described under "Serpentine Drive Belt."
6. Remove radiator inlet and outlet hose clamps, then the hoses from water pump using clamp pliers tool No. J-38185, or equivalent.
7. Remove heater hose clamps, then the hoses from water pump.
8. Remove water pump pulley bolts and pulley.
9. Remove six water pump mounting bolts from engine block, then the water pump.
10. Reverse procedure to install, noting the following:
    a. **On 1997–98 models, torque** water pump mounting bolts to 30 ft. lbs.
    b. **On 1999–2000 models, torque** water pump mounting bolts to 11 ft. lbs., then to 22 ft. lbs.
    c. **On all models, torque** water pump pulley bolts to 90 inch lbs., then to 18 ft. lbs.

RADIATOR

REPLACE

1. Disconnect Intake Air Temperature (IAT) and Mass Air Flow (MAF) sensor connectors.
2. Remove air intake duct/cleaner assembly.
3. Remove mounting bolts and radiator upper support. **Note upper radiator support position in relation to fan shroud assembly for installation.**
4. Raise and support vehicle, then drain coolant into suitable container.
5. Remove electrical connectors and harness from fan shroud.
6. Remove fan shroud.
7. Remove hoses from radiator.
8. **On models equipped with automatic transmission,** remove cooler lines from radiator.
9. **On all models,** remove condenser from radiator and position forward. **It is not necessary to disconnect air conditioning lines from condenser.**
10. Lower and remove radiator.
11. Reverse procedure to install. Tighten mounting bolts to specifications.

FUEL PUMP

REPLACE

1. Relieve fuel system pressure as outlined under "Precautions."
2. Raise and support vehicle.
3. Remove lefthand rear wheel and tire.
4. Clean all fuel line connections before disconnecting.
5. Drain lefthand fuel tank, then mark and disconnect all fuel lines.
6. Cap all fuel lines.
7. Disconnect fuel sender electrical connector.
8. Remove fuel tank strap and shield.
9. Support fuel tank.
10. Remove fuel sender mounting bolts and fuel sender from tank.
11. Note positioning of fuel pump strainer before discarding.
12. Reverse procedure to install, noting the following:
    a. Install new fuel pump strainer, ensuring it is properly positioned as noted during removal.
    b. Align sender cover mark with mark on tank.
    c. Look through tank opening to ensure long side of strainer is visible. It should be approximately one inch from tank opening. If required, rotate sender counterclockwise approximately 90°.
    d. Install sender assembly mounting bolts.
    e. **On 1997 models, torque** sender assembly mounting bolts to 27 inch lbs. in sequence, **Fig. 12.**
    f. **On 1998 models, torque** sender assembly mounting bolts to 26.5 inch lbs. using fuel sender torque tool No. J-42940, or equivalent, in sequence, **Fig. 12.**
    g. **On 1999–2000 models,** hand tighten new breakaway head sender mounting bolts until they are finger

tight, then tighten with suitable wrench until upper heads break off in sequence, **Fig. 12.**

FUEL FILTER

REPLACE

1. Relieve fuel system pressure as outlined under "Precautions."
2. Raise and support vehicle.
3. Clean all fuel filter connections before disconnecting.
4. **On models equipped with automatic transmission,** proceed as follows:
   a. Disconnect stabilizer bar from rear cradle.
   b. Remove exhaust intermediate pipe to muffler bolts.
   c. Lower lefthand muffler.
5. **On all models,** remove fuel filter bracket nut from mounting stud.
6. Disconnect quick-connect fittings from fuel filter, then cap fuel lines.
7. **On 1999–2000 models,** disconnect fuel system ground strap from filter mounting stud.
8. **On all models,** remove fuel filter and bracket, then filter from bracket.
9. Reverse procedure to install. Ensure mounting bracket anti-rotation tab is securely seated into tunnel reinforcement hole.

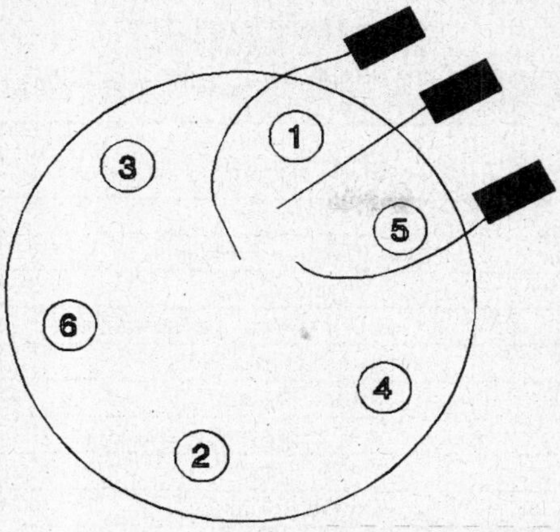

Fig. 12 Fuel sender bolt tightening sequence

TIGHTENING SPECIFICATIONS

Year	Component	Torque/ Ft. Lbs.
1997–2000	A/C Compressor Bracket	37
	A/C Idler Pulley	37
	A/C Tensioner	18
	AIR Pipe To Exhaust Manifold	15
	AIR Righthand Side Pipe Bracket To Cylinder Head	15
	Alternator & Power Steering Pump Bracket	37
	Alternator Rear Bracket	37
	Camshaft Retainer	18
	Camshaft Sensor	18
	Camshaft Sprocket	26
	Connecting Rod Bolts	15①
	Coolant Temperature Gauge Sensor	15
	Crankshaft Bearing Cap Bolts	15③
	Crankshaft Bearing Cap Side Bolts	18
	Crankshaft Bearing Cap Studs	④
	Crankshaft Damper	②
	Crankshaft Oil Deflector	18
	Crankshaft Position Sensor	18
	Cylinder Head Bolts	⑤
	Cylinder Head Coolant Plug	15
	Cylinder Head Core Hole Plug	15
	Drive Belt Idler Pulley	37
	Drive Belt Tensioner	37
	Engine Block Coolant Drain Plugs	44
	Engine Block Heater	30
	Engine Block Oil Gallery Plugs	44
	Engine Flywheel Hub Collar Bolt (Automatic Transmission)	96
	Engine Front Cover	18
	Engine Mount Bracket To Engine Block	37
	Engine Rear Cover	18
	Engine Service Lift Bracket (M8 Bolts)	18
	Engine Service Lift Bracket (M10 Bolts)	37
	Engine Valley Cover	18
	Exhaust Manifold	⑦

Continued

TIGHTENING SPECIFICATIONS—Continued

Year	Component	Torque/ Ft. Lbs.
1997-2000	Flywheel	⑥
	Fuel Injection Fuel Rail	90①
	Ignition Coil	106①
	Ignition Coil Wire Harness Connector	106①
	Intake Manifold Bolts	⑧
	Knock Sensors	15
	Power Steering Pump & Alternator Bracket	37
	Oil Filter	22
	Oil Filter Fitting	40
	Oil Level Indicator Tube	12
	Oil Level Sensor (1997–98)	26
	Oil Level Sensor (1999–2000)	115⑩
	Oil Pan Baffle	106①
	Oil Pan Cover	106①
	Oil Pan Drain Plug	18
	Oil Pan M8 Bolts (Oil Pan To Engine Block & Oil Pan To Front Cover)	18
	Oil Pan M6 Bolts (Oil Pan To Rear Cover)	106①
	Oil Pressure Sensor	15
	Oil Pump Cover	106①
	Oil Pump Relief Valve Plug	106①
	Oil Pump Screen	18
	Oil Pump Screen To Oil Pump	106①
	Oil Pump To Engine Block	18
	Oil Temperature Sensor	15
	Oil Transfer Cover Bolts	106①
	Oxygen Sensor	30
	Power Steering Pump	18
	Power Steering Reservoir Bracket	37
	Spark Plugs (New Cylinder Head)	15
	Spark Plugs (Used Cylinder Head)	11
	Starter Motor	37
	Throttle Body	106①
	Valve Lifter Guide	106①
	Valve Rocker Arm	22
	Valve Rocker Arm Cover	106①
	Vapor Vent Pipe	106①
	Water Inlet Housing	11
	Water Pump	⑨
	Water Pump Cover	11
	Water Pump Pulley	⑨

① — First design, then tighten an additional 60°; Second design, then tighten an additional 75°
② — Refer to "Crankshaft Damper, Replace."
③ — Then tighten an additional 80°.
④ — Then tighten an additional 53°.
⑤ — Refer to "Cylinder Head, Replace."
⑥ — Refer to "Rear Cover, Replace."
⑦ — Refer to "Exhaust Manifold, Replace."
⑧ — Refer to "Intake Manifold, Replace."
⑨ — Refer to "Water Pump, Replace."
⑩ — Inch lbs.

Clutch & Manual Transmission

NOTE: On Air Bag Equipped Models, Refer To "Air Bag System Precautions" Located In The Front Of This Manual For System Disarming & Arming Procedures.

NOTE: Refer To "Computer Relearn Procedures " Located In The Front Of This Manual For Computer Relearn Procedures.

INDEX

ADJUSTMENTS

CLUTCH PEDAL

The clutch release mechanism on these models is hydraulically operated and is not adjustable.

CLUTCH PRESSURE PLATE

Off Vehicle

1. Place clutch pressure plate, with flat surface down, on suitable press.
2. Compress pressure plate diaphragm spring fingers until tension is released from stepped adjusting ring.
3. Place two suitable screwdrivers against two of three stepped adjusting ring tension spring stops, just ahead of adjusting ring tension springs.
4. Rotate stepped adjusting ring counterclockwise until adjusting ring steps are fully adjusted out, then hold in position.
5. Release pressure from pressure plate diaphragm spring fingers.
6. Release adjusting ring tension spring stops.
7. Remove pressure plate from press.

On Vehicle

1. Raise and support vehicle.
2. Remove engine flywheel inspection cover.
3. With assistance, press clutch pedal until tension is released from clutch pressure plate stepped adjusting ring, then continue to hold pedal.
4. Place two suitable screwdrivers against two of three stepped adjusting ring tension spring stops, just ahead of adjusting ring tension springs.
5. Rotate stepped adjusting ring counterclockwise until adjusting ring steps are fully adjusted out, then hold in position.
6. Release clutch pedal.
7. Release adjusting ring tension spring stops.
8. Install flywheel inspection cover, then lower vehicle.

HYDRAULIC SYSTEM SERVICE

HYDRAULIC SYSTEM BLEED

1. Remove clutch master cylinder reservoir cap with diaphragm.
2. Fill clutch master cylinder reservoir with clutch hydraulic fluid part No. 12345347, or equivalent, if required.
3. Raise and support vehicle.
4. Remove intermediate exhaust pipe.
5. Remove driveline tunnel closeout panel.
6. Have an assistant depress clutch pedal fully and hold.
7. Loosen bleeder screw on clutch actuator cylinder to purge air, then tighten bleeder screw.
8. Release clutch pedal.
9. Repeat bleed steps until all air is completely evacuated.
10. Fill clutch master cylinder reservoir, if required.
11. Install driveline tunnel closeout panel in propeller shaft.
12. Install exhaust intermediate pipe, then lower vehicle.

CLUTCH ACTUATING CYLINDER, REPLACE

1. Remove lefthand instrument panel lower insulator panel.
2. Remove clutch master cylinder rod retainer.
3. Remove clutch master cylinder rod from clutch pedal.
4. Raise and support vehicle.
5. Remove clutch actuator cylinder hose from hose retaining clip at rear of engine.
6. Disconnect actuator to master cylinder hose connector using hydraulic clutch line separator tool No. J-36221, or equivalent. Cover hose ends to protect from dirt.
7. Remove driveline support assembly and transaxle.
8. Remove clutch actuator cylinder from driveline support assembly.
9. Reverse procedure to install, noting the following:
   a. Ensure hydraulic hoses are routed away from any interference with other components.
   b. Connect actuator hose to master cylinder hose. After pushing them together, pull outward to ensure they are securely connected. Do not rely on an audible click or visual appearance alone.
   c. Bleed clutch hydraulic system as previously described.

CLUTCH MASTER CYLINDER, REPLACE

1. Remove lefthand instrument panel lower insulator panel.
2. Remove clutch master cylinder rod retainer.
3. Remove clutch master cylinder rod from clutch pedal.
4. Remove windshield washer solvent reservoir.
5. Raise and support vehicle.
6. Remove clutch actuator cylinder hose from hose retaining clip at rear of engine.
7. Disconnect actuator to master cylinder hose connector using hydraulic clutch line separator tool No. J-36221, or equivalent. Cover hose ends to protect from dirt.
8. Lower vehicle.
9. Remove clutch master cylinder reservoir push-in fasteners.
10. Rotate clutch master cylinder counterclockwise 45°.
11. Release clutch master cylinder from dash panel.
12. Remove clutch master cylinder and reservoir.
13. Reverse procedure to install, noting the following:
    a. Ensure hydraulic hoses are routed away from any interference with other components.
    b. Connect actuator hose to master cylinder hose. After pushing them together, pull outward to ensure they are securely connected. Do

not rely on an audible click or visual appearance alone.
c. Bleed clutch hydraulic system as previously described.

CLUTCH

REPLACE

1. Raise and support vehicle.
2. Remove exhaust system.
3. Remove driveline support assembly with transaxle.
4. Remove engine flywheel inspection cover from engine flywheel housing.
5. Loosen visible clutch pressure plate bolts.
6. Rotate engine flywheel and loosen remaining clutch pressure plate bolts.
7. Remove visible clutch pressure plate bolts.
8. Rotate engine flywheel and remove remaining clutch pressure plate bolts.
9. Remove clutch pressure plate and clutch driven plate.
10. Reverse procedure to install, noting the following:
    a. Adjust clutch pressure plate if required as described under "Adjustments."
    b. Align clutch driven plate to pilot bearing using pilot bushing installer tool No. J-38836, or equivalent.
    c. **Torque** clutch pressure plate bolts evenly in four increments to 37 ft. lbs. in a criss cross pattern.

TRANSMISSION

REPLACE

Observe clearance between rear of engine and composite dash panel. Do not let engine rest unsupported against dash panel or damage to the vehicle might result.

1. Remove console.
2. Pry off shift control knob button and retainer.
3. Unscrew shift control knob.
4. Grasp sides of shift control boot and apply light pressure toward shift control lever to release shift boot retaining tabs from instrument panel accessory trim plate.
5. Using light pressure, continue to release remaining boot retaining tabs.
6. Lift boot away from trim plate and remove boot.
7. Remove instrument panel accessory trim plate.
8. Remove shift control closeout boot retaining nuts.
9. Remove shift control closeout boot.
10. Remove shift control assembly.
11. Remove instrument panel lower insulator panel.
12. Remove clutch master cylinder pushrod retainer.
13. Disconnect clutch master cylinder pushrod from clutch pedal.
14. Raise and support vehicle.
15. Remove clutch actuator cylinder hose from hose retaining clip at rear of engine.
16. Disconnect clutch hose connector using clutch line separator tool No. J-36221, or equivalent, then cover hose coupling ends to protect from dirt.
17. Remove rear tires and wheels.
18. Remove intermediate exhaust pipe.
19. Tie muffler assemblies to underbody to keep them positioned aside.
20. Remove driveline tunnel closeout panel.
21. **On models with rear mounted Electronic Brake and Traction Control Module (EBTCM),** proceed as follows:
    a. Remove EBTCM lefthand mounting bracket bolts.
    b. Remove EBTCM lefthand mounting bracket with EBTCM rubber insulators.
    c. Pull lightly to release EBTCM from insulator attached to EBTCM righthand mounting bracket.
    d. Tie off EBTCM to underbody support.
22. **On all models,** remove rear suspension crossmember assembly as described in "Rear Axle & Suspension."
23. Install transmission support fixture tool No. J-42055, or equivalent, to transmission and transmission jack to support fixture.
24. Remove differential to transmission lower nut.
25. Remove transaxle mount bracket to differential bolts.
26. Remove transaxle mount with bracket.
27. Carefully release axle shafts from differential using suitable pry bar.
28. Support axle shafts from underbody.
29. Compress and release four retainers securing wiring harness along driveline support assembly using suitable pliers, then position harness aside.
30. Slowly lower driveline approximately two inches while simultaneously adjusting angle of tilt.
31. Disconnect Vehicle Speed Sensor (VSS) electrical connector.
32. Disconnect wiring harness retainer from stud at differential rear cover.
33. Disconnect wiring harness retainer clip from top of differential.
34. Disconnect electrical connectors at back-up lamp switch, reverse lockout solenoid, gear select (skip shift) solenoid and transmission lubricant temperature sensor.
35. Insert suitable putty knife between edge of shifter bracket on side of driveline support assembly and brake pipe retainer on wall of driveline tunnel.
36. Slowly lower driveline, while simultaneously adjusting angle of tilt and observing relationship between top and rear of differential and lowest part of rear compartment panel floor. Differential should not be lowered more than approximately even with specified body point of reference. Avoid engine to dash panel interference.
37. Release wiring harness from harness retainer along top of transmission.
38. Ensure wiring harness is free from driveline being removed.
39. Support engine under rear of engine oil pan using suitable jack and block of wood to prevent stressing composite dash panel.
40. Remove driveline support assembly to engine flywheel housing mounting bolts.
41. Bend wiring harness bracket away from driveline toward driveline tunnel wall to make clear path for driveline removal.
42. With assistance, insert suitable flat-bladed screwdriver between edge of driveline support assembly and engine flywheel housing, then pry driveline loose from engine.
43. With assistance, lower driveline away from engine until propeller input shaft at front of driveline support assembly just clears engine flywheel housing, then lower completely out of vehicle.
44. Using suitable chain lift, position chain so as not to damage exhaust hangers located on driveline support assembly, then lift driveline off jack.
45. Disconnect transmission support fixture tool No. J-42055, or equivalent, from transmission jack. This will provide stability to assembly while working on bench.
46. Position driveline on workbench with lift still attached.
47. Support driveline assembly and remove lift from driveline.
48. Remove transmission to driveline support assembly bolts and studs.
49. Insert suitable flat-bladed screwdriver between edge of driveline support assembly and transmission, then begin to pry driveline support assembly loose from transmission.
50. Slide differential away from transmission.
51. Remove transmission support fixture tool No. J-42055, or equivalent, if required.
52. Reverse procedure to install, noting the following:
    a. Avoid engine to dash panel interference.
    b. Install new rear suspension crossmember mounting nuts using hand tools.
    c. Ensure clutch hydraulic hoses are routed away from any interference with other components.
    d. Connect clutch actuator hose to master cylinder hose. After pushing them together, pull outward to ensure they are securely connected. Do not rely on an audible click or visual appearance alone.
    e. Bleed clutch hydraulic system as previously described.

TIGHTENING SPECIFICATIONS

Year	Component	Torque/ Ft. Lbs.
1997–2000	Back-Up Lamp Switch	15
	Differential To Transmission	37
	Driveline Support Assembly To Engine Flywheel Housing	37
	EBTCM Lefthand Mounting Bracket	37
	Gear Select Skip Shift Solenoid	30
	Intermediate Exhaust Pipe To Muffler	37
	Rear Shock Absorber Lower Mounting	162
	Rear Suspension Crossmember	81①
	Reverse Lockout Solenoid	30
	Shift Control	22
	Shift Control Closeout Boot Retaining	106②
	Transaxle Mount Bracket To Differential	37
	Transaxle Mount To Rear Suspension Crossmember	37
	Transmission Fluid Drain & Fill Plugs	20
	Transmission Lubricant Temperature Sensor	20
	Transmission Shift Rod Clamp	22
	Transmission To Driveline Support Assembly	37
	Transmission Vent Tube	15

① — Install new nuts. Tighten using hand tools only.
② — Inch lbs.

Rear Axle & Suspension

INDEX

REAR AXLE

REPLACE

Refer to "Clutch & Manual Transmission" or "Automatic Transmissions/Transaxles" for rear axle replacement.

REAR WHEEL SHAFT

REPLACE

1. Apply parking brake, then shift transmission into park or neutral.
2. Raise and support vehicle and remove rear wheel and tire.
3. Insert drift or punch into brake rotor cooling fins and against brake caliper to prevent wheel hub and bearing from turning.
4. Remove spindle nut retaining rear wheel driveshaft to hub.
5. Remove drift or punch.
6. Release parking brake.
7. Remove rear transverse spring as described under "Transverse Spring, Replace."
8. Separate outer tie rod end from knuckle, then position tie rod toward rear of vehicle. **Do not loosen outer tie rod jam nut.**
9. Disconnect wheel speed sensor electrical connector.
10. Disconnect parking brake cable from parking brake lever at rear hub.
11. Remove parking brake cable from bracket, then position toward rear of vehicle.
12. Install rear hub spindle remover tool No. J-42129, or equivalent, onto wheel hub and secure with lugnuts.
13. Begin to disengage driveshaft from wheel hub and bearing. This will give additional clearance to lower ball joint nut.
14. Separate lower ball joint from suspension knuckle.
15. Disengage driveshaft completely from wheel hub and bearing.
16. Support driveshaft, suspension knuckle and upper control arm, then position knuckle toward front.
17. Assemble axle shaft remover, extension and slide hammer tool Nos. J-42128, J-29794 & J-2619-01, or equivalents.
18. Remove driveshaft.
19. Remove rear hub spindle remover tool from wheel hub.
20. Reverse procedure to install.

PROPELLER SHAFT

REPLACE

Refer to "Clutch & Manual Transmission" or "Automatic Transmissions/Transaxles" for rear axle replacement.

HUB & BEARING

REPLACE

1. Raise and support vehicle, then remove tire and wheel.
2. Disconnect wheel speed sensor electrical connector.
3. **On models equipped with Real Time Damping (RTD) suspension,** disconnect RTD position sensor link.

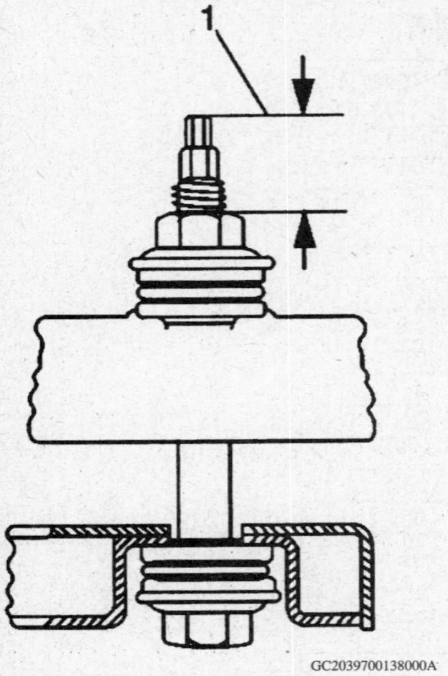

Fig. 1 Spring stud height measurement

4. **On all models,** remove brake caliper and disc rotor.
5. Remove shock absorber solenoid electrical connector.
6. Separate outer tie rod end from suspension knuckle.
7. Remove spindle nut retainer, nut and washer.
8. Separate suspension knuckle from upper control arm.
9. Separate suspension knuckle from lower control arm ball joint stud.
10. Remove suspension knuckle.
11. Remove wheel hub mounting bolts.
12. Remove hub and bearing assembly from suspension knuckle.
13. Reverse procedure to install, noting the following:
    a. **Front and rear hub and bearing assemblies are not interchangeable. Ensure proper replacement part is being installed.**
    b. Tighten all fasteners to specifications.

SPINDLE KNUCKLE

REPLACE

1. Raise and support vehicle.
2. Remove tire and wheel assembly.
3. Disconnect wheel speed sensor electrical connector.
4. **On models equipped with Real Time Damping (RTD) suspension,** disconnect RTD position sensor link.
5. **On all models,** disconnect shock absorber electrical connector.
6. Remove brake caliper and disc rotor.
7. Separate outer tie rod end from suspension knuckle.
8. Remove spindle nut retainer, nut and washer.
9. Separate suspension knuckle from upper control arm.
10. Separate suspension knuckle from lower control arm ball joint stud.
11. Remove suspension knuckle.
12. Reverse procedure to install.

REAR WHEEL SPINDLE

REPLACE

Refer to "Hub & Bearing, Replace" for rear wheel spindle replacement.

SHOCK ABSORBER

REPLACE

1. Raise and support vehicle, then remove tire and wheel.
2. Disconnect shock absorber solenoid electrical connector.
3. Remove lower shock absorber to lower control arm mounting bolt.
4. Remove upper mounting bolts.
5. Remove shock absorber from lower control arm and shock tower.
6. Remove upper insulator retainer and insulator from shock absorber.
7. Reverse procedure to install.

TRANSVERSE LEAF SPRING

REPLACE

1. Raise and support vehicle, then remove both rear tires and wheels.
2. Measure transverse spring stud height, **Fig. 1.**
3. Install transverse leaf spring compressor and adapters, tool Nos. J-33432-A and J-33432-97, or equivalents, **Fig. 2.**
4. Compress spring.
5. Remove spring to control arm mounting nuts, bolts and insulators.
6. Remove spring to crossmember retainer bolts, retainer, spring spacers and insulators.
7. Remove transverse leaf spring.
8. Reverse procedure to install, noting the following:
    a. Set spring stud height to that noted during removal.
    b. **On 1998–2000 models,** ensure spring stud bolt has minimum of two threads showing above nut.
    c. **On all models,** tighten fasteners to specifications.

CONTROL ARM

REPLACE

LOWER

1. Raise and support vehicle, then remove tire and wheel.
2. Remove transverse leaf spring as previously described.
3. Support lower control arm with suitable jack stand, then remove shock absorber to lower control arm mounting bolt.
4. Loosen lower ball joint stud nut.
5. Separate lower ball joint stud from suspension knuckle using separator tool No. J-42188, or equivalent.
6. Remove separator tool and lower ball joint stud nut from suspension knuckle.

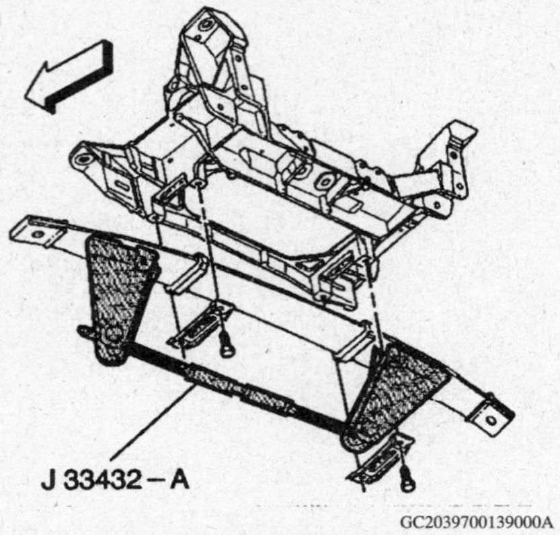

Fig. 2 Transverse leaf spring compressor

7. Remove stabilizer bar link from lower control arm.
8. Mark position of control arm to crossmember cam bolts, washers and nuts, then remove these items.
9. Remove jack stand and control arm.
10. Reverse procedure to install, noting the following:
    a. If required, use hex-head wrench to prevent ball joint stud in place when installing stud nut.
    b. **Torque** stud nut to 15 ft. lbs. to seat stud.
    c. Turn nut an additional 3 ½ flats.
    d. Inspect stud nut for minimum final **torque** of 52 ft. lbs.

UPPER

1. Raise and support vehicle, then remove tire and wheel.
2. Support lower control arm with suitable jack stand.
3. **On models equipped with Real Time Damping (RTD) suspension,** disconnect RTD position sensor link at upper control arm.
4. **On all models,** loosen upper ball joint stud nut, but do not remove it.
5. Separate upper ball joint stud from upper control arm using separator tool No. J-42188, or equivalent.
6. Remove separator tool and stud nut.
7. Remove upper control arm to frame mounting bolts, then the control arm.
8. Reverse procedure to install, noting the following:
    a. If required, use hex-head wrench to prevent ball joint stud in place when installing stud nut.
    b. **Torque** stud nut to 15 ft. lbs. to seat stud.
    c. **On 1997–98 models,** tighten nut an additional 4 flats, then inspect stud nut for minimum final **torque** of 33 ft. lbs.
    d. **On 1999–2000 models,** tighten nut an additional 250°, then inspect stud nut for minimum final **torque** of 41 ft. lbs.

TIE ROD

REPLACE

1. Raise and support vehicle, then remove tire and wheel.

2. Loosen outer tie rod end stud nut, but do not remove it.
3. Separate tie rod end from suspension knuckle using ball joint separator tool No. J-42188, or equivalent.
4. Remove rear suspension adjustment link to crossmember mounting nut.
5. Remove rear suspension adjustment link.
6. Reverse procedure to install. Tighten outer tie rod end stud nut as follows:
   a. **Torque** to 15 ft. lbs.
   b. Tighten an additional 160°.
   c. **Torque** to 33 ft. lbs.

STABILIZER SHAFT

REPLACE

1. Raise and support vehicle, then remove tires and wheels.
2. Remove stabilizer bar link mounting nuts from lower control arms.
3. Remove stabilizer bar to crossmember bracket mounting bolts and bracket.
4. Remove stabilizer bar.
5. Remove stabilizer bar link mounting nuts and shaft links.
6. Reverse procedure to install.

TIGHTENING SPECIFICATIONS

Year	Component	Torque/ Ft. Lbs.
1997–2000	Clutch Actuator Cylinder	106④
	Driveline Support Assembly To Engine Flywheel Housing	37
	Driveline Tunnel Closeout Panel	80④
	EBTCM Lefthand mounting Bracket	37
	Flexplate To Propeller Shaft Rear Bearing	37
	Input Shaft To Front Propeller Shaft Coupler	41
	Lower Control Arm Ball Joint	②
	Lower Control Arm Cam (Front)	107
	Lower Control Arm Cam (Rear)	70
	Outer Tie Rod	⑤
	Outer Tie Rod End Jam	44
	Propeller Input Shaft Front Bearing	26
	Propeller Shaft Hub Clamp	96
	Rear Axle Driveline	①
	Rear Bearing Assembly To Driveline Support Tube	48
	Rear Bearing Assembly To Rear Propeller Shaft Coupler (1997–98)	48
	Rear Bearing Assembly To Rear Propeller Shaft Coupler Bolts (1999–2000)	52
	Rear Crossmember	81③
	Rear Drive Axle Spindle	118
	Rear Exhaust Hanger	37
	Rear Shock Absorber (Lower)	162
	Rear Shock Absorber (Upper)	22
	Rear Spring Anchor Plate (1997–98)	49
	Rear Spring Anchor Plate (1999–2000)	46
	Shift Control	22
	Shift Control Closeout Boot	106④
	Stabilizer Bar Insulator (Lower)	70
	Stabilizer Bar Insulator (Upper)	49
	Stabilizer Bar Link	53
	Tie Rod	50
	Upper Control Arm	81
	Upper Control Arm Ball Joint	②
	Wheel Hub (1997)	70
	Wheel Hub (1998–2000)	96

① — Refer to “Clutch & Manual Transmission” or “Automatic Transmissions/Transaxles” for specifications.
② — Refer to “Control Arm, Replace” for tightening specifications and procedure.
③ — Always install new nuts and tighten them using hand tools only.
④ — Inch Lbs.
⑤ — Refer to “Tie Rod, Replace” for tightening specifications and procedures.

Front Suspension & Steering

NOTE: On Air Bag Equipped Models, Refer To "Air Bag System Precautions" Located In The Front Of This Manual For System Disarming & Arming Procedures.

NOTE: Refer To "Computer Relearn Procedures " Located In The Front Of This Manual For Computer Relearn Procedures.

INDEX

WHEEL BEARING

REPLACE

Refer to "Wheel Hub, Replace" for wheel bearing replacement.

WHEEL HUB

REPLACE

1. Raise and support vehicle, then remove tire and wheel.
2. Remove brake caliper and rotor.
3. Remove stabilizer shaft link from lower control arm.
4. Disconnect wheel speed sensor electrical connector.
5. Support lower control arm with suitable jack stand.
6. Disconnect steering linkage outer tie rod from steering knuckle using separator tool No. J-42188, or equivalent.
7. Loosen upper and lower ball joint stud nuts.
8. Separate steering knuckle from upper and lower control arm using ball joint separator tool No. J-42188, or equivalent.
9. Remove upper and lower ball joint stud nuts.
10. Remove steering knuckle from upper and lower control arms.
11. Remove wheel hub mounting bolts.
12. Remove hub and bearing assembly from steering knuckle.
13. Reverse procedure to install, noting the following:
    a. **Front and rear hub and bearing assemblies are not interchangeable. Ensure proper replacement part is being installed.**
    b. Tighten all fasteners to specifications.

BALL JOINT INSPECTION

1. Raise and support front of vehicle, then position jack stands under lower control arms.
2. Shake tire and wheel assembly while inspecting for stud end movement at knuckle bosses.
3. Shake tire and wheel assembly while inspecting for loose prevailing torque nuts at knuckle bosses.
4. Visually inspect for damaged or worn ball studs and knuckles.
5. Replace ball joint if looseness is indicated.

BALL JOINT

REPLACE

UPPER BALL JOINT

1997

On these models the manufacturer does not provide a specific replacement procedure.

1998–2000

1. Remove steering knuckle as outlined under "Steering Knuckle, Replace."
2. Remove ball joint from knuckle using ball joint remover kit tool Nos. J-9519-E and J-21474-5, or equivalents.
3. install new ball joint into knuckle using tool kit No. J-9519-E and installer tool No. J-28685, or equivalents.
4. **On 1998 models, torque** ball stud nut to 15 ft. lbs., tighten an additional 4 flats, then inspect nut for final **torque** of 33 ft. lbs.
5. **On 1999–2000 models, torque** ball stud nut to 15 ft. lbs., tighten an additional 250°, then inspect nut for final **torque** of 41 ft. lbs.
6. **On all models,** install knuckle onto vehicle.

LOWER BALL JOINT

1997

On these models the manufacturer does not provide a specific replacement procedure.

1998–2000

1. Remove lower control arm as outlined in "Transverse Leaf Spring, Replace."
2. Remove ball joint from control arm using ball joint tool Nos. J-9519-98 and J-9519-E, or equivalents.
3. Install new ball joint into control arm using ball joint tool Nos. J-9519-99 and J-9519-E, or equivalents.
4. **On 1998 models, torque** ball stud nut to 15 ft. lbs., tighten an additional 3 ½ flats, then inspect nut for final **torque** of 41 ft. lbs.
5. **On 1999–2000 models, torque** ball stud nut to 15 ft. lbs., tighten an additional 210°, then inspect nut for final **torque** of 52 ft. lbs.
6. **On all models,** install lower control arm onto vehicle.

SHOCK ABSORBER

REPLACE

REMOVAL

1. Raise and support vehicle, then remove tire and wheel.
2. Remove shock absorber upper mounting nut, insulator retainer and insulator.
3. Remove shock absorber lower mounting nuts.
4. **On 1999–2000 models equipped with heavy duty shock option (FE3),** proceed as follows:
    a. Compress shock absorber from bottom upward using suitable pry bar.

b. Install shock support tool No. J-43822, or equivalent, onto shock to keep it compressed.
5. **On all models,** remove shock absorber from lower control arm and shock tower.
6. Remove shock support tool.
7. Remove insulator and retainer from shock absorber.

INSTALLATION

1. **On models less heavy duty shock option (FE3),** proceed as follows:
   a. Install retainer and insulator to new shock absorber.
   b. Install absorber to upper tower.
   c. Install upper insulator, retainer and nut. Tighten to specifications.
   d. Install absorber lower mounting bolts and nuts. Tighten to specifications.
2. **On 1999–2000 models equipped with heavy duty shock option (FE3),** proceed as follows:
   a. Install shock support tool No. J-43822, or equivalent, onto new shock absorber.
   b. Install absorber onto vehicle.
   c. Install upper insulator, retainer and nut. Tighten to specifications.
   d. Remove shock support tool.
   e. Compress transverse spring using spring compressor tool No. J-33432-A, or equivalent.
   f. Raise lower control arm, then install absorber lower mounting bolts and nuts. Tighten to specifications.
   g. Remove spring compressor tool.
3. **On all models,** install tire and wheel, then lower vehicle.

TRANSVERSE LEAF SPRING

REPLACE

1. Raise and support vehicle, then remove tires and wheels.
2. Measure and record front spring adjuster bolt gap, **Fig. 1.**
3. Install transverse spring compressor tool No. J-33432-A and adapters, or equivalents.
4. Compress transverse spring.
5. Remove lower shock absorber mounting bolts from one lower control arm.
6. Disconnect stabilizer bar link from lower control arm.
7. Loosen lower ball joint nut on control arm, but do not remove it.
8. Separate lower ball joint from steering knuckle using ball joint separator tool No. J-42188, or equivalent.
9. Remove separator tool, ball joint nut and ball joint from steering knuckle. Discard ball joint stud nut.
10. Support lower control arms with suitable jack stands.
11. Mark position of cam bolts for reference.
12. Remove cam bolts from lower control arm.

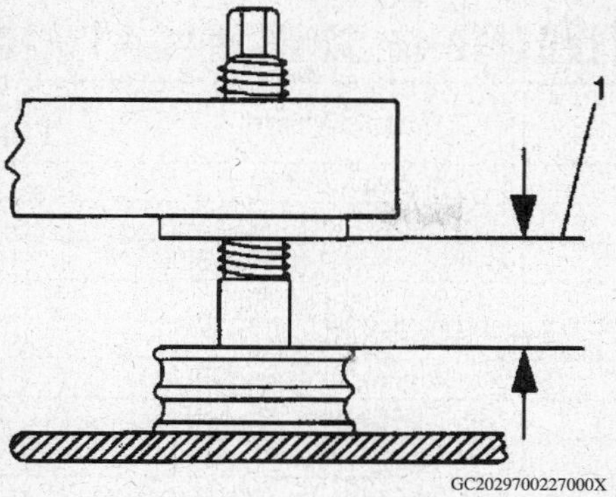

Fig. 1 Transverse spring adjuster gap

13. Remove lower control arm.
14. Remove transverse spring retainers.
15. Remove and discard transverse spring bolts.
16. Remove transverse leaf spring.
17. Remove compressor tool from spring.
18. Reverse procedure to install, noting the following:
    a. Install spring adjuster bolts to height measured previously.
    b. Install cam bolts to position marked previously.
    c. Perform front wheel alignment after assembly.

CONTROL ARM

REPLACE

UPPER CONTROL ARM

1. Raise and support vehicle, then remove tire and wheel.
2. Support lower control arm with suitable jack stand.
3. **On models equipped with Real Time Damping (RTD) suspension,** disconnect RTD sensor link.
4. **On all models,** loosen ball joint stud nut, but do not remove it.
5. Separate upper ball joint stud from upper control arm using ball joint separator tool No. J-42188, or equivalent.
6. Remove tool, nut and ball joint.
7. Remove upper control arm mounting bolts and shims. Note number and position of shims.
8. Remove upper control arm.
9. Reverse procedure to install, noting the following:
   a. **On 1997–98 models, torque** ball stud nut to 15 ft. lbs., tighten an additional 4 flats, then inspect nut for final **torque** of 33 ft. lbs.
   b. **On 1999–2000 models, torque** ball stud nut to 15 ft. lbs., tighten an additional 250°, then inspect nut for final **torque** of 41 ft. lbs.

LOWER CONTROL ARM

Refer to "Transverse Leaf Spring, Replace" for lower control arm replacement procedure.

STEERING KNUCKLE

REPLACE

1. Raise and support vehicle, then remove tire and wheel.
2. Remove brake caliper and rotor.
3. Disconnect stabilizer shaft link from lower control arm.
4. Disconnect wheel speed sensor electrical connector.
5. Support lower control arm with suitable jack stand.
6. Separate outer tie rod ball stud from steering knuckle using ball joint separator tool No. J-42188, or equivalent.
7. Separate upper ball joint stud from upper control arm using separator tool.
8. Separate lower ball joint stud from steering knuckle using separator tool.
9. Remove steering knuckle.
10. Reverse procedure to install.

STABILIZER BAR

REPLACE

1. Raise and support vehicle, then remove tire and wheel.
2. Remove stabilizer bar link nuts and link from stabilizer bar and lower control arm.
3. Remove stabilizer bar insulator clamps from front crossmember.
4. Remove stabilizer bar.
5. Reverse procedure to install.

POWER STEERING GEAR

REPLACE

Refer to "Engine Mount, Replace" in "5.7L Engine" section for power steering gear replacement procedure.

POWER STEERING PUMP

REPLACE

1. **On 1998 models equipped with front-mounted Electronic Brake Control Module and Brake Pressure Modulator Valve (EBTCM/BPMV) and all 1999–2000 models,** remove EBTCM/BPMV and bracket. Position brake pipes aside as required. Cap and plug all open lines.
2. **On all models,** drain power steering fluid into suitable container.
3. Remove power steering fluid reservoir.
4. Remove accessory drive belt.
5. Remove power steering pump pulley using pulley removal tool No. J-25034-B, or equivalent.
6. Disconnect power steering gear inlet hose from power steering pump.
7. Remove power steering pump mounting bolts.
8. Remove power steering pump and bracket.
9. Reverse procedure to install.

TIGHTENING SPECIFICATIONS

Year	Component	Torque/ Ft. Lbs.
1997–2000	Crossmember	81①
	Lower Control Arm	125
	Lower Control Arm Ball Stud	②
	Power Steering Pump	18
	Power Steering Reservoir Bracket	37
	Power Steering Line End Fittings	20
	Shock Absorber (Lower)	21
	Shock Absorber (Upper)	19
	Steering Link Outer Tie Rod End Stud	
	Stabilizer Bar Insulator Clamp (1997–98)	40
	Stabilizer Bar Insulator Clamp (1999–2000)	43
	Stabilizer Bar Link (1997–98)	55
	Stabilizer Bar Link (1999–2000)	53
	Transverse Leaf Spring (1997)	37①
	Transverse Leaf Spring (1998–2000)	46①
	Upper Control Arm (1997)	42
	Upper Control Arm (1998–2000)	48
	Upper Control Arm Ball Stud	②
	Wheel Hub Bearing (1997–98)	70
	Wheel Hub Bearing (1999–2000)	96

① — Always install new bolts and nuts. Do not use old fasteners.

② — Refer "Ball Joint, Replace" for tightening specifications and procedure.

③ — Torque to 15 ft. lbs., tighten an additional 160°, then final torque to 33 ft. lbs.

Wheel Alignment

INDEX

PRELIMINARY INSPECTION

Prior to inspecting or adjusting front suspension alignment, inspect suspension components and wheel bearings for damage or excessive wear and replace as required. Ensure tire pressure is properly adjusted, then raise and release front bumper several times to allow vehicle to assume normal ride height. The following items should be inspected prior to performing wheel alignment procedures:

1. Inspect all tires for proper inflation pressure.
2. Inspect hubs and bearings for excessive wear.
3. Inspect ball joints and tie rod ends for looseness and wear.
4. Inspect for bent wheel rims, wheel runout and faulty tires (belt shifts).
5. Inspect all suspension and steering components for looseness and wear.
6. Inspect for excessive cargo loads.
7. Measure vehicle trim height.

FRONT WHEEL ALIGNMENT

CASTER

1. Loosen lower control arm cam bolt nuts.
2. Rotate cam bolts to caster specification setting.
3. Maintain caster setting while **torquing** cam bolt nuts to 125 ft. lbs.
4. Inspect caster and camber settings after tightening and adjust as required.

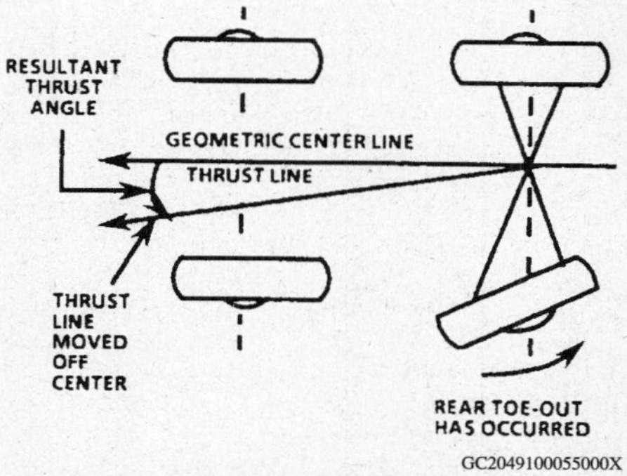

Fig. 1 Vehicle thrust angle

CAMBER

1. Loosen lower control arm cam bolt nuts.
2. Rotate cam bolts to required camber specification setting.
3. Maintain camber setting while **torquing** cam bolt nuts to 125 ft. lbs.
4. Inspect caster and camber settings after tightening and adjust as required.
5. To obtain additional negative camber beyond cam adjustment capability, remove shims from upper control arms.

TOE-IN

1. Loosen jam nut on tie rod.
2. Rotate inner tie rod to toe specification setting.
3. **Torque** jam nut on tie rod end to 50 ft. lbs.
4. Inspect toe setting after tightening and adjust as required.

REAR WHEEL ALIGNMENT

CAMBER

1. Loosen lower control arm cam bolt nuts.
2. Rotate cam bolts to required camber specification setting.
3. Maintain camber setting while **torquing** front cam bolt nut to 107 ft. lbs. and rear cam bolt nut to 71 ft. lbs.
4. Inspect caster and camber settings after tightening and adjust as required.

TOE-IN

1. Loosen rear suspension adjustment link locknut.
2. Rotate inner tie rod to toe specification setting.
3. **Torque** rear suspension adjustment link lock nut to 44 ft. lbs.
4. Inspect toe setting after tightening and adjust as required.

THRUST ANGLE

The vehicle is steered by the front wheels. The path the rear wheels follow is the thrust angle, **Fig. 1.** Thrust angle should be aligned with the vehicle centerline.

VEHICLE RIDE HEIGHT

Refer to **Figs. 2 through 4** for ride height measurements and specifications.

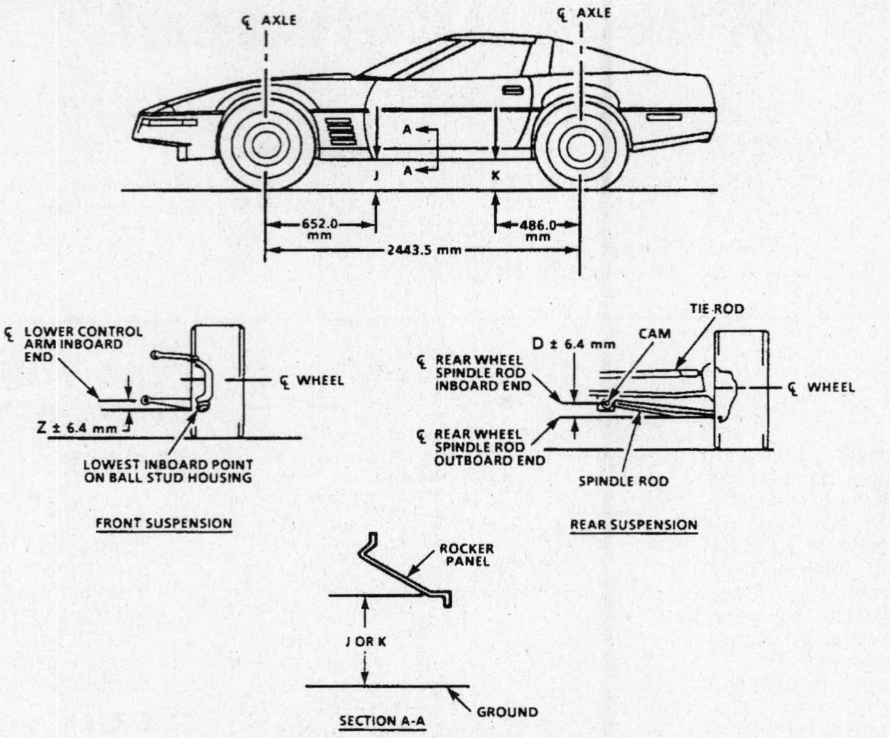

VERTICAL HEIGHTS: "Z" AND "J" DIMENSIONS - LIFT FRONT BUMPER OF VEHICLE UP APPROXIMATELY 38.0 mm. GENTLY REMOVE HANDS AND LET VEHICLE SETTLE ON ITS OWN. REPEAT TWICE FOR A TOTAL OF 3 TIMES. MEASURE "Z" AND "J" DIMENSIONS. PUSH FRONT BUMPER OF VEHICLE DOWN APPROXIMATELY 38.0 mm. GENTLY REMOVE HANDS AND LET VEHICLE RISE ON ITS OWN. REPEAT TWICE FOR A TOTAL OF 3 TIMES. MEASURE "Z" AND "J" DIMENSIONS. TRUE HEIGHTS ARE THE AVERAGE OF THE HIGH AND LOW MEASUREMENTS.

"D" AND "K" DIMENSIONS - SAME PROCEDURE AS "Z" AND "J" DIMENSIONS USING REAR BUMPER.

RECOMMENDED TIRE PRESSURE: TRIM HEIGHT. SET TIRE PRESSURE TO AGREE WITH VEHICLE'S TIRE PRESSURE STICKER FOR LOADING "UP TO VEHICLE CAPACITY."

NOTE: LOAD CONDITIONS: SHIPPING WEIGHT - VEHICLE IS BUILT TO PARTS LIST SPECIFICATIONS INCLUDING COOLANT TO CAPACITY AND 20.8 LITERS (5.5 GALLONS) OF GASOLINE. CURB WEIGHT - VEHICLE IS BUILT TO PARTS LIST SPECIFICATIONS INCLUDING COOLANT TO CAPACITY AND FULL TANK OF GASOLINE.

GC2049200056000X

Fig. 2 Ride height measurement locations

Model	Susp	Eng	Package	Z Height		D Height		J Height		K Height	
				Shipped	Curb	Shipped	Curb	Shipped	Curb	Shipped	Curb
1YY07	FE1	LS1	Base	46mm	44mm ± 5.0mm	114mm	108mm ± 5.0mm	153mm	150mm ± 6.4mm	157mm	151mm ± 6.4mm
1YY07	FE1	LS1	F45	46mm	44mm ± 5.0mm	114mm	108mm ± 5.0mm	153mm	150mm ± 6.4mm	157mm	151mm ± 6.4mm
1YY07	FE3	LS1	Z51	46mm	44mm ± 5.0mm	114mm	108mm ± 5.0mm	153mm	150mm ± 6.4mm	157mm	151mm ± 6.4mm

GC2049700144000A

Fig. 3 Ride height specifications. 1997

Base, F45, Z51	Z Height (Curb)	D Height (Curb)	J Height (Curb)	K Height (Curb)
Service Preferred	44 mm (1.73 in)	108 mm (4.25 in)	152 mm (5.98 in)	157 mm (6.18 in)
Service Allowable	50.4 mm (1.99 in) to 37.6 mm (1.48 in)	114.4 mm (4.50 in) to 101.6 mm (4.0 in)	152 mm (5.98 in)	157 mm (6.18 in)

GC2049800154000X

Fig. 4 Ride height specifications. 1998–2000

ELDORADO, DEVILLE & SEVILLE

NOTE: Refer To Rear Of This Manual For Vehicle Manufacturer's Special Service Tool Suppliers.

INDEX OF SERVICE OPERATIONS

Specifications

GENERAL ENGINE SPECIFICATIONS

Year	Engine Liter	Engine VIN Code②	Fuel Injection System	Bore & Stroke	Compression Ratio	Net H.P. @ RPM③	Maximum Torque Ft. Lbs. @ RPM	Normal Oil Pressure Pounds①
1997 & 2000	4.6L	Y	TPFI	3.66 x 3.31	10.3	275 @ 5600	300 @ 4400	35
	4.6L	9	TPFI	3.66 x 3.31	10.3	300 @ 6000	295 @ 4400	35
1998-99	4.6L	Y	TPFI	3.66 x 3.43	10.3	275 @ 5600	300 @ 4000	35
	4.6L	9	TPFI	3.66 x 3.43	10.3	300 @ 6000	295 @ 4400	35

MPI — Multi-Port Fuel Injection
SPFI — Sequential Port Fuel Injection
TPFI — Tuned Port Fuel Injection

① — At 2000 RPM.
② — The eighth digit denotes engine code.
③ — Ratings are net-as installed in vehicle.

TUNE UP SPECIFICATIONS

Year & Engine, VIN①	Spark Plug Gap	Ignition Timing: Firing Order Fig.④	Ignition Timing: Degrees BTDC	Ignition Timing: Mark Fig.	Curb Idle Speed③	Fast Idle Speed	Fuel Pump Pressure, Psi	Valve Lash
1997–2000								
4.6L/Y	.050	②	10⑤	⑨	⑥	⑥	48–55⑦	⑧
4.6L/9	.050	②	10⑤	⑨	⑥	⑥	48–55⑦	⑧

BTDC — Before top dead center
① — The eighth digit denotes engine code.
② — Cylinder numbering from left to right as viewed from front of vehicle, front bank, 2, 4, 6, 8; rear bank, 1, 3, 5, 7. Firing order 1-2-7-3-4-5-6-8. Refer to **Fig. A** for spark plug wire connections at coil unit.
③ — On auto. trans. models, idle speed is adjusted in Drive. When adjusting idle speed, set parking brake & block drive wheels.
④ — Before disconnecting wires from distributor cap, determine location of No. 1 wire in cap, as distributor position may have been altered from that shown at the end of this chart.
⑤ — Computer controlled, no adjustment.
⑥ — Idle speed is controlled by an idle speed control (ISC) motor or an idle air control (IAC) valve.
⑦ — With shop towel wrapped around fuel pressure valve to prevent fuel spillage, connect a suitable fuel pressure gauge to fuel pressure valve. Check fuel pressure w/ignition switch in the On position, engine not running.
⑧ — Equipped w/non adjustable hydraulic valve lifters.
⑨ — Equipped w/crankshaft position sensor.

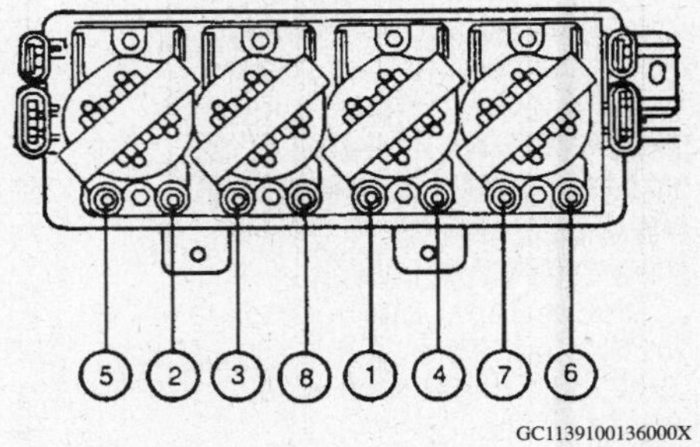

Fig. A

FRONT WHEEL ALIGNMENT SPECIFICATIONS

Year	Model	Caster Angle, Degrees		Camber Angle, Degrees		Total Toe, Degrees①		Ball Joint Inspection
		Limits	Desired	Limits	Desired	Limits	Desired	
1997	DeVille	+1.3 to +3.3④	+2.3④	-.5 to +.5③	0③	0 to +.4	+.2	②
	Eldorado	+1.3 to +3.3④	+2.3④	-.5 to +.5③	0③	0 to +.4	+.2	②
	Seville	+1.3 to +3.3④	+2.3④	-.5 to +.5③	0③	0 to +.4	+.2	②
1998-99	DeVille	+1.3 to +3.3④	+2.3④	-.5 to +.5③	0③	0 to +.4	+.2	②
	Eldorado	+1.3 to +3.3④	+2.3④	-.5 to +.5③	0③	0 to +.4	+.2	②
	Seville	+5.5 to +6.5⑤	+6⑤	-.7 to +.3⑤	-.2⑤	0 to +.4	+.2	②
2000	DeVille	+5.5 to +6.5⑤	+6⑤	-.7 to +.3⑤	-.2⑤	0 to +.4	+.2	②
	Eldorado	+1.3 to +3.3④	+2.3④	-.5 to +.5③	0③	0 to +.4	+.2	②
	Seville	+5.5 to +6.5⑤	+6⑤	-.7 to +.3⑤	-.2⑤	0 to +.4	+.2	②

FWD-Front Wheel Drive
RWD-Rear Wheel Drive
① — Toe-In (+). Toe-Out (-).
② — Refer to "Ball Joint Inspection" in "Front Suspension & Steering."
③ — Cross caster or camber (LH-RH), 0° (+/-.75°).
④ — Cross caster or camber (LH-RH), 0° (+/-1°).
⑤ — Cross caster or camber within .5°.

REAR WHEEL ALIGNMENT SPECIFICATIONS

Year	Model	Camber Angle, Degrees		Total Toe, Degrees①		Thrust Angle, Degrees	
		Limits	Desired	Limits	Desired	Limits	Desired
1997	DeVille	-.8 to +.2②	-.3②	0 to +.4	+.2	-.1 to +.1	0
	Eldorado	-.8 to +.2②	-.3②	0 to +.4	+.2	-.1 to +.1	0
	Seville	-.8 to +.2②	-.3②	0 to +.4	+.2	-.1 to +.1	0
1998-99	DeVille	-.5 to +.5②	0②	0 to +.4	+.2	-.1 to +.1	0
	Eldorado	-.5 to +.5②	0②	0 to +.4	+.2	-.1 to +.1	0
	Seville	③	④	0 to +.4	+.2	-.1 to +.1	0
2000	DeVille	-.8 to +.2	-.3	0 to +.4	+.2	-.1 to +.1	0
	Eldorado	-.5 to +.5②	0②	0 to +.4	+.2	-.1 to +.1	0
	Seville	-.8 to +.2	-.3	0 to +.4	+.2	-.1 to +.1	0

① — Toe-In (+). Toe-Out (-).
② — Cross camber (LH-RH), 0° (+/-.75°).
③ — OnSeville model, –.8 to +.2; On Seville Touring models, –1.1 to –.1. Cross camber (LH-RH), 0° (+/-.5°).
④ — KS, –.3; KY, –.6.

FLUID CAPACITIES & COOLING SYSTEM DATA

Year	Engine/Liter	Coolant Capacity, Qts.	Radiator Cap Relief Pressure, Lbs.	Thermostat Opening Temp., °F	Fuel Tank Gals	Engine Oil Refill Qts. ②	Auto Transaxle Qts.①	
							Drain & Refill	Overhaul
1997	4.6L	12.5	15	188	20	7.5	8	12.6
1998-99	4.6L④	10.7	15	188	20	7.5	11	12.6③
	4.6L⑤	10.7	18	188	20	7.5	11	12.6③
	4.6L⑥	12.5	18	188	18.5	7.5	11	12.6③
2000	4.6L④	12.5	15	188	18.5	7.5	11	12.6③
	4.6L⑤	12.5	18	188	20	7.5	11	12.6③
	4.6L⑥	12.5	⑦	188	18.5	7.5	11	12.6②

① — Approximate, make final check w/dipstick.
② — Includes filter change.
③ — Totally dry, 15 qts.
④ — DeVille.
⑤ — Eldorado.
⑥ — Seville.
⑦ — Radiator cap pressure relief specification is stamped on radiator cap.

LUBRICANT DATA

Year	Model	Lubricant Type		
		Automatic Transaxle	Power Steering	Brake System
1997–2000	All	Dexron III	GM Power Steering Fluid①	Dot 3

① — Or equivalent, meeting GM requirements 1052884.

Electrical

NOTE: On Air Bag Equipped Models, Refer To "Air Bag System Precautions" Located In The Front Of This Manual For System Disarming & Arming Procedures.

NOTE: Refer To "Computer Relearn Procedures" Located In The Front Of This Manual For Computer Relearn Procedures.

INDEX

PRECAUTIONS

AIR BAG SYSTEMS

Refer to "Air Bag System Precautions" in the front of this manual for system disarming and arming procedures.

BATTERY GROUND CABLE

Prior to service, disconnect battery ground cable and isolate as required.

FUSE PANEL & FLASHER LOCATION

ELDORADO, 1997 SEVILLE & 1997-99 DEVILLE

The engine compartment fuse/relay center is located on the front lefthand side of the engine compartment, in front of the strut tower. The LH and RH Maxifuse blocks are located on the front lefthand side of the engine compartment, near the fuse/relay center. The trunk compartment fuse block is located in the front righthand side of the luggage compartment.

The hazard flasher is located under the lefthand side of the instrument panel, near the kick panel. The turn flasher module is located under the lefthand side of the instrument panel, near the knee bolster.

1998–2000 SEVILLE & 2000 DEVILLE

The engine compartment fuse/relay center is located at the right rear of the engine compartment near the power steering pump. The rear fuse block is located in the left rear of passenger compartment under the rear seat.

The hazard/turn flasher is located at the lefthand side of the instrument panel under the knee bolster.

FUEL PUMP RELAY LOCATION

ELDORADO, 1997 SEVILLE & 1997–99 DEVILLE

The fuel pump relay is located on the front lefthand side of the engine compartment, in the fuse/relay center.

1998–2000 SEVILLE & 2000 DEVILLE

The fuel pump relay is located in the left rear of passenger compartment under the rear seat.

RELAY CENTER LOCATION

ELDORADO, 1997 SEVILLE & 1997–99 DEVILLE

The fuse/relay center is located on the front lefthand side of the engine compartment, in front of the strut tower.

1998–2000 SEVILLE & 2000 DEVILLE

The fuse/relay center is located in the left rear of passenger compartment under the rear seat.

STARTER

REPLACE

Refer to **Fig. 1** when replacing starter motor for component location.

1. Remove positive battery cable.
2. Remove intake manifold as outlined under "Intake Manifold, Replace."
3. Remove solenoid and battery cable terminal nuts.
4. Remove starter mounting bolts, then starter.
5. Reverse procedure to install, noting the following:
   a. **Torque** solenoid and battery cable terminal nuts to 5–6 ft. lbs. **Terminal nuts must be properly tightened. failure to do so could result in starter failure due to terminal or cap damage.**
   b. **Torque** starter mounting bolts to 22 ft. lbs.

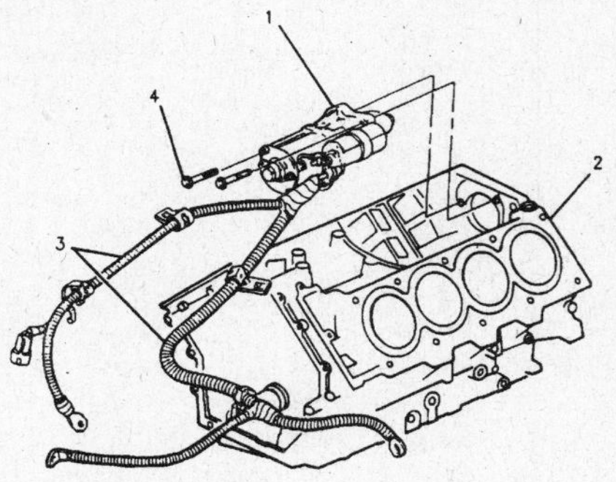

Fig. 1 Starter motor location

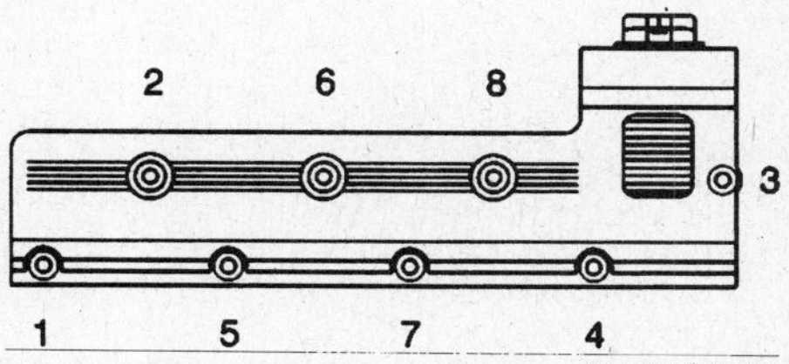

Fig. 2 Ignition control module assembly bolts removal sequence. 2000

COIL PACK

REPLACE

1997–99

1. Remove spark plug wires from ignition control module assembly. Note location of wires for installation reference.
2. Disconnect four electrical connectors from ignition module.
3. Remove ignition control module assembly to rear camshaft cover attaching bolts.
4. Remove module assembly from vehicle.
5. Remove ignition coils from module assembly, then module assembly from bracket.
6. Reverse procedure to install. **Torque** attaching bolts to 9 ft. lbs.

2000

Left Side

1. Remove engine sight shield, oil level indicator then disconnect ignition control module connector.
2. Remove ignition assembly bolts in sequence, **Fig. 2.**
3. Remove ignition assembly then ignition control module.
4. Reverse procedure to install tightening to specifications.

Right Side

1. Remove engine sight shield then disconnect ignition control module connector.
2. **On models with AIR,** disconnect AIR vent solenoid and vacuum hoses then remove AIR assembly.
3. **On all models,** remove ignition assembly bolts in sequence, **Fig. 2.**
4. Remove ignition assembly then ignition control module.
5. Reverse procedure to install tightening to specifications.

IGNITION LOCK

REPLACE

ELDORADO, 1997 SEVILLE & 1997–99 DEVILLE

1. Remove steering wheel as outlined under "Steering Wheel, Replace."
2. Remove turn signal switch as outlined under "Turn Signal Switch, Replace."
3. Remove key from lock, then buzzer switch assembly.
4. Place key in "Lock" position, then remove lock retaining screw, **Fig. 3.**
5. Disconnect electrical connector, retaining clip from housing cover, then withdraw lock cylinder assembly from column.
6. Reverse procedure to install. **Torque** lock retaining screw to 22 inch lbs.

1998–2000 SEVILLE

1. Apply parking brake.
2. Remove radio as outlined under "Radio, Replace."
3. Remove HVAC control head.
4. Turn ignition key to "Run" position.
5. Looking through radio opening, use a suitable flat headed tool to depress lock cylinder retaining tab located on RH lower side of ignition switch, then remove ignition cylinder.
6. Reverse procedure to install.

2000 DEVILLE

1. Remove steering wheel as outlined under "Steering Wheel, Replace."
2. Roll back shift lever seal from upper and lower shrouds.
3. Remove lower steering column shroud

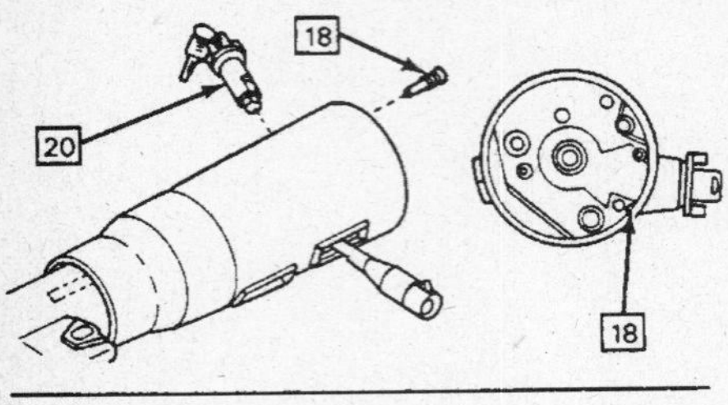

18 SCREW, LOCK RETAINING
20 LOCK CYLINDER SET, STRG COL PASS KEY

GC9129100021000X

Fig. 3 Lock cylinder set removal. Eldorado, 1997 Seville & 1997–99 DeVille

then remove one screw from upper shroud to gain access to lock cylinder access hole.
4. Turn ignition to start position, then using a bent tip awl push down on ignition lock cylinder retaining pin through access hole.
5. Release ignition lock cylinder to run position, then remove by pulling away from steering column.
6. Reverse procedure to install.

IGNITION SWITCH

REPLACE

ELDORADO, 1997 SEVILLE & 1997–99 DEVILLE

Removal

1. **On models with floor shift,** place transmission selector in park and rotate ignition lock to "Run" position.
2. **On all models,** remove left hush panel, lower steering column cover, insulator at toe plate and lower steering column mounting screws.
3. Remove nuts securing upper steering column bracket to instrument panel, then lower column. **Disconnect shift indicator cable and electrical connectors, as needed, prior to lowering column. Do not force column down as it may be damaged.**
4. Remove dimmer switch mounting nut, screw and dimmer switch, then tape actuator rod to steering column.
5. **On models with floor shift,** insert screwdriver into slot in ignition switch inhibitor, depress park-lock cable latch and disconnect cable from inhibitor, **Fig. 4. Ignition switch must be in "Run" position. Do not attempt to disconnect park-lock cable with switch in any other position.** Rotate ignition key to "Off-Lock" position.
6. **On all models,** remove ignition switch stud bolt.
7. Disconnect electrical connector, then remove switch assembly.

Installation

1. Move ignition switch slider to extreme right, then one detent to left to place switch in "Off-Lock" position.
2. Connect electrical connector to ignition switch, install switch assembly on column ensure actuator is properly engaged and **torque** stud bolt to 35 inch lbs.
3. Install dimmer switch assembly, depress switch against actuator and insert 3/32 inch drill into adjustment slot, **Fig. 5,** then **torque** nut and retaining screw to 35 inch lbs.
4. **On models with floor shift,** rotate ignition lock to "Run" position, then install shift-lock cable on inhibitor.
5. **On all models,** reverse procedure to install. **Torque** upper column bracket bolts to 20 ft. lbs. and lower column bolts to 25 ft. lbs.

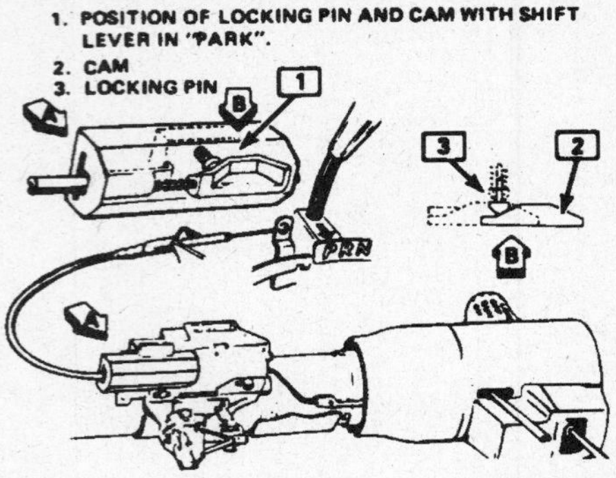

GC9129100022000X

Fig. 4 Park-lock cable (Floor shift). Eldorado, 1997 Seville & 1997–99 DeVille

1998–2000 SEVILLE

1. Apply parking brake.
2. Remove radio as outlined under "Radio, Replace."
3. Remove HVAC control head, then knee bolster.
4. Remove steering column as follows:
   a. Lock steering column using steering wheel anti-rotation pin tool No. J-42640 or equivalent.
   b. Disconnect electrical connections.
   c. Remove upper pinch bolt and nuts securing column to base and instrument panel.
5. Disconnect electrical connections and park lock cable from ignition switch.
6. Remove ignition switch cylinder as outlined under " Ignition Lock, Replace."
7. Remove fasteners for ignition switch located at access hole in steering column opening and through radio opening then remove ignition switch.
8. Reverse procedure to install.

2000 DEVILLE

1. Remove steering column lock cylinder set as outlined under " Ignition Lock, Replace."
2. Remove upper and lower steering column shrouds.
3. Disconnect coded key controller connector, then slide controller from lock module assembly.
4. Disconnect green connector from bottom of ignition switch assembly.
5. Remove lead inside clip on side of ignition switch assembly.
6. Disconnect key alarm connector from lock module assembly, then remove ignition switch assembly.
7. Reverse procedure to install.

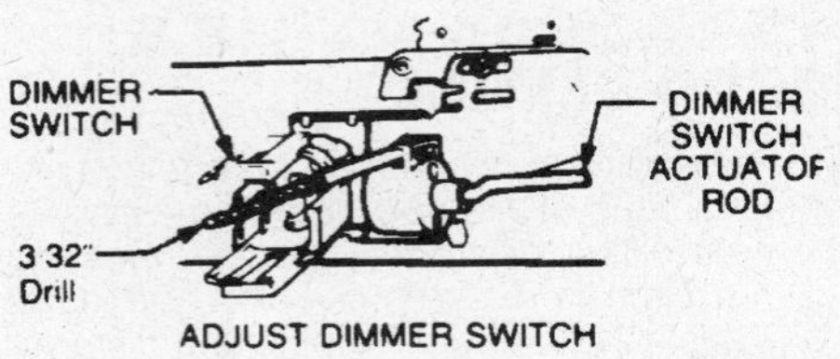

GC9129100023000X

Fig. 5 Dimmer switch installation. Eldorado, 1997 Seville & 1997–99 DeVille

NEUTRAL SAFETY SWITCH

REPLACE

1. Apply parking brake.
2. Shift gear selector to neutral.
3. Disconnect electrical connectors, then remove linkage retaining nut.
4. Disconnect cable and lever.
5. Remove neutral safety switch, **Fig. 6.**
6. Reverse procedure to install, noting the following:
   a. Ensure transaxle is in neutral.
   b. New switches are pre-aligned to neutral position.
   c. If adjustments need to made to an existing switch refer to" Neutral Safety Switch, Adjust."
   d. **Torque** switch bolts to 18 ft. lbs.
   e. **Torque** linkage retaining nut to 15 ft. lbs.

NEUTRAL SAFETY SWITCH

ADJUST

If the pin in the new pre-aligned switch has been sheared or if realigning old switch, switch alignment tool No. J 41545 or equivalent, must be used. Adjust as follows:

1. Insert alignment tool, **Fig. 7,** into two slots on switch.
2. Rotate tool until rear leg of tool falls into slot on switch near hose.
3. Verify tool is seated in all three slots.
4. Remove tool.

HEADLAMP SWITCH

REPLACE

ELDORADO, 1997 SEVILLE & 1997–99 DEVILLE

1. Remove headlamp switch module from instrument panel by firmly pulling outward on headlamp switch knob, **Fig. 8.**
2. Disconnect electrical connector from switch.
3. Reverse procedure to install.

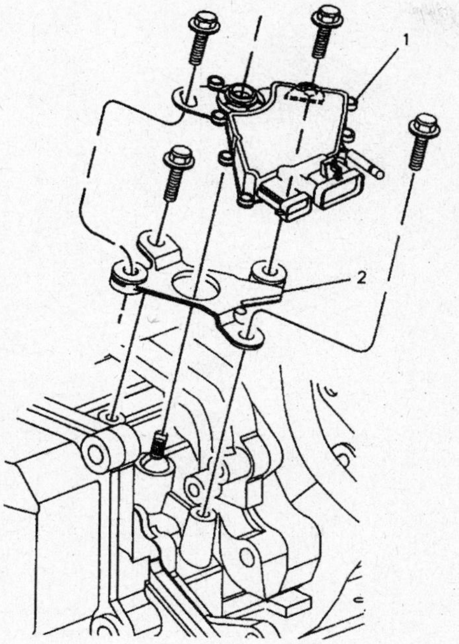

1 PARK/NEUTRAL POSITION SWITCH
2 BRACKET

GC9049600152000X

Fig. 6 Neutral safety switch

1998–2000 SEVILLE & 2000 DEVILLE

1. Remove left instrument panel end cap.
2. Push on rear of switch to remove then disconnect electrical connector.
3. Reverse procedure to install.

TURN SIGNAL SWITCH

REPLACE

ELDORADO, 1997 SEVILLE & 1997–99 DEVILLE

1. Remove steering wheel and inflator module (if equipped), as described under "Steering Wheel, Replace."
2. Remove lower steering column trim cover.
3. Mount spring compressor J–23653 or equivalent on steering shaft, **Fig. 9.**
4. Remove lock plate retaining ring and telescoping wheel components, if equipped.
5. Remove spring compressor.
6. Remove lock plate, canceling cam, upper bearing spring, then upper bearing inner race and seat.
7. Remove multi-function lever.
8. Remove turn signal switch retaining screws, then switch assembly.
9. Reverse procedure to install.

1998–2000 SEVILLE & 2000 DEVILLE

1. Remove steering wheel as outlined under "Steering Wheel, Replace."
2. Remove steering column shrouds.
3. Disconnect then remove multi-function lever.
4. Reverse procedure to install.

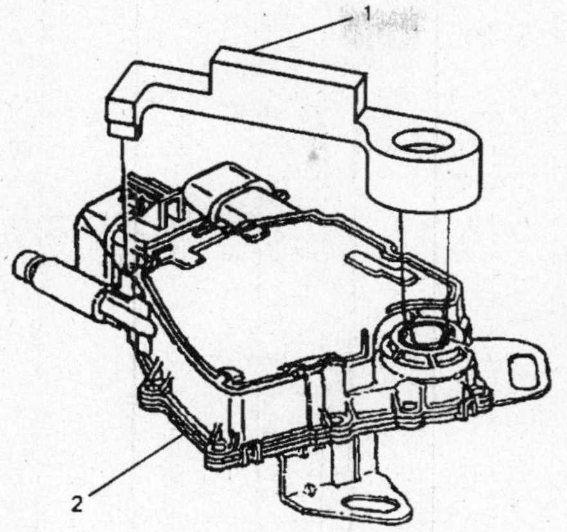

1 ALIGNMENT TOOL
2 PARK/NEUTRAL POSITION SWITCH

GC9049600153000X

Fig. 7 Neutral safety switch adjust

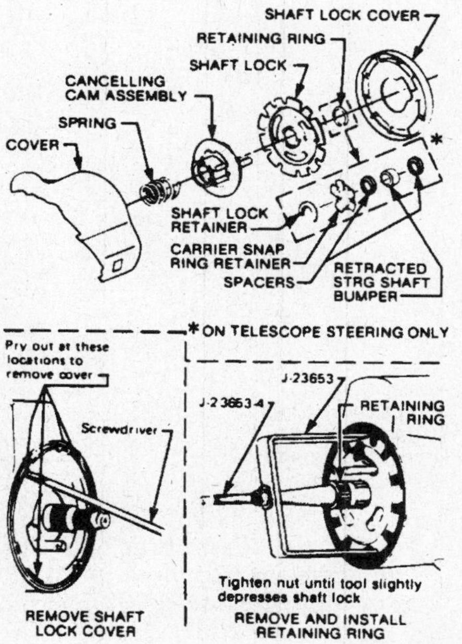

GC9129100024000X

Fig. 9 Lock plate & cancelling cam removal. Eldorado, 1997 Seville & 1997–99 DeVille

DIMMER SWITCH

REPLACE

Refer to "Ignition Switch, Replace" for procedure.

STEERING WHEEL

REPLACE

If the air bag has been deployed, inspect coil for signs of scorching, melting or other damage. Coil must be replaced if damaged.

1. Turn ignition switch to Off position.
2. Remove Torx screws from back of steering wheel.

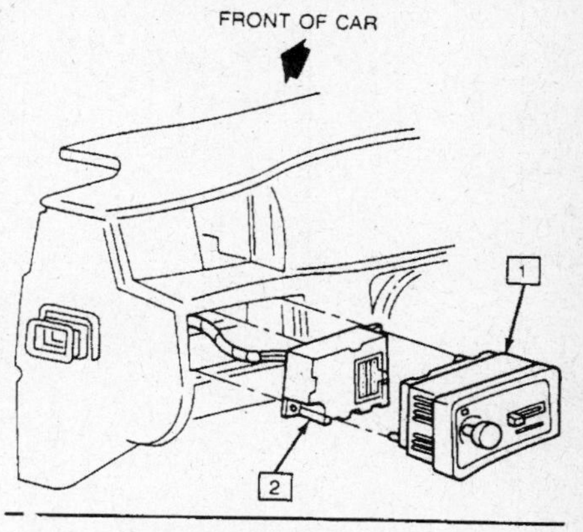

1 HEADLAMP SWITCH
2 TWILIGHT SENTINEL/DRL MODULE

GC9049200098000X

Fig. 8 Headlamp switch replacement. Eldorado, 1997 Seville & 1997–99 DeVille

3. Remove inflator module from wheel. **Always carry live inflator modules with trim cover facing away from you. Never carry module by wiring. Always place module on a flat surface with trim cover facing up.**
4. Remove horn contact by pushing slightly and twisting counterclockwise.
5. Disconnect Connector Position Assurance (CPA) and coil assembly connector from inflator module.
6. Remove steering column shaft nut.
7. Remove steering wheel using puller No. J–1859-03 or equivalent. **Do not thread puller bolts too far in steering wheel. Threading puller bolts too far into steering wheel could damage SIR coil assembly. Four turns is sufficient.**
8. Reverse procedure to install, noting the following:
   a. **Torque** steering wheel shaft nut to 30 ft. lbs.
   b. **Torque** SIR module retaining screws to 27 inch lbs.

INSTRUMENT CLUSTER

REPLACE

1. Remove fuses A5 and B5 from rear compartment fuse panel and fuse A3 from engine compartment fuse panel.
2. Using a small flat-bladed tool, remove defroster grill.
3. Remove sunload and headlamp auto control sensors from defroster grill.
4. Remove three upper trim panel retaining screws, through defroster grill opening.
5. Remove heater and A/C vents from instrument panel.
6. Remove four upper trim panel retaining screws, through vent openings.
7. Remove upper trim panel.
8. Disconnect two electrical connectors from top of instrument panel.
9. Remove four instrument cluster to instrument panel attaching screws, **Fig. 10.**

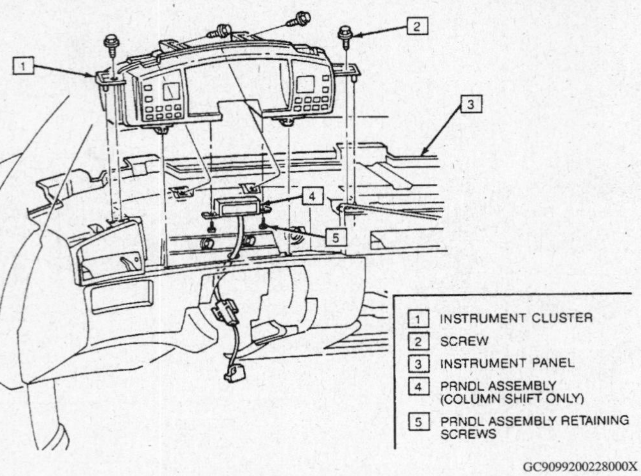

Fig. 10 Instrument cluster removal

10. Raise cluster, remove two screws securing PRNDL mechanism on digital clusters.
11. Remove instrument cluster.
12. Reverse procedure to install.

RADIO

REPLACE

CONSOLE SHIFT

Eldorado, Seville & 1997–99 DeVille

1. Remove shifter trim plate.
2. Remove ashtray assembly.
3. Disconnect Direct Ignition System (DIS).
4. Disconnect electrical connector.
5. Remove screws from radio/HVAC assembly.
6. Disconnect electrical harness, **Fig. 11.**
7. When installing another radio, proceed as follows:
   a. Remove both brackets, **Fig. 12,** from each side of radio.
   b. Remove 16mm plastic loading pin and clip stud from rear of radio.
8. Remove radio.
9. Reverse procedure to install.

2000 DeVille

1. Remove instrument panel center trim plate then remove HVAC control head.
2. Push and hold release tabs on right and left sides of radio then remove from instrument panel.
3. Disconnect antenna lead and electrical connector then remove mounting brackets and studs from radio.
4. Reverse procedure to install.

COLUMN SHIFT

1. Remove radio trim plate.
2. Push in on locking tabs on side of radio and pull out, **Fig. 13.**
3. Remove electrical harness.
4. When installing another radio, proceed as follows:
   a. Remove both brackets, **Fig. 14,** from each side of radio.

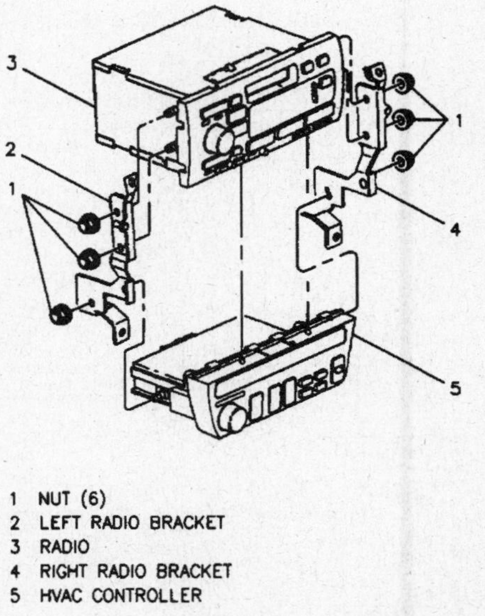

Fig. 12 Radio bracket replacement (Console shift). Eldorado, Seville & 1997–99 DeVille

   b. Remove 16mm plastic loading pin and clip stud from rear of radio.
5. Remove radio.
6. Reverse procedure to install.

WIPER MOTOR

REPLACE

ELDORADO, SEVILLE & 1997–2000 DEVILLE

1. Remove wiper arm assemblies, then air conditioning pipe shroud.
2. Remove shroud air inlet grill panel.
3. Disconnect electrical connectors from wiper motor.
4. Disconnect wiper transmission drive link socket from wiper motor crank arm using tool No. J–39232 or equivalent.
5. Remove air conditioning shroud pipe from wheel house.

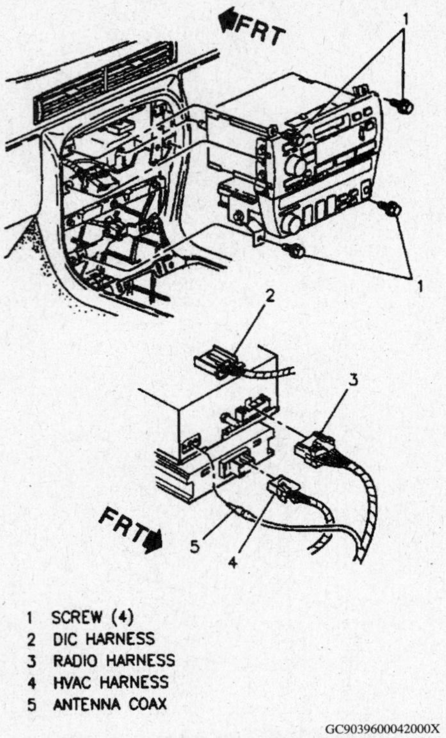

Fig. 11 Radio replacement (Console shift). Eldorado, Seville & 1997–99 DeVille

6. Remove three screws, then wiper motor.
7. Reverse procedure to install.

2000 DEVILLE

1. Remove wipers arms then air inlet grill panel.
2. Remove windshield frame reinforcement fasteners then remove windshield frame reinforcement.
3. Rotate wiper motor crank arm opposite park position by pushing or pulling on transmission linkage.
4. Disconnect wiper motor connector then push harness and grommet through hole in plenum.
5. Remove wiper system drive module fasteners then remove drive module.
6. Using wiper transmission seperator tool No. J-39232 or equivalent, remove drive link from wiper motor crank arm.
7. Remove wiper motor from wiper drive system module.
8. Reverse procedure to install.

WIPER SWITCH

REPLACE

ELDORADO, 1997 SEVILLE & 1997–99 DEVILLE

1. Remove steering wheel as outlined under "Steering Wheel, Replace."
2. Slide connector cover toward front of vehicle, then unplug electrical connector.
3. Push lever in and rotate clockwise ¼ turn and pull out switch.

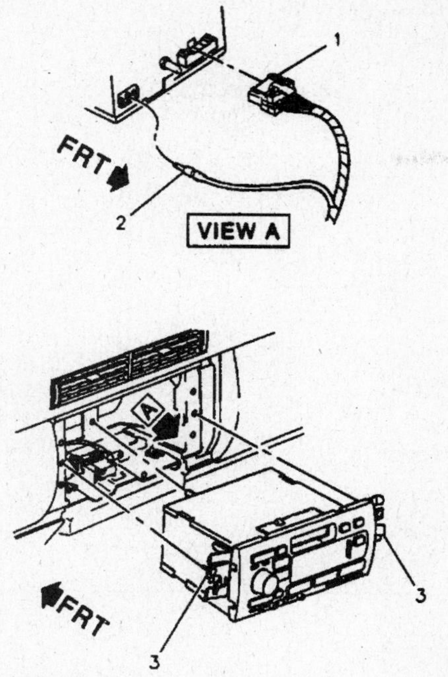

1 HARNESS
2 ANTENNA COAX
3 ALIGNMENT BULLETS AND LOCKING TABS

GC9039600043000X

Fig. 13 Radio replacement. Column shift

4. Reverse procedure to install.

1998–2000 SEVILLE & 2000 DEVILLE

1. Remove steering wheel as outlined under "Steering Wheel, Replace."
2. Remove kneebolster, then steering column nuts.
3. Lower steering column, then remove tilt lever, steering column shrouds and wire harness assembly.
4. **On models with power tilt and telescope** disconnect and remove interface module and harness noting placement of harness.
5. **On all models** depress tabs, then disconnect and remove switch.
6. Reverse procedure to install.

WIPER TRANSMISSION

REPLACE

ELDORADO, SEVILLE & 1997–99 DEVILLE

1. Disconnect battery ground cable, then remove wiper arm assemblies
2. Remove shroud air inlet grille panel.
3. Using tool No. J–39232 or equivalent, remove drive link from wiper motor crank arm.
4. Remove six screws, then wiper transmission assembly.
5. Reverse procedure to install.

2000 DEVILLE

Refer to "Wiper Motor, Replace" for procedure.

BLOWER MOTOR

REPLACE

ELDORADO, 1997 SEVILLE & 1997–99 DEVILLE

Refer to the end of section for blower motor noise.

1. Disconnect battery ground cable.
2. Remove strut tower cross brace.
3. Remove cowl relay center bracket, then disconnect electrical connector and cooling hose from blower motor.
4. Remove MAP sensor mounting bracket.
5. Remove blower motor retaining screws, then tilt blower motor in case to allow fan removal. **Fan must be removed prior to blower motor to prevent fan from bending.**
6. Remove fan retainer and fan from blower motor.
7. Remove blower motor, then blower fan from case.
8. Reverse procedure to install.

1998–99 SEVILLE & 2000 DEVILLE

1. Remove right side sound insulator panel and glove box assembly.
2. Pull back carpet, then remove dash integration module and position aside.
3. Remove blower motor retaining screws, then disconnect and remove blower motor.
4. Reverse procedure to install.

HEATER CORE

REPLACE

ELDORADO, 1997 SEVILLE & 1997–99 DEVILLE

1. Disconnect battery ground cable, then drain cooling system.
2. Remove screws securing glove box module and glove box, then righthand lower sound insulator.
3. Remove programmer as follows:
   a. Remove two ECM bracket mounting screws, then position ECM aside to gain access to rear programmer mounting screw.
   b. Remove threaded rod, then vacuum connector retaining nut from programmer.
   c. Disconnect electrical and vacuum connectors from programmer assembly, then remove three mounting screws and programmer, **Fig. 15.**
4. Disconnect electrical connections from ECM, then remove ECM and mounting bracket from vehicle.
5. Remove heater core cover, then disconnect heater hoses from heater core.
6. Remove two heater core retaining screws, then heater core.
7. Reverse procedure to install. Prior to installing glove box module, adjust air mix door link rod as follows:
   a. Set temperature control for 90° F and allow 1–2 minutes for programmer arm to travel to maximum heat position, **Fig. 16.**

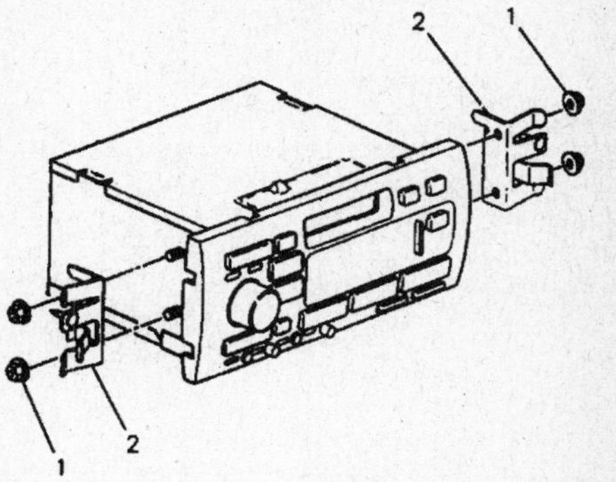

1 NUT (4)
2 LEFT AND RIGHT BRACKET

GC9039600045000X

Fig. 14 Radio bracket replacement. Column shift

   b. Disconnect air mix door link rod from programmer and ensure air mix door operated freely.
   c. Preload air mix door in maximum heat position by pulling rod to seat door against seal, then snap rod into connector on programmer arm, taking care not to disturb position of arm or air mix door.
   d. Set control for 60°F and ensure programmer arm and air mix door travel to maximum cooling position.

1998–99 SEVILLE & 2000 DEVILLE

1. Remove center console as Follows:
   a. Remove storage bins or cd player, then remove cover on floor of storage bin.
   b. Remove console trim plate, then right and left console side trim panels.
   c. Disconnect shift cable from shifter, then remove shift cable from front bracket.
   d. Disconnect park lock electrical connector and remove cable from shifter.
   e. Disconnect electrical connections from console.
   f. Remove console fasteners then console.
2. Remove instrument panel carrier as follows:
   a. Remove instrument panel center trim plate, radio and HVAC control panel.
   b. Remove instrument panel end caps, right sound insulator panel and side window air outlets.
   c. Remove instrument panel upper trim pad, defroster grill and knee bolster.
   d. Disconnect body to instrument panel, radio antenna lead and HVAC harness near blower motor electrical connections.
   e. Remove cigar lighter/ashtray lamp

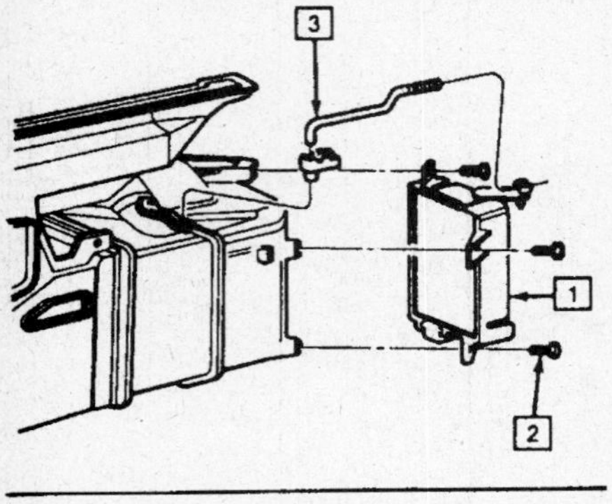

1 PROGRAMMER
2 PROG. MTG. SCREW (3 REQ'D)
3 THREADED ROD

GC9039100034000X

Fig. 15 Programmer mounting bolt locations. Eldorado, 1997 Seville & 1997–99 DeVille

harness from bracket.
   f. Install steering wheel anti-rotation pin tool No. J-42640 or equivalent in steering column.
   g. Remove steering column upper pinch bolt, then disconnect electrical connections and remove steering column.
   h. Disconnect parking brake cable from parking brake pedal assembly.
   i. Remove instrument panel carrier fasteners from center support bracket, steering column support bracket, cowl and hinge pillar, then remove carrier.
3. Remove heater core cover, retaining screws and retaining straps.
4. Disconnect heater hoses from heater core, then remove core.
5. Reverse procedure to install.

EVAPORATOR CORE

REPLACE

ELDORADO, 1997 SEVILLE & 1997–99 DEVILLE

1. Recover refrigerant from system as outlined in " Air Conditioning" section.
2. Drain radiator and cooling system.
3. Remove two bolts from each side of cross-tower support bracket.
4. Remove two nuts from cowl relay center bracket, then position relay bracket aside.
5. Disconnect electrical connectors from power module, blower motor and blower motor resistor.
6. Disconnect both heater core hoses from heater core.
7. Remove evaporator line retaining bracket.
8. Remove evaporator core refrigerant lines. **Cap all open fittings to prevent contamination of system.**
9. Remove heater hose T-connector.
10. Remove two heat shield screws from engine compartment.
11. Raise and support vehicle, then remove remaining two heat shield retaining screws from under vehicle.
12. Remove heat shield, then two A/C module retaining screws.
13. Lower vehicle and remove MAP sensor bracket.
14. Remove diverter valve from righthand side valve cover.
15. Remove two harness hold-down brackets from valve cover.
16. Remove power module, blower motor and sound insulator.
17. Remove A/C module cover screws, module cover, sound insulator and seal.
18. Remove evaporator retaining clamp, then pull evaporator core from evaporator case.
19. Reverse procedure to install, noting the following:
   a. **Torque** module cover retaining screws to 27 inch lbs.
   b. **Torque** line fitting bolt to 18 ft. lbs.
   c. Leak test all refrigerant connections.

1998–99 SEVILLE & 2000 DEVILLE

1. Recover refrigerant from system as outlined in " Air Conditioning" section.
2. Disconnect evaporator lines from core and heater hoses from heater core.
3. Remove center console as outlined under "Heater Core, Replace."
4. Remove instrument panel carrier as outlined under "Heater Core, Replace."
5. Remove evaporator drain, defroster and heater duct assembly.
6. Remove heater and evaporator module.
7. Remove heater and evaporator tube seal, then upper evaporator case.

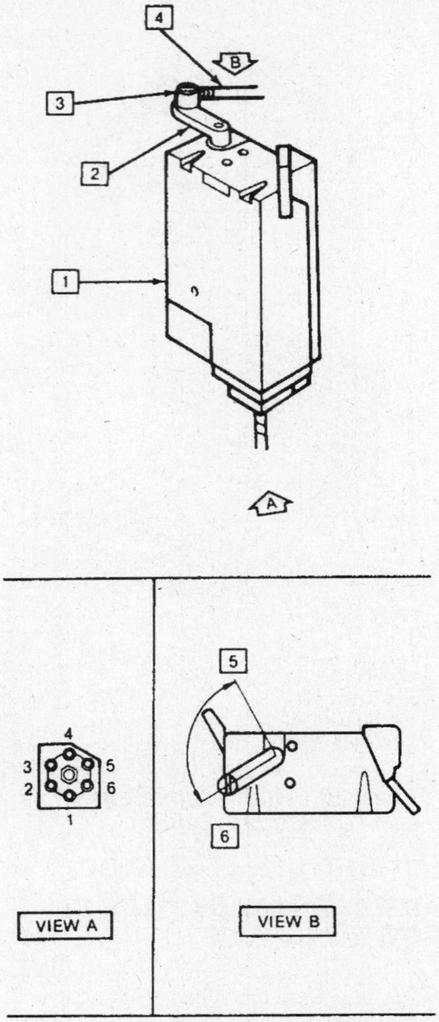

1 PROGRAMMER
2 OUTPUT ARM
3 RETAINER
4 THREADED ROD
5 MAX. A/C POSITION
6 MAX. HEAT POSITION

GC9039100035000X

Fig. 16 Programmer linkage positioning. Eldorado, 1997 Seville & 1997–99 DeVille

8. Remove evaporator core and case seals.
9. Reverse procedure to install.

4.6L Engine

NOTE: On Air Bag Equipped Models, Refer To " Air Bag System Precautions" Located In The Front Of This Manual For System Disarming & Arming Procedures.

NOTE: Refer To "Computer Relearn Procedures " Located In The Front Of This Manual For Computer Relearn Procedures.

INDEX

PRECAUTIONS

AIR BAG SYSTEMS

Refer to "Air Bag System Precautions" in the front of this manual for system disarming and arming procedures.

BATTERY GROUND CABLE

Prior to service, disconnect battery ground cable and isolate as required.

FUEL SYSTEM PRESSURE RELIEF

A small amount of fuel may be released when servicing fuel connections, even after pressure is released. Cover all fuel connections with shop towel before servicing.

1. Turn ignition switch Off.
2. Disconnect battery ground cable.
3. Remove intake manifold top cover.
4. Loosen fuel tank filler cap.
5. Install fuel pressure gauge tool No. J–34730–1A or equivalent, to fuel pressure connection. Wrap shop towel around fitting while connecting gauge.
6. Install bleed hose into approved container, then open valve on gauge to bleed system pressure.

RELEARN PROCEDURES

COMPUTER

Refer to "Computer Relearn Procedure" located in the front of this manual for computer relearn procedures.

THROTTLE POSITION (TP) SENSOR

Ensure nothing is touching or obstructing the accelerator or brake pedals during this procedure.

The TP Sensor Learn Procedure should be performed whenever the TP sensor, the throttle body or the PCM is replaced.

1. Turn ignition to On (engine Off) position.
2. Wait 30 seconds.
3. Turn ignition switch to Lock position.
4. Wait 30 seconds.

IDLE AIR CONTROL

The Idle Air Control Valve (IAC) regulates engine idle speed based on coolant temperature, engine load, battery volage and engine speed. If the IAC disconnected or interrupted, proceed as follows:

1. Coolant temperature must be above 32° F.
2. Vehicle must be in Park.
3. Turn ignition switch to Lock for 20 seconds.

COMPRESSION PRESSURE

When checking compression, lowest cylinder must be within 70 percent of the highest cylinder with a minimum pressure of 140 psi. Perform compression test with engine at normal operating temperature, spark plugs removed and throttle wide open.

ENGINE MOUNT

REPLACE

ELDORADO, 1997 SEVILLE & 1997–99 DEVILLE

1. Remove righthand and lefthand engine cooling fan.
2. Remove right and left torque struts, **Fig. 1.**
3. Install engine support fixture No. J–28467–A. Use only one support at left rear engine bracket.
4. Raise and support vehicle, then remove nuts securing mount to engine cradle, **Fig. 2.**

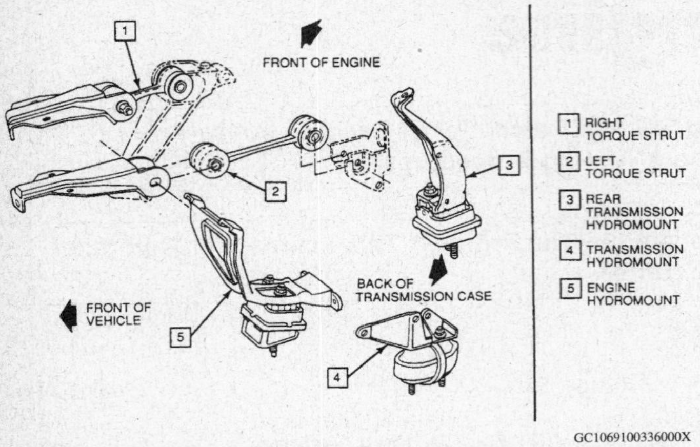

Fig. 1 Engine/transaxle mounts. Eldorado, 1997 Seville & 1997–99 DeVille

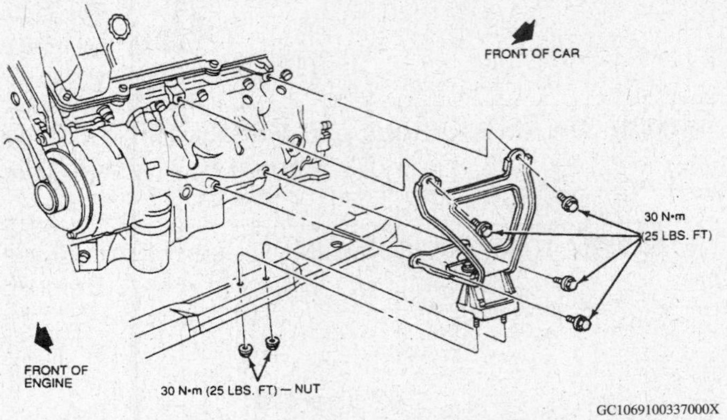

Fig. 2 Front engine mount replacement. Eldorado, 1997 Seville & 1997–99 DeVille

5. Remove bolts securing motor mount bracket to crankcase, then lower vehicle.
6. Remove bolts securing mount to cylinder head and bracket.
7. Raise engine by tightening support chain until mount and bracket can be separated and removed.
8. Reverse procedure to install.

1998–99 SEVILLE & 2000 DEVILLE

Front

1. Remove radiator cooling fans.
2. Install engine lift bracket tool No. J-42504 or equivalent and engine support fixture tool No. J-28467–A or equivalent.
3. Raise and support vehicle, then remove nuts securing mount bracket to engine block.
4. Remove nut securing mount to frame, then lower vehicle.
5. Remove upper bolts securing bracket to engine, then raise engine and remove mount and bracket.
6. Reverse procedure to install tightening to specifications.

Right

1. Raise and support vehicle, then support engine with suitable jack.
2. Remove nut securing mount to bracket, then lower engine slightly.
3. Remove nut and bolts securing mount to frame, then remove mount.
4. Reverse procedure to install tightening to specifications.

ENGINE

REPLACE

1. Release fuel system pressure as outlined under "Precautions."
2. Remove hood, then disconnect both battery cables.
3. Remove air cleaner inlet duct, then drain cooling system.
4. Remove left and right torque struts. Reinstall bolts in torque strut bracket at left front of engine as this will be used as an engine lift point.

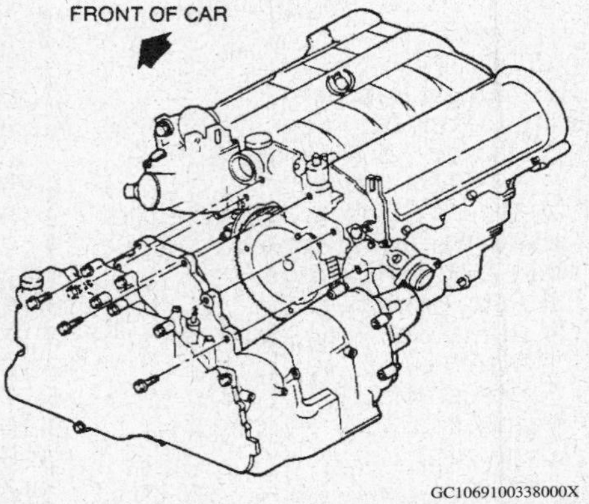

Fig. 3 Bellhousing mounting bolt locations

5. Disconnect radiator hoses from water crossover.
6. Remove both engine cooling fans, then serpentine drive belt.
7. Disconnect cruise control servo connections, then ISC electrical connector.
8. Disconnect throttle cable from throttle body cam.
9. Disconnect shift cable from park/neutral switch and cable bracket at transmission. Remove park/neutral switch.
10. Disconnect power brake vacuum hose, then cylinder head temperature switch.
11. Remove bellhousing bolts, **Fig. 3,** then ignition coils and spark plug wires.
12. Raise and support vehicle, then remove oil pan to transmission brace.
13. Remove torque converter splash shield, then converter to flywheel bolts.
14. Disconnect oil cooler lines at oil filter adapter.
15. Remove A/C compressor. Position compressor aside leaving lines attached.
16. Disconnect electrical connections from harness along lefthand side of engine, **Fig. 4.** Move harness out from behind exhaust manifold.
17. Remove nuts securing motor mount to engine cradle front crossmember, then exhaust pipe.
18. Remove right front wheel, then crankcase to transmission bracket at transmission tail shaft.
19. Disconnect knock sensor, then remove bolts from transmission to cylinder head brace at cylinder head.
20. Lower vehicle, then using fuel line remover No. J–37088 or equivalent, disconnect fuel lines.
21. Disconnect injector harness connector, then hoses from coolant reservoir. Remove coolant reservoir.
22. Disconnect cam position sensor, then heater hoses from water pipes at front of right cylinder head.
23. Disconnect battery cable from junction block, then remove retainer at cylinder head.
24. Disconnect starter cable from junction block, then power steering pump line at pump.
25. Remove power steering line retainer at right front of crankcase, then disconnect rear oxygen sensor connector.
26. Remove screws securing wiring harness retainer to right cam cover. Position harness aside.
27. Connect suitable engine lifting fixture to engine using support hooks at left rear and right rear of engine. Use torque strut bracket at left front of engine for third lift point.
28. Remove engine from vehicle.
29. Reverse procedure to install.

INTAKE MANIFOLD

REPLACE

1. Disconnect battery ground cable.
2. Relieve fuel system pressure as described under "Precautions."
3. Remove four nuts at manifold top cover, **Fig. 5.**
4. Remove front bank spark plug wires.
5. Remove PCV hoses.
6. Remove air intake duct.
7. Disconnect EGR pipe.
8. Disconnect brake booster hose at intake manifold.
9. Disconnect injector harness.
10. Disconnect transaxle vent hose from clip.

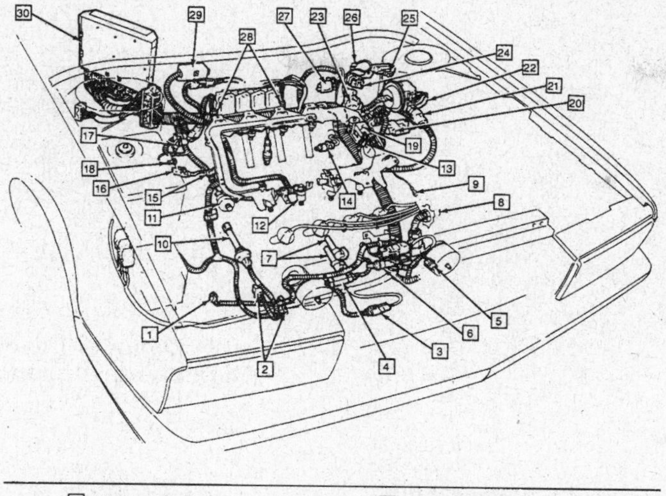

1 COMPRESSOR CLUTCH
2 GENERATOR CONN
3 RIGHT PULLER FAN
4 OIL PRESSURE SWITCH
5 LEFT PULLER FAN
6 O_2 SENSOR
7 CRANKSHAFT POSITION SENSORS (2)
8 TRANSMISSION
9 GROUND
10 OIL LEVEL SWITCH
11 KNOCK SENSOR
12 STARTER
13 MAT SENSOR
14 COOLANT TEMPERATURE SENSOR
15 VEHICLE SPEED SENSOR
16 POWER STEERING PRESSURE SWITCH
17 CAM POSITION SENSOR
18 PCM & DIS GROUNDS
19 MAP SENSOR
20 IDLE SPEED CONTROL
21 THROTTLE POSITION SENSOR
22 CRUISE CONTROL SERVO
23 EGR
24 PARK/NEUTRAL SAFETY SWITCH
25 BRAKE BOOSTER SENSOR
26 SPEED SENSING SWITCH
27 CANISTER PURGE SOLENOID
28 DIS MODULE
29 BATTERY/STARTER JUNCTION BOX
30 POWERTRAIN CONTROL MODULE

GC1069100339000X

Fig. 4 Engine electrical connection locations

11. Remove fuel rail ground wire at rear cylinder head.
12. Disconnect fuel pressure regulator vacuum line.
13. Twist female quick-connect fittings 1/4 turn in each direction to loosen dirt and blow dirt away with compressed air.
14. Use fuel line quick-connect separator tool No. J–37088–A or equivalent, to release locking tabs at fuel rail.
15. Disconnect fuel pipe bracket at EGR valve.
16. Remove throttle body mount bolts.
17. Release locking tabs on fuel rail and pry each injector out of intake manifold using injector remover tool No. J–41081 or equivalent.
18. Remove fuel rail.
19. Remove six bolts, four studs then intake manifold, **Fig. 6.**
20. Reverse procedure to install tightening intake manifold to specifications starting in center and working outward in a circular pattern.

EXHAUST MANIFOLD

REPLACE

LEFT SIDE

1. Remove motor mount as outlined under "Engine Front Mount, Replace."
2. Remove rear alternator bracket, then two bolts at manifold outlet flange.
3. Disconnect oxygen sensor electrical connector, then remove manifold attaching bolts.

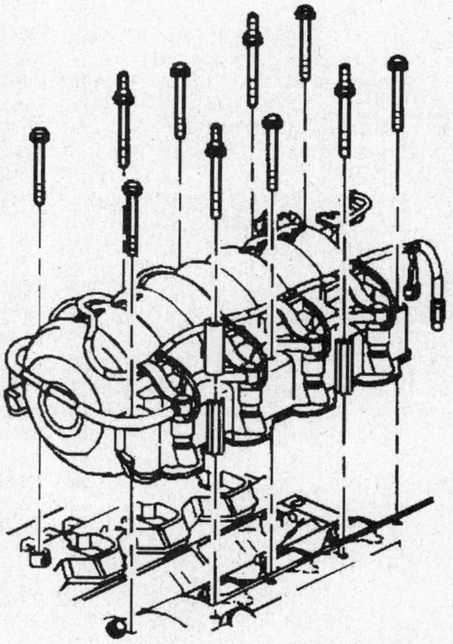

GC1059600108000X

Fig. 6 Intake manifold bolts/studs

4. Remove exhaust manifold, then oxygen sensor.
5. Reverse procedure to install. Coat oxygen sensor threads with high temperature anti-seize compound.

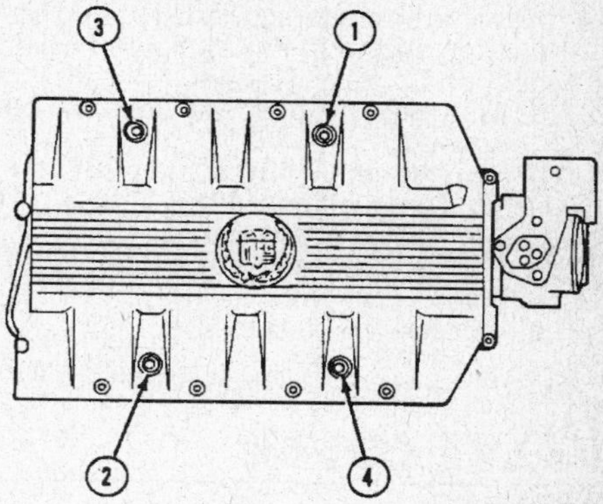

GC1059100076000X

Fig. 5 Intake manifold top cover

RIGHT SIDE

1. Disconnect both battery cables, then rear oxygen sensor and harness clip.
2. Raise and support vehicle, then disconnect exhaust pipe from catalytic converter.
3. Disconnect suspension position sensor at both lower control arms.
4. Support rear crossmember of engine cradle with suitable screw jack, then remove 4 cradle to body bolts.
5. Lower rear of engine cradle.
6. Remove pipe to exhaust manifold and crossover exhaust pipe mounting bolts.
7. Remove right side cylinder head to transaxle brace.
8. Remove exhaust manifold mounting nuts, then exhaust manifold.
9. Reverse procedure to install. Coat oxygen sensor threads with high temperature anti-seize compound.

CYLINDER HEAD

REPLACE

1. Remove intake manifold as described under "Intake Manifold, Replace."
2. Remove cam covers as described under "Valve Cover, Replace."
3. Remove crankshaft damper as described under "Crankshaft Damper, Replace."
4. Remove front cover as described under "Front Cover, Replace."
5. Remove chain tensioner from timing chain for cylinder head being removed.
6. Remove cam sprockets from head being removed. **Timing chains should remain in chain case.**
7. Remove timing chain guide retaining screws through access plugs at front of cylinder head, **Fig. 7.**
8. Remove water crossover, then exhaust manifold as described under "Exhaust Manifold, Replace."
9. Remove cylinder head bolts, then cylinder head and gasket. **When camshafts remain in cylinder head some valves will be open at all times. Do not rest cylinder head on a flat surface with cylinder face down.**

10. Reverse procedure to install. Using sequence shown in **Fig. 8,** tighten cylinder head bolts as follows:
    a. Use new M11 bolts, M6 bolts can be reused.
    b. **Torque** ten M11 bolts to 22 ft. lbs. plus an additional 60.°
    c. Tighten an additional 60.°
    d. Tighten an additional 60° (180° total).
    e. **Torque** M6 bolts to 10 ft. lbs.

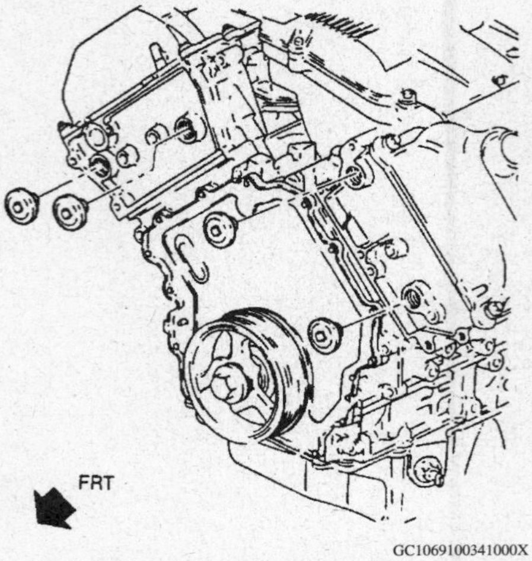

Fig. 7 Chain guide access plug removal

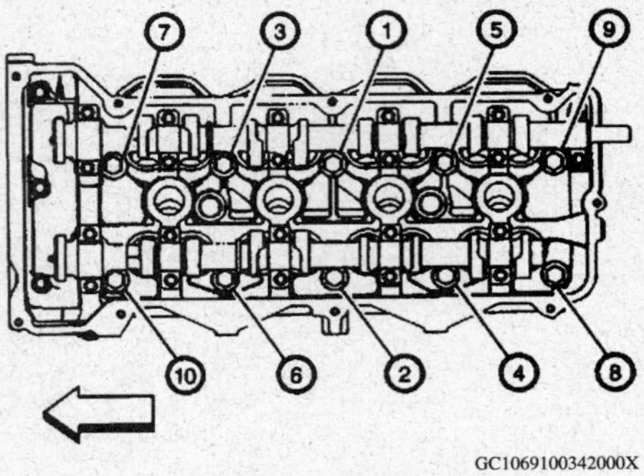

Fig. 8 Cylinder head bolt tightening sequence

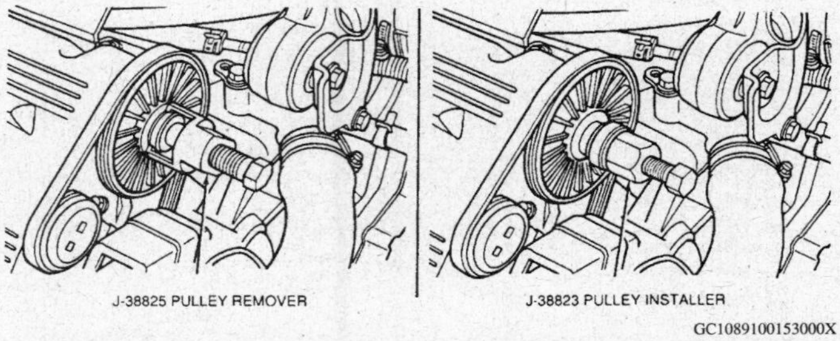

Fig. 9 Water pump pulley removal. Eldorado, 1997 Seville & 1997–99 DeVille

VALVE COVER

REPLACE

ELDORADO, 1997 SEVILLE & 1997–99 DEVILLE

Left Side

1. Disconnect both battery cables, then partially drain cooling system.
2. Disconnect upper radiator hose at water crossover, then spark plug wires.
3. Remove right cooling fan, then disconnect PCV fresh air tube from cam cover.
4. Remove right and left torque struts, then disconnect water pump drive belt.
5. Remove water pump pulley using tools shown in **Fig. 9.**
6. Remove camshaft seal retainer screws, then seal.
7. Disconnect battery cable retainer at front of valve cover, then remove valve cover retaining screws.
8. Remove valve cover as shown in **Fig. 10.**
9. Reverse procedure to install.

Right Side

1. Disconnect both battery cables, then remove tower to tower brace.
2. Raise and support vehicle.
3. Disconnect rear exhaust manifold at converter, then position convertor aside and lower vehicle.
4. Disconnect DIS wiring connectors and mounting bolts, then remove DIS and right bank spark plug wires.
5. Disconnect PCV valve, then remove purge canister solenoid from rear of cover.
6. Remove wiring harness from cover, then cam cover mounting screws.
7. Support front of engine cradle and remove front cradle mounting screws.
8. Remove right and left torque struts.
9. Lower engine cradle to provide clearance at rear of engine compartment.
10. Remove cam cover.
11. Reverse procedure to install.

2000 DEVILLE & SEVILLE

Left Side

1. Remove intake manifold sight shield, then upper filler panel.
2. Partially drain cooling system, then remove radiator hose from water crossover and position aside.
3. Disconnect PCV fresh air tube.
4. Remove ignition coil cassette as outlined under " Coil Pack, Replace," then remove spark plug boots.
5. Remove engine coolant heater wire and position aside.
6. Disconnect generator cooler outlet hose from pipe, then position pipe aside.
7. Remove water pump drive belt shield, then remove water pump drive belt.
8. Remove water pump belt tensioner, then dust cap from end of camshaft.
9. Using water pump drive pulley tool No. J-38825 or equivalent remove water pump drive pulley.
10. Remove camshaft seal and discard.
11. Remove camshaft cover bolts, then lift drive end of camshaft cover and remove reward to clear water pump drive shaft.
12. Reverse procedure to install using new camshaft seal.

Right Side

1. Remove intake manifold sight shield.
2. Disconnect PCV valve, then oxygen sensor wire.
3. Disconnect AIR vent solenoid vacuum tubes and electrical connector, then remove AIR bracket and tube.
4. Remove ignition coil cassette as outlined under " Coil Pack, Replace," then remove spark plug boots.
5. Remove camshaft cover bolts, then camshaft cover.
6. Reverse procedure to install.

VALVE CLEARANCE SPECIFICATIONS

This engine is equipped with hydraulic lifters. Valve adjustment is not necessary.

VALVE ADJUSTMENT

This engine is equipped with hydraulic lifters. Valve adjustment is not necessary.

CRANKSHAFT DAMPER

REPLACE

1. Release tension from accessory drive belt, then raise and support vehicle.
2. Remove right front wheel, then splash shields from wheelwell.
3. Remove brace between engine oil pan and transmission case, then install flywheel holder No. J–39411 or equivalent.
4. Remove balancer bolt, then support engine cradle with suitable jack screw and remove 3 engine cradle bolts at right side of cradle.
5. Disconnect RSS sensor from right-hand lower control arm, then lower engine cradle to obtain clearance below body rail for balancer puller.
6. Install pilot No. J–39344-2 into end of crankshaft.
7. Using puller No. J–38416 or equivalent, remove crankshaft damper.

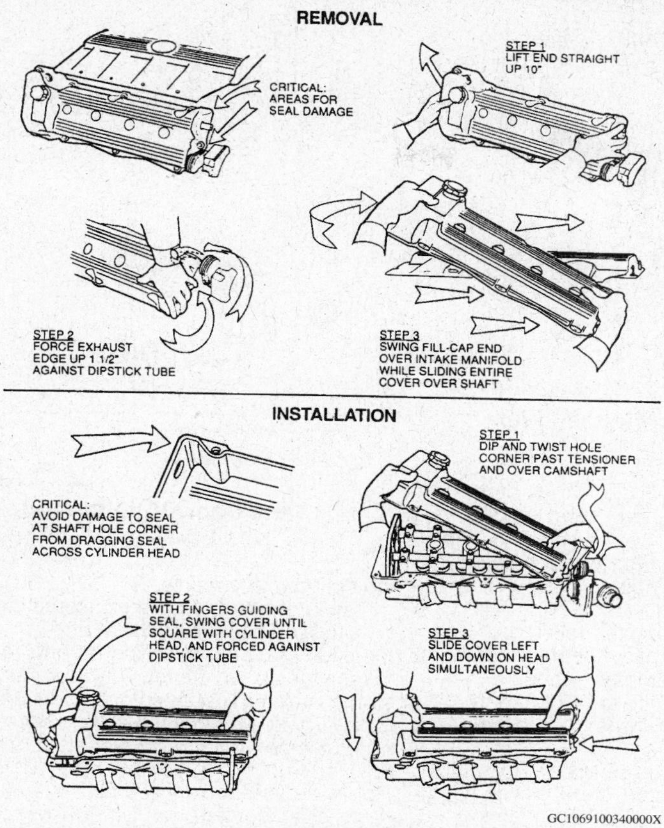
REMOVAL
CRITICAL:
AREAS FOR
SEAL DAMAGE
STEP 1
LIFT END STRAIGHT
UP 10"
STEP 2
FORCE EXHAUST
EDGE UP 1 1/2"
AGAINST DIPSTICK TUBE
STEP 3
SWING FILL-CAP END
OVER INTAKE MANIFOLD
WHILE SLIDING ENTIRE
COVER OVER SHAFT
INSTALLATION
STEP 1
DIP AND TWIST HOLE
CORNER PAST TENSIONER
AND OVER CAMSHAFT
CRITICAL:
AVOID DAMAGE TO SEAL
AT SHAFT HOLE CORNER
FROM DRAGGING SEAL
ACROSS CYLINDER HEAD
STEP 2
WITH FINGERS GUIDING
SEAL, SWING COVER UNTIL
SQUARE WITH CYLINDER
HEAD, AND FORCED AGAINST
DIPSTICK TUBE
STEP 3
SLIDE COVER LEFT
AND DOWN ON HEAD
SIMULTANEOUSLY
GC1069100340000X

Fig. 10 Valve cover replacement. Eldorado, 1997 Seville & 1997–99 DeVille

8. Reverse procedure to install.

FRONT COVER

REPLACE

ELDORADO, 1997 SEVILLE & 1997–99 DEVILLE

1. Remove serpentine drive belt, then bolt securing power steering hose.
2. Remove crankshaft damper as outlined under "Crankshaft Damper, Replace."
3. Remove belt tensioner, then belt idler pulley.
4. Remove front cover mounting bolts, **Fig. 11,** then front cover.
5. Reverse procedure to install.

1998–2000 SEVILLE & 2000 DEVILLE

1. Remove serpentine drive belt.
2. Remove crankshaft damper as outlined under "Crankshaft Damper, Replace."
3. Remove belt tensioner, then belt idler pulley.
4. Raise and support vehicle, then support engine assembly using suitable jack.
5. Remove nuts securing engine mount to engine mount bracket, then nuts securing engine mount bracket to engine.
6. Remove front cover mounting bolts, then front cover.

7. Reverse procedure to install.

FRONT COVER SEAL

REPLACE

1997–99 DEVILLE, ELDORADO & SEVILLE

1. Remove crankshaft damper as outlined under "Crankshaft Damper, Replace."
2. Using screwdriver behind front cover seal, pry out seal. Do not score cover bore for seal or crankshaft.
3. Reverse procedure to install noting the following:
   a. Lubricate seal lips with engine oil and position seal to front cover with garter spring side toward engine.
   b. Using front cover seal installer tool No. J-38818 or equivalent push seal into front cover until tool bottoms on cover.
   c. Ensure installed depth of seal is .30 inch below rear face of front cover around entire seal.

2000 DEVILLE

The crankshaft front oil seal is not serviced as an individual component. When replacing crankshaft front oil seal install a new front cover.

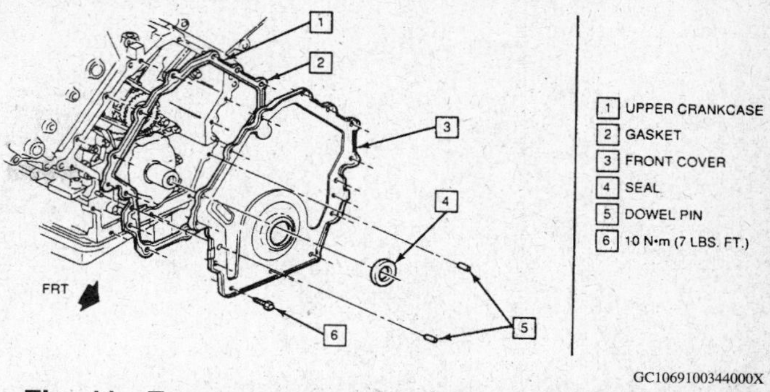
1
2
3
4
5
6
FRT
1 UPPER CRANKCASE
2 GASKET
3 FRONT COVER
4 SEAL
5 DOWEL PIN
6 10 N•m (7 LBS. FT.)
GC1069100344000X

Fig. 11 Front cover replacement. Eldorado, 1997 Seville & 1997–99 DeVille

TIMING CHAIN

REPLACE

PRIMARY

1. Remove engine assembly as described under "Engine, Replace," then place engine assembly on a suitable stand.
2. Remove serpentine drive belt, idler pulley and belt tensioner.
3. Remove front cover as described under "Front Cover, Replace."
4. Remove oil pump assembly as described under "Oil Pump, Replace."
5. Remove valve covers as described under "Valve Cover, Replace."
6. Remove three timing chain tensioners, then all four camshaft sprockets.
7. Remove secondary drive chains from around intermediate shaft sprocket.
8. Remove one bolt from intermediate shaft sprocket and slide gears and primary drive chain off crankshaft and intermediate shaft.
9. Reverse procedure to install, time camshafts as described under "Camshaft, Replace."

SECONDARY

1. Remove front cover as described under "Front Cover, Replace."
2. Remove lefthand valve cover as described under " Valve Cover, Replace."
3. Remove lefthand secondary chain tensioner.
4. Remove lefthand chain guide as described under " Cylinder Head, Replace."
5. Remove lefthand cam sprocket bolts and sprockets.
6. Remove lefthand secondary drive chain, **Fig. 12.**
7. To remove righthand secondary drive chain, refer to steps 2 through 6 and substitute righthand for lefthand.
8. Reverse procedure to install, time camshafts as described under "Camshaft, Replace."

TENSIONER, REPLACE

1. Remove front cover as described in "Front Cover, Replace."
2. Remove two tensioner mounting bolts, then tensioner.
3. Collapse new tensioner as follows:
   a. Rotate ratchet release lever

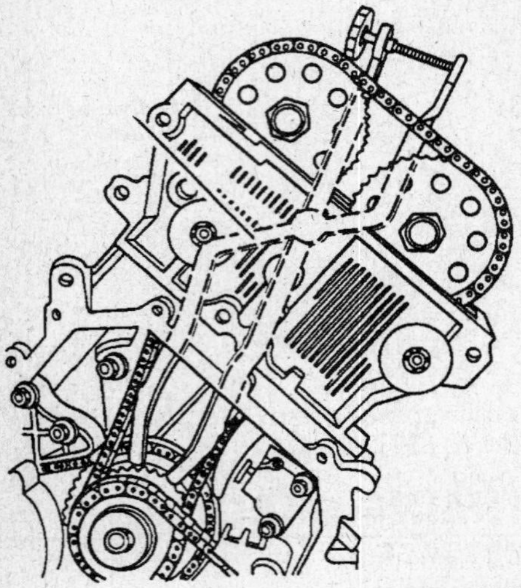

GC1069100343000X

Fig. 12 Drive chain tension

counter clockwise and hold, **Fig. 13.**

b. Collapse tensioner shoe and hold.
c. Release ratchet lever and slowly release pressure on shoe.
d. As ratchet lever moves to first click hold tensioner shoe inward and insert a pin through hole in release lever, **Fig. 14.**

4. Install tensioner and bolts, tighten bolts to specification.
5. Remove retaining pin allowing tensioner shoe to extend.
6. Install front cover.

CAMSHAFT

REPLACE

REMOVAL

1. Remove cam cover as described in "Valve Cover, Replace."
2. Secure cam sprocket to timing chain by installing tie-wraps through sprocket holes. Use four tie-wraps per sprocket. **The sprocket-chain relationship must be maintained throughout this procedure or camshaft timing will be lost and require further engine disassembly to time.**
3. Install cam chain holder tool No. J–38822 or equivalent, behind camshaft sprockets so that it is positioned between chain tensioner and chain guide, **Fig. 12.** Apply tension to tool by tightening tension adjusting screw.
4. Remove both camshaft sprocket bolts. **Note location of cam drive pins in end of camshafts.**
5. Work sprockets off of cams using play in chain.
6. Loosen cam bearing cap bolts a few turns at a time until all valve spring pressure has been released.
7. Remove bolts and bearing caps, then camshaft.

INSTALLATION

1. Apply camshaft prelube part No. 1052365 or equivalent, to face of each cam lobe.

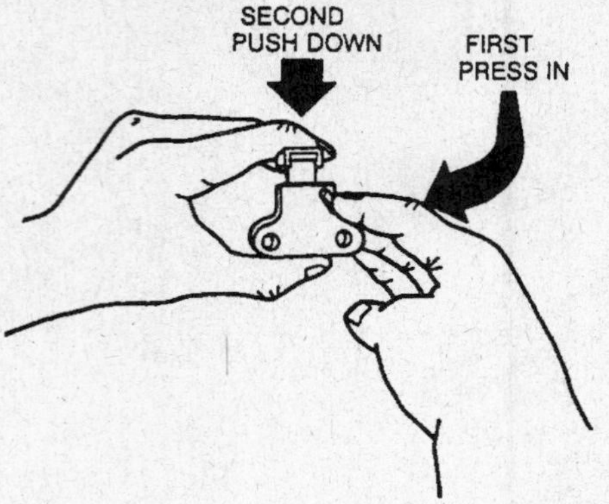

GC1069100345000X

Fig. 13 Tensioner release lever rotation

2. Install camshaft, then position cam bearing caps to cylinder head noting the following:
   a. Arrow on top of bearing cap points towards front of engine.
   b. The "E" mark on top of bearing cap indicates a cap for exhaust cam.
   c. The "I" mark on top of bearing cap indicates a cap for intake cam.
   d. The No. "1" mark on top of bearing cap should be towards front of engine.
3. Loosely install cam bearing cap bolts, then alternately tighten each bearing cap bolt a few turns at a time against valve spring pressure until all bolts are snug.
4. Tighten bearing cap bolts to specification.
5. Rotate camshaft until drive pins are in position to engage cam sprockets over cams, then install retaining bolts. Tighten sprocket bolts to specification.
6. Remove chain holder tool, then tie-wraps from cam sprockets.
7. Install cam cover.

CAMSHAFT TIMING

Setting camshaft timing is necessary whenever the cam drive system has been disturbed such that the relationship between any chain and sprocket has been lost.

1. Remove valve covers as described under "Valve Cover, Replace."
2. Remove front cover as described under "Front Cover, Replace."
3. Remove or retract three chain tensioners. **Tensioners may be in their installed positions but must be fully retracted as described under "Timing Chain, Replace."**
4. Remove oil pump assembly as described in "Oil Pump, Service."
5. Rotate crankshaft until sprocket drive key is at approximately 1 o'clock position.
6. Install crankshaft and intermediate shaft sprockets to primary drive chain with their timing marks aligned as shown in **Fig. 15.**
7. Install crank and intermediate shaft sprockets over their respective shafts.
8. Rotate crankshaft so that crankshaft key engages sprocket without changing timing mark position.

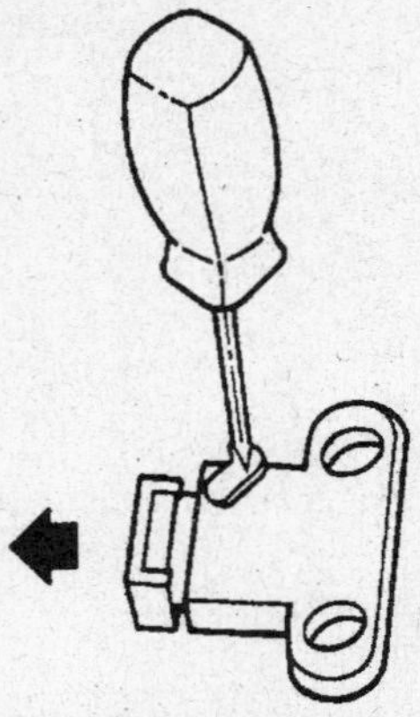

1 RELEASE TO FIRST CLICK
2 INSTALL LOCK PIN

GC1069100346000X

Fig. 14 Tensioner in collapsed position

9. Install intermediate sprocket retaining bolt, tighten bolt to specification.
10. Install primary chain tensioner and release tensioner shoe. Tighten tensioner mounting bolts to specification.
11. Install flywheel holder tool No. J–39411 or equivalent, to lock crankshaft in this position.
12. Route secondary drive chain for left-hand cylinder head over inner row of intermediate shaft teeth.
13. Route secondary drive chain over chain guide and install exhaust cam sprocket to chain so that camshaft drive pin engages sprocket. There should be no slack in lower section of chain and cam drive pin must be perpendicular to cylinder head face as shown in **Fig. 15. RE cam sprocket must contain cam position sensor pickup.**
14. Install intake cam sprocket into chain so sprocket engages cam drive pin while pin remains perpendicular to cylinder head face as shown in **Fig. 15.**
15. A hex is cast into camshafts so that an open end wrench can be used to provide minor repositioning of cams.
16. Loosely install exhaust and intake cam sprocket bolts.
17. Install chain tensioner and release tension on shoe, then tighten tensioner mounting bolts to specifications.
18. Tighten cam sprocket bolts to specifications.
19. Route secondary drive chain for right-hand cylinder head over outer row of intermediate shaft teeth and repeat steps 13 through 18 for righthand cams.

PISTON & ROD ASSEMBLY

Refer to **Fig. 16** for correct piston and rod assembly installation.

Ensure piston and rod assemblies are coated with suitable lubricant before installation.

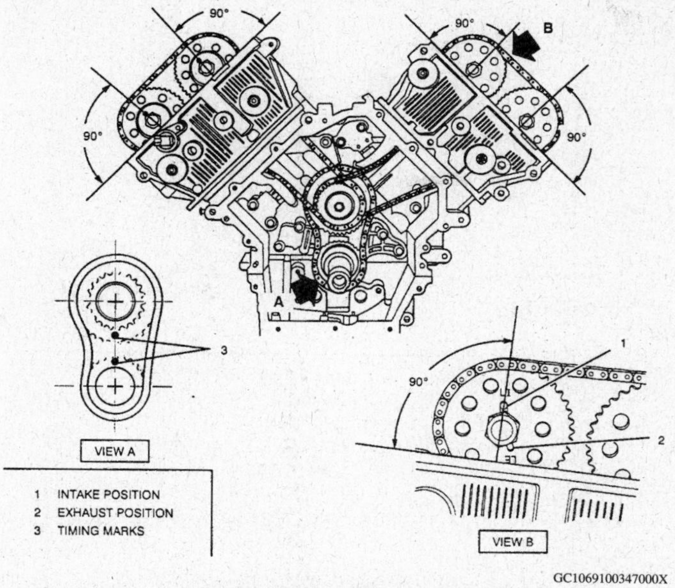

Fig. 15 Camshaft timing procedure

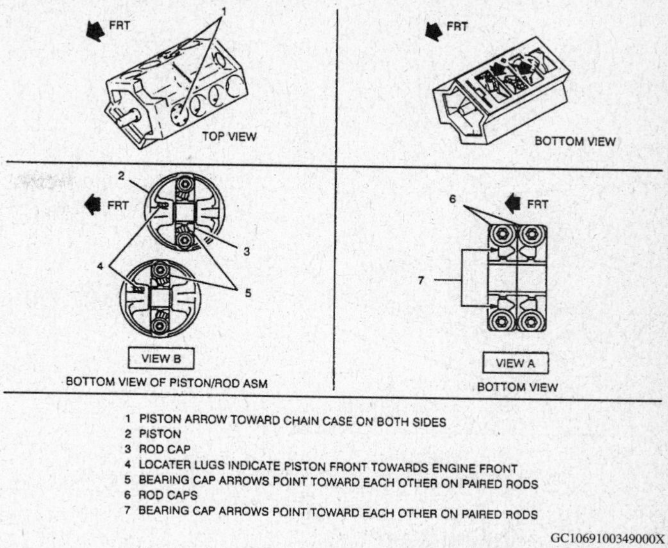

Fig. 16 Piston & rod assembly

MAIN & ROD BEARINGS

Shell type main bearings of steel backed aluminum are used at all positions. The upper halves are all interchangeable, as are all of the lower halves except for the thrust bearings in the No. 3 position. If bearing clearance is greater than .003 inch and new bearings do not reduce the clearance to .0005–.002 inch, a new crankshaft will be required. Undersized bearing are not available and crankshaft grinding is not allowed. When installing main bearing bolts, **torque** bolt Nos. 1–20 to 15 ft. lbs. plus an additional 65° and bolt Nos. 21–28 to 22ft. lbs. using sequence shown in **Fig. 17.** Maximum crankshaft endplay is .019 inch.

Ensure bearings are coated with a suitable lubricant and crankshaft journals are covered completely with lubricant.

CRANKSHAFT REAR OIL SEAL

REPLACE

LIP TYPE SEAL

1. Remove transaxle assembly, refer to "Automatic Transmissions/ Transaxles."
2. Remove eight flywheel mounting bolts, then flywheel.
3. Drill a 1/8 inch hole into metal body of rear main seal, then remove seal using a slide hammer.
4. Place a small dab of RTV sealant at crankcase split line across end of upper/lower crankcase seal.
5. Lubricate new oil seal with engine oil, then slide seal over arbor of seal installation tool No. J–38817 or equivalent.
6. Thread seal-installer tool No. J–38818 or equivalent, in crankshaft flange and install seal by turning handle until tool bottoms against crankcase, **Fig. 18.**

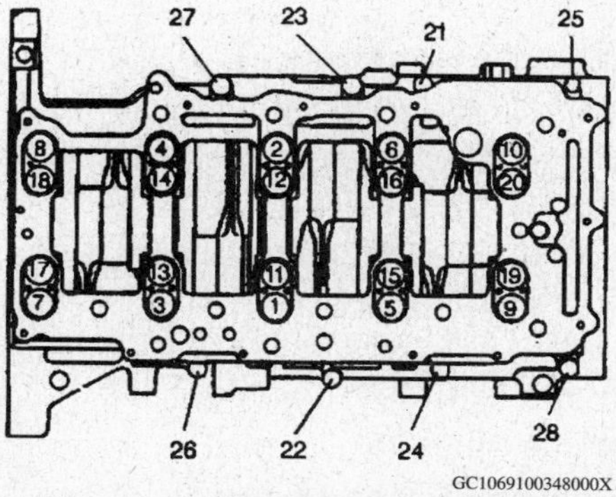

Fig. 17 Main bearing cap bolt tightening sequence

7. Install flywheel and transaxle assembly.

CARTRIDGE TYPE SEAL

1. Remove transaxle assembly, refer to "Automatic Transmissions/ Transaxles."
2. Remove flywheel mounting bolts, then flywheel.
3. Install crankshaft rear oil seal remover tool No. J-42841 or equivalent.
4. Using a variable speed drill with socket adapter, install eight one inch self drilling screws using guide holes in removal tool.
5. With eight removal screws installed remove retaining bolts from removal tool.
6. Install center screw to removal tool, then tighten to pull seal off end of crankshaft.
7. Reverse procedure to install noting the following:
   a. Clean any debris from crankshaft rear oil seal drain, then coat outer diameter of cylinder block with clean engine oil.
   b. **Do not allow engine oil on area where oil seal in to be pressed on crankshaft or on inner diameter of oil seal.** Oil seal has a green coating pre-applied.
   c. Loosen center bolt on crankshaft rear oil seal installer tool No. J-42842 or equivalent, then install on to crankshaft by threading mounting bolts to crankshaft flange.
   d. Install rear oil seal by tightening rear oil seal installer tool until it bottoms against crankcase, then remove rear oil seal installer tool.
   e. Ensure installation depth of crankshaft rear oil seal is equal around circumference.

OIL PAN

REPLACE

1. Remove transaxle assembly, refer to "Automatic Transmissions/ Transaxles."
2. Drain engine oil.
3. Remove oil pan bolts, then pan.
4. Reverse procedure to install, noting the following:
   a. Gasket is reusable unless damaged. **Do not remove gasket from oil pan groove unless replacement is required.**
   b. Using sequence shown in **Fig. 19,** tighten oil pan bolts to specification.

OIL PUMP SERVICE

REMOVAL

1. Remove front cover as described in "Front Cover, Replace."
2. Remove three oil pump mounting bolts, **Fig. 20.**
3. Remove pump and drive spacer.

DISASSEMBLE

1. Remove drive spacer from pump housing, **Fig. 21.**
2. Remove two screws holding pump housing halves together.
3. Remove inner and outer rotors from housing. **Mark mating surfaces.**

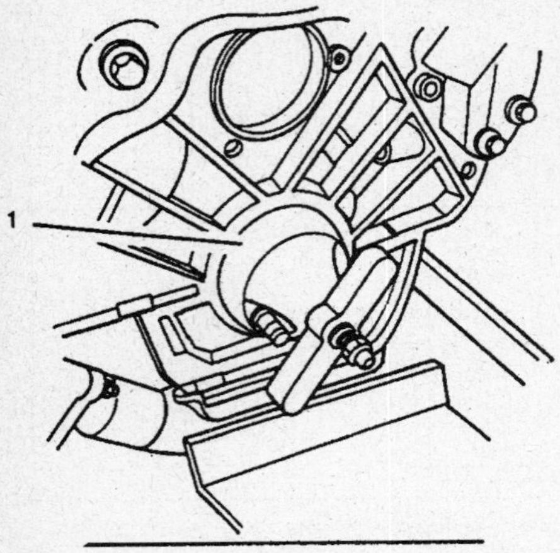

Fig. 18 Rear main seal installation

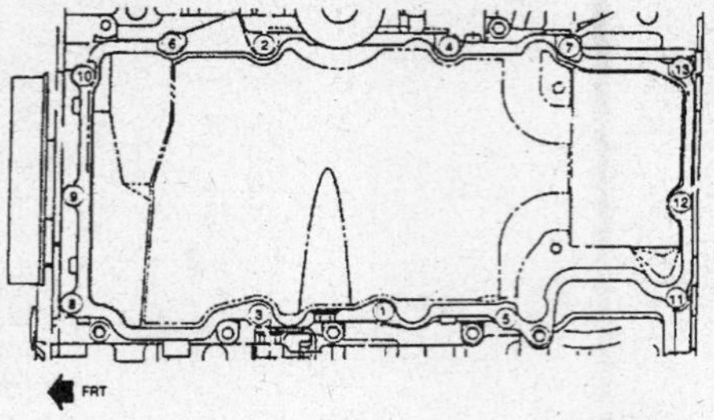

Fig. 19 Oil pan bolt tightening sequence

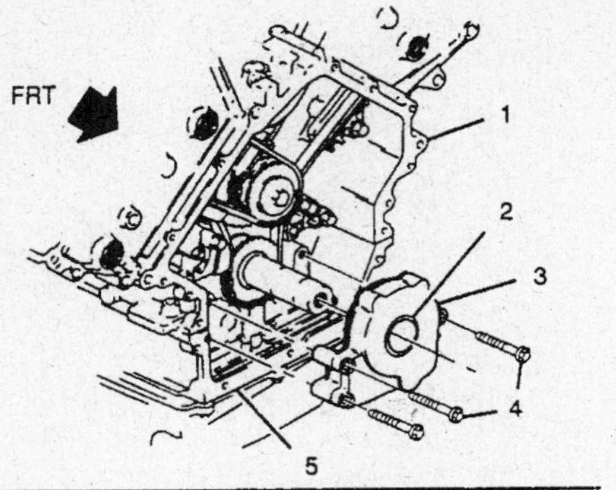

Fig. 20 Oil pump removal

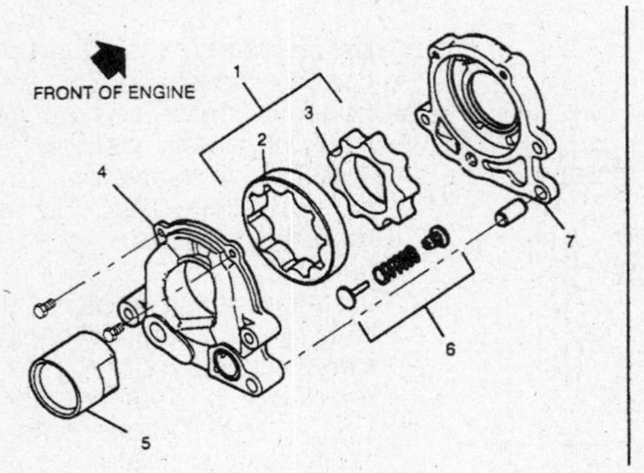

Fig. 21 Exploded view of oil pump

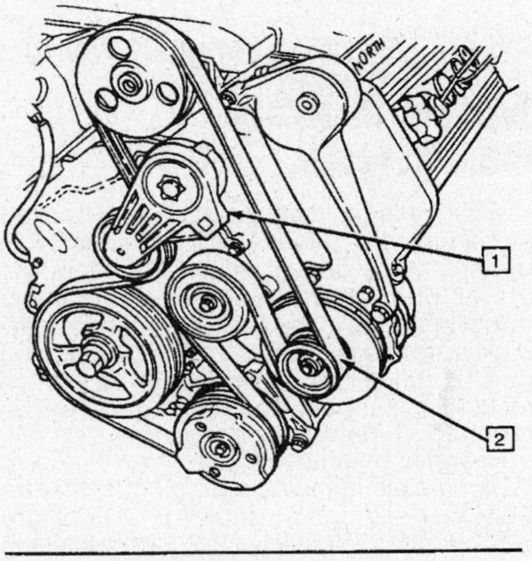

Fig. 22 Serpentine drive belt routing

4. Remove pressure relief valve.

INSPECTION

1. **Internal parts of oil pump are not serviceable, if wear or damage is noted replace entire pump assembly.**
2. Inspect pump housing for nicks, burrs, chips or debris that may cause a leak or binding condition in rotor pocket.
3. Inspect drive or driven rotors for nicks or burrs.
4. Check pump cover and interior surface for excessive wear or score marks.

ASSEMBLE

1. Install inner and outer rotors to pump cover. **Align marks made during pump disassemble procedure.**
2. Install pressure relief valve seat, spring and pilot in pump housing.
3. Assemble housing and cover over locating dial.
4. Insert a ⅜ inch drill bit in pump mounting hole on opposite side to aid in alignment of housing and cover.
5. Install two bolts and **torque** to 9 ft. lbs.

INSTALLATION

1. Install oil pump drive spacer into oil pump from rear so that drive flat engages pump rotor.
2. Position pump over crankshaft, then loosely install bolts.
3. Holding pump up as high as possible, **torque** pump retaining bolts to 7 ft. lbs. plus an additional 35.°
4. Install front cover assembly as described in "Front Cover, Replace."

SERPENTINE DRIVE BELT

1. Rotate drive belt tensioner mechanism upward, away from drive belt using a ½ inch breaker bar.
2. Remove serpentine drive belt.
3. Reverse procedure to install. Refer to **Fig. 22** for serpentine drive belt routing.

COOLING SYSTEM BLEED

This engine does not require a specified bleed procedure. After filling cooling system, run engine to operating temperature with radiator/pressure cap off. Air will then be automatically bled through cap opening.

THERMOSTAT

REPLACE

1. Drain cooling system, then remove front end beauty panel and air cleaner.
2. Remove thermostat housing mounting bolts, then the housing, **Fig. 23.**
3. Remove thermostat and O-ring from housing.
4. Reverse procedure to install.

WATER PUMP

REPLACE

1. Drain cooling system, then remove air cleaner.
2. **On models with AIR,** remove check valve.
3. **On all models,** remove water pump belt cover, then drive belt.
4. Remove radiator outlet hose from thermostat housing, then heater return hose.
5. Using coolant pump remover/installer tool No. J-38816-1A or equivalent, turn pump clockwise to remove from housing, then remove pump from vehicle.
6. Reverse procedure to install.

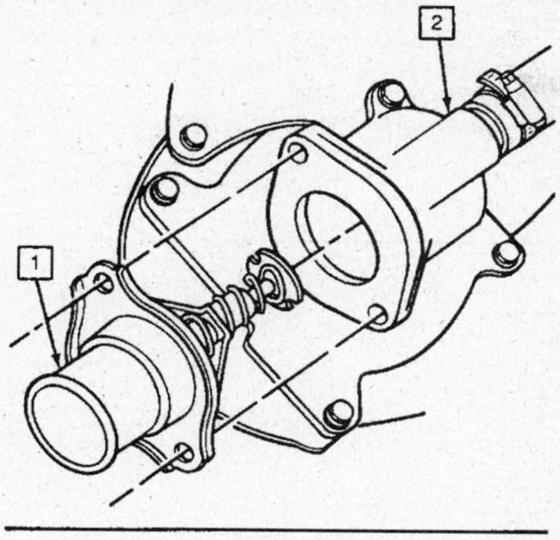

Fig. 23 Thermostat replacement

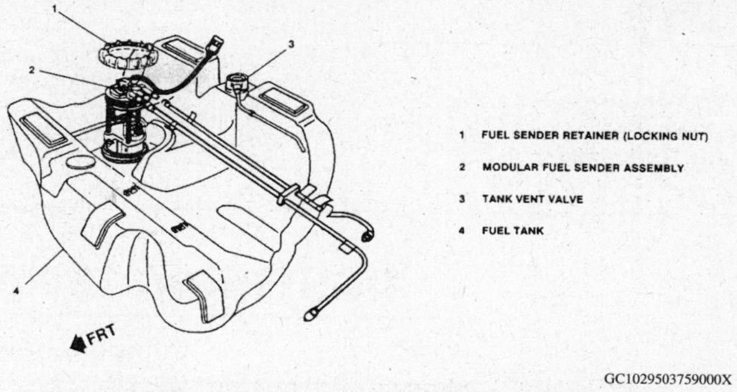

Fig. 24 Modular fuel sending unit/fuel pump removal. Eldorado, 1997 Seville & 1997–99 DeVille

RADIATOR

REPLACE

1. Drain cooling system, then remove plastic radiator support cover.
2. Remove cooling fan, then coolant reservoir hose at filler neck.
3. Disconnect upper and lower radiator hoses.
4. Disconnect oil cooler and transmission cooler lines at radiator.
5. Remove condenser mounting bolts, then pull condenser upward to release feet from tabs located at front of radiator.
6. Remove radiator top support, then radiator.
7. Reverse procedure to install.

FUEL PUMP

REPLACE

ELDORADO, 1997 SEVILLE & 1997-99 DEVILLE

1. Relieve fuel pressure as outlined under "Precautions."
2. Raise and support vehicle, then remove fuel tank.
3. Remove locking nut using tool No. J-39765 or equivalent, **Fig. 24.**
4. Remove modular fuel tank sending unit/fuel pump from tank, then fuel pump from modular fuel sending unit, **Fig. 25.**
5. Reverse procedure to install.

1998-99 SEVILLE & 2000 DEVILLE

1. Relieve fuel pressure as outlined under "Precautions."
2. Drain fuel tank to 3/4 tank full.
3. Remove spare tire cover, jack, spare tire, and rear compartment floor trim.
4. Remove fuel sender access panel.
5. Disconnect quick-connect fittings at fuel sender.
6. Disconnect electrical connections at modular fuel sender and fuel tank pressure sensor.
7. Using fuel sender lock nut wrench tool No. J-39765 or equivalent remove fuel sender retaining ring.
8. Remove fuel sending unit by pulling straight up while pumping fuel from reservoir.
9. Reverse procedure to install using new fuel sender O-ring.

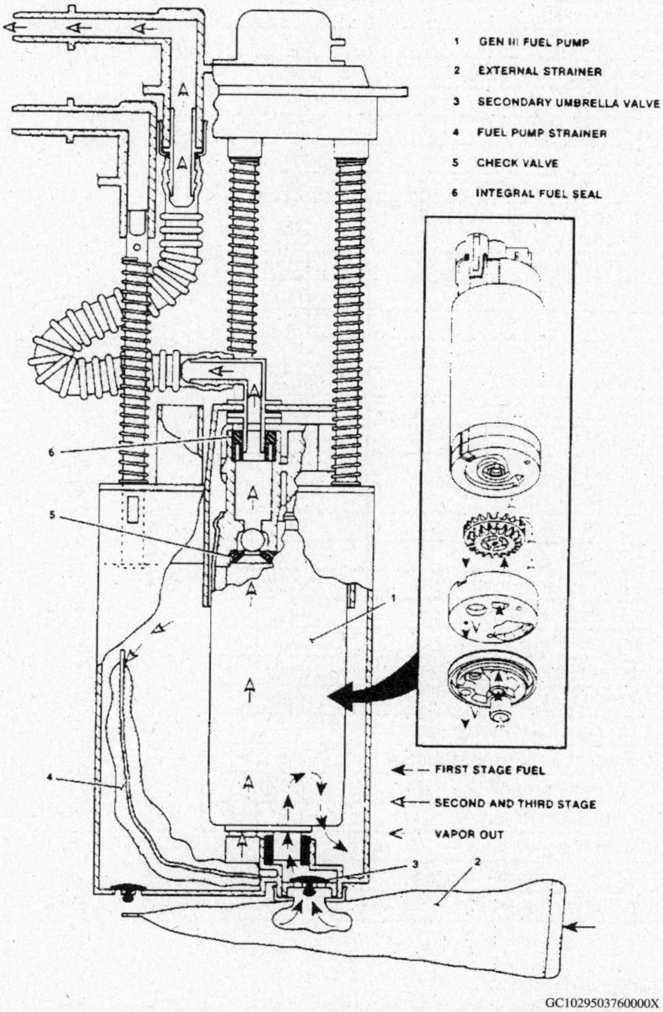

Fig. 25 Fuel pump removal. Eldorado, 1997 Seville & 1997–99 DeVille

FUEL FILTER

REPLACE

1. Disconnect battery ground cable.
2. Release fuel system pressure as outlined under " Precautions."
3. Disconnect fuel filter bracket release tabs.
4. Twist quick-connect fitting ¼ turn in each direction to loosen dirt within fitting.
5. Clean quick-connect fitting at ends of filter.
6. Disconnect quick-connect fittings by squeezing plastic tabs of male end connector and pulling apart.
7. Remove fuel filter.
8. Reverse procedure to install.

TIGHTENING SPECIFICATIONS

Year	Component	Torque/Ft. Lbs.
1997–2000	Belt Tensioner	37
	Cam Cover	89①
	Camshaft Bearing Cap	106①
	Camshaft Drive Chain Tensioner	18
	Camshaft Seal Retainer To Cover	27①
	Camshaft Sprocket	89
	Coolant Drain Plug	72①
	Cooling Fan Mounting Bolts	53①
	Cylinder Head Bolts	③
	Engine Mount Bracket	37
	Engine Mount To Frame	52
	Engine Mount Front	37
	Engine Mount Right	37
	Engine To Transmission	53
	Exhaust Manifold To Cylinder Head Bolt	18
	Exhaust Manifold To Cylinder Head Locknut	18
	Flywheel	11⑤
	Flywheel Housing Cover	80①
	Front Cover	89①
	Fuel Filter Bolt	22
	Ignition Module	80①
	Intake Manifold Bolts	89①
	Intake Manifold Cover Bolts	27①
	Main Bearing Cap Bolts	③
	Oil Filter Adapter	12
	Oil Pan	89①
	Oil Pan Drain Plug	15
	Oil Pump To Lower Crankcase	89①②
	Oil Pump To Suction Pipe	89①
	Oxygen Sensor	30
	Thermostat Housing Bolts	89①
	Throttle Body Bolts	106①
	Torque Strut Bracket To Cylinder Head	37
	Torque Strut Bracket To Water Manifold	18
	Torsional Damper	105④
	Transmission Brace	35
	Water Pump Housing	89①
	Water Pump Pulley Mounting Bolts	22
	Water Pump Stud Nuts	62①

①— Inch pounds.
②— Tighten an additional 35° rotation.
③— Refer to "Cylinder Head, Replace."
④— Tighten an additional 120° rotation.
⑤— Tighten an additional 50° rotation.

Rear Suspension

NOTE: On Air Bag Equipped Models, Refer To "Air Bag System Precautions" Located In The Front Of This Manual For System Disarming & Arming Procedures.

INDEX

PRECAUTIONS

AIR BAG SYSTEMS

Refer to "Air Bag System Precautions" in the front of this manual for system disarming and arming procedures.

BATTERY GROUND CABLE

Prior to service, disconnect battery ground cable and isolate as required.

HUB & BEARING

REPLACE

ELDORADO, 1997 SEVILLE & 1997-99 DEVILLE

1. Raise and support vehicle.
2. Remove tire and wheel assembly.
3. Remove brake caliper attaching bolts and position caliper aside. **Do not suspend caliper by brake line.**
4. Remove rotor retainers, if equipped. Retainers may be discarded after removal.
5. Remove rotor.
6. Remove four hub mounting bolts, then hub and bearing assembly.
7. Reverse procedure to install, tightening to specifications.

1998-2000 SEVILLE & 2000 DEVILLE

1. Raise and support vehicle.
2. Remove wheel and disc brake caliper. **It is not necessary to disconnect hydraulic line from caliper; support caliper assembly from frame to prevent hydraulic line damage.**
3. Remove brake rotor and ABS sensor wire connector.
4. Remove bolts, lift hub and bearing assembly, then the brake shield from control arm, **Fig. 1.**

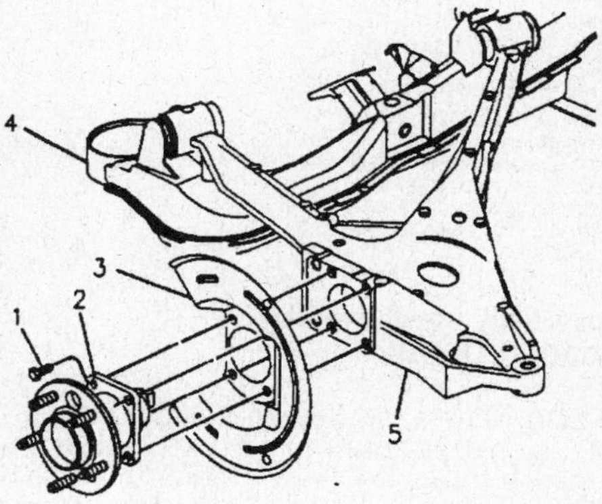

Fig. 1 Hub & bearing replacement. 1998–2000 Seville & 2000 DeVille

5. Reverse procedure to install, tightening to specifications.

REAR SUSPENSION

REPLACE

1998-2000 SEVILLE & 2000 DEVILLE

1. Raise and support vehicle. Remove rear wheels and disconnect exhaust system components as necessary to provide clearance.
2. Remove rear springs as outlined under "Coil Spring, Replace."
3. Remove brake calipers from control arms. **It is not necessary to disconnect hydraulic line at caliper; support caliper from frame to prevent hydraulic line damage.**
4. Disconnect parking brake cables at calipers and at rear suspension support assembly.
5. Disconnect rear suspension support assembly electrical connectors from electrical harness, then the Electronic Level Control (ELC) electrical connector and vent hose.
6. Disconnect ELC air tube from ELC compressor and support rear suspension assembly with a suitable jack, **Fig. 2.**
7. Remove support bracket to body bolts from each side of vehicle.
8. Remove front and rear anchor bolts and lower rear suspension support assembly from vehicle.
9. Reverse procedure to install. Tighten mounting bolts and nuts to specifications.

SHOCK ABSORBER

REPLACE

Refer to **Figs. 3 through 5** when replacing shock absorbers. Inspect upper and lower shock absorber insulators for cracks, tears or other damage. Replace as required.

1. Raise and support vehicle, then remove wheel and tire assembly.
2. Disconnect shock absorber electrical connector from rear suspension support.
3. Support lower control arm with a suitable screw type jack to relieve spring load.
4. Remove lower shock absorber bolt(s), then disconnect electrical connector from top of shock absorber.
5. **On 1997–99 DeVille, 1997 2000 Eldorado & 1997 Seville models,** remove

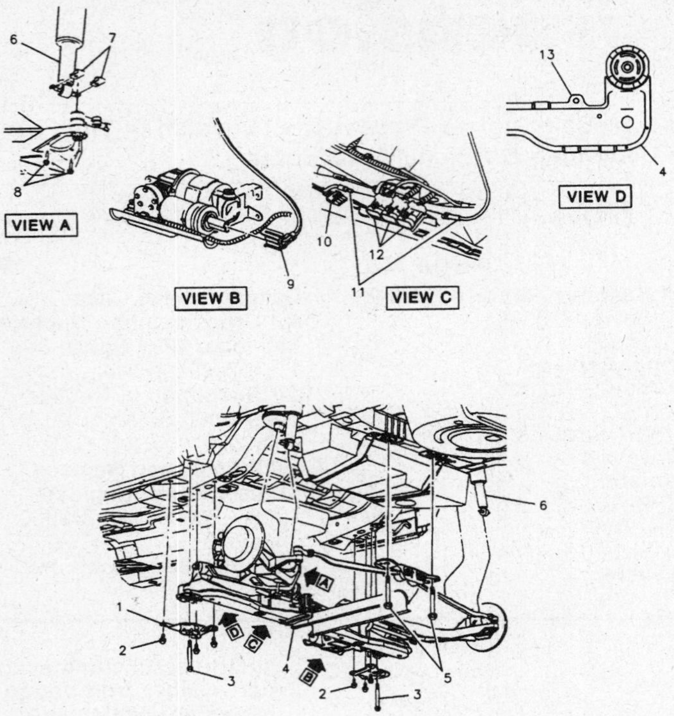

1 SUPPORT BRACKET
2 BOLT 86 N•m (63 LB. FT.)
3 BOLT 191 N•m (141 LB. FT.)
4 REAR SUSPENSION SUPPORT ASSEMBLY
5 BOLT 165 N•m (122 LB. FT.)
6 SHOCK
7 U–NUT
8 BOLT 24 N•m (18 LB. FT.)
9 ELC AIR LINE
10 ELC COMPRESSOR ELECTRICAL CONNECTOR
11 ELC COMPRESSOR VENT TUBE
12 ELECTRICAL CONNECTORS, (ELC HEIGHT SENSOR, FUEL PUMP, ABS HARNESS)
13 GAUGE HOLE

GC2039500109000X

Fig. 2 Rear suspension assembly replacement. 1998–2000 Seville & 2000 DeVille

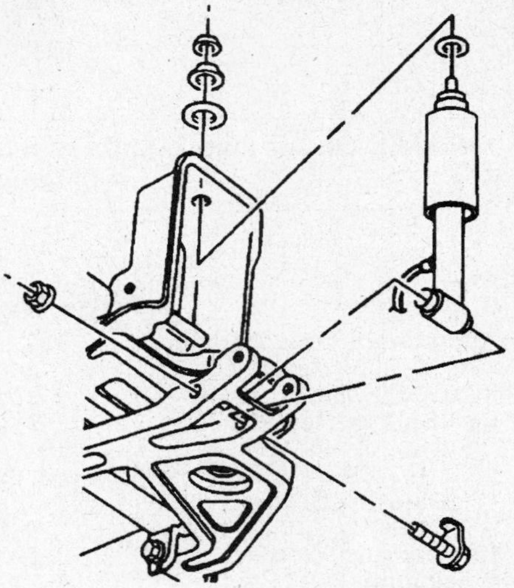

GC2039800140000X

Fig. 3 Shock absorber assembly. Eldorado, 1997 Seville & 1997–99 DeVille

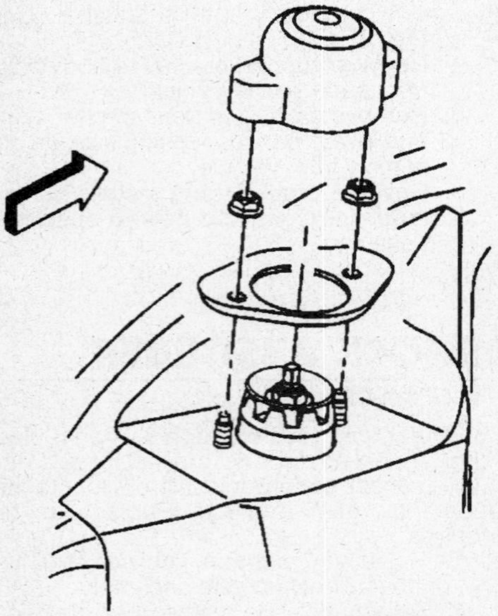

GC2039800143000X

Fig. 4 Shock absorber top mount. 1998–2000 Seville & 2000 DeVille

upper mounting nut, retainer and insulator using tool No. J–35669 or equivalent.

6. **On 1998–2000 Seville & 2000 DeVille** models, pull trunk trim back to gain access to upper shock mount, then remove upper mounting dust cap, nuts and reinforcement.
7. **On all models,** reverse procedure to install, tightening bolts and nuts to specifications.

COIL SPRING

REPLACE

ELDORADO, 1997 SEVILLE & 1997–99 DEVILLE

Refer to "Lower Control Arm, Replace" for coil spring replacement procedures.

1998–2000 SEVILLE & 2000 DEVILLE

Removal

1. Raise and support vehicle.
2. Remove wheel assembly.
3. Support control arm with a suitable jack.
4. Disconnect electronic level control air tube from shock.
5. Remove two bolts securing shock to control arm.
6. Remove cotter pin and hex nut.

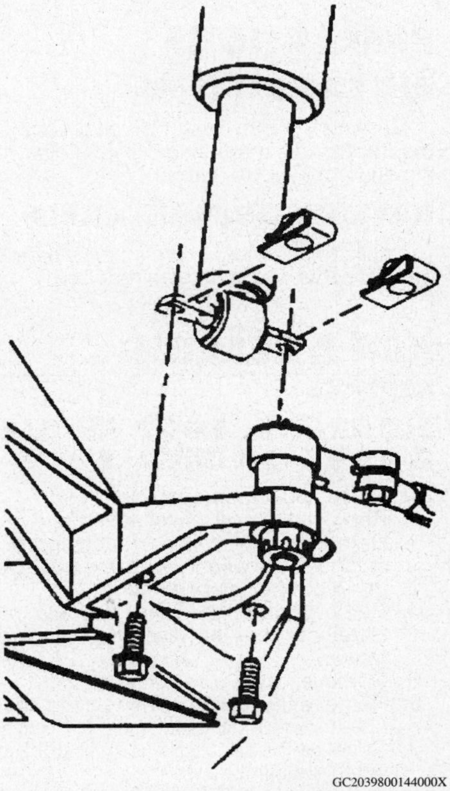

GC2039800144000X

Fig. 5 Shock absorber bottom mount. 1998–2000 Seville & 2000 DeVille

7. Using universal steering linkage puller tool No. J-24319–B, or equivalent, separate adjustment link from knuckle.
8. Lower control arm until it bottoms on support assembly.
9. Using a suitable pry bar, pry under lower spring insulator and remove

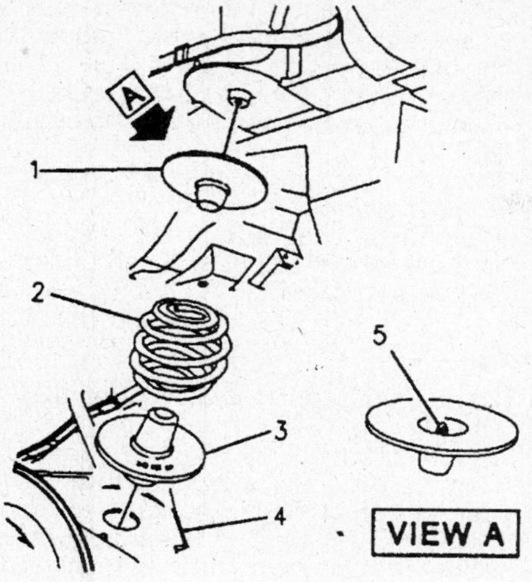

1 JOUNCE BUMPER
2 SPRING
3 LOWER SPRING INSULATOR
4 CONTROL ARM
5 RETAINER

GC2039500111000X

Fig. 6 Coil spring replacement. 1998–2000 Seville & 2000 DeVille

spring with insulator, **Fig. 6.**

10. Remove upper insulator by pulling downward.

Installation

1. Install upper spring insulator in body.
2. Install lower spring insulator in control arm.
3. Install spring, ensuring insulator is seated in control arm.
4. Raise lower control arm and install two shock bolts in control arm.
5. **Torque** shock bolts to 18 ft. lbs.
6. Install adjustment link to control arm and **torque** adjustment link nut to 36 ft. lbs, then an additional ¾ turn. To align the cotter pin, tighten no more than one flat.
7. Connect electronic level control air tube to shock.
8. Install wheel and **torque** lug nuts to 100 ft. lbs. then lower vehicle.

CONTROL ARM

REPLACE

ELDORADO, 1997 SEVILLE & 1997-99 DEVILLE

Lower

1. Raise and support vehicle, then remove wheel and tire assembly.
2. Support inboard end of lower control arm with a suitable transmission jack. Position brackets on jack to securely hold control arm.
3. Remove stabilizer link lower attachment.
4. Remove shock absorber lower attachment.
5. Remove inboard lower control arm nuts and bolts.
6. Slowly lower transmission jack to relieve coil spring pressure.
7. Pull lower control arm down to remove coil spring.
8. Remove lower control arm outboard bolt, then lower control arm.
9. Reverse procedure to install, tightening bolts to specifications.

Upper

1. Raise and support vehicle, then remove wheel and tire assembly.
2. Disconnect electronic level control height sensor connector.
3. Disconnect Road Sensing Suspension (RSS) position sensor and bracket from shock tower.
4. Remove inner and outer upper control arm bolts.
5. Remove upper control arm from vehicle by lifting up and over shock tower.
6. Reverse procedure to install, tightening bolts to specifications.

1998-2000 SEVILLE & 2000 DEVILLE

1. Remove rear suspension support assembly as outlined under " Rear Suspension, Replace."
2. If lefthand control arm is being replaced, remove Electronic Level Control (ELC) height sensor link.
3. Remove stabilizer link bolt and nut and disconnect ABS electrical connector.
4. Remove hub and bearing assembly as outlined under " Hub & Bearing, Replace," then the bolt and nut securing control arm to rear suspension support assembly.
5. Reverse procedure to install, noting the following:
   a. Tighten control arm nuts with vehicle weight resting on rear wheels.
   b. Tighten all bolts and nuts to specifications.

CONTROL ARM BUSHING

REPLACE

1998-2000 SEVILLE & 2000 DEVILLE

Removal

1. Remove control arm as outlined under "Control Arm, Replace," and assemble bushing replacement tools as shown in **Fig. 7.**
2. Tighten nut until bushing is driven from control arm and remove bushing replacement tools.

Installation

1. Start new bushing into control arm with flat on bushing positioned vertically and rearward.
2. Assemble bushing tools as shown in **Fig. 7,** and tighten bolt until bushing is seated fully in control arm.
3. Remove bushing tools and install control arm as outlined under "Control Arm, Replace."

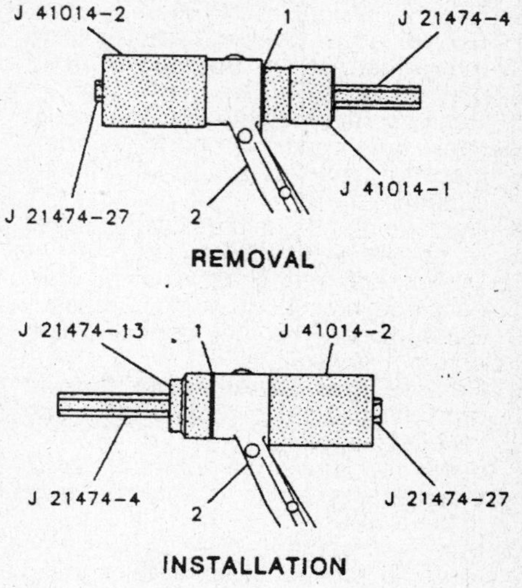

1 BUSHING
2 CONTROL ARM

GC2039500112000X

Fig. 7 Control arm bushing replacement tool installation. 1998–2000 Seville & 2000 DeVille

KNUCKLE

REPLACE

ELDORADO, 1997 SEVILLE & 1997-99 DEVILLE

1. Raise and support vehicle, then remove wheel and tire assembly.
2. Remove caliper and position aside. **Do not allow caliper to hang from hydraulic hose or damage to hose may occur.**
3. Remove rotor, then hub and bearing assembly.
4. Support outboard end of lower control arm with a screw type jack to relieve spring load.
5. Remove lower shock absorber bolt, then stabilizer link from control arm.
6. Remove rear toe link outer bolt and discard.
7. Remove upper and lower control arm outer nuts and bolts.
8. Disconnect speed sensor cable bracket from knuckle, then remove knuckle.
9. Reverse procedure to install replacing rear toe link outer bolt.

REAR CROSSMEMBER

REPLACE

ELDORADO, 1997 SEVILLE & 1997-99 DEVILLE

The rear crossmember (suspension support) can be removed without removing or disconnecting the coil spring, shock absorbers, control arms, knuckles, hub and bearing assemblies or rotors.

1. Raise and support vehicle, then remove wheel and tire assemblies.

2. Remove left caliper and position aside. **Do not allow caliper to hang from hydraulic hose or damage to hose may occur.**
3. Remove intermediate parking brake cable from equalizer and move intermediate cable clear of suspension support.
4. Remove rear brake crossover line and rear brake hose from bracket.
5. Disconnect rear chassis wiring harness from main body wiring harness.
6. Support rear crossmember using suitable jackstand.
7. Remove rear crossmember forward arm bolts, upper mounting bolts and lower insulators.
8. Lower rear crossmember from vehicle slowly, using caution to avoid damage to brake lines.
9. Lower jackstands.
10. Reverse procedure to install, noting the following:
    a. Install both forward bolts in proper direction, with nuts installed on right side of arm.
    b. Cup shaped washer is used on left forward arm bolt only.
    c. Bleed brake system as described under "Brake System, Bleed."

STABILIZER SHAFT

REPLACE

1998–2000 SEVILLE & 2000 DEVILLE

1. Raise and support vehicle, then remove wheels.
2. Remove stabilizer shaft link assembly bolt, nut, retainer and insulators from control arm, **Fig. 8.**
3. Remove clamp bolt and bend open end of clamp upward and remove stabilizer shaft and insulators.
4. Reverse procedure to install, noting the following:

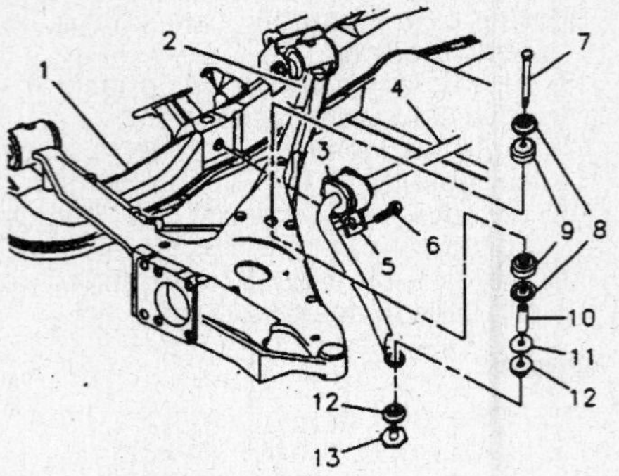

1 REAR SUSPENSION SUPPORT ASSEMBLY	7 BOLT, 13 N•m (115 LB. IN.)
2 CONTROL ARM	8 RETAINER, UPPER
3 INSULATOR, STABILIZER SHAFT	9 INSULATOR, UPPER
4 SHAFT, STABILIZER	10 SLEEVE
5 CLAMP, STABILIZER SHAFT	11 RETAINER, LOWER
6 BOLT, 33 N•m (24 LB. IN.)	12 INSULATOR, LOWER
	13 NUT

GC2039500113000X

Fig. 8 Stabilizer shaft replacement. 1998–2000 Seville & 2000 DeVille

a. Ensure stabilizer shaft is centered before tightening clamp bolt.
b. Tighten all bolts and nuts to specifications.

ADJUSTMENT LINK

REPLACE

1998–2000 SEVILLE

Inner

1. Raise and support vehicle. Remove wheel.
2. Loosen pinch bolt.
3. Support exhaust and rear suspension support assembly with a wood block at least seven inches long.
4. Remove exhaust hangers and rear suspension support assembly mounting bolts.
5. Lower support and exhaust together.
6. Remove cam bolt and nut, then the adjustment link.
7. Remove inner from outer link. Note number of turns for assembly.
8. Reverse procedure to install. Inspect and adjust rear toe as outlined under "Wheel Alignment."

Outer

1. Raise and support vehicle. Remove wheel.
2. Loosen pinch bolt.
3. Remove cotter pin and clotted hex nut.
4. Use universal steering linkage puller tool No. J-24319-B, or equivalent, to separate adjustment link from knuckle. **Do not drive wedge between joint and attached part.**
5. Remove outer from inner link. Note number of turns for assembly.
6. Reverse procedure to install. Inspect and adjust rear toe as outlined under "Wheel Alignment."

2000 DEVILLE

1. Raise and support vehicle, then remove nut from adjustment link.
2. Using universal steering linkage puller tool No. J-24319–B or equivalent, separate adjustment link from control arm.
3. Support exhaust and rear support assembly using a block of wood.
4. Remove exhaust hangers and rear support assembly bolts, then lower support assembly and exhaust together.
5. Remove cam nut and bolt, then remove adjustment link from rear support assembly.
6. Reverse procedure to install. Inspect and adjust rear toe as outlined under "Wheel Alignment."

TIGHTENING SPECIFICATIONS

Component	Torque/Ft. Lbs.
ELDORADO, 1997 SEVILLE & 1997–99 DEVILLE	
Caliper Mounting Bracket Bolts	83
Crossmember Forward Arm Nut (Right Side)	46
Crossmember Forward Arm Nut (Left Side)	75
Crossmember Upper Mounting Bolts	75
Hub Mounting Bolts	53
Lower Control Arm Nut	75
Parking Brake Cable Bracket Bolt	32
Shock Absorber Nut (Lower)	75
Shock Absorber Nut (Upper)	55
Stabilizer Bracket Bolt	44
Stabilizer Link Nut	44
Toe Link Nut (Inner)	42
Toe Link Nut (Outer)	55
Upper Control Arm Nut	42
Wheel Lug Nut	100
1998–2000 SEVILLE & 2000 DEVILLE	
Adjustment Link Pinch Bolt	35
Adjustment Link To Control Arm Nut	36①
Adjustment Link To Rear Suspension Support Assembly	55
Control Arm Nuts	78
ELC Height Sensor Bolts	5
Hub & Bearing Bolts	50
Rear Body Mount Bolts	38
Rear Suspension Support Assembly Bracket Bolts	63
Rear Suspension Support Assembly To Body Rear Bolts	141
Shock Absorber To Control Arm Bolts	18
Shock Tower Mounting Nut	15
Stabilizer Link Bolt	11
Stabilizer Shaft Clamp Bolt	24
Stabilizer Shaft Link Bolt	11
Wheel Lug Nuts	100

① — Plus an additional 1/2 turn.

Front Suspension & Steering

NOTE: On Air Bag Equipped Models, Refer To " Air Bag System Precautions" Located In The Front Of This Manual For System Disarming & Arming Procedures.

INDEX

PRECAUTIONS

AIR BAG SYSTEMS

Refer to "Air Bag System Precautions" in the front of this manual for system disarming and arming procedures.

BATTERY GROUND CABLE

Prior to service, disconnect battery ground cable and isolate as required.

HUB & BEARING

REPLACE

1. Raise and support vehicle, then remove wheel and tire assembly.
2. Using a suitable punch, hold rotor from rotating and remove hub nut and washer.
3. Remove caliper, caliper support and rotor.
4. Separate drive axle as shown, **Fig. 1** from hub using drive axle separator tool No. J–28733–B or equivalent.
5. Remove hub and bearing retaining bolts.
6. Disconnect speed sensor connector, then remove hub and bearing assembly.
7. Reverse procedure to install, tightening bolts to specifications.

BALL JOINT INSPECTION

Replace ball joints if any looseness is detected in the joint or ball joint seal is cut. Complete the following steps in order to inspect ball joint.

1. Raise front of vehicle.
2. Allow suspension to hang free.
3. Grasp tire at top and bottom and move it in and out.
4. Inspect for any horizontal movement in knuckle relative to control arm.
5. Replace ball joint if ball stud is disconnected from knuckle and looseness is detected or ball stud twists in its socket while using finger pressure.
6. Inspect for ball stud tightness in knuckle boss. Shake wheel and feel for movement of stud end or nut at knuckle boss. Replace any worn or damaged ball joints and knuckles.

BALL JOINT

REPLACE

1997–98 DEVILLE, ELDORADO & 1997 SEVILLE

1. Raise and support vehicle.
2. Remove tire and wheel assembly.
3. **On models with road sensing suspension,** disconnect position sensor from lower control arm.
4. **On all models,** remove ball joint from knuckle.
5. Drill out three rivets retaining ball joint. Start with a ¼ inch drill bit, then use a ½ inch bit.
6. Remove ball joint.
7. Reverse procedure to install, noting the following:
   a. **Torque** ball joint nut to 7 ft. lbs. using 90° adapter J–35551 or equivalent.
   b. Tighten nut an additional 120°, noting torque reading.
   c. Tighten nut up to an additional 60° to align holes and install cotter pin. **When tightening nut, minimum torque (as listed in "Tightening Specifications") must be obtained. If minimum torque cannot be obtained, check for stripped threads and repair as needed. If threads are satisfactory, replace ball joint and steering knuckle.**

1998–2000 SEVILLE

The ball joint is not serviced separate the control arm. Refer to "Control Arm, Replace."

1. Raise vehicle allowing control arm to hang free.
2. Remove cotter pin from ball joint and loosen nut.
3. Use ball joint separator remover tool No. J–43828, or equivalent, to remove ball joint from knuckle.
4. Reverse procedure to install.

1999–2000 DEVILLE & ELDORADO

The ball joint is not serviced separate from the control arm. Refer to "Control Arm, Replace."

STRUT

REPLACE

ELDORADO, 1997 SEVILLE & 1997–99 DEVILLE

Care must be taken not to overextend driveshaft Tri-Pot joints when replacing suspension components. Overextending joint could cause separation of internal joint components, resulting in failure of the joint.

1. Remove nuts securing top of strut assembly to body, **Fig. 2.**
2. Raise vehicle and support frame with stands, then remove wheel and tire.
3. Scribe reference marks between strut and steering knuckle as follows:
   a. Scribe strut along lower outboard strut radius (A), **Fig. 3.**
   b. Scribe strut flange on inboard side along curve of knuckle (B).

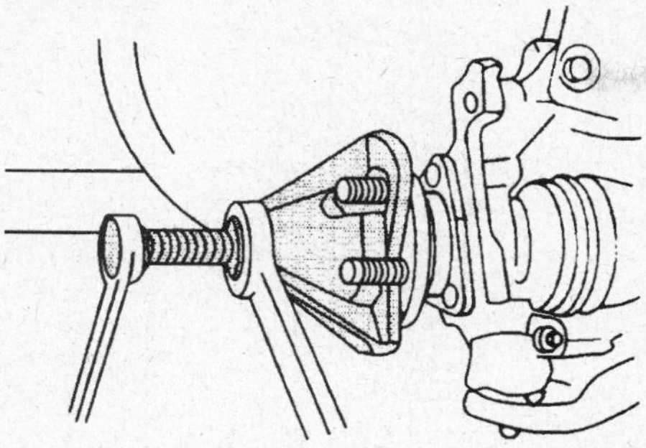

GC2029800229000X

Fig. 1 Drive axle separation

c. Scribe mark along strut/knuckle interface (C).
4. Disconnect brake line bracket from strut.
5. Remove bolt securing strut to stabilizer link, then stabilizer link.
6. Remove bolts securing strut to steering knuckle, support knuckle with wire and remove strut.
7. Reverse procedure to install, aligning scribe marks made during disassembly. tighten nuts and bolts to specifications, then check alignment.

1998–2000 SEVILLE & 2000 DEVILLE

Care should be taken to avoid chipping or cracking spring coating. Failure to observe may result in spring breakage.

1. Remove strut mount bolts at strut to body.
2. Raise vehicle and support vehicle with control arms hanging free.
3. Remove tire and wheel assembly.
4. Disconnect ABS front wheel speed sensor connector.
5. Remove speed sensor bracket from strut.
6. Remove brake line bracket from left-hand strut.
7. Remove strut-to-knuckle bolts. **The knuckle must be retained after strut-to-knuckle bolts have been removed. Failure to observe this may cause ball joint and/or drive axle damage.**
8. Remove strut.
9. Reverse procedures to install, tightening nuts to specification.

STRUT SERVICE

1. Place strut assembly in strut compressor J–34013, **Fig. 4.**
2. Turn compressor forcing screw until spring compresses slightly.
3. Keep dampener shaft from turning with a T-50 Torx bit and remove nut from top of dampener shaft.
4. Using tool J–34013-38 or equivalent, guide dampener shaft out of assembly.
5. Loosen compressor screw while guiding dampener shaft out of assembly, continually loosening compressor screw till strut dampener and spring can be removed. **Be careful to avoid chipping or cracking spring coating when handling front suspension coil spring.**

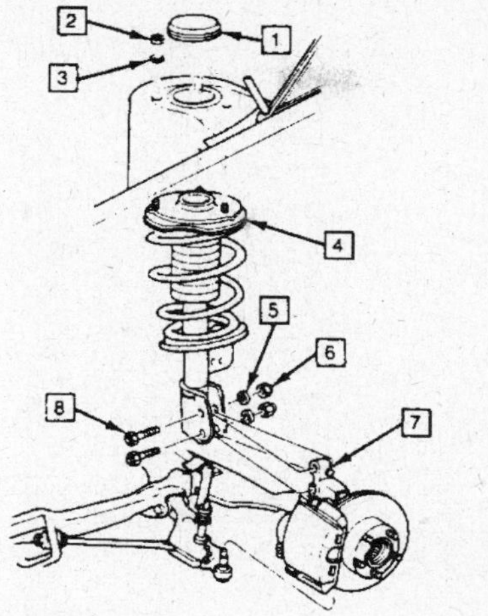

1 COVER
2 NUT 24 N·m (18 FT. LBS.)
3 WASHER
4 STRUT AND SPRING ASSEMBLY
5 WASHER
6 NUT 184 N·m (136 FT. LBS.)
7 KNUCKLE
8 BOLT — INSTALL IN DIRECTION SHOWN

GC2029100133000X

Fig. 2 Steering knuckle & strut replacement. Eldorado, 1997 Seville & 1997–99 DeVille

6. Install strut dampener in strut compressor J–34013 with clamp J–34013-20 clamped on dampener shaft.
7. Install spring over strut in correct position and move assembly upright in strut compressor and install upper locking pin. **Flat on upper spring seat must face out from centerline of vehicle, Fig. 5 or when mounted in strut compressor spring seat faces same direction as steering knuckle mounting flange.**
8. Install rod J–34013-38 or equivalent into strut assembly to guide dampener shaft on reassembly of strut.
9. Start turning compressor screw clockwise on J–34013 while guiding J–34013-38 which will center dampener shaft in assembly.
10. Continue turning compressor screw until dampener shaft threads are visible through top of strut assembly.
11. Install washer and nut, then remove J–34013-20 from dampener shaft.
12. Hold dampener shaft with socket, then tighten dampener shaft nut to specifications.
13. Remove three nuts securing strut assembly to strut compressor, two locking pins at bottom of strut compressor and strut assembly.

CONTROL ARM

REPLACE

ELDORADO, 1997 SEVILLE & 1997–99 DEVILLE

Care must be taken not to overextend driveshaft Tri-Pot joints when replacing

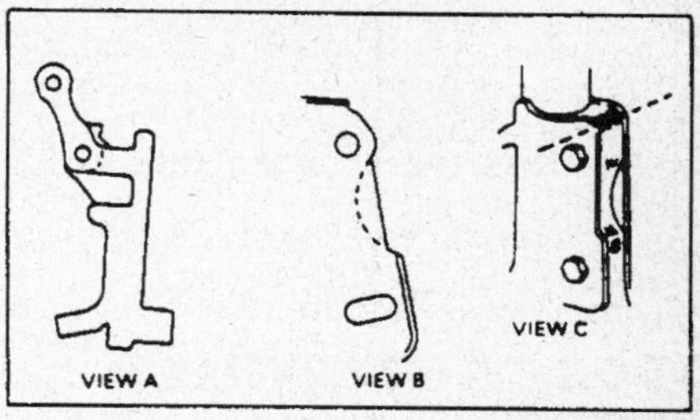

GC2029100134000X

Fig. 3 Steering knuckle & strut alignment marking. Eldorado, 1997 Seville & 1997–99 DeVille

suspension components. Overextending joint could cause separation of internal joint components, resulting in failure of joint.

1. Remove ball joint from steering knuckle as outlined under " Ball Joint, Replace."
2. Remove control arm bushing bolt and brake reaction rod nut, retainer and insulator, **Fig. 6.**
3. Support left side of transaxle with a suitable screw jack and wood block.
4. Remove two transaxle mount nuts, then raise transaxle with screw jack to gain access to control arm bolt.
5. Remove control arm from frame.
6. Reverse procedure to install noting the following:
   a. Install control arm bushing bolt and nut, retainer and insulator but do not tighten bolt.
   b. Tighten bolts to specifications as shown in **Figs. 6 and 7.**

1998–2000 SEVILLE & 2000 DEVILLE

Use only recommended tools for separating ball joint from knuckle. Failure to do so may cause damage to joint and seal.

1. Raise and support vehicle with control arms hanging free. Remove wheel and tire.
2. Disconnect stabilizer link to control arm bolt.
3. Remove cotter pin and loosen nut from ball stud. **Care must be exercised to prevent Tri-Pot joints from being over extended, resulting in separation of internal parts and possible joint failure.**
4. Using ball joint separator tool No. J-43828, or equivalent, remove ball joint from knuckle.
5. Remove mounting bolts and control arm.
6. Reverse procedure to install.

CONTROL ARM BUSHING

REPLACE

ELDORADO, 1997 SEVILLE & 1997–99 DEVILLE

When replacing lower control arm bushings, refer to **Fig. 8.**

1. Remove lower control arm as outlined under "Control Arm, Replace."

2. Install driver, tool No. J–35561-1, receiver No. J–35561-2 and installing cup No. J–35561-3 or equivalents.
3. Press out bushing.
4. Lubricate new bushing with rubber lube.
5. Install tools, then press in new bushing.
6. Install lower control arm.

1998–2000 SEVILLE & 2000 DEVILLE

The rear control bushing is serviced with the control arm and cannot be serviced separately.

1. Remove control arm from vehicle as outlined under " Control Arm, Replace."
2. Assemble bolt assembly tool No. J-21474-27 with a washer through bushing receiver tool No. J-21474-5, or equivalents, with larger diameter end over bushing against control arm, **Fig. 9.**
3. Lubricate bolt threads with high pressure lubricant.
4. Install bushing remover tool No. J-41014-1 (large end facing bushing), thrust bearing and nut tool No. J-21474-4 onto bolt assembly tool No. J-21474-27 or equivalents.
5. Tighten nut until bushing is driven out of control arm.
6. Remove bushing tools.
7. Reverse procedure to install.

STEERING KNUCKLE

REPLACE

1. Remove hub and bearing assembly as outlined under "Hub & Bearing Assembly, Replace."
2. Remove nut securing tie rod, then separate tie rod from knuckle using steering linkage puller tool No. J-24319–B or equivalent.
3. Remove cotter pin and nut securing lower ball joint and separate ball stud from steering knuckle using ball joint separator tool No. J-43828 or equivalent.
4. Remove bolts securing strut to steering knuckle, **Fig. 2,** then steering knuckle.
5. Reverse procedure to install.

STABILIZER BAR

REPLACE

ELDORADO, 1997 SEVILLE & 1997–99 DEVILLE

1. Raise vehicle and support with weight of vehicle resting on frame, not lower control arms.
2. Remove right front wheel and tire.
3. **On models with road sensing suspension,** disconnect position sensor from lower control arm.
4. **On all models,** remove left and right bracket bolts, brackets and insulators, **Fig. 7.**
5. Remove left and right stabilizer links.
6. Disconnect exhaust pipe from rear manifold, raise pipe to gain clearance, then withdraw stabilizer shaft.
7. Reverse procedure to install.

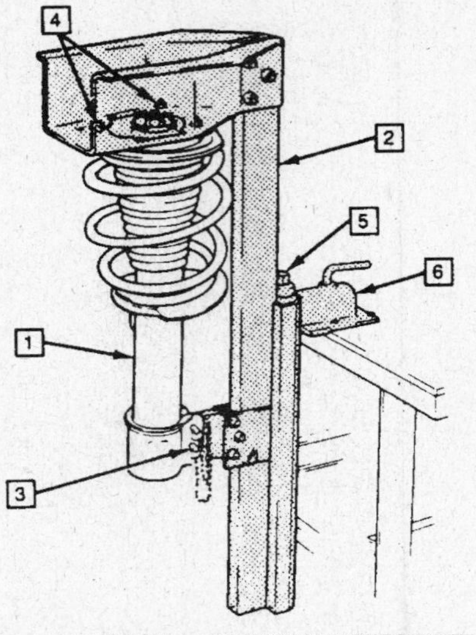

1 STRUT ASSEMBLY
2 STRUT COMPRESSOR J-34013
3 INSTALL LOCKING PINS THROUGH STRUT ASSEMBLY
4 TIGHTEN NUTS TILL FLUSH WITH STRUT COMPRESSOR
5 COMPRESSOR FORCING SCREW
6 HOLDING FIXTURE J3289-20

GC2029100135000X

Fig. 4 Strut assembly installation in strut compressor

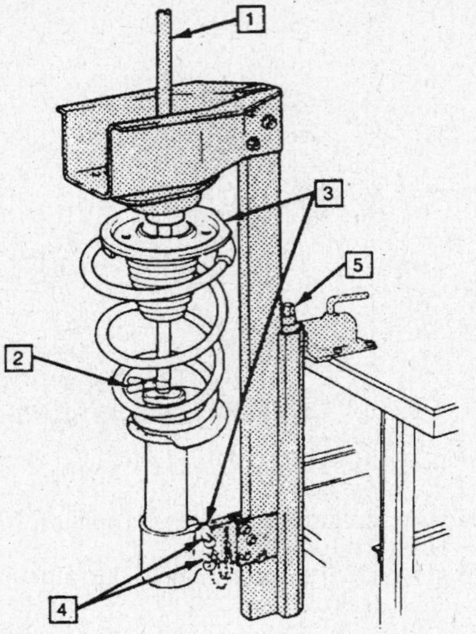

1 ROD J-34013-38 INSTALLED
2 CLAMP J-34013-20 INSTALLED
3 FLAT ON SPRING SEAT MUST FACE SAME DIRECTION AS STEERING KNUCKLE FLANGE
4 BOTH LOCKING PINS INSTALLED
5 COMPRESSOR FORCING SCREW

GC2029100136000X

Fig. 5 Flat on upper spring seat alignment

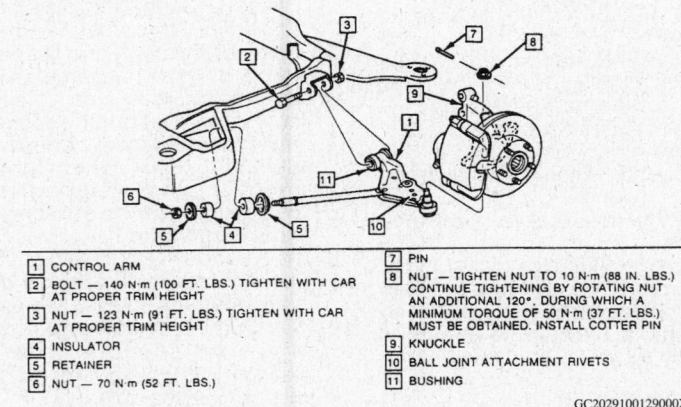

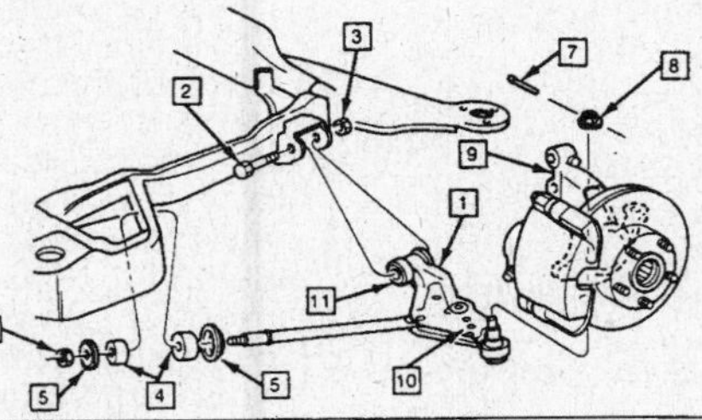

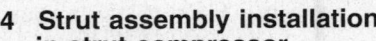

1 CONTROL ARM
2 BOLT — 140 N·m (100 FT. LBS.) TIGHTEN WITH CAR AT PROPER TRIM HEIGHT
3 NUT — 123 N·m (91 FT. LBS.) TIGHTEN WITH CAR AT PROPER TRIM HEIGHT
4 INSULATOR
5 RETAINER
6 NUT — 70 N·m (52 FT. LBS.)
7 PIN
8 NUT — TIGHTEN NUT TO 10 N·m (88 IN. LBS.) CONTINUE TIGHTENING BY ROTATING NUT AN ADDITIONAL 120°, DURING WHICH A MINIMUM TORQUE OF 50 N·m (37 FT. LBS.) MUST BE OBTAINED. INSTALL COTTER PIN
9 KNUCKLE
10 BALL JOINT ATTACHMENT RIVETS
11 BUSHING

GC2029100129000X

Fig. 6 Lower control arm replacement. Eldorado, 1997 Seville & 1997–99 DeVille

1998–2000 SEVILLE & 2000 DEVILLE

1. Raise and support vehicle with control arms hanging free. Remove front wheels and tires.
2. Remove left and righthand stabilizer link bolts.
3. Remove left and righthand stabilizer bar brackets.
4. Use universal steering linkage puller tool No. J-24319-B, or equivalent, to remove lefthand tie rod end from knuckle.
5. Using front ball joint separator tool No. J-36226 or equivalent separate ball joint from steering knuckle.
6. Turn right steering knuckle to left, then guide stabilizer shaft out right side of vehicle in an upward direction.
7. Remove stabilizer shaft out bottom center of vehicle.
8. Reverse procedures to install.

TIE ROD

REPLACE

1998–2000 SEVILLE & 2000 DEVILLE

Inner

1. Remove steering gear as outlined

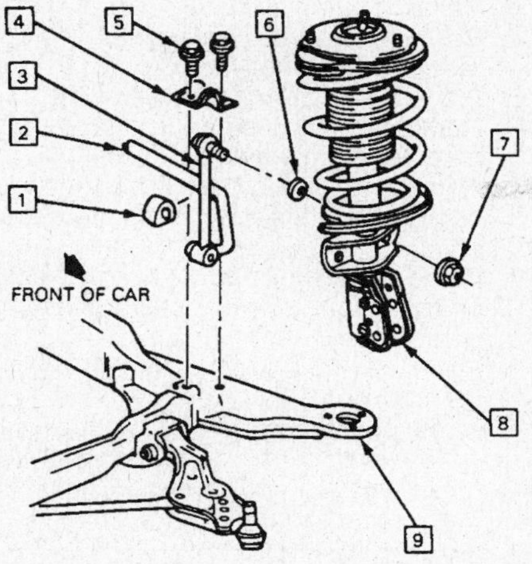

Fig. 7 Stabilizer shaft replacement. Eldorado, 1997 Seville & 1997–99 DeVille

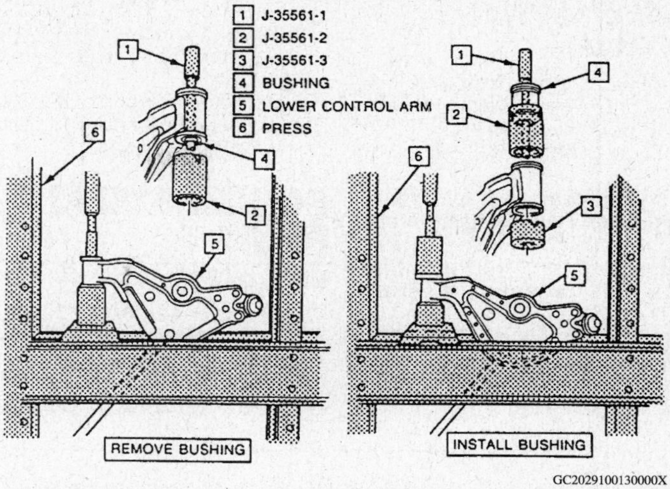

Fig. 8 Lower control arm bushings replacement. Eldorado, 1997 Seville & 1997–99 DeVille

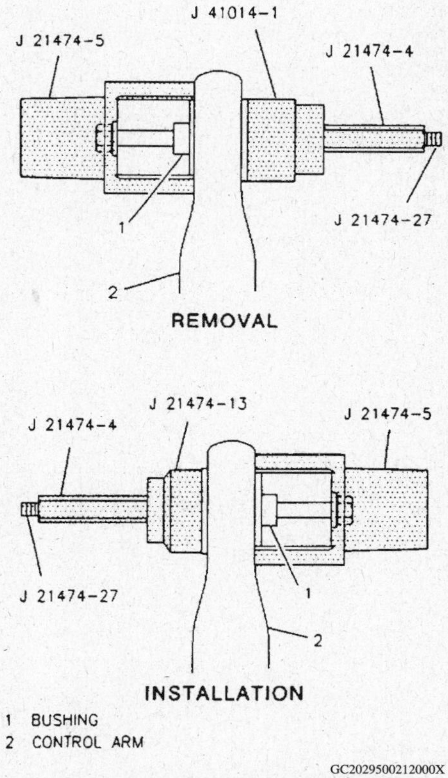

Fig. 9 Control arm bushing replacement. 1998–2000 Seville & 2000 DeVille

under "Power Steering Gear, Replace."
2. Remove outer tie rod.
3. Remove inner tie rod assembly jam nut and end clamp.
4. Remove boot clamp with side cutters and discard.
5. Mark breather tube location on steering gear for assembly.
6. Remove rack and pinion boot and breather tube.
7. Loosen inner tie rod assembly shock dampener and slide back on rack.
8. Hold rack in suitable vice.
9. With one wrench on rack assembly flats and another on inner tire rod housing flats, turn inner tie rod housing counterclockwise and remove.
10. Reverse procedure to install. Gap between rack and housing stakes should be .01 inch.

Outer

1. Remove cotter pin and hex slotted nut.
2. Loosen jam nut.
3. Use universal steering linkage puller tool No. N-24319-01, or equivalent, to remove outer tie rod from steering knuckle.
4. Remove outer from inner tie rod.
5. Reverse procedure to install.

POWER STEERING GEAR

REPLACE

ELDORADO, 1997 SEVILLE & 1997-99 DEVILLE

The front wheels must be positioned straight ahead and the steering wheel locked before proceeding with repair. Failure to do so could result in damage to the clock spring.

1. Disconnect intermediate shaft lower coupling.
2. Raise and support vehicle, then remove left front wheel and tire assembly.
3. Disconnect RSS position sensor and links.
4. Disconnect both tie rod ends from knuckles.
5. Disconnect exhaust Y pipe at converter.
6. Support frame with suitable jackstands.
7. Loosen No. 2 and No. 3 body mount bolts and slightly lower rear of frame. Do not lower any more than is necessary to gain access to steering gear.
8. Remove heat shield, then plastic line retainer.
9. Disconnect both pressure and return lines from steering gear.
10. Disconnect Magnasteer connector.
11. Remove steering gear attachment bolts.
12. Remove steering gear by sliding out to side of vehicle.
13. Reverse procedure to install.

1998–2000 SEVILLE & 2000 DEVILLE

1. Lock steering column by installing lock tool No. J-42640, or equivalent into underside of steering column.
2. Disconnect intermediate shaft lower coupling.
3. Remove right transaxle mount. **Frame must be properly supported before partially lowering. Frame should not be lowered any further than needed to gain access to steering gear.**
4. Disconnect pressure and return pipes from rack and pinion gear.
5. Disconnect Magnasteer electrical connector then remove heat shield.
6. Separate outter tie rod ends from steering knuckle.
7. Remove rack and pinion attaching bolts.
8. Remove rack and pinion assembly.
9. Reverse procedure to install. Tighten bolts to specification.

POWER STEERING PUMP

REPLACE

1. Remove serpentine drive belt, then drain power steering fluid from reservoir.
2. Remove return line from reservoir, then pressure line from pump.
3. Remove pump mounting bolt.
4. Remove power steering pump/reservoir assembly from vehicle.
5. Place assembly in soft jawed vise.
6. Remove power steering pump and reservoir from bracket.
7. Remove retaining clips holding reservoir to power steering pump, then reservoir.
8. Using pulley pulling tool No. J–38825 or equivalent, remove power steering pump pulley.
9. Reverse procedure to install, noting the following:
   a. Reinstall power steering pump pulley using pulley installation tool No. J–38823 or equivalent.

TIGHTENING SPECIFICATIONS

Component	Torque/Ft. Labs.
ELDORADO, 1997 SEVILLE & 1997–99 DEVILLE	
Adjuster Plug Look into	50
Ball Joint To Control Arm	50
Ball Joint To Knuckle	37
Brake Reaction Rod To Frame	58
Caliper Attaching Bolts	63
Caliper Mounting Bracket	83
Control Arm Bushing Nuts	100
Cylinder Line Fittings	20
Dampener Shaft	55
Hub & Bearing To Knuckle	70
Hub To Drive Axle	110
Inner Tie Rod Housing To Rack	74
Intermediate Shaft Pinch Bolts	35
Outer Tie Rod Jam Nut	50
Pinion Locknut	26
Pinion Preload	17④
Power Steering Line Fittings	20
Stabilizer Bracket To Frame	33
Stabilizer Link Nut	41
Strut Mount To Body	18
Strut To Knuckle	75
Strut To Strut Top Mount	①
Tie Rod Nuts	7.5②
Tie Rod Pinch Bolts	41
Wheel Lug Nuts	100
1998–2000 SEVILLE & 2000 DEVILLE	
Ball Joint Nut	89④
Ball Joint To Control Arm Nuts	50
Brake Line & Speed Sensor Bracket Bolts	13
Caliper Mounting Bolts	38
Control Arm Bolt	117
Control Arm Nut	78
Drive Axle Nut	107
Hub & Bearing Bolts	95
Hub Nut	107
Power Steering Gear Hose Connections	20
Power Steering Gear Mounting Bolts	89
Power Steering Pump Bolts	37
Stabilizer Bracket Bolts	24
Stabilizer Shaft Link Nut	11
Strut To Body Attaching Nuts	18
Strut To Knuckle Bolts	136
Tie Rod End To Knuckle Nuts	35–52③
Wheel Lug Nuts	100

① — Torque old design (flanged) nut to 75 ft. lbs. & new design (non-flanged) nut to 55 ft. lbs.

② — Tighten an additional 1/3 turn.

③ — Do not counter-rotate nut for cotter pin insertion.

④ — Inch lbs.

Wheel Alignment

INDEX

FRONT WHEEL ALIGNMENT

ELDORADO, 1997 SEVILLE & 1997-99 DEVILLE

Steering and vibration complaints are not always the result of improper alignment. Another possibility is tire "lead" due to worn or improperly manufactured tires. "Lead" is the vehicles's deviation from a straight path on a level road without pressure on the steering wheel.

Before making any adjustment affecting wheel alignment, make the following checks to ensure correct alignment readings and alignment adjustments.

1. Check all tires for proper inflation pressures and ensure all tires have approximately equal tread wear.
2. Check hub and bearing assemblies for excessive wear, correcting as necessary.
3. Check ball joints and tie rod ends. If they are excessively loose, correct before making adjustment.
4. Check runout of wheels and tires.
5. Check vehicle trim height, correcting as necessary before adjusting alignment.
6. Check for proper operation of Electronic Level Control system.
7. Check strut dampers for proper operation.
8. Check control arms for loose bushings.
9. Check stabilizer bar for loose or missing parts.

Consideration must also be given to excess loads, such as tool boxes or sample cases. If these items are normally carried in vehicle, they should remain in vehicle during alignment adjustments. Consideration should be given to condition of equipment being used to adjust alignment. Follow equipment manufacturer's instructions. Regardless of equipment being used, vehicle must be on level surface, both fore and aft and sideways.

Front Alignment Measurement

Install alignment equipment following equipment manufacturer's instructions. Measure alignment angles, **Fig. 1**, and record the readings. If adjustments are necessary, they must be made in order; caster first, camber second and toe third.

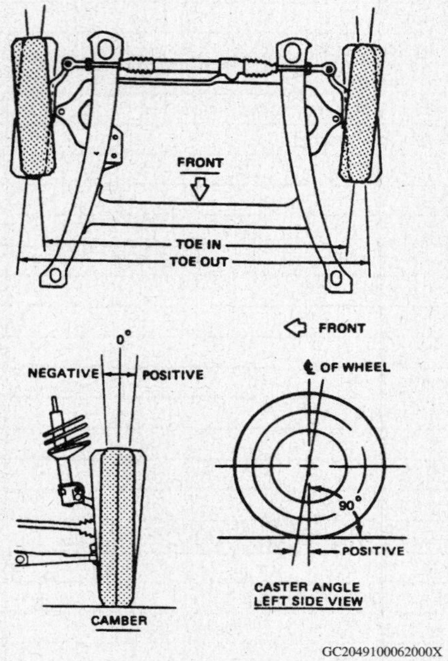

Fig. 1 Front end alignment angles. Eldorado, 1997 Seville & 1997–99 DeVille

Jounce front and rear bumpers three times to normalize suspension prior to measuring angles.

Caster Adjustment

1. Support vehicle by wheels, then loosen top strut mounting nuts and washers.
2. Set caster to specification by moving strut forward or rearward as required. Adjustment sensitivity is approximately .1° per millimeter moved.
3. **Torque** top strut mounting nuts and washers to 18 ft. lbs.

Camber Adjustment

1. Loosen both strut to knuckle bolts just enough to allow movement.
2. Adjust camber by turning camber adjustment bolt, **Fig. 2,** and using camber adjustment tool No. J-39601 or equivalent.
3. **Torque** strut to knuckle nuts to 140 ft. lbs.
4. **Torque** camber adjustment bolt to 7 ft. lbs.

Toe Adjustment

1. Loosen locknut on inner tie rods, **Fig. 3.**
2. Adjust toe by turning inner tie rods.
3. Adjust boots so that they are not twisted.
4. **Torque** locknuts to 46 ft. lbs.

1998-2000 SEVILLE & 2000 DEVILLE

Caster

1. Remove top strut nuts and washers.
2. Raise and support front of vehicle to separate strut from inner wheel housing.
3. Drill two 12/32 inch holes at front and rear of oval strut mounting hole on left and righthand strut towers, **Fig. 4,** and file excess metal to create slotted holes. **Paint exposed metal with rust resistant paint or primer.**
4. Lower front of vehicle.
5. Install strut mounting nuts, but do not tighten at this time.
6. Adjust caster by moving top of strut forward or rearward. A .040 inch position change at tower is approximately .1° change in caster.
7. When caster is within specifications, **torque** strut mounting nuts to 35 ft. lbs.

Camber

1. Raise and support vehicle, then remove both front wheels and tires.
2. Tap out upper and lower strut to knuckle bolts, then separate strut from knuckle.
3. Grind lower bolt hole on struts inner metal plate to match outside plates diameter.
4. File excess metal to make slotted holes, then paint exposed metal with rust resistant paint or primer.
5. Replace strut to knuckle and install bolts but do not tighten at this time.
6. Using camber adjustment tool No. J-39601 or equivalent set chamber to specifications, then tighten bolts to specifications.

Toe

1. Loosen lock nuts on tie rod ends. **Ensure boots are not twisted or damaged during adjustment.**
2. Rotate inner tie rod to adjust toe to specifications.
3. **Torque** lock nuts to 47 ft. lbs.

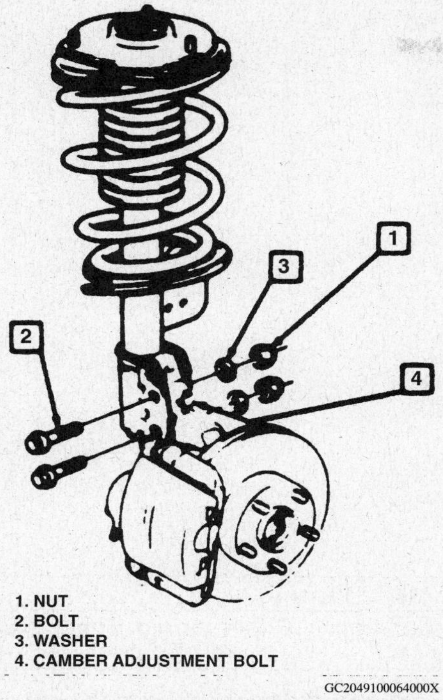

Fig. 2 Front wheel camber adjustment. Eldorado, 1997 Seville & 1997–99 DeVille

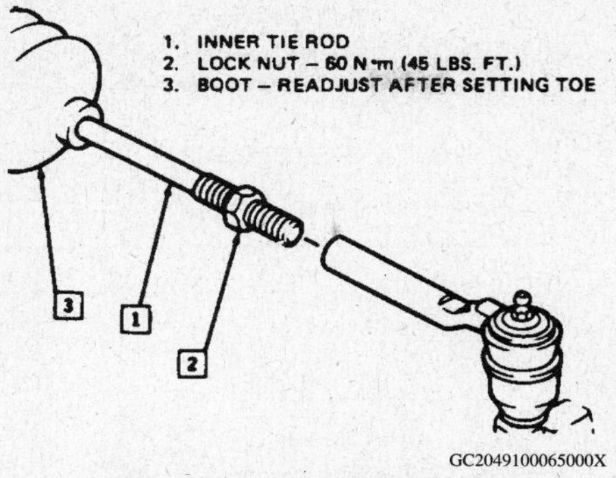

Fig. 3 Front wheel toe adjustment. Eldorado, 1997 Seville & 1997–99 DeVille

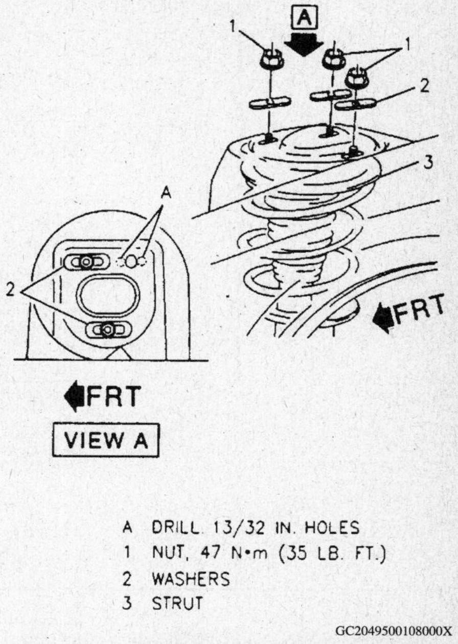

Fig. 4 Front caster adjustment. 1998–2000 Seville & 2000 DeVille

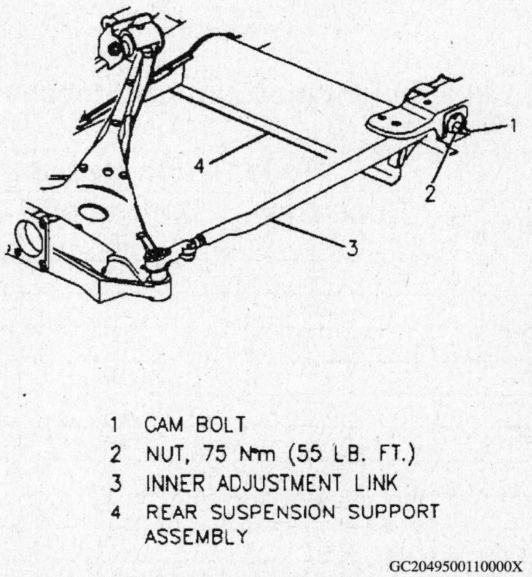

Fig. 5 Rear toe adjustment. 1998–2000 Seville & 2000 DeVille

REAR WHEEL ALIGNMENT

ELDORADO, 1997 SEVILLE & 1997–99 DEVILLE

Rear wheel toe is the only adjustable angle. If camber is not within specifications, inspect for worn or damaged rear suspension components.

Before checking rear trim height or measuring rear alignment angles, the following procedure should be performed to ensure the rear air-adjustable struts are filled with residual pressure only.

1. Place a weight of at least 300 lbs. in vehicle trunk.
2. Turn ignition On, then wait for car leveling light to illuminate.
3. Turn ignition Off and remove weight from trunk.
4. Wait at least 30 seconds for ELC system to exhaust.
5. Roll car forward or backward several complete tire rotations to eliminate effects of tire camber change.
6. Jounce front and rear bumpers 3 times to normalize suspension prior to measuring angles.

Camber Adjustment

1. Loosen front and rear inside control arm mounting bolts.
2. Move control arm to change camber and set to specification.
3. **Torque** control arm mounting bolts to 66 ft. lbs.

Toe Adjustment

1. Loosen inner toe link bolts.
2. Insert screwdriver or prybar between inside rear toe link mounting bolt and rear crossmember assembly.
3. Move toe link to adjust toe and set to specifications.
4. **Torque** toe link mounting bolts to 66 ft. lbs.

1998–2000 SEVILLE & 2000 DEVILLE

Make left and right toe adjustments separately.

1. Loosen inner adjustment link cam nut, **Fig. 5.**
2. Rotate cam bolt using an 18 mm wrench or socket and adjust toe to specifications.
3. **Torque** cam nut to 74 ft. lbs.

VEHICLE RIDE HEIGHT

Refer to **Fig. 6** for ride height measurements and **Fig. 7** for specifications. When checking ride height measurements, fuel tank should be full, tires at should be correct pressure, front seat should be rearward position, truck should be empty except for spare tire and jack and vehicle should be on level ground. If fuel tank is not full, add weight to trunk to compensate for amount fuel vehicle is below the full level.

Prior to checking ride height, lift front bumper upward approximately 1.5 inches and release (3 times), then check front ride height. Push front bumper downward approximately 1.5 inches and release (3 times), then recheck front ride height. Average of both readings to determine vehicle ride height. Check rear ride height in same manner, lifting and pushing rear bumper.

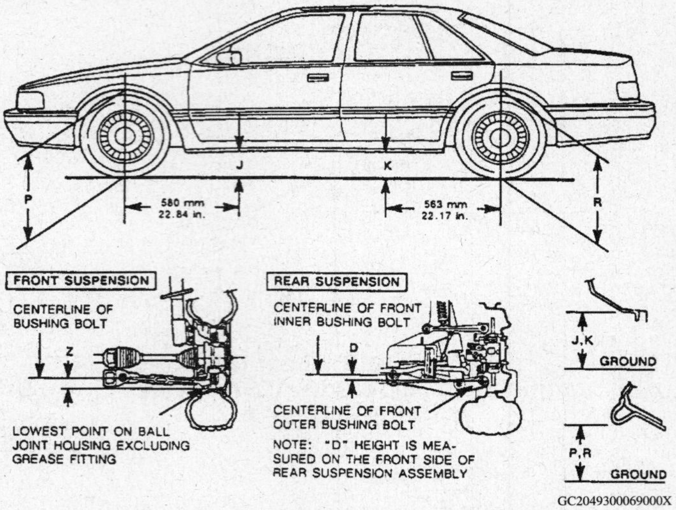

Fig. 6 Ride height measurement locations

Year	Model	Ride Height Measurements In Inches					
		Dimension Z	Dimension D	Dimension J	Dimension K	Dimension P	Dimension R
1997	Eldorado	1.97	1.14	8.66	8.43	28.15	27.91
	DeVille	2.01	1.46	7.56	7.95	27.83	21.38
	DeVille Concours	1.65	1.10	7.17	7.56	27.44	18.19
	Seville SLS	2.20	1.61	9.65	9.65	28.58	28.58
	Seville STS	1.88	1.30	9.33	9.33	28.27	28.27
1998-99	Eldorado	1.97	1.14	8.66	8.43	28.15	27.91
	DeVille	2.01	1.46	7.56	7.95	27.83	21.38
	DeVille Concours	1.65	1.10	7.17	7.56	27.44	18.19
	Seville SLS	1.57	3.39	7.05	9.02	23.62	23.22
	Seville STS	1.18	2.99	6.65	8.58	23.62	23.22
2000	Eldorado	1.97	1.14	8.66	8.43	28.15	27.91
	Deville	1.57	3.39	7.05	9.02	—	—
	Seville	1.57	3.39	7.05	9.02	—	—

Fig. 7 Vehicle ride height specifications

METRO

NOTE: Refer To The Rear Of This Manual For Vehicle Manufacturer's Special Tool Suppliers.

INDEX OF SERVICE OPERATIONS

Specifications

GENERAL ENGINE SPECIFICATIONS

Year	Engine Liter	Fuel System	Bore & Stroke Inches	Comp. Ratio	Net. H.P. @ RPM	Maximum Torque, Ft. Lbs. @ RPM	Normal Oil Pressure, psi
1997	1.0L	TBI	2.91 x 3.03	9.5	55 @ 5700	58 @ 3300	47–61①
	1.3L	TBI	2.91 x 3.03	9.5	70 @ 5500	74 @ 3500	47–61①
1998–2000	1.0L	TBI	2.91 x 3.03	9.5	55 @ 5700	58 @ 3300	47–61
	1.3L	SFI	2.91 x 2.97	9.5	79 @ 6000	75 @ 3000	47–61

TBI — Throttle Body Injection

SFI — Sequential Multi-Port Fuel Injection

① — At 4000 RPM.

TUNE UP SPECIFICATIONS

Year & Engine	Spark Plug Gap	Ignition Timing, BTDC				Curb Idle Speed, RPM		Fast Idle Speed, RPM		Fuel Pump Pressure, psi	Valve Lash
		Firing Order Fig.	Man. Trans.	Auto. Trans.	Mark Fig.	Man. Trans.	Auto. Trans.	Man. Trans.	Auto. Trans.		
1997											
1.0L	.041	A	5①	5①	C	800	850N	③	③	②	④
1.3L	.041	B	5①	5①	C	800	850N	③	③	②	④
1998–2000											
1.0L	.039-.043	A	5①	5①	C	800	850N	③	③	②	④
1.3L	.039-.043	D	⑤	⑤	⑤	800	850N	③	③	⑥	.005–.013

BTDC: Before Top Dead Center

① — When checking ignition timing, connect a jumper wire between diagnostic connector terminals D & E. The diagnostic connector is located next to LH strut tower.

② — To relieve system pressure, remove fuel pump relay from main fuse panel located in engine compartment. Operate engine until fuel supply is depleted. Crank engine several times in 3 second intervals. Remove fuel tank filler cap to release vapor pressure, then reinstall cap. Place ignition switch in Off position, then install fuel pump relay. Attach a suitable fuel pressure test gauge to fuel feed hose. Start engine and check fuel pressure w/engine at idle speed. Fuel pressure should be 13–20 psi. With ignition switch in On position, engine not operating, fuel pressure should be 23–31 psi.

③ — Controlled by an idle speed control motor.

④ — These engines are equipped w/hydraulic valve lash adjusters and no adjustment is required.

⑤ — Equipped w/distributerless ignition. Ignition timing can not be adjusted.

⑥ — With engine running at idle fuel pressure should be 29–34, with ignition switch in On position engine not running fuel pressure should be 39–44 psi.

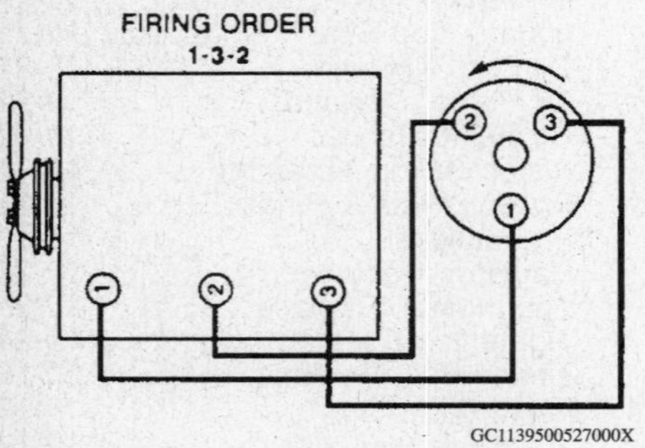

Fig. A

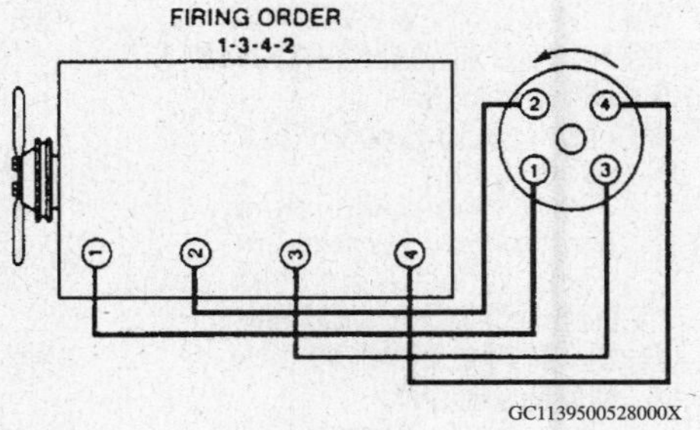

Fig. B

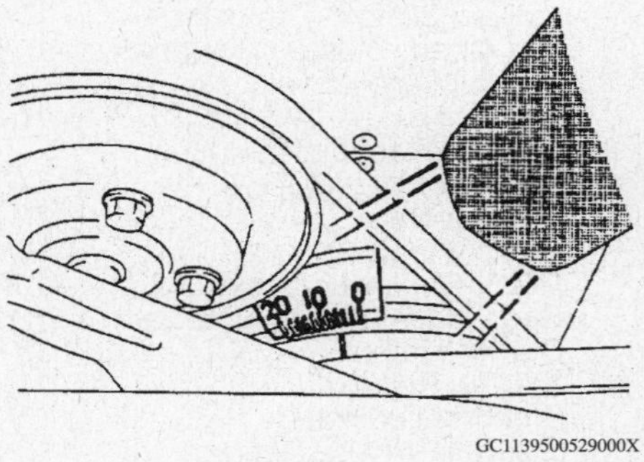

Fig. C

FIRING ORDER 1-3-4-2

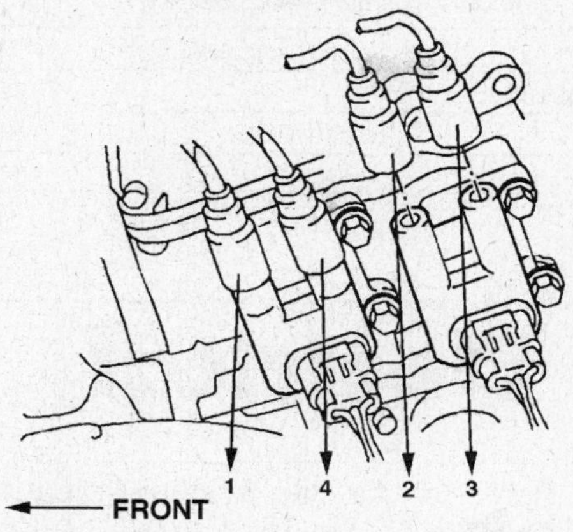

Fig. D

FRONT WHEEL ALIGNMENT SPECIFICATIONS

Year	Models	Caster Angle, Degrees		Camber Angles, Degrees		Total Toe, Degrees	Turning Angle, Degrees		Ball Joint Wear
		Limits	Desired	Limits	Desired		Inner Wheel	Outer Wheel	
1997–2000	All	+1 to +5	+3	–.5 to +1.5	+.5	0 to +.32	38	32	①

① — Refer to "Ball Joint Inspection," in the "Front Suspension & Steering" section, for proper inspection of ball joints.

REAR WHEEL ALIGNMENT SPECIFICATIONS

Year	Camber Angles, Degrees				Total Toe, Degree
	Limits		Desired		
	Left	Right	Left	Right	
1997–2000	–.01 to +1	–.01 to +1	0	0	+.3 to +.6

FLUID CAPACITIES & COOLING SYSTEM DATA

Year	Engine	Coolant Capacity, Qts.		Radiator Cap Relief Pressure, psi	Thermostat Open Temp. °F	Fuel Tank Gals.	Engine Oil Qts.	Transaxle	
		Man. Trans.	Auto. Trans					Man. Pts.	Auto. Qts.①
1997–2000	1.0L	4.13	4.13	12.8	190	10.6	3.5②	5	③
	1.3L	4.9	5	12.8	190	10.6	3.5②	5	③

① — Make final check w/dipstick.
② — Additional oil may be required to bring oil level to full mark when changing oil filter.
③ — Oil pan only, 1.6 qts.; after overhaul less torque converter, 3.7 qts.; after overhaul with new torque converter, 5.2 qts.

LUBRICANT DATA

Year	Lubricant Type			
	Transaxle		Power Steering	Brake System
	Manual	Automatic		
1997–2000	75W-90 GL-4①	Dexron III	Dexron III	DOT 3

① — Synthetic type gear lubricant.

Electrical

NOTE: On Air Bag Equipped Models, Refer To "Air Bag System Precautions" Located In The Front Of This Manual For System Disarming & Arming Procedures.

NOTE: Refer To "Computer Relearn Procedures " Located In The Front Of This Manual For Computer Relearn Procedures.

INDEX

PRECAUTIONS

AIR BAG SYSTEMS

Refer to "Air Bag System Precautions" in the front of this manual for system disarming and arming procedures.

BATTERY GROUND CABLE

Prior to service, disconnect battery ground cable and isolate as required.

FUSE PANEL & FLASHER LOCATION

The main fuse panel (alternator and ignition switch fuses and main fuse for junction fuse panel) is located in the engine compartment on the left hand fender apron. The junction fuse panel (fuses for other components) is located under the left hand side of the instrument panel. The air bag fuse panel, if equipped, is located behind the lefthand side of the instrument panel on the junction block support bracket.

The turn signal and hazard flasher is located under the left hand side of the instrument panel near the fuel panel.

FUEL PUMP RELAY LOCATION

The fuel pump relay is located in the engine compartment relay center at the front lefthand side of the engine compartment next to battery, **Figs. 1 and 2.**

RELAY CENTER LOCATION

The relay center is located at the lefthand side of the engine compartment, near the battery.

STARTER

REPLACE

1. Disconnect solenoid lead and battery cable from starter terminals.
2. Remove two starter attaching bolts, then starter.
3. Reverse procedure to install. **Torque** starter attaching bolts to 17 ft. lbs.

DISTRIBUTOR

REPLACE

1. Disconnect electrical connectors and vacuum lines.
2. Remove distributor cap, then mark rotor position on housing assembly.
3. Mark distributor housing assembly position on engine.
4. Remove distributor flange bolts, then distributor from engine.
5. Reverse procedure to install. Ensure alignment marks match.

IGNITION COIL

REPLACE

1. Disconnect spark plug wires from faulty ignition coil.
2. Disconnect electrical connector from ignition coil.

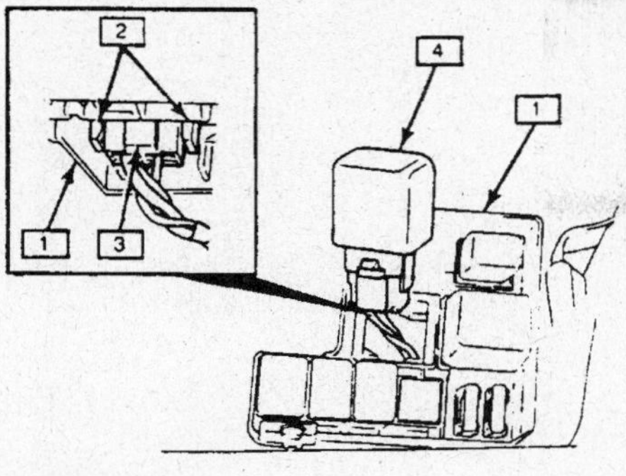

1 MAIN FUSE BOX
2 LOCK TABS
3 FUEL PUMP RELAY ELECTRICAL CONNECTOR
4 FUEL PUMP RELAY

GC1029102746000X

Fig. 1 Fuel pump relay location. 1.0L engine

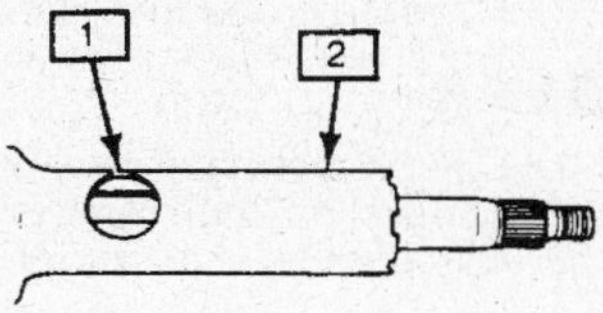

1 STEERING SHAFT
2 STEERING COLUMN

GC9129100030000X

Fig. 4 Steering shaft & column alignment

3. Remove two bolts securing ignition coil, then the ignition coil.
4. Reverse procedure to install, **torque** ignition coil attaching bolts to 8 ft. lbs.

IGNITION SWITCH

REPLACE

REMOVAL

1. Remove turn signal/dimmer switch as outlined under "Turn Signal Switch, Replace."
2. Disconnect ignition switch and key warning electrical connectors.
3. Lift up floor mat at steering shaft and remove steering column coupling cover.
4. Remove upper steering shaft coupling bolt, then connect ignition switch and key warning electrical connectors.
5. Remove steering column attaching nuts, then column assembly.
6. Using a center punch, loosen and remove steering lock attaching bolts, **Fig. 3.**
7. Place ignition switch in ACC or ON position and remove from steering column.

INSTALLATION

1. Position oblong hole on steering shaft at center of hole in steering column, **Fig. 4.**

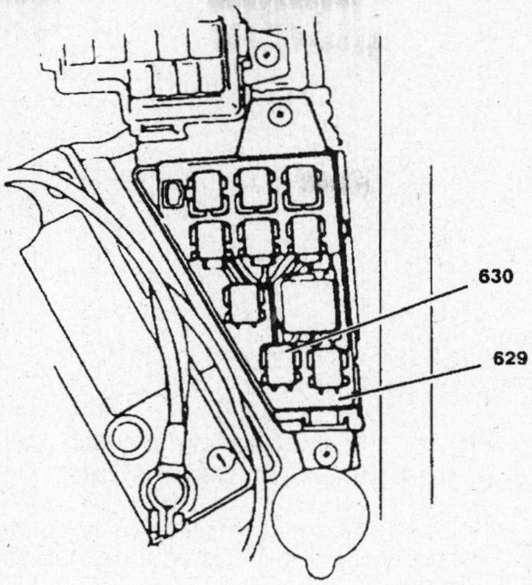

629 RELAY BOX
630 FUEL PUMP RELAY

GC1029503761000X

Fig. 2 Fuel pump relay location. 1.3L engine

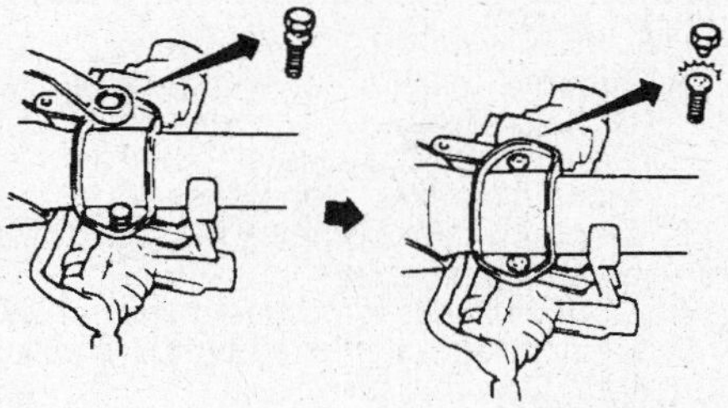

GC9129100031000X

Fig. 5 Ignition switch attaching bolt installation

2. Place ignition switch in ACC or ON position.
3. Position ignition switch to steering column, then place switch in LOCK position.
4. Align ignition switch hub with oblong hole on steering shaft, then rotate steering shaft to ensure it locks.
5. Install replacement ignition switch attaching bolts. Tighten bolts until bolt head breaks off, **Fig. 5.**
6. Place ignition switch in ON or ACC and check for smooth steering shaft rotation. Also check steering shaft lock for proper operation.
7. Align ignition switch hub to steering shaft oblong hole, rotate shaft to ensure steering shaft is locked, **Fig. 6.**
8. Position steering column mounting brackets to mounting studs, then install and **torque** attaching nuts to 10 ft. lbs.
9. Install steering shaft coupling bolt and **torque** to 18 ft. lbs.
10. Install steering shaft coupling cover.
11. Install turn signal/dimmer switch as outlined under "Turn Signal Switch, Replace."

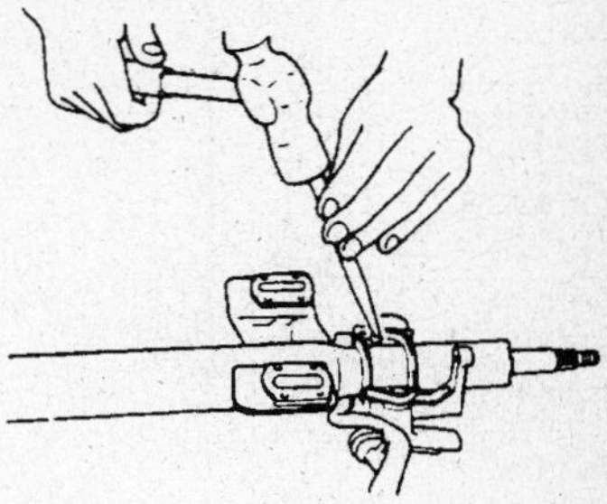

1 CENTER PUNCH (WITH SHARP POINT)
2 IGNITION SWITCH MOUNTING BOLTS

GC9129100029000X

Fig. 3 Ignition switch removal

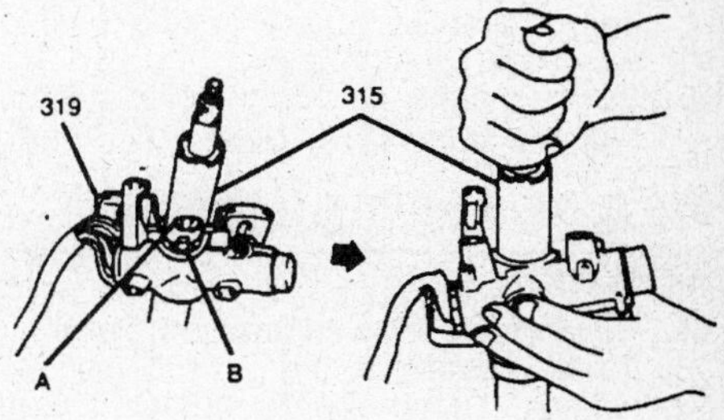

A COLUMN AND SHAFT HOLES
B IGNITION SWITCH HUB
315 STEERING COLUMN
319 IGNITION SWITCH

GC9129500035000X

Fig. 6 Ignition switch hub to steering shaft alignment

CLUTCH START SWITCH

ADJUST

1. Disconnect electrical connector at clutch start switch.
2. Loosen switch locknut, then back off switch adjustment.
3. Connect an ohmmeter between switch terminals.
4. Position clutch pedal at approximately .6 to 1.2 inches from floor and hold.
5. Rotate switch into bracket until ohmmeter just indicates continuity, then tighten locknut. **Torque** locknut to 10 ft. lbs.
6. Connect switch electrical connector.

NEUTRAL SAFETY SWITCH

REPLACE

1. Remove neutral safety switch attaching bolt and switch from transaxle.
2. Place shift lever in Neutral position.
3. Using a screwdriver, position neutral safety switch a shown in **Fig. 7.** Switch should click at this position.
4. Install neutral safety switch to manual shift shaft and loosely install attaching bolt.
5. Rotate switch slightly until a click is

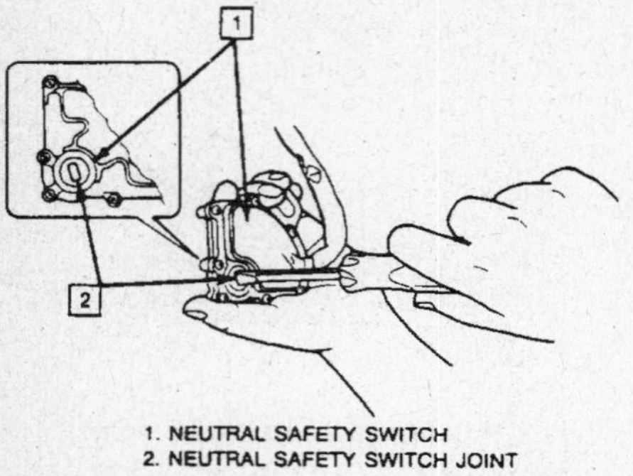

Fig. 7 Positioning neutral safety switch

heard, then **torque** attaching bolt to 9.5–16.5 ft. lbs., **Fig. 8.**

6. Connect electrical connector to switch, then check switch for proper operation.

HEADLAMP SWITCH

REPLACE

1. Remove steering column trim panel.
2. Lower steering column.
3. Remove instrument cluster bezel screws and pull bezel out.
4. Remove headlamp switch from bezel.
5. Remove cluster to instrument panel attaching screws.
6. Pull cluster rearward to reach and disconnect headlamp switch connector.
7. Remove headlamp switch.
8. Reverse procedure to install.

STOP LIGHT SWITCH

REPLACE

Pull up brake pedal and adjust switch position so that clearance between end of thread and brake pedal contact plate A is .02–.04 inch, **Fig. 9.** Tighten locknut.

TURN SIGNAL SWITCH

REPLACE

1. Remove steering wheel, refer to "Steering Wheel, Replace."
2. Remove steering column covers, **Fig. 10.**
3. Disconnect turn signal/dimmer switch electrical connector.
4. Remove turn signal/dimmer switch attaching screws and switch, **Fig. 10.**
5. Reverse procedure to install.

DIMMER SWITCH

REPLACE

Replace dimmer switch as an assembly with the turn signal switch. Refer to "Turn Signal Switch, Replace" for replacement procedure.

STEERING WHEEL

REPLACE

1. Remove air bag inflator module as described in the "Passive Restraints" section.
2. Remove steering wheel nut, then

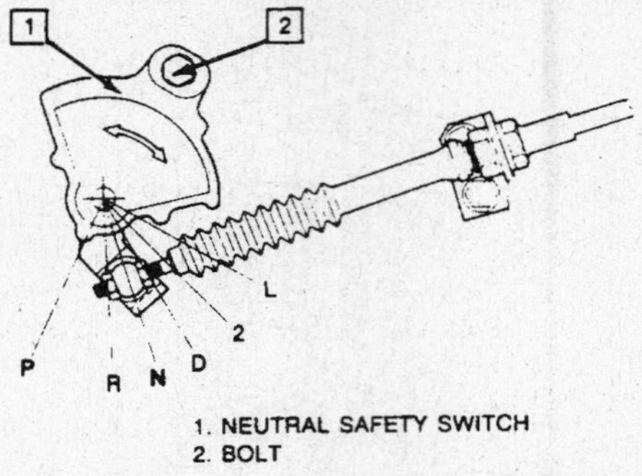

Fig. 8 Neutral safety switch to manual lever installation

place alignment marks on steering shaft and wheel for use during installation.

3. Remove steering wheel using a suitable puller tool.
4. Reverse procedure to install. When installing steering wheel, align marks made during removal. **Torque** steering wheel nut to 24 ft. lbs.

INSTRUMENT CLUSTER

REPLACE

1. Remove cluster lower cover two attaching screws and covers.
2. Remove gauge cluster bezel four attaching screws, then bezel.
3. Depress speedometer plastic tabs to disconnect cable.
4. Remove cluster four attaching screw.
5. Disconnect cluster electrical connectors, then remove cluster.
6. Reverse procedure to install.

RADIO

REPLACE

1. Through glove compartment, disconnect radio and antenna electrical connector.
2. Pull ashtray outward, push downward, then pull ashtray rearward to remove.
3. Remove four instrument panel center trim bezel attaching screws, then the bezel.
4. Through instrument panel ashtray cutout, remove one cross recess screw below rear of radio.
5. Remove radio four attaching screws, then pull radio and mounting brackets rearward.
6. Remove five radio mounting bracket to radio attaching screws, if required, then the radio.
7. Reverse procedure to install.

WIPER MOTOR

REPLACE

FRONT

1. Disconnect connect electrical connector from wiper motor.
2. Remove three wiper motor attaching screws, then nut and washer attaching wiper linkage to motor, **Fig. 11.**
3. Remove wiper motor from vehicle.

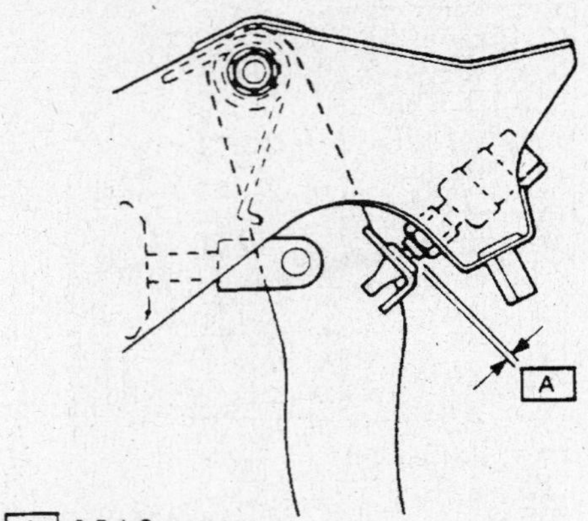

Fig. 9 Stop lamp switch adjustment

4. Reverse procedure to install.

REAR

1. Disconnect hatchback inner door trim panel clips, then remove panel.
2. Disconnect wiper motor electrical connector.
3. Remove wiper motor ground screw, **Fig. 12.**
4. Remove three wiper motor attaching nuts.
5. Disconnect wiper linkage, then remove wiper motor.
6. Reverse procedure to install. **Torque** wiper motor attaching bolts 15 ft. lbs.

WIPER SWITCH

REPLACE

FRONT

1. Remove steering column trim panel.
2. Lower steering column.
3. Remove instrument cluster bezel screws and pull bezel out.
4. Remove wiper switch from bezel.
5. Remove cluster to instrument panel attaching screws.
6. Pull cluster rearward to reach and disconnect wiper switch connector.
7. Remove wiper switch.
8. Reverse procedure to install.

REAR

1. Remove lower steering column trim cover.
2. Remove both steering column attaching nuts and lower steering column.
3. Remove instrument panel cluster trim bezel.
4. Remove rear wiper switch from bezel.
5. Reverse procedure to install.

WIPER TRANSMISSION

REPLACE

FRONT

1. Inspect wiper arms, for proper installation location.
2. Remove wiper arm cover and attaching nut.

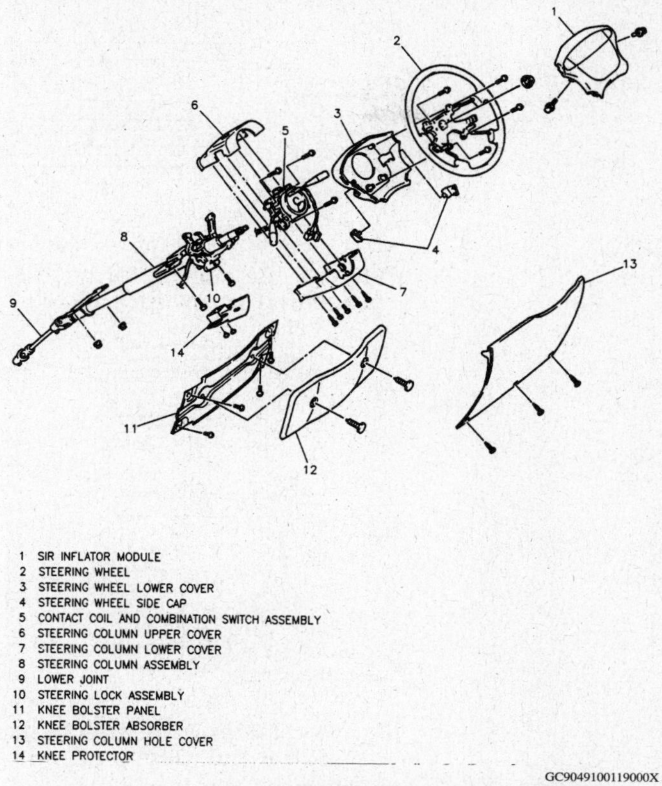

Fig. 10 Turn signal/dimmer switch removal

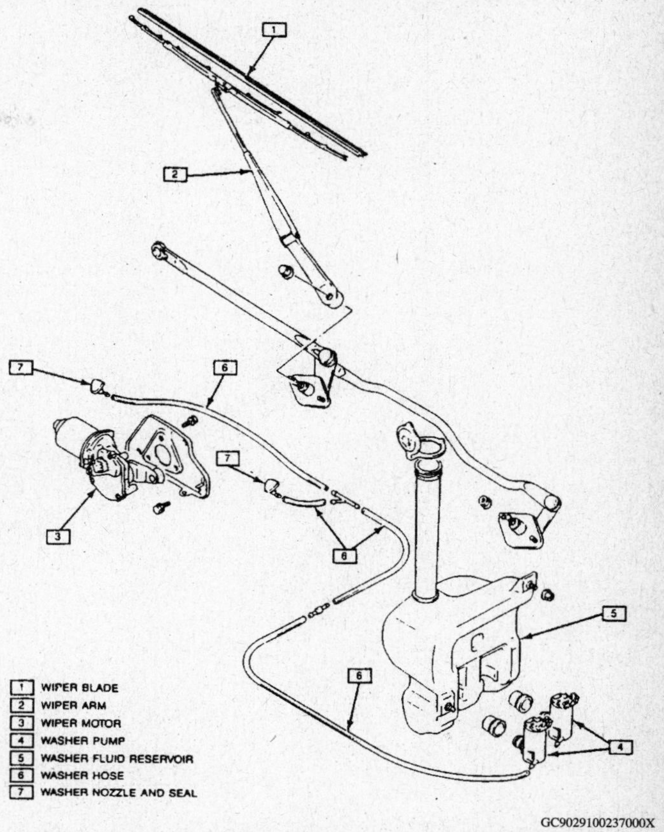

Fig. 11 Front windshield wiper/washer motor & linkage assembly

3. Disconnect 11 cowl vent grill plastic attaching clips, then remove grill.
4. Remove six wiper transmission to cowl attaching nuts.
5. Disconnect wiper motor electrical connector, then remove three motor attaching bolts, pull motor rearward from bulkhead.
6. Pry wiper transmission from motor crank arm, do not disconnect crank arm from motor.
7. Remove wiper motor assembly, then transmission.
8. Reverse procedure to install. **Torque** transmission attaching nuts to 11 ft. lbs.

REAR

1. Inspect wiper arms, for proper installation location.
2. Lift wiper arm nut plastic cover, then remove arm attaching nut.
3. Remove wiper arm from transmission.
4. Remove hatchback door inner trim panel.
5. Disconnect wiper motor electrical connector.
6. Remove motor ground lead attaching screw.
7. Remove motor three attaching nuts, then separate motor from door.
8. Pry transmission from motor crank arm and wiper arm base, then slide transmission rearward to remove.
9. Remove wiper arm base from door, do not disconnect crank arm from motor.
10. Reverse procedure to install. **Torque** wiper arm nut to 15 ft. lbs.

BLOWER MOTOR

REPLACE

1. Depress glove compartment stopper, then pull rearward.
2. Remove glove compartment to instrument panel attaching screws, remove glove compartment.
3. Disconnect ECM electrical connectors, then remove ECM attaching screws and ECM.
4. Disconnect blower motor and blower resistor electrical connectors.
5. Disconnect fresh air control cable from blower motor housing.
6. Remove three blower motor housing attaching bolts, then blower motor housing, **Fig. 13.**
7. Remove air hose and three attaching screws, then separate blower motor from housing, **Fig. 14.**
8. Reverse procedure to install.

HEATER CORE

REPLACE

1. Remove instrument panel as outlined under "Dash Panel Service."
2. Drain coolant into suitable container.
3. Remove heater core clamps and hoses, through engine compartment.
4. Remove blower case to heater case air duct.
5. Remove heater case attaching nuts and bolts **Fig. 15,** then heater case.
6. Remove heater case clip and two attaching screws, then separate case halves, **Fig. 16.**
7. Remove heater core from case.
8. Reverse procedure to install. **Torque** heater case attaching nuts and bolts to 7.5 ft. lbs.

EVAPORATOR CORE

REPLACE

1. Evacuate and recover refrigerant as outlined under "Air Conditioning."
2. Remove blower motor case as outlined under "Blower Motor, Replace."
3. Disconnect A/C amplifier and evaporator thermistor electrical connectors.
4. Disconnect and cap evaporator case refrigerant inlet and outlet pipes.
5. Remove evaporator case drain hose.
6. Remove evaporator case two attaching bolts and one nut, then case.
7. Depress A/C amplifier two lower locking tabs, then slide amplifier upward to remove.
8. Disengage evaporator case clips, to separate case halves.
9. Remove evaporator core from case.
10. Reverse procedure to install. **Torque** evaporator case bolts to 7.5 ft. lbs., inlet pipe nut to 26 ft. lbs. and outlet pipe nut to 33 ft. lbs.

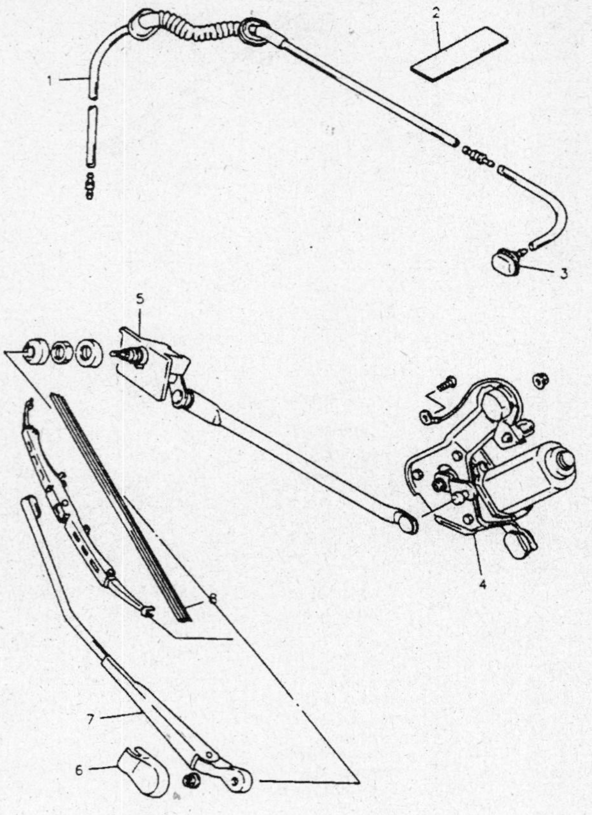

1 REAR WASHER HOSE
2 REAR WASHER HOSE COVER
3 REAR WASHER NOZZLE
4 REAR WIPER MOTOR
5 REAR WIPER LINKAGE
6 REAR WIPER NUT COVER
7 REAR WIPER ARM
8 REAR WIPER BLADE

GC9029500248000X

Fig. 12 Rear windshield wiper motor & linkage assembly

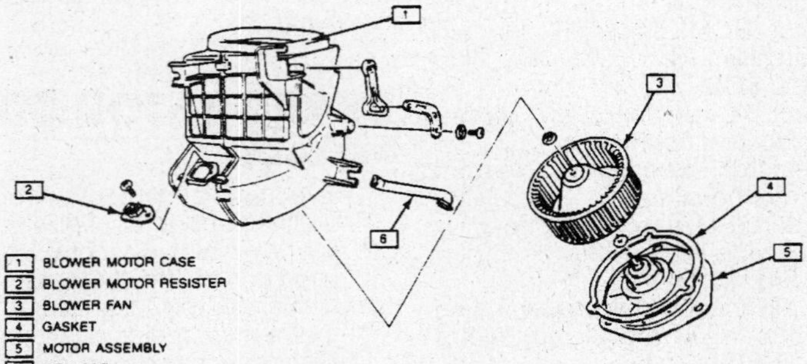

1 BLOWER MOTOR CASE
2 BLOWER MOTOR RESISTER
3 BLOWER FAN
4 GASKET
5 MOTOR ASSEMBLY
6 AIR HOSE

GC7029100069000X

Fig. 14 Blower motor & case assembly

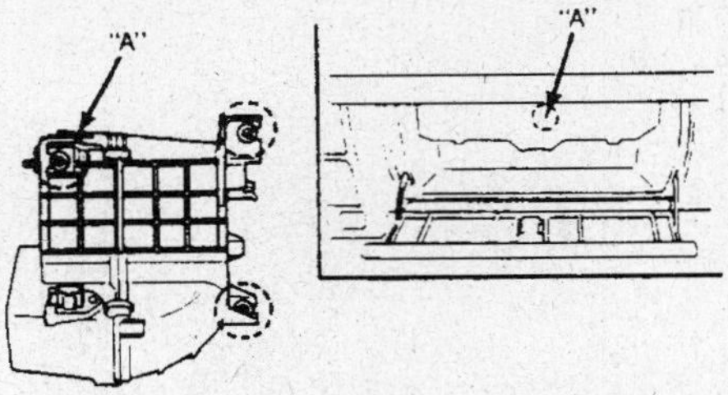

GC7029100068000X

Fig. 13 Blower motor case attaching screw locations

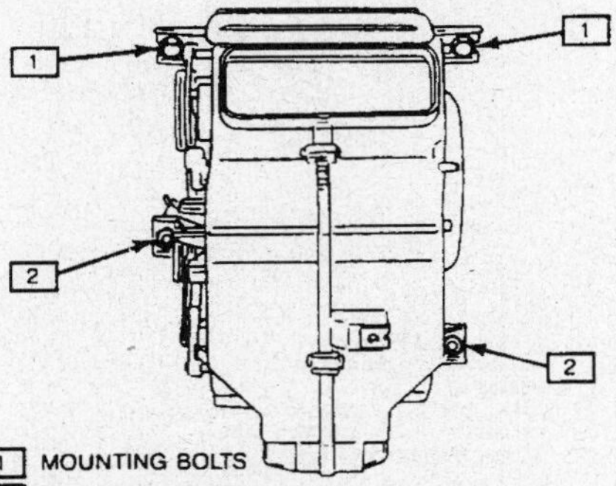

1 MOUNTING BOLTS
2 MOUNTING NUTS

GC7029100071000X

Fig. 15 Heater case attaching bolt & nut locations

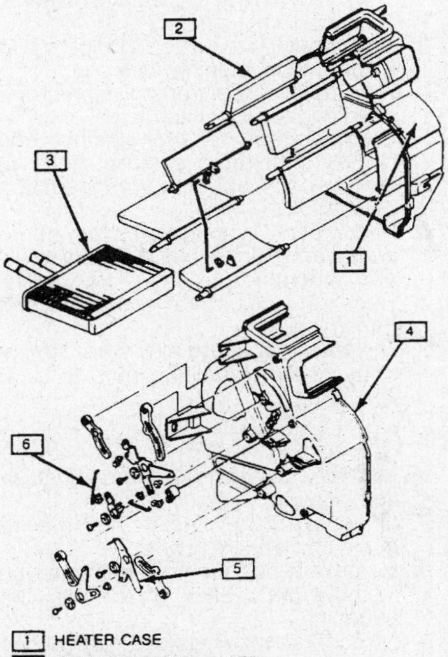

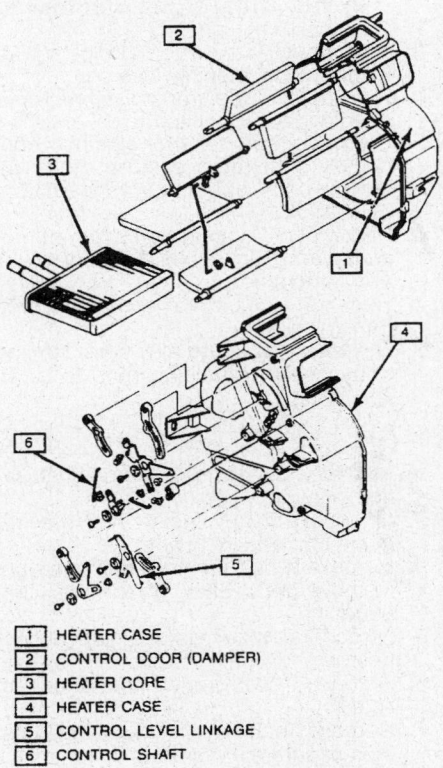

1 HEATER CASE
2 CONTROL DOOR (DAMPER)
3 HEATER CORE
4 HEATER CASE
5 CONTROL LEVEL LINKAGE
6 CONTROL SHAFT

GC7029100072000X

Fig. 16 Exploded view of heater case assembly

1.0L Engine

NOTE: On Air Bag Equipped Models, Refer To "Air Bag System Precautions" Located In The Front Of This Manual For System Disarming & Arming Procedures.

NOTE: Refer To "Computer Relearn Procedures " Located In The Front Of This Manual For Computer Relearn Procedures.

INDEX

PRECAUTIONS

AIR BAG SYSTEMS

Refer to "Air Bag System Precautions" in the front of this manual for system disarming and arming procedures.

BATTERY GROUND CABLE

Prior to service, disconnect battery ground cable and isolate as required.

FUEL SYSTEM PRESSURE RELIEF

1. Loosen fuel filler cap to relieve fuel tank pressure
2. Remove fuel pump relay from relay box located at the lefthand front of the engine compartment, next to the battery. Refer to "Fuel Pump Relay Location" in the "Electrical" section.
3. Crank engine and allow to stall. Crank engine for several seconds more to ensure relief of any remaining fuel.
4. Remove battery ground cable.

COMPRESSION PRESSURE

1. Turn ignition switch to Lock position.
2. Remove spark plugs.
3. Disconnect distributor electrical connector and remove FI fuse from fuse and relay box.
4. Install spark plug port adapter tool No. J 22794, or equivalent and a compression gauge into spark plug hole.
5. **On models equipped with manual transaxle,** depress clutch and accelerator to floor.
6. **On all models,** crank engine and take four pressure readings, noting the highest reading obtained.
7. Compression should increase quickly and evenly. Compression pressure at 250 RPM is 199 psi standard and 156 psi minimum. Maximum allowable pressure difference between any two cylinders at 250 RPM is 14 psi.
8. Repeat compression test procedure for remaining cylinders.
9. After completion, install FI fuse, spark plugs and distributor electrical connector.

ENGINE MOUNT

REPLACE

FRONT

1. Remove engine mount nut, then raise and support vehicle.
2. Support engine using an engine support fixture.
3. Remove engine mount and frame bracket, then mount from bracket.
4. Reverse procedure to install.

REAR

1. Remove engine mount nut, then raise and support vehicle.
2. Remove nut attaching mount to body bracket.
3. Support engine using an engine support fixture.
4. Remove frame bracket, then mount.
5. Reverse procedure to install.

ENGINE

REPLACE

1997

1. Relieve fuel system pressure as outlined under "Precautions."
2. Disconnect windshield washer hose, then remove hood.
3. Remove air cleaner assembly.
4. Drain cooling system, then remove radiator and engine cooling fan.
5. Disconnect high tension lead from ignition coil.
6. Disconnect electrical connector from distributor.
7. Disconnect electrical connectors from coolant temperature sender, engine coolant temperature sensor, engine cooling fan switch and engine oil pressure sender.
8. Disconnect electrical connector from EGR vacuum switching valve.
9. Disconnect electrical connectors from idle speed control valve, throttle position switch, fuel injector and pressure sensor.
10. Disconnect electrical connectors and wiring from alternator and starter motor.
11. Disconnect electrical connector from oxygen sensor.
12. Disconnect battery ground cable from transaxle.
13. **On models with manual transaxle,**

disconnect electrical connector from back-up lamp switch.
14. **On models with automatic transaxle,** disconnect electrical connectors from neutral safety switch, speed sensor and direct clutch and second brake solenoids.
15. **On all models,** disconnect intake manifold to power brake unit vacuum hose.
16. Disconnect evaporative emission canister hoses from intake manifold and tube connections.
17. Disconnect fuel hoses from throttle body.
18. Disconnect heater hoses from engine.
19. Disconnect accelerator cable from throttle body.
20. **On models with manual transaxle,** disconnect clutch cable from fork and housing.
21. **On models with automatic transaxle,** disconnect shift control and fluid pressure control cables from transaxle.
22. **On all models,** disconnect speedometer cable from transaxle.
23. Raise and support vehicle, then disconnect exhaust pipe from exhaust manifold.
24. Drain engine crankcase, then drain fluid from transaxle.
25. **On models with manual transaxle,** disconnect control shaft and extension rod from transaxle.
26. **On all models,** separate drive axles from transaxle. Support drive axles from chassis using wire.
27. **On models with automatic transaxle,** remove engine torque rod bracket from transaxle.
28. **On all models,** lower vehicle and install an engine lifting fixture.
29. Remove engine and transaxle attaching bolts, then engine and transaxle assembly from vehicle.
30. Reverse procedure to install.

1998-2000

1. Relieve fuel system pressure as outlined under "Precautions."
2. Remove both battery cables, battery and battery tray.
3. Drain cooling system into a suitable container.
4. Remove hood.
5. Remove air cleaner assembly.
6. Remove radiator with cooling fan.
7. Disconnect coolant temperature gauge sensor, throttle position sensor and EGR solenoid electrical connectors.
8. Disconnect EGR bypass valve.
9. Disconnect idle speed control solenoid valve, oxygen sensor, fuel injector, MAP sensor and power steering pressure switch electrical connectors.
10. Disconnect ground wires from intake manifold.
11. Disconnect oil pressure switch, alternator and A/C compressor electrical connectors.
12. Disconnect starter solenoid electrical connector.
13. Disconnect back-up lamp switch.
14. Disconnect direct clutch and second brake solenoids.
15. Release main engine harness from clamps.
16. Disconnect the following vacuum hoses:
    a. Front and rear canister purge hoses from intake manifold.
    b. Canister hose from canister pipe.
    c. Pressure sensor hose from intake.
    d. Brake booster hose from intake.
    e. Idle speed control hose from throttle body.
17. Disconnect the following cables:
    a. Accelerator cable from throttle body.
    b. Clutch cable from transaxle.
    c. Shift select cable and throttle valve cable from transaxle.
    d. Speedometer cable from transaxle.
18. Remove inlet and outlet hoses.
19. Remove fuel return and feed hoses from throttle body.
20. Install universal support fixture tool No. J 28467–A with engine support adapters tool No. J 28467–89, or equivalents.
21. Raise and support vehicle.
22. Disconnect exhaust system from exhaust manifold.
23. Remove front pipe/catalytic converter assembly.
24. **On models equipped with manual transaxle** remove gearshift control shaft and extension rod.
25. **On all models** drain engine oil and transaxle fluid into a suitable container.
26. Remove left and right drive axles from transaxle as outlined under "Front Wheel Drive Axle." **It is not necessary to remove driveshafts from steering knuckles.**
27. Remove A/C compressor from bracket and position aside. **Do not disconnect A/C hoses from compressor.**
28. Disconnect power steering hoses from power steering pump.
29. **On models equipped with automatic transaxle** remove torque rod.
30. **On all models** lower vehicle.
31. Remove tool Nos. J 28467–A and J 28467–89, or equivalents and install a suitable engine lifting device.
32. Remove left transaxle mount, right side engine mount and rear engine mount.
33. Remove engine with transaxle from vehicle.
34. Reverse procedure to install tightening all fasteners and filling all fluids to specification.

INTAKE MANIFOLD

REPLACE

1. Relieve fuel system pressure as outlined under "Precautions."
2. Drain cooling system, then remove air cleaner assembly.
3. Disconnect electrical connectors from coolant temperature sender, engine and coolant temperature sensor.
4. Disconnect electrical connector from EGR vacuum switching valve.
5. Disconnect electrical connectors from idle speed control valve, throttle position switch and fuel injector.
6. Disconnect ground wires from intake manifold.
7. Disconnect fuel hoses from throttle body.
8. Disconnect coolant hoses from intake manifold.
9. Disconnect MAP sensor hose from intake manifold.
10. Disconnect evaporative emission hoses from intake manifold and tube.
11. Disconnect power brake unit vacuum hose from intake manifold.
12. Disconnect PCV valve hose from cylinder head cover.
13. Disconnect accelerator cable from throttle body.
14. Disconnect all other electrical connectors and hoses to permit intake manifold and throttle body removal.
15. Remove intake manifold to cylinder head attaching nuts and bolts, then intake manifold and throttle body as an assembly.
16. Reverse procedure to Install.

EXHAUST MANIFOLD

REPLACE

1. Disconnect oxygen sensor electrical connector, then release wiring harness from clamps.
2. Disconnect exhaust pipe from exhaust manifold.
3. Remove exhaust manifold attaching bolts and nuts, then exhaust manifold from cylinder head.
4. Reverse procedure to install.

CYLINDER HEAD

REPLACE

1. Relieve fuel system pressure as outlined under "Precautions."
2. Drain cooling system, then remove air cleaner assembly.
3. Disconnect coil wire from distributor cap.
4. Disconnect distributor electrical connector.
5. Disconnect coolant temperature sender, engine coolant temperature sensor and engine cooling fan switch electrical connectors.
6. Disconnect EGR vacuum switching valve electrical connector.
7. Disconnect idle speed control valve, throttle position switch and fuel injector electrical connectors.
8. Disconnect oxygen sensor electrical connector, then wiring harness from clamps.
9. Disconnect ground wires from intake manifold.
10. Disconnect heater hose from intake manifold and radiator hose from thermostat housing.
11. Disconnect fuel hoses from throttle body.
12. Disconnect MAP sensor hose from intake manifold.
13. Disconnect evaporative emission hoses from intake manifold and tube.
14. Disconnect power brake unit vacuum hose from intake manifold.

15. Disconnect accelerator cable from throttle body.
16. Raise and support vehicle, then disconnect exhaust pipe from exhaust manifold.
17. Lower vehicle, then remove cylinder head cover.
18. Remove cylinder head attaching bolts, then cylinder head.
19. Reverse procedure to install. Tighten cylinder head bolts in several passes in sequence shown in **Fig. 1,** to specifications.

VALVE ARRANGEMENT

FRONT TO REAR

1.0L ....I-E-I-E-I-E

VALVE ADJUSTMENT

These engines are equipped with hydraulic valve lash adjusters and no adjustment is required.

VALVE GUIDES

Valves and valve guides are available in standard size only. The Valve guide can be driven from cylinder bore using valve guide remover tool No. J 37968-1, or equivalent. The valve guide should be driven from the combustion chamber side of the cylinder head out through the valve spring side.

The cylinder head valve guide bore should be reamed with an 11 mm reamer prior to valve guide installation. Heat cylinder head to 176–212°F, then drive valve guide into cylinder head bore using valve guide remover tool No. J 37968-1 and valve guide installer tool No. J 37968-2, or equivalents. Valve guide should be driven in until tool contacts cylinder head. Valve guide protrusion should be .45 inch from cylinder head surface. After installation, ream valve guide with a 5.5 mm reamer.

HYDRAULIC VALVE LASH ADJUSTER SERVICE

Hydraulic valve lash adjusters should not be disassembled.

1. Remove camshaft as outlined under "Camshaft, Replace."
2. Remove hydraulic valve lash adjusters from cylinder head, **Fig. 2.**
3. Check hydraulic valve lash adjusters for wear and damage and replace as necessary.
4. Using a micrometer, measure outside diameter of hydraulic valve lash adjuster. Outside diameter should be 1.2188–1.2194 inches.
5. Measure hydraulic valve lash adjuster bore in cylinder head. Bore diameter should be 1.2205–1.2214 inches.
6. To determine hydraulic valve lash adjuster to cylinder head bore clearance, subtract adjuster outside diameter from cylinder head adjuster bore diameter. Adjuster to bore clearance should be .0010–.0025 inch. If clearance is greater than .0059 inch, replace adjuster or cylinder head as necessary.
7. Place valve lash adjuster in clean engine oil prior to installation. Also pour engine oil through camshaft journal oil holes, until oil is emitted from hydraulic valve lash adjuster oil holes, **Fig. 3.**
8. Apply engine oil to valve lash adjuster, then position adjuster in cylinder head bore and install camshaft.

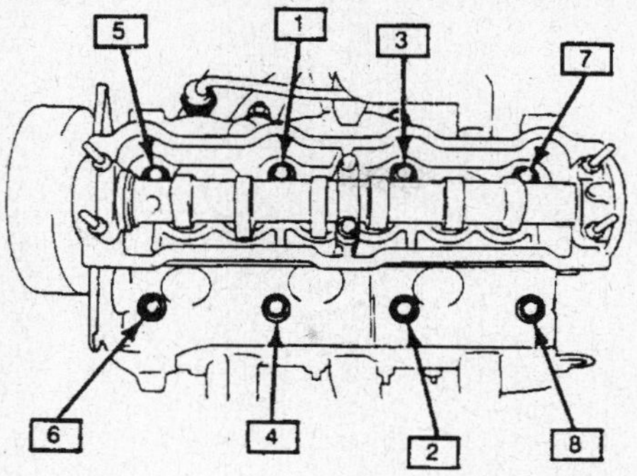

Fig. 1 Cylinder head bolt tightening sequence

TIMING BELT

REPLACE

REMOVAL

1. Raise and support vehicle.
2. Remove fender apron extension from right hand side of vehicle.
3. Remove water pump drive belt, then water pump pulley.
4. Remove four attaching bolts and crankshaft pulley.
5. Remove outer timing belt cover, **Fig. 4.**
6. Align camshaft and crankshaft timing marks, **Fig. 5.**
7. Remove timing belt tensioner, tensioner plate, spring and damper.
8. Remove timing belt.

INSPECTION

Check timing belt for wear and cracks and replace as necessary. Check timing belt tensioner for smoothness of rotation and replace as necessary.

INSTALLATION

1. Position lug on tensioner plate to hole in tensioner, **Fig. 6.**
2. Position tensioner and tensioner plate to engine, then install and hand tighten attaching bolt. Ensure tensioner and tensioner plate move in the same direction, **Fig. 7.** If movement is not as indicated, remove tensioner and reinsert tensioner plate lug into tensioner.
3. Ensure camshaft and crankshaft timing marks are aligned, **Fig. 5.**
4. With tensioner plate pushed upward, install timing belt over camshaft and crankshaft pulleys. **Arrow on timing belt should face toward direction of crankshaft rotation. When installing timing belt, keep drive side of belt free of slack.**
5. Install tensioner spring and damper, then hand tighten tensioner stud.
6. Rotate crankshaft two revolutions clockwise direction to remove slack from belt. **Ensure slack is removed from drive belt and that camshaft and crankshaft timing marks are aligned.**
7. Tighten tensioner stud, then tighten tensioner bolt to specifications.
8. Install timing belt outer cover and crankshaft pulley. **Ensure seal is between oil pump housing and water pump.**
9. Install water pump pulley and drive belt.
10. Install right hand side fender apron extension, then lower vehicle.

CAMSHAFT

REPLACE

This procedure has been revised by a Technical Service Bulletin.

REMOVAL

1. Remove air cleaner assembly, then cylinder head cover.
2. Remove distributor from cylinder head.
3. Remove timing belt as outlined under "Timing Belt, Replace."
4. Position crankshaft sprocket key as shown in, **Fig. 8.**
5. **On models with spoked camshaft timing gear,** position gear so camshaft timing gear pulley pin engages with slot No. 1 on camshaft timing gear, **Fig. 9.**
6. **On all models,** hold camshaft in position by inserting a rod into .39 inch hole in camshaft, then remove camshaft sprocket attaching bolt, **Fig. 10.** Place shop cloth under rod to prevent damage to cylinder head surface.
7. Remove camshaft housings to cylinder head attaching bolts and studs, **Fig. 2.**
8. Remove camshaft from cylinder head. **Hydraulic valve lash adjusters should also be removed and placed in engine oil until installation.**

INSTALLATION

1. Pour engine oil into camshaft journal oil holes until oil is emitted from hydraulic valve lash adjuster holes, **Fig. 3.**
2. Lubricate valve lash adjusters with engine oil and install on cylinder head.
3. Lubricate camshaft with engine oil, then position on cylinder head with sprocket pin hole positioned as shown in **Fig. 11.**
4. On models with spoked (as opposed to solid) camshaft timing gears, install gear so pulley pin engages with slot No. 1 on camshaft timing gear.
5. Lubricate camshaft journal bores in camshaft housing with engine oil.
6. Apply sealant to cylinder head mating surface of camshaft housings No. 1 and No. 3, **Fig. 12.**
7. Position camshaft housings over camshaft and onto cylinder head mating

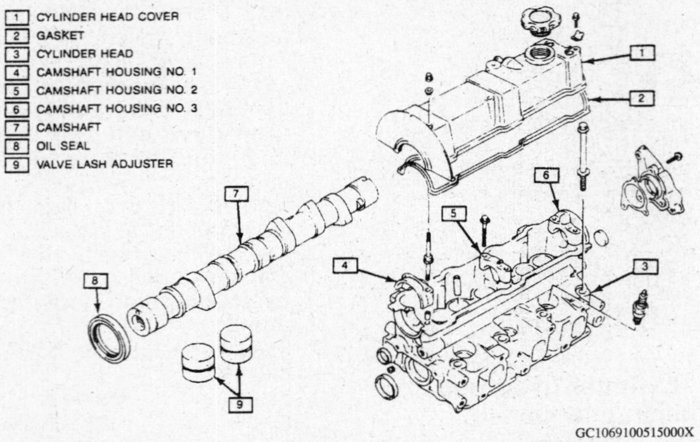

Fig. 2 Camshaft & hydraulic valve lash adjusters

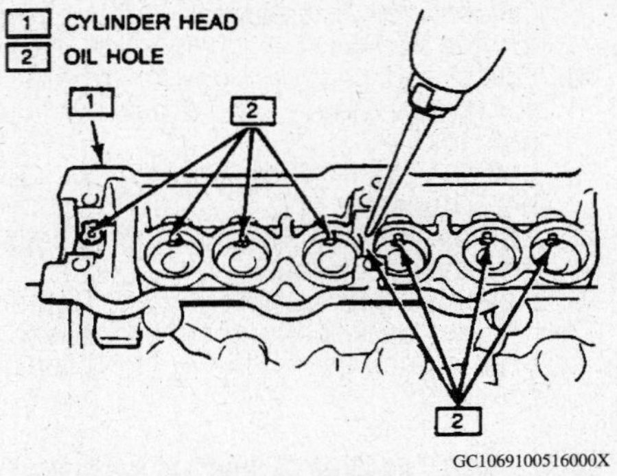

Fig. 3 Applying engine oil to camshaft oil holes

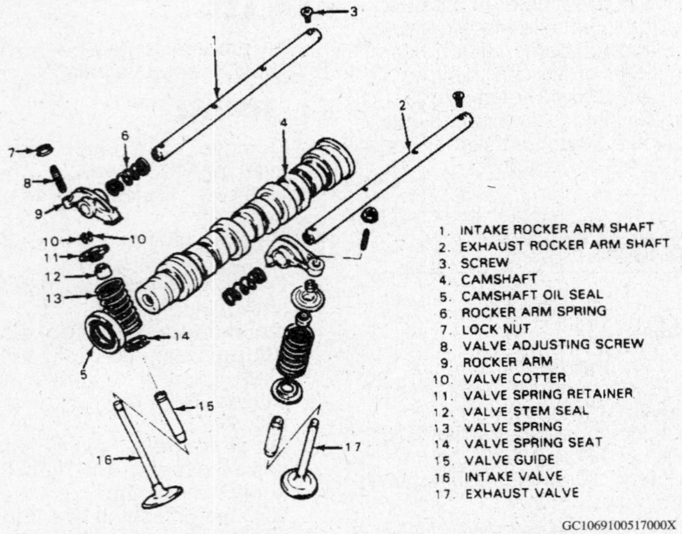

Fig. 4 Timing belt & cover assembly

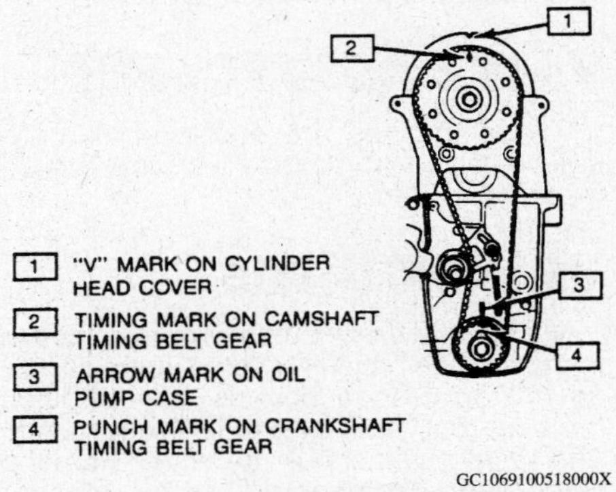

Fig. 5 Camshaft & crankshaft sprocket timing mark alignment

surface. **Arrow on camshaft housing should face camshaft sprocket side of cylinder head.** Camshaft housings are numbered from 1 to 3. The housings are positioned on the cylinder head in numerical order, starting with No. 1 at camshaft sprocket side of cylinder head, **Fig. 13.**

8. Apply engine oil to camshaft housing attaching bolts and studs, then loosely install bolts and studs. Tighten bolts and studs in sequence shown in **Fig. 14,** to specifications.
9. Apply engine oil to camshaft oil seal lip, then install seal. Seal surface should be flush with housing surface.
10. Hold camshaft in position by inserting a rod into .39 inch hole in camshaft, then install and tighten camshaft sprocket attaching bolt, **Fig. 10.** Place shop cloth under rod to prevent damage to cylinder head surface.
11. Install cylinder head cover.
12. Install timing belt as outlined under "Timing Belt, Replace."
13. Install ignition distributor, then install air cleaner assembly.
14. Adjust ignition timing.

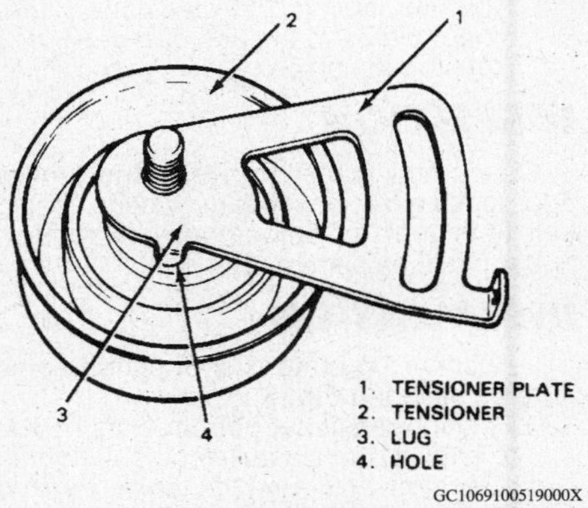

Fig. 6 Tensioner assembly

PISTON & ROD ASSEMBLY

Refer to **Fig. 15** when assembling piston and connecting rod. When installing piston and connecting rod, arrow on piston head should face front of engine and oil hole in connecting rod should face intake manifold. When installing connecting rod cap, arrow on cap should face front of engine.

Measure rod bearing side clearance using a feeler gauge. Connecting rod bearing side clearance should be .0039 to .0078 inch.

PISTONS, PINS & RINGS

Pistons and rings are available in standard size and oversizes of .010 and .020 inch. Piston pins are supplied with pistons in matched sets.

MAIN & ROD BEARINGS

Main and rod bearings are available in standard size and under size of .010 inch. Crankshaft thrust bearings are available in standard size and under size of .005 inch.

CRANKSHAFT REAR OIL SEAL

REPLACE

1. Remove transaxle as outlined under "Transaxle, Replace " in the "Automatic Transaxle" or " Clutch & Manual Transaxle" sections.
2. **On models with manual transaxle,** remove pressure plate and clutch disc.
3. **On all models,** remove flywheel.

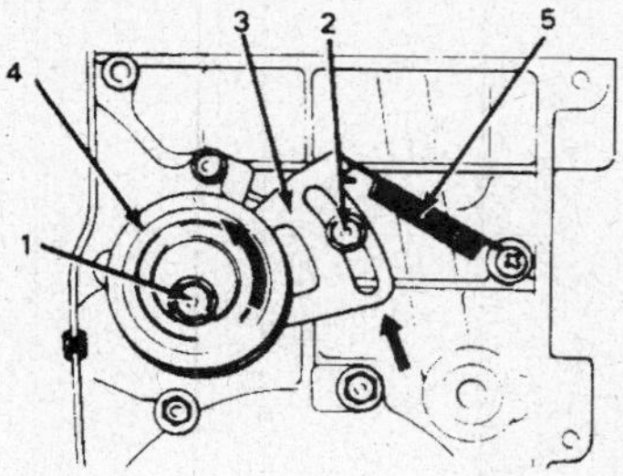

1. TENSIONER BOLT
2. TENSIONER STUD
3. TENSIONER PLATE
4. TENSIONER
5. SPRING

GC1069100520000X

Fig. 7 Tensioner plate movement check

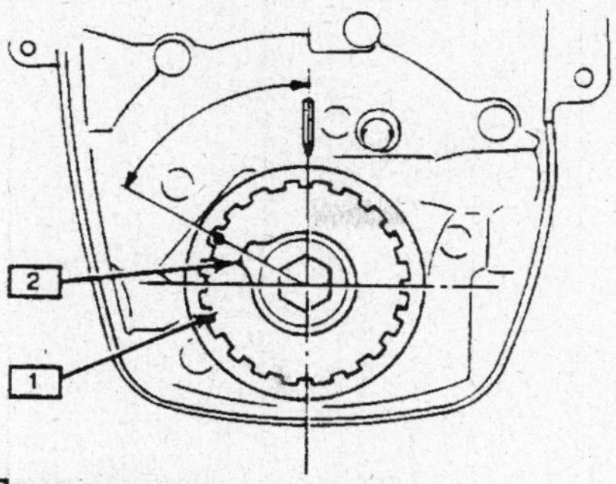

1 CRANKSHAFT TIMING BELT GEAR
2 KEY

GC1069100521000X

Fig. 8 Positioning crankshaft sprocket key

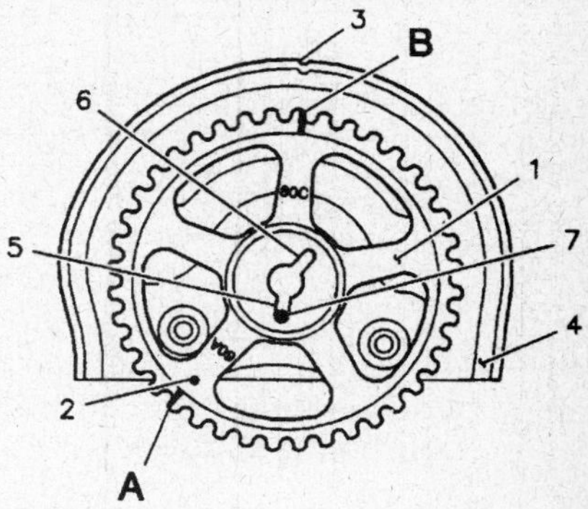

1	CAMSHAFT TIMING PULLEY	5	SLOT NO. 1
2	TIMING MARK	6	SLOT NO. 2
3	"V" MARK	7	PULLEY PIN
4	BELT INSIDE COVER		

GC1069500820000X

Fig. 9 Camshaft timing gear (spoked type)

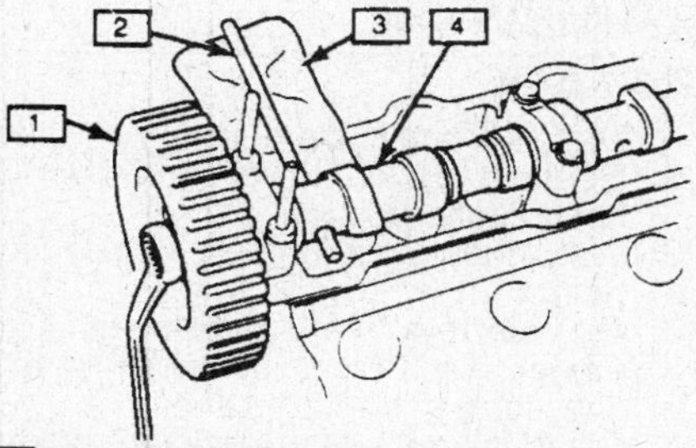

1 CAMSHAFT TIMING BELT GEAR
2 ROD
3 SHOP CLOTH
4 CAMSHAFT

GC1069100522000X

Fig. 10 Camshaft sprocket bolt removal & installation

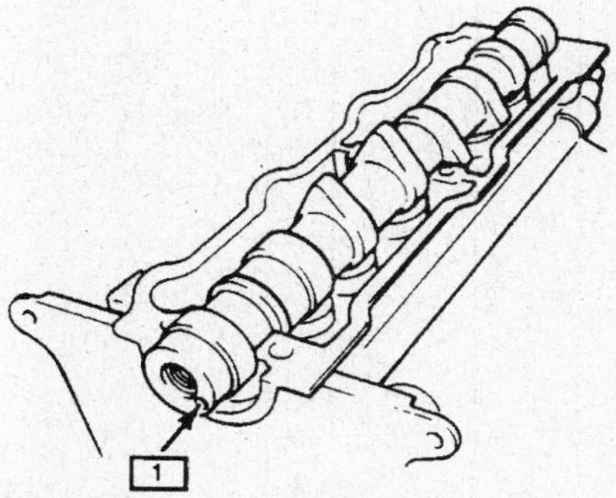

1 TIMING BELT GEAR PIN HOLE

GC1069100523000X

Fig. 11 Position camshaft sprocket pin hole

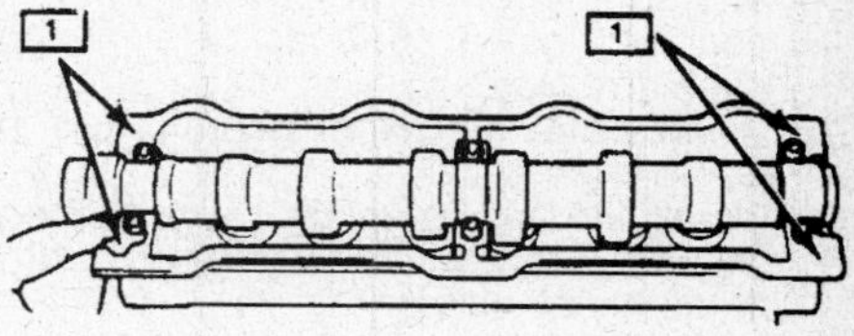

1 APPLY SEALANT

GC1069100524000X

Fig. 12 Camshaft housing to cylinder head surface sealant application

4. Remove seal retainer, then seal from retainer.
5. Reverse procedure to install.

OIL PAN

REPLACE

1. Raise and support vehicle.
2. Drain oil pan.
3. Remove flywheel dust cover.
4. Disconnect exhaust pipe at manifold.
5. Remove oil pan bolts and pan, **Fig. 16.**
6. Remove oil pump screen.
7. Reverse procedure to install. Apply continuous bead of silicon type sealer to oil pan flange inside bolt holes. When tightening oil pan attaching bolts, start at center and working outward. Tighten bolts to specifications.

OIL PUMP

REPLACE

REMOVAL

1. Refer to "Timing Belt, Replace" procedure to remove timing belt.
2. Refer to "Oil Pan, Replace" procedure to remove oil pan.
3. Remove crankshaft timing belt sprocket.
4. Remove alternator mounting bracket, if necessary.

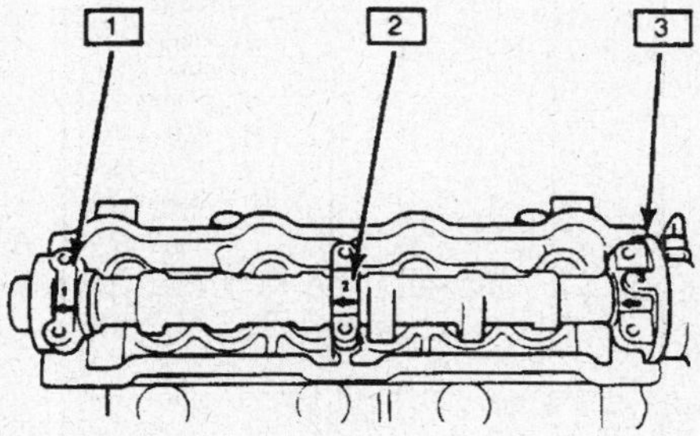

1 NO. 1 HOUSING
2 NO. 2 HOUSING
3 NO. 3 HOUSING

GC1069100525000X

Fig. 13 Camshaft housing locations

5. **On models with A/C,** remove compressor mounting bracket.
6. **On all models,** remove alternator adjusting bolt and upper cover bolt, if necessary.
7. Remove oil pump bolts and pump, **Fig. 17.**

INSTALLATION

1. Install oil pump pins and gasket on engine block.
2. Install oil seal guide tool No. J 34853, or equivalent, onto crankshaft to prevent damage to oil seal lip, **Fig. 18.** Apply engine oil to special tool.
3. Install oil pump onto crankshaft and engine block. Note location of attaching bolts, **Fig. 19. No. 1 bolts are shorter then No. 2 bolts in length.** Install bolts as shown in **Fig. 19,** then **tighten to specifications.**
4. After installing oil pump, check that oil seal lip is not twisted, then remove tool.
5. Install rubber seal between oil pump and water pump, **Fig. 20.**
6. If necessary, trim edges of oil pump seal flush with oil pan mating surface.
7. Install timing belt guide, key and crankshaft timing sprocket. Note that timing belt guide must be installed so that curved side faces oil pump.
8. Install timing belt and tensioner components.
9. Adjust water pump belt tension.
10. Fill crankcase.
11. Run engine to ensure oil pressure is correct.

OIL PUMP SERVICE

1. Remove dipstick tube from oil pump.
2. Remove gear/rotor plate screws and gear plate.
3. Remove outer and inner gears/rotors.
4. Inspect oil seal lip for damage and replace as necessary.
5. Inspect outer and inner gears/rotors,

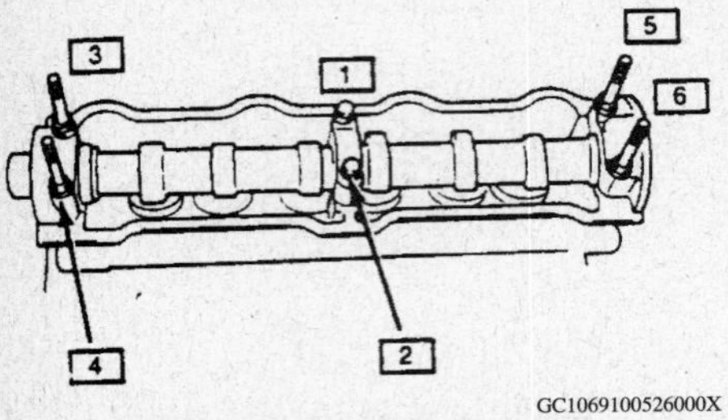

Fig. 14 Camshaft housing bolt tightening sequence

gear/rotor plate and oil pump case for excessive wear or damage.

6. Using feeler gauge, check radial clearance between outer gear/rotor and crescent, **Fig. 21.** If clearance exceeds .0122 inch, replace outer gear/rotor.
7. Using straightedge and feeler gauge, measure side clearance which should not exceed .0059 inch, **Fig. 22.**
8. Wash, clean and dry all oil pump parts.
9. Apply light coat of engine oil to inner and outer gears/rotors, oil seal lip portion and inside surfaces of oil pump case and plate.
10. Install outer and inner gears/rotors in pump case.
11. Install gear/rotor plate and tighten screws securely. Check that gears turn smoothly by hand.
12. Install O-ring in pump case, then dipstick tube.

BELT TENSION DATA

Belt	Belt Deflection Inch①
A/C COMPRESSOR	
All	.28–.35
ALTERNATOR & WATER PUMP	
New	.20–.27
Used	.24–.31

① — With thumb pressure applied.

COOLING SYSTEM BLEED

These engines do not require a specified bleed procedure. After filling cooling system, run engine to operating temperature with radiator/pressure cap off. Air will then be automatically bled through cap opening.

THERMOSTAT

REPLACE

1. Drain cooling system.
2. Remove radiator inlet hose at thermostat housing.
3. Remove thermostat housing and thermostat.
4. Clean both gasket surfaces thoroughly.
5. Reverse procedure to install.

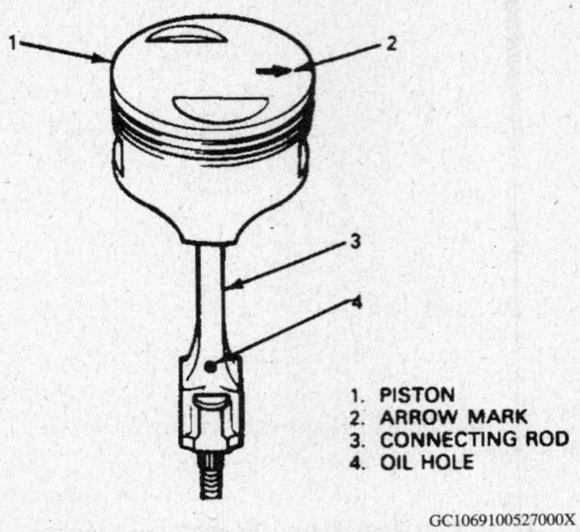

Fig. 15 Piston & connecting rod assembly

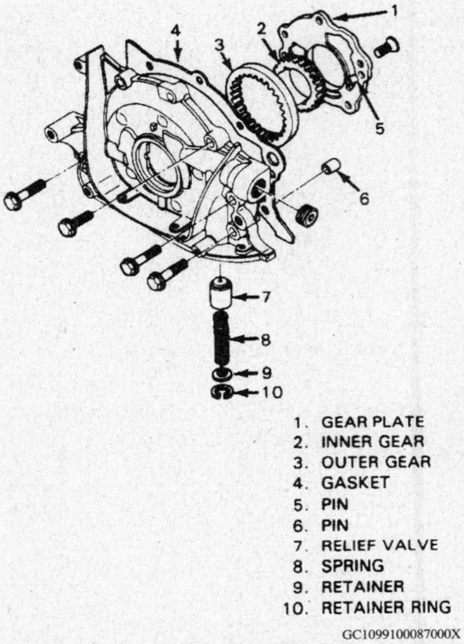

Fig. 17 Rotor type (Trochoid) oil pump

WATER PUMP

REPLACE

1. Drain cooling system.
2. Remove drive belt, water pump pulley, crankshaft pulley, timing belt outside cover, timing belt and timing belt tensioner.
3. Remove water pump attaching bolts and nuts and water pump.
4. Install water pump on engine block.
5. Install rubber seals between water pump and oil pump and between water pump and cylinder head, **Fig. 23.**
6. Install timing belt tensioner, timing belt, timing belt outside cover, crankshaft pulley, water pump pulley and drive belt.
7. Tighten drive belt so it deflects .25–.35 inch on span between water pump pulley and crankshaft pulley.
8. Install valve cover and air cleaner.
9. Fill cooling system.

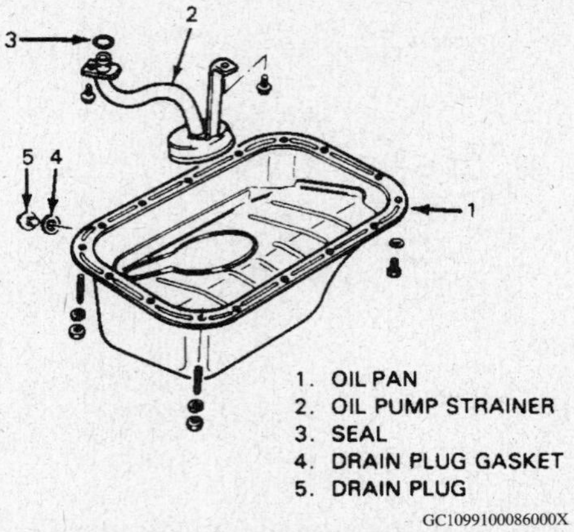

Fig. 16 Oil pan & pick-up tube

RADIATOR

REPLACE

1. Drain cooling system.
2. Remove upper, lower and overflow hoses from radiator.
3. Disconnect cooling fan electrical connector.
4. **On models with automatic transaxle,** disconnect transaxle cooling lines from bottom of radiator.
5. **On all models,** remove upper radiator/fan attaching bolts, then radiator/fan assembly from vehicle.
6. Reverse procedure to install.

FUEL PUMP

REPLACE

1997

1. Relieve fuel system pressure as outlined under "Fuel System Pressure Relief" under "Precautions."
2. Remove rear seat cushion, then disconnect fuel pump and sending unit electrical connectors, then push harness through floor pan grommet.
3. Drain fuel tank, then disconnect inlet hose from fuel filter.
4. Disconnect fuel filler hose from fuel tank.
5. Disconnect vapor hoses and fuel feed and return hoses at fuel tank and pump.
6. Remove fuel tank attaching bolts, then lower fuel tank from vehicle.
7. Remove fuel pump to fuel tank attaching bolts, then fuel pump, **Fig. 24.**
8. Separate fuel pump from motor and sending unit as necessary.
9. Reverse procedure to install.

1998–2000

1. Relieve fuel system pressure as outlined under "Precautions."
2. Remove rear seat cushion, disconnect fuel pump and sending unit electrical connections, then push harness through floor pan grommet.
3. Drain fuel tank.
4. Raise and support vehicle.
5. Remove muffler and exhaust pipe assembly.

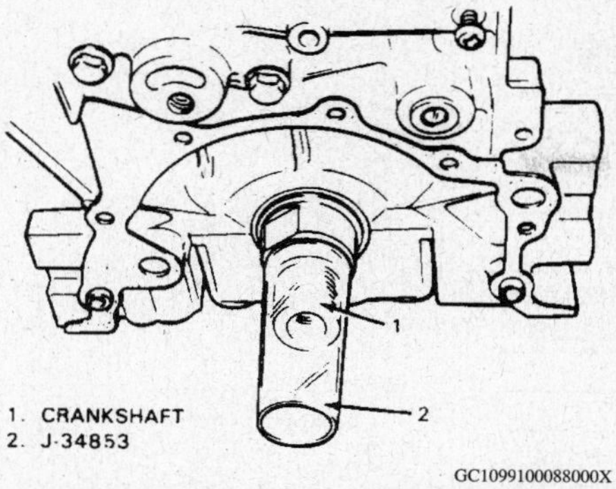

Fig. 18 Crankshaft oil seal guide tool installation

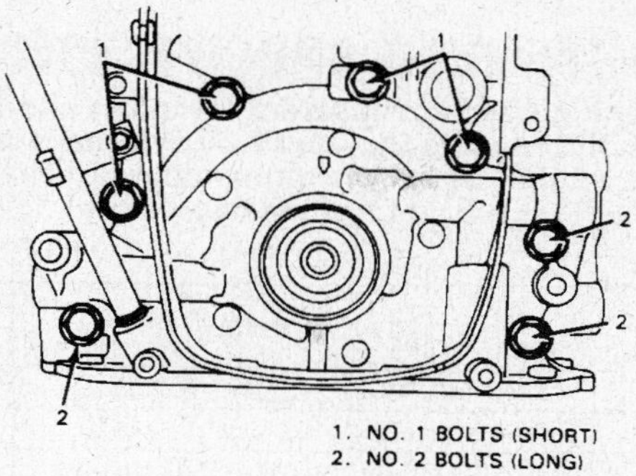

Fig. 19 Oil pump bolt location

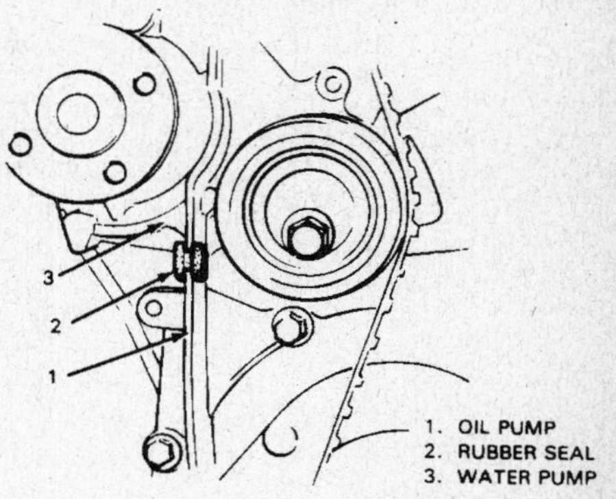

Fig. 20 Rubber seal installation

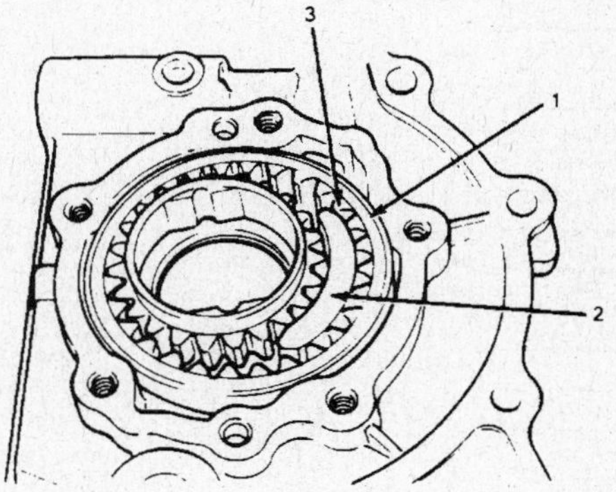

Fig. 21 Oil pump gear radial clearance check. Rotor type similar

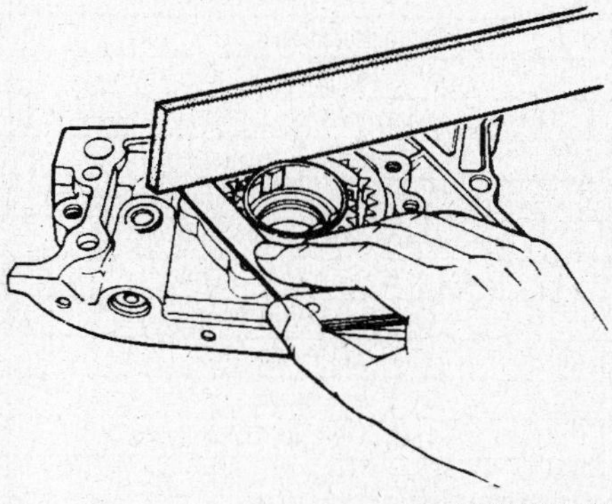

Fig. 22 Oil pump gear side clearance check. Rotor type similar

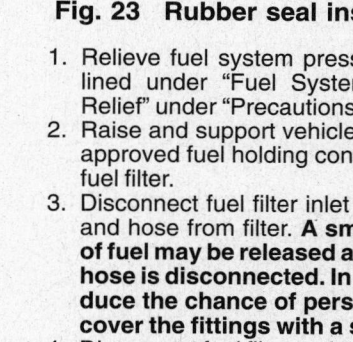

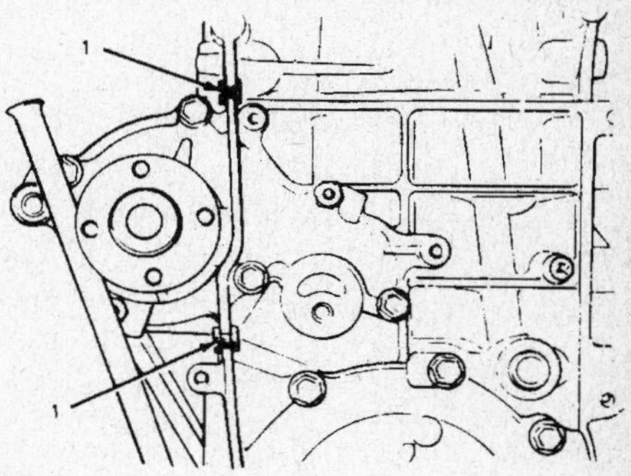

Fig. 23 Rubber seal installation

6. Remove fuel filler neck hose, fuel breather hose, then EVAP canister air inlet hose.
7. Remove parking brake cable and position aside.
8. Remove EVAP canister vapor hose, fuel feed and return hoses at fuel tank and pump.
9. Remove fuel tank attaching bolts, then lower fuel tank from vehicle.
10. Disconnect fuel sender electrical connections and vapor hoses, then fuel feed and return lines.
11. Remove fuel sender assembly from fuel tank.
12. Separate fuel pump from fuel sender assembly as required.
13. Reverse procedure to install.

FUEL FILTER

REPLACE

1997

The fuel filter is located at the lefthand front corner of the fuel tank assembly.

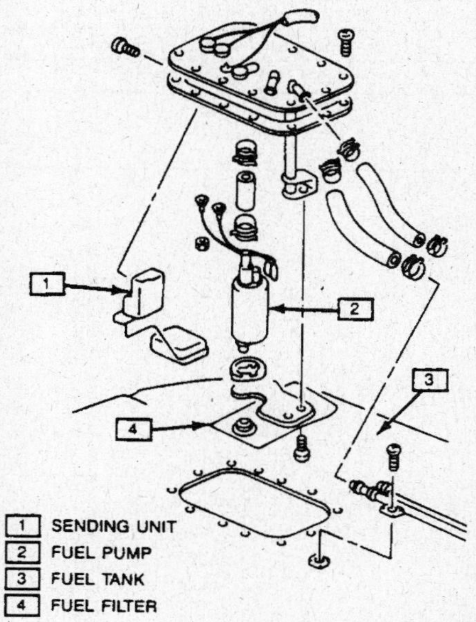

Fig. 24 Electric fuel pump & sending unit removal

1. Relieve fuel system pressure as outlined under "Fuel System Pressure Relief" under "Precautions."
2. Raise and support vehicle, then place approved fuel holding container under fuel filter.
3. Disconnect fuel filter inlet hose clamp and hose from filter. **A small amount of fuel may be released after the fuel hose is disconnected. In order to reduce the chance of personal injury, cover the fittings with a shop towel.**
4. Disconnect fuel filter outlet hose clamp and hose from filter.
5. Remove mounting bracket and filter as an assembly.
6. Reverse procedure to install.

1998–2000

The fuel filter is part of fuel sender assembly located in the fuel tank. The fuel sender assembly must be removed in order to replace fuel sender subassembly that contains fuel filter as outlined under "Fuel Pump, Replace."

TIGHTENING SPECIFICATIONS

Tightening specifications are for clean and lightly lubricated threads only. Dry or dirty threads produce increased friction which prevents accurate measurement of tightness.

Year	Component	Torque/ Ft. Lbs.
1997–2000	Alternator Mounting Bolts & Nuts	17
	Camshaft Housing To Cylinder Head	97①
	Camshaft Sprocket Bolt	44
	Connecting Rod Cap Bolts	26
	Crankshaft Pulley Bolts	12
	Crankshaft Sprocket Bolt	94
	Cylinder Head Bolts	54
	Cylinder Head Cover	97①
	Exhaust Manifold To Cylinder Head	17
	Flywheel To Crankshaft	55
	Ignition Distributor To Cylinder Head	10
	Intake Manifold To Cylinder Head	17
	Main Bearing Cap Bolts	40
	Oil Pan Drain Plug	26
	Oil Pan To Engine	97①
	Oil Pressure Switch	10
	Oil Pump Pickup Tube Bolts	97①
	Oil Pump Rotor Plate Screws	97①
	Oil Pump To Engine	97①
	Spark Plug	21
	Starter Mounting Bolts	17
	Timing Belt Cover Nuts & Bolts	97①
	Timing Belt Tensioner Bolt	20
	Timing Belt Tensioner Stud	97①
	Water Pump To Engine	10

① — Inch lbs.

1.3L Engine

NOTE: On Air Bag Equipped Models, Refer To "Air Bag System Precautions" Located In The Front Of This Manual For System Disarming & Arming Procedures.

NOTE: Refer To "Computer Relearn Procedures " Located In The Front Of This Manual For Computer Relearn Procedures.

INDEX

PRECAUTIONS

AIR BAG SYSTEMS

Refer to "Air Bag System Precautions" in the front of this manual for system disarming and arming procedures.

BATTERY GROUND CABLE

Prior to service, disconnect battery ground cable and isolate as required.

FUEL SYSTEM PRESSURE RELIEF

1. Loosen fuel filler cap to relieve fuel tank pressure.
2. Remove fuel pump relay from relay box located at the lefthand front of the engine compartment, next to the battery. Refer to "Fuel Pump Relay Location" in the "Electrical" section.
3. Crank engine and allow to stall. Crank engine for several seconds more to ensure relief of any remaining fuel.
4. Remove battery ground cable.

COMPRESSION PRESSURE

1. Turn ignition switch to Lock position.
2. Clean debris from spark plug holes if necessary and remove spark plugs.
3. **On 1997 models** disconnect distributor electrical connector and remove FI fuse from fuse and relay box.
4. **On 1998–2000 models** disconnect ignition coils electrical connectors
5. **On all models** install spark plug port adapter tool No. J 22794, or equivalent and a compression gauge into spark plug hole.
6. **On models equipped with manual transaxle,** depress clutch and accelerator to floor.
7. **On all models,** crank engine and take four pressure readings, noting the highest reading obtained.
8. Compression should increase quickly and evenly. Compression pressure at 250 RPM is 199 psi standard and 156 psi minimum. Maximum allowable pressure difference between any two cylinders at 250 RPM is 14 psi.
9. Repeat compression test procedure for remaining cylinders.
10. After completion, install FI fuse, spark plugs and distributor electrical connector.

ENGINE MOUNT

REPLACE

LEFT

1. Remove engine mount nut, then raise and support vehicle.
2. Support engine using an engine support fixture.
3. Remove engine mount and frame bracket, then mount from bracket.
4. Reverse procedure to install.

RIGHT

1. Remove engine mount nut, then raise and support vehicle.
2. Support engine using an engine support fixture.
3. Remove engine mount and frame bracket, then mount from bracket.
4. Reverse procedure to install.

REAR

1. Remove engine mount nut, then raise and support vehicle.
2. Remove nut attaching mount to body bracket.
3. Support engine using an engine support fixture.
4. Remove frame bracket, then mount.
5. Reverse procedure to install.

TORQUE ROD

1. Remove engine mount nut, then raise and support vehicle.
2. Remove nut attaching mount to body bracket.
3. Support engine using an engine support fixture.
4. Remove frame bracket, then mount.
5. Reverse procedure to install.

ENGINE

REPLACE

1997

1. Relieve fuel system pressure as outlined under "Precautions."
2. Disconnect battery cables and remove battery.
3. Disconnect windshield washer hose, then remove hood.
4. Remove air cleaner assembly.
5. Drain cooling system, then remove radiator and engine cooling fan.
6. Disconnect high tension lead from ignition coil.
7. Disconnect electrical connectors from body harness.
8. Disconnect battery ground cable from transaxle.
9. **On models with manual transaxle,** disconnect electrical connector from back-up lamp switch.
10. **On models with automatic transaxle,** disconnect electrical connectors from neutral safety switch and speed sensor.
11. **On all models,** disconnect intake manifold to power brake unit vacuum hose.
12. Disconnect evaporative emission canister hoses from intake manifold and tube connections.
13. Disconnect fuel hoses from throttle body.
14. Disconnect heater hoses from engine.
15. Disconnect accelerator cable from throttle body.
16. **On models with manual transaxle,** disconnect clutch cable from fork and housing.
17. **On models with automatic transaxle,** disconnect shift control and fluid pressure control cables from transaxle.
18. **On all models,** disconnect speedometer cable from transaxle.
19. Raise and support vehicle, then disconnect exhaust pipe from exhaust manifold.
20. Drain engine crankcase, then drain fluid from transaxle.
21. **On models with manual transaxle,** disconnect control shaft and extension rod from transaxle.
22. **On all models,** separate drive axles from transaxle. Suspend drive axles from chassis using wire.
23. **On models with automatic transaxle,** remove engine torque rod bracket from transaxle.
24. **On all models,** lower vehicle and install an engine lifting fixture.
25. Remove engine and transaxle attaching bolts, then engine and transaxle assembly from vehicle.
26. Reverse procedure to install.

1998–2000

1. Relieve fuel system pressure as outlined under "Precautions."
2. Remove both battery cables, battery and battery tray.
3. Drain cooling system into a suitable container.
4. Remove hood.
5. Remove air cleaner assembly.
6. Remove radiator with cooling fan.
7. Disconnect coolant temperature gauge sensor, throttle position sensor and EGR solenoid electrical connectors.
8. Disconnect EGR bypass valve.
9. Disconnect idle speed control solenoid valve, oxygen sensor, fuel injector, MAP sensor and power steering pressure switch electrical connectors.
10. Disconnect ground wires from intake manifold.
11. Disconnect oil pressure switch, alternator and A/C compressor connectors.
12. Disconnect starter solenoid connectors.
13. Disconnect backup lamp switch.
14. Disconnect direct clutch and second brake solenoids.
15. Release main engine harness from clamps.
16. Disconnect following vacuum hoses:
    a. Front and rear canister purge hoses from intake manifold.
    b. Canister hose from canister pipe.
    c. Pressure sensor hose from intake.
    d. Brake booster hose from intake.
    e. Idle speed control hose from throttle body.
17. Disconnect the following cables:
    a. Accelerator cable from throttle body.
    b. Clutch cable from transaxle.
    c. Shift select cable and throttle valve cable from transaxle.
    d. Speedometer cable from transaxle.
18. Remove inlet and outlet hoses.
19. Remove fuel return and feed hoses from throttle body.
20. Install universal support fixture tool No. J 28467–A with engine support adapters tool No. J 28467–89 or equivalents.
21. Raise and support vehicle.
22. Disconnect exhaust system from exhaust manifold.
23. Remove front pipe/catalytic converter assembly.
24. **On models equipped with manual transaxle** remove gearshift control shaft and extension rod.
25. **On all models** drain engine oil and transaxle fluid into a suitable container.
26. Remove left and right drive axles from transaxle as outlined in the "Front Wheel Drive Axle" section. **It is not necessary to remove driveshafts from steering knuckles.**
27. Remove A/C compressor from compressor bracket. **Do not disconnect A/C hoses from compressor.**
28. Disconnect power steering hoses from power steering pump.
29. **On models equipped with automatic transaxle** remove torque rod.
30. **On all models** lower vehicle.
31. Remove tool Nos. J 28467–A and J 28467–89, or equivalents, and install a suitable engine lifting device.
32. Remove left transaxle mount, right side engine mount and rear engine mount.
33. Remove engine with transaxle from vehicle.
34. Reverse procedure to install tightening all fasteners and filling all fluids to specification.

INTAKE MANIFOLD

REPLACE

1997

1. Relieve fuel system pressure as outlined under "Precautions."
2. Drain cooling system, then remove air cleaner assembly.
3. Disconnect electrical connectors from coolant temperature sender, engine and coolant temperature sensor.
4. Disconnect electrical connector from EGR vacuum switching valve.
5. Disconnect electrical connectors from idle speed control valve, throttle position switch, oxygen sensor and fuel injector.
6. Disconnect ground wires from intake manifold.
7. Disconnect fuel hoses from throttle body.
8. Disconnect coolant hoses from intake manifold.
9. Disconnect MAP sensor hose from intake manifold.
10. Disconnect evaporative emission hoses from intake manifold and tube.
11. Disconnect power brake unit vacuum hose from intake manifold.
12. Disconnect PCV valve hose from cylinder head cover.
13. Disconnect accelerator cable from throttle body.
14. Disconnect all other electrical connectors and hoses to permit intake manifold and throttle body removal.
15. Remove intake manifold to cylinder head attaching nuts and bolts, then intake manifold and throttle body as an assembly.
16. Reverse procedure to install, ensuring to install new gasket. Tighten fasteners to specifications.

1998–2000

1. Relieve fuel system pressure as outlined under "Precautions."
2. Drain cooling system into a suitable container.
3. Remove air cleaner assembly.
4. Disconnect ground wires from intake manifold.
5. Disconnect fuel injector, MAP sensor, TP sensor, IAC valve and EVAP canister purge valve electrical connectors, **Fig. 1.**
6. Disconnect wiring harness from retaining clamps.
7. Remove coolant hoses from throttle body.
8. Remove canister purge and brake booster hoses from intake manifold.
9. Remove accelerator cable from throttle body.
10. Remove seven nuts and three bolts from intake manifold.
11. Remove intake manifold with throttle body and wire clamps from cylinder head still attached.
12. Reverse procedure to install. Adjust accelerator cable freeplay as follows:

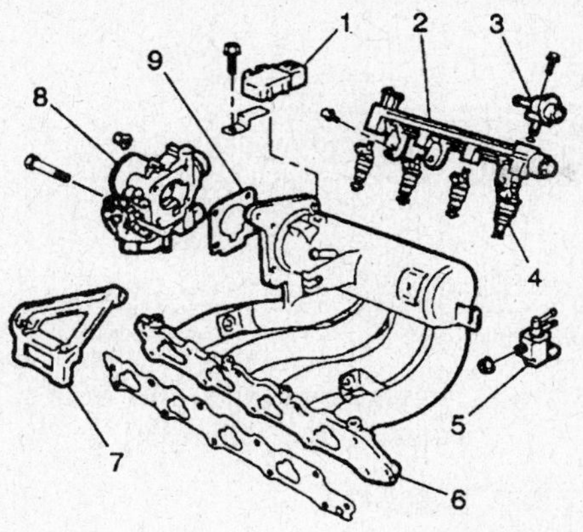

GC1139800681010X

Fig. 1 Intake manifold replacement (Part 1 of 2). 1998–2000

a. Measure accelerator pedal for .08–.27 inch of freeplay with throttle closed, **Fig. 2.**
b. If freeplay is within specifications, go to step e.
c. Loosen accelerator control cable locknut.
d. Turn accelerator control cable adjusting nut in order to obtain .08–.27 inch of freeplay.
e. Depress accelerator pedal to floor.
f. Measure distance, with a suitable feeler gauge between throttle lever and throttle stop.
g. Specifications should be .02–.07 inch.
h. If not within specifications, adjust height of pedal stopper bolt.
i. Operate accelerator control cable from inside of vehicle in order to ensure throttle movement is smooth and not binding.

EXHAUST MANIFOLD

REPLACE

1. Raise and support vehicle.
2. Disconnect catalytic converter from manifold, then lower vehicle.
3. Disconnect oxygen sensor electrical connector, then release wiring harness from clamps.
4. Remove heat shield and engine hanger.
5. Disconnect exhaust pipe from exhaust manifold.
6. Remove exhaust manifold attaching bolts and nuts, then exhaust manifold from cylinder head.
7. Reverse procedure to install, ensuring to install new gasket. Tighten fasteners to specifications.

CYLINDER HEAD

REPLACE

1997

1. Relieve fuel system pressure as outlined under "Precautions."
2. Drain cooling system, then remove air cleaner assembly.

1. MAP SENSOR
2. FUEL RAIL
3. FUEL PRESSURE REGULATOR
4. FUEL INJECTOR
5. EVAP CANISTER PURGE VALVE
6. INTAKE MANIFOLD
7. BRACKET
8. THROTTLE BODY
9. THROTTLE BODY GASKET

GC1139800681020X

Fig. 1 Intake manifold replacement (Part 2 of 2). 1998–2000

3. Remove intake manifold as outlined under "Intake Manifold, Replace."
4. Remove timing belt and tensioner as outlined under "Timing Belt, Replace."
5. Raise and support vehicle, then disconnect exhaust pipe from exhaust manifold.
6. Lower vehicle, then remove cylinder head cover.
7. Remove cylinder head attaching bolts, then cylinder head.
8. Reverse procedure to install. Tighten cylinder head bolts in several passes in sequence shown in **Fig. 3,** to specifications.

1998-2000

1. Relieve fuel system pressure as outlined under "Precautions."
2. Remove intake manifold as outlined under "Intake Manifold, Replace."
3. Remove exhaust manifold as outlined under "Exhaust Manifold, Replace."
4. Remove timing belt and belt tensioner as outlined under "Timing Belt, Replace."
5. Remove valve cover as outlined under "Valve Cover, Replace."
6. Loosen all valve lash adjusting screw locknuts.
7. Turn back valve lash adjusting screw until all valve are closed.
8. Remove head bolts in sequence shown in **Fig. 4. Ensure head bolts are removed in proper sequence to prevent warpage of cylinder head.**
9. Remove cylinder head and discard gasket.
10. Reverse procedure to install, noting the following:
    a. Install cylinder head bolts loosely in order to secure cylinder head.
    b. **Torque** cylinder head bolts evenly and in small increments to 49 ft. lbs. in sequence shown in **Fig. 5.**
    c. Refill cooling system to specification.

VALVE ARRANGEMENT

FRONT TO REAR

1.3L ....I-E-I-E-I-E-I-E

VALVE ADJUSTMENT

1997

These engines are equipped with hydraulic valve lash adjusters and no adjustment is required.

1998-2000

1. Set number one cylinder to top dead center on compression stroke.
2. Ensure camshaft is in proper phase.

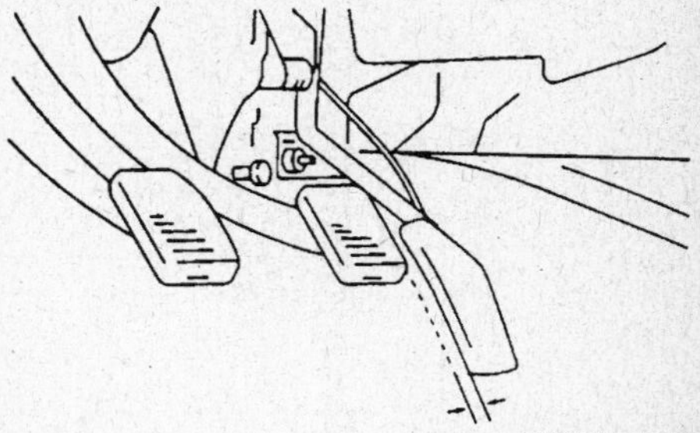

GC1139800682000X

Fig. 2 Accelerator pedal freeplay. 1998–2000

3. Adjust valves 1, 2, 8 and 6 as follows: **Fig. 6.**
    a. Intake valve to .005–.007 inch, cold.
    b. Exhaust valve to .009–.011 inch, cold.
    c. Intake valve to .007–.008 inch, hot.
    d. Exhaust valve to .011–.013 inch, hot.
4. Rotate crankshaft 360.°
5. Adjust valves 3, 4, 7 and 5 as follows: **Fig. 6.**
    a. Intake valve to .005–.007 inch, cold.
    b. Exhaust valve to .009–.01 inch, cold.
    c. Intake valve to .007–.008 inch, hot.
    d. Exhaust valve to .011–.013 inch, hot.

VALVE GUIDES

Valves and valve guides are available in standard size only. The valve guide can be driven from cylinder bore using valve guide remover/installer tool No. J 34834, or equivalent. The valve guide should be driven from the combustion chamber side of the cylinder head out through the valve spring side.

The cylinder head valve guide bore should be reamed with 12 mm reamer tool No. 34831, or equivalent, prior to valve guide installation. Drive valve guide into heated cylinder head bore using valve guide remover/installer tool No. J 34834, or equivalent. Valve guide should be driven in until tool contacts cylinder head. Valve guide protrusion should be .55 inch from cylinder head surface. After installation, ream valve guide with a 7 mm reamer tool No. J 34832, or equivalent.

TIMING BELT

REPLACE

REMOVAL

1. Raise and support vehicle.
2. Remove crankshaft timing pulley.
3. Remove timing belt cover, **Fig. 7.**
4. Align upper and lower timing marks, **Figs. 8 and 9,** by turning crankshaft.
5. Remove tensioner assembly and timing belt.

INSPECTION

Check timing belt for wear and cracks and replace as necessary. Check timing belt tensioner for smoothness of rotation and replace as necessary.

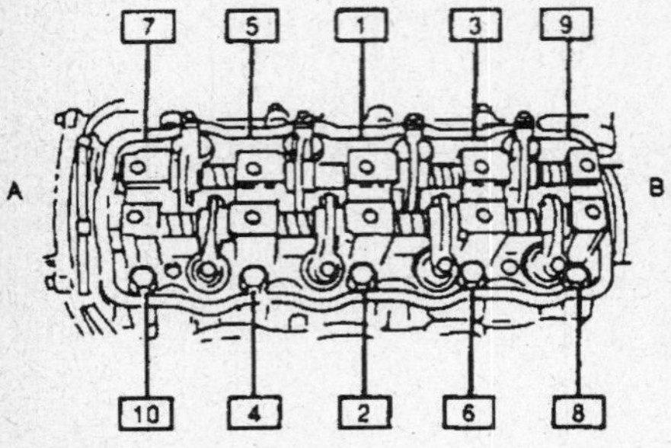

A CAMSHAFT PULLEY SIDE
B DISTRIBUTOR SIDE

GC1069500586000X

Fig. 3 Cylinder head tightening sequence. 1997

INSTALLATION

1. Position lug on tensioner plate to hole in tensioner, **Fig. 10.**
2. Position tensioner and tensioner plate to engine, then install and hand tighten attaching bolt. Ensure tensioner and tensioner plate move in the same direction, **Fig. 11.** If movement is not as indicated, remove tensioner and reinsert tensioner plate lug into tensioner.
3. Ensure camshaft and crankshaft timing marks are aligned,
4. Remove cylinder head cover and completely loosen all valve adjusting screws on intake and exhaust rocker arms. This will permit free rotation of camshaft and prevent damage to valves during timing belt adjustment.
5. With tensioner plate pushed upward, install timing belt over camshaft and crankshaft pulleys. **Arrow on timing belt should face toward direction of crankshaft rotation. When installing timing belt, keep drive side of belt free of slack.**
6. Install tensioner spring and damper, then hand tighten tensioner stud.
7. Rotate crankshaft two revolutions clockwise direction to remove slack from belt. **Ensure slack is removed from drive belt and that camshaft and crankshaft timing marks are aligned.**
8. Tighten tensioner stud, then tensioner bolt to specifications.
9. Install timing belt outer cover and crankshaft pulley. **Ensure seal is between oil pump housing and water pump.**
10. Adjust valve lash, install cylinder head cover and lower vehicle.

CAMSHAFT

REPLACE

1997

Removal

1. **On models with A/C,** remove compressor and bracket.
2. **On all models,** remove air cleaner assembly, then cylinder head cover.
3. Remove distributor from cylinder head.

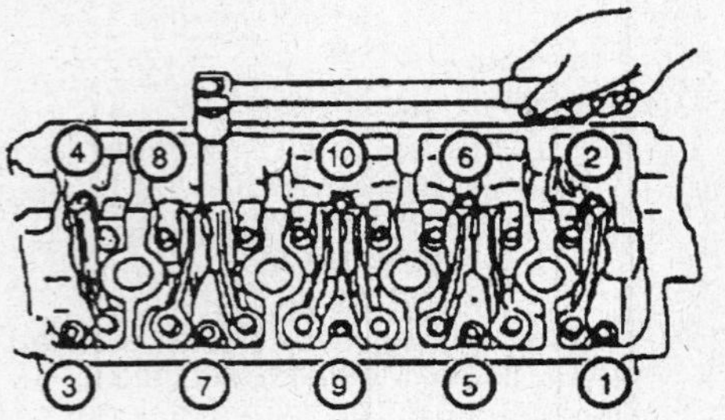

GC1139800683000X

Fig. 4 Cylinder head loosing sequence. 1998–2000

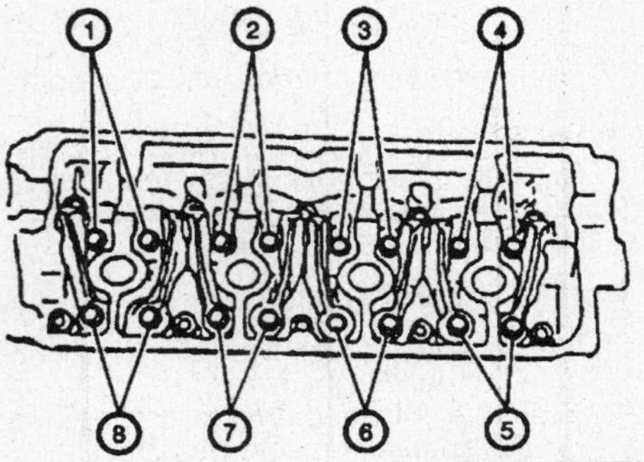

GC1139800677000X

Fig. 6 Valve lash adjustment. 1998–2000

4. Remove rocker arm shafts, springs and rocker arms.
5. Remove timing belt as outlined under "Timing Belt, Replace."
6. Hold camshaft in position by inserting a rod into .39 inch hole in camshaft, then remove camshaft sprocket attaching bolt, **Fig. 12.** Place shop cloth under rod to prevent damage to cylinder head surface.
7. Remove camshaft housings to cylinder head attaching bolts and studs.
8. Remove camshaft from cylinder head.

Installation

1. Lubricate camshaft with engine oil, then position on cylinder head.
2. Rotate crankshaft clockwise and align the punch mark on the crankshaft timing belt gear with the arrow timing mark on the oil pump.
3. Lock camshaft in position by inserting a rod into .39 inch hole in camshaft.
4. Install camshaft timing sprocket to camshaft, ensuring pin on camshaft fits into slot on sprocket. Secure with bolt.
5. Install intake rocker arm shaft with stepped end toward distributor side.
6. Using rocker shaft assembly installer tool No. J 42388, or equivalent, install rocker arms, springs and rocker arm shafts, **Fig. 13.**
7. Tighten rocker shaft assembly in sequence shown in **Fig. 14.**
8. Install cylinder head cover.
9. Install timing belt as outlined under "Timing Belt, Replace."
10. Install ignition distributor, then install air cleaner assembly.
11. **On models with A/C,** install compressor and bracket.

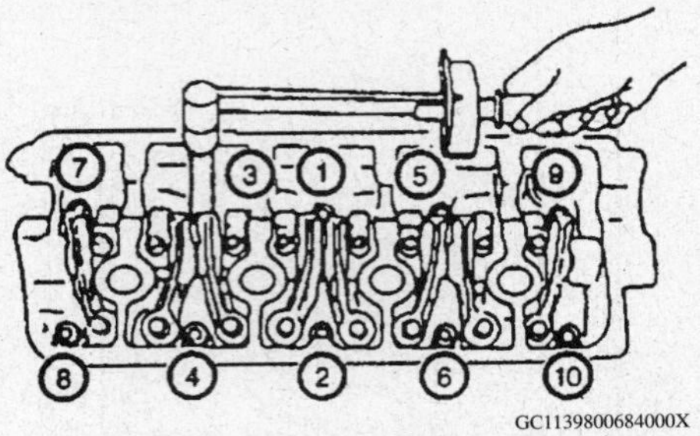

GC1139800684000X

Fig. 5 Cylinder head tightening sequence. 1998–2000

1998–2000

Removal

1. Remove valve cover as outlined under "Valve Cover, Replace."
2. Remove timing belt and timing belt tensioner as outlined under "Timing Belt, Replace."
3. Remove camshaft timing sprocket bolt, then the sprocket.
4. Disconnect cam sensor electrical connector.
5. Disconnect spark plug wires and ignition coil electrical connectors.
6. Remove ignition coils.
7. Remove cam sensor from cylinder head.
8. Loosen all valve adjusting screw lock nuts, back off adjusting screws to allow rocker arms to move freely.
9. Gradually remove twelve camshaft housing bolts in sequence shown in **Fig. 15.**

Installation

1. Apply clean engine oil to camshaft, journals and oil seal.
2. Install camshaft to cylinder head, apply clean engine oil to housing bolts and **torque** housing bolts to 8 ft. lbs. in sequence shown in **Fig. 16.**
3. Install camshaft timing sprocket to camshaft.
4. Ensure pin on camshaft fits slot on sprocket.
5. **Torque** camshaft timing sprocket to 43 ft. lbs.
6. Perform valve lash adjustment as outlined under "Valve Adjustment."
7. Connect cam sensor connector, spark plug wires and ignition coil assemblies.
8. Install timing belt as outlined under "Timing Belt, Replace."
9. Install cylinder head cover as outlined "Valve Cover, Replace."

PISTON & ROD ASSEMBLY

Refer to **Fig. 17** when assembling piston and connecting rod. When installing piston and connecting rod, arrow on piston head should face front of engine and oil hole in connecting rod should face intake manifold. When installing connecting rod cap, arrow on cap should face front of engine.

Measure rod bearing side clearance

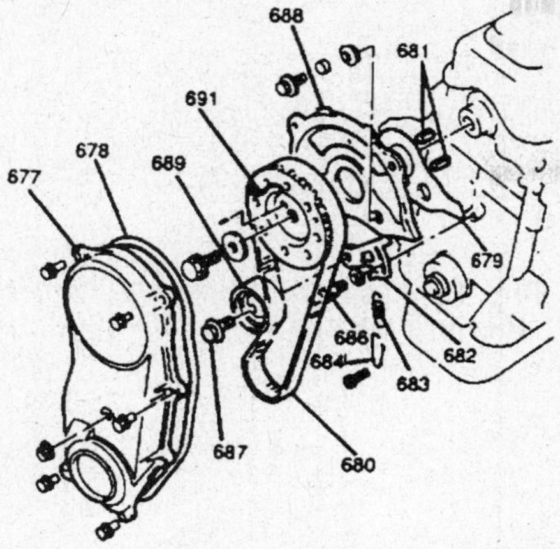

677 TIMING BELT COVER
678 OUTER TIMING BELT COVER GASKET
679 TIMING BELT INNER SEAL
680 TIMING BELT
681 SEAL
682 TENSIONER PLATE
683 TENSIONER SPRING
684 SPRING DAMPER
686 TENSIONER STUD
687 TENSIONER BOLT
688 TIMING BELT INNER COVER
689 TIMING BELT TENSIONER
691 CAMSHAFT TIMING GEAR SPROCKET

GC1069500587000X

Fig. 7 Timing belt assembly

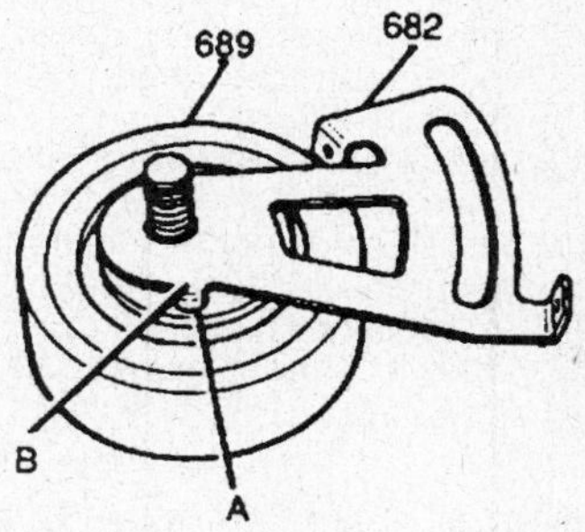

A TIMING BELT TENSIONER HOLE
B TENSIONER PLATE LUG
682 TENSIONER PLATE
689 TIMING BELT TENSIONER

GC1069500590000X

Fig. 10 Timing belt tensioner

using a feeler gauge. Connecting rod bearing side clearance should be .0039 to .0078 inch.

PISTONS, PINS & RINGS

Pistons and rings are available in standard size and oversizes of .0098 and .0197 inch. Piston pins are supplied with pistons in matched sets.

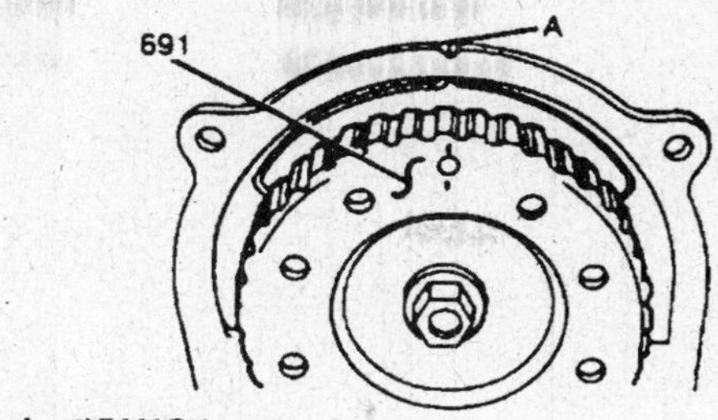

A "V" MARK
691 CAMSHAFT TIMING GEAR SPROCKET

GC1069500588000X

Fig. 8 Camshaft timing mark

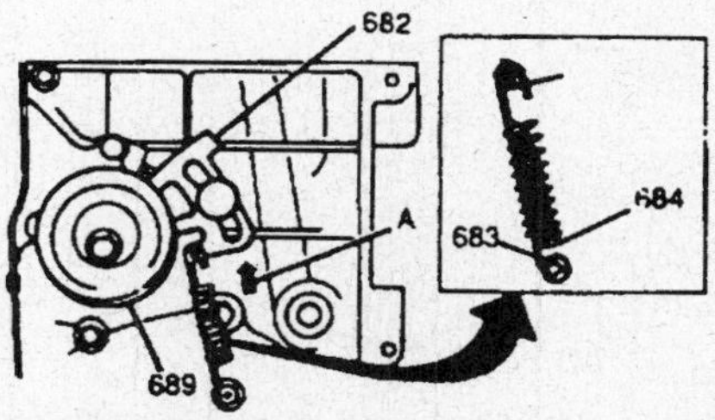

A DIRECTION OF TENSIONER MOVEMENT
682 TENSIONER PLATE
683 TENSIONER SPRING
684 SPRING DAMPER
689 TIMING BELT TENSIONER

GC1069500591000X

Fig. 11 Tensioner adjustment

MAIN & ROD BEARINGS

Main and rod bearings are available in standard size and under size of .010 inch.

CRANKSHAFT REAR OIL SEAL

REPLACE

1. Remove transaxle as outlined under "Transaxle, Replace " in the "Automatic Transaxle" or " Clutch & Manual Transaxle" sections.
2. **On models with manual transaxle,** remove pressure plate and clutch disc.
3. **On all models,** mark flywheel to engine position, then remove flywheel.
4. Remove oil pan as outlined under "Oil Pan, Replace. "
5. Remove seal retainer, then seal from retainer.
6. Reverse procedure to install, ensuring to install new seal.

OIL PAN

REPLACE

1997

1. Raise and support vehicle.
2. Drain engine oil into a suitable container.
3. Remove flywheel dust cover.
4. Disconnect exhaust pipe at manifold.

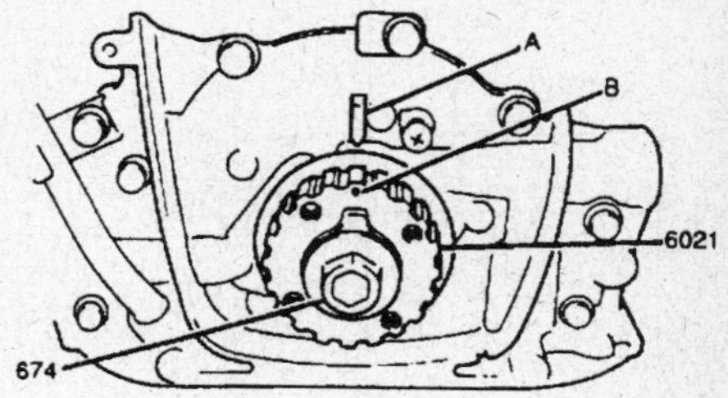

A ARROW MARK ON OIL PUMP CASE
B PUNCH MARK ON CRANKSHAFT TIMING GEAR
674 CRANKSHAFT PULLEY TIMING GEAR BOLT
6021 CRANKSHAFT TIMING GEAR

GC1069500601000X

Fig. 9 Crankshaft timing mark

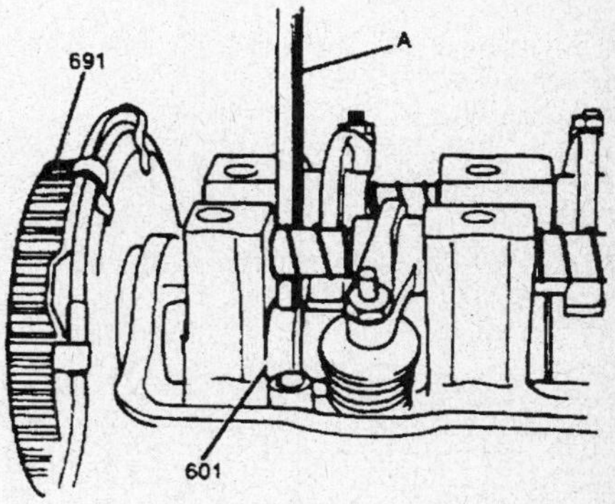

A 10 mm (0.39") ROD
601 CAMSHAFT
691 CAMSHAFT TIMING GEAR SPROCKET

GC1069500592000X

Fig. 12 Camshaft positioning. 1997

5. Remove oil pan bolts and pan, **Fig. 18.**
6. Remove oil pump screen.
7. Reverse procedure to install, ensuring to install new gasket. Apply continuous bead of silicon type sealer to oil pan flange inside bolt holes. When tightening oil pan attaching bolts, start at center and working outward. Tighten bolts to specifications.

1998–2000

1. Raise and support vehicle.
2. Drain engine oil into a suitable container.
3. Remove front pipe/catalytic converter assembly from exhaust manifold, then the resonator/center pipe.
4. Remove crankshaft position sensor.
5. Remove engine oil pan bolts and nuts, then the oil pan.
6. Reverse procedure to install, noting the following:
   a. Apply a continuous bead of silicone part No. 12346240, or equivalent, to engine oil pan mating surface.
   b. **Torque** engine oil pan nuts and bolts to 8 ft. lbs.
   c. **Torque** engine oil drain plug to 26 ft. lbs.

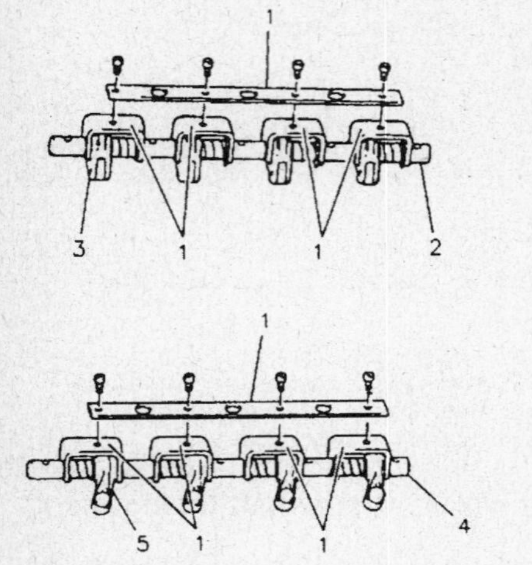

1 J 41388 ROCKER SHAFT ASSEMBLY INSTALLER
2 INTAKE ROCKER SHAFT
3 INTAKE ROCKER ARM
4 EXHAUST ROCKER SHAFT
5 EXHAUST ROCKER ARM

GC1069500593000X

Fig. 13 Rocker shaft installation. 1997

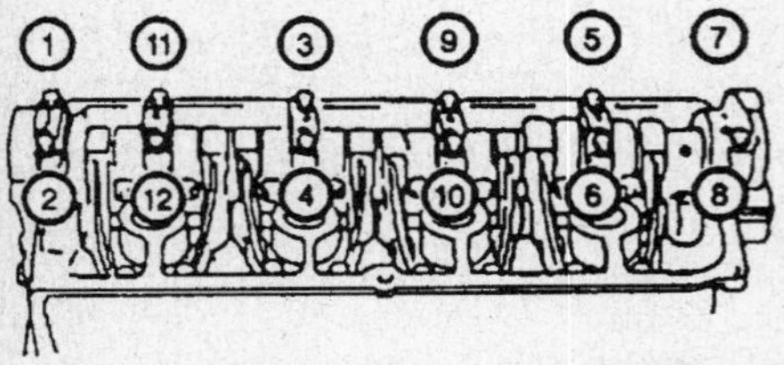

GC1139800687000X

Fig. 16 Camshaft housing bolts tightening sequence. 1998–2000

d. Install a new front pipe/catalytic converter assembly seal.

OIL PUMP

REPLACE

REMOVAL

1. Refer to "Timing Belt, Replace" procedure to remove timing belt.
2. Refer to "Oil Pan, Replace" procedure to remove oil pan.
3. Remove crankshaft timing belt sprocket.
4. Remove alternator mounting bracket, if necessary.
5. Remove A/C compressor mounting bracket, if so equipped.
6. Remove alternator adjusting bolt and upper cover bolt, if necessary.
7. Remove oil pump bolts and pump, **Fig. 19.**

INSTALLATION

1. Install oil pump pins and gasket on engine block.
2. Install oil seal guide tool No. J 34853, or equivalent, onto crankshaft to prevent damage to oil seal lip, **Fig. 20.** Apply engine oil to special tool.
3. Install oil pump onto crankshaft and engine block. Note location of attaching bolts, **Fig. 21. No. 1 bolts are shorter than No. 2 bolts in length.** Install bolts as shown, then tighten to specifications.
4. After installing oil pump, check that oil seal lip is not twisted, then remove tool.
5. Install rubber seal between oil pump and water pump, **Fig. 22.**
6. If necessary, trim edges of oil pump seal flush with oil pan mating surface.
7. Install timing belt guide, key and crankshaft timing sprocket. Note that timing belt guide must be installed so that curved side faces oil pump.
8. Install timing belt and tensioner components.
9. Adjust water pump belt tension.
10. Fill crankcase.
11. Run engine and ensure oil pressure is correct.

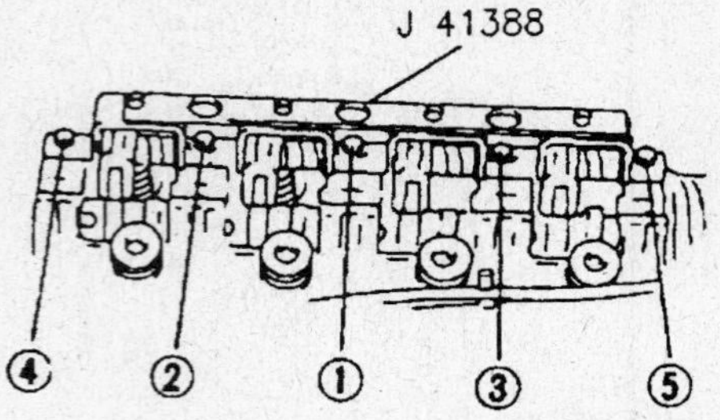

GC1069500594000X

Fig. 14 Rocker shaft tightening sequence. 1997

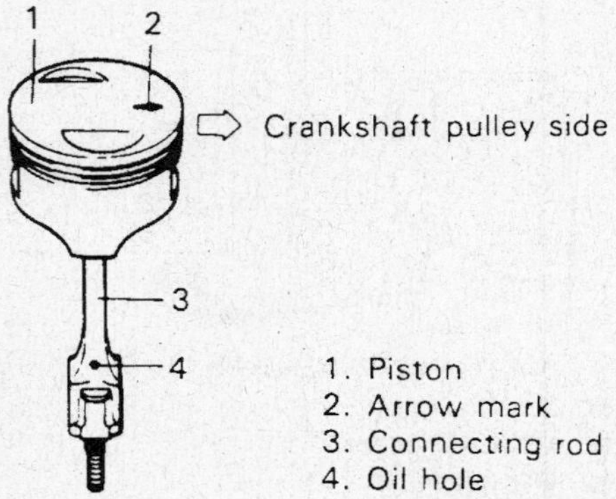

GC1069500595000X

Fig. 17 Piston & connecting rod assembly

OIL PUMP SERVICE

1. Drain oil, then remove dipstick tube from oil pump.
2. Remove rotor plate.
3. Remove outer and inner rotors.
4. Inspect oil seal lip for damage and replace as necessary.
5. Inspect outer and inner rotors, rotor plate and oil pump case for excessive wear or damage.
6. Using feeler gauge, check radial clearance between outer rotor and crescent, **Fig. 23.** If clearance exceeds .0122 inch, replace outer rotor.
7. Using straightedge and feeler gauge, measure side clearance which should not exceed .0059 inch, **Fig. 24.**
8. Wash, clean and dry all oil pump parts.
9. Apply light coat of engine oil to inner and outer rotors, oil seal lip portion and inside surfaces of oil pump case and plate.
10. Install outer and inner rotors in pump case.
11. Install rotor plate and tighten screws securely. Check that gears turn smoothly by hand.
12. Install O-ring in pump case, then dipstick tube.

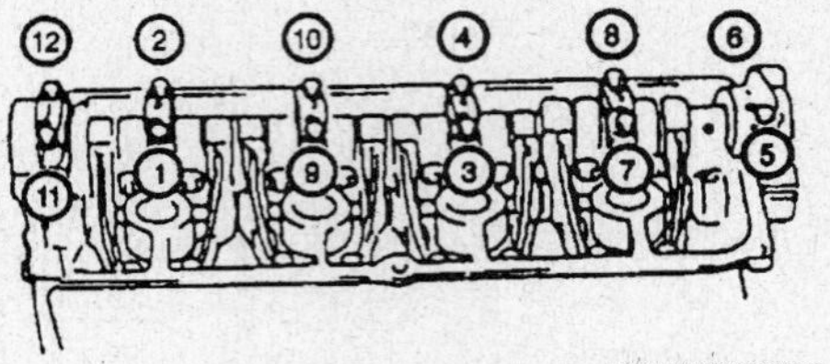

GC1139800686000X

Fig. 15 Camshaft housing bolt loosing sequence. 1998–2000

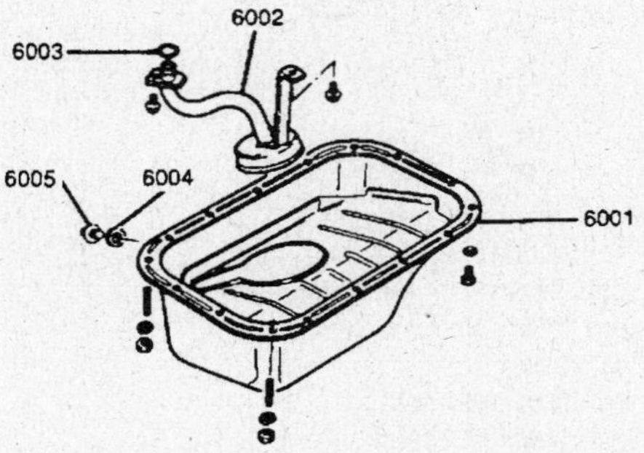

6001 ENGINE OIL PAN
6002 OIL PUMP STRAINER
6003 OIL PUMP STRAINER SEAL
6004 ENGINE OIL DRAIN PLUG GASKET
6005 ENGINE OIL DRAIN PLUG

GC1099500106000X

Fig. 18 Oil pan assembly. 1997

BELT TENSION DATA

Belt	Belt Deflection Inch①
A/C Compressor & Power Steering Pump	.28–.35
Water Pump & Alternator	.25–.32

① — With 22 lbs. pressure applied.

COOLING SYSTEM BLEED

These engines do not require a specified bleed procedure. After filling cooling system, run engine to operating temperature with radiator pressure cap off. Air will then be automatically bled through cap opening.

THERMOSTAT

REPLACE

1. Drain cooling system.
2. Remove radiator inlet hose at thermostat housing.

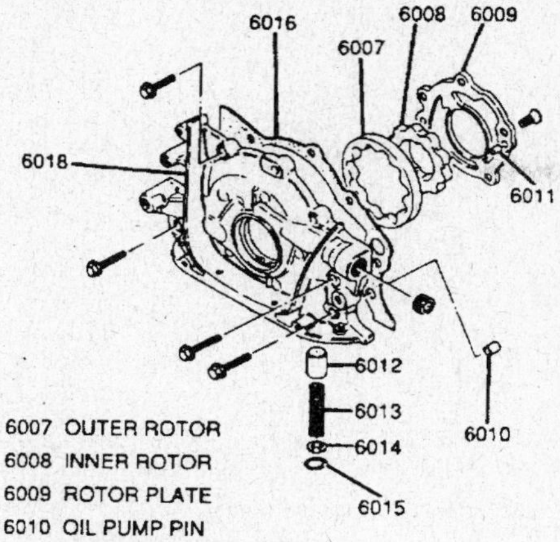

GC1099500107000X

Fig. 19 Rotor type oil pump

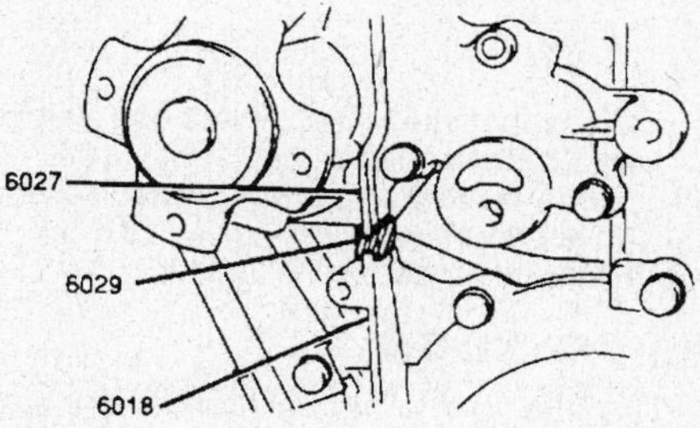

6018 OIL PUMP BODY
6027 COOLANT PUMP
6029 RUBBER SEAL

GC1099500110000X

Fig. 22 Seal installation

3. Remove thermostat housing and thermostat.
4. Clean both gasket surfaces thoroughly.
5. Reverse procedure to install, ensuring to use new gasket.

WATER PUMP

REPLACE

REMOVAL

1. Drain cooling system.
2. Remove air cleaner assembly.
3. **On models with A/C,** remove compressor suction pipe bracket.
4. **On all models,** loosen, but do not remove, water pump bolts.
5. Raise and properly support vehicle.
6. Remove right lower splash shield.
7. **On models with A/C,** remove compressor drive belt.
8. **On all models,** remove lower alternator cover plate, loosen alternator adjusting bolt and remove water pump/alternator drive belt.

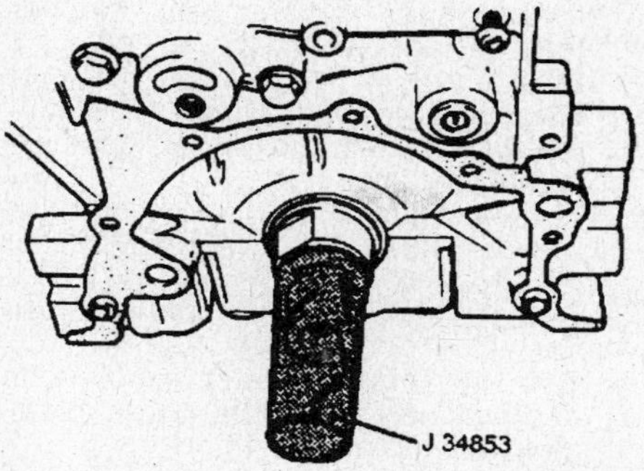

GC1099500108000X

Fig. 20 Crankshaft oil seal guide tool

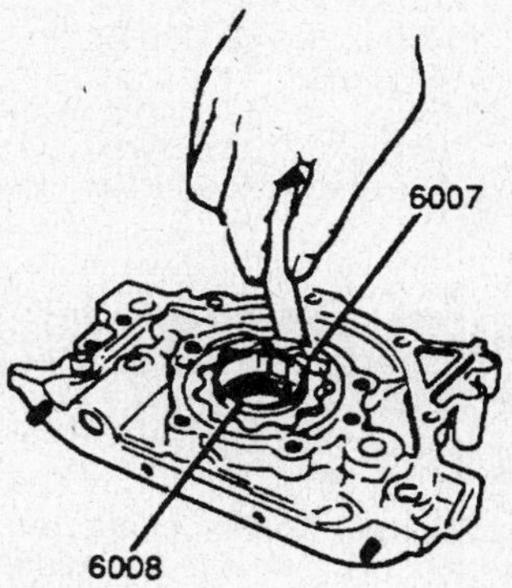

6007 OUTER ROTOR
6008 INNER ROTOR

GC1099500111000X

Fig. 23 Rotor radial clearance inspection

9. Remove crankshaft pulley and water pump pulley.
10. Remove timing belt as outlined under "Timing Belt, Replace."
11. Remove dipstick tube.
12. Remove upper alternator adjusting bracket from water pump.
13. Remove rubber seals from water pump, **Fig. 25.**
14. Remove water pump attaching bolts and nuts and water pump.

INSTALLATION

1. Install water pump on engine block, ensuring to use new gasket.
2. Install rubber seals between water pump and oil pump and between water pump and cylinder head,
3. Install upper alternator adjusting bracket to water pump and tighten to specifications.
4. Install dipstick tube.
5. Install timing belt.
6. Install and hand tighten water pump pulley.
7. Install crankshaft pulley.
8. Install water pump/alternator drive belt and lower alternator cover plate.
9. **On models with A/C,** install compressor drive belt.
10. **On all models,** install right lower splash shield.
11. Lower vehicle.

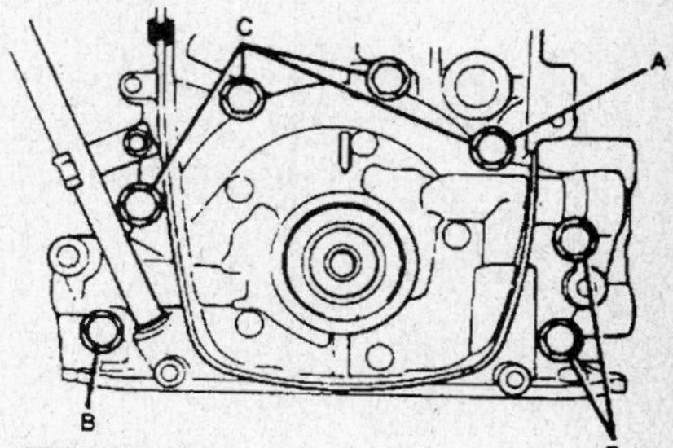

GC1099500109000X

Fig. 21 Oil pump bolt location

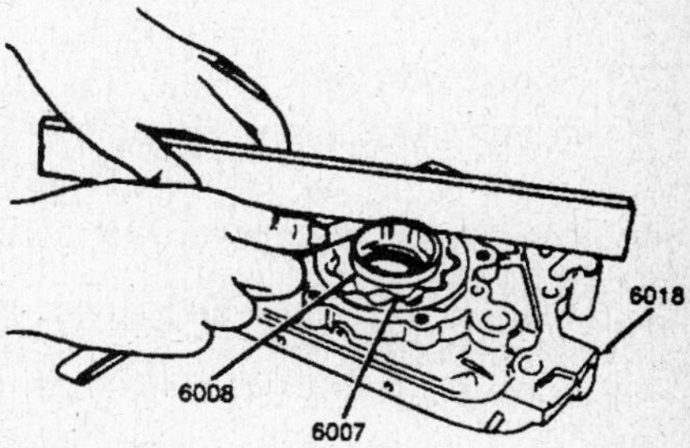

6007 OUTER ROTOR
6008 INNER ROTOR
6018 OIL PUMP BODY

GC1099500112000X

Fig. 24 Rotor side clearance inspection

12. **On models with A/C,** install compressor suction pipe bracket.
13. **On all models,** tighten upper alternator adjustment bolt to specifications.
14. Tighten water pump/alternator drive belt to specifications listed in "Belt Tension Data."
15. Fill cooling system.

RADIATOR

REPLACE

1. Drain cooling system.
2. Remove upper, lower and overflow hoses from radiator.
3. Disconnect cooling fan electrical connector.
4. **On models with automatic transaxle,** disconnect transaxle cooling lines from bottom of radiator.
5. **On all models,** remove upper radiator/fan attaching bolts, then radiator/fan assembly from vehicle.
6. Reverse procedure to install.

FUEL PUMP

REPLACE

1997

1. Relieve fuel system pressure as outlined under "Precautions."
2. Remove rear seat cushion, then disconnect fuel pump and sending unit electrical connectors, then push harness through floor pan grommet.

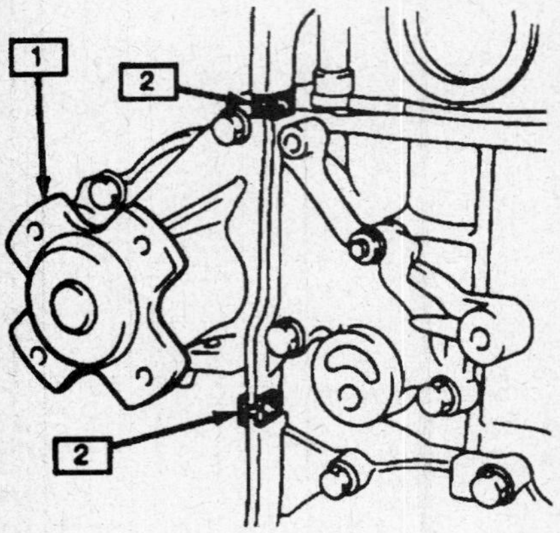

1 COOLANT PUMP
2 RUBBER SEALS

GC1089500243000X

Fig. 25 Water pump rubber seals

3. Drain fuel tank, then disconnect inlet hose from fuel filter.
4. Disconnect fuel filler hose from fuel tank.
5. Disconnect vapor hoses and fuel feed and return hoses at fuel tank and pump.
6. Remove fuel tank attaching bolts, then lower fuel tank from vehicle.
7. Remove fuel pump to fuel tank attaching bolts, then fuel pump, **Fig. 26.**
8. Separate fuel pump from sending unit as necessary.
9. Reverse procedure to install.

1998-2000

1. Relieve fuel system pressure as outlined under "Precautions."
2. Remove rear seat cushion, disconnect fuel pump and sending unit electrical connections, then push harness through floor pan grommet.
3. Drain fuel tank.
4. Raise and properly support vehicle.
5. Remove muffler and exhaust pipe assembly.
6. Remove fuel filler neck hose, fuel breather hose and EVAP canister air inlet hose.
7. Remove parking brake cable and position aside.
8. Remove EVAP canister vapor hose and fuel feed and return hoses at fuel tank and pump.
9. Remove fuel tank attaching bolts, then lower fuel tank from vehicle.
10. Disconnect fuel sender electrical connections and vapor hoses, then fuel feed and return lines.
11. Remove fuel sender assembly from fuel tank.
12. Separate fuel pump from fuel sender assembly as required.
13. Reverse procedure to install.

FUEL FILTER

REPLACE

1997

The fuel filter is located at the lefthand front corner of the fuel tank assembly.

1. Relieve fuel system pressure as outlined under "Precautions."
2. Raise and properly support vehicle, then place approved fuel holding container under fuel filter.
3. Remove parking brake cable bracket bolt and move cable aside
4. Disconnect fuel filter inlet hose clamp and hose from filter. **A small amount of fuel may be released after the fuel hose is disconnected. In order to reduce the chance of personal injury, cover the fittings with a shop towel.**

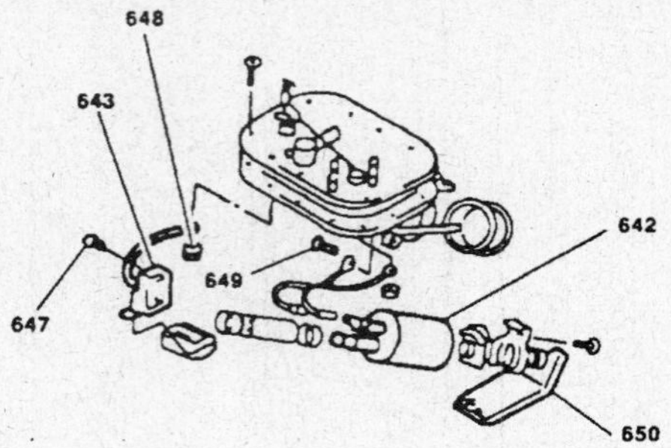

642 FUEL PUMP
643 FUEL GAGE SENDING UNIT
647 FUEL GAGE SENDING UNIT MOUNTING SCREW
648 FUEL GAGE SENDING UNIT LEAD WIRE NUT
649 FUEL PUMP MOUNTING SCREW
650 FUEL PUMP STRAINER

GC1029503762000X

Fig. 26 Fuel pump & sending unit removal

5. Disconnect fuel filter outlet hose clamp and hose from filter.
6. Remove mounting bracket and filter as an assembly.
7. Reverse procedure to install.

1998-2000

The fuel filter is part of fuel sender assembly located in the fuel tank. The fuel sender assembly must be removed in order to replace fuel sender subassembly that contains fuel filter as outlined under "Fuel Pump, Replace."

TIGHTENING SPECIFICATIONS

Tightening specifications are for clean and lightly lubricated threads only. Dry or dirty threads produce increased friction which prevents accurate measurement of tightness.

Year	Component	Torque/ Ft. Lbs.
1997	Air Cleaner Assembly To Cylinder Head	89①
	Alternator Cover	89①
	Alternator Mounting	17
	Alternator Upper Adjustment	17
	Battery Cable To Battery Terminal	89①
	Connecting Rod Cap	26
	Crankshaft Pulley	97①
	Crankshaft Sprocket	96
	Cylinder Head	54
	Cylinder Head Cover	44①
	Exhaust Manifold To Cylinder Head	17
	Engine Mounts	41

Continued

TIGHTENING SPECIFICATIONS—Continued

Tightening specifications are for clean and lightly lubricated threads only. Dry or dirty threads produce increased friction which prevents accurate measurement of tightness.

Year	Component	Torque/ Ft. Lbs.
1997	Flywheel Retaining Bolts (Automatic Transaxle)	45
	Flywheel Retaining Bolts (Manual Transaxle)	57
	Fuel Filter Mounting	11
	Fuel Gauge Sending Unit	89①
	Fuel Tank Mounting	18
	Heat Shield	11
	Ignition Distributor To Cylinder Head	11
	Intake Manifold To Cylinder Head	17
	Lower Rear Mounting Bracket	41
	Main Bearing Cap	40
	Oil Pan Drain Plug	26
	Oil Pan To Engine	97①
	Oil Pressure Switch	10
	Oil Pump Pickup Tube Bolts	97①
	Oil Pump Rotor Plate Screws	97①
	Oil Pump To Engine	97①
	Radiator Lower Mounting	97①
	Radiator Upper Mounting	97①
	Rear Main Seal	106①
	Rocker Arm Mounting	18
	Spark Plug	21
	Starter Mounting	17
	Thermostat Cap	15
	Thermostat Housing	20
	Timing Belt Cover	97①
	Timing Belt Tensioner	20
	Timing Belt Tensioner Stud	97①
	Torque Rod Assembly	41
	Water Pump To Engine	10
	Water Pump Pulley	18
1998–2000	Air Cleaner Assembly To Cylinder Head Bolt	89①
	Camshaft Timing Sprocket Bolts	43
	Connecting Bracket To Rear Mount Nut	41
	Connecting Rod Bearing Cap Nuts	26
	Coolant Pump Pulley Bolts	97①
	Coolant Return Pipe Mounting Bolts	15
	Crankshaft Timing Pulley Bolts	12
	Crankshaft Timing Sprocket Bolt	94
	Cylinder Head to Engine Block Bolts	49
	Engine Oil Drain Plug	26
	Engine Oil Pan Bolts & Nuts	97①
	Exhaust Manifold Bolts & Nuts	17
	Flywheel Retaining Bolts (Automatic Transaxle)	69
	Flywheel Retaining Bolts (Manual Transaxle)	57
	Front Pipe/Catalytic Converter Assembly (To Exhaust Manifold)	37
	Front Pipe/Catalytic Converter Assembly (To Resonator/Center Pipe)	26
	Main Bearing Cap Bolts	40
	Oil Pressure Switch	10

Continued

TIGHTENING SPECIFICATIONS—Continued

Tightening specifications are for clean and lightly lubricated threads only. Dry or dirty threads produce increased friction which prevents accurate measurement of tightness.

Year	Component	Torque/ Ft. Lbs.
1998-2000	Oil Pump Mounting Bolts	97①
	Oil Pump Strainer Bolt	97①
	Rear Main Seal Housing Bolts	97①
	Rocker Arm Shaft Screws	97①
	Timing Belt Cover Nut & Bolts	97①
	Timing Belt Tensioner Bolt	18
	Timing Belt Tensioner Stud	97①
	Torque Rod Bracket Bolts	41

① — Inch lbs.

Clutch & Manual Transaxle

NOTE: On Air Bag Equipped Models, Refer To "Air Bag System Precautions" Located In The Front Of This Manual For System Disarming & Arming Procedures.

NOTE: Refer To "Computer Relearn Procedures " Located In The Front Of This Manual For Computer Relearn Procedures.

INDEX

PRECAUTIONS

AIR BAG SYSTEMS

Refer to "Air Bag System Precautions" in the front of this manual for system disarming and arming procedures.

BATTERY GROUND CABLE

Prior to service, disconnect battery ground cable and isolate as required.

ADJUSTMENTS

CLUTCH PEDAL HEIGHT

Clutch pedal height can be adjusted by turning the clutch pedal stop bolt located at the upper end of the clutch pedal lever, at the pedal bracket. Clutch pedal height should be the same as brake pedal height.

CLUTCH RELEASE ARM PLAY

1. Measure clutch pedal freeplay. Clutch pedal freeplay should be .6 to .8 inch.

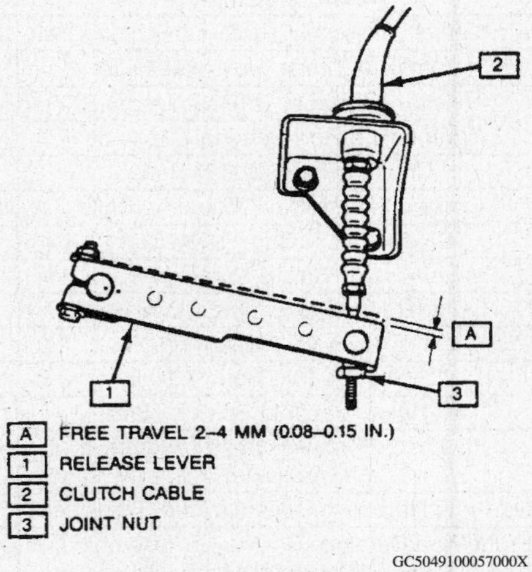

Fig. 1 Clutch cable adjustment

2. If clutch pedal freeplay is not within specifications, adjust clutch cable joint nut to provide a free travel of .08 to .15 inch at release lever, **Fig. 1.**

SHIFT LINKAGE

Check gear shift control lever vertical endplay. Vertical endplay should be 0 to .007 inch. Check distance between instrument panel and gear shift control lever, with transaxle in neutral, **Fig. 2.** Distance should be approximately 4.8 inches, if not adjust.

CLUTCH

REPLACE

1. Refer to "Manual Transaxle, Replace" procedure to remove transaxle.
2. Install suitable tool into pilot bearing to support clutch assembly during removal.
3. Check for X mark or white painted letter on pressure plate and corresponding mark stamped on flywheel. If no markings are found, mark flywheel and pressure plate for assembly purposes.
4. Loosen pressure plate to flywheel attaching bolts 1 turn at a time until spring pressure is released, **Fig. 3.** It may be necessary to use flywheel

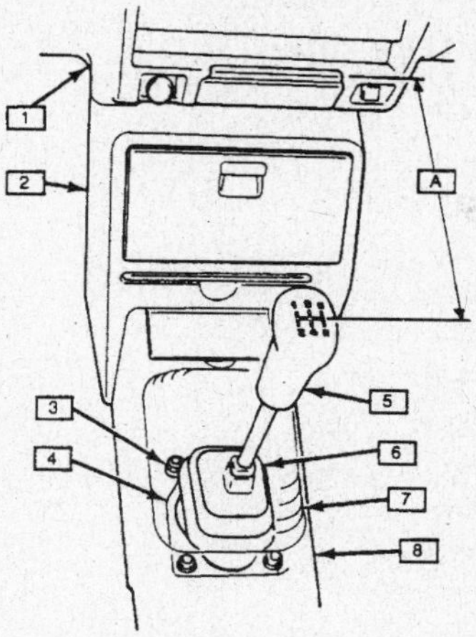

A CONTROL LEVER POSITION DISTANCE
1 INSTRUMENT PANEL
2 CONSOLE BOX
3 CONTROL LEVER HOUSING NUT
4 BOOT COVER
5 CONTROL LEVER KNOB
6 CONTROL LEVER BOOT
7 BOOT NO. 2
8 SHIFT CONTROL LEVER COVER

GC5049100058000X

Fig. 2 Gearshift control lever position

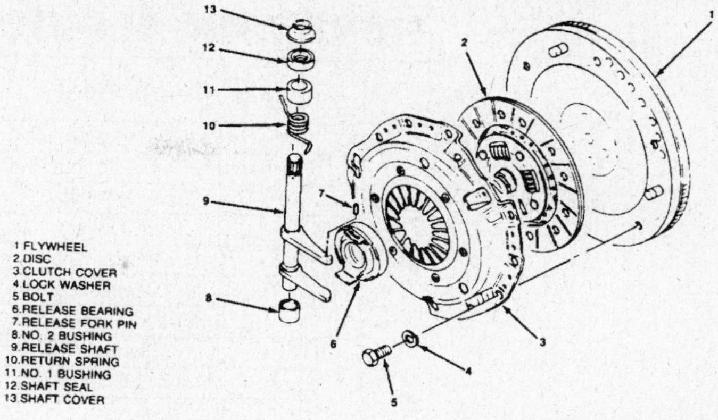

GC5049100059000X

Fig. 3 Clutch assembly

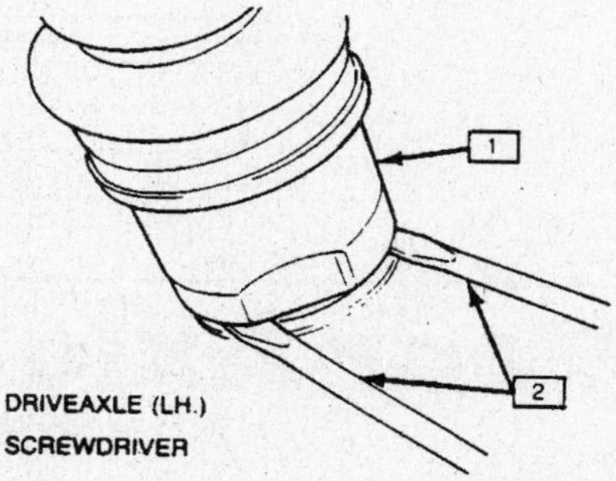

1 DRIVEAXLE (LH.)
2 SCREWDRIVER

GC5049100060000X

Fig. 4 Front drive axle snap ring removal

holder tool No. J 35271, or equivalent to hold flywheel in position when loosening bolts.

5. Remove bolts, pressure plate and clutch disc.
6. Reverse procedure to install. Lubricate splines of transaxle input shaft and pilot bearing surface and release bearing with suitable lithium grease. **Torque** pressure plate cover bolts to 17 ft. lbs.

SHIFT CABLE

REPLACE

1. Remove clutch cable joint nut, then disconnect cable from release arm.
2. Remove clutch cable bracket bolts and bracket.
3. Remove cable attaching bolts at clutch pedal.
4. Remove clutch cable from vehicle.
5. Reverse procedure to install. Refer to "Adjustments" to adjust cable.

TRANSAXLE

REPLACE

1. Disconnect clutch cable from release lever and bracket.
2. Disconnect electrical connectors from transaxle, then remove wiring harness to transaxle attaching brackets.
3. Disconnect speedometer cable from transaxle.
4. Remove upper transaxle attaching bolts.
5. Remove starter motor as outlined under "Starter Motor, Replace."
6. Disconnect vacuum hose from pressure sensor.
7. Install an engine support fixture, then raise and support vehicle.
8. Drain lubricant from transaxle.
9. Disconnect gear shift control lever from gear shift shaft.
10. Remove extension rod nut, then extension rod with washers.
11. Remove attaching nuts and bolts, then exhaust pipe.
12. Remove clutch housing lower cover.
13. Remove left front wheel.
14. Disconnect left tie rod end and ball joint from steering knuckle.
15. Separate drive axles from transaxle, **Fig. 4.** Support drive axles from chassis using wire.
16. Remove lower transaxle to engine attaching bolts and nuts.
17. Support transaxle using a suitable jack.
18. Remove two rear engine attaching nuts, then transaxle left hand mounting bracket attaching nuts and bolts and bracket.
19. Lower transaxle and engine assembly to disconnect assembly from stud bolts at rear engine mounting, then pull transaxle outward toward left hand side to disconnect input shaft from clutch assembly.
20. Lower transaxle, then remove from vehicle.
21. Reverse procedure to install. Lubricate splines of transaxle input shaft and pilot bearing surface and release bearing with suitable lithium grease. When installing transaxle, guide right drive axle into transaxle as it is raised into vehicle. Tighten to specifications.

TIGHTENING SPECIFICATIONS

Year	Component	Torque/ Ft. Lbs.
1997–2000	Back-Up Lamp Switch	17
	Battery Cable To Terminal	89②
	Cable Bracket	21
	Clutch Cover	17
	Clutch Pedal Shaft	15
	Clutch Release Lever	17
	Extension Rod Nut	29
	Flywheel	①
	Gear Shift Control Shaft Bolts & Nuts	15
	Starter	21
	Switch Locknut	10
	Transaxle Hanger	106②
	Transaxle Mounts	44
	Transaxle To Engine Bolts	44
	Transaxle Oil Drain & Filler Plugs	15
	Transaxle Side Cover	106②
	Wheel Lug Nuts	44

① — 1.0L engine, 45 ft. lbs.; 1.3L engine, 57 ft. lbs.
② — Inch lbs.

Rear Axle & Suspension

INDEX

PRECAUTIONS

AIR BAG SYSTEMS

Refer to "Air Bag System Precautions" in the front of this manual for system disarming and arming procedures.

BATTERY GROUND CABLE

Prior to service, disconnect battery ground cable and isolate as required.

HUB & BEARING

REPLACE

1. Raise and support rear of vehicle, then remove wheel.
2. Remove wheel bearing dust cap from brake drum.
3. Using a chisel, unstake wheel bearing nut, then remove wheel bearing nut and washer.
4. Loosen parking brake cable adjusting nuts, then remove plug from backing plate and back off drum brake adjustment.
5. Using a suitable puller, remove brake drum.
6. Using a brass drift, remove wheel bearings from brake drum.

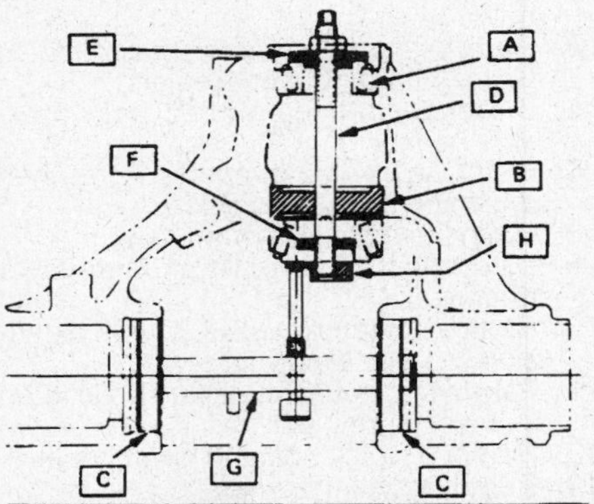

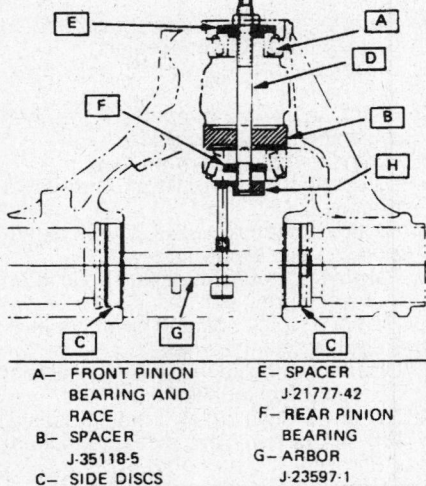

A– FRONT PINION BEARING AND RACE
B– SPACER J-35118-5
C– SIDE DISCS J-21777-45
D– THRU BOLT J-21777-43
E– SPACER J-21777-42
F– REAR PINION BEARING
G– ARBOR J-23597-1
H– GAGE PLATE 35118-2

GC3039100227000X

Fig. 1 Wheel bearing installation

7. Reverse procedure to install, noting the following:
   a. Fill Hub cavity (A), **Fig. 1,** with lithium wheel bearing grease.
   b. Install wheel bearings and spacer using bearing and hub installer tool Nos. J 7079-2 and J 34842, or equivalents. **Wheel bearing should be installed with sealed side facing outward, Fig. 1.**
   c. Install brake drum on spindle. Tighten wheel bearing nut to specifications, then stake nut in position.
   d. After completing installation, adjust drum brake and parking brake.
   e. Bleed and check brake system for proper operation prior to moving vehicle.

STRUT

REPLACE

1. **On two door models,** open hatchback for access to upper strut mounting.
2. **On four door models,** open trunk for access to upper strut mounting.
3. **On all models,** raise and support rear of vehicle, then remove wheel.
4. Support suspension using a suitable jack.
5. Remove strut upper support nuts, then push downward on strut, **Fig. 2.**
6. Remove strut lower attaching bolt, **Fig. 3.**
7. Separate strut from rear suspension

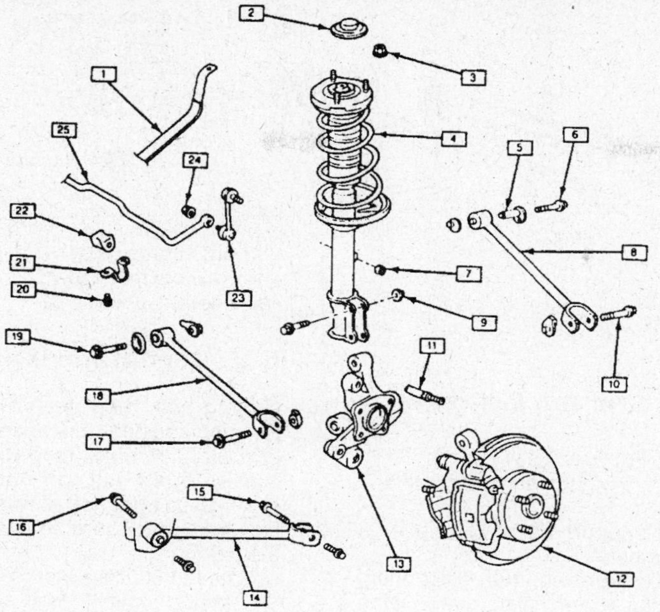

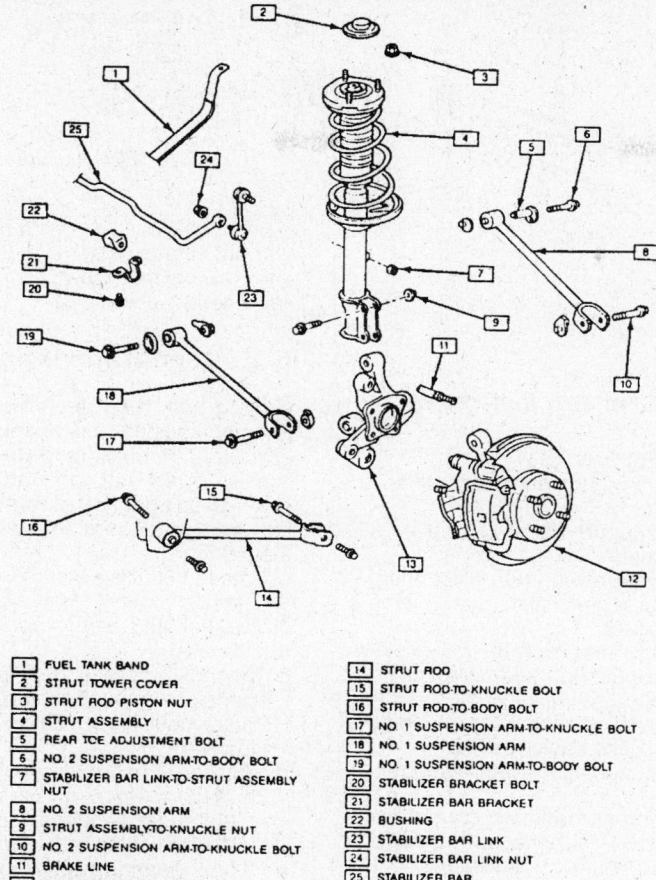

Fig. 2 Strut upper attaching nuts

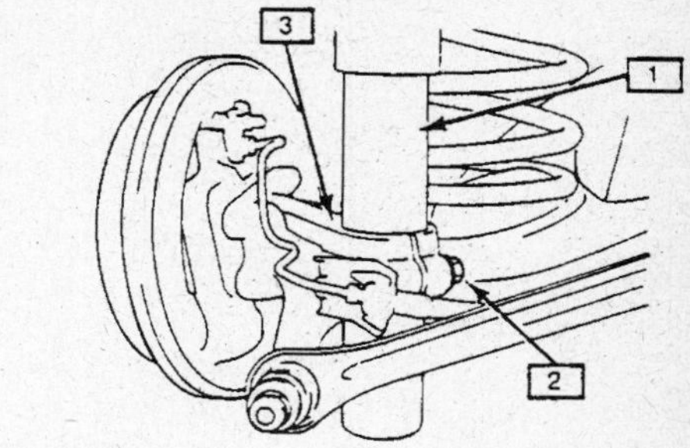

Fig. 3 Strut lower attaching bolt

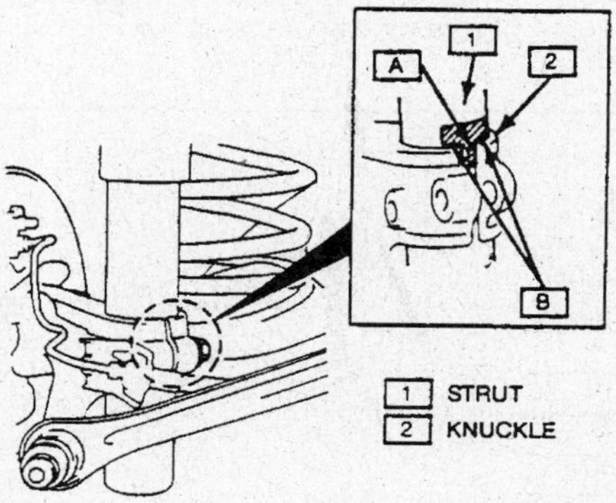

Fig. 4 Strut to rear suspension knuckle position

knuckle, by compressing strut. **If strut is difficult to remove, open slit on knuckle just enough to allow strut removal.**

8. Reverse procedure to install. When installing strut, align projection on strut with slit on rear suspension knuckle, **Fig. 4.**

COIL SPRING

REPLACE

1. Raise and support rear of vehicle, then

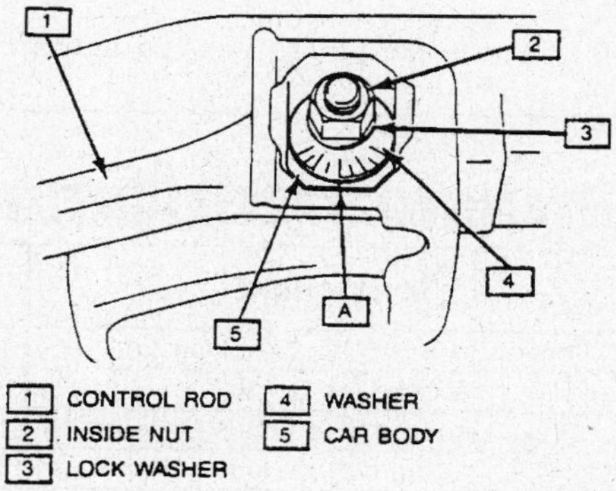

Fig. 5 Control rod inner bolt

remove wheel.

2. Place alignment marks on control rod and control rod washer (A), **Fig. 5,** for setting toe during installation.
3. Remove control rod to body attaching bolt, then separate control rod from bracket.
4. From wheel side of control rod, remove nut from rear suspension knuckle stud, then disconnect control rod.
5. Loosen, but do not remove suspension arm rear attaching nut.
6. Loosen rear suspension knuckle lower attaching nut. Position a suitable jack

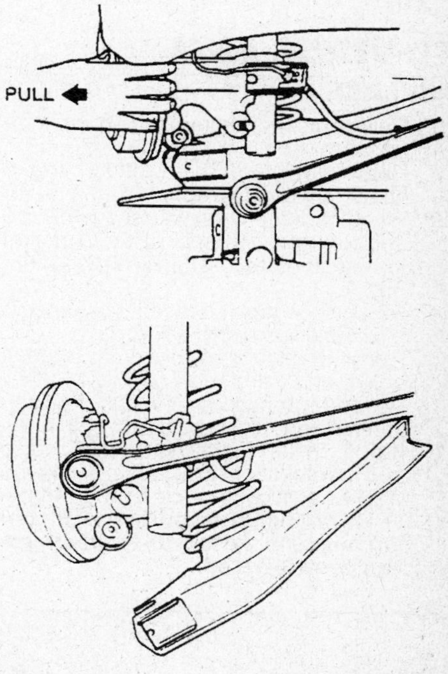

Fig. 6 Coil spring removal

under suspension arm, then remove knuckle lower attaching nut.

7. Raise lower arm slightly to allow removal of rear suspension knuckle lower attaching bolt.
8. Disengage rear suspension knuckle from suspension arm, then carefully lower suspension arm and remove coil spring, **Fig. 6.**
9. Remove remaining suspension arm attaching bolts and nuts and remove suspension arm, if necessary.
10. Reverse procedure to install. When installing spring, position spring end to stepped portion of suspension arm, **Fig. 7.** When installing control rod to body bracket, align marks made on washer and control rod during removal. **Do not tighten control rod or suspension arm attaching nuts and bolts until after vehicle has been lowered.**

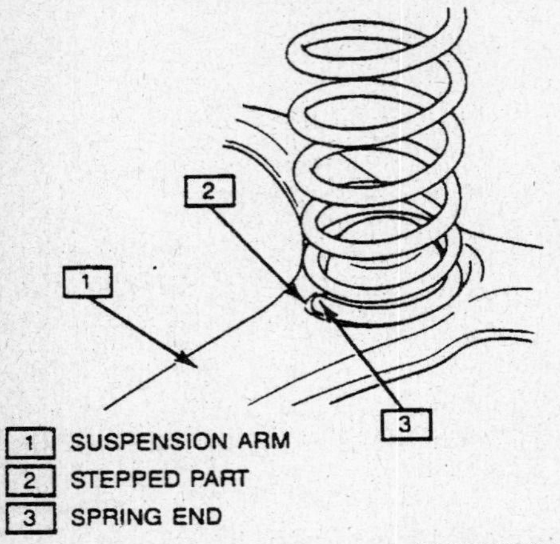

Fig. 7 Coil spring installation

CONTROL ARM

REPLACE

1. Raise and support rear of vehicle, then remove wheel.
2. Remove E-ring, then detach brake hose from control rod.
3. Place alignment marks on control rod and control rod washer at body bracket for setting toe during installation, **Fig. 5.**
4. Remove control rod to rear suspension knuckle attaching nut, **Fig. 8.**
5. Remove control rod to body bracket bolt, then control rod.
6. Reverse procedure to install. Position control rod to vehicle as shown in **Fig. 9.** When installing control rod to body bracket, align marks made on washer and control rod during removal. **Do not tighten control rod attaching nuts and bolts until after vehicle has been lowered.**

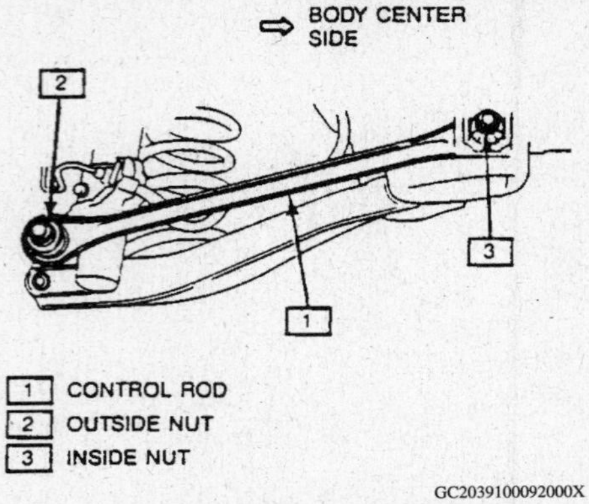

Fig. 8 Control arm installation

KNUCKLE

REPLACE

1. Raise and support rear of vehicle, then remove wheel.
2. Remove brake drum, then disconnect brake hose from rear suspension knuckle bracket.
3. Disconnect brake line from wheel cylinder. Cap brake line and wheel cylinder fitting bore.
4. Remove brake backing plate attaching bolts, then brake backing plate.
5. Position a suitable jack under suspension arm.
6. Place alignment marks on control rod and control rod washer at body bracket for setting toe during installation.
7. Remove control rod to body bracket attaching nut and washer.
8. Remove control rod to rear suspension knuckle stud nut, then control rod.
9. Remove strut to rear suspension knuckle attaching bolt.
10. Remove strut to suspension arm attaching bolt, then separate rear suspension knuckle from suspension arm and strut. **If strut is difficult to remove, open slit on knuckle just enough to allow strut removal.**
11. Reverse procedure to install, noting the following:
    a. When installing control rod to body bracket, align marks made on washer and control rod during removal.
    b. Do not tighten control rod or suspension arm attaching nuts and bolts until after vehicle has been lowered.
    c. Prior to installation, apply sealer to mating surface of brake backing plate and rear suspension knuckle.
    d. When installing brake drum, tighten wheel bearing nut to specification, then stake nut in place using a suitable chisel.
    e. After completing installation, adjust and bleed brake system, then check for proper brake operation before moving vehicle.

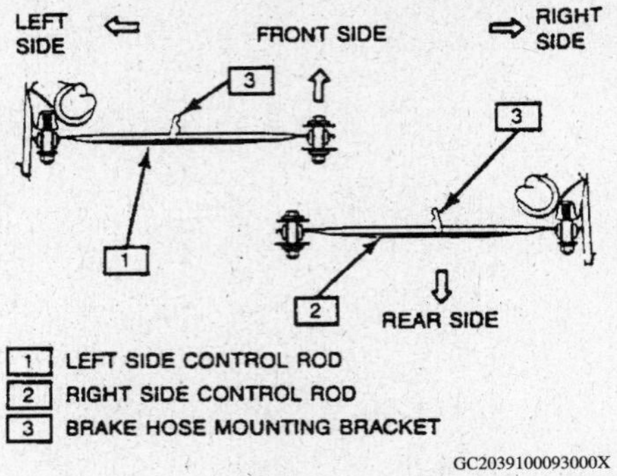

Fig. 9 Control arm installation

TIGHTENING SPECIFICATIONS

Year	Component	Torque/ Ft. Lbs.
1997–2000	Brake Backing Plate Retaining Nuts	17
	Brake Line Bracket	17
	Brake Line Fitting To Wheel Cylinder	12
	Control Rod Nuts	59
	Rear Suspension Knuckle Arm Lower Mounting Nut	27
	Spindle Nut	②
	Stabilizer Mounting	19
	Stabilizer Link To Bar	38
	Stabilizer Link To Control Arm	19
	Strut Lower Mounting Bolt	44
	Strut Support Nut	24
	Strut Upper Nut	37
	Suspension Arm Front Mounting	33
	Suspension Arm To Knuckle	37
	Suspension Arm Rear Nut	27
	Wheel Bearing Retaining Nut	74①
	Wheel Lug Nuts	44

① — Tighten nut, then stake in position.
② — Revised by Technical Service Bulletin: models less ABS, 74 ft. lbs.; models w/ABS, 120 ft. lbs.

Front Suspension & Steering

NOTE: On Air Bag Equipped Models, Refer To "Air Bag System Precautions" Located In The Front Of This Manual For System Disarming & Arming Procedures.

NOTE: Refer To "Computer Relearn Procedures " Located In The Front Of This Manual For Computer Relearn Procedures.

INDEX

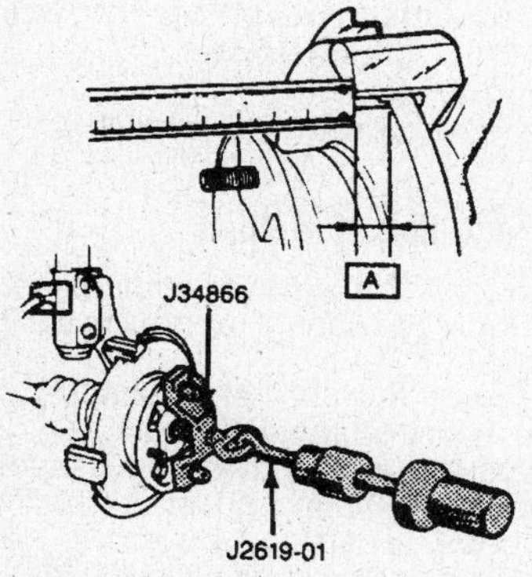

Fig. 1 Hub installation inspection

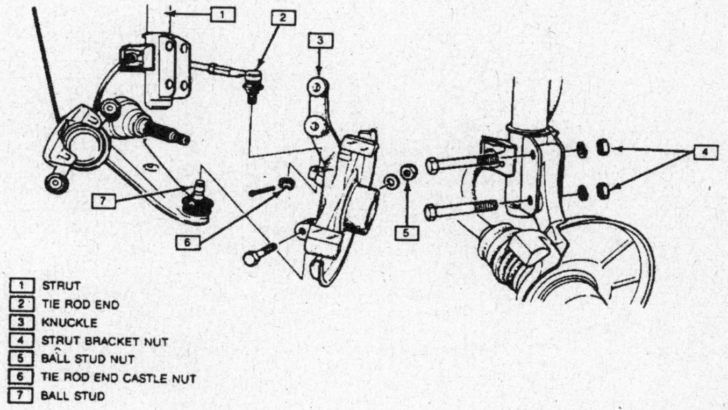

Fig. 2 Steering knuckle removal

PRECAUTIONS

AIR BAG SYSTEMS

Refer to "Air Bag System Precautions" in the front of this manual for system disarming and arming procedures.

BATTERY GROUND CABLE

Prior to service, disconnect battery ground cable and isolate as required.

HUB & BEARING

REPLACE

When checking wheel bearings, raise and support front of vehicle, then rotate wheel to check bearing for smoothness of rotation and noise. Also check wheel bearing endplay with a dial indicator. Wheel bearing endplay should not exceed .016 inch.

REMOVAL

1. Raise and support vehicle, then remove front wheel.
2. Unstake, then remove hub attaching nut.
3. Remove caliper bolts, then caliper with brake line attached. Suspend caliper from chassis with wire.
4. Refer to **Fig. 1,** and measure dimension A for assembly reference. Pull hub out of knuckle.
5. Disconnect tie rod end from knuckle with tie rod end remover tool No. J 21687-02, or equivalent.
6. Remove strut to knuckle bolts and then ball joint stud pinch bolt, **Fig. 2.**
7. Remove knuckle.
8. Using a drift, remove outer, then inner bearing from knuckle.

INSTALLATION

1. Apply suitable grease to balls and oil seal lips of wheel bearings. Fill area A, **Fig. 3,** to approximately 40 percent of capacity with suitable grease.
2. Install wheel bearings using bearing installer tool No. J 34856, or equivalent. **Install wheel bearings with sealed side facing outward. Also ensure spacer is spacer is snug and centered between inner and outer bearings.**
3. Install wheel bearing seal (5), **Fig. 3,** using seal installer tool No. J 34881, or equivalent.
4. Install spacer on hub with bevel side first, **Fig. 4.**
5. Check that wheel bearing spacer bore is aligned with bearing bores. If not, move spacer until aligned.
6. Using plastic hammer, tap hub lightly into knuckle, taking care that alignment is maintained.
7. Using wheel hub installer tool No. J 34856 and handle tool No. J 7079-2, or equivalents, drive hub until dimension A, noted in step 4, is obtained.
8. Install brake caliper.
9. Tighten caliper bolts to specifications.
10. Tighten driveshaft castle nut to specifications

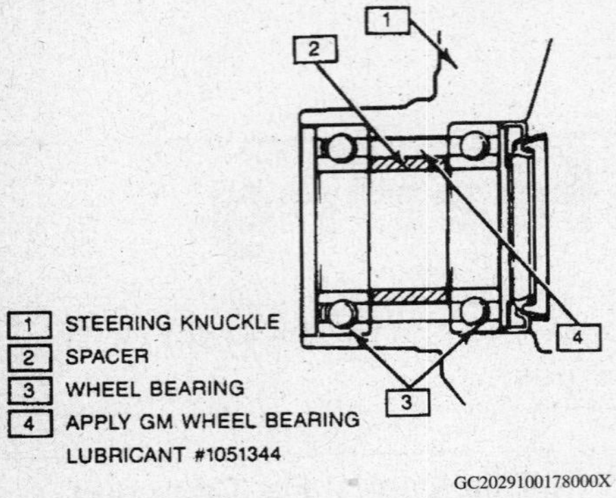

Fig. 3 Steering knuckle hub bearings & seal

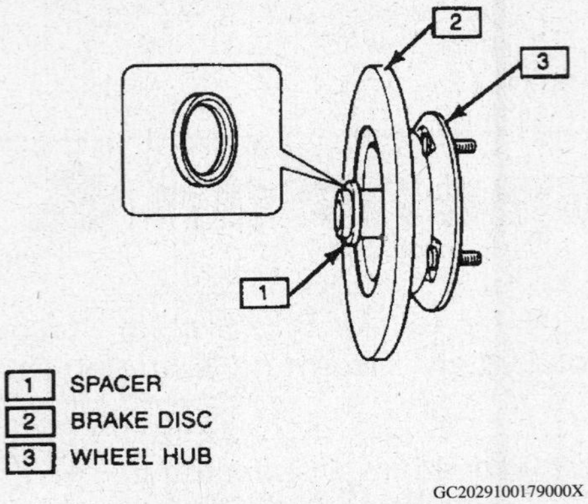

Fig. 4 Wheel hub spacer installation

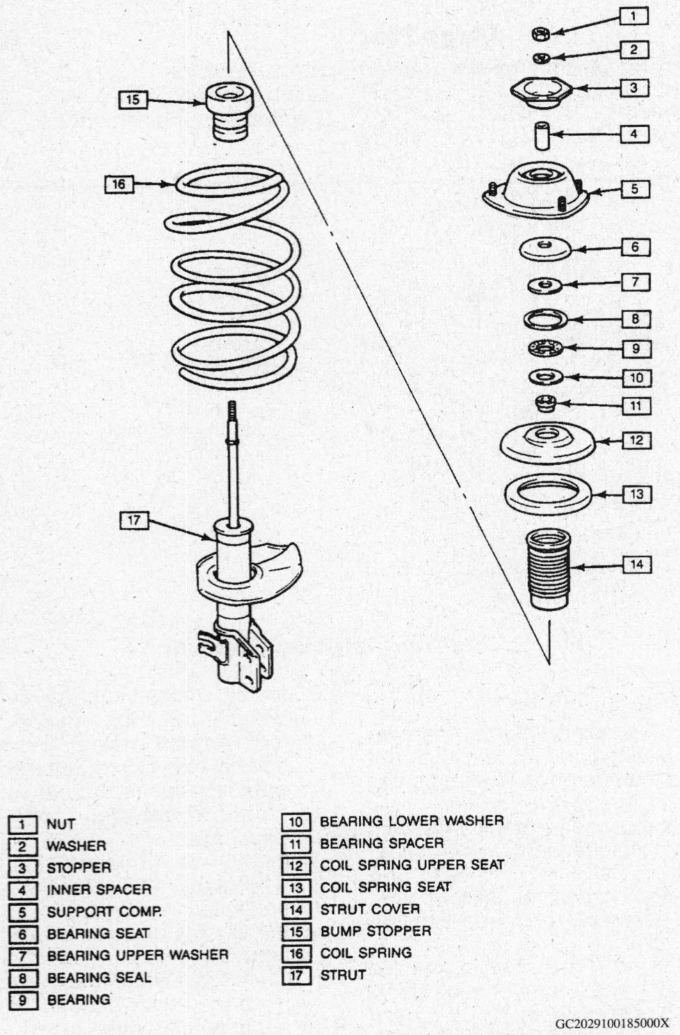

Fig. 6 Exploded view of strut assembly

11. Stake nut in position.
12. Install wheel, then lower vehicle.

STRUT

REPLACE

1. Raise and support vehicle allowing front suspension to hang free.
2. Remove front wheel.
3. Remove E-clip from brake hose and disengage hose from strut bracket, **Fig. 5.**
4. Support lower control arm and knuckle assembly, then remove strut to knuckle bolts.
5. Remove upper strut mount nuts, then strut from vehicle.

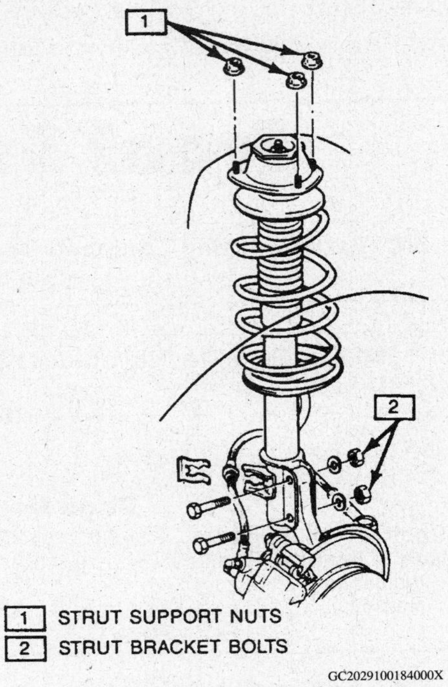

Fig. 5 Strut attaching nut bolt locations

6. Reverse procedure to install.

STRUT SERVICE

1. Mount strut in a spring compressor.
2. Compress spring approximately ½ inch.
3. Remove nut from strut shaft and remove components, **Fig. 6.**
4. Reverse procedure to assemble. Compress spring so strut shaft protrudes through cap by about 1 inch. Tighten nut to specifications.

CONTROL ARM

REPLACE

1. Raise and support vehicle, then remove wheel.
2. Remove ball joint stud to steering knuckle pinch bolt, **Fig. 7.**
3. Remove control arm bracket nut, then bracket bolts.
4. Remove control arm and bracket.
5. If control arm bushing is to be replaced, proceed as follows:
   a. Remove lower control arm as outlined under "Lower Control Arm, Replace."
   b. Press rear bushing from control arm, **Fig. 7.**
   c. Cut flange off front bushing, then press front bushing from control arm, **Fig. 8.**
   d. Apply soap and water to outer surface of front bushing, then press front bushing into control arm until it is centered.
   e. Position rear bushing to control arm, then drive bushing into control arm, **Figs. 9 and 10.**
6. Reverse procedure to install.

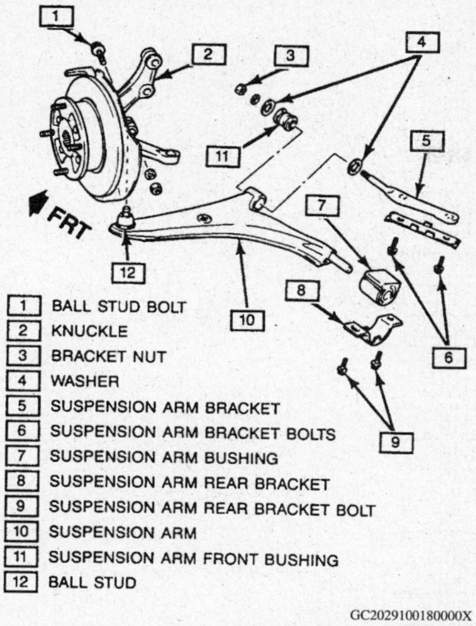

Fig. 7 Lower control arm replacement

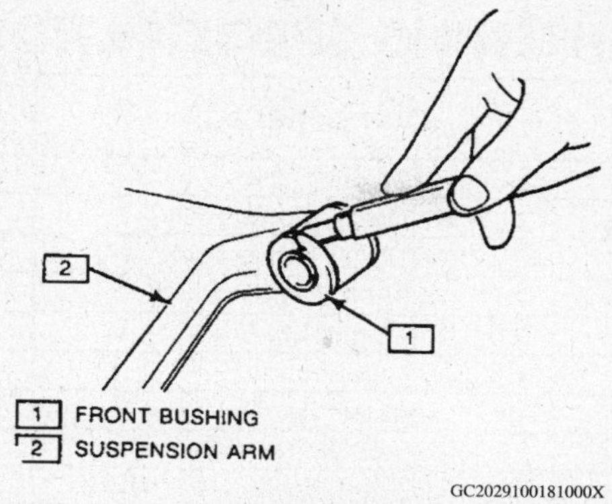

Fig. 8 Cutting flange from control arm front bushing

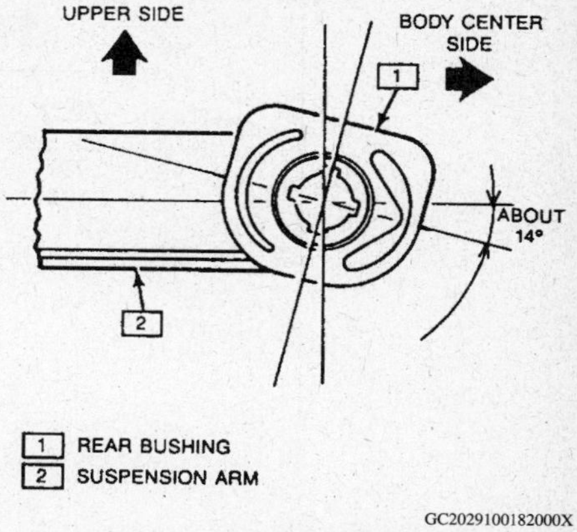

Fig. 9 Rear bushing to control arm installation

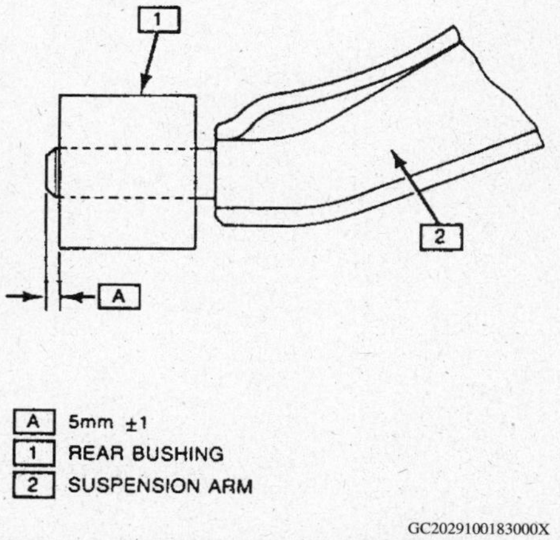

Fig. 10 Rear bushing positioning

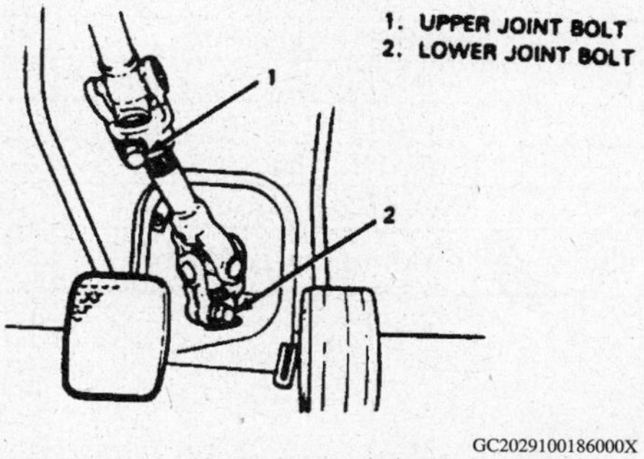

Fig. 11 Steering shaft upper & lower joint bolts

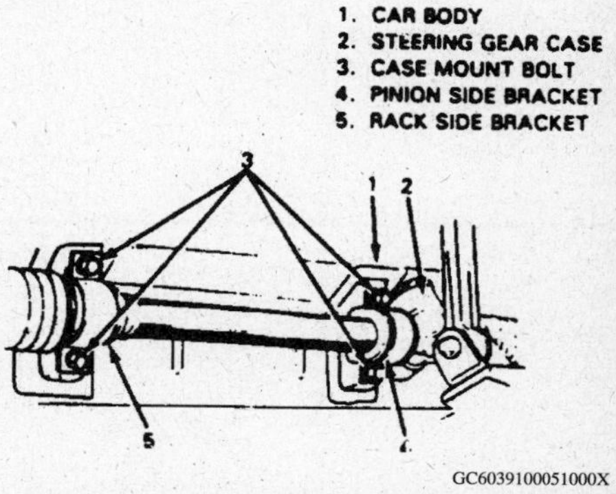

Fig. 12 Steering gear attaching bolts & brackets

MANUAL STEERING GEAR

REPLACE

1. Slide driver's seat rearward.
2. Pull back front part of floor mat on driver's side, then remove steering shaft joint cover.
3. Loosen steering shaft upper joint bolt without removing, **Fig. 11.**
4. Remove steering shaft lower joint bolt and disconnect lower joint from pinion.
5. Raise and properly support vehicle.
6. Remove front wheel and tire assemblies.
7. Remove cotter pins and castle nuts from tie rod ends.
8. Using tie rod end remover tool No. J 21687-02, or equivalent, disconnect tie rods from knuckles.
9. Remove steering gear housing attaching bolts, brackets and steering gear, **Fig. 12.**
10. Reverse procedure to install.

TIGHTENING SPECIFICATIONS

Year	Component	Torque/ Ft. Lbs.
1997–2000	Ball Joint Stud	44
	Brake Caliper To Knuckle	22
	Control Arm Front Bracket	66
	Control Arm Rear Bracket	32
	Front Control Arm Bracket	92
	Hub Bearing	129①
	Stabilizer Bar Link	20
	Stabilizer Bar Mounting	20
	Steering Gear Mounting Bracket	18
	Steering Shaft Coupling	18
	Strut Bracket	59
	Strut Nut	37
	Strut Upper Mounting	21
	Tie Rod Ball	51
	Tie Rod End Castle	32
	Tie Rod End Locknut	32
	Wheel Lug Nuts	44

① — After tightening, stake nut in position.

Wheel Alignment

INDEX

DESCRIPTION

Wheel alignment, is the angular relationship between the wheels, suspension attaching parts and ground. The angle of the knuckle away from the vertical, pointing in or out of wheels, tilt of the wheels from vertical (when viewed from front of vehicle) and tilt of suspension members from vertical (when viewed from side of vehicle), all of these are involved in proper alignment, **Fig. 1**.

CAMBER

Camber is the tilting of front and rear wheels from the vertical when viewed from front of vehicle. When wheels tilt outward at top, camber is positive (+). When wheels tilt inward, camber is negative (MI). Amount of tilt is measured in degrees from the vertical and this is camber angle.

CASTER

Caster is tilting of the front steering axis either forward or backward from the vertical (when viewed from side of vehicle). A backward tilt is positive (+) and a forward tilt is negative (–). On short and long arm type suspensions you cannot see a caster angle without using a special instrument, but if you look straight down from the top of the upper control arm to the ground you would find that ball joints do not line up (fore and aft) when a caster angle other than 0° is present.

TOE

Toe is the turning in or out of wheels. The purpose of toe is to ensure parallel rolling of wheels. Excessive toe-in or toe-out may increase tire wear. Toe also serves to offset small deflections of the suspension which occurs when vehicle is moving.

PRELIMINARY INSPECTION

Steering and vibration problems are not always the result of alignment. An additional problem to be checked is tire lead due to worn or improperly manufactured tires. "Lead" is the deviation of the vehicle from a straight path on a level road without hand pressure on the steering wheel.

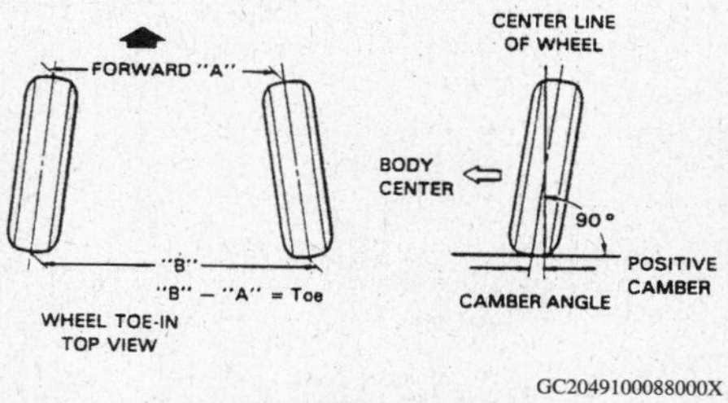

Fig. 1 Suspension geometry

To ensure correct alignment readings and alignment specifications, the following checks and inspections should be made.

1. Check tire for proper inflation and thread wear.
2. Check for loose ball joints and tie rod ends. If excessive looseness is noted, replace defective parts before adjusting toe.
3. Check for wheel runout.
4. Check trim heights. If not within specifications, correct before adjusting toe.
5. Check for loose control arms.
6. Check for loose or missing stabilizer bar components.

FRONT WHEEL ALIGNMENT

CAMBER & CASTER

1. Position vehicle on an alignment fixture following manufacturer's instructions and check caster and camber angles. Bumper should be bounced three times before inspection, to prevent incorrect reading.
2. Camber and caster cannot be adjusted. Should either be found out of specification, locate the cause first.
3. If improper alignment is caused by damaged, worn or loose suspension parts, they should be replaced. If vehicle body or chassis is damaged, it should be repaired.

STEERING ANGLE

When a tie rod or tie rod end is replaced, check toe and steering angle with turning radius gauges. If steering angle is not correct, check right and left tie rods for equal length.

TOE

1. Loosen right and left tie rod end locknuts, **Fig. 2.**
2. Apply grease between tie rods and rack boots.
3. Turn right and left tie rods by the same amount to align toe to specification. **Right and left tie rods should become equal in length.**
4. After adjustment, tighten locknuts and ensure rack boots are not twisted.

REAR WHEEL ALIGNMENT

CAMBER

Camber cannot be adjusted. Should camber be found out of specification, locate the cause. If improper alignment is caused by damaged, worn or loose suspension parts, they should be replaced. If vehicle body or chassis is damaged, it should be repaired.

TOE

The rear wheel toe is adjusted by the inner control arm cam bolt, **Fig. 3.** If toe is found to out of specification, loosen left and right inner control arm cam bolt nuts, then rotate cam bolts by equal amounts to correct toe setting. After completing adjustment, **torque** cam bolt nuts to 51 to 65 ft. lbs.

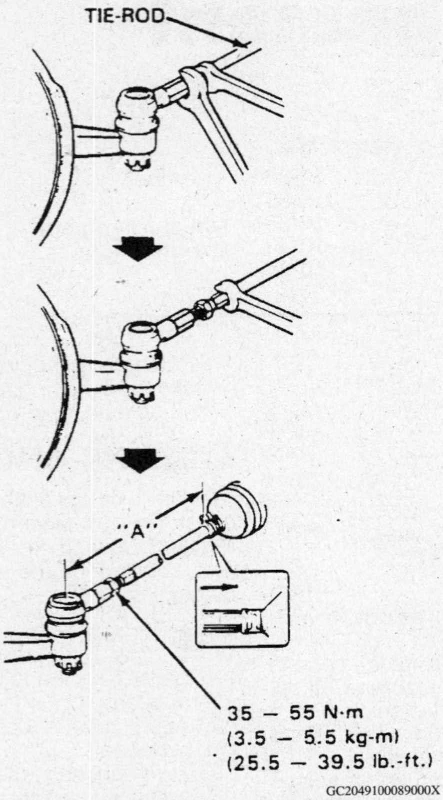

Fig. 2 Front wheel toe adjustment

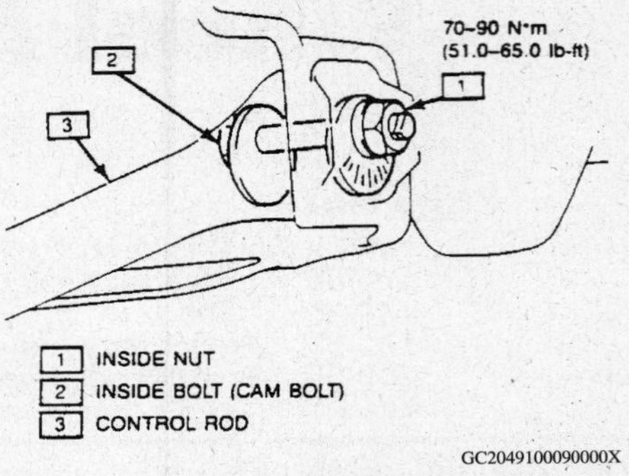

Fig. 3 Rear wheel toe adjustment

PRIZM

NOTE: Refer To Rear Of This Manual For Vehicle Manufacturer's Special Service Tool Suppliers.

INDEX OF SERVICE OPERATIONS

Specifications

GENERAL ENGINE SPECIFICATIONS

Year	Engine		Fuel System	Bore & Stroke, Inch	Compre-ssion Ratio	Net H.P. @ RPM	Maximum Torque, Ft. Lbs. @ RPM	Normal Oil Pressure, psi
	Liter	VIN Code①						
1997	1.6L	6	Fuel Injection	3.19 × 3.03	9.5	105 @ 5800	100 @ 4800	②
	1.8L	8	Fuel Injection	3.19 × 3.37	9.5	115 @ 5600	115 @ 2800	—
1998–2000	1.8L	8	Fuel Injection	3.11 × 3.60	10	120 @ 5600	122 @ 4400	—

① — Eighth digit of the vehicle identification number (VIN) denotes engine code.

② — At idle, 4.3 psi; @ 3000 RPM, 36–71 psi.

TUNE UP SPECIFICATIONS

Year & Engine (VIN)①	Spark Plug Gap, Inch	Ignition Timing BTDC				Curb Idle Speed③		Fast Idle Speed		Fuel Pump Pressure, psi	Valve Clearance, Inch
		Firing Order Fig.②	Man. Trans.	Auto. Trans.	Mark Fig.	Man. Trans.	Auto. Trans.	Man. Trans.	Auto Trans.		
1997											
1.6L (6)	.031	⑥	10°⑤	10°⑤	A	700	700N	④	④	38–44	⑦
1.8L (8)	.031	⑥	10°⑤	10°⑤	A	700	700N	④	④	38–44	⑦
1998											
1.8L (8)	.043	⑧	10°⑤	10°⑤	A	650–750	650–750N	④	④	44–50	⑦
1999–2000											
1.8L (8)	.043	⑧	10°⑤	10°⑤	A	650–750	650–750N	④	④	44–50	⑦

BTDC — Before Top Dead Center
N — Neutral
D — Drive

① — Eighth digit of Vehicle Identification Number (VIN) denotes engine code.

② — Before removing wires from coils or distributor cap, determine location of No. 1 wire, as distributor position may have been altered from that shown at end of this chart.

③ — When adjusting idle speed, set parking brake and block drive wheels.

④ — Electronically controlled.

⑤ — At 700 RPM w/jumper wire connected between terminals of check engine connector. Engine connector is located in the engine compartment on the lefthand inner fender.

⑥ — Cylinder numbering front of engine to rear 1, 2, 3, 4. Firing order, 1-3-4-2. Refer to Fig. B for spark plug wire connections at distributor cap.

⑦ — Intake, .006–.010; exhaust, .010–.014.

⑧ — Cylinder numbering front of engine to rear 1, 2 , 3, 4. Firing order, 1-3-4-2.

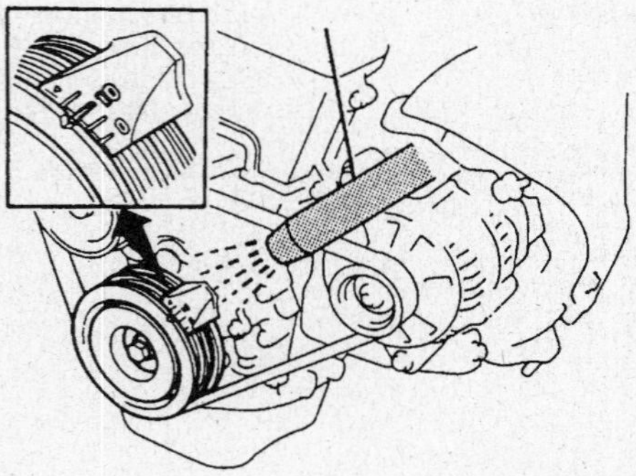

GC1139100157000X

Fig. A

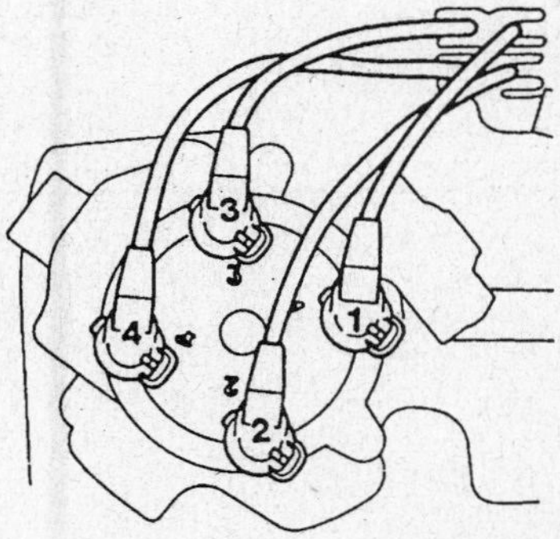

GC1139100156000X

Fig. B

FRONT WHEEL ALIGNMENT SPECIFICATIONS

Year	Model	Caster Angle, Degrees		Camber Angle, Degrees				Toe-In, Inch	Toe Out On Turns, Degrees		Ball Joint Wear
		Limits	Desired	Limits		Desired			Outer Wheel	Inner Wheel	
				Left	Right	Left	Right				
1997	All	+.58 to +2.08	+1.33	–.92 to +.58	–.92 to +.58	–.17	–.17	.08	33	37–41	①
1998–2000	All	+.57 to +2.07	+1.32	–.93 to +.57	–.93 to +.57	–.18	–.18	.04	—	—	②

① — Replace ball joint if any looseness is detected or if ball joint seal is cut.

② — Remove steering knuckle w/hub, then clamp knuckle into suitable soft-jawed vise. Flip ball stud back & forth five times. Install castle nut onto ball joint stud. Rotate nut continuously for one turn every 2–4 seconds, then note torque reading on fifth turn, which should be 9–26 inch lbs. Replace ball joint if reading does not meet specifications.

REAR WHEEL ALIGNMENT SPECIFICATIONS

Year	Model	Camber Angle, Degrees				Toe-In, Inch	Ball Joint Wear
		Limits		Desired			
		Left	Right	Left	Right		
1997–2000	All	–1.67 to –.17	–1.67 to –.17	–.92	–.92	.16	①

① — Replace ball joint if any looseness is detected or if ball joint seal is cut.

FLUID CAPACITIES & COOLING SYSTEM DATA

Year	Engine (VIN) ④	Coolant Capacity, Qts.		Radiator Cap Relief Pressure, Lbs.	Thermo. Opening Temp., Deg. F	Fuel Tank, Gals.	Engine Oil Refill, Qts.	Transaxle Oil	
		Manual Trans.	Auto. Trans.					Man. Trans-axle Qts.	Auto. Transaxle Qts.①
1997	1.6L (6)	6.3	6.2	10.7–14.9	180	13.2	3.1②	1.5	③
	1.8L (8)	6.6	6.4	10.7–14.9	180	13.2	3.7②	1.5	③
1998–2000	1.8L (8)	6.6	⑤	13	180	13.2	3.7②	2	③

① — Approximate. Make final inspection w/dipstick.

② — Filter change, add .2 qt.

③ — Three-speed automatic transaxle, 2.6 qts.; Four-speed automatic transaxle, 3.3 qts.

④ — Eighth digit of Vehicle Identification Number (VIN) denotes engine code.

⑤ — Harrison radiator automatic transaxle, 6.4 qts.; Nippondenso radiator or manual transaxle, 6.6 qts.

LUBRICANT DATA

Year	Model	Lubricant Type			
		Transaxle		Power Steering	Brake System
		Manual	Automatic		
1997	All	75W-90 GL-4	Dexron III	Dexron III	DOT-3
1998–2000	All	①	Dexron III	Dexron III	DOT-3

① — Synthetic manual transmission fluid GM part No. 12346190, or an equivalent 75W-90 GL-4 gear oil.

Electrical

NOTE: On Air Bag Equipped Models, Refer To "Air Bag System Precautions" Located In The Front Of This Manual For System Disarming & Arming Procedures.

NOTE: Refer To "Computer Relearn Procedures " Located In The Front Of This Manual For Computer Relearn Procedures.

INDEX

PRECAUTIONS

AIR BAG SYSTEMS

Refer to "Air Bag System Precautions" in the front of this manual for system disarming and arming procedures.

BATTERY GROUND CABLE

Prior to service, disconnect battery ground cable and isolate as required.

FUSE PANEL & FLASHER LOCATION

Fuse and relay block 1 is located in the lefthand front of the engine compartment, left of the air cleaner. Fuse and relay block 2 is located in lefthand front engine compartment, left of the battery. Fuse and relay block 3 is located in the righthand front engine compartment. On 1998–2000 models, an additional fuse block is located behind an access cover at the lefthand lower end of the instrument panel. The hazard and turn signal flasher is located in Junction Block No. 1 under the lefthand body hinge pillar trim panel. The turn/hazard relay is the tallest of the relays in this block.

RELAY CENTER LOCATION

Fuse and relay block 1 is located in the lefthand front engine compartment, left of the air cleaner. Fuse and relay block 2 is located in lefthand front engine compartment, left of the battery. Fuse and relay block 3 is located in the righthand front engine compartment. On 1998–2000 models, an additional fuse block is located behind an access cover at the lefthand lower end of the instrument panel.

FUEL PUMP RELAY LOCATION

On 1997 models, the circuit opening relay which supplies electrical power to the fuel pump is located on the lefthand center dash support, **Fig. 1.** On 1998–2000 models, the circuit opening relay is located at the lower lefthand side of the passenger compartment, above the kick panel, **Fig. 2.**

STARTER

REPLACE

1997

1. Disconnect IAT sensor electrical connector.
2. Remove air cleaner hose and cap assembly.
3. Remove starter wiring clamp.
4. Disconnect starter motor electrical connectors and positive battery cable.
5. Remove mounting bolts and starter motor.
6. Reverse procedure to install. **Torque** starter mounting bolts to 29 ft. lbs.

1998-2000

1. Remove starter motor upper mounting bolt.
2. Raise and support vehicle.
3. Remove righthand splash shield.
4. Disconnect starter electrical connectors and positive battery cable.
5. Remove lower mounting bolt and starter motor.
6. Reverse procedure to install, noting the following:
   a. **Torque** starter mounting bolts to 27 ft. lbs.
   b. **Torque** positive battery cable to starter mounting nut to 78 inch lbs.

DISTRIBUTOR

REPLACE

1. Disconnect distributor electrical connectors.
2. Remove distributor cap and spark plug wires and position aside.
3. Mark distributor housing and rotor position.
4. Remove distributor mounting bolts.
5. Remove distributor and O-ring from engine.
6. Reverse procedure to install.

IGNITION COIL

REPLACE

1997-99

1. Disconnect spark plug wires from ignition coils.
2. Disconnect two electrical connectors from coils.
3. Remove mounting bolts and coils.
4. Reverse procedure to install. **Torque** ignition coil mounting bolts to 77 inch lbs.

2000

1. Remove mounting bolts and nuts, retainers and engine cover.
2. Disconnect four electrical connectors from coils.
3. Remove coil mounting bolts.

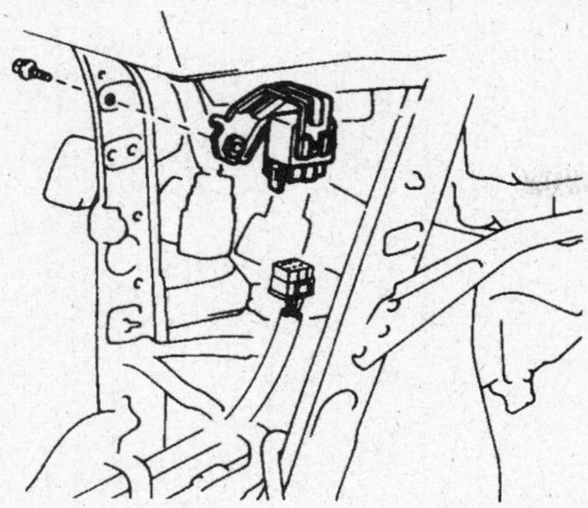

GC1029304879000X

Fig. 1 Circuit opening relay location. 1997

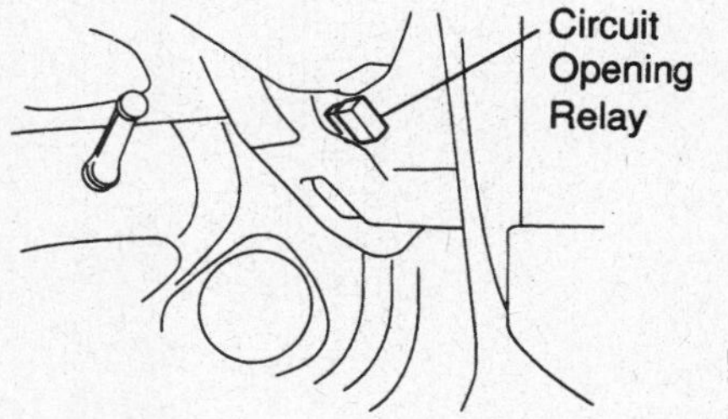

GC1029813133000X

Fig. 2 Circuit opening relay location. 1998–2000

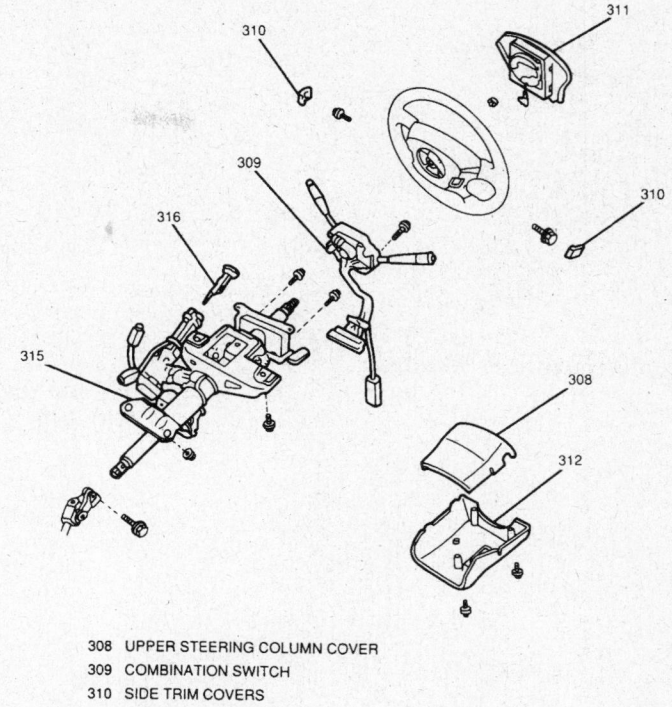

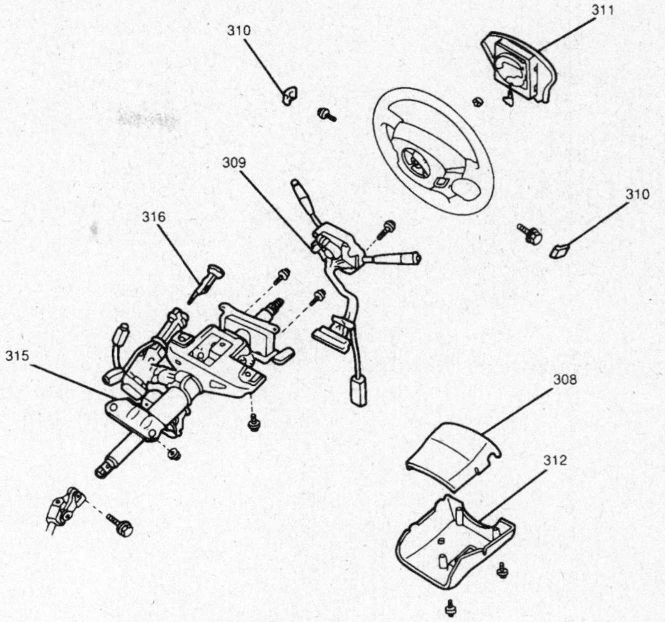

GC6049300175000X

Fig. 3 Steering column exploded view

4. Remove mounting bolts and electrical harness
5. Remove ignition coils.
6. Reverse procedure to install. **Torque** ignition coil mounting bolts to 77 inch lbs.

IGNITION LOCK

REPLACE

1. Remove lower and upper steering column covers, **Fig. 3.**
2. Turn ignition to ACC.
3. push down stop pin and remove cylinder using suitable screwdriver, **Fig. 4.**
4. Reverse procedure to install.

IGNITION SWITCH

REPLACE

1. Remove ignition lock as previously described.
2. Remove knee bolster trim panel and knee bolster, if required.
3. Disconnect ignition switch electrical connector.
4. Remove ignition switch mounting screws.
5. Remove ignition switch from ignition switch housing.
6. Reverse procedure to install.

COMBINATION SWITCH

REPLACE

1. Remove lower and upper steering column covers.
2. Inspect combination switch base for damage. If damage is discovered, replace turn signal, headlamp and washer switch as an assembly.
3. Disconnect electrical connectors as required, then remove combination switch assembly.
4. Reverse procedure to install.

STEERING WHEEL

REPLACE

1. Place front wheels in straight-ahead position, then remove key from lock cylinder.
2. Remove two side trim covers from steering column, **Fig. 3.**
3. Remove two air bag module mounting bolts, release Connector Position Assurance (CPA) and disconnect upper steering column electrical connector, **Fig. 5.**
4. Remove air bag module from steering wheel.
5. Disconnect horn electrical connector.
6. Remove steering wheel mounting nut.
7. Mark end of steering shaft in relation to steering wheel so wheel and shaft can be aligned properly during installation.
8. Remove steering wheel using steering wheel puller tool No. J-1859-A, or equivalent.
9. Reverse procedure to install, noting the following:
   a. Ensure proper position of steering wheel.
   b. **Torque** steering wheel nut to 25 ft. lbs.
   c. Install air bag module and **torque** Torx head screws to 78 inch lbs.

INSTRUMENT CLUSTER

REPLACE

1. Remove instrument cluster bezel screws, then the bezel by disengaging two lower clips.
2. Remove instrument cluster mounting screws, then disconnect all electrical connectors.
3. Carefully remove instrument cluster from instrument panel.
4. Reverse procedure to install.

RADIO

REPLACE

1. Remove instrument panel ashtray.
2. Gently pry and release six accessory trim plate to instrument panel mounting clips, using suitable taped flatbladed tool.
3. Disconnect electrical connectors at cigarette lighter and instrument panel ashtray bulb socket.
4. Remove lighter assembly if required.
5. Remove radio mounting screws.
6. Remove radio from instrument panel.
7. Disconnect radio electrical connections and antenna lead-in cable.
8. Reverse procedure to install.

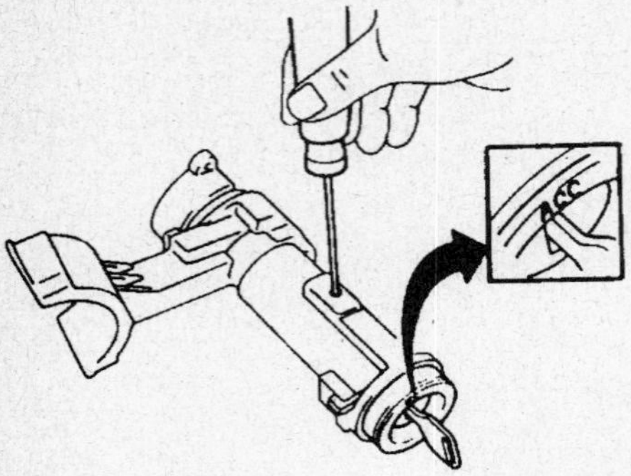

GC9129100028000X

Fig. 4 Ignition cylinder removal

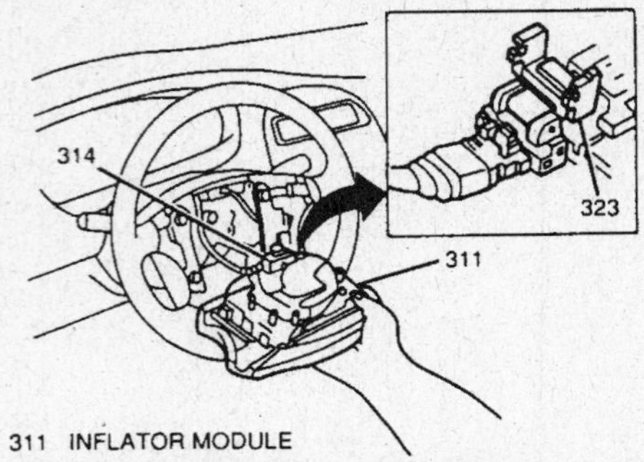

311 INFLATOR MODULE
314 UPPER STEERING COLUMN CONNECTOR
323 CONNECTOR POSITION ASSURANCE (CPA)

GC8019300114000X

Fig. 5 Driver's air bag module removal

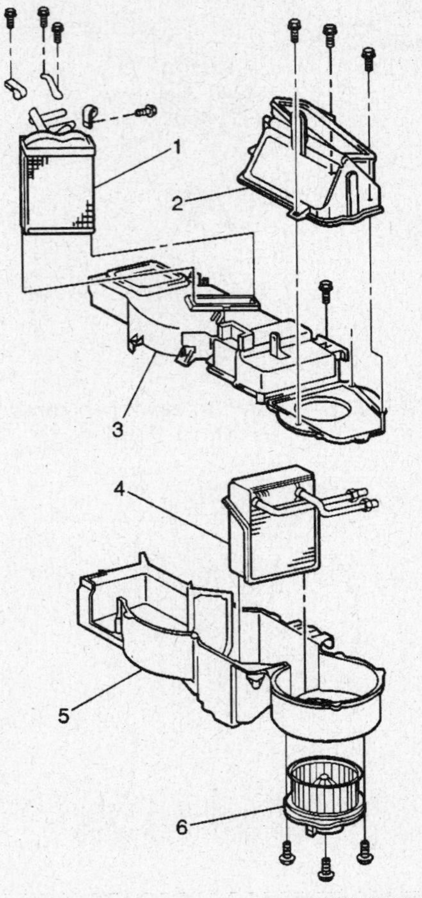

GC7029800595000X

Fig. 7 HVAC module assembly (1: heater core; 2: cover; 3: upper half; 4: evaporator core; 5: lower half; 6: blower motor)

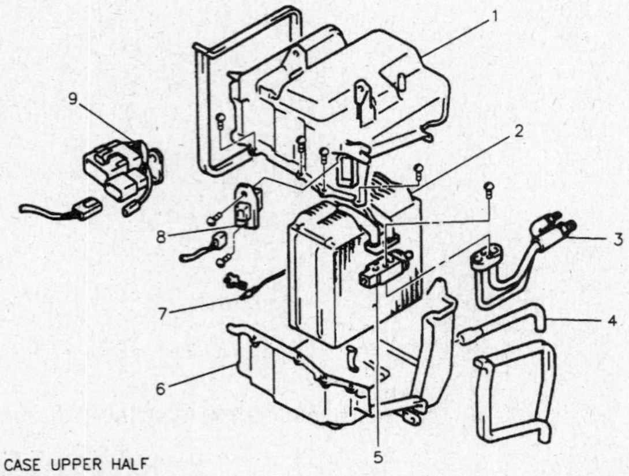

1 EVAPORATOR CASE UPPER HALF
2 EVAPORATOR
3 LIQUID AND SUCTION TUBE
4 DRAIN HOSE
5 EXPANSION VALVE
6 EVAPORATOR CASE LOWER HALF
7 THERMISTOR
8 BLOWER RESISTOR
9 A/C AMPLIFIER

GC7029700594000X

Fig. 6 Evaporator case assembly. 1997

WIPER MOTOR

REPLACE

1. Disconnect wiper motor electrical connector.
2. Remove wiper motor mounting bolts.
3. Disconnect wiper linkage from wiper motor crank arm.
4. Remove wiper motor.
5. Reverse procedure to install.

BLOWER MOTOR

REPLACE

The blower motor is located underneath the instrument panel at the far righthand side of the vehicle. It is accessible through the glove compartment.

1. Remove glove compartment.
2. Disconnect blower motor electrical connector.
3. Remove mounting screws, blower motor and fan assembly.
4. Reverse procedure to install.

HEATER CORE

REPLACE

1. Drain coolant into an suitable container.
2. Recover refrigerant charge.
3. Remove instrument panel as outlined under "Dash Panel Service."
4. Remove instrument panel reinforcement.
5. Disconnect electrical connectors at blower motor, blower motor resistor and A/C compressor control module.
6. Disconnect heater hoses at heater core.
7. **On 1998–2000 models equipped with speed control,** remove servo assembly.
8. **On all models,** remove inlet and outlet tubes from evaporator.
9. Separate rear heater ducts from HVAC module assembly.
10. Remove HVAC module assembly mounting nuts.
11. Carefully pull HVAC module assembly out of vehicle.
12. Remove two heater core brackets, then the heater core from case assembly.
13. Reverse procedure to install.

EVAPORATOR CORE

REPLACE

1997

1. Recover A/C system refrigerant charge.
2. Remove righthand side kick panel and glove compartment assembly.
3. Disconnect evaporator outlet and inlet pipe, then plug hoses and evaporator openings.
4. Disconnect hold-down brackets for inlet and outlet pipes.
5. Remove righthand vent tube.
6. Remove air conditioning amplifier electrical connector, then the amplifier.
7. Disconnect evaporator thermister connector.
8. Remove evaporator case, **Fig. 6.**

9. Separate evaporator case halves, then remove thermister from evaporator.
10. Remove evaporator from case.
11. Reverse procedure to install.

1998–2000

1. Remove heater core as previously described.
2. Remove blower motor cover, **Fig. 7.**
3. Remove HVAC module assembly case halves' mounting screws.
4. Separate case halves.
5. Remove evaporator core.
6. Reverse procedure to install.

1.6L & 1.8L Engines

NOTE: On Air Bag Equipped Models, Refer To "Air Bag System Precautions" Located In The Front Of This Manual For System Disarming & Arming Procedures.

NOTE: Refer To "Computer Relearn Procedures " Located In The Front Of This Manual For Computer Relearn Procedures.

INDEX

PRECAUTIONS

AIR BAG SYSTEMS

Refer to "Air Bag System Precautions" in the front of this manual for system disarming and arming procedures.

BATTERY GROUND CABLE

Prior to service, disconnect battery ground cable and isolate as required.

FUEL SYSTEM PRESSURE RELEASE

1. Loosen fuel filler cap to release fuel tank pressure.
2. **On 1997 models,** remove radio as outlined under "Radio, Replace" in "Electrical" section, to access circuit opening relay.
3. **On all models,** disconnect circuit opening relay electrical connector.
4. Start engine and allow it to run until it stalls from lack of fuel.
5. Crank engine for an additional three seconds to release remaining fuel pressure.
6. Connect circuit opening relay connector, then install radio.
7. Tighten fuel filler cap.

COMPRESSION PRESSURE

1997

Compression readings should be 191 psi at 250 RPM, with a minimum of 142 psi. Maximum difference between cylinders should be 14 psi.

1998–2000

Compression readings should be 218 psi, with a minimum of 145 psi. Maximum difference between cylinders should be 15 psi.

ENGINE MOUNT

REPLACE

1997

1. Support engine assembly using engine support fixture tool No. J-28467-A, or equivalent.
2. Remove cruise control actuator and position aside.
3. Remove cruise control actuator bracket.
4. Disconnect two piece air conditioning pipe bracket.
5. Remove bolts from engine mount bracket and engine mount.
6. Raise and support vehicle.
7. Remove engine splash shields.
8. Remove nuts from underside of engine mount bracket.
9. Lower vehicle.
10. Remove insulator from engine mount bracket.
11. Remove engine mount and bracket. Move A/C pipe to gain clearance.

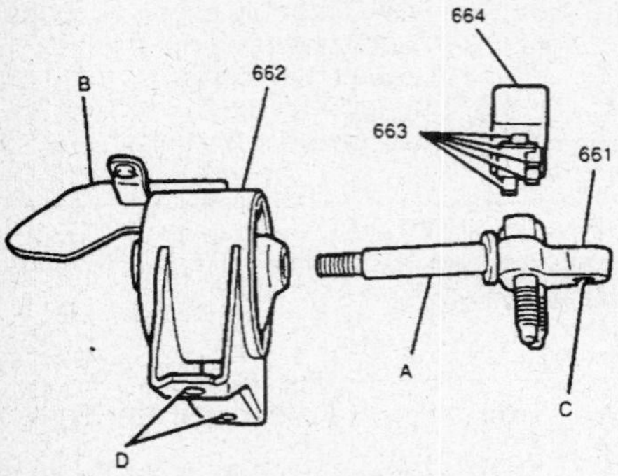

A THROUGH BOLT PART OF ENGINE MOUNT
B BOLT A HOLE
C BOLT B HOLE
B BOLT C HOLES
661 ENGINE MOUNT BRACKET
662 ENGINE MOUNT
663 TANG
664 INSULATOR

GC1069300478000X

Fig. 1 Engine mount replacement. 1997

12. Remove mount through-bolt, then the engine mount, **Fig. 1.**
13. Reverse procedure to install. Tighten mounting bolts to specifications.

1998-2000

1. Raise and support engine using engine support tool No. J-28467-360, or equivalent.
2. Remove three righthand side engine mount to frame bracket bolts.
3. Remove righthand side engine mount to engine bracket bolts.
4. Raise engine slightly in order to provide clearance for engine mount assembly removal.
5. Remove righthand side engine mount.
6. Remove righthand side engine mount to frame bracket from engine mount.
7. Remove righthand side engine mount to engine bracket from engine mount.
8. Reverse procedure to install. Tighten mounting bolts to specifications.

ENGINE

REPLACE

1997

1. Release fuel system pressure as outlined under "Precautions."
2. Drain coolant into an suitable container, engine and transaxle oil into suitable containers.
3. Mark hood hinge position on hood, then remove hood assembly.
4. Remove two splash shields.
5. Disconnect accelerator and kickdown cables.
6. Remove radiator and engine cooling fan assembly.
7. Disconnect required electrical harness and vacuum hose connections.
8. Remove air cleaner hose and air cleaner upper and lower cases.
9. Remove coolant reservoir bracket.
10. Remove washer reservoir.
11. Remove cruise control actuator.
12. Disconnect heater hose from thermostat housing and coolant inlet pipe.

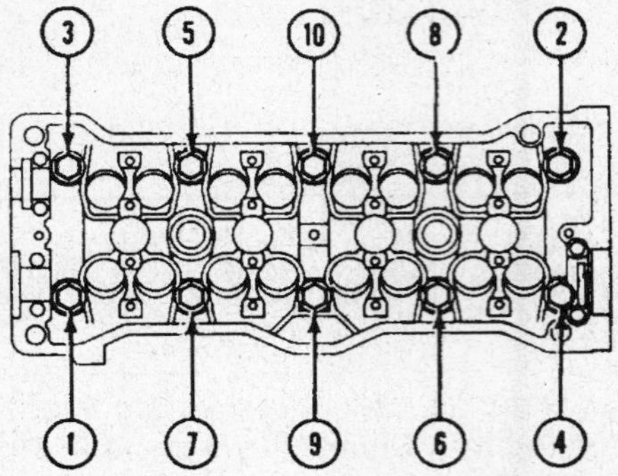

GC1069100481000X

Fig. 2 Cylinder head bolt removal sequence

13. Disconnect fuel feed pipe from fuel rail and intake manifold.
14. Disconnect fuel return hose from fuel pressure regulator.
15. **On models equipped with manual transaxle,** remove clutch release cylinder.
16. **On all models,** disconnect transaxle control cables.
17. Remove lefthand and righthand scuff plates.
18. Remove shift lever knob.
19. Remove knee bolster, glove box door, instrument panel trim bezel, front and rear console and lefthand cowl side trim panel.
20. Remove radio as outlined under "Radio, Replace" in "Electrical" section.
21. Disconnect and remove engine control module.
22. Disconnect cowl panel harness connector and pull harness from cowl panel.
23. Remove air conditioner compressor and power steering oil pump leaving hoses attached. Position compressor aside. **Do not allow compressor or oil pump to be supported by hoses.**
24. Raise and support vehicle.
25. Disconnect front exhaust pipe, exhaust pipe support brackets and oxygen sensor.
26. Disconnect front drive axles as outlined in "Front Wheel Drive Axles" section.
27. Lower vehicle.
28. Attach an engine lifting device to engine, then disconnect engine and transaxle mounts.
29. Ensure all electrical, vacuum and fuel hoses connections are disconnected.
30. Remove engine with transaxle attached.
31. Reverse procedure to install.

1998-2000

1. Release fuel system pressure as outlined under "Precautions."
2. **On models equipped with A/C,** recover refrigerant charge, then position compressor aside with hoses intact.
3. **On all models,** drain coolant and engine oil into suitable containers.
4. Remove washer hose at hood.
5. Make suitable alignment marks as required, then remove hood mounting bolts and hood.

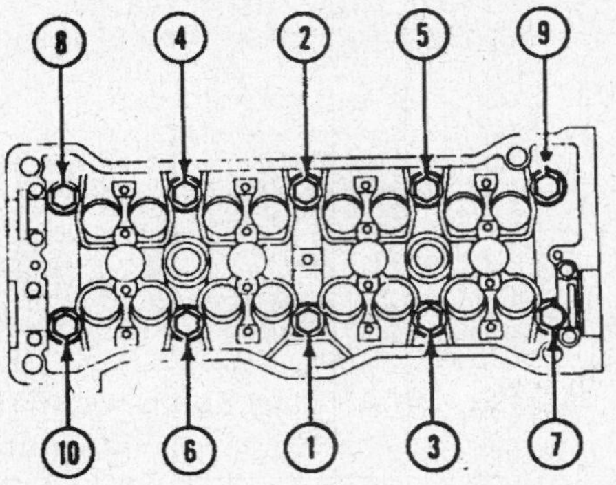

GC1069100482000X

Fig. 3 Cylinder head bolt tightening sequence

6. Remove spark plug wires from spark plugs and position them aside.
7. Remove mounting bolts and ignition coil with plug wires attached.
8. Remove accessory drive belt.
9. **On models equipped with manual transaxle,** proceed as follows:
   a. Remove crankshaft pulley.
   b. Remove alternator.
   c. Remove drive belt tensioner.
10. **On all models,** remove accelerator cable from throttle body.
11. Remove accelerator cable from accelerator cable bracket.
12. **On models equipped with automatic transaxle,** proceed as follows:
    a. Remove transmission Throttle Valve (TV) cable from throttle body.
    b. Remove transmission TV cable from accelerator cable bracket.
13. **On all models,** disconnect Intake Air Temperature (IAT) sensor.
14. Remove air cleaner hose and cap assembly.
15. Remove mounting bolt and Vacuum Switching Valve (VSV) bracket from air cleaner lower case.
16. Remove air filter.
17. Remove mounting bolts and air cleaner lower box.
18. Remove upper radiator hose, then the washer fluid tank mounting bolt. Position washer fluid tank aside.
19. Disconnect washer pump connector and fluid line. Plug line to prevent fluid leakage.
20. Remove upper alternator mounting bolt.
21. Remove mounting bolt, and engine lift hook ground wire.
22. Disconnect all hoses and electrical connectors required to remove engine.
23. Disconnect oxygen sensor electrical connector.
24. Remove mounting nuts, oxygen sensor and gasket.
25. Remove bracket bolts and wiring harness brackets.
26. Free engine harness from its routing and position it aside.
27. Remove lower radiator hose from thermostat housing.
28. Remove upper starter bolt.
29. Remove mounting bolts and lower

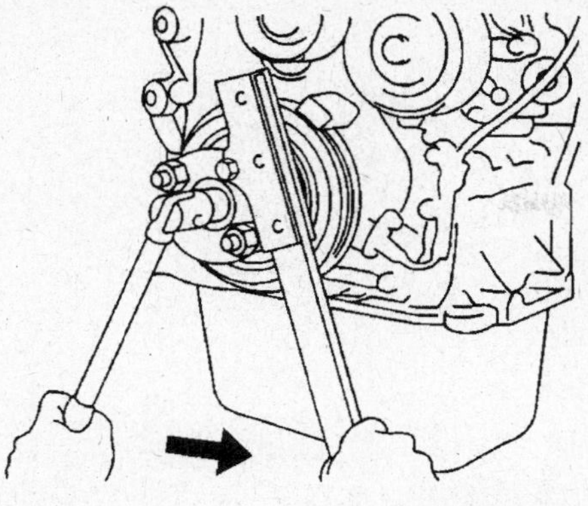

GC1069800985010X

Fig. 4 Crankshaft pulley removal (Part 1 of 2). 1998–2000

splash shield from righthand and lefthand sides of vehicle.

30. Disconnect starter motor electrical connections.
31. Remove lower mounting bolt and starter.
32. **On models equipped with automatic transmission,** remove six torque converter bolts.
33. **On all models,** remove through bolts, nuts and power steering pump.
34. Position power steering pump aside.
35. Remove exhaust pipe to manifold mounting bolts and springs.
36. Remove mounting bolts and axle shaft boot heat shield.
37. Remove four lower transmission to engine mounting bolts, then lower vehicle.
38. Install suitable engine hoist, then remove two upper transmission to engine mounting bolts.
39. Remove mounting bolts, nuts and righthand side mounting insulator.
40. Remove three righthand side engine mounting bolts, then the bracket.
41. Ensure all wires and hoses are positioned aside.
42. Remove engine assembly, then place engine on heavy duty automotive engine stand tool No. J-36854, or equivalent.
43. Reverse procedure to install. Tighten mounting bolts to specifications.

INTAKE MANIFOLD

REPLACE

1997

1. Release fuel system pressure as described under "Precautions."
2. Disconnect vacuum hoses from vacuum sensor on fuel filter, brake booster and A/C actuator hoses.
3. Disconnect exhaust gas recirculation (EGR) solenoid valve and vacuum hose from EGR valve, then remove EGR valve.
4. Remove intake manifold brace.
5. Disconnect fuel return hose from pressure regulator.
6. Disconnect TP sensor and accelerator bracket, then remove throttle body from intake manifold.

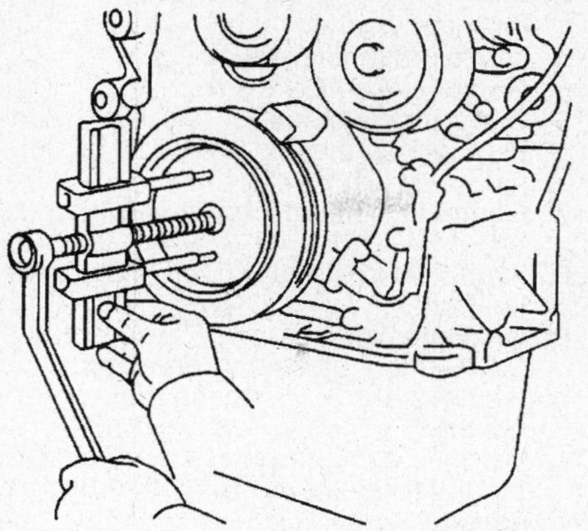

GC1069800985020X

Fig. 4 Crankshaft pulley removal (Part 2 of 2). 1998–2000

7. Remove air intake chamber brace and gasket.
8. Disconnect PCV hoes from cylinder head cover.
9. Remove air intake chamber cover and gasket.
10. Disconnect fuel inlet pipe from fuel rail.
11. Disconnect injector electrical connectors.
12. Remove fuel rail with injectors attached.
13. Remove mounting bolts and intake manifold.
14. Reverse procedure to install.

1998-2000

1. Drain coolant into an suitable container.
2. Disconnect accelerator cable from throttle body.
3. **On models equipped with automatic transaxle,** disconnect TV cable.
4. **On all models,** disconnect IAT sensor electrical connector at air cleaner.
5. Disconnect air cleaner hose from throttle body.
6. Remove air cleaner top assembly.
7. Disconnect following components from throttle body:
   a. Throttle Position Sensor (TPS).
   b. Idle Air Control (IAC) valve connector.
   c. Manifold Absolute Pressure (MAP) sensor connector.
   d. Two coolant bypass hose clamps, then the hoses.
8. Disconnect fuel injector electrical connectors at injectors.
9. Remove mounting bolts and fuel injector wiring harness from intake manifold.
10. Remove mounting bolts and intake manifold support bracket.
11. Disconnect upper radiator hose at radiator. Position hose aside.
12. Remove upper radiator hose support bracket bolt and nut.
13. Remove intake manifold mounting bolts and nuts.
14. Remove upper radiator hose support bracket.
15. Disconnect all vacuum lines at intake manifold.
16. Remove two injector harness support

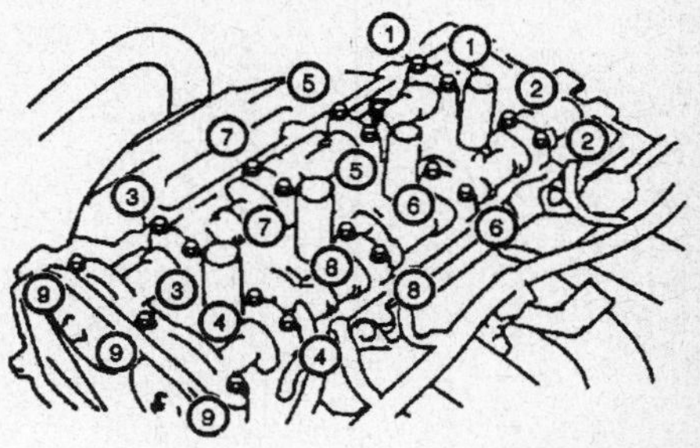

GC1069800986000X

Fig. 5 Camshaft bearing cap loosening sequence. 1998–2000

brackets and intake manifold with throttle body attached from cylinder head.

17. Reverse procedure to install. Tighten mounting bolts to specifications.

EXHAUST MANIFOLD

REPLACE

1997

1. Remove exhaust manifold heat shield or insulator.
2. Raise and support vehicle.
3. Disconnect front exhaust pipe.
4. Remove exhaust manifold support bracket.
5. Lower vehicle.
6. Disconnect oxygen sensor.
7. Remove mounting bolts and exhaust manifold.
8. Reverse procedure to install. Tighten mounting bolts to specifications.

1998-2000

1. Disconnect Heated Oxygen Sensor (HO2S1) electrical connector.
2. Remove oxygen sensor nuts, then the gasket from exhaust pipe.
3. Raise and support vehicle.
4. Remove bolts and springs from exhaust manifold, then the gasket.
5. Remove one bolt from manifold support bracket, then lower vehicle.
6. Remove mounting bolts and upper heat insulator.
7. Remove mounting nuts, exhaust manifold and gasket.
8. Remove mounting bolts and lower heat insulator.
9. Reverse procedure to install.

CYLINDER HEAD

REPLACE

1997

1. Remove camshafts as described under "Camshaft, Replace."
2. Remove vacuum hoses from intake chamber.
3. Remove A/C actuator electrical connector, if equipped.
4. Disconnect EGR solenoid vacuum valve electrical connector.
5. Disconnect vacuum hose from EGR.
6. Remove mounting bolt and EGR valve.

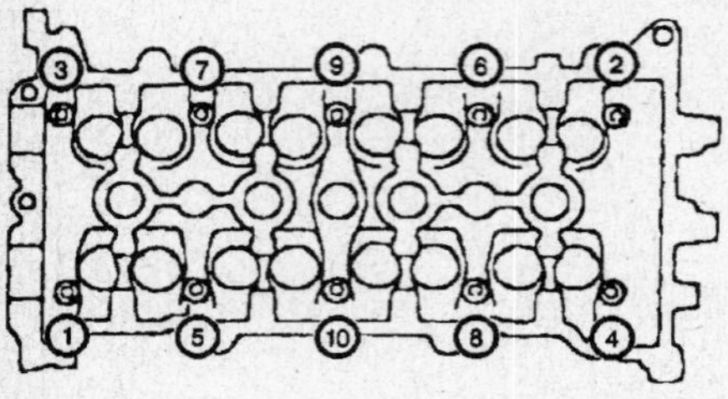

Fig. 6 Cylinder head bolt loosening sequence. 1998–2000

7. Remove engine wire clamp, mounting bolts and intake manifold brace.
8. Remove fuel return hose from pressure regulator.
9. Remove EGR valve and EGR vacuum modulator.
10. Disconnect throttle body position sensor electrical connector.
11. Remove mounting bolts and accelerator bracket.
12. Remove mounting bolts and throttle body.
13. Remove fuel inlet hose clamp bolt, then the air intake chamber brace and gasket.
14. Remove PCV valve, then the vacuum hose from pressure regulator.
15. Remove mounting nuts, bolts and air intake chamber cover.
16. Remove union bolt and two gaskets, then the fuel inlet pipe from fuel rail.
17. Remove fuel injector electrical connectors.
18. Remove fuel rail mounting bolts, then fuel rail with injectors attached.
19. Remove four insulators, then two spacers from cylinder head.
20. Remove mounting bolts and intake manifold.
21. Remove oxygen sensor electrical connector.
22. Remove front pipe to manifold mounting nuts and bolts, then the upper heat insulator.
23. Remove exhaust manifold brace.
24. Remove cylinder head bolts in sequence, **Fig. 2. Note bolt lengths and locations when removing them from head.**
25. Remove cylinder head from dowels.
26. Reverse procedure to install, noting the following:
    a. Install head bolts in proper location.
    b. **Torque** bolts in several passes to 22 ft. lbs. in sequence **Fig. 3.**
    c. Tighten head bolts an additional 90° in sequence.
    d. Final tighten head bolts an additional 90° in sequence.
    e. Tighten all mounting nuts and bolts to specifications.

1998–2000

1. Relieve fuel system pressure as outlined under "Precautions."
2. Drain coolant and engine oil into suitable containers.
3. Remove washer fluid tank mounting bolt, then position tank aside.
4. Disconnect washer pump connector, then the washer pump fluid line. Plug line to prevent fluid leakage.
5. Remove accessory drive belt.
6. Disconnect alternator electrical connector, then the positive cable at alternator.
7. Remove mounting bolts and alternator.
8. Remove accelerator cable from throttle body.
9. Disconnect IAT sensor, TP sensor and MAP sensor electrical connectors.
10. Remove air cleaner hose and cap assembly.
11. Remove coolant bypass hose clamps from throttle body, then the bypass hoses.
12. Disconnect temperature sensor and fuel injector electrical connectors.
13. Remove upper radiator hose.
14. Remove mounting bolts and fuel injector harness from intake manifold. Position harness above intake manifold.
15. Remove mounting bolts and intake manifold support bracket.
16. Disconnect all required vacuum hoses.
17. Remove fuel injector harness brackets.
18. Disconnect oxygen sensor electrical connector.
19. Remove mounting nuts, oxygen sensor and bracket.
20. Raise and support vehicle.
21. Remove mounting bolts and springs from exhaust pipe at manifold.
22. Remove exhaust pipe to manifold seal, then one bolt from exhaust manifold to support bracket.
23. Lower vehicle.
24. Support engine using engine support fixture tool No. J-28467-A, or equivalent.
25. Remove righthand side mounting insulator mounting bolts and nuts.
26. Loosen A/C receiver pinch clamp, then lift A/C receiver in order to access righthand side mounting insulator.
27. Remove righthand side mounting insulator.
28. Disconnect ignition coil electrical connectors.
29. Remove injector fuel rail hold-down clamp, then the spark plug wires from cylinder head cover.
30. Remove mounting bolts and ignition coils with spark plug wires attached.
31. Disconnect fuel line at fuel rail.
32. Remove mounting bolts and ground wires from cylinder head.
33. Position injector harness aside, then remove heater hose at cylinder head water bypass pipe.
34. Remove mounting bolt and camshaft sensor.
35. Remove engine coolant temperature sensor.
36. Remove PCV hoses, then the PCV valve from cylinder head cover.
37. Remove mounting bolts and cylinder head cover.
38. Place No. 1 piston at Top Dead Center (TDC), then align camshaft timing sprockets.

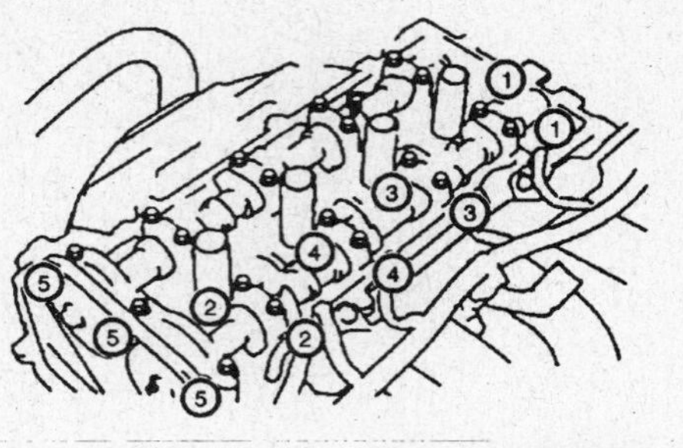

Fig. 7 Intake camshaft cap tightening sequence. 1998–2000

39. Disconnect power steering pressure switch electrical connector.
40. Raise and support vehicle.
41. Remove righthand side lower engine splash shield.
42. Remove through-bolts and power steering pump. Position pump aside.
43. While holding crankshaft pulley, remove bolt and crankshaft pulley, **Fig. 4.**
44. Remove mounting bolt and crankshaft position sensor.
45. Lower vehicle.
46. Remove mounting nut, bolt and drive belt tensioner.
47. Remove mounting bolts and righthand engine mounting bracket.
48. Remove mounting bolts and timing chain tensioner.
49. Remove mounting bolts, nuts and timing chain cover.
50. Remove crank sensor reluctor, then the timing chain slipper bolt and slipper.
51. Remove crankshaft sprocket, then the timing chain.
52. Remove mounting bolts and camshaft sprockets.
53. Remove camshaft bearing cap bolts in sequence, **Fig. 5,** then the bearing caps and camshafts.
54. Remove valve lifters, keeping them in original order.
55. Raise engine using suitable floor jack. **Use wooden block in order to protect oil pan when lifting engine.**
56. Reposition holding fixture.
57. Remove cylinder head bolts in sequence, **Fig. 6,** then the cylinder head.
58. Reverse procedure to install, noting the following:
    a. **On 1999–2000 models, torque** cylinder head bolts to 18 ft. lbs. in sequence, **Fig. 3.**
    b. **On all models, torque** cylinder head bolts to 36 ft. lbs. in sequence.
    c. Tighten bolts an additional 90° using torque angle meter tool No. J-36660, or equivalent, in sequence.
    d. Install intake camshaft.
    e. **Torque** camshaft cap bolts 1–4 to 10 ft. lbs. in sequence, **Fig. 7,** then **torque** bolts (5) to 17 ft. lbs.
    f. Install exhaust camshaft. **Torque** camshaft cap bolts 1– 4 to 10 ft. lbs.

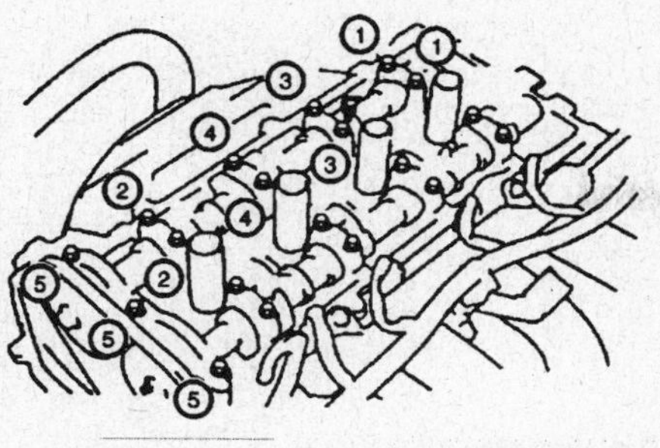

GC1069801050000X

Fig. 8 Exhaust camshaft cap tightening sequence. 1998–2000

in sequence, **Fig. 8,** then **torque** bolts (5) to 17 ft. lbs.

g. Tighten mounting bolts to specifications.

VALVE CLEARANCE SPECIFICATIONS

Year	Engine	Intake	Exhaust
1997–2000	All	.006–.010	.010–.014

VALVE ADJUSTMENT

1997

Measure and adjust valve clearance while the engine is cold.

1. Remove cylinder head cover.
2. Set No. 1 cylinder at TDC on compression stroke.
3. Turn crankshaft to align groove in crankshaft pulley with "0" mark on No. 1 timing belt cover. **Ensure valve lifters on No. 1 cylinder have freeplay. If not, rotate crankshaft pulley 360° and align "0" mark on timing belt cover.**
4. Measure and record valve lash clearance between cam lobe and adjusting shim on No. 1 cylinder intake and exhaust valves, No. 2 cylinder intake and No. 3 cylinder exhaust. Record any clearances which do not meet specifications.
5. Rotate crankshaft pulley 360° and align "0" mark on timing belt cover.
6. Measure and record valve lash clearance between cam lobe and adjusting shim on No. 2 cylinder exhaust valve, No. 3 intake and No. 4 intake and exhaust valves. Record any clearances which do not meet specifications.
7. If clearance is not within specifications, obtain valve clearance adjustment set tool No. J-37141-A, or equivalent.
8. Insert valve spring compression tool No. J-37141-1, or equivalent, between camshaft and lifter adjusting shim. This action will compress valve spring and push lifter down.
9. Insert lifter holding tool No. J-37141-2A, or equivalent, between camshaft and lifter. Position bottom edge of tool on lifter and not on adjusting shim, **Fig. 9.**

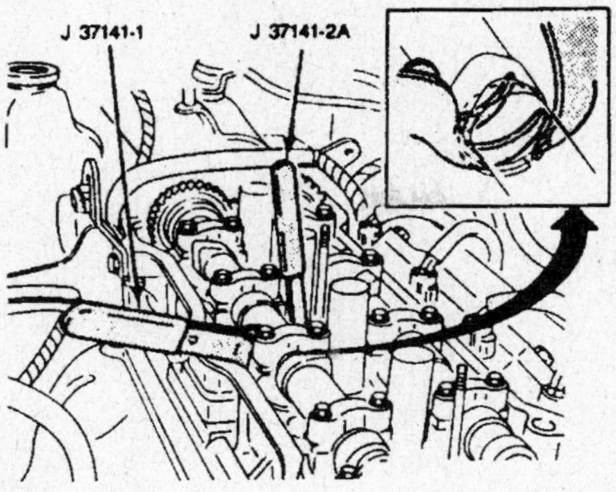

GC1069100488000X

Fig. 9 Valve spring depression. 1997

AVAILABLE SHIMS

Shim No.	Thickness	Shim No.	Thickness
02	2.500 (0.0984)	20	2.950 (0.1161)
04	2.550 (0.1004)	22	3.000 (0.1181)
06	2.600 (0.1024)	24	3.050 (0.1201)
08	2.650 (0.1043)	26	3.100 (0.1220)
10	2.700 (0.1063)	28	3.150 (0.1240)
12	2.750 (0.1083)	30	3.200 (0.1260)
14	2.800 (0.1102)	32	3.250 (0.1280)
16	2.850 (0.1122)	34	3.300 (0.1299)
18	2.900 (0.1142)		

Intake valve clearance (cold):
0.15 – 0.25 mm (0.006 – 0.010 in.)

Example: A 2.800 mm shim is installed and the measured clearance is 0.450 mm. Replace the 2.800 mm shim with shim No. 24 (3.050 mm).

GC1069100490000X

Fig. 11 Valve shim size chart. 1997

10. Remove spring compression tool No. J-37141-1, or equivalent. Lifter holding tool No. J-37141-2A should hold lifter down away from camshaft.
11. Remove adjusting shim with suitable small screwdriver and magnetic finger, **Fig. 10.**
12. Measure thickness of removed shim.
13. Calculate thickness of new shim required by using the following formula:
    a. T = Thickness of shim removed.
    b. A = Valve clearance measured.
    c. N = Thickness of shim required.
    d. For intake valves use formula N = T + (A – .008 inch).
    e. For exhaust valves use formula N = T + (A – .010 inch).
    f. Select shim from **Fig. 11** with thickness as close as possible to calculated value.
14. Install new adjusting shims as required.
15. Depress valve spring using spring compressor tool No. J-37141-1 and remove lifter holding tool No. J-37141-2A, or equivalents.
16. Install cylinder head cover.

1998–2000

Measure and adjust valve clearance while the engine is cold.

1. Remove cylinder head cover.

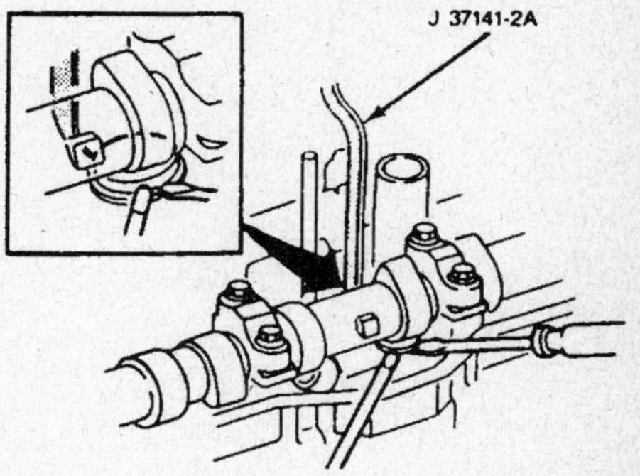

GC1069100489000X

Fig. 10 Adjusting shim removal. 1997

2. Set No. 1 cylinder at TDC on compression stroke.
3. Turn crankshaft to align groove in crankshaft pulley with "0" mark on No. 1 timing belt cover. **Ensure valve lifters on No. 1 cylinder have freeplay. If not, rotate crankshaft pulley 360° and align "0" mark on timing belt cover.**
4. Measure and record valve lash clearance between intake cam lobes and lifters on cylinder Nos. 1 and 2. Record any clearances which do not meet specifications.
5. Measure and record valve lash clearance between exhaust cam lobes and lifters on cylinder Nos. 1 and 3. Record any clearances which do not meet specifications.
6. Rotate crankshaft pulley 360° and align "0" mark on timing belt cover.
7. Measure and record valve lash clearance between intake cam lobes and lifters on cylinder Nos. 3 and 4. Record any clearances which do not meet specifications.
8. Measure and record valve lash clearance between exhaust cam lobes and lifters on cylinder Nos. 2 and 4. Record any clearances which do not meet specifications.
9. If any clearances did not meet specifications, proceed as follows:
    a. Remove valve lifters from offending locations.
    b. Measure removed lifter's thickness, using outside micrometer tool No. J-26900-1, or equivalent.
    c. After measuring lifter's thickness, refer to recorded measurement of that location.
    d. Compare two measurements, then select valve lifter which will provide proper clearance. Lifters are available in 35 different sizes ranging from .1992–.2260 inch in .0008 inch increments.

TIMING BELT COVER

REPLACE

1. Raise and support vehicle.
2. Remove righthand lower stone shield.
3. Lower vehicle.
4. Disconnect engine wiring harness from upper timing belt cover.

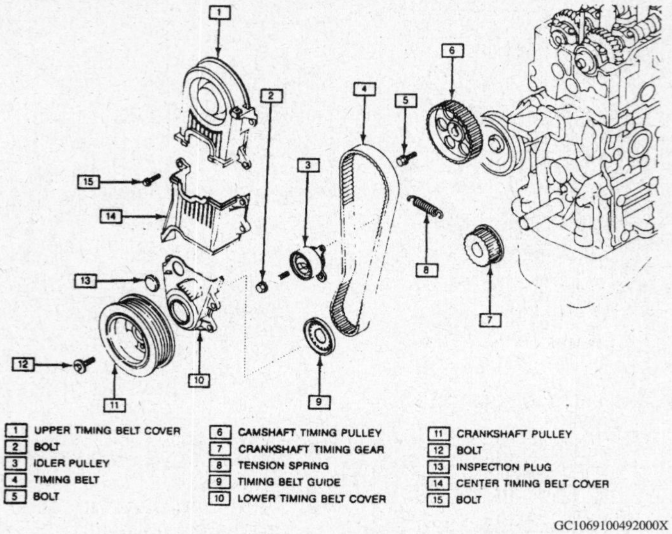

Fig. 12 Timing belt components

5. Remove accessory drive belts.
6. Remove crankshaft pulley using puller tool No. J-1859-03, or equivalent.
7. Remove cylinder head cover and windshield washer reservoir.
8. Support engine using engine support fixture tool No. J-28467-A, or equivalent.
9. Remove righthand engine mount through-bolt.
10. Raise and support vehicle.
11. Remove two rear transaxle mount to main crossmember nuts.
12. Remove two center transaxle mount to center crossmember nuts.
13. Lower vehicle.
14. Raise engine and remove water pump pulley.
15. Remove timing belt covers mounting screws and timing belt covers, **Fig. 12.**
16. Reverse procedure to install.

TIMING BELT & CAMSHAFT TIMING PULLEY

REPLACE

REMOVAL

1. Remove wiper reservoir, cruise control actuator cover and cable.
2. Remove cruise control actuator.
3. Raise and support engine.
4. Remove righthand wheel and wheel housing.
5. Remove accessory drive belts.
6. Lower vehicle.
7. Remove A/C compressor keeping hoses attached. Position compressor aside.
8. Remove A/C compressor bracket.
9. Remove power steering pump keeping hoses attached. Position pump aside.
10. Disconnect alternator and oil pressure switch electrical connections.
11. Remove wiring harness cover and harness from cylinder head.
12. Remove spark plug wires and plugs.
13. Remove PCV hoses from cylinder head covers.
14. Remove cylinder head covers and gaskets.
15. Turn crankshaft to position No. 1 cylinder at TDC on its compression stroke. Valve lifters for No. 1 cylinder should be loose.
16. Disconnect engine ground wire from righthand fender apron.
17. Disconnect engine mounts as previously described.
18. Remove water pump and crankshaft pulleys using puller tool No. J-1859-03, or equivalent.
19. Remove mounting bolts and timing belt covers.
20. Slide timing belt guide from crankshaft.
21. Ensure timing marks are aligned, **Fig. 13.**
22. If timing belt is to be reused, mark timing belt with arrow showing direction of engine rotation.
23. Remove idler pulley bolt, idler pulley and tension spring.
24. Remove timing belt from camshaft and crankshaft timing gears.
25. Remove camshaft timing gear while holding camshaft with hexagonal wrench head, **Fig. 14.**
26. Remove crankshaft timing gear using two suitable flat blade screwdrivers to pry off.

INSTALLATION

1. Install camshaft and crankshaft timing gear aligning keyways on shafts.
2. Tighten camshaft timing gear while holding camshaft with hexagonal wrench head, **Fig. 14.**
3. Install idler pulley and idler pulley spring.
4. Push idler pulley to its extreme lefthand travel and tighten idler pulley.
5. Install timing belt to camshaft and crankshaft timing gears and idler pulley.
6. Loosen idler pulley bolt allowing spring to pull pulley to right.
7. Temporarily install crankshaft pulley bolt and turn crankshaft two complete revolutions clockwise.

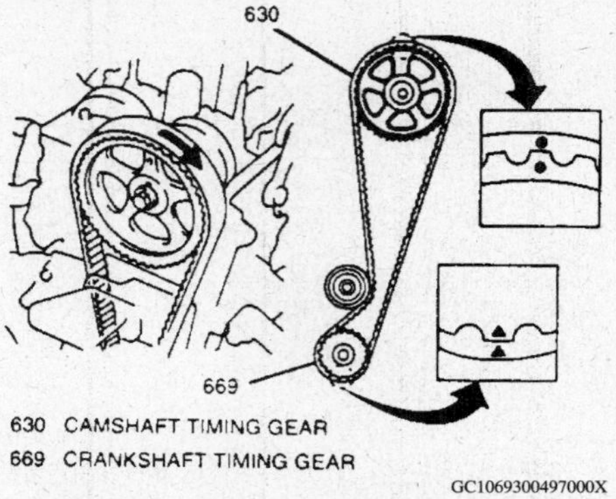

Fig. 13 Engine timing marks

8. Ensure timing marks are still aligned.
9. Measure timing belt deflection, **Fig. 15,** which should be .20–.24 inch with 4.4 lbs. of pressure applied. Replace timing belt if not within specification. If timing belt is within specification, tighten idler pulley.
10. Install timing belt guide, facing cupped side outward.
11. Install timing belt covers starting with lowest cover to highest.
12. Install crankshaft pulley and secure with one bolt.
13. Install engine mount to body.
14. Raise and support vehicle.
15. Install mounting brackets to engine mount.
16. Install righthand side wheel housing and wheel.
17. Lower vehicle.
18. Install A/C pipe bracket and engine ground wire to righthand front fender.
19. Install new cylinder cover gasket and cover.
20. Install PCV hoses, spark plugs and wires.
21. Install engine wiring harness and cover.
22. Connect alternator and oil pressure switch electrical connectors.
23. Install power steering oil pump and air conditioner compressor.
24. Install and adjust accessory drive belts.
25. Install cruise control actuator and windshield washer reservoir.

TIMING CHAIN

REPLACE

1. Drain coolant into an suitable container.
2. Remove windshield washer fluid reservoir mounting bolt. Position reservoir to side.
3. Disconnect windshield washer pump connector, then the fluid line. Plug line to prevent fluid leakage.
4. Remove tension from drive belt tensioner by moving tensioner in clockwise direction.
5. Remove accessory drive belt, then the alternator.
6. Support engine using engine support fixture tool No. J-28467-A, or equivalent.

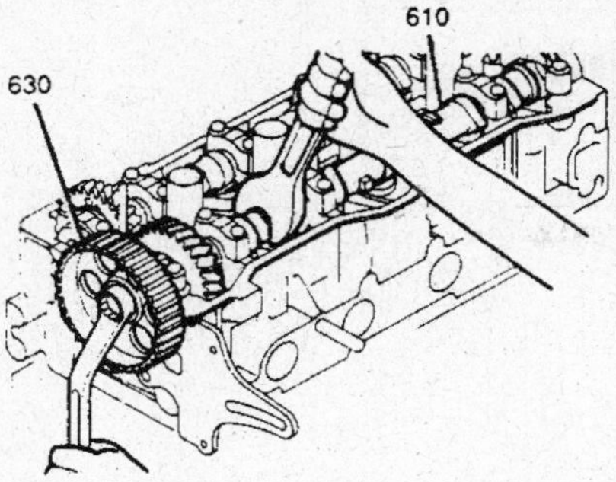

610 EXHAUST CAMSHAFT
630 CAMSHAFT TIMING GEAR

GC1069300498000X

Fig. 14 Camshaft timing gear replacement

7. Remove righthand side engine mount mounting bolts and nuts.
8. Loosen A/C receiver pinch clamp, then lift receiver in order to access righthand side engine mount.
9. Remove righthand side engine mount.
10. Remove cylinder head cover.
11. Rotate No. 1 piston to TDC, then align camshaft timing sprockets.
12. Raise and support vehicle.
13. Remove righthand side lower engine splash shield.
14. Disconnect power steering oil pressure switch electrical connector.
15. Remove through-bolts and power steering pump from mount. Position pump aside with hoses intact.
16. Remove mounting bolt and crankshaft pulley while holding crankshaft pulley, **Fig. 4.**
17. Remove mounting bolt and crankshaft position sensor.
18. Lower vehicle, then remove drive belt tensioner nut.
19. Remove mounting bolt and drive belt tensioner.
20. Remove three mounting bolts and righthand engine mounting bracket.
21. Remove mounting bolts and timing chain tensioner.
22. Remove mounting bolts, nuts and timing chain cover.
23. Remove crankshaft sensor reluctor, then the slipper bolts and slipper.
24. Remove timing chain dampener bolt, dampener, shoe bolts and shoe.
25. Remove crankshaft sprocket, then the timing chain.
26. Reverse procedure to install, noting the following:
    a. Align camshaft timing marks.
    b. Turn crankshaft until crankshaft keyway faces upward.
    c. Tighten mounting bolts to specifications.

CAMSHAFT

REPLACE

1997

Removal

1. Remove cylinder head cover.

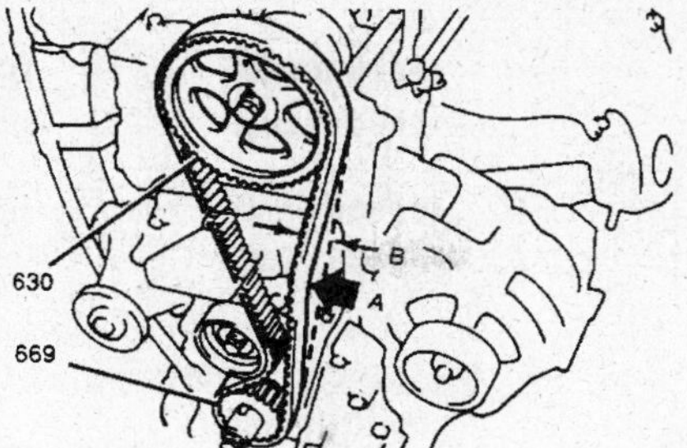

A 20N (4.4 lbs.)
B 5 – 6 mm (0.20 – 0.24")
630 CAMSHAFT TIMING GEAR
669 CRANKSHAFT TIMING GEAR

GC1069300499000X

Fig. 15 Timing belt tension inspection

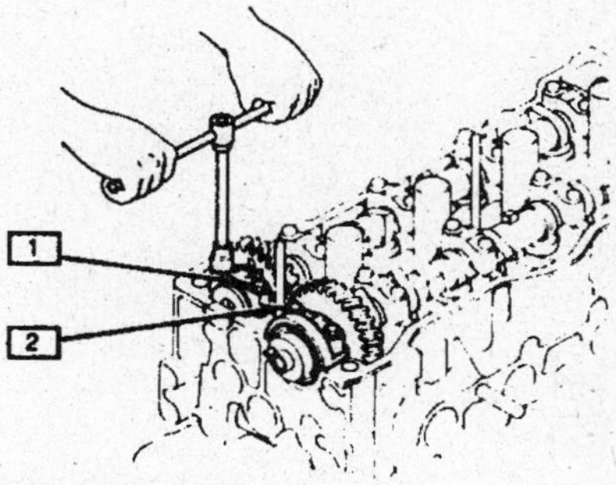

1 INTAKE BEARING CAP BOLT
2 EXHAUST BEARING CAP BOLT

GC1069100503000X

Fig. 17 Number 1 bearing cap bolts

2. Remove timing belt as previously described.
3. Remove camshaft timing gear by holding camshaft with wrench and removing camshaft bolt. **Use caution not to damage camshaft or cylinder head with wrench.**
4. With No. 1 cylinder in TDC position, service bolt hole of intake camshaft gear should be in position, **Fig. 16.**
5. Alternately loosen No. 1 (front) intake and exhaust camshaft bearing cap bolts in several steps, **Fig. 17.**
6. Remove No. 1 bearing caps.
7. Fasten intake camshaft sub-gear to main gear with service bolt, **Fig. 18.**
8. Uniformly loosen each intake camshaft bearing cap bolt in several steps in sequence outlined in **Fig. 19.**
9. Remove intake camshaft bearing caps and camshaft. **The camshaft must be held level while it is being removed. If camshaft is not kept level, portion of cylinder head receiving shaft thrust may crack or be damaged. If camshaft cannot be lifted out straight and level, tighten No. 3 bearing cap and alternately loosen bolts of bearing cap in several steps while pulling up on camshaft gear.**
10. Rotate exhaust camshaft 105° using suitable wrench.
11. Place lockpin in position, **Fig. 20.**
12. Uniformly loosen each exhaust camshaft bearing cap bolt in several steps in sequence outlined in **Fig. 21.**
13. Remove exhaust camshaft bearing caps and camshaft.
14. Disassemble intake camshaft by inserting pins into service holes in camshaft sub-gear, **Fig. 22.**
15. Turn sub-gear clockwise using screwdriver and remove pin C.
16. Remove snap ring, wave washer, camshaft sub gear and camshaft gear spring.
17. Remove exhaust camshaft oil seal.

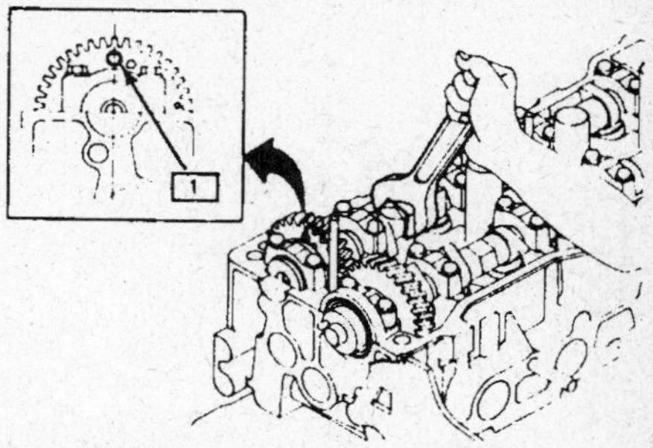

1 SERVICE BOLT HOLE (INTAKE CAMSHAFT)

GC1069100502000X

Fig. 16 Service bolt hole alignment

Installation

1. Install ring, wave washer, camshaft sub-gear and camshaft gear spring.
2. Install pins A and B, **Fig. 22,** into service holes of camshaft sub-gear.
3. Align camshaft drive gear holes and sub-gear using suitable screwdriver, by turning camshaft sub-gear clockwise.
4. Install pin C.
5. Install exhaust camshaft on cylinder head so that No. 1 and No. 3 cam lobes push their valves lifters evenly.
6. Install bearing caps on journals with arrows pointing toward crankshaft pulley.
7. Tighten each bearing cap to specification in several steps in sequence, **Fig. 23.**
8. Apply multi-purpose grease to new exhaust camshaft oil seal and install oil seal using seal installer tool No. J-35403, or equivalent.
9. Position lockpin of exhaust camshaft so that No. 4 cylinder cam lobes push their lifters.
10. Engage intake camshaft gear with exhaust camshaft gear by matching alignment marks.
11. Roll camshaft into position keeping timing gears engaged.
12. Install intake camshaft bearing cap Nos. 2–5 with arrows pointing toward crankshaft pulley. No. 1 bearing cap will be installed later in this procedure.
13. Tighten intake camshaft bearing cap bolts to specifications in several steps in sequence, **Fig. 24.**
14. Remove pins from intake camshaft sub-gear.
15. Install No. 1 bearing cap. If No. 1 bearing cap does not fit properly, push camshaft gear backward by prying apart cylinder head and camshaft gear with suitable pry tool.

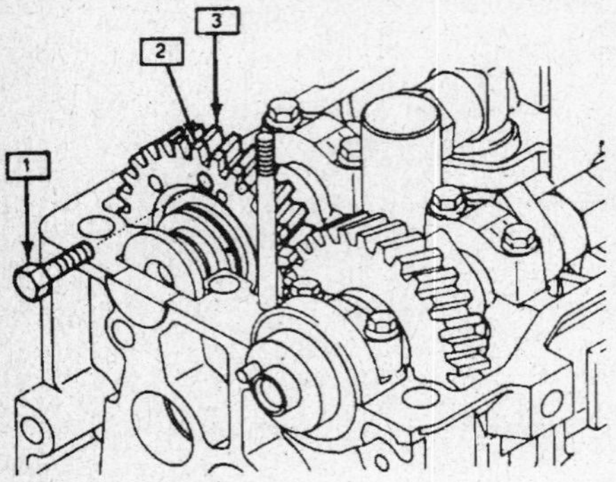

1 SERVICE BOLT
2 SUB-GEAR
3 MAIN GEAR

GC1069100504000X

Fig. 18 Fastening sub-gear to main gear

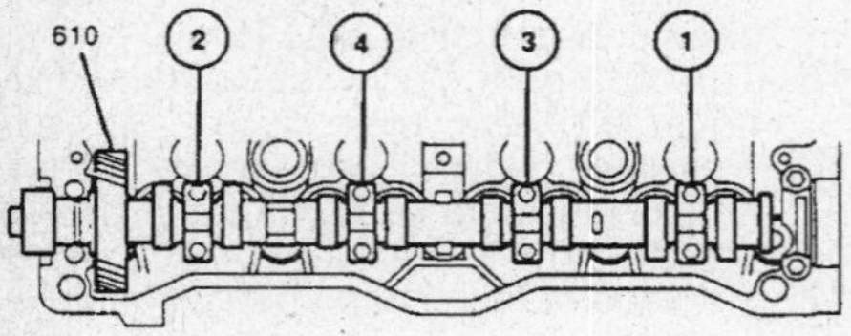

610 EXHAUST CAMSHAFT

GC1069100507000X

Fig. 21 Exhaust camshaft removal sequence

16. Turn exhaust camshaft one revolution from TDC to TDC of No. 1 cylinder.
17. Ensure alignment marks on exhaust and intake gear align.
18. Install camshaft timing gear and secure camshaft, then install timing gear bolt.
19. Install timing belt as previously described.
20. Install cylinder head cover.

1998–2000

Refer to "Cylinder Head, Replace."

PISTON & ROD ASSEMBLY

Assemble pistons to connecting rods as shown, **Fig. 25.**

MAIN & ROD BEARINGS

1997

Main and rod service bearings are available in 5 standard sizes, marked 1–5. If replacing a bearing, replace with one having the same number. If the number of the bearing cannot be determined, select a bearing according to the numbers imprinted on the cylinder block and crankshaft then refer to **Fig. 26** for proper bearing number.

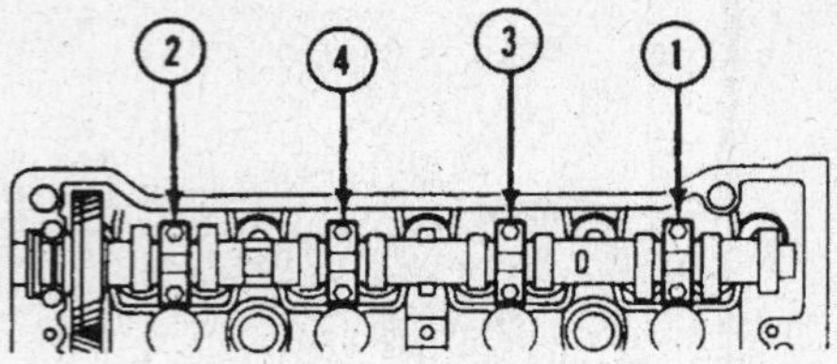

GC1069100505000X

Fig. 19 Intake camshaft removal sequence

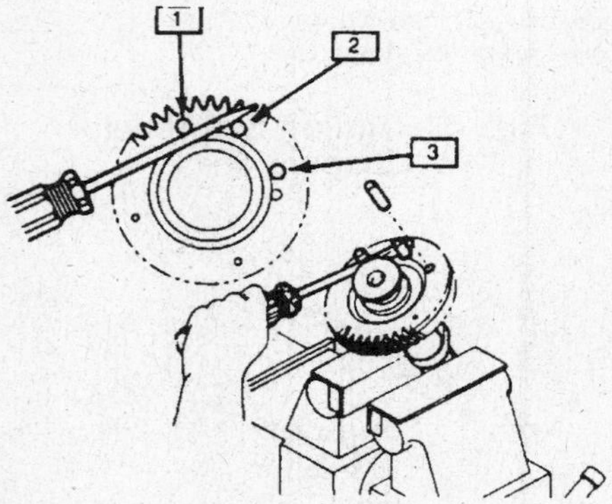

1 PIN A
2 PIN B
3 PIN C

GC1069100508000X

Fig. 22 Exploded view of intake camshaft

1998–2000

Main bearings are available in 4 sizes, marked 1–4. If replacing a bearing, replace with one having the same number. If the number of the bearing cannot be determined, select a bearing according to the numbers imprinted on the cylinder block and crankshaft. For example, a "4" block and a "3" crankshaft equals a "7," which calls for bearing No. 3. Totals 0–2 require bearing No. 1. Totals 3–5 require bearing No. 2. Totals 6–8 require bearing No. 3, and totals 9–11 require bearing No. 4.

Rod bearings are available in 3 sizes, marked 1–3. If replacing a bearing, replace with one having the same number as marked on the connecting rod.

CRANKSHAFT REAR OIL SEAL

REPLACE

1997

1. Remove transaxle.
2. Mark flywheel to crankshaft position, then remove flywheel.
3. Remove rear end plate.
4. Remove rear main oil seal retainer.

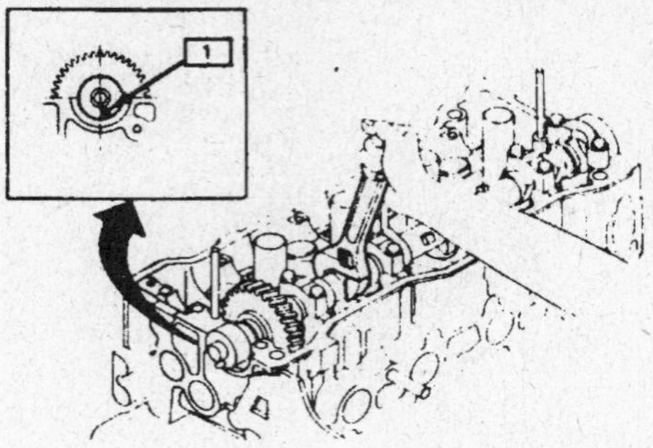

1 KNOCKPIN POSITION

GC1069100506000X

Fig. 20 Knockout pin position

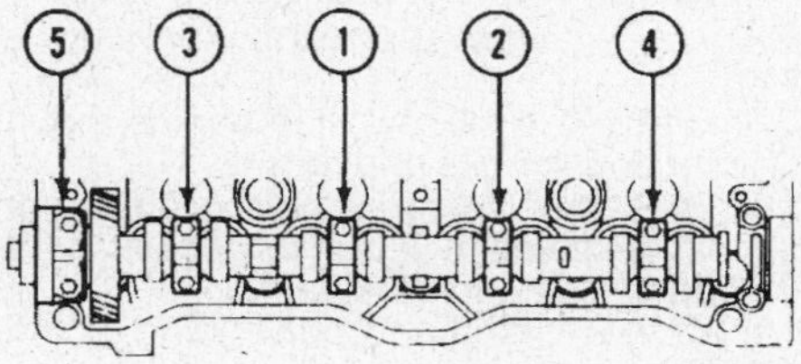

GC1069100509000X

Fig. 23 Exhaust camshaft tightening sequence

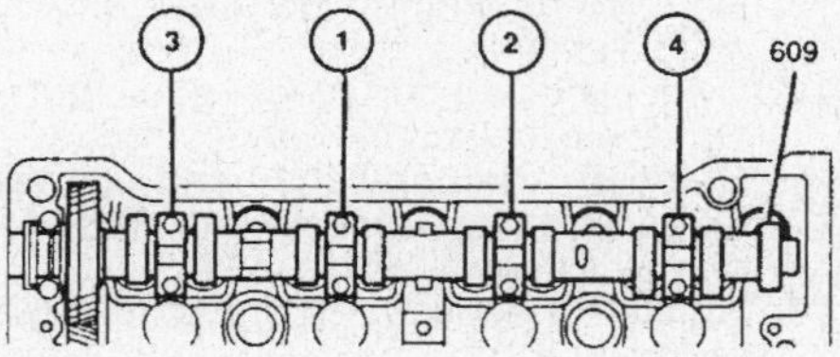

609 INTAKE CAMSHAFT

GC1069100510000X

Fig. 24 Intake camshaft tightening sequence

5. Carefully drive oil seal from retainer using suitable hammer and screwdriver.
6. Install new seal using seal installer tool No. J-35388, or equivalent.
7. Apply wheel bearing grease part No. 1051344, or equivalent, to seal lip.
8. Assemble retainer and rear end plate onto engine, then insert and securely tighten mounting bolts.
9. Assemble flywheel assembly to engine, ensuring marks are properly aligned. Apply sealant part No. 12345493, or equivalent, to bolt threads.
10. Install transaxle.

1998–2000

1. Remove transaxle.
2. Mark flywheel to crankshaft position, then remove flywheel.
3. Remove rear end plate if required.
4. Pry out old seal using suitable screwdriver with tape-wrapped tip.
5. Apply suitable multi-purpose grease to

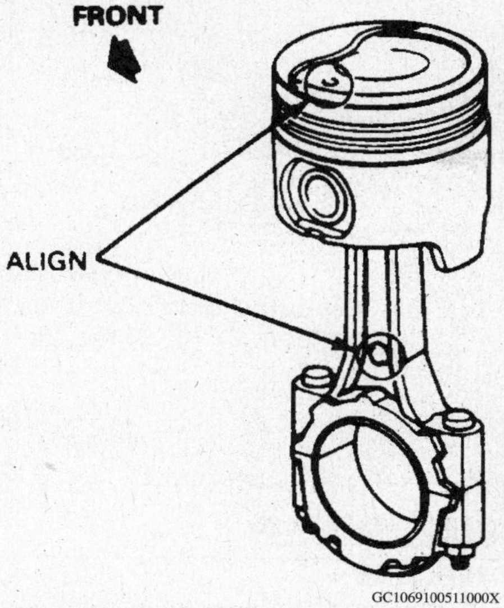

Fig. 25 Piston & rod assembly

new seal's lip.

6. Carefully tap new seal into place until its surface is flush with the retainer edge, using suitable hammer.
7. Assemble flywheel assembly to engine, ensuring marks are properly aligned. Apply sealant part No. 12345493, or equivalent, to bolt threads.
8. Install transaxle.

OIL PAN

REPLACE

1997

1. Raise and support vehicle.
2. Drain engine oil.
3. Remove righthand and lefthand stone covers.
4. Disconnect oxygen sensor connector.
5. Disconnect exhaust pipe from catalytic converter.
6. Disconnect exhaust pipe from exhaust manifold.
7. Remove oil pan bolts and pan.
8. Reverse procedure to install.

1998–2000

1. Raise and support vehicle.
2. Drain engine oil into an suitable container.
3. Remove righthand lower engine splash shield.
4. Remove mounting nuts, bolts and oil pan. **Avoid damaging oil pan contact surface of lower cylinder block.**
5. Remove mounting bolts and oil strainer, if required.
6. Reverse procedure to install, noting the following:
   a. Apply continuous bead of silicone sealant part No. 12346240, or equivalent, to engine oil pan mating surface.
   b. Tighten mounting bolts to specifications.

	NUMBER MARKED								
CYLINDER BLOCK	1			2			3		
CRANKSHAFT	0	1	2	0	1	2	0	1	2
USE BEARING	1	2	3	2	3	4	3	4	5

GC1069701051000X

Fig. 26 Main & rod bearing identification. 1997

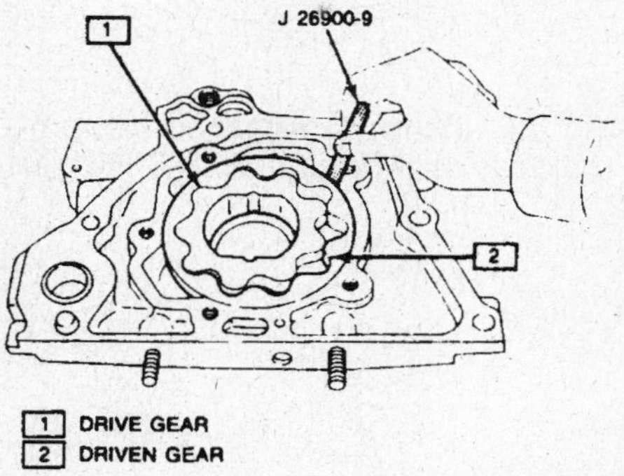

Fig. 28 Oil pump gear to gear clearance inspection. 1997

OIL PUMP

REPLACE

1997

1. Remove timing belt/chain as previously described.
2. Raise and support vehicle.
3. Remove crankshaft timing gear pulley.
4. Remove oil pan if required as previously described.
5. Remove oil pump bolts and oil pump assembly.
6. Reverse procedure to install, noting the following:
   a. Measure driven gear to housing clearance, **Fig. 27.** If clearance is more than .0078 inch, replace oil pump.
   b. Measure drive gear to driven gear clearance, **Fig. 28.** If clearance is more than .0012 inch, replace gear set.
   c. Measure oil pump body to gear clearance, **Fig. 29.** If clearance is more than .004 inch replace oil pump.

1998–2000

1. Remove timing chain as previously described.
2. Remove mounting bolts and pump. Discard gasket.
3. Inspect pump condition as follows:
   a. Measure radial clearance between pump outer gear and housing, **Fig. 30.** Replace outer gear or complete pump if clearance exceeds .0138 inch.
   b. Measure side clearance between pump gears and straightedge, **Fig. 31.** Replace gears if clearance exceeds .0059 inch.
   c. Measure tip clearance between gear tips, **Fig. 32.** Replace gears if clearance exceeds .0138 inch.

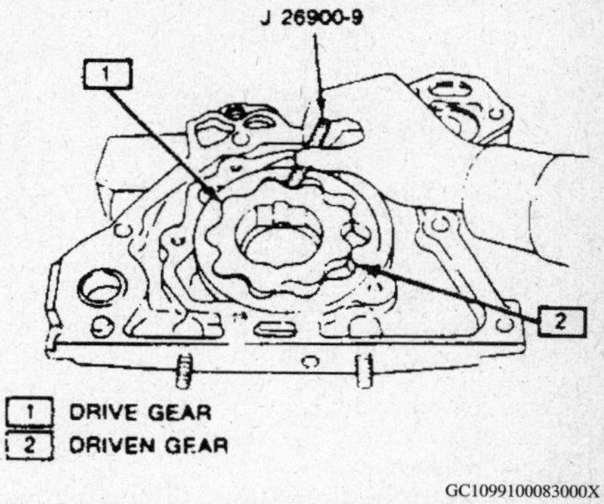

Fig. 27 Oil pump gear to housing clearance inspection. 1997

4. Reverse procedure to install. Tighten mounting bolts to specifications.

BELT TENSION DATA

Year	Engine VIN	Belt	New Ft. Lbs.	Used Ft. Lbs.
1997–2000	6 & 8	Alt.	170–180	95–135
		A/C	①②	①③
		PS	100–121	55–88

① — With 22 lbs. exerted.
② — Deflection of .24–.28 inch.
③ — Deflection of .33–.37 inch.

COOLING SYSTEM BLEED

These engines do not require a specific bleeding procedure. After filling cooling system, bring engine to operating temperature with radiator/pressure cap off. Air will then be automatically bled through cap opening.

THERMOSTAT

REPLACE

1. Drain engine coolant into an suitable container, then disconnect engine coolant switch electrical connector.
2. Remove mounting nuts, housing, thermostat and gasket or O-ring.
3. Ensure gasket or O-ring contact surfaces are clean and free of debris.
4. Reverse procedure to install. Tighten thermostat housing bolts to specifications.

WATER PUMP

REPLACE

1997

1. Drain coolant into an suitable container.
2. Raise and support engine using tool No. J-28467-A, or equivalent.
3. Remove righthand engine mount and insulator as previously described.
4. Remove timing covers.

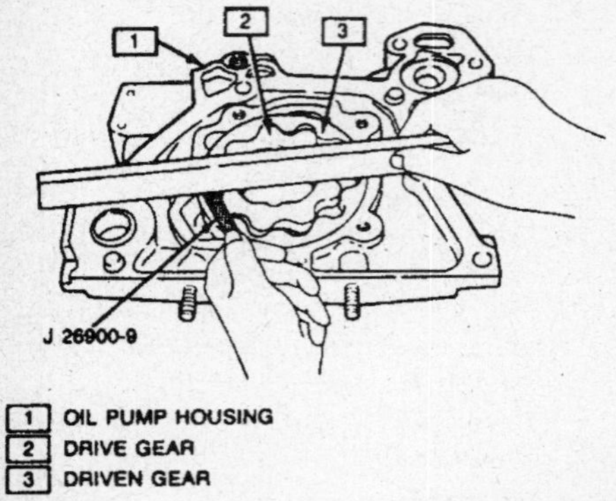

Fig. 29 Oil pump side clearance inspection. 1997

5. **On models equipped with power steering,** remove front transaxle mount.
6. **On all models,** remove radiator fan motor assembly, then the engine wiring harness retainer clip from engine.
7. Remove oil level indicator from guide tube.
8. Remove mounting bolt and guide tube.
9. Remove engine coolant temperature sending unit electrical connector, then the two nuts mounting engine coolant inlet pipe to cylinder block.
10. Loosen hose clamp, then remove coolant inlet pipe.
11. Remove inlet hose from water pump.
12. **On models equipped with power steering,** raise engine.
13. **On all models,** remove mounting bolts, water pump and O-ring.
14. Reverse procedure to install.

1998–2000

1. Drain coolant into an suitable container.
2. Remove engine accessory drive belts.
3. Raise and support vehicle.
4. Remove engine righthand side lower splash shield.
5. Remove mounting bolts, water pump and O-ring.
6. Reverse procedure to install. Tighten mounting bolts to specifications.

RADIATOR

REPLACE

1997

1. Drain coolant into an suitable container.
2. Remove coolant recovery reservoir cap and hoses.
3. Remove upper radiator hose at radiator, **Fig. 33.**
4. Remove lower radiator hose at thermostat housing.
5. Unclip oxygen sensor electrical connector from fan shroud.
6. Raise and properly support vehicle.
7. Remove engine splash shield.
8. Remove lower radiator hose.

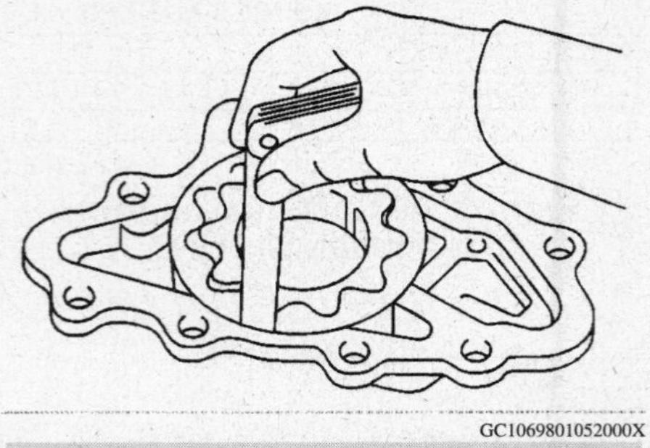

Fig. 30 Oil pump gear to housing clearance inspection. 1998–2000

Fig. 32 Oil pump gear tip clearance inspection. 1998–2000

9. **On models with automatic transaxle,** remove transaxle cooling lines.
10. **On all models,** remove cooling fan electrical connector.
11. Remove radiator fan assembly lower bolts.
12. Lower vehicle.
13. Remove radiator fan assembly upper bolts and fan assembly.
14. Remove radiator support bracket bolts.
15. Remove radiator.
16. Reverse procedure to install.

1998–2000

1. Drain coolant into an suitable container.
2. Raise and support vehicle.
3. Remove engine righthand and lefthand splash shields.
4. **On models equipped with automatic transaxle,** disconnect transaxle fluid cooler hoses at radiator.
5. **On all models,** disconnect radiator lower hose at radiator.
6. Lower vehicle.
7. Remove radiator upper bracket bolts.
8. Disconnect cooling fan electrical connectors.
9. Disconnect radiator upper hose at radiator.
10. Disconnect overflow hose from radiator filler neck.

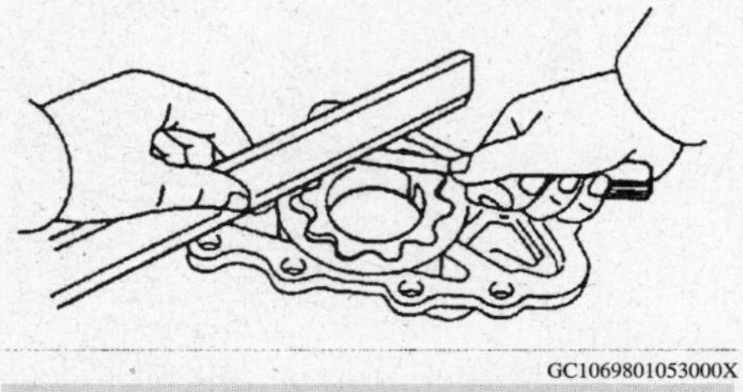

Fig. 31 Oil pump side clearance inspection. 1998–2000

11. Carefully remove radiator and cooling fan assembly.
12. Reverse procedure to install.

FUEL PUMP

REPLACE

1. Release fuel system pressure as outlined in "Precautions. "
2. Remove rear seat cushion, then the floor service hole cover mounting screws and cover.
3. Disconnect fuel sender electrical connector, then the fuel feed hose from sender assembly.
4. Remove fuel return hose from sender assembly.
5. Remove mounting bolts and fuel sender.
6. Remove fuel pump by pulling off lower side of pump from bracket.
7. Disconnect fuel pump electrical connector.
8. Remove rubber cushion from fuel pump, then the fuel pump strainer from fuel pump.
9. Reverse procedure to install.

FUEL FILTER

REPLACE

1997

1. Relieve fuel system pressure as outlined under "Precautions."
2. Remove intake air temperature sensor electrical connector, then loosen air cleaner (ACL) hose clamp bolt.
3. Remove four cap clips from ACL, then ACL hose and cap.
4. Remove evaporative emission hose (EVAP) from EVAP canister.
5. Remove mounting bolt and EVAP canister.
6. Remove fuel feed outlet and outlet lines from fuel filter, then the fuel filter mounting bolts and fuel filter, **Fig. 34.**
7. Reverse procedure to install.

1998–2000

1. Remove fuel pump and level sender assembly as previously described.
2. Remove fuel pump from sender assembly.
3. Separate fuel filter from level sender.
4. Reverse procedure to install.

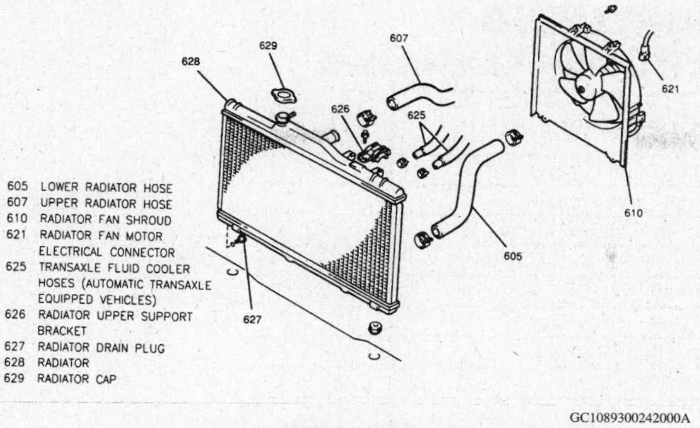

Fig. 33 Radiator removal. 1997

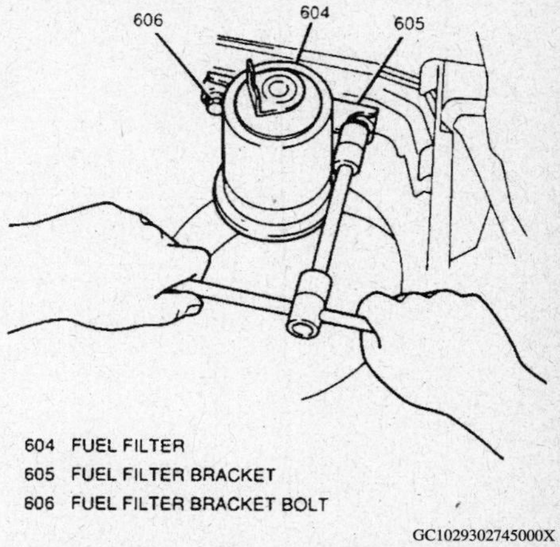

Fig. 34 Fuel filter replacement. 1997

TIGHTENING SPECIFICATIONS

Year	Component	Torque/ Ft. Lbs.
1997	Accelerator Bracket	11
	A/C Compressor Flexible Hose	84–96①
	A/C Pipe Bracket	84–96①
	Actuator	19
	Air Cleaner (ACL) Lower Case	84–96①
	Air Intake Chamber Brace	21
	Air Intake Chamber Cover	14
	Air Pipe	72–84①
	Alternator Bracket	23
	Camshaft Bearing Cap Bolts	106–120①
	Camshaft Timing Gear	43
	Center Support Bearing	45
	Connecting Rod Bearing Cap Nuts	22②
	Coolant Pump	10
	Coolant Pump Pulley	18
	Coolant Reservoir	11
	Crankshaft Pulley	87
	Cruise Control Actuator Bracket	19
	Cylinder Head	③
	EGR Solenoid Valve	106–120①
	EGR Valve To EGR Pipe	43
	EGR Valve To Intake Manifold	106–120①
	Engine Hanger	20
	Engine Mount Bracket	38
	Engine Mount Through Bolts	47
	Engine Mount To Body	19
	Engine Mount To Cylinder Block Brake	38
	Engine Mount To Engine Bracket "A" Bolts	47
	Engine Mount To Engine Bracket "B" Bolts	18
	Engine Mount To Engine Bracket "C" Bolts	47
	Engine Oil Pan	44①
	Exhaust Manifold Brace	29
	Exhaust Manifold	25
	Flywheel (Automatic Transmission)	47
	Flywheel (Manual Transmission)	58

Continued

TIGHTENING SPECIFICATIONS—Continued

Year	Component	Torque/ Ft. Lbs.
1997	Front Pipe Hanger	14
	Front Pipe Support	14
	Front Pipe To Catalytic Converter	32
	Front Pipe To Exhaust Manifold	46
	Fuel Feed Pipe Connector	22
	Fuel Inlet Hose Clamp	84–96①
	Fuel Rail	11
	Guide Tube	72–84①
	Idler Pulley	27
	Insulator	47
	Intake Manifold	14
	Intake Manifold Brace	14
	Lower Engine Reinforcement Brace To Cylinder Block ⑥	47
	Lower Engine Reinforcement Brace To Transaxle ⑤	47
	Lower Heat Insulator	72–84①
	Main Bearing Bolt Caps	44
	Mounting Bracket To Engine	47
	Mounting Bracket To Engine	38
	Oil Drain Plug	25
	Oil Pressure Switch	106–120①
	Oil Pump	16
	Oil Strainer	62①
	Power Steering Pump Bracket	32
	Rear End Plate	49①
	Rear Main Seal	84–96①
	Rotor Plate	84–96①
	Splash Shield	84–96①
	Throttle Body	17
	Timing Belt Cover	62①
	Transaxle To Engine	17
	Union	22
	Upper Heat Insulator	72–84①
	Wheel Housing	11
	Wheel Lug	76
	Wiring Harness Cover	53①
1998–2000	Alternator Bolt (14mm)	18
	Alternator Bolt (17mm)	40
	Axle Shaft Heat Shield	13
	Camshaft Bracket	③
	Camshaft Sensor	11
	Camshaft Sprocket	33
	Connecting Rod Cap Bolts	15②
	Coolant Inlet Pipe	11
	Crankshaft Main Bearing Cap Bolts	④
	Crankshaft Position Sensor	106①
	Crankshaft Pulley	105
	Cylinder Head	③
	Drive Belt Tensioner Bolt	51
	Drive Belt Tensioner Nut	21
	Engine Mounting Bracket	40
	Exhaust Manifold Bracket	26
	Exhaust Manifold Heat Shield	11
	Exhaust Manifold	36

Continued

TIGHTENING SPECIFICATIONS—Continued

Year	Component	Torque/ Ft. Lbs.
1998-2000	Exhaust Pipe	46
	Flywheel (Automatic Transmission)	61
	Flywheel (Manual Transmission)	36②
	Front Transaxle Mount	44
	Front Transaxle Mount Through-Bolt	64
	Fuel Injector Wiring Harness	106①
	Ground Wire	78①
	Guide Tube	84①
	Heat Insulator	106①
	Heated Oxygen Sensor (HO2S, 1999–2000)	30
	Ignition Coil Bracket	78①
	Intake Manifold	13
	Intake Manifold Support Bracket	37
	Lower Transmission To Engine	47
	Mounting Insulator Bolts (Righthand)	47
	Mounting Insulator Nuts (Righthand)	38
	Oil Drain Plug	26
	Oil Pan (1998)	79①
	Oil Pan (1999–2000)	97①
	Oil Pump (1998)	79①
	Oil Pump (1999–2000)	97①
	Oil Strainer (1998)	78①
	Oil Strainer (1999–2000)	97①
	Oxygen Sensor (1998)	14
	Power Steering Pump	29
	Radiator Upper Support Bracket	106①
	Starter (1998)	29
	Starter (1999–2000)	22
	Thermostat Housing	80①
	Timing Chain Cover (10mm)	89①
	Timing Chain Cover (12mm)	13
	Timing Chain Cover (13mm)	14
	Timing Chain Slipper (Lefthand)	80①
	Timing Chain Slipper (Righthand)	20
	Timing Chain Tensioner	89①
	Torque Converter	26
	Washer Fluid Tank	80①
	Water Bypass Pipe To Cylinder Head	80①
	Water Pump Bolts (1998)	10
	Water Pump Bolts (1999–2000)	106①

① — Inch lbs.

② — Tighten an additional 90.°

③ — Refer to "Cylinder Head, Replace."

④ — First pass, 16 ft. lbs.; second pass, 32 ft. lbs.; final pass, 32 ft. lbs. then an additional 90.°

Clutch & Manual Transaxle

NOTE: On Air Bag Equipped Models, Refer To "Air Bag System Precautions" Located In The Front Of This Manual For System Disarming & Arming Procedures.

NOTE: Refer To "Computer Relearn Procedures " Located In The Front Of This Manual For Computer Relearn Procedures.

INDEX

PRECAUTIONS

AIR BAG SYSTEMS

Refer to "Air Bag System Precautions" in the front of this manual for system disarming and arming procedures.

BATTERY GROUND CABLE

Prior to service, disconnect battery ground cable and isolate as required.

ADJUSTMENTS

CLUTCH PEDAL

1. Measure height (4) as shown, **Fig. 1.** If height is not 5.45–5.84 inches, adjust as follows:
   a. Remove lower instrument finish panel and air duct.
   b. Loosen locknut (2).
   c. Turn stopper bolt until clutch pedal height is within 5.12–5.51 inches.
   d. Tighten locknut.
2. Inspect clutch pedal freeplay (3), which should be .197–.591 inch. If freeplay is not as specified, adjust as follows:
   a. Depress clutch pedal until resistance is felt.
   b. Loosen locknut (2).
   c. Turn pushrod (1) until freeplay is within .197–.591 inch.
   d. Tighten locknut.
3. Install air duct and lower instrument panel finish panel.

HYDRAULIC SYSTEM SERVICE

HYDRAULIC SYSTEM BLEED

1. Clean top and sides of reservoir to ensure no foreign material enters system.
2. Remove cap and fill reservoir with proper type of brake fluid.
3. Connect one end of clear vinyl tube to bleeder screw and insert other end of tube into half filled container of brake fluid.
4. Slowly pump clutch pedal several times.
5. While pumping clutch pedal, loosen bleeder screw until fluid starts to runout.
6. Tighten bleeder screw.
7. Repeat procedure until no air bubbles exist in escaping fluid.

CLUTCH PEDAL POSITION SWITCH

REPLACE

1. Disconnect electrical connector from CPP switch.
2. Remove CPP switch from clutch and brake pedal bracket by turning switch counterclockwise.
3. Remove locknut from CPP switch.
4. Reverse procedure to install, noting the following:
   a. Connect digital multimeter tool No. J-39200, or equivalent, to CPP switch electrical connector.
   b. Depress clutch pedal to floor, then let it out .6–1.2 inches from floor.
   c. Adjust CPP switch by threading it into pedal bracket until continuity is seen.
   d. Tighten CPP switch locknut to specifications.

CLUTCH ACTUATOR

REPLACE

1. Raise and support vehicle.
2. Disconnect clutch hydraulic line at actuator.
3. Remove mounting bolts and actuator.
4. Reverse procedure to install. Bleed system as described under "Hydraulic System Bleed."

CLUTCH PEDAL

REPLACE

1. Remove knee bolster.
2. Remove Daytime Running Lamp (DRL) control lamp control module bracket as follows:
   a. Remove instrument panel compartment.
   b. Remove two DRL mounting brackets to instrument panel mounting screws.
   c. Disconnect DRL control module electrical connector.
   d. Remove DRL control module with mounting brackets attached.
3. Remove one screw and lefthand air duct.
4. Remove clutch pedal return spring, then the clevis clip and pin.
5. Disconnect Clutch Pedal Position (CPP) switch electrical connector.
6. Remove clutch pedal assembly bracket to clutch master cylinder mounting nuts.
7. Remove bracket to instrument panel bolts and pedal assembly.
8. Reverse procedure to install. Tighten mounting bolts to specifications.

CLUTCH

REPLACE

1. Remove transaxle assembly.
2. Lock flywheel in place using lock tool No. J-35271, or equivalent.
3. Loosen each set bolt one turn at time until spring tension is released.
4. Remove mounting bolts and pull off clutch assembly.
5. Remove release bearing fork and boot from transaxle.

6. Reverse procedure to install. Tighten bolts to specifications.

TRANSAXLE

REPLACE

1997

1. Support engine using engine support fixture tool No. J-28467-A, or equivalent.
2. Remove battery and battery tray.
3. Remove air cleaner assembly.
4. Disconnect back-up lamp switch.
5. Disconnect ground cable at transaxle.
6. Remove two actuator mounting bolts.
7. Remove actuator line bracket.
8. Remove shift cable retainers, end clips and cables from bracket and position aside.
9. Remove lefthand transaxle mount cover, brace and through-bolt.
10. Remove two upper transaxle to engine bolts.
11. Remove starter assembly.
12. Disconnect speedometer cable.
13. Raise and support vehicle.
14. Remove righthand and lefthand stone shields.
15. Drain transaxle oil.
16. Remove drive axles.
17. Remove three center crossmember to radiator support bolts.
18. Remove front and center mount bolt shields.
19. Remove front, center and rear mount nuts.
20. Remove two center crossmember to main crossmember bolts.
21. Remove exhaust hangers.
22. Support main crossmember using suitable jack.
23. Remove eight main crossmember to underbody bolts.
24. Remove two lower A-frame bracket to underbody bolts. **Lower main crossmember slowly while holding onto center crossmember. Center crossmember will be free to fall at this time and could cause serious bodily injury.**
25. Remove front through-bolt and mount.
26. Remove front mount bracket from transaxle.

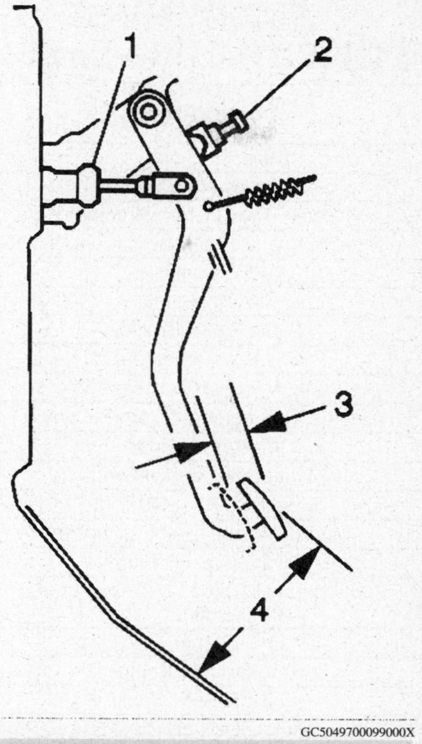

Fig. 1 Clutch pedal adjustment

27. Remove center mount from transaxle.
28. Remove transaxle inspection cover.
29. Remove two lower transaxle bracket to mount bolts.
30. Lower vehicle.
31. Remove remaining transaxle mount to bracket bolts.
32. Lower transaxle to gain clearance to remove transaxle using engine support tool No. J-28467, or equivalent.
33. Remove transaxle mount.
34. Raise and support vehicle.
35. Support transaxle using suitable jack.
36. Remove front and rear lower transaxle to engine bolts.
37. Lower transaxle.
38. Reverse procedure to install.

1998-2000

1. Remove battery, then the air cleaner case assembly.
2. Remove three set bolts from clutch line bracket.
3. Remove mounting bolts, clutch release cylinder and line.
4. Disconnect backup lamp switch and vehicle speed sensor electrical connectors.
5. Disconnect ground cable at transaxle.
6. Disconnect two control cables from transaxle.
7. Remove starter set bolt from transaxle upper side, then the transaxle upper side mounting bolts.
8. Support engine using universal support fixture tool No. J-28467-A, or equivalent.
9. Remove lefthand engine mount mounting bolts
10. Lower transaxle side, then remove lefthand engine mount.
11. Remove front wheels, then raise and support vehicle.
12. Remove lefthand and righthand engine under covers.
13. Drain transaxle fluid into an suitable container.
14. Remove lefthand and righthand driveshafts.
15. Remove mounting bolts and heat insulator.
16. Support suspension crossmember using suitable jack, then remove two stabilizer bar bushing bracket mounting bolts, if equipped.
17. Remove sub-frame and lower suspension arm mounting bolts and nuts.
18. Remove front sub-frame and lower suspension arm.
19. Disconnect electrical connector and wiring from starter.
20. Remove mounting bolt from lower side and starter.
21. Slightly jack up transaxle, then remove four transaxle lower side mounting bolts.
22. Lower transaxle lefthand side, then separate transaxle from engine.
23. Reverse procedure to install. Tighten mounting bolts to specifications.

TIGHTENING SPECIFICATIONS

Year	Component	Torque/Ft. Lbs.
1997	Actuator & Line Bracket	15
	Actuator Assembly Bracket To Instrument Panel	106①
	Back-Up Lamp Switch	15
	Bleeder Screw	96①
	Center Crossmember To Main Crossmember	45
	Center Crossmember To Radiator Support	45
	Center Mount To Transaxle	45
	Center & Rear Mounting	45

Continued

TIGHTENING SPECIFICATIONS—Continued

Year	Component	Torque/Ft. Lbs.
1997	Clutch Cover	14
	Clutch Master Cylinder	106①
	Clutch Pedal Bracket To Instrument Panel	11
	Clutch Pedal Position Switch Locknut	115①
	Flywheel	65
	Front Mount	45
	Front Mount Bracket	45
	Front Mount Through-Bolt	64
	Lower A-Frame To Underbody	159
	Main Crossmember To Underbody	152
	Master Cylinder	106①
	Mount Bracket (Lefthand)	45
	Mount Cover (Lefthand)	45
	Mount Through-Bolt (Lefthand)	64
	Oil Drain & Fill Plugs	96①
	Pedal Bracket Assembly To Instrument Panel	11
	Starter	29
	Transaxle To Engine	34
	Vehicle Speed Sensor	96①
1998–2000	Actuator & Line Bracket	15
	Actuator Assembly Bracket To Instrument Panel	106①
	Back-Up Lamp Switch	17
	Center Crossmember To Main Crossmember	45
	Center Crossmember To Radiator Support	45
	Center Mount To Transaxle	45
	Center & Rear Mounting	45
	Clutch Cover	17
	Clutch Master Cylinder	106①
	Clutch Pedal Bracket To Instrument Panel	11
	Clutch Pedal Position Switch Locknut	115①
	Flywheel	65
	Front Mount	45
	Front Mount Bracket	45
	Lower A-Frame To Underbody	159
	Main Crossmember To Underbody	167
	Master Cylinder Mounting Nuts	15
	Mount Bracket (Lefthand)	45
	Mount Cover (Lefthand)	45
	Mount Through-Bolt (Lefthand)	44
	Oil Drain & Fill Plugs	15
	Pedal Bracket Assembly To Instrument Panel	11
	Starter	27
	Transaxle To Engine (Lower)	34
	Transaxle To Engine (Upper)	11
	Vehicle Speed Sensor	53①

① — Inch lbs.

Rear Axle & Suspension

INDEX

HUB & BEARING

REPLACE

1. Raise and support vehicle, then place jack stands under suspension support.
2. Lower vehicle slightly. Ensure weight rests on suspension supports and not suspension arms.
3. Remove tire and wheel assembly.
4. Remove brake drum.
5. Remove one bolt, then disconnect wheel speed sensor, if equipped.
6. Remove four axle hub and rear suspension knuckle mounting bolts, then the axle hub.
7. Remove and discard O-ring from backing plate.
8. Reverse procedure to install, noting the following:
   a. **On 1998–2000 models,** coat new O-ring with GCLB grease part No. 1051344, or equivalent.
   b. **On all models,** tighten mounting bolts to specifications.

KNUCKLE

REPLACE

1. Remove rear wheel hub as previously described.
2. Remove brake pipe from brake hose and backing plate.
3. Disconnect wheel speed sensor, if equipped.
4. Remove backing plate from rear suspension knuckle.
5. Remove mounting bolt and trailing arm from knuckle.
6. Remove mounting bolt and lateral link from knuckle.
7. Remove mounting bolts, nuts and strut assembly from knuckle.
8. Remove knuckle.
9. Reverse procedure to install, noting the following:
   a. Secure knuckle to strut, then tighten mounting bolts to specifications.
   b. Install lateral links to knuckle and secure with bolt and nut, but do not fully tighten at this time.
   c. Lower vehicle to ground.
   d. Install trailing arm to knuckle. Tighten lateral link mounting bolts to specifications.
   e. Tighten mounting bolts to specifications.

STRUT

REPLACE

1. Remove rear lower seat cushion, then the rear seatback side cushion.
2. Raise and support vehicle, then place jack stands under suspension support.
3. Lower vehicle slightly. Ensure weight rests on jack stands and not suspension arms.
4. Remove rear wheels.
5. Disconnect ABS speed sensor wiring harness clamp from strut assembly.
6. Remove brake pipe from brake hose.
7. Remove clip from brake hose bracket, then the brake hose from brake hose bracket.
8. Connect brake pipe to brake hose to prevent master cylinder reservoir from draining.
9. Disconnect wheel speed sensor wire harness from strut, if equipped.
10. Remove stabilizer shaft joint from strut assembly.
11. Remove strut assembly mounting bolts and nuts from rear suspension knuckle.
12. Remove jack stands from under suspension support.
13. Lower vehicle.
14. Remove strut assembly mounting nuts holding top of strut support.
15. Remove strut assembly.
16. Reverse procedure to install. Tighten mounting bolts to specifications.

COIL SPRING

REPLACE

1. Remove strut assembly as previously described.
2. Mount strut compressor tool No. J-34013 into holding fixture tool No. J-3289-20, or equivalents.
3. Mount strut into compressor tool using strut compressor adapter tool No. J-34013-88, or equivalent.
4. Carefully compress coil spring. **Do not compress too far. This might overload tool and result in severe bodily injury.**
5. Remove strut rod piston nut.
6. Carefully release compressed spring, then remove it from strut.
7. Reverse procedure to assemble.

STABILIZER BAR

REPLACE

1. Raise and support rear of vehicle, then remove rear wheels.
2. Scribe match marks between stabilizer shaft bushings, clamps, shaft and body.
3. Remove brake hose from strut assembly.
4. Remove both stabilizer bar links and bushings.
5. Remove lefthand and righthand stabilizer shaft joints.
6. Remove lefthand and righthand stabilizer shaft bushing retainers.
7. Remove stabilizer shaft bushings.
8. Support fuel tank, then remove bolts from two rear fuel tank bands and allow bands to hang.
9. Support suspension crossmember using suitable jack.
10. Remove six suspension crossmember to body mounting bolts.
11. Lower suspension crossmember.
12. Disconnect hoses from EVAP canister.
13. Disconnect fuel filler neck and vapor hoses from fuel tank.
14. Remove stabilizer shaft by aiming it toward lefthand side of vehicle.
15. Reverse procedure to install. Tighten mounting bolts to specifications.

LATERAL LINK & TRAILING ARM

REPLACE

1997

1. Raise and support vehicle.
2. Remove rear wheels.
3. Remove mounting bolts and trailing arm.
4. Remove mounting nuts and rear lateral links.
5. Remove one bolt and clamp from front exhaust pipe.
6. Disconnect catalytic converter resonator/intermediate pipe and gasket from exhaust pipe.
7. Disconnect oxygen sensor from converter pipe assembly.
8. Disconnect resonator/intermediate pipe from muffler, then remove resonator/intermediate pipe and gasket.
9. Support suspension crossmember using suitable jack.
10. Remove six suspension crossmember to body mounting bolts.
11. Remove outer lateral link bolts and two washers.
12. Lower suspension crossmember.
13. Remove mounting bolts and front lateral link.
14. Reverse procedure to install.

1998–2000

1. Raise and support vehicle.
2. Remove rear tires and wheels.
3. Remove mounting bolts, nuts and trailing arm.
4. Reverse procedure to install, noting the following:
   a. Tighten mounting bolts to specifications.
   b. Jounce vehicle up and down few times to allow suspension to settle into place.
   c. Inspect and adjust wheel alignment as required.

TIGHTENING SPECIFICATIONS

Year	Component	Torque/ Ft. Lbs.
1997–2000	Axle Hub To Knuckle Bolt	59
	Brake Pipe Fittings	11
	Crossmember To Body (1997)	43
	Crossmember To Body , Inner (1998–2000)	14
	Crossmember To Body Outer (1998–2000)	55
	Fuel Tank Band	29
	Lateral Link	89
	Resonator/Intermediate Pipe To Converter	32
	Resonator/Intermediate Pipe To Muffler	14
	Stabilizer Bar Joint To Shaft (1997)	26
	Stabilizer Bar Joint To Shaft (1998–2000)	33
	Stabilizer Shaft Bushing	14
	Strut Assembly	29
	Stabilizer Bar Joint To Strut	33
	Strut To Knuckle	105
	Trailing Arm	67
	Wheel Speed Sensor	69①

① — Inch lbs.

Front Suspension & Steering

NOTE: On Air Bag Equipped Models, Refer To "Air Bag System Precautions" Located In The Front Of This Manual For System Disarming & Arming Procedures.

NOTE: Refer To "Computer Relearn Procedures " Located In The Front Of This Manual For Computer Relearn Procedures.

INDEX

PRECAUTIONS

AIR BAG SYSTEMS

Refer to "Air Bag System Precautions" in the front of this manual for system disarming and arming procedures.

BATTERY GROUND CABLE

Prior to service, disconnect battery ground cable and isolate as required.

DESCRIPTION

The front suspension is a McPherson

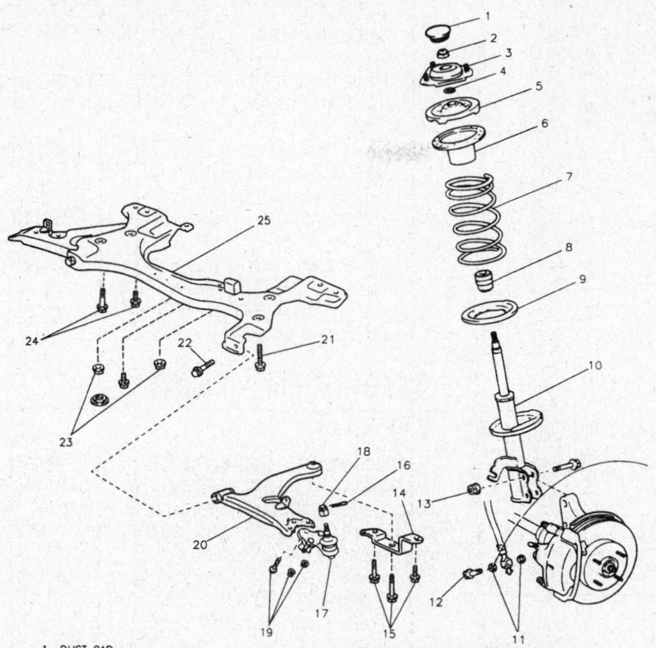

1 DUST CAP
2 STRUT ROD PISTON NUT
3 STRUT SUPPORT
4 DUST SEAL
5 SPRING SEAT
6 UPPER INSULATOR
7 COIL SPRING
8 SPRING BUMPER
9 LOWER INSULATOR
10 STRUT
11 BRAKE LINE GASKETS
12 BRAKE LINE-TO-CALIPER BOLT
13 STRUT MOUNTING NUT AND BOLT
14 LOWER CONTROL ARM RETAINING BRACKET
15 LOWER CONTROL ARM RETAINING BRACKET BOLTS
16 COTTER PIN
17 BALL JOINT
18 BALL JOINT CASTLE NUT
19 BALL JOINT MOUNTING NUT AND BOLT
20 CONTROL ARM
21 CROSSMEMBER MOUNTING BOLTS
22 CROSSMEMBER-TO-CONTROL ARM BOLT
23 CROSSMEMBER MOUNTING NUTS
24 CROSSMEMBER MOUNTING BOLTS
25 SUSPENSION CROSSMEMBER

GC2029700255000X

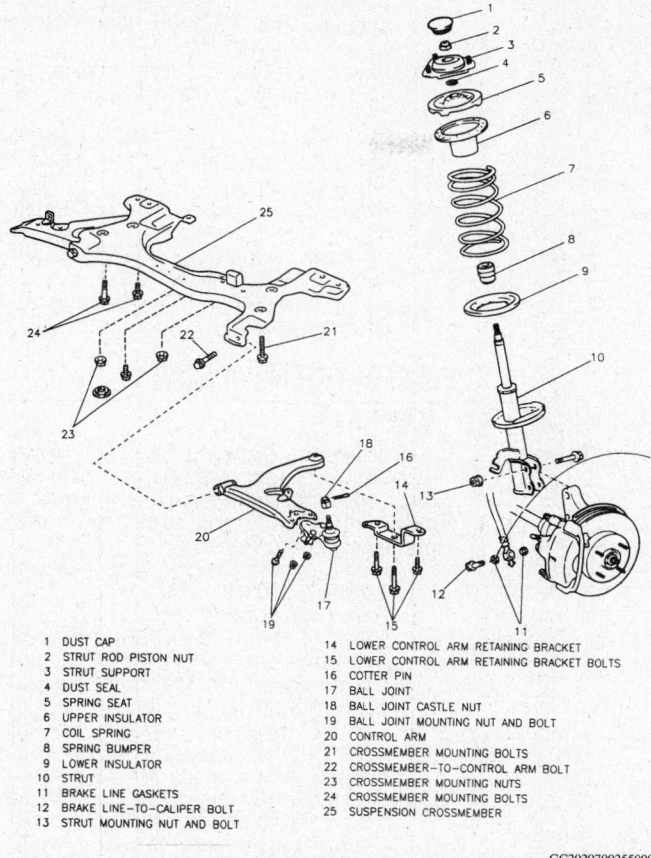

Fig. 1 Disassembled view of front suspension

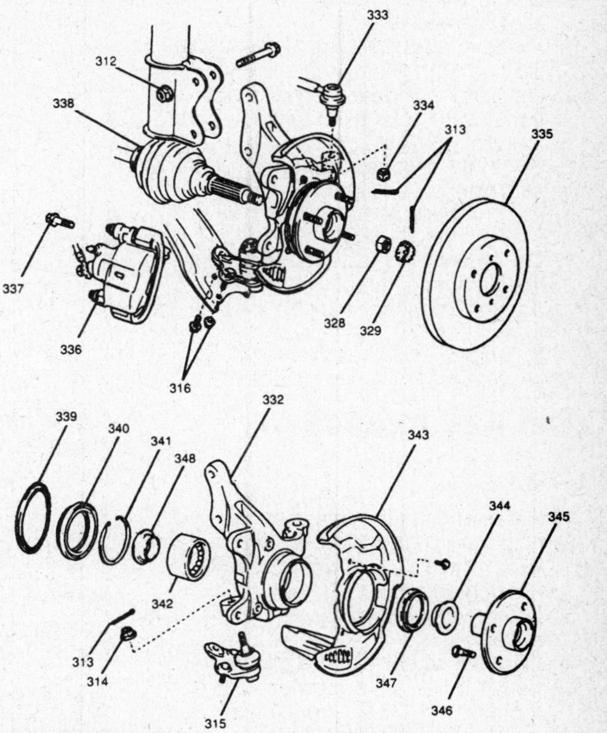

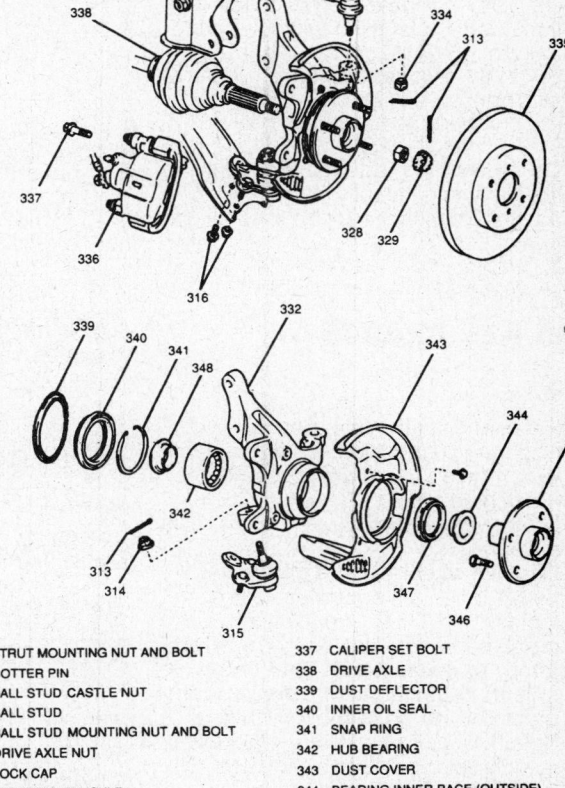

312 STRUT MOUNTING NUT AND BOLT
313 COTTER PIN
314 BALL STUD CASTLE NUT
315 BALL STUD
316 BALL STUD MOUNTING NUT AND BOLT
328 DRIVE AXLE NUT
329 LOCK CAP
332 STEERING KNUCKLE
333 TIE ROD END
334 TIE ROD END NUT
335 BRAKE ROTOR
336 BRAKE CALIPER
337 CALIPER SET BOLT
338 DRIVE AXLE
339 DUST DEFLECTOR
340 INNER OIL SEAL
341 SNAP RING
342 HUB BEARING
343 DUST COVER
344 BEARING INNER RACE (OUTSIDE)
345 AXLE HUB
346 WHEEL STUD
347 OUTER OIL SEAL
348 BEARING INNER RACE (INSIDE)

GC3039700336000X

Fig. 2 Disassembled view of hub & bearing assembly

strut design, **Fig. 1.** The upper end of the strut is anchored to the body by a strut support. The strut and strut support are isolated by a rubber mount. The lower end of the strut is connected to the upper end of the steering knuckle. The lower end of the knuckle is attached to the ball joint, which is attached to the suspension control arm assembly. Movement of the steering wheel is transmitted to the tie rod end and then to the knuckle, turning the wheel and tire assembly.

WHEEL HUB

REPLACE

1. Remove knuckle as outlined under "Steering Knuckle, Replace," then mount into suitable soft-jawed vise.
2. Note installation direction, then remove dust deflector using suitable screwdriver.
3. Remove inner grease seal from knuckle using seal remover tool No. J-26941 and slide hammer tool No. J-23907, or equivalents, **Fig. 2.**
4. Remove inner bearing snap ring and disc brake dust shield.
5. Push out hub using hub remover tool Nos. J-25287 and J-35378, or equivalents.
6. Remove outer bearing race from hub using tools as previously specified.
7. Remove outer grease seal using seal remover tool and slide hammer.
8. **On 1997 models,** remove bearing assembly using bearing remover tool Nos. J-35399 and J-35379, or equivalents.
9. **On 1998–2000 models,** remove bearing assembly using bearing remover tool No. J-22912-01, or equivalent, and suitable press.
10. **On all models,** remove wheel bearing from knuckle, using driver handle tool No. J-8092 and side bearing installer tool No. J-21784, or equivalents, and inner race and receiver cup,
11. Reverse procedure to install, noting the following:
    a. Use bearing installation tool Nos. J-8092 and J-35411, or equivalents, to install hub bearing assembly.
    b. **On 1997 models,** apply Lubriplate part No. 1050109, or equivalent, to outer grease seal lip.
    c. **On 1998–2000 models,** apply GCLB grease part No. 1051344, or equivalent, to outer grease seal lip.
    d. **On all models,** use seal installation tool No. J-35737-01, or equivalent, to install outer grease seal.
    e. Install hub using tool Nos. J-8092 and J-35399, or equivalents.
    f. Use tool No. J-35737-01, or equivalent, to install inner grease seal.
    g. Ensure dust deflector ring faces in its proper direction, then use ring installation tool No. J-35379, or equivalent, to install ring.

BALL JOINT

REPLACE

WITH ABS BRAKES

1. Raise and support vehicle. Place jack stands under suspension crossmember.
2. Lower vehicle slightly so weight of vehicle rests on suspension crossmember and not control arms.
3. Remove steering knuckle with axle hub as previously described.

4. Clamp steering knuckle with axle hub in soft-jawed vise.
5. Remove dust deflector, then the cotter pin and nut.
6. **On 1997 models,** remove ball joint from steering knuckle using separator tool No. J-35413, or equivalent.
7. **On 1998–2000 models,** remove ball joint from steering knuckle using separator tool No. J-24319-B, or equivalent.
8. **On all models,** reverse procedure to install, noting the following:
   a. Tighten mounting bolts to specifications.
   b. Inspect wheel alignment and adjust as required.

LESS ABS BRAKES

1997

1. Raise and support vehicle.
2. Support suspension using suitable jack. Place jack under crossmember, not control arm.
3. Lower vehicle slightly so weight rests on jack.
4. Remove wheel lug nuts and wheel.
5. Install inner drive joint seal protector tool No. J-34754, or equivalent. **Care must be taken not to allow tripod joints to overextend. This could result in separation of internal components and possible join failure.**
6. Separate ball joint from knuckle assembly using ball joint removal tool No. J-35413, or equivalent.
7. Remove two nuts and bolts mounting ball joint and control arm.
8. Remove ball joint.
9. Reverse procedure to install, noting the following:
   a. Tighten knuckle to ball joint nut to specifications.
   b. During installation, always replace self-locking nut and cotter pin with new one.

1998–2000

1. Raise and support vehicle.
2. Support suspension using suitable jack. Place jack under crossmember, not control arm.
3. Lower vehicle slightly so weight rests on jack.
4. Remove knuckle with axle hub.
5. Clamp knuckle in suitable soft-jawed vise.
6. Remove ball joint cotter pin and nut.
7. Remove ball joint from knuckle using separator tool No. J-24319-B, or equivalent.
8. Reverse procedure to install, noting the following:
   a. Tighten knuckle to ball joint nut to specifications.
   b. During installation, always replace self-locking nut and cotter pin with new ones.
   c. Inspect wheel alignment and adjust as required.

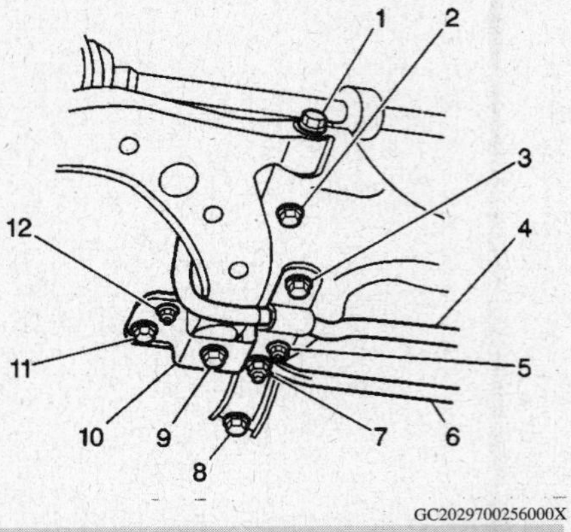

Fig. 3 Front crossmember & control arm fastener tightening sequence

COIL SPRING

REPLACE

Refer to "Strut, Replace" for coil spring replacement procedure.

STRUT

REPLACE

1. Raise and support vehicle.
2. Support suspension using suitable jack. Place jack under suspension supports, not control arm.
3. Lower vehicle slightly so weight rests on jack.
4. **On 1997 models,** install drive joint seal protector tool No. J-34754, or equivalent.
5. **On all models,** remove brake hose from disc brake caliper.
6. Remove clip from brake hose.
7. Remove brake hose from brake hose bracket.
8. Loosen bolts and nuts mounting strut assembly to steering knuckle.
9. Lower vehicle slightly.
10. Remove strut assembly mounting nuts at top of shock tower.
11. Remove strut assembly.
12. Reverse procedure to install, noting the following:
    a. Avoid cracking or scratching spring coating.
    b. Use clean engine oil to coat threads of nuts on lower side of strut assembly.
    c. Install strut lower bolts and nuts, but do not tighten at this time.
    d. Install strut to tower nuts. Tighten to specifications.
    e. Tighten strut lower bolts and nuts to specifications.

COIL SPRING & STRUT SERVICE

1. Remove strut as previously described.
2. Compress spring slightly using strut holding/spring compression tool No. J-34013-B, or equivalent. **Ensure spring seat is secure and will not turn.**
3. Mount compression tool into holding fixture tool No. J-3289-20, or equivalent.
4. Mount strut assembly into holding fixture using adapter tool No. J-34013-88, or equivalent.
5. Remove strut rod dust cap and piston nut.
6. Remove strut support, dust seal, spring seat, upper insulator, coil spring, bumper and lower insulator.
7. Reverse procedure to assemble.

CONTROL ARM

REPLACE

On models equipped with automatic transaxle, it might also be necessary to remove the crossmember, transaxle support, both control arms and stabilizer shaft together as a complete unit.

1. Install engine support fixture tool No. J-28467-360, or equivalent.
2. Raise and support vehicle.
3. Remove lower control arm mounting nuts and bolts.
4. **On models with stabilizer bar,** disconnect stabilizer bar links.
5. **On all models,** remove mounting bolts, nuts and suspension crossmember with control arms attached.
6. Remove mounting bolts. nuts and control arm from crossmember.
7. Reverse procedure to install, noting the following:
   a. Install control arm, but do not tighten mounting bolts at this time.
   b. Install stabilizer shaft and links to control arms, but do not tighten mounting bolts at this time.
   c. Install control arm bracket to crossmember. Tighten mounting bolts to specifications.
   d. Install stabilizer shaft insulator clamps. Tighten nuts to specifications, but do not tighten bolts at this time.
   e. Tighten control arm to knuckle mounting bolts to specifications.
   f. Install suspension support brace. Tighten mounting bolts to specifications.
   g. Install tires and wheels, then lower vehicle to ground.
   h. Raise vehicle on drive-on lift or an alignment rack.
   i. Jounce vehicle up and down few times to allow suspension to settle into place.
   j. Tighten bolt Nos. 9, 1, 3, 11, and 8 in order to specifications **Fig. 3.**
   k. Tighten stabilizer shaft link stud nut to specifications.

CONTROL ARM BUSHING

REPLACE

On these models the control arm bushings are not serviced separately.

Do not attempt to replace them alone. Replace the complete control arm instead.

STEERING KNUCKLE

REPLACE

1997

1. Remove locknut cap and bearing locknut.
2. Remove brake caliper and support with wire.
3. Remove disc brake rotor.
4. Separate tie rod from steering knuckle using tie rod puller tool No. J-6627-A, or equivalent.
5. Remove lower ball joint bolt and nuts and separate it from lower control arm.
6. Remove two strut to steering knuckle nuts.
7. Install drive joint protector tool No. J-34754, or equivalent.
8. Tap driveshaft with suitable plastic hammer and drive out driveshaft.
9. Remove two strut to steering knuckle bolts.
10. Remove steering knuckle assembly.
11. Reverse procedure to install.

1998–2000

1. Raise and support vehicle, then remove tire and wheel.
2. **On models equipped with ABS,** remove sensor from knuckle and position aside.
3. **On all models,** remove front brake hose from strut and position aside.
4. Remove control arm to knuckle bolt and nuts.
5. Remove cotter pin and driveshaft nut retainer from drive axle.
6. Have an assistant step on and hold brake pedal, then remove driveshaft nut.
7. Remove caliper housing and bracket. suspend them with suitable wire or rope.
8. Carefully remove brake rotor. Avoid damaging speed sensor rotor, boot and inner oil seal.
9. Loosen nuts on lower side of strut. Do not remove bolts.
10. Remove outer tie rod cotter pin and nut, then separate tie rod end from knuckle using separator tool No. J-24319-B, or equivalent.
11. Remove nuts and bolts from lower side of strut assembly.
12. Remove knuckle with hub.
13. Remove ball joint cotter pin and nut, then separate ball joint end from knuckle using separator tool No. J-24319-B, or equivalent.
14. Remove hub, bearing and seal as previously described.
15. Reverse procedure to install, noting the following:
    a. Use clean engine oil to coat threads of nuts on lower side of strut assembly.
    b. Install strut lower bolts and nuts, but do not tighten at this time.
    c. Have an assistant step on and hold brake pedal, then tighten driveshaft nut to specifications.
    d. Tighten strut lower bolts and nuts.
    e. Tighten mounting bolts to specifications.

STABILIZER BAR

REPLACE

1. Raise and support vehicle.
2. Remove mounting nuts and stabilizer links.
3. Remove mounting nuts and suspension support brace.
4. Remove mounting bolts and stabilizer bar links from stabilizer shaft.
5. Remove clamp bolts, nuts, studs and stabilizer bar.
6. Reverse procedure to install. Tighten mounting bolts to specifications.

TIE ROD END

REPLACE

Refer to "Power Steering Gear, Replace" for tie rod end replacement procedure.

POWER STEERING GEAR

REPLACE

1997

1. Ensure front wheels are in straight-ahead position, then remove key from ignition.
2. Remove intermediate steering shaft protector.
3. Loosen upper and remove lower intermediate shaft pinch bolts.
4. Open hood and place drain pan under gear assembly.
5. Loosen wheel lug nuts.
6. Raise and support vehicle.
7. Remove both front wheel and tire assemblies.
8. Remove both tie rod ends from knuckles using tie rod remover tool No. J-24319-01, or equivalent.
9. Support transaxle with suitable jack.
10. Remove rear center engine mounting member to body mounting bolts.
11. Remove rear engine mount to mount bracket mounting nut and bolt. Raise and lower rear of transaxle to access steering gear to body mounting nuts and bolts.
12. Disconnect pressure and return lines at steering gear.
13. Remove four gear to body mounting nuts and bolts.
14. Remove gear through access opening.
15. Reverse procedure to install.

1998–2000

1. Ensure front wheels are in straight-ahead position, then remove key from ignition.
2. Remove steering column upper column cover from firewall.
3. Remove steering shaft lower coupling bolt.
4. Remove outlet pipe heat shield.
5. Remove lefthand steering gear inlet and outlet pipe clip bolt.
6. Remove righthand steering gear outlet pipe clip bolt.
7. Remove lefthand steering gear inlet and outlet pipe clip.
8. Place an suitable drain pan under vehicle to catch power steering fluid.
9. Disconnect inlet pipe from steering gear.
10. Disconnect O2S electrical connector, then remove sensor and gasket.
11. Install engine support fixture tool No. J-28467-360, or equivalent.
12. Raise and support vehicle.
13. Remove front tires and wheels.
14. Remove engine righthand and lefthand lower splash shields.
15. Remove driveshaft exhaust heat shield.
16. Remove outer tie rod cotter pin and nut, then the outer tie rods using separator tool No. J-24319-B, or equivalent.
17. Remove front suspension brace.
18. Remove suspension crossmember, transaxle support, control arms and stabilizer shaft together as unit.
19. Remove transaxle rear mount through-bolt and mount.
20. Remove transaxle rear mount bracket.
21. Disconnect exhaust pipe at manifold.
22. Remove steering gear exhaust heat shield.
23. Remove steering gear clamps.
24. Carefully route steering gear to vehicle's righthand side, then lower it and remove it through lefthand side.
25. Remove two insulators from steering gear.
26. Reverse procedure to install, noting the following:
    a. Install new steering gear insulators as required.
    b. Install new exhaust donut.
    c. Tighten mounting bolts to specifications.
    d. Fill reservoir with fresh specified fluid.
    e. Bleed power steering fluid system.
    f. Inspect wheel alignment and adjust as required.

POWER STEERING PUMP

REPLACE

1. Siphon as much power steering fluid from reservoir as possible.
2. Remove pump drive belt.
3. **On 1997 models,** proceed as follows:
    a. Disconnect fluid return hose from pump.
    b. Remove pump upper mounting bolt.
    c. Note their locations, then remove all connections from power steering pressure switch.
4. **On 1998–2000 models,** proceed as follows:
    a. Remove gear inlet hose fitting and inlet pipe from pump.
    b. Remove fluid reservoir hose from pump.
    c. Raise and support vehicle.

d. Remove righthand front tire and wheel.
e. Remove engine righthand lower splash shield.

5. **On all models,** remove pump mounting bolts.
6. Carefully remove power steering pump.
7. Reverse procedure to install, noting the following:
   a. Tighten mounting bolts to specifications.
   b. Fill reservoir with fresh specified fluid.
   c. Bleed power steering fluid system.

TIGHTENING SPECIFICATIONS

Year	Component	Torque/Ft. Lbs.
1997	ABS Hose	21
	ABS Speed Sensor	69①
	ABS Wire Harness	48①
	Axle Nut	159
	Ball Joint To Control Arm	105
	Ball Joint To Steering Knuckle	87
	Brake Caliper To Steering Knuckle Set Bolt	65
	Control Arm Rear Bushing	101
	Control Arm To Suspension Crossmember	161
	Driveshaft Nut	159
	Dust Cover	73①
	Engine Crossmember To Suspension Crossmember Nut A	35
	Engine Crossmember To Suspension Crossmember Bolt B	45
	Engine Crossmember To Suspension Crossmember Nut C	35
	Hub Nut	159
	Rear Control Arm Bushing Bracket Bolt A	108
	Rear Control Arm Bushing Bracket Bolt B	37
	Rear Control Arm Bushing Bracket Nut C	14
	Stabilizer Shaft Bracket	167
	Stabilizer Shaft Link To Stabilizer Shaft	14
	Steering Knuckle To Strut Assembly	203
	Strut Assembly	29
	Suspension Crossmember To Body	152
	Suspension Support Brace	51
	Tie Rod End	36
	Wheel Lug	76
1998–2000	ABS Hose	22①
	ABS Speed Sensor	71①
	ABS Wire Harness	48①
	Axle Nut	166
	Ball Joint To Control Arm	105
	Ball Joint To Steering Knuckle	91
	Brake Caliper To Steering Knuckle Set Bolt	65
	Control Arm Retainer Bracket (Inner)	129
	Control Arm Retainer Bracket (Outer Bolt)	109
	Control Arm Retainer Bracket (Outer Nut)	14
	Control Arm Retainer Bracket (Rear)	91
	Control Arm To Crossmember (Front)	158
	Crossmember Front Outer	167
	Drive Axle Nut	166
	Engine Crossmember To Suspension	45
	Front Suspension Crossmember	42
	Front Transaxle Mount	47
	Stabilizer Shaft Link Nut	33

Continued

TIGHTENING SPECIFICATIONS—Continued

Year	Component	Torque/Ft. Lbs.
1998-2000	Stabilizer Shaft Mount Bracket Front Bolt	167
	Stabilizer Shaft Mount Bracket Nut	14
	Stabilizer Shaft Mount Bracket Stud	109
	Strut Assembly	29
	Strut Rod Piston	34
	Suspension Support Brace	51
	Tie Rod End Nut	36
	Wheel Lug	76

① — Inch lbs.

Wheel Alignment

INDEX

PRECAUTIONS

AIR BAG SYSTEMS

Refer to "Air Bag System Precautions" in the front of this manual for system disarming and arming procedures.

PRELIMINARY INSPECTION

Steering and vibration problems are not always the result of improper alignment. They may also be caused by wheel and tire imbalance or other factors. To ensure proper alignment readings, the following inspections should be done and corrections made before inspecting caster, camber or toe:

1. Inspect all tires for proper inflation pressures and even tread wear.
2. Inspect wheel bearings for looseness.
3. Inspect ball joints and tie rod ends for excessive looseness.
4. Inspect steering gear operation and mounting.
5. Inspect operation of struts.
6. Inspect control arms.
7. Inspect hub and bearing assemblies for excessive wear.

FRONT WHEEL ALIGNMENT

CASTER

Caster cannot be adjusted. Should caster be found out of specification, locate cause first. If components are damaged, bent, loose, dented or worn, they should be replaced. To prevent an improper caster reading, jounce the bumper three times before inspecting.

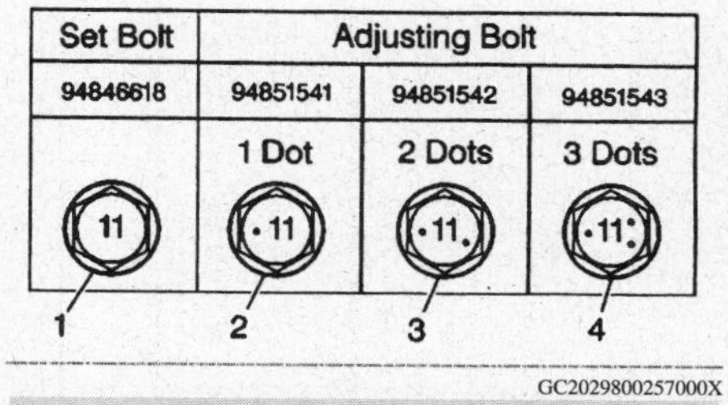

Set Bolt
Adjusting Bolt
94846618
94851541
94851542
94851543
1 Dot
2 Dots
3 Dots
11
11
11
11
1
2
3
4
GC2029800257000X

Fig. 1 Front camber adjustment bolts. 1998–2000

Fig. 2 Front toe adjustment

CAMBER

On 1997 models, camber cannot be adjusted. On 1998–2000 models, camber is adjustable by estimating the amount the camber must be adjusted, selecting the proper combination of bolts from **Fig. 1,** then proceeding as follows:

1. To obtain .25° camber, install bolt No. 1 in upper position and bolt No. 2 in lower position.
2. To obtain .50° camber, install bolt No. 1 in upper position and bolt No. 3 in lower position.
3. To obtain .75° camber, install bolt No. 1 in upper position and bolt No. 4 in lower position.
4. To obtain 1.00° camber, install bolt No. 2 in upper position and bolt No. 4 in lower position.
5. To obtain 1.25° camber, install bolt No. 3 in upper position and bolt No. 4 in lower position.
6. To obtain 1.50° camber, install bolt No. 4 in upper position and bolt No. 4 in lower position.
7. Install bolts, inspect alignment and adjust as required.

TOE-IN

Toe-in is adjusted by changing tie rod length. Loosen boot clamps and slide from the boot assembly. Loosen righthand and lefthand tie rod end locknuts, then turn righthand and lefthand tie rods to align toe-in to specifications. Righthand and lefthand tie rods must be equal in length, **Fig. 2.**

After adjustment, install boot clamps,

tighten nuts to specifications and ensure rack boots are not twisted.

Tighten strut to knuckle nut to specifications, then **torque** tie rod locking nut to 41 ft. lbs.

REAR WHEEL ALIGNMENT

TOE

1. Loosen lefthand and righthand lateral link or tie rod locknuts.
2. Adjust total rear toe by turning adjusting tubes. One revolution of adjusting tube will adjust rear to approximately 1.2.°
3. **On 1997 models,** measure difference between lefthand and righthand lateral link length. Righthand link length must be less than .039 inch difference.
4. **On all models, torque** lateral link or tie rod locknuts to 41 ft. lbs.

CAMBER & CASTER

Rear caster and camber cannot be adjusted. Should camber be found out of specification, locate cause first. If components are damaged, bent loose, dented or worn, they should be replaced. To prevent an improper camber reading, jounce the bumper three times before inspecting. If a tie rod or tie rod end is replaced, inspect toe and steering angle with turning radius gauges. If steering angle is not proper, inspect righthand and lefthand tie rods for equal length. If tie rod length is changed to correct steering, inspect toe once again.

SATURN

INDEX OF SERVICE OPERATIONS

Specifications

GENERAL ENGINE SPECIFICATIONS

Engine/Liter (VIN)①	Fuel Injection System	Bore & Stoke	Compression Ratio	Net H.P. @ RPM	Maximum Torque, Ft. Lbs. @ RPM	Normal Oil Pressure, psi
1997-99						
1.9L SOHC (8)	MPFI	3.23 X 3.54	9.3	100 @ 5000	114 @ 2400	36②
1.9L DOHC (7)	MPFI	3.23 X 3.54	9.5	124 @ 5600	122 @ 4800	36②
2000						
1.9L SOHC (8)	MPFI	3.23 X 3.54	9.3	100 @ 5000	114 @ 2400	36②
1.9L DOHC (7)	MPFI	3.23 X 3.54	9.5	124 @ 5600	122 @ 4800	36②
2.2L DOHC (F)	SPFI	3.38 X 3.72	9.5	137@ 5800	147 @ 4400	65③
3.0L DOHC (R)	SPFI	3.38 X 3.34	10	182 @ 5600	190 @ 3600	21.7④

MPFI — Multi-Point Fuel Injection
SPFI — Sequecial-Point Fuel Injection
DOHC — Dual Overhead Cam
SOHC — Single Overhead Cam

① — Eighth digit of Vehicle Identification Number (VIN) denotes engine code.

② — At 2000 RPM.
③ — At 1000 RPM.
④ — At Idle.

TUNE UP SPECIFICATIONS

Year & Engine/Liter (VIN) ①	Spark Plug Gap	Ignition Timing BTDC				Curb Idle Speed②		Fast Idle Speed②		Fuel Pump Pressure, psi.	Valve Lash, Inch
		Firing Order	Man. Trans.	Auto. Trans.	Mark Fig.	Man. Trans.	Auto. Trans.	Man. Trans.	Auto. Trans.		
1997											
1.9L (8) SOHC MFI	.040	④	⑤	⑤	⑥	750⑦	650D⑦	⑦	⑦	38-44⑧	③
1.9L (7) DOHC MFI	.040	④	⑤	⑤	⑥	850⑦	750D⑦	⑦	⑦	38-44⑧	③
1998-99											
1.9L (8) SOHC MFI	.040	④	⑤	⑤	⑥	750⑦	650/775N⑦	⑦	⑦	40-55⑨	③
1.9L (7) DOHC MFI	.040	④	⑤	⑤	⑥	850/875⑦	750/775N⑦	⑦	⑦	65-94⑨	③
2000											
1.9L (8) SOHC MFI	.040	④	⑤	⑤	⑥	750⑦	650/775N⑦	⑦	⑦	40-55⑨	③
1.9L (7) DOHC MFI	.040	④	⑤	⑤	⑥	850/875⑦	750/775N⑦	⑦	⑦	65-94⑨	③
2.2L (F) DOHC SPFI	.045	④	⑤	⑤	⑥	850/875⑦	750/775N⑦	⑦	⑦	65-75⑨	③
3.0L (R) DOHC SPFI	.039	⑩	—	⑤	⑥	—	750/775N⑦	—	⑦	65-75⑨	③

BTDC — Before Top Dead Center

D — Drive

N — Neutral

① — Eighth digit of Vehicle Identification Number (VIN) denotes engine code.
② — When adjusting idle speed, set parking brake and block drive wheels. Where two idle speeds are listed, higher speed is with idle or A/C solenoid energized.
③ — Equipped w/hydraulic valve lifters.
④ — Cylinder numbering from front of engine to rear 1, 2, 3, 4. Firing order 1-3-4-2. Refer to **Fig. A** for spark plug wire connections at coil unit.
⑤ — Equipped w/Distributorless Ignition System (DIS), no adjustment.
⑥ — Equipped w/crankshaft position sensor.
⑦ — Idle speed is controlled by Idle Air Control (IAC) valve or idle speed control (ISC).
⑧ — Wrap shop towel around fuel pressure test port to prevent fuel spillage, connect suitable fuel pressure gauge to fuel pressure test port. Check fuel pressure with key On and engine Off.
⑨ — Wrap shop towel around fuel pressure test port to prevent fuel spillage, connect suitable fuel pressure gauge to fuel pressure test port. Energize fuel pump using a suitable scan tool & check fuel pressure.
⑩ — 1-2-3-4-5-6.

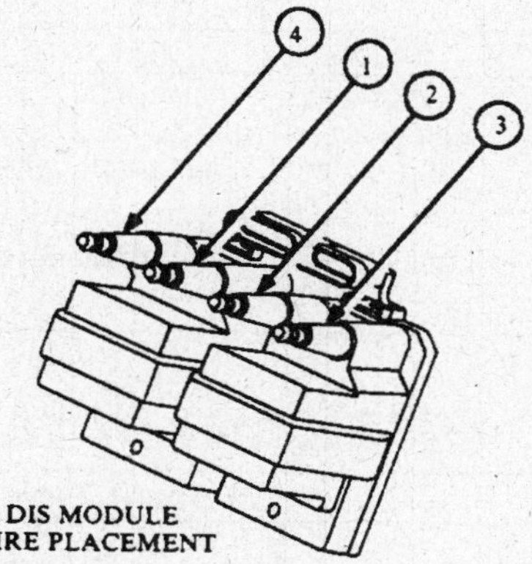

Fig. A

FRONT WHEEL ALIGNMENT SPECIFICATIONS

Engine/Liter	Caster Angle, Degrees①		Camber Angle, Degrees①		Total Toe, Degrees②		Ball Joint Wear
	Limits	Desired	Limits	Desired	Limits	Desired	
S-Series	+1.1 to +2.3	+1.7	-1.2 to +.2	-.5	+.10 to +.30	+.20	③
L-Series	+3.2 to +4.2④	+3.7④	-1.75 to -.50	-.100	+.04 to +.36	+.20	③

① — Cross camber, 0° (+/-1°).
② — Toe-In (+). Toe-Out (-).
③ — Refer to "Ball Joint Inspection" in "Front Suspension & Steering" section.
④ — Caster is not adjustable

REAR WHEEL ALIGNMENT SPECIFICATIONS

Engine	Camber Angle Degrees		Total Toe, Degrees①	
	Limits	Desired	Limits	Desired
S-Series	-1.4 to 0	-.7	+.10 to +.30	+.2
L-Series	-.50 to +.50	-1	+.13 to +.47	+.3

① — Toe-In (+). Toe-Out (-).

FLUID CAPACITIES & COOLING SYSTEM DATA

Engine/Liter ①	Cooling Capacity, Qts.	Radiator Cap Relief Pressure, Lbs.	Thermo. Opening Temp. Deg. F	Fuel Tank Gals.	Engine Oil Refill Qts.③	Transaxle Oil	
						Manual Transaxle Pts.	Auto. Transaxle Qts.②
1997							
1.9L	7	13–20	186	12.8	4	5.2	④
1998-99							
1.9L	7.2	13–17	186	12.1	4	5.2	④
2000							
1.9L	7.2	13–17	186	12.1	4	5.2	④
2.2L	7.4	13–17	194	12.1	5	4	⑤
3.0L	7.8	20–21	188–196	12.1	5	—	⑤

① — Eighth digit of Vehicle Identification Number (VIN) denotes engine code.

② — Approximate, make final check w/dipstick.

③ — Additional oil may be necessary to bring oil level to full mark, when changing oil filter.

④ — Drain & refill, 4 qts.; drain & refill with new filter, 4.2 qts.; total capacity, 7.4 qts.

⑤ — Bottom pan removal, 6.9 qts.; Complete overhaul, 9.5 qts.; total capacity, 12.9 qts.

LUBRICANT DATA

Year	Lubricant Type				
	Transaxle		Power Steering	Brake System	Hydraulic Clutch
	Manual	Automatic			
1997-2000	Dexron III	Dexron III	①	DOT 3	DOT 3

① — Must meet GM specification 9985010.

Electrical

NOTE: On Air Bag Equipped Models, Refer To " Air Bag System Precautions" Located In The Front Of This Manual For System Disarming & Arming Procedures.

NOTE: Refer To "Computer Relearn Procedure " Located In The Front Of This Manual For Computer Relearn Procedures.

INDEX

PRECAUTIONS

AIR BAG SYSTEMS

Refer to "Air Bag System Precautions" in the front of this manual for system disarming and arming procedures.

BATTERY GROUND CABLE

Prior to service, disconnect battery ground cable and isolate as required.

FUSE PANEL & FLASHER LOCATION

S-SERIES

The underhood junction block is located at the lefthand front of the engine compartment at the fender apron. The instrument panel junction block and the flasher module are located behind the center instrument panel, in front of the console.

L-SERIES

The Underhood Fuse Block (UHFB) is located on the rear lefthand side of the engine compartment. The Left Instrument Panel Fuse Block (LIPFB) is located behind the lefthand side kick panel. The Right Instrument Panel Fuse Block (RIPFB) is located behind the righthand side kick panel.

The hazard switch, located in the center of the instrument panel, controls turn signal and hazard lamp flashing.

FUEL PUMP RELAY LOCATION

S-SERIES

The fuel pump relay is located in the Instrument Panel Fuse Block (IPFB), behind the center of the instrument panel.

L-SERIES

The fuel pump relay is located behind the lefthand side kick panel, on the Left Instrument Panel Fuse Block (LIPFB).

RELAY CENTER LOCATION

S-SERIES

Relays are in the located in both the Underhood Junction Block (UHJB) and the Instrument Panel Junction Block (IPJB). Refer to "Fuse Panel & Flasher Location" for junction block locations.

L-SERIES

Relays are located in all three fuse panels, refer to "Fuse Panel & Flasher Location" for fuse block locations.

STARTER

REPLACE

1.9L ENGINE

1. Raise and support vehicle.
2. Disconnect two electrical connectors and position aside, then remove two starter mounting bolts.
3. Pull starter rearward and toward lefthand side of vehicle, then remove from vehicle.
4. Reverse procedure to install, noting the following:
   a. Starter must be guided into flywheel housing and rotated until lower bolt hole in starter flange aligns with mounting hole in engine.

b. **Torque** starter mounting bolts to 27 ft. lbs.
c. **Torque** starter solenoid terminal to 44 inch lbs. and positive terminal to 8 ft. lbs. **Excessive torque will crack solenoid end cap.**

2.2L ENGINE

1. Raise and support vehicle.
2. Disconnect two electrical connectors and position aside.
3. Remove two starter mounting bolts, then the starter.
4. Reverse procedure to install, **torque** starter mounting bolts to 30 ft. lbs.

3.0L ENGINE

1. Raise and support vehicle.
2. Remove right front wheel, then disconnect two electrical connectors.
3. Loosen fastener securing electrical harness bracket to engine block.
4. Remove lower starter mounting bolt, then lower vehicle.
5. Remove upper starter mounting bolt.
6. Move starter right to clear engine block, then left out of flywheel housing.
7. Reverse procedure to install, **torque** starter mounting bolts to 30 ft. lbs.

ALTERNATOR

REPLACE

1.9L ENGINE

1. Remove drive belt.
2. Raise and support vehicle, then remove right hand wheel.
3. Remove right hand wheewell and alternator splash shields, then disconnect field wires.
4. Use alternator output stud wrench tool No. SA9401C, or equivalent, to hold B+ output stud from rotating and disconnect fusible link wire.
5. Remove lower and upper mounting bolts, then alternator through wheel well opening.
6. Reverse procedure to install, noting following:
   a. **Torque** mounting bolts to 24 ft. lbs.
   b. Fusible link wire should be between 10 and 11 o'clock position.
   c. **Torque** positive terminal and alternator splash shield to 8 ft. lbs.

2.2L ENGINE

1. Remove throttle body air duct, then the accessory drive belt.
2. Disconnect two alternator electrical connectors.
3. Remove alternator mounting bolts, then the alternator.
4. Reverse procedure to install, **torque** alternator mounting bolts to 30 ft. lbs.

3.0L ENGINE

1. Remove accessory drive belt, then the belt tensioner.
2. Remove upper alternator to engine block bolts.
3. Raise and support vehicle.
4. Turn steering wheel towards the right to access lower alternator bolt.
5. Remove lower alternator bolt, then lower vehicle.
6. Separate alternator from engine block.
7. Disconnect electrical connectors, then remove alternator.
8. Reverse procedure to install, **torque** alternator mounting bolts to 30 ft. lbs.

COIL PACK

REPLACE

1.9L ENGINE

1. Turn ignition switch to Off position.
2. Note spark plug wire positions for installation reference.
3. Remove spark plug wires from coil towers.
4. Disconnect electrical connector at ignition module.
5. Remove bolts and ignition module.
6. Reverse procedure to install, noting following:
   a. **Torque** bolts to 72 inch lbs.
   b. Push electrical connector until click is heard, then pull back to confirm positive engagement.
   c. Ensure spark plug wires are firmly pressed into boots.
   d. Ensure spark plug wires are oriented properly. Refer to " Tune-Up Specifications."

2.2L ENGINE

1. Turn ignition switch to Off position.
2. Disconnect electrical connector from electronic ignition module.
3. Remove electronic ignition module retaining screws, then the module.
4. Remove coil pack attaching bolts, then the coil pack.
5. Reverse procedure to install, noting the following:
   a. **Torque** coil pack bolts to 84 inch lbs.
   b. **Torque** electronic ignition module retaining screws to 13 inch lbs.

3.0L ENGINE

1. Turn ignition switch to the Off position.
2. Remove upper intake manifold runner as outlined under " Intake Manifold, Replace" in the "3.0L Engine" section.
3. Disconnect electrical connector, then remove ignition coil and gasket.
4. Reverse procedure to install.

IGNITION LOCK

REPLACE

1. Remove ignition lock bezel.
2. Remove upper steering column shroud panel.
3. Insert ignition key to switch.
4. **On S-Series models,** rotate key to the ACC position.
5. **On L-Series models,** rotate key to the START position, then back to the RUN position.
6. **On all models,** depress locking button at top of ignition lock assembly, then remove lock cylinder.
7. Reverse procedure to install.

IGNITION SWITCH

REPLACE

L-SERIES

1. Remove ignition lock cylinder bezel from steering column shroud.
2. Remove steering column upper and lower shrouds.
3. Remove ignition switch to steering column attaching screws.
4. Disconnect ignition switch electrical connector, then remove switch from steering column.
5. Reverse procedure to install, **torque** switch retaining screws to 13 inch lbs.

IGNITION MODULE

REPLACE

S-SERIES

1. Remove steering wheel as outlined under "Steering Wheel, Replace."
2. Remove lefthand side lower filler panel attaching screws.
3. Loosen Data Link Connector (DLC) to filler panel attaching screws, then lower filler panel.
4. Disconnect hood release cable from filler panel, then remove filler panel.
5. Remove airbag module Connector Position Assurance (CPA) retainer.
6. Disconnect connectors from lever control switch, then remove lever control switch from steering column.
7. **On models with automatic transaxle,** disconnect park lock cable from ignition module.
8. **On all models,** disconnect pass lock sensor and ignition switch electrical connectors from ignition module.
9. Remove ignition module shear bolts as follows:
   a. Make a small notch in shear bolt head with a chisel and hammer.
   b. Tap chisel to rotate and loosen bolt.
   c. Remove shear bolts.
10. Remove ignition module assembly from steering column.
11. Reverse procedure to install.

CLUTCH START SWITCH

REPLACE

1. Disconnect clutch switch electrical connector.
2. Remove clutch switch attaching bolt, then the switch.
3. Reverse procedure to install **Torque** clutch switch attaching bolt to 96 inch lbs.

PARK/NEUTRAL POSITION SWITCH

REPLACE

1997 S-SERIES

Refer to "Transaxle Range Switch, Replace" for replacement procedure.

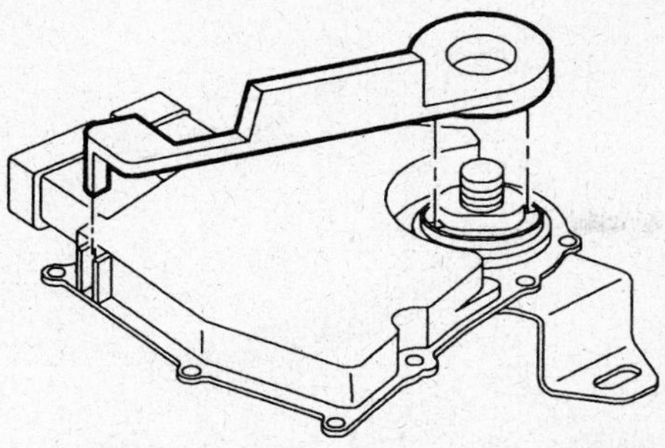

G39030000001000X

Fig. 1 Transaxle range switch alignment. L-Series

TRANSAXLE RANGE SWITCH

REPLACE

S-SERIES

Removal

1. Turn ignition switch off.
2. Remove air cleaner and duct assembly.
3. Disconnect transaxle range switch harness connectors.
4. Disconnect shifter cable from control lever.
5. Place control lever in the full clockwise position.
6. Remove control lever to manual shift shaft retaining nut while holding control lever in place.
7. Remove switch to transaxle case attaching bolts, then the switch from transaxle.

Installation

1. Install switch, then the switch to transaxle case attaching bolts. **Do not tighten bolts at this time.**
2. Install control lever onto manual shaft.
3. While holding control lever, install control lever retaining nut and **torque** to 108 inch lbs.
4. Ensure control lever is in the PARK position by moving lever to the full clockwise position until it clicks and cannot be moved any further.
5. Release control cable assembly adjustment lock tab with a suitable screwdriver.
6. Connect control cable to control lever.
7. Move control cable assembly housing back and forth in adjuster, note endplay.
8. Center control cable assembly in middle of endplay, then depress control cable lock tab.
9. Place transaxle in the DRIVE position.
10. Connect a suitable ohmmeter between transaxle range switch connector terminals.
11. Rotate transaxle range switch toward engine until ohmmeter indicates continuity.
12. **Torque** switch to case attaching bolts to 10 ft. lbs., then ensure continuity still exists between terminals.
13. Connect switch electrical connectors.
14. Install air cleaner and duct assembly.
15. While moving shifter lever to all gear positions, then using a scan tool, ensure each position reads correctly.

L-SERIES

Removal

1. Apply parking brake and place control assembly in the NEUTRAL position.
2. Remove shift control cable from transaxle range switch lever.
3. Disconnect transaxle range switch electrical connectors.
4. Remove range switch lever nut and lever.
5. Remove transaxle range switch to case attaching bolts, then the switch from transaxle.

Installation

1. Ensure transaxle manual shaft is in the NEUTRAL position.
2. Align flats on transaxle shift shaft with flats on transaxle range switch, then install switch.
3. Loosely install switch attaching bolts.
4. Insert transaxle range switch alignment tool No. J41545, or equivalent, over manual shaft, **Fig. 1.**
5. Rotate switch until alignment tool drops into position.
6. **Torque** switch attaching bolts to 15 ft. lbs.
7. Install switch lever and retaining nut, **torque** nut to 26 ft. lbs.
8. Connect switch electrical connectors.
9. Install control cable and ensure vehicle starts only in PARK or NEUTRAL.

MULTI-FUNCTION SWITCH

REPLACE

S-SERIES

1. Remove steering wheel as described under "Steering Wheel, Replace," then Supplemental Inflatable Restraint (SIR) coil assembly as described in "Passive Restraints" section.
2. Remove Connector Position Assurance (CPA) device, then disconnect electrical connectors from multi-function switch, **Fig. 2.**
3. multi-function switch assembly off steering shaft.
4. Reverse procedure to install. Note SIR coil installation precautions included in "Passive Restraints" section.

HEADLAMP/TURN SIGNAL SWITCH

REPLACE

L-SERIES

1. Remove steering wheel as outlined under "Steering Wheel, Replace."
2. Remove ignition switch bezel, then the upper and lower steering column covers.
3. Remove headlamp/turn signal switch from steering column.

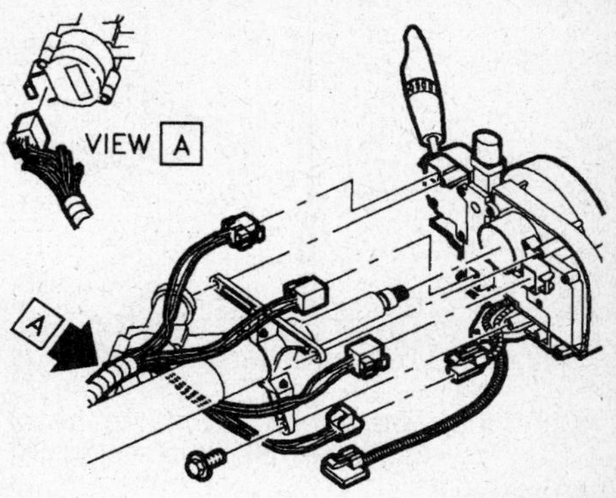

G39049300004000X

Fig. 2 Multi-function switch replacement. S-Series

4. Reverse procedure to install.

S-SERIES

Refer to "Multi-Function Switch, Replace."

STEERING WHEEL

REPLACE

1. Place wheels in straight ahead position.
2. Remove screw caps on steering wheel with flat head screwdriver.
3. Remove inflator module screws.
4. Remove inflator module from steering wheel.
5. Remove integral connector lock device.
6. Disconnect electrical connector and remove inflator module.
7. Disconnect horn switch electrical connector and cruise control electrical connector, if equipped.
8. Remove steering wheel attaching nut.
9. Remove steering wheel with suitable steering wheel puller.
10. Feed electrical wiring through steering wheel and remove steering wheel.
11. Insert yellow tab into SIR coil assembly or use tape to prevent rotating SIR coil.
12. Reverse procedure to install, noting the following:
    a. Install new steering wheel attaching nut and **torque** to 30 ft. lbs.
    b. **Torque** inflator module attaching bolts to 8 ft. lbs.

INSTRUMENT CLUSTER

REPLACE

S-SERIES

1997–99

1. Remove Data Link Connector (DLC) and steering column filler panel screws.
2. Remove hood release cable from lever.
3. Remove steering column filler panel.
4. Disconnect ignition switch electrical connector at right steering column bolt.
5. Remove steering column bolts, then lower column onto front seat.
6. Remove two push pin fasteners in top

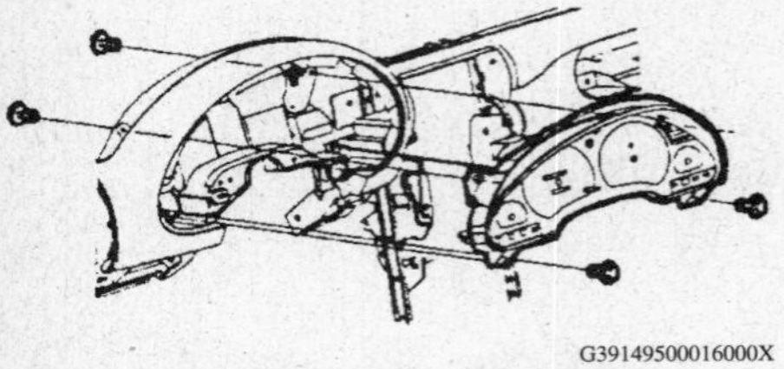

G39149500016000X

Fig. 3 Instrument cluster replacement

portion of instrument cluster trim bezel and pull trim bezel rearward at side clip locations.
7. Remove connector locking pins and disconnect electrical connectors from instrument cluster by depressing tabs on each side of connector.
8. Remove front and rear instrument cluster screws, **Fig. 3.**
9. Remove instrument cluster.
10. Reverse procedure to install. **Torque** steering column bolts to 26 ft. lbs.

2000

1. Remove instrument panel upper trim pad attaching screws, **Fig. 4.**
2. Disengage trim panel retaining clips by grasping edges of trim panel and lifting up.
3. Disengage hook and loop fasteners at rear of upper trim panel by reaching under trim panel and lifting straight up.
4. Raise upper trim panel enough to clear VIN plate.
5. Loosen steering column filler panel attaching bolts. **Do not remove weather strips. Adhesion will be lost if removed.**
6. Remove lefthand side endcap to instrument panel attaching screws.
7. Disengage endcap to instrument panel retaining clips, then remove endcap from instrument panel.
8. Remove upper and lower steering column covers.
9. Lower steering column to its lowest position.
10. Disengage instrument panel bezel retaining clips, then pull bezel outward.
11. Disconnect dimmer/traction control switch assembly electrical connector.
12. Remove instrument panel bezel from instrument panel.
13. Remove instrument cluster retaining screws, then pull cluster away from instrument panel.
14. Disconnect cluster electrical connectors, then remove cluster from instrument panel.
15. Reverse procedure to install.

L-SERIES

1. Remove steering wheel as outlined under "Steering Wheel, Replace."
2. Remove hush panel from under lefthand side of instrument panel.
3. Remove knee bolster panel from under steering column.
4. Remove upper and lower steering column covers.
5. Lower steering column to its lowest position.
6. Remove instrument cluster trim plate

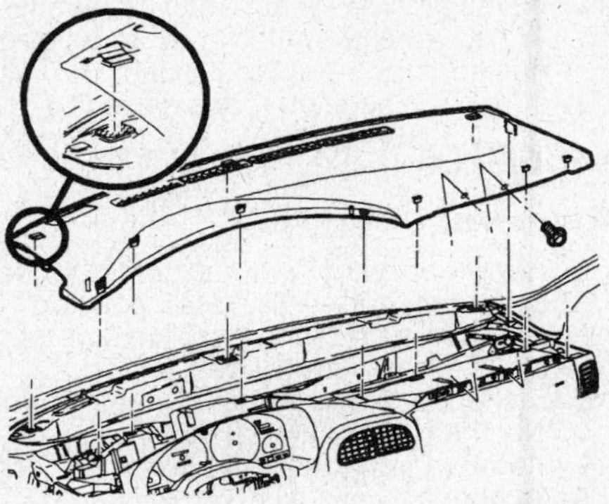

GC9090000051000X

Fig. 4 Upper trim panel removal. 2000 S-Series

attaching screws, then the trim plate.
7. Remove instrument cluster retaining screws, then the cluster.
8. Reverse procedure to install.

RADIO

REPLACE

1. Remove two control cover push pin fasteners and pull radio and heater and air conditioning control cover rearward.
2. Disconnect single traction control, fog lamp and rear defog electrical connector.
3. Remove radio screws.
4. Depress both side spring clips on radio and pull out slightly.
5. Disconnect antenna and electrical connector.
6. **On models equipped with base radio,** remove storage tray by pulling out towards front of radio.
7. **On all models,** remove radio.
8. Reverse procedure to install.

WIPER MOTOR

REPLACE

S-SERIES

1997

1. Remove wiper arm finish cap and attaching screw.
2. Lift wiper blade assembly from windshield, then remove wiper arm from pivot.
3. Remove cowl trim panel, **Fig. 5.**
4. Using a suitable wrench, move wiper motor crank arm to 12 o'clock position to access rear wiper module fasteners.
5. Remove wiper module attaching screws, then lift module to disconnect motor and module electrical connectors.
6. Remove wiper module, then move wiper motor crank arm to 9 o'clock or park position.
7. Remove crank arm nut, then disconnect crank arm from motor shaft.
8. Remove wiper motor attaching nut and bolts, then motor from transmission.

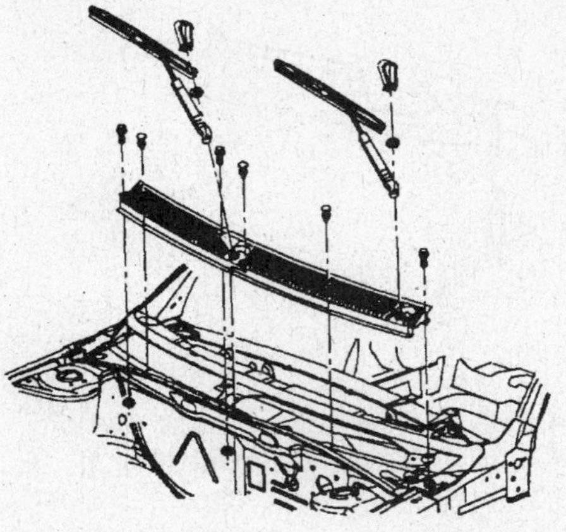

G39149100001000X

Fig. 5 Windshield cowl trim panel removal. S-Series

9. Reverse procedure to install, **torque** wiper motor crank arm on wiper motor shaft to 21 ft. lbs., wiper module to 8 ft. lbs. and wiper arms to 19 ft. lbs.

1998–2000

1. Remove wiper arm finish cap and attaching screw.
2. Lift wiper blade assembly from windshield, then remove wiper arm from pivot.
3. Remove cowl trim panel, **Fig. 5.**
4. Remove instrument panel top cover.
5. Remove defroster duct screws, then position defrost duct aside to allow access to wiper module attaching screws.
6. Place wiper motor arm in 12 o'clock position.
7. Remove wiper module attaching bolts and nuts.
8. Partially remove wiper module, then disconnect electrical connectors from module.
9. Remove wiper module, then place in a suitable vise and remove wiper links from motor arm
10. Remove wiper motor attaching bolts, then motor from module.
11. Reverse procedure to install, **torque** wiper motor to 8 ft. lbs. Install outboard module bolt first, inboard bolt second and **torque** to 13 ft. lbs. Install module nuts and **torque** to 6 ft. lbs.

L-SERIES

1. Remove wiper arm finish cap.
2. Scribe wiper arm positions on windshield using wax pencil or tape.
3. Remove wiper arm retaining nuts, then the wiper arms.
4. Remove weather strip from rear of hood.
5. Remove cowl screen retaining nuts, then the cowl screen **Fig. 6.**
6. Disconnect wiper motor electrical connector.
7. Remove wiper motor retaining bolts, then the wiper motor assembly.
8. Separate wiper motor from transmission assembly.
9. Reverse procedure to install, **torque** wiper motor retaining bolts to 44 inch

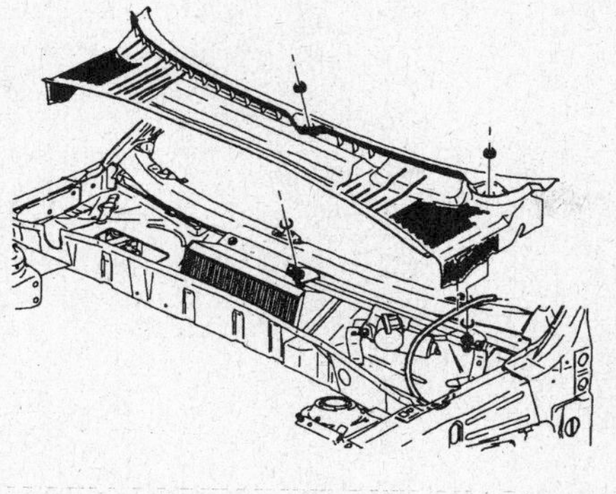

G39029900001100X

Fig. 6 Windshield cowl screen removal. L-Series

lbs. and wiper arm retaining nuts to 21 ft. lbs.

WIPER SWITCH

REPLACE

L-SERIES

1. Remove steering wheel as outlined under "Steering Wheel, Replace."
2. Remove ignition switch bezel, then the upper and lower steering column covers.
3. Remove wiper/washer switch from steering column.
4. Reverse procedure to install.

S-SERIES

Refer to "Multi-Function Switch, Replace."

WIPER TRANSMISSION

REPLACE

Refer to "Wiper Motor, Replace" for wiper motor transmission replacement procedure.

BLOWER MOTOR

REPLACE

S-SERIES

1. Remove right instrument panel lower sound insulator.
2. Disconnect blower motor electrical connector.
3. Remove blower motor attaching screws, then motor.
4. Reverse procedure to install.

L-SERIES

1. Turn ignition switch to the ON position, then select outside air on control head.
2. Remove cowl screen as outlined under "Wiper Motor Replace."
3. Rotate locking tabs outward to release filter assembly, then remove filter.
4. Remove filter housing attaching bolts, then the filter housing.
5. Remove blower motor housing screws, then the housing **Fig. 7.**

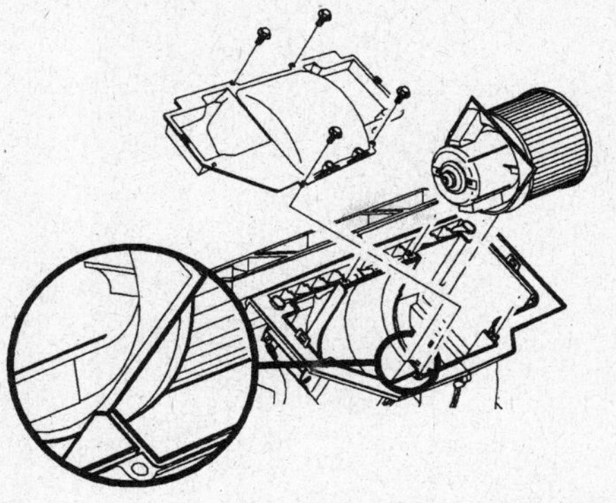

G37029900003400X

Fig. 7 Blower motor removal. L-Series

6. Disconnect blower motor electrical connector, then remove blower motor.
7. Reverse procedure to install, **torque** blower motor housing screws to 9 inch lbs. and filter housing bolts to 31 inch lbs.

HEATER CORE

REPLACE

S-SERIES

1. Drain coolant.
2. Raise and support vehicle.
3. Move heater hose clamps upward, then lower vehicle.
4. Remove heater hoses from core, then blow coolant from heater core with an air hose.
5. Disengage lower instrument panel center trim panels from under instrument panel, then rotate trim panels outward to disengage from front of console assembly.
6. Remove instrument panel lower close-out panel by pulling outward at top edge and rotating downward.
7. Remove lower heater duct attaching screws, then drop duct straight down and slide out sideways, **Fig. 8.**
8. Release temperature cable hold down clip from lower heater core cover by lifting upward on plastic tab while pushing down on top of cable, **Fig. 9.**
9. Slide cable off of temperature door hook, then remove temperature cable.
10. Remove heater core side cover attaching screw, then the side cover.
11. Remove lower heater core cover attaching screws, then the lower cover.
12. Remove lower heater core retainer attaching screw.
13. Remove heater core.
14. Reverse procedure to install.

L-SERIES

1. Drain engine coolant into a suitable container.
2. Remove heater inlet and return hoses.
3. Place end of heater return hose in a container, then apply low air pressure to inlet hose and blow coolant out of heater core.
4. Remove righthand console extension.

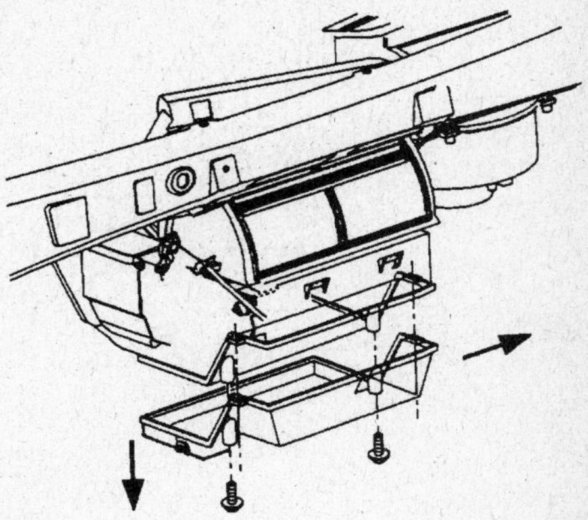

G37029100001000X

Fig. 8 Lower heater duct removal. S-Series

5. Remove heater core pipe to heater core clamps, then the pipe from core end tank **Fig. 10.**
6. Remove core retaining screw, then the strap.
7. Pull center console forward edge outward for access.
8. Pull heater core out of module into passenger foot area **Fig. 11.**
9. Reverse procedure to install.

EVAPORATOR CORE

REPLACE

S-SERIES

1997

1. Recover refrigerant as outlined in "Air Conditioning" section.
2. **On models equipped with DOHC engine,** remove air cleaner cover and air induction hose at intake manifold.
3. **On models equipped with SOHC engine,** remove air cleaner housing.
4. **On all models,** remove suction hose and liquid line from thermal expansion valve.
5. Place protective cover over A/C hoses, lines and expansion module to prevent A/C contamination.
6. Remove thermal expansion valve from evaporator.
7. Raise and support vehicle.
8. Move heater core inlet and outlet clamps up.
9. Lower vehicle.
10. Remove heater core hoses, then using an air hose, blow excess coolant from heater core.
11. Remove instrument panel as outlined in "Dash Panel Service."
12. Lift rear heater duct from mounting bolt, then remove. **Do not remove rear foam seal.**
13. Remove center air outlet duct attaching screws, then duct.
14. Remove windshield defroster nozzle from mode valve assembly, **Fig. 12.**
15. Rotate front of defroster nozzle up and away from windshield, then remove.
16. Remove CPA devices and disconnect blower motor resistor connector.
17. Remove heater and air conditioning

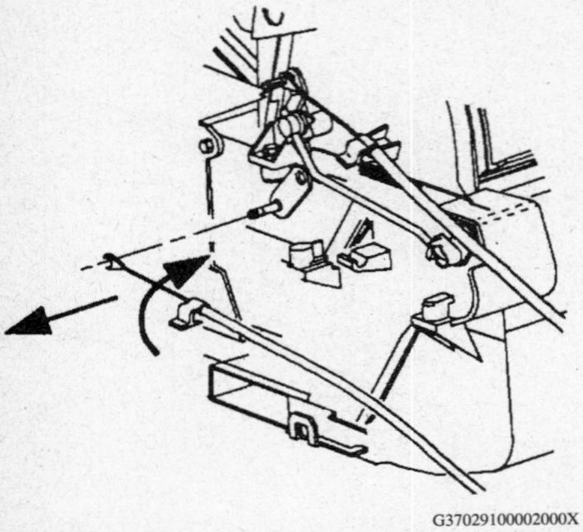

Fig. 9 Temperature cable release. S-Series

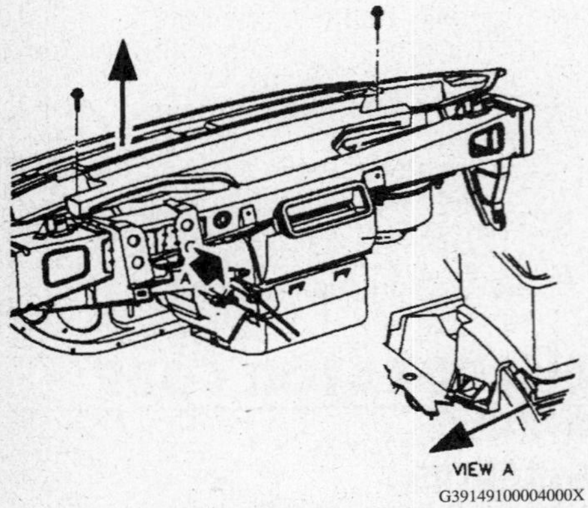

Fig. 12 Windshield defroster nozzle removal. 1997 S-Series

module hold-down clips and disconnect electrical connector.

18. Disconnect blower motor and recirc motor electrical connectors.
19. Remove heater and air conditioning module attaching screws and nuts, then module.
20. Remove and discard drain, heater core pipes, evaporator block and evaporator pipe O-ring front of dash seals, **Fig. 13.**
21. Remove mode valve assembly attaching screws, **Fig. 14,** then lift mode valve assembly upward to remove.
22. Remove upper air inlet case attaching screws, then lift upward to remove, **Fig. 15.**
23. Remove evaporator pipe clamp attaching screws, then lift evaporator upward to remove, **Fig. 16.**
24. Reverse procedure to install, noting following:
    a. **Torque** steering column attaching screws to 33 ft. lbs.
    b. **Torque** thermal expansion valve to evaporator to 8 ft. lbs.
    c. **Torque** thermal expansion valve liquid and suction lines to 19 ft. lbs.

1998–2000

1. Recover refrigerant as outlined in "Air Conditioning" section.
2. Remove air cleaner housing cover and air intake tube.

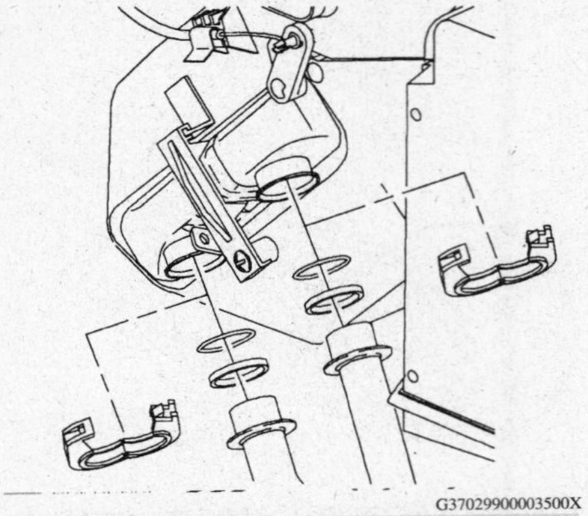

Fig. 10 Heater core pipe removal. L-Series

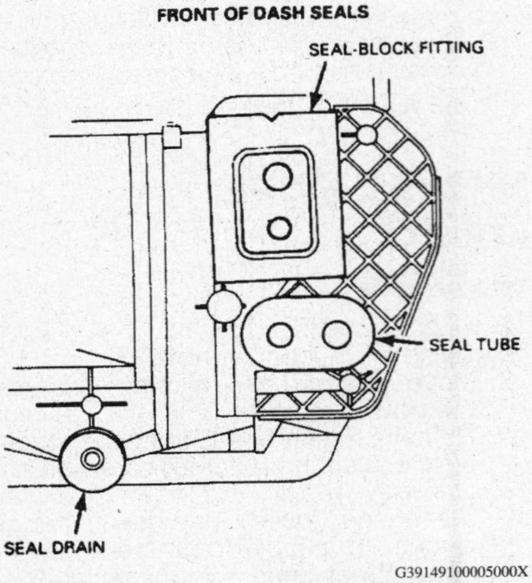

Fig. 13 Front dash seal removal. 1997 S-Series

3. Remove suction hose and liquid line from expansion valve.
4. Remove expansion valve from evaporator.
5. Install protective covers over all A/C lines to prevent system contamination.
6. Drain cooling system, then remove heater inlet hose from engine.
7. Blow remaining coolant from heater core using a suitable air hose.
8. Raise and support vehicle.
9. Remove hoses from heater core, then lower vehicle.
10. Remove instrument panel as outlined in "Dash Panel Service."
11. Remove all wiring harnesses and clips from HVAC module.
12. Disconnect blower and recirc motor electrical connectors.
13. Remove fuel vapor line and clip from HVAC module stud to gain access to nut.
14. Remove three screws and two nuts attaching HVAC module to cowl, **Fig. 17.**
15. Remove HVAC module from vehicle.
16. Remove and discard cowl panel seals.
17. Remove mode valve screws and clips, **Fig. 18.**

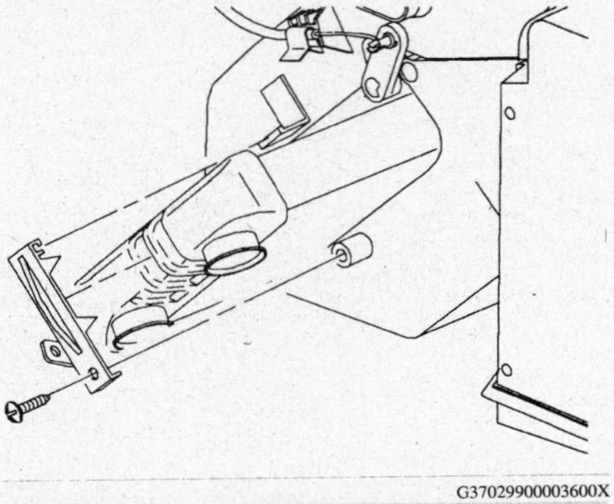

Fig. 11 Heater core removal. L-Series

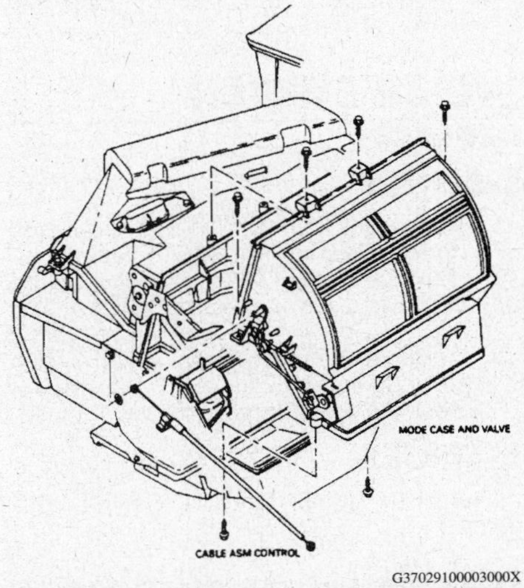

Fig. 14 Mode valve removal. 1997 S-Series

18. Remove mode valve from HVAC module.
19. Remove upper air inlet case from lower case assembly, **Fig. 19.**
20. Remove evaporator tube clamp and screw.
21. Lift evaporator from lower case assembly.
22. Reverse procedure to install, noting the following:
    a. Add 2.25 ounces of PAG oil to new evaporator.
    b. **Torque** HVAC module attaching nuts and screws to 44 inch lbs.
    c. **Torque** steering column attaching bolts to 26 ft. lbs.
    d. **Torque** suction hose and liquid line to 19 ft. lbs.**Use R-12 refrigerant oil to lubricate O-rings. Use of PAG oil can cause premature corrosion of fitting joints.**

L-SERIES

1. Remove blower motor as outlined under "Blower Motor Replace."
2. Recover refrigerant as outlined in "Air Conditioning" section.
3. Remove retaining bolts, then the

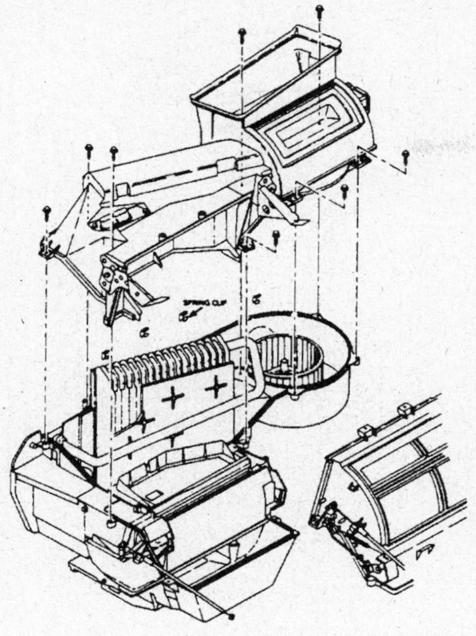

G37029100004000X

Fig. 15 Upper air inlet case removal. 1997 S-Series

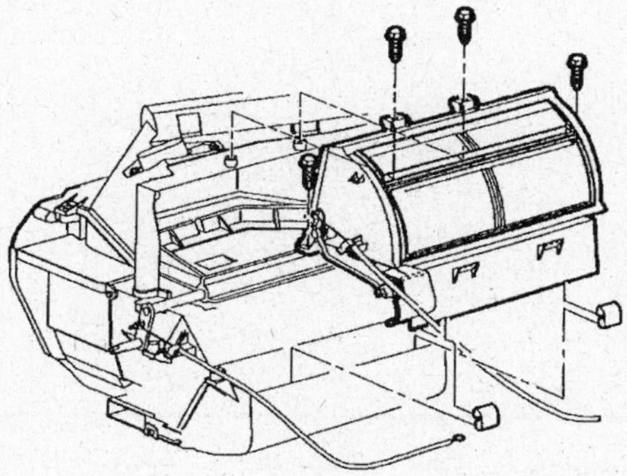

G39149800023000X

Fig. 18 Mode valve removal. 1998–2000 S-Series

suction/liquid line assembly from Thermo Expansion Valve (TXV) **Fig. 20.**

4. Install cap on suction/liquid line hose assembly to prevent spillage.
5. Remove TXV retaining bolts, then install suction/liquid line assembly bolt and hand tighten.
6. Using bolt as handle, remove TXV from evaporator by gently pulling forward, **Fig. 21.**
7. Open glove box door, then remove lamp assembly by pulling on lamp plunger.
8. Disconnect glove box lamp electrical connector.
9. Remove right side instrument panel lower dash insulator retainers.
10. Pull insulator rearward to detach from

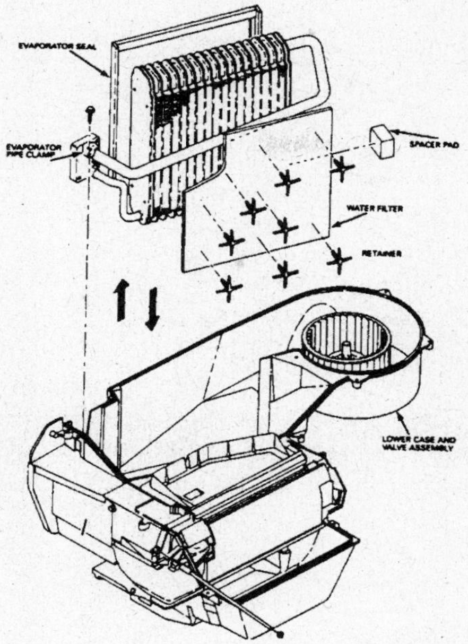

G37029100005000X

Fig. 16 Evaporator removal. 1997 S-Series

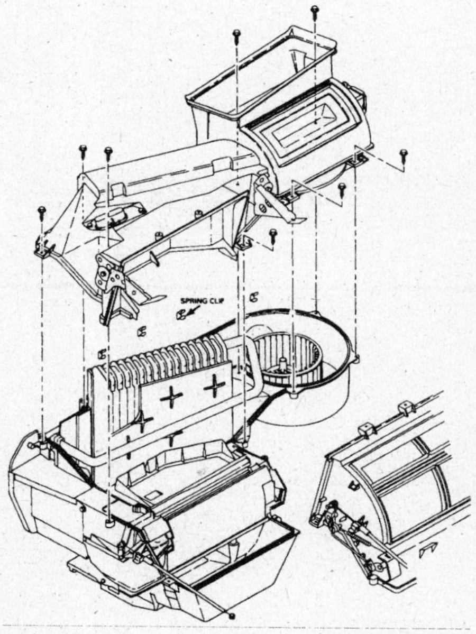

G39149800024000X

Fig. 19 Upper air inlet case removal. 1998–2000 S-Series

forward insulator retainers.

11. Remove right side heater duct assembly retainer, then the duct assembly, **Fig. 22.**
12. Remove glove box door, then the glove box bin fasteners.
13. Slowly tilt glove box bin downward to

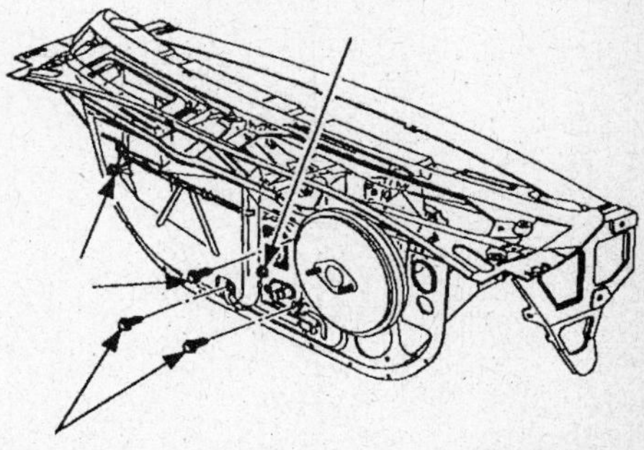

G39149800022000X

Fig. 17 HVAC module fastener location. 1998–2000 S-Series

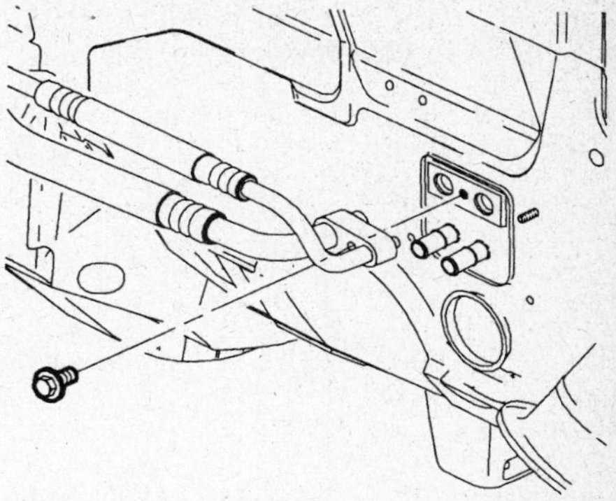

G37029900003700X

Fig. 20 Suction/liquid line assembly removal. L-Series

expose Body Control Module (BCM), **Fig. 23.**

14. Slide BCM module out of attaching slots, then remove glove box bin.
15. Remove hush panel support from front of dash.
16. Locate evaporator access door on right side of module. Entire area inside raised lip is to be cut out.
17. Using a sharp utility knife, cut through module wall following inside of raised bead as guide. **Several passes may be necessary to accomplish this. Fig. 24**
18. Slide evaporator core out through access door opening. Cap pipes to prevent oil spillage.
19. Reverse procedure to install, noting the following:
    a. Add 2.4 ounces of PAG oil to new evaporator.
    b. **Torque** TXV and suction/liquid assembly bolts to 62 inch lbs.
    c. Lubricate O-rings with clean mineral oil.
    d. Apply provided sealant to service door at tongue and groove locations.

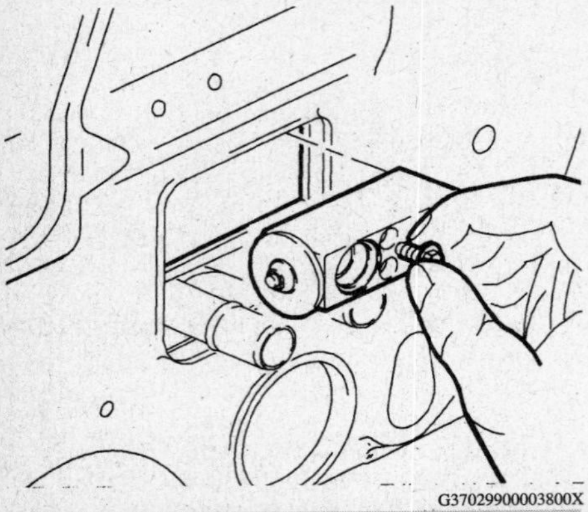

Fig. 21 Thermo Expansion Valve (TXV) removal. L-Series

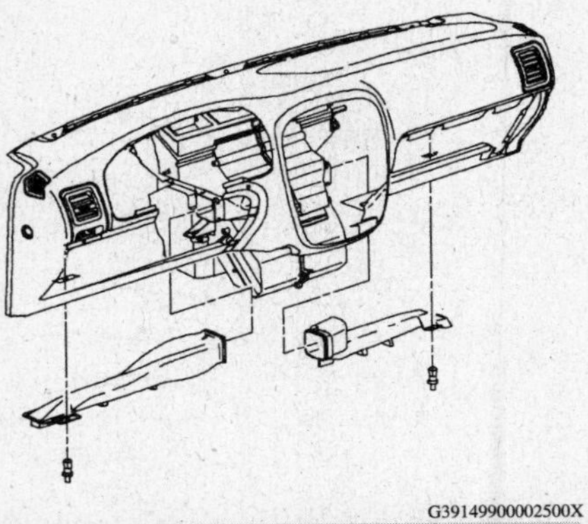

Fig. 22 Heater duct assembly removal. L-Series

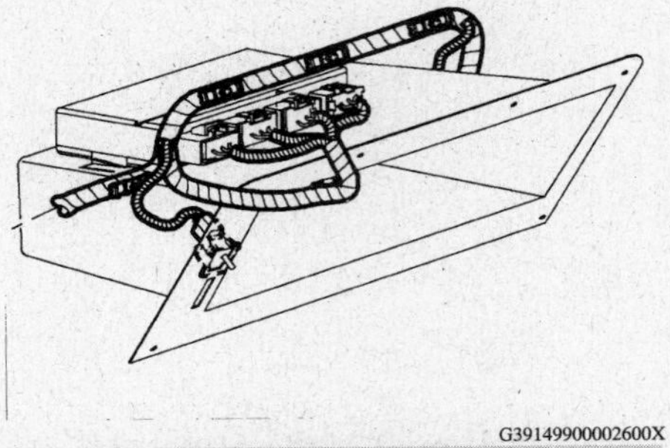

Fig. 23 Body Control Module (BCM) removal. L-Series

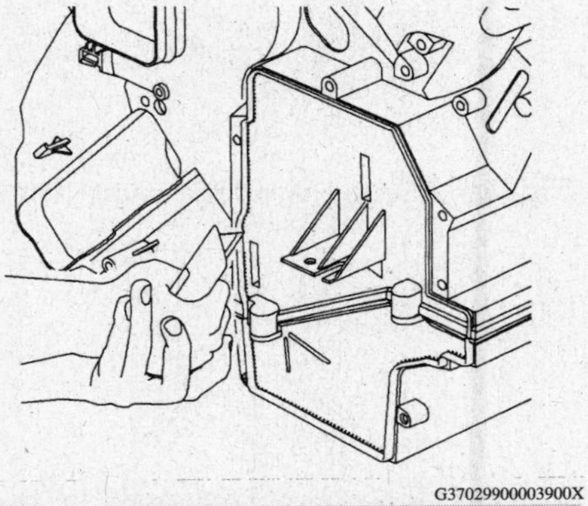

Fig. 24 Evaporator core removal. L-Series

1.9L Engine

NOTE: On Air Bag Equipped Models, Refer To " Air Bag System Precautions" Located In The Front Of This Manual For System Disarming & Arming Procedures.

NOTE: Prior To Performing Any Service Operations Listed In This Section, Consult The "Technical Service Bulletins " Section For Related Information.

NOTE: Refer To "Computer Relearn Procedures " Located In The Front Of This Manual For Computer Relearn Procedures.

INDEX

PRECAUTIONS

AIR BAG SYSTEMS

Refer to "Air Bag System Precautions" in the front of this manual for system disarming and arming procedures.

BATTERY GROUND CABLE

Prior to service, disconnect battery ground cable and isolate as required.

FUEL SYSTEM PRESSURE RELIEF

1. Connect fuel gauge bar kit tool No. SA9127E, or equivalent, to fuel pressure test port using adapter tool No. SA9403E, or equivalent, **Fig. 1.**
2. Place end of bleed hose into a suitable approved container and open valve to bleed system pressure.
3. Once pressure is bled, remove gauge from fuel pressure test port and replace cap.

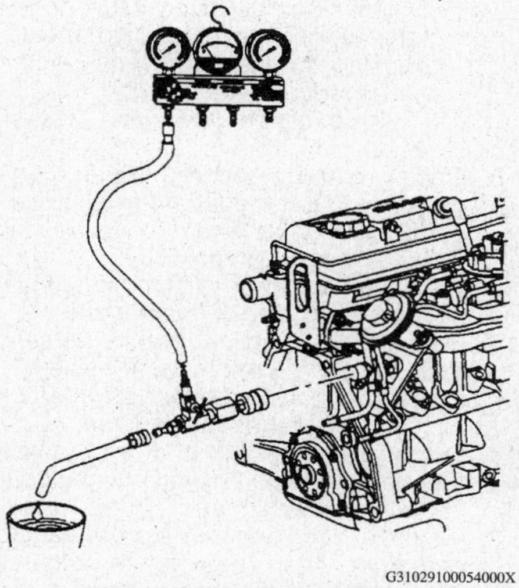

Fig. 1 Fuel pressure bleed

COMPRESSION PRESSURE

1. Start engine and allow to reach normal operating temperature.
2. Turn engine off, then disconnect ignition module harness electrical plug.
3. Remove spark plugs.
4. Install compression gauge tool No. SST SA9127E, or equivalent, in spark plug hole.
5. Ensure battery is charged, then fully open throttle.
6. Measure compression while cranking engine. Cylinder should puff or compression gauge needle should bounce a minimum of 10 times. **Do not crank engine for more than 15 seconds.**
7. Repeat preceding steps for each cylinder.
8. Normal compression pressure is 185–205 psi; minimum pressure is 180 psi.

ENGINE MOUNT

REPLACE

1. Remove two engine mount to midrail bracket attaching nuts, **Fig. 2.**
2. Position a floor jack under oil pan. Using a block of wood between pan and floor jack, raise engine enough to unload mount.
3. Remove three engine to front cover attaching nuts, **Fig. 3,** then engine mount.
4. Reverse procedure to install. Tighten mount to midrail bracket and engine mount to front cover attaching nuts to specifications.

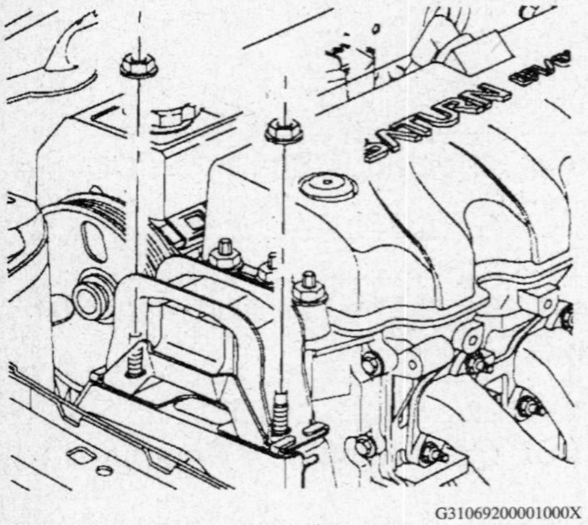

Fig. 2 Engine mount to midrail bracket removal

ENGINE

REPLACE

1. Remove coolant bottle cap, then drain coolant.
2. Relieve fuel system pressure as described under " Precautions."
3. Remove air cleaner assembly.
4. Disconnect the following engine electrical connectors:
   a. Two coolant temperature sensors.
   b. Oxygen sensor and clip, at front transaxle mount bracket.
   c. Idle air control valve.
   d. Two ignition coil connectors.
   e. Throttle position sensor.
   f. Manifold absolute pressure sensor.
   g. EGR solenoid.
   h. Brake booster hose at booster or intake manifold.
   i. Two grounds located rear of cylinder head at transaxle.
   j. Injector connectors.
5. Disconnect the following transaxle connectors:
   a. Neutral safety/selector switch.
   b. Valve body actuator.
   c. Turbine speed sensor.
   d. Temperature sensor.
   e. **On models equipped with manual transaxle,** back-up light switch.
6. **On all models,** disconnect accelerator cables.
7. Bleed residual fuel pressure into a suitable container using gauge bar tool No. SST 9127E, or equivalent, then disconnect fuel lines using fuel line tool No. SA9157E, or equivalent, **Fig. 4. Place a cloth around fitting before disconnecting; cap or suspend open fuel lines to prevent fuel from leaking.**
8. Disconnect upper radiator hose and de-aeration hose at engine.
9. Disconnect A/C compressor and position aside.
10. Pinch tabs to disconnect and plug cooler lines at transaxle, then wrap transaxle cooler line fittings with a cloth.
11. **On models equipped with automatic transaxle,** disconnect shifter cable, **Fig. 5.**
12. **On models equipped with manual**

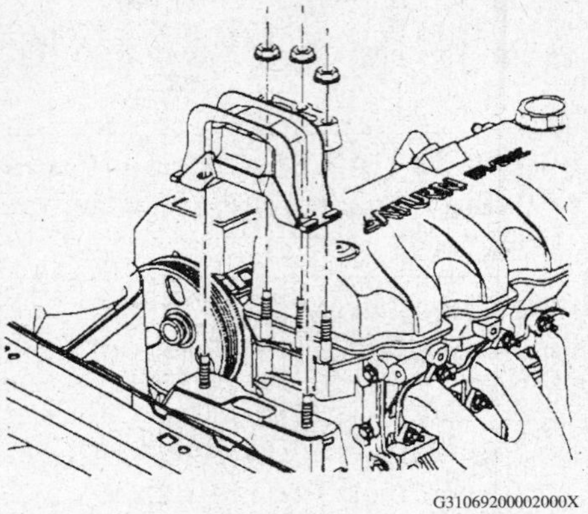

Fig. 3 Engine mount separation from front cover

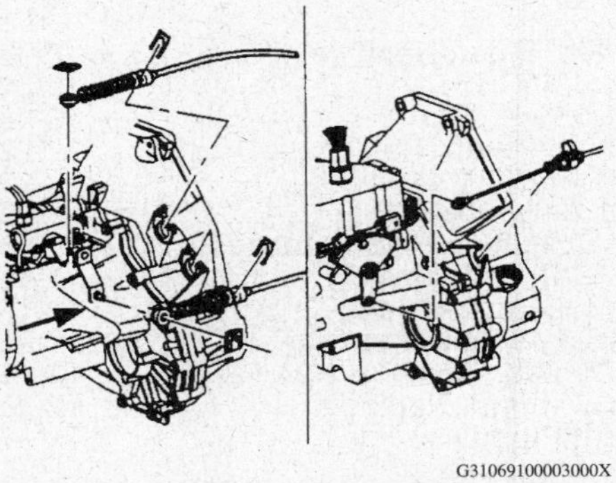

Fig. 5 Transaxle shifter cable removal

transaxle, proceed as follows:
   a. Remove hydraulic damper to clutch housing stud nuts, then slide damper and bracket from studs.
   b. Rotate clutch actuator ¼ turn counterclockwise while pushing toward housing to disengage connector and remove.
   c. Position clutch hydraulic system aside.
13. **On all models,** secure radiator, condenser and fan module to front crossbar using suitable wire.
14. Raise and support vehicle.
15. Remove front wheel assemblies, then front and side shields from cradle.
16. Remove brake caliper bracket attaching bolts, then position caliper aside.
17. Disconnect lower radiator and heater inlet and return hoses at engine.
18. Disconnect steering shaft and power steering pressure switch electrical connector, if equipped.
19. Remove front exhaust pipe, catalytic converter, then powertrain stiffener bracket. **Do not remove torque restrictor bracket to transaxle.**
20. Remove automatic transaxle flywheel cover and torque converter to flexplate attaching bolts.
21. Remove alternator and starter shields.
22. Disconnect the following electrical connectors:
   a. Starter feed.
   b. Alternator feed.
   c. Oil pressure sensor.

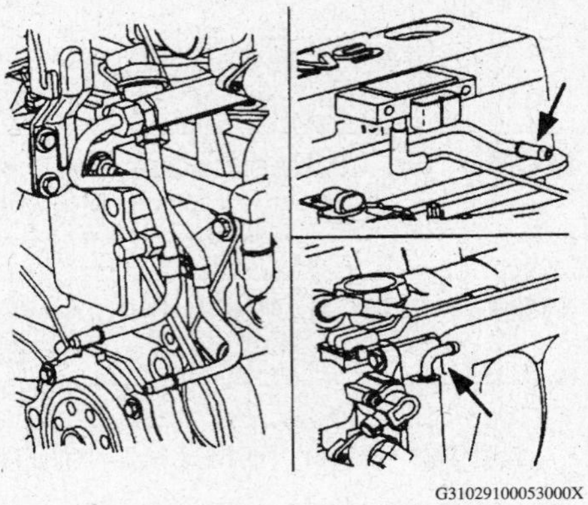

Fig. 4 Fuel line removal

   d. Knock sensor.
   e. Crankshaft position sensor.
   f. EVO solenoid, if equipped.
   g. Vehicle speed sensor.
   h. Canister purge solenoid.
   i. PCM/EC and oxygen sensor.
   j. ABS wheel sensor ground connectors, if equipped.
23. Unclip brake lines from rear of cradle, then remove electrical harness from engine and lower vehicle. Lay electrical harness on underhood junction block and battery cover.
24. Place a 1 x 1 x 2 inch block of wood between torque strut and cradle, **Fig. 6.**
25. Remove upper engine torque axis mount to front cover nuts, then mount to midrail bracket nuts.
26. Position suitable powertrain support dolly and two 4 x 4 x 36 inch wood pieces to support cradle.
27. Remove cradle to body attaching bolts, then lower cradle, ensure two large rear cradle spacers are attached.
28. Install suitable engine lifting equipment.
29. Remove spark plug wire ends at ignition module.
30. Remove power steering pump with bracket, then using wire, attach in upright position to steering gear or cradle.
31. Remove transaxle housing attaching bolts.
32. Remove front engine mount, then disconnect motion restrictor, if required.
33. Place ½ x 1 x 3 inch block of wood below axle shaft.
34. Remove starter bracket.
35. **On models equipped with DOHC engine,** remove intake manifold bracket.
36. **On all models,** remove three axle shaft bracket bolts, then allow bracket to rotate rearward. It may be necessary to lift engine slightly to allow clearance between starter bracket and driveshaft bracket.
37. Place a 4 x 4 x 6 inch block of wood under transaxle housing.
38. Remove engine strut bracket and torque strut assembly. The engine may have to be lifted slightly to allow engine strut removal, **Fig. 7.**
39. Remove four transaxle housing attaching bolts.
40. Lift engine, then install to engine stand.
41. Remove the following:

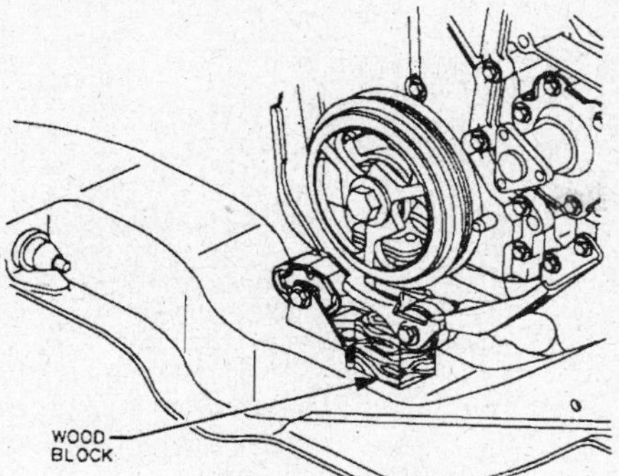

Fig. 6 Support between torque strut & cradle

a. Starter and alternator.
b. Water pump.
c. Oil Pressure sending unit.
d. Knock sensor.
e. Crankshaft position sensor.
f. Clutch assembly (flexplate) and flywheel.
g. Using gasket seal cutter tool No. SST SA9123 E, or equivalent, cut oil pan seal from front cover oil seal rear seal carrier, then remove oil pan and filter.
h. Oil pick up tube.
i. **On models equipped with DOHC engine,** remove baffle plate.

42. **On all models,** reverse procedure to install.

INTAKE MANIFOLD

REPLACE

SOHC ENGINE

1. Drain engine coolant.
2. Remove air cleaner assembly, then disconnect fresh air hose at cam cover.
3. Remove PCV hose.
4. Release fuel system pressure as described under " Precautions."
5. Remove fuel line bracket bolt; then disconnect fuel supply and return line by depressing retaining tabs. Ensure new retainer is used when performing installation procedure.
6. Disconnect throttle cable from throttle body, then remove bracket attaching nuts.
7. Disconnect the following electrical connectors:
   a. Fuel injectors.
   b. Idle air control (IAC).
   c. Throttle position sensor (TPS).
   d. EGR valve.
   e. Manifold absolute pressure sensor.
8. Remove wires with tubes, then position harness onto fuel relay.
9. Disconnect and label vacuum hoses.
10. Disconnect heater hose, then remove cylinder head coolant outlet deaeration line fitting and clamps, then position aside.
11. Remove intake manifold support bracket to block attaching bolt, then accessory drive belt.
12. Remove power steering pump attaching bolts, then position aside.

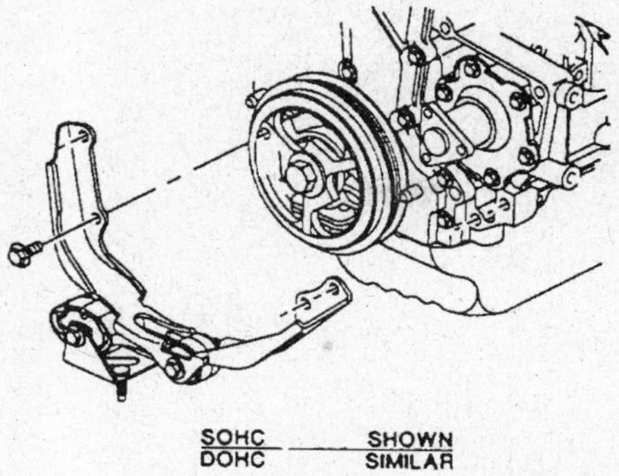

Fig. 7 Engine strut bracket & torque strut removal

13. Remove intake manifold attaching nuts, then manifold and gasket.
14. Reverse procedure to install. Tighten intake manifold attaching nuts to specifications in sequence as shown in **Fig. 8.**

DOHC ENGINE

1. Drain engine coolant.
2. Remove air inlet tube/resonator assembly, then disconnect fresh air hose at cam cover, lift resonator upward to disengage from engine.
3. Remove PCV hose.
4. Relieve fuel system pressure as described under " Precautions."
5. Remove fuel line bracket bolt; then disconnect fuel supply and return lines by depressing plastic retaining tabs of line fitting. Ensure new retainer is used when performing installation procedure.
6. Disconnect throttle cable from throttle body, then remove bracket attaching nuts.
7. Disconnect the following electrical connectors:
   a. Fuel injectors.
   b. Idle air control (IAC).
   c. Throttle position sensor (TPS).
   d. Manifold absolute pressure sensor.
   e. EGR valve.
8. Disconnect heater and de-aeration hoses at intake manifold outlet.
9. Disconnect EGR solenoid vacuum hose.
10. Position electrical harness over brake master cylinder.
11. Remove intake manifold support bracket to block attaching bolt.
12. Remove accessory drive belt.
13. Remove power steering pump attaching bolts, then position aside.
14. Remove upper intake manifold attaching nuts.
15. Raise and support vehicle, then remove lower power steering unit bracket.
16. Remove intake manifold bracket attaching bolt.
17. Disconnect canister purge relay and brake booster vacuum hose.
18. Remove lower intake manifold attaching stud, then lower vehicle and remove manifold.
19. Reverse procedure to install. Tighten

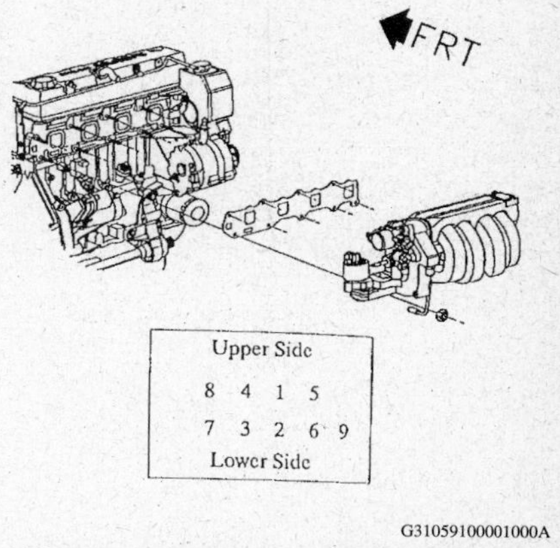

Fig. 8 Intake manifold bolt tightening sequence. SOHC engine

intake manifold attaching nuts to specifications in sequence as shown in **Fig. 9.**

EXHAUST MANIFOLD

REPLACE

1. Raise and support vehicle, then remove nuts securing exhaust pipe to manifold.
2. Lower exhaust pipe and discard gasket, then lower vehicle.
3. Remove A/C compressor and rear compressor bracket.
4. Remove two front exhaust pipe to engine stiffening bracket attaching bolts.
5. Disconnect oxygen sensor electrical connector, then remove sensor.
6. Remove exhaust manifold attaching nuts, then manifold and discard gasket.
7. Reverse procedure to install. Tighten exhaust manifold attaching nuts to specifications in sequence, **Fig. 10.**

CYLINDER HEAD

REPLACE

SOHC ENGINE

1. Remove coolant bottle cap.
2. Drain coolant from engine and radiator.
3. Remove air cleaner and air inlet duct, then disconnect PCV and fresh air hose.
4. Disconnect accelerator cable from throttle lever and bracket from intake manifold.
5. Disconnect the following electrical connectors:
   a. Coolant temperature and PCM connectors.
   b. Injectors.
   c. Idle air control valve.
   d. Manifold air pressure sensor.
   e. Throttle position sensor/switch.
   f. Spark plug wires.
   g. Oxygen sensor.
   h. A/C Compressor.
6. Position electrical harness on underhood junction block.

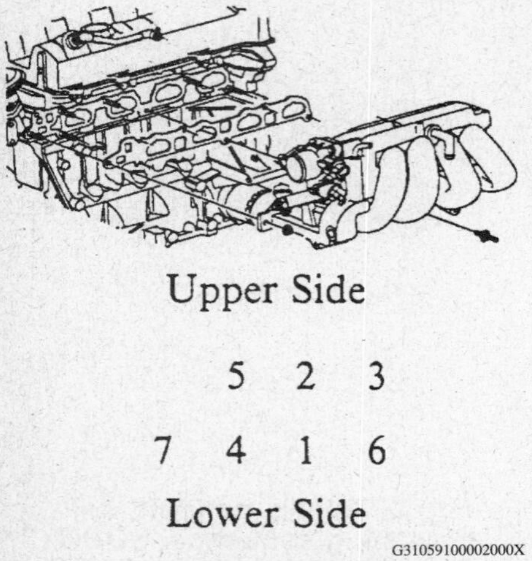

Fig. 9 Intake manifold bolt tightening sequence. DOHC engine

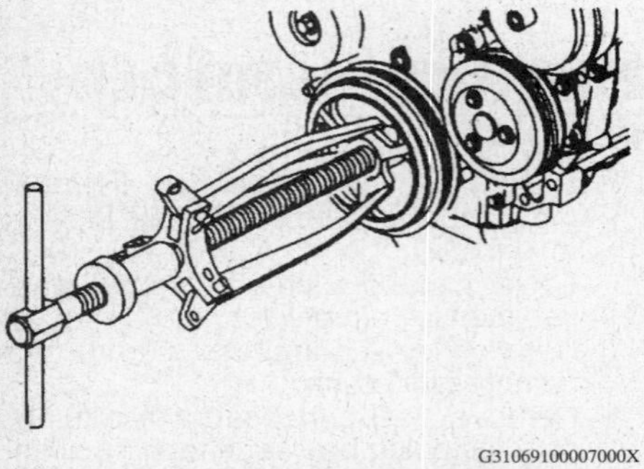

Fig. 12 Crankshaft damper removal

7. Disconnect and label canister purge valve hose and brake booster hose.
8. Disconnect PCV hose at cam cover, fuel regulator vacuum hose and throttle body connector.
9. Disconnect upper radiator hose at cylinder head, heater hose at intake manifold and de-aeration hose at throttle body assembly or intake manifold.
10. Release fuel system pressure as described under " Precautions."
11. Remove fuel line clamp to intake manifold base attaching bolt.
12. Disconnect fuel supply and return lines at throttle body assembly, then remove lower intake manifold support bracket stud.
13. Unclip lower splash shield and place a 1 x 1 x 2 inch block of wood between torque strut and cradle.
14. Remove three right hand upper engine torque axis mount to front cover attaching nuts, allowing engine to rest on block of wood.
15. Remove accessory drive belt.
16. Disconnect de-aeration line at cylinder head water outlet and support bracket then remove rocker cover, **Fig. 11.**
17. Remove three A/C compressor front bracket to cylinder head attaching bolts, then rear bracket attaching bolts. Position compressor aside. **It is not**

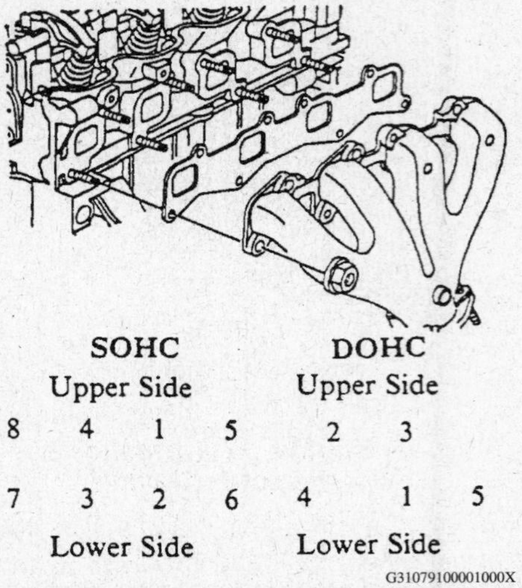

Fig. 10 Exhaust manifold bolt tightening sequence

necessary to recover A/C refrigerant.

18. Remove power steering pump bracket attaching bolts, then position pump aside.
19. Raise and support vehicle, then drain engine oil.
20. Remove right hand wheel and splash shield.
21. Remove drive belt tensioner.
22. Remove crankshaft pulley bolt.
23. Using a universal three jaw puller, **Fig. 12,** while holding damper, remove front crankshaft damper assembly. **Do not pry against cover.**
24. Using crankshaft gear retaining tool No. SA9104 E, or equivalent, with flat side toward crankshaft sprocket, to hold front crankshaft timing sprocket.
25. Remove four front oil pan attaching bolts and front cover attaching bolts.
26. Using RTV cutter tool No. SA9123E, or equivalent, cut RTV seal from front cover.
27. Using front cover pry tangs, remove cover, then remove and discard two oil gallery transfer seals.
28. **Position crankshaft 90° off top dead center (TDC) to ensure pistons will not contact valves during assembly.**
29. Rotate crankshaft clockwise as viewed from crankshaft accessory belt end, ensure timing mark on crankshaft sprocket and keyway align with main bearing cap split line.
30. Remove timing chain, tensioner, guides, camshaft sprocket and chained, using a ⅞ inch wrench to hold camshaft when removing sprocket, **Fig. 13.**
31. Using a six point socket, uniformly loosen and remove ten head bolts in sequence shown, **Fig. 14.**
32. Lift cylinder head from cylinder block dowels.
33. Reverse procedure to install, noting the following:
    a. **When cylinder block or head bolts are replaced, install and torque cylinder head bolts to 48**

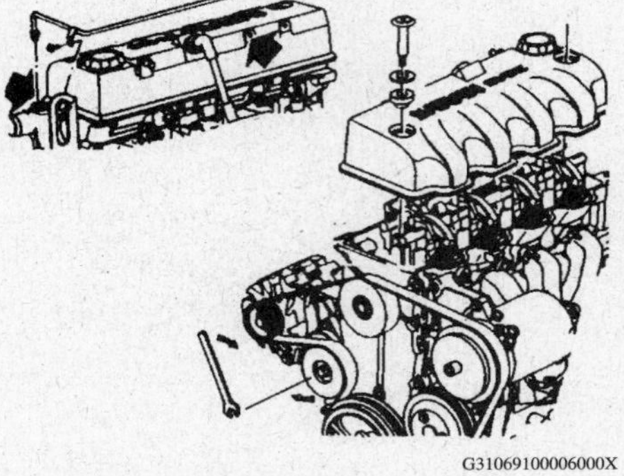

Fig. 11 Valve cover removal. SOHC engine

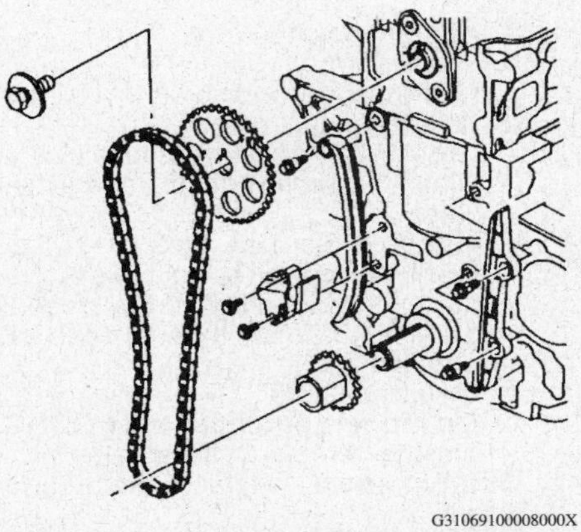

Fig. 13 Timing chain removal. SOHC engine

ft. lbs. in sequence shown in Fig. 15. Remove bolts, then apply a light coating of engine oil to bolt threads before tightening to final specification. This procedure will ensure proper clamp load is achieved.

b. Using sequence shown in **Fig. 15,** tighten cylinder head bolts in three steps: first step, **torque** to 22 ft. lbs.; second step, **torque** to 33 ft. lbs.; third step, install torque angle gauge tool No. SA9140E, or equivalent, then calibrate gauge to zero and turn each bolt an additional 90.°
c. Ensure crankshaft is 90° past TDC, **Fig. 16,** as required, position camshaft to No. 1 TDC by loosely installing sprocket and rotating clockwise until timing pin may be installed, **Fig. 17.**
d. Rotate crankshaft counterclockwise until No. 1 cylinder is TDC, crankshaft sprocket timing mark will align with cylinder block timing mark, **Fig. 18.**
e. One silver link plate aligns to camshaft sprocket pip marks and another paired link plates align with crankshaft sprocket tooth that is located at the 6 o'clock position. Crankshaft sprocket pip mark must be aligned with block timing mark.
f. Place timing chain over camshaft

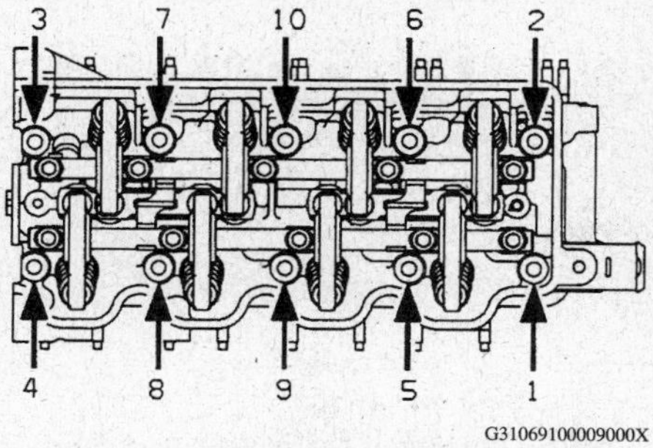

Fig. 14 Cylinder head bolt loosening sequence

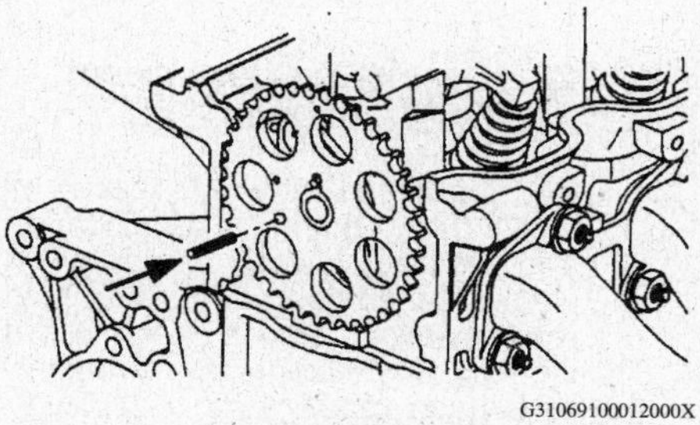

Fig. 17 Camshaft at No. 1 TDC. SOHC engine

sprocket and under crankshaft sprocket, camshaft sprocket FRT letters must face forward, **Fig. 19.**

g. **Keep excess chain slack to chain tensioner side of cylinder block when installing timing chain.**
h. Install camshaft sprocket timing pin, using a 3⁄16 inch drill, **Fig. 17.**
i. Install camshaft washer and bolt, tighten to specifications, while holding cam.
j. Install fixed chain guide and check for clearance between block and head. Ensure guide is installed with FRONT facing away from cylinder block and that chain is tight against guide. Tighten to specification.
k. Install pivoting chain guide and tighten to specification. Check for clearance between block and head. Ensure guide pivots freely.
l. Retract tensioner plunger and hold ratchet using a suitable 1/8 inch drill. Install tensioner and tighten to specification. Remove drill and allow plunger to extend.
m. Verify timing marks.
n. Remove camshaft timing pins.
o. Install crankshaft timing gear retaining tool No. SA9104E, or equivalent.
p. Install front cover and tighten to specification in sequence shown in **Fig. 20.**
q. Pump 6–12 drops of oil through front oil seal drain back hole to ensure hole is not plugged.

DOHC ENGINE

1. Remove coolant bottle cap.
2. Drain coolant from radiator and engine.
3. Remove air cleaner cover and air inlet duct, lift resonator upward to disen-

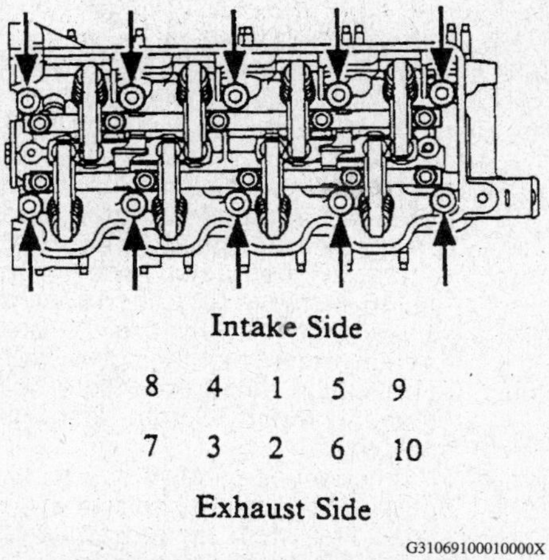

Fig. 15 Cylinder head bolt tightening sequence

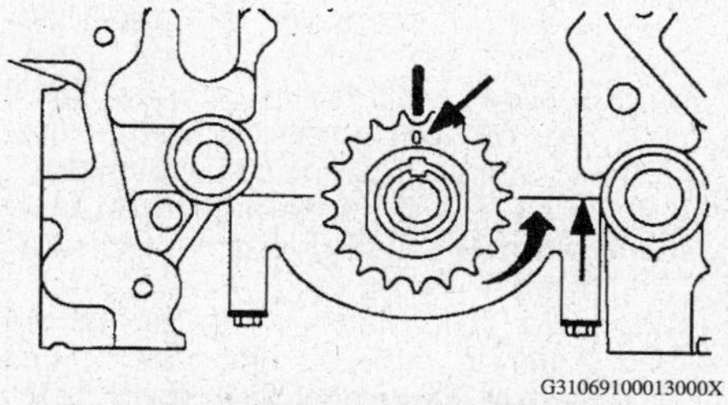

Fig. 18 Crankshaft sprocket & block timing mark

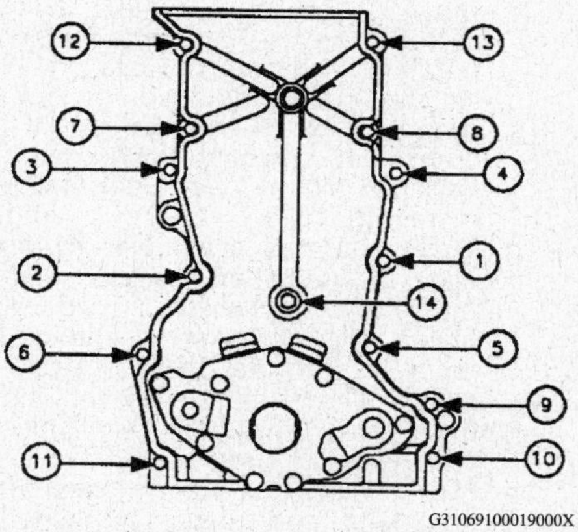

Fig. 20 Front cover tightening sequence. SOHC engine

gage button from engine support bracket.

4. Disconnect cam cover air hose at cam cover.
5. Disconnect accelerator cable from throttle body and intake manifold bracket.
6. Disconnect the following electrical connectors:
   a. Coolant temperature gauge and PCM connectors.
   b. Injector connectors.
   c. Idle air control valve.
   d. Throttle position sensor/switch.
   e. Manifold air pressure sensor.
   f. Oxygen sensor.
   g. Spark plug wires.

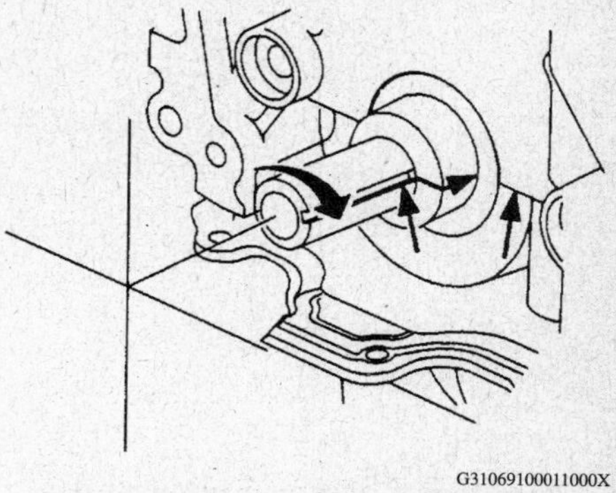

Fig. 16 Crankshaft at 90° past TDC

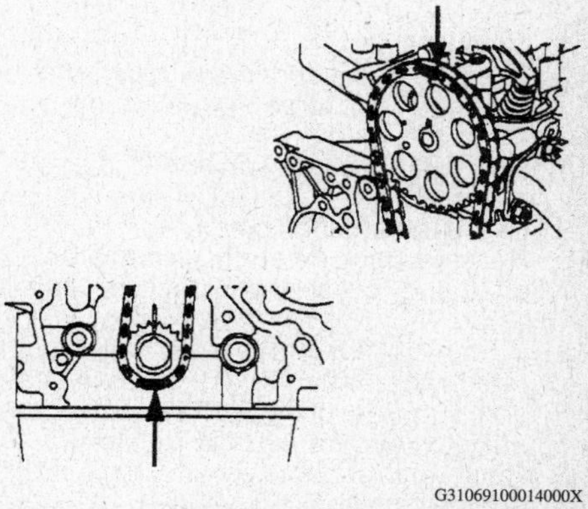

Fig. 19 Timing chain installation. SOHC engine

   h. A/C compressor.
   i. EGR solenoid.
7. Lay electrical harness onto underhood junction block and battery cover.
8. Disconnect and label the following vacuum hoses:
   a. Canister purge valve.
   b. PCV valve at cam cover.
   c. EGR valve.
   d. Fuel regulator, if equipped.
   e. Throttle body connector.
   f. Brake vacuum booster.
9. Disconnect the following hose clamps using clamp tool No. SA911E or equivalent:
   a. Upper radiator hose at cylinder head outlet.
   b. De-aeration hose at intake manifold.
   c. Heater hose at intake manifold or front of dash.
10. Using gauge bar kit tool No. SA9127E, or equivalent, bleed fuel pressure into suitable container.
11. Remove fuel line clamp to intake manifold base attaching bolt.
12. Disconnect fuel supply and return line to fuel rail.
13. Disconnect fuel line at regulator.
14. Remove upper intake manifold support bracket attaching bolt.
15. Unclip lower splash shield and place a 1 x 1 x 2 inch block of wood between torque strut and cradle.
16. Remove three right hand upper engine torque axis mount to front cover attaching nuts, allowing engine to rest on

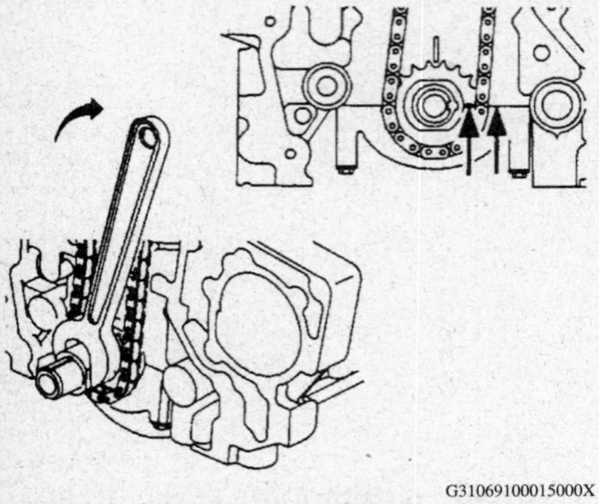

Fig. 21 Crankshaft sprocket & keyway alignment. DOHC engine

block of wood.

17. Remove accessory drive belt and tensioner. Do not remove water pump pulley.
18. Remove accessory drive belt idler pulley.
19. Remove camshaft cover.
20. Remove power steering pump bracket attaching bolts, then position pump aside.
21. Remove A/C compressor front and rear bracket attaching bolts, then position compressor aside. **It is not necessary to recover A/C refrigerant.**
22. Raise and support vehicle, then drain engine oil.
23. Remove right hand wheel and splash shield.
24. Remove intake manifold bracket to intake manifold attaching bolts.
25. Remove front damper assembly bolt while holding damper with a strap wrench or ¾ inch square by 12 inch long piece of wood wedged between damper spoke and lower rear side of front cover.
26. Using a universal three jaw puller, **Fig. 12,** while holding damper, remove front crankshaft damper assembly. **Do not pry against cover.**
27. Disconnect exhaust pipe from exhaust manifold.
28. Install crankshaft gear retaining tool No. SA9104E, or equivalent, with flat side toward sprocket to hold sprocket.
29. Remove four front oil pan bolts, then using RTV cutter tool No. SA9123E, or equivalent, cut seal from front cover.
30. Remove front cover attaching bolts, then use a suitable screwdriver to pry front cover from cylinder block.
31. **Position crankshaft 90° off top dead center to ensure pistons will not contact valves during installation.**
32. Rotate crankshaft clockwise, viewed from crankshaft accessory belt end, ensure timing mark on sprocket and keyway align with main bearing cap split line, **Fig. 21.**
33. Remove timing chain tensioner, guides, camshaft sprockets and chain, then using a ⅞ inch wrench to hold camshaft while removing sprocket bolts. **Do not place fingers or tools between camshaft sprocket and chain during removal or assembly.**
34. Loosen and remove cylinder head bolts in sequence, **Fig. 14.**
35. Lift cylinder head from dowels on engine block, then remove head.
36. Reverse procedure to install, noting the following:
    a. **When cylinder block or head bolts are replaced, install and torque cylinder head bolts to 48 ft. lbs. in sequence shown in Fig. 15.** Remove bolts, then apply a light coating of engine oil to bolt threads before tightening to final specification. This procedure will ensure proper clamp load is achieved.
    b. Using sequence shown in **Fig. 15,** tighten cylinder head bolts in three steps: first step, **torque** to 22 ft. lbs.; second step, **torque** to 37 ft. lbs.; third step, install torque angle gauge tool No. SA9140E, or equivalent, then calibrate gauge to zero and turn each bolt an additional 90.°
    c. Ensure crankshaft is 90° past TDC, **Fig. 16,** then install camshaft timing gears attaching bolts and washer. **"FRT" on sprocket must face forward away from cylinder head.**
    d. Hold camshafts while tightening bolts to specifications. **Do not torque camshaft attaching bolts against 3⁄16 inch timing pins as cylinder head damage may result.**
    e. Rotate camshaft up to No. 1 TDC by rotating camshaft and sprocket until timing pins can be installed.
    f. Rotate crankshaft counterclockwise until No. 1 cylinder is TDC, crankshaft sprocket timing mark will align with cylinder block timing mark, **Fig. 18.**
    g. Two separated silver link plates align to camshaft sprocket pip marks and another two paired link plates align crankshaft sprocket tooth that is located at 6 o'clock position. Crankshaft sprocket pip mark must be aligned with block timing mark.
    h. Place timing chain over camshaft sprockets and under crankshaft sprocket.
    i. **Keep excess chain slack to chain tensioner side (movable guide) of cylinder block when installing timing chain or camshaft sprockets will not be correctly timed.**
    j. Position silver colored link plates over pip mark on cam sprocket, then position crankshaft sprocket tooth that is pointed downward at 6 o'clock position between two silver colored links. Crankshaft sprocket pip mark should be aligned with block timing mark.
    k. Align timing pin holes, crankshaft sprocket pip mark with block mark, colored links with camshaft and crankshaft, **Fig. 22.**
    l. Install fixed guide. Ensure chain is tight against guide.
    m. Install pivoting chain guide. Check for clearance between head and block. Tighten bolt to specification and ensure guide moves freely.
    n. Retract tensioner plunger and hold ratchet lever using a suitable 1/8 inch drill. Install tensioner and tighten bolts to specification.
    o. Remove drill and allow plunger to extend.
    p. Verify all timing marks.
    q. Remove camshaft timing pins.
    r. Install crankshaft retaining tool No. SA9140E, or equivalent.
    s. Install front cover and tighten to specification in sequence shown in **Fig. 23.**
    t. Pump 6–12 drops of oil into oil seal drain back hole and ensure hole is not plugged.

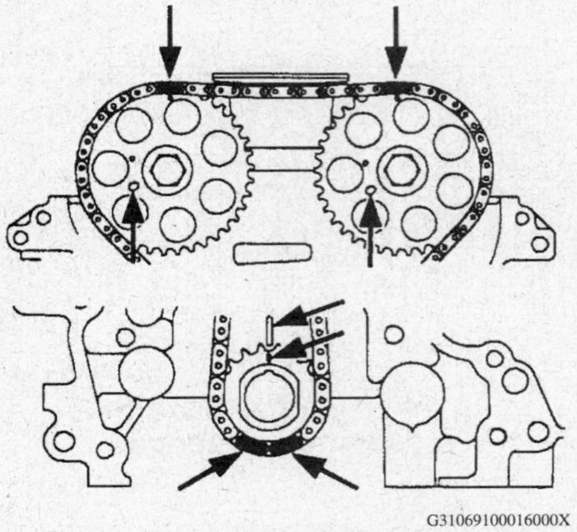

Fig. 22 Crankshaft alignment. DOHC engine

CAMSHAFT LOBE LIFT SPECIFICATIONS

Engine	Intake	Exhaust
SOHC	.2531–.2556	.2531–.2556
DOHC	.3528–.3559	.3409–.3441

VALVE CLEARANCE SPECIFICATIONS

Engine	Stem-To-Guide Clearance, Inch	
	Intake	Exhaust
SOHC	.0010-.0025	.0015-.0032
DOHC	.0010–.0025	.0015–.0032

VALVE ADJUSTMENT

This engine is equipped with hydraulic lifters and no adjustment is required.

VALVE GUIDES

Valve guides are an integral part of the cylinder head and are pressed in. If valve stem clearance becomes excessive, the valve guides must be reamed to the oversize and the oversize valves installed. Valves are available in .010 inch oversize.

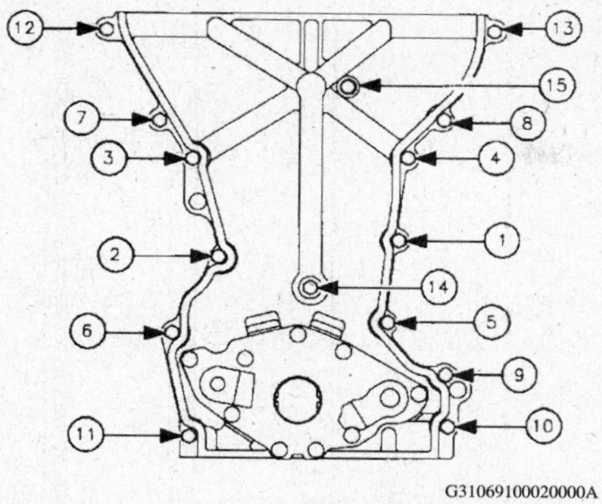

Fig. 23 Front cover tightening sequence. DOHC engine

FRONT COVER

REPLACE

1. Unclip lower splash shield and place a 1 x 1 x 2 inch long block of wood between torque strut and cradle.
2. Remove three right hand upper engine torque axis mount to front cover attaching nuts, allowing engine to rest on block of wood.
3. Remove accessory drive belt, idler pulley, tensioner, crankshaft damper and power steering pump.
4. Remove front cover attaching bolts.
5. Using a screwdriver, pry front cover at upper and lower corners to remove.
6. Reverse procedure to install. Tighten attaching bolts to specifications in sequence, **Figs. 20 and 23.**

TIMING CHAIN

REPLACE

SOHC ENGINE

Refer to "Cylinder Head, Replace" for timing chain replacement procedure. If necessary, timing chain may be inspected as follows:

1. Inspect chain for wear and damaged links.
2. Using ruler, measure chain inner diameter. Standard I.D. is 16.50–16.61 inches and service limit is 16.77 inches, **Fig. 24.**
3. Inspect chain guides for wear and cracks, measure chain track wear. Standard is .0 inch, service limit is .0984 inch, **Fig. 25.**
4. Inspect timing sprocket teeth on crankshaft, camshaft and key for wear. Inspect camshaft thrust plate and sprocket thrust surface for cracks and wear.
5. Inspect tensioner operation, release plunger lock, ensure piston moves freely.
6. Ensure oil feed hole is open, submerge tensioner in oil or solvent, depress plunger and check flow from tensioner body, check cylinder block port for blockage.
7. With timing chain and guides installed,

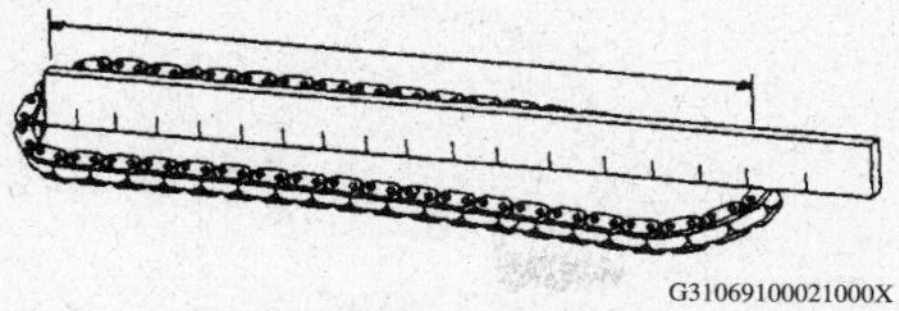

Fig. 24 Timing chain length inspection

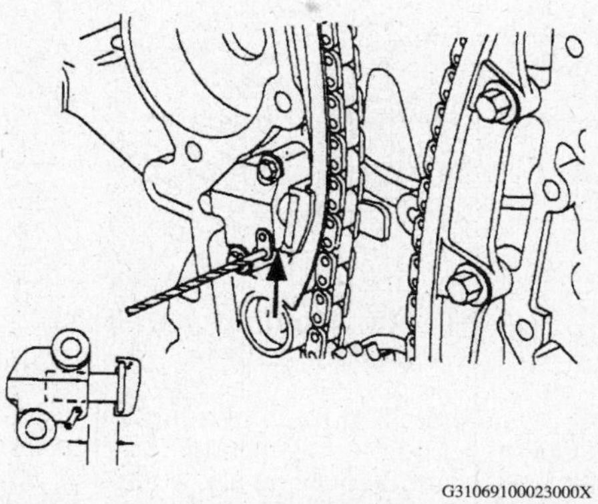

Fig. 26 Timing chain tensioner inspection

measure plunger travel, **Fig. 26.** Standard is .0696–.4380 inch, service limit is .8626 inch.

DOHC ENGINE

Refer to "Cylinder Head, Replace" for timing chain replacement procedure. If necessary, timing chain may be inspected as follows:

1. Inspect chain for wear and damaged links.
2. Using a ruler, measure chain inner diameter, standard I.D. is 22.83–22.95 inches and service limit is 23.15 inches, **Fig. 24.**
3. Inspect chain guides for wear and cracks, measure chain track wear, standard is .0 inch, service limit is .0984 inch, **Fig. 25.**
4. Inspect timing sprocket teeth on crankshaft, camshaft and key for wear. Inspect camshaft thrust plate and sprocket thrust surface for cracks and wear.
5. Inspect tensioner operation, release plunger lock, ensure piston moves freely.
6. Ensure oil feed hole is open, submerge tensioner in oil or solvent, depress plunger and check flow from tensioner body, check cylinder block port for blockage.
7. With timing chain and guides installed, measure plunger travel, **Fig. 26.** Standard is .045–.388 inch, service limit is .8626 inch.

CAMSHAFT

REPLACE

SOHC ENGINE

1. Remove battery cover and battery.
2. Remove camshaft and valve covers, then timing chain, gears and guides as

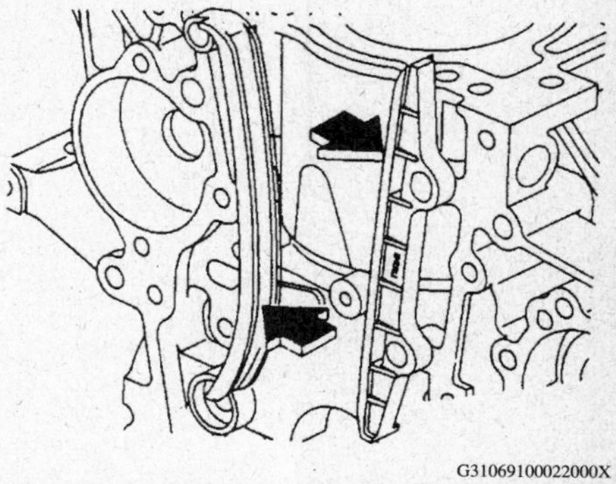

Fig. 25 Timing chain guide track wear

outlined under "Cylinder Head, Replace" in this section.
3. Remove rocker arms and lifter assemblies.
4. Using a suitable driver, push camshaft plug inward, then remove with magnet.
5. Remove camshaft through rear of cylinder head, **Fig. 27.**
6. Reverse procedure to install, noting the following:
   a. Apply Loctite 242, or equivalent, sealant to new cylinder head plug.
   b. Install plug using a suitable bushing driver.

DOHC ENGINE

1. Remove spark plug wires, accessory drive belt, EGR valve solenoid attaching screw, PCV fresh air hose and cam cover assembly.
2. Position No. 1 cylinder to TDC, **Fig. 28,** by aligning damper mark with front cover arrow mark.
3. Prevent camshaft from rotating using a ⅞ inch open end wrench, then remove camshaft timing sprocket attaching bolts and washer.
4. Install front support fixture, aligning two holes in each camshaft sprocket, sprocket adapter and front support fixture.
5. Install but do not tighten fixture mounting nuts, **Fig. 29.**
6. Install suitable camshaft sprocket adapter to each camshaft, but do not tighten pilot bolts, **Fig. 30.**
7. Remove upper timing chain guide and front camshaft bearing caps.
8. While holding camshaft, **torque** sprocket pilot bolts to 18 ft. lbs. using a ⅞ inch wrench.
9. Move camshaft sprocket off end of each camshaft onto sprocket adapter, **Fig. 31.**
10. Install four ⅜ inch nuts and bolts with blocks through camshaft sprocket, sprocket adapter and front support fixture, install steel blocks against rearward side of camshaft sprocket. **Torque** nuts and bolts to 18 ft. lbs.
11. Install two 6 mm front support fixture hex bolts to front cover, **torque** bolts to 7 ft. lbs.
12. While holding camshaft with a ⅞ inch wrench, remove camshaft sprocket pilot bolt.
13. Move cam rearward enough to ensure

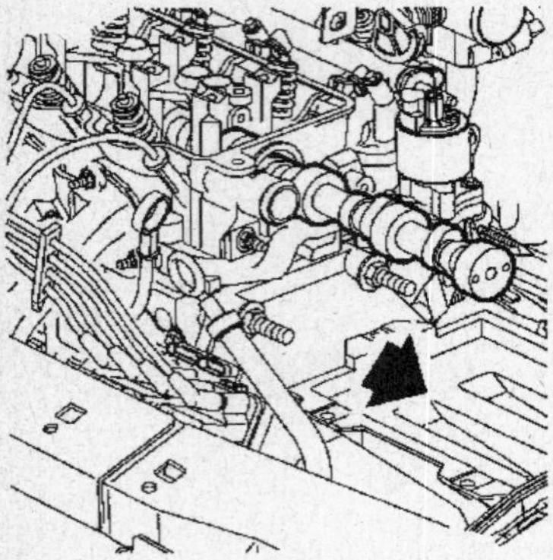

G31069800035000X

Fig. 27 Camshaft removal. SOHC engine

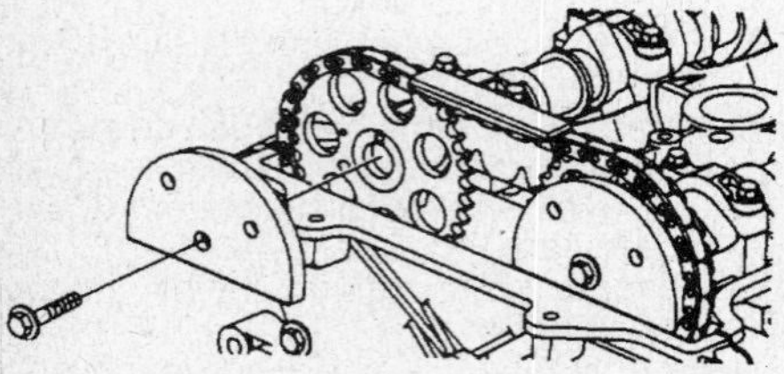

G31069100026000X

Fig. 30 Camshaft support fixture installation. DOHC engine

camshaft end is no longer inside sprocket pilot.

14. Loosen and remove camshaft bearing cap attaching bolts in several passes. **If lifters are removed, keep in order for installation and store with camshaft contact facing downward.**
15. Reverse procedure to install. Tighten camshaft bearing cap and cover bolts to specifications.

PISTON & ROD ASSEMBLY

Assemble the piston and connecting rod by aligning the mark on top of the piston with the front of the engine. Assemble connecting rod to the piston with the bearing tang slots directed toward the exhaust manifold, **Fig. 32.**

PISTONS, PINS & RINGS

Pistons are available in .005 inch (.125 mm) and .0157 inch (.400 mm) oversizes.

To check piston fit in bore, using a micrometer, measure piston diameter at right angle to piston pin hole center line, .20 inch (5 mm) from bottom of piston. Piston diameter plus piston clearance minus .002 inch allowance for finish honing will give piston size to be bored to.

MAIN & ROD BEARINGS

Main and thrust bearings are available in .0005 and .001 inch undersizes, to adjust for correct main journal clearance.

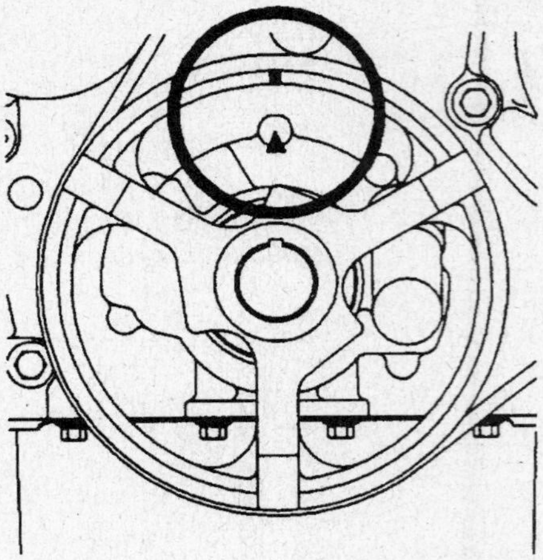

G31069100024000X

Fig. 28 No. 1 cylinder at TDC. DOHC engine

When installing main bearing caps, ensure arrow points towards the front of the engine. Using sequence shown in **Fig. 33, torque** cap bolts to 37 ft. lbs. in several steps.

CRANKSHAFT REAR OIL SEAL

REPLACE

1. Remove transaxle, then the flywheel and cover.
2. If only oil seal requires replacement, proceed as follows:
   a. Insert a suitable screwdriver into pry tangs of seal carrier and remove seal.
   b. Apply engine oil to seal lip and inside diameter of seal carrier.
   c. Install seal using seal installer tool No. SA9121E equivalent.
3. If seal and carrier require replacement, proceed as follows:
   a. Remove oil pan as outlined under "Oil Pan, Replace."
   b. Remove seal carrier.
   c. Remove seal from carrier using a suitable screwdriver and hammer.
   d. Apply engine oil to seal lip and inside of carrier.
   e. Apply an .080 inch diameter bead of RTV, or equivalent to seal carrier.
   f. Install seal carrier and tighten to specification.
   g. Install seal using seal installer tool No. SA9121E, or equivalent.
4. Install transaxle, then flywheel. Tighten to specifications.

OIL PAN

REPLACE

1. Drain engine oil, then remove front exhaust pipe.
2. Remove right side tire, splash shield and vibration damper.
3. Loosen, but do not remove, four front engine mount attaching bolts about ½ inch.
4. Remove oil pan attaching bolts.

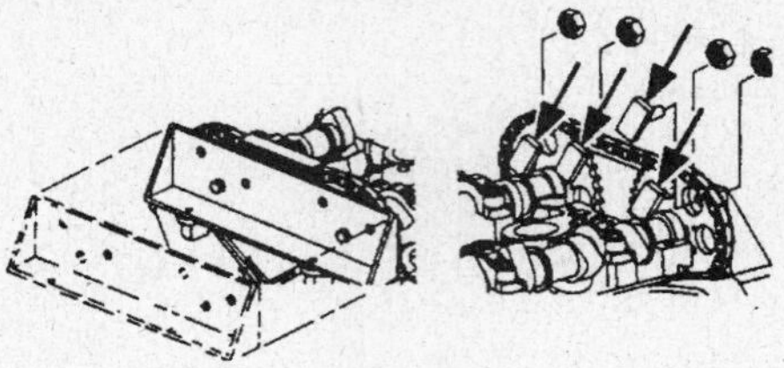

G31069100025000X

Fig. 29 Camshaft front support fixture. DOHC engine

G31069100027000X

Fig. 31 Camshaft removal. DOHC engine

5. Pry front engine mount away from cylinder block to allow oil pan removal.
6. Using RTV removal tool No. SAE9123E, or equivalent, drive sharp edge between pan and block.
7. Drive tool around pan to shear seal, then using a suitable rubber mallet, tap pan sideways to remove.
8. Reverse procedure to install. Apply a .160 inch bead of RTV sealant to inside edge of oil pan groove.

OIL PUMP

REPLACE

1. Raise and support vehicle.
2. Drain engine oil.
3. Remove right hand front wheel assembly and splash shield.
4. Place a 1 x 1 x 2 inch block of wood between torque strut and cradle.
5. Remove drive belt.
6. Remove crankshaft pulley bolt.
7. Using a universal three jaw puller, **Fig. 12,** while holding damper, remove front crankshaft damper assembly. **Do not pry against cover.**
8. Remove idler pulley.
9. Remove power steering pump and position aside.
10. Remove belt tensioner.
11. **On models equipped with SOHC engine,** remove rocker cover.
12. **On models equipped with DOHC engine,** remove cam cover.
13. **On all models,** remove three right hand upper engine torque axis mount to front cover attaching nuts, allowing engine to rest on block of wood.
14. Hold front crankshaft timing sprocket using crankshaft timing gear tool No. SA9104E, or equivalent, with flat side toward crankshaft sprocket.

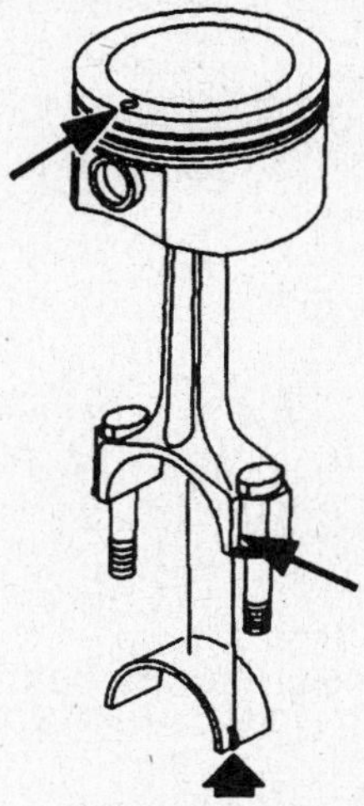

G31069100028000X

Fig. 32 Piston & rod assembly

15. Remove four front oil pan attaching bolts and front cover attaching bolts.
16. Using RTV cutter tool No. SA9123E, or equivalent, cut RTV seal from front cover.
17. Using front cover pry tangs, remove cover, then remove and discard two oil gallery transfer seals.
18. Reverse procedure to install.

OIL PUMP SERVICE

DISASSEMBLE

1. Remove cover plate attaching bolts, then drive and driven rotors.
2. Remove and discard relief valve using tool No. SA9103E, or equivalent.

INSPECTION

1. Inspect body clearance as follows:
   a. Using a feeler gauge, measure clearance between driven rotor and pump body, **Fig. 34.** Standard clearance is .006–.011 inch; maximum clearance is .011 inch.
   b. If clearance is greater than maximum, replace oil pump rotor set.
2. Inspect tip clearance using a feeler gauge between both rotor tips, **Fig. 35.** Maximum clearance is .006 inch.
3. Inspect end to end clearance as follows:
   a. Using a feeler gauge, measure clearance between side of gear rotor assembly and cover plate, **Fig. 36.** Standard clearance is .0016–.0049 inch and maximum clearance is .0050 inch.

ASSEMBLE

1. Using a screwdriver or punch, remove front cover oil seal.
2. Install new oil seal using seal installer tool No. SA9140E, or equivalent, and a suitable press.
3. If relief valve was removed, a new on must be installed. Coat relief valve with engine oil, then using driver tool No. SA9103E, or equivalent and a suitable hammer, install relief valve.

Intake Side

8 4 1 5 9

7 3 2 6 10

Exhaust Side

G31069700076000X

Fig. 33 Main bearing cap bolt tightening sequence

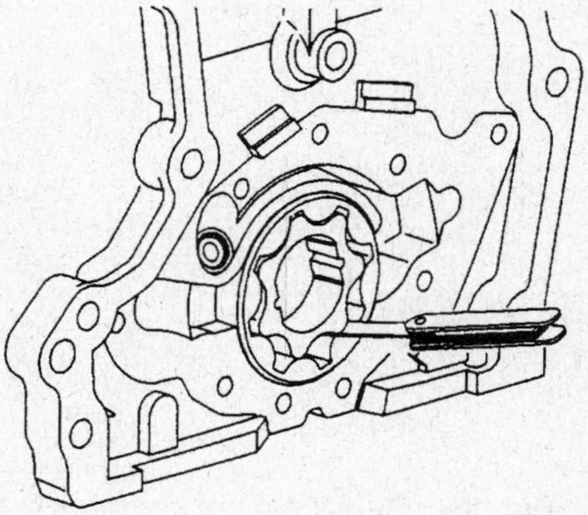

G31099100002000X

Fig. 35 Oil pump tip clearance measurement

4. Pack oil pump assembly with petroleum jelly.
5. Install drive and driven rotors to pump body with chamfer toward front oil seal.
6. Install pump body cover and new bolts. Tighten to specification.

BELT TENSION DATA

Belt	Tension, Lbs.	
	New	Used
Accessory	50–65	45

SERPENTINE DRIVE BELT

BELT ROUTING

Refer to **Figs. 37 and 38** for serpentine belt routing.

TENSIONER, REPLACEMENT

Tensioner internal components are nor serviceable, do not disassemble tensioner.

1. Unclip lower splash shield and place a 1 x 1 x 2 inch long block of wood between torque strut and cradle.
2. Remove three right hand upper engine torque axis mount to front cover attaching nuts, allowing engine to rest on block of wood.
3. Remove belt as outlined under "Belt, Replace" in this section

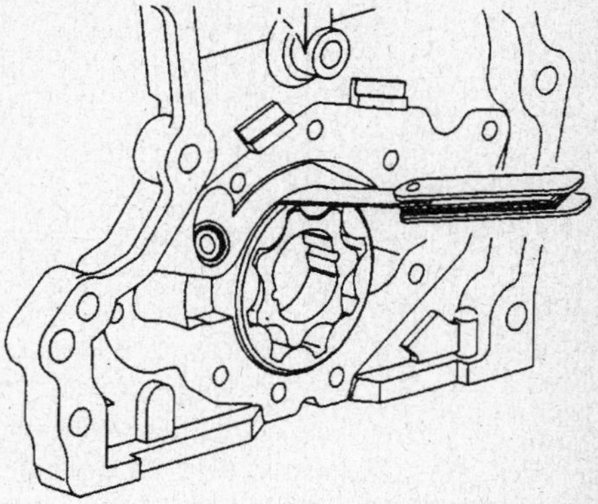

G31099100001000X

Fig. 34 Oil pump body clearance measurement

4. Remove power steering pump with bracket.
5. Remove tensioner upper and lower attaching bolts, **Fig. 39.**
6. Install a pry bar between steel engine mount and steel frame rail, then move engine slightly toward drivers fender, as required, then remove tensioner.
7. Reverse procedure to install.

BELT REPLACEMENT

Removal

1. Using suitable wrench, depress tensioner arm, **Fig. 40.**
2. Remove belt from idler pulley, then accessory pulleys.

Installation

1. Route belt over all pulleys, except front cover idler or A/C compressor.
2. Using suitable wrench, depress tensioner arm, **Fig. 40.**
3. Install belt to idler pulley and A/C compressor.

COOLING SYSTEM BLEED

These engines do not require a special bleed procedure. After filling cooling system, run engine and allow to reach normal operating temperature with pressure cap off. Air will then automatically bleed through cap opening.

THERMOSTAT

REPLACE

REMOVAL

Do not remove pressure cap while engine is running or when engine is still warm.

1. Remove engine drain plug at right front of engine, to drain coolant from radiator, then open draincock at lower part of radiator. Ensure coolant level is below thermostat housing.
2. Disconnect lower radiator hose at thermostat housing using Snap On hose removal tool No. HCP10, or equivalent, then remove two water inlet housing retaining bolts.

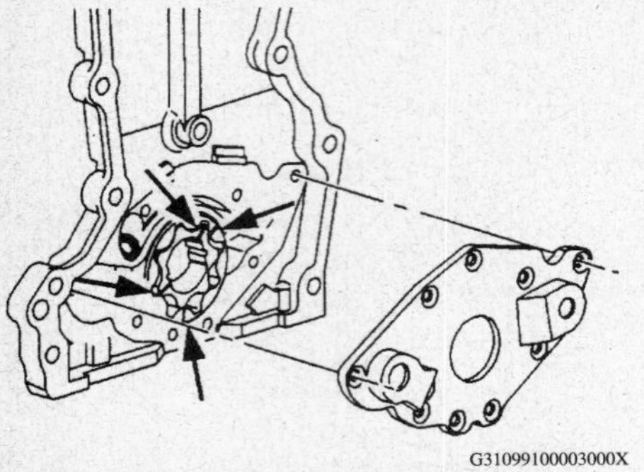

Fig. 36 Oil pump end to end clearance measurement

3. Remove water inlet and thermostat as an assembly, then and discard O-ring.
4. Remove thermostat element with service tool provided with replacement part. The new part will not function correctly if oil comes in contact with part. If oil is found in coolant, flush entire system before replacing thermostat.
5. Ensure no damage or seat deterioration is found within water inlet housing. Use care not to damage machined aluminum surfaces.

INSTALLATION

1. Install new thermostat with service tool provided, ensure tangs are properly seated in legs and piston is correctly positioned in water inlet housing.
2. Install new O-ring on water inlet housing, then water inlet housing, thermostat into cylinder block.
3. Install retaining bolts and tighten to specifications.
4. Close radiator and engine drain plugs and tighten to specification.
5. Install lower radiator hose. Ensure vehicle is on level surface.
6. Fill coolant system using only recommended mixture of 50/50 mixture of water and non phosphate ethylene glycol-base coolant.
7. Start engine and run for several minutes, then fill cooling system surge tank to full cold line.
8. Install pressure cap and check for leaks.

WATER PUMP

REPLACE

1. Drain coolant.
2. Remove accessory drive belt.
3. Raise and support vehicle.
4. Remove right wheel assembly, then inner wheelwell splash shield.
5. Remove A/C compressor attaching bolts, then position aside.
6. Place one inch wood block between crankshaft and water pump pulley, then remove water pump bolts and allow pulley to hang on pump hub.
7. Remove water pump attaching bolts, then water pump and discard gasket.
8. Reverse procedure to install. Tighten water pump bolts to specifications in crossing pattern.

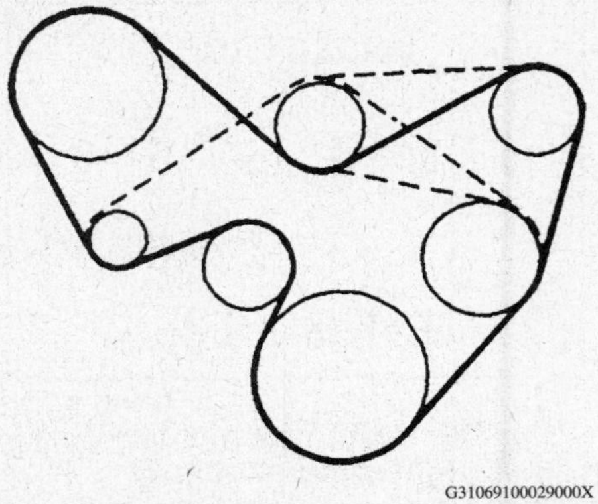

Fig. 37 Serpentine belt routing. SOHC engine

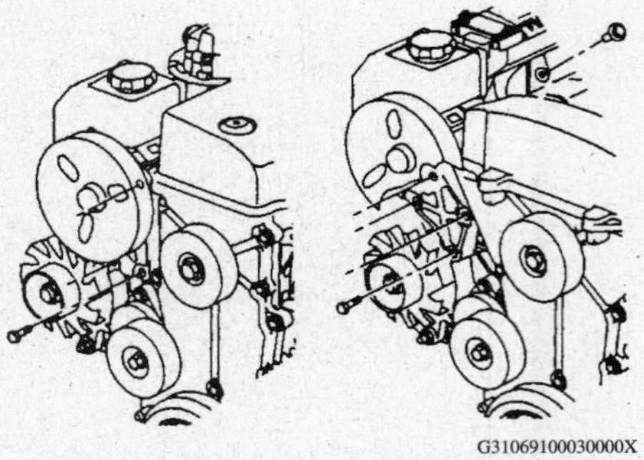

Fig. 39 Belt tensioner removal

RADIATOR

REPLACE

1. Drain cooling system.
2. Remove air intake duct.
3. Remove upper radiator clamp and hose.
4. **On models equipped with automatic transaxle,** remove upper transaxle oil cooler line.
5. **On all models,** remove electric cooling fan assembly.
6. Disconnect lower radiator hose.
7. Raise and support vehicle.
8. Remove lower splash shield.
9. **On models equipped with automatic transaxle,** remove lower transaxle oil cooler line.
10. **On all models,** remove two lower condenser bracket to radiator bolts. Then support condenser to vehicle with wire.
11. Lower vehicle, then remove upper radiator attaching nuts and brackets.
12. **On models equipped with A/C,** remove upper radiator seal.
13. **On all models,** remove radiator from vehicle.
14. Reverse procedure to install.

FUEL PUMP

REPLACE

1997

1. Remove fuel tank as follows:
   a. Remove fuel filler cap.

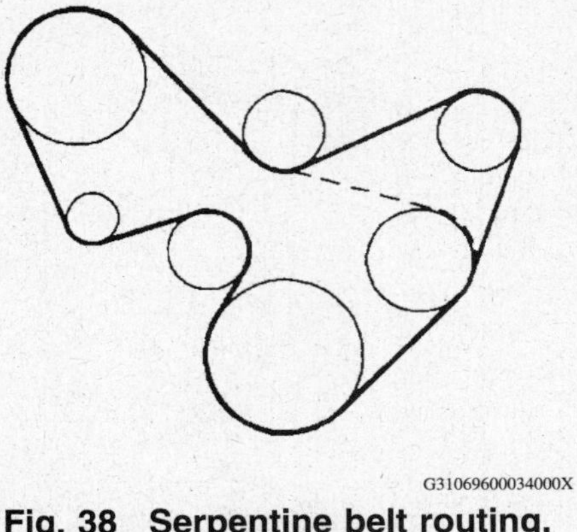

Fig. 38 Serpentine belt routing. DOHC engine

   b. Relieve fuel system pressure as described under " Precautions."
   c. Raise and support rear of vehicle 28 inches higher than front.
   d. Place container below fuel tank fill neck hose, then loosen connecting tube and vent hose clamps.
   e. Wrap a cloth around filler neck connecting tube, then remove tube from tank.
   f. Using a socket extension, push filler neck check ball into fuel tank.
   g. Install siphon hose in fuel tank through fuel filler, then siphon fuel from tank into a container.
   h. Remove fill neck bracket, then disconnect fuel supply and return lines.
   i. Remove fuel tank support straps, then disconnect electrical connector.
   j. Remove fuel tank assembly.
2. Using fuel tank lock ring removal tool No. SA9156E, or equivalent, remove fuel pump module cam lock ring.
3. Lift assembly at 45° angle to remove.
4. Remove and discard large fuel pump module to tank O-ring.
5. Reverse procedure to install. Install a new O-ring between fuel pump module and fuel tank.

1998–2000

When removing fuel system lines and hoses, wrap a suitable shop towel around fitting and have an approved container available to catch any fuel that may spill.

1. Relieve fuel pressure as outlined under "Fuel System Pressure Relief."
2. If fuel pump is operational, drain fuel tank as follows:
   a. Remove air cleaner inlet hose from throttle body.
   b. Disconnect fuel feed line at fuel rail and install fuel adapter fitting tool No. SA309738, or equivalent into fuel line.
   c. Connect one end of a suitable fuel line to adapter and other end to certified fuel handling cart.
   d. Connect a suitable scan tool to data link connector and turn ignition switch ON.
   e. Turn fuel pump on using scan tool

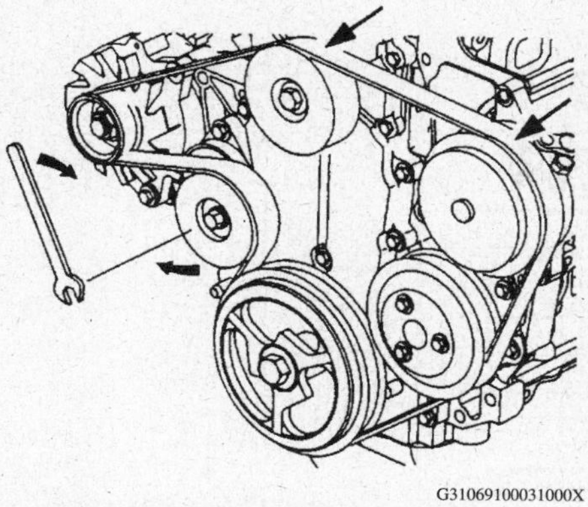

Fig. 40 Belt tensioner arm

and pump fuel into a suitable container.

3. If fuel pump is inoperative, proceed as follows:
   a. Insert siphon hose tool No. SA9804E, or equivalent into fuel filler pipe. **Use of any other type of siphon hose may cause damage to fuel filler check valve.**
   b. Begin fuel siphoning as shown in **Fig. 41.**
4. Remove fuel filler cap and rubber closeout grommet.
5. Remove filler pipe attaching screw.
6. Raise and support vehicle.
7. Remove wheelwell inner cover.
8. Disconnect wiring harness from EVAP vent solenoid.
9. Remove filler pipe lower attaching screw.
10. Disconnect EVAP canister vent pipe at ⅝ inch quick connect to canister hose.
11. Remove fuel filler pipe from fuel tank. Ensure fuel fill check valve is not dislodged from filler pipe.
12. Disconnect fuel feed line from fuel pressure regulator.
13. Disconnect fuel vapor line from quick connect fitting.
14. Remove filter bracket from under brake lines.
15. Place a suitable lifting device under fuel tank and remove two tank strap retaining bolts. Lower tank enough to access fuel pump and tank pressure sensor electrical connectors.
16. Lower fuel tank from vehicle.
17. Disconnect fuel feed and return lines from pressure regulator.
18. Disconnect fuel pump vapor line from fuel tank vent pipe.
19. Using lock ring removal tool No. SA9156E, or equivalent, remove fuel pump retaining ring.
20. Lift pump slightly to disengage tabs, then rotate 90° clockwise until lines are facing 1 o'clock position.
21. Lift pump until bottom is close to tank opening. Tilt pump at a 45° angle toward right side of tank, then lift out.
22. Reverse procedure to install noting the following:
    a. Install new fuel pump "Green" seal. Do not use "Black" seal.
    b. White locator button located on left side of fuel tank should be flush with left side rail when installation is complete.
    c. Replace all plastic fuel line retainers on all lines which were disconnected.
    d. Perform "Service Bay Diagnostic Test" for evaporative emission system using a suitable scan tool.

FUEL FILTER

REPLACE

1997

1. Disconnect fresh air inlet hose from rocker cam cover, then remove air inlet tube.
2. Relieve fuel system pressure as described under " Precautions."
3. Raise and support vehicle, then disconnect quick connect at fuel filter inlet by pinching two plastic tangs together and pulling on fuel line.
4. Loosen fuel filter band clamp fastener, then remove filter from bracket.
5. Reverse procedure to install.

1998–2000

The fuel filter/regulator assembly is located on the underbody near the front left-hand side of the fuel tank.

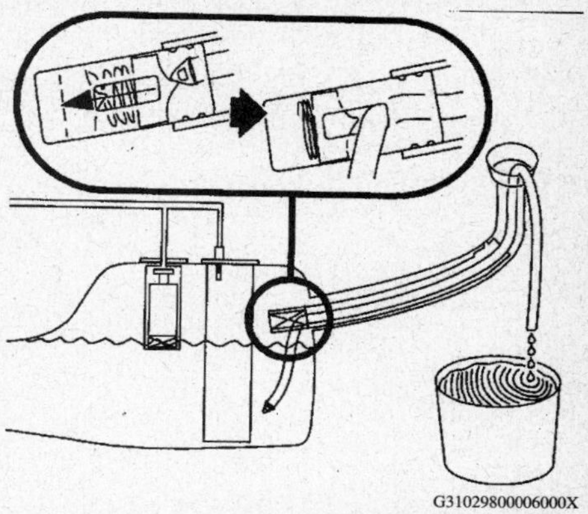

Fig. 41 Fuel tank siphoning. 1998–2000

1. Relieve fuel pressure as outlined under "Precautions. "
2. Raise and support vehicle.
3. Remove fuel filter bracket attaching screws.
4. Unlatch fuel line bundle retaining clip at left side of fuel tank.
5. Disconnect EVAP purge line at 90° quick connect.
6. Slide outlet of filter from support on fuel tank bracket and remove fuel feed line at 90° quick connect.
7. Pivot filter down while moving leg of bracket from under brake lines.
8. Disconnect fuel feed and return lines and remove filter/regulator and bracket assembly.
9. Reverse procedure to install, noting the following:
   a. Install new plastic fuel line retainers to all lines that were removed.
   b. Ensure fuel feed and purge lines are routed on top of emergency brake cable.
   c. Ensure emergency brake cable is secured firmly to underbody to support lines.
   d. Operate fuel pump and inspect system for leaks.
   e. Perform "Service Bay Diagnostic Test" using a suitable scan tool to verify integrity of fuel vapor system.

TIGHTENING SPECIFICATIONS

Year	Component	Torque/Ft. Lbs.
1997– 2000	A/C Compressor Front Bracket To Block	35
	A/C Compressor Front/Rear Bracket To Head	23
	A/C Compressor To Front Bracket	40
	A/C Compressor To Rear Bracket	22
	Accelerator Cable Bracket To Intake Manifold	19
	Air Cleaner Duct Clamp	15①
	Air Cleaner/Resonator Bolts	96①
	Air Cleaner/Resonator Clamps	18①
	Alternator Positive Terminal	84①

Continued

TIGHTENING SPECIFICATIONS—Continued

Year	Component	Torque/Ft. Lbs.
1997-2000	Alternator To Block	24
	Axle Shaft Intermediate Bracket To Block	41
	Battery Cable	13
	Belt Idler Pulley To Front Cover	20
	Belt Tensioner To Block	22
	Block Oil Gallery Plug	22
	Camshaft Bearing Cap To Head (DOHC)	10
	Camshaft Cover To Head (DOHC)	96①
	Camshaft Sprocket To Camshaft	75
	Camshaft Thrust Plate To Head (SOHC)	19
	Canister Band Clamp	31①
	Canister Purge Solenoid To Block	22
	Clutch Pressure Plate To Flywheel	19
	Connecting Rod Cap To Rod	33
	Coolant Drain Plug	22
	Coolant Temperature Sensor	72①
	Cradle To Body	151
	Crankshaft Bearing Cap To Block	⑦
	Crankshaft Damper To Crankshaft	159
	Crankshaft Position Sensor	84①
	Crankshaft Rear Oil Seal Carrier To Block	96①
	Cylinder Head Bolts	③
	De-Aeration Line Fitting To Head	96①
	De-Aeration Line Nut To Head (SOHC)	84①
	EGR Solenoid Bracket (DOHC)	84①
	EGR Solenoid Bracket (SOHC)	19
	EGR Valve	19
	Engine Block Heater To Block	18
	Engine Lift Bracket To Block	22
	Engine Mount To Front Cover	37
	Engine Mount To Midrail Bracket	37
	Engine Support Bracket	23
	ESC Knock Sensor	11
	Exhaust Manifold Studs To Front Pipe	10
	Exhaust Manifold Studs To Head	108①
	Exhaust Manifold To Head (DOHC)	23
	Exhaust Manifold To Head (SOHC)	16
	Exhaust Pipe To Converter	35
	Flexplate To Converter	52
	Flexplate To Crankshaft	44
	Flywheel/Flexplate Cover	84①
	Flywheel To Crankshaft	59
	Front Cover To Block (Center)	84①
	Front Cover To Block (Perimeter)	22
	Front Engine Mount To Block	52
	Fuel Canister Bracket To Frame Rail	22
	Fuel Filter Bracket	72①
	Fuel Line Support Bracket	22
	Fuel Line Support Clip	108①

Continued

TIGHTENING SPECIFICATIONS—Continued

Year	Component	Torque/Ft. Lbs.
1997-2000	Fuel Rail To Intake Manifold	84①
	Fuel Tank Fill Hose	②
	Fuel Tank Fill Pipe Bracket	⑥
	Fuel Tank Straps	35
	Fuel/Vapor Line To Body	27①
	Heater Outlet To Intake Manifold	19
	Heater Return Nipple	37
	Idle Air Control Sensor	28
	Idle Air Control Valve	④
	Ignition Module To Transaxle Case	72①
	Intake Manifold Bracket To Block (LH)	22
	Intake Manifold Bracket To Block (RH) (DOHC)	41
	Intake Manifold Bracket To Manifold (DOHC)	22
	Intake Manifold Bracket To Manifold (SOHC)	21
	Intake Manifold Stud To Fuel Line Clamp (SOHC)	60①
	Intake Manifold Stud To Head	108①
	Intake Manifold Stud To Head (P/S Bracket) (DOHC)	22
	Intake Manifold Stud To Head (P/S Bracket) (SOHC)	16
	Intake Manifold To Head	22
	MAP Sensor	44①
	Motion Restrictor Bracket	40
	Motion Restrictor To Side Of Block	22
	Oil Baffle Plate To Block	41
	Oil Drain Plug	26
	Oil Filter	⑤
	Oil Pan To Block	84①
	Oil Pickup Tube (DOHC)	11
	Oil Pipe Bracket To Baffle Plate	11
	Oil Pipe Bracket To Block (DOHC)	11
	Oil Pipe Bracket To Block (SOHC)	41
	Oil Pressure Sensor	26
	Oil Pump Cover	96①
	Oxygen Sensor	33
	Power Steering Hoses	20
	Power Steering Pump Bracket	28
	Power Steering Pump To Bracket	22
	Power Steering Return Hose Clamp	18①
	Radiator Upper Bracket	96①
	Rear Engine Mount To Block	35
	Rocker Arm Cover To Head (SOHC)	22
	Rocker Arm Shaft To Head	19
	Spark Plug	20
	Starter Motor	27
	Starter Motor Bracket To Axle Shaft	22
	Starter Positive Terminal	96①
	Starter Solenoid Terminal	35①
	Steering Joint To Gear	35
	Stiffening Bracket	40
	Strut To Knuckle	148

Continued

TIGHTENING SPECIFICATIONS—Continued

Year	Component	Torque/Ft. Lbs.
1997-2000	Thermostat Housing To Block	22
	Throttle Body To Air Intake Manifold	23
	Throttle Position Sensor	18①
	Timing Chain Guides	19
	Timing Chain Tensioner	14
	Transaxle Case To Block (Lower)	96
	Transaxle Case To Block (Upper)	66
	Transaxle Lower Mount To Cradle	41
	Transaxle Lower Mount To Transaxle	23
	Transaxle Rear Mount	36
	Vapor Canister To Body	22
	Vehicle Speed Sensor	19①
	Water Pump	22
	Water Pump Pulley	18

DOHC — Dual Over Head Cam
SOHC — Single Over Head Cam
① — Inch lbs.
② — 1997 models, 27 inch lbs.; 1998–2000 models, 35 inch lbs.
③ — Refer to "Cylinder Head, Replace" for bolt tightening procedure.
④ — 1997 models, 18 inch lbs.; 1998–2000 models, 28 inch lbs.
⑤ — Tighten to gasket, then turn an additional ¾–1 turn.
⑥ — 1997 models, 53 inch lbs.; 1998–2000 models, 6 ft. lbs.
⑦ — Refer to "Main & Rod Bearings" for bolt tightening procedure.

2.2L Engine

NOTE: On Air Bag Equipped Models, Refer To " Air Bag System Precautions" Located In The Front Of This Manual For System Disarming & Arming Procedures.

NOTE: Refer To "Computer Relearn Procedures " Located In The Front Of This Manual For Computer Relearn Procedures.

INDEX

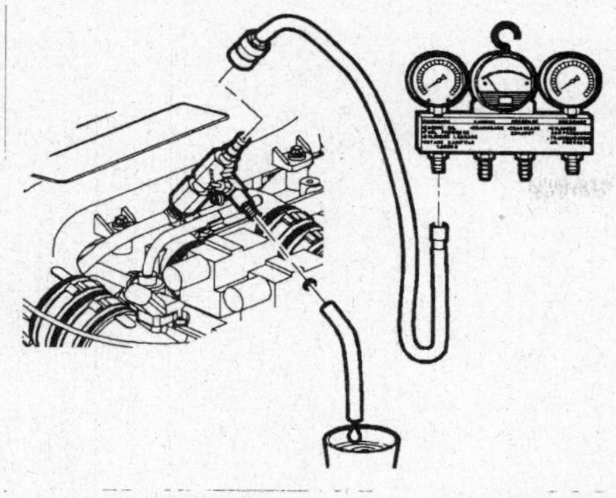

G31029900155000X

Fig. 1 Fuel pressure bleed

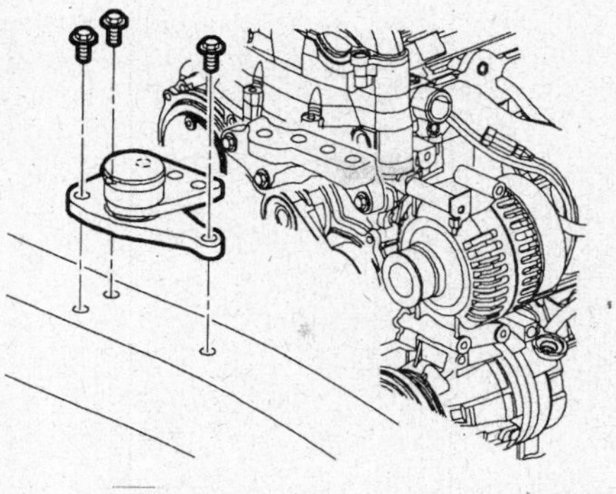

G31069900036000X

Fig. 2 Engine mount removal

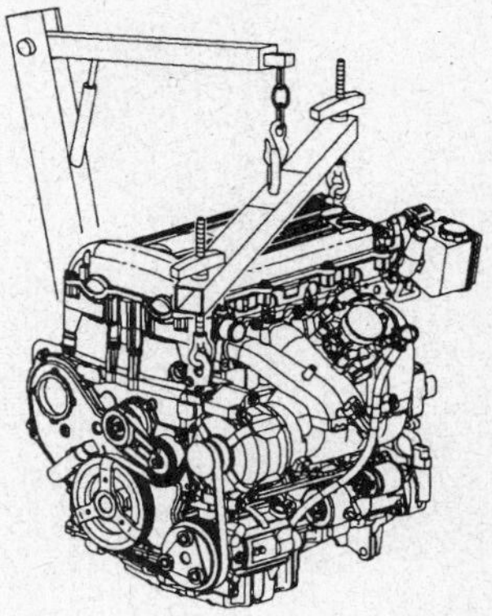

G31069900037000X

Fig. 3 Engine lift hoist attachment

PRECAUTIONS

AIR BAG SYSTEMS

Refer to "Air Bag System Precautions" in the front of this manual for system disarming and arming procedures.

BATTERY GROUND CABLE

Prior to service, disconnect battery ground cable and isolate as required.

FUEL SYSTEM PRESSURE RELIEF

1. Connect gauge bar tool No. 53476, or equivalent, to fuel gauge pressure adapter tool No. 309725, or equivalent, using flexible hose from pressure test kit tool No. SA9127E, or equivalent.
2. Ensure needle valve on pressure kit is closed Off, then connect pressure adapter to fuel line test port, **Fig. 1.**
3. Place end of bleed hose in a suitable approved container and open valve to bleed system pressure.
4. Once pressure is bled, remove gauge from fuel pressure test port and replace cap.

COMPRESSION PRESSURE

1. Start and run engine until it reaches normal operating temperature.
2. Turn engine off, then disconnect wiring from ignition module and remove spark plugs.
3. Install a suitable compression gauge tool in spark plug hole.
4. Ensure battery is charged and throttle is fully open.
5. Crank engine through four compression strokes for each cylinder.
6. Lowest reading cylinder should be within 70% of the highest.
7. No cylinder should read less than 100 psi.
8. Normal compression will build up quickly and evenly to specification in each cylinder.
9. Low compression indicates damaged piston, rings, valves or head gasket.
10. High compression indicates carbon on pistons or combustion chamber.
11. If cylinder compression in one or more cylinders is low, pour one teaspoon of engine oil into cylinder through spark plug hole.
12. Place shop towel over spark plug holes and crank engine for a few seconds without compression gauge or spark plugs installed.
13. Repeat steps 4–6 and measure compression.
14. If adding oil increases compression readings, piston rings leaking.
15. If adding oil does not increase compression, valves or head gasket leaking.
16. Remove compression tester, install spark plugs and tighten to specifications.
17. Connect ignition module wiring and install spark plugs, tighten to specifications.

ENGINE MOUNT

REPLACE

1. Remove air cleaner assembly.
2. Install engine support fixture tool No. SA9150E, or equivalent, to engine.
3. Remove engine mount to bracket fasteners.
4. Remove engine mount to body retaining bolts, **Fig. 2.**
5. Remove engine mount from vehicle.
6. Reverse procedure to install.

ENGINE

REPLACE

AUTOMATIC TRANSAXLE

1. Remove battery, then disconnect main wire feed from fuse block.
2. Disconnect main ground on lefthand fenderwell, then the intake air temperature electrical connector.
3. Remove air cleaner lid, then the inlet duct.
4. Remove air box, then disconnect purge hose from throttle body and position aside.
5. Disconnect the following electrical connectors:
   a. EVAP purge solenoid.
   b. Rear oxygen sensor.
   c. Main wiring harness from master cylinder.
6. Remove cowl cover, then the PCM boot from cowl.
7. Disconnect PCM electrical connector and secure to engine.
8. Remove fuse block lid, then disconnect engine harness main connector from bottom of fuse block.
9. Remove battery tray, then the fuse block tray.
10. Disconnect cruise control and throttle cables.
11. Disconnect brake assist vacuum line from throttle body and position aside.
12. Remove coolant reservoir cap.
13. Relieve fuel pressure as described under "Precautions."
14. Disconnect fuel lines, then the EVAP purge hose at EVAP purge solenoid.
15. Raise and support vehicle.
16. Drain engine coolant into a suitable container.
17. Disconnect heater hoses at lower cowl, then remove starter.
18. Remove torque converter bolts, then the exhaust system from catalytic converter forward.
19. Disconnect tansaxle nose bracket, then remove A/C compressor mounting bolts and secure compressor to frame rail. **It is not required to disconnect A/C lines.**
20. Disconnect lower engine to transaxle bell housing bolts, do not remove upper bolts at this time.
21. Lower vehicle, then remove main hose to coolant reservoir from engine inlet adapter.
22. Remove lower and upper radiator hoses from engine.
23. Drain power steering fluid by removing smaller hose from under reservoir.
24. Disconnect metal power steering line.
25. Attach suitable engine lift hoist to engine lift hooks and support engine weight, **Fig. 3.**

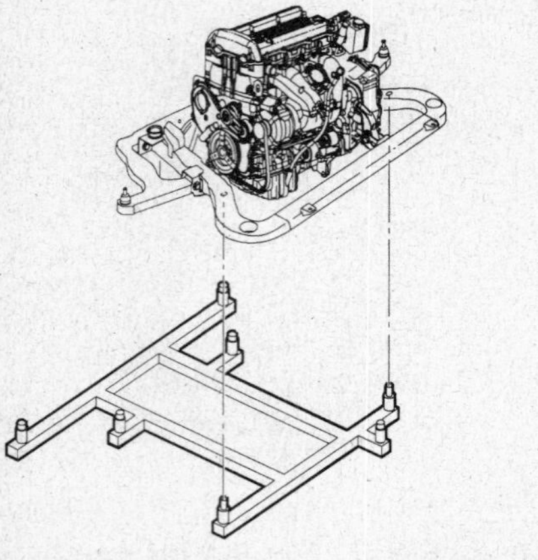

Fig. 4 Frame alignment tool

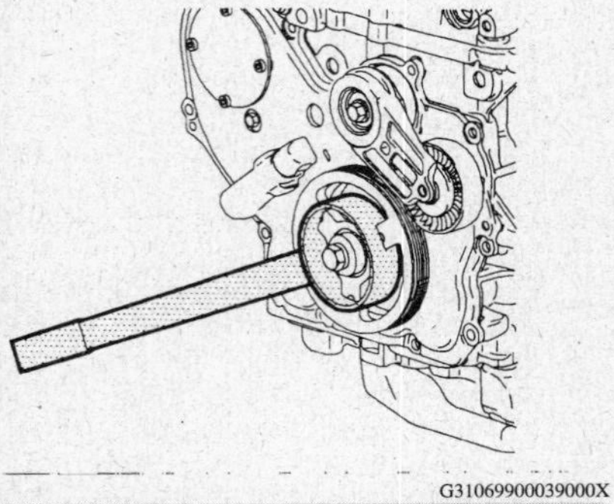

Fig. 7 Crankshaft pulley removal

26. Support weight of transaxle with suitable floor jack or jack stand.
27. Remove right front engine mount from wheel housing, then the engine mount bracket from engine.
28. Remove upper bell housing bolts, then lift engine out of vehicle.
29. Reverse procedure to install, tighten all attaching bolts and nuts to specifications.

MANUAL TRANSAXLE

1. Remove steering gear-to-intermediate shaft pinch bolt, access is from inside vehicle.
2. Remove battery, then disconnect main wire feed from fuse block.
3. Disconnect main ground on lefthand fenderwell, then the intake air temperature electrical connector.
4. Remove air cleaner lid, then the inlet duct.
5. Remove air box, then disconnect purge hose from throttle body and position aside.
6. Disconnect the following engine electrical connectors:
   a. EVAP purge solenoid.
   b. Rear oxygen sensor.
   c. Main harness connector from master cylinder.
   d. Transaxle back-up switch.
7. Remove front of dash cover, then the PCM boot from front of dash.
8. Disconnect PCM electrical connector and secure to engine.
9. Remove fuse block lid, then disconnect engine harness main connector from bottom of fuse block.
10. Remove battery tray, then the fuse block tray.
11. Disconnect cruise control and throttle cables.
12. Disconnect brake assist vacuum line from throttle body and lay aside.
13. Loosen pinch bolt securing control assembly rod to control shaft lever assembly. **Control shaft lever retaining pin has a spring loaded locking feature securing pin in place. If this spring is not depressed before attempting to remove pin, damage to pin will result.**
14. Remove pin retaining control shaft lever to shift control shaft of transaxle.
15. Remove retaining clips securing control shaft lever assembly to transaxle and frame assembly brackets.
16. Remove control shaft lever assembly by pulling straight up from pivot pins.
17. Drain coolant into a suitable container.
18. Remove heater hoses from front-of-dash, then the upper and lower radiator hoses from radiator.
19. Relieve fuel pressure as described under "Precautions."
20. Disconnect fuel lines, then secure radiator to upper radiator support.
21. Raise and support vehicle, then remove right front wheel and tire assembly.
22. Remove right front splash shield, then the left front wheel liner push pin from frame.
23. Install wood blocks between transaxle case and frame, then between crank pulley and frame.
24. Lower vehicle.
25. Disconnect right engine, then left transaxle mounts by removing mount assembly-to-engine/transaxle bolts. Mount brackets will remain on engine and transaxle.
26. Disconnect rear oxygen sensor harness from frame at two attachment points.
27. Remove exhaust manifold pipe from catalytic converter forward.
28. Remove A/C line to frame attachment clip at front of frame. **It is not required to disconnect A/C lines.**

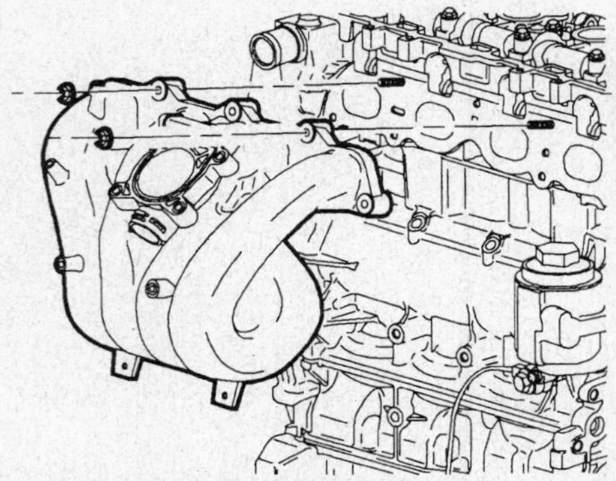

Fig. 5 Intake manifold replacement

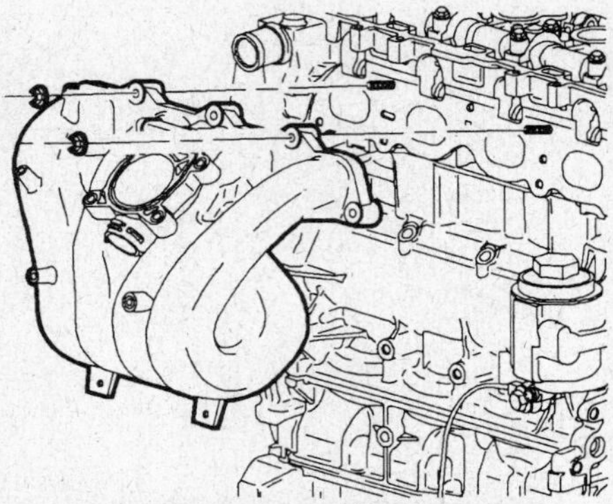

Fig. 6 Exhaust manifold replacement

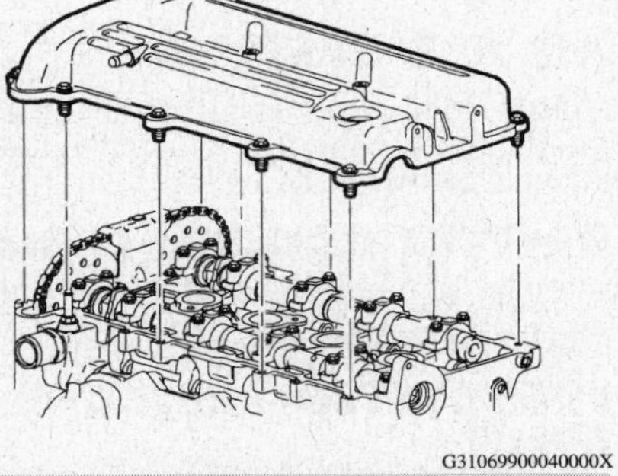

Fig. 8 Camshaft cover assembly removal

29. Remove A/C compressor from engine and secure to cooling module.
30. Remove tie rod-to-steering knuckle bolts, then separate tie rod from steering knuckle assembly using tool No SA91100C or equivalent. Discard tie rod bolts.
31. Remove stabilizer bar links from strut assembly. **Do not attempt to separate ball studs with a wedge type separator tool because seal may be damaged.**
32. Remove lower ball stud bolt, then separate ball from steering knuckle assembly using a suitable tool
33. Remove suspension support assemblies, then suspension support cage nuts from body. Discard cage nuts.
34. Support powertrain and frame with powertrain lifting table and service tool J-43628 or equivalent **Fig. 4.**
35. Remove remaining frame-to-body attaching bolts.
36. Carefully lower powertrain and frame assembly from vehicle.
37. Remove remaining cage nuts and discard.
38. Attach engine lift hoist to engine lift hooks **Fig. 3.**
39. Place a (1¾ inch x 2 inch x 4 inch) and a 1¼ inch x 2 inch x 4 inch) long block of wood under transaxle housing support. **Manual transaxles require engine to be moved approximately 4**

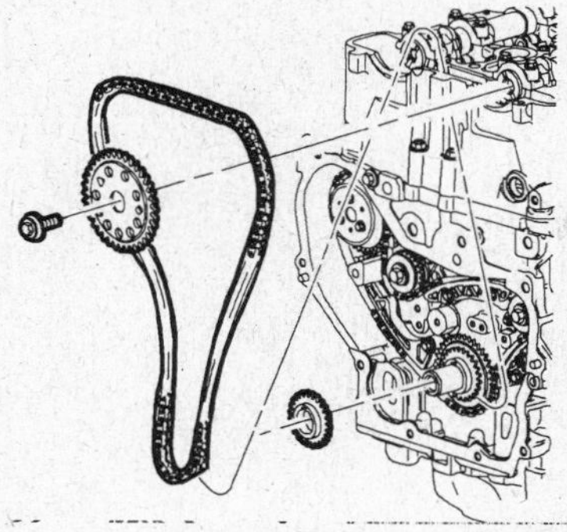

G31069900041000X

Fig. 9 Intake cam sprocket timing chain removal

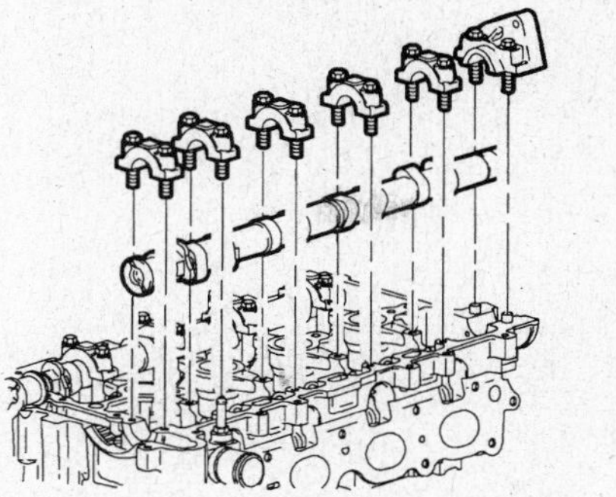

G31069900042000X

Fig. 10 Intake camshaft & bearing caps removal

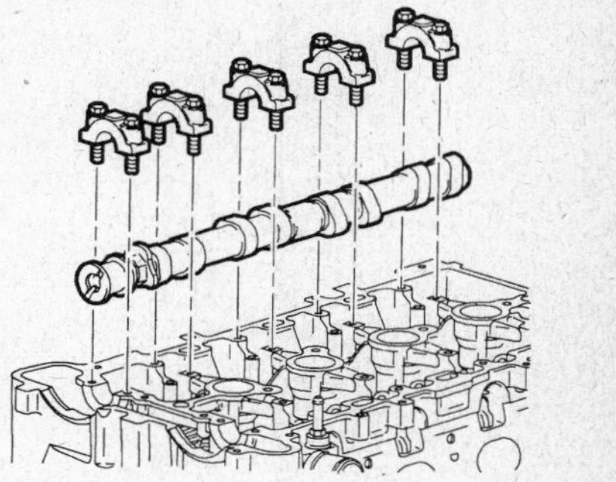

G31069900043000X

Fig. 11 Exhaust camshaft & bearing caps removal

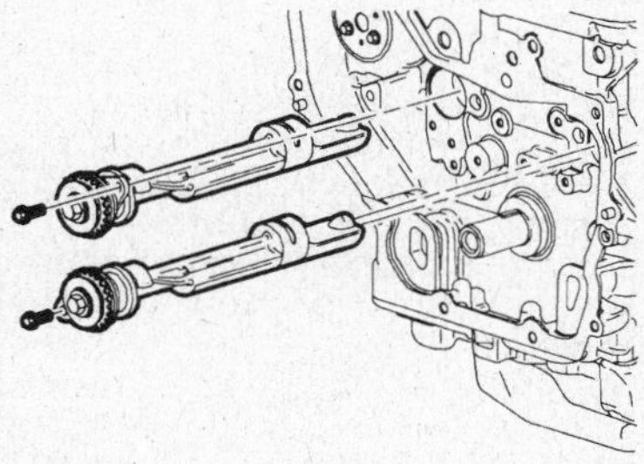

G31069900044000X

Fig. 12 Balance shaft removal

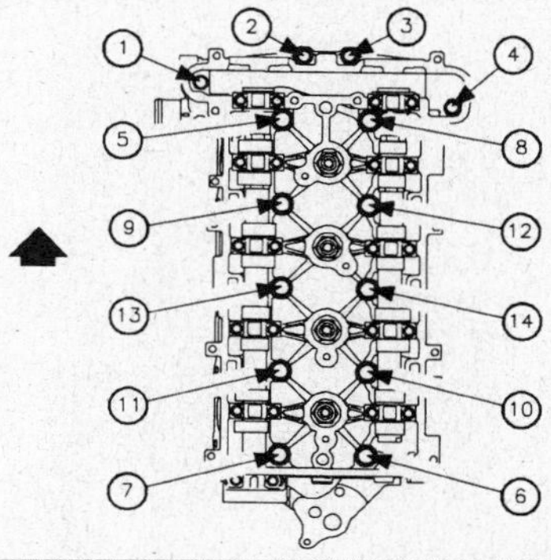

G31069900045000X

Fig. 13 Cylinder head bolt loosening sequence

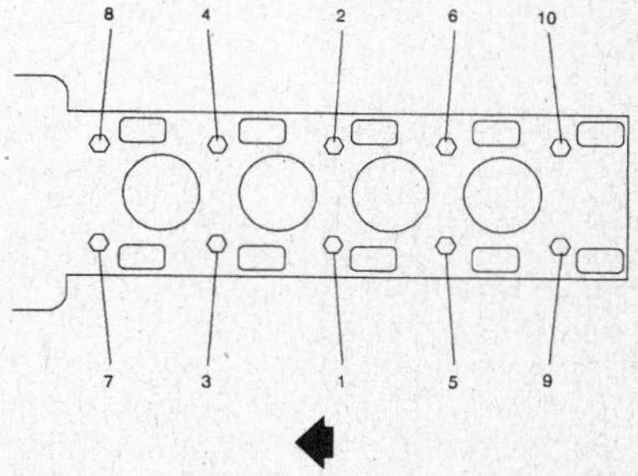

G31069900046000X

Fig. 14 Cylinder head bolt tightening sequence

inches forward in cradle for input shaft disengagement.

40. Remove transaxle bell housing attachment bolts.
41. Carefully lift engine from cradle and mount it on an engine stand or transportation pallet.
42. Reverse procedure to install, tighten all attaching bolts and nuts to specifications.

INTAKE MANIFOLD

REPLACE

Never attempt to remove the intake manifold from a hot engine, allow engine to cool to ambient temperature. Intake manifold is made of a composite plastic and can be damaged if removed when engine is hot.

1. Remove air inlet tube, then air cleaner assembly.
2. Relieve fuel system pressure as described under " Precautions."
3. Disconnect fuel lines using tool Nos. J-37088–1A and J-37088–2A.
4. Disconnect throttle position sensor, IAC and MAP sensor electrical connectors.
5. Disconnect throttle and cruise control cables.
6. Disconnect fuel pressure regulator hose from throttle body and fuel rail.
7. Remove throttle body retaining bolts, then the throttle body.
8. Remove fuel rail assembly.
9. Remove intake manifold retaining bolts and nuts, then the intake manifold **Fig. 5.**
10. Remove intake manifold gasket.
11. If intake manifold needs to be replaced, transfer throttle body and gasket.
12. Reverse procedure to install, tighten nuts and bolts to specifications.

EXHAUST MANIFOLD

REPLACE

1. Remove oxygen sensor from exhaust manifold.
2. Remove exhaust manifold heat shield.
3. Remove exhaust manifold to cylinder head retaining nuts, then exhaust manifold **Fig. 6.**
4. Reverse procedure to install noting the following:
   a. Install new exhaust manifold studs, **torque** exhaust manifold studs to 9 ft. lbs.
   b. **Torque** exhaust manifold to cylinder head nuts to 13 ft. lbs., exhaust manifold heat shield bolts to 18 ft. lbs.
   c. Coat oxygen sensor threads with anti seize compound, Saturn P/N 21485279 or equivalent. **Torque** oxygen sensor to 22 ft. lbs.

CYLINDER HEAD

REPLACE

REMOVAL

1. Remove exhaust manifold as outlined under "Exhaust Manifold Replace."
2. Remove intake manifold as outlined under "Intake Manifold Replace."
3. Install crankshaft pulley holder tool No. J38122, or equivalent, onto crankshaft pulley **Fig. 7.**
4. Remove crankshaft pulley retaining bolt, then the pulley.
5. Remove camshaft cover grounding strap, then the ignition module and coil assembly.
6. Remove camshaft cover assembly, **Fig. 8.**
7. Remove accessory drive belt tensioner as outlined under "Belt Tensioner Replace."
8. Remove engine front cover retaining bolts, then the front cover.
9. Remove upper timing chain guide. **Timing chain tensioner must be removed to unload chain tension before timing chain is removed. If not, timing chain will become cocked and it will be difficult to remove.**
10. Remove timing chain tensioner plunger. **Do not allow any tension on timing chain when loosening camshaft sprocket bolt.**
11. Remove exhaust cam sprocket, use a

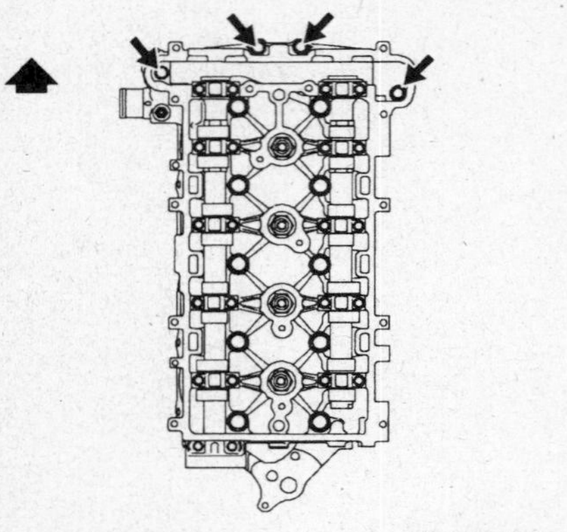

G31069900047000X

Fig. 15 Front cylinder head bolt locations

7/8 open end wrench to hold camshaft in place while loosening camshaft sprocket bolt. Discard bolt.

12. Remove adjustable timing chain guide, then the access plug for fixed timing chain guide bolt.
13. Remove fixed timing guide.
14. Remove intake cam sprocket timing chain through top of cylinder head **Fig. 9.**
15. Remove crankshaft sprocket, then the oiling nozzle.
16. **Remove each bolt on each cap one turn at a time until there is no spring tension on camshaft. Mark bearing caps for installation reference. Keep all of roller finger followers and hydraulic element adjusters in order so they can be reinstalled in their original positions.**
17. Remove intake camshaft bearing cap bolts, then the bearing caps and camshaft, **Fig. 10.**
18. Remove intake camshaft roller finger followers, then the hydraulic element adjusters.
19. Remove exhaust camshaft bearing cap bolts, then bearing caps and camshaft, **Fig. 11.**
20. Remove balance shaft drive chain tensioner, then the adjustable balance shaft chain guide.
21. Remove small balance shaft drive chain guide, then the upper balance shaft chain guide.
22. Remove balance shaft drive chain, then crankshaft drive sprocket.
23. Remove balance bearing carrier bolts, then the balance shafts, **Fig. 12. Keep each balance shaft separate and do not remove front balance shaft bearing bolts.**
24. Remove thermostat and water feed pipe retaining bolts.
25. Remove thermostat housing and water feed pipe from water pump cover. Ensure bolt that goes through the front of the engine block is removed.
26. Remove water pump retaining bolts, then the water pump.
27. Remove cylinder head to block bolts

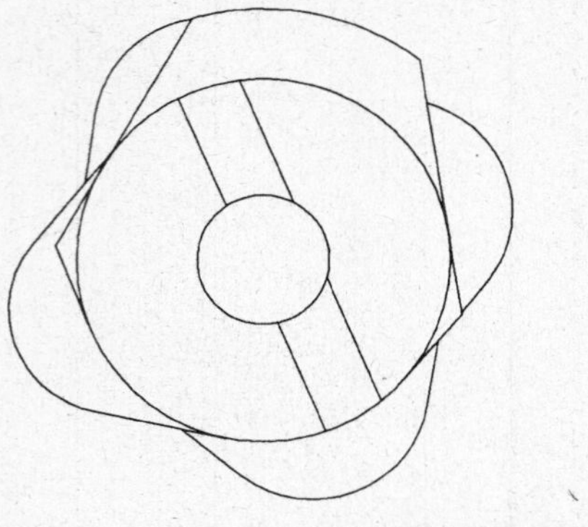

G31069900048000X

Fig. 16 Timing chain sprocket alignment notch position

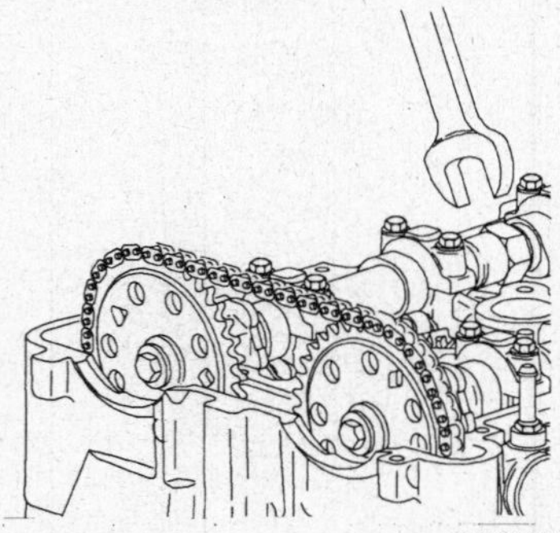

G31069900050000X

Fig. 18 Camshaft sprocket bolts installation

using loosening sequence shown in **Fig. 13.**

28. Remove cylinder head and gasket.

INSTALLATION

1. Install cylinder head gasket to block, then the cylinder head. **Do not use any sealing material, and always use new cylinder head bolts.**
2. Lightly apply clean engine oil to threads and bottom side of flange of head bolt. Allow oil to drain before installation.
3. Using sequence shown in **Fig. 14,** and torque angle gauge tool No. SA9140NE, or equivalent, tighten cylinder head bolts in three steps: First step, **torque** bolts to 22 ft. lbs.; second step, turn each bolt an additional 75°; third step, turn each bolt an additional 185.°
4. Install front cylinder head bolts **Fig. 15, torque** bolts to 18 ft. lbs.
5. Lubricate, then install hydraulic element lash adjusters into their bores in cylinder head.
6. Lubricate valve tips with engine oil supplement, then position roller followers on tip of valve stem and lash adjuster. Ensure roller followers are lubricated.
7. Set intake, then exhaust camshaft on top of roller followers in camshaft bear-

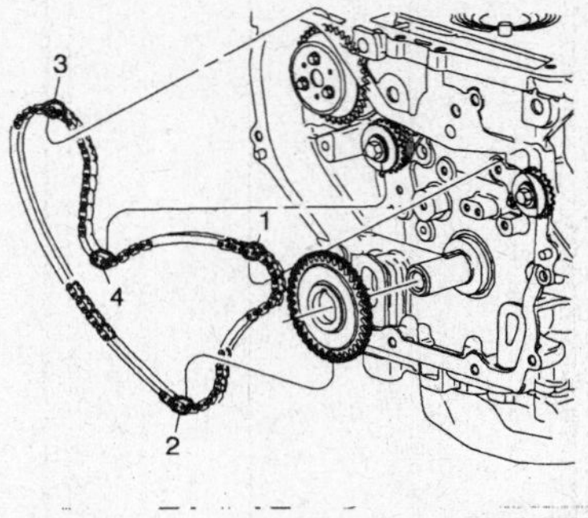

G31069900049000X

Fig. 17 Balance shaft drive chain installation

ing journals. Lubricate with engine oil supplement.

8. Install camshaft bearing caps, then hand start camshaft cap bolts.
9. Timing chain sprocket alignment notch should be oriented to eleven o'clock position **Fig. 16.** Tighten camshaft bearing cap bolts to specifications in increments of three turns until they are seated.
10. Apply 13/64 inch bead, Loctite Anerobic Gasket Maker 578 or equivalent to rear intake camshaft bearing cap. Tighten bolts to specification.
11. Place number one piston to top dead center, then install balance shaft drive chain sprocket on crankshaft.
12. Install balance shafts in their bores, then tighten bolts to specifications.
13. Install water pump, then the water feed tube and thermostat housing to block. Tighten bolts to specifications.
14. Install balance shaft drive chain as follows:
    a. Position chain so copper colored and chrome links are visible **Fig. 17.**
    b. Place copper colored link (1) so it aligns with timing mark on intake side balance shaft sprocket.
    c. Working clockwise around chain, align first chrome link (2) with timing mark on crankshaft drive sprocket (approximately 5 o'clock position on sprocket).
    d. Align last chrome link (3) with timing mark on exhaust side balance shaft drive sprocket, then install balance shaft chain guides.
15. Turn tensioner plunger 30° in its bore and compress plunger until a paper clip can be inserted through hole in plunger body and hole in tensioner plunger.
16. Install timing chain tensioner. Tighten bolt to specification and remove paper clip from balance shaft drive chain tensioner.
17. Install timing chain drive sprocket to crankshaft with timing mark in the 5 o'clock position.
18. Assemble intake camshaft sprocket to timing chain, align timing mark with copper colored link.

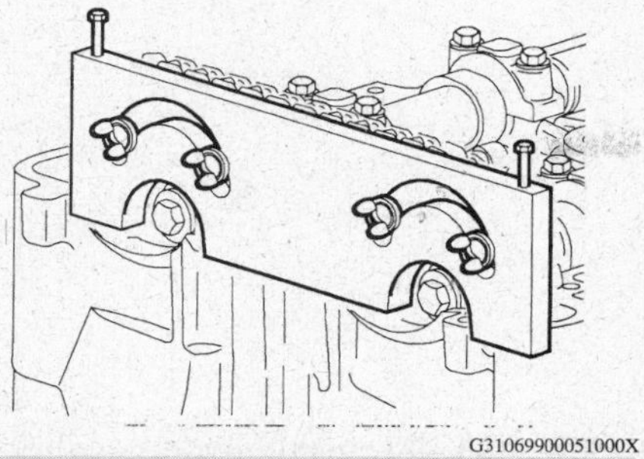

Fig. 19 Camshaft sprocket holding tool installation

19. Lower timing chain through opening in cylinder head.
20. Route timing chain around crankshaft sprocket, then align second link with timing mark on crankshaft sprocket (approximately 5 o'clock position on sprocket).
21. Install intake camshaft sprocket onto intake camshaft, then the new sprocket bolt finger tight. It is not required to align sprocket to camshaft offset notch at this time.
22. Install adjustable timing chain guide through opening in cylinder head, tighten bolt to specification.
23. Install exhaust camshaft sprocket onto exhaust camshaft, then the new sprocket bolt finger tight. Align timing mark on sprocket with silver link.
24. Ensure all colored links and timing marks are aligned.
25. Install fixed chain guide, then the upper timing chain guide.
26. Using a ⅞inch wrench, engage hex on intake and exhaust camshafts, **Fig. 18. Torque** sprocket bolts to 63 ft. lbs. plus an additional 30°.
27. Install a new sealing washer on timing chain tensioner assembly, then the tensioner assembly.
28. Install timing chain oiling nozzle.
29. Apply Loctite threadlocker 242 compound or equivalent, then install timing chain guide bolt access hole plug.
30. Install engine front cover and new gasket.
31. Install accessory drive belt tensioner, then the camshaft cover and gasket. Tighten bolts to specifications.
32. Install crankshaft pulley, then the intake manifold as outlined under "Intake Manifold, Replace."
33. Install exhaust manifold as outlined under "Exhaust Manifold, Replace."

VALVE CLEARANCE SPECIFICATIONS

Stem-To-Guide Clearance, Inch	
Intake	Exhaust
.0012 -.0022	.0016 - .0026

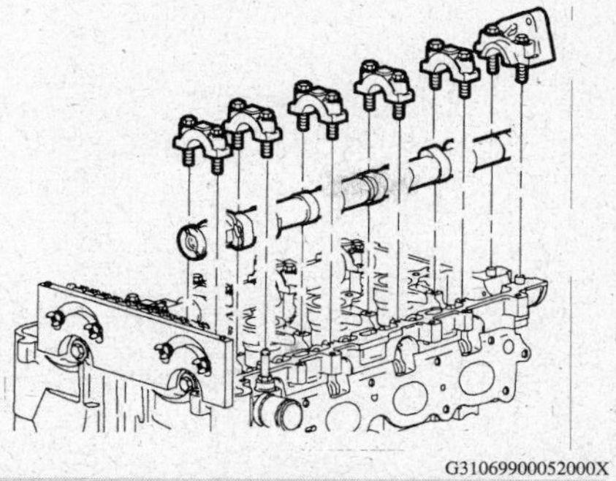

Fig. 20 Camshaft removal

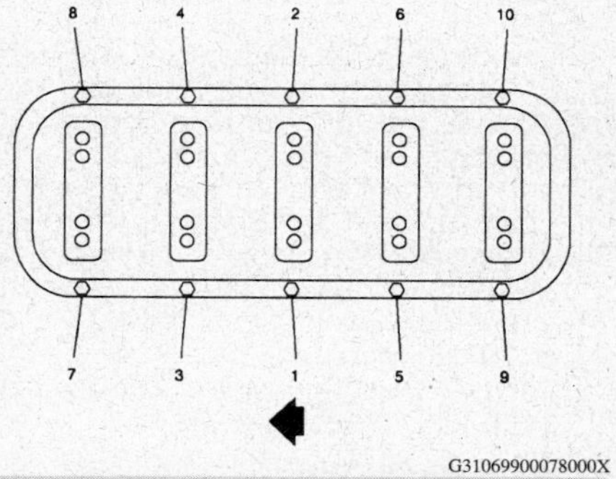

Fig. 22 Lower crankcase outer bolt tightening sequence

VALVE ADJUSTMENT

This engine is equipped with hydraulic lifters and no adjustment is required.

VALVE GUIDES

Valve guides are an integral part of the cylinder head and are pressed in. If valve stem clearance becomes excessive, the valve guides must be hand reamed to the oversize using valve guide reamer tool J-42096, or equivalent. Service valves are available in standard and .075 mm oversize.

FRONT COVER

REPLACE

1. Remove air cleaner assembly, then raise and support vehicle.
2. Drain engine oil into a suitable container, then remove right front wheel and splash shield.
3. Remove engine accessory drive belt as outlined under " Belt Replace."
4. Install crankshaft holder tool J-38122, or equivalent, onto crankshaft pulley.
5. Remove crankshaft pulley and discard bolt.
6. Remove belt tensioner as outlined under "Belt Tensioner Replace."
7. Remove right engine mount as outlined under "Engine Mount Replace."
8. Remove front cover assembly and gasket.

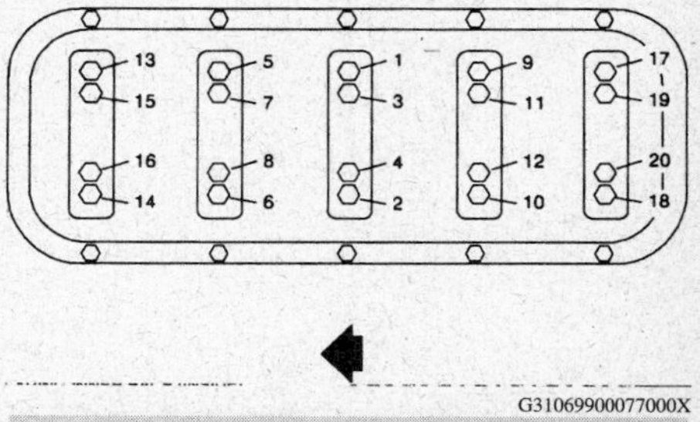

Fig. 21 Lower crankcase inner bolt tightening sequence

9. Reverse procedure to install. Tighten attaching bolts to specifications.

TIMING CHAIN

REPLACE

Refer to "Cylinder Head, Replace" for timing chain replacement.

CAMSHAFT

REPLACE

1. Remove ignition coil, then accessory drive belt, PCV fresh air hose and cam cover assembly.
2. Position piston in the No. 1 cylinder at Top Dead Center (TDC) with intake and exhaust valves closed). **The piston on the No. 1 cylinder must be at Top Dead Center (TDC) when removing or installing camshafts. The timing chain, gears and chain guides could be damaged when air pressure is applied to the cylinder to hold the valves closed.**
3. Remove upper timing chain guide, then the timing chain tensioner.
4. Install camshaft sprocket holding tool No. J-43655, or equivalent, onto cylinder head, **Fig. 19, torque** holding tool to 9 ft. lbs.
5. Hold each camshaft in place using a ⅞ inch open end wrench, then carefully remove camshaft timing sprockets retaining bolts and washers. Discard torque-to-yield bolts.
6. Remove remaining camshaft bearing cap bolts in several passes.
7. Slide camshaft sprockets away from camshafts.
8. Carefully pull camshafts straight up to avoid damaging cylinder head thrust surface, **Fig. 20.**
9. Reverse procedure to install. Tighten attaching bolts to specifications.

PISTON & ROD ASSEMBLY

Install the piston onto the connecting rod with the arrow pointed toward the front of the engine.

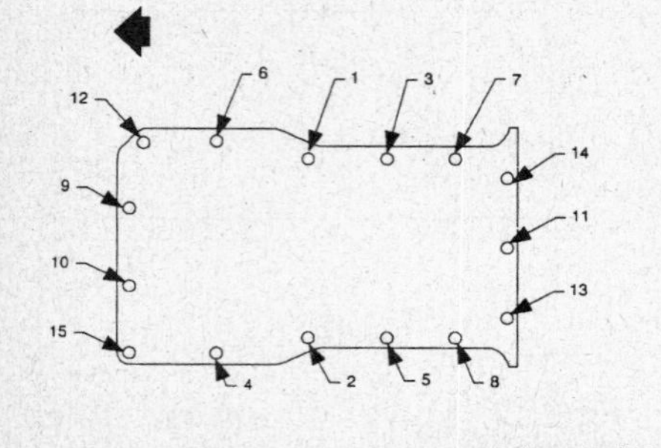

Fig. 23 Oil pan bolt tightening sequence

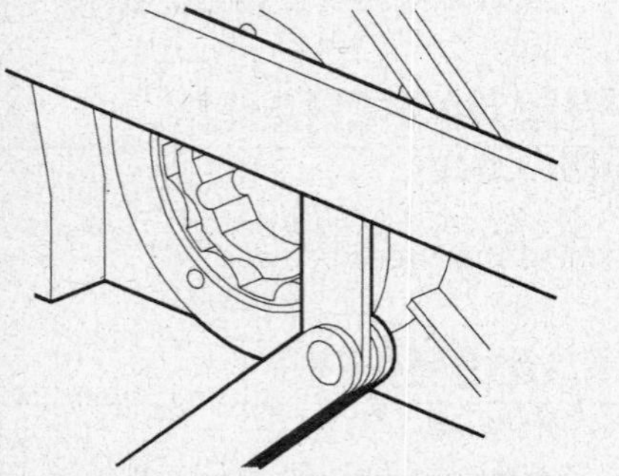

Fig. 26 Oil pump end to end clearance measurement

PISTONS, PINS & RINGS

Replace any pistons that show signs of damage or excessive wear. Piston pin bores and pins must be free of varnish or scuffing. Use an outside micrometer to measure the piston contact areas and piston pin bore. Subtract the measurement of the piston pin bore from the piston pin.

MAIN & ROD BEARINGS

In order to prevent possible cylinder block or crankshaft bearing cap damage when installing crankshaft bearing caps. Use a brass, lead, leather, or an equivalent, soft-faced mallet to install crankshaft bearing caps. Do not use the lower crankcase bolts to pull bearing caps into the seats.

Using lower crankcase inner bolt tightening sequence shown in **Fig. 21, torque** bolts to 15 ft. lbs. Using lower crankcase outer bolt tightening sequence shown in **Fig. 22, torque** bolts to 15 ft. lbs.

CRANKSHAFT REAR OIL SEAL

REPLACE

1. **On models with manual transaxle,** remove transaxle as outlined in "Clutch & Manual Transaxles" section.
2. **On models with automatic transaxle,** remove transaxle as outlined in "Automatic Transaxles" section.
3. **On all models,** remove flywheel and cover.
4. Insert a suitable screwdriver into pry tangs of seal carrier and remove seal.
5. Apply suitable clean engine oil to seal lip and inside diameter of seal carrier.
6. Install seal using seal installer tool No. J-42067, or equivalent.
7. Install transaxle, then the flywheel. Tighten to specifications.

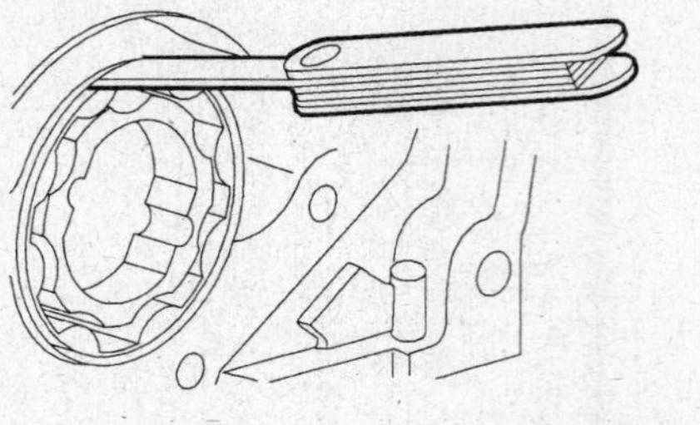

Fig. 24 Oil pump body clearance measurement

OIL PAN

REPLACE

1. Drain engine oil into a suitable container, then remove front exhaust pipe.
2. Remove right front wheel, splash shield and vibration damper.
3. Remove oil pan retaining bolts, then the oil pan at pry points.
4. Reverse procedure to install, noting the following:
   a. Apply a 2 mm bead or RTV Loctite 5900, or equivalent.
   b. Tighten oil pan attaching bolts to specifications in sequence, **Fig. 23.**

OIL PUMP

REPLACE

1. Remove air cleaner assembly, then raise and support vehicle.
2. Drain engine oil into a suitable container, then remove right front wheel and splash shield.
3. Remove accessory drive belt.
4. Remove crankshaft pulley using pulley holding tool No. J-38122, or equivalent.
5. Remove belt tensioner as outlined under "Belt Tensioner, Replace."
6. Install engine support fixture tool No. SA9150E, or equivalent, onto engine.
7. Remove engine mount as outlined under "Engine Mount Replace."
8. Remove front cover bolts, then the 13 mm bolts under water pump cover.
9. Remove front cover assembly and gasket.
10. Reverse procedure to install. Tighten all attaching bolts to specifications.

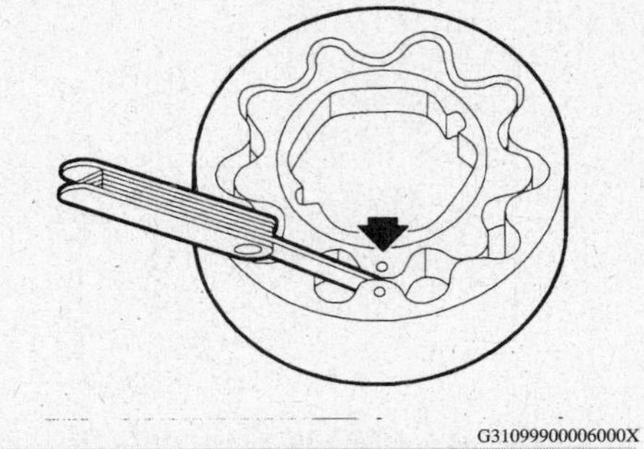

Fig. 25 Oil pump tip clearance measurement

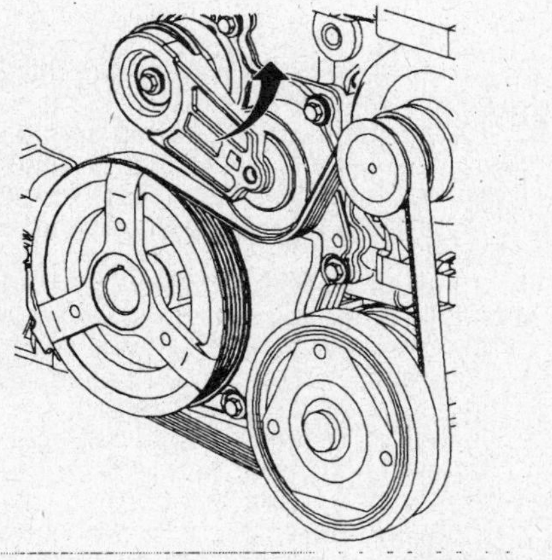

Fig. 27 Serpentine belt routing & removal

OIL PUMP SERVICE

DISASSEMBLE

1. Remove cover plate attaching bolts, then mark drive and driven rotors for assembly reference.
2. Remove drive rotor, then the driven rotor and pressure relief valve.

INSPECTION

1. Using a feeler gauge, measure clearance between driven rotor and pump body **Fig. 24,** maximum clearance is .012 inch. If clearance is greater than maximum, replace oil pump assembly.
2. Inspect tip clearance using a feeler gauge between both tips, **Fig. 25.** Maximum clearance is .006 inch. If clearance is greater than maximum, replace oil pump assembly.
3. Using a feeler gauge, measure clearance between side of drive and driven rotors and oil pump cover plate, **Fig. 26.** Maximum clearance is .003 inch. If clearance is greater than maximum, replace oil pump assembly.

ASSEMBLE

1. Using a screwdriver or punch, remove front cover oil seal.
2. Install new oil seal using oil seal installer tool No. J-35268-A, or equivalent, and a suitable press.
3. Install pressure relief valve, valve

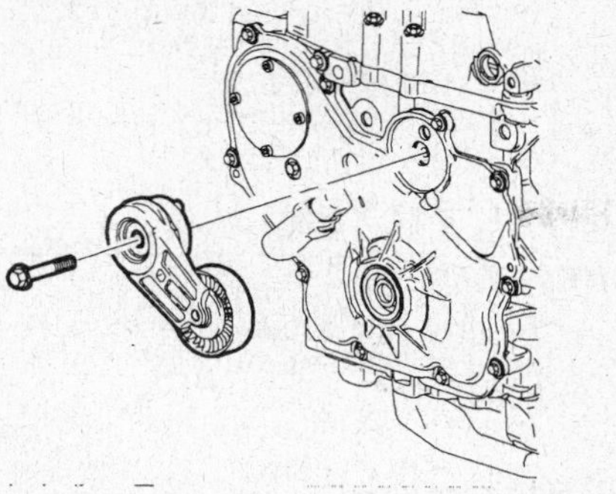

G31069900055000X

Fig. 28 Belt tensioner removal

spring, then the oil pump pressure relief valve plug.
4. Lubricate drive and driven rotors with clean engine oil, then align marks on drive and driven rotors.
5. Install drive and driven rotors into pump body.
6. Fill oil pump with petroleum jelly to prime oil pump.
7. Install oil pump gear cover plate screws.

SERPENTINE DRIVE BELT

BELT ROUTING

Refer to **Fig. 27,** for serpentine belt routing.

TENSIONER REPLACEMENT

The tensioner assembly's internal parts are not serviceable. Do not disassemble tensioner.

1. Depress tensioner arm and remove accessory drive belt.
2. Remove attaching bolts, then the tensioner **Fig. 28.**
3. Reverse procedure to install. Tighten bolts to specification.

BELT REPLACEMENT

Removal

1. Using a 3/8 inch drive breaker bar, depress tensioner arm **Fig. 27.**
2. Remove belt from idler or A/C compressor pulley, then the accessory pulleys.

Installation

1. Route belt around all pulleys, except for idler pulley.
2. Depress tensioner arm using 3/8 inch drive breaker bar.
3. Ensure belt is properly aligned on pulleys, then slip belt over idler pulley.

COOLING SYSTEM BLEED

These engines do not require a special bleed procedure. After filling cooling system, start and run engine until it reaches normal operating temperature with pressure cap off. Air will then automatically bleed through cap opening.

THERMOSTAT

REPLACE

1. Drain engine coolant into a suitable container.
2. Disconnect lower radiator hose at thermostat housing, using Snap-on Tool HCP10, or equivalent. Twist water feed pipe and remove it from water pump.
3. Remove thermostat and water feed assembly bolts, then the thermostat housing bolts.
4. Remove thermostat housing and thermostat element.
5. Discard O-ring. Thermostat will not function correctly once it is contacted by oil. If oil is found in cooling system, it must be flushed and thermostat's cartridge replaced
6. Inspect thermostat components for damage and seat deterioration.
7. Reverse procedure to install.

WATER PUMP

REPLACE

1. Remove air inlet tube, then air cleaner assembly.
2. Drain coolant into a suitable container, then remove exhaust manifold heat shield.
3. Remove thermostat and water feed assembly bolts.
4. Remove water pump sprocket access plate from front cover, then install water pump sprocket holding tool J-43651, or equivalent, **Fig. 29.**
5. Remove retaining bolts accessed from front of engine block.
6. Remove water pump retaining bolts, then the water pump assembly.
7. Reverse procedure to install. Tighten bolts to specifications.

RADIATOR

REPLACE

1. Remove battery, then drain coolant into a suitable container.
2. Disconnect electrical connectors from both cooling fans, then slide electrical connectors out of retainers.
3. Remove pusher fan electrical harness from fan shroud retaining tabs.
4. Remove wiring harness from clamp on fan shroud.
5. **On models equipped with automatic transaxle,** remove upper transaxle cooler lines from radiator end tank, then cap line to prevent oil spillage or contamination.
6. **On all models,** remove upper radiator hose from radiator.
7. Remove fan shroud to radiator bolts, then the shroud assembly.
8. Remove forward wiring harness from retaining clips, then the lower radiator hose from radiator.
9. **On models equipped with automatic transaxle,** remove lower transaxle

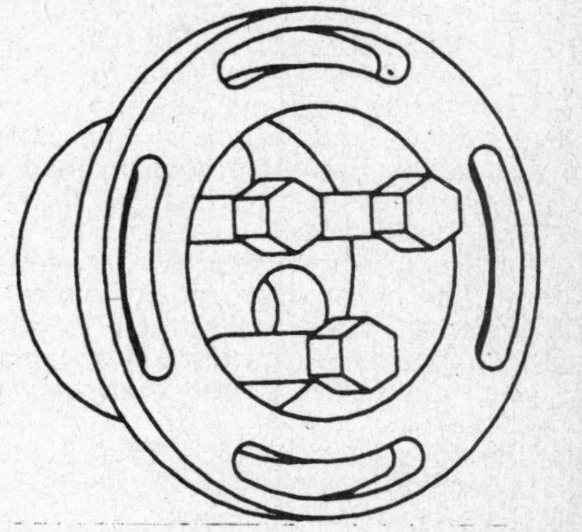

G31089900008000X

Fig. 29 Water pump sprocket holding tool

cooler line, then cap line to prevent oil spillage or contamination.
10. **On all models,** remove radiator upper mount bracket to rail bolts, then the upper bracket and rubber mounts.
11. Using a tie strap, secure condenser away from upper rail.
12. Raise and support vehicle.
13. Remove condenser block to radiator bolts, then the condenser to radiator bolts.
14. Pull condenser and pusher fan assembly down slightly to disengage tabs from radiator.
15. Lower vehicle.
16. Remove radiator from vehicle.
17. Remove upper radiator to condenser gaskets.
18. Reverse procedure to install.

FUEL PUMP

REPLACE

Whenever fuel line fittings are loosened or removed, wrap a shop cloth around the fitting and have an approved container available to collect any fuel.

1. Connect Scan tool to vehicle diagnostic connector, turn ignition to On position.
2. Relieve fuel system pressure as outlined under " Precautions."
3. Raise and support vehicle, keeping scan tool outside of vehicle and accessible.
4. Disconnect fuel feed line at outlet to filter.
5. Install 3/8 x 1/4 inch adapter onto flow/pressure adapter tool No. SA9127E-7, or equivalent, then insert adapter into fuel feed line.
6. Connect one end of a suitable drain hose to other end of adapter, then connect other end of drain hose to a certified fuel handling cart.
7. Turn fuel pump on using scan tool and pump fuel into a suitable container.
8. If fuel pump is inoperative, proceed as follows:
   a. Insert siphon hose guide/funnel into fuel filler pipe.

b. Insert siphon hose J-43290, or equivalent, into guide funnel and fuel filler pipe. Some resistance may be encountered when tip of siphon hose reaches inlet check valve. Repeated probing may be required to slide hose tip through check valve.
c. Begin siphon process and collect fuel into an approved container.
9. Ensure fuel tank is less than ¼ full.
10. Remove exhaust system intermediate pipe, then the rear heat shield retaining bolts.
11. Remove fuel filler pipe lower bracket attaching screw, then disconnect EVAP canister vent hose.
12. Loosen fuel filler pipe hose clamp that is closest to fuel tank, then remove tank ground strap attaching screw located near fuel filter.
13. Disconnect fuel feed line after fuel filter.
14. Disconnect fuel return and EVAP canister purge lines between tank and chassis fuel bundle.
15. Disconnect electrical connectors from fuel tank, then loosen front tank strap bolt, but do not remove.
16. With assistance, remove two rear tank retaining strap bolts.
17. Lower rear half of tank and slide fuel tank downward and rearward, then remove tank from vehicle.
18. Disconnect fuel lines from fuel pump module cover. **To prevent retainer damage, do not attempt to remove retainer with a 12 inch or shorter ratchet/breaker bar.**
19. Remove fuel pump module retainer ring using lock ring service tool No. J-43827, or equivalent.
20. To prevent bending of sending unit float arm, remove sending unit first by pulling retaining clip toward float arm and lifting upward.
21. Carefully lift fuel pump straight up from fuel tank. To disengage fuel pump from fuel pump housing clips must be disengaged at the same time.
22. Discard fuel pump module to tank seal, then remove fuel feed line from bottom of fuel pump cover using removal tool No. J-44078, or equivalent.
23. Disconnect fuel pump electrical connector from fuel pump cover.
24. Inspect fuel tank for metal chips or debris. Remove all contaminants and replace in-line fuel filter before installing a new pump assembly.
25. Reverse procedure to install. Replace all plastic fuel line retainers.

FUEL FILTER

REPLACE

1. Relieve fuel system pressure as outlined under "Precautions."
2. Raise and support vehicle.
3. Remove fuel filter bracket screw, then disconnect fuel lines from inlet and outlet sides of fuel filter.
4. Slide fuel filter out of bracket
5. Reverse procedure, noting the following:
   a. Cycle ignition On for 5 seconds, then Off for 10 seconds.
   b. Repeat previous step twice.
   c. Crank engine until it starts. Maximum starter motor cranking time is 20 seconds.
   d. If engine does not start, repeat steps a through c. Run engine and check system for leaks.

TIGHTENING SPECIFICATIONS

Year	Component	Torque/Ft. Lbs.
2000	A/C Compressor To Block Bolt	18
	Alternator To Block	18
	Battery Hold-Down Bracket	15
	Battery Terminal	13
	Battery Tray Fasteners	11
	Belt Tensioner To Block	37
	Block Oil Gallery Plug	26
	Camshaft Bearing Cap Bolt	96①
	Cam Cover To Head	96①
	Camshaft Sprocket Bolt	23②
	Camshaft Timing Chain Tensioner	44
	Chain Guide Plug	59
	Connecting Rod Bolts	18⑧
	Crankshaft Pulley Bolt	74⑤
	Crankshaft Position Sensor	96①
	Crankshaft Rear Oil Seal Carrier To Block	96①
	Cylinder Head Bolts	③
	EGR Pipe To Cylinder Head Bolt	96①
	EGR Valve	18
	Engine Lift Bracket Front Bolt	18
	Engine Lift Bracket Rear Bolt	18
	Engine Mount Bracket Bolt	66
	Engine Mount To Body Bolt	41
	Exhaust Manifold To Cylinder Head Stud	18
	Exhaust Manifold To Cylinder Head Nut	13
	Exhaust Manifold Pipe Flange Stud	12
	Flexplate Bolt (Automatic Tranaxle)	39⑥

Continued

TIGHTENING SPECIFICATIONS—Continued

Year	Component	Torque/Ft. Lbs.
2000	Flywheel Bolt (Manual Transaxle)	39⑥
	Frame To Body Bolts	75④
	Front Cover To Block	18
	Fuel Fill Neck To Fuel Tank Clamp	44①
	Fuel Filter Bracket	35①
	Fuel Line Bracket	96①
	Fuel Line Support Clip	96①
	Fuel Rail Bracket Stud	96①
	Fuel Tank Straps	15
	Fuel Pressure Regulator	44①
	Heater Shield To Exhaust Manifold	96①
	Idle Air Control Motor Bolts	27①
	Ignition Coil Assembly Bolts	96①
	Intake Camshaft Rear Cap Bolt	18
	Intake Manifold To Cylinder Head Bolt	96①
	Intake Manifold To Cylinder Head Nut	96①
	Intake Manifold To Cylinder Head Stud	53
	Knock Sensor	18
	Lower Crankcase	⑦
	Oil Drain Plug	18
	Oil Pan To Block	18
	Oil Pump Pressure Relief Valve Plug	30
	Oil Pump Cover	53①
	Oxygen Sensor	31
	Power Steering Pump Bolt	18
	Radiator Upper Bracket	53①
	Spark Plug	15
	Starter Motor	37
	Thermostat Housing To Block	96①
	Throttle Body Bolt	96①
	Throttle Body Nut	96①
	Throttle Position Sensor	18①
	Timing Chain Guides	96①
	Timing Chain Nozzle Bolt	96①
	Transaxle Mount Bolts	41
	Transaxle Range Switch Bolts	18
	Transaxle Range Switch Lever Nut	26
	Vent Tube To Cylinder Head Bolt	11
	Water Pump Access Cover Bolt	96①
	Water Pump	18
	Water Pump/Balance Shaft Chain Tensioner	96①
	Water Pump Sprocket	96①

① — Inch lbs.
② — Tighten an additional 30.°
③ — Refer to "Cylinder Head, Replace" for bolt tightening procedure.
④ — Tighten an additional 45.°
⑤ — Tighten an additional 75.°
⑥ — Tighten an additional 25.°
⑦ — Refer to "Main & Rod Bearings" for bolt tightening procedure.
⑧ — Tighten an additional 70.°

3.0L Engine

NOTE: On Air Bag Equipped Models, Refer To " Air Bag System Precautions" Located In The Front Of This Manual For System Disarming & Arming Procedures.

NOTE: Refer To "Computer Relearn Procedures " Located In The Front Of This Manual For Computer Relearn Procedures.

INDEX

PRECAUTIONS

AIR BAG SYSTEMS

Refer to "Air Bag System Precautions" in the front of this manual for system disarming and arming procedures.

BATTERY GROUND CABLE

Prior to service, disconnect battery ground cable and isolate as required.

FUEL SYSTEM PRESSURE RELIEF

With Scan Tool

Start vehicle and locate SPECIAL TESTS, select ECM, then select fuel delivery. Select FUEL PUMP, then command fuel pump off.

Less Scan Tool

Remove schrader valve cap and install fuel pressure gage tool No. SA9127E, or equivalent. Open valve on pressure gage and drain fuel into suitable container.

COMPRESSION PRESSURE

1. Start and run engine until it reaches normal operating temperature, then turn engine off.
2. Remove ignition modules and spark plugs.
3. Connect compression gauge tool No. SA9127E, or equivalent, into spark plug hole.
4. Open throttle fully.
5. Use fully charged battery to crank engine at a minimum of 250 RPM.
6. Measure compression while cranking engine. Prior to reading compression gauge needle should bounce at least ten times.
7. Repeat steps 3–6 for each cylinder.
8. No compression in two or more cylinders indicates damaged timing chain sprockets, camshafts, camshaft key or pins.
9. Minimum compression on any one cylinder should not be less than 70 percent of highest cylinder. No cylinder should read less than 100 psi.
10. Normal compression builds up quickly and evenly to specifications in each cylinder.
11. Low compression indicates damaged piston, rings, valves, or head gasket.
12. High compression indicates carbon on pistons or combustion chamber.
13. If cylinder compression in one or more cylinders is low, pour one teaspoon of engine oil into cylinder through spark plug hole.
14. Place shop towel over spark plug holes and crank engine over a few seconds without compression gauge or spark plugs installed.
15. Repeat steps 3–6 and measure compression.
16. If adding oil increases compression readings, piston rings leaking.
17. If adding oil does not increase compression, valves or head gasket leaking.
18. Remove compression tester, install spark plugs and tighten to specifications.
19. Install ignition modules, spark plugs and connect wires, tighten to specifications.

ENGINE MOUNT

REPLACE

1. Disconnect MAF sensor and remove air box assembly.
2. Remove EVAP purge assembly and position aside.
3. Install engine support fixture and adapter tool Nos. SA9150E and J43405, or equivalents.
4. Remove engine mount, then the mount bracket.
5. Reverse procedure to install, tighten engine mount and bracket to specifications.

ENGINE

REPLACE

1. Disconnect MAF sensor, then remove air cleaner assembly and battery.
2. Remove positive main feed cable at fuse block.
3. Disconnect main TCM connector under cowl cover and position aside.
4. Disconnect inline TCM connector near brake master cylinder.
5. Disconnect A/C pressure connector.
6. Disconnect black engine harness connector from under fuse block, then the lower weather pack connector inside fuse block.
7. Remove fuse block and position aside.
8. Secure engine harness to top of engine.
9. Remove battery tray.
10. Disconnect EVAP purge connector.

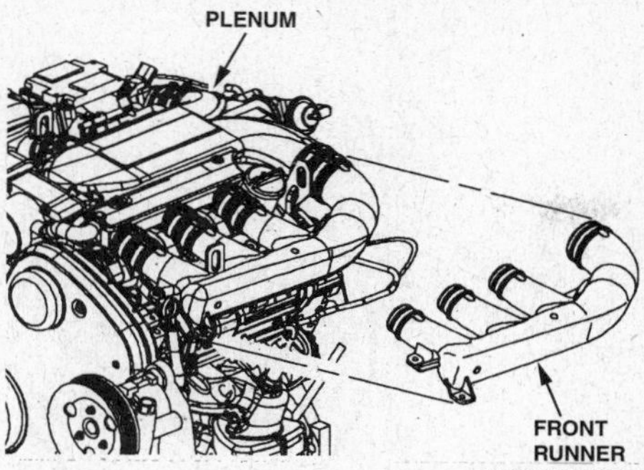

Fig. 1 Upper intake manifold front runner & plenum

11. Disconnect right front speed sensor and secure to engine.
12. Disconnect front oxygen sensor.
13. Disconnect transaxle ground, main connector, shift control and rear ECM connectors.
14. Remove brake booster vacuum hose.
15. Relieve fuel pressure as outlined under "Precautions."
16. Disconnect fuel lines and position aside.
17. Disconnect EVAP purge hose at EVAP purge solenoid.
18. Remove starter, then the torque convertor bolts.
19. Remove exhaust system from catalytic convertor forward.
20. Disconnect transaxle nose bracket.
21. Remove A/C compressor and position aside.
22. Drain engine coolant, then disconnect heater hoses at cowl.
23. Remove lower engine to transaxle bell housing bolts. **Do not remove upper bolts at this time.**
24. Remove main coolant reservoir hose from engine inlet adapter.
25. Remove upper and lower radiator hoses from engine.
26. Remove small hose under power steering fluid reservoir and drain fluid.
27. Disconnect metal power steering line.
28. Remove power steering reservoir and secure to engine.
29. Attach suitable engine lift hoist to engine and support engine weight.
30. Remove right front engine mount and bracket.
31. Remove upper bell housing bolts.
32. Remove engine.
33. Reverse procedure to install, noting the following:
    a. Ensure engine aligns with dowel pins on transaxle.
    b. Tighten to specifications.

INTAKE MANIFOLD

REPLACE

UPPER

1. Remove front runner rubber boot hose clamps using hose clamp pliers tool No. J-43914, or equivalent.
2. Remove front runner, **Fig. 1.**
3. Remove ECM.

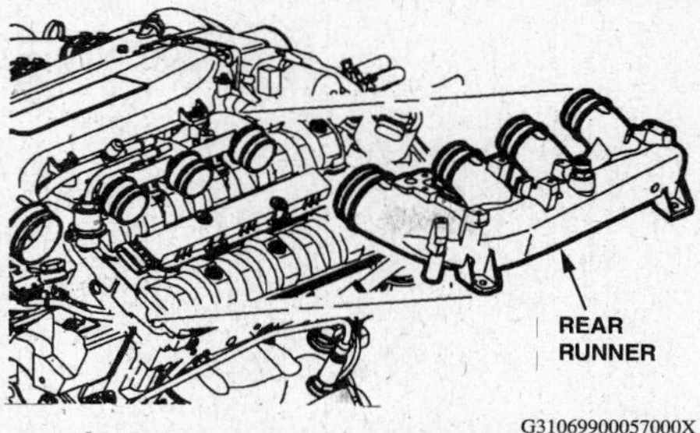

Fig. 2 Upper intake manifold rear runner

4. Remove rear runner rubber boot hose clams using hose clamp pliers tool No. J-43914, or equivalent.
5. Disconnect brake vacuum hose.
6. Disconnect intake plenum switch over valve vacuum hose from switch over valve. Note hose routing for installation reference.
7. Disconnect throttle body vent hose. Note hose routing for installation reference.
8. Remove rear runner, **Fig. 2.**
9. Disconnect throttle body electrical connectors.
10. Remove electrical connector and vacuum hoses from plenum switch over valve solenoid.
11. Remove fuel pressure regulator vacuum hose, then the throttle body heater hoses.
12. Remove plenum.
13. Mask off ports to lower intake.
14. Remove upper intake manifold assembly.
15. Reverse procedure to install.

LOWER

1. Remove upper intake as outlined under "Intake Manifold, Replace."
2. Relieve fuel system pressure as outlined under "Precautions."
3. Remove fuel supply and return hoses from fuel rail using fuel line separator tool No. SA9805E, or equivalent.
4. Disconnect and remove fuel injector harness.
5. Remove fuel rail.
6. Remove lower intake manifold, **Fig. 3.**
7. Remove lower intake manifold spacer.
8. Mask off ports to lower intake manifold spacer.
9. Remove sealing rings.
10. Clean manifold sealing surfaces with nonabrasive cleaner.
11. Reverse procedure to install, noting the following.
    a. Apply Loctite 242, or equivalent to lower intake manifold spacer and lower intake manifold bolts.
    b. Tighten intake manifold and spacer to specifications.

EXHAUST MANIFOLD

REPLACE

1. Remove front oxygen sensor using oxygen sensor socket tool No. J-39194C, or equivalent.

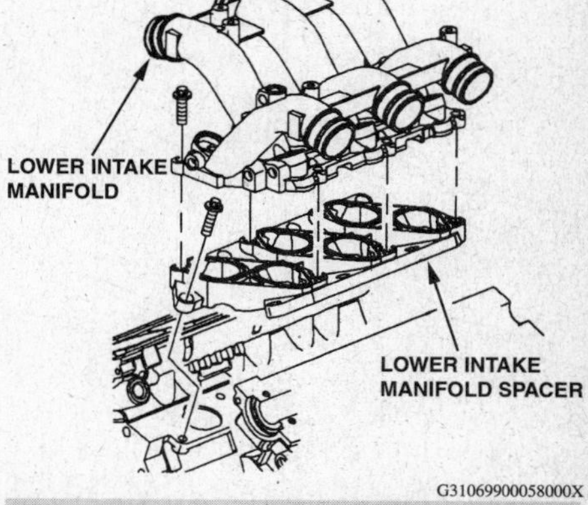

Fig. 3 Lower intake manifold & spacer

2. Remove front exhaust manifold and gasket.
3. Remove rear oxygen sensor using oxygen sensor socket tool No. J-39194C, or equivalent.
4. Disconnect EGR pipe.
5. Remove rear exhaust manifold and gasket.
6. Reverse procedure to install.

CYLINDER HEAD

REPLACE

1. Remove air cleaner assembly.
2. Remove upper and lower intake manifolds as outlined under " Intake Manifold, Replace."
3. Remove coolant intake and heater hoses.
4. Remove coolant bridge and seals, **Fig. 4.**
5. Remove engine ventilation chamber, **Fig. 5.**
6. Drain coolant into a suitable container.
7. Remove upper radiator hose.
8. Remove exhaust manifold heat shield.
9. Remove exhaust pipe to exhaust manifold retaining nuts.
10. Remove front exhaust pipes from exhaust manifolds.
11. Support powertrain with a floor jack under oil pan.
12. Remove front transaxle mount bolt.
13. Raise powertrain with floor jack to gain access to coolant extension housing.
14. Remove oil level indicator tube.
15. Twist and remove coolant extension housing.
16. Remove grounds from front lift bracket.
17. Disconnect oxygen sensor connector.
18. Remove EGR to exhaust manifold pipe.
19. Remove camshaft cover.
20. Remove front timing belt cover as outlined under " Front Cover, Replace."
21. Remove timing belt as outlined under "Timing Belt, Replace."
22. Remove timing belt tensioner bracket.
23. Remove rear timing belt cover as outlined under " Front Cover, Replace."
24. Disconnect camshaft sensor connector.

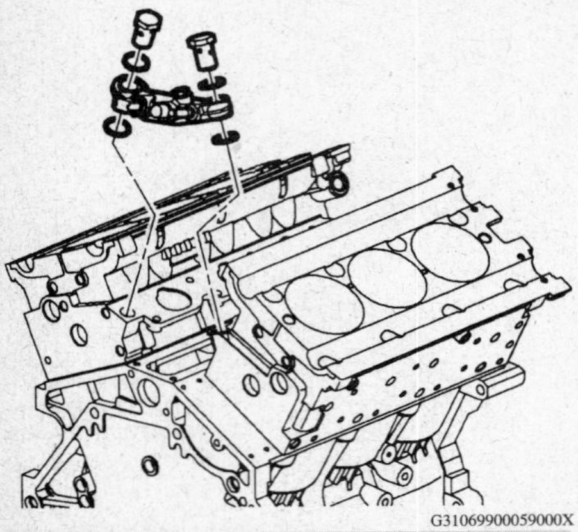

Fig. 4 Coolant bridge removal

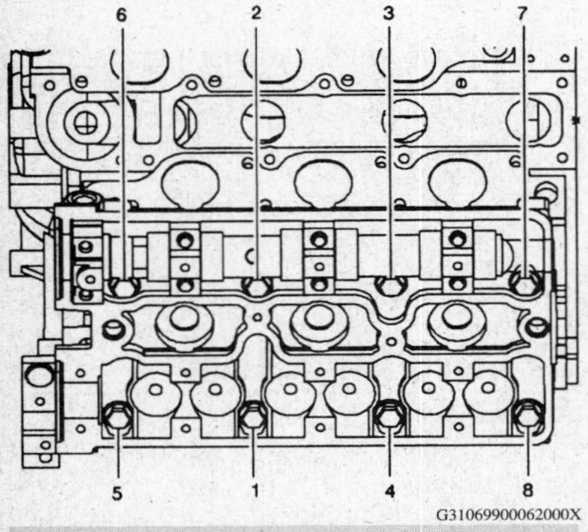

Fig. 7 Cylinder head bolt tightening sequence

25. Remove exhaust camshaft as outlined under "Camshaft, Replace."
26. Using sequence shown in **Fig. 6,** loosen and remove cylinder head bolts in several steps.
27. Remove cylinder head and gasket.
28. Remove exhaust manifold.
29. Clean and inspect cylinder head and sealing surfaces.
30. Reverse procedure to install, noting the following:
    a. Ensure part number imprint on new cylinder head gasket is facing towards the top of the engine.
    b. Using sequence shown in **Fig. 7** and torque angle gauge tool No. SA9140E, or equivalent, tighten cylinder head bolts as follows: first step, **torque** bolts to 18 ft. lbs; second step, an additional 90°; third step, an additional 90°; fourth step, an additional 90°; fifth step, an additional 15.°
    c. Replace sealing rings on coolant pipe and lubricate with coolant.

VALVE COVER

REPLACE

1. Remove upper and lower intake manifolds as outlined under " Intake Manifold, Replace."

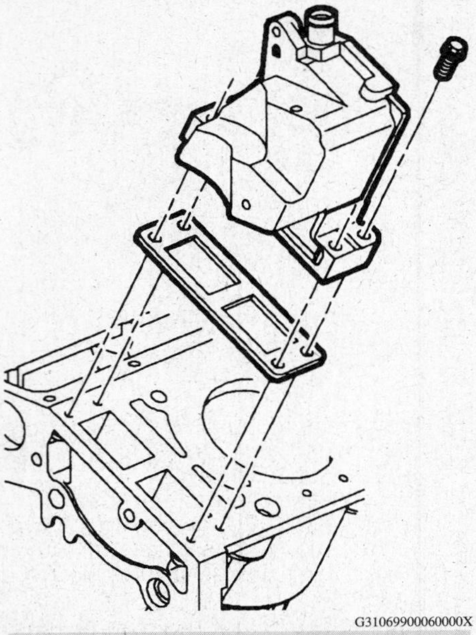

Fig. 5 Engine ventilation chamber removal

2. Remove ignition coils and lift bracket.
3. **On rear cover,** remove knock sensor wire harness and disconnect camshaft position sensor.
4. **On front or rear cover,** remove cover and O-ring seals, ensure all eight O-rings are accounted for.
5. Clean cover and sealing surfaces.
6. Reverse procedure to install, noting the following:
    a. Apply a thin coat of Loctite 5900, or equivalent, to front and rear of cover, **Fig. 8.**
    b. Tighten to specifications.

CAMSHAFT LOBE LIFT SPECIFICATIONS

Exhaust cam lobe lift rise .3409–.3441 inch, minimum service limit is .339 inch.

VALVE ADJUSTMENT

Engine is equipped with hydraulic lifters, no adjustment is required.

FRONT COVER

REPLACE

1. Remove air cleaner assembly.
2. Raise and support vehicle, then remove right front wheel and splash shield.
3. Lower vehicle, then loosen but do not remove water pump pulley bolts.
4. Install engine support fixture and adapters tool Nos. SA9150E and J-43405, or equivalents.
5. Remove serpentine belt as outlined under "Serpentine Drive Belt."
6. Remove water pump and power steering pulleys.
7. Remove serpentine belt tensioner, then remove crankshaft balancer.

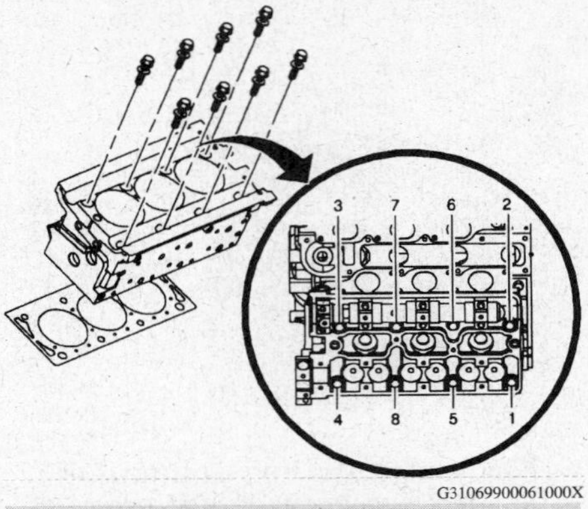

Fig. 6 Cylinder head bolt loosening sequence

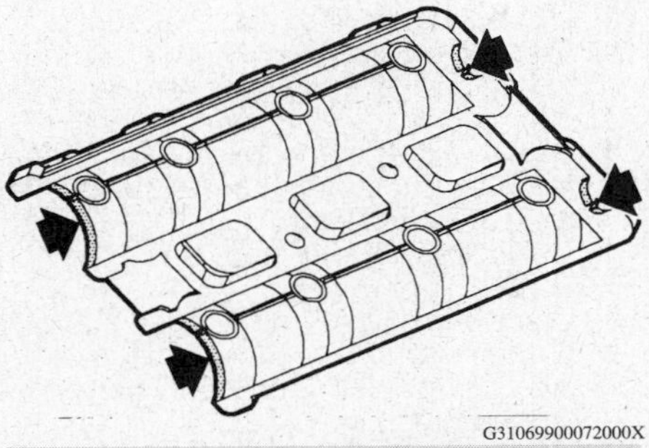

Fig. 8 Valve cover sealant application points

8. Disconnect A/C pressure connector to allow additional slack in harness, then remove wiring harness channel from front cover and position away from front of engine.
9. Remove timing belt front cover.
10. Inspect outer edge sealing strip on front timing cover for cracks or tears and replace as required.
11. Remove timing belt as outlined under "Timing Belt, Replace."
12. To prevent valve to piston contact, rotate crankshaft counterclockwise to 60° BTDC, **Fig. 9.**
13. Remove camshaft gears using camshaft lock tool Nos. J-42069-1 and J-42069-2, or equivalent when initially loosening camshaft bolts, **Fig. 10.**
14. Remove timing belt tensioner bracket.
15. Remove timing belt idler pulley for camshaft Nos. 3 and 4, **Fig. 11.**
16. Remove rear timing belt cover bolts, then the threaded pin and rear timing belt cover.
17. Reverse procedure to install, noting the following:
    a. Install threaded pin with Loctite 242, or equivalent, and tighten to specifications.
    b. Tighten timing belt idler pulley until snug. After final timing belt adjustments are made, tighten to specifications.
    c. Adjust timing belt as outlined under "Timing Belt, Replace."
    d. Install new camshaft gear bolts and

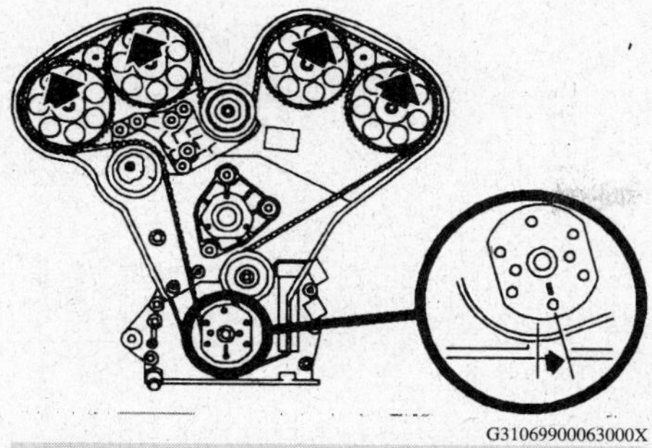

Fig. 9 Crankshaft alignment to 60° BTDC

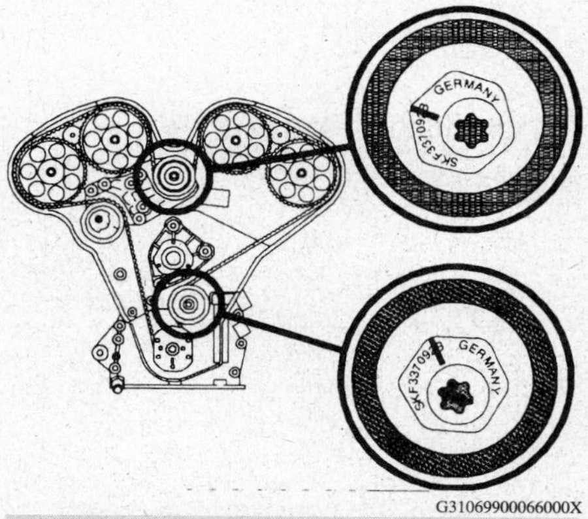

Fig. 12 Upper & lower idler pulleys mark

tighten to specifications.

TIMING BELT

REPLACE

REMOVAL

1. Remove timing belt front cover as outlined under " Front Cover, Replace."
2. Rotate crankshaft using crank hub torx socket tool No. J-42098, or equivalent, until No. 1 cylinder is at 60° BTDC, **Fig. 9.**
3. Install crankshaft locking tool No. J-42069-10, or equivalent.
4. Using crank hub torx socket tool No. J-42098, or equivalent, rotate crankshaft clockwise until No. 1 cylinder is at TDC and tighten lever arm to water pump pulley flange.
5. Ensure alignment of crankshaft is not 180° off. Alignment marks must align with corresponding notches on rear timing belt cover.
6. Install camshaft gear locking tool Nos. J-42069-1 and J-42069-2, or equivalents, **Fig. 10.**
7. Remove upper and lower idler pulleys.
8. Remove timing belt tensioner.
9. Remove timing belt.
10. Do not rotate crankshaft if camshaft locking tools are not in place.
11. Do not rotate camshafts unless crankshaft is at 60° BTDC.

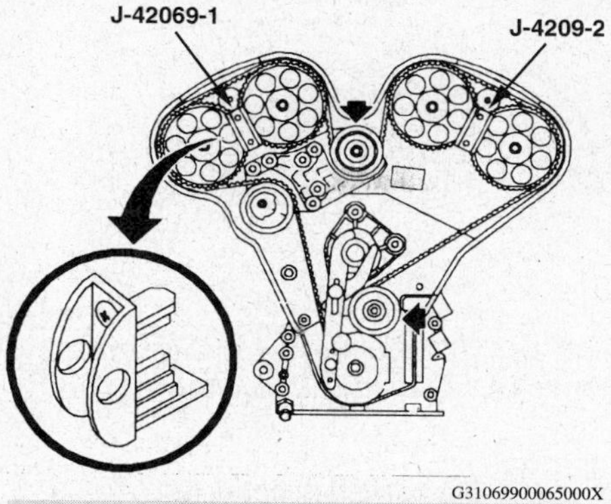

Fig. 10 Camshaft gear locking tool installation

INSTALLATION

1. Remove crankshaft locking tool.
2. Using a felt tip pen, mark furthest point from torx head bolt on upper and lower idler pulleys, **Fig. 12.**
3. Idler pulleys provide adjustment by rotating on an eccentric circle around attachment bolt.
4. Using idler pulley wrench tool No. J-42069-40, or equivalent, install lower idler pulley allowing pulley to rotate with slight resistance.
5. Align marks on timing belt with marks on number 3 and number 4 camshaft sprockets, **Fig. 13.**
6. Route timing belt around lower idler pulley, then around crankshaft sprocket, ensure mark on timing belt aligns with mark on crankshaft sprocket.
7. Using plastic wedge tool No. J-42069-30, or equivalent, lock timing belt to crankshaft sprocket.
8. Route belt around timing belt tensioner, then around No. 1 and No. 2 camshaft sprockets, ensure marks on timing belt align with marks on sprockets.
9. Using idler pulley wrench tool No. J-42069-40, or equivalent, install upper idler pulley, allow pulley to rotate.
10. Install crankshaft locking tool No. J-42069-10, or equivalent, and tighten lever arm to water pump pulley flange.
11. Adjust timing belt tensioner alignment mark ⅛ inch above mark on spring loaded idler, **Fig. 14.**
12. Adjust mark on upper idler pulley to the 10 o'clock position to align No. 1 and No. 2 timing marks close to their settings, then snug but do not fully tighten pulley.
13. Adjust mark on lower idler pulley to the 11 o'clock position to align No. 3 and No. 4 timing marks close to their settings, then snug but do not fully tighten pulley.
14. Remove camshaft locking tools and install checking gage tool No. J-42069–20, or equivalent.
15. Pull timing belt between tensioner and crankshaft sprocket to remove slack between camshaft Nos. 3 and 4 and

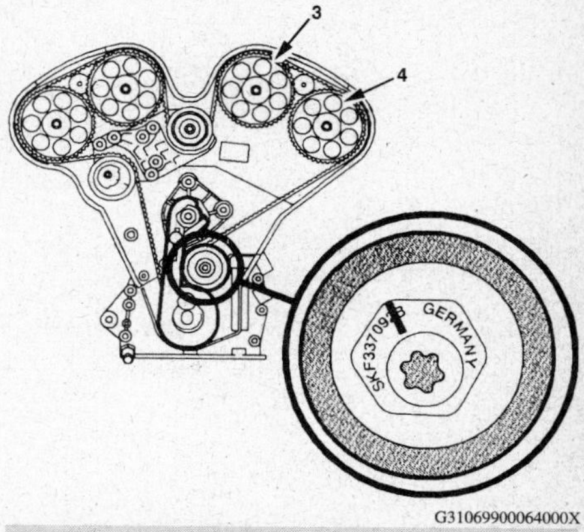

Fig. 11 Camshaft Nos. 3 & 4 idler pulley

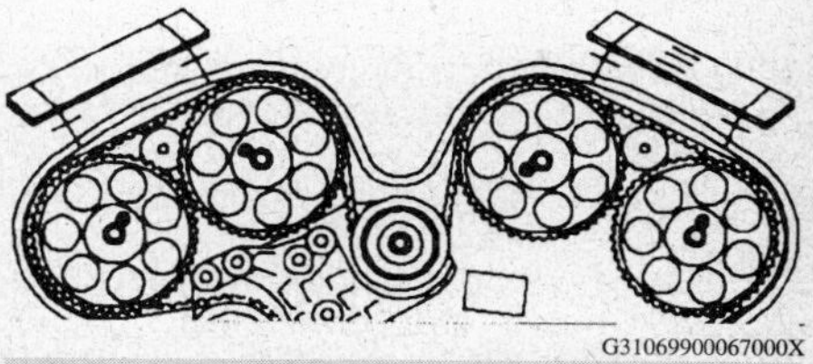

Fig. 13 Timing belt alignment marks

lower idler pulley. Ensure timing marks on camshaft Nos. 3 and 4 are .0394 inch (1 mm) on retard side, **Fig. 15.** If timing marks are not .0394 inch on retard side, turn lower idler clockwise and repeat procedure.

16. Remove crankshaft locking tool.
17. Rotate crankshaft 1¾ turns clockwise and install crankshaft locking tool at TDC. Tighten lever arm to water pump pulley flange. If TDC is passed, do not rotate counterclockwise, rotate crankshaft an additional two turns.
18. Rotate lower idler pulley counterclockwise until timing marks on camshaft sprocket Nos. 3 and 4 align with marks on checking gauge tool.
19. Using idler pulley wrench tool, hold idler pulley and tighten to specifications.
20. Remove crankshaft locking tool.
21. Rotate crankshaft 1¾ turns clockwise and install crankshaft locking tool. Stop at TDC, then tighten lever arm to water pump pulley flange. If TDC is passed, do not rotate counterclockwise, rotate crankshaft an additional two turns.
22. Inspect alignment marks on camshaft Nos. 3 and 4, realign if required.
23. Install checking gauge tool on camshaft Nos. 1 and 2, then install camshaft locking tool on camshaft Nos. 2 and 4.
24. Rotate upper idler pulley counterclockwise until timing marks on camshaft sprocket Nos. 1 and 2 align with marks on checking gauge tool.

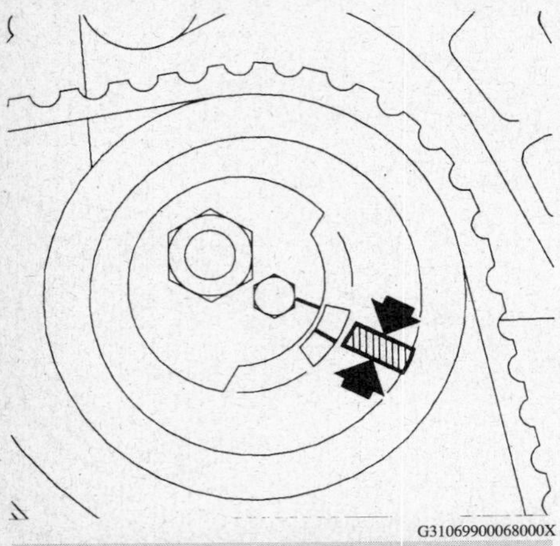

Fig. 14 Timing belt tensioner alignment mark

25. Using idler pulley wrench tool, hold idler pulley and tighten to specifications.
26. Remove camshaft and crankshaft locking tools.
27. Rotate crankshaft 1¾ turns clockwise and install crankshaft locking tool. Stop at TDC, then tighten lever arm to water pump pulley flange. If TDC is passed, do not rotate counterclockwise, rotate crankshaft an additional two turns.
28. Using checking gauge tool, check both pairs of camshaft timing marks, adjust if required.
29. Adjust timing belt tensioner mark ⅛ inch above alignment mark on spring loaded idler, **Fig. 14.**
30. Tighten timing belt tensioner to specifications.
31. Remove crankshaft locking tool and checking gauge tool.
32. Install timing belt front cover as outlined under"Front Cover, Replace."

CAMSHAFT

REPLACE

REMOVAL

1. Remove upper and lower intake manifold as outlined under " Intake Manifold, Replace."
2. Remove air cleaner assembly.
3. Remove timing belt cover as outlined under "Front Cover, Replace."
4. Remove timing belt as outlined under "Timing Belt, Replace."
5. Rotate crankshaft counterclockwise to 60° BTDC to prevent valve to piston contact, **Fig. 9.**
6. Install camshaft locking tool Nos. J-42069-1 and J-42069-2, or equivalents, then remove gear bolt and gear.
7. Ensure camshaft is not under a load from lifters, then remove bearing cap bolts, starting in the center and moving outward in a spiral direction, in stages of ½ to 1 turn.
8. Note code marks on bearing caps as follows:

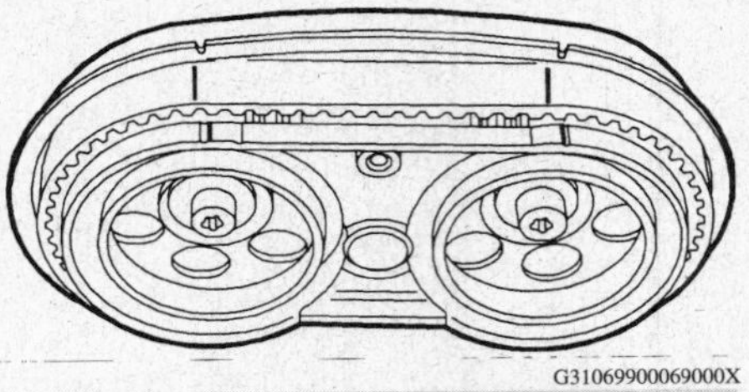

Fig. 15 Timing belt alignment marks retarded .0394 inch (1 mm)

   a. Rear cylinder head (CYL. 1, 3, 5) bearing caps are marked with "L" followed by a number.
   b. Front cylinder head (CYL. 2, 4, 6) bearing caps are marked with "R" followed by a number.
9. Remove camshaft with seal, then clean all bearing and sealing surfaces.

INSTALLATION

1. Lubricate camshaft bearing surfaces with oil.
2. Install camshafts as follows:
   a. **When installing rear exhaust camshaft,** ensure pin points towards the 1 o'clock position.
   b. **When installing rear intake camshaft,** ensure pin points towards the 11 o'clock position.
   c. **When installing front exhaust camshaft,** ensure pin points toward the 12 o'clock position.
   d. **When installing front intake camshaft,** ensure pin points toward 7 o'clock position.
3. Apply sealant Loctite 573, or equivalent, to forward edge of front bearing cap, ensure sealant does not enter oil journal.
4. Install bearing caps in appropriate positions, **Figs. 16 and 17,** and tighten to specifications, starting in center and moving outward in a spiral direction.
5. Coat lip of camshaft seal with engine oil and tap into place using camshaft front seal installer tool No. J-35268-A, or equivalent, ensure seal is fully seated.
6. Install camshaft gear with new bolts and camshaft locking tool, tighten to specifications.
7. Install and adjust timing belt as outlined under "Timing Belt, Replace."
8. Install valve cover as outlined under "Valve Cover, Replace."
9. Install upper and lower intake manifold as outlined under " Intake Manifold, Replace."
10. Install air cleaner assembly.

PISTON & ROD ASSEMBLY

Ensure arrow on piston head faces towards front of engine and bump on connecting rod face towards rear of engine.

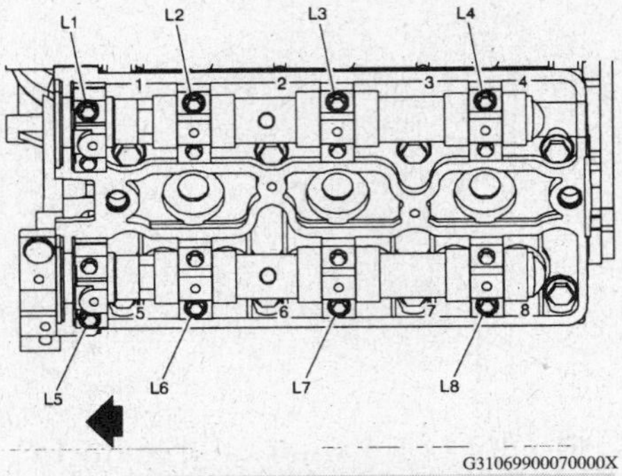

Fig. 16 Rear cylinder head bearing cap locations

PISTONS, PINS & RINGS

1. If cylinders have been honed, a proper size piston must be selected for each bore. Measure cylinder bore after honing and select piston size from corresponding chart, **Fig. 18.**
2. If piston must be separated from connecting rod, note the following:
   a. Using piston pin clip remover/installer tool No. J-43654, or equivalent, remove and install piston pin clips.
   b. Using piston pin remover/installer tool No. SA9101E, or equivalent, remove or install piston from connecting rod.
   c. When assembling piston and rod ensure arrow on top of piston and bump on connecting rod face in opposite directions. Arrow on piston will face front of engine block, bump on connecting rod will face rear of engine block.
3. Use suitable micrometers to measure piston pin bore to piston pin clearance; maximum clearance is .0001–.0003 inch. If clearance is excessive, replace piston and piston pin.
4. After cylinders have been honed, measure piston ring end gap clearances as follows:
   a. Install 1st. and 2nd. compression rings in cylinder bore. Gap should be .0118–.0196 inch.
   b. Install oil control ring in cylinder bore. Gap should be .0157–.0551 inch.
   c. Replace rings if end gap clearance is excessive.
5. Inspect piston ring groove clearance noting the following:
   a. 1st and 2nd compression ring groove clearance should be .0008–.0015 inch.
   b. Oil control ring groove clearance should be .0004–.0012 inch.
   c. Replace piston if ring groove clearance is excessive.
6. When installing rings on piston position as shown, **Fig. 19.**

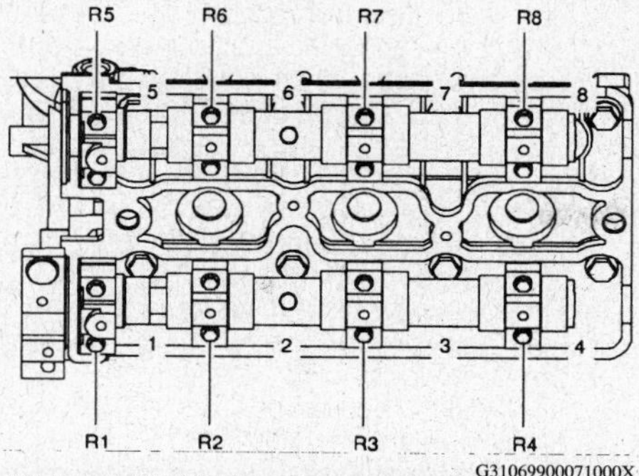

Fig. 17 Front cylinder head bearing cap locations

CYLINDER BORE	PISTON SIZE
(8) 85.976 - 85.985 mm (3.3848 - 3.3852 inch)	(8) 85.940 - 85.950 mm (3.3834 - 3.3838 inch)
(99) 85.985 - 85.995 mm (3.3852 - 3.3856 inch)	(99) 85.950 - 85.960 mm (3.3838 - 3.3842 inch)
(00) 85.995 - 86.005 mm (3.3856 - 3.3860 inch)	(00) 85.960 - 85.970 mm (3.3842 - 3.3846 inch)
(01) 86.005 - 86.015 mm (3.3860 - 3.3864 inch)	(01) 85.970 - 85.980 mm (3.3846 - 3.3850 inch)
(02) 86.015 - 86.025 mm (3.3864 - 3.3868 inch)	(02) 85.980 - 85.990 mm (3.3850 - 3.3854 inch)
† (7 + 0.5) 86.465 - 86.475 mm (3.4041 - 3.4045 inch)	† (7 + 0.5) 86.430 - 86.440 mm (3.4027 - 3.4031 inch)

GC1069700845000X

Fig. 18 Piston selection chart

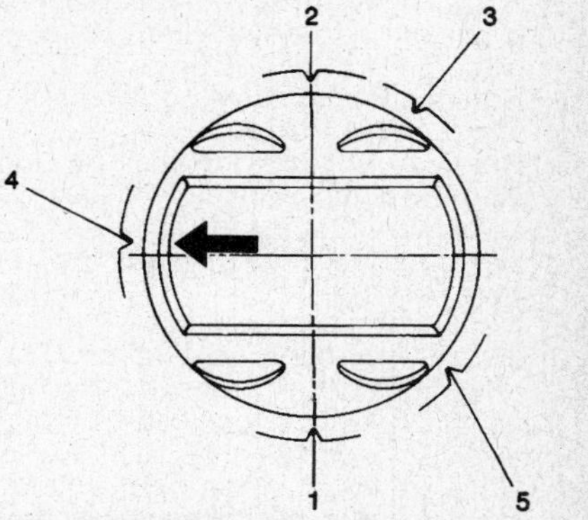

(1) 1st Compression Ring End Gap Location
(2) 2nd Compression Ring End Gap Location
(3) Oil Control Ring Upper Ring End Gap Location
(4) Oil Control Ring Spacer End Gap Location
(5) Oil Control Ring Lower Ring End Gap Location

GC1069700848000X

Fig. 19 Piston ring orientation

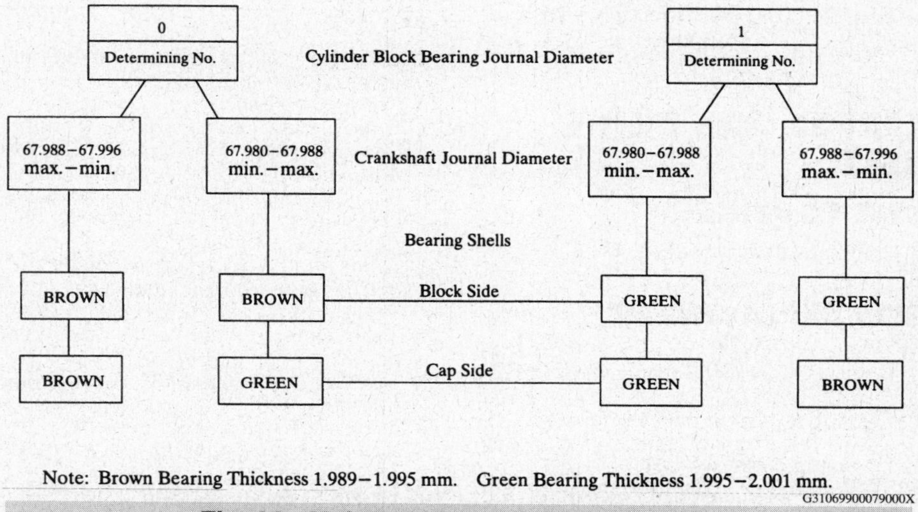

Fig. 20 Main bearing selective fits chart

MAIN & ROD BEARINGS

The crankshaft main bearing caps are numbered 1, 2 and 3 from the front of the engine. The rear bearing cap is not numbered and contains the thrust bearings. The No. 2 and 3 bearing shells do not have oil grooves on the cap sides.

There is a "0" or "1" stamped on the cylinder block oil pan mating flange near the end of each main bearing cap. This is the "Determining No. " The "Determining No." corresponds to each crankshaft main bearing size and color that will be installed. The main journal diameter for a determining No. of "0" is 2.8368–2.8371 inches (72.0000–72.0065 mm). The main journal diameter for a determining No. of "1" is 2.8371–2.8373 inches (72.0065–72.0130 mm). To select the correct main bearing, measure crankshaft main bearing journal diameter, then refer to main bearing selective fits chart shown in **Fig. 20.**

CRANKSHAFT REAR OIL SEAL

REPLACE

1. Remove transaxle as outlined under "Automatic Transaxles. "
2. Counterhold crankshaft with crank hub torx socket tool No. J-42098, or equivalent, then remove flexplate from crankshaft.
3. Center punch steel ring in rear oil seal, then drill small, shallow pilot hole in steel ring.
4. Screw self tapping screw into steel ring, then remove rear oil seal using suitable pliers.
5. Reverse procedure to install, noting the following:
   a. Coat lip of rear oil seal with clean engine oil.
   b. Use rear main oil seal installer tool No. J-42067, or equivalent, to install rear oil seal.
   c. Using torque angle meter tool No. SA9140E, or equivalent, tighten flexplate to specifications.

OIL PAN

REPLACE

1. Remove nose cone bracket bolts from oil pan.
2. Remove lower transaxle flange to oil pan bolts.
3. Remove oil pan using RTV cutter tool No. SA9123E, or equivalent to break pan loose from engine block.
4. Reverse procedure to install using Loctite 5900, or equivalent, 3 mm from inside edge of oil pan. If repair is being performed out of vehicle note the following:
   a. Attach transaxle nose cone bracket to engine to use as a guide for fore and aft alignment.
   b. Use transaxle to engine block or straight edge if transaxle is removed as right and left alignment.
   c. To align fore and aft, install nose cone to oil pan bolts and finger tighten.
   d. To align fore and aft, install transaxle to oil pan bolts or straight edge if transaxle is removed then finger tighten.
   e. Install oil pan bolts using Loctite 242 or equivalent and tighten to specifications.

OIL PUMP

REPLACE

1. Drain coolant.
2. Remove air cleaner assembly.

3. Remove timing belt front and rear covers as outlined under "Front Cover, Replace."
4. Remove timing belt as outlined under "Timing Belt, Replace."
5. Remove A/C compressor and power steering pump then position aside.
6. Pivot alternator aside.
7. Remove oil pan as outlined under "Oil Pan, Replace."
8. Install crank hub holding tool No. J-42065 or equivalent to crankshaft drive gear, then remove drive gear using crank hub torx socket tool No. J-42098 or equivalent.
9. Remove three oil pan housing bolts from oil pump, then remove oil pump.
10. Remove front main oil seal and collar from oil pump.
11. Reverse procedure to install, noting the following:
    a. Use anaerobic sealant Loctite 518 or equivalent to coat pump side of new oil pump gasket.
    b. Install oil pump and align using guide pins. Apply thread sealant Loctite 242 or equivalent to bolts and tighten to specifications.
    c. Coat lip of front main oil seal with clean engine oil, then install using front main seal installer tool No. J-35268-A or equivalent. Ensure seal is seated fully and evenly.
    d. Install new crankshaft drive gear bolt and tighten to specifications.
    e. Tighten A/C compressor, power steering pump and alternator to specifications.
    f. Retighten oil pump to specifications after alternator and drive belt idler pulley for camshafts number 3 and number 4 have been tightened to specifications.
    g. Fill and bleed cooling system as required.

BELT TENSION DATA

1. Allow engine to run for approximately ten minutes with all accessories turned on to ensure engine is warmed up.
2. Rotate tensioner arm clockwise until belt becomes loose, then slowly apply tension back on belt.
3. Marking on tensioner arm must fall within two marks on tensioner body. Replace drive belt if tensioner marks fall outside operating range.
4. Using a calibrated belt tension gauge tool No.SA9181 NE, or equivalent record belt tension at midspan. This check can be performed with engine removed if engine is in vehicle upper engine mount must be removed.
5. Repeat previous steps three times.
6. To determine belt tension, add three recordings together and divide total by three.
7. New belt tension should be 50–65 lbs. Used belt should be at least 45 lbs.

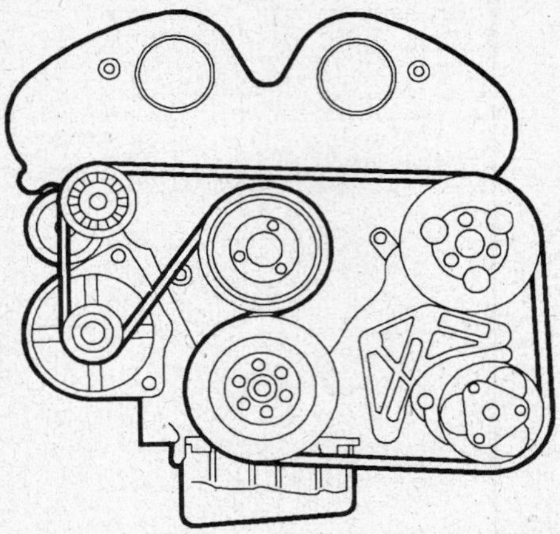

Fig. 21 Serpentine drive belt routing

SERPENTINE DRIVE BELT

BELT ROUTING

Route belt as shown, **Fig. 21.**

BELT REPLACEMENT

1. Remove right front engine mount as outlined under "Engine Mount, Replace."
2. Rotate tensioner pulley clockwise then slide drive belt off tensioner or water pump and remove belt.
3. Reverse procedure to install.

COOLING SYSTEM BLEED

Run engine until thermostat opens, then cycle engine speed from idle to 3000 RPM in 30 second intervals. Add coolant as required to bring level to cold line on reservoir after engine has cooled.

THERMOSTAT

REPLACE

1. Remove thermostat housing extension bolt.
2. Remove thermostat housing extension by pulling it out from thermostat housing.
3. Remove thermostat housing and thermostat.
4. Reverse procedure to install.

WATER PUMP

REPLACE

1. Remove air cleaner inlet duct from throttle body.
2. Remove left front wheel and splash shield.
3. Loosen but do not remove water pump and power steering pump pulley bolts.
4. Remove accessory drive belt as outlined under "Serpentine Drive Belt."
5. Remove water pump and power steering pump pulleys, then drive belt tensioner.
6. Remove front timing belt cover as outlined under " Front Cover, Replace."
7. Remove water pump and O-ring.
8. Reverse procedure to install, noting the following:
    a. Tighten accessory drive belt tensioner to specifications.
    b. Tighten power steering pump and water pump pulleys to specifications after installing drive belt.

RADIATOR

REPLACE

1. Slide fan control module up and off bracket, then position aside.
2. Remove battery.
3. Drain coolant into suitable container.
4. Remove power steering fluid reservoir and position to rear of vehicle.
5. Disconnect both cooling fans and auxiliary water pump, then remove harnesses from fan shroud.
6. Remove upper transaxle cooler line, then unsnap front end tank retainer.
7. Remove upper radiator hose and auxiliary water pump outlet and inlet hoses.
8. Remove fan shroud and forward wiring harness,
9. Remove lower radiator hose, then the lower transaxle cooler line from radiator.
10. Remove upper radiator bracket and mounts, then the radiator hose.
11. Support condenser from upper rail, then remove condenser block bolt from radiator end tank.
12. Remove condenser bolts, then pull condenser and pusher fan assembly down to disengage tabs from radiator.
13. Remove radiator leaving condenser and pusher fan in vehicle, then remove upper and lower radiator to condenser gaskets.
14. Reverse procedure to install, noting the following:
    a. Tighten to specifications.
    b. Fill cooling system as required.

FUEL PUMP

REPLACE

1. Relieve fuel system pressure as outlined under " Precautions."
2. Drain fuel from tank using suitable hand operated pump.
3. Remove exhaust system intermediate pipe with muffler and heat shield.
4. Remove fuel filler pipe lower bracket and disengage filler pipe hose from tank.
5. Disconnect EVAP canister vent hose and quick connect at recirc line.

6. Remove fuel tank grounding strap.
7. Disconnect fuel feed line after fuel filter, then the fuel return and EVAP canister purge lines between tank and chassis fuel bundle.
8. Disconnect electrical connections on fuel tank.
9. With fuel tank supported remove rear tank retaining strap bolts, then the fuel tank.
10. Remove fuel lines from fuel pump module cover.
11. Using a suitable ½ inch breaker bar and lock ring service too No. J-43827, or equivalent remove fuel pump module retaining ring.
12. Disengage fuel pump housing clips, then remove fuel pump from fuel tank.
13. Using fuel clamp pliers tool No. J-44078 or equivalent, remove fuel feed line from bottom of fuel pump, then disconnect fuel pump connector from fuel pump cover.
14. Reverse procedure to install, noting the following:
    a. Install new fuel pump to fuel tank seal.
    b. Using lock ring service tool, install pump cover lock ring with bumps facing away from tank.
    c. Install new retainers into female portion of quick connect fitting on fuel and EVAP canister purge lines.
    d. Tighten fuel tank straps to specification.

FUEL FILTER

REPLACE

1. Relieve fuel system pressure as outlined under " Precautions."
2. Disconnect fuel feed lines, then remove fuel filter.
3. Reverse procedure to install, noting the following:
    a. Install new fuel line retainers into female portion of fuel line fittings.
    b. Tighten fuel filter bracket to specifications.

TIGHTENING SPECIFICATIONS

Year	Component	Torque/Ft. Lbs.
2000	A/C Compressor Bracket Bolt	30
	A/C Compressor Hose Support Strap Bolt	71⑤
	Accelerator Pedal Bracket	89⑤
	Accelerator Pedal Position Sensor	53⑤
	Accessory Bracket, A/C and P/S, Bolt	30
	Accessory Drive Belt Tensioner Bolt	30
	Alternator	30
	Battery Hold Down Bracket	15
	Battery Terminal	13
	Battery Tray Fasteners	11
	Bell Housing Bolts	48
	Belt Tensioner	30
	Camshaft Bearing Cap Bolt	71⑤
	Camshaft Cover Bolt	71⑤
	Camshaft Gear Bolt	37①
	Camshaft Position Sensor	71⑤
	Catalytic Converter Bolt	15
	Catalytic Converter Hanger Bolt	15
	Connecting Rod Cap	26②
	Coolant Bridge Bolt	22
	Crankshaft Balancer Bolt	15
	Crankshaft Main Bearing Cap Bolt	37①
	Crankshaft Torsional Bearing Bridge Bolt	15
	Crankshaft Drive Gear Bolt	184②
	Crankshaft Position Sensor	71⑤
	Crankshaft Reluctor Ring Screw	11
	Crankshaft Sensor Bolt	71⑤
	Cylinder Head Bolt	④
	Drive Belt Tensioner	30
	Engine Control Module	71⑤
	Engine Coolant Temperature Sensor	13
	Engine Mount Bolt	41
	Engine Mount Bracket	41
	Engine Oil Cooler Cover Bolt	22
	Engine Oil Cooler Inlet and Outlet Nut	15
	Engine Rear Cover Bolt	71⑤
	Engine Rear Cover Threaded Pin	89⑤
	Engine Ventilation Chamber Bolt	71⑤

Continued

TIGHTENING SPECIFICATIONS—Continued

Year	Component	Torque/Ft. Lbs.
2000	Exhaust Gas Recirculation Pipe	19
	Exhaust Gas Recirculation Valve	15
	Exhaust Manifold Nut	15
	flexplate Bolt	65
	Front Timing Belt Cover Bolt	48(3)
	Fuel Fill Neck To Fuel Tank Clamp	71(5)
	Fuel Fill Pipe To Body (Lower)	114(5)
	Fuel Fill Pipe To Body (Upper)	35(5)
	Fuel Filter Bracket Bolt	35(5)
	Fuel Line Stone Chip Guard	106(5)
	Fuel Rail Bolt	71(5)
	Fuel Tank Mounting Strap	15
	Fuel Tank Pressure Sensor Nut	18(5)
	Heated Oxygen Sensor 1-Bank Nos. 1 & 2	37
	Heated Oxygen Sensor 2-Bank Nos. 1 & 2	37
	Ignition Coil Bolt	71(5)
	Ignition Module Bolt	71(5)
	Intake Manifold Bolt	15
	Intake Manifold Spacer Bolt	15
	Intake Plenum Bolt	71(5)
	Intake Plenum Switchover Valve	71(5)
	Intake Runner Bolt	71(5)
	Knock Sensors	15
	Main Bearing Cap	37(1)
	Manifold Absolute Pressure Sensor	44(5)
	Negative Battery Cable To Chassis	114(5)
	Oil Cooler Inlet & Outlet Bolt	15
	Oil Filter Cap	19
	Oil Filter Cartridge Housing Drain Plug	89(5)
	Oil Filter Cartridge Housing To Engine Block	33
	Oil Intake Pipe Bolt	71(5)
	Oil Pan Baffle Bolt	71(5)
	Oil Pan Bolt	11
	Oil Pan Drain Plug	19
	Oil Pressure Switch	30
	Oil Pump Bolt	80(5)
	Oxygen Sensors (Exhaust Manifold)	37
	Oxygen Sensors (Lower Exhaust Pipe)	33
	Power Steering Pump Pulley Bolt	15
	Rear Timing Belt Cover Threaded Pin	89(5)
	Rear Timing Cover Bolt	71(5)
	Resonance Chamber Nut	27(5)
	Spark Plug	19
	Starter Assembly	30
	Thermostat Housing Bolt	15
	Throttle Boot Nut (Throttle Position Sensor)	71(5)
	Timing Belt Idler Pulley Bolt	30
	Timing Belt Tensioner Bracket Bolt	30
	Timing Belt Tensioner Fastening Nut	15

Continued

TIGHTENING SPECIFICATIONS—Continued

Year	Component	Torque/Ft. Lbs.
2000	Torque Convertor Bolt	48
	Transaxle Cooler Line (Lower)	36⑤
	Transaxle Cooler Line (Upper)	18
	Transaxle Range Switch Bolts	18
	Tranaxle Range Switch Lever Nut	26
	Water Pump Bolt	19
	Water Pump Pulley Bolt	71⑤
	Wheel Bolt	92
	Wiring Channel Bolt	71⑤

① — Tighten an additional 60,° then an additional 15.°
② — Tighten an additional 45,° then an additional 15.°
③ — Tighten an additional 30,° then an additional 15.°
④ — Refer to "Cylinder Head, Replace" for tighten procedure & specifications.
⑤ — Inch lbs.

Clutch & Manual Transaxle

NOTE: Prior to Performing Any Service Operations Listed In This Section, Consult The "Technical Service Bulletins" Section For Related Information.

INDEX

PRECAUTIONS

AIR BAG SYSTEMS

Refer to "Air Bag System Precautions" in the front of this manual for system disarming and arming procedures.

BATTERY GROUND CABLE

Prior to service, disconnect battery ground cable and isolate as required.

ADJUSTMENTS

CLUTCH PEDAL HEIGHT

The hydraulic clutch system provides automatic clutch adjustment; therefore, there is no adjustment provision. The clutch pedal height can be measured, **Fig. 1,** 4.6–5.4 inches should be indicated. If not, check carpet or floor mat under pedal, a faulty bushing or damaged pedal may be indicated.

HYDRAULIC SYSTEM SERVICE

HYDRAULIC CLUTCH SYSTEM BLEED

1.9L ENGINE

The hydraulic system is serviced as a unit; it has been filled with fluid and bled of air. If the system requires any fluid, check the hydraulic components for leakage. Remove the slave cylinder from the clutch housing and check for leakage at the piston, a slightly wet surface is normal, if excessive, replace system.

Use only DOT 3 brake fluid. **Do not use mineral oil or a paraffin base oil in the hydraulic system as damage to rubber parts will occur.** Clean the cap and sides of reservoir before removing cap, then remove diaphragm. Replace diaphragm and cover after filling.

2.2L ENGINE

Manual Bleed

Use only DOT 3 brake fluid. **Do not use mineral oil or a paraffin base oil in the hydraulic system as damage to rubber parts will occur.**

1. Fill brake fluid reservoir with clean brake fluid.
2. Attach transparent hose over clutch bleeder screw nipple. Submerge other end of hose in a container of brake fluid.
3. Depress and hold down clutch pedal, then loosen clutch bleeder screw on transaxle hydraulic fitting.
4. Allow brake fluid to drain from bleeder screw, then tighten bleeder screw and raise clutch.
5. Repeat steps 3 and 4 until no air bubbles are seen in hose.
6. Check clutch pedal feel for sponginess. If clutch pedal exhibits this feel, repeat bleeding procedure until condition is gone.

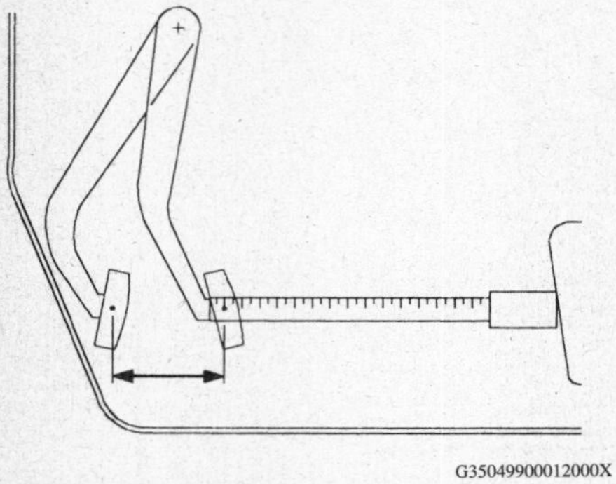

Fig. 1 Clutch pedal height

7. Check fluid level in brake fluid reservoir, add fluid as required.

Pressure Bleed

Use only DOT 3 brake fluid. **Do not use mineral oil or a paraffin base oil in the hydraulic system as damage to rubber parts will occur.**

1. Fill brake fluid reservoir with clean brake fluid.
2. Install bleeder adapter tool No. J-43915 or equivalent to brake fluid reservoir.
3. Connect pressure bleeder to adapter, then charge equipment to 20–25 psi.
4. Attach transparent hose over clutch bleeder screw nipple. Submerge other end of hose in a container of brake fluid.
5. Loosen clutch bleeder screw on transaxle hydraulic fitting, then bleed system until no bubbles are seen in hose.
6. Tighten clutch bleeder screw, check clutch pedal feel for sponginess. If clutch pedal is spongy, repeat bleeding procedure.
7. Remove pressure bleeder equipment, then check fluid level in brake fluid reservoir and add fluid as required.

SLAVE CYLINDER BLEED

2.2L Engine

1. Connect a 18 inch long piece of transparent hose to slave cylinder fitting on transaxle.
2. Depress release bearing on slave cylinder towards clutch housing and release it. Even though release bearing will spring back, slave cylinder piston will remain depressed.
3. Fill hose with 14 inches of DOT 3 brake fluid.
4. Connect vacuum pump SA9180NE with pressure adapter J-35555-92 or equivalents to top of hose.
5. Apply pressure to force brake fluid into slave cylinder, pressure gauge will increase when piston reaches end of travel.
6. Remove vacuum/pressure pump from hose, then depress release bearing. Air bubble will appear in hose.
7. Repeat steps until no air bubbles appear in hose.
8. Leave slave cylinder piston depressed. Drain and remove hose.

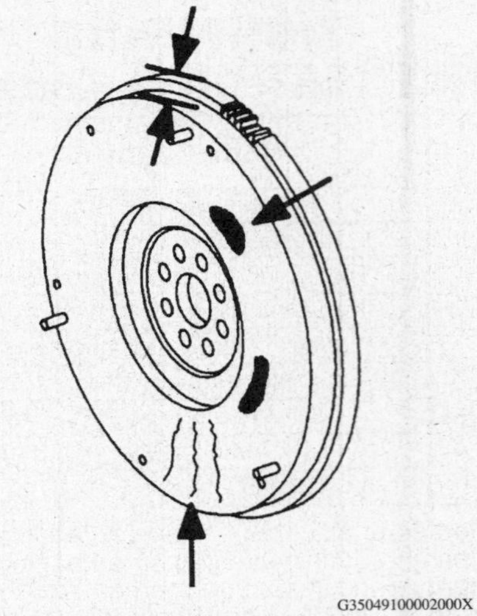

Fig. 2 Pressure plate warpage inspection

CLUTCH HYDRAULIC SYSTEM, REPLACE

1.9L Engine

The clutch hydraulic system must be serviced as a unit; individual components, with the exception of the slave cylinder actuator pushrod retaining strap, cannot be replaced.

1. Block clutch pedal.
2. Remove air induction tube.
3. Remove battery and battery tray if necessary.
4. Rotate actuator 1/4 turn counterclockwise while pushing toward housing to disengage, then remove actuator from clutch housing. **Removal of hydraulic damper prior to actuator removal will result in a broken hydraulic line.**
5. Remove hydraulic damper to clutch housing attaching nuts, then slide damper and bracket assembly from studs.
6. Remove clutch pedal pin to slave cylinder pushrod attaching clip, then disconnect pushrod from pedal.
7. **On models equipped with ABS,** remove brake master cylinder attaching nuts and move cylinder off studs. Ensure brake lines are not damaged during removal.
8. **On all models,** turn slave cylinder about 1/8 turn clockwise, then remove.
9. Reverse procedure to install.

CLUTCH MASTER CYLINDER, REPLACE

2.2L Engine

1. Remove brake fluid reservoir cap, then enough brake fluid to clear passage to clutch cylinder.
2. Disconnect clutch hydraulic line assembly from body retaining clips.
3. Remove clutch hydraulic line assembly from master cylinder and lay aside.
4. Remove left lower I/P close out panel, then master cylinder push rod from clutch pedal.

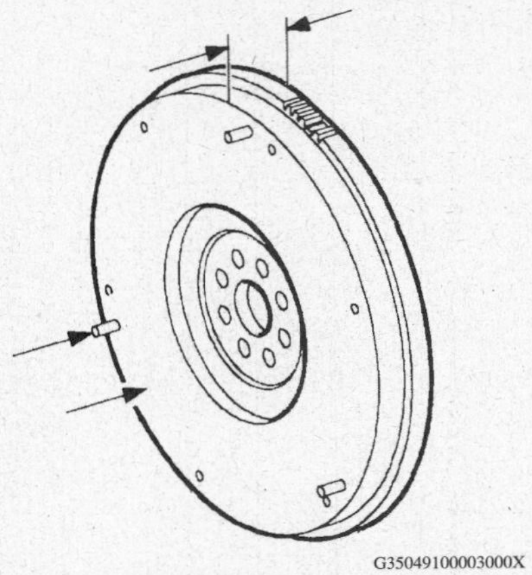

Fig. 3 Flywheel thickness measurement

5. Remove master cylinder retaining nuts, then the master cylinder.
6. Reverse procedure to install, bleed clutch hydraulic system as required. Refer to "Hydraulic Clutch System Bleed", in this section

CLUTCH SLAVE CYLINDER, REPLACE

2.2L Engine

1. Remove transaxle as outlined under "Transaxle Replace."
2. Remove hydraulic line from slave cylinder.
3. Remove slave cylinder bolts, then the slave cylinder.
4. Reverse procedure to install. Use sealant Loctite 592 (P/N21485278) or equivalent on slave cylinder bolts.

CLUTCH

REPLACE

REMOVAL

1. Remove transaxle as outlined under "Transaxle, Replace."
2. Remove unsnap release fork and bearing from ball stud to remove.
3. Slide release bearing from release fork, then check release bearing for excessive play or minimal drag, replace as required. **Do not wash bearing in solvent.**
4. Using a feeler gauge, measure between pressure plate and flywheel; .205–.287 inch should be indicated. If not, replace clutch disc.
5. Remove pressure plate to flywheel attaching bolts in progressive crisscross pattern.
6. Remove pressure plate and clutch disc.

INSPECTION

1. Inspect pressure plate for excessive wear, chatter marks, cracks or overheating, replace as required. **Random black spotting on friction surface is normal.**
2. Using a straightedge and feeler gauge, measure pressure plate warpage, **Fig. 2.** Maximum warpage is .006 inch.

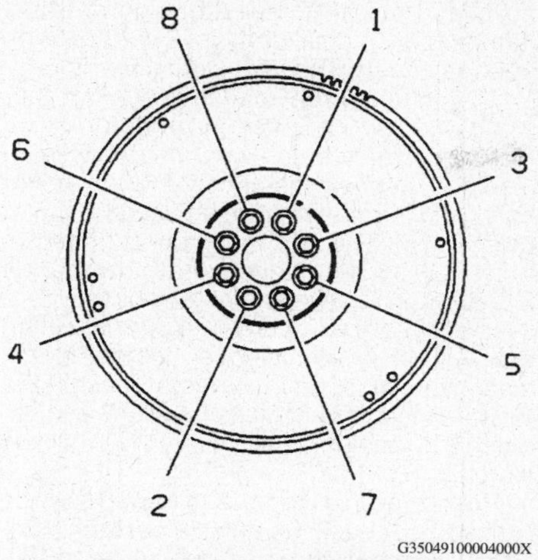

Fig. 4 Flywheel tightening sequence

3. Inspect clutch disc for oil, burn marks and loose damper springs, hub or rivets; replace as required.
4. Inspect flywheel ring gear for wear or damage; replace as required.
5. Measure flywheel thickness, **Fig. 3.** If flywheel is not at least 1.102 inches thick, replace it.
6. Using a dial indicator, measure flywheel runout while pushing crankshaft forward to take up thrust bearing clearance. Maximum runout is .006 inch; replace as required.
7. Remove flywheel to crankshaft attaching bolts, then flywheel.

INSTALLATION

1. Install flywheel to crankshaft attaching bolts, then tighten in sequence, **Fig. 4,** to specifications.
2. Install clutch disc and pressure plate, with pressure plate yellow dot aligned with flywheel mark, then start pressure plate to flywheel bolts.
3. Insert clutch disc alignment tool No. SA9145T, or equivalent, into center hole until it bottoms out in crankshaft.
4. Tighten pressure plate bolts to specifications in crisscross pattern.
5. Remove clutch alignment tool, then install fork clip.
6. Lubricate fork pivot using high temperature grease part No. 21005995, or equivalent, then install release bearing to fork. **Do not lubricate release bearing or quill.**
7. Install release fork and bearing to ball stud.
8. Lubricate input shaft splines, then install transaxle assembly as described under "Transaxle, Replace."

TRANSAXLE

REPLACE

1.9L ENGINE

1. Disconnect battery cables, then raise and support vehicle and remove air induction system.
2. Remove battery hold-down, battery and tray.
3. Remove transaxle strut to midrail bracket and cradle bracket attaching bolts, then loosen transaxle strut to transaxle bracket attaching bolt and position strut aside.
4. Disconnect the following electrical connectors:
   a. Back-up light switch.
   b. Vehicle speed sensor.
   c. Remove and discard vent tube clip.
   d. Two upper clutch housing ground terminals.
   e. Oxygen sensor from clutch housing.
5. Remove upper clutch housing engine bolts.
6. Remove DIS coil attaching screws, then the coil.
7. Remove shift cables from shift arms and clutch housing, **Fig. 5.**
8. Turn clutch slave cylinder ¼ counterclockwise while pushing into clutch housing, then remove cylinder.
9. Remove clutch hydraulic dampener attaching bolts.
10. Using suitable wire, support hydraulic dampener from upper radiator hose.
11. Secure radiator to upper support with mechanics wire.
12. Install engine lifting equipment.
13. Raise and support vehicle, then drain transaxle fluid.
14. Remove front wheels, then right, left and front splash shields.
15. Remove engine mount to cradle attaching nuts.
16. Remove engine strut cradle bracket to cradle fasteners.
17. Remove transaxle to cradle mount.
18. Remove front exhaust pipe.
19. Remove steering gear to cradle attaching bolts and support steering gear with suitable wire.
20. Remove brake line bracket push pin at rear of cradle.
21. Remove engine to transaxle stiffening bracket.
22. Remove clutch housing dust cover.
23. Remove and discard lower ball joint cotter pins, then loosen nut to top of bolt thread.
24. Using ball joint separator tool No. SA9132S, or equivalent, separate ball joint from lower control arm. **Outer CV joint has an ABS speed sensor ring. Failure to use the proper tool will result in loss of ABS or system damage.**
25. Using suitable large screwdriver or pry bar, separate left side axle from transaxle, pull axle slightly rearward and install axle seal protector tool No. SA91112T, or equivalent.
26. Separate right axle from intermediate shaft.
27. **On models equipped with DOHC engine,** remove intake support bracket.
28. **On all models,** remove intake to intermediate shaft support bracket.
29. Remove intermediate shaft to engine block bolts.
30. Slide intermediate shaft from transaxle.
31. Position a suitable powertrain support dolly and two 4 x 4 x 36 inch wood pieces to support cradle.

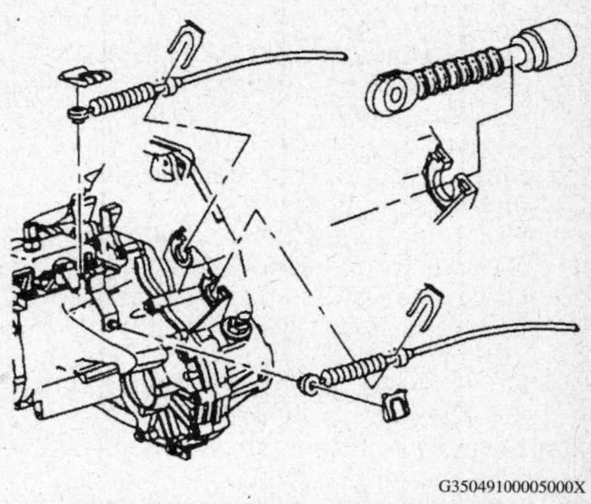

Fig. 5 Shift cable removal

32. Remove cradle to body attaching bolts, then lower cradle, ensure two large rear cradle spacers are attached.
33. Support transaxle with a suitable jack.
34. Remove remaining transaxle to engine bolts and install guide bolt to bottom rear clutch housing bolt hole.
35. Using a screwdriver or pry bar, separate left axle from transaxle. **Do not allow tool to contact or damage axle seal.**
36. Separate transaxle from engine enough to clear intermediate shaft, then lower transaxle to remove.
37. Reverse procedure to install.

2.2L ENGINE

1. Raise and support vehicle, then remove battery.
2. Disconnect battery feed, then coolant hose from underhood fuse block.
3. Release tabs and remove underhood fuse block cover.
4. Release tabs on underhood fuse block, then roll fuse block back to access electrical connectors.
5. Disconnect all connector from fuse block, then lift fuse block off case.
6. Remove harnesses from underhood fuse block case, then case fasteners and case from battery tray.
7. Remove battery tray fasteners, then battery tray.
8. Loosen pinch bolt securing control assembly rod to control shaft lever assembly. **Control shaft lever retaining pin has a spring loaded locking feature securing pin in place. If this spring is not depressed before attempting to remove pin, damage to pin will occur.**
9. Remove pin retaining control shaft lever to shift control shaft of transaxle.
10. Remove retaining clips holding control shaft lever assembly to transaxle and frame assembly bracket.
11. Remove control shaft lever assembly by pulling straight up off pivot pins.
12. Disconnect electrical connector from back up lamp switch, then remove wire harness from transaxle.
13. If hole on top of transaxle has a spring loaded locking pin, remove pin and discard. A new hole will be installed. If hole has a hole plug, remove it and retain for reuse.
14. Remove clutch hydraulic fitting from

transaxle, elevate and secure fitting to prevent excessive loss of brake fluid.
15. Remove upper transaxle to engine mounting bolts, then install engine support fixture to engine.
16. Mark position, then remove left transaxle mount bolts.
17. Remove rear transaxle mount through bolt, the transaxle to frame bolt.
18. Secure radiator to upper support using tie straps, then raise and support vehicle.
19. Remove left front wheel, then the right front lower splash shield.
20. Remove left front wheel liner push pin from frame.
21. Disconnect electrical connector from rear O2 sensor, then remove harness from frame.
22. Remove front transaxle mount through bolt, remaining rear transaxle mount to frame bolts.
23. Remove clip, then A/C line from front of frame.
24. Remove steering gear to frame bolts, then secure steering gear to body.
25. Remove stabilizer bar links from strut assemblies.
26. Remove lower ball stud bolt, then separate ball stud from steering knuckle.
27. Remove suspension support assemblies, then suspension support gage nuts from body. discard cage nuts and support bolts.
28. Support frame assembly using powertrain lifting table tool No. J-43628 or equivalent.
29. Remove four remaining frame to body attaching bolts .
30. Lower frame assembly from vehicle, discard all cage nuts and frame bolts.
31. Remove front transaxle mount, then rear transaxle mount from transaxle.
32. **To prevent damage to CV joint boots, never allow them to contact other parts during removal. Never pull on shaft assembly. When removing right hand axle shaft, transaxle stub shaft may come out of transaxle with axle shaft. When this occurs, inspect axle shaft seal in transaxle for damage and replace if required.**
33. Remove axle shafts from transaxle using a pry bar, leave axle shaft in steering knuckle and secure out of transaxle removal path.
34. Remove A/C line retaining clip and drop A/C line down from body.
35. Drain transaxle fluid into a suitable container, then lower vehicle.
36. Lower left side of powertrain with engine support fixture to allow transaxle to clear engine compartment rail.
37. Remove left transaxle mount bracket from transaxle, then raise vehicle.
38. Remove control shaft lever assembly pivot pin bracket from transaxle case.
39. Support transaxle with a suitable jack, then remove remaining engine to transaxle mounting bolts.
40. Separate transaxle from engine and lower transaxle from vehicle.
41. Reverse procedure to install, noting the following:
    a. Spring loaded locking pin on top of transaxle cannot be reused, install a shift lever hole plug instead.
    b. Bleed system as outlined under "Hydraulic Clutch System Bleed."
    c. Fill transaxle with two quarts of manual transaxle fluid (P/N21018899) or equivalent.

TECHNICAL SERVICE BULLETINS

KNOCKING OR RATTLE NOISE FROM FRONT OF VEHICLE DURING DECELERATION

1997–98

On models built before and including VIN WZ305219 equipped with MP2 or MP3 manual transaxles may experience a knocking or rattle type noise coming from the manual transaxle during moderate to heavy deceleration in any gear. This condition is most noticeable when lifting off of the throttle and decelerating from 4000 RPM and lower.

The gear rattle is caused by insufficient dampening of engine pulsations by the clutch dampening springs. These pulsations allow the unloaded transaxle drive gears to knock against the driven gears. This knocking creates an audible gear rattle.

To address this concern, a long travel damper clutch disc, part No. 21120564 has been released. The new clutch disc is larger than the current clutch disc part No. 21120453, or equivalent. In order to allow clearance for a long travel damper clutch disc, the inner diameter of the clutch cover has been increased and the inside edge of the current flywheel must be chamfered. The new clutch cover part number is 21120582. When servicing a vehicle where it is necessary to replace the current clutch disc with a new long travel damper clutch disc, it is also necessary to machine a chamfer into the current flywheel and replace the original clutch cover with a new clutch cover.

Prior to performing the following service procedure, check the vehicle service history to determine whether the flywheel has already been resurfaced. Due to clearance issues, a resurfaced flywheel and latest design disc are not compatible. The minimum flywheel thickness is 1.11 inches. Using a micrometer, measure flywheel thickness in three places around the circumference of the flywheel. All measurements must be made at the same distance in from the edge of the flywheel and at equal distances from each other. If the flywheel has been resurfaced previously or is less than 1.11 inches in thickness and the clutch disc is being replaced with the long travel damper disc part No. 21120564, or equivalent, it is necessary to replace the flywheel with chamfered flywheel part No. 21120535, or equivalent.

1. Remove clutch cover, clutch disc and flywheel according to procedures outlined in this section.
2. Measure and mark flywheel in area to be machined. Measure 2.4–2.5 inches starting from outside edge of flat portion of flywheel moving towards inside edge of flywheel. The material to be removed is from inside edge of flywheel to measured mark. Total depth of cut should be .12–.16 inch.
3. Install flywheel on to lathe and machine flywheel with cutting tip at 30° angle to flywheel.
4. Install machined flywheel or new flywheel, new clutch disc and new clutch cover according to procedures outlined in this section.

TIGHTENING SPECIFICATIONS

Year	Component	Torque/Ft. Lbs.
1.9L ENGINE		
1997– 2000	Air Box	96⑥
	Clutch Fork Stabilizer	18
	Clutch Housing Dust Cover	84⑥
	Clutch Housing To Engine Bolt (Bottom)	103
	Clutch Housing To Engine Stud (Top)	74
	Clutch Hydraulic Damper Nuts	18

Continued

TIGHTENING SPECIFICATIONS—Continued

Year	Component	Torque/Ft. Lbs.
1.9L ENGINE		
1997-2000	Cradle Bracket To Cradle	52
	Cradle To Body	155
	Down Pipe To Converter	18
	Down Pipe To Exhaust Manifold	23
	Down Pipe To Stiffening Bracket	23
	Engine Strut To Cradle	37
	Flywheel	59
	Ground Terminals To Clutch Housing Studs (Top)	18
	Ignition Module	60⑥
	Intake Support Bracket	22
	Intermediate Shaft Support Bracket	40
	Lower Ball Joint	55
	Lower Transaxle Mount	52
	Pressure Plate	18
	Steering Gear To Cradle	②
	Strut Cradle Bracket To Cradle	52
	Transaxle Bracket To Transaxle	40
	Transaxle Drain Plug	22①
	Transaxle Mount To Case	24
	Transaxle Mount To Cradle	37
	Transaxle Stiffening Bracket	40
	Transaxle Strut To Cradle	52
	Transaxle Strut To Midrail Bracket	37
	Transaxle Strut To Transaxle Bracket	52
	Wheel Lug Nuts	103
2.2L ENGINE		
2000	Ball Stud To Steering Knuckle	75
	Back Up Lamp Switch To Transaxle	18
	Battery Cable Terminals	13
	Battery Hold Down Brackets	15
	Battery Tray	11
	Clutch Master Cylinder Nuts	15
	Clutch Pedal To Front Of Dash	15
	Clutch Pedal To I/P Beam	15
	Clutch Slave Cylinder Bolts	96⑥
	Exhaust Manifold Pipe To Exhaust Manifold Nuts	22
	Exhaust Manifold Pipe To Exhaust Pipe Bolts	15
	Flywheel To Crankshaft	39③
	Frame To Body	60④
	Pressure Plate To Flywheel	11
	Rear Cover To Transaxle	18
	Shift Linkage To Tranaxle	18
	Stabilizer Bar Link To Strut	50
	Steering Gear To Frame	35⑤
	Tie Rod End To Steering Knuckle	45
	Transaxle Case To Clutch Housing	18
	Transaxle Drain Plug	37
	Transaxle Front Mount Through Bolt	41
	Transaxle Mounts To Transaxle	41
	Transaxle Rear Mount Through Bolt	66

Continued

TIGHTENING SPECIFICATIONS—Continued

Year	Component	Torque/Ft. Lbs.
2.2L ENGINE		
2000	Transaxle Rear Mount To Frame	44
	Transaxle To Engine	48
	Underhood Fuse Block Case	84⑥
	Wheel Lug Nut	92

① — Drain plug seal replacement is not necessary.
② — 1997, 40 ft. lbs.; 1998–99, 37 ft. lbs.
③ — Tighten an additional 25.°
④ — Tighten an additional 45°– 60.°
⑤ — Tighten an additional 105.°
⑥ — Inch lbs.

Rear Axle & Suspension

NOTE: On Air Bag Equipped Models, Refer To " Air Bag System Precautions" Located In The Front Of This Manual For System Disarming & Arming Procedures.

NOTE: Prior To Performing Any Service Operations Listed In This Section, Consult The "Technical Service Bulletins " Section For Related Information.

INDEX

PRECAUTIONS

AIR BAG SYSTEMS

Refer to "Air Bag System Precautions" in the front of this manual for system disarming and arming procedures.

BATTERY GROUND CABLE

Prior to service, disconnect battery ground cable and isolate as required.

FASTENER REPLACEMENT

When servicing crossmember and struts, new fasteners should be used during assemble procedures.

HUB & BEARING

REPLACE

DISC BRAKES

1. Raise and support vehicle, then remove wheel assembly.
2. Disconnect ABS wheel speed sensor electrical connector.
3. Remove caliper to knuckle attaching bolts, then hang caliper with wire.
4. Remove brake rotor, then four hub to knuckle attaching bolts, remove hub.
5. Reverse procedure to install. Tighten hub to knuckle bolts, caliper bolts and wheel lug nuts to specifications.

DRUM BRAKES

1. Raise and support vehicle, then remove wheel assembly.
2. **On models equipped with ABS,** disconnect wheel speed sensor harness.
3. **On all models,** remove brake drum, then four hub to knuckle attaching bolts.
4. Remove hub assembly from vehicle.
5. Reverse procedure to install. Tighten hub to knuckle bolts and wheel lug nuts to specifications.

STRUT

REPLACE

S-SERIES

1. Remove rear window trim finish panel.
2. Raise and support vehicle, then remove wheel assembly.
3. Loosen but do not remove steering knuckle to strut attaching nuts.
4. Using a floor jack, support knuckle, then remove upper strut attaching nuts.
5. Disconnect ABS electrical harness from strut.
6. Remove strut to knuckle nuts, then strut.
7. Reverse procedure to install. Replace attaching nuts and tighten to specification.

L-SERIES

1. Raise and support vehicle, then remove wheel assembly.
2. Remove inner wheel liner, then remove shock to knuckle bolt and discard.
3. Remove upper carrier assembly to body bolts.
4. Loosen lower carrier assembly to body bolts until carrier assembly slides out.
5. Reverse procedure to install. Replace attaching bolts and tighten to

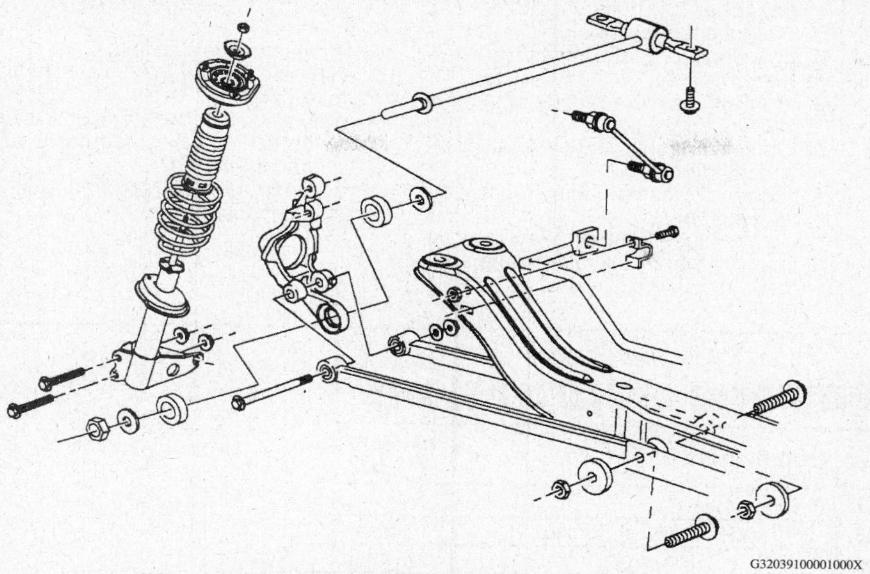

Fig. 1 Exploded view of rear suspension

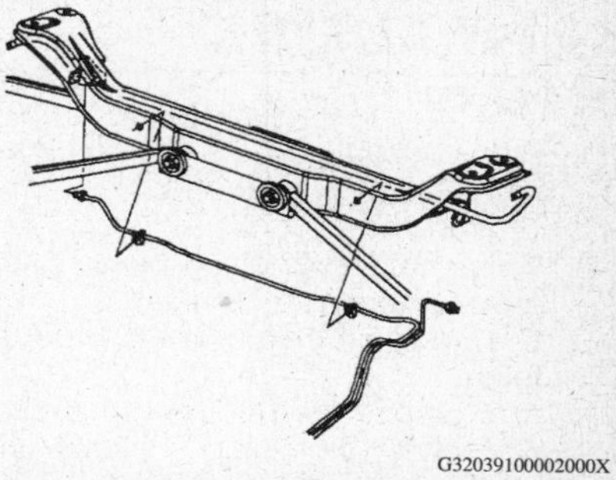

Fig. 2 Brake line removal

specifications.

STRUT SERVICE

1. Mount strut spring compressor tool No. SA9155S, or equivalent, in a suitable holding device, then position strut assembly in compressor.
2. Fasten strut to tool using one strut to knuckle bolt and nut in lower strut mounting hole, then compress spring until upper spring supports are completely unladen.
3. While holding strut shaft in position with a suitable Torx wrench, remove strut shaft nut.
4. Release spring compressor and tilt strut assembly outward, then remove upper spring support and spring from strut.
5. Remove dust shield, then strut from compressor tool.
6. Inspect strut assembly components as follows:
   a. Inspect rubber spring support and dust shield for cracks or deterioration; replace as necessary.
   b. Inspect spring for signs of damage.
   c. Extend and retract strut shaft; if movement is not smooth or resistance is not even, replace strut.
7. Reverse procedure to assemble, noting the following:
   a. Compress spring only enough to install upper washer and shaft nut. **Do not compress spring beyond this point.**
   b. Ensure spring is properly seated in spring supports.
   c. Tighten strut shaft nut to specifications.

KNUCKLE

REPLACE

DISC BRAKES

1. Raise and support vehicle, then remove wheel assembly.
2. Disconnect ABS wheel speed sensor electrical connector.
3. Remove caliper to knuckle attaching bolts. Suspend caliper with mechanics' wire, then remove rotor.
4. Remove hub to knuckle attaching bolts, then hub and backing plate.
5. Loosen but do not remove lateral link to knuckle attaching bolts.
6. Loosen but do not remove strut to knuckle attaching bolts.
7. Remove trailing arm to knuckle attaching nut, then arm to body bolts.
8. Remove lateral link to knuckle attaching nuts, then knuckle to strut bolts and knuckle.
9. Reverse procedure to install.

DRUM BRAKES

1. Raise and support vehicle.
2. Remove wheel assembly and brake drum.
3. Remove hub to knuckle attaching bolts, then hub.
4. Using wire, position brake assembly aside.
5. Loosen but do not remove lateral link and strut to knuckle attaching bolts.
6. Remove trailing arm to knuckle attaching nut, then arm to body bolts, then slide arm from knuckle.
7. Remove link and strut to knuckle attaching bolts, then link.
8. Reverse procedure to install.

TRAILING ARM

REPLACE

1. Raise and support vehicle.
2. Remove wheel assemblies.
3. Remove trailing arm to knuckle attaching nut, **Fig. 1.**
4. Remove trailing arm to body attaching bolts, then slide arm from knuckle.
5. Reverse procedure to install.

SUSPENSION SUPPORT

REPLACE

1. Raise and support vehicle, then remove wheel assemblies.
2. Remove rear exhaust system from resonator back, then heat shield from rear suspension support.
3. Remove upper, then lower control arm to rear axle control arm attaching bolts and discard bolts and nuts.
4. Remove both stabilizer bar links from rear axle control arms.
5. Support rear suspension with a suitable jack stand.
6. Remove four rear suspension support to body bolts, discard bolts.
7. Remove rear suspension support from vehicle.
8. Reverse procedure to install. Tighten new bolts and nuts to specifications.

STABILIZER BAR

REPLACE

S-SERIES

1. Raise and support vehicle, then remove wheel assembly.
2. Position drain container at left rear brake line, then disconnect and plug left brake line.
3. Remove right and left stabilizer bar link to knuckle attaching nuts, then bar to crossmember nuts.
4. Loosen but do not remove lateral link to knuckle attaching bolts, then remove trailing arm to knuckle and arm to body attaching nuts.
5. Slide trailing arm from knuckle, then remove lateral link bolt, swing link downward.
6. Disconnect brake lines from crossmember, **Fig. 2.**
7. Remove stabilizer bar.
8. Reverse procedure to install.

L-SERIES

1. Raise and support vehicle, then remove wheel assemblies.
2. Remove heat shield from rear suspension.
3. Remove left, then right rear stabilizer bar links to rear axle control arm bolts.
4. Remove stabilizer bar to rear suspension attaching bolts, then stabilizer bar from vehicle.
5. Reverse procedure to install. Tighten all bolts to specifications.

LATERAL LINK

REPLACE

1. Remove fuel tank as described under "Fuel Pump, Replace" in "1.9L Engine" section.
2. Raise and support vehicle, then remove wheel assembly.
3. If removing rear lateral link, proceed as follows:
   a. Remove lateral link to knuckle attaching bolt, then lateral link to crossmember bolts, **Fig. 1.**
   b. Remove lateral link.
4. If removing front lateral link, proceed as follows:
   a. Remove rear brake line attaching nut.
   b. Using a suitable jackstand, support crossmember.
   c. Remove crossmember to body attaching bolts.
   d. Lower crossmember, then remove inboard lateral link to crossmember bolt.
   e. Remove lateral link to knuckle attaching bolt.
   f. Remove lateral link.
5. Reverse procedure to install noting the following:
   a. Do not tighten lateral link attaching bolts until crossmember is aligned and tightened.
   b. Ensure wheel alignment is within specification.

TIGHTENING SPECIFICATIONS

Year	Component	Torque/Ft. Lbs.
S-SERIES		
1997– 2000	ABS Electrical Harness	53①
	Brake Line	14
	Crossmember To Body	89
	Front Lateral Link To Crossmember	89
	Front Lateral Link To Knuckle	122
	Hub To Knuckle	63
	Lateral Link To Knuckle	122
	Rear Caliper To Knuckle	63
	Rear Lateral Link To Crossmember	89
	Stabilizer Bar Link To Bracket	30
	Stabilizer Bar To Crossmember	41
	Strut Shaft Nut	37
	Strut To Knuckle	126
	Strut Upper Support Nuts	21
	Trailing Arm To Body	89
	Trailing Arm To Knuckle	74
	Wheel Lug Nut	103
L-SERIES		
2000	Heat Shield To Rear Suspension Support	72①
	Rear Axle Control Bracket	65②
	Rear Brake Drum To Hub	35①
	Rear Brake Hose Bracket To Control Arm	6
	Rear Caliper To Back Plate	59
	Rear Hub To Knuckle	35③
	Stabilizer Bar Clamp	41
	Stabilizer To Control Arm	41
	Strut Carrier To Body	41
	Strut To Knuckle	110③
	Suspension Control Arm To Knuckle	66④
	Suspension Control Arm To Suspension Support	90④
	Suspension Support To Body	66⑤

① — Inch lbs.
② — Tighten an additional 60.°
③ — Tighten an additional 30.°
④ — Tighten an additional 60–75.°
⑤ — Tighten an additional 90–115.°

Front Suspension & Steering

NOTE: On Air Bag Equipped Models, Refer To " Air Bag System Precautions" Located In The Front Of This Manual For System Disarming & Arming Procedures.

NOTE: Prior To Performing Any Service Operations Listed In This Section, Consult The "Technical Service Bulletins " Section For Related Information.

INDEX

PRECAUTIONS

AIR BAG SYSTEMS

Refer to "Air Bag System Precautions" in the front of this manual for system disarming and arming procedures.

BATTERY GROUND CABLE

Prior to service, disconnect battery ground cable and isolate as required.

WHEEL HUB & STEERING KNUCKLE

REPLACE

1. Depress brake pedal, then loosen axle to hub nut.
2. Raise and support vehicle, then remove wheel assembly.
3. Remove caliper to knuckle attaching bolts. Suspend caliper with mechanics wire.
4. Loosen but do not remove knuckle to strut attaching bolts.
5. If rotor is difficult to remove, use two M8 X 1.25 self tapping bolts, to remove, **Fig. 1.**
6. Remove axle nut and washer, then and discard lower control arm ball stud cotter pin.
7. Loosen castle nut until level with top of ball stud.
8. Remove and discard tie rod cotter pin.
9. Remove tie rod and castle nut.
10. Using lower control arm ball stud separator tool No. SA9132S, or equivalent, separate lower control arm from knuckle. **Do not use wedge type tool to separate or ABS speed sensor ring and seal damage may occur.**
11. Remove lower ball joint castle nut, **Fig. 2.**
12. Using tie rod separator tool No. SA91100C, or equivalent, separate tie rod end from steering knuckle.

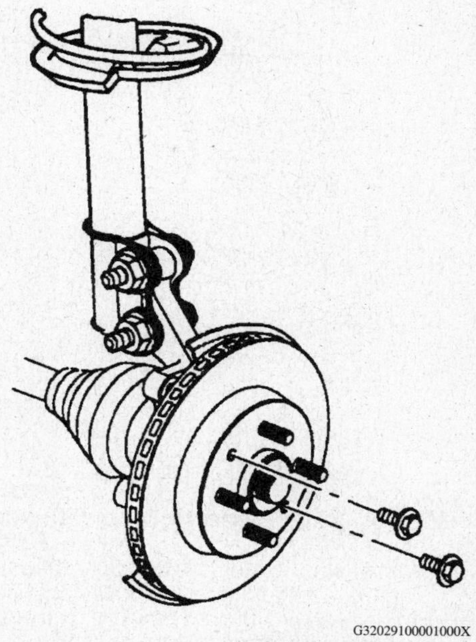

Fig. 1 Brake rotor removal

13. **On models equipped with Anti-Lock Brake System (ABS),** disconnect wheel speed sensor electrical connector.
14. **On all models,** support or suspend drive axle assembly.
15. Remove strut to knuckle attaching bolts, then knuckle and hub assembly. If difficult to separate axle from hub, tap end of drive axle shaft using a block of wood and hammer. **Do not hammer end of axle.**
16. Reverse procedure to install.

HUB & BEARING SERVICE

1. Remove steering knuckle as outlined under "Wheel Hub & Steering Knuckle, Replace."
2. Remove splash shields, then ABS wheel speed sensor.
3. Install wheel bearing/hub removal tool No. SA9159S, or equivalent, **Fig. 3,** then place assembly in a soft jawed vise, **Fig. 4.**
4. Hold hub drive with a wrench. Tighten driver screw to remove hub.
5. Install inner race puller, **Fig. 5,** then remove inner bearing race.
6. Remove steering knuckle from vise, then bridge retainer and bridge.
7. Remove bridge snap ring using snap ring pliers.
8. Using knuckle support tube and small driver, **Fig. 6,** press out bearing.
9. Reverse procedure to assemble.

BALL JOINT INSPECTION

1. Raise and support front of vehicle.
2. Grasp tire at top and bottom, then move bottom of tire in and out.
3. While moving bottom of tire in and out, observe ball joint for any side to side movement.
4. If any side to side movement is noticed, replace lower control arm.

BALL JOINT

REPLACE

LOWER

The ball joint and the lower control arm are serviced as an assembly. Refer to "Control Arm, Replace" for replacement procedure.

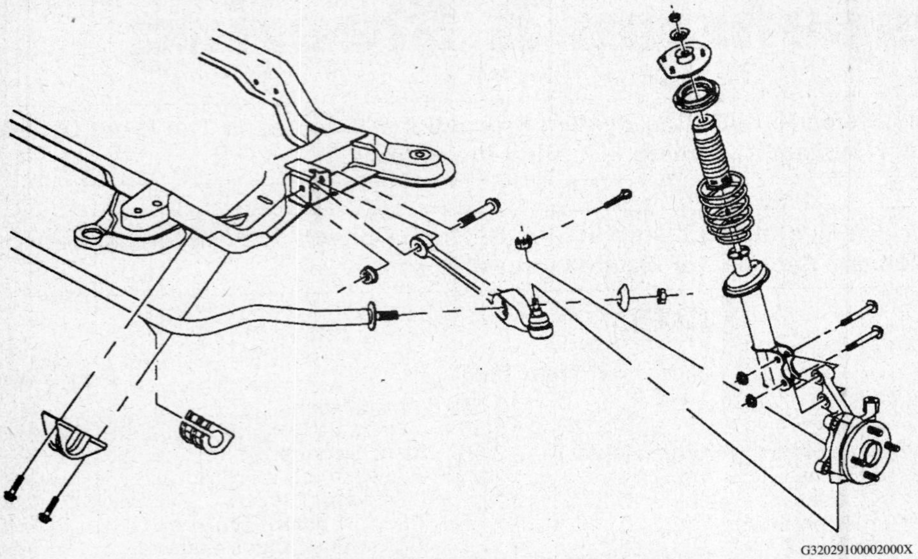

Fig. 2 Exploded view of front suspension

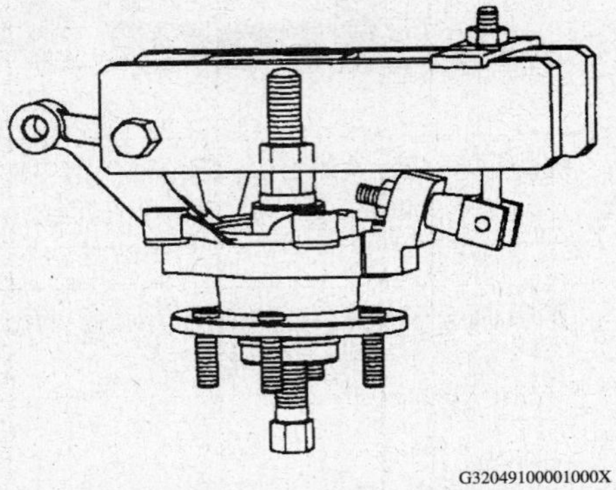

Fig. 3 Wheel bearing/hub removal

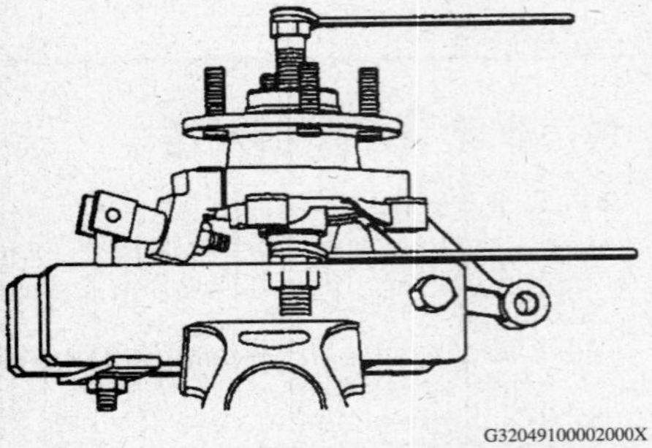

Fig. 4 Hub vise installation

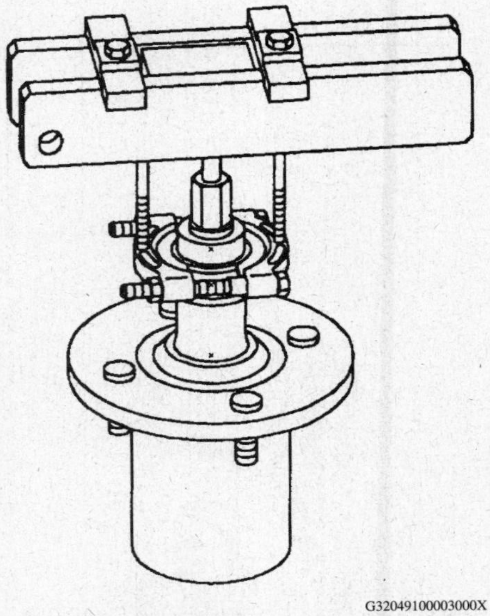

Fig. 5 Inner bearing race removal

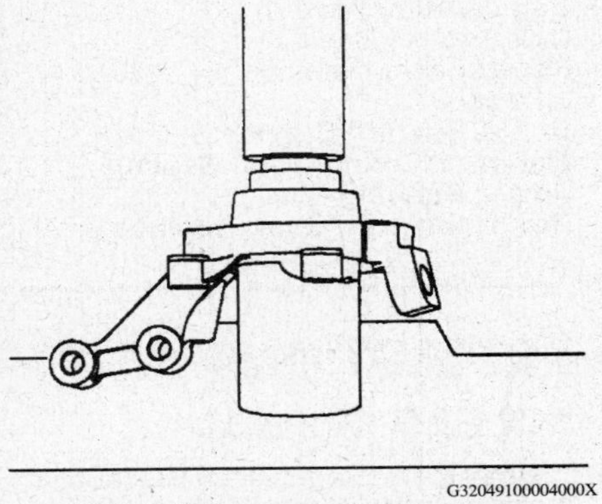

Fig. 6 Bearing removal

COIL SPRING

REPLACE

Refer to "Strut Service" for coil spring replacement procedure.

STRUT

REPLACE

REMOVAL

1. Raise and support vehicle, then remove wheel assembly.
2. **On models equipped with ABS,** disconnect wheel speed sensor electrical connector bracket.
3. **On all models,** loosen but do not remove steering knuckle to strut housing attaching bolts.
4. Place a floor jack below lower control arm and support.
5. Remove and discard upper strut attaching nuts.
6. Slowly raise vehicle, then lower strut assembly.
7. Remove knuckle to housing attaching bolts, **Fig. 2,** then place cloth over CV joint seal.
8. Remove strut assembly.

INSTALLATION

1. Install new upper strut attaching nuts and tighten to specifications.
2. Install strut to steering knuckle attaching bolts and tighten to specifications. **Install new nuts to ensure proper torque retention.**
3. **On models equipped with ABS,** install sensor electrical connector bracket and tighten to specifications.
4. **On all models,** install wheel and tighten lug nuts to specifications.

STRUT SERVICE

DISASSEMBLE

1. Using spring compressor tool No. SA9155C, or equivalent and a suitable holding fixture, compress spring to unload upper strut mount.
2. While holding strut shaft, remove strut shaft nut.
3. Release spring compressor, then tilt strut assembly outward.
4. Remove upper strut assembly, check for damage. replace as required.
5. Remove strut spring and dust shield; inspect for damage and replace as required.
6. Remove strut from holding fixture.

ASSEMBLE

1. Place strut in compressor tool, then attach with strut to knuckle bolt, through lower mounting hole.
2. Extend strut shaft to travel limit.
3. Install dust shield, spring isolator and mount, ensure spring is properly seated in seat and isolator.
4. Compress spring, then install strut shaft attaching nut and tighten to specifications.

CONTROL ARM

REPLACE

LOWER

1. Raise and support vehicle, then remove wheel assembly.
2. Remove and discard lower control arm ball stud cotter pin.
3. Loosen lower control ball stud castle nut until level with top of ball stud.
4. Using lower control arm ball stud separator tool No. SA9132S, or equivalent, separate lower control arm from knuckle. **Do not use wedge type tool or ABS speed sensor ring or seal may be damaged.**

5. Remove lower control arm ball stud castle nut.
6. Remove inner front fender splash shield.
7. Remove lower control arm to cradle attaching nut and bolt, **Fig. 2.**
8. Remove lower control arm to tension strut attaching nut, then arm.
9. Reverse procedure to install.

TENSION STRUT

REPLACE

1. Raise and support vehicle, then remove wheel assembly.
2. Remove and discard lower control arm ball stud cotter pin.
3. Loosen but do not remove left lower control arm ball stud castle nut.
4. For lefthand side of vehicle, proceed as follows:
   a. Using lower control arm ball stud separator tool No. SA9132S, or equivalent, separate lower control arm from steering knuckle. **Do not use wedge type tool or ABS speed sensor ring and seal damage may occur.**
   b. Remove lower control arm ball joint castle nut.
   c. Remove left front inner fender splash shield.
   d. Remove lower control arm to cradle attaching nut and bolt.
5. For right hand side of vehicle, proceed as follows:
   a. Turn wheel left to gain access, then remove tension strut to lower control arm attaching nut and washer.
6. For both sides, remove tension strut to cradle bracket attaching bolts.
7. Remove tension strut and left control arm assembly.
8. Remove control arm to tension strut attaching nut and washer, then separate.
9. Reverse procedure to install.

POWER STEERING GEAR

REPLACE

S-SERIES

1. Raise and support vehicle.
2. Remove and discard tie rod end cotter pins.
3. Remove tie rod end to knuckle castle nuts.
4. Using tie rod separator tool No. SA91100C, or equivalent, remove tie rod end from steering knuckle. **Do not separate joint using wedge-type tool or damage may result.**
5. Remove left inner fender splash shield.
6. Loosen intermediate shaft cover from steering gear, then raise slightly, remove pinch bolt.
7. Disconnect power steering pressure switch, then place drain container below pressure and return hoses.
8. Disconnect pressure and return hoses and allow system to drain.
9. Remove steering gear attaching bolts, then through left fenderwell.

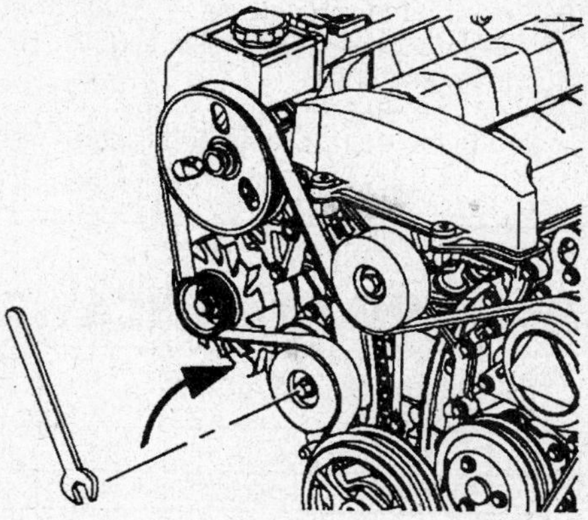
G31069100032000X

Fig. 7 Belt spring tension release. S-Series

10. Reverse procedure to install noting the following:
    a. Install new steering gear attaching nuts.
    b. Apply Loctite 242, or equivalent to pinch bolt.

L-SERIES

Rotating steering wheel while it is disconnected from the steering gear may cause damage to SIR coil.

1. From inside vehicle, remove pinch bolt and disconnect intermediate shaft from steering gear.
2. **On models equipped with 3.0L engine,** remove rear exhaust manifold heat shield.
3. **On all models,** remove rear transaxle mount through bolt, then transaxle mount to frame bolt.
4. Place a suitable drain container under pressure and return hoses at steering gear.
5. Remove hoses from power steering gear and allow to drain.
6. Raise and support vehicle, then remove wheel assemblies.
7. Remove right front lower splash shield.
8. **On models equipped with 3.0L engine,** remove exhaust manifold pipe, then the remaining transaxle mount to frame bolts.
9. **On all models,** remove tie rod end torque prevailing nuts, discard nuts.
10. Separate tie rod end from steering knuckle using tie rod end separator tool No. SA91100C or equivalent.
11. Remove steering gear to frame assembly bolts, then steering gear heat shield.
12. Remove stabilizer bar links from strut assembly, then front suspension support assemblies.
13. Loosen remaining frame to attaching bolts, until there is enough clearance to remove gear through left side wheel opening.
14. Remove steering gear from vehicle.
15. Reverse procedure to install.

POWER STEERING PUMP

REPLACE

S-SERIES

1. Remove power steering pump reservoir fill cap.
2. Raise and support vehicle.
3. Place a drain pan below steering gear hoses.
4. Remove steering gear hoses and allow system to drain. **Do not rotate steering wheel.**
5. Using a suitable box end wrench, relieve spring tension from accessory drive belt, then remove belt, **Fig. 7.**
6. **On models equipped with DOHC engine,** remove pump to intake manifold bracket, then pump to engine block bracket.
7. **On all models,** remove pump to engine block attaching bolts, then raise pump to disconnect EVO electrical connector.
8. Remove pump and hose assembly, then hoses.
9. Reverse procedure to install.

L-SERIES

2.2L Engine

1. Remove power steering pump reservoir fill cap.
2. Place a suitable container under power steering hoses at steering gear.
3. Remove power hoses from steering gear and allow to drain. **Do not rotate steering wheel.**
4. Remove pressure and return hoses at power steering pump, then pump to cylinder head bolts.
5. Remove pump from vehicle.
6. Reverse procedure to install.

3.0L Engine

1. Remove air cleaner assembly, then power steering pulley bolts.
2. Remove accessory drive belt from power steering pump pulley, then pulley.
3. Place a suitable container under power steering pump.
4. Remove power steering pump pressure and return hoses, allow to drain.
5. Remove power steering pump to bracket attaching bolts, then pump from vehicle.
6. Reverse procedure to install.

MANUAL STEERING GEAR

REPLACE

1. Raise and support vehicle.
2. Remove front wheel assemblies.
3. Remove and discard tie rod end cotter pins.
4. Using tie rod separator tool No.

SA91100C, or equivalent, remove tie rod end from steering knuckle. **Do not separate joint with wedge type tool or damage may result.**

5. Remove left inner fender splash shield.
6. Loosen intermediate shaft cover from steering gear, then raise slightly, remove pinch bolt.
7. Remove steering gear cradle attaching bolts, then through left fenderwell.
8. Reverse procedure to install noting the following:
   a. Install new steering gear attaching nuts.
   b. Apply Loctite 242, or equivalent to pinch bolt.

TIGHTENING SPECIFICATIONS

Year	Component	Torque/Ft. Lbs.
S-SERIES		
1997– 2000	ABS Electrical Connector Bracket eri	72③
	Axle To Hub Nut	148
	Ball Joint Stud Castle Nut	55
	Brake Dust Shield	18
	Caliper Bracket To Knuckle	81
	Control Arm To Cradle (Bolt)	92
	Control Arm To Cradle (Nut)	74
	Control Arm To Tension Strut	106
	Hub To Driveshaft Nut	148
	Intermediate Shaft To Steering Gear Pinch Bolt	35
	Power Steering Pressure & Return Line Fittings	20
	Power Steering Pump Bracket	28
	Pump To Engine Block Bolts	28
	Pump To Intake Manifold Bracket (DOHC)	22
	Steering Gear Cradle Bolts	37
	Strut Shaft Nut	37
	Strut To Body	21
	Strut To Steering Knuckle	126
	Tension Strut Bracket To Cradle	103
	Tie Rod End To Steering Knuckle	33
	Upper Strut Mount	21
	Wheel Lug Nuts	103
L-SERIES		
2000	ABS Sensor Bracket To Knuckle	72③
	Caliper Bracket To Knuckle	70
	Control Arm To Frame	65①
	Frame To Body	66②
	Inner Tie Rod To Steering Gear	70
	Intermediate Shaft To Steering Column	20
	Intermediate Shaft To Steering Gear	20
	Power Steering High Pressure Line	20
	Power Steering Pump Pulley	15
	Power Steering Pump To Bracket	15
	Power Steering Pump To Engine	18
	Steering Wheel Nut	30
	Strut Shaft To Body	40
	Strut Shaft To Mount	40
	Stabilizer Bar To Link	50
	Wheel Lug Nut	92

DOHC — Dual Over Head Cam.
① — An additional 75.°
② — An additional 45–60.°
③ — Inch lbs.

Wheel Alignment

INDEX

PRELIMINARY INSPECTION

1. Road test vehicle.
2. Inspect tires for proper inflation, wear pattern or out of round condition.
3. Inspect suspension and steering components for wear and damage.
4. Inspect strut bushings for wear or damage.
5. Inspect vehicle ride height as described under "Vehicle Ride Height" in this section.
6. Wheel alignment should be performed in the following order: rear camber, rear toe, right front camber and caster, left front camber and caster and front toe.

FRONT WHEEL ALIGNMENT

Rear wheel alignment must be set to specifications before front alignment adjustment.

S-SERIES

Caster

1. Lock steering wheel in straight ahead position.
2. Remove and discard upper strut mount attaching nuts.
3. Slide strut forward or rearward to adjust caster. Movement of approximately .157 inch will change caster by about ½.° **Body attachment holes may need to be filed or ground into oval slots to allow enough front to rear strut movement to adjust caster to specifications. Do not exceed .354 inch in slot width.**
4. Install new upper strut mount attaching nuts, then **torque** to 21 ft. lbs.
5. Recheck caster angle.

Camber

1. Lock steering wheel in straight ahead position.
2. Loosen two strut to knuckle fasteners, then pull or push to adjust.
3. If more than 1.5° of camber is needed, check for bent suspension components.
4. If suspension is satisfactory, proceed as follows:
   a. Raise and support vehicle.
   b. Remove wheel assembly.
   c. Remove strut to knuckle attaching bolts, then separate knuckle from strut bracket.
   d. Using a file or grinder, remove material from strut bracket lower hole, **Fig. 1.**
   e. To increase negative camber, remove from outside hole, to increase positive camber, remove from inside hole.
   f. **Torque** strut to knuckle attaching bolts to 126 ft. lbs.
   g. Install wheel assembly and **torque** wheel lug nuts to 103 ft. lbs., then recheck camber setting and lower vehicle.

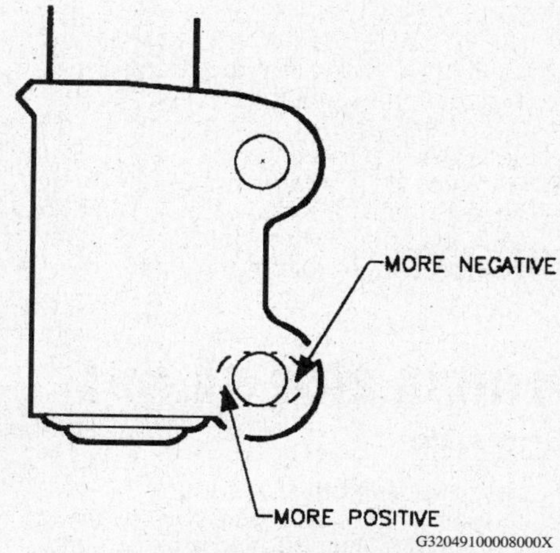

Fig. 1 Front & rear camber adjustment. S-Series

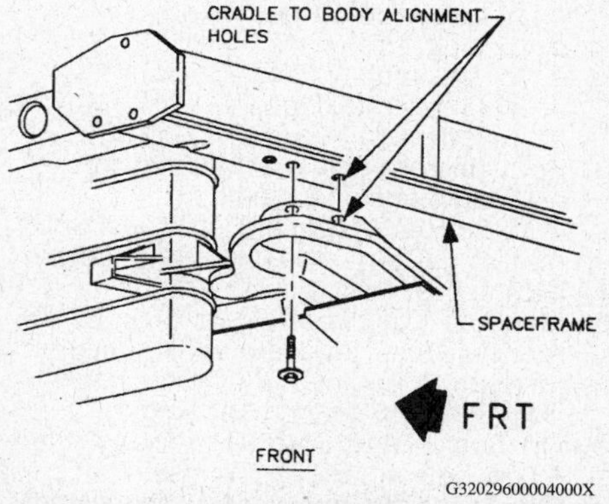

Fig. 2 Cradle alignment. S-Series

Toe-In

1. Lock steering wheel in straight ahead position.
2. Loosen left and right outer tie rod jam nuts.
3. Turn inner tie rod, by flats, to change toe.
4. After adjustment, **torque** outer tie rod end jam nuts 74 ft. lbs.
5. **Ensure seals do not become twisted.**
6. Recheck toe angle.

Cradle

Check cradle to body alignment at two alignment holes using 5⁄16 inch rod, **Fig. 2.** If cradle to body alignment is not correct, loosen cradle fasteners and align cradle to body.

L-SERIES

Caster

Front wheel caster is non adjustable on these vehicles. These angles can be measured but are set by design of the front suspension.

Camber

1. Raise and support vehicle, then remove wheel assemblies.
2. Remove strut to knuckle attaching bolts and discard.
3. Using a file or grinder, remove material from strut bracket lower hole, **Fig. 1.**
4. To increase negative camber, remove from outside hole, to increase positive camber, remove from inside hole.
5. **Torque** strut to knuckle attaching bolts to 37 ft. lbs, then 65 ft. lbs. and turn an additional 65°.
6. Install wheel assembly and **torque** wheel lug nuts to 92 ft. lbs., then lower vehicle and check camber angle. Adjust if required.

Toe-In

For this procedure, refer to the 1.9L engine in this section.

REAR WHEEL ALIGNMENT

S-SERIES

Caster

Rear wheel caster is not adjustable.

Camber

1. Loosen two strut to knuckle fasteners, then pull or push to adjust.

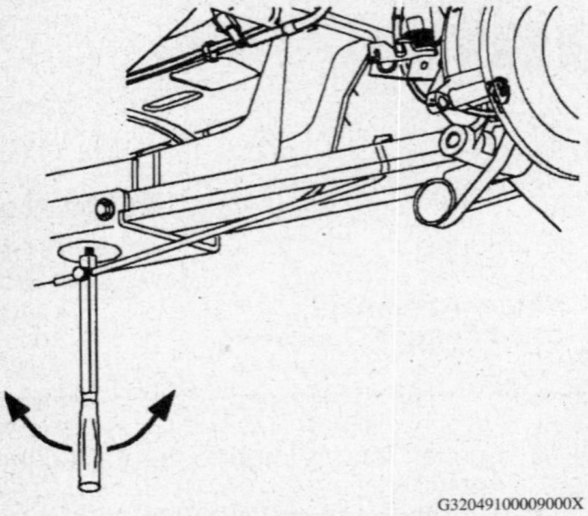

Fig. 3 Rear toe adjustment. S-Series

2. If more then 1.5° of camber is desired, check for bent suspension components.
3. If suspension is good, proceed as follows:
   a. Raise and support vehicle.
   b. Remove wheel assembly.
   c. Remove strut to knuckle attaching bolts, then separate knuckle from strut bracket.
   d. Using a file or grinder, remove material from strut bracket lower hole, **Fig. 1.**
   e. To increase negative camber, remove from outside hole, to increase positive camber, remove from inside hole.
   f. **Torque** strut to knuckle attaching bolts to 126 ft. lbs.
   g. Install wheel assembly and **torque** wheel lug nuts to 103 ft. lbs., then recheck camber setting and lower vehicle.

Toe-In

1. Loosen rearmost lateral link to crossmember attaching bolts.
2. Using rear toe adjusting tool No. SA9158C, or equivalent, move lateral link to adjust, **Fig. 3.**
3. **Torque** lateral link to 89 ft. lbs.
4. Recheck toe, then repeat for other wheel.

L-SERIES

Rear wheel alignment involves setting the toe angle. Rear wheel camber is not adjustable.

Toe-In

1. Remove rear axle control arm bolts and discard.

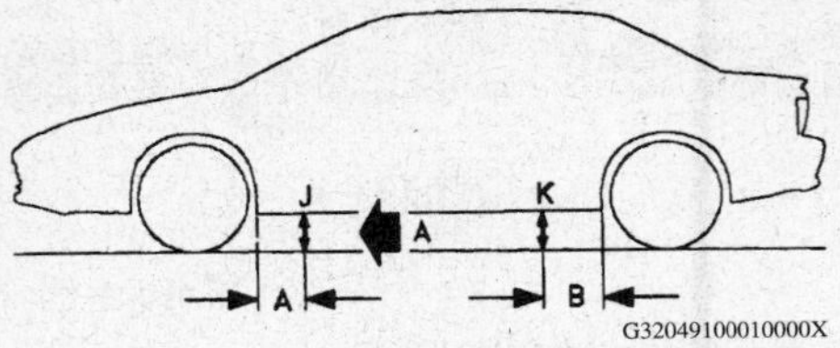

Fig. 4 Vehicle trim height measurement. S-Series

2. Install new bolts, do not tighten at this time but leave inside forward bolt out.
3. Install rear toe adjusting tool No. KM-900 or equivalent into open bolt hole.
4. Using adjusting tool No. KM-900 or equivalent, move rear axle control arm in direction of required toe correction.
5. Snug rear axle control arm bolts, do not tighten at this time.
6. Recheck toe and adjust if required.
7. **Torque** rear axle control arm bolts to 65 ft. lbs., then additional 30°- 45°. Repeat procedure for other rear wheel.

VEHICLE RIDE HEIGHT

S-SERIES

1. Place vehicle on level surface.
2. If fuel tank is not full, the following weight must be added to trunk to simulate a full tank:
   a. 1/8 tank, add 70 lbs.
   b. 1/4 tank, add 60 lbs.
   c. 3/8 tank, add 50 lbs.
   d. 1/2 tank, add 40 lbs.
   e. 5/8 tank, add 30 lbs.
   f. 3/4 tank, add 20 lbs.
   g. 7/8 tank, add 10 lbs.
3. Bounce front and rear suspension to allow suspension to settle.
4. With front tire pressure of 30 psi and rear of 26 psi, measure vehicle ride height, **Fig. 4.**
5. Measure from front (A) or rear (B) of rocker flange, to locate vehicle height measuring points J (front rocker height) and K (rear rocker height).
6. **On Sedan and Wagon models,** A is 4.6 inches and B is 4.1 inches.
7. **On Coupe models,** A is 5.9 inches and B is 5.4 inches.
8. **On all models,** measure vehicle height from level surface, to bottom horizontal surface of rocker panel. **Do not measure from rocker/jacking flange**
9. **On Coupe models,** J should be 7.8–9.1 inches and K should be 7.9–9.4 inches.

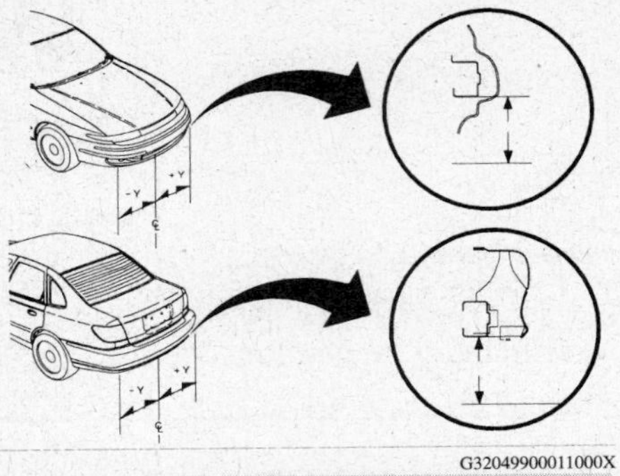

Fig. 5 Vehicle trim height measurement. L-Series

10. **On Sedan models,** J should be 7.8–9.0 inches and K should be 8.0–9.3 inches.
11. **On Coupe SC 1 models with aluminum wheels,** J should be 8.2–9.1 inches and K should be 8.3—9.5 inches.
12. **On Wagon models,** J should be 7.8–9.1 inches and K should be 8.1—9.5 inches.
13. **On all models,** when measuring alignment angles, vehicle trim height must be accurate, if not, add or remove weight until height is correct.

L-SERIES

1. Place vehicle on level surface. Ensure tire pressure is 30 psi for front and rear.
2. If fuel tank is not full, the following weight must be added to trunk to simulate a full tank:
   a. 1/8 tank, add 80 lbs.
   b. 1/4 tank, add 70 lbs.
   c. 3/8 tank, add 60 lbs.
   d. 1/2 tank, add 45 lbs.
   e. 5/8 tank, add 35 lbs.
   f. 3/4 tank, add 20 lbs.
   g. 7/8 tank, add 10 lbs.
3. Bounce front and rear of vehicle a few times to settle suspension.
4. Measure front and rear curb trim height as follows:
   a. Measure distance from ground to locating points –Y and +Y, **Fig. 5.** Right and left locating points are 15.35 inches from centerline of vehicle at front, and 20.86 inches from centerline of vehicle at rear.
   b. Ensure curb trim height is 14.58–16.54 inches at front, and 14.23–16.19 inches at rear.

AIR CONDITIONING

TABLE OF CONTENTS

System Testing

NOTE: On Air Bag Equipped Models, Refer To " Air Bag System Precautions" Located In The Front Of This Manual For System Disarming & Arming Procedures.

INDEX

PRECAUTIONS

General Motors

AIR BAG SYSTEMS

Refer to "Air Bag System Precautions" in the front of this manual for system disarming and arming procedures.

BATTERY GROUND CABLE

Prior to service, disconnect battery ground cable and isolate as required.

SYSTEM

R-134a refrigerant is a non toxic, nonflammable, clear and odorless liquified gas.

R-134a refrigerant is not compatible with R-12 refrigerant. Even small amounts of R-12 in a R-134a system will cause lubricant contamination, compressor failure or improper A/C performance. Never add R-12 to a R-134a system.

Avoid breathing R-134a refrigerant and lubricant vapor or mist. Exposure may irritate eyes, nose and throat. Use only approved service equipment to discharge R-134a systems. Do not heat refrigerant containers with open flame, if container warming is required, place bottom of container in a pail of warm water. R-134a refrigerant will displace oxygen, work only in a well ventilated area to prevent suffocation.

Saturn

Always wear goggles and wrap clean cloth around fittings, valves and connections when performing work that involves opening the refrigerant system. Keep work area well ventilated and do not steam clean or weld on or near any of the air conditioning lines or components. If liquid coolant does touch the eyes, bathe eyes quickly in cold water, then apply a bland disinfectant oil. See an eye doctor.

Before removing and replacing any of the air conditioning refrigeration lines or components, the refrigerant must be completely removed. The refrigerant system may be evacuated and charged using an air conditioning service charging station or a manifold and gauge set with a 30 lb. drum of R134a. **Never charge the air conditioning system through the high pressure side of the system.**

For efficient operation of the air conditioning system, be careful not to contaminate the system with foreign materials, such as dirt, air or moisture. Contamination of the air conditioning system will change the chemical stability of the R134a refrigerant, in turn changing the viscosity of the refrigerant oil. They will also effect pressure, temperature and create corrosion and abnormal wear of moving parts.

DESCRIPTION

General Motors

VARIABLE DISPLACEMENT ORIFICE TUBE SYSTEM

The variable displacement tube (VDOT) system consist of a variable displacement compressor and a fixed expansion tube. The system matches air conditioning demands under all conditions without cycling the compressor clutch. The basic compressor mechanism is a variable angle wobble plate with five axially oriented cylinders. Compressor displacement is controlled by a bellows actuated control valve which

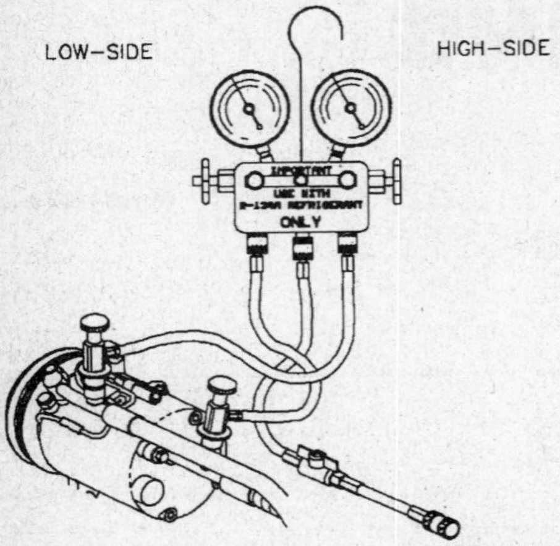

Fig. 1 High & low side Schraeder valve locations

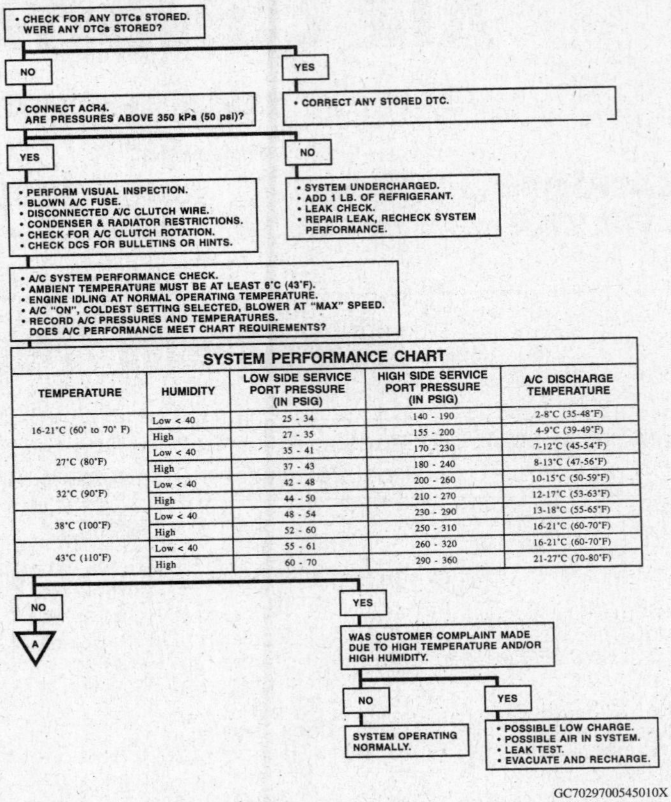

SYSTEM PERFORMANCE CHART

TEMPERATURE	HUMIDITY	LOW SIDE SERVICE PORT PRESSURE (IN PSIG)	HIGH SIDE SERVICE PORT PRESSURE (IN PSIG)	A/C DISCHARGE TEMPERATURE
16-21°C (60° to 70° F)	Low < 40	25 - 34	140 - 190	2-8°C (35-48°F)
	High	27 - 35	155 - 200	4-9°C (39-49°F)
27°C (80°F)	Low < 40	35 - 41	170 - 230	7-12°C (45-54°F)
	High	37 - 43	180 - 240	8-13°C (47-56°F)
32°C (90°F)	Low < 40	42 - 48	200 - 260	10-15°C (50-59°F)
	High	44 - 50	210 - 270	12-17°C (53-63°F)
38°C (100°F)	Low < 40	48 - 54	230 - 290	13-18°C (55-65°F)
	High	52 - 60	250 - 310	16-21°C (60-70°F)
43°C (110°F)	Low < 40	55 - 61	260 - 320	16-21°C (60-70°F)
	High	60 - 70	290 - 360	21-27°C (70-80°F)

Fig. 2 Insufficient A/C cooling troubleshooting (Part 1 of 2)

senses compressor suction pressure, located in the rear head of the compressor. The wobble plate angle and compressor displacement are controlled by the crankcase suction pressure differential. When AC demand is high, and the suction pressure rises above the control point, the valve will maintain a bleed from crankcase to suction, and the compressor will have maximum displacement. When the AC demand is lower, and the suction pressure reaches the control point, the valve will bleed discharge gas into the crankcase and close off a passage from the crankcase to the suction plenum. The angle of the wobble plate is controlled by a force balance on the five pistons. A slight elevation of the crankcase suction pressure differential creates a total force on the pistons resulting in a movement of the wobble plate pivot pin that reduces the plate angle.

Compressor lubrication is accomplished through a system unique to the VDOT system. The crankcase suction bleed is routed through the rotating wobble plate bearing. The rotation acts as an oil separator, which removes some of the oil from the crankcase suction bleed and reroutes it to the crankcase for compressor mechanism lubrication.

Saturn

A/C SYSTEM INSPECTION USING MANIFOLD GAUGE SET

Many of the test procedures in this section require installation of a manifold gauge set. It is important to perform this operation as outlined in order to prevent injury and refrigerant loss. **Always wear goggles and wrap a clean cloth around fittings, valves and connections when performing work that involves opening the refrigerant system.**

Ensure gauges read zero before installing manifold gauge set.

1. Close both hand valves of manifold gauge set.
2. Connect low pressure (blue) gauge hose to suction service port, located on suction pipe, **Fig. 1.**
3. Hand tighten gauge hose nut, then connect adapter to high pressure gauge hose, **Fig. 1.**
4. Connect high pressure (red) gauge hose to discharge service port, located on discharge pipe.
5. Hand tighten adapter hose nut to discharge service port.

TROUBLESHOOTING

General Motors

SYMPTOM DIAGNOSIS CHARTS

Variable Displacement Orifice Tube System

Refer to **Figs. 2 through 5** for symptom troubleshooting charts.

Saturn

Most A/C system faults can be detected by a thorough inspection of the system and components.

1. Check air intake duct, lower air deflector, condenser to radiator seal and rear hood seal for missing or damaged parts.
2. Check outer surfaces of radiator and condenser cores to ensure air flow is not blocked by dirt, leaves or other matter.
3. Check for kinks in hoses and lines and refrigerant leaks using an electronic leak detector.
4. Check for a worn or loose compressor belt or faulty belt tensioner.
5. Check blower motor operation at all speeds.
6. With blower on High, check for equal distribution of air out of all outlets.
7. Check operation of control mode lever and distribution of air from designated outlets.
8. Press "Recirc" button with blower on high. A noticeable increase in air flow and sound should occur. Indicator should illuminate.
9. Start engine and run until normal operating temperature is reached.
10. Check operation of temperature control lever and air outlet temperature from hot to cold.
11. Press "A/C" button. Indicator should illuminate.
12. Check compressor for clutch engagement, slippage or noise.
13. Check electric cooling fan operation with A/C on.
14. Turn A/C off. Compressor clutch should disengage.

PERFORMANCE TEST

General Motors

Remove leaves and debris from front of the condenser core, mounted at the front of

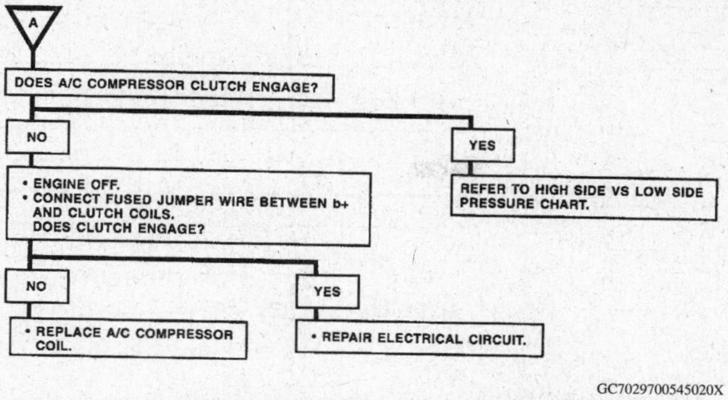

Fig. 2 Insufficient A/C cooling troubleshooting (Part 2 of 2)

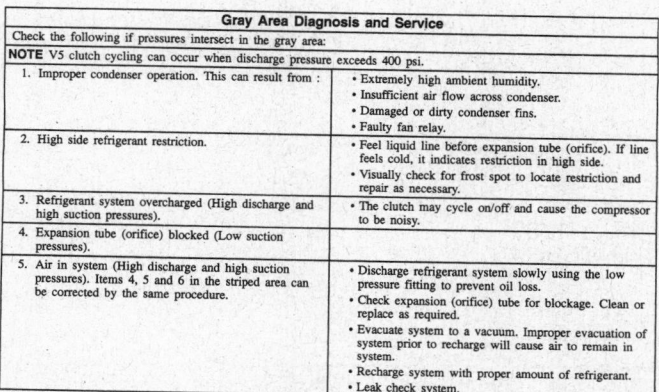

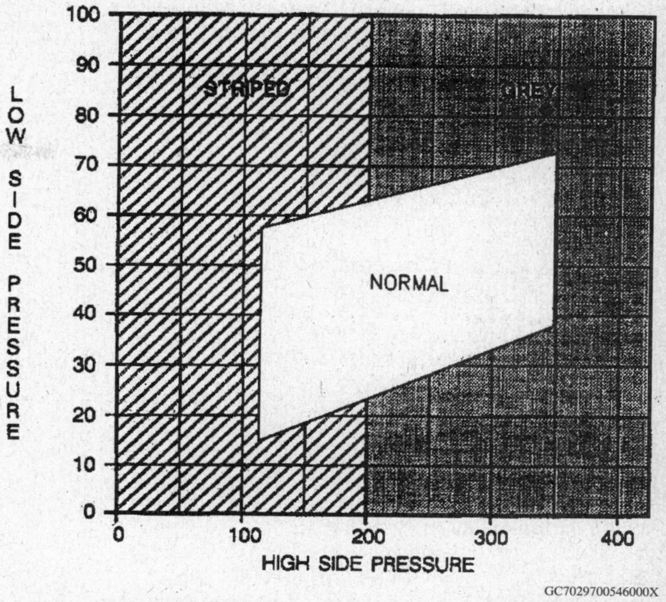

Fig. 3 High side vs. low side pressure chart

Gray Area Diagnosis and Service	
Check the following if pressures intersect in the gray area:	
NOTE V5 clutch cycling can occur when discharge pressure exceeds 400 psi.	
1. Improper condenser operation. This can result from :	• Extremely high ambient humidity. • Insufficient air flow across condenser. • Damaged or dirty condenser fins. • Faulty fan relay.
2. High side refrigerant restriction.	• Feel liquid line before expansion tube (orifice). If line feels cold, it indicates restriction in high side. • Visually check for frost spot to locate restriction and repair as necessary.
3. Refrigerant system overcharged (High discharge and high suction pressures).	• The clutch may cycle on/off and cause the compressor to be noisy.
4. Expansion tube (orifice) blocked (Low suction pressures).	
5. Air in system (High discharge and high suction pressures). Items 4, 5 and 6 in the striped area can be corrected by the same procedure.	• Discharge refrigerant system slowly using the low pressure fitting to prevent oil loss. • Check expansion (orifice) tube for blockage. Clean or replace as required. • Evacuate system to a vacuum. Improper evacuation of system prior to recharge will cause air to remain in system. • Recharge system with proper amount of refrigerant. • Leak check system.

GC7029700547000X

Fig. 4 Gray area diagnosis and service

Striped Area Diagnosis and Service	
Check the following if pressures intersect in the striped area:	
1. Compressor may be internally damaged.	• If suction and discharge pressure are equal and do not change when the A/C mode is turned on and off, the compressor may be internally damaged. • Excess heat at the clutch surfaces or a free wheeling clutch driver are signs of internal compressor damage. • When replacing the compressor, follow component replacement procedures to maintain correct oil charge in the system.
2. Missing expansion tube (orifice).	• Feel liquid line after expansion tube. If line is warm, discharge system and inspect for proper installation of expansion tube. If expansion tube or o-ring is missing replace expansion tube. • If expansion tube is present, remove, clean, or replace tube as necessary and install in system. • Evacuate and charge system.
3. Compressor at minimum stroke.	• If compressor discharge pressures remains only 10-30 psi above suction pressure, compressor may be at minimum stroke. • Run engine at approximately 3000 RPM for three minutes until pressures become normal. During this period, cycle mode lever from vent to A/C every 20 seconds. If no change, perform control valve low load test (step 4).
4. Compressor control valve set improperly. Run low load test to verify. Perform low load test as follows. This procedure is designed to create a low cooling load causing the V5 compressor to go toward minimum stroke which is absolutely necessary for evaluation of control valve set point.	• Start engine and run at fast idle speed. • Open hood, close windows and doors. • Set A/C controls to LOW blower and MAX cooling. • Record and evaluate test results: 1. If suction pressure is 25-35 psi, control valve is functioning properly. 2. If suction pressure is outside limits of 25-35 psi, replace control valve.
5. Refrigerant system undercharged.	• This condition may exist when the suction pressure is below 35 psi during the high load test (step 3). • The suction line before the accumulator will be warm if charge is low. • Add 1 lb. of refrigerant and recheck. Pressures should come into white area. If so, find source of refrigerant leak and repair. • Evacuate and charge system with correct amount of refrigerant.
6. Expansion tube (orifice) blocked.	• Refer to step 5 in the gray area for diagnosis.

GC7029700548000X

Fig. 5 Striped area diagnosis and service

the radiator. All obstructions must be removed, as they will reduce heat transfer and impair the efficiency of the system. Ensure space between the condenser and the radiator is free of foreign matter.

Ensure the evaporator drain is open. The evaporator cools and dehumidifies the air before it enters the passenger compartment. As the core cools the air, moisture condenses on it and is drained through the evaporator water drain tube.

The system should be operated for at least 15 minutes to allow sufficient time for all parts to become completely stabilized. Determine if the system is fully charged by the use of test gauges and sight glass if one is installed on system. Head pressure will read from 180–220 psi or higher, depending upon ambient temperature and the type of unit being tested. The sight glass should be free of bubbles. Low side pressures should read approximately 15–30 psi, depending on the ambient temperature and the unit being tested. The type of control and component installation used on a particular system will directly influence the pressure readings on the high and low sides, **Fig. 6**.

The high side pressure will be affected by the ambient or outside air temperature. Refer to **Fig. 7** for approximate high side pressure readings at various ambient temperatures.

RELATIVE TEMPERATURE OF HIGH & LOW SIDES

The high side of the system should be uniformly hot to the touch throughout. A difference in temperature will indicate a partial blockage of liquid or gas at this point.

The low side of the system should be uniformly cool to the touch with no excessive sweating of the suction line or low side service valve. Excessive sweating or frosting of the low side service valve usually indicates an expansion valve is allowing an excessive amount of refrigerant into the evaporator.

Saturn

SERVICE STALL TEST

Record the manifold gauge pressures and outlet temperature with the following preset vehicle conditions:

1. Install thermometer in right center outlet.
2. Open doors and windows to stabilize interior temperature with outside ambient air temperature.
3. Press "Recirc" button.
4. Set temperature lever to full cold.
5. Select 3rd blower speed.
6. Press "A/C" button.
7. With engine warm, run at 2000 RPM.
8. Continue running until system pressures and outlet temperature stabilize (three to five minutes).
9. Record pressure and temperature.
10. Compare readings to normal system performance charts, **Figs. 8 through 10.**

45 MPH TEST

Recorded manifold gauge pressures and outlet temperature with the vehicle conditions listed under "Service Stall Test," except for the following conditions:

1. "Recirc" off (outside air).
2. Vehicle running at 45 mph with engine fully warm.
3. Compare readings to normal system performance chart, **Figs. 11 through 13.**

Evaporator Pressure Gauge Reading	Evaporator Temperature F°	High Pressure Gauge Reading	Ambient Temperature
0	-21°	45	20°
0.6	-20°	55	30°
2.4	-15°	72	40°
4.5	-10°	86	50°
6.8	- 5°	105	60°
9.2	0°	126	70°
11.8	5°	140	75°
14.7	10°	160	80°
17.1	15°	185	90°
21.1	20°	195	95°
22.5	22°	220	100°
23.9	24°	240	105°
25.4	26°	260	110°
26.9	28°	275	115°
28.5	30°	290	120°
37.0	40°	305	125°
46.7	50°	325	130°
57.7	60°		
70.1	70°		
84.1	80°		
99.6	90°		
116.9	100°		
136.0	110°		
157.1	120°		
179.0	130°		

GC7029100025000X

Fig. 6 Pressure-temperature relationship. Conditions equivalent to 30 mph or 1750 engine RPM. General Motors

Ambient Temp.	High Side Pressure
80	150–170
90	175–195
95	185–205
100	210–230
105	230–250
110	250–270

Fig. 7 High side pressure specifications. General Motors

LEAK TEST

Before beginning any leak test, attach a manifold gauge set and note pressure. If little or no pressure is indicated, a partial charge must be installed. Inspect all connections, compressor head gasket, oil filler plug and compressor shaft seal for leaks.

ELECTRONIC LEAK DETECTORS

Current versions of electronic leak detectors have three settings, one for R-12, one for R-134a and one for gross. The gross setting is for isolating very large leaks already found in one of the other two settings. Refer to operating instructions for the unit being used and observe these general procedures.

1. Move detector probe one inch per second in areas of suspected leaks.
2. Position probe below test point, as refrigerant gas is heavier than air.
3. Inspect service access gauge port valve fittings, particularly when valve caps are missing, as dirt accumulations can destroy the sealing area of valve core when manifold gauge set is attached. Replace missing valve caps after cleaning valve core area. **Valve caps should only be finger tightened. Using pliers to tighten valve caps may distort sealing surface of valve.**
4. Inspect for leaks in manifold gauge set and hoses, as well as the rest of the system.

If the ambient air temperature is . . . DEGREES °F	The pressure gauge should read–(psi) SUCTION	The pressure gauge should read–(psi) DISCHARGE	The right center air should read–(°F) OUTLET °F
70	26~30	115~170	40~48
80	24~28	180~215	42~49
90	22~26	225~270	43~50
100	23~27	275~320	50~56

G37029500025000X

Fig. 8 Service stall test specifications. 1.9L Engine

If the ambient air temperature is . . . DEGREES (°F)	The low side gauge should read . . . SUCTION (psi)	The high side gauge should read . . . DISCHARGE (psi)	The right center air temperature should be . . . OUTLET (°F)
(70)	(29–31)	(105–133)	(41–46)
(80)	(28–30)	(145–160)	(42–45)
(90)	(27–29)	(185–260)	(45–47)
(100)	(26–28)	(225–310)	(46–48)

G37029900040000X

Fig. 9 Service stall specifications. 2.2L engine

If the ambient air temperature is . . . DEGREES (°F)	The low side gauge should read . . . SUCTION (psi)	The high side gauge should read . . . DISCHARGE (psi)	The right center air temperature should be . . . OUTLET (°F)
(70)	(26–29)	(139–185)	(41–46)
(80)	(25–28)	(190–220)	(42–48)
(90)	(25–27)	(225–340)	(45–48)
(100)	(25–27)	(275–340)	(45-53)

G37029900041000X

Fig. 10 Service stall specifications. 3.0L engine

FLAME-TYPE (HALIDE) LEAK DETECTORS

1. Adjust detector flame as low as possible to obtain maximum sensitivity. Ensure copper element is cherry red and not burned away, flame will be almost colorless.
2. Slowly move detector along areas of suspected leaks. A slight leak will cause the flame to change to a bright yellow-green color. A significant leak will be indicated by a brilliant blue flame. Position flame under areas being tested as refrigerant gas is heavier than air. **The presence of dust in the pickup hose may cause a change in the color of the flame. If not recognized, a false diagnosis could be made. Store leak detector in a clean place and ensure hose is free of dust before leak testing.**
3. Inspect the manifold gauge set and hoses for leaks, as well as the rest of the system.
4. Use a small fan to ventilate areas where the leak detector indicates refrigerant constantly. These areas are contaminated with refrigerant and must be ventilated before leak can be pinpointed.

FLUID LEAK DETECTORS

Apply leak detector solution around

NORMAL SYSTEM PERFORMANCE 45 MPH

If the ambient air temperature is . . .	The pressure gauge should read–(psi)	The pressure gauge should read–(psi)	The right center air should read–(°F)
DEGREES °F	SUCTION	DISCHARGE	OUTLET °F
70	29~33	90 ~125	44~48
80	28~32	120~170	44~49
90	26~30	150~200	44~50
100	24~32	180~240	47~53

G37029500026000X

Fig. 11 45 mph test specifications. 1.9L engine

If the ambient air temperature is . . .	The low side gauge should read . . .	The high side gauge should read . . .	The right center air temperature should be . . .
DEGREES (°F)	SUCTION (psi)	DISCHARGE (psi)	OUTLET (°F)
(70)	(30–32)	(92–120)	(42–48)
(80)	(29–31)	(117–150)	(44–50)
(90)	(28–30)	(145–175)	(43–51)
(100)	(28–30)	(185–200)	(43–55)

G37029900043000X

Fig. 13 45 mph test specifications. 3.0L engine

joints to be tested. A cluster of bubbles will form immediately if there is a leak. A white foam that forms after a short while will indicate an extremely small leak. In some confined areas such as sections of the evaporator and condenser, use of an electronic leak detector is recommended.

FLUORESCENT LEAK DETECTORS

The high density black light tool No. J 2848–E, tracer dye injector tool No. J 41436 and tracer dye tool No. J 41447, or equivalent, were developed to detect refrigerant leaks on R-134a systems. **Do not use any other tracer dye in these systems. Another type dye may cause premature compressor failure. Use only a ¼ ounce charge of dye, larger amounts may effect system performance.** After adding tracer dye, clean service valves and all affected surfaces of the dye with GM engine degreaser part No. 1050436, or equivalent, to prevent any false leak diagnosis.

DISCHARGING SYSTEM

General Motors

REFRIGERANT RECOVERY

The refrigerant system must be discharged using an air conditioning refrigerant recovery and recycling system. After completing any necessary repairs the refrigerant system can be evacuated and charged using an air conditioning service charging station. Service fitting caps are color coded for easy reference. Red cap indicates high side port. Blue cap indicates low side port.

Failure to inspect for residual oil from previous recovery can result in adding extra oil to the current vehicle being serviced. This will result in reduced performance and possible compressor damage.

1. Start vehicle and run with the A/C On for two minutes, then attach manifold gauge set to the A/C system, **Fig. 14.** Attach recovery station inlet hose to center fitting of manifold gauge set.
2. Open both valves of manifold gauge set. Ensure refrigerant tank vapor valve and liquid valve are open.
3. Turn main power switch On.
4. Depress compressor start switch. The amber "Compressor On" light will come on and the compressor will start. The compressor will shutoff automatically when recovery is complete.
5. Wait two minutes and inspect for pressure rise. If pressure rise occurs, depress compressor start switch to repeat recovery procedure.
6. To drain receiver dehydrator of A/C system oil, open receiver dehydrator pressurizing valve for 15 seconds to allow compressor discharge pressure back into receiver dehydrator.
7. Open oil drain valve slowly and drain receiver dehydrator. When oil stops draining, close oil drain valve.
8. **Do not allow receiver dehydrator to completely depressurize.**

REFRIGERANT RECYCLING

1. Turn main power switch On.
2. Open both valves on recovery tank.
3. Turn "Recycle Start" switch On. The amber "Recycle On" light will come on and the refrigerant pump will start.
4. Refrigerant will be seen going through the "Moisture Indicator" at start up. If there is a sufficient supply of refrigerant, bubbles will clear after a few seconds. When bubbles clear from " Moisture Indicator," refrigerant pump is operating at maximum efficiency.
5. Allow station to operate until dot in center of " Moisture Indicator" turns green. "Moisture Indicator Dot" should change to a shade indicated on the reference decal. Always run recycling system a minimum of 30 minutes. If "Moisture Indicator" starts out yellow, it could take as long as two hours to turn green, depending on moisture content of refrigerant.
6. Turn Off station when recycling is complete.

If the ambient air temperature is . . .	The low side gauge should read . . .	The high side gauge should read . . .	The right center air temperature should be . . .
DEGREES (°F)	SUCTION (psi)	DISCHARGE (psi)	OUTLET (°F)
(70)	(30–33)	(86–98)	(42–52)
(80)	(30–31)	(110–120)	(43–57)
(90)	(30–31)	(153–170)	(45–49)
(100)	(28–31)	(175–200)	(45–52)

G37029900042000X

Fig. 12 45 mph test specifications. 2.2L engine

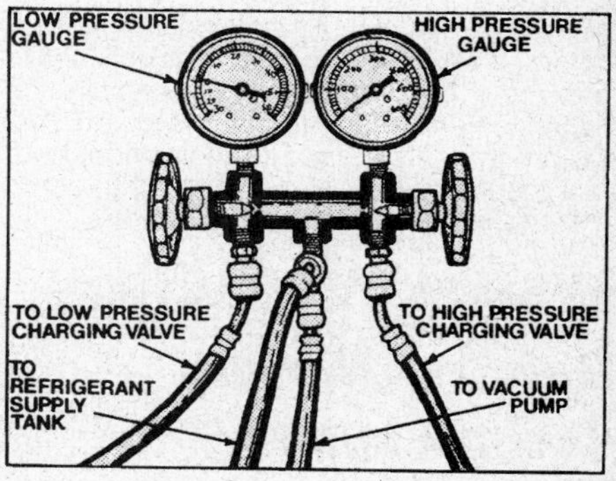

GC7029100026000X

Fig. 14 Manifold gauge set hose connections

REFRIGERANT RECOVERY & RECYCLING OPERATING HINTS

1. When using the recovery station in conjunction with a charging station, attach center port hose of manifold gauge set to inlet port of recovery station, then follow normal operating procedures for recovery/recycling station.
2. When using recovery station in conjunction with an automatic charging station, attach exhaust hose to inlet of recovery station.
3. **On automatic A/C service stations,** a hole has been added at rear of cabinet for access to exhaust hose.
4. **On older type stations,** open front doors of cabinet to reach exhaust hose.
5. **On all models,** after attaching exhaust hose to recovery station, depress main power switch on automatic charging station. Depress exhaust switch. Then follow normal operating procedures for recovery station.
6. Air is automatically vented from recovery tank during recycling. This feature eliminates the need to purge hoses before recovering refrigerant.
7. Operating engine with A/C Off during recovery may reduce recovery time.

8. To help prevent escape of refrigerant to the atmosphere, the recovery station can be attached to a "Dial A Charge" cylinder top vent port when filling the cylinder.
9. Always inspect the recovery station for residual oil from previous recovery.

Saturn

Before removing or replacing any of the A/C refrigerant lines or components, the refrigerant must be completely recovered using an A/C refrigerant recovery and recycling system. Always check the A/C system for pressure with a manifold gauge set to determine if refrigerant is present in the system. Performing recovery on an A/C system that is exposed to the atmosphere as a result of a leak, would allow the recovery station to pull only air into the tank.

SYSTEM EVACUATION

General Motors

VACUUM PUMP

The specification for A/C system pump-down is 28–29½ inches vacuum. This reading can be attained at or near sea level only. For each 1000 feet of altitude, the reading will be 1 inch vacuum lower. As an example, at 5000 feet elevation, only 23–24½ inch of vacuum can be obtained. **The system must be completely discharged before it can be evacuated. Damage to vacuum pump may result if pressurized refrigerant is allowed to enter pump.**

1. With manifold gauge set connected to system, remove cap from vacuum hose connector. Install manifold gauge set center hose to vacuum pump connector. Open low side gauge manifold hand valve only.
2. Ensure low side gauge is calibrated correctly. It should be reading zero. If not, adjust calibration.
3. Evacuate system with the vacuum pump until the low pressure gauge reads at least 28 inches of vacuum.
4. Continue evacuating system for an additional 15 minutes for routine system servicing or 20–30 minutes, if parts have been replaced.
5. When system evacuation is complete, close low side gauge manifold hand valve, then turn vacuum pump off.
6. Verify ability of system to hold vacuum. Watch low side gauge to see that gauge does not rise at a rate faster than 1 inch vacuum every 4–5 minutes. If low side gauge rises at too rapid a rate, install partial charge and leak test.
7. Correct leaks as necessary and evacuate system.
8. If system holds vacuum, charge system with refrigerant.

CHARGING STATION

A vacuum pump is built into the charging station. Complete moisture removal from the system is possible only with a vacuum pump constructed for the purpose.

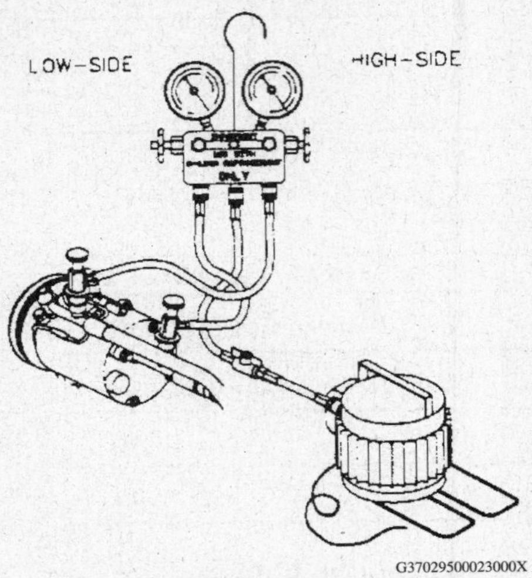

Fig. 15 High & low side Schraeder valve location. Saturn

The system must be completely discharged before it can be evacuated. Damage to the vacuum pump may result if pressurized refrigerant is allowed to enter.

1. Connect hose to vacuum pump, if system was discharged through charging station.
2. Open low side gauge hand valve of charging station.
3. Turn vacuum pump on according to instructions for specific station being used.
4. Evacuate system with the vacuum pump until the low pressure gauge reads at least 28 inches of vacuum. Continue evacuating system for an additional 15 minutes for routine system servicing or 20–30 minutes, if any parts have been replaced.
5. Close low side gauge hand valve, then turn vacuum pump off.
6. Verify ability of system to hold vacuum. Watch low side gauge to see that gauge does not rise at a rate faster than 1 inch vacuum every 4–5 minutes. If low side gauge rises at too rapid a rate, install partial charge and leak test.
7. If system holds vacuum, charge system with refrigerant.

Saturn

1. Connect manifold gauge set and vacuum pump to high and low side Schraeder valves. Refer to **Fig. 15** for valve locations.
2. Turn vacuum pump on and slowly open high and low side valves to pump. Allow system to evacuate for 20–30 minutes. Note vacuum gauge reading.
3. Close high and low side valves. Shut off vacuum pump.
4. Watch low side gauge for vacuum loss (1–3 minutes).
5. If loss is less than 1 inch Hg., from level recorded in previous step, proceed to "Charging System."
6. If vacuum loss is greater than 1 inch Hg., from level recorded in previous step, charge with ½ lb. of R134a refrigerant, depending on system type.
7. Leak test, repair leaks and retest. Disconnect high side adapter from service port and check for vacuum loss before leak testing.

CHARGING SYSTEM

General Motors

CHARGING STATION J-23500-01

Use of the following procedures will prevent charging station from being accidentally exposed to high-side vehicle system pressure.

Use instructions provided with charging station noting the following:

1. Do not connect high pressure line to A/C system.
2. Always keep high pressure valve closed on charging station.
3. Perform all evacuation and charging through low-side pressure service fitting.

DISPOSABLE CANS OR REFRIGERANT DRUM

Never use disposable cans to charge into the high pressure side of the system (compressor discharge port) or into a system that is at high temperature, high system pressures could be transferred into the charging can causing it to explode.

Charging System

1. Start and run engine until normal operating temperature is reached and allow to warm up (choke off, normal idle). Set A/C control lever to OFF.
2. **On all models except Cadillac with display diagnosis,** when 1 lb. of refrigerant has entered system, engage compressor by setting A/C lever to NORM and blower switch to HI to draw in remainder of charge.
3. **On Cadillac models with display diagnosis,** when 1 lb. of refrigerant has entered system, engage compressor by setting climate control panel to AUTO and blower switch to HI to draw in remainder of charge. If system switches to ECON when AUTO is pressed, low refrigerant is indicated, and the compressor will not operate. To obtain compressor operation, clear diagnostic trouble codes and select AUTO again.
4. **On all models,** cooling condenser with a large fan will speed up charging procedure by maintaining condenser temperature below charging cylinder temperature.
5. Close refrigerant supply valve and run engine for 30 seconds to clear lines and gauges.
6. With engine running, remove charging low side hose adapter from accumulator service fitting. Unscrew rapidly to avoid excessive refrigerant loss. **Do not remove a gauge line from its adapter when line is connected to**

A/C system. To disconnect line, always remove line adapter from service fitting. Do not remove charging hose at gauge set while attached to accumulator, as system will be discharged due to depressed Schraeder valve.

7. Replace protective cap on accumulator fitting and turn engine off.
8. Inspect system for leaks.
9. Start engine and inspect for proper system pressures.

Saturn

Never remove a gauge line from its adapter when line is connected to the A/C system. Always remove the line adapter from the service fitting to disconnect a line. Do not remove charging hose at the gauge set while attached to the service low-side fitting. This will result in a complete discharge of the system due to the depressed Schraeder valve in service low-side fitting and may cause personal injury due to escaping refrigerant.

1. Open source valve and allow 1 lb. of liquid R134a to flow into system through low-side service fitting, **Fig. 16.**
2. As soon as 1 lb. has been added to system, start engine, set A/C control to upper outlets, temperature lever to Max cold, blower speed on high and push A/C compressor button to On position (button should illuminate).
3. Slowly draw in remainder of refrigerant charge.

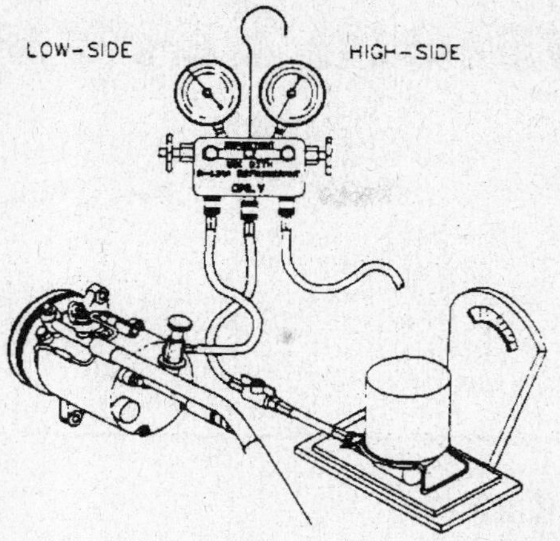

Fig. 16 System charging valve connection. Saturn

4. Turn off source valve and run engine for 30 seconds to clear lines and gauges.
5. With engine running, remove charging low-side hose adapter from suction pipe service fitting. Remove quickly to avoid excess refrigerant escaping from system.
6. Ensure an O-ring seal is inside of caps before installation, because cap is primary seal for A/C service fittings. Failure to tighten cap will result in refrigerant leakage.
7. Install protective caps on service fittings and hand tighten.
8. Turn engine off, then check system for leaks with electronic leak detector.

DRUM METHOD

Place R134a drum on scale and note total weight before charging. Watch scale during charging to determine amount of R134a used.

1. Connect manifold gauge set as follows:
   a. Connect low pressure gauge hose to low pressure service fitting on suction pipe at rear of compressor, **Fig. 16.** Do not connect high pressure line to A/C system.
   b. Connect center hose to R134a source.
2. Open valve on drum to start flow of refrigerant.

CHARGING STATION METHOD

Follow charging station manufacturer's instructions with the following exceptions:

1. Do not connect high pressure line to air conditioning system.
2. Keep high pressure valve on charging station closed at all times.
3. Perform entire evacuation and charge procedure through low-side pressure service fitting on suction pipe, **Fig. 16.**
4. Following these procedures will prevent accidental high-side vehicle system pressure being subjected to charging station in event an error is made in valve sequence during compressor operation to pull in R134a charge.

System Service

INDEX

OIL CHARGE

General Motors

When replacing certain components of an air conditioning system, an oil charge must be added to the system. Refer to " Oil Charge Data Table" for oil charge specifications.

If the refrigerant charge is abruptly lost due to a large refrigerant leak, approximately three ounces of refrigerant oil will be carried out of the system with the refrigerant. Upon replacement of a component which caused a large refrigerant leak, add three ounces of oil to the system plus the amount required for any component replaced as outlined under " Oil Charge Data Table." If possible, add oil directly to the replacement component.

Saturn

ADDING OIL

Adding oil to the A/C system should take place after recovery and before evacuation procedure.

1. Remove refrigeration discharge hose at compressor pipe connection.
2. Pour correct quantity of new Saturn compressor oil, or equivalent, into discharge hose pipe.
3. Always lubricate new O-rings with clean compressor oil prior to assembly.
4. Properly connect hose to compressor with new O-ring. Add new oil to components before installation.

OIL CHARGE REQUIREMENTS

The A/C system requires the use of Saturn Compressor Oil, or equivalent. Refer to the "Specifications" section for system capacity.

New oil quantities must be added to the system during component replacement, as follows:

1. **Compressor:** Remove, drain and measure oil. Drain replacement compressor. Add same amount of new compressor oil as was drained from removed compressor. All new replacement (service) compressors are charged with 2.21 ounces (65cc) of oil.
2. **Evaporator:** For 1.9L engine add 1.14 ounces, for 2.2L and 3.0L engines add 2.4 ounces of new compressor oil.
3. **Condenser:** For 1.9L engine add .75 ounces, for 2.2L and 3.0L engines add 1.3 ounces of new compressor oil.
4. **Receiver-Dehydrator:** For 1.9L engine add 1 ounce, for 2.2L and 3.0L engines add .4 ounce of new compressor oil.

OIL CHARGE DATA TABLE

GENERAL MOTORS

Model	Year	Compressor Model	Oil Charge (Fl. Oz.) When Replacing Component				
			Compressor	Evaporator	Condenser	Accumulator	Receiver & Dehydrator
BUICK							
Century	1997–2000	V-5(1)	(3)	3	1	(4)	—
LeSabre	1997–98	V-5(1)	(3)	3	1	3	—
	1999	V-5(1)	2	3	1	3	—
	2000	V-5(1)	(3)	3	1	3.5	—
Park Ave.	1997–98	V-5(1)	(3)	2	2	3	—
	1999–2000	V-5(1)	2	2	2	3	—
Regal	1997–98	V-5(1)	(3)	3	1	—	(6)
	1999	V-5(1)	(3)	3	1	(4)	—
	2000	V-5(1)	2	3	1	4	—
Riviera	1997–98	V-5(1)	(3)	3	1	3.5	—
	1999	V-5(1)	2	3	1	3	—
Skylark	1997–98	V-5(1)	(3)	3	1	3.5	(6)

Continued

GENERAL MOTORS—Continued

Model	Year	Compressor Model	Oil Charge (Fl. Oz.) When Replacing Component				
			Comp-ressor	Evap-orator	Con-denser	Accum-ulator	Receiver & Dehydrator
CADILLAC							
Catera	1997–98	V-5①	③	3	1	—	⑥
	1999–2000	V-5①	③	3	1	—	1
DeVille	1997–98	HD6/HR6-HE②	2	3	1	3.5	—
	1999	HD6	2	2	1	3	—
	2000	HD6	2.8	1	1	4	—
Eldorado	1997–98	HD6/HR6-HE②	2	3	1	④	—
	1999–2000	HD6	2	2	1	3	—
Seville	1997–98	HD6/HR6-HE②	2	3	1	④	—
	1999–2000	HD6	2.8	1	1	4	—
CHEVROLET/GEO							
Camaro	1997	HD6/HR6-HE②	③	3	1	3.5	⑥
	1998–2000	V-5①	③	3	1	3.5	⑥
Cavalier	1997–98	V-5①	③	3	1	3.5	—
	1999–2000	V-5①	2.8	2	1	3	—
Corvette	1997–98	V-7①	2	3	1	3.5	—
	1999–2000	V-7①	③	3	1	④	—
Impala	2000	V-5①	2	3	1	④	—
Lumina	1997–2000	V-5①	③	3	1	④	⑥
Malibu	1997–98	V-5①	③	3	1	—	⑥
	1999	V-5①	2	3	1	3.5	—
	2000	V-5①	③	3	1	3.5	—
Metro	1997–98	⑨	⑧	.7-1.0	.7-1.0	—	.4
		⑩	⑧	—	.7-1.0	—	.33
	1999–2000	⑩	3	—	.7-1.0	—	.33
Monte Carlo	1997–98	V-5①	③	3	1	—	⑥
	1999	V-5①	③	3	1	④	—
	2000	V-5①	2	3	1	④	—
Prizm	1997	⑤	③	3	⑦	—	3.5
	1998–2000	V-5①	2	2	2	2	—
OLDSMOBILE							
Achieva	1997–98	V-5①	③	3	1	3.5	⑥
Alero	1999–2000	V-5①	2	3	1	3.5	—
Aurora	1997–98	HD6/HR6-HE②	③	3	1	3.5	—
	1999	V-5①	2	2	1	3	—
Cutlass	1997–98	V-5①	③	3	1	—	⑥
	1999	V-5①	2	3	1	3.5	—
Cutlass Supreme	1997	V-5①	③	3	1	—	⑥
Intrigue	1998	V-5①	③	3	1	④	—
	1999–2000	V-7①	③	3	1	④	—
LSS, Regency, 88	1997–98	V-5①	③	3	1	3	—
	1999	V-5①	2	3	1	3	—
PONTIAC							
Bonneville	1997–98	V-5①	③	3	1	3	—
	1999	V-5①	2	3	1	3	—
	2000	V-5①	2	2	2	3	—
Firebird	1997	HD6/HR6-HE②	③	3	1	3.5	⑥
	1998–2000	V-5①	③	3	1	1	⑥
Grand Am	1997–98	V-5①	③	3	1	—	⑥
	1999–2000	V-5①	2	3	1	3.5	—
Grand Prix	1997–98	V-5①	③	3	1	④	⑥
	1999–2000	V-5①	③	3	1	④	—
Sunfire	1997–98	V-5①	③	3	1	3.5	—
	1999–2000	V-5①	2.8	2	1	3	—

① — Variable displacement compressor.
② — Fixed displacement compressor.
③ — Drain oil from old compressor and measure, then drain new compressor. If more than one ounce is drained from old compressor, add same amount to new compressor. If less than one ounce is drained from compressor, add two ounces.
④ — Drain oil from old compressor and measure, then drain new compressor. Add same amount of oil to new compressor as drained from old compressor.
④ — Drain oil from accumulator and measure. Add same amount of oil to new accumulator, plus one ounce. If no oil is drained, add two ounces to new accumulator.
⑤ — Nippondenso 10PA15.
⑥ — Drain oil from receiver and dehydrator assembly and measure. Add same amount of oil to new receiver and dehydrator assembly, plus one ounce.
⑦ — Drain oil from old condenser and measure. If more than .5 ounce is drained from old condenser, add same amount to new condenser. If less than .5 ounce is drained from condenser, add .5 ounce.
⑧ — Replacement compressors contain 2.7 ounces. Drain 1.4 ounces from new compressor before installing.
⑨ — Nippondenso 10 cylinder compressor.
⑩ — Sanden swash type.

OIL LEVEL CHECK

General Motors

Air conditioning oil levels can only be inspected with system discharged and compressor removed from vehicle. Replacement compressor may be shipped with 8–9 ounces of new refrigerant oil. Drain the new oil into a suitable container and retain for later use.

HARRISON HD6/HT6, HD6/HR-6HE 6 CYL., V5 & V7

1. Operate system for several minutes to stabilize system. Turn engine Off.
2. Using a suitable refrigerant recovery/recycling station, discharge the A/C system.
3. Remove compressor from vehicle.
4. Drain and measure refrigerant oil from old compressor through suction and discharge ports, and drain plug.
5. If no compressor oil leaks were noted and more than one ounce of oil is drained, add drained amount using new refrigerant oil.
6. If less than one ounce of oil is drained from compressor, add two ounces of new refrigerant oil.
7. When replacing other A/C components, add specified amount of new refrigerant oil to component as detailed in "Oil Charge Data Table."
8. Install compressor.
9. Evacuate and recharge system, perform leak test.
10. Ensure A/C system is operating properly.

NIPPONDENSO 10 CYLINDER

1. Discharge A/C system using suitable A/C recovery/recycle station.
2. Remove A/C compressor.
3. Drain, measure and discard refrigerant oil from old compressor.
4. Drain refrigerant oil from new compressor.
5. Add new refrigerant oil to replacement compressor equal to amount drained from old compressor.
6. Add specified amount of refrigerant oil to components that are replaced during compressor replacement as detailed in "Oil Charge Data Table."
7. Evacuate and recharge A/C system, perform leak test.
8. Ensure A/C system is operating properly.

Saturn

1. To measure compressor oil, compressor must be removed from engine.
2. Install high and low side compressor oil drain adapter tool Nos. SA9149AC-6 and SA9149AC-5, or equivalents, on low and high side ports.
3. Drain oil into suitable clean container from high side port first and move compressor to a different position to remove all oil possible. Turn compressor over to drain oil from low side port and rotate compressor drive plate in both directions to remove oil from compressor chambers.
4. Move compressor to different positions to remove all oil possible. turn compressor back to high side port to redrain and back to low side port to remove maximum amount of oil. Stop oil draining when oil coming from low and high side ports becomes only drops. Measure oil removed and record.
5. Inspect extracted oil for color change from clear to dark brown or black. Also inspect oil for presence of foreign substances, such as metal filings. If oil extracted is found as mentioned, receiver drier must be replaced.
6. Discard extracted oil properly and replace with specified quantity of new Saturn PAG compressor oil, or equivalent. Refer to " Specifications" for system capacity.

TECHNICAL SERVICE BULLETINS

Saturn

A/C ODOR AT VEHICLE START-UP

1997-98

On some of these models, a musty odor from the A/C system may be present at vehicle start-up. This odor may be caused by microbial growth on the evaporator core. To correct this condition, proceed as follows:

1. Visually inspect A/C evaporator drain for obstructions.
2. Using deodorizing aerosol kit PN 12377951, deodorize evaporator core.
3. Install A/C delayed blower control package PN 12370470.

RATTLE IN ENGINE COMPARTMENT AT IDLE

1997-98

The A/C compressor suction hose may contact the transaxle cover and/or battery tray, causing a rattle condition at idle. This condition exists on 1997 models except for 1997 vehicles built between VINs VZ304167 and VZ314184, which have the foam rubber installed during production and 1998 models built before and including VIN WZ128003.

Apply foam rubber to A/C compressor suction hose conduit as follows:

1. Disconnect front air intake duct assembly at air filter assembly to improve access to A/C compressor suction hose.
2. Remove A/C compressor suction hose conduit from A/C compressor suction hose.
3. Wipe A/C compressor suction hose conduit with alcohol to remove any oil or dirt contamination.
4. Trim a 4½x11¾ inch rectangle piece from a new battery heat shield part No. 21024475, or equivalent.
5. Apply adhesive part No. 10170, or equivalent, to back side of foam piece and to suction hose conduit.
6. Allow enough time for adhesive to flash, then install foam piece to conduit. Align edge of foam piece to opening in conduit and trim off access foam.
7. Install conduit to A/C compressor suction hose, using a mild liquid soap to help installation of conduit to hose.
8. Connect air intake duct.

Specifications

INDEX

A/C SPECIFICATIONS

GENERAL MOTORS

Model	Year	Refrigerant Capacity, Lbs.	Refrigerant Type	Refrigeration Oil			Compressor Clutch Air Gap, Inch
				Viscosity	Total System Capacity, Ounces	Compressor Oil Level	
BUICK							
Century	1997	1.88	R-134a	PAG②	8	①	④
	1998	1.88	R-134a	PAG②	9	①	.015–.020
	1999	1.88	R-134a	PAG②	9	①	.015
LeSabre	1997	2.00	R-134a	PAG②	8	①	.015–.020
	1998	2.00	R-134a	PAG②	9	①	.015–.020
	1999–2000	2.00	R-134a	PAG②	9	①	.015
Park Avenue	1997–98	2.00	R-134a	PAG②	9	①	.015–.020
	1999	2.00	R-134a	PAG②	9	①	.015
Regal	1997	1.88	R-134a	PAG②	8	①	④
	1998	1.88	R-134a	PAG②	9	①	.015–.020
	1999	1.88	R-134a	PAG②	9	①	.015
Riviera	1997–99	2.00	R-134a	PAG②	8	①	.020–.030
Skylark	1997–99	2.25	R-134a	PAG②	9	①	.015–.020
CADILLAC							
Catera	1997	2.60	R-134a	PAG②	9	①	.015
	1998–99	2.56	R-134a	PAG②	9	①	.015–.020
DeVille	1997	2.00	R-134a	PAG②	8	①	.020–.030
	1998	2.00	R-134a	PAG②	9	①	.020–.030
	1999	2.00	R-134a	PAG②	8	①	.020–.030
	2000	2.00	R-134a	③	9	①	—
Eldorado	1997	2.00	R-134a	PAG②	8	①	.020–.030
	1998	2.00	R-134a	PAG②	9	①	.020–.030
	1999	2.00	R-134a	PAG②	8	①	.020–.030
Seville	1997	2.00	R-134a	PAG②	8	①	.020–.030
	1998–99	2.00	R-134a	③	9	①	—
CHEVROLET/GEO							
Camaro	1997	⑤	R-134a	PAG②	8	①	⑥
	1998	1.50	R-134a	PAG②	9	①	⑦
	1999	1.50	R-134a	PAG②	9	①	.015
Cavalier	1997–99	1.50	R-134a	PAG②	9	①	.015–.020
Corvette	1997–99	1.63	R-134a	PAG②	8	①	.015
Impala	2000	1.88	R-134a	PAG②	9	①	.015–.020
Lumina	1997	1.88	R-134a	PAG②	8	①	.015–.020
	1998	1.88	R-134a	PAG②	9	①	.015–.020
	1999	1.88	R-134a	PAG②	9	①	.015
Malibu	1997–98	1.75	R-134a	PAG②	9	①	.015–.020
	1999	1.75	R-134a	PAG②	9.5	①	.016–.020
Metro	1997–98	1.21–1.32	R-134a	PAG②	3.4	①	.014–.025
	1999	1.10–1.32	R-134a	PAG②	3.4	①	—

Continued

GENERAL MOTORS—Continued

Model	Year	Refrigerant Capacity, Lbs.	Refrigerant Type	Refrigeration Oil: Viscosity	Refrigeration Oil: Total System Capacity, Ounces	Refrigeration Oil: Compressor Oil Level	Compressor Clutch Air Gap, Inch
CHEVROLET/GEO							
Monte Carlo	1997	1.88	R-134a	PAG②	8	①	.015–.020
	1998	1.88	R-134a	PAG②	9	①	.015–.020
	1999	1.88	R-134a	PAG②	9	①	.015
Prizm	1997	1.40–1.70	R-134a	PAG②	4.1	①	.014–.025
	1998	1.63	R-134a	PAG②	8	①	.014–.025
	1999	1.65	R-134a	PAG②	8	①	.014–.025
OLDSMOBILE							
Achieva	1997–98	2.25	R-134a	PAG②	9	①	.015–.020
Alero	1999	1.75	R-134a	PAG②	9.5	①	.016–.020
Aurora	1997–99	2.00	R-134a	PAG②	8	①	.015–.020
Cutlass	1997–98	1.75	R-134a	PAG②	9	①	.015–.020
	1999	1.75	R-134a	PAG②	9.5	①	.016–.020
Cutlass Supreme	1997	1.88	R-134a	PAG②	8	①	.015–.020
Intrigue	1998	1.88	R-134a	PAG②	9	①	.015–.020
	1999	1.88	R-134a	PAG②	9	①	.015
LSS, Regency & 88	1997	2.00	R-134a	PAG②	8	①	.015–.020
	1998	2.00	R-134a	PAG②	9	①	.015–.020
	1999	2.00	R-134a	PAG②	9	①	.015
PONTIAC							
Bonneville	1997	2.00	R-134a	PAG②	8	①	.015–.020
	1998	2.00	R-134a	PAG②	9	①	.015–.020
	1999	2.00	R-134a	PAG②	9	①	.015
	2000	2.00	R-134a	PAG②	9	①	.015–.020
Firebird	1997	⑤	R-134a	PAG②	8	①	⑥
	1998	1.50	R-134a	PAG②	9	①	⑦
	1999	1.50	R-134a	PAG②	9	①	.015
Grand Am	1997–98	2.25	R-134a	PAG②	9	①	.015–.020
	1999	1.75	R-134a	PAG②	8	①	.016–.020
Grand Prix	1997	1.88	R-134a	PAG②	8	①	④
	1998	1.88	R-134a	PAG②	9	①	.015–.020
	1999	1.88	R-134a	PAG②	9	①	.015
Sunfire	1997–99	1.5	R-134a	PAG②	9	①	.015–.020

①— "Oil Level" cannot be checked. Refer to total capacity in ounces.
②— On all models except Saturn, use GM PAG refrigerant oil No. 12345923 or equivalent.
③— On 1998–99 Seville & 2000 Deville use SUN PAG oil.
④— Conventional mount compressor, .015–.020 inch; direct mount compressor, .020–.030 inch.
⑤— 3.8L, 1.63 lbs.; 5.7L, 2.00 lbs.
⑥— HD6/HT6 compressor, .020–.030 inch; V5 compressor, .015–.020 inch.
⑦— Models w/ 3.8L engine & V5 compressor, .015–.020 inch. Models w 5.7L engine & V7 compressor, .015 inch.

SATURN

Engine	Refrigerant Type	Refrigerant Capacity, Lbs.	Refrigerant Oil: Total System Capacity, Ounces	Refrigerant Oil: Compressor Oil Level	Compressor Clutch Air Gap, Inch
1997-99					
1.9L	R-134a	1.50	5.07	①	.018–.030
2000					
1.9L	R-134a	1.50	5.07	①	.018–.030
2.2L & 3.0L	R-134a	1.875	7.5	①	.012–.024

① — Oil level cannot be checked. If compressor replacement is necessary, measure amount removed from old compressor, then add same amount to new compressor. Saturn service compressors are charged with 5.07 ounces for 1.9L engine & 7.5 ounces for 2.2L & 3.0L engines.

CHARGING VALVE LOCATION

General Motors

The high pressure charging valve is located either on the high pressure line or the muffler, and the low pressure charging valve is located either on the accumulator or low pressure line.

Saturn

Refer to "System Service" for charging valve locations and illustrations.

BELT TENSION

GENERAL MOTORS

Model	Engine	Belt Tension
BUICK		
Century	2.2L	50–70①
	3.1L	50–70①
LeSabre	3800	50–70①
Park Avenue	3800	50–70①
Regal	3.1L	50–70①
	3800	50–70①
Riviera	3800	50–70①
Skylark	2.3L & 2.4L	50–70①
	3.1L	50–70①
CADILLAC		
Catera	3.0L	50–70①
DeVille	4.6L	110①
Eldorado	4.6L	110①
Seville	4.6L	110①
CHEVROLET/GEO		
Camaro	3.4L	50–70①
	3800	50–70①
	5.7L	105–125①
Cavalier	2.2L	63–77①
	2.3L & 2.4L	50–70①
Corvette	5.7L	60–90①
Lumina	2.2L	63–77①
	3.1L	50–70①
	3.4L	50–70①
	3800	50–70①
Malibu	2.4L	50–70①
	3.1L	50–70①
Metro	1.0L	.28–.35②
	1.3L	.28–.35②
Monte Carlo	3.1L	50–70①
	3.4L	50–70①
	3800	50–70①
Prizm	1.6L	.20–.32②
	1.8L	.20–.32②
OLDSMOBILE		
Achieva	2.3L & 2.4L	50–70①
	3.1L	50–70①
Alero	2.4L & 3.4L	30–50③
Aurora	4.0L	①

Continued

GENERAL MOTORS—Continued

Model	Engine	Belt Tension
OLDSMOBILE		
Cutlass	2.4L	50–70①
	3.1L	50–70①
Cutlass Supreme	3.1L	50–70①
	3.4L	50–70①
Intrigue	3800	50–70①
LSS	3800	50–70 ①
Regency & 88	3800	50–70①
PONTIAC		
Bonneville	3800	50–70①
Firebird	3.4L	50–70①
	3800	50–70①
	5.7L	105–125①
Grand Am	2.3L & 2.4L	50–70①
	3.1L	50–70①
	3.4L	30–50③
Grand Prix	3.1L	50–70①
	3.4L	50–70①
	3800	50–70①
Sunfire	2.2L	63–77①
	2.3L & 2.4L	50–70①

① — Belt tension is controlled automatically by the belt tensioner. If belt tensioner has to operate out of its range to obtain adequate belt tension, replace belt.
② — Belt deflection measured in inches, using 22 lbs. of force.
③ — Belt tension measurement is the average of three measurements.

SATURN

Belt	Tension, Lbs.	
	New	Used
Accessory	50-65	45

COOLING FANS

TABLE OF CONTENTS

Variable Speed Fans, General Motors

INDEX

DESCRIPTION

The fan drive clutch, **Fig. 1,** is a fluid coupling containing silicone oil. Fan speed is regulated by the torque carrying capacity of the silicone oil. The more silicone oil in the coupling, the greater the fan speed. The less silicone oil, the slower the fan speed.

Two types of fan drive clutches are in use. On one, **Fig. 2,** a bi-metallic strip and control piston on the front of the fluid coupling regulates the amount of silicone oil entering the coupling. The bi-metallic strip flexes outward with an increase in surrounding temperature and allows a piston to move outward. The piston opens a valve regulating the flow of silicone oil into the coupling from a reserve chamber. The silicone oil is returned to the reserve chamber through a bleed hole when the valve is closed.

On the other type of fan drive clutch, **Fig. 3,** a heat-sensitive, bi-metal spring connected to an opening plate brings about a similar result. Both units cause the fan speed to increase with a rise in temperature and to decrease as the temperature goes down.

In some cases a Flex-Fan is used instead of a Fan Drive Clutch. Flexible blades vary the volume of air being drawn through the radiator, automatically increasing the pitch at low engine speeds.

Fig. 1 Typical variable speed cooling fan

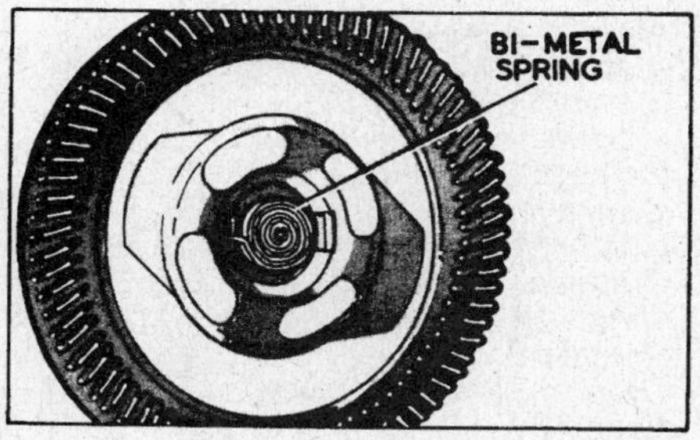

Fig. 3 Variable-speed fan w/ coiled bi-metal thermostatic spring

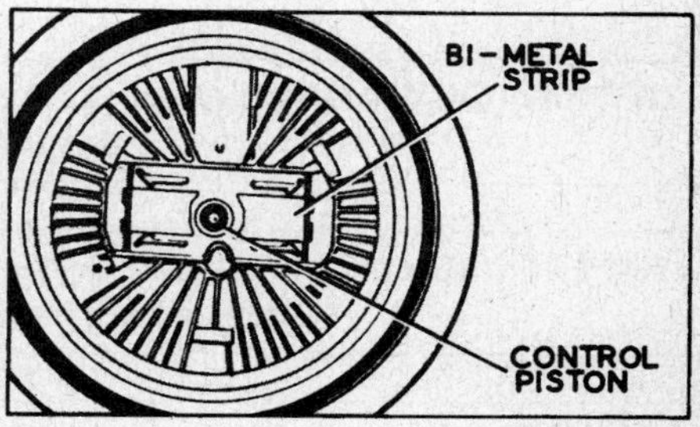

Fig. 2 Variable speed fan w/flat bi-metal thermostatic spring

COMPONENT DIAGNOSIS & TESTING

FAN DRIVE CLUTCH TEST

Do not operate the engine until the fan has been checked for possible cracks and separations.

Run the engine at a fast idle speed (1000 RPM) until normal operating temperature is reached. This process can be expedited by blocking off the front of the radiator with a suitable piece of cardboard. Regardless of temperature, the unit must be operated for at least five minutes before being tested.

Stop the engine and, using a glove or a cloth, immediately check the effort required to turn the fan. If considerable effort is required, it can be assumed that the coupling is operating satisfactorily. If very little effort is required to turn the fan, it is an indication that the coupling is not operating properly and should be replaced.

If the clutch fan is the coiled bi-metal spring type, it may be tested while the vehicle is being driven. To check, disconnect the bi-metal spring, **Fig. 4,** and rotate the spring 90° counterclockwise. This disables the temperature controlled free wheeling feature and the clutch performs like a conventional fan. If this cures the overheating condition, replace the fan clutch.

COMPONENT SERVICE

To prevent silicone fluid from draining into fan drive bearing, do not store or place drive unit on bench with rear of shaft pointing downward.

The removal procedure for either type of

fan clutch assembly is similar for all vehicles. The unit must be unfastened from the water pump, then it may be lifted from the vehicle.

The type of unit shown in **Fig. 2** may be partially disassembled for inspection and cleaning as follows:

1. Remove bolts holding assembly together and separate fan from drive clutch.
2. Remove metal strip on front of fan clutch by pushing one end toward fan clutch body to clear retaining bracket.
3. Push strip aside until its opposite end springs out of place, then remove small control piston.
4. Inspect piston for free movement in coupling device. If piston sticks, clean it with emery cloth. If bi-metal strip is damaged, replace entire unit. **These strips are not interchangeable.**
5. When reassembling, install control piston so that projection on end will contact metal strip, then install metal strip.
6. After reassembly, clean clutch drive with a solvent soaked cloth. Avoid dipping clutch assembly in any type of liquid.
7. Install assembly in vehicle.

The coil spring type of fan clutch cannot be disassembled, serviced or repaired. If it does not function properly, it must be replaced with a new unit.

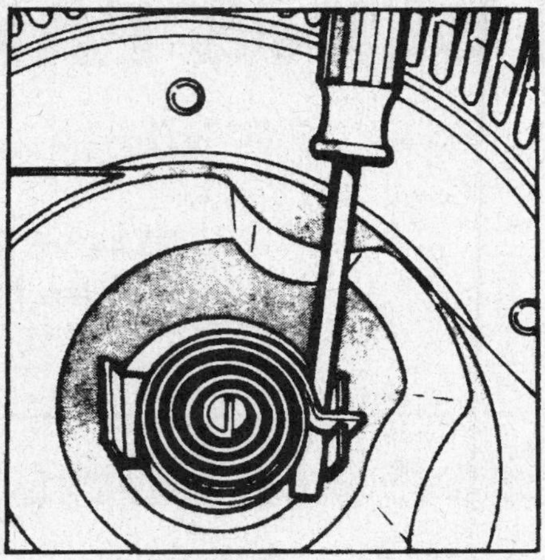

GC1089100035000X

Fig. 4 Bi-metal spring disengagement

Electric Cooling Fans, General Motors

NOTE: On Air Bag Equipped Models, Refer To Air Bag System Precautions Located In The Front Of This Manual For System Disarming & Arming Procedures.

NOTE: "Electrical Symbol & Wire Color Code Identification" Located In The Front Of This Manual Can Be Used As An Aid When Using Wiring Circuits Found In This Section.

NOTE: Refer To "Computer Relearn Procedures" Located In The Front Of This Manual For Computer Relearn Procedures.

INDEX

PRECAUTIONS

AIR BAG SYSTEMS

Refer to "Air Bag System Precautions" in the front of this manual for system disarming and arming procedures.

BATTERY GROUND CABLE

Prior to service, disconnect battery ground cable and isolate as required.

DESCRIPTION

ACHIEVA, CAVALIER, SKYLARK, SUNFIRE & 1997–98 GRAND AM

Cooling fan operation is controlled by the PCM through the fan relay. The PCM uses signals from the engine coolant temperature sensor, intake air temperature sensor, A/C refrigerant pressure sensor and vehicle speed sensor to determine when and how long the fan should operate. The PCM turns the cooling fan on by providing a ground path for the cooling fan control circuit which activates the coolant fan relay.

The relay will be commanded on anytime engine coolant temperature exceeds 223°F, A/C clutch is requested, vehicle speed is less than 38 mph or any Diagnostic Trouble Code (DTC) that causes the MIL lamp to illuminate.

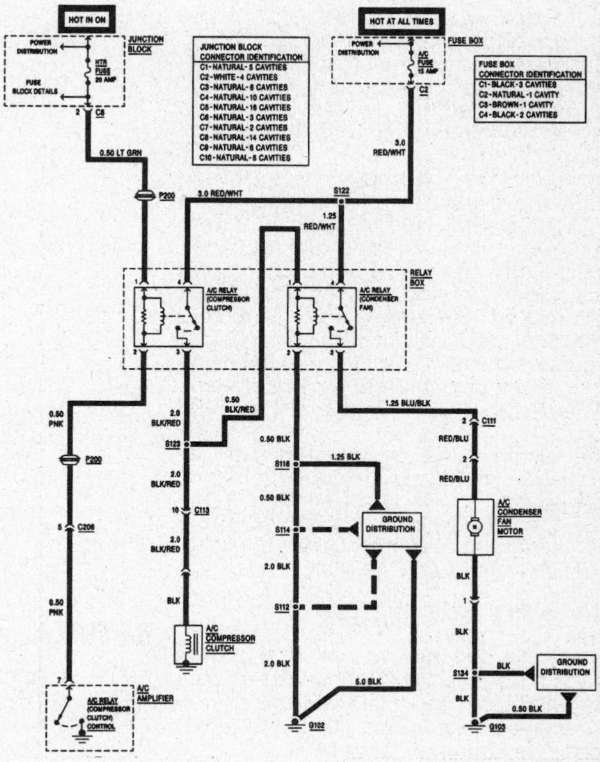

GC1089500273000X

Fig. 1 Wiring diagram (A/C condenser fan). 1997 Metro

ALERO & 1999-2000 GRAND AM

The electric cooling fans are controlled by the Body Control Module (BCM) which enables the fans through the PCM. The PCM enables the ground path for the three cooling fan relays. The relays are used to control the high current flow to power the cooling fan motors.

When minimum cooling is required, the BCM will command the PCM to energize the No. 1 cooling fan relay and since both fans are connected in series through the Mode Control relay, both fans will run at low speed. When maximum cooling is required, the BCM will command the PCM to energize all three cooling fan relays. Power is supplied to the left fan through the No. 1 cooling fan relay and is grounded through the Mode Control relay. The right fan is powered directly through the No. 2 cooling fan relay, causing both fans to run at high speed.

AURORA

The electric cooling fans are used to cool engine coolant flowing through the radiator. They are also used to cool the refrigerant flowing through the A/C condenser.

The electric cooling fans are controlled by the PCM. The PCM controls the ground path for the three cooling fan relays. The relays are used to control the high current flow to power the cooling fan motors. Both fans operate together. When minimum cooling is required, the PCM energizes the low speed cooling fan relay No. 1, and both fans operate at low speed since the fans are connected in series thorough the series/parallel cooling fan relay No. 2. The series/parallel coolant fan relay is a dual position switch and while de-energized, supplies a ground path for the low speed fan circuit. When maximum cooling is required, the PCM energizes all three cooling fan relays. The left hand coolant fan is still power through the low speed cooling fan relay No. 1, but is now grounded through the series/parallel cooling fan relay No. 2 and operates at high speed. The right hand coolant fan is powered directly through the high speed cooling fan relay No. 3 and also operates at high speed.

The low speed cooling fans are controlled by the PCM based on inputs from the A/C system, Engine Coolant Temperature (ECT) sensor and Vehicle Speed Sensor (VSS). The PCM will command low speed fans to turn On when ECT sensor is above 223°F. The PCM will turn the fans Off when the temperature drops about 5°F. The minimum On time for low speed fans is 50 seconds.

The PCM will command high speed fans to turn On at idle when a certain DTC is set, the ECT is above 230°F or the A/C head pressure is above 248 psi. If the high speed fans were turned On by the ECT, the PCM will switch the fans back to low speed when the temperature drops about 5°F. Minimum On time for high speed fans is 30 seconds.

BONNEVILLE, EIGHTY EIGHT, LESABRE, LSS & REGENCY

1997–99

Power for the fan motors is supplied through the Cooling Fan fuse in the LH Maxi fuse block. The cooling fan relays are energized when current supplied by the Cooling Fan fuse flows through the relay coils to ground through the PCM.

During low speed cooling fan operation the PCM supplies a ground path for the low speed cooling fan relay. This closes the low speed relay contacts, allowing current to flow directly to the righthand cooling fan and through a resistor to the lefthand cooling fan.

During high speed cooling fan operation the PCM enables both relays, supplying current directly to both cooling fan relays.

2000

The PCM controls the operation of the cooling fans. This is accomplished by providing a ground path for the cooling fan relay coils within the PCM. The relay contacts will close and complete the circuit between the fusible link at the battery junction block and the fan motors. Whenever the fans are commanded on both fans will be running.

Power for the fan motors is supplied through the Cooling Fan fuse in the righthand Maxi fuse block. The cooling fan relays are energized when current from the Cooling Fan fuse flows through the relay coils to ground through the PCM.

Low speed fan operation will be commanded on anytime engine coolant temperature exceeds 221°F, A/C is requested and ambient temperature is more than 48°F, or A/C pressure is greater than 190 psi.

Before the PCM operates the fans at high speed, it will delay control of the series/parallel and high speed fan relays for six seconds. This six second delay ensures the cooling fan electrical load will not exceed the capacity of the system.

CAMARO & FIREBIRD

Power for the fan motors is supplied through a 40 amp Maxifuse located in the underhood fuse block. The cooling fan relays receive power from a 25 amp fuse located in the underhood fuse block.

During low fan speed operation the PCM supplies a ground path for the No. 1 engine cooling fan relay. This closes the cooling fan relay contacts, allowing current to flow from the 40 amp Maxifuse, through the relays contacts and to left engine cooling fan. The ground path for the left cooling fan is through the No. 3 cooling fan relay and right cooling fan. The result is a series circuit with both fans running at low. The PCM will complete the ground circuit for low speed cooling fan operation anytime engine coolant temperature exceeds 221°F, A/C is requested and ambient temperature is more than 50°F, or A/C pressure is more than 190 psi.

During high speed operation, the PCM supplies a ground path for the No. 1 engine cooling fan relay. After a six second delay, the PCM supplies a ground path for the No. 2 and No. 3 cooling fan relays. The six second delay ensures the cooling fan electrical load will not exceed the capacity of the system. During high speed operation, both coolant fans are supplied current from the 40 amp maxifuse and each cooling fan has its own ground path. The PCM will complete the ground circuit for high speed cooling fan operation anytime engine coolant temperature exceeds 235°F or A/C refrigerant pressure is more than 275 psi.

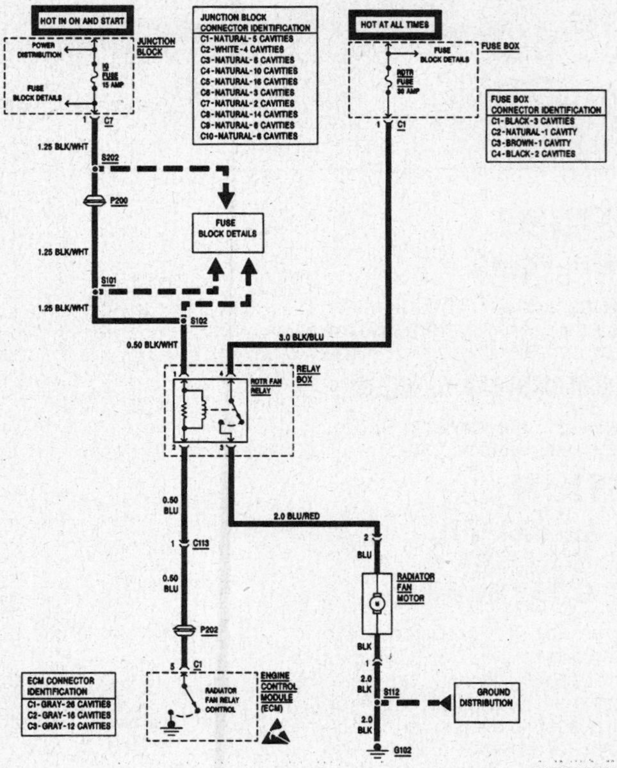

GC1089500274000X

Fig. 2 Wiring diagram (engine cooling fan). 1997 Metro

CATERA

This system consists of one engine coolant fan, two auxiliary coolant fans, two temperature switches, an A/C refrigerant pressure switch, seven fan control relays and a coolant fan resistor.

Battery voltage is supplied to the auxiliary water pump whenever the ignition switch is in the On position. When coolant temperature reaches 212°F (100°C), the primary cooling fan temperature switch stage 1 will close, enabling the Engine Control Module (ECM) relay K48 and the fan control relay K26 to energize. When the ECM relay K48 energizes, battery voltage is applied to the ECM cooling blower. When fan control K26 energizes, battery voltage is applied to the No. 1 and No. 2 auxiliary cooling fans, causing the fans to operate at half speed. The fan control relay K26 will also supply battery voltage to the engine coolant fan through the engine coolant fan resistor. The resistor will cause the engine coolant fan to operate at half speed. The fan control relay K26 will supply battery voltage to the timing control pump through the normally closed contacts of the auxiliary water pump relay K22. This allows the timing control pump to operate. The primary cooling fan temperature switch stage No. 1 contacts will open when the coolant temperature reaches 203°F (95°C). This will turn off all three coolant fans, the ECM blower and the timing control pump, unless the A/C is on.

If the ignition switch is in the OFF position and the coolant temperature is above 212°F (100°C), both auxiliary fans, engine coolant fan and timing control pump will remain on until coolant temperature drops below 203°F (95°C).

CENTURY & REGAL

The engine coolant fan motors receive power from maxifuses located in the underhood electrical center.

During low speed fan operation, the PCM supplies a ground path for the No. 1 Cool Fan relay. This energizes the relay coil, closes the fan relay contacts and supplies current to the primary cooling fan. The ground path for the primary is through the No. 2 Cool Fan relay and secondary fan motor. This results in a series circuit with both fans running at low speed.

To operate the fans at high speed, the PCM first supplies a ground path for the No. 1 Cool Fan relay, then after a three second delay the PCM supplies a ground circuit for the No. 2 and No. 3 Cool Fan relays. This results in a parallel circuit with both fan running at high speed.

CORVETTE

The PCM controls low speed operation by providing a ground path for the Cool Fan 1 relay. This closes the relay switch and allows current to flow from the battery, through the switch to the lefthand cooling fan. The ground circuit for the lefthand fan motor runs through the Cool Fan 3 relay to the righthand cooling fan. This creates a series circuit with both fans running at low speed.

The PCM controls high speed fan operation by providing a ground path for Cool Fan

1, Cool Fan 2 and Cool Fan 3 relays. Providing separate ground paths for the relays creates a parallel circuit, which allows both fans to run at high speed.

CUTLASS & MALIBU

Power for the fan motors is supplied by fuses and relays in the Underhood Electrical Center (U/H BEC). The cooling fan relays are energized when current from the No. 1 and No. 2 Cool Fan fuses flows through the relay coils to ground through the PCM. The No. 1 fan control relay circuit is grounded for low speed fan operation. The No. 1 fan control relay, mode control relay and No. 2 fan control relay are all grounded for high speed fan operation.

During low speed fan operation, the PCM supplies a ground path for the No. 1 fan control relay. This closes the fan control relay contacts, allowing current to flow from the U/H BEC through the relay contacts and to the left cooling fan motor. The ground path for the lefthand cooling fan motor is through the No. 2 fan control relay and righthand cooling fan motor. This results in a series circuit with both fans running at low speed.

During high speed fan operation, the PCM supplies a ground path for the No. 1 fan control relay. The PCM also supplies a ground path for the No. 2 fan control relay and the mode control relay. The No. 1 cooling fan relay is grounded through the Mode Control relay. The right fan is powered directly through the No. 2 cooling fan relay, causing both fans to run at high speed.

CUTLASS SUPREME

Power is supplied to the cooling fan motors through a fusible link and three maxi-fuses located in the underhood electrical center.

To operate the primary cooling fan, the PCM supplies a ground path for the No. 1 fan relay through the Output Driver Module (ODM) B output 1. This closes the relay contacts and current flows through the relay and to the cooling fan.

To operate the secondary cooling fan, the PCM keeps the primary fan operating and supplies a ground path for the No. 2 fan relay. This closes the relay contacts and current flows through the relay and to the cooling fan.

DEVILLE, ELDORADO & SEVILLE

The PCM will command low speed fan operation when engine temperature is in excess of 229°F, transaxle fluid temperature is greater than 302°F, when A/C is requested, or after the vehicle is shutoff and coolant temperature is more than 304°F and system voltage is more than 12 volts the fans will stay on for approximately three minutes.

The PCM will command high fan speed operation when engine coolant temperature is in excess of 234°F, transaxle fluid temperature is greater than 304°F, or when certain DTCs are set.

To operate the fans at low speed the PCM provides a ground path for the Cooling Fan No. 1 relay. This allows current to flow through both cooling fans in a series circuit to ground.

To operate the fans at high speed the PCM provides a ground path for all three cooling fan relays. This changes the circuit to parallel and operates both fans at high speed.

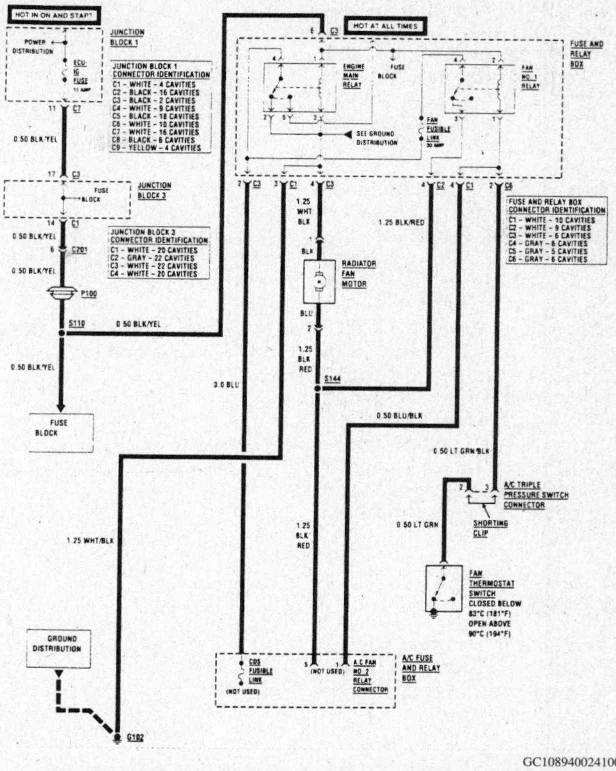

Fig. 3 Wiring diagram. 1997 Prizm less A/C

GRAND PRIX

The cooling fan motors receive power from maxifuses located in the underhood accessory wiring junction block.

During low speed fan operation, the PCM supplies a ground path for the Cool Fan 1 relay. This energizes the relay coil, closes the relay contacts and supplies current to the lefthand cooling fan motor. The ground path for the lefthand cooling fan motor is through the Cool Fan relay and righthand coolant fan motor. This results in a series circuit with both fans running at low speed.

To operate the fans at high speed, the PCM first supplies a ground path for the Cool Fan 1 relay. After a 3–5 second delay, the PCM supplies a ground path for the Cool Fan and Cool Fan 2 relays. The result is a parallel circuit with both fans running at high speed.

IMPALA & 2000 MONTE CARLO

This coolant fan system is equipped with two electric cooling fans and three fan relays which are controlled by the PCM. The relays are wired in a series/parallel arrangement that allows the PCM to operate both fans together at low or high speed.

The PCM controls low fan speed operation by grounding the control circuit for Cool Fan No. 1 relay. The relay supplies current to the No. 1 fan motor. The ground path for the No. 1 fan motor is through the Cool Fan No. 2 relay and the No. 2 fan motor. This results in a series circuit which operates both fans at low speed. The PCM operates the cooling fans at low speed whenever engine coolant temperature exceeds 223°F, A/C operation is requested and ambient temperature is greater than 50°F, A/C refrigerant pressure is greater than 190 psi, or the engine is shutoff and coolant temperature is more than 284.°

To control high speed fan operation, the PCM grounds the control circuit for the Cool Fan No. 1 relay. Then after a three second delay, the PCM grounds the control circuit for Cool Fan No. 2 and No. 3 relays. When the Cool Fan No. 2 relay is energized, both the fans have their own ground path creating a parallel circuit. This parallel circuit causes both fans to operate at high speed. The PCM operates the cooling fans at high speed whenever engine coolant temperature exceeds 230°F, A/C refrigerant pressure exceeds 240 psi.

INTRIGUE

This coolant fan system is equipped with two electric cooling fans and three fan relays which are controlled by the PCM. The relays are wired in a series/parallel arrangement that allows the PCM to operate both fans together at low or high speed.

The PCM controls low fan speed operation by grounding the control circuit for fan relay No. 1. The relay supplies current to the No. 1 fan motor. The ground path for the No. 1 fan motor is through the No. 2 fan relay and the No. 2 fan motor. This results in a series circuit which operates both fans at low speed. The PCM operates the cooling fans at low speed whenever engine coolant temperature exceeds 229°F, A/C operation is requested, or the engine is shutoff and coolant temperature is more than 304°F and system voltage is more than 12 volts. The PCM will shutoff the fans whenever coolant temperature drops below 216°F.

To control high speed fan operation, the PCM grounds the control circuit for the No. 1 fan relay. Then after a three second delay, the PCM grounds the control circuit for the No. 2 and No. 3 fan relays. When the No. 2 fan relay is energized, both the fans have their own ground path creating a parallel circuit. This parallel circuit causes both fans to operate at high speed. The PCM operates the cooling fans at high speed whenever engine coolant temperature exceeds 234°F, A/C refrigerant pressure exceeds 240 psi, or certain Diagnostic Trouble Codes (DTC)s are set.

LUMINA & 1997–99 MONTE CARLO

Power for the cooling fan motors is supplied through a fusible link at the battery junction block. The cooling fans are energized when current flows from the PCM fuse in the No. 1 underhood electrical center and the Fan fuse in the No. 2 underhood electrical center through the relay coils to ground through the PCM.

During low speed fan operation, the PCM supplies a ground path for the No. 1 engine cooling fan relay. This closes the fan relay contacts and allows current to flow to the left engine coolant fan. The ground path for the left cooling fan is the No. 3 cooling fan relay. This results in a series circuit with both cooling fans running at low speed.

During high speed fan operation, the PCM supplies a ground path for the No. 1, No. 2 and No. 3 engine cooling fan relays. With all three relays closed, each fan is supplied current from the battery junction block and has its own ground path.

METRO

Radiator Fan

When ignition switch is in On position, system voltage is applied through ignition fuse to radiator fan switch. Fan switch closes when engine coolant temperature reaches 208°F. With fan switch closed, voltage is applied to radiator fan motor. Since the fan motor is permanently grounded, fan operates as soon as voltage is applied. When temperature falls below 199°F, fan switch opens and voltage to fan motor is interrupted.

A/C Condenser Fan

When ignition switch is in On position, system voltage is applied to dual pressure switch through heater fuse on vehicles equipped with automatic transaxle, or ignition fuse on vehicles equipped with manual transaxle. With dual pressure switch closed, voltage is applied to A/C clutch relay. A/C clutch relay is energized when A/C amplifier grounds coil of relay. With A/C clutch relay energized, voltage is applied through A/C fuse and closed contacts of A/C clutch relay to coil of A/C condenser fan relay. Since A/C condenser fan relay is permanently grounded, relay energizes, contacts close, and voltage is applied to condenser fan. Since condenser fan is permanently grounded, an operates as soon voltage is applied.

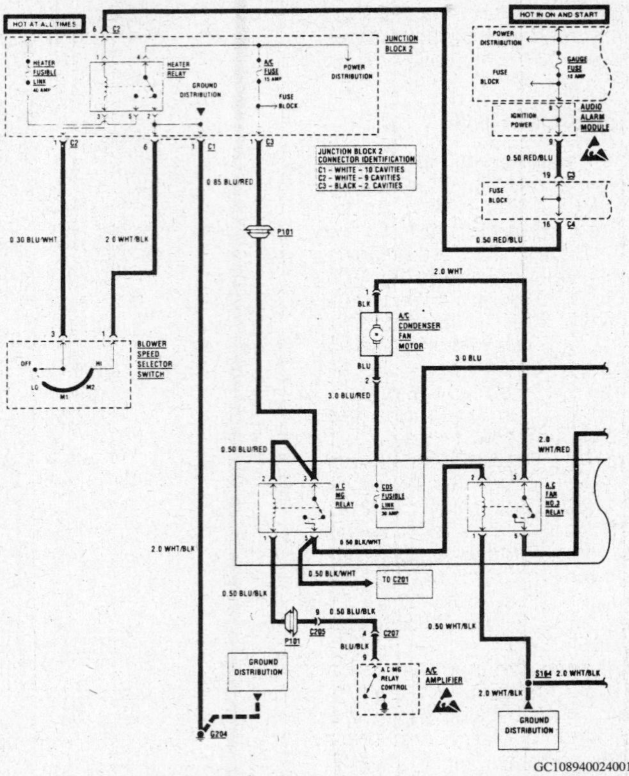

Fig. 4 Wiring diagram (Part 1 of 2). 1997 Prizm with A/C

PARK AVENUE

Power for the cooling fan motors is supplied by the Cool Fan No. 1 and Cool Fan No. 2 Maxi fuses.

During low speed fan operation, the PCM supplies a ground path for the No. 1 Cool Fan relay through the low speed fan control circuit. This energizes the relay coil, closes the relay contacts and supplies current to the primary cooling fan. The ground path for the primary cooling fan is through the No. 2 Cool Fan (series/parallel) relay and secondary cooling fan motor. This results in a series circuit with both fans running at low speed.

To operate the cooling fans at high speed, the PCM first supplies a ground path for No. 1 Cool Fan relay. After a three second delay the PCM supplies a ground path for the No. 2 and No. 3 Cool Fan relays. During high speed operation, both the primary and secondary cooling fans are supplied current through their respective maxifuse and each fan has its own ground.

PRIZM

When the ignition switch is in either the Run or Start positions, system voltage is applied to the coils of the main engine relay and to fan relay 1. Because the main relay is grounded at G108, the relay is energized, its contacts close, and battery voltage is applied through the relay and the radiator fan fusible link to the contacts of fan relay 1.

When engine coolant temperature is below 194°F, the cooling fan temperature switch provides a ground for relay 1, the relay energizes and its contacts are pulled open.

Whenever engine coolant temperature reaches or exceeds 194°F, the cooling fan temperature switch opens, fan relay 1 is de-energized, its contacts close, and system voltage is applied through the relay to the cooling fan motor. Since the fan motor is grounded at G108, it start to operate as soon as voltage is applied.

When engine coolant temperature drops below 194°F, the cooling fan temperature switch closes to ground, fan relay 1 is energized the relay contacts are pulled open and system voltage is no longer applied to the fan motor.

RIVIERA

The No. 1 coolant fan motor receives power from a 40 amp maxifuse. The No. 2 coolant fan motor receives power from a 30 amp maxifuse. Both maxifuses are located in the underhood electrical center.

To operate the fans at low speed, the PCM supplies a ground path for the No. 1 cooling fan relay through the low speed fan control circuit. This energizes the relay coil and supplies current to the primary cooling fan. The ground path for the primary cooling fan is through the No. 2 cooling fan relay and secondary cooling fan motor. This results in a series circuit with both fans running at low speed.

To run the fans at high speed, the PCM first supplies a ground path for the No. 1 cooling fan relay. After a three second delay, the PCM supplies a ground path for the No. 2 and No. 3 cooling fan relays. During high speed fan operation, both the primary and secondary cooling fans are supplied current through their maxifuses and each has its own ground.

TROUBLESHOOTING

EXCEPT METRO

1. Check for open fuses.
2. Check for open fusible links.
3. Check for corrosion on cooling fan and cooling fan relay connectors.
4. Check for clean and tight grounds.

METRO

Preliminary Check

1. Check A/C fuse for open.
2. Check IG fuse for open.
3. Check fusible link "B"for open.
4. Check radiator fan fuse for open.
5. Check engine coolant level.
6. Check A/C system for proper refrigerant charge.
7. Check grounds G101, G104, and G201 are clean and tight.

System Check

1. Run engine until engine coolant temperature reaches 208°F. Cooling fan should run.
2. Turn A/C switch to On position. A/C compressor clutch should engage and a/c condenser fan motor should run.
3. Turn A/C switch to Off position. A/C compressor clutch should disengage and A/C condenser fan motor should stop.

SYSTEM DIAGNOSIS & TESTING

Wiring Diagrams

Refer to **Figs. 1 through 27** for wiring diagrams.

Diagnostic Aids

If the temperature light or gauge indicated overheating, but no boil over is detected, the gauge or light should be checked. The gauge accuracy can also be checked using a scan tool to compare the coolant temperature reading with the gauge reading.

If the engine is actually overheating, and the gauge indicates overheating, but the cooling fan is not operating, the Engine Coolant Temperature (ETC) sensor may have shifted out of calibration and should be replaced.

If the engine is overheating and the cooling fan is operating, the cooling system should be checked.

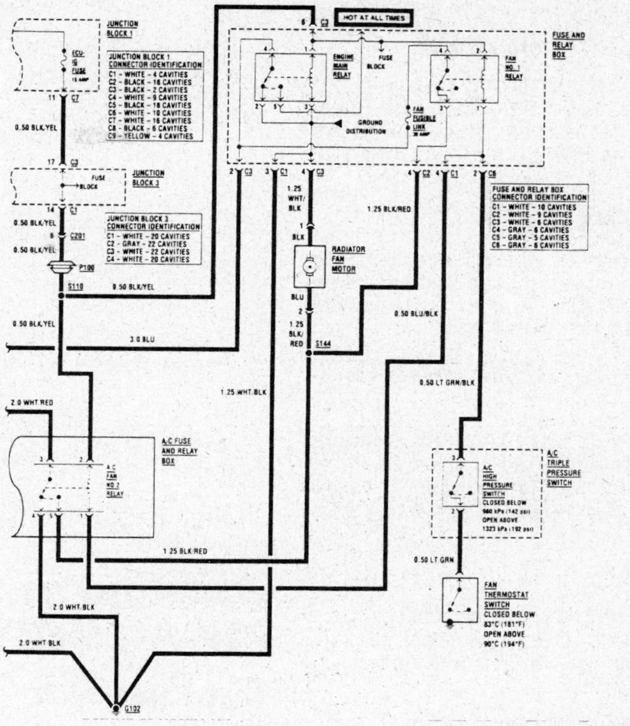

GC1089400240020X

Fig. 4 Wiring diagram (Part 2 of 2). 1997 Prizm with A/C

Diagnostic Tests

ACHIEVA, CAVALIER, SKYLARK, SUNFIRE & 1997-98 GRAND AM

Refer to **Fig. 28** for diagnostic procedures. Refer to "Diagnostic Aids" as previously outlined when referenced by diagnostic tests.

ALERO, CUTLASS, MALIBU & 1999-2000 GRAND AM

Refer to **Fig. 29** for diagnostic procedures. Refer to "Diagnostic Aids" as previously outlined when referenced by diagnostic tests.

AURORA

Refer to **Figs. 30 through 35** for diagnostic procedures. Refer to "Diagnostic Aids" as previously outlined when referenced by diagnostic tests.

BONNEVILLE, EIGHTY EIGHT, LSS, REGENCY & 1997-99 LESABRE

Refer to **Fig. 36** when performing diagnostic procedures. Refer to "Diagnostic Aids" as previously outlined when referenced by diagnostic tests.

CAMARO & FIREBIRD

Refer to **Figs. 37 through 40** for diagnostic procedures. Refer to "Diagnostic Aids" as previously outlined when referenced by diagnostic tests.

CATERA

1997

Refer to **Figs. 41 through 46** when performing diagnostic procedures on these systems. Refer to "Diagnostic Aids" as previously outlined when referenced by diagnostic tests.

1998-2000

Refer to **Figs. 47 through 57** when performing diagnostic procedures on these systems. Refer to "Diagnostic Aids" as previously outlined when referenced by diagnostic tests.

CENTURY & REGAL

Refer to **Figs. 58 through 61** when performing diagnostic procedures on these systems. Refer to "Diagnostic Aids" as previously outlined when referenced by diagnostic tests.

CORVETTE

Refer to **Figs. 62 through 65** for diagnostic procedures. Refer to "Diagnostic Aids" as previously outlined when referenced by diagnostic tests.

CUTLASS SUPREME

Refer to **Fig. 66** when performing diagnostic procedures on these systems. Refer to " Diagnostic Aids" as previously outlined when referenced by diagnostic tests.

ELDORADO, 1997 SEVILLE & 1997–99 DEVILLE

Refer to **Figs. 67 through 78** when performing diagnostic procedures on these systems. Refer to "Diagnostic Aids" as previously outlined when referenced by diagnostic tests.

GRAND PRIX

Refer to **Fig. 79** when performing diagnostic procedures on these systems. Refer to " Diagnostic Aids" as previously outlined when referenced by diagnostic tests.

IMPALA & 2000 MONTE CARLO

Refer to **Figs. 80 through 83** when performing diagnostic procedures on these systems. Refer to "Diagnostic Aids " as previously outlined when referenced by diagnostic tests.

INTRIGUE

Refer to **Fig. 84** for diagnostic procedures. Refer to "Diagnostic Aids" as previously outlined when referenced by diagnostic tests.

LUMINA & 1997–99 MONTE CARLO

Refer to **Fig. 85** when performing diagnostic procedures on these systems. Refer to " Diagnostic Aids" as previously outlined when referenced by diagnostic tests.

METRO

Refer to **Figs. 86 through 88** when performing diagnostic procedures. Refer to "Diagnostic Aids" as previously outlined when referenced by diagnostic tests.

PARK AVENUE

Refer to **Fig. 89** when performing diagnostic procedures.

PRIZM

Refer to **Figs. 90 through 97** when performing diagnostic procedures. Refer to "Diagnostic Aids" as previously outlined when referenced by diagnostic tests.

RIVIERA

Refer to **Fig. 98** for diagnostic procedures.

1998–2000 SEVILLE & 2000 DEVILLE

Refer to **Figs. 99 through 104** when performing diagnostic procedures. Refer to "Diagnostic Aids" as previously outlined when referenced by diagnostic tests.

2000 BONNEVILLE & LESABRE

Refer to **Figs. 105 through 108** when performing diagnostic procedures. Refer to "Diagnostic Aids" as previously outlined when referenced by diagnostic tests.

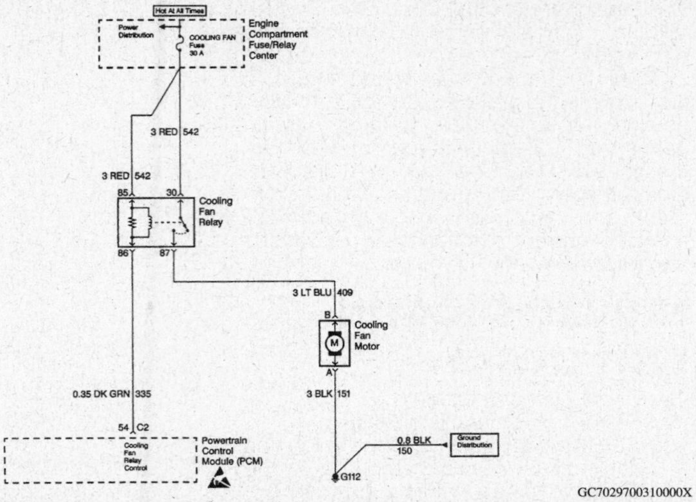

Fig. 5 Wiring diagram. Achieva, Cavalier, Skylark, Sunfire & 1997–98 Grand Am

COMPONENT REPLACEMENT

Cooling Fan

ACHIEVA, SKYLARK & 1997–98 GRAND AM

1. Remove fan attaching bolts, then disconnect fan motor electrical connector.
2. Remove fan assembly.
3. Reverse procedure to install.

ALERO & 1999–2000 GRAND AM

1. Remove A/C line attaching bolt.
2. Remove four upper fan attaching bolts.
3. Raise and support vehicle.
4. Remove four lower fan attaching bolts.
5. Disconnect electrical connector.
6. Remove fan from shroud.
7. Reverse procedure to install.

AURORA & RIVIERA

1. Disconnect wiring harness from fan motor and fan frame.
2. Remove fan guard and hose support as needed.
3. Remove fan assembly from radiator support.
4. Reverse procedure to install.

BONNEVILLE & REGENCY

1. Remove harness from fan motor and fan frame.
2. Remove fan guard and hose support if necessary, then frame to radiator support attaching bolts.
3. Remove fan and frame assembly.
4. Reverse procedure to install.

CAMARO & FIREBIRD

1. Remove air cleaner top.
2. Disconnect wire harness.
3. Remove cooling fan to radiator support bolts.
4. Remove cooling fan assembly.
5. Reverse procedure to install.

CATERA

1. Remove secondary air cutoff bracket bolts, then bracket from cooling fan housing.
2. Remove resonance chamber.
3. Release upper radiator covers self locking tabs.
4. Remove upper radiator covers attaching screws, then covers.
5. Disconnect primary fan motor and primary fan cooling switch electrical connectors.
6. Remove auxiliary water pump from primary fan housing.
7. Remove upper transmission oil cooler fittings.
8. Loosen lower transmission cooler fittings.
9. Remove fan housing bolts, then fan housing from vehicle.
10. Reverse procedure to install.

CAVALIER & SUNFIRE

1997

2.2L & 2.4L Engines

1. Remove air cleaner duct, then disconnect wiring harness from motor and frame.
2. Remove fan assembly from radiator support.
3. Reverse procedure to install.

3.1L Engine

1. Remove air cleaner duct, then air cleaner assembly.
2. Mark latch position for reassembly, then remove primary hood latch.
3. Drain engine coolant to a level below radiator inlet hose at radiator and position aside.
4. **On models with automatic transaxle,** disconnect transaxle cooler lines and position aside.
5. **On all models,** disconnect wiring harness connector at cooling fan, then remove fan assembly from radiator support.
6. Reverse procedure to install.

1998-2000

Primary Cooling Fan

1. Raise and support vehicle, then remove cooling fan mount bolt.
2. Disconnect wiring harness connector from fan motor.
3. Remove cooling fan assembly by pulling out through bottom of vehicle.
4. Reverse procedure to install.

Secondary Cooling Fan

1. Disconnect cooling fan wiring harness electrical connector from fan motor and frame.
2. Remove cooling fan assembly from radiator support.
3. Reverse procedure to install.

CENTURY

PRIMARY FAN

1. Remove air cleaner and resonator assembly.
2. Disconnect cooling fan electrical connector.
3. Remove cooling fan mounting bolts and the fan.
4. Reverse procedure to install.

AUXILIARY FAN

1. Remove grille.
2. Disconnect electrical connector from fan.
3. Remove front end support upper bolts.
4. Remove upper fan mounting bolts.
5. Raise and support vehicle.
6. Remove front support lower bolts.
7. Remove lower fan mounting bolts and the fan.
8. Reverse procedure to install.

CORVETTE

1. Raise and support vehicle, then remove front stabilizer bar bolts.
2. Position front stabilizer bar downward.
3. Disconnect cooling fan motor electrical connectors.
4. Remove wiring harness from fan shrouds.
5. Remove cooling fan assembly mounting bolts.
6. Remove cooling fan assembly from vehicle.
7. Reverse procedure to install.

CUTLASS & MALIBU

1. Remove four fan attaching bolts, then disconnect fan motor electrical connector.
2. Remove fan from shroud.
3. Reverse procedure to install.

CUTLASS SUPREME, GRAND PRIX & REGAL

1. Remove air cleaner assembly.
2. Remove wiring harness from fan motor(s) and fan frame(s).
3. Remove fan frame mounting bolts.
4. Remove fan assembly.

DEVILLE

1. Raise and support vehicle.
2. Disconnect fan electrical connectors.

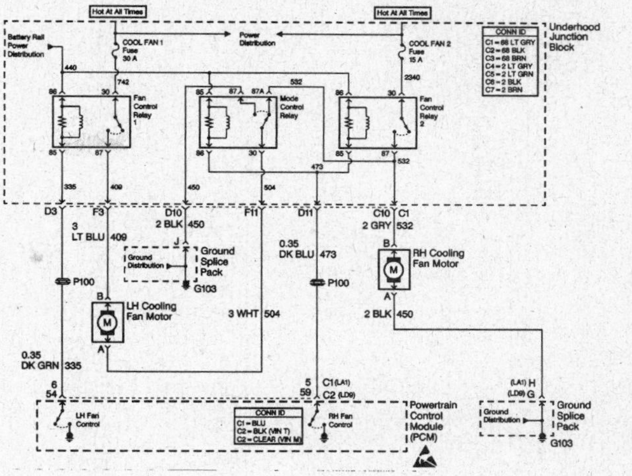

GC1089900393000X

Fig. 6 Wiring diagram. Alero, Cutlass, Malibu & 1999–2000 Grand Am

3. Remove fan to lower cradle attaching screws.
4. Lower vehicle.
5. For right fan, remove A/C accumulator from bracket and position out of the way.
6. Remove air cleaner intake duct.
7. Remove fan to upper radiator mounting panel attaching screws.
8. Remove upper radiator mounting panel.
9. Remove cooling fan(s).
10. Reverse procedure to install.

EIGHTY EIGHT & LSS

1. Remove wiring harness from fan motor and fan frame.
2. Remove fan guard and hose support as necessary.
3. Remove fan assembly from radiator support.
4. Reverse procedure to install.

ELDORADO & SEVILLE

1. **On front cooling fan,** proceed as follows:
   a. Remove plastic radiator cover.
   b. Disconnect fan electrical connector.
   c. Remove right headlamp bracket.
   d. Remove three bolts and cooling fan from vehicle.
2. **On rear cooling fan,** proceed as follows:
   a. Remove upper engine to radiator support torque strut.
   b. Disconnect fan electrical connector.
   c. Disconnect oil cooler bracket from fan.
   d. Remove two upper and lower bolts and fan from vehicle.
3. **On both fans,** reverse procedure to install.

IMPALA, LUMINA & MONTE CARLO

1. Remove air cleaner assembly.
2. Disconnect wiring harness from fan motor(s) and fan frame(s).
3. Remove fan mounting bolts and fan assembly.
4. Reverse procedure to install

METRO

1. Drain cooling system and disconnect upper radiator hose from radiator.
2. Disconnect fan motor electrical connector.
3. Raise and support vehicle, then remove one lower mounting bolt from fan shroud.
4. Lower vehicle and remove two upper cooling fan mounting bolts, then remove fan from vehicle.
5. Reverse procedure to install.

PARK AVENUE & LESABRE

1. Disconnect electrical connector from fan motor and frame.
2. Remove frame to radiator support attaching bolts.
3. Remove fan assembly.
4. Reverse procedure to install.

PRIZM

1. Drain engine coolant from radiator.
2. Disconnect oxygen sensor electrical connector.
3. Remove engine coolant recovery reservoir cap and hoses, then tank.
4. Remove upper radiator hose at radiator.
5. Remove cooling fan mounting bolts, then fan assembly.
6. Reverse procedure to install.

Thermo Switch

METRO

1. Drain cooling system.
2. Remove air cleaner and air inlet tube.
3. Disconnect switch electrical lead, then remove switch from thermostat cap.
4. Reverse procedure to install, wrapping switch threads with sealing tape before installation.

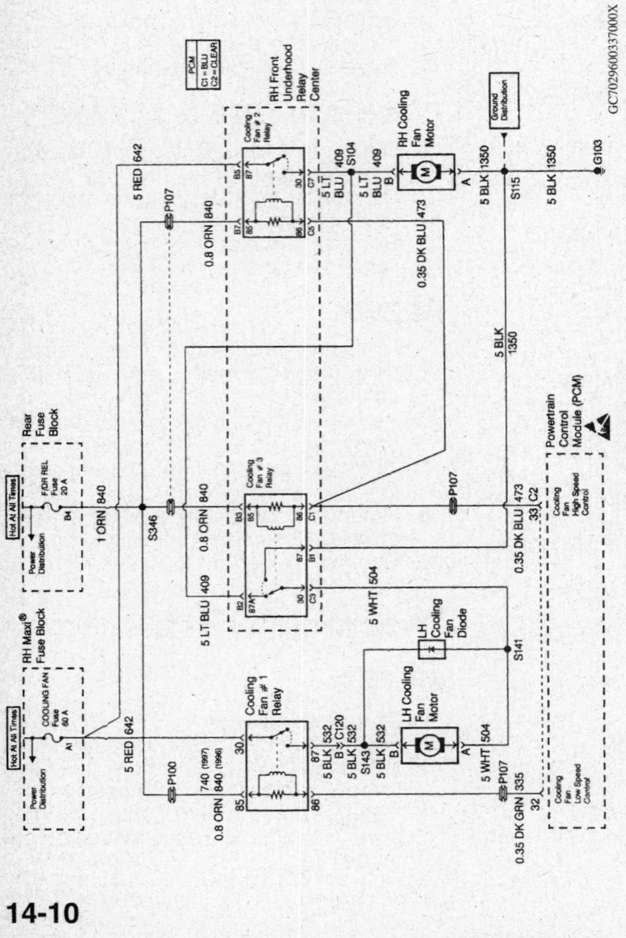

Fig. 7 Wiring diagram. Aurora

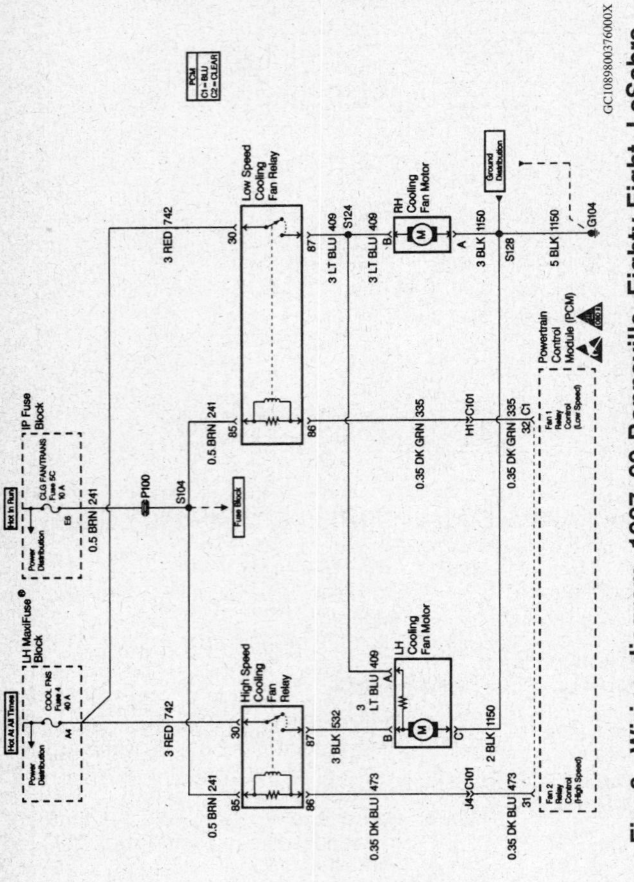

Fig. 8 Wiring diagram. 1997–99 Bonneville, Eighty Eight, LeSabre, LSS & Regency

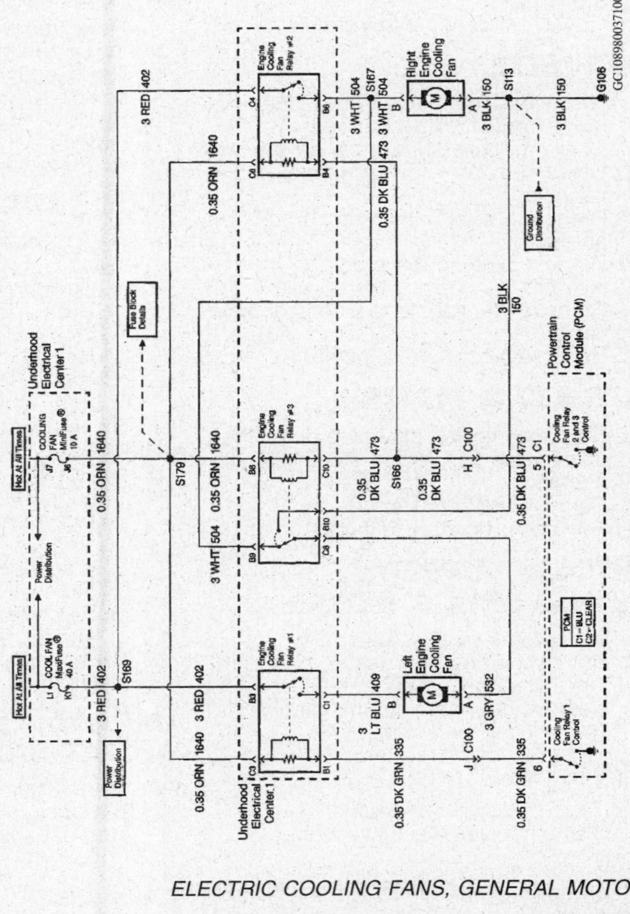

Fig. 9 Wiring diagram. Camaro & Firebird

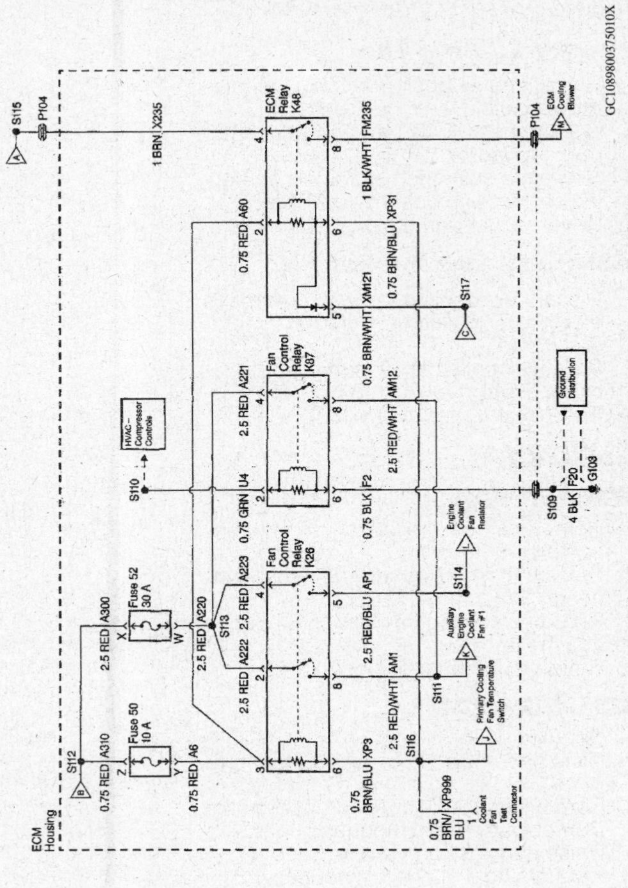

Fig. 10 Wiring diagram (Part 1 of 4). 1997 Catera

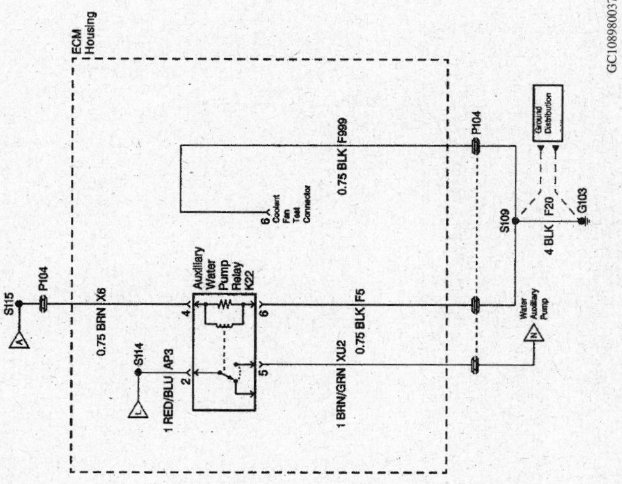

Fig. 10 Wiring diagram (Part 2 of 4). 1997 Catera

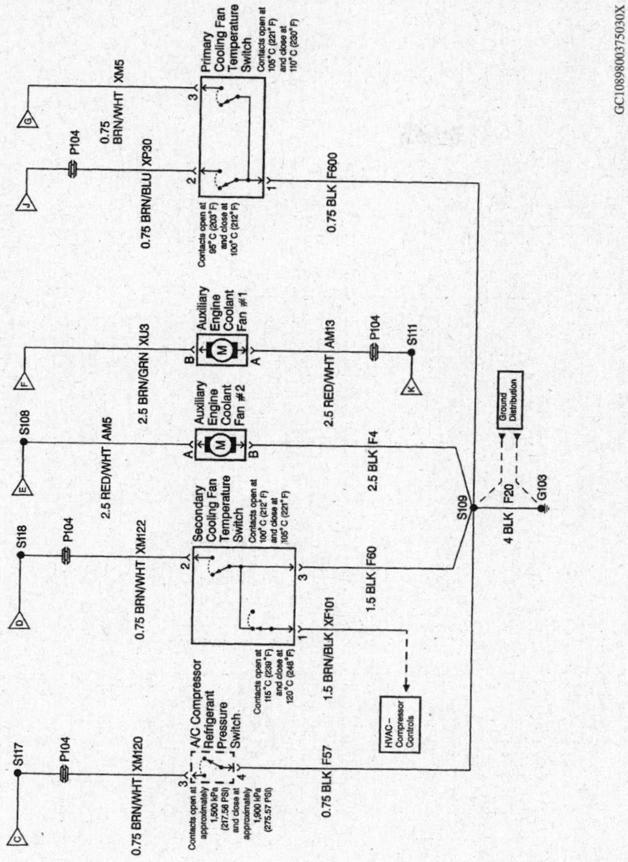

Fig. 10 Wiring diagram (Part 3 of 4). 1997 Catera

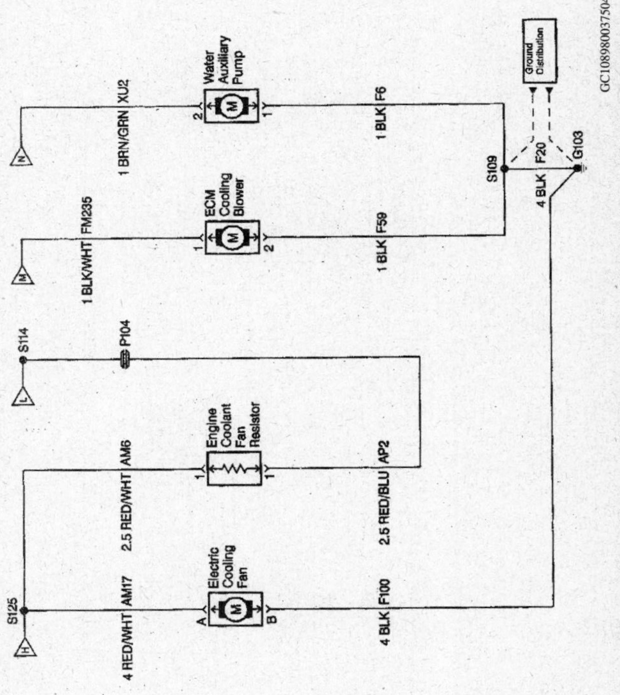

Fig. 10 Wiring diagram (Part 4 of 4). 1997 Catera

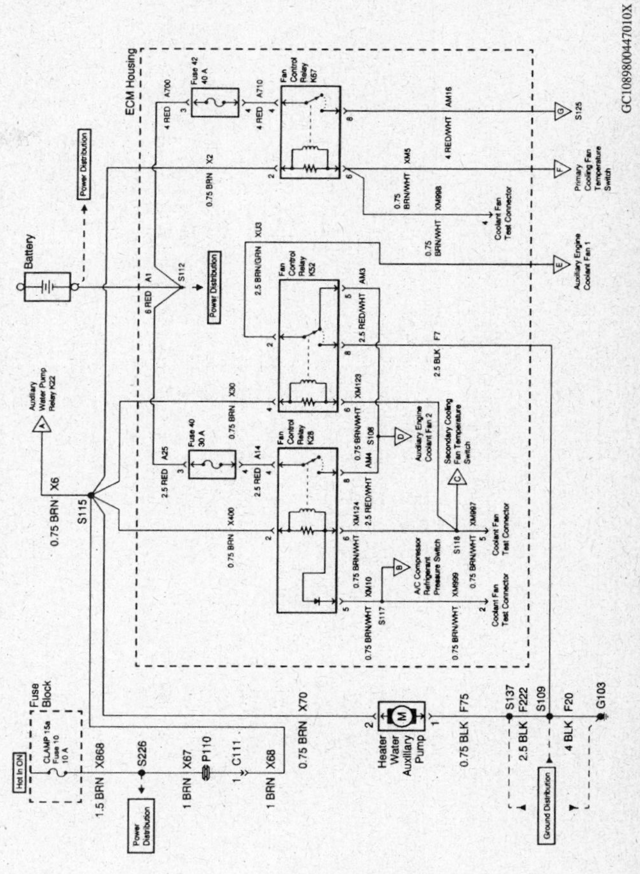

Fig. 11 Wiring diagram (Part 1 of 2). 1998–2000 Catera

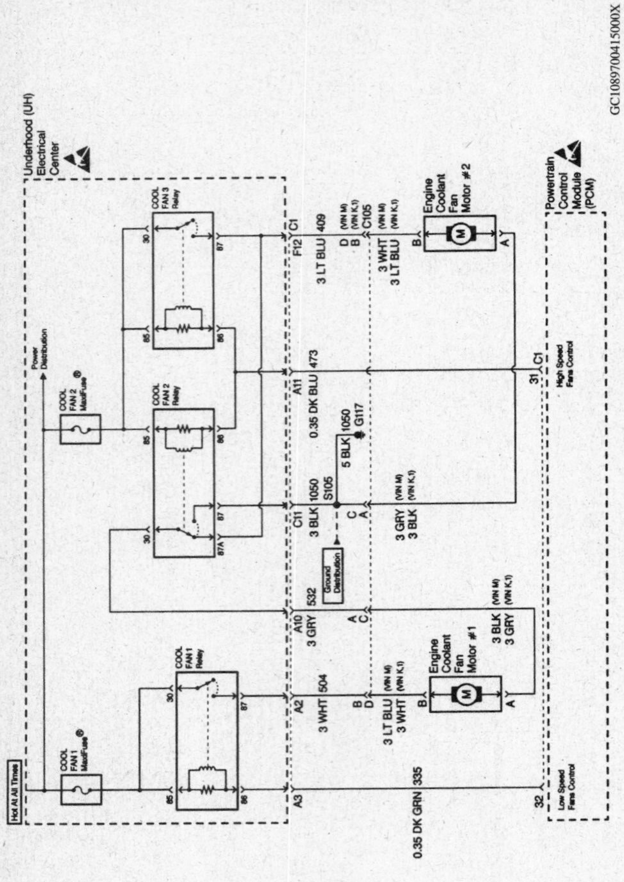

GC1089700415000X

Fig. 12 Wiring diagram. Century & Regal

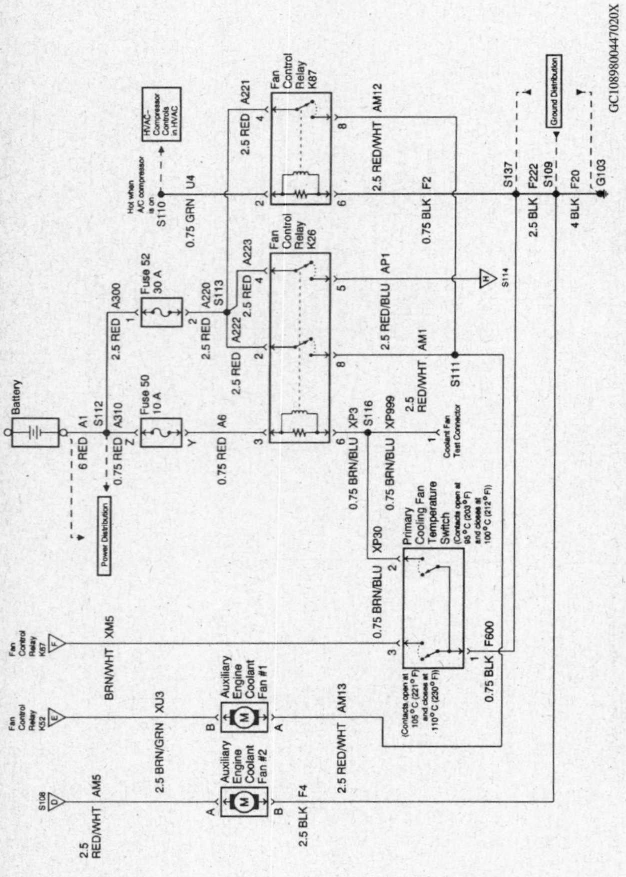

GC1089800447020X

Fig. 11 Wiring diagram (Part 2 of 2). 1998–2000 Catera

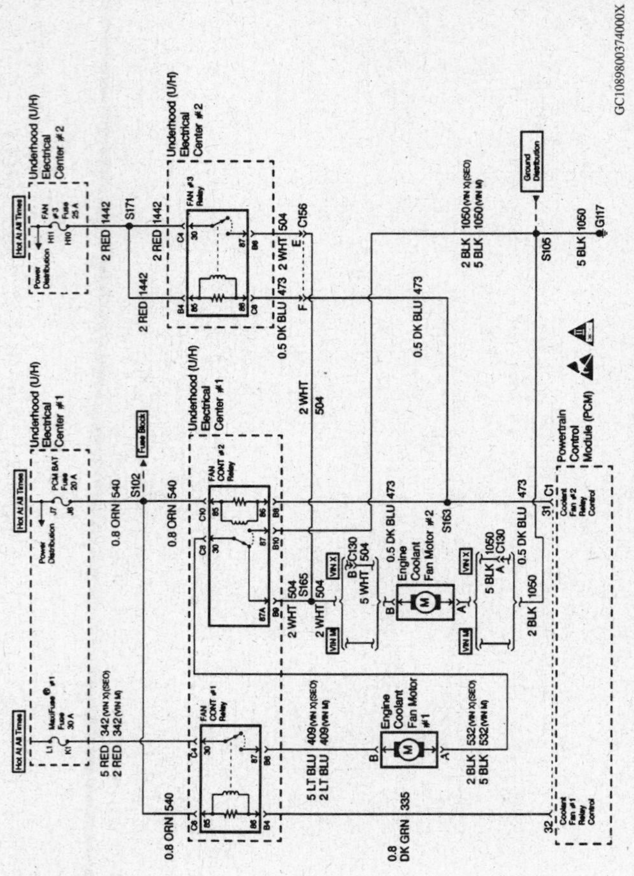

GC1089800374000X

Fig. 14 Wiring diagram. 1997 Lumina & Monte Carlo

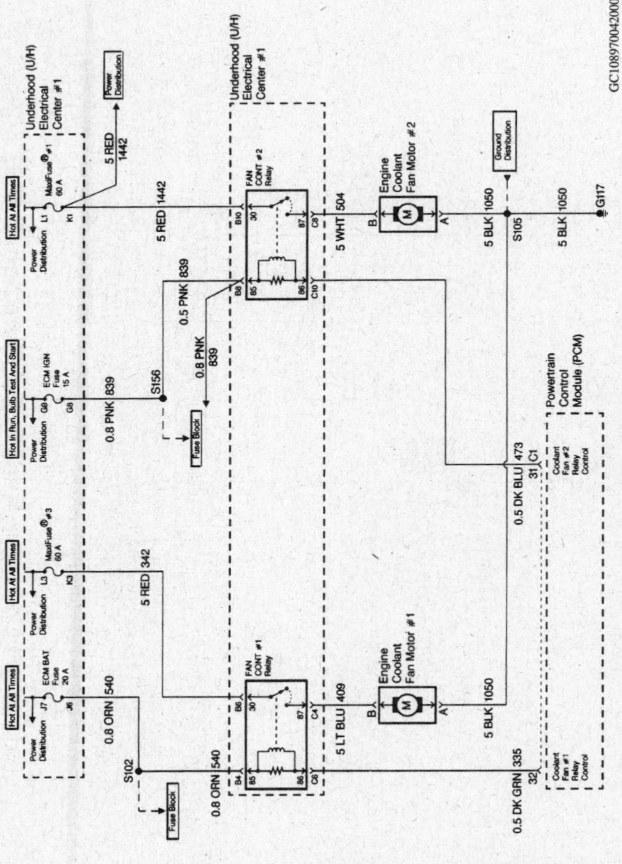

GC1089700420000X

Fig. 13 Wiring diagram. Cutlass Supreme

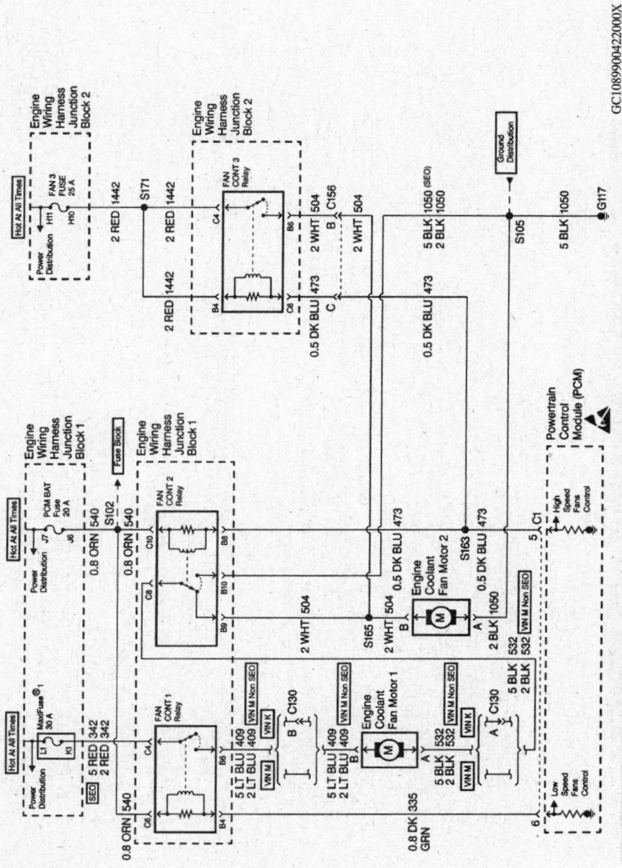

Fig. 15 Wiring diagram. 1998–99 Monte Carlo & 1998–2000 Lumina

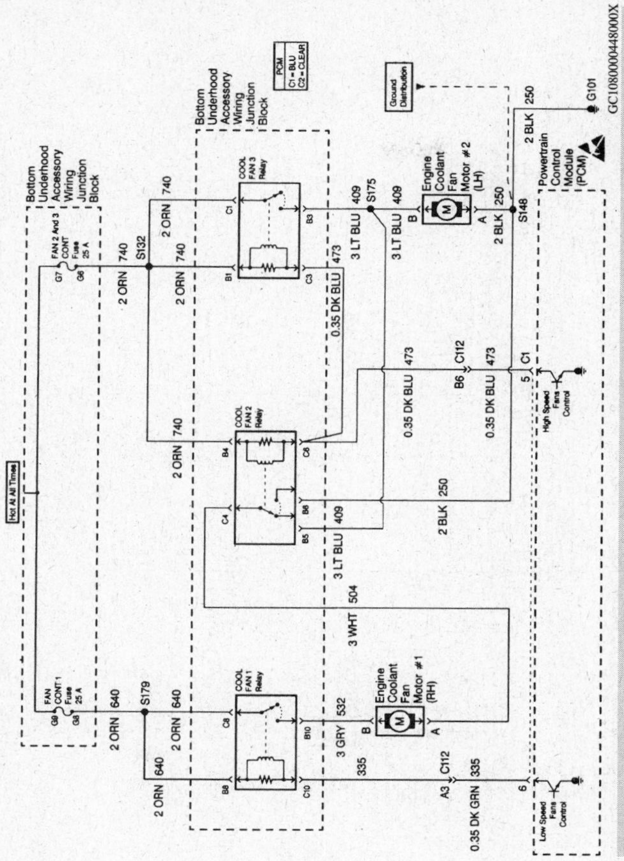

Fig. 16 Wiring diagram. Impala & 2000 Monte Carlo

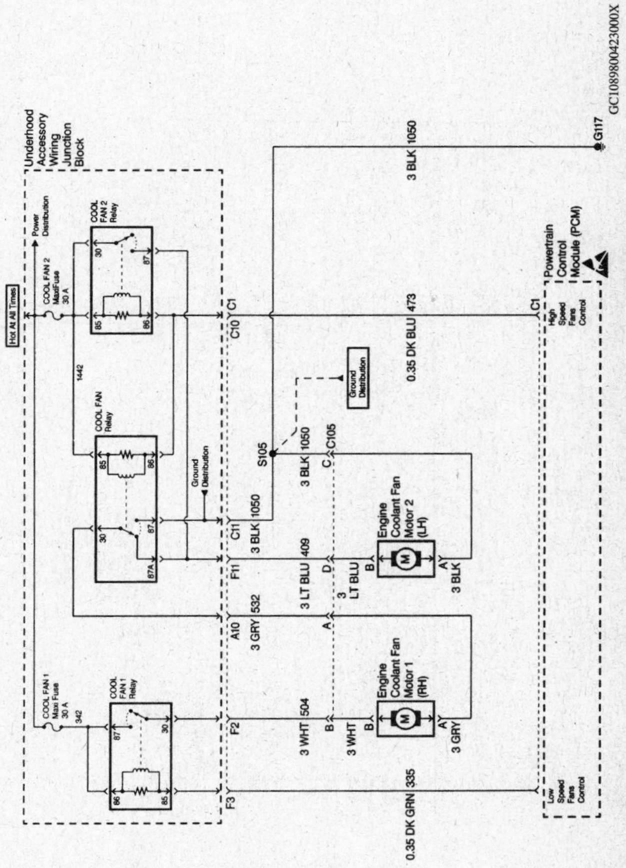

Fig. 17 Wiring diagram. Grand Prix

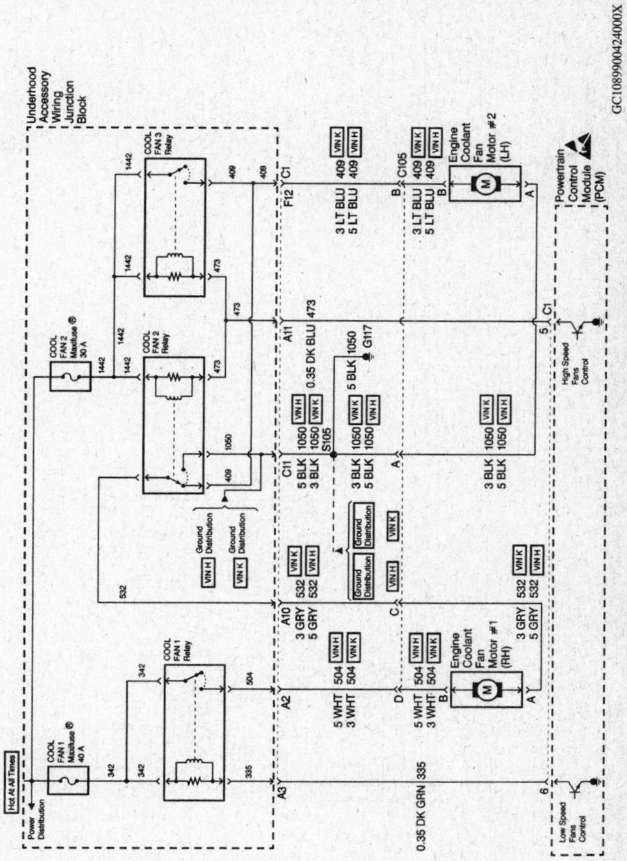

Fig. 18 Wiring diagram. Intrigue

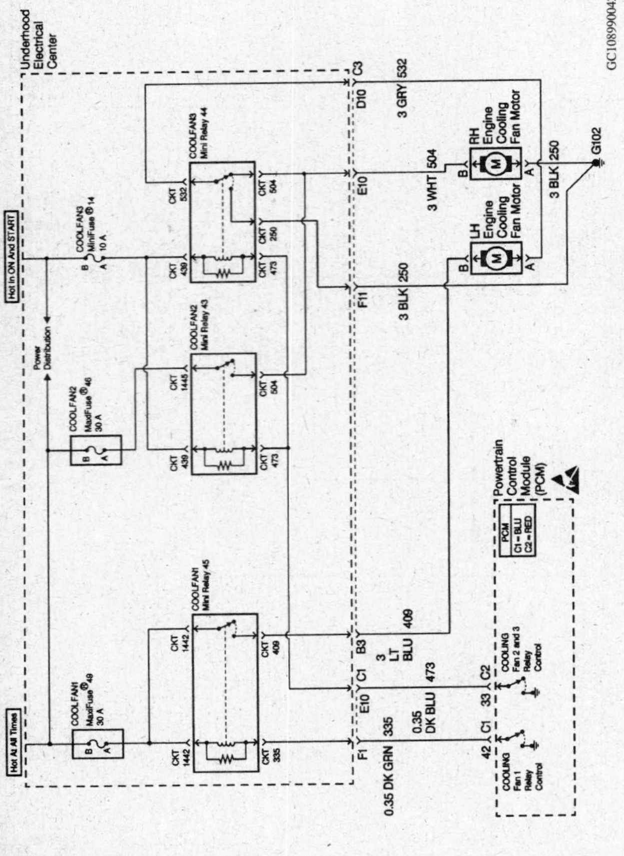

Fig. 19 Wiring diagram. Corvette

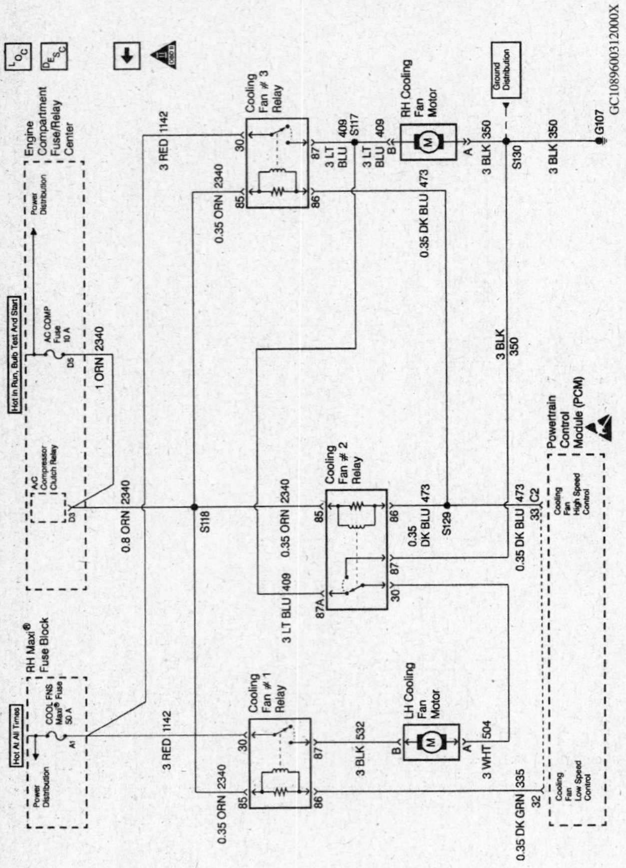

Fig. 20 Wiring diagram. 1997 DeVille, Eldorado & Seville

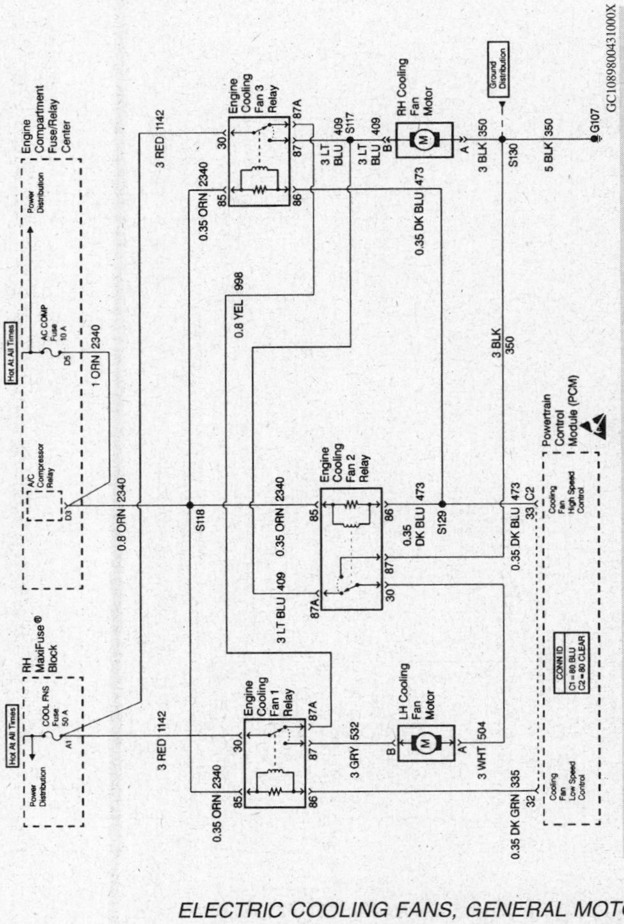

Fig. 21 Wiring diagram. 1998–99 DeVille & 1998–2000 Eldorado

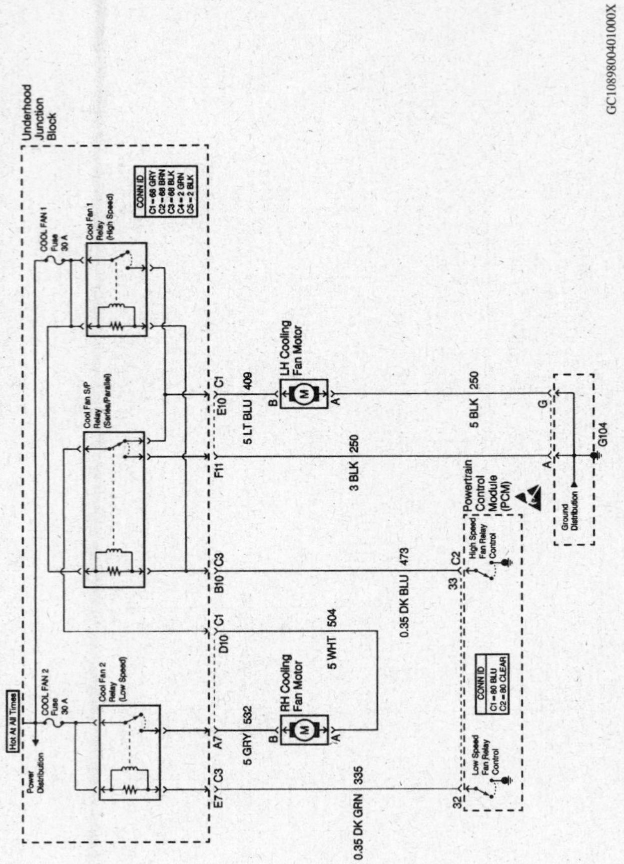

Fig. 22 Wiring diagram. 1998-2000 Seville & 2000 DeVille

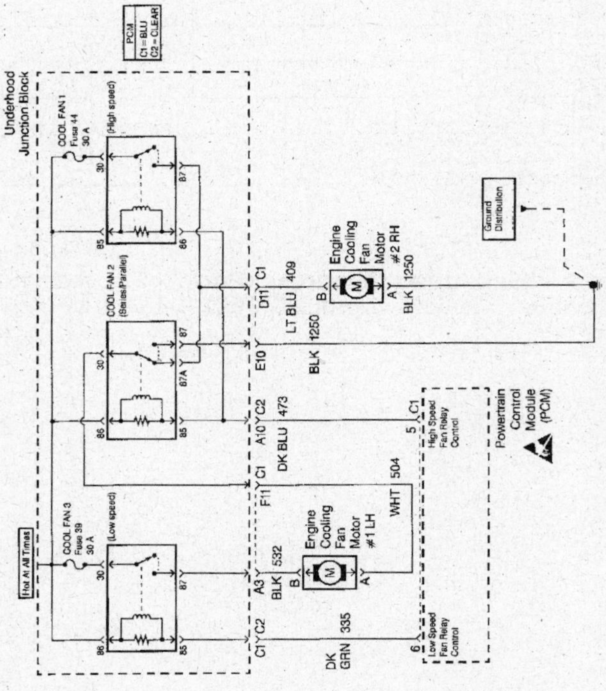

Fig. 23 Wiring diagram. Park Avenue

GC1089800377000X

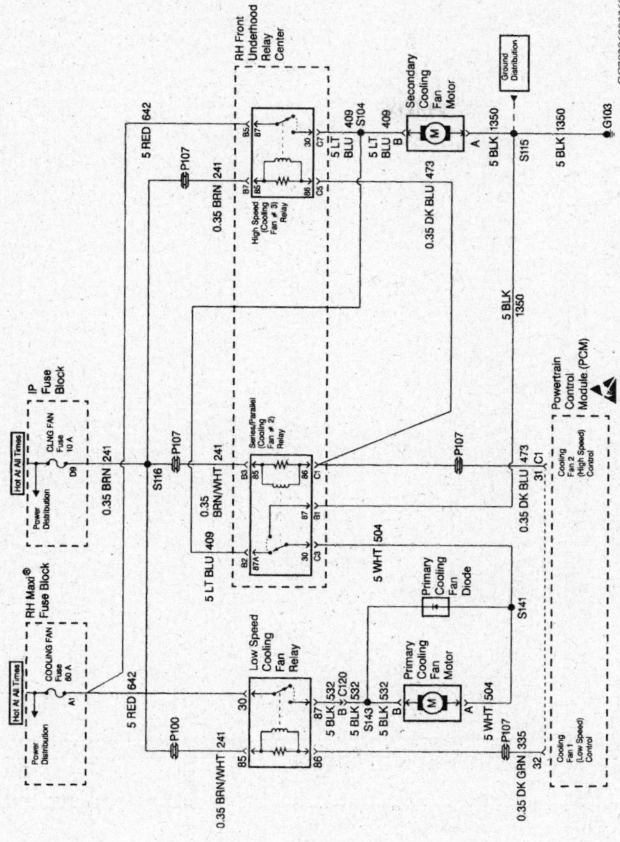

GC7029600336000X

Fig. 24 Wiring diagram. Riviera

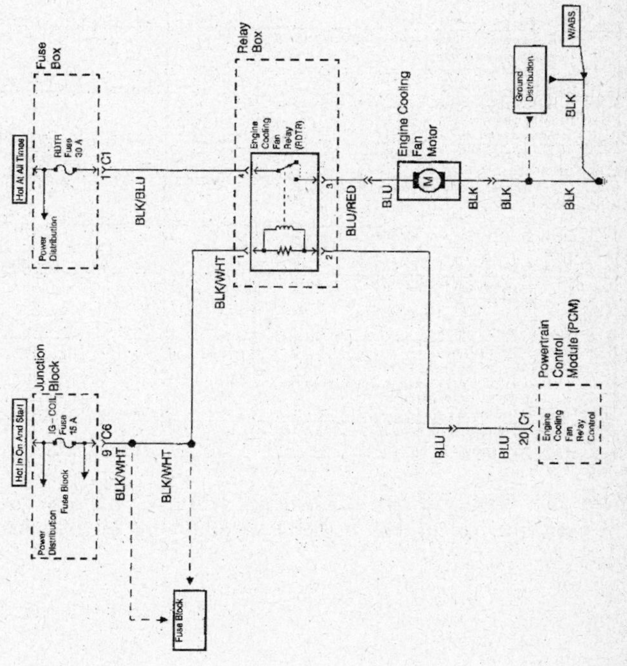

Fig. 25 Wiring diagram. 1998–2000 Metro

GC1089800358000X

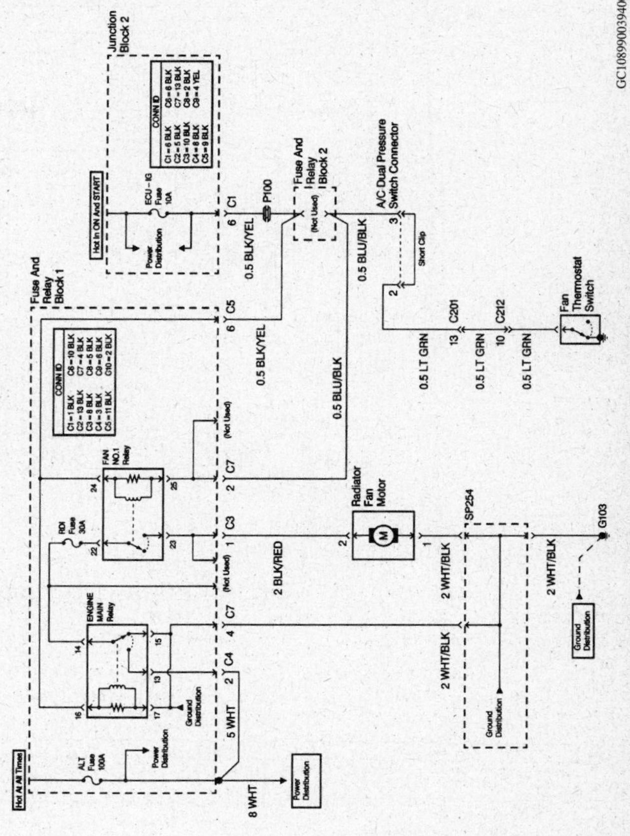

GC1089900394000X

Fig. 26 Wiring diagram. 1998–2000 Prizm

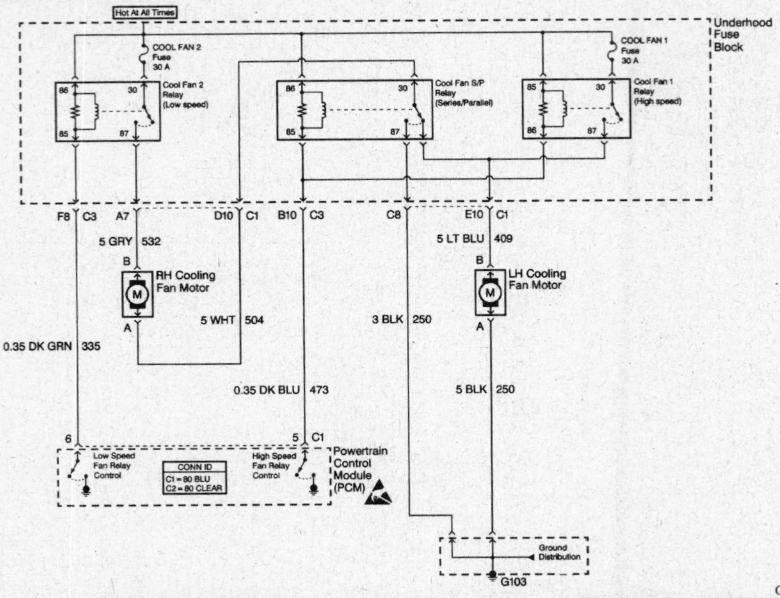

GC1080000438000X

Fig. 27 Wiring diagram. 2000 Bonneville & LeSabre

Step	Action	Value(s)	Yes	No
1	Was the Powertrain On-Board Diagnostic (OBD) System Check performed? Refer to Motor's "Auto Engine Performance & Drivability Manual."	—	*Go to Step 2*	Go to *Powertrain ~~OBD System~~ Check*
2	1. Check the cooling system level. 2. Check the water pump belt condition and tension. Were any repairs necessary?	—	*Go to Step 24*	*Go to Step 3*
3	1. Turn the ignition switch ON, with the engine OFF. 2. Install a scan tool. 3. Engine coolant temperature below the specified value. Is the cooling fan OFF?	98°C (209°F)	*Go to Step 4*	*Go to Step 5*
4	Command the cooling fan relay ON. Is the cooling fan ON?	—	*Go to Step 24*	*Go to Step 6*
5	1. Turn the ignition switch OFF. 2. Disconnect the PCM connectors at the PCM. Is the cooling fan OFF?	—	*Go to Step 23*	*Go to Step 7*
6	1. Disconnect the cooling fan relay electrical connector. 2. With a test light to ground, probe the battery feed circuits. Is the test light ON for both terminals?	—	*Go to Step 8*	*Go to Step 9*
7	1. Disconnect the cooling fan relay electrical connector. 2. With a test light connected to ground, probe the cooling fan battery feed circuit. Does the test light illuminate?	—	*Go to Step 10*	*Go to Step 11*
8	Connect a jumper between the cooling fan relay battery feed and cooling fan battery feed circuits. Is the cooling fan ON?	—	*Go to Step 12*	*Go to Step 13*
9	Repair the open battery feed circuit. Is the action complete?	—	*Go to Step 24*	—
10	Repair the short to B+ in the cooling fan battery feed circuit. Is the action complete?	—	*Go to Step 24*	—
11	Connect the test light to B+ and probe the cooling fan control circuit. Does the test light illuminate?	—	*Go to Step 14*	*Go to Step 22*
12	1. With a test light connected to B+, probe the cooling fan control circuit. 2. Command the cooling fan ON. Does the test light illuminate?	—	*Go to Step 15*	*Go to Step 16*
13	1. Jumper still in place. 2. Disconnect the cooling fan electrical connector. 3. With a test light connected to ground, probe the cooling fan battery feed circuit. Does the test light illuminate?	—	*Go to Step 17*	*Go to Step 18*
14	Repair the short to ground in the cooling fan control circuit. Is the action complete?	—	*Go to Step 24*	—

GC1089600288010X

Fig. 28 Cooling fan diagnosis (Part 1 of 2). Achieva, Cavalier, Skylark, Sunfire & 1997–98 Grand Am

Step	Action	Value(s)	Yes	No
15	Check the terminals to the cooling fan relay and repair as necessary. Was a repair necessary?	—	*Go to Step 24*	*Go to Step 22*
16	Check the cooling fan control circuit for an open or poor connection and repair as necessary. Was a repair necessary?	—	*Go to Step 24*	*Go to Step 23*
17	Connect the test light to B+ and probe the cooling fan ground circuit. Does the test light illuminate?	—	*Go to Step 19*	*Go to Step 20*
18	Repair the open or poor connection in the cooling fan ignition feed circuit. Is the action complete?	—	*Go to Step 24*	—
19	Check for poor connections at the cooling fan electrical connector and repair as necessary. Was a repair necessary.	—	*Go to Step 24*	*Go to Step 21*
20	Repair the open or poor connection in the cooling fan ground circuit. Is the action complete?	—	*Go to Step 24*	—
21	Replace the cooling fan motor. Is the action complete?	—	*Go to Step 24*	—
22	Replace the cooling fan relay. Is the action complete?	—	*Go to Step 24*	—
23	Replace the PCM. Is the action complete?	—	*Go to Step 24*	—
24	1. Turn the ignition switch ON, with the engine OFF. 2. Command the cooling fan ON. Does the cooling turn ON when commanded?	—	System OK	*Go to Step 2*

GC1089600288020X

Fig. 28 Cooling fan diagnosis (Part 2 of 2). Achieva, Cavalier, Skylark, Sunfire & 1997–98 Grand Am

Circuit Description

Power for the fan motors is supplied through the Underhood Bussed Electrical Center (U/H BEC). The cooling fan relays are energized when current flows from the Cool Fan #1 Fuse in the Underhood Bussed Electrical Center (U/H BEC) and Cool Fan #2 fuse in the Underhood Bussed Electrical Center (U/H BEC) through the relay coils to ground through the PCM. The #1 Fan control Relay circuit is grounded for low speed fans operation. The #1 Fan Control Relay control circuit and the Mode control relay (cool fan series) and #2 Fan Control Relay circuits are all grounded for high speed fans operation.

During low speed fans operation the PCM supplies a ground path for the #1 Fan Control Relay. This closes the #1 Fan Control relay contacts, allowing current to flow from the Underhood Bussed Electrical Center (U/H BEC) through the relay contacts to the left hand cooling fan motor. During low speed operation, the ground path for the left hand cooling fan motor is through the #2 Fan Control Relay and the right hand engine cooling fan motor. The result is a series circuit with both cooling fans running at low speed.

During high speed cooling fan operation the PCM supplies a ground path for the #1 Fan control Relay. The PCM also supplies a ground path for #2 Fan Control Relay and the Mode control relay (cool fan series). This closes all three cooling fan relays. During high speed fans operation, both the right and the left hand engine cooling fans are supplied current from the Underhood Bussed Electrical Center (U/H BEC) and each cooling fan has its own ground path.

Diagnostic Aids

Check for the following conditions:

- Poor connection at the PCM, cooling fan relays, or cooling fan motors. Inspect harness connectors for backed out terminals, improper mating, broken locks, improperly formed or damaged terminals, and poor terminal to wire connection.
- Damaged harness. Inspect the wiring harness for damage.

Test Description

Number(s) below refer to the step number(s) on the Diagnostic Table.

2. Stored diagnostic trouble codes may affect engine cooling fans operation. This diagnostic table may lead to improper diagnosis and replacement of good parts if diagnostic trouble codes are present.
6. Ambient temperature must be above 9°C (48°F) before the PCM will enable the cooling fans due to A/C request. The PCM will enable the cooling fans if A/C refrigerant pressure increases regardless of ambient temperature.
77. This vehicle is equipped with a PCM which utilizes an Electrically Erasable Programmable Read Only Memory (EEPROM). When the PCM is being replaced, the new PCM must be programmed.

Step	Action	Value(s)	Yes	No
1	Was the Powertrain On-Board Diagnostic (OBD) System Check performed?	—	*Go to Step 2*	Go to the *Powertrain OBD System Check*
2	Are any PCM DTC(s) stored?	—	Diagnose the PCM DTC(s) first. Go to *Powertrain Control Module Diagnosis*	*Go to Step 3*
3	1. Ensure that the engine coolant temperature is below 100°C (212°F). 2. Turn the A/C *off.* 3. Engine running. 4. Observe the cooling fans. Are the cooling fans running?	—	*Go to Step 32*	*Go to Step 4*
4	1. Command Low Speed Fans *on* using the scan tool output tests function. 2. Observe the cooling fans. Are both cooling fans running at low speed?	—	*Go to Step 5*	*Go to Step 8*

GC102970738201AX

Fig. 29 Cooling fan diagnosis (Part 1 of 9). Alero, Cutlass, Malibu & 1999–2000 Grand Am

Step	Action	Value(s)	Yes	No
5	1. Command high speed fans *on* using the scan tool output tests function. 2. Wait 20 seconds. 3. Observe the cooling fans Are both fans running at high speed?	—	*Go to Step 6*	*Go to Step 58*
6	**Important:** Ambient temperature must be above 9°C (48°F). 1. Exit scan tool output tests. 2. Engine running. 3. Turn the A/C *on.* Are the cooling fans *on?*	—	Go to Diagnostic Aids	*Go to Step 7*
7	View A/C Request on the scan tool. Does A/C Request on the scan tool display Yes?	—	*Go to Step 77*	*Go to A/C Compressor Clutch Control Diagnosis*
8	Is either cooling fan running?	—	*Go to Step 9*	*Go to Step 16*
9	Is the left cooling fan running?	—	*Go to Step 10*	*Go to Step 14*
10	1. Turn *off* the ignition switch. 2. Disconnect the right engine cooling fan. 3. Turn *on* the ignition switch. 4. Command Low speed fans *on* using the scan tool output tests function. 5. Observe the cooling fans. Is the left engine cooling fan running?	—	*Go to Step 11*	*Go to Step 80*
11	Remove the Mode control relay (cool fan series) from the U/H BEC. Is the left engine cooling fan running?	—	*Go to Step 12*	*Go to Step 13*
12	Locate and repair short to ground in CKT 504. Is action complete?	—	*Go to Step 81*	—
13	1. Check CKT 532 for a short to ground. 2. If a problem is found, repair as necessary. Was a problem found?	—	*Go to Step 81*	*Go to Step 70*
14	1. Turn *off* the ignition switch. 2. Disconnect the left engine cooling fan. 3. Turn *on* the ignition switch. 4. Command Low speed fans *on* using the scan tool output tests function. 5. Observe the cooling fans. Is the right engine cooling fan running?	—	*Go to Step 15*	*Go to Step 71*
15	Locate and repair short to battery positive voltage in circuit 532 and 504. If a problem is found repair as necessary. Was a problem found?	—	*Go to Step 81*	*Go to Step 79*

GC102970738201BX

Fig. 29 Cooling fan diagnosis (Part 2 of 9). Alero, Cutlass, Malibu & 1999–2000 Grand Am

Step	Action	Value(s)	Yes	No
16	1. Ignition *on,* engine not running. 2. Remove the #1 Fan Control Relay from the U/H BEC. 3. Probe relay cavity 30 with a test light connected to ground. Is the test light *on?*	—	*Go to Step 18*	*Go to Step 17*
17	1. Identify the cause of no ignition voltage to #1 Cooling Fan Relay cavity 30 • Stalled right engine or left engine cooling fan. • Shorted right engine or left engine cooling fan motor windings. • Short to ground in CKT 342, CKT 532, or CKT 409. • Open in CKT 342. 2. Repair the cause of no ignition voltage to #1 Fan Control Relay. Is action complete?	—	*Go to Step 81*	—
18	Probe #1 Fan Control Relay cavity 86 with a test light connected to ground. Is the test light *on?*	—	*Go to Step 20*	*Go to Step 19*
19	1. Identify the cause of no battery positive voltage to #1 Fan Control Relay cavity 86 • CKT 440 open or shorted to ground. • Shorted #1 Fan Control Relay coil. • Shorted Fan control relay #2 relay coil. • Shorted Mode control relay (cool fan series). • Circuit unrelated to cooling fans. 2. Repair cause of no battery positive voltage to #1 Fan Control Relay cavity 86. Is action complete?	—	*Go to Step 81*	—
20	1. Turn *off* the ignition switch. 2. Disconnect both cooling fans. 3. Connect terminals A and B together at both cooling fan connectors using fused jumpers. 4. Turn *on* the ignition switch. 5. Connect a test light between #1 Fan Control Relay cavities 87 and 30. Is the test light *on?*	—	*Go to Step 21*	*Go to Step 27*
21	1. Connect a test light between #1 Fan Control Relay cavities 85 and 86. 2. Turn *on* the ignition switch. 3. Command Low speed fans *on* using the scan tool output tests function. 4. Observe the test light. Is the test light *on?*	—	*Go to Step 22*	*Go to Step 25*

GC102970738202AX

Fig. 29 Cooling fan diagnosis (Part 3 of 9). Alero, Cutlass, Malibu & 1999–2000 Grand Am

Step	Action	Value(s)	Yes	No
22	1. Turn *off* the ignition switch. 2. Remove the jumpers from the engine cooling fan connectors and reconnect the cooling fans. 3. Install a fused jumper between #1 Fan Control Relay cavities 87 and 30. 4. Turn *on* the ignition switch. 5. Observe the cooling fans. Are both cooling fans running?	—	*Go to Step 23*	*Go to Step 24*
23	1. Check for poor #1 Fan Control Relay connections at the U/H BEC. 2. If a problem is found, repair as necessary. Was a problem found?	—	*Go to Step 81*	*Go to Step 37*
24	1. Check for poor connections at the coolant fan motors. 2. If a problem is found, repair as necessary. Was a problem found?	—	*Go to Step 81*	*Go to Step 63*
25	1. Turn *off* the ignition switch. 2. Disconnect the PCM blue connector C1. 3. Install a fused jumper between #1 Fan Control Relay cavities 86 and 85. 4. Turn *on* the ignition switch. 5. Probe #1 Fan Control Relay control circuit at the PCM harness connector with a test light to ground. Is the test light *on?*	—	*Go to Step 77*	*Go to Step 26*
26	Locate and repair open in the relay control circuit between the PCM and #1 Fan Control Relay cavity 86. Is action complete?	—	*Go to Step 81*	—
27	1. Turn *off* the ignition switch. 2. Remove the jumpers from the cooling fan connectors. 3. Reconnect the cooling fans. 4. Install a fused jumper between #1 Fan Control Relay cavities 87 and 30. 5. Remove the Mode control relay (cool fan series) from the U/H BEC. 6. Probe Mode control relay (cool fan series) cavity 30 with a test light connected to ground. Is the test light *on?*	—	*Go to Step 28*	*Go to Step 31*
28	Connect a test light between Mode control relay (cool fan series) in U/H BEC cavities 30 and 87A. Is the test light *on?*	—	*Go to Step 30*	*Go to Step 29*
29	1. Check for an open in CKT 504 between Mode control relay (cool fan series) cavity 30 and LH Engine Cooling Fan Motor terminal B. 2. If a problem is found, repair as necessary. Was a problem found?	—	*Go to Step 81*	*Go to Step 57*

GC102970738202BX

Fig. 29 Cooling fan diagnosis (Part 4 of 9). Alero, Cutlass, Malibu & 1999–2000 Grand Am

Step	Action	Value(s)	Yes	No
30	1. Check for a poor connection at Mode control relay (cool fan series) in U/H BEC cavities 30 or 87A. 2. If a problem is found, repair as necessary. Was a problem found?	—	*Go to Step 81*	*Go to Step 70*
31	1. Check for an open in #1 Fan Control Relay cavity 87 and left engine cooling fan harness connector terminal B. 2. If a problem is found, repair as necessary. Was a problem found?	—	*Go to Step 81*	*Go to Step 56*
32	Using scan tool, view A/C Request. Does the scan tool display Yes?	—	*Go to A/C Compressor Clutch Control Diagnosis*	*Go to Step 33*
33	Are both cooling fans running at low speed?	—	*Go to Step 34*	*Go to Step 40*
34	Remove #1 Fan Control Relay from the U/H BEC. Are the cooling fans running?	—	*Go to Step 35*	*Go to Step 36*
35	Locate and repair short to voltage in CKT 409. Is action complete?	—	*Go to Step 81*	—
36	Using a test light connected to battery positive voltage, probe #1 Fan Control Relay cavity 86. Is the test light *on?*	—	*Go to Step 38*	*Go to Step 37*
37	Replace #1 Fan Control Relay. Is action complete?	—	*Go to Step 81*	—
38	1. Turn *off* the ignition switch. 2. Disconnect the blue PCM connector. 3. Probe #1 Fan Control Relay cavity 86 with a test light connected to battery positive voltage. Is the test light *on?*	—	*Go to Step 39*	*Go to Step 77*
39	Locate and repair short to ground in the #1 Fan Control Relay control circuit. Is action complete?	—	*Go to Step 81*	—
40	Are both cooling fans running at high speed?	—	*Go to Step 41*	*Go to Step 42*
41	View A/C Pressure on the scan tool. Does the scan tool display voltage less than the specified value?	1.2V	*Go to Step 77*	*Go to Step 44*
42	1. Turn *off* the ignition switch. 2. Disconnect the PCM. 3. Turn *off* the ignition switch. 4. Observe the cooling fans. Is the right engine cooling fan running at high speed?	—	*Go to Step 43*	*Go to Step 77*
43	1. Check for a short to ground in the Mode control relay (cool fan series) Cool and #2 Fan Control Relay control circuit. 2. If a problem is found, repair as necessary. Was a problem found?	—	*Go to Step 81*	*Go to Step 52*

GC102970738203AX

Fig. 29 Cooling fan diagnosis (Part 5 of 9). Alero, Cutlass, Malibu & 1999–2000 Grand Am

Step	Action	Value(s)	Yes	No
44	1. Turn *off* the ignition switch. 2. Disconnect the A/C refrigerant pressure sensor electrical connector. 3. Turn *on* the ignition switch. 4. View A/C Pressure on the scan tool. Does the scan tool display voltage near the specified value?	0V	*Go to Step 46*	*Go to Step 45*
45	Probe the A/C refrigerant pressure signal circuit with a *J 39200* Does the digital multimeter display voltage near the specified value?	0V	*Go to Step 77*	*Go to Step 51*
46	Probe the A/C refrigerant pressure sensor ground with a test light to battery positive voltage. Is the test light *on?*	—	*Go to Step 47*	*Go to Step 49*
47	Probe the A/C refrigerant pressure sensor 5 volt reference circuit with a *J 39200* Does the digital multimeter display voltage near the specified value?	5V	*Go to Step 48*	*Go to Step 50*
48	Replace the A/C refrigerant pressure sensor. Is action complete?	—	*Go to Step 81*	—
49	Locate and repair open or short to voltage in the A/C refrigerant pressure sensor ground circuit. Is action complete?	—	*Go to Step 81*	—
50	Locate and repair open or short to ground in the A/C refrigerant pressure sensor 5 volt reference circuit. Is action complete?	—	*Go to Step 81*	—
51	Locate and repair short to voltage in the A/C refrigerant pressure signal circuit. Is action complete?	—	*Go to Step 81*	—
52	1. Remove the Mode control relay (cool fan series) from the Underhood Bussed Electrical Center (U/H BEC). 2. Observe the cooling fans. Is the right engine cooling fan running at high speed?	—	*Go to Step 53*	*Go to Step 70*
53	Remove the #2 Fan Control Relay from the U/H BEC. Is the right engine cooling fan running at high speed?	—	*Go to Step 54*	*Go to Step 55*
54	Locate and repair short to battery positive voltage in CKT 532. Is action complete?	—	*Go to Step 81*	—
55	Locate and repair short to battery positive voltage in CKT 473. If a problem is found repair as necessary. Was a problem found?	—	*Go to Step 81*	*Go to Step 76*

GC102970738203BX

Fig. 29 Cooling fan diagnosis (Part 6 of 9). Alero, Cutlass, Malibu & 1999–2000 Grand Am

Step	Action	Value(s)	Yes	No
56	1. Check for an open in CKT 504 between #2 Fan Control Relay cavity 30 and left engine cooling fan terminal A. 2. If a problem is found, repair as necessary. Was a problem found?	—	*Go to Step 81*	*Go to Step 79*
57	1. Check for an open in CKT 450 between right engine cooling fan terminal A and ground, or open in CKT 532 from Mode control relay (cool fan series) cavity 87A and RH Cooling Fan Motor cavity B. 2. If a problem is found, repair as necessary. Was a problem found?	—	*Go to Step 81*	*Go to Step 80*
58	1. Ignition *on,* engine not running. 2. Remove the Mode control relay (cool fan series) from the U/H BEC. 3. Install a test light between Mode control relay (cool fan series) cavity 86 and battery positive voltage. 4. Command High speed fans on using the scan tool output controls function. 5. Wait about 5-6 seconds. 6. Observe the test light. Is the test light *on?*	—	*Go to Step 61*	*Go to Step 59*
59	1. Remove the #2 Fan Control Relay from the U/H BEC. 2. Install a test light between #2 Fan Control Relay cavity 85 and battery positive voltage. 3. Command high speed fans on using the scan tool output controls function. 4. Wait 6 seconds. 5. Observe the test light. Is the test light *on?*	—	*Go to Step 78*	*Go to Step 60*
60	1. Turn *off* the ignition switch. 2. Disconnect the PCM. 3. Turn *on* the ignition switch. 4. Check the Mode control relay (cool fan series) and #2 Fan Control Relay control circuit for an open or a short to voltage. 5. If a problem is found, repair as necessary. Was a problem found?	—	*Go to Step 81*	*Go to Step 77*
61	1. Turn *off* the ignition switch. 2. Reinstall the Mode control relay (cool fan series). 3. Disconnect both coolant fan electrical connectors. 4. Turn *on* the ignition switch. 5. Command High speed fans *on* using the scan tool output controls function. 6. Wait about 5-6 seconds. 7. Probe terminal B at the right engine cooling fan connector with a test light to ground. Is the test light *on?*	—	*Go to Step 62*	*Go to Step 64*

GC102970738204AX

Fig. 29 Cooling fan diagnosis (Part 7 of 9). Alero, Cutlass, Malibu & 1999–2000 Grand Am

Step	Action	Value(s)	Yes	No
62	Probe terminal A at the left engine cooling fan connector with a test light to battery positive voltage. Is the test light *on?*	—	*Go to Step 63*	*Go to Step 71*
63	1. Identify cause of inoperative cooling fan. • Open right engine cooling fan motor windings. • Open left engine cooling fan motor windings. • Stalled cooling fan(s). 2. Replace the affected cooling fan motor. Is action complete?	—	*Go to Step 81*	—
64	1. Remove the Mode control relay (cool fan series) from the U/H BEC. 2. Turn *on* the ignition switch. 3. Probe Mode control relay (cool fan series) cavity 85 with a test light connected to ground. Is the test light *on?*	—	*Go to Step 66*	*Go to Step 65*
65	Locate and repair open in the battery positive voltage circuit to Mode control relay (cool fan series). Is action complete?	—	*Go to Step 81*	—
66	Probe Mode control relay (cool fan series) cavity 30 with a test light connected to ground. Is the test light *on?*	—	*Go to Step 68*	*Go to Step 67*
67	Locate and repair open in battery positive voltage circuit to Mode control relay (cool fan series) cavity 30. Is action complete?	—	*Go to Step 81*	—
68	1. Check LH Engine Coolant Fan Motor circuit for an open between Right Engine Coolant Fan terminal B and Mode control relay (cool fan series) cavity 87A. 2. If a problem is found, repair as necessary. Was a problem found?	—	*Go to Step 81*	*Go to Step 69*
69	1. Check for a poor Mode control relay (cool fan series) terminal connections at the U/H BEC. 2. If a problem is found, repair as necessary. Was a problem found?	—	*Go to Step 81*	*Go to Step 70*
70	Replace Mode control relay (cool fan series). Is action complete?	—	*Go to Step 81*	—
71	1. Remove the #2 Fan Control Relay from the U/H BEC. 2. Turn *on* the ignition switch. 3. Probe #2 Fan Control Relay cavity 86 with a test light connected to ground. Is the test light *on?*	—	*Go to Step 73*	*Go to Step 72*
72	Locate and repair open in battery positive voltage circuit to #2 Fan Control Relay cavity 86. Is action complete?	—	*Go to Step 81*	—

GC102970738204BX

Fig. 29 Cooling fan diagnosis (Part 8 of 9). Alero, Cutlass, Malibu & 1999–2000 Grand Am

Step	Action	Value(s)	Yes	No
73	Probe #2 Fan Control Relay cavity 87 in the U/H BEC with a test light to battery positive voltage. Is the test light *on?*	—	*Go to Step 75*	*Go to Step 74*
74	Locate and repair open in circuit between #2 Fan Control Relay cavity 87 and Mode control relay (cool fan series) cavity 87A in the U/H BEC and ground. Is action complete?	—	*Go to Step 81*	—
75	1. Check for poor #2 Fan Control Relay engine terminal connections at the U/H BEC. 2. If a problem is found, repair as necessary. Was a problem found?	—	*Go to Step 81*	*Go to Step 76*
76	Replace the #2 Fan Control Relay in the U/H BEC. Is action complete?	—	*Go to Step 81*	—
77	Replace the PCM. **Important:** The replacement PCM must be programmed. Is action complete?	—	*Go to Step 81*	—
78	Repair open in the Mode control relay (cool fan series) cavity 85 and #2 Fan Control Relay cavity 86 control circuit to PCM. Is action complete?	—	*Go to Step 81*	—
79	Replace the Left Hand Engine Cooling Fan motor. Is action complete?	—	*Go to Step 81*	—
80	Replace the Right Hand Engine Cooling Fan motor. Is action complete?		*Go to Step 81*	
81	1. Engine coolant below 100°C (212°F). 2. A/C *off.* 3. Engine running. Observe the cooling fans. Are the cooling fans running?	—	*Go to Step 32*	*Go to Step 82*
82	1. Command Low speed fans *on* using the scan tool output tests function. 2. Observe the cooling fans. Are both cooling fans running at low speed?	—	*Go to Step 83*	*Go to Step 8*
83	1. Command High speed fans *on* using the scan tool output tests function. 2. Wait 6 seconds. 3. Observe the cooling fans. Are both cooling fans running at high speed?	—	System OK	*Go to Step 58*

GC1029707382050X

Fig. 29 Cooling fan diagnosis (Part 9 of 9). Alero, Cutlass, Malibu & 1999–2000 Grand Am

Step	Action	Value(s)	Yes	No
1	Was the Powertrain On-Board Diagnostic (OBD) System Check performed?	—	*Go to Step 2*	Go to *Powertrain OBD System Check*
2	1. Ensure the engine coolant temperature is between the values specified. 2. Turn HVAC controls to OFF. 3. Start and idle the engine. 4. Using the scan tool select Output Tests and while viewing the Quad Driver 1 display, command All Relays OFF for approximately 15 seconds. 5. Using the scan tool select Output Tests and while viewing the Quad Driver 1 display, command All Relays ON for approximately 15 seconds. Did the Quad Driver 1 display indicate a *Fault*?	5°C - 100°C (41°F - 212°F)	Go to *DTC P1660 Cooling Fan Control Circuits*	*Go to Step 3*
3	With the engine idling turn A/C ON to maximum cooling. Have any other DTC(s) failed this ignition?	—	Go to DTC(s) that are set	*Go to Step 4*
4	1. Turn the engine OFF and the key ON. 2. Ensure engine coolant temperature is below the value specified. 3. Observe fan operation while individually commanding Fan Relay 1 ON, then All Relays ON, then All Relays OFF. • With Fan Relay 1 commanded ON both fans should operate at low speed. • With All Relays commanded ON both fans should operate at high speed. • With All Relays commanded OFF both fans should not operate (unless the PCM detects a fault or high temperature condition). Do both cooling fans operate as commanded?	100°C (212°F)	System OK	*Go to Step 5*
5	Does only Cooling Fan #1 (left) operate with Fan Relay 1 commanded ON then both fans operate when All Relays are commanded ON?	—	*Go to Step 6*	*Go to Step 7*
6	Repair CKT 504 shorted to ground. Is the repair complete?	—	*Go to Step 4*	—
7	Does neither cooling fan operate with Fan Relay 1 commanded ON then only Cooling Fan #2 (right) operate with All Relays commanded ON?	—	*Electric Cooling Fan Diagnosis* (Table 1)	*Go to Step 8*
8	Does neither cooling fan operate with Fan Relay 1 commanded ON then only Cooling Fan #1 (left) operate with All Relays commanded ON?	—	*Electric Cooling Fan Diagnosis* (Table 2)	*Go to Step 9*
9	Do both cooling fans operate with Fan Relay 1 commanded ON then only Cooling Fan #2 (right) operate with All Relays commanded ON?	—	*Electric Cooling Fan Diagnosis* (Table 3)	*Go to Step 10*
10	Do both cooling fans operate with Fan Relay 1 commanded ON then only Cooling Fan #1 (left) operate with All Relays commanded ON?	—	*Electric Cooling Fan Diagnosis* (Table 4)	*Go to Step 11*

GC1089600323020X

Fig. 30 Cooling fan function inspection (Part 2 of 3). Aurora

Circuit Description

To determine if a fault is present perform the Cooling Fan Functional Check. If DTC P1660 is set, or sets during the functional check, it must be diagnosed before proceeding with any of the symptom tables. When the PCM commands low speed fan operation it grounds Cooling Fan Relay 1 which allows current to flow through both cooling fans in a series circuit to ground. If the PCM commands high speed fan operation it grounds all the cooling fan relays, including Fan Relay 1, which changes the circuit to a parallel circuit to ground. If a fault occurs certain symptoms will occur due to the series/parallel circuit design.

The PCM will command fan operation when:

- Low Speed Fan Operation
  - Engine coolant temperature exceeds approximately 106°C (229°F).
  - Transmission fluid temperature exceeds 150°C (302°F).
  - A/C operation is requested.
  - After the vehicle is shut OFF if the coolant temperature at key–off is more than 151°C (304°F) and system voltage was more than 12 volts. The fans will stay ON for approximately 3 minutes.

The fans will switch from low to OFF when the coolant drops below 102°C (216°F).

- High Speed Fan Operation
  - Engine coolant temperature reaches 112°C (234°F).
  - Transmission temperature is more than 151°C (304°F).
  - When certain DTCs set.

The fans will switch from high to low (except DTCs set) when the coolant drops below 106°C (229°F).

- If the cooling fans operate when commanded OFF and DTC P1660 is not set either a cooling fan relay is stuck ON or a cooling fan circuit is shorted to power.
- Whenever a repair is completed repeat the Cooling Fan Functional Check. This will help diagnose possible multiple failures, for example: two water contaminated relays.

Fan Relay Operation Matrix

Operational Mode	OFF	LOW FANS	HIGH FANS
Low Speed Cooling Fan Relay (#1)	De-Energized	Energized	Energized
Series/ Parallel Coling Fan Relay (#2)	De-Energized	De-Energized	Energized
High Speed Cooling Fan (#3)	De-Energized	De-Energized	Energized

*The Series/Parallel Cooling Fan Relay is a dual position switch and while de-energized, supplies a ground path for the low speed fan circuit.

Test Description

Number(s) below refer to the step number(s) on the Functional Table.

1. The Powertrain OBD System Check must be performed first so that mis–diagnosis is avoided, due to the PCM commanding the fans ON due to a DTC set, etc.
2. Checking to see if there is a fault on the cooling fan relay control circuits.
3. Checking to see if any A/C DTCs will set. If A/C DTCs set they must be diagnosed before proceeding with the Cooling Fan Functional Check.
4. Commanding fans ON in sequence to determine the symptom (fault–if any) present.

GC1089600323010X

Fig. 30 Cooling fan function inspection (Part 1 of 3). Aurora

Step	Action	Value(s)	Yes	No
11	Does neither cooling fan operate when Fan Relay 1 is commanded ON and also when All Relays are commanded ON?	—	*Electric Cooling Fan Diagnosis* (Table 5)	*Go to Step 12*
12	Does either cooling fan operate when All Relays is commanded OFF?	—	Go to *Diagnostic Aids*	*Go to Step 4*

GC1089600323030X

Fig. 30 Cooling fan function inspection (Part 3 of 3). Aurora

Step	Action	Value(s)	Yes	No
	DEFINITION: No low speed operation of either cooling fan. High speed operation of right cooling fan only. DTC P1660 is not set.			
1	Was the Cooling Fan Functional Check performed?	—	*Go to Step 2*	*Electric Cooling Fan Diagnosis*
2	1. Disconnect Cooling Fan #1 connector. 2. Using the scan tool select Output Tests then Fan Relays. 3. With the key ON command Relay 1 ON. 4. Using DVM J 39200 measure the voltage to ground at Cooling Fan #1 connector terminal B (harness side). Is the voltage the same or more than the value specified?	10.0 volts	*Go to Step 3*	*Go to Step 6*
3	Jumper Cooling Fan #1 connector terminals A and B together. Does Cooling Fan #2 operate while jumpered?	—	*Go to Step 8*	*Go to Step 4*
4	1. With Cooling Fan #1 connector still jumpered, remove Relay #2. 2. Measure the voltage to ground at Relay #2 terminal 30. Is the voltage the same or more than the value specified?	10.0 volts	*Go to Step 5*	*Go to Step 9*
5	Jumper Relay #2 terminals 30 and 87A together. Does Cooling Fan #2 operate while jumpered?	—	*Go to Step 10*	*Go to Step 11*
6	1. Exit Fan Relays. 2. Remove Relay #1. 3. Measure the voltage to ground at Relay #1 terminal 30. Is the voltage the same or more than the value specified?	10.0 volts	*Go to Step 7*	*Go to Step 12*
7	1. Jumper Fan Relay #1 terminals 30 and 87 together. 2. Measure the voltage to ground at Cooling Fan #1 connector terminal B. Is the voltage to ground the same or more than the value specified?	10.0 volts	*Go to Step 13*	*Go to Step 14*
8	Replace Cooling Fan #1 (left). Is the replacement complete?	—	*Electric Cooling Fan Diagnosis*	—
9	Repair the open in CKT 504 between Cooling Fan #1 and Fan Relay #2. Is the repair complete?	—	*Electric Cooling Fan Diagnosis*	—

GC1089600324010X

Fig. 31 Cooling fan symptom table 1 (Part 1 of 2). Aurora

Step	Action	Value(s)	Yes	No
DEFINITION: No low speed operation of either cooling fan. High speed operation of right cooling fan only. DTC P1660 is not set.				
10	Replace Fan Relay #2. Is the replacement complete?	—	*Electric Cooling Fan Diagnosis*	—
11	Repair the open in CKT 409 between Fan Relay #2 and the CKT 409 splice. Is the repair complete?	—	*Electric Cooling Fan Diagnosis*	—
12	Repair the open in the circuit between Fan Relay #1 terminal 30 and the Maxi fuse. Is the repair complete?	—	*Electric Cooling Fan Diagnosis*	—
13	Replace Fan Relay #1. Is the replacement complete?	—	*Electric Cooling Fan Diagnosis*	—
14	Repair the open in CKT 532 between Fan Relay #1 and Cooling Fan #1. Is the repair complete?	—	*Electric Cooling Fan Diagnosis*	—

GC1089600324020X

Fig. 31 Cooling fan symptom table 1 (Part 2 of 2). Aurora

Step	Action	Value(s)	Yes	No
6	Replace Fan Relay #2. Is the replacement complete?	—	*Electric Cooling Fan Diagnosis*	—
7	Repair the open in the BLK circuit between Cooling Fan #2 (right) terminal A and the splice. Is the repair complete?	—	*Electric Cooling Fan Diagnosis*	—
8	Repair the open in CKT 409 between Cooling Fan #2 (right) the CKT 409 splice and Fan Relay #2. Is the repair complete?	—	*Electric Cooling Fan Diagnosis*	—

GC1089600325020X

Fig. 32 Cooling fan symptom table 2 (Part 2 of 2). Aurora

Step	Action	Value(s)	Yes	No
DEFINITION: Low speed operation of both fans. High speed operation of left cooling fan only. DTC P1660 not set.				
1	Was the Cooling Fan Functional Check performed?	—	*Go to Step 2*	*Electric Cooling Fan Diagnosis*
2	1. Using scan tool select Output Tests then All Relays. 2. With the key ON command All Relays ON. 3. Remove Fan Relay #3. 4. Using DVM J 39200 measure the voltage to ground at Fan Relay #3 terminal 85. Is the voltage the same or more than the value specified?	10.0 volts	*Go to Step 3*	*Go to Step 6*
3	Measure the voltage to ground at Fan Relay #3 terminal 30. Is the voltage the same or more than the value specified?	10.0 volts	*Go to Step 4*	*Go to Step 7*
4	1. Remove Fan Relay #3. 2. Measure the voltage between Fan Relay #3 terminal 86 and Fan Relay #2 terminal 86. Is the resistance the same or less than the value specified?	5 ohms	*Go to Step 5*	*Go to Step 8*
5	1. Reconnect Fan Relay #2. 2. With All Relays still commanded ON, jumper Fan Relay #3 terminals 30 and 87 together. Does Cooling Fan #2 (right) operate while jumpered?	—	*Go to Step 10*	*Go to Step 9*
6	Repair the open in the RED circuit between Fan Relay #3 terminal 30 and the Maxi fuse. Is the repair complete?	—	*Electric Cooling Fan Diagnosis*	—
7	Repair the open in the ORG circuit between Fan Relay #3 terminal 85 and the splice. Is the repair complete?	—	*Electric Cooling Fan Diagnosis*	—
8	Repair the open in CKT 473 between Fan Relay #3 terminal 86 and the CKT 473 splice. Is the repair complete?	—	*Electric Cooling Fan Diagnosis*	—
9	Repair the open in CKT 409 between Fan Relay #3 terminal 87 and the CKT 409 splice. Is the repair complete	—	*Electric Cooling Fan Diagnosis*	—
10	Replace Fan Relay #3. Is the replacement complete?	—	*Electric Cooling Fan Diagnosis*	—

GC1089600327000X

Fig. 34 Cooling fan symptom table 4. Aurora

Step	Action	Value(s)	Yes	No
DEFINITION: No low speed operation of either cooling fan. High speed operation of left cooling fan only. DTC P1660 is not set.				
1	Was the Cooling Fan Functional Check performed?	—	*Go to Step 2*	*Electric Cooling Fan Diagnosis*
2	1. Disconnect Cooling Fan #2 (right) connector. 2. Using the scan tool select Output Tests than Fan Relays. 3. With the key ON, command Fan Relay 1 ON. 4. Jumper Cooling Fan #2 (right) terminals A and B together. Does Cooling Fan #1 (left) operate while jumpered?	—	*Go to Step 5*	*Go to Step 3*
3	1. With Fan Relay 1 still commanded ON remove Fan Relay #2. 2. Jumper Fan Relay #2 terminals 30 and 87A together. Does left cooling fan operate while jumpered?	—	*Go to Step 6*	*Go to Step 4*
4	With Fan Relay #2 still jumpered use DVM J 39200 and measure the voltage to ground at Cooling Fan #2 connector terminal B (harness side). Is the voltage the same or more than the value specified?	10.0 volts	*Go to Step 7*	*Go to Step 8*
5	Replace Cooling Fan #2 (right). Is the replacement complete?	—	*Electric Cooling Fan Diagnosis*	—

GC1089600325010X

Fig. 32 Cooling fan symptom table 2 (Part 1 of 2). Aurora

Step	Action	Value(s)	Yes	No
DEFINITION: Low speed operation of both fans. High speed operation of right cooling fan only. DTC P1660 not set.				
1	Was the Cooling Fan Functional Check performed?	—	*Go to Step 2*	*Electric Cooling Fan Diagnosis*
2	1. Using the scan tool select Output Tests and then Fan Relays. 2. With the key ON select All Relays ON. 3. Remove Fan Relay #2. 4. Using DVM J 39200 measure the voltage to ground at Fan Relay #2 terminal 85. Is the voltage the same or more than the value specified?	10.0 volts	*Go to Step 3*	*Go to Step 5*
3	1. Remove Fan Relay #3. 2. Measure the resistance between Fan Relay #2 terminal 86 and Fan Relay #3 terminal 86. Is the resistance the same or less than the value specified?	5 ohms	*Go to Step 4*	*Go to Step 6*
4	1. Reconnect Fan Relay #3. 2. With All Relays still commanded ON, jumper Fan Relay #2 terminals 30 and 87 together. Do both cooling fans operate while jumpered?	—	*Go to Step 8*	*Go to Step 7*
5	Repair the open in the ORG circuit between Fan Relay #2 terminal 85 and the splice. Is the repair complete?	—	*Electric Cooling Fan Diagnosis*	—
6	Repair the open in CKT 473 between Fan Relay #2 terminal 86 and the CKT 473 splice. Is the repair complete?	—	*Electric Cooling Fan Diagnosis*	—
7	Repair the open in the BLK circuit between Fan Relay #2 terminal 87 and the splice. Is the repair complete?	—	*Electric Cooling Fan Diagnosis*	—
8	Replace Fan Relay #2. Is the replacement complete?	—	*Electric Cooling Fan Diagnosis*	—

GC1089600326000X

Fig. 33 Cooling fan symptom table 3. Aurora

Step	Action	Value(s)	Yes	No
DEFINITION: No fan operation on either high or low speed. DTC P1660 not set.				
1	Did you perform the Cooling Fan Functional Check?	—	Go to *Step 2*	Go to the Cooling Fan Functional Check
2	Check the condition of the cooling fan Maxi fuse. Is the fuse blown?	—	Go to *Step 4*	Go to *Step 3*
3	1. Remove Fan Relay #1. 2. Using DMM J 39200 measure the voltage to ground at Fan Relay #1 terminal 30. Is the voltage the same or more than the value specified?	10 V	Go to *Step 8*	Go to *Step 9*
4	1. Turn the key to LOCK. 2. Replace the Maxi fuse. Does the fuse immediately blow?	—	Go to *Step 10*	Go to *Step 5*
5	1. Turn the key ON. 2. Using the scan tool select Output Tests and then Fan Relays. 3. Command Fan Relay 1 ON. Does the Maxi fuse blow?	—	Go to *Step 11*	Go to *Step 6*
6	Command All Relays ON. Does the Maxi fuse blow?	—	Go to *Step 7*	Fault not present
7	1. Exit Fan Relays. 2. Replace the Maxi fuse. 3. Select Fan Relays and command Fan Relay 1 ON. Is only Cooling Fan #1 (left) operating?	—	Go to *Step 12*	Go to *Step 13*
8	Repair the open in the BLK circuit between both BLK circuit splices or between the BLK circuit splice and ground or the poor/open ground connection. Is the repair complete?	—	*Powertrain Control Module*	—
9	Repair the open in the RED circuit between the Maxi fuse and both relays. Is the repair complete?	—	*Powertrain Control Module*	—
10	Repair the short to ground in the RED circuit between the Maxi fuse and either Fan Relay 1 or Fan Relay 3. Is the repair complete?	—	*Powertrain Control Module*	—
11	Repair the short to ground in CKT 532 between Fan Relay 1 and Cooling Fan #1 (left). Is the repair complete?	—	*Powertrain Control Module*	—
12	Replace Cooling Fan #2 (right). Is the replacement complete?	—	*Powertrain Control Module*	—
13	Replace Cooling Fan #1 (left). Is the replacement complete?	—	*Powertrain Control Module*	—

GC1089900409000X

Fig. 35 Cooling fan symptom table 5. Aurora

Step	Action	Value(s)	Yes	No
1	Was the Powertrain On-Board Diagnostic(OBD) System Check performed?	—	*Go to Step 2*	Go to the *Powertrain OBD System Check*
2	Are any PCM DTC(s) stored?	—	Diagnose the DTCs	*Go to Step 3*
3	1. Engine coolant temperature below 100°C (212°F). 2. Ensure that the A/C is OFF. 3. Engine running. Observe the cooling fans. Are the cooling fans running?	—	*Go to Step 30*	*Go to Step 4*
4	Using scan tool output tests command Fan 1 ON. Do both cooling fans run at low speed?	—	*Go to Step 5*	*Go to Step 8*

GC1089600297010X

Fig. 36 Cooling fan diagnosis (Part 1 of 5). Bonneville, Eighty Eight, LeSabre, LSS & Regency

Step	Action	Value(s)	Yes	No
16	Locate and repair open in CKT 409 to the affected cooling fan motor(s). Is action complete?	—	*Go to Step 46*	—
17	Locate and repair open in the ground circuit to the affected cooling fan motor(s). Is action complete?	—	*Go to Step 46*	—
18	1. Disconnect the high speed cooling fan relay 2. Turn ON the ignition switch. 3. Probe high speed cooling fan relay harness connector terminal 30 with a test light to ground. Is the test light ON?	—	*Go to Step 19*	*Go to Step 29*
19	Probe high speed cooling fan relay harness connector terminal 86 with a test light to ground. Is the test light ON?	—	*Go to Step 20*	*Go to Step 28*
20	1. Connect a fused jumper between high speed cooling fan relay harness connector terminals 30 and 87. 2. Observe the left side cooling fan. Does the left side cooling fan run at high speed?	—	*Go to Step 21*	*Go to Step 24*
21	1. Using the scan tool output control function, select Fan 2 and command the fan ON. 2. Wait 6 seconds. 3. Probe high speed cooling fan harness connector terminal 86 with a test light to B+. Is the test light ON?	—	*Go to Step 42*	*Go to Step 22*
22	1. Turn OFF the ignition switch. 2. Disconnect the PCM. 3. Turn ON the ignition switch. 4. Check the high speed cooling fan relay control circuit for an open or short to voltage between the PCM and the high speed cooling fan relay. 5. If a problem is found, repair as necessary. Was a problem found?	—	*Go to Step 46*	*Go to Step 23*
23	1. Check the high speed cooling fan relay control circuit for a poor terminal connection at the PCM. 2. If a problem is found, repair as necessary. Was a problem found?	—	*Go to Step 46*	*Go to Step 44*
24	1. Disconnect the left side cooling fan motor connector (leave high speed cooling fan relay harness connector terminals 30 and 87 jumpered). 2. Probe the left side cooling fan motor harness connector terminal B with a test light to ground. Is the test light ON?	—	*Go to Step 25*	*Go to Step 27*
25	Connect the test light between left side cooling fan motor harness connector terminals A and B. Is the test light ON?	—	*Go to Step 45*	*Go to Step 26*
26	Locate and repair open in the ground circuit to the left side cooling fan motor. Is action complete?	—	*Go to Step 46*	—
27	Locate and repair open in CKT 532 to the left side cooling fan. Is action complete?	—	*Go to Step 46*	—

GC1089600297030X

Fig. 36 Cooling fan diagnosis (Part 3 of 5). Bonneville, Eighty Eight, LeSabre, LSS & Regency

Step	Action	Value(s)	Yes	No
5	Using scan tool output tests command Fan 2 ON. Does the left side cooling fan run at high speed?	—	*Go to Step 6*	*Go to Step 18*
6	**Important:** Ambient temperature must be above 9°C (48°F). 1. Exit scan tool output tests. 2. Engine running. 3. Turn the A/C ON. Are the cooling fans running?	—	Go to Diagnostic Aids	*Go to Step 7*
7	View the A/C Request display on the scan tool. Does the scan tool display Yes?	—	*Go to Step 44*	*Air Conditioning Diagnosis*
8	1. Turn OFF the ignition switch. 2. Disconnect the low speed cooling fan relay. 3. Turn ON the ignition switch. 4. Probe low speed cooling fan relay harness connector terminal 85 with a test light connected to ground Is the test light ON?	—	*Go to Step 9*	*Go to Step 28*
9	Probe low speed cooling fan relay harness connector terminal 30 with a test light to ground. Is the test light ON?	—	*Go to Step 10*	*Go to Step 29*
10	1. Connect a fused jumper between low speed cooling fan relay harness connector terminals 87 and 30. 2. Observe the cooling fans. Are both cooling fans running at low speed?	—	*Go to Step 11*	*Go to Step 14*
11	1. Using the scan tool output control function, select Fan 1 and command the cooling fans ON. 2. Probe low speed cooling fan harness connector terminal 86 with a test light to B+. Is the test light ON?	—	*Go to Step 40*	*Go to Step 12*
12	1. Turn OFF the ignition switch. 2. Disconnect the PCM. 3. Turn ON the ignition switch. 4. Check the low speed cooling fan relay control circuit for an open or short to voltage between the PCM and the low speed cooling fan relay. 5. If a problem is found, repair as necessary. Was a problem found?	—	*Go to Step 46*	*Go to Step 13*
13	1. Check the low speed cooling fan relay control circuit for a poor terminal connection at the PCM. 2. If a problem is found, repair as necessary. Was a problem found?	—	*Go to Step 46*	*Go to Step 44*
14	1. Disconnect both cooling fan motor 2-way harness connectors (leave low speed cooling fan relay connector terminals 87 and 30 jumpered). 2. Probe terminal B at both cooling fan motor connectors with a test light to ground. Is the test light ON at both cooling fan connectors?	—	*Go to Step 15*	*Go to Step 16*
15	Connect the test light between terminals A and B at both cooling fan connectors. Is the test light ON at both cooling fan connectors?	—	*Go to Step 45*	*Go to Step 17*

GC1089600297020X

Fig. 36 Cooling fan diagnosis (Part 2 of 5). Bonneville, Eighty Eight, LeSabre, LSS & Regency

Step	Action	Value(s)	Yes	No
28	Locate and repair open in ignition feed (CKT 241) to the affected cooling fan relay. Is action complete?	—	*Go to Step 46*	—
29	Locate and repair cause of no battery feed to the affected fan relay cavity 30: • Open or short to ground in CKT 742. • Shorted cooling fan motor windings. • CKT 409 shorted to ground. • CKT 532 shorted to ground. Is action complete?	—	*Go to Step 46*	—
30	Disconnect the high speed cooling fan relay. Is either cooling fan running?	—	*Go to Step 35*	*Go to Step 31*
31	Probe the high speed cooling fan relay harness connector terminal 86 with a test light to B+. Is the test light ON?	—	*Go to Step 32*	*Go to Step 43*
32	Observe A/C Refrigerant Pressure on the scan tool. Is A/C Refrigerant Pressure greater than the specified value?	260 psi (1800 kPa)	Heater Ventilation and Air Conditioning	*Go to Step 33*
33	1. Turn OFF the ignition switch. 2. Disconnect the PCM. 3. Turn ON the ignition switch. 4. Probe the high speed cooling fan relay harness connector terminal 86 with a test light to B+. Is the test light ON?	—	*Go to Step 34*	*Go to Step 44*
34	Locate and repair the short to ground in the high speed cooling fan relay control circuit. Is action complete?	—	*Go to Step 46*	—
35	Disconnect the low speed cooling fan relay. Is either cooling fan ON?	—	*Go to Step 39*	*Go to Step 36*
36	Probe the low speed cooling fan relay harness connector terminal 86 with a test light to B+. Is the test light ON?	—	*Go to Step 37*	*Go to Step 41*
37	1. Turn OFF the ignition switch. 2. Disconnect the PCM. 3. Turn ON the ignition switch. 4. Probe the low speed cooling fan relay harness connector terminal 86 with a test light to B+. Is the test light ON?	—	*Go to Step 38*	*Go to Step 44*
38	Locate and repair the short to ground in the low speed cooling fan relay control circuit. Is action complete?	—	*Go to Step 46*	—
39	Locate and repair short to B+ in affected cooling fan feed CKT 409 or CKT 532. Is action complete?	—	*Go to Step 46*	—
40	1. Check for poor connections at the low speed cooling fan relay. 2. If a problem is found, repair as necessary. Was a problem found?	—	*Go to Step 46*	*Go to Step 41*

GC1089600297040X

Fig. 36 Cooling fan diagnosis (Part 4 of 5). Bonneville, Eighty Eight, LeSabre, LSS & Regency

Step	Action	Value(s)	Yes	No
41	Replace the low speed cooling fan relay. Is action complete?	—	*Go to Step 46*	—
42	1. Check for poor connections at the high speed cooling fan relay. 2. If a problem is found, repair as necessary. Was a problem found?	—	*Go to Step 46*	*Go to Step 43*
43	Replace the high speed cooling fan relay. Is action complete?	—	*Go to Step 46*	—
44	Replace the PCM. **Important:** The replacement PCM must be programmed. Is action complete?	—	*Go to Step 46*	—
45	Replace the affected cooling fan motor. Is action complete?	—	*Go to Step 46*	—
46	1. Engine coolant temperature is below 100°C (212°F). 2. Ensure that the A/C is OFF. 3. Engine running. Are the cooling fans running?	—	*Go to Step 30*	*Go to Step 47*
47	Using scan tool output tests command Fan 1 ON. Do both cooling fans run at low speed?	—	*Go to Step 48*	*Go to Step 8*
48	Using scan tool output tests command Fan 2 ON. Does the left side cooling fan run at high speed?	—	System OK	*Go to Step 18*

GC1089600297050X

Fig. 36 Cooling fan diagnosis (Part 5 of 5). Bonneville, Eighty Eight, LeSabre, LSS & Regency

Step	Action	Value(s)	Yes	No
1	Did you perform the Cooling Fan Functional Check?	—	*Go to Step 2*	Go to Cooling Fan Functional Check
2	Disconnect fan relay #1 Are both fans OFF?	—	*Go to Step 8*	*Go to Step 3*
3	Disconnect fan relay #3 Are both fans OFF?	—	*Go to Step 4*	*Go to Step 10*

GC1089900412010X

Fig. 38 Cooling fan table No. 1 (Part 1 of 2). Camaro & Firebird

Step	Action	Value(s)	Yes	No
4	1. Disconnect the left fan. 2. Probe terminal B of the left fan connector using a *J 34142-B* test lamp that is connected to a good ground. Does the test light illuminate?	—	*Go to Step 11*	*Go to Step 5*
5	Probe terminal A of the left fan connector using a test lamp that is connected to a good ground. Does the test light illuminate?	—	*Go to Step 12*	*Go to Step 6*
6	Probe the cooling fan relay 2 and 3 control circuit (473) at the cooling fan relay #3 connector location (C10) using a test lamp that is connected to B+. Does the test lamp illuminate?	—	*Go to Step 7*	*Go to Step 13*
7	1. Turn OFF the ignition. 2. Leave the test lamp installed. 3. Disconnect the PCM. 4. Turn ON the ignition, with the engine OFF. Is the test lamp still illuminated?	—	*Go to Step 14*	*Go to Step 16*
8	Probe the cooling fan relay 1 control circuit (335) at the cooling fan relay #1 connector location (B1) using the test lamp that is connected to B+. Does the test lamp illuminate?	—	*Go to Step 9*	*Go to Step 13*
9	1. Turn OFF the ignition. 2. Leave the test lamp installed. 3. Disconnect the PCM. 4. Turn ON the ignition, with the engine OFF. Is the test lamp still illuminated?	—	*Go to Step 14*	*Go to Step 16*
10	Repair the RH fan feed circuit (504) for a short to voltage. Did you find and correct the condition?	—	Go to *Cooling Fan Functional Check*	*Go to Step 15*
11	Repair the LH fan feed circuit (409) for a short to voltage. Is the action complete?	—	Go to *Cooling Fan Functional Check*	—
12	Repair the short to voltage in the relay #3 switch feed circuit (532). Is the action complete?	—	Go to *Cooling Fan Functional Check*	—
13	Replace the cooling fan relay #1. Is the action complete?	—	Go to *Cooling Fan Functional Check*	—
14	Repair the relay 2 and 3 control circuit (473) or the relay 1 control circuit (335) for a short to ground. Is the action complete?	—	Go to *Cooling Fan Functional Check*	—
15	Replace the cooling fan relay #2. Is the action complete?	—	Go to *Cooling Fan Functional Check*	—
16	**Important:** Program the replacement PCM. Replace the PCM. Is the action complete?	—	Go to *Cooling Fan Functional Check*	—

GC1089900412020X

Fig. 38 Cooling fan table No. 1 (Part 2 of 2). Camaro & Firebird

Step	Action	Value(s)	Yes	No
1	Did you perform the Powertrain On-Board Diagnostic (OBD) System Check?	—	*Go to Step 2*	Go to *A Powertrain On Board Diagnostic (OBD) System Check*
2	Are any DTCs set?	—	Go to applicable DTC Table	*Go to Step 3*
3	1. Install a scan tool. 2. Engine coolant temperature must be below the specified value for all the fan diagnoses. 3. Turn ON the Ignition, with the engine and A/C OFF. Are the cooling fans OFF?	100°C (212°F)	*Go to Step 4*	Go to Cooling Fan table #1
4	With a scan tool, command the cooling fan relay #1 ON. Are both cooling fans ON?	—	*Go to Step 5*	Go to Cooling Fan table #2
5	With a scan tool, command cooling fan relays #1, #2, and #3 ON. Do both cooling fans switch to high speed?	—	*Go to Step 6*	Go to Cooling Fan table #3
6	1. With a scan tool, exit outputs. 2. Idle the engine leaving the A/C OFF. Are the cooling fans ON?	—	*Go to Step 8*	*Go to Step 7*
7	Turn ON the A/C. Are the cooling fans ON?	—	System OK	*Go to Step 9*
8	Does the scan tool display A/C request as YES?	—	A/C system.	*Go to Step 10*
9	Does the scan tool display A/C request as YES?	—	A/C Refrigerant Pressure Sensor	A/C system.
10	**Important:** Program the replacement PCM. Replace the PCM. Is the action complete?	—	System OK	—

GC1089900411000X

Fig. 37 Cooling fan functional check. Camaro & Firebird

Step	Action	Value(s)	Yes	No
1	Did you perform the Cooling Fan Functional Check?	—	*Go to Step 2*	Go to Cooling Fan Functional Check
2	Did either fan turn ON when cooling fan relay #1 was commanded ON?	—	*Go to Step 3*	*Go to Step 5*
3	1. Install a scan tool. 2. With a scan tool, command cooling fan relay #1 ON. Did the other fan turn OFF?	—	*Go to Step 19*	*Go to Step 4*
4	Disconnect fan relay #2. Did the fan turn OFF?	—	*Go to Step 20*	*Go to Step 21*
5	1. With a scan tool, command cooling fan relay #1 ON. 2. Disconnect fan relay #1. 3. Probe the relay 1 control circuit (335) at the relay #1 connector location (B1) using a *J 34142-B* test lamp that is connected to B+. Does the test lamp illuminate?	—	*Go to Step 6*	*Go to Step 13*
6	Probe both feed circuits (1640 and 402) at the relay 1 connector locations (B3 and C3) using a test lamp that is connected to ground. Does test lamp illuminate for both circuits?	—	*Go to Step 7*	*Go to Step 22*
7	**Important:** Leave jumper in place for remainder of this table. Connect a fused jumper wire between the switch feed circuit (402) and the LH fan feed circuit (409) at the relay #1 connector locations (B3 and C1). Do both fans turn ON?	—	*Go to Step 23*	*Go to Step 8*
8	1. Disconnect the left fan. 2. Probe fan harness connector terminal B with a test lamp that is connected to a good ground, Does the test lamp illuminate?	—	*Go to Step 9*	*Go to Step 24*
9	Connect a second fused jumper wire between the fan harness connector terminals. Is the right fan ON?	—	*Go to Step 16*	*Go to Step 10*
10	1. Reconnect the left fan. 2. Disconnect fan relay #3. 3. Probe the switch feed circuit (532) at the fan relay #3 connector location (C8) using a test lamp that is connected to a good ground. Does the test lamp illuminate?	—	*Go to Step 11*	*Go to Step 25*
11	Using the second jumper wire, jumper the switch ignition feed circuit (532) and the RH fan feed circuit (504) together at relay #3 connector locations (B9 and C8). Do the fans come ON?	—	*Go to Step 26*	*Go to Step 12*
12	1. Reconnect fan relay #3. 2. Disconnect the right fan. 3. Probe fan harness connector terminal B with a test lamp that is connected to a good ground. Is the left fan ON?	—	*Go to Step 16*	*Go to Step 18*

GC1089900413010X

Fig. 39 Cooling fan table No. 2 (Part 1 of 2). Camaro & Firebird

Step	Action	Value(s)	Yes	No
13	1. Test lamp still connected. 2. Turn OFF the ignition. 3. Disconnect the PCM. 4. Probe the cooling fan #1 relay control circuit at the PCM connector, with a fused jumper wire that is connected to a good ground. Is the test lamp ON?	—	*Go to Step 20*	*Go to Step 21*
14	Inspect the PCM connections. Repair faulty connections as necessary. Did you find a problem and correct it?	—	Go to *Cooling Fan Functional Check*	*Go to Step 27*
15	Repair the relay 1 control circuit (335) for an open or shorted to B+. Refer to *Wiring Repairs.* Is the action complete?	—	Go to *Cooling Fan Functional Check*	—
16	Inspect the fan motor ground circuit for a open or the fan motor connections and repair as necessary. Did you find and correct the condition?	—	Go to *Cooling Fan Functional Check*	*Go to Step 17*
17	Replace the fan motor. Is the action complete?	—	Go to *Cooling Fan Functional Check*	—
18	Repair the RH fan feed circuit (504) for an open. Is the action complete?	—	Go to *Cooling Fan Functional Check*	—
19	Replace the fan which was not operating. Is the action complete?	—	Go to *Cooling Fan Functional Check*	—
20	Replace fan relay #2. Is the action complete?	—	Go to *Cooling Fan Functional Check*	—
21	Repair the relay #3 switch feed circuit (532) for a short to ground. Did you find and correct the condition?	—	Go to *Cooling Fan Functional Check*	*Go to Step 26*
22	Repair the open or the grounded circuit for the circuit that did not light. Is the action complete?	—	Go to *Cooling Fan Functional Check*	—
23	Replace fan relay #1. Is the action complete?	—	Go to *Cooling Fan Functional Check*	—
24	Repair the LH fan feed circuit (409) for a open. Is the action complete?	—	Go to *Cooling Fan Functional Check*	—
25	Repair the relay #3 switch feed circuit (532) for a open. Is the action complete?	—	Go to *Cooling Fan Functional Check*	—
26	Replace fan relay #3. Is the action complete?	—	Go to *Cooling Fan Functional Check*	—
27	**Important:** Program the replacement PCM. Replace the PCM. Is the action complete?	—	Go to *Cooling Fan Functional Check*	—

GC1089900413020X

Fig. 39 Cooling fan table No. 2 (Part 2 of 2). Camaro & Firebird

Step	Action	Value(s)	Yes	No
12	Repair the relay 2 and 3 control circuit (473) for an open between fan relay #2 and the splice. Is the action complete?	—	Go to *Cooling Fan Functional Check*	—
13	Repair the open in the relay #2 coil feed circuit (1640). Is the action complete?	—	Go to *Cooling Fan Functional Check*	—
14	Repair the open in the relay #2 switch feed circuit (402). Is the action complete?	—	Go to *Cooling Fan Functional Check*	—
15	Replace the fan relay #2. Is the action complete?	—	Go to *Cooling Fan Functional Check*	—
16	Repair the open in the RH fan feed circuit (504) between fan relay #2 and the splice. Is the action complete?	—	Go to *Cooling Fan Functional Check*	—
17	Repair the fan 2 and 3 relay control circuit (473) for an open or for a short to B+. Is the action complete?	—	Go to *Cooling Fan Functional Check*	—
18	Repair the open in the fan 2 and 3 relay control circuit (473) between fan relay #3 and the splice. Is the action complete?	—	Go to *Cooling Fan Functional Check*	—
19	Repair the open in the ground circuit (150). Is the action complete?	—	Go to *Cooling Fan Functional Check*	—
20	Replace the fan relay #3. Is the action complete?	—	Go to *Cooling Fan Functional Check*	—
21	Repair the open in relay #3 coil feed circuit (1640). Is the action complete?	—	Go to *Cooling Fan Functional Check*	—
22	1. Inspect the PCM connections. 2. Repair faulty connections as necessary. Did you find and correct the condition?	—	Go to *Cooling Fan Functional Check*	*Go to Step 23*
23	**Important:** Program the replacement PCM. Replace the PCM. Is the action complete?	—	Go to *Cooling Fan Functional Check*	—

GC1089900414020X

Fig. 40 Cooling fan table No. 3 (Part 2 of 2). Camaro & Firebird

Step	Action	Value(s)	Yes	No
1	Did you perform the Cooling Fan Functional Check?	—	*Go to Step 2*	Go to *Cooling Fan Functional Check*
2	1. With a scan tool, command cooling fan relay #1 ON. 2. Command cooling fan relays #1, #2, and #3 ON while observing the fans. Did both fans operate with no change?	—	*Go to Step 8*	*Go to Step 3*
3	Did the left fan stop operating?	—	*Go to Step 9*	*Go to Step 4*
4	1. Disconnect fan relay #2. 2. Probe the relay 2 and 3 control circuit (473) at relay #2 connector location (B4) using a *J 34142-B* test lamp that is connected to B+. 3. Command cooling fan relay #2 and #3 ON using a scan tool. Does the test lamp illuminate after several seconds?	—	*Go to Step 5*	*Go to Step 12*
5	Probe the coil feed circuit (1640) at relay #2 connector location (C6) using a test lamp that is connected to a good ground. Does the test lamp illuminate?	—	*Go to Step 6*	*Go to Step 13*
6	Probe the switch feed circuit (402) at the relay #2 connector location (C4) using a test lamp that is connected to a good ground. Does the test lamp illuminate?	—	*Go to Step 7*	*Go to Step 14*
7	Jumper the switch ignition feed circuit (402) and the RH fan feed circuit (504) together at the relay #2 connector locations (C4 and B6). Is the right fan ON?	—	*Go to Step 15*	*Go to Step 16*
8	1. Turn OFF the ignition. 2. Disconnect the PCM. 3. Disconnect fan relay #1. 4. Jumper the switch feed circuit (402) and the LH fan feed circuit (409) together at the relay #1 connector locations (B3 and C1). 5. Turn the ignition ON. 6. Probe the PCM harness connector for the cooling fan relay #2 and #3 control with a fused jumper that is connected to a good ground. Do the fans switch from low to high speed?	—	*Go to Step 22*	*Go to Step 17*
9	1. Disconnect fan relay #3. 2. Probe the relay 2 and 3 control circuit (473) at the relay #3 connector location (C10) using a test lamp that is connected to B+. 3. Command cooling fan relay #2 and #3 ON using a scan tool. Does the test lamp illuminate?	—	*Go to Step 10*	*Go to Step 18*
10	Probe the ground circuit (150) at the relay #3 connector location (B10) using a test lamp that is connected to B+. Does the test lamp illuminate?	—	*Go to Step 11*	*Go to Step 19*
11	Probe the coil feed circuit (1640) at the relay #3 connector location (B8) using a test lamp that is connected to a good ground. Does the test lamp illuminate?	—	*Go to Step 20*	*Go to Step 21*

GC1089900414010X

Fig. 40 Cooling fan table No. 3 (Part 1 of 2). Camaro & Firebird

SYMPTOM	PROCEDURE
Engine coolant fan does not operate	Table #1
Engine coolant fan does not operate at half speed	Table #2
Auxiliary engine coolant fan #1 does not operate	Table #3
Auxiliary engine coolant fan #2 does not operate	Table #4
ECM coolant fan does not operate	Table #5
Timing control pump does not operate.	Table #6
Auxiliary water pump does not operate.	Table #7

GC1089700346000X

Fig. 41 Cooling fan diagnosis symptom table. 1997 Catera

Step	Action	Value(s)	Yes	No
1	1. Locate the test connector within the ECM housing. 2. Using a fused jumper, connect terminal 4 of the test connector to a known good ground. Does the engine coolant fan turn ON?	—	Go to *Step 2*	Go to *Step 3*
2	1. Locate and repair an open or a high resistance in CKTs XM5 or F600. 2. If these CKTs are OK, replace the temperature switch #1. Is the repair or replacement complete?	—	Go to *Step 16*	—
3	1. Disconnect the fan control relay K67 connector. 2. Using the DMM, measure the resistance between terminal 4 of the test connector and terminal 6 of the fan control relay K67. Is the resistance reading within the specified range?	Less than 2 Ω	Go to *Step 5*	Go to *Step 4*
4	Locate and repair an open or a high resistance in CKT XM998. Is the repair complete?	—	Go to *Step 16*	—
5	Using the DMM, measure the voltage between terminal 2 of the fan control relay K67 and a known good ground. Is the voltage reading within the specified range?	B+	Go to *Step 7*	Go to *Step 6*
6	Locate and repair an open or a high resistance in CKT X2. Is the repair complete?	—	Go to *Step 16*	—
7	Using the DMM, measure the voltage between terminal 4 of the fan control relay K67 and a known good ground. Is the voltage reading within the specified range?	B+	Go to *Step 9*	Go to *Step 8*
8	1. Check the intergrity of fuse #42. 2. If the fuse is OK, locate and repair an open or a high resistance in CKTs A710 or A700. Is the repair complete?	—	Go to *Step 16*	—
9	Connect a fused jumper between terminals 4 and 8 of the fan control relay K67 connector. Does the engine coolant fan turn ON?	—	Go to *Step 10*	Go to *Step 11*
10	Replace the fan control relay K67. Is the replacement complete?	—	Go to *Step 16*	—
11	1. Disconnect the engine coolant fan connector. 2. Using the DMM, measure the voltage between terminal A of the engine coolant fan connector and a known good ground. Is the voltage reading within the specified range?	B+	Go to *Step 13*	Go to *Step 12*
12	Locate and repair an open, high resistance or a short to ground in CKTs AM16 or AM17. Is the repair complete?	—	Go to *Step 16*	—

GC1089700347010X

Fig. 42 Table 1, cooling fan inoperative (Part 1 of 2). 1997 Catera

Step	Action	Value(s)	Yes	No
1	1. Locate the test connector within the ECM housing. 2. Using a fused jumper, connect terminal 1 of the test connector to a known good ground. Does the engine coolant fan turn ON at half speed?	—	Go to *Step 2*	Go to *Step 3*
2	1. Locate and repair an open or a high resistance in CKTs XP30 or F600. 2. If these CKTs are OK, replace the temperature switch #1. Is the repair or replacement complete?	—	Go to *Step 18*	—
3	1. Disconnect the fan control relay K26 connector. 2. Using the DMM, measure the resistance between terminal 1 of the test connector and terminal 6 of the fan control relay K26. Is the resistance reading within the specified range?	Less than 2 Ω	Go to *Step 5*	Go to *Step 4*
4	Locate and repair an open or a high resistance in CKTs XP999 or XP3. Is the repair complete?	—	Go to *Step 18*	—
5	Using the DMM, measure the voltage between terminal 3 of the fan control relay K26 and a known good ground. Is the voltage reading within the specified range?	B+	Go to *Step 7*	Go to *Step 6*
6	1. Check the integrity of fuse #50. 2. If fuse #50 is OK, locate and repair an open or a high resistance in CKTs A6 or A310. Is the repair complete?	—	Go to *Step 18*	—
7	Using the DMM, measure the voltage between terminal 4 of the fan control relay K26 and a known good ground. Is the voltage reading within the specified range?	B+	Go to *Step 9*	Go to *Step 8*

GC1089700348010X

Fig. 43 Table 2, cooling fan inoperative at half speed (Part 1 of 2). 1997 Catera

Step	Action	Value(s)	Yes	No
13	Using the DMM, measure the resistance between terminal B of the engine coolant fan connector and a known good ground. Is the resistance reading within the specified range?	Less than 2 Ω	Go to *Step 15*	Go to *Step 14*
14	Locate and repair an open or a high resistance in CKT F100. Is the repair complete?	—	Go to *Step 16*	—
15	Replace the engine coolant fan. Is the replacement complete?	—	Go to *Step 16*	—
16	1. Connect all connectors and components that were disconnected. 2. Verify that the engine coolant fan operates properly. Does the engine coolant fan operate properly?	—	System is OK	Go to *Step 1*

GC1089700347020X

Fig. 42 Table 1, cooling fan inoperative (Part 2 of 2). 1997 Catera

Step	Action	Value(s)	Yes	No
8	1. Check the intergrity of fuse #52. 2. If the fuse is OK, locate and repair an open or a high resistance in CKTs A300, A220 or A223. Is the repair complete?	—	Go to *Step 18*	—
9	Connect a fused jumper between terminals 4 and 5 of the fan control relay K26 connector. Does the engine coolant fan turn ON at half speed?	—	Go to *Step 10*	Go to *Step 11*
10	Replace the fan control relay K26. Is the replacement complete?	—	Go to *Step 18*	—
11	1. Disconnect the engine coolant fan resistor connector. 2. Using the DMM, measure the voltage between terminal 1 of the engine coolant fan resistor connector and a known good ground. Is the voltage reading within the specified range?	B+	Go to *Step 13*	Go to *Step 12*
12	Locate and repair an open, high resistance or a short to ground in CKT AP2. Is the repair complete?	—	Go to *Step 18*	—
13	1. Disconnect the engine coolant fan connector. 2. Using the DMM, measure the resistance between terminal 1 of the engine coolant fan resistor connector and terminal A of the engine coolant fan connector. Is the resistance reading within the specified range?	Less than 2 Ω	Go to *Step 15*	Go to *Step 14*
14	Locate and repair an open or a high resistance in CKTs AM17 or AM6. Is the repair complete?	—	Go to *Step 18*	—
15	Using the DMM, measure the resistance between terminal B of the engine coolant fan connector and a known good ground. Is the resistance reading within the specified range?	Less than 2 Ω	Go to *Step 17*	Go to *Step 16*
16	Locate and repair an open or a high resistance in CKT F100. Is the repair complete?	—	Go to *Step 18*	—
17	1. Check the integrity of the engine coolant fan resistor. If it is open, replace it. 2. If the engine coolant fan resistor is OK, replace the engine coolant fan. Is the repair or replacement complete?	—	Go to *Step 18*	—
18	1. Connect all connectors and components that were disconnected. 2. Verify that the engine coolant fan operates properly at half speed. Does the engine coolant fan operate properly at half speed?	—	System is OK	Go to *Step 1*

GC1089700348020X

Fig. 43 Table 2, cooling fan inoperative at half speed (Part 2 of 2). 1997 Catera

Step	Action	Value(s)	Yes	No
1	1. Locate the test connector within the ECM housing. 2. Using a fused jumper, connect terminal 1 of the test connector to a known good ground. 3. Disconnect the auxiliary engine coolant fan #1 connector. 4. Using the DMM, measure the voltage between terminal A of the auxiliary engine coolant Fan #1 connector and a known good ground while grounding terminal 1 of the test connector. Is the voltage reading within the specified range?	B+	Go to *Step 9*	Go to *Step 2*
2	1. Disconnect the fan control relay K26 connector. 2. Using the DMM, measure the voltage between terminal 3 of the fan control relay K26 connector and a known good ground. Is the voltage reading within the specified range?	B+	Go to *Step 4*	Go to *Step 3*
3	1. Check the integrity of fuse #50. 2. If the fuse is OK, locate and repair an open or a high resistance in CKTs A6 or A310. Is the repair or replacement complete?	—	Go to *Step 10*	—
4	Using the DMM, measure the voltage between terminal 2 of the fan control relay K26 and a known good ground. Is the voltage reading within the specified range?	B+	Go to *Step 6*	Go to *Step 5*
5	1. Check the integrity of fuse #52. 2. If the fuse is OK, locate and repair an open or a high resistance in CKTs A300, A220 or A222. Is the repair complete?	—	Go to *Step 10*	—
6	1. Connect a fused jumper between terminals 2 and 8 of the fan control relay K26 connector. 2. Using the DMM, measure the voltage between terminal A of the auxiliary engine coolant fan #1 connector and a known good ground. Is the voltage reading within the specified range?	B+	Go to *Step 8*	Go to *Step 7*
7	Locate and repair an open or a high resistance in CKTs AM1 or AM13. Is the repair complete?	—	Go to *Step 10*	—
8	Replace the fan control relay K26. Is the replacement complete?	—	Go to *Step 10*	—
9	1. Locate and repair an open or a high resistance in CKTs XP30 or F600. 2. If these CKTs are OK, replace the temperature switch #1. Is the repair or replacement complete?	—	Go to *Step 10*	

GC1089700349010X

Fig. 44 Table 3, auxiliary cooling fan No. 1 inoperative (Part 1 of 2). 1997 Catera

Step	Action	Value(s)	Yes	No
10	1. Locate the test connector within the ECM housing. 2. Using a fused jumper, connect terminal 5 of the test connector to a known good ground. 3. Disconnect the auxiliary engine coolant fan #1 connector. 4. Using the DMM, measure the resistance between terminal B of the auxiliary engine coolant fan #1 connector and a known good ground while grounding terminal 5 of the test connector. Is the resistance reading within the specified range?	Less than 2 Ω	Go to *Step 11*	Go to *Step 12*
11	Replace the auxiliary engine coolant fan #1. Is the replacement complete?	—	Go to *Step 19*	—
12	1. Disconnect the fan control relay K52. 2. Using the DMM, measure the voltage between terminal 4 of the fan control relay K52 and a known good ground. Is the voltage reading within the specified range?	B+	Go to *Step 14*	Go to *Step 13*
13	Locate and repair an open or a high resistance in circuit X30. Is the repair complete?	—	Go to *Step 19*	—
14	Using the DMM, measure the resistance between terminal 8 of the fan control relay K52 and a known good ground. Is the resistance reading within the specified range?	Less than 2 Ω	Go to *Step 16*	Go to *Step 15*
15	Locate and repair an open or a high resistance in CKT F7. Is the repair complete?	—	Go to *Step 19*	—
16	Using the DMM, measure the resistance between terminal 2 of the fan control relay K52 and terminal B of the auxiliary engine coolant fan #1 connector. Is the resistance reading within the specified range?	Less than 2 Ω	Go to *Step 18*	Go to *Step 17*
17	Locate and repair an open or a high resistance in CKT XU3. Is the repair complete?	—	Go to *Step 19*	—
18	1. Locate and repair an open or a high resistance in CKTs XM123, XM997, XM122 or F60. 2. If these CKTs are OK, replace the temperature switch #2. Is the replacement complete?	—	Go to *Step 19*	—
19	1. Connect all connectors that were disconnected. 2. Check the auxiliary engine coolant fan #1 for proper operation. Does the auxiliary engine coolant fan #1 operate properly?	—	System is OK	Go to *Step 1*

GC1089700349020X

Fig. 44 Table 3, auxiliary cooling fan No. 1 inoperative (Part 2 of 2). 1997 Catera

Step	Action	Value(s)	Yes	No
1	1. Locate the test connector within the ECM housing. 2. Using a fused jumper, connect terminal 5 of the test connector to a known good ground. Does the auxiliary engine coolant fan #2 turn ON?	—	Go to *Step 2*	Go to *Step 3*
2	1. Locate and repair an open or a high resistance in CKTs XM122 or F60. 2. If these CKTs are OK, replace the temperature switch #2. Is the repair or replacement complete?	—	Go to *Step 14*	—
3	1. Disconnect the fan control relay K28 connector. 2. Using the DMM, measure the resistance between terminal 5 of the test connector and terminal 6 of the fan control relay K28. Is the resistance reading within the specified range?	Less than 2 Ω	Go to *Step 5*	Go to *Step 4*
4	Locate and repair an open or a high resistance in CKTs XM124 or XM997. Is the repair complete?	—	Go to *Step 14*	—
5	Using the DMM, measure the voltage between terminal 2 of the fan control relay K28 and a known good ground. Is the voltage reading within the specified range?	B+	Go to *Step 7*	Go to *Step 6*
6	Locate and repair an open or a high resistance in CKT X400. Is the repair complete?	—	Go to *Step 14*	—
7	Using the DMM, measure the voltage between terminal 4 of the fan control relay K28 and a known good ground. Is the voltage reading within the specified range?	B+	Go to *Step 9*	Go to *Step 8*
8	1. Check the intergrity of fuse #40. 2. If the fuse is OK, locate and repair an open or a high resistance in CKTs A14 and A25. Is the repair complete?	—	Go to *Step 14*	—
9	Connect a fused jumper between terminals 4 and 8 of the fan control relay K28 connector. Does the auxiliary engine coolant fan #2 turn ON?	—	Go to *Step 10*	Go to *Step 11*
10	Replace the fan control relay K28. Is the replacement complete?	—	Go to *Step 14*	—
11	1. Disconnect the auxiliary engine coolant fan #2 connector. 2. Using the DMM, measure the voltage between terminal A of the auxiliary engine coolant fan #2 connector and a known good ground. Is the voltage reading within the specified range?	B+	Go to *Step 13*	Go to *Step 12*

GC1089700350010X

Fig. 45 Table 4, auxiliary cooling fan No. 2 inoperative (Part 1 of 2). 1997 Catera

Step	Action	Value(s)	Yes	No
12	Locate and repair an open, high resistance or a short to ground in CKTs AM4 or AM 5. Is the repair complete?	—	Go to *Step 14*	—
13	Replace the auxiliary engine coolant fan #2. Is the replacement complete?	—	Go to *Step 14*	—
14	1. Connect all connectors that were disconnected. 2. Check the auxiliary engine coolant fan #2 for proper operation. Does the auxiliary engine coolant fan #2 operate properly?	—	System is OK	go to *Step 1*

GC1089700350020X

Fig. 45 Table 4, auxiliary cooling fan No. 2 inoperative (Part 2 of 2). 1997 Catera

Step	Action	Value(s)	Yes	No
1	1. Locate the test connector within the ECM housing. 2. Using a fused jumper, connect terminal 1 of the test connector to a known good ground. Does the ECM cooling blower turn ON?	—	Go to *Step 2*	Go to *Step 3*
2	1. Locate and repair an open or a high resistance in CKTs XP30 or F600. 2. If these CKTs are OK, replace the temperature switch #1. Is the repair or replacement complete?	—	Go to *Step 14*	—
3	1. Disconnect the ECM relay K48. 2. Using the DMM, measure the voltage between terminal 2 of the ECM relay K48 and a known good ground. Is the voltage reading within the specified range?	B+	Go to *Step 5*	Go to *Step 4*
4	Locate and repair an open or a high resistance in CKT A60. Is the repair complete?	—	Go to *Step 14*	—
5	Using the DMM, measure the voltage between terminal 4 of the ECM relay K48 and a known good ground. Is the voltage reading within the specified range?	B+	Go to *Step 7*	Go to *Step 6*
6	Locate and repair an open or a high resistance in CKT X235. Is the repair complete?	—	Go to *Step 14*	—
7	Connect a fused jumper between terminals 4 and 8 of the ECM relay K48. Does the ECM cooling blower turn ON?	—	Go to *Step 8*	Go to *Step 9*
8	Replace the ECM relay K48. Is the replacement complete?	—	Go to *Step 14*	—

GC1089700351010X

Fig. 46 Table 5, ECM cooling fan inoperative (Part 1 of 2). 1997 Catera

Step	Action	Value(s)	Yes	No
9	1. Disconnect the ECM cooling blower connector. 2. Using the DMM, measure the voltage between terminal 1 of the ECM cooling blower connector and a known good ground. Is the voltage reading within the specified range?	B+	Go to *Step 11*	Go to *Step 10*
10	Locate and repair an open or a high resistance in CKT FM235. Is the repair complete?	—	Go to *Step 14*	—
11	Using the DMM, measure the resistance between terminal 2 of the ECM cooling blower and a known good ground. Is the resistance reading within the specified range?	Less than 2 Ω	Go to *Step 13*	Go to *Step 12*
12	Locate and repair an open or a high resistance in CKT F59. Is the repair complete?	—	Go to *Step 14*	—
13	Replace the ECM cooling blower. Is the replacement complete?	—	Go to *Step 14*	—
14	1. Connect all connectors that were disconnected. 2. Check the ECM cooling blower for proper operation. Does the ECM cooling blower operate properly?	—	System is OK	Go to *Step 1*

GC1089700351020X

Fig. 46 Table 5, ECM cooling fan inoperative (Part 2 of 2). 1997 Catera

Step	Action	Normal Result(s)	Abnormal Result(s)*
4	Check in order to ensure that the auxiliary engine coolant fan #1 and auxiliary engine coolant fan #2 operate at normal speed, when the primary cooling fan temperature switch and the secondary cooling fan temperature switch reach their appropriate temperatures.	1. When the secondary cooling fan temperature switch reaches 105°C (221°F), terminal 2 of the secondary cooling fan temperature switch is grounded, the fan control relays K28 and K52 are energized, and ground is supplied to terminal B of the auxiliary engine coolant fan #1 through fan control relay K52. B+ for the auxiliary engine coolant fan #1 is supplied by the previously energized fan control relay K26. 2. When B+ is supplied to terminal A and ground is supplied to terminal B of the auxiliary engine coolant fan #1, the auxiliary engine coolant fan #1 will operate at normal speed. 3. The fan control relay K28 supplies B+ to terminal A of the auxiliary engine coolant fan #2. Terminal B of the auxiliary engine coolant fan #2 is permanently grounded. The auxiliary engine coolant fan runs at normal speed.	1. The auxiliary engine coolant fan #1 does not operate at normal speed. Refer to *Cooling Fan Inoperative - Auxiliary (Aux Engine Coolant Fan #1 Inop).* 2. The auxiliary engine coolant fan #2 does not operate at normal speed. Refer to *Cooling Fan Inoperative - Auxiliary (Aux Engine Coolant Fan #2 Inop).*
5	Check in order to ensure that the auxiliary engine coolant fan #1 and auxiliary engine fan #2 operate at low speed when the A/C compressor clutch coil is energized.	When the A/C compressor clutch coil is enegized the fan control relay K87 is enegized, and B+ is supplied to terminal A of the auxiliary engine coolant fan #1. The auxiliary engine coolant fan #1 is wired in series with the auxiliary engine coolant fan #2 through the normally closed contacts of the fan control relay K52. The fans will run at low speed until the fan control relay K52 is energized.	The auxiliary engine coolant fan #1 and auxiliary engine coolant fan #2 do not operate at low speed. Refer to *Cooling Fan Inoperative - Auxiliary (A/C Cooling Low Speed).*
6	Check in order to ensure that the auxiliary engine coolant fan #1 and auxiliary engine fan #2 operate at normal speed when the A/C compressor refrigerant pressure switch reaches the appropriate pressure.	When the A/C compressor refrigerant pressure switch reaches 1900 kPa (275 PSI), terminal 3 of the A/C compressor refrigerant pressure switch is grounded, the fan control relay K28 is energized, and the auxiliary engine coolant fan #1 and auxiliary engine coolant fan #2 operate at normal speed.	The auxiliary engine coolant fan #1 and auxiliary engine coolant fan #2 do not operate at normal speed. Refer to *Cooling Fan Inoperative - Auxiliary (A/C Cooling High Speed).*
7	Check in order to ensure that the ECM cooling blower operates at normal speed when the A/C compressor refrigerant pressure switch reaches the appropriate pressure.	When the A/C compressor refrigerant pressure switch reaches 1900 kPa (275 PSI), terminal 3 of the A/C compressor refrigerant pressure switch is grounded, the ECM relay K48 is energized, and the ECM cooling blower operates at normal speed.	The ECM cooling blower does not operate at normal speed. Refer to *ECM Cooling Blower Inoperative.*

GC1089800449020X

Fig. 47 Cooling fan system check (Part 2 of 3). 1998-2000 Catera

Step	Action	Normal Result(s)	Abnormal Result(s)*
1	Check in order to ensure that the electric cooling fan operates at normal speed when the primary cooling fan temperature switch reaches the appropriate temperature.	When the primary cooling fan temperature switch reaches 110°C (230°F), terminal 3 of the primary cooling fan temperature switch is grounded, the fan control relay K67 is energized, and the electric cooling fan operates at normal speed.	The electric cooling fan does not operate at normal speed. Refer to *Cooling Fan Inoperative*
2	Check in order to ensure that the electric cooling fan operates at low speed when the primary cooling fan temperature switch reaches the appropriate temperature.	1. When the primary cooling fan temperature switch reaches 100°C (212°F), terminal 2 of the primary cooling fan temperature switch is grounded, the fan control relay K26 is energized, and the electric cooling fan operates at low speed. 2. The electric cooling fan operates at low speed because the engine coolant fan resistor is in series with the electric cooling fan motor.	The electric cooling fan does not operate at low speed. Refer to *Cooling Fan Inoperative at Low Speed*
3	Check in order to ensure that the auxiliary engine coolant fan #1 and auxiliary engine coolant fan #2 operate at low speed when the primary cooling fan temperature switch reaches the appropriate temperature.	When the primary cooling fan temperature switch reaches 100°C (212°F), terminal 2 of the primary cooling fan temperature switch is grounded, the fan control relay K26 is energized, and B+ is supplied to terminal A of the auxiliary engine coolant fan #1. The auxiliary engine coolant fan #1 is wired in series with the auxiliary engine coolant fan #2 through the normally closed contacts of the fan control relay K52. The fans will run at a lower speed until the fan control relay K52 is energized.	The auxiliary engine coolant fan #1 and auxiliary engine coolant fan #2 do not operate at low speed. Refer to *Cooling Fan Inoperative - Auxiliary (Both Aux Eng Cool Fans Inop)*

GC1089800449010X

Fig. 47 Cooling fan system check (Part 1 of 3). 1998-2000 Catera

Step	Action	Normal Result(s)	Abnormal Result(s)*
8	Check in order to ensure that the water auxiliary pump operates at normal speed when the ignition key is in the ON position.	When the ignition key is turned to the ON position, the auxiliary water pump relay K22 is energized and the water auxiliary pump operates at normal speed.	The water auxiliary pump does not operate at normal speed. Refer to *Water Pump Inoperative - Auxiliary.*
9	Check in order to ensure that the heater water auxiliary pump operates at normal speed when the ignition key is in the ON position.	When the ignition key is in the ON position, B+ is supplied to terminal 2 of the heater water auxiliary pump and the heater water auxiliary pump operates at normal speed.	The heater water auxiliary pump does not operate at normal speed. Refer to *Cooling Fan Circuit Diagnosis (Heater Water Aux Pump Inop).*
* Refer to the appropriate symptom diagnostic table for the applicable abnormal result.			

GC1089800449030X

Fig. 47 Cooling fan system check (Part 3 of 3). 1998-2000 Catera

Step	Action	Value(s)	Yes	No
1	Was the Coolant Fan System Check performed?	B+	*Go to Step 2*	Refer to *Cooling Fan System Check.*
2	1. Disconnect the heater water auxiliary pump connector. 2. Turn the ignition switch to the ON position. 3. Use the DMM to measure the voltage between terminal 2 of the heater water auxiliary pump connector and a known good ground. Is the measured voltage within the specified value?	B+	*Go to Step 4*	*Go to Step 3*
3	1. Locate an open or a high resistance in circuit X70. 2. Repair the open or the high resistance in circuit X70. Is the repair complete?	—	*Go to Step 7*	—
4	Use the DMM to measure the resistance between terminal 1 of the heater water auxiliary pump connector and a known good ground. Is the measured resistance within the specified value?	Less than 5 Ω	*Go to Step 6*	*Go to Step 5*
5	1. Locate an open or a high resistance in circuit F75. 2. Repair the open or the high resistance in circuit F75. Is the repair complete?	—	*Go to Step 7*	—
6	Replace the heater water auxiliary pump. Is the replacement complete?	—	*Go to Step 7*	—
7	1. Connect all connectors and components that were disconnected. 2. Verify the heater water auxiliary pump operates properly? Does the heater water auxiliary pump operate properly?	—	System OK	*Go to Step 1*

GC1089800450000X

Fig. 48 Cooling fan circuit diagnosis (Heater water auxiliary pump inop). 1998-2000 Catera

Step	Action	Value(s)	Yes	No
1	Did you perform the Cooling Fan System Check?	—	*Go to Step 2*	Refer to *Cooling Fan System Check.*
2	1. Turn on the ignition. 2. Locate the coolant fan test connector within the ECM housing. 3. Use a fused jumper to connect terminal 4 of the coolant fan test connector to a known good ground. Does the electric cooling fan turn ON?	—	*Go to Step 3*	*Go to Step 4*
3	1. Locate and repair open or a high resistance in circuits XM5 and/or F600. 2. Replace the primary cooling fan temperature switch if these circuits are OK. Did you complete the repair?	—	*Go to Step 17*	—
4	1. Disconnect the fan control relay K67 connector. 2. Use the DMM in order to measure the resistance between terminal 4 of the coolant fan test connector and terminal 6 of the fan control relay K67. Does the resistance measure near the specified value?	Less than 5 Ω	*Go to Step 6*	*Go to Step 5*
5	1. Locate an open or a high resistance in CKT MX998. 2. Repair the open or the high resistance in CKT MX998. Did you complete the repair?	—	*Go to Step 17*	—
6	Use the DMM in order to measure the voltage between terminal 2 of the fan control relay K67 and a known good ground. Does the voltage measure near the specified value?	B+	*Go to Step 8*	*Go to Step 7*
7	1. Locate an open or a high resistance in CKT X2. 2. Repair the open or the high resistance in CKT X2. Did you complete the repair?	—	*Go to Step 17*	—
8	Use the DMM in order to measure the voltage between terminal 4 of the fan control relay K67 and a known good ground. Does the voltage measure near the specified value?	B+	*Go to Step 10*	*Go to Step 9*
9	1. Check the integrity of fuse #42. 2. If the fuse is OK, locate an open or a high resistance in circuits A710 and/or A700. 3. Repair the open or the high resistance in circuits A710 and/or A700. Did you complete the repair?	—	*Go to Step 17*	—
10	Connect a fused jumper between terminal 4 and terminal 8 of the fan control relay K67 connector. Does the engine coolant fan turn ON?	—	*Go to Step 11*	*Go to Step 12*
11	Replace the fan control relay K67. Did you complete the repair?	—	*Go to Step 17*	—
12	1. Disconnect the electric cooling fan connector. 2. Use the DMM in order to measure the voltage between terminal A of the electric cooling fan connector and a known good ground. Does the voltage measure near the specified value?	B+	*Go to Step 14*	*Go to Step 13*

GC1089800451010X

Fig. 49 Cooling fan inoperative (Part 1 of 2). 1998-2000 Catera

Step	Action	Value(s)	Yes	No
6	Use the DMM in order to measure the voltage between terminal 3 of the fan control relay K26 and a known good ground. Does the voltage measure near the specified value?	B+	*Go to Step 8*	*Go to Step 7*
7	1. Inspect fuse #50 for an open. 2. Locate an open or high resistance in circuits A6 and/or A310. 3. Repair the open or the high resistance in circuits A6 and/or A310. Did you complete the repair?	—	*Go to Step 19*	—
8	Use the DMM in order to measure the voltage between terminal 4 of the fan control relay K26 and a known good ground. Does the voltage measure near the specified value?	B+	*Go to Step 10*	*Go to Step 9*
9	1. Inspect fuse #52 for an open. 2. Locate an open or a high resistance in circuits A300, A220 and/or A223 if the fuse in OK. 3. Repair the open or the high resistance in circuits A300, A220 and/or A223. Did you complete the repair?	—	*Go to Step 19*	—
10	Connect a fused jumper between terminal 4 and terminal 5 of the fan control relay K26 connector. Does the engine coolant fan turn ON at half speed?	—	*Go to Step 11*	*Go to Step 12*
11	Replace the fan control relay K26. Did you complete the repair?	—	*Go to Step 19*	—
12	1. Disconnect the engine coolant fan resistor connector. 2. Use the DMM in order to measure the voltage between terminal 1 of the engine coolant fan resistor connector and a known good ground. Does the voltage measure near the specified value?	B+	*Go to Step 14*	*Go to Step 13*
13	1. Locate an open, high resistance or a short to ground in circuits AP2 and/or AP1. 2. Repair an open, high resistance or a short to ground in circuits AP2 and/or AP1. Did you complete the repair?	—	*Go to Step 19*	—
14	1. Disconnect the electric cooling fan connector. 2. Use the DMM in order to measure the resistance between terminal 1 of the engine coolant fan resistor connector and terminal A of the electric cooling fan connector. Does the resistance measure near the specified value?	Less than 5 Ω	*Go to Step 16*	*Go to Step 15*
15	1. Locate an open or a high resistance in circuits AM17 and/or AM6. 2. Repair the open or the high resistance in circuits AM17 and/or AM6. Did you complete the repair?	—	*Go to Step 19*	—
16	Use the DMM in order to measure the resistance between terminal B of the electric cooling fan connector and a known good ground. Does the resistance measure near the specified value?	Less than 5 Ω	*Go to Step 18*	*Go to Step 17*
17	1. Locate an open or a high resistance in CKT F100. 2. Repair the open or the high resistance in CKT F100. Did you complete the repair?	—	*Go to Step 19*	—

GC1089800452020X

Fig. 50 Cooling fan inoperative at low speed (Part 2 of 3). 1998-2000 Catera

Step	Action	Value(s)	Yes	No
13	1. Locate an open, high resistance or short to ground in circuits AM16 and/or AM17. 2. Repair an open, high resistance or short to ground in circuits AM16 and/or AM17. Did you complete the repair?	—	*Go to Step 17*	—
14	Use the DMM in order to measure the resistance between terminal B of the electric cooling fan connector and a known good ground. Does the resistance measure near the specified value?	Less than 5 Ω	*Go to Step 16*	*Go to Step 15*
15	1. Locate an open or a high resistance in CKT F100. 2. Repair the open or the high resistance in CKT F100. Did you complete the repair?	—	*Go to Step 17*	—
16	Replace the electric cooling fan. Did you complete the repair?	—	*Go to Step 17*	—
17	1. Connect all connectors and components that were previously disconnected. 2. Verify that the electric cooling fan operates properly. Does the electric cooling fan operate properly?	—	Refer to *Cooling Fan System Check.*	*Go to Step 1*

GC1089800451020X

Fig. 49 Cooling fan inoperative (Part 2 of 2). 1998-2000 Catera

Step	Action	Value(s)	Yes	No
1	Did you perform the Cooling Fan Diagnostic System Check?	—	*Go to Step 2*	Refer to *Cooling Fan System Check.*
2	1. Locate the coolant fan test connector within the ECM housing. 2. Use a fused jumper in order to connect terminal 1 of the coolant fan test connector to a known good ground. Does the electric cooling fan turn ON at low speed?	—	*Go to Step 3*	*Go to Step 4*
3	1. Locate an open or a high resistance in circuits XP30 and/or F600. 2. Repair the open or the high resistance in circuits XP30 and/or F600. 3. Replace the primary cooling fan temperature switch if circuits XP30 and F600 are OK. Did you complete the repair?	—	*Go to Step 19*	—
4	1. Disconnect the fan control relay K26 connector. 2. Use the DMM to measure the resistance between terminal 1 of the coolant fan test connector and terminal 6 of the fan control relay K26. Is the measured resistance within the specified value?	Less than 5 Ω	*Go to Step 6*	*Go to Step 5*
5	1. Locate an open or a high resistance in circuits XP999 and/or XP3. 2. Repair the open or the high resistance in circuits XP999 and/or XP3. Did you complete the repair?	—	*Go to Step 19*	—

GC1089800452010X

Fig. 50 Cooling fan inoperative at low speed (Part 1 of 3). 1998-2000 Catera

Step	Action	Value(s)	Yes	No
18	1. Check the integrity of the engine coolant fan resistor. 2. Replace the engine coolant fan resistor if it is open. 3. Replace the electric cooling fan if the engine coolant fan resistor is OK. Did you complete the repair?	—	*Go to Step 19*	—
19	1. Connect all connectors and components that were previously disconnected. 2. Verify that the electric cooling fan operates properly at low speed. Does the electric cooling fan operate properly at low speed?	—	Refer to *Cooling Fan System Check.*	*Go to Step 1*

GC1089800452030X

Fig. 50 Cooling fan inoperative at low speed (Part 3 of 3). 1998-2000 Catera

Step	Action	Value(s)	Yes	No
1	Did you perform the Coolant Fan Diagnostic System Check?	—	*Go to Step 2*	Refer to *Cooling Fan System Check.*
2	1. Disconnect the auxiliary water pump relay K22. 2. Turn on the ignition switch. 3. Use the DMM in order to measure the voltage between terminal 4 of the auxiliary water pump relay K22 connector and a known good ground. Does the voltage measure near the specified value?	B+	*Go to Step 4*	*Go to Step 3*
3	1. Locate an open or a high resistance in CKT X6. 2. Repair the open or the high resistance in CKT X6. Did you complete the repair?	—	*Go to Step 15*	—
4	Use the DMM in order to measure the resistance between terminal 6 of the auxiliary water pump relay K22 connector and a known good ground. Does the resistance measure near the specified value?	Less than 5 Ω	*Go to Step 6*	*Go to Step 5*
5	1. Locate an open or a high resistance in CKT F5. 2. CKT F5. Did you complete the repair?	—	*Go to Step 15*	—
6	1. Locate the coolant fan test connector within the ECM housing. 2. Use a fused jumper to connect terminal 1 of the coolant fan test connector to a known good ground. Does the engine coolant fan turn ON at low speed?	—	*Go to Step 8*	*Go to Step 7*
7	Refer to *Cooling Fan Inoperative at Low Speed* for diagnosis of the electric cooling fan does not operate at low speed. Did you complete the repair?	—	Refer to *Cooling Fan System Check.*	—
8	Use the DMM in order to measure the voltage between terminal 2 of the auxiliary water pump relay K22 connector and a known good ground. Does the voltage measure near the specified value?	B+	*Go to Step 10*	*Go to Step 9*
9	1. Locate an open or a high resistance in CKT AP3. 2. Repair the open or the high resistance in CKT AP3. Did you complete the repair?	—	*Go to Step 15*	—

GC1089800453010X

Fig. 51 Water pump inoperative (Part 1 of 2). 1998-2000 Catera

Step	Action	Value(s)	Yes	No
1	Did you perform the Cooling Fan Diagnostic System Check?	—	*Go to Step 2*	Go to *Cooling Fan System Check*
2	1. Turn the ignition switch to the OFF positon. 2. Locate the coolant fan test connector within the ECM housing. 3. Use a fused jumper to connect terminal 1 of the coolant fan test connector to a known good ground. Does the auxiliary engine coolant fan #1 and fan #2 operate at low speed?	B+	*Go to Step 3*	Go to *Cooling Fan Inoperative - Auxiliary (Both Aux Eng Cool Fans Inop)*
3	1. Turn the ignition switch to the ON position. 2. Disconnect the fan control relay K52 connector. 3. Use the DMM in order to measure the voltage between terminal 4 of the fan control relay K52 connector and a known good ground. Does the voltage measure near the specified value?	B+	*Go to Step 5*	*Go to Step 4*
4	1. Locate a open or a high resistance in circuit X30 2. Repair the open or the high resistance in circuit X30. Did you complete the repair?	—	*Go to Step 8*	—

GC1089800454010X

Fig. 52 Cooling fan inoperative (Auxiliary engine coolant fan No. 1, Part 1 of 2). 1998-2000 Catera

Step	Action	Value(s)	Yes	No
1	Did you perform the Cooling Fan Diagnostic System Check?	—	*Go to Step 2*	Go to *Cooling Fan System Check*
2	1. Turn the ignition switch to the OFF position. 2. Locate the coolant fan test connector within the ECM housing. 3. Use a fused jumper to connect terminal 1 of the coolant fan test connector to a known good ground. Does the auxiliary engine coolant fans #1 and auxiliary engine coolant fan #2 operate at low speed?	B+	*Go to Step 3*	Go to *Cooling Fan Inoperative - Auxiliary (Both Aux Eng Cool Fans Inop)*
3	1. Turn the ignition switch to the ON position. 2. Disconnect the fan control relay K28 connector. 3. Use the DMM in order to measure the voltage between terminal 4 of the fan control relay K28 connector and a known good ground. Does the voltage measure near the specified value?	B+	*Go to Step 5*	*Go to Step 4*
4	1. Check the integrity of fuse #40 2. Locate a open or a high resistance in circuit A14 or A25 if fuse #40 is OK. 3. Repair the open or the high resistance in circuit A14 or A25. Did you complete the repair?	—	*Go to Step 10*	—
5	Use the DMM in order to measure the voltage between terminal 2 of the fan control relay K28 and a known good ground. Does the voltage measure near the specified value?	B+	*Go to Step 7*	*Go to Step 6*
6	1. Locate an open or a high resistance in circuit X400 2. Repair the open or the high resistance in circuit X400. Did you complete the repair?	—	*Go to Step 10*	—

GC1089800455010X

Fig. 53 Cooling fan inoperative (Auxiliary engine coolant fan No. 2, Part 1 of 2). 1998-2000 Catera

Step	Action	Value(s)	Yes	No
10	1. Remove the fused jumper. 2. Install the auxiliary water pump relay K22. 3. Disconnect the water auxiliary pump. 4. Reconnect the fused jumper. 5. Use the DMM in order to measure the voltage between terminal 2 of the water auxiliary pump connector and a known good ground. Does the voltage measure near the specified value?	B+	*Go to Step 12*	*Go to Step 11*
11	1. Locate an open or a high resistance in CKT XU2. 2. Repair the open or the high resistance in CKT XU2. 3. Replace the auxiliary water pump relay K22 if CKT XU2 is OK. Did you complete the repair?	—	*Go to Step 15*	—
12	Use the DMM in order to measure the resistance between terminal 1 of the water auxiliary pump connector and a known good ground. Does the resistance measure near the specified value?	Less than 5 Ω	*Go to Step 14*	*Go to Step 13*
13	1. Locate an open or a high resistance in CKT F6. 2. Repair the open or the high resistance in CKT F6. Did you complete the repair?	—	*Go to Step 15*	—
14	Replace the water auxiliary pump. Did you complete the repair?	—	*Go to Step 15*	—
15	1. Connect all connectors and components that were previously disconnected. 2. Verify that the water auxiliary pump operates properly? Does the water auxiliary pump operate properly?	—	Refer to *Cooling Fan System Check.*	*Go to Step 1*

GC1089800453020X

Fig. 51 Water pump inoperative (Part 2 of 2). 1998-2000 Catera

Step	Action	Value(s)	Yes	No
5	Use the DMM in order to measure the resistance between terminal 8 of the fan control relay K52 and a known good ground. Does the resistance measure near the specified value?	Less than 5Ω	*Go to Step 7*	*Go to Step 6*
6	1. Locate an open or a high resistance in circuit F7 2. Repair the open or the high resistance in circuits F7. Did you complete the repair?	—	*Go to Step 8*	—
7	1. Locate an open or a high resistance in circuits XM123 or XM997. 2. Repair the open or the high resistance in circuits XM123 or XM997. 3. Replace the fan control relay K52 if these circuits are OK. Did you complete the repair?	—	*Go to Step 8*	—
8	1. Connect all connectors and components that were previously disconnected. 2. Check the auxiliary engine coolant fan #1 for proper operation. Does the auxiliary engine coolant fan #1 operate properly?	—	System OK	*Go to Step 1*

GC1089800454020X

Fig. 52 Cooling fan inoperative (Auxiliary engine coolant fan No. 1, Part 2 of 2). 1998-2000 Catera

Step	Action	Value(s)	Yes	No
7	1. Disconnected the auxiliary engine coolant fan #2 connector. 2. Use a DMM in order to measure resistance between terminal 8 of the fan control relay connector and terminal A of the auxiliary engine coolant fan #2 Does the resistance measure near the specified value?	Less than 5Ω	*Go to Step 8*	*Go to Step 9*
8	1. Locate an open or a high resistance in circuits XM124 or XM997. 2. Repair the open or the high resistance in circuits XM124 or XM997. 3. Replace the fan control relay K52 if these circuits are OK. Did you complete the repair?	—	*Go to Step 10*	—
9	1. Locate an open or a high resistance in circuit AM4. 2. Repair the open or the high resistance in circuits AM4. Did you complete the repair?	—	*Go to Step 10*	—
10	1. Connect all connectors and components that were previously disconnected. 2. Check the auxiliary engine coolant fan #2 for proper operation. Does the auxiliary engine coolant fan #2 operate properly?	—	System OK	*Go to Step 1*

GC1089800455020X

Fig. 53 Cooling fan inoperative (Auxiliary engine coolant fan No. 2, Part 2 of 2). 1998-2000 Catera

Step	Action	Value(s)	Yes	No
1	Did you perform the Cooling Fan Diagnostic System Check?	B+	*Go to Step 2*	Go to *Cooling Fan System Check*
2	1. Turn the ignition switch to the ON position. 2. Connect a fused jumper between pin 1 of the coolant fan test connector and a known good ground. 3. Grounding pin 1 of the coolant fan test connector will simulate the closing of the primary cooling fan temperature switch stage 1 contacts, this will energize the fan control relay K26. Does the auxiliary engine coolant fan #1 and auxiliary coolant fan #2 operate at low speed?	—	*Go to Step 3*	*Go to Step 4*
3	1. Locate an open or a high resistance in circuit XP30 or F600. 2. Repair the open or the high resistance in circuit XP30 or F600. 3. Replace the primary cooling fan temperature switch if these circuits are OK. Are the engine cooling fans operating properly?	—	*Go to Step 19*	—
4	1. Disconnect the fused jumper. 2. Disconnect the fan control relay K26 connector. 3. Use the DMM in order to measure the voltage between terminal 3 of the fan control relay K26 connector and a known good ground. Does the voltage measure near the specified value?	B+	*Go to Step 6*	*Go to Step 5*

GC1089800456010X

Fig. 54 Cooling fan inoperative (Both auxiliary engine coolant fans, Part 1 of 3). 1998-2000 Catera

Step	Action	Value(s)	Yes	No
13	1. Locate an open or a high resistance in circuit XU3. 2. Repair the open or the high resistance in circuit XU3 3. Replace the auxiliary engine coolant fan #1 if these circuits are OK. Did you complete the repair?	—	*Go to Step 19*	—
14	Use a DMM in order to measure resistance from terminal B of the auxiliary coolant engine fan #2 connector and a known good ground. Did you measure the resistance near the specified value?	Less than 5Ω	*Go to Step 16*	*Go to Step 15*
15	1. Locate an open or a high resistance in circuit F4. 2. Repair the open or the high resistance in circuits F4 Did you complete the repair?	—	*Go to Step 19*	—
16	1. Remove fan control relay K52 2. With the relay removed determine if the relay contacts are closed. 3. Use a DMM in order to measure resistance between terminal 2 and Terminal 5 of the fan control relay K52. Did you measure the resistance near the specified value?	Less than 5Ω	*Go to Step 17*	*Go to Step 18*
17	1. Locate an open or a high resistance in circuit AM3 or AM5. 2. Repair the open or the high resistance in circuit AM3 or AM5. 3. Replace the auxiliary engine coolant fan #2 if these circuits are OK. Did you complete the repair?	—	*Go to Step 19*	—
18	Replace the fan control relay K52 Did you complete the repair?	—	*Go to Step 19*	—
19	1. Connect all the connectors and components that were disconnected 2. Verify that the auxiliary engine coolant fans #1 and #2 operate properly. Does the auxiliary engine coolant fans #1 and #2 operate properly?	—	System OK	*Go to Step 1*

GC1089800456030X

Fig. 54 Cooling fan inoperative (Both auxiliary engine coolant fans, Part 3 of 3). 1998-2000 Catera

Step	Action	Value(s)	Yes	No
1	Did you perform the Cooling Fan Diagnostic System Check?	—	*Go to Step 2*	Go to *Cooling Fan System Check*
2	1. Turn the ignition switch to the OFF position. 2. Locate the coolant fan test connector within the ECM housing. 3. Use a fused jumper to connect terminal 1 of the coolant fan test connector to a known good ground. Does the auxiliary engine coolant fan #1 and auxiliary engine coolant fan #2 operate at low speed?	B+	*Go to Step 3*	Go to *Cooling Fan Inoperative - Auxiliary (Both Aux Eng Cool Fans Inop)*

GC1089800457010X

Fig. 55 Cooling fan inoperative (A/C cooling low speed, Part 1 of 2). 1998-2000 Catera

Step	Action	Value(s)	Yes	No
5	1. Inspect fuse #50 for an open. 2. Locate an open or a high resistance in circuits A6 and/or A310 if the fuse is OK. 3. Repair the open or the high resistance in circuits A6 and/or A310. Did you complete the repair?	—	*Go to Step 19*	—
6	Use the DMM in order to measure the voltage between terminal 2 of the fan control relay K26 connector and a known good ground. Does the voltage measure near the specified value?	B+	*Go to Step 8*	*Go to Step 7*
7	1. Inspect fuse #52 for an open. 2. Locate an open or a high resistance in circuits A300, A220, and/or A222 if the fuse is OK. 3. Repair the open or the high resistance in circuits A300, A220, and/or A222. Did you complete the repair?	—	*Go to Step 19*	—
8	1. Use a fused jumper to connect terminal 1 of the coolant fan test connector to a known good ground. 2. Use the DMM in order to measure the resistance between terminal 6 of the fan control relay K26 connector and a known good ground. Did you measure the resistance near the specified value?	Less than 5Ω	*Go to Step 10*	*Go to Step 9*
9	1. Locate an open or a high resistance in circuit XP3 or XP999. 2. Repair the open or the high resistance in circuit XP3 or XP999. Did you complete the repair?	—	*Go to Step 19*	—
10	1. Place the fan control relay K26 back in the ECM housing. 2. Leave the fused jumper connected between terminal 1 of the coolant fan test connector and a good ground. 3. Disconnect the auxiliary engine coolant fan #1 connector. 4. Use a DMM in order to measure voltage between terminal A of the auxiliary engine coolant fan #1 and a known good ground. Did you measure the voltage near the specified value?	B+	*Go to Step 12*	*Go to Step 11*
11	1. Locate an open or a high resistance in circuits AM1 or AM13. 2. Repair the open or the high resistance in circuits AM1 or AM13. 3. Replace the fan control relay K26 if these circuits are OK. Did you complete the repair?	—	*Go to Step 19*	—
12	1. Remove the fan control relay K52 2. Connect the auxiliary engine fan #1 connector 3. Use a fused jumper to connect from terminal 2 of the fan control relay K52 to a known good ground. Does the auxiliary engine coolant fan #1 operate?	—	*Go to Step 14*	*Go to Step 13*

GC1089800456020X

Fig. 54 Cooling fan inoperative (Both auxiliary engine coolant fans, Part 2 of 3). 1998-2000 Catera

Step	Action	Value(s)	Yes	No
3	1. Remove the fused jumper. 2. Turn the ignition switch to the ON position. 3. Disconnect the fan control relay K87 connector. 4. Use the DMM in order to measure the voltage between terminal 4 of the fan control relay K87 connector and a known good ground. Does the voltage measure near the specified value?	B+	*Go to Step 5*	*Go to Step 4*
4	1. Locate a open or a high resistance in circuit A221 2. Repair the open or the high resistance in circuit A221. Did you complete the repair?	—	*Go to Step 10*	—
5	Use the DMM in order to measure the resistance between terminal 6 of the fan control relay K87 and a known good ground. Does the resistance measure near the specified value?	Less than 5Ω	*Go to Step 7*	*Go to Step 6*
6	1. Locate an open or a high resistance in circuit F2 2. Repair the open or the high resistance in circuits F2. Did you complete the repair?	—	*Go to Step 10*	—
7	1. Turn the A/C compressor ON 2. Use the DMM in order to measure the voltage between terminal 2 of the fan control relay K87 and a known good ground. Does the voltage measure near the specified value?	B+	*Go to Step 9*	*Go to Step 8*
8	1. Locate an open or a high resistance in circuit U4. 2. Repair the open or the high resistance in circuit U4. 3. Refer to HVAC-Compressor controls for A/C compressor diagnosis if the circuit is OK. Did you complete the repair?	—	*Go to Step 10*	—
9	1. Locate an open or a high resistance in circuits AM12. 2. Repair the open or the high resistance in circuits AM12. 3. Replace the fan control relay K87 if these circuits are OK. Did you complete the repair?	—	*Go to Step 10*	—
10	1. Connect all connectors and components that were previously disconnected. 2. Check the auxiliary engine coolant fan #1 for proper operation. Does the auxiliary engine coolant fans operate at low speed?	—	System OK	*Go to Step 1*

GC1089800457020X

Fig. 55 Cooling fan inoperative (A/C cooling low speed, Part 2 of 2). 1998-2000 Catera

Step	Action	Value(s)	Yes	No
1	Did you perform the Cooling Fan Diagnostic System Check?	—	*Go to Step 2*	Go to *Cooling Fan System Check*
2	1. Turn the A/C compressor ON. 2. Turn the ignition switch to the ON position. 3. Locate the coolant fan test connector within the ECM housing. 4. Use a fused jumper to connect terminal 2 of the coolant fan test connector to a known good ground. Does the Auxiliary fan #1 and Auxiliary fan #2 operate at high speed?	—	*Go to Step 4*	*Go to Step 3*
3	1. Locate an open or a high resistance in circuits XM999 or XM10. 2. Repair the open or the high resistance in circuits XM999 or XM10. 3. Replace the fan control relay K28 if these circuits are OK. Did you complete the repair?	—	*Go to Step 5*	—
4	1. Locate an open or a high resistance in circuit XM120 or circuit F57. 2. Repair the open or the high resistance in circuit XM120 or circuit F57. 3. Replace the A/C compressor refrigerant pressure switch if these circuit are OK. Did you complete the repair?	—	*Go to Step 5*	—
5	1. Connect all connectors and components that were previously disconnected. 2. Check the auxiliary engine coolant fan #1 for proper operation. Does the auxiliary engine coolant fans operate at low speed?	—	System OK	*Go to Step 1*

GC1089800458000X

Fig. 56 Cooling fan inoperative (A/C cooling high speed). 1998-2000 Catera

Step	Action	Value(s)	Yes	No
4	1. Disconnect the ECM relay K48. 2. Use the DMM in order to measure the voltage between terminal 2 of the ECM relay K48 and a known good ground. Does the voltage measure near the specified value?	B+	*Go to Step 6*	*Go to Step 5*
5	1. Locate an open or a high resistance in CKT A60. 2. Repair the open or the high resistance in CKT A60. Did you complete the repair?	—	*Go to Step 15*	—
6	Use the DMM in order to measure the voltage between terminal 4 of the ECM relay K48 and a known good ground. Does the voltage measure near the specified value?	B+	*Go to Step 8*	*Go to Step 7*
7	1. Locate an open or a high resistance in CKT X235. 2. Repair the open or the high resistance in CKT X235. Did you complete the repair?	—	*Go to Step 15*	—
8	Connect a fused jumper between terminal 4 and terminal 8 of the ECM relay K48. Does the ECM cooling blower turn ON?	—	*Go to Step 9*	*Go to Step 10*
9	Replace the ECM relay K48. Did you complete the repair?	—	*Go to Step 15*	—
10	1. Disconnect the ECM cooling blower connector. 2. Use the DMM in order to measure the voltage between terminal 1 of the ECM cooling blower connector and a known good ground. Does the voltage measure near the specified value?	B+	*Go to Step 12*	*Go to Step 11*
11	1. Locate an open or a high resistance in CKT FM235. 2. Repair the open or the high resistance in CKT FM235. Did you complete the repair?	—	*Go to Step 15*	—
12	Use the DMM in order to measure the resistance between terminal 2 of the ECM cooling blower connector and a known good ground. Does the resistance measure near the specified value?	Less than 5 Ω	*Go to Step 14*	*Go to Step 13*
13	1. Locate an open or a high resistance in CKT F59. 2. Repair the open or the high resistance in CKT F59. Did you complete the repair?	—	*Go to Step 15*	—
14	Replace the ECM cooling blower. Did you complete the repair?	—	*Go to Step 15*	—
15	1. Connect all connectors and components that were previously disconnected. 2. Verify that the ECM cooling blower operates properly. Does the ECM cooling blower operate properly?	—	Refer to *Cooling Fan System Check.*	*Go to Step 1*

GC1089800459020X

Fig. 57 ECM cooling blower inoperative (Part 2 of 2). 1998-2000 Catera

Step	Action	Value(s)	Yes	No
1	Did you perform the Coolant Fan Diagnostic System Check?	—	*Go to Step 2*	Refer to *Cooling Fan System Check.*
2	1. Turn on the ignition. 2. Locate the coolant fan test connector within the ECM housing. 3. Use a fused jumper to connect terminal 1 of the coolant fan test connector to a known good ground. Does the ECM cooling blower turn ON?	—	*Go to Step 3*	*Go to Step 4*
3	1. Locate an open or a high resistance in circuits XP30 and/or F600. 2. Repair the open or the high resistance in circuits XP30 and/or F600. 3. Replace the primary cooling fan temperature switch if these circuits are OK. Did you complete the repair?	—	*Go to Step 15*	—

GC1089800459010X

Fig. 57 ECM cooling blower inoperative (Part 1 of 2). 1998-2000 Catera

Step	Action	Value(s)	Yes	No
1	Did you perform the Powertrain On-Board Diagnostic (OBD) System Check?	—	*Go to Step 2*	*Powertrain On Board Diagnostic (OBD) System*
2	Are any DTCs set?	—	Go to applicable DTCs	*Go to Step 3*
3	1. Install a scan tool. 2. Engine coolant temperature must be below the specified value for all the fan diagnoses. 3. Turn on the Ignition, with the engine and A/C off. Are the cooling fans off?	100°C (212°F)	*Go to Step 4*	Go to Cooling Fan table #1
4	With a scan tool, command Low Speed Fans on. Are both cooling fans on?	—	*Go to Step 5*	Go to Cooling Fan table #2
5	**Important:** Allow a 3–5 second delay before determining if the fans have switched from low to high speed. With a scan tool, command High Speed Fans on. Do both cooling fans switch to high speed?	—	*Go to Step 6*	Go to Cooling Fan table #3
6	1. Exit outputs screen on the scan tool. 2. Idle the engine leaving the A/C off. Are the cooling fans on?	—	*Go to Step 8*	*Go to Step 7*
7	Turn on the A/C. Are the cooling fans on?	—	System OK	*Go to Step 9*
8	Does the scan tool display A/C request as YES?	—	Go to *A/C System*	*Go to Step 10*
9	Does the scan tool display A/C request as YES?	—	Go to *A/C System*	Go to *A/C System*
10	**Important:** Program the replacement PCM. Replace the PCM. Is the action complete?	—	System OK	—

GC1089900416000X

Fig. 58 Cooling fan functional check. Century & Regal

Step	Action	Value(s)	Yes	No
1	Did you perform the Cooling Fan Functional Check?	—	*Go to Step 2*	Go to Cooling Fan Functional Check
2	Disconnect Cool Fan 1 Relay. Are both fans off?	—	*Go to Step 8*	*Go to Step 3*
3	Disconnect Cool Fan 3 Relay. Are both fans off?	—	*Go to Step 4*	*Go to Step 10*
4	1. Disconnect the right fan. 2. Probe terminal B of the right fan connector using a *J 34142-B* test lamp that is connected to a known good ground. Does the *J 34142-B* test lamp illuminate?	—	*Go to Step 11*	*Go to Step 5*

GC1089900417010X

Fig. 59 Cooling fan table No. 1 (Part 1 of 2). Century & Regal

Step	Action	Value(s)	Yes	No
5	Probe terminal A of the right fan connector using a *J 34142-B* test lamp that is connected to a known good ground. Does the *J 34142-B* test lamp illuminate?	—	*Go to Step 12*	*Go to Step 6*
6	Probe the High Speed Fans control circuit (473) at the Cool Fan 3 Relay connector in the *Underhood Accessory Wiring Junction Block* using a *J 34142-B* test lamp that is connected to battery positive voltage. Does the *J 34142-B* test lamp illuminate?	—	*Go to Step 7*	*Go to Step 13*
7	1. Turn off the ignition. 2. Leave the *J 34142-B* test lamp installed. 3. Disconnect the PCM. 4. Turn on the ignition, with the engine off. Is the *J 34142-B* test lamp still illuminated?	—	*Go to Step 14*	*Go to Step 16*
8	Probe the Low Speed Fans Control circuit (335) at the Cool Fan 1 Relay connector using the *J 34142-B* test lamp that is connected to battery positive voltage. Does the *J 34142-B* test lamp illuminate?	—	*Go to Step 9*	*Go to Step 13*
9	1. Turn off the ignition. 2. Leave the *J 34142-B* test lamp installed. 3. Disconnect the PCM. 4. Turn on the ignition, with the engine off. Is the *J 34142-B* test lamp still illuminated?	—	*Go to Step 14*	*Go to Step 16*
10	Repair the LH fan feed circuit (504) for a short to voltage. Did you find and correct the condition?	—	Go to Cooling Fan Functional Check	*Go to Step 15*
11	Repair the RH fan feed circuit (409) for a short to voltage. Is the action complete?	—	Go to Cooling Fan Functional Check	—
12	Repair the short to voltage in the Cool Fan 2 Relay feed circuit (532). Is the action complete?	—	Go to Cooling Fan Functional Check	—
13	Replace the Cool Fan 1 Relay. Is the action complete?	—	Go to Cooling Fan Functional Check	—
14	Repair the High Speed Fans Control circuit (473) or the Low Speed Fans Control circuit (335) for a short to ground. Is the action complete?	—	Go to Cooling Fan Functional Check	—
15	Replace the Cool Fan 2 Relay. Is the action complete?	—	Go to Cooling Fan Functional Check	—
16	**Important:** Program the replacement PCM. Replace the PCM. Is the action complete?	—	Go to Cooling Fan Functional Check	—

GC1089900417020X

Fig. 59 Cooling fan table No. 1 (Part 2 of 2). Century & Regal

Step	Action	Value(s)	Yes	No
1	Did you perform the Cooling Fan Functional Check?	—	*Go to Step 2*	Go to Cooling Fan Functional Check
2	Did either fan turn on when Cool Fan 1 Relay was commanded on?	—	*Go to Step 3*	*Go to Step 5*
3	1. Install a scan tool. 2. With a scan tool, command Low Speed Fans on. Did the other fan turn off?	—	*Go to Step 19*	*Go to Step 4*
4	Disconnect Cool Fan 2 Relay. Did the fan turn off?	—	*Go to Step 20*	*Go to Step 21*
5	1. With a scan tool, command Low Speed Fans on. 2. Disconnect Cool Fan 1 Relay. 3. Probe Low Speed Fans Control circuit (335) at the Cool Fan 1 Relay Connector using a *J 34142-B* test lamp that is connected to battery positive voltage. Does the *J 34142-B* test lamp illuminate?	—	*Go to Step 6*	*Go to Step 13*
6	Probe both feed circuits (342) at the Cool Fan 1 Relay Connector locations using a *J 34142-B* test lamp that is connected to ground. Does *J 34142-B* test lamp illuminate for both circuits?	—	*Go to Step 7*	*Go to Step 22*
7	**Important:** Leave jumper in place for remainder of this table. Connect a fused jumper wire between the switch feed circuit (342) and the RH fan feed circuit (409) at the Cool Fan 1 Relay Connector locations. Do both fans turn on?	—	*Go to Step 23*	*Go to Step 8*
8	1. Disconnect the right fan. 2. Probe fan harness connector terminal B with a *J 34142-B* test lamp that is connected to a known good ground. Does the *J 34142-B* test lamp illuminate?	—	*Go to Step 9*	*Go to Step 24*
9	Connect a second fused jumper wire between the right fan harness connector terminals. Is the left fan on?	—	*Go to Step 16*	*Go to Step 10*
10	1. Reconnect the right fan. 2. Disconnect Cool Fan 2 Relay. 3. Probe the switch feed circuit (532) at Cool Fan 2 Relay connector using a *J 34142-B* test lamp that is connected to a known good ground. Does the *J 34142-B* test lamp illuminate?	—	*Go to Step 11*	*Go to Step 25*
11	Using the second jumper wire, jumper the switch feed circuit (532) and the LH fan feed circuit (504) together at Cool Fan 2 Relay connector. Do the fans come on?	—	*Go to Step 26*	*Go to Step 12*
12	1. Reconnect Cool Fan 2 Relay. 2. Disconnect the left fan. 3. Probe left fan harness connector terminal B with a *J 34142-B* test lamp that is connected to a known good ground. Is the right fan on?	—	*Go to Step 16*	*Go to Step 18*

GC1089900418010X

Fig. 60 Cooling fan table No. 2 (Part 1 of 2). Century & Regal

Step	Action	Value(s)	Yes	No
13	1. Keep *J 34142-B* test lamp connected. 2. Turn off the ignition. 3. Disconnect the PCM. 4. Probe the Low Speed Fans Control circuit at the PCM connector, with a fused jumper wire that is connected to a known good ground. Is the *J 34142-B* test lamp on?	—	*Go to Step 20*	*Go to Step 21*
14	Inspect the PCM connections. Repair faulty connections as necessary. Did you find a problem and correct the problem?	—	Go to Cooling Fan Functional Check	*Go to Step 27*
15	Repair the Low Speed Fans Control circuit (335) for an open or shorted to battery positive voltage. Is the action complete?	—	Go to Cooling Fan Functional Check	—
16	Inspect the fan motor ground circuit for a open or the left fan motor connections and repair as necessary. Did you find and correct the condition?	—	Go to Cooling Fan Functional Check	*Go to Step 17*
17	Replace the left fan motor. Is the action complete?	—	Go to Cooling Fan Functional Check	—
18	Repair the RH fan feed circuit (504) for an open. Is the action complete?	—	Go to Cooling Fan Functional Check	—
19	Replace the fan which was not operating. Is the action complete?	—	Go to Cooling Fan Functional Check	—
20	Replace Cool Fan 3 Relay. Is the action complete?	—	Go to Cooling Fan Functional Check	—
21	Repair the Cool Fan 2 Relay feed circuit (532) for a short to ground. Did you find and correct the condition?	—	Go to Cooling Fan Functional Check	*Go to Step 26*
22	Repair the open or the grounded circuit for the circuit that did not light. Is the action complete?	—	Go to Cooling Fan Functional Check	—
23	Replace Cool Fan 1 Relay. Is the action complete?	—	Go to Cooling Fan Functional Check	—
24	Repair the LH fan feed circuit (409) for a open. Is the action complete?	—	Go to Cooling Fan Functional Check	—
25	Repair the Cool Fan 2 Relay feed circuit (532) for a open. Is the action complete?	—	Go to Cooling Fan Functional Check	—
26	Replace Cool Fan 2 Relay. Is the action complete?	—	Go to Cooling Fan Functional Check	—
27	**Important:** Program the replacement PCM. Replace the PCM. Is the action complete?	—	Go to Cooling Fan Functional Check	—

GC1089900418020X

Fig. 60 Cooling fan table No. 2 (Part 2 of 2). Century & Regal

Step	Action	Value(s)	Yes	No
1	Did you perform the Cooling Fan Functional Check?	—	*Go to Step 2*	Go to Cooling Fan Functional Check
2	1. With a scan tool, command Low Speed Fans on. 2. Command High Speed Fans on. Did both fans operate with no change?	—	*Go to Step 8*	*Go to Step 3*
3	Did the left fan stop operating?	—	*Go to Step 9*	*Go to Step 4*
4	1. Disconnect Cool Fan 3 Relay. 2. Probe the High Speed Fans Control circuit (473) at Cool Fan 3 Relay connector using a *J 34142-B* test lamp that is connected to battery positive voltage. 3. Command High Speed Fans on using a scan tool. Does the *J 34142-B* test lamp illuminate after several seconds?	—	*Go to Step 5*	*Go to Step 12*
5	Probe the coil feed circuit (2140) at Cool Fan Relay connector using a *J 34142-B* test lamp that is connected to a known good ground. Does the *J 34142-B* test lamp illuminate?	—	*Go to Step 6*	*Go to Step 13*
6	Probe the switch feed circuit (2140) at the Cool Fan 3 Relay connector using a *J 34142-B* test lamp that is connected to a good ground. Does the *J 34142-B* test lamp illuminate?	—	*Go to Step 7*	*Go to Step 14*
7	Jumper the switch feed circuit (2140) and the LH fan feed circuit (504) together at the Cool Fan 3 Relay connector. Is the left fan on?	—	*Go to Step 15*	*Go to Step 16*
8	1. Turn off the ignition. 2. Disconnect the PCM. 3. Disconnect Cool Fan 1 Relay. 4. Jumper the switch feed circuit (342) and the RH fan feed circuit (409) together at the Cool Fan 1 Relay connector. 5. Turn the ignition on. 6. Probe the PCM harness connector for the High Speed Fans Control circuit with a fused jumper that is connected to a known good ground. Do the fans switch from low to high speed?	—	*Go to Step 22*	*Go to Step 17*
9	1. Disconnect Cool Fan 3 Relay. 2. Probe the High Speed Fans Control Cirucit (473) at the Cool Fan 3 Relay connector using a *J 34142-B* test lamp that is connected to battery positive voltage. 3. Command High Speed Fans on using a scan tool. Does the *J 34142-B* test lamp illuminate?	—	*Go to Step 10*	*Go to Step 18*
10	Probe the ground circuit (1050) at the Cool Fan 2 Relay connector using a *J 34142-B* test lamp that is connected to battery positive voltage. Does the *J 34142-B* test lamp illuminate?	—	*Go to Step 11*	*Go to Step 19*
11	Probe the coil feed circuit (2140) at the Cool Fan 2 Relay connector using a *J 34142-B* test lamp that is connected to a known good ground. Does the *J 34142-B* test lamp illuminate?	—	*Go to Step 20*	*Go to Step 21*
12	Repair the High Speed Fans Control circuit (473) for an open between Cool Fan 3 Relay and the splice. Is the action complete?	—	Go to Cooling Fan Functional Check	—

GC1089900419010X

Fig. 61 Cooling fan table No. 3 (Part 1 of 2). Century & Regal

Step	Action	Value(s)	Yes	No
13	Repair the open in the Cool Fan 3 Relay coil feed circuit (2140). Is the action complete?	—	Go to Cooling Fan Functional Check	—
14	Repair the open in the Cool Fan 3 Relay switch feed circuit (2140). Is the action complete?	—	Go to Cooling Fan Functional Check	—
15	Replace Cool Fan 3 Relay. Is the action complete?	—	Go to Cooling Fan Functional Check	—
16	Repair the open in the LH fan feed circuit (504) between Cool Fan 3 Relay and the splice. Is the action complete?	—	Go to Cooling Fan Functional Check	—
17	Repair the High Speed Fans Control circuit (473) for an open or for a short to battery positive voltage. Is the action complete?	—	Go to Cooling Fan Functional Check	—
18	Repair the open in the High Speed Fans Control circuit (473) between Cool Fan 2 Relay and the splice. Is the action complete?	—	Go to Cooling Fan Functional Check	—
19	Repair the open in the ground circuit (1050). Is the action complete?	—	Go to Cooling Fan Functional Check	—
20	Replace the Cool Fan 2 relay. Is the action complete?	—	Go to Cooling Fan Functional Check	—
21	Repair the open in Cool fan 2 Relay coil feed circuit (2140). Is the action complete?	—	Go to Cooling Fan Functional Check	—
22	1. Inspect the PCM connections. 2. Repair faulty connections as necessary. Did you find and correct the condition?	—	Go to Cooling Fan Functional Check	*Go to Step 23*
23	**Important:** Program the replacement PCM. Replace the PCM. Is the action complete?	—	Go to Cooling Fan Functional Check	—

GC1089900419020X

Fig. 61 Cooling fan table No. 3 (Part 2 of 2). Century & Regal

Step	Action	Value(s)	Yes	No
1	Did you perform the Cooling Fan Functional Check?	—	*Go to Step 2*	Go to Cooling Fan Functional Check
2	1. Turn ON the ignition leaving the engine OFF. 2. Disconnect the cooling fan relay #1. Are both of the cooling fans OFF?	—	*Go to Step 6*	*Go to Step 3*
3	Disconnect the cooling fan relay #3. Are both of the cooling fans OFF?	—	*Go to Step 4*	*Go to Step 5*
4	1. Turn OFF the Ignition. 2. Raise the vehicle. 3. Disconnect the left cooling fan electrical connector. 4. Probe the cooling fan electrical connector terminal B using the test lamp *J 34142-B* connected to ground. 5. Turn ON the ignition leaving the engine OFF. Does the test lamp illuminate?	—	*Go to Step 7*	*Go to Step 8*
5	Disconnect the cooling fan relay #2. Are both of the cooling fans OFF?	—	*Go to Step 10*	*Go to Step 9*
6	Replace the cooling fan relay #1. Is the action complete?	—	Go to Cooling Fan Functional Check	—
7	Repair circuit 409 for a short to B+. Is the action complete?	—	Go to Cooling Fan Functional Check	—
8	Repair circuit 532 for a short to B+. Is the action complete?	—	Go to Cooling Fan Functional Check	—
9	Repair circuit 504 for a short to B+. Is the action complete?	—	Go to Cooling Fan Functional Check	—
10	Replace the cooling fan relay #2. Is the action complete?	—	Go to Cooling Fan Functional Check	—

GC1089900428000X

Fig. 63 Cooling fan table 1. Corvette

Step	Action	Value(s)	Yes	No
1	Did you perform the Powertrain On-Board Diagnostic (OBD) System Check?	—	*Go to Step 2*	Go to *Powertrain On Board Diagnostic (OBD) System Check*
2	Are any DTCs set?	—	Go to applicable DTC Table	*Go to Step 3*
3	**Important:** Engine coolant temperature must be below the specified value for all cooling fan diagnoses. 1. Idle the engine. 2. Turn OFF the A/C. 3. Monitor the A/C Request parameter using the scan tool. Does the scan tool display the A/C request as YES?	100° C (212° F)	*A/C Request Circuit*	*Go to Step 4*
4	1. Turn OFF the ignition. 2. Turn ON the ignition leaving the engine OFF. Are the cooling fans ON?	—	Go to Cooling Fan table #1	*Go to Step 5*
5	Command cooling fan relay #1 ON using a scan tool. Are both cooling fans ON?	—	*Go to Step 6*	Go to Cooling Fan table #2
6	Command cooling fan relays #1, #2 and #3 ON using a scan tool. Do both cooling fans switch to high speed?	—	*Go to Step 7*	Go to Cooling Fan table #3
7	1. Using a scan tool, exit outputs. 2. Idle the engine leaving the A/C OFF. Are the cooling fans ON?	—	Go to Cooling Fan table #1	*Go to Step 8*
8	Turn ON the A/C. Are the cooling fans ON?	—	System OK	*Go to Step 9*
9	Does the scan tool display A/C request as YES?	—	*HVAC* System	*A/C Request Circuit*

GC1089900427000X

Fig. 62 Cooling fan functional check. Corvette

Step	Action	Value(s)	Yes	No
1	Did you perform the Cooling Fan Functional Check?	—	*Go to Step 2*	Go to Cooling Fan Functional Check
2	1. Turn ON the ignition leaving the engine OFF. 2. Disconnect cooling fan relay #1. 3. Probe the cooling fan relay B+ terminal (switch side) at the underhood electrical center using the test lamp *J 34142-B* connected to ground. Does the test lamp illuminate?	—	*Go to Step 3*	*Go to Step 11*
3	**Important:** Leave jumper wire in place for remainder of this table. Jumper the cooling fan relay #1 B+ terminal and load terminals together at the underhood electrical center using a fused jumper wire. Do both fans turn ON?	—	*Go to Step 12*	*Go to Step 4*
4	1. Raise the vehicle. 2. Disconnect the left cooling fan electrical connector. 3. Probe the left cooling fan harness connector terminal B using the test lamp *J 34142-B* connected to ground. Does the test lamp illuminate?	—	*Go to Step 5*	*Go to Step 13*
5	1. Disconnect the cooling fan relay #3. 2. Probe the cooling fan relay #3 terminal for circuit 532 at the underhood electrical center using the test lamp *J 34142-B* connected to B+. Does the test lamp illuminate?	—	*Go to Step 22*	*Go to Step 6*
6	1. Install the cooling fan relay #3. **Important:** Leave the jumper wire in place for remainder of this table. 2. Connect a fused jumper wire between the left cooling fan electrical connector terminals A and B. Does the right cooling fan turn ON?	—	*Go to Step 14*	*Go to Step 7*
7	1. Disconnect the cooling fan relay #3. 2. Probe the cooling fan relay #3 terminal for circuit 532 at the underhood electrical center using the test lamp *J 34142-B* connected to ground. Does the test lamp illuminate?	—	*Go to Step 8*	*Go to Step 16*
8	**Important:** Leave the jumper wire in place for remainder of this table. Connect a fused jumper wire between the cooling fan relay #3 terminals for circuits 532 and 504 at the underhood electrical center. Does the right cooling fan turn ON?	—	*Go to Step 17*	*Go to Step 9*

GC1089900429010X

Fig. 64 Cooling fan table 2 (Part 1 of 2). Corvette

Step	Action	Value(s)	Yes	No
9	1. Disconnect the right cooling fan electrical connector. 2. Probe the right cooling fan electrical connector terminal B using the test lamp *J 34142-B* connected to ground. Does the test lamp illuminate?	—	*Go to Step 10*	*Go to Step 21*
10	Probe the right cooling fan electrical connector terminal A using the test lamp *J 34142-B* connected to B+. Does the test lamp illuminate?	—	*Go to Step 18*	*Go to Step 20*
11	Repair the cooling fan relay B+ supply circuit. Is the action complete?	—	Go to Cooling Fan Functional Check	—
12	Replace the cooling fan relay #1. Is the action complete?	—	Go to Cooling Fan Functional Check	—
13	Repair circuit 409 for an open. Is the action complete?	—	Go to Cooling Fan Functional Check	—
14	1. Inspect for poor connections at the left cooling fan motor. 2. If you find a poor connection, repair the condition as necessary. Did you find and correct the condition?	—	Go to Cooling Fan Functional Check	*Go to Step 15*
15	Replace the LH fan motor. Is the action complete?	—	Go to Cooling Fan Functional Check	—
16	Repair the open in circuit 532 between LH cooling fan connector terminal A and relay #3. Is the action complete?	—	Go to Cooling Fan Functional Check	—
17	Replace the cooling fan relay #3. Is the action complete?	—	Go to Cooling Fan Functional Check	—
18	1. Inspect for poor connections at the right cooling fan motor. 2. If you find a poor connection, repair the condition as necessary. Did you find and correct the condition?	—	Go to Cooling Fan Functional Check	*Go to Step 19*
19	Replace the RH fan motor. Is the action complete?	—	Go to Cooling Fan Functional Check	—
20	Repair the open ground circuit. Is the action complete?	—	Go to Cooling Fan Functional Check	—
21	Repair the open B+ feed circuit to the RH fan motor. Is the action complete?	—	Go to Cooling Fan Functional Check	—
22	Repair the short to ground on the circuit between the left cooling fan motor and relay #3. Is the action complete?	—	Go to Cooling Fan Functional Check	—

GC1089900429020X

Fig. 64 Cooling fan table 2 (Part 2 of 2). Corvette

Step	Action	Value(s)	Yes	No
1	Did you perform the Cooling Fan Functional Check?	—	*Go to Step 2*	Go to Cooling Fan Functional Check
2	1. Turn ON the ignition leaving the engine OFF. 2. Command the cooling fan relays #1, #2 and #3 ON using the scan tool. Is the right fan operating at high speed?	—	*Go to Step 3*	*Go to Step 8*
3	Is the left fan operating at high speed?	—	Go to Cooling Fan Functional Check	*Go to Step 4*
4	1. Remove the cooling fan relay #3. 2. Probe the #3 cooling fan relay B+ supply terminal (coil side) at the underhood electrical center, using the test lamp *J 34142-B* connected to ground. Does the test lamp illuminate?	—	*Go to Step 5*	*Go to Step 11*
5	1. Probe the cooling fan relay #3 control circuit using the test lamp *J 34142-B* connected to B+. 2. Command the cooling fan relays #2 and #3 ON using the scan tool. Does the test lamp illuminate?	—	*Go to Step 6*	*Go to Step 13*
6	Connect a fused jumper wire between the cooling fan relay #3 terminal for circuit 532 and the terminal for circuit 250. Does the left cooling fan turn ON?	—	*Go to Step 16*	*Go to Step 7*
7	Probe the cooling fan relay #3 terminal for circuit 250 at the underhood electrical center using the test lamp *J 34142-B* connected to B+. Does the test lamp illuminate?	—	*Go to Step 17*	*Go to Step 15*
8	1. Turn ON the ignition leaving the engine OFF. 2. Disconnect the cooling fan relay #2. 3. Probe both of the cooling fan relay #2 B+ supply terminals using the test lamp *J 34142-B* connected to ground. Refer to Diagnostic Aids for terminal identification. Does the test lamp illuminate for both terminals?	—	*Go to Step 9*	*Go to Step 11*
9	1. Probe the cooling fan relay #2 control circuit terminal at the underhood electrical center using the test lamp *J 34142-B* connected to B+. 2. Command the cooling fan relays #2 and #3 ON using the scan tool. Does the test lamp illuminate?	—	*Go to Step 10*	*Go to Step 13*
10	Connect a fused jumper wire between the cooling fan relay #2 terminals for circuits 1445 and 504 at the underhood electrical center. Does the right cooling fan turn ON?	—	*Go to Step 12*	*Go to Step 14*

GC1089900430010X

Fig. 65 Cooling fan table 3 (Part 1 of 2). Corvette

Step	Action	Value(s)	Yes	No
11	Repair the cooling fan relay B+ circuit for an open. Is the action complete?	—	Go to Cooling Fan Functional Check	—
12	Replace the cooling fan relay #2. Is the action complete?	—	Go to Cooling Fan Functional Check	—
13	Repair the open cooling fan relay control circuit. Is the action complete?	—	Go to Cooling Fan Functional Check	—
14	Repair circuit 504 for an open. Is the action complete?	—	Go to Cooling Fan Functional Check	—
15	Repair the open ground circuit between the cooling fan relay #3 and the splice. Is the action complete?	—	Go to Cooling Fan Functional Check	—
16	Replace the cooling fan relay #3. Is the action complete?	—	Go to Cooling Fan Functional Check	—
17	1. Inspect for poor connections at the underhood electrical center. 2. Repair the condition as necessary. Is the action complete?	—	Go to Cooling Fan Functional Check	—

GC1089900430020X

Fig. 65 Cooling fan table 3 (Part 2 of 2). Corvette

Step	Action	Value(s)	Yes	No
1	Was the Powertrain On–Board Diagnostic (OBD) System Check performed?	—	*Go to Step 2*	Go to Powertrain OBD System Check
2	Are any PCM DTC(s) stored?	—	Go to applicable DTC table(s)	*Go to Step 3*
3	1. Engine coolant below 100°C (212°F). 2. A/C OFF. 3. Ignition ON. Are the Fans OFF?	—	*Go to Step 4*	*Go to Step 43*
4	Select scan tool Misc. Tests, Relay Control function and command Fan 1 ON. Is Fan 1 ON?	—	*Go to Step 5*	*Go to Step 6*
5	Select scan tool Misc. Tests, Relay Control function and command Fan 2 ON. Is Fan 2 ON?	—	Refer to Diagnostic Aids	*Go to Step 19*
6	1. Remove Fan 1 relay from right underhood electrical center. 2. Ignition ON engine OFF. 3. Connect a test light between cavities 85 and 86 in the relay connector. 4. Select scan tool Misc. Test, Relay Control function and command Fan 1 ON. Is the test light 'ON'?	—	*Go to Step 7*	*Go to Step 15*
7	Check for a blown maxifuse. Is the fuse blown?	—	*Go to Step 19*	*Go to Step 8*
8	1. Connect a test light to ground. 2. Probe cavity 30 in the Fan 1 relay connector. Is the test light ON?	—	*Go to Step 10*	*Go to Step 9*
9	Locate and repair open battery feed circuit to cavity 30 in the Fan 1 relay connector. Is action complete?	—	*Go to Step 56*	—

GC1089700421010X

Fig. 66 Cooling fan diagnosis (Part 1 of 5). Cutlass Supreme

Step	Action	Value(s)	Yes	No
10	1. Ignition OFF. 2. Connect a 20 AMP fused jumper between cavities 30 and 87 in the Fan 1 relay connector. 3. Observe Fan 1. Is Fan 1 running?	—	Go to Step 53	Go to Step 11
11	1. Disconnect the Fan 1 electrical connector. 2. With the 20 AMP fused jumper installed between cavities 30 and 87 in the Fan 1 relay connector, connect a test light the between Fan 1 harness connector terminals Is the test light ON?	—	Go to Step 52	Go to Step 12
12	1. Connect the test light to B+. 2. Probe the Engine Cooling Fan Motor #1 ground circuit at the Fan 1 connector. Is the test light ON?	—	Go to Step 13	Go to Step 14
13	Locate and repair open in the Engine Cooling Fan Motor #1 feed circuit. Is action complete?	—	Go to Step 56	—
14	Locate and repair open in the Engine Cooling Fan Motor #1 ground circuit. Is action complete?	—	Go to Step 56	—
15	1. Connect the test light to ground. 2. Probe cavity 85 at the Fan 1 relay connector. Is the test light ON.	—	Go to Step 16	Go to Step 17
16	1. Ignition OFF. 2. Disconnect the PCM connector. 3. Connect a test light between cavities 85 and 86 at the Fan 1 relay connector. 4. Jumper the Fan 1 relay driver circuit to ground at the PCM connector. Is the test light ON?	—	Go to Step 51	Go to Step 18
17	Locate and repair open in the battery feed circuit to cavity 85 in the Fan 1 relay connector. Is action complete?	—	Go to Step 56	—
18	Locate and repair open in the Fan 1 relay driver circuit. Is action complete?	—	Go to Step 56	—
19	1. Remove 60 AMP maxi fuse #3. 2. Connect a test light to B+. 3. Probe cavity 30 at the Fan 1 relay connector. Is the test light ON?	—	Go to Step 20	Go to Step 21
20	Locate and repair short to ground in the battery feed circuit to cavity 30 in the Fan 1 relay connector. Is action complete?	—	Go to Step 56	—
21	1. Disconnect the Engine Cooling Fan Motor #1 connector. 2. Connect a test light to B+. 3. Probe cavity 87 at the Fan 1 relay connector. Is the test light ON?	—	Go to Step 22	Go to Step 52

GC1089700421020X

Fig. 66 Cooling fan diagnosis (Part 2 of 5). Cutlass Supreme

Step	Action	Value(s)	Yes	No
22	Locate and repair short to ground in the Engine Cooling Fan Motor #1 feed circuit. Is action complete?	—	Go to Step 56	—
23	1. Remove Fan 2 relay from right underhood electrical center. 2. Ignition ON engine OFF. 3. Connect a test light between cavities 85 and 86 in the relay connector. 4. Select scan tool Misc. Test, Relay control function and command Fan 2 ON. Is the test light ON?	—	Go to Step 24	Go to Step 32
24	Check for a blown 60 AMP maxifuse that feeds Fan 2 relay cavity 30. Is the fuse blown?	—	Go to Step 39	Go to Step 25
25	1. Connect a test light to ground. 2. Probe cavity 30 in the Fan 2 relay connector. Is the test light ON?	—	Go to Step 27	Go to Step 26
26	Locate and repair open in feed circuit to Fan 2 relay cavity 30. Is action complete?	—	Go to Step 56	—
27	1. Ignition OFF. 2. Connect a 20 AMP fused jumper between cavities 30 and 87 at the Fan 2 relay connector. 3. Ignition ON. Is Fan 2 ON?	—	Go to Step 54	Go to Step 28
28	1. Disconnect the Engine Cooling Fan motor #2 electrical connector. 2. Connect a 20 AMP fused jumper between cavities 30 and 87 at the Fan 2 relay connector. 3. Connect a test light between the Engine Cooling Fan motor #2 connector terminals Is the test light ON?	—	Go to Step 54	Go to Step 29
29	1. Connect a test light to B+. 2. Probe the ground circuit terminal at the Engine Cooling Fan motor #2 connector. Is the test light ON?	—	Go to Step 30	Go to Step 31
30	Locate and repair open in the Engine Cooling Fan motor #2 feed circuit. Is action complete?	—	Go to Step 56	—
31	Locate and repair open in the Engine Cooling Fan motor #2 ground circuit. Is action complete?	—	Go to Step 56	—
32	Check the fuse that feeds Fan 2 relay cavity 85. Is the fuse blown?	—	Go to Step 33	Go to Step 35
33	1. Remove the fuse that feeds Fan 2 relay cavity 85. 2. Probe cavity 85 at the Fan 2 relay connector with a test light to B+. Is the test light ON?	—	Go to Step 34	Go to Step 55
34	Locate and repair short to ground in the feed circuit to Fan 2 relay cavity 85. Is action complete?	—	Go to Step 56	—

GC1089700421030X

Fig. 66 Cooling fan diagnosis (Part 3 of 5). Cutlass Supreme

Step	Action	Value(s)	Yes	No
35	Probe cavity 85 in the Fan 2 relay connector with a test light to ground. Is the test light ON.	—	Go to Step 36	Go to Step 37
36	1. Ignition OFF. 2. Disconnect the PCM connector. 3. Connect a test light between cavities 85 and 86 at the Fan 2 relay connector. 4. Jumper the Fan 2 relay driver circuit to ground at the PCM connector. Is the test light ON?	—	Go to Step 51	Go to Step 38
37	Locate and repair open in the feed circuit to Fan 2 relay connector cavity 85. Is action complete?	—	Go to Step 56	—
38	Locate and repair open in the Fan 2 driver circuit. Is action complete?	—	Go to Step 56	—
39	1. Remove 60 AMP Maxi fuse #1. 2. Connect a test light to B+. 3. Probe cavity 30 at the Fan 2 relay connector. Is the test light ON?	—	Go to Step 40	Go to Step 41
40	Locate and repair short to ground in the feed circuit to Fan 2 relay connector cavity 30. Is action complete?	—	Go to Step 56	—
41	1. Disconnect the Engine Cooling Fan motor #2 connector. 2. Probe cavity 87 in the Fan 2 relay connector with a test light to B+. Is the test light ON?	—	Go to Step 42	Go to Step 54
42	Locate and repair short to ground in the Engine Cooling Fan motor #2 feed circuit. Is action complete?	—	Go to Step 56	—
43	Are both fans ON?	—	Go to Step 44	Go to Step 45
44	1. Ignition OFF, disconnect A/C pressure sensor. 2. Ignition ON. 3. Using scan tool, monitor A/C Pressure display. Does scan tool indicate A/C pressure at the specified value?	0 psi	Go to Step 49	Go to Step 51
45	Is Fan 1 ON?	—	Go to Step 46	Go to Step 50
46	Using scan tool monitor A/C Pressure. Does scan tool indicate A/C pressure greater than the specified value?	190 psi	Go to Step 47	Go to Step 48
47	1. Disconnect the A/C Pressure sensor. 2. Using scan tool monitor A/C Pressure display. Is A/C pressure display at the specified value	0 psi	Go to Step 49	Go to Step 51
48	Locate and repair short to voltage in the Engine Cooling Fan motor #1 feed circuit. Is action complete?	—	Go to Step 56	—

GC1089700421040X

Fig. 66 Cooling fan diagnosis (Part 4 of 5). Cutlass Supreme

Step	Action	Value(s)	Yes	No
49	Replace the A/C Pressure sensor. Is action complete?	—	Go to Step 56	—
50	Locate and repair short to voltage in the engine cooling Fan motor #2 feed circuit. Is action complete?	—	Go to Step 56	—
51	Replace the PCM. **Important:** The replacement PCM must be programmed. Is Action complete?	—	Go to Step 56.	—
52	Replace the Engine Cooling Fan motor #1 motor. Is action complete?	—	Go to Step 56	—
53	Replace the Fan 1 relay Is action complete?	—	Go to Step 56	—
54	Replace the Engine Cooling Fan motor #2. Is action complete?	—	Go to Step 56	—
55	Replace the Fan 2 relay Is action complete?	—	Go to Step 56	—
56	1. Engine coolant temperature less than 100°C (212°F). 2. A/C select switch OFF. 3. Ignition ON. Are the Fans OFF?	—	Go to Step 57	Go to Step 3
57	Select scan tool Misc. Tests, Relay control function and command Fan 1 ON. Is Fan 1 ON?	—	Go to Step 58	Go to Step 6
58	Select scan tool Misc. Tests, Relay control function and command Fan 2 ON. Is Fan 2 ON?	—	System OK	Go to Step 19

GC1089700421050X

Fig. 66 Cooling fan diagnosis (Part 5 of 5). Cutlass Supreme

Step	Action	Value(s)	Yes	No
1	Was the Powertrain On-Board Diagnostic (OBD) System Check performed?	—	*Go to Step 2*	*Go to Powertrain OBD System Check*
2	1. Ensure the engine coolant temperature is between the values specified. 2. Turn HVAC controls to OFF. 3. Start and idle the engine. 4. Using the scan tool select Output Tests and while viewing the Quad Driver 1 display, command All Relays OFF for approximately 15 seconds. 5. Using the scan tool select Output Tests and while viewing the Quad Driver 1 display, command All Relays ON for approximately 15 seconds. Did the Quad Driver 1 display indicate a *Fault*?	5°C - 100°C (41°F - 212°F)	Go to *DTC P1660 Cooling Fan Control Circuits*	*Go to Step 3*
3	With the engine idling turn A/C ON to maximum cooling. Have any other DTC(s) failed this ignition?	—	Go to DTC(s) that are set	*Go to Step 4*
4	1. Turn the engine OFF and the key ON. 2. Ensure engine coolant temperature is below the value specified. 3. Observe fan operation while individually commanding Fan Relay 1 ON, then All Relays ON, then All Relays OFF. • With Fan Relay 1 commanded ON both fans should operate at low speed. • With All Relays commanded ON both fans should operate at high speed. • With All Relays commanded OFF both fans should not operate (unless the PCM detects a fault or high temperature condition). Do both cooling fans operate as commanded?	100°C (212°F)	System OK	*Go to Step 5*
5	Does only Cooling Fan #1 (left) operate with Fan Relay 1 commanded ON then both fans operate when All Relays are commanded ON?	—	*Go to Step 6*	*Go to Step 7*
6	Repair CKT 504 shorted to ground. Is the repair complete?	—	*Go to Step 4*	—
7	Does neither cooling fan operate with Fan Relay 1 commanded ON then only Cooling Fan #2 (right) operate with All Relays commanded ON?	—	Go to *Electric Cooling Fan Diagnosis* (Table 1)	*Go to Step 8*
8	Does neither cooling fan operate with Fan Relay 1 commanded ON then only Cooling Fan #1 (left) operate with All Relays commanded ON?	—	Go to *Electric Cooling Fan Diagnosis* (Table 2)	*Go to Step 9*
9	Do both cooling fans operate with Fan Relay 1 commanded ON then only Cooling Fan #2 (right) operate with All Relays commanded ON?	—	Go to *Electric Cooling Fan Diagnosis* (Table 3)	*Go to Step 10*
10	Do both cooling fans operate with Fan Relay 1 commanded ON then only Cooling Fan #1 (left) operate with All Relays commanded ON?	—	Go to *Electric Cooling Fan Diagnosis* (Table 4)	*Go to Step 11*

GC1089600313010X

Fig. 67 Cooling fan functional check (Part 1 of 2). 1997 DeVille, Eldorado & Seville

Step	Action	Value(s)	Yes	No
DEFINITION: No low speed operation of either cooling fan. High speed operation of right cooling fan only. DTC P1660 is not set.				
1	Was the Cooling Fan Functional Check performed?	—	*Go to Step 2*	Go to *Electric Cooling Fan Diagnosis*
2	1. Disconnect Cooling Fan #1 connector. 2. Using the scan tool select Output Tests then Fan Relays. 3. With the key ON command Relay 1 ON. 4. Using DVM J 39200 measure the voltage to ground at Cooling Fan #1 connector terminal B (harness side). Is the voltage the same or more than the value specified?	10.0 volts	*Go to Step 3*	*Go to Step 6*
3	Jumper Cooling Fan #1 connector terminals A and B together. Does Cooling Fan #2 operate while jumpered?	—	*Go to Step 8*	*Go to Step 4*
4	1. With Cooling Fan #1 connector still jumpered, remove Relay #2. 2. Measure the voltage to ground at Relay #2 terminal 30. Is the voltage the same or more than the value specified?	10.0 volts	*Go to Step 5*	*Go to Step 9*
5	Jumper Relay #2 terminals 30 and 87A together. Does Cooling Fan #2 operate while jumpered?	—	*Go to Step 10*	*Go to Step 11*
6	1. Exit Fan Relays. 2. Remove Relay #1. 3. Measure the voltage to ground at Relay #1 terminal 30. Is the voltage the same or more than the value specified?	10.0 volts	*Go to Step 7*	*Go to Step 12*
7	1. Jumper Fan Relay #1 terminals 30 and 87 together. 2. Measure the voltage to ground at Cooling Fan #1 connector terminal B. Is the voltage to ground the same or more than the value specified?	10.0 volts	*Go to Step 13*	*Go to Step 14*
8	Replace Cooling Fan #1 (left). Is the replacement complete?	—	Go to *Electric Cooling Fan Diagnosis*	—
9	Repair the open in CKT 504 between Cooling Fan #1 and Fan Relay #2. Is the repair complete?	—	Go to *Electric Cooling Fan Diagnosis*	—

GC1089600314010X

Fig. 68 Table 1, cooling fan symptom diagnosis (Part 1 of 2). 1997 DeVille, Eldorado & Seville

Step	Action	Value(s)	Yes	No
11	Does neither cooling fan operate when Fan Relay 1 is commanded ON and also when All Relays are commanded ON?	—	Go to *Electric Cooling Fan Diagnosis* (Table 5)	*Go to Step 12*
12	Does either cooling fan operate when All Relays is commanded OFF?	—	Go to *Diagnostic Aids*	*Go to Step 4*

GC1089600313020X

Fig. 67 Cooling fan functional check (Part 2 of 2). 1997 DeVille, Eldorado & Seville

Step	Action	Value(s)	Yes	No
DEFINITION: No low speed operation of either cooling fan. High speed operation of right cooling fan only. DTC P1660 is not set.				
10	Replace Fan Relay #2. Is the replacement complete?	—	Go to *Electric Cooling Fan Diagnosis*	—
11	Repair the open in CKT 409 between Fan Relay #2 and the CKT 409 splice. Is the repair complete?	—	Go to *Electric Cooling Fan Diagnosis*	—
12	Repair the open in the circuit between Fan Relay #1 terminal 30 and the Maxi fuse. Is the repair complete?	—	Go to *Electric Cooling Fan Diagnosis*	—
13	Replace Fan Relay #1. Is the replacement complete?	—	Go to *Electric Cooling Fan Diagnosis*	—
14	Repair the open in CKT 532 between Fan Relay #1 and Cooling Fan #1. Is the repair complete?	—	Go to *Electric Cooling Fan Diagnosis*	—

GC1089600314020X

Fig. 68 Table 1, cooling fan symptom diagnosis (Part 2 of 2). 1997 DeVille, Eldorado & Seville

Step	Action	Value(s)	Yes	No
DEFINITION: No low speed operation of either cooling fan. High speed operation of left cooling fan only. DTC P1660 is not set.				
1	Was the Cooling Fan Functional Check performed?	—	*Go to Step 2*	Go to *Electric Cooling Fan Diagnosis*
2	1. Disconnect Cooling Fan #2 (right) connector. 2. Using the scan tool select Output Tests than Fan Relays. 3. With the key ON, command Fan Relay 1 ON. 4. Jumper Cooling Fan #2 (right) terminals A and B together. Does Cooling Fan #1 (left) operate while jumpered?	—	*Go to Step 5*	*Go to Step 3*
3	1. With Fan Relay 1 still commanded ON remove Fan Relay #2. 2. Jumper Fan Relay #2 terminals 30 and 87A together. Does left cooling fan operate while jumpered?	—	*Go to Step 6*	*Go to Step 4*
4	With Fan Relay #2 still jumpered use DVM J 39200 and measure the voltage to ground at Cooling Fan #2 connector terminal B (harness side). Is the voltage the same or more than the value specified?	10.0 volts	*Go to Step 7*	*Go to Step 8*
5	Replace Cooling Fan #2 (right). Is the replacement complete?	—	Go to *Electric Cooling Fan Diagnosis*	—
6	Replace Fan Relay #2. Is the replacement complete?	—	Go to *Electric Cooling Fan Diagnosis*	—

GC1089600315010X

Fig. 69 Table 2, cooling fan symptom diagnosis (Part 1 of 2). 1997 DeVille, Eldorado & Seville

Step	Action	Value(s)	Yes	No
7	Repair the open in the BLK circuit between Cooling Fan #2 (right) terminal A and the splice. Is the repair complete?	—	Go to *Electric Cooling Fan Diagnosis*	—
8	Repair the open in CKT 409 between Cooling Fan #2 (right) the CKT 409 splice and Fan Relay #2. Is the repair complete?	—	Go to *Electric Cooling Fan Diagnosis*	—

GC1089600315020X

Fig. 69 Table 2, cooling fan symptom diagnosis (Part 2 of 2). 1997 DeVille, Eldorado & Seville

Step	Action	Value(s)	Yes	No
DEFINITION: Low speed operation of both fans. High speed operation of right cooling fan only. DTC P1660 not set.				
1	Was the Cooling Fan Functional Check performed?	—	*Go to Step 2*	Go to *Electric Cooling Fan Diagnosis*
2	1. Using the scan tool select Output Tests and then Fan Relays. 2. With the key ON select All Relays ON. 3. Remove Fan Relay #2. 4. Using DVM J 39200 measure the voltage to ground at Fan Relay #2 terminal 85. Is the voltage the same or more than the value specified?	10.0 volts	*Go to Step 3*	*Go to Step 5*
3	1. Remove Fan Relay #3. 2. Measure the resistance between Fan Relay #2 terminal 86 and Fan Relay #3 terminal 86. Is the resistance the same or less than the value specified?	.5 ohms	*Go to Step 4*	*Go to Step 6*
4	1. Reconnect Fan Relay #3. 2. With All Relays still commanded ON, jumper Fan Relay #2 terminals 30 and 87 together. Do both cooling fans operate while jumpered?	—	*Go to Step 8*	*Go to Step 7*
5	Repair the open in the ORG circuit between Fan Relay #2 terminal 85 and the splice. Is the repair complete?	—	Go to *Electric Cooling Fan Diagnosis*	—
6	Repair the open in CKT 473 between Fan Relay #2 terminal 86 and the CKT 473 splice. Is the repair complete?	—	Go to *Electric Cooling Fan Diagnosis*	—
7	Repair the open in the BLK circuit between Fan Relay #2 terminal 87 and the splice. Is the repair complete?	—	Go to *Electric Cooling Fan Diagnosis*	—
8	Replace Fan Relay #2. Is the replacement complete?	—	Go to *Electric Cooling Fan Diagnosis*	—

GC1089600316000X

Fig. 70 Table 3, cooling fan symptom diagnosis. 1997 DeVille, Eldorado & Seville

Step	Action	Value(s)	Yes	No
DEFINITION: No fan operation on either high or low speed. DTC P1660 not set.				
1	Was the Cooling Fan Functional Check performed?	—	*Go to Step 2*	Go to *Electric Cooling Fan Diagnosis*
2	Check the condition of the cooling fan Maxi fuse. Is the fuse blown?	—	*Go to Step 4*	*Go to Step 3*
3	1. Remove Fan Relay #1. 2. Using DVM J 39200 measure the voltage to ground at Fan Relay #1 terminal 30. Is the voltage the same or more than the value specified?	10.0 volts	*Go to Step 8*	*Go to Step 9*
4	1. Turn the key to LOCK. 2. Replace the Maxi fuse. Does the fuse immediately blow?	—	*Go to Step 10*	*Go to Step 5*
5	1. Turn the key ON. 2. Using the scan tool select Output Tests and then Fan Relays. 3. Command Fan Relay 1 ON. Does the Maxi fuse blow?	—	*Go to Step 11*	*Go to Step 6*
6	Command All Relays ON. Does the Maxi fuse blow?	—	*Go to Step 7*	Fault not present
7	1. Exit Fan Relays. 2. Replace the Maxi fuse. 3. Select Fan Relays and command Fan Relay 1 ON. Is only Cooling Fan #1 (left) operating?	—	*Go to Step 12*	*Go to Step 13*
8	Repair the open in the BLK circuit between both BLK circuit splices or between the BLK circuit splice and ground or the poor/open ground connection. Is the repair complete?	—	Go to *Electric Cooling Fan Diagnosis*	—
9	Repair the open in the RED circuit between the Maxi fuse and both relays. Is the repair complete?	—	Go to *Electric Cooling Fan Diagnosis*	—
10	Repair the short to ground in the RED circuit between the Maxi fuse and either Fan Relay 1 or Fan Relay 3. Is the repair complete?	—	Go to *Electric Cooling Fan Diagnosis*	—
11	Repair the short to ground in CKT 532 between Fan Relay 1 and Cooling Fan #1 (left). Is the repair complete?	—	Go to *Electric Cooling Fan Diagnosis*	—
12	Replace Cooling Fan #2 (right). Is the replacement complete?	—	Go to *Electric Cooling Fan Diagnosis*	—
13	Replace Cooling Fan #1 (left). Is the replacement complete?	—	Go to *Electric Cooling Fan Diagnosis*	—

GC1089600318000X

Fig. 72 Table 5, cooling fan symptom diagnosis. 1997 DeVille, Eldorado & Seville

Step	Action	Value(s)	Yes	No
DEFINITION: Low speed operation of both fans. High speed operation of left cooling fan only. DTC P1660 not set.				
1	Was the Cooling Fan Functional Check performed?	—	*Go to Step 2*	Go to *Electric Cooling Fan Diagnosis*
2	1. Using scan tool select Output Tests then All Relays. 2. With the key ON command All Relays ON. 3. Remove Fan Relay #3. 4. Using DVM J 39200 measure the voltage to ground at Fan Relay #3 terminal 85. Is the voltage the same or more than the value specified?	10.0 volts	*Go to Step 3*	*Go to Step 6*
3	Measure the voltage to ground at Fan Relay #3 terminal 30. Is the voltage the same or more than the value specified?	10.0 volts	*Go to Step 4*	*Go to Step 7*
4	1. Remove Fan Relay #3. 2. Measure the voltage between Fan Relay #3 terminal 86 and Fan Relay #2 terminal 86. Is the resistance the same or less than the value specified?	5 ohms	*Go to Step 5*	*Go to Step 8*
5	1. Reconnect Fan Relay #2. 2. With All Relays still commanded ON, jumper Fan Relay #3 terminals 30 and 87 together. Does Cooling Fan #2 (right) operate while jumpered?	—	*Go to Step 10*	*Go to Step 9*
6	Repair the open in the RED circuit between Fan Relay #3 terminal 30 and the Maxi fuse. Is the repair complete?	—	Go to *Electric Cooling Fan Diagnosis*	—
7	Repair the open in the ORG circuit between Fan Relay #3 terminal 85 and the splice. Is the repair complete?	—	Go to *Electric Cooling Fan Diagnosis*	—
8	Repair the open in CKT 473 between Fan Relay #3 terminal 86 and the CKT 473 splice. Is the repair complete?	—	Go to *Electric Cooling Fan Diagnosis*	—
9	Repair the open in CKT 409 between Fan Relay #3 terminal 87 and the CKT 409 splice. Is the repair complete	—	Go to *Electric Cooling Fan Diagnosis*	—
10	Replace Fan Relay #3. Is the replacement complete?	—	Go to *Electric Cooling Fan Diagnosis*	—

GC1089600317000X

Fig. 71 Table 4, cooling fan symptom diagnosis. 1997 DeVille, Eldorado & Seville

Step	Action	Value(s)	Yes	No
1	Did you perform the Powertrain On–Board Diagnostic (OBD) System Check?	—	*Go to Step 2*	Go to *Powertrain On Board Diagnostic (OBD) System Check*
2	1. Ensure the engine coolant temperature is between the values specified. 2. Turn HVAC controls to OFF. 3. Start and idle the engine. 4. Using the scan tool select Output Tests and while viewing the Driver 1 display, command All Relays OFF for approximately 15 seconds. 5. Using the scan tool select Output Tests and while viewing the Driver 1 display, command All Relays ON for approximately 15 seconds. Did the Driver 1 display ever indicate a FAULT?	5°C - 100°C (41°F - 212°F)	*DTC P1660 Cooling Fan Control Circuits*	*Go to Step 3*
3	With the engine idling turn A/C ON to maximum cooling. Have any other DTC(s) failed this ignition?	—	Go to DTC(s) that are set	*Go to Step 4*
4	1. Turn the key to OFF. 2. Disconnect PCM connector C2. 3. Using a test lamp connected to a known good ground probe PCM connector C2 terminals 32 and 33. Does the test lamp illuminate on both terminals?	—	*Go to Step 5*	*Go to Step 14*
5	1. Reconnect PCM connector C2 (if still disconnected). 2. Turn the key ON while leaving the engine OFF. 3. Ensure engine coolant temperature is below the value specified. 4. Observe fan operation while individually commanding Fan Relay 1 ON, then All Relays ON, then All Relays OFF. • With Fan Relay 1 commanded ON both fans should operate at low speed. • With All Relays commanded ON both fans should operate at high speed. • With All Relays commanded OFF both fans should not operate (unless the PCM detects a fault or high temperature condition). Do both cooling fans operate as commanded?	100°C (212°F)	System OK	*Go to Step 6*
6	Does only Cooling Fan #1 (left) operate with Fan Relay 1 commanded ON then both fans operate when All Relays are commanded ON?	—	*Go to Step 7*	*Go to Step 8*
7	Repair CKT 504 shorted to ground. Is the repair complete?	—	*Go to Step 5*	—
8	Does neither cooling fan operate with Fan Relay 1 commanded ON then only Cooling Fan #2 (right) operate with All Relays commanded ON?	—	Go to Cooling Fan Symptom Table 1	*Go to Step 9*
9	Does neither cooling fan operate with Fan Relay 1 commanded ON then only Cooling Fan #1 (left) operate with All Relays commanded ON?	—	Go to Cooling Fan Symptom Table 2	*Go to Step 9*
10	Do both cooling fans operate with Fan Relay 1 commanded ON then only Cooling Fan #2 (right) operate with All Relays commanded ON?	—	Go to Cooling Fan Symptom Table 3	*Go to Step 11*
11	Do both cooling fans operate with Fan Relay 1 commanded ON then only Cooling Fan #1 (left) operate with All Relays commanded ON?	—	Go to Cooling Fan Symptom Table 4	*Go to Step 12*

GC1089800432010X

Fig. 73 Cooling fan functional check (Part 1 of 2). 1998–99 DeVille & 1998–2000 Eldorado

Step	Action	Value(s)	Yes	No
12	Does neither cooling fan operate when Fan Relay 1 is commanded ON and also when All Relays are commanded ON?	—	Go to Cooling Fan Symptom Table 5	*Go to Step 13*
13	Does either cooling fan operate when All Relays is commanded OFF?	—	Go to Diagnostic Aids	*Go to Step 5*
14	Repair the cause of no voltage. Possible cause include the following: • A blown relay supply fuse • An open fan relay • An open cooling fan relay control circuit Is the repair complete?	—	*Go to Step 5*	—

GC1089800432020X

Fig. 73 Cooling fan functional check (Part 2 of 2). 1998–99 DeVille & 1998–2000 Eldorado

Step	Action	Value(s)	Yes	No
DEFINITION: No low speed operation of either cooling fan. High speed operation of right cooling fan only. DTC P1660 is not set.				
1	Was the Cooling Fan Functional Check performed?	—	Go to Step 2	Go to Cooling Fan Functional Check
2	1. Disconnect Cooling Fan #1 connector. 2. Using the scan tool select Output Tests then Fan Relays. 3. With the key ON command Relay 1 ON. 4. Using DMM J 39200 measure the voltage to ground at Cooling Fan #1 connector terminal B (harness side). Is the voltage the same or more than the value specified?	10.0 volts	Go to Step 3	Go to Step 6
3	Jumper Cooling Fan #1 connector terminals A and B together. Does Cooling Fan #2 operate while jumpered?	—	Go to Step 8	Go to Step 4
4	1. With Cooling Fan #1 connector still jumpered, remove Relay #2. 2. Measure the voltage to ground at Relay #2 terminal 30. Is the voltage the same or more than the value specified?	10.0 volts	Go to Step 5	Go to Step 9
5	Jumper Relay #2 terminals 30 and 87A together. Does Cooling Fan #2 operate while jumpered?	—	Go to Step 10	Go to Step 11
6	1. Exit Fan Relays. 2. Remove Relay #1. 3. Measure the voltage to ground at Relay #1 terminal 30. Is the voltage the same or more than the value specified?	10.0 volts	Go to Step 7	Go to Step 12
7	1. Jumper Fan Relay #1 terminals 30 and 87 together. 2. Measure the voltage to ground at Cooling Fan #1 connector terminal B. Is the voltage to ground the same or more than the value specified?	10.0 volts	Go to Step 13	Go to Step 14
8	Replace Cooling Fan #1 (left). Is the replacement complete?	—	Go to Cooling Fan Functional Check	—
9	Repair the open in CKT 504 between Cooling Fan #1 and Fan Relay #2. Is the repair complete?	—	Go to Cooling Fan Functional Check	—

GC1089800433010X

Fig. 74 Cooling fan symptom table 1 (Part 1 of 2). 1998–99 DeVille & 1998–2000 Eldorado

Step	Action	Value(s)	Yes	No
DEFINITION: No low speed operation of either cooling fan. High speed operation of left cooling fan only. DTC P1660 is not set.				
1	Was the Cooling Fan Functional Check performed?	—	Go to Step 2	Go to Cooling Fan Functional Check
2	1. Disconnect Cooling Fan #2 (right) connector. 2. Using the scan tool select Output Tests than Fan Relays. 3. With the key ON, command Fan Relay 1 ON. 4. Jumper Cooling Fan #2 (right) terminals A and B together. Does Cooling Fan #1 (left) operate while jumpered?	—	Go to Step 5	Go to Step 3
3	1. With Fan Relay 1 still commanded ON remove Fan Relay #2. 2. Jumper Fan Relay #2 terminals 30 and 87A together. Does left cooling fan operate while jumpered?	—	Go to Step 6	Go to Step 4
4	With Fan Relay #2 still jumpered use DMM J 39200 and measure the voltage to ground at Cooling Fan #2 connector terminal B (harness side). Is the voltage the same or more than the value specified?	10.0 volts	Go to Step 7	Go to Step 8
5	Replace Cooling Fan #2 (right). Is the replacement complete?	—	Go to Cooling Fan Functional Check	—
6	Replace Fan Relay #2. Is the replacement complete?	—	Go to Cooling Fan Functional Check	—
7	Repair the open in the BLK circuit between Cooling Fan #2 (right) terminal A and the splice. Is the repair complete?	—	Go to Cooling Fan Functional Check	—
8	Repair the open in CKT 409 between Cooling Fan #2 (right) the CKT 409 splice and Fan Relay #2. Is the repair complete?	—	Go to Cooling Fan Functional Check	—

GC1089800434000X

Fig. 75 Cooling fan symptom table 2. 1998–99 DeVille & 1998–2000 Eldorado

Step	Action	Value(s)	Yes	No
DEFINITION: Low speed operation of both fans. High speed operation of left cooling fan only. DTC P1660 not set.				
1	Was the Cooling Fan Functional Check performed?	—	Go to Step 2	Go to Cooling Fan Functional Check
2	1. Using scan tool select Output Tests then All Relays. 2. With the key ON command All Relays ON. 3. Remove Fan Relay #3. 4. Using DMM J 39200 measure the voltage to ground at Fan Relay #3 terminal 85. Is the voltage the same or more than the value specified?	10.0 volts	Go to Step 3	Go to Step 7
3	Measure the voltage to ground at Fan Relay #3 terminal 30. Is the voltage the same or more than the value specified?	10.0 volts	Go to Step 4	Go to Step 6
4	1. Remove Fan Relay #2. 2. Measure the resistance between Fan Relay #3 terminal 86 and Fan Relay #2 terminal 86. Is the resistance the same or less than the value specified?	5 ohms	Go to Step 5	Go to Step 8

GC1089800436010X

Fig. 77 Cooling fan symptom table 4 (Part 1 of 2). 1998–99 DeVille & 1998–2000 Eldorado

Step	Action	Value(s)	Yes	No
10	Replace Fan Relay #2. Is the replacement complete?	—	Go to Cooling Fan Functional Check	—
11	Repair the open in CKT 409 between Fan Relay #2 and the CKT 409 splice. Is the repair complete?	—	Go to Cooling Fan Functional Check	—
12	Repair the open in the circuit between Fan Relay #1 terminal 30 and the Maxi fuse. Is the repair complete?	—	Go to Cooling Fan Functional Check	—
13	Replace Fan Relay #1. Is the replacement complete?	—	Go to Cooling Fan Functional Check	—
14	Repair the open in CKT 532 between Fan Relay #1 and Cooling Fan #1. Is the repair complete?	—	Go to Cooling Fan Functional Check	—

GC1089800433020X

Fig. 74 Cooling fan symptom table 1 (Part 2 of 2). 1998–99 DeVille & 1998–2000 Eldorado

Step	Action	Value(s)	Yes	No
DEFINITION: Low speed operation of both fans. High speed operation of right cooling fan only. DTC P1660 not set.				
1	Was the Cooling Fan Functional Check performed?	—	Go to Step 2	Go to Cooling Fan Functional Check
2	1. Using the scan tool select Output Tests and then Fan Relays. 2. With the key ON select All Relays ON. 3. Remove Fan Relay #2. 4. Using DMM J 39200 measure the voltage to ground at Fan Relay #2 terminal 85. Is the voltage the same or more than the value specified?	10.0 volts	Go to Step 3	Go to Step 5
3	1. Remove Fan Relay #3. 2. Measure the resistance between Fan Relay #2 terminal 86 and Fan Relay #3 terminal 86. Is the resistance the same or less than the value specified?	5 ohms	Go to Step 4	Go to Step 6
4	1. Reconnect Fan Relay #3. 2. With All Relays still commanded ON, jumper Fan Relay #2 terminals 30 and 87 together. Do both cooling fans operate while jumpered?	—	Go to Step 8	Go to Step 7
5	Repair the open in the ORG circuit between Fan Relay #2 terminal 85 and the splice. Is the repair complete?	—	Go to Cooling Fan Functional Check	—
6	Repair the open in CKT 473 between Fan Relay #2 terminal 86 and the CKT 473 splice. Is the repair complete?	—	Go to Cooling Fan Functional Check	—
7	Repair the open in the BLK circuit between Fan Relay #2 terminal 87 and the splice. Is the repair complete?	—	Go to Cooling Fan Functional Check	—
8	Replace Fan Relay #2. Is the replacement complete?	—	Go to Cooling Fan Functional Check	—

GC1089800435000X

Fig. 76 Cooling fan symptom table 3. 1998–99 DeVille & 1998–2000 Eldorado

Step	Action	Value(s)	Yes	No
5	1. Reconnect Fan Relay #2. 2. With All Relays still commanded ON, jumper Fan Relay #3 terminals 30 and 87 together. Does Cooling Fan #2 (right) operate while jumpered?	—	Go to Step 10	Go to Step 9
6	Repair the open in the RED circuit between Fan Relay #3 terminal 30 and the Maxi fuse. Is the repair complete?	—	Go to Cooling Fan Functional Check	—
7	Repair the open in the ORG circuit between Fan Relay #3 terminal 85 and the splice. Is the repair complete?	—	Go to Cooling Fan Functional Check	—
8	Repair the open in CKT 473 between Fan Relay #3 terminal 86 and the CKT 473 splice. Is the repair complete?	—	Go to Cooling Fan Functional Check	—
9	Repair the open in CKT 409 between Fan Relay #3 terminal 87 and the CKT 409 splice. Is the repair complete	—	Go to Cooling Fan Functional Check	—
10	Replace Fan Relay #3. Is the replacement complete?	—	Go to Cooling Fan Functional Check	—

GC1089800436020X

Fig. 77 Cooling fan symptom table 4 (Part 2 of 2). 1998–99 DeVille & 1998–2000 Eldorado

Step	Action	Value(s)	Yes	No
DEFINITION: No fan operation on either high or low speed. DTC P1660 not set.				
1	Was the Cooling Fan Functional Check performed?	—	*Go to Step 2*	Go to Cooling Fan Functional Check
2	Check the condition of the cooling fan Maxi fuse. Is the fuse blown?	—	*Go to Step 4*	*Go to Step 3*
3	1. Remove Fan Relay #1. 2. Using DMM J 39200 measure the voltage to ground at Fan Relay #1 terminal 30. Is the voltage the same or more than the value specified?	10.0 volts	*Go to Step 8*	*Go to Step 9*
4	1. Turn the key to LOCK. 2. Replace the Maxi fuse. Does the fuse immediately blow?	—	*Go to Step 10*	*Go to Step 5*
5	1. Turn the key ON. 2. Using the scan tool select Output Tests and then Fan Relays. 3. Command Fan Relay 1 ON. Does the Maxi fuse blow?	—	*Go to Step 11*	*Go to Step 6*
6	Command All Relays ON. Does the Maxi fuse blow?	—	*Go to Step 7*	Fault not present
7	1. Exit Fan Relays. 2. Replace the Maxi fuse. 3. Select Fan Relays and command Fan Relay 1 ON. Is only Cooling Fan #1 (left) operating?	—	*Go to Step 12*	*Go to Step 13*
8	Repair the open in the BLK circuit between both BLK circuit splices or between the BLK circuit splice and ground or the poor/open ground connection. Is the repair complete?	—	Go to Cooling Fan Functional Check	—

GC1089800437010X

Fig. 78 Cooling fan symptom table 5 (Part 1 of 2). 1998–99 DeVille & 1998–2000 Eldorado

Step	Action	Value(s)	Yes	No
9	Repair the open in the RED circuit between the Maxi fuse and both relays. Is the repair complete?	—	Go to Cooling Fan Functional Check	—
10	Repair the short to ground in the RED circuit between the Maxi fuse and either Fan Relay 1 or Fan Relay 3. Is the repair complete?	—	Go to Cooling Fan Functional Check	—
11	Repair the short to ground in CKT 532 between Fan Relay 1 and Cooling Fan #1 (left). Is the repair complete?	—	Go to Cooling Fan Functional Check	—
12	Replace Cooling Fan #2 (right). Is the replacement complete?	—	Go to Cooling Fan Functional Check	—
13	Replace Cooling Fan #1 (left). Is the replacement complete?	—	Go to Cooling Fan Functional Check	—

GC1089800437020X

Fig. 78 Cooling fan symptom table 5 (Part 2 of 2). 1998–99 DeVille & 1998–2000 Eldorado

Circuit Description:

The engine cooling fan receive power from two separate 30 amp maxifuse located in the Underhood Electrical Center.

During low speed operation, the PCM supplies a ground path for the Cool Fan 1 relay through the Coolant Fan #1 Relay Control circuit. This energizes the relay coil, closes the Fan 1 relay contacts, and supplies current to the primary cooling fan. The ground path for the primary cooling fan is through the series/parallel cooling fan relay (Cool Relay) and secondary cooling fan motor. The result is a series circuit with both fans running at low speed.

To command high speed cooling fan operation the PCM first supplies a ground path for the low speed cooling fan (Cool Fan #1) relay through the Coolant Fan #1 Relay Control circuit. After a 3 second delay, the PCM supplies a ground path for the series/parallel (Cool Relay) and the high speed cooling fan (Cool Fan #2) relays through the Coolant Fan #2 Relay Control circuit. During high speed operation, both the primary and the secondary cooling fans are supplied current through their respective maxifuse and each fan has its own ground path.

Diagnostic Aids

Check for the following conditions:

- Poor connection at the PCM, cooling fan relays, or cooling fan motors. Inspect harness connectors for backed out terminals, improper mating, broken locks, improperly formed or damaged terminals, and poor terminal to wire connection.
- Damaged harness. Inspect the wiring harness for damage.

GC1089700322010X

Fig. 79 Cooling fan diagnosis (Part 1 of 10). Grand Prix

Test Description

Number(s) below refer to the step number(s) on the Diagnostic Table.

2. Stored diagnostic trouble codes may affect engine cooling fans operation. This diagnostic table may lead to improper diagnosis and replacement of good parts if diagnostic trouble codes are present.
6. Ambient temperature must be above 11°C (52°F) before the PCM will enable the cooling fans due to A/C request. The PCM will enable the cooling fans if A/C refrigerant pressure increases regardless of ambient temperature.
77. This vehicle is equipped with a PCM which utilizes an Electrically Erasable Programmable Read Only Memory (EEPROM). When the PCM is being replaced, the new PCM must be programmed.

Step	Action	Value(s)	Yes	No
1	Was the Powertrain On-Board Diagnostic (OBD) System Check performed?	—	*Go to Step 2*	Go to the *Powertrain OBD System Check*
2	Are any PCM DTC(s) stored?	—	Diagnose the PCM DTC(s) first.	*Go to Step 3*
3	1. Ensure that the engine coolant temperature is below 100°C (212°F). 2. Turn OFF the A/C Selector Switch. 3. Engine running. 4. Observe the cooling fans. Are the cooling fans running?	—	*Go to Step 32*	*Go to Step 4*
4	1. Command Fan 1 ON using the scan tool output tests function. 2. Observe the cooling fans. Are both cooling fans running at low speed?	—	*Go to Step 5*	*Go to Step 8*
5	1. Command Fan 2 ON using the scan tool output tests function. 2. Wait 3 seconds. 3. Observe the cooling fans Are both fans running at high speed?	—	*Go to Step 6*	*Go to Step 58*
6	**Important:** Ambient temperature must be above 11°C (52°F). 1. Exit scan tool output tests. 2. Engine running. 3. Turn the A/C ON. Are the cooling fans ON?	—	Go to Diagnostic Aids	*Go to Step 7*
7	View A/C Request on the scan tool. Does A/C Request on the scan tool display Yes?	—	*Go to Step 77*	*PCM Controlled Air Conditioning Diagnosis*
8	Is either cooling fan running?	—	*Go to Step 9*	*Go to Step 16*
9	Is the left cooling fan running?	—	*Go to Step 10*	*Go to Step 14*

GC1089700322020X

Fig. 79 Cooling fan diagnosis (Part 2 of 10). Grand Prix

Step	Action	Value(s)	Yes	No
10	1. Turn OFF the ignition switch. 2. Disconnect the right engine cooling fan. 3. Turn ON the ignition switch. 4. Command Fan 1 ON using the scan tool output tests function. 5. Observe the cooling fans. Is the left engine cooling fan running?		*Go to Step 11*	*Go to Step 80*
11	Remove the engine Cool Fan Relay from the Underhood Electrical Center. Is the left engine cooling fan running?	—	*Go to Step 12*	*Go to Step 13*
12	Locate and repair short to ground in CKT 532. Is action complete?	—	*Go to Step 81*	—
13	1. Check CKT 409 for a short to ground. 2. If a problem is found, repair as necessary and replace Cool Fan 2 maxifuse. Was a problem found?	—	*Go to Step 81*	*Go to Step 76*
14	1. Turn OFF the ignition switch. 2. Disconnect the left engine cooling fan. 3. Turn ON the ignition switch. 4. Command Fan 1 On using the scan tool output tests function. 5. Observe the cooling fans. Is the right engine cooling fan running?	—	*Go to Step 15*	*Go to Step 71*
15	1. Locate and repair the following circuit condition(s): • Short to battery positive in circuit 532 or circuit 504. • Coolant Fan #2 shorted. • Defective engine coolant fan diode. Is action complete?	—	*Go to Step 81*	—
16	1. Ignition On, engine not running. 2. Remove the low speed engine Cool Fan 1 Relay from the Underhood Electrical Center. 3. Probe Cool Fan 1 relay cavity 87 with a test light connected to ground. Is the test light On?	—	*Go to Step 18*	*Go to Step 17*
17	Locate and repair the open in the Cool Fan 1 relay B+ feed to cavity 87. Is action complete?	—	*Go to Step 81*	—
18	Probe Cool Fan 1 relay cavity 86 with a test light connected to ground. Is the test light On?	—	*Go to Step 20*	*Go to Step 19*
19	Locate and repair open in the B+ feed to cavity 86 in the Cool Fan 1 relay connector. Is action complete?	—	*Go to Step 81*	—

GC1089700322030X

Fig. 79 Cooling fan diagnosis (Part 3 of 10). Grand Prix

Step	Action	Value(s)	Yes	No
20	1. Turn OFF the ignition switch. 2. Disconnect both cooling fans. 3. Connect terminals A and B together at both cooling fan connectors using fused jumpers. 4. Turn ON the ignition switch. 5. Connect a test light between Cool Fan 1 relay cavities 87 and 30. Is the test light ON?	—	*Go to Step 21*	*Go to Step 27*
21	1. Connect a test light between Cool Fan 1 relay cavities 85 and 86. 2. Turn ON the ignition switch. 3. Command Fan 1 ON using the scan tool output tests function. 4. Observe the test light. Is the test light ON?	—	*Go to Step 22*	*Go to Step 25*
22	1. Turn OFF the ignition switch. 2. Remove the jumpers from the engine cooling fan connectors and reconnect the cooling fans. 3. Install a fused jumper between Cool Fan 1 relay cavities 87 and 30. 4. Turn ON the ignition switch. 5. Observe the cooling fans. Are both cooling fans running?	—	*Go to Step 23*	*Go to Step 24*
23	1. Check for poor Cool Fan 1 relay connections at the Underhood Electrical Center. 2. If a problem is found, repair as necessary. Was a problem found?	—	*Go to Step 81*	*Go to Step 37*
24	1. Check for poor connections at the coolant fan motors. 2. If a problem is found, repair as necessary. Was a problem found?	—	*Go to Step 81*	*Go to Step 63*
25	1. Turn OFF the ignition switch. 2. Disconnect the PCM blue connector C1. 3. Install a fused jumper between Cool Fan 1 relay cavities 30 and 85. 4. Turn ON the ignition switch. 5. Probe Low Speed Fans circuit (CKT 335) at the PCM harness connector with a test light to ground. Is the test light ON?	—	*Go to Step 77*	*Go to Step 26*
26	Locate and repair open in the Low Speed Fans circuit between the PCM and Cooling Fan 1 relay cavity 86. Is action complete?	—	*Go to Step 81*	—

GC1089700322040X

Fig. 79 Cooling fan diagnosis (Part 4 of 10). Grand Prix

Step	Action	Value(s)	Yes	No
27	1. Turn OFF the ignition switch. 2. Remove the jumpers from the cooling fan connectors. 3. Reconnect the cooling fans. 4. Install a fused jumper between Cool Fan 1 relay cavities 87 and 30. 5. Remove the Cool Fan Relay from the Underhood Electrical Center. 6. Probe Cool Fan Relay cavity 30 with a test light connected to ground. Is the test light On?	—	*Go to Step 28*	*Go to Step 31*
28	Connect a test light between Cool Fan Relay cavities 30 and 87A in the Underhood Electrical Center. Is the test light ON?	—	*Go to Step 30*	*Go to Step 29*
29	1. Check for an open in CKT 409 between Cool Fan Relay cavity 87A and High Speed Fans terminal B. 2. If a problem is found, repair as necessary. Was a problem found?	—	*Go to Step 81*	*Go to Step 57*
30	1. Check for a poor connection at Cool Fan Relay cavities 30 or 87A in the Underhood Relay Center. 2. If a problem is found, repair as necessary. Was a problem found?	—	*Go to Step 81*	*Go to Step 76*
31	1. Check for an open in CKT 504 between Cool Fan 1 relay cavity 30 and left engine cooling fan harness connector terminal B. 2. If a problem is found, repair as necessary. Was a problem found?	—	*Go to Step 81*	*Go to Step 56*
32	Using scan tool, view A/C Request. Does the scan tool display Yes?	—	*PCM Controlled Air Conditioning Diagnosis*	*Go to Step 33*
33	Are both cooling fans running at low speed?	—	*Go to Step 34*	*Go to Step 40*
34	Remove Cool Fan 1 relay from the Underhood Relay Center. Are the cooling fans running?	—	*Go to Step 35*	*Go to Step 36*
35	Locate and repair short to voltage in CKT 504. Is action complete?	—	*Go to Step 81*	—
36	Using a test light connected to B+, probe Cool Fan 1 relay cavity 85. Is the test light On?	—	*Go to Step 38*	*Go to Step 37*
37	Replace Cool Fan 1 relay. Is action complete?	—	*Go to Step 81*	—
38	1. Turn OFF the ignition switch. 2. Disconnect the blue PCM connector. 3. Probe Cool Fan 1 relay cavity 85 with a test light connected to B+. Is the test light On?	—	*Go to Step 39*	*Go to Step 77*

GC1089700322050X

Fig. 79 Cooling fan diagnosis (Part 5 of 10). Grand Prix

Step	Action	Value(s)	Yes	No
39	Locate and repair short to ground in the Low Speed Fans circuit. Is action complete?	—	*Go to Step 81*	—
40	Are both cooling fans running at high speed?	—	*Go to Step 41*	*Go to Step 42*
41	View A/C Pressure on the scan tool. Does the scan tool display voltage less than the specified value?	1.5V	*Go to Step 77*	*Go to Step 44*
42	1. Turn OFF the ignition switch. 2. Disconnect the PCM. 3. Turn ON the ignition switch. 4. Observe the cooling fans. Is the right engine cooling fan running at high speed?	—	*Go to Step 43*	*Go to Step 77*
43	1. Check for a short to ground in the High Speed Fans circuit (CKT 473). 2. If a problem is found, repair as necessary. Was a problem found?	—	*Go to Step 81*	*Go to Step 52*
44	1. Turn off the ignition switch. 2. Disconnect the A/C refrigerant pressure sensor electrical connector. 3. Turn on the ignition switch. 4. View A/C Pressure on the scan tool. Does the scan tool display voltage near the specified value?	0V	*Go to Step 46*	*Go to Step 45*
45	Probe the A/C refrigerant pressure signal circuit with a *J 39200*. Does the digital multimeter display voltage near the specified value?	0V	*Go to Step 77*	*Go to Step 51*
46	Probe the A/C refrigerant pressure sensor ground with a test light to battery positive voltage. Is the test light on?	—	*Go to Step 47*	*Go to Step 49*
47	Probe the A/C refrigerant pressure sensor 5 volt reference B circuit with a *J 39200*. Does the digital multimeter display voltage near the specified value?	5V	*Go to Step 48*	*Go to Step 50*
48	Replace the A/C refrigerant pressure sensor. Is action complete?	—	*Go to Step 81*	—
49	Locate and repair open or short to voltage in the A/C refrigerant pressure sensor ground circuit. Is action complete?	—	*Go to Step 81*	—
50	Locate and repair open or short to ground in the A/C refrigerant pressure sensor 5 volt reference B circuit. Is action complete?	—	*Go to Step 81*	—
51	Locate and repair short to voltage in the A/C refrigerant pressure signal circuit. Is action complete?	—	*Go to Step 81*	—

GC1089700322060X

Fig. 79 Cooling fan diagnosis (Part 6 of 10). Grand Prix

Step	Action	Value(s)	Yes	No
52	1. Remove the Cool Fan 2 relay from the Underhood Electrical Center. 2. Observe the cooling fans. Is the right engine cooling fan running at high speed?	—	*Go to Step 53*	*Go to Step 70*
53	Remove the Cool Fan Relay from the Underhood Electrical Center. Is the right engine cooling fan running at high speed?	—	*Go to Step 54*	*Go to Step 55*
54	Locate and repair short to battery positive voltage in CKT 409. Is action complete?	—	*Go to Step 81*	—
55	Locate and repair short to battery positive voltage in CKT 532. Is action complete?	—	*Go to Step 81*	—
56	1. Check for an open in CKT 532 between Cool Fan Relay cavity 30 and left engine cooling fan terminal A. 2. If a problem is found, repair as necessary. Was a problem found?	—	*Go to Step 81*	*Go to Step 79*
57	1. Check for an open in CKT 1050 between right engine cooling fan terminal A and ground. 2. If a problem is found, repair as necessary. Was a problem found?	—	*Go to Step 81*	*Go to Step 80*
58	1. Ignition ON, engine not running. 2. Remove the Cool Fan 2 relay from the Underhood Electrical Center. 3. Install a test light between Cool Fan 2 relay cavity 86 and battery positive voltage. 4. Command High speed fans on using the scan tool output controls function. 5. Wait approx. 5-6 seconds. 6. Observe the test light. Is the test light on?	—	*Go to Step 61*	*Go to Step 59*
59	1. Remove the Cool Fan Relay from the Underhood Electrical Center. 2. Install a test light between Cool Fan Relay cavity 86 and battery positive voltage. 3. Command high speed fans on using the scan tool output controls function. 4. Wait 6 seconds. 5. Observe the test light. Is the test light ON?	—	*Go to Step 78*	*Go to Step 60*

GC1089700322070X

Fig. 79 Cooling fan diagnosis (Part 7 of 10). Grand Prix

Step	Action	Value(s)	Yes	No
60	1. Turn OFF the ignition switch. 2. Disconnect the PCM. 3. Turn ON the ignition switch. 4. Check the High Speed Fans circuit for an open or a short to voltage. 5. If a problem is found, repair as necessary. Was a problem found?	—	*Go to Step 81*	*Go to Step 77*
61	1. Turn off the ignition switch. 2. Reinstall the Cool Fan 2 relay. 3. Disconnect both coolant fan electrical connectors. 4. Turn on the ignition switch. 5. Command Fan 2 on using the scan tool output controls function. 6. Wait approx. 5-6 seconds. 7. Probe terminal B at the right engine cooling fan connector with a test light to ground. Is the test light on?	—	*Go to Step 62*	*Go to Step 64*
62	Probe terminal A at the left engine cooling fan connector with a test light to B+. Is the test light on?	—	*Go to Step 63*	*Go to Step 71*
63	1. Identify cause of inoperative cooling fan: • Open right engine cooling fan motor windings. • Open left engine cooling fan motor windings. • Stalled cooling fans. 2. Replace the affected cooling fan motor. Is action complete?	—	*Go to Step 81*	—
64	1. Remove the Cool Fan 2 relay from the Underhood Electrical Center. 2. Turn ON the ignition switch. 3. Probe Cool Fan 2 relay cavity 85 with a test light connected to ground. Is the test light on?	—	*Go to Step 66*	*Go to Step 65*
65	1. Locate and repair the following circuit condition(s): • Open in the battery positive feed to the Cool Fan and Cool Fan 2 relays. • Short to ground in the battery positive feed to the Cool Fan and Cool Fan 2 relays. Is action complete?	—	*Go to Step 81*	—
66	Probe Cool Fan 2 relay cavity 30 with a test light connected to ground. Is the test light on?	—	*Go to Step 68*	*Go to Step 67*
67	Locate and repair open in battery positive voltage circuit to Cool Fan 2 relay cavity 30. Is action complete?	—	*Go to Step 81*	—

GC1089700322080X

Fig. 79 Cooling fan diagnosis (Part 8 of 10). Grand Prix

Step	Action	Value(s)	Yes	No
68	1. Check High Speed Fans circuit for an open between right engine cooling fan terminal B and Cool Fan 2 relay cavity 87. 2. If a problem is found, repair as necessary. Was a problem found?	—	*Go to Step 81*	*Go to Step 69*
69	1. Check for a poor Cool Fan 2 relay terminal connections at the Underhood Electrical Center. 2. If a problem is found, repair as necessary. Was a problem found?	—	*Go to Step 81*	*Go to Step 70*
70	Replace Cool Fan 2 relay. Is action complete?	—	*Go to Step 81*	—
71	1. Remove the Cool Fan Relay from the Underhood Electrical Center. 2. Turn ON the ignition switch. 3. Probe Cool Fan Relay cavity 85 with a test light connected to ground. Is the test light on?	—	*Go to Step 73*	*Go to Step 72*
72	Locate and repair open in battery positive voltage circuit to Cool Fan Relay cavity 85. Is action complete?	—	*Go to Step 81*	—
73	Probe Cool Fan Relay cavity 87 in the Underhood Electrical Center with a test light to B+. Is the test light on?	—	*Go to Step 75*	*Go to Step 74*
74	Locate and repair open in circuit between Cool Fan Relay cavity 87 in the Underhood Electrical Center and ground. Is action complete?	—	*Go to Step 81*	—
75	1. Check for poor Cool Fan Relay engine terminal connections at the Underhood Electrical Center. 2. If a problem is found, repair as necessary. Was a problem found?	—	*Go to Step 81*	*Go to Step 76*
76	Replace the Cool Fan Relay in the Underhood Electrical Center. Is action complete?	—	*Go to Step 81*	—
77	Replace the PCM. **Important:** The replacement PCM must be programmed. Is action complete?	—	*Go to Step 81*	—
78	Repair open in the Cool Fan 2 relay control circuit. Is action complete?	—	*Go to Step 81*	—
79	Replace the left engine cooling fan motor. Is action complete?	—	*Go to Step 81*	—

GC1089700322090X

Fig. 79 Cooling fan diagnosis (Part 9 of 10). Grand Prix

Step	Action	Value(s)	Yes	No
80	Replace the right engine cooling fan motor. Is action complete?	—	*Go to Step 81*	—
81	1. Engine coolant below 100°C (212°F). 2. A/C OFF. 3. Engine running. Observe the cooling fans. Are the cooling fans running?	—	*Go to Step 32*	*Go to Step 82*
82	1. Command Fan 1 ON using the scan tool output tests function. 2. Observe the cooling fans. Are both cooling fans running at low speed?	—	*Go to Step 83*	*Go to Step 8*
83	1. Command High speed fans on using the scan tool output tests function. 2. Wait 6 seconds. 3. Observe the cooling fans. Are both cooling fans running at high speed?	—	System OK	*Go to Step 58*

GC1089700322100X

Fig. 79 Cooling fan diagnosis (Part 10 of 10). Grand Prix

Step	Action	Value(s)	Yes	No
1	Did you perform the Powertrain On-Board Diagnostic (OBD) System Check?		Go to Step 2	Powertrain On Board Diagnostic (OBD) System
2	Are any DTCs set?		Go to applicable DTCs	Go to Step 3
3	1 Install a scan tool. 2 Engine coolant temperature must be below the specified value for all the fan diagnoses. 3 Turn ON the Ignition, with the engine and A/C OFF. Are the cooling fans OFF?	100°C (212°F)	Go to Step 4	Go to Cooling Fan table #1
4	With a scan tool, command the low speed cooling fan relay ON. Are both cooling fans ON?		Go to Step 5	Go to Cooling Fan table #2
5	With a scan tool, command the high speed cooling fan relay ON. Does both cooling fans switch to high speed?		Go to Step 6	Go to Cooling Fan table #3
6	1 With a scan tool, exit outputs. 2 Idle the engine leaving the A/C OFF. Are the cooling fans ON?		Go to Step 8	Go to Step 7

GC1080000460010X

Fig. 80 Cooling fan functional check (Part 1 of 2). Impala & 2000 Monte Carlo

Step	Action	Value(s)	Yes	No
6	1 With a scan tool, exit outputs. 2 Idle the engine leaving the A/C OFF. Are the cooling fans ON?		Go to Step 8.	Go to Step 7.
7	Turn ON the A/C. Are the cooling fans ON?		System OK	Go to Step 9
8	Does the scan tool display A/C request as YES?		Go to Cooling Insufficient, A/C System	Go to Step 10
9	Does the scan tool display A/C request as YES?		Go to A Diagnostic System Check	Go to A/C System
10	**Important** **Program the replacement PCM. Refer to** PCM Replacement/Programming **Replace the PCM.** Did you complete the replacement?		System OK	

GC1080000460020X

Fig. 80 Cooling fan functional check (Part 2 of 2). Impala & 2000 Monte Carlo

Step	Action	Value(s)	Yes	No
1	Did you perform the Cooling Fan Functional Check?		Go to Step 2	Go to Cooling Fan Functional Check
2	Disconnect the low speed fan relay. Are both fans OFF?		Go to Step 8	Go to Step 3
3	Disconnect series/parallel fan relay. Are both fans OFF?		Go to Step 4	Go to Step 10
4	1 Disconnect the left fan. 2 Probe the fan feed terminal of the left fan connector using a J 34142-B test lamp that is connected to a good ground. Does the test lamp illuminate?		Go to Step 11	Go to Step 5
5	Probe the series/parallel relay switch feed terminal at the left fan connector using a test lamp that is connected to a good ground. Does the test lamp illuminate?		Go to Step 12	Go to Step 6
6	Probe the series/parallel cooling fan relay control circuit at the series/parallel cooling fan relay connector using a test lamp that is connected to B+. Does the test lamp illuminate?		Go to Step 7	Go to Step 13
7	1 Turn OFF the ignition. 2 Leave the test lamp installed. 3 Disconnect the PCM. 4 Turn ON the ignition, with the engine OFF. Is the test lamp still illuminated?		Go to Step 14	Go to Step 16
8	Probe the low speed cooling fan relay control circuit at the low speed cooling fan relay connector using the test lamp that is connected to B+. Does the test lamp illuminate?		Go to Step 9	Go to Step 13
9	1 Turn OFF the ignition. 2 Leave the test lamp installed. 3 Disconnect the PCM. 4 Turn ON the ignition, with the engine OFF. Is the test lamp still illuminated?		Go to Step 14	Go to Step 16

GC1080000461010X

Fig. 81 Cooling fan table No. 1 (Part 1 of 2). Impala & 2000 Monte Carlo

Step	Action	Value(s)	Yes	No
10	Repair the RH fan feed circuit for a short to voltage. Did you find and correct the condition?		Go to Cooling Fan Functional Check	Go to Step 15
11	Repair the LH fan feed circuit for a short to voltage. Did you find and correct the condition?		Go to Cooling Fan Functional Check	
12	Repair the short to voltage in the series/parallel relay switch feed circuit. Did you find and correct the condition?		Go to Cooling Fan Functional Check	
13	Replace the low speed cooling fan relay. Did you complete the replacement?		Go to Cooling Fan Functional Check	
14	Repair the high speed cooling fan relay control circuit or the low speed cooling fan relay control circuit for a short to ground. Did you find and correct the condition?		Go to Cooling Fan Functional Check	
15	Replace the high speed cooling fan relay. Did you complete the replacement?		Go to Cooling Fan Functional Check	
16	**Important:** **Program the replacement PCM.** Replace the PCM. Did you complete the replacement?		Go to Cooling Fan Functional Check	

GC1080000461020X

Fig. 81 Cooling fan table No. 1 (Part 2 of 2). Impala & 2000 Monte Carlo

Step	Action	Value(s)	Yes	No
1	Did you perform the Cooling Fan Functional Check?		Go to Step 2	Go to Cooling Fan Functional Check
2	Did either fan turn ON when the low speed cooling fan relay was commanded ON?		Go to Step 3	Go to Step 5
3	1 Install a scan tool. 2 Command the low speed cooling fan relay ON. Did the other fan turn OFF?		Go to Step 19	Go to Step 4
4	Disconnect the high speed cooling fan relay. Did the fan turn OFF?		Go to Step 20	Go to Step 21
5	1 With a scan tool, command the low speed cooling fan relay ON. 2 Disconnect the low speed cooling fan relay. 3 Probe the low speed cooling relay control circuit at the e low speed cooling fan relay connector using a J 34142-B test lamp that is connected to B+. Does the test lamp illuminate?		Go to Step 6	Go to Step 13
6	Probe both feed circuits at the low speed cooling fan relay connector using a test lamp that is connected to ground. Does test lamp illuminate for both circuits?		Go to Step 7	Go to Step 22
7	**Important** **Leave jumper in place for remainder of this table.** Connect a fused jumper wire between the switch feed circuit and the LH fan feed circuit at the low speed cooling fan relay connector. Do both fans turn ON?		Go to Step 23	Go to Step 8
8	1 Disconnect the left fan. 2 Probe left fan feed circuit at the fan harness connector terminal with a test lamp that is connected to a good ground. Does the test lamp illuminate?		Go to Step 9	Go to Step 24
9	Connect a second fused jumper wire between the left fan harness connector terminals. Is the right fan ON?		Go to Step 16	Go to Step 10

GC1080000462010X

Fig. 82 Cooling fan table No. 2 (Part 1 of 4). Impala & 2000 Monte Carlo

Step	Action	Values	Yes	No
10	1 Reconnect the left fan. 2 Disconnect the C fan relay. 3 Probe the switch feed circuit at the series/parallel fan relay connector using a test lamp that is connected to a good ground. Does the test lamp illuminate?		Go to Step 11	Go to Step 25
11	Using the second jumper wire, jumper the switch ignition feed circuit and the RH fan feed circuit together at the series/parallel relay connector. Do the fans come ON?		Go to Step 26	Go to Step 12
12	1 Reconnect the series/parallel fan relay. 2 Disconnect the right fan. 3 Probe the fan feed circuit at the fan harness connector terminal with a test lamp that is connected to a good ground. Is the left fan ON?		Go to Step 16	Go to Step 18
13	1 Test lamp still connected. 2 Turn OFF the ignition. 3 Disconnect the PCM. 4 Probe the low speed cooling fan relay control circuit at the PCM connector, with a fused jumper wire that is connected to a good ground. Is the test lamp ON?		Go to Step 20	Go to Step 21
14	Inspect the PCM connections. Repair faulty connections as necessary. Did you find and correct the condition?		Go to Cooling Fan Functional Check	Go to Step 27
15	Repair the low speed fan relay control circuit for an open or short to B+. Did you find and correct the condition?		Go to Cooling Fan Functional Check	

GC1080000462020X

Fig. 82 Cooling fan table No. 2 (Part 2 of 4). Impala & 2000 Monte Carlo

Step	Action	Value(s)	Yes	No
16	Inspect the fan motor ground circuit for an open or the fan motor connections and repair as necessary. Did you find and correct the condition?		Go to Cooling Fan Functional Check	Go to Step 17
17	Replace the fan motor. Did you complete the replacement?		Go to Cooling Fan Functional Check	
18	Repair the RH fan feed circuit for an open. Did you find and correct the condition?		Go to Cooling Fan Functional Check	
19	Replace the fan which was not operating. Did you complete the replacement?		Go to Cooling Fan Functional Check	
20	Replace the high speed fan relay. Did you complete the replacement?		Go to Cooling Fan Functional Check	
21	Repair the series/parallel fan relay switch feed circuit for a short to ground. Did you find and correct the condition?		Go to Cooling Fan Functional Check	Go to Step 26

GC1080000462030X

Fig. 82 Cooling fan table No. 2 (Part 3 of 4). Impala & 2000 Monte Carlo

Step	Action	Value(s)	Yes	No
22	Repair the open or the grounded circuit for the circuit that did not light. Did you find and correct the condition?		Go to Cooling Fan Functional Check	
23	Replace the low speed fan relay. Did you complete the replacement?		Go to Cooling Fan Functional Check	
24	Repair the LH fan feed circuit for an open. Did you find and correct the condition?		Go to Cooling Fan Functional Check	
25	Repair the series/parallel relay switch feed circuit for an open. Did you find and correct the condition?		Go to Cooling Fan Functional Check	
26	Replace the series/parallel fan relay. Did you complete the replacement?		Go to Cooling Fan Functional Check	
27	**Important** **Program the replacement PCM.** Replace the PCM. Did you complete the replacement?		Go to Cooling Fan Functional Check	

GC1080000462040X

Fig. 82 Cooling fan table No. 2 (Part 4 of 4). Impala & 2000 Monte Carlo

Step	Action	Value(s)	Yes	No
1	Did you perform the Cooling Fan Functional Check?		Go to Step 2	Go to Cooling Fan Functional Check
2	1 With a scan tool, command the low speed cooling fan relay ON. 2 Command the high speed cooling fan relay ON while observing the fans. Did both fans operate with no change?		Go to Step 8	Go to Step 3
3	Did the left fan stop operating?		Go to Step 9	Go to Step 4
4	1 Disconnect the high speed fan relay. 2 Probe the high speed fan relay control circuit at the high speed fan relay connector using a J 34142-B test lamp that is connected to B+. 3 Command high speed cooling fan relay ON using a scan tool. Does the test lamp illuminate after several seconds?		Go to Step 5	Go to Step 12
5	Probe the coil feed circuit at the high speed fan relay connector location using a test lamp that is connected to a good ground. Does the test lamp illuminate?		Go to Step 6	Go to Step 13
6	Probe the switch feed circuit at the high speed fan relay connector using a test lamp that is connected to a good ground. Does the test lamp illuminate?		Go to Step 7	Go to Step 14
7	Jumper the switch ignition feed circuit and the RH fan feed circuit together at the high speed fan relay connector. Is the right fan ON?		Go to Step 15	Go to Step 16

GC1080000463010X

Fig. 83 Cooling fan table No. 3 (Part 1 of 4). Impala & 2000 Monte Carlo

Step	Action	Value(s)	Yes	No
8	1 Turn OFF the ignition. 2 Disconnect the PCM. 3 Disconnect low speed fan relay. 4 Jumper the switch feed circuit and the LH fan feed circuit together at the low speed fan relay connector. 5 Turn the ignition ON. 6 Probe the PCM harness connector for the high speed cooling fan relay control circuit with a fused jumper that is connected to a good ground. Does the fans switch from low to high speed?		Go to Step 22	Go to Step 17
9	1 Disconnect the series/parallel fan relay. 2 Probe the high speed fan relay control circuit at the series/parallel fan relay connector using a test lamp that is connected to B+. 3 Command the high speed cooling fan relay ON using a scan tool. Does the test lamp illuminate?		Go to Step 10	Go to Step 18
10	Probe the ground circuit at the series/parallel fan relay connector using a test lamp that is connected to B+. Does the test lamp illuminate?		Go to Step 11	Go to Step 19
11	Probe the coil feed circuit at the series /parallel fan relay connector using a test lamp that is connected to a good ground. Does the test lamp illuminate?		Go to Step 20	Go to Step 21
12	Repair the high speed fan relay control circuit for an open between the high speed fan relay and the splice. Did you find and complete the condition?		Go to Cooling Fan Functional Check	
13	Repair the open in the high speed fan relay coil feed circuit Did you find and complete the condition?		Go to Cooling Fan Functional Check	
14	Repair the open in the high speed fan relay switch feed circuit Did you find and complete the condition?		Go to Cooling Fan Functional Check	

GC1080000463020X

Fig. 83 Cooling fan table No. 3 (Part 2 of 4). Impala & 2000 Monte Carlo

Step	Action	Values	Yes	No
15	Replace the high speed fan relay. Did you complete the replacement?		Go to Cooling Fan Functional Check	
16	Repair the open in the RH fan feed circuit between the high speed fan relay and the splice. Did you find and complete the condition?		Go to Cooling Fan Functional Check	
17	Repair the high speed fan relay control circuit for an open or for a short to B+. Did you find and complete the condition?		Go to Cooling Fan Functional Check	
18	Repair the open in the high speed fan relay control circuit between the series/parallel fan relay and the splice. Did you find and complete the condition?		Go to Cooling Fan Functional Check	
19	Repair the open in the ground circuit. Did you find and complete the condition?		Go to Cooling Fan Functional Check	
20	Replace the series/parallel fan relay. Did you complete the replacement?		Go to Cooling Fan Functional Check	

GC1080000463030X

Fig. 83 Cooling fan table No. 3 (Part 3 of 4). Impala & 2000 Monte Carlo

Step	Action	Value(s)	Yes	No
21	Repair the open in series/parallel fan relay coil feed circuit . Did you find and complete the condition?		Go to Cooling Fan Functional Check	
22	1 Inspect the PCM connections. 2 Repair faulty connections as necessary. Did you find and correct the condition?		Go to Cooling Fan Functional Check	Go to Step 23
23	**Important: Program the replacement PCM.** Replace the PCM. Did you complete the replacement?		Go to Cooling Fan Functional Check	

GC1080000463040X

Fig. 83 Cooling fan table No. 3 (Part 4 of 4). Impala & 2000 Monte Carlo

Step	Action	Value(s)	Yes	No
1	Was the Powertrain On–Board Diagnostic (OBD) System Check performed?	—	*Go to Step 2*	*Powertrain On Board Diagnostic (OBD) System Check*
2	Are any PCM DTC(s) stored?	—	Diagnose the PCM DTC(s) first.	*Go to Step 3*
3	1. Ensure that the engine coolant temperature is below 100°C (212°F). 2. Turn OFF the A/C Selector Switch. 3. Engine running. 4. Observe the cooling fans. Are the cooling fans running?	—	*Go to Step 32*	*Go to Step 4*
4	1. Command Fan 1 ON using the scan tool output tests function. 2. Observe the cooling fans. Are both cooling fans running at low speed?	—	*Go to Step 5*	*Go to Step 8*
5	1. Command Fan 2 ON using the scan tool output tests function. 2. Wait 3 seconds. 3. Observe the cooling fans. Are both fans running at high speed?	—	*Go to Step 6*	*Go to Step 58*
6	**Important:** Ambient temperature must be above 9°C (48°F). 1. Exit scan tool output tests. 2. Engine running. 3. Turn the A/C ON. Are the cooling fans ON?	—	Go to Diagnostic Aids	*Go to Step 7*
7	View A/C Request on the scan tool. Does A/C Request on the scan tool display Yes?	—	*Go to Step 77*	*Go to PCM Controlled A/C Circuit Diagnosis*
8	Is either cooling fan running?	—	*Go to Step 9*	*Go to Step 16*
9	Is the left cooling fan running?	—	*Go to Step 10*	*Go to Step 14*

GC1089900425010X

Fig. 84 Cooling fan diagnosis (Part 1 of 8). Intrigue

Step	Action	Value(s)	Yes	No
10	1. Turn the ignition switch to the OFF position. 2. Disconnect the right engine cooling fan. 3. Turn the ignition switch to the ON position. 4. Command Fan 1 ON using the scan tool output tests function. 5. Observe the cooling fans. Is the left engine cooling fan running?	—	*Go to Step 11*	*Go to Step 80*
11	Remove the engine Cool Fan 2 from the Underhood Electrical Center. Is the left engine cooling fan running?	—	*Go to Step 12*	*Go to Step 13*
12	Locate and repair short to ground in CKT 532. Is action complete?	—	*Go to Step 81*	—
13	1. Check CKT 409 for a short to ground. 2. If a problem is found, repair as necessary and replace Cool Fan 3 maxifuse. Was a problem found?	—	*Go to Step 81*	*Go to Step 76*
14	1. Turn the ignition switch to the OFF position. 2. Disconnect the left engine cooling fan. 3. Turn the ignition switch to the ON position. 4. Command Fan 1 On using the scan tool output tests function. 5. Observe the cooling fans. Is the right engine cooling fan running?	—	*Go to Step 15*	*Go to Step 71*
15	Locate and repair the following circuit condition(s): 1. Short to battery positive in circuit 532 or circuit 504. 2. Coolant fan #2 shorted. 3. Defective engine coolant fan diode. Is action complete?	—	*Go to Step 81*	—
16	1. Ignition On, engine not running. 2. Remove the Cool Fan 1 Relay from the Underhood Electrical Center. 3. Probe cooling fan relay cavity 30 with a test light connected to ground. Is the test light On?	—	*Go to Step 18*	*Go to Step 17*
17	Locate and repair the open in the Cool Fan 1 relay battery positive feed to cavity 30. Is action complete?	—	*Go to Step 81*	—
18	Probe Cool Fan 1 relay cavity 85 with a test light connected to ground. Is the test light On?	—	*Go to Step 20*	*Go to Step 19*
19	Locate and repair open in the battery positive feed to cavity 85 in the Cool Fan 1 relay connector. Is action complete?	—	*Go to Step 81*	—

GC1089900425020X

Fig. 84 Cooling fan diagnosis (Part 2 of 8). Intrigue

Step	Action	Value(s)	Yes	No
20	1. Turn the ignition switch to the OFF position. 2. Disconnect both cooling fans. 3. Connect terminals A and B together at both cooling fan connectors using fused jumpers. 4. Turn the ignition switch to the ON position. 5. Connect a test light between Cool Fan 1 relay cavities 87 and 30. Is the test light ON?	—	Go to Step 21	Go to Step 27
21	1. Connect a test light between Cool Fan 1 relay cavities 85 and 86. 2. Turn the ignition switch to the ON position. 3. Command Fan 1 ON using the scan tool output tests function. 4. Observe the test light. Is the test light ON?	—	Go to Step 22	Go to Step 25
22	1. Turn the ignition switch to the OFF position 2. Remove the jumpers from the engine cooling fan connectors and reconnect the cooling fans. 3. Install a fused jumper between Cool Fan 1 relay cavities 87 and 30. 4. Turn the ignition switch to the ON position. 5. Observe the cooling fans. Are both cooling fans running?	—	Go to Step 23	Go to Step 24
23	1. Check for poor Cool Fan 1 relay connections at the Underhood Electrical Center. 2. If a problem is found, repair as necessary. Was a problem found?	—	Go to Step 81	Go to Step 37
24	1. Check for poor connections at the coolant fan motors. 2. If a problem is found, repair as necessary. Was a problem found?	—	Go to Step 81	Go to Step 63
25	1. Turn the ignition switch to the OFF position. 2. Disconnect the PCM blue connector C1. 3. Install a fused jumper between Cool Fan 1 relay cavities 30 and 86. 4. Turn the ignition switch to the ON position. 5. Probe Low Speed Fans control circuit at the PCM harness connector with a test light to ground. Is the test light ON?	—	Go to Step 77	Go to Step 26
26	Locate and repair open in the Low Speed Fans control circuit between the PCM and Cool Fan 1 relay cavity 86. Is action complete?	—	Go to Step 81	—
27	1. Turn the ignition switch to the OFF position. 2. Remove the jumpers from the cooling fan connectors. 3. Reconnect the cooling fans. 4. Install a fused jumper between Cool Fan 1 relay cavities 87 and 30. 5. Remove the Cool Fan 2 from the Underhood Electrical Center. 6. Probe Cool Fan 2 cavity 30 with a test light connected to ground. Is the test light On?	—	Go to Step 28	Go to Step 31

GC1089900425030X

Fig. 84 Cooling fan diagnosis (Part 3 of 8). Intrigue

Step	Action	Value(s)	Yes	No
28	Connect a test light between Cool Fan 2 cavities 30 and 87A in the Underhood Electrical Center. Is the test light ON?	—	Go to Step 30	Go to Step 29
29	1. Check for an open in CKT 409 between Cool Fan 2 cavity 87A and Engine Coolant Fan Motor #2 terminal B. 2. If a problem is found, repair as necessary. Was a problem found?	—	Go to Step 81	Go to Step 57
30	1. Check for a poor connection at Cool Fan 2 cavities 30 or 87A in the Underhood Relay Center. 2. If a problem is found, repair as necessary. Was a problem found?	—	Go to Step 81	Go to Step 76
31	1. Check for an open in CKT 504 between Cool Fan 1 relay cavity 87 and left engine cooling fan harness connector terminal B. 2. If a problem is found, repair as necessary. Was a problem found?	—	Go to Step 81	Go to Step 56
32	Using scan tool, view A/C Request. Does the scan tool display Yes?	—	PCM Controlled A/C Circuit	Go to Step 33
33	Are both cooling fans running at low speed?	—	Go to Step 34	Go to Step 40
34	Remove Cool Fan 1 relay from the Underhood Relay Center. Are the cooling fans running?	—	Go to Step 35	Go to Step 36
35	Locate and repair short to voltage in CKT 504. Is action complete?	—	Go to Step 81	—
36	Using a test light connected to battery positive voltage, probe Cool Fan 1 relay cavity 86. Is the test light On?	—	Go to Step 38	Go to Step 37
37	Replace Cool Fan 1 relay. Is action complete?	—	Go to Step 81	—
38	1. Turn the ignition switch to the OFF position 2. Disconnect the blue PCM connector. 3. Probe Cool Fan 1 relay cavity 86 with a test light connected to battery positive voltage. Is the test light On?	—	Go to Step 39	Go to Step 77
39	Locate and repair short to ground in the Low Speed Fans control circuit. Is action complete?	—	Go to Step 81	—
40	Are both cooling fans running at high speed?	—	Go to Step 41	Go to Step 42
41	View A/C Pressure on the scan tool. Does the scan tool display voltage less than the specified value?	1.5V	Go to Step 77	Go to Step 44
42	1. Turn the ignition switch to the OFF position. 2. Disconnect the PCM. 3. Turn the ignition switch to the ON position. 4. Observe the cooling fans. Is the right engine cooling fan running at high speed?	—	Go to Step 43	Go to Step 77

GC1089900425040X

Fig. 84 Cooling fan diagnosis (Part 4 of 8). Intrigue

Step	Action	Value(s)	Yes	No
43	1. Check for a short to ground in the High Speed Fans control circuit. 2. If a problem is found, repair as necessary. Was a problem found?	—	Go to Step 81	Go to Step 52
44	1. Turn the ignition switch to the OFF position. 2. Disconnect the A/C refrigerant pressure sensor electrical connector. 3. Turn the ignition switch to the ON position. 4. View A/C Pressure on the scan tool. Does the scan tool display voltage near the specified value?	0V	Go to Step 46	Go to Step 45
45	Probe the A/C refrigerant pressure signal circuit with a *J 39200* Does the digital multimeter display voltage near the specified value?	0V	Go to Step 77	Go to Step 51
46	Probe the A/C refrigerant pressure sensor ground with a test light to battery positive voltage. Is the test light on?	—	Go to Step 47	Go to Step 49
47	Probe the A/C refrigerant pressure sensor 5 volt reference B circuit with a *J 39200* Does the digital multimeter display voltage near the specified value?	5V	Go to Step 48	Go to Step 50
48	Replace the A/C refrigerant pressure sensor. Is action complete?	—	Go to Step 81	—
49	Locate and repair open or short to voltage in the A/C refrigerant pressure sensor ground circuit. Is action complete?	—	Go to Step 81	—
50	Locate and repair open or short to ground in the A/C refrigerant pressure sensor 5 volt reference B circuit. Is action complete?	—	Go to Step 81	—
51	Locate and repair short to voltage in the A/C refrigerant pressure signal circuit. Is action complete?	—	Go to Step 81	—
52	1. Remove the Cool Fan 3 relay from the Underhood Electrical Center. 2. Observe the cooling fans. Is the right engine cooling fan running at high speed?	—	Go to Step 53	Go to Step 70
53	Remove the Cool Fan 2 from the Underhood Electrical Center. Is the right engine cooling fan running at high speed?	—	Go to Step 54	Go to Step 55
54	Locate and repair short to battery positive voltage in CKT 409. Is action complete?	—	Go to Step 81	—
55	Locate and repair short to battery positive voltage in CKT 532. Is action complete?	—	Go to Step 81	—
56	1. Check for an open in CKT 532 between Cool Fan 2 cavity 30 and left engine cooling fan terminal A. 2. If a problem is found, repair as necessary. Was a problem found?	—	Go to Step 81	Go to Step 79

GC1089900425050X

Fig. 84 Cooling fan diagnosis (Part 5 of 8). Intrigue

Step	Action	Value(s)	Yes	No
57	1. Check for an open in CKT 1050 between right engine cooling fan terminal A and ground. 2. If a problem is found, repair as necessary. Was a problem found?	—	Go to Step 81	Go to Step 80
58	1. Ignition ON, engine not running. 2. Remove the Cool Fan 3 relay from the Underhood Electrical Center. 3. Install a test light between Cool Fan 3 relay cavity 86 and battery positive voltage. 4. Command High speed fans on using the scan tool output controls function. 5. Wait approx. 5-6 seconds. 6. Observe the test light. Is the test light on?	—	Go to Step 61	Go to Step 59
59	1. Remove the Cool Fan 2 from the Underhood Electrical Center. 2. Install a test light between Cool Fan 2 cavity 86 and battery positive voltage. 3. Command high speed fans on using the scan tool output controls function. 4. Wait 3 seconds. 5. Observe the test light. Is the test light ON?	—	Go to Step 78	Go to Step 60
60	1. Turn the ignition switch to the OFF position. 2. Disconnect the PCM. 3. Turn the ignition switch to the ON position. 4. Check the High Speed Fans control circuit for an open or a short to voltage. 5. If a problem is found, repair as necessary. Was a problem found?	—	Go to Step 81	Go to Step 77
61	1. Turn the ignition switch to the OFF position 2. Reinstall the Cool Fan 3 relay. 3. Disconnect both coolant fan electrical connectors. 4. Turn the ignition switch to the ON position. 5. Command Fan 2 on using the scan tool output controls function. 6. Wait approx. 3 seconds. 7. Probe terminal B at the right engine cooling fan connector with a test light to ground. Is the test light on?	—	Go to Step 62	Go to Step 64
62	Probe terminal A at the left engine cooling fan connector with a test light to battery positive voltage. Is the test light on?	—	Go to Step 63	Go to Step 71
63	1. Identify cause of inoperative cooling fan: • Open right engine cooling fan motor windings. • Open left engine cooling fan motor windings. • Stalled cooling fan(s). 2. Replace the affected cooling fan motor. Is action complete?	—	Go to Step 81	—

GC1089900425060X

Fig. 84 Cooling fan diagnosis (Part 6 of 8). Intrigue

Step	Action	Value(s)	Yes	No
64	1. Remove the Cool Fan 3 relay from the Underhood Electrical Center. 2. Turn the ignition switch to the ON position. 3. Probe Cool Fan 3 relay cavity 85 with a test light connected to ground. Is the test light on?	—	Go to Step 66	Go to Step 65
65	1. Locate and repair the following circuit condition(s): • Open in the battery positive feed to the Cool and Cool Fan 3 relays. • Short to ground in the battery positive feed to the Cool and Cool Fan 3 relays Is action complete?	—	Go to Step 81	—
66	Probe Cool Fan 3 relay cavity 30 with a test light connected to ground. Is the test light on?	—	Go to Step 68	Go to Step 67
67	Locate and repair open in battery positive voltage circuit to Cool Fan 3 relay cavity 30. Is action complete?	—	Go to Step 81	—
68	1. Check Engine Coolant Fan Motor #2 circuit for an open between right engine cooling fan terminal B and Cool Fan 3 relay cavity 87. 2. If a problem is found, repair as necessary. Was a problem found?	—	Go to Step 81	Go to Step 69
69	1. Check for a poor Cool Fan 3 relay terminal connections at the Underhood Electrical Center. 2. If a problem is found, repair as necessary. Was a problem found?	—	Go to Step 81	Go to Step 70
70	Replace Cool Fan 3 relay. Is action complete?	—	Go to Step 81	—
71	1. Remove the Cool Fan 2 from the Underhood Electrical Center. 2. Turn the ignition switch to the ON position. 3. Probe Cool Fan 2 cavity 85 with a test light connected to ground. Is the test light on?	—	Go to Step 73	Go to Step 72
72	Locate and repair open in battery positive voltage circuit to Cool Fan 2 cavity 85. Is action complete?	—	Go to Step 81	—
73	Probe Cool Fan 2 cavity 87 in the Underhood Electrical Center with a test light to battery positive voltage. Is the test light on?	—	Go to Step 75	Go to Step 74
74	Locate and repair open in circuit between Cool Fan 2 cavity 87 in the Underhood Electrical Center and ground. Is action complete?	—	Go to Step 81	—
75	1. Check for poor Cool Fan 2 engine terminal connections at the Underhood Electrical Center. 2. If a problem is found, repair as necessary. Was a problem found?	—	Go to Step 81	Go to Step 76

GC1089900425070X

Fig. 84 Cooling fan diagnosis (Part 7 of 8). Intrigue

Step	Action	Value(s)	Yes	No
1	Was the Powertrain On-Board Diagnostic (OBD) System Check performed?	—	Go to Step 2	Go to the Powertrain OBD System Check
2	Are any PCM DTC(s) stored?	—	Diagnose the PCM DTC(s) first.	Go to Step 3
3	1. Ensure that the engine coolant temperature is below 100°C (212°F). 2. Turn the A/C *off*. 3. Engine running. 4. Observe the cooling fans. Are the cooling fan(s) running?	—	Go to Step 32	Go to Step 4
4	1. Command Fan 1 *on* using the scan tool output tests function. 2. Observe the cooling fans. Are both cooling fans running at low speed?	—	Go to Step 5	Go to Step 8

GC1089700320010X

Fig. 85 Cooling fan diagnosis (Part 1 of 9). Lumina & 1997–99 Monte Carlo

Step	Action	Value(s)	Yes	No
76	Replace the Cool Fan 2 in the Underhood Electrical Center. Is action complete?	—	Go to Step 81	—
77	Replace the PCM. **Important:** The replacement PCM must be programmed. Is action complete?	—	Go to Step 81	—
78	Repair open in the Cool Fan 3 Relay control circuit. Is action complete?	—	Go to Step 81	—
79	Replace the left engine cooling fan motor. Is action complete?	—	Go to Step 81	—
80	Replace the right engine cooling fan motor. Is action complete?	—	Go to Step 81	—
81	1. Engine coolant below 100°C (212°F). 2. A/C OFF. 3. Engine running. Observe the cooling fans. Are the cooling fans running?	—	Go to Step 32	Go to Step 82
82	1. Command Fan 1 ON using the scan tool output tests function. 2. Observe the cooling fans. Are both cooling fans running at low speed?	—	Go to Step 83	Go to Step 8
83	1. Command High speed fans on using the scan tool output tests function. 2. Wait 6 seconds. 3. Observe the cooling fans. Are both cooling fans running at high speed?	—	System OK	Go to Step 58

GC1089900425080X

Fig. 84 Cooling fan diagnosis (Part 8 of 8). Intrigue

Step	Action	Value(s)	Yes	No
5	1. Command Fan 2 *on* using the scan tool output tests function. 2. Wait 6 seconds. 3. Observe the cooling fans Are both fans running at high speed?	—	Go to Step 6	Go to Step 58
6	**Important:** Ambient temperature must be above 9°C (48°F). 1. Exit scan tool output tests. 2. Engine running. 3. Turn the A/C *on*. Are the cooling fans *on* ?	—	Go to Diagnostic Aids	Go to Step 7
7	View A/C Request on the scan tool. Does A/C Request on the scan tool display Yes?	—	Go to Step 77	Go to A/C Compressor Clutch Control Diagnosis
8	Is either cooling fan running?	—	Go to Step 9	Go to Step 16
9	Is the left cooling fan running?	—	Go to Step 10	Go to Step 14
10	1. Turn *off* the ignition switch. 2. Disconnect the right engine cooling fan. 3. Turn *on* the ignition switch. 4. Command Fan 1 *on* using the scan tool output tests function. 5. Observe the cooling fans. Is the left engine cooling fan running?	—	Go to Step 11	Go to Step 80
11	Remove the engine Fan 2 relay from the Underhood Electrical Center. Is the left engine cooling fan running?	—	Go to Step 12	Go to Step 13
12	Locate and repair short to ground in CKT 532. Is action complete?	—	Go to Step 81	—
13	1. Check CKT 504 for a short to ground. 2. If a problem is found, repair as necessary. Was a problem found?	—	Go to Step 81	Go to Step 70
14	1. Turn *off* the ignition switch. 2. Disconnect the left engine cooling fan. 3. Turn *on* the ignition switch. 4. Command Fan 1 *on* using the scan tool output tests function. 5. Observe the cooling fans. Is the right engine cooling fan running?	—	Go to Step 15	Go to Step 71
15	Locate and repair short to battery positive voltage in circuit 532 and 504. If a problem is found repair as necessary. Was a problem found?	—	Go to Step 81	Go to Step 79

GC1089700320020X

Fig. 85 Cooling fan diagnosis (Part 2 of 9). Lumina & 1997–99 Monte Carlo

Step	Action	Value(s)	Yes	No
16	1. Ignition *on*, engine not running. 2. Remove the low speed engine cooling fan relay #1 from the Underhood Electrical Center. 3. Probe cooling fan relay cavity 30 with a test light connected to ground. Is the test light *on* ?	—	*Go to Step 18*	*Go to Step 17*
17	1. Identify the cause of no battery positive voltage to cooling fan relay #1 cavity 30: • Blown Maxi fuse. If the fuse is blown, locate and correct short circuit. – Stalled right engine or left engine cooling fan. – Shorted right engine or left engine cooling fan motor windings. – Short to ground in CKT 342, CKT 532, or CKT 409. • Open in CKT 342. 2. Repair the cause of no battery positive voltage to Cool Fan 1 relay cavity 30. Is action complete?	—	*Go to Step 81*	—
18	Probe Cool Fan 1 relay cavity 85 with a test light connected to ground. Is the test light *on* ?	—	*Go to Step 20*	*Go to Step 19*
19	1. Identify the cause of no battery positive voltage to Cool Fan 1 relay cavity 85: • Blown fuse. If the fuse is blown, locate short circuit. – CKT 342 open or shorted to ground. – Shorted Cool Fan 1 relay coil. – Shorted Fan 2 relay coil. – Shorted high speed engine Cool Fan 3 relay coil. – Circuit unrelated to cooling fans. 2. Repair cause of no battery positive voltage to Cool Fan 1 relay cavity 85. Is action complete?	—	*Go to Step 81*	—
20	1. Turn *off* the ignition switch. 2. Disconnect both cooling fans. 3. Connect terminals A and B together at both cooling fan connectors using fused jumpers. 4. Turn *off* the ignition switch. 5. Connect a test light between Cool Fan 1 relay cavities 87 and 30. Is the test light ON?	—	*Go to Step 21*	*Go to Step 27*
21	1. Connect a test light between Cool Fan 1 relay cavities 85 and 86. 2. Turn *on* the ignition switch. 3. Command Fan 1 *on* using the scan tool output tests function. 4. Observe the test light. Is the test light *on* ?	—	*Go to Step 22*	*Go to Step 25*

GC1089700320030X

Fig. 85 Cooling fan diagnosis (Part 3 of 9). Lumina & 1997–99 Monte Carlo

Step	Action	Value(s)	Yes	No
22	1. Turn *off* the ignition switch 2. Remove the jumpers from the engine cooling fan connectors and reconnect the cooling fans. 3. Install a fused jumper between Cool Fan 1 relay cavities 87 and 30. 4. Turn *on* the ignition switch. 5. Observe the cooling fans. Are both cooling fans running?	—	*Go to Step 23*	*Go to Step 24*
23	1. Check for poor Cool Fan 1 relay connections at the Underhood Electrical Center. 2. If a problem is found, repair as necessary. Was a problem found?	—	*Go to Step 81*	*Go to Step 37*
24	1. Check for poor connections at the coolant fan motors. 2. If a problem is found, repair as necessary. Was a problem found?	—	*Go to Step 81*	*Go to Step 63*
25	1. Turn *off* the ignition switch. 2. Disconnect the PCM blue connector C1. 3. Install a fused jumper between Cool Fan 1 relay cavities 86 and 85. 4. Turn *on* the ignition switch. 5. Probe Coolant Fan 1 relay control circuit at the PCM harness connector with a test light to ground. Is the test light *on* ?	—	*Go to Step 77*	*Go to Step 26*
26	Locate and repair open in the Coolant Fan 1 relay control circuit between the PCM and Cool Fan 1 relay cavity 86. Is action complete?	—	*Go to Step 81*	—
27	1. Turn *off* the ignition switch. 2. Remove the jumpers from the cooling fan connectors. 3. Reconnect the cooling fans. 4. Install a fused jumper between Cool Fan 1 relay cavities 87 and 30. 5. Remove the Fan 2 relay from the Underhood Electrical Center. 6. Probe Fan 2 relay cavity 30 with a test light connected to ground. Is the test light *on* ?	—	*Go to Step 28*	*Go to Step 31*
28	Connect a test light between Fan 2 relay in Underhood Electrical Center cavities 30 and 87A. Is the test light *on* ?	—	*Go to Step 30*	*Go to Step 29*
29	1. Check for an open in CKT 504 between Fan 2 relay cavity 30 and Engine Coolant Fan Motor #2 terminal B. 2. If a problem is found, repair as necessary. Was a problem found?	—	*Go to Step 81*	*Go to Step 57*
30	1. Check for a poor connection at Fan 2 relay in Underhood Electrical Center cavities 30 or 87A. 2. If a problem is found, repair as necessary. Was a problem found?	—	*Go to Step 81*	*Go to Step 70*

GC1089700320040X

Fig. 85 Cooling fan diagnosis (Part 4 of 9). Lumina & 1997–99 Monte Carlo

Step	Action	Value(s)	Yes	No
31	1. Check for an open in CKT 409 between Cool Fan 1 relay cavity 30 and left engine cooling fan harness connector terminal B. 2. If a problem is found, repair as necessary. Was a problem found?	—	*Go to Step 81*	*Go to Step 56*
32	Using scan tool, view A/C Request. Does the scan tool display Yes?	—	Go to *A/C Compressor Clutch Control Diagnosis* A/C Compressor Clutch Control Diagnosis	*Go to Step 33*
33	Are both cooling fan(s) running at low speed?	—	*Go to Step 34*	*Go to Step 40*
34	Remove Cool Fan 1 relay from the Underhood Electrical Center. Are the cooling fans running?	—	*Go to Step 35*	*Go to Step 36*
35	Locate and repair short to voltage in CKT 409. Is action complete?	—	*Go to Step 81*	—
36	Using a test light connected to battery positive voltage, probe Cool Fan 1 relay cavity 86. Is the test light *on* ?	—	*Go to Step 38*	*Go to Step 37*
37	Replace Cool Fan 1 relay. Is action complete?	—	*Go to Step 81*	—
38	1. Turn *off* the ignition switch 2. Disconnect the blue PCM connector. 3. Probe Cool Fan relay cavity 86 with a test light connected to battery positive voltage. Is the test light *on* ?	—	*Go to Step 39*	*Go to Step 77*
39	Locate and repair short to ground in the Cool Fan 1 relay control circuit. Is action complete?	—	*Go to Step 81*	—
40	Are both cooling fans running at high speed?	—	*Go to Step 41*	*Go to Step 42*
41	View A/C Pressure on the scan tool. Does the scan tool display voltage less than the specified value?	1.2V	*Go to Step 77*	*Go to Step 44*
42	1. Turn *off* the ignition switch. 2. Disconnect the PCM. 3. Turn *off* the ignition switch. 4. Observe the cooling fans. Is the right engine cooling fan running at high speed?	—	*Go to Step 43*	*Go to Step 77*
43	1. Check for a short to ground in the Cool Fan 2 relay and Cool Fan 3 relay control circuit. 2. If a problem is found, repair as necessary. Was a problem found?	—	*Go to Step 81*	*Go to Step 52*

GC1089700320050X

Fig. 85 Cooling fan diagnosis (Part 5 of 9). Lumina & 1997–99 Monte Carlo

Step	Action	Value(s)	Yes	No
44	1. Turn *off* the ignition switch. 2. Disconnect the A/C refrigerant pressure sensor electrical connector. 3. Turn *on* the ignition switch. 4. View A/C Pressure on the scan tool. Does the scan tool display voltage near the specified value?	0V	*Go to Step 46*	*Go to Step 45*
45	Probe the A/C refrigerant pressure signal circuit with a *J 39200* Digital Multimeter connected to the A/C refrigerant pressure sensor ground. Does the digital multimeter display voltage near the specified value?	0V	*Go to Step 77*	*Go to Step 51*
46	Probe the A/C refrigerant pressure sensor ground with a test light to battery positive voltage. Is the test light on?	—	*Go to Step 47*	*Go to Step 49*
47	Probe the A/C refrigerant pressure sensor 5 volt reference circuit with a *J 39200* Digital Multimeter connected to the A/C refrigerant pressure sensor ground. Does the digital multimeter display voltage near the specified value?	5V	*Go to Step 48*	*Go to Step 50*
48	Replace the A/C refrigerant pressure sensor. Is action complete?	—	*Go to Step 81*	—
49	Locate and repair open or short to voltage in the A/C refrigerant pressure sensor ground circuit. Is action complete?	—	*Go to Step 81*	—
50	Locate and repair open or short to ground in the A/C refrigerant pressure sensor 5 volt reference circuit. Is action complete?	—	*Go to Step 81*	—
51	Locate and repair short to voltage in the A/C refrigerant pressure signal circuit. Is action complete?	—	*Go to Step 81*	—
52	1. Remove the Cool Fan 2 relay from the Underhood Electrical Center. 2. Observe the cooling fans. Is the right engine cooling fan running at high speed?	—	*Go to Step 53*	*Go to Step 70*
53	Remove the Fan 3 relay from the Underhood Electrical Center. Is the right engine cooling fan running at high speed?	—	*Go to Step 54*	*Go to Step 55*
54	Locate and repair short to battery positive voltage in CKT 532. Is action complete?	—	*Go to Step 81*	—
55	Locate and repair short to battery positive voltage in CKT 504. If a problem is found repair as necessary. Was a problem found?	—	*Go to Step 81*	*Go to Step 76*
56	1. Check for an open in CKT 532 between Fan 2 relay cavity 30 and left engine cooling fan terminal A. 2. If a problem is found, repair as necessary. Was a problem found?	—	*Go to Step 81*	*Go to Step 79*

GC1089700320060X

Fig. 85 Cooling fan diagnosis (Part 6 of 9). Lumina & 1997–99 Monte Carlo

Step	Action	Value(s)	Yes	No
57	1. Check for an open in CKT 1050 between right engine cooling fan terminal A and ground. 2. If a problem is found, repair as necessary. Was a problem found?	—	*Go to Step 81*	*Go to Step 80*
58	1. Ignition *on*, engine not running. 2. Remove the Cool Fan 2 relay from the Underhood Electrical Center. 3. Install a test light between Cool Fan 2 relay cavity 86 and battery positive voltage. 4. Command High speed fans on using the scan tool output controls function. 5. Wait approx. 5-6 seconds. 6. Observe the test light. Is the test light *on* ?	—	*Go to Step 61*	*Go to Step 59*
59	1. Remove the Fan 3 relay from the Underhood Electrical Center. 2. Install a test light between Fan 3 relay cavity 86 and battery positive voltage. 3. Command high speed fans on using the scan tool output controls function. 4. Wait 6 seconds. 5. Observe the test light. Is the test light *on* ?	—	*Go to Step 78*	*Go to Step 60*
60	1. Turn *off* the ignition switch. 2. Disconnect the PCM. 3. Turn *on* the ignition switch. 4. Check the Cool Fan 2 relay and Cool relay control circuit for an open or a short to voltage. 5. If a problem is found, repair as necessary. Was a problem found?	—	*Go to Step 81*	*Go to Step 77*
61	1. Turn *off* the ignition switch 2. Reinstall the Cool Fan 2 relay. 3. Disconnect both coolant fan electrical connectors. 4. Turn *on* the ignition switch. 5. Command Fan 2 *on* using the scan tool output controls function. 6. Wait approx. 5-6 seconds. 7. Probe terminal B at the right engine cooling fan connector with a test light to ground. Is the test light *on* ?	—	*Go to Step 62*	*Go to Step 64*
62	Probe terminal A at the left engine cooling fan connector with a test light to battery positive voltage. Is the test light *on* ?	—	*Go to Step 63*	*Go to Step 71*
63	1. Identify cause of inoperative cooling fan: • Open right engine cooling fan motor windings. • Open left engine cooling fan motor windings. • Stalled cooling fan(s). 2. Replace the affected cooling fan motor. Is action complete?	—	*Go to Step 81*	—

GC1089700320070X

Fig. 85 Cooling fan diagnosis (Part 7 of 9). Lumina & 1997–99 Monte Carlo

Step	Action	Value(s)	Yes	No
76	Replace the *Cool Fan 3* relay in the Underhood Electrical Center. Is action complete?	—	*Go to Step 81*	—
77	Replace the PCM. **Important:** The replacement PCM must be programmed. Is action complete?	—	*Go to Step 81*	—
78	Repair open in the *Cool Fan* relay cavity 86 and *Cool Fan 2* relay cavity 86 control circuit to PCM. Is action complete?	—	*Go to Step 81*	—
79	Replace the left engine cooling fan motor. Is action complete?	—	*Go to Step 81*	—
80	Replace the right engine cooling fan motor. Is action complete?	—	*Go to Step 81*	
81	1. Engine coolant below 100°C (212°F). 2. A/C *off*. 3. Engine running. 4. Observe the cooling fans. Are the cooling fans running?	—	*Go to Step 32*	*Go to Step 82*
82	1. Command Low Speed Fans *on* using the scan tool output tests function. 2. Observe the cooling fans. Are both cooling fans running at low speed?	—	*Go to Step 83*	*Go to Step 8*
83	1. Command High speed fans *on* using the scan tool output tests function. 2. Wait 6 seconds. 3. Observe the cooling fans. Are both cooling fans running at high speed?	—	System OK	*Go to Step 58*

GC1089700320090X

Fig. 85 Cooling fan diagnosis (Part 9 of 9). Lumina & 1997–99 Monte Carlo

Step	Action	Value(s)	Yes	No
64	1. Remove the high speed engine Cool Fan 2 relay from the Underhood Electrical Center. 2. Turn *on* the ignition switch. 3. Probe Cool Fan 2 relay cavity 85 with a test light connected to ground. Is the test light *on* ?	—	*Go to Step 66*	*Go to Step 65*
65	Locate and repair open in the ignition battery positive voltage circuit to high speed engine Cool Fan 2 relay. Is action complete?	—	*Go to Step 81*	—
66	Probe Cool Fan 2 relay cavity 30 with a test light connected to ground. Is the test light *on* ?	—	*Go to Step 68*	*Go to Step 67*
67	Locate and repair open in battery positive voltage circuit to Cool Fan 2 relay cavity 30. Is action complete?	—	*Go to Step 81*	—
68	1. Check Engine Coolant Fan Motor #1 circuit for an open between right engine cooling fan terminal B and Cool Fan 2 relay cavity 87. 2. If a problem is found, repair as necessary. Was a problem found?	—	*Go to Step 81*	*Go to Step 69*
69	1. Check for a poor Cool Fan 2 relay terminal connections at the Underhood Electrical Center. 2. If a problem is found, repair as necessary. Was a problem found?	—	*Go to Step 81*	*Go to Step 70*
70	Replace Cool Fan 2 relay. Is action complete?	—	*Go to Step 81*	—
71	1. Remove the Fan 3 relay from the Underhood Electrical Center. 2. Turn *on* the ignition switch. 3. Probe Fan 3 relay cavity 85 with a test light connected to ground. Is the test light *on* ?	—	*Go to Step 73*	*Go to Step 72*
72	Locate and repair open in battery positive voltage circuit to Fan 3 relay cavity 85. Is action complete?	—	*Go to Step 81*	—
73	Probe Fan 3 relay cavity 87 in the Underhood Electrical Center with a test light to battery positive voltage. Is the test light *on* ?	—	*Go to Step 75*	*Go to Step 74*
74	Locate and repair open in circuit between Fan 3 cavity 87and Fan 2 relay cavity 87a in the Underhood Electrical Center and ground. Is action complete?	—	*Go to Step 81*	—
75	1. Check for poor Fan 3 relay engine terminal connections at the Underhood Electrical Center. 2. If a problem is found, repair as necessary. Was a problem found?	—	*Go to Step 81*	*Go to Step 76*

GC1089700320080X

Fig. 85 Cooling fan diagnosis (Part 8 of 9). Lumina & 1997–99 Monte Carlo

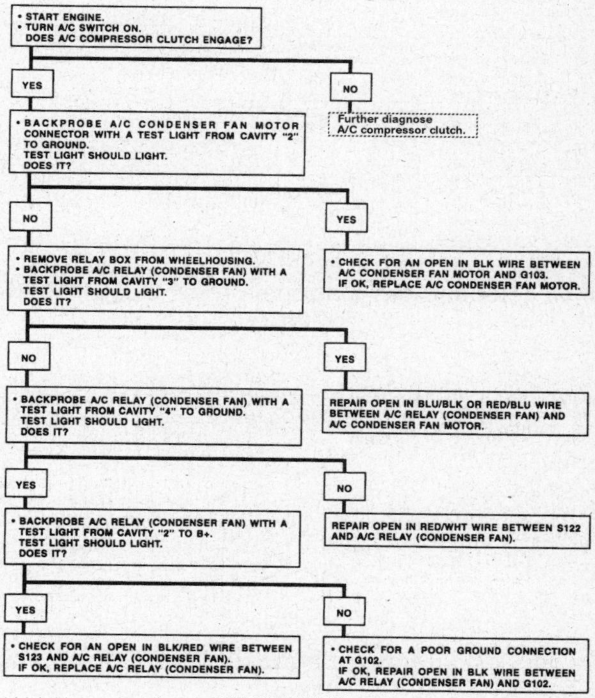

GC1089500275000X

Fig. 86 Chart 1, cooling fan diagnosis (A/C condenser fan motor does not run). 1997 Metro

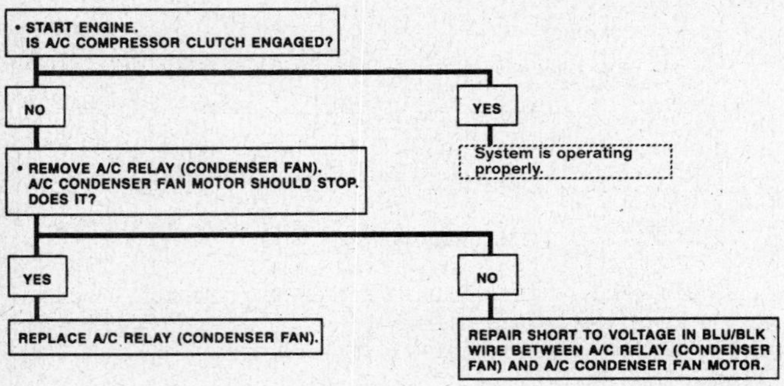

GC1089500276000X

Fig. 87 Chart 1, cooling fan diagnosis (A/C condenser fan motor runs at all times). 1997 Metro

Step	Action	Value(s)	Yes	No
1	Did you perform the Powertrain On-Board Diagnostic System Check?	—	*Go to Step 2*	Go to *Powertrain OBD System Check*
2	1. Start engine and obtain operating temperature. 2. Turn OFF all the accessories. 3. Install a scan tool. 4. Observe the ECT sensor parameter on the scan tool. Does the cooling fan turn ON when ECT reaches above the specified value?	97.5°C (208°F)	*Go to Step 3*	*Go to Step 8*

GC1089800359010X

Fig. 88 Cooling fan diagnosis (Part 1 of 3). 1998–99 Metro

Step	Action	Value(s)	Yes	No
3	Does the cooling fan turn OFF when the ECT drops below the specified value?	92.5°C (199°F)	***"Inspect ECT and ECT wiring."***	*Go to Step 4*
4	1. Check that the ECT is below the specified value. 2. Disconnect the cooling fan relay. Is the cooling fan OFF?	92.5°C (199°F)	*Go to Step 5*	*Go to Step 6*
5	Probe the cooling fan relay connector cavity 2 with a test lamp connected to B+. Did the test lamp illuminate?	—	*Go to Step 7*	*Go to Step 17*
6	Repair the short to voltage in the power feed circuit between the cooling fan relay and the cooling fan motor Is the action complete?	—	*Go to Step 20*	—
7	1. Check for a short to ground in the cooling fan relay control circuit between the PCM and the cooling fan relay. 2. Repair as necessary. Was a repair necessary?	—	*Go to Step 20*	*Go to Step 18*
8	1. Start the engine. 2. Check that the ECT is above the specified value. 3. Disconnect the cooling fan relay. 4. Probe the cooling fan relay connector cavity 2 with a test lamp connected to B+. Did the test lamp illuminate?	97.5°C (208°F)	*Go to Step 9*	*Go to Step 12*
9	Probe the cooling fan relay connector cavity 1 with a test lamp to ground. Did the test lamp illuminate?	—	*Go to Step 10*	*Go to Step 15*
10	Probe the cooling fan relay connector cavity 4 with a test lamp to ground. Did the test lamp illuminate?	—	*Go to Step 11*	*Go to Step 16*
11	Connect a fused jumper wire between the cooling fan relay connector cavities 3 and 4. Is the cooling fan motor ON?	—	*Go to Step 17*	*Go to Step 13*
12	1. Check for a open in the cooling fan relay control circuit between the PCM and the cooling fan relay. 2. Repair as necessary. Was a repair necessary?	—	*Go to Step 20*	*Go to Step 18*
13	1. Check for a open in the power feed circuit between the cooling fan relay and the cooling fan motor. 2. Repair as necessary. Was a repair necessary?	—	*Go to Step 20*	*Go to Step 14*
14	1. Check for an open or a faulty connection in the ground circuit between the cooling fan motor and **ground.** 2. Repair as necessary. Was a repair necessary?	—	*Go to Step 20*	*Go to Step 19*

GC1089800359020X

Fig. 88 Cooling fan diagnosis (Part 2 of 3). 1998–99 Metro

Step	Action	Value(s)	Yes	No
15	Repair the open in the ignition feed circuit between the cooling fan relay terminal 1 and the junction block. Is the action complete?	—	*Go to Step 20*	—
16	Repair the open in the battery feed circuit between the cooling fan relay terminal 4 and the fuse box. Is the action complete?	—	*Go to Step 20*	—
17	Replace the cooling fan relay. Is the action complete?	—	*Go to Step 20*	—
18	Replace the PCM. Is the action complete?	—	*Go to Step 20*	—
19	Replace the cooling fan motor. Is the action complete?	—	*Go to Step 20*	—
20	1. Clear the scan tool information and road test the vehicle within the Freeze Frame conditions that set the DTC. 2. Review the scan tool data and check for DTCs. The repair is complete if no DTCs are stored. Are any DTCs displayed on the scan tool?	—	Go to the Applicable DTC Table	System OK

GC1089800359030X

Fig. 88 Cooling fan diagnosis (Part 3 of 3). 1998–99 Metro

Circuit Description

Power for the cooling fan motors comes from the Cool Fan 1 and Cool Fan 2 Maxi fuses®. The relays are energized when the PCM grounds the fan relay control circuits. The PCM Output Driver Module (ODM) B output 1 (low speed fan control circuit) is grounded for low speed fan operation. PCM ODM B outputs 1 (low speed fan control circuit) and 2 (high speed fan control circuit) are grounded for High Speed operation. The cooling fan system on this vehicle consists of two speed dual speed cooling fans. While in low speed operation, CKT 409 supplies battery positive voltage directly to the right side cooling fan motor. The left side cooling fan motor is supplied battery positve voltage through the right side cooling fan motor, causing both cooling fans to run at low speed. When high speed operation is commanded, the right side fan and left side fans are supplied with their own battery positive voltage feed and ground, causing both cooling fans to run at high speed.

The PCM commands low speed fans operation when the following conditions are present:

- Vehicle speed is less than 58 mph.
- Engine coolant temperature is greater than 100°C (212°F).

OR

- Vehicle speed is less than 40 mph.
- Intake air temperature is greater than 9°C (48°F).
- A/C refrigerant pressure is greater than 190 psi (1300 kPa).

GC1089700330010X

Fig. 89 Cooling fan diagnosis (Part 1 of 10). Park Avenue

For high speed cooling fan operation, the PCM delays control of the high speed cooling fan relay for 6 seconds. The 6 second delay ensures that the cooling fan electrical load will not exceed the capacity of the system. High speed fan operation is commanded when the following conditions are present:

- Vehicle speed is less than 65 mph.
- Engine coolant temperature is greater than 108°C (226°F).

OR

- Vehicle speed is less than 50 mph.
- A/C refrigerant pressure is greater than 260 psi (1800 kPa).

Diagnostic Aids

Check for the following conditions:

- Poor connection at the PCM, cooling fan relays, or cooling fan motors. Inspect harness connectors for backed out terminals, improper mating, broken locks, improperly formed or damaged terminals, and poor terminal to wire connection.
- Damaged harness. Inspect the wiring harness for damage.

Test Description

Number(s) below refer to the step number(s) on the Diagnostic Table.

2. Stored diagnostic trouble codes may affect engine cooling fans operation. This diagnostic table may lead to improper diagnosis and replacement of good parts if diagnostic trouble codes are present.
6. Ambient temperature must be greater than 9°C (48°F) before the PCM will enable the cooling fans due to A/C request. The PCM will enable the cooling fans if A/C refrigerant pressure increases regardless of ambient temperature.
77. This vehicle is equipped with a PCM which utilizes an Electrically Erasable Programmable Read Only Memory (EEPROM). When the PCM is being replaced, the new PCM must be programmed.

Step	Action	Value(s)	Yes	No
1	Was the Powertrain On-Board Diagnostic (OBD) System Check performed?	—	*Go to Step 2*	Go to the *Powertrain OBD System Check*
2	Are any powertrain DTC(s) stored?	—	Diagnose the DTC(s) first.	*Go to Step 3*
3	1. Ensure that the engine coolant temperature is less than 100°C (212°F). 2. Turn the A/C OFF. 3. Engine running. 4. Observe the cooling fans. Are the cooling fan(s) running?	—	*Go to Step 32*	*Go to Step 4*
4	1. Command Fan 1 ON using the scan tool output tests function. 2. Observe the cooling fans. Are both cooling fans running at low speed?	—	*Go to Step 5*	*Go to Step 8*
5	1. Command Fan 2 ON using the scan tool output tests function. 2. Wait 6 seconds. 3. Observe the cooling fans. Are both fans running at high speed?	—	*Go to Step 6*	*Go to Step 58*
6	**Important:** Ambient temperature must be greater than 9°C (48°F). 1. Exit scan tool output tests. 2. Engine running. 3. Turn the A/C ON. Are the cooling fans running?	—	Refer to Diagnostic Aids	*Go to Step 7*

GC1089700330020X

Fig. 89 Cooling fan diagnosis (Part 2 of 10). Park Avenue

Step	Action	Value(s)	Yes	No
7	View A/C Request on the scan tool. Does A/C Request on the scan tool display Yes?	—	Go to Step 77	Refer to *Automatic Temperature Controls*
8	Is either cooling fan running?	—	Go to Step 9	Go to Step 16
9	Is the RH cooling fan running?	—	Go to Step 10	Go to Step 14
10	1. Turn OFF the ignition switch. 2. Disconnect the LH cooling fan. 3. Turn ON the ignition switch. 4. Command Fan 1 ON using the scan tool output tests function. 5. Observe the cooling fans. Is the RH cooling fan running?	—	Go to Step 11	Go to Step 80
11	Remove the series/parallel cooling fan relay from the underhood Bussed Electrical Center. Is the RH cooling fan running?	—	Go to Step 12	Go to Step 13
12	Locate and repair short to ground in CKT 504. Is action complete?	—	Go to Step 81	—
13	1. Check CKT 409 for a short to ground. 2. If a problem is found, repair as necessary. Was a problem found?	—	Go to Step 81	Go to Step 76
14	1. Turn OFF the ignition switch. 2. Disconnect the RH cooling fan. 3. Turn ON the ignition switch. 4. Command Fan 1 ON using the scan tool output tests function. 5. Observe the cooling fans. Is the LH cooling fan running?	—	Go to Step 15	Go to Step 79
15	Replace the RH cooling fan diode. Is action complete?	—	Go to Step 81	—
16	1. Ignition ON, engine not running. 2. Disconnect the low speed cooling fan relay #2. 3. Probe low speed cooling fan relay #2 harness connector cavity 30 with a test light connected to ground. Is the test light ON?	—	Go to Step 18	Go to Step 17

GC1089700330030X

Fig. 89 Cooling fan diagnosis (Part 3 of 10). Park Avenue

Step	Action	Value(s)	Yes	No
23	1. Check for poor connections at the low speed cooling fan relay #2. 2. If a problem is found, repair as necessary. Was a problem found?	—	Go to Step 81	Go to Step 37
24	1. Check for poor connections at the cooling fan motors. 2. If a problem is found, repair as necessary. Was a problem found?	—	Go to Step 81	Go to Step 63
25	1. Turn OFF the ignition switch. 2. Disconnect the PCM blue connector C1. 3. Install a fused jumper between low speed cooling fan relay #2 harness connector cavities 30 and 86. 4. Turn ON the ignition switch. 5. Probe PCM harness connector cavity C1-32 with a test light to ground. Is the test light ON?	—	Go to Step 77	Go to Step 26
26	Repair open in the low speed fans control CKT 335 between the PCM and the low speed cooling fan relay #2. Is action complete?	—	Go to Step 81	—
27	1. Turn OFF the ignition switch. 2. Remove the jumpers from the cooling fan connectors. 3. Reconnect the cooling fans. 4. Install a fused jumper between low speed cooling fan relay #2 harness connector terminals 30 and 87. 5. Remove the series/parallel cooling fan relay from the underhood Bussed Electrical Center. 6. Probe underhood Bussed Electrical Center series/parallel cooling fan relay cavity 30 with a test light connected to ground. Is the test light ON?	—	Go to Step 28	Go to Step 31
28	Connect a test light between Underhood Bussed Electrical Center series/parallel cooling fan relay cavities 30 and 87A. Is the test light ON?	—	Go to Step 30	Go to Step 29
29	1. Check for an open in CKT 409 between underhood Bussed Electrical Center series/parallel cooling fan relay cavity 87A and LH cooling fan terminal B. 2. If a problem is found, repair as necessary. Was a problem found?	—	Go to Step 81	Go to Step 57
30	1. Check for a poor connection at the underhood Bussed Electrical Center series/parallel cooling fan relay cavities 87A or 30. 2. If a problem is found, repair as necessary. Was a problem found?	—	Go to Step 81	Go to Step 76

GC1089700330050X

Fig. 89 Cooling fan diagnosis (Part 5 of 10). Park Avenue

Step	Action	Value(s)	Yes	No
17	1. Identify the cause of no battery positive voltage to low speed cooling fan relay #2 harness connector cavity 30: • Blown fuse. If the fuse is blown, locate and correct short circuit. – Stalled RH or LH cooling fan. – Shorted RH or LH cooling fan motor windings. – Short to ground in CKT 42, CKT 532 or CKT 409. • Open in CKT 42. 2. Repair the cause of no battery positive voltage to low speed cooling fan relay #2 harness connector cavity 30. Diagnosis. Is action complete?	—	Go to Step 81	—
18	Probe low speed cooling fan relay #2 harness connector cavity 86 with a test light connected to ground. Is the test light ON?	—	Go to Step 20	Go to Step 19
19	1. Identify the cause of no battery positive voltage to low speed cooling fan relay #2 harness connector cavity 86: • CKT 001 open. • Poor connection or open in underhood Bussed Electrical Center. 2. Repair cause of no battery positive voltage to low speed cooling fan relay #2 harness connector cavity 86. Is action complete?	—	Go to Step 81	—
20	1. Turn OFF the ignition switch. 2. Disconnect both cooling fans. 3. Connect terminals A and B together at both cooling fan connectors using fused jumpers. 4. Turn ON the ignition switch. 5. Connect a test light between low speed cooling fan relay #2 harness connector cavities 30 and 87. Is the test light ON?	—	Go to Step 21	Go to Step 27
21	1. Connect a test light between low speed cooling fan relay #2 harness connector cavities 85 and 86. 2. Turn ON the ignition switch. 3. Command Fan 1 ON using the scan tool output tests function. 4. Observe the test light. Is the test light ON?	—	Go to Step 22	Go to Step 25
22	1. Turn OFF the ignition switch 2. Remove the jumpers from the engine cooling fan connectors and reconnect the cooling fans. 3. Install a fused jumper between low speed cooling fan relay #2 harness connector cavities 30 and 87. 4. Turn ON the ignition switch. 5. Observe the cooling fans. Are both cooling fans running?	—	Go to Step 23	Go to Step 24

GC1089700330040X

Fig. 89 Cooling fan diagnosis (Part 4 of 10). Park Avenue

Step	Action	Value(s)	Yes	No
31	1. Check for an open in CKT 532 between the low speed cooling fan relay #2 harness connector cavity 87 and RH cooling fan harness connector terminal B. 2. If a problem is found, repair as necessary. Was a problem found?	—	Go to Step 81	Go to Step 56
32	Using scan tool, view A/C Request. Does the scan tool display Yes?	—	Refer to *Automatic Temperature Controls*	Go to Step 33
33	Are both cooling fan(s) running at low speed?	—	Go to Step 34	Go to Step 40
34	Disconnect the low speed cooling fan relay #2. Are the cooling fans running?	—	Go to Step 35	Go to Step 36
35	Locate and repair short to voltage in CKT 532. Is action complete?	—	Go to Step 81	—
36	Using a test light connected to B+, probe low speed cooling fan relay #2 harness connector cavity 85. Is the test light ON?	—	Go to Step 38	Go to Step 37
37	Replace the low speed cooling fan relay #2. Is action complete?	—	Go to Step 81	—
38	1. Turn OFF the ignition switch 2. Disconnect the blue PCM connector C1. 3. Probe low speed cooling fan relay #2 harness connector cavity 85 with a test light connected to B+. Is the test light ON?	—	Go to Step 39	Go to Step 77
39	Locate and repair short to ground in the low speed cooling fan control circuit (CKT 335). Is action complete?	—	Go to Step 81	—
40	Are both cooling fans running at high speed?	—	Go to Step 41	Go to Step 42
41	View A/C High Side Pressure on the scan tool. Does the scan tool display voltage less than the specified value?	1.2V	Go to Step 77	Go to Step 44
42	1. Turn OFF the ignition switch. 2. Disconnect the PCM. 3. Turn ON the ignition switch. 4. Observe the cooling fans. Is the LH cooling fan running at high speed?	—	Go to Step 43	Go to Step 77
43	1. Check for a short to ground in the high spped cooling fans control circuit (CKT 473). 2. If a problem is found, repair as necessary. Was a problem found?	—	Go to Step 81	Go to Step 52
44	1. Turn OFF the ignition switch. 2. Disconnect the A/C refrigerant pressure sensor electrical connector. 3. Turn ON the ignition switch. 4. View A/C High Side Pressure on the scan tool. Does the scan tool display voltage near the specified value?	0V	Go to Step 46	Go to Step 45

GC1089700330060X

Fig. 89 Cooling fan diagnosis (Part 6 of 10). Park Avenue

Step	Action	Value(s)	Yes	No
45	Probe the A/C refrigerant pressure signal circuit with a *J 39200* Digital Multimeter connected to the A/C refrigerant pressure sensor ground. Does the digital multimeter display voltage near the specified value?	0V	*Go to Step 77*	*Go to Step 51*
46	Probe the A/C refrigerant pressure sensor ground circuit with a test light to B+. Is the test light ON?	—	*Go to Step 47*	*Go to Step 49*
47	Probe the A/C refrigerant pressure sensor 5 volt reference circuit B with a *J 39200* Digital Multimeter connected to the A/C refrigerant pressure sensor ground. Does the digital multimeter display voltage near the specified value?	5V	*Go to Step 48*	*Go to Step 50*
48	Replace the A/C refrigerant pressure sensor. Is action complete?	—	*Go to Step 81*	—
49	Locate and repair open or short to voltage in the A/C refrigerant pressure sensor ground circuit. Is action complete?	—	*Go to Step 81*	—
50	Locate and repair open or short to ground in the A/C refrigerant pressure sensor 5 volt reference B circuit. Is action complete?	—	*Go to Step 81*	—
51	Locate and repair short to voltage in the A/C refrigerant pressure signal circuit. Is action complete?	—	*Go to Step 81*	—
52	1. Remove the high speed cooling fan relay #1 from the underhood Bussed Electrical Center. 2. Observe the cooling fans. Is the LH cooling fan running at high speed?	—	*Go to Step 53*	*Go to Step 70*
53	Remove the series/parallel cooling fan relay from the underhood Bussed Electrical Center. Is the LH cooling fan running at high speed?	—	*Go to Step 54*	*Go to Step 55*
54	Locate and repair short to B+ in CKT 409. Is action complete?	—	*Go to Step 81*	—
55	Locate and repair short to B+ in CKT 504. Is action complete?	—	*Go to Step 81*	—
56	1. Check for an open in CKT 504 between series/parallel relay cavity 30 in the underhood Bussed Electrical Center and RH cooling fan terminal A. 2. If a problem is found, repair as necessary. Was a problem found?	—	*Go to Step 81*	*Go to Step 79*

GC1089700330070X

Fig. 89 Cooling fan diagnosis (Part 7 of 10). Park Avenue

Step	Action	Value(s)	Yes	No
57	1. Check for an open in CKT 1250 between LH cooling fan terminal A and ground. 2. If a problem is found, repair as necessary. Was a problem found?	—	*Go to Step 81*	*Go to Step 80*
58	1. Ignition ON, engine not running. 2. Remove the high speed cooling fan relay #1 from the underhood Bussed Electrical Center. 3. Install a test light between high speed cooling fan relay #1 cavity 86 in the underhood Bussed Electrical Center and B+. 4. Command Fan 2 ON using the scan tool output controls function. 5. Wait 6 seconds. 6. Observe the test light. Is the test light ON?	—	*Go to Step 61*	*Go to Step 59*
59	1. Remove the series/parallel cooling fan relay from the underhood Bussed Electrical Center. 2. Install a test light between series/parallel cooling fan relay cavity 86 in the Underhood Bussed Electrical Center and B+. 3. Command Fan 2 ON using the scan tool output controls function. 4. Wait 6 seconds. 5. Observe the test light. Is the test light ON?	—	*Go to Step 78*	*Go to Step 60*
60	1. Turn OFF the ignition switch. 2. Disconnect the PCM. 3. Turn ON the ignition switch. 4. Check the high speed cooling fans control circuit (CKT 473) for an open or a short to voltage between series/parallel cooling fan relay cavity 86 in the underhood Bussed Electrical Center and the PCM. 5. If a problem is found, repair as necessary. Was a problem found?	—	*Go to Step 81*	*Go to Step 77*
61	1. Turn OFF the ignition switch 2. Reinstall the high speed cooling fan relay #1. 3. Disconnect both cooling fan electrical connectors. 4. Turn ON the ignition switch. 5. Command Fan 2 ON using the scan tool output controls function. 6. Wait 6 seconds. 7. Probe terminal B (CKT 409) at the LH cooling fan connector with a test light to ground. Is the test light ON?	—	*Go to Step 62*	*Go to Step 64*
62	Probe terminal A (CKT 504) at the RH cooling fan connector with a test light to B+. Is the test light ON?	—	*Go to Step 63*	*Go to Step 71*

GC1089700330080X

Fig. 89 Cooling fan diagnosis (Part 8 of 10). Park Avenue

Step	Action	Value(s)	Yes	No
63	1. Identify cause of inoperative cooling fan: • Open RH cooling fan motor windings. • Open LH cooling fan motor windings. • Stalled cooling fan(s). 2. Replace the affected cooling fan motor. Is action complete?	—	*Go to Step 81*	—
64	1. Remove the high speed cooling fan relay #1 from the Underhood Bussed Electrical Center. 2. Turn ON the ignition switch. 3. Probe high speed cooling fan relay #1 cavity 85 in the Underhood Bussed Electrical Center with a test light connected to ground. Is the test light ON?	—	*Go to Step 66*	*Go to Step 65*
65	Locate and repair open in the battery positive voltage circuit to high speed cooling fan relay #1. Is action complete?	—	*Go to Step 81*	—
66	Probe high speed cooling fan relay #1 cavity 30 in the Underhood Bussed Electrical Center with a test light connected to ground. Is the test light ON?	—	*Go to Step 68*	*Go to Step 67*
67	Locate and repair open in battery positive voltage circuit to high speed cooling fan relay #1 cavity 30. Is action complete?	—	*Go to Step 81*	—
68	1. Check CKT 409 for an open between LH cooling fan terminal B and high speed cooling fan relay #1 cavity 87 in the Underhood Bussed Electrical Center. 2. If a problem is found, repair as necessary. Was a problem found?	—	*Go to Step 81*	*Go to Step 69*
69	1. Check for poor terminal connections at the high speed cooling fan relay #1. 2. If a problem is found, repair as necessary. Was a problem found?	—	*Go to Step 81*	*Go to Step 70*
70	Replace the high speed cooling fan relay #1. Is action complete?	—	*Go to Step 81*	—
71	1. Remove the series/parallel cooling fan relay. 2. Turn ON the ignition switch. 3. Probe series/parallel cooling fan relay cavity 85 in the Underhood Bussed Electrical Center with a test light connected to ground. Is the test light ON?	—	*Go to Step 73*	*Go to Step 72*
72	Locate and repair open in battery positive voltage circuit to series/parallel cooling fan relay cavity 85 in the Underhood Bussed Electrical Center. Is action complete?	—	*Go to Step 81*	—
73	Probe series/parallel cooling fan relay cavity 30 in the Underhood Bussed Electrical Center with a test light to B+. Is the test light ON?	—	*Go to Step 75*	*Go to Step 74*

GC1089700330090X

Fig. 89 Cooling fan diagnosis (Part 9 of 10). Park Avenue

Step	Action	Value(s)	Yes	No
74	Locate and repair open in CKT 1250 between series/parallel cooling fan relay cavity 87 in the Underhood Bussed Electrical Center cavity and ground. Is action complete?	—	*Go to Step 81*	—
75	1. Check for poor terminal connections at the series/parallel cooling fan relay. 2. If a problem is found, repair as necessary. Was a problem found?	—	*Go to Step 81*	*Go to Step 76*
76	Replace the series/parallel cooling fan relay. Is action complete?	—	*Go to Step 81*	—
77	Replace the PCM. **Important:** The replacement PCM must be programmed. Is action complete?	—	*Go to Step 81*	—
78	Repair open in the high speed cooling fans control circuit (CKT 473) to high speed cooling fan relay #1 cavity 86. Is action complete?	—	*Go to Step 81*	—
79	Replace the RH cooling fan motor. Is action complete?	—	*Go to Step 81*	—
80	Replace the LH cooling fan motor. Is action complete?	*Go to Step 81*		
81	1. Engine coolant less than 100°C (212°F). 2. Ensure that A/C is OFF. 3. Engine running. Observe the cooling fans. Are the cooling fans running?	—	*Go to Step 32*	*Go to Step 82*
82	1. Command Fan 1 ON using the scan tool output tests function. 2. Observe the cooling fans. Are both cooling fans running at low speed?	—	*Go to Step 83*	*Go to Step 8*
83	1. Command Fan 2 ON using the scan tool output tests function. 2. Wait 6 seconds. 3. Observe the cooling fans. Are both cooling fans running at high speed?	—	System OK	*Go to Step 58*

GC1089700330100X

Fig. 89 Cooling fan diagnosis (Part 10 of 10). Park Avenue

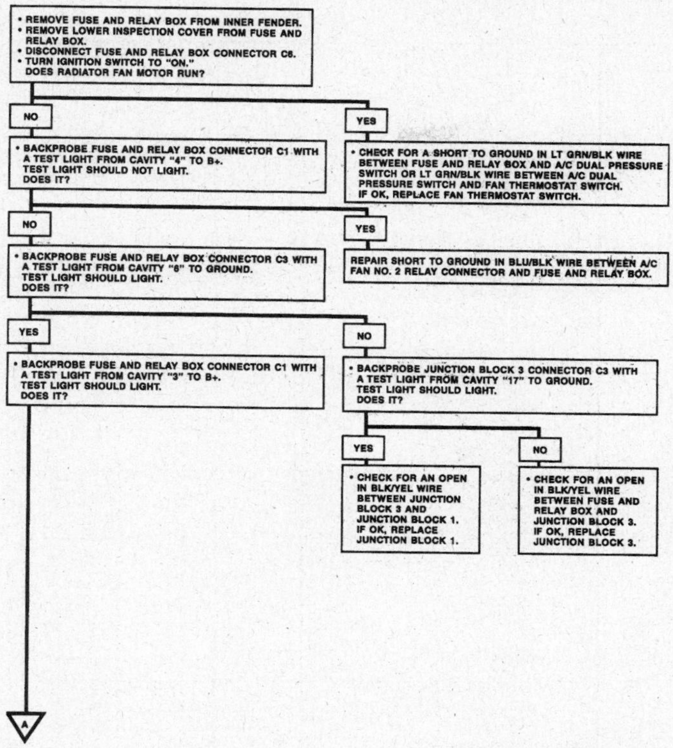

Fig. 90 Chart 1, cooling fan diagnosis (Part 1 of 2). 1997 Prizm

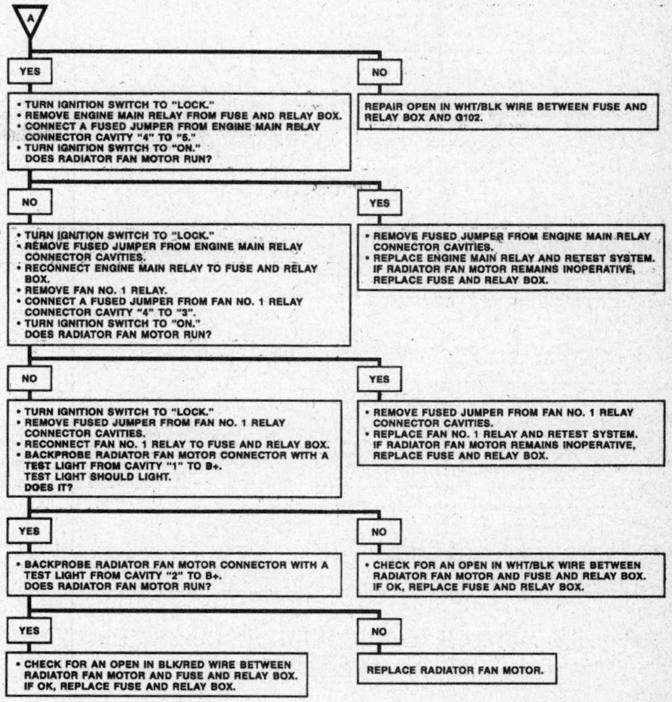

Fig. 90 Chart 1, cooling fan diagnosis (Part 2 of 2). 1997 Prizm

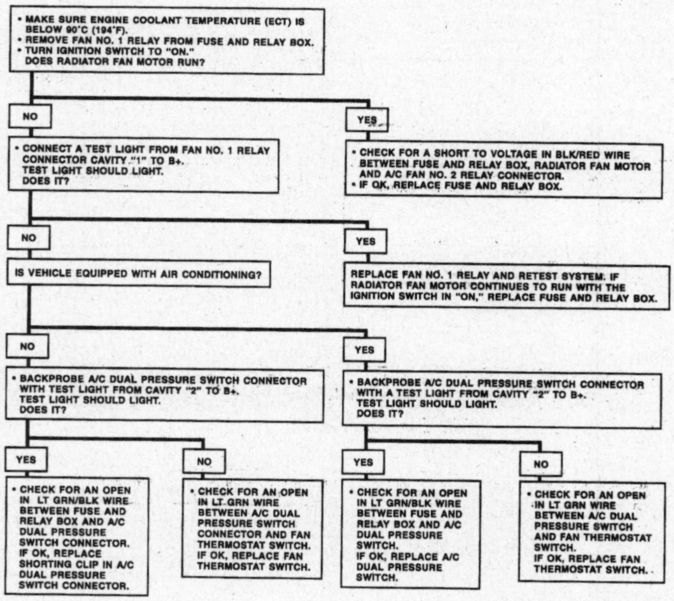

Fig. 91 Chart 2, cooling fan diagnosis. 1997 Prizm

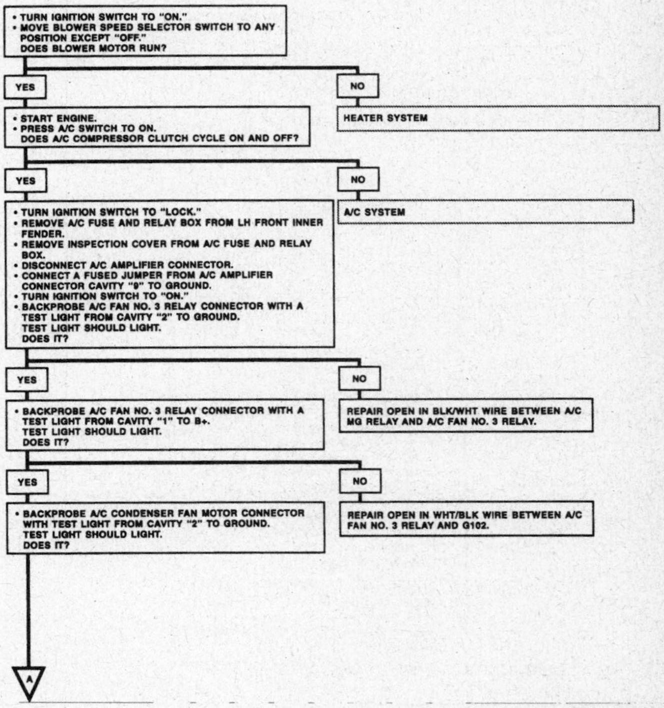

Fig. 92 Chart 3, cooling fan diagnosis (Part 1 of 2). 1997 Prizm

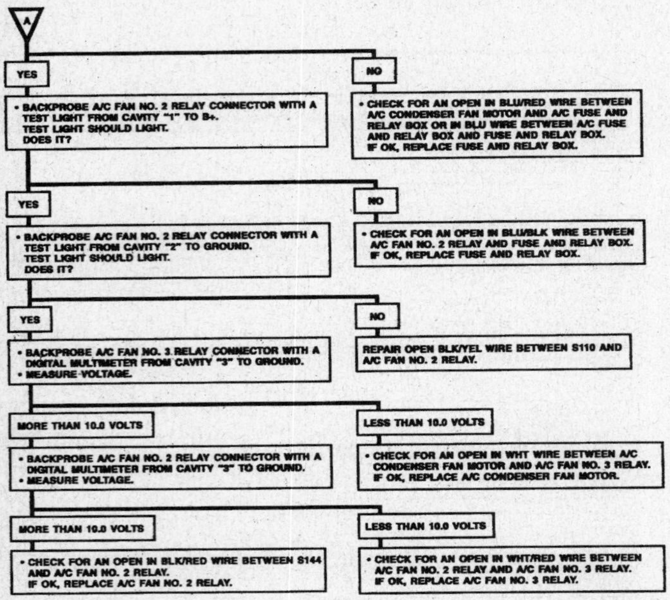
A
YES
NO
• BACKPROBE A/C FAN NO. 2 RELAY CONNECTOR WITH A TEST LIGHT FROM CAVITY "1" TO B+. TEST LIGHT SHOULD LIGHT. DOES IT?
• CHECK FOR AN OPEN IN BLU/RED WIRE BETWEEN A/C CONDENSER FAN MOTOR AND A/C FUSE AND RELAY BOX OR IN BLU WIRE BETWEEN A/C FUSE AND RELAY BOX AND FUSE AND RELAY BOX. IF OK, REPLACE FUSE AND RELAY BOX.
YES
NO
• BACKPROBE A/C FAN NO. 2 RELAY CONNECTOR WITH A TEST LIGHT FROM CAVITY "2" TO GROUND. TEST LIGHT SHOULD LIGHT. DOES IT?
• CHECK FOR AN OPEN IN BLU/BLK WIRE BETWEEN A/C FAN NO. 2 RELAY AND FUSE AND RELAY BOX. IF OK, REPLACE FUSE AND RELAY BOX.
YES
NO
• BACKPROBE A/C FAN NO. 3 RELAY CONNECTOR WITH A DIGITAL MULTIMETER FROM CAVITY "3" TO GROUND.
• MEASURE VOLTAGE.
REPAIR OPEN BLK/YEL WIRE BETWEEN S110 AND A/C FAN NO. 2 RELAY.
MORE THAN 10.0 VOLTS
LESS THAN 10.0 VOLTS
• BACKPROBE A/C FAN NO. 2 RELAY CONNECTOR WITH A DIGITAL MULTIMETER FROM CAVITY "3" TO GROUND.
• MEASURE VOLTAGE.
• CHECK FOR AN OPEN IN WHT WIRE BETWEEN A/C CONDENSER FAN MOTOR AND A/C FAN NO. 3 RELAY. IF OK, REPLACE A/C CONDENSER FAN MOTOR.
MORE THAN 10.0 VOLTS
LESS THAN 10.0 VOLTS
• CHECK FOR AN OPEN IN BLK/RED WIRE BETWEEN S144 AND A/C FAN NO. 2 RELAY. IF OK, REPLACE A/C FAN NO. 2 RELAY.
• CHECK FOR AN OPEN IN WHT/RED WIRE BETWEEN A/C FAN NO. 2 RELAY AND A/C FAN NO. 3 RELAY. IF OK, REPLACE A/C FAN NO. 3 RELAY.

GC1089600336020X

Fig. 92 Chart 3, cooling fan diagnosis (Part 2 of 2). 1997 Prizm

Step	Action	Normal Result(s)	Abnormal Result(s)*
1	• Start and run the engine until the engine coolant temperature reaches 93°C (199°F) • For vehicles with air conditioning refer to the following in HVAC Systems with A/C-Manual: • HVAC System Check • HVAC Blower Controls Schematic • HVAC Compressor/Condenser Fan Controls Schematics	• The main radiator fan motor and the auxiliary radiator fan motor (with A/C only) run at full speed. • The main radiator fan motor and the auxiliary radiator fan motor stop running when the engine coolant temperature drops below 83° C (181° F)	• Cooling Fan Inoperative - Electric • Cooling Fan Inoperative - Auxiliary
2	1 Run the engine until the engine coolant temperature reaches 93°C (199°F) 2 Turn the blower speed selector switch to any position except OFF. 3 Press the A/C switch to ON	• The main radiator fan motor and the auxiliary radiator fan motor run at half speed. • Once the engine coolant temperature reaches 93°C (199°F), the main radiator fan motor and the auxiliary radiator fan motor run at full speed. • If the A/C system pressure exceeds 1520 kPa (220 psi) at the A/C refrigerant pressure switch, the main radiator fan motor and the auxiliary radiator fan motor will run at full speed.	Cooling Fan Inoperative at Low Speed - Electric
3	Press the A/C switch to OFF	The main radiator fan motor and the auxiliary radiator fan motor stop running once the engine coolant temperature drops below 83°C (181°F).	Cooling Fan Runs Continuously - Auxiliary

* Refer to the appropriate symptom diagnostic table for the applicable abnormal result.

GC1089900396000X

Fig. 93 Cooling fan system check. 1998–99 Prizm

1	Was the Cooling Fan System Check performed?		Go to Step 2	Go to Cooling Fan System Check
2	1 Run the engine until operating temperature is reached and the thermostat opens. 2 Stop the engine. 3 Disconnect the auxiliary fan motor connector. 4 Connect a test lamp across the auxiliary fan motor connector. 5 Start the engine. Does the test lamp light?		Go to Step 3	Go to Step 4
3	Replace the auxiliary fan motor. Is the repair complete?		Go to Cooling Fan System Check	
4	Test for battery positive at the auxiliary radiator fan motor connector terminal 2. Is battery voltage present?	B+	Go to Step 8	Go to Step 5
5	Inspect the CDS fuse in fuse and relay block 2 for an open. Is the fuse open ?		Go to Step 6	Go to Step 7
6	Repair the short to ground in the BLU/RED wire between the CDS fuse and the auxiliary radiator fan motor connector terminal 2. Is the repair complete?		Go to Cooling Fan System Check	
7	Repair the open in the BLU wire between the CDS fuse and fuse and relay block 1 OR in the BLU/RED wire between the CDS fuse and the auxiliary fan motor connector terminal 2. Is the repair complete?		Go to Cooling Fan System Check	
8	1 Remove the A/C fan no. 2 relay from fuse and relay block 2. 2 Test for an open between the auxiliary fan motor connector terminal 1 and the A/C fan no. 2 relay cavity 3. 3 Test for an open between the A/C fan no. 2 relay cavity 4 and G104. Was an open found?		Go to Step 10	Go to Step 9
9	Replace the fan no. 2 relay. Is the repair complete?		Go to Cooling Fan System Check	
10	Repair the open. Is the repair complete?		Go to Cooling Fan System Check	

GC1089900397000X

Fig. 94 Auxiliary cooling fan inoperative. 1998–99 Prizm

Step	Action	Value(s)	Yes	No
1	Was the Cooling Fan System Check performed?		Go to Step 2	Go to Cooling Fan System Check
2	1 Run the engine until operating temperature is reached and the thermostat opens. 2 Stop the engine. 3 Disconnect the main fan motor connector. 4 Connect a test lamp across the main fan motor connector. 5 Start the engine. Does the test lamp light?		Go to Step 3	Go to Step 4
3	Replace the main fan motor. Is the repair complete?		Go to Cooling Fan System Check	
4	Test for an open in the WHT/BLK wire between the main fan motor terminal 1 and G103. Was an open found?		Go to Step 17	Go to Step 5
5	Test for an open in the BLK/RED wire between the main fan motor terminal 2 and the fan no. 1 relay terminal 23. Was an open found?		Go to Step 6	Go to Step 7
6	1 Test for an open in the BLK/RED wire between the main fan motor terminal 2 and connector 3 terminal 1 of fuse and relay block 1. 2 Test for an open between connector 3 terminal 1 of fuse and relay block 1 and terminal 23 of the fan no. 1 relay. Is the BLK/RED wire open?		Go to Step 17	Go to Step 14
7	Test for battery voltage at the fan no. 1 relay terminal 22 with the engine running. Is battery voltage present?	B+	Go to Step 15	Go to Step 8
8	Test for an open between terminal 22 of the fan no. 1 relay and terminal 14 of the engine main relay in fuse and relay block 1. Was an open found?		Go to Step 14	Go to Step 9
9	Test for battery voltage at the ENGINE MAIN relay terminal 16 with the engine running. Is battery voltage present?	B+	Go to Step 11	Go to Step 10
10	Test for an open in the BLK/YEL wire between fuse and relay block 1 and fuse and relay block 2 OR in the BLK/YEL wire between fuse and relay block 1 and junction block 2. Was an open found?		Go to Step 17	Go to Step 14

GC1089900398010X

Fig. 95 Main cooling fan inoperative (Part 1 of 2). 1998–99 Prizm

Step	Action	Value(s)	Yes	No
11	Test for battery voltage at terminal 13 of the ENGINE MAIN relay with the engine running. Is battery voltage present?	B+	Go to Step 13	Go to Step 12
12	Test for an open in the WHT wire to connector 4 terminal 2 of fuse and relay block 1. Was an open found?		Go to Step 17	Go to Step 14
13	Test for an open in the WHT/BLK wire between fuse and relay block 1 and G103. Was an open found?		Go to Step 17	Go to Step 16
14	Replace fuse and relay block 1. Is the repair complete?		Go to Cooling Fan System Check	
15	Replace the fan no. 1 relay. Is the repair complete?		Go to Cooling Fan System Check	
16	Replace the engine main relay. Is the repair complete?		Go to Cooling Fan System Check	
17	Repair the open. Is the repair complete?		Go to Cooling Fan System Check	

GC1089900398020X

Fig. 95 Main cooling fan inoperative (Part 2 of 2). 1998–99 Prizm

1	Was the Cooling Fan System Check performed?		Go to Step 2	Go to Cooling Fan System Check
2	1 Start the engine. 2 Move the blower speed selector switch to any position except OFF. Does the blower motor run?		Go to Step 3	HVAC System Check
3	Press the A/C switch to the ON position. Does the A/C compressor clutch engage?		Go to Step 4	HVAC Compressor Clutch Does Not Engage

GC1089900399010X

Fig. 96 Main cooling fan inoperative at low speed (Part 1 of 3). 1998–99 Prizm

4	1 Turn the ignition switch to LOCK. 2 Remove the A/C fan no. 3 relay from fuse and relay block 2. 3 Start the engine. 4 Turn the blower speed selector switch to any position except OFF. 5 Measure the voltage between the A/C fan no. 3 relay cavity 1 and ground. Is the value within the specified range?	B+	Go to Step 6	Go to Step 5
5	Repair the open in the BLK/WHT wire between the A/C fan no. 3 relay cavity 1 and the A/C MG relay cavity 3 in fuse and relay block 2. Is the repair complete?		Go to Cooling Fan System Check	
6	Test for an open in the WHT/BLK between the A/C fan no. 3 relay cavity 2 and G103. Was an open found?		Go to Step 9	Go to Step 7
7	Test for an open in the WHT/RED wire between the A/C fan no. 3 relay cavity 3 and the A/C fan no. 2 relay cavity 5. Was an open found?		Go to Step 9	Go to Step 8
8	Test for an open in the WHT wire between the A/C fan no. 3 relay cavity 5 and fuse and relay block 1. Was an open found?		Go to Step 9	Go to Step 10
9	Repair the open. Is the repair complete?		Go to Cooling Fan System Check	

GC1089900399020X

Fig. 96 Main cooling fan inoperative at low speed (Part 2 of 3). 1998–99 Prizm

10	Replace the A/C fan no. 3 relay. Is the repair complete?		Go to Cooling Fan System Check	

GC1089900399030X

Fig. 96 Main cooling fan inoperative at low speed (Part 3 of 3). 1998–99 Prizm

Step	Action	Value(s)	Yes	No
DEFINITION: The main radiator fan motor and/or the auxiliary radiator fan motor runs continuously with the ignition switch in the RUN position.				
1	Was the Cooling Fan System Check performed?		Go to Step 2	Go to the Cooling Fan System Check
2	Are both fans running continuously?		Go to Step 12	Go to Step 3
3	Is only the main radiator fan motor running continuously?		Go to Step 8	Go to Step 4
4	Is only the auxiliary radiator fan motor running continuously?		Go to Step 5	Go to Step 1
5	1 Ensure that the engine coolant temperature is below 93°C (199°F) 2 Remove the A/C fan no. 2 relay from fuse and relay block 2. 3 Start the engine. 4 Turn the A/C off. Does the auxiliary radiator fan motor run?		Go to Step 6	Go to Step 7
6	Repair the short to ground in the WHT wire between the auxiliary radiator fan motor terminal 1 and fuse and relay block 2. Is the repair complete?		Go to the Cooling Fan System Check	
7	Replace the A/C fan no. 2 relay. Is the repair complete?		Go to the Cooling Fan System Check	
8	1 Ensure that the engine coolant temperature is below 93°C (199°F) 2 Remove the fan no. 1 relay from fuse and relay block 1. 3 Start the engine. 4 Turn the A/C off. Does the main radiator fan motor run?		Go to Step 9	Go to Step 10
9	Repair the short to voltage in the BLK/RED wire between the main radiator fan motor terminal 2 and fuse relay block 1. Is the repair complete?		Go to the Cooling Fan System Check	
10	Test for an open in the BLU/BLK wire between the fan no. 1 relay in fuse and relay block 1 and the A/C fan no. 2 relay in fuse and relay block 2. Was an open found?		Go to Step 18	Go to Step 11
11	Replace the fan no. 1 relay. Is the repair complete?		Go to the Cooling Fan System Check	
12	1 Remove the A/C fan no. 3 relay from fuse and relay block 2. 2 Start the engine. 3 Turn the A/C off. Do both fan motors run?		Go to Step 16	Go to Step 13

GC1089900400010X

Fig. 97 Auxiliary cooling fan runs continuously (Part 1 of 2). 1998–99 Prizm

Step	Action	Value(s)	Yes	No
13	1 Test the A/C MG relay for continuity between terminals 3 and 5. 2 Test the A/C fan no. 3 relay for continuity between terminals 3 and 5. Does continuity exist in either relay?		Go to Step 14	Go to Step 15
14	Replace the faulty relay. Is the repair complete?		Go to the Cooling Fan System Check	
15	Repair the short to B+ in the BLK/WHT wire between the A/C fan no. 3 relay terminal 1 in fuse and relay block 2 and the A/C MG relay terminal 3 in fuse and relay block 2. Is the repair complete?		Go to the Cooling Fan System Check	
16	1 Test for an open in the BLU/BLK wire between the A/C fan no. 2 relay and the A/C refrigerant pressure switch connector. 2 Test for an open in the LT GRN wire between the A/C refrigerant pressure switch connector and the fan control switch. Was an open found?		Go to Step 18	Go to Step 17
17	1 Test for an open in the A/C refrigerant pressure switch, if equipped. 2 Test for an open in the A/C refrigerant pressure switch connector shorting clip, if equipped. Was an open found?		Go to Step 19	Go to Step 20
18	Repair the open/short. Is the repair complete?		Go to the Cooling Fan System Check	
19	1 Replace the A/C refrigerant pressure switch, if equipped. 2 Repair or replace the shorting bar, if equipped. Is the repair complete?		Go to the Cooling Fan System Check	
20	Replace the fan control switch. Is the repair complete?		Go to the Cooling Fan System Check	

GC1089900400020X

Fig. 97 Auxiliary cooling fan runs continuously (Part 2 of 2). 1998–99 Prizm

Circuit Description:

Power for the fan motors is supplied through the Cooling Fan fuse in the RH Maxi fuse block. The cooling fan relays are energized when current flows from the Clng Fan fuse in the IP fuse block through the relay coils to ground through the PCM. The cooling fan 1 control circuit is grounded for low speed fan operation. The cooling fan 1 and cooling fan 2 control circuits are grounded for high speed operation.

During low speed fan operation the PCM supplies a ground path for the low speed cooling fan relay #1. This closes the low speed relay contacts, allowing current to flow from the battery junction block through the relay contacts to the primary cooling fan. During low speed operation, the ground path for the primary cooling fan is through the series/parallel cooling fan relay and secondary cooling fan motor. The result is a series circuit with both fans running at low speed.

To command high speed cooling fan operation the PCM first supplies a ground path for the low speed cooling fan relay through the cooling fan 1 control circuit. After a 6 second delay, the PCM supplies a ground path for the high speed cooling fan relay #3 and the series/parallel cooling fan relay #2 through the cooling fan 2 control circuit. All 3 cooling fan relays are closed for high speed cooling fans operation. During high speed operation, both the primary and the secondary cooling fans are supplied current from the battery junction block and each fan has its own ground path.

Diagnostic Aids

Check for the following conditions:

- Poor connection at the PCM, cooling fan relays, or cooling fan motors. Inspect harness connectors for backed out terminals, improper mating, broken locks, improperly formed or damaged terminals, and poor terminal to wire connection.
- Damaged harness. Inspect the wiring harness for damage.

Test Description

Number(s) below refer to the step number(s) on the Diagnostic Table.

2. Stored diagnostic trouble codes may affect engine cooling fans operation. This diagnostic table may lead to improper diagnosis and replacement of good parts if diagnostic trouble codes are present.
6. Ambient temperature must be greater than 9°C (48°F) before the PCM will enable the cooling fans due to A/C request. The PCM will enable the cooling fans if A/C refrigerant pressure increases regardless of ambient temperature.
77. This vehicle is equipped with a PCM which utilizes an Electrically Erasable Programmable Read Only Memory (EEPROM). When the PCM is being replaced, the new PCM must be programmed.

Step	Action	Value(s)	Yes	No
1	Was the Powertrain On-Board Diagnostic (OBD) System Check performed?	—	*Go to Step 2*	Go to the *Powertrain OBD System Check*
2	Are any powertrain DTC(s) stored?	—	Diagnose the DTC(s) first.	*Go to Step 3*
3	1. Ensure that the engine coolant temperature is less than 100°C (212°F). 2. Turn the A/C OFF. 3. Engine running. 4. Observe the cooling fans. Are the cooling fan(s) running?	—	*Go to Step 32*	*Go to Step 4*
4	1. Command Fan 1 ON using the scan tool output tests function. 2. Observe the cooling fans. Are both cooling fans running at low speed?	—	*Go to Step 5*	*Go to Step 8*

GC1089600329010X

Fig. 98 Cooling fan diagnosis (Part 1 of 10). Riviera

Step	Action	Value(s)	Yes	No
17	1. Identify the cause of no battery positive voltage to low speed cooling fan relay harness connector cavity 30: • Blown fuse. If the fuse is blown, locate and correct short circuit. – Stalled primary or secondary cooling fan. – Shorted primary or secondary cooling fan motor windings. – Short to ground in CKT 642, CKT 532, or CKT 409. – Shorted primary cooling fan diode. • Open in CKT 642. 2. Repair the cause of no battery positive voltage to low speed cooling fan relay harness connector cavity 30. Is action complete?	—	*Go to Step 81*	—
18	Probe low speed cooling fan relay harness connector cavity 85 with a test light connected to ground. Is the test light ON?	—	*Go to Step 20*	*Go to Step 19*
19	1. Identify the cause of no positive voltage to low speed cooling fan relay harness connector cavity 85: • Blown fuse. If the fuse is blown, locate short circuit. – CKT 241 shorted to ground. – Shorted low speed cooling fan relay coil. – Shorted series/parallel cooling fan #2 relay coil. – Shorted high speed cooling fan #3 relay coil. • CKT 241 open. 2. Repair cause of no positive voltage to low speed cooling fan relay harness connector cavity 85. Is action complete?	—	*Go to Step 81*	—
20	1. Turn OFF the ignition switch. 2. Disconnect both cooling fans. 3. Connect terminals A and B together at both cooling fan connectors using fused jumpers. 4. Turn ON the ignition switch. 5. Connect a test light between low speed cooling fan relay harness connector cavities 30 and 87. Is the test light ON?	—	*Go to Step 21*	*Go to Step 27*
21	1. Connect a test light between low speed cooling fan relay harness connector cavities 85 and 86. 2. Turn ON the ignition switch. 3. Command Fan 1 ON using the scan tool output tests function. 4. Observe the test light. Is the test light ON?	—	*Go to Step 22*	*Go to Step 25*

GC1089600329030X

Fig. 98 Cooling fan diagnosis (Part 3 of 10). Riviera

Step	Action	Value(s)	Yes	No
5	1. Command Fan 2 ON using the scan tool output tests function. 2. Wait 6 seconds. 3. Observe the cooling fans Are both fans running at high speed?	—	*Go to Step 6*	*Go to Step 58*
6	**Important:** Ambient temperature must be greater than 9°C (48°F). 1. Exit scan tool output tests. 2. Engine running. 3. Turn the A/C ON. Are the cooling fans running?	—	Refer to Diagnostic Aids	*Go to Step 7*
7	View A/C Request on the scan tool. Does A/C Request on the scan tool display Yes?	—	*Go to Step 77*	*PCM Controlled Air Conditioning Diagnosis*
8	Is either cooling fan running?	—	*Go to Step 9*	*Go to Step 16*
9	Is the primary cooling fan running?	—	*Go to Step 10*	*Go to Step 14*
10	1. Turn OFF the ignition switch. 2. Disconnect the secondary cooling fan. 3. Turn ON the ignition switch. 4. Command Fan 1 ON using the scan tool output tests function. 5. Observe the cooling fans. Is the primary cooling fan running?	—	*Go to Step 11*	*Go to Step 80*
11	Remove the series/parallel cooling fan #2 relay from the RH Underhood Relay Center. Is the primary cooling fan running?	—	*Go to Step 12*	*Go to Step 13*
12	Locate and repair short to ground in CKT 504. Is action complete?	—	*Go to Step 81*	—
13	1. Check CKT 409 for a short to ground. 2. If a problem is found, repair as necessary. Was a problem found?	—	*Go to Step 81*	*Go to Step 76*
14	1. Turn OFF the ignition switch. 2. Disconnect the primary cooling fan. 3. Turn ON the ignition switch. 4. Command Fan 1 ON using the scan tool output tests function. 5. Observe the cooling fans. Is the secondary cooling fan running?	—	*Go to Step 15*	*Go to Step 79*
15	Replace the primary cooling fan diode. Is action complete?	—	*Go to Step 81*	—
16	1. Ignition ON, engine not running. 2. Disconnect the low speed cooling fan relay. 3. Probe low speed cooling fan relay harness connector cavity 30 with a test light connected to ground. Is the test light ON?	—	*Go to Step 18*	*Go to Step 17*

GC1089600329020X

Fig. 98 Cooling fan diagnosis (Part 2 of 10). Riviera

Step	Action	Value(s)	Yes	No
22	1. Turn OFF the ignition switch 2. Remove the jumpers from the engine cooling fan connectors and reconnect the cooling fans. 3. Install a fused jumper between low speed cooling fan relay harness connector cavities 30 and 87. 4. Turn ON the ignition switch. 5. Observe the cooling fans. Are both cooling fans running?	—	*Go to Step 23*	*Go to Step 24*
23	1. Check for poor connections at the low speed cooling fan relay. 2. If a problem is found, repair as necessary. Was a problem found?	—	*Go to Step 81*	*Go to Step 37*
24	1. Check for poor connections at the cooling fan motors. 2. If a problem is found, repair as necessary. Was a problem found?	—	*Go to Step 81*	*Go to Step 63*
25	1. Turn OFF the ignition switch. 2. Disconnect the PCM blue connector C1. 3. Install a fused jumper between low speed cooling fan relay harness connector cavities 30 and 86. 4. Turn ON the ignition switch. 5. Probe PCM harness connector cavity C1-32 with a test light to ground. Is the test light ON?	—	*Go to Step 77*	*Go to Step 26*
26	Repair open in the cooling fan 1 control CKT 335 between the PCM and the low speed cooling fan relay. Is action complete?	—	*Go to Step 81*	—
27	1. Turn OFF the ignition switch. 2. Remove the jumpers from the cooling fan connectors. 3. Reconnect the cooling fans. 4. Install a fused jumper between low speed cooling fan relay harness connector terminals 30 and 87. 5. Remove the series/parallel cooling fan #2 relay from the RH Front Underhood Relay Center. 6. Probe RH Front Underhood Relay Center series/parallel cooling fan #2 relay cavity 30 with a test light connected to ground. Is the test light ON?	—	*Go to Step 28*	*Go to Step 31*
28	Connect a test light between RH Front Underhood Relay Center series/parallel cooling fan #2 relay cavities 30 and 87A. Is the test light ON?	—	*Go to Step 30*	*Go to Step 29*
29	1. Check for an open in CKT 409 between RH Front Underhood Relay Center series/parallel cooling fan #2 relay cavity 87A and secondary cooling fan terminal B. 2. If a problem is found, repair as necessary. Was a problem found?	—	*Go to Step 81*	*Go to Step 57*

GC1089600329040X

Fig. 98 Cooling fan diagnosis (Part 4 of 10). Riviera

Step	Action	Value(s)	Yes	No
30	1. Check for a poor connection at the Underhood Relay Center series/parallel cooling fan #2 relay cavities 87A or 30. 2. If a problem is found, repair as necessary. Was a problem found?	—	*Go to Step 81*	*Go to Step 76*
31	1. Check for an open in CKT 532 between the low speed cooling fan relay harness connector cavity 87 and primary cooling fan harness connector terminal B. 2. If a problem is found, repair as necessary. Was a problem found?	—	*Go to Step 81*	*Go to Step 56*
32	Using scan tool, view A/C Request. Does the scan tool display Yes?	—	*PCM Controlled Air Conditioning*	*Go to Step 33*
33	Are both cooling fan(s) running at low speed?	—	*Go to Step 34*	*Go to Step 40*
34	Disconnect the low speed cooling fan relay. Are the cooling fans running?	—	*Go to Step 35*	*Go to Step 36*
35	Locate and repair short to voltage in CKT 532. Is action complete?	—	*Go to Step 81*	—
36	Using a test light connected to B+, probe low speed cooling fan relay harness connector cavity 86. Is the test light ON?	—	*Go to Step 38*	*Go to Step 37*
37	Replace the low speed cooling fan relay. Is action complete?	—	*Go to Step 81*	—
38	1. Turn OFF the ignition switch 2. Disconnect the blue PCM connector C1. 3. Probe low speed cooling fan relay harness connector cavity 86 with a test light connected to B+. Is the test light ON?	—	*Go to Step 39*	*Go to Step 77*
39	Locate and repair short to ground in the cooling fan 1 control circuit (CKT 335). Is action complete?	—	*Go to Step 81*	—
40	Are both cooling fans running at high speed?	—	*Go to Step 41*	*Go to Step 42*
41	View A/C High Pressure on the scan tool. Does the scan tool display voltage less than the specified value?	1.2V	*Go to Step 77*	*Go to Step 44*
42	1. Turn OFF the ignition switch. 2. Disconnect the PCM. 3. Turn ON the ignition switch. 4. Observe the cooling fans. Is the secondary cooling fan running at high speed?	—	*Go to Step 43*	*Go to Step 77*

GC1089600329050X

Fig. 98 Cooling fan diagnosis (Part 5 of 10). Riviera

Step	Action	Value(s)	Yes	No
53	Remove series/parallel cooling fan #2 relay from the RH Front Underhood Relay Center. Is the secondary cooling fan running at high speed?	—	*Go to Step 54*	*Go to Step 55*
54	Locate and repair short to B+ in CKT 409. Is action complete?	—	*Go to Step 81*	—
55	Locate and repair short to B+ in CKT 504. Is action complete?	—	*Go to Step 81*	—
56	1. Check for an open between series/parallel #2 relay cavity 30 in the RH Front Underhood Relay Center and primary cooling fan terminal A. 2. If a problem is found, repair as necessary. Was a problem found?	—	*Go to Step 81*	*Go to Step 79*
57	1. Check for an open in CKT 1350 between secondary cooling fan terminal A and ground. 2. If a problem is found, repair as necessary. Was a problem found?	—	*Go to Step 81*	*Go to Step 80*
58	1. Ignition ON, engine not running. 2. Remove the high speed cooling fan #3 relay from the RH Front Underhood Relay Center. 3. Install a test light between high speed cooling fan #3 relay cavity 86 in the RH Front Underhood Relay Center and B+. 4. Command Fan 2 ON using the scan tool output controls function. 5. Wait 6 seconds. 6. Observe the test light. Is the test light ON?	—	*Go to Step 61*	*Go to Step 59*
59	1. Remove the series/parallel cooling fan #2 relay from the RH Front Underhood Relay Center. 2. Install a test light between series/parallel cooling fan #2 relay cavity 86 in the RH Front Underhood Relay Center and B+. 3. Command Fan 2 ON using the scan tool output controls function. 4. Wait 6 seconds. 5. Observe the test light. Is the test light ON?	—	*Go to Step 78*	*Go to Step 60*
60	1. Turn OFF the ignition switch. 2. Disconnect the PCM. 3. Turn ON the ignition switch. 4. Check the cooling fan 2 control circuit (CKT 473) for an open or a short to voltage between series/parallel cooling fan #2 relay cavity 86 in the RH Front Underhood Relay Center and the PCM. 5. If a problem is found, repair as necessary. Was a problem found?	—	*Go to Step 81*	*Go to Step 77*

GC1089600329070X

Fig. 98 Cooling fan diagnosis (Part 7 of 10). Riviera

Step	Action	Value(s)	Yes	No
43	1. Check for a short to ground in the cooling fan 2 control circuit (CKT 473). 2. If a problem is found, repair as necessary. Was a problem found?	—	*Go to Step 81*	*Go to Step 52*
44	1. Turn OFF the ignition switch. 2. Disconnect the A/C refrigerant pressure sensor electrical connector. 3. Turn ON the ignition switch. 4. View A/C Pressure on the scan tool. Does the scan tool display voltage near the specified value?	0V	*Go to Step 46*	*Go to Step 45*
45	Probe the A/C refrigerant pressure signal circuit with a *J 39200* Digital Multimeter connected to the A/C refrigerant pressure sensor ground. Does the digital multimeter display voltage near the specified value?	0V	*Go to Step 77*	*Go to Step 51*
46	Probe the A/C refrigerant pressure sensor ground with a test light to B+. Is the test light ON?	—	*Go to Step 47*	*Go to Step 49*
47	Probe the A/C refrigerant pressure sensor 5 volt reference circuit B with a *J 39200* Digital Multimeter connected to the A/C refrigerant pressure sensor ground. Does the digital multimeter display voltage near the specified value?	5V	*Go to Step 48*	*Go to Step 50*
48	Replace the A/C refrigerant pressure sensor. Is action complete?	—	*Go to Step 81*	—
49	Locate and repair open or short to voltage in the A/C refrigerant pressure sensor ground circuit. Is action complete?	—	*Go to Step 81*	—
50	Locate and repair open or short to ground in the A/C refrigerant pressure sensor 5 volt reference B circuit. Is action complete?	—	*Go to Step 81*	—
51	Locate and repair short to voltage in the A/C refrigerant pressure signal circuit. Is action complete?	—	*Go to Step 81*	—
52	1. Remove the high speed cooling fan #3 relay from the RH Front Underhood Relay Center. 2. Observe the cooling fans. Is the secondary cooling fan running at high speed?	—	*Go to Step 53*	*Go to Step 70*

GC1089600329060X

Fig. 98 Cooling fan diagnosis (Part 6 of 10). Riviera

Step	Action	Value(s)	Yes	No
61	1. Turn OFF the ignition switch 2. Reinstall high speed cooling fan #3 relay. 3. Disconnect both cooling fan electrical connectors. 4. Turn ON the ignition switch. 5. Command Fan 2 ON using the scan tool output controls function. 6. Wait 6 seconds. 7. Probe terminal B (CKT 409) at the secondary cooling fan connector with a test light to ground. Is the test light ON?	—	*Go to Step 62*	*Go to Step 64*
62	Probe terminal A (CKT 504) at the primary cooling fan connector with a test light to B+. Is the test light ON?	—	*Go to Step 63*	*Go to Step 71*
63	1. Identify cause of inoperative cooling fan: • Open primary cooling fan motor windings. • Open secondary cooling fan motor windings. • Stalled cooling fan(s). 2. Replace the affected cooling fan motor. Is action complete?	—	*Go to Step 81*	—
64	1. Remove the high speed cooling fan #3 relay from the RH Front Underhood Relay Center. 2. Turn ON the ignition switch. 3. Probe high speed cooling fan #3 relay cavity 85 in the RH Front Underhood Relay Center with a test light connected to ground. Is the test light ON?	—	*Go to Step 66*	*Go to Step 65*
65	Locate and repair open in the ignition positive voltage circuit to high speed cooling fan #3 relay. Is action complete?	—	*Go to Step 81*	—
66	Probe high speed cooling fan #3 relay cavity 87 in the RH Front Underhood Relay Center with a test light connected to ground. Is the test light ON?	—	*Go to Step 68*	*Go to Step 67*
67	Locate and repair open in battery positive voltage circuit to high speed cooling fan #3 relay cavity 87. Is action complete?	—	*Go to Step 81*	—
68	1. Check CKT 409 for an open between secondary cooling fan terminal B and high speed cooling fan #3 relay cavity 30 in the RH Front Underhood Relay Center. 2. If a problem is found, repair as necessary. Was a problem found?	—	*Go to Step 81*	*Go to Step 69*

GC1089600329080X

Fig. 98 Cooling fan diagnosis (Part 8 of 10). Riviera

Step	Action	Value(s)	Yes	No
69	1. Check for poor terminal connections at high speed cooling fan #3 relay. 2. If a problem is found, repair as necessary. Was a problem found?	—	Go to Step 81	Go to Step 70
70	Replace high speed cooling fan #3 relay. Is action complete?	—	Go to Step 81	—
71	1. Remove the series/parallel cooling fan #2 relay. 2. Turn ON the ignition switch. 3. Probe series/parallel cooling fan #2 relay cavity 85 in the RH Front Underhood Relay Center with a test light connected to ground. Is the test light ON?	—	Go to Step 73	Go to Step 72
72	Locate and repair open in battery positive voltage circuit to series/parallel cooling fan #2 relay cavity 85 in the RH Front Underhood Relay Center. Is action complete?	—	Go to Step 81	—
73	Probe series/parallel cooling fan #2 relay cavity 87 in the RH Front Underhood Relay Center with a test light to B+. Is the test light ON?	—	Go to Step 75	Go to Step 74
74	Locate and repair open in CKT 1350 between series/parallel cooling fan #2 relay cavity 87 in the RH Front Underhood Relay Center cavity and ground. Is action complete?	—	Go to Step 81	—
75	1. Check for poor terminal connections at the series/parallel cooling fan #2 relay. 2. If a problem is found, repair as necessary. Was a problem found?	—	Go to Step 81	Go to Step 76
76	Replace the series/parallel cooling fan #2 relay. Is action complete?	—	Go to Step 81	—
77	Replace the PCM. **Important:** The replacement PCM must be programmed. Is action complete?	—	Go to Step 81	—
78	Repair open in the cooling fan 2 control circuit (CKT 473) between the series/parallel cooling fan #2 relay cavity 86 and the high speed cooling fan #3 relay cavity 86. Is action complete?	—	Go to Step 81	—
79	Replace the primary cooling fan motor. Is action complete?	—	Go to Step 81	—
80	Replace the secondary cooling fan motor. Is action complete?	Go to Step 81		

GC1089600329090X

Fig. 98 Cooling fan diagnosis (Part 9 of 10). Riviera

Step	Action	Value(s)	Yes	No
11	Do both cooling fans operate with Fan Relay 1 commanded ON then only Cooling Fan #1 (left) operate with All Relays commanded ON?	—	Go to *Electric Cooling Fan Diagnosis (Cooling Fan Symptom 4)*	Go to Step 12
12	Does neither cooling fan operate when Fan Relay 1 is commanded ON and also when All Relays are commanded ON?	—	Go to *Electric Cooling Fan Diagnosis (Cooling Fan Symptom 5)*	Go to Step 13
13	Does either cooling fan operate when All Relays is commanded OFF?	—	Refer to *Diagnostic Aids*	Go to Step 5
14	Repair the cause of no voltage. Possible cause include the following: • A blown relay supply fuse • An open fan relay • An open cooling fan relay control circuit Is the repair complete?	—	Go to Step 5	—

GC1089800402020X

Fig. 99 Cooling fan functional check (Part 2 of 2). 1998–2000 Seville & 2000 DeVille

Step	Action	Value(s)	Yes	No
	DEFINITION: No low speed operation of either cooling fan. High speed operation of cooling fan #1 (left) only. No DTCs set.			
1	Did you perform the Cooling Fan Functional Check?	—	Go to Step 2	Go to the *Cooling Fan Functional Check*
2	1. Disconnect Cooling Fan #2 (right). 2. Command Fans Low Speed On using the scan tool. 3. Using DMM *J 39200* measure the voltage to ground at Cooling Fan #2 connector terminal B (harness side). Is the voltage the same or more than the value specified?	10.0 volts	Go to Step 3	Go to Step 6
3	Jumper Cooling Fan #2 (right) connector terminals A and B together. Does Cooling Fan #1 operate?	—	Go to Step 8	Go to Step 4
4	1. With Cooling Fan #2 (right) connector still jumpered, remove S/P Relay. 2. Measure the voltage to ground at S/P Relay terminal 30. Is the voltage the same or more than the value specified?	10.0 volts	Go to Step 5	Go to Step 9
5	Jumper S/P Relay terminals 30 and 87A together. Does Cooling Fan #1 (left) operate?	—	Go to Step 10	Go to Step 11
6	1. Command all fans Off using the scan tool. 2. Remove Relay #2. 3. Measure the voltage to ground at Relay #2 terminal 30. Is the voltage the same or more than the value specified?	10.0 volts	Go to Step 7	Go to Step 12
7	1. Jumper Fan Relay #2 terminals 30 and 87 together. 2. Measure the voltage to ground at Cooling Fan #2 (right) connector terminal B. Is the voltage to ground the same or more than the value specified?	10.0 volts	Go to Step 13	Go to Step 14

GC1089800403010X

Fig. 100 Cooling fan symptom 1: no low speed cooling fan operation, high speed left fan only (Part 1 of 2). 1998–2000 Seville & 2000 DeVille

Step	Action	Value(s)	Yes	No
81	1. Engine coolant less than 100°C (212°F). 2. Turn the A/C OFF. 3. Engine running. Observe the cooling fans. Are the cooling fans running?	—	Go to Step 32	Go to Step 82
82	1. Command Fan 1 ON using the scan tool output tests function. 2. Observe the cooling fans. Are both cooling fans running at low speed?	—	Go to Step 83	Go to Step 8
83	1. Command Fan 2 ON using the scan tool output tests function. 2. Wait 6 seconds. 3. Observe the cooling fans. Are both cooling fans running at high speed?	—	System OK	Go to Step 58

GC1089600329100X

Fig. 98 Cooling fan diagnosis (Part 10 of 10). Riviera

Step	Action	Value(s)	Yes	No
1	Was the Powertrain On-Board Diagnostic (OBD) System Check performed?	—	Go to Step 2	Go to *Powertrain OBD System Check*
2	1. Ensure the engine coolant temperature is between the values specified. 2. Turn HVAC controls to OFF. 3. Start and idle the engine. 4. Using the scan tool select Output Tests and while viewing the Driver 1 display, command All Relays OFF for approximately 15 seconds. 5. Using the scan tool select Output Tests and while viewing the Quad Driver 1 display, command All Relays ON for approximately 15 seconds. Did the Driver 1 display ever indicate a *Fault*?	5°C - 100°C (41°F - 212°F)	Go to *DTC P1660 Cooling Fan Control Circuits*	Go to Step 3
3	With the engine idling turn A/C ON to maximum cooling. Have any other DTCs failed this ignition?	—	Go to DTCs that are set	Go to Step 4
4	1. Turn the key to LOCK. 2. Disconnect the PCM connector C2. 3. Using a test lamp connected to a know good ground probe PCM connector C2 terminals 32 and 33. Does the test lamp illuminate on both terminals?	—	Go to Step 5	Go to Step 14
5	1. Reconnect PCM connector C2 (if still Disconnected. 2. Turn the key on while leaving the engine OFF. 3. Ensure engine coolant temperature is below the value specified. 4. Observe fan operation while individually commanding Fan Relay 1 ON, then All Relays ON, then All Relays OFF. • With Fan Relay 1 commanded ON both fans should operate at low speed. • With All Relays commanded ON both fans should operate at high speed. • With All Relays commanded OFF both fans should not operate (unless the PCM detects a fault or high temperature condition). Do both cooling fans operate as commanded?	100°C (212°F)	System OK	Go to Step 6
6	Does only Cooling Fan #1 (left) operate with Fan Relay 1 commanded ON then both fans operate when All Relays are commanded ON?	—	Go to Step 7	Go to Step 8
7	Repair CKT 504 shorted to ground. Is the repair complete?	—	Go to Step 5	—
8	Does neither cooling fan operate with Fan Relay 1 commanded ON then only Cooling Fan #2 (right) operate with All Relays commanded ON?	—	Go to *Electric Cooling Fan Diagnosis (Cooling Fan Symptom 1)*	Go to Step 9
9	Does neither cooling fan operate with Fan Relay 1 commanded ON then only Cooling Fan #1 (left) operate with All Relays commanded ON?	—	Go to *Electric Cooling Fan Diagnosis (Cooling Fan Symptom 2)*	Go to Step 10
10	Do both cooling fans operate with Fan Relay 1 commanded ON then only Cooling Fan #2 (right) operate with All Relays commanded ON?	—	Go to *Electric Cooling Fan Diagnosis (Cooling Fan Symptom 3)*	Go to Step 11

GC1089800402010X

Fig. 99 Cooling fan functional check (Part 1 of 2). 1998–2000 Seville & 2000 DeVille

Step	Action	Value(s)	Yes	No
8	Replace Cooling Fan #2 (right). Is the action complete?	—	Go to the *Cooling Fan Functional Check* for repair verification.	—
9	Repair the open in CKT 504 between Cooling Fan #2 (right) and Fan S/P Relay. Is the action complete?	—	Go to the *Cooling Fan Functional Check* for repair verification.	—
10	Replace S/P Fan Relay. Is the action complete?	—	Go to the *Cooling Fan Functional Check* for repair verification.	—
11	Repair the open in CKT 409 between Fan S/P Relay and the splice. Is the action complete?	—	Go to the *Cooling Fan Functional Check* for repair verification.	—
12	Repair the open power feed circuit to Fan Relay #2 terminal 30. Is the action complete?	—	Go to the *Cooling Fan Functional Check* for repair verification.	—
13	Replace Fan Relay #2. Is the action complete?	—	Go to the *Cooling Fan Functional Check* for repair verification.	—
14	Repair the open in CKT 532 between Fan Relay #2 and Cooling Fan #2 (right). Is the action complete?	—	Go to the *Cooling Fan Functional Check* for repair verification.	—

GC1089800403020X

Fig. 100 Cooling fan symptom 1: no low speed cooling fan operation, high speed left fan only (Part 2 of 2). 1998–2000 Seville & 2000 DeVille

Step	Action	Value(s)	Yes	No
DEFINITION: No low speed operation of either cooling fan. High speed operation of cooling fan #2 (right) only. No DTCs set.				
1	Did you perform the Cooling Fan Functional Check?	—	*Go to Step 2*	Go to the *Cooling Fan Functional Check*
2	1. Disconnect Cooling Fan #1 (left). 2. At the Cooling Fan #1 (left) harness connector, jumper terminals A and B together. 3. Command Fans Low Speed On using the scan tool. Does Cooling Fan #2 (right) operate?	—	*Go to Step 5*	*Go to Step 3*
3	1. Remove Fan S/P Relay. 2. Jumper Fan S/P Relay terminals 30 and 87A together. 3. Command Fans Low Speed On using the scan tool. Does Cooling Fan #2 (right) operate?	—	*Go to Step 6*	*Go to Step 4*
4	With Fan S/P Relay still jumpered use DMM *J 39200* and measure the voltage to ground at Cooling Fan #1 connector terminal B (harness side). Is the voltage the same or more than the value specified?	10.0 volts	*Go to Step 7*	*Go to Step 8*
5	Replace Cooling Fan #1 (left). Is the action complete?	—	Go to the *Cooling Fan Functional Check* for repair verification.	—

GC1089800404010X

Fig. 101 Cooling fan symptom 2: no low speed cooling fan operation, high speed right fan only (Part 1 of 2). 1998–2000 Seville & 2000 DeVille

Step	Action	Value(s)	Yes	No
DEFINITION: Low speed operation of both fans. High speed operation of cooling fan #1 (left) only. No DTCs set.				
1	Did you perform the Cooling Fan Functional Check?	—	*Go to Step 2*	Go to the *Cooling Fan Functional Check*
2	1. Remove Fan S/P Relay. 2. Command High Speed Fans On using the scan tool. 3. Using DMM *J 39200* measure the voltage to ground at Fan S/P Relay terminal 86. Is the voltage the same or more than the value specified?	10.0 volts	*Go to Step 3*	*Go to Step 5*
3	1. Remove Fan Relay #1. 2. Measure the resistance between Fan S/P Relay terminal 85 and Fan Relay #1 terminal 86. Is the resistance the same or less than the value specified?	5 ohms	*Go to Step 4*	*Go to Step 6*
4	1. Reconnect Fan Relay #1. 2. Jumper Fan S/P Relay terminals 30 and 87 together. 3. Command Fans High Speed On using the scan tool. Do both cooling fans operate?	—	*Go to Step 8*	*Go to Step 7*
5	Repair the open power feed circuit to Fan S/P Relay terminal 86. Is the action complete?	—	Go to the *Cooling Fan functional Check* for repair verification.	—
6	Repair the open in CKT 473 between Fan S/P Relay terminal 85 and the splice. Is the action complete?	—	Go to the *Cooling Fan functional Check* for repair verification.	—
7	Repair the open in the ground circuit between Fan S/P Relay terminal 87 and ground. Is the action complete?	—	Go to the *Cooling Fan functional Check* for repair verification.	—
8	Replace Fan S/P Relay. Is the action complete?	—	Go to the *Cooling Fan functional Check* for repair verification.	—

GC1089800405000X

Fig. 102 Cooling fan symptom 3: low speed operation of both fans, high speed left fan only. 1998–2000 Seville & 2000 DeVille

Step	Action	Value(s)	Yes	No
6	Replace Fan S/P Relay. Is the action complete?	—	Go to the *Cooling Fan Functional Check* for repair verification.	—
7	Repair the open ground circuit to Cooling Fan #1 (left). Is the action complete?	—	Go to the *Cooling Fan Functional Check* for repair verification.	—
8	Repair the open in CKT 409 between Cooling Fan #1 (left) and Fan S/P Relay. Is the action complete?	—	Go to the *Cooling Fan Functional Check* for repair verification.	—

GC1089800404020X

Fig. 101 Cooling fan symptom 2: no low speed cooling fan operation, high speed right fan only (Part 2 of 2). 1998–2000 Seville & 2000 DeVille

Step	Action	Value(s)	Yes	No
DEFINITION: Low speed operation of both fans. High speed operation of cooling fan #2 (right) only. No DTCs set.				
1	Did you perform the Cooling Fan Functional Check?	—	*Go to Step 2*	Go to the *Cooling Fan Functional Check*
2	1. Remove Fan Relay #1. 2. Command Fans High Speed On using the scan tool. 3. Using DMM *J 39200* measure the voltage to ground at Fan Relay #1 terminal 85. Is the voltage the same or more than the value specified?	10.0 volts	*Go to Step 3*	*Go to Step 6*
3	Measure the voltage to ground at Fan Relay #1 terminal 30. Is the voltage the same or more than the value specified?	10.0 volts	*Go to Step 4*	*Go to Step 7*
4	1. Remove Fan S/P Relay. 2. Measure the resistance between Fan Relay #1 terminal 86 and Fan S/P Relay terminal 85. Is the resistance the same or less than the value specified?	5 ohms	*Go to Step 5*	*Go to Step 8*
5	Jumper Fan Relay #1 terminals 30 and 87 together. Does Cooling Fan #1 (left) operate?	—	*Go to Step 10*	*Go to Step 9*
6	Repair the open in the power feed circuit to Fan Relay #1 terminal 85. Is the action complete?	—	Go to the *Cooling Fan Functional Check* for repair verification.	—
7	Repair the open in the power feed circuit to Fan Relay #1 terminal 30. Is the action complete?	—	Go to the *Cooling Fan Functional Check* for repair verification.	—
8	Repair the open in CKT 473 between Fan Relay #1 terminal 86 and the splice. Is the action complete?	—	Go to the *Cooling Fan Functional Check* for repair verification.	—
9	Repair the open in CKT 409 between Fan Relay #1 terminal 87 and the splice. Is the action complete	—	Go to the *Cooling Fan Functional Check* for repair verification.	—
10	Replace Fan Relay #1. Is the action complete?	—	Go to the *Cooling Fan Functional Check* for repair verification.	—

GC1089800406000X

Fig. 103 Cooling fan symptom 4: low speed fan operation of both fans, high speed right fan only. 1998–2000 Seville & 2000 DeVille

Step	Action	Value(s)	Yes	No
DEFINITION: No fan operation on either high or low speed. No DTCs set.				
1	Did you perform the Cooling Fan Functional Check?	—	*Go to Step 2*	Go to the *Cooling Fan Functional Check*
2	Check the condition of the cooling fan Maxi fuse. Is the fuse OK?	—	*Go to Step 3*	*Go to Step 4*
3	1. Remove Fan Relay #2. 2. Using DMM *J 39200* measure the voltage to ground at Fan Relay #1 terminal 30. Is the voltage the same or more than the value specified?	10.0 volts	*Go to Step 8*	*Go to Step 9*
4	1. Turn the key to Lock. 2. Replace the Maxi fuse. Does the fuse immediately open?	—	*Go to Step 10*	*Go to Step 5*
5	1. Turn the key On. 2. Command Fans Low Speed On using the scan tool. Does the Maxi fuse open?	—	*Go to Step 11*	*Go to Step 6*
6	Command Fans High Speed On. Does the Maxi fuse blow?	—	*Go to Step 7*	Fault not present
7	1. Command all fans Off using the scan tool. 2. Replace the Maxi fuse. 3. Command Fans Low Speed On. Is only Cooling Fan #2 (right) operating?	—	*Go to Step 12*	*Go to Step 13*
8	Repair the open ground circuit to S/P Relay and Cooling Fan #1. Is the action complete?	—	Go to the *Cooling Fan Functional Check* for repair verification.	—
9	Repair the open power feed circuit to Relays #2 and #1 terminal 30. Is the action complete?	—	Go to the *Cooling Fan Functional Check* for repair verification.	—
10	Repair the short to ground in the power feed circuit to Relays #2 and #1 terminal 30. Is the action complete?	—	Go to the *Cooling Fan Functional Check* for repair verification.	—
11	Repair the short to ground in CKT 532 between Relay #2 and Cooling Fan #2 (right). Is the action complete?	—	Go to the *Cooling Fan Functional Check* for repair verification.	—
12	Replace Cooling Fan #1 (left). Is the action complete?	—	Go to the *Cooling Fan Functional Check* for repair verification.	—
13	Replace Cooling Fan #2 (right). Is the action complete?	—	Go to the *Cooling Fan Functional Check* for repair verification.	—

GC1089800407000X

Fig. 104 Cooling fan symptom 5: no low or high speed fan operation. 1998–2000 Seville & 2000 DeVille

Step	Action	Value(s)	Yes	No
8	Does the scan tool display A/C request as YES?	—	Diagnose A/C system.	*Go to Step 10*
9	Does the scan tool display A/C request as YES?	—	A/C Refrigerant Pressure Sensor	Diagnose A/C system.
10	**Important:** Program the replacement PCM. Replace the PCM. Is the action complete?	—	System OK	—

GC1080000439020X

Fig. 105 Cooling fan functional check (Part 2 of 2). 2000 Bonneville & LeSabre

Step	Action	Value(s)	Yes	No
9	1. Turn OFF the ignition. 2. Leave the test lamp installed. 3. Disconnect the PCM. 4. Turn ON the ignition, with the engine OFF. Is the test lamp still illuminated?	—	*Go to Step 14*	*Go to Step 16*
10	Repair the LH fan feed circuit for a short to voltage. Did you find and correct the condition?	—	Go to Cooling Fan Functional Check	*Go to Step 15*
11	Repair the RH fan feed circuit for a short to voltage. Is the action complete?	—	Go to Cooling Fan Functional Check	—
12	Repair the short to voltage in the series/parallel relay switch feed circuit. Is the action complete?	—	Go to Cooling Fan Functional Check	—
13	Replace the low speed cooling fan relay. Is the action complete?	—	Go to Cooling Fan Functional Check	—
14	Repair the high speed relay control circuit or the low speed relay control circuit for a short to ground. Is the action complete?	—	Go to Cooling Fan Functional Check	—
15	Replace the high speed cooling fan relay. Is the action complete?	—	Go to Cooling Fan Functional Check	—
16	**Important:** Program the replacement PCM. Replace the PCM. Is the action complete?	—	Go to Cooling Fan Functional Check	—

GC1080000440020X

Fig. 106 Cooling fan table 1 (Part 2 of 2). 2000 Bonneville & LeSabre

Step	Action	Value(s)	Yes	No
1	Did you perform the Powertrain On-Board Diagnostic (OBD) System Check?	—	*Go to Step 2*	Go to *A Powertrain On Board Diagnostic (OBD) System Check*
2	Are any DTCs set?	—	Go to applicable DTC Table	*Go to Step 3*
3	1. Install a scan tool. 2. Engine coolant temperature must be below the specified value for all the fan diagnoses. 3. Turn ON the Ignition, with the engine and A/C OFF. Are the cooling fans OFF?	100°C (212°F)	*Go to Step 4*	Go to Cooling Fan table #1
4	With a scan tool, command the low speed cooling fan relay ON. Are both cooling fans ON?	—	*Go to Step 5*	Go to Cooling Fan table #2
5	With a scan tool, command the high speed cooling fan relay ON. Do both cooling fans switch to high speed?	—	*Go to Step 6*	Go to Cooling Fan table #3
6	1. With a scan tool, exit outputs. 2. Idle the engine leaving the A/C OFF. Are the cooling fans ON?	—	*Go to Step 8*	*Go to Step 7*
7	Turn ON the A/C. Are the cooling fans ON?	—	System OK	*Go to Step 9*

GC1080000439010X

Fig. 105 Cooling fan functional check (Part 1 of 2). 2000 Bonneville & LeSabre

Step	Action	Value(s)	Yes	No
1	Did you perform the Cooling Fan Functional Check?	—	*Go to Step 2*	Go to Cooling Fan Functional Check
2	Disconnect the low speed fan relay. Are both fans OFF?	—	*Go to Step 8*	*Go to Step 3*
3	Disconnect the series/parallel fan relay. Are both fans OFF?	—	*Go to Step 4*	*Go to Step 10*
4	1. Disconnect the right fan. 2. Probe the fan feed terminal of the right fan connector using a test lamp that is connected to a good ground. Does the test lamp illuminate?	—	*Go to Step 11*	*Go to Step 5*
5	Probe the series/parallel fan relay switch feed circuit terminal at the right fan connector using a test lamp that is connected to a good ground. Does the test lamp illuminate?	—	*Go to Step 12*	*Go to Step 6*
6	Probe the high speed cooling fan relay control circuit at the series/parallel cooling fan relay connector using a test lamp that is connected to B+. Does the test lamp illuminate?	—	*Go to Step 7*	*Go to Step 13*
7	1. Turn OFF the ignition. 2. Leave the test lamp installed. 3. Disconnect the PCM. 4. Turn ON the ignition, with the engine OFF. Is the test lamp still illuminated?	—	*Go to Step 14*	*Go to Step 16*
8	Probe the low speed cooling fan relay control circuit at the low speed cooling fan relay connector using the test lamp that is connected to B+. Does the test lamp illuminate?	—	*Go to Step 9*	*Go to Step 13*

GC1080000440010X

Fig. 106 Cooling fan table 1 (Part 1 of 2). 2000 Bonneville & LeSabre

Step	Action	Value(s)	Yes	No
1	Did you perform the Cooling Fan Functional Check?	—	*Go to Step 2*	Go to Cooling Fan Functional Check
2	Did either fan turn ON when the low speed cooling fan relay was commanded ON?	—	*Go to Step 3*	*Go to Step 5*
3	1. Install a scan tool. 2. With a scan tool, command the low speed cooling fan relay ON. Did the other fan turn OFF?	—	*Go to Step 19*	*Go to Step 4*
4	Disconnect the high speed fan relay. Did the fan turn OFF?	—	*Go to Step 20*	*Go to Step 21*
5	1. With a scan tool, command the low speed cooling fan relay ON. 2. Disconnect the low speed fan relay. 3. Probe the low speed relay control circuit at the low speed relay connector using a test lamp that is connected to B+. Does the test lamp illuminate?	—	*Go to Step 6*	*Go to Step 13*
6	Probe both feed circuits at the low speed relay connector using a test lamp that is connected to ground. Does test lamp illuminate for both circuits?	—	*Go to Step 7*	*Go to Step 22*

GC1080000441010X

Fig. 107 Cooling fan table 2 (Part 1 of 3). 2000 Bonneville & LeSabre

Step	Action	Value(s)	Yes	No
7	**Important:** Leave jumper in place for remainder of this table. Connect a fused jumper wire between the switch feed circuit and the RH fan feed circuit at the low speed relay connector. Do both fans turn ON?	—	Go to Step 23	Go to Step 8
8	1. Disconnect the right fan. 2. Probe the fan feed circuit at the harness connector with a test lamp that is connected to a good ground. Does the test lamp illuminate?	—	Go to Step 9	Go to Step 24
9	Connect a second fused jumper wire between the fan harness connector terminals. Is the left fan ON?	—	Go to Step 16	Go to Step 10
10	1. Reconnect the right fan. 2. Disconnect the series/parallel fan relay. 3. Probe the switch feed circuit at the series/parallel fan relay connector using a test lamp that is connected to a good ground. Does the test lamp illuminate?	—	Go to Step 11	Go to Step 25
11	Using the second jumper wire, jumper the switch ignition feed circuit and the LH fan feed circuit together at the series/parallel relay connector. Do the fans come ON?	—	Go to Step 26	Go to Step 12
12	1. Reconnect series/parallel fan relay. 2. Disconnect the left fan. 3. Probe fan feed circuit terminal at the harness connector with a test lamp that is connected to a good ground. Is the left fan ON?	—	Go to Step 16	Go to Step 18
13	1. Test lamp still connected. 2. Turn OFF the ignition. 3. Disconnect the PCM. 4. Probe the low speed cooling fan relay control circuit at the PCM connector, with a fused jumper wire that is connected to a good ground. Is the test lamp ON?	—	Go to Step 20	Go to Step 21
14	Inspect the PCM connections. Did you find a problem and correct it?	—	Go to Cooling Fan Functional Check	Go to Step 27
15	Repair the low speed relay control circuit for an open or short to B+. Is the action complete?	—	Go to Cooling Fan Functional Check	—
16	Inspect the fan motor ground circuit for a open or the fan motor connections and repair as necessary. Did you find and correct the condition?	—	Go to Cooling Fan Functional Check	Go to Step 17
17	Replace the fan motor. Is the action complete?	—	Go to Cooling Fan Functional Check	—
18	Repair the LH fan feed circuit for an open. Is the action complete?	—	Go to Cooling Fan Functional Check	—

GC1080000441020X

Fig. 107 Cooling fan table 2 (Part 2 of 3). 2000 Bonneville & LeSabre

Step	Action	Value(s)	Yes	No
1	Did you perform the Cooling Fan Functional Check?	—	Go to Step 2	Go to Cooling Fan Functional Check
2	1. With a scan tool, command the low speed cooling fan relay ON. 2. Command high speed cooling fan relay ON while observing the fans. Did both fans operate with no change?	—	Go to Step 8	Go to Step 3
3	Did the right fan stop operating?	—	Go to Step 9	Go to Step 4
4	1. Disconnect low speed fan relay. 2. Probe the high speed relay control circuit at the high speed relay connector using a test lamp that is connected to B+. 3. Command the high speed cooling fan relay ON using a scan tool. Does the test lamp illuminate after several seconds?	—	Go to Step 5	Go to Step 12
5	Probe the coil feed circuit at the high speed relay connector using a test lamp that is connected to a good ground. Does the test lamp illuminate?	—	Go to Step 6	Go to Step 13
6	Probe the switch feed circuit at the high speed relay connector using a test lamp that is connected to a good ground. Does the test lamp illuminate?	—	Go to Step 7	Go to Step 14

GC1080000442010X

Fig. 108 Cooling fan table 3 (Part 1 of 2). 2000 Bonneville & LeSabre

Step	Action	Value(s)	Yes	No
19	Replace the fan which was not operating. Is the action complete?	—	Go to Cooling Fan Functional Check	—
20	Replace high speed fan relay. Is the action complete?	—	Go to Cooling Fan Functional Check	—
21	Repair the series/parallel relay switch feed circuit for a short to ground. Did you find and correct the condition?	—	Go to Cooling Fan Functional Check	Go to Step 26
22	Repair the open or the grounded circuit for the circuit that did not light. Is the action complete?	—	Go to Cooling Fan Functional Check	—
23	Replace the low speed fan relay. Is the action complete?	—	Go to Cooling Fan Functional Check	—
24	Repair the RH fan feed circuit for an open. Is the action complete?	—	Go to Cooling Fan Functional Check	—
25	Repair the series /parallel relay switch feed circuit for an open. Is the action complete?	—	Go to Cooling Fan Functional Check	—
26	Replace the series/parallel fan relay. Is the action complete?	—	Go to Cooling Fan Functional Check	—
27	**Important:** Program the replacement PCM. Replace the PCM. Is the action complete?	—	Go to Cooling Fan Functional Check	—

GC1080000441030X

Fig. 107 Cooling fan table 2 (Part 3 of 3). 2000 Bonneville & LeSabre

Step	Action	Value(s)	Yes	No
7	Jumper the switch ignition feed circuit and the LH fan feed circuit together at the high speed relay connector. Is the right fan ON?	—	Go to Step 15	Go to Step 16
8	1. Turn OFF the ignition. 2. Disconnect the PCM. 3. Disconnect the low speed fan relay. 4. Jumper the switch feed circuit and the RH fan feed circuit together at the low speed relay connector locations. 5. Turn the ignition ON. 6. Probe the PCM harness connector for the high speed cooling fan relay control circuit with a fused jumper that is connected to a good ground. Do the fans switch from low to high speed?	—	Go to Step 22	Go to Step 17
9	1. Disconnect the series/parallel fan relay. 2. Probe the high speed relay control circuit at the series parallel relay connector using a test lamp that is connected to B+. 3. Command the high speed cooling fan relay ON using a scan tool. Does the test lamp illuminate?	—	Go to Step 10	Go to Step 18
10	Probe the ground circuit at the series /parallel relay connector using a test lamp that is connected to B+. Does the test lamp illuminate?	—	Go to Step 11	Go to Step 19
11	Probe the coil feed circuit at the series /parallel relay connector using a test lamp that is connected to a good ground. Does the test lamp illuminate?	—	Go to Step 20	Go to Step 21
12	Repair the high speed relay control circuit for an open between the high speed fan relay and the splice. Is the action complete?	—	Go to Cooling Fan Functional Check	—
13	Repair the open in the high speed relay coil feed circuit. Is the action complete?	—	Go to Cooling Fan Functional Check	—
14	Repair the open in the high speed relay switch feed circuit. Is the action complete?	—	Go to Cooling Fan Functional Check	—
15	Replace the high speed fan relay. Is the action complete?	—	Go to Cooling Fan Functional Check	—
16	Repair the open in the LH fan feed circuit between the high speed fan relay and the splice. Is the action complete?	—	Go to Cooling Fan Functional Check	—
17	Repair the high speed fan relay control circuit for an open or for a short to B+. Is the action complete?	—	Go to Cooling Fan Functional Check	—
18	Repair the open in the high speed fan relay control circuit between the series/parallel fan relay and the splice. Is the action complete?	—	Go to Cooling Fan Functional Check	—
19	Repair the open in the ground circuit. Is the action complete?	—	Go to Cooling Fan Functional Check	—

GC1080000442020X

Fig. 108 Cooling fan table 3 (Part 2 of 2). 2000 Bonneville & LeSabre

Saturn

NOTE: On Air Bag Equipped Models, Refer To "Air Bag System Precautions" Located In The Front Of This Manual For System Disarming & Arming Procedures.

NOTE: "Electrical Symbol & Wire Color Code Identification" Located In The Front Of This Manual Can Be Used As An Aid When Using Wiring Circuits Found In This Section.

NOTE: Refer To "Computer Relearn Procedures "Located In The Front Of This Manual For Computer Relearn Procedures.

INDEX

DESCRIPTION

On models equipped with A/C, the cooling fan has five unequally spaced blades to provide air flow through the radiator and condenser. the fan is driven by an electric motor which is attached to the radiator support. The fan motor is activated by a coolant temperature switch.

On models less A/C, the cooling fan has four unequally spaced blades that have curled tips to provide minimum noise. A fan shroud is used to prevent recirculation of air around the fan.

SYSTEM DIAGNOSIS & TESTING

Refer to **Figs. 1 through 3,** for electric cooling fan wiring circuit.

COOLING FAN INOPERATIVE

Refer to **Figs. 4 through 6** for electric cooling fan inoperative diagnosis.

COOLING FAN OPERATES CONSTANTLY

Refer to **Figs. 7 and 8** when diagnosing a cooling fan which operates constantly.

COMPONENT REPLACEMENT

COOLING FAN ASSEMBLY

1.9L Engine

1. Remove intake air ducts and disconnect temperature sensor connector.
2. Disconnect wiring harness from cooling fan motor.
3. Loosen and remove top hold-down bolts from cooling fan assembly.

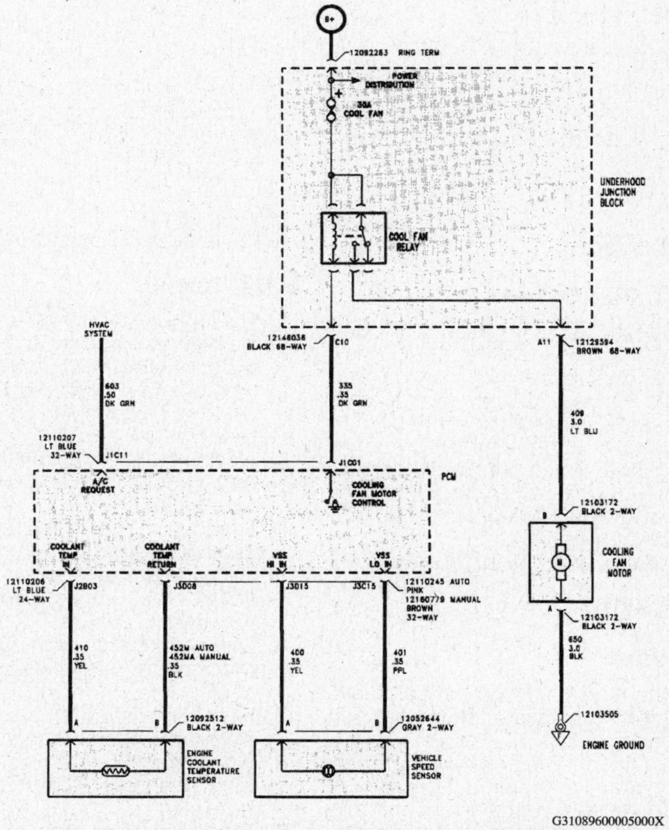

Fig. 1 Cooling fan wiring circuit. 1997–99

4. **On models equipped with automatic transaxle and A/C,** it may be necessary to loosen top transaxle oil cooler line for clearance.
5. **On all models,** lift cooling fan off of lower mounting brackets. Move assembly to left and rotate counterclockwise while lifting upward past upper radiator hose.
6. Remove cooling fan assembly from vehicle.
7. Reverse procedure to install.

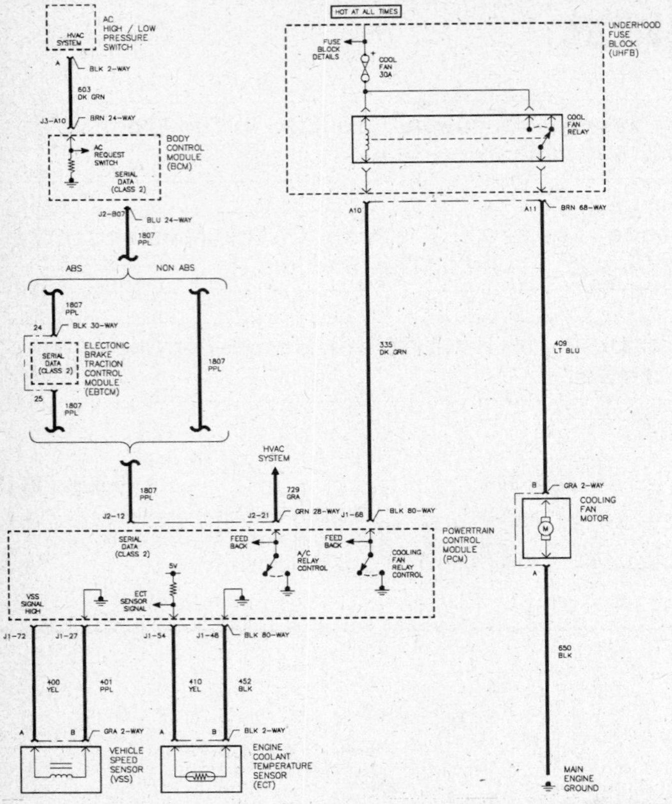

G31089900013000X

Fig. 2 Cooling fan wiring circuit. 2000 w/1.9L engine

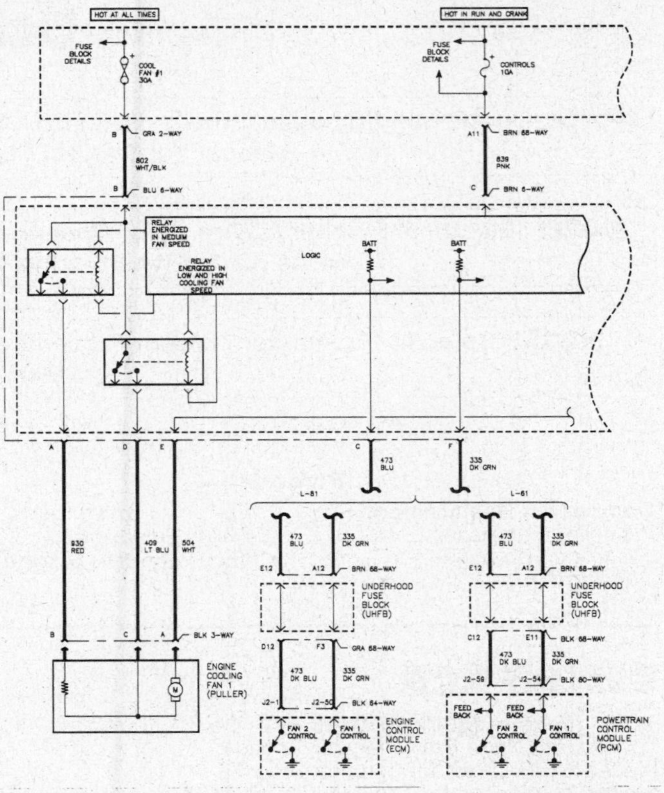

G31089900014010X

Fig. 3 Cooling fan wiring circuit (Part 1 of 3). 2000 w/2.2L & 3.0L engines

PUSHER FAN

2.2L & 3.0L Engines

1. Disconnect pusher fan electrical connector.
2. Release tabs, then remove pusher fan harness from puller fan shroud and push harness clear of radiator end.
3. Raise and support vehicle, then remove pusher fan to condenser retaining nut.
4. Pull lower fan shroud forward, then remove fan.
5. Reverse procedure to install.

PULLER FAN

2.2L Engine

1. Disconnect both cooling fan electrical connectors, then slide connectors out of retainers.
2. Remove pusher fan electrical harness from fan shroud retainer tabs, then wiring harness from clamp on fan shroud.
3. Remove fan shroud to radiator bolts, then fan and shroud assembly.
4. Reverse procedure to install.

3.0L Engine

1. Disconnect battery ground. **It is not required to disconnect fan control module electrical connector.**
2. Remove fan control module by sliding up and off bracket. Lay module and wiring aside.
3. Remove battery insulator cover, then battery hold down and fan control module bracket.
4. Remove battery, then drain engine coolant into a suitable container.
5. Remove power steering fluid reservoir to fan shroud bolts, position reservoir rearward in vehicle.
6. Disconnect both cooling fan electrical connectors, then slide connectors out of retainers.
7. Remove pusher fan electrical harness from fan shroud retainer tabs.
8. Disconnect auxiliary water pump electrical connector, then remove harness from clip.
9. Remove upper transaxle cooler line from radiator, then unsnap from retainer at radiator end.
10. Remove auxiliary water pump outlet hose from radiator, then remove upper radiator hose.
11. Raise and support vehicle, then remove auxiliary water pump inlet hose from radiator.
12. Lower vehicle, then remove fan shroud to radiator bolts.
13. Remove fan and shroud assembly from vehicle.
14. Reverse procedure to install.

COOLING FAN MOTOR

1.9L Engine

1. Remove cooling fan assembly as described under " Cooling Fan Assembly."
2. While holding fan, remove fan blade to motor nut (lefthand thread). Pull fan blade off of motor shaft.
3. Remove screws securing fan motor to shroud.
4. Remove motor from fan shroud.
5. Reverse procedure to install. **Torque** motor nut to 27–44 inch lbs.

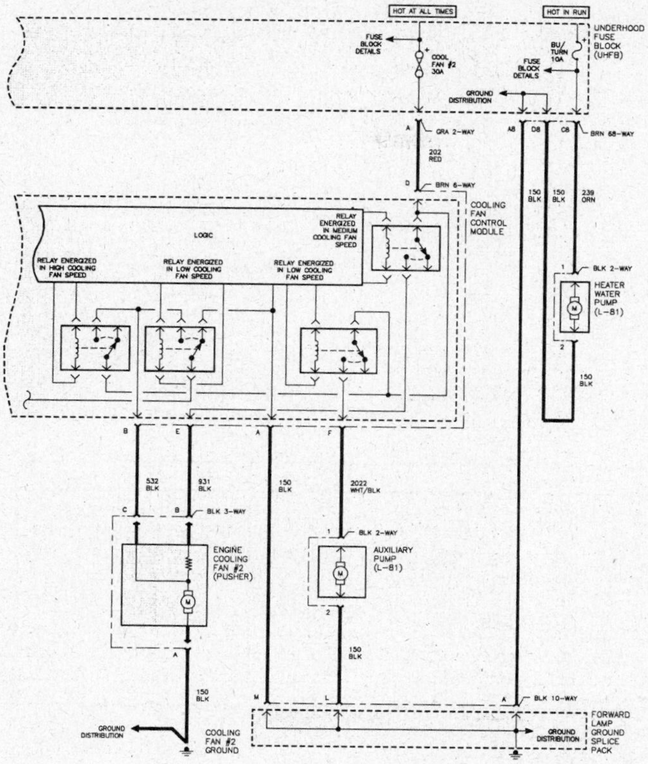

G31089900014020X

Fig. 3 Cooling fan wiring circuit (Part 2 of 3). 2000 w/2.2L & 3.0L engines

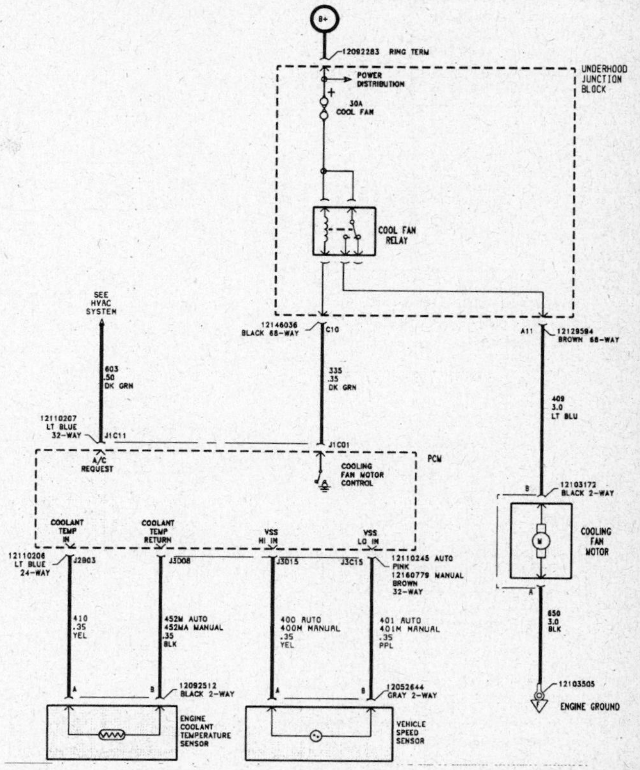

G31089900014030X

Fig. 3 Cooling fan wiring circuit (Part 3 of 3). 2000 w/2.2L & 3.0L engines

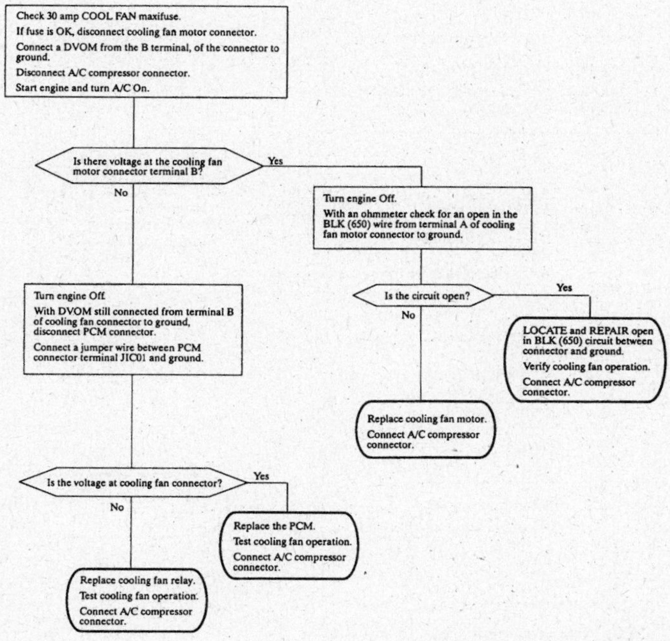

G31089600007000X

Fig. 4 Cooling fan inoperative diagnosis. 1997–99 w/1.9L engine & 2000 w/3.0L engine

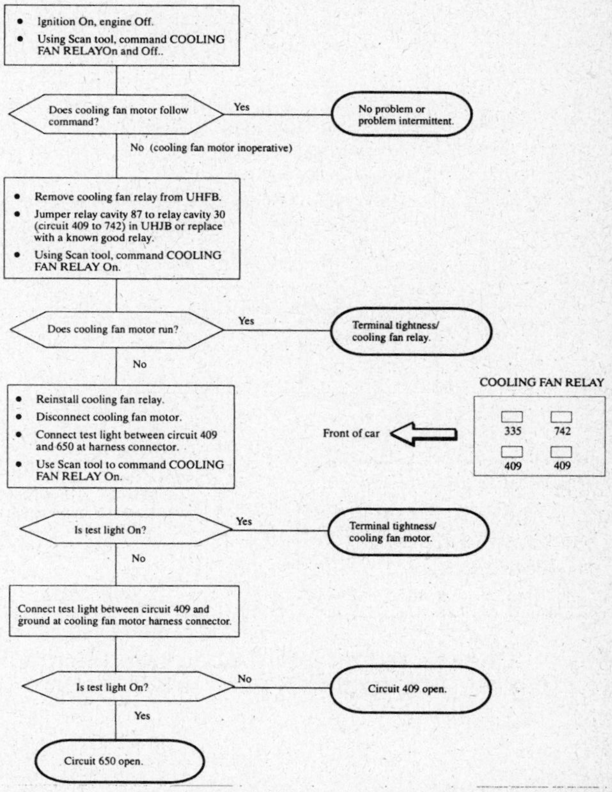

G31089900015000X

Fig. 5 Cooling fan inoperative diagnosis. 2000 w/1.9L engine

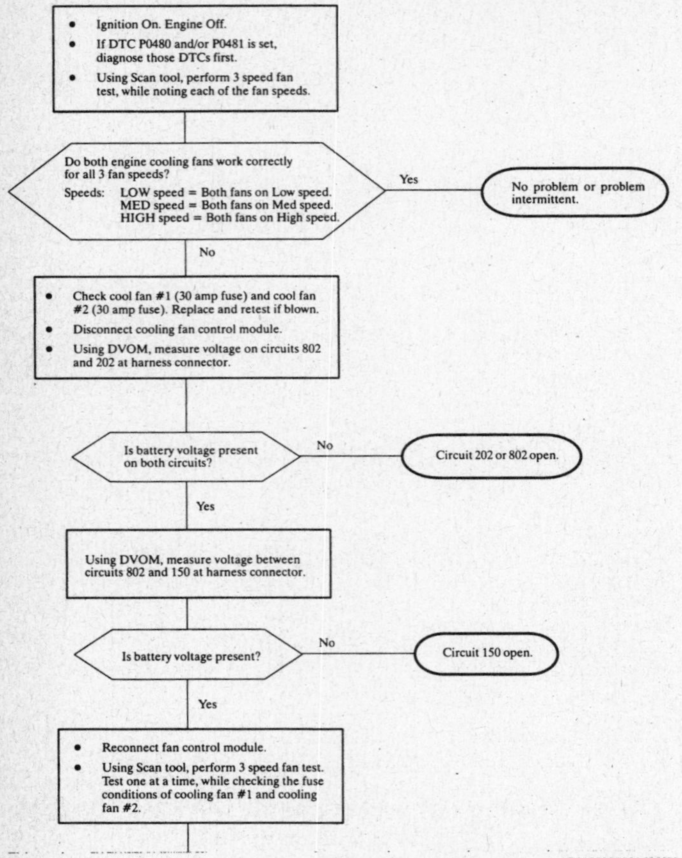

G31089900016010X

Fig. 6 Cooling fan inoperative diagnosis (Part 1 of 2). 2.2L engine

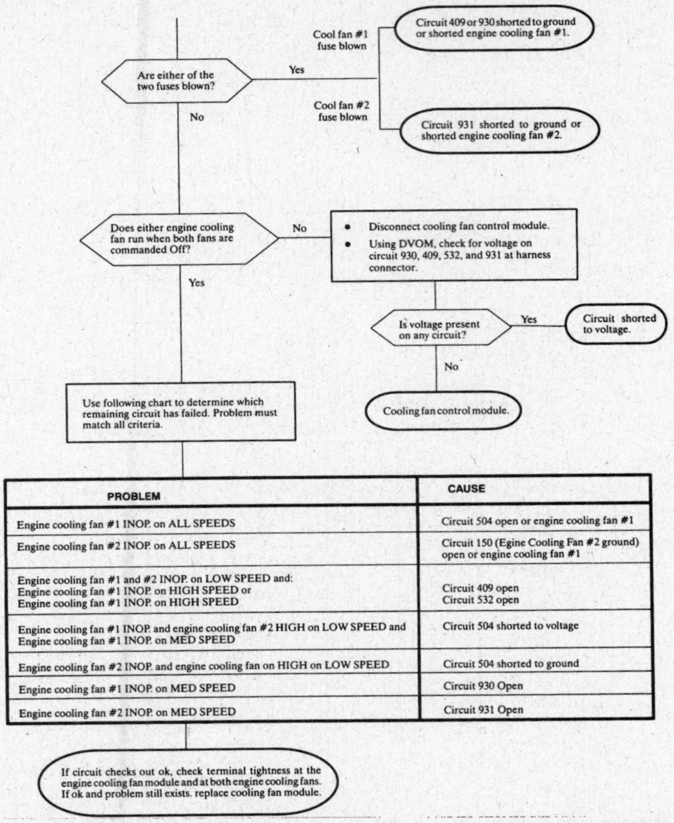

PROBLEM	CAUSE
Engine cooling fan #1 INOP. on ALL SPEEDS	Circuit 504 open or engine cooling fan #1
Engine cooling fan #2 INOP. on ALL SPEEDS	Circuit 150 (Egine Cooling Fan #2 ground) open or engine cooling fan #1
Engine cooling fan #1 and #2 INOP. on LOW SPEED and: Engine cooling fan #1 INOP. on HIGH SPEED or Engine cooling fan #1 INOP. on HIGH SPEED	Circuit 409 open Circuit 532 open
Engine cooling fan #1 INOP. and engine cooling fan #2 HIGH on LOW SPEED and Engine cooling fan #1 INOP. on MED SPEED	Circuit 504 shorted to voltage
Engine cooling fan #2 INOP. and engine cooling fan on HIGH on LOW SPEED	Circuit 504 shorted to ground
Engine cooling fan #1 INOP. on MED SPEED	Circuit 930 Open
Engine cooling fan #2 INOP. on MED SPEED	Circuit 931 Open

G31089900016020X

Fig. 6 Cooling fan inoperative diagnosis (Part 2 of 2). 2.2L engine

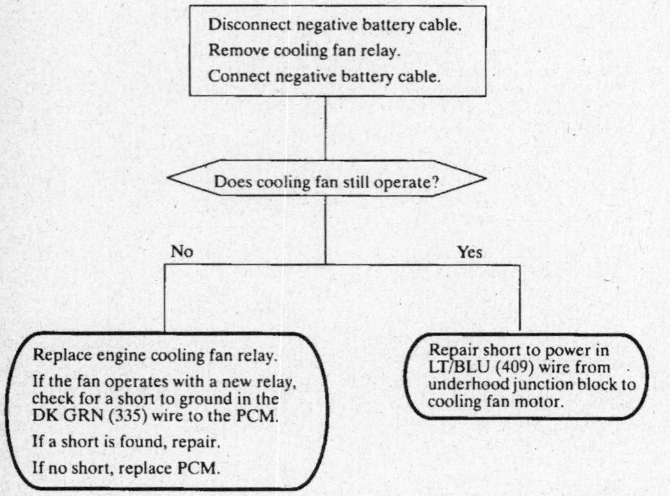

G31089600006000X

Fig. 7 Cooling fan constant operation diagnosis. 1997–99 1.9L engine & 2000 w/3.0L engine

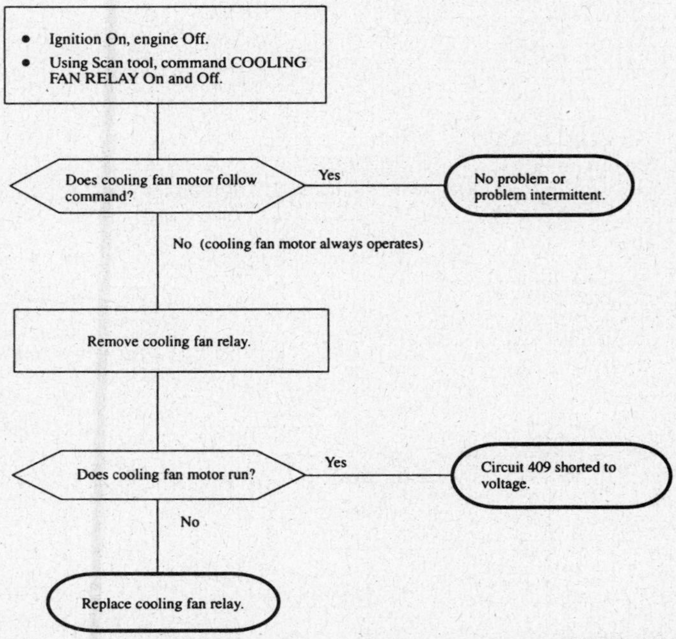

G31089900017000X

Fig. 8 Cooling fan constant operation diagnosis. 2000 w/1.9L engine

STARTER MOTORS

TABLE OF CONTENTS

AC-Delco Starters, General Motors

NOTE: Refer To "Computer Relearn Procedures " Located In The Front Of This Manual For Computer Relearn Procedures.

NOTE: Refer to "Air Bag System Precautions " in the front of this manual for system disarming and arming procedures.

INDEX

APPLICATION CHART

Year	Engine	VIN①	Ident. No.
ACHIEVA, ALERO, GRAND AM & SKYLARK			
1997–98	2.4L	T	10465493
	3.1L	M	10465494
1999-2000	2.4L	T	10465459
	3.4L	E	10465386
AURORA & RIVIERA			
1997–99	3.8L	1	10465309
	3.8L	K	10465309
	4.0L	C	10465294
BONNEVILLE, LESABRE, LSS & 88			
1997	3.8L	K	10465492
	3.8L	1	10455066
1998–2000	3.8L	K	10465421
	3.8L	1	10465309
CAMARO & FIREBIRD			
1997	3.8L	K	10465309
	5.7L	P	10465293
1998–2000	3.8L	K	10465421
	5.7L	G	10465385
CAVALIER & SUNFIRE			
1997	2.2L	4	10465494
	2.4L	T	10465493
1998	2.2L	4	②
	2.4L	T	10465493

Continued

APPLICATION CHART—Continued

Year	Engine	VIN①	Ident. No.
CAVALIER & SUNFIRE			
1999–2000	2.2L	4	10465459
	2.4L	T	10465386
CORVETTE			
1997–2000	5.7L	G	10465385
CUTLASS & MALIBU			
1997	3.1L	M	10465384
	2.4L	T	10465386
1998–99	2.4L	T	10465386
	3.1L	M	10465459
2000	3.1L	M	10465459
CENTURY, CUTLASS SUPREME, GRAND PRIX, INTRIGUE, LUMINA, MONTE CARLO & REGAL			
1997	3.1L	M	10465384
	3.4L	X	10465309
	3.8L	K	10465492
	3.8L	1	10465309
1998–99	3.1L	M	10465459
	3.5L	H	10465422
	3.8L	1	10465309
1998–2000	3.8L	1	10465309
	3.8L	K	10465421
2000	3.1L	J	10465459
DEVILLE, ELDORADO & SEVILLE			
1997–2000	4.6L	9	10465294
	4.6L	Y	10465294
IMPALA			
2000	3.4L	E	PG260 F1
	3.8L	K	PG260 F2
PARK AVENUE			
1997	3.8L	K	10465492
	3.8L	1	10465309
1998–2000	3.8L	1	10465309
	3.8L	K	10465421

①— The eighth digit of VIN denotes engine code.
②— Models w/first design use No. 10465494. Models w/second design use No. 10465459.

PRECAUTIONS

BATTERY GROUND CABLE

Prior to service, disconnect battery ground cable and isolate as required.

DESCRIPTION

SD SERIES

The AC-Delco SD series starter, **Fig. 1**, is a direct drive unit with electromagnetic fields. This starter has an extruded field frame and an overrunning clutch type drive. The overrunning clutch is operated by a solenoid switch mounted to a flange on the drive housing.

The solenoid is attached to the drive end housing by two screws. The cover can be removed to inspect the contacts and contact disc, but the switch is serviced as an assembly only.

Most motors of this type have graphite and oil impregnated bronze bearings which ordinarily require no added lubrication except at time of overhaul when a few drops of light engine oil should be placed on each bearing before assembly.

PG SERIES

The AC-Delco PG series starter, **Fig. 2**, is a planetary gear reduction, permanent magnet field starter. This starter has an anodized steel field frame and an overrunning clutch type drive. The overrunning clutch is operated by a solenoid switch mounted to a flange on the drive housing.

The permanent magnet motor and planetary gear reduction unit allow higher motor RPM while the starter is engaged, for reduced current draw and more efficient operation.

The armature is supported by a ball bearing at the commutator end and is supported within the planetary unit at the drive end. The planetary shaft is supported by a ball bearing within the stationary internal gear at the motor end and a bushing at the opposite end.

TROUBLESHOOTING

SLOW OR NOT CRANKING

Perform the following preliminary inspections to isolate the problem:

1. Turn headlamps On.
2. Ensure headlamps are burning with normal intensity.
3. If headlamps are burning dimly, inspect battery charge condition. Charge or replace as required.
4. If battery is fully charged, operate starter motor.
5. Note whether headlamps go out, dim considerably, or stay bright without starter activating.

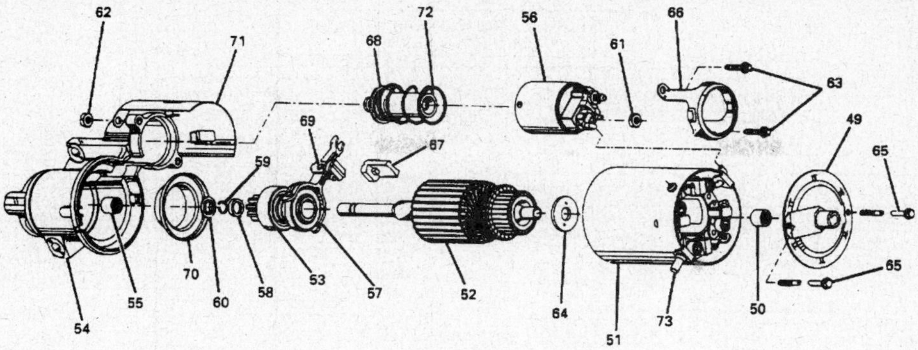

49 FRAME, STARTER COMMUTATOR END
50 BEARING, STARTER ARMATURE COMMUTATOR END
51 FRAME KIT, STARTER WITH FIELD
52 ARMATURE, STARTER
53 DRIVE, STARTER
54 HOUSING, STARTER DRIVE
55 BEARING, STARTER DRIVE SHAFT DRIVE END
56 SWITCH, STARTER SOLENOID
57 LEVER, STARTER SHIFT
58 COLLAR, STARTER DRIVE STOP
59 RETAINER, STARTER DRIVE STOP COLLAR
60 COLLAR, STARTER DRIVE THRUST
61 NUT, STARTER SOLENOID SWITCH OUTER, 10 N·m (89 LB. IN.)
62 NUT, STARTER MOTOR HEAT SHEILD, 8 N·m (71 LB. IN.)
63 BOLT/SCREW, STARTER SOLENOID SWITCH CLAMP, 11 N·m (97 LB. IN.)
64 WASHER, STARTER ARMATURE BRAKE COMMUTATOR END
65 BOLT/SCREW, COMMUTATOR END FRAME, 8.5 N·m (75 LB. IN.)
66 CLAMP, STARTER SOLENOID SWITCH
67 PLUG, STARTER SHIFT LEVER RETAINER
68 PLUNGER, STARTER SOLENOID SWITCH
69 RETAINER, STARTER SHIFT LEVER
70 SHIELD, STARTER DRIVE HOUSING
71 SHIELD, STARTER MOTOR HEAT
72 SPRING, STARTER SOLENOID SWITCH PLUNGER
73 TUBE, STARTER DRAIN

GC1129100028000A

Fig. 1 Exploded view of AC-Delco SD series starter motor (SD260 shown)

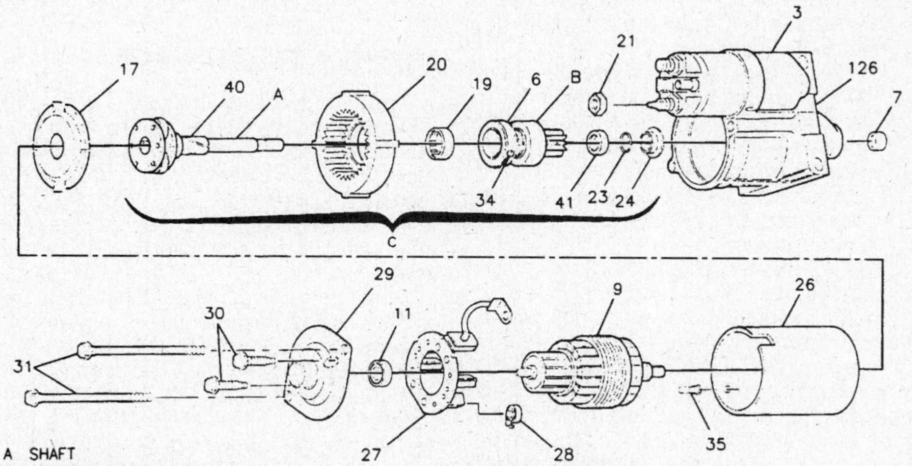

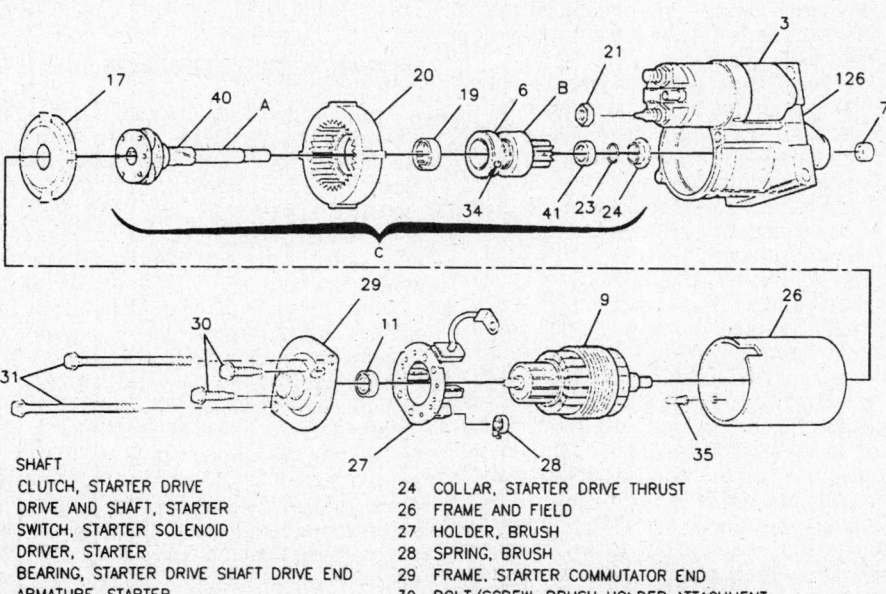

A SHAFT
B CLUTCH, STARTER DRIVE
C DRIVE AND SHAFT, STARTER
3 SWITCH, STARTER SOLENOID
6 DRIVER, STARTER
7 BEARING, STARTER DRIVE SHAFT DRIVE END
9 ARMATURE, STARTER
11 BEARING, COMMUTATOR ENDB BALL
17 SHIELD, PLANETARY GEARS
19 BEARING, INTERNAL GEAR ROLLER
20 GEAR, INTERNAL TOOTH
21 NUT, FIELD LEAD TO SOLENOID
23 RETAINER, STARTER DRIVE STOP COLLAR
24 COLLAR, STARTER DRIVE THRUST
26 FRAME AND FIELD
27 HOLDER, BRUSH
28 SPRING, BRUSH
29 FRAME, STARTER COMMUTATOR END
30 BOLT/SCREW, BRUSH HOLDER ATTACHMENT
31 THROUGH-BOLT/SCREW, STARTER
34 PIN, SHIFT COLLAR
35 TUBE, DRAIN
40 SHAFT AND GEAR
41 COLLAR, STARTER DRIVE STOP
126 HOUSING, STARTER DRIVE

GC1129500067000X

Fig. 2 Exploded view of AC-Delco PG series starter motor (PG250 shown)

6. Refer to the following diagnostic procedures as applicable.

Lamps Go Out

If the lamps go out as the starter switch is closed, it indicates a poor connection between the battery and starter motor.

1. Inspect battery terminals.
2. If corroded, remove, clean and install again.
3. Apply corrosion inhibitor to terminals to retard formation of corrosion.

Lamps Dim

If the lamps dim considerably as the starter switch is closed and the starter operates slowly or not at all, perform the following:

1. Inspect for a discharged battery. Recharge or replace as required.
2. If the battery is fully charged, inspect the engine or the starter motor.
3. Inspect the engine for tight bearings, pistons, or other components.
4. Inspect engine timing and adjust as required.
5. Inspect for heavy engine oil. Low temperatures thicken engine oil and add considerable load to starting system.
6. Inspect starter motor for bent armature, loose pole screws, or worn bearings.
7. Inspect for thrown armature windings or commutator bars.

Lamps Stay Bright, No Cranking Action

Inspect for an open circuit in the starter, the starter switch or control circuit.

1. Place a heavy jumper lead across solenoid main terminals.
2. Starter should engage and operate.
3. If starter fails to perform as indicated, remove and inspect as required.

STARTER DRIVE PROBLEMS

If the starter does not turn over at all or if it drags, inspect the starter or electrical supply system. If the starter is noisy, if it turns but does not engage the engine, or if the starter will not disengage after the engine is started, proceed as follows:

1. Remove starter.
2. Inspect for worn or chipped ring gear or starter pinion.
3. Inspect pinion clearance.
4. Inspect for a bent starter armature shaft. Maximum radial runout is .003 inch.

Drive Clutch Failure

The overrunning clutch is directly activated by a fork and lever. If the clutch will not turn the engine over, inspect for worn out overrunning clutch. Proper meshing of the pinion is controlled by the end clearance between the pinion gear and the starter housing or pinion stop, if used.

1. Inspect and adjust pinion clearance (if applicable).
2. If pinion clearance is non-adjustable, remove starter and inspect for excessive wear of solenoid linkage, shift

lever mechanism, or improper assembly of components.
3. Inspect overrunning clutch for signs of overheating.
4. If clutch shows signs of overheating (bluish color), inspect for rust or gum buildup between armature shaft and drive, or for burred splines.
5. Clean or deburr as required.
6. Overrunning clutches are not serviceable. Replace as required.

Drive Failure

If a Bendix type drive does not engage, inspect the following:

1. Inspect for a broken drive spring, or sheared drive spring bolts.
2. If spring is broken, or spring bolts are sheared off, remove drive and replace damaged components.
3. Inspect screw shaft.
4. If screw shaft threads are gummed or rusty, clean with kerosene or steel wool.
5. Ensure flywheel has adequate ventilation. Inspect breather hole in bottom of flywheel housing and clean if required.
6. If screw shaft threads are clean and rust free, inspect for mechanical failure within the drive itself.

SOLENOID SWITCHES

The solenoid switch on a cranking motor closes the circuit between the battery and the cranking motor and also shifts the drive pinion into mesh with the engine flywheel ring gear. This is done by means of a linkage between the solenoid switch plunger and the shift lever on the cranking motor.

There are two windings in the solenoid: a pull-in winding and a hold-in winding. Both windings are energized when the external control switch is closed. They produce a magnetic field which pulls the plunger in so that the drive pinion is shifted into mesh, and the main contacts in the solenoid switch are closed to connect the battery directly to the cranking motor. Closing the main switch contacts shorts out the pull-in winding since this winding is connected across the main contacts. The magnetism produced by the hold-in winding is sufficient to hold the plunger in, and shorting out the pull-in winding reduces drain on the battery. When the control switch is opened, it disconnects the hold-in winding from the battery. When the hold-in winding is disconnected from the battery, the shift lever spring withdraws the plunger from the solenoid, opening the solenoid switch contacts and at the same time withdrawing the drive pinion from mesh. Proper operation of the switch depends on maintaining a definite balance between the magnetic strength of the pull-in and hold-in windings.

This balance is determined by the size of the wire and the number of turns specified. An open circuit in the hold-in winding or attempts to crank with a discharged battery will cause the switch to chatter.

DIAGNOSIS & TESTING

Refer to **Fig. 3** when diagnosing AC-Delco starter motors.

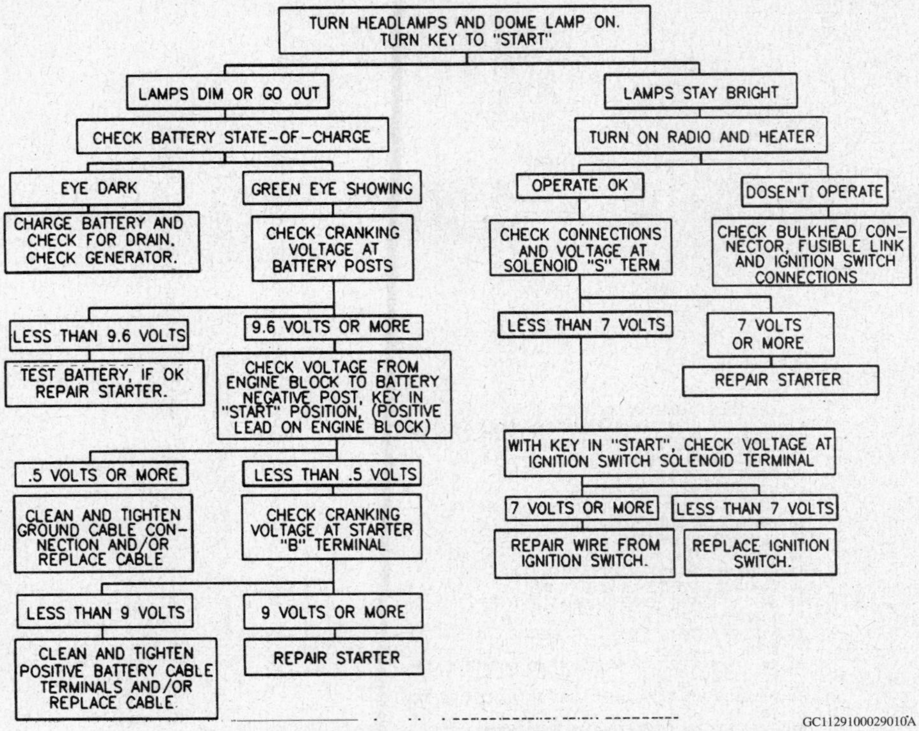

Fig. 3 AC-Delco starter motor diagnosis (Part 1 of 2)

INSPECTING CIRCUIT w/VOLTMETER

Excessive resistance in the circuit between the battery and starter will reduce cranking performance. The resistance can be inspected by using a voltmeter to measure voltage drop in the circuits while the starter is operated. Inspect for the following three conditions:

1. Voltage drop between vehicle frame and grounded battery terminal post.
2. Voltage drop between vehicle frame and starter motor field frame.
3. Voltage drop between insulated battery terminal post and starter motor terminal stud, or the battery terminal stud of the solenoid.

Measurements should show no more than one tenth (.1) volt drop when the starter motor is cranking the engine. Do not use the starter for more than 30 seconds at a time to avoid overheating it.

If excessive voltage drop is found, disconnect the cables, clean the connections, then reconnect the cables. A coating of petroleum jelly on the battery cables and terminal clamps will retard corrosion.

On some models, extra long battery cables may be required due to the location of the battery and starter. This may result in somewhat higher voltage drop than the above recommended .1 volt. To determine the normal voltage drop, test several comparable vehicles and compare the results. If the voltage drop is well above the normal figure for all vehicles inspected, abnormal resistance will be indicated and corrections can be made as required.

FREE SPEED TEST

With the circuit connected as outlined in **Fig. 4,** use a tachometer to measure armature revolutions per minute. Refer to "Starter Specifications" for data. Failure of the motor to perform to specifications may be due to tight or dry bearings, or high resistance connections.

PINION CLEARANCE

There is no provision for adjusting pinion clearance on this type motor. When the shift lever mechanism is properly assembled, the pinion clearance should fall within the limits of .010–.160 inch. If the clearance is not within these limits, inspect for excessive wear of the solenoid linkage or shift lever yoke buttons.

Pinion clearance should be inspected after the motor has been disassembled and assembled again. Disconnect motor field coil connector from solenoid terminal and insulate end. Connect one battery lead to solenoid switch terminal and the other lead to the solenoid frame, **Fig. 5.** Using a jumper lead connected to the solenoid motor terminal, momentarily flash the lead to the solenoid frame. This will shift the pinion into the cranking position until the battery is disconnected.

After energizing the solenoid with the clutch shifted toward the pinion stop retainer, push the pinion back toward the commutator end as far as possible to take up any slack movement, then inspect the clearance with a feeler gauge, **Fig. 6.**

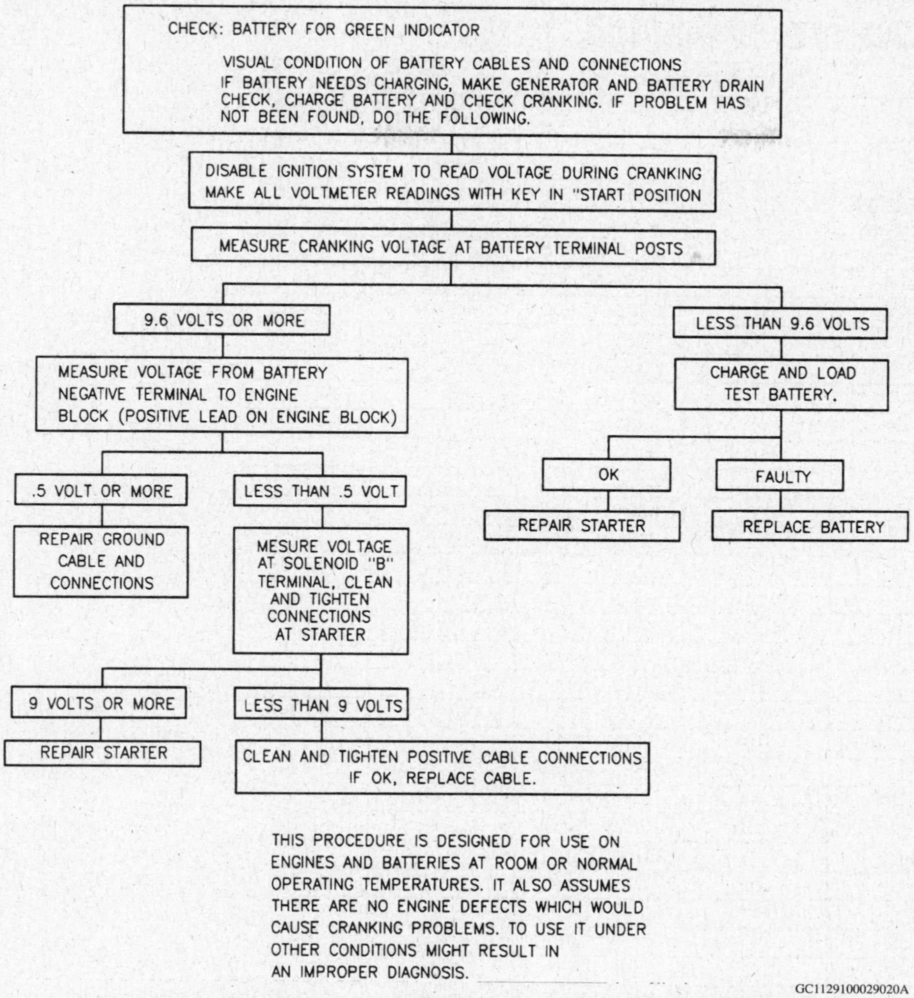
CHECK: BATTERY FOR GREEN INDICATOR
VISUAL CONDITION OF BATTERY CABLES AND CONNECTIONS
IF BATTERY NEEDS CHARGING, MAKE GENERATOR AND BATTERY DRAIN CHECK, CHARGE BATTERY AND CHECK CRANKING. IF PROBLEM HAS NOT BEEN FOUND, DO THE FOLLOWING.
DISABLE IGNITION SYSTEM TO READ VOLTAGE DURING CRANKING
MAKE ALL VOLTMETER READINGS WITH KEY IN "START POSITION
MEASURE CRANKING VOLTAGE AT BATTERY TERMINAL POSTS
9.6 VOLTS OR MORE
LESS THAN 9.6 VOLTS
MEASURE VOLTAGE FROM BATTERY NEGATIVE TERMINAL TO ENGINE BLOCK (POSITIVE LEAD ON ENGINE BLOCK)
CHARGE AND LOAD TEST BATTERY.
OK
FAULTY
.5 VOLT OR MORE
LESS THAN .5 VOLT
REPAIR STARTER
REPLACE BATTERY
REPAIR GROUND CABLE AND CONNECTIONS
MESURE VOLTAGE AT SOLENOID "B" TERMINAL, CLEAN AND TIGHTEN CONNECTIONS AT STARTER
9 VOLTS OR MORE
LESS THAN 9 VOLTS
REPAIR STARTER
CLEAN AND TIGHTEN POSITIVE CABLE CONNECTIONS IF OK, REPLACE CABLE.
THIS PROCEDURE IS DESIGNED FOR USE ON ENGINES AND BATTERIES AT ROOM OR NORMAL OPERATING TEMPERATURES. IT ALSO ASSUMES THERE ARE NO ENGINE DEFECTS WHICH WOULD CAUSE CRANKING PROBLEMS. TO USE IT UNDER OTHER CONDITIONS MIGHT RESULT IN AN IMPROPER DIAGNOSIS.
GC1129100029020A

Fig. 3 AC-Delco starter motor diagnosis (Part 2 of 2)

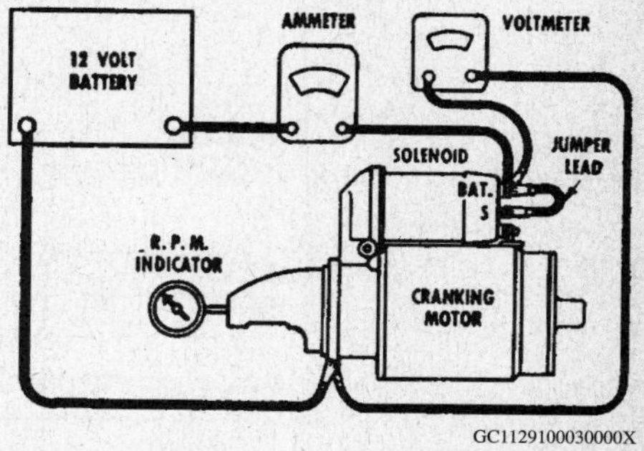
12 VOLT BATTERY
AMMETER
VOLTMETER
SOLENOID
JUMPER LEAD
BAT.
S
R.P.M. INDICATOR
CRANKING MOTOR
GC1129100030000X

Fig. 4 Starter free speed test connections

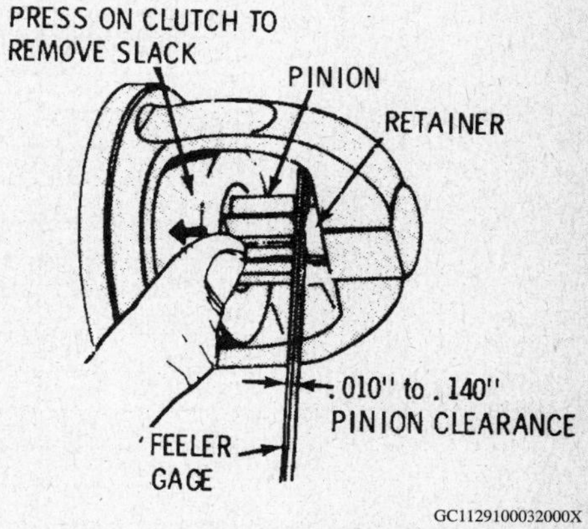
PRESS ON CLUTCH TO REMOVE SLACK
PINION
RETAINER
.010" to .140" PINION CLEARANCE
FEELER GAGE
GC1129100032000X

Fig. 6 Pinion clearance inspection

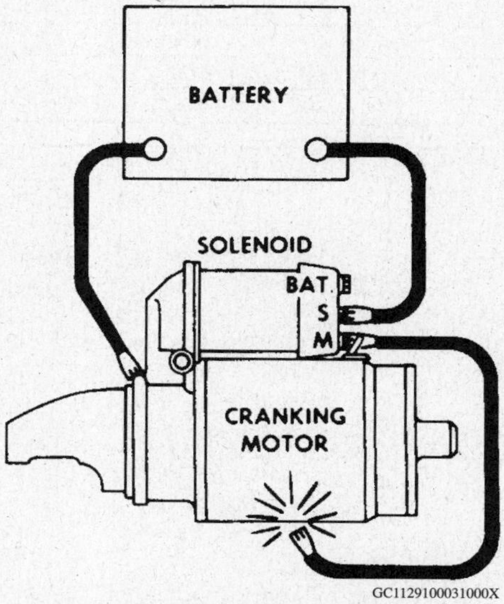
BATTERY
SOLENOID
BAT.
S
M
CRANKING MOTOR
GC1129100031000X

Fig. 5 Starter pinion clearance test connections

STARTER SPECIFICATIONS

Starter Identification No.	Free Speed Test			Solenoid	
	Amps	Volts	RPM	Hold-In Windings, Amps	Pull-In Windings, Amps
PG260 F1	40–90	12	3200–4800	6–12	30–45
PG260 F2	35–85	12	2550–4150	6–12	30–45
10455012	45–75	10	6500–11,000	–	–
10455023	45–75	10	8600–13,000	–	–
10455024	45–74	10	6000–11,900	13–19	23–30
10455045	50–62	10	8500–12,700	13–19	64–76
10455049	52–76	10	6000–12,000	–	–
10455051	45–70	10	6500–11,000	–	–
10455053	45–75	10	6000–11,000	–	–
10455054	45–75	10	6000–11,000	–	–
10455060	45–75	10	6000–11,000	–	–
10455061	45–75	10	6000–11,000	–	–
10455066	45–75	10	8600–13,000	10–20	–
10455067	50–75	10	6000–12,000	–	–
10455069	45–75	10	6000–12,000	–	–
10455309	64–95	10	2825–3275	–	–
10455604	45–90	10	3500–5000	–	–
10455709	45–75	10	8600–12,900	–	–
10465018	60–90	10	2880–3200	10–20	60–85
10465143	65–95	10	2750–3250	–	–
10465293	60–125	11.5	2900–3400	5–15	30–50
10465294	60–120	11.5	2900–3400	5–15	30–50
10465309	60–120	11.5	2900–3400	5–15	30–50
10465384	50–75	10	6000–12,000	—	—
10465385	60–125	11.5	2900–3400	5–15	30–50
10465386	60–120	11.5	2900–3400	—	—
10465391	45–75	10	8600–13,000	—	—
10465421	35–85	12	2550–4150	6–12	30–45
10465422	60–96	11.5	2925–3375	6–12	30–45
10465459	40–90	12	3200–4800	6–12	30–45
10465492	60–120	11.5	2900–3400	5–15	30–50
10465493	50–75	10	6000–12,000	—	—
10465494	50–75	10	6000–12,000	—	—
24503612	45–75	10	6000–11,000	10–20	60–85

AC-Delco Starters, Saturn

INDEX

APPLICATION CHART

Type	Transaxle	Starter Rating, HP (kW)
AC- Delco	Automatic	1.876 (1.4)
	Manual	1.072 (.8)

DESCRIPTION

These planetary gear reduction starters consist of an armature, a frame with permanent magnet poles, a planetary drive mechanism, a solenoid and a housing.

The starters use a planetary gear drive between the armature and motor pinion. The gear drive allows the use of permanent magnets eliminating heat that normally would be produced by coil fields and also simplifies motor construction since there are no internal field coils and connections.

TROUBLESHOOTING

Refer to starting/charging system troubleshooting procedures, **Fig. 1**.

DIAGNOSIS & TESTING

ON-VEHICLE STARTER TEST

Ensure battery is in satisfactory condition before performing test. If battery power is insufficient, the start motor will not function properly.

Electronic system tester tool No. SA9154Z, or equivalent, is required for the following starter system test.

1. Connect red and black tester cables to battery. Place gray inductive current pick-up around positive battery cable.
2. Ensure arrow on gray inductive current pick-up is pointing toward starter motor solenoid.
3. Disable ignition system by disconnecting electrical connection at ignition module.
4. Press "Starter Test" button on system tester.
5. Position tester so display can be seen from driver's seat. When display reads "Crank Engine," turn ignition to Start position.
6. Tester will continue to display "Crank Engine" for 15 seconds.
7. The System Tester will display following information:
   a. **Cranking Amps:** This displays average amperage drawn by starter motor during cranking. Refer to **Fig. 2** for normal operation amperage specifications.
   b. **Cranking Voltage:** This displays average battery voltage during cranking. If voltage is below 9.5 volts, ensure battery is in satisfactory condition and properly charged. Correct cranking voltage and a slow stator indicates loose or corroded cables.
   c. **Good Starter/Bad Starter:** If display reads "Bad Starter," replace starter motor only after determining there is no engine mechanical faults or flywheel binding problems.

30-35
X — Most Probable Cause(s)
• — Possible Causes

COMPLAINT–CONDITION \ CAUSE	Perform AR/BST Starter Test	IGN3 Fuse	Circuit 102A	Circuit 5/6/6B (Manual Trans only)	Circuit 5A/6A/5X (Auto Trans only)	Ignition Switch	Clutch Starter Switch (Manual Trans)	Neutral Starter Switch (Auto Trans)	Starter Motor/Solenoid	Battery	Engine Mechanical	Starter Drive to Flywheel Gap	Extreme Cold	Starter to Engine Surface	Theft Deterrent (RKE) Starter Relay	After market alarm system	Battery Negative Cable	Battery Positive Cable
Starter Dead, No Click from Solenoid		X	X	•	•	•	•	•	X	X					•	•	X	X
Starter Dead, Solenoid Does Click									X	X	•		•					
Starter Cranks Slowly	X								•	X	•		•	•			•	•
Starter Does Not Engage									X			•						
Noisy Starter									X		•	•						

Starter

G31129800008010X

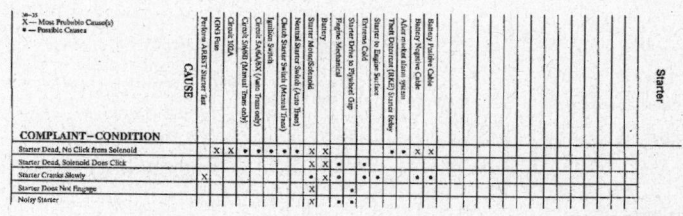

Fig. 1 Troubleshooting (Part 1 of 3)

COMPLAINT/CONDITION	POSSIBLE CAUSE(S)	CORRECTION(S)
No Click, No Crank During Starting.	Faulty or discharged battery.	Check the battery.
	If voltage at the starter solenoid "small" terminal is less than 9 volts, then the control circuit is the probable cause.	Check starter ground: a. paint on mounting surface b. battery negative grounds. c. other loose connections d. Refer to component section
	If voltage at the starter solenoid small terminal is greater than 9 volts, then the motor is the probable cause.	Replace the starter motor.
Click, No Crank During Startup.	If voltage at the starter solenoid small terminal is greater than 6 volts, possible causes could be damaged internal starter ground, excess solenoid temperature, excess voltage drop between the brushes and commutator, or defect at internal solenoid connection.	Check the battery. Replace the starter motor.
	If voltage at the starter solenoid small terminal is greater than 6 volts, a possible cause could be the radial and axial fit between the starter drive gear and flywheel.	Replace starter or flywheel, whichever is found to be damaged.
	Check flywheel runout.	IMPORTANT: Saturn starter motors should not be shimmed.
Starter Motor Continues to Run After Starting.	Starter motor internal short (at contact assembly or solenoid coil) or external short between battery and starter solenoid small terminal or faulty ignition key switch.	Check external ring terminals and wires for possible touching between battery and switch terminal lead. If no external short exists, replace starter motor.
	Internal starter motor damage; either electrical (welded contact, short between motor and battery terminal) or mechanical (contact rod).	Replace starter motor.

G31129800008020X

Fig. 1 Troubleshooting (Part 2 of 3)

CLUTCH START SWITCH

1.9L Engine

1. Check resistance through switch.
2. Circuit should be open with clutch is engaged.
3. Less than two ohms should exist when clutch is fully depressed.

2.2L Engine

1. Disconnect electrical connector from clutch start switch.
2. Using a jumper wire connect terminal A to Terminal B.
3. If engine cranks normal, replace switch.

COMPLAINT/CONDITION	POSSIBLE CAUSE(S)	CORRECTION(S)
High Pitched Whine During Cranking (before the Engine Fires Over), but Engine Cranks and Starts.	The distance between the flywheel and starter drive gear is too great. Check the flywheel for damage such as a bent flywheel or excessive or unusual wear patterns.	Start the engine and carefully touch the outside diameter of the flywheel with chalk or crayon to show high point of tooth runout when the engine is turned off. Turn the engine off and rotate the engine by hand so that the marked teeth are in the area of inspection. If the runout is present, the flywheel may have to be replaced. If no runout exists, check the starter drive gear and starter housing for any unusual conditions that would cause it not to mesh properly. If a problem exists, replace the starter motor. **IMPORTANT:** Saturn starter motors are not shimmed.
High Pitched Whine after Engine Fires Over as Key is being Released (Starter Hang-in, or Solenoid Weak).	The distance between the flywheel and starter drive gear is too small.	Check flywheel runout; if it is acceptable, replace the starter motor. **IMPORTANT:** The starter motor is not shimmed for service.
A Loud Whoop after the Engine Fires Over; but While the Starter is Still Engaged. May Sound like a Siren If Engine is Revved while the Starter is Engaged.	The most probable cause is starter drive assembly.	Replace the starter motor.
A Rumble or Growl, or in Several Cases A Knock as the Starter Motor is Coasting Down to a Stop after Starting the Engine.	The most probable cause is a bent or unbalanced starter armature.	Replace the starter motor.
High Pitched Whine during Starting.	Check the flywheel for damage such as a bent flywheel or unusual wear patterns.	Start the engine and, using chalk, mark the high point of the tooth runout when the engine is turned off. If runout is present, the flywheel may have to be replaced. If no runout exists, the starter drive gear or housing may be preventing the gears from meshing properly. If a condition exists, replace the starter motor.
High Pitched Whine after the Engine Fires over.	Check flywheel runout.	If flywheel runout is acceptable, replace the starter motor.
Rumble or Knock As Starter Motor Coasts Down after Starting.	Starter motor.	Replace the starter motor.

G31129800008030X

Fig. 1 Troubleshooting (Part 3 of 3)

Room Temperature: 5°–27°C (40°–80°F)	80–120 amps
Hot Engine: Coolant above 50°C (120°F)	70 – 110 amps
Cold Engine: 5°C (40°F)	90 – 130 amps

G31129100004000X

Fig. 2 Cranking amperage specifications

NEUTRAL START SWITCH

1. Check resistance through switch from Pin A to Pin B.
2. Circuit should be open when transaxle shifter is in R, 3 or 2.
3. Resistance should be less than 2 ohms when transaxle shifter is in P or N.

TRANSAXLE RANGE SWITCH

1. Disconnect electrical connector transaxle range switch.
2. Using a jumper wire connect terminal E to Terminal G.
3. If engine cranks normal, replace switch.

STARTER SPECIFICATIONS

Type	No Load Test	
	Volts	Amps①
AC-Delco	9.5	80-120

① — At room temperature. Subtract 10 amps for hot engine.

Mitsubishi & Nippondenso Starters

INDEX

APPLICATION CHART

Year	Engine	VIN①	Ident. No.
CATERA & 2000 SATURN			
1997	3.0L	R	④
1998–2000	3.0L	R	90542967
METRO			
1997–98	1.0L②	6	30005925
	1.0L③	6	30005226
	1.3L②	9	30005925
	1.3L③	9	30005226
1999–2000	1.0L②	6	30005925
	1.0L③	6	30005226
	1.3L②	2	30005925
	1.3L③	2	30005563
PRIZM			
1997	1.6L	6	94855154
	1.8L	8	94855154
1998–2000	1.6L	6	94857220
	1.8L	8	94857220

① — The eighth digit of VIN denotes engine code.
② — Automatic transaxle.
③ — Manual transaxle.
④ — Two different starters are used on these models. First design fits models w/numbers through 8216469 on rear of block at bellhousing flange; use part No. 90542532. Second design fits models w/number 8216470 & up on rear of block at bellhousing flange; use part No. 90542967.

PRECAUTIONS

BATTERY GROUND CABLE

Prior to service, disconnect battery ground cable and isolate as required.

DESCRIPTION

Nippondenso starters, **Figs. 1 and 2,** are either conventional or reduction gear types. The conventional type used on manual transmissions consists of a frame and field assembly, an armature assembly, an overrunning clutch assembly, a starter solenoid assembly, a commutator end housing, a brush holder and a shift lever. The reduction gear type starters used on automatic transmissions use all of the above components along with a reduction gear and shock absorber assembly.

TROUBLESHOOTING

SLOW OR NOT CRANKING

1. Turn headlamps On.
2. Ensure headlamps are burning with normal intensity.
3. If headlamps are burning dim, inspect battery charge condition, then charge as required.
4. If battery is fully charged, operate starter motor.
5. Note whether headlamps go out, dim considerably, or stay bright without starter activating.
6. Refer to the following diagnostic procedures as applicable.

Lamps Go Out

If the lamps go out as the starter switch is closed, it indicates a poor connection between the battery and starter motor.

1. Inspect battery terminals.
2. If corroded, remove, clean and reinstall.
3. Apply corrosion inhibitor to terminals to retard formation of corrosion.

Lamps Dim

If the lamps dim considerably as the starter switch is closed and the starter operates slowly or not at all, perform the following:

1. Inspect for a discharged battery, recharge or replace as required.
2. If the battery is fully charged, inspect the engine or the starter motor.
3. Inspect the engine for tight bearings, pistons, or other components.
4. Inspect engine timing, adjust as required.
5. Inspect for heavy engine oil. Low temperatures thicken engine oil and add considerable load to starting system.
6. Inspect starter motor for bent armature, loose pole screws, or worn bearings.

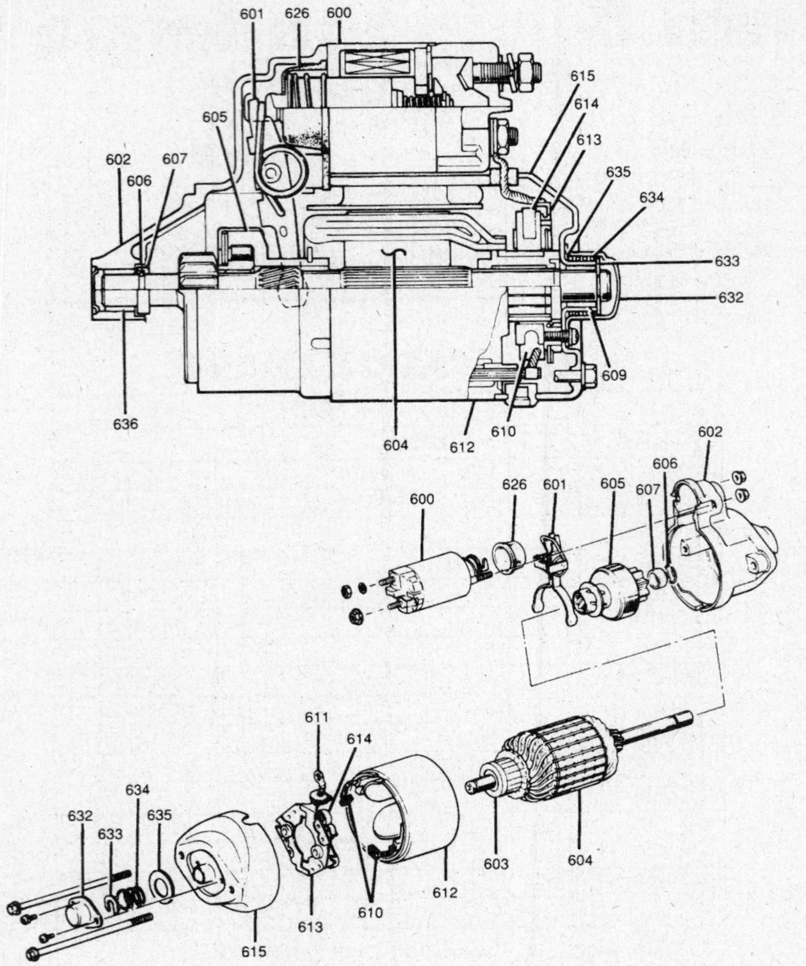

600	SOLENOID	607	ARMATURE STOP RING	615	COMMUTATOR END COVER
601	PINION DRIVE LEVER	609	COMMUTATOR END BUSHING	626	BOOT
602	DRIVE HOUSING	610	BRUSHES	632	COMMUTATOR END CAP
603	COMMUTATOR END	611	FIELD COIL LEAD WIRE	633	ARMATURE PLATE
604	ARMATURE	612	YOKE	634	ARMATURE BRAKE SPRING
605	OVERRUNNING CLUTCH ASSEMBLY	613	BRUSH HOLDER	635	END CAP GASKET
606	ARMATURE RETAINING RING	614	BRUSH SPRINGS	636	DRIVE HOUSING BUSHING

GC1129100033000X

Fig. 1 Exploded view of starter motor. Conventional w/manual transaxle

7. Inspect for thrown armature windings or commutator bars.

Lamps Stay Bright, No Cranking Action

Inspect for an open circuit in the starter, the starter switch or control circuit.

1. Place a heavy jumper lead across solenoid main terminals.
2. Starter should engage and operate.
3. If starter fails to perform as indicated, remove and inspect starter.

STARTER DRIVE PROBLEMS

If the starter does not turn over or if it drags, inspect the starter or electrical supply system. If the starter is noisy, if it turns but does not engage the engine, or if the starter will not disengage after the engine is started, inspect for the following:

1. Worn or chipped ring gear or starter pinion.
2. Improper pinion clearance.
3. Bent starter armature shaft. Maximum radial runout is .003 inch.

Drive Clutch Failure

The overrunning clutch is directly activated by a fork and lever. If the overrunning clutch will not turn engine over, inspect for worn out overrunning clutch. Proper meshing of the pinion is controlled by the end clearance between the pinion gear and the starter housing or pinion stop, if used.

1. Inspect and adjust pinion clearance (if applicable).
2. If pinion clearance is non-adjustable, remove starter and inspect for excessive wear of solenoid linkage, shift lever mechanism, or improper assembly of components.
3. Inspect overrunning clutch for signs of overheating.
4. If clutch shows signs of overheating (bluish color), inspect for rust or gum buildup between armature shaft and drive or for burred splines.
5. Clean or deburr splines as required.
6. Overrunning clutches are not serviceable. Replace as required.

Drive Failure

If a Bendix type drive does not engage, inspect the following:

1. Inspect for a broken drive spring, or for sheared drive spring bolts.
2. If spring is broken, or spring bolts are sheared off, remove drive and replace damaged components.
3. Inspect for screw shaft.

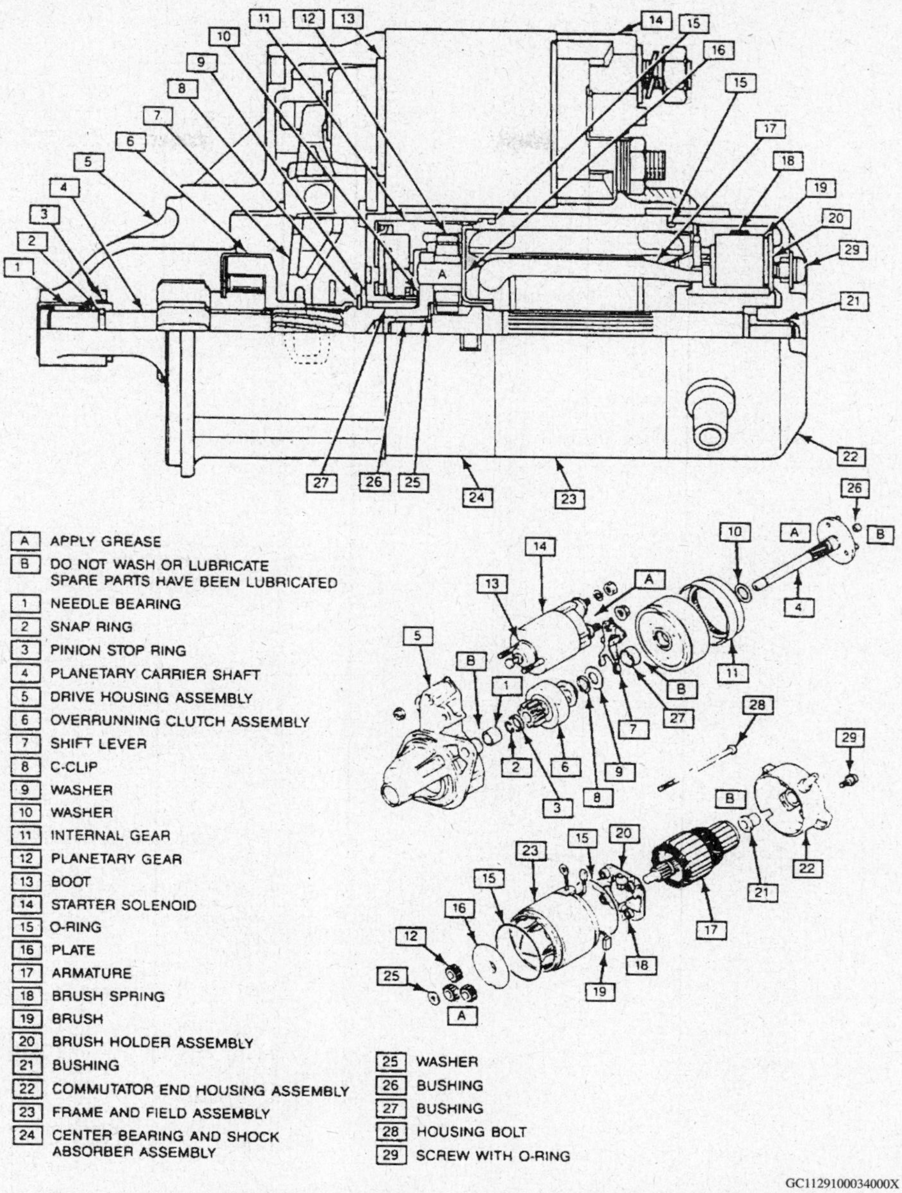

Fig. 2 Exploded view of starter motor. Reduction w/automatic transaxle

4. If screw shaft threads are gummed or rusty, clean with kerosene or steel wool.
5. Ensure flywheel has adequate ventilation. Inspect breather hole in bottom of flywheel housing and clean if required.
6. If screw shaft threads are clean and rust free, look for mechanical failure within the drive itself.

SOLENOID SWITCHES

The solenoid switch on a cranking motor closes the circuit between the battery and the cranking motor and also shifts the drive pinion into mesh with the engine flywheel ring gear. This is done by means of a linkage between the solenoid switch plunger and the shift lever on the cranking motor.

There are two windings in the solenoid: a pull-in and a hold-in. Both windings are energized when the external control switch is closed. They produce a magnetic field which pulls the plunger in so that the drive pinion is shifted into mesh, and the main contacts in the solenoid switch are closed to connect the battery directly to the cranking motor. Closing the main switch contacts shorts out the pull-in winding since this winding is connected across the main contacts. The magnetism produced by the hold-in winding is sufficient to hold the plunger in, and shorting out the pull-in winding reduces battery drain. When the control switch is opened, it disconnects the hold-in winding from the battery. When the hold-in winding is disconnected from the battery, the shift lever spring withdraws the plunger from the solenoid, opening the solenoid switch contacts and at the same time withdrawing the drive pinion from mesh. Proper operation of the switch depends on maintaining a definite balance between the magnetic strength of the pull-in and hold-in windings.

This balance is determined by the size of the wire and the number of turns specified. An open circuit in the hold-in winding or attempts to crank with a discharged battery will cause the switch to chatter.

DIAGNOSIS & TESTING

Refer to **Fig. 3** when troubleshooting these starter motors.

CIRCUIT INSPECTION w/VOLTMETER

Excessive resistance in the circuit between the battery and starter will reduce cranking performance. The resistance can

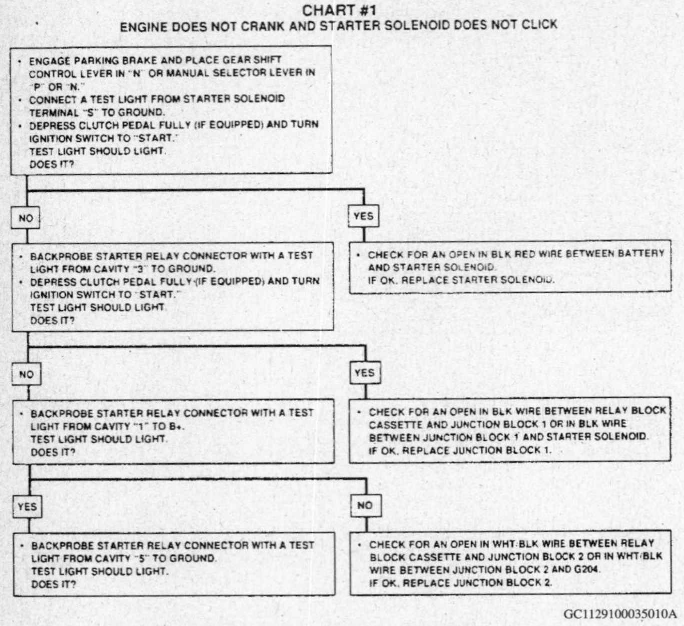

Fig. 3 Diagnosis chart (Part 1 of 4)

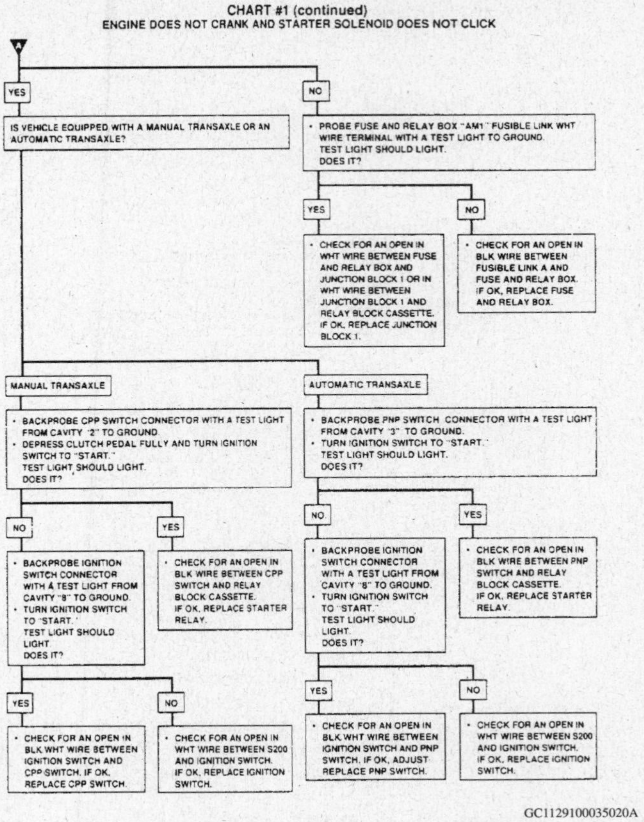

Fig. 3 Diagnosis chart (Part 2 of 4)

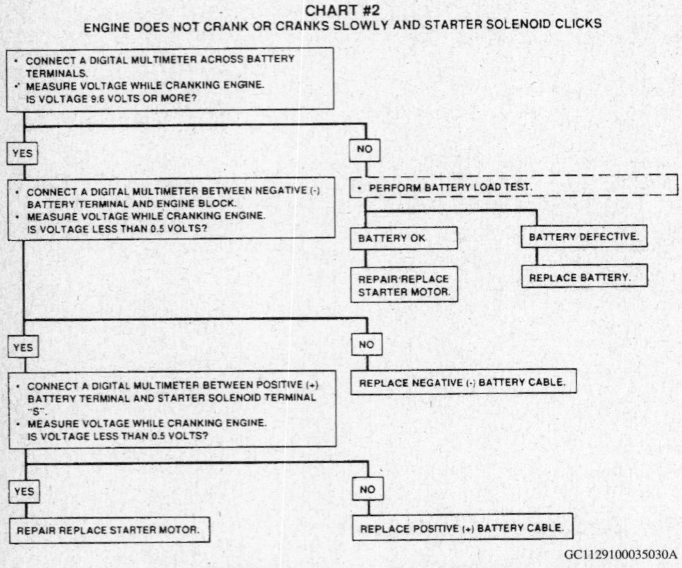

Fig. 3 Diagnosis chart (Part 3 of 4)

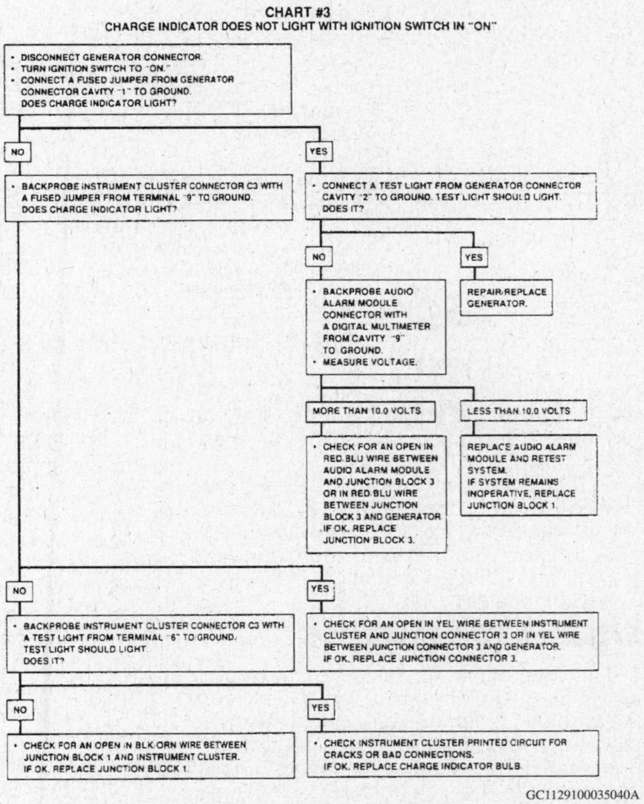

Fig. 3 Diagnosis chart (Part 4 of 4)

be inspected by using a voltmeter to measure voltage drop in the circuits while the starter is operated. Inspect for the following three conditions:

1. Voltage drop between vehicle frame and grounded battery terminal post.
2. Voltage drop between vehicle frame and starter motor field frame.
3. Voltage drop between insulated battery terminal post and starter motor terminal stud, or the battery terminal stud of the solenoid.

Measurements should show no more than one tenth (.1) volt drop when the starter motor is cranking the engine. Do not use the starter for more than 30 seconds at a time to avoid overheating it.

If excessive voltage drop is found, disconnect the cables, clean the connections, then connect the cables again. A coating of petroleum jelly on the battery cables and terminal clamps will retard corrosion.

On some models, extra long battery cables may be required due to the location of the battery and starter. This may result in somewhat higher voltage drop than the above recommended .1 volt. To determine the normal voltage drop, test several comparable vehicles and compare the results. If the voltage drop is well above the normal figure for all vehicles inspected, abnormal resistance will be indicated and corrections can be made as required.

STARTER SPECIFICATIONS

Starter Identification No.	Free Speed Test			Solenoid	
	Amps	Volts	RPM	Hold-In Windings, Amps	Pull-In Windings, Amps
30005925①	75	11	—	—	—
30005226②	60	11	—	—	—
30005563③	60	11	—	—	—
90542532	75	11.5	2900	9.5	51
90542967	—	—	—	—	—
94854717	60–90	11.5	5800–9000	—	—
94855154	60–90	11	—	—	—
94857220	90	11.5	3000	—	—

① — Automatic transaxle.
② — All 1997–98 models w/manual transaxle & 1999–2000 models w/1.0L engine & manual transaxle.
③ — 1999–2000 models w/1.3L engine & manual transaxle.

ALTERNATORS

TABLE OF CONTENTS

Application Chart

Model	Alternator Manufacturer
BUICK	
Century	Delphi
LeSabre	Delphi
Park Avenue	Delphi
Regal	Delphi
Riviera	Delphi
Skylark	Delphi
CADILLAC	
Catera	Bosch
DeVille	Delphi
Eldorado	Delphi
Seville	Delphi
CHEVROLET/GEO	
Camaro	Delphi
Cavalier	Delphi
Corvette	Valeo
Impala	Bosch①
	Delphi
Lumina	Delphi
Malibu	Delphi
Metro	Mitsubishi
Monte Carlo	Delphi
Prizm	Nippondenso
OLDSMOBILE	
Achieva	Delphi
Alero	Delphi
Aurora	Delphi
Cutlass	Delphi
Cutlass Supreme	Delphi
Intrigue	Delphi
LSS, Regency & 88	Delphi
PONTIAC	
Bonneville	Delphi
Firebird	Delphi
Grand Am	Delphi
Grand Prix	Delphi
Sunfire	Delphi
SATURN	
1.9L & 2.2L Engines	Delphi
3.0L Engine	Bosch

① — A Bosch NCB1 125 amp alternator is used for police and taxi options.

Delphi Alternators, General Motors

NOTE: On Air Bag Equipped Models, Refer To " Air Bag System Precautions" Located In The Front Of This Manual For System Disarming & Arming Procedures.

NOTE: Refer To "Computer Relearn Procedure " Located In The Front Of This Manual For Computer Relearn Procedures.

INDEX

APPLICATION CHART

Model	Year	Alternator Model
BUICK		
Century	1997-98	CS-130D
	1999-2000	CS-130DP
LeSabre	1997-98	CS-144
	1999	CS-130
	2000	AD-230 & AD-237
Park Avenue	1997-98	CS-130D
	1999	CS-130DP
	2000	AD-230 & AD-237
Regal	1997–98	CS-130D
	1999-2000	CS-130DP
Riviera	1997–99	CS-144
Skylark	1997-98	①
CADILLAC		
DeVille	1997-98	CS-144
	1999	CS-144 Gen II
	2000	LR 630
Eldorado	1997-98	CS-144
	1999-2000	CS-144 Gen II
Seville	1997	CS-144
	1998-2000	LR-630 Water Cooled
CHEVROLET		
Camaro	1997	②
	1998-2000	CS-130D
Cavalier	1997-2000	CS-130D
Impala	2000	CS-130D
Lumina	1997	CS-130
	1998-2000	③
Malibu	1997-2000	CS-130
Monte Carlo	1997	CS-130
	1998-2000	③
OLDSMOBILE		
Achieva	1997-98	①
Alero	1999-2000	CS-130D
Aurora	1997–99	CS-144

Continued

APPLICATION CHART—Continued

Model	Year	Alternator Model
OLDSMOBILE		
Cutlass	1997–99	CS-130
Cutlass Supreme	1997–99	CS-130
Intrigue	1998-99	CS-144
	2000	AD 237
LSS Regency & 88	1997-98	CS-144
	1999	CS-130
PONTIAC		
Bonneville	1997-98	CS-144
	1999	CS-130
	2000	AD-230 & AD-237
Firebird	1997	CS-130D
		CS-144
	1998-2000	CS-130D
Grand Am	1997-98	①
	1999-2000	CS-130D
Grand Prix	1997–98	CS-130D
	1999-2000	CS130DP
Sunfire	1997–2000	CS-130D

① — 2.4L engine CS-130D, 3.1L engine CS-130
② — 5.7L engine CS-144, 3800 engine CS-130D
③ — Standard application CS130D, optional high output application CS144

PRECAUTIONS

AIR BAG SYSTEMS

Refer to "Air Bag System Precautions" in the front of this manual for system disarming and arming procedures.

BATTERY GROUND CABLE

Prior to service, disconnect battery ground cable and isolate as required.

CHARGING SYSTEM

1. Ensure battery polarity is correct when servicing units. Reversed battery polarity will damage rectifiers and regulators.
2. If booster battery is used for starting, use correct polarity in hook up.
3. When a fast charger is used to charge a vehicle battery, vehicle battery cables should be disconnected unless the fast charger is equipped with a special Alternator Protector, in which case vehicle battery cables need not be disconnected. Fast charger should never be used to start a vehicle as damage to rectifiers will result.
4. Unless this system includes a load relay or field relay, grounding alternator output terminal will damage alternator and/or circuits. This is true even when the system is not in operation since no circuit breaker is used and the battery is applied to the alternator output terminal at all times. The field or load relay acts as a circuit breaker in that it is controlled by the ignition switch.
5. Before making any on vehicle tests of the alternator or regulator, the battery should be checked and the circuit inspected for faulty wiring or insulation. loose or corroded connections and poor ground circuits.
6. Inspect alternator belt tension and condition.
7. The ignition switch should be off and the battery ground cable disconnected before making any test connections to prevent damage to the system.
8. Do not reverse the connections to the alternator.
9. Do not short across or ground any of the terminals in the charging system.
10. Never disconnect the output terminal while the alternator is running.
11. The vehicle battery must be fully charged when testing the charging system.

GENERAL INFORMATION

Alternators are composed of the same functional parts as the conventional D.C. generator but they operate differently. The field is called a rotor and is the turning portion of the unit. The generating part, called a stator, is the stationary member, comparable to the armature in a D.C. generator. The regulator, similar to those used in a D.C. system, regulates the output of the alternator-rectifier system.

The power source of the system is the alternator. Current is transmitted from the field terminal of the regulator through a slip ring to the field coil and back to ground through another slip ring. The strength of the field regulates the output of the alternating current. This alternating current is then transmitted from the alternator to the rectifier where it is converted to direct current.

These alternators employ a three-phase stator winding in which the phase windings are electrically 120° apart. The rotor consists of a field coil encased between interleaved sections producing. When the rotor is energized, a magnetic field with alternate north and south poles is created. By rotating the rotor inside the stator the alternating current is induced in the stator windings. This alternating current is rectified (changed to D.C.) by silicon diodes and brought out to the output terminal of the alternator.

DIODE RECTIFIERS

Six silicon diode rectifiers are used and act as electrical one-way valves. Three of the diodes have ground polarity and are pressed or screwed into a heat sink which is grounded. The other three diodes (ungrounded) are pressed or screwed into and insulated from the end head; these diodes are connected to the alternator output terminal.

Since the diodes have a high resistance to the flow of current in one direction and a low resistance in the opposite direction, they may be connected in a manner which allows current to flow from the alternator to the battery in the low resistance direction. The high resistance in the opposite direction prevents the flow of current from the battery to the alternator. Because of this feature no circuit breaker is required between the alternator and battery.

DESCRIPTION

CS ALTERNATORS

The CS alternator is available in two sizes: CS-130 and CS-144, **Fig. 1.** The numerals denote the outer diameter of the stator laminations in millimeters and the letters CS stand for charging system.

These use a conventional fan mounted next to the pulley to pull air through the assembly for cooling. An internal fan mounted on the rotor pulls air through the slip ring end frame to cool the rectifier, bridge and regulator. Air is expelled through openings in the frame. No periodic maintenance is required.

LR ALTERNATORS

The LR series alternator is available in only one size with an output of 140 amps. The LR series alternator has a liquid cooled end frame. Engine coolant is passed through a tube molded into the end frame next to the electronic components of the alternator. This cooling supplements the air cooling action of the internal fans and helps prevent overheating of the alternator during periods of high electrical demands.

AD ALTERNATORS

The AD alternators are similar to CS type alternators, except that they have dual cooling fans. The AD stand for Air-cooled Dual Internal fan; the 2 is an electric design designator; the 30 or 37 denotes the outside diameter of the stator laminations in millimeters.

SYSTEM OPERATION

CS ALTERNATORS

CS-130 and CS-144 alternators may be used with only two connections. The battery positive BAT terminal must be connected to a battery during operation. The second required connection is through the Powertrain Control Module (PCM) to the indicator light. Three other regulator terminals are available for optional use in vehicle systems. The P terminal is connected to the stator, and may be connected to a tachometer or other device. The F terminal is connected internally to field positive, and may be used as a fault indicator. The S terminal may be connected externally to a voltage, such as battery voltage, to sense voltage to be controlled.

The regulator voltage setting varies with temperature, and limits system voltage by controlling rotor field current. Unlike others regulators, this regulator switches field current On and Off at a fixed frequency about 400 cycles per second. By varying On-Off time, correct average field current is obtained to provide proper system voltage. At high speeds, the On time may be 10% and Off time 90%. At low speeds with high electrical loads, On-Off time may be 90% and 10% respectively.

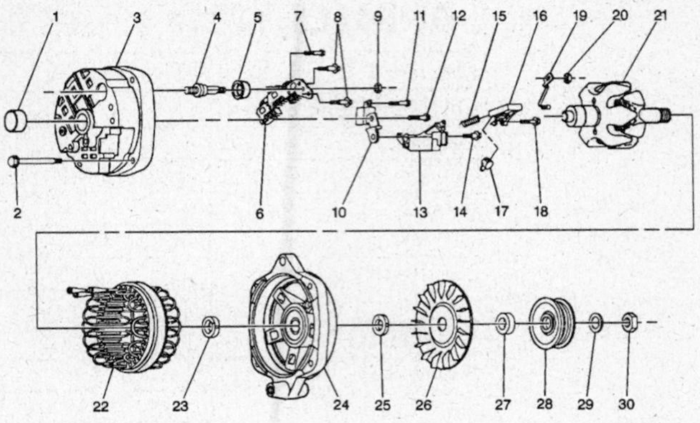

(1) Generator Rotor Slip Ring End Frame Bearing
(2) Generator Through Bolt
(3) Generator Slip Ring End Frame
(4) Generator Battery Terminal Stud
(5) Generator Battery Terminal Sleeve
(6) Generator Rectifier Bridge
(7) Generator Rectifier Bridge Bolt
(8) Generator Rectifier Bridge Bolt (Insulated)
(9) Generator Battery Terminal Nut
(10) Generator Capacitor
(11) Generator Rectifier Bridge Bolt
(12) Generator Capacitor/Rectifier Bolt (Insulated)
(13) Generator Voltage Regulator
(14) Generator Voltage Regulator Attaching Bolt (Insulated)
(15) Generator Brush Spring
(16) Generator Brush Holder
(17) Dust Shield
(18) Generator Brush Holder Bolt
(19) Generator Voltage Regulator Connector Strap
(20) Generator Stator Lead Attaching Nut
(21) Generator Rotor
(22) Generator Stator
(23) Generator Rotor Drive End Bearing Inside Collar
(24) Generator Rotor Drive End Bearing Frame
(25) Generator Rotor Drive End Bearing Outside Collar
(26) Generator Fan
(27) Generator Rotor Drive End Fan Collar
(28) Generator Pulley
(29) Generator Rotor Shaft Drive End Washer
(30) Generator Rotor Shaft Drive End Nut

GC1129700090000X

Fig. 1 Exploded view of CS type alternator

LR ALTERNATORS

The LR series alternator provides the voltage to operate the vehicle's electrical system and to charge the battery through circuit No. 1 (red). When the ignition switch is in the RUN position, voltage is supplied to alternator L terminal by the Powertrain Control Module (PCM), turning on the voltage regulator. The voltage regulator controls current to the rotor, which controls alternator output voltage. When the engine starts, the regulator senses alternator rotation by detecting AC voltage at the stator through an internal wire. Once the engine is running, the regulator varies the field current by controlling the pulse width. The alternator F terminal is connected internally to the voltage regulator and externally to the PCM. The PCM monitors the field voltage on the alternator F terminal.

The PCM turns on the CHARGE indicator lamp by sending a message to the instrument cluster whenever a undervoltage, overvoltage or a stopped alternator is detected.

AD ALTERNATORS

Refer to CS alternators system operation.

DIAGNOSIS & TESTING

CS ALTERNATORS

In-Vehicle Test

When the charging system is operating normally, the indicator lamp will come On when ignition switch is turned On and will go out when the engine starts. If the lamp operates abnormally, or if a undercharge or overcharge battery condition occurs, use the following procedure to diagnose the charging system.

1. Before beginning the test, check the following:
   a. An undercharged battery is often caused by accessories being left on for extended periods of time, or if an accessory lamp stays On. Ensure all lamps and accessories are turned off.
   b. If alternator is noisy check for a loose drive pulley, loose mounting bolts, worn or dirty bearings, defective diodes or a defective stator.
2. Turn ignition switch and all electrical accessory loads off.
3. Connect ammeter in series at alternator output BAT terminal, then connect voltmeter and carbon pile across battery terminal.
4. Connect positive lead of universal electronic CS generator tester tool No. J41450–CS, or equivalent, to alternator output terminal and negative lead to alternator housing. If tester lamp illuminates, proceed to step 5. If tester lamp does not illuminate, proceed as follows:
   a. Using a suitable voltmeter, check voltage between alternator output terminal and battery negative terminal. If battery voltage is indicated, proceed to next step. If battery voltage is not indicated, locate and repair open in alternator output circuit.

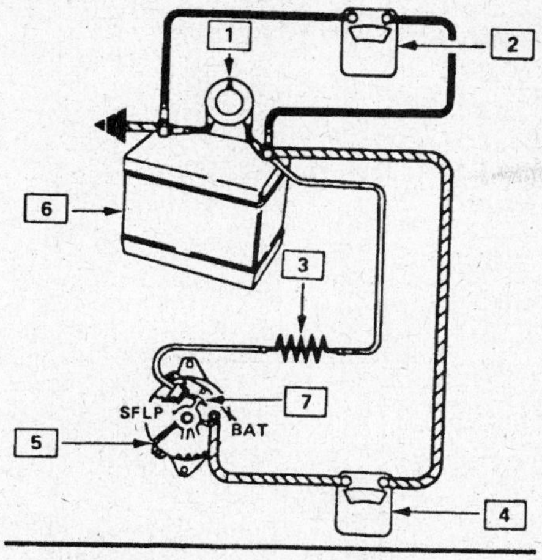

1–CARBON PILE
2–VOLTMETER
3–RESISTOR
4–TESTAMMETER
5–GENERATOR
6–BATTERY
7–CONNECT RESISTOR TO "L" TERMINAL

GC1129100038000X

Fig. 2 Alternator bench check

b. Connect a jumper wire between alternator housing and battery ground terminal. If test lamp illuminates, proceed to step 5. If test lamp does not illuminate, repair open in ground circuit from alternator housing to battery ground terminal.

5. Disconnect alternator connector and connect matching connector of tester to alternator. If red tester lamp illuminates, proceed to step 6. If red tester lamp does not illuminate, proceed as follows:
   a. Disconnect tester lead from alternator.
   b. Turn ignition switch to the RUN position and probe connector terminal "L" of vehicle harness connector with a fused jumper wire.
   c. If fuse does not blow, replace alternator. If fuse blows, repair direct short to battery voltage in terminal "L" circuit, then replace alternator.
6. Turn off all accessories and close doors to ensure there is no load on the battery.
7. Connect positive lead of universal electronic CS generator tester tool No. J–41450–CS, or equivalent, to alternator output terminal and negative lead to alternator housing.
8. Start engine and let engine idle briefly. If red tester lamp does not illuminate, proceed to next step. If red tester lamp illuminates, replace alternator.
9. Increase engine speed to 2500 RPM. If red tester lamp does not illuminate, proceed to next step. If red tester lamp illuminates, replace alternator.
10. With engine speed still at 2500 RPM, turn load on carbon pile load tester to ON and adjust until alternator output is at Load Test value. If red tester lamp does not illuminate, alternator is good. If red tester lamp illuminates, replace alternator.

Step	Action	Value(s)	Yes	No
DEFINITION: Generator on-vehicle test which will test the generator independently from the vehicle wiring.				
2	1. Connect the red alligator clip of a *J 41450-B* CS Generator Electronic Tester to the generator output terminal. (The output wire is attached to the generator with a ring terminal and nut.) 2. Connect the black alligator clip of the *J 41450-B* to the metal generator housing. The green POWER lamp of the tester should light and remain lighted while the tester is being used. Does the green POWER lamp on the tester light?	—	Go to *Step 9*	Go to *Step 3*
3	1. Recheck the alligator clip connections that were made in Step 2. 2. Correct the connections if they were reversed. Does the green POWER lamp on the tester light after the correct connections are verified?	—	Go to *Step 9*	Go to *Step 4*
4	Connect a *J 39200* digital multimeter (DMM) from the generator output terminal to the generator metal housing. Is the measured voltage within the specified range?	Above 12 V	Go to *Step 18*	Go to *Step 5*
5	Use a DMM to check the voltage between the battery terminals. Is the measured voltage within the specified range?	Above 12 V	Go to *Step 6*	Go to *Step 8*

GC1129800091010X

Fig. 3 Charging system test (Part 1 of 5). LR series alternator

Step	Action	Value(s)	Yes	No
6	1. Inspect the circuit between the generator output terminal and the battery positive terminal for a loose connection or open circuit condition. Be sure to check for an open fusible link and/or any blown in-line fuses that may be used on the vehicle. 2. If a loose connection or open circuit was located, repair it. If an open fusible link or blown fuse was found, be sure to check the system for possible causes of a circuit overload, such as a direct B+ short to ground. Is the circuit okay between the generator output terminal and the battery positive terminal?	—	Go to *Step 7*	—
7	Repair the loose connection or open circuit between the battery negative terminal and the generator housing. Is the repair complete?	—	Go to *Step 26*	—
8	1. Inspect the battery. 2. Charge or replace the battery if necessary. Is the battery OK?	—	Go to *Step 26*	—
9	1. Leave the *J 41450-B* alligator clips attached as in Step 2, and disconnect the vehicle 4-way generator connector. 2. Locate the matching 4-way connector of the *J 41450-B* and connect it to the generator. Does the red DIAGNOSTIC lamp on the tester light?	—	Go to *Step 11*	Go to *Step 10*
10	Perform the following test of the DIAGNOSTIC lamp of the *J 41450-B* : 1. Disconnect the *J 41450-B* 4-way connector from the generator, but leave the J41450-B alligator clips connected as in step 2. 2. Prepare a jumper wire with an in-line 100 ohm resistor. The watt rating of the resistor is not important. (An inexpensive 100Ω resistor can be purchased at an electronics supply store.) 3. At one end of the prepared jumper wire, attach a Metri-Pack 150 male terminal probe adapter from a *J 35616-A* Connector Test Adapter Kit. 4. Connect the prepared jumper wire to the *J 41450-B* L terminal (which is called the B terminal on CS 130D, LR, and AD generators). The tester connector terminals are the same as the generator connector terminals, so terminal identification on the *J 41450-B* can be accomplished by referring to Starting and Charging Connector End Views. 5. Connect the other end of the jumper to the battery negative terminal. Does the red DIAGNOSTIC lamp on the tester light when the jumper is connected?	—	Go to *Step 19*	Go to *Step 18*

GC1129800091020X

Fig. 3 Charging system test (Part 2 of 5). LR series alternator

Bench Testing

1. Make connections as shown in **Fig. 2**, however leave the carbon pile disconnected. The ground polarity of the alternator and battery must be the same. The battery must be fully charged. Use a 30–500 ohm resistor between battery and L terminal.
2. Slowly increase alternator speed and observe voltage.
3. If voltage is uncontrolled and increases above 16 volts, the rotor field is shorted, the regulator is defective or both. A shorted rotor field can cause the regulator to become defective. **Battery must be fully charged when making this test.**
4. If voltage is below 16 volts, increase speed and adjust carbon pile obtain maximum amperage output, maintain voltage above 13 volts.
5. If output is within 15 amps of rated output, alternator is satisfactory.
6. If output is not within 15 amps of rated output, alternator is defective and requires repair.

LR ALTERNATORS

Refer to **Fig. 3** for alternator and charging system diagnosis. The LR series alternator is serviced by replacement only.

AD ALTERNATORS

Refer to "CS Alternators" system diagnosis and testing procedure.

Step	Action	Value(s)	Yes	No
11	***Caution: Make sure that the load is completely turned off before connecting or disconnecting a carbon pile load tester to the battery. Otherwise, sparking could ignite battery gasses which are extremely flammable and may explode violently.*** 1. Prior to connecting a carbon pile load tester, make sure that the load dial of the carbon pile tester is turned completely to the OFF position. 2. Connect the cable leads of the carbon pile tester to the battery of the vehicle. 3. Connect an inductive ammeter to the output lead(s) of the generator. Make sure that all output leads pass through the ammeter inductive clip. The carbon pile tester may have its own inductive ammeter, or use a *J 35590* Current Clamp. 4. Start the engine and allow it to idle briefly. Does the red DIAGNOSTIC lamp on the *J 41450-B* light?	—	Go to *Step 19*	Go to *Step 12*
12	Increase the engine speed to 2500 RPM. Does the red DIAGNOSTIC lamp on the *J 41450-B* light?	—	Go to *Step 19*	Go to *Step 13*
13	1. Maintain the engine speed at 2500 RPM. 2. Turn on the load of the carbon pile tester, and increase the load until the generator output is equal to the load test value given in Generator Usage. As the load is increased, is the generator capable of producing the amount of load test current specified in Generator Usage?	—	Go to *Step 14*	Go to *Step 19*
14	Maintain the engine speed at 2500 RPM and continue to operate the generator at the load test value. Is the red DIAGNOSTIC lamp on the *J 41450-B* lit?	—	Go to *Step 19*	Go to *Step 15*
15	1. Maintain the engine speed at 2500 RPM and continue to operate the generator at the load test value. 2. Connect a DMM from the generator output terminal to the battery positive (+) terminal. Is the measured voltage within the specified range?	Above 0.5 V	Go to *Step 22*	Go to *Step 16*
16	1. Maintain the engine speed at 2500 RPM and continue to operate the generator at the load test value. 2. Connect a DMM from the generator metal housing to the battery negative (–) terminal. Is the measured voltage within the specified range?	Above 0.5 V	Go to *Step 23*	Go to *Step 17*
17	***Caution: Make sure that the load is completely turned off before connecting or disconnecting a carbon pile load tester to the battery. Otherwise, sparking could ignite battery gasses which are extremely flammable and may explode violently.*** 1. Disconnect the DMM. 2. Turn OFF the load in the carbon pile tester. 3. Turn the ignition switch to LOCK to stop the engine. 4. Disconnect the carbon pile tester cables from the battery. 5. Disconnect the *J 41450-B* 4-way connector from the generator. 6. Inspect the generator 4-way connector on the vehicle. Does the vehicle have a wire in the L terminal cavity (or B terminal for CS 130D, LR, and AD generators) of the generator 4-way connector?	—	Go to *Step 26*	Go to *Step 24*

GC1129800091030X

Fig. 3 Charging system test (Part 3 of 5). LR series alternator

Step	Action	Value(s)	Yes	No
18	There is an internal problem in the *J 41450-B*. Replace the *J 41450-B*. Has the *J 41450-B* been replaced?	—	Go to *Step 26*	—
19	**Important:** Before generator repair or replacement, the L terminal circuit (if applicable) must be tested for resistance in order to avoid a repeat failure. Disconnect and examine the generator 4-way connector. Is there a wire in the L cavity (or B cavity for CS 130D, LR, and AD generators) of the generator connector?	—	Go to *Step 20*	Go to *Step 24*
20	1. Be sure the 4-way generator connector is disconnected. 2. Turn the ignition key to the RUN position. 3. Connect a fused jumper wire *J 36169-A* (with a 5 amp fuse) from ground to the vehicle 4-way generator connector terminal L (or B terminal for CS 130D, LR, and AD generators). To connect the jumper to the generator, use a Metri-Pack 150 connector test adapter from *J 35616-A*. Refer to Starting and Charging Connector End Views. Does the fuse blow?	—	Go to *Step 21*	Go to *Step 25*
21	There is a short to B+ voltage when the ignition key is in the RUN position. The short may be a result of a miswired condition. The L terminal circuit must be a resistance circuit either through a charge indicator or the PCM. If direct battery voltage is applied to the generator at the L terminal, the regulator will eventually be destroyed, causing a repeat failure. Repair the short to B+ voltage in the L terminal circuit (or B terminal circuit for CS 130D, LR, and AD generators). Is the short circuit repaired?	—	Go to *Step 25*	—
22	1. Turn off the engine. 2. Disconnect the battery negative terminal. 3. Inspect the circuit between the battery positive terminal and the generator output terminal for a high-resistance connection. Disassemble and clean all connections in this circuit. 4. Assemble the connections 5. Connect the battery negative terminal. Is the repair complete?	—	Go to *Step 26*	—
23	1. Turn off the engine. 2. Inspect the ground circuit for high resistance from the battery negative terminal to the generator housing. Disassemble and clean all connections. 3. Assemble the connections Is the repair complete?	—	Go to *Step 26*	—

GC1129800091040X

Fig. 3 Charging system test (Part 4 of 5). LR series alternator

Step	Action	Value(s)	Yes	No
24	The tester turns the generator on in a different way than the vehicle does, so an additional test is necessary. This Step is applicable only for vehicles that do not use an L terminal connection (or B terminal for CS 130D, LR, and AD generators). 1. Remove the 4-way connector from the generator. 2. Measure the generator internal resistance between the L and I/F terminals (B and C terminals for CS 130D, LR, and AD generators). Use Metri-Pack 150 terminal adapters from a *J 35616-A* Connector Test Adapter Kit. The L and I/F terminals are the two middle terminals on the generator. Is the measured resistance within the specified range?	Below 500 Ω	Go to *Step 26*	Go to *Step 25*
25	Repair or replace the generator. Is the repair complete?	—	Go to *Step 26*	—
26	1. Make sure any components removed during diagnosis are installed in place and that all connectors are connected. 2. Repeat the system check. Is the system check complete?	—	System OK	—

GC1129800091050X

Fig. 3 Charging system test (Part 5 of 5). LR series alternator

ALTERNATOR SPECIFICATIONS

Alternator Model	Rated Hot Output Amps
AD-230	105
AD237	105
CS-130	105
CS-130D	105
CS-130 DIF	105
CS-130DP	107
CS-144①	124
CS-144②	150
LR-630	150

① — Except part identification code KG9.
② — Service part identification code KG9.

Delphi Alternators, Saturn

INDEX

APPLICATION CHART

Type	Model
Saturn	CS130
Saturn	CS121

DESCRIPTION

The alternator is constructed of a rotor mounted on bearings in two end frames, a stator assembly, six silicon diodes, an internally mounted voltage regulator and an integral mounted shield. the alternator develops AC voltages which are converted to DC current by a rectifier circuit.

The Powertrain Control Module (PCM) monitors battery voltage and will increase idle speed if battery voltage drops below a calibrated amount.

TROUBLESHOOTING

Refer to **Fig. 1 and 2** for alternator system troubleshooting procedures.

66 X — Most Probable Cause(s)
• — Possible Causes

COMPLAINT–CONDITION / CAUSE	IGN4 Fuse	IGN3 Fuse	IGN1 Fuse	Circuit 15A (Battery Ground)	Circuit 2B	Circuit 3C	Circuit 39C	Circuit 25/25A	I/P Cluster	Generator	Ignition Switch	Excessive Electrical Load	Constant Running at Low RPM	Loose Belt	Broken Belt	Loose Mounting Bolts	Parasitic Load	Fusible Link Circuit 2C
Charge Warning Telltale Lamp Does Not Light	X		X		X	X	X	X	•	•	•							
Charge Warning Telltale Lamp stays on with Engine on								X	•	•		•	•	•	•			
Battery is Undercharged				X	X					•		•	•	•	•		X	X
Battery is Overcharged										X								
Lights Dim at Idle												X	•	•	X			•
Lights Dim at Over 1000 RPM										•				X	•	•		
Mechanical Noise										•				X		•		
Radio Noise/Hum or Whistle										X								
Output Exceeds 16V																		

G31129500007000X

Fig. 1 Alternator system troubleshooting chart

DIAGNOSIS & TESTING

PRECAUTIONS

Before connecting any test equipment to alternator, ensure engine is stopped, ignition switch is in Off position and drive belt is at correct tension. Refer to "Belt Tension Data" in the section for tension specifications.

CHARGING SYSTEM LIGHT FUNCTION TEST

1. Turn ignition key to Off position. Charge indicator lamp should be off.
2. Turn ignition key to On position. Charge indicator lamp should be on.
3. Crank engine. Charge indicator lamp should turn off and stay off once engine is running.

ALTERNATOR TEST

Electronic system tester tool No. SA9154Z, or equivalent, is required for the following starter system test.

1. Clean battery terminals and attach electronic system tester clamps to appropriate terminals.
2. Clamp current probe to wire leading to battery ground terminal. Arrow on probe should point toward battery.
3. Press "Charging System Test." Display should show correct number of cylinders.
4. Run engine at 2000 RPM until display flashes "Maintain 2000 RPM."
5. Hold at 2000 RPM until counter counts down from ten seconds.
6. When ten seconds are over, run engine at idle until display reads "Maintain Idle." Hold this momentarily until display reads "Test Complete."
7. Press "Continue" to see results. Electronic System Tester will display voltage and current output of alternator as follows:
   a. Voltage output should be above 13 volts.
   b. Current output should be a minimum of 60 amps.
8. If alternator does not meet specifications, proceed as follows:
   a. Verify battery is charged sufficiently and ensure electrical system is not excessively loaded.
   b. If battery has sufficient charge, electrical loads are not excessive and alternator performance is still not as specified, replace alternator.
   c. Repeat test to verify alternator is functioning properly.

COMPLAINT/CONDITION	POSSIBLE CAUSE(S)	CORRECTION(S)
High Pitch Whine with High Electrical Loads	– Magnetic noise from generator	– Verify additional electrical loads from accessories (e.g., cell phone, CB radio, radar detector, etc.).
	– Bearing noise	– Disconnect regulator connector if the whine is no longer present; tighten to specification all generator mounting bolts. Reconnect regulator; if whine still exists, replace generator.
Squeal, Click, Chirp, or Squeak Seems To Follow Engine rpm	– Serpentine belt	– Spray belt dressing on serpentine belt. If noise goes away, replace belt.
	– Generator bearing noise or rotor rub	– Check belt tension and ensure all belted accessories are tight. If noise is still present, replace generator.

G31129900009000X

Fig. 2 Alternator system troubleshooting chart

ALTERNATOR SPECIFICATIONS

Type	Model	Max. Rated Output, Amps	Temp. Deg. F	Approx. Output Amps @ RPM
Saturn	CS121& CS130	96	81	91 @ 2000
			221	71 @ 2000.

Bosch Alternators

NOTE: On Air Bag Equipped Models, Refer To " Air Bag System Precautions" Located In The Front Of This Manual For System Disarming & Arming Procedures.

NOTE: Refer To "Computer Relearn Procedure " Located In The Front Of This Manual For Computer Relearn Procedures.

INDEX

APPLICATION CHART

Model	Year	Rated Hot Output Amps.
Catera	1997–2000	120
Impala	2000	125

GENERAL INFORMATION

Refer to "Delphi Alternators" for general information.

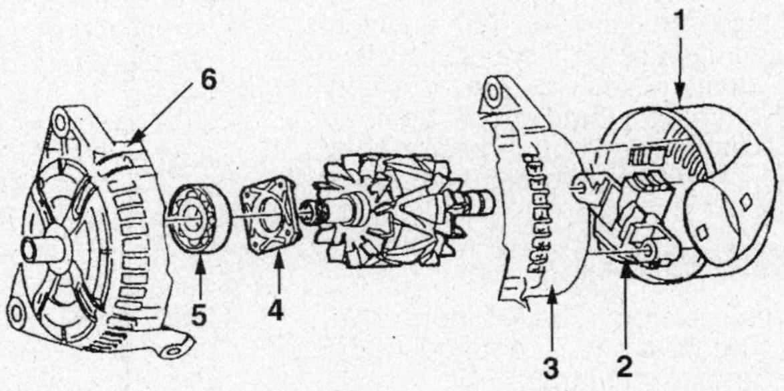

1. REAR CAP
2. REGULATOR
3. REAR COVER
4. FRONT BEARING RETAINER
5. FRONT BEARING
6. FRONT COVER
7. ARMATURE

GC11298000800000X

Fig. 1 Exploded view of Bosch alternator

PRECAUTIONS

AIR BAG SYSTEMS

Refer to "Air Bag System Precautions" in the front of this manual for system disarming and arming procedures.

BATTERY GROUND CABLE

Prior to service, disconnect battery ground cable and isolate as required.

CHARGING SYSTEM

1. Ensure battery polarity is correct when servicing units. Reversed battery polarity will damage rectifiers and regulators.
2. If booster battery is used for starting, use correct polarity in hook up.
3. When a fast charger is used to charge a vehicle battery, the vehicle battery cables should be disconnected unless the fast charger is equipped with a special Alternator Protector, in which case the vehicle battery cables need not be disconnected. Fast charger should never be used to start a vehicle as damage to rectifiers will result.
4. Unless the system includes a load relay or field relay, grounding the alter nator output terminal will damage the alternator and/or circuits. This is true even when the system is not in operation since no circuit breaker is used and the battery is applied to the alternator output terminal at all times. The field or load relay acts as a circuit breaker in that it is controlled by the ignition switch.
5. Before making any on vehicle tests of the alternator or regulator, the battery should be checked and the circuit inspected for faulty wiring or insulation. loose or corroded connections and poor ground circuits.
6. Inspect alternator belt tension and condition.
7. The ignition switch should be off and the battery ground cable disconnected before making any test connections to prevent damage to the system.
8. Do not reverse the connections to the alternator.
9. Do not short across or ground any of the terminals in the charging system.
10. Never disconnect the output terminal while the alternator is running.
11. The vehicle battery must be fully charged when testing the charging system.

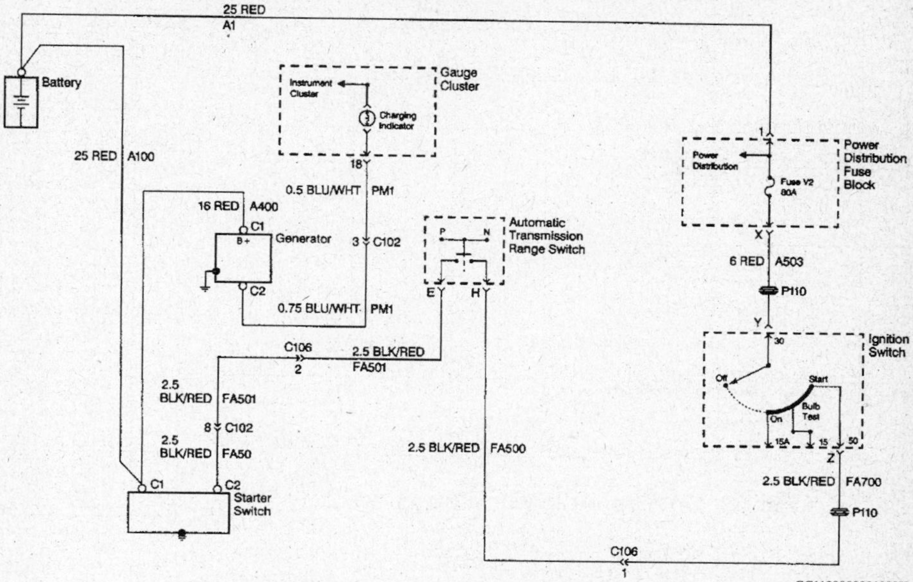

GC1129800081000X

Fig. 2 Charging system wiring diagram. Catera

Step	Action	Value(s)	Yes	No
1.	1. Disconnect the generator connector C2. 2. Turn the ignition switch to the ON position. 3. Use the DMM to measure the voltage between the generator connector C2 and a known good ground. Is the measured voltage within the specified value?	B+	*Go to Step 3*	*Go to Step 2*
2	1. Locate an open or a high resistance in circuit PM1. 2. Repair the open or the high resistance in circuit PM1. Is the repair complete?	—	*Go to Step 8*	—
3	Disconnect generator connector C1. 2. Use the DMM to measure the voltage between the generator connector C1 and a known good ground. Is the measured voltage within the specified value?	B+	*Go to Step 5*	*Go to Step 4*
4	1. Locate an open or a high resistance in circuits A100 and/or A400. 2. Repair the open or the high resistance in circuits A100 and/or A400. Is the repair complete?	—	*Go to Step 5*	—

GC1129800082010X

Fig. 3 Battery is undercharged or overcharged (Part 1 of 2)

Step	Action	Value(s)	Yes	No
5	1. Reconnect the generator connector. 2. Turn OFF all the accessories. 3. Run the engine at fast idle. 4. Use the DMM to measure the voltage between the positive and the negative terminals of the battery. Is the measured voltage within the specified value?	12.5–14.5V	*Go to Step 7*	*Go to Step 6*
6	Repair or replace the generator. Is the repair or replacement complete?	—	*Go to Step 8*	—
7	1. Load test the generator. 2. Replace the battery if the generator passed the load test. Is the replacement complete?	—	*Go to Step 8*	—
8	1. Connect all of the connectors and components that were disconnected. 2. Verify that the generator operates properly. Does the generator operate properly?	—	System OK	*Go to Step 1*

GC1129800082020X

Fig. 3 Battery is undercharged or overcharged (Part 2 of 2)

DESCRIPTION

CATERA

The Bosch alternator is a 120 amp output alternator. The main components are the rotor, field coil, regulator and rectifier bridge, **Fig. 1.** The alternator is water cooled. The coolant hose runs directly from the radiator to the alternator housing. No periodic maintenance is required.

IMPALA

The Bosch alternator is a 125 amp output alternator. The main components are the rotor, field coil, rectifier bridge and a digital regulator.

SYSTEM OPERATION

A regulator supplies current to the field coil of the rotor. When the field coil is supplied with voltage, a magnetic field is created. As the rotor turns, this magnetic field creates AC voltage and current in the stator windings. The AC voltage and current is converted to DC by a rectifier bridge which is available to the vehicle's electrical system.

DIAGNOSIS & TESTING

CATERA

Refer to wiring diagram **Fig. 2** and diagnosis charts **Figs. 3 through 5** for charging system diagnosis.

IMPALA

Refer to wiring diagram **Fig. 6** and diagnosis charts **Fig. 7** for charging system diagnosis.

Step	Action	Value(s)	Yes	No
1	1. Disconnect generator connector C2. 2. Turn the ignition switch to the ON position. Is the charging indicator lamp illuminated?	—	*Go to Step 3*	*Go to Step 2*
2	Repair or replace the generator. Is the repair or replacement complete?	—	*Go to Step 6*	—
3	Disconnect connector C102. Is the charging indicator lamp illuminated?	—	*Go to Step 5*	*Go to Step 4*
4	1. Locate the short to ground in circuit PM1 between the generator connector C2 and connector C102 terminal 3. 2. Repair the short to ground in circuit PM1. Is the repair complete?	—	*Go to Step 6*	—
5	1. Locate a short to ground in circuit PM1 between the gauge cluster connector terminal 18 and connector C102 terminal 3. 2. Repair the short to ground in circuit PM1 between the gauge cluster connector terminal 18 and connector C102 terminal 3. 3. Replace the gauge cluster if circuit PM1 is OK. Is the repair or replacement complete?	—	*Go to Step 6*	—
6	1. Connect all connectors and components that were disconnected. 2. Verify that the charging indicator lamp operates properly. Does the charging indicator lamp operate properly?	—	System OK	*Go to Step 1*

GC1129800083000X

Fig. 4 Charge indicator always on

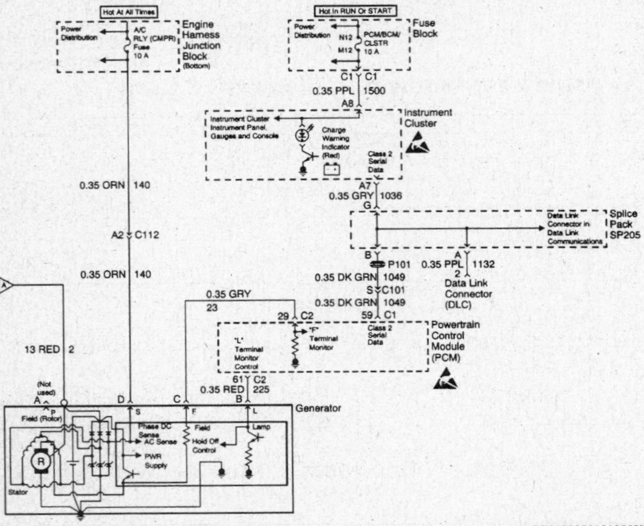

GC1120000101000X

Fig. 6 Charging system wiring diagram. Impala

Step	Action	Value(s)	Yes	No
1	1. Disconnect generator connector C2. 2. Attach a fused jumper from the generator connector C2 to ground. 3. Turn the ignition switch to the ON position. Is the charging indicator lamp illuminated?	—	*Go to Step 2*	*Go to Step 3*
2	Repair or replace the generator. Is the repair or replacement complete?	—	*Go to Step 6*	—
3	1. Disconnect connector C102. 2. Attach a fused jumper between terminal 3 of connector C102 and a known good ground. Is the charging indicator lamp illuminated?	—	*Go to Step 4*	*Go to Step 6*
4	1. Locate an open or a high resistance in circuit PM1 between terminal 3 of connector C102 and the generator connector C2. 2. Repair the open or the high resistance in circuit PM1 between terminal 3 of connector C102 and the generator connector C2. Is the repair complete?	—	*Go to Step 6*	—
5	1. Locate an open or a high resistance in circuit PM1 between terminal 3 of connector C102 and terminal 18 of the gauge cluster connector. 2. Repair the open or the high resistance in circuit PM1 between terminal 3 of connector C102 and terminal 18 of the gauge cluster connector. 3. Replace the gauge cluster if circuit PM1 is OK. Is the repair or replacement complete?	—	*Go to Step 6*	—
6	1. Connect all of the connectors and components that were disconnected. 2. Verify that the charging indicator operates properly. Does the charging indicator lamp operate properly?	—	System OK	*Go to Step 1*

GC1129800084000X

Fig. 5 Charge indicator inoperative

Step	Action	Value(s)	Yes	No
1	**Inspect battery & starting system.** **Are systems operating properly?**		Go to Step 2	**Repair or replace components as needed**
2	Connect the J 41450-B to the generator. Does the green POWER lamp on the tester light?		Go to Step 4	Go to Step 3
3	Measure the voltage from the output terminal of the J 41450-B to the metal housing of the generator. Does the voltage measure greater than the specified value?	12 V	Go to Step 12	Go to Step 4
4	1 Disconnect the generator harness connector. 2 Locate the matching harness connector on the J 41450-B and connect it to the generator. Does the red DIAGNOSTIC lamp on the tester light?		Go to Step 6	Go to Step 5
5	**Notice:** The J 41450-B connector terminals are the same as the generator connector terminals. 1 Disconnect the J 41450-B harness connector from the generator. 2 Prepare a jumper wire with an in-line 100Ω resistor. 3 Attach a Metri-Pack 150 male terminal probe adapter from a J 35616-A 4 Connect the jumper wire between the L terminal of the J 41450-B and a good ground. Does the red DIAGNOSTIC lamp on the tester light?		Go to Step 15	Go to Step 13

GC1120000102010X

Fig. 7 Charging system test (Part 1 of 3). Impala

Step	Action	Value(s)	Yes	No
6	**Caution** **Make sure that the load is completely turned off before connecting or disconnecting a carbon pile load tester to the battery. Otherwise, sparking could ignite battery gasses which are extremely flammable and may explode violently.** 1 Connect a carbon pile tester to the vehicle. 2 Connect an inductive ammeter to the output circuit of the generator. 3 Start the engine and allow it to idle briefly. Does the red DIAGNOSTIC lamp on the tester light?		Go to Step 15	Go to Step 7
7	Increase the engine speed to 2500 RPM. Does the red DIAGNOSTIC lamp on the tester light?		Go to Step 15	Go to Step 8
8	1 Maintain the engine speed at 2500 RPM. 2 Turn on the load of the carbon pile tester and increase the load until the generator output is equal to the load test value. Is the generator output greater than the load test value?		Go to Step 9	Go to Step 15
9	Maintain the engine speed at 2500 RPM and continue to operate the generator at the load test value. Does the red DIAGNOSTIC lamp on the tester light?		Go to Step 15	Go to Step 10
10	1 Maintain the engine speed at 2500 RPM and continue to operate the generator at the load test value. 2 Measure the voltage from the output terminal of the generator to the positive terminal on the front relay block. Does the voltage measure greater than the specified value?	0.5 V	Go to Step 15	Go to Step 11

GC1120000102020X

Fig. 7 Charging system test (Part 2 of 3). Impala

Step	Action	Value(s)	Yes	No
11	1 Maintain the engine speed at 2500 RPM and continue to operate the generator at the load test value. 2 Measure the voltage from the housing of the generator to a good ground. Does the voltage measure greater than the specified value?	0.5 V	Go to Step 15	Go to Step 13
12	There is an internal problem in the J 41450-B . Replace the J 41450-B . Has the J 41450-B been replaced?		Go to Step 2	
13	Test the output circuit of the generator for a high resistance or an open. Did you find and correct the condition?		Go to Step 17	Go to Step 14
14	Test the ground circuit of the generator for a high resistance or an open. Did you find and correct the condition?		Go to Step 17	Go to Step 15
15	Inspect for poor connections at the harness connector of the generator. Did you find and correct the condition?		Go to Step 17	Go to Step 16
16	Replace the generator. Is the repair complete?		Go to Step 17	
17	Operate the system for which the symptom occurred. Does the symptom reoccur?		Go to Step 2	System OK

GC1120000102030X

Fig. 7 Charging system test (Part 3 of 3). Impala

ALTERNATOR SPECIFICATIONS

Model	Year	Rated Hot Output Amps	Regulated Voltage	Brush Length Minimum, Inch	Commulator Diameter Minimum, Inch
Catera	1997–2000	120	14.7–15	.315	1.228
Impala	2000	125	—	—	—

Mitsubishi & Nippondenso Alternators

NOTE: On Air Bag Equipped Models, Refer To " Air Bag System Precautions" Located In The Front Of This Manual For System Disarming & Arming Procedures.

NOTE: Refer To "Computer Relearn Procedure " Located In The Front Of This Manual For Computer Relearn Procedures.

INDEX

APPLICATION CHART

Model	Year	Manufacturer	Rated Hot Output Amps.
Metro	1997-2000	Mitsubishi	55
Prizm	1997–98	Nippondenso	70
	1999-2000	Nippondenso	80

GENERAL INFORMATION

Refer to "Delphi Alternators" for general information.

PRECAUTIONS

AIR BAG SYSTEMS

Refer to "Air Bag System Precautions" in the front of this manual for system disarming and arming procedures.

BATTERY GROUND CABLE

Prior to service, disconnect battery ground cable and isolate as required.

CHARGING SYSTEM

1. Ensure battery polarity is correct when servicing units. Reversed battery polarity will damage rectifiers and regulators.
2. If booster battery is used for starting, use correct polarity in hook up.
3. When a fast charger is used to charge a vehicle battery, the vehicle battery cables should be disconnected unless the fast charger is equipped with a special Alternator Protector, in which case the vehicle battery cables need not be disconnected. Fast charger should never be used to start a vehicle as damage to rectifiers will result.
4. Unless the system includes a load relay or field relay, grounding the alternator output terminal will damage the alternator and/or circuits. This is true even when the system is not in operation since no circuit breaker is used and the battery is applied to the alternator output terminal at all times. The field or load relay acts as a circuit breaker in that it is controlled by the ignition switch.
5. Before making any on vehicle tests of the alternator or regulator, the battery should be checked and the circuit inspected for faulty wiring or insulation. loose or corroded connections and poor ground circuits.
6. Inspect alternator belt tension and condition.
7. The ignition switch should be off and the battery ground cable disconnected before making any test connections to prevent damage to the system.
8. Do not reverse the connections to the alternator.
9. Do not short across or ground any of the terminals in the charging system.
10. Never disconnect the output terminal while the alternator is running.
11. The vehicle battery must be fully charged when testing the charging system.

DESCRIPTION

These alternators have IC integral solid state regulators, **Figs. 1 and 2.** All regulator components are enclosed into a solid mold and are attached to the slip ring end frame along with the brush holder assembly. The alternator voltage setting cannot be adjusted.

The alternator rotor bearings contain enough grease to eliminate the need for periodic lubrication. Two brushes carry current through the two slip rings to the field coil mounted on the rotor.

The stator windings are assembled on the inside of a laminated core that form part of the alternator frame. The rectifier bridge contains six diodes which electrically change stator A.C. voltage into D.C. voltage. The neutral diodes serve to convert the voltage fluctuation at the neutral point to direct current for increasing generator output.

DIAGNOSIS & TESTING

SYSTEM TEST

1. Connect a voltmeter across the battery.
2. Start engine and allow to run at 2,000 RPM, then check reading of voltmeter. Voltmeter should read at least 13.5 volts.
3. If voltage reading is not as specified, disconnect battery ground cable.
4. Disconnect alternator B terminal wire.
5. Connect ammeter red lead to alternator B terminal and black lead to disconnected B terminal wire.

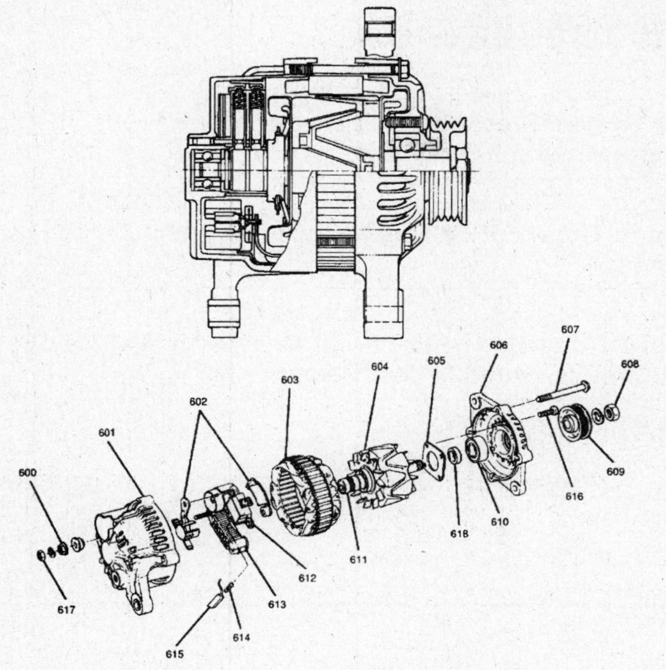

Fig. 1 Exploded view of Mitsubishi alternator

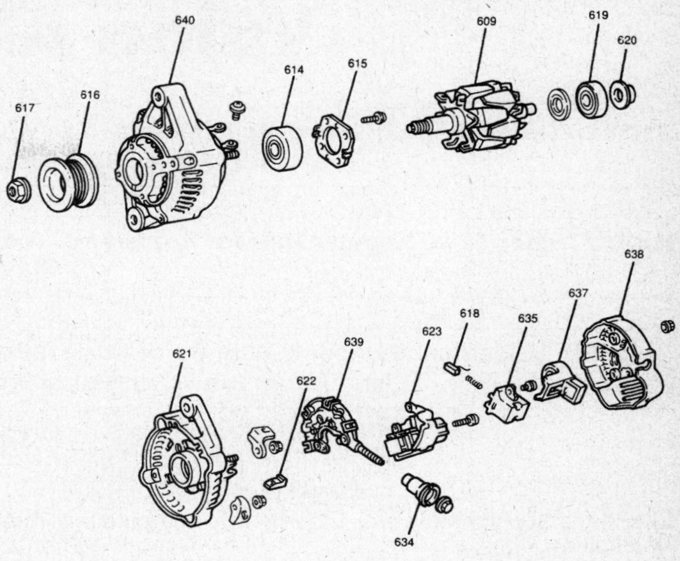

Fig. 2 Exploded view of Nippondenso alternator

6. Connect a voltmeter between alternator B terminal and chassis ground.
7. Connect battery ground cable, then start engine and turn On all accessories.
8. Operate engine at sufficient RPM (approximately 2000 RPM) to obtain maximum alternator current output.
9. If current reading is not within 10 amps of maximum rated output or voltage reading is not 13.5 to 16 volts, repair alternator.

REGULATOR TEST

1. Connect a voltmeter and fast charger to battery.
2. Turn ignition switch On and slowly increase charge rate. Indicator lamp in vehicle will begin to dim when voltage setting is reached.
3. Observe voltmeter, light should dim at 13.5 –16.0 volts.
4. If no voltage is present, replace voltage regulator.

ALTERNATOR SPECIFICATIONS

Model	Year	Alternator Manufacturer	Rated Hot Output Amps	Regulated Voltage
Metro	1997–2000	Mitsubishi	55	14.7–15
Prizm	1997–98	Nippondenso	70	13.5–15
	1999-2000	Nippondenso	80	13.5-15

Valeo Alternators

NOTE: On Air Bag Equipped Models, Refer To " Air Bag System Precautions" Located In The Front Of This Manual For System Disarming & Arming Procedures.

NOTE: Refer To "Computer Relearn Procedure " Located In The Front Of This Manual For Computer Relearn Procedures.

NOTE: "Electrical Symbol & Wire Color Code Identification" Located In The Front Of This Manual May Be Used As An Aid When Using Wiring Circuits Found In This Section.

INDEX

APPLICATION CHART

Model	Year	Rated Output Amps.
Corvette	1997–2000	70-110

GENERAL INFORMATION

Refer to "Delphi Alternators" for general information.

PRECAUTIONS

AIR BAG SYSTEMS

Refer to "Air Bag System Precautions" in the front of this manual for system disarming and arming procedures.

BATTERY GROUND CABLE

Prior to service, disconnect battery ground cable and isolate as required.

CHARGING SYSTEM

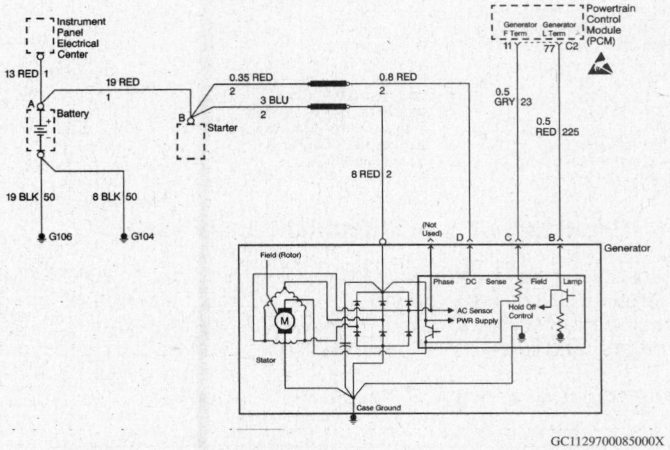

Fig. 1 Charging system wiring diagram

1. Ensure battery polarity is correct when servicing units. Reversed battery polarity will damage rectifiers and regulators.
2. If booster battery is used for starting, use correct polarity in hook up.
3. When a fast charger is used to charge a vehicle battery, the vehicle battery cables should be disconnected unless the fast charger is equipped with a special Alternator Protector, in which case the vehicle battery cables need not be disconnected. Fast charger should never be used to start a vehicle as damage to rectifiers will result.
4. Unless the system includes a load relay or field relay, grounding the alternator output terminal will damage the alternator and/or circuits. This is true even when the system is not in operation since no circuit breaker is used and the battery is applied to the alternator output terminal at all times. The field or load relay acts as a circuit breaker in that it is controlled by the ignition switch.
5. Before making any on vehicle tests of the alternator or regulator, the battery should be checked and the circuit inspected for faulty wiring or insulation. loose or corroded connections and poor ground circuits.
6. Inspect alternator belt tension and condition.
7. The ignition switch should be off and the battery ground cable disconnected before making any test connections to prevent damage to the system.
8. Do not reverse the connections to the alternator.
9. Do not short across or ground any of the terminals in the charging system.
10. Never disconnect the output terminal while the alternator is running.
11. The vehicle battery must be fully charged when testing the charging system.

DESCRIPTION

The Valeo alternator is available in one size with a maximum output of 110 amps. The main components are the rotor, regulator and rectifier bridge. No periodic maintenance is required.

DIAGNOSIS & TESTING

Refer to wiring diagram **Fig. 1** and diagnosis charts **Figs. 2 through 5** for charging system diagnosis.

Step	Action	Normal Result(s)	Abnormal Result(s)*
1	1. Inspect the battery for proper installation. 2. Inspect the battery for cracking or other damage. 3. Inspect the battery terminals for proper connection. 4. Inspect the battery terminals for excessive corrosion. 5. Inspect the battery cables for proper installation. 6. Check that all ground connections are clean and tight. 7. Inspect the battery hydrometer (eye) for a green dot. 8. Connect a DMM between the battery's positive and negative terminals. 9. Ensure that any aftermarket accessory equipment is de-energized. 10. Observe the battery voltage.	1. The battery is properly installed. 2. The battery is free from physical damage. 3. The battery terminals are free from corrosion. 4. The battery cables are properly connected. 5. The battery cables are properly installed. 6. The battery hydrometer displays a green dot. 7. Battery voltage is approximately between 11.5 to 13.0 volts.	• Battery Hydrometer Displays Dark or Yellow Dot. • Common Causes of Battery Failure. • Battery is undercharged (refer to Battery Charging).
2	1. Remove the DMM from the battery terminals. 2. Perform a load test on the battery	Battery maintains a specified voltage level according to the Battery Temperature vs. Voltage Drop table.	Battery does not maintain the specified voltage level during the load test, replace the battery

GC1129700089010X

Fig. 2 Charging system check (Part 1 of 2)

Step	Action	Normal Result(s)	Abnormal Result(s)*
3	1. Install the scan tool to the diagnostic link connector. 2. Turn the ignition switch to the ON position. 3. Select display DTC function with the scan tool. 4. Check for any stored PCM, BCM, or communication DTCs related to theft deterrent, starting or charging system operation.	No DTCs are stored in memory or current status.	• DTC is stored in memory or current status (refer to appropriate DTC table). • Scan Tool Does Not Communicate with Component.
4	1. Start the engine and allow it to idle in PARK. 2. Press the HVAC MODE control button until the LOWER floor position is displayed. 3. Depress the fan control button until the fan reaches high speed. 4. Turn the headlamp switch to the ON position (headlights ON). 5. Move the wiper switch to the HI position (maintain some moisture on the windshield while the wipers are in operation). 6. Maintain engine speed between 800 and 1000 RPMs. 7. Connect a DMM between the battery positive terminal and negative terminal. 8. Observe the voltage reading at the DMM.	1. The generator operates without unusual noises. 2. The battery indicator light on the instrument cluster extinguishes after the engine is started. 3. The SERVICE ENGINE SOON malfunction indicator lamp extinguishes when the engine starts. 4. The DMM reads approximately between 12.0 and 16.0 volts while the engine is idling.	• Battery is Undercharged or Overcharged (Low/High Voltage Message). • Indicator-Always ON (Charge System Fault Message). • Voltmeter Displaying High or Low.

GC1129700089020X

Fig. 2 Charging system check (Part 2 of 2)

Step	Action	Value(s)	Yes	No
	DEFINITION: The vehicle's charging system has begun to either undercharge or overcharge the battery. The regulated voltage has dropped below 13.5 volts or raised above 15.5 volts with the vehicle in normal operation. The Instrument Panel Cluster (IPC) has detected this condition through monitoring the Ignition 1 voltage at the IPC connector terminal A13. If the voltage reading at the IPC terminal A13 falls out of the normal range, the IPC will inform the driver by illuminating across the Driver's Information Center either the LOW VOLTAGE or HIGH VOLTAGE warning message. The voltmeter indicator may or may not indicate abnormal voltage readings. If PCM fault codes P0562 or P0563 exist, diagnose those first before proceeding with this table. Always ensure that a good battery is installed in the vehicle, charging system operation depends heavily on the battery condition.			
1	Were you sent here from the Charging System Check?	—	*Go to Step 2*	Go to Charging System Check
2	Load test the battery. Does the battery pass the load test?	—	*Go to Step 5*	*Go to Step 3*
3	1. Recharge the battery. 2. After charging, load test the battery again. Does the battery pass the load test?	—	*Go to Step 5*	*Go to Step 4*
4	Replace the battery. Is the repair complete?	—	Go to Charging System Check	—
5	1. Start the engine and allow it to idle in Park. 2. Load the electrical system by turning on the headlights and the high blower. 3. Connect a DMM between the battery terminals. 4. Measure the available voltage at the battery with the engine running and the electrical system under load. Is the voltage within the specified values?	10.0-14.0V	*Go to Step 6*	*Go to Step 11*
6	1. Turn the ignition switch to the OFF position. 2. Disconnect the instrument panel cluster connector. 3. Return the ignition switch to the ON position. 4. Connect a DMM between ground and the instrument panel cluster terminal A13. 5. Measure the available voltage at the instrument panel cluster terminal A13. Is the voltage within the specified values?	10.0-14.0V	*Go to Step 7*	*Go to Step 8*
7	Replace the instrument panel cluster (IPC). Is the repair complete?	—	Go to Charging System Check	—
8	Check the IPC MiniFuse #19 fuse for an open circuit. Is this fuse open?	—	*Go to Step 9*	*Go to Step 10*
9	Repair a short to ground in CKT 139. Is the repair complete?	—	Go to Charging System Check	—
10	Repair the open in CKT 139. Is the repair complete?	—	Go to Charging System Check	—
11	1. Connect a DMM between the BATTERY terminal (CKT 2-large red wire) in the back of the generator and ground. 2. Measure the available voltage at the BATTERY terminal (CKT 2-large red wire) in the back of the generator. Is the voltage within the specified values?	10.0-14.0V	*Go to Step 15*	*Go to Step 12*
12	Check the fusible link at the starter motor between the medium gauge blue wire (CKT 2) and the heavy gauge red wire (CKT 2). See wiring schematic for further detail. Is the fusible link open?	—	*Go to Step 13*	*Go to Step 14*

GC1129700086010X

Fig. 3 Battery is undercharged or overcharged (Part 1 of 3)

Step	Action	Value(s)	Yes	No
13	Repair a short to ground in CKT 2 (13 red wire) between the generator BATTERY terminal and the fusible link. Is the repair complete?	—	Go to Charging System Check	—
14	Repair an open in CKT 1 (19 red wire), CKT 2 (3 blue wire) or CKT 2 (13 red wire) between the generator BATTERY terminal and the positive battery terminal. Is the repair complete?	—	Go to Charging System Check	—
15	1. Disconnect the generator connector. 2. Connect a DMM between the generator connector terminal D (CKT 2-medium red wire) and ground. 3. Measure the available voltage at the generator connector terminal D (CKT 2-medium red wire). Is the voltage within the specified values?	10.0-14.0V	*Go to Step 19*	*Go to Step 16*
16	Check the fusible link at the starter motor between the small gauge grey wire (CKT 2) and the medium gauge red wire (CKT 2). See wiring schematic for further detail. Is the fusible link open?	—	*Go to Step 17*	*Go to Step 18*
17	Repair a short to ground in CKT 2 (1 red wire) between the generator connector terminal D and the fusible link. Is the repair complete?	—	Go to Charging System Check	—
18	Repair an open in CKT 1 (19 red wire), CKT 2 (0.5 grey wire) or CKT 2 (1 red wire) between the generator connector terminal D and the positive battery terminal. Is the repair complete?	—	Go to Charging System Check	—
19	1. Disconnect the powertrain control module connector C2. 2. Connect a DMM between the generator connector terminal C (CKT 23) and the powertrain control module connector C2 terminal 11. 3. Measure CKT 23 for continuity between these two connectors. Is CKT 23 continuous between the generator connector and the powertrain control module connector C2?	—	*Go to Step 20*	*Go to Step 22*
20	1. Powertrain control module connector C2 and generator connector are still disconnected. 2. Connect the DMM between the generator connector terminal C (CKT 23) and ground. 3. Measure CKT 23 for continuity to ground. Is CKT 23 shorted to ground?	—	*Go to Step 23*	*Go to Step 21*
21	1. Powertrain control module connector C2 and generator connector are still disconnected. 2. DMM still connected between the generator connector terminal C (CKT 23) and ground. 3. Turn the ignition switch to the ON position. 4. Measure CKT 23 for available voltage. Is CKT 23 shorted to battery power?	—	*Go to Step 24*	*Go to Step 25*

GC1129700086020X

Fig. 3 Battery is undercharged or overcharged (Part 2 of 3)

Step	Action	Value(s)	Yes	No
22	Repair the open in CKT 23 between the generator connector and the powertrain control module connector C2. Is the repair complete?	—	Go to Charging System Check	—
23	Repair the short to ground in CKT 23 between the generator connector and the powertrain control module connector C2. Is the repair complete?	—	Go to Charging System Check	—
24	Repair the short to battery power in CKT 23 between the generator connector and the powertrain control module connector C2. Is the repair complete?	—	Go to Charging System Check	—
25	1. Connect a DMM between the generator connector terminal B (CKT 225) and the powertrain control module connector C2 terminal 77. 2. Measure CKT 225 for continuity between these two connectors. Is CKT 225 continuous between the generator connector and the powertrain control module connector C2?	—	*Go to Step 26*	*Go to Step 28*
26	1. Powertrain control module connector C2 and generator connector are still disconnected. 2. Connect the DMM between the generator connector terminal B (CKT 225) and ground. 3. Measure CKT 225 for continuity to ground. Is CKT 225 shorted to ground?	—	*Go to Step 29*	*Go to Step 27*
27	1. Powertrain control module connector C2 and generator connector are still disconnected. 2. DMM still connected between the generator connector terminal B (CKT 225) and ground. 3. Turn the ignition switch to the ON position. 4. Measure CKT 225 for available voltage. Is CKT 225 shorted to battery power?	—	*Go to Step 30*	*Go to Step 31*
28	Repair the open in CKT 225 between the generator connector and the powertrain control module connector C2. Is the repair complete?	—	Go to Charging System Check	—
29	Repair the short to ground in CKT 225 between the generator connector and the powertrain control module connector C2. Is the repair complete?	—	Go to Charging System Check	—
30	Repair the short to battery power in CKT 225 between the generator connector and the powertrain control module connector C2. Is the repair complete?	—	Go to Charging System Check	—
31	Replace the generator. Is the repair complete?	—	Go to Charging System Check	—

GC1129700086030X

Fig. 3 Battery is undercharged or overcharged (Part 3 of 3)

Step	Action	Value(s)	Yes	No
	DEFINITION: A charging system fault has been detected by the Powertrain Control Module (PCM). The PCM monitors CKT 225 at connector C2 terminal 77. If the incorrect voltage reading is detected at connector C2 terminal 77, the PCM will send a Class 2 message to the IPC indicating a charging system fault. The CHARGE SYSTEM FAULT warning message will then illuminate across the Driver's Information Center. The voltmeter indicator may or may not indicate abnormal voltage readings. If PCM fault codes P0562 or P0563 exist, diagnose those first before proceeding with this table. Always ensure that a good battery is installed in the vehicle, charging system operation depends heavily on the battery condition.			
1	Were you sent here from the Charging System Check?	—	*Go to Step 2*	Go to Charging System Check
2	Load test the battery. Does the battery pass the load test?	—	*Go to Step 5*	*Go to Step 3*
3	1. Recharge the battery. 2. After charging, load test the battery again. Does the battery pass the load test?	—	*Go to Step 5*	*Go to Step 4*
4	Replace the battery. Is the repair complete?	—	Go to Charging System Check	—
5	1. Start the engine and allow it to idle in Park. 2. Load the electrical system by turning on the headlights and the high blower. 3. Connect a DMM between the battery terminals. 4. Measure the available voltage at the battery with the engine running and the electrical system under load. Is the voltage within the specified values?	10.0-14.0V	*Go to Step 6*	*Go to Step 11*
6	1. Turn the ignition switch to the OFF position. 2. Disconnect the powertrain control module connector C2. 3. Return the ignition switch to the ON position. 4. Connect a DMM between ground and: • the powertrain control module connector C2 terminal 61. • the powertrain control module connector C2 terminal 20. • the powertrain control module connector C2 terminal 19. 5. Measure the available voltage at these powertrain control module terminals. Is the voltage within the specified values?	10.0-14.0V	*Go to Step 7*	*Go to Step 8*
7	Replace the Powertrain Control Module (PCM). Is the repair complete?	—	Go to Charging System Check	—
8	Check the following fuses for an open cirucit. • PCMB MiniFuse #23 • PCM MiniFuse #16 Is either of these fuses open?	—	*Go to Step 9*	*Go to Step 10*
9	Repair a short to ground in the circuit relative to the open fuse. • CKT 340 = PCMB MiniFuse #23 • CKT 239 = PCM MiniFuse #16 Is the repair complete?	—	Go to Charging System Check	—

GC1129700087010X

Fig. 4 Charge indicator always on (Part 1 of 4)

Step	Action	Value(s)	Yes	No
10	Repair the open in the circuit relative to the PCM terminal lacking voltage. • CKT 340 = PCM connector C2 terminals 20 and 61 • CKT 239 = PCM connector C2 terminal 19 Is the repair complete?	—	Go to Charging System Check	—
11	1. Connect a DMM between the BATTERY terminal (CKT 2-large red wire) in the back of the generator and ground. 2. Measure the available voltage at the BATTERY terminal (CKT 2-large red wire) in the back of the generator. Is the voltage within the specified values?	10.0-14.0V	*Go to Step 15*	*Go to Step 12*
12	Check the fusible link located down at the starter motor between the medium gauge blue wire (CKT 2) and the heavy gauge red wire (CKT 2). Is the fusible link open?	—	*Go to Step 13*	*Go to Step 14*
13	Repair a short to ground in CKT 2 (13 red wire) between the generator BATTERY terminal and the fusible link. Is the repair complete?	—	Go to Charging System Check	—
14	Repair an open in CKT 1 (19 red wire), CKT 2 (3 blue wire) or CKT 2 (13 red wire) between the generator BATTERY terminal and the positive battery terminal. Is the repair complete?	—	Go to Charging System Check	—
15	1. Disconnect the generator connector. 2. Connect a DMM between the generator connector terminal D (CKT 2-medium red wire) and ground. 3. Measure the available voltage at the generator connector terminal D (CKT 2-medium red wire). Is the voltage within the specified values?	10.0-14.0V	*Go to Step 19*	*Go to Step 16*
16	Check the fusible link located down at the starter motor between the small gauge grey wire (CKT 2) and the medium gauge red wire (CKT 2). Is the fusible link open?	—	*Go to Step 17*	*Go to Step 18*
17	Repair a short to ground in CKT 2 (1 red wire) between the generator connector terminal D and the fusible link. Is the repair complete?	—	Go to Charging System Check	—
18	Repair an open in CKT 1 (19 red wire), CKT 2 (0.5 grey wire) or CKT 2 (1 red wire) between the generator connector terminal D and the positive battery terminal. Is the repair complete?	—	Go to Charging System Check	—
19	1. Disconnect the powertrain control module connector C2. 2. Connect a DMM between the generator connector terminal C (CKT 23) and the powertrain control module connector C2 terminal 11. 3. Measure CKT 23 for continuity between these two connectors. Is CKT 23 continuous between the generator connector and the powertrain control module connector C2?	—	*Go to Step 20*	*Go to Step 22*

GC1129700087020X

Fig. 4 Charge indicator always on (Part 2 of 4)

Step	Action	Value(s)	Yes	No
20	1. Powertrain control module connector C2 and generator connector are still disconnected. 2. Connect the DMM between the generator connector terminal C (CKT 23) and ground. 3. Measure CKT 23 for continuity to ground. Is CKT 23 shorted to ground?	—	*Go to Step 23*	*Go to Step 21*
21	1. Powertrain control module connector C2 and generator connector are still disconnected. 2. DMM still connected between the generator connector terminal C (CKT 23) and ground. 3. Turn the ignition switch to the ON position. 4. Measure CKT 23 for available voltage. Is CKT 23 shorted to battery power?	—	*Go to Step 24*	*Go to Step 25*
22	Repair the open in CKT 23 between the generator connector and the powertrain control module connector C2. Is the repair complete?	—	Go to Charging System Check	—
23	Repair the short to ground in CKT 23 between the generator connector and the powertrain control module connector C2. Is the repair complete?	—	Go to Charging System Check	—
24	Repair the short to battery power in CKT 23 between the generator connector and the powertrain control module connector C2. Is the repair complete?	—	Go to Charging System Check	—
25	1. Connect a DMM between the generator connector terminal B (CKT 225) and the powertrain control module connector C2 terminal 77. 2. Measure CKT 225 for continuity between these two connectors. Is CKT 225 continuous between the generator connector and the powertrain control module connector C2?	—	*Go to Step 26*	*Go to Step 28*
26	1. Powertrain control module connector C2 and generator connector are still disconnected. 2. Connect the DMM between the generator connector terminal B (CKT 225) and ground. 3. Measure CKT 225 for continuity to ground. Is CKT 225 shorted to ground?	—	*Go to Step 29*	*Go to Step 27*
27	1. Powertrain control module connector C2 and generator connector are still disconnected. 2. DMM still connected between the generator connector terminal B (CKT 225) and ground. 3. Turn the ignition switch to the ON position. 4. Measure CKT 225 for available voltage. Is CKT 225 shorted to battery power?	—	*Go to Step 30*	*Go to Step 31*
28	Repair the open in CKT 225 between the generator connector and the powertrain control module connector C2. Is the repair complete?	—	Go to Charging System Check	—
29	Repair the short to ground in CKT 225 between the generator connector and the powertrain control module connector C2. Is the repair complete?	—	Go to Charging System Check	—

GC1129700087030X

Fig. 4 Charge indicator always on (Part 3 of 4)

Step	Action	Value(s)	Yes	No
30	Repair the short to battery power in CKT 225 between the generator connector and the powertrain control module connector C2. Is the repair complete?	—	Go to Charging System Check	—
31	Replace the generator. Is the repair complete?	—	Go to Charging System Check	—

GC1129700087040X

Fig. 4 Charge indicator always on (Part 4 of 4)

Step	Action	Value(s)	Yes	No
19	1. Disconnect the powertrain control module connector C2. 2. Connect a DMM between the generator connector terminal C (CKT 23) and the powertrain control module connector C2 terminal 11. 3. Measure CKT 23 for continuity between these two connectors. Is CKT 23 continuous between the generator connector and the powertrain control module connector C2?	—	Go to Step 20	Go to Step 22
20	1. Powertrain control module connector C2 and generator connector are still disconnected. 2. Connect the DMM between the generator connector terminal C (CKT 23) and ground. 3. Measure CKT 23 for continuity to ground. Is CKT 23 shorted to ground?	—	Go to Step 23	Go to Step 21
21	1. Powertrain control module connector C2 and generator connector are still disconnected. 2. DMM still connected between the generator connector terminal C (CKT 23) and ground. 3. Turn the ignition switch to the ON position. 4. Measure CKT 23 for available voltage. Is CKT 23 shorted to battery power?	—	Go to Step 24	Go to Step 25
22	Repair the open in CKT 23 between the generator connector and the powertrain control module connector C2. Is the repair complete?	—	Go to Charging System Check	—
23	Repair the short to ground in CKT 23 between the generator connector and the powertrain control module connector C2. Is the repair complete?	—	Go to Charging System Check	—
24	Repair the short to battery power in CKT 23 between the generator connector and the powertrain control module connector C2. Is the repair complete?	—	Go to Charging System Check	—
25	1. Connect a DMM between the generator connector terminal B (CKT 225) and the powertrain control module connector C2 terminal 77. 2. Measure CKT 225 for continuity between these two connectors. Is CKT 225 continuous between the generator connector and the powertrain control module connector C2?	—	Go to Step 26	Go to Step 28
26	1. Powertrain control module connector C2 and generator connector are still disconnected. 2. Connect the DMM between the generator connector terminal B (CKT 225) and ground. 3. Measure CKT 225 for continuity to ground. Is CKT 225 shorted to ground?	—	Go to Step 29	Go to Step 27
27	1. Powertrain control module connector C2 and generator connector are still disconnected. 2. DMM still connected between the generator connector terminal B (CKT 225) and ground. 3. Turn the ignition switch to the ON position. 4. Measure CKT 225 for available voltage. Is CKT 225 shorted to battery power?	—	Go to Step 30	Go to Step 31

GC1129700088030X

Fig. 5 Voltmeter displaying high or low (Part 3 of 4)

Step	Action	Value(s)	Yes	No
DEFINITION: The voltmeter is indicating abnormal voltage readings. The Instrument Panel Cluster (IPC) monitors Ignition 1 voltage at the IPC connector terminal A13. If the voltage reading at the IPC terminal A13 falls out of the normal range, the IPC should inform the driver by illuminating across the Driver's Information Center either the LOW VOLTAGE or HIGH VOLTAGE warning message. If PCM fault codes P0562 or P0563 exist, diagnose those first before proceeding with this table. Always ensure that a good battery is installed in the vehicle, charging system operation depends heavily on the battery condition.				
1	Were you sent here from the Charging System Check?	—	Go to Step 2	Go to Charging System Check
2	Load test the battery. Does the battery pass the load test?	—	Go to Step 5	Go to Step 3
3	1. Recharge the battery. 2. After charging, load test the battery again. Does the battery pass the load test?	—	Go to Step 5	Go to Step 4
4	Replace the battery. Is the repair complete?	—	Go to Charging System Check	—
5	1. Start the engine and allow it to idle in Park. 2. Load the electrical system by turning on the headlights and the high blower. 3. Connect a DMM between the battery terminals. 4. Measure the available voltage at the battery with the engine running and the electrical system under load. Is the voltage within the specified values?	10.0-14.0V	Go to Step 6	Go to Step 11
6	1. Turn the ignition switch to the OFF position. 2. Disconnect the instrument panel cluster connector. 3. Connect one DMM between the battery terminals. 4. Connect another DMM between ground and the instrument panel cluster terminal A13. 5. Start the engine and allow it to idle in Park. 6. Load the electrical system by turning on the headlights and the high blower. 7. Compare the voltage readings at the instrument panel cluster terminal A13 to the voltage reading at the battery. Are the voltage readings within 0.1 to 1.5 volts of each other?	—	Go to Step 7	Go to Step 8
7	Replace the instrument panel cluster (IPC). Is the repair complete?	—	Go to Charging System Check	—
8	Check the IPC MiniFuse #19 fuse for an open circuit. Is this fuse open?	—	Go to Step 9	Go to Step 10

GC1129700088010X

Fig. 5 Voltmeter displaying high or low (Part 1 of 4)

Step	Action	Value(s)	Yes	No
9	Repair a short to ground in CKT 139 between the IPC and the instrument panel electrical center. Is the repair complete?	—	Go to Charging System Check	—
10	Repair the open or high resistance in CKT 139 between the IPC and the instrument panel electrical center. Is the repair complete?	—	Go to Charging System Check	—
11	1. Connect a DMM between the BATTERY terminal (CKT 2-large red wire) in the back of the generator and ground. 2. Measure the available voltage at the BATTERY terminal (CKT 2-large red wire) in the back of the generator. Is the voltage within the specified values?	10.0-14.0V	Go to Step 15	Go to Step 12
12	Check the fusible link located down at the starter motor between the medium gauge blue wire (CKT 2) and the heavy gauge red wire (CKT 2). Is the fusible link open?	—	Go to Step 13	Go to Step 14
13	Repair a short to ground in CKT 2 (13 red wire) between the generator BATTERY terminal and the fusible link. Is the repair complete?	—	Go to Charging System Check	—
14	Repair an open in CKT 1 (19 red wire), CKT 2 (3 blue wire) or CKT 2 (13 red wire) between the generator BATTERY terminal and the positive battery terminal. Is the repair complete?	—	Go to Charging System Check	—
15	1. Disconnect the generator connector. 2. Connect a DMM between the generator connector terminal D (CKT 2-medium red wire) and ground. 3. Measure the available voltage at the generator connector terminal D (CKT 2-medium red wire). Is the voltage within the specified values?	10.0-14.0V	Go to Step 19	Go to Step 16
16	Check the fusible link located down at the starter motor between the small gauge grey wire (CKT 2) and the medium gauge red wire (CKT 2). Is the fusible link open?	—	Go to Step 17	Go to Step 18
17	Repair a short to ground in CKT 2 (1 red wire) between the generator connector terminal D and the fusible link. Is the repair complete?	—	Go to Charging System Check	—
18	Repair an open in CKT 1 (19 red wire), CKT 2 (0.5 grey wire) or CKT 2 (1 red wire) between the generator connector terminal D and the positive battery terminal. Is the repair complete?	—	Go to Charging System Check	—

GC1129700088020X

Fig. 5 Voltmeter displaying high or low (Part 2 of 4)

Step	Action	Value(s)	Yes	No
28	Repair the open in CKT 225 between the generator connector and the powertrain control module connector C2. Is the repair complete?	—	Go to Charging System Check	—
29	Repair the short to ground in CKT 225 between the generator connector and the powertrain control module connector C2. Is the repair complete?	—	Go to Charging System Check	—
30	Repair the short to battery power in CKT 225 between the generator connector and the powertrain control module connector C2. Is the repair complete?	—	Go to Charging System Check	—
31	Replace the generator. Is the repair complete?	—	Go to Charging System Check	—

GC1129700088040X

Fig. 5 Voltmeter displaying high or low (Part 4 of 4)

ALTERNATOR SPECIFICATIONS

Model	Year	Rated Hot Output Amps
Corvette	1997–2000	110

STEERING COLUMNS

TABLE OF CONTENTS

General Motors

INDEX

STEERING COLUMN EXPLODED VIEWS

Model	Year	Type		Shifter Position		SIR	Page No.	Fig. No.
		Standard	Tilt	Column	Floor			
Achieva & Skylark	1997-98	X	—	—	X	—	17-12	19
		—	X	—	X	X	17-13	20
Alero	1999-2000	—	X	—	X	X	17-5	5
Aurora & Riviera	1997-99	—	X	X	—	X	17-14	21
		—	X	—	X	X	17-15	22
Bonneville & LeSabre, LSS, & 88	1997–99	—	X	X	—	X	17-20	27
		—	X	—	X	X	17-21	28
Bonneville & LeSabre	2000	—	X	X	—	X	17-23	31
Camaro & Firebird	1997-2000	—	X	—	X	X	17-16	23
Catera	1997-2000	—	X	—	X	X	17-25	32
Cavalier & Sunfire	1997-2000	X	—	—	X	X	17-26	34
		—	X	—	X	X	17-27	35
Century	1997-2000	—	X	X	—	X	17-36	46
Corvette①	1997-2000	—	X	—	X	X	17-17	24
		—	X	—	X	X	17-18	25
		—	X	—	X	X	17-19	26
Cutlass & Malibu	1997-2000	—	X	—	X	X	17-28	36
Cutlass Supreme	1997	—	X	X	—	X	17-37	47
		—	X	—	X	X	17-38	48
DeVille, Eldorado & Seville	1997-2000	—	X	X	—	X	17-30	39
		—	X	—	X	X	17-31	40

Continued

STEERING COLUMN EXPLODED VIEWS—Continued

Model	Year	Type		Shifter Position		SIR	Page No.	Fig. No.
		Standard	Tilt	Column	Floor			
Grand Am	1997-2000	X	—	—	X	—	17-12	19
		—	X	—	X	X	17-13	20
Grand Prix, Intrigue & Regal	1997-2000	—	X	—	X	X	17-34	45
		—	X	X	—	X	17-36	46
Impala	2000	—	X	X	—	X	17-11	16
		—	X	—	X	X	17-11	16
Lumina & Monte Carlo	1997-2000	—	X	X	—	X	17-37	47
		—	X	—	X	X	17-38	48
Metro	1997-2000	X	—	—	X	—	17-42	61
Park Avenue	1997-2000	—	X	X	—	X	17-44	65
Prizm	1997-2000	—	X	—	X	X	17-45	66
Regency	1997–99	—	X	X	—	X	17-20	27
		—	X	—	X	X	17-21	28

① — Fig 23, non telescoping with sensor; fig 24, non telescoping without sensor; fig 25, telescoping.

PRECAUTIONS

AIR BAG SYSTEMS

Refer to "Air Bag System Precautions" in the front of this manual for system disarming and arming procedures.

BATTERY GROUND CABLE

Prior to service, disconnect battery ground cable and isolate as required.

SERVICE

Use only the specified screws, bolts and nuts during the mandatory assembling sequence and tighten to specifications to ensure proper breakaway action of column under impact. Avoid using excessively long bolts as they may prevent a portion of the steering column from collapsing under impact.

When removing or installing, steering wheel, ignition switch or lock, turn signal switch, adjusting transmission linkage, or installing and adjusting neutral-start or back-up light switch, refer to appropriate car chapter.

If a shift tube shows a sheared plastic injection, a new shift tube must be installed. If a steering shaft shows a sheared plastic, but it is not bent, it can be repaired by using a Service Steering Shaft Repair Kit part No. 7810077. The kit contains instructions and dimensions for all steering columns. On some models, the attaching brackets will shear under impact and must also be replaced.

STEERING COLUMN DAMAGE

When the steering column is removed from the vehicle, it is extremely susceptible to damage. Dropping the steering column assembly on its end could collapse the steering shaft assembly or loosen plastic injections that keep the steering column assembly rigid. Leaning on the steering column assembly could cause the jacket to bend or deform. Any of these conditions could impair the steering column assembly's collapsible design. If the steering wheel must be removed, use only the specified steering wheel puller and steering wheel puller bolts. Never hammer on the end of the shaft.

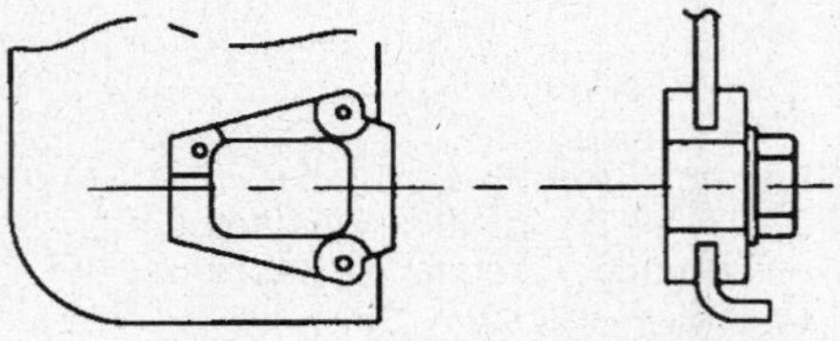

GC4069800253000X

Fig. 1 Inspecting for looseness on steering column bracket assembly

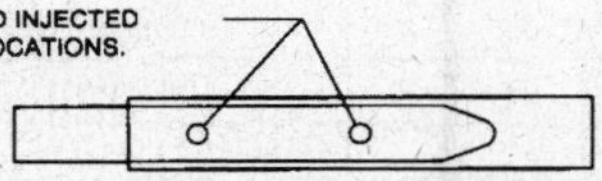
CHECK FOR SHEARED INJECTED
PLASTIC AT THESE LOCATIONS.

GC4069800254000X

Fig. 3 Inspecting for sheared plastic

SIR COIL DAMAGE

The front wheels of the vehicle must be in a straight ahead position and the steering column must be in the locked position before disconnecting the steering column or intermediate shaft. Failure to follow these procedures will cause improper alignment of some components during installation and result in damage to the SIR coil assembly.

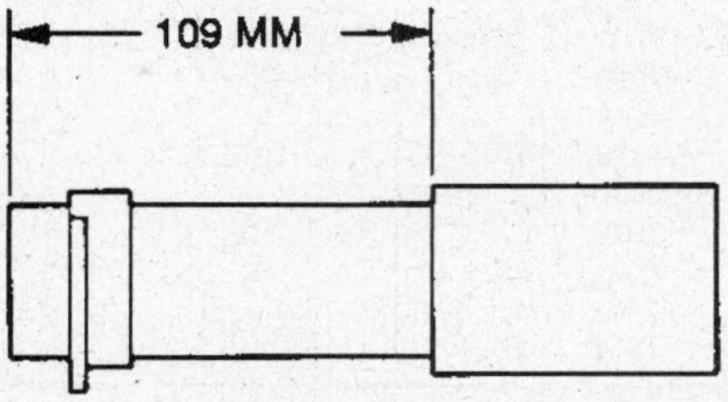
109 MM

GC4069800255000X

Fig. 2 Jacket assembly collapse measurement

STEERING COLUMN COLLISION DAMAGE

Vehicles involved in accidents resulting in frame damage, major body or sheet metal damage, or where steering column has been impacted, or where supplemental inflatable restraints systems deployed, may also have a damaged or misaligned steering column. Inspect the following components when performing service operations on steering columns

1. Inspect capsules on steering column bracket assembly, all must be securely seated in bracket slots and inspected for any looseness when pushed or pulled by hand, **Fig. 1.** If bracket is not as indicated, replace bracket or jacket assembly.
2. Inspect for jacket assembly collapse by measuring distance from lower edge of upper jacket,**Fig. 2.** If measured dimensions are not as specified, replace jacket assembly.
3. Visually inspect steering column for sheared plastic, **Fig. 3.**

Condition	Cause
The lock system does not lock.	• A broken lock bolt spring • A worn lock bolt spring • A damaged sector • A damaged lock cylinder • A burr on the lock bolt • A damaged housing • A damaged rack • Interference between the bowl and the rack coupling • A binding ignition switch • A restricted actuator rod • The sector is installed incorrectly. • The shift lever is not in the PARK position. • The park lock cable is incorrectly adjusted. • The park lock components are damaged.

Condition	Cause
The lock system sticks in START.	• A deformed actuator rod • *High Lock Effort Between the Off Lock Positions*

Condition	Cause
The key cannot be removed in the OFF-LOCK position.	• The ignition switch is not set correctly. • A damaged lock cylinder • An improperly adjusted linkage • The shift lever is not in the PARK position.

Condition	Cause
The lock cylinder can be removed without depressing the retainer.	A missing lock cylinder retaining screw

Condition	Cause
The lock cylinder effort between OFF and OFF-LOCK is high.	A distorted rack

Condition	Cause
The lock bolt hits the shift lock in the OFF position and the PARK position.	The ignition switch is set incorrectly.

GC6049900276010X

Fig. 4 Steering column troubleshooting chart (Part 1 of 5)

Condition	Causes
A high lock effort exists.	• The lock cylinder is damaged. • The ignition switch is damaged. • A rack preload spring is broken. • A rack preload spring is broken. • Burrs exist on the following items: – The sector – The rack – The housing – The support – The actuator rod coupling • The sector shaft is bent. • A rack is damaged. • The housing is extreme misaligned to the cover. • A coupling slot in the rack is distorted. • An actuator rod is damaged. • The ignition switch mounting bracket is bent. • An actuator rod is restricted. • The key cut is damaged. • The key cut is incorrect. • The park lock cable is incorrectly adjusted. • The park lock components are damaged.

Condition	Causes
Noise is present in the steering column.	• The pinch bolts are loose in the intermediate shaft coupling. • The column is misaligned • The contact ring is not lubricated. • The bearing lacks lubrication. • The column components are loose. • The steering shaft bearings are worn. • The steering shaft bearings are broken. • The shaft lock snap ring is not seated. • The spherical joint is not lubricated. • The dust seal is rubbing the column shaft coupling. • The contact ring is worn. • The contact ring is damaged. • The brushes are worn. • The brushes are damaged. • The lock bolt is bolt. • The lock bolt is improperly lubricated.

GC6049900276020X

Fig. 4 Steering column troubleshooting chart (Part 2 of 5)

4. If steering shaft shows sheared plastic, replace steering shaft.
5. Remove inflatable restraint coil assembly and allow to hang freely.
6. Using a suitable dial indicator at lower end of steering shaft, rotate steering wheel and measure runout.
7. Runout must not exceed .063 inch. If measurement is not as indicated, replace steering shaft.

TROUBLESHOOTING

Refer to **Fig. 4** for steering column troubleshooting.

STEERING COLUMN

REPLACE

ACHIEVA, 1997-98 GRAND AM & SKYLARK

1. Remove inflator module as outlined in "Passive Restraints."
2. Remove left lower insulator panel, then the lower steering column filler panel.
3. Disconnect two yellow two-way SIR connectors, then remove steering wheel.
4. Remove tilt lever, then the upper and lower steering column covers.
5. Disconnect lock cylinder wire from connector, then the headlamp switch and windshield wiper switch connectors.
6. Disconnect park lock/brake transmission shift interlock cable from ignition switch, then remove upper flexible column bolt.
7. Remove column bracket support bolts, then the steering column.
8. Reverse procedure to install, noting the following:
   a. **Torque** pinch bolt to 30 ft. lbs.
   b. Ensure steering shaft is centered in mast jacket, reposition column as necessary, then **torque** mounting bolts to 20 ft. lbs.

ALERO & 1999-2000 GRAND AM

1. Remove inflator module as outlined in "Passive Restraints."
2. Remove steering wheel, **Fig. 5.**
3. Remove tilt lever as needed.
4. Remove three upper steering column cover screws, then the cover.
5. Remove three lower steering column cover screws, then the cover.
6. Disconnect headlamp switch and windshield wiper switch.
7. Disconnect cruise control electrical connector.
8. Remove instrument panel trim plate, then the instrument cluster.
9. Cut plastic wire wrap, then route SIR coil wiring out of way.
10. Remove left lower sound insulator.
11. Position upper intermediate shaft boot out of way, then remove upper shaft pinch bolt.
12. Remove lower steering column bracket support bolts.
13. Loosen upper column bolts.
14. Spread lower steering column intermediate shaft joint apart with a screwdriver.
15. Remove upper column bolts.
16. Rotate steering column 45° counterclockwise, then remove the steering column.
17. Reverse procedure to install, noting the following:
    a. **Torque** upper and lower column bracket support bolts to 19 ft. lbs.
    b. **Torque** upper intermediate shaft pinch bolt to 16 ft. lbs.
    c. **Torque** steering wheel nut to 30 ft. lbs.

AURORA & RIVIERA

1. Remove inflator module as outlined in "Passive Restraints."
2. Remove air bag module and steering wheel, **Fig. 6.**
3. Remove knee bolster and reinforcement bracket.
4. **On models equipped with column shift,** remove shift lever cable.
5. **On models equipped with console shift,** unlock ignition and remove park lock cable, then lock ignition.
6. **On all models,** disconnect steering column wiring harness connector from main body wiring harness.
7. Disconnect steering column shaft from intermediate shaft, position seal as needed.
8. Loosen but do not remove two nuts at lower steering column support.
9. Support column and remove two nuts at upper steering column support. Discard clips at upper steering column support, if present.
10. Remove steering column from vehicle.

Condition	Causes
High steering shaft effort exists.	• The column is misaligned. • The dust sel is improperly installed. • The dust seal is deformed. • The upper bearing is damaged. • The lower bearing is damaged. • The intermediate steering shaft universal joint is tight. • The shroud is rubbing on the column cover.

Condition	Causes
Lash exists in the steering column.	• The IP-to-column mounting bolts for the upper bracket are loose. • The IP-to-column mounting bolts for the lower bracket are loose. • The weld nuts on the jacket are broken. • The IP upper bracket capsule is sheared. • The shoes in the housing are loose. • The tilt head pivot pins are loose. • The shoe lock pin in the support is loose. • The support screws are loose. • The upper bracket-to-jacket bolts in the column are loose. • The lower bracket-to-jacket bolts in the column are loose. • The lower bracket-to-adapter screws are loose. • The bearing assembly mounting screws are loose. • The IP-to-jacket mounting bolts are loose.

Condition	Causes
The steering wheel is loose.	• Excessive clearance exists between the pivot pin diameters and the holes in the support or in the housing. • The anti-lash spring in the spheres is damaged. • The anti-lash spring in the spheres is missing. • The upper bearing is not seated in the housing. • The inner race seal is missing from the upper bearing. • The support screws are loose. • The bearing preload spring is missing. • The bearing preload spring is broken.

Condition	Causes
The steering wheel is loose in every other tilt position.	• A loose fit exists between the shoe and the shoe pivot pin. • The shoe is not free in the slot.

GC6049900276030X

Fig. 4 Steering column troubleshooting chart (Part 3 of 5)

Condition	Causes
The steering wheel does not lock in any tilt position.	• The shoe seized on the pivot pin. • Burrs are present in the shoe grooves. • Dirt is present in the shoe grooves. • The shoe lock spring is weak. • The shoe lock spring is broken.

Condition	Causes
The steering wheel does not return to the top tilt position.	• The pivot pins are binding. • The wheel tilt spring is broken. • The wheel tilt spring is weak. • The turn signal switch wires are too tight.

Condition	Causes
Noise is present when tilting the column.	• The upper tilt bumpers are worn. • The tilt spring rubs in the housing.

Condition	Causes
The turn signal will not indicate lane change.	• The lane change pressure pad is broken. • The spring hanger is broken. • The lane change spring is broken. • The lane change spring is missing. • The lane change spring is misproportioned. • The base is jammed. • The wires are jammed.

Condition	Causes
The turn signal will not stay in the turn position.	• Foreign material is impeding movement of the yoke. • Loose parts are impeding movement of the yoke. • A detent is broken. • A detent is missing. • A canceling spring is broken. • A canceling spring is missing.

GC6049900276040X

Fig. 4 Steering column troubleshooting chart (Part 4 of 5)

Condition	Causes
The turn signal will not cancel.	• The switch mounting screws are loose. • A switch is broken. • The anchor bosses are broken. • A detent is broken. • A return is broken. • A canceling spring is broken. • A detent is missing. • A return is missing. • A canceling spring is missing. • A detent is out-of-position. • A return is out-of-position. • A canceling spring is out-of-position. • A cancelling cam is worn.

Condition	Causes
The turn signal is difficult to operate.	• A turn signal lever screw is loose. • A yoke is broken. Replace the switch. • A yoke is distorted. Replace the switch. • The springs are loose. • The springs are mispositioned. • Interference caused by foreign material exists. • The turn signal switch mounting screws are loose.

Condition	Causes
The electrical system will not function.	• The ignition switch is damaged. • The ignition switch is improperly adjusted. • A loose connection at the ignition switch exists. • A loose connection at the column connectors exists.

Condition	Causes
The switch cannot be set correctly.	• The switch actuator rod is deformed. • The sector is engaged in the wrong rack tooth.

GC6049900276050X

Fig. 4 Steering column troubleshooting chart (Part 5 of 5)

11. Reverse procedure to install, noting the following:
    a. Loosely install nuts on lower support bracket studs, position steering column into vehicle and slide lower support onto nuts.
    b. **Torque** pinch bolt to 35 ft. lbs.
    c. **Torque** upper and lower support nuts to 20 ft. lbs.
    d. **Torque** wiring harness connector to 6 ft. lbs.

BONNEVILLE, LESABRE, LSS, REGENCY & 88

1. Remove inflator module as outlined in "Passive Restraints," then the steering wheel.
2. Remove trim plate and knee bolster deflector.
3. **On models equipped with column shift,** disconnect shift indicator cable.
4. **On all models,** loosen column support bracket bolts.
5. Remove steering column support brace bolt, **Fig. 7,** then the brace.
6. Disconnect steering column wiring harness, **Fig. 8.** then support column and remove two support bracket bolts.
7. **On models equipped with column shift,** disconnect shift control cable from actuator, and as needed, from slot in lower column bracket.
8. **On models equipped with console shift,** disconnect park lock cable from ignition switch inhibitor.
9. **On all models,** position seal as necessary, then loosen or remove upper intermediate steering shaft pinch bolt.
10. Disconnect steering column shaft from intermediate steering shaft.
11. Remove steering column from vehicle.
12. Reverse procedure to install, noting the following:
    a. Hand start one bolt into lower right position of steering column support bracket.
    b. **Torque** pinch bolt to 35 ft. lbs.
    c. **Torque** lower support brace bolt to 7 ft. lbs.
    d. **Torque** upper and lower support bracket to 20 ft. lbs.
    e. **Torque** wiring harness connector to 42 inch lbs.

CAMARO & FIREBIRD

1. Remove lefthand instrument panel insulator, then the knee bolster and deflector.
2. Remove inflator module as outlined in "Passive Restraints," then the steering wheel.
3. Remove intermediate steering shaft

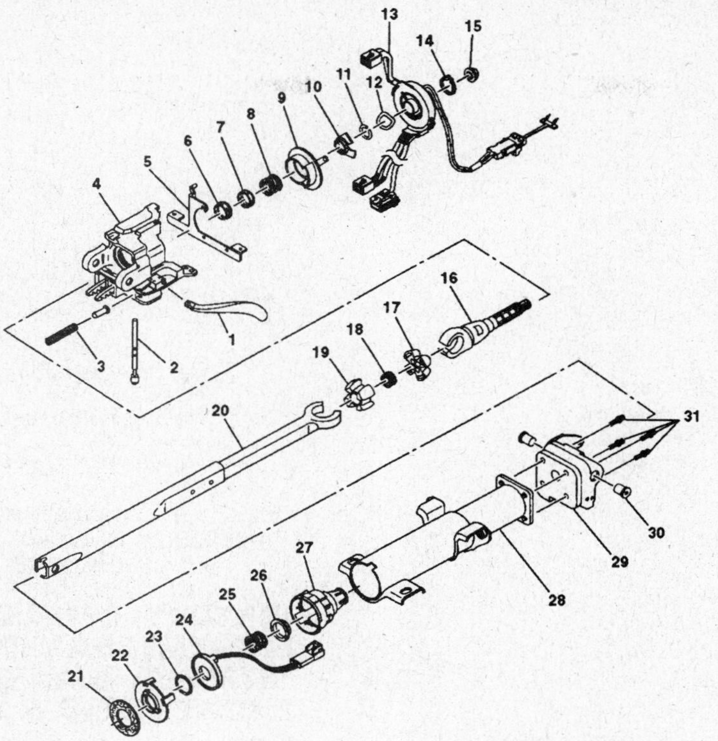

(1) Tilt Lever
(2) Anti-Rotation Pin
(3) Tilt Spring and Guide
(4) Bearing and Housing Assembly
(5) Switch Adapter Plate
(6) Upper Bearing Spring
(7) Upper Bearing Inner Race Seat
(8) Upper Bearing Spring
(9) Turn Signal Cancel Cam Assembly
(10) Cam Orientation Plate
(11) Bearing Retainer
(12) Wave Washer
(13) SIR Coil Assembly
(14) Snap Ring
(15) Flanged Prevailing Torque Nut
(16) Race and Upper Shaft Assembly
(17) Centering Sphere
(18) Joint Preload Spring
(19) Centering Sphere
(20) Lower Shaft Assembly

GC6049900252000X

Fig. 5 Exploded view of tilt steering column. Alero

bolt from steering gear coupling shaft and column, **Fig. 9,** then the cover from dash panel.

4. Disconnect electrical connectors, then remove nuts and shims from steering column support.
5. **On models equipped with automatic transmission,** disconnect park lock cable from ignition switch.
6. **On all models,** remove steering column from vehicle.
7. Reverse procedure to install, noting the following:
   a. **Torque** steering column support nuts to 18 ft. lbs.
   b. **Torque** electrical connectors to 14 ft. lbs.

CATERA

If service replacement steering column is being installed, do not remove the anti-rotation pin until after the column has been connected to the steering gear. Removing the anti-rotation pin before the column is connected to the steering gear may cause damage to the SIR coil.

1. Disable SIR system as outline in "Air Bag System Disarming and Arming."
2. Remove inflator module as outlined in "Passive Restraints, " then the steering wheel.
3. Remove SIR coil.
4. Remove ignition lock cylinder.
5. Disconnect and remove theft deterrent immobilizer.
6. Remove ignition switch, windshield washer switch, and turn signal switch.
7. Remove driver's knee bolster and sound insulator.
8. Remove coupler bolt from steering column shaft connection.
9. Separate coupler enough to allow for shaft removal.
10. Remove forward support strap nut.
11. Using a suitable chisel, rotate forward support strap shear bolt to remove.
12. Remove rear support bracket bolt.
13. Pull steering column straight back through dash assembly.
14. Reverse procedure to install noting the following:
    a. **Torque** rear support bracket bolt to 16 ft. lbs.
    b. **Torque** forward support strap nut to 16 ft. lbs.
    c. **Torque** new forward support shear bolt to 15 ft. lbs.
    d. **Torque** steering column shaft connector bolt to 16 ft. lbs.

CAVALIER & SUNFIRE

1. Remove inflator module as outlined in "Passive Restraints, " then the steering wheel.
2. Remove left lower sound insulator, then the side instrument panel covers.
3. Remove instrument panel pad by removing one screw from defroster vent, one screw from under defroster vent, one screw on each side panel, two screws in glove box toward left rear, and three screws along top of glove box.
4. Remove tilt lever, then the upper and lower column covers as outlined under "Column Cover, Disassemble."
5. Disconnect cruise control, headlamp switch and windshield wiper switch connectors, then the ignition switch.
6. Disconnect "Passlock" cylinder connector.
7. **On models equipped with automatic transaxle,** disconnect park lock/brake transmission shift interlock cable from lock cylinder housing assembly.
8. **On all models,** remove upper flexible joint pinch bolt, then the left side wire harness retainer clip, **Fig. 10.**
9. Loosen lower column bracket support bolts, then remove upper column support bolts.
10. Using a suitable screwdriver, spread lower steering column flexible joint apart, then remove steering column from vehicle.
11. Reverse procedure to install, noting the following:
    a. **Torque** upper and lower column support bolts to 20 ft. lbs.
    b. **Torque** pinch bolt to 30 ft. lbs.

CORVETTE

1. Remove inflator module as outlined in "Passive Restraints, "
2. Turn steering wheel to the left to access upper intermediate steering shaft pinch bolt, then remove pinch bolt.
3. Turn steering wheel until wheels are in straight ahead position, then lock steering column.
4. Remove steering wheel, then the tilt lever.
5. Remove left knee bolster trim panel, then the knee bolster.
6. Disconnect electrical connectors from column, then remove lower steering column support plate nuts, **Fig. 11.**

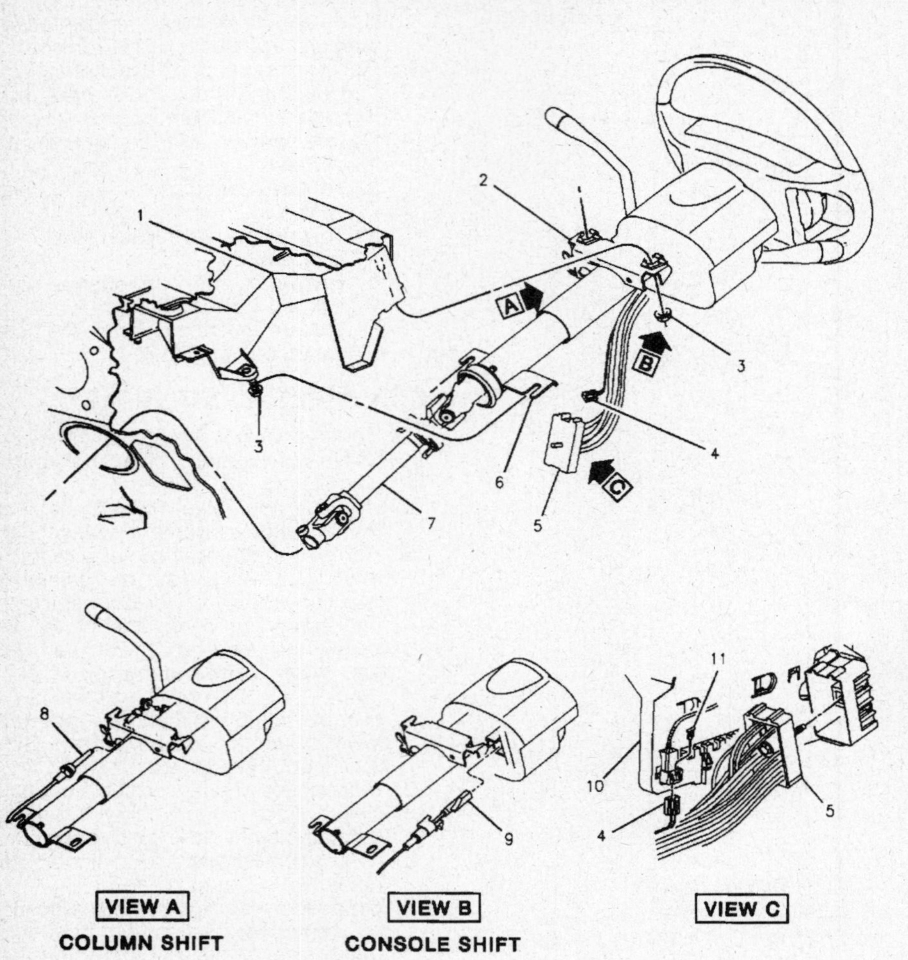

1 BRACKET, STEERING COLUMN SUPPORT
2 SUPPORT, STEERING COLUMN UPPER
3 NUT, 27 N•m (20 LB. FT.)
4 CONNECTOR, SIR
5 CONNECTOR, STEERING COLUMN WIRING HARNESS
6 SUPPORT, STEERING COLUMN LOWER
7 INTERMEDIATE STEERING SHAFT
8 SHIFT LEVER CABLE
9 PARK LOCK CABLE
10 BRACKET, MULTIUSE MODULE
11 CONNECTOR, POSITION ASSURANCE (CPA)

GC6049500173000X

Fig. 6 Steering column replacement. Aurora & Riviera

7. Remove upper steering column bracket nuts, then remove steering column from vehicle.
8. Reverse procedure to install, noting the following:
   a. **Torque** upper steering column bracket nuts and lower steering column support plate nuts to 17 ft. lbs.
   b. **Torque** pinch bolt to 35 ft. lbs.

CUTLASS & MALIBU

1. Remove inflator module as outlined in "Passive Restraints," then the steering wheel.
2. Remove column covers as outlined under "Column Cover, Replace."
3. Remove tilt lever, then disconnect cruise control, headlamp and windshield wiper switch connectors.
4. Remove instrument panel trim plate, then the instrument cluster.
5. Remove left lower sound insulator, then disconnect SIR coil wiring harness and cut plastic zip tie.
6. Position upper intermediate shaft boot aside, then remove shaft pinch bolt.
7. Loosen steering column bracket support bolts, **Fig. 12,** then loosen upper column bolts.
8. Spread lower steering column intermediate shaft joint apart using screwdriver, then remove upper column bolts.
9. Rotate column counterclockwise approximately 45°, then remove column from vehicle.
10. Reverse procedure to install, noting the following:
    a. **Torque** upper and lower column support bracket bolts to 18 ft. lbs.
    b. **Torque** intermediate shaft pinch bolt to 16 ft. lbs.
    c. **Torque** steering wheel nut to 30 ft. lbs.

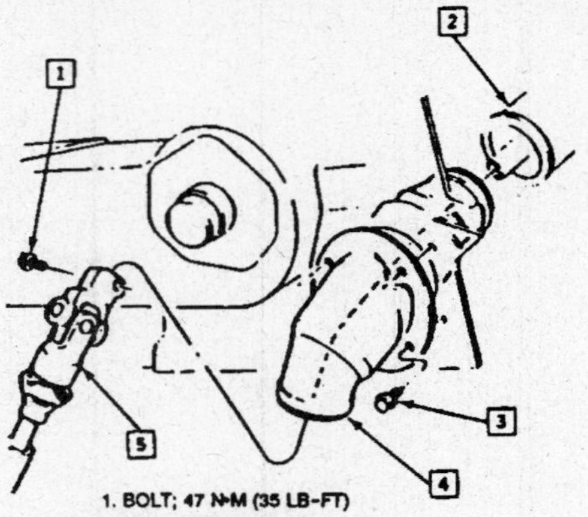

1. BOLT; 47 N•M (35 LB-FT)
2. STEERING COLUMN
3. SCREW (4); 2.4 N•M (21 LB-IN)
4. SEAL ASSEMBLY
5. INTERMEDIATE SHAFT ASSEMBLY

GC6049100044000X

Fig. 7 Intermediate shaft & boot installation. Bonneville, LeSabre, LSS & 88

CENTURY, CUTLASS SUPREME, GRAND PRIX, INTRIGUE, LUMINA, MONTE CARLO & REGAL

1. Remove inflator module as outlined in "Passive Restraints," then the steering wheel.
2. Remove lefthand instrument panel insulator.
3. **On Century and Regal models,** remove knee bolster bracket.
4. **On all models,** remove trim panel below steering column.
5. Push top of intermediate shaft seal down, **Fig. 13,** then remove upper intermediate steering shaft pinch bolt.
6. **On models equipped with console shift,** disconnect shift indicator cable end and casing from shift cam and automatic transmission control indicator adjuster, or park lock cable.
7. **On models equipped with column shift,** disconnect transaxle shift cable from ball stud on steering column and transaxle shift cable casing from steering column bracket.
8. **On all models,** remove lower steering column bolts, then the upper steering column bolts.
9. Disconnect electrical connector, then remove steering column from vehicle.
10. Reverse procedure to install, noting the following:
    a. **Torque** upper and lower steering column bolts to 18 ft. lbs.
    b. **Torque** pinch bolt to 35 ft. lbs.

DEVILLE, ELDORADO & SEVILLE

1. Remove inflator module as outlined in "Passive Restraints."
2. Remove knee bolster and steering column reinforcement plate.
3. Disconnect electrical connectors from column.
4. Remove pinch bolt from intermediate shaft, **Fig. 14.**

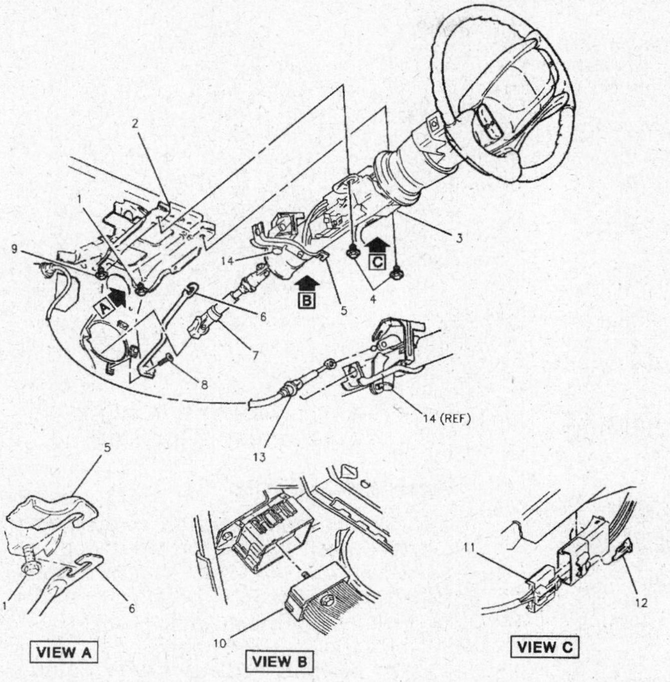

1 BOLT/SCREW, STEERING COLUMN SUPPORT BRACKET 27 N•m (20 LB. FT.)
2 STEERING COLUMN SUPPORT BRACKET
3 UPPER SUPPORT BRACKET
4 BOLT/SCREW 27 N•m (20 LB. FT.)
5 LOWER SUPPORT
6 BRACE, STEERING COLUMN LOWER SUPPORT
7 INTERMEDIATE SHAFT
8 BOLT/SCREW 9.5 N•m (84 LB. IN.)
9 BOLT/SCREW 27 N•m (20 LB. FT.)
10 CONNECTOR, STEERING COLUMN WIRING HARNESS
11 CONNECTOR, (YELLOW) STEERING COLUMN 2-WAY
12 RETAINER
13 CABLE, SHIFT CONTROL (COLUMN SHIFT)
14 SOLENOID, BRAKE TRANSMISSION SHIFT INTERLOCK

GC6049100045000A

Fig. 8 Steering column replacement. Bonneville, LeSabre, LSS & 88

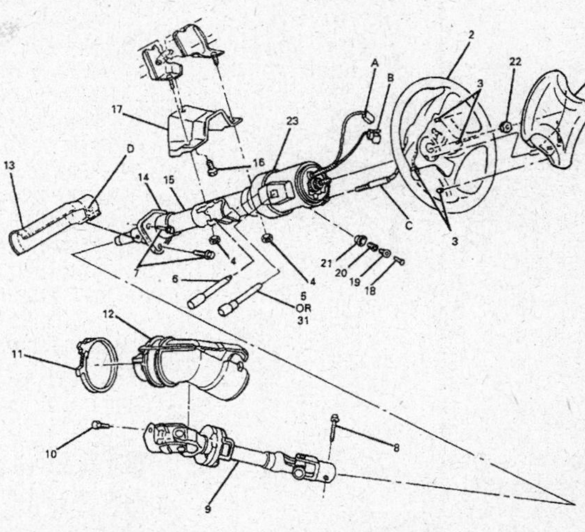

A CONNECTOR, RADIO ASSEMBLY ELECTRICAL (PONTIAC ONLY)
B CONNECTOR, SIR COIL ASSEMBLY ELECTRICAL
C LEAD, HORN
D BUTTON, STEERING GEAR COUPLING HEAT SHIELD
1 MODULE ASSEMBLY, INFLATABLE RESTRAINT STEERING WHEEL
2 WHEEL ASSEMBLY, STEERING
3 BOLT/SCREW, STEERING WHEEL
4 NUT, STEERING COLUMN UPPER SUPPORT
5 LEVER ASSEMBLY, TURN SIGNAL AND HEADLAMP DIMMER SWITCH AND CRUISE CONTROL ACTUATOR AND WINDSHIELD WIPER AND WINDSHIELD WASHER
6 LEVER ASSEMBLY, STEERING COLUMN TILT WHEEL RELEASE
7 BOLT/SCREW, STEERING COLUMN
8 BOLT/SCREW, INTERMEDIATE STEERING SHAFT
9 SHAFT ASSEMBLY, STEERING GEAR COUPLING
10 BOLT/SCREW, INTERMEDIATE STEERING SHAFT
11 CLAMP, STEERING GEAR COUPLING SHIELD
12 BOOT, STEERING GEAR
13 SHIELD, STEERING GEAR COUPLING HEAT
14 COVER ASSEMBLY, STEERING COLUMN DASH PANEL
15 COLUMN ASSEMBLY, STEERING
16 BOLT/SCREW, STEERING COLUMN GUIDE,
17 GUIDE, STEERING COLUMN
18 BOLT/SCREW, HAZARD WARNING SWITCH KNOB
19 BUTTON, HAZARD WARNING SWITCH
20 SPRING, HAZARD WARNING SWITCH KNOB
21 KNOB, HAZARD WARNING SWITCH
22 NUT, STEERING WHEEL
23 SEALER, STEERING COLUMN
31 LEVER ASSEMBLY, TURN SIGNAL AND HEADLAMP DIMMER SWITCH AND WINDSHIELD WIPER AND WINDSHIELD WASHER

GC6049100052000A

Fig. 9 Steering column replacement. Camaro & Firebird

5. Remove lower support bracket from vehicle.
6. Remove upper column support from instrument panel, then the column from vehicle.
7. Reverse procedure to install, noting the following:
   a. Install column in vehicle and support at upper bracket with two bolts, **Fig. 15,** do not tighten at this time.
   b. **Torque** pinch bolt to 35 ft. lbs.
   c. **Torque** upper and lower column support bolts to 20 ft. lbs., then the lower bracket to column screws to 12 ft. lbs.

IMPALA

Do not support steering column by only the lower or upper support bracket. Damage to column lower bearing adapter could result.

1. Disarm air bag system as outlined under "Precautions."
2. Remove inflator module as outlined in "Passive Restraints."
3. Remove steering wheel, **Fig. 16.**
4. Remove lefthand instrument panel insulator.
5. Remove trim panel below steering column.
6. Remove steering column knee bolster.
7. Remove steering column intermediate shaft from steering column.
8. Remove shift indicator cable, casing from shift cam and automatic control indicator adjuster or park lock cable.
9. Disconnect transaxle range selector cable from ball stud on steering column.
10. Remove transaxle shift cable casing from steering column bracket by depressing two tabs.
11. Disconnect steering column electrical connectors.
12. Loosen steering column electrical connector bolt.
13. Separate two steering column electrical connector halves.
14. Remove lower steering column mounting bolts.
15. Remove upper steering column mounting bolts, then the steering column.
16. Reverse procedure to install, noting the following:
    a. **When installing steering column to intermediate shaft, ensure shaft is seated prior to pinch bolt installation.**
    b. **Torque** pinch bolt to 35 ft. lbs.
    c. **Torque** steering column retaining bolts to 18 ft. lbs. Tighten right side lower bolt first, then left side lower bolt , left side upper nut and right side upper nut.

METRO

1. Remove inflator module as outlined in "Passive Restraints," then the steering wheel.
2. Remove knee bolster, then loosen two upper steering column support bolts and lower column slightly.
3. Disconnect SIR coil and combination switch connectors, then remove upper and lower steering column covers by removing screws from lower cover, **Fig. 17.**
4. Remove SIR coil and combination switch, then disconnect ignition wiring connectors at junction block.
5. Pull aside steering shaft joint cover, then remove steering shaft joint upper pinch bolt.
6. Remove lower steering column mounting nuts, then the upper steering column mounting bolts.
7. Lower steering column, then disconnect shift interlock cable from ignition switch.
8. Remove steering column from vehicle, then the ignition switch from steering column assembly.
9. Reverse procedure to install, noting the following:
   a. **Torque** lower steering column mounting nuts to 10 ft. lbs.
   b. **Torque** steering shaft joint upper pinch bolt to 18 ft. lbs.
   c. **Torque** upper steering column mounting bolts to 10 ft. lbs.

PARK AVENUE

1. Remove inflator module as outlined in "Passive Restraints," then the steering wheel.
2. Push in hazard button, then remove

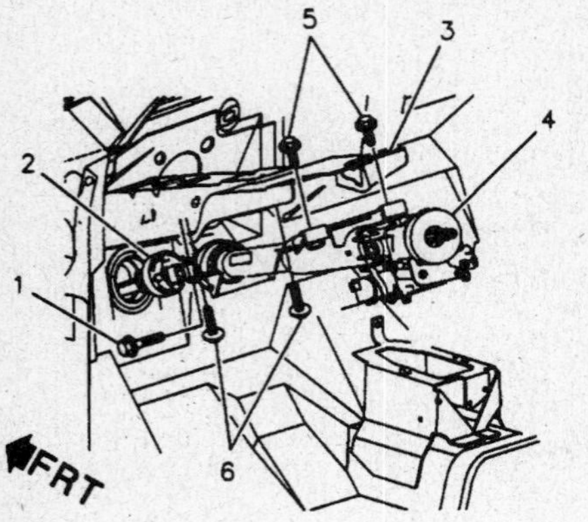

1 UPPER PINCH BOLT
2 FLANGE AND STEERING COUPLING
3 UPPER COLUMN SUPPORT
4 STEERING COLUMN
5 UPPER COLUMN BOLT
6 LOWER COLUMN BOLT

GC6049700227000X

Fig. 10 Steering column replacement. Cavalier & Sunfire

knee bolster and bracket.

3. **On models equipped with column shift,** remove shift lever cable.
4. **On models equipped with console shift,** unlock ignition and remove park lock cable, then lock ignition.
5. **On all models,** disconnect steering column electrical connectors, then remove upper intermediate shaft pinch bolt, **Fig.18.**
6. Remove steering column shaft from intermediate shaft, loosen but do not remove two nuts at lower steering column support.
7. Support steering column and remove two nuts at upper steering column support. **Discard clips at upper steering column support. These clips are for assembly plant usage only.**
8. Remove lower steering column support nuts, then the steering column from vehicle.
9. Reverse procedure to install, noting the following:
   a. **Torque** pinch bolt to 35 ft. lbs.
   b. **Torque** upper and lower support nuts to 20 ft. lbs.
   c. **Torque** wiring harness connector to 6 ft. lbs.

PRIZM

1. Remove inflator module as outlined in "Passive Restraints."
2. Remove steering wheel.
3. Unclip left front carpet retainer, then loosen two screws and disconnect hood release lever from knee bolster.
4. Remove two trim caps, then the four bolts securing knee bolster to the instrument panel.
5. Pull out instrument panel left-side ventilation duct.
6. Loosen five screws and remove upper and lower steering column trim covers.
7. Disconnect steering column electrical connectors.
8. Remove steering column pinch bolt.
9. Remove two bolts and nuts, then the steering column from the instrument panel.
10. Reverse procedure to install, noting the following:
    a. **Torque** steering column mounting bolts to 19 ft. lbs.
    b. **Torque** steering column pinch bolt to 26 ft. lbs.
    c. **Torque** knee bolster bolts to 7 ft. lbs.

STEERING COLUMN SERVICE

ACHIEVA, 1997-98 GRAND AM & SKYLARK

STANDARD COLUMN

Refer to **Fig. 19** when servicing these steering columns.

Steering Column Covers

1. Remove three screws from lower steering column cover, then separate column covers by snapping apart.
2. Reverse procedure to install.

Turn Signal Switch

Refer to the "Electrical" section of the "Achieva, Grand Am & Skylark" chassis chapter, for turn signal switch replacement.

Wash/Wipe Switch

Refer to the "Electrical" section of the "Achieva, Grand Am & Skylark" chassis chapter, for wash/wipe switch replacement.

Ignition Switch

Refer to the "Electrical" section of the "Achieva, Grand Am & Skylark" chassis chapter, for ignition switch replacement.

Interlock Solenoid

1. Remove steering wheel as outlined in the "Electrical" section of the "Achieva, Grand Am & Skylark" chassis chapter.
2. Place shifter lever in Park position, then the ignition key in Off-Lock position and remove key.
3. Disconnect wire connector from interlock solenoid assembly.
4. Remove interlock solenoid mounting screws, then the interlock solenoid assembly.
5. Reverse procedure to install. **Torque** mounting screws to 21 inch lbs.

Lock Cylinder

Refer to the "Electrical" section of the "Achieva, Grand Am & Skylark" chassis chapter, for ignition lock replacement.

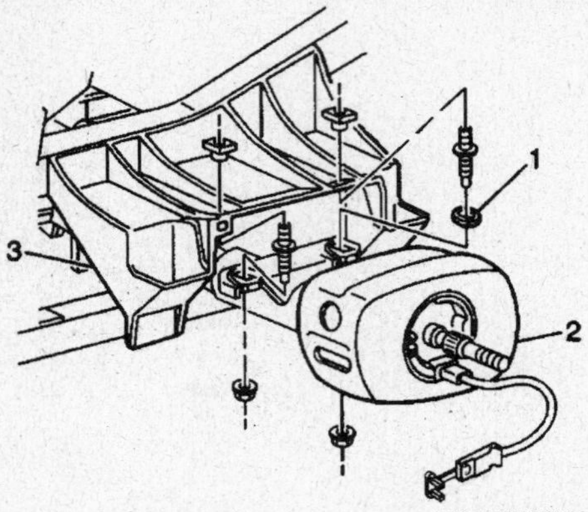

GC6049700228000X

Fig. 11 Steering column replacement. Corvette

Park Lock Cable

1. Remove steering wheel as outlined in the "Electrical" section of the "Achieva, Grand Am & Skylark" chassis chapter.
2. Place key in RUN position, then disconnect park lock cable from lock cylinder housing assembly.
3. **On models equipped with column shift,** disconnect park lock cable from shift gate assembly.
4. **On all models,** reverse procedure to install, noting the following:
   a. Place key in RUN position and shift lever in PARK position.
   b. Snap connector body of cable assembly to lock cylinder, ensure locking tab is fully engaged into lock cylinder housing.
   c. **On models equipped with column shift,** place key in Off-Lock position and pull key half way out of lock cylinder housing.
   d. **On all models,** route cable end fitting through park lock latch, then depress adjuster button and snap cable adjuster assembly to shift gate assembly.
   e. Snap cable into cable retainer, then depress adjuster button and pull cable sheathing towards lock cylinder to remove lash from system.
   f. Release sheathing, then release button.

Column Jacket Bushing, Orientation Plate Cam, Turn Signal Cancel Cam, Upper Bearing Spring, Bearing, Column Shaft, Column Housing & Jacket

1. Remove steering wheel as outlined in the "Electrical" section of the "Achieva, Grand Am & Skylark" chassis chapter.
2. Remove steering column from vehicle as outlined under "Steering Column, Replace."

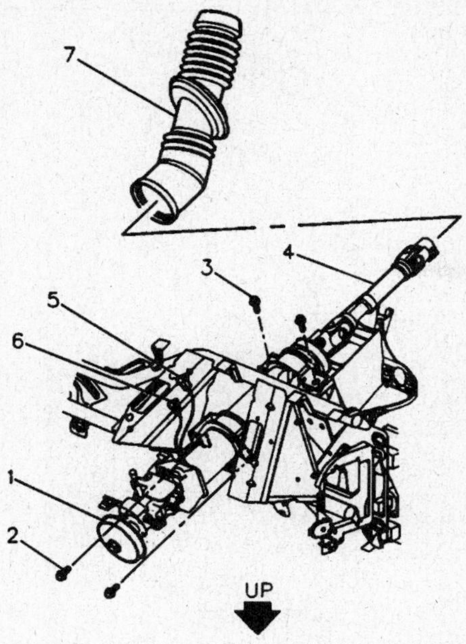

(1) Coil, SIR
(2) Bolt, Steering Column (Lower)
(3) Bolt, Steering Column (Upper)
(4) Intermediate Shaft
(5) Connection, SIR
(6) Connector, Cruise
(7) Intermediate Shaft Boot

GC6049700224000X

Fig. 12 Steering column replacement. Cutlass & Malibu

3. Remove SIR coil and allow to hang freely
4. Remove steering column from vehicle as outlined previously.
5. Remove shaft lock retaining ring using lock plate compressor No. J 23653–SIR or equivalent. Dispose of ring.
6. Remove shaft lock, turn signal cancel cam, and upper bearing spring and spacer.
7. Remove steering column jacket bushing assembly, then the steering column shaft assembly from lower end of steering column jacket assembly.
8. Remove bushing assembly and retaining ring from steering shaft assembly.
9. Reverse procedure to install.

TILT COLUMN

Refer to **Fig. 20** when servicing these steering columns. Refer to "Standard Column" for procedures not found in this section.

Column Jacket Bushing, Orientation Plate Cam, Turn Signal Cancel Cam, Upper Bearing Spring, Bearing, Column Shaft, Column Housing & Column Jacket

1. Remove steering wheel as outlined in the "Electrical" section of the "Achieva, Grand Am & Skylark" chassis chapter.
2. Remove SIR coil assembly.
3. Remove steering column assembly as previously outlined.
4. Put key in Run position, push on locking tab on end of lock cable, then remove the cable.
5. Remove wire restraint clip from bottom of steering column jacket support assembly.
6. Tilt column to Up position.
7. Using a Phillips head screwdriver, push tilt wheel spring retainer down and turn counterclockwise to release.
8. Remove column jacket bushing assembly ort position sensor and bushing assembly from jacket assembly.
9. Move shift lever to Park position.
10. Using tool No. J–21854–01, remove two pivot pins.
11. Install and pull tilt arm to disengage steering wheel lock shoes from dowel pins in steering column jacket support assembly.
12. Remove bearing and housing assembly with steering shaft assembly.
13. Reverse procedure to install.

ALERO & 1999–2000 GRAND AM

Refer to **Fig. 5** when servicing the steering column.

TILT SPRING

1. Use tilt lever to move tilt column into up position.
2. Pry spring upward until a bulge occurs and most of spring tension is removed.
3. Secure locking spring with locking pliers.
4. Continue prying on spring until tilt spring disengages from post on steering column support assembly and steering column housing and bearing assembly.
5. Remove tilt spring guide from tilt spring.
6. Reverse procedure to install.

STEERING COLUMN TILT HEAD ASSEMBLY

1. Remove steering column as outline previously.
2. Remove SIR coil.
3. Compress cam orientation plate using lock plate compressor No. J–23653–SIR and cam orientation plate adapter No. J– 42137 or equivalents.
4. Remove and dispose of bearing retainer.
5. Remove cam orientation plate.
6. Remove turn signal cam assembly.
7. Remove upper bearing spring, inner race seat, and inner race.
8. Remove pivot pins using pivot pin remover No. J– 21854–1 or equivalent.
9. Pull tilt arm to disengage steering wheel lock shoes from dowel pins in steering column support assembly.
10. Remove bearing and housing assembly.
11. Reverse procedure to assemble, noting the following:
    a. Lubricate pivot pins with grease.
    b. Press pivot pins until seated, and stake at three locations.

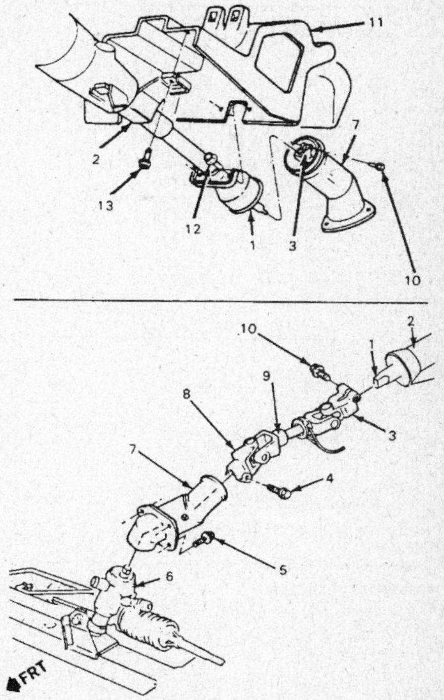

1 STEERING SHAFT-LOWER END
2 STEERING COLUMN ASSEMBLY
3 INTERMEDIATE SHAFT COUPLING-UPPER
4 PINCH BOLT-LOWER COUPLING
5 SCREW
6 STEERING GEAR
7 SEAL-INTERMEDIATE SHAFT
8 INTERMEDIATE SHAFT COUPLING-LOWER
9 INTERMEDIATE SHAFT
10 PINCH BOLT-UPPER COUPLING
11 BRACKET-BRAKE PEDAL
12 BOLT-LOWER STEERING COLUMN
13 BOLT-UPPER STEERING COLUMN

GC6049100057000X

Fig. 13 Steering column replacement. Century, Cutlass Supreme, Grand Prix, Intrigue, Lumina, Monte Carlo & Regal

LOWER STEERING SHAFT, LOWER BEARING & COLUMN JACKET

1. Remove steering column as outlined previously.
2. Remove steering shaft seal from sensor retainer.
3. Remove sensor retainer from end of steering shaft assembly.
4. Remove lower spring retainer, steering wheel speed sensor assembly, and lower bearing spring and seat from steering shaft assembly:
5. Remove adapter and bearing assembly from steering column jacket assembly.
6. Remove upper tilt head components as outlined previously.
7. Remove steering shaft assembly from steering column support assembly.
8. Remove four Torx head screws from steering column support assembly.
9. Remove steering column support assembly from steering column jacket assembly.

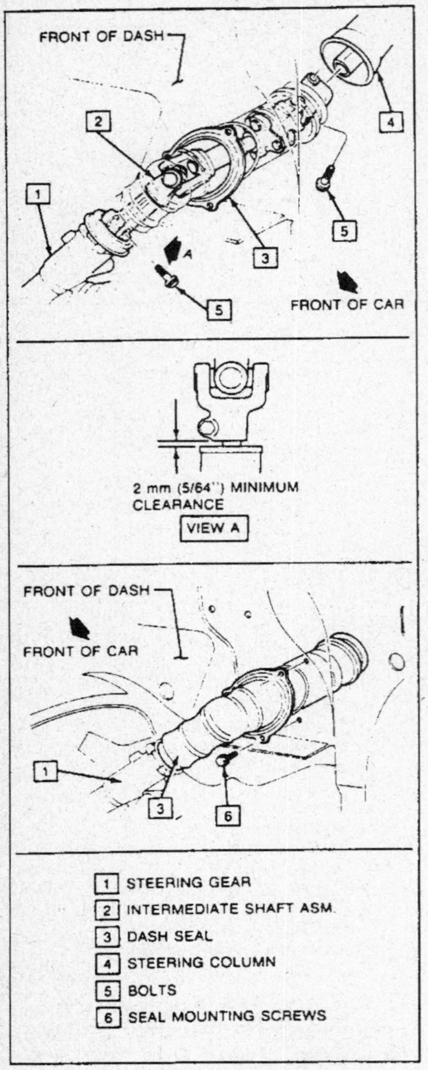

GC6049100048000X

Fig. 14 Intermediate shaft & boot. DeVille, Eldorado & Seville

10. Mark the race and upper shaft assembly, then the lower steering shaft assembly to ensure proper assembly.
11. Tilt race and upper shaft assembly 90° toward each other.
12. Disengage and remove race and upper shaft assembly.
13. Remove centering sphere from race and upper shaft assembly by rotating centering sphere 90°.
14. Lift centering sphere out of race and upper shaft assembly
15. Remove joint preload spring from centering sphere.
16. Inspect centering sphere and joint preload spring, replace parts as necessary.
17. Reverse procedure to install, noting the following:
    a. Grease centering sphere with lithium grease.
    b. Assemble centering sphere and joint preload spring assembly using centering sphere installer tool No. J 41688 or equivalent.
    c. Apply lithium grease to exposed shaft engagement areas.

SIR COIL CENTERING

The SIR coil assembly will become uncentered if the steering column is separated from the steering gear and rotates, or if the centering spring is pushed down and the hub rotates while the coil is removed from the steering column. To center the coil, perform the following procedure:

1. Remove coil assembly from steering column.
2. Hold coil with bottom facing upward.
3. Depress spring lock and rotate hub counterclockwise until it stops.
4. Ensure coil ribbon is wound against center hub.
5. Rotate coil hub clockwise approximately 2½ turns.
6. Release spring lock between locking tabs.

AURORA & RIVIERA

Refer to **Figs. 21 and 22** when servicing these steering columns.

STEERING COLUMN COVERS

1. Lower or remove steering column as outlined under " Steering Column, Replace,"
2. Disable SIR system.
3. **On 1997–98 models,** proceed as follows:
    a. Remove three self tapping screws from upper cover.
    b. Remove upper cover, then the pan head screw.
    c. Remove tilt knob lever, then the shift lever seal.
    d. Remove close out knob by prying locking tabs from bearing and housing assembly.
    e. Remove three tapping screws from lower cover, then the cover.
4. **On 1999 models,** proceed as follows:
    a. Steering wheel must be in 12 o'clock position, then place column on a modular column holding fixture tool No. J–41352 or equivalent.
    b. Remove upper, then lower tapping screws and column cover.
5. **On all models,** reverse procedure to install, noting the following:
    a. **Torque** for 1997–98 upper and lower tapping screws to 46 inch lbs, then 1999 upper and lower tapping screws to 5 inch lbs.
    b. **Torque** pan head screw to 30 inch lbs.

TURN SIGNAL SWITCH

Refer to the "Electrical" section of the "Aurora & Riviera" chassis chapter, for turn signal switch replacement.

WASH/WIPER SWITCH

Refer to the "Electrical" section of the "Aurora & Riviera" chassis chapter, for wash and wiper switch replacement.

IGNITION SWITCH

Refer to the "Electrical" section of the "Aurora & Riviera" chassis chapter for ignition switch replacement.

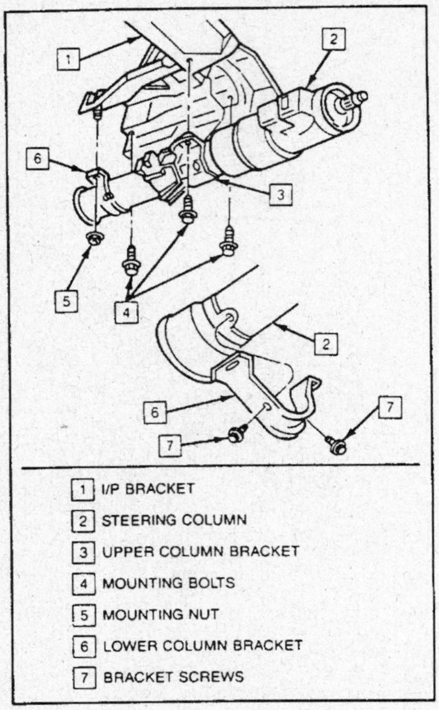

GC6049100049000X

Fig. 15 Steering column installation. DeVille, Eldorado & Seville

INTERLOCK SOLENOID

Column Shift

1. Remove steering wheel as outlined in the "Electrical " section of the "Aurora & Riviera" chassis chapter.
2. Remove upper and lower column covers as outlined under "Steering Column Covers."
3. Remove two tapping screws from bottom of bearing and housing assembly.
4. Disconnect interlock solenoid wire connector from turn signal and multifunction switch assembly wire harness.
5. Remove interlock solenoid assembly.
6. Reverse procedure to install. **Torque** mounting screws to 15 inch lbs.

LOCK CYLINDER

Refer to the "Electrical" section of the "Aurora & Riviera" chassis chapter for ignition lock cylinder replacement.

PARK LOCK CABLE

1. Remove steering wheel as outlined in the "Electrical " section of the "Aurora & Riviera" chassis chapter.
2. Remove upper and lower column covers as outlined in " Steering Column Covers."
3. Remove park lock cable as follows:
    a. Turn key to Run position.
    b. Press in locking tab on end of cable, then remove cable from bottom of bearing and housing assembly
    c. Pry locking tab on opposite end of

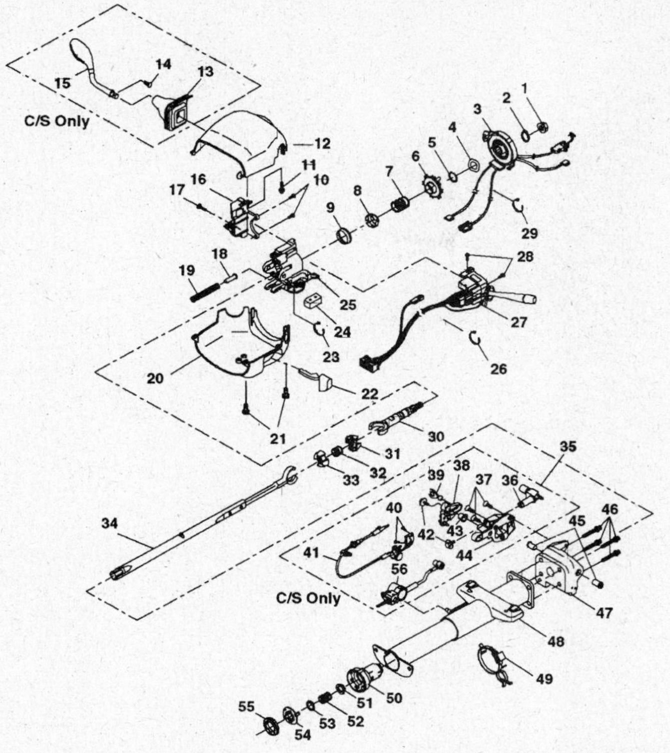

GC6040000291010X

Fig. 16 Exploded view of steering column (Part 1 of 2). Impala

1. Hexagon Nut
2. Retaining Ring
3. SIR Coil Assembly
4. Wave Washer
5. Bearing Retainer
6. Turn Signal Cancel Cam Assembly
7. Upper Bearing Spring
8. Upper Bearing Inner Race Seat
9. Inner Race
10. Flat Head Screw
11. Pan Head Tapping Screw
12. Upper Shroud
13. Shift Lever Seal
14. Shift Lever Screw
15. Automatic Transmission Control Lever Assembly
16. Switch Mounting Bracket
17. Flat Head Screw
18. Spring Guide
19. Tilt Spring
20. Lower Shroud
21. TORX® Head Screw
22. Tilt Lever Assembly
23. Wire Harness Strap
24. Spacer
25. Steering Column Tilt Head
26. Wire Harness Strap
27. Turn Signal And Multifunction Switch Assembly
28. Pan Head Tapping Screw
29. Wire Harness Strap
30. Race And Upper Shaft Assembly
31. Centering Sphere
32. Joint Preload Spring
33. Centering Sphere
34. Lower Steering Shaft Assembly
35. Linear Shift Assembly
36. Shift Lever Clevis
37. Flat Head 6-Lobed Socket Tapping Screw
38. Cable Shift Cam Assembly
39. Ball and Actuator
40. Oval Head 6-Lobed Socket Tapping Screw
41. Park Lock Cable Assembly
42. Hex Flange Head Bolt
43. Cam Bushing
44. Gear Shift Lever Assembly Support Bracket
45. Pivot Pin
46. TORX® Head Screw
47. Steering Column Support Assembly
48. Steering Column Jacket Assembly
49. Wire Harness Strap
50. Adapter and Bearing Assembly
51. Lower Bearing Seat
52. Lower Bearing Spring
53. Lower Spring Retainer
54. Sensor Retainer
55. Steering Shaft Seal
56. Electrical (BTSI) Actuator

GC6040000290020X

Fig. 16 Exploded view of steering column (Part 2 of 2). Impala

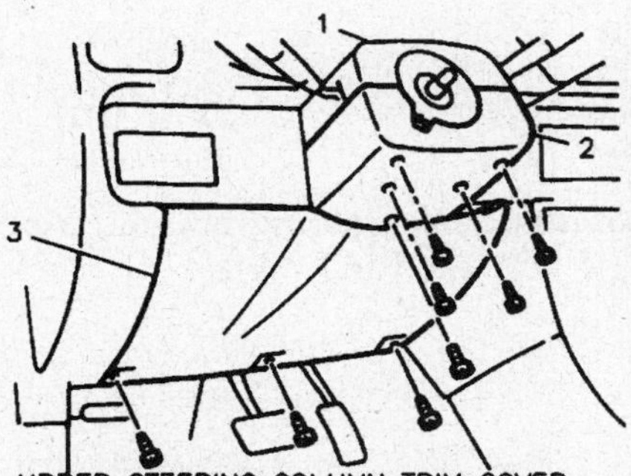

1 UPPER STEERING COLUMN TRIM COVER
2 LOWER STEERING COLUMN TRIM COVER
3 HOLE TRIM COVER

GC6049700225000X

Fig. 17 Steering column cover replacement. Metro

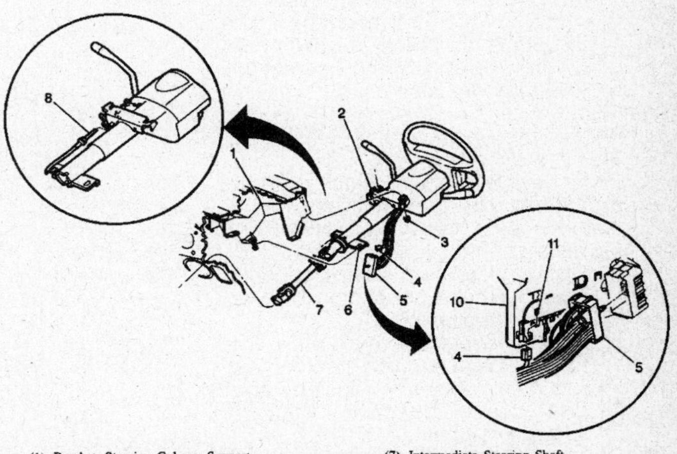

(1) Bracket, Steering Column Support
(2) Support, Steering Column Upper
(3) Nut
(4) Connector, SIR
(5) Connector, Steering Column Wiring Harness
(6) Support, Steering Column Lower
(7) Intermediate Steering Shaft
(8) Shift Lever Cable
(9) Park Lock Cable
(10) Bracket, Multiuse Module
(11) Connector, Position Assurance (CPA)

GC6049700226000X

Fig. 18 Steering column replacement. Park Avenue

cable and remove cable from linear shift base adapter.
   d. Remove wire cable from park lock latch.
4. Place shift lever in Neutral position.
5. If necessary, remove shift lever spring as follows:
   a. Pry off shift lever spring leg.
   b. Remove shift lever clip from shift lever pin.
   c. Remove shift lever pin with drift.
   d. Remove shift lever spring with linear shift lever assembly.
6. Remove three flat head tapping screws.
7. Remove linear shift base adapter from column.
8. Remove transaxle cable from ball stud on linear shift base adapter.
9. Reverse procedure to install, ensuring to **torque** flat hat head tapping screws to 7 ft. lbs.

UPPER HEAD HOUSING COMPONENTS, SHAFT LOCK, TURN SIGNAL CANCEL CAM, UPPER BEARING SPRING, UPPER BEARING INNER RACE SEAT & INNER RACE

1. Remove steering wheel as outlined in the "Electrical" section of the "Aurora & Riviera" chassis chapter.
2. Remove SIR coil assembly.
3. Remove shaft lock retaining ring using lock plate compressor tool No. J–23653-SIR, or equivalent, to push down shaft lock. Discard ring.
4. Remove shaft lock, then the turn signal cancel cam assembly.
5. Remove upper bearing spring, upper bearing inner race seat and inner race.
6. Remove tilt lever bracket.
7. Reverse procedure to install.

1997–99 BONNEVILLE, CAMARO, CORVETTE, FIREBIRD, LESABRE, LSS, REGENCY & 88

Refer to **Figs. 23 through 28** for exploded view of steering columns.

COIL, SHAFT LOCK, TURN SIGNAL CANCELLING CAM, UPPER BEARING SPRING & SEAT, INNER RACE, TURN SIGNAL SWITCH, BUZZER SWITCH & LOCK CYLINDER SET

1. Remove inflator module as outlined in "Passive Restraints, " then the coil assembly retaining ring.
2. Remove coil assembly and let hang freely, then the wave washer.
3. Using compressor tool No. J– 23653–SIR, or equivalent, remove shaft lock retaining ring lock plate, then the shaft lock.
4. Remove turn signal cancel cam assembly, then the upper bearing spring.
5. Remove upper bearing race seat, then the inner race.
6. Remove turn signal switch assembly as outlined in " Electrical" section of appropriate chassis chapter.
7. Remove coil assembly as follows:
   a. **On Bonneville, LeSabre, LSS, Regency and 88 models,** disconnect "RSWC" connector from turn signal harness.
   b. **On all models,** remove wire protector, then the wire harness strap.
   c. Attach a length of mechanics wire to both coil terminal connectors to aid in reassembly, then gently pull wire through column.
8. Remove key from pass key lock cylinder set, then the buzzer switch assembly.
9. Insert key in pass key lock cylinder, then remove lock retaining screw.
10. Remove pass key lock cylinder and harness as follows:
    a. Disconnect terminal connector from bulkhead connector, then remove wire protector.
    b. Attach a length of mechanics wire to aid in reassembly, then remove retaining clip from housing cover and gently pull wire harness through column.
11. Reverse procedure to install, noting the following:
    a. **Torque** pass key lock cylinder retaining screw to 22 inch lbs.
    b. **Torque** signal switch assembly screws to 30 inch lbs.
    c. **Torque** signal switch arm screws to 20 inch lbs.

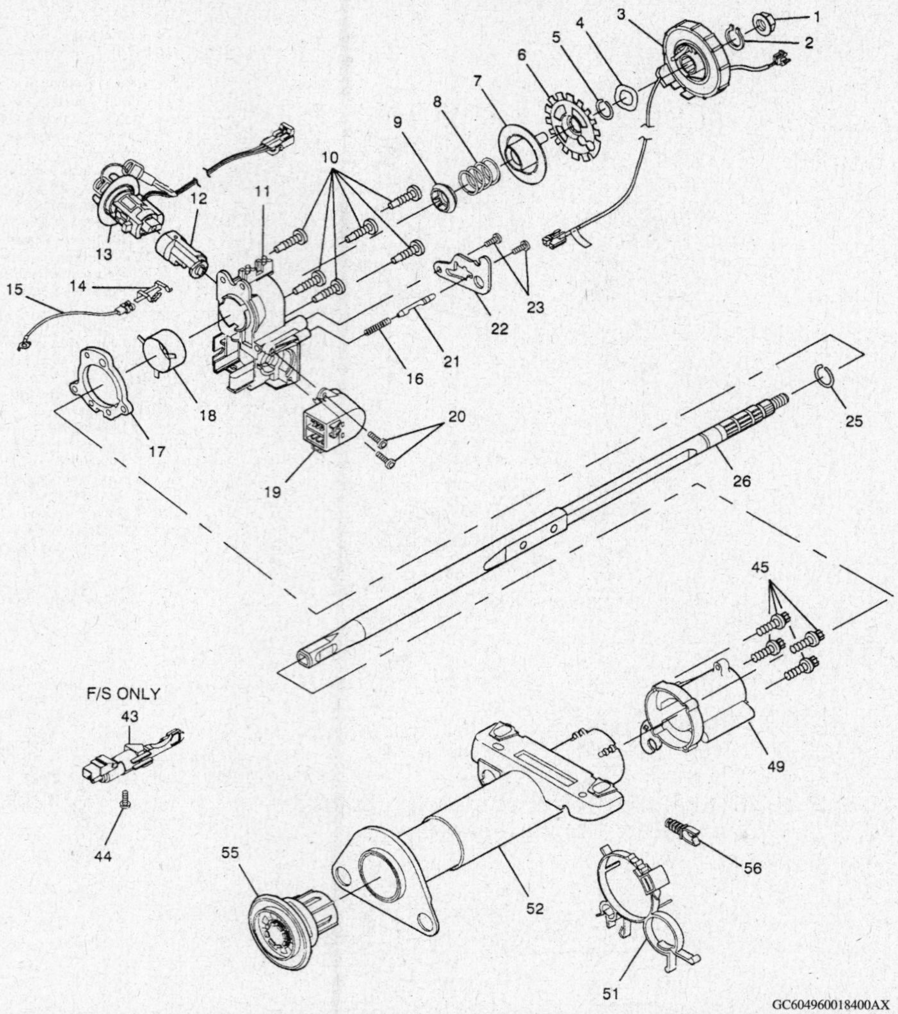

Fig. 19 Exploded view of standard steering column. Achieva, Grand Am & Skylark (Part 1 of 2)

LOCK HOUSING COVER, COVER END CAP, PIVOT & SWITCH, DIMMER SWITCH ROD ACTUATOR & TILT SPRING

1. Disassemble coil, shaft lock, turn signal cancel cam, upper bearing spring and seat, inner race turn signal switch, buzzer switch and lock cylinder set as outlined previously.
2. Remove lock cover housing end cap.
3. Remove lock housing cover attaching screws and the cover, then the tilt lever.
4. Remove base plate and dimmer switch rod actuator, then gently pull pivot switch wiring harness through column housing and gear shift lever bowl.
5. **On models equipped with cruise control,** unplug connector from base plate and remove multi-function lever.
6. **On all models,** remove pivot pin, then the pivot and switch assembly.
7. Remove spring retainer, then the spring and spring guide.
8. Reverse procedure to install, noting the following:
   a. Coat spring guide and spring with lithium grease and install them, then install spring retainer.
   b. Install lock housing cover, tighten screw in 12 o'clock position first, screw in 8 o'clock position second and screw in 3 o'clock position third, then **torque** screws to 8 ft. lbs. in same order.

1- NUT, HEX LOCKING (M14x1.5)
2- RING, RETAINING
3- COIL ASM, SIR
4- WASHER, WAVE
5- RING, RETAINING
6- LOCK, SHAFT
7- CAM ASM, T/SIG CANCEL
8- SPRING, UPPER BEARING
9- SPACER, UPPER BEARING
10- SCREW, ADAPTER
11- HOUSING ASM, STRG COLUMN
12- ACTUATOR ASM, IGNITION LOCK
13- LOCK CYL SET, STRG COLUMN
14- SPRING, LOCK PRE-LOAD
15- STRAP , GROUND
16- SPRING, LOCK BOLT
17- PLATE, MOUNTING
18- RETAINER, BEARING
19- SWITCH ASM, IGNITION
20- SCREW, TAPPING
21- BOLT ASM, LOCK
22- BRACKET, LOCK BOLT SUPPORT
23- SCREW, TAPPING
25- RING, RETAINING
26- SHAFT ASM, STEERING
43- ELEC PARK LOCK, STRG COL
44- SCREW, TAPPING
45- SCREW, SUPPORT
49- ADAPTER, SUPPORT MOUNTING
51- STRAP, WIRE
52- JACKET ASM, STRG COL
54- BOLT, FLNG HEX HD (M8X1.25)
55- BUSHING ASM, COLUMN JACKET
56- CLIP, WIRE RESTRAINT

GC604960018400BX

Fig. 19 Exploded view of standard steering column. Achieva, Grand Am & Skylark (Part 2 of 2)

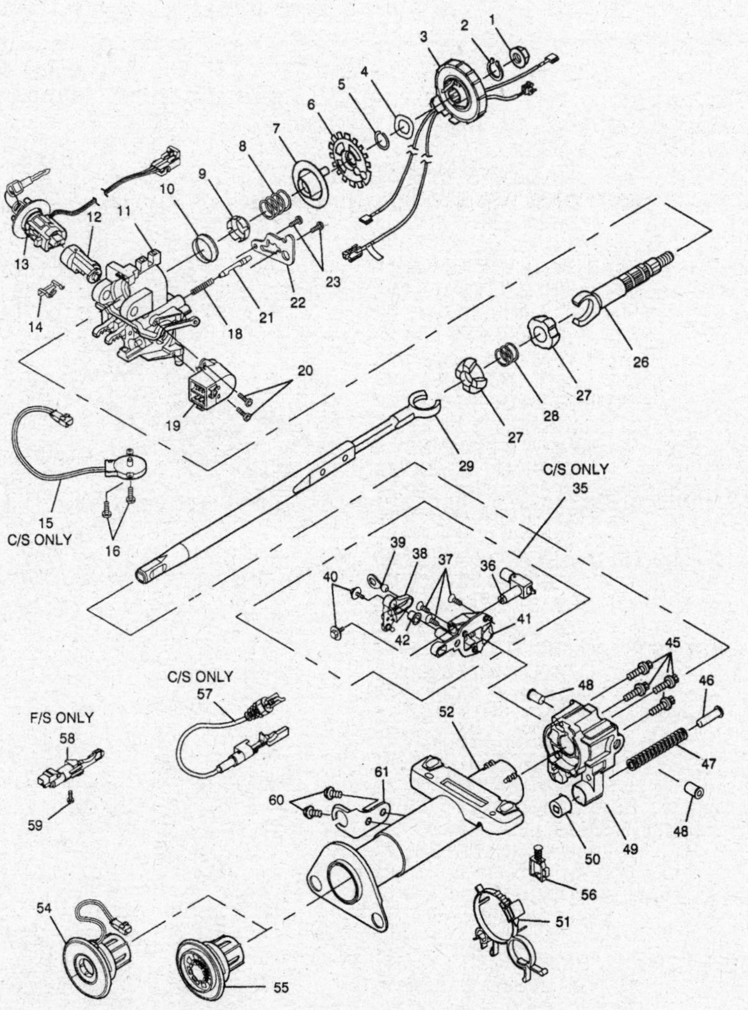

Fig. 20 Exploded view of tilt steeeering column. Achieva, Grand Am & Skylark w/SIR (Part 1 of 2)

1- NUT, HEX LOCKING (M14x1.5)
2- RING, RETAINING
3- COIL ASM, SIR
4- WASHER, WAVE
5- RING, RETAINING
6- LOCK, SHAFT
7- CAM ASM, TURN SIG CANCEL
8- SPRING, UPPER BEARING
9- SEAT, UPPER BEARING INNER RACE
10- RACE, INNER
11- HOUSING ASM, BRG &
12- ACTUATOR ASM, IGNITION LOCK
13- LOCK CYL SET, STRG COLUMN
14- SPRING, LOCK PRELOAD
15- SOLENOID ASM, INTERLOCK
16- SCREW, TAPPING
18- SPRING, LOCK BOLT
19- SWITCH ASM, IGNITION
20- SCREW, TAPPING
21-BOLT ASM, LOCK
22-BRACKET, LOCK BOLT SUPPORT
23-SCREW, TAPPING
26-SHAFT ASM, RACE & UPPER
27-SPHERE, CENTERING
28-SPRING, JOINT PRELOAD
29-SHAFT ASM, LOWER
35-SHIFT ASM, LINEAR
36-CLEVIS, SHIFT LEVER
37-SCREW, FLAT HD TAPPING
38-CAM ASM, CABLE SHIFT
39-ACTUATOR ASM, BALL
40-BOLT, HEX FLANGE HEAD
41-BRACKET, GS LEVER ASM SUPPORT
42-BUSHING,CAM
45-SCREW, SUPPORT
46-GUIDE, SPRING
47-SPRING, TILT WHEEL
48-PIN, PIVOT
49-SUPPORT ASM, STRG COL JACKET
50-RETAINER, SPRING
51-STRAP, WIRE
52-JACKET ASM, STRG COL
54-BUSHING ASM, POSITION SENSOR &
55-BUSHING ASM, COLUMN JACKET
56-CLIP, WIRE RESTRAINT
57-CABLE ASM, PARK LOCK
58-ELECTRIC PARK LOCK, STRG COL
59-SCREW, TAPPING
60-BOLT, FLANGED
61-BRACKET, CABLE SUPPORT

Fig. 20 Exploded view of tilt steering column. Achieva, Grand Am & Skylark w/SIR (Part 2 of 2)

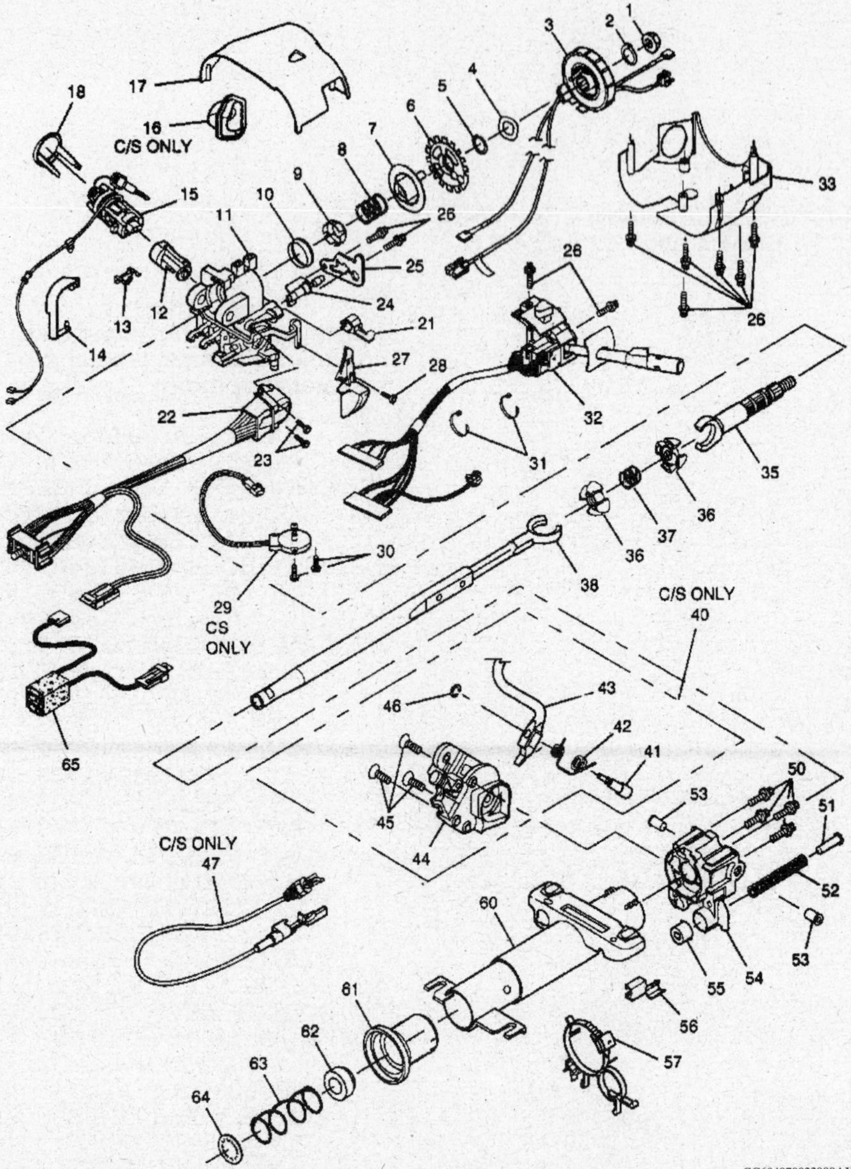

GC604970022900AX

Fig. 21 Exploded view of steering column w/column shift (Part 1 of 2). Aurora & Riviera

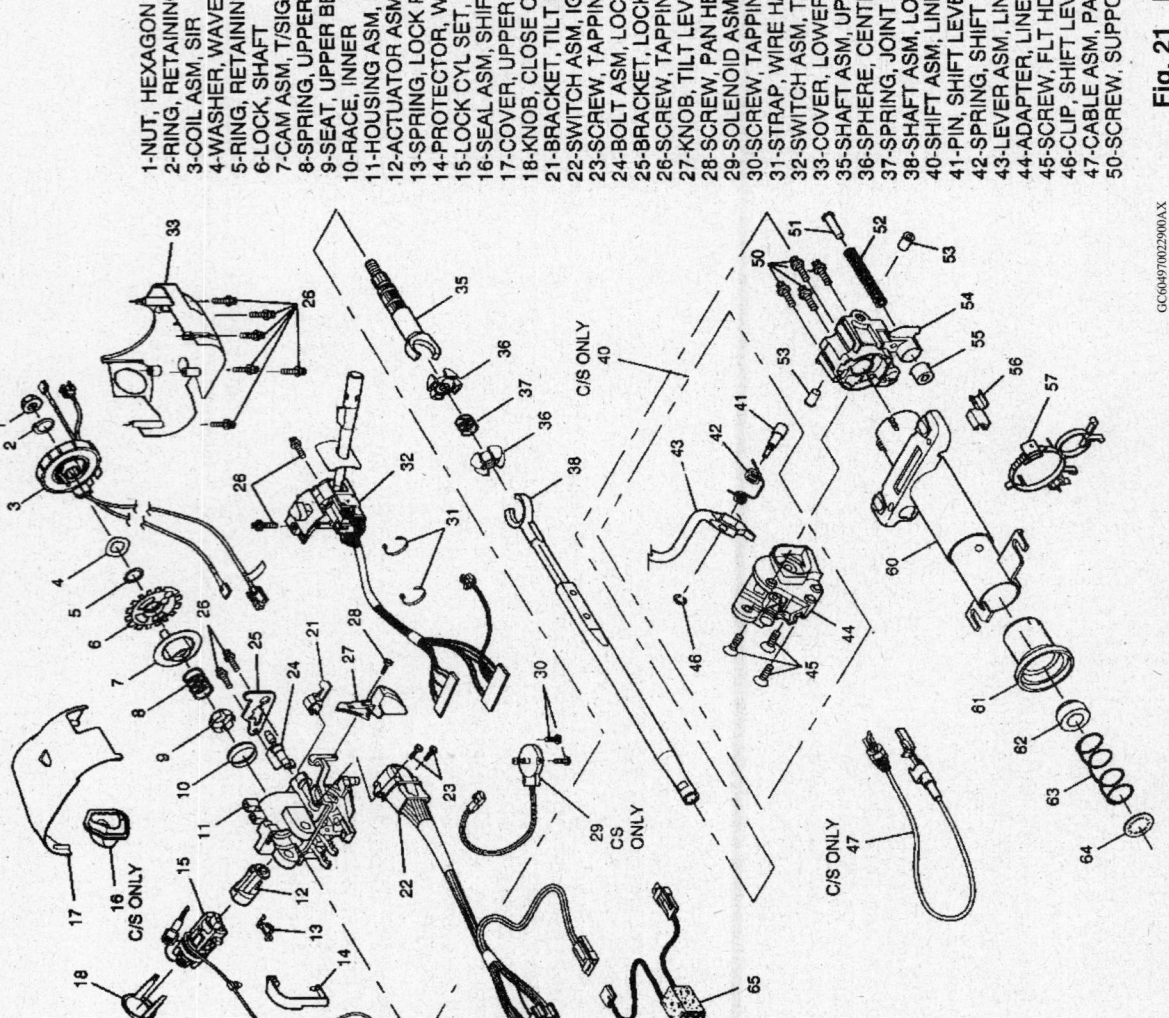

1-NUT, HEXAGON LOCKING (M14x1.5)
2-RING, RETAINING
3-COIL ASM, SIR
4-WASHER, WAVE
5-RING, RETAINING
6-LOCK, SHAFT
7-CAM ASM, T/SIG CANCEL
8-SPRING, UPPER BEARING
9-SEAT, UPPER BEARING INNER RACE
10-RACE, INNER
11-HOUSING ASM, BRG &
12-ACTUATOR ASM, IGNITION LOCK
13-SPRING, LOCK PRE-LOAD
14-PROTECTOR, WIRING
15-LOCK CYL SET, STRG COLUMN
16-SEAL ASM, SHIFT LEVER
17-COVER, UPPER
18-KNOB, CLOSE OUT
21-BRACKET, TILT LEVER
22-SWITCH ASM, IGN & KEY ALARM
23-SCREW, TAPPING
24-BOLT ASM, LOCK
25-BRACKET, LOCK BOLT SUPPORT
26-SCREW, TAPPING
27-KNOB, TILT LEVER
28-SCREW, PAN HEAD
29-SOLENOID ASM, INTERLOCK
30-SCREW, TAPPING
31-STRAP, WIRE HARNESS
32-SWITCH ASM, T/S & MULTIFUNC
33-COVER, LOWER
35-SHAFT ASM, UPPER
36-SPHERE, CENTERING
37-SPRING, JOINT PRELOAD
38-SHAFT ASM, LOWER STRG
40-SHIFT ASM, LINEAR
41-PIN, SHIFT LEVER
42-SPRING, SHIFT LEVER
43-LEVER ASM, LINEAR SHIFT
44-ADAPTER, LINEAR SHIFT BASE (NC)
45-SCREW, FLT HD TAPPING
46-CLIP, SHIFT LEVER
47-CABLE ASM, PARK LOCK
50-SCREW, SUPPORT
51-GUIDE, SPRING
52-SPRING, TILT WHEEL
53-PIN, PIVOT
54-SUPPORT ASM, STRG COL JACKET
55-RETAINER, SPRING
56-CLIP, WIRE RESTRAINT
57-STRAP, WIRE HARNESS
60-JACKET ASM, STRG COL
61-BEARING ASM, ADAPTER &
62-SEAT, LOWER BEARING
63-SPRING, LOWER BEARING
64-RETAINER, LOWER SPRING
65-HARNESS ASM, JUMPER

GC604970022900BX

Fig. 21 Exploded view of steering column w/column shift (Part 2 of 2). Aurora & Riviera

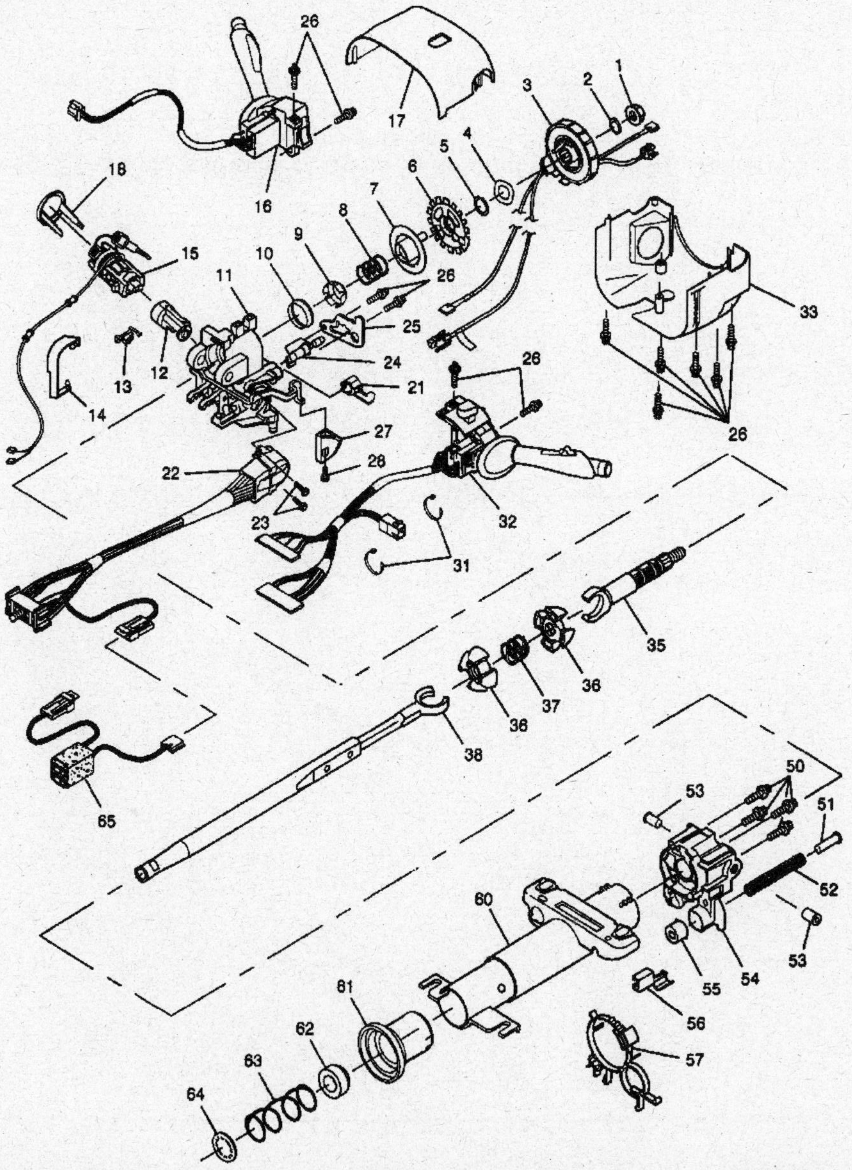

Fig. 22 Exploded view of steering column w/floor shift (Part 1 of 2). Aurora & Riviera

1- NUT, HEXAGON LOCKING (M14x1.5)
2- RING, RETAINING
3- COIL ASM, SIR
4- WASHER, WAVE
5- RING, RETAINING
6- LOCK, SHAFT
7- CAM ASM, T/SIG CANCEL
8- SPRING, UPPER BEARING
9- SEAT, UPPER BEARING INNER RACE
10- RACE, INNER
11- HOUSING ASM, BRG &
12- ACTUATOR ASM, IGNITION LOCK
13- SPRING, LOCK PRE-LOAD
14- PROTECTOR, WIRING
15- LOCK CYL SET, STRG COLUMN
16- SWITCH ASM, PIVOT & (PULSE)
17- COVER, UPPER
18- KNOB, CLOSE OUT
21- BRACKET, TILT LEVER
22- SWITCH ASM, IGN & KEY ALARM
23- SCREW, TAPPING
24- BOLT ASM, LOCK
25- BRACKET, LOCK BOLT SUPPORT
26- SCREW, TAPPING
27- KNOB, TILT LEVER
28- SCREW, PAN HEAD
31- STRAP, WIRE
32- SWITCH ASM, T/S & MULTIFUNC
33- COVER, LOWER
35- SHAFT ASM, UPPER
36- SPHERE, CENTERING
37- SPRING, JOINT PRELOAD
38- SHAFT ASM, LOWER STRG
50- SCREW, SUPPORT
51- GUIDE, SPRING
52- SPRING, WHEEL TILT
53- PIN, PIVOT
54- SUPPORT ASM, STRG COL JACKET
55- RETAINER, SPRING
56- CLIP, WIRE RESTRAINT
57- STRAP, WIRE HARNESS
60- JACKET ASM, STRG COL
61- BEARING ASM, ADAPTER &
62- SEAT, LOWER BEARING
63- SPRING, LOWER BEARING
64- RETAINER, LOWER SPRING
65- HARNESS ASM, JUMPER

GC604970023000BX

Fig. 22 Exploded view of steering column w/floor shift (Part 2 of 2). Aurora & Riviera

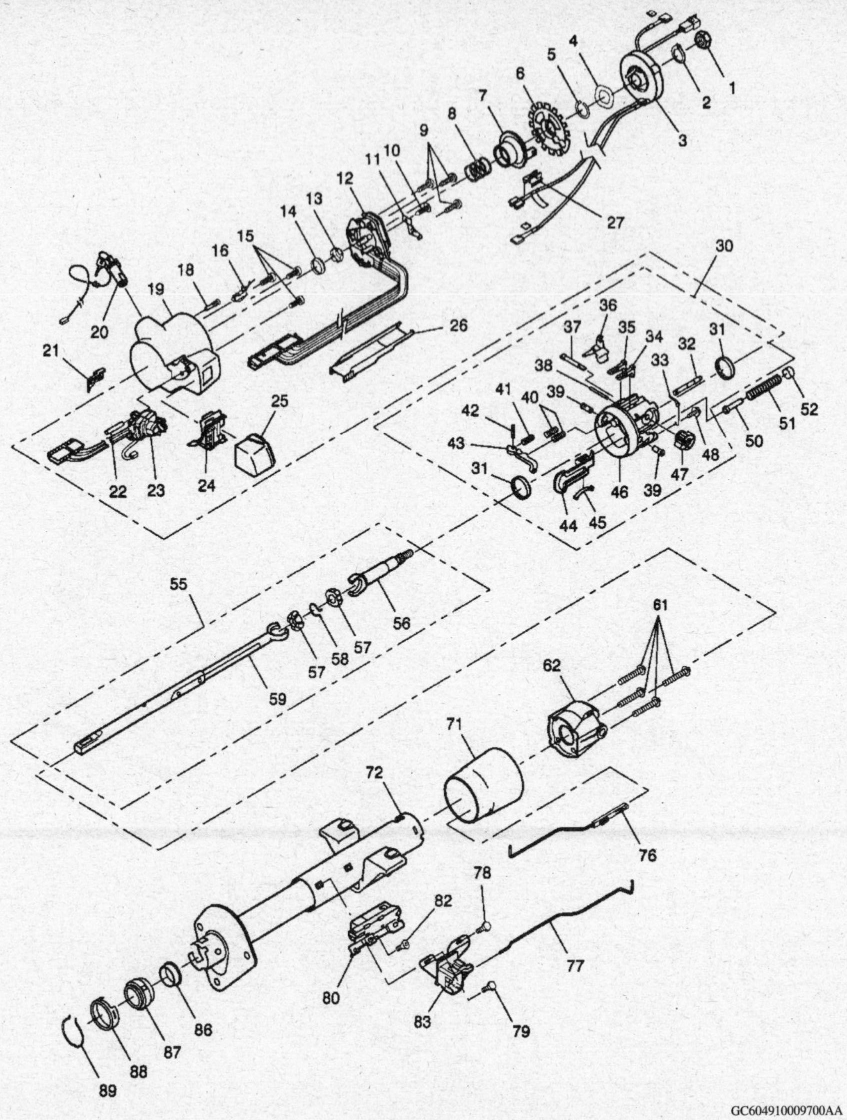

GC604910009700AA

Fig. 23 Exploded view of steering column (Part 1 of 2). Camaro & Firebird

1- NUT, HEX LOCKING (M14x1.5)
2- RING, RETAINING
3- COIL ASM, INFL RESTRAINT
4- WASHER, WAVE
5- RING, RETAINING
6- LOCK, SHAFT
7- CAM ASM, TURN SIG CANCEL
8- SPRING, UPPER BEARING
9- SCREW, BNDG HD CR RECESS
10- SCREW, RD WASH HD (M4.2x1.41)
11- ARM ASM, SIGNAL SWITCH
12- SWITCH ASM, TURN SIGNAL
13- SEAT, UPPER BRG INNER RACE
14- RACE, INNER
15- SCREW, PAN HD SOC TAP
16- SWITCH ASM, BUZZER
18- SCREW, LOCK RETAINING
19- COVER ASM, LOCK HOUSING
20- LOCK CYLINDER SET, STRG COL PASS KEY
21- ACTUATOR, DIMMER SW ROD
22- PIN, SWITCH ACTUATOR PIVOT
23- SWITCH ASM, PIVOT & (PULSE)
24- BASE PLATE, COL HSG CVR END
25- CAP, COL HSG COVER END
26- PROTECTOR, WIRING
27- SHROUD, CONNECTOR
30- HOUSING ASM, STRG COLUMN
31- BEARING ASM
32- BOLT, LOCK
33- SPRING, LOCK BOLT
34- SHOE, STEERING WHEEL LOCK
35- SHOE, STEERING WHEEL LOCK
36- SHIELD, WIRE PROTECTOR
37- SHAFT, DRIVE
38- PIN, DOWEL
39- PIN, PIVOT
40- SPRING, SHOE
41- SPRING, RELEASE LEVER
42- PIN, RELEASE LEVER
43- LEVER, SHOE RELEASE
44- RACK, SWITCH ACTUATOR
45- SPRING, RACK PRELOAD
46- HOUSING, STRG COLUMN
47- SECTOR, SWITCH ACTUATOR
48- SCREW, HEX WASHER HEAD
50- GUIDE, SPRING
51- SPRING, WHEEL TILT
52- RETAINER, SPRING
55- SHAFT ASM, STEERING COLUMN
56- SHAFT ASM, RACE & UPPER
57- SPHERE, CENTERING
58- SPRING, JOINT PRELOAD
59- SHAFT ASM, LOWER STEERING
61- SCREW, SUPPORT
62- SUPPORT ASM, STRG COL HSG
71- SHROUD, STRG COLUMN HOUSING
72- JACKET ASM, STRG COL
76- ACTUATOR ASM, IGNITION SWITCH
77- ROD, DIMMER SWITCH
78- SCREW, WASH HD (#10-24X.25)
79- SCREW, HEX WASH HD TAP
80- SWITCH ASM, IGNITION
82- SCREW, FLT HD (#10-24X.31)
83- SWITCH ASM, DIMMER
86- ADAPTER, LOWER BEARING
87- BEARING ASM
88- RETAINER, BEARING ADAPTER
89- CLIP, LOWER BEARING ADAPTER

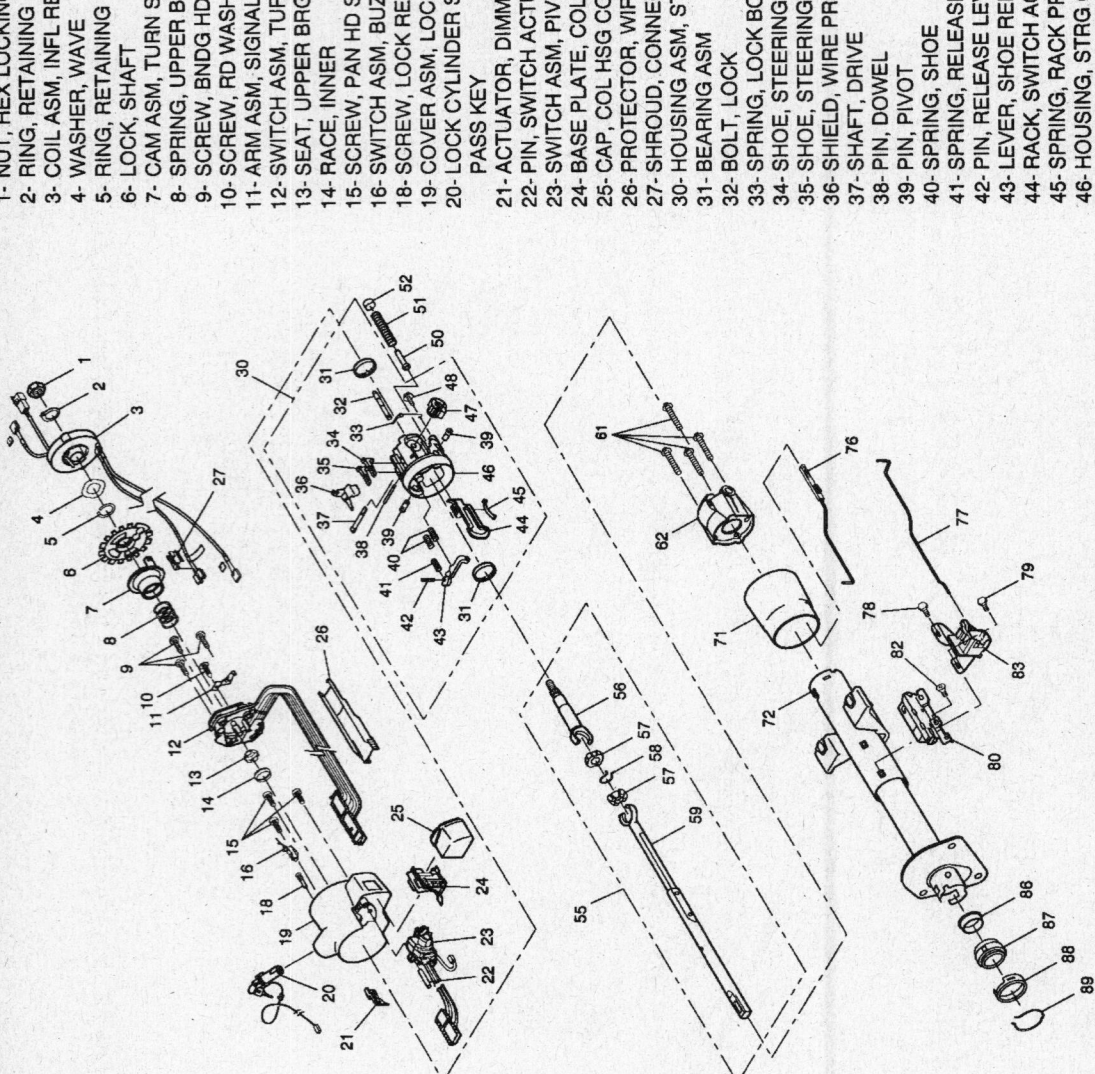

Service Kits

201- RACK SERV KIT, COL SECTOR & -INCLUDES: 14,31,33,44,47,48
202- SPRING SERV KIT, TILT COLUMN -INCLUDES: 13,14,39,50,51,52
203- COIL SERV KIT, INFL RESTRAINT -INCLUDES: 3,4,27
204- SPHERE SERV KIT, TILT COLUMN -INCLUDES: 57,58
205- GREASE SERV KIT, (SYNTHETIC)

GC604910009700BA

Fig. 23 Exploded view of steering column (Part 2 of 2). Camaro & Firebird (Part 2 of 2)

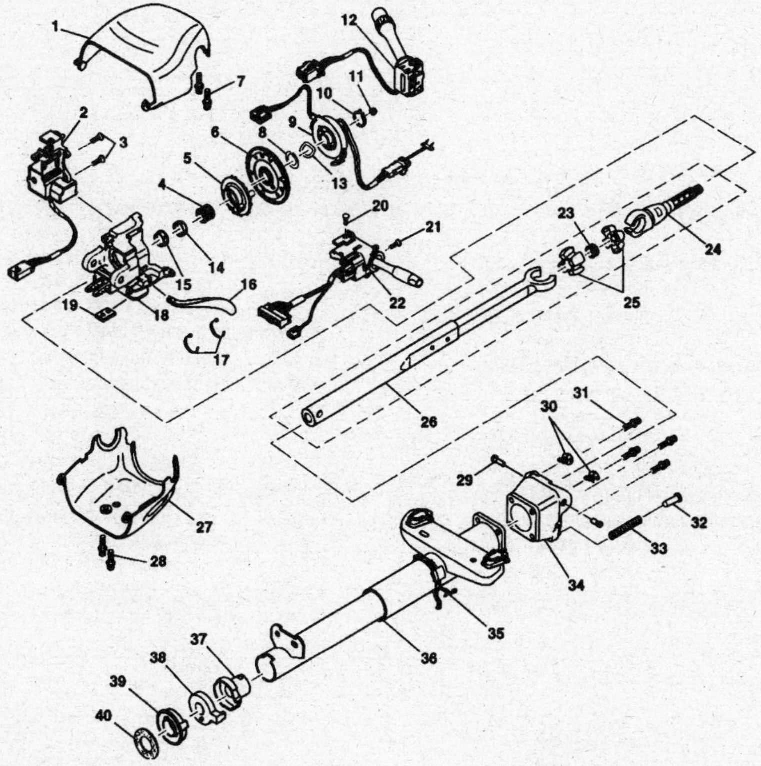

(1) Upper Shroud
(2) Electric Column Lock
(3) Pan Head Tapping Screw
(4) Upper Bearing Spring
(5) Turn Signal Cancel Cam Assembly
(6) Shaft Lock Shield Assembly
(7) Torx Head Screw
(8) Bearing Retainer
(9) SIR Coil Assembly
(10) Retaining Ring
(11) Flanged Prevailing Torque Nut
(12) Pivot and Pulse Switch Assembly
(13) Wave Washer
(14) Upper Bearing Inner Race Seat
(15) Inner Race
(16) Tilt Lever
(17) Wire Harness Straps
(18) Steering Column Tilt Head Assembly
(19) Wire Harness Spacer
(20) Pan Head Tapping Screws
(21) Pan Head Tapping Screws
(22) Turn Signal and Multifunction Switch Assembly

GC6049900277010X

Fig. 24 Exploded view of steering column (Part 1 of 2). Corvette Non Telescoping w/sensor

(23) Joint Preload Spring
(24) Race and Upper Shaft Assembly
(25) Centering Sphere
(26) Lower Steering Shaft Assembly
(27) Lower Shroud
(28) TORX® Head Screw
(29) Pivot Pin
(30) Tilt Bumper
(31) TORX® Head Screw
(32) Spring Guide
(33) Tilt Spring
(34) Steering Column Support Assembly
(35) Wire Harness Strap
(36) Steering Column Jacket Assembly
(37) Adapter and Bearing Assembly
(38) High Resolution Steering Wheel Position Sensor Assembly
(39) Sensor Retainer
(40) Steering Shaft Seal

GC6049900277020X

Fig. 24 Exploded view of steering column (Part 2 of 2). Corvette Non Telescoping w/sensor

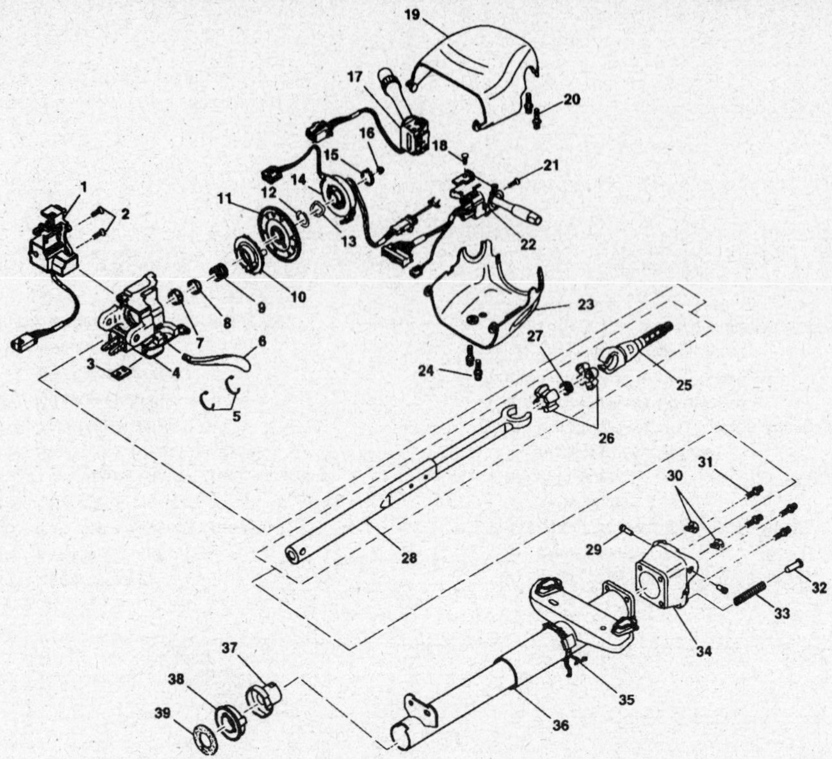

(1) Electric Column Lock
(2) Pan Head Tapping Screws
(3) Wire Harness Spacer
(4) Steering Column Tilt Head Assembly
(5) Wire Harness Straps
(6) Tilt Lever
(7) Inner Race
(8) Upper Bearing Inner Race Seat
(9) Upper Bearing Spring
(10) Turn Signal Cancel Cam Assembly
(11) Shaft Lock Shield Assembly
(12) Bearing Retainer
(13) Wave Washer
(14) SIR Coil Assembly
(15) Retaining Ring
(16) Flanged Prevailing Torque Nut
(17) Pivot and Pulse Switch Assembly
(18) Pan Head Tapping Screws
(19) Upper Shroud
(20) TORX® Head Screw
(21) Pan Head Tapping Screws
(22) Turn Signal and Multifunction Switch Assembly
(23) Lower Shroud
(24) Torx Head Screw
(25) Race and Upper Shaft Assembly

GC6049900278010X

Fig. 25 Exploded view of steering column (Part 1 of 2). Corvette Non Telescoping less sensor

(26) Centering Sphere
(27) Joint Preload Spring
(28) Lower Steering Shaft Assembly
(29) Pivot Pin
(30) Tilt Bumper
(31) TORX® Head Screw
(32) Spring Guide
(33) Tilt Spring
(34) Steering Column Support Assembly
(35) Wire Harness Strap
(36) Steering Column Jacket Assembly
(37) Adapter and Bearing Assembly
(38) Sensor Retainer
(39) Steering Shaft Seal

GC6049900278020X

Fig. 25 Exploded view of steering column (Part 2 of 2). Corvette Non Telescoping less sensor

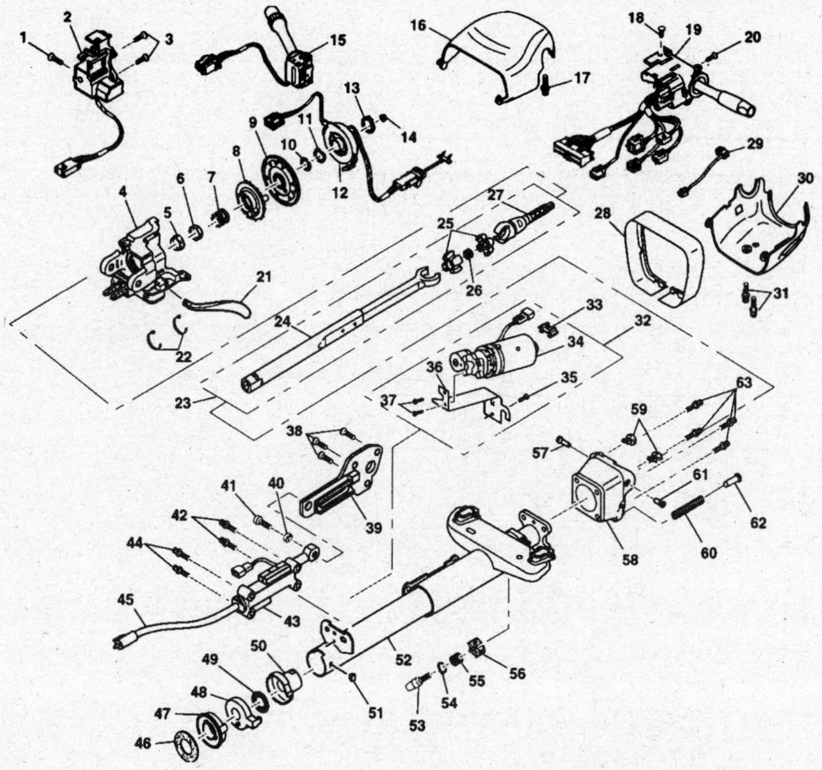

(1) Pan Head Tapping Screws
(2) Electric Column Lock
(3) Pan Head Tapping Screws
(4) Steering Column Tilt Head Assembly
(5) Inner Race
(6) Upper Bearing Inner Race Seat
(7) Upper Bearing Spring
(8) Turn Signal Cancel Cam Assembly
(9) Shaft Lock Shield Assembly
(10) Bearing Retainer
(11) Wave Washer
(12) SIR Coil Assembly
(13) Retaining Ring
(14) Flanged Prevailing Torque Nut
(15) Pivot and Pulse Switch Assembly
(16) Upper Shroud
(17) TORX® Head Screw
(18) Pan Head Tapping Screws
(19) Turn Signal and Multifunction Switch Assembly
(20) Pan Head Tapping Screws
(21) Tilt Lever
(22) Wire Harness Strap
(23) Steering Shaft Assembly
(24) Lower Steering Yoke Assembly
(25) Centering Sphere

GC6049900279010X

Fig. 26 Exploded view of steering column (Part 1 of 2). Corvette Telescoping

(26) Joint Preload Spring
(27) Race and Upper Shaft Assembly
(28) Steering Column Close Out Shroud
(29) Telescoping Switch Assembly
(30) Lower Shroud
(31) Pan Head Tapping Screw
(32) Telescope Motor and Bracket Assembly
(33) Connector Clip
(34) Telescope Drive Motor Assembly
(35) Pan Head Tapping Screws
(36) Telescope Drive Bracket
(37) Pan Head Tapping Screws
(38) Flat Head 6–Lobed Soc Tap Screw
(39) Telescope Adapter Assembly
(40) Telescope Drive Ball
(41) Telescope Drive Bolt
(42) TORX® Head Screw
(43) Telescope Actuator Assembly
(44) TORX® Head Screw
(45) Cable Assembly
(46) Steering Shaft Seal
(47) Sensor Retainer
(48) Hi Resolution Steering Wheel Position Sensor Assembly
(49) Lower Spring Retainer
(50) Adapter and Bearing Assembly
(51) Switch Housing Blocking Plug
(52) Telebearing and Jacket Assembly
(53) Shoulder Bolt
(54) Retaining Ring
(55) Compression Spring
(56) Anti Rotation Ball
(57) Pivot Pin
(58) Steering Column Support Assembly
(59) Tilt Bumper
(60) Tilt Spring
(61) Pivot Pin
(62) Spring Guide
(63) Support Screw

GC6049900279020X

Fig. 26 Exploded view of steering column (Part 2 of 2). Corvette Telescoping

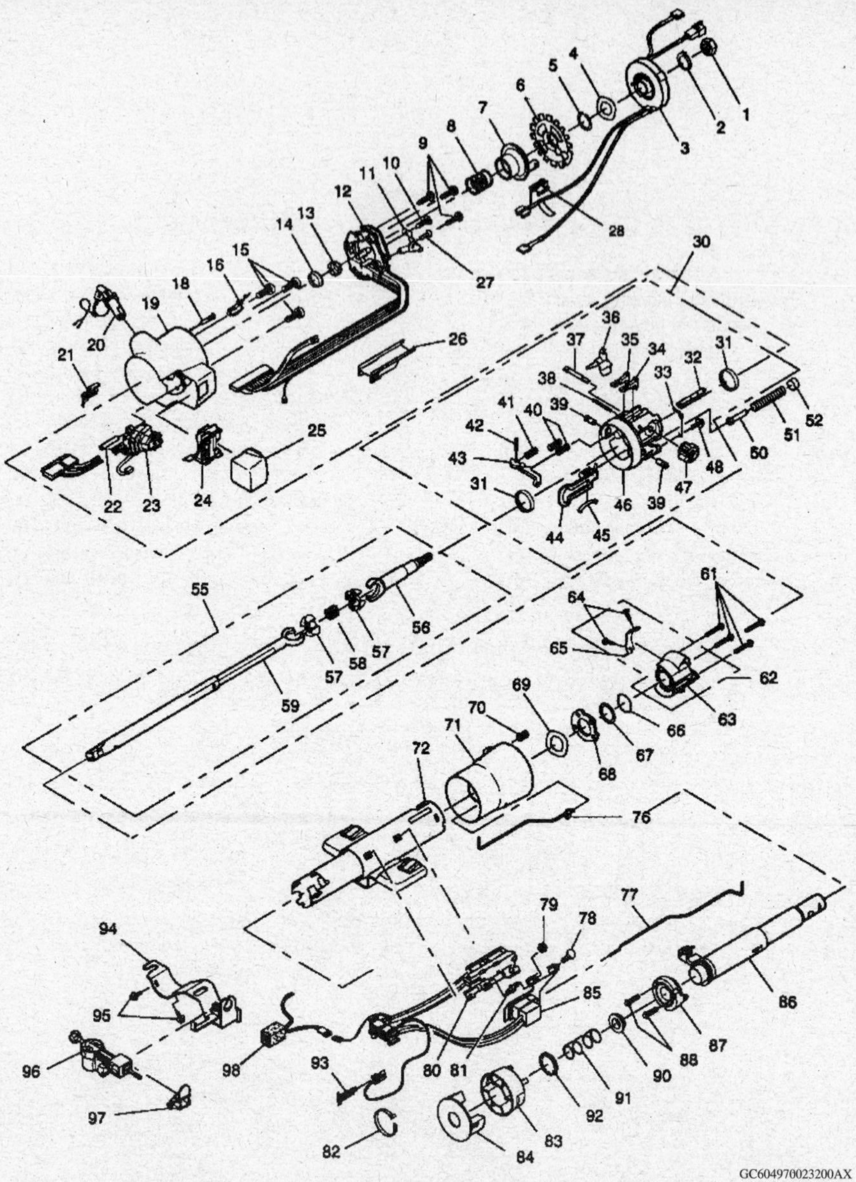

Fig. 27 Exploded view of steering column (Part 1 of 2). 1997–99 Bonneville & LeSabre, LSS, Regency & 88 w/column shift

1-NUT, HEX LOCKING (M14x1.5)
2-RING, RETAINING
3-COIL ASM, SIR
4-WASHER, WAVE
5-RING, RETAINING
6-LOCK, SHAFT
7-CAM ASM, TURN SIG CANCEL
8-SPRING, UPPER BEARING
9-SCREW, BNDG HD CR RECESS
10-SCREW, C/S TAPPING (#8-18X.75)
11-ARM ASM, SIGNAL SWITCH
12-SWITCH ASM, TURN SIGNAL
13-SEAT, UPPER BRG INNER RACE
14-RACE, INNER
15-SCREW, PAN HD SOC TAP
16-SWITCH ASM, BUZZER
18-SCREW, LOCK RETAINING
19-COVER ASM, LOCK HOUSING
20-LOCK CYLINDER SET, STRG COL (PASS KEY)
21-ACTUATOR, DIMMER SW ROD
22-PIN, SWITCH ACTUATOR PIVOT
23-SWITCH ASM, PIVOT & (PULSE)
24-BASE PLATE, COL HSG CVR END
25-CAP, COL HSG COVER END
26-PROTECTOR, WIRING
27-SCREW, FLT HD TAPPING
28-SHROUD, CONNECTOR
30-HOUSING ASM, STRG COLUMN
31-BEARING ASM
32-BOLT, LOCK
33-SPRING, LOCK BOLT
34-SHOE, STRG WHEEL LOCK
35-SHOE, STRG WHEEL LOCK
36-SHIELD, WIRE PROTECTOR
37-SHAFT, DRIVE
38-PIN, DOWEL
39-PIN, PIVOT
40-SPRING, SHOE
41-SPRING, RELEASE LEVER
42-PIN, RELEASE LEVER
43-LEVER, SHOE RELEASE
44-RACK, SWITCH ACTUATOR
45-SPRING, RACK PRELOAD
46-HOUSING, STRG COLUMN
47-SECTOR, SWITCH ACTUATOR
48-SCREW, HEX WASHER HEAD
50-GUIDE, SPRING
51-SPRING, WHEEL TILT
52-RETAINER, SPRING
55-SHAFT ASM, STEERING
56-SHAFT ASM, RACE & UPPER
57-SPHERE, CENTERING
58-SPRING, JOINT PRELOAD
59-SHAFT ASM, LOWER STEERING
61-SCREW, SUPPORT
62-SUPPORT ASM, STRG COL HSG
63-SUPPORT, STRG COL HSG
64-SCREW, OVL HD CROSS RECESS
65-GATE, SHIFT LEVER
66-RING, SHIFT TUBE RETAINING
67-WASHER, THRUST
68-PLATE, LOCK
69-WASHER, WAVE
70-SPRING, SHIFT LEVER
71-BOWL ASM, GEARSHIFT LEVER
72-JACKET ASM, STRG COL
76-ACTUATOR ASM, IGN SWITCH
77-ROD, DIMMER SWITCH
78-SCREW, WASH HD (#10-24x.25)
79-NUT, HEXAGON (#10-24)
80-SWITCH ASM, IGNITION & DIMR
81-STUD, DIMR & IGN SW MTG
82-STRAP, WIRE HARNESS
83-RETAINER, BEARING & SEAL
84-WASHER ASM, RETAINER
85-SWITCH ASM, DIMMER
86-TUBE ASM, SHIFT
87-BEARING ASM, ADAPTER &
88-SCREW, HEX WASHER HD TAP
90-SEAT, LOWER BEARING
91-SPRING, LOWER BEARING
92-RETAINER, LOWER SPRING
93-CONNECTOR, AXIAL POSN ASSUR
94-SUPPORT, STRG COL LOWER
95-BOLT, HEX FLNG HD (M6x1x14)
96-ACTUATOR, ELECTRICAL (BTSI)
97-CLIP, ADJUSTMENT RETAINING
98-HARNESS ASM, JUMPER

GC604970023200BX

Fig. 27 Exploded view of steering column (Part 2 of 2). 1997–99 Bonneville & LeSabre, LSS, Regency & 88 w/column shift

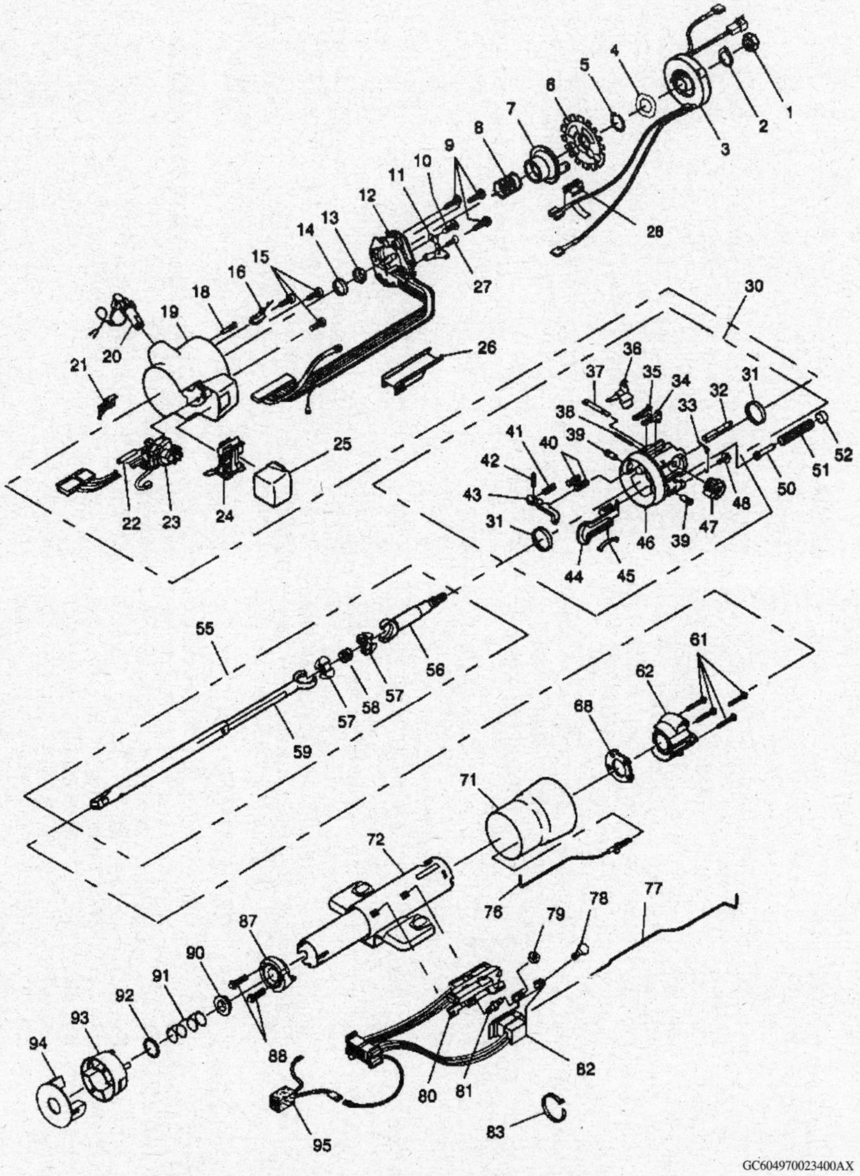

GC604970023400AX

Fig. 28 Exploded view of steering column (Part 1 of 2). 1997–99 Bonneville, LSS, Regency & 88 w/floor shift

1-NUT, HEX LOCKING (M14x1.5)
2-RING, RETAINING
3-COIL ASM, INFL RESTRAINT
4-WASHER, WAVE
5-RING, RETAINING
6-LOCK, SHAFT
7-CAM ASM, TURN SIG CANCEL
8-SPRING, UPPER BEARING
9-SCREW, BNDG HD CR RECESS
10-SCREW, C/S TAPPING (8-18X.75)
11-ARM ASM, SIGNAL SWITCH
12-SWITCH ASM, TURN SIGNAL
13-SEAT, UPPER BRG INNER RACE
14-RACE, INNER
15-SCREW, PAN HD SOC TAP
16-SWITCH ASM, BUZZER
18-SCREW, LOCK RETAINING
19-COVER ASM, LOCK HOUSING
20-LOCK CYLINDER SET, STRG COL (PASS KEY)
21-ACTUATOR, DIMMER SW ROD
22-PIN, SWITCH ACTUATOR PIVOT
23-SWITCH ASM, PIVOT & (PULSE)
24-BASE PLATE, COL HSG CVR END
25-CAP, COL HSG COVER END
26-PROTECTOR, WIRING
27-SCREW, FLT HD TAPPING
28-SHROUD, CONNECTOR
30-HOUSING ASM, STRG COLUMN
31-BEARING ASM
32-BOLT, LOCK
33-SPRING, LOCK BOLT
34-SHOE, STRG WHEEL LOCK
35-SHOE, STRG WHEEL LOCK
36-SHIELD, WIRE PROTECTOR
37-SHAFT, DRIVE
38-PIN, DOWEL
39-PIN, PIVOT
40-SPRING, SHOE
41-SPRING, RELEASE LEVER
42-PIN, RELEASE LEVER
43-LEVER, SHOE RELEASE
44-RACK, SWITCH ACTUATOR
45-SPRING, RACK PRELOAD
46-HOUSING, STRG COLUMN
47-SECTOR, SWITCH ACTUATOR
48-SCREW, HEX WASHER HEAD
50-GUIDE, SPRING
51-SPRING, WHEEL TILT
52-RETAINER, SPRING
55-SHAFT ASM, STEERING
56-SHAFT ASM, RACE & UPPER
57-SPHERE, CENTERING
58-SPRING, JOINT PRELOAD
59-SHAFT ASM, LOWER STEERING
61-SCREW, SUPPORT
62-SUPPORT ASM, STRG COL HSG
68-PLATE, LOCK
71-SHROUD, STRG COL HSG
72-JACKET ASM, STRG COL
76-ACTUATOR ASM, IGN SWITCH
77-ROD, DIMMER SWITCH
78-SCREW, WASH HD (#10-24x.25)
79-NUT, HEXAGON (#10-24)
80-SWITCH ASM, IGN & DIMMER
81-STUD, DIMR & IGN SW MTG
82-SWITCH ASM, DIMMER
83-STRAP, WIRE HARNESS
87-BEARING ASM, ADAPTER &
88-SCREW, HEX WASHER HD TAP
90-SEAT, LOWER BEARING
91-SPRING, LOWER BEARING
92-RETAINER, LOWER SPRING
93-RETAINER, BEARING & SEAL
94-WASHER ASM, RETAINER
95-HARNESS ASM, JUMPER

GC604970023400BX

Fig. 28 Exploded view of steering column (Part 2 of 2). 1997–99 Bonneville, LSS, Regency & 88 w/floor shift

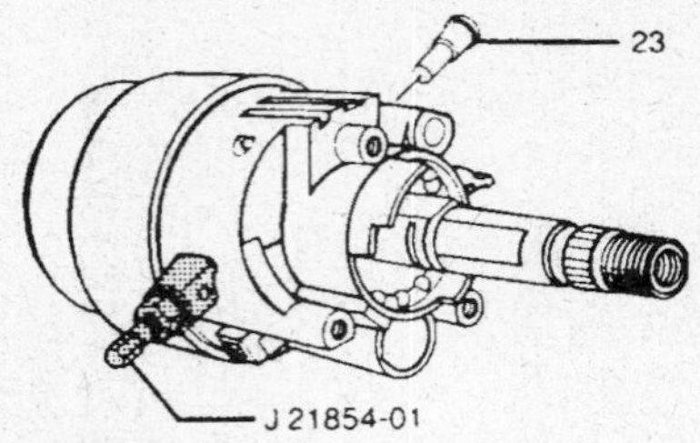

23 PIN, PIVOT

GC6049100092000X

Fig. 29 Pivot pin removal. Bonneville, Camaro, Corvette, DeVille, Firebird, LeSabre, LSS, Park Avenue & 88

COLUMN HOUSING, LOCK SHOES, ACTUATOR SECTOR, SWITCH ACTUATOR RACK, BEARINGS & LOCK BOLT

1. Disassemble coil, shaft lock, turn signal cancel cam, upper bearing spring and seat, inner race turn signal switch, buzzer switch and lock cylinder set as outlined previously.
2. Disassemble lock housing cover, cover end cap, pivot and switch, dimmer switch rod actuator and tilt spring as outlined previously.
3. Remove lock housing cover attaching screws and the cover, then the tilt lever.
4. Remove cover housing end cap, base plate and dimmer switch rod actuator, then gently pull pivot switch wire harness through column housing and gear shift lever bowl.
5. **On models equipped with cruise control,** unplug connector from base plate and remove multi-function lever.
6. **On all models,** remove spring retainer, then the spring and spring guide.
7. Using pivot pin removal tool No. J-21854-01, or equivalent, remove pivot pins, **Fig. 29,** then install tilt lever.
8. Remove column housing assembly by pulling back on tilt lever and pulling housing down and away from column.
9. Remove bearing assembly, then the hex head screw.
10. Remove lock bolt spring and lock bolt, then the switch actuator rack and rack preload spring.
11. Remove driveshaft, then the switch actuator sector.
12. Remove release lever pin, then the shoe release lever.
13. Remove release lever spring, then the dowel pin.
14. Remove steering wheel lock shoes, then the lock shoe springs.
15. Reverse procedure to install.

SHAFT, COLUMN HOUSING SUPPORT, SHIFT TUBE, IGNITION SWITCH, DIMMER SWITCH & LOWER BEARING

1. Remove inflator module as outlined in "Passive Restraints."
2. Remove washer head screw, **Fig. 30,** then the hex nut and ground wire with ring terminal from stud.
3. Remove dimmer switch assembly from dimmer switch rod, then the wiring harness strap.
4. Disconnect positive assurance terminal connector from bulkhead connector, then the dimmer switch wires from positions 4B, 5B and 5C of bulkhead connector.
5. Reverse procedure to install, noting the following:
   a. Connect dimmer switch wires; Tan — 4B; Green — 5B; Yellow — 5 C.
   b. **Torque** dimmer switch assembly screw and nut to 35 inch lbs.

2000 BONNEVILLE & LESABRE

Refer to **Fig. 31,** for exploded view of steering column.

COIL ASSEMBLY

1. Remove steering column as outlined under "Steering Column, Replace."
2. Remove inflator module as outlined under "Passive Restraints."
3. Remove steering wheel as outlined under "Electrical"
4. Remove upper and lower steering column shrouds.
5. Remove wire harness straps, then the wire harness assembly from wire restraint clip.
6. Remove black SIR connector from fused jumper assembly connector.
7. Using snap ring pliers remove retaining ring, then the SIR coil assembly.
8. Remove wave washer.
9. Reverse procedure to assemble.

LINEAR SHIFT ASSEMBLY

1. Remove steering column as outlined under "Steering Column, Replace."
2. Remove inflator module as outlined under "Passive Restraints."
3. Remove steering wheel as outlined under "Electrical"
4. Remove upper and lower steering column shrouds.
5. Remove wire harness straps, then the wire harness assembly from wire restraint clip.
6. Disconnect shift lever electrical connector, then slide shift lever seal up shift lever and remove lever retaining screw.
7. Remove shift lever, then disconnect and remove electric BTSI actuator from steering column.
8. Lock cylinder should be in Off-lock position.
9. Remove three flat head six lobed socket tap screws, then the linear shift assembly from steering column.
10. Reverse procedure to assemble. Tighten to specification.

TILT SPRING

The tilt spring and guide are under pressure and could become a projectile. During disassembly and assembly procedures, secure the tilt spring. Exercise caution when removing or installing the tilt spring and guide, as bodily injury may result.

1. Remove upper and lower steering column shrouds.
2. Use tilt lever to tilt steering column in

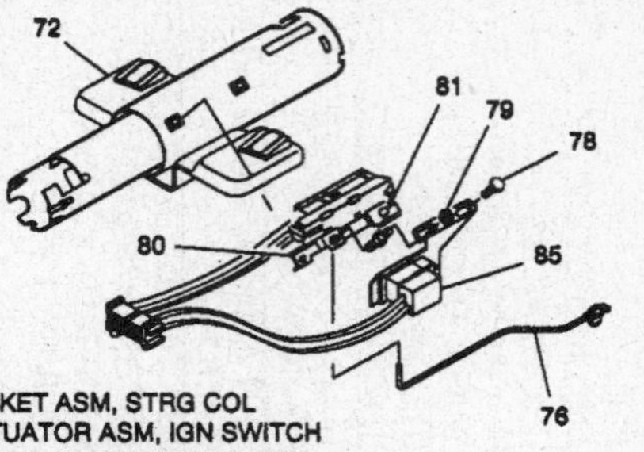

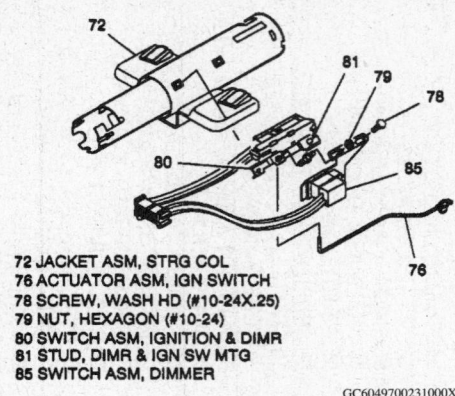

72 JACKET ASM, STRG COL
76 ACTUATOR ASM, IGN SWITCH
78 SCREW, WASH HD (#10-24X.25)
79 NUT, HEXAGON (#10-24)
80 SWITCH ASM, IGNITION & DIMR
81 STUD, DIMR & IGN SW MTG
85 SWITCH ASM, DIMMER

GC6049700231000X

Fig. 30 Ignition & dimmer switch replacement. Bonneville, Camaro, Corvette, Firebird, LeSabre, LSS, Regency & 88

"UP" position.

3. Pry tilt spring until a bulge occurs and most of tilt spring tension is removed.
4. Secure tilt spring and continue to pry until tilt spring disengages from post on steering wheel column assembly and column tilt head assembly.
5. Remove tilt spring guide from tilt spring.
6. Reverse procedure to assemble.

LOCK MODULE ASSEMBLY

1. Remove coded key controller, then the ignition and key alarm switch assembly.
2. Remove upper tilt head components as described under "Steering Column Tilt Head Housing."
3. Lock cylinder should be in Off-lock position.
4. Insert a small screwdriver into slot on lock module assembly, push against locking tab to remove.
5. Disconnect park lock cable assembly.
6. Remove three pan head tapping screws, then the lock module assembly.
7. Reverse procedure to assemble. Adjust park lock cable assembly as follows:
   a. Use gear shift lever to put column in park position.
   b. Put ignition switch in off-lock position. Remove key.
   c. Unlock adjuster ring on park lock cable assembly with park lock cable pliers tool no. J 41396.
   d. Pull on cable until park lock latch contacts gear shift lever. Release cable.
   e. Lock adjuster ring securely in place on park lock cable assembly with cable pliers.

STEERING COLUMN TILT HEAD HOUSING

1. Remove SIR as described under "Coil Assembly" in this section.
2. Remove, then dispose of bearing retainer using bearing remover tool No. J 23653–SIR or equivalent.
3. Remove shaft lock shield assembly,

then the turn signal cancel cam assembly.
4. Remove upper bearing spring, then the upper bearing inner race seat.
5. Remove inner race.
6. Reverse procedure to assemble.

STEERING SHAFT, LOWER BEARING & JACKET

1. Remove upper tilt head components as described under " Steering Column Tilt Head Housing."
2. Disconnect electrical connector from pivot and pulse switch assembly if required.
3. Press on locking tabs of pivot and pulse switch assembly, then pull out pivot and pulse switch assembly out of mounting bracket.
4. Remove screws, then the mounting bracket.
5. Remove turn signal and multi-function switch assembly.
6. Remove tilt spring, then the linear shift assembly, shift lever and BTSI actuator.
7. Remove two pivot pins from steering column support assembly using pivot pin remover tool No. J– 21854–1 or equivalent.
8. Remove dual triangle Sensor assembly if equipped.
9. Remove boot seal, then the steering shaft seal.
10. Remove sensor retainer, then the steering shaft seal.
11. Remove three flat head screws, then the cable support bracket.
12. Remove tilt head assembly with lower steering shaft still attached from steering column support assembly.
13. Remove tilt head assembly from steering shaft assembly.
14. Mark race and upper shaft and lower steering shaft to ensure proper assembly. Failure to assemble properly will cause steering wheel to be tuned 180°.
15. Reverse procedure to assemble.

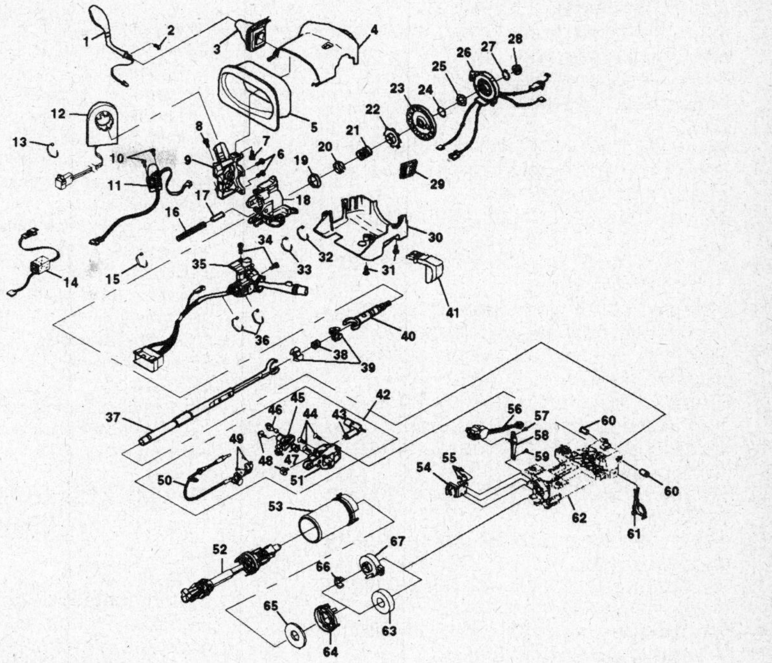

(1) Automatic Transmission Control Lever Assembly
(2) Shift Lever Screw
(3) Shift Lever Seal
(4) Upper Shroud
(5) Steering Column Closeout Shroud
(6) Pan Head Tapping Screw
(7) TORX® Head Screw
(8) Pan Head Tapping Screw
(9) Lock Module Assembly
(10) Tapping Screw
(11) Ignition & Key Alarm Switch Assembly
(12) Coded Key Controller
(13) Wire Harness Strap
(14) Fused Jumper Assembly
(15) Wire Harness Strap
(16) Tilt Spring
(17) Spring Guide
(18) Steering Column Tilt Head Assembly
(19) Inner Race
(20) Upper Bearing Inner Race Seat
(21) Upper Bearing Spring
(22) Turn Signal Cancel Cam Assembly
(23) Shaft Lock Sheild Assembly
(24) Bearing Retainer
(25) Wave Washer
(26) SIR Coil Assembly
(27) Retaining Ring

GC6049900286010X

Fig. 31 Exploded view of steering column (Part 1 of 2). 2000 Bonneville & LeSabre w/column shift

CATERA

Refer to **Fig. 32** for exploded view of steering column.

STEERING COLUMN HOUSING

1. Remove signal switch housing screws, then the signal switch housing.
2. Remove heads from lock housing shear bolts using a ¼ inch drill bit.
3. Remove lock housing from steering column housing assembly, then the shear bolts from the lock housing using a suitable pair of locking type pliers.
4. Remove retaining ring using lock plate compressor tool No. J–23653–SIR, with a compressor plate adapter tool No. J–23653–91, or equivalents.
5. Remove spring retainer, upper bearing spring, inner race seat and inner race.
6. Insert a No. 2 Phillips head screwdriver into square opening in tilt spring retainer, **Fig. 33,** then depress tilt spring retainer and turn screwdriver to unlock tilt spring retainer.
7. Remove tilt spring retainer and tilt spring by pushing spring out towards front of column.
8. Remove pivot pins using pivot pin remover tool No. J– 21854–01, or equivalent, then pull tilt lever forward to release tilt shoes from column support assembly.
9. Remove steering column assembly.
10. Reverse procedure to install, ensuring to use a new retaining ring.

LOWER STEERING SHAFT, LOWER BEARING & COLUMN JACKET

1. Remove steering column housing as outlined under " Steering Column Housing."
2. Remove steering shaft assembly from steering column housing support and jacket assembly. **Make alignment marks on upper and lower steering shaft assemblies prior to disassembly.**
3. Remove bearing assembly, then the steering column housing support screws and column support housing.
4. Disconnect upper and lower steering shaft assemblies by tilt upper steering shaft 90° from lower steering shaft.
5. Rotate centering sphere 90°, then lift centering sphere away from upper steering shaft.
6. Remove shaft preload spring from centering sphere.
7. Reverse procedure to install, noting the following:
   a. Install a new centering sphere and preload spring, using a centering sphere installer tool No. J 41688, or equivalent, and a vise.
   b. **Torque** signal switch housing screws to 35 inch lbs.

CAVALIER & SUNFIRE

STANDARD COLUMN

Refer to **Fig. 34** when servicing these steering columns.

Shaft Lock, Turn Signal Cancel Cam, Upper Bearing Spring, Thrust Washer, Buzzer Switch & Column Lock Cylinder Set

1. Remove inflator module as outlined in "Passive Restraints. "
2. Remove steering wheel as outlined in the "Electrical " section of the "Cavalier

& Sunfire" chassis chapter.
3. Remove shaft lock cover, then the shaft lock retaining ring using plate compressor tool No. J-23653-SIR, or equivalent, to depress shaft lock. Discard ring.
4. Remove shaft lock, turn signal cancelling cam assembly, upper bearing spring and thrust washer.
5. Move turn signal to the right turn position.
6. Remove multi-function lever and hazard knob assembly.
7. Remove screw and signal switch arm, then the turn signal switch screws.
8. Remove turn signal switch assembly and allow switch to hang freely.
9. Remove key from lock cylinder set, then the buzzer switch assembly.
10. Install key in lock cylinder and turn to Lock position.
11. Remove retaining screw, then the lock cylinder set.
12. Reverse procedure to install, noting the following:
    a. **Torque** lock cylinder set retaining screw to 40 inch lbs.
    b. **Torque** turn signal switch assembly screws to 30 inch lbs.
    c. **Torque** signal switch arm screw to 20 inch lbs.

(28) Hexagon Locking Nut
(29) Shroud Protector
(30) Lower Shroud
(31) Pan Head Tapping Screw
(32) Wire Harness Strap
(33) Wire Harness Strap
(34) Pan Head Tapping Screw
(35) Turn Signal and Multifunction Switch
(36) Wire Harness Strap
(37) Lower Steering Shaft Assembly
(38) Joint Preload Spring
(39) Centering Sphere
(40) Race and Upper Shaft Assembly
(41) Tilt Lever Assembly
(42) Linear Shift Assembly
(43) Shift Lever Clevis
(44) Cam Bushing
(45) Flat Head 6–Lobed Socket Tapping Screw
(46) Cable Shift Cam Assembly
(47) Hex Flanged Head Bolt
(48) Ball and Actuator Assembly
(49) Oval Head 6–Lobed Socket Tapping Screw
(50) Park Lock Cabel Assembly
(51) Gear Shift Lever Assembly Support Bracket
(52) Intermediate Steering Shaft Assembly
(53) Boot Seal
(54) Cable Support Bracket
(55) Flat Head Screw
(56) Electrical BTSI Actuator
(57) Pan Head Tapping Screw
(58) BTSI Mounting Bracket Assembly
(59) Pan Head Tapping Screw
(60) Pivot Pin
(61) Wire Restraint Clip
(62) Steering Column Support Assembly
(63) Steering Shaft Seal
(64) Sensor Retainer
(65) Steering Shaft Seal
(66) Sensor Locator
(67) Sensor Steer Sensor Assembly

GC6049900286020X

Fig. 31 Exploded view of steering column (Part 2 of 2). 2000 Bonneville & LeSabre w/column shift

Steering Shaft, Turn Signal Switch, Column Housing, Switch Actuator Pivot, Spring & Bolt, Bearing, Switch Actuator Sector & Ignition Switch Actuator

1. Remove inflator module as outlined in "Passive Restraints."
2. Remove steering wheel as outlined in the "Electrical" section of the "Cavalier & Sunfire" chassis chapter.
3. Remove steering column from vehicle as outlined under "Steering Column, Replace."
4. Inspect steering column for damage.
5. Remove steering shaft assembly, then the retaining ring from shaft.
6. Inspect column shaft assembly for damage.
7. Remove four support bolts, then the steering column support bracket assembly.
8. Remove wiring protector, turn signal switch assembly, washer head screw and hex nut.
9. Remove dimmer switch, dimmer switch rod and switch mounting stud.
10. Remove ignition switch, two cross recess screws and ignition switch inhibitor housing assembly.
11. Remove cover screws and lock housing cover assembly with floor shift lever bowl and shift bowl shroud. Pull housing cover from jacket and remove upper bearing retainer.
12. Remove three cross recess screws, floor shift lever bowl with shift bowl shroud, then the shroud from bowl.
13. If necessary, disassemble steering column housing as follows:
    a. Remove switch actuator rack with spring and bolt assembly, then the spring and bolt assembly from switch actuator rack.
    b. Remove switch actuator rod from rack, then the spring thrust washer from spring and bolt assembly.
    c. Remove switch actuator sector, rack preload spring, switch actuator pivot pin and switch actuator pivot assembly.
    d. Remove bearing retaining bushing using a punch, then the bearing assembly using a punch.
14. Reverse procedure to install, noting the following:
    a. **Torque** switch actuator pivot pin to 27 inch lbs.
    b. Assemble spring and bolt assembly with switch actuator rack to housing assembly. **First tooth of rack must interact with first and second tooth of sector. With rack fully inserted, block tooth of sector will rest in block tooth of rack.**
    c. **Torque** three cross recess screws to 17 inch lbs.
    d. **Torque** cover screws in clockwise order to 47 inch lbs.
    e. **Torque** ignition switch and mounting stud to 35 inch lbs.
    f. **Torque** dimmer switch screw and nut to 35 inch lbs.
    g. **Torque** steering column support bracket assembly bolts to 22 ft. lbs.

TILT COLUMN

Refer to **Fig. 35** when servicing these steering columns.

Shaft Lock, Turn Signal Cancel Cam, upper Bearing Spring, Upper Bearing Inner Race Seat, Inner Race, Buzzer Switch & Column Lock Cylinder Set

1. Remove inflator module as outlined in "Passive Restraints."
2. Remove steering wheel as outlined in the "Electrical" section of the "Cavalier & Sunfire" chassis chapter.
3. Remove shaft lock cover, then the shaft lock retaining ring using plate compressor J-23653-C, or equivalent, to depress shaft lock. Discard ring.
4. Remove shaft lock, turn signal cancelling cam assembly, upper bearing spring, upper bearing inner race seat and inner race.
5. Move turn signal to the right turn position.
6. Remove multi-function lever and hazard knob assembly.
7. Remove screw and signal switch arm, then the turn signal switch screws.
8. Remove turn signal switch assembly and allow switch to hang freely.
9. Remove key from lock cylinder set, then the buzzer switch assembly.
10. Install key in lock cylinder and turn to Lock position.
11. Remove lock retaining screw, then the lock cylinder.
12. Reverse procedure to install, noting the following:
    a. **Torque** lock cylinder retaining screw to 22 inch lbs.
    b. **Torque** turn signal switch assembly screws to 30 inch lbs.
    c. **Torque** signal switch arm screw to 20 inch lbs.

Lock Housing Cover, Column Housing Cover End Cap, Pivot & Pulse Switch, Dimmer Switch Rod Actuator & Tilt Spring

1. Remove inflator module as outlined in "Passive Restraints."
2. Remove steering wheel as outlined in the "Electrical" section of the "Cavalier & Sunfire" chassis chapter.
3. Remove tilt lever, cover screws and lock housing cover assembly. Let cover hang freely.
4. Remove column housing cover end cap with dimmer switch rod actuator, then the actuator from end cap.
5. Remove switch actuator pivot pin, then the pivot and pulse switch assembly.
6. Remove spring retainer using a cross

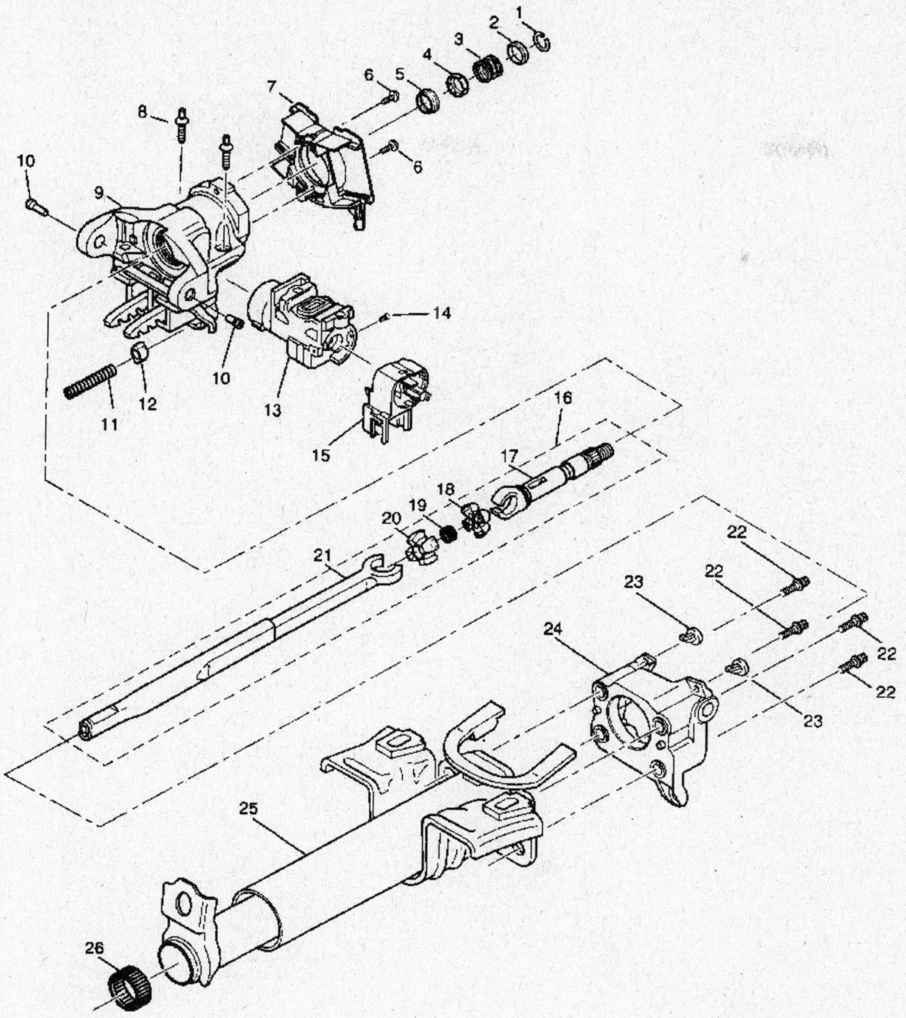

1. Ring, Retaining
2. Retainer, Spring
3. Spring, Upper Bearing
4. Seat, Inner Race
5. Race, Inner
6. Screw, Support
7. Housing, Signal Switch
8. Bolt, Shear
9. Housing, Steering Column
10. Pin, Pivot
11. Spring, Wheel Tilt
12. Retainer, Spring
13. Housing Asm, Lock Ay A/Trns
14. Screw, Set
15. Switch Asm, Ignition
16. Shaft Assembly, Steering
17. Shaft Assembly, Race and Upper
18. Sphere, Centering
19. Spring, Joint Preload
20. Sphere, Centering
21. Shaft Assembly, Lower Steering
22. Screw, Support
23. Bumper
24. Support, Strging Column Housing
25. Jacket Asm, Steering Column
26. Bearing Assembly, Lower Shaft

GC6049700242000X

Fig. 32 Exploded view of steering column. Catera

recess head screwdriver to push retainer down and turn clockwise to release.

7. Remove spring and spring guide.
8. Reverse procedure to install, noting the following:
   a. Install lock housing cover assembly and mounting screws. Tighten screw in 12 o'clock position first, screw in 8 o'clock position second, and screw in 3 o'clock position third. **Torque** screws in same order to 80 inch lbs.

Turn Signal Switch, Column Housing, Steering Wheel Lock Shoe, Switch Actuator Sector, Switch Actuator Rack, Bearing, Lock Bolt, Steering Shaft & Column Housing Support

1. Remove inflator module as outlined in "Passive Restraints."
2. Remove steering wheel as outlined in the "Electrical" section of the "Cavalier & Sunfire" chassis chapter.

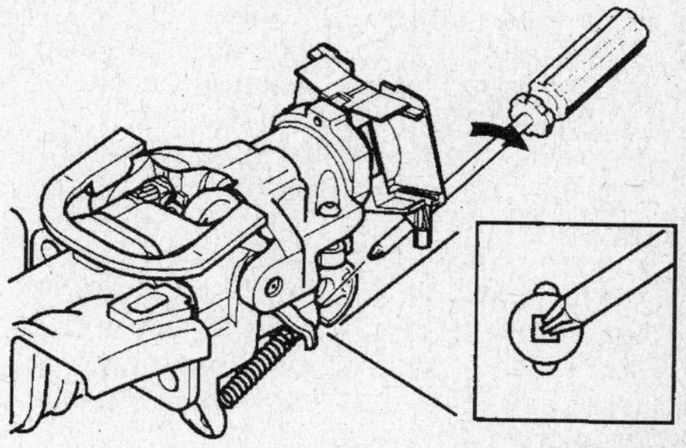

GC6049700243000X

Fig. 33 Tilt spring replacement. Catera

3. Remove steering column from vehicle as outlined under " Steering Column, Replace."
4. Inspect steering column for damage.
5. Disassemble lock housing cover, column housing cover end cap, pivot and pulse switch, dimmer switch rod actuator and tilt spring as previously outlined.
6. Remove turn signal switch assembly with lock housing cover assembly from steering column.
7. Remove four bolts and support bracket from steering column, then the wiring protectors and gently pull wire harness through column.
8. Remove pivot pins using pivot pin removal tool No. J-21854-01, or equivalent, then install tilt lever.
9. Remove steering column housing assembly, pull back on tilt lever and pull steering column housing assembly down and away from column.
10. If necessary, disassemble steering column housing as follows:
    a. Remove bearing assembly, hex head screw, lock bolt spring, lock bolt, switch actuator rack and rack preload spring.
    b. Remove driveshaft, switch actuator sector, then the release lever pin using lock shoe and release lever pin remover/installer tool No. J-22635, or equivalent.
    c. Remove shoe release lever, release lever spring, then the dowel pin using lock shoe and release lever pin remover/installer.
    d. Remove lock shoes and shoe springs.
11. If necessary, assemble steering column housing as follows:
    a. Install shoe springs and lock shoes, then the dowel pin using lock shoe and release lever pin remover/installer.
    b. Install release lever spring, shoe release lever, then the release lever pin using lock shoe and release lever pin remover/installer.
    c. Install switch actuator sector, driveshaft and rack preload spring, then assemble switch actuator rack to actuator sector.
    d. Assemble bearing assembly lubricated with lithium grease to column housing using steering column housing bearing installer tool No. J-38639 and driver handle tool No.

J-8092, or equivalents.
e. Install lock bolt, lock bolt spring and hex head screw. **Torque** screw to 35 inch lbs.
12. Remove steering column jacket bushing, then the steering column shaft assembly.
13. Inspect steering column shaft assembly for damage, then mark upper shaft assembly and lower steering shaft assembly to ensure proper assembly.
14. If necessary, disassemble steering column shaft assembly as follows:
   a. Disassemble upper shaft assembly from lower steering shaft assembly. Tilt 90° to each other and disengage.
   b. Disassemble centering sphere from upper shaft assembly. Rotate sphere 90° and slip out.
   c. Remove joint preload spring from centering sphere.
15. If necessary, assemble steering column shaft assembly as follows:
   a. Install joint preload spring to centering sphere, then lubricate centering sphere with lithium grease, slip into upper shaft assembly and rotate sphere 90.°
   b. Install upper shaft assembly to lower steering shaft assembly. Align marks and tilt assemblies 90° to each other.
16. Remove support screws, then the column housing support assembly with dimmer switch rod from steering column jacket assembly. Remove rod from support.
17. Remove lock plate from steering column jacket assembly, then the steering column housing shroud.
18. Remove hex nut and screw, then the dimmer switch assembly from rod.
19. Remove mounting stud and ignition switch assembly with switch actuator assembly.
20. Remove switch actuator assembly from switch assembly, then the two pan head screws from ignition switch and ignition switch inhibitor housing assembly.
21. Remove ignition switch inhibitor from ignition switch.
22. Reverse procedure to install, noting the following:
   a. **Torque** support assembly mounting screws to 6 ft. lbs.
   b. **Torque** ignition switch mounting stud to 35 inch lbs.
   c. **Torque** two pan head screws to 30 inch lbs.
   d. **Torque** dimmer switch screw and nut to 35 inch lbs.
   e. **Torque** support bracket bolts to 22 ft. lbs.

CUTLASS & MALIBU

Refer to **Fig. 36,** for exploded view of steering column.

STEERING COLUMN COVERS

1. Remove tilt lever, then the three screws from lower steering column cover.
2. Separate column covers by snapping apart.
3. Reverse procedure to install.

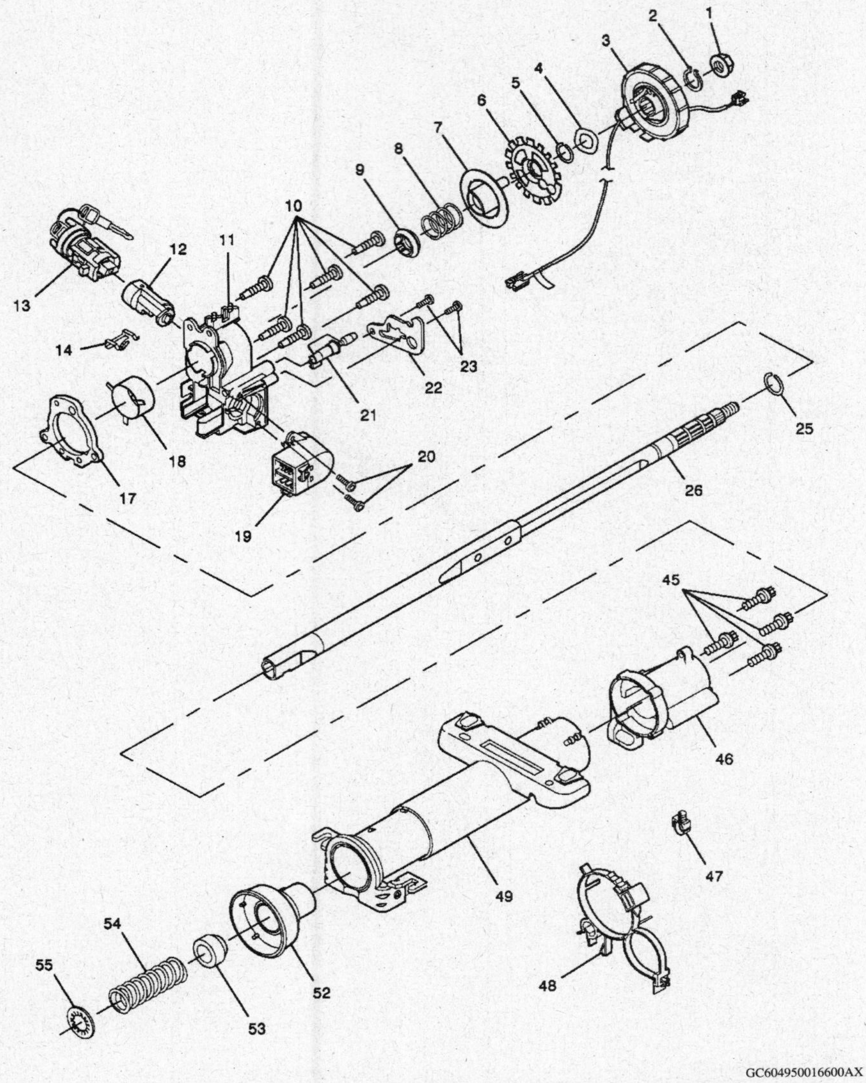

Fig. 34 Exploded view of standard steering column (Part 1 of 2). Cavalier & Sunfire

COIL ASSEMBLY

1. Remove steering column as outlined under "Steering Column, Replace."
2. Remove inflator module as outlined under "Passive Restraints."
3. Remove steering wheel as outlined under "Electrical " section of the "Achieva, Cutlass, Grand Am, Malibu & Skylark" chassis chapter.
4. Remove nut and coil assembly retaining ring, then the coil assembly.
5. Remove wave washer.
6. Reverse procedure to install.

SHAFT LOCK, TURN SIGNAL CANCEL CAM, TILT SPRING, UPPER BEARING SPRING, UPPER BEARING INNER RACE SEAT, INNER RACE, PIVOT PINS & STEERING COLUMN HOUSING

1. Remove coil assembly as outlined under "Coil Assembly."
2. Remove retaining ring using lock plate compressor tool No. J–23653–SIR, or equivalent, then dispose of retaining ring.
3. Remove turn signal cancel cam orientation plate, then the turn signal cancel cam assembly.
4. Remove tilt spring and guide, then the upper bearing spring.
5. Remove upper bearing inner race seat, then the inner race.
6. Remove two pivot pins using pivot pin remover tool No. J–21854–01, or equivalent.
7. Pull tilt arm to disengage steering wheel lock shoes from dowel pins in steering column support assembly, then remove steering column housing and bearing assembly.
8. Reverse procedure to install.

STEERING COLUMN SHAFT ASSEMBLY

1. Remove upper tilt head components

as outlined under " Shaft Lock, Turn Signal Cancel Cam, Tilt Spring, Upper Bearing spring, Upper Bearing Inner Race Seat, Inner Race, Pivot Pins & Steering Column Housing. "

2. Remove steering shaft seal and sensor retainer, then the lower bearing seat, lower bearing spring and lower spring retainer, **Fig. 37.**
3. Remove adapter and bearing assembly from jacket assembly, then remove steering shaft assembly from steering column jacket assembly.
4. Remove lower steering shaft assembly from race and upper shaft assembly, then the centering sphere from upper shaft by rotating sphere 90° and slipping out, **Fig. 38.**
5. Remove shaft preload spring from centering sphere.
6. Reverse procedure to install, noting the following:
   a. Install a new centering sphere and preload spring, using a centering sphere installer tool No. J 41688, or equivalent, and a vise.
   b. Install lower bearing seat, lower bearing spring and lower spring retainer, compressing lower bearing spring to a length of .91–.94 inches, between lower bearing seat and lower spring retainer.

DEVILLE, ELDORADO & SEVILLE

The steering wheel must be straight and the column in the Lock position. **Care must be taken when handling column with a live inflator module. Never point bag deploy surface toward you, and never stand column on steering wheel. Accidental deployment in these positions may cause injury. Always face bag deploy surface toward open space to allow for unrestricted expansion.**

Refer to **Figs. 39 and 40** for steering column service procedures.

UPPER COLUMN

The upper column consists of the following components: air bag coil assembly, shaft lock, turn signal cancelling cam assembly, upper bearing spring, upper bearing inner race seat, inner race, turn signal switch assembly, buzzer switch assembly and the steering column pass key lock cylinder set.

1. Remove inflator module and steering wheel as outlined in " Steering Column, Replace.".
2. Remove coil assembly retaining ring, then the coil assembly.
3. Remove wave washer, then using compressor tool No. J-23653-C, or equivalent, to push down shaft lock, remove shaft lock retaining ring.
4. Remove shaft lock, then the turn signal cancelling cam assembly.
5. Remove upper bearing spring and upper bearing inner race seat.
6. Remove inner race, then move turn signal to Right Turn position (up).
7. Remove multi-function lever and hazard knob assembly.
8. Remove signal switch arm, then the

1-NUT, HEX LOCKING (M14x1.5)
2-RING, RETAINING
3-COIL ASM, SIR
4-WASHER, WAVE
5-RING, RETAINING
6-LOCK, SHAFT
7-CAM ASM, T/SIG CANCEL
8-SPRING, UPPER BEARING
9-SPACER, UPPER BEARING
10-SCREW, ADAPTER
11-HOUSING ASM, STRG COLUMN
12-ACTUATOR ASM, IGNITION LOCK
13-LOCK CYL SET, STRG COLUMN
14-SPRING, LOCK PRE-LOAD
17-PLATE, MOUNTING
18-RETAINER, BEARING
19-SWITCH ASM, IGNITION
20-SCREW, TAPPING
21-BOLT ASM, LOCK
22-BRACKET, LOCK BOLT SUPPORT
23-SCREW, TAPPING
25-RING, RETAINING
26-SHAFT ASM, STEERING
45-SCREW, SUPPORT
46-ADAPTER, SUPPORT MOUNTING
47- CLIP, WIRE RESTRAINT
48-STRAP, WIRE
49-JACKET ASM, STRG COL
52-BEARING ASM, ADAPTER &
53-SEAT, LOWER BEARING
54-SPRING, LOWER BEARING
55-RETAINER, LOWER SPRING

Service Kits

201-GREASE SERV KIT, (SYNTHETIC)

GC604950016600BX

Fig. 34 Exploded view of standard steering column (Part 2 of 2). Cavalier & Sunfire

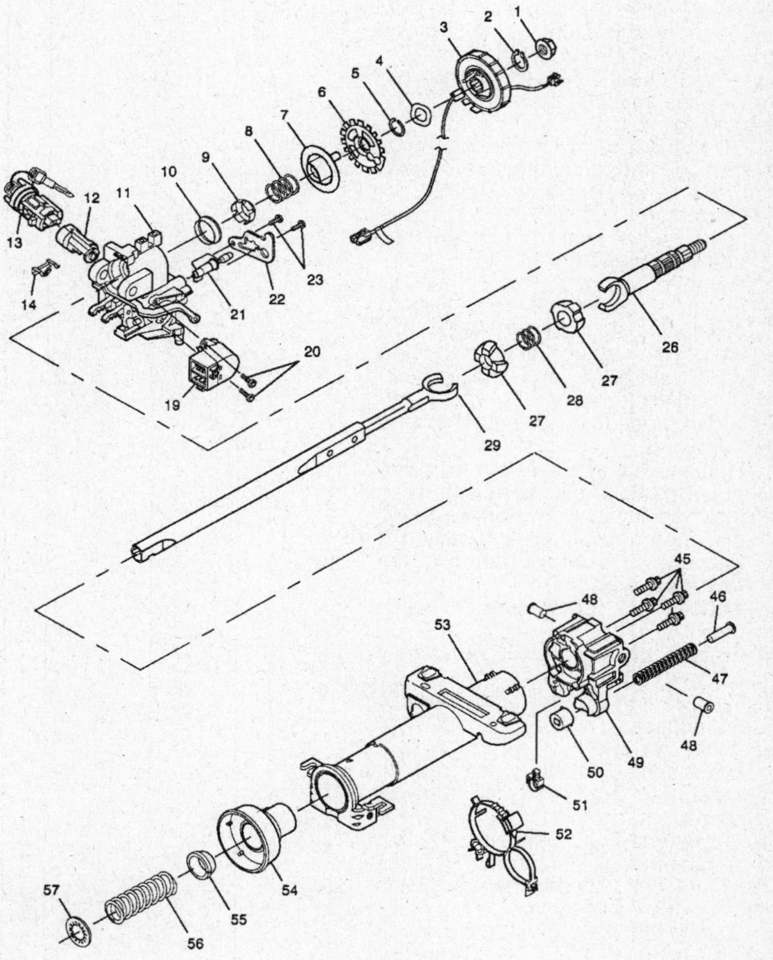

GC604950016700AX

Fig. 35 Exploded view of tilt steering column (Part 1 of 2). Cavalier & Sunfire

turn signal switch screws.

9. Remove turn signal switch assembly as follows:
   a. Disconnect turn signal switch connector from the bulkhead connector.
   b. Remove wiring protector.
   c. Gently pull wire harness through column.
10. **Coil assembly will become uncentered if the steering column is separated from the steering gear and is allowed to rotate; or if the centering spring is pushed down, letting the hub rotate while the coil is removed from the steering column.**
11. Remove inflatable restraint coil assembly with wire harness from the coil assembly as follows:
    a. Remove the coil terminal from the vehicle harness.
    b. Remove yellow connector shroud from the black terminal connector.
    c. Remove wiring protector.
    d. Attach a length of mechanics wire to the coil terminal connector to aid in assembling.
    e. Gently pull wire through column.
12. Remove key from pass key lock cylinder set, **Fig. 41.**
13. Remove buzzer switch assembly, then reinsert key in pass key in lock cylinder. Ensure key is in Lock position.
14. Remove lock retaining screw, then remove pass key lock cylinder and harness as follows:
    a. Disconnect pivot switch connector from bulkhead connector and remove 13-way secondary lock.
    b. Disconnect two terminals of pass key wire harness from cavities 12 and 13 of switch connector.
    c. Remove wiring protector, then attach a piece of mechanics wire to terminal to aid in assembling.
    d. Remove retaining clip from housing cover and gently pull wire harness through column.
15. Reverse procedure to install, noting the following:
    a. Route wire from pass key lock cylinder, **Fig. 42,** and snap retaining clip into hole in housing. **Failure to do so may result in component damage or malfunction of pass key lock cylinder.**
    b. **Torque** lock retaining screw to 22 inch lbs.
    c. **Torque** turn signal switch assembly screw to 30 inch lbs.
    d. **Torque** signal switch arm screws to 20 inch lbs.
    e. While holding coil assembly, depress spring lock to rotate hub in direction of arrow, **Fig. 43,** until is stops.
    f. Rotate coil hub in opposite direction approximately 2 ½ turns. Release spring lock between locking tabs in front of arrow, **Fig. 43.**
    g. Align opening in coil with horn tower and "locating bump" between two tabs on housing cover, **Fig. 44.**

HOUSING COVER

The housing cover consists of the follow-

1- NUT, HEX LOCKING (M14x1.5)
2- RING, RETAINING
3- COIL ASM, SIR
4- WASHER, WAVE
5- RING, RETAINING
6- LOCK, SHAFT
7- CAM ASM, T/SIG CANCEL
8- SPRING, UPPER BEARING
9- SEAT, UPPER BEARING INNER RACE
10- RACE, INNER
11- HOUSING ASM, BRG &
12- ACTUATOR ASM, IGNITION LOCK
13- LOCK CYL SET, STRG COLUMN
14- SPRING, LOCK PRE-LOAD
19- SWITCH ASM, IGNITION
20- SCREW, TAPPING
21- BOLT ASM, LOCK
22- BRACKET, LOCK BOLT SUPPORT
23- SCREW, TAPPING
26- SHAFT ASM, RACE & UPPER
27- SPHERE, CENTERING
28- SPRING, JOINT PRELOAD
29- SHAFT ASM, LOWER
45- SCREW, SUPPORT
46- GUIDE, SPRING
47- SPRING, WHEEL TILT
48- PIN, PIVOT
49- SUPPORT ASM, STRG COL
50- RETAINER, SPRING
51- CLIP, WIRE RESTRAINT
52- STRAP, WIRE
53- JACKET ASM, STRG COL
54- BEARING ASM, ADAPTER &
55- SEAT, LOWER BEARING
56- SPRING, LOWER BEARING
57- RETAINER, LOWER SPRING

Service Kits

201- SPRING SERV KIT, TILT COLUMN
-INCLUDES: 9,10,47
202- SPHERE SERV KIT, TILT COLUMN
-INCLUDES: 27,28
203- GREASE SERV KIT, (SYNTHETIC)

GC604950016700BX

Fig. 35 Exploded view of tilt steering column (Part 2 of 2). Cavalier & Sunfire

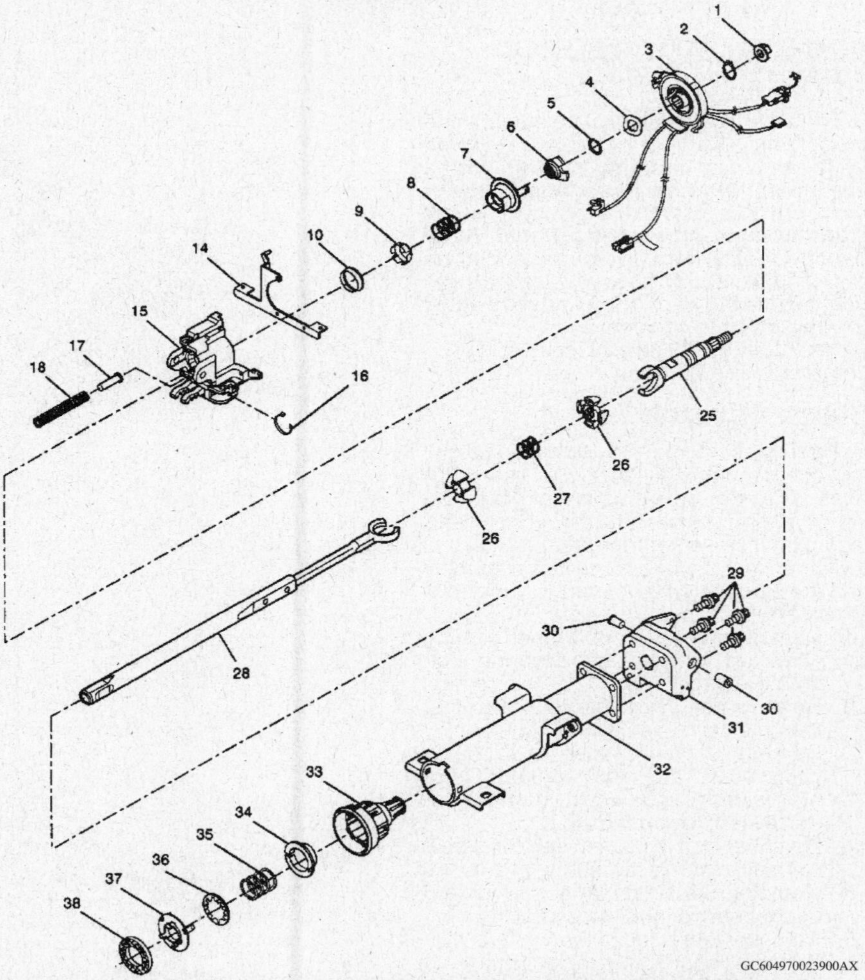

GC604970023900AX

Fig. 36 Exploded view of steering column (Part 1 of 2). Cutlass & Malibu

1-NUT, HEXAGON LOCKING (M14x1.5)
2-RING, RETAINING
3-COIL ASM, SIR (2 CONDUCTOR)
3-COIL ASM, SIR (6 CONDUCTOR)
4-WASHER, WAVE
5-RING, RETAINING
6-PLATE, CAM ORIENTATION
7-CAM ASM, T/SIG CANCEL
8-SPRING, UPPER BEARING
9-SEAT, UPPER BEARING INNER RACE
10-RACE, INNER
14-PLATE, SWITCH ADAPTER
15-HOUSING & BEARING ASM, STRG COL
16-STRAP, WIRE HARNESS
17-GUIDE, SPRING
18-SPRING, TILT
25-SHAFT ASM, RACE & UPPER
26-SPHERE, CENTERING
27-SPRING, JOINT PRELOAD
28-SHAFT ASM, LOWER
29-SCREW, TORX HEAD
30-PIN, PIVOT
31-SUPPORT ASM, STRG COL
32-JACKET ASM, STRG COL
33-BEARING ASM, ADAPTER &
34-SEAT, LOWER BEARING
35-SPRING, LOWER BEARING
36-RETAINER, LOWER SPRING
37-RETAINER, SENSOR
38-SEAL, STRG SHAFT

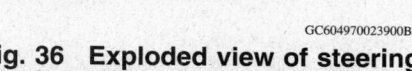

GC604970023900BX

Fig. 36 Exploded view of steering column (Part 2 of 2). Cutlass & Malibu

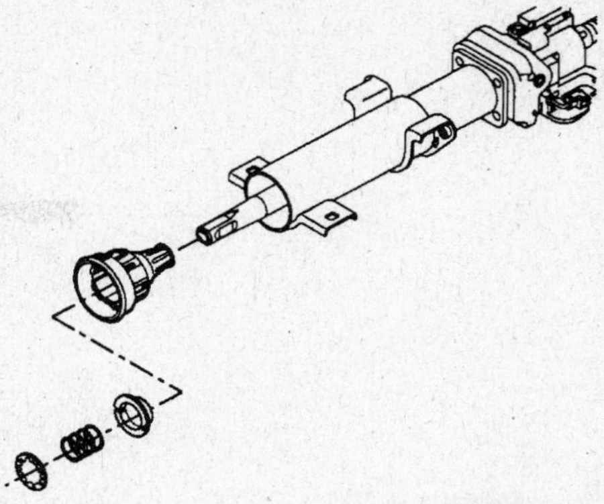

GC6049700240000X

Fig. 37 Steering column shaft assembly. Cutlass & Malibu

ing components: lock housing cover assembly, column housing cover end cap, pivot & pulse switch assembly, dimmer switch rod actuator and the tilt spring assembly.

1. Remove upper column as outlined under "Upper Column " disassembly procedures.
2. Remove housing end cap.
3. Remove cruise control and multi-function lever connectors from base plate and disconnect.
4. Remove multi-function lever.
5. Remove cover screws, then remove the tilt lever.
6. Remove lock housing cover assembly.
7. Remove base plate and dimmer switch rod actuator.
8. Remove switch actuator pivot pin, then the pivot and pulse switch assembly as follows:
   a. Allow switch to hang freely if removal is not required.
   b. Disconnect pivot and switch connector from bulkhead connector.
   c. Gently pull wire harness through column.
9. Remove spring retainer, spring and spring guide.
10. Reverse procedure to install, ensuring to tighten lock housing cover screws in 12 o'clock position first, 8 o'clock position second, and the screw in the 3 o'clock position last. **Torque** screws in same order to 80 inch lbs.

MID COLUMN

The mid column consists of the following components: steering column housing assembly, steering wheel lock shoe, switch actuator sector, switch actuator rack, bearing assembly, lock bolt, steering column housing support assembly, steering shaft assembly and the shift tube assembly.

1. Remove steering column from vehicle as outlined under "Steering Column, Replace."
2. Perform all disassembling steps outlined under "Housing Cover."
3. Remove pivot pins using pivot pin removal tool No. J-21854-01, or equivalent. Install tilt lever.
4. Remove steering column housing assembly. Pull back on tilt lever and pull steering column housing assembly down and away from column.
5. Remove the following components to disassemble the steering column housing assembly:
   a. Bearing assembly.
   b. Wire abrasion shield.
   c. Hex head screw.
   d. Lock bolt spring.
   e. Lock bolt.
   f. Switch actuator rack and rack preload spring.
   g. Driveshaft.
   h. Switch actuator sector.
   i. Release lever pin using lock shoe and release lever pin tool No. J-22635, or equivalent.
   j. Shoe release lever.
   k. Release lever spring.
   l. Dowel pin using lock show and release lever pin tool No. J-22635, or equivalent.
   m. Lock shoes and shoe springs.
6. Remove lower spring retainer.
7. Remove bearing and seal retainer.
8. Remove lower spring retainer.
9. Remove lower bearing spring and lower bearing seat.
10. Remove hex head bolts, then the adapter and bearing assembly.

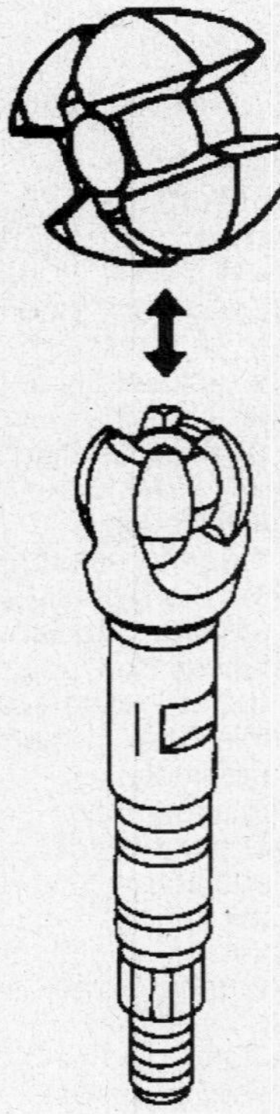

Fig. 38 Lower steering shaft assembly. Cutlass & Malibu

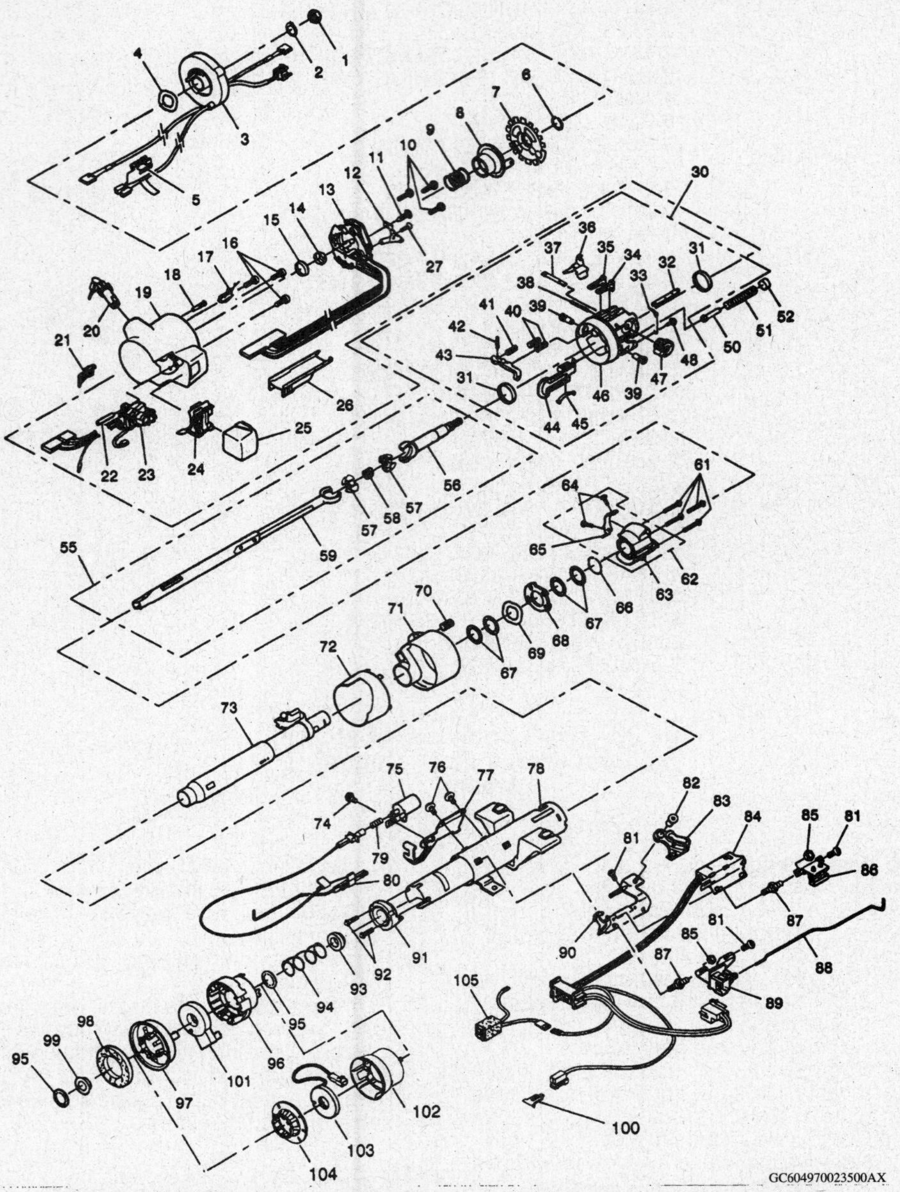

Fig. 39 Exploded view of steering column (Part 1 of 2). DeVille, Eldorado & Seville w/column shift

1 - NUT, HEXAGON LOCKING (M14x1.5)
2 - RING, RETAINING
3 - COIL ASM, SIR
4 - WASHER, WAVE
5 - SHROUD, CONNECTOR
6 - RING, RETAINING
7 - LOCK, SHAFT
8 - CAM ASM, T/SIG CANCEL
9 - SPRING, UPPER BEARING
10 - SCREW, BNDG HD CR RECESS
11 - SCREW, RD WASH HD (M4.2x1.41)
12 - ARM ASM, SIGNAL SWITCH
13 - SWITCH ASM, TURN SIGNAL
14 - SEAT, UPPER BRG INNER RACE
15 - RACE, INNER
16 - SCREW, PAN HD 6 LOBED SOC TAP
17 - SWITCH ASM, BUZZER
18 - SCREW, LOCK RETAINING
19 - COVER ASM, LOCK HOUSING
20 - LOCK CYLINDER SET, STRG COL
21 - ACTUATOR, DIMMER SW ROD
22 - PIN, SWITCH ACTUATOR PIVOT
23 - SWITCH ASM, PIVOT & (PULSE)
24 - BASE PLATE, COL HSG CVR END
25 - CAP, COL HSG COVER END
26 - PROTECTOR, WIRING
27 - SCREW, FLAT HEAD TAPPING
30 - HOUSING ASM, STRG COLUMN
31 - BEARING ASM
32 - BOLT, LOCK
33 - SPRING, LOCK BOLT
34 - SHOE, STEERING WHEEL LOCK
35 - SHOE, STEERING WHEEL LOCK
36 - SHIELD, WIRE PROTECTOR
37 - SHAFT, DRIVE
38 - PIN, DOWEL
39 - PIN, PIVOT
40 - SPRING, SHOE
41 - SPRING, RELEASE LEVER
42 - PIN, RELEASE LEVER
43 - LEVER, SHOE RELEASE
44 - RACK, SWITCH ACTUATOR
45 - SPRING, RACK PRELOAD
46 - HOUSING, STRG COLUMN
47 - SECTOR, SWITCH ACTUATOR
48 - SCREW, HEX WASHER HEAD
50 - GUIDE, SPRING
51 - SPRING, WHEEL TILT
52 - RETAINER, SPRING
55 - SHAFT ASM, STEERING
56 - SHAFT ASM, RACE & UPPER
57 - SPHERE, CENTERING
58 - SPRING, JOINT PRELOAD
59 - SHAFT ASM, LOWER STEERING
61 - SCREW, SUPPORT
62 - SUPPORT ASM, STRG COL HSG
63 - SUPPORT, STRG COL HSG
64 - SCREW, OVL HD CROSS RECESS
65 - GATE, SHIFT LEVER
66 - RING, SHIFT TUBE RETAINING
67 - WASHER, THRUST
68 - PLATE, LOCK
69 - WASHER, WAVE
70 - SPRING, SHIFT LEVER
71 - BOWL ASM, GEARSHIFT LEVER
72 - SHROUD, GEARSHIFT BOWL
73 - TUBE ASM, SHIFT
74 - SCREW, HEX WASH HD (#10-24X.25)
75 - SOLENOID ASM, INTERLOCK
76 - SCREW, WASH HD (#10-24X.25)
77 - BRACKET, SOLENOID
78 - JACKET ASM, STRG COL
79 - SPRING, BALL JOINT
80 - ACTUATOR ASM, IGNITION SWITCH
81 - SCREW, TORX WASHER HEAD
82 - RETAINER, CAM
83 - CAM ASM, CABLE SHIFT
84 - SWITCH ASM, IGNITION
85 - NUT, HEXAGON (#10-24)
86 - ADJUSTER ASM, PRNDL
87 - STUD, DIMR SW MTG
88 - ROD, DIMMER SWITCH
89 - SWITCH ASM, DIMMER
90 - BRACKET ASM, STUD &
91 - BEARING ASM, ADAPTER &
92 - SCREW, HEX WASHER HD TAP
93 - SEAT, LOWER BEARING
94 - SPRING, LOWER BEARING
95 - RETAINER, LOWER SPRING
96 - ADAPTER, STRG SENSOR
97 - RETAINER, SENSOR
98 - SEAL, STEERING SHAFT
99 - BUSHING, SEAL RETAINING
100 - CONNECTOR, AXIAL POSN ASSURANCE
101 - SENSOR ASM, HI RES STRG WHL POSN
102 - RETAINER, BEARING
103 - SENSOR ASM, STRG WHL POSN
104 - DAMPENER ASM, ROTATIONAL
105 - HARNESS ASM, JUMPER

GC604970023500BX

Fig. 39 Exploded view of steering column (Part 2 of 2). DeVille, Eldorado & Seville w/column shift

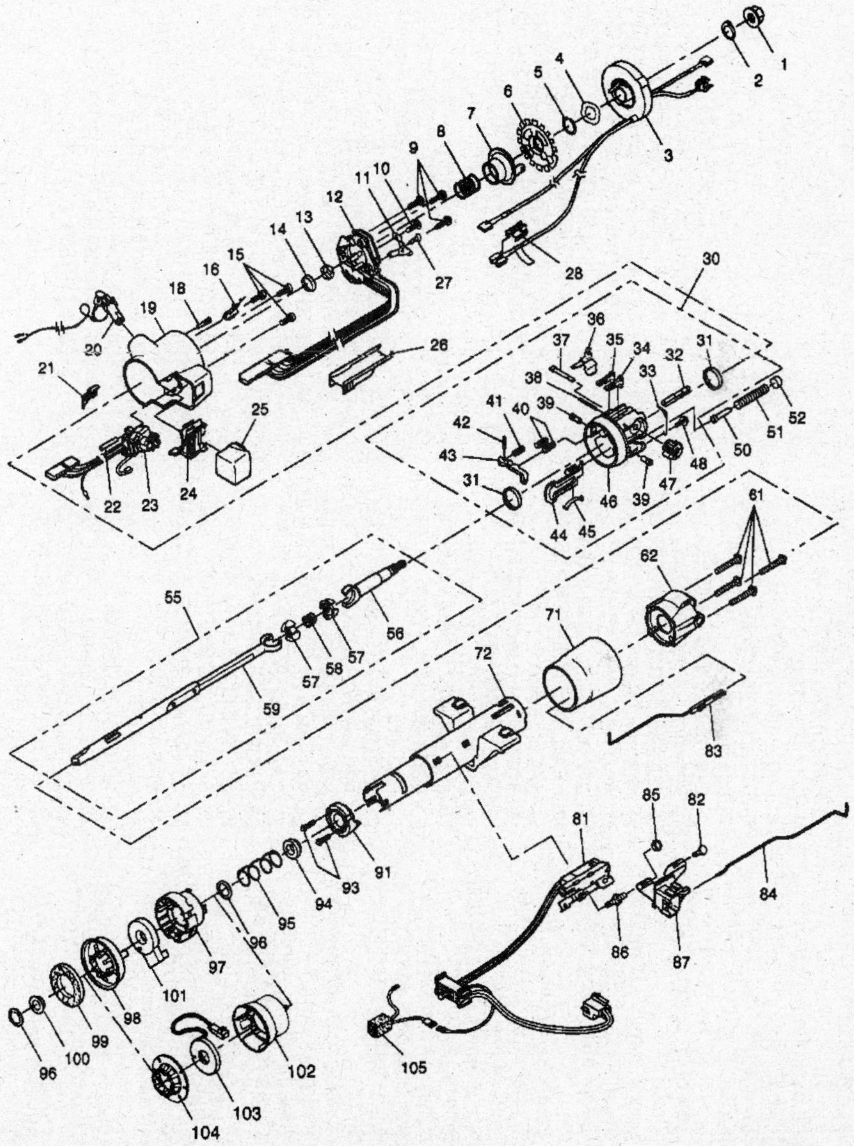

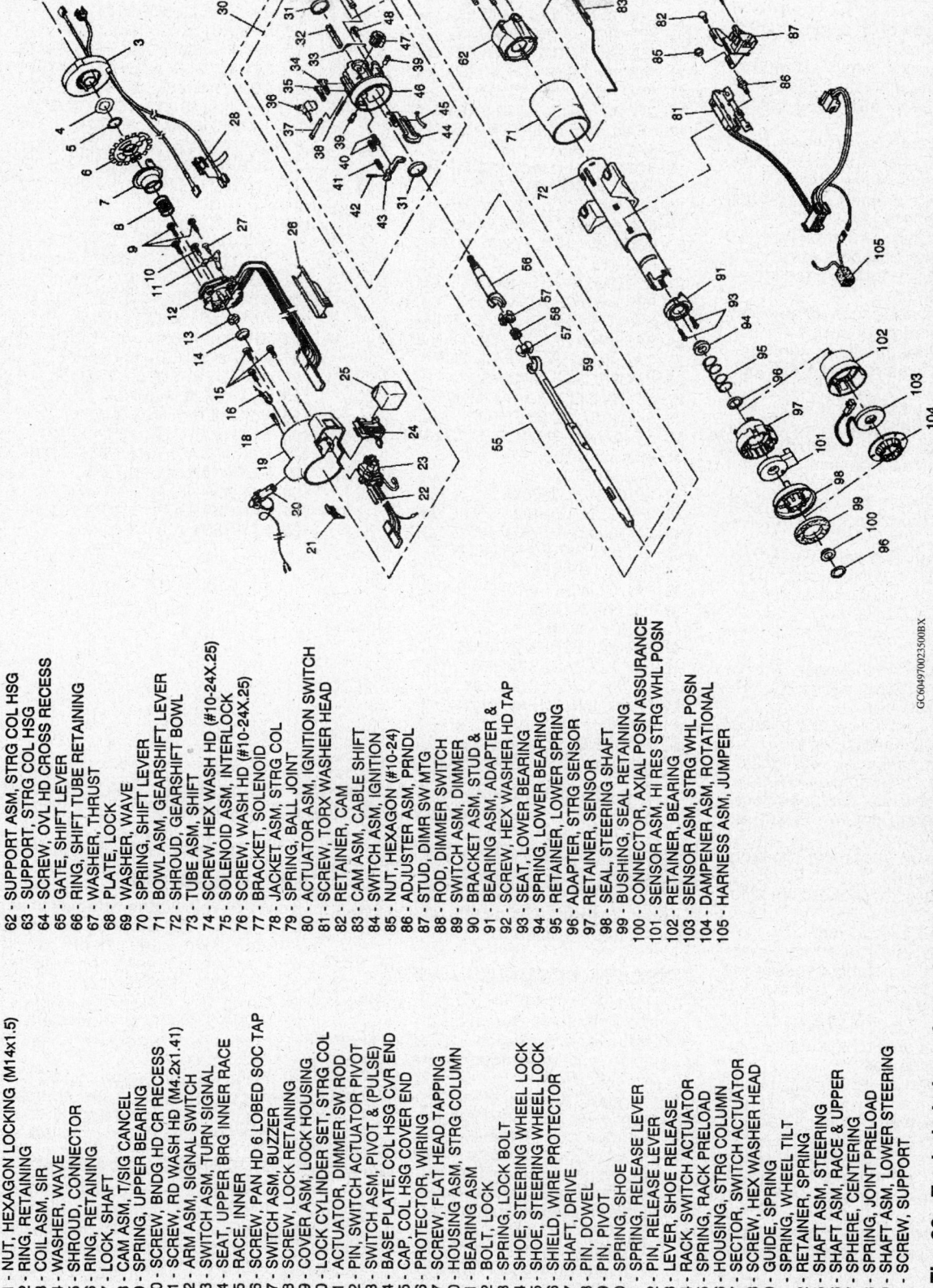

GC604970023600AX

Fig. 40 Exploded view of steering column (Part 1 of 2). DeVille, Eldorado & Seville w/console shift

11. Remove steering column shaft assembly.
12. Mark upper shaft assembly and lower steering shaft assembly to ensure proper assembly. Failure to assemble properly will cause steering wheel to be turned 180.°
13. Disassemble steering column shaft assembly as follows:
    a. Separate upper shaft assembly from lower steering shaft assembly. Tilt 90° to each other and disengage.
    b. Separate centering sphere from upper shaft assembly by rotating sphere 90° and sliding out.
    c. Remove joint preload spring from centering sphere.
14. Remove support screws, then remove column housing support assembly with dimmer switch rod from the steering column jacket.
15. Remove oval head recess screws and shift lever gate from support.
16. Remove shift tube retaining ring, then the two thrust washers and the lock plate.
17. Remove wave washer and two thrust washers, then the gearshift lever bowl assembly with the gearshift bowl shroud and shift tube assembly.
18. Remove shroud from bowl.
19. Remove shift lever spring, then the shift tube from the bowl. Use a press is necessary.
20. Remove hex nut and pan head screw securing PRNDL adjuster assembly.
21. Remove PRNDL adjuster bracket and the dimmer switch assembly.
22. Remove dimmer and ignition switch mounting stud.
23. Remove ignition switch assembly from ignition switch actuator assembly.
24. Remove cam retainer.
25. Remove pan head screw and dimmer and ignition switch mounting stud.
26. Remove cable assembly with ignition switch actuator assembly as follows:
    a. Remove cable clip from upper location of steering column jacket assembly.
    b. Remove cable mounting clip from solenoid bracket.
    c. Remove ball joint socket from solenoid.
    d. Remove ball joint spring.
27. Remove hex washer head screw securing interlock solenoid assembly and solenoid bracket to steering column jacket assembly.
28. Remove hex washer head screws securing solenoid bracket to steering column jacket assembly.
29. Reverse procedure to install, noting the following:
    a. **Torque** solenoid bracket screws to 35 inch lbs.
    b. **Torque** bracket assembly screw and stud to 35 inch lbs.
    c. **Torque** cable shift cam retainer to 35 inch lbs.
    d. **Torque** gate screws to 33 inch lbs.
    e. **Torque** support assembly screws to 88 inch lbs.
    f. **Torque** hex head screws to 30 inch lbs.

1- NUT, HEX LOCKING (M14x1.5)
2- RING, RETAINING
3- COIL ASM, SIR
4- WASHER, WAVE
5- RING, RETAINING
6- LOCK, SHAFT
7- CAM ASM, T/SIG CANCEL
8- SPRING, UPPER BEARING
9- SCREW, BNDG HD CR RECESS
10- SCREW, RD WASH HD (M4.2x1.41)
11- ARM ASM, SIGNAL SWITCH
12- SWITCH ASM, TURN SIGNAL
13- SEAT, UPPER BRG INNER RACE
14- RACE, INNER
15- SCREW, PAN HD 6 LOBED SOC TAP
16- SWITCH ASM, BUZZER
18- SCREW, LOCK RETAINING
19- COVER ASM, LOCK HOUSING
20- LOCK CYLINDER SET, STRG COL PASS KEY
21- ACTUATOR, DIMMER SWITCH ROD
22- PIN, SWITCH ACTUATOR PIVOT
23- SWITCH ASM, PIVOT & (PULSE)
24- BASE PLATE, COL HSG CVR END
25- CAP, COL HSG COVER END
26- PROTECTOR, WIRING
27- SCREW, FLT HD TAPPING
28- SHROUD, CONNECTOR
30- HOUSING ASM, STRG COLUMN
31- BEARING ASM
32- BOLT, LOCK
33- SPRING, LOCK BOLT
34- SHOE, STEERING WHEEL LOCK
35- SHOE, STEERING WHEEL LOCK
36- SHIELD, WIRE PROTECTOR
37- SHAFT, DRIVE
38- PIN, DOWEL
39- PIN, PIVOT
40- SPRING, SHOE
41- SPRING, RELEASE LEVER
42- PIN, RELEASE LEVER
43- LEVER, SHOE RELEASE
44- RACK, SWITCH ACTUATOR
45- SPRING, RACK PRELOAD
46- HOUSING, STRG COLUMN
47- SECTOR, SWITCH ACTUATOR
48- SCREW, HEX WASHER HEAD
50- GUIDE, SPRING
51- SPRING, WHEEL TILT
52- RETAINER, SPRING
55- SHAFT ASM, STEERING
56- SHAFT ASM, RACE & UPPER
57- SPHERE, CENTERING
58- SPRING, JOINT PRELOAD
59- SHAFT ASM, LOWER STEERING
61- SCREW, HEX WASHER HD TAPPING
62- SUPPORT ASM, STRG COL HSG
71- SHROUD, STRG COLUMN HSG
72- JACKET ASM, STRG COL
81- SWITCH ASM, COL LOCK & IGN
82- SCREW, WASH HD (#10-24X.25)
83- ACTUATOR ASM, IGNITION SWITCH
84- ROD, DIMMER SWITCH
85- NUT, HEXAGON (#10-24)
86- STUD, DIMR & IGN SW MTG
87- SWITCH ASM, DIMMER
91- BEARING ASM, ADAPTER &
93- SCREW, HEX WASHER HD TAP
94- SEAT, LOWER BEARING
95- SPRING, LOWER BEARING
96- RETAINER, LOWER SPRING
97- ADAPTER, STRG SENSOR
98- RETAINER, SENSOR
99- SEAL, STEERING SHAFT
100- BUSHING, SEAL RETAINING
101- SENSOR ASM, HI RES STRG WHL POSN
102- RETAINER, BEARING
103- SENSOR ASM, STRG WHL POSN
104- DAMPENER ASM, ROTATIONAL
105- HARNESS ASM, JUMPER

GC604970023600BX

Fig. 40 Exploded view of steering column (Part 2 of 2). DeVille, Eldorado & Seville w/console shift

CENTURY, GRAND PRIX, INTRIGUE & REGAL

Refer to **Figs. 45 and 46** for exploded view of steering column.

STEERING COLUMN COVERS

1. Remove inflator module as outlined under "Passive Restraints."
2. Remove intermediate steering shaft pinch bolt, then the steering column from vehicle.
3. Remove tilt lever, then the lower column cover pan head tapping screws.
4. Remove lock cylinder.
5. Remove lower column cover, then the upper column cover Torx head screws.
6. Remove upper column cover.
7. Reverse procedure to install, noting the following:
    a. **Torque** upper column cover Torx head screws to 12 inch lbs.
    b. **Torque** lower column cover pan head tapping screws to 30 inch lbs.
    c. **Torque** pinch bolt to 35 ft. lbs.

UPPER COLUMN

1. Remove steering column cover as outlined under " Steering Column Cover," then the steering wheel.
2. Remove coil assembly retaining ring, then the coil assembly.
3. Using lock plate compressor tool No. J–23653–SIR, or equivalent, remove shaft lock retaining ring, then the shaft lock plate.
4. Remove turn signal cancel cam, then the upper bearing spring, upper bearing inner race seat and inner race.
5. Reverse procedure to install.

MID COLUMN (COLUMN SHIFT)

1. Remove steering column cover as outlined under " Steering Column Cover."
2. Remove cam assembly hex head bolt, then the ball and actuator assembly.
3. Disconnect park lock cable, then remove park lock cable oval head tap screws.

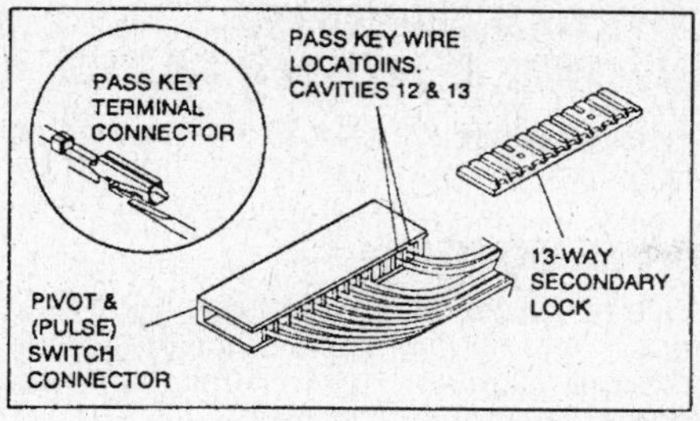

GC6049300112000X

Fig. 41 Pass key wire connection locations. Eldorado, Seville & DeVille

4. Remove shift lever clevis, then the park lock cable from the support bracket.
5. Disconnect BTSI actuator arm from outer shift cable ball stud, then the transaxle shift cable from inner ball stud.
6. Remove cam assembly hex head bolt, then the cable shift cam assembly.
7. Remove cam bushing, then the cam assembly flat head tap screws.
8. Remove gearshift lever assembly support bracket.
9. Reverse procedure to install, noting the following:
   a. **Torque** cam assembly flat head tap screws to 7 ft. lbs.
   b. **Torque** cam assembly hex head bolt to 13 ft. lbs.
   c. **Torque** park lock cable oval head tap screws to 58 inch lbs.

LOWER COLUMN

1. Remove steering guide assemblies from steering column jacket, then the steering column covers as outlined under "Steering Column Covers."
2. Remove turn signal and multi-function switch.
3. Remove linear shift assembly as follows:
   a. Remove cam assembly hex head bolt, then the ball and actuator assembly.
   b. Disconnect park lock cable, then remove park lock cable oval head tap screws.
   c. Remove shift lever clevis.
4. Pry up on tilt spring and spring guide until a bulge appears and most spring tension is removed.
5. Secure spring with a suitable pair of locking pliers, then continue to pry until spring disengages from post. **Tilt spring and spring guide are under pressure and could cause injury if not secured with a suitable pair of locking pliers.**
6. Remove spring guide from spring.
7. Remove steering shaft seal and sensor retainer from adapter and bearing assembly, then the lower spring retainer, lower bearing spring and lower bearing seat.
8. Remove adapter and bearing assembly from steering column jacket.
9. Using pivot pin removal tool No J-21854-01, or equivalent, remove pivot pins.

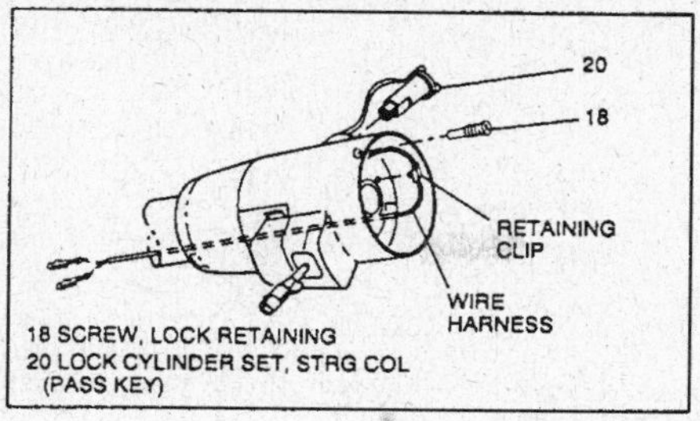

GC6049300113000X

Fig. 42 Pass key wire installation. Eldorado, Seville & DeVille

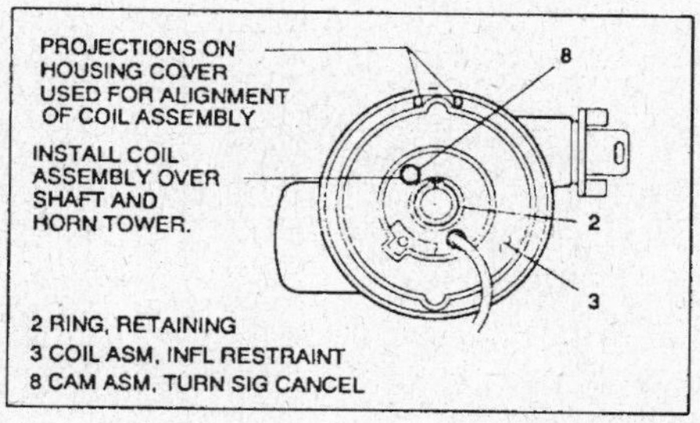

GC6049300115000X

Fig. 44 Coil assembly installation. Eldorado, Seville & DeVille

10. Remove steering column tilt head assembly with steering shaft by installing and pulling tilt arm to disengage steering wheel lock shoes from dowel pins in steering column support.
11. Disconnect upper and lower steering shaft assemblies by tilting upper steering shaft 90° from lower steering shaft.
12. Rotate centering sphere 90°, then lift centering sphere away from upper steering shaft.
13. Remove shaft preload spring from centering sphere.
14. Reverse procedure to install, noting the following:
    a. Install a new centering sphere and preload spring, using a centering sphere installer tool No. J 41688, or equivalent, and a vise.
    b. **Torque** steering column support Torx head screws to 14 ft. lbs.
    c. **Torque** lower steering column cover pan head tapping screws to 5 ft. lbs.

SHAFT LOCK SHIELD, TURN SIGNAL CAM, UPPER BEARING SPRING, UPPER BEARING INNER RACE SEAT & INNER RACE

1. Remove SIR coil and let hang freely.
2. Using lock plate compressor tool No. J 23653–SIR or equivalent, push down on shaft lock assembly to remove. Discard ring.
3. Remove shaft lock shield assembly.
4. Remove turn signal cancel cam.
5. Remove upper bearing spring, inner race seat, and inner race.
6. Reverse procedure to install.

LOCK MODULE ASSEMBLY

1. Remove shaft lock shield, turn signal

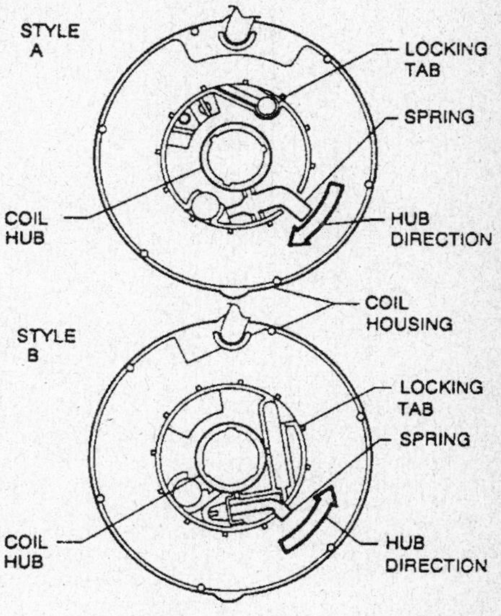

GC6049300114000X

Fig. 43 Coil assembly centering. Eldorado, Seville & DeVille

cam, upper bearing spring, upper bearing inner race seat, and inner race as outlined previously.
2. Put lock cylinder in Off-Lock position and gear shift into Park position.
3. Insert small blade screwdriver into slot in lock module assembly.
4. Push against locking tab on end of cable assembly and remove.
5. Pry retaining clip on alarm switch with a small blade screwdriver.
6. Rotate alarm switch ¼ turn and remove.
7. Remove two tapping screws from ignition and key alarm switch assembly, let switch hang freely.
8. **Lock bolt assembly is under slight spring pressure from lock bolt spring. Hold lock bolt in place while removing lock module assembly.**
9. Remove three pan head tapping screws, then the lock module assembly.
10. Remove lock bolt assembly with lock bolt spring.
11. Remove spring from lock bolt.
12. Remove lock cylinder.
13. Reverse procedure to install.

ELECTRIC PARK LOCK

1. Remove transmission fuse No. 24 in instrument panel fuse panel.
2. Remove filler plug on bottom of lower shroud.
3. Insert a small screwdriver into hole and push up on manual override of electric park lock.
4. Turn key to Lock position, and remove.
5. Remove upper and lower steering column covers as outlined previously.
6. Remove torque head screw and black connector.
7. Remove electronic park lock from the lock module with a small screwdriver.
8. Reverse procedure to install.

TILT SPRING

Tilt spring and spring guide are under

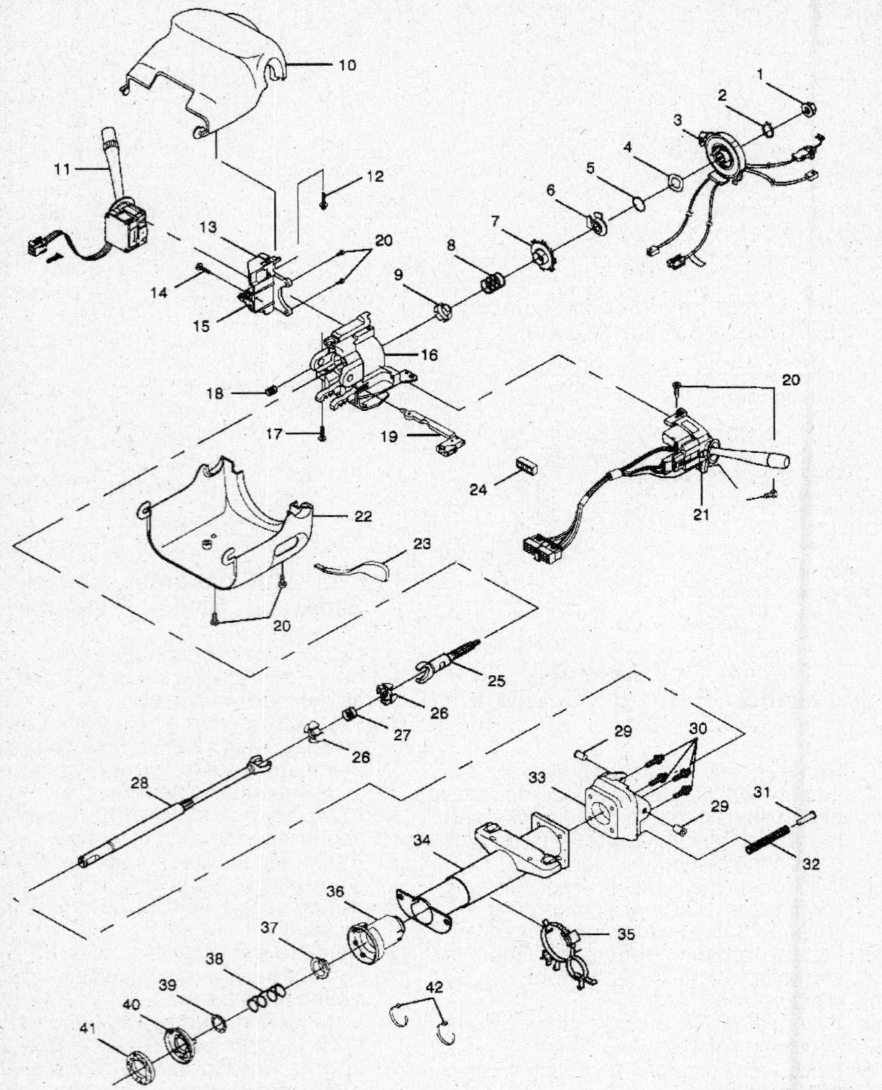

Fig. 45 Exploded view of steering column (Part 1 of 2). Intrigue & Grand Prix w/floor shift

pressure. During removal and installation secure spring with locking pliers. Exercise caution when removing or installing spring guide, as bodily injury may result.

1. Disable SIR system as outlined in "Air Bag System Disarming."
2. Remove two pan head self tapping screws from lower shroud.
3. Tilt shroud down and slide back to disengage locking tabs, then remove shroud.
4. Tilt column to up position.
5. Pry spring up until a bulge occurs and most of spring tension is removed.
6. Secure spring with locking pliers and continue prying until spring disengages from post on steering column.
7. Remove spring guide from tilt spring.
8. Reverse procedure to install.

LINEAR SHIFT ASSEMBLY

Linear shift assembly may be removed as an assembly or certain components may be disassembled as necessary to do repairs. Remove or disassemble only those components necessary to do repairs.

1. Remove upper and lower covers as outlined previously.
2. Place lock cylinder in Off-Lock position and gear shift in Park position.
3. Insert a small blade screwdriver into slot in lock module assembly.
4. Push against locking tab on end of cable to release and remove park lock cable assembly.
5. Pry actuator arm of electrical actuator from outer shift cable ball stud on cable shift cam assembly and mounting pin on jacket.
6. Remove transaxle cable from inner shift cable ball stud on cable shift cam assembly.
7. Shift column to Neutral position to gain access to lower self tapping screw.
8. Remove three self tapping screws, then the linear shift assembly.
9. Reverse procedure to install.

CUTLASS SUPREME, LUMINA & MONTE CARLO

Refer to **Figs. 47 and 48** when servicing this column.

UPPER COLUMN

Do not allow steering column to be supported only by the upper or lower support brackets. Damage to the column lower bearing adapter could result.

1. Disable the SIR system as outlined in "Air Bag System Disarming and Arming."
2. Remove the SIR assembly retaining ring.
3. Remove wave washer.
4. Using lock plate compressor tool No. J–23653–SIR, or equivalent, push down on shaft lock. Remove and dispose of bearing retainer.
5. Remove turn signal cancelling cam assembly.
6. Remove upper bearing spring, inner race seat, and inner race.
7. Remove multi-function lever.
8. Using fingers, push top and bottom edges of housing end cover cap out of slots in housing.
9. Remove round head washer screw, and flathead screw.
10. Remove pivot and pulse dimmer switch connector from bulkhead connector.
11. Using a screwdriver, pry on the upper and lower wings of switch body, **Fig. 49.**
12. Remove wiring protector and wire harness clamp from tab inside housing, pull wire harness from column.
13. With a small screwdriver, pry knob from hazard warning switch.
14. Place turn signal switch in Right Turn position.
15. Remove three binding head cross recess screws.
16. Remove turn signal switch and allow to hang freely.
17. Remove wiring protector from SIR coil and attach a length of mechanics wire to coil terminal terminals. Wire will be used to ease reassembly.
18. Remove coil and pull wires through column.
19. Remove key from lock cylinder set.
20. Remove buzzer switch assembly.
21. Reinsert key and move switch to Lock position.
22. Remove steering lock cylinder set retaining screw.
23. Remove terminal of pass key wiring harness from vehicle wire harness.
24. Remove wiring protector.
25. Attach a length of mechanics wire to terminal for ease of reassembly.
26. Remove steering column lock cylinder set retaining clip, pull lock and wiring harness through steering column.
27. Remove three pan head six lobed socket tapping screws.
28. Remove tilt lever, lock housing cover and sleeve assembly, and wire protector shield.
29. Seat counterbore of tilt spring compressor No. J 39246 or equivalent,

over end race and upper shaft assembly.

30. Thread and seat standard flanged previously torqued nut on to race and upper shaft assembly, **Fig. 50,** to secure tool.
31. Align square extension on end of tool bolt with square hole in spring retainer and seat.
32. Rotate tool bolt clockwise with wrench until it contacts surface of tool block.
33. Spring retainer must be compressed approximately ¼ inch into steering column housing.
34. Rotate hexagon section on end of tool bolt counterclockwise approximately ¼ turn.
35. Unscrew tool boot until spring and spring retainer are loose and free of tool.
36. Remove spring retainer, tilt spring and spring guide.
37. Reverse procedure to install, noting the following:
    a. Refer to **Fig. 51,** for proper wire routing.
    b. **Torque** cylinder lock retaining screw to 22 inch lbs.
    c. **Torque** turn signal switch assembly mounting screws to 31 inch lbs.
    d. Set steering shaft so that block tooth on race and upper shaft assembly is at the 12 o'clock position, wheels should be straight ahead.
    e. Set steering column lock cylinder set to Lock position.
    f. **SIR coil assembly will become uncentered if steering column is allowed to rotate or centering spring is pushed down, letting hub rotate while coil is removed from column. If this occurs, refer to Fig. 52,** and perform the following:
        1. Position vehicle wheels straight ahead.
        2. Remove coil assembly.
        3. Hold coil assembly with bottom up.
        4. While holding coil assembly, depress spring lock to rotate hub in direction of arrow until it stops.
        5. Coil ribbon should be wound up snug against center hub.
        6. Rotate coil hub in opposite direction approximately 2½ turns.
        7. Release spring lock between locking tabs.
38. If new SIR coil is being installed, assemble pre-centered coil assembly to steering column. Remove and dispose of centering tab.
39. Sir coil assembly wires must be kept tight with no slack while installing SIR coil assembly. Failure to do so may cause wires to be kinked near shaft lock area and cut when steering wheel is turned.

1-NUT, FLANGED PREVAIL TORQUE
2-RING, RETAINING
3-SIR, COIL ASSEMBLY
4-WASHER, WAVE
5-RING, RETAINING
6-SHIELD, SHAFT LOCK
7-CAM, T/S CANCEL
8-SPRING, UPPER BEARING
9-SEAT, UPPER BEARING
10-SHROUD, UPPER
11-SWITCH ASM, PIVOT & PULSE
12-SCREW, TORX HEAD
13-BRACKET, SWITCH MOUNTING
14-SCREW, TORX HEAD
16-TILT HEAD ASM, STRG COLUMN
17-SCREW, TORX HEAD
18-SPRING, TILT LEVER
19-LEVER ASM, SHOE RELEASE
20-SCREW, PAN HEAD TAPPING
21-SWITCH ASM, T/S MULTIFUNCTION
22-SHROUD, LOWER
23-LEVER ASM, TILT
24-SPACER, WIRE HARNESS
25-SHAFT ASM, RACE & UPPER
26-SPHERE, CENTERING
27-SPRING, JOINT PRELOAD
28-SHAFT ASM, LOWER STRG
29-PIN, PIVOT
30-SCREW, TORX HEAD
31-SPRING, GUIDE
32-SPRING, TILT
33-SUPPORT ASM, STRG COLUMN
34-JACKET ASM, STRG COLUMN
35-STRAP, WIRE HARNESS
36-BEARING ASM, ADAPTER &
37-SEAT, LOWER BEARING
38-SPRING, LOWER BEARING
39-RETAINER, LOWER SPRING
40-RETAINER, SENSOR
41-SEAL, STRG SHAFT
42-STRAP, WIRE HARNESS

GC604980024600BX

Fig. 45 Exploded view of steering column (Part 2 of 2). Intrigue & Grand Prix w/floor shift

MID COLUMN

1. Disable the SIR system as outlined in "Air Bag Disarming and Arming."
2. Remove steering column from vehicle.
3. Perform steps two through 36 as outlined in "Upper Column."
4. Remove pivot pins using pivot pin remover No. J– 21854–01 or equivalent.
5. Reinstall tilt lever.
6. Pull back on tilt lever and pull steering column housing assembly down and away from column.
7. Remove sensor retainer.
8. Remove steering wheel speed sensor assembly from adapter and bearing assembly.
9. Remove and dispose of lower spring retainer.
10. Remove lower spring.
11. Remove lower bearing seat.
12. Remove adapter and bearing assembly.
13. Remove steering shaft assembly.
14. Disassemble lower steering shaft assembly from race and upper shaft assembly.
15. Tilt lower steering shaft assembly 90° to race and upper shaft assembly and disengage.
16. Remove housing support assembly.
17. Remove shift lever gate from steering column housing support.
18. Remove shift tube retaining ring and two thrust washers.
19. Turn gearshift lever bowl assembly clockwise to 4 o'clock position.
20. Push lock plate with thumb and rotate counterclockwise until loose.
21. Remove wave washer, two thrust washers, and cam retainer.
22. Remove gearshift lever bowl assembly with shift tube assembly.
23. Remove shift lever spring from bowl, then the shift tube from bowl using a suitable press.
24. Remove shift bowl protector from gearshift lever bowl assembly.
25. Remove park position switch assembly from stud and bracket assembly.
26. Remove PRNDL adjuster bracket.
27. Remove ignition switch assembly from ignition switch actuator assembly.
28. Remove BTSI cable assembly from interlock solenoid assembly and ignition switch actuator assembly.
29. Ensure BTSI cable assembly remains straight and does not become kinked during removal and installation.

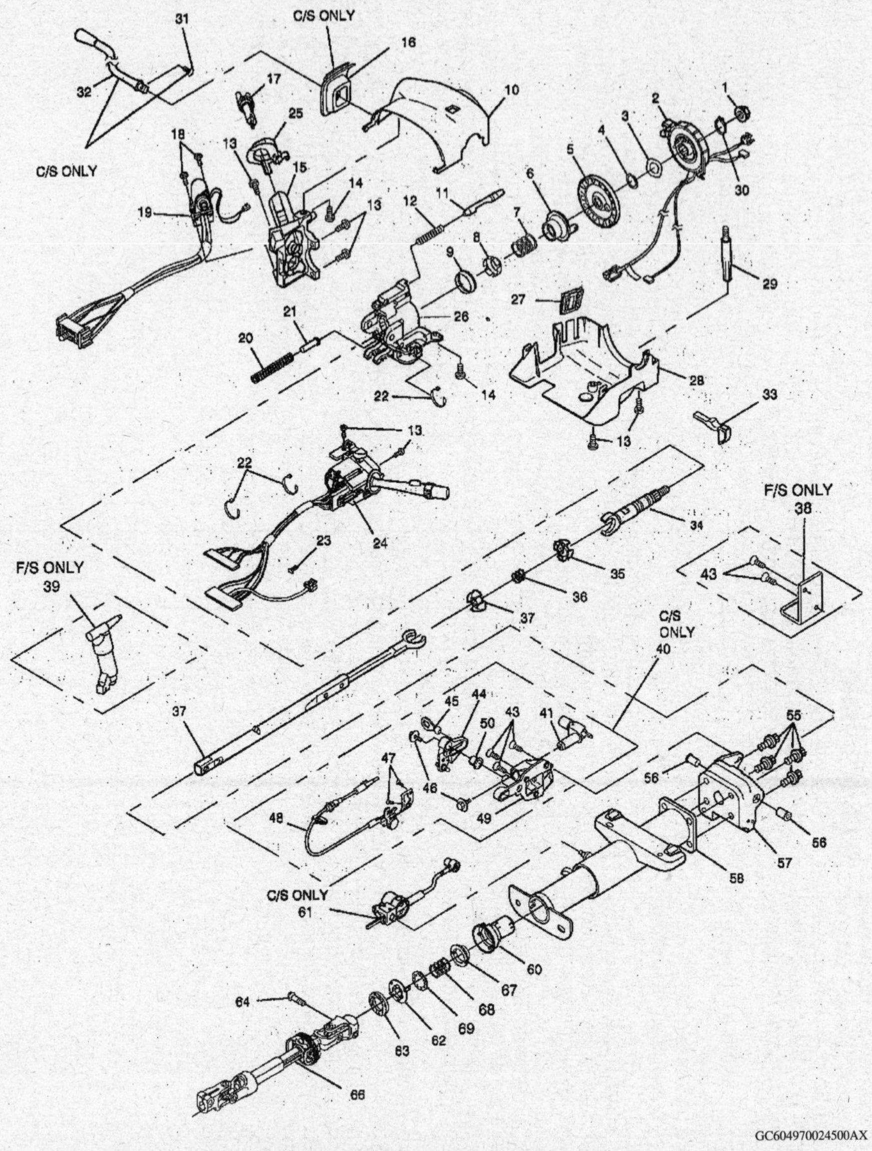

Fig. 46 Exploded view of steering column (Part 1 of 2). Century, Grand Prix & Regal w/column shift

1-NUT, HEXAGON LOCKING (M14x1.5)
2-COIL ASM, SIR
3-WASHER, WAVE
4-RING, RETAINING
5-SHIELD ASM, SHAFT LOCK
6-CAM ASM, T/SIG CANCEL
7-SPRING, UPPER BEARING
8-SEAT, UPPER BEARING INNER RACE
9-RACE, INNER
10-SHROUD, UPPER
11-BOLT ASM, LOCK
12-SPRING, LOCK BOLT
13-SCREW, PAN HD TAPPING
14-SCREW, TORX HEAD
15-ASM, LOCK MODULE
16-SEAL, SHIFT LEVER
17-LOCK CYL SET, STRG COLUMN
18-SCREW, TAPPING
19-SWITCH ASM, IGN & KEY ALARM
20-SPRING, TILT
21-GUIDE, SPRING
22-STRAP, WIRE HARNESS
23-CONNECTOR, AXIAL POSN ASSUR
24-SWITCH ASM, T/S & MULTIFUNCTION
25-RING, TRIM
26- TILT HEAD ASM, STRG COL
27-PROTECTOR, SHROUD
28-SHROUD, LOWER
29-STUD, SHROUD MOUNTING
30-RING, RETAINING
31- SCREW, SHIFT LEVER
32-LEVER ASM, A/TRNS CONTROL
33-LEVER ASM, TILT
34-SHAFT ASM, RACE & UPPER
35-SPHERE, CENTERING
36-SPRING, JOINT PRELOAD
37-SHAFT ASM, LOWER STRG
38-STRAP REINFORCEMENT, STRG
39-ELEC PARK LOCK, STRG COL
40-SHIFT ASM, LINEAR
41-CLEVIS, SHIFT LEVER
43-SCREW, FLAT HD 6-LOBED SOC TAP
44-CAM ASM, CABLE SHIFT
45-ACTUATOR ASM, BALL &
46-BOLT, HEX FLANGE HEAD
47-SCREW, OVAL HD 6-LOBED SOC TAP
48-CABLE ASM, PARK LOCK
49-BRACKET, G/S LEVER ASM SUPPORT
50-BUSHING, CAM
55-SCREW, TORX HEAD
56-PIN, PIVOT
57-SUPPORT ASM, STRG COL
58-JACKET ASM, STRG COL
60-BEARING ASM, ADAPTER &
61-ACTUATOR, ELECTRICAL (BTSI)
62-RETAINER, SENSOR
63-SEAL, STEERING SHAFT
64-BOLT, PINCH
65-SHAFT ASM, INTER STRG
66-SHAFT ASM, INTER STRG
67-SEAT, LOWER BEARING
68-SPRING, LOWER BEARING
69-RETAINER, LOWER SPRING

GC604970024500BX

Fig. 46 Exploded view of steering column (Part 2 of 2). Century, Grand Prix & Regal w/column shift

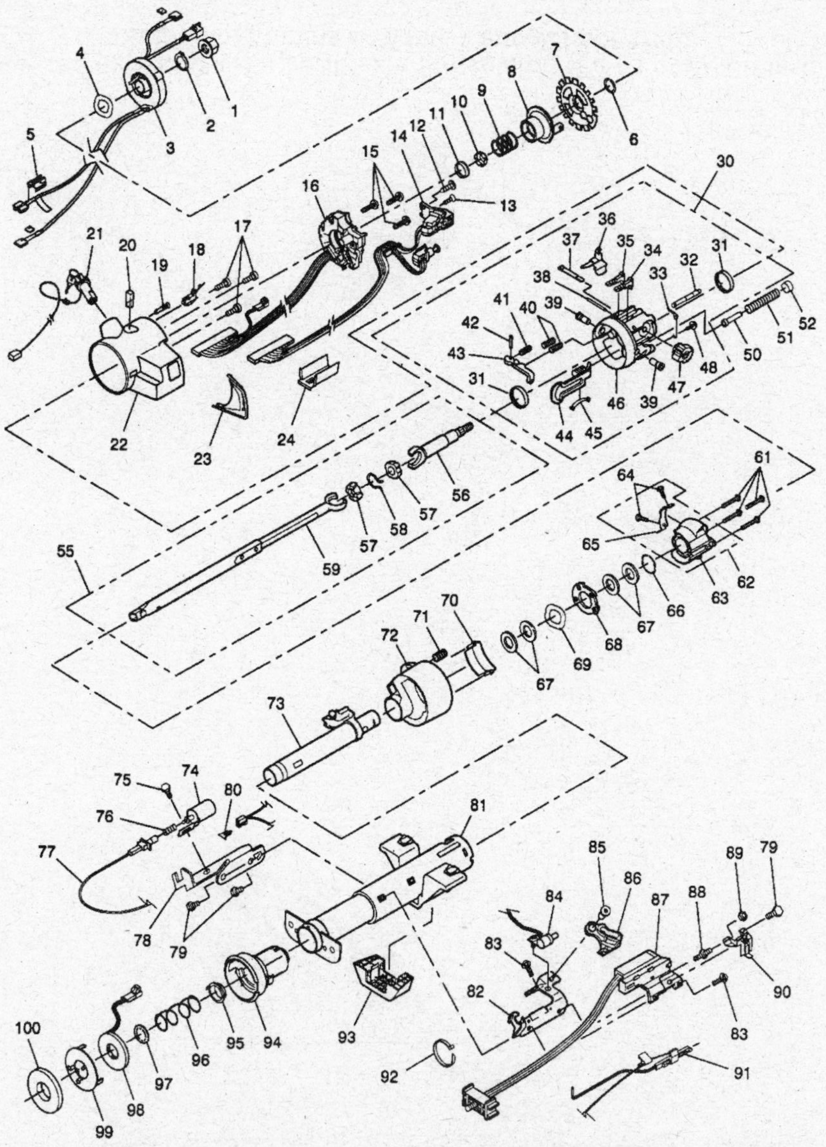

Fig. 47 Exploded view of tilt steering column (Part 1 of 2). Cutlass Supreme, Lumina & Monte Carlo w/column shift

1-NUT, HEXAGON LOCKING (M14x1.5)
2-RING, RETAINING
3-COIL ASM, SIR
4-WASHER, WAVE
5-SHROUD, CONNECTOR
6-RING, RETAINING
7-LOCK, SHAFT
8-CAM ASM, T/SIG CANCEL
9-SPRING, UPPER BEARING
10-SEAT, UPPER BRG INNER RACE
11-RACE, INNER
12-SCREW, RD WASH HD (M4.2X1.41)
13-SCREW, FLAT HEAD
14-SW ASM, PIVOT & (PULSE-DIMMER)
15-SCREW, BNDG HD CR RECESS
16-SWITCH ASM, TURN SIGNAL
17-SCREW, PAN HD 6-LOBED SOC TAP
18-SWITCH ASM, BUZZER
19-SCREW, LOCK RETAINING
20-KNOB, HAZARD WARNING SW
21-LOCK CYLINDER SET, STRG COL
22-COVER & SLEEVE ASM, LOCK HSG
23-CAP, HSG COVER END
24-PROTECTOR, WIRING
30-HOUSING ASM, STRG COLUMN
31-BEARING ASM
32-BOLT ASM, SHAFT LOCK
33-SPRING, LOCK BOLT
34-SHOE, STEERING WHEEL LOCK
35-SHOE, STEERING WHEEL LOCK
36-SHIELD, PROTECTOR WIRE
37-SHAFT, DRIVE
38-PIN, DOWEL
39-PIN, PIVOT
40-SPRING, SHOE
41-SPRING, RELEASE LEVER
42-PIN, RELEASE LEVER
43-LEVER ASM, SHOE RELEASE
44-RACK, SWITCH ACTUATOR
45-SPRING, RACK PRELOAD
46-HOUSING, STRG COLUMN
47-SECTOR, SWITCH ACTUATOR
48-SCREW, HEX WASHER HEAD
50-GUIDE, SPRING
51-SPRING, WHEEL TILT
52-RETAINER, SPRING
55-SHAFT ASM, STEERING
56-SHAFT ASM, RACE & UPPER
57-SPHERE, CENTERING
58-SPRING, JOINT PRELOAD
59-SHAFT ASM, LOWER STEERING
61-SCREW, SUPPORT
62-SUPPORT ASM, STRG COL HSG
63-SUPPORT, STRG COL HSG
64-SCREW, OVL HD CROSS RECESS
65-GATE, SHIFT LEVER
66-RING, SHIFT TUBE RETAINING
67-WASHER, THRUST
68-PLATE, LOCK
69-WASHER, WAVE
70-PROTECTOR, SHIFT BOWL
71-SPRING, SHIFT LEVER
72-BOWL ASM, GEARSHIFT LEVER
73-TUBE ASM, SHIFT
74-SOLENOID ASM, INTERLOCK
75-SCREW, HEX WASHER HEAD
76-SPRING, BALL JOINT
77-CABLE ASM, BTSI
78-BRACKET, SOLENOID ADAPTER
79-SCREW, HEX WASH HD (#10-24X0.25)
80-CONNECTOR, AXIAL POSN ASSUR
81-JACKET ASM, STRG COL
82-BRACKET ASM, STUD &
83-SCREW, TORX WASHER HEAD
84-SWITCH ASM, PARK POSITION
85-RETAINER, CAM
86-CAM ASM, CABLE SHIFT
87-SWITCH ASM, IGNITION
88-STUD, DIMR SW MOUNTING
89-NUT, HEXAGON (#10-24)
90-ADJUSTER ASM, PRNDL
91-ACTUATOR ASM, IGNITION SWITCH
92-STRAP, WIRE HARNESS
93-CAPSULE,STRG COL SUPPORT
94-BEARING ASM, ADAPTER &
95-SEAT, LOWER BEARING
96-SPRING, LOWER BEARING
97-RETAINER, LOWER SPRING
98-SENSOR ASM, STRG WHL SPD
99-RETAINER, SENSOR
100-SEAL, STEERING SHAFT

Service Kits

201-RACK SERV KIT, COL SECTOR &
-INCLUDES: 11,31,33,44,47,48
202-SPRING SERV KIT, TILT COLUMN
-INCLUDES: 10,11,39,50,51,52
203-COIL ASM SERV KIT, SIR
-INCLUDES: 3,4,5
204-SPHERE SERV KIT, TILT COLUMN
-INCLUDES: 57,58
205-GREASE SERV KIT, (SYNTHETIC)

GC604940016900BX

Fig. 47 Exploded view of tilt steering column (Part 2 of 2). Cutlass Supreme, Lumina & Monte Carlo w/column shift

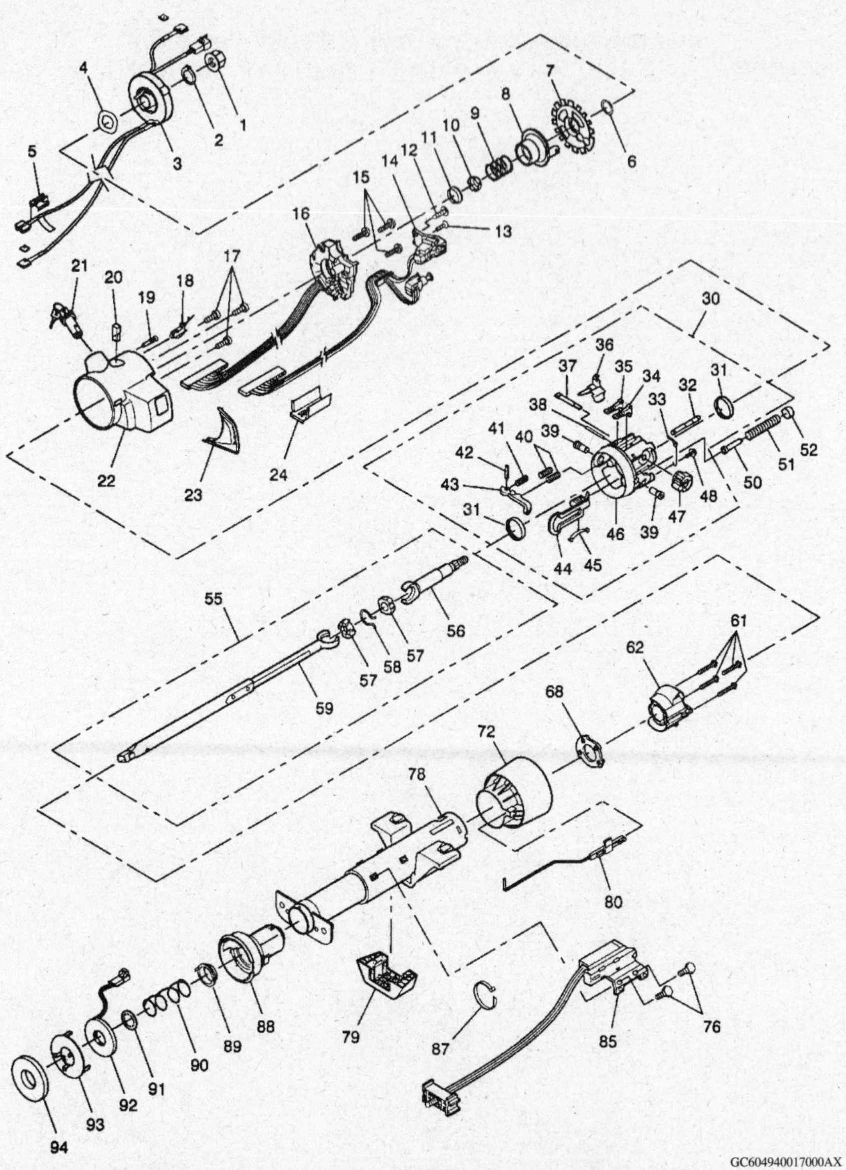

Fig. 48 Exploded view of tilt steering column (Part 1 of 2). Cutlass Supreme, Lumina & Monte Carlo w/floor shift

1-NUT, HEXAGON LOCKING (M14x1.5)
2-RING, RETAINING
3-COIL ASM, SIR
4-WASHER, WAVE
5-SHROUD, CONNECTOR
6-RING, RETAINING
7-LOCK, SHAFT
8-CAM ASM, T/SIG CANCEL
9-SPRING, UPPER BEARING
10-SEAT, UPPER BRG INNER RACE
11-RACE, INNER
12-SCREW, RD WASH HD (M4.2X1.41)
13-SCREW, FLAT HEAD
14-SW ASM, PIVOT & (PULSE-DIMMER)
15-SCREW, BNDG HD CR RECESS
16-SWITCH ASM, TURN SIGNAL
17-SCREW, PAN HD 6-LOBED SOC TAP
18-SWITCH ASM, BUZZER
19-SCREW, LOCK RETAINING
20-KNOB, HAZARD WARNING SW
21-LOCK CYLINDER SET, STRG COL
22-COVER & SLEEVE ASM, LOCK HSG
23-CAP, HSG COVER END
24-PROTECTOR, WIRING
30-HOUSING ASM, STRG COLUMN
31-BEARING ASM
32-BOLT ASM, SHAFT LOCK
33-SPRING, LOCK BOLT
34-SHOE, STEERING WHEEL LOCK
35-SHOE, STEERING WHEEL LOCK
36-SHIELD, PROTECTOR WIRE
37-SHAFT, DRIVE
38-PIN, DOWEL
39-PIN, PIVOT
40-SPRING, SHOE
41-SPRING, RELEASE LEVER
42-PIN, RELEASE LEVER
43-LEVER ASM, SHOE RELEASE
44-RACK, SWITCH ACTUATOR
45-SPRING, RACK PRELOAD
46-HOUSING, STRG COLUMN
47-SECTOR, SWITCH ACTUATOR
48-SCREW, HEX WASHER HEAD
50-GUIDE, SPRING
51-SPRING, TILT
52-RETAINER, SPRING
55-SHAFT ASM, STEERING
56-SHAFT ASM, RACE & UPPER
57-SPHERE, CENTERING
58-SPRING, JOINT PRELOAD
59-SHAFT ASM, LOWER STEERING
61-SCREW, SUPPORT
62-SUPPORT ASM, STRG COL HSG
68-PLATE, LOCK
72-SHROUD, STRG COL
76-SCREW, WASH HD (#10-24X0.25)
78-JACKET ASM, STRG COL
79-CAPSULE, STRG COL SUPPORT
80-ACTUATOR ASM, IGNITION SWITCH
85-SWITCH ASM, COLUMN LOCK & IGN
87-STRAP, WIRE HARNESS
88-BEARING ASM, ADAPTER &
89-SEAT, LOWER BEARING
90-SPRING, LOWER BEARING
91-RETAINER, LOWER SPRING
92-SENSOR ASM, STRG WHL SPD
93-RETAINER, SENSOR
94-SEAL,STEERING SHAFT

Service Kits

201-RACK SERV KIT, COL SECTOR &
-INCLUDES: 11,31,33,44,47,48
202-SPRING SERV KIT, TILT COLUMN
-INCLUDES: 10,11,39,50,51,52
203-COIL SERV KIT, INFL RESTRAINT
-INCLUDES: 3,4,5
204-SPHERE SERV KIT, TILT COLUMN
-INCLUDES: 57,58
205-GREASE SERV KIT, (SYNTHETIC)

GC604940017000BX

Fig. 48 Exploded view of tilt steering column (Part 2 of 2). Cutlass Supreme, Lumina & Monte Carlo w/floor shift

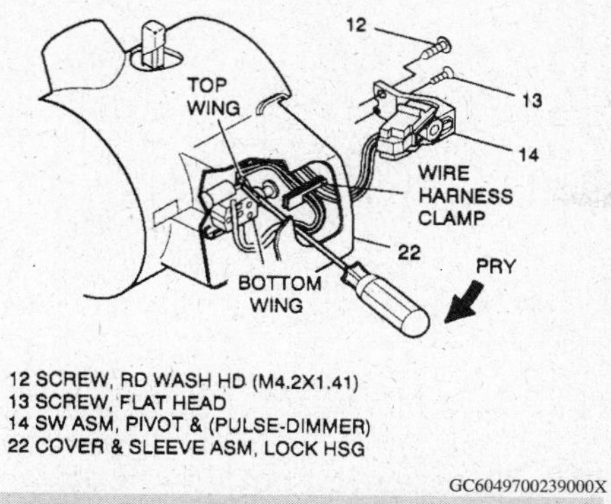

Fig. 49 Pivot & pulse dimmer switch removal. Cutlass Supreme, Lumina & Monte Carlo

LOWER COLUMN

1. Disable the SIR system as outline in "Air Bag System Disarming and Arming."
2. Remove axial position assurance connector and vehicle wire harness connector from interlock solenoid assembly.
3. Remove BTSI cable assembly from interlock solenoid assembly. Ensure BTSI cable assembly does not become kinked during removal. Remove interlock solenoid assembly.

STEERING COLUMN HOUSING ASSEMBLY

Remove only those components necessary to do repairs.

1. To disassemble the steering column housing assembly, remove the following:
   a. Switch actuator rack.
   b. Rack preload spring.
   c. Hexagon washer head screw.
   d. Lock bolt spring and shaft lock bolt assembly, **Fig. 53.**
   e. Switch actuator sector.
   f. Drive shaft.
   g. Bearing assembly.
   h. Release lever pin, using lock shoe and release lever pin remover and installer No. J 22635 or equivalent.
   i. Shoe release lever assembly, **Fig. 54.**
   j. Release lever spring.
   k. Dowel pin using tool No. J 22635 or equivalent.
   l. Steering wheel lock shoes.
   m. Shoe springs.

STEERING SHAFT ASSEMBLY

1. Tilt race and upper and lower steering shaft assembly 90° to each other and disengage.
2. Rotate centering sphere 90° and slip out.
3. Remove joint preload spring from centering sphere, **Fig. 55.**

CENTERING SPHERE

1. Remove old centering spring and sphere.
2. Clean and inspect, replace components as necessary.
3. Grease sphere with lithium grease. Grease lower half of sphere in upper shaft assembly engagement areas.
4. Grease upper half of sphere in shaft engagement areas opposite to greased areas of lower half of sphere.
5. Place centering sphere installer tool No. J 41688 or equivalent, in a vise.
6. Place bottom half of centering sphere, spring, top half of centering sphere, and the driver in the installer tool, **Fig. 56.**
7. Compress spring and rotate driver 90° in clockwise direction.
8. Ensure feet of driver slide into grooves in base. Rotate driver until arms lock in place.
9. Once sphere is locked in place, attach race and upper shaft assembly.
10. After race and upper shaft assembly is attached to centering sphere, rotate shaft 90° downward to lock centering sphere in place.
11. Remove centering sphere installer and the race and upper shaft assembly from vise.
12. Disassemble tool by separating the base, then remove shaft and sphere assembly.
13. Apply lithium grease to exposed shaft engagement area and install lower shaft assembly.

IGNITION SWITCH ASSEMBLY

1. Disable the SIR system as outlined in "Air bag System Disarming & Arming."
2. Remove steering column from vehicle as outlined previously.
3. Remove PRNDL adjuster bracket.
4. Remove Torx washer head screws, dimmer switch mounting stud, then the ignition switch assembly from ignition switch actuator assembly.
5. Remove turn signal switch assembly connector from bulkhead connector.
6. Remove pivot and pulse dimmer switch assembly connector from bulkhead connector.
7. Install ignition switch assembly to steering column jacket assembly with ignition switch assembly in Off-Lock position.
8. New ignition switch assembly will be pinned in Off-lock position. Remove plastic pin after switch is assembled to column.
9. Move slider switch to extreme right position.
10. Move slider switch one detent to left Off-lock position.
11. Install 3/32 inch drill bit in hole on switch to limit travel.
12. Install ignition switch assembly to ignition switch actuator assembly.
13. Install dimmer switch mounting stud, **torque** to 35 inch lbs.
14. Install Torx washer head screw, **torque** to 35 inch lbs.
15. Remove drill bit from ignition switch.
16. Install remaining components in reverse order of removal.

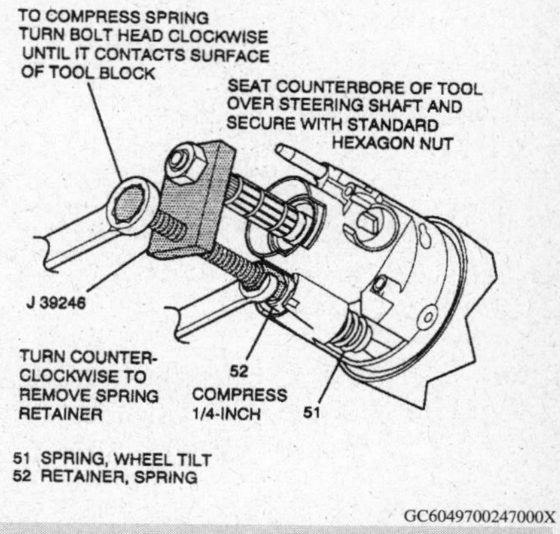

Fig. 50 Tilt spring assembly removal. Cutlass Supreme, Lumina & Monte Carlo

ADAPTER & BEARING ASSEMBLY, STEERING WHEEL SPEED SENSOR ASSEMBLY

1. Disable the SIR system as outlined in "Airbag System Disarming and Arming."
2. Remove steering column from vehicle as outlined previously.
3. Remove sensor retainer, then the steering shaft seal from the retainer.
4. Remove steering wheel speed sensor assembly from adapter and bearing assembly.
5. Remove and dispose of lower spring retainer.
6. Remove lower bearing spring and seat.
7. Remove adapter and bearing assembly.
8. Lubricate inner surface of lower bearing with lithium grease.
9. Install adapter and bearing assembly, lower bearing seat, and lower bearing spring.
10. Install new lower spring retainer and press retainer onto steering shaft assembly until spring retainer is flush with adapter and bearing assembly, **Fig. 57.**

IMPALA

Refer to **Fig. 16** when servicing this steering column.

INTERMEDIATE STEERING SHAFT

1. Raise and support vehicle.
2. Position intermediate steering shaft seal in order to provide access to lower pinch bolt.
3. Remove intermediate steering shaft lower pinch bolt from power steering gear stub shaft, **Fig. 58. Front wheels must be maintained in straight ahead position and steering column must be in Lock position before disconnecting steering column or intermediate shaft.**

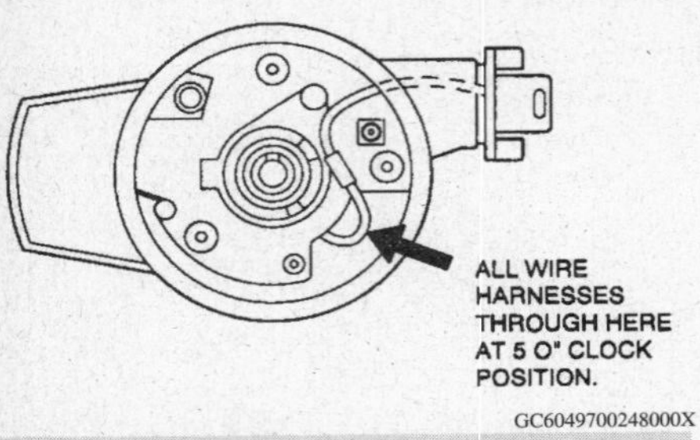

Fig. 51 Wire harness routing. Cutlass Supreme, Lumina & Monte Carlo

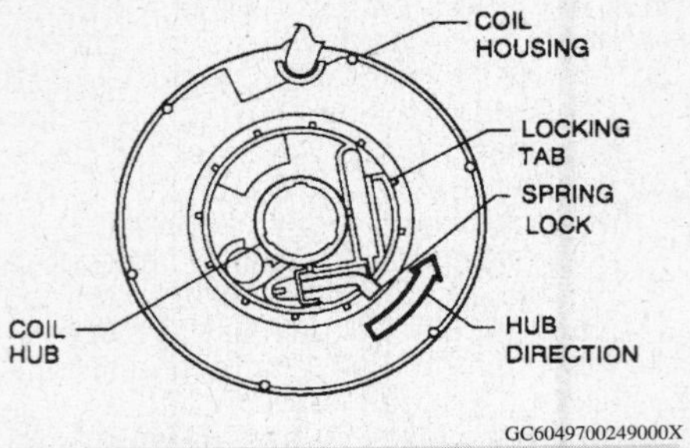

Fig. 52 Centering SIR coil. Cutlass Supreme, Lumina & Monte Carlo

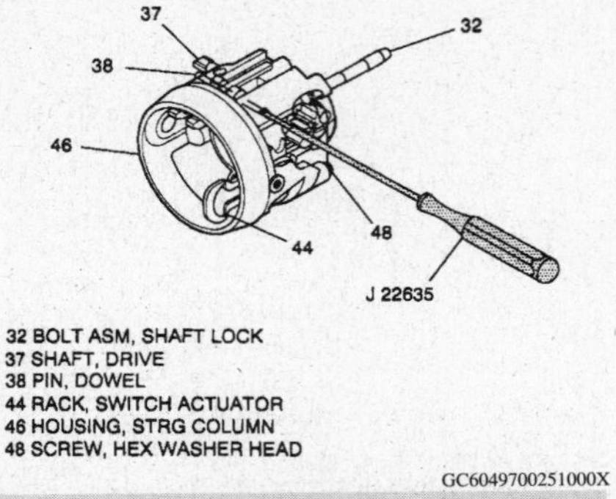

Fig. 53 Steering column housing assembly. Cutlass Supreme, Lumina & Monte Carlo

4. Remove intermediate steering shaft from power steering gear stub shaft.
5. Lower vehicle.
6. Remove left instrument panel insulator.
7. Reposition intermediate steering shaft seal to gain access to upper pinch bolt.
8. Remove intermediate steering shaft from steering column.
9. Disconnect intermediate steering shaft from steering column.
10. Remove intermediate shaft.
11. Reverse procedure to install. **Torque** pinch bolts to 35 ft. lbs.

STEERING COLUMN TRIM COVER

1. Disarm air bag system as outlined under "Precautions."
2. Remove tilt lever.
3. Remove ignition lock cylinder.
4. Remove steering column trim cover retaining screws from steering column trim covers, then the trim covers, **Figs. 59 and 60.**
5. Reverse procedure to install, noting the following:
   a. **Torque** upper trim cover retaining screws 13 inch lbs.
   b. **Torque** lower trim cover retaining screws 31 inch lbs.

STEERING WHEEL CONTROL SWITCH

1. Disarm air bag system as outlined under "Precautions."
2. Remove inflator module as outlined in "Passive Restraints."
3. Remove steering wheel controls, wire harness from retainers in steering wheel aluminum insert and plastic back shroud.
4. Remove cruise control switch bezel to steering wheel insert retaining screw.
5. Disconnect electrical connector from back of cruise control switch.
6. Remove steering wheel controls switch and bezel assembly from steering wheel.
7. Reverse procedure to install.

TILT LEVER

Removal

1. Rock tilt lever back and forth to remove it from steering column.
2. Pull lever away from steering column.

Installation

1. Press tilt wheel lever into place.
2. Ensure tilt lever operates properly.

METRO

Refer to **Figs. 61 through 63** when servicing this steering column.

SIR COIL, TURN SIGNAL & DIMMER SWITCH

1. Remove inflator module as outlined in "Passive Restraints."
2. Remove steering wheel as outlined under "Electrical" section of "Metro" chassis chapter.
3. Remove knee bolster, then loosen two upper steering column mounting bolts and lower column slightly.
4. Remove upper and lower steering column covers, then disconnect coil assembly and combination switch electrical connectors.
5. Loosen switch electrical harness wire bands on lower steering column, then remove coil assembly and combination switch screws.
6. Remove coil assembly and combination switch.
7. Disconnect all wiring connectors at junction block, then pull back forward section of driver's side floor carpet.
8. Move aside steering shaft joint cover by hand, then remove steering shaft joint upper pinch bolt and lower column.
9. Disconnect shift interlock cable from ignition switch, then remove steering column from vehicle.
10. Remove ignition switch from steering column assembly.
11. Reverse procedure to install, noting the following:
    a. **Torque** upper and lower steering column mounting nuts to 10 ft. lbs.
    b. **Torque** pinch bolt to 18 ft. lbs.

STEERING COLUMN LOCK

Remove steering wheel as outlined in "Steering Column, Replace" in this section.

1. Remove ignition switch attaching screw, then the switch.
2. Remove ignition key warning switch attaching screws, then the switch.
3. Loosen and remove two steering column lock retaining bolts using a suitable center punch, **Fig. 64. When using center punch do not damage aluminum parts of lock assembly.**
4. Turn ignition key to On or ACC position, then remove lock assembly from steering column.
5. Reverse procedure to install.

PARK AVENUE

Refer to **Fig. 65,** for exploded view of steering column.

STEERING COLUMN COVERS

1. Remove inflator module as outlined under "Passive Restraints."
2. Remove tilt lever, then the two pan head tapping screws from lower column cover.
3. Tilt lower column cover downward, then slide back cover to disengage from locking tabs, then remove column cover protector.
4. Remove two upper column cover Torx head screws, then the upper column cover.
5. Reverse procedure to install, noting the following:
   a. **Torque** upper column cover to 13 inch lbs.
   b. **Torque** two pan head tapping screws to 5 ft. lbs.

COIL ASSEMBLY, SHAFT LOCK, TURN SIGNAL CANCEL CAM, UPPER BEARING SPRING, UPPER BEARING INNER RACE SEAT & INNER RACE

1. Remove column covers as outlined under "Steering Column Cover."
2. Remove inflator module as outlined under "Passive Restraints."
3. Remove three wire harness straps from steering column wiring harness, then the coil assembly retaining ring.
4. Remove coil assembly, then the wave washer.
5. Using lock plate compressor tool No. J–23653–SIR, or equivalent, remove retaining ring, then the shaft lock.
6. Remove turn signal cancel cam assembly, then the upper bearing spring.
7. Remove upper bearing inner race seat, then the inner race.
8. Reverse procedure to install.

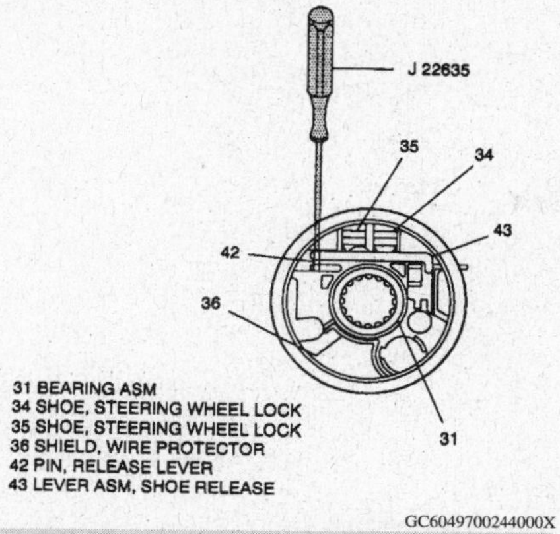

GC6049700244000X

Fig. 54 Lock housing cover components. Cutlass Supreme, Lumina & Monte Carlo

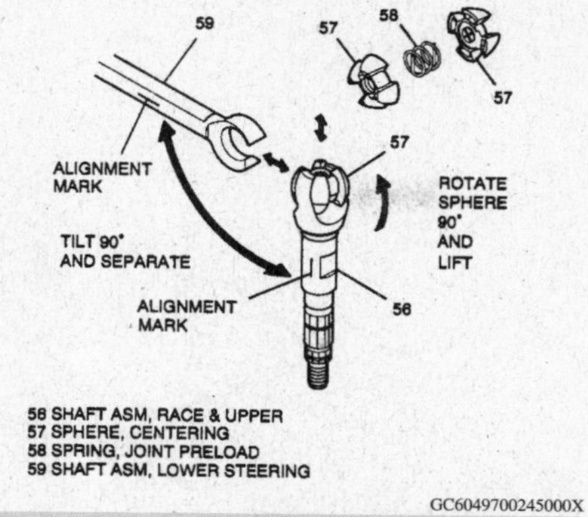

GC6049700245000X

Fig. 55 Steering shaft components. Cutlass Supreme, Lumina & Monte Carlo

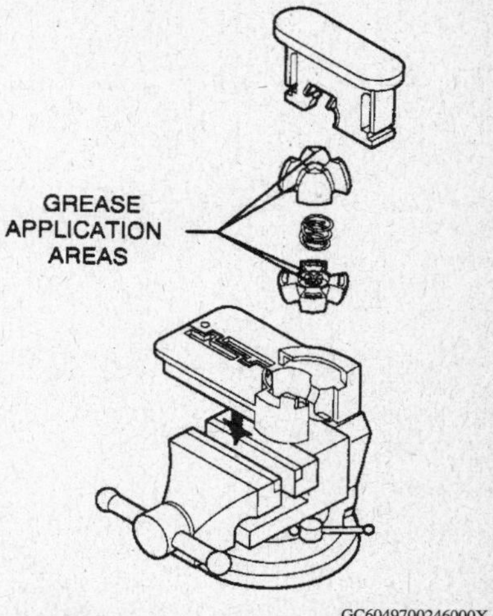

GC6049700246000X

Fig. 56 Centering sphere installation tool. Cutlass Supreme, Lumina & Monte Carlo

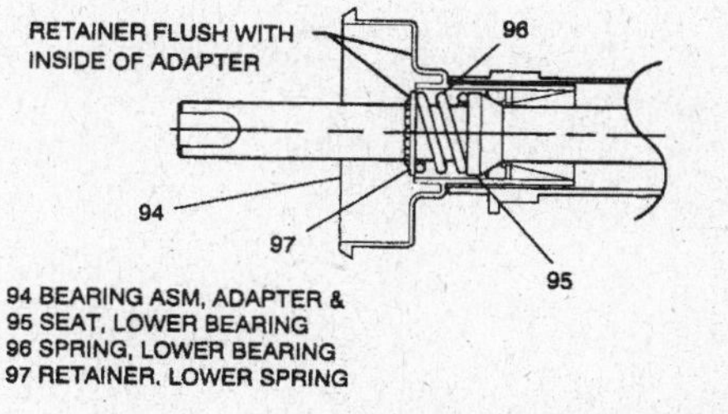

GC6049700250000X

Fig. 57 Spring height measurement. Cutlass Supreme, Lumina & Monte Carlo

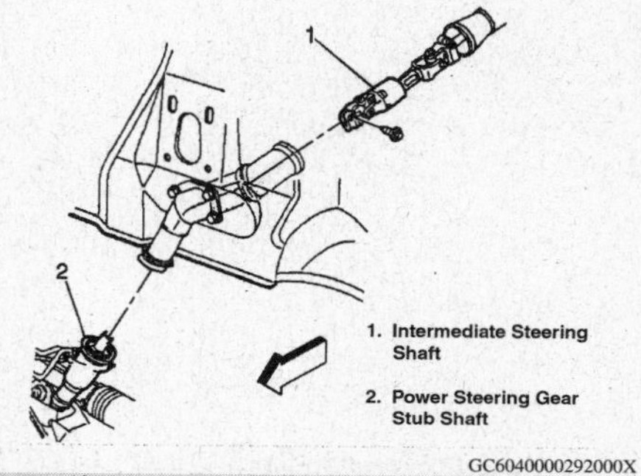

GC6040000292000X

Fig. 58 Intermediate steering shaft replacement. Impala

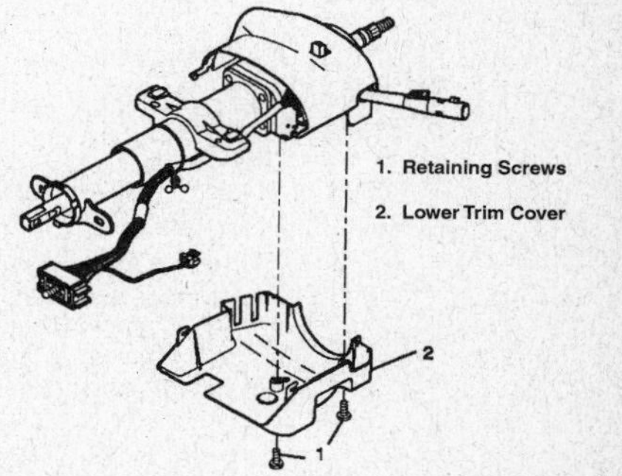

GC6040000293000X

Fig. 59 Steering column trim cover replacement (Lower). Impala

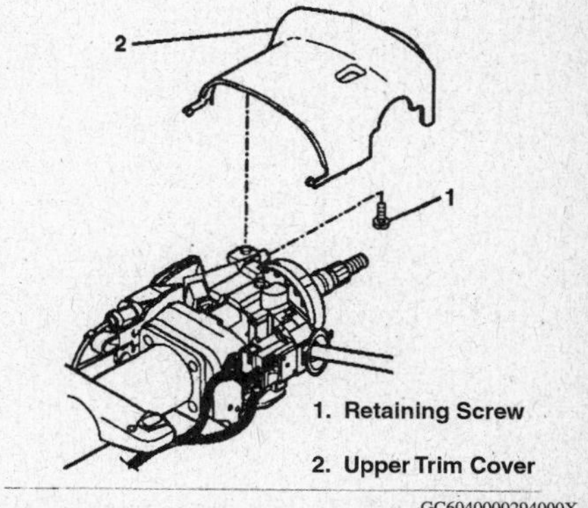

GC6040000294000X

Fig. 60 Steering column trim cover replacement (Upper). Impala

LINEAR SHIFT, SHIFT LEVER CLEVIS, PARK LOCK CABLE, G/S LEVER, BALL & ACTUATOR ASSEMBLY

1. Remove steering column as outlined under "Steering Column, Replace."
2. Tilt column to center position, then remove two pan head tapping screws from lower column cover.
3. Remove lower column cover, then the two Torx head screws from upper column cover.
4. Remove upper column cover, then remove shift lever.
5. Remove shift lever seal, then the park lock cable assembly from lock module assembly.
6. Pry actuator arm of electrical actuator from outer shift cable ball stud on cable shift cam assembly and mounting pin on jacket.
7. Remove hex flanged head bolt, then the ball and actuator assembly.
8. Lifting up on shift gate, rotate shift lever clevis, then remove clevis from gearshift lever assembly support bracket.
9. Pry locking ring off of park lock cable assembly, then move park lock latch to gain access to lower oval head tap screw.
10. Remove two oval head tap screws from shift gate, then the park lock cable assembly.
11. Pry transaxle shift cable from inner ball stud on cable shift cam assembly, then remove hex head bolt.
12. Remove cam bushing from cable shift cam assembly, then the three flat head tap screws.
13. Remove gearshift lever assembly support bracket.
14. Reverse procedure to install, noting the following:
    a. **Torque** flat head tap screws to 7 ft. lbs.
    b. **Torque** hex head bolt to 14 ft. lbs.
    c. **Torque** oval head tap screws to 58 inch lbs.

PRIZM

The steering column cannot be serviced, a faulty column can only be replaced.

Refer to **Fig. 66** for exploded view of steering column.

1. Disconnect combination switch electrical connector.
2. Loosen four screws and remove combination switch from steering column.
3. Remove ignition switch housing as follows:
    a. Using a suitable center punch, mark center of the tapered-head bolts securing the ignition switch housing.
    b. Using a .12–.16 inch (3–4 mm) drill bit, drill into tapered-head bolts.
    c. Remove two tapered-head bolts using a suitable bolt extractor, then remove the ignition switch housing.
4. Remove main shaft, noting the following:
    a. Using suitable snap ring pliers, remove upper snap ring.
    b. Remove shaft from steering column tube.
    c. Remove snap ring from shaft.
5. Reverse procedure to install, ensuring to tighten tapered-head bolts until heads snap off.

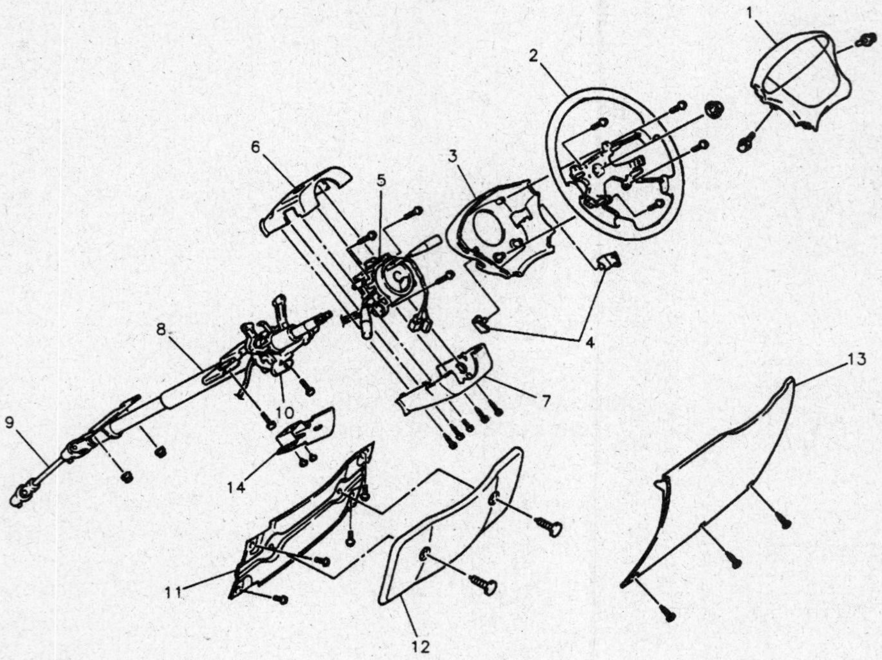

1 SIR INFLATOR MODULE
2 STEERING WHEEL
3 STEERING WHEEL LOWER COVER
4 STEERING WHEEL SIDE CAP
5 CONTACT COIL AND COMBINATION SWITCH ASSEMBLY
6 STEERING COLUMN UPPER COVER
7 STEERING COLUMN LOWER COVER
8 STEERING COLUMN ASSEMBLY
9 LOWER JOINT
10 STEERING LOCK ASSEMBLY
11 KNEE BOLSTER PANEL
12 KNEE BOLSTER ABSORBER
13 STEERING COLUMN HOLE COVER
14 KNEE PROTECTOR

GC6049500190000X

Fig. 61 Exploded view of steering column. Metro

REMOVAL

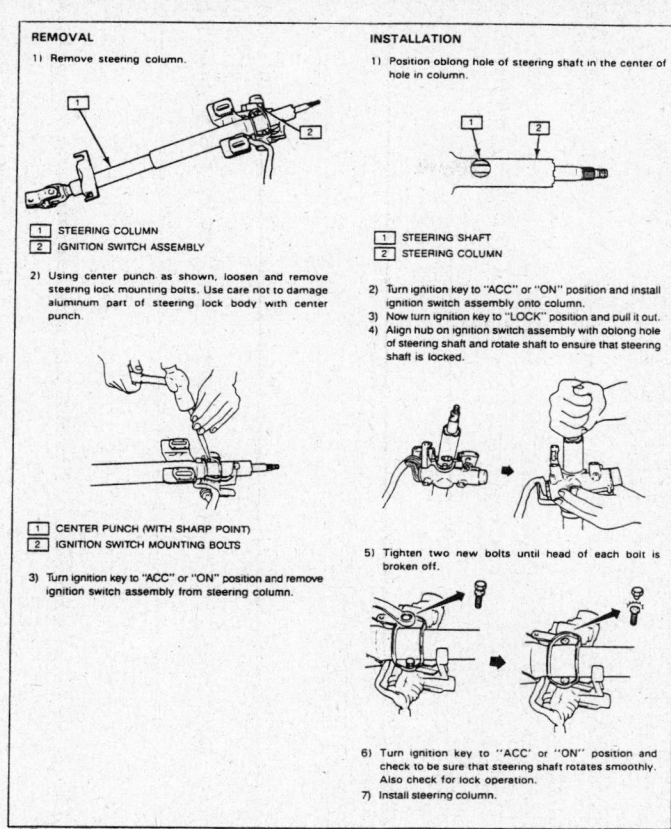

1) Remove steering column.

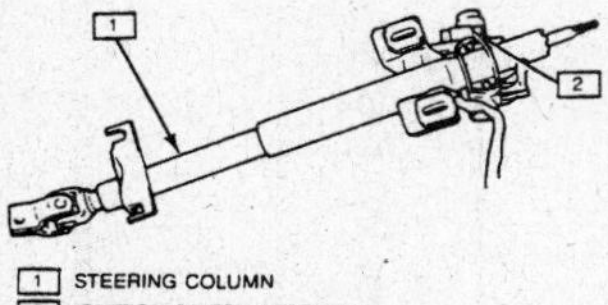

1 STEERING COLUMN
2 IGNITION SWITCH ASSEMBLY

2) Using center punch as shown, loosen and remove steering lock mounting bolts. Use care not to damage aluminum part of steering lock body with center punch.

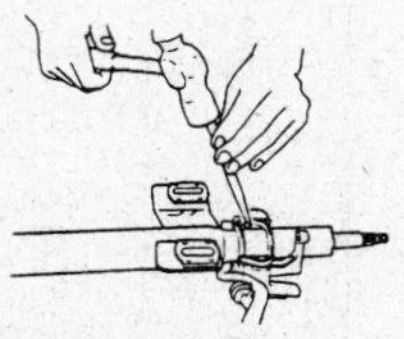

1 CENTER PUNCH (WITH SHARP POINT)
2 IGNITION SWITCH MOUNTING BOLTS

3) Turn ignition key to "ACC" or "ON" position and remove ignition switch assembly from steering column.

INSTALLATION

1) Position oblong hole of steering shaft in the center of hole in column.

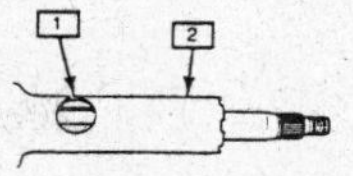

1 STEERING SHAFT
2 STEERING COLUMN

2) Turn ignition key to "ACC" or "ON" position and install ignition switch assembly onto column.
3) Now turn ignition key to "LOCK" position and pull it out.
4) Align hub on ignition switch assembly with oblong hole of steering shaft and rotate shaft to ensure that steering shaft is locked.

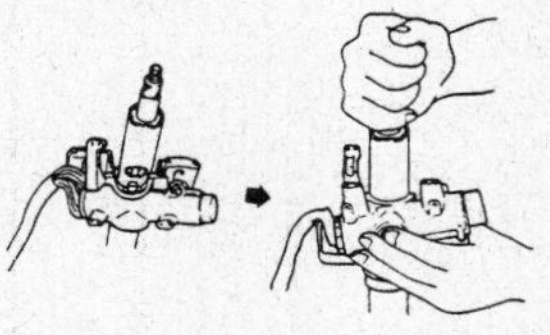

5) Tighten two new bolts until head of each bolt is broken off.

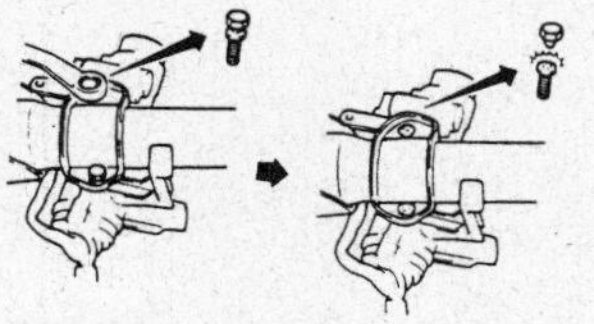

6) Turn ignition key to "ACC" or "ON" position and check to be sure that steering shaft rotates smoothly. Also check for lock operation.
7) Install steering column.

GC6049100120000X

Fig. 62 Steering lock replacement. Metro

REMOVAL

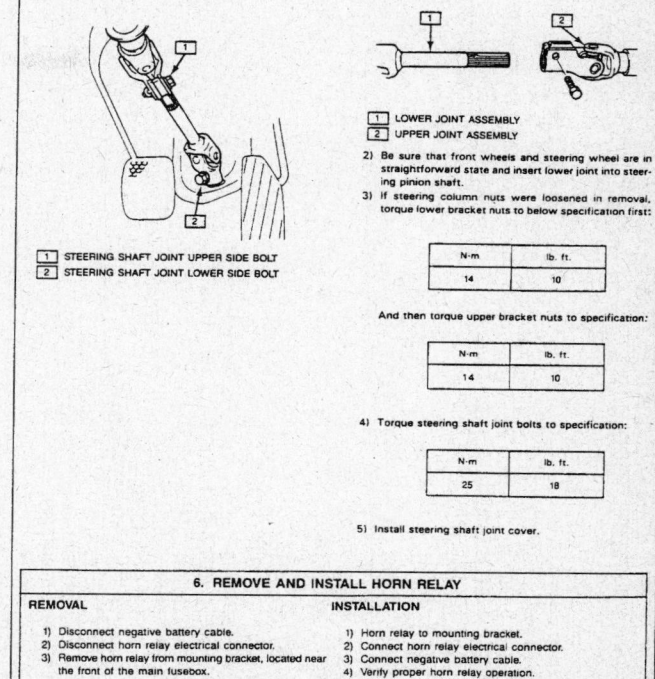

1) Set front wheels in the straightforward state and remove steering shaft joint cover.
2) Remove steering shaft joint bolts.

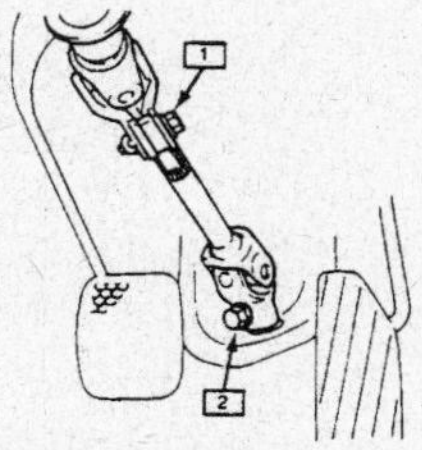

1 STEERING SHAFT JOINT UPPER SIDE BOLT
2 STEERING SHAFT JOINT LOWER SIDE BOLT

INSTALLATION

1) Align flat part of lower joint shaft with bolt hole of upper joint as shown. Then insert lower joint shaft into upper joint.

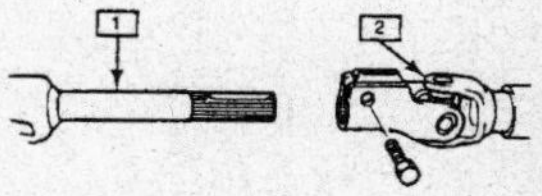

1 LOWER JOINT ASSEMBLY
2 UPPER JOINT ASSEMBLY

2) Be sure that front wheels and steering wheel are in straightforward state and insert lower joint into steering pinion shaft.
3) If steering column nuts were loosened in removal, torque lower bracket nuts to below specification first:

N·m	lb. ft.
14	10

And then torque upper bracket nuts to specification:

N·m	lb. ft.
14	10

4) Torque steering shaft joint bolts to specification:

N·m	lb. ft.
25	18

5) Install steering shaft joint cover.

6. REMOVE AND INSTALL HORN RELAY

REMOVAL

1) Disconnect negative battery cable.
2) Disconnect horn relay electrical connector.
3) Remove horn relay from mounting bracket, located near the front of the main fusebox.

INSTALLATION

1) Horn relay to mounting bracket.
2) Connect horn relay electrical connector.
3) Connect negative battery cable.
4) Verify proper horn relay operation.

GC6049100121000X

Fig. 63 Steering shaft lower joint & horn relay replacement. Metro

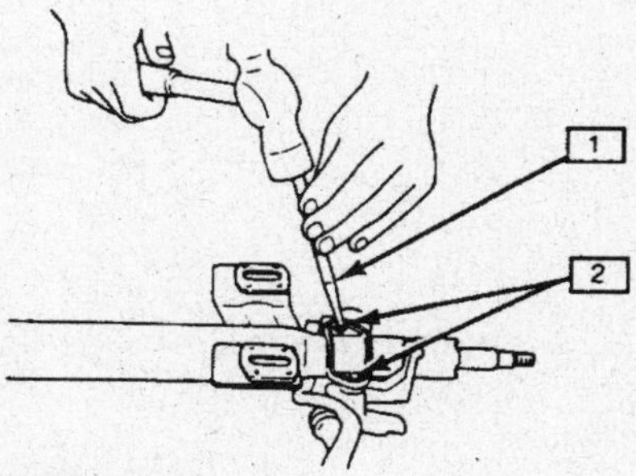

1 CENTER PUNCH
2 STEERING COLUMN LOCK BOLTS

GC6049100124000X

Fig. 64 Steering column lock bolts removal. Metro

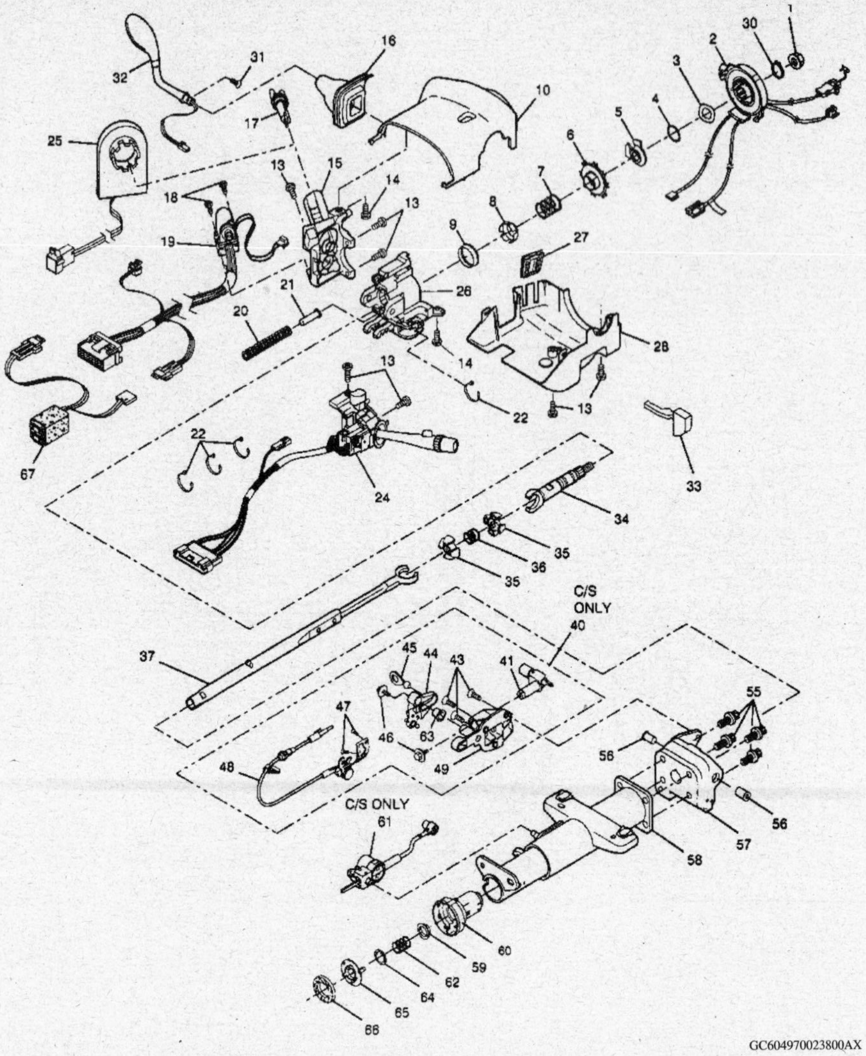

GC604970023800AX

Fig. 65 Exploded view of steering column (Part 1 of 2). Park Avenue

1-NUT,FLANGED PREVAIL TORQUE
2-COIL ASM, SIR
3-WASHER, WAVE
4-RING, RETAINER
5-SHIELD ASM, SHAFT LOCK
6-CAM ASM, T/SIG CANCEL
7-SPRING, UPPER BEARING
8-SEAT, UPPER BEARING INNER RACE
9-RACE, INNER
10-SHROUD, UPPER
11-BOLT ASM, LOCK
12-SPRING, LOCK BOLT
13-SCREW, PAN HD TAPPING
14-SCREW, TORX HEAD
15-ASM, LOCK MODULE
16-SEAL, SHIFT LEVER
17-LOCK CYL SET, STRG COLUMN
18-SCREW, TAPPING
19-SWITCH ASM, IGN & KEY ALARM
20-SPRING, TILT
21-GUIDE, SPRING
22-STRAP, WIRE HARNESS
24-SWITCH ASM, T/S & MULTIFUNCTION
25-CONTROL CODED KEY
26-TILT HEAD ASM, STRG COL
27-PROTECTOR, SHROUD
28-SHROUD, LOWER
29-STUD, SHROUD MOUNTING
30-RING, RETAINING
31-SCREW, SHIFT LEVER
32-LEVER ASM, A/TRNS CONTROL
33-LEVER ASM, TILT
34-SHAFT ASM, RACE & UPPER
35-SPHERE, CENTERING
36-SPRING, JOINT PRELOAD
37-SHAFT ASM, LOWER STRG
40-SHIFT ASM, LINEAR
41-CLEVIS, SHIFT LEVER
43-SCREW, FLAT HD 6-LOBED SOC TAP
44-CAM ASM, CABLE SHIFT
45-ACTUATOR ASM, BALL &
46-BOLT, HEX FLANGE HEAD
47-SCREW, OVAL HD 6-LOBED SOC TAP
48-CABLE ASM, PARK LOCK
49-BRACKET, G/S LEVER ASM SUPPORT
55-SCREW, TORX HEAD
56-PIN, PIVOT
57-SUPPORT ASM, STRG COL
58-JACKET ASM, STRG COL
59-SEAT, LOWER BEARING
60-BEARING ASM, ADAPTER &
61-ACTUATOR, ELECTRICAL (BTSI)
62-SPRING, LOWER BEARING
63-BUSHING, CAM
64-RETAINER, LOWER SPRING
65-RETAINER, SENSOR
66-SEAL, STEERING SHAFT
67-HARNESS ASM, JUMPER

GC604970023800BX

Fig. 65 Exploded view of steering column (Part 2 of 2). Park Avenue

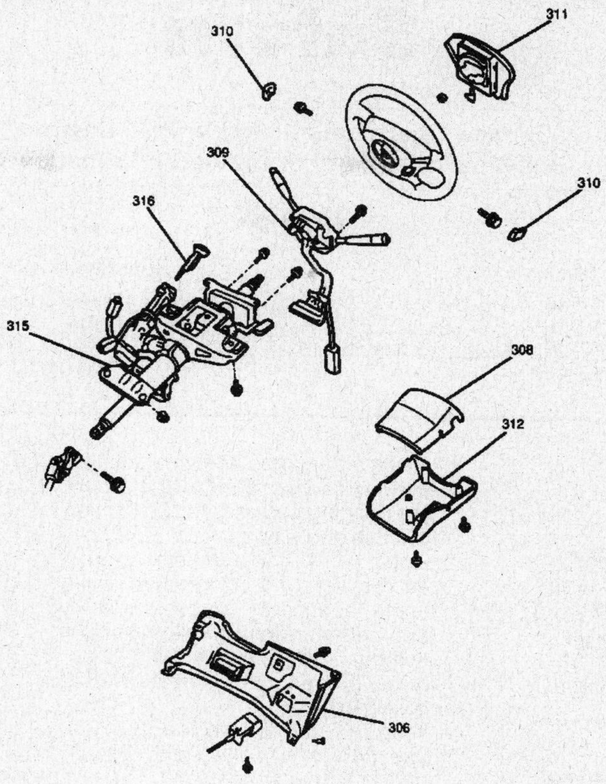

306 KNEE BOLSTER
308 UPPER STEERING COLUMN COVER
309 COMBINATION SWITCH
310 SIDE TRIM COVERS
311 INFLATOR MODULE
312 LOWER STEERING COLUMN COVER
315 STEERING COLUMN ASSEMBLY
316 IGNITION SWITCH

GC6049700237000X

Fig. 66 Exploded view of steering column. Prizm

Saturn

NOTE: Prior To Performing Any Service Operations Listed In This Section, Consult The "Technical Service Bulletins" Section For Related Information.

INDEX

PRECAUTIONS

AIR BAG SYSTEMS

Refer to "Air Bag System Precautions" in the front of this manual for system disarming and arming procedures.

BATTERY GROUND CABLE

Prior to service, disconnect battery ground cable and isolate as required.

STEERING COLUMN

REPLACE

S-SERIES

1. Remove steering wheel as described in "Electrical" section and Supplemental Inflatable Restraint (SIR) coil as described in "Passive Restraints" section.
2. Remove steering column lower filler panel screws and loosen Data Link Connector (DLC) screws, then pull filler panel outward and down.
3. Disconnect hood release cable from handle as follows:
   a. Release cable housing retainer.
   b. Pull cable and housing downward until cable can pass through cutout in handle, then slide cable out of handle.
4. Remove steering column lower filler panel, then multi-function switch as described in "Electrical" section.
5. Disconnect ignition switch electrical connector at steering column upper support bracket if necessary.
6. **On models equipped with automatic transmission,** disconnect park lock cable from ignition module if equipped.
7. **On all models,** remove intermediate shaft bolt and disconnect shaft from column.
8. Remove upper and lower column attaching bolts and nuts.
9. Disconnect harness clamps from steering column, then remove from vehicle.
10. If a new column is to be installed, ignition module must be removed as follows:
    a. Place steering column in a suitable soft-jawed vise; then, using a center punch, mark center of ignition module shear bolts.
    b. Drill a 1/8 inch hole in bolts at each center mark, then remove bolts using a suitable screw extractor and separate ignition module from column.
11. Reverse procedure to install, noting the following:
    a. When installing ignition module, use new shear bolts and tighten until bolt heads break off.
    b. **On 1997 models, torque** intermediate shaft bolt to 30 ft. lbs.
    c. **On 1998–2000 models, torque** intermediate shaft bolt to 34 ft. lbs.

L-SERIES

1. Remove steering wheel as described in "Electrical" section and Supplemental Inflatable Restraint (SIR) coil as described in "Passive Restraints" section.
2. Remove HVAC duct, then knee bolster.
3. Disconnect the following electrical connectors:
   a. Wiper/washer and headlamp/turn signal switches.
   b. Ignition switch at left of steering column.
   c. Interlock solenoid at right of steering column.
   d. Ignition switch at right of steering wheel.
4. Remove wiper/washer, then headlamp/turn signal switches.
5. Remove signal switch housing, then upper intermediate shaft bolt and disconnect shaft from steering column.
6. Remove lower, then upper steering column support bolts and nuts.
7. Remove steering column from vehicle.
8. If a new column is to be installed, ignition module must be removed as follows:
   a. Place steering column in a suitable soft-jawed vise; then, using a center punch, mark center of ignition module shear bolts.
   b. Drill a 1/8 inch hole in bolts at each center mark, then remove bolts using a suitable screw extractor and separate ignition module from column.
9. Reverse procedure to install noting the following:
   a. When installing ignition module, use new shear bolts and tighten until bolt heads break off.
   b. **Torque** upper, lower and intermediate shaft pinch bolts to 20 ft. lbs.
   c. **Torque** signal switch housing bolt to 14 inch lbs.

STEERING COLUMN SERVICE

The steering column is serviced only as an assembly. If a steering column fault or defect is found, replacement is required.

TECHNICAL SERVICE BULLETINS

BUZZING NOISE FROM STEERING COLUMN

1997-98

On 1997–98 models up to and including VIN WZ166759, a buss noise can emit from the steering column. This noise may be present when driving over bumps at 15–25 mph.

Drive vehicle over a bumpy gravel surface. The noise may only be present at a specific angle of the steering wheel. It may be necessary to turn the steering wheel off-center when driving. The steering wheel should be held lightly to duplicate the condition. When noise is present, pressing inward on the steering wheel, toward the front of the vehicle will reduce the noise.

If the noise is reduced, condition is caused by excessive lash in lower steering column bearing. Replace steering column as outlined in this section.

MANUAL STEERING GEARS

TABLE OF CONTENTS

Metro

INDEX

DESCRIPTION

The rack and pinion steering system consists of two main components, the rack and the pinion. The motion of turning the steering wheel is transferred to the pinion. The rotary motion of the pinion is then transferred through the pinion teeth which mesh with teeth on the rack, which gives the rack linear motion. The linear motion is then transmitted through the inner and outer tie rods to the steering knuckles which turn the wheels.

STEERING GEAR SERVICE

Refer to **Fig. 1** when servicing steering gear assembly.

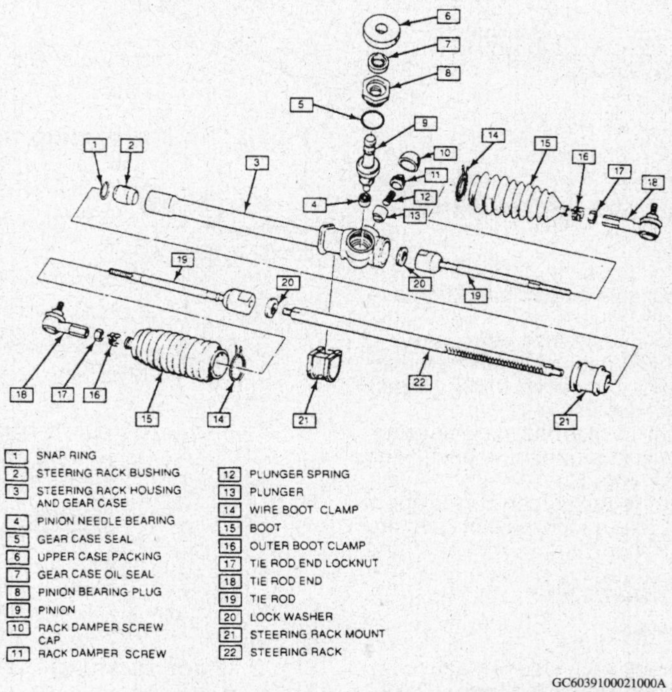

Fig. 1 Exploded view of manual rack & pinion steering assembly

STEERING PINION

Disassemble

1. Remove rack damper screw cap and damper screw.
2. Remove rack plunger spring and rack plunger.
3. Remove steering gear case packing.
4. Using pinion bearing plug socket tool No. J-41378 or equivalent, remove pinion bearing plug with oil seal.
5. Tap in position, **Fig. 2,** with a plastic hammer to separate pinion assembly from housing.

Inspection

1. Inspect pinion teeth for wear or damage.
2. Inspect oil seal for wear or damage.
3. Inspect plunger spring, screw cap, screw and plunger for wear or damage.
4. Inspect gear case packing for damage.

Assemble

1. Apply grease to pinion teeth and gear case oil seal lip.
2. Install pinion assembly.
3. Install pinion case seal and bearing plug, then tighten plug to specifications.
4. Install oil seal and gear case packing.
5. Install rack plunger, plunger spring and damper screw.
6. After tightening damper screw, back it off 90° and check rotational torque of pinion. Pinion turning torque should be 9.0–12.96 inch lbs., **Fig. 3.**

STEERING RACK

Disassemble

1. Remove boot wires and clips, then slide boots toward tie rod end.
2. Unbend tie rod lock washers and remove tie rods. Mark left and right tie rods.
3. Remove rack plunger and pinion assembly as described under "Steering Pinion," disassemble.
4. Remove rack from gear case, **Fig. 4.**

Inspection

1. Inspect steering rack for deflection and rack teeth for wear or damage. Rack deflection should not exceed .016 inch.

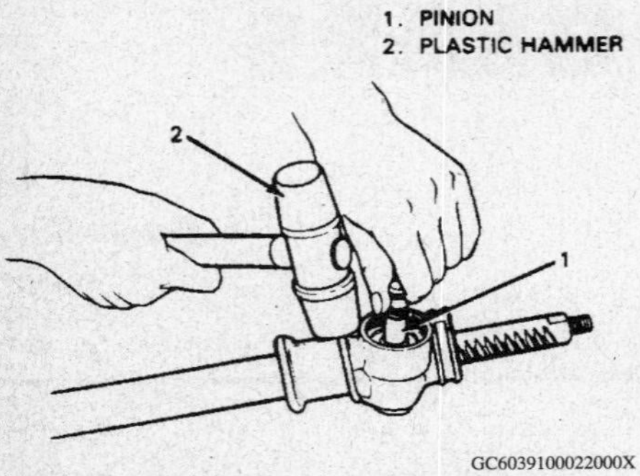

Fig. 2 Separating pinion from housing

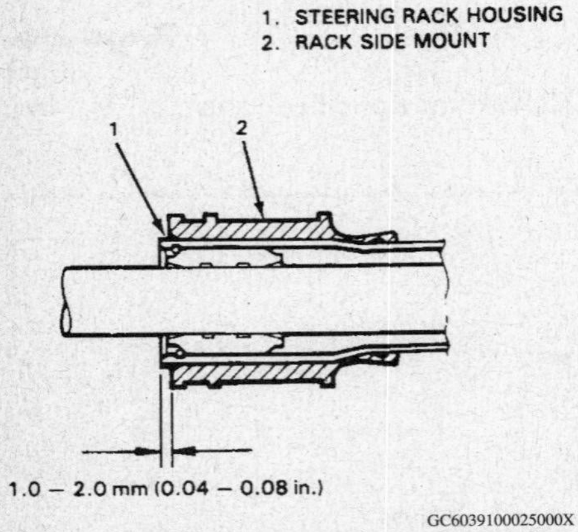

Fig. 5 Rack side mount position

Assemble

1. Apply a suitable lithium based grease to rack teeth surface.
2. Install rack into steering gear case.
3. Install pinion assembly and plunger assembly as described under "Steering Pinion," assemble.
4. Install boot to steering rack housing. Ensure rack side mount is positioned as shown in **Fig. 5.**
5. Install tie rods and tighten nuts to specification. Ensure lock washer tabs are bent down

PINION BEARING

Disassemble

1. Remove rack from steering gear case as described under "Steering Rack," disassemble.
2. Remove pinion bearing using puller tools Nos. J-34839 and J-6125-1B, **Fig. 6,** or equivalents.

Inspection

Check pinion bearing for wear or damages.

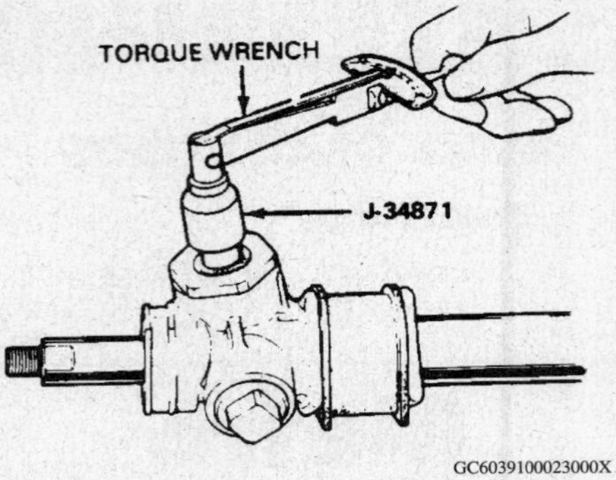

Fig. 3 Pinion torque check

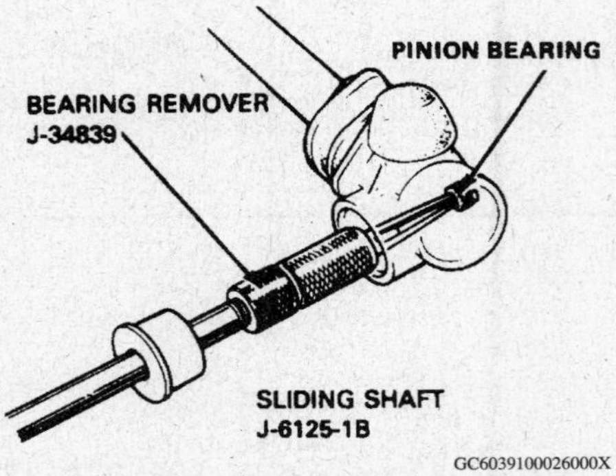

Fig. 6 Pinion bearing removal

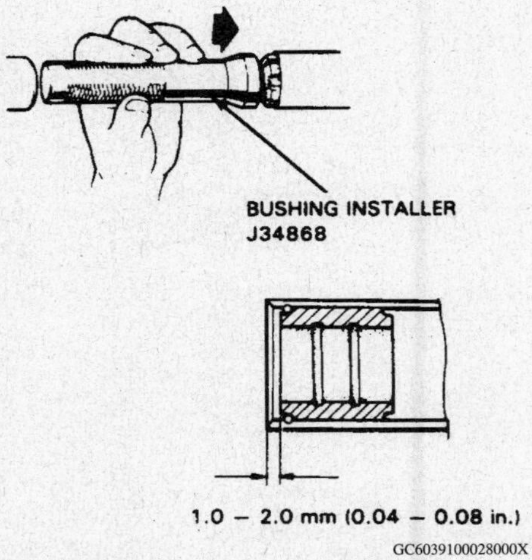

Fig. 8 Rack bushing installation

Assemble

1. Apply a suitable lithium based grease to pinion bearing rollers.
2. Press fit pinion bearing into gear case using bearing installer tool No. J-34840, or equivalent.
3. After bearing has been installed, ensure rollers are installed properly.
4. Refer to "Steering Rack," assemble, for steering rack installation.

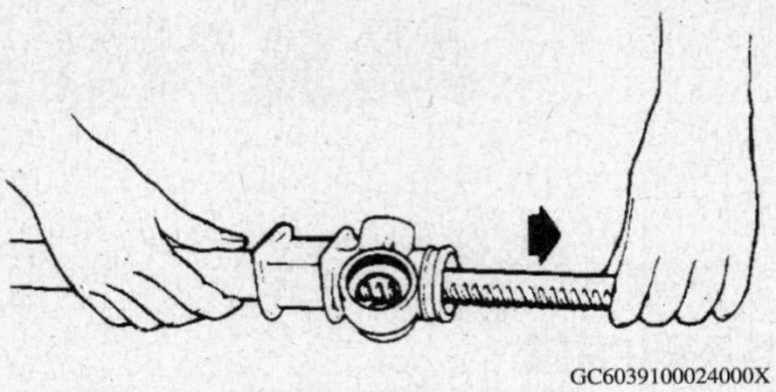

Fig. 4 Rack from gear case removal

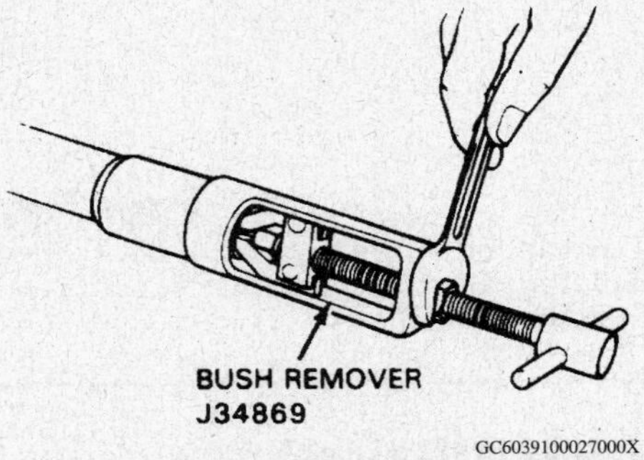

Fig. 7 Rack bushing removal

RACK BUSHING

Removal

1. Remove rack from steering gear case as described under "Steering Rack," disassemble.
2. Remove snap ring. **When removing bushing, be careful not to pull bushing while holding gear case in vise as the housing may come off gear case.**
3. Remove bushing from rack housing using puller tool No. J-34869, or equivalent, **Fig. 7.**

Inspection

Inspect bushing for wear or damage.

Installation

1. Apply a suitable lithium based grease to inner surface of bushing.
2. Using bushing installer tool No. J-34868, or equivalent, install bushing into rack housing. Ensure bushing to housing clearance is as shown, **Fig. 8.**
3. Install snap ring.
4. Install steering rack assembly as described under "Steering Rack," assemble.

TIGHTENING SPECIFICATIONS

Component	Torque, Ft. Lbs.
Adjuster Plug Locknut	70
Flange & Coupling Pinch Bolt	18
Coupling To Column Pinch Bolt	18
Outer Tie Rod Jam Nut	32
Pinion Preload	9–13①
Steering Gear Mounting Bracket Bolts	18
Steering Shaft Joint Bolts	18
Tie Rod Ball Nut (1997)	63
Tie Rod Ball Nut (1998–99)	51
Tie Rod End Castle Nuts	32
Tie Rod End Locknuts	32

① — Inch lbs.
② — 1997, 63 ft. lbs.; 1998-99, 51 ft. lbs.

Saturn

INDEX

Complaint/Condition	Possible Cause(s)	Correction(s)
Hard Steering	Front tire(s) improperly inflated.	Inflate tire(s) correctly.
	Improperly adjusted, improperly lubricated or damaged steering gear.	Adjust, lubricate (check for damaged seals) or replace steering gear.
	Worn or binding lower control arm ball stud(s).	Replace lower control arm(s).
	Worn or binding inner or outer tie rod end(s).	Replace inner or outer tie rod end(s).
	Worn or binding upper strut mount(s).	Replace mount(s).
	Worn or binding intermediate shaft joint(s).	Replace intermediate shaft.
	Binding within steering column or intermediate shaft boot.	Correct condition.
Poor return of steering wheel to center	Front tire(s) improperly inflated.	Inflate tire(s) correctly.
	Improperly adjusted, improperly lubricated or damaged steering gear.	Adjust, lubricate (check for damaged seals) or replace steering gear.
	Worn or binding lower control arm ball stud(s).	Replace lower control arm(s).
	Worn or binding inner or outer tie rod end(s).	Replace inner or outer tie rod end(s).
	Worn or binding upper strut mount(s).	Replace mount(s).
	Worn or binding intermediate shaft joint(s).	Replace intermediate shaft.
	Binding within steering column or intermediate shaft boot.	Correct condition.
	Incorrect front wheel caster.	Adjust front wheel caster.
Excessive free play in steering	Wheel bearing(s) worn.	Replace wheel bearing(s).
	Steering gear mounting bolt(s) loose.	Tighten bolt(s).
	Steering gear out of adjustment or worn.	Adjust or replace steering gear.
	Inner or outer steering tie rod(s) worn.	Replace tie rod(s).
	Lower control arm ball stud(s) worn.	Replace lower control arm(s).
	Tension strut bushings worn.	Replace bushings.
Rattle clunking noise in steering	Inner or outer tie rod end(s) worn.	Replace tie rod end(s).
	Steering gear out of adjustment or worn.	Adjust or replace steering gear.
	Intermediate shaft joint(s) worn.	Replace intermediate shaft.
	Steering gear mounting bolt(s) loose.	Tighten bolt(s).
	Worn wheel bearing(s).	Replace wheel bearing(s).

G34029100079000X

Fig. 1 Steering system troubleshooting

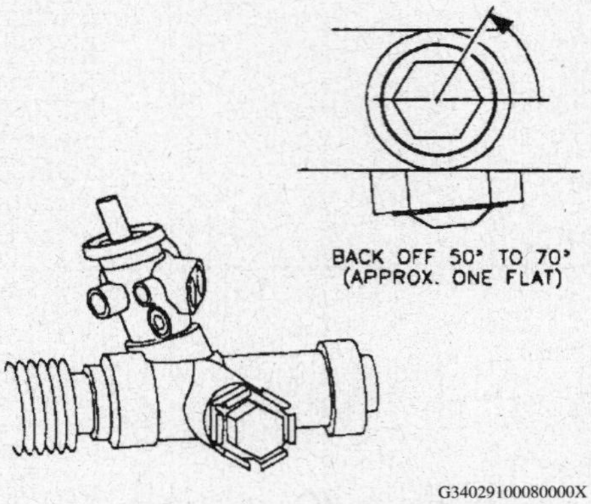

Fig. 2 Bearing preload adjustment

DESCRIPTION

The manual steering system is a rack and pinion design. The major components of the steering system are the steering wheel, steering column and shaft, intermediate shaft, manual steering gear, tie rods and steering knuckles.

When the steering wheel is turned, the steering shaft turns the intermediate shaft which turns the pinion of the steering gear. The gear teeth on the pinion mesh with the mating teeth on the straight rack inside the steering gear. Rotation of the pinion converts to a straight-line motion of the rack across the vehicle that moves the tie rods either left or right. This motion causes the steering knuckle to pivot either clockwise or counterclockwise, steering the front wheels.

TROUBLESHOOTING

Refer to **Fig. 1** for manual steering system troubleshooting.

ADJUSTMENTS

BEARING PRELOAD

The following adjustment should be made with the front wheels raised and the steering wheel centered.

1. Loosen adjuster plug locknut on steering gear housing.
2. Turn adjuster plug clockwise until it bottoms in steering gear housing, **Fig. 2.**
3. **Torque** adjuster plug to 9 ft. lbs.
4. Back-off adjuster plug 50° (approximately one flat of nut).
5. **Torque** locknut, while holding adjuster plug, to 52 ft. lbs.
6. Check steering wheel return following adjustment.

STEERING GEAR SERVICE

Steering gear must be serviced as an assembly.

POWER STEERING

TABLE OF CONTENTS

Application Chart

Model	Year	Power Steering Type
BUICK		
Century	1997–2000	Saginaw Rack & Pinion①
LeSabre	1997–2000	Saginaw Rack & Pinion①
Park Avenue	1997–2000	Saginaw Rack & Pinion①
Regal	1997–2000	Saginaw Rack & Pinion①
Riviera	1997–99	Saginaw Rack & Pinion②
Skylark	1997–98	Saginaw Rack & Pinion①
CADILLAC		
Catera	1997–2000	Saginaw Rotary Valve②
DeVille	1997–2000	Saginaw Rack & Pinion②
Eldorado	1997–2000	Saginaw Rack & Pinion②
Seville	1997–2000	Saginaw Rack & Pinion②
CHEVROLET		
Camaro	1997–2000	Saginaw Rack & Pinion
Cavalier	1997–2000	Saginaw Rack & Pinion
Corvette	1997–2000	Saginaw Rack & Pinion②
Impala	2000	Saginaw Rack & Pinion
Lumina	1997–2000	Saginaw Rack & Pinion
Malibu	1997–2000	Saginaw Rack & Pinion
Metro	1997–2000	Saginaw Rack & Pinion
Monte Carlo	1997–2000	Saginaw Rack & Pinion
Prizm	1997–2000	Toyota
OLDSMOBILE		
Achieva	1997–98	Saginaw Rack & Pinion①
Alero	1999–2000	Saginaw Rack & Pinion①
Aurora	1997–99	Saginaw Rack & Pinion②
Cutlass	1997–99	Saginaw Rack & Pinion
Cutlass Supreme	1997	Saginaw Rack & Pinion①
Eighty-Eight	1997–99	Saginaw Rack & Pinion①
Intrigue	1998–2000	Saginaw Rack & Pinion②
LSS	1997–99	Saginaw Rack & Pinion①
Regency	1998	Saginaw Rack & Pinion①

Continued

Model	Year	Power Steering Type
PONTIAC		
Bonneville	1997–2000	Saginaw Rack & Pinion①
Firebird	1997–2000	Saginaw Rack & Pinion
Grand Am	1997–2000	Saginaw Rack & Pinion①
Grand Prix	1997–2000	Saginaw Rack & Pinion①
Sunfire	1997–2000	Saginaw Rack & Pinion
SATURN		
All	1997–2000	Saturn

① — Optional Variable Effort Steering (VES) system.
② — Standard VES system.

Power Steering Pressure Specifications

Model	Engine	Maximum Pressure Reading, Gauge Valve Open	Minimum Pressure Reading, Gauge Valve Closed
Achieva	2.3L, 2.4L , 3.1L & 3.3L	150	1000
Alero	2.4L & 3.4L	150	1000
Aurora	4.0L	200	1500
Bonneville	3800	80–125	1500
Camaro	3800 & 5.7L	150	1300
Catera	3.0L	150	1600
Cavalier	2.2L & 2.4L	150	1000
Century	3.1L & 3800	80–125	1000
Corvette	5.7L	150	1250
Cutlass	3.1L	150	1000
Cutlass Supreme	3.1L	150	1000
DeVille	4.6L	①	②
Eighty Eight	3800	150	1000
Eldorado	4.6L	200	1500
Firebird	3800 & 5.7L	150	1300
Grand Am	2.4L, 3.1L & 3.4L	150	1000
Grand Prix	3.1L & 3800	80–125	1000
Impala	3.4L & 3800	150	1250
Intrigue	3.5L & 3800	150	1000
LeSabre	3800	80–125	1500
LSS	3800	80–125	1500
Lumina	3.1L, 3.4L & 3800	80–125	1000
Malibu	2.4L & 3.1L	150	1000
Metro	1.0L & 1.3L	142	924
Monte Carlo	3.1L, 3.4L & 3800	150	1000
Park Avenue	3800	200	1500
Prizm	1.6L & 1.8L	—	924
Regal	3.1L & 3800	80–125	1000
Regency	3800	150	1000
Riviera	3800	200	1500
Seville	4.6L	①	②
Skylark	2.3L, 2.4L, 3.1L & 3.3L	150	1000
Sunfire	2.2L & 2.4L	150	1000

① — 1997 models, 200 psi; 1998–2000 models, 150 psi.
② — 1997 models, 1500 psi; 1998–2000 models, 1700 psi.

Power Steering Pumps, General Motors

INDEX

PRECAUTIONS

AIR BAG SYSTEMS

Refer to "Air Bag System Precautions" in the front of this manual for system disarming and arming procedures.

BATTERY GROUND CABLE

Prior to service, disconnect battery ground cable and isolate as required.

DIAGNOSIS & TESTING

SYSTEM PRESSURE TEST

When performing system test procedures, power steering pressures can easily exceed 1000 psi. Extreme caution must be exercised when performing these tests to prevent personal injury.

Except Catera, Metro & Prizm

1. Disconnect pressure hose at pump. Use a suitable container to catch any fluid leakage.
2. Connect a spare pressure hose to pump.
3. Connect pressure gauge tools and components illustrated in **Figs. 1 and 2,** or power steering system analyzer tool No. J-25323-A or equivalent to both hoses.
4. Open valve on gauge.
5. Start engine and allow system to reach normal operating temperature.
6. Inspect fluid level and ensure it is at proper level. Add fluid as required.
7. When engine is at operating temperature, pressure reading on gauge should be 80–125 psi with a maximum as described under "Power Steering Pressure Specifications." If pressure is more than maximum specification, inspect hoses for restrictions.
8. **Do not leave valve fully closed for more than 5 seconds or pump could be damaged.** Fully close valve three times, noting the following:
   a. Three readings should be within 50 psi of each other.
   b. If pressure readings are at least minimum as described under "Power Steering Pressure Specifications" and are within 50 psi of each other, pump is functioning properly.

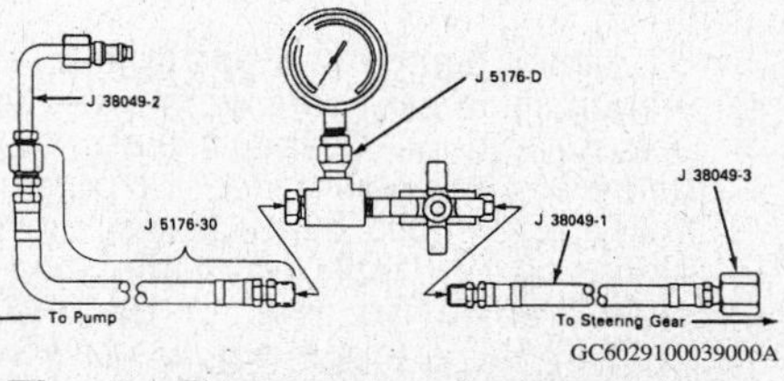

Fig. 1 Power steering pressure gauge connections. Except DeVille, Eldorado & Seville

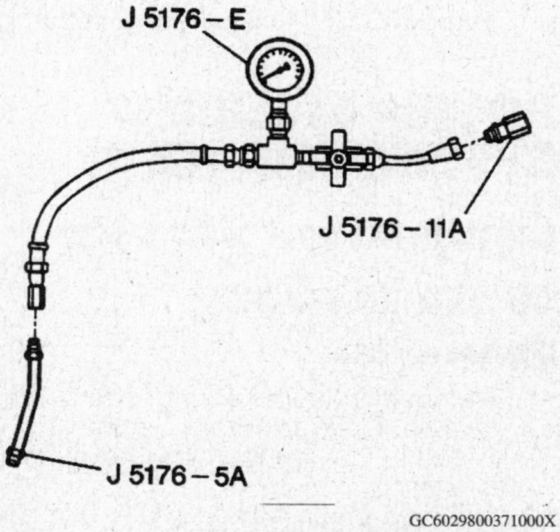

Fig. 3 Power steering pressure gauge connections. Catera

   c. If pressure readings are at least minimum as described under "Power Steering Pressure Specifications," but not within 50 psi of each other, flow control valve is sticking and needs to be removed and cleaned. Burrs can be removed using crocus cloth.
9. If pressure readings are within specifications, leave valve open and turn steering wheel to both stops. If pressure at stops is not same as maximum pressure as described under "Power Steering Pressure Specifications," the steering gear is leaking internally.
10. Turn engine off and remove testing gauge and hoses.
11. Connect pressure hose and inspect fluid level.

Catera

1. Disconnect power steering pump pressure hose from pump. Use a suitable container to catch any fluid leakage.

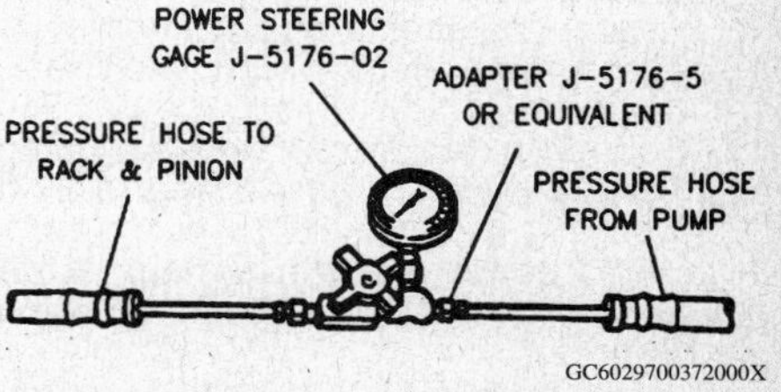

Fig. 2 Power steering pressure gauge connections. DeVille, Eldorado & Seville

2. Connect pressure tester adapter tool No. J-5176-5A, or equivalent to pump, **Fig. 3.**
3. Connect pressure tester to power steering pressure hose using pressure test adapter tool No. J-5176-11A, or equivalent.
4. Open valve on pressure tester.
5. Bleed power steering system as outlined under "Power Steering System Service."
6. Start engine and allow it to reach normal operating temperature.
7. Pressure should be no more than 150 psi with engine at idle and valve open. If pressure is more than specified, inspect for following conditions:
   a. Inspect hoses and pipes for restrictions or kinks.
   b. Inspect valve on steering gear inlet hose fitting for proper operation.
   c. Inspect valve on steering gear inlet hose fitting for restriction.
8. **Do not leave valve fully closed for more than 5 seconds or damage to pump could result.** Close valve on gauge three times, noting the following:
   a. Each reading should be at least 1600 psi and be within 50 psi of each other.
   b. If pressure readings are as specified and within 50 psi of each other, pump is operating properly.
   c. If pressure readings are below 1600 psi, replace pump.
9. With valve in open position, turn steering wheel to both stops, noting the following:
   a. Pressure reading should be same as maximum pressure reading as

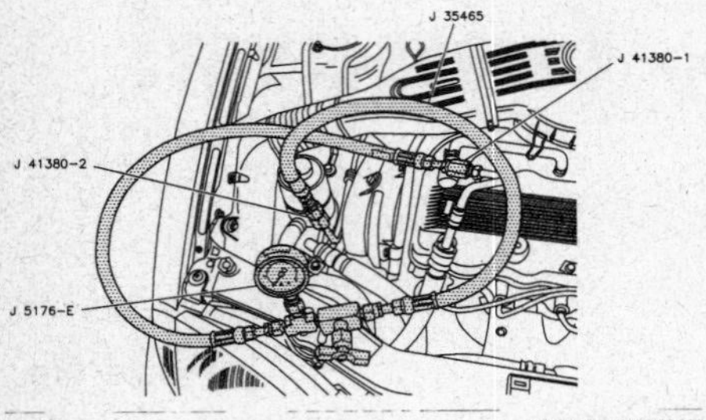

Fig. 4 Power steering pressure gauge connections. Metro

described under "Power Steering Pressure Specifications."
 b. If pressure is not as specified, steering gear is leaking internally.
10. Turn engine off, then remove pressure test tools.
11. Connect pump pressure hose to pump.
12. **Torque** pressure hose fitting to 21 ft. lbs.
13. Bleed power steering system as described under "Power Steering System Service."

Metro

1. Remove one 10 mm bolt retaining high pressure hose and pipe to core support, then disconnect hose to high pressure pipe at core support.
2. Install pressure gauge tool No. J-5176-E, pressure tester adapter hose tool No. J-35465 and pressure tester adapter kit tool No. J-41380, or equivalents as follows:
   a. Connect gauge side of pressure gauge to pressure hose from pump.
   b. Connect valve side of gauge to pressure line to rack, **Fig. 4.**
3. Bleed power steering system as described under "Power Steering System Bleed."
4. Start engine, then turn steering wheel from righthand and lefthand stops two or three times.
5. Ensure fluid level is at proper level.
6. Turn off engine and ensure fluid temperature is at least 176° F.
7. Start and run engine at idle.
8. Inspect pressure, noting the following:
   a. With valve open and engine idling, pressure reading should be no more than 142 psi.
   b. If pressure reading is more than 142 psi, inspect hoses for restrictions or control valve for damage.
9. **Do not leave valve closed for more than 10 seconds or pump damage could result.** Inspect fluid pressure reading with valve closed, noting the following:
   a. If pressure reading is below 825 psi, repair or replace power steering pump.
   b. If pressure gauge reading is higher than 924 psi, possible cause is malfunction of relief valve.
10. With engine idling and valve open, turn steering wheel to full right or full left and read pressure, noting the following:
   a. Pressure should be no lower than 825 psi and no higher than 924 psi.
   b. If reading is lower than 825 psi, repair or replace rack and pinion.
   c. If reading is higher than 924 psi, repair or replace relief valve.

Prizm

1. Disconnect pressure line from gear housing.
2. Connect pressure gauge tool No. J-5176 and gauge adapter tool No. J-35465, or equivalents to power steering system, **Fig. 5.**
3. Bleed system, then start engine and turn steering wheel from righthand to lefthand stops two or three times.
4. Shut off engine and ensure fluid temperature is at least 176°F and reservoir is full.
5. Start engine and run at idle speed.
6. Inspect fluid pressure with valve on pressure gauge closed. If pressure is below 924 psi, power steering pump is faulty and must be repaired or replaced as required. **Do not keep valve closed for more than 5 seconds. This could damage power steering system.**
7. Open valve on power steering gear and record pressure reading at 1000 RPM and at 3000 RPM. If there is more than 71 psi difference between 1000 and 3000 RPM inspections, repair or replace steering gear valve.

POWER STEERING SYSTEM SERVICE

Component Service

CB SERIES PUMP

Disassemble

1. Remove power steering pump from vehicle. Refer to "Front Suspension & Steering" in the appropriate chassis chapter.
2. Remove union fitting with O-ring and O-ring seal, **Fig. 6.**
3. Remove control valve assembly and flow control spring.
4. Protect driveshaft with shim stock and remove driveshaft seal by cutting with small chisel. Discard seal.
5. Remove end cover retaining ring by inserting punch in access hole.
6. Gently push on driveshaft to assist in removing end cover, O-ring, pressure plate spring, pump ring, pump vanes and driveshaft subassembly.
7. Remove O-ring from housing.
8. Note orientation of pump ring holes and dowel pins.
9. Remove dowel pins, then driveshaft seal if not previously removed.
10. Remove pressure plate, pressure plate spring and O-ring from end cover.
11. Remove shaft retaining ring from driveshaft, then the pump rotor and thrust plate.

Inspection

1. Clean all components in clean power steering fluid, then dry thoroughly.

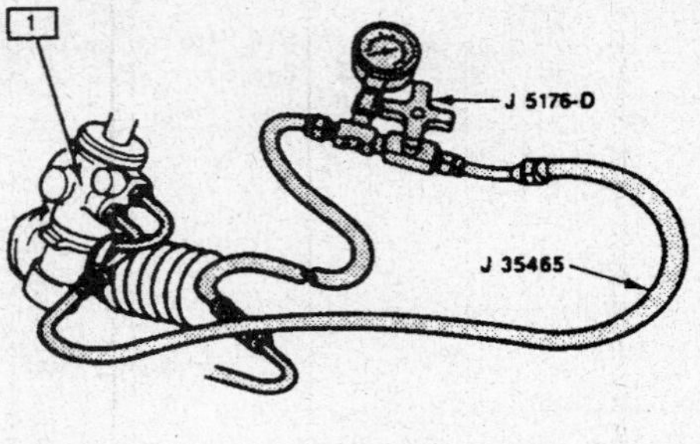

Fig. 5 Power steering pressure gauge connections. Prizm

2. Inspect pump ring, vanes, thrust plate, pressure plate and driveshaft for scoring, pitting or chatter marks, replacing components as required.

Assemble

1. Lubricate new driveshaft seal with power steering fluid, then using seal installer tool No. J-7728, or equivalent, press driveshaft seal into pump housing.
2. Install pump ring dowel pins into housing.
3. Install thrust plate and pump rotor onto driveshaft, **Fig. 7.**
4. Install new shaft retaining ring onto driveshaft.
5. Install driveshaft subassembly into housing.
6. Install pump ring with holes positioned properly onto dowel pins, **Fig. 7,** in housing.
7. Install vanes into pump rotor.
8. Lubricate new O-ring (large) with power steering fluid and install O-ring into end cover.
9. Install pressure plate and pressure plate spring.
10. Lubricate new O-ring (small) and install O-ring into end cover.
11. Lubricate outer edge of end cover with power steering fluid and press end cover into housing.
12. Insert retaining ring into groove in housing with ring opening near access hole opening.

TC SERIES PUMP

Refer to **Fig. 8** for service procedures on this power steering pump.

Power Steering System Bleed

EXCEPT AURORA & RIVIERA

Bleed power steering system after any component replacement, fluid line disconnection or in case of steering system noise. Bleed system to prevent pump damage, stop steering noise and to ensure proper system operation. Inspect steering system before bleeding, looking for power steering lines touching frame, body or engine. Also

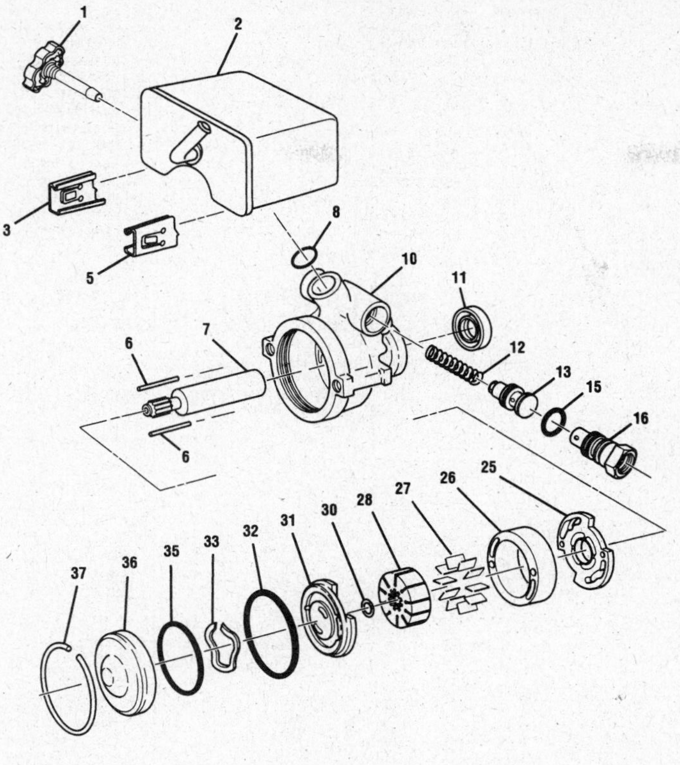

1 - CAPSTICK ASM, RESERVOIR
2 - RESERVOIR ASM, HYD PUMP (TYPICAL)
3 - CLIP, RESERVOIR RETAINING (LH)
5 - CLIP, RESERVOIR RETAINING (RH)
6 - PIN, PUMP RING DOWEL
7 - SHAFT, DRIVE
8 - SEAL, O-RING
10 - HOUSING ASM, HYD PUMP
11 - SEAL, DRIVE SHAFT
12 - SPRING, FLOW CONTROL
13 - VALVE ASM, CONTROL
15 - SEAL, O-RING
16 - FITTING, O-RING UNION
25 - PLATE, THRUST
26 - RING, PUMP
27 - VANE
28 - ROTOR, PUMP
30 - RING, SHAFT RETAINING
31 - PLATE, PRESSURE
32 - SEAL, O-RING
33 - SPRING, PRESSURE PLATE
35 - SEAL, O-RING
36 - COVER, END
37 - RING, RETAINING

GC6029700405000X

Fig. 6 Exploded view of CB series power steering pump

inspect all hose connections for looseness or leaks and tighten as required.

On 1997 models, refer to **Fig. 9** for proper bleeding procedure.

On 1998–2000 models, proceed as follows:

1. Remove power steering pump reservoir cap.
2. Fill reservoir with proper fluid to the "full cold" level.
3. Connect vacuum pump tool No. J-35555 and power steering bleeder adapter tool No. J-43485, or equivalents to reservoir filler neck as illustrated in **Fig. 10.**
4. Apply a maximum vacuum of 20 inches, then wait 5 minutes.
5. Inspect vacuum level after the 5 minute break, which typically will drop 2–3 inches. If vacuum does not remain steady, refer to "Special Bleeding Conditions."
6. Install reservoir cap, then start and idle engine.
7. Stop engine, then inspect power steering fluid level.
8. Wait another 5 minutes, then repeat previous two steps until fluid level has stabilized.
9. Start and idle engine, then turn steering wheel 180–360° degrees in both directions 5 times. **Do not turn wheel all the way to the stops.**
10. Stop engine, then inspect power steering fluid level again.
11. Connect vacuum pump and power steering bleeder adapter to reservoir filler neck as illustrated in **Fig. 10.**
12. Apply a maximum vacuum of 20 inches, then wait 5 minutes.
13. Inspect vacuum level after the 5 minute break, which typically will drop 2–3 inches. If vacuum does not remain steady, refer to "Special Bleeding Conditions."

SPECIAL BLEEDING CONDITIONS

1. If vacuum continued to drop during bleeding procedure, remove power steering pressure and return hoses from power steering pump.

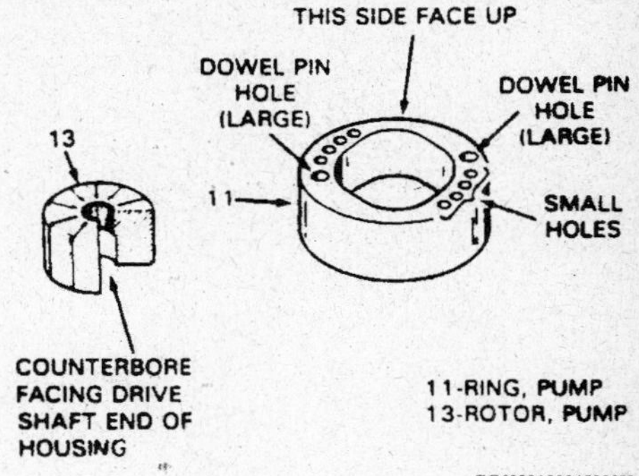

GC6029100045000X

Fig. 7 Rotor and/or pump ring installation. CB series power steering pump

2. Install plugs from power steering bleeder adapter tool No. J-43485, or equivalents into power steering pump pressure and return ports.
3. Connect vacuum pump and power steering bleeder adapter to reservoir filler neck as illustrated in **Fig. 10.**
4. Apply a maximum vacuum of 20 inches.
5. **If vacuum drops again,** repair or replace power steering pump as required. **If vacuum holds steady,** proceed as follows:
   a. Inspect power steering fluid and ensure it is free of bubbles and is not discolored.
   b. Replace return hose clamps and O-rings.
   c. Replace pressure hose O-rings and reservoir to pump O-ring.
   d. Repeat bleeding procedure from very beginning.
   e. Drive vehicle approximately 10 miles on a smooth, flat surface to ensure power steering system reaches full operating temperature.

AURORA & RIVIERA

1. Turn ignition Off.
2. Raise and support front of vehicle until tires clear the ground.
3. Rotate steering wheel to full lefthand turn.
4. Fill power steering fluid reservoir to "full cold" level. Leave reservoir cap off at this time.
5. Turn steering wheel lock to lock at least 40 times with engine stopped while an assistant inspects fluid level and condition. **Ensure fluid level remains at "full cold" level. Trapped air might cause fluid to overflow. Clean up any spills immediately.**
6. If any bubbles appear, inspect for loose fluid line connections and correct as required.
7. Start and idle engine, ensuring fluid is kept at proper level.
8. Install reservoir cap.
9. Turn steering wheel until front tires reach center position.
10. Lower the vehicle and allow engine to idle for two minutes.
11. Turn steering wheel in both directions

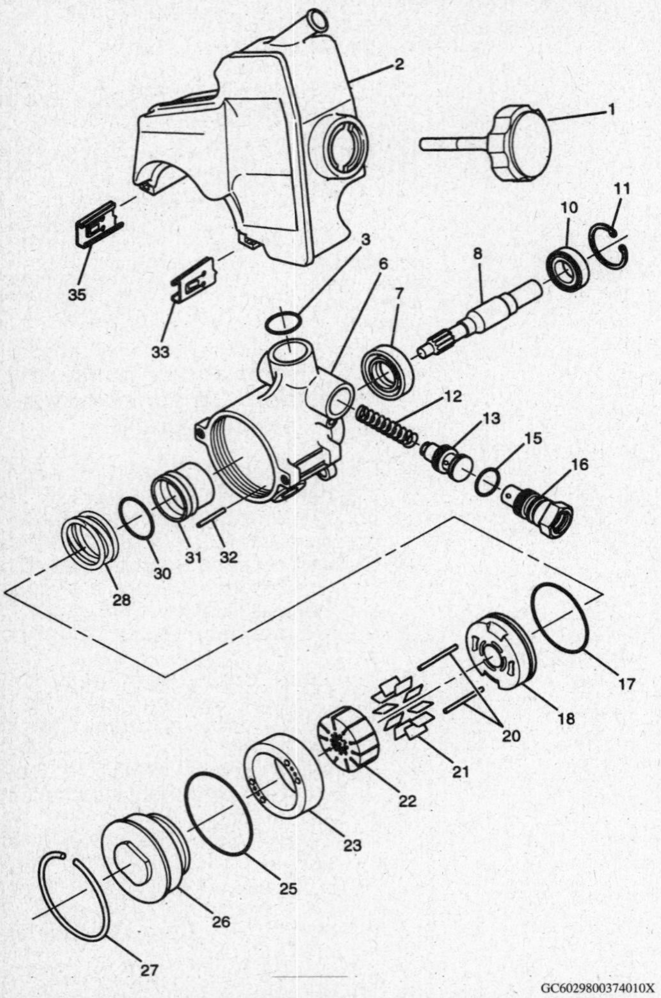
2
1
11
10
8
35
3
6
7
33
12
13
15
16
31
32
30
28
17
18
20
21
22
23
25
26
27
GC6029800374010X

Fig. 8 Power steering pump assembly overhaul (Part 1 of 2). TC Series

Key No.	Part Name	Key No.	Part Name
1	CAPSTICK ASM, RESERVOIR	20	PIN, PUMP RING DOWEL (2)
2	RESERVOIR ASM, HYD PUMP	21	VANE (10)
3	SEAL, O-RING	22	ROTOR, PUMP
6	HOUSING ASM, HYD PUMP	23	RING, PUMP
7	SEAL, DRIVE SHAFT	25	SEAL, O-RING
8	SHAFT, DRIVE	26	PLATE ASM, THRUST
10	BEARING ASM, BALL	27	RING, THRUST PLATE RETAINING
11	RING, RETAINING	28	SPRING, PRESSURE PLATE
12	SPRING, FLOW CONTROL	30	SEAL, O-RING
13	VALVE ASM, CONTROL	31	SLEEVE ASM
15	SEAL, O-RING	32	PIN, DOWEL
16	FITTING, O-RING UNION	33	CLIP, RESERVOIR RETAINING (RH)
17	SEAL, O-RING	35	CLIP, RESERVOIR RETAINING (LH)
18	PLATE, PRESSURE		

GC6029800374020X

Fig. 8 Power steering pump assembly overhaul (Part 2 of 2). TC Series

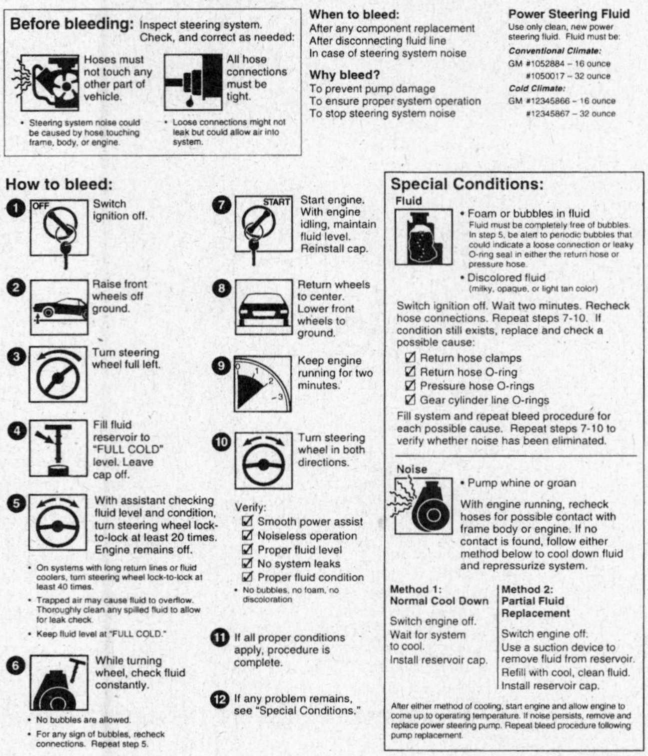
Before bleeding: Inspect steering system. Check, and correct as needed:
Hoses must not touch any other part of vehicle.
• Steering system noise could be caused by hose touching frame, body, or engine.
All hose connections must be tight.
• Loose connections might not leak but could allow air into system.
When to bleed:
After any component replacement
After disconnecting fluid line
In case of steering system noise
Why bleed?
To prevent pump damage
To ensure proper system operation
To stop steering system noise
Power Steering Fluid
Use only clean, new power steering fluid. Fluid must be:
Conventional Climate:
GM #1052884 – 16 ounce
#1050017 – 32 ounce
Cold Climate:
GM #12345866 – 16 ounce
#12345867 – 32 ounce
How to bleed:
1 Switch ignition off.
OFF
2 Raise front wheels off ground.
3 Turn steering wheel full left.
4 Fill fluid reservoir to "FULL COLD" level. Leave cap off.
5 With assistant checking fluid level and condition, turn steering wheel lock-to-lock at least 20 times. Engine remains off.
• On systems with long return lines or fluid coolers, turn steering wheel lock-to-lock at least 40 times.
• Trapped air may cause fluid to overflow. Thoroughly clean any spilled fluid to allow for leak check.
• Keep fluid level at "FULL COLD."
6 While turning wheel, check fluid constantly.
• No bubbles are allowed.
• For any sign of bubbles, recheck connections. Repeat step 5.
7 Start engine. With engine idling, maintain fluid level. Reinstall cap.
START
8 Return wheels to center. Lower front wheels to ground.
9 Keep engine running for two minutes.
10 Turn steering wheel in both directions.
Verify:
☑ Smooth power assist
☑ Noiseless operation
☑ Proper fluid level
☑ No system leaks
☑ Proper fluid condition
• No bubbles, no foam, no discoloration
11 If all proper conditions apply, procedure is complete.
12 If any problem remains, see "Special Conditions."
Special Conditions:
Fluid
• Foam or bubbles in fluid
Fluid must be completely free of bubbles. In step 5, be alert to periodic bubbles that could indicate a loose connection or leaky O-ring seal in either the return hose or pressure hose.
• Discolored fluid
(milky, opaque, or light tan color)
Switch ignition off. Wait two minutes. Recheck hose connections. Repeat steps 7-10. If condition still exists, replace and check a possible cause:
☑ Return hose clamps
☑ Return hose O-ring
☑ Pressure hose O-rings
☑ Gear cylinder line O-rings
Fill system and repeat bleed procedure for each possible cause. Repeat steps 7-10 to verify whether noise has been eliminated.
Noise
• Pump whine or groan
With engine running, recheck hoses for possible contact with frame body or engine. If no contact is found, follow either method below to cool down fluid and repressurize system.
Method 1: Normal Cool Down
Switch engine off.
Wait for system to cool.
Install reservoir cap.
Method 2: Partial Fluid Replacement
Switch engine off.
Use a suction device to remove fluid from reservoir.
Refill with cool, clean fluid.
Install reservoir cap.
After either method of cooling, start engine and allow engine to come up to operating temperature. If noise persists, remove and replace power steering pump. Repeat bleed procedure following pump replacement.
GC6029600116000X

Fig. 9 Power steering system bleed procedure. 1997

and ensure it rotates smoothly and noiselessly.

12. Ensure fluid remains at proper level, has no bubbles, foam or discoloration and does not leak.
13. If bubbles, discoloration or foam appear in fluid, proceed as follows:
    a. Turn ignition Off.
    b. Wait 2 minutes, then inspect hose connections again.
    c. Start and idle engine while maintaining fluid at proper level.
    d. Install reservoir cap.
    e. Turn steering wheel in both directions and ensure it rotates smoothly and noiselessly.
    f. If a fluid fault condition persists, inspect and replace return hose clamps and O-rings, pressure hose O-rings and gear cylinder line O-rings.
14. If pump groans or whines, idle engine and inspect for hose contact and interference with the body, engine and frame. Correct as required.
15. If no hose contact or interference is found, proceed as follows:
    a. Stop engine and allow power steering system to cool off.
    b. Using a suitable suction device, siphon fluid from reservoir.
    c. Refill reservoir with cool, clean specified power steering fluid.
    d. Install reservoir cap, then start engine and bring to operating temperature.
16. If noises persist, replace power steering pump assembly, then repeat bleeding procedure.

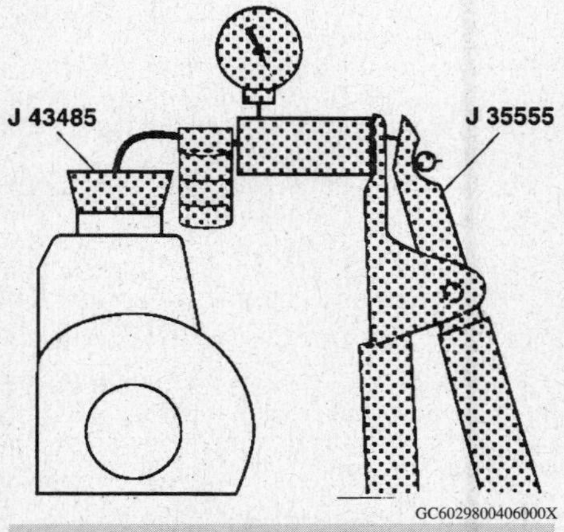
J 43485
J 35555
GC6029800406000X

Fig. 10 Power steering bleeder tool installation in reservoir

Saginaw Rack & Pinion Power Steering Gear Less Speed Sensitive Steering, General Motors

INDEX

PRECAUTIONS

AIR BAG SYSTEMS

Refer to "Air Bag System Precautions" in the front of this manual for system disarming and arming procedures.

BATTERY GROUND CABLE

Prior to service, disconnect battery ground cable and isolate as required.

DESCRIPTION

POWER STEERING GEAR

This power steering gear assembly incorporates an integral tube and housing containing a pinion shaft and steering rack. The tube and housing are joined by a plastic injection-bonding process. The pinion shaft is supported in the housing by thrust bearings and bushings. A bushing and bulkhead assembly supports the steering in the tube.

A rotary-type valve body is used to control the hydraulic steering assist. Fluid under pressure is directed to the gear housing and into the valve body. The valve body then directs fluid to the power cylinder.

A spool valve, connected to the stub shaft by a locating pin, rotates within the valve body. Fluid directional passages, machined into the spool valve, are aligned with fluid passages in the valve body as the spool valve rotates. Fluid is directed through these passages, into either side of the power cylinder through the externally mounted oil lines.

DIAGNOSIS & TESTING

EXTERNAL LEAK INSPECTION

1. With engine off, wipe entire power steering system clean and dry.
2. Ensure fluid level is at proper level.
3. Start engine, then turn steering wheel from stop to stop a few times. Do not hold at stop for a long period.
4. Find exact area of leak and repair as required, **Fig. 1.**

POWER STEERING SYSTEM SERVICE

Component Service

POWER STEERING GEAR

DISASSEMBLE

Refer to **Figs. 2 through 4** for service procedures.

OUTER TIE ROD

1. Remove prevailing torque nut or cotter pin and hex slotted nut from outer tie rod assembly, **Figs. 5 and 6.**
2. **On Achieva, Skylark and 1997–98 Grand Am models,** proceed as follows:
   a. Loosen outer tie rod pinch bolts, then separate outer tie rod from steering knuckle using steering linkage puller, tool No. J-24319-01, or equivalent.
   b. Remove outer tie rod from tie rod adjuster.
3. **On all models except Achieva, Skylark and 1997–98 Grand Am,** proceed as follows:
   a. Loosen jam nut, then remove outer tie rod from steering knuckle using steering linkage remover tool No. J-24319-01, or equivalent.
   b. Remove outer tie rod from inner tie rod.
4. **On all models,** reverse procedure to install, noting the following:
   a. **On 1998–2000 Century, Grand Prix and Regal models, torque** prevailing nut to tie rod end to 22 ft. lbs., then rotate an additional 120°.
   b. **On all models except 1998–2000 Century, Grand Prix and Regal, torque** hex slotted nut to 35 ft. lbs. with a maximum of 52 ft. lbs. to install cotter pin. **Do not back off nut when installing cotter pin.**
   c. **On all models,** adjust toe by turning inner tie rod.
   d. **Torque** jam nut against outer tie rod to 50 ft. lbs.

INNER TIE ROD

ACHIEVA, SKYLARK & 1997–98 GRAND AM

1. Remove and dispose of lock plate from inner tie rod bolts, **Fig. 7.**
2. Remove inner tie rod bolt.
3. Slide out and remove inner tie rod between bolt support plate and rack and pinion boot. **If both inner tie rods are to be removed, after removing the first tie rod, install bolt again to keep rack and pinion and other components aligned.**
4. Reverse procedure to install, noting the following:
   a. Ensure center housing cover washers are fitted into rack and pinion boot.
   b. Install new lock plate with notches in proper position over flats of inner tie rod bolts.
   c. Tighten inner tie rod bolts to specifications.

EXCEPT ACHIEVA, SKYLARK & 1997–98 GRAND AM

Removal

Rack must be held during inner tie rod removal to prevent internal gear damage.

1. Remove rack and pinion steering assembly from vehicle.
2. Remove outer tie rod from inner tie rod assembly, then rack and pinion boot.
3. Place wrench on flat of rack assembly and place wrench on flats of inner tie rod housing, **Fig. 8.**
4. Rotate housing counterclockwise until inner tie rod separates from rack.

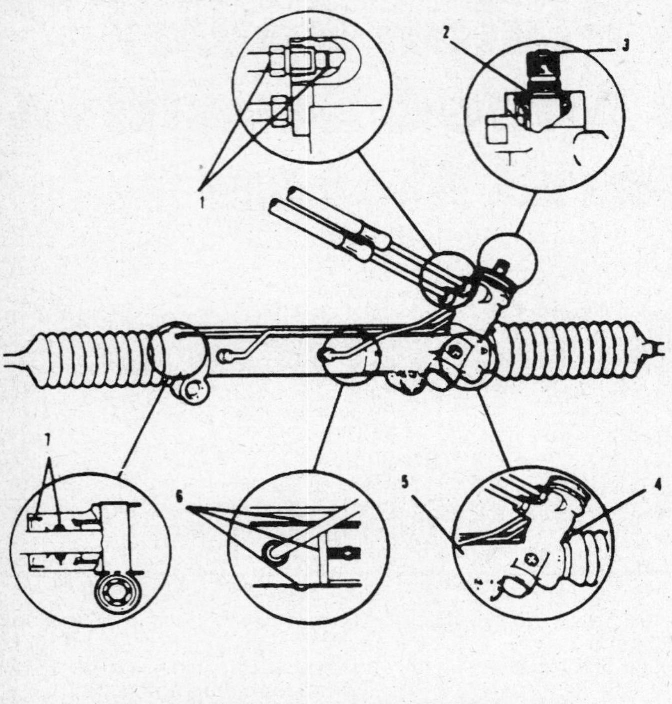

1 TIGHTEN FITTING TO 27 N m (20 LB FT) IF LEAKAGE PERSISTS, REPLACE O-RING SEAL IF LEAKAGE IS DUE TO DAMAGED THREADS, REPAIR FITTING NUT OR REPLACE LINE AS REQUIRED IF HOUSING THREADS ARE BADLY DAMAGED, REPLACE HOUSING
2 REPLACE DUST AND STUB SHAFT SEALS
3 IF LEAKAGE IS OBSERVED BETWEEN TORSION BAR AND STUB SHAFT, PARTIAL GEAR REPLACEMENT WILL BE REQUIRED
4 IF LEAKAGE IS OBSERVED AT DRIVER SIDE AND IS NOT AFFECTED BY THE DIRECTION OF TURN, PARTIAL GEAR REPLACEMENT WILL BE REQUIRED
5 IF LEAKAGE IS OBSERVED AT THE HOUSING END AND SPURTS WHEN BOTTOMED IN LEFT TURN, PARTIAL GEAR REPLACEMENT WILL BE REQUIRED
6 PARTIAL GEAR REPLACEMENT MAY BE REQUIRED
7 IF LEAKAGE IS OBSERVED AT PASSENGER SIDE, IT IS NECESSARY TO REPLACE WITH A PARTIAL GEAR ASSEMBLY.

GC6029700407000X

Fig. 1 Power rack & pinion steering gear leak diagnosis

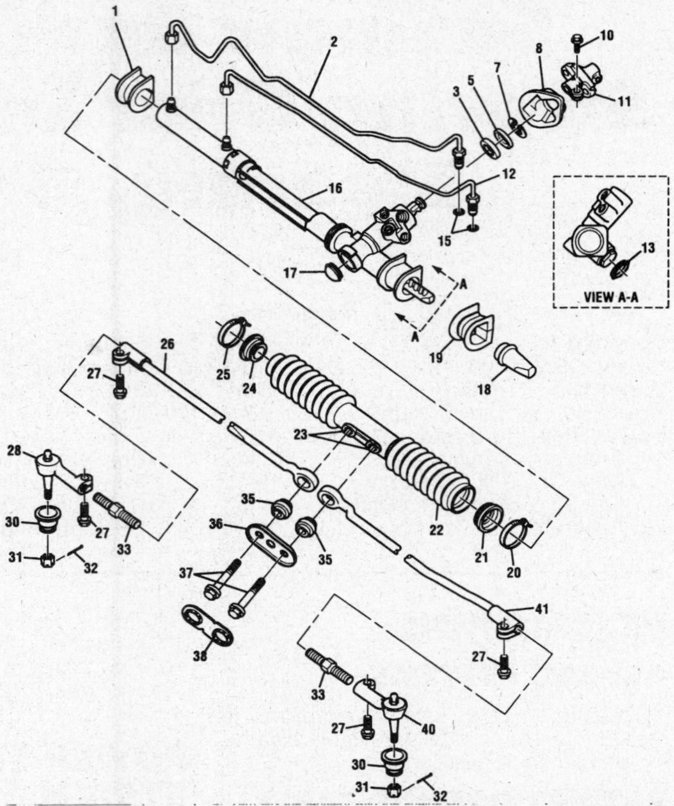

GC6029700408010X

Fig. 2 Exploded view of power rack & pinion assembly (Part 1 of 2). Achieva, Skylark & 1997–98 Grand Am

1 - GROMMET, MOUNTING
2 - LINE ASM, CYLINDER (LT)
3 - ANNULUS ASM, BEARING
5 - SEAL, STUB SHAFT
7 - RING, RETAINING
8 - SEAL, DASH
10 - BOLT, PINCH
11 - COUPLING, FLANGE & STEERING
12 - LINE ASM, CYLINDER (RT)
13 - NUT, ADJUSTER PLUG LOCK
15 - SEAL, O-RING
16 - HOUSING, RACK & PINION
17 - COVER, DUST
18 - COVER, HOUSING END
19 - GROMMET, MOUNTING
20 - CLAMP, BOOT
21 - BUSHING, BOOT RETAINING
22 - BOOT, RACK & PINION
23 - WASHER, CENTER HOUSING COVER (PART OF 22)
24 - BUSHING, BOOT RETAINING
25 - CLAMP, BOOT
26 - ASSEMBLY, INNER TIE ROD
27 - BOLT, PINCH
28 - ASSEMBLY, OUTER TIE ROD
30 - SEAL, TIE ROD
31 - NUT, HEX SLOTTED
32 - PIN, COTTER
33 - ADJUSTER, TIE ROD
35 - BUSHING, INNER PIVOT
36 - PLATE, BOLT SUPPORT
37 - BOLT, INNER TIE ROD
38 - PLATE, LOCK
40 - ASSEMBLY, OUTER TIE ROD
41 - ASSEMBLY, INNER TIE ROD

GC6029700408020X

Fig. 2 Exploded view of power rack & pinion assembly (Part 2 of 2). Achieva, Skylark & 1997–98 Grand Am

Installation

Rack must be held during inner tie rod installation to prevent internal gear damage.

1. Install inner tie rod on rack and tighten to specifications, **Fig. 9.**
2. Support rack and housing of inner tie rod assembly, then stake both sides of inner tie rod housing to flats on rack, **Fig. 10.**
3. Inspect both stakes by inserting a .010 inch feeler gauge between rack and housing stake. **When properly staked, feeler gauge must not pass between rack and housing stakes.**
4. Slide shock damper over housing until it engages.
5. Install boot and rack outer tie rod, then the rack and pinion assembly to vehicle.

RACK BEARING PRELOAD

EXCEPT ACHIEVA, SKYLARK & 1997–98 GRAND AM

On all models except 1998–2000 Century, Grand Prix and Regal, make adjustment with front wheels raised and steering wheel centered. Ensure steering wheel returns to center position after adjustment.

On 1998–2000 Century, Grand Prix and Regal models, make adjustment with the steering rack assembly removed from the vehicle.

1. Loosen locknut, then turn adjuster plug clockwise until it bottoms in housing, then back off 50–70.°
2. Tighten locknut to specifications while holding adjuster plug.

ACHIEVA, SKYLARK & 1997–98 GRAND AM

On Vehicle Adjustment

Make adjustment with front wheels raised and steering wheel centered. Ensure the steering wheel returns to the center position after adjustment.

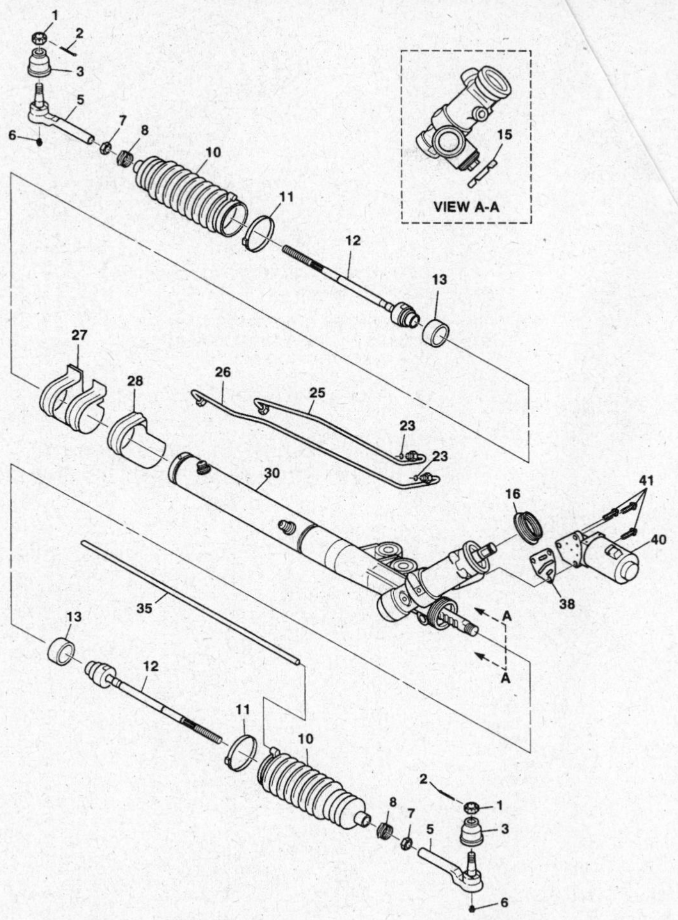

1 - NUT, HEXAGON SLOTTED
2 - PIN, COTTER
3 - SEAL, TIE ROD & END HSG
5 - ROD ASM, OUTER TIE
6 - FITTING, LUBRICATION
7 - NUT, METRIC HEX (M14X1.5)
8 - CLAMP, TIE ROD END
10 - BOOT, RACK & PINION
11 - CLAMP, SEAL RETAINING
12 - ROD ASM, INNER TIE
13 - RING, SHOCK DAMPENER
15 - NUT, ADJUSTER PLUG LOCK
16 - ADAPTER, SEAL
23 - SEAL, O-RING
25 - LINE ASM, CYLINDER (RT)
26 - LINE ASM, CYLINDER (LT)
27 - BRACKET ASM, MOUNTING
28 - GROMMET, MOUNTING
30 - GEAR ASM, RACK & PINION (PARTIAL)
35 - TUBE, BREATHER
38 - GASKET, MANIFOLD
40 - MANIFOLD ASM, CONTROL VALVE &
41 - SCREW, PAN HD 6-LOBED SOC (M6X1)

GC6029600115000X

Fig. 3 Exploded view of power rack & pinion assembly. Except Achieva, Camaro, Firebird, Skylark, 1997–98 Grand Am & Intrigue

1 - NUT, HEXAGON SLOTTED
2 - PIN, COTTER
3 - SEAL, TIE ROD
5 - ROD ASM, OUTER TIE
6 - FITTING, LUBE (90 DEG ELBOW)
7 - NUT, METRIC HEX (M14 X 1.5)
8 - CLAMP, TIE ROD END
10 - BOOT, RACK & PINION
11 - CLAMP, SEAL RETAINING
12 - ROD ASM, INNER TIE
13 - RING, SHOCK DAMPENER
15 - NUT, ADJUSTER PLUG LOCK
16 - ADAPTER, SEAL
17 - RING, RETAINING
20 - SEAL, STUB SHAFT
21 - BEARING ANNULUS ASM, NEEDLE
23 - SEAL, O-RING (4.50 I.D.)
25 - LINE ASM, CYLINDER (RT)
26 - LINE ASM, CYLINDER (LT)
30 - GEAR ASM, RACK & PINION (PARTIAL)
32 - NUT, HEX LOCK
33 - COVER, DUST
35 - CLIP, PIPE
36 - BUSHING, STEERING GEAR
37 - SLEEVE, STEERING GEAR BUSHING

GC6029700409020X

Fig. 4 Exploded view of power rack & pinion assembly (Part 2 of 2). Camaro & Firebird

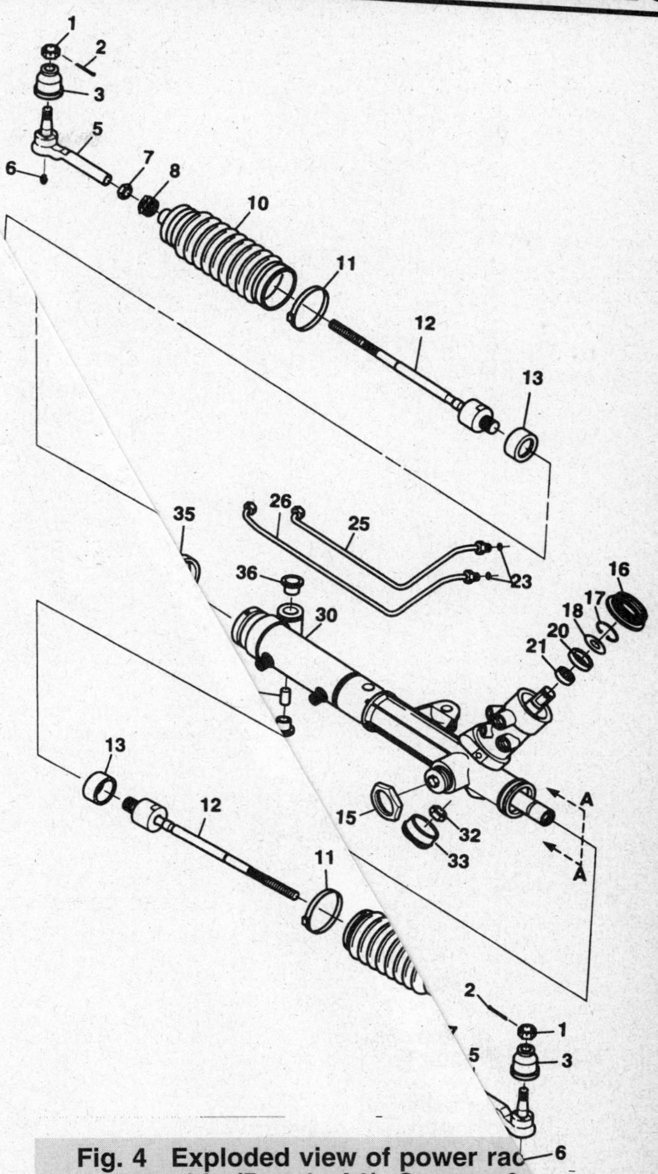

GC6029700409010X

Fig. 4 Exploded view of power rac... assembly (Part 1 of 2). Camaro & ...

...n

1. Loosen locknut, turn a... clockwise until it bottoms i... then back off 35–45.°
2. Tighten adjuster plug locknut t... fications while holding adjuster p...

RACK, PINION BOOT & BREATHER TUBE

EXCEPT ACHIEVA, SKYLARK & 1997-98 GRAND AM

Removal

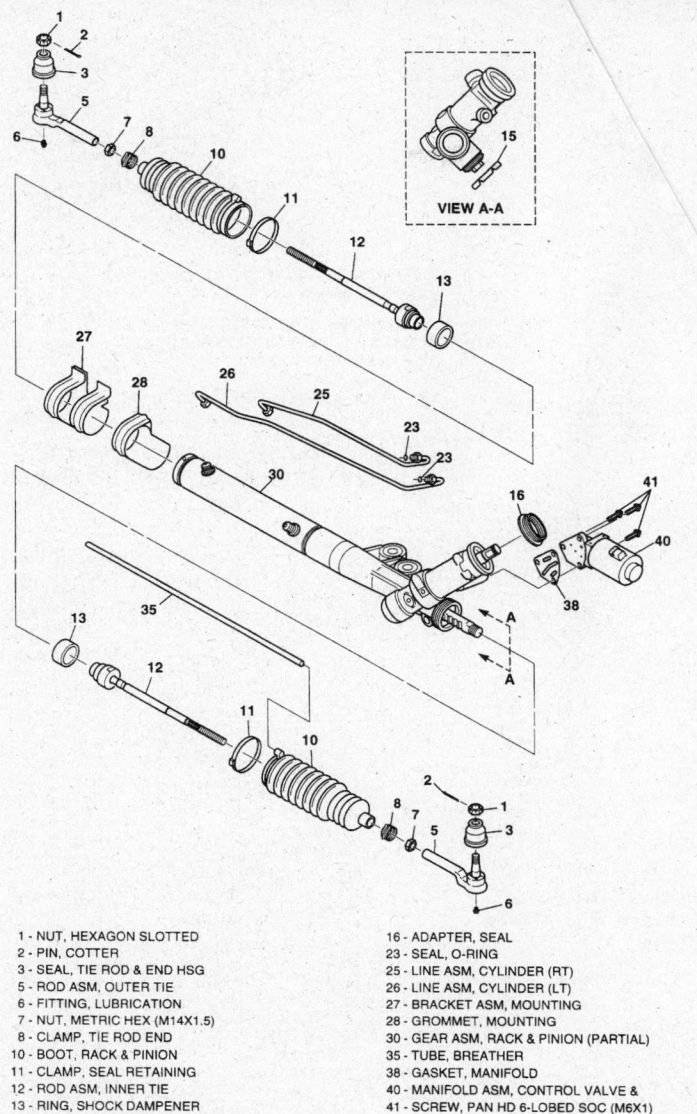

1. Remove outer tie rod.
2. Remove hex jam nut from inner tie rod assembly.
3. Remove tie rod end clamp, **Fig. 11,** then remove and discard boot clamp with side cutters.
4. Mark location of breather tube on

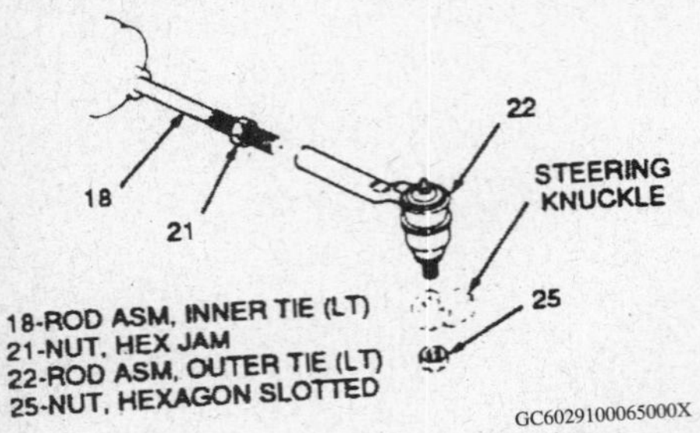

Fig. 5 Outer tie rod replacement. Except Achieva, Skylark & 1997–98 Grand Am

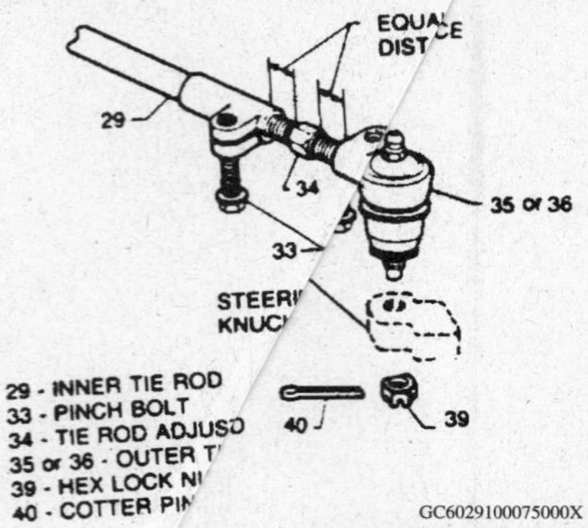

Fig. 6 er tie rod replacement. kylark & 1997–98 Grand Achiev Am

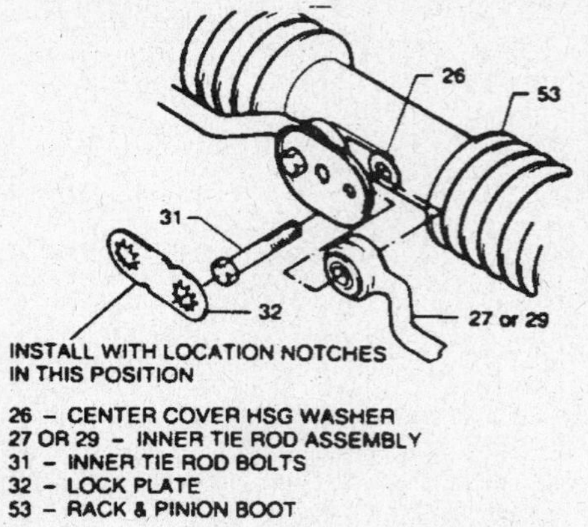

Fig. 7 Inner tie rod assembly. Achieva, Skylark & 1997–98 Grand Am

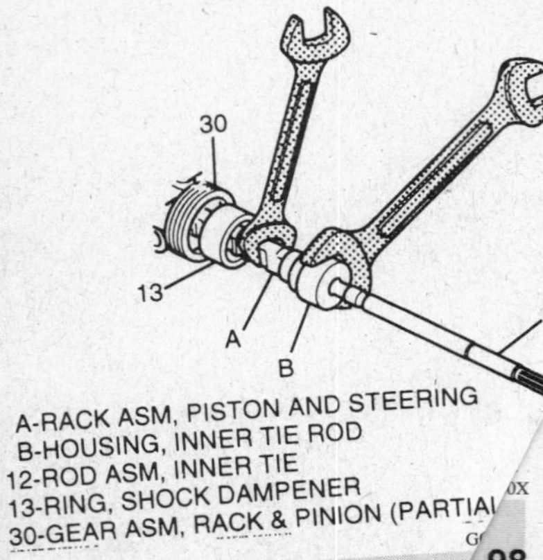

Fig. 8 Inner tie rod re -98 Except Achieva, Skylark Grand Am

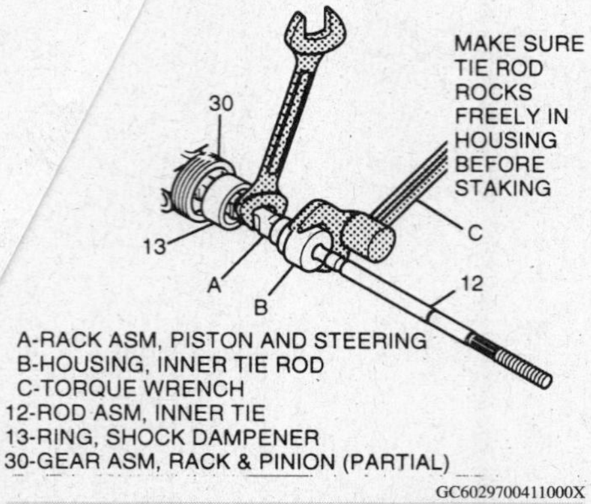

Fig. 9 Inner tie rod installation. Except Achieva, Skylark & 1997-98 Grand Am

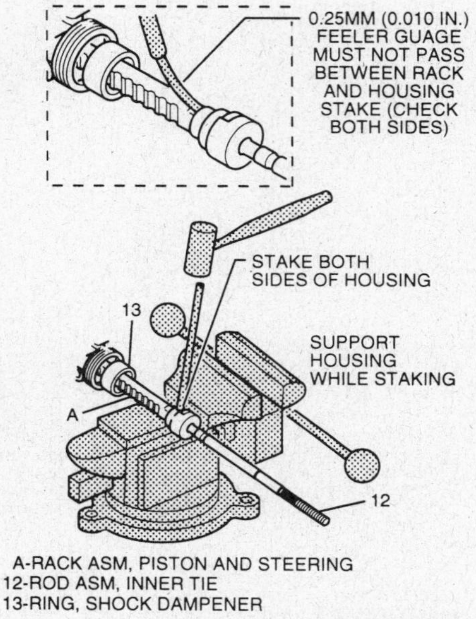

Fig. 10 Inner tie rod staking procedure. Except Achieva, Skylark & 1997-98 Grand Am

e, then re-
e.
housing before rem
move boot and br

Installation

nto boot.
tie rod or hous-

1. Install new bc
2. Apply greas ther tube.
   ing, **Fig. 12** sing until seated in
3. Align and ng.
4. Install b mp on boot and crimp.
   housin end clamp on boot and
5. Posi ers.
6. Pos
   se

AL, DUST SEAL & ANNULUS

PIN B CHIEVA, SKYLARK & 3 GRAND AM

I

ove rack and pinion steering assembly from vehicle.
Remove adjuster plug locknut from adjuster plug, **Fig. 13.**
3. Remove adjuster plug from housing, then the adjuster spring and rack bearing.
4. Remove retaining ring from valve bore of housing, then the dust cover, **Fig. 14.**
5. Holding stub shaft, remove hex locknut from pinion and valve assembly. **Stub shaft must be held to prevent damage to pinion teeth.**

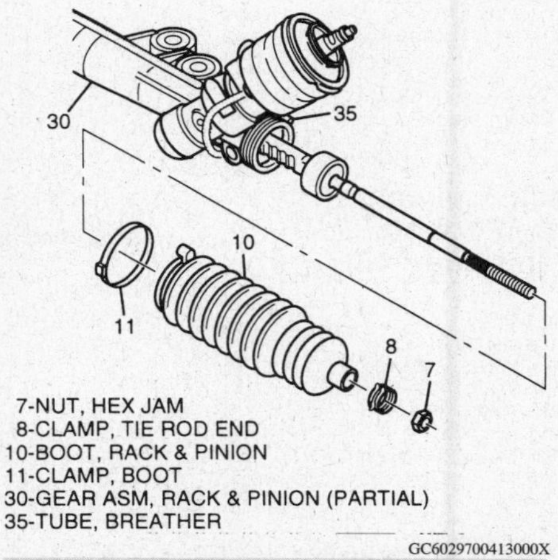

Fig. 11 Boot replacement. Except Achieva, Skylark & 1997-98 Grand Am

6. Using an arbor press, **Fig. 15,** press on threaded end of pinion until it is possible to remove stub shaft, dust seal, stub shaft seal and annulus bearing.

Installation

1. While holding valve stub shaft, install hex locknut onto pinion. Tighten locknut to specifications. **If stub shaft is not held, damage to pinion teeth will occur.**
2. Install dust cover to gear assembly.
3. Install stub shaft bearing annulus assembly onto valve stub shaft.
4. Install seal protector tool No. J-29810, or equivalent onto valve stub shaft.
5. Apply a small amount of grease between seals, then install stub shaft seal and dust seal over protector and into gear assembly.
6. Install retaining ring into groove in gear assembly.
7. Lubricate stub shaft and dust seal area with grease.
8. Coat rack bearing, adjuster spring and adjuster plug with lithium base grease and install gear assembly.
9. Adjust assembly as follows:

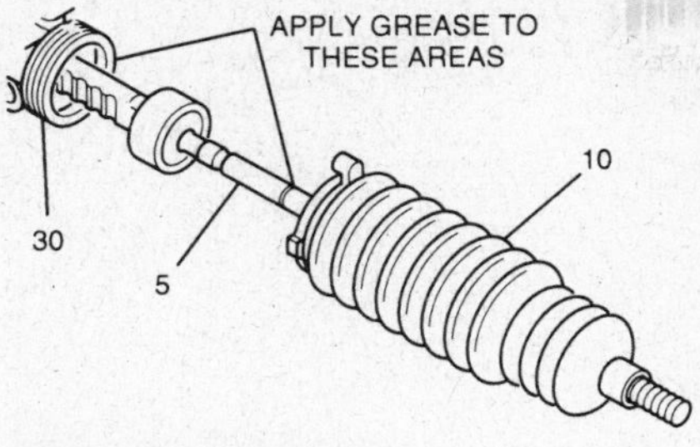

5-ROD ASM, INNER TIE
10-BOOT, RACK & PINION
30-GEAR ASM, RACK & PINION (PARTIAL)
GC6029700414000X

Fig. 12 Boot seal application. Except Achieva, Skylark & 1997-98 Grand Am

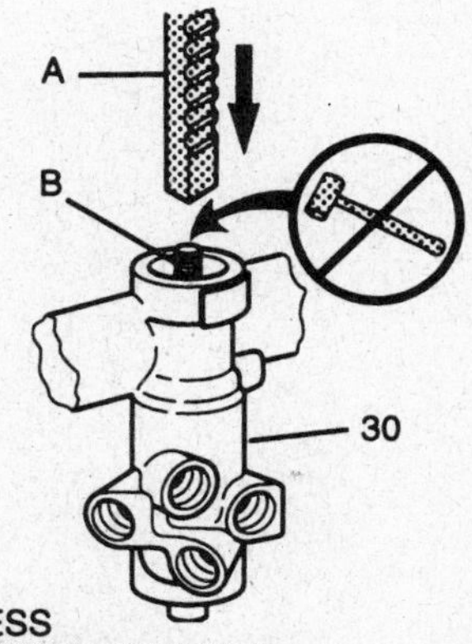

A-ARBOR PRESS
B-THREADED END OF PINION
30-GEAR ASM, RACK & PINION (PARTIAL)
GC6029700417000X

Fig. 15 Stub shaft, dust seal & stub shaft seal removal. Except Achieva, Skylark & 1997–98 Grand Am

a. With rack centered in gear assembly, turn adjuster plug clockwise until it bottoms in gear assembly, then back off 50–70.°
b. Measure rotational torque on pinion. Maximum pinion preload torque should be 16 inch lbs.

10. Install adjuster plug locknut to adjuster plug.
11. Tighten adjuster plug firmly against gear assembly while holding adjuster plug stationary.
12. Install rack and pinion assembly.

INNER PIVOT BUSHINGS

ACHIEVA, SKYLARK & 1997–98 GRAND AM

Refer to **Figs. 16 and 17** for removal and installation procedures.

FLANGE & STEERING COUPLING ASSEMBLY

ACHIEVA, SKYLARK & 1997–98 GRAND AM

1. Remove rack and pinion assembly from vehicle.

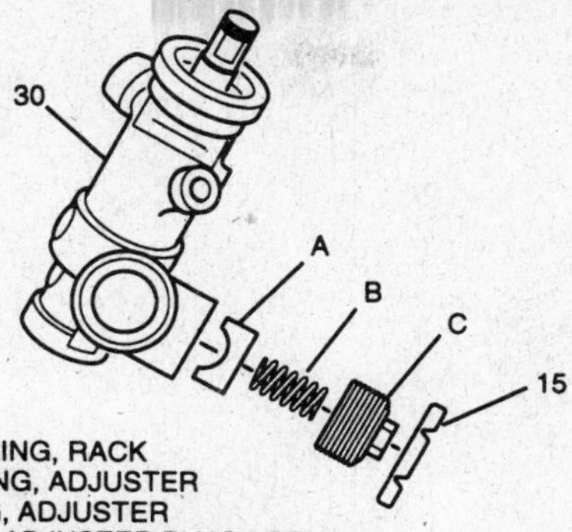

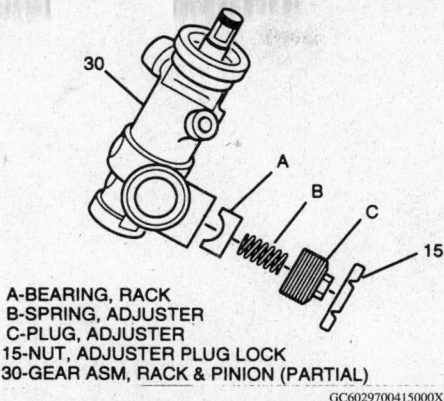

A-BEARING, RACK
B-SPRING, ADJUSTER
C-PLUG, ADJUSTER
15-NUT, ADJUSTER PLUG LOCK
30-GEAR ASM, RACK & PINION (PARTIAL)
GC6029700415000X

Fig. 13 Rack bearing removal. Except Achieva, Skylark & 1997–98 Grand Am

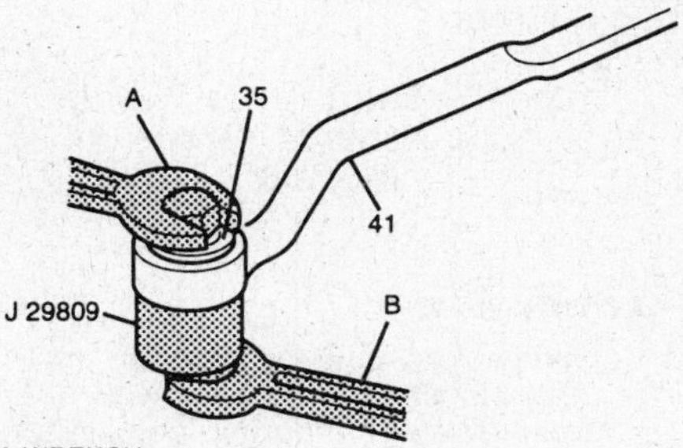

A-WRENCH
B-WRENCH
35-BUSHING, PIVOT
41-ASSEMBLY, INNER TIE ROD
GC6029200418000X

Fig. 16 Inner pivot bushing removal. Achieva, Skylark & 1997–98 Grand Am

2. Remove pinch bolt from flange and steering coupling assembly, then the coupling, **Fig. 18.**
3. Reverse procedure to install. **Torque** pinch bolt to 30 ft. lbs.

HYDRAULIC CYLINDER LINES

ACHIEVA, SKYLARK & 1997–98 GRAND AM

Refer to **Fig. 2** for replacement procedure. Ensure new O-rings are installed. **Torque** line fittings at valve end to 14 ft. lbs. **Torque** line fittings at cylinder end to 20 ft. lbs.

RACK GUIDE

ACHIEVA, SKYLARK & 1997–98 GRAND AM

Removal

1. Remove rack and pinion steering assembly from vehicle.
2. Remove lock plate from inner tie rod bolts and discard, **Figs. 2 and 19.**
3. Remove inner tie rod bolts, bolt support plate, cylinder lines and inner tie rod assemblies.
4. Cut and remove mounting grommet

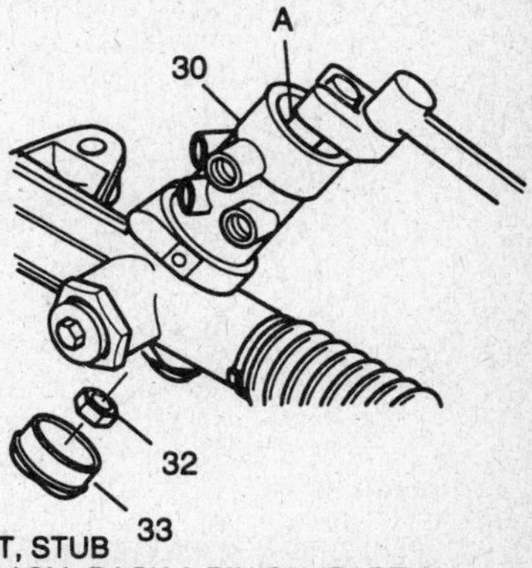

A-SHAFT, STUB
30-GEAR ASM, RACK & PINION (PARTIAL)
32-NUT, HEX LOCK
33-COVER, DUST
GC6029700416000X

Fig. 14 Retaining ring & locknut removal. Except Achieva, Skylark & 1997–98 Grand Am

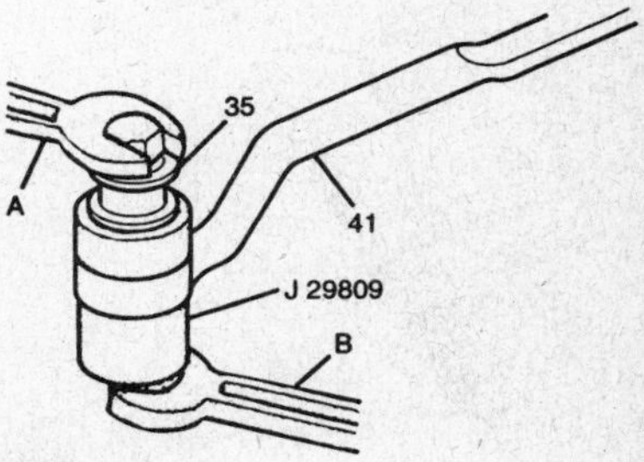

A-WRENCH
B-WRENCH
35-BUSHING, PIVOT
41-ASSEMBLY, INNER TIE ROD
GC6029200419000X

Fig. 17 Inner pivot bushing installation. Achieva, Skylark & 1997–98 Grand Am

and boot clamp.

5. Slide boot retaining bushing from rack and pinion boot, then boot assembly from rack and pinion housing.
6. Insert rack guide assembly from rod and rack assembly if required.

Installation

1. Slide boot retaining bushing from rack and pinion housing.
2. Slide new boot clamp on rack and pinion boot, then install boot retaining bushing into rack and pinion boot.
3. Install rack guide on rack.
4. Coat inner lip of boot retaining bushing lightly with grease, then install boot on housing. Ensure center housing cover washers are in place on boot.
5. Install inner tie rod bolts through cover washers and rack and pinion boot. Screw into rack lightly.
6. Slide boot and boot retaining bushing until seated in bushing groove in housing. Crimp new boot clamp.
7. Slide other end of boot into boot groove on cylinder end of housing.
8. Slide other end of boot into boot

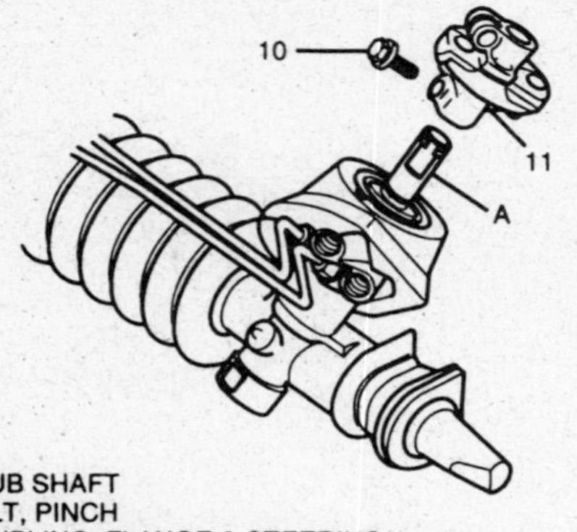

A-STUB SHAFT
10-BOLT, PINCH
11-COUPLING, FLANGE & STEERING

GC6029200420000X

Fig. 18 Flange & steering coupling assembly. Achieva, Skylark & 1997–98 Grand Am

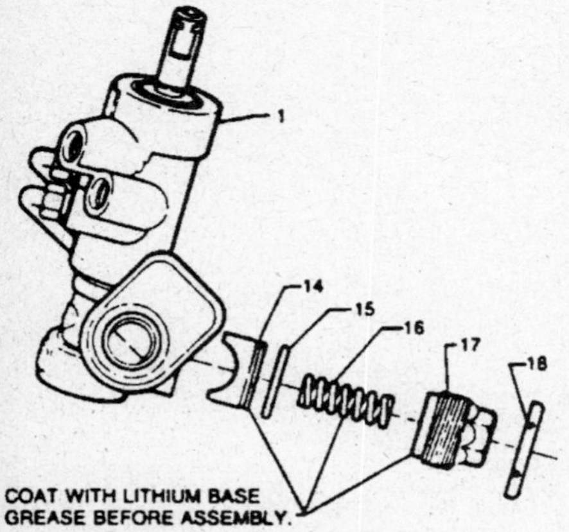

1 – HOUSING ASSEMBLY
14 – RACK BEARING
15 – O-RING SEAL
16 – ADJUSTER SPRING
17 – ADJUSTER PLUG
18 – ADJUSTER PLUG LOCK NUT

GC6029100082000X

Fig. 21 Rack bearing assembly. Achieva, Skylark & 1997–98 Grand Am

groove on cylinder end of housing and crimp new boot clamp. **Bridge of boot clamp must be crimped over split in boot retaining bushing to ensure proper sealing, Fig. 20.**

9. Install new lock plate with notches in proper position over flats of inner tie rod bolts.

RACK BEARINGS

ACHIEVA, SKYLARK & 1997–98 GRAND AM

Removal

1. Remove rack and pinion assembly from vehicle.
2. Remove adjuster plug nut from adjuster plug, then adjuster plug from housing, **Fig. 21.**
3. Remove adjuster spring and rack bearing with O-ring seal attached.

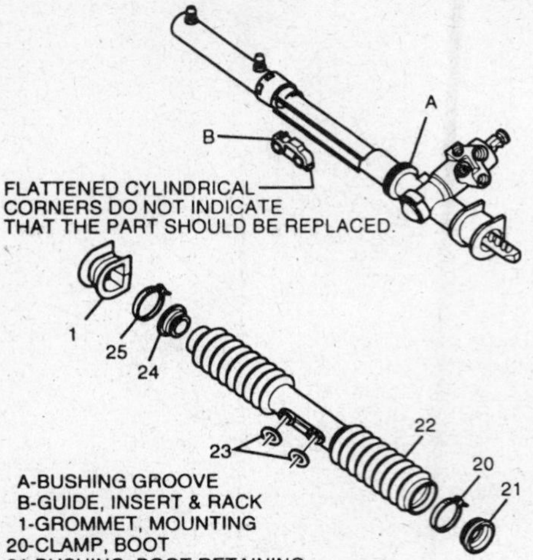

A-BUSHING GROOVE
B-GUIDE, INSERT & RACK
1-GROMMET, MOUNTING
20-CLAMP, BOOT
21-BUSHING, BOOT RETAINING
22-BOOT, RACK & PINION
23-WASHER, CENTER HOUSING COVER
24-BUSING, BOOT RETAINING
25-CLAMP, BOOT

GC6029200421000X

Fig. 19 Boot & rack guide assembly. Achieva, Grand Am & Skylark

Installation

1. Coat components with lithium grease, then install rack bearing with O-ring seal adjuster spring and adjuster plug into housing.
2. With rack centered in housing, turn adjuster plug clockwise until it bottoms in housing, then back off 35–45° and measure pinion torque. Maximum pinion preload torque is 16 inch lbs.
3. Install locknut to adjuster plug and tighten to specifications while holding adjuster plug stationary, **Fig. 22.**

STUB SHAFT SEALS & UPPER BEARING

ACHIEVA, SKYLARK & 1997–98 GRAND AM

Removal

1. Remove rack and pinion assembly from vehicle.
2. Remove retaining ring and dust cover, **Fig. 23.**
3. While holding stub shaft, remove locknut from pinion. **If stub shaft is not held, damage to pinion teeth will occur.**
4. Using suitable press equipment, press on threaded end of pinion until flush with ball bearing assembly. Complete removal of valve and pinion assembly is not required.
5. Remove stub shaft dust seal, stub shaft seal and stub shaft bearing annulus assembly from valve end of housing.

Installation

1. Install annulus assembly into gear.
2. Place seal protector tool No. J-29810, or equivalent onto stub shaft and install stub shaft seal and stub shaft dust seal

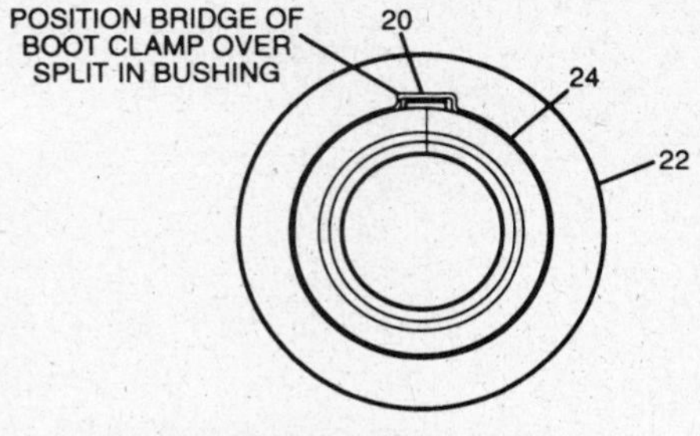

A-SPLIT IN BOOT RETAINING BUSHING
20-CLAMP, BOOT
22-BOOT, RACK & PINION
24-BUSHING, BOOT RETAINING

GC6029200422000X

Fig. 20 Boot clamp position. Achieva, Skylark & 1997–98 Grand Am

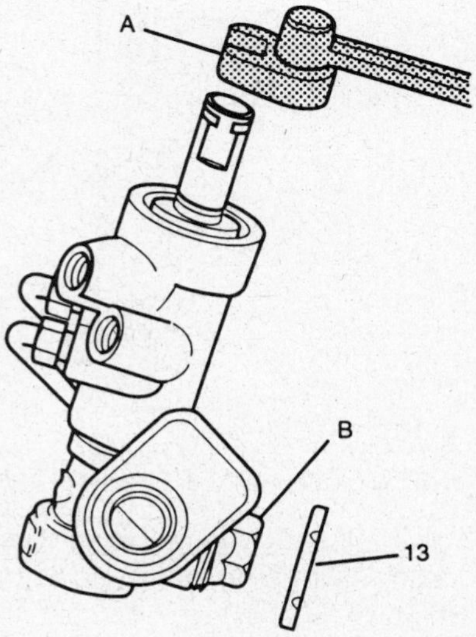

A-9/16" (14 MM) CROWFOOT WRENCH
B-PLUG, ADJUSTER
13-NUT, ADJUSTER PLUG LOCK

GC6029200423000X

Fig. 22 Rack bearing adjustment. Achieva, Skylark & 1997–98 Grand Am

over protector and into housing.

3. While holding the stub shaft firmly, seat pinion locknut and tighten to specifications.

BOOT OR RACK GUIDE

ACHIEVA, SKYLARK & 1997–98 GRAND AM

1. Cut off righthand hand mounting grommet and boot clamps, **Fig. 2.**
2. Slide boot retaining bushing from rack and pinion boot.
3. Slide boot assembly from rack and pinion housing.
4. Remove insert and rack guide assembly as required.
5. Slide boot retaining bushing from rack and pinion boot.

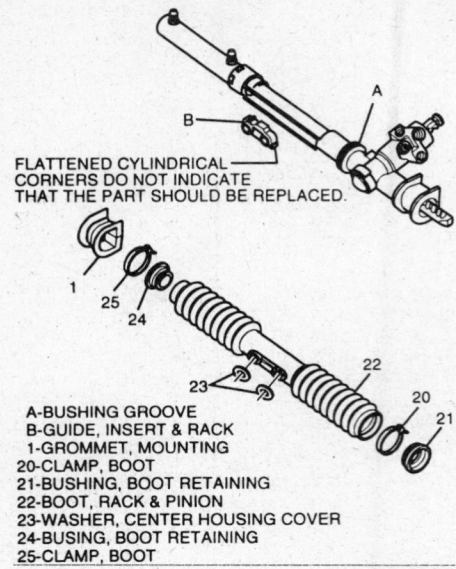

6. Slide new boot clamp onto rack and pinion boot.
7. Insert boot retaining bushing into rack and pinion boot.
8. Coat inner lip of boot retaining bushing lightly with suitable grease to facilitate assembly, then slide assembly onto housing assembly.
9. Ensure center housing cover washers are in place on rack and pinion boot.
10. Insert inner tie rod bolt through center housing cover washers, then the insert and rack guide and lightly thread bolt into rod and rack assembly to keep components in proper alignment.
11. Place boot retaining bushing onto cylinder tube of rack and pinion assembly, then slide into end of rack and pinion boot.
12. Slide boot clamp over cylinder end of housing and position on rack and pinion boot.
13. Slide rack and pinion boot and boot retaining bushing until seated in bushing groove in housing.
14. Position boot clamp on rack and pinion boot and crimp clamp.
15. Position bridge of boot clamp over split in boot retaining bushing and crimp clamp. **Bridge of boot clamp must be crimped over split in boot retaining bushing to ensure proper sealing.**

TIGHTENING SPECIFICATIONS

Component	Torque/Ft. Lbs.
EXCEPT CENTURY, CUTLASS SUPREME, GRAND PRIX, IMPALA, LUMINA, MONTE CARLO & REGAL	
Adjuster Plug Locknut	50
Hex Locknut	22
Hex Nut	50
Hexagon Slotted Nut	35
Inner Tie Rod Housing To Rack	70
Tie Rod Jam Nut	50
CENTURY, CUTLASS SUPREME, GRAND PRIX, LUMINA, MONTE CARLO & REGAL	
Adjuster Plug Locknut	55
Inner Tie Rod Housing To Rack	74
Tie Rod End Nuts (1997 Century, Grand Prix & Regal)	18①
Tie Rod End Nuts (1997 Cutlass Supreme, Lumina & Monte Carlo)	84②④
Tie Rod End Nuts (1998–2000)	22③
Tie Rod Jam Nut	50
IMPALA	
Fluid Cooler Pipe Bolt	84④
Inner Tie Rod	74
Intermediate Shaft Pinch Bolts	35
Steering Gear Cylinder Line Fittings	12.6
Steering Gear Mounting Bolts	59
Steering Gear Valve End Fittings	20
Steering Pump Mounting Bolts	25
Tie Rod End Nuts	22③
Tie Rod Jam Nuts	50

① — Tighten an additional 180°.

② — Tighten an additional 210°.

③ — Tighten an additional 120°.

④ — Inch lbs.

Saginaw Rack & Pinion Power Steering Gear w/Speed Sensitive Steering, General Motors

NOTE: "Electrical Symbol & Wire Color Code Identification" Located In The Front Of This Manual May Be Used As An Aid When Using Wiring Circuits Found In This Section.

INDEX

PRECAUTIONS

AIR BAG SYSTEMS

Refer to "Air Bag System Precautions" in the front of this manual for system disarming and arming procedures.

BATTERY GROUND CABLE

Prior to service, disconnect battery ground cable and isolate as required.

DESCRIPTION

Speed sensitive steering (Variable Effort or Magnasteer) varies the driver effort required to steer as vehicle speed changes. At low speeds, the system provides maximum power assist. At higher speeds, steering effort is increased to provide firmer steering and directional stability. Variable steering effort is accomplished by reducing power steering fluid flow from the pump as vehicle speed increases. When the vehicle is stationary, the system provides maximum flow. The speed sensitive steering system is made up of an Electronic Brake Control Module (EBCM) or Electronic Brake Traction Control Module (EBCTM), power steering fluid flow actuating device, steering wheel speed sensor, power rack and pinion and power steering pump.

Except for differences in valve machining, the design of the speed sensitive power rack and pinion assembly is the same as for the non-speed sensitive power rack and pinion.

DIAGNOSIS & TESTING

Accessing Diagnostic Trouble Codes

Diagnostic Trouble Codes (DTCs) must be read using a suitably programmed scan tool. There are no provisions for flash code diagnostics.

1. Turn ignition Off.
2. Connect suitably programmed scan tool to Data Link Connector (DLC).
3. Turn ignition On.
4. Select scan tool's Special Functions.
5. Read and record DTCs.

Diagnostic Trouble Code Interpretation

Refer to **Fig. 1** for diagnostic trouble code interpretation.

Code	Description
C0450	Steering Assist Control Actuator Circuit Malfunction
C0455	Steering Position Sensor Circuit Malfunction
C1241	Speed Sensitive Steering Circuit Malfunction
C1243	Steering Wheel Position Sensor Circuit Malfunction
C1273	Actuator Circuit Open Or Shorted To Ground
C1274	Actuator Circuit Shorted Or Solenoid Shorted

Fig. 1 Diagnostic trouble code interpretation

Wiring Diagrams

Refer to **Figs. 2 through 14** for wiring diagrams.

Diagnostic Tests

Refer to **Fig. 15** for diagnostic tests. Refer to **Figs. 16 through 18** for system inspections and **Figs. 19 through 38** for diagnostic trouble code tests.

Clearing Diagnostic Trouble Codes

DTCs cannot be cleared by disconnecting EBTCM or battery cables. Follow the scan tool manufacturer's instructions to clear DTCs.

POWER STEERING SYSTEM SERVICE

Component Service

POWER STEERING GEAR

Disassemble

Refer to **Figs. 39 through 42** for procedures. On Achieva, Skylark and 1997–98 Grand Am models, refer to "Saginaw Rack & Pinion Power Steering Gear Less Speed Sensitive Steering." For procedures not contained in this section, refer to "Saginaw Rack & Pinion Power Steering Gear Less Speed Sensitive Steering."

EBCM

1. Disconnect EBCM from bracket using pressure tabs.

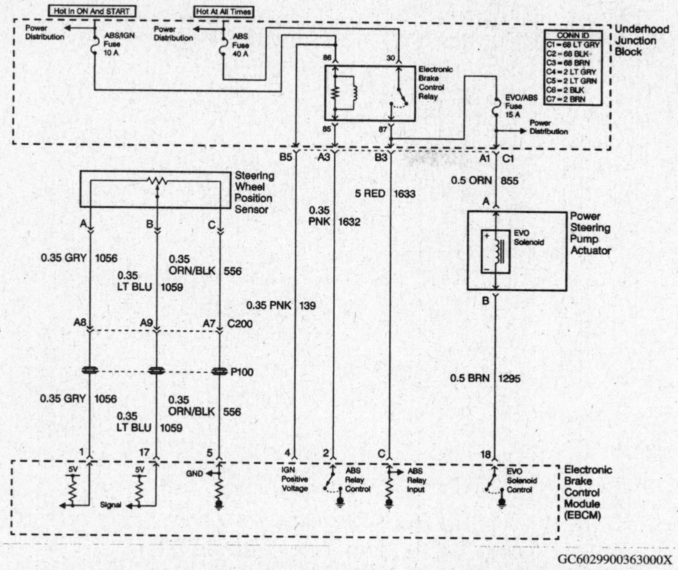

Fig. 2 Wiring diagram. Alero & 1999–2000 Grand Am

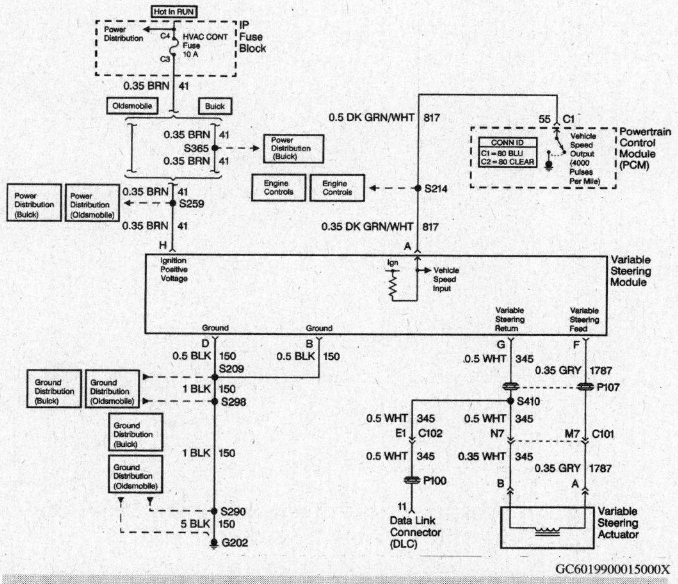

Fig. 4 Wiring diagram. 1999 Aurora & Riviera

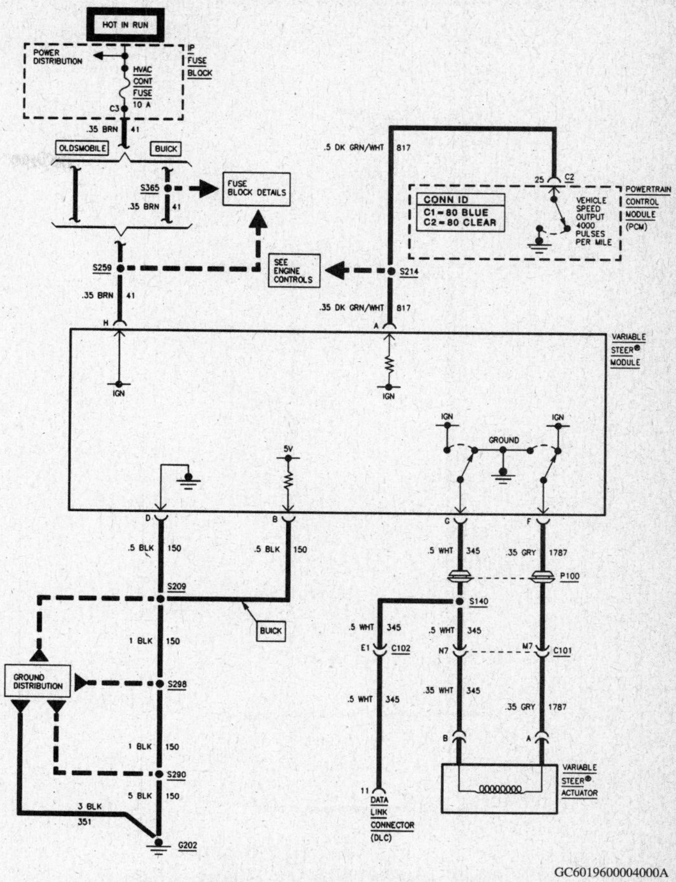

Fig. 3 Wiring diagram. 1997–98 Aurora & Riviera

2. Disconnect EBCM electrical connectors.
3. Remove EBCM.
4. Reverse procedure to install.

VARIABLE EFFORT STEERING PROGRAMMING

Bonneville, Eighty Eight, LeSabre, LSS, Park Avenue & Regency

Refer to **Fig. 43** for variable effort steering programming procedures.

Seville

Refer to **Fig. 44** for variable effort steering programming procedures.

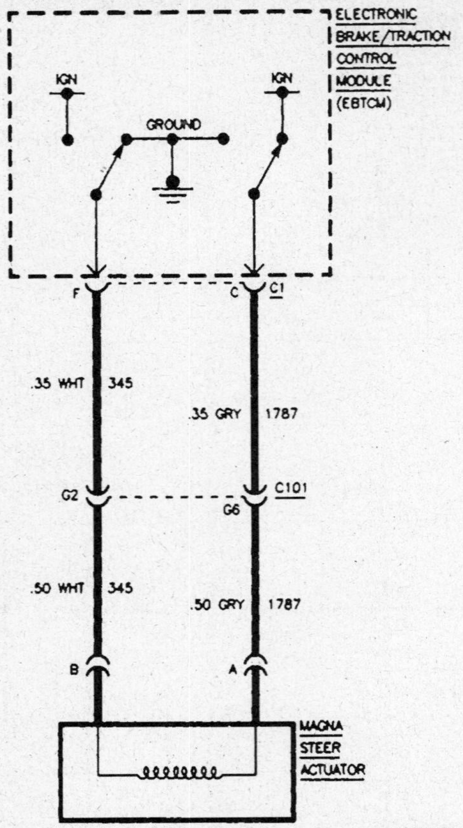

Fig. 5 Wiring diagram. Bonneville, Eighty Eight, LSS, LeSabre, Park Avenue & Regency

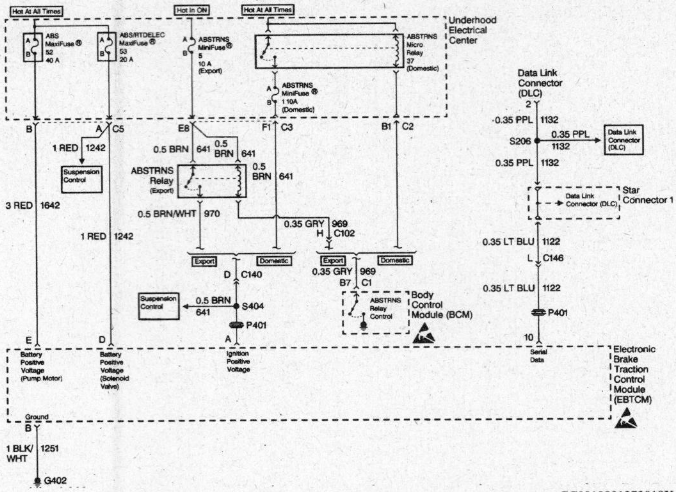

Fig. 6 Wiring diagram (Part 1 of 2). 1997–98 Corvette w/rear mounted EBTCM

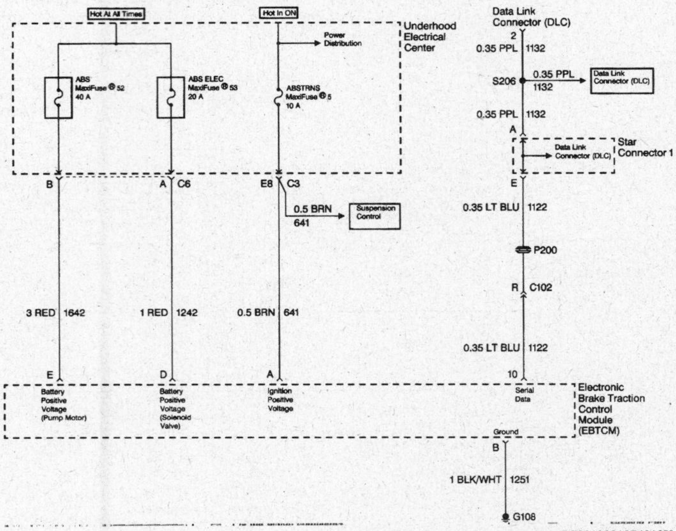

Fig. 7 Wiring diagram (Part 1 of 2). 1997–98 Corvette w/front mounted EBTCM

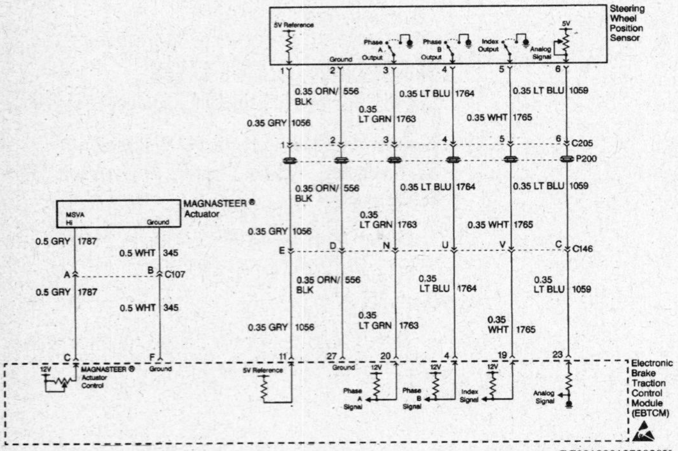

Fig. 6 Wiring diagram (Part 2 of 2). 1997–98 Corvette w/rear mounted EBTCM

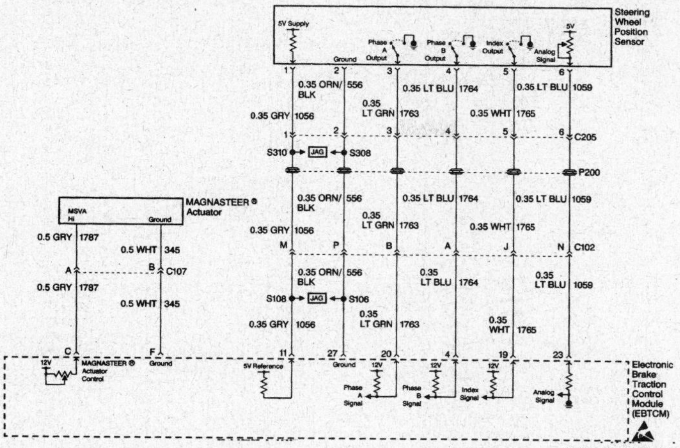

Fig. 7 Wiring diagram (Part 2 of 2). 1997–98 Corvette w/front mounted EBTCM

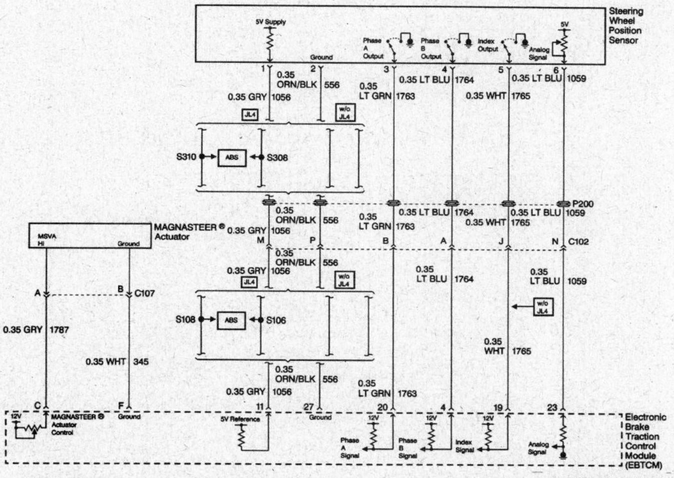

Fig. 8 Wiring diagram (Part 2 of 2). 1999–2000 Corvette

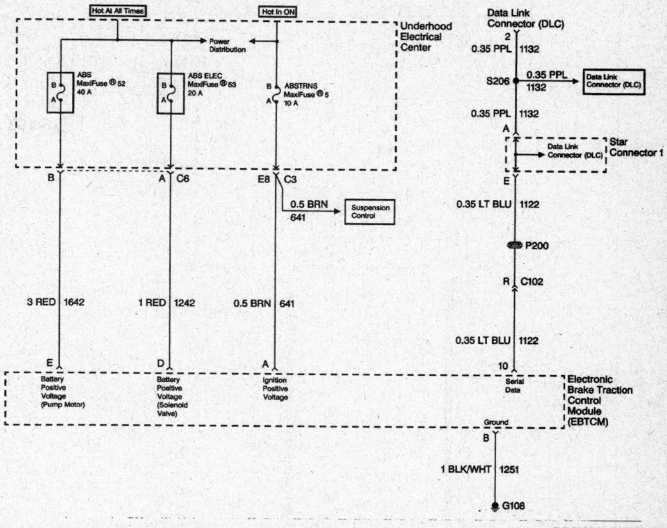

Fig. 8 Wiring diagram (Part 1 of 2). 1999–2000 Corvette

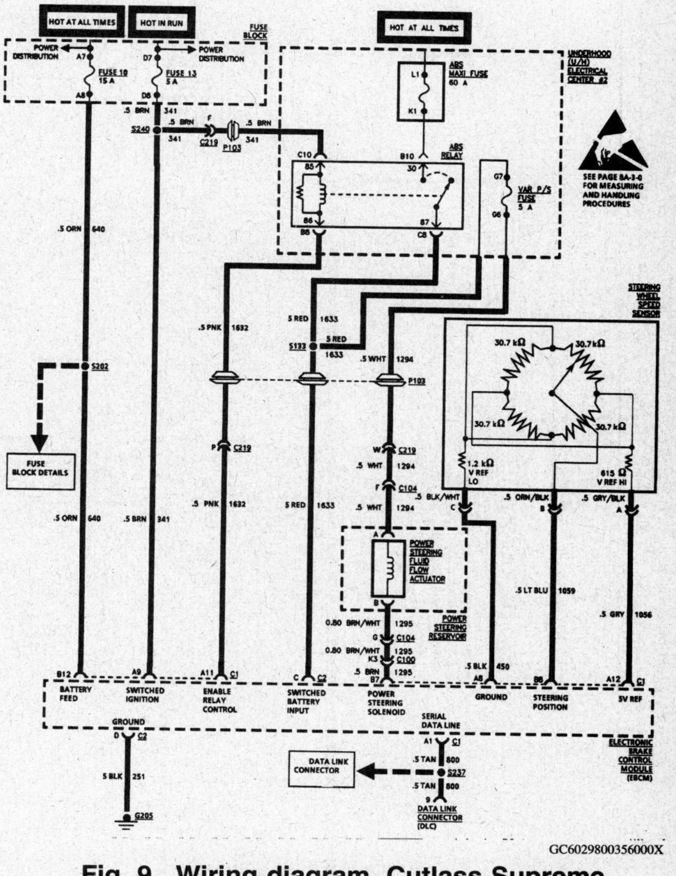

Fig. 9 Wiring diagram. Cutlass Supreme, Lumina & Monte Carlo

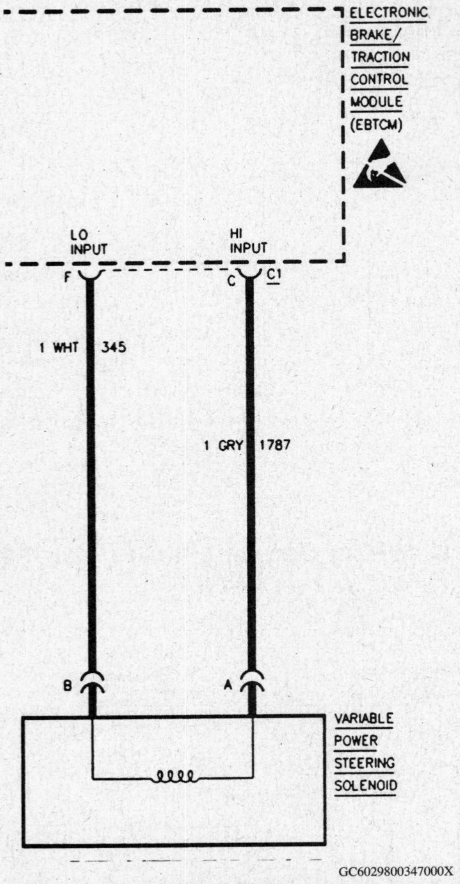

Fig. 10 Wiring diagram. DeVille & Eldorado

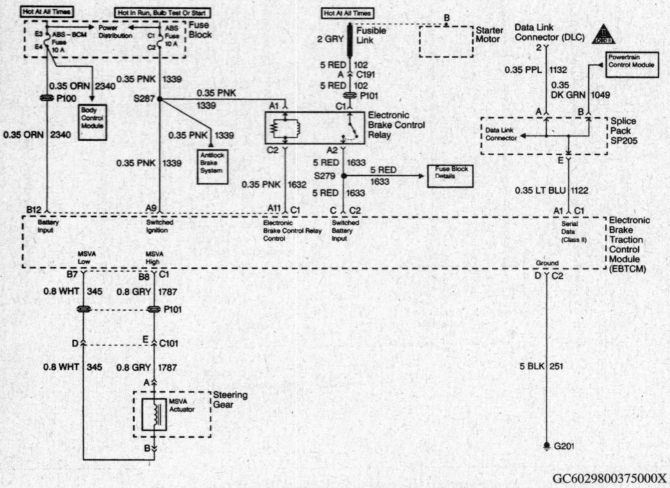

Fig. 12 Wiring diagram. 1998 Intrigue

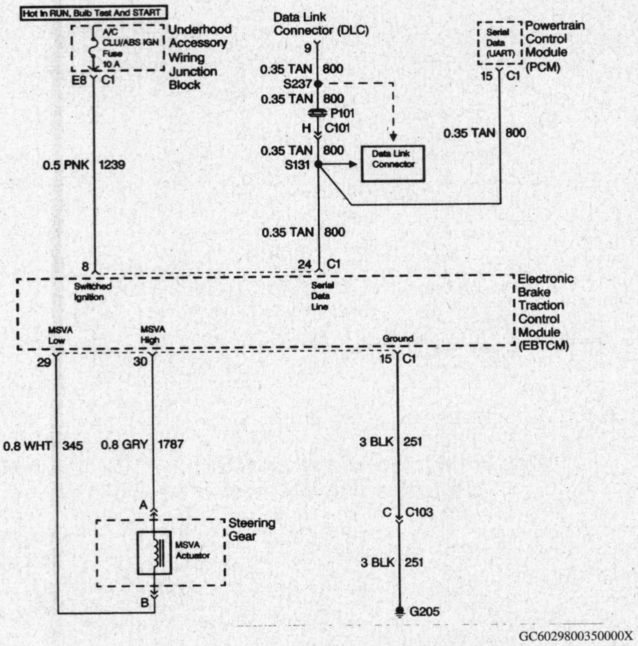

Fig. 11 Wiring diagram. Grand Prix

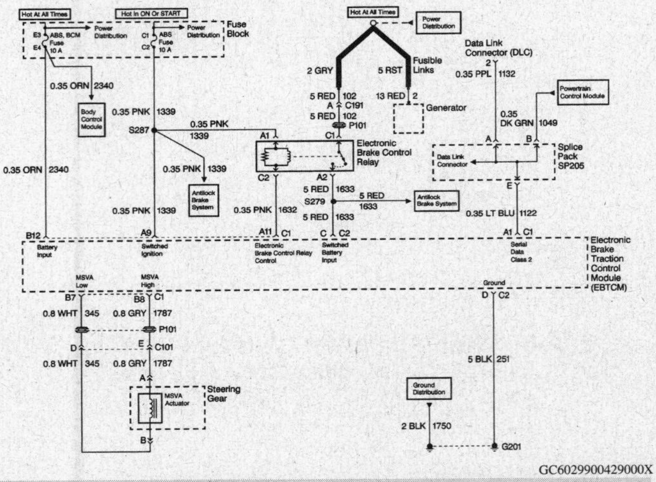

Fig. 13 Wiring diagram. 1999 Intrigue

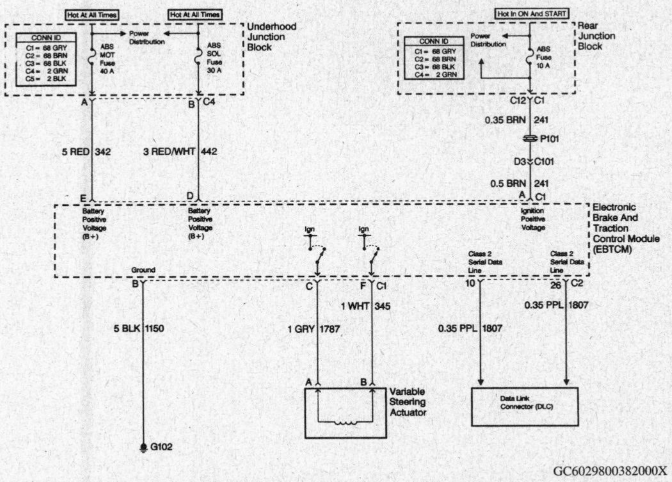

Fig. 14 Wiring diagram. Seville

DIAGNOSTIC CHART INDEX

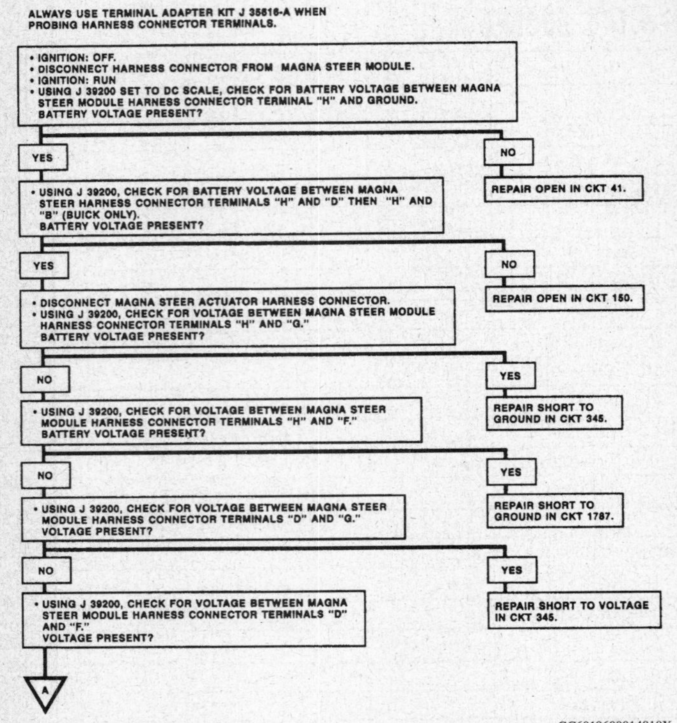

GC6019600014010X

Fig. 15 Test 1: Too Heavy, Too Light Or No Effort Assist (Part 1 of 2). Aurora & Riviera

ACTION	NORMAL RESULTS
Engine running, turn steering wheel right then left.	Steering wheel turns with minimal effort.
Connect scan tool, perform Variable Power Steering function test.	Steering wheel effort varies as test is performed.
Drive vehicle, turn steering wheel right then left.	As vehicle speed increases, the level of effort to turn steering wheel also increases.

GC6029800379000X

Fig. 16 System Inspection. Bonneville, Eighty Eight, LeSabre, LSS, Regency, & Park Avenue

ACTION	NORMAL RESULTS
[1] • Engine is running. • Turn steering wheel right then left.	Steering wheel turns with minimal effort.
[2] • Connect scan tool. • Perform Magna Steer® function test.	Steering wheel effort varies as test is performed.
[3] • Drive vehicle. • Turn steering wheel right then left.	As vehicle speed increases, the level of effort required to turn steering wheel also increases.

GC6029800378000X

Fig. 17 System Inspection. DeVille & Eldorado

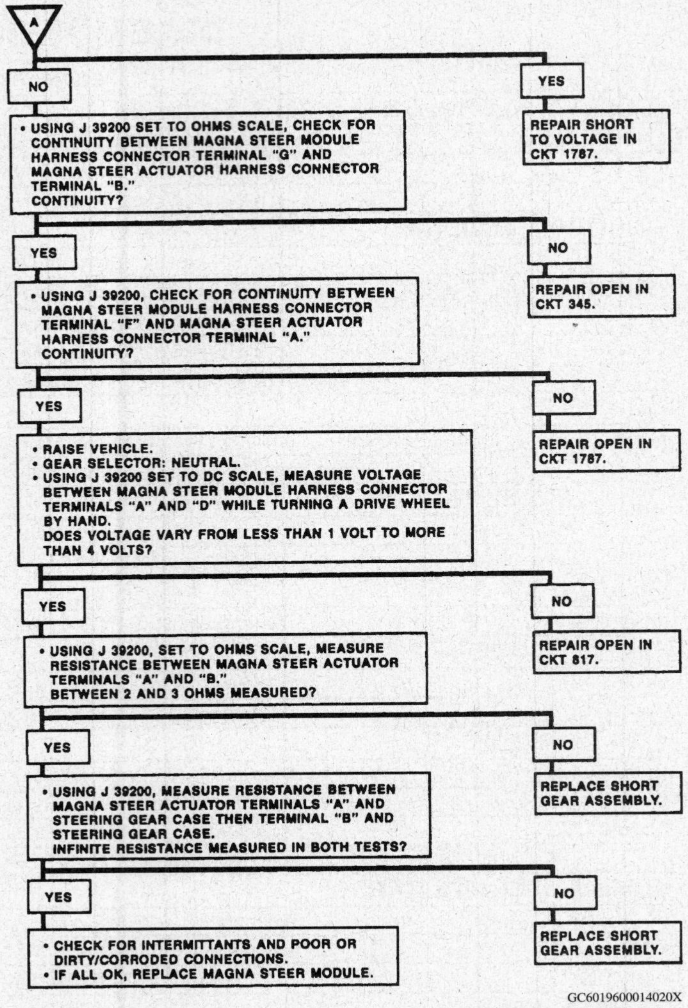

GC6019600014020X

Fig. 15 Test 1: Too Heavy, Too Light Or No Effort Assist (Part 2 of 2). Aurora & Riviera

Step	Action	Value(s)	Yes	No
1	Plug a scan tool into the Data Link Connector (DLC). Does the scan tool communicate with the Electronic Brake/Traction Control Module (EBTCM)?	—	*Go to Step 2*	*No Communication with EBCM/EBTCM*
2	1. Connect a scan tool to the Data Link Connector (DLC). 2. Run the Magna® Steer Electrical system test. Did the system pass?	—	Refer to *Variable Effort Steering Programming*	*Go to Step 3*
3	Check for DTC C1241-Variable Power Steering Circuit Malfunction. Is DTC C1241 set?	—	Refer to *DTC C1241 Magnasteer Malfunction*	Refer to *Variable Effort Steering Programming*

GC6029800381000X

Fig. 18 System Inspection. Seville

Step	Action	Value(s)	Yes	No
1	Was the ABS Diagnostic System Check performed?	—	Go to Step 2	Refer to Anti-Lock Brakes
2	1. Turn the ignition to the OFF position. 2. Disconnect the EBTCM harness connector. 3. Install the J39700 Universal Pinout Box using the J39700-530 cable adapter to the EBTCM harness connector only. 4. Using the J 39200 DMM, measure the resistance between the J 39700 terminals 29 and 30. Is the resistance within the specified range?	7 - 19 Ω	Go to Step 11	Go to Step 3
3	1. Disconnect the 2-way MAGNASTEER actuator connector. 2. Measure the resistance between the MAGNASTEER actuator pins A and B. Is the resistance within the specified range?	7 - 15 Ω	Go to Step 5	Go to Step 4
4	Replace the MAGNASTEER actuator. Has the repair been made and the system rechecked?	—	Refer to Anti-Lock Brakes	—
5	Measure the resistance between the J39700 terminal 29 and MAGNASTEER actuator harness connector terminal B. Is the resistance within the specified range?	0 - 2 Ω	Go to Step 7	Go to Step 6
6	Repair the open or the high resistance circuit 345. Is the circuit repair complete?	—	Refer to Anti-Lock Brakes	—
7	Measure the resistance between the J39700 terminal 30 and MAGNASTEER actuator harness connector terminal A. Is the resistance within the specified range?	0 - 2 Ω	Go to Step 9	Go to Step 8
8	Repair a poor connection or an open in circuit 1787. Has the repair been made and the system rechecked?	—	Refer to Anti-Lock Brakes	—

GC6029800351010X

Fig. 19 Code C0450: Steering Assist Control Actuator Circuit Malfunction (Part 1 of 3). Grand Prix

Step	Action	Value(s)	Yes	No
9	Measure the resistance between the J39700 terminals 29 and 30. Is the resistance within the specified range?	OL (Infinite)	Go to Step 22	Go to Step 10
10	Repair the short between circuit 345 and circuit 1787 Has the repair been made and the system rechecked?	—	Refer to Anti-Lock Brakes	—
11	Measure the resistance between the J39700 terminals 15 and 29. Is the resistance within the specified range?	OL (Infinite)	Go to Step 17	Go to Step 12
12	1. Disconnect the 2-way MAGNASTEER actuator connector. 2. Measure the resistance between the J39700 terminals 15 and 29. Is the resistance within the specified range?	OL (Infinite)	Go to Step 14	Go to Step 13
13	Repair the short to ground in circuit 345. Has the repair been made and the system rechecked?	—	Refer to Anti-Lock Brakes	—
14	Measure the resistance between the J39700 terminal 15 and 30. Is the resistance within the specified range?	OL (Infinite)	Go to Step 16	Go to Step 15
15	Repair the short to ground in circuit 1787. Has the repair been made and the system rechecked?	—	Refer to Anti-Lock Brakes	—
16	Measure the resistance between the MAGNASTEER actuator pin A and the steering gear case. Is the resistance within the specified range?	OL (Infinite)	Go to Step 22	Go to Step 4
17	1. Turn the ignition switch to the RUN position with the engine OFF. 2. Measure the voltage between J39700 terminals 15 and 29. Is the voltage within the specified range?	0 - 1 V	Go to Step 22	Go to Step 18
18	1. Disconnect the 2-way MAGNASTEER actuator connector. 2. Measure the voltage between J39700 terminals 15 and 29. Is the voltage within the specified range?	0 - 1 V	Go to Step 20	Go to Step 19
19	Repair the short to voltage in circuit 345. Has the repair been made and the system rechecked?	—	Refer to Anti-Lock Brakes	—
20	Measure the voltage between J39700 terminals 15 and 30. Is the voltage within the specified range?	0 - 1 V	Go to Step 22	Go to Step 21
21	Repair the short to voltage in circuit 1787. Has the repair been made and the system rechecked?	—	Refer to Anti-Lock Brakes	—

GC6029800351020X

Fig. 19 Code C0450: Steering Assist Control Actuator Circuit Malfunction (Part 2 of 3). Grand Prix

Step	Action	Value(s)	Yes	No
22	1. Turn the ignition switch to the OFF position. 2. Inspect EBTCM harness connectors and 2-way MAGNASTEER actuator harness connector for damage or corrosion which may result in an open or short with all connectors connected. Is there any evidence of damage or corrosion?	—	Go to Step 23	Go to Step 24
23	Repair as necessary. Has the repair been made and the system rechecked?	—	Refer to Anti-Lock Brakes	—
24	1. Reconnect all connectors. 2. Test drive the vehicle to a speed greater than 40 km/h (25 mph). Does the DTC C0450 reset?	—	Go to Step 25	Go to Step 26
25	Replace the EBTCM. Has the repair been made and the system rechecked?	—	Refer to Anti-Lock Brakes	—
26	Problem is intermittent.	—	—	—

GC6029800351030X

Fig. 19 Code C0450: Steering Assist Control Actuator Circuit Malfunction (Part 3 of 3). Grand Prix

Step	Action	Value(s)	Yes	No
1	Was the Variable Effort Steering System Check performed?	—	Go to *Step 2*	Refer to Steering System Inspection
2	1. Turn the ignition switch to the OFF position. 2. Disconnect the Electronic Brake and Traction Control Module (EBTCM) harness connector. 3. Install the *J 39700* Universal Pinout Box using the J 39700-530 cable adaptor to the EBTCM harness connector only. 4. Use the *J 39200* DMM in order to measure the resistance between the following components: • *J 39700* terminal 29 • *J 39700* terminal 30 Is the resistance within the specified range?	1.6 - 3.1Ω	Go to *Step 11*	Go to *Step 3*
3	1. Disconnect the two-way MAGNASTEER® actuator connector. 2. Using *J 39200* DMM, measure the resistance between the following components: • MAGNASTEER® actuator pin A • MAGNASTEER® actuator pin B Is the resistance within the specified range?	1.6 - 3.1Ω	Go to *Step 5*	Go to *Step 4*
4	Replace the MAGNASTEER® actuator. Is the repair complete?	—	Refer to Steering System Inspection	—
5	Using *J 39200* DMM, measure the resistance between the following components: • The *J 39700* terminal 29 • The MAGNASTEER® actuator harness connector terminal B Is the resistance within the specified range?	0–2Ω	Go to *Step 7*	Go to *Step 6*
6	Repair the open or high resistance in CKT 345. Is the repair complete?	—	Refer to Steering System Inspection	—
7	Using *J 39200* DMM, measure the resistance between the following components: • The *J 39700* terminal 30 • The MAGNASTEER® actuator harness connector terminal A Is the resistance within the specified range?	0–2Ω	Go to *Step 9*	Go to *Step 8*
8	Repair the open or high resistance in CKT 1787. Is the repair complete?	—	Refer to Steering System Inspection	—
9	Using *J 39200* DMM, measure the resistance between the following components: • The *J 39700* terminal 29 • The *J 39700* terminal 30 Is the resistance within the specified range?	OL (Infinite)	Go to *Step 22*	Go to *Step 10*

GC6029900430010X

Fig. 20 Code C0450: Steering Assist Control Actuator Circuit Malfunction (Part 1 of 3). 1999 Intrigue

Step	Action	Value(s)	Yes	No
10	Repair the short between CKT 345 and CKT 1787. Is the repair complete?	—	Refer to Steering System Inspection	—
11	Using *J 39200* DMM, measure the resistance between the following components: • The *J 39700* terminal 15 • The *J 39700* terminal 29 Is the resistance within the specified range?	OL (Infinite)	Go to *Step 17*	Go to *Step 12*
12	1. Disconnect the two-way MAGNASTEER® actuator connector. 2. Using *J 39200* DMM, measure the resistance between the following components: • The *J 39700* terminal 15 • The *J 39700* terminal 29 Is the resistance within the specified range?	OL (Infinite)	Go to *Step 14*	Go to *Step 13*
13	Repair the short to ground in CKT 345. Is the repair complete?	—	Refer to Steering System Inspection	—
14	Using *J 39200* DMM, measure the resistance between the following components: • The *J 39700* terminal 15 • The *J 39700* terminal 30 Is the resistance within the specified range?	OL (Infinite)	Go to *Step 16*	Go to *Step 15*
15	Repair the short to ground in CKT 1787. Is the repair complete?	—	Refer to Steering System Inspection	—
16	Using *J 39200* DMM, measure the resistance between the following components: • The MAGNASTEER® actuator pin A • The steering gear case Is the resistance within the specified range?	OL (Infinite)	Go to *Step 22*	Go to *Step 4*
17	1. Turn the ignition switch to the ON position with the engine OFF. 2. Using *J 39200* DMM, measure the voltage between the following components: • The *J 39700* terminal 15 • The *J 39700* terminal 29 Is the voltage within the specified range?	0–1V	Go to *Step 22*	Go to *Step 18*
18	1. Disconnect the two-way MAGNASTEER® actuator connector. 2. Using *J 39200* DMM, measure the voltage between the following components: • The *J 39700* terminal 15 • The *J 39700* terminal 29. Is the voltage within the specified range?	0–1V	Go to *Step 20*	Go to *Step 19*
19	Repair the short to voltage in CKT 345. Is the repair complete?	—	Refer to Steering System Inspection	—

GC6029900430020X

Fig. 20 Code C0450: Steering Assist Control Actuator Circuit Malfunction (Part 2 of 3). 1999 Intrigue

Step	Action	Value(s)	Yes	No
1	Was the Variable Effort Steering System Check performed?	—	*Go to Step 2*	Refer to Steering System Inspection
2	1. Point the front wheels straight ahead. 2. Using a scan tool check the Steering Wheel Position Sensor Analog voltage. Is the voltage within the range specified within the value(s) column?	2–3 V	*Go to Step 4*	*Go to Step 3*
3	Is the voltage in the range specified within the values(s) column?	0.15–4.84 V	*Go to Step 5*	*Go to Step 9*
4	Replace the EBTCM. Is the repair complete?	—	Refer to Steering System Inspection	—
5	1. Turn the ignition switch to the OFF position. 2. Disable the Supplemental Inflatable Restraint (SIR). 3. Remove the Inflatable Restraint Steering Wheel Module Coil. 4. Remove the Intermediate Steering Shaft. 5. Turn the ignition switch to the ON position, engine off. 6. Using a scan tool monitor the Steering Wheel Position Sensor analog voltage as you rotate the steering column shaft. 7. Turn the steering column shaft until the analog voltage is close to 2.5 volts. Does the analog voltage move smoothly to, or close to, 2.5 volts?	—	*Go to Step 7*	*Go to Step 6*
6	Replace the Steering Wheel Position Sensor. Is the replacement complete?	—	Refer to Steering System Inspection	—

GC6029900431010X

Fig. 21 Code C0455: Steering Position Sensor Circuit Malfunction (Part 1 of 3). 1999 Intrigue

Step	Action	Value(s)	Yes	No
20	Using *J 39200* DMM, measure the voltage between the following components: • The *J 39700* terminal 15 • The *J 39700* terminal 30 Is the voltage within the specified range?	0–1V	Go to *Step 22*	Go to *Step 21*
21	Repair the short to voltage in CKT 1787. Is the repair complete?	—	Refer to Steering System Inspection	—
22	1. Turn the ignition switch to the OFF position. **Important:** Damage or corrosion may result in an open or short with all of the connectors connected. 2. Inspect the EBTCM harness connectors for the following conditions: • Damage • Corrosion **Important:** Damage or corrosion may result in an open or short with all of the connectors connected. 3. Inspect the two-way MAGNASTEER® actuator harness connector for the following conditions: • Damage • Corrosion Do the connectors exhibit signs of corrosion or damage?	—	Go to *Step 23*	Go to *Step 24*
23	1. Repair the damaged or corroded harness connectors in the EBTCM. 2. Repair the damaged or corroded two-way MAGNASTEER® actuator harness connector. Is the repair complete?	—	Refer to Steering System Inspection	—
24	1. Reconnect all of the connectors. 2. Test drive the vehicle to a speed greater than 40 km/h (25 mph). Did the DTC C0450 reset?	—	Go to *Step 25*	Refer to Steering System Inspection
25	Replace the EBTCM. Is the repair complete?	—	Refer to Steering System Inspection	—

GC6029900430030X

Fig. 20 Code C0450: Steering Assist Control Actuator Circuit Malfunction (Part 3 of 3). 1999 Intrigue

Step	Action	Value(s)	Yes	No
7	1. Leave the steering column shaft centered at 2.5 volts. 2. Turn the ignition switch to the OFF position. 3. Install the Intermediate Steering Shaft. 4. Install the Inflatable Restraint Steering Wheel Module Coil. 5. Enable the SIR. Is the repair complete?	—	*Go to Step 8*	—
8	1. Turn the ignition switch to the ON position, engine off. 2. Using a scan tool clear DTC C0455. 3. Drive vehicle above 30 Km/h (18 mph) for several minutes in a straight line. 4. Using a scan tool check for DTC C0455. Did DTC C0455 set as a current DTC?	—	*Go to Step 4*	Refer to Steering System Inspection
9	1. Turn the Ignition switch to the OFF position. 2. Disconnect the EBTCM. 3. Install the *J 39700* Universal Pinout Box using the J 39700-530 cable adapter to the EBTCM harness connector and the EBTCM. 4. Turn the ignition switch to the ON position, engine off. 5. Using *J 39200* DMM, measure the voltage between ground and terminal 26 of *J 39700.* Is the voltage within the range specified in the value(s) column?	0.15–4.84 V	*Go to Step 4*	*Go to Step 10*
10	1. Turn the ignition switch to the OFF position. 2. Disconnect the Steering Wheel Position Sensor connector. 3. Turn the ignition switch to the ON position, engine off. 4. Using the *J 39200* DMM, measure the voltage between ground and terminal 1 of the Steering Wheel Position Sensor harness connector. Is the voltage within the range specified in the value(s) column?	4.75–5.25 V	*Go to Step 11*	*Go to Step 18*
11	Using *J 39200* DMM, measure the resistance between the Steering Wheel Position Sensor harness connector terminal 2 and a good ground. Is the resistance within the range specified in the value(s) column?	0–5 Ω	*Go to Step 12*	*Go to Step 24*
12	1. Turn the Ignition switch to the ON position, engine off. 2. Using the *J 39200* DMM, measure the voltage at terminal 6 of the Steering Wheel Position Sensor harness connector. Is the voltage within the range specified in the value(s) column?	Above 1 V	*Go to Step 13*	*Go to Step 14*
13	Repair CKT 1059 for a short to voltage, being sure to check for a short to CKT 1056. Is the repair complete?	—	Refer to Steering System Inspection	—
14	1. Turn the ignition switch to the OFF position. 2. Disconnect the J 39700-530 cable adapter from the EBTCM leaving the J 39700-530 cable adapter connected to the EBTCM harness connector. 3. Using *J 39200* DMM, measure the resistance between terminals 26 and 15 of *J 39700.* Is the resistance within the range specified within the value(s) column?	OL (Infinite)	*Go to Step 16*	*Go to Step 15*

GC6029900431020X

Fig. 21 Code C0455: Steering Position Sensor Circuit Malfunction (Part 2 of 3). 1999 Intrigue

Step	Action	Value(s)	Yes	No
15	Repair CKT 1059 for a short to ground, being sure to check for a short to CKT 556. Is the repair complete?	—	Refer to Steering System Inspection	—
16	1. Connect a jumper wire between terminals 26 and 18 of *J 39700*. 2. Using *J 39200* DMM, measure the resistance between the Steering Wheel Position Sensors harness connector terminals 2 and 6. Is the resistance within the range specified within the value(s) column?	0–5 Ω	*Go to Step 6*	*Go to Step 17*
17	Repair CKT 1059 for an open or high resistance. Is the repair complete?	—	Refer to Steering System Inspection	—
18	Using the *J 39200* DMM, measure the voltage at terminal 1 of the Steering Wheel Position Sensor harness connector. Is the voltage in the range specified in the value(s) column?	above 5.25 V	*Go to Step 19*	*Go to Step 20*
19	Repair CKT 1056 for a short to battery. Is the repair complete?	—	Refer to Steering System Inspection	—
20	1. Turn the ignition switch to the OFF position. 2. Disconnect the J 39700-530 cable adapter from the EBTCM leaving the J 39700-530 cable adapter connected to the EBTCM harness connector. 3. Connect a jumper wire between terminals 28 and 15 of *J 39700*. 4. Using *J 39200* DMM, measure the resistance between the Steering Wheel Position Sensor harness connector terminal 1 and a good ground. Is the resistance within the range specified within the value(s) column?	0–5 Ω	*Go to Step 22*	*Go to Step 21*
21	Repair CKT 1056 for an open or high resistance. Is the repair complete?	—	Refer to Steering System Inspection	—
22	1. Remove the jumper wire from *J 39700*. 2. Using *J 39200* DMM, measure the resistance between the Steering Wheel Position Sensor harness connector terminal 1 and a good ground. Is the resistance within the range specified in the values column?	OL (infinite)	*Go to Step 4*	*Go to Step 23*
23	Repair CKT 1056 for a short to ground. Is the repair complete?	—	Refer to Steering System Inspection	—
24	1. Turn the ignition switch to the OFF position. 2. Disconnect the J 39700-530 cable adapter from the EBTCM leaving the J 39700-530 cable adapter connected to the EBTCM harness connector. 3. Using the *J 39200* DMM, measure the resistance between the *J 39700* terminal 18 and terminal 2 of the Steering Wheel Position Sensor harness connector. Is the resistance within the range specified in the value(s) column?	0-5Ω	*Go to Step 4*	*Go to Step 25*
25	Repair CKT 556 for an open or high resistance. Is the repair complete?	—	Refer to Steering System Inspection	—

GC6029900431030X

Fig. 21 Code C0455: Steering Position Sensor Circuit Malfunction (Part 3 of 3). 1999 Intrigue

Step	Action	Value(s)	Yes	No
11	1. Reconnect the Variable Power Steering Solenoid connector. 2. Using J39200, measure the resistance between terminals C and F of J39700. Is the resistance within the specified range?	1.6 - 3.1 Ω	Go to Step 17	Go to Step 12
12	Is the resistance less than the range specified in the value(s) column?	-	Go to Step 13	Go to Step 14
13	Repair CKT 1787 (GRY) and 345 (WHT) for a short together.	-	Go to System Check.	-
14	1. Connect a fused jumper wire between terminals C and B of J39700. 2. Disconnect the Variable Power Steering Solenoid. 3. Using J39200, measure the resistance between the Variable Power Steering Solenoid harness connector terminal A and a good ground. Is the resistance within the specified range?	0 - 5 Ω	Go to Step 15	Go to Step 16
15	Repair CKT 345 (WHT) for an open. Is the wire repair complete?	-	Go to System Check.	-
16	Repair CKT 1787 (GRY) for an open. Is the wire repair complete?	-	Go to System Check.	-
17	1. Turn the ignition switch to the RUN position. 2. Using J39200, measure for voltage at terminal C of J39700. Is the voltage within the specified range?	above 1 volt	Go to Step 18	Go to Step 19
18	Repair CKT 1787 (GRY) for a short to voltage. Is the repair complete?	-	Go to System Check.	-
19	Using J39200, measure for voltage at terminal F of J39700. Is the voltage within the specified range?	above 1 volt	Go to Step 20	Go to Step 21
20	Repair CKT 345 (WHT) for a short to voltage. Is the repair complete?	-	Go to System Check.	-
21	Replace the EBTCM. Is the module replacement complete?	-	Go to System Check.	-

GC6029800355020X

Fig. 22 Code C1241: Speed Sensitive Steering Circuit Malfunction (Part 2 of 2). 1998 Bonneville, Eighty Eight, LeSabre, LSS, Park Avenue & Regency

Step	Action	Value(s)	Yes	No
1	Was the Steering Controls Diagnostic System Check performed?	-	Go to Step 2	Go to System Check.
2	Inspect wiring and connectors for damage. Is physical damage evident?	-	Go to Step 3	Go to Step 4
3	Repair as necessary. Is repair complete?	-	Go to System Check.	-
4	1. Disconnect Variable Power Steering Solenoid connector. 2. Using J39200, measure the resistance between terminals A and B on the Variable Power Steering Solenoid. Is the resistance within the specified range?	1.6 - 3.1 Ω	Go to Step 5	Go to Step 6
5	1. Using J39200, measure the resistance between terminal A and a good ground. 2. Using J39200, measure the resistance between terminal B and a good ground. Was the resistance of either measurement within the specified range?	-	Go to Step 6	Go to Step 7
6	Replace the Variable Power Steering Solenoid. Is the actuator replacement complete?	-	Go to System Check.	-
7	1. Turn the ignition switch to the OFF position. 2. Disconnect the Electronic Brake/Traction Control Module (EBTCM) connector C1. 3. Install a J39700 universal pinout box using J39700-25 cable adapter to the EBTCM harness only. 4. Using J39200, measure the resistance between terminals C and B of J39700. Is the resistance within the specified range?	Less than OL	Go to Step 8	Go to Step 9
8	Repair CKT 1787 (GRY) for a short to ground. Is the repair complete?	-	Go to System Check.	-
9	Using J39200, measure the resistance between terminals F and B of J39700. Is the resistance within the range specified?	Less than OL	Go to Step 10	Go to Step 11
10	Repair CKT 345 (WHT) for a short to ground. Is the repair complete?	-	Go to System Check.	-

GC6029800355010X

Fig. 22 Code C1241: Speed Sensitive Steering Circuit Malfunction (Part 1 of 2). 1998 Bonneville, Eighty Eight, LeSabre, LSS, Park Avenue & Regency

Step	Action	Value(s)	Yes	No
1	Did you perform the Variable Effort Steering System Inspection?	—	Go to *Step 2*	Refer to System Inspection
2	Inspect the wiring and the connectors for damage. Is physical damage evident?	—	Go to *Step 3*	Go to *Step 4*
3	Repair damage to the wiring and connectors. Did you complete the repair?	—	Refer to System Inspection	—
4	1. Turn OFF the ignition. 2. Disconnect the EBCM/EBTCM connector. 3. Install the *J 39700* universal pinout box using the *J 39700 - 25* cable adapter to the EBCM/EBTCM harness connector only. 4. Use the *J 39200* DMM to measure the resistance between the *J 39700* terminal C and terminal F. Is the resistance within the specified range?	1.6–3.1 Ω	Go to *Step 19*	Go to *Step 5*
5	1. Disconnect the variable steering actuator connector. 2. Use the *J 39200* to measure the resistance between the variable steering actuator terminal A and terminal C. Is the resistance within the specified range?	1.6–3.1 Ω	Go to *Step 6*	Go to *Step 12*
6	Use the *J 39200* to measure the resistance between the *J 39700* terminal C and the variable steering actuator connector terminal A. Is the resistance less than the specified value?	0.5 Ω	Go to *Step 7*	Go to *Step 13*
7	Use the *J 39200* to measure the resistance between the *J 39700* terminal F and the variable steering actuator connector terminal B. Is the resistance less than the specified value?	0.5 Ω	Go to *Step 8*	Go to *Step 14*
8	Use the *J 39200* to measure the resistance between the *J 39700* terminal F and a good ground. Is the resistance less than the specified value?	OL	Go to *Step 15*	Go to *Step 9*
9	Use the *J 39200* to measure the resistance between the *J 39700* terminal F and a good ground. Is the resistance greater than the specified value?	1 V	Go to *Step 16*	Go to *Step 10*
10	Use the *J 39200* to measure the resistance between the *J 39700* terminal C and a good ground. Is the resistance less than the specified value?	OL	Go to *Step 17*	Go to *Step 11*
11	Use the *J 39200* to measure the resistance between the *J 39700* terminal C and a good ground. Is the resistance greater than the specified value?	1 V	Go to *Step 18*	Go to *Step 19*
12	Replace the variable steering actuator. Did you complete the repair?	—	Refer to System Inspection	—
13	Repair the open in CKT 1787. Did you complete the repair?	—	Refer to System Inspection	—
14	Repair the open in CKT 345. Did you complete the repair?	—	Refer to System Inspection	—

GC6029900426010X

Fig. 23 Code C1241: Speed Sensitive Steering Circuit Malfunction (Part 1 of 2). 1999–2000 Bonneville, Eighty Eight, LeSabre, LSS, Park Avenue & Regency

Step	Action	Value(s)	Yes	No
15	Repair the short to ground in CKT 345. Did you complete the repair?	—	Refer to System Inspection	—
16	Repair the short to voltage in CKT 345. Did you complete the repair?	—	Refer to System Inspection	—
17	Repair the short to ground in CKT 1787. Did you complete the repair?	—	Refer to System Inspection	—
18	Repair the short to voltage in CKT 1787. Did you complete the repair?	—	Refer to System Inspection	—
19	Replace the EBCM/EBTCM. Did you complete the repair?	—	Refer to System Inspection	—

GC6029900426020X

Fig. 23 Code C1241: Speed Sensitive Steering Circuit Malfunction (Part 2 of 2). 1999–2000 Bonneville, Eighty Eight, LeSabre, LSS, Park Avenue & Regency

Step	Action	Value(s)	Yes	No
12	Using *J 39200* DMM, measure the resistance between terminals C and B of *J 39700.* Is the resistance within the range specified in the value(s) column?	OL (infinite)	*Go to Step 19*	*Go to Step 13*
13	1. Disconnect the Magnasteer Actuator. 2. Using *J 39200* DMM, measure the resistance between terminal A and ground of the Magnasteer Actuator Connector. Is the resistance within the range specified in the value(s) column?	OL (infinite)	*Go to Step 14*	*Go to Step 11*
14	Using *J 39200* DMM, measure the resistance between terminals F and B of *J 39700.* Is the resistance within the range specified in the value(s) column?	OL (infinite)	*Go to Step 16*	*Go to Step 15*
15	Repair CKT 345 for a short to ground. Is the repair complete?	—	Refer to ABS	—
16	Using *J 39200* DMM, measure the resistance between terminals C and B of *J 39700.* Is the resistance within the range specified in the value(s) column?	OL (infinite)	*Go to Step 17*	*Go to Step 18*
17	Malfunction is intermittent. Inspect all connectors and harnesses for damage that may result in a short to ground when connected. Is the repair complete?	—	Refer to ABS	—
18	Repair CKT 1787 for a short to ground. Is the repair complete?	—	Refer to ABS	—
19	1. Disconnect the Magnasteer Actuator. 2. Turn the ignition switch to the ON position, engine off. 3. Using *J 39200* DMM, measure the voltage at terminal F of *J 39700.* Is the voltage within the range specified in the value(s) column?	Above 1V	*Go to Step 20*	*Go to Step 21*
20	Repair CKT 345 for a short to voltage. Is the repair complete?	—	Refer to ABS	—
21	Using *J 39200* DMM, measure the voltage at terminal C of *J 39700.* Is the voltage within the range specified in the value(s) column?	Above 1V	*Go to Step 22*	*Go to Step 23*
22	Repair CKT 1787 for a short to voltage. Is the repair complete?	—	Refer to ABS	—
23	Replace the EBTCM. Is the replacement complete?	—	Refer to ABS	—

GC6029800360020X

Fig. 24 Code C1241: Speed Sensitive Steering Circuit Malfunction (Part 2 of 2). Corvette w/Rear Mounted EBCM

Step	Action	Value(s)	Yes	No
1	Was the ABS Diagnostic System Check performed?	—	*Go to Step 2*	Refer to ABS
2	1. Inspect the Magnasteer wiring and connectors for damage. 2. Inspect the Magnasteer Actuator for looseness or damage. Is physical damage of Actuator evident?	—	*Go to Step 3*	*Go to Step 4*
3	Repair as necessary. Is the repair complete?	—	Refer to ABS	—
4	1. Turn the ignition switch to the OFF position. 2. Disconnect the EBTCM. 3. Install the *J 39700* Universal Pinout Box using the *J 39700-25* cable adapter to the EBTCM harness connector only. 4. Using *J 39200* DMM, measure the resistance between terminals C and F of *J 39700.* Is the resistance within the range specified in the value(s) column?	2–3Ω	*Go to Step 12*	*Go to Step 5*
5	1. Disconnect the Magnasteer Actuator. 2. Using *J 39200* DMM, measure the resistance between terminals A and B of the Magnasteer Actuator Connector. Is the resistance within the range specified in the value(s) column?	2–3Ω	*Go to Step 6*	*Go to Step 11*
6	1. Connect a jumper between the Magnasteer Actuator harness connector terminal A and ground. 2. Using *J 39200* DMM, measure the resistance between terminals C and B of *J 39700.* Is the resistance within the range specified in the value(s) column?	0–5Ω	*Go to Step 8*	*Go to Step 7*
7	Repair CKT 1787 for an open or high resistance. Is the repair complete?	—	Refer to ABS	—
8	1. Connect a jumper between the Magnasteer Actuator harness connector terminal B and ground. 2. Using *J 39200* DMM, measure the resistance between terminals F and B of *J 39700.* Is the resistance within the range specified in the value(s) column?	0–5Ω	*Go to Step 10*	*Go to Step 9*
9	Repair CKT 345 for an open or high resistance. Is the repair complete?	—	Refer to ABS	—
10	Malfunction is intermittent. Inspect all connectors and harnesses for damage that may result in an open or high resistance when connected. Is the repair complete?	—	Refer to ABS	—
11	Replace the Power Steering Gear. Is the replacement complete?	—	Refer to ABS	—

GC6029800360010X

Fig. 24 Code C1241: Speed Sensitive Steering Circuit Malfunction (Part 1 of 2). Corvette w/Rear Mounted EBCM

Step	Action	Value(s)	Yes	No
1	Was the ABS Diagnostic System Check performed?	—	*Go to Step 2*	Refer to ABS
2	1. Inspect the Magnasteer wiring and connectors for damage. 2. Inspect the Magnasteer Actuator for looseness or damage. Is physical damage of Actuator evident?	—	*Go to Step 3*	*Go to Step 4*
3	Repair as necessary. Is the repair complete?	—	Refer to ABS	—
4	1. Turn the ignition switch to the OFF position. 2. Disconnect the EBTCM. 3. Install the *J 39700* Universal Pinout Box using the *J 39700-25* cable adapter to the EBTCM harness connector only. 4. Using *J 39200* DMM, measure the resistance between terminals C and F of *J 39700.* Is the resistance within the range specified in the value(s) column?	2–3Ω	*Go to Step 12*	*Go to Step 5*
5	1. Disconnect the Magnasteer Actuator. 2. Using *J 39200* DMM, measure the resistance between terminals A and B of the Magnasteer Actuator Connector. Is the resistance within the range specified in the value(s) column?	2–3Ω	*Go to Step 6*	*Go to Step 11*
6	1. Connect a jumper between the Magnasteer Actuator harness connector terminal A and ground. 2. Using *J 39200* DMM, measure the resistance between terminals C and B of *J 39700.* Is the resistance within the range specified in the value(s) column?	0–5Ω	*Go to Step 8*	*Go to Step 7*
7	Repair CKT 1787 for an open or high resistance. Is the repair complete?	—	Refer to ABS	—
8	1. Connect a jumper between the Magnasteer Actuator harness connector terminal B and ground. 2. Using *J 39200* DMM, measure the resistance between terminals F and B of *J 39700.* Is the resistance within the range specified in the value(s) column?	0–5Ω	*Go to Step 10*	*Go to Step 9*
9	Repair CKT 345 for an open or high resistance. Is the repair complete?	—	Refer to ABS	—
10	Malfunction is intermittent. Inspect all connectors and harnesses for damage that may result in an open or high resistance when connected. Is the repair complete?	—	Refer to ABS	—
11	Replace the Power Steering Gear. Is the replacement complete?	—	Refer to ABS	—

GC6029800361010X

Fig. 25 Code C1241: Speed Sensitive Steering Circuit Malfunction (Part 1 of 2). Corvette w/Front Mounted EBCM

Step	Action	Value(s)	Yes	No
12	Using *J 39200* DMM, measure the resistance between terminals C and B of *J 39700*. Is the resistance within the range specified in the value(s) column?	OL (infinite)	*Go to Step 19*	*Go to Step 13*
13	1. Disconnect the Magnasteer Actuator. 2. Using *J 39200* DMM, measure the resistance between terminal A and ground of the Magnasteer Actuator Connector. Is the resistance within the range specified in the value(s) column?	OL (infinite)	*Go to Step 14*	*Go to Step 11*
14	Using *J 39200* DMM, measure the resistance between terminals F and B of *J 39700*. Is the resistance within the range specified in the value(s) column?	OL (infinite)	*Go to Step 16*	*Go to Step 15*
15	Repair CKT 345 for a short to ground. Is the repair complete?	—	Refer to ABS	—
16	Using *J 39200* DMM, measure the resistance between terminals C and B of *J 39700*. Is the resistance within the range specified in the value(s) column?	OL (infinite)	*Go to Step 17*	*Go to Step 18*
17	Malfunction is intermittent. Inspect all connectors and harnesses for damage that may result in a short to ground when connected. Is the repair complete?	—	Refer to ABS	—
18	Repair CKT 1787 for a short to ground. Is the repair complete?	—	Refer to ABS	—
19	1. Disconnect the Magnasteer Actuator. 2. Turn the ignition switch to the ON position, engine off. 3. Using *J 39200* DMM, measure the voltage at terminal F of *J 39700*. Is the voltage within the range specified in the value(s) column?	Above 1V	*Go to Step 20*	*Go to Step 21*
20	Repair CKT 345 for a short to voltage. Is the repair complete?	—	Refer to ABS	—
21	Using *J 39200* DMM, measure the voltage at terminal C of *J 39700*. Is the voltage within the range specified in the value(s) column?	Above 1V	*Go to Step 22*	*Go to Step 23*
22	Repair CKT 1787 for a short to voltage. Is the repair complete?	—	Refer to ABS	—
23	Replace the EBTCM. Is the replacement complete?	—	Refer to ABS	—

GC6029800361020X

Fig. 25 Code C1241: Speed Sensitive Steering Circuit Malfunction (Part 2 of 2). Corvette w/Front Mounted EBCM

Step	Action	Value(s)	Yes	No
1	Was the Variable Effort Steering System Check performed?	—	*Go to Step 2*	REFER TO SYSTEM CHECK
2	Inspect wiring and connectors for damage. Is physical damage evident?	—	*Go to Step 3*	*Go to Step 4*
3	Repair wiring as necessary. Is repair complete?	—	REFER TO SYSTEM CHECK	—
4	1. Turn ignition OFF. 2. Disconnect the Variable Steering Actuator connector. 3. Using a DMM, measure the resistance between Variable Steering Actuator connector terminals A and B. Is the resistance within the specified value?	1.6–3.1 Ω	*Go to Step 5*	*Go to Step 6*
5	1. Using a DMM, measure the resistance between Variable Steering Actuator connector terminal A and ground. 2. Using a DMM, measure the resistance between Variable Steering Actuator connector terminal B and ground. Was the resistance within the specified value?	Less than OL	*Go to Step 6*	*Go to Step 7*
6	Replace the Variable Steering Actuator. Is the repair completed?	—	REFER TO SYSTEM CHECK	—
7	1. Disconnect the EBTCM connector. 2. Install a J39700 universal pinout box using J39700-25 cable adapter to the EBTCM harness only. 3. Using a DMM, measure the resistance between terminals C and B of J39700. Is the resistance within the specified range?	Less than OL	*Go to Step 8*	*Go to Step 9*
8	Repair CKT 1787 (GRY). Is repair completed?	—	REFER TO SYSTEM CHECK	—
9	Using a DMM, measure the resistance between F and B of the J39700. Is the resistance within the specified value?	Less than OL	*Go to Step 10*	*Go to Step 11*
10	Repair CKT 345 (WHT). Is the repair completed?	—	REFER TO SYSTEM CHECK	—
11	1. Reconnect the Variable Steering Actuator. 2. Using a DMM, measure the resistance between terminals C and F of J39700. Is the resistance within the specified value?	1.6–3.1 Ω	*Go to Step 14*	*Go to Step 12*
12	Is the resistance less than the specified value?	1.6–3.1 Ω	*Go to Step 8*	*Go to Step 13*

GC6029800349010X

Fig. 27 Code C1241: Speed Sensitive Steering Circuit Malfunction (Part 1 of 2). 1997–98 Seville

Step	Action	Value(s)	Yes	No
1	1. Turn the ignition switch to the OFF position. 2. Disconnect the Electronic Brake/Traction Control Module (EBTCM). 3. Disconnect the Variable Power Steering Solenoid. 4. Using a DMM, measure voltage at the Variable Power Steering Solenoid connector terminal B and B+. Is any voltage measured?	—	Go to Step 2	Go to Step 3
2	Repair the short to ground in the wire. Has the repair been made and the system rechecked?	—	System OK	—
3	Using a DMM, measure voltage at the Variable Power Steering Solenoid connector terminal B and ground. Is any voltage measured?	—	Go to Step 4	Go to Step 5
4	Repair the short to B+ in the wire. Has the repair been made and the system rechecked?	—	System OK	—
5	Using a DMM, measure voltage at the Variable Power Steering Solenoid connector terminal A and B+. Is any voltage measured?	—	Go to Step 2	Go to Step 6
6	Using a DMM, measure voltage at the Variable Power Steering Solenoid connector terminal A and ground. Is any voltage measured?	—	Go to Step 4	Go to Step 7
7	1. Reconnect the EBTCM. 2. Using a DMM, measure voltage at the Variable Power Steering Solenoid connector terminal B and B+. Is the voltage level acceptable?	9-14V	Go to Step 8	Go to Step 9
8	Using a DMM, measure voltage at the Variable Power Steering Solenoid connector terminal A and B+. Is the voltage level acceptable?	9-14V	Go to Step 10	Go to Step 11
9	Using a DMM, measure voltage at the EBTCM connector C1 terminal F and B+. Is the voltage level acceptable?	9-14V	Go to Step 12	Go to Step 13
10	Replace the Variable Power Steering Solenoid. Has the repair been made and the system rechecked?	—	System OK	—
11	Using a DMM, measure voltage at the EBTCM connector C1 terminal C and B+. Is the voltage level acceptable?	9-14V	Go to Step 12	Go to Step 13
12	Repair the open in the wire. Has the repair been made and the system rechecked?	—	System OK	—
13	Replace the EBTCM. Has the repair been made and the system rechecked?	—	System OK	—

GC6029800348000X

Fig. 26 Code C1241: Speed Sensitive Steering Circuit Malfunction. DeVille & Eldorado

Step	Action	Value(s)	Yes	No
13	1. Connect a fused jumper between terminals C and B of J39700. 2. Using a DMM, measure the resistance between the Variable Steering Actuator harness connector terminal A and ground. Is the resistance within the specified range?	0–5 Ω	*Go to Step 10*	*Go to Step 8*
14	1. Turn the ignition switch to the ON position. 2. Using a DMM, measure the voltage at terminal C of J39700. Is the voltage within the specified range?	Above 1 volt	*Go to Step 8*	*Go to Step 15*
15	Using a DMM, measure the voltage at terminal F of J39700. Is the voltage within the specified value?	Above 1 volt	*Go to Step 10*	*Go to Step 16*
16	Replace the EBTCM. Is the repair completed?	—	REFER TO SYSTEM CHECK	—

GC6029800349020X

Fig. 27 Code C1241: Speed Sensitive Steering Circuit Malfunction (Part 2 of 2). 1997–98 Seville

Step	Action	Value(s)	Yes	No
1	Did you perform the Variable Effort Steering System Inspection?	—	Go to *Step 2*	Refer to System Inspection
2	Inspect the wiring and the connectors for damage. Is physical damage evident?	—	Go to *Step 3*	Go to *Step 4*
3	Repair damage to the wiring and connectors. Did you complete the repair?	—	Refer to System Inspection	—
4	1. Turn OFF the ignition. 2. Disconnect the EBTCM connector. 3. Install the *J 39700* universal pinout box using the *J 39700-25* cable adapter to the EBTCM harness connector only. 4. Use a *J 39200* DMM in order to measure the resistance between terminal C and terminal F of the *J 39700*. Is the resistance within the specified range?	1.6–3.1 Ω	Go to *Step 19*	Go to *Step 5*
5	1. Disconnect the variable steering actuator connector. 2. Use a *J 39200* DMM in order to measure the resistance between the variable steering actuator terminal A and terminal B. Is the resistance within the specified range?	1.6–3.1 Ω	Go to *Step 6*	Go to *Step 12*
6	Use a *J 39200* DMM in order to measure the resistance between terminal C of the *J 39700* and the variable steering actuator connector terminal A. Is the resistance less than the specified value?	0.5 Ω	Go to *Step 7*	Go to *Step 13*
7	Use a *J 39200* DMM in order to measure the resistance between terminal F of the *J 39700* and the variable steering actuator connector terminal B. Is the resistance less than the specified value?	0.5 Ω	Go to *Step 8*	Go to *Step 14*
8	Use a *J 39200* DMM in order to measure the resistance between terminal F of the *J 39700* and a good ground. Is the resistance less than the specified value?	OL	Go to *Step 15*	Go to *Step 9*
9	Use a *J 39200* DMM in order to measure the voltage between terminal F of the *J 39700* and a good ground. Is the voltage greater than the specified value?	1 V	Go to *Step 16*	Go to *Step 10*
10	Use a *J 39200* DMM in order to measure the resistance between terminal C of the *J 39700* and a good ground. Is the resistance less than the specified value?	OL	Go to *Step 17*	Go to *Step 11*
11	Use a *J 39200* DMM in order to measure the voltage between terminal C of the *J 39700* and a good ground. Is the voltage greater than the specified value?	1 V	Go to *Step 18*	Go to *Step 19*
12	Replace the variable steering actuator. Did you complete the repair?	—	Refer to System Inspection	—
13	Repair the open in CKT 1787 (GRY). Did you complete the repair?	—	Refer to System Inspection	—

GC6029900425010X

Fig. 28 Code C1241: Speed Sensitive Steering Circuit Malfunction (Part 1 of 2). 1999–2000 Seville

Step	Action	Value(s)	Yes	No
1	Was the ABS Diagnostic System Check performed?	—	Go to Step 2	Refer to Anti-Lock Brakes
2	1. Start the engine. 2. Using a scan tool, select DATA LIST and monitor the steering wheel sensor voltage while rotating the steering wheel from stop-to-stop. Is the voltage within the range specified?	0-.5V	Go to Step 5	Go to Step 3
3	Is the voltage from Step 2 within the range specified in the Value(s) column?	4.7-5V	Go to Step 14	Go to Step 4
4	Does the voltage from Step 2 vary?	—	Go to Step 21	Go to Step 1
5	1. Turn the ignition switch to the OFF position. 2. Disconnect the steering wheel position sensor. 3. Disconnect the ECBM harness connector. 4. Using the J 39200, measure the resistance between the ECBM harness connector terminals 17 and 5. Is the resistance within the range specified in the Value(s) column?	Infinite	Go to Step 6	Go to Step 29
6	Using the J 39200, measure the resistance between the ECBM harness connector terminals 1 and 5. Is the resistance within the range specified in the Value(s) column?	Infinite	Go to Step 7	Go to Step 30
7	Using the J 39200, measure the resistance between the ECBM harness connector terminal 17 and ground. Is the resistance within the range specified in the Value(s) column?	Infinite	Go to Step 8	Go to Step 31
8	Using the J 39200, measure the resistance between the ECBM harness connector terminal 1 and ground. Is the resistance within the range specified in the Value(s) column?	Infinite	Go to Step 9	Go to Step 32
9	Using the J 39200, measure the resistance between the ECBM harness connector terminal 1 and the steering wheel position sensor harness connector terminal A. Is the resistance within the range specified in the Value(s) column?	0-2 Ω	Go to Step 10	Go to Step 33
10	Using the J 39200, measure the resistance between the ECBM harness connector terminal 17 and the steering wheel position sensor harness connector terminal B. Is the resistance within the range specified in the Value(s) column?	0-2 Ω	Go to Step 11	Go to Step 34

GC6029800352010X

Fig. 29 Code C1243: Steering Wheel Position Sensor Circuit Malfunction (Part 1 of 5). Achieva, Alero, Grand Am & Skylark

Step	Action	Value(s)	Yes	No
14	Repair the open in CKT 345 (WHT). Did you complete the repair?	—	Refer to System Inspection	—
15	Repair the short to ground in CKT 345 (WHT). Did you complete the repair?	—	Refer to System Inspection	—
16	Repair the short to voltage in CKT 345 (WHT). Did you complete the repair?	—	Refer to System Inspection	—
17	Repair the short to ground in CKT 1787 (GRY). Did you complete the repair?	—	Refer to System Inspection	—
18	Repair the short to voltage in CKT 1787 (GRY). Did you complete the repair?	—	Refer to System Inspection	—
19	Replace the EBTCM. Did you complete the repair?	—	Refer to System Inspection	—

GC6029900425020X

Fig. 28 Code C1241: Speed Sensitive Steering Circuit Malfunction (Part 2 of 2). 1999–2000 Seville

Step	Action	Value(s)	Yes	No
11	Inspect the ECBM harness connector terminals 1 and 17 and all steering wheel position sensor terminals for poor terminal contact. Is poor terminal contact evident?	—	Go to Step 35	Go to Step 12
12	1. Reconnect the ECBM harness connector. 2. Turn the ignition switch to the RUN position. 3. Using the J 39200, measure the voltage between the steering wheel position sensor harness connector terminals A and C. Is the voltage greater than the value listed in the Value(s) column?	4.0V	Go to Step 41	Go to Step 13
13	1. Turn the ignition switch to the OFF position. 2. Inspect CKTs 1056, 1059, and 556 for damage which may result in shorts between the circuits or shorts to ground. Repair damage if evident. 3. Reconnect all connectors. 4. Turn the ignition switch to the RUN position. Is DTC C1243 set as a current DTC?	—	Go to Step 42	Refer to Anti-Lock Brakes
14	1. Turn the ignition switch to the OFF position. 2. Disconnect steering wheel position sensor. 3. Turn the ignition switch to the RUN position. Does the scan tool display the steering wheel position sensor voltage within the range specified in the Value(s) column?	0-1V	Go to Step 15	Go to Step 16
15	Using the J 39200, measure the resistance between the steering wheel sensor harness connector terminal C and ground. Is the resistance within the range specified in the Value(s) column?	0-5 Ω	Go to Step 41	Go to Step 18
16	1. Turn the ignition switch to the OFF position. 2. Disconnect ECBM harness connector. 3. Turn the ignition switch to the RUN position. 4. Using the J 39200, measure the voltage between the ECBM harness connector terminal 17 and ground. Is the voltage within the range specified in the Value(s) column?	0-1V	Go to Step 17	Go to Step 38
17	1. Turn the ignition switch to the OFF position. 2. Inspect CKT 1059 for any damage which may result in a short to voltage with all connectors connected. Repair any damage if evident. 3. Reconnect all connectors. 4. Turn the ignition switch to the RUN position. Is DTC C1243 set as a current DTC?	—	Go to Step 42	Refer to Anti-Lock Brakes

GC6029800352020X

Fig. 29 Code C1243: Steering Wheel Position Sensor Circuit Malfunction (Part 2 of 5). Achieva, Alero, Grand Am & Skylark

Step	Action	Value(s)	Yes	No
18	1. Turn the ignition switch to the OFF position. 2. Disconnect ECBM harness connector. 3. Using the J 39200, measure the resistance between the steering wheel position sensor harness connector terminal C and the ECBM harness connector terminal 5. Is the resistance within the range specified in the Value(s) column?	0-2 Ω	Go to Step 19	Go to Step 36
19	1. Turn the ignition switch to the RUN position. 2. Using the J 39200, measure the voltage between the ECBM harness connector terminal 5 and ground. Is the voltage within the range specified in the Value(s) column?	0-1V	Go to Step 20	Go to Step 37
20	1. Turn the ignition switch to the OFF position. 2. Inspect the ECBM harness connector and the steering wheel position sensor terminals for poor terminal contact. Replace any terminals with poor terminal contact. 3. Inspect all steering wheel position sensor circuits for damage which may result in a short to voltage or an open with all connectors connected. Repair damage if evident. 4. Reconnect all connectors. 5. Turn the ignition switch to the RUN position. Is DTC C1243 set as a current DTC?	—	Go to Step 42	Refer to "Diagnosis & Testing" in "Anti-lock Brakes"
21	1. Turn the ignition switch to the RUN position. 2. Using the J 39200, measure the voltage by backprobing between the steering wheel position sensor harness connector terminals A and C. Is the voltage within the the range listed in the Value(s) column?	4.5-5.5V	Go to Step 22	Go to Step 23
22	1. Turn the ignition switch to the OFF position. 2. Disconnect the steering wheel position sensor. 3. Turn the ignition switch to the RUN position. 4. Using the J39200, measure the voltage by backprobing between the steering wheel position sensor harness connector terminals A and C. Is the voltage within the the range listed in the Value(s) column?	4.5-5.5V	Go to Step 27	Go to Step 41
23	1. Turn the ignition switch to the OFF position. 2. Disconnect the ECBM harness connector. 3. Disconnect the steering wheel position sensor harness connector. 4. Measure the resistance between the ECBM harness connector terminals 1 and 17. Is the resistance within the range specified in the Value(s) column?	Infinite	Go to Step 24	Go to Step 40

GC6029800352030X

Fig. 29 Code C1243: Steering Wheel Position Sensor Circuit Malfunction (Part 3 of 5). Achieva, Alero, Grand Am & Skylark

Step	Action	Value(s)	Yes	No
33	Repair the open or high resistance in CKT 1056. Is the repair complete?	—	Refer to Anti-Lock Brakes	—
34	Repair the open or high resistance in CKT 1059. Is the repair complete?	—	Refer to Anti-Lock Brakes	—
35	Replace the terminals that exhibit poor contact. Is the repair complete?	—	Refer to Anti-Lock Brakes	—
36	Repair the open or high resistance in CKT 556. Is the repair complete?	—	Refer to Anti-Lock Brakes	—
37	Repair the short to voltage in CKT 556. Is the repair complete?	—	Refer to Anti-Lock Brakes	—
38	Repair the short to voltage in CKT 1059. Is the repair complete?	—	Refer to Anti-Lock Brakes	—
39	Repair the short to voltage in CKT 1056. Is the repair complete?	—	Refer to Anti-Lock Brakes	—
40	Repair the short between CKTs 1056 and 1059. Is the repair complete?	—	Refer to Anti-Lock Brakes	—
41	Replace the steering wheel position sensor. Is the repair complete?	—	Refer to Anti-Lock Brakes	—
42	Replace the ECBM. Is the repair complete?	—	Refer to Anti-Lock Brakes	—

GC6029800352050X

Fig. 29 Code C1243: Steering Wheel Position Sensor Circuit Malfunction (Part 5 of 5). Achieva, Alero, Grand Am & Skylark

Step	Action	Value(s)	Yes	No
24	Using the MIN/MAX function of the J 39200, measure the resistance between the steering wheel position sensor terminals A and B while rotating the steering wheel slowly from stop-to-stop. Is the resistance within the range specified in the Value(s) column?	390-12,000 Ω	Go to Step 25	Go to Step 41
25	1. Inspect CKTs 1056 and 1059 for damage which may result in a short between the two circuits with all connectors connected. Repair damage if evident. 2. Reconnect all connectors. 3. Being very careful not to move the steering wheel, turn the ignition switch to the RUN position. Is DTC C1243 set as a current DTC?	—	Go to Step 42	Go to Step 26
26	Turn the steering wheel slowly from stop-to-stop. Is DTC C1243 set as a current DTC?	—	Go to Step 41	Refer to Anti-Lock Brakes
27	1. Turn the ignition switch to the OFF position. 2. Disconnect the ECBM harness connector. 3. Turn the ignition switch to the RUN position. 4. Using the J 39200, measure the voltage between the ECBM harness connector terminal 1 and ground. Is the voltage within the the range listed in the Value(s) column?	4.5-5.5V	Go to Step 39	Go to Step 28
28	1. Turn the ignition switch to the OFF position. 2. Inspect CKT 1056 for any damage which may result in a short to voltage with all connectors connected. Repair any damage if evident. 3. Reconnect all connectors. 4. Turn the ignition switch to the RUN position. Is DTC C1243 set as a current DTC?	—	Go to Step 42	Refer to Anti-Lock Brakes
29	Repair the short between CKTs 1059 and 556. Is the repair complete?	—	Refer to Anti-Lock Brakes	—
30	Repair the short between CKTs 1056 and 556. Is the repair complete?	—	Refer to Anti-Lock Brakes	—
31	Repair the short to ground in CKT 1059. Is the repair complete?	—	Refer to Anti-Lock Brakes	—
32	Repair the short to ground in CKT 1056. Is the repair complete?	—	Refer to Anti-Lock Brakes	—

GC6029800352040X

Fig. 29 Code C1243: Steering Wheel Position Sensor Circuit Malfunction (Part 4 of 5). Achieva, Alero, Grand Am & Skylark

Step	Action	Value(s)	Yes	No
1	Was the ABS Diagnostic System Check performed?	—	Go to Step 2	Refer to ABS
2	1. Start the engine. 2. Using a scan tool, select DATA LIST and monitor steering wheel sensor voltage while rotating steering wheel stop-to-stop. Is the voltage within range specified?	0-0.5V	Go to Step 5	Go to Step 3
3	Is the voltage from Step 2 within range specified?	4.7-5V	Go to Step 14	Go to Step 4
4	Does the voltage from Step 2 vary?	—	Go to Step 21	Go to Step 1
5	1. Turn the ignition switch to the OFF position. 2. Disconnect the steering wheel speed sensor. 3. Disconnect the EBCM harness connectors. 4. Using the J 39200, measure the resistance between EBCM harness C1 terminals B8 and A8. Is the resistance within range specified?	OL (Infinite)	Go to Step 6	Go to Step 29
6	Using the J 39200, measure the resistance between EBCM harness C1 terminals A12 and A8. Is the resistance within range specified?	OL (Infinite)	Go to Step 7	Go to Step 30
7	Using the J 39200, measure the resistance between EBCM harness connector C1 terminal B8 and ground. Is the resistance within range specified?	OL (Infinite)	Go to Step 8	Go to Step 31
8	Using the J 39200, measure the resistance between EBCM harness connector C1 terminal A12 and ground. Is the resistance within range specified?	OL (Infinite)	Go to Step 9	Go to Step 32
9	Using the J 39200, measure the resistance between EBCM harness connector C1 terminal A12 and steering wheel speed sensor harness connector terminal A. Is the resistance within range specified?	0-2 Ω	Go to Step 10	Go to Step 33
10	Using the J 39200, measure the resistance between EBCM harness connector C1 terminal B8 and steering wheel speed sensor harness connector terminal B. Is the resistance within range specified?	0-2 Ω	Go to Step 11	Go to Step 34
11	Inspect EBCM harness connector C1 terminals A12 and B8 and all steering wheel speed sensor terminals for poor terminal contact. Is poor terminal contact evident?	—	Go to Step 35	Go to Step 12

GC6029800357010X

Fig. 30 Code C1243: Steering Wheel Position Sensor Circuit Malfunction (Part 1 of 5). Lumina & Monte Carlo

Step	Action	Value(s)	Yes	No
12	1. Reconnect the EBCM harness connectors. 2. Turn the ignition switch to the RUN position. 3. Using the J 39200, measure the voltage between steering wheel speed sensor harness connector terminals A and C. Is the voltage greater than the value listed?	4.0V	Go to Step 41	Go to Step 13
13	1. Turn the ignition switch to the OFF position. 2. Inspect CKTs 1056, 1059, and 450 for damage which may result in shorts between the circuits or shorts to ground. Repair damage if evident. 3. Reconnect all connectors. 4. Turn the ignition switch to the RUN position. Is DTC C1243 set as a current DTC?	—	Go to Step 42	Refer to ABS
14	1. Turn the ignition switch to the OFF position. 2. Disconnect steering wheel speed sensor. 3. Turn the ignition switch to the RUN position. Does the scan tool display the steering wheel speed sensor voltage within range specified?	0-1V	Go to Step 15	Go to Step 16
15	Using the J 39200, measure the resistance between the steering wheel sensor harness connector terminal C and ground. Is the resistance within range specified?	0-5 Ω	Go to Step 41	Go to Step 18
16	1. Turn the ignition switch to the OFF position. 2. Disconnect the EBCM harness connectors. 3. Turn the ignition switch to the RUN position. 4. Using the J 39200, measure the voltage the EBCM harness connector C1 terminal B8 and ground. Is the voltage within range specified?	0-1V	Go to Step 17	Go to Step 38
17	1. Turn the ignition switch to the OFF position. 2. Inspect CKT 1059 for damage which may result in a short to voltage with all connectors connected. Repair damage if evident. 3. Reconnect all connectors. 4. Turn the ignition switch to the RUN position. Is DTC C1243 set as a current DTC?	—	Go to Step 42	Refer to ABS
18	1. Turn the ignition switch to the OFF position. 2. Disconnect the EBCM harness connectors. 3. Using the J 39200, measure the resistance between the steering wheel speed sensor harness connector terminal C and the EBCM harness connector C1 terminal A8. Is the resistance within range specified?	0-2 Ω	Go to Step 19	Go to Step 36
19	1. Turn the ignition switch to the RUN position. 2. Using the J 39200, measure the voltage between the EBCM harness connector C1 terminal A8 and ground. Is the voltage within range specified?	0-1V	Go to Step 20	Go to Step 37

GC6029800357020X

Fig. 30 Code C1243: Steering Wheel Position Sensor Circuit Malfunction (Part 2 of 5). Lumina & Monte Carlo

Step	Action	Value(s)	Yes	No
27	1. Turn the ignition switch to the OFF position. 2. Disconnect the EBCM harness connectors. 3. Turn the ignition switch to the RUN position. 4. Using the J 39200, measure the voltage between the EBCM harness connector C1 terminal A12 and ground. Is the voltage greater than the value listed?	4.5-5.5V	Go to Step 39	Go to Step 28
28	1. Turn the ignition switch to the OFF position. 2. Inspect CKT 1056 for damage which may result in a short to voltage with all connectors connected. Repair damage if evident. 3. Reconnect all connectors. 4. Turn the ignition switch to the RUN position. Is DTC C1243 set as a current DTC?	—	Go to Step 42	Refer to ABS
29	Repair short between CKTs 1059 and 450. Is the repair complete?	—	Refer to ABS	—
30	Repair short between CKTs 1056 and 450. Is the repair complete?	—	Refer to ABS	—
31	Repair short to ground in CKT 1059. Is the repair complete?	—	Refer to ABS	—
32	Repair short to ground in CKT 1056. Is the repair complete?	—	Refer to ABS	—
33	Repair open or high resistance in CKT 1056. Is the repair complete?	—	Refer to ABS	—
34	Repair open or high resistance in CKT 1059. Is the repair complete?	—	Refer to ABS	—
35	Replace the terminals that exhibit poor contact. Is the repair complete?	—	Refer to ABS	—
36	Repair open or high resistance in CKT 450. Is the repair complete?	—	Refer to ABS	—
37	Repair short to voltage in CKT 450. Is the repair complete?	—	Refer to ABS	—
38	Repair short to voltage in CKT 1059. Is the repair complete?	—	Refer to ABS	—

GC6029800357040X

Fig. 30 Code C1243: Steering Wheel Position Sensor Circuit Malfunction (Part 4 of 5). Lumina & Monte Carlo

Step	Action	Value(s)	Yes	No
20	1. Turn the ignition switch to the OFF position. 2. Inspect EBCM harness connector and steering wheel speed sensor terminals for poor terminal contact. Replace any terminals with poor terminal contact. 3. Inspect all steering wheel speed sensor circuits for damage which may result in a short to voltage or an open with all connectors connected. Repair damage if evident. 4. Reconnect all connectors. 5. Turn the ignition switch to the RUN position. Is DTC C1243 set as a current DTC?	—	Go to Step 42	Refer to ABS
21	1. Turn the ignition switch to the RUN position. 2. Using the J 39200, measure the voltage by backprobing between the steering wheel speed sensor harness connector terminals A and C. Is the voltage greater than the value listed?	4.5-5.5V	Go to Step 22	Go to Step 23
22	1. Turn the ignition switch to the OFF position. 2. Disconnect the steering wheel speed sensor. 3. Turn the ignition switch to the RUN position. 4. Repeat Step 21. Is the voltage greater than the value listed?	4.5-5.5V	Go to Step 27	Go to Step 41
23	1. Turn the ignition switch to the OFF position. 2. Disconnect the EBCM harness connectors. 3. Disconnect the steering wheel speed sensor harness connector. 4. Measure the resistance between EBCM harness connector C1 terminals A12 and B8. Is the resistance within range specified?	OL (Infinite)	Go to Step 24	Go to Step 40
24	Using the MIN/MAX function of the J 39200, measure the resistance between the steering wheel speed sensor terminals A and B while rotating the steering wheel slowly stop-to-stop. Is the resistance within range specified?	390-12,000 Ω	Go to Step 25	Go to Step 41
25	1. Inspect CKTs 1056 and 1059 for damage which may result in a short between the two circuits with all connectors connected. Repair damage if evident. 2. Reconnect all connectors. 3. Being very careful not to move steering wheel, turn the ignition switch to the RUN position. Is DTC C1243 set as a current DTC?	—	Go to Step 42	Go to Step 26
26	Turn the steering wheel slowly stop-to-stop. Is DTC C1243 set as a current DTC?	—	Go to Step 41	Refer to ABS

GC6029800357030X

Fig. 30 Code C1243: Steering Wheel Position Sensor Circuit Malfunction (Part 3 of 5). Lumina & Monte Carlo

Step	Action	Value(s)	Yes	No
39	Repair short to voltage in CKT 1056. Is the repair complete?	—	Refer to ABS	—
40	Repair short between CKTs 1056 and 1059. Is the repair complete?	—	Refer to ABS	—
41	Replace the steering wheel speed sensor. Is the repair complete?	—	Refer to ABS	—
42	Replace the EBCM. Is the repair complete?	—	Refer to ABS	—

GC6029800357050X

Fig. 30 Code C1243: Steering Wheel Position Sensor Circuit Malfunction (Part 5 of 5). Lumina & Monte Carlo

Step	Action	Value(s)	Yes	No
1	Was the ABS Diagnostic System Check performed?	—	Go to Step 2	Refer to ABS
2	1. Turn the ignition switch to the RUN position. 2. Using the scan tool, select MISC. TESTS, select VES MANUAL CONTROL function, and command EVO actuator ON. Is the feedback current greater than the value listed in the Value(s) column?	100 mA	Go to Step 14	Go to Step 3
3	1. Turn the ignition switch to the OFF position. 2. Disconnect the ECBM harness connector. 3. Disconnect the 2-way EVO actuator connector. 4. Using the J 39200, measure the resistance between the 2-way EVO actuator harness connector terminal B and the ECBM harness connector terminal 18. Is the resistance within the range specified in the Value(s) column?	0-2 Ω	Go to Step 4	Go to Step 10
4	Using the J 39200, measure the resistance between the ECBM harness connector terminal 18 and ground. Is the resistance within the range specified in the Value(s) column?	Infinite	Go to Step 5	Go to Step 11
5	Using the J 39200, measure the resistance between the 2-way EVO actuator harness connector terminal A and the ECBM harness connector terminal C. Is the resistance within the range specified in the Value(s) column?	0-2 Ω	Go to Step 6	Go to Step 12
6	Using the J 39200, measure the resistance between the ECBM harness connector terminal C and ground. Is the resistance within the range specified in the Value(s) column?	Infinite	Go to Step 7	Go to Step 13
7	1. Reconnect the EVO actuator connector. 2. Using the J 39200, measure the resistance between the ECBM harness connector terminal 18 and ground. Is the resistance within the range specified in the Value(s) column?	Infinite	Go to Step 8	Go to Step 15
8	Using the J 39200, measure the resistance between the ECBM harness connector terminals 18 and C. Is the resistance within the range specified in the Value(s) column?	7-19 Ω	Go to Step 9	Go to Step 15

GC6029800353010X

Fig. 31 Code C1273: Actuator Circuit Open Or Shorted To Ground (Part 1 of 2). Achieva, Alero, Grand Am & Skylark

Step	Action	Value(s)	Yes	No
9	1. Inspect the ECBM harness connector and the 2-way EVO actuator harness connector for poor terminal contact or corrosion. Replace any terminals with poor terminal contact or corrosion. 2. Inspect CKT 1295 for damage which may result in a short to ground or an open with all connectors connected. Repair the damage if evident. 3. Reconnect all connectors. 4. Turn the ignition switch to the RUN position. Is DTC C1273 set as a current DTC?	—	Check wiring circuit for damage or loose connections	Check wiring circuit for damage or loose connections
10	Repair the open or high resistance in CKT 1295. Is the repair complete?	—	Refer to ABS	—
11	Repair the short to ground in CKT 1295. Is the repair complete?	—	Refer to ABS	—
12	Repair the open or high resistance in CKT 1294/1633. Is the repair complete?	—	Refer to ABS	—
13	Repair short to ground in CKT 1633/1294 or 855. Is the repair complete?	—	Refer to ABS	—
14	Malfunction is intermittent.	—	Go to Diagnostic Aids	Go to Diagnostic Aids
15	Replace the EVO actuator. Is the repair complete?	—	Refer to ABS	—
16	Replace the ECBM. Is the repair complete?	—	Refer to ABS	—

GC6029800353020X

Fig. 31 Code C1273: Actuator Circuit Open Or Shorted To Ground (Part 2 of 2). Achieva, Alero, Grand Am & Skylark

Step	Action	Value(s)	Yes	No
1	Was the ABS Diagnostic System Check performed?	—	Go to Step 2	Refer to ABS
2	1. Turn the ignition switch to the RUN position. 2. Using the scan tool, select MISC. TESTS, select VES MANUAL CONTROL function and command VES actuator ON. Is the feedback current greater than the value listed?	100 mA	Go to Step 14	Go to Step 3
3	1. Turn the ignition switch to the OFF position. 2. Disconnect the EBCM harness connectors. 3. Disconnect the 2-way MSVA actuator connector. 4. Using the J 39200, measure the resistance between the 2-way MSVA actuator harness connector terminal B and the EBCM harness connector C1 terminal B7. Is the resistance within range specified?	0-2 Ω	Go to Step 4	Go to Step 10
4	Using the J 39200, measure the resistance between the EBCM harness connector C1 terminal B7 and ground. Is the resistance within range specified?	OL (Infinite)	Go to Step 5	Go to Step 11
5	Using the J 39200, measure the resistance between the 2-way MSVA actuator harness connector terminal A and the EBCM harness connector C1 terminal B8. Is the resistance within range specified?	0-2 Ω	Go to Step 6	Go to Step 12
6	Using the J 39200, measure the resistance between the EBCM harness connector C1 terminal B8 and ground. Is the resistance within range specified?	OL (Infinite)	Go to Step 7	Go to Step 13
7	1. Reconnect the MSVA actuator connector. 2. Using the J 39200, measure the resistance between the EBCM harness connector C1 terminal B7 and ground. Is the resistance within range specified?	OL (Infinite)	Go to Step 8	Go to Step 15
8	Using the J 39200, measure the resistance between the EBCM harness connector C1 terminal B7 and C1 terminal B8. Is the resistance within range specified?	7-19 Ω	Go to Step 9	Go to Step 15

GC6029800376010X

Fig. 32 Code C1273: Actuator Circuit Open Or Shorted To Ground (Part 1 of 2). 1998 Intrigue

Step	Action	Value(s)	Yes	No
9	1. Inspect EBCM harness connectors and 2-way MSVA actuator harness connector for poor terminal contact or corrosion. Replace any terminals with poor terminal contact or corrosion. 2. Inspect CKT 345 for damage which may result in a short to ground or an open with all connectors connected. Repair the damage if evident. 3. Reconnect all connectors. 4. Turn the ignition switch to the RUN position. Is DTC C1273 set as a current DTC?	—	Go to Step 16	Go to Step 14
10	Repair open or high resistance in CKT 345. Is the repair complete?	—	Refer to ABS	—
11	Repair short to ground in CKT 345. Is the repair complete?	—	Refer to ABS	—
12	Repair open or high resistance in CKT 1787. Is the repair complete?	—	Refer to ABS	—
13	Repair short to ground in CKT 1787. Is the repair complete?	—	Refer to ABS	—
14	Malfunction is intermittent.	—	—	—
15	Replace the MSVA actuator. Is the repair complete?	—	Refer to ABS	—
16	Replace the EBCM. Is the repair complete?	—	Refer to ABS	—

GC6029800376020X

Fig. 32 Code C1273: Actuator Circuit Open Or Shorted To Ground (Part 2 of 2). 1998 Intrigue

Step	Action	Value(s)	Yes	No
1	Was the ABS Diagnostic System Check performed?	—	*Go to Step 2*	Perform ABS Inspection
2	1. Turn the ignition switch on. 2. Using scan tool, command the Variable Effort Steering (VES) actuator on. Refer to *Scan Tool* manufacturer's instructions for more information. 3. Observe the feedback current on the scan tool. Is the feedback current greater than the value listed?	100 mA	*Go to Step 16*	*Go to Step 3*
3	1. Turn the ignition switch off. 2. Disconnect the Electronic Brake Traction Control Module (EBTCM) harness connectors. 3. Disconnect the MSVA actuator connector. 4. Using a DMM, measure the resistance between the MSVA actuator harness connector terminal B and the EBTCM harness connector C1 terminal B7. Is the measured resistance within the specified range?	Less than 2Ω	*Go to Step 4*	*Go to Step 10*
4	Using a DMM, measure the resistance between the EBTCM harness connector C1 terminal B7 and ground. Is the measured resistance within the specified range?	∞	*Go to Step 5*	*Go to Step 11*
5	Using a DMM, measure the resistance between the MSVA actuator harness connector terminal A and the EBTCM harness connector C1 terminal B8. Is the measured resistance within the specified range?	Less than 2Ω	*Go to Step 6*	*Go to Step 12*
6	Using a DMM, measure the resistance between the EBTCM harness connector C1 terminal B8 and ground. Is the measured resistance within the specified range?	∞	*Go to Step 7*	*Go to Step 13*

GC6029900432010X

Fig. 33 Code 1273: Actuator Circuit Open Or Shorted To Ground (Part 1 of 2). 1999 Intrigue

Step	Action	Value(s)	Yes	No
7	1. Reconnect the MSVA actuator connector. 2. Using a DMM, measure the resistance between the EBTCM harness connector C1 terminal B7 and ground. Is the measured resistance within the specified range?	∞	*Go to Step 8*	*Go to Step 14*
8	Using a DMM, measure the resistance between the EBTCM harness connector C1 terminal B7 and C1 terminal B8. Is the measured resistance within the specified range?	7–19Ω	*Go to Step 9*	*Go to Step 14*
9	1. Inspect the EBTCM harness connectors and the MSVA actuator harness connector for poor terminal contact or corrosion. Replace any terminals with poor terminal contact or corrosion. 2. Inspect circuit 345 for damage which may result in a short to ground or an open with all connectors connected. Repair the damage if evident. 3. Reconnect all the connectors. 4. Turn the ignition switch on. 5. Clear Diagnostic Trouble Codes (DTCs) 6. Check for DTCs Is DTC C1273 set as a current DTC?	—	*Go to Step 15*	*Go to Step 16*
10	Repair poor connection or open in circuit 345. Is the repair complete?	—	*Go to Step 17*	—
11	Repair short to ground in circuit 345. Is the repair complete?	—	*Go to Step 17*	—
12	Repair poor connection or open in circuit 1787. Is the repair complete?	—	*Go to Step 17*	—
13	Repair short to ground in circuit 1787. Is the repair complete?	—	*Go to Step 17*	—
14	Replace the MSVA actuator. Is the repair complete?	—	*Go to Step 17*	—
15	Replace the EBTCM. Is the repair complete?	—	*Go to Step 17*	—
16	The malfunction is not present at this time. this DTC. Is the action complete?	—	System OK	—
17	1. Turn the ignition switch off. 2. Reconnect connectors/components removed. Is the action complete?	—	Perform ABS Inspection	—

GC6029900432020X

Fig. 33 Code 1273: Actuator Circuit Open Or Shorted To Ground (Part 2 of 2). 1999 Intrigue

Step	Action	Value(s)	Yes	No
1	Was the ABS Diagnostic System Check performed?	—	Go to Step 2	Refer to ABS
2	1. Turn the ignition switch to the RUN position. 2. Using the scan tool, select MISC. TESTS, select VES MANUAL CONTROL function and command VES actuator ON. Is the feedback current greater than the value listed?	100mA	Go to Step 14	Go to Step 3
3	1. Turn the ignition switch to the OFF position. 2. Disconnect the EBCM harness connectors. 3. Disconnect the 2-way power steering fluid flow actuator connector. 4. Using the J 39200, measure the resistance between the 2-way power steering fluid flow actuator harness connector terminal B and the EBCM harness connector C1 terminal B7. Is the resistance within range specified?	0-2 Ω	Go to Step 4	Go to Step 10
4	Using the J 39200, measure the resistance between the EBCM harness connector C1 terminal B7 and ground. Is the resistance within range specified?	OL (Infinite)	Go to Step 5	Go to Step 11
5	Using the J 39200, measure the resistance between the 2-way power steering fluid flow actuator harness connector terminal A and the EBCM harness connector C2 terminal C. Is the resistance within range specified?	0-2 Ω	Go to Step 6	Go to Step 12
6	Using the J 39200, measure the resistance between the EBCM harness connector C2 terminal C and ground. Is the resistance within range specified?	OL (Infinite)	Go to Step 7	Go to Step 13
7	1. Reconnect the power steering fluid flow actuator connector. 2. Using the J 39200, measure the resistance between the EBCM harness connector C1 terminal B7 and ground. Is the resistance within range specified?	OL (Infinite)	Go to Step 8	Go to Step 15
8	Using the J 39200, measure the resistance between the EBCM harness connectors C1 terminal B7 and C2 terminal C. Is the resistance within range specified?	7-19 Ω	Go to Step 9	Go to Step 15

GC6029800358010X

Fig. 34 Code C1273: Actuator Circuit Open Or Shorted To Ground (Part 1 of 2). Lumina & Monte Carlo

Step	Action	Value(s)	Yes	No
9	1. Inspect EBCM harness connectors and 2-way power steering fluid flow actuator harness connector for poor terminal contact or corrosion. Replace any terminals with poor terminal contact or corrosion. 2. Inspect CKT 1295 for damage which may result in a short to ground or an open with all connectors connected. Repair the damage if evident. 3. Reconnect all connectors. 4. Turn the ignition switch to the RUN position. Is DTC C1273 set as a current DTC?	—	Go to Step 16	Go to Step 14
10	Repair open or high resistance in CKT 1295. Is the repair complete?	—	Refer to ABS	—
11	Repair short to ground in CKT 1295. Is the repair complete?	—	Refer to ABS	—
12	Repair open or high resistance in CKT 1633/1294. Is the repair complete?	—	Refer to ABS	—
13	Repair short to ground in CKT 1633/1294. Is the repair complete?	—	Refer to ABS	—
14	Malfunction is intermittent.	—	—	—
15	Replace the power steering fluid flow actuator. Is the repair complete?	—	Refer to ABS	—
16	Replace the EBCM. Is the repair complete?	—	Refer to ABS	—

GC6029800358020X

Fig. 34 Code C1273: Actuator Circuit Open Or Shorted To Ground (Part 2 of 2). Lumina & Monte Carlo

Step	Action	Value(s)	Yes	No
1	Was the ABS Diagnostic System Check performed?	—	Go to Step 2	Refer to ABS
2	1. Turn the ignition switch to the OFF position. 2. Disconnect the ECBM harness connector. 3. Turn the ignition switch to the RUN position. 4. Using the J 39200, measure the voltage between the ECBM harness connector terminal 18 and ground. Is the voltage within the range specified in the Value(s) column?	0-1V	Go to Step 3	Go to Step 6
3	1. Turn the ignition switch to the OFF position. 2. Using the J 39200, measure the resistance between the ECBM harness connector terminals 18 and C. Is the resistance within the range specified in the Value(s) column?	7-19 Ω	Go to Step 4	Go to Step 5
4	1. Inspect the ECBM harness connector and the 2-way EVO actuator harness connector for damage which may result in a short to voltage or an open with all connectors connected. Repair the damage if evident. 2. Reconnect all connectors. 3. Start the engine. Wait 10 seconds. Does DTC C1274 set as a current DTC?	—	Go to Step 10	Go to Step 8
5	1. Disconnect the 2-way EVO actuator connector. 2. Using the J 39200, measure the resistance between the ECBM harness connector terminals 18 and C. Is the resistance within the range specified in the Value(s) column?	Infinite	Go to Step 9	Go to Step 7
6	Repair the short to voltage in CKT 1295. Is the repair complete?	—	Refer to ABS	—
7	Repair the short between CKTs 1295 and 1294/1633. Is the repair complete?	—	Refer to ABS	—
8	Malfunction is intermittent.	—	—	—
9	Replace the EVO actuator. Is the repair complete?	—	Refer to ABS	—
10	Replace the ECBM. Is the repair complete?	—	Refer to ABS	—

GC6029800354000X

Fig. 35 Code C1274: Actuator Circuit Shorted Or Solenoid Shorted. Achieva, Alero, Grand Am & Skylark

Step	Action	Value(s)	Yes	No
8	Malfunction is intermittent.	—	—	—
9	Replace the MSVA actuator. Is the repair complete?	—	Refer to ABS	—
10	Replace the EBCM. Is the repair complete?	—	Refer to ABS	—

GC6029800377020X

Fig. 36 Code C1274: Actuator Open Or Shorted Or Solenoid Shorted (Part 2 of 2). 1998 Intrigue

Step	Action	Value(s)	Yes	No
1	Was the ABS Diagnostic System Check performed?	—	Go to Step 2	Refer to ABS
2	1. Turn the ignition switch to the OFF position. 2. Disconnect the EBCM harness connectors. 3. Turn the ignition switch to the RUN position. 4. Using the J 39200, measure the voltage between the EBCM harness connector C1 terminal B7 and ground. Is the voltage within range specified?	0-1V	Go to Step 3	Go to Step 6
3	1. Turn the ignition switch to the OFF position. 2. Using the J 39200, measure the resistance between the EBCM harness connector C1 terminal B7 and C1 terminal B8. Is the resistance within range specified?	7-19 Ω	Go to Step 4	Go to Step 5
4	1. Inspect EBCM harness connectors and 2-way MSVA actuator harness connector for damage which may result in a short to voltage or an open with all connectors connected. Repair the damage if evident. 2. Reconnect all connectors. 3. Start the engine. Wait 10 seconds. Does DTC C1274 set as a current DTC?	—	Go to Step 10	Go to Step 8
5	1. Disconnect the 2-way MSVA actuator connector. 2. Using the J 39200, measure the resistance between the EBCM harness connectors C1 terminal B7 and C1 terminal B8. Is the resistance within range specified?	OL (Infinite)	Go to Step 9	Go to Step 7
6	Repair short to voltage in CKT 345. Is the repair complete?	—	Refer to ABS	—
7	Repair short between CKTs 345 and 1787. Is the repair complete?	—	Refer to ABS	—

GC6029800377010X

Fig. 36 Code C1274: Actuator Open Or Shorted Or Solenoid Shorted (Part 1 of 2). 1998 Intrigue

Step	Action	Value(s)	Yes	No
1	Was the ABS Diagnostic System Check performed?	—	*Go to Step 2*	Perform ABS Inspection
2	1. Turn the ignition switch off. 2. Disconnect the Electronic Brake Traction Control Module (EBTCM) harness connectors. 3. Turn the ignition switch on. 4. Using a DMM, measure the voltage between the EBTCM harness connector C1 terminal B7 and ground. Is the measured voltage within the specified range?	Less than 2V	*Go to Step 3*	*Go to Step 6*
3	1. Turn the ignition switch off. 2. Using a DMM, measure the resistance between the EBTCM harness connector C1 terminal B7 and C1 terminal B8. Is the measured resistance within the specified range?	7–19Ω	*Go to Step 4*	*Go to Step 5*
4	1. Inspect the EBCM harness connectors and the MSVA actuator harness connector for damage which may result in a short to voltage or an open with all the connectors connected. Repair the damage if evident. 2. Reconnect all the connectors. 3. Clear Variable Effort Steering (VES) Diagnostic Trouble Codes (DTCs). 4. Start the engine. Wait 10 seconds. 5. Check for VES DTCs. Does DTC C1274 reset as a current DTC?	—	*Go to Step 9*	*Go to Step 10*
5	1. Disconnect the MSVA actuator connector. 2. Using a DMM, measure the resistance between the EBTCM harness connectors C1 terminal B7 and C1 terminal B8. Is the measured resistance within the specified range?	∞	*Go to Step 8*	*Go to Step 7*
6	Repair short to voltage in circuit 345. Is the repair complete?	—	*Go to Step 11*	—
7	Repair short between circuits 345 and 1787. Is the repair complete?	—	*Go to Step 11*	—
8	Replace the MSVA actuator. Is the repair complete?	—	*Go to Step 11*	—

GC6029900433010X

Fig. 37 Code C1274: Actuator Open Or Shorted Or Solenoid Shorted (Part 1 of 2). 1999 Intrigue

Step	Action	Value(s)	Yes	No
9	Replace the EBTCM. Is the repair complete?	—	*Go to Step 11*	—
10	The malfunction is not present at this time. Is the action complete?	—	System OK	—
11	1. Turn the ignition switch off. 2. Reconnect connectors/components removed. Is the action complete?	—	Perform ABS Inspection	—

GC6029900433020X

Fig. 37 Code C1274: Actuator Open Or Shorted Or Solenoid Shorted (Part 2 of 2). 1999 Intrigue

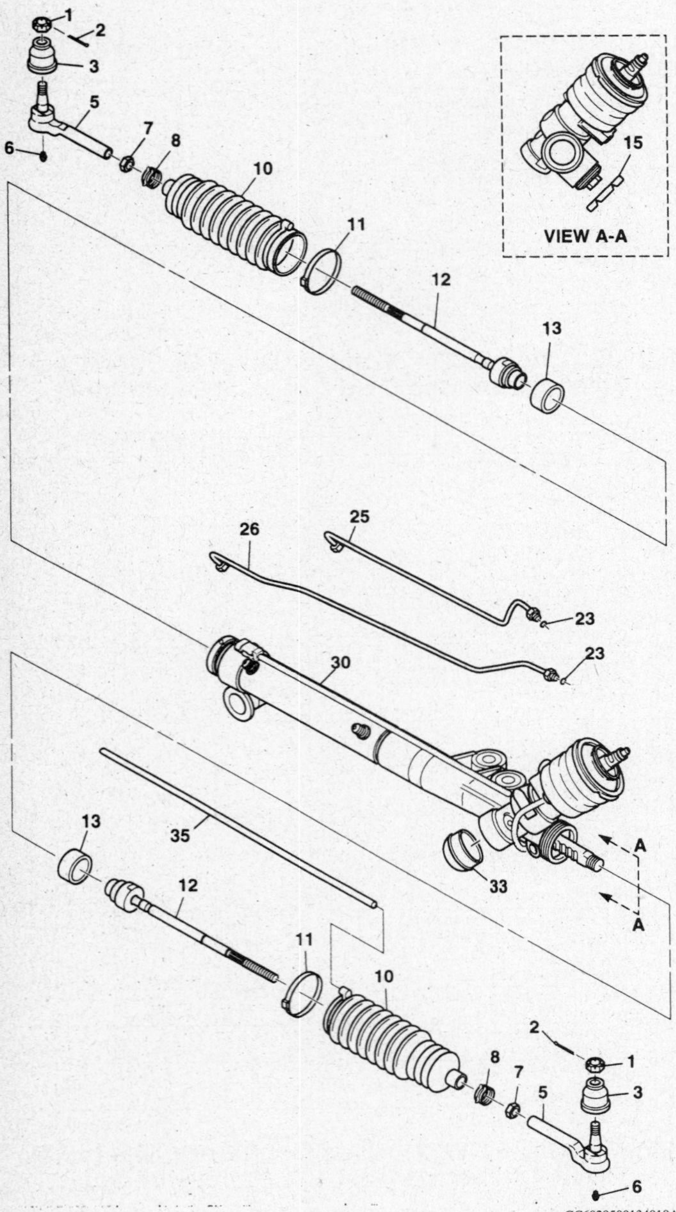

GC6029500134010A

Fig. 39 Exploded view of power rack & pinion assembly (Part 1 of 2). Aurora & Riviera

Step	Action	Value(s)	Yes	No
1	Was the ABS Diagnostic System Check performed?	—	Go to Step 2	Refer to ABS
2	1. Turn the ignition switch to the OFF position. 2. Disconnect the EBCM harness connectors. 3. Turn the ignition switch to the RUN position. 4. Using the J 39200, measure the voltage between the EBCM harness C1 terminal B7 and ground. Is the voltage within range specified?	0-1V	Go to Step 3	Go to Step 6
3	1. Turn the ignition switch to the OFF position. 2. Using the J 39200, measure the resistance between the EBCM harness connectors C1 terminal B7 and C2 terminal C. Is the resistance within the range specified?	7-19 Ω	Go to Step 4	Go to Step 5
4	1. Inspect EBCM harness connectors and 2-way power steering fluid flow actuator harness connector for damage which may result in a short to voltage or an open with all connectors connected. Repair the damage if evident. 2. Reconnect all connectors. 3. Start the engine. Wait 10 seconds. Does DTC C1274 set as a current DTC?	—	Go to Step 10	Go to Step 8
5	1. Disconnect the 2-way power steering fluid flow actuator connector. 2. Using the J 39200, measure the resistance between the EBCM harness connectors C1 terminal B7 and C2 terminal C. Is the resistance within range specified?	OL (Infinite)	Go to Step 9	Go to Step 7
6	Repair short to voltage in CKT 1295. Is the repair complete?	—	Refer to ABS	—
7	Repair short between CKTs 1295 and 1294/1633. Is the repair complete?	—	Refer to ABS	—
8	Malfunction is intermittent.	—	—	—
9	Replace the power steering fluid flow actuator. Is the repair complete?	—	Refer to ABS	—
10	Replace the EBCM. Is the repair complete?	—	Refer to ABS	—

GC6029800359000X

Fig. 38 Code C1274: Actuator Circuit Shorted Or Solenoid Shorted. Lumina & Monte Carlo

1 - NUT, HEXAGON SLOTTED
2 - PIN, COTTER
3 - SEAL, TIE ROD
5 - ROD ASM, OUTER TIE
6 - FITTING, LUBRICATION
7 - NUT, HEX JAM
8 - CLAMP, TIE ROD END
10 - BOOT, RACK & PINION
11 - CLAMP, BOOT
12 - ROD ASM, INNER TIE
13 - RING, SHOCK DAMPENER
15 - NUT, ADJUSTER PLUG LOCK
23 - SEAL, O-RING
25 - LINE ASM, CYLINDER (RH)
26 - LINE ASM, CYLINDER (LH)
30 - GEAR ASM, RACK & PINION (PARTIAL)
33 - COVER, DUST (ADD)
35 - TUBE, BREATHER

GC6029500134020A

Fig. 39 Exploded view of power rack & pinion assembly (Part 2 of 2). Aurora & Riviera

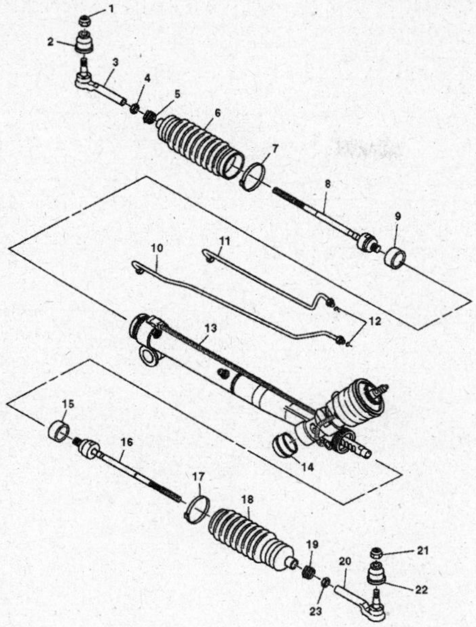

(1) Prevailing Torque Nut
(2) Tie Rod Seal
(3) Outer Tie Rod Assembly
(4) Hex Jam Nut
(5) Tie Rod End Clamp
(6) Rack and Pinion Boot
(7) Boot Clamp
(8) Inner Tie Rod Assembly
(9) Shock Dampener Ring
(10) Cylinder Line Assembly (LH)
(11) Cylinder Line Assembly (RH)
(12) O-ring Seal
(13) Rack and Pinion Gear Assembly (Partial)
(14) Dust Cover
(15) Shock Dampener Ring
(16) Inner Tie Rod Assembly
(17) Boot Clamp
(18) Rack and Pinion Boot
(19) Tie Rod End Clamp
(20) Outer Tie Rod Assembly
(21) Prevailing Torque Nut
(22) Tie Rod Seal
(23) Hex Jam Nut

GC6029800362000X

Fig. 40 Exploded view of power rack & pinion assembly. Corvette & Intrigue

1 - NUT, HEXAGON SLOTTED
2 - PIN, COTTER
3 - SEAL, TIE ROD
5 - ROD ASM, OUTER TIE
7 - NUT, HEX JAM
8 - CLAMP, TIE ROD END
10 - BOOT, RACK & PINION
11 - CLAMP, BOOT
12 - ROD ASM, INNER TIE
13 - RING, SHOCK DAMPENER
15 - NUT, ADJUSTER PLUG LOCK
16 - ADAPTER, SEAL
17 - RING, RETAINING
20 - SEAL, STUB SHAFT
21 - ANNULUS ASM, BEARING
22 - PLUG ASM, O-RING
23 - SEAL, O-RING
25 - LINE ASM, CYLINDER (RH)
26 - LINE ASM, CYLINDER (LH)
27 - BRACKET ASM, MOUNTING
28 - GROMMET, MOUNTING
30 - GEAR ASM, RACK & PINION (PARTIAL)
32 - NUT, HEX LOCK
33 - COVER, DUST
35 - TUBE, BREATHER

GC6029800386020X

Fig. 41 Exploded view of power rack & pinion assembly (Part 2 of 2). DeVille, Eldorado & Seville

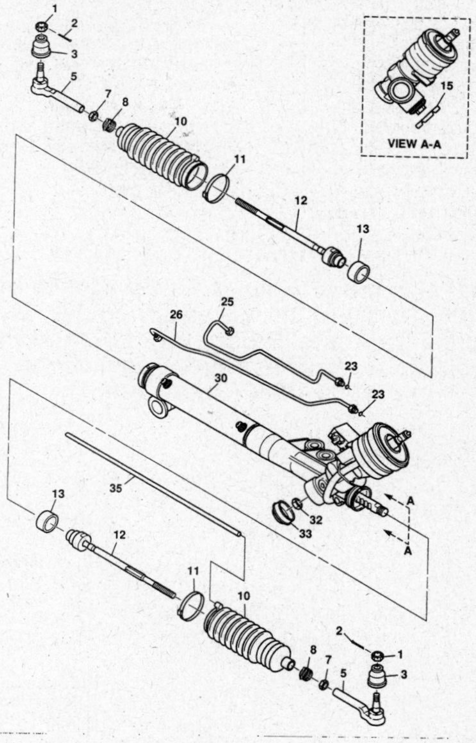

GC6029800386010X

Fig. 41 Exploded view of power rack & pinion assembly (Part 1 of 2). DeVille, Eldorado & Seville

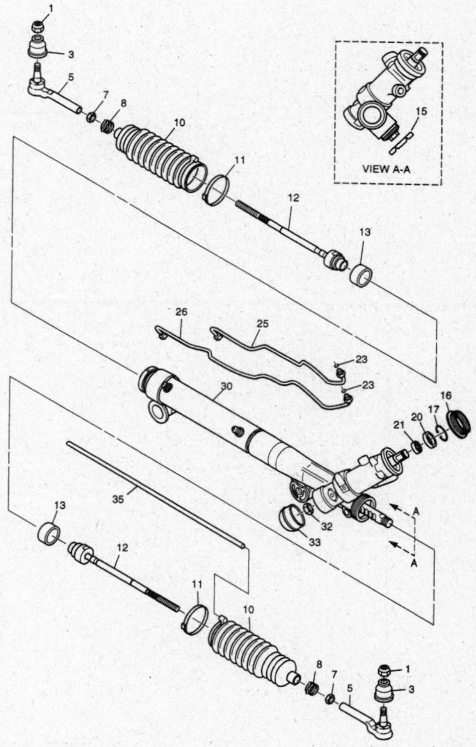

GC6029800385010X

Fig. 42 Exploded view of power rack & pinion assembly (Part 1 of 2). Alero, Bonneville, Century, Cutlass Supreme, Eighty-Eight, Grand Prix, LeSabre, LSS, Park Avenue, Regal, Regency & 1999–2000 Grand Am

1 - NUT, HEX TORQUE PREVAILING
3 - SEAL, TIE ROD
5 - ROD ASM, OUTER TIE
7 - NUT, HEX JAM
8 - CLAMP, TIE ROD END
10 - BOOT, RACK & PINION
11 - CLAMP, BOOT
12 - ROD ASM, INNER TIE
13 - RING, SHOCK DAMPENER
15 - NUT, ADJUSTER PLUG LOCK
16 - ADAPTER, SEAL
17 - RING, RETAINING
20 - SEAL, STUB SHAFT
21 - ANNULUS BEARING ASM
23 - SEAL, O-RING
25 - LINE ASM, CYLINDER (RH)
26 - LINE ASM, CYLINDER (LH)
30 - GEAR ASM, RACK & PINION (PARTIAL)
32 - NUT, HEX LOCK
33 - COVER, DUST
35 - BREATHER TUBE

GC6029800385020X

Fig. 42 Exploded view of power rack & pinion assembly (Part 2 of 2). Alero, Bonneville, Century, Cutlass Supreme, Eighty-Eight, Grand Prix, LeSabre, LSS, Park Avenue, Regal, Regency & 1999–2000 Grand Am

Step	Action	Scan Tool Display
1	1. Connect a scan tool to the data link connector (DLC). 2. Input the vehicle information and select Chassis.	• Delco Bosch ABS/TCS • Magna Steer
2	Select Magna Steer.	• Diagnostics • Recalibration
3	Select Recalibration.	• Magna Steer Recalibration Procedure - Ensure that the ignition is ON and the engine is OFF. • Press ENTER to Start.
4	Press ENTER.	Is the VIN correct?
5	Select YES.	Does the vehicle have Magna Steer RPO # <NV8 ?
6	Select YES.	Is the vehicle equipped with the Gran Touring Package RPO # <Y56 ?
7	Select YES.	Recal with the FACTORY STANDARD calibration
8	Select NO.	Select the calibration: • More firm • Factory calibration • Less firm
9	Select the desired response mode.	• Magna Steer Recalibration Procedure is complete. • Press EXIT in order to return to the menu.
10	Exit the scan tool.	Reprogramming is complete.

GC6029900427000X

Fig. 43 Variable effort steering programming. Bonneville, Eighty Eight, LeSabre, LSS, Park Avenue & Regency

Action	Result
1. Install a *Scan Tool.* 2. Input the vehicle information and select Chassis.	• ABS/TCS/ICCS • Magna Steer
Select Magna Steer.	• Diagnostics • Recalibration
Select Recalibration.	Magna Steer Recalibration Procedure - Be sure Ignition is ON Engine OFF Press [ENTER] to Start
Press [ENTER].	Is VIN Correct?
Select YES.	Factory Standard Calibration Will Be Used For This VIN. Press [ENTER] to Start
Press [ENTER].	Magna Steer Recalibration Procedure is complete Press [EXIT] to Return to Menu.
Exit the scan tool.	Reprogramming is complete.

GC6019800016000X

Fig. 44 Variable effort steering programming. Seville

Saginaw Rotary Valve Power Steering Gear, General Motors

INDEX

Code	Description
21	No Speed Signal
22	Solenoid Short To Ground/Open
23	Power Steering Control Module Malfunction

Fig. 1 Diagnostic trouble code interpretation

PRECAUTIONS

AIR BAG SYSTEMS

Refer to "Air Bag System Precautions" in the front of this manual for system disarming and arming procedures.

BATTERY GROUND CABLE

Prior to service, disconnect battery ground cable and isolate as required.

DESCRIPTION

The Saginaw rotary valve steering gear incorporates a recirculating ball system in which steel balls act as a rolling thread between a steering worm shaft and the rack piston.

Variable Effort Steering (VES) or Speed Sensitive Steering (SSS) is a power steering system varies the steering effort required to steer the vehicle at different speeds. At low speeds, the system provides maximum power assist. At higher speeds, increased steering effort will provide firmer steering (road feel) and direction stability. The power steering control module uses speed input from the Electronic Braking Traction Control Module (EBTCM) to control the power steering fluid flow control valve actuator. The power steering fluid flow control valve actuator utilizes a pintle valve to control fluid flow to the steering gear.

DIAGNOSIS & TESTING

Accessing Diagnostic Trouble Codes

Diagnostic Trouble Codes (DTCs) may be read using a suitably programmed scan tool. There are no provisions for flash code diagnostics.

1. Turn ignition Off.
2. Connect suitably programmed scan tool to Data Link Connector (DLC).
3.
4. Turn ignition On. Select scan tool's Special Functions.
5. Turn ignition On.
6. Turn ignition On. Select scan tool's Special Functions.
7. Read and record DTCs.

Diagnostic Trouble Code Interpretation

Refer to **Fig. 1** for diagnostic trouble code interpretation.

Wiring Diagrams

Refer to **Fig. 2** for wiring diagram.

Diagnostic Tests

Refer to **Fig. 3** for system inspection and **Figs. 4 through 6** for diagnostic trouble code tests.

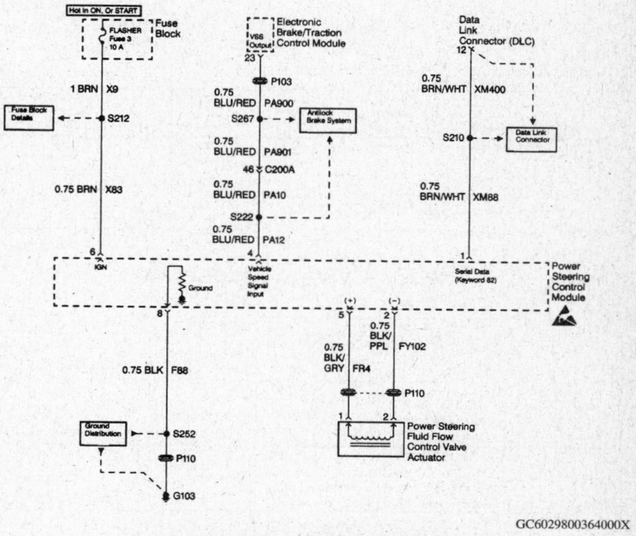

Fig. 2 Wiring diagram

Clearing Diagnostic Trouble Codes

DTCs cannot be cleared by disconnecting EBTCM or battery cables. Follow the scan tool manufacturer's instructions to clear DTCs.

POWER STEERING SYSTEM SERVICE

POWER STEERING CONTROL MODULE

1. Twist self-locking screws to allow for front of sound insulator to drop down, **Fig. 7.** Remove sound insulator.
2. Disconnect control module electrical connectors, **Fig. 8.**
3. Remove power steering control module.
4. Reverse procedure to install.
5. Reverse procedure to install.

Step	Action	Value(s)	Yes	No
1	1. Prepare the vehicle for a road test. 2. Check the power steering fluid level. 3. Check the power steering belt tension. 4. Check the tire inflation. 5. Road test the vehicle using various parking maneuvers and a level stretch of highway. Does the steering force lessen when parking and require more force as the vehicle speed increases?	—	*Go to Step 3*	*Go to Step 2*
2	Was the problem found and repaired?	—	*Go to Step 9*	—
3	1. The procedure for reading DTCs is to use the scan tool. 2. When reading DTCs, follow the instructions that are supplied by the scan tool manufacturer. 3. Connect the scan tool to the data link connector (DLC). 4. Establish communication with the power steering control module. Does the scan tool communicate with the power steering control module?	—	*Go to Step 5*	*Go to Step 4*
4	*ST Does Not Communicate with PS Control Module*	—	—	—
5	Are there any current DTCs displayed?	—	*Go to Step 6*	*Go to Step 7*
6	1. If DTC 21 is present, refer to *DTC 21.* 2. If DTC 22 is present, refer to *DTC 22*. 3. If DTC 23 is present, refer to *DTC 23*. Go to the appropriate table to diagnose the DTC.	—	—	—
7	Are any history or intermittent codes displayed?	—	*Go to Step 8*	*Go to Step 9*
8	Locate and repair the problem. Was the intermittent problem found and repaired?	—	*Go to Step 9*	—
9	1. Connect all connectors and components that were disconnected. 2. Install the scan tool. 3. Check for any current or history or intermittent DTCs. Are there any current or history or intermittent DTCs present?	—	*Go to Step 1*	System OK

GC6029800380000X

Fig. 3 System Inspection

Step	Action	Value(s)	Yes	No
1	Was the Variable Effort Steering System Check performed?	—	*Go to Step 2*	Refer to System Check
2	1. Connect the scan tool to the data link connector (DTC). 2. Check for a current DTC 22. Is a current DTC 22 displayed?	—	*Go to Step 3*	*Go to Step 4*
3	1. Remove the power steering control module (PSCM). 2. Use a DMM to measure the resistance across terminals 2 and 5 of the module connector. Is the measured resistance within the specified value?	7–8 Ω	*Go to Step 6*	*Go to Step 7*
4	Check for a history or an intermittent DTC 22. Is a history or an intermittent DTC 22 displayed?	—	*Go to Step 5*	*Go to Step 6*
5	1. Locate an intermittent in circuits FR4 and/or FY102. 2. Repair the intermittent in circuits FR4 and/or FY102. Is the repair complete?	—	*Go to Step 10*	—
6	1. Use the DMM to measure the resistance between terminal 2 of the PSCM connector and a known good ground. 2. Use the DMM to measure the resistance between terminal 5 of the PSCM connector and a known good ground. Is the measured resistance for both measurements within the specified value?	OL	*Go to Step 8*	*Go to Step 9*
7	1. Locate an open or a high resistance in circuits FR4 and/or FY102. 2. Repair the open or the high resistance in circuits FR4 and/or FY102. 3. Replace the power steering fluid flow control valve actuator if these circuits are OK. Is the repair or replacement complete?	—	*Go to Step 10*	—
8	1. Check power and ground circuits to the module. 2. Replace the power steering control module if power and ground is OK. Is the replacement complete?	—	*Go to Step 10*	—

GC6029800366010X

Fig. 5 Code 22: Solenoid Circuit Short To Ground/ Open (Part 1 of 2)

Step	Action	Value(s)	Yes	No
1	Was the Variable Effort Steering System Check performed?	—	*Go to Step 2*	Check Speedometer
2	Does the speedometer operate properly?	—	*Go to Step 3*	Check Speedometer
3	1. Disconnect the power steering control module connector. 2. Raise the drive wheels. 3. Turn the ignition switch to the ON position. 4. Use the DMM, on the AC scale, to measure the voltage between terminals 4 and 8 of the power steering control module connector while rotating the LH rear wheel. Is the measured voltage within the specified value?	Greater than 1 VAC	*Go to Step 5*	*Go to Step 4*
4	1. Locate an open or a high resistance in circuit PA12. 2. Repair the open or the high resistance in circuit PA12. Is the repair complete?	—	*Go to Step 6*	—
5	Replace the power steering control module. Is the replacement complete?	—	*Go to Step 6*	—
6	1. Connect all connectors and components that were disconnected. 2. Road test the vehicle. 3. After road test, install the scan tool again. 4. Check for DTC 21. Is DTC 21 present?	—	*Go to Step 1*	System OK

GC6029800365000X

Fig. 4 Code 21: No Speed Signal

Step	Action	Value(s)	Yes	No
9	1. If any continuity readings were observed, locate a short to ground in circuits FR4 and/or FY102. 2. Repair the short to ground in circuits FR4 and/or FY102. Is the repair complete?	—	*Go to Step 10*	—
10	1. Connect all connectors or components that were disconnected. 2. Road test the vehicle. 3. After the road test, install the scan tool again. 4. Check for DTC 22. Is DTC 22 displayed?	—	*Go to Step 1*	System OK

GC6029800366020X

Fig. 5 Code 22: Solenoid Circuit Short To Ground/ Open (Part 2 of 2)

Step	Action	Value(s)	Yes	No
1	Was the Variable Effort Steering System Check performed?	—	*Go to Step 2*	Refer to System Check
2	1. Remove the power steering control module (PSCM). 2. Turn the ignition switch to the ON position. 3. Use a DMM to measure the voltage between terminal 6 of the PSCM connector and a known good ground. Is the measured voltage within the specified value?	B+	*Go to Step 4*	*Go to Step 3*
3	1. Locate an open or a high resistance in circuit X83. 2. Repair the open or the high resistance in circuit X83. Is the repair complete?	—	*Go to Step 7*	—
4	Use the DMM to measure the resistance between terminal 8 of the PSCM connector and a known good ground. Is the measured resistance within the specified value?	Less than 5 Ω	*Go to Step 6*	*Go to Step 5*
5	1. Locate an open or a high resistance in circuit F88. 2. Repair the open or the high resistance in circuit F88. Is the repair complete?	—	*Go to Step 7*	—
6	Replace the power steering control module. Effort Steering. Is the replacement complete?	—	*Go to Step 7*	—
7	1. Connect all of the connectors and components that were disconnected. 2. Road test the vehicle. 3. Install the scan tool after the road test. 4. Check for DTC 23. Is DTC 23 displayed?	—	*Go to Step 1*	System OK

GC6029800367000X

Fig. 6 Code 23: Power Steering Control Module Malfunction

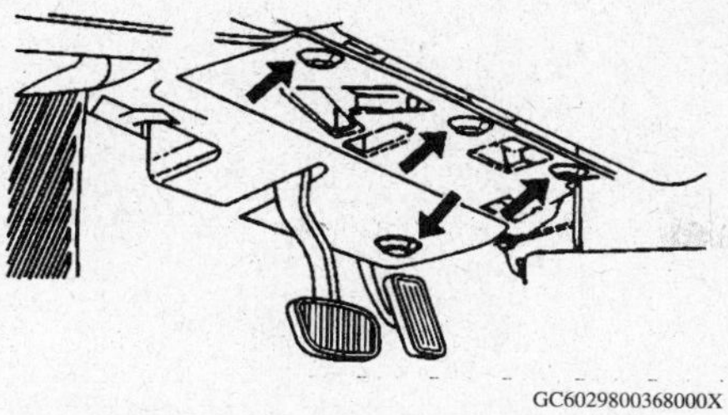

Fig. 7 Sound insulator self-locking screws location

FLOW CONTROL VALVE ACTUATOR

1. Remove steering gear as described under "Front Suspension & Steering" in the appropriate chassis section of this service manual.
2. Remove flow control valve actuator retaining screws, then the flow control valve actuator.
3. Reverse procedure to install. Tighten flow control valve actuator retaining screws to specifications.

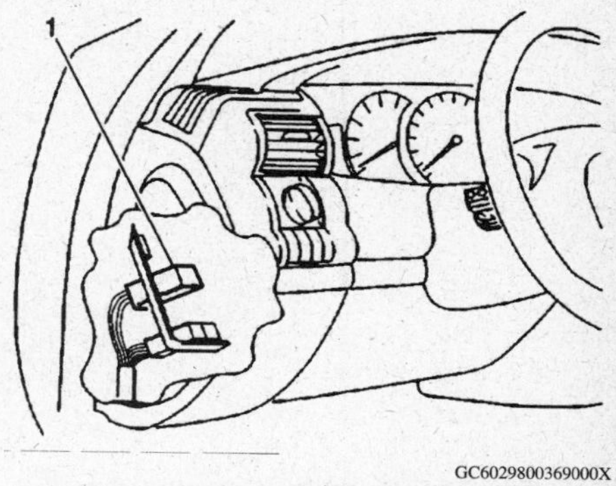

Fig. 8 Power steering control module location

TIGHTENING SPECIFICATIONS

Component	Torque/Ft. Lbs.
Ball Stud Nut (1997–98)	44
Ball Stud Nut (1999–2000)	44①
Flow Control Valve Actuator	27②
Idler Arm Bolts	44
Tie Rod Adjuster Clamp Bolt	11
Steering Gear Bolts	30
Steering Gear Coupler Bolt	16

① — Plus an additional 52°.
② — Inch lbs.

Toyota Rack & Pinion Power Steering Gear, Prizm

INDEX

PRECAUTIONS

AIR BAG SYSTEMS

Refer to "Air Bag System Precautions" in the front of this manual for system disarming and arming procedures.

BATTERY GROUND CABLE

Prior to service, disconnect battery ground cable and isolate as required.

DESCRIPTION

This steering system converts rotary motion to linear motion as follows: when the steering wheel is turned, rotary motion is transferred to the steering shaft, the shaft joint and rack pinion. The pinion teeth mesh with teeth on the rack and the rotary motion is transferred to the rack and changed to linear motion. The linear force is then transmitted through the tie rods to the steering knuckles which steer the front wheels.

POWER STEERING SYSTEM SERVICE

STEERING GEAR

REMOVAL

1. Ensure front wheels are in straight-ahead position, then turn ignition to Lock.
2. Remove steering column upper cover bolts from firewall.
3. **On 1997 models,** place matchmarks on steering shaft joint and control valve shaft, then remove joint assembly.
4. **On 1998–2000 models,** remove steering column shaft lower coupling pinch bolt.
5. **On all models,** remove power steering fluid outlet pipe heat shield.
6. Remove lefthand and righthand steering gear inlet and outlet pipe clips and bolts.
7. Locate a suitable drain pan to collect power steering fluid spillage.
8. Disconnect inlet and outlet pipes from steering gear.
9. Remove oxygen sensor as required.

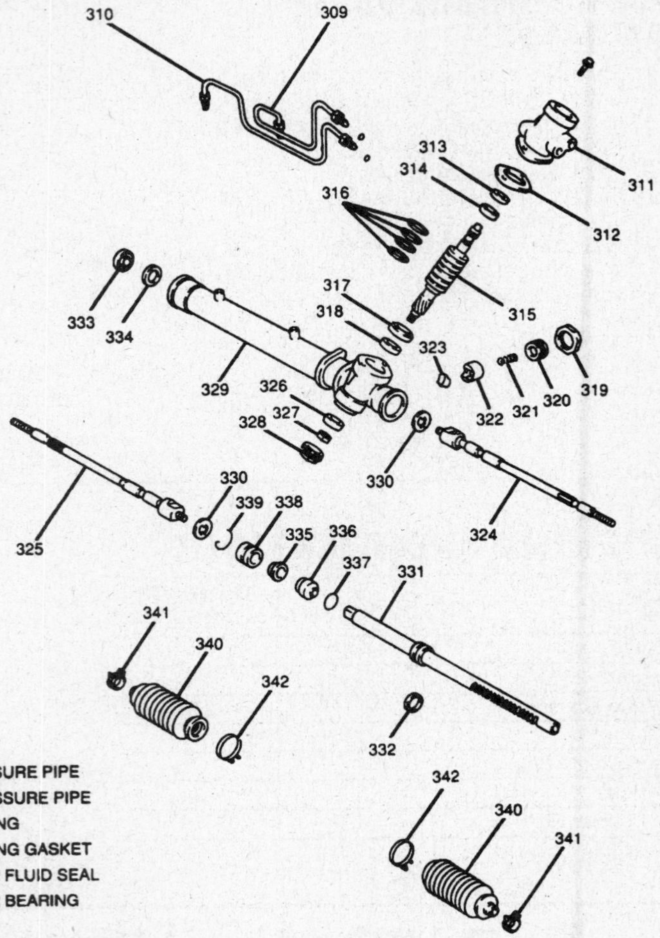

309 LEFT TURN FLUID PRESSURE PIPE
310 RIGHT TURN FLUID PRESSURE PIPE
311 CONTROL VALVE HOUSING
312 CONTROL VALVE HOUSING GASKET
313 CONTROL VALVE UPPER FLUID SEAL
314 CONTROL VALVE UPPER BEARING
315 CONTROL VALVE
316 CONTROL VALVE TEFLON· SEAL RINGS
317 STEERING RACK HOUSING UPPER BEARING
318 CONTROL VALVE LOWER FLUID SEAL
319 RACK GUIDE SPRING CAP LOCKNUT
320 RACK GUIDE SPRING CAP
321 RACK GUIDE SPRING
322 RACK GUIDE
323 RACK GUIDE SEAT
324 LEFT TIE ROD
325 RIGHT TIE ROD
326 CONTROL VALVE LOWER BEARING
327 CONTROL VALVE LOCKNUT
328 RACK HOUSING CAP
329 RACK HOUSING
330 CLAW WASHER
331 STEERING RACK
332 STEERING RACK TEFLON· SEAL RING
333 STEERING RACK INNER FLUID SEAL
334 STEERING RACK INNER SPACER
335 STEERING RACK OUTER FLUID SEAL
336 STEERING RACK OUTER SPACER
337 STEERING RACK OUTER SPACER O-RING
338 CYLINDER END STOPPER
339 CYLINDER END STOPPER WIRE
340 TIE ROD BOOT
341 OUTER BOOT CLAMP
342 INNER BOOT CLAMP

GC6029300112000A

Fig. 1 Exploded view of Toyota (Prizm) power rack & pinion steering gear assembly

Discard the gasket.
10. Install engine support tool No. J-28467-360, or equivalent.
11. Raise and support vehicle.
12. Remove engine righthand and lefthand lower splash shields.
13. Remove driveshaft exhaust heat shield.
14. Remove front tires and wheels.
15. Using puller tool No. J-24319-B, or equivalent, remove outer tie rods.
16. **On 1998–2000 models,** proceed as follows:
    a. Remove front suspension brace nuts, then the brace.
    b. Remove front suspension crossmember, transaxle support, control arms and front stabilizer shaft as a complete unit.
    c. Remove rear transaxle mount through-bolt, then the mount.
    d. Remove rear transaxle mount bracket bolts, then the bracket.
17. **On all models,** disconnect exhaust pipe from manifold.
18. Remove steering gear boot heat shield.
19. Remove steering gear clamp fasteners, then the clamps.
20. **On 1997 models,** carefully slide steering gear out through righthand wheelwell opening.
21. **On 1998–2000 models,** move steering gear to righthand side of vehicle, then lower and remove from lefthand side.
22. **On all models,** remove insulators from steering gear.

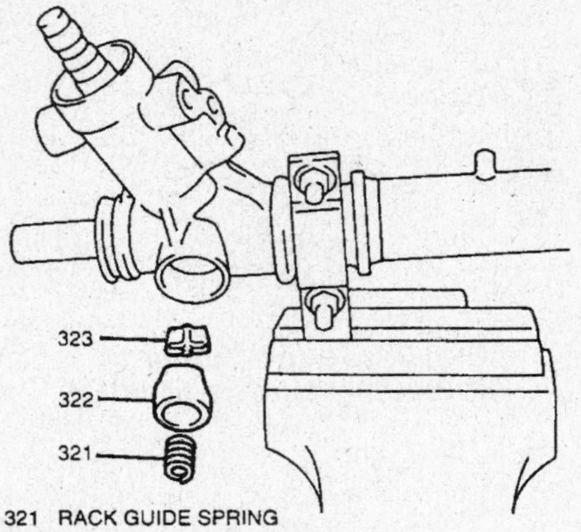

321 RACK GUIDE SPRING
322 RACK GUIDE
323 RACK GUIDE SEAT

GC6029300113000X

Fig. 2 Rack guide, spring & seat removal. 1997

DISASSEMBLE

1997

1. Remove steering unit, **Fig. 1,** from vehicle and place in suitable soft-jawed vise.
2. Remove righthand and lefthand turn pressure pipes between valve housing and cylinder using injection line wrench tool No. J-29698-A, or equivalent.
3. Place match marks on tie rod ends and tie rods, then remove tie rod ends.
4. Remove both rack boots.
5. Unstake claw washers retaining both tie rods to steering rack, then remove using tie rod housing wrench tool No. J-35414 and steering rack end wrench tool No. J-35418, or equivalents.
6. Remove steering rack guide cap nut, cap, spring, rack guide and seat using rack guide spring cap wrench tool No. J-35309-2 and spring cap locknut wrench tool No. J-35692, or equivalents, **Fig. 2.**
7. Remove control valve locknut from control using pinion preload socket tool No. J-35428, or equivalent to hold control valve stationary.
8. Remove dust cover from top of pinion gear, then two bolts, control valve housing and gasket from steering rack housing, **Fig. 3.**
9. Turn cylinder end stopper using cylinder end stopper end wrench tool No. J-39901, or equivalent until both ends of cylinder end stopper wire appear in slot on top of steering rack housing.
10. Turn cylinder end stopper using cylinder end stopper end wrench so that loose end of cylinder end stopper wire is fed out of slot on top of steering rack

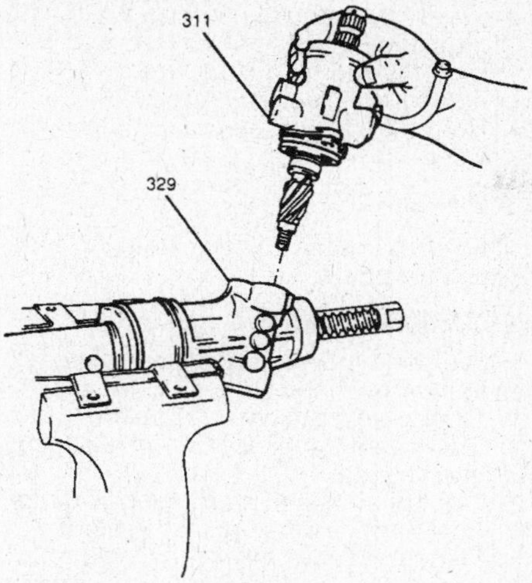

Fig. 3 Control valve housing removal. 1997

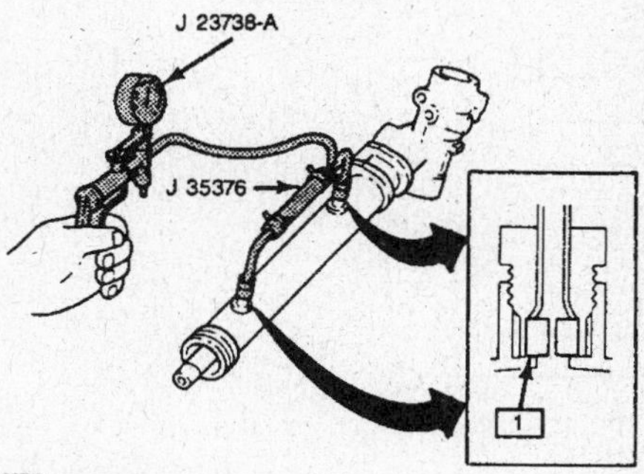

Fig. 6 Steering rack fluid seal integrity inspection

housing.

11. Remove cylinder end stopper wire and cylinder end stopper from steering rack housing, **Fig. 4.** Install a rack seal protector tool No. J-36595, or equivalent onto toothed portion on steering rack to protect inner steering rack fluid seal.
12. Remove steering rack and steering rack outer spacer from steering rack housing.
13. Remove steering rack outer fluid seal from outer spacer.
14. Remove O-ring from steering outer spacer.
15. Remove steering rack inner fluid seal and spacer from steering rack housing using rack cylinder seal remover tool No. J-35434-1 with drive handle tool No. J-35434-2, or equivalents.
16. Remove steering rack housing lower bearing from steering rack housing using a brass drift punch and hammer.
17. Remove steering rack upper bearing using a control valve bearing remover tool No. J-39902 with driver handle tool No. J-35434-2, or equivalents.
18. Clean all disassembled components. **Do not use a wire brush.**
19. Inspect rack bar for corrosion, pits,

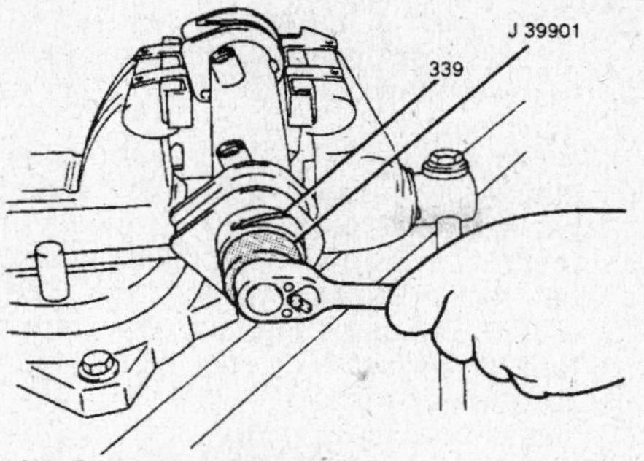

Fig. 4 Cylinder end stopper wire removal

scratches, dents, teeth wear or damage.

20. Measure steering rack runout using dial indicator tool set No. J-8001, or equivalent. If runout is greater than .0118 inch, replace steering rack.

1998–2000

Do not disassemble the steering gear on these models.

ASSEMBLE

1997

1. Install steering rack housing upper bearing into steering rack housing using control valve bearing stopper tool No. J-39903 and driver handle tool No. J-7079-2, or equivalents, **Fig. 5.**
2. Install steering rack inner fluid seal and spacer into steering rack housing using rack seal protector tool No. J-36595, or equivalent and steering rack.
3. Place rack seal protector tool over toothed portion of steering rack, then slide fluid seal and spacer over protector tool and onto steering rack.
4. Install steering rack into steering rack housing and tap gently with plastic mallet until inner fluid seal and spacer have been seated.
5. Remove rack seal protector tool from steering rack.
6. Install new O-ring onto steering rack outer spacer.
7. Install new steering rack outer fluid seal into steering rack outer spacer.
8. Install cylinder end stopper into steering rack housing as follows:
   a. Turn cylinder end stopper using cylinder end stopper wrench tool No. J-39901, or equivalent until wire end hole appears in slot on top of steering rack housing.
   b. Place hooked end of cylinder end stopper wire into wire end of hole of cylinder end stopper and turn cylinder end stopper using cylinder end stopper wrench while feeding cylinder end stopper wire into slot on top of steering rack housing.
   c. Continue to turn cylinder end stopper until both ends of cylinder end stopper wire are no longer visible.
9. Inspect steering rack fluid seal integrity using cylinder pressure tester tool No.

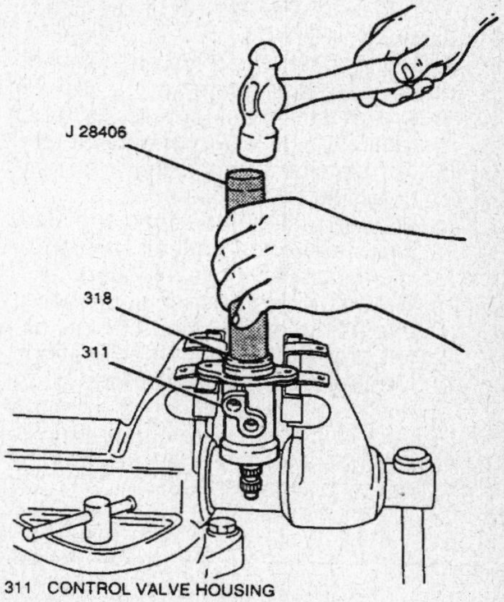

Fig. 5 Steering rack housing upper bearing installation

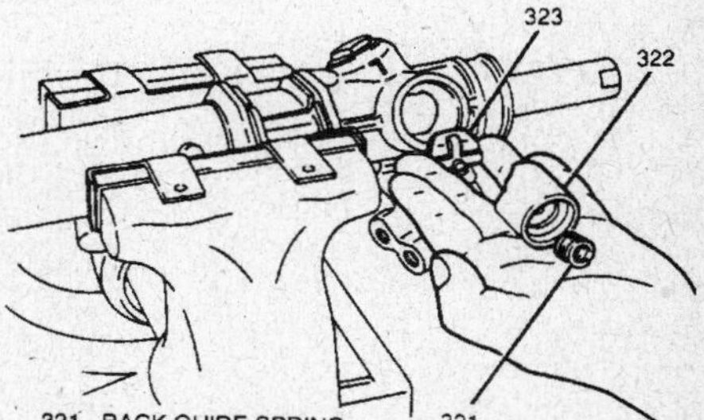

Fig. 7 Rack guide, spring & seat installation. 1997

J-35376, or equivalent and suitable vacuum pipe, **Fig. 6.**

10. Apply 15 inches of vacuum to steering rack housing and observe vacuum pump. If pressure tester indicates a loss of vacuum, inspect steering rack inner and outer fluid seals.
11. Install new control valve housing gasket and control valve housing onto steering rack housing, then **torque** two bolts to 13 ft. lbs.
12. Install dust cover onto top of pinion gear.
13. Install steering rack housing lower bearing and new control valve locknut onto control valve using pinion preload socket tool No. J-35428, or equivalent to hold control valve stationary.
14. Apply Loctite pipe sealant part No. 12346004, or equivalent to threaded portion of rack housing cap.
15. Install housing cap into steering rack housing, then **torque** to 43 ft. lbs., **Fig. 7.** Apply Loctite pipe sealant to threaded portion of rack guide spring cap.
16. Install rack guide spring cap into steering rack housing using locknut wrench

tool No. J-35309-2, or equivalent, then **torque** to 18 ft. lbs.

17. Adjust total pinion preload as follows:
    a. Loosen rack guide spring cap 15° (1/24 of a turn) using locknut wrench tool No. J-35309-2, or equivalent.
    b. Turn pinion shaft to right and left one rotation each.
    c. Loosen rack guide spring cap using locknut wrench until all tension on rack guide spring is released.
    d. Gradually tighten rack guide spring cap using locknut wrench until pinion preload is within specifications.
    e. Measure total pinion preload (starting torque) using pinion preload socket tool No. J-35428, or equivalent and a torque wrench. Standard pinion preload should be 7–12.4 ft. lbs.
18. Install rack guide spring cap locknut onto rack guide spring cap using locknut wrench tool No. J-35309-2, or equivalent.
19. While holding rack guide spring cap stationary, **torque** rack guide spring cap locknut to 43 ft. lbs.
20. Install tie rods onto steering rack using tie rod housing wrench tool No. J-35414 and steering rack end wrench tool No. J-35418, or equivalents, then **torque** tie rods to 61 ft. lbs.
21. Stake both claw washers, then slide both tie rod boots toward steering rack housing.
22. Install inner and outer boot clamps to both boots.
23. Inspect righthand and lefthand turn fluid pressure pipe O-rings for cuts or other damage, replacing as required.
24. Install righthand and lefthand turn fluid pressure pipes to power steering gear, then **torque** fluid pressure pipe flare nuts to 10 ft. lbs.
25. Remove power steering gear from vise.

1998–2000

Do not disassemble the steering gear on these models.

INSTALLATION

Reverse removal procedure to install, noting the following:

1. Replace exhaust flange gasket.
2. Install a new gasket when installing oxygen sensor.
3. Tighten all fasteners to specifications.
4. Bleed power steering fluid system.
5. Inspect for and correct any leakage.

TIGHTENING SPECIFICATIONS

Component	Torque/Ft. Lbs.
Front Suspension Brace Nuts	51
Inner Tie Rod Housing To Rack (1997–99)	32
Inner Tie Rod Housing To Rack (2000)	46
Inner Tie Rod Pinch Bolts (1997)	36
Inner Tie Rod Pinch Bolts (1998–2000)	46
Outer Tie Rod Jam Nut	41
Outer Tie Rod Castle Nut (1997)	61
Outer Tie Rod Castle Nut (1998–2000)	①
Power Steering Inlet Hose Fitting (1998–2000)	40
Power Steering Line Fittings (1997)	10
Steering Gear Mounting Bolts & Nuts	52
Steering Shaft Lower Coupling Bolt	26
Transaxle Rear Mount Bolts	57
Transaxle Rear Mount Through-Bolts	64

① — Torque to 36 ft. lbs. Rotate an additional 1/6 turn or 52 ft. lbs. to align cotter pin slots. Do not back nut off for cotter pin installation.

Saturn

NOTE: Prior To Performing Any Service Operations Listed In This Section, Consult The "Technical Service Bulletins " Section For Related Information.

INDEX

DESCRIPTION

STEERING SYSTEM

The power steering system is a rack and pinion design featuring a constant flow or electronic variable orifice (EVO) system. Vehicles equipped with a DOHC engine utilize the EVO system while models equipped with the SOHC engine utilize the constant flow design.

Unlike conventional power steering systems, the EVO feature adjusts the amount of steering assist according to the speed of the vehicle, which is monitored by a vehicle speed sensor (VSS). This information is read electronically by the Powertrain Control Module (PCM), which commands the EVO actuator to control the power steering pump output flow.

At low speeds, where high levels of assist are desired, the EVO actuator is opened more widely, providing more flow to the steering gear and greater assist. At higher speeds, the actuator is closed further, providing less pump flow and less steering assist and improved road feeling. All of the additional flow of the pump that is not needed by the gear is allowed to return to the reservoir through a bypass.

EVO ACTUATOR

The EVO actuator is a 10 ohm linear solenoid. The PCM controls the current to the high and low side of the actuator so current control is retained in the presence of any output fault condition.

The control of the actuator is accomplished by pulse width modulating (PWM) voltage to the actuator ad monitoring the actual current flow. The PCM varies the PWM signal in order to make the actual current equal to the desired current.

TROUBLESHOOTING

Refer to **Fig. 1** for power steering system troubleshooting.

DIAGNOSIS & TESTING

HYDRAULIC SYSTEM TEST

1. Disconnect high pressure line at steering gear and install power steering system tester tool No. SA9134C, or equivalent.
2. Open gate valve on power steering system tester.
3. Run engine until it has reached normal operating temperature. Replace any power steering fluid lost during tester installation, then bleed system if necessary.
4. With engine idling, record pressure and flow rate. If pressure reading is greater than 150 psi, stop engine and check power steering lines for restrictions. **Do not turn steering wheel while performing this test.**
5. Slowly close gate valve until 700 psi is indicated on power steering tester. Record pressure and flow rate.
6. Flow rate should not drop more than 1 gallon per minute from recorded flow rate.
7. If flow rate drops more than 1 gallon per minute, replace ring, rotor and vanes in pump. Also inspect pressure plate and thrust plates for wear.
8. Completely close and open gate valve three times. **Do not close gate valve for more than five seconds at a time.** Record fluid pressure each time valve is closed.
9. If all three readings are not within 50 psi, replace flow control valve.
10. With gate valve open, increase engine speed to 1600 RPM and record fluid pressure and flow rate. **Do not turn steering wheel.**
11. Flow rate should not vary more than 1 gallon per minute from flow rate recorded in step 4.
12. Ensure flow control valve moves freely in pump housing. Inspect valve for burrs.
13. Turn steering wheel completely to left, then completely to right. Record fluid pressure and flow rate at each stop.
14. If flow rate is greater then 1 gallon per minute, steering gear is leaking internally and must be replaced.

EVO SUBSYSTEM TEST

1. Disconnect high pressure line at power steering pump and install Power Steering System Tester tool No. SA9134C, or equivalent.
2. Connect a Powertrain Diagnostic Tool (PDT) to ALDL diagnostic port. Follow tool manufacturer's instructions.
3. Open gate valve on steering system tester.
4. Run engine until normal operating temperature is reached. Replace any power steering fluid lost during tester installation, then bleed system if necessary.
5. Select "EVO Subsystem Test" using PDT tool, in special test menu.
6. Using PDT, command EVO actuator to provide "full assist." Record power steering fluid flow rate, as indicated on power steering system tester. If flow rate is not between 2.35–2.85 gallons per minute, replace EVO actuator.
7. Using PDT, command EVO actuator to provide "no assist. " Record fluid flow rate, as indicated on steering tester. If flow rate is not between .4–.9 gallons per minute, replace EVO actuator.

POWER STEERING SYSTEM SERVICE

Component Service

POWER STEERING PUMP OVERHAUL

Disassemble

1. Remove power steering pump from vehicle.
2. Remove reservoir retaining clips from reservoir assembly.
3. Remove reservoir from housing.
4. Remove O-ring seal from pump housing, then pulley using puller tool No. SA9162C, or equivalent.
5. Remove three power steering pump to bracket fasteners and remove bracket from pump.
6. Remove EVO actuator assembly using removal tool No. SA9116C, or equivalent.
7. Remove flow control valve and spring.

COMPLAINT/CONDITION	POSSIBLE CAUSE(S)	CORRECTION(S)
Hard Steering	Front tire(s) improperly inflated.	Inflate tire(s) correctly.
	Improperly adjusted, improperly lubricated or damaged steering gear.	Adjust, lubricate (check for damaged boots), or replace steering gear.
	Worn or binding lower control arm ball stud(s).	Replace lower control arm(s).
	Worn or binding inner or outer tie rod(s).	Replace inner or outer tie rod end(s).
	Worn or binding upper strut mount(s).	Replace mount(s).
	Worn or binding intermediate shaft joint(s).	Replace intermediate shaft.
	Accessory drive belt loose.	Check accessory drive belt tension.
	Power steering fluid level low.	Add power steering fluid.
	Insufficient power steering pump pressure.	Repair or replace power steering pump.
	Faulty EVO actuator.	Replace EVO actuator.
	Restricted or leaking power steering hoses.	Replace hoses or tighten hose connections.
	High internal leakage in steering gear.	Replace steering gear.
	Excessive front wheel caster.	Perform alignment.
	Binding within steering column or intermediate shaft boot.	Correct condition.
Poor return of steering wheel to center.	Front tire(s) improperly inflated.	Inflate tire(s) correctly.
	Improperly adjusted, improperly lubricated, or binding steering gear.	Adjust, lubricate (check for damaged boots), or replace steering gear.
	Incorrect front wheel caster.	Perform alignment.
	Worn or binding inner or outer tie rod end(s).	Replace inner or outer tie rod end(s).
	Worn or binding upper strut mount(s).	Replace mount(s).
	Worn or binding intermediate shaft joint(s).	Replace intermediate shaft.
	Binding within steering column or intermediate shaft boot.	Correct condition.

G36029100001010A

Fig. 1 Power steering system troubleshooting (Part 1 of 3)

COMPLAINT/CONDITION	POSSIBLE CAUSE(S)	CORRECTION(S)
Excessive free play in steering.	Wheel bearing(s) worn.	Replace wheel bearing(s).
	Steering gear mounting bolt(s) loose.	Tighten bolt(s).
	Steering gear out of adjustment or worn.	Adjust or replace steering gear.
	Worn inner or outer steering tie rod(s).	Replace tie rod(s).
	Lower control arm ball stud(s) worn.	Replace lower control arm(s).
	Front stabilizer bar bushings worn.	Replace bushings.
Rattle and/or clunking noise in steering	Inner or outer tie rod end(s) worn.	Replace inner or outer tie rod end(s).
	Steering gear out of adjustment or worn.	Adjust or replace steering gear.
	Intermediate shaft joint(s) worn.	Replace intermediate shaft.
	Steering gear mounting bolt(s) loose.	Tighten bolt(s).
	Worn wheel bearing(s).	Replace wheel bearing(s).
Momentary increase in steering effort when steering wheel is turned quickly with system at warm operating temperature.	High internal leakage in steering gear.	Replace steering gear.
	Low power steering fluid level.	Correct power steering fluid level.
	Insufficient pump pressure.	Repair or replace power steering pump.
	Damaged EVO actuator.	Replace actuator.
	EVO electrical circuit malfunction.	Correct condition.
Steering wheel surges or jerks when turning at low speeds.	Insufficient power steering pump pressure.	Repair or replace power steering pump.
	High internal leakage in steering gear.	Replace steering gear.
	Loose accessory drive belt.	Check accessory drive belt tension.
Insufficient system pressure – caused by pump.	Flow control valve stuck or inoperative.	Free or replace flow control valve.
	EVO system malfunction.	Refer to EVO system diagnosis.
	Pressure plate not flat against pump ring.	Correct condition.
	Worn pump ring.	Replace pump ring.
	Scored pressure plate, thrust plate, or rotor.	Replace components.
	Vane(s) sticking in rotor slot(s).	Clean rotor/vanes or replace component(s).
	Cracked or broken thrust or pressure plate.	Replace components.

G36029100001020A

Fig. 1 Power steering system troubleshooting (Part 2 of 3)

COMPLAINT/CONDITION	POSSIBLE CAUSE(S)	CORRECTION(S)
Insufficient system pressure – caused by steering gear.	Leaking steering gear piston seals or inner rack seal.	Replace steering gear.
Growling noise in power steering pump.	Excessive back pressure in hoses or steering gear caused by restriction.	Eliminate restriction.
	Scored pressure plate, thrust plate, or rotor.	Replace component(s)
	Worn pump ring.	Replace pump ring.
	Air in power steering fluid.	Add power steering fluid and bleed system.
	Pump mounting loose.	Tighten pump mounting.
Rattling noise in power steering pump.	Vane(s) sticking in rotor slot(s).	Clean rotor/vanes or replace component(s).
Swishing noise in power steering pump.	Damaged flow control valve.	Replace flow control valve.
Whining noise in power steering pump.	Pump shaft being scored.	Replace pump.

G36029100001030A

Fig. 1 Power steering system troubleshooting (Part 3 of 3)

8. Remove retaining ring, **Fig. 2,** as follows:
   a. Use a C-clamp (one side on end cover, other on pump driveshaft) to depress end cover, easing removal of retaining ring.
   b. Insert a piece of wood between C-clamp and pump driveshaft.
   c. Place a punch into pump housing access hole and remove retaining ring.
9. Push on driveshaft to assist in removing end cover.
10. Remove internal pump components in two groups, **Fig. 3,** as follows:
    a. Remove end cover, O-ring, pressure plate spring and pressure plate.
    b. Remove driveshaft with pump rotor, pump vanes, pump ring, thrust plate and shaft retaining ring.
11. Remove O-ring seal (A), two dowel pins (B) and driveshaft seal (C) from pump housing, **Fig. 4.**
12. Remove pressure plate, pressure plate spring and O-ring from end cover.
13. Remove shaft retaining ring from driveshaft.
14. Remove pump rotor, pump vanes, pump ring and thrust plate from driveshaft, **Fig. 5.**
15. Separate pump rotor, pump vanes and pump ring.
16. Clean all parts with new power steering fluid.
17. Inspect pump ring, pump vanes, thrust plate and driveshaft for scoring, pitting or chatter marks.
18. Replace any damaged components. Do not attempt to remove damage with abrasive cleaners.
19. A wavy pattern on pump ring face will be present with low mileage and should not be mistaken for premature wear or damage.

Assemble

1. Lubricate driveshaft with new power steering fluid.
2. Install new driveshaft seal into pump housing using a suitably sized socket as a driver.
3. Install thrust plate and pump rotor onto driveshaft.
4. Install driveshaft/rotor/thrust plate assembly into housing, **Fig. 6.**
5. Install pump ring dowel pins into pump housing through thrust plate. Install pump ring (with holes correctly positioned onto dowel pins) into housing, **Fig. 7.**
6. Pump ring face has a indentation on one side near dowel hole. The ring must be installed with the indentation facing up. **If ring is installed upside down, pump will not function.**
7. Install vanes into pump rotor. Vanes may be installed in either direction.
8. Lubricate new pump housing O-ring with power steering fluid and install into groove in housing.
9. Align pressure plate dowel holes with dowel pins and install plate into housing.
10. Position pressure plate spring against

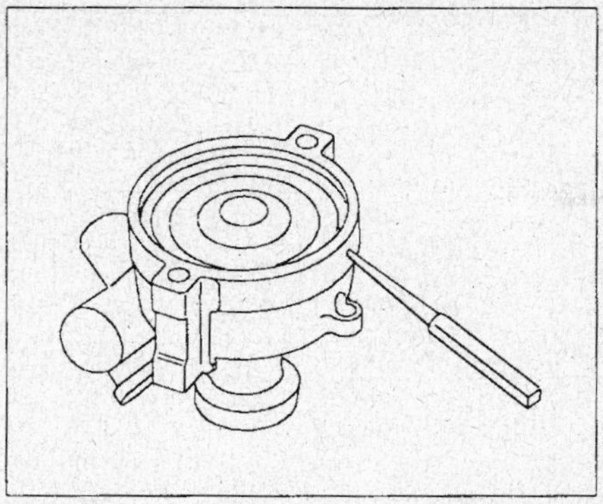

G36029100005000X

Fig. 2 Pump retaining ring removal

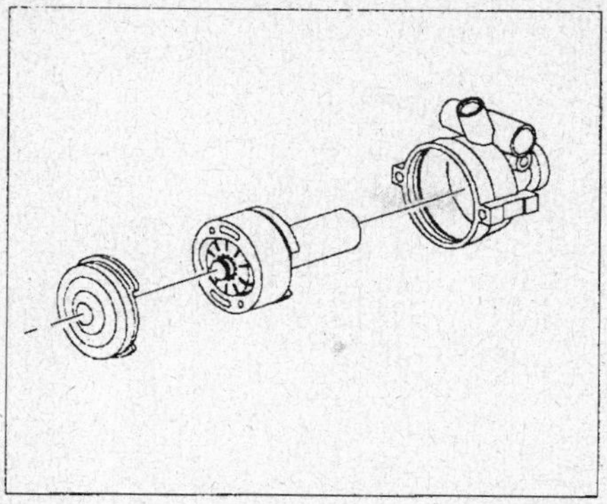

G36029100006000X

Fig. 3 Pump internal component removal

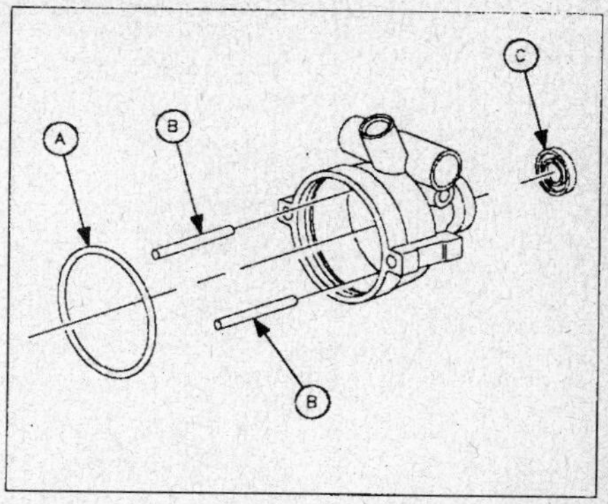

G36029100007000X

Fig. 4 Pump housing O-ring seal, dowel pins and driveshaft seal removal

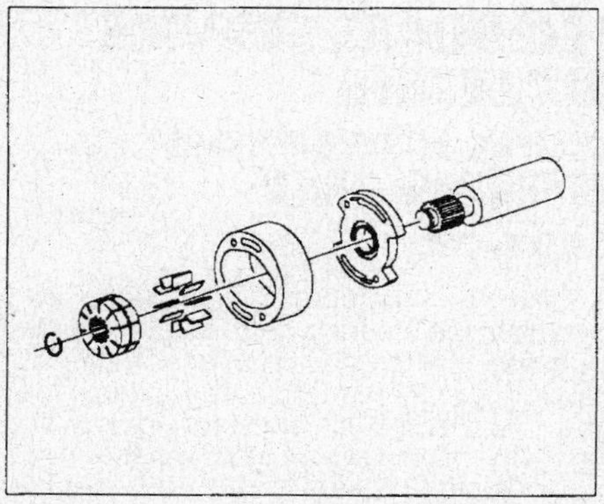

G36029100008000X

Fig. 5 Removing rotor, vanes, ring and thrust plate from driveshaft

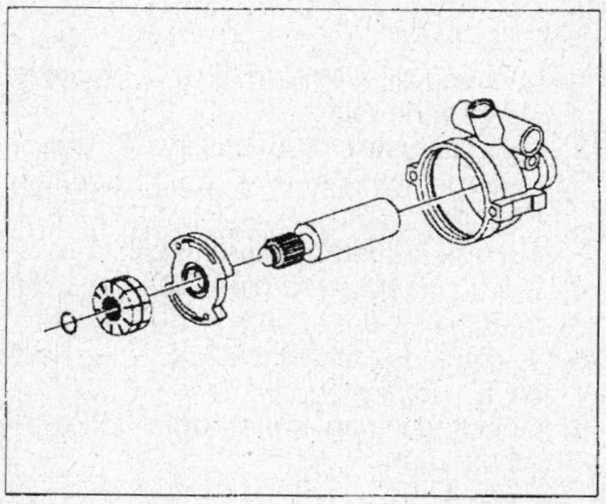

G36029100009000X

Fig. 6 Driveshaft/rotor/thrust plate assembly

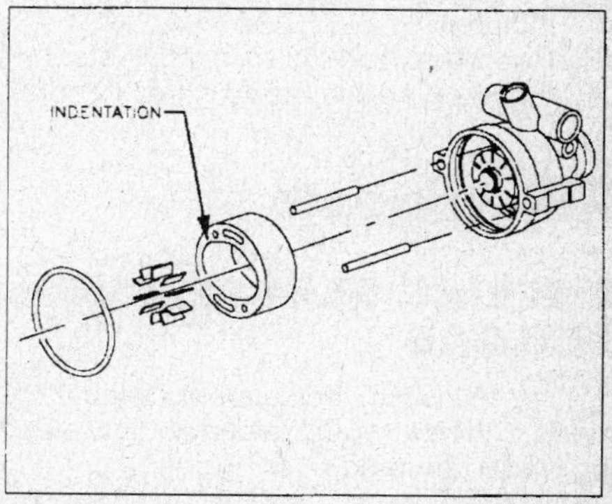

G36029100010000X

Fig. 7 Pump ring dowel pins & pump ring assembly

pressure plate. Lubricate new end cover O-ring with power steering fluid and install onto end cover, **Fig. 8.**

11. Lubricate outer edge of end cover with power steering fluid, then press end cover into pump housing.
12. Install retaining ring into groove in pump housing, with ring opening near access hole in housing. Ensure ring is fully seated in housing groove.
13. Install three O-ring seals onto EVO actuator, if removed during disassembly procedure. **Install three seals (A, B and C) in correct position as shown in Fig. 9.**
14. Correctly position EVO actuator and discharge fitting to pump assembly, **Fig. 10.**
15. **Torque** EVO actuator to 46 ft. lbs. using installation tool No. SA9116C, or equivalent, **Fig. 10.**
16. Install power steering pump bracket onto power steering pump with three fasteners. **Torque** to 28 ft. lbs.
17. Install pump pulley using installation tool No. SA9162C, or equivalent.
18. Lubricate new reservoir O-ring with power steering fluid and install onto reservoir.
19. Install reservoir into pump housing. Push reservoir straight into housing, then install retaining clips.

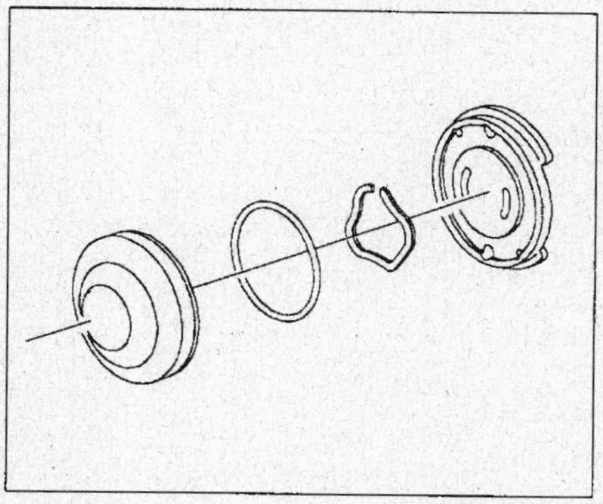

G36029100011000X

Fig. 8 Pressure plate assembly

20. Install pump on engine and bleed power steering system as described in this section.

ELECTRONIC VARIABLE ORIFICE (EVO) ACTUATOR, REPLACE

1. Remove pump from vehicle, then disconnect EVO electrical connector locating clip.
2. Remove EVO actuator assembly using socket removal tool No. SA91116C, or equivalent, **Fig. 10.** Do not pivot socket tool during removal.
3. Remove discharge fitting from actuator.
4. Remove three O-ring seals from actuator. Note size and location of O-ring seals.
5. Reverse procedure to install, noting the following:
   a. Refer to **Fig. 9.**
   b. **Torque** EVO actuator to 46 ft. lbs.
   c. Install pump and bleed power steering system as described in this section.

Power Steering System Bleed

1. With engine off, front wheels raised and turned completely toward left side, check reservoir fluid level. Add fluid if necessary.
2. Bleed system by turning wheels from side to side several times without contacting stops.
3. Start engine and check fluid level. Add fluid if necessary.
4. Return steering wheel to straight ahead position, lower front wheels and

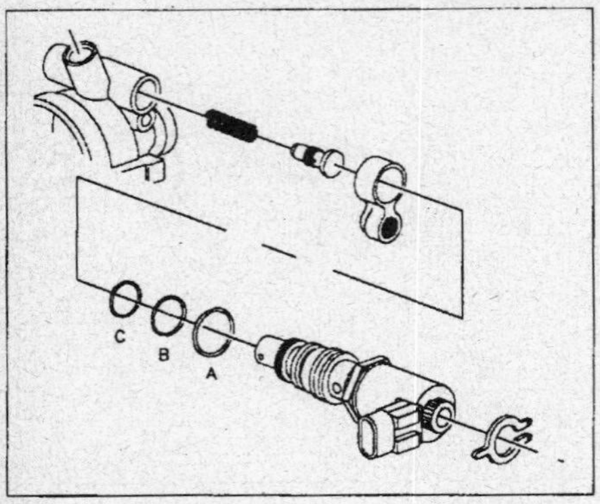

G36029100004000X

Fig. 9 EVO actuator O-ring locations

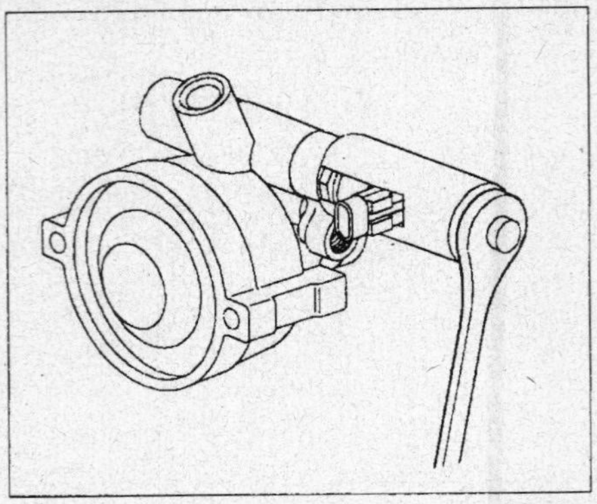

G36029100003000X

Fig. 10 EVO actuator replacement

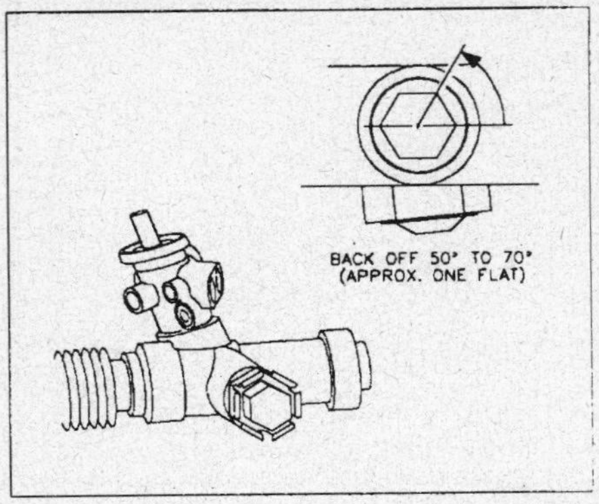

G36029100002000X

Fig. 11 Steering gear bearing preload adjustment

allow engine to idle for two to three minutes.

5. Road test vehicle to ensure steering functions normally and is free of noise.

Adjustments

STEERING GEAR BEARING PRELOAD

The following adjustment should be made with front wheel raised and the steering wheel centered.

1. Loosen adjuster plug locknut on steering gear housing.
2. Turn adjuster plug clockwise until it bottoms in steering gear housing, **Fig. 11.**
3. **Torque** adjuster plug to 9 ft. lbs.
4. Back off adjuster plug 50° (approximately one flat of nut).
5. **Torque** locknut to 52 ft. lbs. while holding adjuster plug.
6. Check steering wheel return following adjustment.

TECHNICAL SERVICE BULLETINS

CLUNK NOISE FROM STEERING GEAR

1997–98

On 1997–98 models a clunk noise may emit from the steering gear. This noise may be present when driving over variations in pavement at 5–10 mph. This condition may be caused by insufficient steering gear preload. Check and adjust steering gear bearing preload as outlined under "Adjustments" in this section.

DISC BRAKES

NOTE: On Air Bag Equipped Models, Refer To "Air Bag System Precautions" Located In The Front Of This Manual For System Disarming & Arming Procedures.

TABLE OF CONTENTS

Application Chart

Model	Year	Front/Rear Brakes	Application
BUICK			
Century	1997–2000	Front	AC Delco Single Piston Type 2
	1997–2000	Rear	AC Delco Single Piston Type 1
LeSabre	1997–2000	Front	AC Delco Single Piston Type 2
Park Avenue	1997–2000	Front	AC Delco Single Piston Type 2
	1997–2000	Rear	AC Delco Single Piston Type 2
Regal	1997–2000	Front	AC Delco Single Piston Type 2
	1997–2000	Rear	AC Delco Single Piston Type 1
Riviera	1997–99	Front	AC Delco Single Piston Type 2
	1997–99	Rear	AC Delco Single Piston Type 2
Skylark	1997–98	Front	AC Delco Single Piston Type 2
CADILLAC			
Catera	1997–2000	Front	AC Delco Single Piston Type 2
	1997–2000	Rear	AC Delco Dual Piston
DeVille	1997–2000	Front	AC Delco Single Piston Type 2
	1997–2000	Rear	AC Delco Single Piston Type 2
Eldorado	1997–2000	Front	AC Delco Single Piston Type 2
	1997–2000	Rear	AC Delco Single Piston Type 2
Seville	1997–2000	Front	AC Delco Single Piston Type 2
	1997–2000	Rear	AC Delco Single Piston Type 2
CHEVROLET			
Camaro	1997	Front	AC Delco Single Piston Type 2
	1997–2000	Rear	PBR Single Piston
	1998–2000	Front	AC Delco Dual Piston
Cavalier	1997–2000	Front	AC Delco Single Piston Type 2

Continued

Model	Year	Front/Rear Brakes	Application
CHEVROLET			
Corvette	1997–2000	Front	PBR Dual Piston
	1997–2000	Rear	PBR Single Piston
Impala	2000	Front	AC Delco Single Piston Type 2
		Rear	AC Delco Single Piston Type 2
Lumina	1997–99	Front	AC Delco Dual Piston
	2000	Front	AC Delco Single Piston Type 2
	1997–2000	Rear	AC Delco Single Piston Type 2
Malibu	1997–2000	Front	AC Delco Single Piston Type 2
Monte Carlo	1997–99	Front	AC Delco Dual Piston
	2000	Front	AC Delco Single Piston Type 2
	1997–2000	Rear	AC Delco Single Piston Type 2
CHEVROLET/GEO			
Metro	1997–2000	Front	Aisin Seiki Type 1
Prizm	1997–99	Front	Toyota/GM
OLDSMOBILE			
Achieva	1997–98	Front	AC Delco Single Piston Type 2
Alero	1999–2000	Front	AC Delco Single Piston Type 2
		Rear	AC Delco Single Piston Type 2
Aurora	1997–99	Front	AC Delco Single Piston Type 2
	1997–99	Rear	AC Delco Single Piston Type 2
Cutlass	1997–99	Front	AC Delco Single Piston Type 2
Cutlass Supreme	1997	Front	AC Delco Dual Piston
	1997	Rear	AC Delco Single Piston Type 2
Intrigue	1998–2000	Front	AC Delco Single Piston Type 2
	1998–2000	Rear	AC Delco Single Piston Type 1
LSS	1997–99	Front	AC Delco Single Piston Type 2
Regency	1997–99	Front	AC Delco Single Piston Type 2
Eighty-Eight	1997–99	Front	AC Delco Single Piston Type 2
PONTIAC			
Bonneville	1997–2000	Front	AC Delco Single Piston Type 2
Firebird	1997	Front	AC Delco Single Piston Type 2
	1997–2000	Rear	PBR Single Piston
	1998–2000	Front	AC Delco Dual Piston
Grand Am	1997–2000	Front	AC Delco Single Piston Type 2
	1997–2000	Rear	AC Delco Single Piston Type 2
Grand Prix	1997–2000	Front	AC Delco Single Piston Type 2
	1997–2000	Rear	AC Delco Single Piston Type 1
Sunfire	1997–99	Front	AC Delco Single Piston Type 2
SATURN			
All	1997–2000	All	All

Aisin-Seiki Single Piston Front Disc Brake (Type 1)

INDEX

PRECAUTIONS

1. Grease or any other foreign material must be kept off brake linings, caliper, surfaces of disc and external surfaces of hub during service procedures.
2. Handling brake disc and caliper should be done in a way to avoid deformation of disc and nicking or scratching brake linings.
3. If inspection reveals worn or damaged rubber piston seals, they should be replaced.
4. During removal and installation of a wheel assembly, be sure not to interfere with or damage caliper splash shield or bleeder screw.
5. Front wheel bearing preload should be adjusted to specifications.
6. Ensure vehicle is centered on hoist before servicing any front end components to avoid bending or damaging disc splash shield on full righthand or lefthand wheel turns.
7. Before vehicle is moved after any brake service work, obtain a firm brake pedal.
8. Assembly bolts of two piece caliper housings should not be disturbed unless caliper requires service.

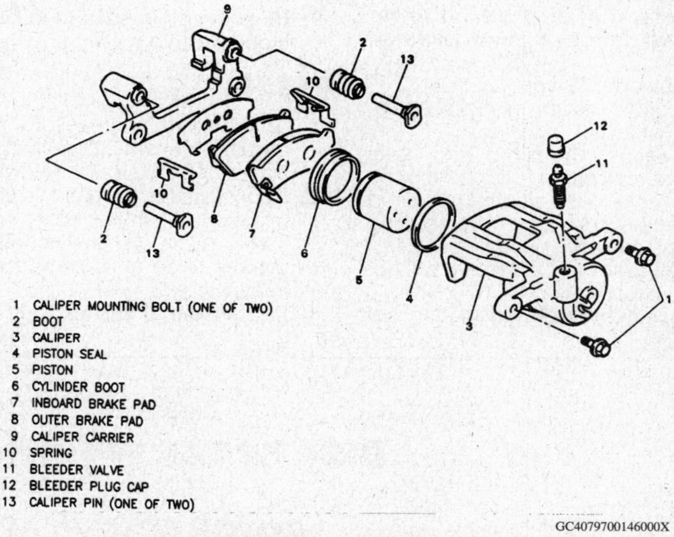

Fig. 1 Exploded view of disc brake caliper assembly. Metro

DESCRIPTION

This single piston sliding caliper assembly, **Fig. 1,** is mounted to a support bracket by two slide pins. The caliper assembly slides on the two mounting pins. Upon brake application, fluid pressure against the piston forces the inboard shoe and lining assembly against the inboard side of the disc. This action causes the caliper assembly to slide until the outboard lining comes into contact with the disc.

TROUBLESHOOTING

BRAKE ROUGHNESS

The most common cause of brake chatter on disc brakes is a variation in thickness of the disc. If roughness or vibration is encountered during highway operation or if pedal pulsation is experienced at low speeds, the disc may have excessive thickness variation. To inspect for this condition, measure the disc at 12 points with a micrometer at a radius approximately one inch from edge of disc. If thickness measurements vary by more than .0005 inch, the disc should be replaced with a new one.

Excessive lateral runout of braking disc may cause a piston "knocking back," possibly creating increased pedal travel and vibration when brakes are applied.

Before inspecting the runout, the wheel bearings should be adjusted. The adjustment is very important and will be required at the completion of the test to prevent bearing failure. Adjust the wheel bearings as outlined in the appropriate "Front Suspension & Steering" chassis section.

BRAKE PAD SERVICE

1. Remove approximately 2⁄3 of brake fluid from master cylinder.
2. Raise and support vehicle.
3. Mark relationship between front wheel and axle, then remove wheel and tire assembly.
4. Remove two caliper slide pins from bracket.
5. Unfasten caliper and support with a length of rope or wire, leaving hydraulic lines connected.
6. Remove brake pads, shims, wear indicators and retainers, **Fig. 1.**
7. Reverse procedure to install.

CALIPER SERVICE

REMOVAL

1. Remove approximately 2⁄3 of brake fluid from master cylinder.
2. Raise and support vehicle.
3. Mark relationship between front wheel and axle, then remove wheel and tire assembly.
4. If caliper assembly is to be serviced, remove inlet fitting attaching bolt, copper washer, and inlet fitting from caliper housing. Plug opening in inlet fitting to prevent fluid loss and contamination. **Do not crimp brake hose, since this may damage internal structure of hose. If only shoe and lining assemblies are to be replaced, do not disconnect brake line fitting from caliper.**
5. Remove caliper slide pins and caliper. If only shoe and lining assemblies are to be replaced, suspend caliper from chassis using suitable hanger. **Do not allow caliper to hang by brake hose.**
6. Remove shoe and lining assembly.

7. Remove bracket attaching bolts, then the bracket.
8. Remove slide pin boot from bracket.

DISASSEMBLE

1. Drain brake fluid from caliper.
2. Use clean shop towels to pad interior of caliper assembly, then remove piston by directing compressed air into caliper brake hose inlet hole, **Fig. 2. Use just enough air pressure to ease piston out of bore. Do not place fingers in front of piston for any reason when applying compressed air. This could result in serious personal injury.**
3. Remove dust boot from piston.
4. Using a small piece of wood or plastic, remove piston seal from bore. **Do not use a metal tool of any kind to remove seal since it may damage bore.**
5. Remove bleeder valve.
6. Inspect piston for scoring, nicks, corrosion, and wear.
7. Inspect caliper housing and seal groove for corrosion, nicks, scoring and excessive wear. Use crocus cloth to polish away corrosion from housing bore. Replace caliper housing if corrosion in and around seal groove will not clean up with crocus cloth.
8. Clean all parts with denatured alcohol then dry with unlubricated compressed air.
9. Blow out all passages in housing and bleeder valve.

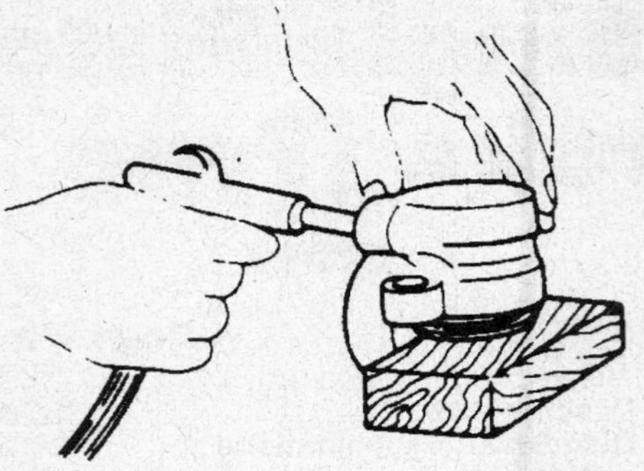

Fig. 2 Caliper piston removal

ASSEMBLE

1. Apply suitable grease to piston seal and cylinder wall, then install the seal. Ensure piston seal is not twisted.
2. Apply suitable grease to sliding portion of piston and install dust boot.
3. Insert edge of dust boot into boot groove, then slowly force piston fully into cylinder.
4. Install bleeder valve.

INSTALLATION

1. Apply suitable grease to inner face of slide pin boot.
2. Install slide pin boot to bracket.
3. Install bracket and attaching bolts.
4. Install shoe and lining assembly. Ensure wear indicators are located on trailing edge of shoe assemblies during forward wheel rotation.
5. Install caliper assembly to bracket. Tighten attaching bolts to specifications.
6. Attach hose to caliper.
7. Install wheel and tire assembly, then lower the vehicle.
8. Fill master cylinder to proper level and bleed brakes as described in the "Hydraulic Brake Systems" chapter. **Before moving vehicle, pump brake pedal several times to ensure it is firm. Do not move vehicle until a firm pedal is obtained.**

ROTOR

REPLACE

1. Remove caliper assembly from rotor as described under " Brake Pad Service."
2. Remove rotor from wheel hub.
3. Reverse procedure to install.

DISC BRAKE SPECIFICATIONS

ROTOR SPECIFICATIONS

Model	Year	Nominal Thickness, Inch	Minimum Refinish Thickness, Inch	Maximum Lateral Runout, Inch	Maximum Scoring Depth, Inch	Maximum Thickness Variation, Inch
Metro	1997	.670	.59	.004	.015	.0039
	1998–2000	—	.59	.004	.015	.0039

TIGHTENING SPECIFICATIONS

Component	Torque/Ft. Lbs.
Bleeder Valve	89①
Brake Hose Union Bolt	17
Brake Pipe Fittings	12
Caliper Mounting Bracket	29–43
Caliper Mounting Slide Pins	22

① — Inch lbs.

AC-Delco Single Piston Front Disc Brake (Type 2)

INDEX

PRECAUTIONS

1. Grease or any other foreign material must be kept off brake linings, caliper, surfaces of disc and external surfaces of hub during service procedures.
2. Handling brake disc and caliper should be done in a way to avoid deformation of disc and nicking or scratching brake linings.
3. If inspection reveals worn or damaged rubber piston seals, they should be replaced.
4. During removal and installation of a wheel assembly, ensure not to interfere with or damage caliper splash shield, or bleeder screw.
5. Front wheel bearing preload should be adjusted to specifications.
6. Ensure vehicle is centered on hoist before servicing any front end components to avoid bending or damaging disc splash shield on full righthand or lefthand wheel turns.
7. Before vehicle is moved after any brake service work, be sure to obtain a firm brake pedal.
8. Assembly bolts of two piece caliper housings should not be disturbed unless caliper requires service.

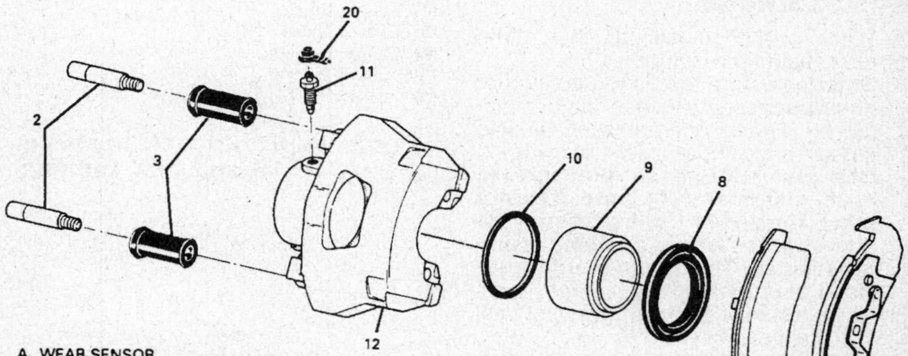

A WEAR SENSOR
2 BOLT/SCREW WITH SLEEVE, FRONT BRAKE CALIPER
3 BUSHING, FRONT BRAKE CALIPER BOLT
5 PAD ASSEMBLY, FRONT DISC BRAKE OUTER
7 PAD ASSEMBLY, FRONT DISC BRAKE INNER
8 BOOT, FRONT BRAKE CALIPER PISTON
9 PISTON, FRONT BRAKE CALIPER
10 SEAL, FRONT BRAKE CALIPER PISTON
11 VALVE, FRONT BRAKE CALIPER BLEEDER
12 HOUSING, FRONT BRAKE CALIPER
20 CAP, FRONT BRAKE CALIPER BLEEDER VALVE

GC4079100054000X

Fig. 1 Exploded view of caliper. Achieva, Alero, Cavalier, Eighty-Eight, Grand Am, LeSabre, LSS, Regency, Skylark, Sunfire & 1997 Camaro, Catera, Firebird & Park Avenue

DESCRIPTION

The caliper has a single piston and is mounted to the support bracket by two mounting bolts, **Figs. 1 through 3.** The caliper assembly slides on the two mounting bolts. Upon brake application, fluid pressure against the piston forces the inboard shoe and lining assembly against the inboard side of the disc. This action causes the caliper assembly to slide until the outboard lining comes into contact with the disc. As pressure builds up the linings are pressed against the disc with increased force.

TROUBLESHOOTING

BRAKE ROUGHNESS

The most common cause of brake chatter on disc brakes is a variation in disc thickness. If roughness or vibration is encountered during highway operation or if pedal pulsation is experienced at low speeds, the disc may have excessive thickness variation. To inspect for this condition, measure the disc at 12 points with a micrometer at a radius approximately one inch from edge of disc. If thickness measurements vary by more than .0005 inch, the disc should be replaced with a new one.

Excessive lateral runout of braking disc may cause a piston "knocking back," possibly creating increased pedal travel and vibration when brakes are applied.

Before inspecting the runout, the wheel bearings should be adjusted. The adjustment is very important and will be required at the completion of the test to prevent bearing failure. Adjust the wheel bearings as outlined in the appropriate "Front Suspension & Steering" chassis section.

BRAKE PAD SERVICE

1. Remove caliper as outlined under "Caliper Service."
2. Remove brake pads and pad retainers from caliper bracket, **Figs. 1 through 3.**
3. Reverse procedure to install.

CALIPER SERVICE

REPLACEMENT

1. Remove approximately ⅔ of brake fluid from master cylinder.
2. Raise and support front of vehicle, then remove wheel and tire assembly.
3. Using suitable C-clamp, push piston back into caliper bore, **Fig. 4.**
4. If caliper assembly is being removed for service, remove inlet fitting attaching bolt, copper washer, and inlet fitting from caliper housing. Plug opening in inlet fitting to prevent fluid loss and contamination. **Do not crimp brake hose since this may damage hose's internal structure. If only shoe and**

lining assemblies are to be replaced, do not disconnect brake line fitting from caliper.

5. **On Catera models,** carefully separate sensor from inner brake pad, **Fig. 5,** by placing a small screwdriver between lower section of sensor and brake pad.
6. **On all models,** remove caliper mounting bolts, **Fig. 6.** If bolts show signs of corrosion, replace them when installing caliper assembly.
7. Remove caliper assembly from disc. If only shoe and lining assemblies are to be replaced, use a length of rope or wire to suspend caliper from spring coil. Never allow caliper to hang from brake hose.
8. Reverse procedure to install. Tighten fasteners to specifications.

DISASSEMBLE

1. Clean outside of caliper, then drain brake fluid from caliper.
2. Use clean shop towels to pad interior of caliper assembly, then remove piston by directing compressed air into caliper brake hose inlet hole, **Fig. 7. Use just enough air pressure to ease piston out of bore. Do not place fingers in front of piston for any reason when applying compressed air. This could result in serious personal injury.**
3. Using a screwdriver, remove dust boot from caliper bore, **Fig. 8.**
4. Using a small piece of wood or plastic, remove piston seal from bore. **Do not use a metal tool of any kind to remove seal since it may damage bore.**
5. Remove bleeder valve.
6. Inspect piston for scoring, nicks, corrosion, and wear and replace as needed.
7. Inspect caliper housing and seal groove for corrosion, nicks, scoring and excessive wear, then use crocus cloth to polish away corrosion from housing bore.
8. Replace caliper housing if corrosion in and around seal groove will not clean up with crocus cloth.
9. Clean all parts with denatured alcohol and dry with unlubricated compressed air.
10. Blow out all passages in housing and bleeder valve.
11. Reverse procedure to assemble. Be sure to properly seat dust boot using installer tool No. J-36349, or equivalent, **Fig. 9.**

ROTOR

REPLACE

1. Raise and support vehicle, then remove tire and wheel assembly.
2. Remove caliper assembly from rotor as described in " Caliper Service."
3. Remove caliper assembly mounting bracket attaching bolts, then the mounting bracket.
4. Remove rotor from hub and bearing assembly.
5. Reverse procedure to install.

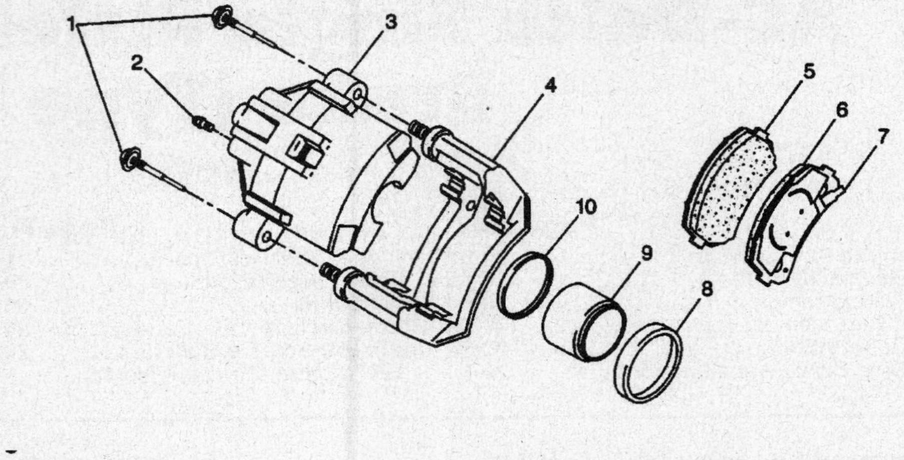

(1) Caliper Bolts
(2) Bleeder Valve
(3) Caliper Housing
(4) Caliper Bracket
(5) Inboard Pad
(6) Outboard Pad
(7) Wear Sensor
(8) Caliper Boot
(9) Piston
(10) Piston Seal

GC4079700137000X

Fig. 2 Exploded view of caliper. Aurora, Century, DeVille, Eldorado, Grand Prix, Intrigue, Regal, Riviera & Seville

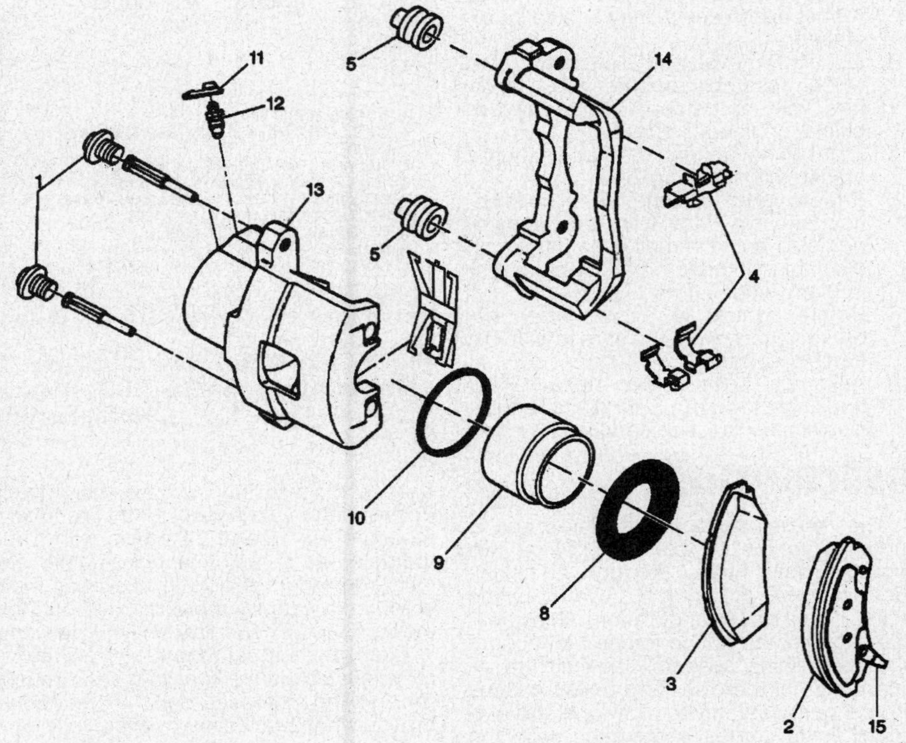

(1) Bolt and Slide Pin Assemblies
(2) Outboard Brake Pad
(3) Inboard Brake Pad
(4) Clips, Brake Pad
(5) Boot, Brake Pin Slide
(8) Seal, Brake Caliper Dust
(9) Piston, Brake Caliper
(10) Seal, Brake Caliper Piston
(11) Cap, Brake Bleeder Screw
(12) Screw, Brake Bleeder
(13) Caliper, Brake
(14) Bracket, Caliper to Knuckle
(15) Wear Sensor

GC4079700138000X

Fig. 3 Exploded view of caliper. Cutlass & Malibu

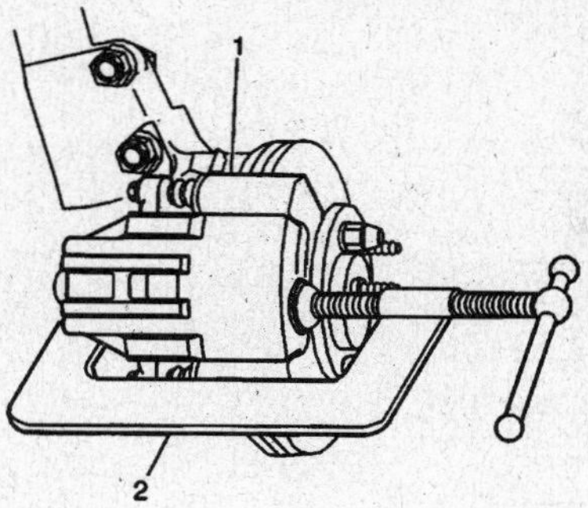

(1) Caliper
(2) C-Clamp

GC4079700136000X

Fig. 4 Piston compression

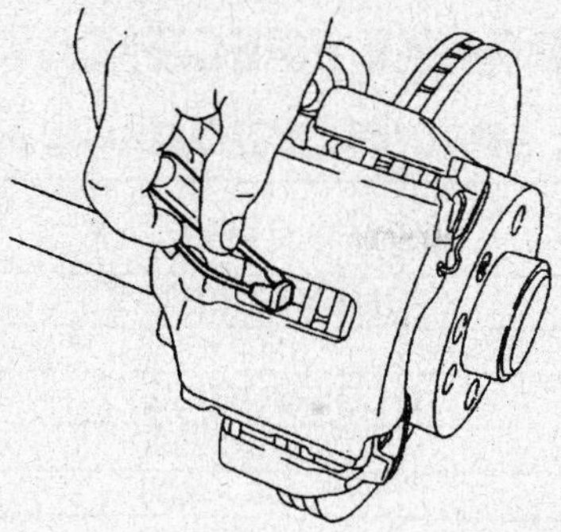

GC4079700140000X

Fig. 5 Brake pad sensor removal. Catera

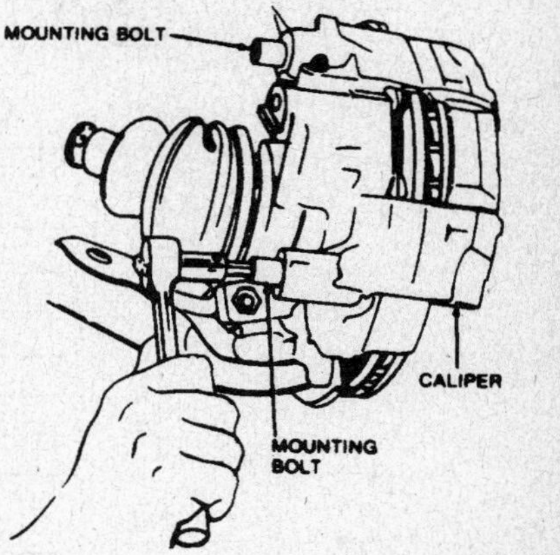

GC4079100059000X

Fig. 6 Caliper mounting bolts replacement

TECHNICAL SERVICE BULLETINS

1997 AURORA, DEVILLE, ELDORADO, PARK AVENUE, RIVIERA & SEVILLE

Brake Noise From Front Brakes

On these models, a grunting, groaning, grinding or crunching noise may be heard when applying the brakes at low speeds (0–35 mph).

To correct this condition, replace front brake pads with new pads part No. 18024961. A slight squeal may still be heard with new brake pads.

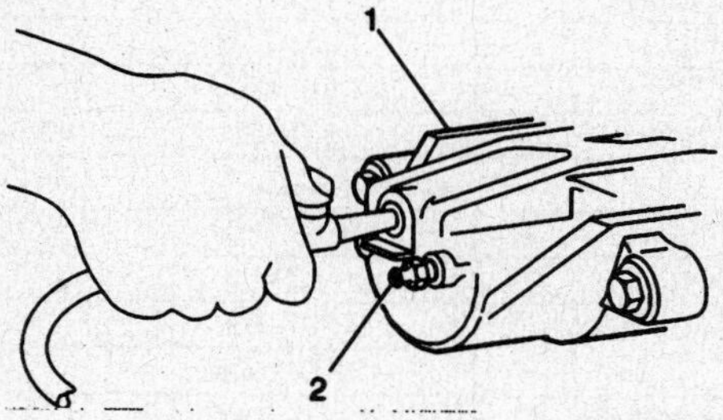

GC4079700147000X

Fig. 7 Caliper piston removal

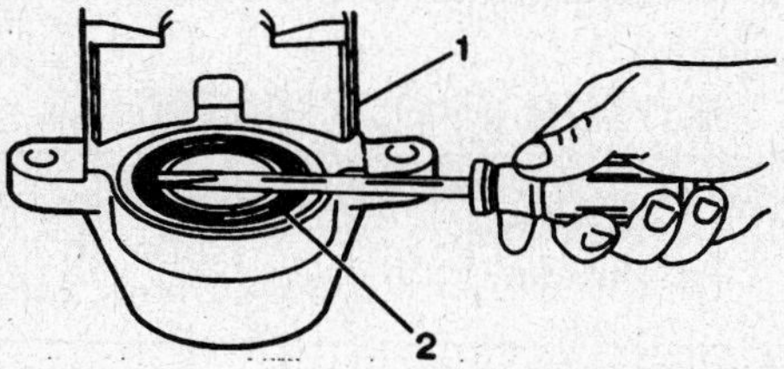

GC4079700148000X

Fig. 8 Dust boot removal

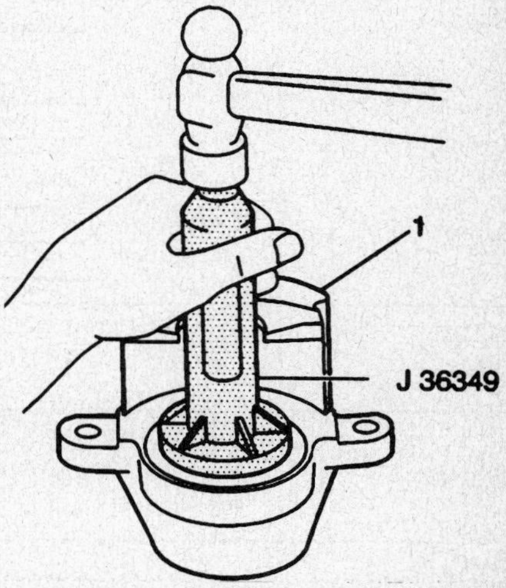

GC4079700149000X

Fig. 9 Dust boot installation in caliper

DISC BRAKE SPECIFICATIONS

CALIPER SPECIFICATIONS

Model	Year	Caliper Bore Dia. Inch
BUICK		
Century	1997–2000	2.50
LeSabre	1997–2000	2.52
Park Avenue	1997–2000	2.52
Regal	1997–2000	2.50
Riviera	1997–99	2.52
Skylark	1997–98	2.24
CADILLAC		
Catera	1997–2000	2.24
DeVille	1997–2000	2.52
Eldorado	1997–2000	2.52
Seville	1997–2000	2.52
CHEVROLET		
Camaro	1997	2.50
Cavalier	1997–2000	2.24

Continued

DISC BRAKE SPECIFICATIONS

CALIPER SPECIFICATIONS—Continued

Model	Year	Caliper Bore Dia. Inch
CHEVROLET		
Malibu	1997–2000	2.36
OLDSMOBILE		
Achieva	1997–98	2.24
Alero	1999-2000	2.36
Aurora	1997–99	2.52
Cutlass	1997	2.36
	1998–99	—
Eighty-Eight	1997–99	2.52
Intrigue	1998–2000	2.50
LSS	1997–99	2.52
Regency	1997–99	2.52
PONTIAC		
Bonneville	1997–2000	2.52
Firebird	1997	2.50
Grand Am	1997–98	2.24
	1999-2000	2.36
Grand Prix	1997–2000	2.50
Sunfire	1997–2000	2.24

ROTOR SPECIFICATIONS

Model	Year	Nominal Thickness, Inch	Minimum Refinish Thickness, Inch	Thickness Variation (Parallelism), Inch	Lateral Runout (T.I.R.), Inch
BUICK					
Century	1997–2000	1.27	1.25	.0005	.003
LeSabre	1997–2000	1.267	1.224	.0005	.002
Park Avenue	1997–2000	1.267	1.224	.0005	.002
Regal	1997–2000	1.27	1.25	.0005	.003
Riviera	1997–99	1.267	1.224	.0005	.002
Skylark	1997–98	.806	.786	.0005	.003
CADILLAC					
Catera	1997–2000	1.102	1.043	.0005	.001
DeVille	1997–2000	1.267	1.224	.0005	.002
Eldorado	1997–2000	1.267	1.224	.0005	.002
Seville	1997–2000	1.267	1.224	.0005	.002
CHEVROLET					
Camaro	1997	1.260	1.250	.0005	.005
Cavalier	1997–2000	.786	.751	.0005	.003
Malibu	1997–2000	1.031	.987	.0005	.003
OLDSMOBILE					
Achieva	1997–98	.806	.786	.0005	.003
Alero	1999–2000	1.270	1.250	.0005	.003
Aurora	1997–99	1.267	1.224	.0005	.002
Cutlass	1997–99	1.031	.987	.0005	.003
Eighty-Eight	1997–99	1.260	1.224	.0005	.002
Intrigue	1998–2000	1.27	1.25	.0005	.003
LSS	1997–99	1.260	1.224	.0005	.002
Regency	1997–99	1.260	1.224	.0005	.002
PONTIAC					
Bonneville	1997–2000	1.267	1.224	.0005	.002

Continued

ROTOR SPECIFICATIONS—Continued

Model	Year	Nominal Thickness, Inch	Minimum Refinish Thickness, Inch	Thickness Variation (Parallelism), Inch	Lateral Runout (T.I.R.), Inch
PONTIAC					
Firebird	1997	1.260	1.250	.0005	.005
Grand Am	1997–98	.806	.786	.0005	.003
	1999-2000	1.270	1.250	.0005	.003
Grand Prix	1997–2000	1.27	1.25	.0005	.003
Sunfire	1997–2000	.786	.751	.0005	.003

TIGHTENING SPECIFICATIONS

Component	Torque/Ft. Lbs.
Brake Hose To Caliper (Achieva, Alero, Cavalier, Grand Am, Skylark, Sunfire & 1997 Camaro & Firebird)	32
Brake Hose To Caliper (Catera)	30
Brake Hose To Caliper (Century, Cutlass, Intrigue, Malibu, Regal)	40
Brake Hose To Caliper (Aurora, Bonneville, DeVille, Eighty-Eight, Eldorado, LSS, LeSabre, Park Avenue, Regency, Riviera & Seville)	33
Caliper Bleeder Screw (Except Catera)	115②
Caliper Bleeder Screw (Catera)	80.5②
Caliper Bracket Mounting Bolts (Except Catera)	137
Caliper Bracket Mounting Bolts (Catera)	70①
Caliper Mounting Bolts (Except Achieva, Alero, Bonneville, Catera, Eighty-Eight, Grand Am, LeSabre, LSS, Regency & Skylark)	63
Caliper Mounting Bolts (Achieva, Alero, Bonneville, Cavalier, Eighty-Eight, Grand Am, LeSabre, LSS, Regency, Skylark, Sunfire & 1997 Camaro & Firebird)	38
Caliper Mounting Bolts (Catera)	22
Rotor Setscrew (Catera)	35②
Wheel Speed Sensor Mounting Bolt	96②
Wheel Lug Nuts (Except Catera)	100
Wheel Lug Nuts (Catera)	80

① — Rotate an additional 37°.

② — Inch lbs.

AC-Delco Dual Piston Front Disc Brake

INDEX

PRECAUTIONS

1. Grease or any other foreign material must be kept off brake linings, caliper, surfaces of disc and external surfaces of hub during service procedures.
2. Handling brake disc and caliper should be done in a way to avoid deformation of disc and nicking or scratching brake linings.
3. If inspection reveals worn or damaged rubber piston seals, they should be replaced.
4. During removal and installation of a wheel assembly, ensure not to interfere with or damage caliper splash shield, or bleeder screw.
5. Front wheel bearings preload should be adjusted to specifications.
6. Ensure vehicle is centered on hoist before servicing any front end components to avoid bending or damaging disc splash shield on full righthand or lefthand wheel turns.
7. Before vehicle is moved after any brake service work, obtain a firm brake pedal.
8. Assembly bolts of two piece caliper housings should not be disturbed unless caliper requires service.

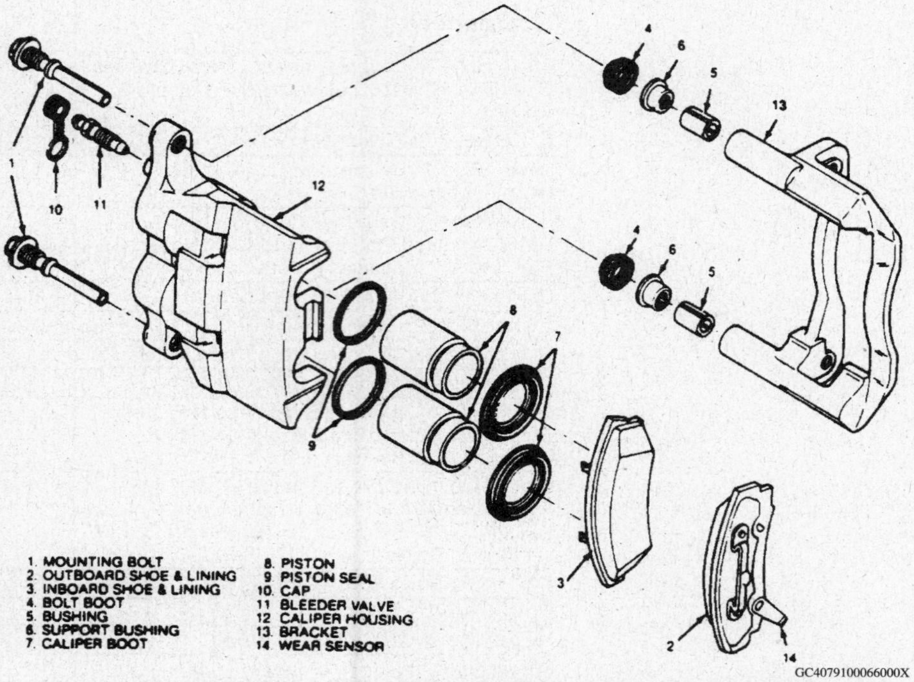

Fig. 1 Exploded view of AC-Delco 3242 series dual piston caliper

DESCRIPTION

This dual piston sliding caliper, **Fig. 1,** is comprised of two interconnected bores and is attached to a mounting bracket with two mounting bolts. Hydraulic pressure acting on the bottom of the caliper bores forces the pistons outward, enabling the caliper to slide inward, thereby clamping the brake shoes against the rotor.

TROUBLESHOOTING

BRAKE ROUGHNESS

The most common cause of brake chatter on disc brakes is a variation in disc thickness. If roughness or vibration is encountered during highway operation or if pedal pulsation is experienced at low speeds, the disc may have excessive thickness variation. To inspect for this condition, measure the disc at 12 points with a micrometer at a radius approximately one inch from edge of disc. If thickness measurements vary by more than .0005 inch, the disc should be replaced with a new one.

Excessive lateral runout of braking disc may cause a piston "knocking back," possibly creating increased pedal travel and vibration when brakes are applied.

Before inspecting the runout, the wheel bearings should be adjusted. The adjustment is very important and will be required at the completion of the test to prevent bearing failure. Adjust the wheel bearings as outlined in the appropriate "Front Suspension & Steering" chassis section.

BRAKE PAD SERVICE

1. Remove caliper as described under "Caliper Service."
2. Lift upward on outward shoe retaining spring of outboard shoe until it clears center lug, then remove shoe from caliper.
3. Pull inboard shoe outward to disengage retainer springs from pistons, then remove inboard shoe from caliper.
4. Reverse procedure to install, noting the following:
   a. Install inboard shoe into caliper. Ensure retainer spring tangs are fully positioned into pistons.
   b. Snap outboard shoe retaining spring over housing center lug, then install outboard shoe into caliper.

CALIPER SERVICE

REMOVAL

1. Siphon enough brake fluid out of master cylinder to bring fluid level to ⅓ full to avoid fluid overflow when caliper pistons are pushed back into bores.
2. Raise and support vehicle, then remove front wheels.

3. Mark relationship between wheel to hub and bearing assembly.
4. Using a suitable C-clamp and, if required, a block of wood, push pistons back together into caliper bores.
5. If caliper assembly is to be serviced, remove inlet fitting attaching bolt, copper washer, and inlet fitting from caliper housing. Plug opening in inlet fitting to prevent fluid loss and contamination. **Do not crimp brake hose, as this may damage internal structure of hose. If only shoe and lining assemblies are to be replaced, do not disconnect brake line fitting from caliper.**
6. Remove two mounting bolts, then the caliper. If only shoe and lining assemblies are to be replaced, suspend caliper from chassis using suitable rope or wire. **Do not allow caliper to hang by brake hose.**

DISASSEMBLE

1. Remove caliper assembly as described under "Caliper Service," then drain brake fluid from caliper.
2. Position shop towel in interior part of caliper, then slowly apply compressed air to inlet port and remove pistons. **It is imperative that one piston be partially installed to facilitate removal of second piston from bore. A pad or wooden spacer may be used to prevent complete removal of first piston.**
3. Remove piston boots from caliper bores, then using suitable wooden or plastic tool, pry piston seals from caliper bore grooves. **Do not use a metal tool of any kind to remove seal since it may damage bore.**
4. Remove bleeder valve from caliper.
5. Inspect piston for scoring, nicks, corrosion, and wear.
6. Inspect caliper housing and seal grooves for corrosion, nicks, scoring and excessive wear. Use crocus cloth to polish away corrosion from housing bore. Replace caliper housing if corrosion in and around seal grooves will not clean up with crocus cloth.
7. Clean all parts with denatured alcohol and dry with unlubricated compressed air.

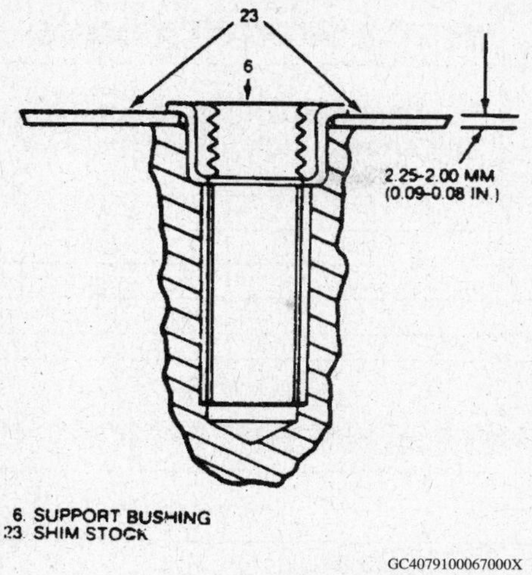

Fig. 2 Support bushing installation

8. Blow out all passages in housing and bleeder valve.

MOUNTING BRACKET SERVICE

Removal

1. Remove caliper as described under "Caliper Service."
2. Using suitable Torx bit, remove mounting bracket attaching bolts and mounting bracket.

Bushing & Boot Replacement

1. Remove mounting bracket from vehicle.
2. Remove bolt boots from support bushings, **Fig. 1.**
3. Clamp bracket in a suitable vise, then pry support bushings from inner bushings in bracket ears with small screwdriver.
4. Using a paper clip, pull inner bushings from mounting bracket ears.
5. Lubricate inner bushings with silicone based grease, then install bushings flush with bracket ears.
6. Position an .080–.090 inch thick shim stock on bracket ear face, then drive support bushings into inner bushings, **Fig. 2.** When properly installed, bushing should protrude .080–.090 inch above bracket ear face.
7. Snap new bolt boots over support bushing lip.

Installation

1. Coat mounting bracket attaching bolt threads with Loctite sealant, or equivalent.
2. Align mounting bracket holes, then install mounting bracket and tighten attaching bolts to specifications.

ASSEMBLE

1. Install bleeder valve.
2. Lubricate piston seals with clean brake fluid, then carefully install seals into caliper bore grooves. **Ensure seals are not twisted.**
3. Lubricate boots and install onto pistons, then push pistons fully into caliper bores.
4. Seat boots into caliper bores using boot seal installer tool No. J-36349, or equivalent.

INSTALLATION

1. Position caliper over rotor and onto mounting bracket.
2. Lubricate entire length of mounting bolts with silicone based grease, then install bolts and tighten to specifications.
3. If inlet fitting was removed, install fitting using new copper washer.
4. Install front wheels, fill master cylinder to proper level, then bleed brake as described in the "Hydraulic Brake Systems" chapter. **Before moving vehicle, pump brake pedal several times to ensure it is firm. Do not move vehicle until a firm pedal is obtained.**

ROTOR

REPLACE

1. Raise and support vehicle, then remove tire and wheel assembly.
2. Remove caliper and caliper mounting bracket as described under "Caliper Service."
3. Remove rotor from hub and bearing assembly.
4. Reverse procedure to install.

DISC BRAKE SPECIFICATIONS

CALIPER SPECIFICATIONS

Model	Year	Caliper Bore Dia. Inch
Camaro & Firebird	1998–2000	2.50
Cutlass Supreme, Lumina & Monte Carlo	1997–99	1.654

ROTOR SPECIFICATIONS

Model	Year	Nominal Thickness, Inch	Minimum Thickness, Inch	Thickness Variation (Transverse Runout), Inch	Maximum Lateral Runout, Inch
Camaro & Firebird	1998–2000	1.260	1.223	.0005	.005
Cutlass Supreme	1997	1.039	.987	.0005	.003
Lumina & Monte Carlo	1997–98	1.039	.987	.0005	.003
	1999	1.270	1.250	.0005	.003

TIGHTENING SPECIFICATIONS

Component	Torque/Ft. Lbs.
CAMARO & FIREBIRD	
Brake Hose To Caliper Inlet Fitting Bolt	30
Brake Pipe Connection	11
Caliper Bleeder Valve (1998)	115①
Caliper Bleeder Valve (1999)	105.5①
Caliper Mounting Bracket Bolt (1998)	162
Caliper Mounting Bracket Bolt (1999)	74
Caliper Slide Bolt	23
CUTLASS SUPREME LUMINA & MONTE CARLO	
Brake Hose To Caliper Inlet Fitting Bolt (1997–98)	33
Brake Hose To Caliper Inlet Fitting Bolt (1999)	40
Brake Pipe Connection	11
Caliper Bleeder Valve (1997–98)	115①
Caliper Bleeder Valve (1999)	105.5①
Caliper Mounting Bracket Bolt (1997–98)	148
Caliper Mounting Bracket Bolt (1999)	137
Caliper Slide Bolt	80

① — Inch lbs.

PBR Dual Piston Front Disc Brake

INDEX

PRECAUTIONS

1. Grease or any other foreign material must be kept off brake linings, caliper, surfaces of disc and external surfaces of hub during service procedures.
2. Handling brake disc and caliper should be done in a way to avoid deformation of disc and nicking or scratching brake linings.
3. If inspection reveals worn or damaged rubber piston seals, they should be replaced.
4. During removal and installation of a wheel assembly, ensure not to interfere with or damage caliper splash shield, or bleeder screw.
5. Front wheel bearings preload should be adjusted to specifications.
6. Ensure vehicle is centered on hoist before servicing any front end components to avoid bending or damaging disc splash shield on full righthand or lefthand wheel turns.
7. Before vehicle is moved after any brake service work, obtain a firm brake pedal.
8. Assembly bolts of two piece caliper housings should not be disturbed unless caliper requires service.

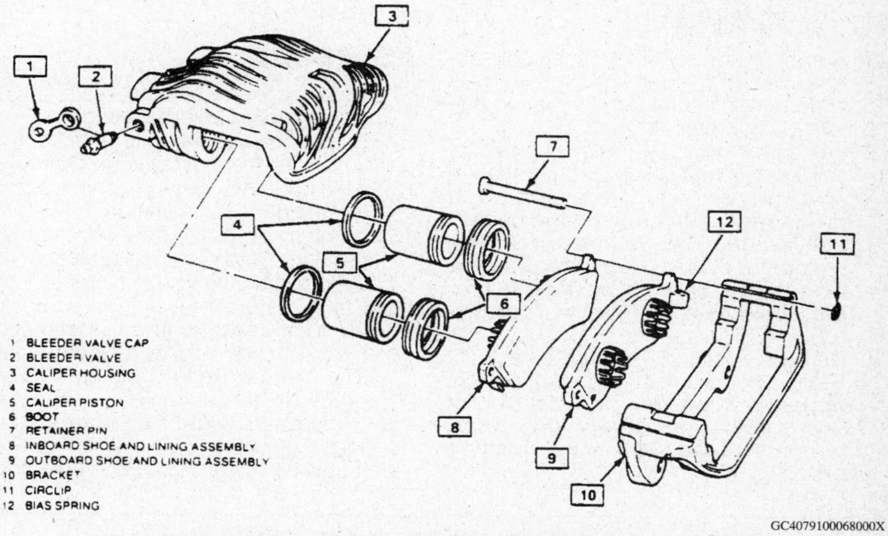

Fig. 1 Exploded view of PBR dual piston front caliper

DESCRIPTION

This front caliper, **Fig. 1,** consists of dual pistons and an aluminum housing which is suspended on the shoe and lining assemblies. Hydraulic pressure, created by applying force to the brake pedal, acts equally against the pistons and the bottom of the caliper bores to move the pistons outward. This action slides the caliper inward, resulting in a clamping action on the brake rotor. This clamping action forces the linings against the rotor, creating the friction required to stop the vehicle.

TROUBLESHOOTING

BRAKE ROUGHNESS

The most common cause of brake chatter on disc brakes is a variation in disc thickness. If roughness or vibration is encountered during highway operation or if pedal pulsation is experienced at low speeds, the disc may have excessive thickness variation. To inspect for this condition, measure the disc at 12 points with a micrometer at a radius approximately one inch from edge of disc. If thickness measurements vary by more than .0005 inch, the disc should be replaced with a new one.

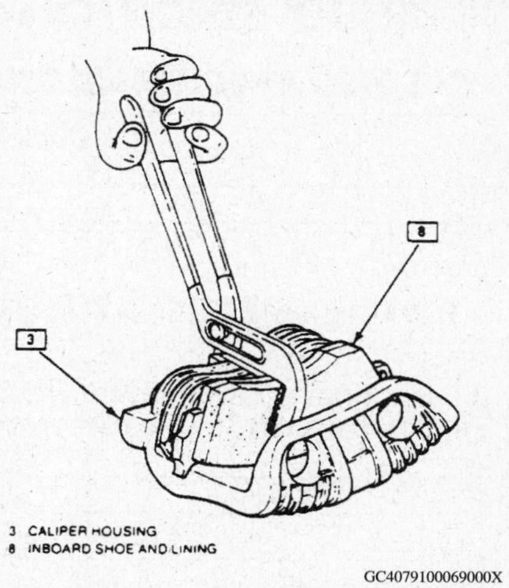

Fig. 2 Piston retraction in caliper bores

Excessive lateral runout of braking disc may cause a piston "knocking back," possibly creating increased pedal travel and vibration when brakes are applied.

Before inspecting the runout, the wheel bearings should be adjusted. The adjustment is very important and will be required at the completion of the test to prevent bearing failure. Adjust the wheel bearings as outlined in the appropriate "Front Suspension & Steering" chassis section.

BRAKE PAD SERVICE

REMOVAL

1. Remove brake caliper as described under "Caliper Service."
2. Position suitable pliers over caliper and center of inboard shoe and lining, **Fig. 2,** then squeeze pliers to bottom pistons in caliper bores.
3. Remove shoe and lining assemblies.

INSTALLATION

1. Install inboard shoe and lining.
2. Ensure tangs on shoe fully engage pistons. When properly installed, shoe should be flush with piston.
3. Install outboard shoe and lining into caliper housing. Ensure insulators are fully seated into holes in outboard side of housing.
4. Install caliper as outlined under "Caliper Service."

CALIPER SERVICE

REMOVAL

1. Remove ⅔ of total brake fluid capacity from master cylinder reservoir.

2. Raise and support vehicle, then remove tire and wheel assembly.
3. If caliper requires overhaul, remove inlet fitting attaching bolt, then disconnect inlet fitting from caliper housing.
4. Discard both gaskets, then plug openings in inlet fitting and caliper to prevent loss or contamination of fluid. **Do not crimp brake hose since this may damage hose's internal structure.**
5. Remove caliper guide pin bolts, then the caliper from rotor and caliper mounting bracket. If only shoe and linings require replacement, suspend caliper from upper control arm to prevent damage to brake hose.

DISASSEMBLE

1. Remove shoe and lining assemblies.
2. Pad interior of caliper housing with shop towels to prevent damage to pistons during removal.
3. Position shop towel in interior part of caliper, then slowly apply compressed air to inlet port and remove pistons. **It is imperative that one piston be partially installed to facilitate removal of second piston from bore. A pad or wooden spacer may be used to prevent complete removal of first piston.**
4. Remove dust boots from pistons.
5. Using a small piece of wood or plastic, remove piston seal from bore. **Do not use a metal tool of any kind to remove seal since it may damage bore.**
6. Remove bleeder valve cap and bleeder valve.
7. Inspect piston for scoring, nicks, corrosion, and wear.
8. Inspect caliper housing and seal groove for corrosion, nicks, scoring and excessive wear.
9. Use crocus cloth to polish away corrosion from housing bore. Replace caliper housing if corrosion in and around seal groove will not clean up with crocus cloth.
10. Clean all parts with denatured alcohol, then dry with unlubricated compressed air.
11. Blow out all passages in housing and bleeder valve.

ASSEMBLE

1. Install cap onto bleeder valve, then install bleeder valve into caliper.
2. Using clean brake fluid, lubricate piston seals, then install seals into caliper bore grooves. Ensure seals are not twisted during installation.
3. Using clean brake fluid, lubricate caliper bores and piston assemblies.
4. Install boot over end of piston.
5. Place piston into caliper bore, then push downward until fully bottomed in bore. Ensure boot is properly seated into groove around piston and into groove in caliper bore.
6. Repeat step 3 and 4 for remaining piston.
7. Install shoes and linings as described in this section, then bleed brake system.

INSTALLATION

1. Ensure guiding surfaces on shoe and lining assemblies and mounting bracket are seated properly, then position caliper over rotor and onto mounting bracket.
2. Press caliper housing downward to compress bias springs (12), **Fig. 1,** then install new retainer pin and circlip. **Two sets of retainer pins are available for service, one for base calipers and one for heavy duty. Since circlip grooves are cut in different positions, ensure proper retainer pin is used.**
3. If caliper was overhauled, connect inlet fitting using new gaskets, then bleed brake system as required.
4. Install wheel and tire assembly, then lower the vehicle.
5. Fill master cylinder to proper level, then pump brake pedal to bring pads into contact with brake rotor.

ROTOR

REPLACE

1. Remove caliper as described under "Caliper Service."
2. Remove caliper mounting bracket attaching bolts, then the mounting bracket.
3. Remove rotor from hub assembly.
4. Reverse procedure to install.

DISC BRAKE SPECIFICATIONS

CALIPER SPECIFICATIONS

Model	Year	Caliper Bore Dia. Inch
Corvette	1997–2000	1.50

ROTOR SPECIFICATIONS

Model	Year	Nominal Thickness, Inch	Minimum Refinish Thickness, Inch	Thickness Variation (Parallelism), Inch	Lateral Runout (T.I.R.), Inch
Corvette	1997–98	1.260	1.200	.0005	.006
	1999–2000	1.260	1.205	.0005	.003

TIGHTENING SPECIFICATIONS

Component	Torque/Ft. Lbs.
Brake Hose To Caliper	30
Caliper Bleeder Screw	108①
Front Caliper Mounting Bracket (1997)	160
Front Caliper Mounting Bracket (1998–2000)	125
Wheel Lug Nuts	100

① — Inch lbs.

AC-Delco Dual Piston Rear Disc Brake

INDEX

PRECAUTIONS

1. Grease or any other foreign material must be kept off brake linings, caliper, surfaces of disc and external surfaces of hub during service procedures.
2. Handling brake disc and caliper should be done in a way to avoid deformation of disc and nicking or scratching brake linings.
3. If inspection reveals rubber piston seals are worn or damaged, they should be replaced.
4. During removal and installation of a wheel assembly, ensure not to interfere with or damage caliper splash shield, or bleeder screw.
5. Front wheel bearings preload should be adjusted to specifications .
6. Ensure vehicle is centered on hoist before servicing any front end components to avoid bending or damaging disc splash shield on full righthand or lefthand wheel turns.
7. Before vehicle is moved after any brake service work, ensure to obtain a firm brake pedal.
8. Assembly bolts of two piece caliper housings should not be disturbed unless caliper requires service.

DESCRIPTION

The rear disc brake caliper contains opposing dual pistons in a two piece cast iron housing which bolts directly to the mounting flange of the rear suspension lower trailing arm. Hydraulic pressure, created by applying force to the brake pedal, acts equally against all surfaces of both pistons and both piston bore cavity surfaces. The parking brake application is completely independent of the hydraulic braking system.

TROUBLESHOOTING

BRAKE ROUGHNESS

The most common cause of brake chatter on disc brakes is a variation in thickness of the disc. If roughness or vibration is encountered during highway operation or if pedal pulsation is experienced at low speeds, the disc may have excessive thickness variation. To inspect for this condition, measure the disc at 12 points with a micrometer at a radius approximately one inch from edge of disc. If thickness measurements vary by more than .0005 inch, the disc should be replaced with a new one.

Excessive lateral runout of braking disc may cause a piston "knocking back," possibly creating increased pedal travel and vibration when brakes are applied.

Before inspecting the runout, the wheel bearings should be adjusted. The adjustment is very important and will be required at the completion of the test to prevent bearing failure. Adjust the wheel bearings as outlined in the appropriate "Front Suspension & Steering" chassis section.

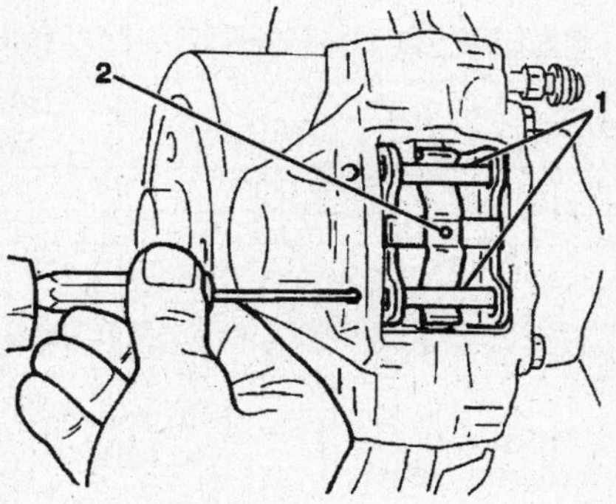

(1) Rear Brake Caliper Retaining Pins
(2) Rear Brake Caliper Spring Retainer

GC4079700141000X

Fig. 1 Rear brake pad removal. Catera

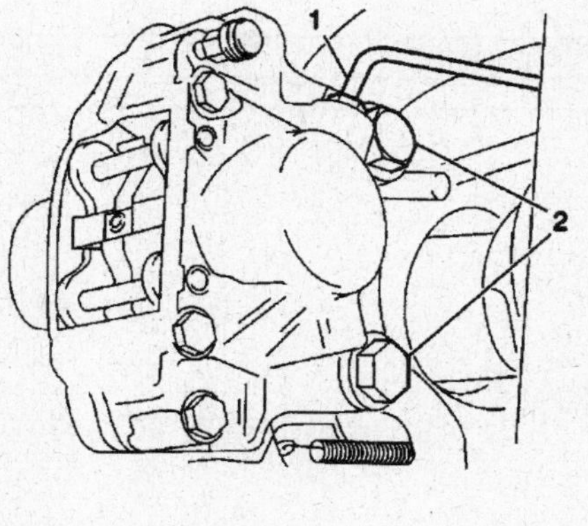

(1) Rear Brake Caliper Pipe
(2) Rear Brake Caliper Bolt

GC4079700142000X

Fig. 2 Rear brake caliper removal. Catera

BRAKE PAD SERVICE

1. Remove approximately ⅓ of brake fluid from master cylinder.
2. Raise and support vehicle, then remove wheel and tire assembly.
3. Using a screwdriver, gently pry between rotor and each brake pad to bottom each piston in its bore.
4. Remove brake caliper retaining pins from brake caliper, **Fig. 1**, then the brake pads.
5. Reverse procedure to install.

CALIPER SERVICE

REPLACEMENT

1. Remove brake pads as outlined under "Brake Pad Service, " then the rear caliper pipe, **Fig. 2.**
2. Remove rear brake caliper bolts, then the caliper from rotor.
3. Reverse procedure to install. Tighten rear brake caliper bolts and brake pipe fitting to specifications.

DISASSEMBLE

1. Install piston retainer tool No. J-22429, or equivalent on opposite cylinder to be removed.
2. Remove piston by directing dry filtered compressed air into fluid channel port of caliper housing, then cover exposed bore with tool No. J-22429, or equivalent, and remove opposing piston using dry unlubricated compressed air.
3. Using a small piece of wood or plastic, remove piston seal from bore. **Do not use a metal tool of any kind to remove seal since it may damage bore.**
4. Remove bleeder valve cap and rear brake caliper bleeder valve.

ASSEMBLE

1. Install new bleeder valve and cap, then the new piston seals lubricated with clean brake fluid.
2. Install dust boots lubricated with clean brake fluid onto pistons, then the pistons into caliper housing bores.
3. With pistons bottomed in bores, ensure outer edge of dust boots are around caliper housing embossments.

ROTOR

REPLACE

1. Remove caliper as outlined under "Caliper Service, " then the rotor setscrew.
2. Remove rotor from vehicle.
3. Reverse procedure to install.

TECHNICAL SERVICE BULLETINS

1997 CATERA

Brake Squeal Noise

On these models, a squeal noise may be heard from rear brakes when the brakes are applied. The noise may be most pronounced when braking in reverse and/or when the weather conditions are cold and damp.

To correct this condition, replace the rear brake calipers with second design calipers, part No. 90543586 for lefthand, or part No. 90543587 for the righthand. Vehicles after VIN breakpoint VR908949 are already equipped with second design calipers.

DISC BRAKE SPECIFICATIONS

CALIPER SPECIFICATIONS

Model	Year	Caliper Bore Dia. Inch
Catera	1997–2000	1.57

ROTOR SPECIFICATIONS

Model	Year	Nominal Thickness, Inch	Minimum Refinish Thickness, Inch	Thickness Variation (Parallelism), Inch	Lateral Runout (T.I.R.), Inch
Catera	1997–2000	.433	.393	.0005	.004

TIGHTENING SPECIFICATIONS

Component	Torque/Ft. Lbs.
Rear Brake Caliper Bolts	59
Rear Brake Caliper Pipe	12

AC-Delco Single Piston Rear Disc Brake (Type 1)

INDEX

PRECAUTIONS

1. Grease or any other foreign material must be kept off brake linings, caliper, surfaces of disc and external surfaces of hub during service procedures.
2. Handling brake disc and caliper should be done in a way to avoid deformation of disc and nicking or scratching brake linings.
3. If inspection reveals worn or damaged rubber piston seals, they should be replaced.
4. During removal and installation of a wheel assembly, ensure not to interfere with or damage caliper splash shield, or bleeder screw.
5. Front wheel bearings preload should be adjusted to specifications.
6. Ensure vehicle is centered on hoist before servicing any front end components to avoid bending or damaging disc splash shield on full righthand or lefthand wheel turns.
7. Before vehicle is moved after any brake service work, ensure to obtain a firm brake pedal.
8. Assembly bolts of two piece caliper housings should not be disturbed unless caliper requires service.

DESCRIPTION

The caliper has a single piston, **Fig. 1**, and is mounted to the support bracket by two mounting bolts. The caliper assembly slides on the two mounting bolts. Upon brake application, fluid pressure against the piston forces the inboard shoe and lining assembly against the inboard side of the disc. This action causes the caliper assembly to slide until the outboard lining comes into contact with the disc. As pressure builds up the linings are pressed against the disc with increased force.

TROUBLESHOOTING

BRAKE ROUGHNESS

The most common cause of brake chatter on disc brakes is a variation in disc thickness. If roughness or vibration is encountered during highway operation or if pedal pulsation is experienced at low speeds, the disc may have excessive thickness variation. To inspect for this condition, measure the disc at 12 points with a micrometer at a radius approximately one inch from edge of disc. If thickness measurements vary by more than .0005 inch, the disc should be replaced with a new one.

Excessive lateral runout of braking disc may cause a piston "knocking back," possibly creating increased pedal travel and vibration when brakes are applied.

Before inspecting the runout, the wheel bearings should be adjusted. The adjustment is very important and will be required at the completion of the test to prevent bearing failure. Adjust the wheel bearings as outlined in the appropriate "Front Suspension & Steering" chassis section.

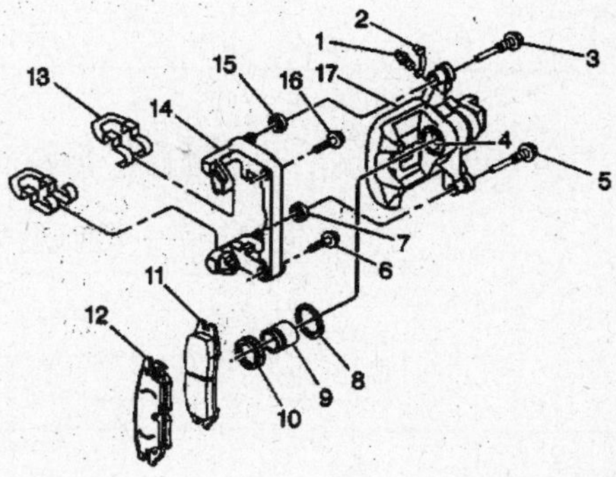

(1) Valve, Caliper Bleeder
(2) Cap, Bleeder Valve
(3) Bolt, Caliper
(4) Caliper Bore
(5) Bolt, Caliper
(6) Bolt, Caliper Bracket
(7) Boot, Caliper
(8) Seal, Caliper Piston
(9) Piston, Caliper
(10) Boot, Caliper Piston
(11) Pad, Inner
(12) Pad, Outer
(13) Clips, Retainer
(14) Bracket, Caliper
(15) Boot, Caliper
(16) Bolt, Caliper Bracket
(17) Housing, Caliper

GC4079700143000X

Fig. 1 Exploded view of rear caliper. Century, Grand Prix, Intrigue & Regal

BRAKE PAD SERVICE

1. Remove ⅔ of brake fluid from master cylinder reservoir.
2. Raise and support vehicle.
3. Mark relationship of wheel to axle flange, then remove wheel and tire assembly.
4. Using a suitable C-clamp, compress caliper piston enough for clearance, then remove upper caliper bolt.
5. Pivot caliper body down in order to access the pads. **Do not remove the caliper body.**
6. Remove brake pads and pad clips from caliper bracket.
7. Reverse procedure to install. Tighten caliper bolt to specifications.

CALIPER SERVICE

REPLACEMENT

1. Remove ⅔ of brake fluid from master cylinder reservoir.
2. Raise and support vehicle.
3. Mark relationship of wheel to axle flange, then remove wheel and tire assembly.
4. Using a suitable C-clamp, compress caliper piston enough for clearance.
5. Remove brake hose from caliper plug openings in caliper and brake hose to prevent fluid loss and contamination.
6. Remove caliper bolts, then the caliper housing from rotor and caliper bracket.
7. Reverse procedure to install. Tighten fasteners to specifications.

DISASSEMBLE

1. Pad interior of caliper assembly with a

clean shop towel, then remove piston assembly using low pressure compressed air into caliper inlet hole. **Do not place fingers in front of piston in an attempt to catch or protect piston when applying compressed air. This could result in serious injury.**
2. Using a small screwdriver, pry up one end of boot ring and work boot ring out of caliper groove.
3. Using a small wooden or plastic tool, remove piston seal from caliper bore groove.
4. Remove bleeder valve and bleeder valve cap.
5. Clean all parts in clean denatured alcohol, then dry with unlubricated low pressure compressed air.
6. Blow out all passages in caliper body and bleeder valve.
7. Inspect piston assembly for nicks, cracks, wear or corrosion.
8. Inspect piston bore for scoring, nicks, wear or corrosion. Use crocus cloth to polish out light corrosion. Replace caliper if any heavy corrosion is found. **Do not hone caliper bore.**
9. Inspect seal groove for nicks or burrs.
10. Inspect boots for cuts, tears or deterioration.

ASSEMBLE

1. Install bleeder valve and bleeder valve cap. Tighten to specifications.
2. Install new lubricated piston seal into caliper bore grooves, then the piston boot onto piston.
3. Lubricate piston with clean brake fluid, then install piston and boot into bore of caliper.
4. Install piston ring. Ensure outside edge of piston boot is seated smoothly in counterbore of caliper body.
5. Install caliper.

ROTOR

REPLACE

1. Remove caliper assembly as described under "Caliper Service."
2. Remove caliper mounting bracket attaching bolts, then the mounting bracket.
3. Remove rotor from hub and bearing assembly.
4. Reverse procedure to install.

DISC BRAKE SPECIFICATIONS

CALIPER SPECIFICATIONS

Model	Year	Caliper Bore Dia. Inch
All	1997–2000	1.50

ROTOR SPECIFICATIONS

Model	Year	Nominal Thickness, Inch	Minimum Refinish Thickness, Inch	Discard Thickness, Inch	Thickness Variation, Inch	Lateral Runout (T.I.R.), Inch
All	1997–2000	.430	.410	.350	.0001	.003

TIGHTENING SPECIFICATIONS

Component	Torque/Ft. Lbs.
Brake Hose To Caliper	40
Caliper Bleeder Screw (1997–98)	96①
Caliper Bleeder Screw (1999-2000)	62①
Caliper Bracket Bolts	92
Caliper Mounting Bolts	32

① — Inch lbs.

AC-Delco Single Piston Rear Disc Brake (Type 2)

INDEX

PRECAUTIONS

1. Grease or any other foreign material must be kept off brake linings, caliper, surfaces of disc and external surfaces of hub during service procedures.
2. Handling brake disc and caliper should be done in a way to avoid deformation of disc and nicking or scratching brake linings.
3. If inspection reveals rubber piston seals are worn or damaged, they should be replaced.
4. During removal and installation of a wheel assembly, ensure not to interfere with or damage caliper splash shield, or bleeder screw.
5. Front wheel bearings preload should be adjusted to specifications.
6. Ensure vehicle is centered on hoist before servicing any front end components to avoid bending or damaging disc splash shield on full righthand or lefthand wheel turns.
7. Before vehicle is moved after any brake service work, obtain a firm brake pedal.
8. Assembly bolts of two piece caliper housings should not be disturbed unless caliper requires service.

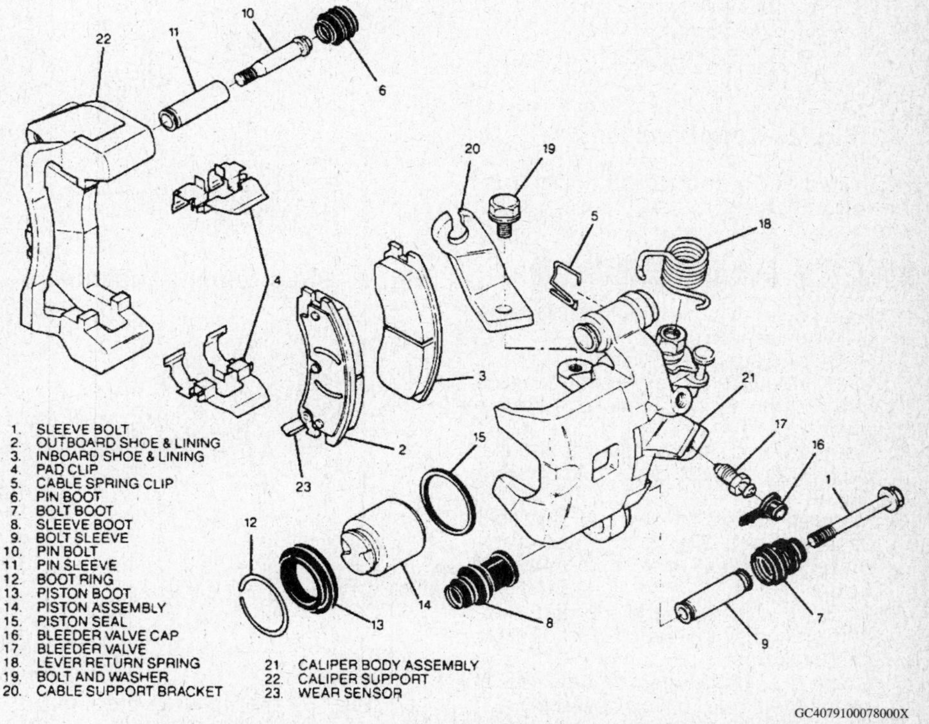

Fig. 1 Disassembled view of AC-Delco single piston rear disc brake caliper. Type 2

DESCRIPTION

The caliper assembly, **Fig. 1,** has a single bore and is mounted to the support bracket with two mounting bolt and sleeve assemblies. Hydraulic pressure created by applying the brake pedal is converted by the caliper to a stopping force. This force acts equally against the piston and the bottom of the piston bore to move the piston outward and to slide the caliper inward resulting in a clamping action. This clamping action presses the linings against the rotor, creating friction to stop the vehicle.

When the parking brake is applied, the external caliper parking brake lever moves and rotates a spindle within the caliper housing. As the spindle rotates, a connecting rod is pushed against an internal adjusting screw which is threaded into a sleeve nut in the piston assembly. This causes the piston assembly to move outward bringing the inboard shoe and lining assembly against the rotor. As the inboard shoe and lining contacts the rotor, a reaction force causes the caliper housing to slide inward pressing the outboard shoe and lining against the rotor.

The piston assembly contains a self adjusting mechanism to keep the parking brake in proper adjustment. As the linings are worn, the piston moves through the seal to maintain proper lining to rotor clearance. The parking brake adjusts to proper clearances through an internal sleeve nut that rotates and moves as one unit with the piston.

TROUBLESHOOTING

BRAKE ROUGHNESS

The most common cause of brake chatter on disc brakes is a variation in disc thickness. If roughness or vibration is encountered during highway operation or if pedal pulsation is experienced at low speeds, the disc may have excessive thickness variation. To inspect for this condition, measure the disc at 12 points with a micrometer at a radius approximately one inch from edge of disc. If thickness measurements vary by more than .0005 inch, the disc should be replaced with a new one.

Excessive lateral runout of braking disc may cause a piston "knocking back," possibly creating increased pedal travel and vibration when brakes are applied.

Before inspecting the runout, the wheel bearings should be adjusted. The adjustment is very important and will be required at the completion of the test to prevent bearing failure. Adjust the wheel bearings

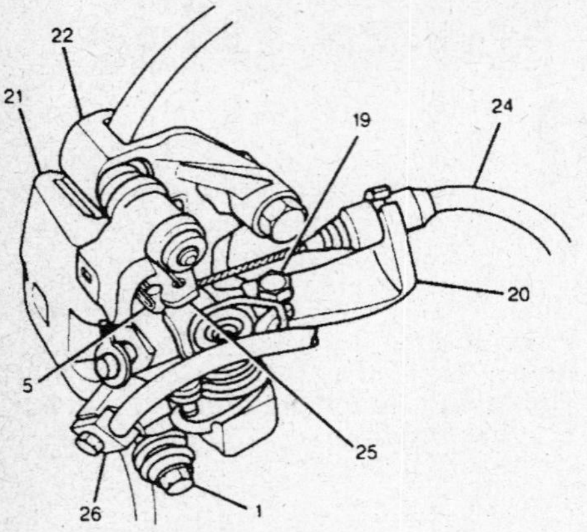

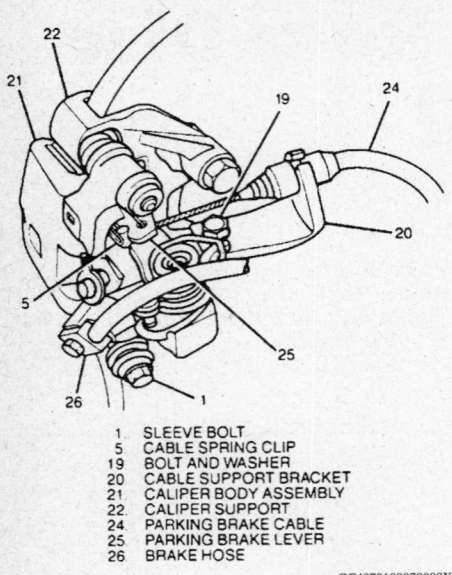

1. SLEEVE BOLT
5. CABLE SPRING CLIP
19. BOLT AND WASHER
20. CABLE SUPPORT BRACKET
21. CALIPER BODY ASSEMBLY
22. CALIPER SUPPORT
24. PARKING BRAKE CABLE
25. PARKING BRAKE LEVER
26. BRAKE HOSE

GC4079100079000X

Fig. 2 Caliper assembly

as outlined in the appropriate "Front Suspension & Steering" chassis section.

BRAKE PAD SERVICE

1. Remove ⅔ of brake fluid from master cylinder reservoir.
2. Raise and support vehicle.
3. Mark relationship of wheel to axle flange, then remove wheel and tire assembly.
4. Remove bolt and washer attaching cable support bracket to caliper body, **Fig. 2.**
5. Remove sleeve bolt and pivot caliper assembly up, **Fig. 3. Do not completely remove caliper assembly body.**
6. Remove outboard and inboard shoe and linings, then two pad clips from caliper support.
7. Using a suitable spanner type tool in piston slots, turn piston assembly and thread it into caliper body assembly.
8. After bottoming piston, lift inner edge of boot next to piston assembly and press out any trapped air.
9. Ensure slots in end of piston are positioned as shown in **Fig. 4** before pivoting caliper body assembly down over shoe and linings in caliper support. Use suitable spanner type tool to turn piston as required.
10. Install pad clips, outboard and inboard shoe and linings in caliper support. **Ensure wear sensor is on outboard shoe positioned downward at leading edge of rotor during forward wheel rotation.**
11. Pivot caliper body assembly down over shoe and lining assemblies. Ensure not to damage piston boot on inboard shoe.
12. After caliper body is in position, inspect installation of pad clips again. If required, use a small screwdriver to reseat or center pad clips on support abutments.

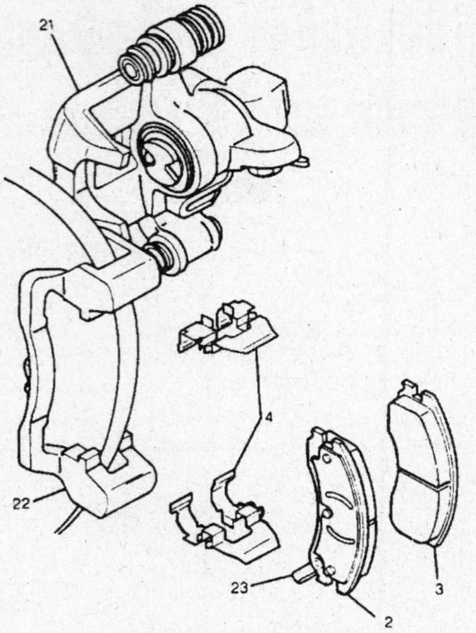

2. OUTBOARD SHOE & LINING
3. INBOARD SHOE & LINING
4. PAD CLIP
21. CALIPER BODY ASSEMBLY
22. CALIPER SUPPORT
23. WEAR SENSOR

GC4079100083000X

Fig. 3 Shoe & lining installation

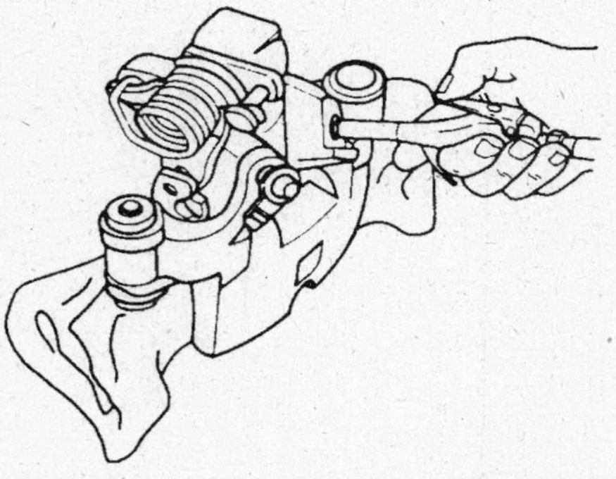

GC4079100080000X

Fig. 5 Removing piston

13. Install sleeve bolt and **torque** to 20 ft. lbs.
14. Install cable support bracket and **torque** bolt to 32 ft. lbs.
15. Install wheels and tires, aligning previous marks, then lower the vehicle.
16. Apply approximately 175 lbs. of force to brake pedal three times to seat shoe and linings against rotor.

CALIPER SERVICE

REPLACEMENT

1. Raise and support vehicle.
2. Mark relationship of wheel to axle flange, then remove wheel and tire assembly.
3. Remove brake hose from caliper, **Fig. 2.** Plug openings in caliper and brake hose to prevent fluid loss and contamination.
4. Lift up on end of cable spring to free

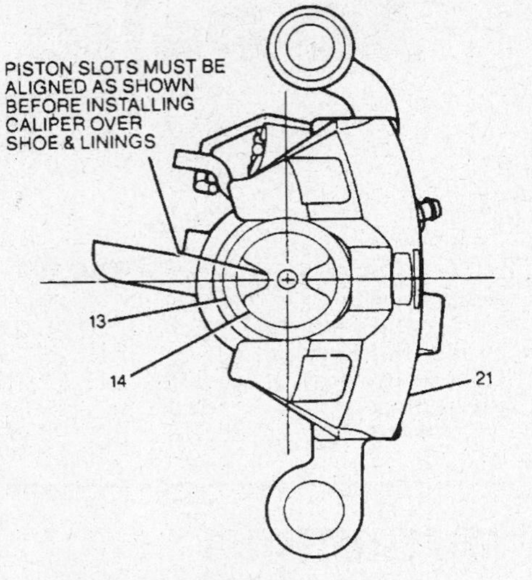

13. PISTON BOOT
14. PISTON ASSEMBLY
21. CALIPER BODY ASSEMBLY

GC4079100084000X

Fig. 4 Positioning piston slots

end of cable from lever, then disconnect parking brake cable from lever.

5. Remove bolt and washer attaching cable support bracket to caliper body assembly.
6. Remove sleeve bolt and caliper body assembly.
7. Reverse procedure to install, noting the following:
   a. **Torque** sleeve bolt to 20 ft. lbs.
   b. **Torque** cable support bracket to 32 ft. lbs.
   c. Bleed brakes.

DISASSEMBLE

1. Remove caliper from vehicle as described under "Caliper Service."
2. Pad interior of caliper assembly with a clean shop towel, then remove piston assembly using low pressure compressed air into caliper inlet hole, **Fig. 5. Do not place fingers in front of piston in an attempt to catch or protect piston when applying compressed air. This could result in serious injury.**
3. Using a small screwdriver, pry up one end of boot ring, **Fig. 6.** Work boot ring out of caliper groove.
4. Using a small wooden or plastic tool, remove piston seal from caliper bore groove.
5. Remove bleeder valve and bleeder valve cap.
6. If lever return spring replacement is required, remove by using a screwdriver to disengage return spring from parking brake lever, then unhook spring from stopper pin, **Fig. 7.**
7. Remove pin boot and pin bolt, then the bolt sleeve and sleeve bolt from caliper body.
8. Remove pin bolt and pin sleeve from caliper support.
9. Clean all parts in clean denatured alcohol, then dry with unlubricated low pressure compressed air.
10. Blow out all passages in caliper body

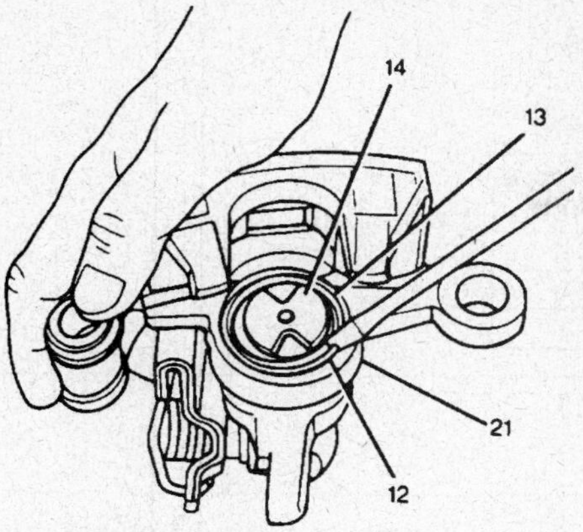

12. BOOT RING
13. PISTON BOOT
14. PISTON ASSEMBLY
21. CALIPER BODY ASSEMBLY

GC4079100081000X

Fig. 6 Removing boot ring

and bleeder valve.

11. Inspect piston assembly for nicks, cracks, wear or corrosion.
12. Inspect piston bore for scoring, nicks, wear or corrosion. Use crocus cloth to polish out light corrosion. Replace caliper if any heavy corrosion is found. **Do not hone caliper bore.**
13. Inspect seal groove for nicks or burrs.
14. Inspect boots for cuts, tears or deterioration.
15. Inspect bolt sleeve and pin sleeve for corrosion or damage. **Do not attempt to polish away corrosion.**

ASSEMBLE

1. Lubricate pin sleeve with silicone grease, then install pin bolts and pin sleeve to caliper support.
2. Lubricate sleeve boot with silicone grease, then compress lip on sleeve boot and push it through caliper body assembly until lip emerges and seals on inboard face of caliper ear.
3. Lubricate push bolt sleeve with silicone grease, then push it in through lip end of boot until boot seats in sleeve groove at other end.
4. Install bolt boot onto caliper body.
5. Install small end of pin boot over pin sleeve until boot seats in pin groove.
6. If removed, position new lever return spring with hook end around stopper pin, then pry other end of spring over lever.
7. Install bleeder valve and bleeder valve cap.
8. Lubricate new piston seal with clean brake fluid and install in groove in caliper bore. Ensure it is not twisted.
9. Install piston boot onto piston assembly.
10. Lubricate piston assembly with clean brake fluid.
11. Start piston assembly in by hand, then thread into bottom of caliper bore using spanner type tool in slots in end of piston assembly.
12. Ensure outside edge of piston boot is smoothly seated in counterbore of caliper body assembly.
13. Work boot ring into groove near open end of caliper bore using care not to pinch piston boot between boot ring and caliper body.
14. After installing ring, lift inner edge of boot next to piston assembly and press out any trapped air. Boot must lay flat.
15. Install caliper on vehicle as described under "Caliper Service."

ROTOR

REPLACE

1. Remove caliper assembly as described under "Caliper Service."
2. Remove caliper mounting bracket attaching bolts, then the mounting bracket.
3. Remove rotor from hub and bearing assembly.
4. Reverse procedure to install. Adjust parking brake as described under "Adjustments."

ADJUSTMENTS

PARKING BRAKE

1. Cycle brake system as follows:
   a. Apply service brake with a pedal force of 150 lbs. and release.
   b. Fully apply parking brake using approximately 125 lbs. of force on final stroke, and release.
   c. Apply and release parking brake two additional times as described above.
2. Inspect parking brake pedal assembly for full release by turning ignition On and observing brake warning lamp, which should be off.

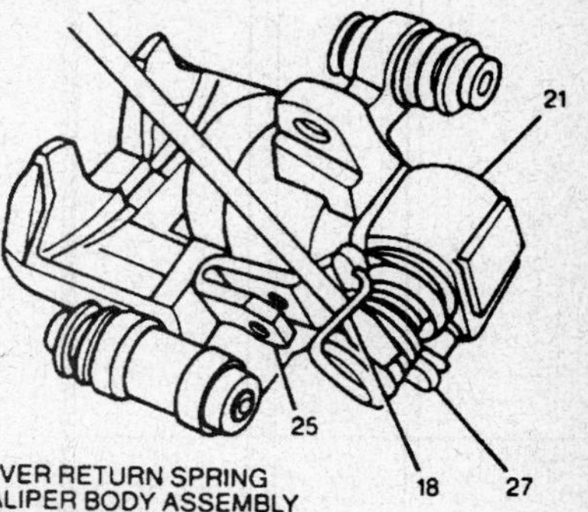

18. LEVER RETURN SPRING
21. CALIPER BODY ASSEMBLY
25. PARKING BRAKE LEVER
27. STOPPER PIN

GC4079100082000X

Fig. 7 Removing lever return spring

3. If brake warning lamp is on and parking brake appears to be fully released, operate manual pedal release lever and pull downward on front park brake cable to remove slack from pedal assembly.
4. Raise and support vehicle.
5. Inspect parking brake levers on rear calipers, noting the following:
   a. Levers should be against stops on caliper housing.
   b. If levers are not against stops, inspect for binding in rear brake cables and position levers against stops.
6. Tighten parking brake cable at adjuster until either lefthand or righthand lever begins to move off of stop.
7. Loosen adjuster until lever which moved off of stop in step four is again resting on stop. **Both levers should be resting on caliper stops after completing this step.**
8. Operate parking brake several times to inspect adjustment.
9. A firm pedal feel should be obtained by pumping pedal less than one stroke.
10. Inspect lefthand and righthand caliper levers. Both levers must be resting on stops after adjustment of parking brake.
11. Inspect operation of parking brake. If possible, place vehicle on a grade and inspect parking brake holding ability.

DISC BRAKE SPECIFICATIONS

CALIPER SPECIFICATIONS

Model	Year	Caliper Bore Dia. Inch
Alero & Grand Am	1999–2000	1.50
Aurora & Riviera	1997–99	1.50
Cutlass Supreme	1997	1.65
DeVille	1997–2000	1.50

Continued

DISC BRAKE SPECIFICATIONS

CALIPER SPECIFICATIONS—Continued

Model	Year	Caliper Bore Dia. Inch
Eldorado & Seville	1997–2000	1.50
Lumina & Monte Carlo	1997–99	1.65
Park Avenue	1999-2000	1.50

ROTOR SPECIFICATIONS

Model	Year	Nominal Thickness, Inch	Minimum Refinish Thickness, Inch	Discard Thickness, Inch	Thickness Variation, Inch	Lateral Runout (T.I.R.), Inch
Alero & Grand Am	1999-2000	.433	.410	.350	.0005	—
Aurora & Riviera	1997–99	.433	.423	.374	.0005	.002
Cutlass Supreme	1997	.492	.444	.370	.0005	.003
DeVille	1997–98	.433	.389	.374	.0005	.002
	1999-2000	.433	.423	.374	.0005	.002
Eldorado & Seville	1997–98	.433	.389	.374	.0005	.002
	1999-2000	.433	.423	.374	.0005	.002
Lumina & Monte Carlo	1997	.492	.444	.429	.0005	.003
	1998–99	.492	.444	.370	.0005	.003
Park Avenue	1999-2000	.433	.423	.374	.0005	.002

TIGHTENING SPECIFICATIONS

Component	Torque/Ft. Lbs.
Brake Hose To Caliper	32
Caliper Bleeder Screw	108①
Caliper Bracket Mounting Bolts	83
Caliper Mounting Bolts	63
Master Cylinder To Booster	22
Wheel Lug Nuts	100
Wheel Speed Sensor Mounting Bolt	108①

① — Inch lbs.

PBR Single Piston Rear Disc Brake

INDEX

PRECAUTIONS

1. Grease or any other foreign material must be kept off brake linings, caliper, surfaces of disc and external surfaces of hub during service procedures.
2. Handling brake disc and caliper should be done in a way to avoid deformation of disc and nicking or scratching brake linings.
3. If inspection reveals worn or damaged rubber piston seals, they should be replaced.
4. During removal and installation of a wheel assembly, ensure not to interfere with or damage caliper splash shield, or bleeder screw.
5. Front wheel bearings preload should be adjusted to specifications.
6. Ensure vehicle is centered on hoist before servicing any front end components to avoid bending or damaging disc splash shield on full righthand or lefthand wheel turns.
7. Before vehicle is moved after any brake service work, obtain a firm brake pedal.
8. Assembly bolts of two piece caliper housings should not be disturbed unless caliper requires service.

DESCRIPTION

This rear caliper, **Fig. 1**, consists of a single piston and an aluminum housing which is suspended in a mounting bracket through two slide pins. Hydraulic pressure, created by applying force to the brake pedal, acts equally against the piston and the bottom of the caliper bore to move the piston outward. This action slides the caliper inward, resulting in a clamping action on the brake rotor. This clamping action forces the linings against the rotor, creating the friction required to stop the vehicle.

The parking brake mechanism on this caliper is completely independent of the hydraulic brake system. When the parking brake is applied, the lever on the caliper causes the pushrod, actuating collar and clamp rod assembly to move outward. This causes the caliper to move inward, mechanically forcing the linings against the rotor.

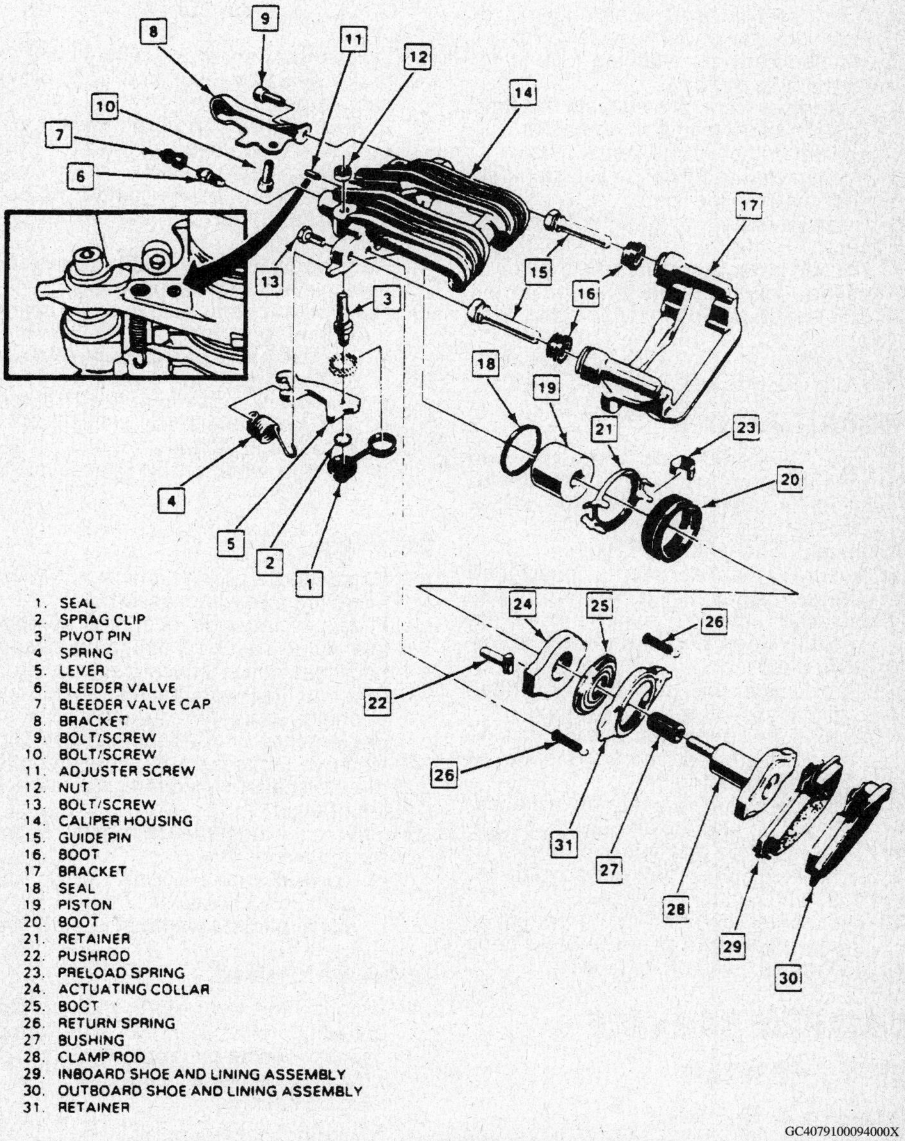

Fig. 1 Typical exploded view of PBR single piston rear caliper

TROUBLESHOOTING

BRAKE ROUGHNESS

The most common cause of brake chatter on disc brakes is a variation in disc thickness. If roughness or vibration is encountered during highway operation or if pedal pulsation is experienced at low speeds, the disc may have excessive thickness variation. To inspect for this condition, measure the disc at 12 points with a micrometer at a radius approximately one inch from edge of disc. If thickness measurements vary by more than .0005 inch, the disc should be replaced with a new one.

Excessive lateral runout of braking disc

may cause a piston " knocking back," possibly creating increased pedal travel and vibration when brakes are applied.

Before inspecting the runout, the wheel bearings should be adjusted. The adjustment is very important and will be required at the completion of the test to prevent bearing failure. Adjust the wheel bearings as outlined in the appropriate "Front Suspension & Steering" chassis section.

BRAKE PAD SERVICE

REMOVAL

1. Remove ⅔ of total brake fluid capacity from master cylinder reservoir.
2. Raise and support vehicle, then remove tire and wheel assembly.
3. Install two wheel retaining nuts to retain rotor in position.
4. Position one end of a suitable C-clamp against inlet fitting bolt and other end against outboard shoe and lining.
5. Tighten clamp, **Fig. 2,** until piston fully bottoms in caliper bore.
6. Remove upper guide pin bolt and discard.
7. Loosen lower guide pin bolt, then pivot caliper downward on lower guide pin bolt to expose shoe and lining assemblies.
8. Remove shoes and linings from mounting bracket.

INSTALLATION

1. Install outboard shoe and lining onto mounting bracket. Ensure insulator on shoe is positioned toward caliper housing.
2. Install inboard shoe and lining.
3. Ensure wear sensor is positioned nearest caliper piston. When properly installed, sensor should be in trailing position when wheel is rotated in forward direction.
4. Pivot caliper into position over shoes and linings, noting the following:
   a. Ensure springs on outboard shoe do not protrude through inspection hole in housing.
   b. If protrusion is evident, lift caliper housing and adjust position of outboard shoe and lining.
5. Install and tighten new upper guide pin bolt, then tighten lower bolt.
6. Fill master cylinder to proper level, then pump brake pedal to bring pads into contact with brake rotor.

CALIPER SERVICE

REPLACEMENT

Camaro & Firebird

1. Raise and support vehicle, then disconnect park brake cable at equalizer.
2. Remove tire and wheel assemblies, then install two wheel nuts to retain rotor.
3. If caliper is to be overhauled, remove brake hose fitting bolt/screw, brake hose and brake hose gasket.
4. If return spring coils are open, remove park brake lever return spring.

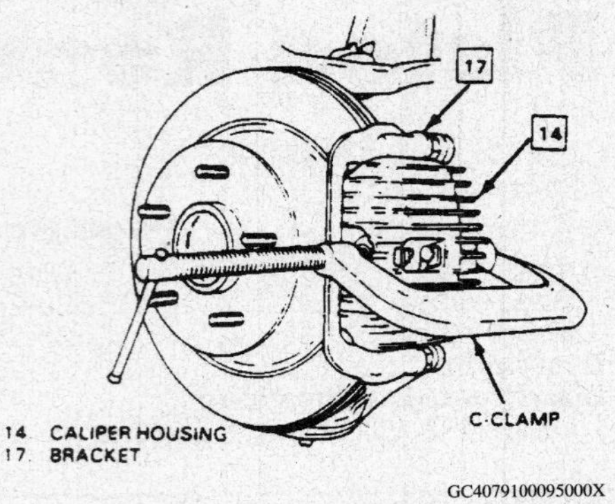

Fig. 2 Piston compression in caliper bore

5. Disconnect park brake cable from park brake actuator lever and park brake cable bracket.
6. If required, remove vibration dampener nut and vibration dampener from park brake cable bracket.
7. Remove brake caliper guide pin bolt and discard, then the rear caliper bolt and discard.
8. Remove rear brake caliper from rotor and caliper mounting plate.
9. Reverse procedure to install, noting the following:
   a. **Torque** brake caliper guide pin bolt to 27 ft. lbs.
   b. **Torque** rear caliper bolt to 22 ft. lbs.
   c. **Torque** brake hose fitting bolt or screw to 22 ft. lbs.
   d. **Torque** vibration dampener nut to 37 ft. lbs.

Corvette

1. Raise and support vehicle, then remove tire and wheel assembly.
2. If caliper requires overhaul, remove inlet fitting attaching bolt, then disconnect inlet fitting from caliper housing.
3. Discard the two gaskets, then plug openings in inlet fitting and caliper to prevent loss or contamination of fluid.
4. Remove brake caliper guide pin bolts, then the caliper from rotor and mounting bracket.
5. Reverse procedure to install, noting the following:
   a. **Torque** brake caliper guide pin bolts to 23 ft. lbs.
   b. **Torque** inlet fitting bolt to 30 ft. lbs.

DISASSEMBLE

1. Remove the two return springs from actuating collar, then pull collar out of caliper housing and remove clamp rod (28) and bushing (27), **Fig. 1.**
2. Discard bushing.
3. Bend back boot retainer tabs, then remove retainers (21, 31), boots (20, 25) and pushrod (22) from actuating collar.
4. Remove preload spring (23) from retainer (31), then discard retainers and boots.
5. Use clean shop towels to pad interior of caliper assembly, then remove piston by directing compressed air into caliper brake hose inlet hole, **Use just enough air pressure to ease piston out of bore. Do not place fingers in front of piston for any reason when applying compressed air. This could result in serious personal injury.**
6. Using a small piece of wood or plastic, remove piston seal from bore. **Do not use a metal tool of any kind to remove seal since it may damage bore.**
7. Remove bleeder valve cap and bleeder valve.
8. Remove seal (1), sprag clip (2) and lever (5) from pivot pin (3), then discard sprag clip.
9. Clean all metal components with suitable solvent, then dry with compressed air.
10. Inspect parking brake lever components, piston, caliper bore and mounting bracket for scoring, excessive wear or corrosion.

ASSEMBLE

1. Using clean brake fluid, lubricate piston seal, then install seal into caliper bore groove. Ensure seal is not twisted during installation.
2. Using clean brake fluid, lubricate caliper bore and piston.
3. Place piston into caliper bore, then push downward until fully bottomed in bore.
4. Apply lubricant provided in repair kit to actuating collar (24), then install pushrod (22), new boots (20, 25) and new retainers (21, 31) onto collar, **Fig. 1.**
5. Clamp retainers firmly against collar, then bend tabs on retainer (21) to hold assembly together.
6. Connect preload spring (23) onto retainer (31).
7. Apply lubricant provided in repair kit to clamp rod (28), then slide rod through holes in boot (25) and actuating collar (24). Ensure boot is firmly positioned against reaction plate on clamp rod.
8. Lubricate new compliance bushing (27), then install bushing onto clamp rod (28).
9. Lubricate grooved bead of inner boot (20), boot groove in caliper housing and actuating collar with lubricant provided in repair kit.
10. Push clamp rod to bottom of piston mating hole, then pull actuating collar (24) and seat inner boot (20) into boot groove in caliper housing.
11. Ensure pushrod (22) is positioned in hole in caliper housing, then install bleeder cap and valve.
12. If removed, install pivot pin (3) and new nut (12) onto caliper. Tighten nut to specifications, then lubricate parking brake lever (5) and pivot pin.
13. Install pivot pin seal (1), parking brake lever and new sprag clip (2).
14. Ensure teeth of sprag clip face away from lever, then snap seal cap over pivot pin.
15. Install two collar return springs (26) onto retainer (31). Ensure retainer enters springs at end of second coil.
16. Install adjustment screw (11) into caliper housing until actuating collar is parallel to piston bore face of housing.

17. Lubricate guide pins with suitable grease, then slide boots onto pins.
18. Fill boots with grease, then install into mounting bracket. Ensure boots are properly positioned in grooves in pins and mounting bracket.
19. Install caliper and bleed brake system, then adjust parking brake free travel as described under "Caliper Service."

ROTOR

REPLACE

1. Remove caliper as described under "Caliper Service."
2. Remove caliper mounting bracket attaching bolts, then the mounting bracket.
3. Remove rotor from hub and bearing assembly.
4. Reverse procedure to install. Adjust parking brake as described under "Adjustments" if required.

ADJUSTMENTS

PARKING BRAKE

1. Release parking brake lever, then raise and support vehicle.
2. Remove rear wheels, then install lug nuts on two opposite wheel studs to hold brake rotor in position.
3. Back caliper pistons into bores.
4. Loosen parking brake cable adjusting nut until there is no tension on parking brake shoes.
5. Turn each brake rotor until parking brake shoe star adjuster is visible through hole in rotor.
6. Adjusting one side at a time, tighten adjuster until rotor cannot be turned by hand, then back star wheel off 5–7 notches. **Adjust parking brake shoes by inserting a suitable tool through hole in rotor. On driver's side, tighten adjuster by moving tool handle upward. On passenger's side, tighten adjuster by moving tool handle downward.**
7. Install rear wheels and pull parking lever up two notches.
8. Tighten cable adjusting nut at equalizer until there is drag on wheels.
9. Release parking brake lever and inspect adjustment. No drag should be felt when rotating wheels.

DISC BRAKE SPECIFICATIONS

CALIPER SPECIFICATIONS

Model	Year	Caliper Bore Dia. Inch
CHEVROLET		
Camaro	1997–2000	1.595
Corvette	1997–2000	1.600
PONTIAC		
Firebird	1997–2000	1.595

ROTOR SPECIFICATIONS

Model	Year	Nominal Thickness, Inch	Minimum Refinish Thickness, Inch	Thickness Variation (Parallelism), Inch	Lateral Runout (T.I.R.), Inch
Camaro & Firebird	1997–98	.787	.733	.0005	.006
	1999–2000	1.020	.980	.0005	.003
Corvette	1997–2000	1.020	.980	.0005	.003

TIGHTENING SPECIFICATIONS

Component	Torque/Ft. lbs.
Brake Hose To Caliper	①
Caliper Bleeder Screw	108②
Front Caliper Mounting Bracket (1997)	160
Front Caliper Mounting Bracket (1998–2000)	125
Rear Caliper Mounting Bracket (1997)	160
Rear Caliper Mounting Bracket (1998–2000)	125
Rear Lower Guide Pin Bolt	①
Rear Pivot Pin Nut	16
Rear Upper Guide Pin Bolt	①
Wheel Lug Nuts	100

①— Refer to "Caliper Service" for tightening specifications.
②— Inch lbs.

Toyota/GM Single Piston Caliper

INDEX

PRECAUTIONS

1. Grease or any other foreign material must be kept off brake linings, caliper, surfaces of disc and external surfaces of hub during service procedures.
2. Handling brake disc and caliper should be done in a way to avoid deformation of disc and nicking or scratching brake linings.
3. If inspection reveals worn or damaged rubber piston seals, they should be replaced.
4. During removal and installation of a wheel assembly, ensure not to interfere with or damage caliper splash shield, or bleeder screw.
5. Front wheel bearing preload should be adjusted to specifications.
6. Ensure vehicle is centered on hoist before servicing any front end components to avoid bending or damaging disc splash shield on full righthand or lefthand wheel turns.
7. Before vehicle is moved after any brake service work, ensure to obtain a firm brake pedal.
8. Assembly bolts of two piece caliper housings should not be disturbed unless caliper requires service.

DESCRIPTION

The caliper is a single bore design and is mounted to a carrier assembly. Hydraulic pressure, created by applying brake pedal, is converted by caliper to a stopping force. This force acts equally against the piston and bottom of caliper bore to move the piston outward and to slide caliper inward resulting in a clamping action on the rotor. The clamping action forces linings against the rotor, creating friction required to stop the vehicle.

TROUBLESHOOTING

BRAKE ROUGHNESS

The most common cause of brake chatter on disc brakes is a variation in disc thickness. If roughness or vibration is encountered during highway operation or if pedal pulsation is experienced at low speeds, the disc may have excessive thickness variation. To inspect for this condition, measure the disc at 12 points with a micrometer at a radius approximately one inch from edge of disc. If thickness measurements vary by more than .0005 inch, the disc should be replaced with a new one.

Excessive lateral runout of braking disc may cause a piston "knocking back," possibly creating increased pedal travel and vibration when brakes are applied.

Before inspecting the runout, the wheel bearings should be adjusted. The adjustment is very important and will be required at the completion of the test to prevent bearing failure. Adjust the wheel bearings as outlined in the appropriate "Front Suspension & Steering" chassis section.

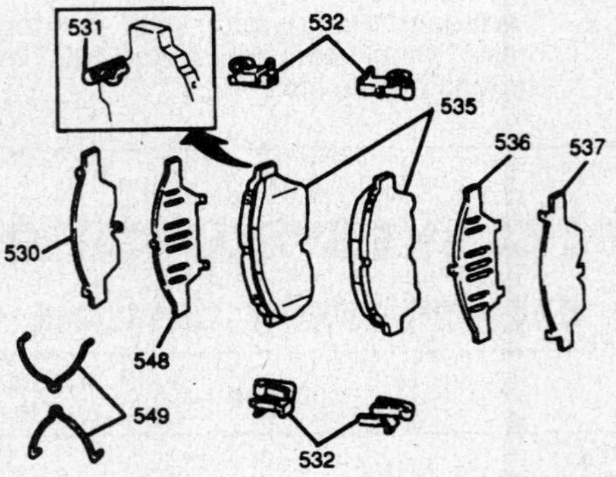

530 ANTI-SQUEAL SHIM (INBOARD)
531 PAD WEAR INDICATOR PLATE
532 ANTI-RATTLE SPRINGS
535 BRAKE PADS
536 ANTI-SQUEAL SHIM (INNER OUTBOARD)
537 ANTI-SQUEAL SHIM (OUTBOARD)
548 ANTI-SQUEAL SHIM (INNER INBOARD)
549 ANTI-SQUEAL SPRINGS

GC4079700150000X

Fig. 1 Brake pad assembly

BRAKE PAD SERVICE

REMOVAL

Replace brake pads on one wheel at a time to prevent opposite side caliper piston from being forced out of bore.

1. Remove caliper as described under "Caliper Service, " leaving brake hose connected, and secure caliper aside.
2. Remove anti-rattle clips, then the brake pads, **Fig. 1.**
3. Remove pad wear indicator plates and anti-squeal shims.
4. Remove support plates.

INSTALLATION

1. Install new support plates on caliper mounting bracket.
2. Install new wear indicators and anti-squeal shims on each pad, **Fig. 1,** then position pads in caliper mounting bracket. **Ensure arrow on wear indicator is pointing in rotating direction of rotor.**
3. Install anti-rattle springs.
4. Seat piston in caliper bore, then install caliper and mounting bolts. Tighten bolts to specifications.
5. Fill master cylinder, then bleed brakes as outlined in the "Hydraulic Brake Systems" chapter.

CALIPER SERVICE

REMOVAL

1. Siphon ⅔ of brake fluid from master cylinder.
2. Raise and support vehicle, then remove wheels.
3. Reinstall two wheel nuts to retain rotor, then remove caliper mounting bolts, **Fig. 2.**
4. Remove union nut securing brake hose to caliper and drain fluid into a suitable container. **If caliper is only being removed for brake pad replacement, do not disconnect brake hose.**
5. Compress piston as needed, then remove caliper. If brake hose remains connected, secure caliper aside to prevent hose from being stretched.

DISASSEMBLE

1. Remove two caliper slide bushings, four dust boots and spacer collars, **Fig. 2.**
2. Pry out caliper dust boot retaining ring, then remove dust boot.
3. Place clean shop towels in caliper web to protect piston, then apply compressed air to caliper fluid inlet to force piston from bore. **Keep fingers clear of caliper web when removing piston. Use only enough air pressure to ease piston out of bore or piston may be damaged.**
4. Remove piston seal from caliper bore. Ensure not to mar machined surface of caliper.
5. Remove bleeder valve.

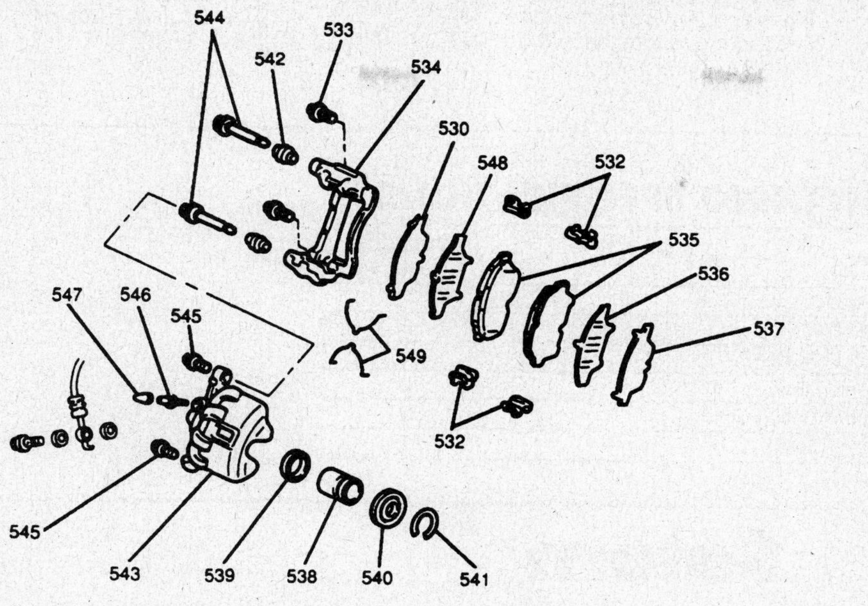

530 ANTI-SQUEAL SHIM (INBOARD)
532 ANTI-RATTLE SPRINGS
533 CALIPER CARRIER BOLTS
534 CALIPER CARRIER
535 BRAKE PADS
536 ANTI-SQUEAL SHIM (INNER OUTBOARD)
537 ANTI-SQUEAL SHIM (OUTBOARD)
538 PISTON
539 PISTON SEAL
540 PISTON BOOT
541 CALIPER SET RING
542 DUST BOOTS
543 CALIPER HOUSING
544 SLIDE PINS
545 CALIPER MOUNTING BOLTS
546 BLEEDER SCREW
547 CAP
548 ANTI-SQUEAL SHIM (INNER INBOARD)
549 ANTI-SQUEAL SPRINGS

GC4079700151000X

Fig. 2 Exploded view of Toyota/GM brake caliper

6. Clean components with alcohol and wipe dry with clean, lint free shop towels.
7. Blow out caliper body and fluid passages with clean, filtered compressed air.
8. Inspect caliper and piston for damage, distortion, excessive wear and pitting.
9. Replace mounting bolts, collars and caliper slides if they are damaged or worn.

ASSEMBLE

1. Apply lithium soap base glycol grease to components, **Fig. 3.**
2. Install piston seal in caliper. Ensure seal is squarely seated in groove.

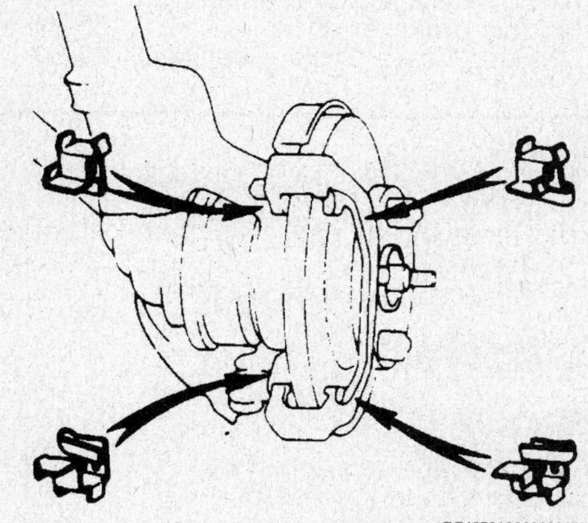

GC4079100099000X

Fig. 4 Caliper support installation

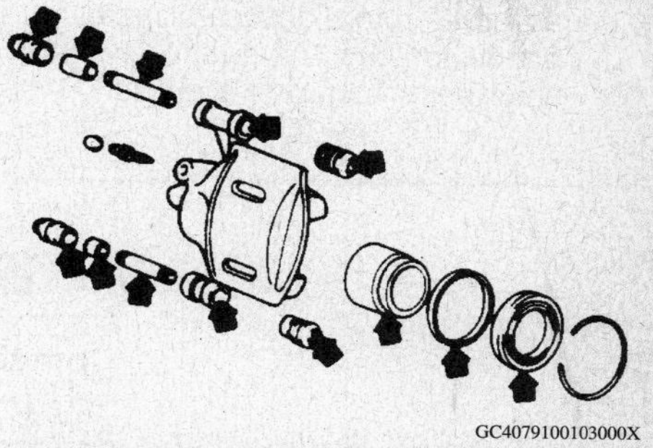

GC4079100103000X

Fig. 3 Caliper piston installation

3. Press piston into bore. Ensure piston enters bore straight.
4. Seat piston dust boot in caliper groove, then install retaining ring.
5. Install two collars and four slide bushing dust boots, **Fig. 2,** rotating boots as they are pressed in to ensure they are fully seated.
6. Install slide bushings through dust boots. Ensure boots remain seated in caliper grooves.

INSTALLATION

1. Seat piston in caliper bore. Ensure not to damage piston.
2. Ensure support plates, **Fig. 4,** and anti-rattle springs are properly positioned, then mount caliper over rotor onto mounting bracket.
3. Install caliper mounting bolts and tighten to specifications.
4. Install brake hose and mounting bolts, using new copper gaskets, then tighten bolts to specifications.
5. Fill master cylinder, then bleed brake system as outlined in the "Hydraulic Brake Systems" chapter.

ROTOR

REPLACE

1. Remove caliper as described under "Caliper Service. "
2. Remove anti-rattle springs from caliper carrier.
3. Remove caliper carrier mounting bolts, then the caliper carrier.
4. Remove brake rotor from wheel hub. If rotor cannot be removed by hand, install two 8 mm bolts into rotor. Tightening bolts will force rotor off wheel hub.
5. Reverse procedure to install.

DISC BRAKE SPECIFICATIONS

ROTOR SPECIFICATIONS

Model	Year	Nominal Thickness, Inch	Minimum Refinish Thickness, Inch①	Thickness Variation (Parallelism), Inch	Lateral Runout (T.I.R.), Inch
Prizm	1997–2000	.866	.787	.0005	.002

① — All brake rotors have a discard dimension cast into them. This is a wear dimension, not a refinish dimension. Any rotor that does not meet specifications should be discarded.

TIGHTENING SPECIFICATIONS

Component	Torque/Ft. Lbs.
ABS Wheel Speed Sensor Bolt	72①
Bleeder Valve (1997)	80.5①
Bleeder Valve (1998–99)	72①
Brake Hose Union Bolt	22
Caliper Carrier Mounting Bolts	65
Caliper Mounting Bolts	25

① — Inch lbs.

Saturn

NOTE: Prior To Performing Any Service Operations Listed In This Section, Consult The "Technical Service Bulletins " Section For Related Information.

INDEX

BRAKE SYSTEM BLEED

Refer to "Hydraulic Brake Systems" for manual and pressure bleeding procedures.

BRAKE PAD SERVICE

S-Series

FRONT

1. Raise and support vehicle.
2. Remove front wheel assemblies.
3. Remove caliper lockpin.
4. Pivot caliper upward around guide pin.
5. Remove brake pads.
6. Remove two pad clips from caliper support.
7. Reverse procedure to install.

REAR

1. Raise and support vehicle.
2. Remove wheel assemblies.
3. Remove caliper lockpin and guide pin.
4. Remove caliper from support and suspend with mechanics wire.
5. Remove brake pads from caliper support.
6. Remove two pad clips from caliper support.
7. Reverse procedure to install.

L-Series

FRONT

1. Raise and support vehicle.
2. Remove front wheel assemblies.
3. Pry off locking plate, then remove brake pressure hose from strut.
4. Remove pad retainer spring, then caliper-to-bracket guide pins and caliper assembly.
5. Remove inboard, then outboard brake pads from caliper assembly.
6. Reverse procedure to install.

REAR

1. Raise and support vehicle.
2. Remove rear wheel assemblies.
3. Drive out brake pad retaining pins from outside-to-inside, then remove pins, retaining spring and pads.
4. Reverse procedure to install.

CALIPER SERVICE

S-Series

FRONT

REPLACEMENT

1. Raise and support vehicle.
2. Remove wheel assemblies.
3. Disconnect caliper brake fluid lines and plug opening.
4. Remove caliper lockpin, guide pin and pin boots.
5. Remove caliper from caliper support, ensure not to damage pin boots.
6. Remove brake pads.
7. Remove two pad clips from caliper support.
8. Reverse procedure to install.

OVERHAUL

Disassemble

1. Inspect lockpin and guide pin boots for damage. replace as required.
2. Inspect piston boot and lockpin for damage, replace as required.

3. Using a small screwdriver, remove piston boot ring and boot.
4. Pad caliper interior with a suitable cushion, then apply non-lubricated compressed air to caliper inlet hole to remove piston.
5. Remove piston seal, then bleeder valve and cap.
6. Clean all parts in clean denatured alcohol, then dry with non-lubricated compressed air, then blow out all caliper body and bleeder valve passages.
7. Inspect piston for damage, replace as required.
8. Inspect caliper bore for damage, slight corrosion may be removed using suitable crocus cloth, if damage is excessive, replace caliper. **Do not hone caliper bore.**
9. Inspect seal groove for damage, replace as required.

Assemble

1. Install bleeder valve.
2. Lubricate piston seal using clean brake fluid, then install, ensure seal is not twisted.
3. Install lubricated piston boot to piston.
4. Install lubricated piston to body, push piston to bottom of bore.
5. Install boot ring, ensure piston boot outer edge is smoothly seated in counterbore, work boot ring into groove near open end of caliper bore. **Do not pinch piston ring between boot ring and body.**
6. Lift piston boot inner edge to release trapped air, then install caliper and bleed brake system.

REAR

REPLACEMENT

1. Raise and support vehicle.
2. Remove wheel assemblies.
3. Disconnect caliper brake fluid lines and plug opening.
4. Slip parking brake cable end from brake lever; then, using cable release tool No. SA9151BR, or equivalent, remove cable outer housing.
5. Remove caliper lockpin and guide pin.
6. Remove caliper from caliper support, ensure not to damage pin boots.
7. Remove lockpin and guide pins from caliper support.
8. Reverse procedure to install.

OVERHAUL

Disassemble

1. Inspect lockpin and guide pin boots for damage, replace as required.
2. Inspect piston boot and lockpin for damage, replace as required.
3. Using a small screwdriver, remove piston boot ring and boot.
4. Pad caliper interior with suitable cushion, then apply non-lubricated compressed air to caliper inlet hole to remove piston **Fig. 1.**
5. Remove piston seal, then bleeder valve and cap.
6. Clean all parts in clean denatured alcohol, then dry with non-lubricated compressed air, then blow out all caliper body and bleeder valve passages.
7. Inspect piston for damage, replace as required.
8. Inspect caliper bore for damage, slight corrosion may be removed using suitable crocus cloth, if damage is excessive, replace caliper. **Do not hone caliper bore.**
9. Inspect seal groove for damage, replace as required.

Assemble

1. Install bleeder valve and cap.
2. Lubricate piston seal using clean brake fluid, then install, ensure seal is not twisted.
3. Install lubricated piston boot to piston.
4. Install lubricated piston to body, push piston by hand, then install piston installation tool No. SA91110NE, or equivalent, to piston slots, rotate piston clockwise to install, **Fig. 2.**
5. Install boot ring, ensure piston boot outer edge is smoothly seated in counterbore, work boot ring into groove near open end of caliper bore. **Do not pinch piston ring between boot ring and body.**
6. Lift piston boot inner edge to release trapped air, then install caliper and bleed brake system.

L-Series

FRONT

REPLACEMENT

1. Raise and support vehicle, then remove wheel assemblies.
2. Remove brake hose from caliper and plug opening.
3. Remove brake pad retaining spring from caliper, then caliper-to-bracket guide pins.
4. Remove caliper from support bracket, then pads from caliper.
5. Reverse procedure to install.

OVERHAUL

Disassemble

1. Inspect guide pin sleeves and covers for damage, replace as required.
2. Inspect boot for deterioration, if damaged overhaul caliper.
3. Using a small screwdriver, remove piston boot ring and boot.
4. Pad caliper interior with a suitable cushion, then apply non-lubricated compressed air to caliper inlet hole to remove piston.
5. Remove piston seal, then bleeder valve and cap.
6. Clean all parts in clean denatured alcohol, then dry with non-lubricated compressed air, then blow out all caliper body and bleeder valve passages.
7. Inspect piston for damage, replace as required.
8. Inspect caliper bore for damage, noting the following:
   a. Slight corrosion may be removed using suitable crocus cloth.
   b. If damage is excessive, replace caliper.
   c. **Do not hone caliper bore.**
   d.
9. Inspect seal groove for damage, replace as required.

Assemble

1. Install bleeder valve.
2. Lubricate piston seal using clean brake fluid, then install. Ensure seal is not twisted.
3. Install lubricated piston boot to piston.
4. Install lubricated piston to body, push piston to bottom of bore.
5. Install boot ring, noting the following:
   a. Ensure piston boot outer edge is smoothly seated in counterbore.
   b. Work boot ring into groove near open end of caliper bore.
   c. **Do not pinch piston ring between boot ring and body.**
6. Lift piston boot inner edge to release trapped air, then install caliper and bleed brake system.

REAR

REPLACEMENT

1. Raise and support vehicle, then remove wheel assemblies.
2. Drive out brake pad retaining pins from outside-to-inside, then remove pins, retaining spring and pads.
3. Remove brake pipe from caliper and plug opening.
4. Remove caliper to rear axle control arm fasteners, then caliper assembly.
5. Reverse procedure to install.

OVERHAUL

Disassemble

The rear caliper has a dual piston design. The caliper must not be completely disassembled, only disassemble one piston at a time.

1. Carefully pry out piston boot clamp using a small screwdriver, then remove piston boot.
2. Pad caliper interior with suitable cushion, then apply non-lubricated compressed air to caliper inlet hole to remove piston.
3. Remove piston seal, then bleeder valve and cap.
4. Clean all parts in clean denatured alcohol, then dry with non-lubricated compressed air.
5. Blow out all caliper body and bleeder valve passages.
6. Inspect piston for damage, replace as required.
7. Inspect caliper bore for damage, noting the following:
   a. slight corrosion may be removed using suitable crocus cloth.
   b. If damage is excessive, replace caliper.
   c. **Do not hone caliper bore.**
8. Inspect seal groove for damage, replace as required.

Assemble

1. Install bleeder valve and cap.
2. Lubricate piston seal using clean brake fluid, then install. Ensure seal is not twisted.
3. Install lubricated piston boot to piston.

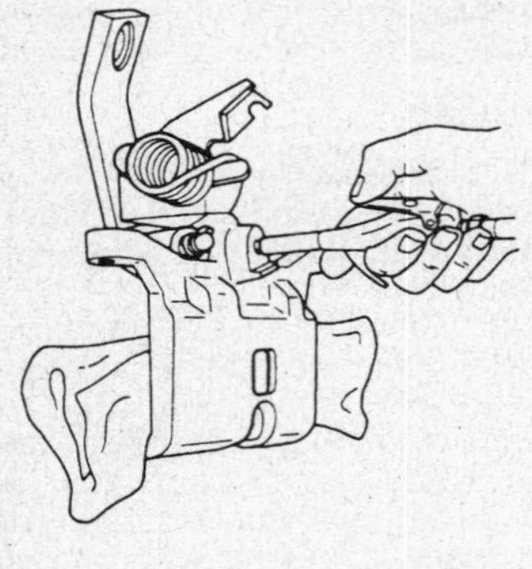

G34079100003000X

Fig. 1 Rear caliper piston removal

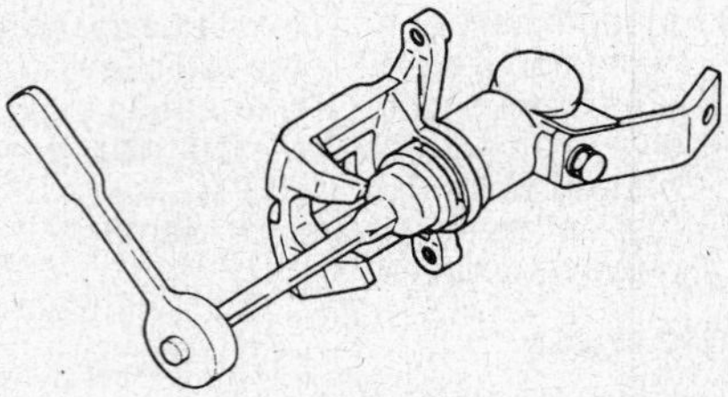

G34079100004000X

Fig. 2 Rear caliper piston installation. S-Series

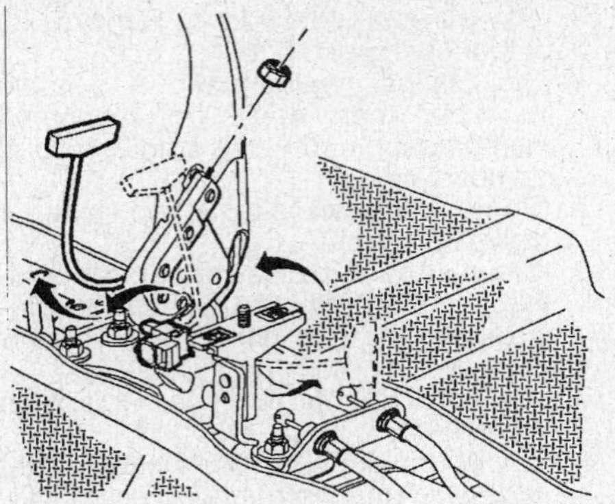

G34079800005000X

Fig. 3 Parking brake equalizer cable removal

4. Insert lubricated piston into body, then install caliper and bleed brake system.

ROTOR

REPLACE

S-SERIES

1. Raise and support vehicle.
2. Remove road wheel.
3. Remove caliper support to knuckle bolts, then and suspend caliper from strut spring with wire.
4. Remove rotor.
5. Reverse procedure to install. Tighten caliper bolts to specifications.

L-SERIES

1. Raise and support vehicle, then remove wheel assemblies.
2. Pry off locking plate, then remove brake pressure hose from strut.
3. Remove caliper bracket to steering knuckle bolts, then suspend caliper using wire.
4. Remove rotor retaining screw, then rotor.
5. Reverse procedure to install.

PARKING BRAKE SERVICE

PARKING BRAKE EQUALIZER CABLE, REPLACE

1. Remove center console as outlined in "Dash Panel Service" section.
2. Remove adjuster nut, then cables from equalizer assembly, **Fig. 3.**
3. Place parking brake lever to highest position.
4. Lift equalizer cable over parking brake indicator switch and swing forward. Pull cable down and out of parking brake lever.
5. Reverse procedure to install. Adjust parking brake cable.

PARKING BRAKE CABLE, REPLACE

S-SERIES

1. Remove center console as outlined in "Dash Panel Service" section.
2. Loosen adjuster nut.
3. Remove parking brake cables from equalizer, then from parking brake base.
4. Remove rear seat bottom cushion, then pull back carpet.
5. Raise and support vehicle.
6. Remove parking brake cable grommet from floor pan.
7. Remove parking brake cable attaching brackets and tie strap.
8. Disconnect cable end from caliper. Remove cable from bracket using parking brake release tool No. SA9151BR, or equivalent.
9. Remove cable from vehicle.
10. Reverse procedure to install. Adjust parking brake cable.

L-SERIES

1. Release parking brake.
2. Remove parking brake boot by squeezing boot in sides while pulling upwards.
3. Loosen parking brake adjuster nut to provide ample slack in brake cable.
4. Raise and support vehicle, then disconnect exhaust resonator from exhaust manifold pipe.
5. Remove exhaust pipe to body insulator, then lower exhaust resonator pipe and muffler assembly from vehicle.
6. Remove exhaust heat shield, then disengage parking brake cable from rear parking brake cable and discard clips.
7. Disengage front parking brake cable from equalizer.
8. Remove cable body attachment points.
9. Reverse procedure to install. Adjust parking brake cable as outlined under "Adjustments," in this section

PARKING BRAKE SHOES, REPLACE

1. Raise and support vehicle, then remove rear wheel assemblies.
2. Remove rear caliper to rear axle control arm bolts, then suspend caliper using wire.
3. Remove rotor retaining screw, then rotor.
4. Remove return springs from parking brake shoes, then brake shoe hold down retainers.
5. Remove parking brake shoes and adjuster.
6. Reverse procedure to install. Adjust parking brake as outlined under "Adjustments," in this section

ADJUSTMENTS

PARKING BRAKE

S-SERIES

1. Lift parking brake lever, then remove cover attaching screw and cover.
2. Raise and support vehicle.
3. Pull parking brake lever to first click.
4. Tighten adjuster nut until moderate drag is felt at both rear wheels when turned by hand.
5. Pull up on parking brake lever until twelfth or thirteenth click is heard. Repeat 3 to 4 times.
6. Ensure no drag exists when parking brake is in rest position.
7. Pull lever to first click and ensure moderate drag exists at both rear wheels. Repeat procedure until adjustment is correct.

L-SERIES

1. Remove parking brake boot by squeezing boot in sides while pulling upwards.
2. Raise and support vehicle, then remove rear wheel assemblies.
3. Access to parking brake adjuster is through a hole in front face of rotor.
4. Turn adjuster at rear rotor until brake disc locks. Turn back adjuster until brake disc just moves freely.
5. Pull parking brake lever to third click.
6. Tighten adjuster nut until heavy drag is felt at both rear wheels when turned by hand.
7. Apply and release parking brake several times. There should be no drag when parking brake lever is in rest position.
8. Pull lever to third click and ensure heavy drag exists at both rear wheels. Repeat procedure until adjustment is correct.

TECHNICAL SERVICE BULLETINS

REAR DISC BRAKE NOISE/ PULSATION

1997-98

On models equipped with rear disc brakes (JL9), built up to and including WZ223951, may exhibit disc brake grind/ growl, squeak/squeal noise and/or pulsation during slow braking.

Brake noise may be caused by vibration of brake components and/or contact between the disc brake pad and rotor during stopping. Some intermittent brake noises are normal. In high corrosion areas of the country, semi-metallic pads, interacting with the rear rotor, may contribute to the corrosion process leaving a rear disc brake pad shaped "footprint" on the rotor. This may cause rear disc brake pulsation. In addition, the pulsation may be caused by thickness variation worn into the rotor by the disc brake pads. The new disc brake pads, installed on 1998 vehicles built after WZ223951, cause less rotor thickness variation as a result of wear.

Replace rear disc brake pads with new non-asbestos organic rear disc brake pads part No. 21013126, or equivalent, according to procedures outlined in this section.

DISC BRAKE SPECIFICATIONS

New Thickness		Minimum Refinish Thickness①		Discard Thickness		Thickness Variation (Parallelism)	Lateral Runout (T.I.R.)
Front	Rear	Front	Rear	Front	Rear		
S-SERIES							
.71	.44	.633	.37	.625	.35	.0005	.0024
L-SERIES							
.98	.39	.900	.35	.870	.31	.0003	.0010

① — All brake rotors have a discard dimension cast into them. This is a wear dimension, not a refinish dimension. Any rotor that does not meet specifications should be discarded.

TIGHTENING SPECIFICATIONS

Component	Torque/Ft. Lbs.
S-SERIES	
Backing Plate To Knuckle②	63
Bleed Valve	96③
Brake Hose To Caliper	36
Brake Lever To Floor Nut	23
Brake Line To Brake Hose	18
Brake Line To Master Cylinder	24
Caliper Lock & Guide Pins	27
Caliper Mount Bracket①	81
Caliper To Caliper Support①	27
Caliper To Knuckle②	63
Wheel Lug Nuts	103
Wheel Speed Sensor To Knuckle	84③
L-SERIES	
Bleed Valve①	17③
Bleed Valve②	72③
Brake Hose To Brake Pipe	13
Brake Hose To Brake Caliper	30
Brake Pipe To Caliper	12
Brake Lever To Floor Nut	84③
Caliper to Bracket Guide Pins	22
Caliper To Steering Knuckle	70
Caliper To Rear Axle Control Arm	59
Exhaust Heat Shield	35③
Wheel Lug Nuts	92
Wheel Speed Sensor To Knuckle	72③

① — Front.
② — Rear.
③ — Inch lbs.

DRUM BRAKES

TABLE OF CONTENTS

Application Chart

Model	Application
BUICK	
Century	Type 5
LeSabre	Type 5
Skylark	Type 1
CHEVROLET/GEO	
Camaro	Type 2
Cavalier	Type 1
Lumina	Type 5
Malibu	Type 5
Metro	Type 4
Prizm	Type 3
OLDSMOBILE	
Achieva	Type 1
Alero	Type 5
Cutlass	Type 5
Eighty Eight	Type 5
LSS	Type 5
Regency	Type 5
PONTIAC	
Bonneville	Type 5
Firebird	Type 2
Grand Am (1997–98)	Type 1
Grand Am (1999-2000)	Type 5
Sunfire	Type 1
SATURN	
All	Type 6

Types 1 & 2

INDEX

PRECAUTIONS

When working on or around brake assemblies, care must be taken to prevent breathing asbestos dust, as many manufacturers incorporate asbestos fibers in the production of brake linings. During routine service operations the amount of asbestos dust from brake lining wear is at a low level due to a chemical breakdown during use, and a few precautions will minimize exposure.

1. Do not sand or grind brake linings unless suitable local exhaust ventilation equipment is used to prevent excessive asbestos exposure.
2. Wear a suitable respirator approved for asbestos dust use during all repair procedures.
3. When cleaning brake dust from brake components, use a vacuum cleaner with a highly efficient filter system. If a suitable vacuum cleaner is not available, use a water soaked rag. **Do not use compressed air or dry brush to clean brake components.**
4. Keep work area clean using same equipment as for cleaning brake components.
5. Properly dispose of rags and vacuum cleaner bags by placing them in plastic bags.
6. Do not smoke or eat while working on brake systems. **Never use gasoline, kerosene, alcohol, motor oil, transmission fluid, or any fluid containing mineral oil to clean brake system components. These fluids will damage the rubber caps and seals. If system contamination is suspected, inspect brake fluid in the reservoir for dirt, discoloration, or separation (breakdown) of the brake fluid into distinct layers. Drain and flush the hydraulic system with clean brake fluid if contamination is suspected.**

INSPECTION

1. Inspect components for damage or wear. Replace as required.
2. Inspect wheel cylinder boots for tears, cuts or heat damage. Replace as required.
3. **On type 1 brakes,** remove wheel cylinder links. If fluid spills from boot center hole, replace wheel cylinder.
4. **On type 2 brakes,** use a small screwdriver to pry center hole of boot away from piston. If fluid spills from center hole, replace wheel cylinder.
5. **On both types,** light fluid coatings on piston within cylinder is considered normal.
6. Inspect backing plate for evidence of axle seal leakage. If leakage exists, refer to individual car chapters for axle seal replacement procedures.
7. Inspect backing plate attaching bolts and ensure they are tight.
8. Using fine emery cloth or other suitable abrasive, clean rust and dirt from shoe contact surface on backing plate.

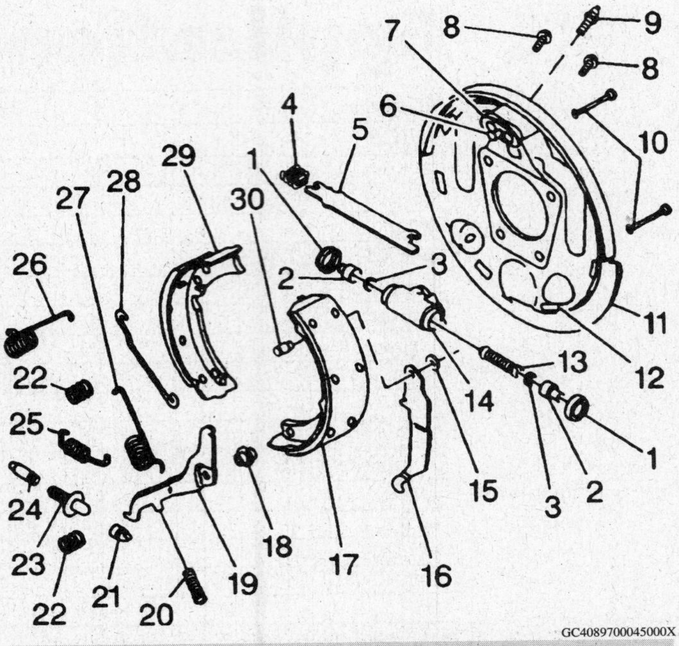

Fig. 1 Drum brake assembly (Type 1). 1-boot, 2-piston, 3-seal, 4-strut spring, 5-strut, 6-shoe retainer, 7-anchor pin, 8-bolt, 9-bleeder screw, 10-hold-down pins, 11-backing plate, 12-shoe contact points, 13-piston spring, 14-cylinder, 15-retainer ring, 16-parking brake lever, 17-secondary shoe, 18-sleeve, 19-actuator lever, 20-return spring, 21-socket, 22-hold-down spring, 23-star wheel, 24-pivot nut, 25-adjuster spring, 26-return spring

BRAKE DRUMS

Any time the brake drums are removed for brake service, the braking surface diameter should be inspected with a suitable brake drum micrometer at several points to determine if they are within the safe oversize limit stamped on the brake drum outer surface. If the braking surface diameter exceeds specifications, the drum must be replaced. If the braking surface diameter is within specifications, drums should be cleaned and inspected for cracks, scores, deep grooves, taper, out-of-round and heat spotting. If drums are cracked or heat spotted, they must be replaced. Minor scores should be removed with sandpaper. Grooves and large scores can only be removed by machining with special equipment, as long as the braking surface is within specifications stamped on brake drum outer surface. Any brake drum sufficiently out-of-round to cause vehicle vibration or noise while braking or showing taper should also be machined, removing only enough stock to true up the brake drum.

After a brake drum is machined, wipe the braking surface diameter with a denatured alcohol soaked cloth. If one brake drum is machined, the other should also be machined to the same diameter to maintain equal braking forces.

BRAKE LININGS & SPRINGS

Inspect brake linings for excessive wear, damage, oil, grease or brake fluid contamination. If any of the above conditions exists, brake linings should be replaced. Do not attempt to replace only one set of brake shoes; they should be replaced as an axle set only to maintain equal braking forces. Examine brake shoe webbing, hold-down and return springs for signs of overheating indicated by a slight blue color. If any component exhibits overheating signs, replace hold-down and return springs with new ones. Overheated springs lose their pull and could cause brake linings to wear out prematurely. Inspect all springs for sags, bends and external damage and replace as required.

Inspect hold-down retainers and pins for bends, rust and corrosion. If any of the above is found, replace as required.

BACKING PLATE

Inspect backing plate shoe contact surface for grooves that may restrict shoe movement and cannot be removed by lightly sanding with emery cloth or other suitable abrasive. If backing plate exhibits above condition, it should be replaced. Also inspect for signs of cracks, warpage and excessive rust, indicating need for replacement.

ADJUSTER MECHANISM

Inspect all components for rust, corrosion, bends and fatigue. Replace as required. **On adjuster mechanism equipped with adjuster cable,** inspect cable for kinks, fraying or elongation of eyelet and replace as required.

PARKING BRAKE CABLE

Inspect parking brake cable end for kinks, fraying and elongation and replace as required. Use a small hose clamp to compress clamp where it enters backing plate to remove it.

BRAKE SERVICE

REMOVAL

1. Raise and support rear of vehicle, then remove tire and wheel assembly.

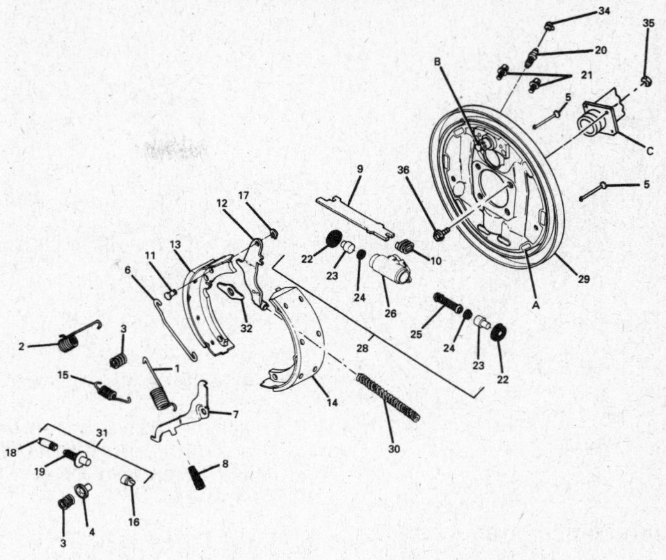

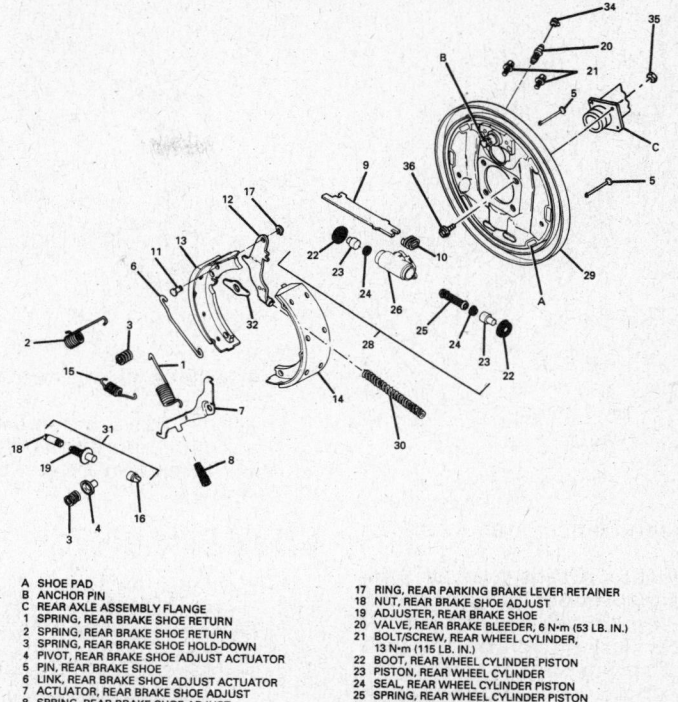

A SHOE PAD
B ANCHOR PIN
C REAR AXLE ASSEMBLY FLANGE
1 SPRING, REAR BRAKE SHOE RETURN
2 SPRING, REAR BRAKE SHOE RETURN
3 SPRING, REAR BRAKE SHOE HOLD-DOWN
4 PIVOT, REAR BRAKE SHOE ADJUST ACTUATOR
5 PIN, REAR BRAKE SHOE
6 LINK, REAR BRAKE SHOE ADJUST ACTUATOR
7 ACTUATOR, REAR BRAKE SHOE ADJUST
8 SPRING, REAR BRAKE SHOE ADJUST ACTUATOR RETURN
9 STRUT, REAR PARKING BRAKE LEVER
10 SPRING, REAR PARKING BRAKE LEVER STRUT
11 PIN, REAR PARKING BRAKE LEVER PIVOT
12 LEVER ASSEMBLY, REAR PARKING BRAKE
13 SHOE, REAR BRAKE PRIMARY
14 SHOE, REAR BRAKE SECONDARY
15 SPRING, REAR BRAKE SHOE ADJUST
16 SOCKET, REAR BRAKE SHOE ADJUST
17 RING, REAR PARKING BRAKE LEVER RETAINER
18 NUT, REAR BRAKE SHOE ADJUST
19 ADJUSTER, REAR BRAKE SHOE
20 VALVE, REAR BRAKE BLEEDER, 6 N•m (53 LB. IN.)
21 BOLT/SCREW, REAR WHEEL CYLINDER, 13 N•m (115 LB. IN.)
22 BOOT, REAR WHEEL CYLINDER PISTON
23 PISTON, REAR WHEEL CYLINDER
24 SEAL, REAR WHEEL CYLINDER PISTON
25 SPRING, REAR WHEEL CYLINDER PISTON
26 BODY, REAR WHEEL CYLINDER
28 CYLINDER, REAR WHEEL
29 PLATE, REAR BRAKE BACKING
30 SPRING, PARKING BRAKE CABLE RETURN
31 ADJUSTER ASSEMBLY, REAR BRAKE SHOE
32 GUIDE, REAR BRAKE SHOE
34 CAP, BLEEDER VALVE
35 NUT, REAR BRAKE BACKING PLATE, 58 N•m (43 LB. FT.)
36 BOLT/SCREW, REAR BRAKE BACKING PLATE

GC4089300042000B

Fig. 2 Drum brake assembly. Type 2

2. Mark drum and axle hub, then remove brake drum. If brake lining is dragging on brake drum, back off brake adjustment by rotating adjustment screw. Refer to individual car chapter for procedure. **If brake drum is rusted or corroded to axle flange and cannot be removed, lightly tap axle flange to drum mounting surface with a suitable hammer.**
3. Using brake spring removal and installation tool Nos. J-8049 or J-29840, or their equivalents, unhook primary and secondary return springs, **Figs. 1 and 2. Observe location of brake components being removed to aid during installation.**
4. Remove brake hold-down springs with suitable tool.
5. Lift actuating lever, then unhook and remove actuating link from anchor pin.
6. Remove actuating lever(s) and return spring.
7. Spread shoes apart and remove parking brake strut and spring.
8. Disconnect parking brake cable from lever, then remove brake shoes from backing plate.
9. Separate brake shoes by removing adjusting screw and spring, then unhook parking brake lever from shoe assembly.
10. Clean dirt from brake drum, backing plate and all other components. **Do not use compressed air or dry brush to clean brake components. Many brake components contain asbestos fibers which, if inhaled, can cause serious injury. Clean brake components with a water soaked rag or a suitable vacuum cleaner to minimize airborne dust.**

INSTALLATION

1. Lubricate parking brake lever fulcrum with suitable brake lubricant, then attach lever to brake shoe. Ensure lever operates smoothly.
2. Connect brake shoes with adjusting screw spring, then position adjusting screw. **Ensure adjusting screw star wheel does not contact adjusting screw spring after installation and also ensure righthand thread adjusting screw is installed on lefthand side of vehicle and lefthand thread adjusting screw is installed on righthand side of vehicle. When brake shoe installation is completed, ensure star wheel lines up with adjusting hole in backing plate.**
3. Lubricate backing plate shoe contact surfaces with suitable brake lubricant, then the area where parking brake cable contacts backing plate.
4. Install brake shoes on backing plate while engaging wheel cylinder links (if equipped) with shoe webbing. Connect parking brake cable to parking brake lever. **The primary shoe (short**

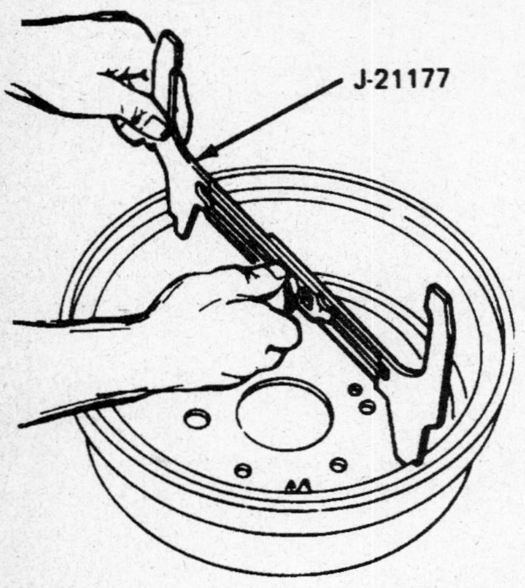
J-21177
GC4089100019000X

Fig. 3 Brake drum measurement

lining) faces towards front of vehicle. The end without the strut spring should engage parking brake lever and secondary shoe. The end with the strut spring should engage the primary shoe.**

5. Install actuating levers, actuating link and return spring, **Figs. 1 and 2.**
6. Install hold-down springs with suitable tool.
7. Install primary and secondary shoe return springs using brake spring pliers or equivalent.
8. Using suitable brake drum to shoe gauge, measure brake drum inside diameter. Adjust brake shoes to dimension obtained on outside portion of gauge.
9. Install brake drum, wheel and tire assembly.
10. If any hydraulic connections have been opened, bleed brake system.
11. Adjust parking brake. Refer to individual car chapters for procedures.
12. Inspect all hydraulic lines and connections for leakage and repair as required.
13. Inspect master cylinder fluid level and replenish as required.
14. Inspect brake pedal for proper feel and return.
15. Lower vehicle and road test. **Do not severely apply brakes immediately after installation of new brake linings or permanent damage may occur to linings, and/or brake drums may become scored. Brakes must be used moderately during first several hundred miles of operation to ensure proper burnishing of linings.**

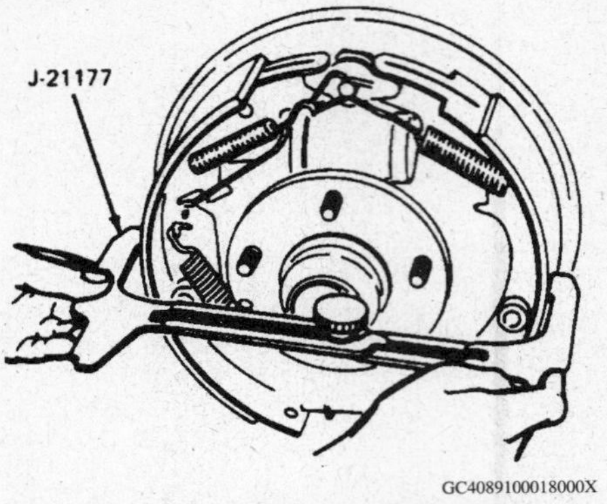
J-21177
GC4089100018000X

Fig. 4 Brake shoe measurement

ADJUSTMENTS

These brakes have self-adjusting shoe mechanisms that ensure proper lining-to-drum clearances at all times. The automatic adjusters operate only when the brakes are applied as the vehicle is moving rearward.

An initial adjustment is required after the brake shoes have been relined or replaced, or when the length of the adjusting screw has been changed during service operations.

Frequent usage of an automatic transmission forward range to halt reverse vehicle motion may prevent the automatic adjusters from functioning, thereby inducing low pedal heights. Should low pedal heights be encountered, it is recommended that numerous forward and reverse stops be made until satisfactory pedal height is obtained. **If a low pedal condition cannot be corrected by making numerous reverse stops (provided the hydraulic system is free of air) it indicates that the self-adjusting mechanism is not functioning. Therefore, it will be necessary to remove the brake drum, clean, free up and lubricate the adjusting mechanism. Then adjust the brakes as follows, ensuring the parking brake is fully released.**

SERVICE BRAKE

Brake adjustment cannot be performed with the drums installed. The following procedure is mandatory after new linings are installed, or when the length of the brake shoe adjusting screw has been changed.

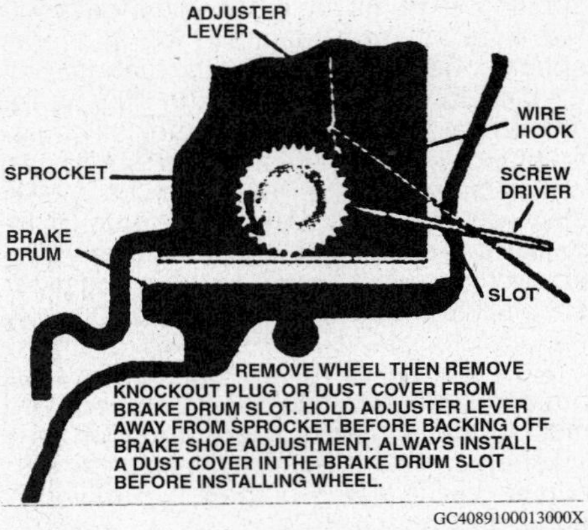
ADJUSTER LEVER
WIRE HOOK
SPROCKET
SCREW DRIVER
BRAKE DRUM
SLOT
REMOVE WHEEL THEN REMOVE KNOCKOUT PLUG OR DUST COVER FROM BRAKE DRUM SLOT. HOLD ADJUSTER LEVER AWAY FROM SPROCKET BEFORE BACKING OFF BRAKE SHOE ADJUSTMENT. ALWAYS INSTALL A DUST COVER IN THE BRAKE DRUM SLOT BEFORE INSTALLING WHEEL.
GC4089100013000X

Fig. 5 Brake shoe adjustment

1. With brake drums removed, position the caliper as shown in **Fig. 3** to the inside diameter of the drum, then tighten the clamp screw.
2. Position brake shoe end of the caliper tool over the brake shoes as shown in **Fig. 4.**
3. Rotate gauge slightly around shoes to ensure gauge contacts linings at largest diameter.
4. **On Type 1 brakes,** adjust brake shoes until their outside diameter is .030 inch less than that of drum's inside diameter. **If it is necessary to back off the brake shoe adjustment, it will be necessary to hold the adjuster lever away from the adjuster screw, Fig. 5.**
5. **On Type 2 brakes,** adjust brake shoes until their outside diameter is .050 inch less than that of drum's inside diameter. **If it is necessary to back off the brake shoe adjustment, it will be necessary to hold the adjuster lever away from the adjuster screw, Fig. 5.**

PARKING BRAKE

On these brake systems, no adjustment is necessary. These models have a self-adjusting parking brake system and it should not be adjusted or modified in any way.

On Type 1 brakes, fully applying and releasing the parking brake 4–6 times the system will perform its self-adjustment procedure.

On Type 2 brakes, the parking brake adjusts automatically by pulling on the parking brake lever.

DRUM BRAKE SPECIFICATIONS

Model	Brake Drum Inside Dia. Inch	
	Nominal	Maximum
BUICK		
Skylark	7.877	7.899
CHEVROLET		
Camaro	9.500	9.590

Continued

DRUM BRAKE SPECIFICATIONS—Continued

Model	Brake Drum Inside Dia. Inch	
	Nominal	Maximum
CHEVROLET		
Cavalier	7.877	7.899
OLDSMOBILE		
Achieva	7.877	7.899
PONTIAC		
Firebird	9.500	9.590
Grand Am	7.877	7.899
Sunfire	7.877	7.899

TIGHTENING SPECIFICATIONS

Component	Torque/Ft. Lbs.
ACHIEVA, CAVALIER, CENTURY GRAND AM, SKYLARK & SUNFIRE	
Wheel Cylinder Bleeder Screw	60①
Wheel Cylinder Line Fitting	18
Wheel Cylinder To Backing Plate	15
Wheel Lug Nuts	100
CAMARO & FIREBIRD	
Backing Plate To Axle Housing Nut	43
Pivot Pin Nut	16
Wheel Cylinder Bleeder Screw	53①
Wheel Cylinder Line Fitting	13
Wheel Lug Nuts	81

① — Inch lbs.

Type 3

INDEX

PRECAUTIONS

When working on or around brake assemblies, care must be taken to prevent breathing asbestos dust, as many manufacturers incorporate asbestos fibers in the production of brake linings. During routine service operations the amount of asbestos dust from brake lining wear is at a low level due to a chemical breakdown during use, and a few precautions will minimize exposure.

1. Do not sand or grind brake linings unless suitable local exhaust ventilation equipment is used to prevent excessive asbestos exposure.
2. Wear a suitable respirator approved for asbestos dust use during all repair procedures.
3. When cleaning brake dust from brake components, use a vacuum cleaner with a highly efficient filter system. If a suitable vacuum cleaner is not available, use a water soaked rag. **Do not use compressed air or dry brush to clean brake components.**
4. Keep work area clean using same equipment as for cleaning brake components.
5. Properly dispose of rags and vacuum cleaner bags by placing them in plastic bags.
6. Do not smoke or eat while working on brake systems. **Never use gasoline, kerosene, alcohol, motor oil, transmission fluid, or any fluid containing mineral oil to clean brake system components. These fluids will damage the rubber caps and seals. If system contamination is suspected, inspect brake fluid in the reservoir for dirt, discoloration, or separation (breakdown) of the brake fluid into distinct layers. Drain and flush the hydraulic system with clean brake fluid if contamination is suspected.**

INSPECTION

1. Inspect brake drum, shoes, strut, auto adjuster lever, springs and backing plate for wear, distortion, cracks or other abnormal conditions.
2. If any components are of doubtful strength or quality due to damage, heat discoloration, stress or wear, replace them.
3. Measure brake drum inside diameter and the brake shoe lining thickness.
4. Inspect lining and drum for proper contact.

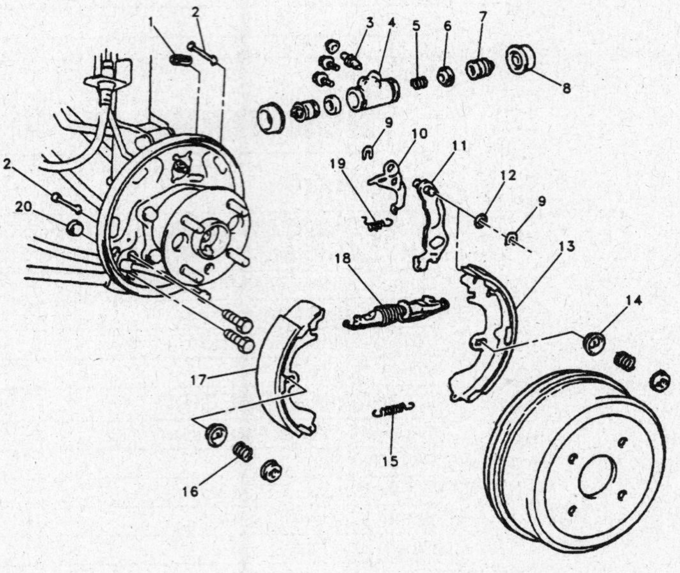

Fig. 1 Drum brake assembly

BRAKE DRUMS

Any time the brake drums are removed for brake service, the braking surface diameter should be inspected with a suitable brake drum micrometer at several points to determine if they are within the safe oversize limit stamped on the brake drum outer surface. If the braking surface diameter exceeds specifications, the drum must be replaced. If the braking surface diameter is within specifications, drums should be cleaned and inspected for cracks, scores, deep grooves, taper, out-of-round and heat spotting. If drums are cracked or heat spotted, they must be replaced. Minor scores should be removed with sandpaper. Grooves and large scores can only be removed by machining with special equipment, as long as the braking surface is within specifications stamped on brake drum outer surface. Any brake drum sufficiently out-of-round to cause vehicle vibration or noise while braking or showing taper should also be machined, removing only enough stock to true up the brake drum.

After a brake drum is machined, wipe the braking surface diameter with a denatured alcohol soaked cloth. If one brake drum is machined, the other should also be machined to the same diameter to maintain equal braking forces.

BRAKE LININGS & SPRINGS

Inspect brake linings for excessive wear, damage, oil, grease or brake fluid contamination. If any of the above conditions exists, brake linings should be replaced. Do not attempt to replace only one set of brake shoes; they should be replaced as an axle set only to maintain equal braking forces.

Examine brake shoe webbing, hold-down and return springs for signs of overheating indicated by a slight blue color. If any component exhibits overheating signs, replace hold-down and return springs with new ones. Overheated springs lose their pull and could cause brake linings to wear out prematurely. Inspect all springs for sags, bends and external damage and replace as required.

Inspect hold-down retainers and pins for bends, rust and corrosion. If any of the above is found, replace as required.

BACKING PLATE

Inspect backing plate shoe contact surface for grooves that may restrict shoe movement and cannot be removed by lightly sanding with emery cloth or other suitable abrasive. If backing plate exhibits above condition, it should be replaced. Also inspect for signs of cracks, warpage and excessive rust, indicating need for replacement.

ADJUSTER MECHANISM

Inspect all components for rust, corrosion, bends and fatigue. Replace as required. On adjuster mechanism equipped with adjuster cable, inspect cable for kinks, fraying or elongation of eyelet and replace as required.

PARKING BRAKE CABLE

Inspect parking brake cable end for kinks, fraying and elongation and replace as required. Use a small hose clamp to compress clamp where it enters backing plate to remove.

BRAKE SERVICE

REMOVAL

1. Raise and support vehicle.
2. Mark relationship of wheel to axle, then remove wheel and tire assembly.
3. Remove brake drum. If drum is difficult to remove, insert screwdriver through hole in backing plate and hold automatic adjusting lever away from adjusting bolt, then, using a second screwdriver, reduce brake shoe adjustment.
4. Remove return spring, **Fig. 1.**
5. Remove hold-down spring, retainers and pin retaining front shoe.
6. Disconnect anchor spring from front shoe, then remove front shoe.
7. Remove anchor spring.
8. Remove hold-down spring, retainers and pin retaining rear shoe.

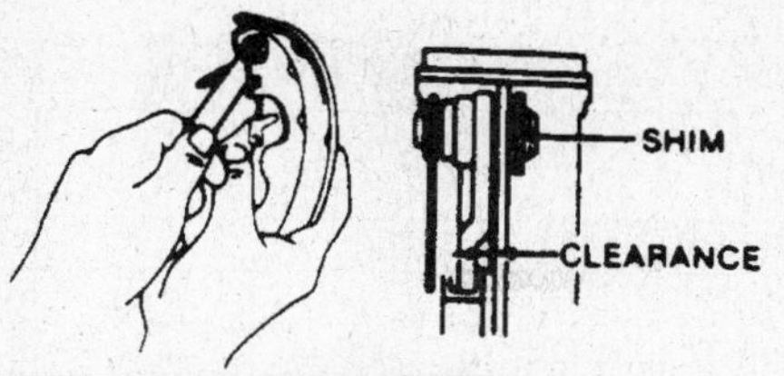

SHIM THICKNESS	
THICKNESS	THICKNESS
0.2 MM (0.008 IN.)	0.5 MM (0.020 IN.)
0.3 MM (0.012 IN.)	0.6 MM (0.024 IN.)
0.4 MM (0.016 IN.)	0.9 MM (0.035 IN.)

GC4089100025000X

Fig. 2 Lever to shoe clearance inspection

9. Using screwdriver, disconnect parking brake cable from anchor plate.
10. Using pliers, disconnect parking brake cable from lever and remove rear shoe together with strut.
11. Remove adjusting lever spring, then the strut together with return spring.
12. Remove parking brake lever and automatic adjusting lever from rear shoe by prying out "C" washer and removing shims and levers.
13. Clean dirt from brake drum, backing plate and all other components. **Do not use compressed air or dry brush to clean brake components. Many brake components contain asbestos fibers which, if inhaled, can cause serious injury. Clean brake components with a water soaked rag or a suitable vacuum cleaner to minimize airborne dust.**

INSTALLATION

1. Apply white lithium grease part No. 1050109, or a suitable equivalent to backing plate brake shoe contact points, anchor plate brake shoe contact points, strut and adjusting bolt contact points and the strut and brake shoe contact points.
2. Install parking brake lever and automatic adjusting lever to rear shoe as follows:
   a. Temporarily install levers and shim with a new " C" washer.
   b. Using feeler gauge, measure clearance between shoe and lever, **Fig. 2.**
   c. If clearance is not 0–.0138 inch, adjust by installing replacement shim.
   d. Using pliers, stake "C" washer.
3. Set strut and return spring in place on rear shoe and install adjusting lever spring.
4. Install rear shoe as follows:
   a. Using pliers, connect parking brake cable to lever.
   b. Pass parking brake cable through notch in anchor plate.
   c. Set rear shoe in place with end of shoe inserted in wheel cylinder and other end in anchor plate.
   d. Install hold-down spring, retainers and pin.
5. Install front shoe as follows:
   a. Install anchor spring between front and rear shoes.
   b. Set front shoe in place with end of shoe inserted in wheel cylinder and the strut in place.
   c. Install hold-down spring, retainers and pin.
   d. Connect return spring.
6. Inspect operation of automatic adjuster mechanism as follows:
   a. Move parking brake lever of rear shoe back and forth and ensure adjusting bolt turns. If bolt does not turn, inspect brakes for improper installation.
   b. Adjust strut length to shortest possible distance.
   c. Install brake drum.
   d. Pull parking brake lever all the way up until a clicking sound can no longer be heard.
7. Inspect clearance between brake shoes and drum. Remove drum and measure brake drum inside diameter and diameter of brake shoes.
8. If clearance is not .024 inch, inspect parking brake system.
9. Install brake drum and the wheel and tire assembly.
10. Fill master cylinder as required and bleed brake system.
11. Inspect for fluid leakage.

ADJUSTMENTS

SERVICE BRAKE

Adjustment is accomplished automatically by pulling the parking brake lever all the way up until a clicking sound can no longer be heard.

PARKING BRAKE

1. Ensure parking brake lever travel is proper by pulling parking brake lever all the way up and counting the number of clicks.
2. Parking brake lever travel should be 4–7 clicks. If not, remove console, loosen locknut and turn adjusting nut until proper travel is achieved.

DRUM BRAKE SPECIFICATIONS

Model	Brake Drum Inside Dia. Inch	
	Nominal	Maximum
Prizm	7.874	7.913

TIGHTENING SPECIFICATIONS

Component	Torque/Ft. Lbs.
Brake Line To Wheel Cylinder Fitting	11
Hub Retaining Bolts	59
Wheel Cylinder Bleeder Screw	72①
Wheel Cylinder Retaining Bolts (1997)	96①
Wheel Cylinder Retaining Bolts (1998–2000)	89①
Wheel Lug Nuts	76

① — Inch lbs.

Type 4

INDEX

PRECAUTIONS

When working on or around brake assemblies, care must be taken to prevent breathing asbestos dust, as many manufacturers incorporate asbestos fibers in the production of brake linings. During routine service operations the amount of asbestos dust from brake lining wear is at a low level due to a chemical breakdown during use, and a few precautions will minimize exposure.

1. Do not sand or grind brake linings unless suitable local exhaust ventilation equipment is used to prevent excessive asbestos exposure.
2. Wear a suitable respirator approved for asbestos dust use during all repair procedures.
3. When cleaning brake dust from brake components, use a vacuum cleaner with a highly efficient filter system. If a suitable vacuum cleaner is not available, use a water soaked rag. **Do not use compressed air or dry brush to clean brake components.**
4. Keep work area clean using same equipment as for cleaning brake components.
5. Properly dispose of rags and vacuum cleaner bags by placing them in plastic bags.
6. Do not smoke or eat while working on brake systems. **Never use gasoline, kerosene, alcohol, motor oil, transmission fluid, or any fluid containing mineral oil to clean brake system components. These fluids will damage the rubber caps and seals. If system contamination is suspected, inspect brake fluid in the reservoir for dirt, discoloration, or separation (breakdown) of the brake fluid into distinct layers. Drain and flush the hydraulic system with clean brake fluid if contamination is suspected.**

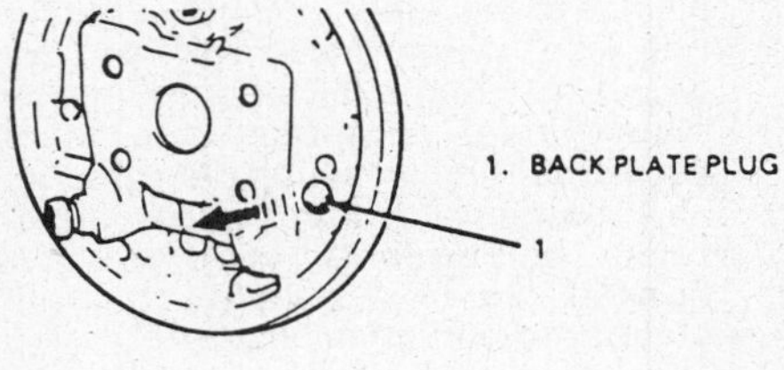

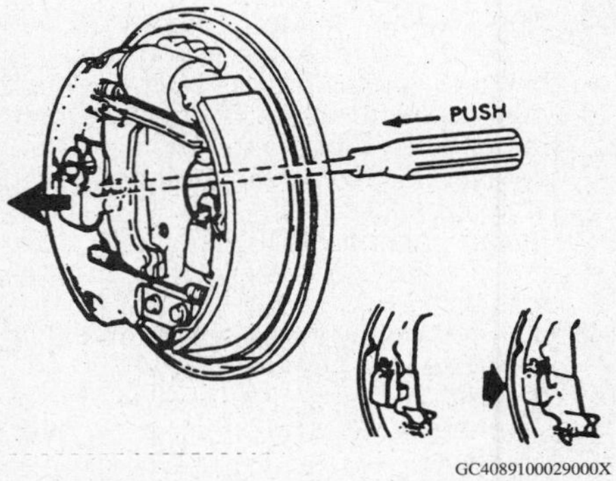

Fig. 1 Backing plate plug removal

INSPECTION

1. If any components are of doubtful strength or quality due to heat discoloration, or are worn, replace them.
2. Inspect wheel cylinder dust boots for signs of excessive wear or damage. If any leakage is apparent replace or rebuild wheel cylinder.
3. Clean dirt and/or rust from brake drum, backing plate and all other components. **Do not use compressed air or dry brush to clean brake components. Many brake components contain asbestos fibers which, if inhaled, can cause serious injury. Clean brake components with a water soaked rag or a suitable vacuum cleaner to minimize airborne dust.**

BRAKE DRUMS

Any time the brake drums are removed for brake service, the braking surface diameter should be inspected with a suitable brake drum micrometer at several points to determine if they are within the safe oversize limit stamped on the brake drum outer surface. If the braking surface diameter exceeds specifications, the drum must be replaced. If the braking surface diameter is within specifications, drums should be cleaned and inspected for cracks, scores, deep grooves, taper, out-of-round and heat spotting. If drums are cracked or heat spotted, they must be replaced. Minor scores should be removed with sandpaper. Grooves and large scores can only be removed by machining with special equipment, as long as the braking surface is within specifications stamped on brake drum outer surface. Any brake drum sufficiently out-of-round to cause vehicle vibration or noise while braking or showing taper should also be machined, removing only enough stock to true up the brake drum.

After a brake drum is machined, wipe the braking surface diameter with a denatured alcohol soaked cloth. If one brake drum is machined, the other should also be machined to the same diameter to maintain equal braking forces.

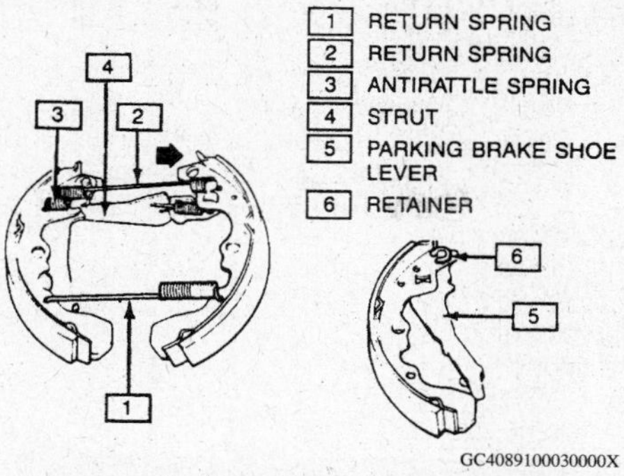

Fig. 2 Brake shoe return spring identification

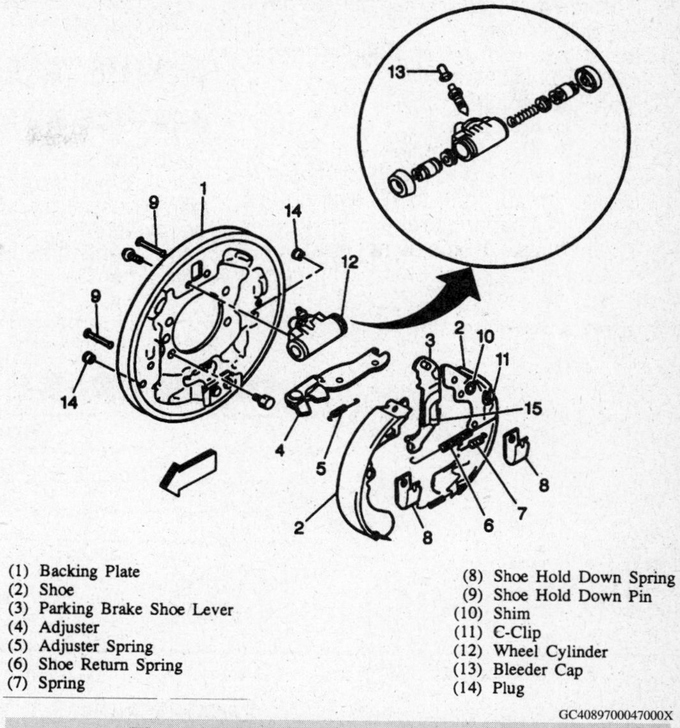

Fig. 3 Rear brake unit assembly

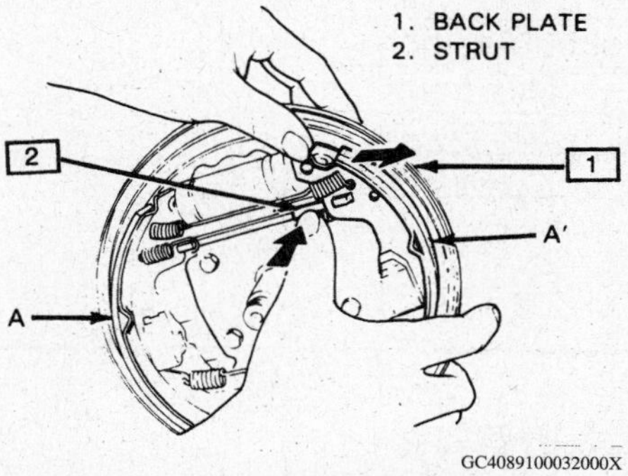

Fig. 4 Brake lining installation

BRAKE LININGS & SPRINGS

Inspect brake linings for excessive wear, damage, oil, grease or brake fluid contamination. If any of the above conditions exists, brake linings should be replaced. Do not attempt to replace only one set of brake shoes. They should be replaced as an axle set only to maintain equal braking forces. Examine brake shoe webbing, hold-down and return springs for signs of overheating indicated by a slight blue color. If any component exhibits overheating signs, replace hold-down and return springs with new ones. Overheated springs lose their pull and could cause brake linings to wear out prematurely. Inspect all springs for sags, bends and external damage and replace as required.

Inspect hold-down retainers and pins for bends, rust and corrosion. If any of the above is found, replace as required.

BACKING PLATE

Inspect backing plate shoe contact surface for grooves that may restrict shoe movement and cannot be removed by lightly sanding with emery cloth or other suitable abrasive. If backing plate exhibits above condition, it should be replaced. Also inspect for signs of cracks, warpage and excessive rust, indicating need for replacement.

ADJUSTER MECHANISM

Inspect all components for rust, corrosion, bends and fatigue. Replace as required. **On adjuster mechanism equipped with adjuster cable,** inspect cable for kinks, fraying or elongation of eyelet and replace as required.

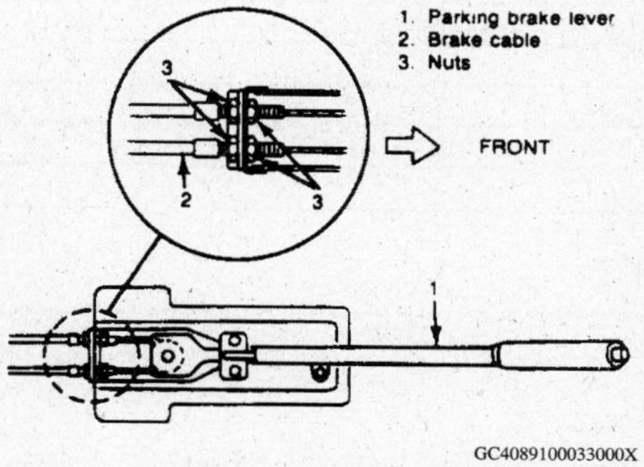

Fig. 5 Parking brake adjustment

PARKING BRAKE CABLE

Inspect parking brake cable end for kinks, fraying and elongation and replace as required. Use a small hose clamp to compress clamp where it enters backing plate to remove.

BRAKE SERVICE

REMOVAL

1. Raise and support vehicle.
2. Remove spindle cap by hammering lightly at three points around cap.
3. Remove cotter pin or unfasten staked portion of nut, then remove castle nut and washer.
4. Loosen parking brake cable adjusting nuts.
5. Remove backing plate plug, **Fig. 1.**
6. Insert screwdriver into plug hole until it contacts shoe hold-down spring, then push in direction shown, **Fig. 1.** This pushes hold-down spring up and releases parking brake shoe lever from hold-down spring, resulting in added clearance between shoe and drum.
7. **On models equipped with ABS,** install two 8 mm bolts into drum, then tighten them to remove drum from hub.
8. **On models less ABS,** using slide hammer tool No. J-2619-01 and brake drum remover tool No. J-34866, or their equivalents, pull off brake drum.
9. **On all models,** remove brake shoe hold-down springs by turning hold-down pins.
10. Disconnect parking brake cable from parking brake shoe lever and remove brake shoes.
11. Remove spring (1) in **Fig. 2,** pull primary shoe in direction of arrow and disengage strut (4) and return spring (2).
12. Disconnect return spring (3) from shoe.
13. Disconnect parking brake shoe lever from shoe.

INSTALLATION

1. Apply white lithium grease part No. 1050109, or a suitable equivalent to backing plate brake shoe contact points and to anchor plate brake shoe contact points.
2. Assemble brake shoes, levers and springs as shown in **Fig. 3.**
3. Push shoe hold-down springs down into place. Turn hold-down pins to engage springs.
4. To minimize dimension "A-A," **Fig. 4,** push strut towards backplate while pushing out on shoe as shown.

5. Position tab of spring clip behind parking brake lever.
6. Install brake drum and tighten castle nut to specifications.
7. Install cotter pin.
8. Install spindle cap.
9. Install wheel.
10. Depress brake pedal several times to obtain proper drum to shoe clearance and adjust parking brake.
11. Ensure brake drums do not drag.
12. Lower the vehicle and test brake operation.

ADJUSTMENTS

SERVICE BRAKE

Adjustment is accomplished automatically by applying brake pedal 3–5 times with 66 lbs. of pressure. Brake pedal should be cycled 3–5 times when replacement components are installed to ensure proper adjustment.

PARKING BRAKE

The parking brake lever should be adjusted so lever comes up 3–6 notches with 44 lbs. of pull applied.

Adjust travel by loosening adjustment nuts, **Fig. 5.**

DRUM BRAKE SPECIFICATIONS

Model	Brake Drum Inside Dia. Inch	
	Nominal	Maximum
Metro①	7.09	7.16
Metro②	7.87	7.95

① — 2–Door.

② — 4–Door.

TIGHTENING SPECIFICATIONS

Component	Torque/Ft. Lbs.
Backing Plate Mounting Bolts	17
Bleeder Valve	89①
Brake Fluid Pipe Nut	12
Hub Assembly Spindle Nut	58–87
Wheel Lug Nuts	44

① — Inch lbs.

Type 5

INDEX

DESCRIPTION

This brake assembly operates with fewer components, but is equal to other drum brake systems in performance. In this assembly, a single spring holds both shoe and lining to the backing plate and acts as a retractor spring for the shoe and lining assemblies, **Fig. 1**.

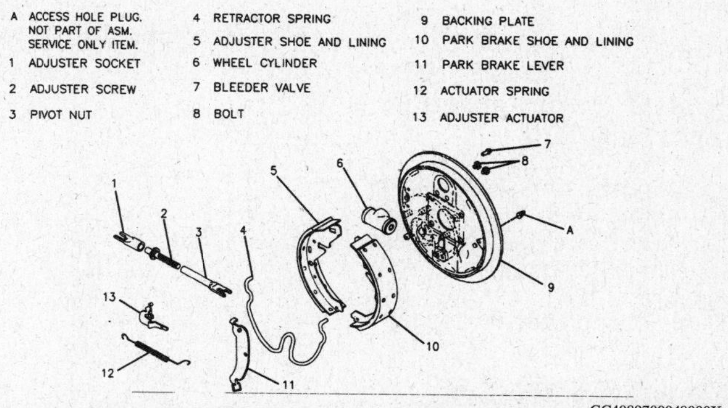

Fig. 1 Brake drum assembly

PRECAUTIONS

When working on or around brake assemblies, care must be taken to prevent breathing asbestos dust, as many manufacturers incorporate asbestos fibers in the production of brake linings. During routine service operations the amount of asbestos dust from brake lining wear is at a low level due to a chemical breakdown during use, and a few precautions will minimize exposure.

1. Do not sand or grind brake linings unless suitable local exhaust ventilation equipment is used to prevent excessive asbestos exposure.
2. Wear a suitable respirator approved for asbestos dust use during all repair procedures.
3. When cleaning brake dust from brake components, use a vacuum cleaner with a highly efficient filter system. If a suitable vacuum cleaner is not available, use a water soaked rag. **Do not use compressed air or dry brush to clean brake components.**
4. Keep work area clean using same equipment as for cleaning brake components.
5. Properly dispose of rags and vacuum cleaner bags by placing them in plastic bags.
6. Do not smoke or eat while working on brake systems. **Never use gasoline, kerosene, alcohol, motor oil, transmission fluid, or any fluid containing mineral oil to clean brake system components. These fluids will damage the rubber caps and seals. If system contamination is suspected, inspect brake fluid in the reservoir for dirt, discoloration, or separation (breakdown) of the brake fluid into distinct layers. Drain and flush the hydraulic system with clean brake fluid if contamination is suspected.**

INSPECTION

1. If any components are of doubtful strength or quality due to heat discoloration, or are worn, replace them.
2. Inspect wheel cylinder dust boots for signs of excessive wear or damage. If any leakage is apparent replace wheel cylinder.
3. Clean dirt and/or rust from brake drum, backing plate and all other components. **Do not use compressed air or dry brush to clean brake components. Many brake components contain asbestos fibers which, if inhaled, can cause serious injury. Clean brake components with a water soaked rag or a suitable vacuum cleaner to minimize airborne dust.**

BRAKE DRUMS

Any time the brake drums are removed for brake service, the braking surface diameter should be inspected with a suitable brake drum micrometer at several points to determine if they are within the safe oversize limit stamped on the brake drum outer surface. If the braking surface diameter exceeds specifications, the drum must be replaced. If the braking surface diameter is within specifications, drums should be cleaned and inspected for cracks, scores, deep grooves, taper, out-of-round and heat spotting. If drums are cracked or heat spotted, they must be replaced. Minor scores should be removed with sandpaper. Grooves and large scores can only be removed by machining with special equipment, as long as the braking surface is within specifications stamped on brake drum outer surface. Any brake drum sufficiently out-of-round to cause vehicle vibration or noise while braking or showing taper should also be machined, removing only enough stock to true up the brake drum.

After a brake drum is machined, wipe the braking surface diameter with a denatured alcohol soaked cloth. If one brake drum is machined, the other should also be machined to the same diameter to maintain equal braking forces.

BRAKE LININGS & SPRINGS

Inspect brake linings for excessive wear, damage, oil, grease or brake fluid contamination. If any of the above conditions exists, brake linings should be replaced. Do not attempt to replace only one set of brake shoes. they should be replaced as an axle set only to maintain equal braking forces. Examine brake shoe webbing, hold-down and return springs for signs of overheating indicated by a slight blue color. If any component exhibits overheating signs, replace hold-down and return springs with new ones. Overheated springs lose their pull and could cause brake linings to wear out prematurely. Inspect all springs for sags, bends and external damage and replace as required.

Inspect hold-down retainers and pins for bends, rust and corrosion. If any of the above is found, replace as required.

BACKING PLATE

Inspect backing plate shoe contact surface for grooves that may restrict shoe

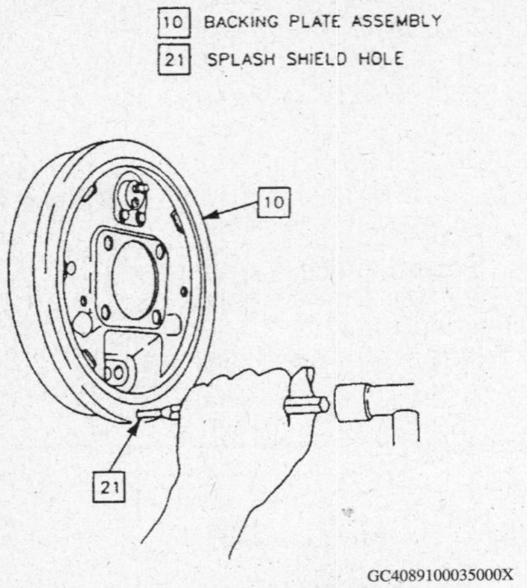

Fig. 2 Loosening drum through splash shield

movement and cannot be removed by lightly sanding with emery cloth or other suitable abrasive. If backing plate exhibits above condition, it should be replaced. Also inspect for signs of cracks, warpage and excessive rust, indicating need for replacement.

ADJUSTER MECHANISM

Inspect all components for rust, corrosion, bends and fatigue. Replace as required. **On adjuster mechanism equipped with adjuster cable,** inspect cable for kinks, fraying or elongation of eyelet and replace as required.

PARKING BRAKE CABLE

Inspect parking brake cable end for kinks, fraying and elongation and replace as required. Use a small hose clamp to compress clamp where it enters backing plate to remove.

BRAKE SERVICE

REMOVAL

1. Raise and support vehicle.
2. Mark relationship of wheel to axle, then remove wheel and tire assembly.
3. Remove brake drum. If drum is difficult to remove, proceed as follows:
   a. Ensure parking brake is released.
   b. Back off parking brake cable adjustment.
   c. Remove access hole plug from backing plate, insert screwdriver through hole and push parking brake lever off its stop.
   d. Insert punch through hole in splash shield **Fig. 2,** tap on punch to loosen drum, then remove drum.
4. Remove actuator spring using brake tool No. J-38400, or equivalent to pry loop end of spring from adjuster actuator, **Fig. 3. Do not over stretch the spring as this will reduce its effectiveness.**
5. Remove end of retractor spring from adjuster shoe and lining assembly, **Fig. 4. Keep finger away from retractor spring to prevent pinching.**

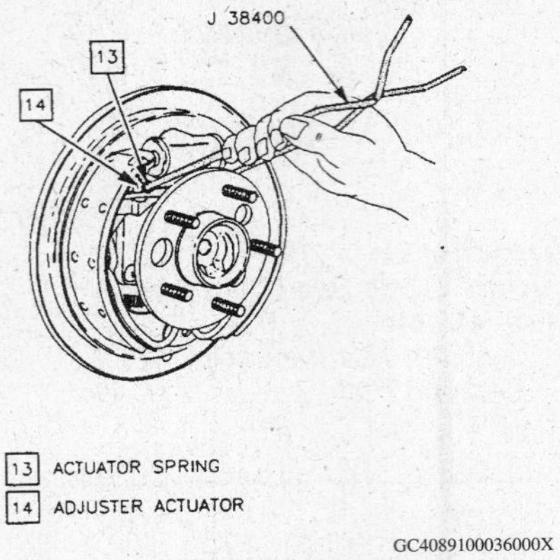

Fig. 3 Actuator spring removal

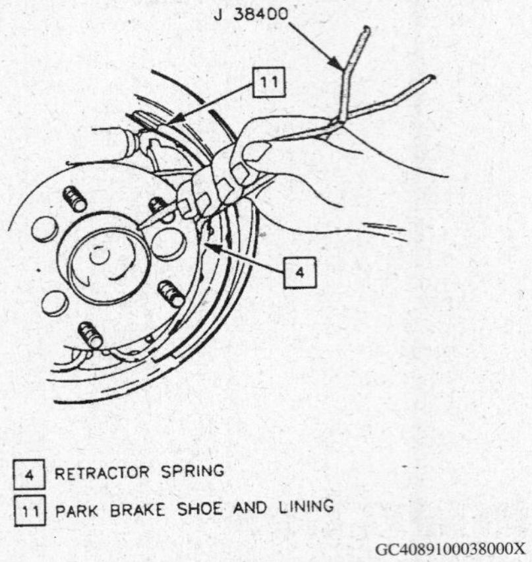

Fig. 5 Spring end installation onto shoe web

6. Remove adjuster shoe and lining assembly, adjuster actuator, then the adjusting screw assembly.
7. Remove park brake lever from shoe assembly, do not remove parking brake cable from lever unless parking brake lever is being replaced.
8. Remove retractor spring from park brake shoe and lining.
9. Pry end of retractor spring toward axle using brake tool, until it snaps off shoe web onto backing plate. Remove park brake shoe.

INSTALLATION

1. Using brake lubricant No. 1052196, or equivalent, lubricate raised shoe pads on backing plate, anchor surfaces on backing plate and adjuster screw threads.
2. Install retractor spring if removed by hooking center spring section under tab on anchor.
3. Install park shoe and lining assembly as follows:
   a. Place shoe on backing plate.
   b. Using brake tool No. J-38400, or equivalent, pull end of retractor spring up to rest on web of brake shoe, **Fig. 5.**
   c. Pull end of retractor spring over until it locks into slot of brake shoe, **Fig. 6.**
4. Install park brake lever.
5. Install adjuster screw and adjuster

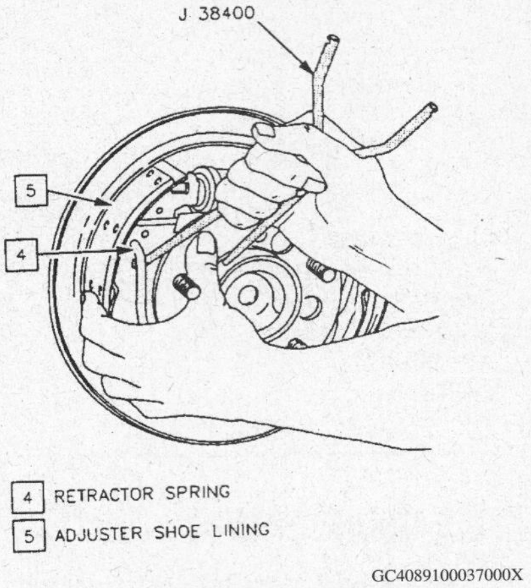

Fig. 4 Retractor spring disengagement

shoe as follows:
   a. Place shoe on backing plate.
   b. Using brake tool, pull end of retractor spring up to rest on web of brake shoe.
   c. Pull end of retractor spring over until if locks into slot of brake shoe.
6. Install adjuster actuator by spreading shoes using brake tool, **Fig. 7,** then move actuator into place.
7. Install actuator spring.
8. Adjust brakes using suitable adjustment tool. The shoes' outer diameter should be .050 inch less than inside diameter of each drum.
9. Install drums, wheels and tires, aligning marks made during removal.

ADJUSTMENTS

SERVICE BRAKE

1. Raise and support vehicle.
2. Mark relationship of wheel to axle, then remove wheel and tire assembly.
3. Remove brake drum. If drum is difficult to remove, proceed as follows:
   a. Ensure parking brake is released.
   b. Back off parking brake cable adjustment.
   c. Remove access hole plug from backing plate, insert screwdriver through hole and push parking brake lever off its stop.
   d. Insert punch through hole in splash shield **Fig. 2,** tap on punch to loosen drum, then remove drum.
4. Measure inside diameter of drum using tool Nos. J-21177-A or J-22364-01, or their equivalents.
5. Adjust by turning star wheel adjuster. Lining diameter should be .050 inch less than inside diameter of each drum.
6. Install drums, wheels and tires.
7. Lower the vehicle, then tighten wheel lug nuts to specifications.

PARKING BRAKE

1. Adjust brakes as outlined in "Service Brake Adjustment."
2. Apply and release parking brake five times to six clicks.

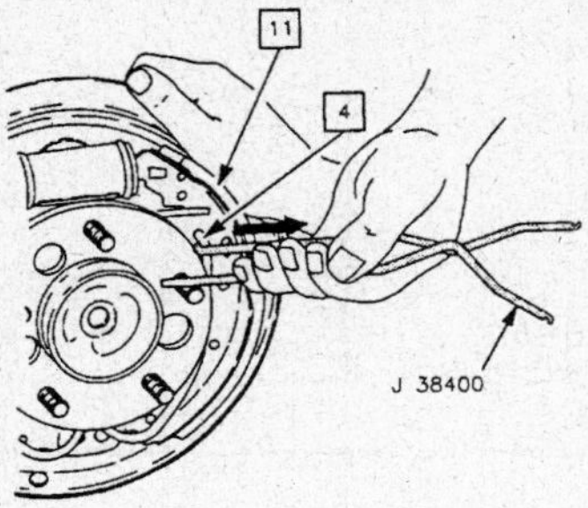

4 RETRACTOR SPRING
11 PARK BRAKE SHOE AND LINING

GC4089100039000X

Fig. 6 Spring end installation into shoe slot

3. Ensure pedal is fully released by turning ignition On. The brake warning lamp should be off.
4. If brake warning lamp is lit, operate pedal release lever and pull downward on front parking brake cable.
5. Raise and support vehicle, then remove access hole plug.
6. Adjust cable until a ⅛ inch drill bit can be inserted through access hole into space between shoe web and park lever, **Fig. 8.** Proper adjustment is when a ⅛ inch drill bit will fit in the space but a ¼ inch bit will not.

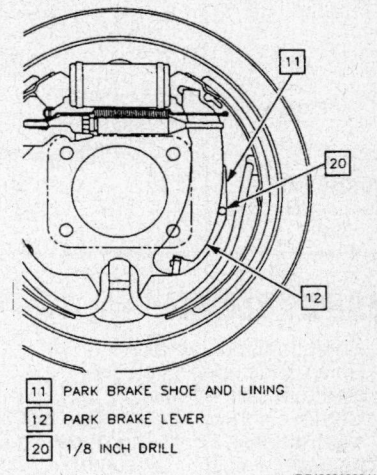

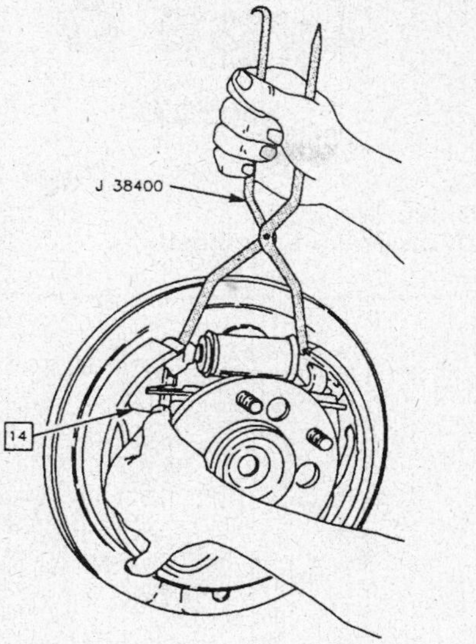

14 ADJUSTER ACTUATOR

GC4089100040000X

Fig. 7 Shoe spreading to install adjuster actuator

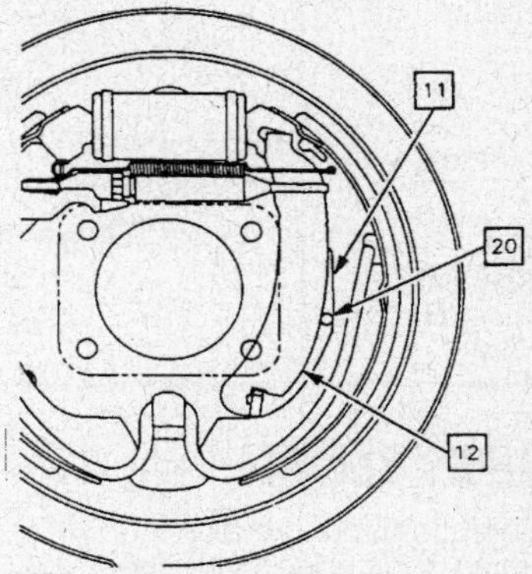

11 PARK BRAKE SHOE AND LINING
12 PARK BRAKE LEVER
20 1/8 INCH DRILL

GC4089100041000X

Fig. 8 Parking brake adjustment

7. Release brake, then ensure wheels rotate freely.
8. Replace access hole plug, then lower the vehicle.

DRUM BRAKE SPECIFICATIONS

Model	Drum Brake Inside Dia. Inch	
	Nominal	Maximum
BUICK		
Century	8.863	8.920
LeSabre	8.863	8.920
CHEVROLET		
Lumina	8.863	8.920
Malibu	8.900	8.909
OLDSMOBILE		
Alero	8.863	8.920
Cutlass	8.900	8.909
LSS	8.863	8.920
Eighty Eight	8.863	8.920
Regency	8.863	8.920
PONTIAC		
Bonneville	8.863	8.920
Grand Am (1999-2000)	8.863	8.920

TIGHTENING SPECIFICATIONS

Component	Torque/Ft. Lbs.
Wheel Cylinder Bleeder Screw (Alero & Grand Am)	115①
Wheel Cylinder Bleeder Screw (Bonneville, Eighty Eight, LeSabre, LSS & Regency)	89①
Wheel Cylinder Bleeder Screw (Cutlass & Malibu)	62①
Wheel Cylinder Line Fitting	11
Wheel Cylinder To Backing Plate	108①
Wheel Lug Nuts	100

① — Inch lbs.

Type 6

INDEX

INSPECTION

1. Release parking brake.
2. Raise and support vehicle.
3. Remove rear wheels.
4. Remove brake drum. **Do not pry against brake backing plate.**
5. Inspect adjuster assembly, ensure screw threads turn smoothly into nut over full threaded length.
6. Inspect wheel cylinder for damage, leakage or seizure; replace as required.

BRAKE SERVICE

1. Release parking brake.
2. Raise and support vehicle.
3. Remove rear wheels.
4. Remove brake drum. **Do not pry against brake backing plate.**
5. Remove lower return spring, **Fig. 1.**
6. Remove adjuster spring.
7. Remove leading brake shoe hold-down, spring and pin.
8. Remove adjuster assembly and lever.

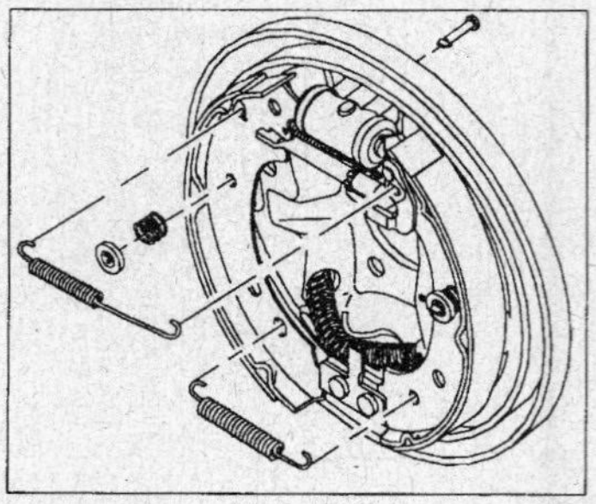

G34089100001000X

Fig. 1 Rear brake assembly

If difficult, pull leading shoe toward front of vehicle, then or turn star wheel on adjuster to shorten length.

9. Twist shoe from upper return spring engagement to remove.
10. Remove parking brake shoe upper return spring.
11. Remove park brake shoe hold-down cup, spring and pin.
12. Push park brake lever into cable spring to remove park brake cable from lever.
13. Remove park brake lever retainer and wave washer and separate from park brake shoe.
14. Reverse procedure to install noting the following:
    a. Lubricate adjuster assembly, adjuster lever surface, backing plate at shoe contact pads and park brake lever pin and brake shoe web contact surface.
    b. Using brake drum clearance tool No. SA91109NE, or equivalent, drum inner diameter, then measure brake shoe assembly outer diameter, adjust brake adjuster to obtain .050 inch measurement less than drum inner diameter.

ADJUSTMENTS

PARKING BRAKE

Refer to "Adjustments" under " Disc Brakes" for parking brake adjustment.

DRUM BRAKE SPECIFICATIONS

Brake Drum I.D., Inch	Minimum Refinish Diameter, Inch	Discard Diameter, Inch
S-SERIES		
7.87	7.90	7.93
L-SERIES		
9.05	9.08	9.09

TIGHTENING SPECIFICATIONS

Component	Torque/Ft. Lbs.
Backing Plate To Knuckle	63
Bleed Valve	66①
Brake Line To Brake Hose	18
Brake Line To Wheel Cylinder	36
Brake Pipe To Union	14
Wheel Cylinder To Backing Plate	84①
Wheel Lug Nuts	92

① — Inch lbs.

HYDRAULIC BRAKE SYSTEMS

TABLE OF CONTENTS

General Motors

INDEX

DESCRIPTION

FRONT & REAR SPLIT SYSTEM

When the brake pedal is depressed, both the primary (front brake) and the secondary (rear brake) master cylinder pistons are moved simultaneously to exert hydraulic fluid pressure on their respective systems, **Fig. 1**.

If the rear (secondary) brake system fails, initial brake pedal movement will cause the unrestricted secondary piston to bottom in the master cylinder bore. Primary piston movement will displace hydraulic fluid in the primary section of the master cylinder to actuate the front brake system.

If the front (primary) brake system fails, initial brake pedal movement will cause the unrestricted primary piston to bottom out against the secondary piston. Continued downward movement of the brake pedal moves the secondary piston to displace hydraulic fluid in the rear brake system to actuate the rear brakes.

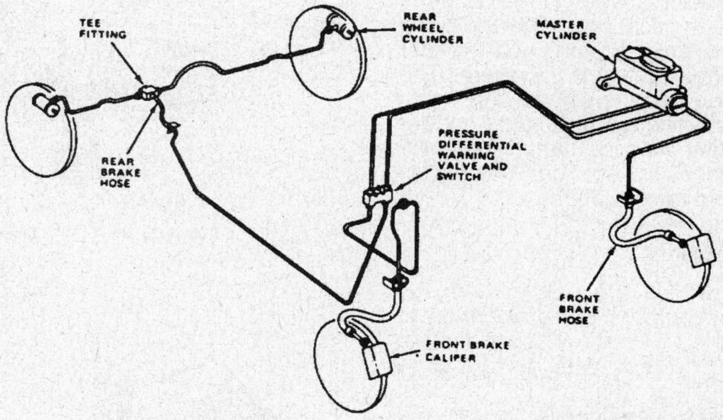

GC4099100014000X

Fig. 1 Front & rear split brake system

DIAGONALLY SPLIT SYSTEM

This system operates on the same principle as conventional front and rear split systems, using primary and secondary master cylinders which move simultaneously to exert hydraulic pressure on their respective systems. The hydraulic brake lines on this system, however, have been diagonally split front to rear (left front to right rear and right front to left rear) in place of separate lines to the front and rear wheels, **Fig. 2**.

In the event of a system failure, the remaining non-failed system will do all the braking on one front wheel and one rear wheel, maintaining 50% of the total braking force.

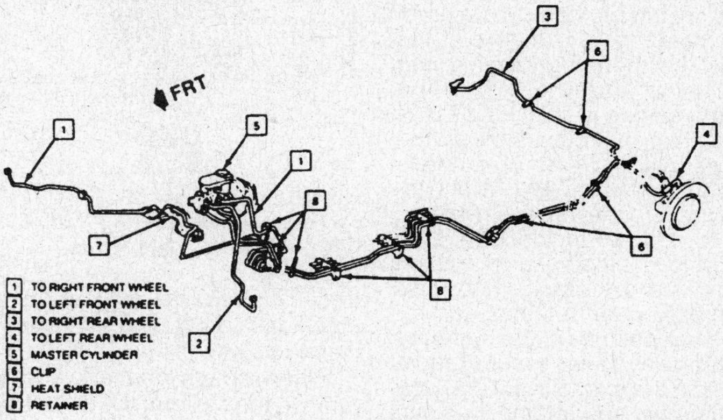

GC4099100015000X

Fig. 2 Diagonally split brake system

COMPONENTS

Warning Lamp

The warning lamp should illuminate when the ignition switch is in the start position, and turn off when the switch returns to run. If the brake lamp remains on after the ignition returns to run, check fluid level in master cylinder reservoir and inspect parking brake. If the warning lamp does not turn on during cranking, check for defective bulb or blown fuse.

Fluid Level Sensor

This sensor, mounted on the master cylinder, will activate the brake warning lamp if a low brake fluid level is detected. The lamp will turn off once the fluid level is corrected.

Brake Warning Lamp Switches

In **Fig. 3,** as pressure falls in one system, the other system's normal pressure forces the piston to the inoperative side, contacting the switch terminal, causing the warning lamp on the instrument panel to glow.

The switch, **Fig. 4,** is mounted directly in the master cylinder assembly. Whenever there is a specified differential pressure, the switch piston will activate the brake failure warning switch and cause the brake warning lamp to glow.

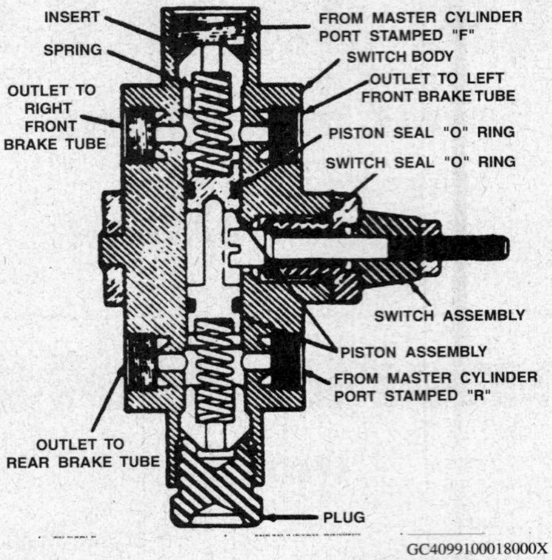

Fig. 3 Pressure differential valve & brake warning lamp switch

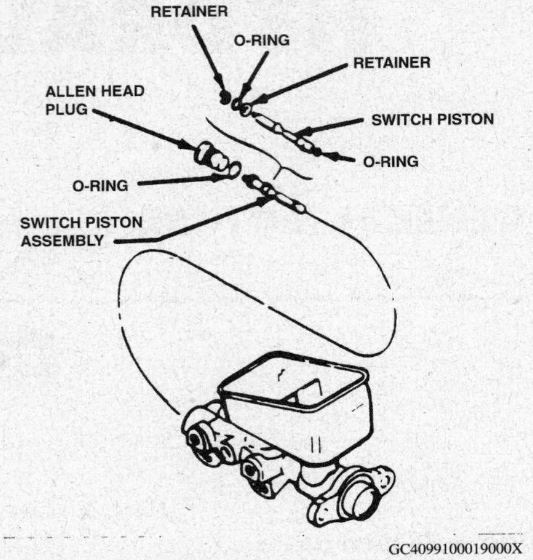

Fig. 4 Dual master cylinder w/built in warning lamp switch

Combination Valve

The combination valve, **Fig. 5,** is a metering valve, failure warning switch, and a proportioner in one assembly and is used on disc brake applications. The metering valve delays front disc braking until the rear drum brake shoes contact the drum. The failure warning switch is actuated in event of front or rear brake system failure, in turn activating a dash warning lamp. The proportioner balances front to rear braking action during rapid deceleration.

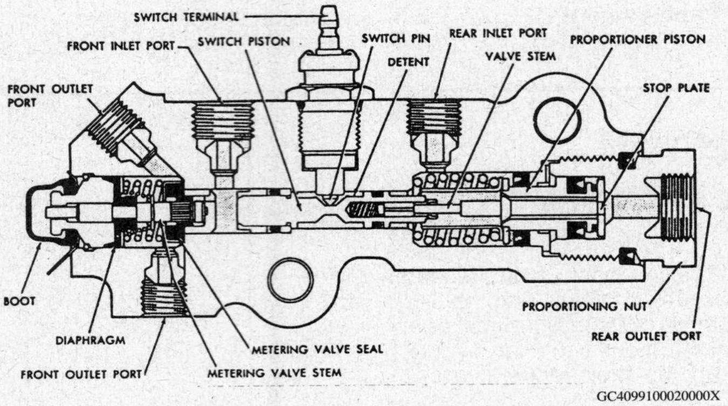

Fig. 5 Combination valve

Metering Valve

When the brakes are not applied, the metering valve permits the brake fluid to flow through the valve allowing the fluid to expand and contract with temperature changes.

When the brakes are initially applied, the metering valve stem moves to the left, preventing fluid to flow through the valve to the front disc brakes. This is accomplished by the smooth end of the metering valve stem contacting the metering valve seal lip at 4 to 30 psi, **Fig. 6.** The metering valve spring holds the retainer against the seal until a predetermined pressure is produced at the valve inlet port which overcomes the spring pressure and permits hydraulic pressure to actuate the front disc brakes, **Fig. 7.** The increased pressure into the valve is metered through the valve seal, to the front disc brakes, producing an increased force on the diaphragm. The diaphragm then pulls the pin, in turn pulling the retainer, and reduces the spring pressure on the metering valve seal. Eventually, the pressure reaches a point at which the spring is pulled away by the diaphragm pin and retainer, leaving the metering valve unrestricted, permitting full pressure to pass through the metering valve.

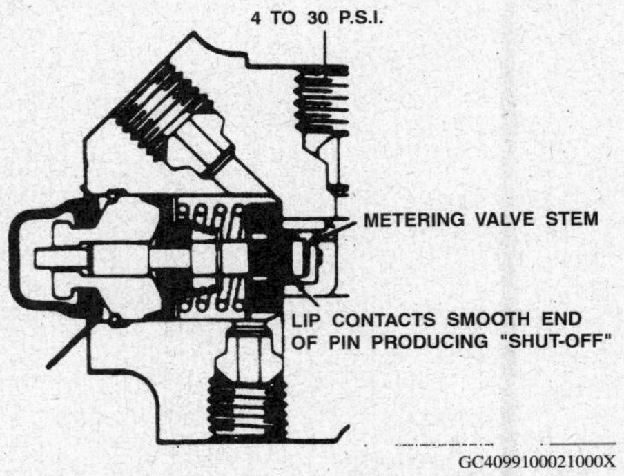

Fig. 6 Metering valve. Initial braking

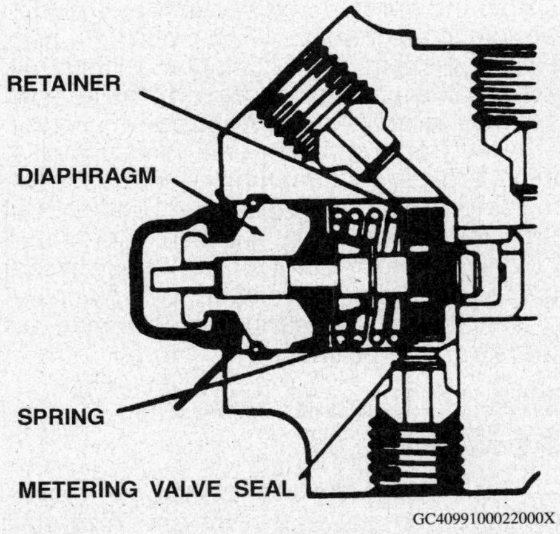

Fig. 7 Metering valve. Continued braking

Failure Warning Switch

If the rear brake system fails, the front system pressure forces the switch piston to the right, **Fig. 8.** The switch pin is then forced up into the switch, completing the electrical circuit and activates the dash warning lamp.

When repairs are made and pressure returns to the system, the piston moves to the left, resetting the switch. The detent on the piston requires approximately 100–450 psi to permit full reset of the piston. In event of front brake system failure, the piston moves to the left and the same sequence of events is followed as for rear system failure except the piston resets to the right.

Proportioning Or Pressure Control Valve

During rapid deceleration, a portion of vehicle weight is transferred to the front wheels. This resultant loss of weight at rear wheels must be compensated for to avoid early rear wheel skid. The proportioner or pressure control valve reduces rear brake

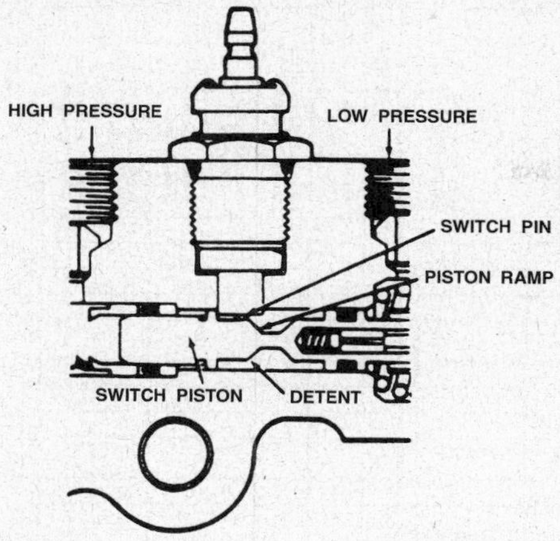

GC4099100023000X

Fig. 8 Failure warning switch. Rear system failure

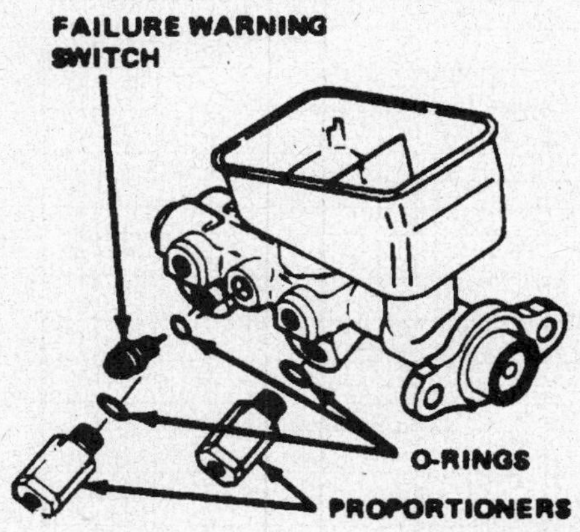

GC4099100026000X

Fig. 11 Proportioners installed in master cylinder

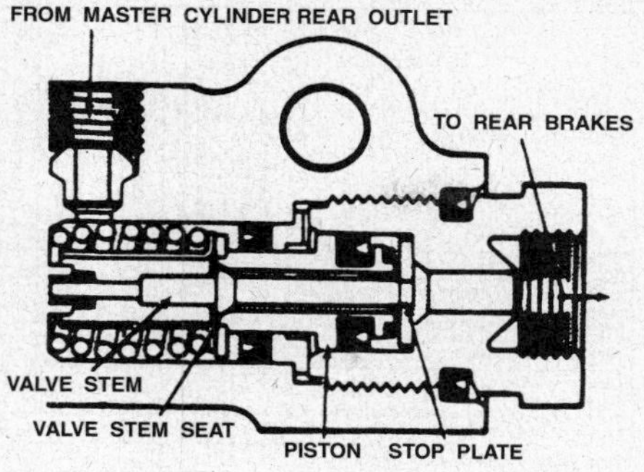

GC4099100024000X

Fig. 9 Proportioner. Rapid deceleration

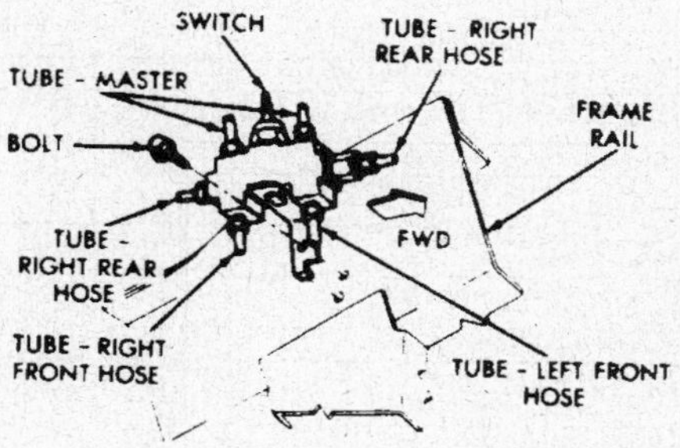

GC4099100027000X

Fig. 12 Distribution switch. Diagonally split brake systems

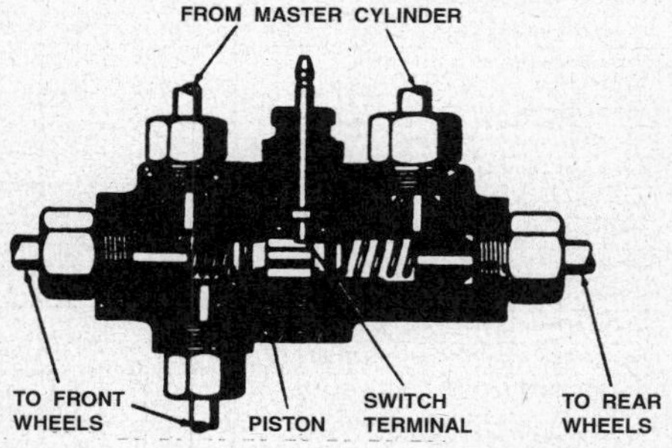

GC4099100029000X

Fig. 14 Brake distribution switch. Failed

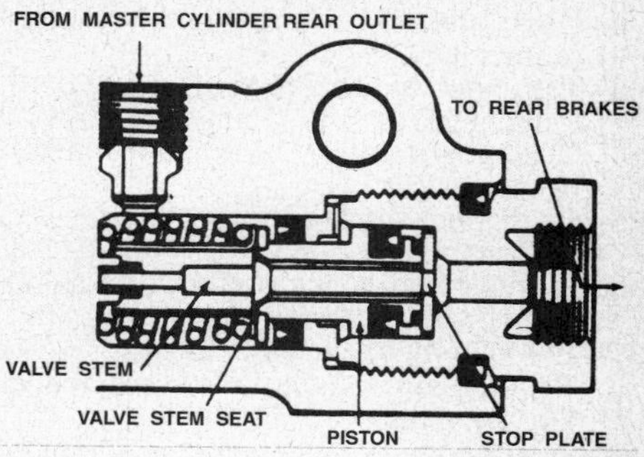

GC4099100025000X

Fig. 10 Proportioner. Normal braking

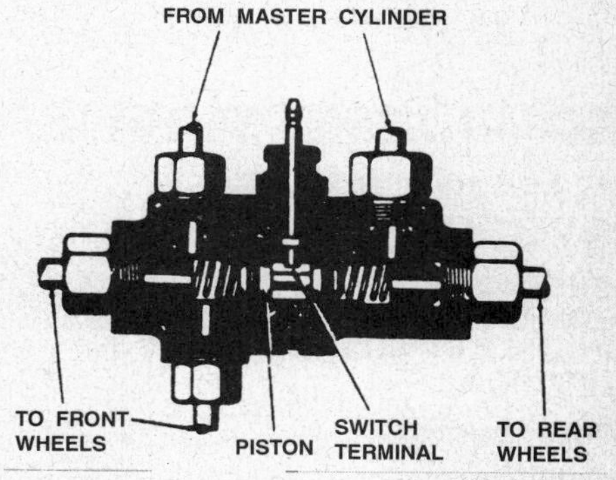

GC4099100028000X

Fig. 13 Brake distribution switch. Normal

system pressure, delaying rear wheel skid. When the proportioner or pressure control valve is incorporated in the combination valve assembly, pressure developed within the valve acts against the large end of the piston, overcoming the spring pressure, moving the piston left, **Fig. 9.** The piston then contacts the stem seat and restricts line pressure through the valve.

During normal braking operation, the proportioner or pressure control valve is not functional. Brake fluid flows into the proportioner or pressure control valve between the piston center hole and the valve stem, through the stop plate and to the rear brakes. Spring pressure loads the piston during normal braking, causing it to rest against the stop plate, **Fig. 10.**

On diagonally split brake systems, two proportioners or pressure control valves are used. One controls the left rear brake, the other the right rear brake. The proportioners or pressure control valves are installed in the master cylinder rear brake outlet ports, **Fig. 11.**

Brake Distribution Valve & Switch

This switch assembly, **Fig. 12,** is used on some diagonally split brake systems and Corvette four wheel disc brake systems. It is connected to the outlet ports of the master cylinder and to the brake warning lamp and warns the driver if either the primary or secondary brake system has failed.

When hydraulic pressure is equal in both primary and secondary brake systems, the switch remains centered, **Fig. 13.** If pressure fails in one of the systems, the piston moves toward the inoperative side, **Fig. 14.** The shoulder of the piston contacts the switch terminal, providing a ground and lighting the warning lamp.

TROUBLESHOOTING

When troubleshooting the hydraulic brake system, perform the following checks and inspections as outlined below. If problem still exists within system, refer to **Figs. 15 and 16.**

MASTER CYLINDER INTERNAL FLUID LEAKAGE CHECK

Start engine and depress the brake pedal. If the pedal gradually falls under constant pressure, the hydraulic system may be leaking. Raise the vehicle on a lift and check all tubing lines and backing plates for signs of leakage. It may be necessary to lift or remove the carpeting or floor mats to check for booster or master cylinder leakage.

ROAD TEST

When testing brakes, ensure the road is level and dry. Test brakes at both light and heavy pedal pressure. Do not lock up brakes or slide tires during a brake test.

Check the tires on the vehicle before performing a brake test. Tires should be equally inflated, identical in size and with equal tread pattern. Excessive camber and caster will cause the brakes to pull. An overloaded vehicle will also brake erratically.

DIAGNOSIS & TESTING

Refer to **Fig. 17** for diagnosis chart.

COMPONENT REPLACEMENT

MASTER CYLINDER

1. Disconnect retainer and electrical connector from fluid level sensor.

2. Drain brake fluid from master cylinder reservoir.
3. Plug hose to prevent fluid loss or contamination.
4. Disconnect brake pipes from master cylinder.
5. Plug open pipes to prevent fluid loss or contamination.
6. Remove two master cylinder retaining nuts, then the master cylinder.
7. Remove reservoir, if necessary.
8. Reverse procedure to install, noting the following:
   a. **Torque** master cylinder retaining nuts to 20 ft. lbs.
   b. **Torque** brake pipe fittings to 11 ft. lbs.
   c. Bleed hydraulic system as described under "Brake System Bleed."

COMPONENT SERVICE

MASTER CYLINDER OVERHAUL

EXCEPT AURORA, BONNEVILLE, EIGHTY-EIGHT, LESABRE, LSS, PARK AVENUE, REGENCY & RIVIERA

Disassemble

Refer to **Figs. 18 and 19** when performing the following procedures.

1. Remove master cylinder from vehicle as follows:
   a. Disconnect and plug hydraulic lines.
   b. Remove two master cylinder attaching nuts, then the master cylinder.
2. Remove reservoir cover and diaphragm. Discard old brake fluid in reservoir.
3. Inspect cover and diaphragm.
4. Remove fluid level switch, if equipped.
5. **On models with compact master cylinder,** remove proportioner valve assembly, **Fig. 19.**
6. **On all models,** depress primary piston and remove lock ring.
7. Plug primary fluid outlet (outlet nearest to cowl when master cylinder is installed), then apply compressed air into secondary fluid outlet to remove primary and secondary pistons.
8. Remove spring retainer and seals from secondary piston.
9. Clamp master cylinder in a vise, **Fig. 20,** then remove reservoir using a pry bar.
10. Remove reservoir grommets.
11. Inspect master cylinder bore for corrosion. **Do not use abrasive material on master cylinder bore.**

Assemble

Clean all parts not included in repair kit with brake fluid. **Do not dry with compressed air.** Lubricate all rubber parts with clean brake fluid prior to installation.

1. Lubricate new reservoir grommets with silicone brake lube, then press grommets into master cylinder body. Ensure grommets are properly seated.
2. Lay reservoir upside down on flat, hard surface.
3. Press master cylinder body onto reservoir using rocking motion.
4. Install new seals on secondary piston, then the spring retainer.
5. Install spring and secondary piston assembly into cylinder.
6. Install primary piston.
7. Depress primary piston into cylinder, then install lock ring.
8. Install fluid level switch, if equipped.
9. **On models with compact master cylinder,** install proportioner valve assembly, **Fig. 19.**
10. **On all models,** install diaphragm into reservoir cover, then install cover onto reservoir.
11. Install master cylinder and bleed brake system.

CAUSE \ SYMPTOM	Excessive Brake Pedal Travel	Brake Pedal Travel Gradually Increases	Excessive Brake Pedal Effort	Excessive Braking Action	Brakes Slow To Respond	Brakes Slow To Release	Brakes Drag	Uneven Braking Action (Side To Side)	Uneven Braking Action (Front To Rear)	Scraping Noise From Brakes	Brakes Squeak During Application*	Brakes Squeak During Stop*	Brakes Chatter (Roughness)	Brakes Groan At End Of Stop*	Brake Warning Lamp Glows During Stop
Leaking Brake Line or Connection	X	XX							X						XX
Leaking Wheel Cylinder or Piston Seal	X	XX		X				X							X
Leaking Master Cylinder	X	XX													X
Air in Brake System	XX								X						XX
Contaminated or Improper Brake Fluid					X	X	X								X
Leaking Vacuum System			XX		X										
Restricted Air Passage in Power Head			X		XX	X									
Damaged Power Head			X	X	X	X	X								
Improperly Assembled Power Head Valving			X	X	X	X	XX								
Worn Out Brake Lining-Replace			X	X				X	X	X	X	X		X	
Uneven Brake Lining Wear-Replace and Correct	X			X				X	X	X	X	XX		X	X
Glazed Brake Lining			XX		X			X	X		X	X			
Incorrect Lining Material-Replace			X	X				X	X			X		X	
Contaminated Brake Lining-Replace				XX				XX	XX	X	X	X		X	
Linings Damaged by Abusive Use-Replace			X	XX				X	X	X	X	X		X	
Excessive Brake Lining Dust			X	XX				XX	XX		X	XX		X	
Heat Spotted or Scored Brake Drums or Rotors				X				X	X		X	X	XX	X	
Out-of-Round or Vibrating Brake Drums												X	XX		
Improper Thickness Variation on Brake Rotors													XX		
Excessive Lateral Run-Out													X		
Faulty Automatic Adjusters	X						X	X	X						X
Incorrect Wheel Cylinder Sizes			X	X				X	X						
Weak or Incorrect Brake Shoe Retention Springs				X		X	XX	X	X	XX	X	XX			
Brake Assembly Attachments-Missing or Loose	X						X	X	X	X		X	X	X	
Insufficient Brake Shoe Guide Lubricant						X	X	X	X	XX	XX				
Restricted Brake Fluid Passage or Sticking Wheel Cylinder Piston		X	X		X	X	X	X	X						
Faulty Metering Valve	X		X	X	X	X	X		X						X
Brake Pedal Linkage Interference or Binding			X		X	XX	XX								
Improperly Adjusted Parking Brake							X								
Drums Tapered or Threaded										XX					
Incorrect Front End Alignment								XX							
Incorrect Tire Pressure								X	X						
Incorrect Wheel Bearing Adjustment	X									X			X		
Loose Front Suspension Attachments								X		XX			X	X	
Out-of-Balance Wheel Assemblies													XX		
Operator Riding Brake Pedal	X	X	X				X		X					X	
Improperly Adjusted Booster Pushrod	X					X	XX								X
Sticking Wheel Cylinder or Caliper Pistons			X			X	X	X	X						
Faulty Proportioning Valve			X		X	X	X								

XX — Indicates more probable cause(s) X — Indicates other causes *May be a normal condition.

GC4099100030010X

Fig. 15 Brake diagnosis chart. Front disc/rear drum system

AURORA, BONNEVILLE, EIGHTY-EIGHT, LESABRE, LSS, PARK AVENUE, REGENCY & RIVIERA

These master cylinders are not serviceable. Master cylinder must be replaced as a complete unit. **Do not attempt to overhaul the master cylinder.**

CORVETTE

1. Remove reservoir cap and diaphragm from reservoir.
2. Drain fluid, then remove master cylinder prime pipe clamp and prime pipe.
3. Remove reservoir retaining screw and reservoir, **Fig. 21.**
4. Remove reservoir O-rings from reservoir wells.
5. Slightly depress piston and remove retaining ring with retaining ring pliers.

6. Invert cylinder so reservoir wells face downward.
7. Depress primary and secondary pistons with a brass rod or wooden dowel until fully bottomed in bore. Secondary stop pin should fall freely from cylinder.
8. Gently bump open end of cylinder body against a piece of wood to dislodge primary piston, then remove primary piston.
9. Gently bump open end of cylinder body against a piece of wood to dislodge secondary piston and center valve assembly, then remove secondary piston. **Do not remove or disturb screw which retains primary spring to secondary piston. This has been set to a predetermined height and will severely affect cylinder performance if setting is changed.**
10. Remove secondary return spring from secondary piston assembly.
11. Remove spring retainer from secondary piston using a small screwdriver to lift crimp to allow retainer to slide off piston, **Fig. 22.**
12. Remove center valve plunger and spring from secondary piston.
13. Remove seal retainer using a sharp knife or razor blade to cut and remove plastic retaining cup retaining ring from primary piston, **Fig. 23.**
14. Remove recuperating guide.
15. Remove all rubber seals from both pistons, **Figs. 24 and 25. Take extreme care not to damage any surfaces on piston, particularly areas where seals seat.**
16. Remove pressure differential switch assembly. **Do not disassemble spring or probe from switch body.**
17. Remove end plug and O-ring. **Care must be taken not to lose small electrical bias spring located just inside end plug.**
18. Remove warning switch assembly from master cylinder assembly. **Keep warning switch and probe together as an assembly.**
19. Remove end plug, O-ring and electrical bias spring.
20. Gently tap cylinder body against a piece of wood to dislodge proportioning valve spool assembly, then remove proportioning valve spool assembly including O-ring and spacer. **Do not disassemble proportioning valve, it is serviced as an assembly only.**
21. **The proportioning valve is prelubricated with a special grease, do not use a cleaning solution to clean it or parts included in repair kit. Clean all other parts in denatured alcohol. Use filtered unlubricated compressed air to dry all parts and passages within the cylinder.**
22. Reverse procedure to assemble, ensure all seals and parts are lubricated with clean brake fluid.

CAUSE / SYMPTOM	Excessive Brake Pedal Travel	Brake Pedal Travel Gradually Increases	Excessive Brake Pedal Effort	Excessive Braking Action	Brakes Slow To Respond	Brakes Slow To Release	Brakes Drag	Uneven Braking Action (Side To Side)	Uneven Braking Action (Front To Rear)	Scraping Noise From Brakes	Brakes Squeak During Application*	Brakes Squeak During Stop*	Brakes Chatter (Roughness)	Brakes Groan At End Of Stop*	Brake Warning Lamp Glows
Leaking Brake Line or Connection	X	XX	X						X						XX
Leaking Piston Seal	X	XX	X	X				X	X						X
Leaking Master Cylinder	X	XX	X						X						X
Air in Brake System	XX		X						X						XX
Contaminated or Improper Brake Fluid	X				X	X	X	X	X						X
Leaking Vacuum System			XX		X										
Restricted Air Passage in Power Head		X	X		XX	X									
Damaged Power Head		X	X	X	X	XX									
Worn Out Brake Lining			X	X				X	X	X	X	X		X	
Uneven Brake Lining Wear-Replace	X			X				X	X	X	X	XX		X	X
Glazed Brake Lining			XX		X			X	X		X	X			
Incorrect Lining Material-Replace			X	X		X		X	X			X		X	
Contaminated Brake Lining-Replace				XX		X		XX	XX	X	X	X		X	
Linings Damaged by Abusive Use-Replace			X	XX				X	X	X	X	X		X	
Heat Spotted or Scored Discs				X				X	X		X	X	XX	X	
Improper Thickness Variation	X												XX		
Excessive Lateral Run-Out	X												X		
Automatic Adjuster Problem	X	X					X	X	X						X
Brake Assembly Attachments-Missing or Loose	X						X	X	X	X		X	X	X	
Restricted Brake Fluid Passage		X	X		X	X	X	X	X						X
Improperly Adjusted Stoplamp Switch Or Cruise Control Vacuum Dump							X								
Metering Valve Problem		X	X	X	X	X	X		X						X
Proportioning Valve Problem		X	X	X	X	X	X		X						X
Brake Pedal Linkage Interference or Binding			X		X	XX	XX								
Improperly Adjusted Parking Brake							X		X						
Improper Length Booster Pushrod	X			X		X	XX		X						
Incorrect Front End Alignment								XX							
Incorrect Tire Pressure								X	X						
Incorrect Wheel Bearing Adjustment	X									X			X		
Loose Front Suspension Attachments							X	X		XX			X	X	
Out-of-Balance Wheel Assemblies													XX		
Operator Riding Brake Pedal			X				X		X					X	
Sticking Caliper or Wheel Cylinder Pistons					X	X	XX	X	X						
Park Brake Switch Circuit Grounded															XX
Park Brake Not Releasing						X		X							XX

XX — Indicates more probable cause(s)

X — Indicates other causes

*May be a normal condition.

GC4099100030020X

Fig. 16 Brake diagnosis chart. Four wheel disc system

WHEEL CYLINDER OVERHAUL

1. Raise and support vehicle.
2. Remove wheel, drum and brake shoes.
3. Disconnect hydraulic line at wheel cylinder. **Do not pull metal line away from cylinder, as this may kink or bend line.** Line will separate from cylinder when cylinder is moved away from brake backing plate.
4. Remove wheel cylinder to brake plate attaching screws, then the wheel cylinder.
5. Remove boots, pistons, springs and cups from cylinder, **Fig. 26.**
6. Clean all parts with brake fluid.
7. Inspect cylinder bore. A scored bore may be honed as long as the diameter is not increased by more than .005 inch.
8. Ensure hands are clean before proceeding with assembly.
9. Lubricate cylinder wall and rubber cups with brake fluid, then install springs, cups, pistons and boots in housing.
10. Wipe end of hydraulic line to remove any foreign matter, then place wheel cylinder in position.
11. Enter tubing into cylinder and start threads on fitting.
12. Secure cylinder to backing plate, then complete tightening of tubing fitting.
13. Install brake shoes, drum and wheel.
14. Bleed brake system, then adjust brakes.

BRAKE SYSTEM BLEED

MANUAL

Pressure bleeding is recommended for all hydraulic systems. However, if a pressure bleeder is unavailable, use the following procedure. **Brake fluid damages painted surfaces. Immediately clean any spilled fluid.**

1. Remove vacuum reserve by pumping brakes several times with engine off.
2. Fill master cylinder reservoir with clean brake fluid. **Do not let reservoir fall below half full during bleeding procedure.**
3. If necessary, bleed master cylinder as follows:
   a. Loosen master cylinder forward brake line connection until fluid flows from reservoir, then tighten brake line.

b. Instruct an assistant to slowly depress brake pedal one time and hold.
c. Loosen front brake line connection and purge air from cylinder.
d. Tighten connection and slowly release brake pedal.
e. Wait 15 seconds, then repeat until all air is purged.
f. Bleed rearward brake line connection by repeating steps a through e.

4. Loosen, then retighten bleeder valves at all four wheels.
5. Bleed calipers or wheel cylinders in sequence outlined under "Bleed Sequence."
6. Place one end of a transparent tube over bleeder valve, then submerge other end of tube into transparent container filled with clean brake fluid, **Fig. 27.**
7. Have assistant slowly depress brake pedal one time and hold.
8. Loosen bleeder valve and purge air from wheel cylinder or caliper. Tighten bleeder screw and slowly release pedal.
9. Wait 15 seconds, then repeat steps 7 and 8 until all air is bled from system.

PRESSURE

1. Loosen, then tighten bleeder valves at all four wheels.
2. Using a diaphragm type pressure bleeder, install suitable bleeder adapter to master cylinder, **Fig. 28.**
3. Charge bleeder ball to 20–25 psi.
4. Connect pressure bleeder line to adapter.
5. Open line valve on pressure bleeder, then depress bleed-off valve on adapter until a small amount of brake fluid is released.
6. Raise and support vehicle.
7. Bleed calipers or wheel cylinders in sequence outlined under " Bleed Sequence."
8. Place one end of a transparent tube over bleeder valve, then submerge other end of tube into transparent container filled with clean brake fluid, **Fig. 27.**
9. Open bleeder valve ½ to ¾ turn and allow fluid to flow into container until all air is purged from line.

BLEED SEQUENCE

Rear wheel drive models: if manual bleeding, RR-LR-RF-LF; if pressure bleeding, bleed front brakes together and rear brakes together.

The same types of brake trouble are encountered with power brakes as with standard brakes. Before checking power brake system for source of trouble, refer to the brake system diagnosis charts. After these possible causes have been eliminated, check for cause as outlined below:

HARD PEDAL

CAUSE	CORRECTION
Broken or damaged hydraulic brake pipes.	Inspect and replace as necessary.
Vacuum failure.	Check for: Faulty vacuum check valve or grommet. Replace. Collapsed or damaged vacuum hose. Replace. Plugged or loose vacuum fitting. Repair. Faulty air valve seal or support plate seal. Replace. Damaged floating control valve. Replace. Bad stud welds on front or rear housing or power head. Replace unless easily repaired.
Faulty diaphragm.	Replace.
Restricted air filter element.	Replace.
Worn or distorted reaction plate or levers.	Replace plate or levers.
Cracked or broken power pistons or retainer.	Replace power pistons and piston rod retainer.

GRABBY BRAKES (Apparent Off-On Condition)

CAUSE	CORRECTION
Broken or damaged hydraulic brake pipes.	Inspect and replace as necessary.
Insufficient fluid in master cylinder.	Fill reservoirs with approved brake fluid. Check for leaks.
Faulty master cylinder seals.	Repair or replace as necessary.
Cracked master cylinder casting.	Replace.
Leaks in pipes or connections at disc brake calipers or wheel cylinders.	Inspect and repair as necessary.
Air in hydraulic system.	Bleed system.

BRAKES FAIL TO RELEASE

CAUSE	CORRECTION
Blocked passage in power piston.	Inspect and repair or replace as necessary.
Air valve sticking shut.	Check for proper lubrication of air valve "O" ring.
Broken piston return spring.	Replace.
Broken air valve spring.	Replace.
Tight pedal linkage.	Repair or replace as necessary.

GC4099100031000X

Fig. 17 Power brake diagnosis chart

Front wheel drive models: RR-LF-LR-RF.

HYDRAULIC SYSTEM FLUSH

If brake fluid is old, contaminated, or whenever new hydraulic system parts are installed, the system must be flushed. Bleed brakes, allowing at least one quart of clean brake fluid to pass through system. Any rubber parts in the hydraulic system which were exposed to contaminated fluid must be replaced.

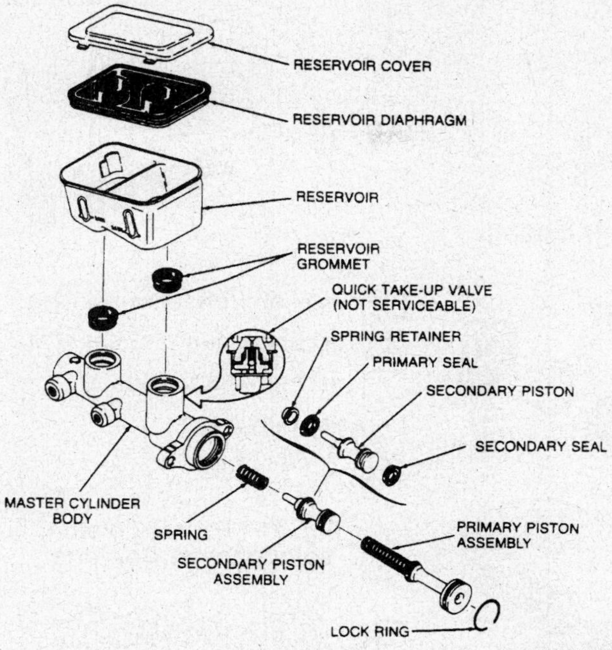

GC4099100034000X

Fig. 18 Dual master cylinder assembly. Composite type

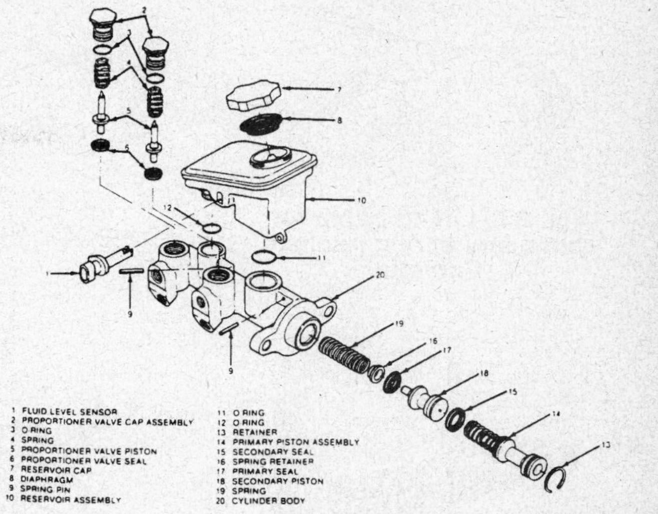

GC4099100035000X

Fig. 19 Compact master cylinder assembly

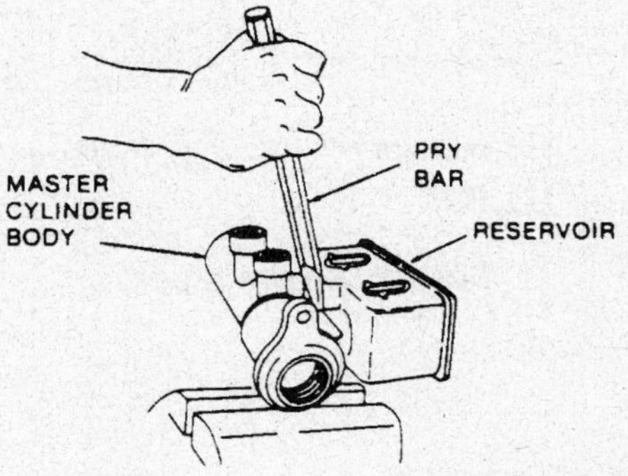

GC4099100036000X

Fig. 20 Master cylinder reservoir removal. Composite type

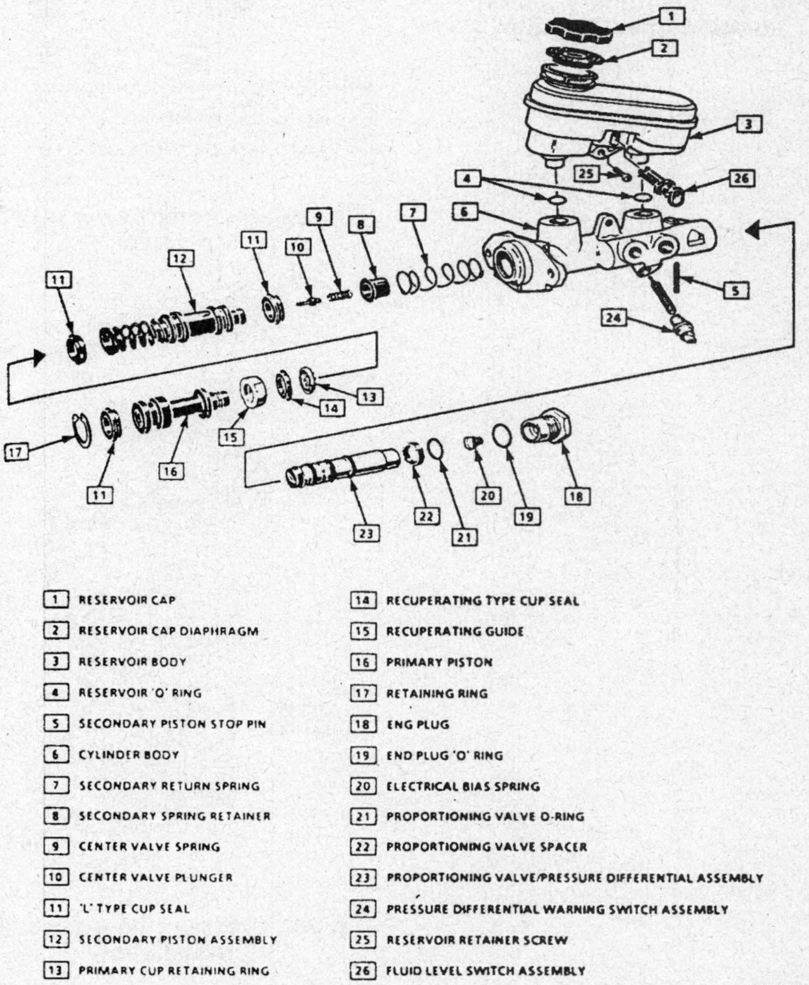

GC4099200037000X

Fig. 21 Composite master cylinder. Corvette

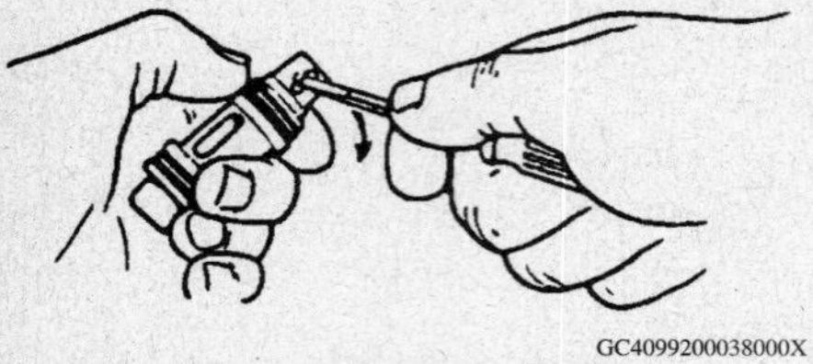

GC4099200038000X

Fig. 22 Lifting crimp on secondary spring retainer. Corvette

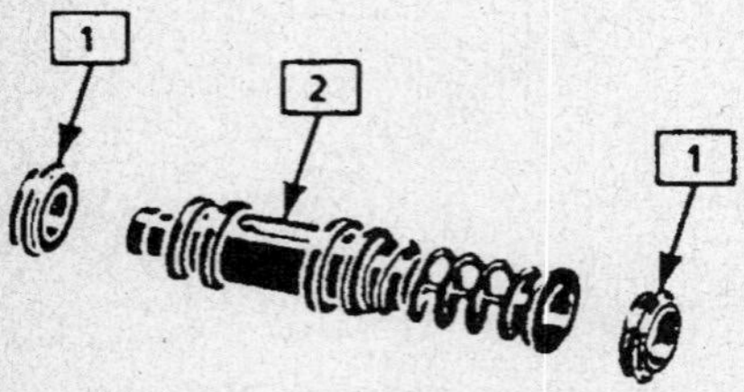

1 'L' TYPE CUP SEAL
2 SECONDARY PISTON ASSEMBLY

GC4099200041000X

Fig. 25 Secondary piston components. Corvette

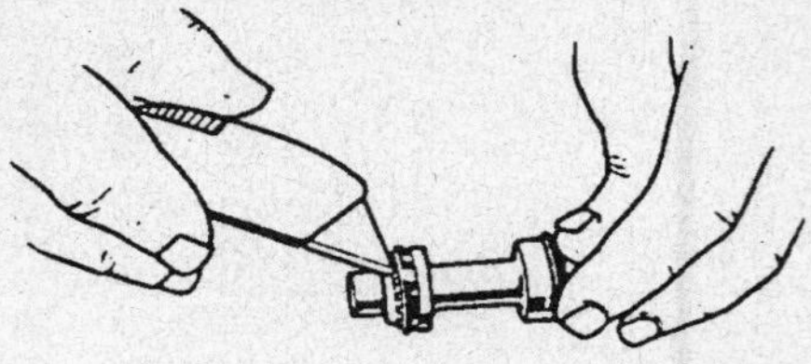

GC4099200039000X

Fig. 23 Seal retainer cutting. Corvette

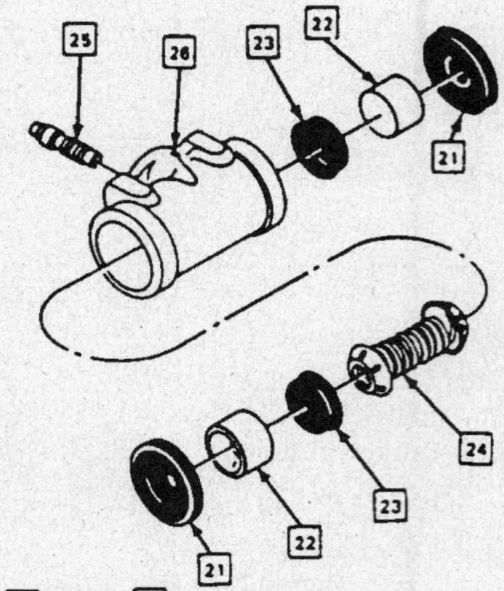

21	BOOT	24	SPRING ASSEMBLY
22	PISTON	25	BLEEDER VALVE
23	SEAL	26	CYLINDER BODY

GC4099100042000X

Fig. 26 Exploded view of wheel cylinder

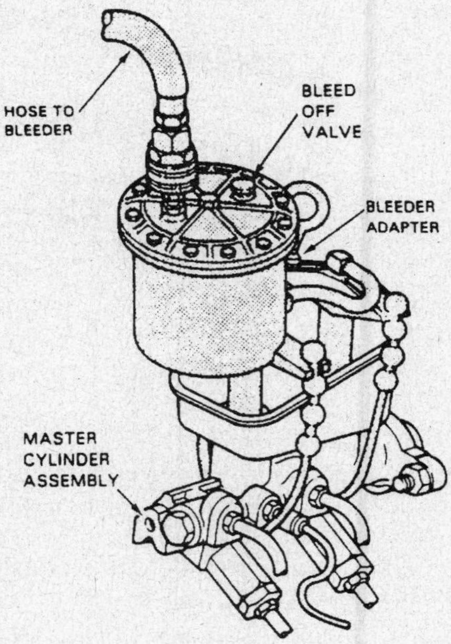

GC4099100033000X

Fig. 28 Pressure bleeder adapter installation

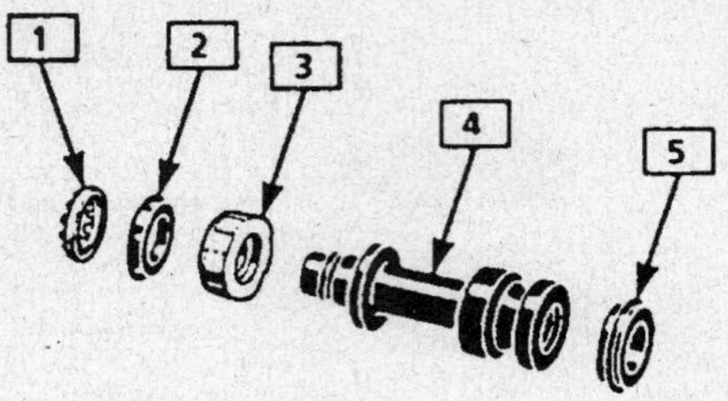

1 PRIMARY CUP RETAINING RING
2 RECUPERATING TYPE CUP SEAL
3 RECUPERATING GUIDE
4 PRIMARY PISTON
5 'L' TYPE CUP SEAL

GC4099200040000X

Fig. 24 Primary piston components. Corvette

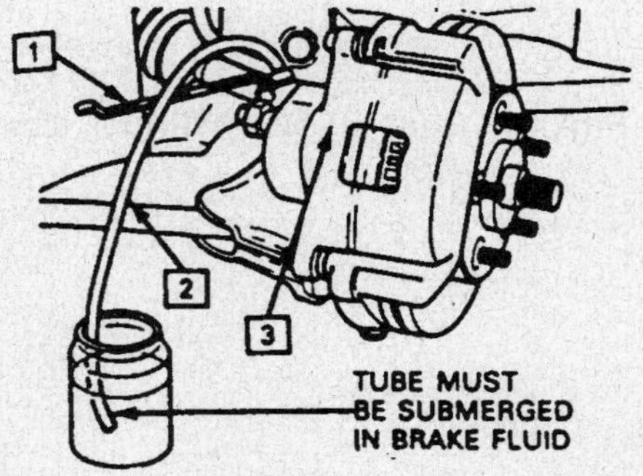

1 BLEEDER WRENCH 3 CALIPER
2 TUBE

GC4099100032000X

Fig. 27 Brake bleed

HYDRAULIC BRAKE SYSTEM SPECIFICATIONS

Model	Year	Master Cylinder Bore Dia., Inch	Front Caliper Bore Dia., Inch	Rear Caliper Bore Dia., Inch	Wheel Cylinder Bore Dia., Inch
BUICK					
Century	1997–98	1.000	2.500	1.500	.874
LeSabre	1997–98	1.000④	2.520	—	.937
	1999	1.000④	2.500	—	.937
	2000	1.000④	2.500	1.500	—
Park Avenue	1997–98	1.000④	2.520	1.500	—
	1999–2000	1.000④	2.500	1.500	—
Regal	1997–98	1.000	2.500	1.500	—
Riviera	1997–98	1.000④	2.520	1.500	—
Skylark	1997–98	.874	2.244	—	.689
CADILLAC					
Catera	1997–99	①	2.244	1.574	—
DeVille	1997–98	1.000	2.500	1.500	.937
	1999	1.000	2.500	1.500	—
Eldorado	1997–2000	1.000	2.500	1.500	—
Seville	1997	1.000	2.520	1.500	.937
CHEVROLET/GEO					
Camaro	1997–98	1.000	2.500	1.595	.810
Cavalier	1997–2000	.874	2.244	—	.689
Corvette	1997–99	.930	1.500③	1.590	—
Lumina	1997–99	.945	1.654	—	.874
Malibu	1997–2000	1.000	2.362	—	.874
Metro	1997–98	.810	1.889	—	.685
Monte Carlo	1997–99	.945	1.654	—	.874
Prizm	1997	②	2.128	—	.688
OLDSMOBILE					
Achieva	1997–98	.874	2.244	—	.689
Alero	1999–2000	1.000	2.36	1.50	.874
Aurora	1997–98	1.000④	2.520	1.500	—
Cutlass	1997–98	1.000	2.362	—	.874
Cutlass Supreme	1997	.945	1.654	1.500	—
Eighty-Eight	1997–98	1.000④	2.500	—	.937
	1999	1.000④	2.500	—	.937
Intrigue	1998	1.000	2.500	1.500	—
LSS	1997–98	1.000④	2.500	—	.937
Regency	1997–98	1.000④	2.500	—	.937
PONTIAC					
Bonneville	1997–98	1.000④	2.500	—	.937
	1999	1.000④	2.500	—	.937
	2000	1.000	2.500	1.500	—
Firebird	1997–98	1.000	2.500	1.595	.810
Grand Am	1997–98	.874	2.244	—	.689
	1999–2000	1.000	2.36	1.50	.874
Grand Prix	1997–98	1.000	2.500	1.500	—
Sunfire	1997–2000	.874	2.244	—	.689

① — Primary piston, .960 inch; secondary piston, .812 inch.

② — Less ABS, .812 inch; w/ABS, .875 inch.

③ — Dual piston caliper.

④ — Master cylinder cannot be overhauled.

Saturn

INDEX

DESCRIPTION

These vehicles use a diagonally split hydraulic system, **Fig. 1.** This system combines the left front and right rear brake on one hydraulic circuit, while the right front and left rear are on the other.

Installed in master cylinder are integral brake proportioning valves, which limit the fluid pressure to the rear brakes after a predetermined rear brake pressure has been reached. These valves are used to minimize the occurrence of rear wheel lock-up when the brakes are applied and the vehicle is lightly loaded in the rear.

A brake fluid level sensor, located in the brake fluid reservoir, will activate the brake warning lamp if the brake fluid becomes low. After the brake fluid level is corrected and a moderately high brake pedal force is applied, the brake warning lamp should go off.

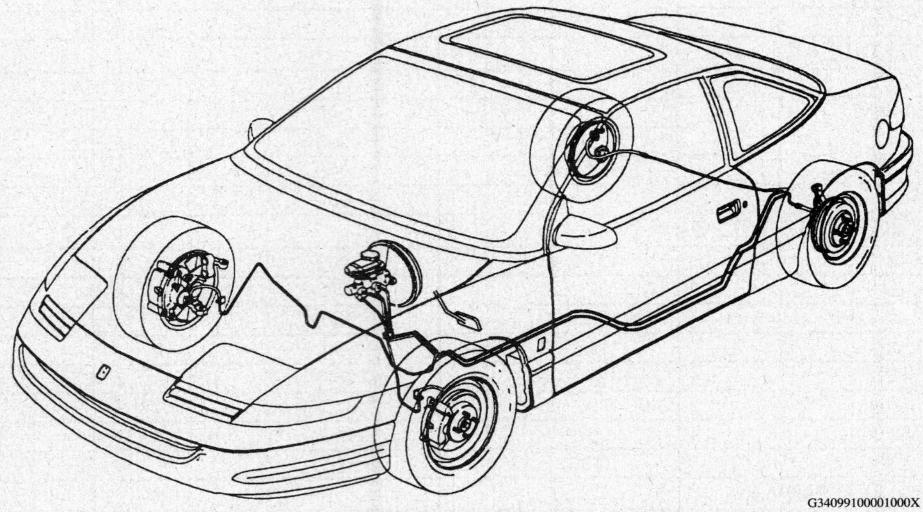

Fig. 1 Diagonally split brake system

TROUBLESHOOTING

When troubleshooting the hydraulic brake system, perform the following checks and inspections. If a fault still exists within the system, refer to the brake system diagnosis chart, **Fig. 2,** and the troubleshooting chart, **Fig. 3.**

ROAD TESTING

When testing brakes, ensure the road is level and dry. Test brakes at both light and heavy pedal pressure. Do not lock up brakes or slide tires during a brake test.

Check the tires on the vehicle before performing a brake test. Tires should be equally inflated, identical in size and of equal tread pattern. Excessive camber and caster will cause the brakes to pull. An overloaded vehicle will also brake erratically.

FLUID LEAKS

Start engine and depress the brake pedal. If the pedal gradually falls under constant pressure, the hydraulic system may be leaking. Raise and support vehicle and check all tubing lines and backing plates for signs of leakage. It may be necessary to lift or remove the carpeting or floor mats to check for booster or master cylinder leakage.

COMPONENT REPLACEMENT

MASTER CYLINDER

1. Remove brake fluid level sensor electrical connector from master cylinder reservoir.
2. Remove brake line fitting nuts from master cylinder. **Plug open lines and fittings to prevent brake fluid loss and contamination.**
3. Remove two master cylinder to brake booster attaching nuts and master cylinder.
4. Reverse procedure to install.

FLUID RESERVOIR

S-SERIES

1. Remove master cylinder from vehicle as described under " Master Cylinder" in this section.
2. Wipe reservoir cap clean, remove cap and inspect reservoir cap and diaphragm for cuts, nicks or deformation. Replace damaged parts as necessary.
3. Drain brake fluid from reservoir.
4. **On models equipped with anti-lock brakes,** remove modulator and motor pack from master cylinder.
5. **On all models,** remove brake fluid level sensor.
6. Place master cylinder in vice. **Do not clamp on master cylinder body.**
7. Drive out spring pins using a ⅛ inch punch, **Fig. 4.**
8. Pull reservoir out of cylinder body, then remove O-rings from grooves in reservoir bayonets, **Fig. 5.**
9. Clean reservoir with clean denatured alcohol and inspect reservoir for cracks or deformation. Replace reservoir if damaged.
10. Reverse procedure to install using new O-rings.

L-SERIES

1. Remove master cylinder from vehicle as described under " Master Cylinder" in this section.
2. Unclip reservoir hold down clamps, then remove reservoir by pulling upward.
3. Reverse procedure to install.

COMPONENT SERVICE

MASTER CYLINDER OVERHAUL

Disassemble

1. Remove master cylinder from vehicle as described under " Component Replacement."
2. Wipe reservoir cap clean, remove cap and inspect reservoir cap and diaphragm for cuts, nicks or deformation. Replace damaged parts as necessary.

18

X — Most Probable Cause(s)
• — Possible Causes

COMPLAINT–CONDITION / CAUSE	Low Brake Fluid Level	Leaking Brak Pipe or Connection	Leaking Wheel Cylinder or Piston Seal	Leaking Master Cylinder	Air in Brake System	Contaminated or Improper Brake Fluid	Leaking Vacuum System	Restricted Air Passage in Vacuum Booster	Damaged Vacuum Booster	Worn Out Brake Lining	Glazed Brake Lining	Uneven Brake Lining Wear	Incorrect Lining Material	Contaminated Brake Lining	Excessive Brake Lining Dust	Heat Spotted/Scored Drums/Rotors	Out–of–Round Brake Drums	Excessive Rotor Thickness Variation	Excessive Rotor/Hub Lateral Runout	Faulty Automatic Adjusters	Weak or Incorrect Brake Shoe Springs	Brake Asm. Bolts Missing or Loose	Insufficient Brake Shoe Guide Lubricant	Restricted Fluid Passage	Sticking Wheel Cylinder/Caliper Piston	Incorrect Stoplamp Switch Adjustment	Brake Pedal Linkage Interference/Binding	Improperly Adjusted Park Brake	Park Brake Cable Seized	Drum Tapered or Threaded	Operator Riding Brake Pedal	Improper Booster Pushrod Length	Caliper Not Sliding Freely
Excessive Brake Pedal Travel	•	•	•	•	X							•							•	•		•									•	•	•
Brake Pedal Travel Gradually Increases		X	X	X																											•		
Excessive Brake Pedal Effort	•						X	•	•	•	X		•		•									•	•		•				•		
Excessive Braking Action			•						•	•		•	•	X	X	•					•												
Brakes Slow to Respond						•	•	X	•		•													•	•		•						
Brakes Slow to Release						•		•	•												•		•	•	•		X		•			•	
Brakes Drag						•			•											•	•	•	•	•	•	X	•	X	•		•	X	X
Uneven Braking Action (Side–to–Side)		•	•							•	•	•	•	X	X	•				•	•	•	•	•	•								
Uneven Braking Action (Front–to–Rear)		•			•					•	•	•	•	X	X	•				•	•	•	•	•	•				•		•		
Scraping Noise from Brakes										•		•		•	•						X	•	X							X			•
Brakes Squeak During Application										•	•	•		•	•	•			•		•		X										
Brakes Squeak During Stop										•	•	•	•	•	X	•	•				X	•									•		
Brakes Pulsate (Roughness)																X	X	X	•			•				•							X
Brakes Groan at End of Stop										•			•	•	•	•						•											
Brake Warning Lamp Glows	X	•	•	•																													

G34099100002000A

Fig. 2 Brake diagnosis chart

Complaint/Condition	Possible Cause(s)	Correction(s)
Pedal Feel		
Excessive Pedal Travel	Air in brake system.	Bleed brake system.
	Front or rear brakes not adjusting to lining wear.	Check adjuster mechanism and replace or repair as needed.
	Leaking wheel cylinder or caliper piston seal.	Replace wheel cylinder or overhaul caliper
	Leaking at brake line or hose connections.	Tighten connection. Replace line or hose.
	Internal master cylinder seal leak.	Overhaul or replace master cylinder.
	Uneven lining wear or damaged lining.	Replace lining.
	Rotor or drum out of specifications (i.e. rotor too thin, parallelism, out of round, bell shaped etc.).	Replace rotor, or drum.
	Improper vacuum booster to master cylinder length.	Replace booster and pushrod.
Pedal Creeps Down	Internal master cylinder seal leak or defective master cylinder bore.	Repair or replace master cylinder.
	Leaking wheel cylinder or caliper piston seal.	Replace wheel cylinder or overhaul caliper
	Leaking at brake line or hose connections.	Tighten connection. Replace lines or hose.
	Damaged vacuum booster check valve or grommet.	Replace check valve and grommet.
Pedal Pulses	Rotor or drum out of specifications (i.e. lateral runout, parallelism, out of round, bell shaped etc.).	Replace or turn rotor or drum.
	Worn out linings or linings wearing unevenly.	Replace linings.
	Wheel bearings worn.	Replace wheel bearing.
	Damaged suspension, knuckle or axle.	Replace defective parts.

G34099100003010X

Fig. 3 Brake pedal feel troubleshooting chart (Part 1 of 6)

3. Drain brake fluid from reservoir.
4. **On models equipped with anti-lock brakes,** remove modulator and motor pack from master cylinder.
5. **On all models,** remove brake fluid level sensor.
6. Remove reservoir as described under "Component Replacement."
7. While depressing master cylinder piston, remove retainer clip, **Fig. 6.**
8. Apply low pressure non-lubricated compressed air into upper brake fluid output port, **Fig. 7.** This will facilitate removal of primary and secondary piston assemblies as well as spring and spring retainer.
9. Clean all parts with clean denatured alcohol. Dry with unlubricated, low pressure compressed air. Blow out all passages in cylinder body.
10. Inspect pistons and seals for nicks, cuts, cracks, wear or corrosion. Replace all worn or damaged parts.
11. Inspect master cylinder bore for scoring or corrosion. If cylinder bore is damaged, replace master cylinder. Do not hone master cylinder bore.

Assemble

1. Lubricate secondary seal and master cylinder bore with clean brake fluid.
2. Install spring and secondary piston assembly into master cylinder bore, **Fig. 8.**
3. Lubricate primary seal and master cylinder bore with clean brake fluid.
4. Install primary piston assembly into master cylinder bore.
5. While depressing master cylinder piston, install retainer clip.
6. Install reservoir as described under "Fluid Reservoir."
7. Install brake fluid level sensor.
8. **On models equipped with anti-lock brakes,** install modulator and motor pack from master cylinder.
9. **On all models,** install master cylinder into vehicle as described under "Component Replacement."

BRAKE SYSTEM BLEED

Brake fluid is corrosive to painted surfaces. Care must be taken not to allow brake fluid to come in contact with painted surfaces on vehicle.

Complaint/Condition	Possible Cause(s)	Correction(s)
Excessive Pedal Effort	Leaking or damaged vacuum booster (i.e. cut diaphragm, restricted vacuum hose, damaged vacuum check valve, cracked power piston, restricted air passages)	Replace booster.
	Worn out brake linings (glazed)	Replace linings.
	Damage to braking surface of rotor or drum.	Replace rotor or drum.
	Crimped brake line or collapsed brake hose.	Replace line or hose.
	Engine out of specifications.	Check engine to specification.
Pedal Goes to the Floor	Low fluid level, large amount of air in system.	Bleed brake system.
	Broken brake line or brake hose.	Replace line or hose.
	Cut, torn or nicked master cylinder secondary seals.	Repair or replace master cylinder.
	Brake pedal not connected to push rod.	Check connection and repair.
	Wheel cylinder or caliper piston falls out.	Check assembly and repair.

G34099100003020X

Fig. 3 Brake pedal feel troubleshooting chart (Part 2 of 6)

Complaint/Condition	Possible Cause(s)	Correction(s)
Performance		
Brake Pull Left/Right	Caliper pistons sticking.	Overhaul caliper and replace piston.
	Loose wheel bearings or suspension attachments.	Replace wheel bearings or tighten suspension attachments.
	Worn suspension components.	Replace suspension components.
	Loose steering or steering gear.	Repair or replace steering components.
	Uneven wear on tires, tires not properly inflated or incorrect tires for vehicle.	Check tire and replace if necessary.
	Uneven worn linings.	Replace linings.
	Front suspension out of line.	Align suspension.
	Restricted brake line or hose.	Replace line or hose.
Brakes Grab	Contaminated brake linings.	Replace linings.
	Damage to braking surface of rotors or drums.	Replace rotors or drums.
	Rotor or drum out of specifications (i.e. lateral runout, parallelism, out of round, bell shaped, etc.).	Replace or turn rotor or drum.
	Damaged vacuum booster.	Replace booster.
Brakes Drag	Caliper pistons stuck.	Overhaul caliper and replace piston.
	Corroded caliper bolts. Caliper will not retract.	Replace bolts and bolt boots.
	Compensating port or bypass hole in master cylinder clogged.	Clean master cylinder and rebuild.
	Worn or damaged drum brake return springs.	Replace drum brake springs.
	Contaminated or improper brake fluid, rubber seals are swollen.	Flush brake system and replace all rubber parts including hoses.
	Parking brake not releasing.	Check cable and cable attachments.
	Self-adjusters over adjusting for lining wear.	Overhaul or replace adjusters.
	Improper vacuum booster push rod length.	Gage booster push rod and replace if needed.
Brake Action Uneven (Front – Rear)	Uneven wear on tires, tires improperly inflated or incorrect tires installed.	Check tires and replace if needed.
	Proportioning valve not functioning properly.	Replace master cylinder.
	Linings wearing unevenly front to rear.	Replace linings.
	Fluid leak in system.	Check system for leaks and repair or replace components.
	Hot spots or worn surface on drum or rotor.	Replace drum or rotor.

G34099100003040X

Fig. 3 Brake pedal feel troubleshooting chart (Part 4 of 6)

Complaint/Condition	Possible Cause(s)	Correction(s)
Noise		
Squeal/Scrape While Not Braking	Worn linings, sensor scraping on rotor (normal).	Replace linings.
	Loose drum brake component (spring, lever, adjuster, etc.).	Check drum brake and repair.
	Loose front suspension attachments.	Tighten attachments or replace.
	Caliper interference with rotor.	Check clearance and repair.
	Bent or cracked suspension parts.	Replace components.
	Drum or rotor contacting backing plate or dust shield.	Check clearance and repair.
Squeal/Scrape While Braking	Linings worn out, shoe contacting drum or rotor.	Replace linings.
	Lack of lubrication on backing plate or on adjuster screw.	Lubricate backing plate or adjuster screw.
	Lack of lubrication on caliper sliding surfaces.	Lubricate.
	Lack of lubrication on brake pedal attachments.	Lubricate.
	Damage to insulator between disc brake shoe and caliper piston.	Replace insulator and pads as needed.
	Hot spots or worn surface on drum or rotor.	Replace rotor or drum.
	Weak hold down springs or worn drum brake components.	Replace drum brake springs.
Chatters/Rattles	Hot spots or worn surface on drum or rotor.	Replace drum or rotor.
	Rotor or drum out of specifications (i.e. lateral runout, parallelism, out of round, bell shaped, etc.).	Replace or turn rotor or drum.
	Lining contaminated with foreign substances.	Replace linings.
	Linings wearing unevenly.	Replace linings.
	Bent or loose brake shoes.	Replace show and linings.
	Weak or broken retractor springs.	Replace drum brake springs.
	Loose brake cable, brake line, or ABS wiring.	Check cable or line connection and tighten or replace as needed.
Groans (at/near stop)	Linings worn out.	Replace linings.
	Incorrect or damaged lining material.	Replace linings.
	Hot spots or worn surface on drum or rotor.	Replace drum or rotor.
	Cracked or bent knuckle or suspension parts.	Replace suspension component.
	Loose suspension.	Tighten suspension or replace.

G34099100003030X

Fig. 3 Brake pedal feel troubleshooting chart (Part 3 of 6)

Complaint/Condition	Possible Cause(s)	Correction(s)
Brakes Slow to Release	Caliper piston sticking.	Overhaul caliper and replace piston.
	Corroded caliper bolts. Caliper will not retract.	Replace bolts and bolt boots.
	Contaminated or improper brake fluid, rubber seals are swollen.	Flush brake system and replace all rubber parts including hoses.
	Worn caliper piston seals.	Overhaul calipers.
	Worn or damaged drum brake return springs.	Replace drum brake springs.
	Worn or damaged master cylinder seals.	Overhaul master cylinder.
	Damage to mechanical action of brake pedal.	Check pedal and repair or replace.
Slow Response/Excessive Stopping Distance	Rotor not turned to proper surface finish.	Check rotor surface finish and turn rotor or replace.
	Linings not adjusting properly, damaged self-adjusters or worn piston seal.	Overhaul drum brake or caliper.
	Caliper pistons sticking.	Overhaul caliper and replace piston.
	Worn or glazed linings.	Replace linings.
	Proportioning valve not functioning properly.	Replace master cylinder.
Odor	Linings over heated.	
	Lining contaminated with foreign substances.	Replace lining.
Poor Fuel Economy	Linings over heated.	
	Egg shaped drum or bent rotor/knuckle.	Replace drum, rotor or knuckle.

G34099100003050X

Fig. 3 Brake pedal feel troubleshooting chart (Part 5 of 6)

Complaint/Condition	Possible Cause(s)	Correction(s)
Telltale		
Red (Brake) Telltale On	Park brake on.	Release park brake.
	Low brake fluid level in master cylinder (check for leaks).	Fill reservoir. Check for leaks.
	Improperly adjusted park brake switch.	Check park brake switch connection and adjustment.
	Damaged park brake switch or switch circuit.	Replace switch or repair circuit.
	Antilock brake system (ABS) problem	Refer to ABS
Amber (ABS) Telltale On (Solid/Flashing)	Refer to ABS	
Parking Brake		
Does Not Hold	Park brake not adjusted properly.	Adjust park brake.
	Brakes not adjusting properly.	Check brake adjusters and repair or replace as needed.
	Linings worn out.	Replace linings.
	Linings contaminated with foreign material.	Replace linings.
	Cable disconnected from lever.	Connect cable.
	Lever bent or loose.	Replace lever.
	Cable slipping.	Replace cable.
Does Not Release	Park brake cables binding.	Check cable and cable attachments.
	Release lever broken or binding.	Replace park brake lever.
Parking Brake Lever Hard to Apply	Lack of lubrication on apply mechanism.	Lubricate apply mechanism.
	Park brake cables binding.	Check cables and cable attachments.

G34099100003060X

Fig. 3 Brake pedal feel troubleshooting chart (Part 6 of 6)

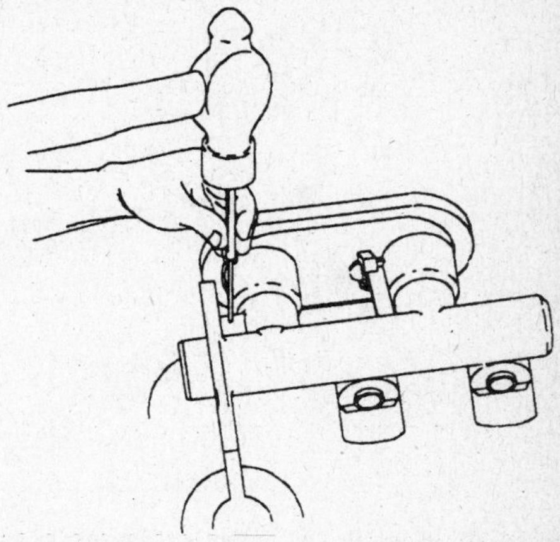

G34099100005000X

Fig. 4 Master cylinder reservoir spring pin removal. S-Series

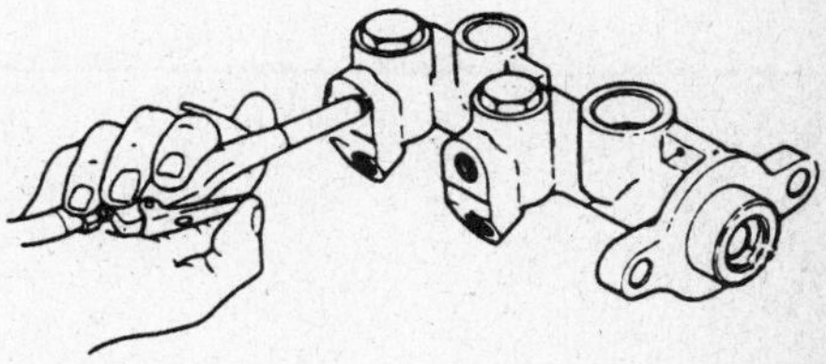

G34099100008000X

Fig. 7 Master cylinder piston removal

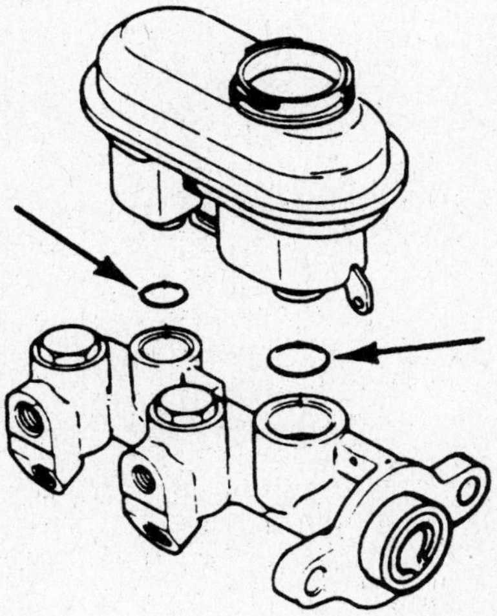

G34099100006000X

Fig. 5 Reservoir & O-ring removal from cylinder body. S-Series

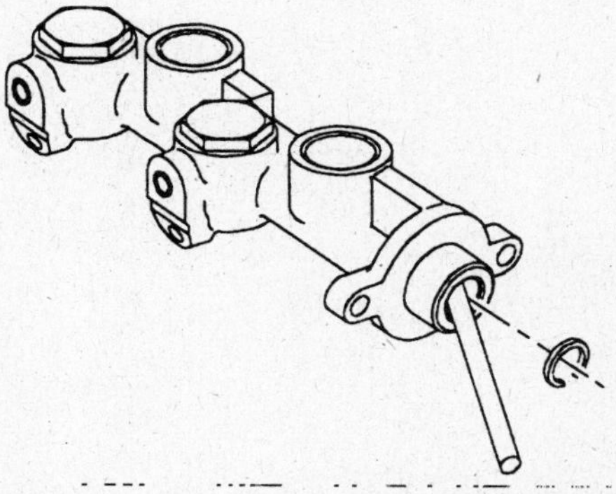

G34099100007000X

Fig. 6 Master cylinder retainer clip removal

When bleeding the brake system, always bleed right rear wheel circuit first, followed by the left front, left rear and, finally, right front.

MANUAL BLEED

1. Fill master cylinder reservoir with DOT 3 type brake fluid. Keep reservoir at least half full during bleeding procedure.
2. If master cylinder is suspected to have air trapped inside, it must be bled before bleeding brake lines. Bleed master cylinder as follows:
   a. Depress brake pedal slowly one time and hold.
   b. Loosen front brake line at master cylinder and allow brake fluid to flow from front master cylinder port, then tighten front brake line to master cylinder.
   c. Repeat sequence until all air is removed from master cylinder bore.
3. Loosen, then slightly retighten bleeder valves at all four wheels. Repair any broken, stripped or frozen valves at this time.
4. Proceed to appropriate wheel first and follow RR-LF-LR-RF bleeding sequence.
5. Place transparent tube over bleeder valve, then allow tube to hang down into transparent container. Ensure end of tube is submerged in clean brake fluid.
6. Instruct an assistant to slowly depress brake pedal one time and hold.
7. Crack open bleeder valve, purging air from cylinder. Retighten bleeder screw and slowly release pedal.
8. Repeat steps 6 and 7 until all air is bled from system.
9. Check fluid level after bleeding each wheel and fill as necessary.

PRESSURE BLEED

Pressure bleeding equipment must be the diaphragm type. It must have a rubber diaphragm between the air supply and the brake fluid to prevent air, moisture and other contaminants from entering brake system.

1. Clean brake fluid reservoir cap and area around cap, then remove cap.
2. Fill master cylinder reservoir with DOT 3 type brake fluid.
3. Install bleeder adapter tool No. SA9150BR, or equivalent, on brake fluid reservoir, **Fig. 9.**
4. Connect pressure bleeder to adapter and set pressure to 20–25 psi.
5. Loosen front brake line at master cylinder and allow brake fluid to flow from front master cylinder port until all air is bled, then tighten front brake line to master cylinder.
6. Open each bleeder valve until all air is bled, then tighten bleeder screw.
7. Remove pressure bleeder and ensure fluid level is full.

HYDRAULIC BRAKE SYSTEM FLUSH

If brake fluid is old, rusty or contaminated or whenever new parts are installed in hydraulic system, the system must be flushed. Bleed brakes, allowing at least one quart of clean brake fluid to pass through system. Any rubber parts in hydraulic system which were exposed to contaminated fluid must be replaced.

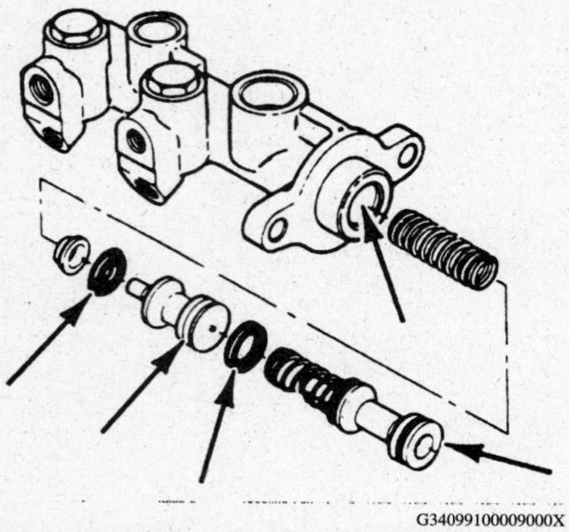

Fig. 8 Master cylinder piston & seal installation

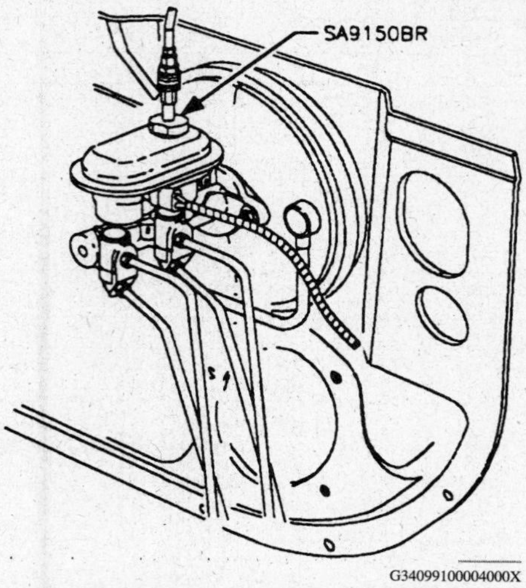

Fig. 9 Brake pressure bleeder adapter installation

POWER BRAKE UNITS

INDEX

APPLICATION CHART

Model	Power Brake Type
BUICK	
Century	AC-Delco Tandem Diaphragm
LeSabre	AC-Delco Tandem Diaphragm
Park Avenue	AC-Delco Tandem Diaphragm
Regal	AC-Delco Tandem Diaphragm
Riviera	AC-Delco Tandem Diaphragm
Skylark	AC-Delco Tandem Diaphragm
CADILLAC	
DeVille	AC-Delco Tandem Diaphragm
Eldorado	AC-Delco Tandem Diaphragm
Seville	AC-Delco Tandem Diaphragm
CHEVROLET/GEO	
Camaro	AC-Delco Tandem Diaphragm
Cavalier	AC-Delco Tandem Diaphragm
Corvette	AC-Delco Tandem Diaphragm
Impala	AC-Delco Tandem Diaphragm
Lumina	AC-Delco Tandem Diaphragm
Malibu	AC-Delco Tandem Diaphragm
Metro	AC-Delco Single Diaphragm
Monte Carlo	AC-Delco Tandem Diaphragm
Prizm	Toyota/GM Single Diaphragm
OLDSMOBILE	
Achieva	AC-Delco Tandem Diaphragm
Alero	AC-Delco Tandem Diaphragm
Aurora	AC-Delco Tandem Diaphragm
Cutlass	AC-Delco Tandem Diaphragm
Cutlass Supreme	AC-Delco Tandem Diaphragm
Intrigue	AC-Delco Tandem Diaphragm
LSS	AC-Delco Tandem Diaphragm
Regency	AC-Delco Tandem Diaphragm
88	AC-Delco Tandem Diaphragm
PONTIAC	
Bonneville	AC-Delco Tandem Diaphragm
Firebird	AC-Delco Tandem Diaphragm
Grand Am	AC-Delco Tandem Diaphragm
Grand Prix	AC-Delco Tandem Diaphragm
Sunfire	AC-Delco Tandem Diaphragm

PRECAUTIONS

1. After disassembling a power brake unit, soak all metal components in solvent.
2. Use only alcohol on components containing rubber. After the components have been thoroughly cleaned and rinsed in solvent, they should be washed again in clean alcohol before assembly.
3. Use compressed air to blow dirt and cleaning fluid from the recesses and internal passages.
4. Always use all the components furnished in the repair kit.
5. **Use extreme caution when disassembling power assist mechanisms. If internal spring tension is suddenly released it could cause damage or personal injury.**

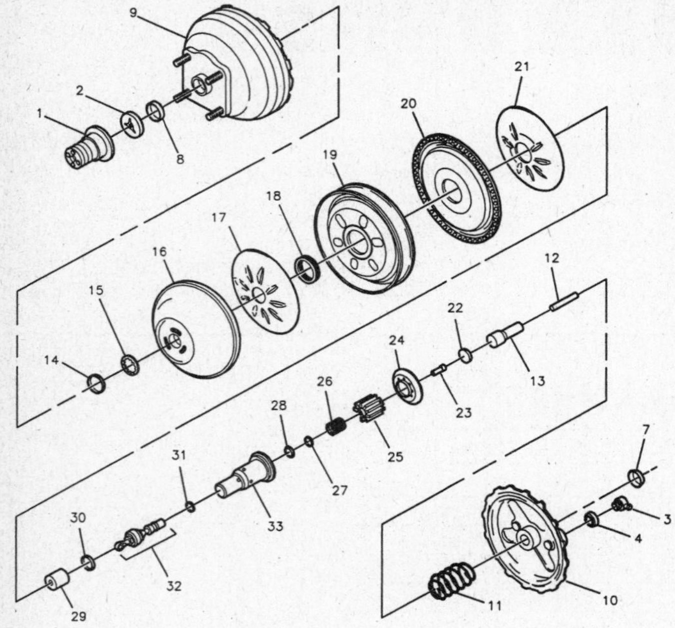

1	BOOT	11	RETURN SPRING	18	SECONDARY PISTON BEARING	26	AIR VALVE SPRING
2	AIR FILTER	12	PISTON ROD (GAGED)	19	HOUSING DIVIDER	27	REACTION BUMPER
3	VACUUM CHECK VALVE	13	REACTION RETAINER	20	SECONDARY DIAPHRAGM	28	RETAINING RING
4	GROMMET	14	AIR SILENCER	21	SECONDARY SUPPORT PLATE	29	SILENCER
7	FRONT HOUSING SEAL	15	DIAPHRAGM RETAINER	22	REACTION DISC	30	RETAINER
8	PRIMARY PISTON BEARING	16	PRIMARY DIAPHRAGM	23	REACTION PISTON	31	O-RING
9	REAR HOUSING	17	PRIMARY SUPPORT PLATE	24	REACTION BODY RETAINER	32	AIR VALVE PUSH ROD ASSEMBLY
10	FRONT HOUSING			25	REACTION BODY	33	POWER PISTON

GC4099700059000X

Fig. 1 Exploded view of AC-Delco tandem diaphragm booster

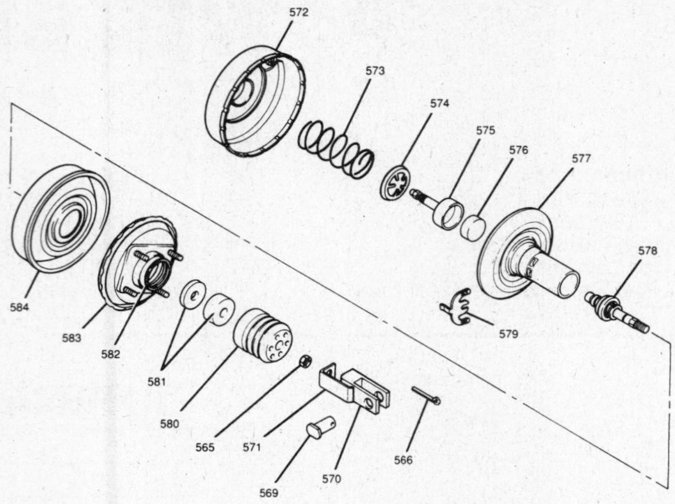

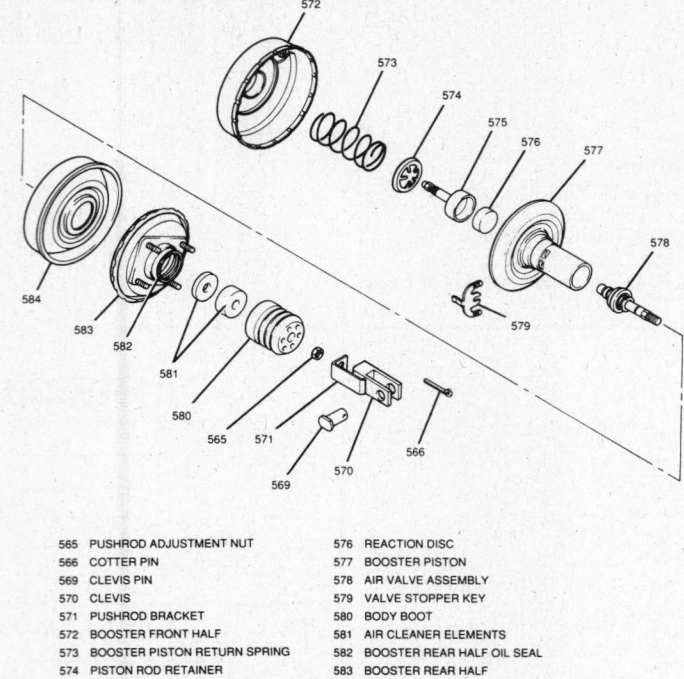

565	PUSHROD ADJUSTMENT NUT	576	REACTION DISC
566	COTTER PIN	577	BOOSTER PISTON
569	CLEVIS PIN	578	AIR VALVE ASSEMBLY
570	CLEVIS	579	VALVE STOPPER KEY
571	PUSHROD BRACKET	580	BODY BOOT
572	BOOSTER FRONT HALF	581	AIR CLEANER ELEMENTS
573	BOOSTER PISTON RETURN SPRING	582	BOOSTER REAR HALF OIL SEAL
574	PISTON ROD RETAINER	583	BOOSTER REAR HALF
575	PISTON ROD	584	DIAPHRAGM

GC4099400052000A

Fig. 2 Exploded view of AC-Delco single diaphragm booster

DESCRIPTION

AC-DELCO TANDEM DIAPHRAGM TYPE

This unit utilizes a vacuum power chamber, consisting of a front and rear shell, housing divider, front and rear diaphragm, plate assemblies, hydraulic pushrod and a diaphragm return spring, **Fig. 1.**

In normal operating mode, with service brakes in released position, the booster operates with vacuum on both sides of its diaphragms. When brakes are applied, air at atmospheric pressure is admitted to one side of each diaphragm to provide power assist. When the service brake is released, atmospheric air is shut off from one side of each diaphragm. The air is then drawn from the booster through the vacuum check valve to the vacuum source.

AC-DELCO SINGLE DIAPHRAGM TYPE

The AC-Delco power booster assembly, **Fig. 2,** is located along the bulkhead in the lefthand side engine compartment, between the brake pedal and master cylinder. It is designed to take advantage of the vacuum produced by the engine. The applied force created when brake pedal is applied is mechanically increased with assistance of engine vacuum.

TOYOTA/GM SINGLE DIAPHRAGM TYPE

The Toyota/GM single diaphragm type booster assembly, **Fig. 3,** is located between the master cylinder and brake pedal. When the brake pedal is depressed, the force is transmitted to the master cylinder piston through the valve operating rod, booster air valve, reaction disc and piston rod. The force of the booster piston is developed due to the pressure difference between the front and rear chambers.

TROUBLESHOOTING

BRAKES GRAB

1. Contaminated, worn or faulty brake linings.
2. Drum or brake rotor out-of-round.
3. Faulty brake booster.

HARD PEDAL/BRAKES INEFFICIENT

1. Contaminated, glazed or faulty brake linings.
2. Frozen caliper piston.
3. Faulty vacuum pump, or leak in booster vacuum supply system.
4. Faulty brake booster.

SLOW OR NO RELEASE

1. Faulty pushrod adjustment.
2. Bind in linkage.

ADJUSTMENTS

BRAKE PEDAL

TOYOTA/GM SINGLE DIAPHRAGM TYPE

1. With engine running and brake pedal in rest position, measure distance between face of pedal and floor mat.
2. **On 1997 models,** distance should be 5.65–6.05 inches.
3. **On 1998–99 models,** distance should be 5.850–6.244 inches.
4. **On all models,** if distance is not as specified, adjust pedal height as follows:
   a. Remove lefthand lower instrument panel trim section and air duct.
   b. Loosen stop lamp switch sufficiently to access for pedal adjustment.
   c. Loosen locknut and rotate pedal pushrod as needed to obtain specified pedal height, then tighten locknut.
   d. Adjust position of brake lamp switch so that plunger lightly contacts pedal stopper and brake lamps are off when pedal is released.
   e. Inspect pedal free travel.
5. With engine stopped, depress brake

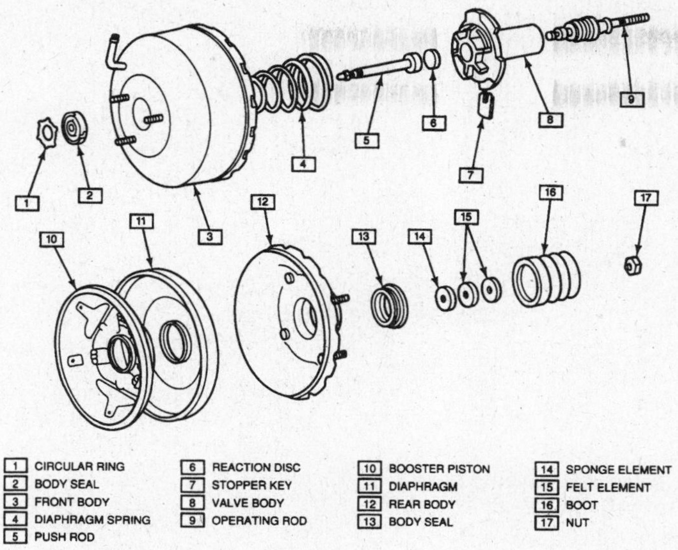

Fig. 3 Exploded view of Toyota/GM brake booster

pedal several times to ensure there is no vacuum pressure in booster.

6. Release pedal, then press pedal down until the beginning of resistance is felt, measuring the pedal travel. **Pedal free travel is the amount that the brake booster air valve is moved by the pedal pushrod.**
7. If pedal travel is not .12–.24 inch, adjust pedal freeplay as follows:
   a. Adjust pedal free travel by loosening locknut and rotating pedal pushrod.
   b. Ensure brake lamp switch and pedal height are properly adjusted, then start engine and confirm that free travel still exists.
   c. Inspect pedal reserve distance.
8. Release parking brake, then start engine.
9. Depress brake pedal with an applied force of 110 lbs., then measure distance from face of pedal to floor mat.
10. **On 1997 models,** pedal reserve distance should be at least 2.76 inches.
11. **On 1998–99 models,** pedal reserve distance should not be more than 3.35 inches.
12. **On all models,** if pedal reserve distance does not meet specifications, inspect and repair brake system as needed.

PUSHROD

Proper adjustment of the master cylinder pushrod is required to ensure proper operation of the power brake system. A pushrod that is too long will cause the master cylinder piston to close off the compensating port, preventing hydraulic pressure from being released and resulting in brake drag. A pushrod that is too short will cause excessive brake pedal travel and cause groaning noises to come from the booster when the brakes are applied. A properly adjusted pushrod that remains assembled to the booster with which it was matched during production should not require service adjustment. However, if the booster, master cylinder or pushrod are serviced, the pushrod may require adjustment.

There are two methods that can be used to inspect for proper pushrod length and installation. These are the gauge method and air method. Usually, if the power unit pushrod requires adjustment, use the power unit repair kit gauge. The gauge measures from the end of the pushrod to the power unit shell.

GAUGE METHOD

AC-Delco Tandem Diaphragm Type

The master cylinder pushrod length is fixed and is usually only inspected after the unit has been overhauled. This procedure can be performed with the unit removed from the vehicle if a suitable vacuum source is available.

1. Assemble booster unit and install pushrod, ensuring pushrod is fully seated.
2. Apply 20 inches or maximum engine vacuum to booster.
3. Position gauge tool No. J-37839, or equivalent over pushrod as shown in **Fig. 4.**
4. If output button length is not within limits of gauge, replace booster assembly.
5. Install power unit and inspect adjustment, ensuring master cylinder compensating port is open with engine running and brake pedal released.

AC-Delco Single Diaphragm Type

This unit is used on Metro models. The length of the booster piston rod is adjusted to provide specified clearance between the piston rod end and master cylinder piston. Before making an adjustment, push piston rod several times to ensure reaction disc is in place. Ensure gasket is installed to master cylinder and keep inside of booster at atmospheric pressure.

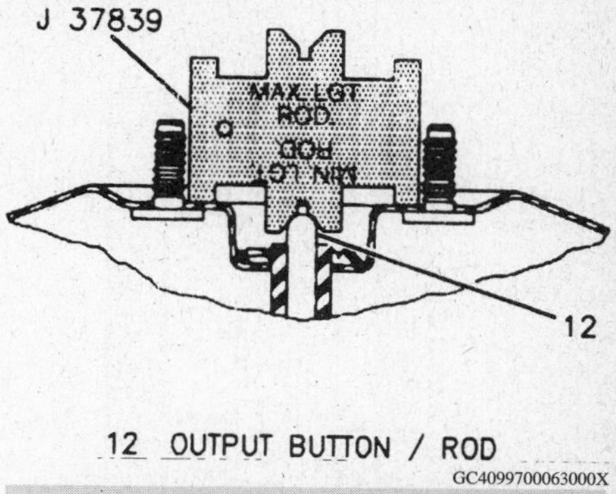

Fig. 4 Master cylinder measurement. AC-Delco tandem diaphragm type

1. Place booster pin rod gauge tool No. J-39567, or equivalent, on master cylinder (1) and push pin until it contacts piston (2), **Fig. 5.**
2. Turn tool upside down and place it on booster. Adjust booster piston rod length until rod end contacts pin head.
3. Adjust clearance by turning adjusting bolt (4) of piston rod (3), **Fig. 6.** There should be no clearance between the booster piston rod and the gauge tool (2).
4. Measure pushrod clevis length, which should be 3.92–3.96 inches, **Fig. 7.**
5. Adjust pushrod clevis length as required, then **torque** locknut to 18 ft. lbs.

Toyota/GM Single Diaphragm Type

This unit is used on Prizm models. The length of the booster piston rod is adjusted to provide specified clearance between the piston rod end and master cylinder piston. Before making an adjustment, push piston rod several times to ensure reaction disc is in place. Ensure gasket is installed to master cylinder and keep inside of booster at atmospheric pressure.

1. Place booster pin rod gauge tool No. J-39567, or equivalent, on master cylinder (1) and push pin until it contacts piston (2), **Fig. 5.**
2. Push gauge tool's pin down until it contacts master cylinder piston.
3. Remove gauge tool from master cylinder.
4. Turn tool upside down and place it on booster assembly.
5. Adjust clearance, **Fig. 6.** There should be no clearance between the booster piston rod and the gauge tool

AIR METHOD

1. Ensure master cylinder attaching nuts are tight.
2. Remove master cylinder filler cap.
3. With brake released, force compressed air into the hydraulic outlet of the master cylinder. **Regulate air pressure to a value of approximately 5 psi to prevent spraying brake fluid from master cylinder. Care must be taken not to allow brake**

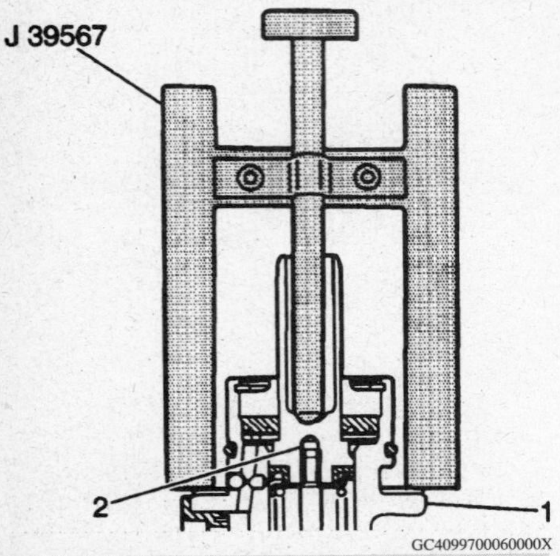

Fig. 5 Master cylinder adjustment tool. AC-Delco & Toyota/GM single diaphragm type

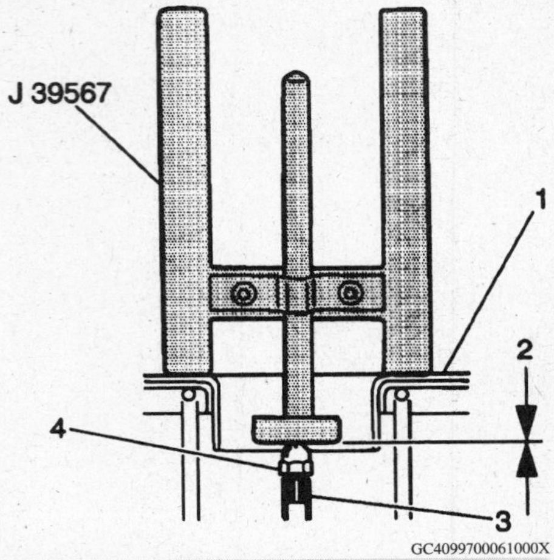

Fig. 6 Booster piston rod adjustment. AC-Delco & Toyota/ GM single diaphragm type

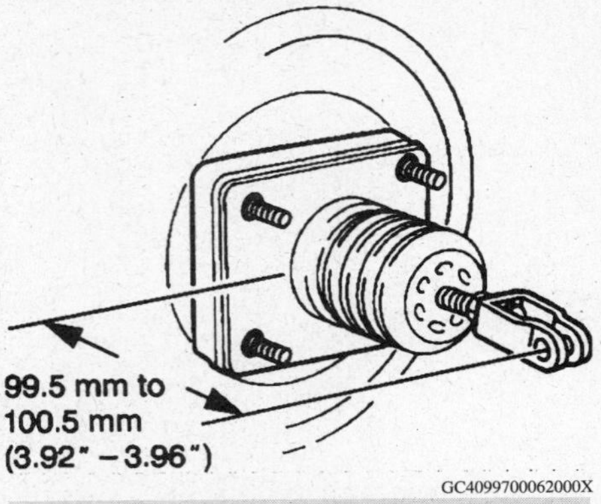

Fig. 7 Pushrod clevis length adjustment. AC-Delco & Toyota/ GM single diaphragm type

fluid to contact painted surfaces of vehicle, skin or eyes, as damage or personal injury will result.

4. If air passes through the compensating port, which is the smaller of the two holes in the bottom of the master cylinder reservoir, the adjustment is satisfactory.
5. If air does not flow through the compensating port, adjust the pushrod as required, either by means of the adjustment screw (if provided) or by adding shims between the master cylinder and power unit shell until the air flows freely.
6. Connect brake lines and bleed system.

GENERAL SERVICE

Two basic types of power assist mechanisms are used: vacuum assist diaphragm assemblies, which use engine vacuum or, in some cases vacuum pressure developed by an external vacuum pump. The second type is a hydraulic pressure assist mechanism, which use pressure developed by an external pump (usually the power steering pump). Both systems act to increase the force exerted on the master cylinder piston by the operator. This in turn increases the hydraulic pressure delivered to the wheel cylinders while decreasing driver effort required to obtain acceptable stopping performance.

Vacuum assist units are similar in operation and get their energy by opposing engine vacuum to atmospheric pressure. A piston and cylinder, flexible diaphragm (bellows) utilize this energy to provide brake assistance. The fundamental difference between these types of vacuum assist systems lies simply in how the diaphragm within the power unit is suspended when the brakes are not applied.

In order to properly diagnose vacuum assist system malfunctions it is important to know whether the diaphragm within a power unit is air suspended or vacuum suspended. Air-suspended units are under atmospheric pressure until the brakes are applied. Engine vacuum is then admitted, causing the piston or diaphragm to move (or the bellows to collapse). Vacuum-suspended types are balanced with engine vacuum until the brake pedal is depressed, allowing atmospheric pressure to unbalance the unit and apply force to the brake system.

Regardless of whether the brakes are vacuum or hydraulically assisted, certain general service procedures apply. Only specified, clean brake fluid should be used in brake systems. On hydro-boost systems, use of the specified hydraulic fluid in the boost circuit is essential to proper system operation. Care must be taken not to mix the fluids of the two separate operating circuits. Use of improper fluids or contaminated fluid will cause damage to the seals and valves.

POWER BRAKE UNIT SERVICE

This brake booster is not serviceable and should be replaced as an assembly.

AUTOMATIC TRANSMISSIONS/ TRANSAXLES

TABLE OF CONTENTS

Application Chart

Model	Type
1997	
Achieva, Grand Am & Skylark	4T60-E
Aurora, DeVille, Eldorado & Seville	4T80-E
Bonneville, Eighty-Eight, LSS, LeSabre, Park Avenue & Regency	4T60-E
Camaro & Firebird	4L60-E
Catera	4L30-E
Cavalier & Sunfire	3T40 & 4T40-E
Century & Cutlass Supreme	4T60-E
Corvette	4L60-E
Cutlass & Malibu	4T40 & 4T40–E
Grand Prix, Lumina, Monte Carlo & Regal	4T60-E & 4T65-E
Metro	Aisin-Seiki
Prizm	A131L/A245E
Riviera	4T65-E
Saturn	S-Series 4-Speed
1998	
Achieva, Grand Am & Skylark	4T60-E
Aurora, DeVille, Eldorado & Seville	4T80-E
Bonneville, Eighty-Eight, LeSabre, LSS, Park Avenue & Regency	4T65-E
Catera	4L30-E
Camaro & Firebird	4L60-E
Cavalier & Sunfire	3T40 & 4T40-E
Century	4T60-E
Corvette	4L60-E
Cutlass & Malibu	4T40-E
Intrigue	4T65-E

Continued

Model	Type
1998	
Grand Prix, Lumina, Monte Carlo & Regal	4T60-E & 4T65-E
Metro	Aisin-Seiki
Prizm	A131/A245-E
Riviera	4T65-E
Saturn	S-Series 4-Speed
1999	
Alero & Grand Am	4T40-E/4T45-E
Aurora, DeVille, Eldorado & Seville	4T80-E
Bonneville, Eighty-Eight, LeSabre, LSS & Park Avenue	4T60-E/4T65-E
Camaro & Firebird	4L60-E
Catera	4L30-E
Cavalier & Sunfire	4T40-E/3T40
Century	3T40/4T60-E/4T65-E
Corvette	4L60-E
Cutlass & Malibu	4T40-E
Grand Prix	4T60-E/4T65-E
Intrigue	4T65-E
Lumina & Monte Carlo	3T40, 4T60-E & 4T65-E
Metro	Aisin-Seiki
Prizm	A245E/A131L
Regal	4T60-E/4T65-E
Riviera	4T65-E
Saturn	S-Series 4-Speed
2000	
Alero & Grand Am	4T40-E/4T45-E
Bonneville, LeSabre & Park Avenue	4T65-E
Camaro & Firebird	4L60-E
Catera	4L30-E
Cavalier & Sunfire	4T40-E/3T40
Century	4T65-E
Corvette	4L60-E
DeVille, Eldorado & Seville	4T80-E
Grand Prix	4T65-E
Intrigue	4T65-E
Impala, Lumina & Monte Carlo	4T65-E
Malibu	4T40-E
Metro	Aisin-Seiki
Prizm	A245E/A131L
Regal	4T65-E
Saturn	L-Series 4-Speed
	S-Series 4-Speed

Aisin Warner A131L Automatic Transaxle

NOTE: On Air Bag Equipped Models, Refer To " Air Bag System Precautions" Located In The Front Of This Manual For System Disarming & Arming Procedures.

NOTE: Refer To "Computer Relearn Procedures " Located In The Front Of This Manual For Computer Relearn Procedures.

INDEX

PRECAUTIONS

AIR BAG SYSTEMS

Refer to "Air Bag System Precautions" in the front of this manual for system disarming and arming procedures.

BATTERY GROUND CABLE

Prior to service, disconnect battery ground cable and isolate as required.

IDENTIFICATION

The transaxle identification number (1) is located on the top of the transaxle case above the left drive axle, **Fig. 1.**

DESCRIPTION

The torque converter is equipped with an integral lock-up clutch. For higher performance, greater fuel economy and quietness, a high efficiency torque converter, wider gear ratio, compact high-precision valve body, high efficiency oil pump and a light weight durable integral transaxle case are used.

TROUBLESHOOTING

Refer to **Figs. 2 through 13** for troubleshooting.

MAINTENANCE

Refer to "Lubricant Data Chart" in the appropriate chassis chapter of this manual for transmission fluid specifications.

FLUID CHECK

1. Start engine and allow transaxle fluid to reach 158–176°F.
2. Position vehicle on level surface and set parking brake.
3. With engine idling and brake pedal depressed, move shift lever through all positions.
4. Remove transaxle dipstick, wipe clean and replace.
5. Remove dipstick again. Ensure fluid is at HOT level.
6. Refer to "Lubricant Data Chart" for capacities.

FLUID CHANGE

Refer to "Lubricant Data Chart" in the appropriate chassis chapter of this manual for transmission fluid specifications.

1. Raise and support vehicle.
2. Remove splash shield.
3. Place a suitable container under transaxle, then remove plug and drain fluid.
4. Remove bolts, oil pan and gasket.
5. Remove bolts, filter screen and gasket.
6. Clean screen and magnets with suitable solvent and dry thoroughly.
7. Install new gasket, screen and mounting bolts. Tighten bolts to specifications.
8. Install new gasket, oil pan and mounting bolts. Tighten bolts to specifications.
9. Install new drain plug and tighten to specifications.
10. Install splash shield, then lower vehicle and fill transaxle.
11. Start engine and move selector lever through all ranges, ending in P position.
12. With engine idling, check and adjust fluid level.

ADJUSTMENTS

THROTTLE VALVE (TV) CABLE

1. Inspect TV cable for deflection or looseness.
2. Ensure TV is in fully closed position.
3. Measure TV cable boot to inner cable stopper (4) clearance using a feeler gauge, **Fig. 14.** If clearance is more than .04 inch, proceed to next step.
4. Adjust TV cable boot to inner cable stopper clearance by turning adjustment nuts (1,2) until clearance is as specified. Tighten TV cable adjusting nut to specification.

IN-VEHICLE REPAIRS

VALVE BODY, REPLACE

Removal

1. Raise and support vehicle.
2. Clean area around oil pan, then drain transmission fluid.
3. Remove oil pan, gasket and oil strainer.
4. Remove mounting bolts, bracket and oil apply tube.
5. Remove oil tubes using a suitable screwdriver and manual detent spring.
6. Remove mounting bolts and manual valve assembly.
7. Remove valve body to cable bracket retaining bolt, then disconnect throttle cable.
8. Remove mounting bolts, valve body, governor, apply gasket and governor oil gasket.

Installation

1. Install governor oil gasket, governor

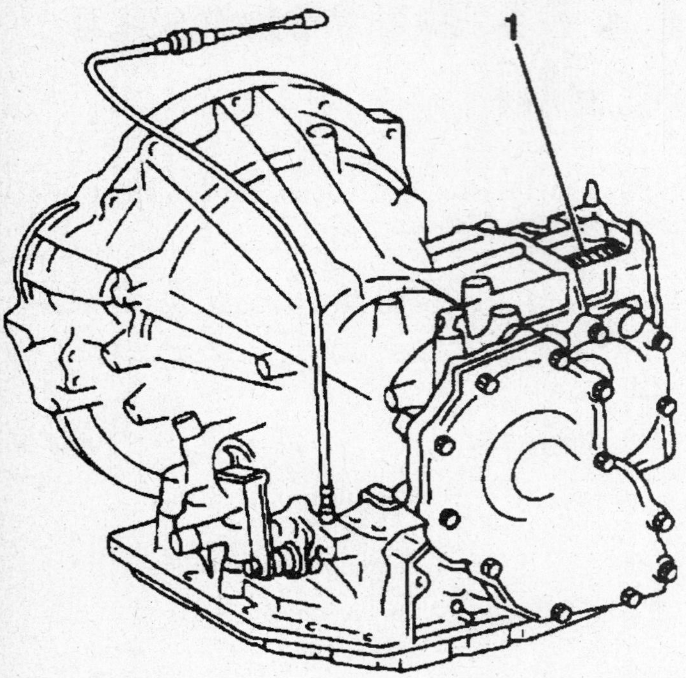

Fig. 1 Transaxle identification number plate location

Problem	Action
Low fluid.	Add fluid.
TV cable out of adjustment, binding or damaged.	Adjust or replace throttle valve cable.
Shift select cable out of adjustment, biding or damaged.	Adjust or replace shift select cable.
Manual valve binding or sticking.	Inspect valve body.
Throttle valve binding or sticking.	Inspect valve body.
B2 control valve binding or sticking.	Inspect valve body.
Accumulator(s) pistons damaged or leaking.	Inspect accumulator pistons.
Accumulator(s) seals cut or damaged.	Inspect accumulator seals.
Accumulator(s) broken or distorted springs.	Inspect accumulator springs.
Incorrect line pressure.	Perform line pressure diagnosis.

GC5029800944000X

Fig. 2 Harsh engagement into any drive range

and governor apply gasket.

2. Hold valve body in place, manually retain cam in downward position and slip cable end into slot.
3. Position valve body into place and install, then finger tighten mounting bolts. Tighten bolts to specification. **retaining bolt lengths (mm) are indicated in Fig. 15.**
4. Align manual valve with pin on manual valve lever and install manual valve body.
5. Insert and finger tighten retaining bolts. Tighten to specification. **Retaining bolt lengths (mm) are indicated in Fig. 16.**
6. Install detent spring, then insert and finger tighten retaining bolts. Tighten retaining bolts to specification.
7. Ensure manual lever is in contact with center of roller at tip of detent spring and install oil tubes.
8. Install apply tube bracket and oil strainer.
9. Insert magnet into oil pan, then install oil pan with new gasket.
10. Insert oil pan retaining bolts and tighten to specification.
11. Install drain plug with new gasket and tighten to specification.
12. Fill transaxle to specifications and ensure proper fluid level.

TV CABLE, REPLACE

Removal

1. Loosen TV cable jam nuts.
2. Disconnect throttle cable from bracket and throttle plate.
3. Remove neutral start and back-up switch.
4. Remove valve body as described in this section, then the throttle cable end from throttle pressure valve cam.
5. Pull cable from transaxle case.

Installation

1. Insert cable into transaxle case and install retaining plate and bolt.
2. Install valve body as described in this section.
3. Bend cable to a radius of approximately 7.87 inches, **Fig. 17.**
4. Lightly pull inner cable from housing until a slight resistance is felt and hold in position.
5. Stake stopper onto inner cable so that .031–.059 inch clearance exists between stop and cable housing. **Cable stop is not staked in place on replacement cable.**
6. Connect throttle cable to throttle linkage and adjust cable as described in this section.
7. Install neutral safety switch and manual shift lever.
8. Adjust switch as described in this section.
9. Ensure transaxle fluid level is to specifications.

GOVERNOR VALVE, REPLACE

1. Raise and support vehicle.
2. Remove transaxle cover and lefthand driveshaft.
3. Remove governor cover and O-ring.
4. Remove governor body with thrust washer.
5. Remove washer and governor body adapter.
6. Reverse procedure to install.

SECOND BRAKE SERVO ASSEMBLY, REPLACE

Removal

1. Raise and support vehicle.
2. Drain fluid from transaxle.
3. Remove shift cable bracket at transaxle.
4. Install second brake servo compressor tool No. J-35549-A, or equivalent, then compress second brake servo.
5. Remove second brake servo snap ring and second brake servo compressor.
6. Remove cover.
7. Remove piston and outer spring.

Installation

1. Insert piston, less outer spring, then install snap ring.
2. Install brake apply rod tool No. J-35679, or equivalent, and observe groove on plunger of tool.
3. Push button on tool, **Fig. 18.** This allows tool to push brake apply rod into case. If groove is visible, piston stroke is correct (.059–.118 inch). If stroke is greater than specified, replace piston rod with 2.870 inch or 2.811 inch rod as needed.
4. Remove snap ring, then install piston and outer spring.
5. Install spring compressor tool No. J-35549, or equivalent, to compress spring, then insert snap ring.
6. Install cover and shift cable bracket.
7. Lower vehicle.

BRAKE TRANSMISSION SHIFT INTERLOCK, REPLACE

The automatic transmission control lever solenoid is part of the brake transmission shift interlock system. The solenoid prevents the vehicle from shifting out of Park position unless brake is applied.

1. Remove rear console assembly.
2. Disconnect electrical connector from shift interlock solenoid.
3. Remove indicator bulb.
4. Remove two shift indicator cover retaining bolts.
5. Raise and rotate shift indicator cover to access two retaining screws on shift interlock solenoid.
6. Remove two shift interlock retaining screws, then the shift interlock solenoid.
7. Reverse procedure to install.

MANUAL SELECTOR, REPLACE

1. Remove center console.

Problem	Action
Fluid level is low.	Add fluid.
TV cable is out of adjustment, binding or damaged.	Adjust or replace throttle valve cable..
Shift select cable is out of adjustment, biding or damaged.	Adjust or replace shift select cable.
Throttle valve is binding or sticking.	Inspect valve body.
Primary regulator valve is binding or sticking.	Inspect valve body.
Accumulator pistons are damaged or leaking.	Inspect accumulator pistons.
Accumulator seals are cut or damaged.	Inspect accumulator seals.
Accumulator springs are broken or distorted.	Inspect accumulator springs.
Forward clutch discs are worn.	Replace forward clutch discs.
Forward clutch piston or seal is leaking or damaged.	Inspect forward clutch piston seal.
Input shaft O-rings are cut or damaged.	Inspect input shaft O-ring.
One-way clutch is not holding or damaged.	Inspect one-way clutch.
Fluid pressure is incorrect.	Perform line pressure diagnosis.

GC5029800945000X

Fig. 3 Slips in first gear

Problem	Action
Throttle valve cable is out of adjustment, binding or damaged.	Adjust or replace throttle valve cable.
Throttle valve is binding or sticking.	Inspect valve body.
1-2 shift valve is binding or sticking.	Inspect valve body.
Primary regulator valve is binding or sticking.	Inspect valve body.
Intermediate servo seals are cut or damaged.	Inspect intermediate servo seals.
Intermediate servo piston is binding or sticking.	Inspect intermediate servo piston.
2nd brake band is worn or out of alignment.	Inspect 2nd brake band.
Fluid pressure is incorrect	Perform line pressure diagnosis.

GC5029800946000X

Fig. 4 First gear only

Problem	Action
Fluid level is low.	Add fluid.
Throttle valve cable out of adjustment, binding or damaged.	Adjust or replace throttle valve cable.
Throttle valve binding or sticking.	Inspect valve body.
1-2 shift valve binding or sticking.	Inspect valve body.
Primary regulator valve binding or sticking.	Inspect valve body.
Intermediate servo seals are cut or damaged.	Inspect valve body.
Intermediate servo piston is binding or sticking.	Inspect intermediate servo seals.
Intermediate servo piston rod is not engaged.	Inspect intermediate servo piston.
2nd brake band is worn or out of alignment.	Inspect 2nd brake band.
Internal damage to torque converter.	Replace torque converter.
Forward clutch discs are worn.	Replace forward clutch discs.
Forward clutch piston or seal are leaking or damaged.	Inspect forward clutch piston and seal.
Input shaft O-rings are cut or damaged.	Inspect input shaft O-rings.
Fluid pressure is incorrect.	Perform line pressure diagnosis.

GC5029800947000X

Fig. 5 Slipping or rough 1-2 shift

Problem	Action
Fluid level is low.	Add fluid.
Throttle valve cable out of adjustment, binding or damaged.	Adjust or replace throttle valve cable.
Throttle valve binding or sticking.	Inspect valve body.
2-3 shift valve binding or sticking.	Inspect valve body.
Primary regulator valve binding or sticking.	Inspect valve body.
Intermediate servo piston binding or sticking.	Inspect intermediate servo seals.
Intermediate servo piston rod not engaged.	Inspect intermediate servo piston.
2nd brake band not releasing.	Inspect 2nd brake band.
Torque converter internal damage.	Replace torque converter.
Direct clutch discs are worn.	Replace direct clutch discs.
Direct clutch piston or seal is leaking or damaged.	Inspect direct clutch piston and seal.
Fluid pressure is incorrect.	Perform line pressure diagnosis.

GC5029800948000X

Fig. 6 No 2-3 shift or 2-3 shift slipping

Problem	Action
Fluid level is low.	Add fluid.
Throttle valve cable out of adjustment, binding or damaged.	Adjust or replace throttle valve cable.
Valve body spacer plate or gaskets damaged or not positioned correctly.	Inspect valve body.
Throttle valve is binding or sticking.	Inspect valve body.
Check balls omitted or not positioned correctly.	Inspect valve body.
Internal damage to torque converter.	Replace torque converter.
Direct clutch piston or seal leaking or damaged.	Inspect direct clutch piston and seal.
Fluid pressure is incorrect.	Perform the line pressure diagnosis.

GC5029800949000X

Fig. 7 High or low shift points

Problem	Action
Throttle valve is cable out of adjustment, binding or damaged.	Adjust or replace throttle valve cable.
Throttle valve is binding or sticking.	Inspect valve body.
1-2 shift valve is binding or sticking.	Inspect valve body.
2-3 shift valve is binding or sticking.	Inspect valve body.
Primary regulator is valve binding or sticking.	Inspect valve body.
Valve springs are broken or distorted.	Inspect valve body.
Valve body casting is damaged or porous.	Inspect valve body.
Intermediate servo piston is binding or sticking.	Inspect intermediate servo piston.
Intermediate servo piston seals are cut or damaged.	Inspect intermediate servo piston seals.
Intermediate servo piston rod is binding.	Inspect intermediate sero piston rod.
2nd brake band is worn or out of alignment.	Replace 1st-reverse brake clutch discs.
1st-reverse brake clutch discs worn.	Replace 1st-reverse brake clutch.
1st-reverse brake piston or seal is leaking or damaged.	Inspect 1st-reverse brake piston.
One-way clutch not holding or damaged.	Inspect one-way clutch.

GC5029800950000X

Fig. 8 No part throttle or delayed downshifts

Problem	Action
Shift select cable is out of adjustment, binding or damaged.	Adjust or replace shift select cable.
Manual valve is binding or sticking.	Inspect valve body.
1-2 shift valve is binding or sticking.	Inspect valve body.
2-3 shift valve is binding or sticking.	Inspect valve body.
Valve springs are broken or distorted.	Inspect valve body.
Valve body casting is damaged or porous.	Inspect valve body.
Intermediate servo piston is binding or sticking.	Inspect intermediate servo piston.
Intermediate servo piston seals are cut or damaged.	Inspect intermediate servo piston seals.
Intermediate servo piston rod is binding.	Inspect intermediate servo piston rod.
2nd brake band is worn or out of alignment.	Inspect 2nd brake band.
1st-reverse brake clutch disc worn.	Replace 1st-reverse brake clutch discs.
1st-reverse brake piston or seal leaking or damaged.	Inspect 1st-reverse brake piston.
One-way clutch not holding or damaged.	Inspect one-way clutch.

GC5029800951000X

Fig. 9 No engine braking or 3-2-1 manual downshift

Problem	Action
Fluid level is low.	Add fluid.
Shift select cable is out of adjustment, binding or damaged.	Adjust or replace shift select cable.
Valve body spacer plate or gaskets not positioned correctly or damaged.	Inspect valve body.
Check balls omitted or not positioned correctly.	Inspect valve body.
Manual valve binding or sticking.	Inspect valve body.
Manual valve link disconnected.	Inspect manual valve link.
Direct clutch piston or seals leaking or damaged.	Inspect direct clutch piston and seals.
Incorrect line pressure.	Perform Line Pressure Test diagnosis.

GC5029800952000X

Fig. 10 No reverse or slips in reverse

Problem	Action
Fluid pump is internally leaking.	Inspect fluid pump.
Fluid pump drive and driven gears worn or damaged.	Repair fluid pump drive and driven gears.
Fluid pump cover seal rings cut or damaged.	Inspect fluid pump seal rings.
Fluid pump body or cover casting is porous or damaged.	Repair/replace fluid pump.
Throttle valve cable out of adjustment, binding or damaged.	Adjust or replace throttle valve cable.
Throttle valve cable link is loose or disconnected.	Inspect throttle valve cable link.
Valve body spacer plate or gaskets not positioned correctly or damaged.	Inspect valve body.
Check balls omitted or not positioned correctly or damaged.	Inspect valve body.
Manual valve binding or sticking.	Inspect valve body.
Manual valve link is disconnected.	Inspect manual valve link.
Primary regulator valve binding or sticking.	Inspect valve body.
Case internal leak in forward clutch fluid circuit.	Repair and replace case.
Case internal leak in direct clutch fluid circuit.	Repair and replace case.
Case fluid passages blocked or restricted.	Repair and replace case.

GC5029800953000X

Fig. 11 Fluid pressure high or low

Problem	Action
Shift select cable is out of adjustment, binding or damaged.	Adjust shift select cable.
Parking lock rod, pawl or spring is faulty.	Inspect parking lock assembly.

GC5029800954000X

Fig. 12 No Park or ratcheting noise in Park

Problem	Action
Low or no fluid.	Add fluid.
Shift cable out of adjustment, binding or damaged.	Adjust or replace select cable.
Parking lock pawl mechanism locked or frozen.	Inspect parking lock pawl.
Broken torque converter to flywheel bolts.	Replace bolts.
Torque converter stator one-way clutch no holding.	Replace torque converter.
Torque converter failure.	Replace torque converter.
Valve body spacer plate or gaskets improper position or damaged.	Inspect valve body.
Check balls omitted or improper position.	Inspect valve body.
Manual valve binding or sticking.	Inspect valve body.
Manual valve link disconnected.	Inspect manual valve linkage.
Incorrect line pressure.	Perform line pressure diagnosis.

GC5029800955000X

Fig. 13 Unable to run in all ranges

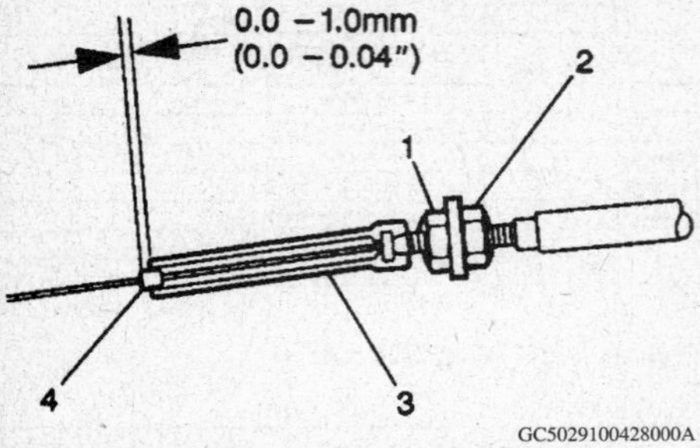

Fig. 14 TV cable adjustment

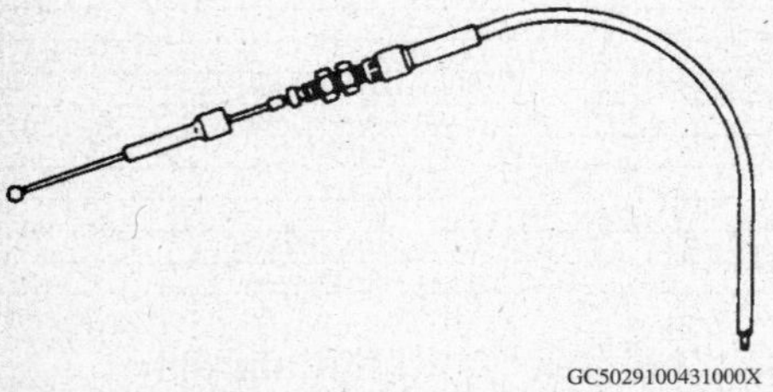

Fig. 17 TV cable positioning for stopper installation

2. Remove one spring clip (2), then the shift select cable (1) from manual selector lever, **Fig. 19.**
3. Remove one E-clip (2) and shift select cable (1) from manual selector base, **Fig. 20.**
4. Remove four manual selector retaining bolts, then the manual selector.
5. Reverse procedure to install. Tighten manual selector bolts to specification.

TRANSAXLE

REPLACE

1. Disconnect Intake Air Temperature (IAT) sensor electrical connector.
2. Remove air cleaner cover and filter.
3. Loosen air cleaner intake tube clamp.
4. Remove three air cleaner retaining bolts, then the air cleaner.
5. Disconnect Park/Neutral Position (PNP) switch electrical connector.
6. Disconnect solenoid wire harness electrical connector.
7. Remove ground strap from transaxle case, then loosen TV cable locknut.
8. Disconnect throttle cable from throttle linkage and TV cable bracket.
9. Disconnect vehicle speed sensor electrical connector.
10. Remove shift select cable from manual lever.
11. Remove E-clip, then the shift select cable from shift select cable bracket.
12. Remove TV cable guide bracket from transaxle case.
13. Remove two upper transaxle to engine retaining bolts.
14. Remove starter.
15. Install universal support fixture tool No. J–28467-A, or equivalent.
16. Remove two retaining bolts, then the left transaxle mounting bracket reinforcement from transaxle.
17. Remove one left transaxle mounting bracket retaining bolt.
18. Raise and support vehicle, then place

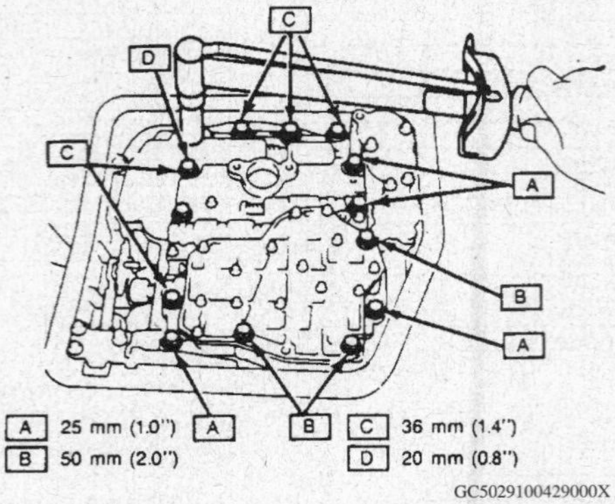

Fig. 15 Valve body bolt identification

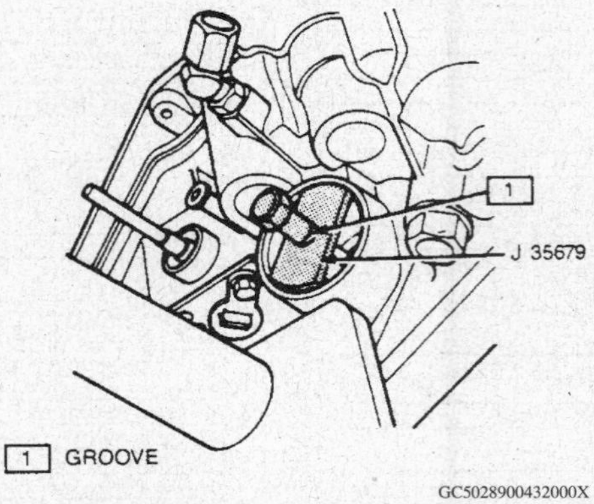

Fig. 18 Second brake servo plunger installation

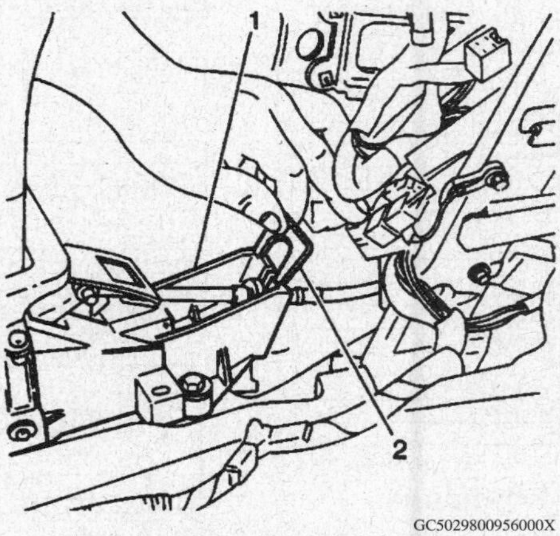

Fig. 20 Shift cable to selector base removal

a suitable container under transaxle.

19. Remove transaxle drain plug and drain fluid.
20. Remove differential drain plug and drain fluid from differential case.
21. Remove left and right splash shields from vehicle.
22. Remove two hose clamps, then the inner and outer fluid cooler hoses from fluid cooler pipes at transaxle. **Plug fluid cooler hoses to prevent fluid leakage.**
23. Remove two retaining bolts from left transaxle mounting bracket.
24. Remove front wheels.

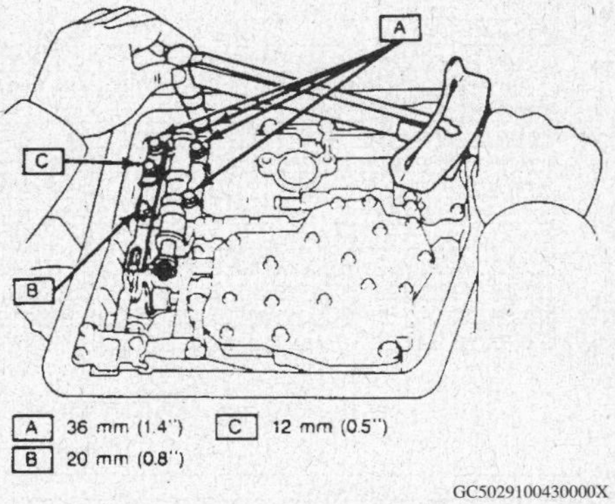

Fig. 16 Manual valve body bolt identification

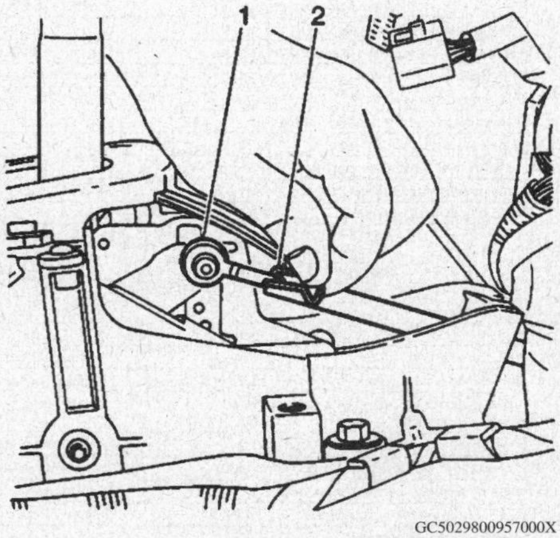

Fig. 19 Shift cable to selector lever removal

25. Remove right and left drive axles.
26. Remove two retaining bolts from exhaust pipe support, then one nut and exhaust pipe support from center crossmember.
27. Remove two retaining bolts from front exhaust pipe to three way catalytic converter mating flange.
28. Disconnect electrical connector from oxygen sensor at front exhaust pipe.
29. Remove two front exhaust pipe to exhaust manifold retaining bolts, then the front exhaust pipe.
30. Remove crossmember plastic access cover from center crossmember.
31. Remove two front transaxle mount retaining bolts, then three rear transaxle mount retaining nuts.
32. Remove front suspension crossmember retaining bolts, then the front suspension crossmember.
33. Support transmission using a suitable hydraulic transmission jack.
34. Remove engine reinforcement brace retaining bolts, then the engine reinforcement brace.
35. Remove flywheel access cover, then the flywheel to torque converter retaining bolts.
36. Remove two lower transaxle to engine retaining bolts, then the transaxle.
37. Reverse procedure to install. Tighten bolts to specification.

TIGHTENING SPECIFICATIONS

Year	Component	Torque/ Ft. Lbs.
1997–2000	Cable End Bolt	15
	Center Crossmember To Main Crossmember Bolts	45
	Center Crossmember To Radiator Support Bolts	45
	Center Mount Mounting Nuts	45
	Center Mount To Transaxle Bolts	45
	Detent Spring Attaching Bolt	72①
	Differential Check Fill Plug	29
	Differential Fill & Drain Plug	29
	Drain Plug	29
	Exhaust Hanger Bracket Nuts	10
	Fill Tube To Case Bolt	96①
	Front, Center & Rear Mount Bolts	45
	Front Mount Bolts	45
	Front Mount Bracket Bolts	13
	Front Mount Through Bolt	64
	Governor Cover Bolts	96①
	Left Mount Brace Bolts	13
	Left Mount Through Bolt	66
	Lower A-Frame To Underbody Bolts	94
	Lower Mount To Bracket Bolts	45
	Lower Starter Motor Bolt	29
	Lower Transaxle Mount Bolts	45
	Main Crossmember To Underbody Bolts	152
	Manual Lever Cap Nut	84①
	Manual Valve & Manual Detent Spring Bolts	84①
	Mount Cover & Brace Bolts	13
	Neutral Start Switch Bolts	72①
	Oil Apply Tube Retainer Bolts	44①
	Oil Cooler Line Nuts	20
	Oil Cooler Pipe Fittings	15
	Oil Filter Bolts	84①
	Oil Pan Bolts	44①
	Oil Pan Drain Plug Bolt	29
	Oil Pump Bolts	16
	Rear Mount Through Bolt	64
	Shift Control Assembly Bolts	15
	Shift Control Bolts	15
	Side Case Cover Bolts	44①
	Switch Retaining Bolt	84①
	Throttle Valve Cable Adjusting Nut	72①
	Throttle Valve Cable Housing Locknuts	84①
	Torque Converter Bolts	14
	Transaxle Fluid Drain Plug	29
	Transaxle To Engine Bolts	47
	Upper Mount To Bracket Bolts	45
	Upper Starter Bolt	29
	Upper Transaxle Mount Bracket Bolt	45
	Valve Body Bolts	84①
	Wheel Lug Nuts	76

① — Inch lbs.

Aisin Warner A245E Automatic Transaxle

NOTE: On Air Bag Equipped Models, Refer To " Air Bag System Precautions" Located In The Front Of This Manual For System Disarming & Arming Procedures.

NOTE: Refer To "Computer Relearn Procedures " Located In The Front Of This Manual For Computer Relearn Procedures.

INDEX

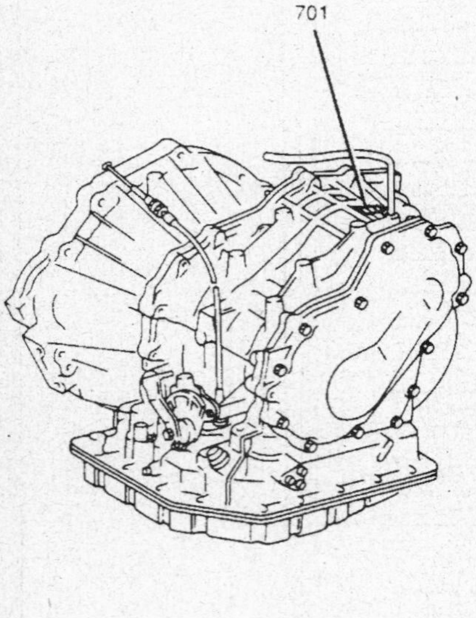

701 TRANSAXLE IDENTIFICATION NUMBER LOCATION

GC5029300438000X

Fig. 1 Transaxle identification number location

PRECAUTIONS

AIR BAG SYSTEMS

Refer to "Air Bag System Precautions" in the front of this manual for system disarming and arming procedures.

BATTERY GROUND CABLE

Prior to service, disconnect battery ground cable and isolate as required.

IDENTIFICATION

The A245E four-speed automatic transaxle identification number is located on top of the transaxle case in front of the vent tube, **Fig. 1.**

DESCRIPTION

The A245E transaxle is equipped with an integral lock-up mechanism, fuel consumption has been reduced and power output increased by more precise shift control and monitoring of the throttle opening angle.

TROUBLESHOOTING

Refer to **Figs. 2 through 10** for troubleshooting.

Problem	Action
The Fluid is contaminated.	Flush and add fresh fluid.
Torque converter is faulty.	Replace torque converter.
Transaxle is faulty.	Overhaul transaxle.

GC5029800958000X

Fig. 2 Fluid discolored or smells burnt

MAINTENANCE

Refer to "Aisin Warner A131L Automatic Transaxle."

ADJUSTMENTS

THROTTLE VALVE (TV) CABLE

Refer to "Adjustments" in the " Aisin Warner A131L Automatic Transaxle" for procedure.

IN-VEHICLE REPAIRS

BRAKE TRANSMISSION SHIFT INTERLOCK, REPLACE

Refer to "Adjustments" in the " Aisin Warner A131L Automatic Transaxle" for procedure.

MANUAL SELECTOR, REPLACE

Refer to "Adjustments" in the " Aisin Warner A131L Automatic Transaxle" for procedure.

VALVE BODY & ACCUMULATOR, REPLACE

1. Raise and support vehicle.
2. Remove six bolts and lefthand splash shield from vehicle.
3. Place a drain pan or suitable container under transaxle oil pan.
4. Remove drain plug and drain transaxle fluid, then remove transaxle fluid pan. **When removing transaxle oil pan, use caution to not damage mating surfaces. Use a rubber mallet and wooden block if pan is frozen to transaxle; do not use metal objects (crow bar, screwdriver, etc.) to free pan.**
5. Remove filter and screen from valve body.
6. Disconnect solenoid electrical connectors from shift solenoid Nos. 1 and 2 and TCC solenoid, **Fig. 11.**
7. Remove bolt and solenoid wire harness clip from valve body and detent spring.
8. Remove TV cable from throttle valve cam. **B2 accumulator, check ball and spring may drop from transaxle during valve body removal. B2 accumulator is under intense spring pressure and may push valve body down after valve body bolts are loosened.**

Problem	Action
Low or no fluid.	Add fluid.
Shift cable out of adjustment, binding or damaged.	Adjust or replace select cable.
Parking lock pawl mechanism locked or frozen.	Inspect parking lock pawl.
Broken torque converter to flywheel bolts.	Replace bolts.
Torque converter stator one-way clutch no holding.	Replace torque converter.
Torque converter failure.	Replace torque converter.
Valve body spacer plate or gaskets improper position or damaged.	Inspect valve body.
Check balls omitted or improper position.	Inspect valve body.
Manual valve binding or sticking.	Inspect valve body.
Manual valve link disconnected.	Inspect manual valve linkage.
Incorrect line pressure.	Perform line pressure diagnosis.

GC5029800959000X

Fig. 3 Unable to Run in all ranges

Problem	Action
Low fluid.	Add fluid.
TV cable out of adjustment, binding or damaged.	Adjust or replace throttle valve cable.
Shift select cable out of adjustment, biding or damaged.	Adjust or replace shift select cable.
Manual valve binding or sticking.	Inspect valve body.
Throttle valve binding or sticking.	Inspect valve body.
B2 control valve binding or sticking.	Inspect valve body.
Accumulator(s) pistons damaged or leaking.	Inspect accumulator pistons.
Accumulator(s) seals cut or damaged.	Inspect accumulator seals.
Accumulator(s) broken or distorted springs.	Inspect accumulator springs.
Incorrect line pressure.	Perform line pressure diagnosis.

GC5029800960000X

Fig. 4 Harsh engagement into any drive range

Problem	Action
Throttle valve cable out of adjustment.	Adjust throttle valve cable.
Faulty throttle vavle cable and cam.	Inpsect throttle valve cable and cam.
Faulty accumulator pistons.	Inspect accumulator pistons.
Faulty valve body.	Inspect valve body.
Faulty transaxle.	Overhaul transaxle.

GC5029800961000X

Fig. 5 Harsh downshift

Problem	Action
Valve body is faulty.	Inspect valve body.
Shift solenoid is faulty.	Inspect shift solenoid.
Fault within electronic control system.	Perform Powertrain On-Board Diagnostic (OBD) system check

GC5029800962000X

Fig. 6 No downshift when coasting

Problem	Action
Throttle valve cable is faulty.	Inspect throttle valve cable.
Valve body is faulty.	Inspect valve body.
Transaxle is faulty.	Overhaul transaxle.
Shift solenoid is faulty.	Inspect shift solenoid.
Fault within electronic control system.	Perform Powertrain On-Board Diagnostic (OBD) system check

GC5029800963000X

Fig. 7 Downshift occurs too quickly or too late

Problem	Action
Shift solenoid is Faulty.	Inspect shift solenoid.
Fault within electronic control system.	Perform Powertrain On-Board Diagnostic (OBD) system check
Faulty valve body.	Inspect valve body.
Throttle valve cable is faulty.	Inspect throttle valve cable.

GC5029800964000X

Fig. 8 No OD-3, 3-2 or 2-1 kickdown

Problem	Action
Shift solenoid is faulty.	Inspect shift solenoid.
Fault within electronic control system.	Perform Powertrain On-Board Diagnostic (OBD) system check
Valve body is faulty.	Inspect valve body.
Transaxle is faulty	Inspect the transaxle.

GC5029800965000X

Fig. 9 No engine braking in 2 or L range

Problem	Action
Shift select cable out of adjustment.	Adjust shift select cable.
Faulty parking lock pawl and spring.	Inspect cam and spring.

GC5029800966000X

Fig. 10 Vehicle does not hold in Park range.

9. Remove 17 bolts, **Fig. 12,** then the valve body from transaxle while simultaneously disconnecting manual valve link from manual lever.
10. Remove check ball body and spring from transaxle and B2 accumulator piston and spring. **When using compressed air to remove components from transaxle case, air pressure should never exceed 14 psi.**
11. Remove C2, C1 and C3 accumulator pistons and springs from transaxle case by slowly applying low pressure compressed air into accumulator apply passages, **Figs. 13 through 15.**
12. Reverse procedure to install. Inspect transaxle case for nicks or scars, accumulator seals for cuts or damage and accumulator pistons for cracks or porosity.

TV CABLE, REPLACE

1. Loosen TV cable locknut and adjust nut, **Fig. 16.**
2. Disconnect TV cable from TV linkage and TV cable bracket, then from cable guide bracket at top of transaxle.
3. Raise and support vehicle.
4. Remove lefthand splash shield.
5. Disconnect Park/Neutral Position (PNP) switch from transaxle and place a drain pan or suitable container under transaxle fluid pan.
6. Drain transaxle fluid, then remove transaxle pan.
7. Disconnect TV cable from throttle valve cam at valve body.
8. Remove cable retaining bolt and cable.
9. Inspect TV cable for fraying, kinks, excessive wear or damage.
10. **New TV cables do not have a staked TV cable stopper. A new stopper must be staked if using a new cable.** To stake cable stopper, proceed as follows:
    a. Bend cable to a radius of approximately 7.87 inches, **Fig. 17.**
    b. Lightly pull inner cable from housing until a slight resistance is felt and hold in position.
    c. Stake stopper onto inner cable so that .031–.059 inch clearance exists between stop and cable housing.
11. Reverse procedure to install.

TRANSAXLE

REPLACE

1. Remove battery, hold down bracket and tray.
2. Disconnect Intake Air Temperature (IAT) connector.
3. Remove air cleaner cover and air cleaner.
4. Disconnect solenoid wire harness electrical connector from solenoid wire harness.
5. Disconnect PNP switch connector.
6. Remove ground strap from transaxle case and loosen TV cable locknut and adjust nut.
7. Disconnect TV cable from throttle linkage and TV cable bracket.
8. Disconnect Vehicle Speed Sensor (VSS) electrical connector.
9. Remove shift select cable from manual lever and shift select cable bracket.
10. Remove cable guide bracket from transaxle case, then the upper transaxle to engine bolts.
11. Remove upper starter motor retaining bolt from starter motor.
12. Remove lefthand transaxle mounting bracket reinforcement bolts, then the bracket from transaxle.
13. Remove bolt from lefthand transaxle mounting bracket.
14. Raise and support vehicle.
15. Place a drain pan or suitable container under transaxle fluid pan, then drain transaxle fluid.
16. Remove starter positive terminal nut, positive battery cable and electrical connector from starter.
17. Remove lower starter retaining bolt, then the starter.
18. Remove both splash shields and plug fluid cooler pipes to prevent transaxle fluid cooler leakage.
19. Remove inner and outer cooler hoses and pipes at transaxle.
20. Remove bolts from lefthand transaxle mounting bracket.

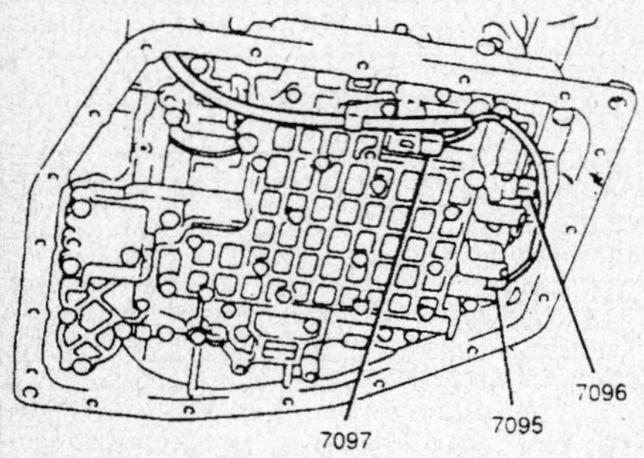

7095 SHIFT SOLENOID NO. 1 ELECTRICAL CONNECTOR
7096 SHIFT SOLENOID NO. 2 ELECTRICAL CONNECTOR
7097 TORQUE CONVERTER CLUTCH (TCC) SOLENOID ELECTRICAL CONNECTOR

GC5029300439000X

Fig. 11 Solenoid electrical connectors

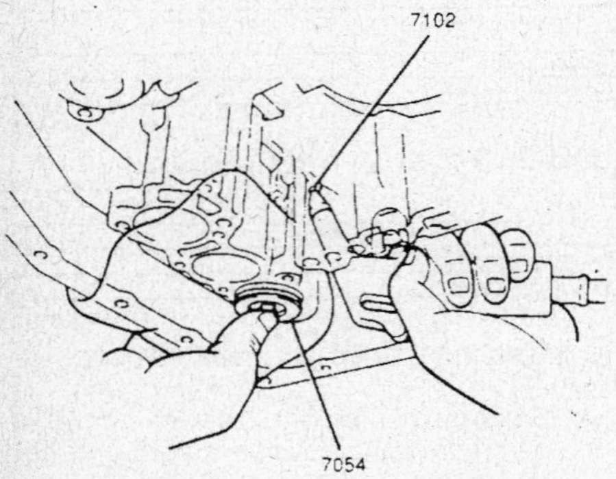

7054 C1 ACCUMULATOR PISTON
7102 C1 ACCUMULATOR APPLY PASSAGE

GC5029300442000X

Fig. 14 C1 accumulator piston & spring removal

21. Remove both front wheel assemblies.
22. Remove both drive axles.
23. Remove exhaust pipe support bolts and center crossmember.
24. **On models equipped with Federal emissions,** remove front exhaust pipe to three way catalytic converter mating flange bolts.
25. **On models equipped with California emissions,** remove front exhaust pipe to warm up three way catalytic converter mating flange nuts, then the front exhaust pipe.
26. **On all models,** remove front exhaust pipe to exhaust manifold mating flange nuts, then the front exhaust pipe.
27. Remove center crossmember plastic access cover from center crossmember, then the bolts and nuts from front transaxle mount.
28. Remove front suspension and center crossmembers, then support transaxle with a suitable jack.
29. Remove flywheel access cover from engine rear end plate, then the flywheel to torque converter retaining bolts.
30. Remove drain pan from underneath transaxle.
31. Remove lower transaxle to engine retaining bolts.
32. Disconnect transaxle from engine by carefully moving transaxle away from engine toward lefthand side of engine compartment and very slowly lowering hydraulic jack ensuring no obstructions exist.
33. Reverse procedure to install.

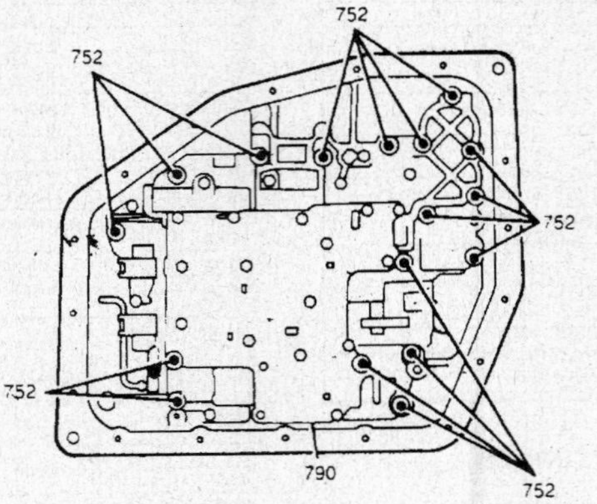

752 VALVE BODY ASSEMBLY BOLTS
790 VALVE BODY ASSEMBLY

GC5029300440000X

Fig. 12 Valve body bolt location

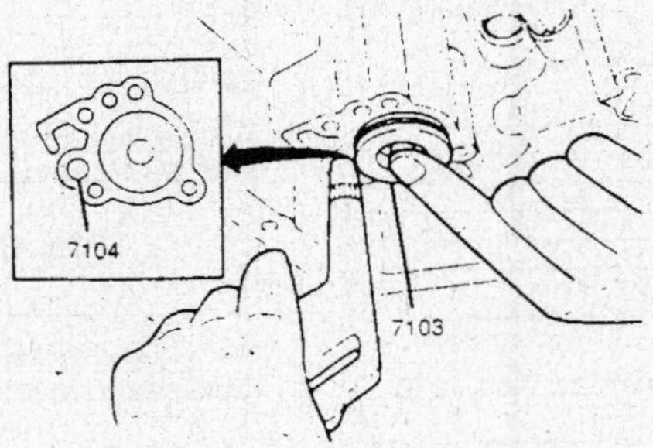

7103 C3 ACCUMULATOR PISTON
7104 C3 ACCUMULATOR APPLY PASSAGE

GC5029300443000X

Fig. 15 C3 accumulator piston & spring removal

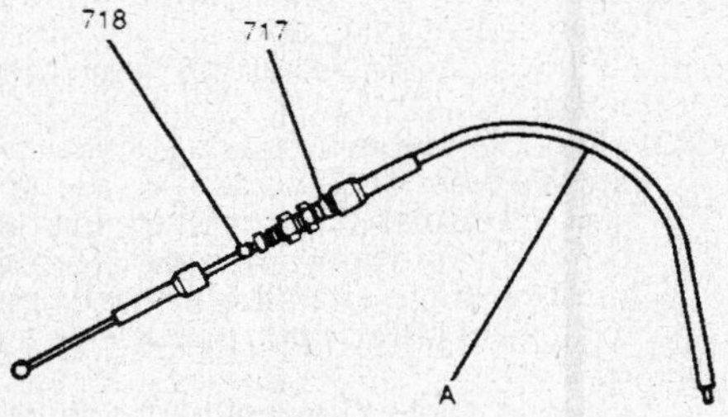

A 200 mm (7.87") RADIUS
717 TV CABLE
718 TV CABLE STOPPER

GC5029300445000X

Fig. 17 TV cable stopper staking

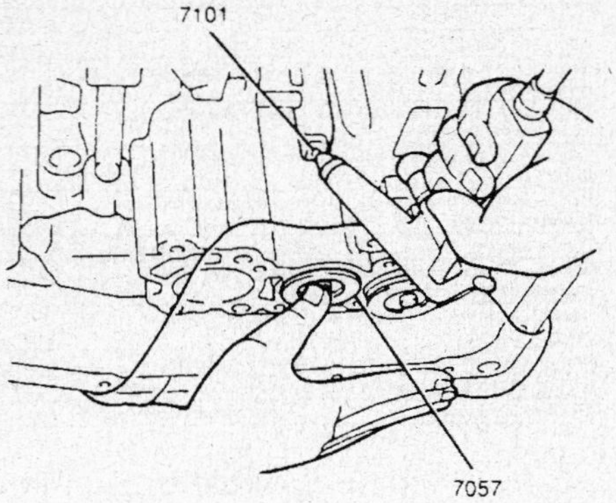

7057 C2 ACCUMULATOR PISTON
7101 C2 ACCUMULATOR APPLY PASSAGE

GC5029300441000X

Fig. 13 C2 accumulator piston & spring removal

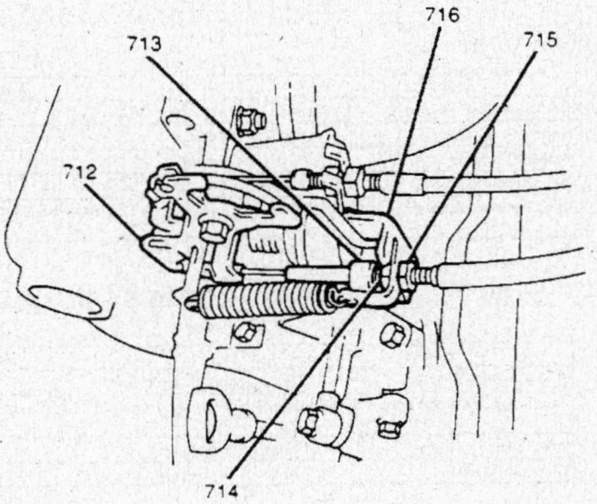

712 THROTTLE VALVE LINKAGE
713 OUTER CABLE BOOT
714 TV CABLE ADJUST NUT
715 TV CABLE LOCKNUT
716 TV CABLE BRACKET

GC5029300444000X

Fig. 16 TV cable locknut & adjust nut location

TIGHTENING SPECIFICATIONS

Year	Component	Torque/ Ft. Lbs.
1997–2000	Air Cleaner Bolts	44①
	Axle Nut	129
	Ball Stud	44
	Battery Ground Cable	11
	Battery Hold-Down Bracket Bolt	44①
	Battery Hold-Down Bracket Nut	72①
	Bulkhead Grommet Bolt	15
	Center Crossmember Rear Bolt & Nuts	45
	Detent Spring Bolts	84①
	Direct Clutch Solenoid Retaining Bolt	35①
	Drain Plug	17
	Driveshaft Nut	129
	Fluid Filter Screen Bolts	84①
	Flywheel To Torque Converter Bolts	14
	Front Exhaust Pipe Support Bolts	14
	Front Exhaust Pipe Support Nuts & Bolts	14
	Front Exhaust Pipe To Exhaust Manifold Nuts	46
	Front Exhaust Pipe To Three Way Catalytic Converter Mating Flange Bolts	32
	Front Exhaust Pipe To Warm Up Three Way Catalytic Converter Mating Flange Nuts	46
	Front Suspension Crossmember Bolts	152
	Front Transaxle Mount Bolts	35
	Front Transaxle Mount Through Bolt & Nut	64
	Ground Strap Bolt	10
	Hub Nut	129
	Interlock Cable	10
	Left Transaxle Mounting Bracket Bolts	35
	Left Transaxle Mounting Bracket Reinforcement Bolts	15
	Left Transaxle Mount Through Bolt	64
	Lower Engine Reinforcement Brace Bolts	47
	Oil Pan	53①
	Oil Strainer Attaching Bolt	53①
	Park Neutral Position	48①
	Rear Transaxle Mount Nuts	42
	Rear Transaxle Mount Through Bolt	64
	Selector Lever Housing Nut	25
	Second Gear Brake Solenoid Retaining Bolt	35①
	Solenoid Wire Harness Clip Bolt	53①
	Solenoid Wire Harness Retaining Bolt	53①
	Solenoid Wire Harness Retaining Plate & Bracket Bolt	15
	Speedometer Driven Gear Retaining	11
	Splash Shield Bolts	44①
	Starter Motor Positive Terminal Nut	44①
	Starter Motor Retaining Bolts	29
	Transaxle Fluid Drain Plug	13
	Transaxle Fluid Pan Bolts	43①
	Transaxle To Engine Bolts	47
	Transmission Control Module Retaining Bolt	11
	TV Cable Guide Bracket Bolt	72①
	TV Cable Locknut	72①
	TV Cable Retaining Bolt	72①
	Valve Body	84①
	Vehicle Speed Sensor	53①

① — Inch lbs.

Aisin Seiki Automatic Transaxle

NOTE: On Air Bag Equipped Models, Refer To " Air Bag System Precautions" Located In The Front Of This Manual For System Disarming & Arming Procedures.

NOTE: Refer To "Computer Relearn Procedures " Located In The Front Of This Manual For Computer Relearn Procedures.

INDEX

PRECAUTIONS

AIR BAG SYSTEMS

Refer to "Air Bag System Precautions" in the front of this manual for system disarming and arming procedures.

BATTERY GROUND CABLE

Prior to service, disconnect battery ground cable and isolate as required.

IDENTIFICATION

The transaxle identification number is located on the top center of the transaxle assembly, **Fig. 1.**

TROUBLESHOOTING

1. Ensure engine coolant is at normal operating temperature.
2. Ensure engine idle speed is 800–900 RPM.
3. Ensure transaxle fluid level is correct and at normal operating temperature.
4. Ensure accelerator cable, oil pressure control cable and selector cable are properly adjusted.
5. Ensure gear shift control system wiring is in good condition.
6. Ensure vacuum switch hose is properly connected.
7. Refer to **Fig. 2,** for transaxle troubleshooting.

MAINTENANCE

Refer to "Lubricant Data Chart" in the appropriate chassis chapter of this manual for transmission fluid specifications.

FLUID CHECK

1. Drive vehicle for approximately 15 minutes to bring fluid to normal operating temperature.
2. With vehicle on level surface, apply parking brake and block drive wheels.
3. With selector lever in Park, start engine and move selector lever through each range and return to Park.
4. Remove dipstick and check fluid level.
5. Fluid level should be between two "HOT" marks on dipstick.
6. Add fluid as required to bring fluid to specified level.

FLUID CHANGE

Under normal driving conditions, fluid should be changed and oil strainer cleaned every 100,000 miles. Under harsh driving conditions fluid should be changed every 15,000 miles. To service, proceed as follows:

1. Raise and support front of vehicle.
2. Remove plug and drain fluid into a suitable container.
3. Remove oil pan retaining bolts, then the oil pan.
4. Remove oil strainer retaining bolts, then the oil strainer.
5. Clean strainer and oil pan in solvent. Engine magnet in oil pan is positioned directly below oil strainer.
6. Install oil strainer and retaining bolts. Tighten bolts to specification.
7. Install oil pan using new gasket. Tighten retaining bolts to specification. **Two of the oil pan retaining bolts have crossed grooves on the bolt head. When installing these two bolts, coat threads with sealant and install in positions shown in Fig. 3.**
8. Lower vehicle and fill oil pan.
9. Check fluid level as previously described and adjust as necessary.

ADJUSTMENTS

THROTTLE VALVE (TV) CABLE

1. Inspect accelerator cable for play and adjust as required.
2. Start engine and allow it to run at idle speed until operating temperature is reached.
3. Remove TV cable adjustment cover.
4. Measure TV cable boot to inner stopper clearance. If clearance is more than .02 inch, adjust TV cable, **Fig. 4.**
5. Turn TV cable adjustment nuts "A" until correct clearance is obtained. If correct clearance cannot be obtained using adjustment nuts "A" , use adjustment nuts " B."

PARK/NEUTRAL POSITION (PNP) SWITCH

1. Remove park/neutral position switch from transaxle as described under "Park/Neutral Position Switch, Replace."
2. Move transaxle lever to Neutral position.
3. Using a flat-bladed screwdriver, turn park/neutral switch joint clockwise or counterclockwise until a distinct click is heard in position **Fig. 5.**
4. Install PNP switch to transaxle as described under " Park/Neutral Position Switch, Replace."

IN-VEHICLE REPAIRS

BRAKE TRANSAXLE SHIFT INTERLOCK, REPLACE

1. Remove selector knob to selector lever retaining screws, **Fig. 6.**

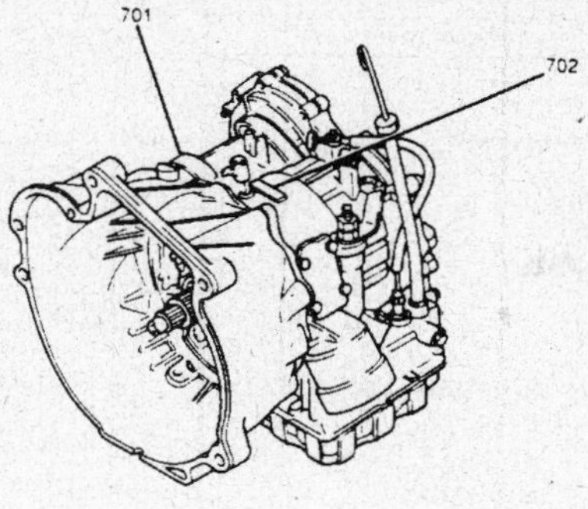

701 TRANSAXLE CASE
702 TRANSAXLE IDENTIFICATION NUMBER LOCATION

GC5029200461000X

Fig. 1 Transaxle identification number location

CONDITION	INSPECT COMPONENT	FOR CAUSE
HARSH ENGAGEMENT INTO ANY FORWARD RANGE	FLUID LEVEL INDICATOR	– LOW FLUID LEVEL
	TV CABLE	– MISADJUSTED, BINDING OR DAMAGED
	SHIFT SELECT CABLE	– MISADJUSTED, BINDING OR DAMAGED
	VALVE BODY	– MANUAL VALVE BINDING OR STICKING – THROTTLE VALVE BINDING OR STICKING – B2 CONTROL VALVE BINDING OR STICKING
	ACCUMULATORS	– PISTONS DAMAGED OR LEAKING – SEALS CUT OR DAMAGED – BROKEN OR DISTORTED SPRINGS
	FLUID PRESSURE	– INSPECT FOR CAUSES OF HIGH OR LOW FLUID PRESSURE
SLIPS IN 1ST GEAR	FLUID LEVEL INDICATOR	– LOW FLUID LEVEL
	TV CABLE	– MISADJUSTED, BINDING OR DAMAGED
	SHIFT SELECT CABLE	– MISADJUSTED, BINDING OR DAMAGED
	VALVE BODY	– THROTTLE VALVE BINDING OR STICKING – PRIMARY REGULATOR VALVE BINDING OR STICKING
	ACCUMULATORS	– PISTONS DAMAGED OR LEAKING – SEALS CUT OR DAMAGED – BROKEN OR DISTORTED SPRINGS
	FORWARD CLUTCH	– CLUTCH DISCS WORN – FORWARD CLUTCH PISTON OR SEAL LEAKING OR DAMAGED – INPUT SHAFT O-RINGS CUT OR DAMAGED
	ONE-WAY CLUTCH	– NOT HOLDING OR DAMAGED
	FLUID PRESSURE	– INSPECT FOR CAUSES OF HIGH OR LOW FLUID PRESSURE

GC5029300495010X

Fig. 2 Troubleshooting chart (Part 1 of 6)

CONDITION	INSPECT COMPONENT	FOR CAUSE
1ST GEAR ONLY — NO UPSHIFT	TV CABLE	– MISADJUSTED, BINDING OR DAMAGED
	VALVE BODY	– THROTTLE VALVE BINDING OR STICKING – 1–2 SHIFT VALVE BINDING OR STICKING – PRIMARY REGULATOR VALVE BINDING OR STICKING
	INTERMEDIATE SERVO	– SEALS CUT OR DAMAGED – PISTON BINDING OR STICKING – PISTON ROD NOT ENGAGED
	2ND BRAKE BAND	– WORN OR MISALIGNED
	FLUID PRESSURE	– INSPECT FOR CAUSES OF HIGH OR LOW FLUID PRESSURE
SLIPPING OR ROUGH 1–2 UPSHIFT	FLUID LEVEL INDICATOR	– LOW FLUID LEVEL
	TV CABLE	– MISADJUSTED, BINDING OR DAMAGED
	VALVE BODY	– THROTTLE VALVE BINDING OR STICKING – 1–2 SHIFT VALVE BINDING OR STICKING – PRIMARY REGULATOR VALVE BINDING OR STICKING
	INTERMEDIATE SERVO	– SEALS CUT OR DAMAGED – PISTON BINDING OR STICKING – PISTON ROD NOT ENGAGED
	2ND BRAKE BAND	– WORN OR MISALIGNED
	TORQUE CONVERTER	– INTERNAL DAMAGE
	FORWARD CLUTCH	– CLUTCH DISCS WORN – FORWARD CLUTCH PISTON OR SEAL LEAKING OR DAMAGED – INPUT SHAFT O-RINGS CUT OR DAMAGED
	FLUID PRESSURE	– INSPECT FOR CAUSES OF HIGH OR LOW FLUID PRESSURE

GC5029300495020X

Fig. 2 Troubleshooting chart (Part 2 of 6)

2. Remove mounting screws and center console.
3. Remove manual selector bulb socket from manual selector cover.
4. Remove manual selector cover to selector lever retaining screws.
5. Remove retainer clip and clevis pin, then disconnect shift select cable from selector lever.
6. Disconnect interlock cable end from key release plate on manual selector.
7. Remove interlock cable to selector assembly retaining bolt, then disconnect cable from assembly.
8. Disconnect shift lock solenoid electrical connector located under carpet.
9. Raise and support vehicle.
10. Remove selector lever assembly housing seat retaining nuts.
11. Lower vehicle, then remove selector lever housing and selector lever from floor.
12. Reverse procedure to install, noting the following:
    a. Tighten selector lever housing seat nuts to specification.
    b. Adjust interlock cable as outlined under "Interlock Cable, Replace."
    c. Adjust shift select cable as outline under "Shift Select Cable, Replace."
    d. Apply lithium grease under solenoid lock plate **Fig. 7.**

SHIFT SELECT CABLE, REPLACE

1. Remove selector lever knob to selector lever retaining screws.
2. Remove mounting screws and center console.
3. Remove manual selector cover lamp bulb socket from selector cover, **Fig. 8.**
4. Remove selector cover to selector lever retaining screws.
5. Remove retainer clip and clevis pin, then disconnect shift select cable from selector lever.
6. Remove front carpet retainers and pull back carpet.
7. Remove retaining clip and shift select cable from transaxle retaining bracket.
8. Remove nut and disconnect shift select cable from manual shift lever.

CONDITION	INSPECT COMPONENT	FOR CAUSE
NO 2–3 SHIFT OR 2–3 SHIFT SLIPPING	FLUID LEVEL INDICATOR	– LOW FLUID LEVEL
	TV CABLE	– MISADJUSTED, BINDING OR DAMAGED
	VALVE BODY	– THROTTLE VALVE BINDING OR STICKING – 2–3 SHIFT VALVE BINDING OR STICKING – PRIMARY REGULATOR VALVE BINDING OR STICKING
	INTERMEDIATE SERVO	– PISTON BINDING OR STICKING – PISTON ROD BINDING
	2ND BRAKE BAND	– NOT RELEASING
	TORQUE CONVERTER	– INTERNAL DAMAGE
	DIRECT CLUTCH	– CLUTCH DISCS WORN – DIRECT CLUTCH PISTON OR SEAL LEAKING OR DAMAGED
	FLUID PRESSURE	– INSPECT FOR CAUSES OF HIGH OR LOW FLUID PRESSURE
HIGH OR LOW SHIFT POINTS	FLUID LEVEL INDICATOR	– LOW FLUID LEVEL
	TV CABLE	– MISADJUSTED, BINDING OR DAMAGED
	VALVE BODY	– SPACER PLATE OR GASKETS MISPOSITIONED OR DAMAGED – THROTTLE VALVE BINDING OR STICKING – CHECK BALLS OMITTED OR MISPOSITIONED
	TORQUE CONVERTER	– INTERNAL DAMAGE
	FORWARD CLUTCH	– FORWARD CLUTCH PISTON OR SEAL LEAKING OR DAMAGED – INPUT SHAFT O-RINGS CUT OR DAMAGED
	DIRECT CLUTCH	– DIRECT CLUTCH PISTON OR SEAL LEAKING OR DAMAGED
	FLUID PRESSURE	– INSPECT FOR CAUSES OF HIGH OR LOW FLUID PRESSURE

GC5029300495030X

Fig. 2 Troubleshooting chart (Part 3 of 6)

CONDITION	INSPECT COMPONENT	FOR CAUSE
NO PART THROTTLE OR DELAYED DOWNSHIFT	TV CABLE	– MISADJUSTED, BINDING OR DAMAGED
	VALVE BODY	– THROTTLE VALVE BINDING OR STICKING – 2–3 SHIFT VALVE BINDING OR STICKING – 1–2 SHIFT VALVE BINDING OR STICKING – PRIMARY REGULATOR VALVE BINDING OR STICKING – BROKEN OR DISTORTED VALVE SPRINGS – DAMAGED OR POROUS VALVE BODY CASTING
	INTERMEDIATE SERVO	– PISTON BINDING OR STICKING – PISTON SEALS CUT OR DAMAGED – PISTON ROD BINDING
	2ND BRAKE BAND	– WORN OR MISPOSITIONED
	1ST-REVERSE BRAKE	– CLUTCH DISCS WORN – 1ST-REVERSE BRAKE PISTON OR SEAL LEAKING OR DAMAGED
	ONE-WAY CLUTCH	– NOT HOLDING OR DAMAGED
NO ENGINE BRAKING OR 3–2–1 MANUAL DOWNSHIFT	SHIFT SELECT CABLE	– MISADJUSTED, BINDING OR DAMAGED
	VALVE BODY	– MANUAL VALVE BINDING OR STICKING – 2–3 SHIFT VALVE BINDING OR STICKING – 1–2 SHIFT VALVE BINDING OR STICKING – PRIMARY REGULATOR VALVE BINDING OR STICKING – BROKEN OR DISTORTED VALVE SPRINGS – DAMAGED OR POROUS VALVE BODY CASTING
	INTERMEDIATE SERVO	– PISTON BINDING OR STICKING – PISTON SEALS CUT OR DAMAGED – PISTON ROD BINDING
	2ND BRAKE BAND	– WORN OR MISPOSITIONED
	1ST-REVERSE BRAKE	– CLUTCH DISCS WORN – 1ST-REVERSE BRAKE PISTON OR SEAL LEAKING OR DAMAGED
	ONE-WAY CLUTCH	– NOT HOLDING OR DAMAGED

GC5029300495040X

Fig. 2 Troubleshooting chart (Part 4 of 6)

CONDITION	INSPECT COMPONENT	FOR CAUSE
NO REVERSE OR SLIPS IN REVERSE	FLUID LEVEL INDICATOR	– LOW FLUID LEVEL
	SHIFT SELECT CABLE	– MISADJUSTED, BINDING OR DAMAGED
	VALVE BODY	– SPACER PLATE OR GASKETS MISPOSITIONED OR DAMAGED – CHECK BALLS OMITTED OR MISPOSITIONED – MANUAL VALVE BINDING OR STICKING – MANUAL VALVE LINK DISCONNECTED
	DIRECT CLUTCH	– DIRECT CLUTCH PISTON OR SEAL LEAKING OR DAMAGED
	FLUID PRESSURE	– INSPECT FOR CAUSES OF HIGH OR LOW FLUID PRESSURE
FLUID PRESSURE HIGH OR LOW (VERIFY WITH GAGE — REFER TO "LINE PRESSURE TEST" PROCEDURE EARLIER IN THIS SECTION)	FLUID PUMP	– INTERNAL FLUID PUMP LEAK – FLUID PUMP DRIVE AND DRIVEN GEARS WORN OR DAMAGED – FLUID PUMP COVER SEAL RINGS CUT OR DAMAGED – FLUID PUMP BODY OR COVER CASTING POROUS OR DAMAGED
	TV CABLE	– TV CABLE LINK LOOSE OR DISCONNECTED – MISADJUSTED, BINDING OR DAMAGED
	VALVE BODY	– SPACER PLATE OR GASKETS MISPOSITIONED OR DAMAGED – CHECK BALLS OMITTED OR MISPOSITIONED – MANUAL VALVE BINDING OR STICKING – MANUAL VALVE LINK DISCONNECTED – PRIMARY REGULATOR VALVE BINDING OR STICKING
	CASE	– INTERNAL LEAK IN FORWARD CLUTCH FLUID CIRCUIT – INTERNAL LEAK IN DIRECT CLUTCH FLUID CIRCUIT – FLUID PASSAGES BLOCKED OR RESTRICTED

GC5029300495050X

Fig. 2 Troubleshooting chart (Part 5 of 6)

CONDITION	INSPECT COMPONENT	FOR CAUSE
NO PARK OR RATCHETING NOISE IN PARK	SHIFT SELECT CABLE	– MISADJUSTED, BINDING OR DAMAGED
	LOCK PAWL SPRING	– DISCONNECTED OR BROKEN
	PARKING LOCK ROD	– DISCONNECTED OR BROKEN
	PARKING LOCK PAWL	– LOOSE OR DISCONNECTED
	LOCK PAWL SPRING	– WEAK OR DAMAGED
VEHICLE DOES NOT MOVE IN ANY RANGE — FORWARD OR REVERSE	FLUID LEVEL INDICATOR	– LITTLE OR NO FLUID
	SHIFT SELECT CABLE	– MISADJUSTED, BINDING OR DAMAGED
	PARKING LOCK PAWL	– MECHANISM LOCKED OR FROZEN
	TORQUE CONVERTER	– BROKEN TORQUE CONVERTER-TO-FLYWHEEL BOLTS – STATOR ONE-WAY CLUTCH NOT HOLDING – INTERNAL DAMAGE
	VALVE BODY	– SPACER PLATE OR GASKETS MISPOSITIONED OR DAMAGED – CHECK BALLS OMITTED OR MISPOSITIONED – MANUAL VALVE BINDING OR STICKING – MANUAL VALVE LINK DISCONNECTED
	FLUID PRESSURE	– INSPECT FOR CAUSES OF HIGH OR LOW FLUID PRESSURE

GC5029300495060X

Fig. 2 Troubleshooting chart (Part 6 of 6)

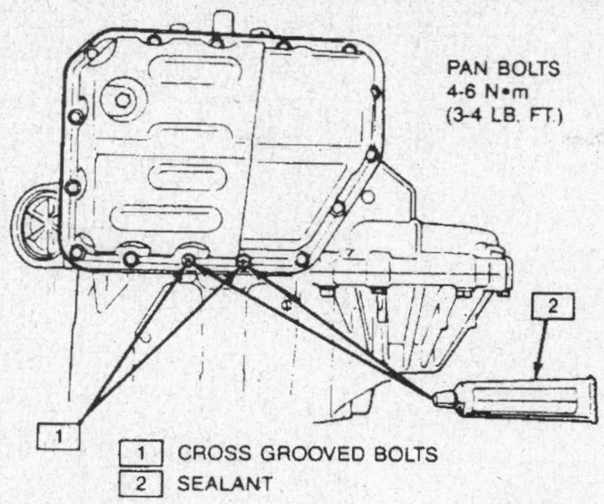

GC5029100465000X

Fig. 3 Oil pan installation

9. Remove bolts from bulkhead grommet and pull shift select cable out of bulkhead from engine compartment side of bulkhead.
10. Reverse procedure to install, noting the following:
    a. Tighten bulkhead grommet bolts to specification.
    b. After connecting shift select cable to transaxle retaining bracket, tighten adjustment nut "A" by hand until it contacts shift select cable joint, **Fig. 9.**
    c. Using an open end wrench, tighten adjustment nut " B" until it is jammed against manual shift select cable joint.
    d. Apply lithium grease to shift select cable clevis pin.

PARK/NEUTRAL POSITION SWITCH, REPLACE

1. Disconnect park/neutral position switch electrical connector.
2. Remove position switch wiring harness from retaining clips.
3. Remove switch to transaxle retaining bolt.
4. Reverse procedure to install. Adjust position switch described under "Adjustments."

INTERLOCK CABLE, REPLACE

Removal

1. Remove selector lever knob to selector lever retaining screws.
2. Remove center console retaining screws, then the center console.
3. Remove manual selector cover lamp bulb socket from selector cover.
4. Remove selector cover to selector lever retaining screws.
5. Disconnect interlock cable end from key release plate on manual selector, **Fig. 10.**
6. Remove interlock cable retaining bolt.
7. Disconnect interlock cable from selector lever housing bracket.
8. Remove front carpet retainers and pull back front carpet.
9. Remove upper and lower steering column covers.
10. Remove upper and lower steering column mounting nuts, then lower steering column.
11. Remove screw and interlock cable retaining clamp from ignition switch.
12. Push release shaft in at ignition switch lock mechanism.
13. Remove cable end from ignition switch and interlock cable from vehicle.

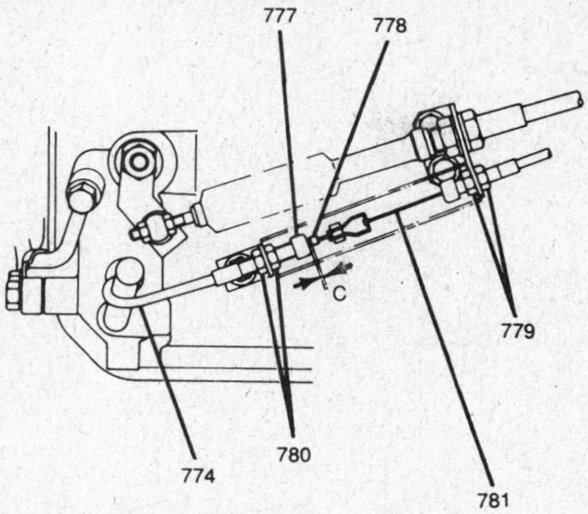

C 0.0–0.5 mm (0.0–0.02")
774 TV CABLE ASSEMBLY
777 TV CABLE BOOT
778 INNER CABLE STOPPER
779 ACCELERATOR CABLE ADJUSTMENT NUTS "B"
780 TV CABLE ADJUSTMENT NUTS "A"
781 ACCELERATOR CABLE

GC5029300477000X

Fig. 4 TV cable adjustment

Installation

1. Install cable into vehicle and route it to ignition switch.
2. Push release shaft in at ignition switch and insert cable end.
3. Attach interlock cable retaining clamp to ignition switch and secure with screw.
4. Reposition steering column, then install retaining nuts.
5. Install steering column covers.
6. Refit front carpet and install carpet retainers.
7. Attach interlock cable to selector lever housing bracket.
8. Attach cable end to key release plate.
9. Move selector lever to Park position and hold selector button in.
10. Rotate key release plate and insert a small screwdriver through key release plate to hold it in position, **Fig. 11.**
11. Allow retaining spring to position interlock control bracket.
12. Tighten interlock cable bolt to specification.
13. Ensure when selector lever is in Park position, ignition key can be moved from ACC to Lock and ignition key can be removed from ignition switch.
14. Ensure when selector lever is in any position other than P that ignition switch cannot be turned to ACC or Lock position.
15. Install manual selector cover onto selector lever.
16. Install manual selector cover lamp bulb socket into cover.
17. Install console and selector knob.

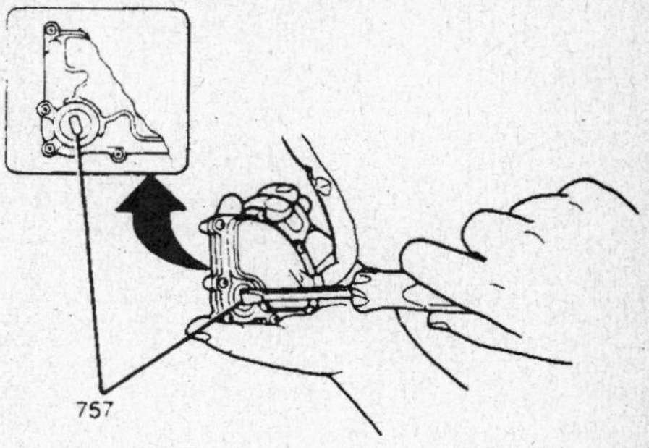

757 PNP SWITCH JOINT

GC5029300482000X

Fig. 5 Park/Neutral position switch adjustment

SHIFT LOCK SOLENOID, REPLACE

Removal

1. Remove selector lever knob to selector lever retaining screws.
2. Remove center console retaining screws and center console.
3. Remove selector lever upper cover and lower cover.
4. Disconnect shift solenoid electrical connector located under carpet.
5. Remove shift lock solenoid retaining screws and shift lock solenoid from selector lever housing, **Fig. 12.**

Installation

1. Move selector lever to Park position.
2. Apply lithium grease to upper and lower edges of solenoid lock plate.
3. Attach shift lock solenoid to selector lever housing and hand tighten two retaining screws.
4. Connect shift lock solenoid electrical connector.
5. Adjust shift lock solenoid so that it operates as follows:
    a. When ignition switch is turned off, solenoid is not actuated.
    b. When ignition switch is turned on and brake pedal is depressed, solenoid is actuated and solenoid lock plate should be positioned as shown in **Fig. 12.**
    c. There should be no clearance between solenoid lock plate and selector lever.
    d. If manual override is enabled with ignition switch in the OFF position, selector lever can be moved to any range or position.
6. Tighten shift lock solenoid retaining screws. **Ensure selector lever locks in P position and cannot be shifted to any other position.**
7. Install lower cover onto selector lever.
8. Install upper cover onto selector lever.
9. Install console and selector lever knob.

TV CABLE, REPLACE

1. Remove TV cable adjustment cover, **Fig. 13.**
2. Disconnect TV cable from accelerator cable and bracket assembly.

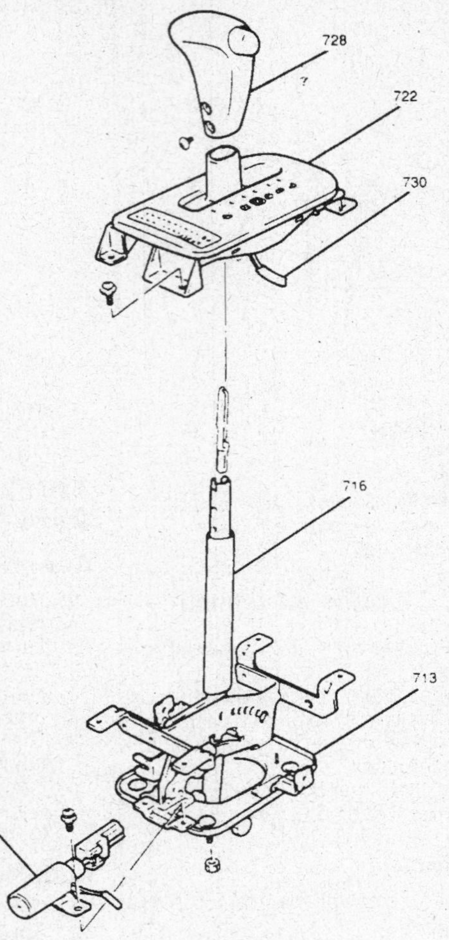

713 SELECTOR LEVER HOUSING
716 SELECTOR LEVER
722 SELECTOR COVER
728 SELECTOR LEVER KNOB
730 INDICATOR LAMP
732 SHIFT LOCK SOLENOID

GC5029300478000X

Fig. 6 Manual selector assembly

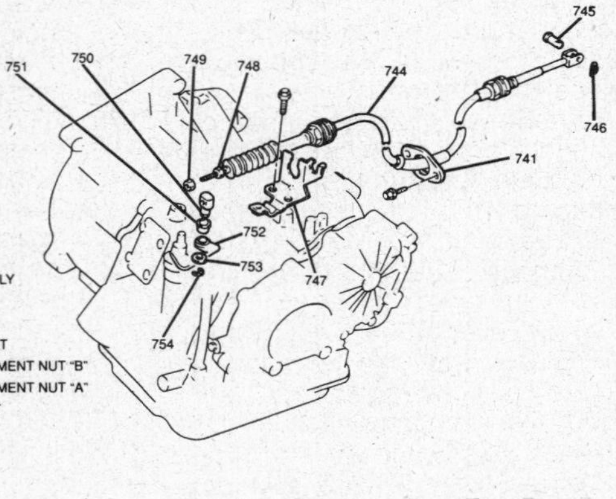

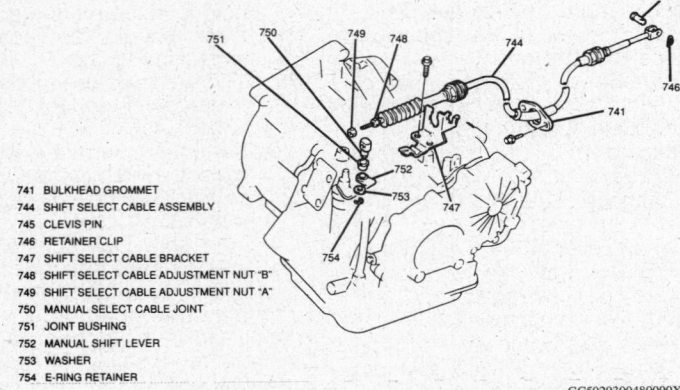

741 BULKHEAD GROMMET
744 SHIFT SELECT CABLE ASSEMBLY
745 CLEVIS PIN
746 RETAINER CLIP
747 SHIFT SELECT CABLE BRACKET
748 SHIFT SELECT CABLE ADJUSTMENT NUT "B"
749 SHIFT SELECT CABLE ADJUSTMENT NUT "A"
750 MANUAL SELECT CABLE JOINT
751 JOINT BUSHING
752 MANUAL SHIFT LEVER
753 WASHER
754 E-RING RETAINER

GC5029300480000X

Fig. 8 Shift select cable assembly

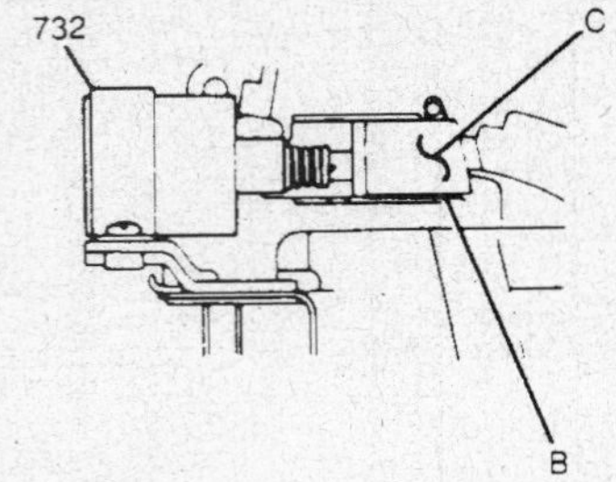

B LITHIUM GREASE
C MANUAL OVERRIDE SOLENOID LOCK PLATE
732 SHIFT LOCK SOLENOID

GC5029300479000X

Fig. 7 Solenoid lock plate

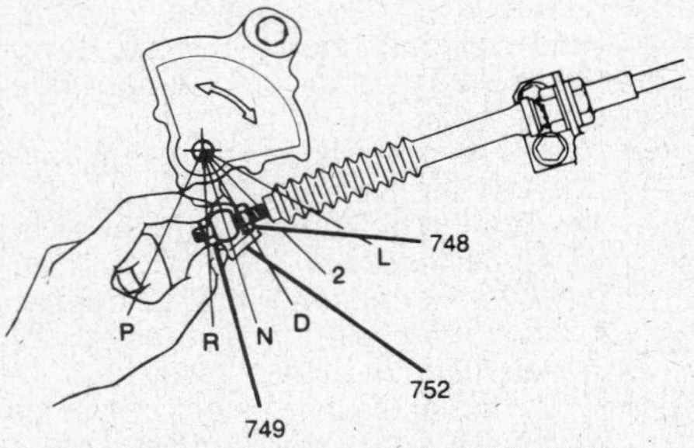

748 SHIFT SELECT CABLE ADJUSTMENT NUT "B"
749 SHIFT SELECT CABLE ADJUSTMENT NUT "A"
752 MANUAL SHIFT LEVER

GC5029300481000X

Fig. 9 Shift select cable installation

3. Raise and support vehicle.
4. Remove transaxle drain plug and drain fluid from transaxle.
5. Remove transaxle oil pan guard, oil pan and gasket.
6. Disconnect TV cable from throttle valve cam.
7. Reverse procedure to install, noting the following:
   a. Adjust TV cable as described under "Adjustments."
   b. Tighten fluid pan bolts and drain plug to specification.

TRANSAXLE CONTROL MODULE, REPLACE

1. Disconnect Transaxle Control Module (TCM) electrical connectors.
2. Remove retaining bolts and TCM from under lefthand side of instrument panel, **Fig. 14.**
3. Reverse procedure to install. Tighten TCM retaining bolts to specification.

INTERMEDIATE SERVO, REPLACE

1. Raise and support vehicle.
2. Remove three transaxle fluid pan bolts **Fig. 15.**
3. Install piston cover depressor tool No. J-35534, or equivalent, onto transaxle oil pan, **Fig. 16.**
4. Tighten adjustment bolt on tool until servo cover snap ring can be removed.
5. Remove servo cover snap ring and slowly loosen adjustment bolt.

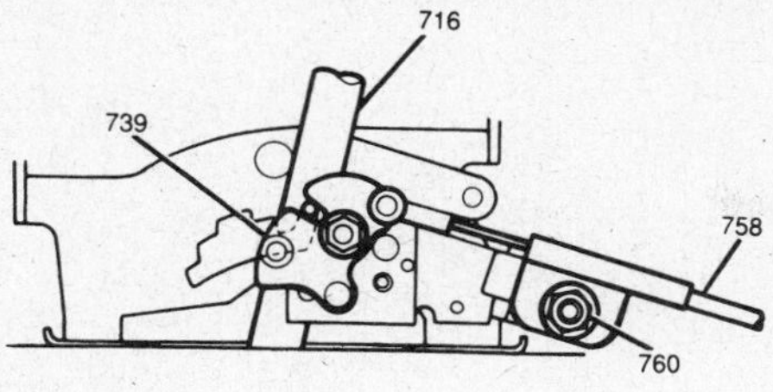

716 SELECTOR LEVER
739 KEY RELEASE PLATE
758 INTERLOCK CABLE ASSEMBLY
760 INTERLOCK CABLE BOLT

GC5029300483000X

Fig. 10 Interlock cable & manual selector assembly

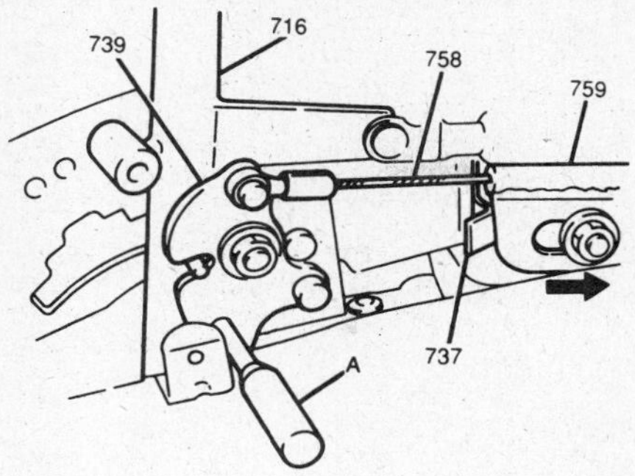

A SMALL SCREWDRIVER
716 SELECTOR LEVER
737 RETAINING SPRING
739 KEY RELEASE PLATE
758 INTERLOCK CABLE
759 INTERLOCK CABLE BRACKET

GC5029300484000X

Fig. 11 Interlock cable adjustment

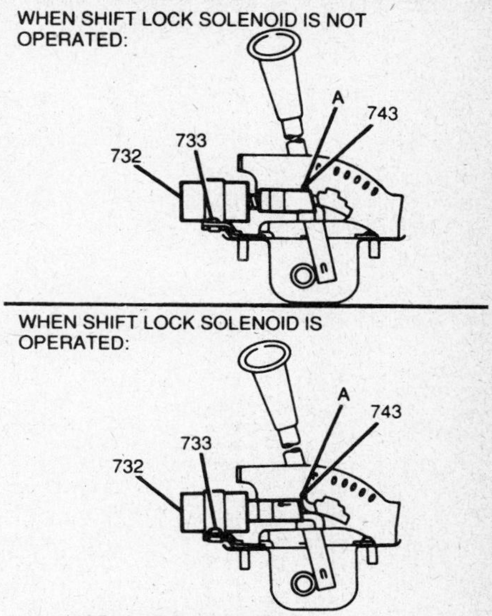

A APPLY LITHIUM GREASE
732 SHIFT LOCK SOLENOID
733 SHIFT LOCK SOLENOID RETAINING SCREW
743 DETENT PIN

GC5029300485000X

Fig. 12 Shift lock solenoid operation

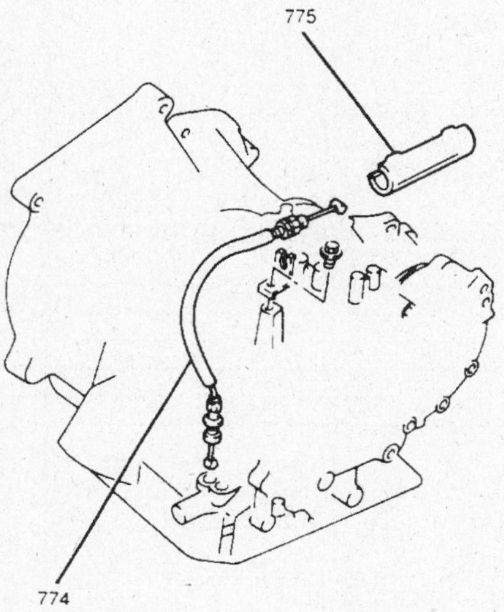

774 TV CABLE ASSEMBLY
775 TV CABLE ADJUSTMENT COVER

GC5029300486000X

Fig. 13 TV cable & adjustment cover

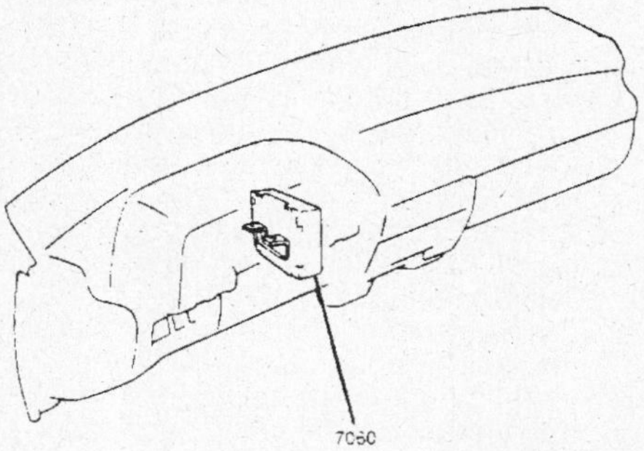

GC5029300487000X

Fig. 14 Transaxle control module location

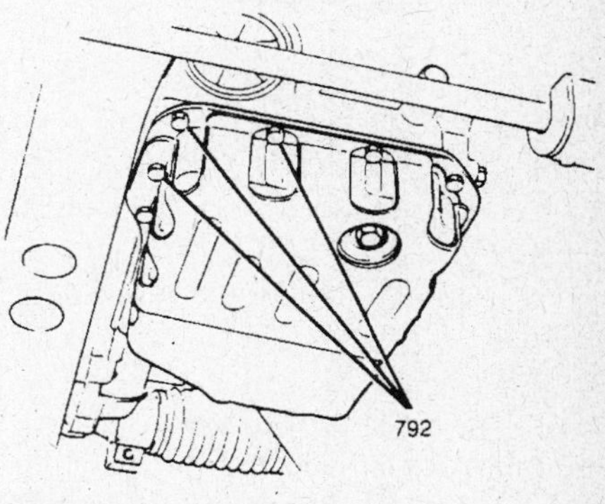

792 TRANSAXLE FLUID PAN BOLTS

GC5029300488000X

Fig. 15 Transaxle fluid pan bolts

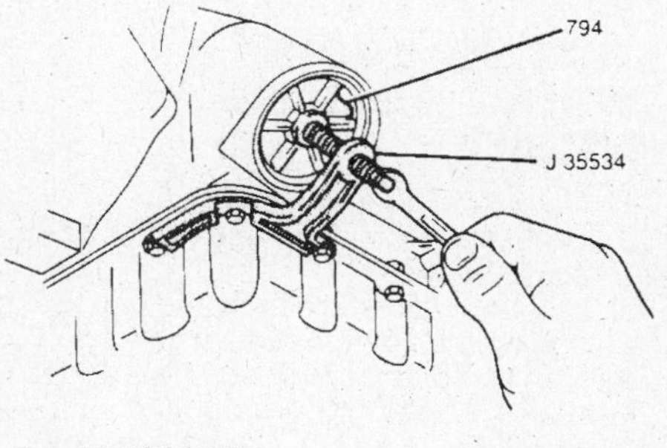

794 SERVO COVER

GC5029300489000X

Fig. 16 Piston cover depressor tool installation

6. Remove servo cover, servo piston, springs and piston rod, **Fig. 17.**
7. Reverse procedure to install. Apply transmission fluid liberally to all servo components prior to installation.

DRIVE AXLE SHAFT FLUID SEAL, REPLACE

1. Raise and support vehicle.
2. Remove wheel cover or center cap.
3. Unstake drive axle nut, and remove drive axle nut and washer.
4. Remove tire and wheel assembly.
5. Drain transaxle fluid and install two boot protectors tool No. J-28712, or equivalent, onto inner and outer drive axle boots.
6. Using a suitable screwdriver, pry differential side joint away from transaxle and remove differential side gear snap ring.
7. Remove ball stud and nut, and separate steering knuckle from control arm.
8. Remove drive axle assembly by removing differential side joint from differential side gear.
9. Remove drive axle fluid seal from transaxle.
10. Reverse procedure to install, noting the following:
    a. Use axle shaft seal installer tool No. J-35538, or equivalent, to install seal.
    b. Coat transaxle oil pan drain plug with Loctite pipe sealant part No. 1052080, or equivalent.
    c. Tighten drain plug to specification.

VALVE BODY & ACCUMULATOR, REPLACE

Removal

1. Raise and support vehicle.
2. Drain transaxle fluid, then remove oil pan and gasket.
3. Disconnect direct clutch and 2nd brake solenoid electrical connectors.
4. Using a suitable screwdriver, pry forward clutch accumulator and 2nd brake fluid pipes from lower valve body.
5. Disconnect TV cable from throttle valve cam.
6. Remove retaining bolts and fluid filter screen.
7. Remove valve body retaining bolts, **Fig. 18.**
8. Remove forward clutch and 2nd brake accumulators from transaxle case by covering accumulator bores with a

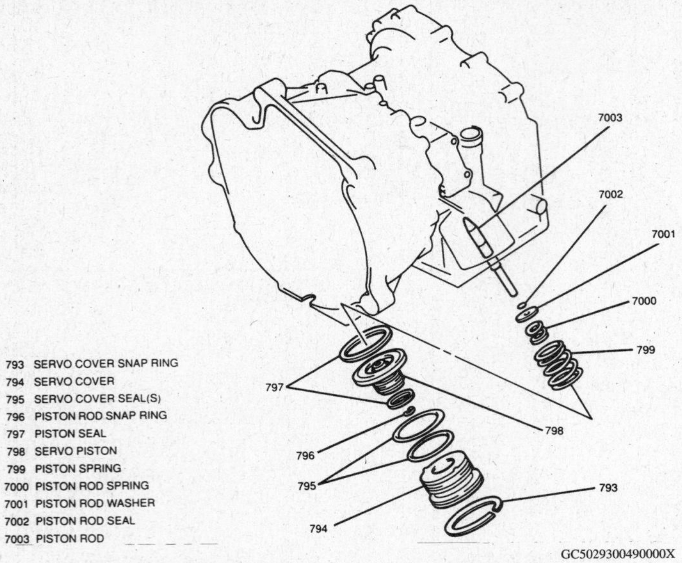

Fig. 17 Intermediate servo components

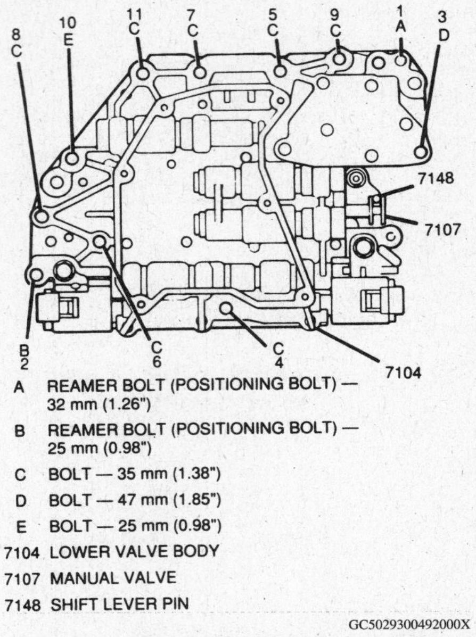

Fig. 18 Valve body bolt locations

BOLT	LENGTH	PIECES
A	29.5 mm (1.16")	6
B	38 mm (1.49")	6
C	44 mm (1.73")	2
D	REAMER BOLT	2

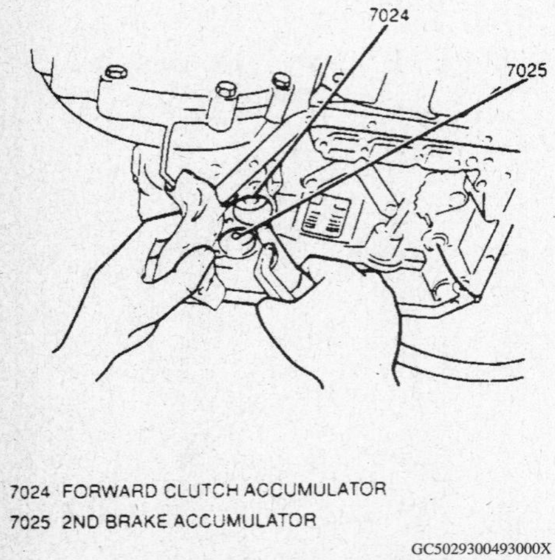

Fig. 19 Accumulator removal

cloth and slowly applying low pressure compressed air into fluid pressure passage, **Fig. 19.**

Installation

Torque sequence and specification is very important to valve body operation. If bolts are tightened at random, valve bores may become distorted and inhibit valve operation. Make sure all parts are clean and free of damage prior to their installation. When installing valve body to case, make sure accumulators and springs are in their correct positions and all valve body bolts are installed according to length and position. Do not use air powered tools when installing valve body.

1. Apply Transjel transmission assembly lubricant No. J-36850, or equivalent, to seals, and install forward clutch and 2nd brake accumulators in case bores.
2. Install valve body into transaxle case aligning manual valve with shift lever pin.
3. Install and hand tighten valve body bolts in their correct position, **Fig. 20.**
4. Tighten bolts A and B to specifications first, then tighten remaining bolts to specifications in a diagonal pattern.
5. Install fluid filter screen and tighten bolts to specification.
6. Attach TV cable to throttle valve cam.
7. Install forward clutch accumulator and 2nd brake fluid pipes.
8. Connect direct clutch and 2nd brake solenoid connectors.
9. Install oil pan with new oil pan gasket and tighten pan bolts to specification.
10. Coat transaxle oil pan drain plug with Loctite pipe sealant part No. 1052080, or equivalent, install and tighten to specification.
11. Fill transaxle with fluid and check level.

SHIFT SOLENOIDS & WIRING HARNESS, REPLACE

1. Raise and support vehicle.
2. Drain transaxle fluid and remove transaxle oil pan.
3. Disconnect direct clutch and 2nd brake solenoid electrical connectors.
4. Remove direct clutch solenoid and 2nd brake solenoid mounting bolts, **Fig. 21.**
5. Remove solenoid wiring harness retaining nut and plate.
6. Pull wiring harness out of transaxle case.
7. Reverse procedure to install, noting the following:
   a. Tighten bolts to specifications.
   b. Coat transaxle oil pan drain plug with Loctite pipe sealant part No. 1052080, or equivalent.
   c. Fill transaxle with fluid and check level.

TRANSAXLE

REPLACE

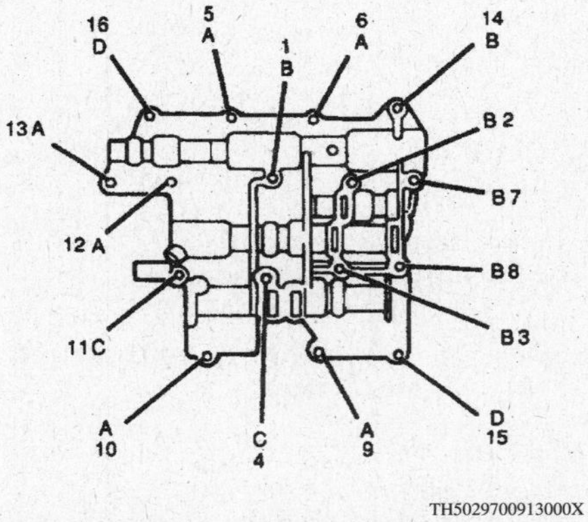

Fig. 20 Upper valve body bolt tightening sequence

1. Remove hood retaining bolts, then hood assembly.
2. Remove battery hold down bolt, then the bracket and battery.
3. Remove adjustment cover and TV cable, then the adjustment nut and shift select cable.
4. Remove engine wire harness bracket, then the vehicle speed sensor, shift solenoid harness and transaxle range switch electrical connectors.
5. Remove clip and speedometer cable, then the clamps and inlet and outlet fluid cooler hoses. Plug hoses to prevent fluid leakage.
6. Remove starter motor.
7. Remove upper rear transaxle bulkhead retaining bolt, rear mount through bolt and nut, and upper engine retaining bolts.
8. Remove ground cable from transaxle.

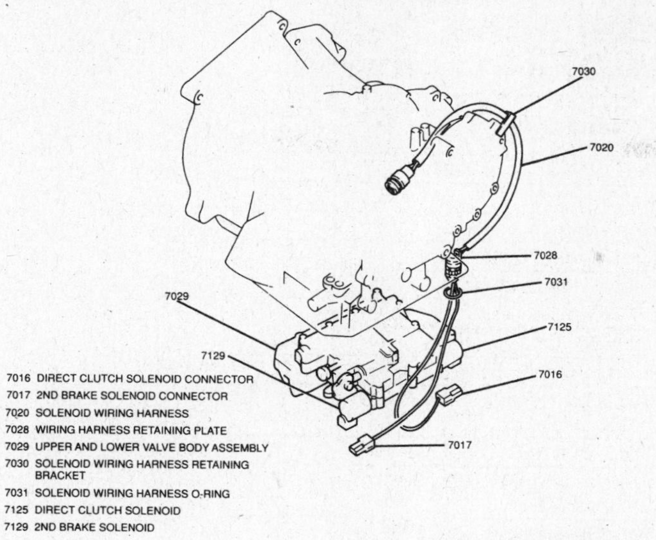

Fig. 21 Shift solenoids & wiring harness

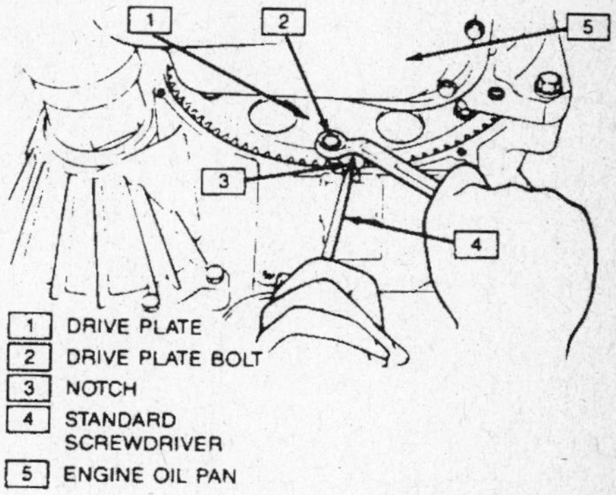

Fig. 22 Driveplate bolt removal

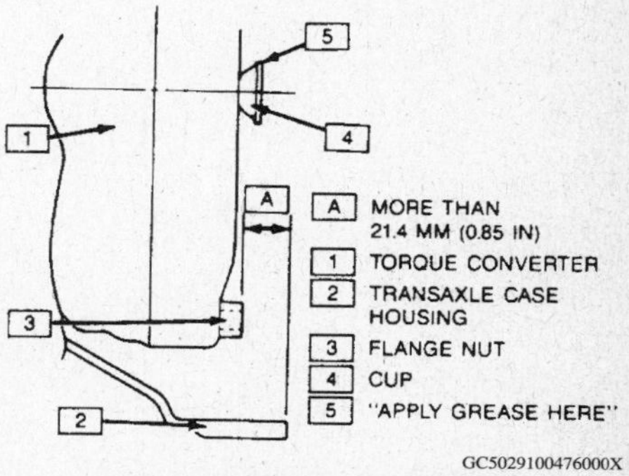

Fig. 23 Torque converter installation

9. Install universal support fixture tool No. J-28467-A and adapters, or equivalent, then raise and support vehicle.
10. Drain transaxle fluid into suitable container.
11. Remove front wheel assemblies, then righthand and lefthand splash shields.
12. Remove right and lefthand ball stud nuts and bolts, then separate control arms from steering knuckles.
13. Install drive axle boot protector tool No. J-28712, or equivalent, on differential side and wheel side joints of both axles.
14. Remove wheel center cap, cotter pin and driveshaft nut, then the wheel nuts and wheel assembly.
15. Remove snap ring from spline of differential side joint using a suitable screwdriver.
16. Remove stabilizer bar bracket bolts and ball stud bolt, then the ball stud from steering knuckle by pulling down on stabilizer bar.
17. Disconnect inboard joint from differential side gear and wheel side joint from steering knuckle.
18. Remove drive axle assemblies.
19. Remove bolts and rear engine torque rod, then the bolts and flywheel cover from transaxle case housing.
20. Using a suitable screwdriver in notch provided to hold driveplate, remove torque converter mounting bolts, **Fig. 22.**
21. Remove exhaust hanger bracket and lower rear engine mount bulkhead bolt.
22. Remove nuts and bolts, then the rear engine mount bracket.
23. Lower vehicle and slightly lower engine.
24. Raise and support vehicle, then support transaxle with suitable hydraulic jack.
25. Remove bolts and lefthand transaxle mount and bracket.
26. Remove lower retaining bolt, nut and stud.
27. Move transaxle toward lefthand side of engine compartment, then remove transaxle.
28. Reverse procedure to install noting the following:
    a. Apply suitable grease around torque converter center cup.
    b. Measure distance A, **Fig. 23.** Distance should measure more than .85 inch. If distance is less than specified, converter installation is improper and must be corrected.
    c. Guide righthand drive axle into differential side gear as transaxle is being raised.
    d. After installing inboard joints into differential side gear, push inboard joints into side gears until snap rings on drive axles engage side gears.
    e. Adjust oil pressure control cable if necessary.
    f. Fill transaxle with fluid.
    g. Tighten to specification.

TIGHTENING SPECIFICATIONS

Year	Component	Torque/ Ft. Lbs.
1997–2000	Automatic Transaxle Controller Retaining Bolts	11
	Ball Stud Nuts & Bolts	44
	Direct Clutch Solenoid Retaining Bolt	35①
	Engine Wiring Harness Bracket Bolts	12
	Filler Tube Bracket & Screen Bolt	53①
	Flywheel Cover Bolts	84①
	Flywheel To Torque Converter Bolts	14
	Inlet & Outlet Union Bolts	16
	Lefthand Transaxle Mount Bracket Bolts & Retaining Nuts	40

Continued

TIGHTENING SPECIFICATIONS—Continued

Year	Component	Torque/ Ft. Lbs.
1997-2000	Lower Engine To Transaxle Retaining Bolt	40
	Lower Rear Engine Mount To Bulkhead Bolt	40
	Lower Valve Body Bolts	9
	Lower Valve Body Cover Bolts	35①
	Rear Engine Mount Bracket Bolts & Nuts	40
	Rear Engine Torque Rod Assembly Bolts	40
	Second Brake Solenoid Retaining Bolt	35①
	Selector Lever Assembly Housing Seat Nuts	11.5
	Shift Lever Back-up & Neutral Safety Switch Mounting Bolt	17
	Shift Select Cable Bulkhead Grommet Bolts	15
	Solenoid Wiring Harness Retaining Bracket Bolt & Nut	15
	Speedometer Driven Gear Case Bolt	11
	Starter Motor Bolts	17
	Transaxle Cooler Pipe Retaining Bracket Bolt	20
	Transaxle Drain Plug	17
	Transaxle Fluid Pan Bolts	53①
	Upper Rear Transaxle Mount To Bulkhead Bolt	40
	Upper Transaxle To Engine Retaining Bolts	40
	Upper Valve Body Bolts	53①
	Vehicle Speed Sensor Retaining Bolt	17

① — Inch lbs.

Turbo Hydra-Matic 3T40 Automatic Transaxle

NOTE: On Air Bag Equipped Models, Refer To " Air Bag System Precautions" Located In The Front Of This Manual For System Disarming & Arming Procedures.

NOTE: Refer To "Computer Relearn Procedures " Located In The Front Of This Manual For Computer Relearn Procedures.

INDEX

PRECAUTIONS

AIR BAG SYSTEMS

Refer to "Air Bag System Precautions" in the front of this manual for system disarming and arming procedures.

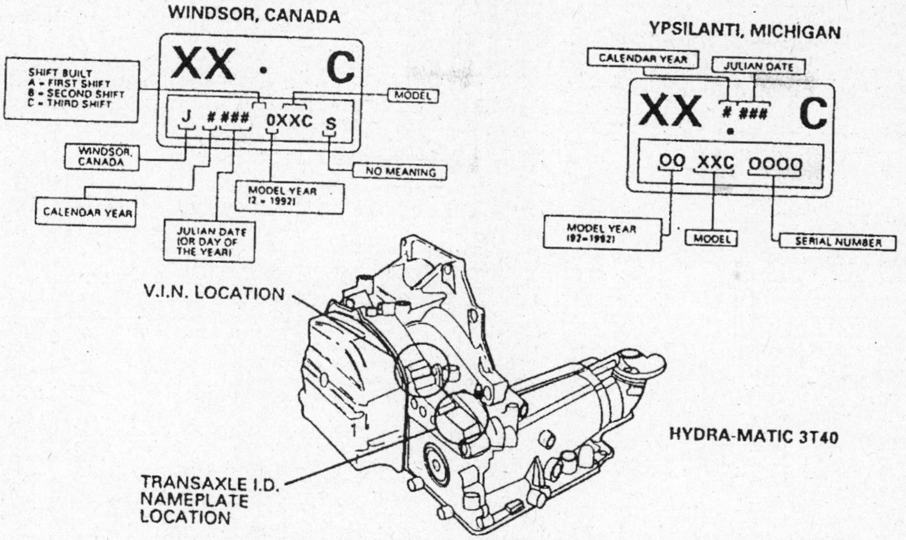

Copyrighted Material Reprinted with Permission from Hydra-Matic Div., GM Corp.

TH5028800099000X

Fig. 1 Transaxle identification

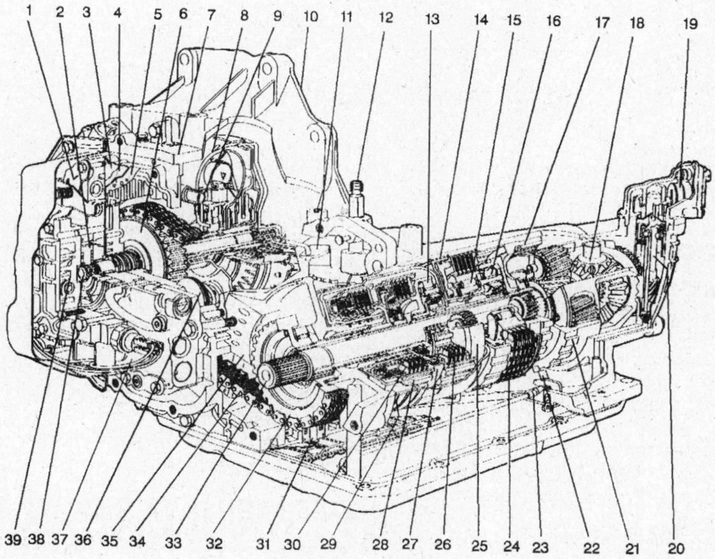

Legend

(1) Throttle Lever and Bracket Assembly
(2) Pump Rotor
(3) Gasket, Spacer Plate
(4) Spacer Plate
(5) Gasket, Spacer Plate
(6) Drive Sprocket
(7) Case Cover
(8) Torque Converter
(9) Manual Valve
(10) Case
(11) Manual Detent Lever
(12) Manual Shaft
(13) Input Planetary Gear Set
(14) Low and Reverse Clutch Housing
(15) Roller Clutch
(16) Reaction Planetary Gear Set
(17) Final Drive Internal Gear
(18) Differential Assembly
(19) Speedometer Drive Gear
(20) Governor Assembly
(21) Reaction Internal Gear
(22) Parking Lock Pawl
(23) Parking Lock Pawl
(24) Low and Reverse Clutch Plate Assembly
(25) Input Internal Gear
(26) Forward Clutch Plate Assembly
(27) Forward Clutch Housing
(28) Direct Clutch Housing
(29) Intermediate Band
(30) Direct Clutch Plate Assembly
(31) Intermediate Servo Piston
(32) Driven Sprocket
(33) Output Shaft
(34) Drive Link Assembly
(35) Driven Support Sprocket
(36) 1-2 Accumulator Piston
(37) Control Valve and Pump Assembly
(38) Pump Shaft
(39) Auxiliary Valve Body

GC5029800800000X

Fig. 2 Cross-section view of 3T40 transmission

BATTERY GROUND CABLE

Prior to service, disconnect battery ground cable and isolate as required.

IDENTIFICATION

This transaxle may be identified by a model tag attached to the case exterior, **Fig. 1.**

DESCRIPTION

The hydra-matic 3T40 transmission, **Fig. 2,** is a fully automatic unit for front wheel drive vehicles. The 3T40 provides three forward gear ranges and a reverse. Throttle opening controls oil pressure and shift points. The 3T40 transmission consists of a four element hydraulic torque converter, a compound planetary gear set, a dual sprocket and drive link assembly, three multiple disc clutches, one roller clutch, an intermediate band assembly, a valve body assembly and a vane type oil pump.

TROUBLESHOOTING

Refer to **Figs. 3 through 30** for troubleshooting charts.

BRAKE TRANSAXLE SHIFT INTERLOCK (BTSI) SYSTEM

1. Verify brake light operation.
2. If brake lights do not operate, refer to **Fig. 31** for wiring diagrams and **Figs. 32 and 33** for diagnostic procedures.
3. Check for proper installation of aftermarket equipment or for broken or partially broken wires inside of insulation. This could cause system failures, but not be indicated in a continuity or voltage check.

MAINTENANCE

Refer to "Lubricant Data Chart" in the appropriate chassis chapter of this manual for transaxle fluid specifications.

FLUID LEVEL CHECK

When checking fluid level, the fluid will be higher on the indicator when the transmission is cold. The fluid will drop when checked at operating temperature.

1. Start and operate engine for 15 minutes or until transmission fluid reaches operating temperature of 190-220° F.
2. Park vehicle on level surface, then apply parking brake and chock wheels.
3. With engine idling and brake pedal depressed, move shift lever through each gear range, ending in Park position.
4. Check fluid level, color and condition.

FLUID CHANGE

1. Raise and support vehicle, then position a drain pan under oil pan.
2. Remove front and side oil pan retaining bolts and loosen rear pan retaining bolts.
3. Pry oil pan loose from transaxle case and allow fluid to drain.
4. Remove remaining retaining bolts, oil

Checks	Cause
Oil Level	Low
TV Cable	• Not adjusted properly • Wrong cable
Oil Pressure	Check for causes of high or low oil pressure.
Forward Clutch	• Restricted feed • Burned clutch plates
Driven Sprocket Support	Rough machine surface
Case Cover Gasket	Incorrect gasket

GC5029800801000X

Fig. 3 Chatters/slips in first gear

Checks	Cause
Direct Clutch	• Burned clutch plates • Seal ring is off the piston • Exhaust check ball is sticking
Lo and Reverse Clutch	• Housing cup plug assembly is restricted or not fully seated • Leaking seals
Lo and Reverse Pipe	O-ring seal is damaged or missing
Case to Cover Gasket	• Incorrect (the driven sprocket support height is wrong) • Damaged or leaking

GC5029800802010X

Fig. 4 Slips in reverse or no reverse (Part 1 of 2)

Checks	Cause
Lo and Reverse Clutch	Burned plates
Manual Valve	A fallen out retainer clip
Low Line Pressure	Check the causes of low line pressure

GC5029800802020X

Fig. 4 Slips in reverse or no reverse (Part 2 of 2)

Checks	Cause
Manual Linkage	Misadjusted
TV Cable	Misadjusted, unhooked, bound, or broken
Oil Level	Low
Governor or Speed Sensor (depending on model)	• The cover is worn • A thrust washer is missing • The governor seal is worn or cut • The governor spring is not seated • The governor weights are binding on the pin • A ball is missing • The governor driven gear is stripped
Intermediate Servo	• The apply pin is incorrect or sticking • Seals are cut, damaged, or missing • The piston is sticking or is damaged • Porosity in the case servo bore
Control Valve Assembly	• Valves are sticking • Spacer plate gaskets are leaking or are incorrectly installed
Valve Body Spacer	• The governor feed orifice to the 1-2 and 2-3 shift valve is plugged • The drive to governor orifice is plugged
Intermediate Band	Burned or worn
Case Cover	• Porosity • Undrilled holes • Missing cup plugs • The second oil passage is leaking
Case	• Leaks in the governor passage or pipe • Leaks in the second oil passage

GC5029800803000X

Fig. 5 No upshift, delayed upshift or full throttle upshift

pan and gasket. Thoroughly clean pan before reinstalling.

5. Remove and discard screen and O-ring seal.
6. Install replacement screen and O-ring seal, locating screen against dipstick stop.
7. Install gasket on oil pan, then install oil pan and tighten retaining bolts to specification.
8. Lower vehicle and add fluid.
9. With selector in Park, parking brake applied and engine at idle speed and operating temperature, check fluid level and add fluid as necessary. **Do not race engine. Move shift lever through ranges and back to P position.**

ADJUSTMENTS

PARK/LOCK CABLE

1. Place floor shift lever in Park position.
2. Place ignition in lock position.
3. Unseat body housing lock from body housing.
4. Ensure there is no gap between metal terminal stop and protruding end of blue plastic collar. If a gap exists, adjust position of park/lock cable.
5. Ensure blue plastic collar is flush or recessed .04 inch within ignition park/lock housing. If collar position is not as specified, adjust position of park/lock cable.
6. Adjust outer cable conduit to obtain proper location of white plastic housing in ignition switch. Ensure body housing is still attached to shift control mounting bracket.
7. Seat body housing lock in body housing while holding outer cable conduit in position.

THROTTLE VALVE (TV) CABLE

1997-98

1. Depress and hold readjustment tab.
2. Pull cable conduit out until slider mechanism hits stop.
3. Release button.
4. Remove floor mat.
5. Firmly depress accelerator pedal to wide open throttle position.
6. Ensure cable moves freely. Cable may appear to function properly with engine stopped and cold, recheck after engine is hot.

1999 & 2000

1. Depress and hold readjustment tab.
2. Pull cable conduit out until slider mechanism hits stop.
3. Release button.
4. Position a 17 mm socket and torque wrench onto throttle body pulley cam assembly.
5. Rotate torque wrench to wide open throttle position, then **torque** to 62-69 inch lbs. Audible clicks will be heard during this step.
6. Release applied pressure on torque wrench.
7. Remove torque wrench and socket.
8. Ensure cable moves freely. Cable may appear to function properly with engine stopped and cold, recheck after engine is hot.

IN-VEHICLE REPAIRS

AUXILIARY VALVE BODY, VALVE BODY & OIL PUMP ASSEMBLY, REPLACE

1. Remove TV cable from transmission.
2. Remove transmission mount bracket.
3. Remove valve body cover retaining bolts, then the cover and gasket.
4. Remove TCC solenoid to valve body retaining bolt, then the TCC solenoid.
5. Remove TCC solenoid wiring connector from case connector, then disconnect wires from pressure switches.
6. Remove TV lever retaining bolts from valve body, then the TV lever and cable link.
7. Ensure six check balls are not lost during removal procedure and that green bolt is not removed at this time.
8. Remove remaining valve body to case attaching bolts, then the valve body.
9. Remove green bolt.
10. Separate valve body from oil pump
11. Remove check ball behind control valve assembly.
12. Reverse procedure to install. Tighten bolts to specification.

INTERMEDIATE SERVO & ACCUMULATOR CHECK VALVE, REPLACE

1. Raise and support vehicle.
2. Remove transaxle oil pan and gasket, then the screen and O-ring.
3. Remove reverse oil pipe retaining brackets, intermediate servo cover and gasket.
4. Remove accumulator valve and spring.
5. Remove intermediate servo assembly.
6. Reverse procedure to install

GOVERNOR, REPLACE

1. Raise and support vehicle.
2. Disconnect VSS lead from transaxle.
3. Remove mounting bolts and VSS housing.
4. Remove O-ring.
5. Remove governor assembly, governor shaft screen assembly and seal, **Fig. 34.**
6. Reverse procedure to install.

Checks	Cause
Oil Level	High or Low
TV Cable	Misadjusted, unhooked, bound, or broken
Oil Pressure	Check for causes of high or low oil pressure.
Intermediate Servo	• Seals are cut, damaged, or leaking • The piston is damaged • The servo bore in the case is damaged • The apply pin is too long or too short • The servo orifice bleed cup plug is missing • A leak exists between the servo apply pin and the case
Intermediate Band (606)	The servo band apply pin is binding

GC5029800804010X

Fig. 6 Slipping or rough 1-2 shift (Part 1 of 2)

Checks	Cause
TV Link	Link is bent or is wrong
Control Valve Assembly	• The TV plunger is binding • The shift TV valve is binding • The 1-2 accumulator valve is binding
1-2 Accumulator	• Binding 1-2 accumulator piston • Broken 1-2 accumulator spring • The piston seal or groove is damaged • The 1-2 accumulator bore is damaged
Spacer Plate	• The spacer plate or the gasket is incorrect • The gasket is incorrectly installed
Case	The second oil passage is leaking
Case Cover	The second oil passage is leaking

GC5029800804020X

Fig. 6 Slipping or rough 1-2 shift (Part 2 of 2)

Checks	Cause
Oil Level	Incorrect level
TV Valve	Misadjusted, unhooked, bound, or broken
Manual Linkage	Misadjusted
Oil Pressure	(Check for causes of high or low oil pressure)
Direct Clutch	Plugged accumulator exhaust port
Direct Clutch Exhaust #1 Checkball	Mispositioned or missing
Control Valve Assembly	• Binding plunger and throttle valve • Binding shift TV valve

GC5029800805000X

Fig. 7 2-3 shift rough or delay

Checks	Cause
Oil Level	Incorrect level
TV Cable	Misadjusted, unhooked, bound, or broken
Manual Linkage	Misadjusted
Oil Pressure	(Check for causes of high or low oil pressure)
Intermediate Servo	• The Piston to case oil seal is damaged • The servo piston is damaged • The servo bore in the case is damaged
Accumulator Exhaust Check Valve	Not seating in the case
Spacer Plate	• The direct clutch feed orifice is plugged or restricted • The spacer plate or the gaskets are leaking, damaged, or incorrectly installed • Incorrect spacer plate
Checkball #5	Not seating or missing

GC5029800806010X

Fig. 8 2-3 shift soft, slips or early (Part 1 of 2)

PARKING PAWL SHAFT, REPLACE

1. Raise and support vehicle.
2. Remove transaxle oil pan.
3. Remove oil strainer and filter seal.
4. Remove fluid level indicator stop.
5. Remove rod retainer and parking lock bracket.
6. Remove clip, pin, rod and spring.
7. Reverse procedure to install.

TRANSAXLE SIDE CASE COVER, REPLACE

1. Remove transmission bracket.
2. Remove valve body cover and gasket as described under " Auxiliary Valve Body, Valve Body & Oil Pump Assembly, Replace."
3. Disconnect TCC wire from case connector.
4. emove valve body retaining bolts, n the valve body from oil pump.
5. nove oil pump assembly retaining , then the oil pump from case
6. ve oil pump drive shaft.
7. e valve body spacer plate, then cer plate gaskets.
8. t case cover retaining bolts, ase cover.
9. In pi 12 x 1.95 x 14 bolts in dowel p d tighten equally in order to R ver loose.
10. bocedure to install. Tighten fication.

TV CA EPLACE

Remo

1. Ren tor c e end from accelera- sembly slot.
2. Rem brac conduit end from sing locking tangs.
3. Rem straps routing clips or
4. Remo ing bo transaxle retain- transa cable cover at isible.
5. Remo then re ansaxle link, se seal.

Installation

1. Install a new seal into transaxle case hole.
2. Install transaxle end of cable to TV link.
3. Install TV cable bolt and washer assembly to transaxle. Tighten bolt to specification.
4. Install TV cable routing clips and straps.
5. Install TV cable conduit end to bracket.
6. Install TV cable into accelerator control lever assembly slot.
7. Pull on upper end of cable, noting the following:
   a. Cable should travel a short distance with light resistance caused by small return spring on TV lever.
   b. When releasing upper end of TV cable, cable should return to zero TV position.
8. Adjust TV cable as described under "Adjustments."

VEHICLE SPEED SENSOR (VSS), REPLACE

1. Raise and support vehicle.
2. Disconnect speed sensor lead from transaxle.
3. Remove speed sensor housing retaining bolts, then the housing and O-ring.
4. Reverse procedure to install.

TRANSAXLE

REPLACE

1. **On models equipped with 2.2L engine,** remove intake air duct.
2. **On all models,** remove TV cable as outlined under "TV Cable, Replace."
3. Remove shift cable and bracket.
4. Remove vacuum lines.
5. Disconnect electrical connectors.
6. **On models equipped with 2.2L engine,** remove power steering pump and position aside.
7. **On all models,** remove filler tube.
8. Support engine and transaxle assembly using engine support fixture tool No. J28467-360, or equivalent.
9. Remove top transaxle to engine retaining bolts.
10. Raise and support vehicle.
11. Remove front wheels.
12. Remove left splash shield.
13. Remove front ABS wheel speed sensors, then the harness from left suspension support.
14. Remove lower ball joints from knuckle, then the stabilizer shaft links.
15. Remove front air deflector.
16. Remove left suspension support.
17. Remove drive axles.
18. Remove engine to transaxle brace.
19. Remove converter cover retaining bolts, then the cover.
20. Remove starter.
21. Remove flywheel to torque converter retaining bolts.
22. Remove transaxle oil cooler pipes.
23. Remove ground wires from engine to transaxle bolt.
24. Remove cooler pipe brace, then the exhaust brace.
25. Remove engine and transaxle mount retaining bolts.
26. Support transaxle with a suitable transaxle jack.
27. Remove transaxle mount to body retaining bolts.
28. Remove heater core hose pipe brace to transaxle nut and bolt.
29. Remove remaining transaxle to engine retaining bolts.
30. Remove transaxle assembly.
31. Reverse procedure to install. Tighten bolts to specification.

Checks	Cause
Case Cover	• Porosity is in the direct clutch case cover passage • Case cover gaskets are incorrect • The driven sprocket support passages are interconnected, leaking, or restricted • The driven sprocket support oil seal rings are damaged or are missing • The sleeve is loose or is out of position
Direct Clutch	• A leaking checkball • A damaged checkball capsule • Damaged or missing seals • A cracked or damaged housing or piston • A missing or incorrect apply ring • The wrong number of clutch plates

GC5029800806020X

Fig. 8 2-3 shift soft, slips or early (Part 2 of 2)

Checks	Cause
Spacer Plate	The spacer plate or the gaskets are leaking, are damaged, or are incorrectly installed
Case to Governor Shaft Sleeve	Damaged or missing
Direct Clutch	• The checkball is leaking • The checkball capsule is damaged • The seals are damaged or missing • The housing or the piston is cracked or damaged • The backing plate snap ring is out of the groove • The clutch plates are damaged or are missing

GC5029800807020X

Fig. 9 No 2-3 shift or 2-3 shift delay (Part 2 of 2)

Checks	Cause
Oil Level	Incorrect level
Oil Pressure	(Check the cause of low oil pressure)
Converter, Drive Sprocket Support Bushings	Converter drainback
Turbine Shaft	The scarf seals are damaged or are leaking

GC5029800809000X

Fig. 11 Delay in drive and reverse

Checks	Cause
Driven Sprocket Support	The sleeve is turned
Oil Pressure	(See causes of low oil pressure)
Manual Linkage	The manual valve is not moving
Driven Sprocket Support	• The drive oil passage is blocked in the driven sprocket support or the gasket • The sleeve is loose or is mislocated
Case Cover	A leak exists in the drive oil passage
Forward Clutch	Plates are burned or damaged
Control Valve Assembly	The valve body pipe is leaking or missing

GC5029800811000X

Fig. 13 No drive in forward ranges

Checks	Cause
Oil Level	• Incorrect level • External leaks
Forward Clutch	The feed in the input shaft is restricted (may occur with a cold engine at a fast engine idle)
Case Cover	• A leak has occurred between the case cover and the driven sprocket support passages • Incorrect gaskets are between the case cover and the driven sprocket support passages

GC5029800813000X

Fig. 15 No drive in drive ranges

Checks	Cause
Intermediate Servo	• The apply pin is wrong or is sticking • The seals are cut, are damaged, or are missing • The piston is sticking or is damaged • Porosity is in the case servo bore
Accumulator Exhaust Valve	The valve is sticking, not seating
Control Valve Assembly	The 1-2 shift valve is sticking
Spacer Plate	• The gaskets are incorrectly installed • The governor feed to the 1-2 shift valve is blocked • The intermediate band apply feed orifice is blocked • Wrong spacer plate

GC5029800815010X

Fig. 17 Shifts 1-3, misses second (Part 1 of 2)

Checks	Cause
Oil Level	Incorrect level
TV Valve	Misadjusted, unhooked, bound, or broken
Manual Linkage	Misadjusted
Governor or Governor Cover (depending on model)	• The cover is worn • A thrust washer is missing • The governor seal is worn or cut • The governor spring is not seated • The governor weights are binding on a pin • A ball is missing • The governor driven gear is stripped
Intermediate Servo	• The piston to case oil seal is damaged • The servo piston is damaged • The servo bore in the case is damaged
Accumulator Exhaust Check Valve	The valve is not seating in the case
Case	• The direct clutch accumulator cup plug is leaking or missing • The case to governor shaft sleeve is missing or is damaged • The center gasket is leaking
Case Cover	• The case cover bolts are loose • The driven sprocket support passages are interconnected, are leaking or are restricted • The driven sprocket support oil seal rings are damaged or are missing • The sleeve is loose or is out of position
Throttle Lever and Bracket Assembly	Binding
TV Link	Wrong, unhooked, or binding TV link
Control Valve Assembly	• The 2-3 shift valve or the 2-3 TV valve are sticking • The shift TV valve is sticking • The governor feed to the 2-3 shift valve is restricted • The direct clutch feed orifice is restricted • The #5 checkball is missing or is mislocated

GC5029800807010X

Fig. 9 No 2-3 shift or 2-3 shift delay (Part 1 of 2)

Checks	Cause
Auxiliary Valve Body	Missing or clogged TCC auxiliary valve body filter

GC5029800808000X

Fig. 10 Engine stalls during reverse or drive engagement

Checks	Cause
Lo Roller Clutch	• Springs are missing • Rollers are galled or are missing

GC5029800810000X

Fig. 12 No drive in drive or intermediate range

Checks	Cause
Oil Level	Incorrect level
Torque Converter	The converter to flex plate bolts are missing
Oil Pressure	• The pressure regulator valve is sticking in the bushing • Pump seals are worn • The oil pump shaft is broken
Differential	The differential is damaged or broken up
Drive Link	• The drive link is broken • An object is between the drive link and the sprocket
Manual Valve	A retainer clip is fallen out
Manual Linkage	Misadjusted
Input Shaft	The shaft is loose or has broken away from the forward clutch drum
Reaction Carrier	The carrier is broken at the lo roller clutch cam

GC5 00X

Fig. 14 No drive in all ranges

Checks	Cause
Governor	• Springs are distorted or out of place • Governor weights are binding on the pin
Control Valve Assembly	• The 1-2 shift valve is sticking in the upshifted position • The 1-2 throttle valve is sticking in the upshifted positior

00X

Fig. 16 Second speed start

Checks	Cause
Case	The intermediate servo apply passage (second oil) is blo
Case Cover	The intermediate servo apply passage (second oil) is bl
Intermediate Band	• The band is improperly installed • The band is burned or broken

020X

Fig. 17 Shifts 1-3, misses second (

Checks	Cause
Governor or Governor Cover (depending on model)	• The Governor cover is worn • The thrust washer is missing • The governor seal is worn or cut • The governor spring is not seated • The governor weights are binding on the pin • A ball is missing • The governor driven gear is stripped
Intermediate Servo	The intermediate servo is sticking
Direct Clutch Orifice Controlled by #2 Checkball	Restricted orifice
1-2 Accumulator	• The piston is missing • A seal is leaking

GC5029800816000X

Fig. 18 Shifts 3-1 at high speeds for passing gear

Checks	Cause
Manual Linkage	Misadjusted
Lo and Reverse Clutch	• The lo and reverse pipe is leaking • The piston seals are leaking
Control Valve Assembly	The lo blow off valve assembly is damaged

GC5029800818000X

Fig. 20 No overrun braking in Low

Checks	Cause
Direct Clutch Center Seal	Center seal is missing in the direct clutch

GC5029800820000X

Fig. 22 Binding in third gear

Checks	Cause
Definition: Additionally, a popping noise similar to popcorn popping	
Oil Pump System	• Verify that the noise is internal to the oil pump during a preliminary oil pressure check. An increase in line pressure will vary an oil pump noise • Pump cavitation is indicated by bubbles on the fluid level indicator • Check the transmission fluid strainer for a filter seam leak • Check the transmission fluid strainer seal for proper positioning or for a cut seal

GC5029800822000X

Fig. 24 Whine noise varying with RPM or fluid pressure

Checks	Cause
Definition: Additionally, noise is most noticeable under light throttle	
Drive Link Assembly System	Verify a noise from the sprockets or the drive link assembly (chain) by placing your left foot on the brake and by moving the gear selector from Park or Neutral to Drive or Reverse. If the noise stops, check the remaining items in this list.
Drive Link (Chain) Assembly	Stretched
Drive Sprocket and Driven Sprocket	Broken or sheared teeth
Drive and Driven Sprocket Support Bearing Assemblies	Bearing race or roller bearing surfaces are rough or pitted
Drive Sprocket Support and Driven Sprocket Support	Bearing outer race support is rough or nicked

GC5029800824000X

Fig. 26 Whine/growl noise that changes w/vehicle speed

Checks	Cause
Reaction Gear Set	—
Reaction Internal Gear	Gears are worn or pitted
Reaction Carrier Assembly	The thrust washer or the thrust bearing mating surfaces are rough or pitted.
Reaction Sun Gear	—
Reaction Sun Gear to Reaction Internal Gear Thrust Bearing	Thrust bearing races or roller bearing surfaces are rough or pitted

GC5029800826000X

Fig. 28 Noise in second

Checks	Cause
TV Cable	Misadjusted, unhooked, bound, or broken
Throttle Cable Assembly	Not opening throttle sufficiently
Control Valve Assembly	• The shift TV valve is binding • The TV valve is binding
Space Plate	• Spacer plate holes are plugged • The gasket is mispositioned or damaged

GC5029800817000X

Fig. 19 No full throttle downshift

Checks	Cause
Intermediate Servo	The oil seal ring is missing or is damaged
Intermediate Band	The band is mispositioned, broken, or burned
1-2 Accumulator	The accumulator piston or pin is missing or damaged

GC5029800819000X

Fig. 21 No intermediate range

Checks	Cause
Definition: A whine which may be RPM or load sensitive, or ceases when the TCC engages	
Torque Converter	Verify that the noise is internal to the torque converter by placing your left foot on the brake with the gear selector in drive. Then momentarily stall the engine. The torque converter noise increases under load.

GC5029800821000X

Fig. 23 Noise in all ranges

Checks	Cause
• Trace Cooler Pipes • Check for binding or contact at the Radiator other than the Cooler Pipe Connectors	Verify a pressure buzz by watching for a needle vibration on the pressure gage. A road test may be necessary.

GC5029800823000X

Fig. 25 Buzz noise or high frequency rattle sound

Checks	Cause
Definition: Noise is related to vehicle speed. Whine may diminish or go away after an upshift to Second Gear	
Input Gear Set	—
Input Internal Gear	Gears are worn or pitted
Input Carrier Assembly	The thrust washer mating surfaces are rough or pitted
Input Sun Gear	—

GC5029800825000X

Fig. 27 Noise in first or reverse

Checks	Cause
Definition: Noise may occur in First, Second, or Third	
Final Drive Gear Set	—
Final Drive Internal Gear	—
Differential Carrier	—
Final Drive Sun Gear	—
Differential Pinions	—
Differential Side Gears	• Gears are worn or pitted • The thrust washer or the thrust bearing mating surfaces are rough or pitted
Final Drive Sun Gear to Final Drive Internal Gear Thrust Bearing	—
Final Drive Sun Gear to Differential Carrier Thrust Bearing	Thrust bearing races or roller bearing surfaces are rough or pitted
Differential Carrier to Case thrust Bearing	—

GC5029800827000X

Fig. 29 Final drive noise or hum under light throttle

Checks	Cause
Definition: Between 25-40 mph under coast or drive operation	
Lo and Reverse Clutch Pack	• Steel plates are not flat • Clutch pack clearance • Parallel grooved fiber plates
Case	Excess plate-to-case clearance due to case machining

GC5029800828000X

Fig. 30 Metallic rattle noise in second or third gear

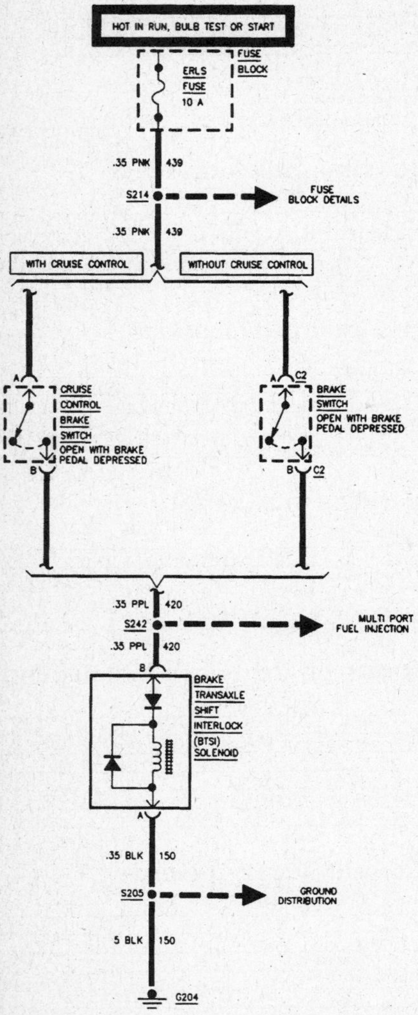

GC5029700829000X

Fig. 31 BTSI wiring diagram

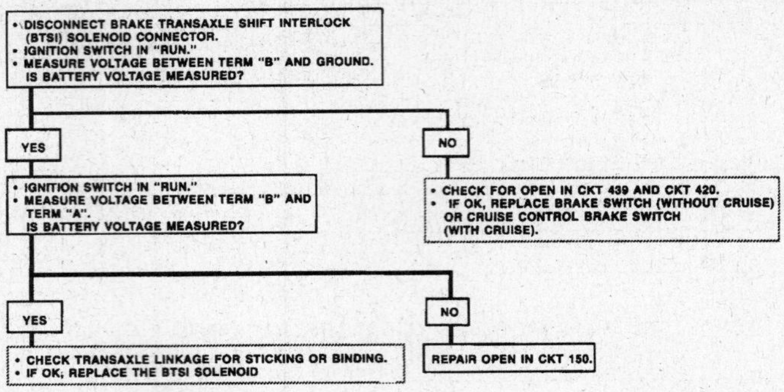

GC5029700830000X

Fig. 32 Gear selector shifts out of Park w/ignition switch in Run and brake pedal not depressed

Step	Action	Value(s)	Yes	No
1	1. Disconnect the Brake Transaxle Shift Interlock (BTSI) Solenoid connector. 2. Turn the Ignition Switch to the RUN position. 3. Use the DMM to measure the voltage in cirucit 420 between the Brake Transaxle Shift Interlock (BTSI) Solenoid connector terminal B and ground. Is the measured voltage within specified range?	B+	Go to Step 2	Go to Step 3
2	Use the DMM to measure the voltage in cirucit 420 between the Brake Transaxle Shift Interlock (BTSI) Solenoid connector terminal B and terminal A. Is the measured voltage within specified range?	B+	Go to Step 7	Go to Step 8
3	1. Disconnect the Brake Switch connector C2 or the Cruise Control Brake Switch. 2. Use the DMM to measure the resistance in circuit 420 between the Brake Transaxle Shift Interlock (BTSI) Solenoid connector terminal B and the Brake Switch connector C2 terminal B or the Cruise Control Brake Switch connector terminal B. Is the measured resistance within the specified range?	0 - 2 Ω	Go to Step 5	Go to Step 4
4	Repair the open circuit condition in circuit 420 between the Brake Transaxle Shift Interlock (BTSI) Solenoid connector terminal B and the Brake Switch connector C2 terminal B or the Cruise Control Brake Switch connector terminal B. Is the repair complete?	—	System OK	—
5	Use the DMM to measure the voltage in circuit 439 between the Brake Switch connector C2 terminal A or the Cruise Control Brake Switch connector terminal A and ground. Is the measured resistance within the specified range?	0 - 2 Ω	Go to Step 9	Go to Step 6

GC5029800831010X

Fig. 33 Gear selector does not shift out of Park w/brake pedal depressed and ignition switch in Run position (Part 1 of 2)

Step	Action	Value(s)	Yes	No
6	Repair the open circuit condition in circuit 439 between the Brake Switch connector C2 terminal A or the Cruise Control Brake Switch connector terminal A and the Fuse Block. Is the repair complete?	—	System OK	—
7	Check the Transaxle Linkage for sticking or binding. Does the Transaxle Linkage stick or bind?	—	Refer to Transaxle.	Go to Step 10
8	Repair the open circuit condition in circuit 150 between the Brake Transaxle Shift Interlock (BTSI) Solenoid and ground. Is the repair complete?	—	System OK	—
9	Replace the Brake Switch or the Cruise Control Brake Switch. Is the repair complete?	—	System OK	—
10	Replace the BTSI solenoid. Is the repair complete?	—	System OK	—

GC5029800831020X

Fig. 33 Gear selector does not shift out of Park w/brake pedal depressed and ignition switch in Run position (Part 2 of 2)

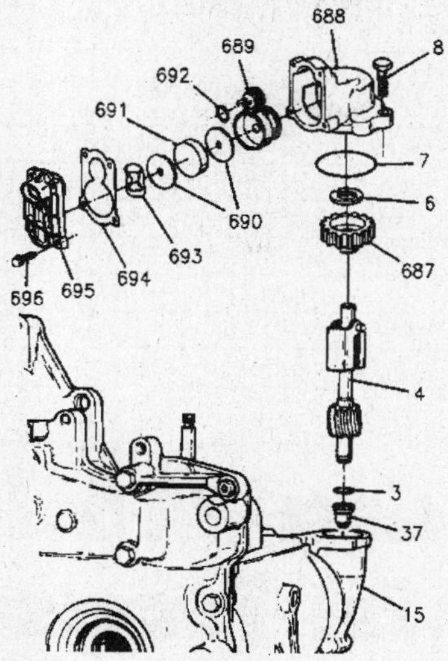

3 FLUID SEAL RING
4 COMPLETE GOVERNOR ASM.
6 GEAR/COVER THRUST BEARING ASM.
7 "O" RING SEAL
8 GOVERNOR COVER TO CASE COVER
15 CASE ASSEMBLY
37 GOV. SHAFT SLEEVE AND SCREEN ASM.
39 GOVERNOR COVER BEARING ASSEMBLY
687 SPEED SENSOR ROTOR
688 SPEED SENSOR HOUSING
689 COIL ASSEMBLY
690 WASHER
691 MAGNET
692 "O" RING SEAL
693 WAVE SPRING WASHER
694 COVER GASKET
695 HOUSING COVER
696 BOLT

TH5029500946000X

Fig. 34 Governor assembly

TIGHTENING SPECIFICATIONS

Year	Component	Torque/ Ft. Lbs.
1997–2000	Axle Nut	184
	Case Cover To Case	18
	Cooler Connector	23
	Governor Cover To Case	96①
	Intermediate Servo Cover	96①
	Oil Pan & Valve Body Cover	96①
	Parking Lock Bracket To Case	18
	Pipe Extension Bolt	41
	Pipe Retainer To Case	18
	Pressure Switch	96①
	Pump Cover To Case Cover	18
	TCC Solenoid Valve To Valve Body	96①
	Throttle Valve Cable To Case	72①

Continued

TIGHTENING SPECIFICATIONS—Continued

Year	Component	Torque/ Ft. Lbs.
1997-2000	Transaxle Mount To Body	49
	Transaxle Support	55
	Transaxle To Engine Brace	32
	Transaxle To Engine Mount	71
	Valve Body	96①
	Valve Body To Sprocket Support	18
	Vehicle Speed Sensor	96①

① — Inch lbs.

Turbo Hydra-Matic 4L30-E Automatic Transmission

NOTE: On Air Bag Equipped Models, Refer To " Air Bag System Precautions" Located In The Front Of This Manual For System Disarming & Arming Procedures.

NOTE: Refer To "Computer Relearn Procedures " Located In The Front Of This Manual For Computer Relearn Procedures.

INDEX

PRECAUTIONS

AIR BAG SYSTEMS

Refer to "Air Bag System Precautions" in the front of this manual for system disarming and arming procedures.

BATTERY GROUND CABLE

Prior to service, disconnect battery ground cable and isolate as required.

IDENTIFICATION

Refer to **Fig. 1** for transmission identification.

DESCRIPTION

The 4L30-E transmission is a four-speed automatic with a torque converter clutch that provides a direct coupling to the engine when desired, **Fig. 2.** Gear changes, line pressure and torque converter clutch operation are controlled by a separate Transmission Control Module (TCM). There are three driver-selectable, shift programs.

TROUBLESHOOTING

Refer to **Fig. 3** for troubleshooting.

MAINTENANCE

Refer to "Lubricant Data Chart" in the appropriate chassis chapter of this manual for transmission fluid specifications.

FLUID CHECK

This transmission does not have a dipstick.

1. Ensure transmission fluid is at normal operating temperature (113–185°F), which is usually obtained after 15 miles of highway driving.
2. Place transmission range selector in Park position and apply parking brake.
3. Wait for engine to cool to ambient temperature.
4. Raise and support vehicle.
5. Start engine, move gear select through all gears and return to Park position.
6. With engine idling, remove transmission oil pan fill plug.
7. Fluid level should be at plug opening's lower edge. Use suitable oil suction gun to add fluid as necessary.
8. Install oil plug and lower vehicle.

FLUID CHANGE

1. Raise and support vehicle, then place suitable container under oil pan.
2. Remove bolts from front and sides of pan and loosen rear pan bolts.
3. Separate oil pan from transmission case by lightly tapping pan with suitable rubber mallet and flat-bladed screwdriver, then drain fluid.
4. Remove rear bolts, pan and gasket.

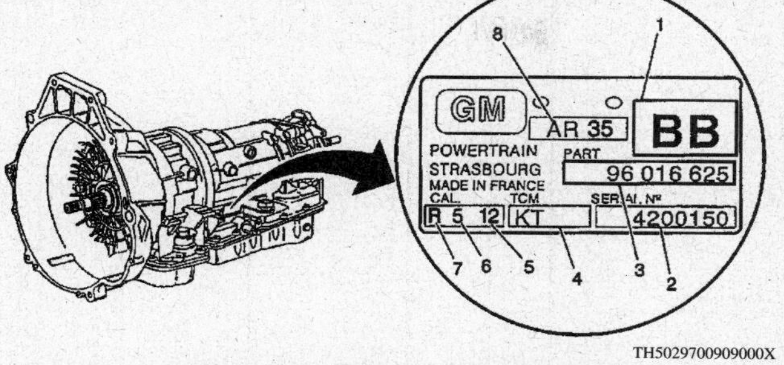

TH5029700909000X

Fig. 1 Transmission identification

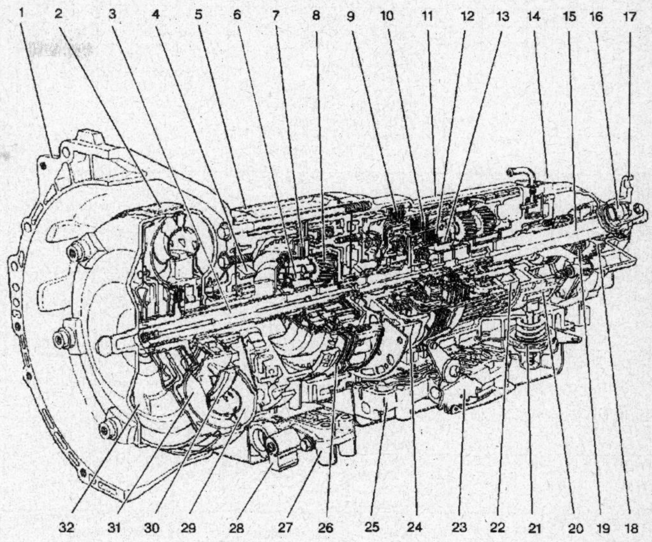

TH5029800910000X

Fig. 2 Cross-section view of 4L30-E transmission

Condition	Cause	Inspect Component
Engine Cannot Be Started	• Selector Lever Is Not In Position **P** or **N** • Selector Lever Position Switch/Shift Linkage Is Incorrectly Adjusted • Fluid Pump Is Blocked • Torque Converter Is Blocked	• Place Selector Lever In Position **N** • Adjust Selector Lever Position Switch/Shift Linkage • Remove Pump, Clean And Repair As Necessary • Remove Converter And Repair/Replace As Necessary
Selector Lever Position **P** Cannot Be Engaged	• Selector Lever Position Switch/Shift Linkage Is Incorrectly Adjusted • Shift Gate At Selector Lever Position **P** Damaged	• Adjust Selector Lever Position Switch/Shift Linkage • Replace Shift Gate
Rattling Noises In The Transmission	• Parking Lock Return Spring Worn	• Replace Parking Lock Return Spring
Vehicle Cannot Be Driven, Rear Wheels Locked	• Parking Lock Return Spring Worn	• Replace Parking Lock Return Spring
Delay In Shifting From **N** To **D**	• Transmission Fluid Level Too Low • Fluid Pressure Too Low • Brake Band Valve Jammed	• Perform Fluid Checking • Perform Line Pressure Checking • Replace Brake Band Valve
Slips Or Shudders In 1ST Gear	• Transmission Fluid Pressure Too Low • Torque Converter Defective • Loss Of Fluid In Circuit Between Accumulator And Brake Band • Incorrectly Adjusted Brake Band • Defective Free Wheel (Planetary Set Or 4TH Gear Unit) • Fluid Loss In Converter Clutch Fluid Circuit	• Perform Line Pressure Checking • Replace Torque Converter • Search For Leaking Part And Replace • Adjust Brake Band • Replace Free Wheel (Planetary Set Or 4TH Gear Unit) • Search For Leaking Part And Replace
No Reverse Gear	• Selector Lever Position Switch/Shift Linkage Is Incorrectly Adjusted (Only Recognizable When Transmission Is Removed And Disassembled) • Clutch For Reverse Gear Defective	• Adjust Selector Lever Position Switch/Shift Linkage • Replace Clutch For Reverse Gear
Driving In Selector Lever Position **N**	• Selector Lever Position Switch/Shift Linkage Is Incorrectly Adjusted • Brake Band Adjustment Too Tight	• Adjust Selector Lever Position Switch/Shift Linkage • Adjust Brake Band
Coarse Shifting From **N** To **D**	• Brake Band Valve Blocked Or Defective • Cable Connection To Pressure Regulator Defective • Pressure Regulator Defective	• Repair Cable • Replace Pressure Regulator

TH5029700911010X

Fig. 3 Troubleshooting (Part 1 of 4)

Condition	Cause	Inspect Component
Poor Acceleration	• Engine Performance Is Degraded • Winter Program Is Selected • Default Mode Is Active • Torque Converter Is Defective	• Inspect Powertrain OBD System Check • Check Winter Program Selection • Inspect Transmission OBD System • Replace Torque Converter
No 1-2 Upshift	• Selector Lever In Position 1 • Selector Lever Position Switch/Shift Linkage Is Incorrectly Adjusted • Solenoid Valve For 1-2/3-4 Shift Or ON-OFF Valve In Valve Body Assembly Blocked • Loss Of Fluid In Clutch C2 Or In Fluid Circuit (Only Recognizable When Transmission Is Removed And Disassembled)	• Adjust Selector Lever Position Switch/Shift Linkage • Search For Leaking Part And Replace
Difficulty In Shifting Between 1-2 Gear	• Incorrect Fluid Pressure In Clutch C2 • Accumulator Valve For 1-2 Shift Blocked Or Leaking • Loss Of Fluid In Clutch C2 Or In Fluid Circuit (Only Recognizable When Transmission Is Removed And Disassembled) • Incorrect Main Pressure	• Perform Fluid Pressure Check • Replace Accumulator Valve • Search For Leaking Part And Replace • Perform Fluid Pressure Check Outlined In This Section
No 2-3 Upshift	• Selector Lever In Position **2** • Selector Lever Position Switch/Shift Linkage Is Incorrectly Adjusted • Solenoid Valve For 2-3 Shift Or ON-OFF Valve In Valve Body Assembly Defective	• Adjust Selector Lever Position Switch/Shift Linkage
Difficulty In Shifting Between 2-3 Gear	• Incorrectly Adjusted Brake Band • Loss Of Fluid In Return Line Between Accumulator And Brake Band • Loss Of Fluid In Clutch C3 Or In Fluid Circuit • Brake Band Valve Defective Or Blocked • Incorrect Fluid Pressure	• Adjust Brake Band • Replace Brake Band Valve • Search For Leaking Part And Replace • • Perform Fluid Pressure Check

TH5029700911020X

Fig. 3 Troubleshooting (Part 2 of 4)

5. Remove retaining bolts and filter.
6. Clean case, front adapter case and oil pan gasket surfaces with suitable solvent and air dry.
7. Install oil pan and retaining bolts. Tighten bolts to specification.
8. Fill transaxle to lower edge of oil pan fill plug opening, then install plug and tighten to specifications.
9. Lower vehicle and check fluid level.

TRANSAXLE OIL COOLER FLUSH

Refer to "Turbo Hydra-Matic 4T80-E Automatic Transaxle. "

ADJUSTMENTS

SHIFT LEVER ROD

1. Place shift lever in Park position.
2. Raise and support vehicle.
3. Loosen adjustment bolt to allow adjuster to slide freely.
4. Hold selector against rear stop and tighten adjustment bolt to specifications.
5. Lower vehicle and ensure engine starts when selector is in Park or Neutral positions only.

TRANSMISSION CONTROL SELECTOR SWITCH

1. Apply parking brake and position selector in Neutral position.
2. Raise and support vehicle.
3. Remove transmission and selector lever position switch covers.
4. Remove transmission selector lever nut and intermediate lever.

Condition	Cause	Inspect Component
No 3-4 Upshift	• Selector Lever In Position **3** • Selector Lever Position Switch/Shift Linkage Is Incorrectly Adjusted • Solenoid Valve For 1-2/3-4 Shift Or ON-OFF Valve In Valve Body Assembly Defective • Loss Of Hydraulic Fluid In Clutch C4 Or In Fluid Circuit	• Adjust Selector Lever Position Switch/Shift Linkage • Search For Leaking Part And Replace
Difficulty In Shifting Between 3-4 Gear	• Loss Of Fluid In Clutch C4 Or In Fluid Circuit • Incorrect Fluid Pressure • Bridging 4TH Gear Clutch (4TH Gear Lockup Clutch) Cannot Be Released	• Search For Leaking Part And Replace • Perform Fluid Pressure Check • Overhaul/Replace Transmission
No Engagement Of Torque Converter Clutch	• Solenoid Valve For Converter Clutch Defective • Interruption In Signal Circuit • Fluid Loss In Fluid Circuit Of Converter Clutch	• Search For Leaking Part And Replace
Rattling In Torque Converter Clutch	• Torque Converter Clutch Defective • Fluid Pressure Inadequate	• Replace Torque Converter • Perform Fluid Pressure Check
Torque Converter Clutch Cannot Be Released	• Solenoid Valve For Converter Clutch Defective • Return Line Blocked	• Clean/Replace Line
Vibration In 2ND Gear	• Solenoid Valve Of Converter Clutch Jammed In Position Active So That Converter Clutch Is Engaged	• Replace Solenoid Valve
No Sport Program	• Tip Switch Defective • Electrical Circuit Interruption	• Inspect Sport Mode Indicator Lamp/Selector Switch Diagnosis In Section 7
No Winter Program	• Tip Switch Defective • Electrical Circuit Interruption	• Inspect Winter Mode Indicator Lamp/Selector Switch
No Kickdown Function	• Kickdown Switch Defective • Electrical Circuit Interruption	
No Downshift Possible	• 1-2/3-4 Or 2-3 Shift Solenoid Valves Defective Or ON-OFF Valve In Valve Body Assembly Locked	

TH5029700911030X

Fig. 3 Troubleshooting (Part 3 of 4)

Condition	Cause	Inspect Component
No Engine Braking With Selector Lever In Position **D** And Transmission In 3RD Gear Or Selector Lever In Position **3** And Transmission In 3RD Gear Or Selector Lever In Position **2** And Transmission In 2ND Gear Or Selector Lever In Position **1** And Transmission In 1ST Gear	• Bridging Clutch For 4TH Gear (4TH Gear Lockup Clutch) Defective Or Loss Of Fluid In Fluid Circuit	• Overhaul/Replace Transmission
Transmission Overheating, Fluid Leaking From Transmission Ventilation	• Transmission Fluid Level Too High • Torque Converter Clutch Not Functioning • Extreme Load In Default Mode Or In Winter Mode	• Perform Fluid Checking • Repair/Replace Converter Clutch

TH5029700911040X

Fig. 3 Troubleshooting (Part 4 of 4)

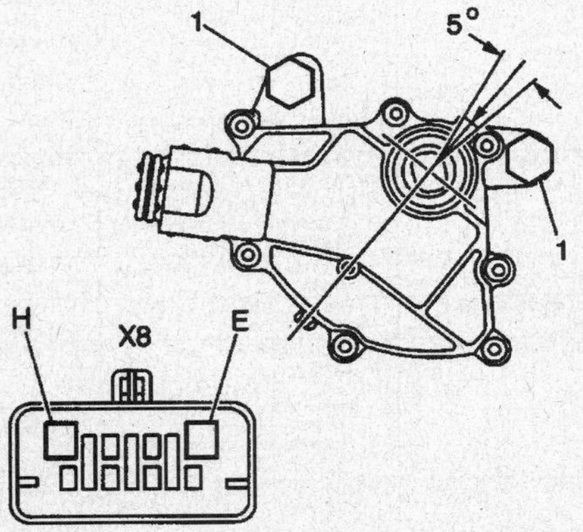

TH5029700912000X

Fig. 4 Mode switch adjustment

5. Disconnect mode switch electrical connector.
6. Connect multimeter to mode switch electrical connector terminals E and H, **Fig. 4.**
7. Loosen mounting bolts and rotate mode switch in both directions to determine electrical contact range.
8. Position switch in middle of range.
9. Reverse procedure to install.

THIRD CLUTCH SERVO PISTON

1. Hold adjusting sleeve with wrench and loosen lock nut.
2. **Torque** adjusting screw to 40 inch lbs.
3. Loosen adjusting screw five turns.
4. Hold adjusting sleeve and screw, then **torque** locknut to 14 ft. lbs.

IN-VEHICLE REPAIRS

BRAKE TRANSMISSION SHIFT INTERLOCK (BTSI) SOLENOID, REPLACE

1. Remove floor console, parking brake and shift selector boots.
2. Remove low and second blockout switch, then the transmission control indicator and shift plate.
3. Raise and support vehicle.
4. Remove BTSI solenoid retaining screw.
5. Lower vehicle.
6. Remove electrical connector and BTSI solenoid.
7. Reverse procedure to install. Tighten bolts to specifications.

AUTOMATIC TRANSMISSION CONTROL ASSEMBLY, REPLACE

1. Remove console and mounting nuts, then the rear air duct front and console rear supports.
2. Slide rear air duct to rear and disconnect automatic transmission control electrical connector.
3. Raise and support vehicle.
4. Remove clip and slide rod off shift lever.
5. Lower vehicle and drill out rivets, then remove automatic transmission control assembly.
6. Reverse procedure to install. Tighten bolts to specifications.

DRIVE FLANGE & CASE EXTENSION SEAL, REPLACE

1. Raise and support vehicle.
2. Remove bolts and use a suitable screwdriver to pry propeller shaft coupling away from drive flange.
3. Hold drive flange with rear hub holding tool No. J-42066, or equivalent, and remove retaining nut.
4. Remove flange and pry out seal with a suitable screwdriver.
5. Reverse procedure to install, noting the following:
   a. Use transmission extension housing seal installer tool No. J-42080, or equivalent, to install new seal.
   b. Use new drive flange nut.
   c. Tighten nuts and bolts to specifications.

CASE EXTENSION, REPLACE

1. Raise and support vehicle.
2. Support transmission with suitable transmission jack.
3. Remove body bolts and crossmember, then the mount bolts and mount.
4. Remove drive flange as described under "Drive Flange & Case Extension Seal, Replace."
5. Remove mounting bolts and catalytic converter support bracket.
6. Remove electrical connector, mounting bolt and speed sensor. Do not pry sensor out.
7. Remove oxygen sensor harness clips.
8. Remove mounting bolts, extension and gasket.
9. Remove speed sensor ring and extension seal.
10. Use suitable size spacer to press bearing out of extension case rear.
11. Reverse procedure to install. Tighten bolts to specifications.

SOLENOID VALVES, REPLACE

The 2-3 shift, 1-2/3-4 shift and band control solenoid valves are located in the main case. The Torque Convert Clutch (TCC) and force motor solenoid valves are located in the front case.

1. Remove oil pan and filter as outlined under "Maintenance."

2. Remove solenoid valve electrical connectors.
3. Use suitable pliers to remove retaining pin, then the valves.
4. Reverse procedure to install.

TRANSMISSION CONTROL MODULE (TCM)

1. Remove righthand side sound insulator panel and retainer.
2. Remove side floor air outlet and glove compartment.
3. Remove mounting nuts, pull TCM away from studs.
4. Reverse procedure to install.

TRANSMISSION

REPLACE

1. Raise and support vehicle.
2. Remove shift lever rod.
3. Remove mounting bolts and use suitable small screwdriver to pry propeller shaft coupling from drive flange.
4. Remove upper and lower oil pan and bell housing access hole plugs.
5. Mark flex plate and torque converter for assembly, then remove retaining bolts.
6. Squeeze and slide clamps from connection, then remove oil cooler inlet and outlet pipes from center pipes.
7. Disconnect oxygen sensor connectors.
8. Remove catalytic converters.
9. Remove transmission housing to engine oil pan bolts.
10. Install suitable transmission support.
11. Remove crossmember to mount nuts, then the crossmember to body bolts and crossmember.
12. Lower transmission to access housing to engine block bolts.
13. Remove transmission ventilation hose, transmission control selector switch, adapter case, main case, speed sensor and harness clip connectors.
14. Support front of engine.
15. Remove housing to engine block bolts and transmission.
16. Flush oil cooler as outlined under "Maintenance."
17. Reverse procedure to install, noting the following:
    a. Apply suitable thread locking compound to housing to engine block bolts.
    b. Tighten nuts and bolts to specifications.
    c. Adjust shift lever rod as outlined under "Adjustments."

TIGHTENING SPECIFICATIONS

Year	Component	Torque/ Ft. Lbs.
1997–2000	Catalytic Converter Support	15
	Catalytic Converter To Muffler	30
	Console Rear Support	35①
	Drive Flange Nut	74
	Flex Plate	22
	Force Motor Solenoid Valve	84①
	Front Oil Pan	96①
	Oil Cooler Fittings At Radiator	18
	Oil Cooler Inlet	18
	Oil Cooler Outlet	22
	Oil Pan	96①
	Oil Pan Fill Plug	33
	Oil Pressure Test Hole Plug	108①
	Propeller Shaft Coupling	70
	Rear Air Duct Front Support	72①
	Shift Lever Rod Adjustment	72①
	TCC Solenoid Valve	84①
	Transmission Case Extension Nut	15
	Transmission Case Extension Bolt	23
	Transmission Control Selector Switch	10
	Transmission Crossmember To Body	33
	Transmission Crossmember To Mount	15
	Transmission Housing To Engine Block	44
	Transmission Housing To Engine Oil Pan	15
	Transmission Mount	30
	Transmission Oil Filter	15
	Transmission Speed Sensor	84①

① — Inch Lbs.

Turbo Hydra-Matic 4L60-E Automatic Transmission

NOTE: On Air Bag Equipped Models, Refer To " Air Bag System Precautions" Located In The Front Of This Manual For System Disarming & Arming Procedures.

NOTE: Refer To "Computer Relearn Procedures " Located In The Front Of This Manual For Computer Relearn Procedures.

INDEX

PRECAUTIONS

AIR BAG SYSTEMS

Refer to "Air Bag System Precautions" in the front of this manual for system disarming and arming procedures.

BATTERY GROUND CABLE

Prior to service, disconnect battery ground cable and isolate as required.

IDENTIFICATION

The 4L60-E transmission has a metal identification nameplate attached to the case exterior or a stamped identification number on the pan rail, **Fig. 1.**

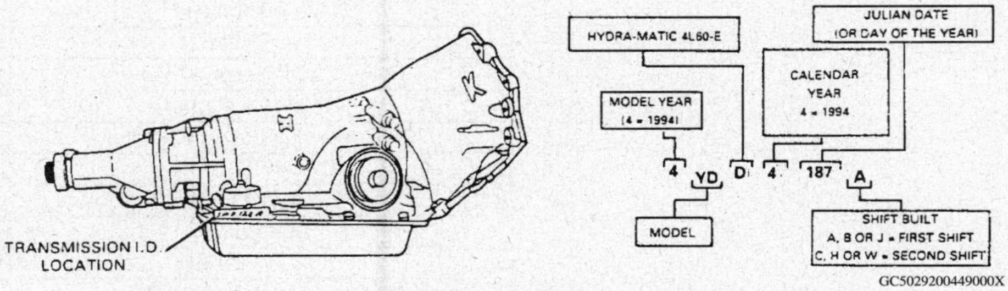

Fig. 1 Transmission identification number location

DESCRIPTION

The 4L60-E **Fig. 2** is an electronically controlled transmission consisting of a three-element hydraulic torque converter with the addition of a converter clutch. A Power Control Module (PCM) manages engine and transmission functions as a single system. The PCM retards engine spark for an instant during each gear shift which reduces engine torque as the gear is engaged. After the shift is completed, spark is advanced and torque is brought to normal operating levels. Shifting is accomplished by sensor-driven servos located within the transmission valve body.

Also two planetary gear sets, five multiple-disc type clutches, two roller or one-way clutches and a band are used which provide the friction elements to produce four forward speeds, the last of which is overdrive.

The torque converter, through oil, couples the engine power to the gear sets and hydraulically provides additional torque multiplication when required. Also, through the converter clutch, the converter drive and driven members operate as one unit when applied, providing mechanical drive from the engine through the transmission.

The gear ratio changes are fully automatic in relation to the vehicle speed and engine torque. Vehicle speed and engine torque are directed to the transmission providing the proper gear ratio for maximum efficiency and performance at all throttle openings.

A hydraulic system pressurized by a variable capacity vane-type pump, provides the operating pressure required for the operation of the friction elements and automatic controls.

TROUBLESHOOTING

Refer to **Figs. 3 through 30** for troubleshooting.

MAINTENANCE

Refer to "Lubricant Data Chart" in the appropriate chassis chapter of this manual for transmission fluid specifications.

FLUID CHECK

Fluid level should be checked at every engine oil change. Frequency of change for transmission fluid is dependent on the type of driving conditions in which the vehicle is used. If the transmission is subjected to severe service such as: use in heavy city traffic when the outside temperature regularly reaches 90°F, use in very hilly or mountainous areas, commercial use such as taxi or delivery service, the fluid should be changed every 15,000 miles. Otherwise, change the fluid every 100,000 miles. To check fluid at operating temperature (190°–200°F), which is obtained only after 15 miles of highway-type driving:

1. Apply parking brake and block wheels.
2. Place selector lever in Park position and start, but do not race, engine.
3. Move selector lever through each range pausing three seconds in each.
4. Check fluid immediately with selector lever in Park, engine running at slow idle, and vehicle on level surface. Fluid level should be at full hot mark.

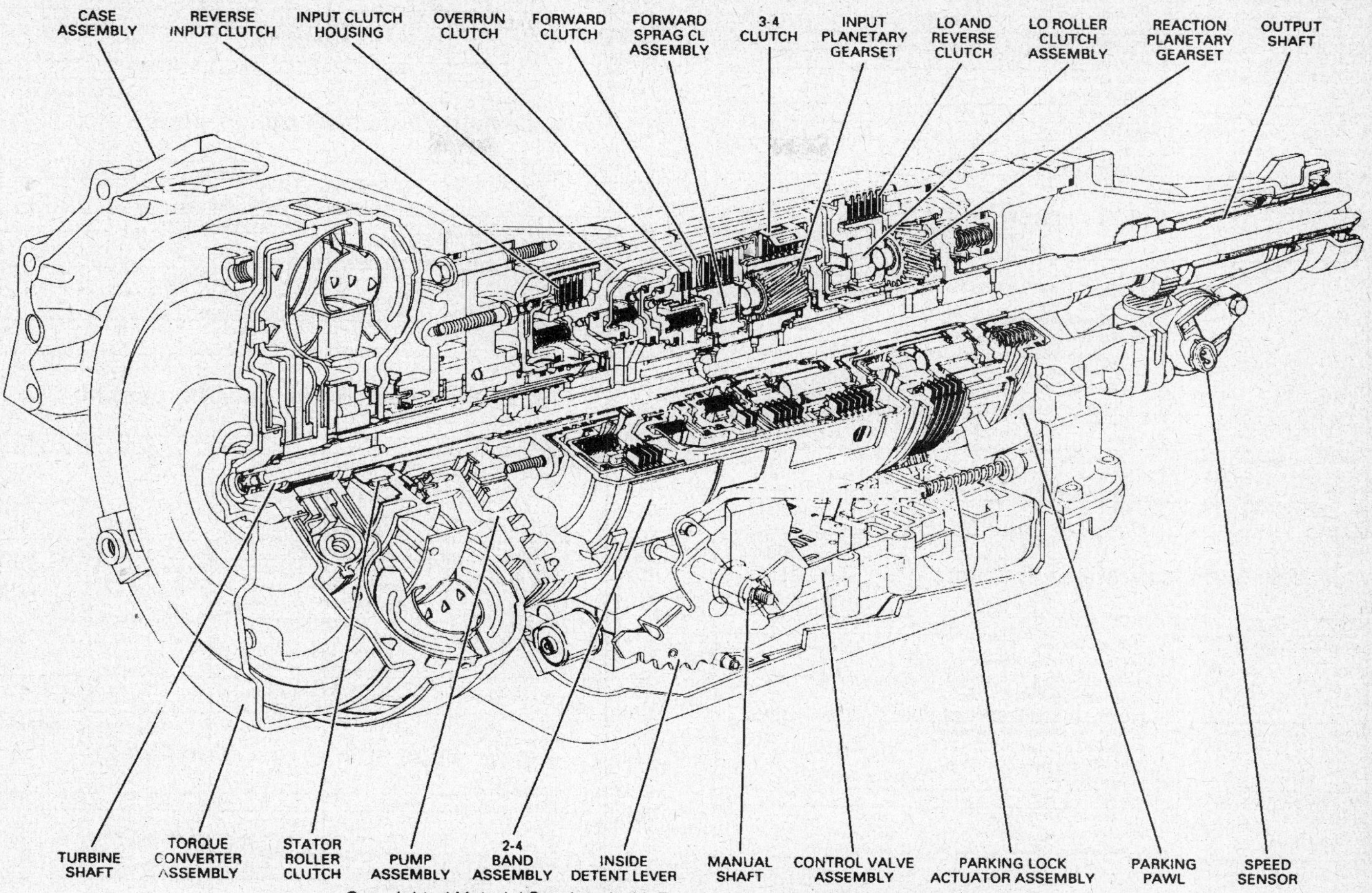

TH5029400481000X

Fig. 2 Cross-sectional view of transmission

Checks	Causes
Oil Pump Assembly	• Pressure regulator valve stuck • Pressure regulator valve spring • Rotor guide omitted or misassembled • Rotor cracked or broken • Reverse boost valve or sleeve stuck, damaged or incorrectly assembled • Orifice hole in pressure regulator valve plugged • Sticking slide or excessive rotor clearance • Pressure relief ball not seated or damaged • Porosity in pump cover or body • Wrong pump cover • Pump faces not flat • Excessive rotor clearance
Oil Filter	• Intake pipe restricted by casting flash • Cracks in filter body or intake pipe • O-ring seal missing, cut or damaged • Wrong grease used on rebuild
Control Valve Body	• Manual valve scored or damaged • Spacer plate or gaskets incorrect, misassembled or damaged • Face not flat • 2-3 Shift valve stuck • Checkballs omitted or misassembled
Pressure Control Solenoid	Damage to pins
Transmission Fluid Pressure Manual Valve Position Switch	• Contamination • Damaged seals
Case	Case to control valve body face not flat
System Voltage	• 12 volts not supplied to transmission • Electrical short (pinched solenoid wire) • Solenoid not grounded

GC5029800864000X

Fig. 3 Oil pressure high or low

FLUID CHANGE

1. Raise and support vehicle.
2. Place a suitable drain pan under transmission.
3. Clean any dirt around check/fill plug, then remove check/fill plug and allow fluid to drain.
4. Support transmission oil pan.
5. Remove oil pan retaining bolts, then the oil pan.
6. Loosely install check/fill plug.
7. Lightly tap oil pan or pry in order to loosen pan.
8. Drain remaining fluid from pan.
9. Remove filter by pulling down with a twisting motion. **Note position of filter before removal to aid installation.**
10. Remove filter seal.
11. Reverse procedure to install, noting the following:
    a. Remove all gasket material from oil pan and case surfaces.
    b. Coat new filter seal with transmission assembling lubricant part No. J36850, or equivalent.
    c. Tighten oil pan bolts to specification.

ADJUSTMENTS

SHIFT CONTROL CABLE

Camaro & Firebird

1. Place transmission shift control lever into park, then apply parking brake.
2. Raise and support vehicle.
3. Position transmission range selector lever to park by rotating range selector lever clockwise until it reaches full mechanical stop position.
4. Snap transmission shift cable into bracket with cable adjustment button up.

Checks	Causes
Throttle Position Sensor	Open or shorted circuit
Vehicle Speed Sensor	Open or shorted circuit
Pressure Switch Assembly	• Contamination • Damaged seals
Trans Fluid Temperature Sensor	Open or shorted circuit
Engine Coolant Temperature Sensor	Open or shorted circuit
Pressure Control Solenoid	• Damage to pins • Contamination

GC5029800865000X

Fig. 4 Harsh shifts

Checks	Causes
Case	• Porous or damaged valve body pad • 2-4 Servo Assembly – 2-4 accumulator porosity – Damaged servo piston seals – Apply pin damaged or improper length • 2-4 Band Assembly – Burned – Anchor pin not engaged
Throttle Position Sensor	• Disconnected • Damage
Vehicle Speed Sensor	• Disconnected • Damaged • Bolt not tightened
4WD Low Switch	• Disconnected • Damaged

GC5029800866020X

Fig. 5 Inaccurate shift points (Part 2 of 2)

Checks	Causes
Forward Clutch Assembly	• Clutch plates worn • Porosity or damage in forward clutch piston • Forward clutch piston inner and outer seals missing, cut or damaged • Damaged forward clutch housing • Forward clutch housing retainer and ball assembly not sealing or damaged
Forward Clutch Accumulator	• Piston seal missing, cut or damaged • Piston out of its bore • Porosity in the piston or valve body • Stuck abuse valve
Input Housing and Shaft Assembly	Turbine shaft seals missing, cut or damaged
Valve Body	• 1-2 Accumulator valve stuck • Face not flat, damaged lands or interconnected passages • Spacer plate or gaskets incorrect, mispositioned or damaged

GC5029800868010X

Fig. 7 Slips in first gear (Part 1 of 2)

Checks	Causes
Valve Body Assembly	• 1-2 Shift valve train stuck • Gaskets or spacer plate incorrect, mispositioned or damaged • 1-2 Accumulator valve stuck • Face not flat
2-4 Servo Assembly	• Apply pin too long or too short • 2nd servo apply piston seal missing, cut or damaged • Restricted or missing oil passages • Servo bore in case damaged
2nd Accumulator	• Porosity in 1-2 accumulator housing or piston • Piston seal or groove damaged • Nicks or burrs in 1-2 accumulator housing • Missing or restricted oil passage
2-4 Band	Worn or mispositioned
Oil Pump Assembly or Case	Faces not flat

GC5029800869000X

Fig. 8 Slipping or rough 1-2 shift

Checks	Causes
2nd Accumulator	• Porosity in 1-2 accumulator housing or piston • Piston seal or groove damaged • Nicks or burrs in 1-2 accumulator housing • Missing or restricted oil passage
2-4 Band	Worn or mispositioned
Oil Pump Assembly or Case	Faces not flat

GC5029800870020X

Fig. 9 No 2-3 shift or 2-3 shift slips, rough or hunting (Part 2 of 2)

Checks	Causes
System Voltage	• 12 volts not supplied to transmission • Electrical short (pinched solenoid wire) • Solenoid not grounded
3-2 Control Solenoid (394)	• Shorted or damaged • Contamination • Damaged Seal

GC5029800872000X

Fig. 11 Third gear only

Checks	Causes
Oil Pump Assembly	• Stuck pressure regulator valve • Sticking pump slide
Valve Body Assembly	Spacer plate or gaskets misassembled, damaged or incorrect

GC5029800866010X

Fig. 5 Inaccurate shift points (Part 1 of 2)

Checks	Causes
Valve Body	• The 1-2 Shift valve is sticking • The spacer plate or gaskets are mispositioned or damaged
Case	The case to valve body face is damaged or is not flat
Shift Solenoid Valves	• Stuck or damaged • Faulty electrical connection
2-4 Servo Assembly	• The apply passage case is restricted or blocked • Nicks or burrs on the servo pin or on the pin bore in the case • Fourth servo piston is installed backwards
2–4 Band Assembly	• The 2–4 band is worn or damaged • The band anchor pin is not engaged

GC5029800867000X

Fig. 6 First gear range only, no upshift

Checks	Causes
Low Roller Clutch	• Damage to lugs to inner ramps • Rollers not free moving • Inadequate spring tension • Damage to inner splines • Lube passage plugged
Torque Converter	Stator roller clutch not holding
1-2 Accumulator Assembly	• Porosity in piston or 1-2 Accumulator cover and pin assembly • Damaged ring grooves on piston • Piston seal missing, cut or damaged • Valve body to spacer plate gasket at 1-2 Accumulator cover, missing or damaged • Leak between piston and pin • Broken 1-2 Accumulator spring
Line Pressure	Refer to *Oil Pressure High or Low*
2-4 Servo Assembly	4th Servo piston in backwards

GC5029800868020X

Fig. 7 Slips in first gear (Part 2 of 2)

Checks	Causes
Valve Body Assembly	• 1-2 Shift valve train stuck • Gaskets or spacer plate incorrect, mispositioned or damaged • 1-2 Accumulator valve stuck • Face not flat
2-4 Servo Assembly	• Apply pin too long or too short • 2nd servo apply piston seal missing, cut or damaged • Restricted or missing oil passages • Servo bore in case damaged

GC5029800870010X

Fig. 9 No 2-3 shift or 2-3 shift slips, rough or hunting (Part 1 of 2)

Checks	Causes
Shift Solenoid Valves (379)	• Sediment is in the valves • The electrical connection is faulty • Damaged seal

GC5029800871000X

Fig. 10 Second/third gear only or first/fourth gears only

Checks	Causes
3-2 Control Solenoid	• Shorted or damaged • Contamination • Damaged Seal

GC5029800873000X

Fig. 12 3-2 flare or tie-up

Checks	Causes
Oil Pump Assembly	• Pump cover retainer and ball assembly omitted or damaged • Faces not flat
Valve Body Assembly	• Valves stuck – 2-3 Shift valve train – Accumulator valve – 1-2 Shift valve train – 3-2 Control valve • Spacer plate or gaskets incorrect, mispositioned or damaged
2-4 Servo Assembly	• Incorrect band apply pin • Missing or damaged servo seals • Porosity in piston, cover or case • Damaged piston seal grooves • Plugged or missing orifice cup plug

GC5029800874010X

Fig. 13 No 3-4 shift, slips or rough 3-4 shift (Part 1 of 2)

Checks	Causes
Case	• 3rd Accumulator retainer and ball assembly leaking • Porosity in 3-4 accumulator piston or bore • 3-4 Accumulator piston seal or seal grooves damaged • Plugged or missing orifice cup plug • Restricted oil passage
Input Housing Assembly	Refer to Slipping 2-3 Shift
2-4 Band Assembly	Worn or misassembled

GC5029800874020X

Fig. 13 No 3-4 shift, slips or rough 3-4 shift (Part 2 of 2)

Checks	Causes
Input Housing Assembly	• 3-4 Apply ring stuck in applied position • Forward clutch not releasing • Turbine shaft seals missing, cut or damaged
Manual Valve Link	Disconnect
Valve Body Assembly	• 2-3 Shift valve stuck • Manual linkage not adjusted • Spacer plate and gaskets incorrect, mispositioned or damaged • Lo overrun valve stuck • Orificed cup plug restricted, missing or damaged

GC5029800876010X

Fig. 15 No part throttle or delayed downshifts (Part 1 of 2)

Checks	Causes
Valve Body Assembly	• Orifice cup plug missing • Checkball missing

GC5029800877000X

Fig. 16 Harsh garage shift

Checks	Causes
Electrical	• 12 volts not supplied to transmission • Outside electrical connector damaged • Inside electrical connector, wiring harness or solenoid damaged • Electrical short (pinched solenoid wire) • Solenoid not grounded
Torque Converter Clutch	Internal damage

GC5029800879010X

Fig. 18 No TCC apply (Part 1 of 2)

Checks	Causes
Input Housing Assembly	• 3-4 Apply ring stuck in applied position • Forward clutch not releasing • Turbine shaft seals missing, cut or damaged
Manual Valve Link	Disconnect
Valve Body Assembly	• 2-3 Shift valve stuck • Manual linkage not adjusted • Spacer plate and gaskets incorrect, mispositioned or damaged • Lo overrun valve stuck • Orificed cup plug restricted, missing or damaged
Reverse Input Clutch Assembly	• Clutch plate worn • Reverse input housing and drum assembly cracked at weld • Clutch plate retaining ring out of groove • Return spring assembly retaining ring out of groove • Seals cut or damaged • Restricted apply passage • Porosity in piston • Belleville plate installed incorrectly • Excessive clutch plate travel • Oversized housing
Lo and Reverse Clutch	• Clutch plates worn • Porosity in piston • Seals damaged • Return spring assembly retaining ring mispositioned • Restricted apply passage

GC5029800875000X

Fig. 14 No reverse or slips in reverse

Checks	Causes
Reverse Input Clutch Assembly	• Clutch plate worn • Reverse input housing and drum assembly cracked at weld • Clutch plate retaining ring out of groove • Return spring assembly retaining ring out of groove • Seals cut or damaged • Restricted apply passage • Porosity in piston • Belleville plate installed incorrectly • Excessive clutch plate travel • Oversized housing
Lo and Reverse Clutch	• Clutch plates worn • Porosity in piston • Seals damaged • Return spring assembly retaining ring mispositioned • Restricted apply passage

GC5029800876020X

Fig. 15 No part throttle or delayed downshifts (Part 2 of 2)

Checks	Causes
External Linkage	Not adjusted properly
Valve Body Assembly	• 4-3 Sequence valve stuck • Checkball mispositioned • Spacer plate and gaskets incorrect, damaged or mispositioned
Input Clutch Assembly	• Turbine shaft oil passages plugged or not drilled • Turbine shaft seal rings damaged • Turbine shaft sealing balls loose or missing • Turbine shaft sealing balls loose or missing • Porosity in forward or overrun clutch piston • Overrun piston seals cut or damaged • Overrun piston checkball not sealing

GC5029800878000X

Fig. 17 No overrun braking, manual 3-2-1

Checks	Causes
Oil Pump Assembly	• Converter clutch valve stuck or assembled backwards • Converter clutch valve retaining ring mispositioned • Pump to case gasket mispositioned • Orifice cup plug restricted or damaged • Solenoid O-ring seal cut or damaged • High or uneven bolt torque (pump body to cover)
Input Housing and Shaft	• Turbine shaft O-ring seal cut or damaged • Turbine shaft retainer and ball assembly restricted or damaged
Transmission Fluid Pressure Manual Valve Position Switch	• Contamination • Damaged seals
Control Valve Body Assembly	• TCC signal valve stuck • Solenoid O-ring leaking
Solenoid Screen	Blocked
TCC Solenoid Valve	Internal damage
Engine Speed Sensor	Internal damage
Engine Coolant Temperature Sensor	Internal damage
Automatic Transmission Fluid Temperature Sensor	Internal damage
Brake Switch	Internal damage

GC5029800879020X

Fig. 18 No TCC apply (Part 2 of 2)

Checks	Causes
Electrical	• 12 volts not supplied to transmission • Outside electrical connector damaged • Inside electrical connector, wiring harness or solenoid damaged • Electrical short (pinched solenoid wire) • Solenoid not grounded
Converter	Internal damage
Oil Pump Assembly	• Converter clutch valve stuck or assembled backwards • Converter clutch valve retaining ring mispositioned • Pump to case gasket mispositioned • Orifice cup plug restricted or damaged • Solenoid O-ring seal cut or damaged • High or uneven bolt torque (pump body to cover)
Input Housing and Shaft	• Turbine shaft O-ring seal cut or damaged • Turbine shaft retainer and ball assembly restricted or damaged
Pressure Switch Assembly	• Contamination • Damaged seals
Valve Body Assembly	• TCC signal valve stuck • Solenoid O-ring leaking
Solenoid Screen	Blocked

GC5029800880000X

Fig. 19 TCC shudder

Checks	Causes
TCC Solenoid Valve	• External ground • Clogged exhaust orifice
Converter	Internal damage
Valve Body Assembly	The converter clutch apply valve is stuck in the apply position
Oil Pump Assembly	The converter clutch valve is stuck
PCM	External ground

GC5029800881000X

Fig. 20 No TCC release

Checks	Causes
Forward Clutch Sprag Assembly	The sprag assembly is installed backwards

GC5029800883000X

Fig. 22 Second gear start

Checks	Causes
Oil Pump	Chamber in pump body rotor pocket
Miscellaneous	Fluid level—overfilled

GC5029800885000X

Fig. 24 Oil out the vent

Checks	Causes
Parking Pawl	The parking pawl return spring is weak, damaged, or misassembled

GC5029800887000X

Fig. 26 Ratcheting noise

Checks	Causes
Torque Converter	• The stator roller clutch is not holding • The converter is not bolted to the flex plate

GC5029800889000X

Fig. 28 No drive in drive range

Checks	Causes
Torque Converter	Converter drainback

GC5029800891000X

Fig. 30 Delay in drive & reverse

Checks	Causes
Forward Clutch	The clutch does not release
Manual Valve Link	Disconnected
Case	• The face is not flat • Internal leakage exists

GC5029800882000X

Fig. 21 Drives in Neutral

Checks	Causes
Parking Linkage	• Actuator rod assembly bent or damaged • Actuator rod spring binding or improperly crimped • Actuator rod not attached to inside detent lever • Parking lock bracket damaged or not torqued properly • Inside detent lever not torqued properly • Parking pawl binding or damaged

GC5029800884000X

Fig. 23 No Park

Checks	Causes
Oil Pump	Chamber in pump body rotor pocket
Miscellaneous	Fluid level—overfilled

GC5029800886000X

Fig. 25 Vibration in reverse and whining noise in Park

Checks	Causes
Torque Converter	The converter to flex plate bolts are missing

GC5029800888000X

Fig. 27 No drive in all ranges

Checks	Causes
Torque Converter	• The welded seam is leaking • The converter hub is damaged
Torque Converter Seal	• The seal assembly is damaged • The garter spring is missing

GC5029800890000X

Fig. 29 Front oil leak

5. Snap shift cable onto range selector lever pin, then press cable adjustment button down.
6. Insert retainer to fitting of shift cable.
7. Lower vehicle.

Corvette

1. Raise and support vehicle.
2. Shift transmission into Neutral position.
3. Using a flat bladed screwdriver, pry to release transmission shift control cable adjustment lock.
4. Ensure transmission floor shift control and transmission are in neutral detent position.
5. Press to secure transmission shift control cable adjustment lock and lower vehicle.
6. Check cable adjustment by rotating control lever through detents.

IN-VEHICLE REPAIRS

CONTROL VALVE BODY & PRESSURE SWITCH, REPLACE

1. Raise and support vehicle.
2. Remove oil pan and gasket
3. Remove oil filter and filter seal.
4. Disconnect electrical connectors from control valve body components.
5. Remove TCC solenoid bolts and solenoid assembly with O-ring seal.
6. Remove wiring harness retaining bolts and set harness aside, **Fig. 31.**
7. Remove manual detent spring assembly retaining bolt.
8. Remove remaining control valve body retaining bolts.
9. Remove manual valve link and control valve body.
10. Reverse procedure to install, noting the following:
    a. Before installing valve body, ensure valve body and transmission case check balls are in their correct location. Refer to **Figs. 32 and 33** for check ball locations.
    b. Install all control valve body bolts.
    c. Using spiral sequence, **Fig. 34,** tighten bolts to specification. **If bolts are tightened in a random sequence, valve bores may be distorted and will inhibit valve operation.**

VEHICLE SPEED SENSOR, REPLACE

Camaro & Firebird

1. Raise and support vehicle.
2. Disconnect speed sensor electrical connector.
3. Remove speed sensor retaining bolt, **Fig. 35.**
4. Remove speed sensor and O-ring seal.
5. Reverse procedure to install. Tighten speed sensor retaining bolt to specification.

Corvette

1. Raise and support vehicle.

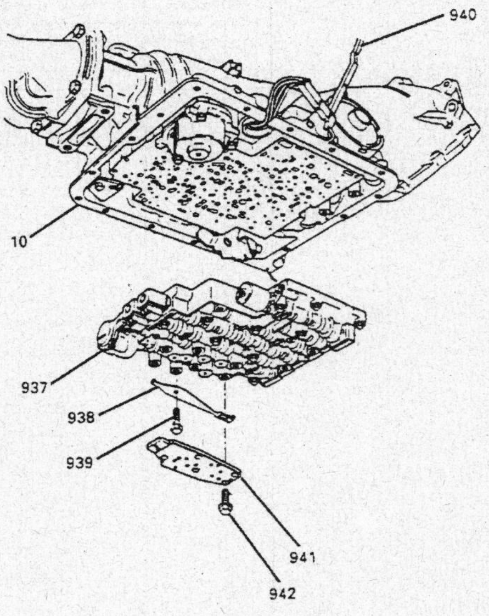

10 CASE, TRANSMISSION
937 VALVE ASSEMBLY, CONTROL BODY
938 SPRING ASSEMBLY, MANUAL DETENT
939 BOLT/SCREW, MANUAL DETENT SPRING
940 SOLENOID ASSEMBLY, WIRING HARNESS AND
941 SWITCH ASSEMBLY, TRANSMISSION PRESSURE
942 BOLT/SCREW, PRESSURE SWITCH ASSEMBLY

GC5029400450000X

Fig. 31 Control valve & pressure switch assembly

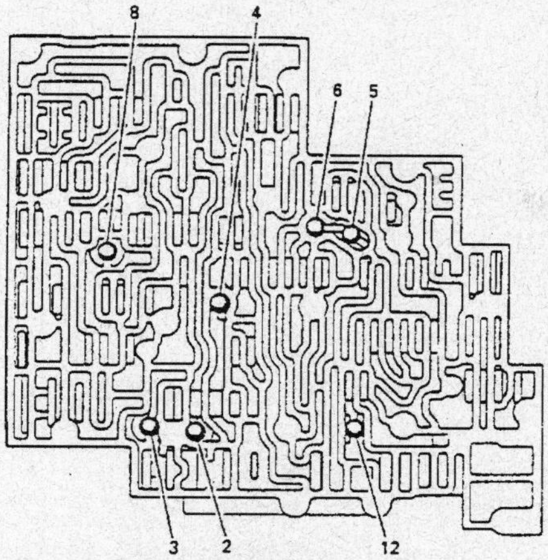

2 BALL, #2 CHECK (3RD ACCUMULATOR)
3 BALL, #3 CHECK (REVERSE INPUT)
4 BALL, #4 CHECK (3-4 CLUTCH EXHAUST)
5 BALL, #5 CHECK (OVERRUN CLUTCH FEED)
6 BALL, #6 CHECK (OVERRUN CLUTCH CONTROL)
8 BALL, #8 CHECK (1-2 UPSHIFT)
12 BALL, #2 CHECK (FORWARD CLUTCH ACCUM.)

GC5029400457000X

Fig. 32 Control valve body check ball locations

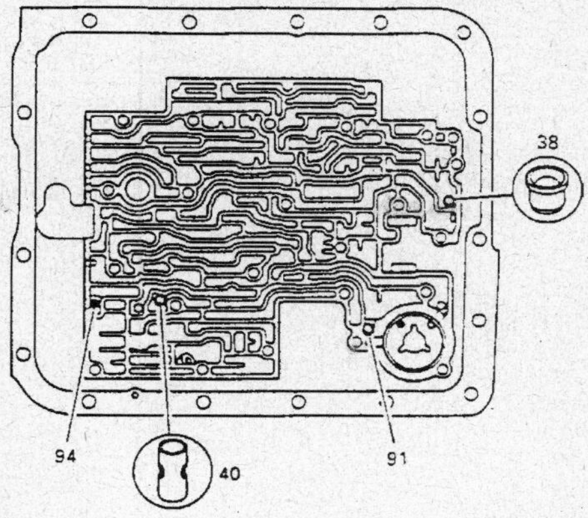

38 PLUG, TRANSMISSION CASE (ACCUM. BLEED)
40 RETAINER AND BALL ASSEMBLY, 3RD ACCUM.
91 NO. 1 CHECKBALL
94 SCREEN, TCC

GC5029400458000X

Fig. 33 Transmission case check ball locations

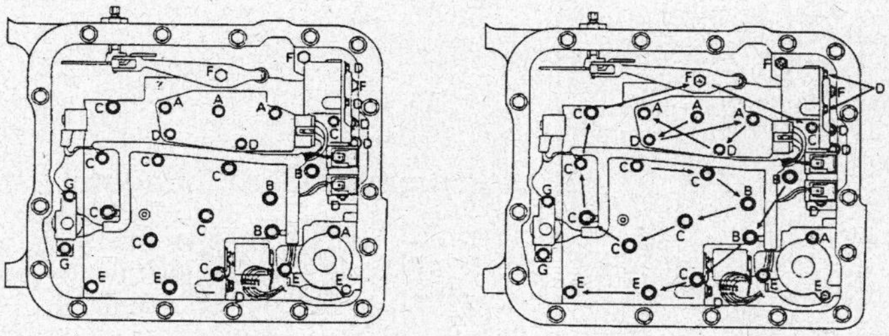

A M6 X 1.0 X 65.0
B M6 X 1.0 X 54.4
C M6 X 1.0 X 47.5
D M6 X 1.0 X 18.0
E M6 X 1.0 X 35.0
F M8 X 1.25 X 20.0
G M6 X 1.0 X 12.0

GC5029400451000X

Fig. 34 Control valve body bolts & tightening pattern

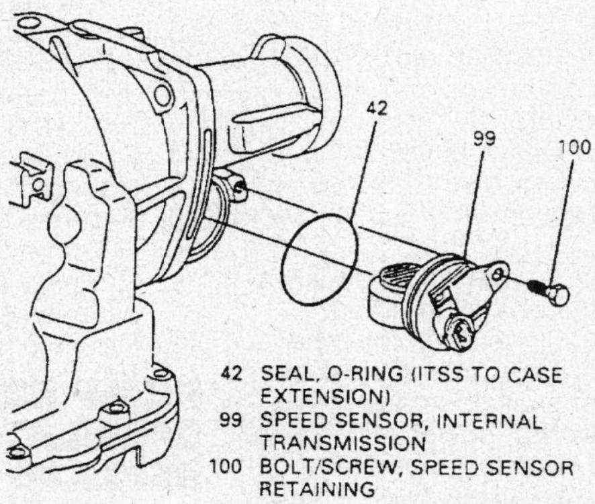

42 SEAL, O-RING (ITSS TO CASE EXTENSION)
99 SPEED SENSOR, INTERNAL TRANSMISSION
100 BOLT/SCREW, SPEED SENSOR RETAINING

GC5029400452000X

Fig. 35 Vehicle speed sensor

2. Remove righthand muffler assembly, then disconnect electrical connector from vehicle speed sensor.
3. Remove retaining bolt, then the vehicle speed sensor from rear axle differential case by lifting up and out of hole.
4. Reverse procedure to install. Tighten bolt to specification.

ACCUMULATOR, REPLACE

1. Raise and support vehicle.
2. Remove oil pan and gasket.
3. Remove oil filter and filter seal.
4. Remove control valve body as described under "Control Valve Body & Pressure Switch, Replace."
5. Remove accumulator cover bolts, **Fig. 36.**
6. Remove 1–2 accumulator cover, piston and spring.
7. Remove spacer plate support bolts.
8. Remove spacer plate and spacer plate gaskets.
9. Remove 3-4 accumulator spring, piston and pin.
10. Remove accumulator assembly.
11. Reverse procedure to install, noting the following:
    a. When installing 3-4 accumulator piston onto pin, piston legs must face valve body.
    b. When installing case and valve body gaskets, case gasket will be marked with a C and valve body gasket will be marked with a V.
    c. Tighten spacer plate support bolts to specification.

CONTROL & SHIFT SOLENOIDS, REPLACE

1. Raise and support vehicle.
2. Remove oil pan, oil filter and filter seal.
3. Remove accumulator cover bolts.
4. Remove 1–2 accumulator cover, piston and spring.
5. Disconnect control and shift solenoid electrical connectors.
6. Remove pressure control solenoid retainer bolt, retainer and solenoid, **Fig. 37.**
7. Remove shift solenoid retainers and shift solenoids.
8. Remove 3–2 control solenoid retainer and control solenoid.
9. Reverse procedure to install.

TCC SOLENOID & WIRING HARNESS, REPLACE

Corvette

1. Raise and support vehicle.
2. Remove righthand muffler assembly.
3. Remove transmission oil pan, oil filter and seal.
4. Disconnect external wiring harness connector from transmission pass through connector by squeezing fore and aft flats on connector in order to release locking tabs.
5. Remove 1-2 accumulator cover bolts, cover, piston and piston spring.
6. Disconnect electrical connectors and remove TCC PWM solenoid retainer.
7. Remove TCC PWM solenoid from control valve body.

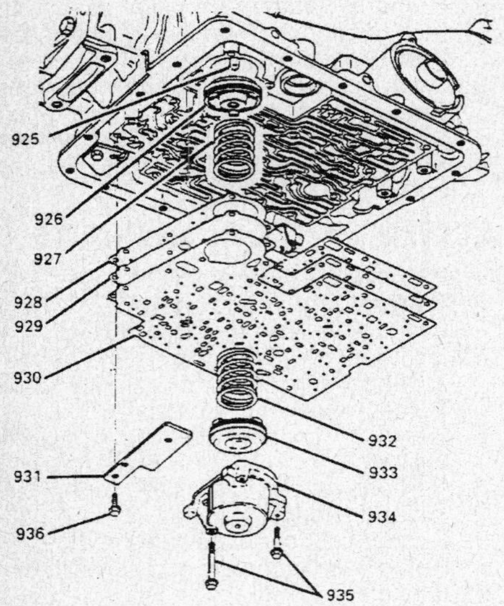

925 PIN, ACCUMULATOR PISTON
926 PISTON, 3-4 ACCUMULATOR
927 SPRING, 3-4 ACCUMULATOR
928 GASKET, SPACER PLATE TO CASE
929 PLATE, VALVE BODY SPACER
930 GASKET, SPACER PLATE TO VALVE BODY
931 PLATE, SPACER PLATE SUPPORT
932 1-2 ACCUMULATOR
933 1-2 ACCUMULATOR
934 COVER AND PIN ASSEMBLY, 1-2 ACCUMULATOR
935 BOLT/SCREW, ACCUMULATOR COVER
936 BOLT/SCREW, SPACER PLATE SUPPORT

GC5029400453000X

Fig. 36 Accumulator assembly

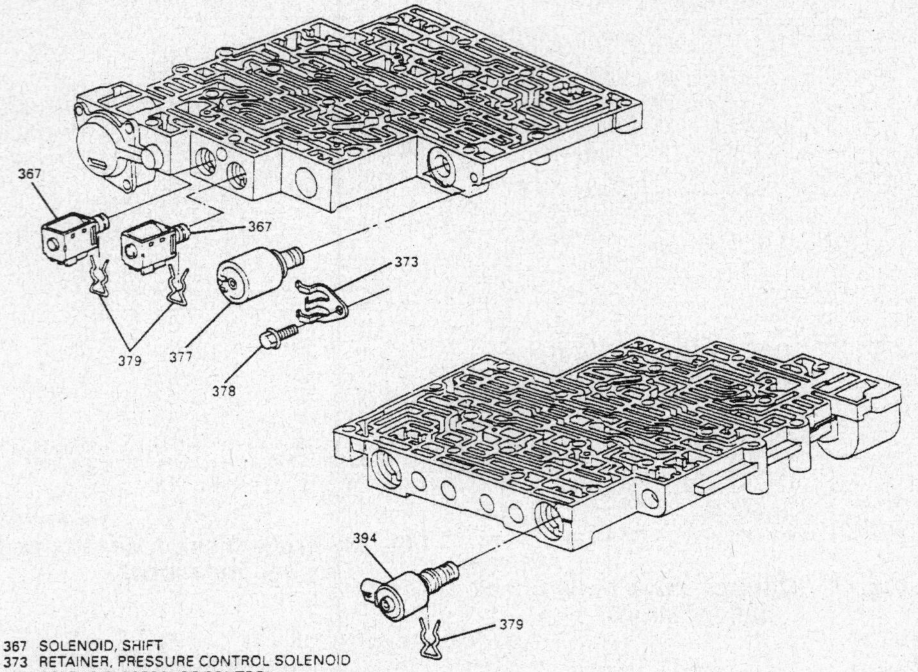

367 SOLENOID, SHIFT
373 RETAINER, PRESSURE CONTROL SOLENOID
377 SOLENOID, PRESSURE CONTROL
378 BOLT/SCREW, PRESSURE CONTROL SOLENOID RETAINER, 11 N•m (97 LB. IN.)
379 RETAINER, SOLENOID
394 SOLENOID, 3-2 CONTROL

GC5029400454000X

Fig. 37 Electrical component locations

8. Remove pressure control solenoid retainer bolt, retainer and solenoid from control valve body.
9. Remove TCC solenoid bolts and wiring harness bolts.
10. Remove pass-through electrical connector from transmission case by positioning small end of power piston seal protector and diaphragm retainer installer tool No. J-28458, or equivalent, over top of connector, then twisting tool to release four tabs while at same time pulling harness through case.
11. Remove TCC solenoid with wiring harness from transmission case.
12. Reverse procedure to install, noting the following:
    a. Tighten TCC solenoid retaining bolt to specification.
    b. Tighten pressure control solenoid retaining bolt to specification.
    c. When installing 1-2 accumulator piston to accumulator cover, piston legs must face towards case.
    d. Tighten accumulator retaining bolts to specification.

Camaro & Firebird

1. Raise and support vehicle.
2. Remove exhaust crossover pipe to exhaust manifold retaining nuts.
3. Remove exhaust pipe to catalytic converter retaining bolts and nuts.
4. Remove catalytic converter and crossover pipe assembly.
5. Remove transmission oil pan, oil filter and seal.
6. Disconnect external wiring harness connector from transmission pass through connector.

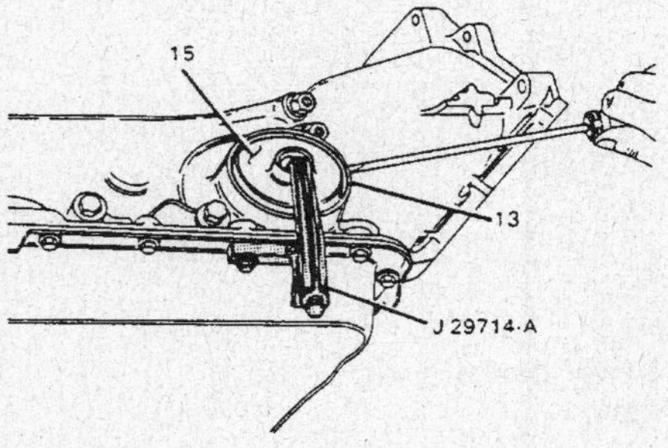

13 RING, 2-4 BAND SERVO COVER RETAINING
15 COVER, 2-4 BAND SERVO

GC5029400455000X

Fig. 38 Servo cover removal

7. Remove accumulator cover bolts, 1-2 accumulator cover, piston and spring.
8. Disconnect component electrical connectors.
9. Remove pressure control solenoid retainer bolt, retainer and solenoid.
10. Remove TCC solenoid retaining bolts.
11. Remove pass-through electrical connector from transmission case by positioning small end of power piston seal protector and diaphragm retainer installer tool No. J-28458, or equivalent, over top of connector, then twisting tool to release four tabs while at same time pulling harness through case.
12. Remove TCC solenoid with wiring harness from transmission case.
13. Reverse procedure to install, noting the following:
    a. Tighten solenoid retaining bolt to specification.
    b. Tighten pressure control solenoid retaining bolt to specification.
    c. When installing 1-2 accumulator piston to accumulator cover, piston legs must face towards case.
    d. Tighten accumulator retaining bolts to specification.

2-4 SERVO ASSEMBLY, REPLACE

1. Remove exhaust system as described under "TCC Solenoid & Wiring Harness, Replace."
2. Remove transmission oil pan bolt below servo cover, **Fig. 38.**
3. Install servo cover depressor tool No. J-29714-A, or equivalent, on oil pan and install bolt included with tool, **Fig. 38.**
4. Depress servo cover and remove retaining ring.
5. Remove tool from oil pan.
6. Remove cover and seal ring.
7. Remove servo piston and bore apply pin assembly.
8. Reverse procedure to install.

PUMP PRESSURE REGULATOR VALVE, REPLACE

1. Raise and support vehicle.
2. Remove transmission oil pan and gasket.
3. Compress pressure regulator valve with a small screwdriver, **Fig. 39.**
4. Remove retaining ring and slowly release spring tension.
5. Remove pressure regulator bore plug, valve, spring and guide.

6. Reverse procedure to install.

REAR OIL SEAL, REPLACE

1. Remove exhaust system as described under "TCC Solenoid & Wiring Harness, Replace."
2. Support transmission with suitable jack.
3. Remove driveline support bolts, washers and nuts.
4. Position driveline support aside to gain clearance.
5. Mark relationship of propeller shaft to pinion yoke, then disconnect rear universal joint by removing propeller shaft retainers. **Tape bearing cups to trunnion to prevent dropping and loss of roller bearings.**
6. Slide slip yoke from transmission and remove propeller shaft from vehicle.
7. Remove rear oil seal from transmission rear case extension.
8. Reverse procedure to install.

TRANSMISSION

REPLACE

CAMARO & FIREBIRD

1. Remove air intake duct and disconnect electrical connector from intake air temperature sensor.
2. Remove transmission fluid level indicator.
3. Raise and support vehicle.
4. Remove catalytic converter, then the range selector lever cable from transmission.
5. Remove center support bearing from torque arm and propeller shaft.
6. Support rear axle with jack and remove rear axle torque arm.
7. Remove starter motor and loosen righthand side rear engine mount bracket bolts.
8. Remove mounting bolts and transmission support braces from vehicle.
9. Remove transmission converter cover bolts and cover.
10. Remove torque converter bolts retaining flywheel to torque converter.
11. Remove oil cooler pipes at transmission, then disconnect transmission electrical connectors.
12. Support transmission and remove transmission bolts.
13. Remove transmission fluid fill tube and separate transmission from engine.
14. Attach torque converter holding fixture tool No. J-21366, or equivalent, to transmission to retain torque converter when moving transmission.
15. Lower transmission from vehicle.
16. Reverse procedure to install.

CORVETTE

1. Raise and support vehicle.
2. Remove rear tire and wheel assemblies.
3. Shift transmission into Neutral position and remove intermediate exhaust pipe.
4. Tie off lefthand muffler assembly to underbody to support out of way.

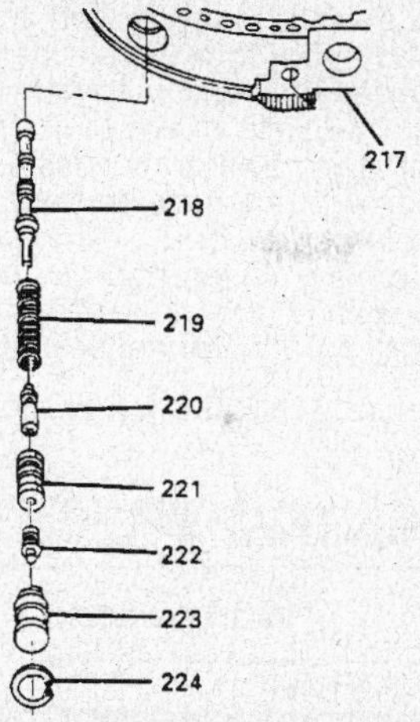

217 PUMP ASSEMBLY, AUTOMATIC TRANSMISSION OI
218 VALVE, PRESSURE REGULATOR
219 SPRING, PRESSURE REGULATOR VALVE
220 VALVE, REVERSE BOOST
221 BUSHING, REVERSE BOOST VALVE
222 VALVE, TV BOOST
223 BUSHING, TV BOOST VALVE
224 RING, TV BOOST VALVE BUSHING RETAINER

GC5029400456000X

Fig. 39 Pump pressure regulator valve assembly

5. Remove righthand muffler assembly and driveline tunnel closeout panel.
6. Using a suitable flat bladed screwdriver, remove rear bellhousing access plug.
7. Match mark transmission flexplate to transmission torque converter through access hole in rear bellhousing.
8. Remove transmission flexplate bolts and two plug bolts from front of driveline support assembly.
9. Propeller input shaft front bearing positioning bolts are intended to remain tightened to specification and in place until instructed in installation procedure.
10. Install two bolts, M10–1.5 X 55 mm, or longer, in place of plug bolts. Long bolts retain the propeller input shaft front bearing in its original position during removal and installation. **Torque** propeller input shaft front bearing positioning bolts to 26 ft. lbs.
11. Using a suitable flat bladed screwdriver, remove engine flywheel housing access plug.
12. Loosen propeller shaft hub clamp bolt and rotate engine at flywheel, if necessary for alignment.
13. Shift transmission into Park position and remove nuts retaining transmission shift cable bracket to transmission.
14. Disconnect transmission shift control cable from transmission shift lever by unsnapping cable.
15. Reposition transmission shift cable and bracket.
16. Remove electronic brake and traction control module (EBTCM) lefthand mounting bracket bolts.
17. Remove EBTCM lefthand mounting bracket with EBTCM rubber insulators.
18. Pull lightly to release EBTCM from insulator attached to EBTCM righthand mounting bracket. Tie off EBTCM to underbody to support out of way.
19. Remove rear transverse spring and support lower control arm with a straight jack.
20. Disconnect outer tie rod end from suspension knuckle and shock absorber lower retaining bolt.
21. Disconnect lower ball joint from suspension knuckle.
22. Remove straight jack from control arm. Repeat previous steps to other side suspension components.
23. Install transmission support fixture tool No. J-42055, or equivalent, with transmission jack to transmission.
24. Disconnect wring harness and brake pipe clip retainers from rear suspension crossmember.
25. Remove differential to transmission lower nut. Removing nut at this time will aid in separating differential from transmission after driveline has been removed from vehicle.
26. Remove transmission mount to rear crossmember nuts.
27. Position transmission jack under rear suspension crossmember and firmly secure crossmember to jack.
28. By hand, remove rear suspension crossmember retaining nuts.
29. With aid of an assistant, slowly lower rear suspension crossmember away from vehicle frame rails and remove crossmember.
30. Remove transmission mount bracket to differential bolts, then the transmission mount bracket.
31. Using a pry bar, release axle shafts from differential.
32. Tie off axle shafts to underbody to support out of way.
33. Using pliers, compress and release four retainers securing wiring harness along driveline support assembly and push harness out of way.
34. Slowly lower driveline approximately two inches, while adjusting angle of tilt in order to access electrical connectors.
35. Disconnect vehicle speed sensor and wiring harness retainer from stud at differential rear cover.
36. Disconnect wiring harness retainer clip from top of differential.
37. Have an assistant guide front of driveline during removal of driveline from vehicle.
38. Slowly lower driveline while adjusting angle of tilt and pulling driveline away from engine until propeller input shaft at front of driveline support assembly just clears engine flywheel housing.
39. Slowly lower driveline completely out of vehicle.
40. Position chain fall, or equivalent, of a lift device in a way which will protect transmission oil cooler rear pipes and rear exhaust hangers located on driveline support assembly.
41. Using lift device, raise driveline to relieve weight from transmission jack.
42. Disconnect support fixture from transmission jack only. Support fixture will provide stability to driveline components while working on a bench.

43. Position driveline on a workbench with lift device still attached, and support driveline support assembly and differential from additional balance.
44. Remove lift device from driveline and disconnect transmission oil cooler rear pipes from fittings on transmission.
45. Remove transmission to driveline support bolts, insert a suitable flat bladed screwdriver or similar tool between support assembly and transmission, and begin to pry driveline support assembly loose from transmission.
46. Slowly slide driveline support assembly away from transmission while supporting transmission torque converter to transmission.
47. Remove differential to transmission bolts and nuts.
48. Use care when separating differential from transmission to not damage transmission output shaft seal in differential plate. Slowly slide differential from transmission.
49. Remove differential plate from differential.
50. Remove transmission from support fixture.
51. Reverse procedure to install.

TIGHTENING SPECIFICATIONS

Year	Component	Torque/ Ft. Lbs.
CAMARO & FIREBIRD		
1997–2000	Accumulator Cover	96①
	Auxiliary Valve Body Bolt	96①
	Case Extension Bolt	26
	Control Valve Body	96①
	Filler Tube To Transmission Case②	35
	Filler Tube To Transmission Case③	55
	Floorshift Control Bolt	44①
	Flywheel Cover	84①
	Manual Shift Detent Assembly	16
	Neutral Safety/Back-up Lamp Switch	18①
	Oil Cooler Connector At Radiator	20
	Oil Cooler Connector At Transmission	28
	Oil Pan Bolts	12
	Pressure Control Solenoid Retainer	96①
	Shift Cable Nut	11
	Spacer Plate Support	96①
	TCC Solenoid Valve	96①
	Torque Converter Bolts	46
	Transmission Case Extension To Transmission	26
	Transmission Mount To Transmission Bolt	40
	Transmission Mount To Transmission Support Nut	35
	Transmission Support To Frame Bolt	40
	Transmission To Engine Bolt③	35
	Transmission To Engine Bolts②	70
	TV Cable To Transmission Bolt	84①
	Valve Body Bolts	96①
	Vehicle Speed Sensor	96①
	Vehicle Speed Sensor Retainer	84①
	Wheel Lug Nuts	81
CORVETTE		
1997–2000	Accumulator Cover Bolts	96①
	Control Valve Body Bolts	96①
	Differential To Transmission Bolts & Nuts	37
	Driveline Support Assembly To Engine Flywheel Housing Bolts	37
	Driveline Support Assembly Front Plug Bolts	37
	EBTCM Lefthand Mounting Bracket Mounting Bolts	37
	Flexplate To Torque Converter Bolts	47
	Floor Shift Control Retaining Nuts	84①
	Fluid Check/Fill Plug	22
	Intermediate Shaft Lower coupling Bolt	25
	Oil Pan Bolts	96①

Continued

TIGHTENING SPECIFICATIONS—Continued

Year	Component	Torque/ Ft. Lbs.
CORVETTE		
1997-2000	Park/Neutral Position Switch Mounting Bolts	20
	Propeller Input Shaft Front Bearing Positioning Bolts	26
	Propeller Shaft Hub Clamp Bolt	96
	Rear Shock Absorber Lower Mounting Bolt	162
	Rear Suspension Crossmember Mounting Nuts	81
	TCC Solenoid Retaining Bolts	96①
	Transmission Mount Bracket To Differential Bolts	37
	Transmission Mount To Rear Suspension Crossmember Nuts	37
	Transmission Range Selector Lever Nuts	15
	Transmission Shift Control Cable Bracket Retaining Nuts	15

① — Inch lbs.
② — V8 engine.
③ — V6 engine.

Turbo Hydra-Matic 4T40-E/4T45-E Automatic Transaxle

NOTE: On Air Bag Equipped Models, Refer To " Air Bag System Precautions" Located In The Front Of This Manual For System Disarming & Arming Procedures.

NOTE: Refer To "Computer Relearn Procedures " Located In The Front Of This Manual For Computer Relearn Procedures.

INDEX

PRECAUTIONS

AIR BAG SYSTEMS

Refer to "Air Bag System Precautions" in the front of this manual for system disarming and arming procedures.

BATTERY GROUND CABLE

Prior to service, disconnect battery ground cable and isolate as required.

IDENTIFICATION

The transaxle identification tag is located on the rear righthand side of the transaxle housing, **Fig. 1**.

DESCRIPTION

The 4T40-E transaxle, **Fig. 2,** is a fully automatic electronically controlled front wheel drive transaxle with four forward gear ranges including overdrive and one reverse gear range. Oil pressure is supplied by a variable displacement vane type oil pump. Two shift solenoids, operated by the PCM, control shift points and TCC apply rates, which are influenced by various sensor inputs. The transaxle unit includes a three element hydraulic torque converter and lockup clutching element, four multiple disc clutch packs, roller clutch,

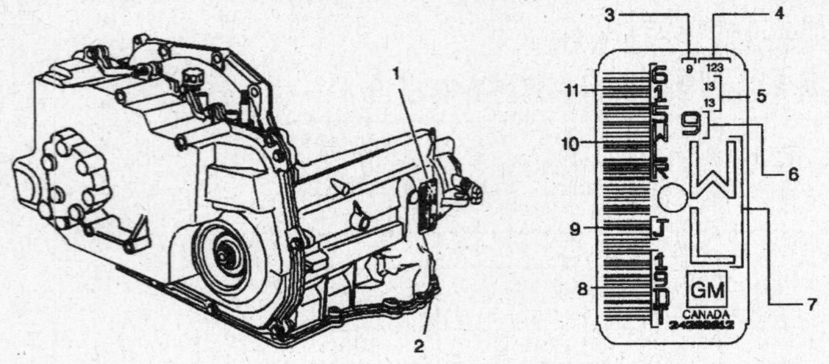

(1) Transmission ID Location
(2) VIN Location
(3) Calendar Year (9 = 1999)
(4) Julian Date
(5) Shift and Line Number
(6) Calendar Year (9 = 1999)
(7) Model
(8) Serial Number in Base Code 31
(9) J = Windsor Plant
(10) Broadcast Code
(11) Transmission (4T40-E)

TH5029600810000A

Fig. 1 Transaxle identification tag location

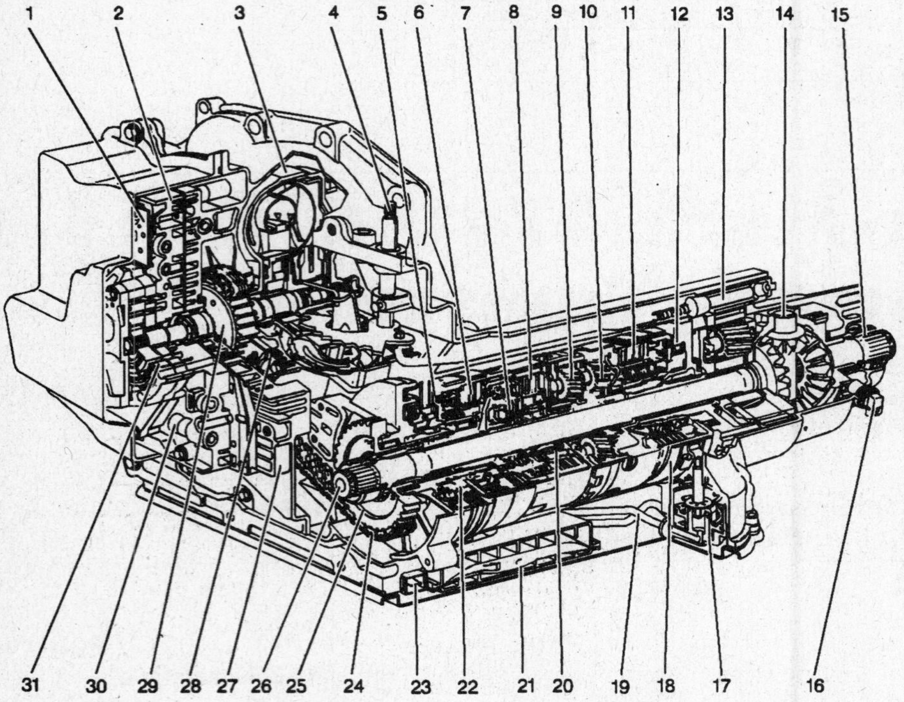

(1) TFP Manual Valve Position Switch Assembly
(2) Control Valve Body Assembly
(3) Torque Converter Assembly
(4) Manual Shaft and Detent Lever Assembly
(5) 2nd Clutch
(6) Reverse Clutch
(7) Coast Clutch
(8) Direct Clutch
(9) Reaction Planetary Gear Set
(10) Input Planetary Gear Set
(11) Forward Clutch
(12) Lo Roller Clutch
(13) Parking Lock Actuator Assembly
(14) Differential and Final Drive Assembly
(15) Output Stub Shaft
(16) Output Speed Sensor
(17) Lo/Reverse Servo Assembly
(18) Lo/Reverse Band
(19) Oil Feed Tube Assembly
(20) Input Sprag Clutch Assembly
(21) Oil Filter Assembly
(22) 2nd Roller Clutch
(23) Oil Level Control Valve
(24) Drive Link Assembly
(25) Driven Sprocket
(26) Output Shaft
(27) Channel Plate Assembly
(28) Input Speed Sensor
(29) Drive Sprocket
(30) Control Valve Body Assembly
(31) Oil Pump Assembly

TH5029600811000A

Fig. 2 Cross sectional view of 4T40-E transaxle

sprag clutch, two bands and a compound reaction planetary gearset. Power is transmitted to the drive wheels from the planetary gear through a final drive gearset and differential assembly.

TROUBLESHOOTING

Refer to **Figs. 3 through 39** for troubleshooting.

BRAKE TRANSAXLE SHIFT INTERLOCK (BTSI)

1. Verify brake light operation.
2. If brake lights do not operate, refer to **Figs. 40 and 41** for wiring diagrams and **Figs. 42 through 44** for diagnostic procedures.
3. Check for proper installation of aftermarket equipment or for broken or partially broken wires inside of insulation. This could cause system failures, but not be indicated in a continuity or voltage check.

FLUID PRESSURE CHECK

This transaxle uses a vane type pump to produce hydraulic pressure and a transaxle pressure control solenoid at the pressure regulator valve to control pressure after it leaves the pump. The transaxle pressure control solenoid is controlled by an electrical signal that ranges from 0–1.1 amp. 1.1 amp corresponds to a minimum line pressure of approximately 45–55 psi. Zero amps corresponds to a maximum line pressure of approximately 140–180 psi in overdrive. Refer to **Fig. 45** for inspection.

MAINTENANCE

Refer to "Lubricant Data Chart" in the appropriate chassis chapter of this manual for transaxle fluid specifications.

FLUID LEVEL CHECK & CHANGE

Start engine and drive vehicle approximately 15 miles or until the transaxle reaches operating temperature of 180–200°F.

1. Allow engine to run at idle speed for three to five minutes with accessories off.
2. Apply brake and move shift lever through all gear ranges, pausing three seconds in each range.
3. Place shift lever in Park position.
4. Raise and support vehicle.
5. Place oil container under check plug.
6. Check that oil level is at bottom of oil check hole. Because transaxle operates over a range of fluid levels, fluid may or may not drain out of screw hole when screw is removed.
7. If fluid drains through screw hole, transaxle may have been overfilled. When fluid stops draining, fluid level is correct and check plug may be installed.

Checks	Action
Oil Level	High or Low; correct as required
• Pressure Regulator Valve • Springs • Boost Valve	Stuck
Pressure Control Solenoid	• Leak, damaged O-rings • Loose connector, damaged pins • Contaminated
Torque Signal Regulator Valve	Stuck
Transmission Wiring Harness	• Loose connector at the vehicle harness • Short
Pressure Switch Assembly	• Loose connector • Damaged or missing O-ring
Throttle Position Sensor	• Damaged, sticking, disconnected • An intermittent open or a shorted circuit
Oil Filter	Clogged, broken, or loose
Oil Filter Seal	Leaking
Cooler Lines	Clogged or restricted
Cooler Line Seals	Leaking
Oil Pump	Damaged, sticking, porous, or leaking
Oil Pump Drive Shaft	Damaged
Pressure Relief Valve	Damaged spring or missing ball
• Transmission Case • Valve Body • Channel Plate	• Porosity, leaking circuits • Flatness of machined surfaces

GC5029900764000X

Fig. 3 High or low line pressure

Checks	Action
Shift Solenoids	• Contamination • An intermittent open or a shorted circuit
Throttle Position Sensor	• Damaged, disconnected • An intermittent open or a shorted circuit
Vehicle and Input Speed Sensors	• Damaged, disconnected or loose • An intermittent open or a shorted circuit

GC5029900765000X

Fig. 4 Inaccurate/inconsistent shift points

Checks	Action
Line Pressure	High (Refer to *High or Low Line Pressure*)
Checkballs	Missing; no orificed apply
Accumulators	• Springs or piston binding; no accumulation • Accumulator valve is stuck
Clutch Housing Retainer and Ball Assemblies	Plugged

GC5029900766000X

Fig. 5 Harsh shifts

Checks	Action
Reverse Clutch	No apply or slipping
Piston and Seal Assembly	Binding, cracked, or leaking
Inner Seal	Plugged orifice
Clutch Plates	Worn friction or broken splines
Snap Ring	Out of position
Housing	Cracked, plugged feed holes, or broken tangs
Housing Retainer and Ball Assembly	Missing or out of position
Springs	Binding
Reverse Clutch Fluid Routing	Fluid leak or restriction
Driven Sprocket Support	• Leaking seal rings • Porosity, damage, misalignment
Channel Plate and Gasket, and Valve Body, Gaskets, and Channel Plate	Porosity, fluid leak across the channels, misalignment, damage, or fluid restriction
Low and Reverse Band and Servo	No apply or slipping
Servo Piston	Broken or binding
Servo Piston Seals	Leaking
Servo Pin and Springs	Binding
Servo Cover	Broken, loose, or leaking
Low and Reverse Band	Broken, worn, or out of position
Anchor Pin	Broken
Fluid Feed Tubes	• Broken, bent, or plugged • Missing or leaking seal rings
Transmission Case	Porosity, fluid leak, or restriction
Shift Linkage	Disconnected or misaligned
Manual Valve and Link	Disconnected or misaligned
#1 Checkball	Missing (no low band fluid)
Fluid Level	Low
Fluid Pressure	Low (Refer to *High or Low Line Pressure*)

GC5029900767000X

Fig. 6 No reverse or slips in reverse

Checks	Action
Forward Clutch	No apply or slipping
Piston and Seal Assembly	Binding, cracked, or leaking
Inner Seal	Plugged orifice
Clutch Plates	Worn friction, or broken splines
Snap Ring	Out of position
Housing	Cracked, or plugged feed holes
Housing Retainer and Ball Assembly	Missing or out of position
Springs	Binding
Input Sprag	Damaged or not holding
Lo Roller Clutch	Damaged or not holding
Forward Clutch Fluid Routing	Fluid leak or restriction
Oil Feed Tubes	• Bent, broken, or plugged • Leaking seal rings

GC5029900768010X

Fig. 7 No first gear, slips in first gear (Part 1 of 2)

Checks	Action
Forward Clutch Support	• Porosity • Leaking or damaged seal rings • Plugged feed holes
Channel Plate and Gasket	• Porosity • Misalignment • Fluid leaking across the channels • Restriction
PSA	Leaking drive switch O-ring
1-2 Shift Solenoid Valve	• Failed OFF • Leaking
1-2 Shift Valve	Stuck in upshifted position
2-3 Shift Solenoid Valve	• Failed ON • Plugged exhaust
• Manual Valve • Shift Linkage	Misalignment
Torque Converter	Stator roller clutch is not holding
Line Pressure	Low Pressure (Refer to *High or Low Line Pressure*)

GC5029900768020X

Fig. 7 No first gear, slips in first gear (Part 2 of 2)

Checks	Action
Second Clutch	No apply or slipping
Piston and Seal Assembly	Binding, cracked, or leaking
Clutch Plates	Worn friction or broken splines
Snap Ring	Out of position
Spring	Binding
Driven Sprocket Support	Damaged, leaking, porous
Second Clutch Fluid Routing	Fluid leak or restriction
• Valve Body • Gaskets and Spacer Plate • Channel Plate and Gasket • Driven Sprocket Support	• Porosity • Misalignment • Loose or restricted • Fluid leak across the channels
Second Roller Clutch	Damaged, not holding
1-2 Shift Solenoid Valve	• Stuck ON • Plugged
Forward Clutch	Low capacity shows up in Second Gear
Line Pressure	Low pressure (Refer to *High or Low Line Pressure*)
1-2 Accumulator	• Leak at the piston seal • Channel plate or case porosity
1-2 Accumulator Valve	Stuck
2-3 Shift Valve	Stuck in an upshifted position
PSA	Malfunction (Electrical or Hydraulic)

GC5029900769000X

Fig. 8 No second gear, slips in second gear

8. If fluid does not drain through screw hole, transaxle fluid level may have been low. Add fluid at vent cap location in half liter (1 pint) increments until oil level is at bottom of oil check hole.
9. Install oil check plug and tighten to specifications.
10. Lower vehicle.

OIL FILTER & SEAL REPLACEMENT

1. Raise and support vehicle.
2. Drain transaxle fluid.
3. Remove transaxle oil pan and gasket.
4. Remove oil filter assembly.
5. Using a small screwdriver, remove filter neck seal from transaxle case and discard. Ensure not to score case during seal removal.
6. Reverse procedure to install, noting the following:
   a. Oil pan gasket may be reused, unless sealing ribs are damaged.
   b. Install new oil filter and seal. Tap

Checks	Action
Direct Clutch	No apply or slipping
Piston and Seal Assembly	Binding, cracked, or leaking
Clutch Plates	Worn friction or broken splines
Snap Ring	Out of position
Springs	Binding
Direct & Coasting Housing and Input Shaft	• Damaged or cracked • Restricted feed holes
Housing Retaining and Ball Assembly	Missing or loose
Direct Clutch Fluid Routing	Fluid leak or restriction
• Valve Body • Gaskets & Spacer Plate • Channel Plate & Gasket • Driven Sprocket Support	• Porosity • Misalignment • Looseness • Fluid Restriction • Fluid leak across the channels
Driven Sprocket support Seals	Leaking
Input Shaft	• Leaking seals • Damaged or misaligned sleeve
2-3 Shift Solenoid Valve	• Stuck OFF • Leaking
2-3 Accumulator	• A leak at a piston seal • Channel plate or case porosity
2-3 Accumulator Valve	Stuck
Line Pressure	Low pressure (Refer to *High or Low Line Pressure*)
3-4 Shift Valve	Stuck in upshifted position
PSA	Malfunction (Electrical or Hydraulic)

GC5029900770000X

Fig. 9 No third gear, slips in third gear

Checks	Action
Intermediate/Fourth Band & Servo	No apply or slipping
Servo Piston	Broken or binding
Servo Piston Seals	Leaking
Servo Pin and Springs	Binding
Servo Cover	Broken, loose, or leaking
Band	Broken, worn, or out of position
Case	Cracked at the band seat
Band Apply Fluid Routing	Fluid leak and fluid restricting
• Valve Body • Gaskets & Spacer Plate • Channel Plate • Case	• Porosity • Misalignment • Fluid leak across the channels

GC5029900772010X

Fig. 11 No fourth gear, slips in fourth gear (Part 1 of 2)

Checks	Action
1-2 Shift Solenoid Valve	• Stuck OFF • Leaking
3-4 Shift Valve	Stuck in the downshifted position
Manual Valve	Misaligned in Manual Third gear
3-4 Accumulator	• A leak at the piston seal • Channel plate or case porosity
3-4 Accumulator Valve	Stuck
Line Pressure	Low pressure (Refer to *High or Low Line Pressure*)
Direct Clutch	A low capacity will cause a failure in the Fourth gear
PSA	Malfunction (Hydraulic or Electrical)

Fig. 12 No fourth gear, slipss in fourth gear (Part 1 of 2)

Checks	Action
Torque Converter	• Broken lugs or a failed lug weld • Sheared lug bolts • Worn turbine shaft splines • An internal failure • A cracked cover at the weld
Wheel Drive Shafts	• Damaged • Worn or loose splines
Turbine Shaft	Stripped splines
Oil Pump	Seized or broken pump gears
Oil Pump Shaft	Broken or stripped splines
Filter and Filter Seal	Plugged or missing
Fluid Level	Low
Shift Linkage	Disconnected
Drive/Driven Sprockets and Drive Chain	Broken
Planetary Gears	Failure or lack of lube
Final drive	Gear failure or lack of lube
Channel Plate and Gasket	Damaged, leaking, or misaligned
Valve Body, Gaskets, and Spacer Plate	Damaged, leaking, or misaligned
• Forward Sprag Clutch • Forward Clutch • Low Roller Clutch	Damaged or not holding (Refer to *No First Gear, Slips in First Gear*)
Hydraulic System	• Tie up • Fluid circuit leaks

GC5029900773000X

Fig. 13 Loss Of Drive

Checks	Action
Fluid Level	Low
Shift Solenoids	• Second gear start failed OFF • 2-3 Shift solenoid Valve failed ON
TCC System	The TCC is stuck ON or is dragging
Torque Converter	Contaminated or damaged

GC5029900774000X

Fig. 14 Loss of power

Checks	Action
1-2 Shift Valve	Stuck in the down shifted position

GC5029900771000X

Fig. 10 Second gear only

Checks	Action
1-2 Shift Solenoid Valve	• Stuck OFF • Leaking
3-4 Shift Valve	Stuck in the downshifted position
Manual Valve	Misaligned in Manual Third gear
3-4 Accumulator	• A leak at the piston seal • Channel plate or case porosity
3-4 Accumulator Valve	Stuck
Line Pressure	Low pressure (Refer to *High or Low Line Pressure*)
Direct Clutch	A low capacity will cause a failure in the Fourth gear
PSA	Malfunction (Hydraulic or Electrical)

Fig. 11 No fourth gear, slips in fourth gear (Part 2 of 2)

Checks	Action
1-2 Shift Solenoid Valve	• Stuck OFF • Leaking
3-4 Shift Valve	Stuck in the downshifted position
Manual Valve	Misaligned in Manual Third gear
3-4 Accumulator	• A leak at the piston seal • Channel plate or case porosity
3-4 Accumulator Valve	Stuck
Line Pressure	Low pressure (Refer to *High or Low Line Pressure*)
Direct Clutch	A low capacity will cause a failure in the Fourth gear
PSA	Malfunction (Hydraulic or Electrical)

GC5029900772020X

Fig. 12 No fourth gear, slips in fourth gear (Part 2 of 2)

Checks	Action
TCC System	The TCC is stuck ON or is dragging
TCC Solenoid Valve	• Stuck ON • Solenoid exhaust is plugged
TCC Regulated Apply Valve	Stuck in the apply position

GC5029900775000X

Fig. 15 Engine stall

Checks	Action
2-3 Shift Solenoid Valve	• Stuck in OFF • Leaking solenoid • Electrical malfunction
2-3 Shift Valve	Stuck in downshifted position
Direct Clutch	Failed clutch (released)

GC5029900776000X

Fig. 16 First & second gears only

Checks	Action
2-3 Shift Solenoid Valve	• Stuck ON • Solenoid is plugged • Electrical malfunction
1-2 and 2-3 Shift Valves	Both are stuck in an upshifted position

GC5029900777000X

Fig. 17 Third & fourth gears only

Checks	Action
1-2 Shift Solenoid Valve	• Stuck ON • The solenoid is plugged • Electrical malfunction

GC5029900778000X

Fig. 18 First & fourth gears only

Checks	Action
1-2 Shift Solenoid Valve	• Stuck OFF • The solenoid is leaking • Electrical malfunction

GC5029900779000X

Fig. 19 Second & third gears only

Checks	Action
Parking Lock Actuator Assembly	• Bent or damaged rod • Binding or broken spring • The rod is not attached to the detent lever
Detent Roller and Spring	• The bolt is not torqued, or loose • Bent or damaged
Detent Lever	• Damaged or loose • A manual shaft pin is missing
Manual Valve	• Misaligned • The manual valve to detent lever link is bent
Parking Lock Pawl	• Damaged • Broken tooth
Park Lock Gear	• Damaged teeth • Damaged splines
Park Pawl Spring	Broken or missing
Shift Linkage	Misadjusted

GC5029900780000X

Fig. 20 No Park

Checks	Action
Parking Pawl	The return spring is damaged, weak, or misassembled

GC5029900781000X

Fig. 21 Ratcheting noise

Checks	Action
Coast Clutch	No apply
Intermediate or Fourth Band	No apply
Pressure Switch Assembly	Leaking or inoperative
Vehicle Speed Sensor	Reads 0 mph

GC5029900783000X

Fig. 23 No engine braking; manual second & second gear

Checks	Action
Forward Clutch (Drives Forward)	Not releasing
Reverse Clutch and Lo & Reverse Servo (Drives in Reverse)	Both are not releasing
Manual Valve and Linkage	Misaligned

GC5029900785000X

Fig. 25 Drives in Neutral

Checks	Action
Indicator Linkage	Misadjusted
Detent Spring and Roller Assembly	• Broken or missing • Loose bolt
Manual Valve	Not connected to the detent lever

GC5029900787000X

Fig. 27 Shift indicator indicates wrong gear selection

Checks	Action
Torque Converter	• Out of balance • Internal Failure
Transmission or Engine	Misaligned
Output or Stub Shafts	• Out of balance • Worn or damaged bushings
Turbine Shaft	• Out of balance • Worn bushings

GC5029900789000X

Fig. 29 Vibration

Checks	Action
Definition: A high pitch whine which will intensify with engine RPM or which is sensitive to the oil pressure	
Oil Pump System	Verify that the noise is internal to the oil pump during a preliminary oil pressure check. An increase in line pressure will vary an oil pump noise.

GC5029900791000X

Fig. 31 High pitch whine

Checks	Action
Definition: A Buzz or High Frequency Rattle	
Trace Cooler Pipes (Check for binding or contact at the Radiator, other than at the Cooler Pipe connectors).	Verify a pressure buzz by watching for a needle vibration of the pressure guage. A road test may be necessary.

GC5029900793000X

Fig. 33 Buzz or high frequency rattle

Checks	Action
Definition: A Whine or Growl that increases and fades with vehicle speed and is most noticeable under light acceleration	
Drive Link Assembly System	Verify that the noise comes from the sprockets or the from the drive link assembly (chain) by placing your left foot on the brake and by moving the gear selector from PARK or REVERSE. If the noise stops, check the following items: • Drive Chain • Drive Sprocket • Driven Sprocket • Drive Sprocket Support • Driven Sprocket Support
Drive Chain	Stretched
Drive Sprocket and Driven Sprocket	• Broken or sheared teeth • Nicked or scored bearing surfaces • The bearing race or roller bearing surfaces on the gear support inner bearing are rough or pitted • A damaged bearing
Drive Sprocket Support and Driven Sprocket Support	The bearing outer race support is rough or nicked

GC5029900794000X

Fig. 34 Whine or growl

Checks	Action
Coast Clutch	No apply or slipping
Piston and Seal Assembly	Binding, cracked, or leaking
Clutch Plates	Worn friction or broken splines
Springs	Binding
Direct & Coast Clutch Housing and Input Shaft	• Damaged or cracked • Fluid feed holes are restricted
Housing Retainer and Ball Assembly	Missing or loose
Coast Clutch Fluid Routing	Fluid leak or restriction
• Valve Body Gaskets and Spacer Plate • Channel Plate and Gasket • Driven Sprocket Support	• Porosity • Misalignment • Looseness • Fluid restriction • Fluid leak across the channels
Driven Sprocket Support Seals	Leaking
Input Shaft	• Leaking seals • Damaged or misaligned sleeve
Oil Level or Line Pressure	Low Pressure (Refer to *High or Low Line Pressure*)
3-4 Shift Valve	Stuck in Fourth gear position (No coast clutch apply)
Manual Valve or Shift Linkage	Misaligned

GC5029900782000X

Fig. 22 No engine braking; all manual ranges

Checks	Action
Coast Clutch	No apply
Lo and Reverse Servo	No apply
Pressure Switch Assembly	Leaking or inoperative
#1 Checkball	Missing

GC5029900784000X

Fig. 24 No engine braking; manual first & first gear

Checks	Action
Manual Valve to Detent Lever Link	• Broken or missing • Disconnected from the manual valve
Manual Valve to Link Clip	Disconnected
Manual Valve	Stuck
Shift Linkage	Disconnected
Valve Body, Channel Plate and Case	Blocked fluid channels

GC5029900786000X

Fig. 26 No gear selection

Checks	Action
Fluid	• Degraded fluid • Contaminated (Antifreeze) • The transmission is overfilled
Cooler Lines	Plugged
Transmission Oil Filter	Clogged or cracked
Filter Seal	Leaking
Side Cover Seal	Damaged
Engine	Overheated
Vehicle	Overloaded
Oil Level Control Valve	Damaged or loose

GC5029900788000X

Fig. 28 Fluid foaming

Checks	Action
Definition: In All Ranges: a whine which may be sensitive to RPM load, or which ceases when the TCC engages	
Torque Converter	Verify that the noise is internal to the torque converter by placing your left foot on the brake with the gear or selector in DRIVE. Momentarily stall the engine. Torque Converter noise increases under load.

GC5029900790000X

Fig. 30 RPM sensitive whine

Checks	Action
Definition: A Popping noise, similar to popcorn popping	
Oil Pump System	• Inspect for pump cavitation, indicated by bubbles in fluid • Inspect the transmission fluid filter for a leaky seam • Inspect the transmission fluid filter seal for improper positioning or for a cut seal

GC5029900792000X

Fig. 32 Popping noise

Checks	Action
Definition: A Final Drive Noise or Hum is most noticeable under light throttle acceleration or turns	
• Final Drive Gear Set • Final Drive Internal Gear	• Worn planet pinions • Worn washers • Worn or damaged teeth
• Differential Carrier • Differential Side Gears	• Worn or pitted gears • A damaged thrust washer

GC5029900795000X

Fig. 35 Final drive hum

Checks	Action
Definition: Noise in 1st, 2nd, 3rd, or 4th	
• Final Drive Sun Gear • Final Drive Pinions	Worn or damaged gears

GC5029900796000X

Fig. 36 Noise in forward ranges

Checks	Action
Definition: Noise only in certain gear ranges	
Determine the power flow and the applicable components that may be causing this noise.	

GC5029900797000X

Fig. 37 Noise in random ranges

Checks	Action
TCC Solenoid	• Internal failure • A plugged fluid exhaust • An external ground
Torque Converter	Internal failure
TCC Regulated Apply Valve and TCC Control Valve	Stuck in the TCC apply position

GC5029900798000X

Fig. 38 No torque converter clutch release

Checks	Action
Engine Coolant Temp Sensor	Malfunction

GC5029900799000X

Fig. 39 Torque converter clutch apply w/cold engine

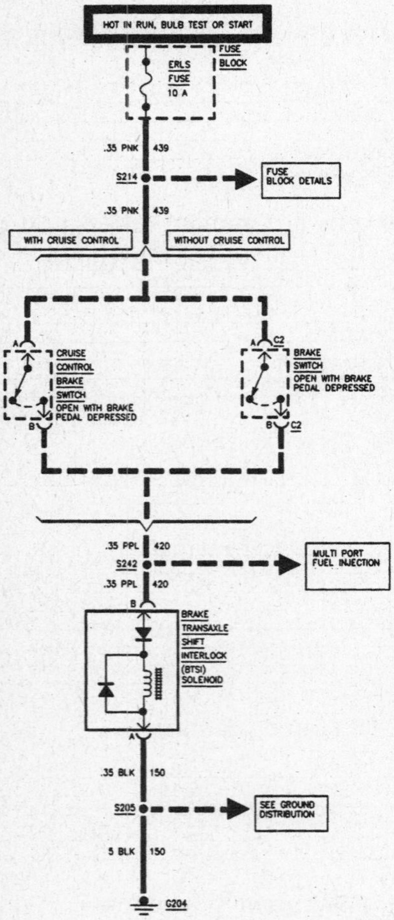

TH5019600254000X

Fig. 40 BTSI wiring diagram. Cavalier & Sunfire

gently and evenly on seal to prevent damage to case bore or seal.

c. Tighten pan bolts to specifications.

ADJUSTMENTS

PARK LOCK CABLE

1. Place floor shift lever in Park position.
2. Place ignition switch in lock position.
3. Unseat body housing lock from body housing.
4. Ensure there is no gap between metal terminal stop and protruding end of white plastic collar. If a gap exists, adjust position of park/lock cable.
5. Ensure white plastic collar is flush or recessed about .04 inch with ignition park/lock housing. If collar is not in proper location, adjust position of park/lock cable.
6. Adjust outer cable conduit in order to obtain proper location of white plastic housing in ignition switch.
7. Ensure body housing is still attached to shift control mounting bracket.
8. Seat body housing lock in body housing while holding outer cable conduit in position.
9. Inspect park/lock control cable as described under " In-Vehicle Repairs."

IN-VEHICLE REPAIRS

OIL PAN, REPLACE

1. Raise and support vehicle.
2. Loosen oil pan retaining bolts.
3. Place a suitable container under oil pan, then drain oil.
4. Remove oil pan retaining bolts, then the oil pan and gasket.
5. Reverse procedure to install. Tighten oil pan retaining bolts to specification.

VEHICLE SPEED SENSOR, REPLACE

1. Raise and support vehicle.
2. Disconnect electrical connector.
3. Remove speed sensor retaining bolt, **Fig. 46.**
4. Remove speed sensor from case extension.
5. Remove O-ring from speed sensor.
6. Reverse procedure to install. Replace O-ring.

OIL FEED PIPES & GASKETS, REPLACE

1. Raise and support vehicle.
2. Remove transaxle oil pan as described in this section, then the filter assembly.
3. Remove four bolts retaining oil feed pipe assembly to transaxle, **Fig. 47.**
4. Remove oil feed pipe assembly, then the eight seals.
5. Reverse procedure to install, noting the following:
   a. Inspect pipes for plugged passages, bends or cracks.
   b. Inspect seal rings and replace if cut, swelled or damaged.

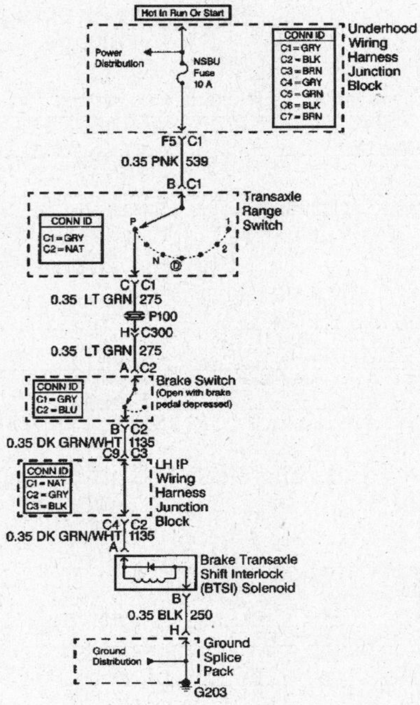

TH5029800941000X

Fig. 41 BTSI wiring diagram. Cutlass & Malibu

   c. Replace oil pan gasket if damaged.
   d. Tighten bolts to specifications.

PARK LOCK CONTROL CABLE, REPLACE

Removal

1. Remove console.
2. Remove left sound insulator.
3. Remove knee bolster.
4. Loosen lower steering column bracket bolts, then lower steering column.
5. Place transaxle shift lever in Park position.
6. Place ignition in Run position. **Do not proceed to next step with key in any other position.**
7. Insert a screwdriver blade into slot provided in ignition switch inhibitor.
8. Depress cable latch, then pull control cable from inhibitor.
9. Push cable connector lock button at shifter base to up position.
10. Snap cable from park/lock lever pin.
11. Depress two cable latches, then remove control cable latches from automatic transaxle control.
12. Remove control cable clips.

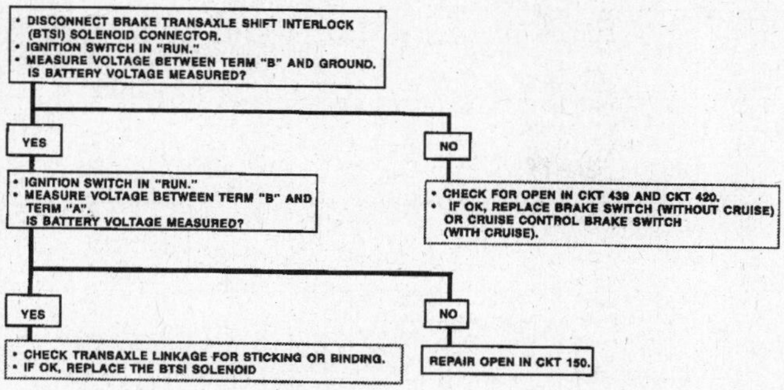

TH5019600255000X

Fig. 42 BTSI diagnosis chart (gear selector shifts out of Park w/ignition switch in Run position & brake pedal not depressed). Cavalier & Sunfire

Step	Action	Value(s)	Yes	No
1	1. Disconnect the Brake Switch connector C2. 2. Turn the Ignition Switch to the RUN position. Can the Transaxle be shifted out of PARK?	—	Go to Step 2	Go to Step 3
2	Check the adjustment of the Brake Switch, if OK replace the Brake Switch. Is repair complete?	—	System OK	—
3	Disconnect the LH IP Wiring Harness Junction Block connector C3. Can the Transaxle be shifted out of PARK?	—	Go to Step 4	Go to Step 5

TH5029800942010X

Fig. 43 BTSI diagnosis chart (gear selector does not shift out of Park w/ignition switch in Run position & brake pedal depressed, Part 1 of 2). Cutlass & Malibu

Step	Action	Value(s)	Yes	No
4	Repair the short to B+ in circuit 1135 between the LH IP Wiring Harness Junction Block and the Brake Switch. Is repair complete?	—	System OK	—
5	Disconnect the LH IP Wiring Harness Junction Block connector C2. Can the Transaxle be shifted out of PARK?	—	Go to Step 6	Go to Step 7
6	Replace the LH IP Wiring Harness Junction Block. Is repair complete?	—	System OK	—
7	Disconnect the Brake Transaxle Shift Interlock (BTSI) Solenoid connector. Can the Transaxle be shifted out of PARK?	—	Go to Step 8	Go to Step 9
8	Repair the short to B+ in circuit 1135 between the LH IP Wiring Harness Junction Block and the Brake Transaxle Shift Interlock (BTSI) Solenoid. Is repair complete?	—	System OK	—
9	Replace the Brake Transaxle Shift Interlock (BTSI) Solenoid. Is repair complete?	—	System OK	—

TH5029800942020X

Fig. 43 BTSI diagnosis chart (gear selector does not shift out of Park w/ignition switch in Run position & brake pedal depressed, Part 2 of 2). Cutlass & Malibu

Step	Action	Value(s)	Yes	No
1	1. Disconnect the Transaxle Range Switch connector C1. 2. Turn the Ignition Switch to the RUN position. 3. Connect a test lamp between terminal B of the Transaxle Range Switch connector C1 and ground. Does the test lamp light?	—	Go to Step 2	Go to Step 3
2	Connect a fused jumper between terminal B and terminal C of the Transaxle Range Switch connector C1. Can the Transaxle be shifted out of PARK?	—	Go to Step 4	Go to Step 5
3	Backprobe the Underhood Wiring Harness Junction Block connector C1 with a test lamp between terminal F5 and ground. Does the test lamp light?	—	Go to Step 6	Go to Step 7
4	1. Reconnect the Transaxle Range Switch connector C1. 2. Backprobe the Brake Switch connector C2 with a test lamp between terminal A and ground. Does the test lamp light?	—	Go to Step 8	Go to Step 9

TH5029800943010X

Fig. 44 BTSI diagnosis chart (gear selector shifts out of Park w/ignition switch in Run position & brake pedal not depressed, Part 1 of 3). Cutlass & Malibu

Installation

When installing a new park/lock cable, keep the shipping cover gauge attached until instructed to detach it. The shipping cover gauge will aid in the proper positioning of cable.

1. Ensure cable lock button is in Up position, then place shift lever in Park position.
2. Snap control cable connector into automatic transaxle control.
3. Place ignition in Run position. **Do not insert cable with key in any other position.**
4. Snap control cable into inhibitor housing until snap lock is seated.
5. Remove shipping cover gauge.
6. Place ignition in Lock position.
7. Snap control cable end onto shift park/lock lever pin.
8. Push cable connector hose forward in order to remove any slack.
9. With no load applied to connector nose, snap cable connector lock button down. Ensure proper operation of park/lock control cable before installing steering column to instrument panel.
10. Raise and connect steering column bracket bolts.
11. Tighten column bracket bolts.
12. Install knee bolster, then the left sound insulator.
13. Install console.

Function Inspection

1. Ensure there is no gap between metal terminal stop and protruding end of white plastic collar. If a gap exists, adjust position of park/lock cable.
2. Ensure white plastic collar is flush or .04 inch recessed within park/lock housing. If collar position is not as specified, adjust position of park/lock cable.
3. Ensure terminal stop on column end of park/lock cable is touching white collar that protrudes from ignition switch.
4. Place ignition in Lock position.
5. Place floor shift lever into Park position.
6. Ensure terminal stop is in correct position as described in step 3.
7. Check white plastic collar travel as follows:
   a. Ensure ignition remains in Lock position.
   b. Ensure floor shift lever remains in Park position.
   c. Gently depress park/lock button on floor shift lever until resistance is felt.
   d. Ensure white plastic collar travels no more than .06 inch. **Floor shift lever must not come out of Park.**
8. Place ignition switch in On position, then check for proper movement of floor shift lever through all gear ranges.
9. While moving shift lever through drive gears, ensure ignition cannot be turned to lock position.
10. Ensure key can be removed with ignition in Lock position and floor shift lever in Park position.
11. If one or more inspections have failed, adjust park/lock cable as described under "Adjustments" and recheck.

SERVO ASSEMBLY, REPLACE

1. Raise and support vehicle.
2. Remove oil pan as described in this section.
3. Remove servo cover bolts and cover, **Figs. 48 and 49.**
4. Remove snap ring, piston assembly, sealing ring and servo spring.
5. Reverse procedure to install.

CASE SIDE COVER, REPLACE

1. Remove park/neutral position switch.
2. Raise and support vehicle.
3. Remove left front wheel.
4. Remove inner splash shield.

Step	Action	Value(s)	Yes	No
5	Check the adjustment of the Transaxle Range Switch. If OK, replace the Transaxle Range Switch. Is repair complete?	—	System OK	—
6	Repair the open in circuit 539 between the Underhood Wiring Harness Junction Block and the Transaxle Range Switch. Is repair complete?	—	System OK	—
7	Replace the Underhood Wiring Harness Junction Block. Is repair complete?	—	System OK	—
8	Backprobe the Brake Switch connector C2 with a test lamp between terminal B and ground. Does the test lamp light?	—	Go to Step 10	Go to Step 11
9	Repair the open in circuit 275 between the Transaxle Range Switch and the Brake Switch. Is repair complete?	—	System OK	—
10	Backprobe the LH IP Wiring Harness Junction Block connector C3 with a test lamp between terminal C9 and ground. Does the test lamp light?	—	Go to Step 12	Go to Step 13
11	Check the adjustment of the Brake Switch, if OK replace the Brake Switch. Is repair complete?	—	System OK	—
12	Backprobe the LH IP Wiring Harness Junction Block connector C2 with a test lamp between terminal C4 and ground. Does the test lamp light?	—	Go to Step 14	Go to Step 15
13	Repair the open in circuit 1135 between the Brake Switch and the LH IP Wiring Harness Junction Block. Is repair complete?	—	System OK	—
14	1. Disconnect the Brake Transaxle Shift Interlock (BTSI) Solenoid connector. 2. Connect a test lamp between terminal A of the Brake Transaxle Shift Interlock (BTSI) Solenoid connector and ground. Does the test lamp light?	—	Go to Step 16	Go to Step 17
15	Replace the LH IP Wiring Harness Junction Block. Is repair complete?	—	System OK	—

TH5029800943020X

Fig. 44 BTSI diagnosis chart (gear selector shifts out of Park w/ignition switch in Run position & brake pedal not depressed, Part 2 of 3). Cutlass & Malibu

5. Remove tie rod end from knuckle.
6. Remove stabilizer shaft link from lower control arm.
7. Remove ball joint from steering knuckle.
8. Remove drive axle from transaxle.
9. Remove pinch bolt from intermediate shaft. **Failure to disconnect intermediate shaft from rack and pinion steering gear stub shaft can result in damage to steering gear or intermediate shaft. This could cause loss of steering control.**
10. Remove intermediate shaft from steering gear.
11. Position transaxle jack under transaxle oil pan, then raise jack until it supports transaxle.
12. Remove three frame to body retaining bolts on left side.
13. Lower transaxle to gain access to case side cover.
14. Remove oil cooler pipes at case.
15. Remove case side cover retaining bolts, then the side cover.
16. Reverse procedure to install. Tighten bolts to specification.

Step	Action	Value(s)	Yes	No
16	Connect a test lamp between terminal A and terminal B of the Brake Transaxle Shift Interlock (BTSI) Solenoid connector. Does the test lamp light?	—	Go to Step 18	Go to Step 19
17	Repair the open in circuit 1135 between the LH IP Wiring Harness Junction Block and the Brake Transaxle Shift Interlock (BTSI) Solenoid. Is repair complete?	—	System OK	—
18	Replace the Brake Transaxle Shift Interlock (BTSI) Solenoid. Is repair complete?	—	System OK	—
19	Repair the open in circuit 250 between the Brake Transaxle Shift Interlock (BTSI) Solenoid and Ground Splice Pack G203. Is repair complete?	—	System OK	—

TH5029800943030X

Fig. 44 BTSI diagnosis chart (gear selector shifts out of Park w/ignition switch in Run position & brake pedal not depressed, Part 3 of 3). Cutlass & Malibu

Line pressures are calibrated for two sets of gear ranges – Drive-Park-Neutral and Reverse. This allows the transaxle line pressure to be appropriate for different pressure needs in different gear ranges:

Gear Range	Nominal Line Pressure Range
Drive, Park or Neutral	50 - 160 PSI 345 – 1103 KPA
Reverse	58 - 186 PSI 400 – 1282 KPA

Before performing a line pressure check, verify that the pressure control solenoid is receiving the correct electrical signal from the PCM:

1. Install a scan tool.
2. Start the engine and set parking brake.
3. Check for a stored pressure control solenoid diagnostic trouble code, and other diagnostic trouble codes.
4. Repair vehicle if necessary.

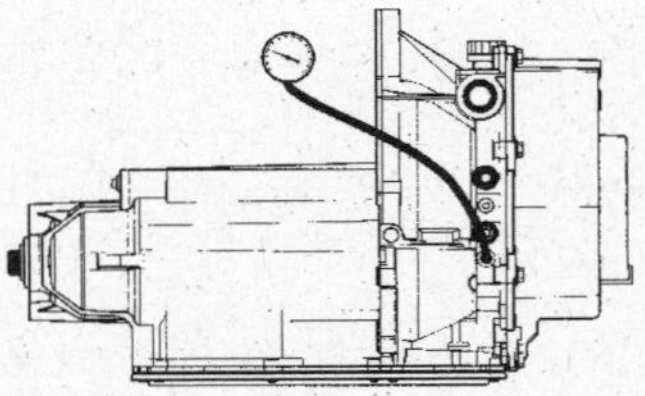

Inspect
- Fluid level
- Manual linkage

Install or Connect
- TECH 1 Scan tool
- Oil pressure gage at line pressure tap

5. Put gear selector in Park and set the parking brake.
6. Start engine and allow it to warm up at idle.
7. Access the "PCS Control" test on the TECH 1 scan tool.
8. Increase DESIRED PCS in 0.1 Amp increments and read the corresponding line pressure on the pressure gage. (Allow pressure to stabilize for 5 seconds after each current change.)
9. Compare data to the Drive-Park-Neutral line pressure chart below.

***NOTICE** Total test running time should not exceed 2 minutes, or transaxle damage could occur.

CAUTION Brakes must be applied at all times to prevent unexpected vehicle motion.

If pressure readings differ greatly from the line pressure chart, refer to the Diagnosis Charts contained in this section.

The TECH 1 scan tool is only able to control the pressure control solenoid in Park and Neutral with the vehicle stopped. This protects the clutches from extremely high or low pressures in Drive or Reverse ranges.

Pressure Control Solenoid Current (Amp)	Approximate Line Pressure (PSI)
0.00	152 - 160
0.10	149 - 151
0.30	141 - 143
0.50	124 - 127
0.60	111 - 115
0.70	97 - 101
0.80	81 - 84
0.90	64 - 67
0.95	56 - 58
1.00	50 - 51
1.05	50
1.10	50

NOTE: Pressures are at 70°C and vary with temperature. Pressure drops as temperature increases.

TH5019600241000X

Fig. 45 Line pressure inspection

STUB AXLE SHAFT, RIGHTHAND OUTPUT AXLE SHAFT OIL SEALS & SLEEVES, REPLACE

1. Raise and support vehicle.
2. Remove tire and wheel assembly.
3. Remove inner splash shield and separate tie rod from steering knuckle.
4. Remove ball joint from steering knuckle.
5. Remove drive axle assembly.
6. Remove snap ring from stub axle shaft. Discard snap ring.
7. Pull lightly on shaft and rotate it until output shaft snap ring at differential seats in taper on differential side gear.
8. Remove stub shaft from transaxle using slide hammer tool No. J-6125

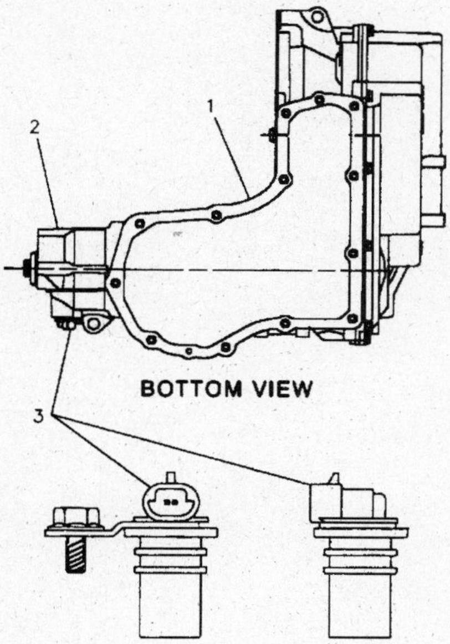

1 TRANSAXLE BOTTOM PAN
2 TRANSAXLE ASSEMBLY
3 VEHICLE SPEED SENSOR

TH5029600814000X

Fig. 46 Vehicle speed sensor

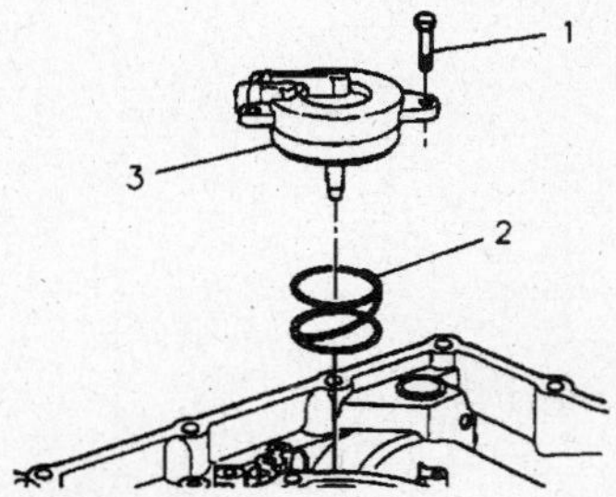

1 BOLT, SERVO COVER
2 SPRING, SERVO RETURN (INTERMEDIATE/4TH)
3 COVER, SERVO (INTERMEDIATE/4TH)

TH5029600816000X

Fig. 49 Intermediate/4th servo

and shaft removal tool No. J-38868, or equivalents, **Fig. 50.**

9. Remove sleeve from stub shaft using puller tool No. J-41227, or equivalent, **Fig. 51.**
10. Remove righthand axle seal from transaxle using seal removal tool No. J-23129 and slide hammer tool No. J-6125, or equivalents.
11. Remove transaxle side cover assembly.
12. Remove sleeve from output shaft using puller tool No. J-41227, or equivalent, **Fig. 51.**
13. Reverse procedure to install, noting the following:
    a. Lubricate seal lip with a light wipe of transaxle fluid and install new seal using seal tool No. J-41102, or equivalent.
    b. Install shaft sleeves with sleeve installer tool No. 41228, or equivalent.
    c. Install two new snap rings on stub shaft.
    d. Carefully guide axle shaft past lip seal. **To prevent damage to seal, do not allow shaft splines to contact any portion of seal lip surface.**

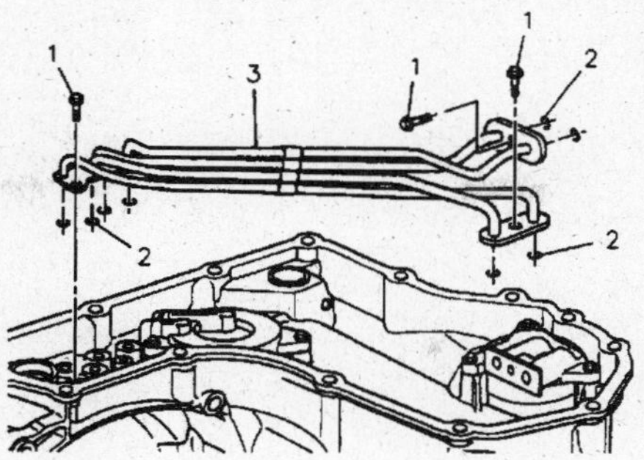

1 BOLT, TUBE ASSEMBLY
2 SEAL, OIL FEED TUBE ASSEMBLY
3 TUBE ASSEMBLY, OIL FEED

TH5029600823000X

Fig. 47 Oil feed pipe assembly

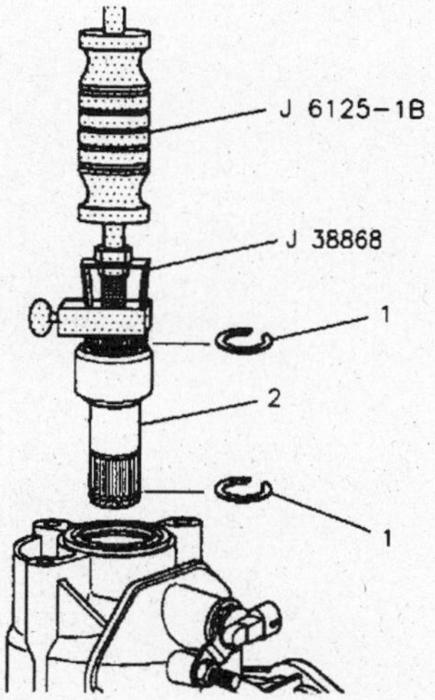

1 RING, OUTPUT/STUB SHAFT SNAP
2 SHAFT, OUTPUT STUB

TH5029600825000X

Fig. 50 Stub shaft removal

TRANSAXLE

REPLACE

1997 CUTLASS & MALIBU

1. Remove air cleaner assembly.
2. Remove shift linkage from transaxle.
3. Remove electrical wiring connections from transaxle.
4. Install engine support fixture tool No. J-28467–360, or equivalent.
5. Remove upper transaxle to engine bolts.
6. Raise and support vehicle.

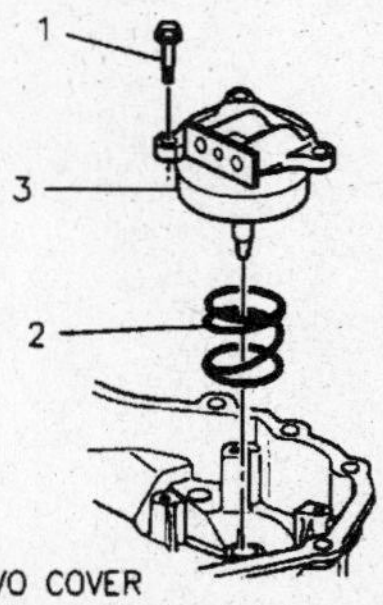

1 BOLT, SERVO COVER
2 SPRING, SERVO RETURN (LO/REVERSE)
3 COVER, SERVO (LO/REVERSE)

TH5029600815000X

Fig. 48 Low/Reverse servo

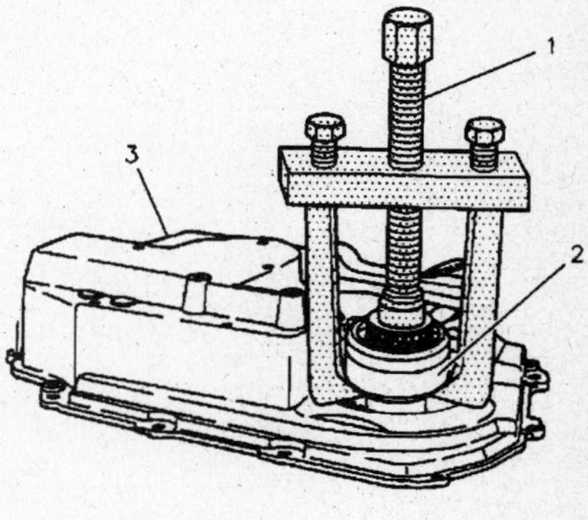

1 J 41227
2 SLEEVE, OUTPUT/STUB SHAFT
3 TRANSAXLE

TH5029600826000X

Fig. 51 Sleeve removal

7. Remove both front wheels.
8. Remove right and lefthand splash shields.
9. Remove both front wheel speed sensors and harness from lefthand side suspension support.
10. Remove both outer tie rods from steering knuckle assembly using tie rod removal tool No. J-24319-B, or equivalent.
11. Remove both ball joints from steering knuckle assembly using knuckle removal tool No. J-38892, or equivalent.
12. Remove front suspension support brace.
13. Support suspension support assembly retaining bolts and assembly.
14. Lower suspension support assembly enough to disconnect steering coupling and both power steering fluid lines.
15. Remove both drive axles from transaxle support.
16. Remove engine to transaxle brace.
17. Remove shift cable bracket.
18. Remove starter.
19. Remove transaxle converter cover.
20. Mark flywheel to torque converter relationship for reassembly.
21. Remove torque converter to flywheel bolts.
22. Remove transaxle cooler pipes.

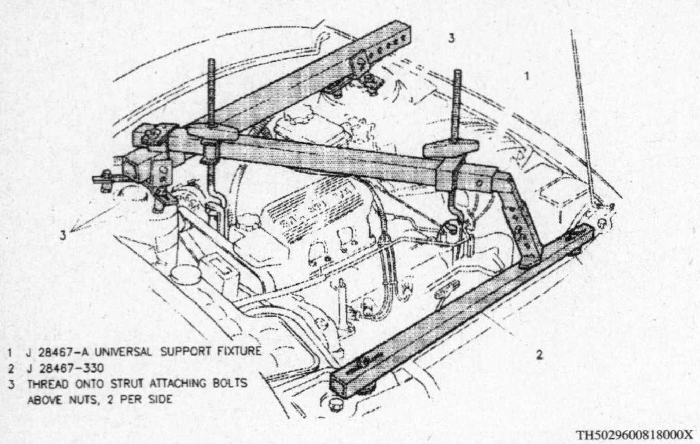

Fig. 52 Engine support fixture installation

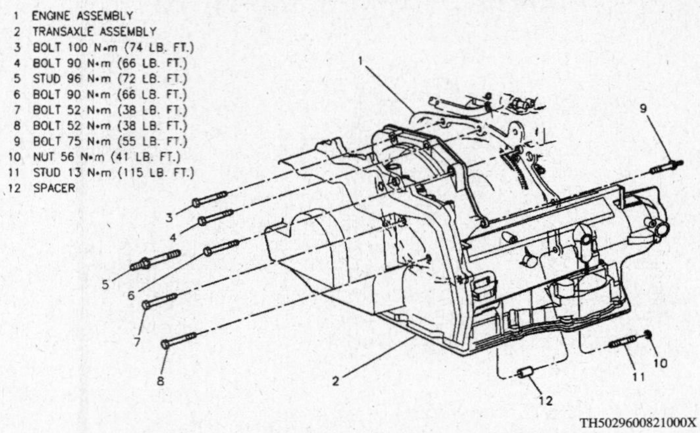

Fig. 53 Transaxle to engine bolts

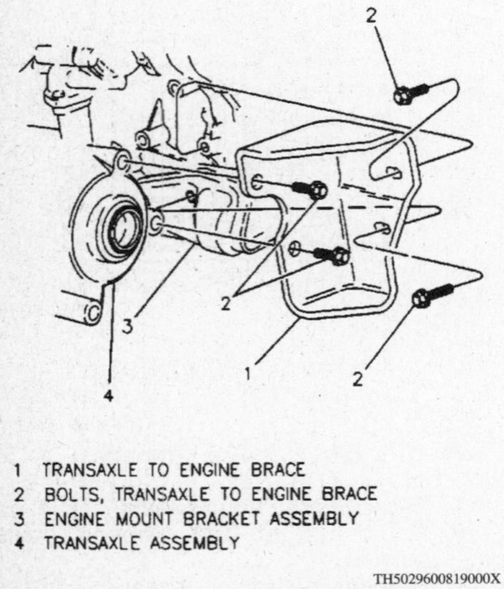

Fig. 54 Engine to transaxle brace

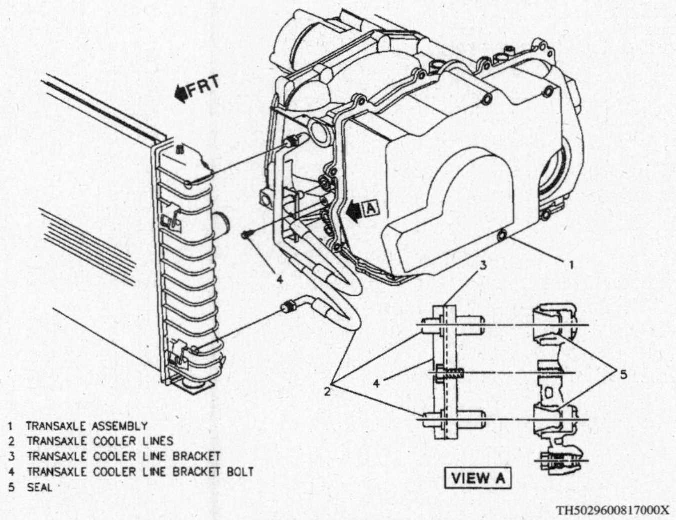

Fig. 55 Transaxle oil cooler lines

23. Remove brake hose bracket from body.
24. Remove transaxle mount pipe expansion bolt.
25. Remove transaxle mount to body bolts and lower vehicle.
26. Lower transaxle with engine support fixture enough to remove transaxle.
27. Raise and support vehicle.
28. Support transaxle and remove transaxle to engine bolts.
29. Remove transaxle assembly.
30. Reverse procedure to install.

ALERO, GRAND AM & 1998-2000 CUTLASS & MALIBU

1. Support engine using engine support fixture tool No. J28467-360, or equivalent.
2. Support transaxle with a suitable safety stand.
3. Raise vehicle. Ensure pressure is off transaxle mounts.
4. Remove splash shield.
5. Remove air cleaner and duct assembly from throttle body.
6. Remove wire harness from upper transaxle mount bracket.
7. Remove upper transaxle mount.
8. Remove shifter cable.
9. Remove ground cables from transaxle mounting studs.
10. Disconnect park/neutral switch connector.
11. Remove transaxle vent tube, then the rear transaxle mount.
12. Raise and support vehicle.
13. Drain transaxle fluid.
14. Remove both front wheels.
15. Remove left front inner splash shield.
16. Remove front ABS wheel speed sensor connectors.
17. Remove left side harness from its routing.
18. Remove flywheel housing cover bolts, then the housing cover.
19. Remove vehicle speed sensor.
20. Remove torque converter bolts.
21. Remove left and right ball joint nuts.
22. Remove left suspension support retaining bolts.
23. Remove drive axles.
24. Remove front lower transaxle mount bolts, then the front lower transaxle mount.
25. Attach transaxle case to support stand.
26. Remove transaxle to engine mount bolts.
27. Remove transaxle from vehicle.
28. Reverse procedure to install. Tighten bolts to specification.

CAVALIER & SUNFIRE

1997

1. Remove intake air duct.
2. Disconnect TV cable.
3. Disconnect shift cable and remove bracket.
4. Disconnect vacuum lines and electrical connectors.
5. Remove power steering pump and set aside.
6. Remove filler tube.
7. Install engine support fixture No. J-28467-A, or equivalent, **Fig. 52.**
8. Remove top engine to transaxle bolts, **Fig. 53.**
9. Raise and support vehicle.
10. Remove both front tire and wheel assemblies.

11. Remove lefthand splash shield.
12. Remove both front ABS wheel speed sensors and harness from lefthand suspension support.
13. Remove both lower ball joints and stabilizer shaft links.
14. Remove front air deflector and lefthand suspension support.
15. Remove both drive axles.
16. Remove engine to transaxle brace, **Fig. 54.**
17. Remove transaxle converter cover.
18. Remove starter and flywheel to torque converter bolts.
19. Disconnect transaxle cooler lines, **Fig. 55.**
20. Disconnect ground wires.
21. Remove cooler pipe brace and exhaust brace.
22. Remove bolts from engine and transaxle mount, **Fig. 56.**
23. Support engine with a suitable jack and remove transaxle mount to body bolts.
24. Remove core hose pipe brace.
25. Remove remaining engine to transaxle bolts.
26. Remove transaxle assembly.
27. Reverse procedure to install.

1998-2000

1. Remove air cleaner assembly.
2. Remove shift linkage from transaxle.
3. Disconnect wiring connections from transaxle.
4. Support engine using engine support fixture tool No. J28467-360, or equivalent.
5. Remove upper transaxle to engine retaining bolts.
6. Raise and support vehicle.

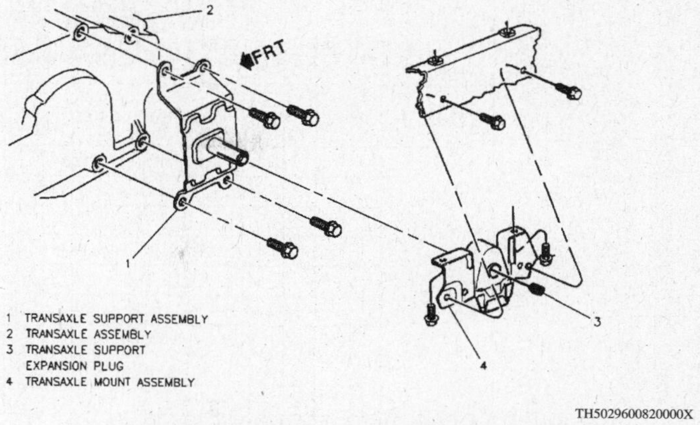

Fig. 56 Transaxle mount assembly

7. Remove both front wheel assemblies.
8. Remove left and right splash shields.
9. Remove front ABS wheel speed sensors, then disconnect harness from left side suspension support.
10. Remove outer tie rods from steering knuckle assembly.
11. Remove ball joints from knuckle assembly.
12. Remove front suspension support brace retaining bolts, then the support brace.
13. Remove engine mount strut from strut mount bracket.
14. Remove suspension support assembly retaining bolts and lower suspension support assembly.
15. Disconnect steering coupling and power steering fluid lines from suspension support assembly, then remove suspension support assembly.
16. Remove drive axles from transaxle.
17. Remove engine to transaxle brace, then the shift cable bracket.
18. Remove starter, then the transaxle converter cover.
19. Mark flywheel to torque converter for reassembly, then remove torque converter to flywheel bolts.
20. Remove transaxle cooler pipes, then the brake hose bracket to body.
21. Remove transaxle mount to body bolts.
22. Lower vehicle, then the transaxle with engine support fixture enough to remove transaxle.
23. Raise vehicle and support transaxle.
24. Remove transaxle to engine retaining bolts, then the transaxle.
25. Reverse procedure to install.

TIGHTENING SPECIFICATIONS

Year	Component	Torque/ Ft. Lbs.
1997–2000	Case Cover	18
	Case Side Cover	21
	Channel Plate To Case & Channel Plate To Driven Sprocket Support Bolts	10
	Control Valve Assembly Bolts	108②
	Converter Shield	18
	Cooler Pipes At Case	72②
	Cooler Pipes At Radiator	15–30
	Cowl Bolts	17②
	Flexplate To Torque Converter	46
	Flywheel Housing	90②
	Flywheel To Torque Converter	46
	Frame To Body	83
	Front Suspension Support Brace	49
	Neutral Position Safety Switch To Case	18
	Oil Check Plug	10
	Oil Feed Pipe Bolts	108②
	Oil Pan Retaining Bolts	10
	Oil Pump Bolts	108②
	Pressure Switch Assembly Bolts	108②
	Second Clutch Switch	96②

Continued

TIGHTENING SPECIFICATIONS—Continued

Year	Component	Torque/ Ft. Lbs.
1997-2000	Servo Cover Bolts	108②
	Shift Cable Bracket Bolt	18
	Shift Cable Bracket Nut	37
	Shift Lever To Transaxle Nut	15
	Spacer Plate Support Bolts	10
	Speed Sensor Housing To Case	96②
	TCC Solenoid Bolt To Auxiliary Valve Body	96②
	Third Clutch Pressure Switch	96②
	Transaxle Case Side Cover Bolts	21①
	Transaxle Oil Pan To Case	96②
	Transaxle To Engine Mount Bolts	③
	TV Cable To Case	80
	Vehicle Speed Sensor	96②
	Wire Harness Retainer Bolt	108②

① — In star pattern.
② — Inch lbs.
③ — On Alero, Grand Am & 1998-99 Cutlass & Malibu models, 55 ft. lbs.; on Cavalier, Sunfire & 1997 Cutlass & Malibu, 66 ft. lbs.

Turbo Hydra-Matic 4T60-E & 4T65-E Automatic Transaxles

NOTE: On Air Bag Equipped Models, Refer To " Air Bag System Precautions" Located In The Front Of This Manual For System Disarming & Arming Procedures.

NOTE: Refer To "Computer Relearn Procedures " Located In The Front Of This Manual For Computer Relearn Procedures.

NOTE: Prior To Performing Any Service Operations Listed In This Section, Consult The "Technical Service Bulletins " Section For Related Information.

INDEX

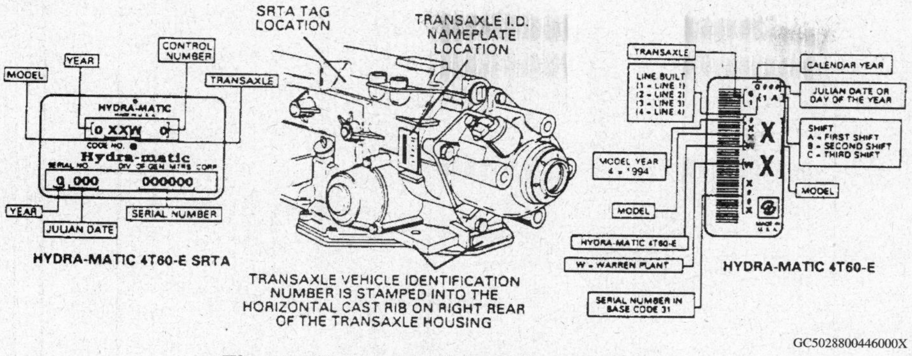

Fig. 1 Transaxle identification plate

PRECAUTIONS

AIR BAG SYSTEMS

Refer to "Air Bag System Precautions" in the front of this manual for system disarming and arming procedures.

BATTERY GROUND CABLE

Prior to service, disconnect battery ground cable and isolate as required.

IDENTIFICATION

This transaxle may be identified by codes stamped into the horizontal cast rib on the righthand rear side of the transaxle housing, **Fig. 1**.

DESCRIPTION

The 4T60-E and 4T65-E transaxles **Fig. 2** are fully automatic units which provide four forward speeds including an overdrive top gear. The transmission units include a three element hydraulic torque converter and lock-up clutching element, four multiple disc clutch, two bands and a compound reaction planetary gear set. Power transmitted to the drive wheels from the planetary gear through a final drive gear set and differential assembly.

The converter is designed to provide torque multiplication during acceleration and at slow vehicle speed, and lock-up during normal operation for increase operating economy. Operation of the converter lock-up is controlled automatically by the engine fuel system electronic control module. In addition, the converter drives the vane type oil pump by means of a shaft splined to the converter cover.

The torque converter hydraulically couples the engine to the planetary gears through a turbine and shaft assembly which drives the transmission output shaft by means of a drive link chain and sprockets.

TROUBLESHOOTING

4T60-E TRANSAXLE

Refer to **Figs. 3 through 34** for 4T60-E troubleshooting procedures.

4T65-E TRANSAXLE

Refer to **Figs. 35 through 63** for 4T65-E troubleshooting procedures.

BRAKE TRANSAXLE SHIFT INTERLOCK (BTSI)

1. Verify brake light operation.
2. If brake lights do not operate, refer to **Fig. 64** for wiring diagram and **Fig. 65** for diagnostic procedure.
3. Check for proper installation of after-market equipment or for broken or partially broken wires inside of insulation. This could cause system failures, but not be indicated in a continuity or voltage check.

MAINTENANCE

Refer to "Lubricant Data Chart" in the appropriate chassis chapter of this manual for transmission fluid specifications.

FLUID CHECK

To check fluid, drive vehicle for at least 15 minutes to bring fluid to operating temperature (200°F). With vehicle on a level surface and engine idling in Park and parking brake applied, move the shift lever through each gear range ending in park, the level on the dipstick should be at the FULL mark. To bring the fluid level from the ADD mark to the FULL mark requires one pint of fluid. If vehicle cannot be driven sufficiently to bring fluid to operating temperature, the level on the dipstick should be between the two dimples on the dipstick with fluid temperature at 70°F. Note that the two dimples are located above the FULL mark.

An early change to a darker color from the usual red color and/or a strong odor that is usually associated with overheated fluid is normal and should not be considered as a positive sign of required maintenance or unit failure.

When adding fluid, do not overfill, as foaming and loss of fluid through the vent may occur as the fluid heats up. Also, if fluid level is too low, complete loss of drive may occur especially when cold, which can cause transmission failure.

Every 100,000 miles, the oil should be drained, the oil pan removed, the screen cleaned and fresh fluid added. For vehicles subjected to more severe use such as heavy city traffic especially in hot weather, prolonged periods of idling or towing, this maintenance should be performed every 15,000 miles.

FLUID CHANGE

This procedure has been modified by a Technical Service Bulletin.

1. Raise and support vehicle.
2. Position drain pan under oil pan.
3. Remove front and side oil pan retaining bolts and loosen rear pan retaining bolts.
4. Carefully pry oil pan loose from transaxle case and allow fluid to drain.
5. Remove remaining retaining bolts, oil pan and gasket. Thoroughly clean pan before reinstalling.
6. Remove and discard screen and O-ring seal.
7. Install replacement screen and O-ring seal, locating screen against dipstick stop.
8. Install gasket on oil pan and apply Loctite 242, or equivalent, to oil pan bolts to prevent leakage.
9. Tighten oil pan bolts to specification.
10. Lower vehicle and add fluid.
11. With selector in Park, parking brake applied and engine at idle speed and operating temperature, check fluid level and add fluid as necessary. **Do not race engine or move shift lever through ranges.**

ADJUSTMENTS

SHIFT CONTROL CABLE

Acheiva, Cavalier, Skylark & 1997-98 Grand Am

1. Apply parking brake and block wheels.
2. Position range selector into Neutral position.
3. Lift up range selector cable locking button.
4. Remove range selector cable end from transaxle range selector level, **Fig. 66.**
5. Position transaxle range selector lever into L position. Obtain L position by rotating transaxle range selector lever toward front of vehicle until it stops.
6. Snap range selector cable end onto transaxle range selector lever.
7. Press range selector cable locking button down into locked position.
8. Position range selector lever into Park position.
9. Remove wheel blocks and release parking brake.

Bonneville, LeSabre, LSS, Park Avenue, Regency, Riviera & Eighty-Eight

NOTE: Adjust shift cable only when transaxle and gear selector are in Neutral position. Failure to do so may result in shift cable misalignment.

1. Apply parking brake and remove shift cable terminal from transaxle manual shaft lever pin.
2. Lift lock button. Ensure adjuster is free to move.

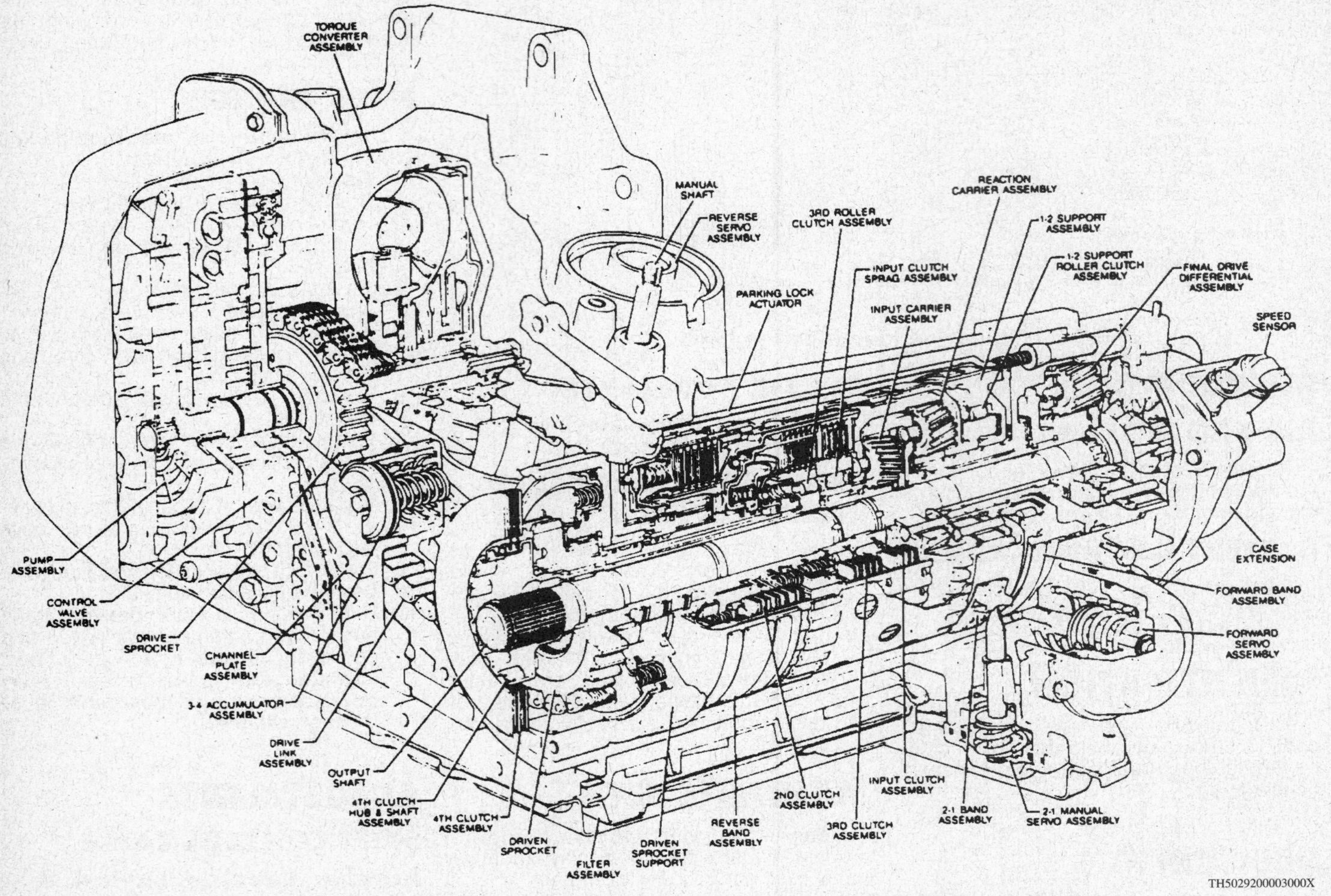

Fig. 2 Turbo Hydra-Matic 4T60–E & 4T65-E automatic transaxles

3. Place manual shaft lever in Neutral position by rotating fully counter clockwise to Park position and rotating two audible clicks clockwise to desired position.
4. Place gear selector in Neutral position.
5. Grasp shift cable terminal and pull toward pin on manual shaft lever.
6. Shift cable adjuster spring should compress as terminal is moved toward pin.
7. Attach pin to lever by pushing downward until it snaps.
8. Press adjuster lock button down flush with adjuster body.
9. Shift to Park position and release parking brake while applying service brakes.
10. Start engine and ensure all indicated gear positions match vehicle response.

Century, Cutlass Supreme, Grand Prix, Impala, Intrigue, Lumina, Monte Carlo & Regal

NOTE: Adjust shift cable only when transaxle and gear selector are in Neutral position. Failure to do so may result in shift cable misalignment.

1. Apply parking brake and disconnect shift cables at both ends.
2. Do not attempt to separate metal couplings. Both cable sections will be damaged if two metal couplings are disconnected.
3. Push up to adjustment position to release adjuster until cable housings separate.
4. Depress adjuster clip once. This mobilizes adjuster housing toward transaxle end fitting.
5. Position end fittings so they slide together until parts can be felt coming together and locking.
6. Depress adjuster clip completely. This locks cable into adjusted position.
7. Pull conduit in opposite direction to ensure full system adjustment of shift cable.
8. Ensure conduit is fully engaged.
9. Horseshoe clip with tab is not flush when not fully engaged.
10. Install shift cable retainer and wiring harness clip or strap.
11. Start engine and ensure all indicated gear positions match vehicle response.

IN-VEHICLE REPAIRS

VALVE BODY, REPLACE

1. Raise and support vehicle.
2. Drain transaxle fluid into a suitable container and remove case side cover.
3. Remove oil pump.
4. Remove bolts, valve body and gasket while keeping spacer plate with transaxle.
5. Reverse procedure to install. **Do not use impact type tools to install valve body.** Tighten valve body bolts to specifications shown, **Fig. 67.**

ACCUMULATOR, REPLACE

1. Raise and support vehicle.
2. Drain transaxle fluid into a suitable container and remove oil pan.
3. Remove oil filter and seal, then the accumulator cover retaining bolts and cover.
4. Remove accumulator piston, oil seal and spring.
5. Reverse procedure to install.

REVERSE SERVO, REPLACE

1. Remove air cleaner assembly and exhaust crossover pipe.
2. Raise driver's side of car so it is higher than differential side. This will ensure reverse band is in proper location.
3. Depress servo cover, and remove snap ring, servo cover, servo piston, sealing ring, apply pin and servo spring, **Fig. 68.**
4. Reverse procedure to install.

Checks	Cause
Oil Level	Overfilled transmission
Foaming Transmission Oil	• Contaminated with antifreeze • Engine overheating • Lube pipes leaking
Foaming Oil Filter or Seal	• Damaged seal assembly • Cracked or damaged filter assembly
Thermo Element in the Case	• Does not close when hot • Not insulated correctly • Incorrect pin heights
Upper Channel Plate Gasket	Damaged or incorrectly installed gasket
Drive Sprocket Support	Plugged drain back holes

GC5029800832000X

Fig. 3 Oil out of vent or foaming. 4T60-E

Checks	Cause
Oil Level	Low: correct
Oil Pressure	Low: Refer to High or Low Oil Pressure
Manual Linkage	Misadjusted or disconnected
1-2 Shift Solenoid valve or TCC Solenoid valve	Malfunctioned or mislocated
Forward Servo Assembly	Damaged piston or seal
1/2 Roller Clutch	Damaged
Drive Axles	Disengaged
Oil Pump Assembly	Damaged: Refer to High or Low Oil Pressure
#3 Checkball	Missing
Torque Converter	Stator roller clutch (vehicle moves, but vehicle is very sluggish)
Drive Link Assembly	• Damaged or broken drive link chain • Damaged sprockets
Input Clutch Assembly	• Burned or missing clutch plates • Damaged piston or seals • Leaking housing checkball assembly • Damaged input shaft seals • Blocked feed passages on the input shaft
Input Sprag, Input Sun Gear Assembly	• Improper assembly • Damaged sprag: roll over
Input Carrier, Reaction Carrier Assembly	• Damaged pinions • Damaged internal gear • Damaged sun gear
Output Shaft	• Damaged shaft • Misassembled with axles
Forward Band Assembly	• Burned • Band apply pin is mislocated with the band (Assembly will still move in Manual Lo gear and in Manual Second gear)
Parking Pawl	Broken spring, the pawl remains engaged
Final Drive Assembly, or Final Drive Sun Gear Shaft	Damaged side gear, gears, pinion, or internal gear

GC5029800836000X

Fig. 7 No drive in drive range. 4T60-E

Checks	Cause
Oil Pressure	Refer to Causes of High or Low Oil Pressure
1-2 Accumulator Piston, Cover, and Springs	• Improperly torqued cover bolts • Damaged piston or seal • Damaged spring • Damaged or mispositioned gaskets • Low torque of bolts • Piston and Springs installed upside down
Control Valve Assembly	• Stuck 1-2 Accumulator valve • Mislocated or missing 1-2 Accumulator bushing retainer
#2 Checkball	Mislocated
Driven Sprocket Support	• Rolled or twisted seal for the driven sprocket support ring • Worn sleeve in the second clutch housing
Fluid Level	Low
Filter	Cracked or damaged

GC5029800838000X

Fig. 9 Harsh or soft 1-2 shift feel. 4T60-E

Checks	Cause
Second Clutch	• Worn fiber plates • Leaking check valve ball • Cut seal • Damaged steel plates • Mispositioned snap ring
Driven Sprocket Support	• Damaged seal rings

GC5029800840000X

Fig. 11 Shudder 1-2 shift. 4T60-E

Checks	Cause
2-3 Shift Solenoid ON Failure	• Foreign material in the solenoid • The PCM signal is grounded • Pinched solenoid return wire to ground

GC5029800842000X

Fig. 13 First & second gear only, 2-3 solenoid stuck on. 4T60-E

Checks	Cause
Oil Level	High or low; correct as required
Vacuum Line	Leaking, pinched, disconnected, or cut
Modulator	Leaks or damaged diaphragm (A bent modulator will not function correctly)
Modulator Valve	Nicked, scored, or cut valve
Oil Pump Assembly	• Slide stuck, seals damaged, vanes damaged • Pump drive shaft damaged
Pressure Regulator Valve or Springs	Nicked or scored valve; damaged springs
Pressure Relief Valve	Damaged spring; missing ball

GC5029800833000X

Fig. 4 High or low oil pressure. 4T60-E

Checks	Cause
Fluid Level	Low
Cooler Checkball	Not seating, allowing converter to drain back
Reverse Servo Assembly	A cut or damaged seal
Input Shaft and Housing Assembly	Damaged retainer and ball assembly
Forward Servo Assembly	• Damaged or mislocated Seal • Damaged or cut seal
Input Clutch Outer Piston Seal	Damaged or cut/rolled seal

GC5029800834000X

Fig. 5 Delayed engagement. 4T60-E

Checks	Cause
Fluid Level	Low: correct
Vacuum Line	Pinched, slowing vacuum response
Modulator	Damaged
Oil Pressure	See causes of low pressure
Modulator Valve	Stuck or binding
Forward Servo Assembly	Damaged or missing cushion spring or retainer
Forward Servo Piston	Damaged seal
Oil Filter	Plugged
Filter Seal	Cut or damaged

GC5029800835010X

Fig. 6 Slips in drive (Part 1 of 2). 4T60-E

Checks	Cause
Forward Servo Seal	• Leaking, damaged, or missing seal • Low torque of bolts
Torque Converter	Stator roller clutch not holding
Bolt	Low torque allowing leakage for driven sprocket support
Input Clutch Assembly	• Leaks at ball capsule or seals • Damaged seals
Pump Assembly	• Sticking slide • Leak at the slide seals
1-2 Shift Solenoid, TCC solenoid	Malfunctioned or mislocated

GC5029800835020X

Fig. 6 Slips in drive (Part 2 of 2). 4T60-E

Checks	Cause
Control Valve Assembly	• Stuck or binding 1-2 Shift valve • Mispositioned or damaged space plate or gaskets
Driven Sprocket Support	Damaged oil seals
Second Clutch Assembly	• Damaged clutch plates • Damaged piston or seals • Misassembled parts
Reverse Reaction Drum	Damaged splines

GC5029800837000X

Fig. 8 First gear only. 4T60-E

Checks	Cause
Spacer Plate	Wrong Spacer Plate
1-2 Accumulator Seal	Cut seal
1-2 Accumulator Valve	Stuck valve

GC5029800839000X

Fig. 10 Harsh or soft 2-1 shift feel. 4T60-E

Checks	Cause
Possible diagnostic trouble code set	• Check service bulletins • Incorrect tooth count on VS Sensor Rotor • Wrong PROM • Wrong final drive ratio or model
Possible diagnostic trouble code set	• Wrong PROM • Check Service Bulletins
Possible Diagnostic trouble code set	• Check service bulletins • Wrong PROM

GC5029800841000X

Fig. 12 High or low upshift or downshift speed. 4T60-E

Checks	Cause
1-2 Shift Solenoid ON Failure	• Foreign material in the solenoid • The PCM signal is grounded • Pinched solenoid return wire to ground

GC5029800843000X

Fig. 14 First & fourth gear only, 1-2 solenoid stuck on. 4T60-E

Checks	Cause
1-2 Shift Solenoid OFF Failure	• Insufficient force of the solenoid • Foreign material is plugging the filter • The PCM is not grounding • Failure of the O-ring • No supply voltage to the 1-2 Shift Solenoid • Wires are not connected to the solenoid

GC5029800844000X

Fig. 15 Second & third gear only, 1-2 solenoid stuck off. 4T60-E

Checks	Cause
Third Roller Clutch Assembly	• Damaged cage • Rollers out of the cage • Damaged springs • Misassembled input sun gear shaft • No third gear in Manual Lo • No engine braking in Manual Lo

GC5029800845020X

Fig. 16 No 2-3 shift (Part 2 of 2). 4T60-E

Checks	Cause
PCM and Transmission Wiring	• Loose connector • Corroded connector • Defective PCM
Generator and Wiring	• Loose connector • Corroded connector • Defective generator
Speed Sensor and Wiring	• Loose connector • Corroded connector • Defective speed sensor
PCM and Wiring 1-2 and 2-3 Shift Solenoid Valves	• Loose connector • Corroded connector • Defective quad driver

GC5029800847000X

Fig. 18 Third gear only. 4T60-E

Checks	Cause
2-3 Shift Solenoid for OFF Failure	• Foreign material and plugging in the filter • Insufficient force of the solenoid • O-ring failure • An open wire from the shift solenoid to the PCM • The PCM is not grounding • No supply voltage to the solenoid • Wires are not connected to the solenoid

GC5029800849000X

Fig. 20 Third & fourth gear operation. 4T60-E

Checks	Cause
Possible diagnostic trouble code set	Refer to High or Low Oil Pressure
Accumulator Cover and Piston	• Damaged seals • Missing springs
#10 Checkball	Missing
Control Valve Assembly	Stuck 3-4 accumulator valve
3-4 Accumulator Spring Package	Present 3-4 accumulator spring
Control Valve Assembly	Missing #10 checkball
3-4 Accumulator Seal	Cut seal
3-4 Accumulator Valve	Stuck valve
Control Valve Assembly	Missing #10 checkball
3-4 Accumulator Seal	Cut seal
3-4 Accumulator Valve	Stuck valve

GC5029800851000X

Fig. 22 Harsh or soft 3-4/4-3 shift feel. 4T60-E

Checks	Cause
1-2 Shift Solenoid valve or TCC Solenoid valve	Malfunctioned or walked out solenoid
Reverse Reaction Drum	Damaged splines
Input Sprag	Refer to No Drive
Input and Reaction Carriers	Refer to No Drive

GC5029800852020X

Fig. 23 No reverse (Part 2 of 2). 4T60-E

Checks	Cause
Oil Pressure	Refer to High or Low Oil Pressure
Reverse Servo Assembly	Damaged seal
Reverse Reaction Drum	Damaged splines

GC5029800854000X

Fig. 25 Slips in reverse. 4T60-E

Checks	Cause
Control Valve Assembly	• Stuck 2-3 shift valve • Stuck 3-2 manual downshift valve
Channel Plate Gasket	Mispositioned or damaged
Driven Sprocket Support	Blocked Third clutch passage
Input Housing and Shaft Assembly	• Damaged seals • Blocked oil passages
Third Clutch Assembly	• Burned clutch plates • Damaged piston or seals • Damaged checkball assembly in the piston

GC5029800845010X

Fig. 16 No 2-3 shift (Part 1 of 2). 4T60-E

Checks	Cause
Possible Diagnostic trouble code set	Refer to High or Low Oil Pressure
#4 Checkball	Mislocated for a soft shift
#9 Checkball	Mislocated for a harsh shift
2-3 Accumulator Piston, Gaskets, and Seals	• Missing springs • Cut seal • Damaged gaskets • Low torque of bolts
Control Valve Assembly	Missing #9 checkball
2-3 Accumulator Valve	Stuck valve
Control Valve Assembly	Missing #9 checkball
2-3 Accumulator Valve	Stuck valve

GC5029800846000X

Fig. 17 Harsh or soft 2-3/3-2 shift feel. 4T60-E

Checks	Cause
2-3 Shift Solenoid Valve	The solenoid is mislocated from the control valve assembly

GC5029800848000X

Fig. 19 Fourth gear starts. 4T60-E

Checks	Cause
Control Valve Assembly	• Stuck 3-4 shift valve • Stuck 4-3 manual downshift valve
Fourth Clutch Shaft	Damaged spline
Fourth Clutch Assembly	• Burned clutch plates • Damaged piston or seals • Mislocated clutch plates or piston
Shift Cable	Adjust the shift cable

GC5029800850000X

Fig. 21 No 3-4 shift. 4T60-E

Checks	Cause
Oil Pressure	Refer to High or Low Oil Pressure
Reverse Servo	• Misassembled servo • Damaged piston or seal • Missing cushion spring or retainers
Oil Pump Assembly	Refer to No Drive
Drive Link Assembly	Refer to No Drive
Reverse Band	• Burned or damaged reverse band • Mislocated band apply pin
Input Clutch	Refer to No Drive

GC5029800852010X

Fig. 23 No reverse (Part 1 of 2). 4T60-E

Checks	Cause
Final Drive Internal Gear	Deformed or dented parking pawl
Reverse Servo Pin and Bore	Misalignment of pin to bore

GC5029800853000X

Fig. 24 Locked up in drive/reverse. 4T60-E

Checks	Cause
Final Drive Internal Gear	• Park pawl spring • Parking pawl • Parking gear
Actuator Assembly	Damaged spring
Shift Cable	Adjustment to the shift cable

GC5029800855000X

Fig. 26 No Park range. 4T60-E

Checks	Cause
Modulator or Lines	Loss of vacuum due to damaged lines or modulator
Reverse Servo Cushion Spring	Broken or wrong spring
Control Valve Assembly	• Missing #5 checkball, results in harsh reverse • Missing #6 checkball, results in harsh drive
Forward Servo Cushion Spring	Broken or wrong spring
Spacer Plate	Thermal element does not close when the element is warm, causing harsh Neutral to Drive

GC5029800856000X

Fig. 27 Harsh Neutral to reverse or harsh Neutral to drive. 4T60-E

Checks	Cause
Control Valve Assembly	Stuck 1-2 shift valve
Second Clutch Housing and Drum assembly	• Scored drum surface • Hot spots caused by band slipping
Reverse Band Assembly	Burned fiber material
#5 Checkball	Missing or mislocated checkball
Servo Cushion Spring	Damaged or wrong spring

GC5029800857000X

Fig. 28 Second gear starts. 4T60-E

Checks	Cause
TCC Solenoid Valve	The TCC solenoid valve does not exhaust
Control Valve Assembly	The converter clutch valve is stuck in apply position
TCC Screen	Missing screen, allowing foreign material to stick the TCC solenoid ON

GC5029800859000X

Fig. 30 Converter clutch does not release. 4T60-E

Checks	Cause
TCC PWM Solenoid Valve for OFF Failure	• Foreign material in TCC PWM solenoid valve • No PCM signal • Insufficient force of PWM • Failure of the O-rings • Open wire • No supply voltage to the TCC PWM solenoid valve

GC5029800861000X

Fig. 32 Harsh converter clutch (TCC) apply. 4T60-E

Checks	Cause
Verify Proper PCM Operation and Vehicle Wiring	Improper operation or wiring
Wiring Harness	• Damaged or loose connector • Pinched wires • Inoperative TCC Solenoid valve
Control Valve Assembly	• Stuck converter clutch valve • Stuck converter clutch regulator valve
TCC Solenoid Valve	Leaking solenoid O-ring
Solenoid Screen	Blocked screen
Torque Converter	Inspect the converter
Turbine Shaft	Damaged seals
Oil Pump Drive Shaft	Damaged seal
Channel Plate	Damaged or unseated blow off checkball for the converter clutch
TCC Solenoid Valve for OFF Failure	• Foreign material and plugging in the filter • Insufficient force • O-ring failure • No PCM signal • Open wire • No supply voltage to the TCC solenoid valve • Improperly molded solenoid housing, which causes the solenoid to separate from the control valve assembly
TCC Solenoid Valve for ON Failure	• Foreign material • Pinched wire • Grounded PCM signal
Brake Switch (No TCC Apply)	• No supply voltage • Corroded connector • Corroded switch contact • Loose connector • Pinched wire
PRNDL Circuit Problem	• Loose connector • Corroded connector • Corroded switch contact • Pinched wire • PRNDL connector wires A and B are switched around, if PRNDL indicates anything but D3 or D4
Coolant Temperature Sensor	• Corroded Connector • Incorrect resistance • Loose connector • Pinched wire

GC5029800863000X

Fig. 34 No TCC apply. 4T60-E

Checks	Cause
2-1 Manual Band	Burned or glazed fiber material
Apply Pin	Not engaging 2-1 manual band
Seals	• Cut or damaged • Missing filter, which allows foreign material to damage the seal and the bore
Gaskets	Damaged gaskets
Bolts	Low torque

GC5029800858000X

Fig. 29 No engine braking in manual second or low range. 4T60-E

Checks	Cause
TCC Solenoid Valve for ON Failure	• Foreign material • Pinched solenoid wire to ground • PCM signal is grounded

GC5029800860000X

Fig. 31 Converter clutch stuck on in third and fourth gears. 4T60-E

Checks	Cause
Control Valve Assembly	Stuck regulator valve in the converter clutch
Turbine Shaft	• Damaged or missing seals • Damaged or unseated blow off checkball for the converter clutch
Channel Plate	Regulator valve in the converter clutch
Drive Sprocket Support	Worn bushing
Torque Converter	Worn or glazed fiber material (replace the converter)

GC5029800862000X

Fig. 33 Converter clutch apply rough, slips or shudders. 4T60-E

Checks	Cause
DEFINITION: Transmission main line pressure that is determined to be high or low. Refer to *Line Pressure Check Procedure.*	
Automatic transmission fluid level (low pressure only)	Low fluid level
Thermo element assembly (low pressure only)	• The thermo element plate pins are misadjusted • The thermo element or the thermo element plate is out of position, missing, or damaged — causing low fluid level in the oil pan
Oil filter and seal assembly	• The oil filter assembly is missing or damaged • The oil filter seal assembly is missing or damaged (low pressure only)
Wiring harness assembly	The wiring harness assembly is disconnected or damaged
Oil pump assembly	• The following components are worn or damaged (low pressure only): – the oil pump cover – the oil pump body – the oil pump vane ring – the oil pump rotor – the oil pump vanes – the oil pump slide oil seal ring – the oil pump slide O-ring seal – the oil pump slide • The oil pump slide is binding (high pressure only) • The oil pump prime springs or the oil pump slide pivot pin is missing or damaged (low pressure only) • The oil pump slide seal or the oil pump slide seal support is missing or damaged (high pressure only)
Pressure control solenoid valve assembly	• The pressure control solenoid valve assembly is damaged • The solenoid valve O-ring seals are missing or damaged • The valve retainer is missing or damaged
Torque signal regulator valve assembly	• The torque signal regulator valve is binding or damaged • The valve retainer is missing or damaged
Pressure regulator valve assembly	• The pressure regulator valve is binding or is damaged • The pressure regulator valve springs is missing or damaged • The reverse boost valve is binding or is damaged (high pressure only) • The line boost valve is binding or is damaged (high pressure only) • The valve retainer is missing or is damaged
Actuator feed limit valve assembly (low pressure only)	• The actuator feed limit valve is binding or is damaged • The actuator feed limit valve spring is missing or is damaged • The actuator feed limit valve spring retainer is missing or damaged
Low blow off valve assembly (low pressure only)	• The low blow off valve spring is missing or is damaged • The low blow off ball valve is missing, binding, or is damaged • The low blow off valve spring retainer is missing or is damaged

GC5029901025000X

Fig. 35 Incorrect line pressure. 4T65-E

FORWARD SERVO, REPLACE

1. Install engine support fixture tool No. J-28467-A, engine support fixture adapter tool No. J-28467-90 and engine support adapter leg tool No. J-36462, or equivalents.
2. Raise and support vehicle.
3. Remove power steering rack and pinion heat shield.
4. Remove power steering rack and pinion retaining bolts and hang steering rack from exhaust pipe flange.
5. Disconnect transaxle and engine mounts.
6. Support rear of frame with jackstand, loosen front frame and rear frame bolts.
7. Lower frame from jackstand and disconnect power steering lines from righthand side of frame.
8. Remove servo cover bolts, servo cover, servo piston, sealing ring, apply pin, servo spring retainer and servo spring, **Fig. 68.**
9. Reverse procedure to install.

TRANSAXLE

REPLACE

ACHIEVA, SKYLARK & 1997-98 GRAND AM

1. Remove air intake duct.
2. Remove shift linkage from transmission.
3. Disconnect vacuum modulator line at modulator.

Checks	Cause
DEFINITION: Gear engagement that takes longer than three seconds when the engine is idling in Park or Neutral, and the gear selector is moved to Drive or Reverse range.	
Automatic transmission fluid level	Low fluid level
Transmission main line pressure	Low transmission main line pressure
Reverse band servo assembly (Reverse engagement only)	The reverse band servo piston oil seal ring is damaged or rolled
Forward band servo assembly (Drive engagement only)	The forward band servo piston oil seal ring is damaged or rolled
Control valve body assembly (Reverse engagement only)	The reverse servo boost valve is binding or is damaged
Control valve body assembly (Drive engagement only)	The forward servo boost valve is binding or is damaged
Control valve body spacer plate assembly (Drive engagement only)	The thermal element is damaged or is not functioning properly
TCC blowoff ball valve assembly	The TCC blowoff ball valve is not seating — causing torque converter drain back)
Input clutch assembly	• The input clutch housing oil seal rings are damaged or rolled • The input clutch housing assembly sealing surfaces are damaged • The input clutch housing ball check valve assembly is plugged or damaged • The input clutch inner piston seal is damaged or rolled • The input clutch outer piston seal is damaged or rolled • The input clutch piston assembly sealing surfaces are damaged

GC5029901026000X

Fig. 36 Delayed park to reverse/drive engagement. 4T65-E

Checks	Cause
DEFINITION: A large engine RPM increase is noted with little or no vehicle forward speed increase during the following conditions: • The engine is running • The transmission is in Drive range • The vehicle is stopped or moving slowly • The vehicle brakes are not applied • The throttle is opened 25% or greater	
Automatic transmission fluid level	Low fluid level
Transmission main line pressure	Low transmission main line pressure
Manual linkage	Misadjusted
Oil filter assembly	• The oil filter assembly is missing, plugged, or damaged • The oil filter seal assembly is missing or damaged
Accumulator and manual 2 - 1 band servo assembly	• A loose or damaged forward band servo oil pipe • Loose manual 2 - 1 band servo cover or accumulator cover bolts • Missing or damaged manual 2 - 1 servo cover gasket • A damaged accumulator cover spacer plate assembly
Forward band servo assembly	• A servo piston oil seal ring is missing or is damaged • A servo piston is damaged or is stuck in the servo cover • The servo piston cushion spring or the retainer is missing or damaged • The servo piston pin is not engaged to the forward band assembly • The forward band assembly is worn or burned • The forward band assembly is disengaged from the anchor pin • The anchor pin is loose or missing
Control valve body assembly	The #3 Ball check valve is missing
Torque converter assembly	The torque converter assembly stator clutch is not holding
Drive link assembly	• The drive link assembly is broken • The drive/driven sprockets are damaged
Input clutch assembly	• The input clutch sprag assembly is damaged or misassembled • The input clutch housing oil seal rings are missing or are damaged • The input clutch housing ball check valve assembly is missing or is damaged • The input clutch piston inner/outer seals are missing or are damaged • The input clutch piston is damaged • The input clutch plates are worn
1 - 2 clutch roller assembly	The 1 - 2 clutch roller assembly is damaged
Input and reaction carrier assemblies	The input carrier assembly or the reaction carrier assembly components are damaged
Differential carrier assembly	• The park pawl assembly is broken or damaged • The sun gear shaft, the internal gear assembly, or the carrier assembly components are damaged

GC5029901028000X

Fig. 38 Slips in drive or no drive. 4T65-E

Checks	Cause
DEFINITION: The vehicle cannot be moved forward or backward during the following conditions: • The engine is running • The transmission is in Drive or Reverse range • The vehicle brakes are not applied • The throttle is closed (idling)	
Manual linkage	Misadjusted
Input and reaction carrier assemblies	The input carrier assembly or the reaction carrier assembly components are damaged
Differential carrier assembly	• The park pawl assembly is broken or damaged • The sun gear shaft, the internal gear assembly, or the carrier assembly components are damaged

GC5029901030000X

Fig. 40 Locked up in drive/reverse. 4T65-E

Checks	Cause
DEFINITION: Gear engagement that is harsh when the engine is idling in Park or Neutral, and the gear selector is moved to Drive or Reverse range.	
Transmission main line pressure	High transmission main line pressure
Reverse band servo assembly (Reverse engagement only)	The reverse band servo piston cushion spring is broken or is missing
Forward band servo assembly (Drive engagement only)	The forward band servo piston cushion spring is broken or is missing
Transmission case cover ball check valve Reverse engagement only)	#5 Ball check valve is mislocated or is missing
Transmission case cover ball check valve (Drive engagement only	#6 Ball check valve is mislocated or is missing
Control valve body assembly (Reverse engagement only)	Reverse servo boost valve is binding or is damaged
Control valve body assembly (Drive engagement only)	Forward servo boost valve is binding or is damaged
Control valve body spacer plate assembly (Drive engagement only)	The thermal element is damaged or is not functioning properly

GC5029901027000X

Fig. 37 Harsh park to reverse/drive engagement. 4T65-E

Checks	Cause
DEFINITION: A large engine RPM increase is noted with little or no vehicle rearward speed increase during the following conditions: • The engine is running • The transmission is in Reverse range • The vehicle is stopped or moving slowly • The vehicle brakes are not applied • The throttle is opened 25% or greater	
Automatic transmission fluid level	Low fluid level
Transmission main line pressure	Low transmission main line pressure
Manual linkage	Misadjusted
Oil filter assembly	• The oil filter assembly is missing, plugged, or damaged • The oil filter seal assembly is missing or damaged
Reverse band servo assembly	• A servo piston oil seal ring is missing or is damaged • A servo piston is damaged or is stuck in the case bore • The servo piston cushion springs or the retainer is missing or damaged • The servo piston pin is not engaged to the reverse band assembly • The reverse band assembly is worn or burned • The reverse band assembly is disengaged from the anchor pin band • The anchor pin is loose or missing
Torque converter assembly	The torque converter assembly stator clutch is not holding
Drive link assembly	• The drive link assembly is broken • The drive/driven sprockets are damaged
Input clutch assembly	• The input clutch sprag assembly is damaged or misassembled • The input clutch housing oil seal rings are missing or are damaged • The input clutch housing ball check valve assembly is missing or is damaged • The input clutch piston inner/outer seals are missing or are damaged • The input clutch piston is damaged • The input clutch plates are worn
Reverse reaction drum	The reverse reaction drum splines are damaged
Input and reaction carrier assemblies	The input carrier assembly or the reaction carrier assembly components are damaged
Differential carrier assembly	• The park pawl assembly is broken or damaged • The sun gear shaft the internal gear assembly, or the carrier assembly components are damaged

GC5029901029000X

Fig. 39 Slips in reverse or no reverse. 4T65-E

Checks	Cause
DEFINITION: One of the two following conditions occur: • The transmission range selector cannot be moved into Park • The vehicle can move forward or backward more than one meter (3 ft) after the transmission range selector is moved into Park	
Manual linkage	Misadjusted
Differential carrier assembly	The park pawl assembly is broken or damaged
Park pawl actuator assembly	• The actuator assembly is damaged • The actuator guide is damaged or debris is present

GC5029901031000X

Fig. 41 No park range. 4T65-E

Checks	Cause
DEFINITION: One of the two following conditions occurs during a first to second gear steady throttle upshift, or a second to first gear coast, or a light to moderate throttle detent downshift: • Harsh shift fee — an unacceptable quick gear change occurs • Soft shift feel — an unacceptable long gear change occurs	
Automatic transmission fluid level (soft shift only)	Low fluid level
Transmission main line pressure	Low or high transmission main line pressure
Oil filter assembly (soft shift only)	• The oil filter assembly is missing, plugged, or damaged • The oil filter seal assembly is missing or damaged
1 - 2 accumulator assembly	• Misassembled (upside down) 1 - 2 accumulator assembly • Damaged or missing 1 - 2 accumulator piston oil seal ring • A damaged or missing 1 - 2 accumulator piston cushion spring or outer spring • A stuck or binding 1 - 2 accumulator piston • Debris in the passages of the accumulator cover spacer plate
Control valve body assembly	• Debris in the passages of the control valve body or spacer plate assembly • Missing or mislocated #2 ball check valve • Misassembled 1 - 2 accumulator valve line-up • Stuck or binding 1 - 2 accumulator valve • Damaged or missing 1 - 2 accumulator valve spring • Missing, damaged, or misassembled 2 - 3 accumulator valve bushing bore plug or retainers
Driven sprocket support assembly (soft shift only)	• A damaged second clutch housing oil seal rings or the four lobe oil seal ring seals • Worn or damaged second clutch housing bushings
Second clutch assembly	• Missing or not seated second clutch basking plate retaining ring • Missing or misassembled second clutch backing plate • Worn, damaged, or misassembled clutch plates • Missing or not seated second clutch spring retaining ring • A damaged spring assembly or piston • A missing or damaged second clutch housing ball check valve assembly • A damaged second clutch housing assembly

GC5029901032000X

Fig. 42 Harsh or soft 1 - 2 shift feel. 4T65-E

Checks	Cause
DEFINITION: One of the two following conditions occurs during a third to fourth gear steady throttle upshift, or a fourth to third gear coast, or a light to moderate throttle detent downshift: • Harsh shift feel — an unacceptable quick gear change occurs • Soft shift feel — an unacceptable long gear change occurs	
Automatic transmission fluid level (soft shift only)	Low fluid level
Transmission main line pressure	Low or high transmission main line pressure
Oil filter assembly (soft shift only)	• The oil filter assembly is missing, plugged, or damaged • The oil filter seal assembly is missing or damaged
3 - 4 accumulator assembly	• Misassembled (upside down) 3 - 4 accumulator assembly • Damaged or missing 3 - 4 accumulator piston oil seal ring • A damaged or missing 3 - 4 accumulator piston outer spring • A stuck or binding 3 - 4 accumulator piston • A damaged 3 - 4 accumulator piston cylinder or O-ring seal

GC5029901034010X

Fig. 44 Harsh or soft 3 - 4/4 - 3 shift feel (Part 1 of 2). 4T65-E

Checks	Cause
DEFINITION: An upshift or a downshift (or TCC apply) that occurs at a speed outside of the calibrated range. Refer to *Shift Speed.*	
ECM/PCM calibration information	Incorrect calibration in the ECM/PCM
Throttle Position (TP) sensor	Misadjusted or faulty TP sensor

GC5029901035000X

Fig. 45 High or low upshift or downshift speed. 4T65-E

Checks	Cause
DEFINITION: The transmission only provides first and fourth gear in Drive range. The shift pattern as the vehicle accelerates from a stop is 1 - 1-4 - 4. First gear ratio is 2.921:1 and fourth gear ratio is 0.705:1	
Control valve body assembly	• A faulty 1 - 2. 3 - 4shift solenoid valve assembly is stuck On • Debris is found in the control valve body or the spacer plate assembly

GC5029901037000X

Fig. 47 First and fourth gear only (1 -2 solenoid stuck on). 4T65-E

Checks	Cause
DEFINITION: The transmission only provides second and third gear in Drive range. The shift pattern as the vehicle accelerates from a stop is 2 - 2-3 - 3. Second gear ratio is 1.568:1 and third gear ratio is 1.000:1	
Control valve body assembly	• A faulty 1 - 2. 3 - 4 shift solenoid valve assembly is stuck Off • A missing or damaged shift solenoid valve O-ring seal • Plugged or damaged solenoid valve screen/seal assembly • Debris is found in the control valve body or the spacer plate assembly
Case cover assembly	A stuck, binding, or missing actuator feed limit valve line-up

GC5029901038000X

Fig. 48 Second and third gear only (1 -2 solenoid stuck off). 4T65-E

Checks	Cause
DEFINITION: One of the two following conditions occurs during a second to third gear steady throttle upshift, or a third to second gear coast, or a light to moderate throttle detent downshift: • Harsh shift fee — an unacceptable quick gear change occurs • Soft shift feel — an unacceptable long gear change occurs	
Automatic transmission fluid level (soft shift only)	Low fluid level
Transmission main line pressure	Low or high transmission main line pressure
Oil filter assembly (soft shift only)	• The oil filter assembly is missing, plugged, or damaged • The oil filter seal assembly is missing or damaged
2 - 3 accumulator assembly	• Misassembled (upside down) 2 - 3 accumulator assembly • Damaged or missing 2 - 3 accumulator piston oil seal ring • A damaged or missing 2 - 3 accumulator piston cushion spring or outer spring • A stuck or binding 2 - 3 accumulator piston • Debris in the passages of the accumulator cover spacer plate
Control valve body assembly	• Debris in the passages of the control valve body or spacer plate assembly • Missing or mislocated #4 or #9 ball check valves • Misassembled 2 - 3 accumulator valve line-up • Stuck or binding 2 - 3 accumulator valve • Missing, damaged, or misassembled 2 - 3 accumulator valve bushing bore plug, or retainers
Driven sprocket support assembly (soft shift only)	A plugged third clutch oil passage in the driven sprocket support assembly
Third clutch assembly	• The input clutch housing oil seal rings are missing or are damaged • The third clutch ball check valve assembly is missing or is damaged • The third clutch piston is damaged • The third clutch piston inner seal is missing or damage • The third clutch plates are worn or misassembled

GC5029901033000X

Fig. 43 Harsh or soft 2 - 3/3 - 2 shift feel. 4T65-E

Checks	Cause
Control valve body assembly	• Debris in the passages of the control valve body or spacer plate assembly • Misassembled 3 - 4 accumulator valve line-up • Stuck or binding 3 - 4 accumulator valve • Missing, damaged, or misassembled 3 - 4 accumulator valve spring or retainer
Driven sprocket support assembly (soft shift only)	• A missing or damaged fourth clutch orifice • A damaged driven sprocket support assembly
Fourth clutch assembly	• Worn, damaged, or misassembled clutch plates • A missing or not seated fourth clutch spring retaining ring • A damaged spring assembly or piston • Worn or damaged fourth clutch piston seals

GC5029901034020X

Fig. 44 Harsh or soft 3 - 4/4 - 3 shift feel (Part 2 of 2). 4T65-E

Checks	Cause
DEFINITION: The transmission only provides first and second gear in Drive range. The shift pattern as the vehicle accelerates from a stop is 1 - 2-2 - 1. First gear ratio is 2.921:1 and second gear ratio is 1.568:1	
Control valve body assembly	• A faulty 2 - 3 shift solenoid valve asembly is stuck On • Debris is found in the control valve body or the spacer plate assembly

GC5029901036000X

Fig. 46 First and second gear only (2 - 3 solenoid stuck on). 4T65-E

Checks	Cause
DEFINITION: The transmission only provides third and fourth gear in Drive range. The shift pattern as the vehicle accelerates from a stop is 4 - 3-3 - 4. Third gear ratio is 1.000:1 and fourth gear ratio is 0.705:1	
Control valve body assembly	• A faulty 2 - 3 shift solenoid valve assembly is stuck Off • A missing or mislocated 2 - 3 shift solenoid valve and retainer • A missing or damaged shift solenoid valve O-ring seal • Plugged or damaged solenoid valve screen/seal assembly • Debris is found in the control valve body or the spacer plate assembly

GC5029901039000X

Fig. 49 Third and fourth gear only (2 - 3 solenoid stuck off). 4T65-E

Checks	Cause
DEFINITION: The transmission only provides first gear in Drive range. The vehicle accelerates from a stop in first gear and does not upshift. First gear ratio is 2.921:1	
Control valve body assembly	• The 1 - 2 shift valve is stuck or binding • Debris is found in the control valve body or the spacer plate assembly • The spacer plate and gaskets are misassembled
Second clutch assembly	• A missing or not seated second clutch backing plate retaining ring • A missing or misassembled second clutch backing plate • Worn, damaged, or misassembled clutch plates • A missing or not seated second clutch spring retaining ring • A damaged spring assembly or piston • A missing or damaged second clutch housing ball check valve assembly • A damaged second clutch housing assembly
Reverse reaction drum	Damaged splines of the reverse reaction drum

GC5029901040000X

Fig. 50 First gear only. 4T65-E

Checks	Cause
DEFINITION: The transmission only provides third gear in Drive range. The vehicle accelerates from a stop in third gear and does not upshift. Third gear ratio is 1.000:1	
Control valve body assembly	• Debris is found in the control valve body or the spacer plate assembly • The spacer plate and gaskets are misassembled

GC5029901042000X

Fig. 52 Third gear only. 4T65-E

Checks	Cause
DEFINITION: A large engine RPM increase is noted in first gear, Drive range, with little or no vehicle forward speed increase. Second, third, and fourth gear operation are normal. Shifts into first gear are soft or do not occur. First gear ratio is 2.921:1	
Automatic transmission fluid level	Low fluid level
Transmission main line pressure	Low transmission main line pressure
Oil filter assembly	• The oil filter assembly is missing, plugged, or damaged • The oil filter seal assembly is missing or is damaged
Accumulator and manual 2 - 1 band servo assembly	• A loose or damaged forward band servo oil pipe • Loose manual 2 - 1 band servo cover of accumulator cover bolts • A missing or a damaged manual 2 - 1 servo cover gasket • A damaged accumulator cover spacer plate assembly
Forward band servo assembly	• The servo piston oil seal ring is missing or damaged • The servo piston is damaged or stuck in the servo cover • The servo piston cushion spring or the retainer is missing or damaged • The servo piston pin is not engaged to the forward band assembly • The forward band assembly is worn or burned • The forward band assembly is disengaged from the anchor pin • The band anchor pin is loose or missing
Control valve body assembly	• The 1 - 2 shift valve is stuck or binding • The #3 ball check valve is missing
Input clutch assembly	• The input clutch sprag assembly is damaged or misassembled • The input clutch housing oil seal rings are missing or damaged • The input clutch housing ball check valve assembly is missing or damaged • The input clutch piston inner/outer seals are missing or damaged • The input clutch piston is damaged • The input clutch plates are worn
1 - 2 clutch roller assembly	The 1 - 2 clutch roller assembly is damaged

GC5029901044000X

Fig. 54 Slipping or no first gear. 4T65-E

Checks	Cause
DEFINITION: A large engine RPM increase is noted in third gear, Drive range, with little or no vehicle forward speed increase. First, second, and fourth gear operation are normal. Shifts into third gear are soft or do not occur. Third gear ratio is 1.000:1.	
Automatic transmission fluid level	Low fluid level
Transmission main line pressure	Low transmission main line pressure
Oil filter assembly	• The oil filter assembly is missing, plugged, or damaged • The oil filter seal assembly is missing or is damaged
Control valve body assembly	• The 2 - 3 shift valve or the 3 - 2 manual downshift valve is stuck or binding • Debris is found in the passages of the control valve body or of the spacer plate assembly • The #4 or the #9 ball check valve is missing or mislocated
Driven sprocket support assembly	A plugged third clutch oil passage in the driven sprocket support assembly
Third clutch assembly	• Input clutch housing oil seal rings are missing or damaged • The third clutch ball check valve assembly is missing or damaged • The third clutch piston is damaged • The third clutch piston inner seal is missing or damaged • The third clutch plates are worn or misassembled
Third clutch sprag assembly	• The sprag was misassembled (backwards) on the inner race • A damaged third clutch sprag assembly

GC5029901046000X

Fig. 56 Slipping or no third gear. 4T65-E

Checks	Cause
DEFINITION: The transmission only provides second gear in Drive range. The vehicle accelerates from a stop in second gear and does not upshift. Second gear ratio is 1.568:1	
Control valve body assembly	• The 1 - 2 shift valve is stuck or binding • Debris is found in the control valve body or the spacer plate assembly • The spacer plate and gaskets are misassembled
Input carrier assembly	• A damaged input sun gear • Damaged input carrier planetary pinions

GC5029901041000X

Fig. 51 Second gear only. 4T65-E

Checks	Cause
DEFINITION: The transmission only provides fourth gear in Drive range. The vehicle accelerates from a stop in fourth gear and does not upshift. Third gear ratio is 1.000:1	
Control valve body assembly	• Debris is found in the control valve body or the spacer plate assembly • The spacer plate and gaskets are misassembled

GC5029901043000X

Fig. 53 Fourth gear only. 4T65-E

Checks	Cause
DEFINITION: A large engine RPM increase is noted in second gear, Drive range, with little or no vehicle forward speed increase. First, third, and fourth gear operation are normal. Shifts into second gear are soft or do not occur. Second gear ratio is 1.568:1.	
Automatic transmission fluid level	Low fluid level
Transmission main line pressure	Low transmission main line pressure
Oil filter assembly	• The oil filter assembly is missing, plugged, or damaged • The oil filter seal assembly is missing or is damaged
Control valve body assembly	• The 1 - 2 shift valve is stuck or binding • Debris is found in the passages of the control valve body or of the spacer plate assembly
Driven sprocket support assembly	• Damaged second clutch housing oil seal rings • Damaged four lobe oil seal ring seals • Worn or damaged second clutch housing bushings
Second clutch assembly	• Missing or not seated second clutch backing plate retaining ring • Missing or misassembled second clutch backing plate • Worn, damaged, or misassembled clutch plates • Missing or not seated second clutch spring retaining ring • Damaged spring assembly or piston • Missing or damaged second clutch housing ball check valve assembly • Damaged second clutch housing assembly

GC5029901045000X

Fig. 55 Slipping or no second gear. 4T65-E

Checks	Cause
DEFINITION: A large engine RPM increase is noted in fourth gear, Drive range, with little or no vehicle forward speed increase. First, second, and third gear operation are normal. Shifts into fourth gear are soft or do not occur. Fourth gear ratio is 0.705:1.	
Automatic transmission fluid level	Low fluid level
Transmission main line pressure	Low transmission main line pressure
Oil filter assembly	• The oil filter assembly is missing, plugged, or damaged • The oil filter seal assembly is missing or is damaged
Control valve body assembly	• The 3 - 4 shift valve or the 4 - 3 manual downshift valve is stuck or binding • Debris is found in the passages of the control valve body or of the spacer plate assembly
Case cover assembly	Distortion or damage occurs at the manual valve or at the case cover causing PRN oil leak
Driven sprocket support assembly	A plugged third clutch oil passage in the driven sprocket support assembly
Fourth clutch assembly	• The clutch plates are worn, damaged, or misassembled • A missing or not seated fourth clutch spring retaining ring • A damaged spring assembly or piston • Worn or damaged fourth clutch piston seals
Third clutch sprag assembly	• The sprag was misassembled (backwards) on the inner race • A damaged third clutch sprag assembly

GC5029901047000X

Fig. 57 Slipping or no fourth gear. 4T65-E

Checks	Cause
DEFINITION: A large engine RPM increase and forward vehicle speed decrease do not immediately occur when the transmission is shifted from third or fourth gear in Drive or Manual Third range to either first or second gear, Manual Second, or Low range.	
Accumulator and manual 2 - 1 band servo assembly	• A loose or damaged manual 2 - 1 band servo oil pipe • Loose manual 2 - 1 band servo cover or accumulator cover bolts • A damaged accumulator cover spacer plate assembly • A damaged or missing servo piston seal or a servo piston cylinder O-ring seal • A missing servo exhaust screen assembly, allowing debris into the cylinder • A misassembled manual 2 - 1 servo assembly
Manual 2 - 1 band assembly	• A band assembly that is worn or burned • A band assembly that is disengaged from the anchor pin • A band anchor pin that is loose or missing

GC5029901048000X

Fig. 58 No engine braking in manual second or low range. 4T65-E

Checks	Cause
DEFINITION: No difference in RPM is noted between the engine speed and the transmission input (turbine) speed in any transmission range. This condition may also cause the engine to stall when the vehicle is slowed to a stop or when the transmission is shifted from Park or Neutral range into Reverse or Drive range.	
Control valve body assembly	• The TCC control valve or the TCC regulatcr apply valve is stuck or binding • The spacer plate and gaskets are misassembled or contain incorrect parts
Torque converter assembly	A faulty torque converter assembly : the pressure plate is stuck in the applied position

GC5029901049000X

Fig. 59 Converter clutch stuck on in all gears. 4T65-E

Checks	Cause
DEFINITION: No difference in RPM is noted between the engine speed and the transaxle input (turbine) shaft speed in second, third and fourth gear, DRIVE range. TCC is not ON in first gear and the engine does not stall when the vehicle slows to a stop or is shifted from PARK or NEUTRAL range to REVERSE or DRIVE range.	
Control valve body assembly	• The TCC PWM solenoid valve assembly is faulty (stuck ON) • The spacer plate and gaskets are misassembled or contain incorrect parts • The PWM internal O-ring is missing or damaged

GC5029901050000X

Fig. 60 Converter clutch stuck on in 2nd, 3rd and 4th gear. 4T65-E

Checks	Cause
DEFINITION: An unacceptably quick TCC apply or release occurs in third or fourth gear, Drive or Manual third range, with the throttle held steady.	
Control valve body assembly	• The TCC regulator apply valve is stuck or binding • The TCC regulator apply valve spring is missing or damaged • The TCC control valve spring is missing or damaged • The spacer plate and gaskets are misassembled or contain incorrect parts
Torque converter assembly	A faulty torque converter assembly

GC5029901051000X

Fig. 61 Harsh converter clutch (TCC) apply or release. 4T65-E

Checks	Cause
DEFINITION: An unacceptably long TCC apply occurs in third or fourth gear, Drive or Manual Third range, with the throttle held steady. This can cause a momentary rapid jerking sensation in the vehicle during the TCC apply.	
Control valve body assembly	• The TCC regulator apply valve is stuck or binding • The TCC regulator apply valve spring is missing or damaged • The spacer plate and gaskets are misassembled or contain incorrect parts
Case cover assembly	The TCC blowoff ball valve or the spring is damaged or is not seating
Turbine shaft assembly	• The turbine shaft O-ring seal is damaged or is missing • The turbine shaft oil seal rings are damaged or missing • The turbine shaft is damaged
Drive sprocket support assembly	The turbine shaft bushing is worn or damaged
Torque converter assembly	The torque converter assembly is faulty

GC5029901052000X

Fig. 62 Converter clutch apply rough, slips or shudders. 4T65-E

Checks	Cause
DEFINITION: A large difference in RPM is noted between the engine speed and the transmission input (turbine) speed in third or fourth gear, Drive or Manual Third range when the TCC is commanded On by the PCM.	
Control valve body assembly	• The TCC PWM solenoid valve assembly is stuck Off • The TCC control valve or the TCC regulator apply valve is stuck or binding • The #10 ball check valve is missing or is mislocated • The spacer plate and gaskets are misassembled or contain incorrect parts
Case cover assembly	The TCC blowoff ball valve or the spring is damaged or is not seating
Turbine shaft assembly	• The turbine shaft O-ring seal is damaged or is missing • The turbine shaft oil seal rings are damaged or missing • The turbine shaft is damaged
Drive sprocket support assembly	The turbine shaft bushing is worn or damaged
Torque converter assembly	The torque converter assembly is faulty

GC5029901053000X

Fig. 63 No TCC apply. 4T65-E

4. Disconnect electrical connectors from torque converter clutch, park/neutral position switch and shift solenoid.
5. Support engine using engine support fixture tool No. J28467-360, or equivalent.
6. Remove two top transmission to engine retaining bolts.
7. Remove rubber hose from transmission to vent pipe, then the remaining upper engine to transmission retaining bolts.
8. Raise and support vehicle, then remove both front wheels.
9. Remove right and left splash shield.
10. Remove both front ABS wheel speed sensors and harness from left side suspension support.
11. Remove both ball joints from control arms, then the left stabilizer shaft link pin bolt.
12. Remove left stabilizer shaft frame bushing clamp nuts.
13. Remove left suspension support assembly, then the drive axles.
14. Remove engine to transmission brace, then the starter motor.
15. Remove transmission converter cover, then the heater core hose pipe brace to transmission nut and bolt.
16. Remove torque converter to flywheel retaining bolts. Using a scribe, mark flywheel to torque converter relationship for proper installation.
17. Remove oil level indicator and fill tube, then the transmission oil cooler pipes. Plug pipes to prevent leakage.
18. Remove vehicle speed sensor, then the vacuum reserve tank.
19. Position a suitable transmission jack under transmission.
20. Remove transmission mount to body retaining bolts, then remove remaining engine to transmission retaining bolts.
21. Remove transmission.
22. Reverse procedure to install.

BONNEVILLE, LSS, LESABRE, REGENCY & EIGHTY-EIGHT,

1. Disconnect cross brace from struts towers as follows:
   a. Loosen bar assembly through-bolts.
   b. Remove inboard strut nuts.
   c. Remove brace assembly.
   d. Install inboard strut nuts.
2. Remove air intake duct.
3. Remove cruise control cable at throttle body, then the vacuum hoses at servo and servo assembly.
4. Remove shift control linkage mounting bracket at transaxle and lever at manual shaft.
5. Disconnect wiring connectors at transaxle park/neutral position switch, back up lamp switch, transaxle electrical connector and vehicle speed sensor.
6. Remove fuel pipe retainers and disconnect vacuum modulator hose at modulator.
7. Remove top three transaxle to engine bolts and install engine support fixture. **"Load" support fixture by tightening wing nuts several turns to relieve tension on frame and mounts.**
8. Raise and support vehicle.
9. Remove front wheel and ball joint assemblies.
10. Separate control arms from steering knuckles. **Drive axle seal protector tool No. J-34754, or equivalent, should be modified and installed on any drive axle prior to service. Failure to observe this can result in damage and possible joint failure.**
11. Remove righthand drive axle from transaxle only. Do not remove from hub/knuckle assembly.
12. Remove lefthand drive axle from transaxle and hub/knuckle assembly.
13. Support transaxle with jackstand and remove lefthand front transaxle mount.
14. Remove torque strut bracket from transaxle and lefthand rear transaxle mount to transaxle bolts.
15. Remove transaxle brace from engine bracket and stabilizer shaft link to control arm bolt.
16. Remove flywheel cover bolts, flywheel cover and flywheel to converter bolts. Mark flywheel to converter relationship to ensure proper installation.
17. Remove bolts retaining rear frame member to front frame dog leg.
18. Remove front lefthand frame to body retaining bolts and front lefthand frame dog leg to righthand frame member bolts.
19. Remove frame assembly by swinging aside and supporting with suitable

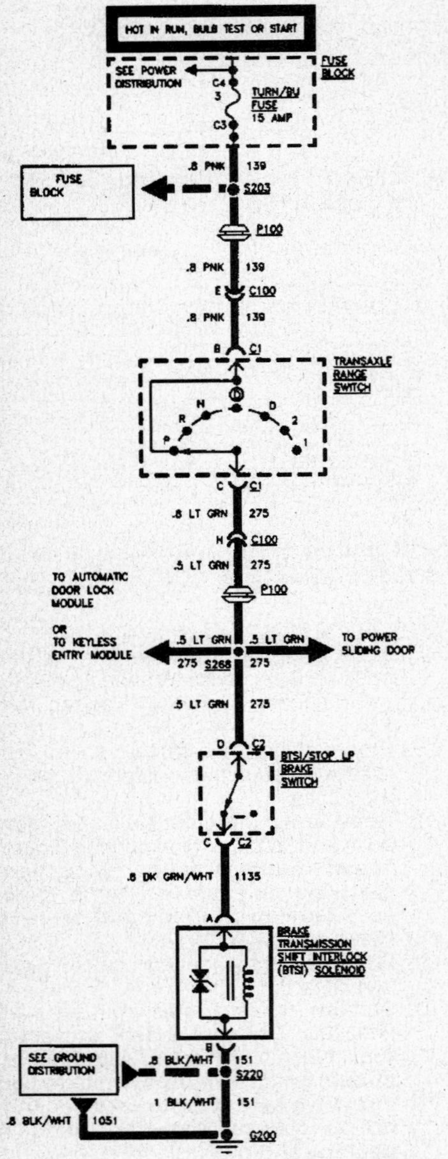

Fig. 64 BTSI wiring diagram

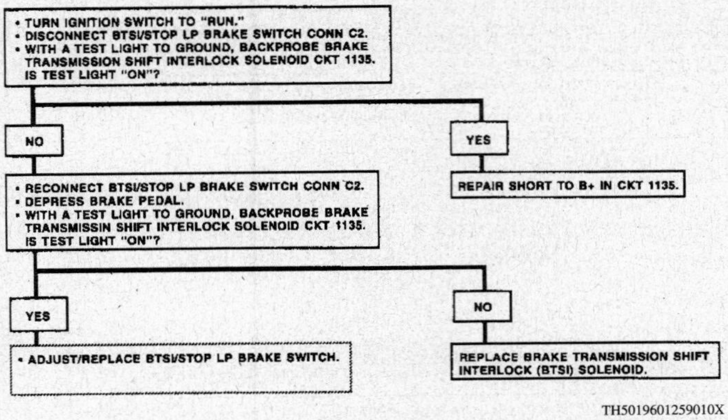

Fig. 65 BTSI diagnosis chart (Part 1 of 2)

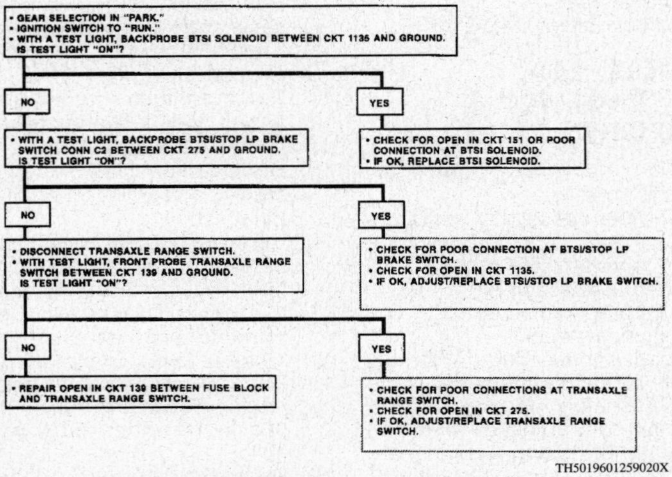

Fig. 65 BTSI diagnosis chart (Part 2 of 2)

stand, then disconnect cooler pipes at transaxle.

20. Remove remaining transaxle to engine retaining bolts. **One bolt is located between transaxle case and engine block and is installed in opposite direction.**
21. Lower transaxle away from vehicle.
22. Reverse procedure to install.

CENTURY, CUTLASS SUPREME, GRAND PRIX, IMPALA, INTRIGUE, MONTE CARLO, LUMINA & REGAL

1. Remove throttle body air inlet duct.
2. Install engine support adapter tool No. J-28467-90, or equivalent
3. Install engine support fixture tool No. J-28467-A, or equivalent.
4. Install engine support adapter leg set tool No. J-36462, or equivalent.
5. Remove engine mount struts and wiring harness connectors from transaxle.
6. Remove auto transaxle range selector cable from park/neutral position switch.
7. Remove auto transaxle range selector cable and bracket from transaxle, then the park/neutral position switch.
8. Remove transaxle fluid filler tube.
9. Remove upper transaxle bolts and wiring harness grounds.
10. Raise and support vehicle.
11. Remove front wheel and tire assemblies.
12. Remove engine splash shields.
13. Remove both tie rod ends from steering knuckles.
14. Remove power steering gear heat shield.
15. Remove power steering gear retaining bolts and power steering gear from frame.
16. Secure power steering gear with wire, then remove power steering cooler line clamps from frame.
17. Remove engine mount lower nuts.
18. Remove lower ball joints from steering knuckles.
19. Remove torque converter cover and starter motor.
20. Remove torque converter bolts and drain transaxle fluid.

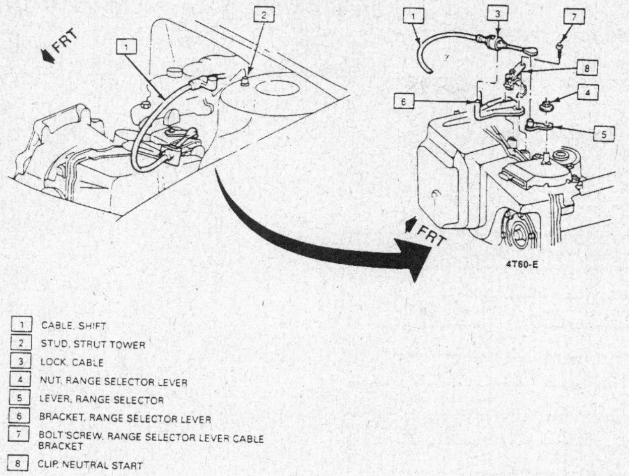

GC5029400448000X

Fig. 66 Shift control cable adjustment

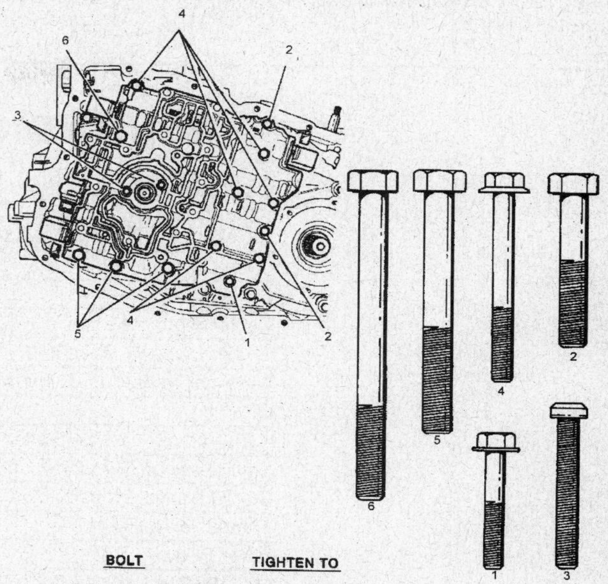

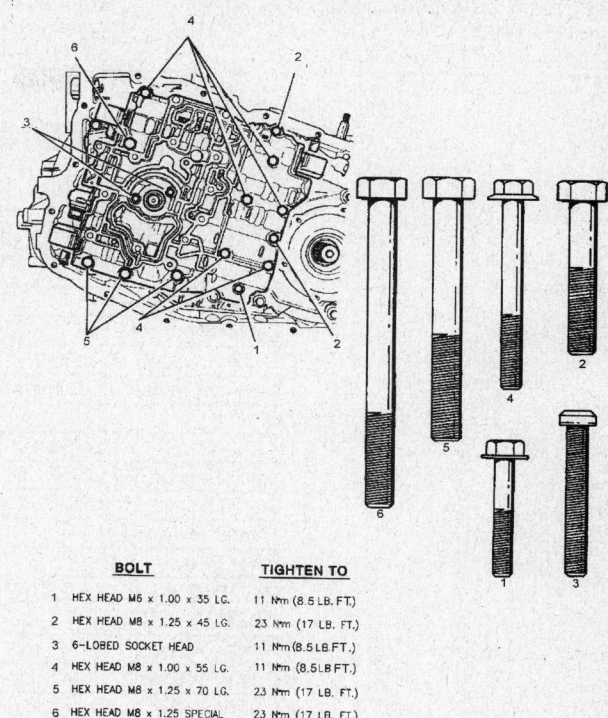

	BOLT	TIGHTEN TO
1	HEX HEAD M6 x 1.00 x 35 LG.	11 N·m (8.5 LB. FT.)
2	HEX HEAD M8 x 1.25 x 45 LG.	23 N·m (17 LB. FT.)
3	6-LOBED SOCKET HEAD	11 N·m (8.5 LB. FT.)
4	HEX HEAD M8 x 1.00 x 55 LG.	11 N·m (8.5 LB. FT.)
5	HEX HEAD M8 x 1.25 x 70 LG.	23 N·m (17 LB. FT.)
6	HEX HEAD M8 x 1.25 SPECIAL	23 N·m (17 LB. FT.)

TH5029600944000X

Fig. 67 Valve body bolt tightening specifications

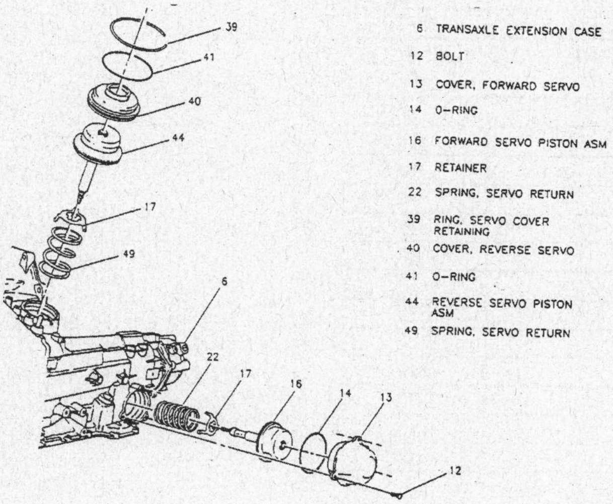

TH5029200023000X

Fig. 68 Reverse & forward servo

21. Remove transaxle cooler hoses from transaxle.
22. Disconnect drive axles from transaxle and secure to steering knuckles and struts.
23. Disconnect wheel speed sensor and vehicle speed sensor wiring harness connectors.
24. Support transaxle and frame, then remove transaxle brace.
25. Remove lower transaxle bolt and stud.
26. Remove frame to body bolts, then lower transaxle and frame from vehicle.
27. Remove transaxle from frame.
28. Reverse procedure to install.

PARK AVENUE & RIVIERA

1. Remove air cleaner cover and disconnect transaxle electrical connector.
2. Disconnect shift control cable bracket with cable attached.
3. Remove top transaxle case bolts and top bolt from rear transaxle mount.
4. Remove lefthand steering gear mount bolts.
5. Disconnect O2 sensor connector.
6. Install engine support fixture tool No. J-28467–A, or equivalent.
7. Load fixture by tightening wing nuts several turns to relieve tension on frame and mounts.
8. Raise and support vehicle.
9. Remove wheel and tire assemblies.
10. Remove lefthand splash shield assembly.
11. Remove power steering line bracket from engine frame.
12. Remove righthand splash shield and lefthand transaxle mount from engine frame.
13. Remove righthand transaxle mount from frame.
14. Remove righthand steering rack mount bolts from engine frame.
15. Secure steering gear to exhaust with wire.
16. Disconnect transaxle cooler lines from engine frame.
17. Remove sway bar mounts from lower control arms.
18. Separate lower ball joints from steering knuckles and hand tighten ball joint nuts.
19. Remove engine frame bolts.
20. Remove ball joint nuts and lower engine frame.
21. Remove drive axles from transaxle.
22. Remove cover and torque converter bolts.
23. Mark flywheel to torque converter position for proper assembly.
24. Disconnect input speed sensor connectors.
25. Remove engine to transaxle bracket.
26. Remove transaxle fluid filler tube.
27. Remove rear engine mount and remaining transaxle bolts.
28. Remove transaxle from vehicle.
29. Reverse procedure to install.

TECHNICAL SERVICE BULLETINS

INTERMITTENT NEUTRAL CONDITION AT HIGHWAY SPEEDS

1997

On these models, there may be an intermittent Neutral condition at highway speeds or in fourth gear.

This condition may be caused by 3-2 manual downshift valve sticking. To correct this condition, proceed as follows:

1. Inspect fluid and pan for signs of distressed clutches or debris.
2. Remove and disassembly 1-2 and 2-3 accumulator housing assembly.
3. Inspect housing for signs of scoring,

sediment or abnormalities that might cause debris.

4. Repair as necessary.
5. Inspect 2-3 and 3-2 valve line. If valves are scored, replace control valve body.

TIGHTENING SPECIFICATIONS

Component	Torque/Ft. Lbs.
ACHIEVA, SKYLARK & 1997-98 GRAND AM	
Case Cover	18
Case Side Cover	96①
Cooler Pipes At Case	16
Cooler Pipes At Radiator	20
Flywheel To Torque Converter Bolts	46
Oil Pan	96–108①
Park/Neutral Position Switch To Case	18
Shift Lever To Transaxle Nut	15
Speed Sensor Housing To Case	96①
Transaxle To Engine	66
Valve Body To Case	15–20
BONNEVILLE, LESABRE, LSS, PARK AVENUE & EIGHTY-EIGHT	
Flywheel Cover	11
Governor Cover	11
Left Front And righthand Rear Mount To Transaxle	40
Left Rear Mount To Transaxle	30
Neutral Start & Back-Up Switch	20
Oil Cooler Lines At Radiator	20
Oil Cooler Lines At Transaxle	16
Starter Bolts	32
Throttle Cable To Transaxle	72①
Torque Converter Bolts	46
Transaxle Mount To Frame Nuts	30
Transaxle To Engine Bolts	55
Wheel Lug Nuts	100
CENTURY	
Bracket To Transaxle Bolt	41
Channel Plate Attaching Bolts	41
Console Shift Control Assembly Nut	18
Fill Tube Bolt	18
Flywheel Cover Bolts	84①
Governor Housing Bolts	96①
Modulator retaining bolt	20
Mount To Bracket Nut	35
Oil Pan Bolts	12
Park/Neutral Switch Bolts	21
Shift Control Bracket	18
Shift Control Lever	15
TCC Solenoid Screws	10
Torque Converter Bolts	46
Transaxle Case Side Cover	10
Transaxle Cooler Pipe Clip Bolt	35
Transaxle Cooler Pipe To Radiator	13
Valve Body Bolts	10
Wheel Lug Nuts	100
CUTLASS SUPREME, GRAND PRIX, IMPALA, INTRIGUE, LUMINA, MONTE CARLO & REGAL	
Auxiliary Oil Cooler Bolt	18
Auxiliary Oil Cooler Nut	84①
Bracket To Transaxle Front Bolts	35

Continued

TIGHTENING SPECIFICATIONS—Continued

Component	Torque/Ft. Lbs.
CUTLASS SUPREME, GRAND PRIX, IMPALA, INTRIGUE, LUMINA, MONTE CARLO & REGAL	
Bracket To Transaxle Top Bolt	61
Console Shift Control Nut	18
Engine To Transaxle Brace Bolt	35
Fill Tube Bolt	18
Flywheel Cover Bolt	84①
Governor Housing Bolts	96①
Modulator Retaining Bolt	18
Mount To Support Nut	35
Neutral Start Switch	18
Oil Cooler Line Clip Bolt	35
Oil Cooler Line To Radiator	13
Oil Pan Bolts	13
Oil Scoop Retaining Bolt	72①
Shift Control Bracket	18
Shift Control Lever	15
Support Frame Bolt	38
Support Frame Nut	32
TCC Solenoid Screws	10
Throttle Cable Bolt	84①
Torque Converter Bolt	44
Transaxle Case Side Cover	10
Transaxle To Engine Bolts	55
Valve Body Bolts	10
Wheel Lug Nuts	100
RIVIERA	
Accumulator Assembly Attaching Bolt	20
Auxiliary Oil Cooler Pipe Fitting	20
Brace To Engine Bracket Bolt	37
Brace To Transaxle Bolt	33
Bracket To Transaxle Mount Nut	30
Case Extension Bolt	27
Case Side Cover Bolt	7–10
Engine Bracket To Engine Bolt	70
Engine To Transaxle Bolt	55
Extension Cover Bolt	22–30
Filler Tube Bracket Bolt	15
Flywheel Cover Bolt	10
Frame Nut	30
Frame To Body Bolt	83
Front Side Of Bracket To Transaxle Bolt/Stud	47
Front Top Of Bracket To Transaxle/Engine Bolt	55
Modulator Bolt	15–20
Neutral Start Switch Bolt	20
Neutral Start Switch Shift Lever Nut	15
Oil Cooler Line Ball Check Fitting At Transaxle	43
Oil Cooler Line To Radiator	20
Oil Cooler Line To Transaxle	33
Oil Pan Bolt	12–13
Oil Scoop Bolt	44–97①
Rear Top Of Bracket To Transaxle Bolt	43
Shift Control Cable Bracket To Transaxle	18
Shift Lever To Neutral Start Switch	15
Speed Sensor To Case Extension Bolt	96①

Continued

TIGHTENING SPECIFICATIONS—Continued

Component	Torque/Ft. Lbs.
RIVIERA	
Starter Bolts	32
Torque Converter Bolts	46②
Transaxle Mount To Body Rail Bolt	37
Transaxle To Body Rail Mount, Bracket to Transaxle Bolt	55
Transaxle To Body Rail Mount, Nut	29
Transaxle To Engine Bolt	55
Transaxle To Subframe Mount Bolt	75
Transaxle To Subframe Mount, Bracket to Engine Bolt	42
Transaxle To Subframe Mount, Bracket to Frame Bolt & Nuts	53
Wheel Lug Nuts	100

① — Inch lbs.
② — Tighten in two steps.

Turbo Hydra-Matic 4T80-E Automatic Transaxle

NOTE: On Air Bag Equipped Models, Refer To " Air Bag System Precautions" Located In The Front Of This Manual For System Disarming & Arming Procedures.

NOTE: Refer To "Computer Relearn Procedures " Located In The Front Of This Manual For Computer Relearn Procedures.

NOTE: Prior To Performing Any Service Operations Listed In This Section, Consult The "Technical Service Bulletins " Section For Related Information.

INDEX

PRECAUTIONS

AIR BAG SYSTEMS

Refer to "Air Bag System Precautions" in the front of this manual for system disarming and arming procedures.

BATTERY GROUND CABLE

Prior to service, disconnect battery ground cable and isolate as required.

IDENTIFICATION

Refer to **Fig. 1** for transaxle identification location.

DESCRIPTION

The 4T80–E transaxle, **Fig. 2,** is a fully automatic electronically controlled transaxle. It has four forward ranges, including overdrive. Two shift solenoids, operated by the PCM, control shift points. Oil pressure is supplied by three gear type oil pumps and regulated by a transaxle pressure control solenoid (force motor) which is controlled by the PCM. Shift schedule and TCC apply rates, which are influenced by many sensor inputs, are controlled by the PCM.

TROUBLESHOOTING

Refer to **Figs. 3 through 54** for troubleshooting.

BRAKE TRANSAXLE SHIFT INTERLOCK (BTSI)

Refer to wiring diagrams, **Figs. 55 through 57** and diagnosis charts, **Figs. 58 through 60,** to diagnose the BTSI system.

For the 1998–2000 Seville, Brake Transaxle Shift Interlock (BTSI) is an integral part of the Park Lock Cable and can not be serviced separately. Refer to "Park Lock Cable Replacement," in this section.

MAINTENANCE

Refer to "Lubricant Data Chart" in the appropriate chassis chapter of this manual for transmission fluid specifications.

FLUID CHECK

Cold Transaxle Fluid

This procedure is valid when vehicle is cold, has not been driven and transmission fluid temperature is between 70–90°F. The vehicle should be parked on a level surface. Approximately five minutes are available to finish this procedure before cold temperature is exceeded and test becomes invalid.

1. Apply brake and start engine.
2. Hold brake and move shifter through each gear range, pausing three seconds in each. Return shifter to Park.
3. Apply parking brake and allow engine to idle for two to three minutes.
4. For remainder of test, shifter should be in Park, parking brake should be applied and foot brake NOT applied (foot brake will affect oil level).
5. Remove dipstick and wipe clean, then insert dipstick for three seconds and pull out.
6. Check both sides of dipstick. Fluid level on lower side must be in cold range of indicator.
7. If level is in cold range, no level adjustment is necessary.
8. If level is not in cold range, add fluid until level reaches middle of cold range. Transaxle will need to be warmed and fluid level checked again. Refer to "Hot Transaxle Fluid" checking procedure.

Hot Transaxle Fluid

Wait at least 30 minutes before checking transaxle fluid if the vehicle has been driven when the outside temperature is above 90°F, at high speed for an extended period of time and/or in heavy traffic (especially in hot weather). To obtain an accurate reading, the fluid must be at normal operating temperature (180°–200°F). Bring the vehicle up to operating temperature by driving about 15 miles when outside temperature is above 50 if.

1. Park vehicle on level surface and place shifter in Park.
2. Apply brake, move shifter through each gear range, pausing for three seconds in each range and place shifter in Park.
3. Apply parking brake and allow engine to idle for three to five minutes.
4. For remainder of test, shifter should be in Park, parking brake should be applied and foot brake should NOT be on applied (foot brake will affect oil level).
5. Remove dipstick and wipe clean, then insert dipstick for three seconds and pull out.
6. Check both sides of dipstick. Fluid level on lower side must be in hot range of indicator.
7. If level is in hot range, no level adjustment is necessary.
8. If level is not in hot range, add fluid until level reaches middle of hot range.

FLUID CHANGE

1. Raise and support vehicle, then place drain pan under transaxle oil pan.
2. Loosen bottom pan bolts in proper sequence, **Figs. 61 through 63** and drain fluid into drain pan.
3. Removing oil pan will only partially drain transaxle fluid. Remaining fluid is held in side cover and torque converter; removing drain plug in case after fluid pan removal will drain fluid from side cover. It is not necessary to drain torque converter during most service procedures.
4. Remove oil pan and transaxle case bolts, pan and gasket.
5. Remove left and righthand scavenger screens, **Fig. 64.**
6. Inspect oil pan and transaxle case for dents or nicks in sealing surface, replacing if damaged.
7. Inspect bolts for thread damage.
8. Reverse procedure to install, noting the following:
   a. Install new fluid pan gasket.
   b. Add transaxle fluid. Refer to "Fluid Check" as outlined.
   c. Reset transaxle oil life indicator if complete fluid change was necessary. Refer to "Resetting Transaxle Oil Life Indicator" as outlined.

RESETTING TRANSAXLE OIL LIFE INDICATOR

The PCM maintains a value for transaxle oil life which indicates the percentage of oil life remaining and is calculated based on transaxle temperature and speed. When the vehicle is new, the transaxle oil life is 100%; as mileage accumulates, oil life will eventually decrease to 0%. When the value reaches 1%, the CCDIC displays the message CHANGE TRANSAXLE OIL.

The oil life indicator should be reset to 100% when transaxle oil is changed or when the transaxle is replaced. Transaxle oil life value should be recorded prior to PCM replacement and programmed into the new PCM. To reset the transaxle oil life indicator, proceed as follows:

1. Turn ignition switch to Run position.
2. Display TRANSAXLE OIL LIFE on driver information center.
3. Press and hold Reset until oil life changes to 100%.

TRANSAXLE OIL COOLER FLUSH

Use cooler flusher tool No. J-35944, **Fig. 65,** and flushing solution funnel tool No. J-35944-20, or equivalents. Do not substitute the recommended flushing solution. The use of other solutions can result in damage to the tool, components or other improper flushing of the cooler. **Air supply must be equipped with a water/oil filter and must not exceed 120 psi. Excess air pressure may rupture the flushing tool or cooler, causing personal injury.**

1. Fill flushing tool No. J-35944–A, or equivalent, with 20–21 ounces of flushing solution J-35944-20, or equivalent. **Do not overfill.**
2. Secure cap and pressurize can to 80–120 psi.
3. Connect discharge hose to transaxle fitting end of oil cooler pipe that goes to top fitting at radiator and clip discharge hose into drain container.
4. Mount flushing tool to undercarriage using hook provided.
5. Connect hose from flushing tool to remaining oil cooler pipe and with water valve (on flushing tool) in Off position, connect water hose from water supply to flushing tool.
6. Open water supply at faucet and switch water valve (on flushing tool) to On position and allow water to flow through oil cooler for 10 seconds. **If water does not flow through cooler, do not continue with flushing procedure; cooling system may be plugged. Excess pressure may cause personal injury. Replacement of cooler pipe and/or cooler may be necessary.**
7. Switch water valve (on flushing tool) to Off position and clip discharge hose into a five gallon pail with a lid, or place

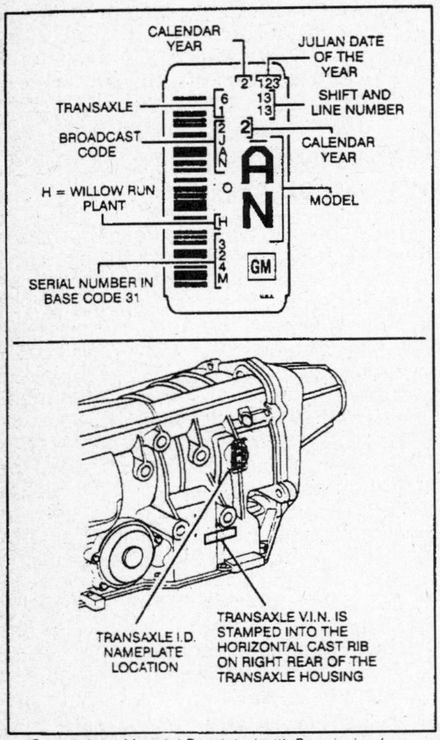

Copyrighted Material Reprinted with Permission from Hydra-Matic Div., GM Corp.

THA059000035000X

Fig. 1 Transaxle identification location

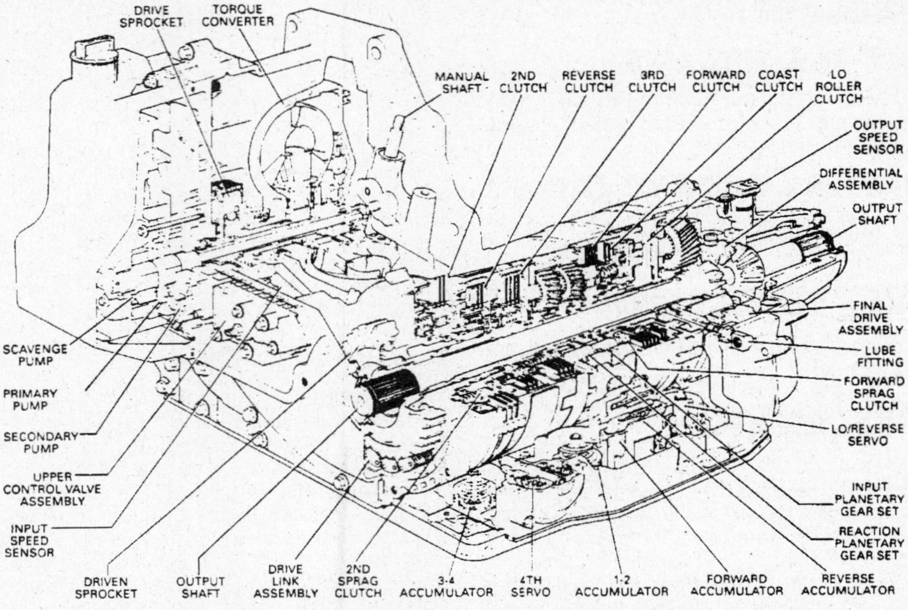

Copyrighted Material Reprinted with Permission from Hydra-Matic Div., GM Corp.

THA059300036000X

Fig. 2 Cross-sectional view of 4T80-E transaxle

Checks	Action
DEFINITION: High Line Pressure	
Pressure Reg. Valve	Stuck at high torque signal due to undersized bore, sediment or Pressure Control Solenoid failure.
Pressure Control Solenoid (PCS)	• Failed OFF, intermittent short • Loose connector
PCS Feed Valve	Stuck
Pressure Reg. Boost Valve	Stuck open
TFP Val. Position Sw.	Loose connector
Transmission Wiring Harness	Loose connection at vehicle harness
Checkballs	Missing
Final Drive Internal Gear Snap Ring	Missing
Actuator Feed Limit Valve	Stuck open

GC5029800892000X

Fig. 3 Harsh shifts

Checks	Action
DEFINITION: Inadequate Lube or Low Line Pressure	
Scavenge Pump Body	Leakage at the gasket or pump body
Scavenge Pipe	Restriction
Scavenge Pipe Seal	Damaged, cut or leaking
Primary Pump Body	Leakage at the gasket or pump body
Scavenge Screens	Clogged
Pressure Reg. Valve	Stuck due to sediment
Secondary Pump Body	Leakage at the gasket or pump body
Transmission Fluid	Low level
Cooler Lines	Clogged or restricted

GC5029800893000X

Fig. 4 Low line pressure

Checks	Action
1-2 Shift Solenoid Valve	• Stuck OFF • Pinched wire to ground
Pressure Control Solenoid	• Inoperative • Leakage • Pinched wire to ground
Starts at HI Line only, Driven Sprocket Support	Staked checkball missing

GC5029800894000X

Fig. 5 Second gear starts

a shop towel over end of discharge hose to prevent splash. **Discharge will foam when solution and water mix.**

8. Switch water valve (on flushing tool) to On position and depress trigger on handle. **Use bale clip provided on handle to hold trigger.**
9. Flush cooler for two minutes while applying air to air valve for 3–5 seconds. **Apply air at 15–20 seconds intervals to create surging action.**
10. Release trigger and switch water valve (on flushing tool) to Off position and disconnect hoses from cooler pipes.
11. Reverse positions and reconnect and reconnect to cooler pipes to back flush system.
12. Repeat Steps 8 and 9 and release trigger and allow water to flow to rinse oil cooler for one minute.
13. Switch water valve (on flushing tool) to Off position and turn off water supply at faucet.
14. Dry system with compressed air for two minutes (minimum) or until there is no moisture coming from discharge hose. Use an air chuck clip, if available.
15. **Excess residual moisture may corrode cooler, pipes and damage transaxle. If Steps 14 through 18 cannot be completed at this time, use a squirt type oil can filled with transmission fluid to rinse cooler and pipes.**
16. Connect cooler feed pipe to transaxle (top connector is feed, bottom connector is cooler return).
17. Attach discharge hose to cooler return pipe and place into oil drain container.
18. Fill transaxle to appropriate level with transmission fluid (Dexron IIE).
19. Start engine and allow to run for 30 seconds. A minimum of two quarts must flow through discharge hose.
20. If fluid flow is not sufficient, disconnect oil feed line at radiator and restart engine and check flow rate. If flow rate is

Checks	Action
Fluid Level	Too high or too low
Line Pressure	Too low
Scavenge Pump	Gears worn or broken
Primary Pump	Gears worn or broken
Scavenge Pipe	Debris in pipe
Scavenge Pipe Seal	Cut or damaged
Reverse Clutch Seals	Cut, damaged or leaking
Reverse Clutch Plates	Damaged or burned
Reverse Band	Damaged, burned, slipping
Reverse Servo Piston	Damaged or cracked
Reverse Servo Seals	Cut, damaged or leaking
Reverse Servo Pin	Binding, too short
Reverse Band Anchor Pins	Loose, missing

GC5029800895000X

Fig. 6 Transmission slips in reverse

Checks	Action
Checkballs	Missing from FWD/coast clutch
Lo/Rev Servo Apply Pin	Apply pin damage
1-2 Shift Valve	Stuck in upshifted position
FWD/CC Support Seals	Damaged
FWD/CC Studs	Damaged, broken
Lo Roller Clutch	Worn or damaged
1-2 Shift Solenoid Valve	• Debris, or failed OFF • Pinched or damaged wires, inoperative
Forward Clutch Piston	Damaged or cracked

GC5029800897010X

Fig. 8 No first, second, third or fourth (Part 1 of 2)

Checks	Action
2nd Clutch Plates	Burned or damaged
2nd Clutch Piston/Seals	• Cracked or damaged • Rolled, damaged or leaking
2nd Clutch Return Springs	Broken, out of position
2nd Sprag	Damaged, not holding
1-2 Shift Solenoid Valve	Stuck ON
1-2 Shift Valve	Stuck in 1st gear

GC5029800898000X

Fig. 9 No second or third gear

Checks	Action
1-2 Shift Solenoid Valve	• Inoperative • Debris • Pinched wires
4th Band	Burned, slipping, missing
4th Servo Pin	Broken, seized
4th Servo Piston	Damaged
4th Servo Seals	Rolled, cut or damaged
4th Servo Cover	Cracked
3-4 Shift Valve Bore Plug	Misassembled

GC5029800900000X

Fig. 11 No fourth gear

Checks	Action
1-2 and 2-3 Shift Solenoid Valves	• O-ring seal damage • No compression

GC5029800902000X

Fig. 13 Inconsistent shifts

Checks	Action
Oil Transfer Sleeve	Misaligned
Drive Link Assembly	Broken, slipping
Drive and Driven Sprockets	Damaged
Drive Axle	Splines damaged

GC5029800904000X

Fig. 15 No engine braking

Checks	Action
4th Band	Slipping, burned
4th Band Servo Pin	Stuck, broken
4th Servo Piston	Damaged, cracked
4th Servo Seals	Cut, rolled or damaged
Coast Clutch Plates	Burned, damaged
Coast Clutch Seal/Checkball	Cut, worn or nicked
Transmission Fluid Pressure Manual Valve Position Switch	Inoperative
Coast Clutch Support Seals	Damaged, missing

GC5029800906000X

Fig. 17 No overrun braking in second gear

Checks	Action
Line Pressure	Too low
Pressure Control Solenoid	Stuck ON
Pressure Control Solenoid Clamp	Broken clamp causing leakage
Calibration Prom	Incorrect

GC5029800896000X

Fig. 7 Soft shifts

Checks	Action
Forward Clutch Piston Seals	Rolled, cut or damaged
Support Housing Seal Rings	Leaking, damaged or cut
Forward Sprag	Damaged, not holding
Checkball No. 8	Missing

GC5029800897020X

Fig. 8 No first, second, third or fourth (Part 2 of 2)

Checks	Action
3-4 Shift Valve Bore Plug	Misassembled
Driven Sprocket Support	Exhaust valve cup plug or valve improperly installed
3rd Clutch Plates	Burned, splines damaged
3rd Clutch Piston	Cracked, damaged, checkball damage
3rd Clutch Seals on Piston	Cut or rolled
Checkballs	Missing or stuck
2-3 Shift Solenoid Valve	• Debris • Wires pinched or damaged • Inoperative
1-2 Shift Solenoid Valve	• Debris • Wires pinched or damaged • Inoperative

GC5029800899000X

Fig. 10 No third gear

Checks	Action
Lo Roller Clutch	Worn or damaged
Forward Sprag	Damaged, not holding
Oil Transfer Sleeve	Misaligned, damaged, leaking
Forward Clutch Plates	Burned, damaged
Forward Clutch Piston Seals	Leaking, cut or rolled
Detent Lever	Misaligned
FWD/Coast Housing	Broken or spline damage
Forward Clutch Piston	Cracked or damaged
1-2 and/or 2-3 Shift Solenoid Valve	• Debris • Pinched or damaged wires • Inoperative
Manual Valve	Misaligned
Checkball in Housing	Leaking

GC5029800901000X

Fig. 12 No first gear

Checks	Action
2-3 Shift Solenoid Valve	• Stuck ON • Pinched wire to ground

GC5029800903000X

Fig. 14 Third & fourth gears only

Checks	Action
Coast Clutch Plates	Burned or damaged
Coast Clutch Seal/Checkball	Cut, worn or nicked
Forward Clutch Housing	• Splines damaged • Housing cracked
Fluid Level	• Low • Stuck in upshift position
3-4 Shift Valve	Debris, stuck
1-2 Shift Solenoid Valve	Debris, stuck

GC5029800905000X

Fig. 16 No overrun braking in third gear

Checks	Action
Transmission Fluid Pressure Manual Valve Position Switch	Inoperative
Coast Clutch Plates	Burned, damaged
Coast Clutch Seal/Checkball	Cut, worn or nicked
Checkball No. 6	Missing
Lo/Reverse Band	Slipping, burned, damaged
Lo/Reverse Servo Piston	Damaged, seized
Lo/Reverse Servo Seals	Leaking, rolled

GC5029800907000X

Fig. 18 No engine braking in first gear

Checks	Action
DEFINITION: Forward Motion in Neutral	
Manual Valve	Mispositioned or stuck
Forward Clutch Springs	Jammed
Forward Clutch Piston	Jammed
Forward Clutch Plates	Seized or jammed
Forward Clutch Housing	Feed hole plugged, inspect tower
Forward/Coast Clutch Support Hub	Holes plugged
Shift Linkage	• Mispositioned • Disconnected

GC5029800908000X

Fig. 19 Forward motion in Neutral

Checks	Action
Torque Converter	• Broken lug, failed lug weld • Sheared lug bolts • Worn turbine shaft splines • Low fluid • Pump hub cracked or broken • Internal failure • Closure weld failure • Cover cracked at weld
Scavenger, Primary Pumps	Seized, broken pump gears
Pump Shaft	Broken
Channel Plates	Damaged
Gaskets	Damaged
Scavenge Pipe Seal	Damaged or missing
Drive and Driven Sprockets	Broken
Drive Link Assembly	Broken
Driven Sprocket Support	Damaged, porosity, leaking
Final Drive	Damaged, splines worn
Final Drive Pinions	• Spalled pins or pinions • Lack of lube
Forward Sprag Clutch	Worn, broken or locked
Forward/Coast Clutch Support	No lube
Manual Valve and Link	Not attached to detent lever
Turbine Shaft	Dislodged, stripped splines

GC5029800911000X

Fig. 22 Loss of drive

Checks	Action
Manual Valve	Not engaged to detent lever
Detent Roller Pin	Missing, damaged
Detent Roller	Broken or disconnected
Detent Spring	Broken or disconnected
Manual Detent Pivot	Loose or missing
Manual Shaft	Flats not parallel
Indicator Linkage	Misadjusted

GC5029800914000X

Fig. 25 Shift lever indicates wrong gear

Checks	Action
Turbine Shaft to Drive Sprocket Support O-Ring Seal	Worn or damaged
TCC Solenoid Valve	Malfunction
Transmission Fluid	Low
Converter Feed Limit Valve	Sticking

GC5029800916000X

Fig. 27 Soft TCC apply

Checks	Action
Transmission Fluid Temperature Sensor	Shorted

GC5029800917000X

Fig. 28 Early TCC engagement

Checks	Action
Converter Feed Limit Valve	Valve is stuck open, due to sediment or undersized bore

GC5029800919000X

Fig. 30 Converter ballooning

Checks	Action
TCC	Stuck ON or dragging
TCC Solenoid Valve	• Stuck ON • Pinched wire to ground • Inoperative
Converter Feed Limit Valve	Stuck open
Turbine Shaft	Spline damaged

GC5029800909000X

Fig. 20 Engine stall

Checks	Action
Transmission	Low fluid
1-2 and 2-3 Shift Solenoid Valves	2nd gear starts
TCC System	TCC Stuck ON or dragging
Torque Converter	Debris
Turbine Shaft	Bushing damage

GC5029800910000X

Fig. 21 Loss of power

Checks	Action
Manual Valve	• Not engaged to detent lever • Stuck in wrong position
Transmission Range Switch	Not working, mispositioned

GC5029800912000X

Fig. 23 Engine starts in gear

Checks	Action
Detent Lever	Nut loose or missing
Manual Valve	Stuck
Spacer Plate/Gaskets	Blocked holes
Control Valve Bodies, Channel Plate, Case	Blocked channels

GC5029800913000X

Fig. 24 No gear selection

Checks	Action
TCC Solenoid Valve	• Stuck OFF • O-ring failed • No voltage to solenoid • Poor connection
PCM	No signal to solenoid
Brake Switch	• Contact corroded • Poor connection • Pinched wire • Misadjusted • No supply voltage
TCC Control Valve	Stuck OFF due to sediment or undersized bore
TCC Regulating Valve	Stuck OFF due to sediment or undersized bore
TCC Feed Valve	Stuck OFF due to sediment or undersized bore
3rd Clutch Filter Screen	Clogged
Turbine Shaft to Drive Sprocket Support O-Ring Seal	• Damaged or leaking • Worn
Torque Converter	• Ballooning • TCC not engaging fully or slipping

GC5029800915000X

Fig. 26 No TCC apply

Checks	Action
TCC Solenoid Valve	Stuck ON due to debris
Converter Feed Limit Valve	Stuck ON due to debris

GC5029800918000X

Fig. 29 TCC not disengaging

Checks	Action
Drive Sprocket Support	• Broken or detached from case • Spline damage

GC5029800920000X

Fig. 31 No torque multiplication

Checks	Action
Reaction Carrier Shell	Missing, teeth damaged
Lo/Reverse Anchor Pin	Anchor pin broken or not positioned
Driven Sprocket Support	• Porosity or broken • Feed holes blocked
Driven Sprocket Support Seals	Leaking
Driven Sprocket Support Bolts	Loose, not in grooves, mislocated
Reverse Band	Broken, worn not anchored
Reverse Band Apply Pin	• Too short or binding in case • Broken
Reverse Clutch Piston	Binding in case
Reverse Clutch Piston Seals	Leaking, damaged or worn
Checkball in Piston	Missing
Case Cover Gaskets	Damaged or displaced
Case Cover	Damaged
Fluid Pressure	Too low
Reverse Clutch Steel Plates	Splines worn
Reverse Clutch Fiber Plates	Splines or friction material worn
Reverse Clutch Spring Assembly	Jammed
Reverse Clutch Housing	Cracked
Snap Ring	Out

GC5029800921000X

Fig. 32 No reverse

Checks	Action
Transmission Fluid Pressure Manual Valve Position Switch	Inoperative
Pressure Regulator Boost Valve	Stuck in bushing
Lateral Accelerometer	Circuit Malfunction — Scewed Sensor

GC5029800923000X

Fig. 34 Extended or delayed upshifts

Checks	Action
Torque Converter	• Loose lug bolts • Out of balance • Internal failure
Transmission/Engine	Misaligned
Case Extension	Axle support bushing worn

GC5029800925000X

Fig. 36 Noise

Checks	Action
DEFINITION: A high pitch whine which will intensify with engine RPM or which is Oil Pressure sensitive	
Oil Pump System	Verify that the noise is internal to the oil pump during a preliminary oil pressure check. An increase in line pressure will vary an oil pump noise.

GC5029800927000X

Fig. 38 Whine noise varying with RPM or fluid pressure

Checks	Action
Trace cooler pipes and check for binding or contact at the radiator other than the cooler pipe connectors	Verify pressure buzz by watching for a needle vibration on the pressure gauge. Road test may be necessary.

GC5029800929000X

Fig. 40 Buzz noise or high frequency rattle sound

Checks	Action
DEFINITION: A final drive noise or hum that is most noticeable under light throttle acceleration or turns	
• Final Drive Gear Set	• Worn, planet pinions or washers
• Final Drive Internal Gear	• Worn, tooth damage
• Differential Carrier	• Gears worn or pitted
• Differential Side Gears	• Thrust washer damage

GC5029800931000X

Fig. 42 Final drive noise or hum noise

Checks	Action
Torque Converter	• Out of balance • Internal failure
Transmission/Engine	Misaligned
Case Extension	Axle support bushing worn
Turbine Shaft	Worn bushing
Output Shaft	Out of balance

GC5029800933000X

Fig. 44 Vibration diagnosis

Checks	Action
Seal on Indicator	• Cut or nicked • Missing

GC5029800935000X

Fig. 46 Leak at fluid fill indicator

Checks	Action
Detent Spring	Weak or broken
Detent Lever	Mislocated or broken
Actuator Rod	• Bent • Guide damaged
Park Pawl Pivot Pin	Missing
Parking Lock Gear	Damaged teeth
Park Pawl	Damaged tooth
Manual Linkage	Misadjusted or disconnected

GC5029800922000X

Fig. 33 Does not stay in Park

Checks	Action
Cooler Circuit Lines	Blocked or leaking
Cooler Fittings	Blocked or leaking
Spacer Plate/Gaskets	Holes missing, off location
Scavenger Pipe	• Damaged, clogged • Poor seal at pipe
Control Valve Bodies	Loose, broken or missing bolts
Transmission Fluid Filter	Sitting in side cover
Filter Seal	Cut damaged neck seal
Left and Right Scavenge Screens	Clogged or not seated in case

GC5029800924000X

Fig. 35 Transaxle seized

Checks	Action
DEFINITION: A whine which may be RPM load sensitive or which ceases when the TCC engages	
Torque Converter	Verify that the noise is internal to the torque converter by placing your left foot on the brake with the gear selector in Drive. Momentarily stall the engine. Torque converter noise increases under load.

GC5029800926000X

Fig. 37 Noise in all ranges

Checks	Action
DEFINITION: A popping noise similar to popcorn popping	
Oil Pump System	• Pump cavitation, indicated by bubbles on fluid level indicator • Transmission fluid strainer for filter seam leak • Transmission fluid strainer seal for proper positioning or cut seal

GC5029800928000X

Fig. 39 Popping noise

Checks	Action
DEFINITION: A whine or growl that increases and fades with vehicle speed and is most noticeable under light acceleration	
Drive Link Assembly System	Verify noise from sprockets and/or drive link assembly chain by placing your left foot on the brake and moving the gear selector from Park or Reverse. If the noise stops, check items below:
Drive Link Assembly Chain	Stretched
Drive Sprocket and Driven Sprocket	• Teeth broken or sheared • Bearing surfaces nicked or scored • Bearing race or roller bearing surfaces on gear Support Inner Bearings rough or pitted • Bearing damage
Drive Sprocket Support and Driven Sprocket Support	Bearing outer race support rough or nicked

GC5029800930000X

Fig. 41 Whine/growl noise that changes w/vehicle speed

Checks	Action
Final Drive Sun Gear	Gears worn or damaged
Final Drive Pinions	Gears worn or damaged

GC5029800932000X

Fig. 43 Noise in first, second, third or fourth

Checks	Action
Bottom Pan	Damaged or not flat
Bottom Pan Gasket	Damaged or off location
Case	Porosity or cracked
Bottom Pan to Case Bolts	• Flange inside out, damage • High or low torque

GC5029800934000X

Fig. 45 Leak at bottom pan

Checks	Action
Vehicle Speed Sensor O-Ring Seal	Cut, nicked or missing

GC5029800936000X

Fig. 47 Leak at vehicle speed sensor

Checks	Action
Electrical connector	• Damaged or not seated • Cut or nicked • Missing, porosity
O-Ring Seal	• Damaged or not seated • Cut or nicked • Missing, porosity
Case	Porosity or cracked

GC5029800937000X

Fig. 48 Leak at electrical connector

Checks	Action
Case extension	Porosity or cracked
Case	Porosity or cracked
Case Extension to Case Seal	• Cut or nicked • Missing
Case Extension to Case Bolts	• Low torque • Missing

GC5029800939000X

Fig. 50 Leak at case extension

Checks	Action
Converter Hub Seal Assembly	• Cut, nicked or worn • Missing garter spring
Torque Converter Bolt	• Low torque • Damaged hub

GC5029800941000X

Fig. 52 Leak at converter seal

Checks	Action
Transmission Fluid	• Contaminated with antifreeze • Transmission overfilled
Engine	Overheated
Transmission Fluid Filter	Cracked or not seated
Filter Seal	Damaged or not seated
Vehicle	Overloaded
Left and Right Scavenge Screens	Clogged

GC5029800943000X

Fig. 54 Fluid foaming

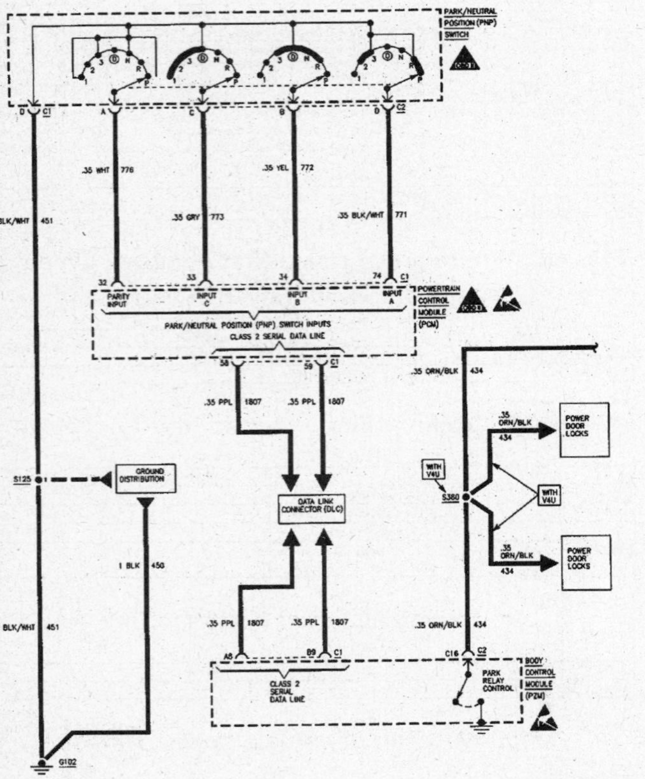

GC5029700587010X

Fig. 55 BTSI system wiring circuit (Part 1 of 2). 1997 DeVille, Eldorado & Seville

Checks	Action
Cooler Connectors	• Stripped threads • Damaged flare, seal damage • High or low torque
Case	• Stripped threads • Porosity • Debris in threads

GC5029800938000X

Fig. 49 Leak at cooler connections

Checks	Action
Manual Shaft Seal	• Cut or nicked • Not seated
Linkage	Misadjusted

GC5029800940000X

Fig. 51 Leak at manual shift

Checks	Action
Tri-Pot Joint	Corrosion on Tri-Pot housing at mating surface

GC5029800942000X

Fig. 53 Leak at drive axle seal

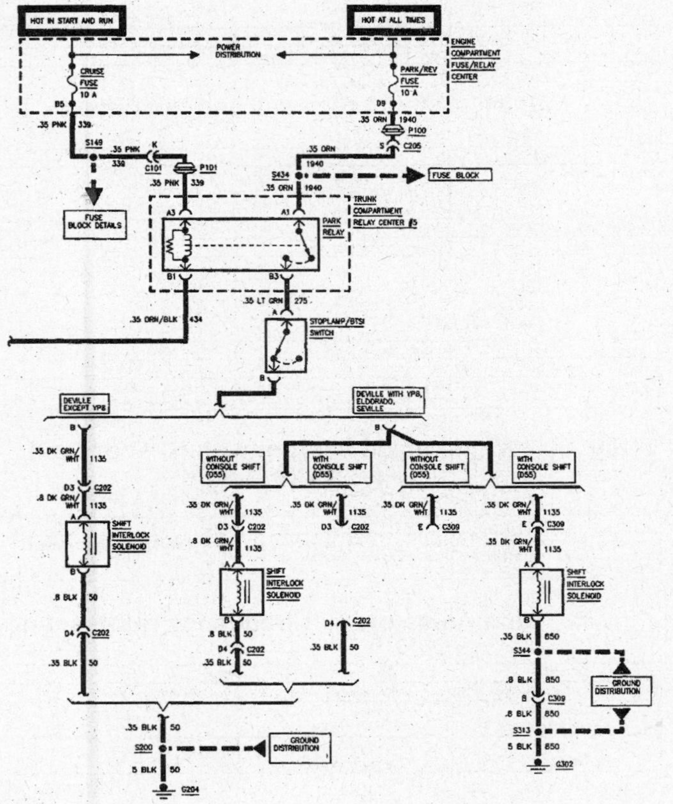

GC5029700587020X

Fig. 55 BTSI system wiring circuit (Part 2 of 2). 1997 DeVille, Eldorado & Seville

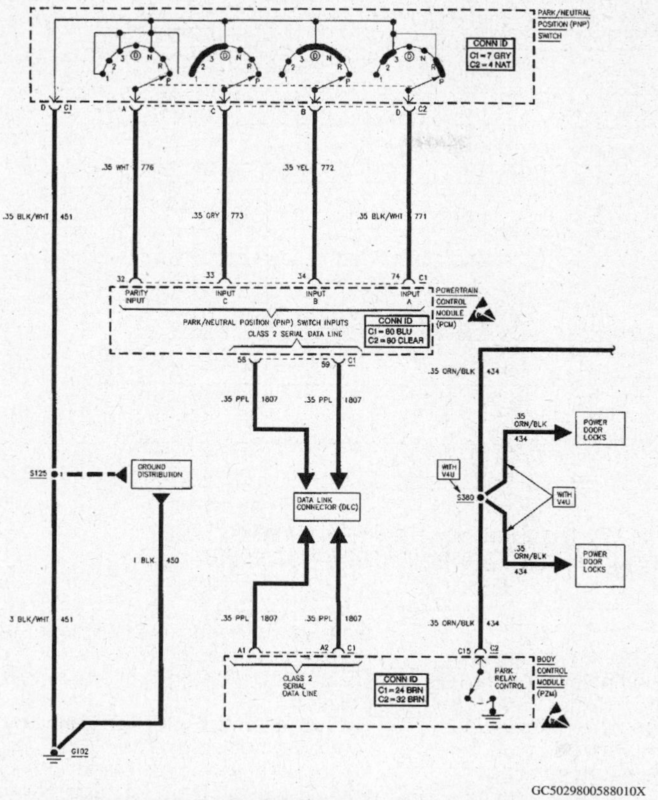

GC5029800588010X

Fig. 56 BTSI system wiring circuit (Part 1 of 2). 1998-99 DeVille & Eldorado

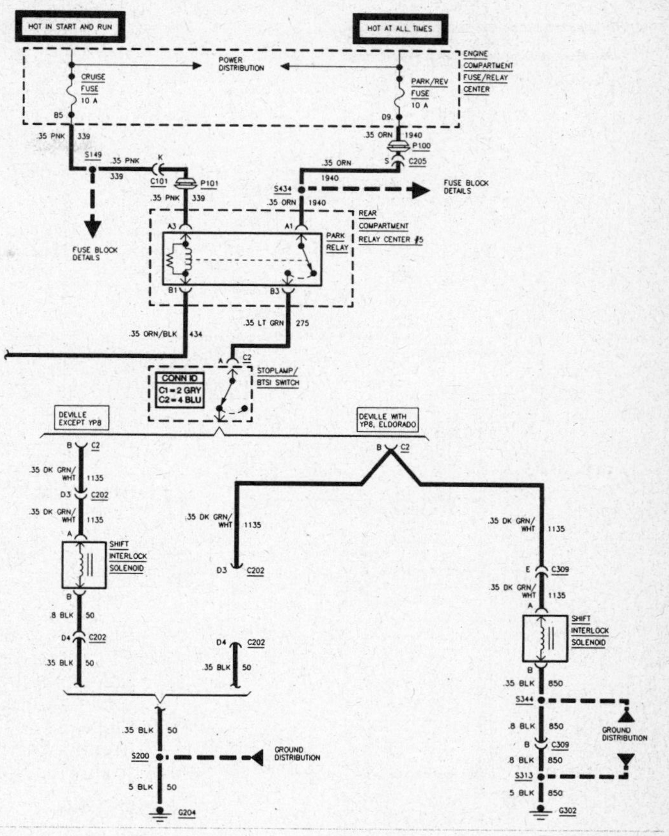

GC5029800588020X

Fig. 56 BTSI system wiring circuit (Part 2 of 2). 1998-99 DeVille & Eldorado

not sufficient, inspect oil cooler feed and transaxle for cause. If flow rate is sufficient, repeat oil cooler flushing and fluid flow check procedures. If flow is not sufficient, replace oil cooler.

21. Remove discharge hose and connect cooler return pipe to transaxle and fill transaxle to proper fluid level as outlined.
22. Thoroughly clean flushing tool with water. **Do not store tool with flushing solution in tank.**

RESETTING TRANSAXLE ADAPTS

The PCM maintains five transaxle adapt parameters for transaxle control. The line pressure control system has the ability to continuously adapt line pressure thereby compensating for normal wear of clutch plates, seals and springs. The five types of transaxle adapts are: upshift adapt (monitors automatic transaxle input shaft speed sensor and vehicle speed sensor to monitor when shift occurs), steady state adapt (monitors speed sensor inputs after a shift to calculate amount of slippage in that gear), garage shift adapt (monitors speed sensor inputs to calculate if shift occurs too fast or too slow), WOT 1-2 adapt (monitors VSS and RPM during a 1-2 WOT shift), learn tap (accelerated PLM learn mode, technician must road test vehicle for 15 minutes, normal time 2–3 hours). The transaxle may experience harsh, soft or mushy shifts for up to two days after adapt parameters have been reset. Transaxle adapts must be reset when a transaxle overhaul or replacement has taken place. To reset PCM adapts, proceed as follows:

1. Connect a suitable scan tool to DLC.
2. Select miscellaneous test.
3. Select A/T outputs and clear or reset all adapts.

ADJUSTMENTS

SHIFT CONTROL CABLE

Aurora, Deville, Eldorado & 1997 Seville

1. Remove air cleaner duct and housing.
2. Use a flat head screwdriver to pry lock button on shifter cable to unlocked position, **Fig. 66.**
3. Place transaxle shifter in Neutral and select Neutral position at lever on transaxle manual shaft.
4. Depress lock button on shifter cable into Locked position, **Fig. 66.**
5. Install air cleaner duct and housing.

1998–2000 Seville

1. Move driver's seat to its most rearward position, then remove left side console trim plate.
2. Move shifter lever to N neutral position, then insert socket through hole in side of console and loosen shift control cable adjustment nut **Fig. 67.**
3. Shift cable will set self adjust at this point. No other adjustment is needed.
4. Tighten shift control cable adjustment nut to specification, then install left side console trim plate.

PARK LOCK CABLE

1. Place park/lock cable adjuster into unlocked position.
2. Pull cable forward to remove slack and release cable.
3. Move cable adjuster rearward 1/16 inch from previous position. Hold cable in position and place park/lock cable adjuster to locked position.
4. If shift lever moves from Park with key in lock position or if key will not return to lock position, repeat adjustment procedure as necessary.

IN-VEHICLE REPAIRS

SHIFT CONTROL CABLE

DEVILLE, ELDORADO & SEVILLE

Removal

Refer to **Figs. 66 and 69** when servicing shifter cable.

1. Remove air cleaner duct and housing if necessary and disconnect shifter cable at lever on transaxle manual shaft.
2. Disconnect shifter cable at bracket on transaxle, then remove retaining bolts and bracket at transaxle (if bracket replacement is necessary), **Fig. 68.**

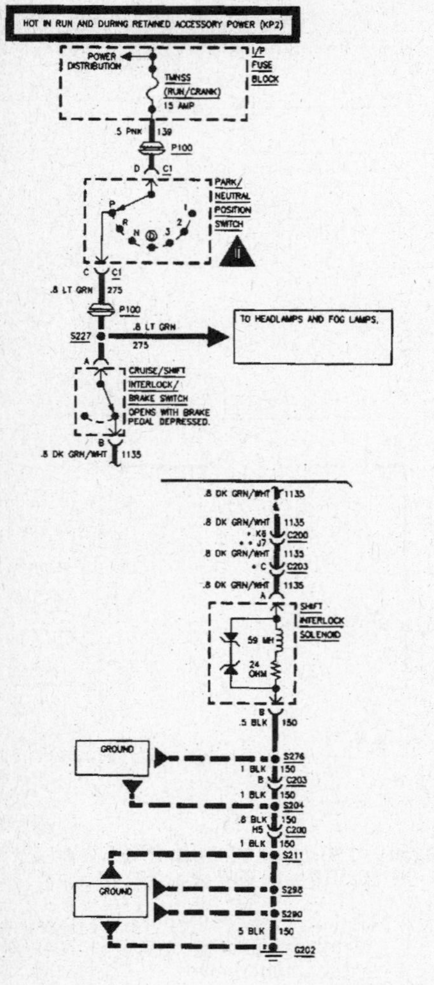

GC5029500516000X

Fig. 57 BTSI system wiring circuit. Aurora

3. Remove shifter knob and console trim plate in passenger compartment, **Fig. 69.**
4. Disconnect shifter cable at shifter assembly.
5. Loosen carpet attachments on front lefthand side of passenger compartment to allow access to cable routing.
6. Remove cable grommet through cowl and cable from vehicle.

Installation

1. Install cable through cowl and grommet into cowl, then route cable under carpet and attach carpet in front lefthand side of passenger compartment.
2. Connect shifter cable at shifter assembly and install trim plate and shifter knob in passenger compartment.
3. Install cable bracket and retaining bolts at transaxle (if bracket replacement was necessary) and tighten bolts to specification.
4. Connect shifter cable at bracket on transaxle and at lever on transaxle manual shaft.
5. Use a flat head screwdriver to pry lock button on shifter cable to unlocked position, **Fig. 66.**
6. Place transaxle shifter in Neutral and select Neutral position at lever on transaxle manual shaft.
7. Depress lock button on shifter cable into Locked position, **Fig. 66.**
8. Install air cleaner duct and housing.

Brake Transaxle Shift Interlock (BTSI) System Check

Step	Action	Normal Results	Abnormal Results
1	With the ignition in RUN and engine not running, attempt to shift vehicle out of PARK.	Vehicle does not shift out of PARK.	Vehicle Shifts Out Of PARK Without Brake Pedal Pressed.
2	Press brake pedal and attempt to shift vehicle out of PARK.	Vehicle shifts out of PARK.	Vehicle Does Not Shift Out Of PARK With Brake Pedal Pressed.

Vehicle Shifts Out Of PARK Without Brake Pedal Pressed

Step	Action	Value(s)	Yes	No
1	Connect a scan tool to the data link connector (DLC) and retrieve PZM DTCs. Is PZM DTC B2502 or B2503 present?	—	Body Control Module	Go to Step 2
2	1. Turn ignition switch to RUN with engine not running. 2. Remove park relay. 3. Check for voltage from park relay connector terminal A1 to ground. Is battery voltage present?	9 - 12V	Go to Step 4	Go to Step 3
3	Repair open or short to ground in CKT 1940 (ORN). Is the circuit repair complete?	—	System OK	—
4	Check for voltage from park relay connector terminal A3 to ground. Is battery voltage present?	9 - 12V	Go to Step 6	Go to Step 5
5	Repair open or short to ground in CKT 339 (PNK). Is the circuit repair complete?	—	System OK	—

GC5029800589010X

Fig. 58 BTSI troubleshooting (Part 1 of 3). 1997 DeVille, Eldorado, Seville & 1998-99 DeVille & Eldorado

AURORA

When servicing shifter cable refer to **Figs. 66 and 70.**

1. Remove cable end cap from transaxle park/neutral position switch lever.
2. Disconnect cable from bracket by prying up on lock button to unlocked position.
3. Remove lefthand I/P sound insulator.
4. Remove console center trim panel.
5. Disconnect shift control cable from floor shift assembly.
6. Reverse removal procedure to install, noting the following:
   a. Use a flathead screwdriver to pry lock button on shifter cable to unlocked position, **Fig. 66.**
   b. Place transaxle shifter in Neutral by rotating selector shaft clockwise from Park to Reverse and Neutral.
   c. Select Neutral position at lever on transaxle manual shaft.
   d. Depress lock button on shifter cable into LOCKED position, **Fig. 66.**

PARK LOCK CABLE (CONSOLE SHIFT)

REMOVAL

Refer to **Figs. 66 and 69** when servicing park/lock (console shift) cable.

1. Place shifter in Park and remove lefthand instrument panel sound insulator. Loosen lefthand front carpet to allow access to park/lock cable routing.
2. **On Seville models,** disconnect BTSI electrical connector.
3. **On Deville and Eldorado models,** remove steering column reinforcement plate and steering column bolts, then lower steering column.
4. **On all models.** turn ignition key to Run position.
5. **Do not attempt with ignition key in any other position than Run.** Slip a flat head screwdriver blade into ignition switch inhibitor slot and depress cable latch, then pull park/lock cable from inhibitor.
6. Remove radio and console trim plates if necessary.
7. Disconnect park/lock cable at shifter assembly.
8. Remove park/lock cable from vehicle.

INSTALLATION

1. Using a flat head screwdriver, pry lock button of park/lock cable into Unlocked position and connect park/lock cable at shifter assembly.
2. With shifter in Park and ignition key in Run, snap park/lock cable into inhibitor housing.
3. **Do not with ignition key in any other position than Run.** Turn key to Lock position and snap cable end onto pin of shifter lever.
4. Push park/lock cable toward shifter lever assembly to remove slack.
5. Push lock button on park/lock cable down into locked position.
6. With shifter in Park and ignition key in Lock position, ensure shifter cannot move to another position. Ignition key should not be removable from its cylinder.
7. Turn ignition key to Run position and move shifter to Neutral. Ensure ignition key cannot be turned to Lock position.
8. If checks in Steps 7 and 8 are OK, proceed with procedure. If checks are not OK, readjust park/lock cable beginning with Step 1.
9. **On Deville and Eldorado models,** raise steering column and install bolts and reinforcement plate
10. **On Seville models,** connect BTSI electrical connector.

Step	Action	Value(s)	Yes	No
6	1. Connect a fused jumper between park relay connector terminals A1 and B3. 2. Attempt to shift vehicle out of PARK. Is the gear shifter locked?	—	Go to Step 16	Go to Step 7
7	1. Disconnect stoplamp/BTSI switch connector 2. Check voltage at stoplamp/BTSI switch connector terminal A to ground. Is battery voltage present?	9 - 12V	Go to Step 9	Go to Step 8
8	Repair open CKT 275 (LT GRN). Is the circuit repair complete?	—	System OK	—
9	Connect a test lamp across stoplamp/BTSI switch connector C2 terminals A and B. Does the test lamp light?	—	Go to Step 11	Go to Step 10
10	Check that the stoplamp/BTSI switch is properly adjusted and that connector C2 terminals are clean and tight. If OK, replace stoplamp/BTSI switch. Is replacement complete?	—	System OK	—
11	1. Reconnect stoplamp/BTSI switch connector 2. Disconnect shift interlock solenoid connector. 3. Check for voltage at shift interlock solenoid connector terminal A to ground. Is battery voltage present?	9 - 12V	Go to Step 13	Go to Step 12
12	Repair open in CKT 1135 (DK GRN/WHT). Is the circuit repair complete?	—	System OK	—
13	Connect a test lamp across shift interlock solenoid connector terminals A and B. Does the test lamp light?	—	Go to Step 15	Go to Step 14
14	Repair open CKT 50 (BLK) or CKT 850 (BLK). Is the circuit repair complete?	—	System OK	—
15	Check that the shift interlock solenoid connector terminals are clean and tight. If OK, replace shift interlock solenoid. Is the replacement complete?	—	System OK	—
16	1. Remove fused jumper and reconnect park relay. 2. Using scan tool, enter PZM data. Does the PZM, as monitored by the scan tool, indicate that the vehicle is in PARK?	—	Go to Step 17	Engine Controls
17	1. Turn ignition OFF. 2. Disconnect body control module (PZM) connector C2. 3. Turn ignition to RUN. 4. Connect a fused jumper from PZM connector C2 terminal C16 to ground. 5. Attempt to shift the vehicle out of PARK. Is the gear shifter locked?	—	Go to Step 21	Go to Step 18

GC5029800589020X

Fig. 58 BTSI troubleshooting (Part 2 of 3). 1997 DeVille, Eldorado, Seville & 1998-99 DeVille & Eldorado

11. **On all models,** install console and radio trim plates and secure lefthand front carpet and lefthand instrument panel sound insulator.

BRAKE-TRANSAXLE SHIFT INTERLOCK (BTSI), REPLACE

On 1998–2000 Seville, BTSI is an integral part of the Park Lock Cable and can not be serviced separately.

1. Remove shifter knob and console trim plate, **Fig. 69.**
2. Disconnect electrical connector and BTSI solenoid at shifter assembly.
3. Reverse procedure to install.

VALVE BODY, REPLACE

Refer to **Fig. 71** when servicing lower control valve.

Step	Action	Value(s)	Yes	No
18	Check CKT 434 (ORN/BLK) for an open. Is the circuit OK?	—	Go to Step 20	Go to Step 19
19	Repair open CKT 434 (ORN/BLK). Is the circuit repair complete?	—	System OK	—
20	Check park relay for poor terminal contact. If OK, replace park relay. Is the replacement complete?	—	System OK	—
21	Check body control module (PZM) connector C2 for poor terminal contact. If OK, replace PZM. Is the replacement complete?	—	System OK	—

Vehicle Does Not Shift Out Of PARK With Brake Pedal Pressed

Step	Action	Value(s)	Yes	No
1	Connect a scan tool to the data link connector (DLC) and retrieve PZM DTCs. Is PZM DTC B2502 or B2503 present?	—	Go to Body Control Module (PZM) Diagnosis	Go to Step 2
2	1. Disconnect stoplamp/BTSI switch connector C2. 2. Attempt to shift vehicle out of PARK. Is gear shifter unlocked?	—	Go to Step 3	Go to Step 4
3	Check that stoplamp/BTSI switch is properly adjusted and that connector C2 terminals are clean and tight. If OK, replace stoplamp/BTSI switch. Is the replacement complete?	—	System OK	—
4	Check for voltage at shift interlock solenoid connector terminal B. Is battery voltage present?	9 - 12V	Go to Step 5	Go to Step 6
5	Repair short to battery voltage in CKT 1135 (DK GRN/WHT). Is the circuit repair complete?	—	System OK	—
6	Check that shift interlock solenoid connector terminals are clean and tight. If OK, replace the shift interlock solenoid. Is the repair complete?	—	System OK	—

GC5029800589030X

Fig. 58 BTSI troubleshooting (Part 3 of 3). 1997 DeVille, Eldorado, Seville & 1998-99 DeVille & Eldorado

CHART #1
GEAR SELECTOR SHIFTS OUT OF PARK WITH IGNITION SWITCH IN RUN AND BRAKE PEDAL NOT PRESSED

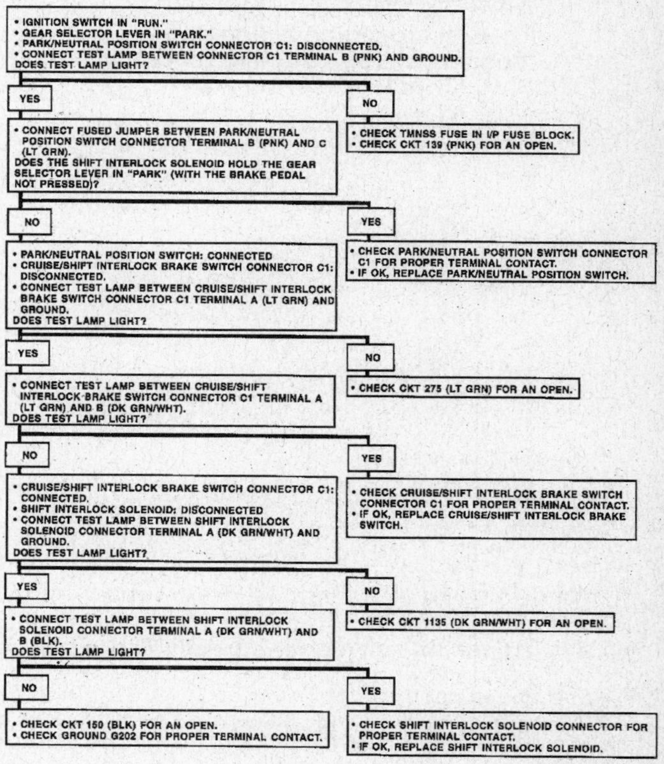

GC5029800590000X

Fig. 59 Transaxle shifts out of Park w/ignition switch in Run position & brake pedal not pressed. Aurora

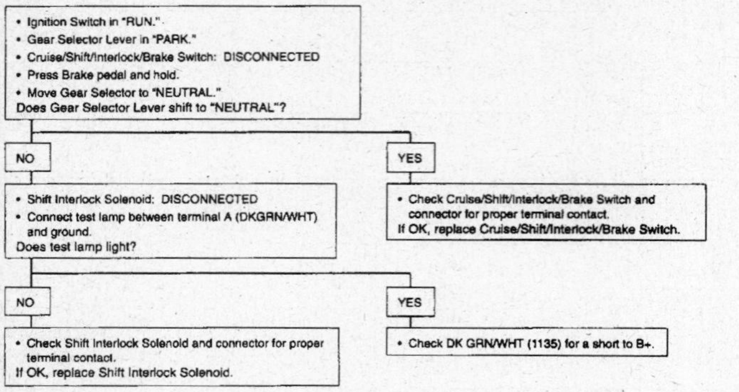

GC5029500520000X

Fig. 60 Transaxle does not shift out of Park w/brake pedal depressed & ignition switch in Run position. Aurora

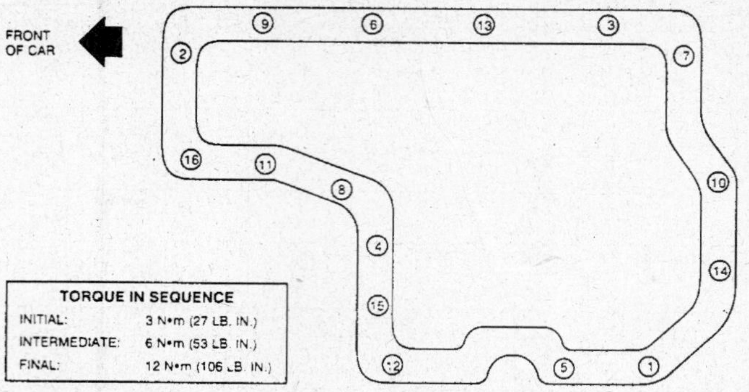

Copyrighted Material Reprinted with Permission from Hydra-Matic Div., GM Corp.

THA059000037000X

Fig. 61 Transaxle bottom pan bolt loosening & tightening sequence. 1997 Aurora

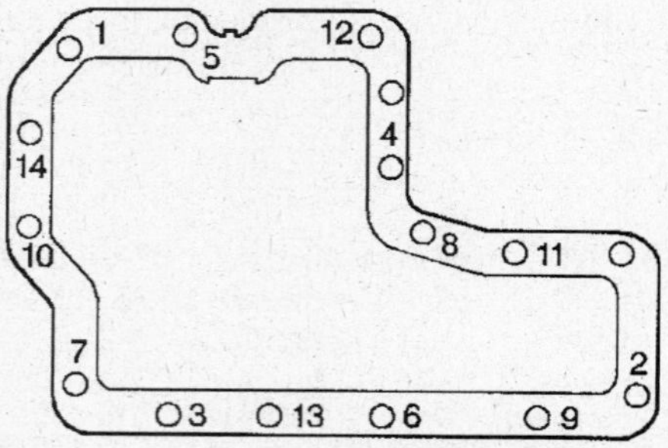

TH5029800945000X

Fig. 62 Transaxle bottom pan bolt loosening & tightening sequence. 1997 DeVille, Eldorado & 1998–99 Aurora

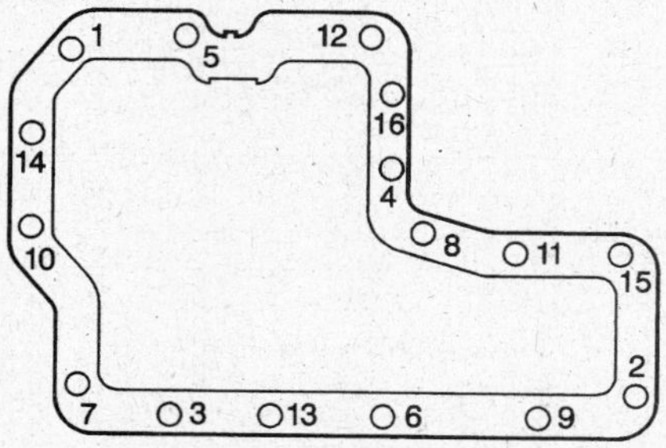

GC5029901054000X

Fig. 63 Transaxle bottom pan loosening & tightening sequence. 1998-2000 Deville & Eldorado

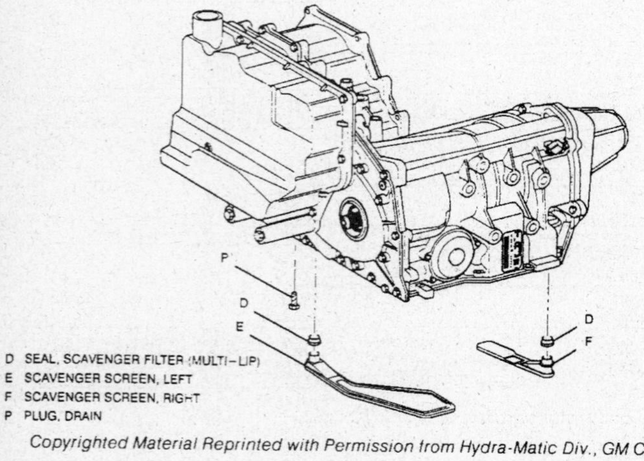

Copyrighted Material Reprinted with Permission from Hydra-Matic Div., GM Corp.

TH5029300511000X

Fig. 64 Transaxle scavenger screens & drain plug

1. Raise and support vehicle, then remove bottom pan, scavenger screens and seals as described in this section.
2. Using a small screwdriver, bend back small tabs to disconnect shift solenoids A, B and transaxle pressure switch connectors, **Fig. 72.**
3. Disconnect manual valve linkage clip with a small screwdriver.
4. Disconnect wiring harness from retaining clips on lower controls assembly.
5. Remove oil transfer plate.
6. Remove bolts and two nuts using 10 mm socket. **Do not remove five bolts in lower channel plate, Fig. 73.**
7. Remove lower channel plate, valve and accumulator assemblies from case.
8. Position low reverse band using a .02–.03 inch shim, **Fig. 74.**
9. Place lower controls against forward support studs.
10. Hand start bolts into channel plate and remove shim stock.
11. Place oil transfer plate over open gasket area. Hand start bolts to hold plate in place, noting installation order.
12. Install two nuts on forward support studs and tighten bolts and nuts to specification.
13. Connect manual valve to detent lever.
14. Route harness over spacer plate rib and detent lever and snap into retaining clips on lower controls assembly.
15. Connect wiring harness to shift solenoids A and B and transaxle pressure sensor.
16. Install scavenger screens, lip seals, bottom pan and gasket as described in this section.
17. Add transaxle fluid as necessary. Reset transaxle oil life indicator if a complete fluid change was necessary.

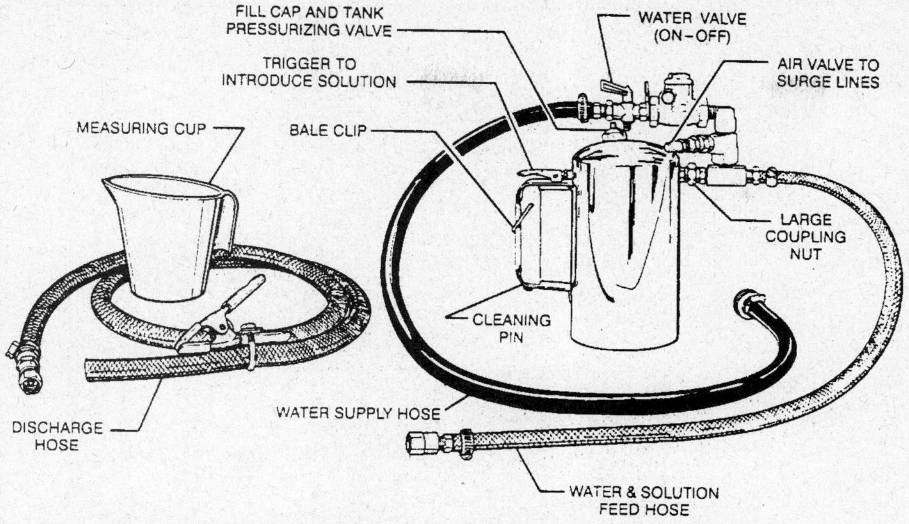

TH5029300524000X

Fig. 65 Transaxle oil cooler flushing tool

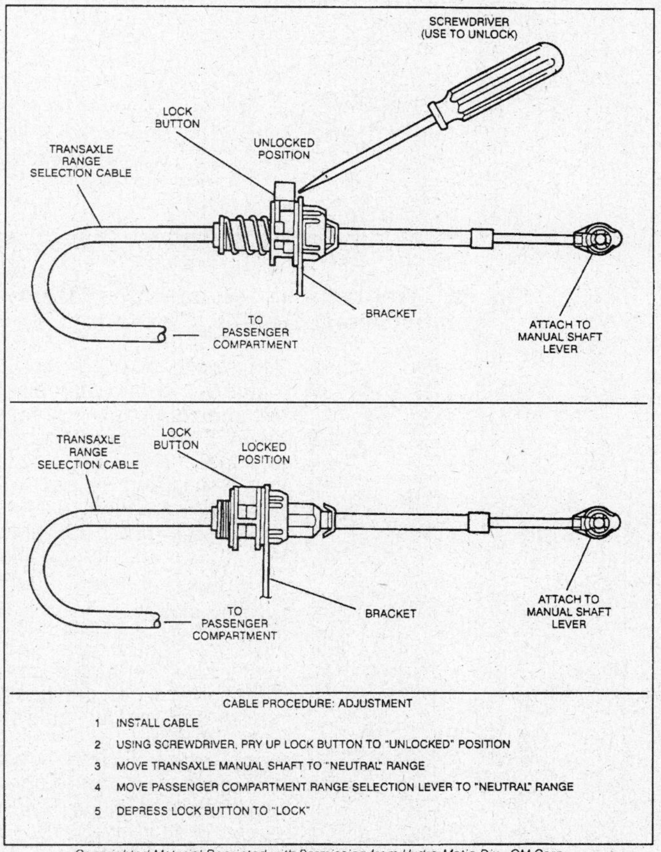

TH5029300522000X

Fig. 66 Transaxle shift control cable adjustment. Aurora, Deville, Eldorado & 1997 Seville

SOLENOIDS A & B (1-2 & 2-3 SHIFT SOLENOIDS), REPLACE

Refer to **Fig. 71** when servicing shift solenoid assemblies.

1. Raise and support vehicle, then remove bottom pan and gasket, scavenger screens and seals as described in this section.
2. Remove lower controls assembly.
3. Remove transaxle pressure switch manifold bolts, then the transaxle pressure switch manifold.
4. Remove lower control valve assembly and gasket from lower channel plate.
5. Remove solenoids A and B retaining clips and solenoids.
6. Reverse procedure to install, noting the following:
   a. Add transaxle fluid as outlined.
   b. Reset transaxle oil life indicator, if a complete fluid change was necessary.

1-2, 3-4, FORWARD & REVERSE ACCUMULATORS, REPLACE

REMOVAL

1. Raise and support vehicle, then remove bottom pan and gasket, scavenger screens and lip seals as described in this section.
2. Remove lower controls assembly.
3. Remove nine bolts (three from channel side).
4. Remove accumulator housing from channel plate, then the check balls. **Do not lose check balls.**
5. Remove spring.
6. Remove accumulator piston top snap rings from housing side, then the 1–2 and 3–4 accumulator assemblies.
7. Remove five accumulator housing cover bolts and accumulator housing cover and gasket.
8. Remove forward accumulator assembly and reverse accumulator assembly.

INSPECTION

1. Inspect accumulator pins for straightness by rolling on a flat surface.
2. Inspect accumulator seals for tearing or roll over and snap rings for overexpansion
3. Inspect accumulator bores for scratches or nicks.
4. Replace gasket and inspect springs for cracking or damage.

INSTALLATION

Use a light coat of transmission fluid to lubricate all seals before installing accumulator assemblies.

1. Install forward accumulator assembly and reverse accumulator assembly.
2. Install new gasket and accumulator housing cover.

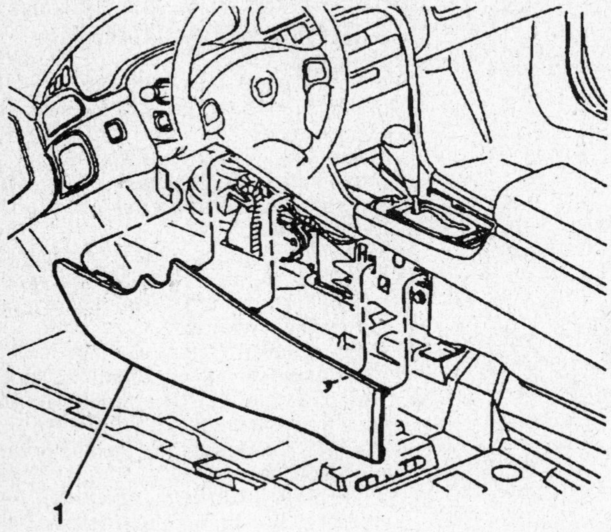

GC5029901055000X

Fig. 67 Transaxle shift control cable adjustment. 1998-2000 Seville

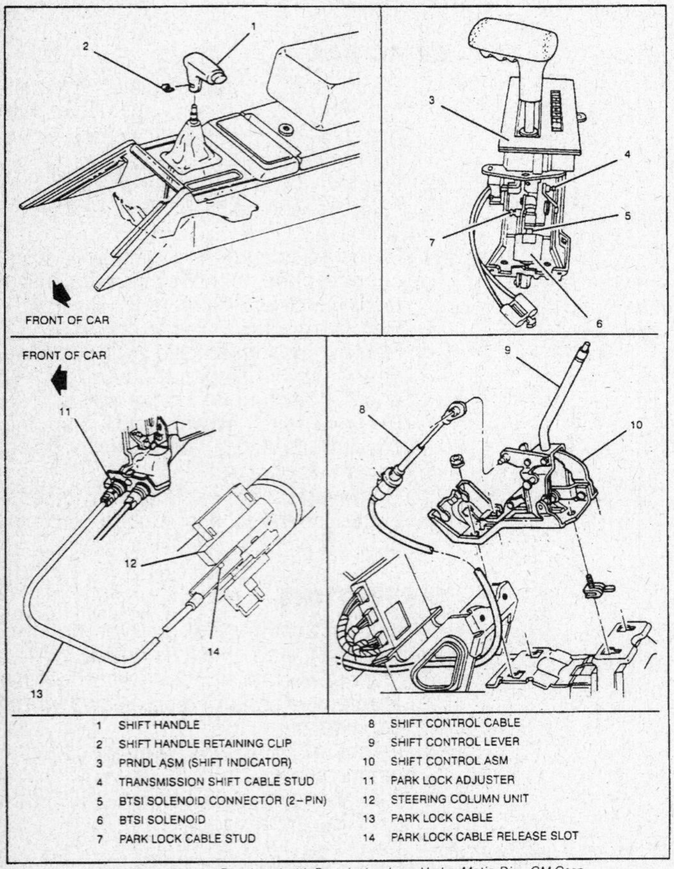

TH5029300521000X

Fig. 69 Transaxle range control system, passenger compartment. DeVille, Eldorado & Seville

3. Install accumulator housing cover bolts and tighten bolts to specification.
4. Install 1-2 accumulator pin. Retain with two snap rings.
5. Install 1-2 accumulator spring, piston and seal.

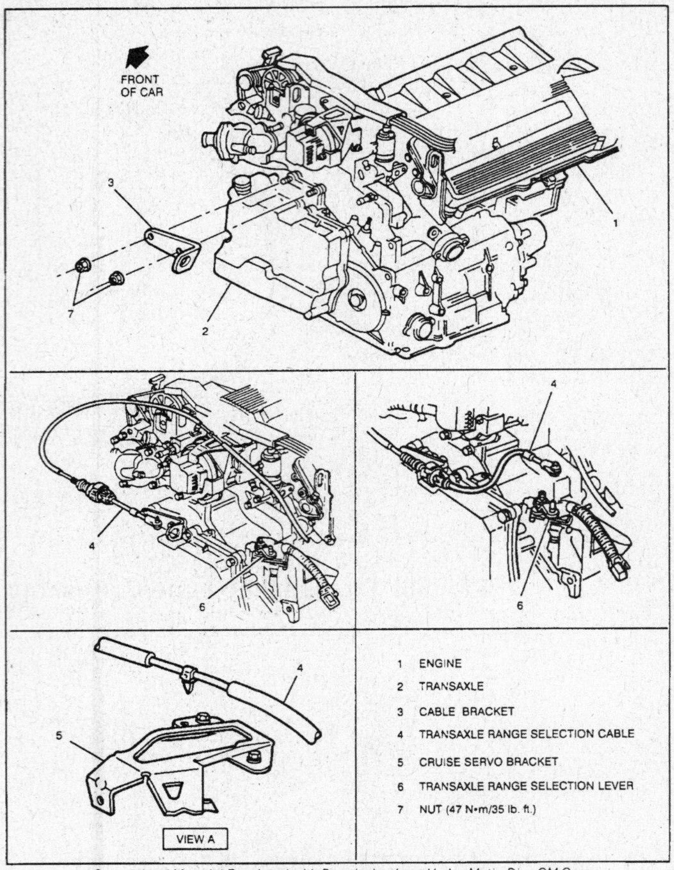

TH5029300520000X

Fig. 68 Transaxle range control system, engine compartment. DeVille, Eldorado & Seville

6. Install snap ring and spring.
7. Install 3-4 accumulator pin. Retain with two snap rings.
8. Install 3-4 accumulator spring, piston and seal.
9. Install snap ring.
10. Install check balls.
11. Install guide pins J-39630-2, or equivalent, for accumulator housing, then the accumulator housing to lower channel plate.
12. Remove guide pins and install remaining bolts. Tighten bolts to specification.
13. Install lower controls assembly.
14. Install bottom pan and gasket, scavenger screens and lip seals as described in this section.
15. Add transaxle fluid as necessary.
16. Reset transaxle oil life indicator, if a complete fluid change was necessary.

LOWER VALVE ASSEMBLY, SPACER PLATE & CHANNEL PLATE, REPLACE

1. Raise and support vehicle, then remove bottom pan and gasket, scavenger screens and seals as described in this section.
2. Remove lower controls assembly.
3. Remove nine accumulator housing bolts (three from channel plate side).
4. Remove accumulator housing from

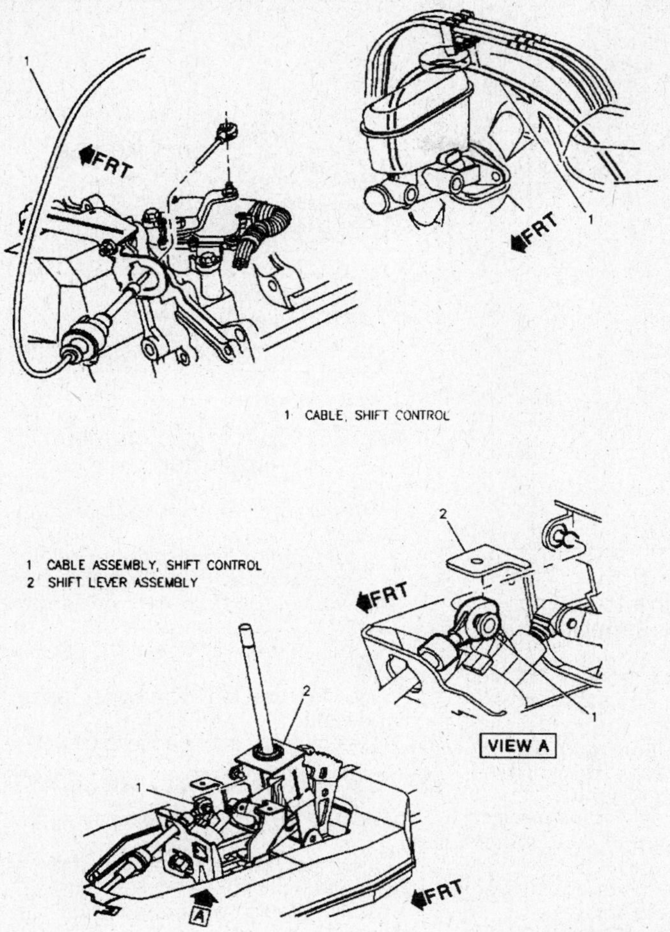

GC5029500786000X

Fig. 70 Shift control cable & shift lever assembly. Aurora

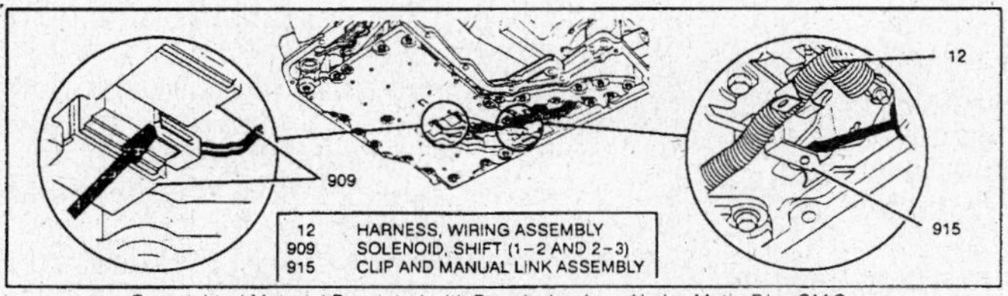

Copyrighted Material Reprinted with Permission from Hydra-Matic Div., GM Corp.

TH5029300527000X

Fig. 72 Disengaging connector tabs

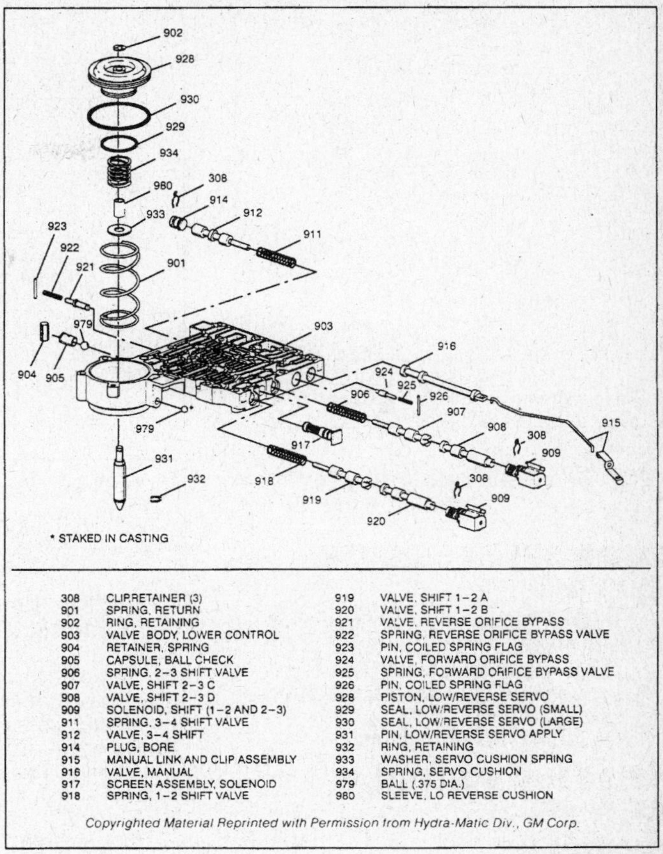

* STAKED IN CASTING
308 CLIP,RETAINER (3)
901 SPRING, RETURN
902 RING, RETAINING
903 VALVE BODY, LOWER CONTROL
904 RETAINER, SPRING
905 CAPSULE, BALL CHECK
906 SPRING, 2–3 SHIFT VALVE
907 VALVE, SHIFT 2–3 C
908 VALVE, SHIFT 2–3 D
909 SOLENOID, SHIFT (1–2 AND 2–3)
911 SPRING, 3–4 SHIFT VALVE
912 VALVE, 3–4 SHIFT
914 PLUG, BORE
915 MANUAL LINK AND CLIP ASSEMBLY
916 VALVE, MANUAL
917 SCREEN ASSEMBLY, SOLENOID
918 SPRING, 1–2 SHIFT VALVE
919 VALVE, SHIFT 1–2 A
920 VALVE, SHIFT 1–2 B
921 VALVE, REVERSE ORIFICE BYPASS
922 SPRING, REVERSE ORIFICE BYPASS VALVE
923 PIN, COILED SPRING FLAG
924 VALVE, FORWARD ORIFICE BYPASS
925 SPRING, FORWARD ORIFICE BYPASS VALVE
926 PIN, COILED SPRING FLAG
928 PISTON, LOW/REVERSE SERVO
929 SEAL, LOW/REVERSE SERVO (SMALL)
930 SEAL, LOW/REVERSE SERVO (LARGE)
931 PIN, LOW/REVERSE SERVO APPLY
932 RING, RETAINING
933 WASHER, SERVO CUSHION SPRING
934 SPRING, SERVO CUSHION
979 BALL (.375 DIA.)
980 SLEEVE, LO REVERSE CUSHION

Copyrighted Material Reprinted with Permission from Hydra-Matic Div., GM Corp.

TH5029300530000X

Fig. 71 Exploded view of lower controls assembly

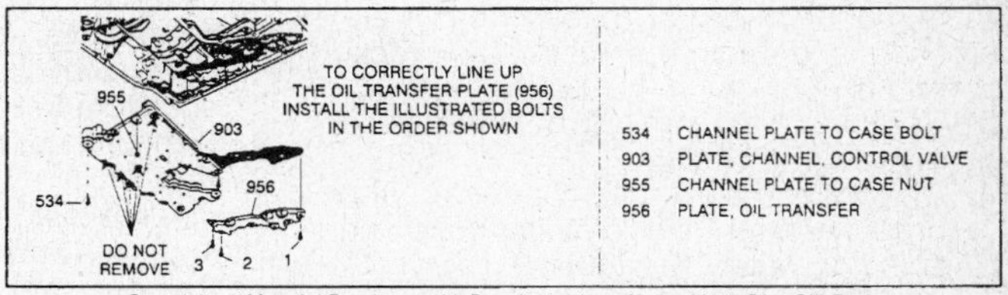

TO CORRECTLY LINE UP THE OIL TRANSFER PLATE (956) INSTALL THE ILLUSTRATED BOLTS IN THE ORDER SHOWN

Copyrighted Material Reprinted with Permission from Hydra-Matic Div., GM Corp.

TH5029300528000X

Fig. 73 Oil transfer, channel & control valve plates

channel plate and four check balls.

5. Remove transaxle pressure switch manifold bolts and manifold.
6. Remove eleven bolts (two on channel plate side) and lower control valve assembly and gasket from lower channel plate.
7. Remove four check balls.
8. Remove manual valve link and clip and manual valve.
9. Remove lo/reverse servo piston retaining ring. Push lo/reverse apply pin to remove servo assembly.
10. Remove return spring and clip and push out servo pin.
11. Remove servo cushion spring and spring washer. **Inspect check valves for movement.**
12. Remove clips and shift solenoids A and B and solenoid screen.
13. Remove 1–2 shift valves A and B and 1–2 shift valve spring.
14. Remove 2–3 shift valves C and D and 2–3 shift valve spring.
15. Remove coiled spring pin.
16. Remove forward bypass valve spring and forward bypass valve.
17. Remove retaining clip and bore plug.
18. Remove 3–4 shift valve, 3–4 shift valve spring and coiled spring pin.
19. Remove reverse orifice bypass valve spring and reverse orifice bypass valve.
20. Remove retaining sleeve.
21. Remove ball check capsule and checkball.
22. Remove bolts and plate from channel plate.
23. Remove spacer plate and gasket.
24. Inspect servo seals for roll over, tearing or cuts.
25. Inspect springs for damage and retaining clips for overexpansion.
26. Inspect all valve and piston bores for nicks and wear.
27. Inspect lo/reverse servo apply pin for straightness by rolling on flat surface.
28. Inspect solenoid screen for particles or damage.
29. Inspect checkball in valve body for freedom of movement.
30. Inspect valve body channel plate passages for debris.
31. Reverse procedure to install, noting the following:
    a. Install guide pins **Figs. 75 through 78.**
    b. Remove guide pins and install retaining bolts as needed.

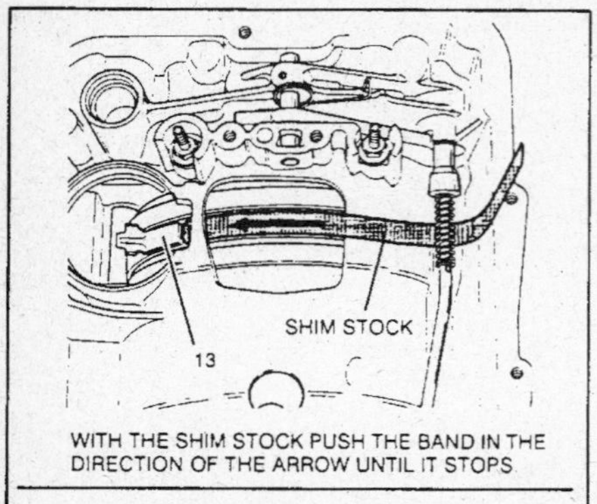

TH5029300529000X

Fig. 74 Positioning low/reverse band

ROAD SPEED SENSOR, REPLACE

1. Raise and support vehicle, then remove righthand front wheel.
2. Disconnect electrical connector at sensor, then remove retaining bolt and sensor, **Fig. 79.**
3. Reverse procedure to install.

SELECTOR SWITCH, REPLACE

REMOVAL

1. Remove air cleaner duct and housing, then disconnect shifter cable at lever on transaxle manual shaft.
2. Disconnect shifter cable from transaxle and remove shifter cable bracket, **Fig. 68.**
3. Remove retaining nut and transaxle manual shaft lever.
4. Disconnect electrical connector and hose, then remove retaining bolts and selector switch, **Fig. 80.**

INSTALLATION

1. Install transaxle range switch and retaining bolts finger tight, then rotate transaxle manual shaft to Neutral position.
2. Rotate range switch so service gauge pin can be installed, **Fig. 80.** Tighten transaxle range switch bolts to specification.
3. Remove service gauge pin and connect electrical connector and hose.
4. Install transaxle manual shaft lever and tighten retaining nut to specification.
5. Install shift cable bracket onto transaxle and connect cable.
6. Install shift cable at lever on transaxle manual shaft.
7. Install air cleaner duct and housing.

4TH SERVO, REPLACE

1. Raise and support vehicle.
2. Remove exhaust system as necessary.
3. Remove steering gear retaining bolts from lefthand side of gear.

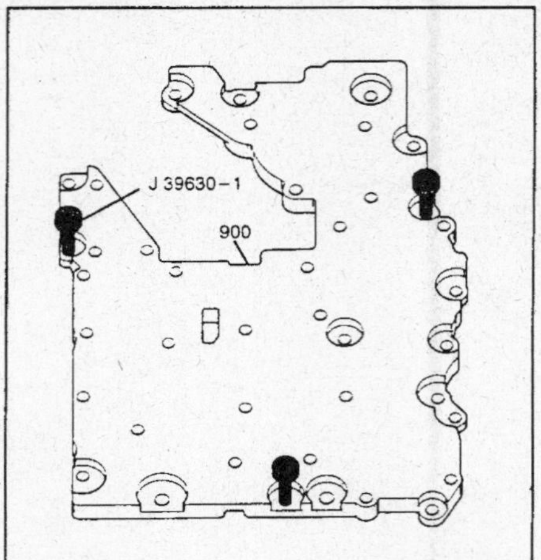

TH5029300531000X

Fig. 75 Guide pins to lower channel plate installation

4. Remove through bolt from righthand side of steering gear and support gear as necessary.
5. Remove retaining clamp from power steering lines and support transmission with a suitable jackstand.
6. Remove righthand transmission mount bolts and support rear frame with a suitable jackstand.
7. Remove rear frame bolts and lower frame to gain access to servo.
8. Remove three bolts, **Fig. 81.** Hold servo cover in place until all bolts are removed. If cover is not held in place, apply pin will damage bore in case.
9. Remove cover and servo assembly, **Fig. 81.**
10. Inspect piston for cracking and check apply pin and springs for damage.
11. Remove seal and servo cover seal.
12. Remove snap ring, pin and springs.
13. Reverse procedure to install, noting the following:
    a. Install new seal onto piston and pin, small spring, retainer, snap ring and seal to cover.
    b. Install 4th servo and large spring into cover. **Ensure tab on piston is aligned with notch in case bore (early models).**
    c. Ensure flat spring is centered between bosses on cover (early models). A light mark may be scribed on top of piston for a reference. **Do not mark side of piston or a fluid leak or binding condition may result.**
    d. Install cover retaining screws. Hand start screws and tighten in a star pattern to specification.
    e. Add transmission fluid as necessary.

SCAVENGER SCREENS & LIP SEALS, REPLACE

1. Raise and support vehicle, then re-

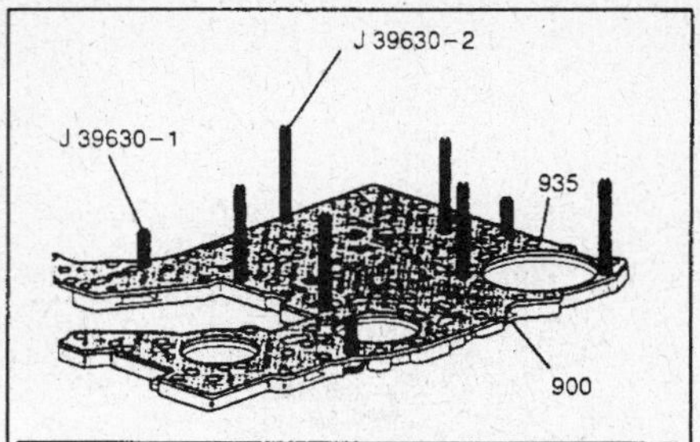

Copyrighted Material Reprinted with Permission from Hydra-Matic Div., GM Corp.

TH5029300532000X

Fig. 76 Spacer plate/gasket installation

move bottom pan as described in this section.
2. Remove left and/or righthand scavenger screens and seals with small screwdriver. **Do not score or damage case.**
3. Inspect screen lip seals for nicks or cuts.
4. Clean or replace scavenger screen and install.
5. Install pan as described in this section.

DRIVE AXLE SEAL, REPLACE

Refer to **Fig. 82** when removing drive axle.

1. Raise and support vehicle, then remove wheel and tire.
2. Install suitable seal protector on outer joint.
3. Remove hub nut. Insert drift or screwdriver into caliper and rotor to prevent rotor from turning.
4. Remove ball joint cotter pin and nut and loosen joint using suitable ball joint separator.
5. Remove drive axle from hub using suitable front hub spindle remover and move strut and knuckle rearward.
6. Remove drive axle from transaxle with suitable prybar.
7. Use screwdriver to pry outer seal from transaxle and use pliers to remove remaining housing of drive axle seal from transaxle.
8. Inspect transaxle case for damage after removing seal.
9. Clean drive axle seal mating surface on housing with crocus cloth.
10. Install drive axle seal using axle seal installer tool No. J-39051, or equivalent, and hammer.
11. If installing righthand drive axle, install suitable axle seal protector so it can be pulled out after drive axle is installed.
12. Install drive axle into transaxle. Ensure drive axle snap ring is properly seated by grasping inner joint housing and pulling outboard. **Do not pull on drive axle.** Driveshaft will remain in place when snap ring is properly seated.
13. Install drive axle into hub and bearing assembly.
14. Connect ball joint to knuckle. **Torque** ball joint nut to 7 ft. lbs. and tighten an

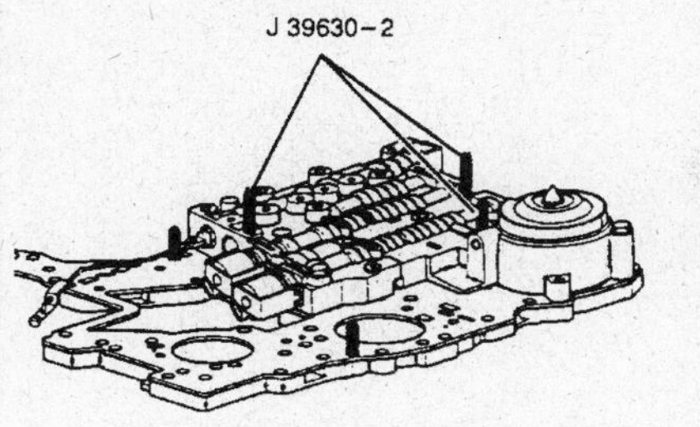

TH5029300533000X

Fig. 77 Lower valve body installation

additional 120° (two flats). When tightening nut, a minimum **torque** of 37 ft. lbs. must be obtained. If 37 ft. lbs. cannot be obtained, inspect for stripped threads. If threads are OK, replace ball joint and knuckle. If required, turn nut up to an additional 60° (one flat) to allow for installation of cotter pin.

15. Install hub nut and tighten to specification. Prevent drive axle from turning by inserting a screwdriver into rotor fins.
16. Remove seal protector. If a axle seal protector was installed, remove it by pulling inline with handle. Ensure it is completely removed and no pieces are left inside of transaxle.
17. Install wheel and tire and lower vehicle.

CASE EXTENSION & SCAVENGER PIPE, REPLACE

REMOVAL

1. Raise and support vehicle, then remove righthand front wheel assembly and splash shields.
2. Remove Real Time Damping (RTD) sensor from lower control arm.
3. Disconnect righthand stabilizer link, righthand tie rod and righthand ball joint from steering knuckle.
4. Remove righthand drive axle.
5. Support transaxle using suitable support fixture.
6. Disconnect power steering pressure switch connector and wiring harness.
7. Disconnect righthand transaxle mount and bracket connector and wiring harness, then remove righthand transaxle to engine bracket and heat shield.
8. Disconnect VSS connector and ground from case.
9. Remove case extension bolts and stud using a torque wrench and case extension and seal, **Fig. 83.** Seal may remain in extension.
10. Remove roller thrust bearing and selective washer and bolt.
11. Remove scavenger pipe by prying on differential, then remove seal.
12. Inspect scavenger tube for damage and clogging.
13. Inspect case extension and case mating surfaces for scoring and damage.

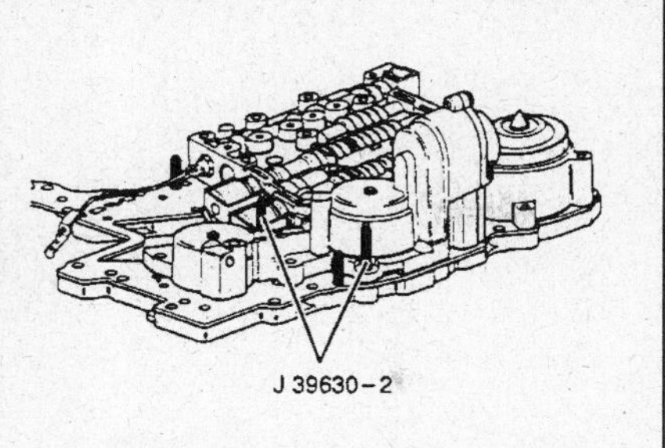

TH5029300534000X

Fig. 78 Accumulator assembly installation

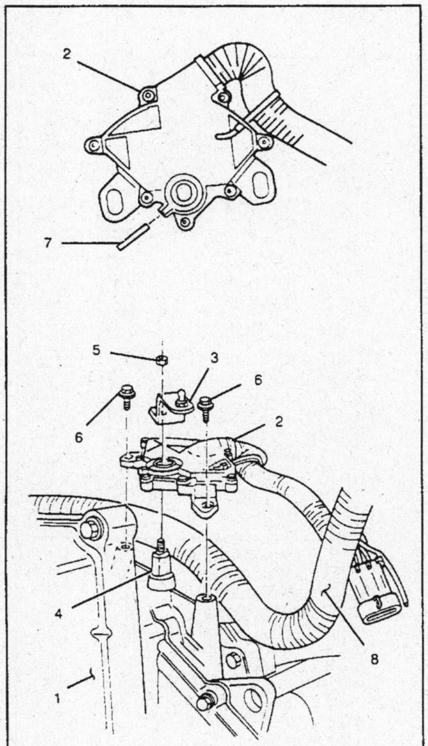

1 TRANSAXLE
2 TRANSAXLE RANGE SWITCH
3 RANGE SELECTION LEVER
4 TRANSAXLE MANUAL SHAFT
5 NUT (20 N•m/15 LB. FT.)
6 BOLT (28 N•m/21 LB.FT.)
7 SERVICE GAUGE PIN (2.34MM/3/32 IN.)
8 ENGINE WIRING HARNESS

TH5029300523000X

Fig. 80 Selector switch replacement

INSTALLATION

1. Install scavenger tube seal into case,

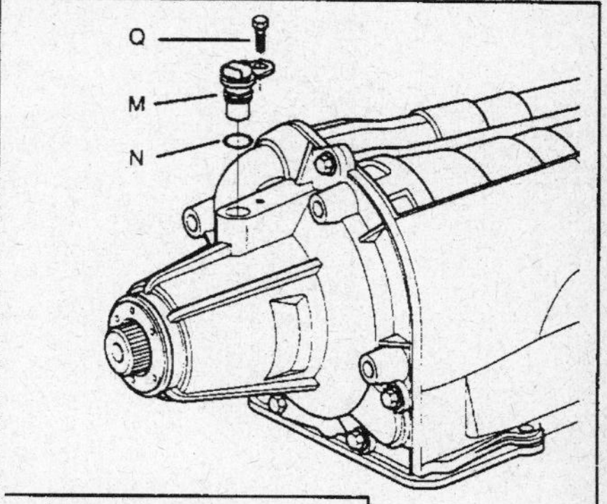

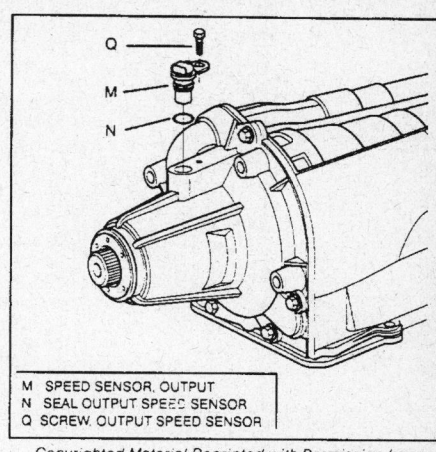

M SPEED SENSOR, OUTPUT
N SEAL OUTPUT SPEED SENSOR
Q SCREW, OUTPUT SPEED SENSOR

TH5029300525000X

Fig. 79 Road speed sensor replacement

Fig. 83 and tap scavenger tube into case using a plastic hammer to ensure fit. Pipe rib will remain exposed.

2. Install scavenger bolt and tighten to specification.
3. Install selective washer and thrust roller bearing onto differential output shaft.
4. Insert case extension seal into case extension and install case extension onto case.
5. Using star pattern, install bolts and stud with stud in 11 o'clock position. Tighten bolts to specification.
6. Connect VSS connector and ground to case.
7. Install righthand transaxle to engine bracket.
8. Install heat shield and righthand transaxle mount and bolts.
9. Install power steering pressure switch connector and wiring harness.
10. Remove transaxle support.
11. Install drive axle.
12. Connect righthand ball joint, righthand tie rod and righthand stabilizer link to steering knuckle.
13. Install RTD sensor to lower control arm.
14. Install splash shields and wheel assembly.
15. Add transmission fluid as necessary.

MANUAL SHAFT/PARK ACTUATOR, REPLACE

REMOVAL

Refer to **Fig. 84** when servicing the manual shaft/park lock actuator assemblies.

1. Remove transaxle range switch.
2. Raise and support vehicle.
3. Remove bottom pan and gasket, scavenger screens and seals as described in this section.
4. Remove lower controls assembly.
5. Remove detent spring. Grasp detent roller end of spring with pliers to remove.
6. Remove detent roller bolt, pivot arm, sleeve and washer.

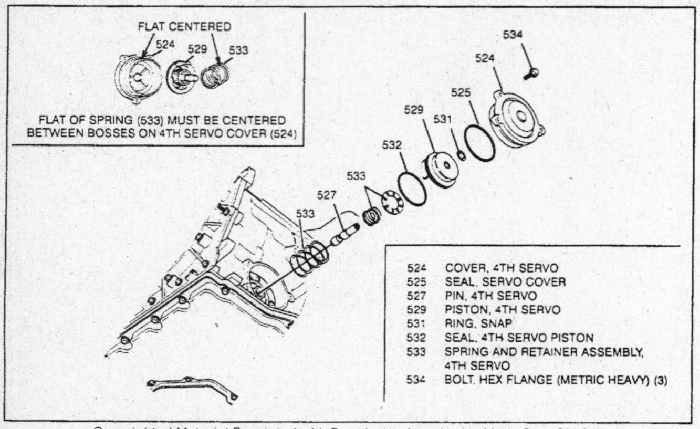

TH5029300526000X

Fig. 81 Exploded view of 4th servo assembly

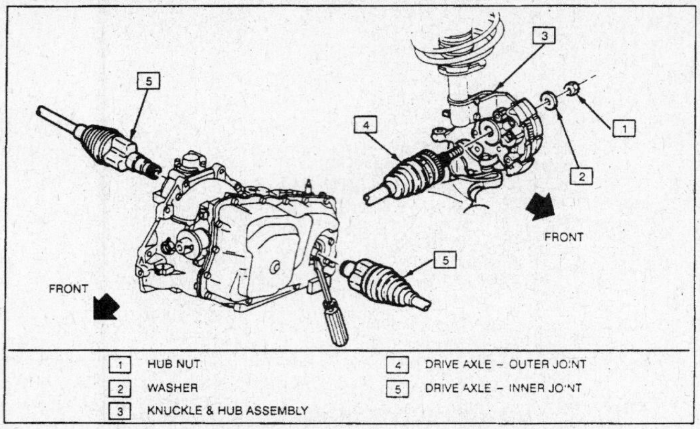

TH5029300536000X

Fig. 82 Drive axle removal

7. Remove manual shaft nut. **Detent lever must be held in place when removing nut to prevent damage to actuator rod.**
8. Remove detent lever and actuator rod. Discard detent lever.
9. Remove manual shaft and lower vehicle.
10. Remove seal and washer.
11. Inspect actuator guide for excessive wear and actuator rod for cracked end, bent rod or broken spring.

INSTALLATION

1. Install new manual shaft seal into case.
2. Raise and support vehicle.
3. Install manual shaft and seat manual shaft (flush with case) seal with appropriate socket.
4. Attach new detent lever and actuator rod to manual shaft and hold detent lever in place with a screwdriver to prevent bending of actuator rod.
5. Install manual shaft nut and tighten to specification.
6. Install detent roller washer, pivot arm and sleeves.
7. Install detent roller assembly bolt and tighten to specification.
8. Install detent return spring to detent roller assembly and manual shaft.
9. Install lower controls assembly.
10. Install bottom pan and gasket, scavenger screens and lip seals.
11. Lower vehicle.
12. Add transaxle fluid as necessary.
13. If complete fluid change was necessary, reset transaxle oil life indicator as described in this section.

PARKING PAWL, SPRING & SLEEVE, REPLACE

REMOVAL

Refer to **Fig. 85** when servicing parking pawl assembly.

1. Raise and support vehicle.
2. Remove bottom pan and gasket, scavenger screen and seals as described in this section.
3. Remove lower controls assembly.
4. Remove final drive assembly as described in this section.

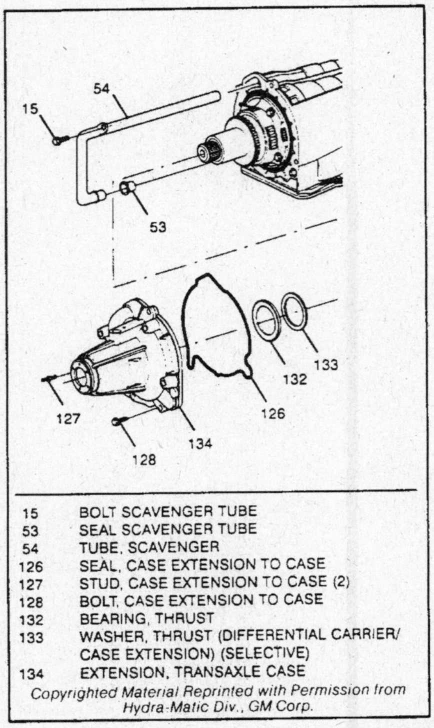

TH5029300537000X

Fig. 83 Exploded view of case extension & scavenger pipe

5. Move manual shaft from Park position.
6. Drive out pivot pin retaining pin.
7. Drive parking pawl pivot pin towards extension housing with pin punch. Push down on spring while driving shaft out.
8. Remove parking pawl and spring.
9. Remove park/lock sleeve using a rubber mallet. Drive out towards case extension portion of case.

INSPECTION

1. Inspect parking pawl tooth for damage.
2. Inspect parking pawl spring for over expansion
3. Inspect pivot pin for scorning and excessive wear.

INSTALLATION

1. Place pawl in case slot and attach spring to pawl.
2. Insert pivot pin through spring and pawl. Hook end of spring locates on case and square end of top of parking pawl.
3. Install retaining pin using a hammer and pin punch and install actuator sleeve.
4. Install final drive assembly described in this section.
5. Install lower controls assembly.
6. Install bottom pan and gasket, scavenger screens and lip seals as described in this section.
7. Lower vehicle.
8. Add transmission fluid and reset transaxle oil life indicator as described in this section.

CONVERTER COVER, REPLACE

1. Raise and support vehicle.
2. Remove engine to transaxle brace bolts and torque converter cover bolt and cover.
3. Reverse procedure to install. Tighten torque converter cover bolt and engine to transaxle brace bolt to specification.

FINAL DRIVE

1. Remove case extension described in this section.
2. Using a suitable torque wrench, remove differential housing bolts. Ensure transmission is in Park position.
3. Remove differential housing, differential gear snap ring, gear and thrust washer.
4. Remove final drive carrier, thrust bearing and sun gear.
5. Remove snap ring and final drive internal gear.
6. Reverse procedure to install.

TRANSAXLE

REPLACE

Refer to **Figs. 86 through 88** when removing and installing transaxle.

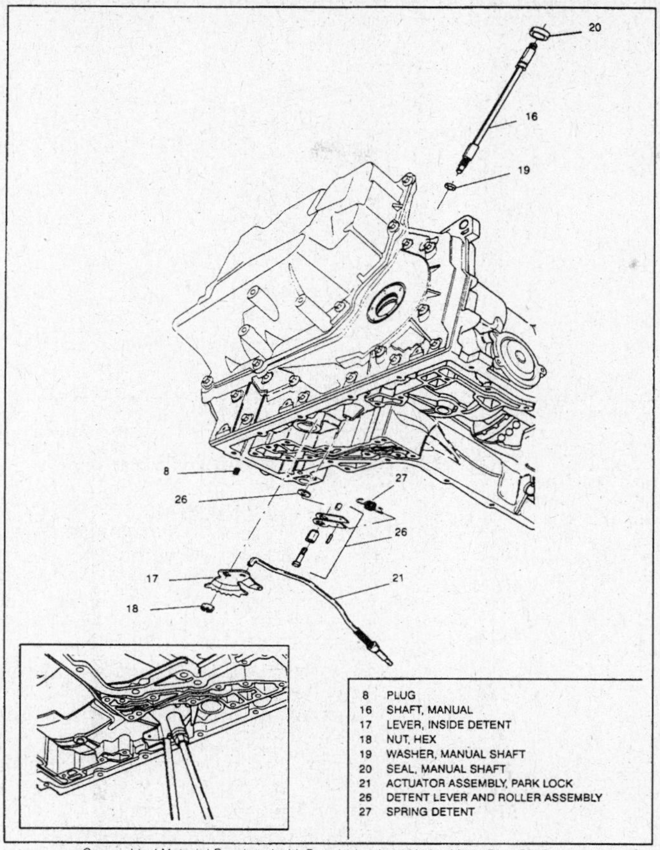

Copyrighted Material Reprinted with Permission from Hydra-Matic Div., GM Corp.

TH5029300535000X

Fig. 84 Exploded view of manual shift & detent lever assembly

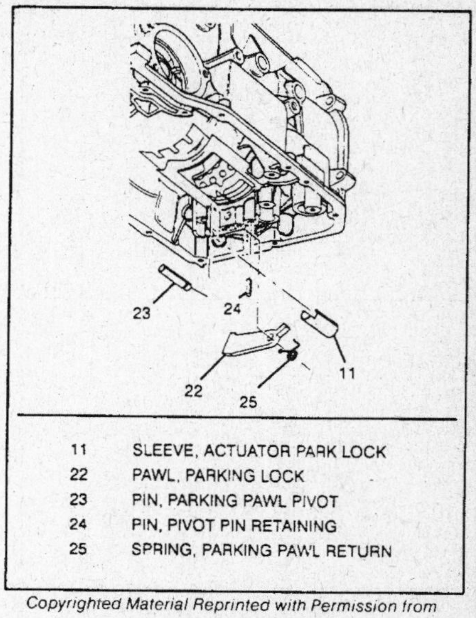

Copyrighted Material Reprinted with Permission from Hydra-Matic Div., GM Corp.

TH5029300540000X

Fig. 85 Parking pawl & actuator sleeve components

DEVILLE & ELDORADO

1. Remove headlamp housing upper filler panel and diagonal brace.
2. Remove air cleaner assembly and disconnect shifter cable and bracket at transaxle.
3. Remove torque struts.
4. Disconnect oil cooler lines and oil sending line at transaxle.
5. Remove two upper bellhousing bolts.
6. Disconnect power steering hose at auxiliary cooler. Plug cooler holes and return hose to prevent fluid leakage and contamination.
7. Install engine support fixture J-28467, or equivalent, and raise powertrain until weight is off mounts.
8. Raise and support vehicle, then remove both front wheel and splash shield assemblies.
9. Disconnect both front suspension position sensors from lower control arms and position aside.
10. Separate both tie rods from steering knuckles and both ball joints from struts.
11. Remove both drive axles from hubs and transaxle.
12. Disconnect power steering filter at cradle.
13. Remove A/C splash shield from frame.
14. Remove ABS modulator from bracket and support.
15. Remove engine oil pan to transaxle bracket.
16. Remove torque converter cover and flywheel to converter bolts. Mark flywheel to converter position for assembly purposes.
17. Remove powertrain mount nuts from cradle.
18. Rotate steering intermediate shaft until steering gear stub shaft clamp bolt is accessible through lefthand wheel opening.
19. Remove clamp bolt through lefthand wheel opening.
20. Remove steering intermediate shaft from steering gear. **Failure to disconnect intermediate shaft from rack and pinion stub shaft can result in damage to steering gear and/or intermediate shaft. This damage could result in loss of steering control which could cause personal injury. Do not rotate steering wheel or move position of steering gear when intermediate shaft is disconnected; SIR coil in steering column will become uncentered. If coil becomes uncentered, it may be damaged during vehicle operation.**
21. Disconnect electrical harness from front of cradle and support rear of cradle with a jackstand.
22. Remove four rear cradle bolts and lower jack stand enough to gain access to power steering gear heat shield and return line fitting.
23. Remove power steering gear heat shield and return line at gear. Plug steering gear and pressure line to avoid leakage and contamination.
24. Disconnect power steering electrical connector.
25. Raise jack stand and install one rear cradle bolt on each side to finger tightness to support cradle. Remove jack stand.
26. Support frame and remove six frame mount bolts.
27. Lower frame and/or raise vehicle with steering gear attached.
28. Disconnect transaxle, VSS, ground strap and transaxle harness from transaxle clip connectors
29. Disconnect fuel line bundle from transaxle.
30. Remove left and righthand transaxle mount and bracket assemblies from transaxle.
31. Install transaxle support fixture tool No. J-28664, or equivalent.
32. Remove engine to transaxle heat shield and bracket, then two engine to transaxle bolts.
33. Lower transaxle.
34. Disconnect manual shaft linkage and neutral start switch.
35. Disconnect speed sensor and oil return pipe.
36. Reverse procedure to install, noting the following:
    a. Install six frame mount bolts in following order: lefthand side No. 2 mount bolt into body, lefthand side No. 1 mount bolt into body and remaining bolts in no specific order. Tighten six frame mount bolts to

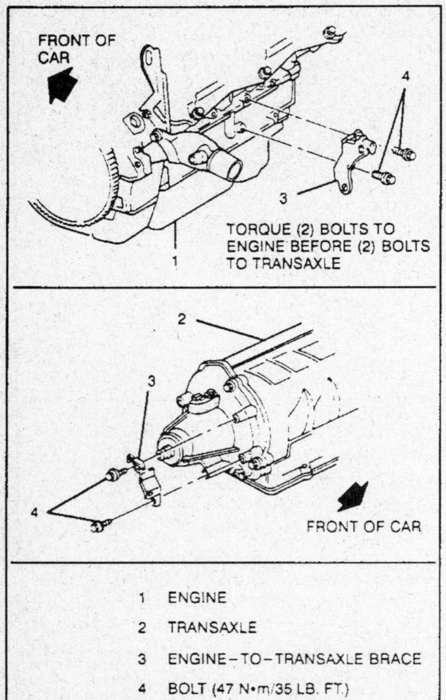

Copyrighted Material Reprinted with Permission from Hydra-Matic Div., GM Corp.

TH5029300543000X

Fig. 86 Engine to transaxle brace removal

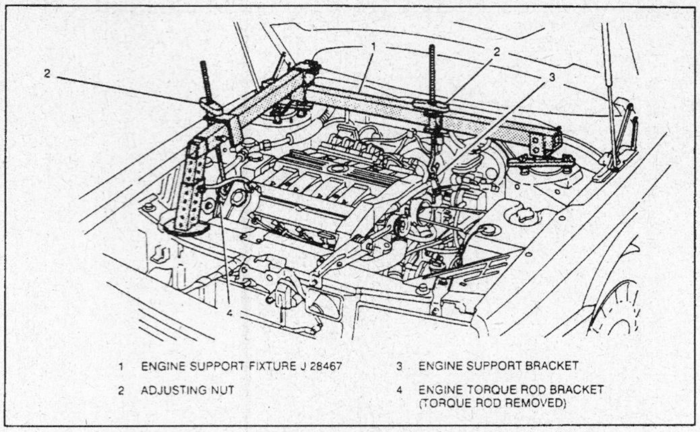

Copyrighted Material Reprinted with Permission from Hydra-Matic Div., GM Corp.

TH5029300544000X

Fig. 87 Engine support fixture installation

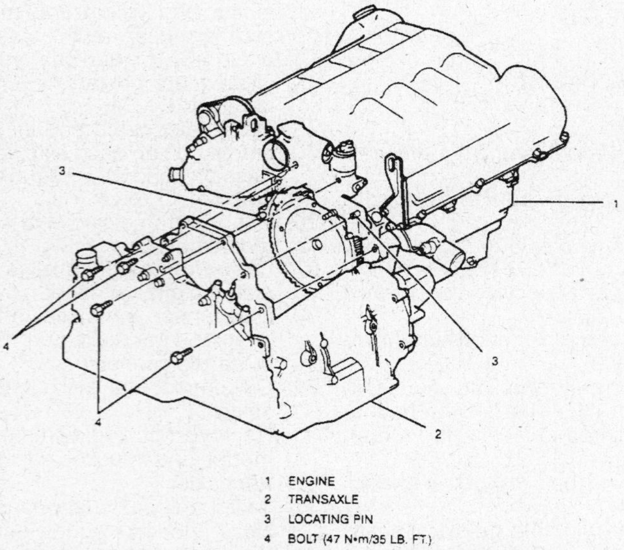

Copyrighted Material Reprinted with Permission from Hydra-Matic Div., GM Corp.

TH5029300545000X

Fig. 88 Transaxle to engine attachment locations

specifications.

b. Flush transaxle oil cooler.
c. Adjust transaxle range switch.
d. Adjust range control cable as outlined.
e. Bleed power steering system.
f. Add transmission fluid.
g. Check front suspension alignment, set toe as necessary.
h. Reset transaxle adapts.
i. Reset transaxle oil life indicator.

AURORA

1. Remove shift control cable and bracket at transaxle.
2. Remove manual shaft lever and transaxle range selector switch.
3. Install engine support fixture tool No. J-28467, or equivalent, and raise powertrain until weight is off mounts.
4. Drain cooling system.
5. Remove vacuum line at brake booster and transaxle vent hose.
6. Disconnect transaxle and power steering gear electrical connectors.
7. Disconnect upper and lower transaxle cooler lines.
8. Remove bracket retaining nut at transaxle.
9. Disconnect coolant bypass tube at thermostat housing.
10. Remove right and lefthand transaxle mount bolts.
11. Raise and support vehicle, then remove both front wheel and splash shield assemblies.
12. Remove outer tie rods and ball joints from steering knuckles.
13. Remove lefthand and righthand drive axle nuts and drive axles from hub.
14. Remove righthand and lefthand drive axles from transaxle.
15. Remove oil pan to transaxle bracket.
16. Remove torque converter cover and torque converter to flywheel bolts.
17. Remove complete exhaust system as necessary.
18. Support transaxle using a suitable jack.
19. Remove steering rack to righthand transaxle mount bolts.
20. Remove bolts and righthand transaxle mount.
21. Remove power steering lines and brackets as necessary.
22. Remove mounting bolt and righthand steering rack.
23. Remove support frame and knock sensor shield.
24. Remove engine to transaxle brace and transaxle mount to bracket retaining nuts.
25. Disconnect electrical connectors from neutral safety switch.
26. Remove rear transaxle mount bracket and engine to transaxle retaining bolts.
27. Remove bolts and frame.
28. Lower transaxle from vehicle.
29. Reverse procedure to install.

SEVILLE

1. Drain cooling system.
2. Remove upper filler panel.
3. Remove air cleaner upper plenum and intake tube.

4. Remove surge tank inlet and outlet pipes.
5. Disconnect oil cooler lines at cooler, then the oil sending line at transaxle. Plug hoses to prevent leakage.
6. Disconnect shift cable from shift linkage.
7. Remove shift linkage assembly from transaxle.
8. Remove upper transaxle to engine retaining bolts.
9. Support engine using engine support fixture tool No. J28467-360, or equivalent.
10. Raise left side of powertrain (Transaxle side) 1 inch above resting position.
11. Raise and support vehicle, then remove both front tires.
12. Remove lower splash shield.
13. Remove both front suspension position sensor links from lower control arms and position them aside.
14. Remove both stabilizer links from lower control arms. Allow stabilizer shaft to sit loosely on engine frame.
15. Remove both stabilizer shaft insulator brackets from engine frame.
16. Remove drive axle nuts, then separate axles from hub.
17. Remove both tie rod cotter pins and nuts, then separate tie rods from steering knuckles.
18. Remove both lower ball joint cotter pins and nuts, then separate ball joints from steering knuckles.
19. Remove drive axles.
20. Remove Brake Pressure Modulator Valve (BPMV) and bracket from engine frame.
21. Remove rear transaxle mount bracket retaining bolts from left frame rail.
22. Remove left and right engine mount retaining nuts from engine frame.
23. Remove steering rack retaining bolts from engine frame.
24. Remove brake line and power steering line retainers from engine frame.
25. Remove post oxygen sensor heat shield, then disconnect post oxygen sensor.
26. Disconnect one center exhaust hanger to allow easy movement of exhaust in rearward direction.
27. Remove catalytic converter brace.
28. Lower vehicle, then support engine frame using engine support table tool No. J-35580, or equivalent.
29. Remove six engine fame mount retaining bolts from engine frame.
30. Fully separate tie rod ends and lower ball joints from steering knuckles.
31. Raise vehicle slowly away from engine frame.
32. Remove engine frame and support table from under vehicle.
33. Remove steering rack heat shield from rack.
34. Disconnect power steering lines from steering rack.
35. Remove right rear engine to transaxle bracket upper retaining bolts and bracket.
36. Remove right transaxle mount bracket lower retaining bolts and bracket from transaxle. Support steering rack in a position that allows access to bracket bolts.
37. Remove steering rack.
38. Remove right front engine to transaxle brace bolt, nut, brace and heat shield.
39. Remove right front engine to transaxle bracket.
40. Remove engine oil pan to transaxle bracket, then the torque converter cover brace and cover.
41. Remove flywheel to torque converter bolts. Mark flywheel to torque converter relationship for installation.
42. Disconnect all transaxle electrical connectors.
43. Remove engine to transaxle heat shield and bracket.
44. Support transaxle using a suitable transaxle jack.
45. Remove engine to transaxle retaining bolts.
46. Separate transaxle from engine, then lower transaxle.
47. Reverse procedure to install.

TECHNICAL SERVICE BULLETINS

TCC BUSS OR MOAN

AURORA, DEVILLE, ELDORADO & SEVILLE

1997

On these models there may be a buzz or moan at 28–34 mph, at or near minimum throttle upshift speeds for one second when TCC applies.

This condition may be caused by TCC control valve and enable valve lineups in upper control valve body. This condition does not affect driveability, operation or durability. To correct this condition, install revised case cover assembly spacer plate and upper control valve body with revised remanufactured kit, part No. 24209915.

DELAYED OR NO ENGINE BRAKING IN D3

AURORA, DEVILLE, ELDORADO & SEVILLE

1998

On these models, there may be a no engine braking condition or a several second delay when the shift lever is placed in the D3 position.

This condition may be caused by coast clutch apply fluid being restricted within the forward clutch piston assembly, which is the housing for the coast clutch piston. To correct this condition, install revised forward clutch piston assembly with revised remanufactured kit part No. 24213271.

TIGHTENING SPECIFICATIONS

Year	Component	Torque/ Ft. Lbs.
1997–2000	A/C Splash Shield	35
	Accumulator Cover Bolts (8 mm)	6–10
	Actuator Rod Nut	20–25
	Axle Nut	110
	Ball Joint Nut	⑤
	Bottom Pan Bolts	②
	Case Cover Bolts & Studs	20
	Case Extension Bolt (10 mm)	15–20
	Case Extension Bolts (Except 10 mm Bolt) & Stud	37–40
	Case To Forward Clutch Support Studs	14–20
	Channel Plate To Accumulator Housing Bolts (10 mm)	6–10
	Channel Plate To Lower Control Valve Body Bolt (10 mm)	6–10
	Cooler Fitting	19–21

Continued

TIGHTENING SPECIFICATIONS—Continued

Year	Component	Torque/ Ft. Lbs.
1997-2000	Detent Roller Assembly Bolt	6–10
	Differential Housing Bolts	52–56
	Drive Axle Hub Nuts	110
	Drive Sprocket Support Bolts	8–10
	Engine Oil Pan To Transaxle Bracket③	35
	Engine Oil Pan To Transaxle Bracket④	104①
	Engine To Transaxle Brace & Heat Shield	35
	Engine To Transaxle Lower Bolts	55
	Flywheel To Converter Bolt	44
	Hub Nut	110
	Lower Control Valve Body To Channel Plate Bolts (10 mm)	6–10
	Manual Shaft Nut	15
	Oil Transfer Plate Bolts & Nuts	6–10
	Power Steering Pressure Hose Fitting	20
	Pressure Control (PC) Solenoid (Bolt)	8–10
	Pump Assembly Bolts	8–10
	Range Control Cable Bracket Bolts	108①
	Scavenge Bolt	6–10
	Scavenge Pump Body Cover Bolts (10 mm)	8–10
	Side Cover Bolt (13 mm)	15–20
	Side Cover Bolts (15 mm)	37–40
	Spacer Plate Support To Channel Plate Bolts (8mm)	6–10
	Speed Sensor Bolt	6–10
	Stabilizer Link To Strut Nuts	49
	Steering Intermediate Shaft To Steering Gear Bolt	35
	Temperature Sensor	30①
	Torque Converter Cover Bolts	108①
	Transaxle Mount Bolts	35
	Transaxle Mount Bracket Bolts	35
	Transaxle Range Control Cable Brackets	35①
	Transaxle Range Switch	104①
	Upper Control Valve Assembly Bolts	8–10
	Wiring Harness Bolts	8–10
	4th Servo Cover Bolts	6–10

①— Inch Lbs.

②— Torque bolt to 27 inch lbs., then to 53 inch lbs. & finally to 9 ft. lbs.

③— Cadillac.

④— Aurora.

⑤— Refer to "Drive Axle Seal, Replace."

Saturn S–Series 4–Speed Automatic Transaxle

NOTE: On Air Bag Equipped Models, Refer To " Air Bag System Precautions" Located In The Front Of This Manual For System Disarming & Arming Procedures.

NOTE: Refer To "Computer Relearn Procedure " Located In The Front Of This Manual For Computer Relearn Procedures.

INDEX

PRECAUTIONS

AIR BAG SYSTEMS

Refer to "Air Bag System Precautions" in the front of this manual for system disarming and arming procedures.

BATTERY GROUND CABLE

Prior to service, disconnect battery ground cable and isolate as required.

IDENTIFICATION

The transaxle identification plate is located on the torque converter housing, **Fig. 1.**

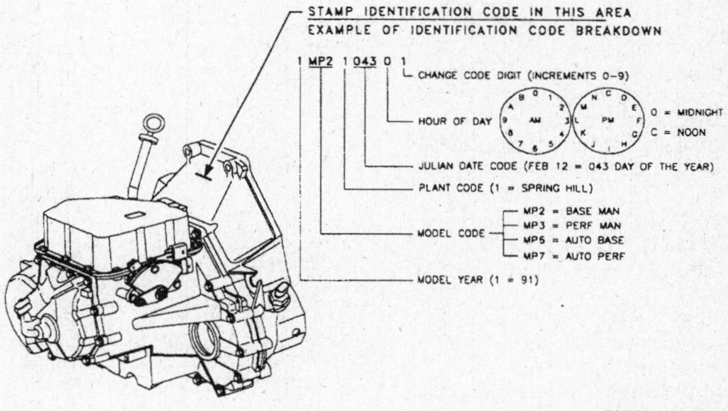

G35029100001000X

Fig. 1 Transaxle identification

DESCRIPTION

This four speed transaxle is a fully automatic unit consisting of four multiple disc clutches, a four element torque converter with a lock up clutch, 1st gear sprag clutch and a servo actuated dog clutch.

The transaxle uses and electronic control system. The unit uses five electrohydraulic actuators in conjunction with a powertrain control module (PCM) and its sensors to control shift timing, shift feel and on-board diagnostics.

TROUBLESHOOTING

Refer to **Fig. 2** for transaxle troubleshooting, **Fig. 3** for brake/transaxle shift Interlock (BTSI) system troubleshooting and **Fig. 4** for shift model selector troubleshooting.

MAINTENANCE

FLUID CHECK

1. Start engine and allow to reach normal operating temperature.
2. Position vehicle on level surface.
3. Apply parking brake.
4. Move selector through all gears.
5. Move gear selector to P (park) position.
6. Allow engine to idle for three minutes with accessories off.
7. Check fluid level, color and condition.

FLUID CHANGE

1. Fluid may be drained when operating temperature of 190–200°F is reached.
2. Turn engine off, then raise and support vehicle.
3. Remove transaxle drain plug, then allow fluid five minutes to drain.
4. Install new drain plug washer and drain plug, then **torque** plug to 22 ft. lbs.
5. Fill transaxle with to correct fluid level.

IN-VEHICLE REPAIRS

SELECTOR SWITCH, REPLACE

Removal

1. Remove air induction tube.
2. Remove air filter box, then lift resonator upward to disengage from service support bracket if necessary.
3. Disconnect gear selector switch electrical connector.
4. Remove control lever shaft attaching nut, then manual lever, noting position.
5. Remove two selector switch to transaxle case attaching bolts, then switch.

Installation

1. Install switch to transaxle, then install switch to case attaching bolt and finger tighten.
2. Install manual lever to control shaft attaching nut, then tighten to specifications.
3. Adjust switch as follows:
   a. Place transaxle in D4 position, then using a suitable ohmmeter check for continuity across selector switch terminals, if continuity is not indicated, rotate switch toward engine until continuity is present.
   b. Tighten switch to case attaching

bolts to specifications, then recheck for continuity. Failure to rotate switch toward engine to achieve continuity may result in a DTC.

4. Install cable to control lever, then adjust cable as outlined under "Shift Cable, Replace."
5. Connect switch electrical connector.
6. Install air induction tube and tighten attaching bolts to specifications.

SHIFT CABLE, REPLACE

Removal

1. Remove console assembly as outlined under "Dash Panel Service."
2. Position shifter in second gear, then disconnect cable end from shifter.
3. Depress two cable tabs on cable housing, then remove cable from shifter assembly.
4. Remove air induction tube.
5. Disconnect cable from shifter lever.
6. Depress two cable retaining tabs, then remove cable from converter housing.
7. Raise and support vehicle.
8. Remove cable grommet from front of dash, then two attaching nuts and feed grommet plate through dash hole.

Installation

1. Feed cable and plate through front of dash, then install plat and tighten attaching nuts to specifications.
2. Connect cable to shift lever assembly.
3. Install cable housing to shifter assembly.
4. Install console assembly.
5. Install cable to converter housing.
6. Ensure transaxle and shifter are in park position.
7. Release cable adjustment lock tab, using a screwdriver, to pry lock tab up, then lift with hand.
8. Connect cable to shift lever, then install retainer.
9. Move cable housing back and forth in adjuster, noting endplay:
   a. Center cable housing in middle of endplay.
   b. Press in lock tab.
   c. Verify correct operation.
10. Install air induction tube.

X — Most Probable Cause(s)
• — Possible Causes

COMPLAINT–CONDITION / CAUSE	MAT	CTS	Dis. Primary	Dis. Secondary	Fuel Delivery System	EGR System	TPS	MAP Sensor	Eng. Vac.	Engine Mech. System	PCM/TC Calibration	Trans. 1st Gear Hyd./Mech.	Trans. Line Act. System	Trans. 2nd Act. System	Trans. 3rd Act. System	Trans. 4th Act. System	Trans. TCC Act. System	Trans. Hydra/Mech.	Trans. Perf/Norm Sw.	Shift to 2 Lt. Circuit	PRNDL Sel. Circuit	Brake Switch Circuit	Trans. Master Enable Circuit	Clutch Clearance	Gear Clearance Incorrect	1st Clutch Defective	2nd Clutch Defective	3rd Clutch Defective	4th Clutch Defective	Park Pawl Mech.	Reverse Fork Mech.	TCC Defective	Input Shaft Nut
Trans Hard Up-Shift:	X	•	•		•	X	•	X			•		X					•	•		•			X			•						
1st–2nd													X	•													•	•					
2nd–3rd													X	•	•													•	•				
3rd–4th													X		•	•																	
Trans Vibration:			•		•												X	X															
While Cruising				•	•												•	X															
Idling			•		•					•								X															
Accelerating			•		•												•	X															
Cold Ambient			•		•												•	X															
Normal Operating Temperature			•		•												•	X															
Cold Engine		X	•		•												•	•															
Decelerating						•											•	X															
Accessory Load			•		•												•	X															
Under Load			•		•												•	X															
Always			•		•												•	X															
Trans Shudder:			•	•	•	•				•				•	•	•	•	•															
Acceleration				X										•	•	•	•																
Normal Operating Temperature				•													•	•															
Deceleration																	•	•															
Braking																						•											
Under Load			•	X	•	•				•				•	•	•	•	•															
2nd Gear				X										•			X	•															
3rd Gear			X			•									•		X	•															
4th Gear				X		X										•	X	•															
Reverse				•										•				X															

G35029100061010X

Fig. 2 Transaxle troubleshooting chart (Part 1 of 2)

X — Most Probable Cause(s)
• — Possible Causes

COMPLAINT–CONDITION / CAUSE	MAT	CTS	Dis. Primary	Dis. Secondary	Fuel Delivery System	EGR System	TPS	MAP Sensor	Eng. Vac.	Engine Mech. System	PCM/TCM Calibration	Trans. 1st Gear Hyd./Mech.	Trans. Line Act. System	Trans. 2nd Act. System	Trans. 3rd Act. System	Trans. 4th Act. System	Trans. TCC Act. System	Trans. Hydra/Mech.	Trans. Perf/Norm Sw.	Shift to 2 Lt. Circuit	PRNDL Sel. Circuit	Brake Switch Circuit	Trans. Master Enable Circuit	Clutch Clearance	Gear Clearance Incorrect	1st Clutch Defective	2nd Clutch Defective	3rd Clutch Defective	4th Clutch Defective	Park Pawl Mech.	Reverse Fork Mech.	TCC Defective	Input Shaft Nut
Trans Hard Downshift			•				•						X						•		•						•	•	•				
Accelerating													X						X								•	•	•				
Decelerating													X				X		X														
Shift to Two (2) Light													X				X																
Trans Slipping:													X	•	•	•	•									•	•	•	•			•	
Accelerating													X	•	•	•	•									•	•	•	•				
Normal Operating Temperature												•	X	•	•	•	•																
Cold Engine													X	•	•	•	•									•	•	•	•				
From Launch												•	X																				
1st Gear													X													X							
2nd Gear														X													X						•
3rd Gear															X													•					
4th Gear																X													•				
Reverse														X				X									X						
TCC																	X														X		
Trans Gear Missing:													X	•	•	•	•				•		•			•	•	•	•			X	
Reverse														•													X				X		•
Drives in Neutral																								X	•	•	•	•	•				
Trans No Park																														X			
Trans Stuck In Park																														X			
Trans Hunting/Gears, TCC:		•					X	X	X		•	•		X	X	X	X		•		•	X											
While Cruising		•					X	X	X		•				•																		
Cold Engine		X					•	•	•					•	•	•	•		•														
Under Load							X	X	X				•	•	•	•	•				•												

G35029100061020X

Fig. 2 Transaxle troubleshooting chart (Part 2 of 2)

PARK LOCK CABLE, REPLACE

Removal

1. Remove console as outlined under "Dash Panel Service."
2. Remove lower column cover attaching screws, upper cover and ignition cylinder.
3. Remove lower cover.
4. Release park lock cable retaining tabs, then remove from ignition module.
5. Disconnect cable from control base and remove.
6. If vehicle is equipped with an ignition module tie strap, ignition module must be replaced along with park lock cable. Refer to " Steering Column, Replace" for replacement of ignition module.

Installation

1. Install new cable and route under HVAC module fin.
2. Route under accelerator pedal bracket retaining clip.
3. Install cable to control base.
4. Install cable to ignition module.
5. Install upper and lower covers and ignition cylinder.
6. Adjust park lock cable as follows:
   a. Place shift control lever to P position.
   b. Remove key from ignition lock cylinder.
   c. Remove front cup holder assembly to access cable.
   d. Lift park lock cable adjustment lock tab.
   e. Depress control shift lever button and release 3 times to move cable into position.

X — Most Probable Cause(s)
• — Possible Causes

COMPLAINT – CONDITION / CAUSE	Turn Signal 7.5 A Fuse	Ignition 10A Fuse	Circuit 350W	Circuit 102A	Circuit 3	Circuit 139H	Circuit 1135	BTSI Solenoid	Park/Neutral Position Switch	Brake Switch	Ignition Switch
Shifts Out of Park/Ignition On/Brake Off	X	•	•	•	•	•	•	•	•	•	•
Does Not Shift Out of Park/Ignition On/Brake On								•		X	

G35029300067000X

Fig. 3 Brake/transaxle shift Interlock (BTSI) troubleshooting chart

X — Most Probable Cause(s)
• — Possible Causes

COMPLAINT – CONDITION / CAUSE	IGN 1 Fuse	Open Circuit 3C	Faulty IGN Switch	Open Right Side Body Ground	Open Circuit 350Y	Open Circuit 350A	Faulty Shift Mode Select	Open Circuit 553B	Open Circuit 553	Ground Circuit 553B	Ground Circuit 553	Ground Circuit 122Y	TCC	Open Circuit 39B
PDT Indicates Correct Position														
LED, Doesn't Operate	X	•	•				•							•
PDT Indicates Norm Only														
Light Doesn't Operate				•	•	•	•							
PDT Indicates Norm Mode Only														
LED, Light Operate							•	•	•					
PDT Indicates Perf Mode Only														
LED On All the Time										•	•	•		
LED, Light Operate													•	

G35099700070000X

Fig. 4 Shift mode selector troubleshooting chart

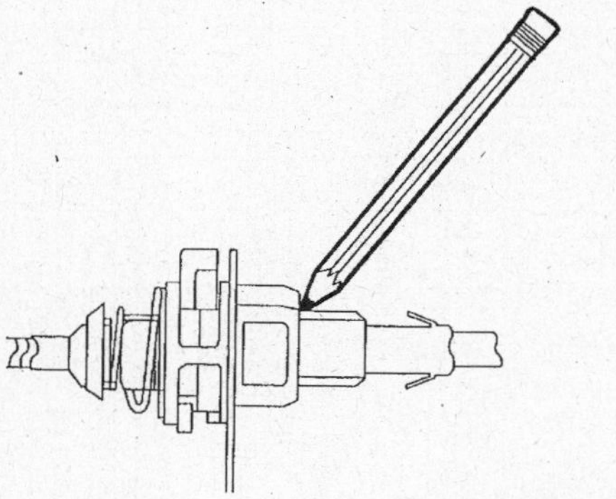

G35029800071000X

Fig. 5 Park lock cable adjustment

f. Place a mark on slider next to lock body as shown in **Fig. 5.**
g. Move cable toward control base assembly .049 inch.
h. When correct gap is obtained, depress lock tab.
i. Apply parking brake.
j. Depress shift control lever button and attempt to move shifter from P position. If shift lever moves from P position, repeat adjustment procedure.
k. Place key into ignition cylinder and turn to RUN position.
l. Depress brake pedal and shift control lever from P position.
m. Release brake pedal, then attempt to turn ignition key to LOCK position. If key moves to LOCK position, repeat adjustment procedure.

VALVE BODY, REPLACE

Removal

1. Remove air cleaner and hose assembly.
2. Remove battery and tray.
3. Loosen transaxle connector bolt, then disconnect electrical connector.
4. **On models equipped with ABS,** remove master cylinder to booster attaching nuts, lift cylinder slightly to remove valve body cover, then position cylinder back on booster studs.
5. **On all models,** remove valve body cover attaching bolts.
6. Remove eleven valve body to case bolts as shown in **Fig. 6.**

Installation

1. Lower valve body to case, then install manual link to manual valve.
2. Refer to **Fig. 7** for valve body bolt location.
3. Clean and lubricate attaching bolts with Dexron II, or equivalent.
4. Install and finger tighten valve body to case dowel bolts, **Fig. 8.**
5. Tighten valve body bolts in sequence, **Fig. 9,** to specifications.
6. Tighten valve body to case attaching bolts in sequence, **Fig. 10,** to specifications.
7. Using suitable carburetor cleaner, clean valve body cover gasket surface, then install valve body cover attaching bolts and tighten to specifications in sequence as shown in **Fig. 11.**
8. **On models equipped with ABS,** install master cylinder to booster attaching nuts, then tighten to specifications.
9. **On all models,** connector transaxle electrical connector, then tighten connector attaching bolt to specifications.
10. Install battery tray, then tighten attaching bolts to specifications.
11. Install battery and battery shield attaching bolts, then tighten to specifications.
12. Connect battery terminals. **Connect positive terminal first to prevent arcing.**

TRANSAXLE

REPLACE

1. Remove air induction tube.
2. Remove air cleaner assembly.
3. Remove transaxle strut to midrail bracket attaching bolt.
4. Loosen transaxle strut to transaxle bracket bolt and pivot strut to side.
5. Remove battery and battery tray.
6. Disconnect the following electrical connectors:
   a. Actuator connector.
   b. Vehicle and turbine speed sensor.
   c. Transaxle temperature sensor.
   d. Selector switch connector.
   e. Two ground terminals from top two converter housing bolts.

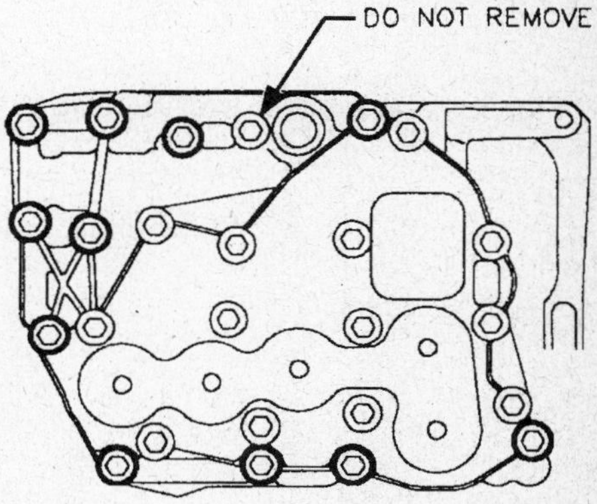

G35029100058000X

Fig. 6 Valve body to case bolt removal

   f. Ground wire from neutral safety switch.
7. Remove top two converter housing to engine bolts.
8. Disconnect spark plug wires from coil towers.
9. Remove electrical connectors from electronic ignition module.
10. Remove and discard DIS module to housing attaching bolts, then module.
11. Secure radiator to upper radiator support with mechanics wire.
12. Install engine support bar tool No. SA9105E, or equivalent.
13. Raise and support vehicle, then drain transaxle fluid.
14. Remove front wheel assemblies.
15. Remove right, left and front splash shields.
16. Remove engine strut cradle bracket to cradle attaching bolts.
17. Remove transaxle mount to cradle attaching bolt.
18. Remove front exhaust pipe.
19. Remove steering gear to cradle attaching bolts, then support gear using suitable mechanics wire.
20. Remove brake line pushpin from rear of cradle.
21. Remove stiffening brace.
22. Remove converter housing dust cover,

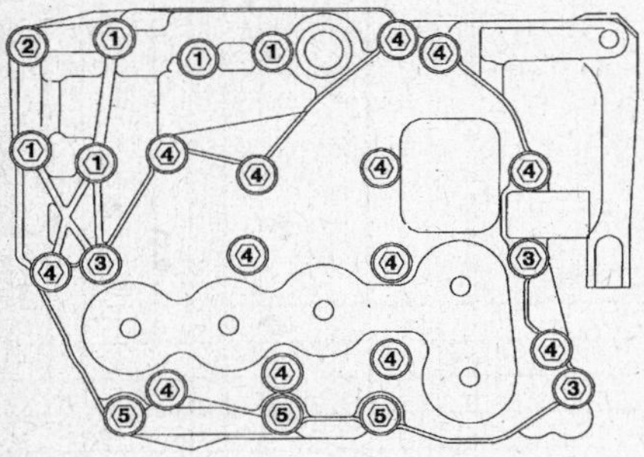

BOLT NO.	LENGTH (mm)	QUANTITY
1	50.0	5
2	57.0 DWL	1
3	83.0 DWL	3
4	75.0	13
5	65.0	3

NOTE: BOLT NUMBERS ARE NOT ON THE BOLTS.

G35029100004000A

Fig. 7 Valve body bolt location

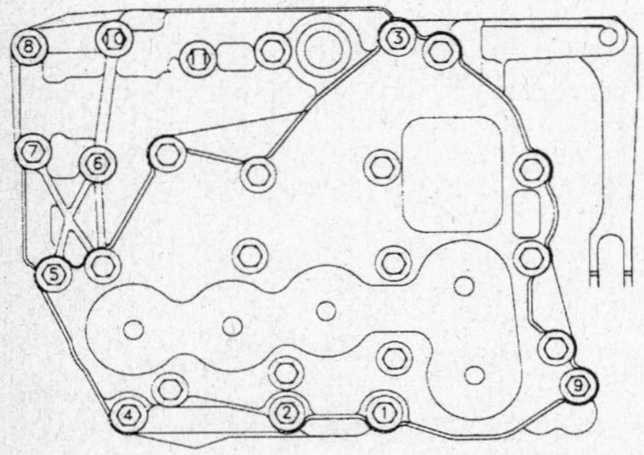

G35029100006000X

Fig. 10 Valve body to case bolt tightening sequence

then converter to flywheel attaching bolts.

23. Remove ball joint cotter pins.

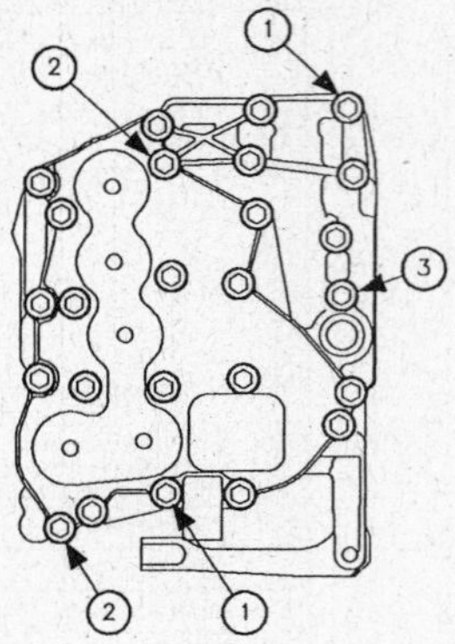

G35029800072000X

Fig. 8 Valve body dowel bolt location

24. Using ball joint separating tool No. SA9332S, separate lower ball joints from steering knuckles.
25. Using a suitable pry bar, separate left axle from transaxle.
26. Install seal protector tool No. SA91112T, or equivalent to axle seal and remove axle.
27. Separate right axle from intermediate shaft.
28. **On models equipped with DOHC engine,** remove intake manifold support bracket.
29. **On all models,** remove intermediate shaft to engine block attaching bolts.
30. Remove intermediate shaft from transaxle.
31. Using a suitable powertrain support and two 4 inch by 4 inch by 36 inch pieces of lumber, support cradle.
32. Disconnect transaxle cooler lines from transaxle.
33. Remove four cradle to body bolts, then lower cradle from vehicle.
34. Support transaxle with a suitable jack.
35. Remove remaining torque converter housing bolts.
36. Separate transaxle from engine, lower transaxle enough to reach shifter cable.

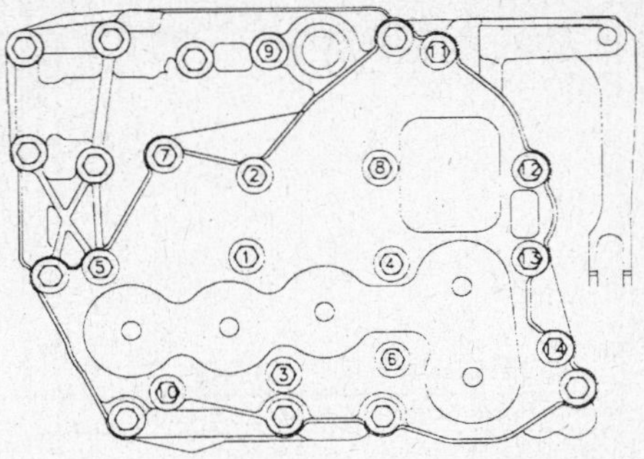

G35029100005000X

Fig. 9 Valve body bolt tightening sequence

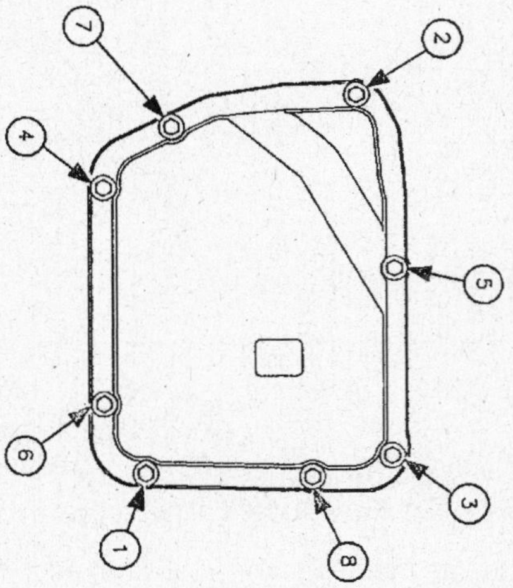

G35029800073000X

Fig. 11 Valve body cover bolt tightening sequence

37. Disconnect shift cable, then lower transaxle from vehicle.
38. Reverse procedure to install. Tighten nuts and bolts to specifications.

TIGHTENING SPECIFICATIONS

Year	Component	Torque/ Ft. Lbs.
1997–2000	Air Cleaner Box To Battery Tray	84①
	Brake Master Cylinder To Booster	20
	Converter Housing To Case (Short)	18
	Converter Housing To Case (Long)	21
	Cradle To Body	155
	Distributorless Ignition System (DIS) Module	72①
	Dust Cover To Converter Housing	96①
	Engine Strut Bracket To Cradle	37
	Exhaust Down Pipe To Catalytic Converter	18
	Exhaust Down Pipe To Exhaust Manifold	23
	Flywheel To Crankshaft	44
	Ground Terminal To Converter Housing	18
	Input Shaft Clamp	111

Continued

TIGHTENING SPECIFICATIONS—Continued

Year	Component	Torque/ Ft. Lbs.
1997-2000	Intake Bracket	22
	Intermediate Shaft Bracket	40
	Lower Ball Joint Nut	55②
	Shifter To Floor	19
	Steering Rack To Cradle	37
	Torque Converter To Flexplate	52
	Transaxle Drain Plug	22
	Transaxle Electrical Connector Bolt	27①
	Transaxle Mount To Cradle	37
	Transaxle Mount To Transaxle	24
	Transaxle Oil Indicator Tube	108①
	Transaxle To Engine Bolts	103
	Transaxle To Engine Studs	74
	Valve Body Cover Bolt	108①
	Valve Body To Case	96①
	Wheel Lug Nuts	103

①— Inch lbs.
②— Tighten, then align nut slot to cotter pin hole.

Saturn L-Series 4–Speed Automatic Transaxle

NOTE: On Air Bag Equipped Models, Refer To " Air Bag System Precautions" Located In The Front Of This Manual For System Disarming & Arming Procedures.

NOTE: Refer To "Computer Relearn Procedure " Located In The Front Of This Manual For Computer Relearn Procedures.

INDEX

PRECAUTIONS

AIR BAG SYSTEMS

Refer to "Air Bag System Precautions" in the front of this manual for system disarming and arming procedures.

BATTERY GROUND CABLE

Prior to service, disconnect battery ground cable and isolate as required.

IDENTIFICATION

The transaxle identification plate is located on the rear of the transaxle case, **Fig. 1**.

DESCRIPTION

This transaxle is a fully automatic front wheel drive electronically controlled transaxle. It provides four forward ranges that includes overdrive and a reverse gear range.

The PCM/TCM controls shift points by using two shift solenoids. A vane type pump supplies oil pressure. The PCM/TCM regulates oil pressure by means of pressure control solenoid (PCS).

TROUBLESHOOTING

Refer to **Fig. 2** for transaxle troubleshooting, **Figs. 3 and 4** for Brake Transaxle Shift Interlock (BTSI) system.

MAINTENANCE

FLUID CHECK

1. Start engine and allow to reach normal operating temperature.

2. Position vehicle on level surface.
3. Apply parking brake.
4. Move selector through all gears.
5. Move gear selector to P (park) position.
6. Allow engine to idle for three minutes with accessories off.
7. Check fluid level, color and condition.

FLUID CHANGE

1. Fluid may be drained when operating temperature of 190–200°F is reached.
2. Turn engine off, then raise and support vehicle.
3. Remove transaxle drain plug, then allow fluid five minutes to drain.
4. Install new drain plug washer and drain plug, then **torque** plug to 22 ft. lbs.
5. Fill transaxle with to correct fluid level.

IN-VEHICLE REPAIRS

TRANSAXLE RANGE SWITCH, REPLACE

Refer to "Electrical" section of the "Saturn" chassis chapter for switch replacement.

CONTROL CABLE ASSEMBLY, REPLACE

Removal

1. Remove console assembly as outlined under "Dash Panel Service."
2. Using a screwdriver disconnect control cable from control assembly, then remove control cable retaining clip.
3. Depress tabs on control cable, then remove cable from control assembly.
4. Disconnect control cable from transaxle range switch lever, then remove control cable retaining clip.
5. Depress tabs on control cable, then remove cable from control cable bracket.
6. Remove control cable grommet from dash panel, then cable from vehicle.

Installation

1. Guide control cable through pass-through in dash panel.
2. Press cable into pass through hole in dash panel, then route cable through cable bracket on powertrain mount and secure into bracket.
3. Install control cable retaining clip, then connect cable end to control assembly lever.
4. Connect control cable to pin on control assembly, then secure cable into control assembly by pushing into place.
5. Install control cable retaining clip.
6. Install console assembly.
7. Adjust cable as follows:
   a. Move control assembly into Park position, then disconnect control cable from transaxle range switch lever.
   b. Ensure range switch lever is in park position by moving lever counterclockwise until it clicks and cannot be moved any further.
   c. Release control cable assembly adjustment lock tab at control cable bracket on rear of powertrain mount.

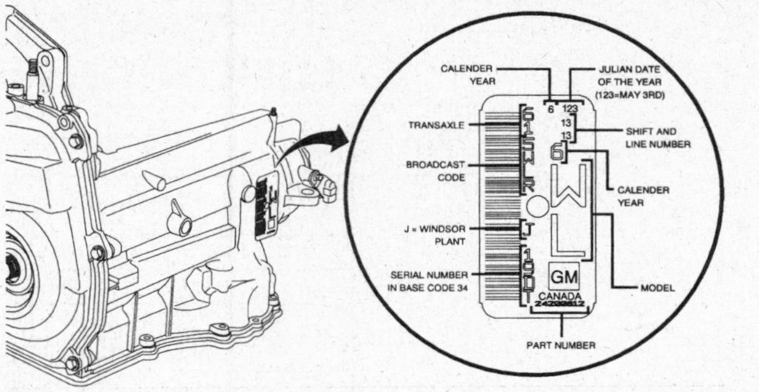

G35029900090000X

Fig. 1 Transaxle identification

   d. Use a screwdriver or pick to pry up lock tab and lift **Fig. 5.**
   e. Connect control cable end to transaxle range switch lever.
   f. Depress lock tab on control cable assembly, then verify for proper operation.

VALVE BODY, REPLACE

Removal

1. Remove battery hold down bracket and battery.
2. Remove underhood fuse block and battery tray as outlined under "Engine Replace."
3. Remove wire harness from transaxle case side cover, then upper transaxle case side cover bolts.
4. Install engine support fixture assembly to engine.
5. Mark position, then remove left transaxle mount bolts.
6. Remove left transaxle mount from engine compartment rail.
7. Remove frame assembly as outlined under "Clutch And Manual Transaxle," and "Frame Assembly Removal."
8. Remove left drive axle from transaxle using a pry bar. Remove axle retaining ring from output shaft and discard.
9. Leave axle in steering knuckle, tie axle up and position aside.
10. Remove power steering lines from bracket on left side transaxle, then the bracket.
11. Remove remaining transaxle case side bolts, then the cover and gaskets.
12. Remove oil pump bolts, then oil pump assembly and shaft **Fig. 6.**
13. Disconnect electrical connectors from the following:
    a. Pressure control solenoid and 1-2, 2-3 shift solenoids **Fig. 7.**
    b. TFP switch assembly and TCC solenoid.
14. Remove TFP switch from valve body. TFP switch O-rings are reusable if not damaged, and should remain with switch.
15. Remove remaining control valve body bolts, then the valve body assembly **Fig. 8.**
16. Remove and discard valve body to spacer plate gasket.
17. Remove spacer plate support, then spacer plate with filter and discard spacer plate to channel plate gasket. **Check balls may fall out of channel plate assembly. Retain ball with petroleum jelly.**

Installation

1. Ensure checkball are in proper locations on channel plate **Fig. 9.**
2. Install new spacer plate to channel plate gasket, then spacer plate with filter attached.
3. Hand start spacer plate support bolts, then install spacer plate support.
4. Install new valve body to spacer plate gasket, then valve body assembly onto gasket.
5. Hand start valve body assembly bolts to hold valve body in place.
6. Install TFP switch assembly onto control valve body.
7. Install remaining control valve body retaining bolts **Figs. 10 and 11,** hand start bolts.
8. Connect transaxle wiring harness connectors to TFP switch assembly, Pressure control, 1-2 and 2-3 solenoids.
9. Install oil pump shaft into control valve body assembly, oil pump onto oil pump shaft and valve body.
10. Install transaxle case side gaskets and seals, then driven sprocket thrust washer and retain with petroleum jelly.
11. **Axle seal protector tool No. J 41102 or equivalent must be used on output shaft of transaxle to protect axle seal from damage when installing case side cover. Failure to do so may cause damage to seal.**
12. Install axle seal protector tool No. J41102 on output shaft, then side cover assembly onto transaxle case.
13. Install lower transaxle side cover bolts, then left transaxle mount bracket to transaxle.
14. Install power steering lines to left transaxle mount bracket.
15. In order to prevent damage to axle shaft, add grease (P/N 7843867) or equivalent to shaft prior to installation.
16. Install new axle retaining clip on output, then untie axle shaft and install into transaxle.
17. Install frame assembly, then transaxle shaft to engine compartment rail.
18. Remove engine support fixture, then

COMPLAINT/CONDITION	POSSIBLE CAUSE(S)	CORRECTION(S)
Vibration	Torque Converter (55) out of balance	Replace torque converter.
	Missing or loose torque converter bolts/lugs	Tighten/replace faulty components.
	Internal failure of torque converter	Replace torque converter.
	Output (94) or stub shafts (58) out of balance	Replace shaft as needed.
	Output or stub shaft bushings worn	Replace bushings as needed.
	Turbine shaft out of balance	Replace turbine shaft as needed.
	Turbine shaft bushings worn	Replace bushings as needed.
RPM sensitive whine (in all ranges) which may be sensitive to RPM load, or which ceases when the TCC engages	Torque converter faulty (55)	Verify that noise is internal to torque converter by placing your left foot on the brake with the gear selector in Drive. Momentarily stall engine. If noise increases under load, replace torque converter.
High pitch whine (in all ranges) which will intensify with engine RPM or which is sensitive to the oil pressure	Oil pump faulty	Verify that noise is internal to oil pump during a preliminary oil pressure check. If an increase in line pressure causes an increase in noise, replace oil pump.
Popping noise similar to popcorn popping	Oil pump system faulty and is allowing air into the system	First inspect transaxle fluid filter for a leaky seam. Replace fluid filter and fluid filter seal.
		Next, inspect transaxle fluid filter seal for improper positioning or for a cut seal. Replace fluid filter and fluid filter seal.
		Inspect oil level control valve for proper operation or obstructions.
		Finally, inspect for pump cavitation, indicated by bubbles in fluid. Replace pump if cavitation found.
Buzz or high frequency rattle	Transaxle oil cooler line assembly is kinked	Verify a pressure buzz by watching for a needle vibration of the pressure gage. A road test may be necessary. Refer to "Road Test" procedure in this service manual. If pressure variation is found, inspect oil cooler lines. Repair/replace as necessary.
	Binding or contact at radiator, other than at cooler pipe connectors	Inspect transaxle oil cooler line assembly routing and determine where contact is. Repair/replace components as needed.

G35029900091010X

Fig. 2 Transaxle troubleshooting chart (Part 1 of 2)

COMPLAINT/CONDITION	POSSIBLE CAUSE(S)	CORRECTION(S)
A whine or growl that increases and fades with vehicle speed and is most noticeable under light acceleration	Drive link assembly system	Verify that noise comes from sprockets or from drive link assembly (chain) by placing your left foot on the brake and by moving the gear selector from Park or Neutral. If the noise stops, check the following items.
	Drive chain (36) stretched	Replace drive chain.
	Drive sprocket (37) and/or driven sprocket (91) has broken or sheared teeth	Replace faulty sprocket.
	Drive sprocket support (43) and/or driven sprocket support (95) has nicked or scored bearing surfaces	Replace faulty sprocket support.
Final drive noise is a noise or hum which is most noticeable under light throttle acceleration or turns	Final drive and differential assembly could have worn final drive planet pinion gears (714)	Inspect final drive planet pinion gear, replace as necessary.
	Final drive and differential assembly could have worn pinion thrust washers (710)	Inspect pinion thrust washers, replace as necessary.
	Final drive sun gear (115) worn or has damaged teeth	Inspect final drive sun gear, replace as necessary.
	Final drive internal gear (118) is worn or has damaged teeth	Inspect final drive internal gear, replace as necessary.
	Final drive and differential assembly has worn or pitted differential pinion gears (707)	Inspect differential pinion gears, replace as necessary.
	Final drive and differential assembly has worn or pitted differential side gears (709)	Inspect differential side gears, replace as necessary.
	Final drive and differential assembly has damaged differential pinion thrust washers (710)	Inspect differential pinion thrust washers, replace as necessary.
	Final drive and differential assembly has damaged differential side gear thrust washers (708)	Inspect differential side gear thrust washers, replace as necessary.
Noise in all forward ranges: 1st, 2nd, 3rd, and 4th	Worn or damaged final drive sun gear (115)	Inspect final drive sun gear, replace as necessary.
	Worn or damaged final drive planet pinion gear (711)	Inspect final drive planet pinion gears, replace as necessary.
Noise heard only in certain gear ranges (Random Noise)	Refer to "Range Reference Chart" in the Specifications portion of this service manual. Determine power flow and applicable components that may be causing noise.	
Ratcheting noise	Parking lock pawl return spring is damaged, weak or misassembled	Inspect forward clutch support assembly, repair/replace as necessary

G35029900091020X

Fig. 2 Transaxle troubleshooting chart (Part 2 of 2)

CIRCUIT DESCRIPTION

The brake transmission shift interlock (BTSI) solenoid is energized by the body control module (BCM) switching circuit 816 to ground while ignition is in RUN. When energized, the BTSI solenoid will allow shifting from PARK. A condition for shifting from PARK is the foot brake must be applied. The BCM receives this information over the serial data link from the engine controller. The BTSI solenoid will allow shifting from PARK when ignition is in ACCY position without a brake pedal input.

The BCM also monitors ignition 1 circuit 339 and ignition 2 circuit 743, to determine if the ignition switch is in the RUN or ACC position.

DTC SET CONDITIONS

- Ignition in RUN
- Foot brake is not applied
- Circuit 816 is shorted to ground or open

DIAGNOSTIC AIDS

- Check for poor connection at the BCM. Inspect harness connectors for backed out terminals, improper terminal mating, broken connector locks, improperly formed or damaged terminals and poor terminal to wire connection (terminal crimped over wire insulation and not conductors).
- Inspect wiring harness for damage. Check for broken or chaffed insulation.
- If fault is suspected to be intermittent, wiggling harness wiring may help in locating fault.

G35029900092010X

Fig. 3 Brake/transaxle shift interlock (BTSI) voltage low chart (Part 1 of 2)

install upper transaxle side cover bolts.
19. Install wire harness to transxale case side cover.
20. Install battery tray and underhood fuse block.
21. Install battery, then battery hold down bracket.
22. Start engine, warm up transaxle and check for fluid leaks.

TRANSAXLE

REPLACE

1. Remove battery hold down bracket and battery.
2. Remove underhood fuse block and battery tray as outlined under "Engine Replace."
3. Disconnect control cable from transaxle range switch lever using a screwdriver.
4. Remove control cable bracket from rear powertrain mount. Tie cable and bracket to dash panel.
5. Remove electrical connector, then ground wire and all wiring attachments from transaxle.
6. Disconnect transaxle range switch electrical connectors, then remove upper engine to transaxle bolts.
7. **On models equipped with 3.0L engine,** remove accessory drive belt from alternator, then accessory drive belt tensioner assembly and alternator.
8. **On all models,** disconnect output speed sensor electrical connector, then remove harness from mounting stud.
9. Install engine support fixture to engine.
10. Remove frame assembly as outlined under "Clutch And Manual Transaxle," and "Frame Assembly Removal."
11. Pry out axle shafts from transaxle, leaving axle shafts in steering knuckles and secure away from transaxle removal path.

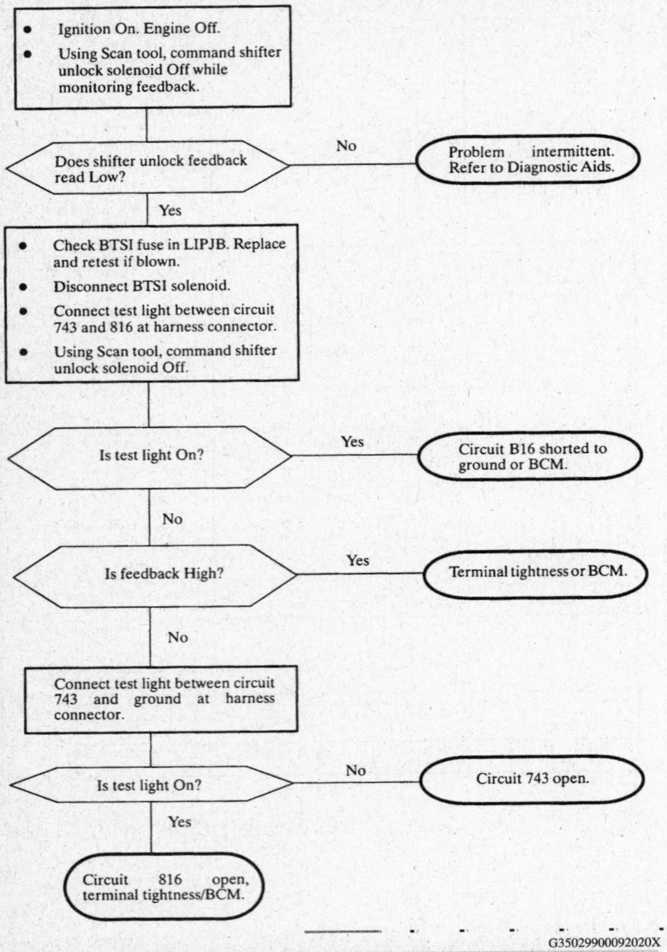

Fig. 3 Brake/transaxle shift interlock (BTSI) voltage low chart (Part 2 of 2)

CIRCUIT DESCRIPTION

The brake transmission shift interlock (BTSI) solenoid is energized by the body control module (BCM) switching circuit 816 to ground while ignition is in RUN. When energized, the BTSI solenoid will allow shifting from PARK. A condition for shifting from PARK is the foot brake must be applied. The BCM receives this information over the serial data link from the engine controller. The BTSI solenoid will allow shifting from PARK when ignition is in the ACCY position without a brake pedal input.

The BCM also monitors ignition 1 circuit 339 and ignition 2 circuit 743 to determine if the ignition switch is in the RUN or ACC position.

DTC SET CONDITIONS

- Ignition in RUN or ACCY position
- Foot brake is applied
- Circuit 816 is shorted to battery voltage

DIAGNOSTIC AIDS

- Inspect wiring harness for damage. Check for broken or chaffed insulation.
- If fault is suspected to be intermittent, wiggling harness wiring may help in locating fault.

G35029900093010X

Fig. 4 Brake/transaxle shift interlock (BTSI) voltage high chart (Part 1 of 2)

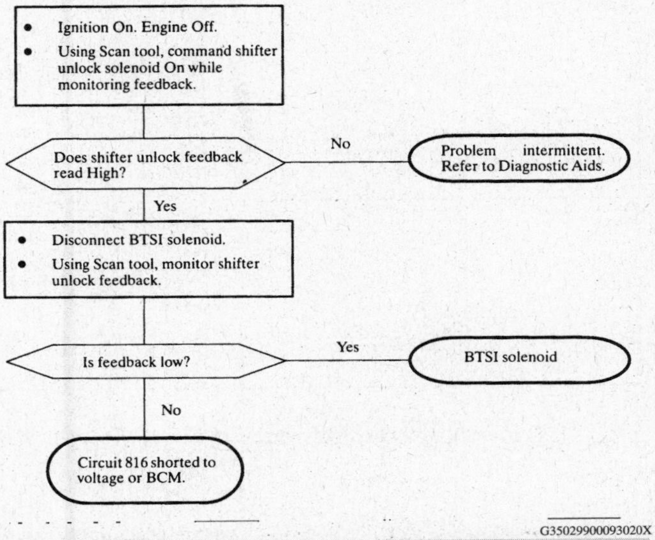

Fig. 4 Brake/transaxle shift interlock (BTSI) voltage high chart (Part 2 of 2)

12. **On models equipped with 3.0L engine,** remove wiring harness mounting bracket from rear of engine block for access to starter.
13. **On all models,** remove engine to transaxle bracket, then starter electrical connectors.
14. Remove flexplate to torque converter bolts using torque converter tool No. J-44014 or equivalent.
15. Remove oil cooler line assembly from transaxle.
16. Remove lower two engine to transaxle mounting bolts, then lower vehicle.
17. Mark position of left transaxle mount, then remove bolts.
18. Raise and support vehicle.
19. Slide hydraulic lift table under transaxle.
20. Lower vehicle slowly until transaxle is on hydraulic lift table. Place a wood block between barrel of transaxle and surface of table.
21. Remove remaining engine to transaxle mounting bolts.
22. Slide transaxle away from engine assembly, then raise vehicle from transaxle.
23. Reverse procedure to install. Tighten nuts and bolts to specifications.

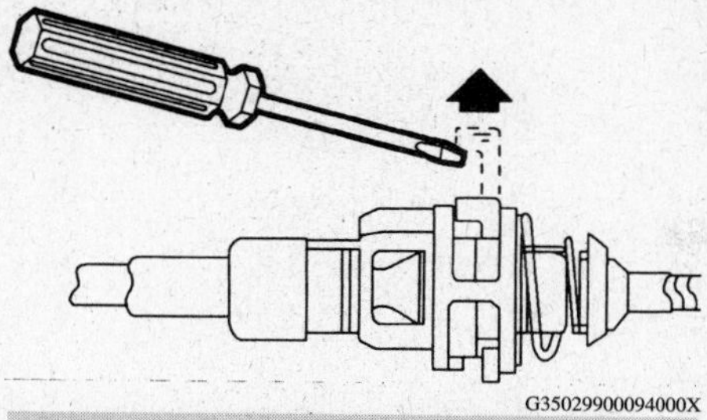

Fig. 5 Control cable assembly adjustment

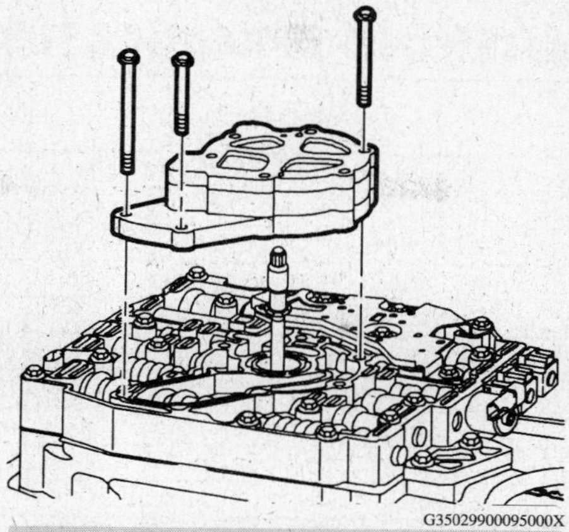

Fig. 6 Oil pump assembly & shaft removal

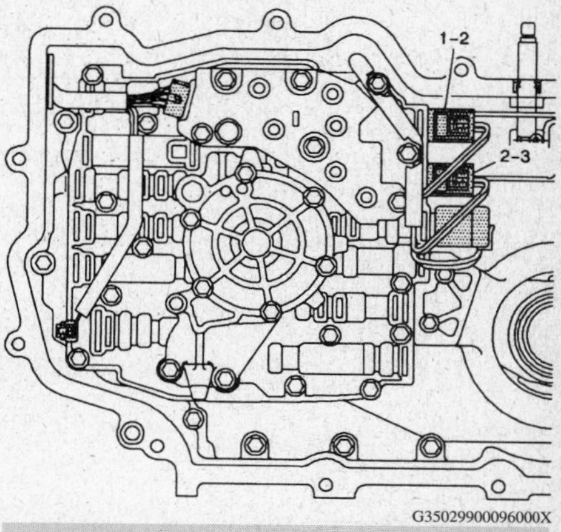

Fig. 7 1-2 & 2-3 shift solenoid harness connectors

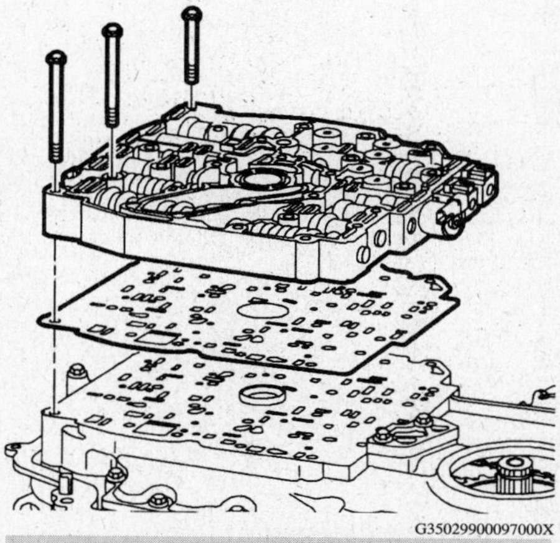

Fig. 8 Valve body removal

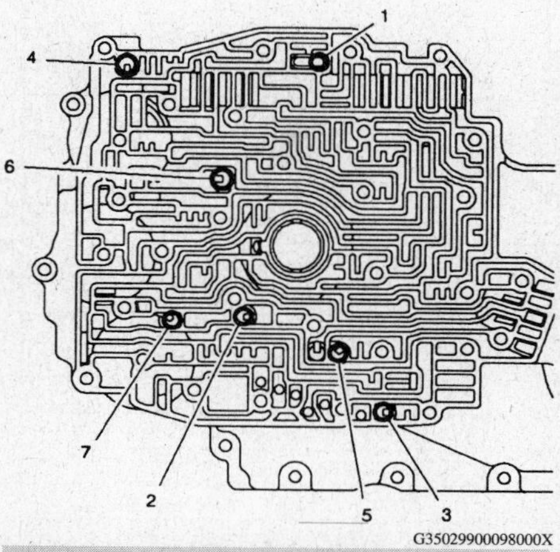

Fig. 9 Channel plate checkball locations

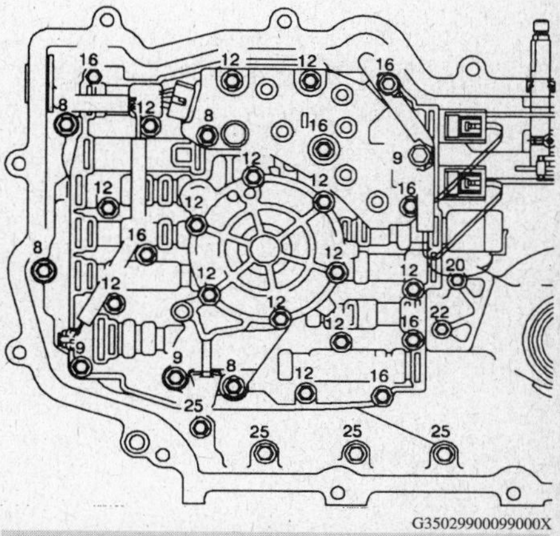

Fig. 10 Valve body bolt locations

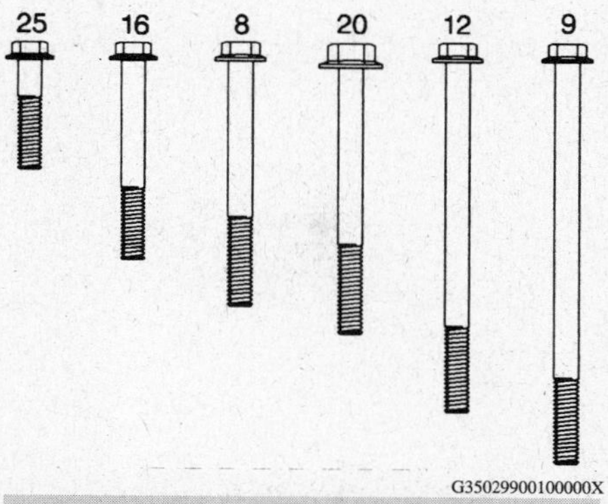

Fig. 11 Valve body bolt identification

TIGHTENING SPECIFICATIONS

Year	Component	Torque/ Ft. Lbs.
2000	Accessory Drive Belt Tensioner Bolt	30
	Aternator	30
	Channel Plate To Case	10
	Channel Plate To Driven Sprocket Support	10
	Control Assembly To Floor Pan	72①
	Control Cable Mounting Bracket	15
	Control Valve Body To Case	108①
	Engine To Transaxle	48
	Engine To Tranaxle Bracket	26
	Flexplate To Torque Converter	33
	Oil Pump	108①
	Output Speed Sensor	96①
	Power Steering Line To Left Transaxle Mount	84①
	Side Cover To Transaxle Case	15
	Spacer Plate Support	10
	Starter Assembly	30
	Transaxle Cooler Line Fittings	18
	Transaxle Mount (Front) Through Bolt	41
	Transaxle To Engine Compartment Rail	15
	Transaxle To Mount Bracket	66
	Transaxle Mount To Mount Bracket	41
	Transaxle Mount (Rear) Through Bolt	66
	Transaxle Mounts (Front & Rear) to Transaxle	66
	Transaxle Range Switch	15
	Transaxle Range Switch Lever	26
	Wire Harness Attachment	15
	Wiring Harness Retainer	108①
	Wheel Log Nut	92

① — Inch lbs.

FRONT WHEEL DRIVE AXLES

TABLE OF CONTENTS

General Motors

INDEX

PRECAUTIONS

BATTERY GROUND CABLE

Prior to service, disconnect battery ground cable and isolate as required.

GENERAL PRECAUTIONS

On models equipped with tripod joints on inboard axles, care must be taken not to overextend joints. When either or both ends are disconnected, overextending the tripod joint could result in internal joint separation.

On vehicles equipped with ball type constant velocity inboard joints, install inner drive joint seal protector tool No. J-34754, or equivalent, on inboard seal and install axle boot protector tool No. J-28712, or equivalent, on outboard seal if necessary. On vehicles equipped with tripod inboard joints, install axle boot seal protector tool No. J-28712, or equivalent, on outboard seal and tool No. J-33162, or equivalent, on inboard seal, if necessary.

DESCRIPTION

Front wheel drive systems, **Figs. 1 through 6,** consist of left and right drive axles. The drive axles have three major components; inboard constant velocity (CV) joint, axle shaft and outboard constant velocity (CV) joint.

The inboard CV joint is connected to the transaxle and may use a tripod joint, double offset joint or a ball type joint. Either type joint allows the drive axle to move with the suspension. The outboard CV joint uses a ball type constant velocity joint. The ball type joint allows the drive axle to move with steering and suspension movements.

TROUBLESHOOTING

CLICKING NOISE IN TURNS

Worn or damaged outboard joint, cut or damaged seals.

CLUNK WHEN ACCELERATING FROM COAST TO DRIVE

Worn or damaged constant velocity joint.

SHUDDER OR VIBRATION DURING ACCELERATION

1. Excessive CV joint angle due to incorrect toe in or incorrect trim height.
2. Worn or damaged inboard or outboard CV joints.
3. Sticking tripod joint spider assembly.

VIBRATION AT HIGHWAY SPEEDS

1. Out-of-balance front tires or wheels.
2. Out-of-round front tires.
3. Worn CV joint.
4. Binding or tight CV joint.

DRIVESHAFT

REPLACE

ACHIEVA, ALERO, CAVALIER, CUTLASS, GRAND AM, MALIBU, SKYLARK & SUNFIRE

Prior to removal of drive axle assembly, cover all sharp edges in area of drive axle with shop towel so that seal is not damaged during removal.

1. Raise and support vehicle, then remove wheel and tire assembly.
2. Disconnect tie rod from steering knuckle.
3. Insert a drift or punch into caliper and rotor to prevent rotor from turning.
4. Remove drive axle nut and washer.
5. Remove ball joint cotter pin and nut, then loosen joint using ball joint separator tool No. J -38892, or equivalent.
6. **On models equipped with ABS,** disconnect ABS sensor wire
7. **On all models,** disconnect stabilizer link, then separate joint using a suitable ball joint separator.
8. Disconnect axle from hub and bearing using front hub spindle tool No.

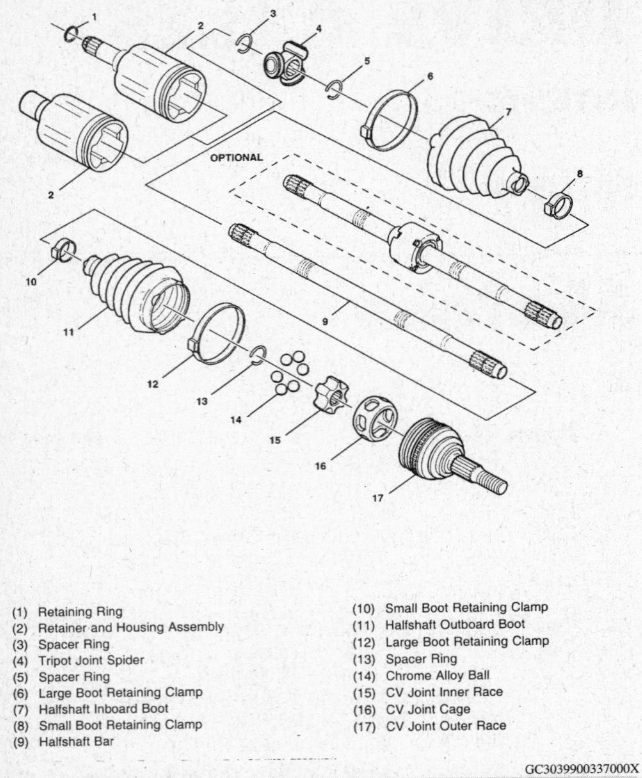

Fig. 1 Exploded view of front drive axle assembly. Cavalier & Sunfire

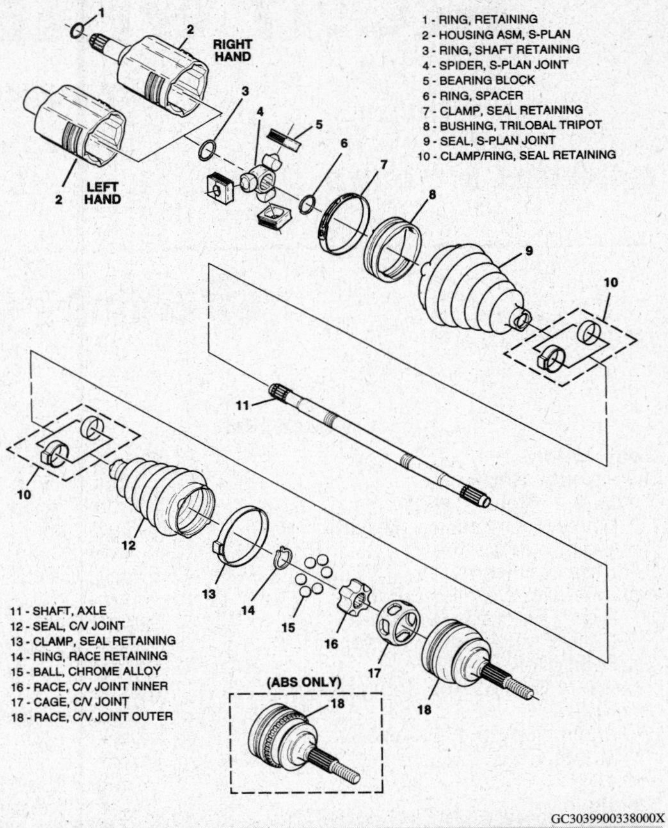

Fig. 2 Exploded view of front drive axle assembly. 1997 Seville & 1997–98 DeVille & Eldorado

J-28733, or equivalent, then move strut and knuckle assembly rearward.

9. Reverse procedure to install. Tighten fasteners to specifications.

AURORA & RIVIERA

Removal

1. Raise and support vehicle, then remove wheels.
2. Remove stabilizer shaft link assembly bolt.
3. Remove ball joint cotter pin and nut, then loosen joint using ball joint removal tool No. J-36226, or equivalent.
4. Separate joint with pry bar between suspension support and lower control arm.
5. Insert suitable drift or screwdriver into caliper and rotor to prevent rotor from turning, then remove hub nut.
6. Using puller tool No. J-28733-B, or equivalent, separate axle from hub.
7. Move strut and knuckle rearward.
8. Using puller tools No. J-33008 and J-2619-01, or equivalents, remove drive axle from transaxle.

Installation

1. If installing right side drive axle, install protector tool No. J-37292-B, or equivalent, so that it may be removed after drive axle is installed.
2. Install drive axle into transaxle by placing a suitable screwdriver into groove on joint housing and tapping until axle is seated.
3. Insert drive axle into hub and bearing, then install new hub nut.
4. Insert a suitable drift or screwdriver into caliper and rotor to prevent rotor from turning, then tighten axle nut to specification.
5. Attach ball joint to knuckle and tighten to specification.
6. Install stabilizer shaft link assembly and tighten to specification.
7. Remove protector tool No. J-37292-B, or equivalent.
8. Install wheels and lower vehicle.

BONNEVILLE, DEVILLE, EIGHTY EIGHT, ELDORADO, LESABRE, LSS, PARK AVENUE, REGENCY & SEVILLE

Removal

1. Raise and support vehicle, then remove tire and wheel assembly.
2. Install a brass drift or a screwdriver to prevent rotor from turning.
3. Remove axle nut and washer.
4. Remove stabilizer shaft or link from control arm.
5. Remove nut from ball joint, then separate ball joint from steering knuckle using separator tool No. J-36226, or equivalent.
6. Remove drive axle from hub and bearing assembly using front hub spindle remover tool No. J-28733-A, or equivalent.
7. Remove drive axle from transaxle using axle shaft remover puller tools No. J-33008, J-29794 and slide hammer tool No. J-2619-01, or equivalents, if necessary.

Installation

1. Install drive axle into transaxle using seal protector tool No. J-37292-B, or equivalent
2. Seat snap ring by placing a screwdriver into groove on joint housing and tapping until seated.
3. Grasp inner housing and pull outward. If snap ring is properly seated, axle will remain in place.
4. Install drive axle into hub and bearing assembly.
5. Install lower ball joint to steering knuckle and tighten to specifications.
6. Install stabilizer shaft or link to control arm and tighten to specifications.
7. Insert a screwdriver or drift into caliper and rotor to prevent rotor from turning.
8. Install new hub nut and washer and tighten to specification.
9. Install tire and wheel assembly, then lower vehicle.

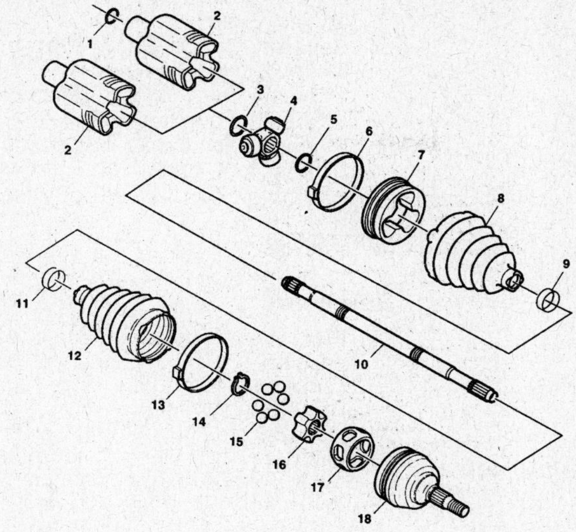

(1) Retaining Ring
(2) Retainer and Housing Assembly
(3) Shaft Retaining Ring
(4) Tripot Spider Assembly
(5) Spacer Ring
(6) Boot Retaining Clamp
(7) Tripot Trilobal Bushing
(8) Halfshaft Inboard Boot
(9) Swage Ring
(10) Halfshaft Bar
(11) Swage Ring
(12) Halfshaft Outboard Boot
(13) Boot Retaining Clamp
(14) Race Retaining Ring
(15) Chrome Alloy Ball
(16) CV Joint Inner Race
(17) CV Joint Cage
(18) CV Joint Outer Race

GC3039900339000X

Fig. 3 Exploded view of front drive axle assembly. Except Cavalier, Metro, Prizm, Sunfire & 1997 Seville & 1997–98 DeVille & Eldorado

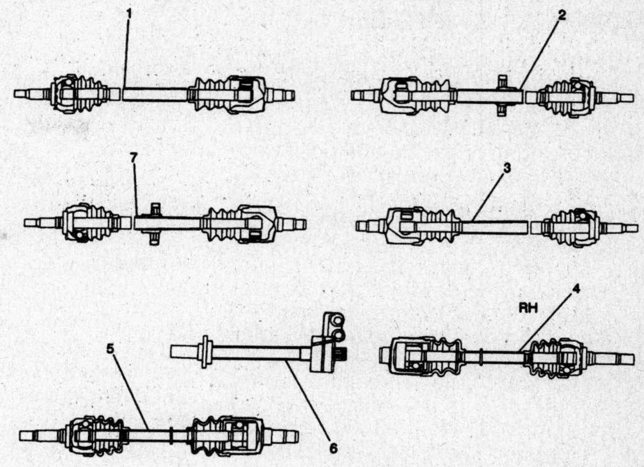

(1) Left Drive Axle Shaft (Automatic Transaxle)
(2) Right Drive Axle Shaft (Automatic Transaxle)
(3) Right Drive Axle Shaft (Manual Transaxle 1.0 L Vehicles Only)
(4) Right Drive Axle Shaft (Manual Transaxle 1.3 L Vehicles Only)
(5) Left Drive Axle Shaft (Manual Transaxle 1.3 L Vehicles Only)
(6) Right Inner Drive Axle Shaft Support Arbor (Manual Transaxle)
(7) Left Drive Axle Shaft (Manual Transaxle 1.0 L Vehicles Only)

GC3039900340000X

Fig. 4 Cutaway view of front drive axle assembly. Metro

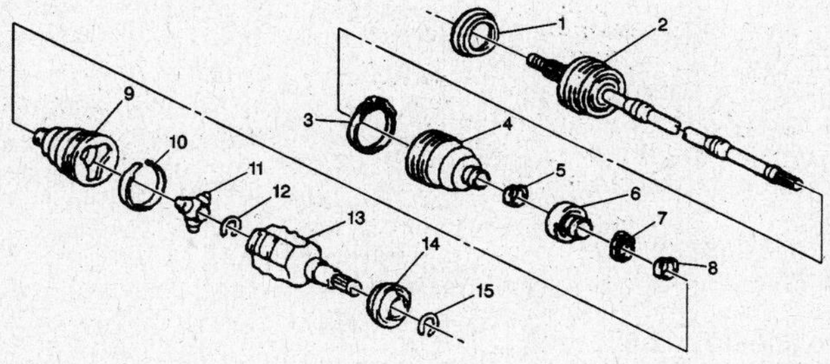

(1) Outer Joint Seal
(2) Outer Joint
(3) Outer Boot Clamp
(4) Outer Boot
(5) Outer Boot Clamp
(6) Damper (RH Shaft Only)
(7) Damper Clamp
(8) Inner Boot Clamp
(9) Inner Boot
(10) Inner Boot Clamp
(11) Tripot Joint
(12) Snap Ring
(13) Inner Joint Housing
(14) Inner Joint Seal
(15) Snap Ring

GC3039900341000X

Fig. 5 Exploded view of front drive axle assembly. Prizm

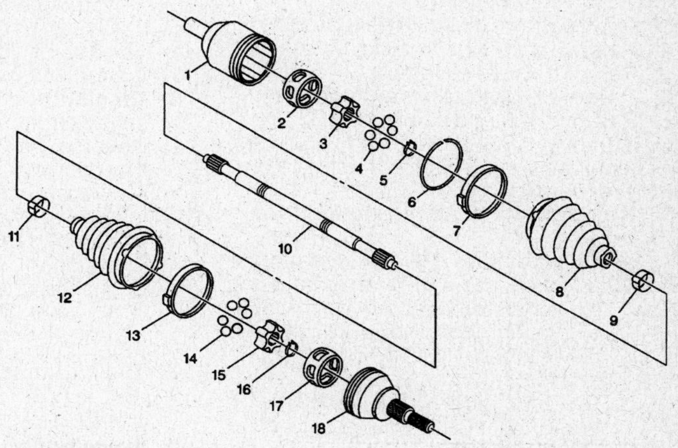

1. Inner Joint Outer Race
2. Inner Joint Cage
3. Inner Joint Inner Race
4. Ball Bearings
5. Inner Joint Inner Race Retaining Snap Ring
6. Inner Joint Outer Race Retaining Ring
7. Inner Joint Large Seal Clamp
8. Inner Joint Seal
9. Inner Joint Small Seal Clamp
10. Axle Shaft
11. Outer Joint Small Seal Clamp
12. Outer Joint Seal
13. Outer Joint Large Seal Clamp
14. Ball Bearings
15. Outer Joint Inner Race
16. Outer Joint Retaining Ring
17. Outer Joint Cage
18. Outer Joint Outer Race

GC3030000370000X

Fig. 6 Exploded view of front drive axle assembly. Impala

CENTURY, GRAND PRIX, INTRIGUE & REGAL

1. Raise and support vehicle, then remove tire and wheel assembly.
2. Remove stabilizer link.
3. Remove front wheel drive axle nut.
4. Insert a drift or flat bladed tool into caliper and rotor to prevent rotor from turning.
5. Disconnect tie rod from steering knuckle.
6. Disconnect ball joint from steering knuckle using ball joint/stud separator tool No. J-41820, or equivalent.
7. Remove axle shaft, noting the following:
   a. **On right side drive axle,** separate drive axle from transaxle using axle shaft tool No. J-3308, extension tool No. J-29794 and puller tool No. J-2619-01, or equivalents.
   b. **On left side drive axle,** using frame for leverage, separate drive axle from transaxle with a screwdriver or prybar in groove provided on inner joint.
8. **On both sides,** reverse procedure to install, noting the following:
   a. Install a new front wheel drive axle nut.
   b. Tighten fasteners to specifications.

CUTLASS SUPREME, LUMINA & MONTE CARLO

1. Remove front wheel drive axle nut.
2. Raise and support vehicle.
3. Remove wheel assembly.
4. Remove brake caliper and rotor.
5. Remove hub and bearing.
6. Remove ABS sensor retaining bolt, then position ABS sensor aside to prevent damage.
7. Remove axle shaft, noting the following:
   a. **On right side drive axle,** separate drive axle from the transaxle using axle shaft remover tool No. J-3308, extension tool No. J-29794 and puller tool No. J-2619-01, or equivalents.
   b. **On left side drive axle,** using frame for leverage, separate drive axle from transaxle with a screwdriver or prybar in groove provided on inner joint.
8. **On both sides,** remove drive axle bearing through knuckle.
9. Reverse procedure to install, noting the following:
   a. Install axle seal protector tool No. J-37292-A, or equivalent, to right side of transaxle in a position so it can be pulled out after drive axle is installed.
   b. Tighten fasteners to specification.

METRO

1. Raise and support vehicle.
2. **On models with ABS,** remove ABS wheel speed sensor.
3. **On all models,** remove wheel and tire assembly.

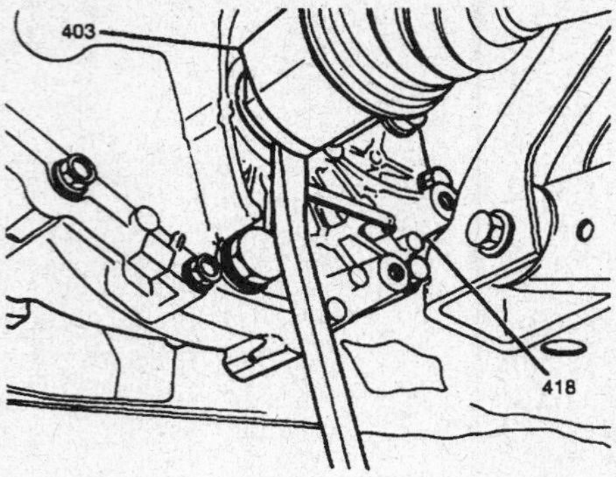

403 DIFFERENTIAL-SIDE JOINT HOUSING
418 TRANSAXLE ASSEMBLY

GC3039600278000X

Fig. 7 Inner joint removal. Metro & Prizm

4. Unstake, then remove driveshaft nut and washer.
5. Remove ball joint pinch bolt, then pry ball joint from knuckle.
6. **On models except sedan,** pry inboard driveshaft joints from transaxle using a pry bar or large screwdriver, **Fig. 7.**
7. **On sedan models,** remove drive axle as follows:
   a. Pry lefthand side inboard driveshaft joint from transaxle using a large screwdriver.
   b. Using a suitable soft mallet, tap at base of right inner joint to remove from intermediate driveshaft.
8. **On all models,** remove drive axle assembly from steering knuckle.
9. Reverse procedure to install, noting the following:
   a. Clean front wheel bearing seal, then apply grease to seal.
   b. Check seal for breakage or deterioration, replace if necessary.
   c. Install wheel side joint to steering knuckle, then the differential-side joint to the transaxle.
   d. Push drive axle into transaxle by hand until snap ring is seated in spline.
   e. Tighten fasteners to specification.
   f. Stake axle nut.

PRIZM

1. Raise and support vehicle.
2. Remove hub nut cap, then the cotter pin, hub nut and washer.
3. Remove tie rod end nut, then separate tie rod from steering knuckle using tie rod end puller tool No. J-6627-A, or equivalent.
4. Remove ball joint mounting nuts from control arm, then separate knuckle and ball joint from control arm.
5. Using a suitable soft face hammer, remove drive axle from hub assembly. If shaft is difficult to remove, use crankshaft gear puller tool No. J-25287, or equivalent.
6. Remove drive axle assembly from transaxle by gently prying between transaxle case and joint with a suitable pry bar, **Fig. 7.**
7. Reverse procedure to install, noting the following:
   a. Install drive axle in transaxle first, then the hub assembly.
   b. Ensure joint snap ring is seated in transaxle.
   c. Tighten fasteners to specification.

IMPALA

Removal

1. Place transmission in Park or Neutral position.
2. Apply parking brake.
3. Raise and support vehicle.
4. Remove tire and wheel assembly.
5. Insert a drift or punch into brake rotor cooling fins and against caliper to prevent wheel hub and bearing from turning.
6. Remove spindle nut retaining rear wheel drive shaft to hub.
7. Remove drift or punch.
8. Release parking brake.
9. Remove rear transverse spring.
10. Separate outer tie rod end from knuckle and position tie rod toward rear of vehicle. **Do not loosen outer tie rod jam nut.**
11. Disconnect wheel speed sensor electrical connector.
12. Disconnect parking brake cable from parking brake lever.
13. Remove parking brake cable from bracket and reposition toward rear.
14. Install rear hub spindle removal tool No. J42129, or equivalent, onto wheel hub and secure it with wheel lugs.
15. Partially disengage driveshaft from wheel hub and bearing.
16. Separate lower ball joint from suspension knuckle.
17. Disengage driveshaft completely from wheel hub and bearing.
18. Support driveshaft.
19. Support suspension knuckle and upper control arm, then position knuckle toward front of vehicle.
20. Assemble axle shaft removal tool No. J42128, extension tool No. J29794 and slide hammer tool No. J2619-01, or equivalents.
21. Install axle shaft removal tool No. J42128, or equivalent, evenly onto rear beveled surface of driveshaft inner joint housing.
22. Disengage driveshaft from rear axle differential, then remove tool assembly.

Installation

1. Position driveshaft to rear axle differential output shaft. **Ensure to support driveshaft until it is completely installed.**
2. Align and guide driveshaft onto differential output shaft.
3. Engage driveshaft fully onto differential output shaft.

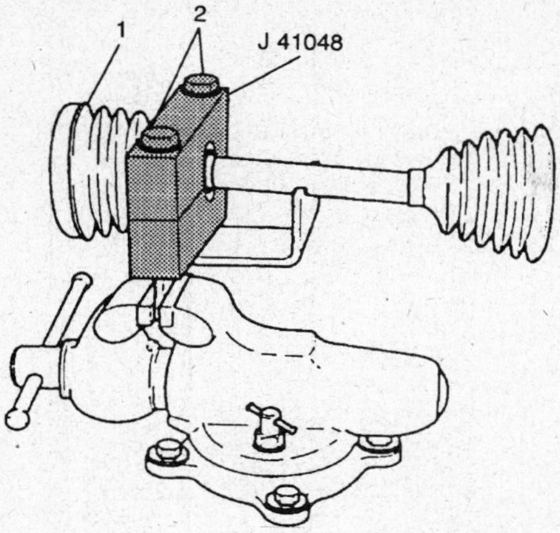

GC3039900315000X

Fig. 8 Small wage tool installation. Except Cavalier, Metro, Sunfire & Prizm

4. Ensure driveshaft is fully seated on differential output shaft.
5. Position suspension knuckle to driveshaft.
6. Align and guide driveshaft into wheel hub and bearing. **Do not seat fully.**
7. Connect lower ball joint to suspension knuckle.
8. Install parking brake cable into bracket.
9. Connect parking brake cable to parking brake lever.
10. Connect wheel speed sensor electrical connector.
11. Connect outer tie rod end to suspension knuckle.
12. Install rear transverse spring.
13. Set parking brake.
14. Insert a drift or punch into brake rotor cooling fins and against caliper to prevent wheel hub and bearing from turning.
15. Install driveshaft retaining nut, noting the following:
    a. Slowly tighten nut to draw driveshaft to wheel hub and bearing.
    b. **Torque** drive axle spindle nut 118 ft. lbs.
16. Remove drift or punch.
17. Release parking brake.
18. Install wheel and tire assembly.
19. Lower vehicle.

DRIVESHAFT SERVICE

Except Cavalier, Metro, Prizm & Sunfire

INNER TRIPOD JOINT

DISASSEMBLE

When halfshaft is removed for any reason, the transmission sealing surface (Tripod male/female shank of compartment) should be inspected for corrosion. If corrosion is present, surface should be cleaned using crocus cloth or suitable equivalent. Refer to **Figs. 2 and 3** when performing the following procedure.

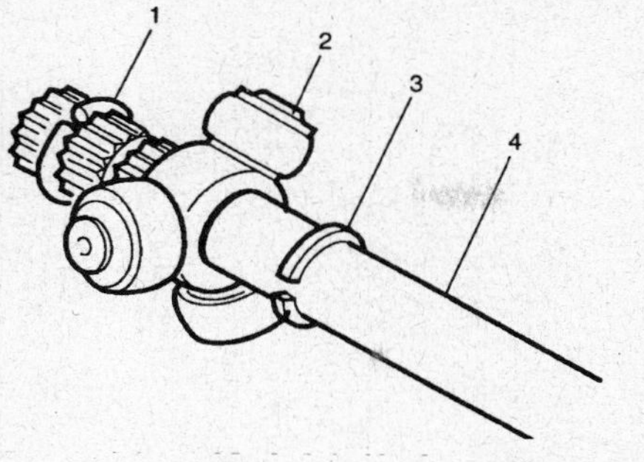

GC3039900316000X

Fig. 9 Inner tripod joint assemble. Except Cavalier, Metro, Sunfire & Prizm

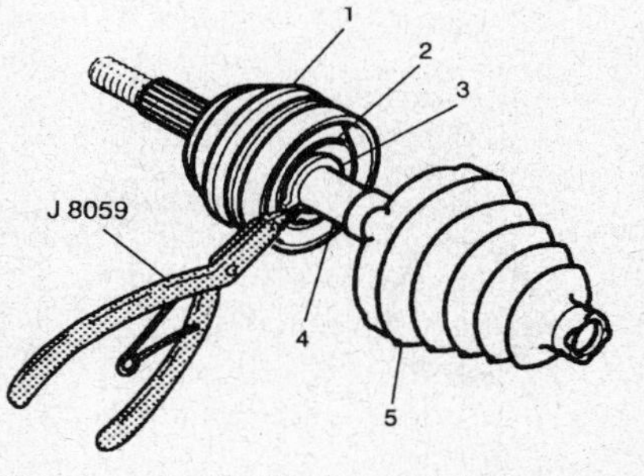

GC3039900318000X

Fig. 11 Outer CV joint disassemble. Except Cavalier, Sunfire & Prizm

1. Use a hand grinder, or equivalent, to cut through swage ring. Use care not to damage tripod housing.
2. Remove large boot retaining clamp from tripod joint using a suitable side cutter, then discard clamp.
3. Disconnect inboard boot from trilobal tripod bushing at large diameter.
4. Slide boot away from joint along shaft.
5. Remove housing from tripod joint spider and shaft.
6. Remove trilobal tripod bushing from housing.
7. Spread spacer ring using snap ring pliers No. J-8059, or equivalent.
8. Slide spacer ring and tripod joint spider backward on shaft.
9. Remove retaining ring from groove on shaft.
10. Slide tripod joint spider assembly off shaft.

ASSEMBLE

1. Place new small boot clamp onto small end of joint boot.
2. Slide clamp and boot onto shaft.
3. Position small end of joint boot into joint boot groove on shaft.
4. Mount lower part of small swage tool No. J-41048, or equivalent, in a vise, **Fig. 8.**
5. Position outboard end (1) of shaft assembly in small swage tool.
6. Align top of boot neck on bottom die using indicator.
7. Place top half of small swage tool on lower half.
8. Ensure there are no pinch points on inboard boot. This could cause damage to inboard boot.
9. Insert bolts (2) and hand tighten.
10. Ensure inboard boot, housing and swage ring are all aligned.
11. Tighten each bolt (2) 180° at a time until both sides are bottomed.
12. Install spacer ring (2) beyond second ring using snap ring pliers tool No. J-8059, or equivalent, **Fig. 9.**
13. Ensure counterbored face on joint spider (2) faces toward end of shaft (4).
14. Slide joint spider assembly (2) toward spacer ring (1) as far as it will go.
15. Install retaining ring in groove of shaft.
16. Slide joint spider assembly back towards end of bar, then reseat spacer ring in groove.
17. Place half of grease from service kit in inboard boot, then use remaining grease to repack housing.
18. Install trilobal bushing to housing.
19. Position larger new boot retaining clamp on inboard boot, then slide housing over spider assembly on shaft.
20. Slide large diameter of inboard boot with clamp in place over outside of trilobal tripod bushing, then locate lip of boot in groove.
21. Ensure shaft inboard boot is not dimpled, stretched out or deformed in any way.
22. Position joint assembly at proper vehicle dimension using seal clamp tool No. J-35910, or equivalent, **Fig. 10.**
23. Align inboard boot (3), tripod housing (1) and large boot retaining clamp (2).
24. Crimp boot retaining clamp using seal clamp tool to specifications.

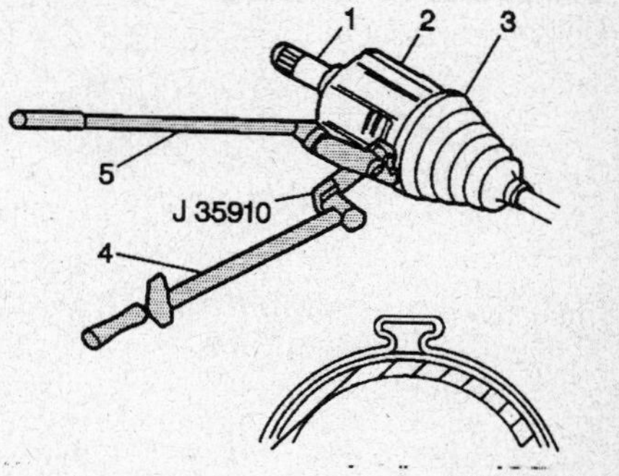

GC3039900317000X

Fig. 10 Inner tripod joint alignment. Except Cavalier, Metro, Sunfire & Prizm

OUTER CONSTANT VELOCITY (CV) JOINT

DISASSEMBLE

1. Remove large and small boot retaining clamps from CV joint with a suitable side cutter. Discard clamps.
2. Disconnect outboard boot (5) from CV joint outer race (1) at large diameter and slide boot away form joint, **Fig. 11.**
3. Wipe grease from face of CV joint inner race.
4. Spread ears on race retaining ring (3) using snap ring pliers No. J-8059, or

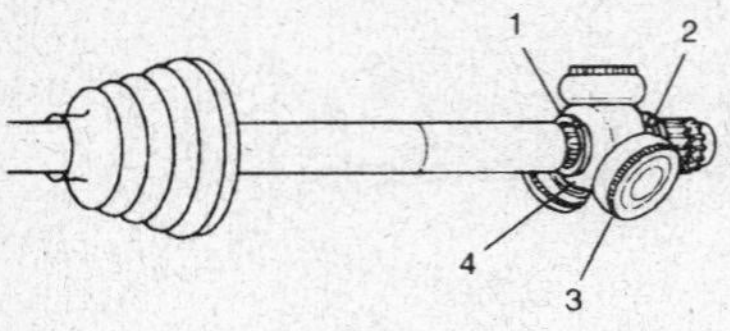

Fig. 12 Inner tripod joint. Cavalier & Sunfire

equivalent, then remove CV joint assembly from shaft.
5. Remove shaft outboard boot (5) from shaft.
6. Using a brass drift and hammer, tap on CV joint cage until it is tilted enough to remove first chrome alloy ball.
7. Tilt cage in opposite direction to remove opposing ball. Repeat until all six balls are removed.
8. Position CV joint cage and inner race 90° to centerline of outer race, then align joint cage windows with lands of outer race.
9. Remove CV joint cage and inner race from outer race.
10. Rotate CV joint inner race 90° to centerline of joint cage. Ensure lands of joint inner race are aligned with windows of CV joint cage.
11. Pivot inner race into cage window, then remove inner race.

ASSEMBLE

1. Install new boot retaining clamp on neck of shaft outboard boot.
2. Slide outboard boot onto shaft and position neck of boot in boot groove on shaft.
3. Crimp boot retaining clamp using seal clamp tool No. J-35910, or equivalent, to specifications.
4. Place a light coat of grease from service kit on ball grooves of inner and outer races.
5. Hold inner race 90° to centerline of cage with lands of inner race aligned with windows of cage, then install inner race into cage.
6. Hold cage and inner race 90° to centerline of outer race and align cage windows with lands of outer race. Ensure retaining ring side of inner race faces compartment bar.
7. Install cage and inner race into outer race.
8. Install first chrome ball, then tilt cage in opposite direction to install opposing ball. Repeat until all six balls are in place.
9. Place half amount of grease supplied with kit inside outboard boot, then use remaining grease to pack CV joint.
10. Push CV joint onto shaft until retaining ring is seated in groove on shaft. Ensure CV boot is not dimpled, stretched out or out of shape in any way.
11. Slide large diameter of outboard boot with large boot retaining clamp in place over outside CV joint outer race, then locate boot lip in groove on CV joint outer race.

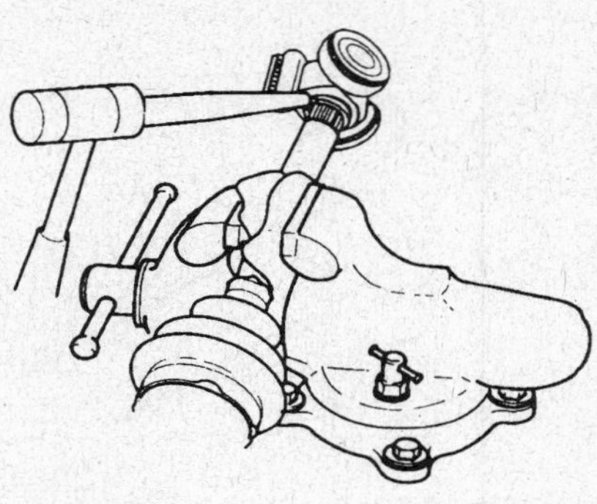

Fig. 13 Tripod joint removal. Cavalier & Sunfire

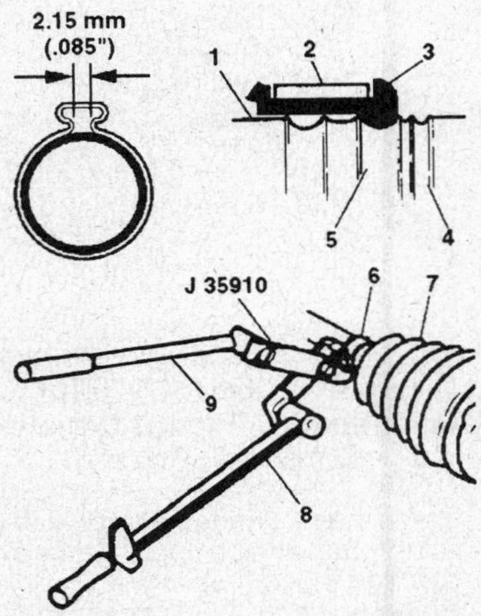

Fig. 15 Tripod boot installation. Cavalier & Sunfire w/free motion joint

12. Crimp boot retaining clamp using seal clamp tool to specifications.

Cavalier & Sunfire

INNER TRIPOD JOINT

DISASSEMBLE

1. Remove and discard small and large retaining clamps from inboard boot.
2. Separate housing assembly from boot at large diameter end.
3. Slide boot away from joint along axle shaft.
4. Remove and discard spacer ring (2), **Fig. 12,** from end of axle using suitable snap ring pliers.
5. Place a brass drift on the area of the tripod spider next to the axle shaft, **Fig. 13.**
6. Tap on brass drift to remove tripod spider assembly from axle.
7. Remove spacer ring (1), **Fig. 12,** from shoulder of axle with suitable snap ring pliers.
8. Clean tripod balls, needle roller and housing with suitable solvent, dry thoroughly.
9. Remove boot from axle shaft and inspect joint boot, spider, housing, tripod balls, needle rollers and retaining ring for wear or damage.
10. Replace components as necessary.

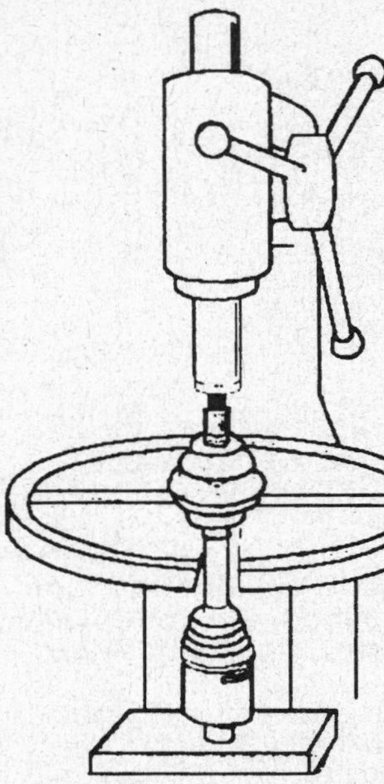

Fig. 14 Driveshaft orientation in arbor press. Cavalier & Sunfire w/tripod joint

ASSEMBLE

1. Install new boot retaining clamp on neck of boot.
2. Do not crimp boot at this time.
3. Clean axle shaft with wire brush to remove rust and corrosion from boot grooves.
4. Slide tripod boot onto axle passing boot grooves on CV end of axle shaft.
5. Install new spacer ring and the tripod spider assembly onto axle.
6. Place axle assembly onto arbor press with tripod spider assembly on press plate and CV joint assembly under press head, **Fig. 14.**
7. Lower arbor press head onto CV joint assembly until tripod spider is next to spacer ring. Do not exceed 4000 lbs. of pressure during this procedure.
8. Remove axle assembly from arbor press.
9. Place new spacer ring in groove at end of axle.
10. Slide tripod boot onto groove in axle, **Fig. 15.**
11. Crimp small boot retaining clamp using seal clamp tool No. J-35910, or equivalent.
12. Place approximately 1/4 of grease from service kit in boot. Use remainder to repack housing.
13. Slide housing over spider assembly, engage tripod boot.
14. End of tripod boot must be next to boot

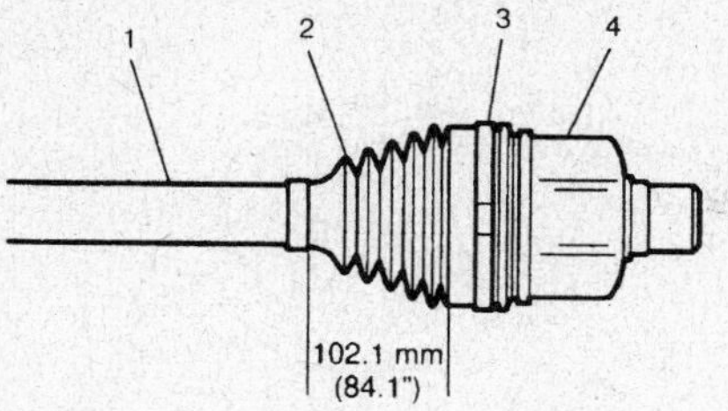

GC3039900350000X

Fig. 16 Joint assembly dimension. 1998-99 Cavalier & Sunfire w/tripod joint

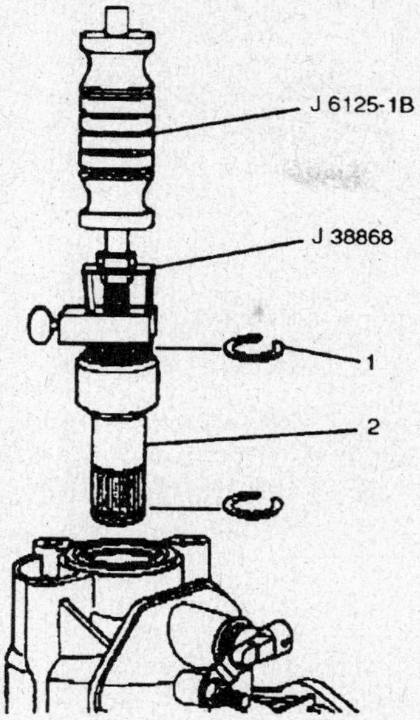

GC3039900342000X

Fig. 17 Slide hammer & stub shaft removal tool. Cavalier & Sunfire w/free motion joint

GC3039900343000X

Fig. 18 Tripod spacer ring removal. Cavalier & Sunfire w/free motion joint

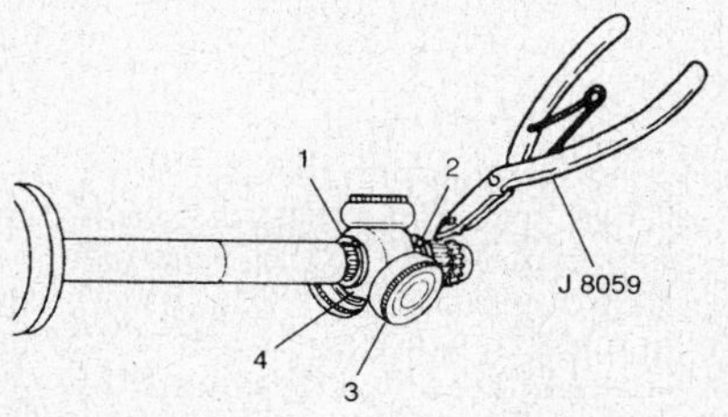

GC3039900345000X

Fig. 19 Tripod joint spider installation. Cavalier & Sunfire w/free motion joint

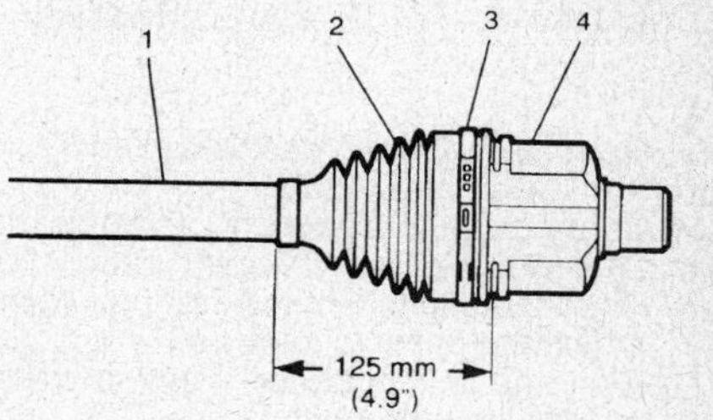

GC3039900346000X

Fig. 20 Inboard boot. Cavalier & Sunfire w/free motion joint

stop on housing.

15. Position joint assembly at proper dimension, **Fig. 16.**
16. Boot must not be dimpled, stretched or distorted.
17. Align boot, housing and retaining clamp, then crimp large clamp with seal clamp tool.

FREE MOTION JOINT

DISASSEMBLE

The transaxle stub shaft may disengage from the transaxle during the axle tripod removal. If the transaxle stub shaft disengages, perform the following procedure to separate the shaft from the tripod housing:

1. Connect stub shaft removal tool No. J-38868, or equivalent, to snap ring groove on stub shaft and connect impact slide hammer No. J-6125-1B, or equivalent, to stub shaft removal tool, **Fig. 17.**
2. Use slide hammer to remove shaft from tripod housing.
3. Install new snap rings onto stub shaft.
4. Install stub axle into transaxle.
5. Remove small boot & large boot retaining clamps from CV joint with a suitable side cutter. Discard clamps.
6. Separate tripod boot from trilobal tripod bushing at large diameter end.
7. Slide boot away from joint along upper halfshaft.
8. Remove housing from tripod joint spider and halfshaft.
9. Spread spacer ring with snap ring pliers No. J-8059, or equivalent, then slide spacer ring and tripod joint spider back on compartment, **Fig. 18.**
10. Remove compartment retaining ring and slide tripod joint spider assembly off of halfshaft.
11. Clean tripod balls, needle rollers and housing with suitable solvent.
12. Remove trilobal tripod bushing from housing.
13. Remove spacer ring and boot from halfshaft.
14. Inspect compartment inboard boot, tripod joint spider assembly, housing, trilobal tripod bushing, tripod balls and needle rollers for damage or wear and replace as necessary.

ASSEMBLE

1. Install new small boot retaining clamp on neck of tripod boot.
2. Do not crimp retaining clamp.
3. Clean axle with wire brush to remove any rust or corrosion in boot mounting area.
4. Slide tripod boot onto axle, position neck of tripod boot in boot groove, **Fig. 15.**
5. Crimp boot retaining clamp using seal clamp tool No. J-35910, or equivalent, to 100 ft. lbs., **Fig. 15.**
6. Install spacer ring on axle beyond second groove.
7. Slide tripod joint spider assembly (3) toward spacer ring as far as it will go.
8. Ensure counterbored face of tripod joint spider (4) faces end of axle, **Fig. 19.**
9. Install retaining ring (2) in groove of axle using suitable snap ring pliers.
10. Slide tripod joint spider assembly towards end of axle and reseat spacer ring in groove of halfshaft.
11. Place approximately half of grease from service kit in inboard boot. Use remainder of grease to repack housing.
12. Ensure bushing is flush with face of housing.
13. Install trilobal tripod bushing to housing.
14. Position larger new clamp on inboard boot (2), **Fig. 20.**
15. Slide housing (4) over tripod joint spider assembly on axle (1).
16. Slide large diameter of inboard boot (2), with large clamp in place, over outside of trilobal tripod bushing.
17. Locate lip of boot in groove and position joint assembly at proper position, **Fig. 20.**
18. Inboard boot must not be dimpled, stretched or distorted.
19. Using earless seal clamp tool No. J-35566, or equivalent, secure boot retaining clamp.

OUTER CONSTANT VELOCITY (CV) JOINT

2.4L ENGINE & 4T40E TRANSMISSION

Disassemble

1. Remove large and small retaining clamps from CV joint with suitable side cutters, discard clamps.
2. Separate boot from CV joint and slide up axle shaft.
3. Wipe grease away from face of inner CV race.
4. Spread ears on retaining ring (17), **Fig. 21,** with snap ring pliers No. J-8059, or equivalent.

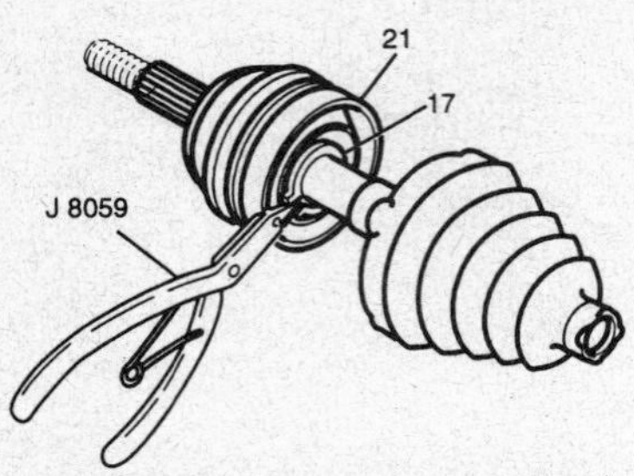

17-RING, RACE RETAINING
21-RACE, C/V JOINT OUTER

GC3039900351000X

Fig. 21 CV joint race retaining ring. Cavalier & Sunfire w/2.4L engine & 4T40E transmission

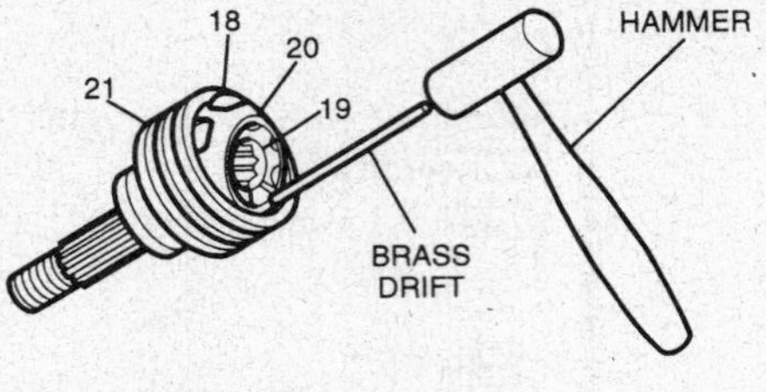

18-BALL, CHROME ALLOY
19-RACE, C/V JOINT INNER
20-CAGE, C/V JOINT
21-RACE. C/V JOINT OUTER

GC3039900352000X

Fig. 22 CV joint ball removal. Cavalier & Sunfire w/2.4L engine & 4T40E transmission

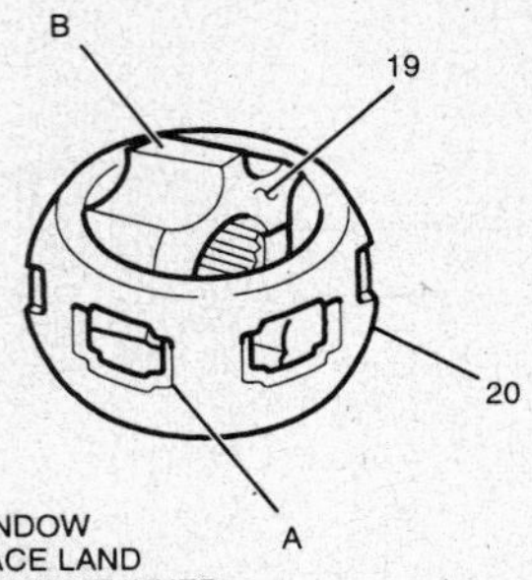

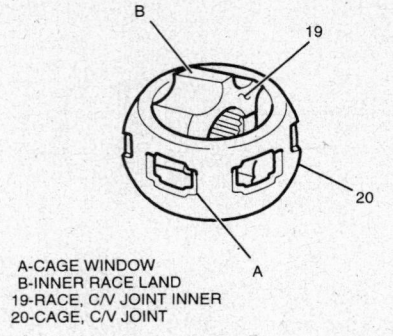

A-CAGE WINDOW
B-INNER RACE LAND
19-RACE, C/V JOINT INNER
20-CAGE, C/V JOINT

GC3039900353000X

Fig. 23 CV joint ball installation. Cavalier & Sunfire w/2.4L engine & 4T40E transmission

5. Remove CV joint assembly and boot from axle shaft.
6. Use a suitable brass drift and hammer to gently tap on CV joint cage (20), **Fig. 22,** until it is tilted enough to remove first chrome alloy ball.
7. Tilt cage in opposite direction to remove opposing ball.
8. Repeat this process until all six balls are removed from cage.
9. Position cage (20), **Fig. 23,** and inner race (19) 90° to centerline of outer race and align cage windows with lands of outer race
10. Rotate inner race 90° to centerline of cage with lands of inner race aligned with windows of cage.
11. Pivot inner race into cage window and remove inner race.
12. Clean inner and outer race assemblies, cage and balls with suitable solvent, then dry thoroughly.

Assemble

1. Install new small retaining clamp onto boot, do not tighten clamp at this time.
2. Slide boot onto axle shaft and position neck of seal into seal groove on axle.
3. Crimp seal retaining clamp with seal clamp tool No. J-35910, or equivalent to specification.
4. Put a light coat of grease from service kit on ball grooves of inner race and outer race.
5. Hold inner race 90° to centerline of cage with lands of inner race aligned with windows of cage and insert inner race into cage.
6. Hold cage and inner race 90° to centerline of outer race and align cage windows with lands of outer race.
7. Install cage and inner race into outer race.
8. Ensure retaining ring side of inner race is facing axle shaft.
9. Insert first chrome ball then tilt cage in opposite direction to insert opposing ball.
10. Repeat this process until all six balls are in place.
11. Place approximately one half of grease from service kit inside seal and pack CV joint with remaining grease.
12. Push CV joint onto axle shaft until retaining ring is seated in groove on axle shaft.
13. Slide large diameter of seal with large boot retaining clamp in place over outside of CV joint race and locate seal lip in groove on race.
14. Seal must not be dimpled, stretched or deformed.
15. Crimp boot retaining band to specification using seal clamp tool No. J-35910, or equivalent.

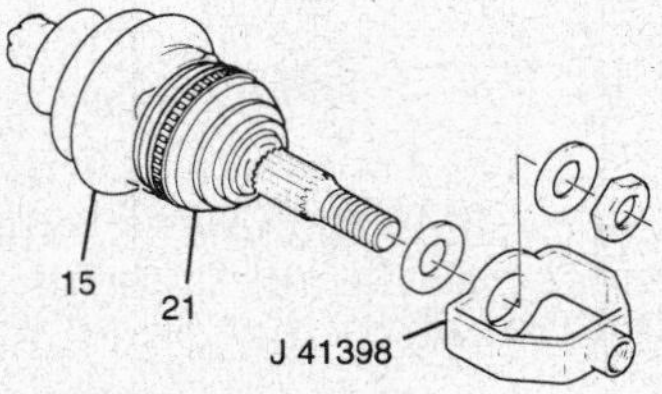

15-SEAL, DRIVE AXLE OUTBOARD
21-RACE, C/V JOINT OUTER

GC3039900354000X

Fig. 24 CV joint removal tool. Cavalier & Sunfire w/2.2L engine w/3T40 & 4T40E transmissions & 2.2L & 2.4L engines w/5 speed manual transmission

WITH 2.2L ENGINE & 3T40 OR 4T40E TRANSMISSION & 2.2L & 2.4L ENGINES w/5 SPEED MANUAL TRANSMISSION

Disassemble

1. Remove large and small CV boot retaining clamps with suitable side cutters, discard clamps.
2. Separate boot from CV joint at large end and slide seal away from joint along axle shaft.
3. Wipe grease away from face of inner CV race.
4. Clamp axle in vise.
5. Attach CV puller tool No. J-41398, or equivalent, to threaded area of outer race, **Fig. 24.**
6. Attach slide hammer tool No. J-2619–01, or equivalent, onto end of CV puller tool.
7. Spread ears in race retaining ring with suitable snap ring pliers.
8. While spreading ring, use slide hammer to remove CV joint from axle.
9. Remove seal from axle, then the slide hammer and CV puller from CV joint.
10. Use a brass drift and hammer to gently tap on the CV joint cage until it is tilted enough to remove first chrome ball.
11. Tilt cage in opposite direction and repeat procedure.
12. Remove all six balls from CV joint.
13. Position cage and inner race 90° to centerline of outer race and align cage windows with lands of outer race.
14. Remove cage and inner race from outer race.
15. Rotate inner race 90° to centerline of cage with lands of inner race aligned with windows of cage.
16. Pivot inner race into cage window and remove inner race.
17. Clean inner and outer race assemblies, cage and balls with suitable solvent, dry thoroughly.

Assemble

1. Apply a light coat of grease from service kit to ball grooves of inner race and outer race.
2. Hold inner race 90° to centerline of cage with lands of inner race aligned with windows of cage and insert race into cage.
3. Hold cage and race 90° to centerline of outer race and align cage windows with lands of outer race.
4. Install cage and inner race into outer race.
5. Ensure retaining ring side of inner race faces toward axle shaft.
6. Insert first chrome ball, then tilt cage in opposite direction and insert opposing ball.
7. Repeat this process until all six balls have been installed.
8. Pack CV joint with approximately one half of grease supplied in service kit.
9. Install new small retaining ring on neck of CV boot, do not crimp at this time.
10. Clean axle shaft with wire brush to remove rust and corrosion from CV boot mounting grooves.

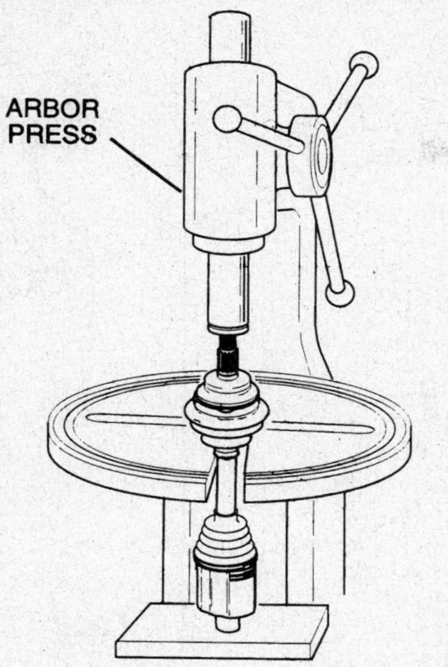

GC3039900355000X

Fig. 25 CV joint installation. Cavalier & Sunfire w/2.2L engine w/3T40 & 4T40E transmissions & 2.2L & 2.4L engines w/5 speed manual transmission

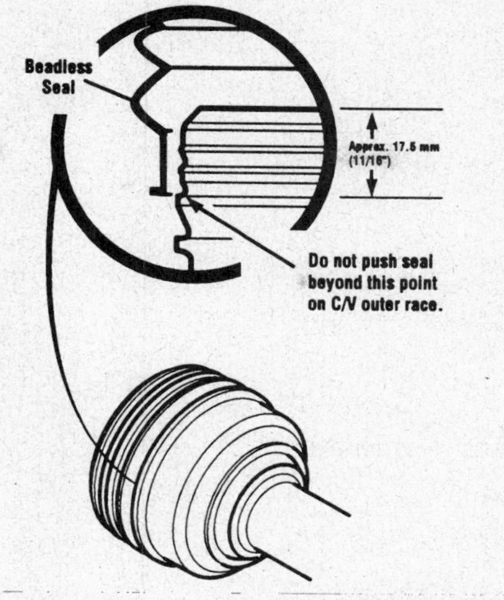

GC3039900356000X

Fig. 26 CV outer joint installation measurement. Cavalier & Sunfire w/2.2L engine w/3T40 & 4T40E transmissions & 2.2L & 2.4L engines w/5 speed manual transmission

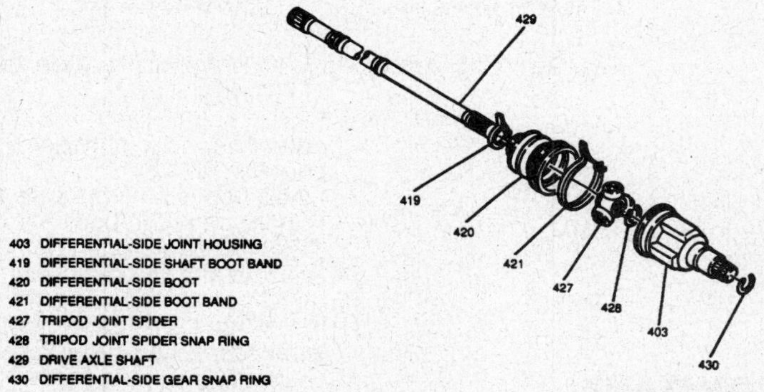

GC3039600280000X

Fig. 27 Exploded view of tripod inner joint. Metro

11. Slide CV joint boot onto drive axle shaft.
12. Position large retaining clamp around CV joint boot.
13. While supporting tripod assembly, place drive axle assembly into arbor press with CV assembly under the press head, **Fig. 25.**
14. Press head onto CV joint assembly until press cannot move any further, do not exceed 4000 psi of pressure.
15. Remove axle assembly from arbor press.
16. Place neck of CV joint boot into seal groove on drive axle shaft.
17. Using seal clamp tool No. J-35910, or equivalent, crimp small retaining clamp.
18. Place remaining grease from service kit inside boot.
19. Measure up approximately 11⁄16 of an inch from bottom edge of CV outer joint assembly, **Fig. 26.**
20. Slide large diameter of seal with clamp in place over outside of CV joint and locate seal lip to ridge as previously measured.
21. Seal must not be dimpled, twisted or deformed.
22. Using seal clamp tool No. J-35910, or equivalent, crimp large clamp to specification.

Metro

INNER TRIPOD JOINT

DISASSEMBLE

Place match marks on all components before removal from shaft.

1. Remove large band from boot, **Fig. 27,** then pull boot back from joint.
2. Slide outer housing from tripod spider.
3. Remove spider retaining snap ring from shaft, then the spider.
4. Remove small band from boot, then the boot from shaft.

ASSEMBLE

1. Clean components thoroughly, then lubricate with 2.8–3.5 oz. of suitable joint grease.
2. Ensure match marks are aligned.
3. Install boot with small clamp to shaft.
4. Install spider, then the snap ring.
5. Install outer housing, then the boot to outer housing
6. Ensure boot is not stretched, collapsed, twisted or kinked when tightening boot bands.

DOUBLE OFFSET JOINT

DISASSEMBLE

Place match marks on all components before removal from shaft.

1. Remove large band from boot, **Fig. 28,** then pull boot back from outer joint housing.
2. Remove snap ring from joint outer housing, then the outer housing from shaft.
3. Remove roller ball guide snap ring from shaft, then the roller ball guide from shaft.
4. Remove balls from cage.
5. Rotate ball guide in cage 90° until flats align, then rotate guide and remove from cage.
6. Remove small band from boot, then the boot from shaft.

ASSEMBLE

1. Clean components thoroughly, then lubricate joint components with 1.0–1.4 oz. of suitable joint grease. Pack joint housing and boot with remaining grease.
2. Ensure match marks are aligned.
3. Install boot with small band to shaft.
4. Assemble cage and balls to ball guide.
5. Install ball guide to shaft and secure with snap ring.
6. Install outer housing over ball guide assembly, then secure with snap ring.
7. Install boot and large band to outer housing.
8. Ensure boot is not stretched, collapsed, twisted or kinked when installing boot bands.

Prizm

INNER TRIPOD JOINT

DISASSEMBLE

Place match marks on all components before removal from shaft.

1. Secure axle assembly in a soft-jawed vise.
2. Remove boot retaining clamps, **Fig. 29.**
3. Remove boot from outer housing, then outer housing from shaft.
4. Remove tripod retaining ring using snap ring pliers.

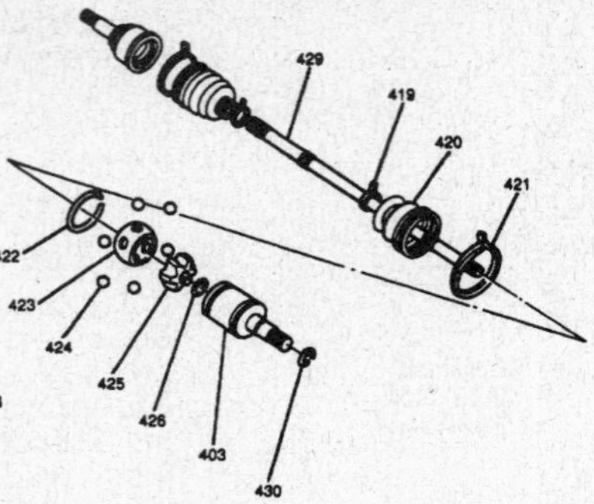

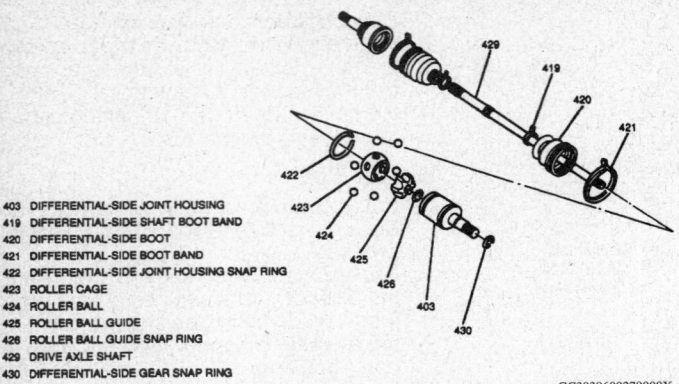

Fig. 28 Exploded view of double offset inner joint. Metro

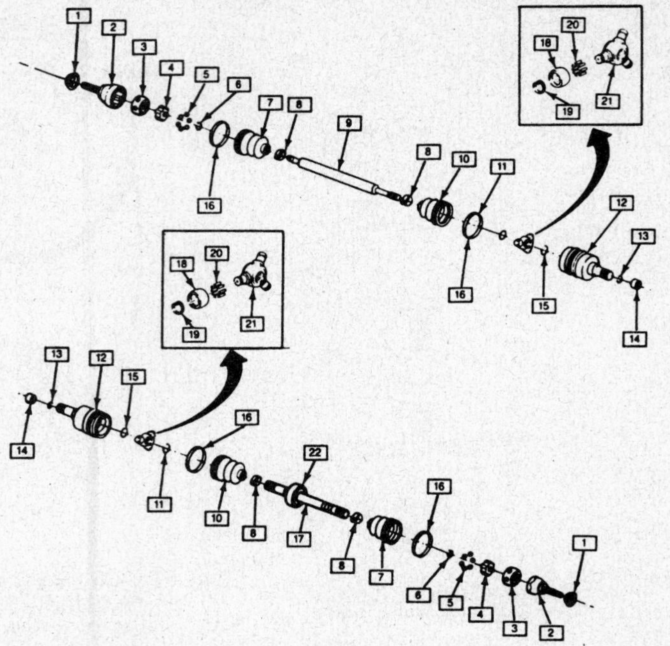

Fig. 29 Exploded view of front drive axle assembly. Prizm

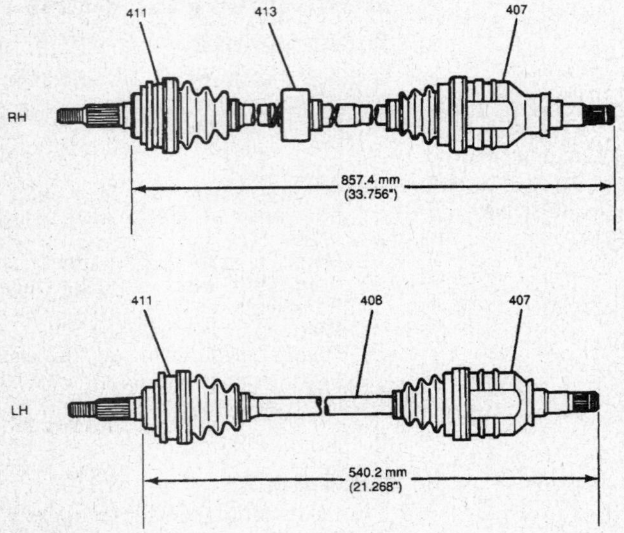

Fig. 30 Axle length. Prizm

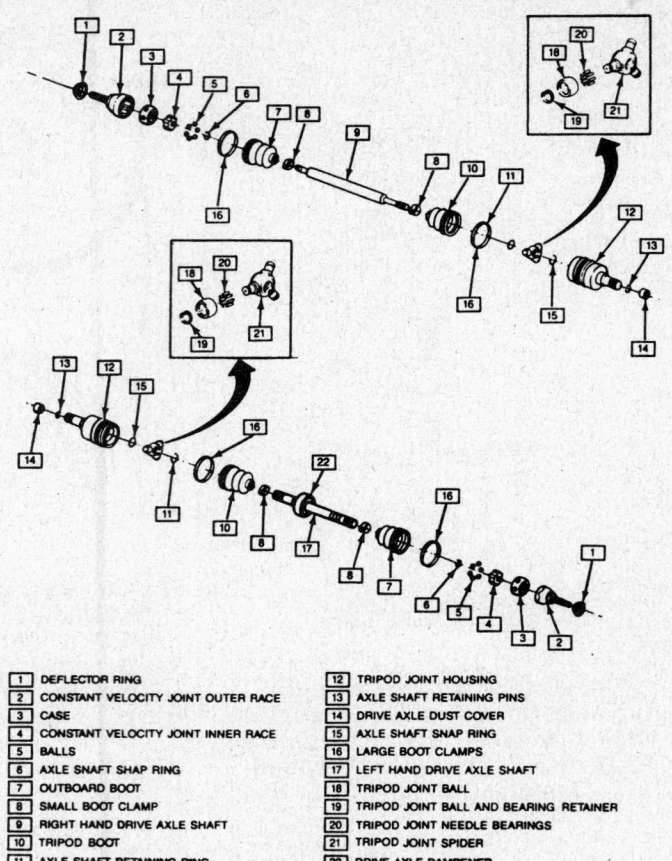

5. Remove tripod from shaft.
6. Remove boot from shaft.

ASSEMBLE

1. Apply GM grease part No. 7845393, or equivalent, to tripod housing and spider joint.
2. Install boot clamp on drive axle shaft, **Fig. 29,** then the boot. Do not tighten clamp at this time.
3. Install spider joint assembly on drive axle using a brass drift and hammer, then the snap ring.
4. Install outer housing onto spider assembly.
5. Install axle shaft snap ring into outer housing.
6. Connect boot and boot clamp to tripod outer housing.
7. Refer to **Fig. 30** for axle length specifications when installing and tightening boot clamps.
8. Ensure boot is not stretched, collapsed, twisted or kinked when installing boot bands.

OUTER CONSTANT VELOCITY (CV) JOINT

DISASSEMBLE

Place match marks on all components before removal from shaft.

1. Secure axle assembly in a soft-jawed vise.
2. Remove boot retaining clamps, **Fig. 29.**
3. Pull boot back from outer housing.
4. While compressing axle shaft snap ring with suitable snap ring pliers, pull or tap outer joint from shaft.
5. Rotate inner race and ball cage until balls can be removed.
6. Rotate inner race in ball cage until flats align, then remove inner race.
7. Rotate ball cage until flats align, then remove from outer housing.
8. Remove boot from axle shaft.

ASSEMBLE

1. Apply GM grease part No. 7845393, or equivalent, to joint housing and components.
2. Install boot clamp on drive axle shaft, **Fig. 29,** then the boot. Do not tighten clamp at this time.
3. Assemble inner race, ball cage and balls into outer housing.
4. Install new axle shaft snap ring into inner race, then slide assembly onto shaft until snap ring seats.
5. Connect boot and boot clamp to joint outer housing.
6. Refer to **Fig. 30** for axle length specifications when installing and tightening boot clamps.
7. Ensure boot is not stretched, collapsed, twisted or kinked when installing boot bands.

INTERMEDIATE SHAFT

REPLACE

ACHIEVA, CAVALIER, GRAND AM, SKYLARK & SUNFIRE

1. Install engine support tool No. J-28467-A, or equivalent.
2. Remove driveshaft as described under "Driveshaft, Replace."
3. Remove intermediate driveshaft support bracket to engine retaining bolts, then the intermediate shaft assembly.

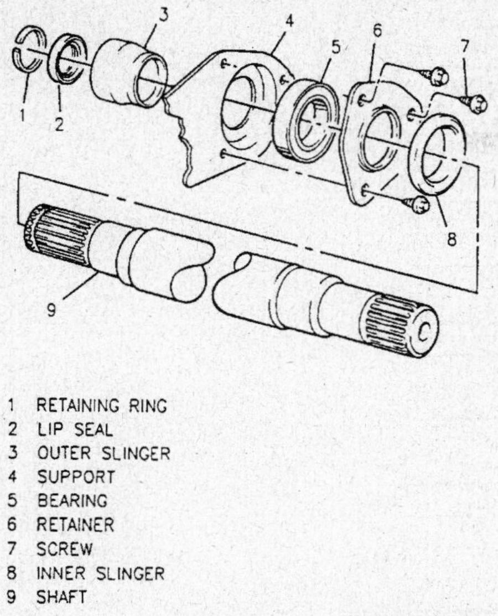

Fig. 31 Exploded view of intermediate shaft. Achieva, Cavalier, Grand Am, Skylark & Sunfire

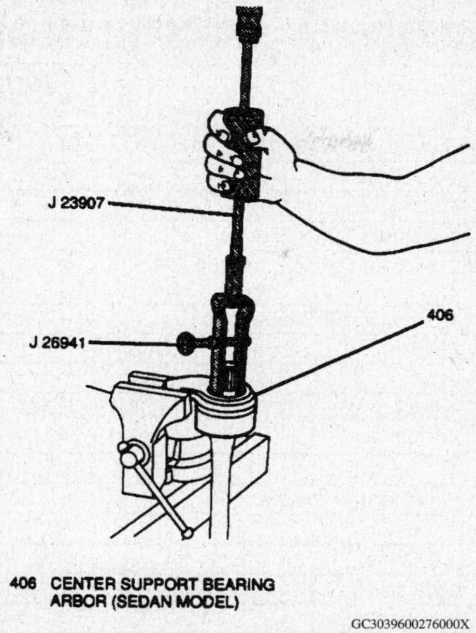

Fig. 32 Intermediate driveshaft support seal removal. Metro

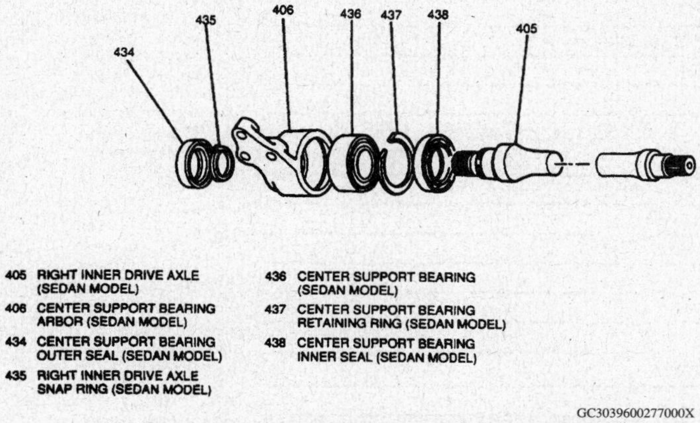

Fig. 33 Exploded view of intermediate driveshaft support. Metro

4. Reverse procedure to install, noting the following:
   a. Tighten intermediate driveshaft support bolts to specifications.
   b. Coat splines of intermediate shaft with chassis grease.

METRO

1. Remove righthand drive axle as described under "Driveshaft, Replace."
2. Remove intermediate driveshaft support bearing mounting bolts.
3. Pry intermediate driveshaft from transaxle using a suitable screwdriver or prybar, **Fig. 7.**
4. Reverse procedure to install.

INTERMEDIATE SHAFT SERVICE

ACHIEVA, CAVALIER, GRAND AM, SKYLARK & SUNFIRE

Disassemble

1. Remove retaining ring and lip seal, **Fig. 31.**
2. Using split plate tool No. J-22912-1, or equivalent, behind inner slinger, press shaft from bearing.
3. Remove retainer from support screws.
4. Using replacer tool No. J-23694, or equivalent, press bearing from support.

Assemble

1. Press bearing into support using press arbor plate across bearing.
2. Using split plate tool No. J-22912-1, or equivalent, press inner slinger on shaft.
3. Install retainer over shaft.
4. Place support with bearing on press arbor plate and press shaft into bearing until bearing inner race contacts chamfer on shaft. **Do not press bearing beyond where chamfer begins on shaft.**
5. Using split plate, press outer slinger on shaft.
6. Apply sealer to outer slinger and shaft joint, then install lip seal using seal installer tool No. J-34115, or equivalent.
7. Install retaining ring.
8. Install retainer to support. Tighten fasteners to specifications

METRO

Disassemble

1. Support intermediate driveshaft bearing arbor in a suitable vise.
2. Remove outer bearing seal using puller tool No. J-26942 with slide hammer tool No. J-23907, or equivalents, **Fig. 32.**
3. Remove driveshaft to bearing snap ring, **Fig. 33.**
4. Using gear puller tool No. J-28888-D, or equivalent, press driveshaft from bearing.
5. Turn bearing arbor over and secure in vise.
6. Remove inner bearing seal using puller tool No. J-26942 with slide hammer tool No. J-23907, or equivalents.
7. Remove bearing to arbor retaining snap ring.
8. Remove bearing from arbor.

Assemble

1. Secure arbor into a suitable vise.
2. Place bearing into arbor, then install snap ring, **Fig. 33.**
3. Install inner seal using driver tool No. J-37751, or equivalent. **Ensure seal is installed with garter spring facing out.**
4. Lubricate seal lips with a suitable grease.
5. Using a suitable press, install intermediate driveshaft into bearing.
6. Install driveshaft snap ring.
7. Install outer seal using driver tool No. J-37751, or equivalent. **Ensure seal is installed with garter spring facing out.**
8. Lubricate seal lips with a suitable grease.

TIGHTENING SPECIFICATIONS

Component	Torque/Ft. Lbs.
ACHIEVA, SKYLARK & 1997 GRAND AM	
Axle Nut	[7]
Ball Joint To Steering Knuckle	41-48
Intermediate Driveshaft Support Bolts	48
Intermediate Driveshaft Retainer To Support Screws	89[2]
Inner/Outer CV Joint Small Seal Clamp	100
Stabilizer Link Nut	22
Wheel Lug Nuts	100
ALERO & 1998-2000 CUTLASS, GRAND AM & MALIBU	
Axle Nut	284
Ball Joint To Steering Knuckle Nut	41–50
Large Joint Seal Clamp	130
Small Joint Seal Clamp	100
Stabilizer Link Assembly Nut	13
Tie Rod To Knuckle Nut	15[3]
Wheel Lug Nuts	100
AURORA, PARK AVENUE & RIVIERA	
Axle Nut	[1]
Ball Joint To Steering Knuckle Nut	[5]
Inner/Outer CV Joint Large Seal Clamp	130
Stabilizer Link Assembly Nut	13
Wheel Lug Nuts	100
BONNEVILLE, EIGHTY EIGHT, LESABRE, LSS & REGENCY	
Axle Nut	107
Ball Joint To Steering Knuckle	[5]
Inner/Outer CV Joint large Seal Clamp	130
Stabilizer Shaft Bracket Bolt	35
Stabilizer Shaft Link Nut	13
Wheel Lug Nuts	100
CAVALIER & SUNFIRE	
Axle Nut	[6]
Ball Joint To Knuckle Nut	41-48
Inner/Outer CV Joint Small Seal Clamp	100
Intermediate Driveshaft Support Bolts	49
Intermediate Shaft Retainer To Support Screws	84[2]
Stabilizer Link Assembly Nut	13
Wheel Lug Nuts	100
CENTURY, GRAND PRIX, INTRIGUE & REGAL	
Axle Nut	118
Ball Joint To Steering Knuckle Nut	40
Inner/Outer CV Joint Large Seal Clamp	130
Stabilizer Shaft Bracket Bolt	35
Stabilizer Link Assembly Nut	17
Wheel Lug Nuts	100
CUTLASS SUPREME, LUMINA & MONTE CARLO	
Axle Nut	159
Inner /Outer CV Joint Large Seal Clamp	130
Stabilizer Bar Clamp Bolts	35
Stabilizer Link Assembly Nut	13
Wheel Lug Nuts	100
DEVILLE, ELDORADO & 1997 SEVILLE	
Axle Nut	110
Ball Joint To Steering Knuckle Nut	37

Continued

TIGHTENING SPECIFICATIONS—Continued

Component	Torque/Ft. Lbs.
DEVILLE, ELDORADO & 1997 SEVILLE	
Inner/Outer CV Joint large Seal Clamp	130
Stabilizer Bracket To Frame	33
Stabilizer Link Nut	41
Wheel Lug Nuts	100
IMPALA	
Axle Nut	159
Ball Joint To Steering Knuckle Nut	50
Inner/Outer CV Joint Large Seal Clamp	130
Stabilizer Link Assembly Nut	17
METRO	
Automatic Transaxle Drain Bolt	17
Axle Nut	129
Ball Joint Pinch Bolt	44
Intermediate Driveshaft Support Bolts	44
Manual Transaxle Drain Bolt	21
Wheel Lug Nuts	44
PRIZM	
ABS Speed Sensor	71②
Axle Nut	⑦
Lower Control Arm To Ball Joint Bolts	105
Tie Rod Nut	40
Wheel Lug Nuts	76
1997 CUTLASS & MALIBU	
Axle Nut	192
Ball Joint To Knuckle Nut	41–50
Large CV Joint Seal Clamp	130
Small CV Joint Seal Clamp	100
Stabilizer Link Assembly Nut	13
Tie Rod To Knuckle Nut	15④
Wheel Lug Nuts	100
1998-99 SEVILLE	
Axle Nut	107
Ball Joint To Knuckle Nut	⑤
Inner/Outer CV Joint Large Seal Clamp	130
Stabilizer Bracket Bolts	28
Stabilizer Link Nuts	13
Wheel Lug Nuts	100

① — 1997–98 models, 107 ft. lbs.; 1999–2000 models, 118 ft. lbs.

② — Inch lbs.

③ — 1998–2000 Cutlass & Grand Am models, tighten an additional 180°; 1999–2000 Alero & Grand Am models, tighten first to 33 ft. lbs., then to 50 ft. lbs.

④ — Tighten an additional 90.°

⑤ — Tighten to 88 inch lbs., then tighten two flats to 41 ft. lbs. minimum.

⑥ — 1997 models, 185 ft. lbs.; 1998–2000 models, 144 ft. lbs.

⑦ — 1997 models, 159 ft. lbs.; 1998–2000 models, 166 ft. lbs.

Saturn

INDEX

DESCRIPTION

The drive axle assembly, **Fig. 1,** consists of a tri-pot joint and an outer constant velocity (CV) joint, connected to an axle shaft. The outer CV joint has the ability to swivel, while the tri-pot joint has the ability to both swivel and move in and out. The right side of the vehicle incorporates an intermediate shaft, allowing the left and right axle shafts to be of equal length.

The drive axle should be inspected periodically for damage and wear.

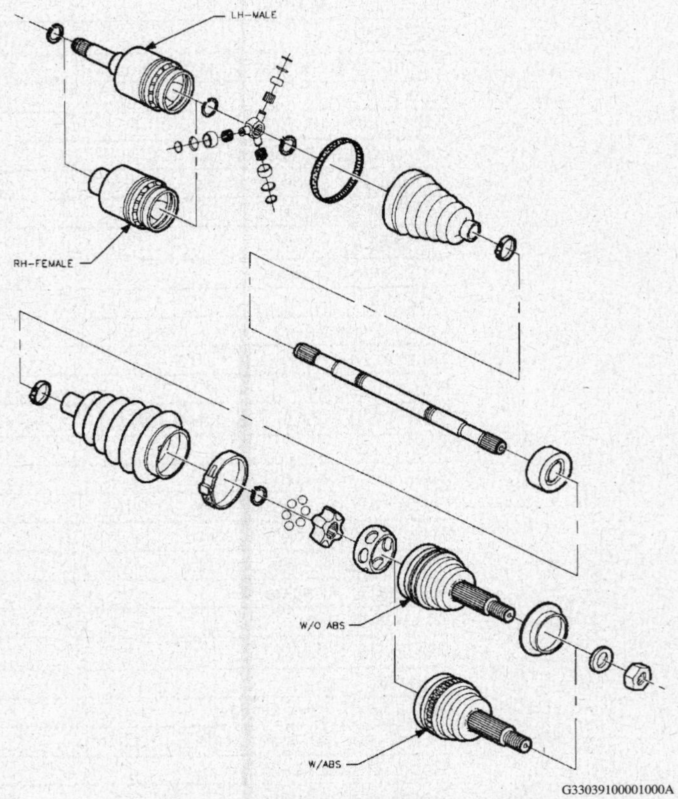

Fig. 1 Disassembled view of driveshaft

TROUBLESHOOTING

CLICKING NOISE IN TURNS

Worn or damaged outboard joint(s).

CLUNK WHEN ACCELERATING FROM COAST TO DRIVE

Worn or damaged inboard tri-pot joint(s).

SHUDDER OR VIBRATION DURING ACCELERATION

1. Excessive CV joint angle.
2. Incorrect toe in or out.
3. Incorrect trim height.
4. Worn or damaged inboard or outboard CV joint(s).

VIBRATION AT HIGHWAY SPEEDS

1. Out of balance front tires or wheels.
2. Out of round front tires.
3. Worn CV joint(s).
4. Binding or tight CV joint(s).

DRIVESHAFT

REPLACE

REMOVAL

1. Depress brake pedal and loosen drive axle nut.
2. Raise and support vehicle, then remove front wheel and front inner splash shield. **If left drive axle or intermediate shaft is being removed, drain fluid from transaxle.**
3. Remove drive axle nut and washer, **Fig. 2.**
4. Remove and discard lower control arm to steering knuckle cotter pin.
5. Loosen lower control arm to steering knuckle castle nut to point where top of castle nut is even with top of ball stud. **Do not remove castle nut at this time.**
6. Separate lower control arm from steering knuckle, using removal tool No. SA9132S, or equivalent, **Fig. 3.** Do not use a wedge type tool to separate joint.
7. Remove and discard outer tie rod cotter pin, then tie rod end castle nut.
8. Separate tie rod end from steering knuckle, using removal tool No. SA91100C, or equivalent, **Fig. 4. Do not use a wedge type tool to separate joint.**
9. Remove lower control arm to steering knuckle castle nut.
10. Position a long pry bar at proper cradle and tension strut locations, then pull down on pry bar, separating lower control arm ball stud from steering knuckle, **Fig. 5.** Pull steering knuckle away from ball stud.
11. While pulling knuckle/strut assembly away from vehicle, pull outer end of drive axle out of wheel hub. If difficulty is encountered separating axle from hub, tap on end of drive axle shaft using a block of wood and a hammer, **Fig. 6.**
12. Support or suspend drive axle assembly with mechanics wire, **Fig. 7.**
13. **When removing right side drive axle,** remove drive axle from intermediate shaft by tapping axle at correct location with a hammer, using a block of wood between hammer and drive axle,

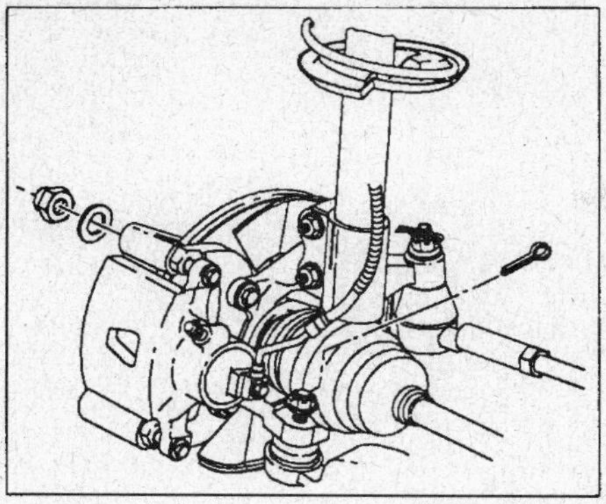

G33039100002000X

Fig. 2 Driveshaft nut & washer removal

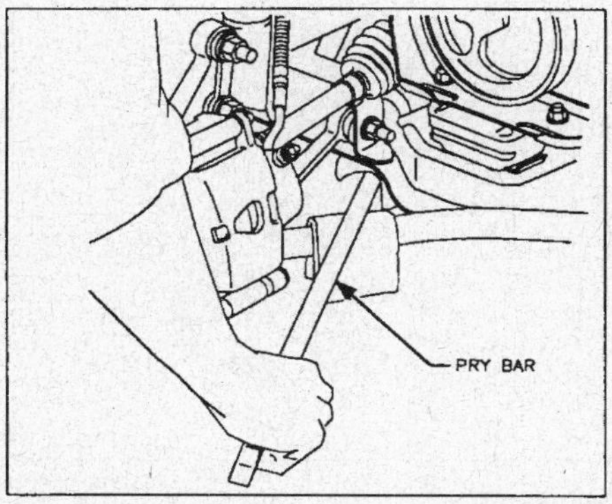

G33039100005000X

Fig. 5 Lower ball joint separation from steering knuckle

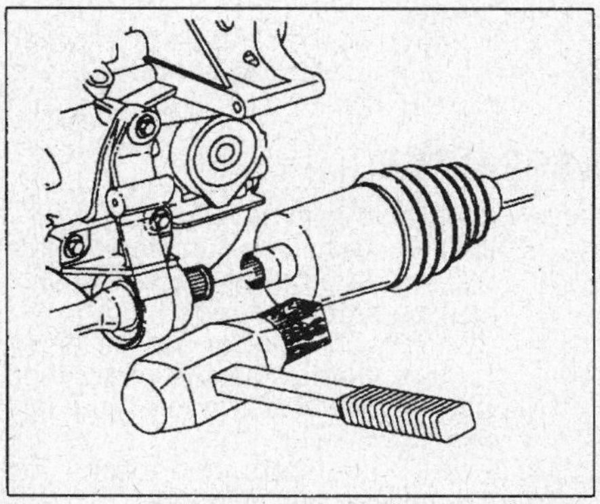

G33039100008000X

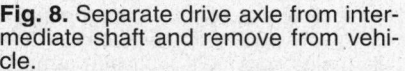

Fig. 8 Right drive axle removal from intermediate shaft

Fig. 8. Separate drive axle from intermediate shaft and remove from vehicle.

14. **When removing left side drive axle,** remove drive axle by inserting a large screwdriver at correct location and prying axle out of transaxle, **Fig. 9. When inserting screwdriver between transaxle and drive axle, do not contact transaxle oil seal.** Remove drive axle from vehicle.

INSTALLATION

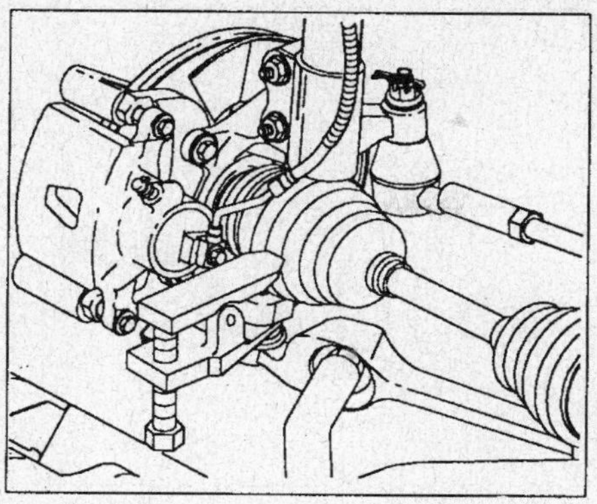

G33039100003000X

Fig. 3 Lower ball joint separation

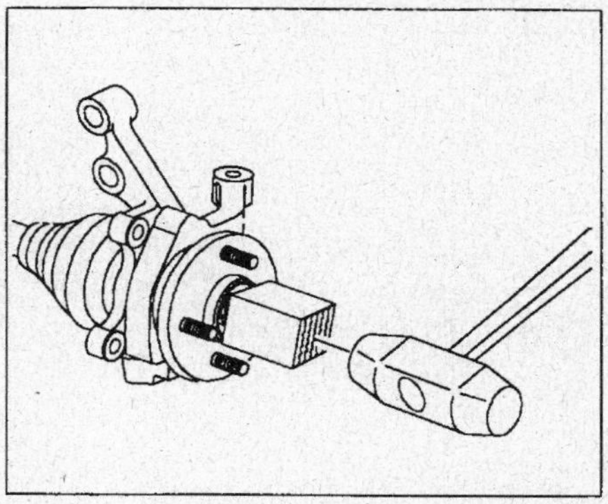

G33039100006000X

Fig. 6 Axle separation from hub

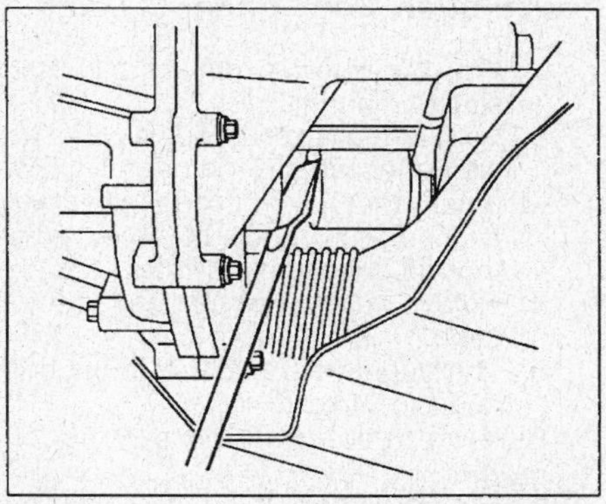

G33039100009000X

Fig. 9 Left drive axle removal from transaxle

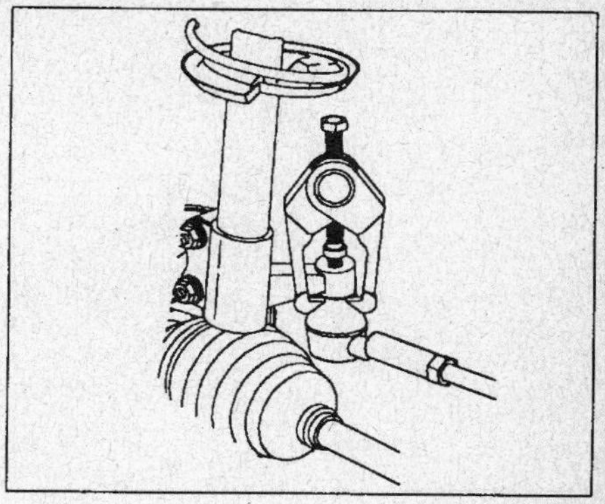

G33039100004000X

Fig. 4 Outer tie rod end separation

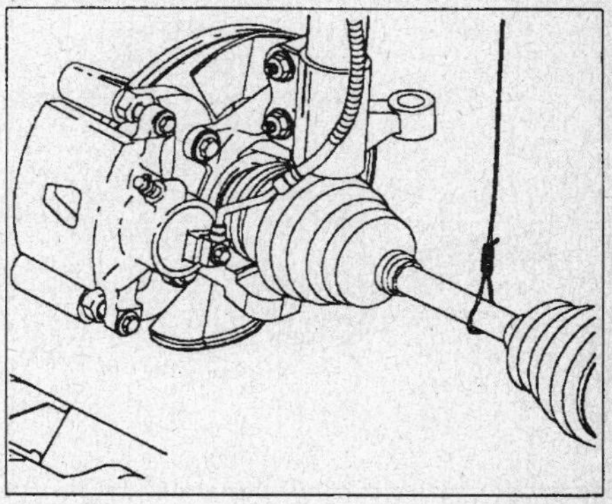

G33039100007000X

Fig. 7 Drive axle assembly support

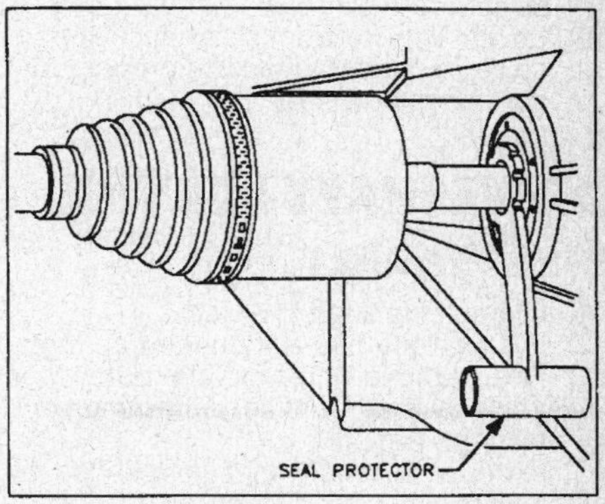

G33039100010000X

Fig. 10 Transaxle seal protector installed in transaxle

1. **When installing left side drive axle,** install transaxle seal protector tool No. SA91112T, or equivalent, into transaxle, **Fig. 10.**
2. After drive axle splines have safely passed transaxle oil seal, remove seal protector and fully seat drive axle into transaxle.
3. **When installing right side drive axle,** insert inner end of drive axle onto outer end of intermediate driveshaft and push firmly to engage axle retaining ring.
4. **When installing both drive axles,** insert outer end or drive axle into wheel hub. Do not install drive axle to hub washer or nut at this time.
5. Install lower control arm ball stud into steering knuckle. Install ball stud castle nut but do not tighten at this time.
6. Install tie rod end to steering knuckle with castle nut and new cotter pin. **Torque** castle nut to 33 ft. lbs.
7. **Torque** ball joint stud castle nut to 55 ft. lbs. and install new cotter pin.
8. Install new axle to hub washer and nut. **Torque** axle nut to 148 ft. lbs.
9. Install front inner fender splash shield.
10. **Remove rust or corrosion from wheel mounting surfaces and brake rotors and drums. Failure to do so can cause wheel lug nuts to loosen in service.**
11. Position wheel onto hub and install

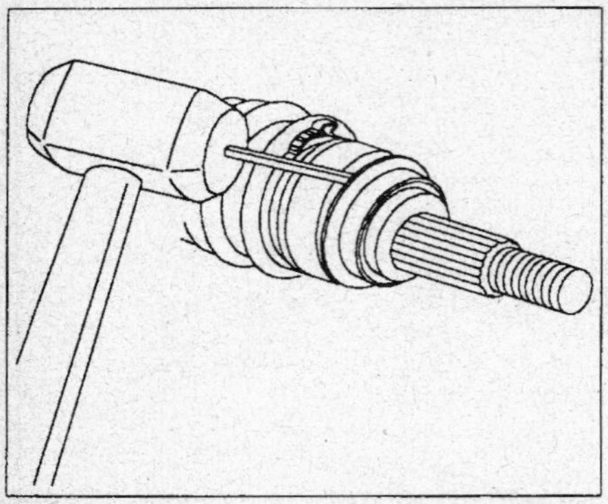

G330391000110000X

Fig. 11 Deflector ring removal from axle

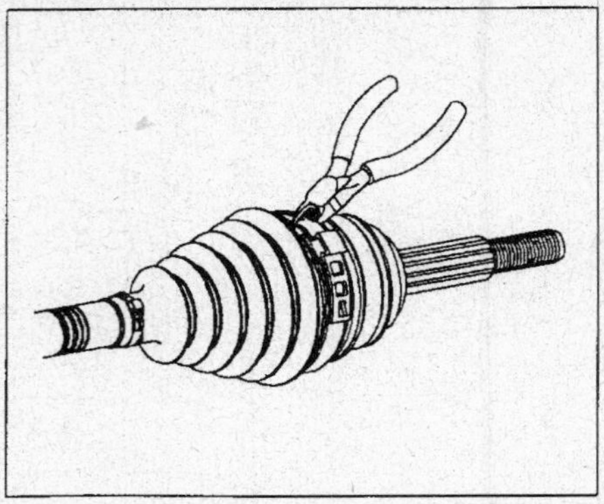

G330391000120000X

Fig. 12 Outer CV joint retaining clamp removal

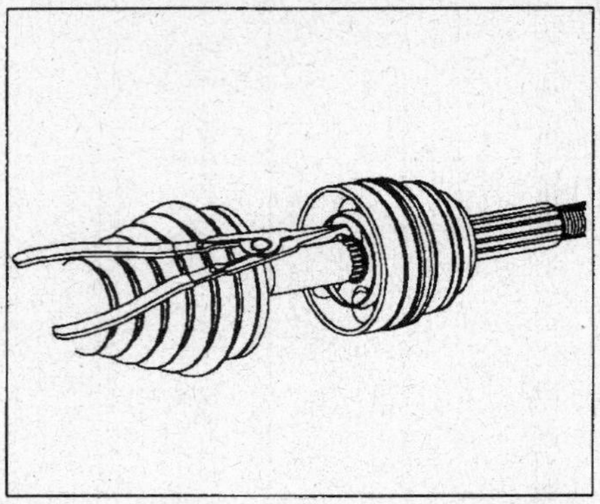

G330391000130000X

Fig. 13 Race retaining ring

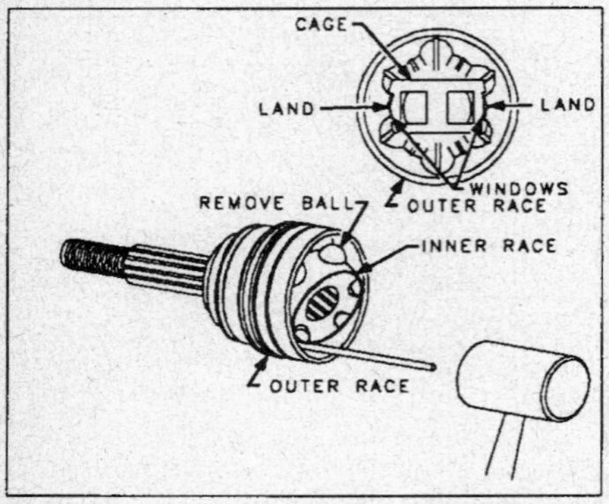

G330391000140000X

Fig. 14 CV joint ball removal

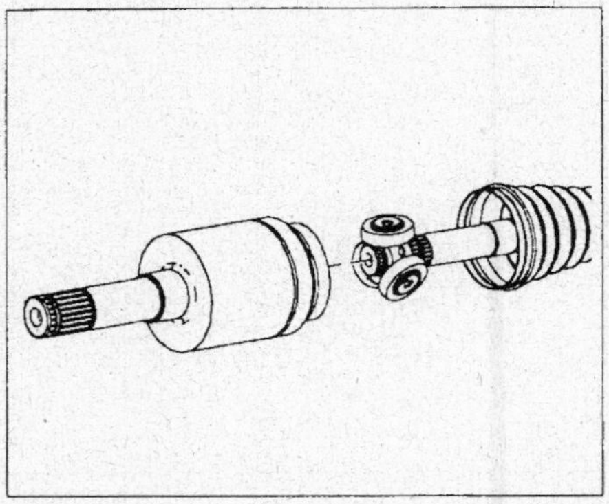

G330391000150000X

Fig. 15 Tri-pot housing separation from spider & shaft

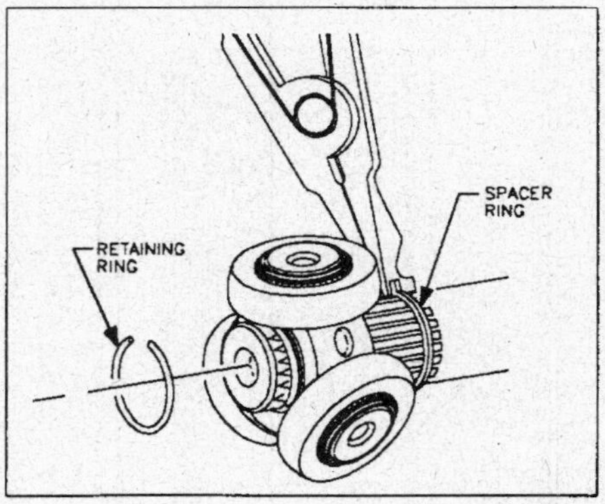

G330391000160000X

Fig. 16 Spider assembly retaining ring removal from shaft

wheel nuts. **Torque** nuts in a crossing pattern to 103 ft. lbs.

12. Lower vehicle from hoist and fill transaxle to correct level with proper lubricant, if necessary.

DRIVESHAFT SERVICE

DISASSEMBLY

1. Clamp axle shaft in a vise.
2. If drive axle has a damaged deflector ring, remove ring from CV outer race using a brass drift and hammer and discard, **Fig. 11.**
3. Remove outer CV joint and seal as follows:
   a. Cut seal retaining clamps on CV joint seal with side cutters or a flat screw driver. Disengage outer band from inner band at retainer peg and discard clamp, **Fig. 12.**
   b. Separate joint seal from CV joint race at large diameter and slide seal along axle shaft away from joint.
   c. Wipe excess grease from face of CV inner race.
   d. Spread ears on race retaining ring with snap ring pliers No. SA9198C or equivalent and remove CV joint assembly from axle shaft, **Fig. 13.**
   e. Remove axle seal from shaft.
4. Disassemble CV joint as follows:
   a. Using a brass drift, tap on cage until tilted enough to remove first ball, **Fig. 14.** Remove remaining balls in similar manner.
   b. With all balls removed, pivot cage and inner race 90° to center line of outer race with cage windows aligned with lands of outer race, then lift out cage and inner race.
   c. Rotate inner race up and out of cage.
   d. Thoroughly clean all CV joint parts and allow to dry.
5. Remove tri-pot joint and seal as follows:
   a. Cut eared seal retaining clamp on tri-pot seal using side cutters and discard.
   b. Remove and discard clamp using a small bladed screwdriver.
   c. Separate seal from tri-pot housing at large diameter and slide seal along axle shaft away from joint.
   d. Wipe excess grease from face of tri-pot spider and inside of tri-pot housing, then remove tri-pot housing from spider and shaft, **Fig. 15.**
   e. Spread spacer ring with snap ring tool No. SA9198C, or equivalent and slide spacer ring and tri-pot spider back on axle, **Fig. 16.**
   f. Remove spider retaining ring from groove on axle shaft and slide spider assembly off shaft. **Handle tri-pot spider assembly with care. Tri-pot balls and needle rollers mat separate from spider trunnions.**
   g. Remove seal from axle shaft, then thoroughly degrease housing and allow to dry.

ASSEMBLY

1. Assembly CV joint as follows:
   a. Inspect parts for unusual wear, cracks and other damage. Replace joint assembly if needed.
   b. Place a light coat of grease on all inner and outer race grooves, then insert and rotate inner race into cage.
   c. Install cage and inner race into outer race with windows of cage aligned with lines of outer race.
   d. Install balls using a brass drift to rotate and position cage and inner race.
   e. Pack assembled joint with grease provided with service kit.
2. Install outer CV joint and seal as follows:
   a. Install small retaining clamp on neck of new seal. Do not crimp.
   b. Slide seal onto axle shaft and locate neck of seal in proper position in seal groove on axle shaft.
   c. Crimp seal retaining clamp with crimping tool No. SA9203C, or equivalent, **Fig. 17.** Check clamp location during crimp operation to ensure it is positioned correctly around entire circumference.

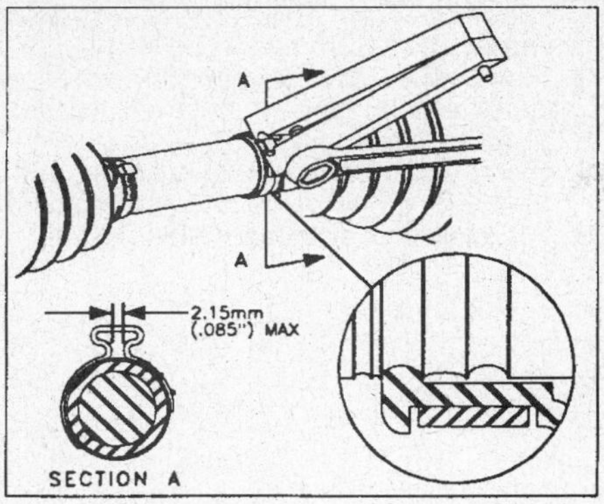

G33039100017000X

Fig. 17 Small CV joint retaining clamp crimp

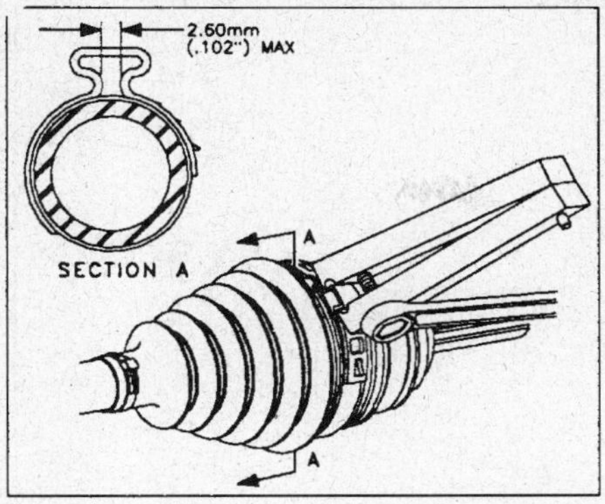

G33039100018000X

Fig. 18 Large CV joint retaining clamp crimp

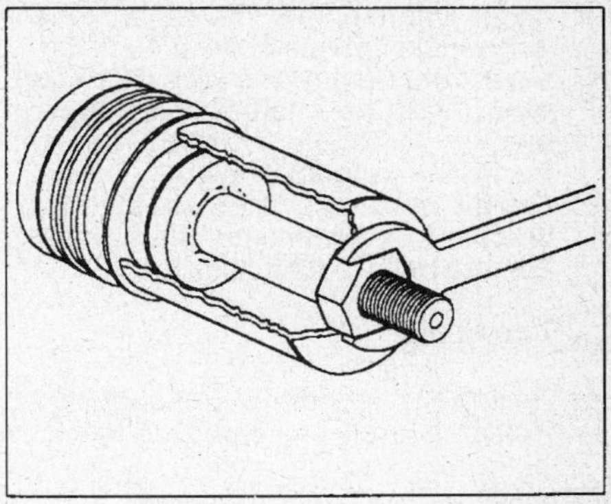

G33039100019000X

Fig. 19 Deflector ring installation

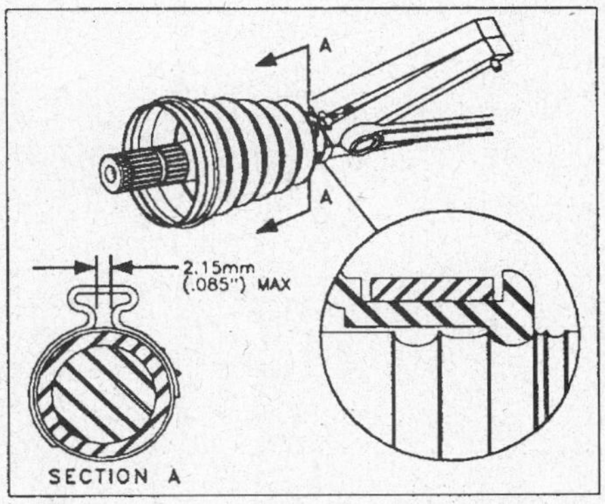

G33039100020000X

Fig. 20 Small tri-pot seal retaining ring crimp

d. Measure clamp ear end gap dimension and recrimp if necessary.
e. Place approximately half of grease provided in kit, inside seal and pack CV with remaining grease.
f. Position large seal retaining clamp around seal. **Ensure retaining ring side of inner race faces axle shaft prior to installation.**
g. Push CV joint onto axle shaft until retaining ring is seated in groove on axle shaft.
h. Slide large diameter of seal over outside of CV joint race and locate lip of seal in housing groove.
i. Crimp seal retaining clamp with crimping tool No. SA9203C, or equivalent, **Fig. 18.** Check clamp location during crimp operation to ensure it is positioned correctly around entire circumference.
j. Measure clamp ear end gap dimension and recrimp if necessary.
k. Position deflecting ring at CV joint outer race, if removed.
l. Using axle deflector ring installer tool No. SA9160C, or equivalent, and a M20 x 1.0 nut, tighten nut until deflector bottoms against shoulder of CV outer race, **Fig. 19.**

3. Install tri-pot joint and seal as follows:
   a. Inspect tri-pot joint components for unusual wear, cracks and other damage and replace if needed.
   b. Clean shaft. If rust is present in seal mounting area, remove rust with wire brush.
   c. Install small seal retaining clamp on neck of seal. Do not crimp.
   d. Slide seal onto shaft and locate neck of seal in proper position in seal groove on axle shaft.
   e. Crimp seal retaining clamp with crimping tool No. SA9203C, or equivalent, **Fig. 20.** Check clamp location during crimp operation to ensure it is positioned correctly around entire circumference.
   f. Measure clamp ear end gap dimension and recrimp if necessary, then install spacer ring on axle shaft and beyond second groove.
   g. Slide tri-pot spider assembly past spider retaining ring groove. **Ensure counterbored surface of tri-pot spider faces end of shaft after installation.**
   h. Install spider retaining ring in groove of axle shaft with snap ring tool No. SA9198C, or equivalent, then slide tri-pot spider towards end of shaft and reseat spacer ring in groove on axle.
   i. Place approximately half of grease provided in kit in side seal and use remainder to pack tri-pot housing.
   j. Install new convolute retainer over seal. **Joint must be assembled with convolute retainer in position. Seal damage will result if joint is not assembled to correct dimension.**
   k. Position seal retaining clamp around large diameter of seal, then slide tri-pot housing over tri-pot spider assembly on shaft.
   l. Slide large diameter of seal over outside of tri-pot housing and locate lip of seal in housing groove.
   m. Position tri-pot assembly at proper vehicle dimension, **Fig. 21.**
   n. Place large seal retaining clamp around seal and close with crimping tool No. SA9161C, or equivalent, **Fig. 22.**

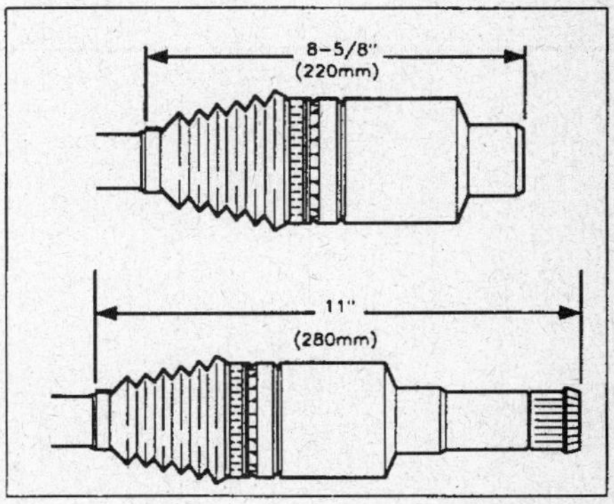

G33039100021000X

Fig. 21 Tri-pot assembly at proper vehicle dimension

INTERMEDIATE SHAFT

REPLACE

S-Series

REMOVAL

1. Remove right side driveshaft as described under " Driveshaft, Replace."
2. **On models equipped with DOHC engine,** remove intermediate shaft support bracket to intake manifold bracket fasteners.
3. **On all models,** remove starter motor bracket to intermediate shaft bracket fastener as necessary.
4. Remove intermediate shaft support bracket to engine block fasteners.
5. Remove intermediate drive assembly from vehicle.

INSTALLATION

1. Install transaxle seal protector tool No. SA91112T, or equivalent, **Fig. 10.**
2. Install intermediate driveshaft into transaxle. **Do not contact oil seal with shaft splines. Splines can damage oil seal.**
3. After intermediate driveshaft splines have safely passed transaxle oil seal, remove seal protector and fully seat intermediate driveshaft into transaxle.

4. Install intermediate driveshaft to engine block. **Torque** bolts to 40 ft. lbs.
5. **On models equipped with DOHC engine,** install intermediate shaft support bracket to intake manifold bracket. **Torque** bolts to 33 ft. lbs.
6. **On all models,** install starter motor bracket to intermediate shaft bracket. **Torque** bolts to 22 ft. lbs.

L-Series

1. Remove lower Left I/P closeout panel.
2. **Rotating steering wheel while it is disconnected from steering gear may cause damage to SIR coil.**
3. Remove intermediate shaft to steering gear pinch bolt, then intermediate shaft to steering column pinch bolt.
4. Remove intermediate shaft from vehicle.
5. Reverse procedure to install.

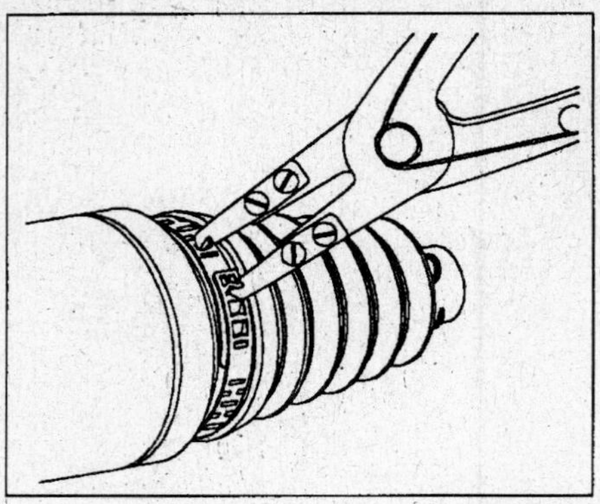
G33039100022000X

Fig. 22 Tri-pot large retaining clamp installation

DRIVE AXLES

INDEX

APPLICATION CHART

Model	Gear Ratio	Ring Gear Diameter, Inch
Camaro	2.73	7.62
	3.08	7.62
	3.23	7.62
	3.42	7.62
Catera	3.90	7.40
Corvette	2.73	7.62
	3.15	7.62
	3.42	7.62
Firebird	2.73	7.62
	3.08	7.62
	3.23	7.62
	3.42	7.62

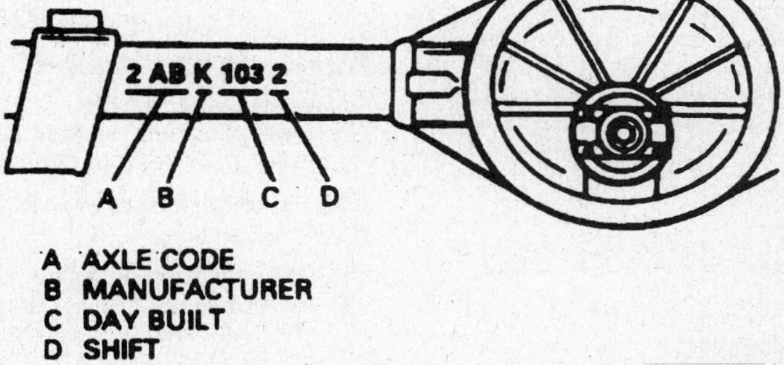

Fig. 1 Axle identification. 1997 Camaro & Firebird

IDENTIFICATION

CAMARO & FIREBIRD

Axle identification numbers can be found stamped on the righthand front section of the axle shaft housing, **Figs. 1 and 2.** Production option codes are also located on the service parts identification label.

CORVETTE

Axle identification numbers can be found on a tag, located on the side of the differential carrier, **Fig. 3.**

DESCRIPTION

STANDARD SEMI-FLOATING AXLE w/HYPOID TYPE DIFFERENTIAL

The standard rear axle is a semi-floating hypoid rear axle. When the vehicle turns a corner, the differential allows the outer rear wheel to turn faster than inner wheel. The inner wheel, turning slower with respect to the outer wheel, slows its side differential pinion gear. The differential pinion gears roll around the slowed side differential pinion gear, driving the other differential pinion gear and wheel at a faster pace.

On Camaro and Firebird models equipped with the standard axle and anti-lock brakes (ABS), a single rear wheel speed sensor is located on the differential carrier behind the ring gear. A wheel speed sensor mounts on the top of the axle housing opposite the reluctor wheel.

LIMITED SLIP AXLE w/AUBURN CONE & DANA TRAC-LOK TYPE DIFFERENTIALS

Limited slip rear axles have several definitive operating characteristics. An understanding of these characteristics is required to aid in diagnosis.

The energizing force comes from the thrust side of the gears. Consequently, a free spinning wheel may not have enough resistance to driving torque to apply the clutch packs or cones. If this occurs, applying the parking brake a few notches will provide enough resistance to energize the cones.

Energizing the cones is independent of acceleration, therefore a very slow application of the throttle on starting is recommended to provide maximum traction by preventing "breakaway" of either tire.

All rear axle components of vehicles with limited slip rear axle are interchangeable with those equipped with the standard rear axle, except for the differential case. It is similar in all respects to the standard differential case with the addition of cone clutches splined to each side gear. The differential case is non-serviceable and must be replaced as a unit.

LIMITED SLIP AXLE w/ZEXEL TORSEN TYPE DIFFERENTIAL

The limited slip rear axle differential found on 1999–2000 Camaro and Firebird models is the Zexel Torsen differential. Unlike previous limited slip differentials, the Torsen assembly does not utilize cone clutches, but rather a system of close tolerance gears. With normal operation, both tires and wheels rotate at equal speeds while vehicle is being driven straight ahead. An equal driving force is delivered to each wheel during straight ahead driving. When turning a corner, the inside wheel requires extra driving force. This unequal driving

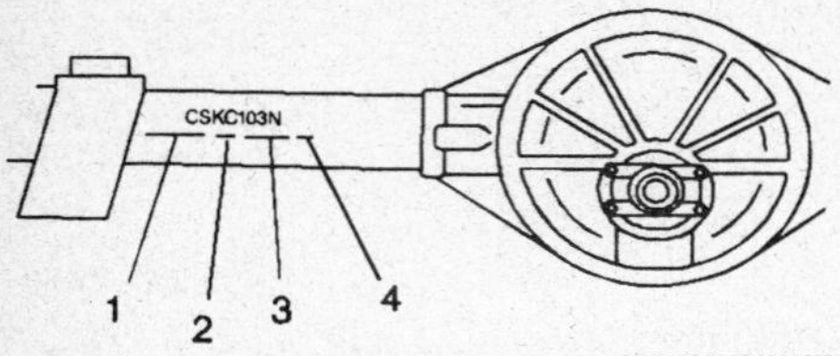

GC3039800360000X

Fig. 2 Axle identification. 1998–2000 Camaro & Firebird (1-axle code, 2-manufacturer's code, 3-build date, 4-shift)

force results in a compensation of inside and outside axles by differential.

All rear axle components of vehicles with limited slip rear axle are interchangeable with those equipped with the standard rear axle, except for the differential case. The differential case is non-serviceable and must be replaced as a unit.

On models equipped with limited slip axles, anti-lock brakes (ABS) and Traction Control system (TCS), rear wheel speed sensors are mounted on the axle shafts behind the axle flange. Reluctor wheels are integral with the axle shafts and are not serviced separately. The entire axle must be replaced if reluctor wheel replacement is required.

TROUBLESHOOTING

PRELIMINARY INSPECTIONS

Before the rear axle is to be serviced, ensure the source of the problem is the rear axle itself and not originating in other sources such as noise from the tires, road surface, engine, transmission, wheel bearings, muffler or body components. Perform the following procedures to inspect for other sources that could be mistaken for axle noise:

1. Ensure rear axle lubricant is at the proper level and type, then select a level asphalt road to reduce tire and body noise.
2. After vehicle has been driven far enough to warm lubricant, note at which speed the noise occurs then stop vehicle. With vehicle in neutral run engine slowly through the RPM range that the noise occurred to determine if noise was caused by the exhaust or powertrain.
3. Inspect for tire noise by temporarily inflating all tires to approximately 50 psi for test purposes only. Drive vehicle on a level asphalt road and note if a change in noise occurs compared to noise while tires are inflated at normal pressure. After test is completed ensure tires are inflated to manufacturer's specifications.
4. Inspect the front and rear wheel bearings by lightly applying the brakes while keeping vehicle speed steady. If the noise diminishes, inspect front and rear wheel bearings by jacking up the front wheels, then spinning or shaking them to determine if bearings are loose. Replace if required.
5. With vehicle jacked up, inspect for metal to metal contact between the spring and the spring opening in the frame, upper and lower control arm bushings and frame and axle housing brackets. Ensure there is no metal to metal contact between the floor of the body and the frame. Replace bushings or rubber insulators if required.

REAR AXLE NOISES

CAMARO & FIREBIRD

After noise has been determined to be in the axle and not from other sources, inspect for the specific type of axle noise as follows:

Rough Growl Or Grating

1. Faulty pinion or rear axle case side bearing.

Chatter On Turns

1. Wrong lubricant in axle.
2. Clutch cones worn, if applicable.

Knock At Low Speeds

1. Worn universal joint.
2. Side gear hub counterbore in the differential case worn oversize.

Clunk While Accelerating Or Decelerating

1. Worn differential case.
2. Excessive clearance between the axle shaft and side gear splines.
3. Excessive clearance between side gear hub and counterbore in case.
4. Excessive drive pinion and ring gear backlash.
5. Worn pinion and side gear teeth.
6. Worn thrust washers.

Constant Scraping Noise At Low Speeds

1. Faulty or worn pinion bearing.

Constant Whine While Driving

1. Faulty or worn ring and pinion gear.

Groan In Forward Or Reverse

1. Wrong lubricant in axle.

Whine Louder While Turning

1. Faulty or worn axle side gear and/or pinion.

CATERA

Refer to **Fig. 4** for differential noise diagnosis.

CORVETTE

Refer to **Fig. 5** for differential noise diagnosis.

LIMITED SLIP AXLE OPERATION

EXCEPT 1999–2000 CAMARO & FIREBIRD

Improper operation is often indicated by clutch slipping or grabbing which produces

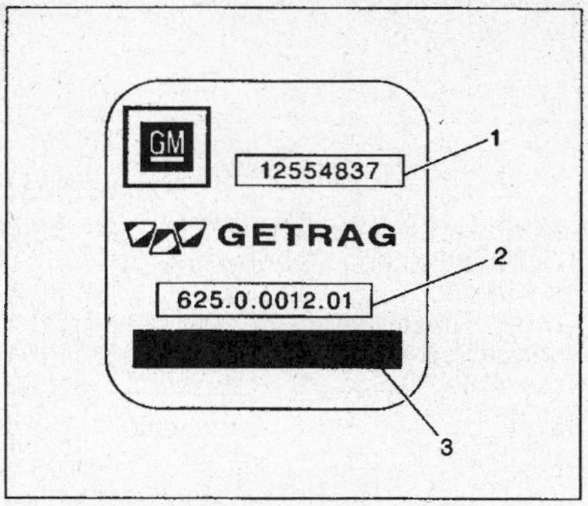

(1) GM Part Number
(2) Getrag Part Number
(3) Serial Number

Available Axle Ratios

GM P/N	Axle Ratio	Transmission
12551769	342	Manual
12554837	273 (Base)	Automatic
12556313	315 (Optional)	Automatic

GC3039700290000X

Fig. 3 Axle identification. Corvette

a whirring or chattering noise. These noises do not always indicate an axle failure but could be from lack of proper lubrication or normal noise when axle clutches are engaged during certain road conditions. Since the operational life of the limited slip unit is dependent on equal rotation of the wheels while driving straight ahead, it is important that there is no major difference in rear wheel tire size, air pressure or wear pattern, otherwise the vehicle may swerve during acceleration. If limited slip differential problems are not caused by the above, inspect for proper operation as follows:

Auburn Cone Type Differential

1. With parking brake released and automatic transmission in park or manual transmission in gear, raise both tires off the floor.
2. Remove hubcap or wheel disc and install axle shaft puller tool No. J-21579, or equivalent to either wheel with ½ × 13 adapter tool No. J-2619-01, or equivalent.
3. Using a suitable torque wrench, measure torque required to rotate one wheel, which should be 125–225 ft. lbs.
4. Place transmission in neutral position, then lower one rear tire to the ground.
5. Measure torque required to rotate the raised wheel.
6. **On 1997–98 Camaro and Firebird models,** torque should be 44–66 ft. lbs.
7. **On all models,** the differential case must be replaced as a unit if proper specifications are not obtained.

Dana Trac-Lok Type Differential

1. With automatic transmission in park and manual transmission in gear, raise

Condition	Cause
Noise is the same in drive or coast.	• Road noise. • Tire noise. • Front wheel bearing noise. • Rear wheel bearing noise. • Incorrect driveline angles.
Noise changes on a different type of road.	1. Road noise. 2. Tire noise.
Noise tone is lower as the vehicle speed is lowered.	Tire noise.
Noise is produced with the vehicle standing and driving.	• Engine noise. • Automatic transmission noise.
Vibration	• Unbalanced propeller shaft. • Damaged propeller shaft. • Tire unbalance. • Worn universal joint in the propeller shaft. • Incorrect driveline angles.
A knock or a click approximately every two revolutions of the rear wheel.	Rear wheel bearing.
Noise is most pronounced on turns.	• Rear wheel bearing. • Worn rear tie rod ends.
A continuous low pitch whirring or scraping noise starting at a relatively low speed.	Differential drive pinion gear inner or outer bearing noise.
Drive noise, coast noise, or float noise.	Differential ring gear and differential drive pinion gear noise.
Clunk on acceleration or deceleration	• A worn differential drive pinion gear or differential side gear hub counterbore worn oversize. • A worn universal joint on propeller shaft.
Groan in forward or reverse	• Wrong axle lubricant in axle. • Differential drive pinion gear bearing worn.
Clunk or knock on rough road operation.	Worn rear tie rod ends.

GC3039700298000A

Fig. 4 Differential noise diagnosis. Catera

Concern	Probable Cause
The noise is the same in drive or when coasting	• Road noise • Tire noise • Front wheel bearing noise
The noise changes on the different type of road surfaces	• Road noise • Tire noise
The noise tone lowers as the vehicle speed is decreased	• Tire noise • Worn bearings • Worn gear set
A similar noise is produced with the vehicle either standing or when driving	• Engine noise • Transmission noise
The noise is most pronounced on turns	Differential side gear and pinion
A continuous low pitch whirring or scraping noise starting at a relatively low speed	Pinion bearing
Drive noise, coast noise or float noise	Ring and pinion gear
A clunk on acceleration or deceleration	Worn differential shaft in case
A groan in forward or reverse	Incorrect rear axle lubricant in the differential
A chatter on turns	• Wrong rear axle lubricate in the differential • Clutch plates worn • No friction modifier in the lubricant
A clunk or knock when driving on a rough road surface	Excessive end play of yoke shafts to differential shaft

GC3039700291000A

Fig. 5 Differential noise diagnosis. Corvette

rear of vehicle until one rear tire is off the ground.

2. Remove rear wheel assembly, then attach side hammer assembly tool No. J-2619-01 and axle shaft remover tool No. J-21579, or equivalents, to axle shaft flange and a ½ inch × 13 bolt into adapter.
3. Raise other tire off the ground and attach torque wrench to side hammer assembly tool No. J-2619-01, or equivalent, then measure torque required to rotate axle shaft. If reading is less than 48 ft. lbs., remove and repair the differential unit.

DISASSEMBLE

DIFFERENTIAL

CAMARO & FIREBIRD

Drum Brakes

1. Remove axle housing drain plug or rear cover and drain fluid into an approved container, **Fig. 6.**
2. Remove rear axle assembly. Refer to appropriate chassis chapter for procedure.
3. Remove rear brake pipe assemblies from rear brake cylinders, then disconnect center hose assembly from junction block.
4. Remove rear brake assemblies from housing, then rear axle shaft bearings and seals.
5. Remove rear backing plates, then differential case and differential drive pinion gear.

Disc Brakes

A shim may be installed between the rear brake caliper mounting plate and axle shaft tube flange on housing. This shim centers the rear brake caliper and pads over the brake rotor, ensuring even brake pad assembly pressure during braking. This shim may have to be changed when the housing is replaced.

1. Remove axle housing drain plug or rear cover and drain fluid into an approved container, **Fig. 6.**
2. Remove rear axle assembly. Refer to appropriate chassis chapter for procedure.
3. Remove rear brake pipe assemblies from rear brake hose junction block, then junction block from housing.
4. Remove rear brake pipe and hose assemblies from housing.
5. Remove brake shaft bearing assemblies and seals, then caliper anchor brackets and mounting plates.
6. Remove shim, if installed.
7. Remove differential case, then differential drive pinion gear.

CATERA

1. Remove rear axle assembly as outlined in "Catera " chassis chapter.
2. Mount differential into holding fixture tool No. J-3289-20, or equivalent.
3. Remove rear axle housing cover bolts, then rear axle housing cover.
4. Using suitable prybar, remove drive axle seals.
5. Using rear axle housing cover bolts, install side bearing preload clamp plate tool No. J-42143, or equivalent onto righthand side of rear axle housing cover, **Fig. 7.**
6. Install side bearing preload clamp plate tool No. J-42143, or equivalent onto righthand differential side bearing outer race. Tighten clamp only enough to relieve a significant amount of bearing preload from snap ring.
7. Tighten clamp onto side bearing preload clamp tool No. J-42149, or equivalent.
8. Use a hammer and a drift to rotate rear axle differential adjuster ring so that ring opening is accessible.
9. Use suitable heavy duty snap ring pliers to remove adjuster snap ring from righthand bearing cover.
10. Remove side bearing preload clamp tool and side bearing preload clamp plate tool from rear axle housing.
11. Using suitable heavy duty snap ring pliers, remove adjuster ring from lefthand side of rear axle housing.
12. Using a suitable rubber-faced mallet and a piece of wood, drive out righthand differential side bearing outer race from cover opening of differential.

Inspect differential side bearing seal on outer race for damage, replace as required.

13. Lightly tap carrier through righthand side bearing bore using a rubber mallet and a piece of wood to drive lefthand side differential bearing outer race out of housing. Inspect differential side bearing seal on outer race for damage, replace as required.
14. Remove differential carrier from rear axle housing.
15. Using a rubber mallet, remove drive pinion from differential carrier.
16. Remove drive pinion seal from differential carrier, then drive pinion outer bearing from bearing bore.
17. Remove drive pinion gear inner bearing from pinion gear.
18. Remove pinion bearing outer races from rear axle housing.

CORVETTE

1. Remove rear axle assembly as outlined in the "Rear Axle & Suspension" section of the "Corvette" chassis chapter.
2. **On models equipped with automatic transmission,** remove differential carrier seal plate from front of differential carrier housing, then O-ring. Discard O-ring.
3. **On all models,** remove differential carrier mount.
4. Remove fill plug washer and fill tag.
5. Remove drain plug, allowing fluid to drain into an approved container.
6. Remove vehicle speed sensor bolt, then speed sensor.
7. Remove righthand side differential carrier cover bolts, then the cover and O-ring seal, **Fig. 8.** Discard O-ring.
8. Install two 10 mm nuts onto righthand side transmission mounting stud and remove stud from block.
9. Remove righthand side transmission stud mount bolts, then stud mount from the differential carrier.
10. Remove righthand side output shaft snap ring.
11. Using differential housing lifting tool No. J-42155, or equivalent, remove differential case assembly from differential carrier.
12. Remove differential carrier cover bolts, then rear cover and O-ring seal. Discard O-ring.
13. Remove pinion cartridge bolts.
14. Using heat gun tool No. J-25070, or equivalent, heat differential carrier around pinion cartridge
15. Remove pinion cartridge from differential carrier by threading two long bolts into pinion cartridge.
16. Remove pinion cartridge O-ring seal. Discard O-ring.
17. Remove pinion cartridge shim pack from differential carrier. **Tag shim pack to indicate its installation position.**
18. Remove lefthand side differential carrier cover bolts, then the cover and O-ring. Discard O-ring. .

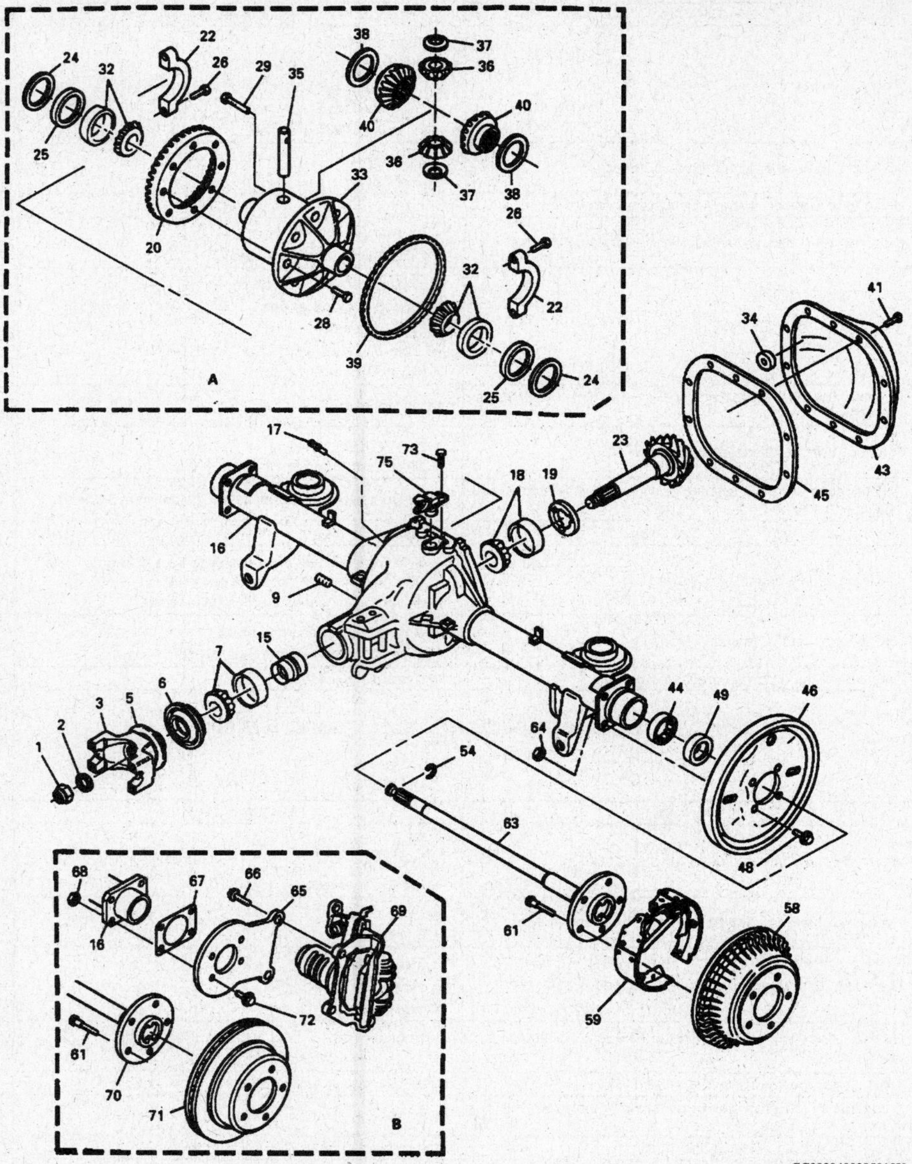

GC3039400285010X

Fig. 6 Exploded view of standard rear axle (Part 1 of 2). Camaro & Firebird

A DIFFERENTIAL
B OPTIONAL DISC BRAKE
1 NUT, DIFFERENTIAL DRIVE PINION GEAR
2 WASHER, DIFFERENTIAL DRIVE PINION GEAR
3 YOKE, DIFFERENTIAL DRIVE PINION GEAR
5 DEFLECTOR, DIFFERENTIAL DRIVE PINION GEAR DIRT
6 SEAL, DIFFERENTIAL DRIVE PINION GEAR
7 BEARING, DIFFERENTIAL DRIVE PINION GEAR OUTER
9 PLUG, REAR AXLE HOUSING DRAIN
15 SPACER, DIFFERENTIAL DRIVE PINION GEAR BEARING
16 HOUSING, REAR AXLE
17 VENT, REAR AXLE
18 BEARING, DIFFERENTIAL DRIVE PINION GEAR INNER
19 SHIM, DIFFERENTIAL DRIVE PINION GEAR
20 GEAR, DIFFERENTIAL RING
22 CAP, DIFFERENTIAL CARRIER BEARING
23 GEAR, DIFFERENTIAL DRIVE PINION
24 SHIM, DIFFERENTIAL BEARING
25 SPACER, DIFFERENTIAL BEARING
26 BOLT/SCREW, DIFFERENTIAL BEARING CAP
28 BOLT/SCREW, DIFFERENTIAL RING GEAR
29 BOLT/SCREW, DIFFERENTIAL PINION GEAR SHAFT LOCK
32 BEARING, DIFFERENTIAL
33 CASE, DIFFERENTIAL
34 MAGNET, REAR AXLE HOUSING CHIP COLLECTING
35 SHAFT, DIFFERENTIAL PINION GEAR
36 GEAR, DIFFERENTIAL PINION
37 WASHER, DIFFERENTIAL PINION GEAR THRUST
38 WASHER, DIFFERENTIAL SIDE GEAR THRUST
39 WHEEL, REAR WHEEL SPEED SENSOR RELUCTOR
40 GEAR, DIFFERENTIAL SIDE
41 BOLT/SCREW, REAR AXLE HOUSING
43 COVER, REAR AXLE HOUSING
44 BEARING, REAR AXLE SHAFT
45 GASKET, REAR AXLE HOUSING COVER
46 PLATE, REAR BRAKE BACKING
48 BOLT/SCREW, REAR BRAKE BACKING
49 SEAL, REAR AXLE SHAFT BEARING
54 LOCK, REAR AXLE SHAFT
58 DRUM, REAR BRAKE
59 BRAKE, REAR
61 BOLT/SCREW, REAR WHEEL
63 SHAFT REAR AXLE (DRUM BRAKE ASSEMBLIES)
64 NUT, REAR BRAKE BACKING PLATE
65 PLATE, REAR BRAKE CALIPER MOUNTING
66 BOLT/SCREW, CALIPER MOUNTING
67 SHIM, AXLE TUBE FLANGE
68 NUT, REAR BRAKE CALIPER MOUNTING PLATE
69 CALIPER, REAR BRAKE
70 SHAFT, REAR AXLE (DISC BRAKE ASSEMBLIES)
71 ROTOR, REAR BRAKE
72 BOLT/SCREW, REAR BRAKE BACKING PLATE
73 BOLT/SCREW, SENSOR PLUG MOUNTING
75 SENSOR, WHEEL SPEED

GC3039400285020X

Fig. 6 Exploded view of standard rear axle (Part 2 of 2). Camaro & Firebird

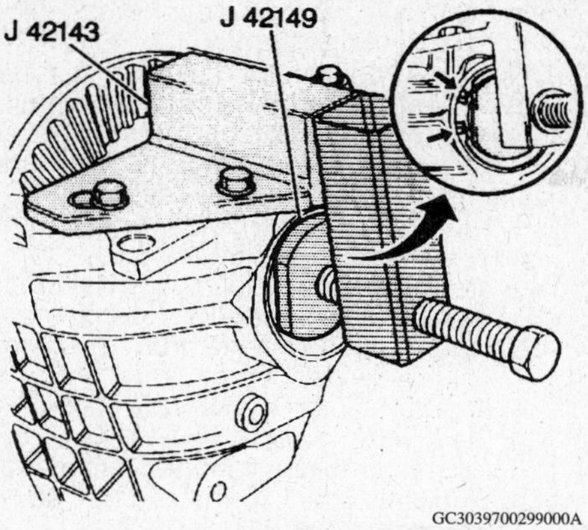

Fig. 7 Preload clamp tool installation. Catera

DRIVE PINION

CAMARO & FIREBIRD

1. Scribe reference mark between drive pinion and driveshaft yoke.
2. Hold yoke with suitable tool, then remove pinion nut and yoke. **Replace yoke if it shows wear in the seal-to-flange contacting surface.**
3. Install pinion removal tool No. J-22536, or equivalent to end of pinion shaft, then using a suitable hammer, tap pinion shaft out of pinion housing. **Apply heavy hand pressure onto tool to keep outer drive pinion gear bearing seated. Hold gear end of pinion shaft when removing to prevent it from falling from axle housing. Remove and discard pinion nut and collapsible spacer.**
4. Remove front and rear bearing races from pinion housing using drift positioned in race slots and hammer.
5. Remove rear pinion bearing using an arbor press and adapters. Measure and record thickness of shim which is found under rear bearing.

CATERA

1. Inspect differential drive pinion gear inner and outer bearing preload.
2. Shake differential drive pinion gear inner and outer bearing to inspect for drive pinion gear looseness if there is no preload reading. Detective bearings or a worn pinion flange could cause looseness.
3. Remove differential drive pinion flange.
4. Using a suitable rubber-faced dead blow hammer, drive pinion gear from differential housing.
5. Remove pinion gear bearing spacer from pinion gear.
6. Remove pinion gear inner bearing from drive pinion gear.

CORVETTE

1. Use a punch to unstake drive pinion nut from drive pinion.
2. Using spanner wrench tool No. J-42163 and pinion gear holder tool No. J-42164, or equivalents, remove drive pinion nut from drive pinion.
3. Using a hydraulic press, V-blocks and side gear compressor tool No. J-42162, or equivalent, remove drive pinion bearing, drive pinion housing and bearing spacer from drive pinion. Discard bearing and spacer. **Drive pinion bearings and spacer must be replaced as a set.**
4. Using a hydraulic press, side gear compressor tool No. J-42162 and front pinion bearing remover tool No. J-42166, or equivalents, remove front drive pinion bearing from drive pinion. Discard bearing.
5. Using a hydraulic press and bearing race remover tool No. J-42194, or equivalent, remove front drive pinion bearing inner race from drive pinion housing. Discard bearing race.
6. Using a hydraulic press and bearing race remover tool No. J-42194, or equivalent, remove rear drive pinion bearing outer race from drive pinion housing. Discard bearing race.

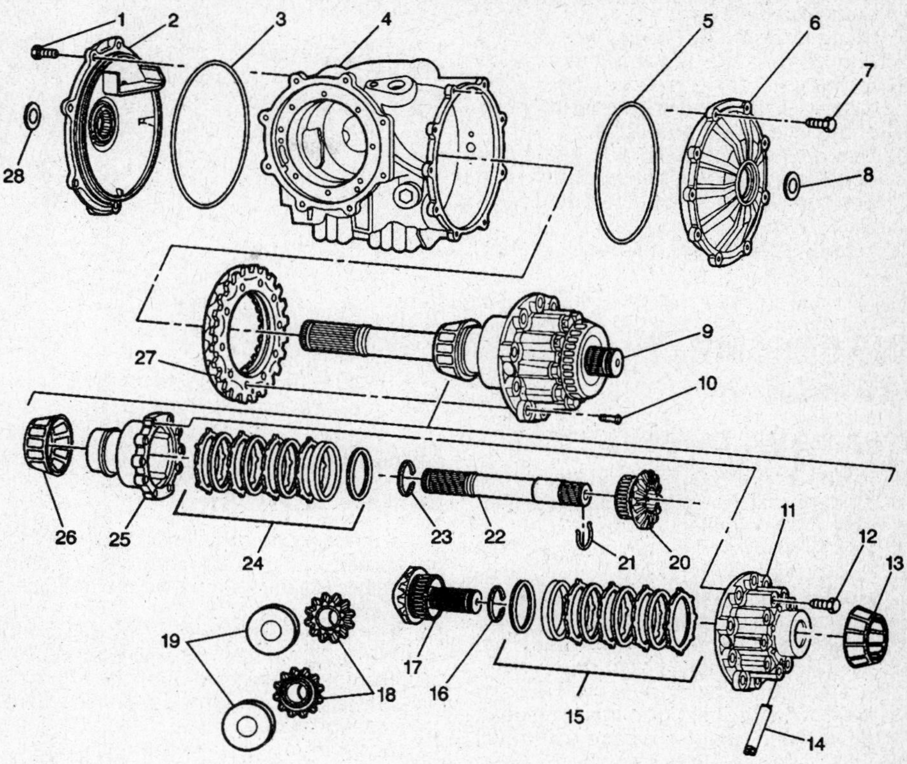

(1) Bolt
(2) Left Side Cover
(3) O-Ring Seal
(4) ifferential Carrier
(5) O-Ring Seal
(6) Right Side Cover
(7) Bolt
(8) Output Shaft Oil Seal
(9) Differential Case Assembly
(10) Bolt
(11) Right Side Differential Case
(12) Bolt
(13) Bearing
(14) Pin
(15) Clutch Pack
(16) C-Clip
(17) Right Output Gear and Shaft
(18) Side Gears
(19) Side Gear Washers
(20) Left Output Gear
(21) C-Clip
(22) Left Output Shaft
(23) C-Clip
(24) Clutch Pack

GC3039700363000X

Fig. 8 Exploded view of differential assembly. Corvette

RING GEAR & DIFFERENTIAL HOUSING

CATERA

1. Clamp differential carrier in a soft jawed vise.
2. Remove ring gear bolts.
3. Using a suitable dead blow hammer and a brass drift, separate gear from differential carrier.
4. Using a suitable drift and hammer, drive out pinion shaft from side of carrier at machined recession in shaft.
5. Remove pinion gear shaft retaining ring from differential carrier.
6. Clamp counterpiece of pinion side gear alignment tool No. J-42178, or

equivalent in a vise.

7. Place carrier onto counterpiece with ring gear flange towards the bottom, facing up.
8. Attach ½ inch drive ratchet to drive shaft pinion gear (2), **Fig. 9.**
9. Use ratchet to rotate pinion gears and accompanying washer from installed position while holding differential carrier (1), **Fig. 9.**
10. Remove shims from differential carrier.

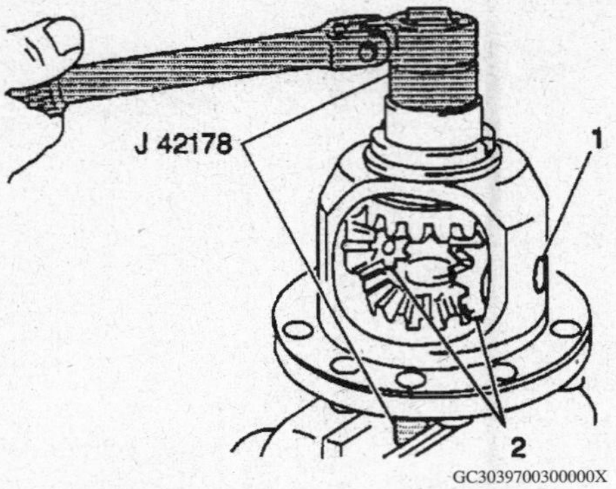

Fig. 9 Pinion & side gear removal. Catera

SUBASSEMBLY SERVICE

STANDARD DIFFERENTIAL

1. If side carrier bearings are to be replaced, remove bearings using a suitable bearing puller.
2. Remove differential pinion shaft lock bolt and the pinion shaft.
3. Remove differential pinions and thrust washers, side gears and side gear thrust washers, noting installation position for assembly. Keep thrust washers with respective gears.
4. Remove ring gear bolts, then ring gear, driving ring gear from case using drift and hammer. **Ring gear bolts have lefthand hand threads. Do not pry between ring gear and case since mating surfaces will be damaged.**
5. Inspect components as outlined in "Cleaning & Inspection" and replace as required.
6. Install thrust washers on side gears and mount side gears in case. **Lubricate all components with specified gear lubricant prior to assembly.**
7. Position one differential pinion (less thrust washer) between side gears and rotate gears until pinion is directly opposite case loading opening.
8. Install other pinion with pinion shaft holes aligned, then rotate side gears and ensure pinions align with shaft openings in case.
9. When pinions are properly aligned, rotate pinions toward loading opening just enough to allow thrust washer installation and install washers.
10. Align pinions with shaft opening in case, insert pinion shaft through case, then install new lock bolt. It is not necessary to torque lock bolt at this time.
11. Ensure ring gear and case mating surfaces are clean and free from burrs, mount gear on case, install two new retaining bolts at opposite sides of gear and alternately tighten bolts to draw gear on case.
12. Install remaining ring gear bolts hand tight and ensure gear is squarely seated on case. **Always use new bolts of proper type when installing ring gear. Do not use old bolts again.**
13. Alternately **torque** ring gear bolts to 89 ft. lbs.
14. Press side bearings onto case. If old bearings are used again, ensure they are installed in their original positions.

LIMITED SLIP

Camaro & Firebird

On these models the limited slip differential cannot be serviced separately. If damaged, the differential must be replaced as a unit.

1. Remove case side bearings using tool No. J-22888-20A, or equivalent.
2. Remove all but two opposite ring gear attaching bolts, then loosen the two remaining bolts.
3. Loosen ring gear by tapping on bolts, then remove ring gear from differential.
4. This limited slip rear axle case is not serviceable. If differential case is not satisfactory, replace complete assembly.

Corvette

1. Remove ring gear to differential case attaching bolts.
2. Using a brass punch and hammer, separate ring gear from differential case.
3. Using a hydraulic press with righthand side differential bearing remover tool No. J-42159 and side gear compressor tool No. J-42162, or equivalents, remove righthand differential case side bearing from case. Discard bearing.
4. Remove differential case bolts, then separate righthand differential case from lefthand differential case.
5. Remove lefthand output shaft from differential case.
6. Remove lefthand clutch pack from differential case, noting the following:
   a. Friction discs and plates develop specific wear patterns. Keep plates and discs in specific order in which they were removed.
   b. Inspect clutch plates and discs. If any plate or disc shows wear or scoring, replace the complete pack.
   c. Tag clutch pack to indicate its installation position.
7. Using a hydraulic press with suitable V-blocks and side gear compressor tool No. J-42162, or equivalent, remove lefthand differential case side bearing.
8. Remove C-clip from lefthand output shaft, then the output shaft from side gear.
9. Using a hydraulic press and side gear compressor tool, remove cross pin from righthand differential.
10. Note position of spider gears for installation reference, then remove them from righthand differential case.
11. Remove righthand output shaft and side gear from differential case.
12. Remove righthand clutch pack from differential case, noting the following:
    a. Friction discs and plates develop specific wear patterns. Keep plates and discs in specific order in which they were removed.
    b. Inspect clutch plates and discs. If any plate or disc shows wear or scoring, replace the complete pack.
    c. Tag clutch pack to indicate its installation position.

CLEANING & INSPECTION

1. Clean components in solvent and blow dry with compressed air, noting the following:
   a. Keep all components in order to ensure proper assembly.
   b. Do not use brush when cleaning bearings.
   c. Do not spin dry bearings since they will be damaged.
   d. Lightly lubricate components after cleaning to retard corrosion.
2. Inspect gears for cracks, chipped teeth, wear and scoring and damaged bearing or mounting surfaces. Replace gears that are damaged or excessively worn. **Ring gear and pinion must be replaced as an assembly.**
3. Inspect differential case for cracks, damage, worn side gear bores and scored bearing surfaces and replace as required.
4. Inspect housing for scored bearing mount surfaces, cracks and distortion and replace as required.
5. Inspect bearing rollers and races for pitting, scoring, overheating and damage.
6. Mate bearing with race and inspect operation.
7. Replace any bearing that is damaged, excessively worn or that fails to operate smoothly.
8. Mount differential case along with side bearings and ring gear in housing and measure runout with side bearings adjusted for zero preload and a dial indicator positioned against machined edge of ring gear.
9. If runout exceeds .003 inch and gear cannot be positioned to eliminate runout, ring gear and/or case should be replaced.

ADJUSTMENTS

DIFFERENTIAL SIDE BEARING PRELOAD

Camaro & Firebird

On these models, side bearing preload should be set before pinion is installed. If pinion is installed, remove ring gear.

1. Ensure bearing bores in housing and bearing caps are clean and free from burrs.
2. Measure production shims or service spacer and shim packs removed during disassembly to determine approximate thickness of shims required for installation. **Do not use cast iron production shims more than once as they may break during installation. If service spacers and shims were previously installed, they can be used again.**
3. In addition to .170 inch service spacers for each side, refer to chart, **Fig. 10,** and select service shim thickness required based on measurements made in previous step.
4. Place outer races over side bearings, mount differential assembly in housing and insert service spacer between each bearing race and housing with chamfered edge against housing.
5. Install lefthand bearing cap to retain case assembly and tighten bolts hand tight so that case can be moved while inspecting adjustments. **A bearing cap bolt can be installed in lower righthand bearing cap hole to prevent case from dropping while performing shim adjustments.**
6. Select one or two shims totaling thickness calculated in step 3 and insert them between righthand bearing cap and service spacer.
7. Insert progressively larger feeler gauges between shim and service spacer until noticeable increase in drag can be felt, pushing gauge down until it contacts housing bore to obtain proper reading. **Rotate case while inserting gauges to ensure even readings.**
8. The gauge used just before additional drag is felt is proper thickness to obtain "zero preload." By starting with a thin gauge a sense of feel can be obtained for the original light drag caused by the weight of the case, allowing the drag caused by the beginning of preload to be recognized. **It will be necessary to work case in and out and to the left in order to insert feeler gauges.**
9. When the proper gauge thickness has been determined to obtain zero preload, remove bearing cap, case assembly service spacers and shim pack.
10. Select two service shims of approximate equal thickness whose total thickness is equal to the thickness of the shims installed in step 6 plus the thickness of the feeler gauge used to obtain zero preload.
11. Shims selected during this procedure allow differential assembly to be installed at zero preload, the equivalent of a "slip-fit " in case, during backlash adjustment. Final preload is not added until backlash has been adjusted.

Catera

1. Install side bearing preload clamp tool No. J-42143, or equivalent onto rear axle housing cover surfaces, **Fig. 7.** Tighten cover bolts until fully seated.

4.32 mm (0.170") SERVICE DIFFERENTIAL BEARING SPACER	
TOTAL THICKNESS OF BOTH PRODUCTION DIFFERENTIAL BEARING SHIMS REMOVED	TOTAL THICKNESS OF SERVICE DIFFERENTIAL BEARING SHIMS TO BE USED AS A STARTING POINT
10.57 mm (0.416")	1.52 mm (0.060")
10.92 mm (0.430")	1.78 mm (0.070")
11.18 mm (0.440")	2.03 mm (0.080")
11.43 mm (0.450")	2.29 mm (0.090")
11.68 mm (0.460")	2.54 mm (0.100")
11.94 mm (0.470")	2.79 mm (0.110")
12.19 mm (0.480")	3.05 mm (0.120")
12.45 mm (0.490")	3.30 mm (0.130")
12.70 mm (0.500")	3.56 mm (0.140")
12.95 mm (0.510")	3.81 mm (0.150")
13.21 mm (0.520")	4.06 mm (0.160")
13.46 mm (0.530")	4.32 mm (0.170")
13.97 mm (0.550")	4.83 mm (0.190")

GC3039100217000A

Fig. 10 Service shim thickness chart

2. Install side bearing preload clamp plate tool No. J-42149, or equivalent between side bearing race and side bearing clamp tool.
3. Install dial indicator tool No. J-8001, or equivalent onto side bearing clamp tool No. J-42143, or equivalent with indicator button resting on ring gear surface.
4. Install differential carrier with bearing races into rear axle housing.
5. Using suitable heavy duty snap ring pliers, install lefthand adjuster ring.
6. Install snap rings of various thickness until there is no movement of the differential carrier indicated by the dial indicator.
7. Add an additional .005 inch shim to each side in adjuster ring thickness. Total preload should be .010 inch.
8. If it is necessary to vary adjuster ring thickness once side bearing preload has been established, always maintain the same total thickness between the two snap rings to maintain preload. For example, if it was required that .002 inch be removed from lefthand side adjuster ring thickness to properly establish backlash, .002 inch must be added to righthand side adjuster ring thickness in order to maintain side bearing preload.
9. Using differential side bearing alignment kit tool No. J-42178, or equivalent and a suitable inch pound torque wrench, measure differential carrier rotating torque. With bearing lubricated, rotating torque should be 4.5–6.5 inch lbs.

Corvette

1. Place depth gauge tool No. J-42168-7, or equivalent onto flat of gauge block tool No. J-42168-2, or equivalent, **Fig. 11.**
2. Place depth gauge tool plunger tip against bottom of differential carrier bearing bore. Tighten setscrew to lock plunger into place.
3. Install gauge block tool No. J-42168-6, or equivalent onto gauge plate tool No. J-42168-5, or equivalent with proper gear step closest to the outer edge.
4. Install gauge plate tool into a suitable vise, **Fig. 12.**
5. Mount ring gear and case assembly onto gauge plate tool. Ensure lefthand side bearing seats in the lefthand side bearing race.
6. Place depth gauge tool No. J-42168-7, or equivalent onto back face of ring gear.
7. Measure distance between J-42168-7 and J-42168-6, **Fig. 12.**
8. Determine proper shim thickness, then tag lefthand side bearing shim pack for assembly as follows:
   a. The ring gear value stamping is in millimeters.
   b. If ring gear has a zero (0) stamping, the measured value is the shim thickness.
   c. If ring gear has a plus (+) or minus (–) value stamped on it, add or subtract that value from feeler gauge reading to calculate shim thickness.
9. Remove J-42168-2 and J-42168-12 from differential housing.
10. Using a suitable hydraulic press and race installer tool No. J-42172, or equivalent, install righthand side cover bearing race, **Fig. 13.**
11. Using a suitable hydraulic press and race installer tool, install lefthand side bearing race and shim pack into differential housing.
12. Place differential carrier onto ring gear holder tool No. J-42173, or equivalent.
13. Using differential case lifting tool No. J-42155, or equivalent, install ring gear and case into differential carrier.
14. Install righthand side differential carrier cover and bolts. **Torque** to 18 ft. lbs.
15. Position a dial indicator onto end of righthand axle shaft, **Fig. 14.**
16. Grip output shaft and move up and down to measure total travel, **Fig. 15.**
17. Add .004 inch to measurement from previous step. This is righthand side outer bearing race shim pack size.
18. Remove righthand side differential carrier cover and bolts.
19. Using hydraulic press and bearing race remover tool No. J-42194, or equivalent, remove righthand side outer bearing race.
20. Install righthand side outer bearing race and shim pack.
21. Using hydraulic press and race installer tool No. J-42172, or equivalent, install bearing race.
22. Using hydraulic press and bearing installer tool No. J-42157, or equivalent, install lefthand side output shaft bearing into cover.
23. Using seal installer tool No. J-36797, or equivalent, install lefthand side axle seal into cover.
24. Using differential case lifting tool No. J-42155, or equivalent, remove ring gear and case from differential housing.

DRIVE PINION DEPTH

Camaro & Firebird

1. Install pinion bearing races in housing using a suitable driver.
2. Lubricate pinion bearings and install bearings in races.

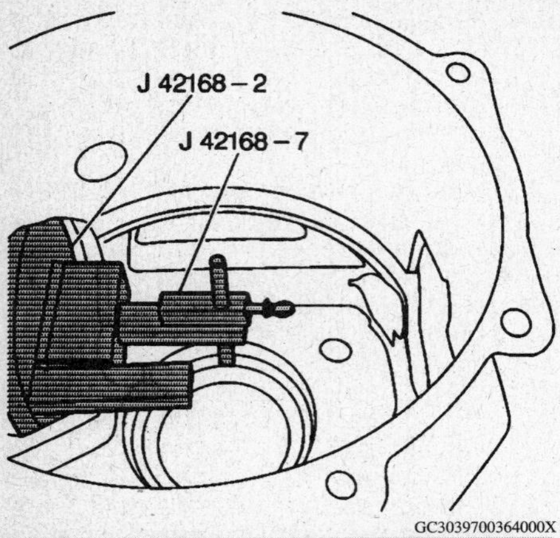

Fig. 11 Depth gauge & block setup. Corvette

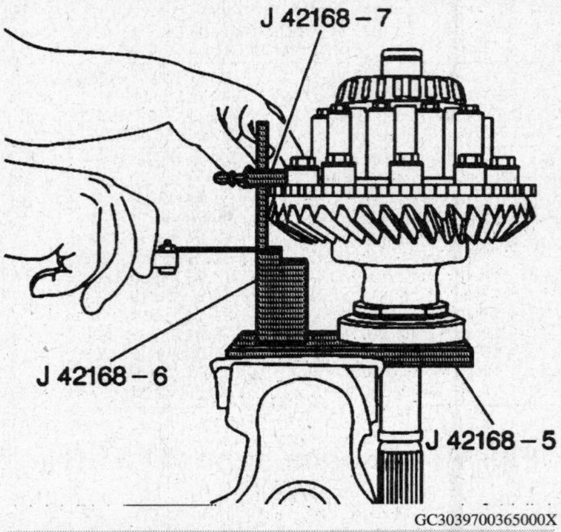

Fig. 12 Gauge plate tool installation in vise. Corvette

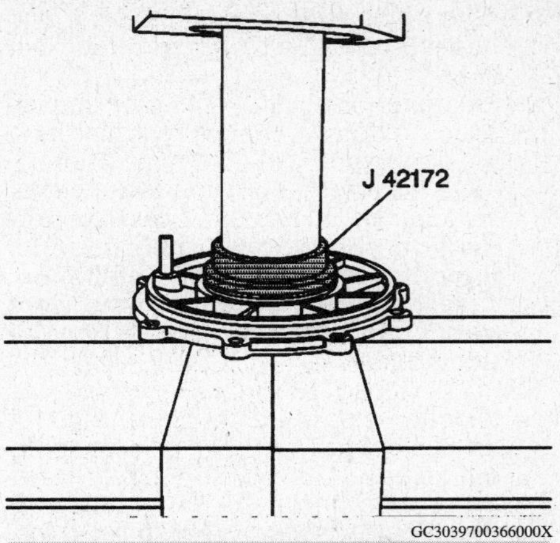

Fig. 13 Righthand side cover bearing race installation. Corvette

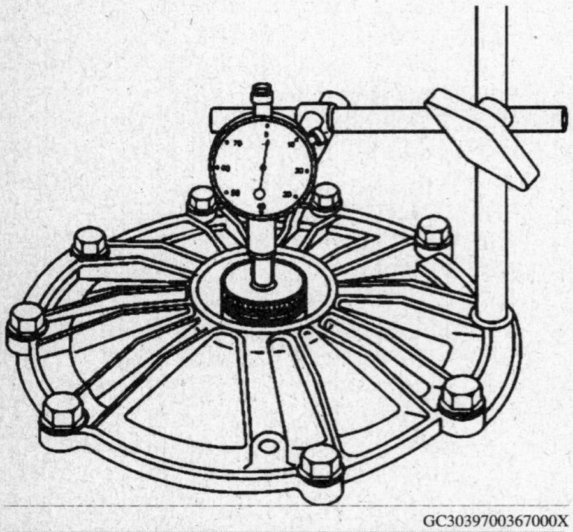

Fig. 14 Dial indicator installation onto righthand axle shaft. Corvette

3. Mount depth gauging tools in housing as outlined in **Fig. 16,** noting the following:
   a. Assemble gauge plate onto preload stud.
   b. Hold pinion bearings in position, insert stud through rear bearing and pilot and front bearing and pilot, then install retaining nut and tighten nut until snug.
   c. Rotate tool to ensure bearings are properly seated.
   d. Hold preload stud and tighten nut until 20 inch lbs. of torque is required to rotate stud. **To prevent damage to bearing, tighten nut in small increments, measuring rotating torque after each adjustment.**
   e. Mount side bearing discs on arbor, using step for disc that corresponds to base of housing.
   f. Mount arbor and plunger assembly in housing, ensuring side bearing discs are properly seated.
   g. Install bearing caps, then **torque** cap bolts to 55 ft. lbs. to prevent bearing discs from moving, **Fig. 17.**
4. Mount dial indicator on arbor stud with indicator contact button bearing against top of arbor plunger.
5. Preload indicator ½ inch against plunger and secure to arbor mounting stud in this position.
6. Place arbor plunger on gauge plate, rotating plate as required so that plunger rests directly on button corresponding to ring gear size.
7. Slowly rock plunger rod back and forth across button while observing dial indicator.
8. At point on button where indicator registers greatest deflection, zero dial indicator. **Perform above two steps several times to ensure proper setting.**
9. Once verified zero reading is obtained, swing plunger aside until it is clear of gauge plate button and record dial indicator reading. **Indicator will now read required pinion depth shim thickness for a "nominal" pinion.**
10. Record dial indicator's reading at pointer position. This will indicate proper drive pinion gear shim to install. As an example, if pointer moved .067 inch counterclockwise to a reading of .033 inch, this translates to a .033 inch shim thickness.
11. Remove gauging tools and pinion bearings from housing, noting installation position of bearings.

Catera

1. When replacing differential ring and pinion set, it is important to note that the replacement drive pinion gear will have markings on the gear face, **Fig. 18.**
2. Markings indicate adjustments that need to be made to shim thickness as a result of gear production tolerances.
3. Check value, indicated in hundredths of a millimeter (+22 = .22 mm), shows how deep the drive pinion should be installed relative to the drive pinion zero line. Compare this value with the value stamped on the original pinion gear to decide which size shim should be installed.

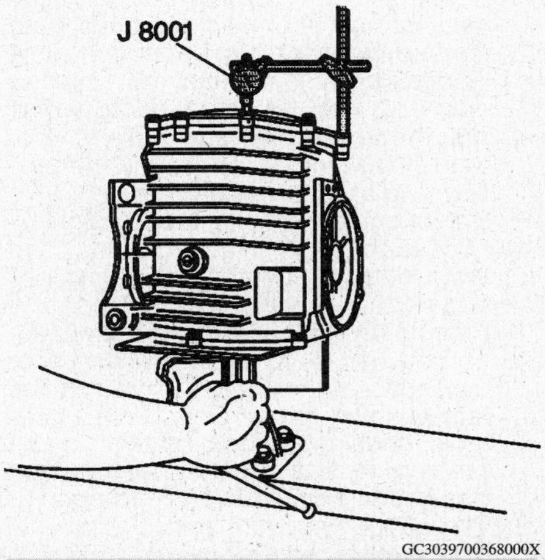

Fig. 15 Output shaft total travel measurement. Corvette

4. Pairing value (2628) is stamped on pinion gear and ring gear. This marking identifies a matched gear set.
5. Underline value does not come into play during service.

Corvette

1. Install gauge cylinder tool No. J-42168-1 and gauge block tool No. J-42168-2, or equivalents into differential housing in the lefthand side bearing race location, **Fig. 19.**
2. Using a feeler gauge, measure distance between tip of gauge cylinder tool No. J-42168-1 and gauge block tool No. J-42168-2, or equivalents. **If the pinion gear has a plus (+) or minus (–) number (metric value) stamped on the end, the shim thickness must be adjusted by that amount.**
3. Subtract measured value from .10826 inch (2.75 mm). The value of .10826 inch is the shim thickness required if the pinion has a zero stamped on the end.
4. Refer to pinion shim selection chart,

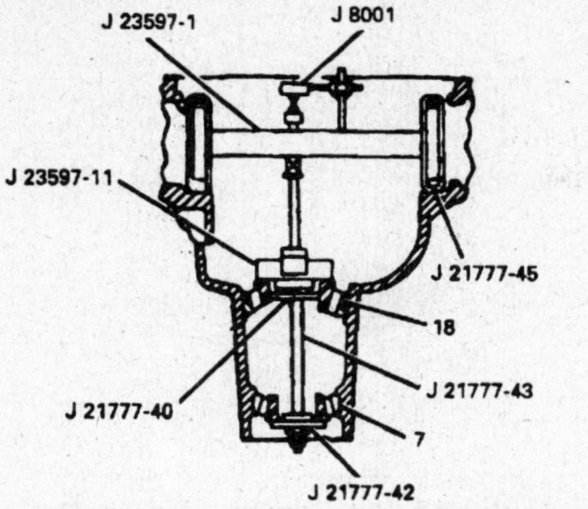

7 BEARING, DIFFERENTIAL DRIVE PINION GEAR OUTER
18 BEARING, DIFFERENTIAL DRIVE PINION GEAR INNER
GC3039700361000X

Fig. 16 Pinion gauge tool installation. Camaro & Firebird

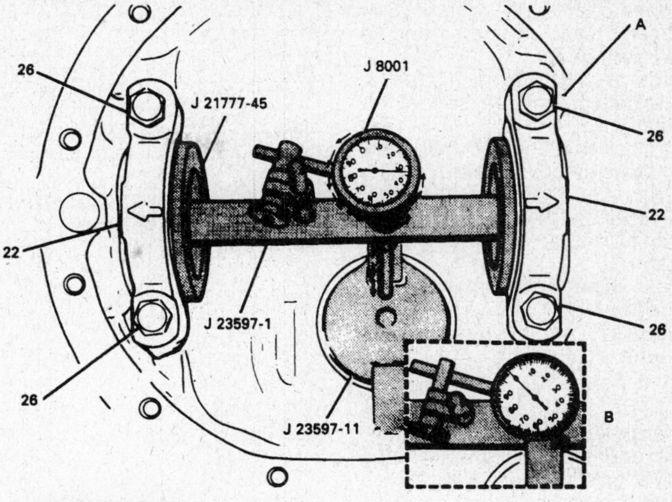

A OFF GAGE BLOCK
B ON GAGE BLOCK
22 CAP, DIFFERENTIAL CARRIER BEARING
26 BOLT/SCREW, DIFFERENTIAL CARRIER BEARING CAP
GC3039700362000X

Fig. 17 Pinion depth inspection. Camaro & Firebird

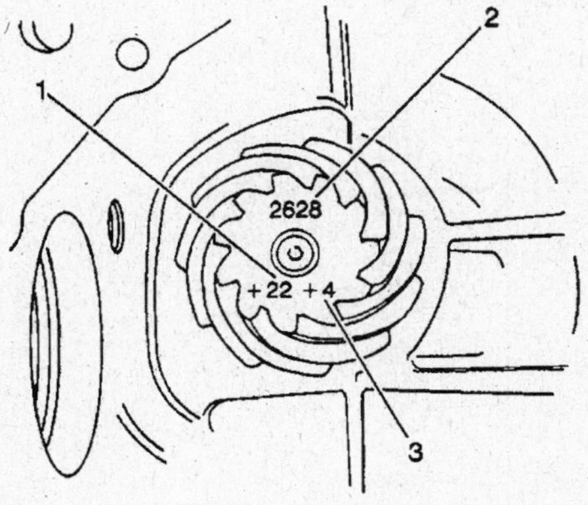

1. CHECK VALUE
2. PAIRING VALUE
3. UNDERLINE VALUE

GC3039700301000X

Fig. 18 Drive pinion gear face adjustment markings. Catera

Fig. 20, for available shim sizes.

5. Remove gauge cylinder and gauge block tools from carrier.

ASSEMBLE

DIFFERENTIAL

Camaro & Firebird

1. Ensure pinion depth and bearing preload are properly adjusted, as described under "Adjustments."
2. Install differential case assembly and selected side bearing shims as described under "Adjustments."
3. Install bearing caps in proper position, then **torque** cap bolts to 55 ft. lbs.
4. Rotate assembly to ensure bearings are properly seated.
5. Mount dial indicator on housing with plunger bearing against tooth on ring gear, **Fig. 21.** Use small contact button on indicator plunger so that contact can be made at heel end of tooth and position dial indicator with plunger in-line with gear rotation and perpendicular to gear tooth.
6. Hold pinion stationary and rock ring gear back and forth while reading backlash on indicator.
7. Measure backlash at three evenly spaced positions around ring gear and record readings. **If backlash varies by more than .002 inch at any position, inspect ring gear installation and runout and correct as required.**
8. If backlash is not within specifications, remove differential case assembly and bearing shims keeping shims in order.
9. Backlash is adjusted by increasing thickness of one shim while decreasing thickness of opposite side shim by the same amount in order to maintain proper side bearing preload. Select shims to adjust backlash as follows:
   a. If backlash is excessive, increase thickness of shim on gear tooth side and decrease thickness of shim on opposite side by the same amount.
   b. If backlash is less than specified, decrease thickness of shim on gear tooth side while increasing thickness of opposite shim by the same amount. **Each .002 inch change in shim thickness alters backlash by .001 inch.**
10. Install differential assembly, shims and bearing caps. **Torque** bearing cap bolts to 55 ft. lbs., then inspect backlash again and adjust as required.
11. If side bearing preload was set to zero during side bearing preload adjustment, proceed as follows:
    a. Remove both bearing caps and shim packs, keeping shim packs in respective lefthand or righthand positions.
    b. Select lefthand side differential preload shim from specifications chart and insert shim between lefthand bearing race and spacer, then install lefthand bearing cap with bolts hand tight.

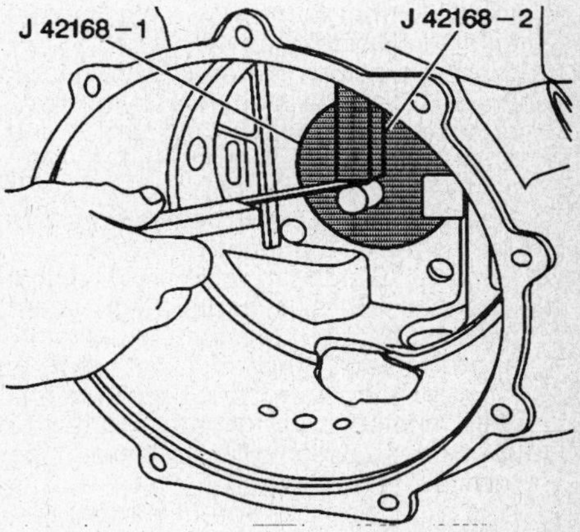

GC3039700293000A

Fig. 19 Pinion depth measurement. Corvette

    c. Select righthand side differential preload shim from specifications chart and insert shim between righthand bearing race and spacer using a soft faced hammer.
    d. Install righthand bearing cap, then **torque** all cap bolts to 55 ft. lbs.
12. Ensure ring gear teeth are clean and free from oil, then coat both drive and coast side of each tooth with marking compound.
13. Apply braking force to "load" ring gear, then rotate driveshaft yoke with wrench so that ring gear rotates one full revolution in each direction. **Test made without "loading" gears will not yield satisfactory pattern. Excessive gear rotation is not recommended.**
14. Compare gear tooth pattern with **Fig. 22,** and correct assembly adjustments as required.

15. When proper gear tooth contact pattern has been obtained, clean marking compound from gears.
16. Install axles and driveshaft. Refer to appropriate sections of this manual for axle installation.
17. Install rear cover using RTV or new gasket and **torque** cover bolts to 22 ft. lbs.
18. Install fluid drain plug and **torque** to 26 ft. lbs., then fill rear axle with appropriate lubricant.
19. **On models equipped with limited slip differential,** add limited slip additive No. 1052358, or equivalent to rear axle lubricant.

Catera

1. Place differential carrier (1) on differential side and pinion alignment tool No. J-42178, or equivalent, **Fig. 23.**
2. Install counterpiece of alignment tool into opposing differential carrier bore.
3. Install new pinion gear retaining ring onto differential carrier.
4. Coat pinion gears and shims with rear axle lubricant.
5. Install thicker shim (that with notches around outer edge) toward carrier.
6. Install thinner (conical) washer toward differential side gear.
7. Place shims on differential side gears.
8. Place differential side gears with previously installed shims into carrier and onto both pieces of alignment tool No. J-42178, or equivalent.
9. Coat pinion gears and conical washers with rear axle lubricant.
10. Engage pinion gears and conical washers with side gears. Align gears and washers so that they are exactly opposite each other in carrier window.
11. Move pinion gear conical washers forward in intended rotational direction to start or lead pinion gears into mounting position.
12. Use a ratchet to rotate alignment tool to draw pinion gears into position. **Ensure conical gears also move into position.** It may be necessary to use a small drift and hammer to assist washers into position.
13. Using a suitable dead blow hammer, drive rear axle gear shaft into carrier bore.
14. Attach a torque wrench to alignment tool No. J-42178, or equivalent and measure rotating torque, which should be 11–22 ft. lbs.
15. Heat ring gear to 212°F. **Do not overheat.**
16. Aligning bolt holes, install ring gear onto carrier.
17. Install new ring gear bolts, then using sequence outlined in **Fig. 24, torque** bolts to 85 ft. lbs.
18. Lubricate carrier side bearings and carrier bearing surface.
19. Press side bearing onto carrier using a suitable press.
20. Install inner and outer pinion bearing outer races into housing.
21. Install drive pinion gear inner bearing onto drive pinion gear.
22. Install drive pinion seal into differential.
23. Install drive pinion, then carrier into rear axle housing.
24. Using drive axle seal driver tool No. J-26234, or equivalent, drive axle seals into bearing cups.
25. Install rear axle cover, then **torque** the bolts to 44 ft. lbs.

mm	in
0.200	0.0078
0.250	0.0098
0.300	0.0118
0.500	0.0196
1.000	0.0393

GC3039700294000X

Fig. 20 Pinion adjustment shims. Corvette

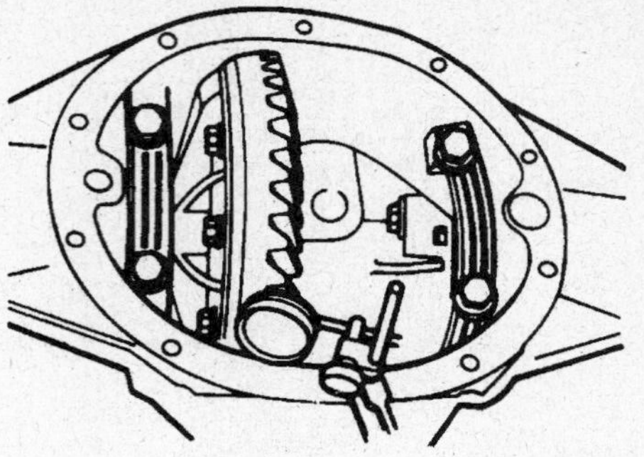

GC3039100221000X

Fig. 21 Ring gear & pinion backlash inspection. Camaro & Firebird

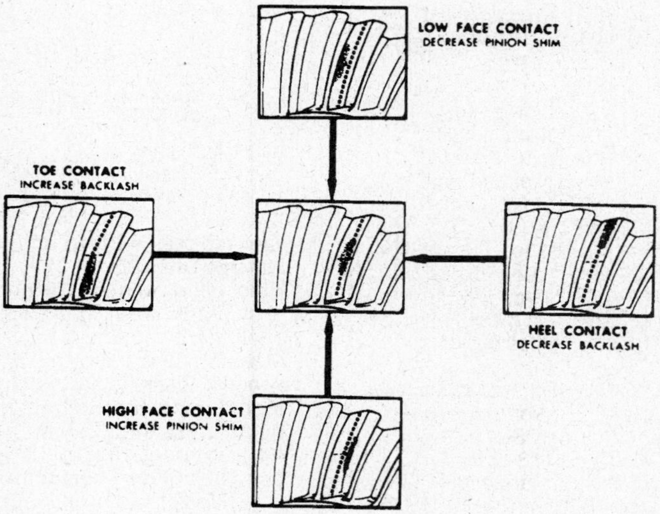

GC3039100222000X

Fig. 22 Gear tooth contact pattern inspection. Camaro & Firebird

Corvette

1. Install righthand clutch pack into differential case. Install steel plates and friction discs alternately, thicker friction washer, concave washer, then steel washer.
2. Install righthand output shaft and spider gears into differential case.
3. Using a hydraulic press and side gear compressor tool No. J-42162, or equivalent, install cross pin into differential case.
4. Install lefthand output shaft into side gear, then C-clip onto lefthand output shaft.
5. Using bearing installer tool No. J-42160, or equivalent, install lefthand differential case side bearing.
6. Install lefthand clutch pack into differential case. Install steel plates and friction discs alternately, thicker friction washer, concave washer, then steel washer.
7. Install lefthand output shaft and side gear into differential case.
8. Install lefthand differential case to righthand differential case.
9. Install differential case bolts, then **torque** to 41 ft. lbs.
10. Install ring gear onto differential case.
11. Using ring gear holder tool No. J-42173 or, equivalent, to support differential case, install ring gear bolts. **Torque** bolts to 144 ft. lbs.
12. Using bearing installer tool No. J-42160, or equivalent, install righthand differential case side bearing.
13. Install gauge block tool No. J-42168-2 and plug tool No. J-42168-12, or equivalents into drive pinion location of differential carrier.
14. Place depth gauge tool No. J-42168-7, or equivalent, onto flat end of gauge block tool No. J-42168-2, or equivalent, **Fig. 25.**
15. Place tip of plunger on depth gauge tool No. J-42168-7, or equivalent against bottom of bearing bore in differential carrier. Tighten set screw to lock plunger in place.
16. Install gauge block tool No. J-42168-6,

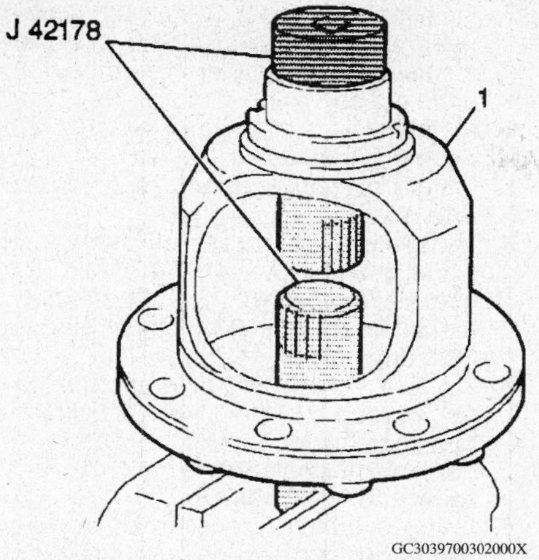

Fig. 23 Differential carrier alignment. Catera

or equivalent onto gauge plate tool No. J-42168-5, or equivalent, with proper gear step closest to outer edge.

17. Place ring gear and case assembly onto gauge plate tool No. J-42168-5, or equivalent, **Fig. 26.**
18. Remove depth gauge tool No. J-42168-7, or equivalent. If ring gear has a plus (+) or minus (–) number (metric value) stamped on the side the shim thickness must be adjusted by that amount.
19. Using a feeler gauge, measure distance between plunger tip of depth gauge tool No. J-42168-7 and gauge block tool No. J-42168-6, or equivalents, **Fig. 26.** This distance is the shim thickness required if ring gear has a zero stamped on the side.
20. Remove gauge block tool No. J-42168-2 and plug tool No. J-42168-12.
21. Install lefthand side shim pack into housing.
22. Using bearing race installer tool No. J-42172, or equivalent, install lefthand side outer bearing race into carrier.
23. Using a hydraulic press and output shaft bearing installer tool No. J-42157, or equivalent, install output shaft bearing into lefthand differential carrier cover.
24. Using seal installer tool No. J-36797, or equivalent, install new output shaft oil seal into lefthand differential carrier cover.
25. Install new O-ring seal into lefthand cover, then the cover bolts. **Torque** to 18 ft. lbs.
26. Place differential carrier on rear gear holder tool No. J-42173, or equivalent.
27. Using differential case lifting tool No. J-42155, or equivalent, install ring gear and case assembly into differential carrier.
28. Install righthand side differential carrier cover and cover bolts. **Torque** bolts to 18 ft. lbs.
29. Position measuring tool No. J-8001, or equivalent onto end of righthand axle shaft, **Fig. 27.**
30. Move output shaft up and down and

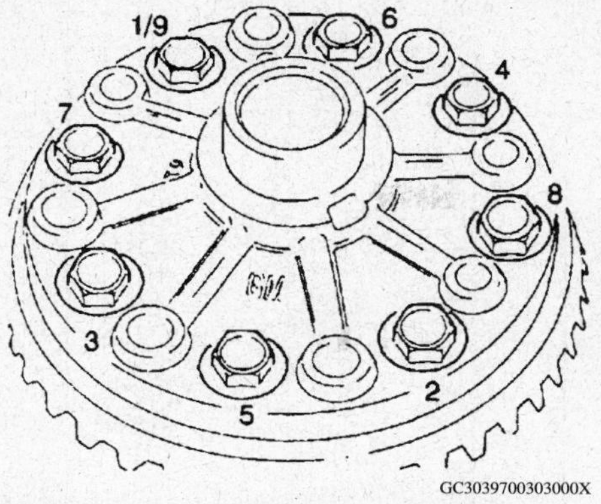

Fig. 24 Ring gear bolt tightening sequence. Catera

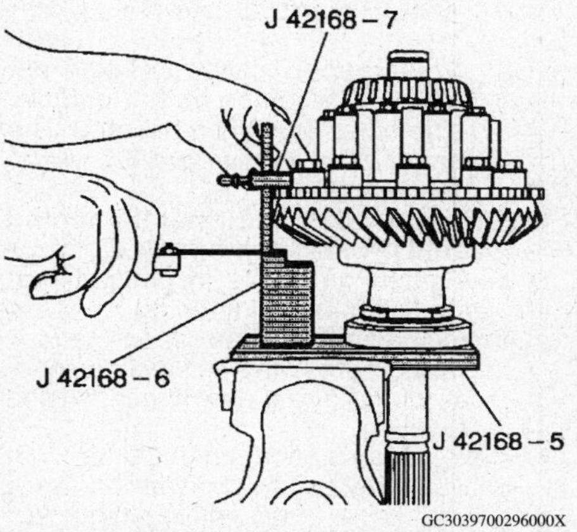

Fig. 26 Differential side bearing adjustment. Corvette

measure total travel. To obtain proper size shim, add .004 inch to total travel measurement.

31. Using a hydraulic press and bearing race remover tool No. J-42194, or equivalent, remove righthand side outer bearing race.
32. Install righthand side shim pack into differential carrier cover.
33. Using a hydraulic press and bearing race installer tool No. J-42172, or equivalent, install righthand side outer bearing race.
34. Using a hydraulic press and bearing installer tool No. J-42157, or equivalent, install righthand side output shaft bearing.
35. Using seal installer tool No. J-36797, or equivalent, install righthand side output shaft oil seal into carrier cover.
36. Using differential case lifting tool No. J-42155, or equivalent, remove ring gear and case assembly from differential carrier.
37. Install lefthand side carrier cover with new O-ring, then the cover bolts. **Torque** bolts to 18 ft. lbs.
38. Install drive pinion shim pack onto pinion cartridge.
39. Lubricate new pinion cartridge O-ring seal with clean engine oil, then install O-ring into groove on pinion cartridge.
40. Using heat gun tool No. J-25070, or equivalent, heat differential carrier

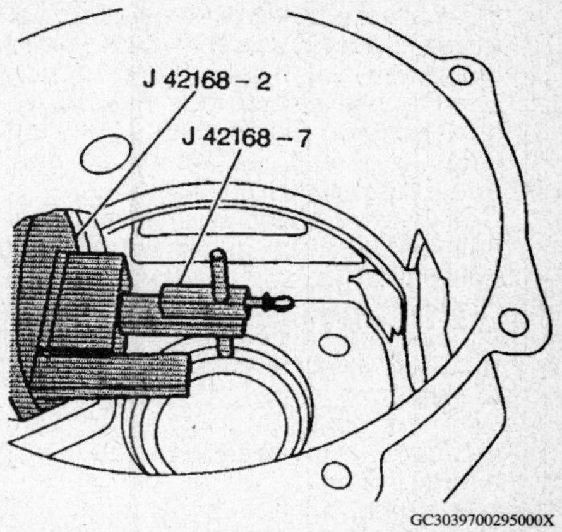

Fig. 25 Depth gauge installation. Corvette

around drive pinion cartridge opening, then install drive pinion cartridge into differential carrier.

41. Install drive pinion cartridge bolts. **Torque** bolts to 41 ft. lbs.
42. Using a torque wrench and pinion gear holder tool No. J-42164, or equivalent, measure pinion rotating torque, which should not exceed 22 inch lbs.
43. Install rear differential cover, magnet, O-ring and rear cover bolts. **Torque** bolts to 7.4 ft. lbs.
44. Using differential case lifting tool No. J-42155, or equivalent, install differential case assembly into carrier.
45. Install C-clip onto righthand output shaft.
46. Install righthand side transmission stud mount and bolts. **Torque** bolts to 7 ft. lbs.
47. Install righthand side transmission mounting stud. **Torque** stud to 31 ft. lbs.
48. Install righthand side differential carrier cover, O-ring and cover bolts. **Torque** bolts to 18 ft. lbs.
49. Install vehicle speed sensor and bolt. **Torque** bolt to 7.4 ft. lbs.
50. Install axle lubricant drain plug. **Torque** plug to 26 ft. lbs.
51. Fill differential with synthetic axle lubricant part No. 12378261 and limited slip additive part No. 1052358, or equivalent.
52. Install axle lubricant fill tag, washer and plug. **Torque** plug to 26 ft. lbs.

DRIVE PINION

Camaro & Firebird

1. Install selected shim onto pinion shaft, lubricate rear pinion bearing with specified axle lubricant, then press rear bearing onto pinion using suitable spacers.
2. Install new collapsible spacer onto pinion shaft, then insert pinion assembly into housing.
3. Lubricate front pinion bearing, install bearing into housing and tap bearing over pinion shaft with a drift while assistant holds pinion in place. **Old pinion nut and a large washer can be used to seat front bearing on pinion,**

but care must be taken not to collapse spacer if this method is used.

4. Install new pinion seal in housing, coat seal lips with grease, then mount driveshaft yoke on pinion shaft, lightly tapping yoke until several pinion shaft threads protrude from yoke.
5. Coat rear of pinion washer with suitable sealer, then install washer and new pinion nut.
6. Hold driveshaft yoke with suitable tool, then alternately tighten pinion nut and rotate pinion until endplay is reduced to zero.
7. When endplay is reduced to zero, measure pinion bearing preload using a torque wrench.
8. Nut should be further tightened only slightly and preload should be inspected after each tightening. Exceeding preload specifications will compress the collapsible spacer too far and require installation of a new spacer. Set preload at 15–30 inch lbs. on new inner and outer bearing assemblies or 10–15 inch lbs. on used assemblies. Rotate drive pinion several times to ensure inner and outer baring assemblies have been seated, then measure preload again. If preload has been reduced by rotating drive pinion gear, reset preload to specifications.

Catera

1. Lubricate differential drive pinion gear outer bearing with suitable axle lubricant.
2. Using drive handle tool No. J-8092 and outer race installer tool No. J-42147, or equivalents, install drive pinion gear outer bearing outer race into housing.
3. Install drive pinion gear outer bearing, then the pinion seal.
4. Install pinion shim into housing.
5. Using driver handle tool No. J-8092 and pinion bearing race installer tool No. J-8608, or equivalents, install inner bearing race into housing.
6. Lubricate differential drive pinion gear inner bearing and drive pinion gear shaft with rear axle lubricant.
7. Using a suitable press, install differential drive pinion gear inner bearing onto drive pinion gear.
8. Install pinion seal, then drive pinion gear into housing.
9. Install drive pinion gear inner bearing onto drive pinion gear.
10. Install pinion gear bearing spacer onto drive pinion gear.
11. Install drive pinion gear into rear axle housing and set pinion depth.
12. Install drive pinion seal, noting the following:

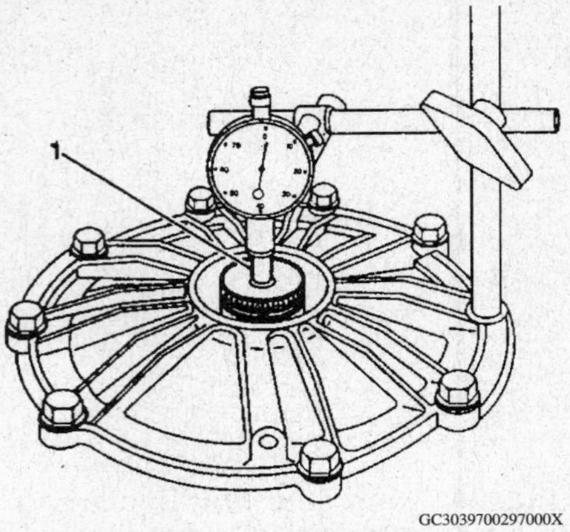

Fig. 27 RH axle bearing adjustment. Corvette

   a. Preload specification is being approached when no further endplay is detected and when holder will no longer pivot freely as drive pinion gear is rotated.
   b. **Do not attempt further tightening until preload is inspected.**
   c. Tighten nut while inspecting preload after each tightening.
   d. Exceeding preload specifications will compress the collapsible spacer too far and a new spacer will be required.

13. Hold pinion flange, then tighten nut until endplay begins to disappear while intermittently rotating drive pinion gear to seat inner and outer bearings.
14. **On new bearings,** set preload to 9–15 inch lbs.
15. **On used bearings,** set preload to 8–11 inch lbs.
16. Rotate drive pinion gear several times to ensure inner and outer bearings have been seated.
17. Measure preload again and adjust as required.

Corvette

Drive pinion bearings and spacer must be replaced as a set.

1. Using a hydraulic press and bearing race installer tool No. J-42172, or equivalent, install front drive pinion bearing inner race into drive pinion housing.
2. Using a hydraulic press and bearing race installer tool No. J-42170, or equivalent, install rear drive pinion bearing outer race into drive pinion housing.
3. Using a hydraulic press, pinion bearing installer tool No. J-42160 and pinion gear holder tool No. J-42164, or equivalents, install front pinion bearing onto drive pinion.
4. Install drive pinion and bearing into drive pinion housing.
5. Install drive pinion bearing spacer onto drive pinion.
6. Using a hydraulic press, pinion bearing installer tool No. J-42160 and pinion gear holder tool No. J-42164, or equivalents, install rear drive pinion bearing onto drive pinion.
7. Using a ¾ inch torque wrench, spanner wrench tool No. J-42163 and pinion gear holder tool No. J-42164, or equivalents, install drive pinion nut and **torque** to 392 ft. lbs.
8. Using a punch, stake areas of drive pinion nut into two notches in end of drive pinion.

RING GEAR & DIFFERENTIAL HOUSING

Catera

1. Clamp pinion alignment tool No. J-42178, or equivalent, into vise.
2. Place differential carrier onto special tool with ring gear flange facing downward.
3. Place counterpiece of pinion alignment tool into opposing differential carrier bore.
4. Install new differential pinion gear retaining ring into carrier.
5. Install shims on side gears, placing thicker shim toward carrier and thinner washer toward side gear.
6. Place side gears with shims into carrier and onto pinion alignment tool.
7. Engage pinion gears and washers, ensuring that they are opposite each other.
8. Move pinion gear washers forward in intended rotational direction, leading pinion gears into position.
9. Using ratchet, rotate pinion alignment tool to draw pinion gears into position.
10. Using deadblow hammer, drive pinion gear shaft into carrier bore and through pinion gears and washers.
11. Attach torque wrench to pinion alignment tool and inspect rotational torque. Acceptable rotational torque reading is between 11 and 22 ft. lbs.
12. Heat ring gear to 212° F, then install onto differential carrier. Ensure all bolt holes are aligned.
13. Torque ring gear bolts in sequence outlined, **Fig. 24,** to 85 ft. lbs.

DRIVE AXLE SPECIFICATIONS

CAMARO & FIREBIRD

Year	Axle Model	Ring Gear Diameter, Inch	Ring Gear Backlash, Inch	Pinion Bearing Preload, Inch Lbs.		Total Assembly Preload, Inch Lbs.		Side Bearing Preload, Inch Lbs.		Differential Bearings, Inch Lbs.	
				New	Used	New	Used	New	Used	Used	New
1997–2000	GM	7.62	.005–.009	15–30	10–15	32–55	16–28	—	—	—	—

CATERA

Year	Model	Ring Gear Back Lash, Inch	Pinion Bearing Preload, Inch Lbs.		Differential Assembly Preload, Inch Lbs.①
			New Bearings	Used Bearings	
1997–2000	All	.004–.008	9–15	8–11	4.5–6.5

① — Without pinion gear in housing.

CORVETTE

Year	Axle Model	Carrier Type	Ring Gear Backlash		Pinion Bearing Preload		Side Gear Preload	
			Method	Adjustment, Inch	Method	New Bearings Inch Lbs.	Method	Adjustment, Inch
1997–2000	Getrag	Integral	Shims	①	Shims	①	Shims	①

① — Adjustment is determined by markings on ring gear & pinion set.

ENGINE REBUILDING SPECIFICATIONS

TABLE OF CONTENTS

General Motors

NOTE: For Engine Tightening Specifications, Refer To The Engine Section In The Appropriate Chassis Chapter Of This Manual.

INDEX

CYLINDER HEAD, VALVE GUIDE & VALVE SEATS

All Measurements Given In Inches Unless Otherwise Specified

Engine Liter/ VIN	Year	Cylinder Head Warpage Limit	Cylinder Head Overall Thickness	Valve Guides			Valve Seats			
				Standard Inside Diameter	Stem To Guide Clearance		Seat Angle	Seat Width		Runout
					Intake	Exhaust		Intake	Exhaust	
1.0L/6	1997–99	.002	—	.2165–.2170	.0008–.0022	.0018–.0028	45°	.0512–.0590	.0512–.0590	.031
1.3L/9	1997	.002	—	.2756–.2761	.0008–.0019	.0014–.0025	45°	.0512–.0590	.0512–.0590	.031
1.3L/9	1998–99	.002	—	.2159–.2169	.0002–.0018	.0012–.0027	45°	.0433–.0512	.0433–.0512	.031
1.6L/6	1997–98	.002	—	.2366–.2374	.0010–.0031	.0012–.0039	45°	.0470–.0630	.0470–.0630	—
1.8L/8	1997–99	.002	—	.2366–.2374	.0010–.0031	.0012–.0039	45°	.0470–.0630④	.0470–.0630④	—
2.2L/4	1997	②	—	—	.0010–.0027	.0014–.0031	46°	.0490–.0590	.0630–.0750	.0012
	1998–99	②	—	.275–.276	.0007–.0020	.0014–.0029	45°	.110	.138	.0014
2.4L/T	1997	.003	—	—	.0010–.0028	.0015–.0032	①	.0370–.0748	.0370–.0748	.0015
	1998–99	.003	—	—	.0009–.0025	.0009–.0025	45°	.0370–.0748	.0370–.0748	.0015
3.0L/R	1997–99	.002	—	.2362–.2367	.0012–.0022	.0016–.0026	45°	.0394–.0551	.0551–.0709	—
3.1L/M	1997–99	②	—	—	.0010–.0027	.0010–.0027	45°	.0610–.0710	.0670–.0790	.0010
3.4L/E	1999	—	—	—	.0010–.0027	.0010–.0027	45°	.0610–.0710	.0670–.0790	.0001
3.4L/X	1997	②	—	—	.0011–.0026	.0018–.0033	46°	.0492–.0591	.0630–.0748	.0030

Continued

CYLINDER HEAD, VALVE GUIDE & VALVE SEATS—Continued

All Measurements Given In Inches Unless Otherwise Specified

Engine Liter/ VIN	Year	Cylinder Head Warpage Limit	Cylinder Head Overall Thickness	Valve Guides			Valve Seats			
				Standard Inside Diameter	Stem To Guide Clearance		Seat Angle	Seat Width		Runout
					Intake	Exhaust		Intake	Exhaust	
3.5L/H	1999	.002	—	.235	.0010–.0030	.0020–.0040	45.75°	.0165–.0322	.0511–.0668	.0014
3.8L/K, 1	1997–2000	②	—	—	.0015–.0032	.0015–.0032	45°	.0600–.0800	.0900–.1100	.0020
4.0L/C	1997	.002③	—	.2350	.0010–.0030	.0020–.0040	46°	.0170–.0330	.0270–.0430	.0020
	1998–99	.002③	—	.2350	.0011–.0027	.0011–.0027	46°	.0170–.0330	.0270–.0430	.0020
4.6L/Y, 9	1997–2000	.002	—	.2350	.0010–.0030	.0020–.0040	46°	.0170–.0330	.0270–.0430	.0020
5.7L/P	1997	.004	—	—	.0010–.0037	.0010–.0047	46°	.030–.050	.060–.080	.0020
5.7L/G	1997–99	.004	—	—	.0010–.0037	.0010–.0037	46°	.0400	.0700	.0020

①— Intake valve, 46°; exhaust valve 45.5°.

②— Maximum surface refinish, .010 inch.

③— If warpage is more than .008 inch, replace head.

④— 1998–99, .049 inch.

VALVE SPRINGS

All Measurements Given In Inches Unless Otherwise Specified.

Engine Liter/VIN	Year	Free Length	Installed Height	Seated Pressure Pounds @ Inches	Comp. Pressure Pounds @ Inches	Out Of Square Limit
1.0L/6	1997–99	1.614–1.665	1.280	46–52 @ 1.28	—	.079
1.3L/9	1997	1.894–1.941	1.630	50–64 @ 1.63	—	.079
1.3L/9	1998–99	1.4500	1.24	21–28 @ 1.24	—	.079
1.6L/6	1997–98	1.669	1.250	37 @ 1.25	—	.079
1.8L/8	1997	1.669	1.250	37 @ 1.25	—	.079
	1998–99	1.8070	1.323	31–35 @ 1.323	—	.079
2.2L/4	1997	1.950	1.710	75–81 @ 1.71	220–236 @ 1.278	—
	1998–99	1.91	1.60	73–81 @ 1.60	201–215 @ 1.175	—
2.4L/T	1997–99	—	.980–1.000	50–55 @ 1.44	122–133 @ 1.062	—
3.0L/R	1997–99	—	1.540	57 @ 1.338	—	—
3.1L/M	1997–99	1.890	1.701	75 @ 1.701	230 @ 1.260	—
3.4L/E	1999	1.890	1.701	75 @ 1.701	230 @ 1.260	—
3.4L/X	1997	1.6551	1.400	65 @ 1.40	160 @ 1.03	—
3.5L/H	1999	1.663	1.377	47–52 @ 1.377	130–142 @ .964	—
3.8L/K, 1	1997	1.981	1.690–1.720	80 @ 1.75	210 @ 1.315	—
	1998–2000	1.960	1.690–1.720	75 @ 1.72	228 @ 1.277	—
4.0L/C	1997–98	1.591	1.190	46 @ 1.19	92 @ .854	—
	1999	1.591	1.190	53 @ 1.19	109 @ .854	—
4.6L/Y	1997–98	1.591	1.190	46 @ 1.19	92 @ .854	—
	1999–2000	1.591	1.190	53 @ 1.19	109 @ .823	—
4.6L/9	1997–99	1.591	1.190	53 @ 1.19	109 @ .823	—
5.7L/P	1997	2.020	1.780	81–89 @ 1.78	245–264 @ 1.330	—
5.7/G	1997–99	2.080	1.800	76 @ 1.80	220 @ 1.320	—

VALVES

All Measurements Given In Inches Unless Otherwise Specified.

Engine Liter/VIN	Year	Stem Diameter		Valve Stem Installed Height	Valve Lash		Face Angle	Margin①
		Intake	Exhaust		Intake	Exhaust		
1.0L/6	1997–99	.2148–.2157	.2142–.2148	—	⑥	⑥	45°	②
1.3L/9	1997	.2742–.2748	.2737–.2742	—	⑥	⑥	45°	—
	1998–99	.2152–.2157	.2142–.2148	—	⑥	⑥	45°	—
1.6L/6	1997–98	.2350–.2356	.2348–.2354	—	.006–.010③	.010–.014③	45°	.020
1.8L/8	1997	.2350–.2356	.2348–.2354	—	.006–.010③	.010–.014③	45°	.020
	1998–99	.2154–.2159	.2152-.–2157	—	.006–.010③	.010–.014③	45°	—
2.2L/4	1997–99	—	—	—	.001–.003	.001–.003	45°	.031
2.4L/T	1997–99	.2331–.2339	.2326–.2334	.9787–1.0024	—	—	④	.0098
3.0L/R	1997–99	.2344–.2350	.2341–.2346	—	—	—	45°	—
3.1L/M	1997–99	—	—	1.701	⑩	⑩	45°	⑪
3.4L/E	1999	—	—	—	⑥	⑥	45°	⑪
3.4L/X	1997	—	—	⑨	⑥	⑥	45°	.029
3.5L/H	1999	.2331–.2339	.2331–.2339	—	⑥	⑥	45°	⑫
3.8L/K, 1	1997–2000	—	—	1.935–1.975	⑥	⑥	45°	.025
4.0L/C	1997–99	2331–.2339	2331–.2339	⑦	⑥	⑥	45°	⑧
4.6L/Y,9	1997–2000	.2331–.2339	.2331–.2339	⑦	—	—	45°	⑧
5.7L/P	1997	—	—	—	⑤	⑤	45°	—
5.7L/G	1997–99	.3130–.3140	.3130–.3140	—	⑥	⑥	45°	—

① — Minimum.
② — Intake, .02 inch; exhaust, .027 inch.
③ — Cold.
④ — Intake valve, 46°; exhaust valve, 45.5°.
⑤ — Zero lash plus or minus 1 1/4 turns.
⑥ — Hydraulic lifters, zero lash.
⑦ — Intake, 1.389–1.453 inches; Max. 1.463 inches. Exhaust, 1.332–1.392 inches; Max. 1.402 inches. Measured from top of stem to head.
⑧ — Intake, .005 inch; exhaust, .030 inch.
⑨ — Intake, 1.654 inches, plus or minus .019 inch; Exhaust, 1.653 inches, plus or minus .019 inch.
⑩ — Zero lash plus 1 1/2 turns.
⑪ — Intake, .083 inch; Exhaust, .106 inch.
⑫ — Intake, .0354 inch; exhaust, .0432 inch.

CAMSHAFT

All Measurements Given In Inches Unless Otherwise Specified.

Engine Liter/ VIN	Year	Camshaft Journal Diameter	Maximum Journal Runout	Camshaft Bearing Clearance	Camshaft Endplay	Rocker Arm Oil Clearance	Lifter Bore Diameter	Lifter Diameter	Lifter To Bore Clearance
1.0L/6	1997–99	①	.0039	.0008–.0024	—	—	1.2205–1.2214	1.2188–1.2194	.0010–.0025
1.3L/9	1997–99	③	.0039	.0020–.0059⑤	—	.0005–.0035⑥	—	—	—
1.6L/6	1997–98	②	.0012	.0014–.0028	.0043	—	1.2205–1.2215	1.2191–1.2195	.0009–.0028
1.8L/8	1997	.9035–.9041	.0012	.0014–.0028	.0043	—	—	—	—
	1998–99	.9035–.9041	.0016	—	—	—	1.2205–1.2215	1.2191–1.2195	.0009–.0028
2.2L/4	1997–99	1.8680–1.8690	—	.0010–.0039⑦	—	—	—	—	—
2.4L/T	1997–99	④	—	.0019–.0043	.0009–.0088	—	1.3381–1.3393	1.3369–1.3375	.0006–.0023
3.0L/R	1997–99	1.0990–1.1010	—	.0015–.0020	.0016–.0057	—	—	—	—
3.1L/M	1997–99	1.8680–1.8690	.0010	.001–.0039	—	—	—	—	—
3.4L/E	1999	1.8680–1.8690	.0010	.0010–.0039	—	—	—	—	—

Continued

CAMSHAFT—Continued

All Measurements Given In Inches Unless Otherwise Specified.

Engine Liter/ VIN	Year	Camshaft Journal Diameter	Maximum Journal Runout	Camshaft Bearing Clearance	Camshaft Endplay	Rocker Arm Oil Clearance	Lifter Bore Diameter	Lifter Diameter	Lifter To Bore Clearance
1.0L/6	1997–99	①	.0039	.0008–.0024	—	—	1.2205–1.2214	1.2188–1.2194	.0010–.0025
3.4L/X	1997	2.1643–2.1654	—	.0019–.0040	—	—	—	—	—
3.5L/H	1999	1.0610–1.0620	.0020	.0016–.0033	—	—	.4727-.–4736	.4716–.4721	.0014–.0016
3.8L/K, 1	1997	1.7850–1.7860	—	.0005–.0035	—	—	—	—	—
	1998–2000	1.8462–1.8448	—	.0016–.0047	—	—	—	—	—
4.0L/C	1997–99	1.0610–1.0620	.0009	.0020–.0030	—	—	1.2992	1.2970–1.2980	.0010–.0030
4.6L/Y,9	1997–99	1.0610–1.0620	—	.0020–.0030	—	—	1.2992	1.2970–1.2980	.0010–.0030
	2000	1.0610–1.0620	—	.0020–.0030	—	—	.4727–.4736	.4716–.4721	.0014–.0016
5.7L/P	1997	1.8677–1.8697	—	—	.0004–.0120	—	—	—	—
5.7L/G	1997–99	2.1640–2.1660	.0020	—	.0010–.0120	—	—	—	—

① — Journal No. 1, 1.0220–1.0228 inches; journal No. 2 & 3, 1.1795–1.1803 inches.

② — Journal No. 1, .9822–.9829 inch; journal No. 2, 3, 4 & 5, .9035–.9041 inch.

③ — Working from front to rear of camshaft, diameter No. 1 dual journals 1.7373–1.7381 inches; diameter No. 2 journal 1.7451–1.7640 inches; diameter No. 3 journal 1.7350–1.7539 inches; diameter No. 4 journal 1.7609–1.7618 inches; diameter No. 5 journal 1.7687–1.7697 inches.

④ — Journal No. 1, 1.5720–1.5728 inches; journal No. 2, 3, 4 & 5, 1.3751–1.3760 inches.

⑤ — 1998–99, .0016–.0047 inch.

⑥ — 1998–99, .0001–.0035 inch.

⑦ — 1998–99, .0005–.0035 inch.

CRANKSHAFT, BEARINGS & RODS

All Measurements Given In Inches Unless Otherwise Specified.

Engine Liter/ VIN	Year	Crankshaft: Standard Journal Diameter: Main Bearing	Crankshaft: Standard Journal Diameter: Crank Pin	Crankshaft: Out of Round All①	Crankshaft: Taper All①	Bearing Clearance: Main Bearings	Bearing Clearance: Connecting Rod Bearings	Bearing Clearance: Thrust Bearing Clearance	Connecting Rod Side Clearance
1.0L/6	1997–99	②	1.6529–1.6535	.00040	.00040	.0008–.0015	.0012–.0019	.0044–.0122	.0039–.0078
1.3L/9	1997–99	②	1.6529–1.6535	.00040	.00040	.0008–.0023	.0012–.0031	—	.0039–.0137
1.6L/6	1997–98	④	—	.00320	.00320	.0006–.0039	.0008–.0031	.0006–.0118	.0059–.0098
1.8L/8	1997	④	—	.00020	.00020	.0006–.0039	.0008–.0031	.0006–.0118	.0008–.0031
	1998–99	⑦	—	.0004	.0004	.0002–.0014	.0008–.0031	.0016–.0118	.0063–.0157
2.2L/4	1997–99	2.4945–2.4954	1.9983–1.9994	.00190	.00190	.0006–.0019	.0010–.0031	.0020–.0070	.0039–.0149
2.4L/T	1997	2.3634–2.3626	1.8887–1.8897	.00020	.00020	.0005–.0030	.0005–.0020	—	.0059–.0177
	1998–99	2.3622–2.3631	1.8887–1.8897	.00020	.00030	.0004–.0023	.0004–.0026	—	.0059–.0177
3.0L/R	1997–99	2.6763–2.6766	1.9270–1.9280	.00120	—	.0006–.0017	.0005–.0024	—	.0027–.0110
3.1L/M	1997–99	2.6473–2.6483	1.9987–1.9994	.00020	.00020	.0008–.0025	.0007–.0024	.0012–.0030	.0070–.0170

Continued

CRANKSHAFT, BEARINGS & RODS—Continued

All Measurements Given In Inches Unless Otherwise Specified.

Engine Liter/ VIN	Year	Crankshaft				Bearing Clearance			Connecting Rod Side Clearance
		Standard Journal Diameter		Out of Round All①	Taper All①	Main Bearings	Connecting Rod Bearings	Thrust Bearing Clearance	
		Main Bearing	Crank Pin						
3.4L/E	1999	2.6473–2.6483	1.9987–1.9994	.00020	.00020	.0008–.0025	.0007–.0024	.0012–.0030	.0070–.0170
3.4L/X	1997	2.6472–2.6479	1.9987–1.9994	.00020	.00020	.0008–.0025	.0007–.0024	.0013–.0030	.0071–.0173
3.5L/H	1999	2.7550–2.7560	2.1829–2.1835	.00016	.00015	.0006–.0018	.0009–.0020	—	.004–.013
3.8L/K, 1	1997	2.4988–2.4998	2.2487–2.2499	.00030	.00030	.0008–.0022	.0008–.0022	.0030–.0110	.0030–.0150
	1998–2000	2.4988–2.4998	2.2487–2.2499	.00025	.00035	⑥	.0005–.0026	—	.0040–.0200
4.0L/C	1997–99	2.5335–.2.5337	2.1239–2.1245	.00016	.00015	.0006–.0020	.0010–.0030	—	—
4.6L/Y,9	1997–2000	2.5335–2.5337	2.1239–2.1245	.00016	.00016	.0006–.0025	.0010–.0030	—	.0080–.0200
5.7L/P	1997	⑤	2.0978–2.0998	.0002	.0002	③	.0013–.0035	.0020–.0080	.006–.024
5.7L/G	1997–99	2.558–2.559	2.0991–2.0999	.00031	.00078	.0007–.00212	.0006–.0025	—	.00433–.0200

① — Maximum.
② — The counter weights of No. 1 cylinder have four stamped numbers, they indicate journal diameters at bearing caps respectively. No. 1, 1.7714–1.7716 inches; No. 2, 1.7712–1.7714 inches & No. 3, 1.7710–1.7712 inches.
③ — Journal No. 1, .0010–.0020 inch; journal No. 2, 3 & 4, .0090–.0025 inch; journal No. 5, .0015–.0030 inch.
④ — Stamping No. 0, 1.8895–1.8898 inches; stamping No. 1, 1.8893–1.8895 inches; stamping No. 2, 1.8891–1.8893 inches.
⑤ — Diameter No. 1, 2.4484–2.4493 inches; diameter No. 2, 3 & 4, 2.4481–2.4491 inches; journal No. 5, 2.4479–2.4491 inches.
⑥ — No 1. bearing clearance, .0070–.0016 inch; Nos. 2, 3 and 4, .0009–.0018 inch.
⑦ — Stamping No. 0, 1.8897–1.8898 inches; stamping No. 1, 1.8896–1.8897 inches; stamping No. 2, 1.8895–1.8896 inches; stamping No. 3, 1.8894–1.8895 inches; stamping No. 4, 1.8893–1.8894 inches; stamping No. 5, 1.8892–1.8893 inches.

PISTONS, PINS & RINGS

All Measurements Given In Inches Unless Otherwise Specified.

Engine Liter/ VIN	Year	Piston Diameter (Std.)	Piston Clearance	Piston Pin Diameter①	Piston Pin To Piston Clearance	Piston Ring End Gap②		Piston Ring Side Clearance	
						Comp.	Oil	Comp.	Oil
1.0L/6	1997–99	2.9122–2.9130	.0008–.0015	—	—	.0079–.0276	.0079–.0708	③	—
1.3L/9	1997–99	⑧	.0008–.0015	㉑	—	.0079–.0276	.0079–.0708	.0014–.0027	.0008–.0023
1.6L/6	1997–98	⑩	.0008–.0015	—	—	.0413	.0413	⑤	—
1.8 /8	1997	⑩	.0008–.0015	.8264–.8267	.0004–.0005	⑭	.0413	—	—
	1998–99	3.1073–3.1077	.0026–.0039	.7876–.7879	㉒	㉓	.0059–.0157	㉔	—
2.2L/4	1997	—	.0007–.0017	.8000–.8002	.0003–.0007	.0100–.0200	.0100–.0400	.0019–.0027	.0019–.0082
	1998–99	—	.0022–.0034	.8001–.8002	.0003–.0008	㉕	.010–.030	㉖	.0005–.0087
2.4L/T	1997	3.6203–3.6210	.0007–.0020	.8659–.8661	.00007–.00043	⑦	.0157–.0551	⑥	—
	1998–99	3.5404–3.5420	.0010–.0031	.8659–.8661	.00008–.00043	⑦	.0098–.0299	⑥	—

Continued

PISTONS, PINS & RINGS—Continued

All Measurements Given In Inches Unless Otherwise Specified.

Engine Liter/ VIN	Year	Piston Diameter (Std.)	Piston Clearance	Piston Pin Diameter①	Piston Pin To Piston Clearance	Piston Ring End Gap②		Piston Ring Side Clearance	
						Comp.	Oil	Comp.	Oil
3.0L/R	1997–99	⑮	.0010-.0018	.8267	.0001–.0003	.0118–.0196	0.157–.0551	.0008–.0015	.0004–.0012
3.1L/M	1997–99	3.5029–3.5040	.0013–.0027	.9052–.9060	.0004–.0008	⑬	.0098–.050	.0020–.0033	.0080
3.4L/E	1999	3.6209–3.6216	.0013–.0027	.9052–.9054	.0004–.0008	.0060–.0140	.0098–.050	.0020–.0033	.008
3.4L/X	1997	3.6215–3.6220	.0008–.0020	.9052–.9054	.0006–.0018	④	.0098–.0299	.0013–.0031	.0011–.0081
3.5L/H	1999	3.521–3.522	.0010–.0025	.8265–.8267	.0001–.0006	⑰	.0100–.0300	.0016–.0037	⑫
3.8L/K, 1	1997–98	—	.0004–.0020	.8659–.8661	.0003–.0009	⑪	.0100–.0300	.0013–.0031	.0009–.0079
3.8L/K	1999–2000	—	.004–.0020⑲	.8659–.8661	.00008–.00051	⑳	.0100–.0300	.0013–.0031	.0009–.0079
3.8L/ 1	1999	—	.0008–.0039⑲	.9053–.9055	.00026–.00061	⑳	.0100–.0300	.0013–.0031	.0009–.0079
4.0L/C	1997–98	—	.0008–.0020	.8650–.8660	—	⑨	.0100–.0300	.0020–.0040	⑫
	1999	3.4230–3.4240⑱	.0008.–0020	.8650–.8660	—	⑨	.0100–.0300	.0016–.0037	⑫
4.6L/Y,9	1997–98	3.6597–3.6603㉗	.0008–.0020	.8650–.8660	—	⑰	.0100–.0300	.0016–.0037	⑫
	1999–2000	3.6597–3.6603㉗	.0008–.0020	.8650–.8660	—	⑰	.0100–.0300	.0016–.0037	⑫
5.7L/P	1997	—	.0010–.0027	.9270–.9271	.0004–.0010	.0010–.0035	.0010–.0065	.0019–.0035	.0020–.0080
5.7L/G	1997–99	3.8962–3.8969	.0007–.00212	.9447–.9448	.0004–.00078	.0090–.0149	.0070–.0271	⑯	.0004–.0087

① — Pistons & pins are matched set & should be replaced as an assembly.
② — Maximum.
③ — Top ring, .0012–.0027 inch; 2nd ring, .0008–.0023 inch.
④ — Top ring, .008–.018 inch; 2nd ring, .022–.032 inch.
⑤ — Top ring, .0018–.0033 inch; 2nd ring, .0012–.0028 inch.
⑥ — Top ring, .0016–.0031 inch; 2nd ring, .0012–.0028 inch.
⑦ — Top ring, .006–.012 inch; 1997 2nd ring, .0119–.0161 inch; 1998–99 2nd ring, .0098–.0157 inch.
⑧ — There are two standard sizes of pistons marked with a No. on top. No. 1, 2.9126–2.9130 inches; No. 2, 2.9120–2.9126 inches in diameter.
⑨ — Top ring .010–.016 inch; 2nd ring .014–.020 inch.
⑩ — There are three standard sizes of pistons marked with a No. on top. No. 1, 3.1852–3.1856 inches; No. 2, 3.1856–3.1860 inches; No. 3, 3.1860–3.1864 inches.
⑪ — Top ring, .012–.022 inch; 2nd ring, .030–.040 inch.
⑫ — Zero clearance; side sealing ring.
⑬ — Top ring, .006–.014 inch; 2nd ring, .020–.028 inch.
⑭ — Top ring, .0413 inch; lower ring, .0472 inch.
⑮ — Fit designation stamped on top of piston: (8) 3.3834–3.3838 inches; (99) 3.3838–3.3842 inches; (00) 3.3842–3.3846 inches; (01) 3.3846–3.3850 inches; (02) 3.3850–3.3854 inches.
⑯ — Top ring, .0016–.0033 inch; 2nd ring, .0016–.0031 inch.
⑰ — Top ring, .010–.016 inch; 2nd ring, .014–.020 inch.
⑱ — Measured 46mm from top of piston.
⑲ — Measured 41mm from top of piston.
⑳ — Top ring, .010–.018; 2nd ring, .023–.033 inch.
㉑ — 1998–99 .7479–.7480 inch
㉒ — Interference fit.
㉓ — Top ring, .0098–.0138 inch; lower ring, .0138–.0197 inch.
㉔ — Top ring, .0012–.0028 inch; lower ring, .0012–.0028 inch.
㉕ — Top ring, .010–.020 inch; lower ring, .0012–.0177 inch.
㉖ — Top ring, .0020–.0035 inch; lower ring, .0016–.0031 inch.
㉗ — Measured 1.58 inch from top of piston.

CYLINDER BLOCK

All Measurements Given In Inches Unless Otherwise Specified.

Engine Liter/VIN	Year	Cylinder Bore Diameter (Std.)	Cylinder Bore Taper Max.	Cylinder Bore Out of Round Max.
1.0L/6	1997–99	①	.0039	.0039
1.3L/9	1997–99	①	.0040	.0040
1.6L/6	1997–98	3.1980–3.2177	.0005	.0050
1.8L/8	1997	3.1890–3.2177	.0050	.0050
	1998–99	3.1102–3.1107	.0039	.0039
2.2L/4	1997–99	3.5036–3.5043	.0005	.0005
2.4L/T	1997–99	3.5430–3.5435	.0003	.0004
3.0L/R	1997–99	③	.0003	.0026
3.1L/T,M	1997–99	3.5046–3.5053	.0005	.0008
3.4L/E	1999	3.6228–3.6235	.0004	.0003
3.4L/X	1997	3.6228–3.6235	.00051	.0004
3.5L/H	1999	3.5230④	.0004	.0004
3.8L/K, 1	1997–98	3.8000	.001	.001
	1999–2000	3.8000	.0010	.0010
4.0L/C	1997–98	3.43⑤	.0040	.0040
	1999	3.4240–3.4250④	.0040	.0040
4.6L/Y,9	1997	3.66⑤	.0004	.0008
	1998–99	3.4240–3.4250④	.0040	.0040
	2000	3.6611-3.6617④	.0040	.0040
5.7L/P	1997	4.0007–4.0017	②	.0020
5.7L/G	1997–99	3.8970–3.8980	.0007	—

① — Cylinder bore diameter Nos. are stamped on top of block in sequence. No. 1, 2.9138–2.9142 inches & No. 2, 2.9134–2.9138 inches.

② — Thrust side, .0005 inch; relief side, .0010 inch.

③ — Fit designation stamped on block: (8) 3.3848– 3.3852 inches; (99) 3.3852–3.3856 inches; (00) 3.3856–3.3860 inches; (01) 3.3860–3.3864 inches; (02) 3.3864–3.3868 inches.

④ — At 1.614 inch below deck surface.

⑤ — At 1.97 inch below deck surface.

OIL PUMP

All Measurements Given In Inches Unless Otherwise Specified.

Engine Liter/ VIN	Year	Gear Backlash	Gear To Body Clearance	Gear End-play①	Gear Pocket		Pump Gear Thickness	Pump Gear Diameter	Relief Valve To Body Clearance
					Depth	Diameter			
1.0L/6	1997–99	—	.012	.006	—	—	—	—	—
1.3L/9	1997–99	—	.012	.006	—	—	—	—	—
1.6L/6	1997–98	.0030–.0140	.004	.008	—	—	—	—	—
1.8L/8	1997	.0010–.0140	.003–.008	.001–.040	—	—	—	—	—
	1998–99	.0138	.0138	.0059	—	—	—	—	—
2.2L/4	1997–99	.0040–.0080	.002–.003	.002–.007	1.1950–1.1980	1.5030–1.5060	.6727–.6731	1.498–1.500	.0015–.0035
2.4L/T	1997–98	.0091–.0201	—	—	.6736–.6756	2.1273–2.1292	.6727–.6731	—	—
	1999	.0029–.0055	—	—	.6023–.6043	1.7730–1.7750	.5994–.6003	—	—
3.0L/R	1997–99	②	②	②	②	②	②	②	②
3.1L/M③	1997–99	.0040–.0080	.001–.003	.002–.005	1.2020–1.2040	1.5030–1.5050	1.1990–1.2000	1.4980–1.5000	.0015–.0035
3.4L/E	1999	.0037–.0077	.001–.003	.002–.005	1.2020–1.2040	1.5030–1.5050	1.1990–1.2000	1.4980–1.5000	.0015–.0035
3.4L/X	1997	.0040–.0080	.003–.004	.002–.006	1.2020–1.2050	1.5040–1.5060	1.1990–1.2000	1.4980–1.5000	.0015–.0035
3.5L/H	1999	—	—	—	—	—	—	—	—
3.8L/K, 1	1997–2000	.0060	.008–.015	.001–.0035	.4610–.4625	3.5080–3.5120	—	—	.0015–.0030
4.0L/C	1997–99	—	—	—	—	—	—	—	—
4.6L/Y,9	1997–2000	②	②	②	②	②	②	②	②
5.7L/P	1997	②	②	②	②	②	②	②	②
5.7L/G	1997–99	②	②	②	②	②	②	②	②

① — Measured between pump cover & end of gears using straightedge & feeler gauge.
② — Pump components are not serviced separately. If any component is damaged or worn, pump should be replaced.
③ — Cast iron body pump.

Saturn

INDEX

CYLINDER HEAD, VALVE GUIDE & VALVE SEATS

All Specifications Given In Inches Unless Otherwise Specified.

Engine/Liter	Cylinder Head Warpage Limit	Cylinder Head Overall Thickness	Valve Guides			Valve Seats			
			Standard I.D.	Stem To Guide Clearance		Seat Angle, Deg.	Seat Width		Runout
				Intake	Exhaust		Intake	Exhaust	
1.9L SOHC	①	4.4440–4.4540	.2751–.2761	.0010–.0025	.0015–.0032	44.5–45.5°	.0394–.0512	.0512–.0630	—
1.9L DOHC	①	4.4449–4.4527	.2750–.2760	.0010–.0025	.0015–.0032	44.5–45.5°	.0394-.0512	.0512-.0630	—
2.2L DOHC	.020	—	.2362–2367	.0012.–.0022	.0016–.0026	45°	.031	.031	.0020
3.0L DOHC	.0020/3.937	5.272–5.280	—	.0012.–.0022	.0016–.0026	45°	.0394-.0551	.0551-.0709	—

SOHC — Single Overhead Cam
DOHC — Dual Overhead Cam

① — Longitudinal deck, .0040 inch; transverse deck, .0020 inch.

VALVE SPRINGS

All Specifications Given In Inches, Unless Otherwise Specified.

Engine/Liter	Free Length	Seated Press., Lbs. @ Inches	Comp. Press., Lbs. @ Inches	Out Of Square Limit
1.9L SOHC	1.8898–1.9134	76–87 @ 1.61	202–211 @ 1.280	.100
1.9L DOHC①	1.6100	66–77 @ 1.34	163–180 @ .984	.100
1.9L DOHC②	1.6100	55-65 @ 1.38	126-142 @ .984	.100
1.9L DOHC③	1.56	42–48 @ 1.221	99–109 @ .874	.100

SOHC — Single Overhead Cam
DOHC — Dual Overhead Cam

① — 1997 models.
② — 1998–99 models.
③ — 2000 models.

VALVES

All Specifications Given In Inches, Unless Otherwise Specified.

Engine/Liter	Stem Diameter		Clearance①		Face Angle	Margin Min.
	Intake	Exhaust	Intake	Exhaust		
1.9L SOHC③	.2736–.2741	.2736–.2741	.0010–.0025	.0015-.0032	44.75–45.25°	②
1.9L SOHC④	.2736–.2741	.2736–.2740	.0010–.0025	.0015-.0032	44.75–45.25°	②
1.9L DOHC③	.2736–.2741	.2729–.2736	.0010–.0025	.0015–.0032	45.00–45.50°	.0295
1.9L DOHC④	.2736–.2740	.2726–.2736	.0010–.0025	.0015–.0032	45.00–45.50°	②
2.2L DOHC	.2362–.2367	.2362–.2367	.0012–.0022	.0016–.0026	45°	.031
3.0L DOHC	.2344–.2350	.2341–.2346	.0012–.0022	.0016–.0026	45°	⑤

SOHC — Single Overhead Cam
DOHC — Dual Overhead Cam
① — Between valve guide bushing & valve.
② — Intake width, .0350 inch; exhaust width, .0390 inch.
③ — 1997 models.
④ — 1998–2000 models.
⑤ — Intake width, .0394 inch; exhaust width, .0551 inch.

CAMSHAFT

All Specifications Given In Inches, Unless Otherwise Specified.

Engine/Liter	Camshaft Journal Diameter	Maximum Journal Runout	Camshaft Bearing Clearance	Camshaft Endplay	Rocker Arm Oil Clearance	Lifter Bore Diameter	Lifter Diameter	Lifter To Bore Clearance
1.9L SOHC	1.7480–1.7490	.0020–.0028	.0020–.0040	.0028–.0079	—	—	.8420–.8427	.0007–.0024
1.9L DOHC	1.1398–1.1406	.0020–.0040	.0021–.0030	.0020–.0080	—	—	1.2976–1.2982	.0010–.0026
2.2L DOHC	1.0604–1.0614	—	.0016–.0034	.0016–.0057	—	—	.8215–.8236	.0007–.0024
3.0L DOHC	1.0990–1.0100	—	.0015–.0020	.0016–.0057	—	—	1.2976–1.2982	.0010–.0026

SOHC — Single Overhead Cam
DOHC — Dual Overhead Cam

CRANKSHAFT, BEARINGS & RODS

All Specifications Given In Inches, Unless Otherwise Specified.

Engine/ Liter	Crankshaft				Bearing Clearance			Connecting Rod	
	Standard Journal Diameter		Out Of Round, All①	Taper, All①	Main Bearings	Connecting Rod Bearings	Thrust Bearing Clearance	Pin Bore Diameter	Side Clearance
	Main Bearing	Crank Pin							
1.9L	2.2438–2.2444	1.8500–1.8508	.0004	.0004	.0002–.0020	.0001–.0021	.0020-.0089	.7679–.7685	.0065–.0171
2.2L	2.2045–2.2050	1.9291–1.9297	.0026	.0026	.0012–.0026	.0004–.0016	.0011–.0027	.7872–.7874	.0028–.0146
3.0L	②	1.9270–1.9190	.0012	.0012	.0006–.0017	.0005–.0024	—	1.9271–.928	.0027–.0110

① — Maximum.

② — Standard size green,2.6763–2.6766; standard size brown, 2.6766–2.6770.

PISTONS, PINS & RINGS

All Specifications Given In Inches, Unless Otherwise Specified.

Engine/ Liter	Piston Diameter (Std.)①	Piston Clearance	Piston Pin Diameter②③	Piston Pin To Piston Clearance	Piston Ring End Gap, Min.		Piston Ring Side Clearance	
					Comp.	Oil	Comp.	Oil
1.9L	3.2270–3.2277	④	.7676–.7677	.0001–.0004	.0098	.0197	⑤	—
2.2L	3.3845–3.3851	.0004–.0016	.7875–.7877	.0001–.0005	⑦	.010–.030	.0012–.0027	—
3.0L	3.3834–3.3828	.0001–.0003	.8267	.0010–.0018	.0118–.0196	.0157–.0551	.0008–.0015	.0004–.0012

① — Measured @ .20 inch from bottom of piston.

② — Pistons & pins are matched set & should be replaced as an assembly.

③ — Minimum.

④ — Bore 1, 2 & 3, .0002–.0017 inch; bore 4, .0006–.0021 inch.

⑤ — Top ring, .0016–.0035 inch; 2nd ring, .0012–.0031 inch.

⑥ — Measured @ .57 inch from bottom of piston.

⑦ — Top ring,.008–.016 inch; 2nd ring, .014–.022.

CYLINDER BLOCK

All Specifications Given In Inches, Unless Otherwise Specified.

Engine/Liter	Cylinder Bore Dia. (Std.)	Cylinder Bore Taper, Max.	Cylinder Bore Out Of Round, Max.
1.9L	①	.0020	.0020
2.2L	3.3855–3.3861	.0004	.0004
3.0L	3.3848–3.3852	.0003	.0026

① — Cylinder bores 1, 2 & 3, 3.2280–3.2287 inches; cylinder bore No. 4, 3.2283–3.2291 inches.

OIL PUMP

All Specifications Given In Inches, Unless Otherwise Specified.

Engine/Liter	Body To Side Clearance	Gear To Body Clearance	Tip Clearance	Gear Pocket		Pump Gear Thickness	Pump Gear Diameter	Relief Valve To Body Clearance
				Depth	Diameter			
1.9L	.0060-.0110	.0016-.0049	.0060	—	—	—	—	—
2.2L	.012	.003	.006	—	—	—	—	—
3.0L	.011	①	.006	—	—	—	—	—

① — Inner gear to housing, .003 inch;
outer gear to housing, .004 inch.

DECIMAL & MILLIMETER EQUIVALENTS

Inch	Inch	mm
1/64	.015625	.397
1/32	.03125	.794
3/64	.046875	1.191
1/16	.0625	1.587
5/64	.078125	1.984
3/32	.09375	2.381
7/64	.109375	2.778
1/8	.125	3.175
9/64	.140625	3.572
5/32	.15625	3.969
11/64	.17185	4.366
3/16	.1875	4.762
13/64	.203125	5.159
7/32	.21875	5.556
15/64	.234375	5.953
1/4	.25	6.350
17/64	.265626	6.747
9/32	.28125	7.144
19/64	.296875	7.541
5/16	.3125	7.937
21/64	.328125	8.334
11/32	.34375	8.731

Inch	Inch	mm
23/64	.359375	9.128
3/8	.375	9.525
25/64	.390625	9.922
13/32	.40625	10.319
27/64	.421875	10.716
7/16	.4375	11.113
29/64	.453125	11.509
15/32	.46875	11.906
31/64	.484375	12.303
1/2	.5	12.700
33/64	.515625	13.097
17/32	.53125	13.494
35/64	.546875	13.890
9/16	.5625	14.287
37/64	.578125	14.684
19/32	.59375	15.081
39/64	.609375	15.478
5/8	.625	15.875
41/64	.640625	16.272
21/32	.65625	16.669
43/64	.671875	17.065

Inch	Inch	mm
11/16	.6875	17.462
45/64	.703125	17.859
23/32	.71875	18.265
47/64	.734375	18.653
3/4	.75	19.505
49/64	.765625	19.447
25/32	.78125	19.884
51/64	.796875	20.240
13/16	.8125	20.637
53/64	.828125	21.034
27/32	.84375	21.431
55/64	.859375	21.828
7/8	.875	22.225
57/64	.890625	22.622
29/32	.90625	23.019
59/64	.921875	23.415
15/16	.9375	23.812
61/64	.953125	24.209
31/32	.96875	24.606
63/64	.984375	25.003
1	1	25.400

Special Service Tools

Throughout this manual references are made to and illustrations may depict the use of special tools required to perform certain jobs. These special tools can generally be ordered through the dealers of the make vehicle being serviced. It is also suggested that you check with local automotive supply firms as they also supply tools manufactured by other firms that will assist in the performance of these jobs. The vehicle manufacturers special tools are supplied by:

Chrysler Corporation . . . . Miller Special Tools
SPX Corporation
23400 Industrial Park Court
Farmington Hills, Michigan 48335

Ford Motor Company . . . . Owatonna Tool Company
Owatonna, Minnesota 55060

General Motors Corporation . . . . Kent-Moore
SPX Corporation
28635 Mound Rd.
Warren, Michigan 48092-3499

MANUAL INFORMATION LOCATOR

Front Wheel Drive Models

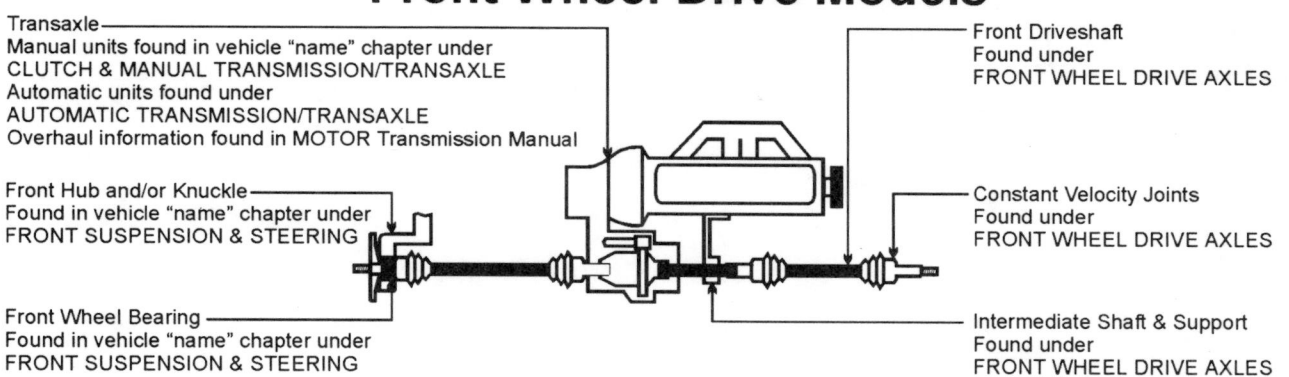

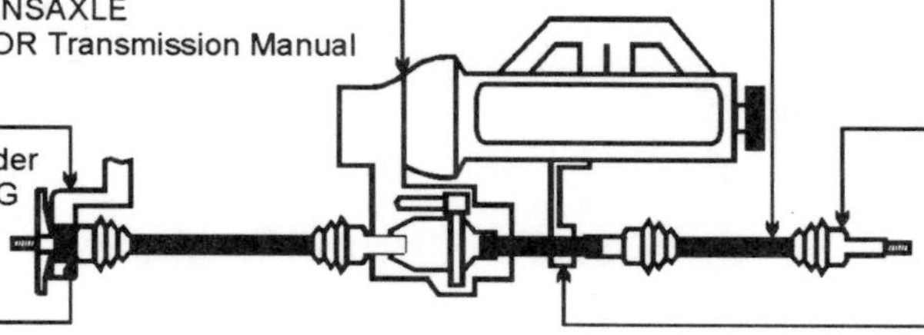

All Wheel Drive Models

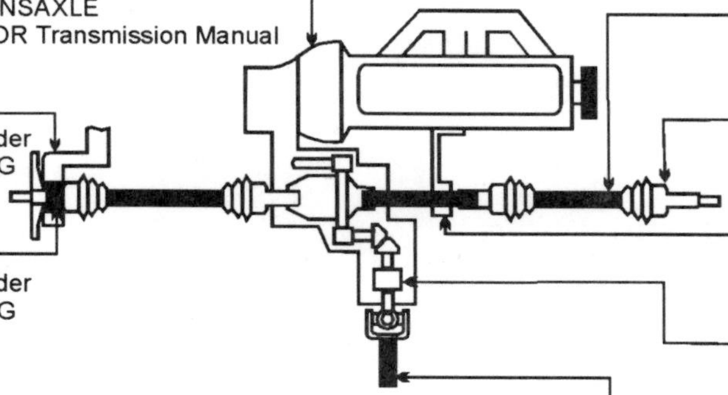

For rear drive components of All Wheel Drive refer to Rear Wheel Drive illustration

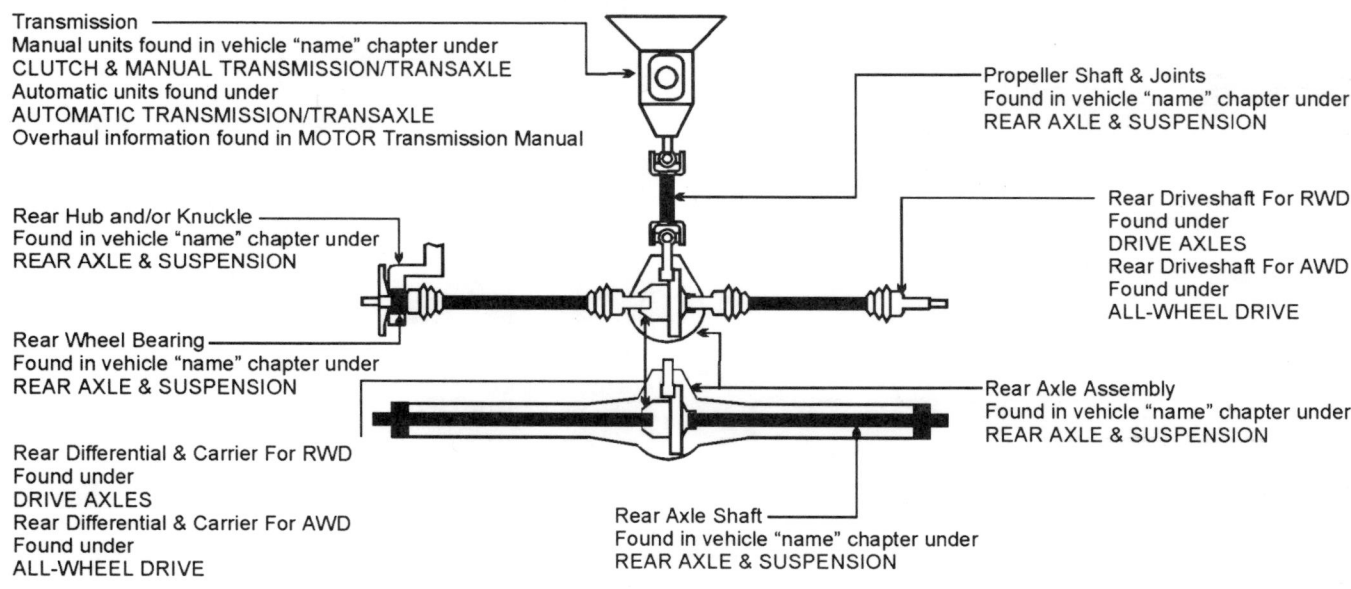

Rear Wheel Drive Models

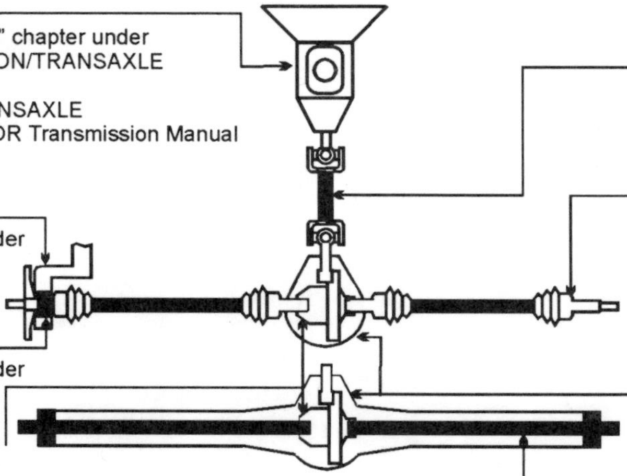

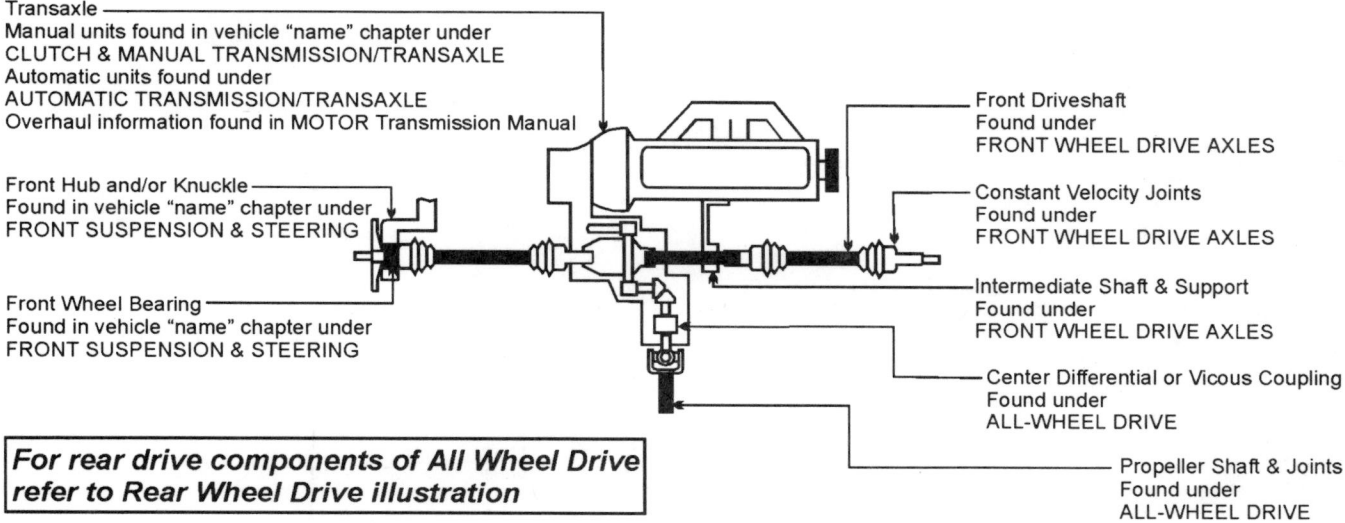

MANUAL INFORMATION LOCATOR—Continued

Operation/Subject/Topic	Auto Repair Manual, Vol. 1	Auto Repair Manual, Vol. 2	Domestic Engine Performance & Driveability Manual
Air Bags	—	X	—
Air Bag System Precautions	X	X	X
Air Conditioning	X	—	—
AIR Systems	—	—	X
All-Wheel Drive Systems	X	—	—
Alternator Specifications	X	—	—
Alternator Systems	X	—	—
Anti-Lock Brake Systems	—	X	—
Automatic Seat Belts	—	X	—
Automatic Transaxle In-Vehicle Service	X	—	—
Automatic Transmission In-Vehicle Service	X	—	—
Axle Shaft Service	X	—	—
Back-Up Light Switch, Replace	X	—	—
Balance Shaft Service	X	—	—
Ball Joint Service	X	—	—
Belt Tension Data	X	—	—
Blower Motor, Replace	X	—	—
Brake Booster Service	X	—	—
Brake Service	X	—	—
Camber Adjustment	X	—	—
Camshaft Service	X	—	—
Capacity Data	X	—	—
Caster Adjustment	X	—	—
Catalytic Converters	—	—	X
Clutch Service	X	—	—
Clutch Start Switch, Replace	X	—	—
Coil Pack, Replace	X	—	X
Coil Spring, Replace	X	—	—
Compression Check	X	—	X
Compression Pressures	X	—	X
Computer Relearn Procedures	X	X	X
Computerized Engine Control Systems	—	—	X
Control Arm Service	X	—	—
Cooling System Bleed	X	—	—
Cooling System Data	X	—	—
Crankshaft Pulley, Replace	X	—	—
Crankshaft Rear Oil Seal Service	X	—	—
Cruise Control Systems	—	X	—
Cylinder Block Specifications	X	—	—
Cylinder Head Service	X	—	—
Cylinder Head Specifications	X	—	—
Cylinder Head, Replace	X	—	—
Cylinder Liner, Replace	X	—	—
Dash Panel Service	—	X	—
Differential Service	X	—	—
Dimmer Switch, Replace	X	—	—
Disc Brake Service	X	—	—
Distributor Service	—	—	X
Distributor, Replace	X	—	X
Distributorless Ignition Systems	—	—	X
Drive Axle Service	X	—	—
Drive Belt Tension Data	X	—	—
Drum Brake Service	X	—	—
EGR System	—	—	X
Electric Engine Cooling Fans	X	—	—
Electric Fuel Pumps	X	—	X
Electrical Symbol Identification	X	X	X
Electronic Fuel Injection	—	—	X
Electronic Ignition	—	—	X
Electronic Instrumentation	—	—	X
Electronic Level Controls	—	X	—
Emission Control Application Charts	—	—	X
Emission Controls	—	—	X
Emission Vacuum Hose Routings	—	—	X
Engine Compartment Reference Diagrams	—	—	X
Engine Cooling Fans	X	—	—
Engine Control Module, Replace	—	—	X
Engine Control Unit, Replace	—	—	X
Engine Front Cover Service	X	—	—
Engine Mounts, Replace	X	—	—
Engine Oil Seal Service	X	—	—
Engine Rebuilding Specifications	X	—	—
Engine Repairs	X	—	—
Engine Sensor Location	—	—	X
Engine Sensor Replacement	—	—	X
Engine Sensor Specifications	—	—	X
Engine System Identification Charts	—	—	X
Engine Tightening Specifications	X	—	—
Engine, Replace	X	—	—
Evaporator Core, Replace	X	—	—
Exhaust Gas Recirculation (EGR) Systems	—	—	X
Exhaust Manifold, Replace	X	—	—
Fast Idle Speed Adjustment	—	—	X
Federal Air Quality Standards	—	—	X
Flasher Location	X	—	—
Front Drive Axle Service	X	—	—
Front Wheel Alignment	X	—	—
Fuel Control System Identification	—	—	X
Fuel Filter, Replace	X	—	—
Fuel Injection Systems	—	—	X
Fuel Injector Cleaning Procedures	—	—	X
Fuel Injector, Replace	—	—	X
Fuel Pump Pressure Specifications	X	—	X
Fuel Pump Pressure Test	—	—	X
Fuel Pump Relay Location	X	—	X
Fuel Pump Replacement	X	—	X
Fuse Panel Location	X	—	—
General Engine Specifications	X	—	—
Headlight Switch, Replace	X	—	—
Heated Air Cleaners	—	—	X
Heater Core, Replace	X	—	—
Hub & Bearing Assembly Service	X	—	—
Hydraulic Brake System Service	X	—	—
Hydraulic Engine Cooling Fans	X	—	—
Hydraulic Valve LIfter Service	X	—	—
Idle Mixture Adjustments	—	—	X
Idle Speed Adjustments	—	—	X
Ignition Lock, Replace	X	—	—
Ignition Switch, Replace	X	—	—
Ignition System Application	—	—	X
Ignition Timing Procedures	—	—	X
Instrument Cluster, Replace	X	—	—
Intake Manifold, Replace	X	—	—
Intermittent Malfunction Computer Diagnosis	—	—	X
Knock Sensor, Replace	—	—	X
Leaf Spring, Replace	X	—	—
Lift Point Illustrations	X	X	—
Locking Differential Service	X	—	—
Locking Hub Service	X	—	—
Lower Ball Joint, Replace	X	—	—